# The Princeton Encyclopedia of Poetry and Poetics

# The Princeton Encyclopedia of Poetry and Poetics

Fourth Edition

EDITOR IN CHIEF

## Roland Greene
*Stanford University*

GENERAL EDITOR

## Stephen Cushman
*University of Virginia*

ASSOCIATE EDITORS

### Clare Cavanagh
*Northwestern University*

### Jahan Ramazani
*University of Virginia*

### Paul Rouzer
*University of Minnesota*

ASSISTANT EDITORS

Harris Feinsod
*Northwestern University*

David Marno
*University of California, Berkeley*

Alexandra Slessarev
*Stanford University*

PRINCETON UNIVERSITY PRESS

PRINCETON AND OXFORD

Published by Princeton University Press, 41 William Street, Princeton, New Jersey 08540

In the United Kingdom: Princeton University Press, 6 Oxford Street, Woodstock, Oxfordshire OX20 1TW

Based on the original edition. Alex Preminger, editor, Frank J. Warnke and O. B. Hardison, Jr., associate editors.

*Cover art:* Jiri Kolar, *Love Poem,* 1964, collage. Photo: Jiri Lammel. Courtesy of the Museum Kampa / The Jan and Meda Mládek Foundation Collection

Library of Congress Cataloging-in-Publication Data

The Princeton encyclopedia of poetry and poetics / Roland Greene, editor in chief ; Stephen Cushman, general editor ; Clare Cavanagh, Jahan Ramazani, Paul Rouzer, associate editors ; Harris Feinsod, David Marno, Alexandra Slessarev, assistant editors.—4th ed.

     p. cm.

  Rev. ed. of : The Princeton encyclopedia of poetry and poetics / Alex Preminger and T.V.F. Brogan, co-editors ; Frank J. Warnke, O.B. Hardison, Jr., and Earl Miner, associate editors. 1993.

  Includes bibliographical references and index.

  ISBN 978-0-691-13334-8 (cloth : alk. paper)—ISBN 978-0-691-15491-6 (pbk. : alk. paper)  1. Poetry—Dictionaries. 2. Poetics—Dictionaries.  3. Poetry—History and criticism.  I. Greene, Roland Arthur.  II. Cushman, Stephen, 1956-  III. Cavanagh, Clare.  IV. Ramazani, Jahan, 1960–  V. Rouzer, Paul F.  VI. Feinsod, Harris. VII. Marno, David.  VIII. Slessarev, Alexandra.  IX. Princeton encyclopedia of poetry and poetics.

  PN1021.N39  2012

808.1'03—dc23 2012005602

British Library Cataloging-in-Publication Data is available

This book has been composed in Adobe Garamond Pro with Myriad Display

Printed on acid-free paper. ∞

press.princeton.edu

Printed in the United States of America

10 9 8 7 6 5 4

# Contents

# Preface

Poetics, the theoretical and practical study of poetry, is among the oldest disciplines in the West, one of those founded by Aristotle along with ethics, logic, and political science. *The Princeton Encyclopedia of Poetry and Poetics* is the comprehensive guide to this rich field. This edition of the *Encyclopedia* significantly develops the past three editions of 1965, 1974, and 1993. Of the more than 1,100 articles, some incorporate and expand their antecedents in those editions, bringing their topics into the present with fresh scholarship and new perspectives. Some 250 entries are entirely new, in response to the changes that poetry and poetics have undergone in the last twenty years. Most articles on major topics have been not only made current but reconceived, in most cases to accommodate a closer attention to poetics. The scope of the *Encyclopedia* has always been worldwide, concerning (as the original editors put it) the history, theory, technique, and criticism of poetry from earliest times to the present.

## The Plan of the Encyclopedia

The solid foundation of the previous editions has offered us the opportunity to enhance coverage without compromising the traditional attention to European and especially English-language poetry and poetics. This edition expands coverage of international poetries, avant-gardes and movements, and the many phenomena, from cognitive poetics to poetry slams to digital poetry that have gained momentum since 1993. Latin America, East and South Asia, Africa, and Eastern Europe are represented here by an infusion of new entries and specialist contributors who present not only the broad canvas of national and regional literary history but the granular detail of informed scholarship.

For instance, to complement the general article on the poetry of the United States, new entries address such topics as the Black Mountain school, the Fireside poets, confessional poetry, and the San Francisco Renaissance. Spanish America is represented by a general essay on the hemispheric tradition in poetry as well as by discrete entries on the poetries of Mexico, Peru, Argentina, Chile, and many other countries. And both sets of articles converse with an authoritative new entry on the poetry of the indigenous Americas, which is in turn augmented by pieces on Guaraní, Inuit, and Navajo poetries, among others. Asian poetry and poetics receive substantial new investments in critical discussion, notably in entries concerning the popular poetry of China, Chinese poetic drama, the influential tenth-century Japanese collection known as the *Kokinshū,* and the poetry of Cambodia, among others. The coverage of India now involves not only a general entry on the poetry of the subcontinent but many more articles on the history and tradition of poetic forms and styles in various languages from Hindi to Gujarati to Sanskrit. Africa and Eastern Europe see a new measure of attention to countries, languages, movements, and styles.

This wave of locality and specificity changes the character of the *Encyclopedia,* and brings into the book a wide-ranging cast of contributors, new approaches, and topics of different dimensions. It permitted us to reduce the size and scope of many of the larger entries on national poetries. Free of the obligation to define every episode and movement, the authors of articles on topics such as the poetry of England or the poetry of Spain have been encouraged to delineate a literary history in bold strokes; their narratives are complemented by new items on the particular histories of such topics as Georgianism and neo-Gongorism, respectively. The perspectives of omnibus entries on the poetry of Spanish America or of India still have an important place in this edition, offering the reader both a wide view and a close focus.

Moreover, we have challenged the tacit assumption of many handbooks that general poetic terms may be treated through English-language examples only. A large number of general entries here are written by scholars of poetries other than English—a Hispanist on pastoral, a scholar of the French Renaissance on epideixis, a Persianist on panegyric.

The *Encyclopedia* includes five kinds of entries: terms and concepts; genres and forms; periods, schools, and movements; the poetries of nations, regions, and languages; and poetry in relation to other cultural forms, disciplines, and social practices such as linguistics, religion, and science. It does not contain entries on poets or works, but discusses these in the context of the larger topics to which they are related. While the A-to-Z format tends to obscure the integrity of these five categories, each one entails certain obligations and challenges.

Terminology makes for one of the most technically exacting aspects of the project. The *Encyclopedia* remains the authoritative source for brief definitions of particular terms or expansive treatments of broad topics, such as the exhaustive treatment of rhyme. Entries on concepts such as structuralism or speech act theory are designed to engage with poetry over other kinds of literature or writing. This category is home to transhistorical terms such as cento, eclogue, and *gai saber;* fundamental topics in the history of criticism such as emotion and imagination; and critical concepts of wide application such as ethnopoetics and organicism. From its entries one could assemble a history of ideas in and about poetry.

The rubrics of genre and form often shade into one another, but at the same time they tend to follow complementary logics of openness and limitation, respectively. Most entries on genres, such as those on the *alba* and the *paraclausithyron,* follow the evolution of their objects to the present day, while many entries on forms locate them in their original settings of language, epoch, and culture. Nonetheless, the reader will encounter a number of entries that do both, as well as bracing new essays on the concepts of genre and form.

Coverage of periods, schools, and movements has been deepened for this edition, both as a category in itself and within the other categories. For example, postmodern poetry of the United States entails new entries on (among other topics) projective verse, composition by field, Language poetry, and absorption, some contributed by poet-critics in the tradition of William Carlos Williams's entry on the "variable foot" for the 1965 edition. Again, the focus is on poetics. Our entry on naturalism, skewed toward the poetic application of that concept, is very different from an article of the same title in a handbook of general literary criticism or theory.

The fourth category, the poetries of nations, regions, and languages, is a customary strength of the *Encyclopedia;* many readers have found the past editions a reliable source for introductions to unfamiliar literatures. In this edition we have tried to devise topics that accommodate the histories of national poetries while taking account of local or transnational differences, and that follow languages out of national borders. The results for our nomenclature are described below. Multiple language traditions found within a nation or region are treated as much as is practical, though never fully enough to trace the poetic complexity of modern, multicultural societies.

Finally, the articles concerned with poetry in relation to disciplines, culture, and society—for titles, such entries often take the form of "religion and poetry" or "science and poetry"—have been focused on the implications for the history of poetry as opposed to history in a more general sense. (Depending on the topic and the contributor's approach, some conceptual entries draw a relation to poetics rather than to poetry: thus "anthropology and poetry" but "linguistics and poetics.") From these articles, one could build a history of poetry's relations to the intellectual and cultural world at large.

Of course, these five rubrics are provisional, and many items could move among them. All of the main categories now include entries that reflect on category making, such as "colonial poetics" and "national poetry." A longstanding rubric, "Western poetics," has been answered not by a corresponding omnibus entry for the non-Western world but by new articles on Chinese, Japanese, Sanskrit, and other poetics. Many items are tacitly engaged with one another and might be read in counterpoint (e.g., "criticism," "interpretation," and "hermeneutics," or "imitation," "mimesis," and "representation"); some of these, such as the new set called "poetry as artifact," "poetry as fiction," "poetry as information," and "poetry as knowledge," make a sweeping overview of complementary approaches. (Several other entries continue that overview under various titles: poetry as commodity in "Frankfurt school" and as object of faith in "belief and poetry," and the several entries on terms such as "poem," "text," and "work.") And many important items, such as "politics and poetry," "postcolonial poetics," and of course "poetry," straddle the divisions of the book.

As every reader will notice, this book has been conceived to enable cross-coverages and contradictions insofar as these facts register the current condition of poetry studies. The significance of Whitman or Ḥāfiẓ, the idea of poetic genius, and the continuing implications of the New Criticism are too multifarious to fit into one or two entries. The reader will find these and many other topics in several articles, often from the perspectives of distinctive fields or interests. An index, the first in the history of the *Encyclopedia,* makes such collations part of the experience of this book.

As the fourth edition of a book that has been in print since 1965, this project carries its history within itself; many entries include the names of past contributors whose entries have been augmented and brought up to date. Every item in the 1993 edition was evaluated by the team of editors.

Some were dropped, while many more were assigned to readers and prospective contributors who were invited to assess the received material. In some cases an old entry stands on its substance while requiring only a new bibliography, which the editors have provided. In others, we publish a collaboration between past and present contributors that could take place only between the covers of this *Encyclopedia*. The majority of articles, and nearly all of the most prominent ones, have been entirely reconceived by new contributors.

Some six years in the making, this project is also the portrait of a discipline—the worldwide field of poetry studies—in the process of development. It attempts to address the permanent questions in the field, such as the nature of the poetic, while giving some attention to topics that seem to belong to the present and the near future, such as conceptual writing and documentary poetics; it also involves a decided effort on the editors' part to devote resources to topics, such as exegetical interpretation and archetypal criticism, that are currently unfashionable but seem likely to be revived in new manners. No doubt in twenty years the values of this fourth edition will appear in a historical light, but in any case we have chosen both to acknowledge and to transcend the present moment as far as possible. Finally, however, such a project can be only what its population of authors—a cross-section of scholars of poetry around the world—want it to be.

## The Conventions of the Fourth Edition

One of the longstanding strengths of the *Encyclopedia* is its coverage of the poetries of the world. The present edition attempts to make a distinction between poetries that are based in nations or territories and those that are based in language, international cultures, or diasporas—no doubt sometimes an ambiguous difference, but nonetheless one that seems worth making. The entry on the poetry of France is discrete from those on the various francophone poetries of Africa, Canada, or the Caribbean, while Persian poetry is best approached as a single topic with international ramifications. The "poetry of England" and the "poetry of the United States" as topics are preferable to "English" or "American" poetry, with their uncertain but expansive outlines. In its coverage of the British Isles, the former entry is complemented by articles on Welsh, Scottish, and Irish poetries, while the latter is cross-referenced to companion pieces on U.S. poetries wholly or partly in other languages that can claim their own fields of study,

such as French-language, Chicana/o, and Asian American poetry. An entry such as "German poetry" takes a linguistic rather than a national approach, but is complemented by entries on Austria, Switzerland, and the Low Countries that follow geopolitical contours and discuss discrete languages within those outlines. In many cases the contributors made the final determination of what to call their entries, which no doubt produces some asymmetries that reflect the differences in the fields represented here.

For example, Walther von der Vogelweide, a poet who wrote in Middle High German, is treated in "German poetry" as the first important political poet in the language, in "poetry of Austria" for his residence in Vienna and service to Duke Frederick I, in "Minnesang" and "Spruchdichtung" for his generic affiliations, in "Meistersinger" for his influence—and in "biography and poetry" as the subject of one of the first biographies of a medieval poet. The result is a comprehensive, multivocal account of many of the signal events in world poetry, from the Occitan troubadours to the *modernismo* of Rubén Darío to the visual and material poetries of the past fifty years.

Translations are generally given within parentheses, without quotation marks if no other words appear in the parenthetical matter, but set off within quotation marks when some qualification is needed, as in the form of many etymologies: e.g., arsis and thesis (Gr., "raising and lowering"). Translated titles generally appear in the most comprehensive articles, such as those on national poetries or important developments such as "modernism"; entries of smaller scope often give original titles without translation, although contributors have the discretion to translate titles where it clarifies the argument to do so. (We tolerate inconsistency that reflects to some degree the field at hand: thus some major entries, such as "baroque" or "Renaissance poetics," do not translate titles at all; others such as "love poetry" give only translated titles.) Translated titles of books are given in italics when the title refers to an actual English translation: e.g. the Georgian poet Shota Rustaveli's *Vepkhis tqaosani* (*The Man in the Panther's Skin*). For poems, translated titles are given with quotation marks when the translation has been published under that title, but without quotation marks when the translated title is ad hoc.

This convention sometimes entails reproducing a non-literal rendering that appears in a published translation, such as Boccaccio's *Trattatello in laude di Dante* as *Life of Dante,* or the Guatemalan poet Otto René Castillo's *Vámonos patria a caminar* as

*Let's Go!* We believe that the value of indicating an extant translation outweighs the occasional infelicity. At the same time, it is likely we have overlooked some published translations, and many new ones will appear over the life of this book.

Dates of the lives and works of poets and critics often appear in the most comprehensive entries on a given topic (e.g. a regional entry such as "poetry of the Low Countries" or a major movement such as "poststructuralism"), showing up less often as topics become narrower. Dates of works in the age of print refer to publication unless otherwise indicated.

Articles contain two types of cross-references: those that appear within the body of an entry (indicated with asterisks or in parentheses with small capitals), and those that follow an entry, just before the bibliographies. If the former are often topics that extend the fabric of the definition at hand, the latter often indicate adjacent topics of broader interest. Of course, both kinds of cross-reference hold out the danger of infinite connection: nearly every entry could be linked to many others, and the countless usages of terms such as *line, metaphor,* and *poetics* cannot all be linked to the entries concerned with those terms. Accordingly we have tried to apply cross-references judiciously, indicating where further reading in a related entry really complements the argument at hand.

The bibliographies are intended as guides to relevant scholarship of the distant and recent past, not only as lists of works cited in the entries. The bibliographies have been lightly standardized, but some entries—say, those that narrate the development of a field—gain from citing works of scholarship in their original iterations (John Crowe Ransom's essay "Criticism, Inc." in its first appearance in the *Virginia Quarterly Review* of 1937) or in their original languages—while many others choose to cite later editions or translations into English as a convenience for the reader.

The deliberately limited standardization of the volume allows the reader to observe the conditions and assumptions that are native to each national literature, topic, or approach represented: something as fundamental as what "classical" or "hermeticism" means, or as technical as where one finds an important essay by Roman Jakobson, may appear differently at several places in the book. One might learn a great deal by noticing these facts—in effect, by interpreting the *Encyclopedia* itself as a living document of the discipline that unites us across languages, periods, and methods, namely the study of poetry and poetics.

## The State of the Field

As a discipline, poetics is undergoing a renewal. In the past it was sometimes conceived as an antiquarian field, a vehicle for broadly theoretical issues in literature, or a name for poets' reflections on their practice. Recently, however, the discipline has turned more explicitly toward historical and cross-cultural questions. In the United States, research groups on poetics at several universities have contributed to this momentum, as have digital projects that render the materials of historical and international poetries readily available and make new kinds of conversation possible. Ventures such as this *Encyclopedia,* new and old at once, contribute to this conversation by introducing scholars to one another, by opening local topics to comparative attention, and most of all by providing information and perspective.

For two generations *The Princeton Encyclopedia of Poetry and Poetics* has been the common property of the worldwide community of poetry scholars. We are proud to bring it, renewed, to another generation.

# Acknowledgments

The fourth edition of *The Princeton Encyclopedia of Poetry and Poetics* has been a collective work of the worldwide community of poetry scholars over several years. It began at the instigation of Anne Savarese, executive editor for reference at Princeton University Press, whose judgment and taste have conditioned the project at every stage. At the Press, Claire Tillman-McTigue and Diana Goovaerts kept the assembly of authors in contact with the editors, and the editors in touch with one another. Ellen Foos, production editor for the volume, was unfailingly patient with wayward editors and stretched deadlines. Mary Lou Bertucci copyedited the text and is responsible for matters of consistency.

The editors gratefully acknowledge the help of the research assistants who have been involved with the *Encyclopedia* over the years: Sarah Bishop, Lauren Boehm, Maia Draper, Jaime Lynn Farrar, Suzanne Ashley King, Elizabeth Molmen, Frank Rodriguez, Whitney Trump, and Daniel Veraldi. At Stanford University, R. Lucas Coe maintained communications with the Press.

The heart of the book, its 1,100 articles, were conceived, evaluated, and improved by the gathering of contributors, whose names appear elsewhere in the front matter. Many of them read and commented anonymously on the work of others. Some did much more, especially Walter G. Andrews, Yigal Bronner, Marisa Galvez, Joseph Lease, Marjorie Perloff, and Haun Saussy.

The scholars, poets, and others who did not write articles for this edition but nonetheless advised the project are a distinguished roster, and this book belongs to them as well: Txetxu Aguado, Jaime Alazraki, David Atwell, Shahzad Bashir, Stephen C. Berkwitz, Paula Blank, Elisabeth Boyi, Dominic Parviz Brookshaw, Marina Brownlee, Ardis Butterfield, Melanie Conroy, Neil Corcoran, Mary Thomas Crane, John Dagenais, Wai Chee Dimock, Craig Dworkin, Lazar Fleishman, Barbara Fuchs, Christina Galvez, Forrest Gander, J. Neil Garcia, Simon Gaunt, Michael Gluzman, Fabian Goppelsröder, Margaret Greer, Timothy Hampton, Benjamin Harshav, Waïl Hassan, Héctor Hoyos, Jasmine Hu, Alex Hunt, Witi Ihimaera, Kate Jenckes, F. Sionil Jose, Smaro Kamboureli, Sarah Kay, Maurice Kilwein Guevara, Seth Kimmel, Paul Kiparsky, Rachel Lee, Seth Lerer, Chris Mann, Annabel Martín, John Maynard, Natalie Melas, Farzaneh Milani, Ignacio Navarrete, Patricia Parker, Michael Predmore, Phoebe Putnam, Margaret Reid, Joan Ramon Resina, Alicia Rios, Hollis Robbins, Janice Ross, David Rubin, Susan Schultz, David Shulman, Richard Sieburth, Barbara Herrnstein Smith, Sidonie Smith, Ann Smock, Willard Spiegelman, Susan Stephens, Marlene van Niekerk, Susanne Woods, Kevin Young, Shu Yi Zhou, and Jan Ziolkowski.

Finally, we gratefully acknowledge the following authors, publishers, and agents for granting us permission to use brief selections from the copyrighted material listed below. Great care has been taken to trace all the owners of copyrighted material used in this book. Any inadvertent omissions pointed out to us will be gladly acknowledged in future printings.

Alurista for five lines of his poem "Mis ojos hinchados."

Arte Público Press for ten lines of "Guitarreros" by Américo Paredes, from *Between Two Worlds,* copyright © 1991 by Arte Público Press; and four lines of "Emily Dickinson" by Lucha Corpi, from *Palabras de Mediodia/Noon Words,* copyright © 1980 by Arte Público Press. Both reprinted by permission of Arte Público Press.

Gordon Brotherston for six lines of his translation of Preuss's musings on the Witoto; six lines of his translation of a traditional Quechua hymn; and twelve lines of his translation from the Nahuatl of an excerpt from *Cuauhtitlan Annals.*

The University of California Press for five lines of "The Box" by Robert Creeley, from *The Collected Poems of Robert Creeley, 1945–1960,* copyright © 2006 by the Regents of the University of California; and two lines of "Two Voices" by Khalil Gibran from *An Anthology of Modern Arabic Poetry,* edited by Hamid Algar and Mounah Khouri, copyright © 1974 by the Regents of the University of California. Both reprinted by permission of the University of California Press.

Cambridge University Press for three lines of "Eulogy" by al-Mutanabbi, from *Poems of al-Mutanabbi,* translated by A. J. Arberry, copyright © 1967 by Cambridge University Press; and three lines by al-Khansa, from *Arabic Poetry: A Primer for Students,* translated by A. J. Arberry, copyright © 1965 by Cambridge University Press. Both reprinted by the permission of Cambridge University Press.

Coach House Books for four lines from *Eunoia,* by Christian Bök (Coach House Books, 2001, updated 2009).

Columbia University Press for six lines of "Tansim ka, or, Song of a Loyal Heart" from *Early Korean Literature: Selections and Introductions,* by David R. McCann, copyright © 2000 Columbia University Press; twelve lines of "Azaleas," six lines of "Winter Sky," and eighteen lines of "Grasses," each from *The Columbia Anthology of Modern Korean Poetry,* edited by David R. McCann, copyright © 2004 Columbia University Press. All reprinted by permission of the publisher.

Jayne Cortez for eight lines of "If the Drum Is a Woman," copyright © 2011 by Jayne Cortez.

Faber and Faber Ltd. for two lines of "The Hollow Men" by T. S. Eliot from *Collected Poems 1909–1962* by T. S. Eliot, copyright © 1974 by Faber and Faber, Ltd.; three lines of "The Fragment" by Seamus Heaney, from *Electric Light,* copyright © 2001 by Seamus Heaney and reprinted by permission of Faber and Faber, Ltd.; "In a Station of the Metro" by Ezra Pound, from *Personae,* copyright © 1926 by Ezra Pound; and "Red Wheel Barrow" by William Carlos Williams, from *The Collected Poems: Volume I, 1909–1939,* copyright © 1938 by William Carlos Williams. All reprinted by permission of Faber and Faber, Ltd.

Rafael Jesús González for eleven lines of his poem "The Coin (Ars Poetica)" from *El hacedor de juegos/The Maker of Games* (San Francisco: Casa Editorial, 1977; 2nd edition, 1987), copyright © 2012 by Rafael Jesús González. Reprinted by permission of the author.

Graywolf Press for thirteen lines of "John Col" by Elizabeth Alexander from *The Venus Hottentot,* copyright © 1990 by the Rector and Visitors of the University of Virginia.

Harvard University Press for five lines of "Artifice of Absorption" from *A Poetics* by Charles Bernstein, Cambridge, Mass.: Harvard University Press, copyright © 1992 by Charles Bernstein; four lines of *The Kalevala: Or, Poems of the Kalevala District,* compiled by Elias Lönnrot, translated by Francis Peabody Magoun, Jr., Cambridge, Mass.: Harvard University Press, copyright © 1963 by the President and Fellows of Harvard College. Both reprinted by permission of the publisher.

University of Hertfordshire Press for twelve lines from an untitled poem translated by Iren Kertesz-Wilkinson, published in *Romani Culture and Gypsy Identity,* edited by T. A. Acton and G. Mundy, University of Hertfordshire Press, 1997; nine lines of "O Land, I Am Your Daughter" by Bronislawa Wajs and four lines of "Roads of the Roma" by Leksa Manus, both published in *The Roads of the Roma: A PEN Anthology of Gypsy Writers,* copyright © 1998 by PEN American Center, University of Hertfordshire Press.

Henry Holt and Company for two lines of "The Gift Outright" from *The Poetry of Robert Frost,* edited by Edward Connery Lathem, copyright © 1969 by Henry Holt and Company, copyright © 1942 by Robert Frost, copyright © 1970 by Lesley Frost Ballantine. Reprinted by permission of Henry Holt and Company, LLC.

Houghton Mifflin Harcourt Publishing Company for excerpts from "The Hollow Men" from *Collected Poems 1909–1962* by T. S. Eliot, copyright © 1936 by Harcourt, Inc. and renewed by T. S. Eliot; and eight lines of "It Is Dangerous to Read Newspapers" from *Selected Poems I, 1965–1975* by Margaret Atwood, copyright © 1976 by Margaret Atwood. Both reprinted by permission of Houghton Mifflin Harcourt Publishing Company. All rights reserved.

Robert Huey for permission to reprint five lines of his translation of "Shinkokinshū" by Fujiwara Teika.

Phoebe Larrimore Literary Agency for eight lines of "It Is Dangerous to Read Newspapers" by Margaret Atwood, used by permission of the author. Available in the following collections: In the United States, *Selected Poems I, 1965–1975,* published by Houghton Mifflin, copyright © Margaret Atwood 1976; in Canada, *Selected Poems, 1966–1984,* published by McClelland and Stewart, copyright © Margaret Atwood 1990; in the UK, *Eating Fire,* published by Virago Books, copyright © Margaret Atwood 1998.

Ian Monk for excerpts from his poems "A Threnodialist's Dozen" and "Elementary Morality."

James T. Monroe for his translation of "Envoie to a Love Poem" from *Hispano-Arabic Poetry: A Student Anthology,* published by the University of California Press, 1974.

José Montoya for six lines of his poem "El Louie."

New Directions Publishing Corporation for five lines of "The Five Day Rain" by Denise Levertov, from *Collected Earlier Poems 1940–1960,* copyright © 1960 by Denise Levertov; four lines of "Poems" by Dylan Thomas, from *Collected Poems,* copyright © 1952 by Dylan Thomas; five lines of "Epigram (After the Greek)" by H. D. (Hilda Doolittle), from *Collected Poems, 1912–1944,* copyright © 1982 by The Estate of Hilda Doolittle; "In a Station of the Metro" by Ezra Pound, from *Personae,* copyright © 1926 by Ezra Pound; and "Red Wheel Barrow" by William Carlos Williams, from *The Collected Poems: Volume I, 1909–1939,* copyright

© 1938 by New Directions Publishing Corp. All reprinted by permission of New Directions Publishing Corp.

Nightwood Editions for six lines of "language (in)habits" from *Forage* by Rita Wong, published by Nightwood Editions, 2007; http://www.night woodeditions.com.

Oxford University Press for eight lines of "It Is Dangerous to Read Newspapers" from Margaret Atwood, *The Animals in that Country,* copyright © 1969 Oxford University Press Canada. Reprinted by permission of the publisher.

Burton Raffel for his translation of a *pantun,* the traditional Malay four-line verse.

Random House for four lines of "River Snow" from *The Anchor Book of Chinese Poetry,* edited by Tony Barnstone and Chou Ping, copyright © 2005 by Tony Barnstone and Chou Ping. Used by permission of Anchor Books, a division of Random House, Inc.

Lynne Rienner Publications for five lines of "Lazarus 1962" by Khalil Hawi from *Naked in Exile: The Threshing Floors of Hunger,* translated by Adnan Haydar and Michael Beard, © 1984. Reprinted by permission of Lynne Rienner Publications.

Sonia Sanchez for four lines of her poem "a / coltrane / poem."

Maekawa Sajuro for five lines of an untitled poem from *Shokubutsusai* by Maekawa Samio, translated by Leith Morton.

Simon & Schuster, Inc., for three lines of "Leda and the Swan," reprinted by the permission of Scribner, a Division of Simon & Schuster, Inc., from *The Collected Works of W. B. Yeats, Volume 1: The Poems, Revised* by W. B. Yeats, edited by Richard J. Finneran, copyright © 1928 by the Macmillan Company, renewed 1956 by Georgie Yeats. All rights reserved.

Society of Biblical Literature for six lines of "Kirta," from *Ugaritic Narrative Poetry,* edited by Simon B. Parker, copyright © 1997. Reprinted by permission of the Society of Biblical Literature.

Talon Books for twenty-one lines of "Naked Poems" from *Selected Poems: The Vision Tree* copyright © 1982 Phyllis Webb, Talon Books, Vancouver, B.C. Reprinted by permission of the publisher.

University of Virginia Press for four lines of "A Warm Day in Winter" by Paul Laurence Dunbar from *The Collected Poetry of Paul Laurence Dunbar,* edited by Joanne M. Braxton, copyright © 1993 Rector and Visitors of the University of Virginia. Reprinted by permission of the University of Virginia Press.

Wesleyan University Press for eight lines of "Spring Images" by James Wright from *Collected Poems,* copyright © 1971 by James Wright; eleven lines of "Altazor" by Vincente Huidobro, translated by Eliot Weinberger, copyright © 2004 by Eliot Weinberger. Both reprinted by permission of Wesleyan University Press.

# Topical List of Entries

# Bibliographical Abbreviations

**Abrams** M. H. Abrams, *The Mirror and the Lamp: Romantic Theory and the Critical Tradition*, 1953

**AION-SL** *Annali dell'Istituto Universitario Orientale di Napoli: sezione filologico-letteraria*

**AJP** *American Journal of Philology*

**AJS** *American Journal of Semiotics*

**AL** *American Literature*

**Allen** W. S. Allen, *Accent and Rhythm*, 1973

**Analecta hymnica** *Analecta hymnica medii aevi*, ed. G. M. Dreves, C. Blume, and H. M. Bannister, 55 v., 1886–1922

**Attridge, Poetic Rhythm** D. Attridge, *Poetic Rhythm: An Introduction*, 1995

**Attridge, Rhythms** D. Attridge, *The Rhythms of English Poetry*, 1982

**Auerbach** E. Auerbach, *Mimesis: The Representation of Reality in Western Literature*, trans. W. R. Trask, 1953

**Beare** W. Beare, *Latin Verse and European Song*, 1957

**Bec** P. Bec, *La Lyrique Française au moyen âge (XIIe–XIIIe siècles): Contribution à une typologie des genres poétiques médiévaux*, 2 v., 1977–78

**Benjamin** W. Benjamin, "The Work of Art in the Age of Mechanical Reproduction," *Illuminations*, trans. H. Zohn, 1968

**BGDSL (H)** *Beiträge zur Geschichte des deutschen Sprache und Literatur (Halle)*

**BGDSL (T)** *Beiträge zur Geschichte des deutschen Sprache und Literatur (Tübingen)*

**BHS** *Bulletin of Hispanic Studies*

**BJA** *British Journal of Aesthetics*

**Bowra** C. M. Bowra, *Greek Lyric Poetry from Alcman to Simonides*, 2d ed., 1961

**Bridges** R. Bridges, *Milton's Prosody*, rev. ed., 1921

**Brogan** T.V.F. Brogan, *English Versification, 1570–1980: A Reference Guide with a Global Appendix*, 1981

**Brooks** C. Brooks, *The Well Wrought Urn*, 1947

**Brooks and Warren** C. Brooks and W. P. Warren, *Understanding Poetry*, 3d ed., 1960

**Carper and Attridge** T. Carper and D. Attridge, *Meter and Meaning: An Introduction to Rhythm*, 2003

**CBEL** *Cambridge Bibliography of English Literature*, ed. F. W. Bateson, 4 v., 1940; v. 5, *Supplement*, ed. G. Watson, 1957

**CBFL** *A Critical Bibliography of French Literature*, gen. ed. D. C. Cabeen and R. A. Brooks, 6 v., 1947–1994

**CE** *College English*

**Chambers** F. M. Chambers, *An Introduction to Old Provençal Versification*, 1985

**Chatman** S. Chatman, *A Theory of Meter*, 1965

**CHCL** *Cambridge History of Classical Literature*, v. 1, *Greek Literature*, ed. P. E. Easterling and B.M.W. Knox, 1985; v. 2, *Latin Literature*, ed. E. J. Kenney and W. V. Clausen, 1982

**CHEL** *Cambridge History of English Literature*, ed. A. W. Ward and A. R. Waller, 14 v., 1907–16

**CHLC** *Cambridge History of Literary Criticism*, 9 v., 1989–2005

**Chomsky and Halle** N. Chomsky and M. Halle, *The Sound Pattern of English*, 1968

**CJ** *Classical Journal*

**CL** *Comparative Literature*

**CML** *Classical and Modern Literature*

**Corbett** E.P.J. Corbett, *Classical Rhetoric for the Modern Student*, 3d ed., 1990

**CP** *Classical Philology*

**CQ** *Classical Quarterly*

**Crane** *Critics and Criticism, Ancient and Modern*, ed. R. S. Crane, 1952

**CritI** *Critical Inquiry*

**Crusius** F. Crusius, *Römische Metrik: ein Einführung*, 8th ed., rev. H. Rubenbauer, 1967

**Culler** J. Culler, *Structuralist Poetics: Structuralism, Linguistics, and the Study of Literature*, 1975

**Cureton** R. D. Cureton, *Rhythmic Phrasing in English Verse*, 1992

**Curtius** E. Curtius, *European Literature and the Latin Middle Ages*, trans. W. R. Trask, 1953

**CW** *Classical World*

**DAI** *Dissertation Abstracts International*

**Dale** A. M. Dale, *The Lyric Meters of Greek Drama*, 2d ed., 1968

**DDJ** *Deutsches Dante-Jahrbuch*

**de Man** P. de Man, *Blindness and Insight: Essays in the Rhetoric of Contemporary Criticism*, 2d ed., 1983

**Derrida** J. Derrida, *Of Grammatology*, trans. G. C. Spivak, 2d ed., 1998

**DHI** *Dictionary of the History of Ideas*, ed. P. P. Weiner, 6 v., 1968–74

**Dronke** P. Dronke, *Medieval Latin and the Rise of European Love Lyric*, 2d ed., 2 v., 1968

**Duffell** M. J. Duffell, *A New History of English Metre*, 2008

**E&S** *Essays and Studies of the English Association*

**ELH** *ELH* (formerly *English Literary History*)

**Eliot, Essays** T. S. Eliot, *Selected Essays*, rev. ed., 1950

**Elwert** W. T. Elwert, *Französische Metrik*, 4th ed., 1978

**Elwert, Italienische** W. T. Elwert, *Italienische Metrik*, 2d ed., 1984

**Empson** W. Empson, *Seven Types of Ambiguity*, 3d ed., 1953

**ENLL** *English Language and Linguistics*

**Fabb et al.** N. Fabb, D. Atridge, A. Durant, and C. MacCabe, *The Linguistics of Writing*, 1987

**Faral** E. Faral, *Les arts poétique du XIIe et du XIIIe siècles*, 1924

**Finch and Varnes** *An Exaltation of Forms: Contemporary Poets Celebrate the Diversity of Their Art*, ed. A. Finch and K. Varnes, 2002

**Fish** S. Fish, *Is There a Text in This Class? The Authority of Interpretive Communities*, 1980

**Fisher** *The Medieval Literature of Western Europe: A Review of Research, Mainly 1930–1960*, ed. J. H. Fisher, 1965

**FMLS** *Forum for Modern Language Studies*

**Fontanier** P. Fontanier, *Les figures du discourse*, 1977

**Fowler** A. Fowler, *Kinds of Literature: An Introduction to the Theory of Genres and Modes*, 1982

**Frye** N. Frye, *Anatomy of Criticism: Four Essays*, 1957

**FS** *French Studies*

**Gasparov** M. L. Gasparov, *Sovremennyj russkij stix: Metrika i ritmika*, 1974

**Gasparov, History** M. L. Gasparov, *A History of European Versification*, trans. G. S. Smith and M. Tarlinskaja, 1996

**GRLMA** *Grundriss der romanischen Literaturen des Mittelalters*, ed. H. R. Jauss and E. Köhler, 11 v., 1968–

**Group μ** Group μ (J. Dubois, F. Edeline, J.-M. Klinkenberg, P. Minguet, F. Pire, H. Trinon), *A General Rhetoric*, trans. P. B. Burrell and E. M. Slotkin, 1981

**Halporn et al.** J. W. Halporn, M. Ostwald, and T. G. Rosenmeyer, *The Meters of Greek and Latin Poetry*, 2d ed., 1980

**Hardie** W. R. Hardie, *Res Metrica*, 1920

**HJAS** *Harvard Journal of Asiatic Studies*

**Hollander** J. Hollander, *Vision and Resonance: Two Senses of Poetic Form*, 2d ed., 1985

**Hollier** *A New History of French Literature*, ed. D. Hollier, 1989

**HQ** *Hopkins Quarterly*

**HR** *Hispanic Review*

**HudR** *Hudson Review*

**ICPhS** *International Congress of Phonetic Sciences* (journal)

**IJCT** *International Journal of Classical Tradition*

**JAAC** *Journal of Aesthetics and Art Criticism*

**JAC** *JAC: A Journal of Rhetoric, Culture, and Politics*

**JAF** *Journal of American Folklore*

**Jakobson** R. Jakobson, *Selected Writings*, 8 v., 1962–88

**Jakobson and Halle** R. Jakobson and M. Halle, *Fundamentals of Language*, 1956

**JAOS** *Journal of American Oriental Society*

**Jarman and Hughes** *A Guide to Welsh Literature*, ed. A. O. H. Jarman and G. R. Hughes, 2 v., 1976–79

**Jeanroy** A. Jeanroy, *La Poésie lyrique des Troubadours*, 2 v., 1934

**Jeanroy, Origines** A. Jeanroy, *Les origines de la poésie lyrique en France au moyen âge*, 4th ed., 1965

**JEGP** *Journal of English and Germanic Philology*

**JFLS** *Journal of French Language Studies*

**JHS** *Journal of Hellenic Studies*

**JL** *Journal of Linguistics*

**Jour. P. Society** *Journal of Polynesian Society*

**JPhon** *Journal of Phonetics*

**Kastner** L. E. Kastner, *A History of French Versification*, 1903

**Keil** *Grammatici Latini*, ed. H. Keil, 7 v., 1855–80; v. 8, *Anecdota helvitica: Supplementum*, ed. H. Hagen, 1870

**Koster** W.J.W. Koster, *Traité de métrique greque suivi d'un précis de métrique latine*, 5th ed., 1966

**KSMB** *Keats-Shelley Journal*

**KR** *Kenyon Review*

**L&S** *Language and Speech*

**Lang** *Language*

**Lang&S** *Language and Style*

**Lanham** R. A. Lanham, *A Handlist of Rhetorical Terms*, 2d ed., 1991

**Lausberg** H. Lausberg, *Handbook of Literary Rhetoric: A Foundation for Literary Study*, trans. M. T. Bliss, A. Jansen, and D. E. Orton, 1998

**Le Gentil** P. Le Gentil, *La Poésie lyrique espagnole et portugaise à la fin du moyen âge*, 2 v., 1949–53

**Lewis** C. S. Lewis, *The Allegory of Love*, 1936

**LingI** *Linguistic Inquiry*

**Lord** A. B. Lord, *The Singer of Tales*, 2d ed., 2000

**Lote** G. Lote, *Histoire du vers française*, 9 v., 1940

**M&H** *Medievalia et Humanistica: Studies in Medieval and Renaissance Culture*

**Maas** P. Maas, *Greek Metre*, trans. H. Lloyd-Jones, 3d ed., 1962

**Manitius** M. Manitius, *Geschichte der lateinischen Literatur des Mittelalters*, 3 v., 1905–36

**Mazaleyrat** J. Mazaleyrat, *Éléments de métrique française*, 3d ed., 1981

**Meyer** W. Meyer, *Gesammelte Abhandlungen zur mittellateinischen Rhythmik*, 3 v., 1905–36

**MGG** *Die Musik in Geschichte und Gegenwart: Allegemeine Enzyklopaedia der Musik*, ed. F. Blume, 16 v., 1949–79

**MGH** *Monumenta germaniae historica*

**MHRA** Modern Humanities Research Association

**Michaelides** S. Michaelides, *The Music of Ancient Greece: An Encyclopaedia*, 1978

**MidwestQ** *Midwest Quarterly*

**Migne, PG** *Patrologiae cursus completus, series graeca*, ed. J. P. Migne, 161 v., 1857–66

**Migne, PL** *Patrologiae cursus completus, series latina*, ed. J. P. Migne, 221 v., 1844–64

**Miner et al.** E. Miner, H. Odagiri, and R. E. Morrell, *The Princeton Companion to Classical Japanese Literature*, 1986

**MLN** *Modern Language Notes*

**MLQ** *Modern Language Quarterly*

**MLQ (London)** *Modern Language Quarterly (London)*

**MLR** *Modern Language Review*

**Morier** H. Morier, *Dictionnaire de poétique et de rhétorique*, 5th ed., rev. and exp., 1998

**Morris-Jones** J. Morris-Jones, *Cerdd Dafod*, 1925, rpt. with index, 1980

**MP** *Modern Philology*

**Murphy** J. J. Murphy, *Rhetoric in the Middle Ages: A History of Rhetorical Theory from St. Augustine to the Renaissance*, 1974

**N&Q** *Notes & Queries*

**Navarro** T. Navarro, *Métrica española: Reseña histórica y descriptiva*, 6th ed., 1983

**NER/BLQ** *New England Review / Bread Loaf Quarterly*

**New CBEL** *New Cambridge Bibliography of English Literature*, ed. G. Watson and I. R. Willison, 5 v., 1969–77

**New Grove**  *New Grove Dictionary of Music and Musicians*, ed. S. Sadie, 20 v., 1980

**Nienhauser et al.**  W. H. Nienhauser, Jr., C. Hartman, Y. W. Ma, and S. H. West, *The Indiana Companion to Traditional Chinese Literature*, 1986

**NLH**  *New Literary History*

**NM**  *Neuphilologische Mitteilungen (Bulletin of the Modern Language Society)*

**Norberg**  D. Norberg, *Introduction a l'étude de la versification latine médiévale*, 1958

**Norden**  E. Norden, *Die antike Kunstprosa*, 9th ed., 2 v., 1983

**OED**  *Oxford English Dictionary*

**OL**  *Orbis Litterarum: International Review of Literary Studies*

**Olson**  C. Olson, "Projective Verse," *Collected Prose*, ed. D. Allen and B. Friedlander, 1997

**Omond**  T. S. Omond, *English Metrists*, 1921

**P&R**  *Philosophy and Rhetoric*

**Parry**  M. Parry, *The Making of Homeric Verse*, ed. A. Parry, 1971

**Parry, History**  T. Parry, *A History of Welsh Literature*, trans. H. I. Bell, 1955

**Patterson**  W. F. Patterson, *Three Centuries of French Poetic Theory: A Critical History of the Chief Arts of Poetry in France (1328–1630)*, 2 v., 1935

**Pauly-Wissowa**  *Paulys Realencyclopädie der classischen Alterumswissenschaft*, ed. A. Pauly, G. Wissowa, W. Kroll, and K. Mittelhaus, 24 v. (A–Q), 10 v. (R–Z, Series 2), and 15 v. (Supplements), 1894–1978

**PBA**  *Proceedings of the British Academy*

**Pearsall**  D. Pearsall, *Old English and Middle English Poetry*, 1977

**PMLA**  *Publications of the Modern Language Association of America*

**PoT**  *Poetics Today*

**PQ**  *Philological Quarterly*

**PsychologR**  *Psychological Review*

**Puttenham**  G. Puttenham, *The Arte of English Poesie*, ed. F. Whigham and W. A. Rebhorn, 2007

**QJS**  *Quarterly Journal of Speech*

**Raby, Christian**  F.J.E. Raby, *A History of Christian-Latin Poetry From the Beginnings to the Close of the Middle Ages*, 2d ed., 1953

**Raby, Secular**  F.J.E. Raby, *A History of Secular Latin Poetry in the Middle Ages*, 2d ed., 2 v., 1957

**Ransom**  *Selected Essays of John Crowe Ransom*, ed. T. D. Young and J. Hindle, 1984

**Reallexikon I**  *Reallexikon der deutschen Literaturgeschichte*, 1st ed., ed. P. Merker and W. Stammler, 4 v., 1925–31

**Reallexikon II**  *Reallexikon der deutschen Literaturgeschichte*, 2d ed., ed. W. Kohlschmidt and W. Mohr (v. 1–3), K. Kanzog and A. Masser (v. 4), 1958–84

**Reallexikon III**  *Reallexikon der deutschen Literaturwissenschaft*, 3d ed, ed. H. Fricke, K. Frubmüller, J.-D. Müller, and K. Weimar, 3 v., 1997–2003

**REL**  *Review of English Literature*

**RES**  *Review of English Studies*

**Richards**  I. A. Richards, *Principles of Literary Criticism*, 1925

**RLC**  *Revue de littérature compareé*

**RPh**  *Romance Philology*

**RQ**  *Renaissance Quarterly*

**RR**  *Romanic Review*

**SAC**  *Studies in the Age of Chaucer*

**Saintsbury, Prose**  G. Saintsbury, *A History of English Prose Rhythm*, 1912

**Saintsbury, Prosody**  G. Saintsbury, *A History of English Prosody, from the Twelfth Century to the Present Day*, 2d ed., 3 v., 1961

**Saisselin**  R. G. Saisselin, *The Rule of Reason and the Ruses of the Heart: A Philosophical Dictionary of Classical French Criticism, Critics, and Aesthetic Issues*, 1970

**Sayce**  O. Sayce, *The Medieval German Lyric, 1150–1300: The Development of Its Themes and Forms in Their European Context*, 1982

**Scherr**  B. P. Scherr, *Russian Poetry: Meter, Rhythm, and Rhyme*, 1986

**Schipper**  J. M. Schipper, *Englische Metrik*, 3 v., 1881–88

**Schipper, History**  J. M. Schipper, *A History of English Versification*, 1910

**Schmid and Stählin**  W. Schmid and O. Stählin, *Geschichte der griechischen Literatur*, 7 v., 1920–48

**Scott**  C. Scott, *French Verse-Art: A Study*, 1980

**Sebeok**  *Style in Language*, ed. T. Sebeok, 1960

**SEL**  *Studies in English Literature 1500–1900*

**ShQ**  *Shakespeare Quarterly*

**Sievers**  E. Sievers, *Altgermanische Metrik*, 1893

**SIR**  *Studies in Romanticism*

**Smith**  *Elizabethan Critical Essays*, ed. G. G. Smith, 2 v., 1904

**Snell**  B. Snell, *Griechesche Metrik*, 4th ed., 1982

**SP**  *Studies in Philology*

**Spongano**  R. Spongano, *Nozioni ed esempi di metric italiana*, 2d ed., 1974

**SR**  *Sewanee Review*

**Stephens**  *The Oxford Companion to the Literature of Wales*, ed. M. Stephens, 1986

**TAPA**  *Transactions of the American Philological Association*

**Tarlinskaja**  M. Tarlinskaja, *English Verse: Theory and History*, 1976

**Terras**  *Handbook of Russian Literature*, ed. V. Terras, 1985

**Thieme**  H. P. Thieme, *Essai sur l'histoire du vers française*, 1916

**Thompson**  J. Thompson, *The Founding of English Metre*, 2d ed., 1989

**Trypanis**  C. A. Trypanis, *Greek Poetry from Homer to Seferis*, 1981

**TPS**  *Transactions of the Philological Society*

**TSL**  *Tennessee Studies in Literature*

**TSLL**  *Texas Studies in Literature and Language*

**Vickers**  B. Vickers, *Classical Rhetoric in English Poetry*, 2d ed., 1989

**Vickers, Defence**  B. Vickers, *In Defence of Rhetoric*, 1988

**VP**  *Victorian Poetry*

**VQR**  *Virginia Quarterly Review*

**Weinberg**  B. Weinberg, *A History of Literary Criticism in the Italian Renaissance*, 2 v., 1961

**Wellek**  R. Wellek, *A History of Modern Criticism, 1750–1950*, 8 v., 1955–92

**Wellek and Warren**  R. Wellek and A. Warren, *Theory of Literature*, 3d ed., 1956

**Welsh**  A. Welsh, *Roots of Lyric*, 1978

**West**  M. L. West, *Greek Metre*, 1982

***WHB***  *Wiener Humanistische Blätter*

**Wilamowitz**  U. von Wilamowitz-Moellendorf, *Griechesche Verkunst*, 1921

**Wilkins**  E. H. Wilkins, *A History of Italian Literature*, rev. T. G. Bergin, 1974

**Williams and Ford**  J.E.C. Williams and P. K. Ford, *The Irish Literary Tradition*, 1992

**Wimsatt**  *Versification: Major Language Types*, ed. W. K. Wimsatt, 1972

**Wimsatt and Beardsley**  W. K. Wimsatt and M. C. Beardsley, "The Concept of Meter: An Exercise in Abstraction," *PMLA* 74 (1959); rpt. in *Hateful Contraries*, W. K. Wimsatt, 1965

**Wimsatt and Brooks**  W. K. Wimsatt and C. Brooks, *Literary Criticism: A Short History*, 1957

***YFS***  *Yale French Studies*

***YLS***  *Yearbook of Langland Studies*

***ZCP***  *Zeitschrift für celtische Philologie*

***ZDA***  *Zeitschrift für deutsches Altertum*

***ZFSL***  *Zeitschrift für französische Sprache und Literatur*

***ZRP***  *Zeitschrift für Romanische Philologie*

***ZVS***  *Zeitschrift für Vergleichende Sprachforschung*

# General Abbreviations

The abbreviations below are used throughout the volume to conserve space. General abbreviations may also show plural forms, e.g., "cs." for "centuries."

**Af.** African
**Af. Am.** African American
**Am.** American
**anthol.** anthology
**Ar.** Arabic
**Assoc.** Association

**b.** born
**bibl.** bibliography
**Brit.** British

**c./cs.** century
**ca.** *circa*, about
**cf.** *confer*, compare
**ch.** chapter
**cl.** classical
**contemp.** contemporary
**crit.** criticism

**d.** died
**devel./devels.** development
**dict.** dictionary
**diss.** dissertation

**ed./eds.** edition, editor, edited by
**e.g.** *exempla gratia*, for example
**Eng.** English
**esp.** especially
**et al.** *et alii*, and others
**Eur.** European

**ff.** following
**fl.** *floruit*, flourished
**Fr.** French

**Ger.** German
**Gr.** Greek

**Heb.** Hebrew
**hist./hists.** history

**IE** Indo-Euopean
**i.e.** *id est*, that is
**incl.** including
**intro./intros.** introduction
**Ir.** Irish
**It.** Italian

**jour./jours.** journal

**lang./langs.** language
**Lat.** Latin
**ling.** linguistics, linguistic
**lit./lits.** literature
**lit. crit.** literary criticism
**lit. hist.** literary history

**ME** Middle English
**med.** medieval
**MHG** Middle High German
**mod.** modern
**ms./mss.** manuscript

**NT** New Testament

**OE** Old English
**OF** Old French
**OHG** Old High German
**ON** Old Norse
**OT** Old Testament

**p./pp.** page
**pl.** plural
**Port.** Portuguese
**postmod.** postmodern
**premod.** premodern
**pseud.** pseudonym
**pub.** published

**r.** reigned
**Ren.** Renaissance
**rev.** revised
**Rev.** Review
**rhet./rhets.** rhetoric
**rpt.** reprinted
**Rus.** Russian

**sing.** singular
**Sp.** Spanish
**supp.** supplement(ed)

**temp.** temporary
**trad./trads.** tradition
**trans.** translation, translated

**v.** volume(s)

# Contributors

This list includes all contributors credited in this edition of the encyclopedia, including some whose articles from the previous edition have been updated by the editors or other contributors. Those with names preceded by a dagger (†) are deceased.

**Gémino H. Abad,** English (emeritus), University of the Philippines

**Hazard Adams,** English and Comparative Literature (emeritus), University of Washington

**†Percy G. Adams,** English, University of Tennessee

**Cécile Alduy,** French, Stanford University

**†Fernando Alegría,** Spanish and Portuguese, Stanford University

**Joseph Allen,** Asian Languages and Literatures, University of Minnesota

**Roger M. A. Allen,** Arabic Languages and Literatures (emeritus), University of Pennsylvania

**Robert Alter,** Hebrew and Comparative Literature, University of California, Berkeley

**Charles Altieri,** English, University of California, Berkeley

**Hélio J. S. Alves,** Portuguese and Comparative Literature, University of Evora

**Walter Andrews,** Ottoman and Turkish Literature, University of Washington

**†Robert P. apRoberts,** English, California State University, Northridge

**Francesco Marco Aresu,** Italian, Stanford University

**Samuel G. Armistead,** Spanish (emeritus), University of California, Davis

**†John Arthos,** English, University of Michigan

**Robert Ashmore,** East Asian Languages and Cultures, University of California, Berkeley

**Paul S. Atkins,** Asian Languages and Literature, University of Washington

**†Stuart Atkins,** German and Comparative Literature, University of California, Santa Barbara

**Derek Attridge,** English and Related Literature, University of York

**Harry Aveling,** Asian Studies, La Trobe University

**Jan Baetens,** Cultural Studies, University of Leuven

**Timothy Bahti,** German and Comparative Literature (emeritus), University of Michigan

**James O. Bailey,** Slavic Languages and Literature (emeritus), University of Wisconsin– Madison

**Peter S. Baker,** English, University of Virginia

**Henryk Baran,** Slavic Studies, University at Albany, State University of New York

**Alessandro Barchiesi,** Classics, Stanford University

**Vincent Barletta,** Iberian and Latin American Cultures, Stanford University

**Jeffrey Barnouw,** English (emeritus), University of Texas

**Henry J. Baron,** English, Calvin College

**Mark Barr,** English, St. Mary's University

**Shadi Bartsch,** Classics, University of Chicago

**Catherine Bates,** English and Comparative Literature, University of Warwick

**Guinn Batten,** English, Washington University in Saint Louis

**Gary Beckman,** Hittite and Mesopotamian Studies, University of Michigan

**†Ernst H. Behler,** Germanics and Comparative Literature, University of Washington

**Margaret H. Beissinger,** Slavic Languages and Literatures, Princeton University

**Esther G. Belin,** Writing, Fort Lewis College

**Alexandra G. Bennett,** English, Northern Illinois University

**Sandra L. Bermann,** Comparative Literature, Princeton University

**Charles Bernstein,** English, University of Pennsylvania

**Eleanor Berry,** independent scholar

**†Jess B. Bessinger,** English, New York University

**Krzysztof Biedrzycki,** Polish Literature, Jagiellonian University

**Stanley S. Bill,** Slavic Languages and Literatures, Northwestern University

**Lloyd Bishop,** French (emeritus), Virginia Polytechnic Institute and State University

**Jenny Björklund,** Center for Gender Research, Uppsala University

**Josiah Blackmore,** Spanish and Portuguese, University of Toronto

**Kirstie Blair,** English Literature, University of Glasgow

**C. D. Blanton,** English, University of California, Berkeley

**Mutlu Konuk Blasing,** English, Brown University

**†Morton W. Bloomfield,** English, Harvard University

**Frederick L. Blumberg,** Comparative Literature, Stanford University

**Lev Blumenfeld,** Linguistics, Carleton University

**Fredric Bogel,** English, Cornell University

**Willard Bohn,** Foreign Languages (emeritus), Illinois State University

**Roy C. Boland,** Spanish and Latin American Studies, University of Sydney

**Annika Bostelmann,** German, Institute of Rostock

**Enric Bou,** Linguistics and Comparative Cultures, Ca'Foscari University of Venice

**Betsy Bowden,** English, Rutgers University, Camden

**Claire Bowen,** English, Dickinson College

**Katherine Bowers,** Slavic Languages and Literatures, Northwestern University

**Matthieu Boyd,** Literature, Fairleigh Dickinson University

**Jeremy Braddock,** English, Cornell University

**Gordon Braden,** English, University of Virginia

**Anthony Bradley,** English (emeritus), University of Vermont

**Ross Brann,** Near Eastern Studies, Cornell University

**Laurence A. Breiner,** English, Boston University

**Karen Britland,** English, University of Wisconsin–Madison

Claudia Brodsky, Comparative Literature, Princeton University

Jacqueline Vaught Brogan, English, University of Notre Dame

†T.V.F. Brogan, independent scholar

Yigal Bronner, South Asian Languages and Civilizations, University of Chicago

Gordon Brotherston, Languages, Linguistics, and Cultures, University of Manchester

Kristina Vise Browder, English, Troy University

Catherine Brown, Spanish, University of Michigan

†Huntington Brown, English, University of Minnesota

Katherine A. Brown, French, Skidmore College

†Merle E. Brown, English, University of Iowa

†Juan Bruce-Novoa, Spanish and Portuguese, University of California, Irvine

Benjamin Bruch, Celtic Languages and Literature, Celtic Institute of North America

Matilda Tomaryn Bruckner, French, Boston College

Horst Brunner, German Philology, University of Wuerzburg

Gerald L. Bruns, English (emeritus), University of Notre Dame

Patrick Buckridge, Humanities, Griffith University

Sidney Burris, English, University of Arkansas

John Burt, English, Brandeis University

Stephen Burt, English, Harvard University

Christopher Bush, French and Comparative Literary Studies, Northwestern University

Michel Byrne, Celtic and Gaelic, University of Glasgow

Lorraine Byrne Bodley, Music, National University of Ireland, Maynooth

Thomas Cable, English (emeritus), University of Texas

Kolter M. Campbell, Slavic Languages and Literatures, Northwestern University

Marta Ortiz Canseco, Philology, University of Alcalá

David Caplan, English, Ohio Wesleyan University

Thomas Carper, English (emeritus), University of Southern Maine

Antonio Carreño, Hispanic Studies, Brown University

Meredith Walker Castile, English, Stanford University

Clare Cavanagh, Slavic Languages and Literatures, Northwestern University

Max Cavitch, English, University of Pennsylvania

Mary Ann Caws, Comparative Literature, English, and French, Graduate Center, City University of New York

Natalia Cecire, Fox Center for Humanistic Inquiry, Emory University

Seeta Chaganti, English, University of California, Davis

†Frank M. Chambers, French, University of Arizona

Jennifer Chang, English, University of Virginia

Kang-i-Sun Chang, East Asian Languages and Literatures, Yale University

Jack Chen, Asian Languages and Cultures, University of California, Los Angeles

Patrick Cheney, English and Comparative Literature, Pennsylvania State University

David H. Chisholm, German Studies (emeritus), University of Arizona

Elżbieta Chrzanowska-Kluczewska, English Philology, Jagiellonian University

Odile Cisneros, Spanish, Portuguese, and Latin American Studies, University of Alberta

Michael P. Clark, English, University of California, Irvine

†Dorothy Clotelle Clarke, Spanish and Portuguese, University of California, Berkeley

Albrecht Classen, German Studies, University of Arizona

Michelle Clayton, Comparative Literature, Spanish and Portuguese, University of California, Los Angeles

Katharine Cleland, English, Pennsylvania State University

James M. Cocola, English, Worcester Polytechnic Institute

Michael C. Cohen, English, University of California, Los Angeles

Ann Baynes Coiro, English, Rutgers University

A. Thomas Cole, English (emeritus), Yale University

Claire Colebrook, English, Pennsylvania State University

Stephen Collis, English, Simon Fraser University

Gregory G. Colomb, English, University of Virginia

David A. Colón, English, Texas Christian University

Anne E. Commons, East Asian Studies, University of Alberta

J. E. Congleton, Humanities and Sciences (emeritus), University of Findlay

Eleanor Cook, English (emerita), University of Toronto

†Robert Cook, English, University of Iceland

G. Burns Cooper, English, University of Alaska, Fairbanks

Rita Copeland, Classical Studies, English and Comparative Literature, University of Pennsylvania

Ian D. Copestake, British Culture, University of Bamberg

François Cornilliat, French, Rutgers University

†Procope S. Costas, Classical Studies, Brooklyn College, City University of New York

Bonnie Costello, English, Boston University

†Ronald S. Crane, English Language and Literature, University of Chicago

Johaina Crisostomo, independent scholar

Holly Crocker, English Language and Literature, University of South Carolina

Jennifer Croft, Comparative Literary Studies, Northwestern University

Joanna Crow, School of Modern Languages, Bristol University

Cheryl A. Crowley, Russian and East Asian Languages and Cultures, Emory University

Isagani R. Cruz, Literature and Philippine Languages (emeritus), De La Salle University

Jonathan Culler, English, Cornell University

Stephen Cushman, English, University of Virginia

Maria Damon, English, University of Minnesota

†Phillip Damon, English and Comparative Literature, University of California, Berkeley

Michael Dash, French, Social and Cultural Analysis, New York University

Ian Davidson, English and Comparative Literature, Northumbria University

Michael Davidson, English, University of California, San Diego

Kathleen Davis, English, University of Rhode Island

Dirk de Geest, Literary Theory, University of Leiden

Jonathan Decter, Sephardic Studies, Brandeis University

Andrew M. Devine, Classics, Stanford University

Jeroen Dewulf, German, University of California, Berkeley

Vinay Dharwadker, Languages and Cultures of Asia, University of Wisconsin–Madison

Thibaut d'Hubert, South Asian Languages and Civilizations, University of Chicago College

Joanne Diaz, English, Illinois Wesleyan University

Terence Diggory, English, Skidmore College

Connor Doak, Slavic Languages and Literatures, Northwestern University

Jeffrey Dolven, English, Princeton University

Daniel G. Donaghue, Old English Studies, Harvard University

Neil H. Donahue, German and Comparative Literature, Hofstra University

Christopher Donaldson, Comparative Literature, Stanford University

David F. Dorsey, independent scholar

Edward Doughtie, English (emeritus), Rice University

Johanna Drucker, Information Studies, University of California, Los Angeles

Andrew Dubois, English, University of Toronto

Heather Dubrow, English, Fordham University

Martin J. Duffell, Iberian and Latin American Studies, Queen Mary, University of London

Dianne Dugaw, English, University of Oregon

Francois Dumont, Literature, University of Laval

†Charles W. Dunn, Celtic Languages and Literatures (emeritus), Harvard University

Rachel Blau DuPlessis, English, Temple University

Sascha Ebeling, South Asian Languages and Civilizations, University of Chicago

Jonathan P. Eburne, Comparative Literature and English, Pennsylvania State University

Robert R. Edwards, English, Pennsylvania State University

Sveinn Yngvi Egilsson, Icelandic and Comparative Cultural Studies, University of Iceland

Robert G. Eisenhauer, independent scholar

Helen Regueiro Elam, English, University at Albany, State University of New York

Jonathan Elmer, English, Indiana University

†Gerald F. Else, Classical Studies, University of Michigan

Robert Elsie, independent scholar

Lori Emerson, English, University of Colorado

James Engell, English and Comparative Literature, Harvard University

†Alfred Garvin Engstrom, French, University of North Carolina, Chapel Hill

†Alan W. Entwistle, Hindi, University of Washington

†Alvin A. Eustis, French, University of California, Berkeley

David Evans, Modern Languages, University of St. Andrews

†Robert O. Evans, English and Comparative Literature (emeritus), University of New Mexico

Raphael Falco, English, University of Maryland, Baltimore County

Walter Farber, Near Eastern Languages and Civilizations, University of Chicago

Ibrahim Fathy, independent scholar

Harris Feinsod, English, Northwestern University

Frances Ferguson, English, Johns Hopkins University

Margaret W. Ferguson, English, University of California, Davis

Patrick ffrench, French, King's College London

Annie Finch, Creative Writing, University of Southern Maine

Jordan Finkin, Oriental Studies (Hebrew), University of Oxford

†Harold Fisch, English, Bar-Ilan University

†Solomon Fishman, English, University of California, Davis

†Wolfgang Bernhard Fleischman, Comparative Literature, Montclair State College

†Robert Harter Fogle, English, University of North Carolina, Chapel Hill

†Stephen F. Fogle, English, Adelphi Suffolk College

†John Miles Foley, Classical Studies, University of Missouri

Stephen Foley, English and Comparative Literature, Brown University

Patrick K. Ford, Celtic Languages and Literatures, Harvard University

Benjamin Foster, Near Eastern Languages and Civilizations, Yale University

Alastair Fowler, Rhetoric and English Literature (emeritus), University of Edinburgh

Elizabeth Fowler, English, University of Virginia

Nicholas Frankel, English, Virginia Commonwealth University

Lisa Freinkel, Comparative Literature, University of Oregon

Amanda L. French, Center for History and New Media, George Mason University

†Bernard J. Fridsma, Germanic Languages (emeritus), Calvin College

Debra Fried, English, Cornell University

Nila Friedberg, Russian, Portland State University

†Albert B. Friedman, English, Claremont Graduate University

Norman Friedman, English (emeritus), Queens College, City University of New York

Dmitry Frolov, Arabic Philology, Moscow State University

Paul H. Fry, English, Yale University

†Joseph G. Fucilla, Romance Languages, Northwestern University

Robert Dennis Fulk, English, Indiana University

Graham Furniss, Languages and Cultures of Africa, University of London

Thomas Furniss, English, University of Strathclyde

René Galand, French (emeritus), Wellesley College

Miguel Ángel Garrido Gallardo, Literary Theory, Spanish National Research Council, Madrid

Marisa Galvez, French, Stanford University

Linda Garber, Women's and Gender Studies, Santa Clara University

Ariadna García-Bryce, Spanish, Reed College

Leonardo García-Pabón, Romance Languages, University of Oregon

Thomas Gardner, English, Virginia Polytechnic Institute

Boris Gasparov, Slavic Languages and Literature, Columbia University

Mary Malcolm Gaylord, Romance Languages and Literatures, Harvard University

Sophie Gee, English, Princeton University

Stephen A. Geller, Bible, Jewish Theological Seminary

Natalie Gerber, English, State University of New York, Fredonia

E. Michael Gerli, Spanish, University of Virginia

Edwin Gerow, Religion and Humanities (emeritus), Reed College

†Robert J. Getty, Classics, University of North Carolina

Denise Gigante, English, Stanford University

Brian Glavey, English Language and Literature, University of South Carolina

Leon Golden, Classics (emeritus), Florida State University

Lorrie Goldensohn, independent scholar

Alan Golding, English, University of Louisville

Robert P. Goldman, South and Southeast Asian Studies, University of California, Berkeley

†Ulrich K. Goldsmith, German, University of Colorado

David Goldstein, English, York University

Kevis Goodman, English, University of California, Berkeley

Sverker Göransson, Literature, University of Gothenburg

†Lewis H. Gordon, Italian and French, Brown University

Rüdiger Görner, Germanic Studies, Queen Mary, University of London

Stathis Gourgouris, Classics, Columbia University

George G. Grabowicz, Ukranian Literature, Harvard University

Kenneth J. E. Graham, English Language and Literature, University of Waterloo

Phyllis Granoff, Religious Studies, Yale University

Erik Gray, English, Columbia University

Stephen Gray, independent scholar

Roland Greene, Comparative Literature, Stanford University

Edward L. Greenstein, Bible, Bar-Ilan University

Tobias B. Gregory, English, Catholic University of America

†Michelle Grimaud, French, Wellesley College

Anne Marie Guglielmo, Comparative Literature, Stanford University

Hans Ulrich Gumbrecht, Comparative Literature, Stanford University

Kathryn Gutzwiller, Classics, University of Cincinnati

Janet Hadda, English (emerita), University of California, Los Angeles

†Vernon Hall, Comparative Literature, University of Wisconsin–Madison

Charles Hallisey, Buddhist Literatures, Harvard Divinity School

Stephen Halliwell, Greek, University of St. Andrews

James W. Halporn, Classical Studies, Indiana University

†Albert W. Halsall, French, Carleton University

Russell G. Hamilton, Portuguese, Brazilian, and Lusophone African Literatures, Vanderbilt University

Hannibal Hamlin, English, Ohio State University

William L. Hanaway, Near Eastern Languages and Civilizations (emeritus), University of Pennsylvania

Kristin Hanson, English, Universitiy of California, Berkeley

†O. B. Hardison, English, Georgetown University

David Hargreaves, Linguistics, Western Oregon University

William E. Harkins, Slavic Languages, Columbia University

William Harmon, English and Comparative Literature (emeritus), University of North Carolina, Chapel Hill

Joseph Harris, English, Harvard University

Robert L. Harrison, independent scholar

Henry Hart, English, College of William and Mary

Kevin Hart, Religious Studies, University of Virginia

Lauran Hartley, Tibetan Studies Librarian, Columbia University

Charles O. Hartman, English, Connecticut College

Ruth Harvey, Modern Languages, Literatures, and Cultures, Royal Holloway, University of London

Ernst Haüblein, independent scholar

Edward R. Haymes, German, Cleveland State University

Kenneth Haynes, Comparative Literature and Classics, Brown University

Gregory Hays, Classics, University of Virginia

Wade Heaton, English, Southeastern Louisiana University

Ulf Hedetoft, Nationality and Migration Studies, University of Copenhagen

Wolfhart Heinrichs, Arabic, Harvard University

Ursula K. Heise, English, Stanford University

Gustav Heldt, East Asian Languages, Literatures, and Cultures, University of Virginia

James S. Helgeson, French and Francophone Studies, University of Nottingham

Benjamin A. Heller, Spanish, University of Notre Dame

Sarah-Grace Heller, French, Ohio State University

Elizabeth K. Helsinger, Art History, University of Chicago

Omaar Hena, English, Wake Forest University

†Stephen E. Henderson, Afro-American Studies and English, Howard University

†C. John Herington, Classics, Yale University

Brenda Hillman, English, Saint Mary's College of California

Kenneth Hiltner, English, University of California, Santa Barbara

Daniel Hoffman, English (emeritus), University of Pennsylvania

Tyler Hoffman, English, Rutgers University, Camden

Norman N. Holland, English (emeritus), University of Florida

John Holmes, English Language and Literature, University of Reading

†Urban T. Holmes, Romance Languages, University of North Carolina, Chapel Hill

Bruce Holsinger, English, University of Virginia

Marianne Hopman, Classics, Northwestern University

†Roger A. Hornsby, Classics, University of Iowa

H. Mack Horton, East Asian Languages and Cultures, University of California, Berkeley

Vittorio Hösle, German and Russian Languages and Literatures, University of Notre Dame

Peter Howarth, School of English and Drama, Queen Mary, University of London

Laura L. Howes, English, University of Tennessee, Knoxville

Thomas John Hudak, Linguistics, Arizona State University

Robert Huey, Japanese Literature, University of Hawai'i, Manoa

Shaun F. D. Hughes, Comparative Literature, Purdue University

Kathryn Hume, Comparative Literature, Stanford University

Jerry Hunter, Welsh, Bangor University

Walter Hunter, English, University of Virginia

Linda Hutcheon, English and Comparative Literature, University of Toronto

Wilt L. Idema, Chinese Literature, Harvard University

Luis Miguel Isava, Literatura, Universidad Simón Bolívar

Fernando Iturburu, Spanish, State University of New York, Plattsburgh

Linda Ivanits, Russian and Comparative Literature, Pennsylvania State University

†Ivar Ivask, Modern Languages, University of Oklahoma

Oren Izenberg, English, University of Illinois, Chicago

Virginia Jackson, English, University of California, Irvine

Alessandro Michelangelo Jaker, Linguistics, Stanford University

Alison James, Romance Languages and Literatures, University of Chicago

Gerald J. Janecek, Russian and Eastern Studies (emeritus), University of Kentucky

Hanna Janiszewska, English, Stanford University

Nicholas Jenkins, English, Stanford University

D. B. S. Jeyaraj, independent scholar

Ramya Chamalie Jirasinghe, independent scholar

Christopher Johnson, Comparative Literature, Harvard University

Eleanor Johnson, English and Comparative Literature, Columbia University

Jeffrey Johnson, English Language and Literature, Daito Bunka University

Eileen Tess Johnston, English, United States Naval Academy

Aled Llion Jones, Department of Celtic Languages and Literatures, Harvard University

†Charles W. Jones, English, University of California, Berkeley

Meta DuEwa Jones, English, University of Texas

William R. Jones, English and Philosophy, Murray State University

Elise Bickford Jorgens, English (emerita), College of Charleston

Walter Jost, English, University of Virginia

Cathy L. Jrade, Spanish and Portuguese, Vanderbilt University

Gregory Jusdanis, Greek and Latin, Ohio State University

Steven Justice, English, University of California, Berkeley

Ananya Jahanara Kabir, Humanities, University of Leeds

Andrew Kahn, Russian Literature, University of Oxford

†Sholom J. Kahn, English, Hebrew University of Jerusalem

Rayna Kalas, English, Cornell University

Julie Kane, English, Northwestern State University of Louisiana

Paul Kane, English, Vassar College

Ruth Kaplan, English, Quinnipiac University

Matthew T. Kapstein, Philosophy of Religions and History of Religions, University of Chicago Divinity School

Robert Kaufman, Comparative Literature, University of California, Berkeley

Nanor Kebranian, Armenian Literature, Columbia University

Edmund Keeley, English (emeritus), Princeton University

Eric Keenaghan, English, University at Albany, State University of New York

Jennifer Keith, English, University of North Carolina, Greensboro

Lynn Keller, English, University of Wisconsin–Madison

William J. Kennedy, Comparative Literature, Cornell University

Dov-Ber Kerler, Jewish Studies, Indiana University

Martin Kern, East Asian Studies, Princeton University

Sachin C. Ketkar, English, Maharaja Sayajrao University of Baroda

Arthur F. Kinney, English, University of Massachusetts, Amherst

Clare R. Kinney, English, University of Virginia

Gwen Kirkpatrick, Spanish and Portuguese, Georgetown University

Peter Kirkpatrick, English, University of Sydney

Matthew G. Kirschenbaum, English, University of Maryland

Dodona Kiziria, Slavic Languages and Literatures (emeritus), Indiana University

Conor Klamann, Slavic Languages and Literatures, Northwestern University

Christopher Kleinhenz, French and Italian, University of Wisconsin–Madison

Peter Kline, English, James Madison University

David Knechtges, Asian Languages and Literature, University of Washington

Nisha Kommattam, South Asian Languages and Civilizations, University of Chicago

Alireza Korangy Isfahani, Department of Middle Eastern and South Asian Languages and Cultures, University of Virginia

David Kovacs, Classics, University of Virginia

Christina Kramer, Slavic Languages and Literatures, University of Toronto

Christopher Krentz, English, University of Virginia

†Murray Krieger, English, University of California, Irvine

Theresa Krier, English, Macalester College

Efraín Kristal, Comparative Literature, University of California, Los Angeles

Jelle Krol, Tresoar Friesland Historical and Literary Center

Dean Krouk, Languages and Literatures, St. Olaf College

Paul K. Kugler, Inter-regional Society of Jungian Analysis

Jill Kuhnheim, Spanish and Portuguese, University of Kansas

Aaron Kunin, English, Pomona College

Christoph Küper, English Linguistics, University of Vechta

Leslie Kurke, Classics and Comparative Literature, University of California, Berkeley

William Kuskin, English, University of Colorado

David Kutzko, Classics, Western Michigan University

Catherine Labio, English, University of Colorado

Dov Landau, Hebrew and Comparative Literature, Bar-Ilan University

George Lang, French, University of Ottawa

Susan S. Lanser, English, Brandeis University

Ilse Laude-Cirtautas, Russian, East European and Central Asian Studies, University of Washington

Marc D. Lauxtermann, Byzantine and Modern Greek Language and Literature, University of Oxford

Sarah Lawall, Comparative Literature (emerita), University of Massachusetts

Joseph Lease, Writing and Literature, California College of the Arts

John Leavitt, Anthropology, University of Montreal

Meredith Lee, German (emerita), University of California, Irvine

Young-Jun Lee, Korean Literature, Kyung Hee University

Catherine Léglu, Medieval Studies, University of Reading

†Ilse Lehiste, Linguistics, Ohio State University

Vincent B. Leitch, English, University of Oklahoma

Keith D. Leonard, Literature, American University

Laurence D. Lerner, English, Vanderbilt University

Rolf Lessenich, English, American, and Celtic Studies (emeritus), University of Bonn

Gayle Levy, French, University of Missouri, Kansas City

Jennifer Lewin, Writing, Boston University

Franklin D. Lewis, Persian Language and Literature, University of Chicago

Rhiannon Lewis, English, Stanford University

Tracy K. Lewis, Portuguese, State University of New York, Oswego

Joel Lidov, Classics, Graduate Center, City University of New York

Eva Lilja, Comparative Literature, University of Gothenburg

Ian K. Lilly, European Languages and Literatures, University of Auckland

John Lindow, Scandinavian, University of California, Berkeley

Ursula Lindqvist, Scandinavian, Harvard University

Lawrence Lipking, English, Northwestern University

Rene Felix Lissens, Dutch and German Literature (emeritus), St. Ignatius University

Daiva Litvinskaitė, Slavic and Baltic Languages and Literatures, University of Illinois, Chicago

Ernesto Livon-Grosman, Hispanic Studies, Boston College

Ernesto Livorni, Comparative Literature, University of Wisconsin–Madison

†D. Myrddin Lloyd, National Library of Scotland

Jonathan Loesberg, Literature, American University

Yelena Lorman, Comparative Literary Studies, Northwestern University

Paul Losensky, Comparative Literature, Indiana University

Tina Lu, East Asian Languages and Literatures, Yale University

†Katharine Luomala, Anthropology, University of Hawai'i

David B. Lurie, Japanese History and Literature, Columbia University

Sverre Lyngstad, English (emeritus), New Jersey Institute of Technology

John MacInnes, School of Scottish Studies (emeritus), University of Edinburgh

Armando Maggi, Italian Literature, University of Chicago

John L. Mahoney, English (emeritus), Boston College

Lawrence Manley, English, Yale University

Jenny C. Mann, English, Cornell University

Joshua K. Mann, English, Stanford University

Michael L. Manson, Literature, American University

Abednego M. Maphumulo, Modern and Oral Literature, University of Kwa-Zulu

Kathleen N. March, Spanish, University of Maine

Samuel Mareel, Dutch Literature, Ghent University

David Marno, English, University of California, Berkeley

John Henry Marshall, Romance Philology (emeritus), University of London

Keavy Martin, English, University of Alberta

Meredith Martin, English, Princeton University

†Wallace Martin, English, University of Toledo

Timothy J. Materer, English, University of Missouri

Timothy Mathews, French and Comparative Criticism, University College London

Jonathan Mayhew, Spanish and Portuguese, University of Kansas

Krystyna Mazur, American Studies, University of Warsaw

Nicholas F. Mazza, Social Work, Florida State University

Pamela McCallum, English, University of Calgary

David R. McCann, Korean Literature, Harvard University

Russ McDonald, English and Comparative Literature, Goldsmiths, University of London

Kevin McFadden, Virginia Foundation for the Humanities

Jerome McGann, English, University of Virginia

Meredith McGill, English, Rutgers University

Robin McGrath, independent scholar

Arvind Krishna Mehrotra, independent scholar

Julie S. Meisami, Persian, University of Oxford

Louis Menand, English, Harvard University

Edward Mendelson, English and Comparative Literature, Columbia University

†Lore Metzger, English, Emory University

Talya Meyers, English, Stanford University

Leah Middlebrook, Comparative Literature and Spanish, University of Oregon

Peter Middleton, English, University of Southampton

†Rigo Mignani, Romance Languages, Binghamton University, State University of New York

Laurent Mignon, Turkish, University of Oxford

Cristianne Miller, English, University at Buffalo, State University of New York

John F. Miller, Classics, University of Virginia

Tyrus Miller, Literature, University of California, Santa Cruz

†Earl Miner, English and Comparative Literature, Princeton University

W. J. T. Mitchell, English and Art History, University of Chicago

Ivan Mladenov, Literature, Bulgarian Academy of Sciences

K. Silem Mohammad, English and Writing, Southern Oregon University

Reidulf K. Molvaer, independent scholar

Steven Monte, English, College of Staten Island, City University of New York

Robert L. Montgomery, English (emeritus), University of California, Irvine

Colin H. Moore, Comparative Literature, Stanford University

Anna H. More, Spanish and Portuguese, University of California, Los Angeles

Adelaide Morris, English, University of Iowa

Saundra Morris, English, Bucknell University

Gary Saul Morson, Slavic Languages and Literatures, Northwestern University

Leith Morton, English, Tokyo Institute of Technology

Ian Frederick Moulton, Interdisciplinary Humanities and Communication, Arizona State University

Paula M. L. Moya, English, Stanford University

Jan-Dirk Müller, German Philology, Ludwig Maximilians University of Munich

H. Adlai Murdoch, French, University of Illinois, Urbana-Champaign

Walton Muyumba, English, University of North Texas

C. M. Naim, South Asian Languages and Civilizations (emeritus), University of Chicago

James Naughton, Czech and Slovak, University of Oxford

Sharon Diane Nell, Modern Languages and Literatures, Loyola University Maryland

Barbara Barney Nelson, Languages and Literature, Sul Ross State University

Virgil P. Nemoianu, English and Philosophy, Catholic University of America

Carole E. Newlands, Classics, University of Colorado

J. K. Newman, Classics (emeritus), University of Illinois

Peter Nicholls, English, New York University

B. Ashton Nichols, English, Dickinson College

Jan Krogh Nielsen, Danish, University of Washington

James Nohrnberg, English, University of Virginia

Carrie Noland, French and Italian, University of California, Irvine

Barnaby Norman, French, King's College London

Michael North, English, University of California, Los Angeles

Ranjini Obeyesekere, Anthropology (emerita), Princeton University

†Michael Patrick O'Connor, Semitics, Catholic University of America

Mari Jose Olaziregi, Basque Studies, University of the Basque Country

Jeff Opland, Languages and Cultures of Africa, University of London

†Ants Oras, English, University of Florida

Martin Orwin, Somali and Amharic School of Oriental and African Studies, University of London

†Richard H. Osberg, English, Santa Clara University

Andrew L. Osborn, English, University of Dallas

Iztok Osojnik, independent scholar

Stephen Owen, Comparative Literature, Harvard University

William D. Paden, French (emeritus), Northwestern University

Kirsten Blythe Painter, independent scholar

Lucy B. Palache, independent scholar

Anne Paolucci, Council on National Literature

†Henry Paolucci, Government and Politics (emeritus), St. John's University

†Douglass S. Parker, Classics, University of Texas, Austin

Walter Ward Parks, independent scholar

James Parsons, Music, Missouri State University

Deven M. Patel, South Asia Studies, University of Pennsylvania

Dipti R. Pattanaik, English, Ravenshaw University

Mark Payne, Classics, University of Chicago

Victoria Pedrick, Classics, Georgetown University

Stephen Penn, English, University of Stirling

Jeffrey M. Perl, Humanities, Bar-Ilan University

Marjorie Perloff, English (emerita), Stanford University

†Laurence Perrine, English, Southern Methodist University

Charles A. Perrone, Portuguese and Luso-Brazilian Culture and Literatures, University of Florida

Curtis Perry, English, University of Illinois, Chicago

†Erskine A. Peters, English, University of Notre Dame

Guillaume Peureux, French, University of California, Davis

Ineke Phaf-Rheinberger, African Literature and Culture, Humboldt University, Berlin

Chantal Phan, French, University of British Columbia

Allen W. Phillips, Spanish (emeritus), University of California, Santa Barbara

Natalie Phillips, English, Stanford University

Noam Pines, Comparative Literature, Stanford University

†Arshi Pipa, Italian and Albanian, University of Minnesota

William Bowman Piper, English (emeritus), Rice University

Elizabeth W. Poe, French, Tulane University

Jean-Jacques Poucel, French, Southern Connecticut State University

†Alex Preminger, independent scholar

Jenifer Presto, Comparative Literature and Russian, University of Oregon

Yopie Prins, English, University of Michigan

Joseph Pucci, Classics and Comparative Literature, Brown University

Marc Quaghebeur, Archives and Museum of Literature, Brussels

William H. Race, Classics, University of North Carolina, Chapel Hill

Burton Raffel, English (emeritus), University of Louisiana, Lafayette

Jahan Ramazani, English, University of Virginia

Esperanza Ramirez-Christensen, Japanese Literature, University of Michigan

Virginia Ramos, Comparative Literature, Stanford University

Arnold Rampersad, English (emeritus), Stanford University

Velcheru Narayana Rao, Languages and Cultures of Asia (emeritus), University of Wisconsin–Madison

Suresh Raval, English, University of Arizona

Mohit K. Ray, English (emeritus), Bardwan University

Brian M. Reed, English, University of Washington

†Erica Reiner, Eastern Languages, University of Chicago

Timothy J. Reiss, Comparative Literature (emeritus), New York University

Elizabeth Renker, English, Ohio State University

Eric J. Rettberg, English Language and Literature, University of Virginia

Alena Rettová, Swahili Literature and Culture, School of Oriental and African Studies, University of London

Maria G. Rewakowicz, Slavic Languages and Literatures, University of Washington

Eliza Richards, English and Comparative Literature, University of North Carolina, Chapel Hill

Alan Richardson, English, Boston College

Hallie Smith Richmond, English, University of Virginia

Francois Rigolot, French and Italian, Princeton University

Tulku Thondup Rinpoche, Buddhayana Foundation

Elias L. Rivers, Spanish, Stony Brook University

Hugh Roberts, English, University of California, Irvine

Françoise Robin, independent scholar

Jenefer Robinson, Philosophy, University of Cincinnati

Peter Robinson, English Language and Literature, University of Reading

Emily Rohrbach, English, Northwestern University

Philip Rollinson, English, University of South Carolina

Armando Romero, Romance Languages and Literatures, University of Cincinnati

Susan Rosenbaum, English, University of Georgia

Jason Rosenblatt, English, Georgetown University

Patricia A. Rosenmeyer, Classics, University of Wisconsin–Madison

Sven H. Rossel, Comparative Literature, University of Washington

David J. Rothman, Creative Writing, Western State College of Colorado

Phillip Rothwell, Spanish and Portuguese, Rutgers University

Paul Rouzer, Asian Languages and Literatures, University of Minnesota

Christopher Rovee, English, Stanford University

†Beryl Rowland, English, University of Victoria

David Lee Rubin, French (emeritus), University of Virginia

Charles Russell, American Studies, Rutgers University, Newark

Elizabeth Sagaser, English, Colby College

Ramon Saldivar, English, Stanford University

David Salter, English Literature, University of Edinburgh

Graham Sanders, Classical Chinese Literature, University of Toronto

Stephanie Sandler, Slavic Languages and Literatures, Harvard University

Rosa Sarabia, Spanish and Portuguese, University of Toronto

Edith Sarra, East Asian Languages and Cultures, Indiana University

Haun Saussy, Comparative Literature, University of Chicago

Olive L. Sayce, Modern Languages, University of Oxford

Jennifer Scappettone, English Language and Literature, University of Chicago

Raymond P. Scheindlin, Medieval Hebrew Literature, Jewish Theological Seminary

†Bernard N. Schilling, English and Comparative Literature, University of Rochester

Stephanie Schmidt, Iberian and Latin American Cultures, Stanford University

Michael Schoenfeldt, English, University of Michigan

Richard Scholar, Modern Languages, University of Oxford

Stephen Schryer, English, University of New Brunswick

Russell G. Schuh, Linguistics, University of California, Los Angeles

Joshua Scodel, English and Comparative Literature, University of Chicago

Clive Scott, European Literature (emeritus), University of East Anglia

Matthew Scott, English Language and Literature, University of Reading

Andrew Seal, American Studies, Yale University

Jacobo Sefami, Spanish and Portuguese, University of California, Irvine

†A. Lytton Sells, French and Italian, Indiana University

Alexander Sens, Classics, Georgetown University

Shafiq Shamel, English, Stanford University

†Marianne Shapiro, Comparative Literature, Brown University

Robert B. Shaw, English, Mount Holyoke College

Vered Karti Shemtov, Hebrew Language and Literature, Stanford University

Charles P. Shepherdson, English, University at Albany, State University of New York

Anna Shields, Chinese Literature, University of Maryland, Baltimore County

Rimvydas Silbajoris, Slavic (emeritus), Ohio State University

Juris Silenieks, French (emeritus), Carnegie Mellon University

†Isidore Silver, Humanities, Washington University in Saint Louis

†Joseph H. Silverman, Spanish, University of California, Santa Cruz

Kirsti K. Simonsuuri, Comparative Literature, University of Helsinki

James Simpson, French, University of Glasgow

Amardeep Singh, English, Lehigh University

Alexandra Slessarev, English, Stanford University

Thomas O. Sloane, Rhetoric (emeritus), University of California, Berkeley

Edgar Slotkin, English and Comparative Literature, University of Cincinnati

James Smethurst, Afro-American Studies, University of Massachusetts, Amherst

Guntis Šmidchens, Scandinavian Studies, University of Washington

†A. J. M. Smith, English, Michigan State University

Barbara Herrnstein Smith, Comparative and English Literature, Duke University and Brown University

Ivo Smits, Area Studies (Japan), Leiden University

Rupert Snell, Asian Studies, University of Texas, Austin

Angela Sorby, English, Marquette University

Tamar Sovran, Hebrew Language, Tel Aviv University

Lisa Russ Spaar, English, University of Virginia

Ezra Spicehandler, Hebrew Literature (emeritus), Hebrew Union College

Willard Spiegelman, English, Southern Methodist University

G. Gabrielle Starr, English, New York University

Timothy Steele, English, California State University, Los Angeles

Peter Steiner, Slavic Languages and Literatures, University of Pennsylvania

†Martin Steinmann, English, University of Illinois, Chicago

Laurence D. Stephens, Classics, University of North Carolina, Chapel Hill

Malynne Sternstein, Slavic Languages and Literatures, University of Chicago

Robert S. Stilling, English, University of Virginia

Richard P. Sugg, English, Florida International University

Robert Sullivan, English, University of Hawai'i

Luke Sunderland, French, University of Cambridge

Tae-kyung T. E. Sung, English, University of California, Irvine

†Roy Arthur Swanson, Classics, University of Wisconsin

Jeffrey S. Sychterz, English, Fayetteville State University

Meredith Ramirez Talusan, Comparative Literature, Cornell University

G. Thomas Tanselle, English and Comparative Literature (emeritus), Columbia University

Bronwen Tate, Comparative Literature, Stanford University

Miles Taylor, English, Le Moyne College

Frances Teague, English, University of Georgia

Gordon Teskey, English and American Literature, Harvard University

†Robert Donald Thornton, English, State University of New York, New Paltz

Galin Tihanov, Comparative Literature, Queen Mary, University of London

Francisco Tomsich, independent scholar

Humphrey Tonkin, Humanities (emeritus), University of Hartford

Chandrakant Topiwala, independent scholar

Steven C. Tracy, Afro-American Studies, University of Massachusetts, Amherst

Wesley Trimpi, English (emeritus), Stanford University

Reuven Tsur, Hebrew Literature, Tel Aviv University

Gary Tubb, South Asian Languages and Civilizations, University of Chicago

Herbert F. Tucker, English, University of Virginia

Leslie Ullman, Creative Writing (emerita), University of Texas, El Paso

Michael Ursell, Literature, University of California, Santa Cruz

Quang Phu Van, Vietnamese, Yale University

W. J. van Bekkum, Semitic Languages and Cultures, University of Groningen

John Van Sickle, Classics, Brooklyn College, City University of New York

Anton Vander Zee, English, Stanford University

Valeria Varga, Central Eurasian Studies, Indiana University

Daniel Veraldi, independent scholar

Aida Vidan, Slavic Languages and Literatures, Harvard University

Robert Vilain, German, University of Bristol

Louise Viljoen, Afrikaans and Dutch, University of Stellensbosch

Robert von Hallberg, English and Comparative Literature, University of Chicago

Michael Wachtel, Slavic Languages and Literatures, Princeton University

David A. Wacks, Spanish, University of Oregon

Mara R. Wade, Germanic Languages and Literatures, University of Illinois, Urbana-Champaign

Amanda Walling, English, University of Hartford

Christopher Warley, English, University of Toronto

†Frank J. Warnke, Comparative Literature, University of Georgia

James Perrin Warren, English, Washington and Lee University

William Waters, Modern Languages and Comparative Literature, Boston University

Amanda Watson, Research and Instruction Librarian, Connecticut College

Roderick Watson, English (emeritus), University of Stirling

Jessica Weare, English, Stanford University

Ruth Helen Webb, History, Classics, and Archaeology, Birkbeck College, University of London

Anthony K. Webster, Anthropology, Southern Illinois University

†Uriel Weinrich, Yiddish, Columbia University

Madeline Weinstein, English, Harvard University

†Edward R. Weismiller, English, George Washington University

Philip Weller, Music, University of Nottingham

Colin Wells, English, St. Olaf College

Andrew Welsh, English, Rutgers University

William Wenthe, English, Texas Tech University

Winthrop Wetherbee, Humanities (emeritus), Cornell University

†Rachel Wetzsteon, English, William Paterson University

Bridget Whearty, English, Stanford University

Philip White, English, Centre College

Steven F. White, Spanish and Portuguese, St. Lawrence University

Simon Wickham-Smith, Russian, East European, and Central Asian Studies, University of Washington

†John Ellis Caerwyn Williams, Welsh and Celtic University, College of Wales

Rhian Williams, English and Scottish Language and Literature, University of Glasgow

James I. Wimsatt, English (emeritus), University of Texas, Austin

Michael Winkler, German Studies (emeritus), Rice University

James A. Winn, English, Boston University

Rosemary (Gates) Winslow, English, Catholic University of America

Steven Winspur, French and Italian, University of Wisconsin–Madison

†Tibor Wlassics, Italian, University of Virginia

Susan J. Wolfson, English, Princeton University

Allen G. Wood, French and Comparative Literature, Purdue University

Dafydd Wood, Comparative Literature, University of Texas

James Robert Wood, English, Stanford University

Malcolm Woodland, English, University of Toronto

W. B. Worthen, Theatre, Barnard College

George T. Wright, English (emeritus), University of Minnesota

Teri Shaffer Yamada, Asian Studies, California State University, Long Beach

Michelle Yeh, Chinese, University of California, Davis

Timothy Yu, English, University of Toronto

†Lawrence J. Zillman, English, University of Washington

Marc Zimmerman, Modern and Classical Languages, University of Houston

Eliza Zingesser, French, Princeton University

Robert Zydenbos, Institute of Indiology, Ludwig Maximilian University of Munich

# The Princeton Encyclopedia of Poetry and Poetics

**ABECEDARIUS,** abecedarian (med. Lat. term for an ABC primer). An alphabetic *acrostic, a poem in which each line or stanza begins with a successive letter of the alphabet. The abecedarius was often a spiritual or meditative device in the ancient world, used for prayers, hymns, and prophecies, but it also has an inveterate role as a tool for teaching children language. In divine poetry, not only the word but even letters and sounds, given pattern, bear mystical significance and incantatory power—as do numbers (see NUMEROLOGY). The abecedarius, only one of several such forms, has had a special appeal as a literalization of the alpha-omega trope.

The earliest attested examples are Semitic, and abecedarii held an esp. important place in Heb. religious poetry, to judge from the dozen-odd examples in the OT. The best known of these is Psalm 119, which is made of 22 octave stanzas, one for each letter of the Heb. alphabet, all lines of each octave beginning with the same letter. The more common stanzaic type, however, is that used by Chaucer for his "ABC," where only the first line of the stanza bears the letter (cf. the ornate initials of illuminated mss.). Psalms 111–12 represent the astrophic type, wherein the initials of each successive line form the alphabet. In the comparable Japanese form, *Iroha mojigusari,* the first line must begin with the first and end with the second character of the alphabet, the second with the second and third, and so on. A number of abecedarii are extant in cl. and Alexandrian Gr., but they were also popular in Byzantine Gr. and are copious in med. Lat.: St. Augustine's well-known abecedarian psalm against the Donatists (Migne, *PL* 43.23 ff.) is the earliest known example of med. rhythmical verse.

As a mod. instructive device for children, the abecedarius has seen many familiar forms. In Eng., the best-known abecedarius is the song "'A'—You're Adorable," by Buddy Kaye, Fred Wise, and Sidney Lippman (1948).

■ K. Krumbacher, *Geschichte der byzantinischen litteratur,* 2d ed. (1897); C. Daux, *Le Chant abécédaire de St. Augustin* (1905); H. Leclercq, "Abécédaire," *Dictionnaire d'archéologie chrétienne,* ed. F. Cabrol (1907); Meyer, v. 2, ch. 6; F. Dornseiff, *Das Alphabet in Mystik und Magie,* 2d ed. (1925), sect. 14; R. Marcus, "Alphabetic Acrostics in the Hellenistic and Roman Periods," *Journal of Near Eastern Studies* 6 (1947); Raby, *Secular.*
                                    T.V.F. BROGAN; D. A. COLÓN

**ABSORPTION**. A term for the process of a reader's deep engagement with a poem, marked by a lack of self-consciousness about the materiality of the reading process. Poetic rhythm is often used to enhance the experience of deep absorption in a poem; this is most marked in such hypnotically rhythmic poems as

S. T. Coleridge's "Kubla Khan," but the condition is also achieved by a range of representational and material devices that pull the reader into a poem. Absorption typically works by unifying the sound, form, and theme of a poem into a construct that the reader perceives as seamless. Absorption may extend to such effects as a heightened sense of the poem as fiction and an identification with the *persona.

Various modernist modes, incl. *collage, parataxis, and *cacophony, are often understood as disrupting the readability of poems. Such modes may seem to make the reader self-conscious about negotiating the compositional structures of the poem and, by so doing, theatricalize (in Fried's term) the experience of reading. Bertolt Brecht's "alienation effect" (*verfremdungseffekt*), a term he first used in the 1930s, provides a useful model for breaking the identification of the spectator with the spectacle under *modernism, esp. as this term relates to the Rus. Formalist Viktor Shklovsky's 1917 discussion of *ostranenie* or *defamiliarization. Both *verfremdungseffekt* and *ostranenie* are antiabsorptive devices.

Neither absorption nor its converses—impermeability, unreadability, disruption—are inherent poetic values; rather, they suggest approaches to reading and listening. The difference is not as much an essence as a direction: a centrifugal (projective) poetic field versus a centripetal (introjective) one. Poems that attempt to be conventionally absorbing in form and content run the risk of becoming tedious and boring—that is, highly unabsorbing—esp. when they rely on traditional forms and themes that may seem outmoded to historically conscious readers. In contrast, many seemingly antiabsorptive gestures, incl. discontinuity, cut-ups, and opacity, may create rhythmically charged, hyper-engaging poems. Moreover, the active use of linguistic materiality—the reader's or listener's acute awareness of the verbal materials and structures of the poem—may contribute to multilevel, supercharged poetic absorption. It seems evident that absorption is historically conditioned: for some readers and listeners, depending on the period and particular poems, *dissonance will be more absorbing than *consonance or *euphony. Indeed, lit. hist. might be seen as incl. cycles of change in readers' affective responses to emerging acoustic, structural, and thematic dimensions of poetry. The shock of the new for some is the invigorating tonic of the contemporary for others. Modernist and avant-garde poetics that emphasize fragmentation, discontinuity, visual materiality, incompleteness, boredom, or noise often do so in order to open new possibilities for "verbivocovisual" (James Joyce's word from *Finnegans Wake*) engagement of all the senses. Such poetics often explore the chordal possibilities that result from incommensurability, rather than unity, among the levels of form, rhythm, and content; under the sign of overlay and palimpsest, discrepant and impermeable elements of a poem can be recognized as pleats and folds. Temporal, thematic, and stylistic disjunction may form, dissolve, and reform into shifting constellations (to use Benjamin's term) that are open possibilities for a reader's or a listener's absorption into the newly emerging force field of the poem.

See AVANT-GARDE POETICS, DIFFICULTY, LANGUAGE POETRY, PRESENCE.

■ B. Brecht, "Brecht on Theater," trans. J. Willett (1977); C. Bernstein, "Artifice of Absorption," in *A Poetics* (1991); V. Shklovsky, "Art as Device" (1917) in *Theory of Prose*, trans. B. Sher (1991); Michael Fried, "Art and Objecthood" in *Art and Objecthood* (1997); W. Benjamin, "The Doctrine of the Similar" (1933), trans. R. Livingstone, *Selected Writings*, ed. M. W. Jennings et al., v. 2, (1999); R. Tsur, *"Kubla Khan"—Poetic Structure, Hypnotic Quality, and Cognitive Style* (2006).

C. BERNSTEIN

**ACCENT.** In Eng., accent is the auditory prominence perceived in one syllable as compared with others in its vicinity. Accent and stress are often treated as synonymous, though some literary scholars and linguists distinguish the two terms according to a variety of criteria. Disagreements persist about the source and acoustical nature of syllabic prominence—loudness, volume, *pitch, *duration, or some combination of factors—but they are arguably of peripheral relevance to the understanding of accent within Eng. poetics.

The phenomena of accent vary among langs. and the poetics associated with them. The Eng. lexical contrast between *convict* as noun and as verb has no parallel in Fr. (Sp. resembles Eng. in this regard, while Finnish resembles Fr.) For Fr. speakers, stress contours are perceived on the level of the phrase or clause, and learning Eng. entails acquiring the ability to hear contrastive accent in words, just as a Japanese speaker learning Eng. must acquire the distinction between the liquids *l* and *r*. A consequence is that, while Fr. *meters count only *syllables, Eng. meters conventionally also govern the number and distribution of accents.

In Eng. speech, accent operates in various ways on scales from the word (*convict*) through the sentence. As the units grow larger, accent becomes increasingly available to choice and conscious use for rhetorical emphasis. One step beyond the accents recorded in dicts. is the difference between "Spanish teacher" as a compound (a person who teaches Sp.) and as a phrase (a teacher from Spain). Eng. phonology enjoins stronger accent on "Spanish" in the compound and "teacher" in the phrase.

These lexical accents and differences in accent between compounds and phrases are "hardwired" into the Eng. lang. Beyond those, speakers exercise more deliberate choice when they employ contrasting accent to create rhetorical or logical emphases that are intimately entwined with semantic context. In the opposition Chicago White Sox vs. Chicago Cubs, it is the variable rather than the fixed element that receives the accent. Consequently, the question "Are you a fan of the Chicago *Cubs*?" accords with what we know about the world of baseball, while "Are you a fan of the *Chicago* Cubs?" implies a Cubs team from some other city. This kind of contrastive stress, so dynamic in Eng. speech, also plays a variety of important roles in the poetic manipulation of lang., perhaps esp. in how written poetry contrives to convey the rhetorical and intonational contours of speech. When a line break, for instance, encourages the reader to place an accent on some word where it would not normally be expected, the emphasis may suggest an unanticipated logical contrast. This foregrounding of accent may have rhetorical implications: "The art of losing isn't hard to master; / so many things seem filled with the intent / to *be* lost that their loss is no disaster" (emphasis inferred; Elizabeth Bishop, "One Art"); "The sound of horns and motors, which shall bring / Sweeney to Mrs. Porter [not Actaeon to Diana] in the spring" (T. S. Eliot, *The Waste Land*).

Within the specific realm of traditional Eng. metrical verse, words are treated as bearing an accent if they are short polysyllables (whose stress can be looked up in a dict.) or monosyllables that belong to an open class (noun, verb, adjective, adverb, interjection). Other syllables tend to be unstressed. Yet several factors can alter this perception. One is the kind of rhetorical force created by contrastive stress, esp. in the volatile case of pronouns. Another, more pervasive influence arises from the complex interaction between the abstract, narrowly constrained pattern of meter and the concrete, highly contingent *rhythm of the spoken words. This fundamental distinction—meter and rhythm are related similarly to "the human face" and "a human's face"—crucially conditions how we perceive accent; it accounts for some difficulties that an unpracticed reader of metrical verse, though a native of Eng. speech, may have in locating the accents in a line.

Some of the confusion surrounding the term may be reduced if we recognize that *accent* names phenomena on two different levels of abstraction, the acoustical and the metrical. There is an analogy with phonemes. Speakers of Eng. unconsciously insert a puff of air after the *p* in *pan*, but not in *span*. The difference can be detected by using acoustic instruments or by holding a palm in front of the mouth, yet is not detected by speakers in the absence of exceptional attention. The *p* in both cases represents the same phoneme, the same distinctive feature in the Eng. phonetic system—a system that does not merely divide the continuous acoustic stream of speech but abstracts from it a small set of three or four dozen discrete items. Similarly, various acoustical phenomena (pitch, loudness, etc.) give rise to an indefinitely large number of degrees and perhaps even kinds of accent; yet within a metrical context, the accustomed reader—analogous to a native speaker—reduces this continuum to an abstraction of (usually) two opposed values, stressed vs. unstressed. (The analogy fails to capture how the reader is simultaneously aware of a continuum of stress weights in the speech rhythm and a binary feature in the metrical pattern, both embodied in a single set of words.)

Differences of accent between compounds and phrases, or introduced for the sake of rhetorical contrast, which operate prominently within the larger manifold of rhythm, make no difference on the level of meter. "Spanish teacher" in either sense would be scanned as two *trochees, and the stronger stress on one word or the other has no specifically metrical effect. The four degrees of stress adopted by Chatman and others from Trager and Smith, while useful in the phonological analysis of Eng. and in the poetic understanding of rhythm, are unnecessary in the specifically metrical treatment of accent. The "four levels" represent an intermediate abstraction, as does the more traditional compromise of secondary stress or the hovering accent of Brooks and Warren. "Trager and Smith . . . demonstrated that stress and pitch are much more complex and variable phenomena than could be accounted for by the binary unstress-stress relation of traditional prosody" (Bradford 1994)—but this important truth should not mislead us into trying to weld speech rhythm and metrical pattern into an unwieldy whole, rather than hearing their interplay.

Readers are sensitive to a far wider range of rhythmic phenomena in poetry than those that are encoded within a metrical system. The nuanced stress patterns of speech, though they are foregrounded in nonmetrical or *free verse, do not disappear from the reader's awareness in metrical verse with its two-valued feature of accent. Rather, the give and take between the claims of meter and rhythm become a major source of auditory richness. Syllables may be heard as stressed either because of their prominence in speech or because of their position within the metrical line.

Any of the kinds of speech accent—lexical, phrasal, rhetorical—may coincide with a stressed position within the metrical line (as in the even-numbered positions within an *iambic *pentameter); or the speech and metrical accents may be momentarily out of phase. Within the accentual-syllabic system of Eng. metrics, these possibilities give rise to a repertoire of more or less common or striking variations. When speech accents occur in metrically unstressed positions, they give rise to metrical *substitutions of one foot for another, such as the trochee or the *spondee for the iamb:

/  x                    /     /
Singest of summer in full-throated ease

When metrical accents occur where no speech accent is available to embody them, the syllable receives "promoted" stress. The conjunction in the middle of W. B. Yeats's line, "We loved each other and were ignorant," which might pass unstressed in speech, exhibits this kind of promoted accent. It may render the verse line different from and semantically richer than its speech equivalent. The metrical expectation of accent in this position in the line is presumably the initial cause of the promotion; whether the rhetorical point—

that love and ignorance are not at odds as one might think, but inextricable—is an effect or another kind of cause would be difficult to decide.

The phonological and metrical understandings of accent can sometimes even be directly at odds. In a compound word like *townsman*, the second syllable is not unstressed (its vowel is not reduced to schwa). Phonologically, then, the syllable sequence "townsman of" presents three descending levels of stress. In A. E. Housman's line, however, "Townsman of a stiller town," the reader hears "of" with an accent created or promoted by the underlying metrical pattern of iambic *tetrameter; and in comparison, the syllable "-man" is heard as unstressed. The case is complicated by the copresence of other details: because the line is headless, e.g., we know not to scan the initial compound word as a spondee only once we get the following syllables ("a still-"); the unambiguous accent on the last of those syllables (confirmed by the final alternation, "-er town") anchors the whole iambic matrix and retrospectively clarifies the metrical role of "Townsman of." Complications of this kind are typical in the interaction between metrical pattern and speech rhythms and constitute a primary reason for apparent ambiguities of accent in lines of Eng. verse.

*See* DEMOTION, PROMOTION.

■ G. L. Trager and H. L. Smith Jr., *An Outline of English Structure* (1951); W. K. Wimsatt and M. C. Beardsley, "The Concept of Meter: An Exercise in Abstraction," *PMLA* 74 (1959), Brooks and Warren; Chatman, chaps. 3, 4, appendix; N. Chomsky and M. Halle, *The Sound Pattern of English* (1968); M. Halle and S. J. Keyser, *English Stress* (1971); R. Vanderslice and P. Ladefoged, "Binary Suprasegmental Features and Transformational Word-Accentuation Rules," *Lang* 48 (1972); P. Kiparsky, "Stress, Syntax, and Meter," *Lang* 51 (1975); M. Liberman and A. S. Prince, "On Stress and Linguistic Rhythm," *LingI* 8 (1977); E. O. Selkirk, *Phonology and Syntax* (1984); B. Hayes, "The Prosodic Hierarchy in Meter," *Phonetics and Phonology*, ed. P. Kiparsky and G. Youmans (1989); R. Bradford, *Roman Jakobson* (1994).

C. O. HARTMAN

**ACCENTUAL-SYLLABIC VERSE.** In Eng. poetry that is not written in *free verse, the most common and traditional metrical system is called "accentual-syllabic" because it combines a count of *syllables per line with rules for the number and position of *accents in the line.

Metrical systems in different langs. measure lines by various linguistic elements and combinations of elements. Some systems are based on counting a single kind of element (syllables in Fr., monosyllabic words in Chinese). Others—such as the Lat. quantitative meters and the accentual-syllabic system used in mod. Eng., mod. Gr., Ger., and many other langs.—coordinate two different measures, such as syllables and their length or syllables and their stress. Cl. theorists provided a method of analyzing these meters by dividing them into feet, small units defined by various permutations of the two kinds of elements. Thus, the iamb orders a slack syllable and a stressed one (in Eng.) or a short syllable and a long one (in Lat.), while the *trochee reverses the iamb's order and the *anapest extends the iamb by doubling the initial weak syllable position.

Two-element *meters tend to maintain the stability of the lines' measure without as much rigidity in adherence to the meter's defining rules as single-element meters require. Consequently, much of the richness of variation in a two-element meter such as the accentual-syllabic can be captured at least crudely by analysis of substituted feet, metrical inversions, promoted stresses, and similar concepts that build on the notion of the *foot. This variety can be sketched or roughly diagrammed by *scansion of the lines.

Particular meters in such a two-element system are conventionally named by combining an adjectival form of the name of the base foot (iambic, dactylic, trochaic, etc.) with a noun made of a Lat. number word plus "-meter": trimeter, tetrameter, pentameter, hexameter, and so on.

*See* DEMOTION, PROMOTION, PROSODY, SUBSTITUTION.

C. O. HARTMAN

**ACCENTUAL VERSE.** Verse organized by count of stresses, not by count of *syllables. Many prosodists of the 18th, 19th, and early 20th cs. looked upon most med. verse, a large amount of Ren. verse, and all popular verse down to the present as loose, rough, or irregular in number of syllables and in placement of stresses; from this assumption (not demonstration), they concluded that regulated count of stresses was the only criterion of the *meter. Schipper, e.g., effectually views most ME and mod. Eng. four-stress verse as descended from OE alliterative verse. But in this, he misconceived the nature of OE prosody (see ENGLISH PROSODY, GERMANIC PROSODY). Other prosodists, too, have lumped together verse of very different rhythmic textures drawn from widely different social registers and textual contexts, treating all of them under the general rubric of accentual verse. This generalization masks differences that should probably be characterized in metrical (and not merely more broadly rhythmic) terms. Ideally, we would isolate the similarities among species of accentual verse and then identify either features or gradations in strictness of form that differentiate them. No clear theoretical foundation has been established to accomplish this.

Several varieties of accentual verse have been proposed in the Western langs.: (1) folk verse as opposed to art verse, i.e., the large class of popular (e.g., greeting card) verse, *nursery rhymes, college cheers and chants, slogans, logos, and *jingles—both Malof and Attridge rightly insist on the centrality of the four-stress line here; (2) *ballad and *hymn meter, specifically the meter of the Eng. and Scottish popular ballads and of the metrical psalters in the Sternhold-Hopkins

line; (3) popular *song—an extremely large class; (4) literary imitations of genuine ballad meter such as the *Christabel meter; (5) genuine *oral poetry, which indeed seems to show a fixed number of stresses per line but, in fact, is constructed by lexico-metrical formulaic phrases (see FORMULA); (6) simple *doggerel, i.e., lines that hardly scan at all except for stress count, whether because of authorial ineptitude, scribal misprision, textual corruption, or reader misperception—there are many scraps of late med. verse that *seem* to be so; (7) literary verse (often stichic) that is less regular than accentual-syllabic principles would demand but clearly not entirely free, e.g., the four-stress lines that Helen Gardner has pointed out in T. S. Eliot's *Four Quartets*; (8) Ger. *knittelvers*, both in a freer, late med. variety subsequently revived for literary and dramatic purposes by J. W. Goethe and Bertholt Brecht, and in a stricter, 16th-c. variety (*Hans-Sachs verse*) in octosyllabic couplets; and (9) Rus. *dol'nik* verse, a 20th-c. meter popularized by Alexander Blok, mainly in three-stress lines (interestingly, this form devolved from literary verse, not folk verse as in Eng. and Ger.). In all the preceding, there has been an assumption that accentual verse is isoaccentual; if one defines it more broadly (organized only on stresses but not always the same number per line), one would then admit Ger. *freie Rhythmen* and *freie Verse* and possibly Fr. 19th-c. *vers libéré*. But these verge on *free verse.

When Robert Bridges, the Eng. poet and prosodist, studied accentual verse at the turn of the 20th c., he believed he discovered a paradox in claims that accentual verse works by counting the natural stresses in the line. For example, despite S. T. Coleridge's claims that "Christabel" is in a "new" *meter* and that every line in it will be found to have exactly four stresses, the poem actually contains a number of problematic lines, like "How drowsily it crew," which cannot by any reasonable standard carry four natural accents. Of this line Bridges remarks: "In stress-verse this line can have only two accents . . . but judging from other lines in the poem, it was almost certainly meant to have three, and if so, the second of these is a conventional accent; it does not occur in the speech but in the metre, and has to be imagined because the metre suggests or requires it; and it is plain that *if the stress is to be the rule of the metre, the metre cannot be called on to provide the stress*" (italics added). For Bridges, the definition of true "accentual verse" is that it operates on only two principles: "*the stress governs the rhythm*" and "*the stresses must all be true speech-stresses*" (Bridges set these sentences in all capitals). This two-part definition, he asserts, strictly distinguishes accentual verse from *accentual-syllabic verse, in which it is the function of the meter to establish and preserve in the mind's ear a paradigm, an abstract pattern, such that, if the line itself does not supply the requisite number of accents, the pattern shall supply them mentally. But Bridges's view is complicated by the dominance of accentual-syllabism in so much mod. Eng. verse that poets and readers may hear promoted stresses even in a mostly accentual context. In many poems by Elizabeth

Bishop, such as "The Fish" (three-stress), e.g., the near regularity of accent counts encourages us to fill out some shorter lines with stresses that, while strong relative to surrounding syllables, would not be heard in the speech rhythm of the line (see RELATIVE STRESS PRINCIPLE); analyzing the verse as either strictly accentual or as consistently but roughly accentual-syllabic requires acknowledging exceptions, but calling the result "free verse" ignores important gestures toward regularity.

In Eng. as in other Teutonic langs., accentual verse has some claim to being fundamental; it is "the simplest, oldest, and most natural poetic measure in English" (Gioia). It lies near the root of poetry, as it were, and near the point where poetry and music diverge (and reconverge in song). It comes closer than accentual-syllabic meters to manifesting the *beat that defines the term *meter* in the musical sense of that word. Perhaps partly for this reason, versions of accentual verse (measuring lines in four, three, or even two stresses) have been popular alongside mod. free verse, sometimes only notionally distinct from it.

See ALLITERATION, BALLAD METER, EQUIVALENCE, VERSIFICATION. See also NUMBER(S).

■ Schipper; Bridges, "Appendix on Accentual Verse"; G. Saintsbury, *History of English Prosody* (1906–10); W. Kayser, *Kleine deutsche Versschule* (1946); H. Gardner, *The Art of T. S. Eliot* (1949); J. Bailey, "The Stress-Meter of Goethe's *Der Erlkönig,*" *Lang&S* 2 (1969); J. Malof, *A Manual of English Meters* (1970), chaps. 3–4; M. G. Tarlinskaja, "Meter and Rhythm of Pre-Chaucerian Rhymed Verse," *Linguistics* 121 (1974) and *English Verse: Theory and History* (1976); Scott; Brogan, 319–37; Attridge; Scherr; D. Gioia, "Accentual Verse," http://www.danagioia.net/essays/eaccentual.htm.

T.V.F. BROGAN; C. O. HARTMAN

**ACEPHALOUS** (Gr., "headless"). A term used for lines of verse that are missing an initial syllable (Ger. *fehlende Auftakt,* suppression of the *anacrusis). Though it is undeniable that, in some runs of regular *accentual-syllabic verse, occasional lines will be found that are simply missing their first syllables, whether from design or defect of textual transmission, the claims that have most often been made about the concept of acephaly have been made on more sweeping grounds, involving metrical phenomena that are, in fact, capable of varying interpretation. It used to be held, e.g., that there are some eight or nine acephalous lines in Chaucer, incl.—depending on how one treats final *e,* hence, how one scans—the first line of the "General Prologue" in the *Canterbury Tales.* It was also claimed that a missing first syllable changes rising rhythm to falling—see Schipper (see also RISING AND FALLING RHYTHM). Many temporal and musical theories of *meter are congenial to the notion of acephalous lines as important variants rather than simply defects, but such theories are not now widely accepted. If, however, acephaly, as foreclipping, is disputed, the converse phenomenon, *catalexis, the cutting off of

final syllables, is very well attested; but this may, in fact, be unrelated.

■ Schipper; Brogan, K106, K125, K150, K344; Dale, 22 ff.; G. T. Wright, *Shakespeare's Metrical Art* (1988).

T.V.F. BROGAN

**ACMEISM.** A Rus. poetic circle formed in 1912 in reaction against mystical *symbolism, the reigning movement of the prior decade. Founded by Nikolai Gumilev and Sergei Gorodetsky, the acmeist coterie included Anna Akhmatova, Osip Mandelstam, Vladimir Narbut, and Mikhail Zenkevich, all of whom produced poems of a widely divergent nature. The Gr. term *akmē* denotes not only "apex" but "point" and "edge," evoking the group's interest in precision and sharpness. Eschewing the symbolist notion of the poet as an inward-looking dreamer, the acmeists saw poetry as a craft and the poet as an artisan who carves out exact meanings of words with his "hammer." For this reason, they advocated architectural "equilibrium" rather than the musical "vagueness" of symbolism. The notion of equilibrium informed their entire program: the acmeists aimed for a balance between past and present, between the poet's inner world and the external, tangible world. They proposed evolutionary rather than revolutionary change, positioning themselves against their radical contemporaries, the Rus. futurists. In contrast to the futurist rejection of the past, Mandelstam later defined acmeism as a "yearning for world culture." While *futurism discarded mimetic representation in favor of fragmentation and wordplay, and symbolism depicted objects as vehicles to a higher sphere, acmeism espoused a poetics of palpability and precision: the acmeist poet depicts the earthly object with heightened clarity, attempting to view it as if for the first time, like Adam. (This idea was underscored by acmeism's alternate name, "Adamism.") Acmeism thus embodied a broader international phenomenon of the 1910s: a tempered *modernism that forged a middle ground between poetic trad. and avant-garde radicalism. The strongest exemplars of this, Rus. acmeism and Anglo-Am. *imagism, both sought inspiration in Chinese poetry, Gr. and Roman imagery, the *Parnassians, and the Fr. poet Théophile Gautier. Both groups adopted the metaphor of "hardness" to imply their twin goals of restrained self-expression and rigorous technique. The movements' leaders, the acmeist Gumilev and the imagist Ezra Pound, both modeled at least some of their principles on the spare, chiseled verse of their female companions: Anna Akhmatova and H.D. (Hilda Doolittle). The outbreak of World War I effectively put an end to acmeism, although attempts were later made to resurrect it. Its most significant members, Akhmatova and Mandelstam, never repudiated the movement, yet their late work differs greatly from their acmeist poems of the 1910s.

See AVANT-GARDE POETICS; RUSSIA, POETRY OF.

■ B. Eikhenbaum, *Anna Akhmatova* (1922); R. Timenchik, "Zametki ob akmeizme" (Notes on Acmeism), *Russian Literature* 7–8 (1974); D. Mickiewicz, "The Acmeist Conception of the Poetic Word," *Russian Lan-*

*guage Journal*, suppl. issue (1975); E. Rusinko, "Russian Acmeism and Anglo-American Imagism," *Ulbandus Review* 1 (1978); V. Zhirmunsky, "Symbolism's Successors" (1916), *The Noise of Change*, ed. S. Rabinowitz (1986); R. Eshelman, *Nikolaj Gumilev and Neoclassical Modernism* (1993); C. Cavanagh, *Osip Mandelstam and the Modernist Creation of Tradition* (1995); J. Doherty, *The Acmeist Movement in Russian Poetry* (1995); O. Lekmanov, *Kniga ob akmeizme* (Book about Acmeism, 1998); K. Painter, *Flint on a Bright Stone: Precision and Restraint in American, Russian, and German Modernism* (2006).

K. PAINTER

**ACROSTIC** (Gr., "at the tip of the verse"). A poem in which the first letter of each line or stanza spells out either the alphabet (an *abecedarius*); a name, usually of the author or the addressee (a patron, a beloved, a saint); or the title of the work (e.g., Plautus; Ben Jonson's *The Alchemist*). On occasion, the initials spell out a whole sentence—the oldest extant examples of this sort are seven Babylonian texts dating from ca. 1000 BCE, which use the first syllable of each ideogram. By far the most common form reveals, while it purports to conceal, the author's name, as in the acrostic Cicero claims Ennius wrote or François Villon's acrostic to his mother that spells "Villone." The spelling is usually straightforward but may be in anagram for the sake of concealment. If the medial letter of each line spells out a name, the poem is a mesostich; if the final letter, a telestich; if both initials and finals are used, a double acrostic (two of the Babylonian acrostics are such); if all three, a triple acrostic. Finals may also be in reverse order. In any case, the aesthetic of the acrostic is clandestine, as its signs are virtually invisible to rhythm and sense, and is meant to be received by seeing the text on the page.

The visual aesthetic of acrostics relates to other clever forms, including *carmina quadrata*; the deft word-square *intexti* of Hrabanus Maurus (ca. 784–856), such as the grid that bears "Magnentius Rhabanus Maurus hoc opus fecit" (Magnentius Rhabanus Maurus made this work)—with a mod. analogue in Edward Taylor's poem to Elizabeth Fitch—and *carmina figurata* or pattern poetry, alongside which acrostics are commonly found in ancient texts (e.g., the *Greek Anthology*). In Asia, acrostics are found in both Chinese poetry (ring poems, wherein one can begin reading at any character) and Japanese poetry (*kakushidai* and *mono no na*).

Acrostics are the kind of mannered *artifice that will be popular in any silver-age poetry; they flourished in Alexandria and in the Middle Ages, being written by Boniface, Bede, Fortunatus, Giovanni Boccaccio, Eustache Deschamps, and Clément Marot among many. Commodian has a book of 80 acrostics, the *Instructiones*; not only is Aldhelm's *De laudibus virginitatis* a double acrostic made out of its first line, but the last line is the first line read backward, forming a box. The longest acrostic is apparently Boccaccio's *Amorosa visione*, which spells out three entire sonnets. In the Ren., Joachim du Bellay excepted the ingenious acrostic and anagram from his sweeping dismissal of med. Fr. verse forms. Sir John Davies wrote a posy of 26 acrostics to Queen Elizabeth (*Hymnes of Astraea*, 1599). The mod. disparagement begins as early as Joseph Addison (*Spectator* no. 60), but the acrostic was very popular among the Victorians, appearing in the last chapter of Lewis Carroll's *Through the Looking Glass*. In E. A. Poe's valentine poem to Frances Sargent Osgood, her name is spelled by the first letter of the first line, the second letter of the second line, and so on in a diagonal pattern across the page.

In vernacular conversation, this process of elevating initials into a higher script to produce acronyms (snafu, gulag)—now especially common with the proliferation of instant messaging and online chat—has evolved a growing shorthand vocabulary. But even in the early Christian Church, the symbol of the fish is such an acronym: the initials of the five Gr. words in the phrase "Jesus Christ, God's Son, Savior" spell out the Gr. word for fish, *ichthys*.

*See* ANAGRAM.

■ A. Kopp, "Das Akrostichon als kritische Hilfsmittel," *Zeitschrift für deutsche Philologie* 32 (1900); Kastner; K. Krumbacher, "Die Acrostichis in der griechischen Kirchenpoesie," *Sitzungsberichte der königlichbayerische Akad. der Wiss., philos.-philol.-hist. Klasse* (1904); H. Leclercq, "Acrostiche," *Dictionnaire d'archéologie chrétienne*, ed. F. Cabrol (1907); E. Graf, "Akrostichis," Pauly-Wissowa; R. A. Knox, *Book of Acrostics* (1924); F. Dornseiff, *Das Alphabet in Mystik un Magie*, 2d ed. (1925); Lote, 2.305; *Reallexikon II*; W. G. Lambert, *Babylonian Wisdom Literature*, ch. 3 (1960); R.F.G. Sweet, "A Pair of Double Acrostics in Akkadian," *Orientalia* 38 (1969); T. Augarde, *Oxford Guide to Word Games* (1984); Miner et al., pt. 4; W. Stephenson, "The Acrostic 'fictio' in Robert Henryson's 'The Testament of Cresseid' (58–63)," *Chaucer Review* 29.2 (1994); M.A.S. Carter, "Vergilium Vestigare: Aeneid 12.587–8," *CQ* 52.2 (2002); D. L. Norberg, *An Introduction to the Study of Medieval Latin Versification* (2004); J. Danielewicz, "Further Hellenistic Acrostics: Aratus and Others," *Mnemosyne* 58.3 (2005); E. Assis, "The Alphabetic Acrostic in the Book of Lamentations," *Catholic Biblical Quarterly* 69.4 (2007); J. Partner, "Satanic Visions and Acrostics in *Paradise Lost*," *Essays in Criticism* 57.2 (2007).

T.V.F. BROGAN; D. A. COLÓN

**ADDRESS.** Under the heading of *address* in poetry come not only the listeners a poem invokes or implies and the inanimate things or dead people to whom it may speak, but the entire communicative context that such a work projects. The contextual embeddedness of address includes its reference to a situation of utterance (called *deixis*) but also the ways in which that situation participates in artistic *convention; the poem's own hist. and fate as a text; and social practices governing literary production and circulation.

Most written poems do not acknowledge that they are written rather than sung or spoken, but only a minority adhere throughout to a representation of one-to-one, face-to-face address. A poem may say "you" (or use the vocative) to more than one addressee; allude to auditors overhearing; call on objects or abstractions in an *apostrophe; convey that its ostensible target is not paying *attention; or leave doubt as to who is meant by "you." Poems may also show no ling. markers of address whatever and yet point to their reception in ways that show resemblance to the explicit hailing of a reader (e.g., in Shakespeare's sonnet 65, "in black ink my love may still shine bright").

Most sentences in conversation or in a letter do not include the word *you* but are pragmatically indistinguishable from those that do: context, not a pronoun, makes it clear to all who is speaking to whom in what situation. Short written poems usually lack this kind of disambiguating context, leaving them strikingly underspecified for address. In ling. terminology, the person meant to hear or read is the *target*, whereas *addressee* means only the person designated by the pronoun *you*. These need not coincide: thus, a parent may say "you" to an infant while expecting uptake chiefly from an overhearing, targeted spouse; or a criticism of John can be made more provoking by taking the sham form of address to Mary while John, the target, is standing by; but in lit. crit., the term *address* often serves for both. To avoid an overtechnical idiom, the present entry continues to use *address* in this double sense; the term *target* is not established in poetry crit., and the sense intended should be clear in the examples that follow. (For this and other helpful distinctions, see Goffman 1981; Levinson 1983, 1988; Clark 1992.)

Consideration of address in poetry takes place against the background of a critical trad. that could seem to deny that poetic addresses are in any sense effectual. P. B. Shelley's *Defence of Poetry* (1821) styles the poet as "a nightingale, who sits in darkness and sings to cheer its own solitude with sweet sounds; his auditors are as men entranced by the melody of an unseen musician, who feel that they are moved and softened, yet know not whence or why." John Stuart Mill's celebrated 1833 remark in "What Is Poetry?" that "poetry is *over*heard. . . . [T]he peculiarity of poetry appears to us to lie in the poet's utter unconsciousness of a listener" likewise seems to rule out the possibility of poetic address to any real audience beyond the self, since "poetry is feeling confessing itself to itself, in moments of solitude." (A few sentences later in the same essay, Mill shifts his image slightly, writing now not of the "utter unconsciousness" that an audience is present but of the poet's success in "excluding . . . every vestige" of such consciousness from the poem: "The actor knows that there is an audience present; but if he acts as though he knew it, he acts ill." The ease with which Mill moves between these apparently contradictory models can be taken to point not to a muddle but to an insight: the kind of distinction we make in theater between, say, Hamlet, who does not and cannot share the theater audience's ontological space, and the actor playing Hamlet, who does but works to make it seem as though he does not, is often elusive in poetry, notwithstanding critical postulates of the poetic speaker or

"lyric I." This slipperiness, in turn, has consequences for understanding poetic address, since, without such distinct levels, it can be difficult even to be sure what counts as being addressed in a poem or who if anyone may be covertly or explicitly included as a bystander or in any of various oblique ways "meant.") Influential though Shelley's and Mill's romantic view of the singing or soliloquizing poet has been (also through later inflections of it by T. S. Eliot and Northrop Frye), this model does not account well for poems addressing a patron, friend, beloved, or the reader. Poems addressed to a contemporary of the poet predominate in Gr. and Lat. poetry and are plentiful in other trads.; they might also be thought closest to quotidian speech or writing. But, in fact, writing a poem to someone (like singing a song to him or her), even when—as in W. C. Williams's "This Is Just to Say"—the poem seems to approximate daily communication, actually brings that communication to a temporary halt; poetry suspends relationship in order to present it. Poems addressing contemporaries are marked by this fact. Moreover, insofar as a poem is not only a message but also a thing (see ARTIFACT), it by its nature looks beyond any single hearer. Eliot's poem "A Dedication to My Wife" formulates the double fact: "These are private words addressed to you in public." It is not that the one-to-one address is mere pretense; the words of an intimate poem are private, even as their articulation as poetry binds and ritualizes them in more-than-private ways.

The vast corpus of Eur. poetry in the *courtly love and Petrarchan trads. (see PETRARCHISM) makes vivid illustration of another, related dimension of address: the intertextual one. Here the stylized appeal to (e.g.) a hard-hearted mistress is first of all an element of the trad. and only secondarily—if at all—an address to a genuine hearer. The effect of the sometimes self-conscious conventionality is to produce a *you* whose function is at least as much display as it is communication. Where we posit or know of a historical person who may have been meant, that person will have found herself in one or another relation to the textual and intertextual *you* that is a version of her. Each such poem will "mean" a real person or generate a fictive one to a different degree and in its own ways.

The character of each poem's individual address has an effect, in turn, on the extent to which it is appropriate to emphasize the notion of the reader as an overhearer. A poem whose explicit addressee cannot hear might be assumed to be targeting theatrically some other audience of eavesdroppers instead. Address to absent or dead persons is, presumably for this reason, traditionally grouped with apostrophes to objects and abstractions. But, in fact, poetic address to the absent and dead varies greatly in tone and effect, from the customary pomp of public-sounding addresses to great men of past ages, to Constantine Cavafy's surprisingly intimate addresses to them (as in "Ides of March"), to Sylvia Plath's riddling whimsy in addressing her unborn child ("You're"), to the deep longing of some poems of address to a deserting lover or the beloved dead. Poems of this last sort that are convincing in the intensity of their focus on the lost addressee may not stand to gain from introducing the idea of an overhearer.

Address to a reader, by contrast, might seem to bring a poem into clear alignment with the norms of one-to-one communication, but, in fact, it too is attended by many complexities. One example will show a number of these. When Stefan George's volume *Das Jahr der Seele* (The Year of the Soul, 1897) opens autumnally with a poem whose first line is "Komm in den totgesagten park und schau" (Come to the park they say is dead and look), nothing rules out address to an unnamed companion of the poet who is here invited into a really existing park—in which case we readers seem mere overhearers, ratified or not. But as the book's *invitatio*, the poem must be in equal measure a direct appeal to its reader as it asks the addressee to "take the deep yellow, the soft grey / from birch and from boxwood" and "twine" them gently with fading flowers "in an autumnal vision." In George's programmatic *decadence, the park must also represent the book itself, as it also represents Eur. high culture, refined and enervated, at the fin de siècle. The poem's eight imperatives, all instructions for the visitor in a certain garden, form at the same time a collective proposal to the reader for particular cultural stances and acts of mind. There are still more complications to identifying the poem's addressee if we know that George's *Das Jahr der Seele* was artisanally printed in only 206 copies for an exclusive male circle, a historical audience to which no present reader can be admitted. On the other hand, George's disdain for the broader reading public of his time went hand in hand with his keen sense of art's bid to endure through time, i.e., to find later readers. But are you the later reader so addressed? The complications of reader address vary widely among eras, poets, and individual poems, but they are seldom absent.

When a poem offers insufficient cues for readers to be certain of the communicative situation it posits, or addresses a "you" whose identity is ambiguous, contextual factors and practices of reading guide readers' sense of poetry's addressedness as much as or more than textual cues do. Poems in a sequence may, e.g., show quite different relations to addressees when read individually from when taken together. Knowledge of literary-historical context may also be decisive in shaping a reader's sense of a poem's energies of address. Even architectural hist. may come to bear: it has, e.g., been suggested with respect to the poetry of early mod. England, an era whose domestic architecture is said to have made privacy a rare and fleeting experience, that alertness to the possible presence of side participants (bystanders or eavesdroppers) may significantly change our readings of poems that looked rather different when read through romantic presuppositions of the speaker's solitude (Dubrow). Much work remains to be done in shedding historical light on poetic address in individual poets, eras, and trads. But even the fullest contextualizing labors will leave some residue of ambiguous address, not least because poets have recognized the artistic fruitfulness of poetry's communicative uncertainties and sometimes

made them integral. Moreover, address in general is not only a feature or property of texts; since it is the axis of communication, its workings are peculiarly dependent on the reader's uptake.

Address plays a distinctive enough role in the work of a few poets that it has attracted special critical attention there. Crit. of Walt Whitman, e.g., has provided several investigations of address to a reader, few poets having dwelt so insistently as Whitman on their poems' contact with readers in a later time. Paul Celan's poems return often to a "you" who sometimes seems to be the deity in whom the poems may or may not show belief, but at other times may be the reader or a Buberian principle of addressable personhood in humans generally. And the work of John Ashbery, where pronouns come and go bewilderingly, plays persistently with the tendency of an unidentified "you" to arrest or unsettle the reader. Such highly ambiguous address is in some ways a special case; but in another way, the lability of reference in Ashbery's work exhibits in concentrated form the freedom that poetry gains through its characteristic detachment from the contexts of use that ordinarily govern lang., a detachment and freedom nowhere more palpable than in poetry's unleashed powers of address.

*See* EPITAPH, MONOLOGUE, VOICE.

■ T. S. Eliot, "The Three Voices of Poetry," *On Poetry and Poets* (1957); Frye; E. Goffman, "Footing," *Forms of Talk* (1981); B. Costello, "John Ashbery and the Idea of the Reader," *Contemporary Literature* 23 (1982); J. Culler, "Apostrophe," *The Pursuit of Signs* (1982); W. R. Johnson, *The Idea of Lyric* (1982); S. C. Levinson, *Pragmatics* (1983); N. Frye, "Approaching the Lyric," and H. F. Tucker, "Dramatic Monologue and the Overhearing of Lyric," *Lyric Poetry: Beyond New Criticism*, ed. C. Hošek and P. Parker (1985); K. Larson, *Whitman's Drama of Consensus* (1988); S. C. Levinson, "Putting Linguistics on a Proper Footing," *Erving Goffman: Exploring the Interaction Order*, ed. P. Drew and A. Wootton (1988); C. Altieri, "Life after Difference: The Positions of the Interpreter and the Positionings of the Interpreted," *Canons and Consequences* (1990); H. Clark, *Arenas of Language Use* (1992); O. Mandelstam, "On the Addressee," *The Complete Critical Prose*, trans. J. G. Harris and C. Link (1997); W. Waters, *Poetry's Touch: On Lyric Address* (2003); V. Jackson, *Dickinson's Misery: A Theory of Lyric Reading* (2005); H. Vendler, *Invisible Listeners* (2005); H. Dubrow, *The Challenges of Orpheus* (2008).

W. WATERS

**ADONIC** (Adoneus, *versus Adonius*). In Gr. and Lat. poetry, an *aeolic or dactylic clausula that took the form of the last two feet of the dactylic hexameter, i.e., $- \cup \cup - -$, and took its name from the refrain of the song to the god Adonis: *o tŏn Ādōnīn* (Sappho, fr. 168 [Lobel-Page]). According to the Alexandrian grammarians, the adonic formed the fourth line of the *sapphic strophe, although often there is no word end between the third and fourth lines (which suggests the two lines were metrically one), as is true in Lat. also—e.g., Horace, *Odes* 1.2.19 ff.: *u/xorius amnis* (– / – ∪ ∪ – –). But Horace seems to have followed the Alexandrians, for usually there is word end between the sapphic *hendecasyllable and the adonic, and twice there is hiatus. Adonics appear together with other aeolic cola (see COLON) in Plautus and Seneca. Columbanus (sixth c.) wrote adonics; Boethius combined the *hemiepes with the adonic (*Consolation of Philosophy* 1.2). The adonic verse was also used in stichic poems (see STICHOS) and in strophes of various lengths in med. Lat. verse, in both quantitative and rhythmic meters.

■ Norberg; Crusius; C. Questa, *Introduzione alla metrica di Plauto* (1967); Halporn et al.

J. W. HALPORN

**ADYNATON.** The impossibility device: the rhetorical figure for magnifying an event by comparison with something impossible, e.g., "I'd walk a million miles for one of your smiles" (Al Jolson, "My Mammy"); cf. "Hell will freeze over before . . ." and the closely related figure of the impossibility of finding the right words (*aporia), i.e., the "inexpressibility topos," e.g., "Words fail me"; "I can't begin to tell you how much . . ." In Gr. and Lat. lit., the two most common varieties of adynaton are the "sooner than" type, which claims that the impossible will come true sooner than the event in question will take place, and the "impossible-count" type, referring to unimaginable numbers—for instance, of sands on the shore or stars in the sky. These varieties are uncommon in the lit. of the Middle Ages. By contrast, OF writers cultivated a different brand known as the *fatras, dealing with impossible or ridiculous accomplishments. Occitan poets used an allied form made popular by Petrarch's sonnet "Pace non trovo e non ho da far guerra." The Gr. and Lat. types were, however, abundantly revived by Petrarchan poets all over Europe, who made use of them either to emphasize the cruelty of the lady or to affirm their love. In Shakespeare's *Antony and Cleopatra*, Antony employs adynaton to dramatize his intent to remain in Egypt despite his Roman responsibilities: "Let Rome in Tiber melt and the wide arch / Of the rang'd empire fall. Here is my space" (1.1.33). Adynaton may also be used negatively to assert a contrary impossibility, as in Shakespeare's *Richard II*: "Not all the water in the rough rude sea, / Can wash the balme off from an anointed King" (3.2.54–55). Other famous examples include those found in Andrew Marvell's "To His Coy Mistress," Robert Browning's "Up at a Villa—Down in the City," W. H. Auden's "As I Walked Out One Evening," and, strikingly, in Louis MacKay's "Ill-Tempered Lover." In East Asian poetry, varieties of adynata are used as a rhetorical device in the poetry of praise. The poems and hymns of blessing and sacrifice in the *Book of Songs*, the oldest extant anthol. of Chinese poetry, use magnificent similes and numbers, and a Middle Korean poem, "Song of the Gong," uses the myth of the impossible ("when the roasted chestnut sprouts, then . . ."). Richard Lanham's position, that adynaton is "sometimes a confession that words fail us," would tend to place the figure in the category of metalogisms characterized by Group μ as the suppression of units of expression, i.e., among figures like *litotes, *aposiopesis, reticentia, and silence. Adynaton, thus, might also serve the function of promising rather than maintaining silence.

■ R. H. Coon, "The Reversal of Nature as a Rhetorical Figure," *Indiana Univ. Studies* 15 (1928); H. V. Canter, "The Figure Adynaton in Greek and Latin Poetry," *AJP* 51 (1930); E. Dutoit, *Le Thème de l'adynaton dans la poésie antique* (1936); Curtius 94–98, 159 ff.; L. C. Porter, *La Fatrasie et le fatras* (1960); Group μ; C. Petzsch, "Tannhäusers Lied IX in C und in cgm 4997. Adynatonkatalog und Vortragsformen," *Euphorion* 75 (1981)—on impossibility catalogs; M. Shapiro, "The Adynaton in Petrarch's Sestinas," *Dante, Petrarch, Boccaccio*, ed. A. S. Bernardo and A. L. Pellegrini (1983); Lanham.

A. W. HALSALL; T.V.F. BROGAN

**AEOLIC,** aristophaneus. The name usually given to a class of ancient Gr. lyric meters, so called because first attested in the poems of Sappho and Alcaeus, which were composed in the Aeolic dialect. Common to all forms labeled aeolic is the sequence – ∪ ∪ – ∪ – , which appears occasionally as a *colon by itself but much more frequently is preceded and/or followed by a single *anceps (syllable either long or short), or preceded by the so-called aeolic base (a double anceps in Sappho and Alcaeus, elsewhere either – x , x – , or ∪ ∪ ). Iambic or trochaic may precede or follow within the same colon, and the – ∪ ∪ – sequence may be expanded into either a dactylic – ∪ ∪ – ∪ ∪ – (∪ ∪ –) or a choriambic – ∪ ∪ – – ∪ ∪ – (– ∪ ∪ –). Typical examples are

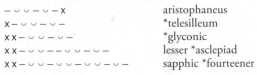

| | |
|---|---|
| – ∪ ∪ – ∪ – x | aristophaneus |
| x – ∪ ∪ – ∪ – | *telesilleum |
| x x – ∪ ∪ – ∪ – | *glyconic |
| x x – ∪ ∪ – – ∪ ∪ – ∪ – | lesser *asclepiad |
| x x – ∪ ∪ – ∪ ∪ – ∪ ∪ – ∪ – | sapphic *fourteener |

The aeolic sequence – ∪ ∪ – ∪ – may be terminally shortened into – ∪ ∪ – x, most notably in the pherecratean (x x – ∪ ∪ – x) and reizianum (x – ∪ ∪ – x), as well as replaced by – x – ∪ ∪ – , usually in the glyconic equivalent known as the choriambic dimeter (see CHORIAMB): x x – x – ∪ ∪ – . The latter name is somewhat misleading, however, suggesting as it does a compound out of two independent parts. Genuine dimeters in which the second element is a choriamb do exist, but the first section is either an iamb or another choriamb, and they are more closely related to pure iambic *dimeters (x – ∪ – x – ∪ –) or the mixed form – ∪ ∪ – – ∪ – than they are to aeolic. There also exists a catalectic form (see CATALEXIS) of the latter, externally identical with the aeolic – ∪ ∪ – ∪ – x and called, like it, an aristophaneus; but all such dimeters are foreign to the versification of Alcaeus and Sappho. They appear first in Anacreon and have close affinities with the *ionic sequences characteristic of him, one of which, ⌣ ⌣ – ⌣ – ⌣ – –, is actually known as the *anacreontic.

*See* GREEK POETRY, MELIC POETRY.

■ D. L. Page, *Sappho and Alcaeus* (1955); Maas, sect. 54; D. S. Raven, *Greek Metre* (1962); Dale, ch. 9–10; D. Korzeniewski, *Griechische Metrik* (1968); Halporn et al.; Snell; West, 29 ff.; K. Itsumi, "The 'Choriambic Dimeter' in Euripides," *CQ* 76 (1982), and "The Glyconic in Tragedy," *CQ* 78 (1984)—fundamental for the two forms discussed; A. M. Laguna Ortiz, "Nueva descripción funcional de los eolocoriambos de Alceo y Safo," *Cuadernos de filología clásica: estudios griegos e indoeuropeos* 7 (1997).

A. T. COLE

**AESTHETICISM.** A term originally used in the early 19th c. to label an attention to the sensuous elements of art in opposition to its social responsibilities, thus applied in contemp. reviews to Alfred, Lord Tennyson's early poems; more famously, the term for a literary, philosophical, and cultural movement of the later 19th c. that came to be identified with the phrase "art for art's sake." From that movement, in the 20th c., the term came to be identified with a belief that art is autonomous and has intrinsic value. Although in a broad sense, those beliefs characterize much formative aesthetic theory in 18th-c. England and 19th-c. Germany, from Anthony Ashley Cooper, the third Earl of Shaftesbury (1671–1713) through Immanuel Kant, Friedrich Schiller, and even G.W.F. Hegel, the early Victorian connotation of irresponsible attention to the sensuous element in art, at the expense of social awareness, remained tied to the term, even for mid-20th-c. formalists (see FORMALISM) who shared most of the fundamental aesthetic beliefs of aestheticism.

Tracing either the roots or the boundaries of aestheticism as a movement in 19th-c. England is difficult since that term, as well as "the aesthetic movement," often referred to a set of loose alliances around a common resistance to mid-Victorian aesthetic and social beliefs. The central intellectual statement of the movement is Walter Pater's *Studies in the History of the Renaissance* (1873), particularly its "Conclusion," which in its original version contained the most famous utterance of the phrase "art for art's sake," though that phrase in Eng. goes back at least to A. C. Swinburne's book on William Blake. Through Swinburne and also directly, Pater might have found the phrase and certainly did find many ideas about art in the Fr. symbolist movement (the phrase "*l'art pour l'art*" occurs in Victor Cousin as early as 1818). But Pater was also well read in the Ger. aesthetic theorizing of the late 18th and early 19th cs., and his essay on Johann Winckelmann shows not only a knowledge of that critic but an extended consideration of Hegel's *Lectures on Aesthetics*. More important for the movement's intellectual and cultural influence, however, Pater absorbed the aesthetic and literary theories of John Ruskin and Matthew Arnold, while resisting Ruskin's moral evaluations and Arnold's insistence on an objective view of culture and art, thus giving intellectual definition to aestheticism as a theory

of a specific type of apprehension—one he claimed made life valuable. At the most basic level, following Kant's idea that one perceives beauty when one perceives an object as having purposiveness without purpose and Hegel's objectification of Kant in defining art as the embodiment of the idea of beauty, Pater defined aesthetic apprehension as a particular mode of perception that allows one to live with more intense awareness and sees art as the mode best prepared to give that apprehension. He took from both Ruskin and Arnold an insistence that art and culture could act as a perspective from which to evaluate society but intentionally stripped from each the moral earnestness, making his own aesthetic critique more resistant to Victorian moral and social norms and thus provoking charges of hedonism and irresponsibility.

Although Pater gave aestheticism its intellectual definition as a movement, by the time his book appeared, it was already a broad set of practices and beliefs. Although *Pre-Raphaelitism as a theory of painting originally denoted an antagonism to academic and cl. compositions and forms in favor of a return both to nature and to the intensity and color that these painters saw in art before Raphael, by the 1860s—when it had become associated with aestheticism—the movement also referred to the particular style of female beauty in the paintings, most famously of D. G. Rossetti. When one adds to these principles a greater attention to ornament; an ethic of craft; an attention to the status of aesthetic objects as popularized by William Morris's extrapolation of Ruskin's theories; and an association of later Victorian poets such as Swinburne, Rossetti, and Morris either antagonistically as the *"fleshly school" or as "Aesthetic Poetry" (Pater's title for a review of Morris, for which the "Conclusion" to *The Renaissance* was originally written), it becomes possible to see a constellation of intellectual positions and styles in painting, poetry, and art objects that in different ways challenged mid-Victorian moral and aesthetic standards. As an example of the associations the movement could evoke, the murderous heroine of Mary Braddon's phenomenally popular novel *Lady Audley's Secret* has a portrait done that depicts her as a Pre-Raphaelite beauty, with that association meant to inform us of a dangerous aspect to her beauty. By 1883, Gilbert and Sullivan could satirize the movement in expansive strokes in their operetta *Patience* and expect the audience to get the joke.

A more subversive and hidden strand of aestheticism was its connection with homosexuality both as a practice and as an association with Hellenism at Oxford in the 1870s and 1880s (see Dowling). Pater was turned down for a promotion at Oxford in the wake of a long-suppressed scandal regarding his relations with an undergraduate. He had been satirized as the sexually ambiguous Mr. Rose in W. H. Mallock's *The New Republic* and, when he revised the "Conclusion" to *The Renaissance* in 1888, largely toning down some of the phrases most associated with his aestheticism, he gave as a reason that "it might possibly mislead some of those young men into whose hands it might fall." This strand of the movement becomes particularly important to Pater's famous student Oscar Wilde, who brings together the intellectual, cultural, and scandalous aspects of aestheticism in ways that account for its vexed afterlife in 20th-c. lit. hist. Wilde, in such essays as "The Critic as Artist" and "The Decay of Lying," gave Pater's aesthetic theories, through ironies and paradoxes, a more challenging edge. His book *The Soul of Man under Socialism* gave to aestheticism a more explicit set of political implications (though not ones that would have been shared by Pater or other aesthetes before Wilde). Perhaps most significantly for the larger culture, his plays in the early to mid-1890s, ending with *The Importance of Being Earnest*, coupled with a notorious public persona, entertained and challenged a middle-class audience with sharp ironies at its beliefs and practices (see Gagnier). His trial and conviction for gross indecency (the 1885 Criminal Law Amendment Acts term for recriminalizing male homosexual acts) effectively captured all these strands of aestheticism under a penumbra of homophobia that affected its understanding for almost the next 100 years.

One might think, for instance, that given its relations with *symbolism and its roots in Kantian aesthetics, Pater's program would have filiations in T. S. Eliot's poetic thought, influenced as he was by Fr. symbolism, and in mid-century formalism, affected as it was by Kantian ideas of purposiveness without purpose. But Eliot's writing on Pater is famously dismissive, and the *New Criticism barely has a word to say about him. M. C. Beardsley, in *Aesthetics*, divides aestheticism into one aspect that he treats as truism—that art should not be judged according to moral, political, or other extraneous criteria—and another that he considers "a form of fanaticism," the view that "maintains the supreme value of art over everything else." Meanwhile, though Wilde's reputation as an author—largely for *Earnest* and *The Picture of Dorian Gray*—remained high, it was generally scrubbed of any mention of his sexuality. In the last decades of the 20th c., theoretical movements such as deconstruction, feminism, and queer theory have brought closer attention to Pater, Wilde, and the other strands of aestheticism, though with the antagonism of these movements to formalism, often at the expense of the aesthetic theory within aestheticism. More recent studies, including work reviving fiction and poetry directly influenced by aestheticism, have also started to rectify this problem.

■ M. C. Beardsley, *Aesthetics* (1966); D. De Laura, *Hebrew and Hellene in Victorian England* (1969); M. Levey, *The Case of Walter Pater* (1978); R. Gagnier, *Idylls of the Marketplace* (1986); R. Ellmann, *Oscar Wilde* (1988); C. Williams, *Transfigured World* (1989); R. Dellamora, *Masculine Desire* (1990); J. Loesberg, *Aestheticism and Deconstruction* (1991); L. Dowling, *Hellenism and Homosexuality in Victorian Oxford* (1996); E. Hanson, *Decadence and Catholicism* (1997); K. A. Psomiades, *Beauty's Body* (1997); Y. Prins, *Victorian Sappho* (1999); T. Shaffer, *The Forgotten Female Aesthetes* (2000); J. Siegel, *Desire and Excess* (2000).

J. LOESBERG

**AFFECT.** When Wimsatt and Beardsley published "The Affective Fallacy" in 1949, the term *affective* was not widespread in lit. crit., though the phenomena they were examining—the range of emotive, psychological, even physiological responses to literary lang.—had been the subject of much discussion. The adjective *affective* (from the noun *affect*, "a feeling or subjective experience accompanying a thought or action," "an emotion, a mood" [*OED*]) provides Wimsatt and Beardsley a label beneath which a great deal of poetic theory—from Aristotle and Longinus through Edmund Burke and S. T. Coleridge to I. A. Richards and Max Eastman—can be both gathered in one place and held skeptically at arm's length. The "affective fallacy," they argue, is the "confusion between the poem and its *results*," a confusion leading directly to "impressionism and relativism," an unacceptable confusion for a self-styled "objective criticism." As the invocation of objectivity can suggest, *affect* as a term in poetic theory registers crit.'s uneasy engagement with science. In its mod. usage, *affect* enters the Eng. lexicon through the scientific psychology of the late 19th c. As an explicitly scientific term, *affect* insists both on its distinction from numerous apparent synonyms—e.g., emotion or mood—and on its higher level of generality than the particular affects—e.g., anxiety, disgust, joy—that it collectively designates. In psychoanalysis, affects (anxiety or melancholy, for instance) are central to Sigmund Freud's project of the description of unconscious motivations yet finally remain subordinated to the analysis of representations, the latter being understood to be more amenable to scientific control (Green). The term *affect* thus seems to treat the phenomena to which it refers with a scientifically skeptical distance, even as it incites the further drawing of distinctions—precisely its function in Wimsatt and Beardsley's essay, as they rename Aristotelian or Coleridgean theory as kinds of affective crit.

Modernist poetics, of which the "The Affective Fallacy" is perhaps the acme, emerges within a horizon defined by scientific psychology (see MODERNISM). Richards openly advocates a "co-operation of psychology and literary criticism" in the service of the regulation of "dangers both of a false understanding of the sense" of poems "and of a distorted development of feeling" about them. T. S. Eliot famously distinguishes between emotions and feelings: "The business of the poet is not to find new emotions, but to use the ordinary ones and, in working them up into poetry, to express feelings which are not in actual emotions at all." Emotion here is the property of psychological individuals, while "floating feelings" are what are catalyzed in poems and belong no longer to either author or reader: "Poetry is not a turning loose of emotion, but an escape from emotion." Eliot's attack on the idea of the poet as an expressive personality is made, like Richards's "practical criticism," in the name of science: it is only when a poet achieves "depersonalization that art may be said to approach the condition of science." While neither Richards nor Eliot uses the term *affect*—like some contemp. writers, they prefer "feelings"—their stated desire to "approach the condition of science" by way of describing an "escape from emotion" (with all the subjectivism that implies) into a more free-floating, and more subtly differentiated, realm of response is part of the hist. of the term *affect* in poetic theory. Massumi, to name one contemp. legatee, works out from findings in experimental psychology to argue, like Eliot, for an "autonomy of affect" vis-à-vis "emotions."

Wimsatt and Beardsley turned their scientific skepticism esp. against the overreaching of scientific approaches to literary understanding: "The gap between various levels of physiological experience and the recognition of value remains wide, in the laboratory or out." For the past several decades, however, researchers have been narrowing this "gap," with its implied opposition between affective "experience" and poetic or semantic "value." The "affective stylistics" of Fish's "reader-response" crit. refuses to separate experience and value. The meaning of a poem cannot be separated from the experience of reading it, *pace* Wimsatt and Beardsley: John Milton's *Paradise Lost* produces *as its meaning* an affective experience of being "surprised by sin." Approaching the issue from psychology, Tomkins both granted affects an autonomy they were not allowed in the classic Freudian drive system and tied them more essentially to human cognition and intention: "for human subjects value is any object of affect," he states sweepingly. More recently, Damasio, a neurologist, has described the detailed interdependence of cognition and affect. Damasio, too, leverages a distinction between emotions and feelings, though for him the former is a bodily response to the environment, while the latter is a perception of this body state.

For some literary critics, the scientific lexicon has held out the promise of an improved crit. Sedgwick and Frank applaud the descriptive richness of Tomkins's eight (or more) primary affects, and the invitation to descriptive taxonomy has been taken up by such critics as Altieri, who sees feelings, emotions, passions, and moods as analytically separable subdivisions of affect, each capable of shedding light on specific poetic and literary effects. Ngai's subtle study of "ugly feelings" in mod. and avant-garde lit., while not esp. interested in scientific research on affect, also takes up the joys of taxonomic innovation: the prose experiments of Samuel Beckett and Gertrude Stein, she tells us, induce an affect of "stuplimity" in their readers. Affective responses to rhythm and rhyme have been analyzed through the prism of a *cognitive poetics (Tsur), and in general there has been a great deal of work in recent years at the intersection of philosophy, scientific psychology, neuroscience, and lit. crit. Some have attempted to synthesize this work into a full-blown account of emotion and its interrelations with the arts (Robinson), while others have emphasized particular issues such as emotional expression in the arts (Wollheim). Some history-minded critics have shown skepticism about the emotions. Reddy tries to navigate between rhetorically and biologically based perspectives on affect in his discussion of 18th-c. sentimentality. Gross and Pinch, by contrast, both insist that discourses of emotion and affect are just that—discourses, the products of rhetorical innovation and trad.: affects serve as a kind of social currency, a thesis bolstered by social-constructionist anthropological research such as Abu-Lughod's study of the role of poetry among Bedouin women. Pinch's analysis of 18th-c. discussions of affect and emotion returns us to Eliot's distinction between (personal) emotions and feelings or affects that seem "impersonal" (7): "Not always lodged within the private, inner lives of individual persons, [feelings] rather circulate among persons as somewhat autonomous substances" (1). The distinction between (subjective, personal) emotions and expression and a more inchoate, but no less powerful, region of affects is esp. relevant to the theory and crit. of the *lyric, whether challenged by avant-garde practitioners (Silliman et al.) or by literary historians insisting that Sappho's passion (Prins) or Dickinson's "misery" (Jackson) are not affective properties of these two poets, but the result of their uptake in critical trads. Stewart, on the other hand, insists that "lyric" has precisely as its crucial task the mediation of individual affective expressivity and the context-independence of trad., lang., and historical address. Lyric is not the mere expression of private emotions, Stewart agrees, but it gives form to what Eliot might call "feelings" and what contemp. crit. often calls "affects," that have "escaped" the measure of the individual body, person, or subject.

■ T. S. Eliot, "Tradition and the Individual Talent," *The Sacred Wood* (1920); I. A. Richards, *Practical Criticism* (1929); W. K. Wimsatt and M. C. Beardsley, "The Affective Fallacy," *The Verbal Icon* (1954); S. Fish, *Surprised by Sin* (1967), and "Literature in the Reader: Affective Stylistics," *Is There a Text in This Class?* (1980); L. Abu-Lughod, *Veiled Sentiments: Honor and Poetry in a Bedouin Society* (1986); A. Green, "Conceptions of Affect," *On Private Madness* (1986); R. Wollheim, *Painting as an Art* (1987); R. Silliman, C. Harryman, L. Hejinian, S. Benson, B. Perelman, and B. Watten, "Aesthetic Tendency and the Politics of Poetry: A Manifesto," *Social Text* 19–20 (1988); R. Tsur, *Toward a Theory of Cognitive Poetics,* 2d ed. (2008); *Shame and Her Sisters,* ed. A. Frank and E. Sedgwick (1995), esp. S. Tomkins, "What Are Affects?" and E. Sedgwick and A. Frank, "Shame in the Cybernetic Fold"; A. Pinch, *Strange Fits of Passion* (1996); A. Damasio, *The Feeling of What Happens* (1999); Y. Prins, *Victorian Sappho* (1999); W. M. Reddy, *The Navigation of Feeling* (2001); P. Fisher, *The Vehement Passions* (2003); B. Massumi, "The Autonomy of Affect," *Parables for the Virtual* (2002); S. Stewart, *Poetry and the Fate of the Senses* (2002); C. Altieri, *The Particulars of Rapture* (2003); S. Ngai, *Ugly Feelings* (2005); V. Jackson, *Dickinson's Misery* (2005); J. Robinson, *Deeper Than Reason* (2005); D. Gross, *The Secret History of Emotion* (2006).

J. ELMER

**AFFECTIVE FALLACY.** "The Affective Fallacy" is the title of a 1949 essay by William K. Wimsatt, Jr. and Monroe C. Beardsley. It follows their 1946 essay, "The Intentional Fallacy." The two critics use the term to designate any approach to lit. that comments upon the emotional, imaginative, or physiological effects of a poem upon one or more readers. The outcome is that the poem itself tends to disappear as an object of study. In particular, since readers' aesthetic reactions to poetry are influenced by different factors, affective crit. often slips into *impressionism and relativism. Wimsatt and Beardsley instead call for an objective crit. focused on the poem as an autonomous verbal icon.

Like the preceding essay, "The Affective Fallacy" was a crucial statement of New Critical orthodoxy. In particular, the essay's argument was crucial to the Am. New Critics' efforts to professionalize literary studies. Wimsatt and Beardsley, thus, orient their essay against two modes of crit. that represented weak models of literary professionalism. The first is the scientific study of the emotive effects of lit. pioneered by I. A. Richards. This approach erodes literature's disciplinary distinctiveness, culminating in a positivistic study of reader psychology. The second mode is the literary appreciation typical of middlebrow publications like the Book-of-the-Month Club. This crit., the authors argue, is a mass-cultural version of the more sophisticated *affect criticism of the romantic era.

In the 1970s, the affective fallacy was revisited by *reader-response critics, who argued on epistemological, linguistic, and artistic grounds for an affective or subjective crit. that focuses on the relation between poem and reader. Nevertheless, Wimsatt and Beardsley's disavowal of affective crit. as a subprofessional endeavor continues to influence the ways in which critics envisage the distinction between professional and lay readings of literary texts, esp. as reflected in pedagogy.

*See* INTENTIONAL FALLACY, NEW CRITICISM, READER.

■ W. K. Wimsatt and M. C. Beardsley, "The Intentional Fallacy" and "The Affective Fallacy," *The Verbal Icon* (1954); S. Fish, *Is There a Text in This Class?* (1980).

S. SCHRYER

**AFFLATUS.** (cl. Lat., "a blowing or breathing on," also "breeze," or "blast" from wind, animals, humans; also *adflatus*). Cicero, *De divinatione* 2.57.117, writes of a blowing out of the earth, "adflatus e terra," in a passage skeptical of the Delphic Oracle; also, sometimes with a negative connotation, as in Ovid, *Metamorphoses* 7.551, "adflatu . . . nocent," where the breath of those dying of plague pollutes the air. But this negative sense did not carry into later lit. Instead, the figurative sense is found, meaning *"inspiration" or "breathing in" of the divine spirit; this sense, too, is classical and can be found in Cicero (*De natura deorum* 2.66), as well as in Horace and Virgil. At *Aeneid* 6.50–51, Virgil describes the Sibyl as frenzied, disheveled with prophetic fever, and physically inflated: "adflata est numine quando / iam propriore dei" (since she felt the god's power breathing nearer). This sense of the proximity of power, along with the transformation of the inspired figure, accompanies the term in later usage in the Neo-Lat. era. But *afflatus* never became a common term. In its rare appearances, *afflatus* was virtually interchangeable with

*furor divinus* (divine frenzy) and, in the realm of poetry, **furor poeticus*. E.g., *Numine afflatur* is the inscription under the medallion for Poetry in the vault to Raphael's Stanza Della Segnatura in the Vatican (Curtius).

■ Curtius; C. J. Steppich, *Numine Afflatur: Die Inspiration des Dichters im Denken der Renaissance* (2002).

R. FALCO

## AFRICA, POETRY OF

I. English
II. French
III. Portuguese
IV. Indigenous. *See* EGYPT, POETRY OF; ETHIOPIA, POETRY OF; HAUSA POETRY; SOMALI POETRY; SWAHILI POETRY; XHOSA POETRY; ZULU POETRY.

**I. English.** With the end of the colonial period and the advance of literacy and higher education in Africa came a rapid efflorescence of Af. poetry written in Eng. This poetry displays the variety to be expected in so diverse a continent. Like other examples of *postcolonial poetics, Af. poetry in Eng. develops out of the fusion of indigenous trads. with the literary inheritances transmitted through the colonial lang. It is responsive to local idioms, values, and hist. and at the same time remakes for Af. experience the forms and styles imported through Eng. from the Brit. Isles, America, and elsewhere. The adoption of the Eng. lang. for Af. purposes, while advantageous to writers who wish to be heard by an international audience, is fraught with political significance. Some Af. critics contend that poetry written in a historically imperialist lang. cannot be fully disassociated from colonialism's oppressive legacy.

Af. poetry written in Eng. is often seen as divided between poetry that is locally rooted and influenced by Af. oral trads. and cosmopolitan poetry, which is indebted primarily to Western literary trads. The work of Af. poets, however, complicates this distinction, since even the most cosmopolitan poets, such as the Nigerian poet Wole Soyinka, also draw on local oral trads., and even the most local, such as the Ugandan poet Okot p'Bitek (1931–82), also make use of Western literary models. In the wake of colonialism and under the influence of globalization, Af. poetry in Eng. is inextricable from Brit., Ir., Am., and other influences, even when in revolt against the West's values and cultural forms. Conversely, in the West, the descendants of enslaved Africans and economic migrants have fundamentally shaped poetry.

The first poem in the sequence "Heavensgate" (1962, rev. 1964) by Nigerian poet Christopher Okigbo (1932–67) serves as an example of the enmeshment of Af. and Western poetics in sub-Saharan Africa. The poet invokes the Igbo river goddess, near the village where he grew up: "Before you, mother Idoto / naked I stand." Reaffirming his affinity with native culture, Okigbo grounds his poem in local religion and flora (naked, he leans on the oilbean tree, sacred to Idoto, a totem for her worship). At the same time, his *diction (referring to himself as "a prodigal" further in the poem) and rhet. ("Before you, mother Idoto") also recall the Christianity that missionaries imported into Igboland.

The lyric is shaped by the Roman Catholicism in which Okigbo was brought up, incl. prayers to the Virgin Mary and the story of the prodigal son. The poem's final lines, which cry out to a native divinity, paradoxically echo Psalm 130 ("Out of the depths have I cried unto thee, O Lord") and Psalm 5 ("Give ear to my words, O Lord. . . . Hearken unto the voice of my cry").

Although Af. poets are indebted to religious, lyric, and other cultural forms from the West, they seldom lose their awareness of Africa's rich oral trads. A poem such as Okot p'Bitek's *Lawino* (1966) relies on Acholi *songs, *proverbs, *repetitions, idioms, and oral address, even as it also draws on the model of the Western long poem (Okot has cited H. W. Longfellow's *Hiawatha* as a key influence). An aggrieved village woman inveighs against her husband for forsaking his local culture and being too enamored of Western ways: "Listen, Ocol, you are the son of a Chief, / Leave foolish behavior to little children." In her book-length complaint, Lawino repeatedly brandishes an Acholi proverb that warns against uprooting the pumpkin; in so doing, she emphasizes the importance of preserving the household, as well as the oral trads. that sustain it.

Between the poles marked out by Okigbo's highly literary, allusive, syntactically complex early poetry and Okot's orally based poetics of song, praise (see EPIDEICTIC POETRY), and *invective, Af. poetry has discovered a multitude of ways to mediate the oral and scribal, the local and global, the socially urgent protest and the private meditation. Indeed, as an Oxford-trained anthropologist influenced by Longfellow and the Bible, Okot cannot be reduced to simple nativism. And as a poet who absorbs drum rhythms and praise song into his later work, Okigbo—who died fighting for an independent Biafra—should not be seen as a Westernized sellout. Under the influence of intensified global communication, trade, education, and travel, younger poets work in ever-more deeply hybrid and transnational forms. The South Af. Lesego Rampolokeng (b. 1965), e.g., draws on a global array of influences, incl. rap musicians (see HIP-HOP POETICS), the Af. Am. Last Poets, Jamaican dub poet Mutabaruka, and Jamaican-born Brit. reggae poet Linton Kwesi Johnson, to mount a vehement social critique of his country both before and after apartheid.

From the period of Af. decolonization, first formally achieved in anglophone Africa with Ghana's independence in 1957, to today's struggle against both external economic imperialism and the internalized colonialism of dictators and tyrants, oral and other traditional poetry has strongly influenced Af. Eng. poems. The imprint of Af. oral culture is visible in such fundamental elements as the poet's stance as defender of communal values; allusions to the hist., customs, and artifacts of the culture; and the architectonic features adapted from praise song, proverbial tale, *epic, invective, and indigenous prayer. Experiments in the transmutation of traditional Af. poetic forms into Eng. vary with the culture represented.

Arising in the aftermath of *modernism, much Af. Eng. poetry eschews *meter and *rhyme in favor of *free verse, often ornamented by *alliteration and *assonance, although rap's influence has spawned intensely rhymed and rhythmic verse. Poems that are meant to speak to, or for, Af. communities avoid extended *conceits unless they are buttressed by hard or sardonic reason or concrete *imagery.

A. *West Africa.* West Africa, particularly Nigeria and Ghana, has the oldest and most influential trad. of sophisticated poetry in Eng. This *lyric poetry combines audacious leaps of thought and individualized expression with social responsibility; it privileges the metaphysical, religious, and social concepts of its own society, although it also draws on concepts indigenous to Eur. cultural hist. When social protest is overt, it is usually presented with intellectual and artistic complexity rather than simplistic fervor. Exemplary Nigerian poets and their principal works include the country's oldest active poet Gabriel Okara (b. 1921; *The Fisherman's Invocation* [1978], written against the background of civil war); Christopher Okigbo (*Labyrinths* [1971], incl. the prophetic sequence "Path of Thunder"); J. P. Clark (b. 1935; *Reed in the Tide* [1965], incl. autobiographical poems; *Casualties* [1970], concerning the war between Nigeria and Biafra; *A Decade of Tongues* [1981]; *State of the Union* [1981], about Nigeria's socioeconomic and political problems in an international context); the philosopher and polemicist Chinweizu (b. ca. 1935; *Invocations and Admonitions* [1986]); the Nobel laureate Wole Soyinka (b. 1934; *Idanre* [1967], based on Yoruba mythology; *Shuttle in the Crypt* [1971]; *Mandela's Earth and Other Poems* [1988]; and a number of plays that contain poetry); Odia Ofeimun (b. 1947; *The Poet Lied* [1989], *Dreams at Work* [2000]); Niyi Osundare (b. 1947; *Village Voices* [1984], *The Eye of the Earth* [1986], *Waiting Laughters* [1990], *The Word Is an Egg* [2004]); and Tanure Ojaide (b. 1948; *Labyrinths of the Delta* [1986], *The Endless Song* [1988], *In the House of Words* [2006]).

Among Ghanaians, experiments in the trans. and adaptation of indigenous poetic forms have been common, as in the works of Kofi Awoonor (b. 1935; *Rediscovery* [1964], in which Ewe funeral *dirges are brought into Eng.; *Night of My Blood* [1971], both autobiographical and political; *Ride Me, Memory* [1973], in which a Ghanaian abroad reflects on his country; *The House by the Sea* [1978]; *Guardians of the Sacred Word* [1978], a collection of Ewe poetry); Kofi Anyidoho (b. 1947; *Elegy for the Revolution* [1978], *A Harvest of Our Dreams* [1985], *Ancestral Logic and Caribbean Blues* [1992]); and Atukwei (John) Okai (b. 1941; *The Oath of the Fontomfrom* [1971], whose title poem refers to a royal drum that beats out the hist. of a society; *Lorgorligi Logarithms* [1974]; *Freedom Symphony* [2008], love poems). Closer to Western trads. of sensibility and structure are others such as Kwesi Brew (1924–2007; *The Shadows of Laughter* [1968], *African Panorama* [1981], *Return of No Return* [1995], *The Clan of the Leopard* [1996]), A. W. Kayper-Mensah (1923–80; *The Dark Wanderer* [1970]; *The Drummer in Our Time* [1975], concerning Africa's view of Europe; *Sankofa: Adinkra Poems* [1976]; *Proverb

*Poems* [1976]), and Frank Kobina Parkes (1932–2004; *Songs from the Wilderness* [1965]).

A notable poet of Gambia was Lenrie Peters (1932–2009; *Satellites* [1967], poems about human rights in the broadest sense; *Katchikali* [1971], which takes its name from a sacred place in Bakau, where the coast of Gambia juts into the North Atlantic; *Selected Poetry* [1981]).

Prominent poets of Sierra Leone include Syl Cheney-Coker (b. 1945; *Concerto for an Exile* [1973]; *The Graveyard Also Has Teeth* [1980]; *The Blood in the Desert's Eyes* [1990]) and Lemuel Johnson (1940–2002; *Highlife for Caliban* [1973]; *Hand on the Navel* [1978]).

B. *East Africa.* East Af. poetry is dominated by two styles. One originated in Okot p'Bitek's trans. and adaptation of his own Acholi poetry. Okot (*Song of Lawino*, the lament of a rural wife over encroaching Westernization; *Song of Ocol* [1970], her husband's reply; "Song of Prisoner" [1971], a commentary on Kenyan politics; "Song of Malaya" [1971], a critique of sexual morality) was probably the most widely read poet of Africa in the later 20th c. Through long rhetorical *monologues usually narrated by a victim of modernization, these poems express social commentary with lucid, graphic imagery, humorous irony, and paradoxical common sense. Another Ugandan poet who makes extensive use of Af. proverbs and folk culture is Okello Oculi (b. 1942; *Orphan* [1968], an allegorical account of Af. culture's removal from traditional values; *Malak* [1976], a narrative poem about the dictator Idi Amin's Uganda; *Kookolem* [1978], about the intersection of social and domestic oppression; *Song for the Sun in Us* [2000]).

An alternative style, more obviously indebted to West Af. poetry, uses *asyndeton, subtle *imagery, and erudite *allusions to convey a mordant and individualized vision of mod. life. It includes a wider range of subjects, tones, and frames of reference. Preeminent poets include the Kenyan Jared Angira (b. 1947; *Juices* [1970]; *Silent Voices* [1972]; *Soft Corals* [1973]; *Cascades* [1979]; *The Years Go By* [1980]), the Ugandan, Richard Ntiru (b. 1946; *Tensions* [1971]), and the South Sudanese Taban lo Liyong (b. 1939; *Meditations in Limbo* [1970]; *Frantz Fanon's Uneven Ribs* [1971]; *Another Nigger Dead* [1972]; *Ballads of Underdevelopment* [1976]; *Another Last Word* [1990]).

C. *Southern Africa.* Before the abolition of apartheid, Eng.-lang. South Af. poetry was most concerned with subjugation, courage, poverty, prisons, revolt, and the private griefs of public injustice. South Af. poets writing in Eng. before the 1970s were often exiles, whose works, therefore, also reflected Brit. or Am. experience—e.g., Arthur Nortje (1942–70; *Dead Roots* [1973]), Cosmo Pieterse (b. 1930; *Echo and Choruses: "Ballad of the Cells"* [1974]), and esp. Dennis Brutus (1924–2009; *Sirens, Knuckles and Boots* [1963]; *Letters to Martha and Other Poems from a South African Prison* [1968]; *Poems from Algiers* [1970]; *A Simple Lust* [1973], the collection that marked Brutus's turn from artifice toward a *plain style; *China Poems* [1975]; *Stubborn*

*Hope* [1978]; *Salutes and Censures* [1982]; *Leafdrift* [2005]). In Brutus's poetry, the speaker is often an observer combining passionate concern with reflective distance, and the imagery portrays monstrous abuse in natural and social settings of oblivious serenity. Even after the ending of apartheid, Brutus continued to write poetry that championed a more just social order than South Africa achieved as a new democracy.

The experimental adaptation of regional Af. forms to original poetry in the Eng. lang. is well represented by the work of Mazisi Kunene (1930–2006; *Zulu Poems* [1970]; *Emperor Shaka the Great: A Zulu Epic* [1979], an adaptation of a traditional epic; *Anthem of the Decades* [1981]; and *The Ancestors and the Sacred Mountain* [1982]).

Keroapetse Kgositsile (b. 1938; *Spirits Unchained* [1969]; *For Melba* [1970]; *My Name Is Afrika* [1971]; *The Present Is a Dangerous Place to Live* [1975]; *To the Bitter End* [1995]; *This Way I Salute You* [2004]) and the broadly popular Oswald Mtshali (b. 1940; *Sounds of a Cowhide Drum* [1971]; *Fireflames* [1980]) are forerunners of the dramatic change in and copious output of Af. poetry after 1970. The influence of Af. Am. musical and poetic forms, esp. *jazz, rap, *blues, and the renaissance of the 1960s, looking back to the *Harlem Renaissance, is often evident (see AFRICAN AMERICAN POETRY). Immediacy may be reinforced by incl. phrases from South Af. langs. or Afrikaans or by directly addressing the reader as a compatriot. Major writers include poets who wrote in solidarity with the Black Consciousness movement's emphasis on the affirmation of black cultural values in the face of state-based terror and oppression, such as Mongane Serote (b. 1944; *Yakhal'Inkomo* [1972]; *Tsetlo* [1974]; *No Baby Must Weep* [1975]; *Behold Mama, Flowers* [1978]; *The Night Keeps Winking* [1982]; *Freedom Lament and Song* [1997]; *History Is the Home Address* [2004]); Sipho Sepamla (1932–2007; *Hurry Up to It!* [1975]; *The Soweto I Love* [1977]; *From Gorée to Soweto* [1988]); Mafika Pascal Gwala (b. 1946; *Jol'iinkomo* [1977]; *No More Lullabies* [1982]); James Matthews (b. 1929; *Cry Rage* [1972]; *No Time for Dreams* [1977]; *Flames and Flowers* [2000]; *Age Is a Beautiful Phase* [2008]); Daniel P. Kunene (b. 1923; *Pirates Have Become Our Kings* [1978]; *A Seed Must Seem to Die* [1981]); and the jazz-influenced Wopko Pieter Jensma (b. 1939; *Sing for Our Execution* [1973]; *Where White Is the Colour Where Black Is the Number* [1974]; *I Must Show You My Clippings* [1977]).

Postapartheid poets in South Africa include Ingrid de Kok (b. 1951; *Familiar Ground* [1988], *Transfer* [1997], *Terrestrial Things* [2002]), Kelwyn Sole (b. 1951; *The Blood of Our Silence* [1988], *Projections in the Past Tense* [1992], *Love That Is Night* [1998], *Mirror and Water Gazing* [2001]), Gail Dendy (b. 1957; *Assault and the Moth* [1993]), Gabeba Baderoon (b. 1969; *The Dream in the Next Body* [2005], *The Museum of Ordinary Life* [2005], *A Hundred Silences* [2006]), and the performance poet Rampolokeng (*Horns for Hondo* [1990], *Rap Master Supreme—Word Bomber in the Extreme* [1997], *The Bavino Sermons* [1999]). See SOUTH AFRICA, POETRY OF.

Politics and economics have denied a wide international audience to the poetry of South Africa's anglophone neighbors. Malawian figures include David Rubadiri (b. 1930; *An African Thunderstorm* [2004]), Frank M. Chipasula (b. 1949; *Visions and Reflections* [1972]; *O Earth Wait for Me* [1984]; *Nightwatcher, Nightsong* [1986]; *Whispers in the Wings* [2001]), Jack Mapanje (b. 1944; *Of Chameleons and Gods* [1981], *Beasts of Nalunga* [2007]), and Steve Chimombo (b. 1945; *A Referendum of the Forest Creatures* [1993], *Napolo and Other Poems* [2009]).

Notable Zambian poets are Richard A. Chima (b. 1945; *The Loneliness of a Drunkard* [1973]) and Patu Simoko (b. 1951; *Africa Is Made of Clay* [1978]).

Zimbabwe has produced copious poetry reflecting both the price of liberating warfare and the consequences of victory. Preeminent poets include Samuel Chimsoro (b. 1949; *Smoke and Flames* [1978]), Musaemura Zimunya (b. 1949; *Thought Tracks* [1982], *Kingfisher, Jikinya and Other Poems* [1982], *Country Dawns and City Lights* [1985]), Mudereri Kadhani (b. 1952; *Quarantine Rhythms* [1976]), Chenjerai Hove (b. 1956; *Up in Arms* [1982], *Red Hills of Home* [1984], *Blind Moon* [2004]), and Freedom Nyamubaya (b. 1960; *On the Road Again* [1986]).

With important national and individual differences, the poetry of southern Africa still has an identifiable character. It is often premised on an intense affinity for the land and, through that, a close union between the spiritual and physical worlds. Nature is presented as a manifestation of religious forces but is also treated with a more direct, nonsymbolic sensibility than in other Af. poetry. Poet and *personae are more closely identified with their community through a diction that relies on direct *address to the reader as putative interlocutor, conversational *apostrophe, quiet humor, *anaphora, and avoidance of strident effects. Esoteric lyricism and declamation are both rare. The stresses that urban cultures impose on rural life and on personal values and identity are common themes, as well as the systemic effects of colonial and postcolonial hegemony. In form and themes, the poetry of this region adapts Eng. to provide sophisticated but unaffected articulation of traditional Af. worldviews in a context of rapid social change.

Af. poetry in Eng. displays an immense cultural and personal variety. Sometimes written in an engaged and earnest tone, frequently leavened by humor, it maintains close identification with communal values and experience while conveying personal perceptions and global influences. Inventively hybridizing Eng. poetic forms with indigenous cultural resources, Af. poetry in Eng. is true to a mod. Af. experience that straddles Western and Af. metaphysical, ethical, and aesthetic visions.

**II. French**. The rise of Af. poetry in Fr. cannot be understood without reference to the slave trade and the subsequent colonization of Africa, the cultural politics France and Belgium imposed during their years of occupation, and multiple forms of resistance to these conditions.

It is no accident that New World writers are usually included in studies and anthols. of Af. poetry in Fr. Both Africans and Af. Americans had to confront the same racist oppression. They accordingly made common cause and sought out each other for inspiration and readership, despite real differences. Hence, the importance of Harlem Renaissance figures such as Langston Hughes and Claude McKay to the founders of *Negritude, the first coherent Af. literary and intellectual movement, which can be dated to the 1930s. Of the founders of the first important literary review, *L'Étudiant Noir* (The Black Student), Aimé Césaire (1913–2008) of Martinique, Léon G. Damas (1912–78) of French Guiana, and Léopold Sédar Senghor (1906–2001) of Senegal, only the last was from Africa itself, and all three were students in Paris. This tendency toward cross-fertilization with other black lits. made Af. poetry in Fr. intercontinental in scope. Though Césaire and Senghor and later poets repeatedly demonstrated their mastery of Fr. trad., they were drawn both to other lits. from what was then called the third world and to indigenous Af. lits. The desire to embrace and renew traditional Af. poetic practice, expressed rhetorically by the proponents of Negritude, has become increasingly important among subsequent generations, who are, however, aware of the difficulties such hybrid literary forms present.

There is no exhaustive definition for the term *Negritude*. Coined by Césaire in his 1939 *Cahier d'un retour au pays natal* (*Notebook of a Return to the Native Land*), it was, in his words, "the simple recognition of the fact that one is black, the acceptance of this fact and of our destiny as blacks, of our history and our culture." Yet there is nothing simple about this statement; its implications are manifold, and the poetry that sought to express it took many different forms, from Damas's explosive *Pigments* (1937) to Césaire's virulent defense of black culture in his *Cahier* to Senghor's lofty exaltation of Af. values beginning with his 1945 *Chants d'ombre* (*Shadow Songs*). The landmark anthol. of Negritude poetry came three years later, Senghor's *Anthologie de la nouvelle poésie nègre et malgache de langue française* (Anthology of New Black and Malagasy Poetry in the French Language, 1948), with its influential preface by Jean-Paul Sartre, "Orphée noir" ("Black Orpheus").

In Sartre's view, Negritude was but an antithesis, a second phase of reaction to white racism that, while defending the specificity of black culture, did so in view of a final synthesis, the transition to a universal (in Sartre's version, proletarian) culture with no oppressors and, ultimately, no specificity. Sartre's perspective was at odds with that of Senghor himself, who had in mind a less politicized universality, but the former set the grounds for Frantz Fanon's typology of postcolonial cultures in *Les Damnés de la terre* (*The Wretched of the Earth*, 1961), one on which most interpretations of postcolonial lit. hist. implicitly repose: a dialectical movement from a colonial period of slavish imitation of Western models to a period of revolt, exemplified by Negritude, and then a postindependence period in which Africans have taken control of their own culture, though not without outside interference.

Damas died relatively young, but Senghor and Césaire lived until the 21st c., and the canonical status of their version of Negritude has been confirmed by Senghor's weighty *Oeuvres complètes* (Complete Works, 2006) and the volumes that marked Césaire's 90th birthday in 2003. Yet, already in 1966, the anthol. by the publisher Présence Africaine, *Nouvelle somme de poésie du monde noir* (A New Survey of the Poetry of the Black World), can be seen as a more ambiguous and ambitious poetic project than those rooted in early Negritude. Foremost among the poets from that generation was Tchicaya U'Tamsi (1931–88), whose dense and difficult oeuvre combined contemp. techniques with an anguished concern for the Congo and the ravages of neocolonialism, esp. in his 1962 *Epitomé*. The number of retrospective eds. that followed his death is a mark of his influence, and it is often against the dominating figure of Tchicaya that later Af. Fr.-lang. poets are measured, not only his fellow Congolese (Brazzaville) J. B. Tati-Loutard (b. 1939, *Oeuvres poétiques* [2007]) and Sony Labou Tansi (1947–95), but, e.g. the Ivorian Jean-Marie Adiaffi (b. 1941), and the Senegalese Amadou Lamine Sall (b. 1951) and Hamidou Dia (b. 1953).

Over the past three decades, Af. poetry in Fr., while still continental in scope, has become more self-consciously local, more often related to the national trads. of the individual poets. Starting with Tati-Loutard's 1976 *Anthologie de la littérature congolaise d'expression française* (Anthology of Congolese Literature in French), there began to appear critical works and collections of poetry representing the increasingly self-defining national lits. of Benin (1984), Cameroon (1982), Gabon (1978), the Ivory Coast (1983), and Togo (1980), among others. This parceling up of a subcontinent into national lits. reflects the rise of distinct national identities across Africa and inevitably points to conflicts among them. In time, *African literature* will seem as broad and as vague a concept as *European literature*, the internal differences within Africa nuancing the abstract and often racially defined concept of a single continental-wide identity.

One prominent thematic thread of contemp. Af. poetry in Fr. is the experience of exile or emigration, which has affected not only the intellectual elite that write and read poetry in Fr. but Africans of all origins from across the continent. This contemp. state of exile can readily be related back to the original diasporic displacement brought about by the slave trade, hence, the continuing relevance of Césaire's *Cahier* and the preoccupation with Af. cultural identity both at home and in the growing Af. communities around the world, in Europe but also in the Americas. It is, thus, not at all uncommon for a Congolese poet like Alain Mabanckou (b. 1966) to find inspiration not only in his homeland but in the large Af. community in Paris, and thereafter among Af.-Americans in Los Angeles. Similarly, Véronique Tadjo (b. 1955) was born in Paris but was raised in the Ivory Coast, which continues to inspire her poetry. Rare in fact is the Af. poet writing in Fr. who does not have a foothold on two continents: the Senegalese Babacar Sall (Dakar/Paris), Léopold Congo Mbemba (Brazzaville/Paris), and Amadu

Elimane Kane (Senegal/Paris). This is as much the case for female as for male poets, Tanella Boni (Abidjan/Toulouse) and Clémentine Faïk-Nzuji (Kinshasa/Brussels) being additional salient cases among the former.

Many observers think that, despite the continuing hegemony of Paris as a cultural center, writing in Fr. outside France is destined to assume as important a role as writing in Eng. beyond the U.S. and Britain. Af. poetry in Fr. is arguably one of the richest sources of this *littérature-monde* (lit. of the world in Fr.). This is a less categorical claim perhaps than that made by Sartre in 1948—that Af. and Antillean poetries were the only true "revolutionary" poetries of those times. But the variety of poetic experience conveyed by Af. poets in Fr. confirms that Af. cultures can speak universally with force and authenticity (see CARIBBEAN POETRY [French]; FRANCE, POETRY OF).

**III. Portuguese.** Af. poetry in Port. is often known as Lusophone Af. poetry, although some resist the term *Lusophone*, claiming it contains colonial overtones. This was arguably the first Af. poetry in a Eur. lang. to be published. Some facetious critics claim the 16th-c. Port. national bard Luís de Camões as the first Port. Af. poet, pointing to his descriptions of the continent in his literary epic *The Lusiads* (1572). The question of who qualifies as an Af. poet of Port. expression became contentious in the period immediately following the independence of the former colonies (1973–75), when the newly formed nations sought to define their own literary *canons and claim historical roots that contested Port. cultural hegemony.

It is generally accepted that José da Silva Maia Ferreira (1827–81?), born in Angola and of Port. heritage, was the first poet pub. in Port.-speaking Africa when he released his *Espontaneidades da minha alma* (Outpourings from My Soul) in 1849. The work is probably the first collection of poems printed in the sub-Saharan region. With the independence of Angola, Mozambique, Cape Verde, Guinea-Bissau, and São Tomé e Príncipe, five increasingly diverse national poetries were born, written mainly in Port. but also, in the case of Cape Verde, Guinea-Bissau, and São Tomé, in local Port.-based creoles.

Precursors of these national poetics, such as Silva Maia Ferreira; Joaquim Cordeiro da Matta (1857–94), a black Angolan poet; and Caetano da Costa Alegre (1864–90) from the island of São Tomé, wrote verse modeled on Eur. styles and themes, though often informed by an Af. consciousness. Some wrote verse reflecting their sense of social reformism and dedication to Port. liberalism. They did not propose independence for the colonies so much as a more progressive Port. empire. Beginning in the 1930s in the Cape Verde Islands and in the 1950s in Angola and Mozambique, however, poems of cultural legitimization and growing social protest, fanned by the winds of nationalism, characterized the literary movements initiated by members of an emerging black and *mestiço* (mixed-race) intelligentsia and their Af.-born or -raised white allies.

On the largely mestiço Cape Verde Islands, a trio of poets—Jorge Barbosa (1902–71), Oswaldo Alcântara (pseud. of Baltasar Lopes da Silva, 1907–89), and Manuel Lopes (1907–2005)—founded in 1936 what became known as the *Claridade* movement, named after the group's arts and culture journal. Under the influence of Brazilian modernism and northeast regionalism, they codified the islands' Creole ethos, giving artistic expression to the prevailing Cape Verdean themes of solitude, the sea, drought, and emigration. This generation reacted to the universalism of poets such as José Lopes (1871–1962), who as well as publishing poetry in Port., wrote poems in Fr. and Eng. and defended the concept of a global Port. nation.

In the Angolan cities of Benguela and esp. Luanda, a thinly veiled nationalist poetics emerged (censorship and police repression precluded outspoken militancy) among black, mestiço, and a few white poets, some of whom would form the nucleus of the Movement of the Liberation of Angola (MPLA), founded in 1956. Poets like Agostinho Neto (1922–79), who was Angola's first president; Viriato da Cruz (1928–73); António Jacinto (1924–91); Fernando Costa Andrade (1936–2009); and Mário António Fernandes de Oliveira (1934–89) produced poems that called for an independent Angola. Many militant poets, in Mozambique as well as Angola, were also guerrilla fighters. Others fled into exile or paid for their militancy with imprisonment.

Throughout the 1960s until the 1974 military coup that toppled the colonial government in Lisbon, much Af. poetry in Port. was produced underground. Militants distributed their poems clandestinely or published them abroad. Neto wrote surreptitiously in his prison cell in Portugal and managed to smuggle his poems out of the Aljube prison to Kinshasa, Dar es Salaam, Milan, and Belgrade, where they were published in bilingual eds. Only after independence did these poets emerge from secrecy and "return" legitimately to Angola.

In Mozambique, during the two decades before national independence, a few Europeans produced poetry that was a conscious part more of Port. lit. than of Mozambique's incipient cultural expression. Starting in the 1960s, these Euro-Mozambicans, most notably Rui Knopfli (1933–97), born and raised in the colonial city of Lourenço Marques (now Maputo), sought to represent the essence of an Afro-Eur. experience. After Mozambican independence, a debate raged within the new nation's cultural elite as to whether the work of poets like Knopfli belonged in an emerging national canon, with most considering him Port. rather than Mozambican, a position he contested. As might be expected, a poetry of Af. cultural and racial essentialism, whether by black or mixed-race Mozambicans, coincided with the rise of nationalism in the 1950s and 1960s. The mestiço poets José Craveirinha (1922–2003) and Noémia de Sousa (1926–2003) both wrote a number of memorable poems of cultural revindication. Many of the arguments used to exclude Knopfli from the Mozambican canon, most notably his absence from postindependence Mozambique, could equally well apply to de Sousa, who spent much of her life in

Europe. However, few readers contest her place in the poetic canon of Mozambique.

Craveirinha, Mozambique's most celebrated writer, is considered one of the greatest Port.-lang. poets of the 20th c. In 2001, he won the Prémio Camões, the highest award granted for lifetime literary contributions to the Port. lang. Unlike many Mozambican poets of his generation, who allowed their political dogmas to dictate their aesthetic programs, Craveirinha repeatedly demonstrated how a profound lyricism could serve the political causes he supported. He was capable of exceptionally moving love poetry as well as political demands to address inequalities and social injustice.

Many of the Port. Af. poets who wrote in the years leading to independence spent some of their formative years in Lisbon. Not surprisingly, Lusophone Negritude poetry appeared there, where these poets shared ideas and influences. Most notably, Francisco José Tenreiro (1921–63), a mestiço from the island of São Tomé who lived most of his life in the Port. capital, emerged as the greatest writer of Negritude poetry in Port. Under the influence of the Harlem Renaissance, Afro-Cuban Negrism, and francophone poets such as Senghor and Césaire, Tenreiro wrote the poems published posthumously as *Coração em África* (My Heart in Africa, 1964).

Some Angolan writers have proclaimed that their poetry was born in the struggle for liberation, while Negritude was conceived in defeat as a Eur.-based phenomenon that had little to do with Africa. During the decade of anticolonialist wars in Angola, Mozambique, and Guinea-Bissau, poetry became increasingly combative and tendentious. Marcelino dos Santos (b. 1929), a high-ranking member of the Mozambique Liberation Movement (Frelimo), who became its vice president, was at the forefront of militant poets who wrote pamphletary verse that, during the protracted war, served as a didactic instrument as well as a goad to political mobilization. Not noted for its aestheticism, the poetry of this generation is a valuable historical document tracing the ideological concerns of the liberation movement.

In the early years after independence, a multiracial array of poets began seeking new ways to capture poetically the changed realities of their nations. In Angola, Manuel Rui (b. 1941) emerged as one of the most important poetic voices of his generation, writing the verses of the Angolan national *anthem. He later concentrated on prose but always in a highly poeticized way. Similarly, Mia Couto (b. 1955) of Mozambique is a poet who became more famous for his extremely lyrical prose. His ling. innovation is so profound and celebrated that it is difficult to categorize him as anything other than a poet. Alda do Espírito Santo (1926–2010), like Rui in Angola, provided the lyrics of the national anthem of São Tomé e Príncipe and became a major literary and political presence in her nation, rising to become the speaker of São Tomé's parliament. In most of the newly independent nations, poetry and politics went hand in hand. This politicized poetry had been born of the independence struggles and continued in the early years of independence in the service of the state. However, it soon became obvious to the practitioners of poetry that the new realities of independence demanded a different kind of poetics, and the next generation of poets became less aligned with, or compromised by, the failings of the liberation movements now in power.

The imperative of new poetic discourses reflecting a changed political reality led Rui, along with fellow Angolans such as Arlindo Barbeitos (b. 1940), Rui Duarte de Carvalho (1941–2010), Jofre Rocha (b. 1941), and David Mestre (1948–97), to experiment with new styles of poetry, which followed political prescriptions less and challenged aesthetic boundaries more. Two of these poets, Duarte de Carvalho and Mestre, were born in Portugal, where Mestre died. In Mozambique, Rui Nogar (1933–93) and Luis Carlos Patraquim (b. 1953); in Cape Verde, Corsino Fortes (b. 1933), Oswaldo Osório (b. 1937), and Arménio Vieira (b. 1941); in Guinea-Bissau, Helder Proença (b. 1956); and in São Tomé, Frederico Gustavo dos Anjos (b. 1954) have all attempted, with varying degrees of success, to shift poetic boundaries away from a collective voice of protest to a more introspective interrogation of the poetic self. In Angola, Duarte de Carvalho has experimented with an integrated form of Af. oral expression and Brazilian *concrete poetry, as well as repeatedly playing with the boundaries between literary genres.

Since independence, a number of poets have emerged in each of the five Port.-speaking Af. countries, inflecting the Port. lang. in ways that are often indebted to oral trads. local to their nations. At the same time, from the 1980s onward, and perhaps in response to a nascent questioning of the failure to realize the promises of independence, poetry from Port.-speaking Africa has taken a decidedly self-interrogating turn. Salient practitioners of this different type of poetics, which owes much to Af. and Eur. heritages but also to the political failures and civil strife, include the following: from Angola, Rui Augusto (b. 1958), Ana Paula Tavares (b. 1952), José Luís Mendonça (b. 1955), and Ana de Santana (b. 1960); from Mozambique, Luís Carlos Patraquim, Hélder Muteia (b. 1960), Armando Artur (b. 1962), and Eduardo White (b. 1964); and from Cape Verde, José L. Hopffer Almada (b. 1960), who organized *Mirabilis*, an anthol. of work by some 60 island poets (pub. 1991). Tavares's work has become increasingly popular and more sophisticated. Alongside Conceição Lima (b. 1961) from São Tomé, Vera Duarte (b. 1952) and Dina Salústia (b. 1941) from Cape Verde, and Odete Costa Semedo (b. 1959) from Guinea-Bissau, Tavares has demonstrated that successful and popular poetry in Port.-speaking Africa is no longer the preserve of men. Indeed, women have produced some of the most innovative poetry in the Port. lang. in recent years.

*See* BRAZIL, POETRY OF; COLONIAL POETICS; ORAL POETRY; PORTUGAL, POETRY OF.

■ **English**. *Anthologies*: *West African Verse*, ed. D. Nwoga (1966); *Poems from East Africa*, ed. D. Cook et al. (1971); *The Word Is Here: Poetry from Modern Africa*, ed. K. Kgositsile (1973); *Poems of Black Africa*, ed. W. Soyinka (1975); *A World of Their Own: South African Poets of the Seventies*, ed. S. Gray (1976); *Introduction to East African Poetry*, ed. J. Kariara et al. (1977); *Zimbabwean Poetry in English*, ed. K. Z. Muchemwa (1978); *African Poetry in English*, ed. S. H. Burton et al. (1979); *Summons: Poems from Tanzania*, ed. R. S. Mabala (1980); *Somehow We Survive*, ed. S. Plumpp (1982); *The Return of the Amasi Bird*, ed. T. Couzens et al. (1982); *A New Book of African Verse*, ed. J. Reed et al. (1984); *The Heritage of African Poetry*, ed. I. Okpewho (1984); *When My Brothers Come Home: Poems from Central and Southern Africa*, ed. F. M. Chipasula (1985); *The Fate of Vultures*, ed. M. Zimunya et al. (1989); *The Heinemann Book of African Poetry in English*, ed. A. Maja-Pearce (1990); *The New African Poetry*, ed. T. Ojaide and T. M. Sallah (1999); *The Penguin Book of Modern African Poetry*, ed. G. Moore and U. Beier, 5th ed. (2007); *Bending the Bow: An Anthology of African Love Poetry*, ed. F. Chipasula (2009). ***Bibliographies***: *Bibliography of Creative African Writing*, ed. J. Janheinz et al. (1971); *Black African Literature in English*, ed. B. Lindfors (1979); *New Reader's Guide to African Literature*, ed. H. M. Zell et al., 2d ed. (1983); *Supplement to Black African Literature in English*, 1977–1982, ed. B. Lindfors (1985); *Companion to South African English Literature*, ed. D. Adey et al. (1986). **Criticism and History**: A. Roscoe, *Mother Is Gold: A Study of West African Literature* (1971); O. R. Dathorne, *The Black Mind: A History of African Literature* (1974); K. Awoonor, *The Breast of the Earth* (1975); R. N. Egudu, *Four Modern West African Poets* (1977); A. Roscoe, *Uhuru's Fire: African Literature East to South* (1977); G. Moore, *Twelve African Writers* (1980); K. L. Goodwin, *Understanding African Poetry: A Study of Ten Poets* (1982); J. Alvarez-Pereyre, *The Poetry of Commitment in South Africa*, trans. Clive Wake (1984); A. Z. Davies and F. Stratton, *How to Teach Poetry: An African Perspective* (1984); T. O. McLoughlin and F. R. Mhonyera, *Insights: An Introduction to the Criticism of Zimbabwean and Other Poetry* (1984); T. Olafioye, *Politics in African Poetry* (1984); U. Barnett, *A Vision of Order: A Study of Black South African Literature in English (1914–1980)* (1985); *European-Language Writing in Sub-Saharan Africa*, ed. A. S. Gérard, 2 v. (1986); R. Fraser, *West African Poetry: A Critical History* (1986); A. McClintock, "'Azikwelwa' (We Will Not Ride): Politics and Value in Black South African Poetry," *CritI* 13 (1987); E. Ngara, *Ideology and Form in African Poetry* (1990); K. A. Appiah, *In My Father's House* (1992); T. Ojaide, "New Trends in Modern African Poetry," *Research in African Literatures* 26 (1995); *Companion to African Literatures*, ed. D. Killam and R. Rowe (2000); A. Irele, *The African Imagination* (2001); J. Ramazani, *The Hybrid Muse: Postcolonial Poetry in English* (2001); R. S. Patke, *Postcolonial Poetry in English* (2006); A. A. Roscoe, *The Columbia Guide to Central African Literature in English since 1945* (2007); S. Gikandi and E. Mwangi, *The Columbia Guide to East African Literature in English* *since 1945* (2007); J. Ramazani, *A Transnational Poetics* (2009); S. Egya, "Art and Outrage: A Critical Survey of Recent Nigerian Poetry in English," *Research in African Literatures* 42 (2011).

■ **French**. *Anthologies*: *Anthologie négro-africaine*, ed. L. Kesteloot (1967); *Poètes d'Afrique et des Antilles*, ed. H. Dia (2002); *Nouvelle anthologie africaine: La poesie*, ed. J. Chevrier (2002); *Nouvelle anthologie africaine II: La poesie*, ed. J. Chevrier (2006). *Criticism and History*: R. Cornevin, *Littératures d'Afrique noire de langue française* (1976); A. S. Gérard, *European-Writing in Sub-Saharan Africa*, 2 v. (1986); *Dictionnaire des oeuvres littérature négro-africaines de langue française*, ed. A. Kom (1983); A. Rouch and G. Clavreuil, *Littératures nationales d'écriture française* (1986); J. Chevrier, *Littérature nègre* (1999); "Que peut la poésie aujourd'hui?" spec. iss. *Africultures* 24 (2000); P. Nganang, *Manifeste d'une nouvelle littérature africaine* (2007); L. Kesteloot, *Les écrivains noirs de langue française*, 2d ed. (2010).

■ **Portuguese**. *Anthologies*: *No reino de Caliban: Antologia panorâmica da poesia africana de expressão portuguesa*, ed. M. Ferreira, 3 v. (1975–86); *Antologia temática de poesia africana*, ed. M. de Andrade, 2 v. (1976–79); *Poems from Angola*, ed. and trans. M. Wolfers (1979); *A Horse of White Clouds*, ed. and trans. D. Burness (1989); *For Vasco: Poems from Guinea-Bissau*, trans. A.R.L. Fernandes et al. (2006). *Bibliography*: *Bibliografia das literaturas africanas de expressão portuguesa*, ed. G. Moser and M. Ferreira (1983). *Criticism and History*: G. Moser, *Essays in Portuguese-African Literature* (1969); R. Hamilton, *Voices from an Empire: A History of Afro-Portuguese Literature* (1975); M. Ferreira, *Literatura africana de expressão portuguesa*, 2 v. (1977); R. Hamilton, *Literatura africana, literatura necessária*, 2 v. (1981–83); *The Postcolonial Literature of Lusophone Africa*, ed. P. Chabal et al. (1996).

D. F. Dorsey, J. Ramazani (Eng.); G. Lang (Fr.); R. G. Hamilton, P. Rothwell (Port.)

**AFRICAN AMERICAN POETRY.** Af. Am. poetry began, to all intents and purposes, with the improbable appearance in 1773 in London of *Poems on Various Subjects, Religious and Moral by Phillis Wheatley, Negro Servant to Mr. John Wheatley of Boston, in New England*. From one point of view, the appearance of this book was a minor event. From another perspective, it was historic. The event was minor in that *Poems on Various Subjects* followed somewhat mechanically the values and practices of Brit. literary masters of the age; in addition, the presence of several occasional pieces set in New England added to its provincial air. But *Poems on Various Subjects* also broke new ground. Only the second book of verse pub. by an Am. woman, following the Eng.-born Anne Bradstreet's achievement a century before, it posed a serious challenge to key assumptions most white people held at that time about the mental capacity of blacks. Accordingly, *Poems on Various Subjects* included an affidavit from 18 eminent white men of Boston, incl. John Hancock and the governor of the colony, Thomas Hutchinson, attesting to the fact that—*mirabile dictu*—the volume was the work of

"PHILLIS, a young Negro girl." They had grilled her, and she had passed their test.

These men enacted the skepticism, crippling at its worst, bracing at its best, with which white America regarded—and to some extent still regards—the black poet. In turn, Wheatley anticipated, if mainly in token ways, some of the basic, abiding concerns of black poets to come. In her verse, she recorded both her discomfort with her identity as a black Am. (one born in Africa) and her determination to succeed as an artist. In poems such as "To the University of Cambridge, in New England" and "On Being Brought from Africa to America," she contested the prevailing belief that blacks were essentially worthless except as chattel slaves. Pagan Africa, she conceded, was indeed "the land of errors, and *Egyptian* gloom," but Christianity granted blacks a chance at divine redemption, even if slavery itself had made deliverance possible. So, too, in the secular sphere, she knew that writing and publishing poetry empowered blacks at a time when they possessed little power. Their accomplished poems showed the world that blacks, incl. slaves or servants, deserved far more than white society allowed them. In fact, Wheatley's standing as a poet enabled her in 1776 to visit and be cordially received by General George Washington (whom she eulogized in a poem) at his encampment near Cambridge, Massachusetts. Finally, in addressing certain poems to other blacks, incl. "To S.M., A Young African Painter, on Seeing His Works," Wheatley also revealed a hunger for community based on race pride that spoke to the social insecurity and even loneliness that marked, and would continue to mark, the lives of many black poets in America.

By the time she died in 1784, Wheatley was all but forgotten. (As part of a sweeping indictment of the quality of black life, Thomas Jefferson dismissed her poetry as "below criticism.") Nevertheless, a thin line of writers kept the idea of the black Am. poet alive. In North Carolina, George Moses Horton, a slave allowed unusual freedom, became the first black explicitly to attack slavery in verse—although most of his poems are trite. In publishing three volumes of verse, incl. his first, *The Hope of Liberty* (1829) and the misleadingly titled *Naked Genius* (1865), Horton saw his career overlap with the age of radical abolitionism but without catching its transforming fire. Not so with two other notable black poets of this time. In 1853, when James M. Whitfield published *America and Other Poems*, his piece "America" denounced his nation as a land "of blood, crime, and wrong." Frances Ellen Watkins Harper's *Poems on Miscellaneous Subjects*, appearing the following year and endorsed by the abolitionist zealot William Lloyd Garrison, protested the treatment of black women in particular. Harper's "The Slave Mother," didactic and sentimental but invaluable as propaganda, led to a long career in service to civil rights through poetry (albeit poetry mainly of a preachy kind), fiction, and journalism that was esp. bold in its attacks on lynching.

Black poets, incl. Whitfield and Harper, starting out in the antebellum years, fell far short of the historic achievement of the authors of prose slave narratives. This relatively novel form fueled abolitionist fervor, as in the impact of *Narrative of the Life of Frederick Douglass, an American Slave, Written by Himself* (1845), while also achieving a measure of literary distinction. The slave narrative would shape the Af. Am. novel just as it directly shaped Harriet Beecher Stowe's epochal *Uncle Tom's Cabin*. However, it seemed to have little effect on black poetry. Nor were black poets of the age moved by Walt Whitman's *Leaves of Grass* (1855); most, like their white counterparts, held to old-fashioned notions about the ideal form and content of verse. Black poetry produced a Whitman, but Albery A. Whitman of Springfield, Ohio, although prolific, vigorous, and visionary at his best, was captive to archaic notions about diction and stanza forms. Following the Civil War, far from growing with their new freedom, black poets seemed to enter the doldrums.

That period of stagnation ended with the arrival of Paul Laurence Dunbar of Ohio. Dunbar became the first black poet to gain a national audience. He also became a treasured poet among black Ams. because of his loving portraits of black life. Dunbar seized on two major literary trends. One was the so-called plantation trad., in which romantic notions about slavery, incl. myths about kind masters and mistresses and their happy "darkies," helped white America to close the book on the Civil War. The other was the vogue of Am. regionalism, accompanied by a keen interest in dialect. Both were epitomized in fiction by Mark Twain's *Adventures of Huckleberry Finn* (1883) and in poetry by the verse of James Whitcomb Riley of Indiana, who exerted a strong influence on Dunbar. With his collections *Oak and Ivy* (1893), *Major and Minors* (1895), and the best-selling *Lyrics of Lowly Life* (1896), for which William Dean Howells wrote an intro., Dunbar became renowned both for dialect poems about black life and also for poems written in standard Eng. on more elevated, putatively universal themes. Eventually, the tension between these two areas began to demoralize him. When Howells expressed in his preface a preference for Dunbar's dialect verse, which captured for him what he saw as the true range of the black sensibility—between the poles of "appetite" and "emotion"—Dunbar mourned his fate as a black poet. "The Poet" bares his anguish over the fact that, despite his labors to write poems on "universal" themes in cultivated lang., the world insensitively "turned to praise / A jingle in a broken tongue."

*Dialect poetry came to dominate black poetry, just as the plantation trad. widely caricatured black life and culture. The irony was that the plantation trad. and the vogue of dialect verse coincided with the legalization, through crucial U.S. Supreme Court decisions of 1895 and 1896 in particular, of racial segregation in America. Black poets were aware of this irony. Dunbar's friend James D. Carrothers, who also excelled at the form, made clear in his poem "At the Closed Gate of Justice" his anguished belief that "To be a Negro in a day like this / Demands forgiveness." As with Dunbar, however, writing dialect verse made Carrothers's reputation as a poet. *Century* magazine and other leading white jours. published his work. Nevertheless, the tension between dialect and standard Eng. persisted, as may be seen in any comparison of Carrothers's amusing dialect piece "Me 'n' Dunbar" to his elegy of 1912, "Paul Laurence Dunbar."

Dialect verse sponsored by the plantation trad. was doomed. It did not survive far into the new century, esp. as antiblack repression, epitomized by the brazen lynching of blacks, intensified—and black resistance grew. The militancy of intellectuals such as W.E.B. Du Bois played a strong role in its demise. In *The Souls of Black Folk* (1903), a landmark prose work that helped to define mod. Af. Am. character and psychology, Du Bois electrified black intellectuals and artists with his identification of a dramatic "double-consciousness" as innate to Af. Am. life. He identified the key quality of the Af. Am. as his or her "two-ness—an American, a Negro; two souls, two thoughts, two unreconciled strivings; two warring ideals in one dark body, whose dogged strength alone keeps it from being torn asunder." He published only a few of his poems, but work such as his fierce, almost dithyrambic "A Litany of Atlanta" (following the Atlanta Riot of 1906) and "The Song of the Smoke" were *free-verse protests that helped to destabilize the hold exerted by dialect and plantation caricatures.

Other poets of this period contested dialect in different ways. William Stanley Braithwaite, a starched black Bostonian who became nationally respected as the ed. of more than 30 anthols. of verse, incl. an annual anthol. of Am. magazine verse, admired Dunbar as a poet. Nevertheless, his first volume, *Lyrics of Life and Love* (1904), showed his kindred devotion to the major Eng. romantic poets, whose work indeed inspired most black Am. poets. Seeking to be mod., Braithwaite also absorbed the influence of contemp. Am. writers such as E. A. Robinson. However, the result typically was charming, gently moving, often expertly written poetry that, avoiding the subject of race, lacked blood and sinew. Fenton Johnson of Chicago, who published three collections of verse, incl. *Visions of the Dusk* (1915) and *Songs of the Soil* (1916), also admired Dunbar. With the trauma of World War I, however, he became perhaps the first black poet to follow a recognized version of aesthetic *modernism. Familiar with Harriet Monroe's Chicago-based *Poetry* magazine and thus exposed to the esoteric work of T. S. Eliot and Ezra Pound, he hewed instead to the populist line of modernism preferred by Edgar Lee Masters and Carl Sandburg. Johnson's poems in this vein, lamenting the effects of civilization in a sometimes cynical tone, helped to finish off dialect verse among younger black poets.

Another key poet in this transitional period around World War I was Claude McKay. In his native Jamaica, inspired largely by Dunbar and despite his own wide reading, he had published two volumes of dialect verse. Moving to New York, however, he fell in with modernist literary leaders such as Robinson, Waldo Frank, and Floyd Dell. He became an editor at Dell's *Liberator* magazine. In the process, McKay abandoned dialect. His volumes *Spring in New Hampshire* (1919) and *Harlem Shadows* (1922) showed off McKay's lyric power, but in explosive *sonnets (he believed in the form) such as "If We Must Die," "White House," "To the White Fiends," and "America," he also vented his rage against racism and the hypocrisy endemic to America. "If We Must Die," written following the deadly antiblack Chicago Riots of 1919, thrilled aspiring black poets and became his signature piece. McKay set new standards for verse as a vehicle for black protest—although "If We Must Die" makes no specific mention of race, nation, or politics.

Finally, in some respects, the most important transitional figure was the poet, novelist, diplomat, and NAACP leader James Weldon Johnson, a Floridian settled in New York City. In his preface to his key anthology of 1923, *The Book of American Negro Poetry* (rev. 1931), Johnson declared dialect verse dead. Later, he would credit his own rejection of the form to a belated but shattering reading of Walt Whitman's *Leaves of Grass*. Johnson published several stately poems in praise of Af. Am. hist. and culture. His best-known pieces are probably "O Black and Unknown Bards," about the composers of the black spirituals, and the text of "Lift Ev'ry Voice and Sing," the so-called black Am. national *anthem. Johnson understood the higher aims of dialect poets, even if he no longer wished to be one. In 1927, when his book of free verse, *God's Trombones*, offered seven sermons as delivered by old-time black preachers, he sought to capture, esp. in "The Creation" (a sermon based on Genesis), the rhetorical and rhythmic virtuosity of the black sermonic trad. without recourse to the traditional markers of black illiteracy.

In the early years of the so-called *Harlem Renaissance, which spanned most of the 1920s and early 1930s, poetry played a decisive role. Replacing the tension between standard Eng. and dialect verse was a not entirely unrelated clash between a devotion to traditional notions concerning poetry and a contrary passion for contemp. black mass culture. This clash played itself out most dramatically in the contrast between the work of Countee Cullen and Langston Hughes. Extravagantly admiring the Eng. poets John Keats (as in "To John Keats, Poet, at Spring Time") and A. E. Housman, Cullen saw the lang. of lower-class urban black culture as inimical to true poetry. He also nursed a mournful sense of his identity as a black poet, as his title "The Shroud of Color" suggests. His sonnet "Yet Do I Marvel" ends with the speaker amazed that an inscrutable God should have done "this curious thing: / To make a poet black, and bid him sing!" The sense of a self-destructive conflict between being black and Am. haunts his major poem, "Heritage" ("What is Africa to me? / Copper sun and scarlet sea . . ."). This poem also hints at its persona's possibly conflicted sexuality; but the themes of gayness, lesbianism, and bisexuality were topics that few white and virtually no black poets dared to treat at that time. Nevertheless, with his first volume, *Color* (1925), Cullen established his reputation

as a harbinger of a new day in black poetry, one rooted in youth and modernity.

Hughes saw poetry differently. He built his early reputation on a succession of poems, such as his signature "The Negro Speaks of Rivers," that calmly asserted the beauty, integrity, and history of the Af. Am. people. Such work dominated his first book, *The Weary Blues* (1926), but his second, *Fine Clothes to the Jew* (1927), broke new ground with its privileging of the *blues as its major influence. Condemned in the black press for seeming to endorse the semiliterate, sexually unrestrained culture of the urban black poor, the book put in place some key elements of future black verse. Above all, Hughes saw black music, esp. the blues (which he had used only tentatively in *The Weary Blues*), as the core of his mature aesthetic. Later he recalled how he had tried to write poems shaped by black music. "Like the waves of the sea," he wrote in *The Big Sea* (1940), "coming one after another, always one after another, like the earth moving around the sun, night, day—night, day—night, day, forever, so is the undertow of black music with its rhythm that never betrays you, its strength like the beat of the human heart, its humor, and its rooted power." The blues emphasized the pain of black life but also typically a mordant wit and an exuberant embrace of life. In this way, ordinary blacks converted pain into art. Dialect returned to black poetry but in a new form. Now it expressed rage and despair where, as Hughes saw it, sophisticated literary forms often filtered and finally betrayed such emotions.

Virtually the full range of the black Am. lang. and life experience was now at the disposal of black poets, even if only a few explored it. One of these poets was the Howard University professor Sterling Brown. His sole volume, *Southern Road* (1932), built on the blues foundation with poems such as "Ma Rainey," about one of the most famous blues performers. Most other poets of the era, esp. the women writers, stuck to the genteel. Angelina Weld Grimké and Georgia Douglas Johnson offered largely sentimental poems about love and the loss of love; and younger writers such as Anne Spencer and Helene Johnson also found it hard to surrender their "respectability." In poems such as "Before the Feast of Shushan" and "At the Carnival," Spencer showed the keenest interest in "high" modernism among the writers of the Harlem Renaissance. A devout Christian, Arna Bontemps created a poetry of meditation and spiritual concern largely unprecedented in black verse since the 18th c. His "Mourning at Bethesda," which links spiritual loss to the effects of the involuntary African Diaspora, became one of the most admired poems of the Harlem Renaissance.

A victim of the Great Depression, the movement faded into what became virtually a lost decade for Af. Am. poetry. Most of the published poets seemed to shut up shop; Hughes shifted to writing radical socialist propaganda poems such as "Goodbye Christ" and "Good Morning Revolution." Four new talents in particular rose to fill the void. In 1942, Margaret Walker won a Yale Younger Poets award for her slender volume *For My People*. Its title poem is a rhythmic affirmation of love and respect for the black masses, incl. black women. Although Walker did not build on this success as a poet, about the same time Gwendolyn Brooks launched a career that would keep her near the center of black Am. poetry for decades to come. In her first volume, *A Street in Bronzeville* (1945), she explored black life in a corner of Chicago, where she lived most of her life. Four years later, in 1949, she published *Annie Allen*, which won her a Pulitzer Prize. This was easily the most prestigious honor ever given to a black Am. poet. Brooks offered a new fusion in Af. Am. poetry. Influenced both by writers such as Hughes and by the high modernist trad. then epitomized perhaps by Robert Lowell, she moved as a poet between relative simplicity and, as in "The Sundays of Satin-Legs Smith" ("Inamoratas, with an approbation, / Bestowed his title. Blessed his inclination . . ."), a complexity of prosody, learned *allusion, and sustained *irony basically novel to black Am. poetry. Brooks brought intelligence and life experience to her poetry. Early pieces such as "kitchenette building" (about the struggles of the poetic imagination when the poet must suffer the trials of a typical lower-income housewife) and "the mother" (about the psychological trauma of abortions) explored the realities of city life in a fashion new to black poetry. Anchored in Chicago, Brooks was alert to national issues and trends. Her poetry continued to grow as that of other writers withered. Faced by the intimidating Black Power movement of the 1960s, she threw in her lot with the young. The result was well-received volumes such as *Primer for Black Folks* and *Black Love*, although her best poetry had come almost certainly before the turbulent 1960s.

If Brooks made sure she modified and domesticated some of the key techniques of high modernism, Melvin B. Tolson came to commit himself to its most arcane, esoteric, and bewildering aspects. In the 1930s, he wrote a relatively conventional collection of poetic portraits of Harlem life published some 30 years later as *Harlem Gallery* (1965) and *A Gallery of Harlem Portraits* (1979). In 1944, his book *Rendezvous with America* drew on the success of its best-known poem, "Dark Symphony," a solemn but fairly conventional paean to black achievement. However, a government commission from Liberia to produce a long poem in honor of the centenary of the republic founded by Am. exslaves led to the most daring modernist venture in Af. Am. poetry: *Libretto for the Republic of Liberia* (1953). This volume, densely studded in almost every line with abstruse allusions and parodic wordplay, appeared with a tribute to its author by Allen Tate, among the elite poets and critics of poetry. Tate hailed Tolson as peerless in his fusion of the black experience with the most complex lang. of modernism.

The fourth member of this transitional quartet was Robert Hayden of Detroit, Michigan. Influenced by his deep reading in historical material as part of the Federal Writers' Project of the late 1930s, Hayden published *Heart-Shape in the Dust* (1940). His career then took a fortuitous turn when, as a graduate student at the University of Michigan, he studied with W. H. Auden, a visiting professor. Hayden's understanding of poetry and hist. began to mature. Shaped also by the pacifist universalism of his Baha'i faith, he brought a visionary but firmly grounded quality to his meditations on race, hist., and everyday life. His best work includes finely wrought and yet viscerally powerful poems about slavery such as "Middle Passage" and "Runagate Runagate." Later he applied a perhaps even more refined moral and artistic consciousness in writing poems about contemp. life, such as the *elegy "El Hajj Malik El-Shabazz" about Malcolm X's spiritual evolution and tragic end. His mastery as a writer may be seen in the late volumes *The Night Blooming Cereus* (1972) and *Angle of Ascent: New and Selected Poems* (1975). In 1976, the Library of Congress appointed him its Consultant in Poetry, the first Af. Am. to hold that position.

By this time, almost all the older writers, incl. Hayden, were under severe fire from militant younger blacks inspired, starting in 1965, by the Black Power and *Black Arts movements. Both movements preached an exclusionary version of black identity and hostility toward white culture. The most powerful figure in the arts was the poet, dramatist, and editor Amiri Baraka, who changed his name from LeRoi Jones to emphasize his African nationalist identity. Once a disciple of the Beat movement (see BEAT POETRY), Baraka (as LeRoi Jones) had lived with his wife, Hettie Cohen, in Greenwich Village, New York, where they edited the Beat arts journal *Jugen*. His first book of poetry, *Preface to a Twenty-Volume Suicide Note* (1961), presented a charming, sometimes whimsical sensibility fortified by a keen intelligence and a studied interest in popular culture as well as formal experimentation. Following the assassination of Malcolm X in 1965, however, Jones abandoned these connections and moved to Harlem, where he tried to establish a repertory company based on Black Arts principles. Now he wrote a different, far more aggressive kind of poetry. Indebted in matters of form to W. C. Williams and to the iconoclastic Beat master Allen Ginsberg, as well as to the disruptive music of jazz performers such as John Coltrane, Baraka demanded a new black poetry of ruthless militancy—"poems that kill," he declared. In addition to whites, he targeted blacks who, in his opinion, had failed to purge themselves of their allegiances to white culture. His manifesto poem "Black Art," laced with obscene words and images of violence and degradation, offered an almost apocalyptic view of race relations in America. His poetry of this period is featured in his *Black Magic: Poetry 1961–1967*, pub. in 1969.

Poetry exploded in popularity within the black community. Seldom, if ever, had the art been integrated so thoroughly in America into a major social movement. The Chicago-based poet Don L. Lee, later Haki Madhubuti, saw his slender volume *Don't Cry, Scream!* (1969), published by his own Third World Press, sell about 100,000 copies. A plethora of other slender volumes with a similar agenda—to assert black rage and independence from whites—was almost greedily consumed by a mass of readers hungry for the Black Power and Black Arts messages. The major publisher of such volumes, often in cheap paperback form, was the astute ed. Dudley Randall's Broadside Press of Detroit. Established white presses, once indifferent if not hostile to black writers, began to seek out Af. Am. poets.

For a while, the similarities between the poets seemed far more prominent than their differences; a choir seemed to be singing almost exclusively about rage, injustice, black solidarity, and the desire for revenge. But this relative uniformity slowly gave way to the individualism necessary for the growth of art. The conversion of Amiri Baraka from black nationalism to Marxism-Leninism-Maoism epitomized the desire of the younger poets for growth and further change. Pride in black culture and their black selves was not negotiable, but some of these poets increasingly offered work shaped more by their individual integrity than by political ideology. Key aspects of the school of so-called *confessional poetry, with its emphasis on individualism, blended in their approach to poetry with the techniques encouraged by Baraka's earlier example.

The new poets, emerging over a relatively short period, included Alice Walker, Mari Evans, Etheridge Knight, Audre Lorde, June Jordan, Clarence Major, Ishmael Reed, Michael S. Harper, Jayne Cortez, Lucille Clifton, and Carolyn Rodgers. Each produced multiple volumes of verse. (Some, such as Walker, Lorde, Major, and Reed, excelled also in prose.) Almost all wrote free verse only; rhyme and forms such as the sonnet seemed obsolete or perhaps treacherous. Nevertheless, there was variety. If the lang. of the street was important to poets such as Sonia Sanchez and Cortez, others aimed for only a modest infusion of the vernacular in their lines. The iconoclastic Reed helped to take black poetry toward aspects of *postmodernism. Jordan's progressive politics (less dogmatic than Baraka's but no less trenchant) offered an implicit critique of black nationalism—but so did the broadening vistas of the new Af. Am. poet.

Gender became a major line of division as black nationalism transformed and matured with richer sources of inspiration. Building (unconsciously perhaps) on Gwendolyn Brooks's foundation, black women poets began to explore the variegated territory of feminism (see FEMINIST APPROACHES TO POETRY). In contesting the dominance of males, which most women had accepted, sometimes meekly, at the height of Black Power, women poets essentially changed the face of the new black poet. The same unspoken tension would result, in the area of fiction, in the material triumph of novelists such as Alice Walker, Gloria Naylor, Terry McMillan, and Toni Morrison over their male counterparts. The tension also figured in the extraordinary success on the stage in 1975 of the poet Ntozake Shange's verse play *for colored girls who have considered suicide, when the rainbow is enuf.*

Perhaps nothing underwrote the lives and careers of black poets, and assured the growth of black poetry, as much as did the acquisition by many of these writers of comfortable niches in colleges and universities as teachers of creative writing or black literary studies. This step was part of the post–World War II growth of creative writing as a field in colleges and universities, as well as a result of the changes that brought many black students to predominantly white colleges with the success of the civil rights movement. Plagued by the same economic deprivation that afflicted black Ams. as a whole over the centuries, the most successful black poets finally were assured of a room of their own.

Over the most recent generation, Af. Am. poets, some of them veterans from the 1960s, others born at that time, have shown that the line begun tentatively in the 18th c. with Phillis Wheatley has come to rich fruition. They continue to win honors and awards that reflect the fact that their work, anchored for the most part in their people's culture, nevertheless resounds with universal implications. As a body, these poets possess intellectual depth to match their technical skills. Rita Dove not only won the Pulitzer Prize for poetry for her third published collection, *Thomas and Beulah* (1986), but served as *poet laureate of the United States from 1993 to 1995. Yusef Komunyakaa won the Pulitzer Prize for poetry in 1994 for his volume *Neon Vernacular*. From an earlier generation, Lucille Clifton, whose first collection had come out in 1969, won the National Book Award in 2000 for *Blessing the Boats: New and Selected Poems, 1988–2000*. In 2007, Natasha Trethewey won the Pulitzer Prize for *Native Guard*, poems about black Union soldiers in Mississippi during the Civil War. Maya Angelou recited a poem at the first inauguration of President Bill Clinton, and Elizabeth Alexander did the same when President Barack Obama was inaugurated in 2009.

Perhaps the single most significant institutional devel. in black poetry at the turn of the millennium has been the growth of the Cave Canem collective. This organization was founded in 1996 by the poets (and professors) Cornelius Eady and Toi Derricotte, with the aim of protecting and nurturing Af. Am. poetry and poets. To Derricotte and Eady, black poets on the whole were underrepresented and isolated in most universities, despite their progress as a group. Within ten years, Cave Canem had become national in scope, with a board of directors, a regular and varied set of programs that includes an annual summer retreat for younger poets, and the direct or indirect support of almost every leading Af. Am. poet. It supports both those writers based in academic institutions and those inspired or excited by more popular, democratic forms, incl. the *poetry slam. Cave Canem, most importantly, appears to have the backing, formally or informally, of almost every eminent black poet. This group includes the jazz-inspired experimenter and sometimes Language poet Nathaniel Mackey (*Eroding Witness*, 1985; *Song of Udhra*, 1993; and *Whatsaid Serif*, 1998); Carl Phillips, whose *Speak*

*Low* (2009) was his tenth pub. book of poetry and who teaches Classics as well as creative writing; and Harryette Mullen, whose *Muse & Drudge* (1995) and *Sleeping with the Dictionary* (2002) show her extraordinary range of influences, from blues to erudition. On such a foundation, the future health of Af. Am. poetry, a form born in slavery and alienation, seems assured.

■ **Anthologies:** *In Search of Color Everywhere: A Collection of African-American Poetry*, ed. E. Miller (1994); C. Major, *The Garden Thrives: Twentieth-Century African-American Poetry* (1996); A. L. Nielsen, *Black Chant: Languages of African-American Postmodernism* (1997); *Giant Steps: The New Generation of African American Writers*, ed. K. Young (2000); *The Norton Anthology of African American Literature*, ed. H. L. Gates Jr. and N. Y. McKay, 2d ed. (2004); *A Different Image: The Legacy of Broadside Press: An Anthology*, ed. G. House, R. Weatherstone, A. M. Ward (2004); J. V. Gabbin, *Furious Flower: African American Poetry from the Black Arts Movement to the Present* (2004); *Every Goodbye Ain't Gone: An Anthology of Innovative Poetry by African Americans*, ed. A. L. Nielsen and L. Ramey (2006); *Gathering Ground: A Reader Celebrating Cave Canem's First Decade*, ed. T. Derricotte and C. Eady (2006); *The Oxford Book of African American Poetry*, ed. A. Rampersad (2006); *Rainbow Darkness: An Anthology of African American Poetry*, ed. K. Tuma (2006); *Shadowed Dreams: Women's Poetry of the Harlem Renaissance*, ed. M. Honey, 2d ed. rev. (2006); *Brother to Brother: New Writings by Black Gay Men*, ed. E. Hemphill (2007).

■ **Biographies:** R. M. Farnsworth, *Melvin B. Tolson, 1898–1966* (1984); A. Rampersad, *The Life of Langston Hughes*, 2 v. (1986, 1988); W. F. Cooper, *Claude McKay* (1987); C. E. Kerman and R. Eldridge, *The Lives of Jean Toomer* (1987); M. J. Boyd, *Discarded Legacy* (1994)—on the life of Frances E. W. Harper; A. De Veaux, *Warrior Poet: A Biography of Audre Lorde* (2004).

■ **Criticism and History:** *The New Negro*, ed. A. Locke (1925); W. H. Robinson, *Early Black American Poets* (1969); N. I. Huggins, *Harlem Renaissance* (1971); S. Henderson, *Understanding the New Black Poetry: Introduction and Anthology* (1973); M. A. Richmond, *Bid the Vassal Soar* (1974); E. Redmond, *Drumvoices: The Mission of Afro-American Poetry: A Critical History* (1976); W. Sollors, *Amiri Baraka / LeRoi Jones: The Quest for a Populist Modernism* (1978); D. L. Lewis, *When Harlem Was in Vogue* (1981); *Dictionary of Literary Biography: Afro-American Poets since 1955*, ed. T. Harris and T. M. Davis (1985); G. T. Hull, *Color, Sex & Poetry: Three Women Writers of the Harlem Renaissance* (1987); J. R. Sherman, *Invisible Poets: Afro-Americans of the Nineteenth Century*, 2d ed. (1989); D. H. Melhem, *Heroism in the New Black Poetry: Introductions and Interviews* (1990); *The Road before Us: 100 Gay Black Poets*, ed. A. Saint (1991); *African-American Poetry of the Nineteenth Century*, ed. J. R. Sherman (1992); F. S. Foster, *Written by Herself: Literary Production of Early African American Writers* (1993); *The Oxford Companion to African American Literature*, ed. W. L. Andrews, F. S. Foster, T. Harris (1997); "Database of Twentieth-Century African-American Poetry" (1998), Chadwyck-Healey, http://collections.chadwyck.com/marketing/home_20aap.jsp; F. P. Brown, *Performing the Word: African American Poetry as Vernacular Culture* (1999); J. E. Smethurst, *The New Red Negro: The Literary Left and African American Poetry, 1930–1946* (1999); L. Thomas, *Extraordinary Measures: Afrocentric Modernism and Twentieth-Century American Poetry* (2000); B. Dorsey, *Spirituality, Sensuality, Literality: Blues, Jazz, and Rap as Music and Poetry* (2000); D. Bruce, *The Origins of African American Literature, 1680–1865* (2001); *African American Poets: Lives, Works, and Sources*, ed. J. O. Pettis (2002); T. Bolden, *Afro-Blue: Improvisations in African American Poetry and Culture* (2004); J. S. Gray, *Race and Time: American Women's Poetics from Antislavery to Racial Modernity* (2004); C. Clarke, *"After Mecca": Women Poets and the Black Arts Movement* (2005); K. D. Leonard, *Fettered Genius: The African American Bardic Poet from Slavery to Civil Rights* (2006); A. M. Mance, *Inventing Black Women: African American Women Poets and Self-Representation, 1877–2000* (2007); L. Ramey, *Slave Songs and the Birth of African American Poetry* (2008).

A. RAMPERSAD; M. D. JONES

**AFRIKAANS POETRY.** *See* SOUTH AFRICA, POETRY OF.

**AGRARIANS.** Agrarianism, a literary and political movement in the U.S. South of the late 1920s and early 1930s, argued that the future of the region lay not with industrial devel. and cultural modernization but with independent, small-farm agriculture and with the traditionalism in culture and religion that its proponents associated with agricultural economies. Many key names in the Agrarian movement, such as Robert Penn Warren (1905–89), Allen Tate (1899–1979), John Crowe Ransom (1888–1974), and Donald Davidson (1893–1968), had earlier been associated with the *Fugitives, but the two movements are distinct, since the Fugitives did not have a political cast. The key texts of the Agrarian movement are two collections of essays, *I'll Take My Stand* (1930) and *Who Owns America?* (1936). Agrarianism has influenced the poetry and fiction of the South down to the present.

The Agrarians, opposing the advocates of the New South, argued that industrialization would bring in its train not prosperity but new forms of exploitation; that economic modernization would yield only materialism, deracination, and social alienation; and that cultural modernization would lead to a tyranny of thought over feeling and of abstraction over concrete experience. The Agrarians placed the small farmer at the center of southern life and culture, arguing that the life and trads. of the small farmer offered kinds of economic and spiritual fulfillment unavailable to urban modernity. The political claims Agrarians made are essentially arguments about culture, not about economics. The agrarian life, they believed, requires an unsentimental appreciation of the power of nature, a skeptical insight into human limitation and fallenness, and an essentially religious respect for the dark mystery of transcendence, all values they felt to be in short supply in the capitalist world. Their South was the yeoman South that Thomas Jefferson had idealized in *Notes on the State of Virginia*, not the planter South of the antebellum era, and their hostility to capitalism likewise had a Jeffersonian flavor. As a political program, Agrarianism ranks with other crank economic and political theories of the 1930s such as Social Credit, and, like Social Credit, its relevance today is mostly as a source of insight into the literary works produced by some of its advocates. On the whole, their thinking owed more to W. B. Yeats and, esp., to Leo Tolstoy, than to any disciplined study of politics, economics, or hist.

Agrarian strains of thought continue to play a role in Am. conservatism, mediated by the writings of Richard Weaver and M. E. Bradford. The thought of the historian Eugene Genovese has, since the 1990s, taken a turn sympathetic toward Agrarianism. And important southern writers of succeeding generations such as Flannery O'Connor and Wendell Berry inherited something of Agrarianism in their sensibilities. Early 21st-c. manifestations of "green" lit. and crit. also share some features—such as hostility to capitalist materialism and respect for the otherness of nature—with Agrarianism.

*See* ENVIRONMENT AND POETRY.

■ P. K. Conkin, *The Southern Agrarians* (1988); P. V. Murphy, *The Rebuke of History: The Southern Agrarians and American Conservative Thought* (2001); *The Southern Agrarians and the New Deal,* ed. E. S. Bingham and T. A. Underwood (2001).

J. BURT

**AGUDEZA** (Sp., "acuteness"). Arguably the word that best conveys the Sp. *baroque in its literary, philosophical, and ideological valences, *agudeza* is often translated as "wit" or "witticism." In the 17th c., however, it was far from mere wordplay. The verbal agudeza is the product of a keen mod. mind sharpened on social, economic, and spiritual disillusionments (*desengaños*) and saturated in a culture of perspectivism and a general rationalist distancing from earlier passions and beliefs.

Agudeza is not restricted to sophisticated aphorisms and *conceits. Strictly speaking, those are *conceptos*, although the terms are subject to slippage. While *agudeza* is sometimes used for *concepto*, it also refers to the capacity to grasp the intricate and subtle correspondences that inform an elaborate *metaphor, as well as to the correspondences themselves. It is thus as closely bound to *ingenio* (ingenium) as it is to *concepto*. Indeed, the principal theorist of agudeza, the urbane Jesuit Baltasar Gracián, understood the three to work in concert—a fact indicated by title of his *Arte de ingenio, tratado de la Agudeza. En que se explican todos los modos y diferencias de Conceptos* (1642), the work that became his better-known *Agudeza y arte de ingenio* (1648).

Seventeenth-c. Sp. lit. is rife with examples. In the sonnet by Francisco de Quevedo that begins "Si mis párpados, Lisi, labios fueran" (Lisi, were my eyelids lips), the lover's eyes drink down Lisi's beauties as if they had dropsy ("Tus bellezas, hidrópicos, bebieran"). The long trad. by which eyes are the windows (*cristales*) of the soul, combined with a similar custom that compares water to crystal, provides the ground for the concepto in the second quatrain: "cristales, sedientos de cristales . . . alimentando su morir, vivieran" (crystals thirsting for crystals . . . they would live by feeding on their own death). The agudeza of the poem is enhanced by Quevedo's sense for *rhythm, *assonance, and *paradox, as well as his consciousness of the times. The third stanza describes the lover as sustained by this "invisible comercio" (invisible commerce). Is this a fantasy of Petrarchan true love or a paid transaction? Either way, the poem encodes central preoccupations for Golden Age Sp. wit.

*See* INVENTION, WIT.

■ A. Maravall, *Culture of the Baroque*, trans. T. Cochran (1986); E. Hidalgo-Serna, *El pensamiento ingenioso en Gracián* (1993); *Rhetoric and Politics: Baltasar Gracián and the New World Order*, ed. N. Spadaccini and J. Talens (1997); D. Castillo, *A(wry) Views* (2001).

L. MIDDLEBROOK

**AIR** (1) Described as a "musico-poetic miniature" by Fischlin, *air* (ayre, Fr. *air de cour*) most aptly refers to a style of song that flourished in courtly social circles in England and France in the 16th and 17th cs. Airs are typically solo songs (though sometimes printed in such a way that they can be accompanied by additional singers), accompanied by a lute or other plucked instrument and featuring a refined and intimate style appropriate to the courts in which they were sung. A hallmark of the genre is clear presentation of the text, sometimes with illustrative musical devices highlighting specific words. Many airs take their lyrics from the noted poets of the day; many are Petrarchan, and most are love songs; many are strophic (see STROPHE); and they range in quality from exquisite gems to cliché-ridden rhymes. These stylistic features distinguish the air from other types of song that coexisted with it (e.g., Eng. *ballad, Eng. or It. *madrigal) or that evolved into more dramatic or elaborate vocal compositions (Ger. *lied, It. aria). (2) By extension, *air* frequently designates a melody or tune, apart from any harmony or accompaniment, and thus a musical composition, usually brief, in which the melody is dominant. In the same courtly circles, an air was sometimes an instrumental dance tune with a prominent melody. (3) *Air* has also come to be associated with the texts or lyrics, especially of the Eng. variety, which themselves have been the subject of stylistic and historical investigation in the 20th and 21st cs. (4) In the writings of some of the late 16th- and 17th-c. Eng. musical theorists such as Thomas Morley and Charles Butler, *air* denotes the mode or key of a piece.

*See* MUSIC AND POETRY, SONG.

■ T. Morley, *A Plaine and Easie Introduction to Practicall Musicke* (1597); C. Butler, *Principles of Musick*

(1636); P. Warlock, *The English Ayre* (1926); *Roger North on Music*, ed. J. Wilson (1959); U. Olshausen, *Das lautenbegleitete Sololied in England um 1600* (1963); *Lyrics from English Airs, 1596–1622*, ed. E. Doughtie (1970); I. Spink, *English Song* (1974); N. Fortune and D. Greer, "Air," *New Grove*; E. Jorgens, *The Well-Tun'd Word* (1982); L. Schleiner, *The Living Lyre in English Verse* (1984); E. Doughtie, *English Renaissance Song* (1986); W. Maynard, *Elizabethan Lyric Poetry and Its Music* (1986); L. Auld, "Text as Pre-text: French Court Airs," *Literature and the Other Arts*, ed. D. L. Rubin (1993); D. Fischlin, *In Small Proportions* (1998).

E. B. JORGENS

**AKKADIAN POETRY.** *See* ASSYRIA AND BABYLONIA, POETRY OF.

**ALAṂKĀRA** (Sanskrit, "ornamentation"). A category of figure in *Sanskrit poetics entailing many possible aesthetic effects incl. *simile (*upamā*) and *metaphor (*rūpaka*). In his *Nāṭyaśāstra* (ca. before 200 BCE), the poetic theorist Bharata mentions only four such figures; in addition to upamā and rūpaka, there are *dīpaka* (illumination) and *yamaka* (repetition of phonetically similar words or syllables). The rhetorician Bhāmaha in his *Kāvyālaṃkāra* (written 6th or 7th c. CE) presents *Alaṃkāraśāstra*, or the science of poetics, as an independent discipline. Since the two important components of the *Kāvyaśarīra* (body of poetry) were supposed to be *śabda* (word) and *artha* (meaning), the sonic and the semantic, the alaṃkāras were divided into two categories: *śabdālaṃkāra* (those based on phonetic form) and *arthālaṃkāra* (those based on meaning). Rudraṭa (fl. 9th c.) divides śabdālaṃkāra into five subcategories. Sometime in the 11th c., Bhoja added a third category: *ubhayālaṃkāra*, a poetic figure that involves both the sonic and the semantic. Ruyyaka divided alaṃkāras into seven classes on the basis of their semantic content and the construction of meaning. By the time of Mammaṭa (fl. 11th c.), the number rises to 61.

A traditional question has been whether alaṃkāra is integral to the poem or is added simply to make a statement charming. To be functional and not merely decorative, an alaṃkāra must come *ab intra* and be organically integrated into the poem. Mukherji points out, on the authority of the 9th-c. author Vāmana, that the alaṃkāra "is not to be taken in its literary sense of poetic figures only: it conveys, as well, the idea of poetic beauty in general, and that constitutes the real connotation of the term."

■ Daṇḍin, *Kāvyādarśa* (1924); Vāmana, *Kāvyālaṃkārasūtra* (1928). Bharata, *Nāṭyaśāstra* (1950); P. V. Kane, *Sāhityadarpaṇa: Paricchedas I, II, X Arthālaṃkāra with Exhaustive Notes* (1965); Rudraṭa, *Kāvyālaṃkāra* (1965); Ruyyaka, *Alaṃkārasarvaśva* (1965); R. Mukherji, *Literary Criticism in Ancient India* (1966); Bhāmaha, *Kāvyālaṃkāra* (1970); *Dhvanyāloka of Ānandavardhana*, ed. K. Krishnamoorthy (1974); S. K. De, *History of Sanskrit Poetics* (1976); K. Kapoor, *Literary Theory: Indian Conceptual Framework* (1998); B. Pal, *Alaṃkāra-Vicintā* (2007).

M. K. RAY

**AL-ANDALUS, POETRY OF.** Opinions are divided as to whether the Ar. poetry of the Iberian peninsula is truly distinctive within the general field of Ar. poetry. Some scholars point to the prominence of specific themes, such as *nature and descriptions of flowers and gardens, as well as to the two types of strophic poem that originated in Al-Andalus (see STROPHE), as evidence of the distinctiveness of Ar. poetry; some (Pérès, García Gómez [1946], Armistead [1980], Monroe) claim that it reflects a native Iberian trad. preserved continuously from the Roman period and reemerging later in the poetry of Spain and Portugal. Others point to the continuity of the forms, rhetorical patterns, and themes prevailing in Al-Andalus with those of the Abbasid Empire (750–1258): most poems are *monorhymed, are set in quantitative meter according to certain canonical patterns (see CLASSICAL PROSODY, QUANTITY), are phrased in cl. Ar., and employ the rhetorical figures associated with neoclassical Abbasid verse.

The literary dependence of Al-Andalus on Abbasid Baghdad is epitomized in the career of Abū al-Ḥassan ʿAlī ibn Nafayni (known as Ziryāb), a 9th-c. CE Iranian polymath who, arriving in Córdoba, used the prestige of his origins to set the court fashions in poetry, music, and manners in accordance with those of Baghdad. By the time of the establishment of the Umayyad caliphate of Córdoba in ca. 930 CE, the strophic *muwashshaḥ* had emerged as a distinctive local contribution to Ar. poetry, the only strophic form ever to be cultivated to any great extent by poets writing in cl. Ar. The originator of the genre is thought to be either Muḥammad Maḥmud al-Qabrī (ca. 900 CE) or Ibn ʿAbd Rabbihi (ca. 860–940 CE).

The muwashshaḥ consists of five to seven strophes, each in two parts (*ghuṣn* [pl. *aghṣān*] and *simṭ* [pl. *asmāṭ*]). The aghṣān all have the same metrical and rhyming patterns, but the rhyme sound changes from strophe to strophe; the asmāṭ are uniform in meter and in rhyme sound throughout the poem. The poem tends to begin with an opening simṭ. The final simṭ, around which the whole poem was probably composed, is the much-discussed *kharja*. The kharja is written either in vernacular Ar., in Ibero-Romance, or in some combination of the two; and it is generally believed to be a quotation from vernacular songs otherwise lost. Of great interest to Romance philologists as the earliest attestations of lyric poetry in any Ibero-Romance lang., the kharjas are thought by some to point to the existence of Iberian popular poetry predating the Muslim conquest (711 CE), supporting the theory of a continuous Iberian element in Andalusi poetry; but aside from the kharjas themselves, no such poetry is extant.

The metrics of the muwashshaḥ may also point to Romance origin. Though the poems can be scanned in conformity with the quantitative principles of Ar. poetry (*ārūḍ*), the metrical patterns only rarely correspond to the canonical ones, and the kharja often resists quantitative analysis altogether. The metrical principle underlying the muwashshaḥ is believed by many to be syllabic (García Gómez 1975, Monroe), though others maintain that it is quantitative, having arisen through the evolution of the *qaṣīda. Both Hartmann and Stern pointed out that Eastern poets occasionally varied the qaṣīda's monorhyme by subdividing each of the two *hemistichs with *internal rhyme; the result was the pattern *bbba*, with *a* representing the constant rhyme. When a whole poem has the *bbba* pattern, each line is a miniature stanza. Thus, a subtype of the qaṣīda may have developed into an entirely new verse type. This shift may have occurred under the influence of Romance verse forms reflected in the *villancico* and the *rondeau*, for unlike cl. Ar. verse, the muwashshaḥ was sung, and Romance musical patterns seem to have played at least some part in shaping it. Another possible source is the stanzaic musammaṭ form, which is first attested to in the poetry of Abū Nuwās (d. 815 CE).

Another class of poems thought to be derived from earlier Romance models has survived in the *urjūza* poems on historical themes developed by Ibn ʿAbd Rabbihi and others; these are long poems composed of rhyming *distichs in a nonclassical quantitative meter known as *rajaz*. Neither the form nor the theme was an Andalusi invention, however; they were, instead, a direct imitation of an Abbasid model, and these 9th- and 10th-c. poems do not seem to have created a lasting genre.

Though poetry is reported to have been an important feature of Andalusi culture, esp. in the Cordoban court, as it was throughout the Ar.-speaking world, little has survived from the 8th and 9th cs., and what remains is conventional in terms of theme, imagery, and verse patterns. Under the caliphate, however, Córdoba flourished as a literary center, and Andalusi poetry began to outshine even that of the East. The bulk of the poetry was courtly *panegyric and lampoon in qaṣīda form, but *love poetry was extremely popular, as were descriptions of wine and wine drinking, gardens, and ascetic verse. Great poets include Ibn Hānī (ca. 937–73), Ibn Darrāj al-Qasṭallī (fl. ca. 980), and al-Sharīf al-Ṭalīq (d. 1009). The latter two cultivated flower poetry, which was to become a specialty of later Andalusi poets. They employ an increasingly ornate rhetorical style (*badīʿ*) that originated in the East and is associated with the Abbasid master Abū Tammām (788–845).

The decline of the Cordoban caliphate (1009–31) and the period of the Ṭāʾifa kingdoms (1031–91) saw the greatest achievements of Andalusi poetry. Ibn Shuhayd (fl. ca. 1035) composed a body of passionate and pessimistic verse, as well as an unusual treatise on the nature of poetry in which the narrator visits and converses with the familiar spirits of dead poets. In contrast to the prevailing doctrine of poetry as a learned craft of rhetorically ornamented speech, he propounds an idea of individual poetic inspiration. The theologian and legist Ibn Ḥazm (994–1064) wrote mostly short love verses, more conventional in style, but embodying a spiritual ideal of love closely resembling that of the *troubadours and worked out in detail in his prose treatise. Their younger contemporary Ibn Zaydūn (1003–71) composed a body of very individual poetry, esp. the *odes arising out of his celebrated love affair with the princess

Walāda bint al-Mustakfī (1001–80; also an accomplished poet) that reflect the spiritual ideals of love developed by Ibn Ḥazm. It is from this period, the late 11th c., that muwashshaḥ texts are preserved.

Under the Ṭāʾifa kings, the city states of Al-Andalus vied with each other for preeminence in the arts, esp. poetry. Seville became the city of poets par excellence, boasting the presence of the mature Ibn Zaydūn, Ibn ʿAmmār (1031–86), Ibn al-Labbana (d. 1113), and Ibn Hamdīs (ca. 1056–1133); its last Arab ruler, al-Muʿtamid Ibn ʿAbbād (1040–95), the patron of all these, was himself a gifted poet. This efflorescence of poetry was partly made possible by a policy of relative religious tolerance common at the Ṭāʾifa courts, but the Almoravids (1091–1145) introduced a fundamentalist regime that suppressed secular arts. A few great poets, trained in the earlier period, flourished, such as the nostalgic nature poet Ibn Khafāja (1058–1138), Ibn ʿAbdūn (d. 1134) of Évora, the muwashshaḥ poet Abū al-Abbas al-Amā al-Tutīlī (d. 1126), and the opaque Ibn al-Zaqqāq (1100–33); but it was also an age of *anthologists. Nevertheless, the period saw the invention, probably by Ibn Bājja (early 12th c.), of the *zajal* (see ZÉJEL) and its full flowering in the works of Ibn Quzmān (1078–1160). These are strophic poems, similar to muwashshaḥ in that the strophes have one element whose rhyme changes from strophe to strophe and another with constant rhyme, but the lang. is colloquial Andalusi Ar., the final simṭ is not different from the rest of the poem, and there may be more than seven strophes; the asmāṭ also have only half the number of lines in the opening simṭ. The vulgar lang. of the zajal complements its theme, the bawdy, colorful life of taverns and streets, observed and turned into lit. by sophisticated poets of aristocratic origin who mock the conventions of courtly love and courtly poetry. The form was probably adapted from vulgar poetry. Apparently as a secondary devel., a type of zajal arose resembling the muwashshaḥ in everything but lang. Both types are already present in the works of Ibn Quzmān.

Under the Almohads (1145–1223), there was a revival of poetry: the great poets were al-Ruṣāfī (d. 1177); the converted Jew Abū Ishāq Ibrāhīm ibn Sahl of Seville (1212–52); Ḥāzim al-Qarṭājannī (1211–85), whose work on the theory of poetry was also influential; and a famous woman poet, Ḥafsa bint al-Ḥajj al-Rakuniyya (1135–91). The most original devel., however, was the mystical poetry of Ibn ʿal-Arabī (1165–1240), which derived its imagery from secular love poetry and its diction from the highly metaphorical style of the age. The final political phase of Al-Andalus, the Kingdom of Granada (1248–1492), produced a few important poets, incl. Ibn al-Khaṭīb (1313–74) and Ibn Zamrak (1333–93), whose poems embellish the Alhambra.

The similarity of some of the strophic patterns of Arabo-Andalusi poetry and the notions of love sung by Andalusi poets to those of the troubadours has led some to see Ar. poetry as the inspiration of the troubadours (Nykl). The exact relationship of Andalusi poetry to the troubadour lyric continues to be the subject of intense scholarly debate (Boase, Menocal 1987), as also is the problem of the zajal's influence on the Galician-Port. *cantigas.

See ARABIC POETRY; MEDIEVAL POETRY; PORTUGAL, POETRY OF; SPAIN, POETRY OF.

■ M. Hartmann, *Das arabische Strophengedicht* (1897); A. Cour, *Un poète arabe d'Andalousie: Ibn Zaídoûn* (1920); R. Menéndez Pidal, "Poesía árabe y poesía europea," *Bulletin hispanique* 40 (1938); E. García Gómez, *Un eclipse de la poesía en Sevilla* (1945) and *Poemas arábigoandaluces*, 3d ed. (1946); A. R. Nykl, *Hispano-Arabic Poetry and Its Relations with the Old Provençal Troubadours* (1946); A. J. Arberry, *Moorish Poetry* (1953); Ibn Ḥazm, *The Ring of the Dove*, trans. A. J. Arberry (1953); H. Pérès, *La poésie andalouse en arabe classique au XIe siècle*, 2d ed. (1953); P. Le Gentil, *Le Virelai et le villancico* (1954); S. Fiore, *Über die Beziehungen zwischen der arabischen und der fruhitalienischen Lyrik* (1956); P. Le Gentil, "La Strophe zadjalesque, les khardjas et le problème des origines du lyrisme roman," *Romania* 84 (1963)—judicious review of research to 1963; W. Heinrichs, *Arabische Dichtung und Griechische Poetik* (1969); Ibn Shuhayd, *Treatise of Familiar Spirits and Demons*, ed. and trans. J. T. Monroe (1971); E. García Gómez, *Todo Ben Quzman* (1972); J. M. Solà-Solé, *Corpus de poesía mozárabe* (1973); J. T. Monroe, *Hispano-Arabic Poetry* (1974); S. M. Stern, *Hispano-Arabic Strophic Poetry* (1974); M. Frenk, *La jarchas mozárabes y los comienzos de la lírica románica* (1975); E. García Gómez, *Las jarchas de la serie árabe en su marco*, 2d ed. (1975); R. Scheindlin, *Form and Structure in the Poetry of al-Muʿtamid Ibn ʿAbbad* (1975); L. F. Compton, *Andalusian Lyrical Poetry and Old Spanish Love Songs* (1976); R. Boase, *The Origin and Meaning of Courtly Love* (1977); R. Hitchcock, *The Kharja: A Critical Bibliography* (1977); M. Frenk, *Estudios sobre lírica antigua* (1978); E. García Gómez, *El libro de las banderas de los campeones de Ibn Saʿid al Magribi*, 2d ed. (1978); S. G. Armistead, "Some Recent Developments in Kharja Scholarship," *La Corónica* 8 (1980); *GRLMA* 2.1.46–73; M. R. Menocal, "The Etymology of Old Provençal *trobar, trobador*," *RPh* 36 (1982–83); Ibn Quzmān, *El cancionero hispanoárabe*, trans. F. Corriente Córdoba (1984); M. R. Menocal, *The Arabic Role in Medieval Literary History* (1987); D. C. Clarke, "The Prosody of the Hargas," *La Corónica* 16 (1987–88); M. J. Rubiera Mata, *Poesía femenina hispanoárabe* (1989); C. Addas, "L'œuvre poétique d'Ibn ʿArabî et sa réception," *Studia Islamica* 91 (2000); A. P. Espósito, "The Monkey in the Jarcha: Tradition and Canonicity in the Early Iberian Lyric," *Journal of Medieval and Early Modern Studies* 30 (2000); T. Rosen, "The Muwashshah," *The Literature of Al-Andalus*, ed. M. R. Menocal, R. Scheindlin, and M. Sells (2000); S. G. Armistead, "Kharjas and Villancicos," and R. K. Farrin, "The 'Nūniyya' of Ibn Zaydūn: A Structural and Thematic Analysis," *Journal of Arabic Literature* 34 (2003); F. Corriente, "Again on (Partially) Romance Andalusi 'Kharajāt," *Journal of Arabic Literature* 35 (2004); H. L. Heijkoop and Otto Zwartjes, *Muwuššuḥ, Zajal, Kharja: Bibliography of Strophic Poetry and Music from Al-Andalus and Their Influence in East and West* (2004).

R. P. SCHEINDLIN; V. BARLETTA

**ALBA** (Occitan, Sp., "dawn"; OF *aube, aubade*; Galician-Port. *alva*; Ger. *Tagelied*). A dawn song about adulterous love, expressing one or both lovers' regret over the coming of dawn after a night of love. A third voice, a watchman, may announce the coming of dawn and the need for the lovers to separate. An Occitan *alba* may contain a dialogue (or serial monologues) between lover and beloved or a lover and the watchman or a combination of monologue with a brief narrative intro. The voices may fear the jealous husband ( *gilos* ) and the lovers' secret being discovered. In its staging of a secret, consummated love under the threat of the coming of dawn, the alba, unlike the *canso*, imagines a love of mutual but nonetheless illicit attraction. The alba has no fixed metrical form, but in Occitan each stanza usually ends with a *refrain that contains the word *alba*. The earliest examples date from the end of the 12th c. By the turn of the 13th c., the alba belongs to the technical vocabulary of *troubadours and later appears in the grammatical manual *Doctrina de compondre dictats* (late 13th c.).

Various theories of origins remain hypothetical. The earliest attributed alba, Giraut de Bornelh's "Reis glorios, verais lums e clartatz," bears a melodic resemblance to the Lat. hymn to the Virgin, "Ave maris stella" (ca. 9th c.) and the 11th-c. Occitan *versus* "O Maria, Deu maire"; this song as well as an earlier bilingual Lat.-Occitan alba ("Alba de Fleury-sur-Loire") attests to the likely dialogue between the secular alba and the long trad. of Lat. religious dawn hymns such as those by Prudentius (ca. 348–405) and Ambrose (4th c.) that figure dawn as announcing the light of salvation. In Mozarabic *zéjels and *kharjas, songs about the parting of lovers incorporating the word *alba* suggest a relation with an independent Romance trad. that exerted an influence on the Occitan alba. Likewise, the courtly Occitan alba perhaps developed in conjunction with a popular pan-Romance lyric trad. that includes OF *chanson de femme* and the Galician-Port. *cantigas d'amigo* (see CANTIGA), as well as similar Catalan, Sp., and It. compositions. This trad. consists of dialogue or women's songs about separation, the arrival of dawn signaled by light and bird's song, and the risk of being seen; the adulterous situation of the husband or presence of a watchman seems to have been a significant devel. of the genre (Jeanroy). The watchman plays an important role as mediator between the two symbolic worlds of night (illicit love in an enclosed space) and day (courtly society, *lauzengiers* or evil gossips or enemies of love; Saville). Eng. examples can be found in Chaucer (*Troilus and Criseyde*, 3.1415–1533, 1695–1712 and "Reeve's Tale" 4236–47), Shakespeare (*Romeo and Juliet* 3.5.1–64), John Donne ("The Sun Rising," "The Good Morrow"), and Robert Browning ("Parting at Morning"). In the 20th c., the genre was attempted by

Ezra Pound ("Alba"), W. H. Auden ("Aubade"), Philip Larkin, ("Aubade"), and Robert Creeley ("Alba").

■ **Anthologies**: *Eos: An Enquiry into the Theme of Lovers' Meetings and Partings at Dawn in Poetry*, ed. A.T. Hatto (1965); *Et ades sera l'alba. Angoisse de l'aube: Recueil des chansons d'aube des troubadours*, ed. G. Gouiran (2005).

■ **Criticism and History**: Jeanroy; R. E. Kaske, "An Aube in the *Reeve's Tale*," *ELH* 26 (1959), and "The Aube in Chaucer's *Troilus*," *Troilus and Criseyde and the Minor Poems, Chaucer Criticism 2*, ed. R. J. Schoeck and J. Taylor (1961); J. Saville, *The Medieval Erotic Alba* (1972); D. Rieger, *GRLMA* 2.1B (1979); E. W. Poe, "The Three Modalities of the Old Provençal Dawn Song," *RPh* 37 (1984), and "New Light on the *Alba*: A Genre Redefined," *Viator* 15 (1984); H. U. Seeber, "Intimität und Gesellschaft. Zur Renaissance der Aubade in der englischen Lyrik des 20. Jahrhunderts," *Gattungsprobleme in der anglo-amerikanischen Literatur*, ed. R. Borgmeir (1986); T. F. Cornejo, *La canción de alba en la lírica románica medieval* (1999); F. Bauer, "L'aube et la nuit," *Revue des langues romanes* 110 (2006); C. Chaguinian, "L'alba dans le système des genres troubadouresques: Réflexions sur le rapport des troubadours à la production non troubadouresque," *Cahiers de Civilisation Médiévale* 50 (2007).

M. Galvez

**ALBANIA, POETRY OF.** Albanian is an IE lang. spoken in Albania, Kosovo, and surrounding areas in the southwestern part of the Balkan Peninsula. Albania attained its independence in 1912 after five centuries as part of the Ottoman Empire.

The beginnings of written verse in Albania are strongly linked to the Catholic Church. Pjetër Budi (1566–1622), from the Mati area, trained for the priesthood at the Illyrian College of Loretto, south of Ancona in Italy, and was later bishop of Sapa and Sarda in the Zadrima region. His major publication, a catechism titled *Dottrina Christiana* (Christian Doctrine, 1618), has an appendix of 53 pages of religious poetry in Albanian, some 3,000 lines. This verse, incl. both trans. from Lat. and original Albanian poems in quatrain form, is octosyllabic, which is the standard in Albanian folk verse. Budi prefers biblical themes, eulogies, and universal motifs such as the inevitability of death. Though his rhymes are not always elegant, his verse evinces an authenticity of feeling and genuine human concern for the sufferings of a misguided world.

The Ottoman invasion and occupation of Albania, starting in the late 14th c., brought about the gradual demise of this early Catholic poetry. It was replaced by *aljamiado* verse, written in Ar. script and strongly influenced by Islamic culture. Muslim poets wrote initially in Ottoman Turkish, but by the mid-18th c., they were experimenting in Albanian as well. Among the leading literary figures of this period was Nezim Frakulla (ca. 1680–1760), from the Fier region. Nezim writes proudly that he was the first person to compose a *\*divan* in Albanian: "Who bade the *divan* speak Albanian? / Nezim has made it known, / Who bade clarity speak in Albanian? / Nezim has made it human." About 110 of his poems are preserved, all replete with vocabulary of Turkish and Persian origin.

Leaving aside the Italo-Albanian poets of southern Italy, such as Giulio Variboba (1724–88), Nicola Chetta (ca.1740–1803), Girolamo De Rada (1814–1903), and Giuseppe Serembe (1844–1901), who all made substantial contributions to the evolution of Albanian verse, we first note a revival of verse in Albania itself in the late 19th c., during the *Rilindja* period of national renaissance. Among the leading figures of this movement for national identity and political autonomy were Pashko Vasa (1825–92) of Shkodra, whose poem *O moj Shqypni, e mjera Shqypni* (O Albania, Poor Albania), a stirring appeal for national awakening, was written in the dramatic years of the League of Prizren, 1878–80; and Naim Frashëri (1846–1900), now widely regarded as Albania's national poet. Frashëri's verse, pub. for the most part while he was living in Constantinople and very popular among Albanians at the time, included *\*pastoral lyrics in the trad. of Virgil, heavily laden with the imagery of his mountain homeland; historical epics; and Bektashi religious verse.

A qualitative step forward occurred in the early decades of the 20th c., when the Albanian lang. first became widespread in education and publishing. Though the romantic nationalism of the Rilindja period was still popular, other themes were introduced, incl. love poetry, which initially caused quite a scandal. Among the leading poets of the early decades were Anton Zako Çajupi (1866–1930), who was active in Egypt; Ndre Mjeda (1866–1937) of Shkodra, whose collection *Juvenilia* (1917), influenced by the 19th-c. It. classics, included *\*sonnets and other verse in refined meters; and Asdreni (1872–1947), from the southeastern Korça region, whose first three verse collections were well received.

The greatest figure of Albanian verse before World War II was Gjergj Fishta (1871–1940), whose 15,000-line verse epic of Albanian history, *Lahuta e Malcís* (*The Highland Lute*, 1937), caused him to be revered as the Albanian Homer. When the Communists took power in 1944, his work was swiftly repressed, and the very mention of his name was taboo for 46 years.

Two poets, entirely different from one another, may be regarded as the vanguards of modernity in Albanian lit. The messianic Migjeni (1911–38) of Shkodra turned away from the beauty of the Albanian mountains and the sacred trads. of the nation to devote his verse to the social realities of despair and ubiquitous squalor, against which he rose in defiance. His slender collection *Vargjet e Lira* (Free Verse, 1944), pub. posthumously, represented a literary revolution and a breath of fresh air that did away with the trads. of romantic nationalism for good. Lasgush Poradeci (1899–1987), a pantheistic poet from Pogradec on Lake Ohrid, studied the ever-changing moods of the lake to offer crystalline verse in southern Albanian folk style.

Albanian written culture and verse reached a zenith in the 1930s and early 1940s. A mod. lit. had been created, and the nation had come of age. However, it was a brief blossoming in the shadow of an apocalypse. The Stalinist takeover and purges under dictator Enver Hoxha (1908–85) caused terror in intellectual circles and snuffed out imaginative writing in the country for almost 20 years. Only Martin Camaj (1925–92), in Bavarian exile, and the unfettered poets of Kosovo were left to build on established trads.

By the early 1960s, a new generation of poets in Albania, led by Fatos Arapi (b. 1930), Dritëro Agolli (b. 1931), and Ismail Kadare (b. 1936), managed to slip elements of aesthetic finesse into their volumes of obligatory and otherwise stale partisan poetry. There was no thaw in Albanian verse during the Communist period (1944–89); but cautious openings, ever so slight, enabled some verse of quality to be published, and it immediately caught the imagination of the beleaguered public.

Ideological restrictions vanished when the Stalinist regime imploded in 1989–90, and chaos reigned in the little Balkan country for a decade. Yet, despite the harsh conditions of a free-market economy, contemp. poetry lost none of its fundamental importance in Albanian national culture. Well into the 21st c., verse collections still account for more than 50% of literary output. Albania is and remains a land of poets.

■ G. Schirò, *Storia della letteratura albanese* (1959); A. Pipa, *Albanian Literature: Social Perspectives* (1978) and *Contemporary Albanian Literature* (1991); *An Elusive Eagle Soars: Anthology of Modern Albanian Poetry*, ed. R. Elsie (1993); R. Elsie, *History of Albanian Literature* (1995) and *Studies in Modern Albanian Literature and Culture* (1996); A. Zotos, *Anthologie de la poésie albanaise* (1998); R. Elsie, *Albanian Literature: A Short History* (2005); *Songs of the Frontier Warriors, Kёngë Kreshnikёsh: Albanian Epic Verse* (2004) and *Lightning from the Depths: An Anthology of Albanian Poetry* (2008) ed. and trans. R. Elsie and J. Mathie-Heck.

R. ELSIE

**ALCAIC.** An *aeolic *strophe named after Alcaeus of Lesbos (fl. early 6th c. BCE) that consists of two 11-syllable lines (alcaic *hendecasyllables) having the form x – ᴗ – x – ᴗ ᴗ – ᴗ – followed by a third line that is a rhythmic extension of the first two: x – ᴗ – x – ᴗ x – ᴗ ᴗ – ᴗ ᴗ – ᴗ – – (Snell). The Alexandrian grammarians separated the third line into two parts, after the ninth position, creating a four-line stanza, the third line of nine syllables ( x – ᴗ – x – ᴗ – –) and the fourth of ten ( – ᴗ ᴗ – ᴗ ᴗ – ᴗ – –). The first two lines, the hendecasyllables, are known as greater alcaics, the decasyllable (fourth line) as a lesser alcaic. Horace, who used this strophe more than any other in his *Odes* (37 times), seems to have regarded it as a four-line stanza, allowing *hiatus between third and fourth lines (e.g., *Odes* 2.14.3–4). Horace's alcaic strophe was used by med. poets: Hilary of Poitiers (4th c. CE) in his first *hymn created a stanza consisting of a *glyconic alternating with either an alcaic hendecasyllable or an *asclepiad; Prudentius (ca. 348–405) used the alcaic hendecasyllable for stichic verse; and the hendeca-

syllable in quatrains, devised by Ennodius (late 5th c.), became the most used alcaic form of the Middle Ages. It was adapted in It. by Gabriello Chiabrera (1552–1638), Paolo Rolli (1687–1765), and Giovanni Fantoni (1755–1807). Like Chiabrera, Ren. metrists in England and France attempted imitations of alcaics on both accentual and quantitative principles. In 18th-c. Germany, F. G. Klopstock ("An meine Freunde," "An Fanny") composed 17 alcaic *odes, as did Friedrich Hölderlin ("An die Parzen," "Der Main"), August von Platen, and others in the 19th. Alfred, Lord Tennyson's alcaic ode to John Milton ("O mighty-mouth'd inventor of harmonies") makes the most serious effort of his age to reproduce the cl. rules for quantitative *scansion without replacing *quantity by stress; and Tennyson considered the *In Memoriam stanza related to the alcaic. By contrast, Arthur Clough and A. C. Swinburne wrote accentual alcaics. Trans. of cl. alcaics in the 20th c. include examples by Richmond Lattimore (*Greek Lyrics*, 1955) and J. B. Leishman's trans. of Horace (1956).

*See* CLASSICAL METERS IN MODERN LANGUAGES.

■ F. V. Graeser, *De stropha alcaica* (1865); E. Brocks, "Die Fortleben der alkäische Strophe," *Germanisch-Romanische Monatsschrift* 13 (1925); O. Francabandera, *Contribuzioni alla storia dell'alcaica* (1928); Norberg; Bowra; W. Bennett, *German Verse in Classical Metres* (1963); Koster; N. A. Bonavia-Hunt, *Horace the Minstrel* (1969); R.G.M. Nisbet and M. Hubbard, *A Commentary on Horace: "Odes" Book I* (1970); E. Schäfer, *Deutscher Horaz* (1976); Halporn et al.; Snell; West; D. Schaller, "Der alkäische Hendekasyllabus im frühen Mittelalter," *Mittellateinisches Jahrbuch* 19 (1984); R. Warren, "Alcaics in Exile: W. H. Auden's 'In Memory of Sigmund Freud,'" *Philosophy and Literature* 20 (1996); J. Talbot, "Tennyson's Alcaics: Greek and Latin Prosody and the Invention of English Meters," *SP* 101 (2004).

R. A. SWANSON; J. W. HALPORN; T.V.F. BROGAN

**ALCMANIC VERSE.** A final *colon in the *strophe of the *Partheneion* of the Gr. lyric poet Alcman (7th c. BCE) which can take two forms: – ᴗ ᴗ – ᴗ ᴗ – ᴗ – – or – ᴗ ᴗ – ᴗ ᴗ – ᴗ ᴗ – (West). The latter, a dactylic tetrameter brachycatalectic, is the one to which the term usually refers, although some scholars call the full dactylic tetrameter the alcmanic and the catalectic dactylic tetrameter the *archilochian (Klingner).

■ *Horatius: Opera*, ed. F. Klingner, 3d ed. (1959); Maas; Halporn et al.; Snell; West.

J. W. HALPORN

**ALEATORY POETICS.** No work of art can exclude chance entirely, in the sense of bringing all aspects of the work under the creator's conscious control. Aleatory poetics, however, deliberately engages with chance as a compositional principle. The category encompasses a wide range of practices, including automatic writing, techniques of cut-up and *collage, combinatorial forms, and systems of random or probabilistic selection and ordering. Although it is possible to identify premod. antecedents (e.g., the combinatorial works of some *rhétoriqueur* poets in the 15th and 16th cs.), the exploration of chance procedures becomes central to much 20th-c. experimental practice, reaching a high point at two key moments: first in the 1910s and 1920s, then in the 1950s and 1960s.

The poetry and poetics of Stéphane Mallarmé anticipate the widespread artistic investigation of chance, yet they are in many respects supremely *anti*-aleatory. For Mallarmé, chance is both the precondition for poetry's existence and that which poetry strives to transcend without ever abolishing it. This is the core insight of the poem *Un coup de dés* (A Throw of the Dice, 1897). Mallarmé's unfinished *Livre* (Book), the unbound pages of which would have been subject to multiple permutations, points forward to later experiments in mobile form. It also illustrates a set of paradoxes: the withdrawal of the poet, reduced to the role of "operator," effaces the contingency of authorial subjectivity to establish the absolute authority of the "Book," and the opening of the literary work to a plurality of readings fuses with the notion of an absolute and total meaning (see BOOK, POETIC).

Mallarmé's *Un coup de dés* was not widely disseminated until a 1914 republication, by which time it was both a precursor and contemporary to new avant-garde chance procedures. Tristan Tzara's recipe for making a Dadaist poem by cutting out words from a newspaper article and drawing them out of a bag (1920) eschewed the authorial control of the Mallarméan approach (see DADA). Dadaist manipulations of chance may be interpreted either as forms of anti-art that aggressively reject meaning or as attempts to uncover mystical truths (as the Dada artist Hans [Jean] Arp came to see them); they may be experiments in depersonalization or quests for the unconscious self (Tzara's claim that "the poem will resemble you" is perhaps not entirely ironic). Less equivocal is the surrealist attitude that tends to merge chance and necessity, whether through the practice of automatic writing that suspends the conscious will in order to uncover the deeper workings of the psyche or through the investigation of "objective chance," defined by André Breton in *L'Amour fou* (Mad Love, 1937) as "the form of manifestation of exterior necessity which traces its path in the human unconscious." The surrealist word collage game known as the *cadavre exquis* (exquisite corpse) offers a variant on Tzara's method that produces unexpected but grammatically correct sentences (see SURREALISM). In a slightly different vein, Raymond Roussel's writing procedures, which use polysemous phrases or homophonic pairings of sentences to generate narratives, exploit the element of chance inherent in lang. itself (see POLYSEMY).

The hist. of aleatory poetics parallels devels. in the visual arts, beginning with the "canned chance" of Marcel Duchamp's *Trois stoppages étalon* (Three Standard Stoppages, 1913), produced by dropping three meter-long threads onto strips of canvas, then gluing them into place. In the wake of *cubism and *expressionism, artists explored the external or the psychological workings of chance by means of collage or automatism: examples include Arp's practice of dropping and pasting pieces of torn paper, André Masson's automatic drawings, and Max Ernst's use of decalcomania (transferring paint between two surfaces) and *frottage* (rubbing with a pencil over a textured surface). In the 1940s and 1950s, artists often emphasized spontaneous brushwork or the dripping of paint (the tachism of Jean Dubuffet and Pierre Soulages; the action painting of Jackson Pollock, Franz Kline, and Willem de Kooning), while Robert Rauschenberg created "combines" of found objects. In lit., techniques of collage or combination often break up narrative continuity: versions of the cut-up technique pioneered by Tzara have been adopted by writers such as the lettrist poet Gil J. Wolman (see LETTRISME); the painter, poet, and performance artist Brion Gysin; and the novelist William S. Burroughs. Marc Saporta's *Composition No. 1* (1962) is an unbound novel whose pages may be shuffled, and Julio Cortázar's *Rayuela* (Hopscotch, 1966) offers the reader several possible paths through the text.

It is not until the 1950s and 1960s that the adjective *aleatory*, or sometimes *aleatoric* (from the Latin *alea*, a die, dice), began to be applied to works of art, specifically to musical compositions. The term is somewhat ambiguous, referring in the broadest sense to works that are partially undetermined by the composer, either in their composition or in their performance (or both). An example of the first type— i.e., of works that involve chance in composition but have a determinate final form—is John Cage's *Music of Changes* for piano (1951), composed using coin flipping to select musical parameters among charts modeled after the Chinese *I Ching* (Book of Changes). The second category—of works that are indeterminate with respect to performance—includes Pierre Boulez's Third Piano Sonata (1955–57), which allows the performer freedom in ordering the composed sections, and Karlheinz Stockhausen's *Klavierstück XI* (1956), which has billions of possible combinations. Forms of indeterminacy range from coin flipping to the use of imprecise notation that reduces the composer's control over sounds (Morton Feldman's *Intersection* and *Projection* series, Earle Brown's *December 1951*), and from the combination and assembling of fragments by the performer (Stockhausen, Boulez) to stochastic methods that involve complex probability calculations (Iannis Xenakis). In a narrower sense, the notion of aleatory music is a polemical concept: Boulez, whose aesthetic aims remain close to Mallarmé's conception of the Book, applies the term to works in which chance is directed and absorbed, in opposition to the supposedly anarchic indeterminacy of Cage's chance operations.

Notwithstanding this local terminological quarrel, Cage is the central figure in the hist. of aleatory poetics. His work bridges music and the other arts—both in his own practice as composer and poet and through collaborations, notably with Rauschenberg and with the choreographer Merce Cunningham.

Influenced by both Dada and Cage, the artists associated with the Fluxus network continued the investigation of chance methods across different media. La Monte Young's proto-Fluxus compilation *An Anthology of Chance Operations* includes pieces by Cage as well as poetry, compositions, and essays by Claus Bremer, Earle Brown, Joseph Byrd, Walter De Maria, Henry Flynt, Ray Johnson, Yoko Ono, Dick Higgins, Toshi Ichiyanagi, Jackson Mac Low, Richard Maxfield, Nam June Paik, Emmett Williams, and Christian Wolff, among others. *Indeterminacy as a feature of performance predominates in this collection, where the texts are notations to be interpreted. Fluxus composer and artist George Brecht uses the term *chance-imagery* to refer to "our formation of images resulting from chance, wherever these occur in nature" (*Chance-Imagery*, 1966), thus calling into question the distinction between nature and art. Daniel Spoerri's *Topographie Anecdotée du Hasard* (Anecdoted Topography of Chance, 1962) maps, catalogs, and describes the objects lying on the artist's table and the memories associated with them, thus suggesting an approach to the indeterminate core of personhood.

Jackson Mac Low was among the most consistently vital practitioners of aleatory poetry. Influenced by Cage and inspired by Zen Buddhism, Mac Low employed chance operations (random digits, dice, playing cards) to select words, with the aim of minimizing the role of the ego in poetic composition. He developed methods that he characterized as "deterministic yet nonintentional," most notably the techniques of *acrostic and "diastic" "reading-through text selection," which involve searching a source text for words or other verbal units that contain (as their first letter or in other positions) the successive letters of a "seed text" (*Stanzas for Iris Lezak* [1960], *Asymmetries* [1960–61], *The Pronouns* [1964], *Words nd Ends from Ez* [1981–83]). Mac Low's methods belong to what is often termed "procedural poetics" (Perloff), in which *constraint determines the generative principles of composition. A strict distinction between aleatory and deterministic procedures may be less useful in this context than a reflection on the problem of nonintentionality and unpredictability that is at the heart of such practices and their critical reception.

Devels. in technology since the 1950s, such as the application of probability-based algorithms, have offered new possibilities for the exploitation of specific types of randomness. In the 1960s, a group led by the semiotician Max Bense at the Technische Hochschule in Stuttgart experimented in "stochastic texts" based on probability distributions. Theo Lutz used a computer program to produce simple sentences from a repertory of 100 words from Franz Kafka's *The Castle*. This project of generative aesthetics unites formal experimentation with scientific inquiry into lang.

The work of the *Oulipo or *Ouvroir de littérature potentielle* (Workshop for Potential Literature) high-lights the contentiousness of the notion of aleatory poetics. The Oulipo explores the use of various constraints and procedures in writing. Reacting fiercely to critics who categorize the group's methods as aleatory, the Oulipo insists that its approach is "anti-chance." It defines itself against surrealist automatism and (to a lesser degree) against the experimental stochastic lit. of Bense's Stuttgart school. Nevertheless, although Oulipo writers seem uninterested in automatism, coin flipping, and stochastics, some Oulipian methods may be deemed aleatory (in accordance with the musical application of the term) in the place that they assign to the reader. This is the case for Raymond Queneau's *Cent mille milliards de poèmes* (Hundred Thousand Billion Poems, 1961), a work in which the lines of ten original sonnets may be combined to produce $10^{14}$ sonnets. Furthermore, even a rule-based method such as "S+7," which entails replacing each noun in a given text with the seventh one following it in a given dict., involves a certain suspension or at least displacement of authorial intention (as with Mac Low's deterministic operations).

By eschewing complete control of the writing process or by opening up the text to the reader's intervention, aleatory poetics challenges the very definition of the literary work. Chance methods sometimes emulate natural processes, as in John Cage's introduction of the ambient environment into the space of the performance. In this regard, they may be understood as realist in intent or situated within an avant-garde trad. that challenges the divide between art and life. They have sometimes been interpreted as a response or parallel to devels. in science, from Werner Heisenberg's uncertainty principle to chaos theory, but they can also be theorized in terms of revelation of the unconscious, spontaneous expression, or escape from the confines of bias and personal preference. The ambiguities of aleatory poetics—between art and anti-art, playfulness and mysticism, system and randomness, nature and *artifice, the subjective and the impersonal—encapsulate many of the tensions at the heart of avant-garde and experimental writing.

*See* AVANT-GARDE POETICS.

■ T. Lutz, "Stochastiche Texte," *Augenblick* 4 (1959); J. Cage, *Silence* (1961); H. Richter, *Dada* (1965); A. Breton, *Manifestoes of Surrealism*, trans. R. Seaver and H. R. Lane (1969); M. Duchamp, *Salt Seller*, ed. M. Sanouillet and E. Peterson (1973); E. Köhler, *Der literarische Zufall* (1973); M. Nyman, *Experimental Music* (1974); H. Watts, *Chance: A Perspective on Dada* (1979); *Oulipo: A Primer of Potential Literature*, ed. and trans. W. F. Motte (1986); U. Eco, *The Open Work*, trans. A. Cancogni (1989); P. Boulez, "Alea," *Stocktakings from an Apprenticeship*, trans. S. Walsh (1991); M. Perloff, *Radical Artifice* (1991); T. Tzara, *Seven Dada Manifestos and Lampisteries*, trans. B. Wright (1992); *The Boulez-Cage Correspondence*, trans. R. Samuels (1993); J. Cage *I–IV* (1997); *Oulipo Compendium*, ed. H. Mathews and A. Brotchie (1998); Y. Uno, "Aleatoric Processes," *Encyclopedia of Aesthetics*, ed. M. Kelly (1998), Oxford Art Online, http://www.oxfordartonline.com/ subscriber/article/opr/t234/e0016; P. Griffiths, "Aleatory," *Grove Music Online, Oxford Music Online*, http://www.oxfordmusiconline.com/subscriber/article/grove/music/00509; J. Mac Low, *Thing of Beauty*, ed. A. Tardos (2008).

A. JAMES

## ALEXANDRIANISM

**I. Alexandria**, founded in 331 BCE at the mouth of the Nile by Alexander the Great, was the wealthy and cosmopolitan capital of the Ptolemaic dynasty (Fraser). Seeking to demonstrate their place as the true heirs to the Gr. heritage, the Ptolemies founded a museum (literally, shrine of the Muses) to which they attracted scholars and scientists from all over the Gr.-speaking world. The museum was accompanied by an enormous library in which the Ptolemies aimed at accumulating all Gr. writing of earlier periods. Some of the scholars who were charged with the classification, textual crit., and interpretation of archaic and cl. Gr. lit. in that institution also wrote poetry of their own.

**II. Connotations of Alexandrianism**. Befitting the inhabitants of a large commercial metropolis, in antiquity *Alexandrian* could imply impudence or wit (Quintilian, *Institutio oratoria* 1.2.7). In mod. parlance, the adjective is typically used to denote the highly self-conscious, self-referential, and allusive style that characterizes the compositions of scholar-poets resident at the museum and library. In this sense, the term is slightly misleading, since the literary qualities associated with Alexandrian lit. are shared by the work of some poets of the Hellenistic age (roughly defined as the period from the death of Alexander until the defeat of the last Ptolemy in 31 BCE) who had no known association with the city. As our understanding of Hellenistic poetry has grown, the precise nuance of the term *Alexandrianism*, which has sometimes been used pejoratively to denote an overly precious or pretentious style, has changed.

**III. Hellenistic Poetry and Alexandrianism**. The stylistic qualities associated with Alexandrianism are well represented by the work of Callimachus of Cyrene (ca. 305–240 BCE), a highly productive scholar-poet working under the patronage of the early Ptolemies. In the *proem to his *Aetia*, an elegiac poem in four books in which he describes the origins of a variety of obscure local trads., Callimachus defends himself against literary rivals, whom he terms *Telchines*, for not having written a long poem on kings and heroes (frag. 1 Pfeiffer). This passage, which had a remarkable influence on Roman poetry (see sect. IV below), led to the view that Callimachus (who himself composed an epic

poem titled *Hecale*) rejected the writing of large-scale *epic poetry and instead favored shorter forms, but the oppositions set up in the proem are about stylistic rather than generic differences. His stated preference for brevity need not entail a rejection of longer poetic forms but rather a preference for poetry in which each word was chosen with the utmost care and precision. Callimachus was acutely aware of the traditional generic associations of discrete words and phrases and of the formal conventions of particular genres, and much of the interest of his often very witty poems lies in his self-conscious awareness and manipulation of these conventions.

Callimachus and contemporaries such as Theocritus and Apollonius of Rhodes were intensely self-conscious about their place in a long trad. tracing back to Homer and sought to demonstrate their knowledge of earlier lit. while simultaneously emphasizing their independence from it. To this end, they regularly engage with specific passages of a wide range of earlier poetry, incl. the Homeric poems, whose prominence in the trad. lends them particular importance. Hellenistic poets regularly reuse Homeric lang. while subtly varying it, evoke verses whose interpretation was debated by contemp. scholars, or allude in meaningful ways to Homeric scenes. Such evocation of the literary past calls attention to the author's own departure from it. Even the four-book epic *Argonautica* of Apollonius of Rhodes, the most superficially Homeric of surviving Alexandrian poetry (scholars once believed, wrongly, that Apollonius and Callimachus feuded about the propriety of writing epic), incorporates elements from other *genres, incl. *tragedy, and represents its principal hero, Jason, as a figure quite different from the traditional heroes of the *Iliad* and the *Odyssey*, despite sharing certain qualities with them. The "reduction" of heroic figures and scenes is, indeed, a common feature of Alexandrian poetry: thus, Theocritus's Cyclops is shown not as a horrible monster but as a haplessly love-stricken youth, while Heracles' killing of the Nemean lion in Callimachus's *Aetia* is juxtaposed and set in parallel to the war Molorchus wages on field mice.

This approach to lit. was evident in all genres: Theocritus's *idylls play on the intersection of high and low forms, incl. mime and other drama, as well as epic; Callimachus's iambi locate the poet in a trad. deriving from Hipponax but also explicitly defend the intermingling of elements drawn from different genres; literary *epigrams play on the boundaries between funerary and dedicatory verse inscriptions and archaic *elegy and *lyric.

**IV. Alexandrian Imagery**. In addition to the *Aetia* prologue, Callimachus's surviving work, much of it recovered on papyrus during the course of the last century, contains several other passages that self-referentially comment on his literary program; similarly programmatic passages may be found in the work of other poets, incl. the idylls of Theocritus. Cumulatively, several themes found in these passages reappear in later poetry as markers of Alexandrianism: an emphasis on Hesiod as a stylistic precursor; the treatment of water (rather than wine), esp. that from Mt. Helicon, as a source of poetic *inspiration and a concomitant focus on fresh water; the claim that the poet is treading a narrow, difficult, or original path; the opposition of the poet to a broader crowd, representing those who reject the stylistic qualities he advocates; qualitative and quantitative oppositions involving length, sound, and weight, in which the poet's own work is represented as brief, fine, clear, or light rather than lengthy, muddy, loud, or weighty; the refusal (*recusatio; see Wimmel) to meet conventional expectations (the "warning Apollo" motif, later modified to the promise to write epic "one day" or to the referral of a patron's request for such epic to another, and by implication, better poet); the representation of poetry as the object of intense labor, *ponos* (cf. Theocritus 7.51).

**V. Alexandrianism in Rome**. The rise of Roman political power throughout the Mediterranean coincided with the flowering of Alexandria and its literary culture, and Alexandrianism was an important strand of the pervasive influence that Gr. lit. exerted on Roman poetry from its inception. Alexandrianism is evident in the work of the trilingual Ennius and marked in Lucilius (Puelma Piwonka) and *Neoteric writers such as Catullus and Calvus, whose work included short epics written in the refined manner of the Alexandrian poets.

The discovery of the *Aetia* prologue in the early 20th c. made it clear that a number of passages of Roman poetry—incl. Virgil's influential sixth *eclogue, numerous programmatic passages of Roman elegy (esp. Propertius), Horatian lyric and *satire, and the proem to Ovid's *Metamorphoses*—drew on and adapted to a new context Callimachus's apology for not singing about kings and heroes. Although mod. critics have often conceived of Alexandrianism largely in relation to the question of the status of epic as an acceptable literary form, the influence of Alexandrian poetics was far broader.

Beyond formal issues, Roman poets adapted the highly allusive strategies of Alexandrianism as well as its self-conscious concern with the tension between rupture and continuity with the past. In this sense, Virgil's *Aeneid*, an epic that draws on the work of a range of Gr. models incl. Apollonius and Callimachus, is a quintessentially Alexandrian poem. Moreover, recent work has revealed the role that Alexandrian representations of the Egyptian capital and its rulers played for Roman poets as they faced Rome's growing power and the consolidation of political authority under a single ruler. In this sense, Alexandrianism is not merely an aesthetic phenomenon but a means by which Roman poets explored the values of their own cosmopolitan city, its empire, and rulers.

**VI. Alexandrianism in Modern Literature**. Alexandrianism is an enduring phenomenon. Fr. practitioners and theorists such as Paul Valéry and Stéphane Mallarmé show many parallels with ancient ideas (Howald). Am. poets such as Ezra Pound and T. S. Eliot reveal an interest in *allusion and a complicated relationship to traditional forms such as epic (in their case, John Milton). More broadly, the self-conscious tension between continuity and discontinuity with the past (as understood in both historical and literary terms) that pervades Alexandrian poetry finds many parallels in contemp. lit.

*See* CLASSICAL POETICS, GREEK POETRY.

■ **Criticism and History**: U. von Wilamowitz, *Hellenistische Dichtung in der Zeit des Kallimachos*, 2 v. (1924); J. U. Powell, *Collectanea Alexandrina* (1925); E. Howald, *Der Dichter Kallimachos von Kyrene* (1948); M. Puelma Piwonka, *Lucilius und Kallimachos* (1949); W. Wimmel, *Kallimachos in Rom* (1960); G. N. Knauer, *Die Aeneis und Homer* (1964); J. K. Newman, *Augustus and the New Poetry* (1967)—appendix, "Alexandrianism in Modern English Poetry"; R. Pfeiffer, *History of Classical Scholarship* (1968); P. M. Fraser, *Ptolemaic Alexandria*, 3 v. (1972); R. Häussler, *Das historische Epos der Griechen und Römer bis Virgil* (1976); and *Das historische Epos von Lucan bis Silius und seine Theorie* (1978); R. D. Brown, "Lucretius and Callimachus," *Illinois Classical Studies* 7 (1982); *Supplementum Hellenisticum*, ed. H. Lloyd-Jones and P. Parsons (1983); J. K. Newman, *The Classical Epic Tradition* (1986); *A Hellenistic Anthology*, ed. N. Hopkinson (1988); G. O. Hutchinson, *Hellenistic Poetry* (1988); A. Cameron, *Callimachus and His Critics* (1995); D. Nelis, *Vergil's Aeneid and the Argonautica of Apollonius of Rhodes* (2001); S. Stephens, *Seeing Double: Intercultural Poetics in Ptolemaic Alexandria* (2003); M. Fantuzzi and R. Hunter, *Tradition and Innovation in Hellenistic Poetry* (2004).

■ **Primary Texts**: *Select Papyri III: Lit. Papyri*, ed. D. L. Page (1950); *Theocritus*, ed. A.S.F. Gow (1952); *Callimachus: Aetia, Iambi, Hecale and Other Fragments*, ed. and trans. C. A. Trypanis (1958); *Callimachus*, ed. R. Pfeiffer, 2 v. (1965–69).

J. K. NEWMAN; A. SENS

**ALEXANDRINE**. The grand line of Fr. poetry since the 16th c., the alexandrine is made of 12 countable vowels (or 13 vowels in a feminine verse line: see MASCULINE AND FEMININE) and divided in two *hemistichs (6-6), as in the following lines from Sonnet 31 of *Les Regrets* (1558) by Joachim du Bellay:

Heureux qui, comme Ulysse, + a fait un beau voyage
   1   2  3   4    5 6     7 8 9  10  11 12(13)
(Happy the man who, like Ulysses, completed a great
  voyage)

   Ou comme cestuy-là+ qui conquit la toison
   1 2   3 4 5 6    7 8   9 10 11 12
   (Or like he who won the Golden Fleece)

Although its name comes from the *Roman d'Alexandre* (The Romance of Alexander, 1170), the alexandrine had been used previously in the *Pèlerinage de Charlemagne* (The Pilgrimage of Charlemagne, 1150). Hypotheses about its origins are numerous (from the most credible to the least, as follows: imitation of Lat. verse; length matched to the number of syllables that can be read in one breath; combination of two six-syllable lines). As the longest Fr. cl. verse line, it was at first seen as resembling discourse in prose; du Bellay, for instance, wrote the *Regrets* in alexandrines because his book was meant to express an intimate and informal type of inspiration. Considered to be less noble than the more common ten-syllable line, the alexandrine was associated primarily with popular poetry. In 1572, Pierre de Ronsard wrote in the preface to the *Franciade*, "It would have been much easier to write my book in alexandrines, since this is the longest verse line, were it not for the scruple that they sound too much like prose." Nevertheless, between the 16th and 17th cs., the alexandrine became not only the most widely used verse line in Fr. poetry but the preferred form of elevated and even "noble" genres such as *epic and *tragedy. Thus, a name that referred to the med. heroic poem was elevated to the status of national symbol and eventually came to typify Fr. poetry overall (Halévy). In reality, Ronsard's reluctance to espouse the alexandrine bears witness to its success after 1555, when it began to displace the ten-syllable line as the new *vers héroïque*. This agreement on what had become the most common verse line in Fr. poetry of the Ren. illustrates the dedication of poets in their efforts to forge a national lang.

Since the exact number of syllables that speakers of Fr. can routinely identify with certainty in a given verse line is limited to eight or fewer, the alexandrine is heard not as a whole but as two hexasyllabic units. But the cl. 6-6 alexandrine is just one of the possible 12-syllable meters in Fr., along with 8-4, 4-4-4, 3-5-4, 5-7, and 7-5, all of which appeared during the second half of the 19th c. Strictly speaking, the designation "alexandrine" should be reserved for 6-6 lines and not all dodecasyllabic lines.

Given its status as the favorite Fr. meter, the alexandrine has always been criticized. Poets and theorists of the 18th c. (e.g., François Neuf-Château, Toussaint Rémond de Saint Mard, Jean-François Marmontel, Louis-Séastien Mercier, André Chénier, Jean-Antoine Roucher) judged its structure to be too rigid, an obstacle to the expression of poets' voices and passions. Traditional theatrical declamation of the line, which was based on a rising tone for the first six syllables and a falling tone for the final six, was felt to be monotonous and little conducive to rhythm (Lote 1940). Later, Hugo heroically claimed he had "disloqué ce grand niais d'alexandrin" (dislocated the alexandrine, that great simpleton [*Les Contemplations*, 1856]). Though in his poetry Hugo never changed the alexandrine's fundamental 6-6 structure, even as he straddled line-limits (through *rejets* and *enjambments*), he launched a radical change that some romantics demanded. Subsequent generations from Charles Baudelaire to Arthur Rimbaud, including such figures as Paul Verlaine and Théodore de Banville but excluding Gérard de Nerval and Théophile Gautier, investigated ways to renew the "grand vers" by inventing new scansions that first could accommodate the 6-6 structure ("mesures d'accompagnement"; Cornulier 1995): alternative scansions appeared, such as the 8-4 as

in "Comme César pour un sourire, Ô Cléopâtre" (Like Caesar for a smile, O Cleopatra; Verlaine, "Lettre," *Fêtes galantes*, 1869); the 4-8 as in "Entendez-vous? C'est la marmite qu'accompagne / L'horloge du tic-tac allègre de son pouls" (Do you hear? It is the pot / That accompanies the blithe pulse of the clock; Verlaine, "L'Auberge," *Jadis et naguère*, 1881); the 4-4-4 as in "Mais de ceci, pour mon malheur, ne sachant rien" (But knowing nothing about this, unfortunately; Charles-Marie Leconte de Lisle, "Le corbeau," *Poèmes barbares*, 1862); and the rare 3-5-4 as in "Ô malheur ! je me sens frémir, la vieille terre . . ." (Oh misfortune! I tremble, the old earth . . .; "Qu'est-ce pour nous, mon coeur . . ." Rimbaud, *Derniers vers*, 1872). Then, increasingly bold in their line construction, poets weakened the usual syntactic pause of the *caesura by placing in the sixth position words that could not receive vocal emphasis, such as the proclitic article *un*: "Chacun plantant, comme *un* outil, son bec impur" (Each [bird] planting his unclean beak as if it were a tool; "Un voyage à Cythère," Baudelaire, *Les Fleurs du mal*, 1857).

Experiments with the alexandrine (but also with the decasyllable) led to the emergence of *vers libre* (free verse) at the turn of the 20th c. But in spite of free verse's liberties, poets have maintained a system of echoes and resemblances with the alexandrine, which remains the most prominent poetic line in Fr.

*See* FRENCH PROSODY, SYLLABIC VERSE.

■ G. Lote, *L'Alexandrin d'après la phonétique expérimentale* (1919); J. Roubaud, *La Vieillesse d'Alexandre* (1978); B. de Cornulier, *Théorie du vers* (1982); S. P. Verluyten, "Analyse de l'alexandrin: Mètre ou rythme?" in *Le Souci des apparences*, ed. M. Dominicy (1989); H. Morier, "L'Alexandrin classique était bel et bien un tétramètre," in *Langue, littérature du XVIIᵉ et du XVIIIᵉ siècle* (1990); G. Lote, *Histoire du vers français* (VIII) (1994[1953]); B. de Cornulier, *Art poëtique* (1995); J.-M. Gouvard, *Critique du vers* (2000); O. Halévy, "La vie d'une forme: l'alexandrin renaissant (1452–1573)," *L'Information littéraire* (2004); J. Gros de Gasquet, *En disant l'alexandrin renaissant* (2006); G. Peureux, *La Fabrique du vers* (2009).

G. Peureux

**ALLAEOSTROPHA.** The Gr. term *alloiostropha* is used by Hephaestion to describe one type of *apolelymena* (literally, released or free verse—verse that does not exhibit a repeated pattern of any sort). Apolelymena too short to constitute what Hephaestion regards as a single *strophe are called *astropha* (*astrophic*); those that do not exhibit any single recognizable pattern of division into strophes are *atmeta* (indivisibles); and those composed of two or more contrasting strophes are *heterostropha* (composed of strophes of which the one is different from the other) if there are only two such strophes and *alloiostropha* (different strophied) if there are more than two. John Milton uses the term, spelled *allaeostropha* (for reasons unknown), in the preface to *Samson Agonistes* to describe verse in irregular *stanzas. Hephaestion was published in Adrien Turnèbe's ed. in 1553, a work that Milton almost surely would have known,

it being the only ed. available in the 17th c. and He-
phaestion the standard authority for all ancient met-
rical doctrine.

*See* HETEROMETRIC, ODE, STICHOS.

■ Maas, sects. 30, 71, 72; West, 135–37.

A. T. COLE

## ALLEGORY

I. Uses of the Term
II. Allegory in the Modern World
III. Allegorizing
IV. Historical Development
V. Dialectic of the Visible and the Invisible

**I. Uses of the Term**. There are three senses in which
crit. uses the term *allegory* (Gr. *allegoria*; ἄλλος "other"
+ ἀγορεύειν "public speaking"): (1) as an entire work of
art, "*an* allegory"; (2) as a pattern of images, "an allegory
*of* "; and (3) as arbitrary interpretation, where something
is read "*as* an allegory" of something else. In the first, alle-
gory is a literary or artistic genre in which the entire work
of art is presented as secondary with respect to its mean-
ing, eliciting interpretation throughout. In the second,
traditional, symbolic figures, often *personifications, are
used to give visible form to abstract concepts and pro-
cesses. Such figures appear most often within allegorical
works of the kind just described, but they also appear
in other media and genres. In the third, often called al-
legorizing, nonallegorical works are interpreted as if in-
tended to be allegories, as when *The Odyssey* is asserted
to be an allegory of the journey of the soul through
the world or when the Israelites' passing through the
Red Sea is asserted to be an allegory of baptism.

In an allegory of the first kind, the immediate nar-
rative—the story of a knight named Redcrosse, e.g.—
is presented as a covering or veil behind which the
real meaning is concealed, or so we are to suppose.
The immediate narrative is relatively incoherent on
its own and densely symbolic. We think of the narra-
tive in comparison with writing: just as written letters
are secondary to the sounds for which they stand, so
the elements of the immediate narrative of an allegory
seem to stand for something else. For this reason, the
immediate narrative is spoken of (by an inaccurate
analogy) as the "literal" meaning and what it hides as
the "figural" or represented meaning. Although the
figural meaning is supposed to be concealed, there
are many clues to what it is: personified abstractions
(Disdain, Mr. Worldly-Wise), traditional symbols
(the Anchor of Hope, the Torch of Ire), significant
topography (the Wandering Wood, the Hill of Dif-
ficulty), and elaborately semiotic architectural struc-
tures (the Castle of Perseverance, the House of Pride).

Such hints provide the general contexts of mean-
ing within which interpretation is to occur (moral,
historical, political, religious), leaving the reader to fill
in and organize details. An allegory arouses *hermeneu-
tic anxiety* and supplies instructions for *interpretative
play*. By engaging in such play, the reader builds a co-
herent structure of meaning that is then imagined to
have been hidden in advance and to have been merely
discovered by the reader. Hermeneutic anxiety and

interpretative play are allegory's primary aesthetic ef-
fects. They are complemented by a sense of penetrating
through the text toward a singularity—Dante would
call it a *punto*—that is at the heart of the mystery of the
world. Only there may one rest from interpretation.
We may refer to this last as *the narcosis of repose in the
truth*. Thus, the three phases of response to an allegory
are *hermeneutic anxiety*, *interpretative play*, and *narcosis
of repose in the truth*.

How does an allegory differ from a *fable, a beast
fable by Aesop, e.g.? The fable makes sense on its own
as narrative and is moralized only at the end. But an al-
legory is a relatively incoherent narrative that demands
interpretation throughout in order to make it cohere.

The best-known allegories were composed in the
Middle Ages and the Ren.: Guillaume de Lorris and
Jean de Meun's *Roman de la Rose*, Christine de Pi-
zan's *City of Women* (parodically refashioned by the
filmmaker Federico Fellini in *Città di donne*), Dante's
*Divine Comedy*, William Langland's *Piers Plowman*,
Edmund Spenser's *Faerie Queene*, and John Bunyan's
*Pilgrim's Progress*.

Some scholars with a narrower view of allegory, no-
tably Auerbach, have argued that Dante's *Comedy* is
not an allegory, or is only partly so, because his nar-
rative is mimetically real, not secondary with respect
to its meaning, as de Meun's narrative is (e.g, de Meun
portrays the sexual act as a pilgrim's putting his staff in
the hole of a shrine). Still, Dante's *Comedy* elicits in-
terpretation throughout and brings us to a singularity
where we experience the narcosis of repose in the truth.
In fact, all the masters of allegory, incl. great painters
such as Peter Paul Rubens, strain against the conven-
tions of the genre by making their imaginative worlds
as real as the transcendent meaning to which they refer.
For almost 1,000 years, from late antiquity to the late
Ren., allegory was reputed the truest form of artistic
expression, giving visible form to *invisibilia*, which are
more real than what we can see.

**II. Allegory in the Modern World**. We should not
suppose allegory is confined to the past or is only of
antiquarian interest. It is impossible to understand
mod. culture without allegory, first, because allegori-
cal imagery (*allegory* in our second sense of the word)
has spilled over into the mod. world, appearing on the
coats of arms of states, on public monuments, in po-
litical cartoons, on commercial products, and on the
Internet. Andy Warhol, painter of the Brillo box and
of the Campbell's Soup can and of famous images of
Jacqueline Kennedy and Mao Zedong, recognized that,
with the explosion of reproducible images in mod. cul-
ture, flat images become portentous icons.

Something very like allegory (in our first sense of
the word) thrives in high culture, too. There are some
affinities with allegory in the terrifying fables of Franz
Kafka, notably "In the Penal Colony," with its violent
scene of writing on the body. A great deal of mod. po-
etry, with its incoherent syntax and its allusive sense of
a mystery withheld, has affinities with allegory, arous-
ing hermeneutic anxiety, engaging us in interpretative
play, and delivering the narcosis of repose in the truth.

Ezra Pound's *Cantos* arouses hermeneutic anxiety and demands the same kind of reading, interpretative play, as does allegory. Although there is less use of allegory in film than one might expect, given how well suited to allegory the visual character of the medium is, Fellini's films are a striking exception. He develops an elaborate system of allegorical imagery that grows in complexity from one film to the next. For the great prophet of modernity, Charles Baudelaire, allegory is the only means of expressing the alienation of the spirit from the material conditions of urban life, conditions to which the spirit remains nevertheless bound, as the allegorical sign is arbitrarily bound to its meaning.

Similar affinities are found in mod. painting and sculpture, from the abstracted but emotionally powerful figures in Pablo Picasso's *Guernica* to the riddling iconography of Jasper Johns. The contemp. Ger. artist Anselm Kiefer works self-consciously in the allegorical trad., drawing on an astonishing range of contingent discourses (alchemy, astrology, Kabbalah, the Bible, Germanic myth, and mod. poetry) to build monumental works that arouse hermeneutic anxiety and elicit interpretative play—and aesthetic narcosis. Examples are the vast installation *Sternenfall* ("'Disaster'" or "'Falling Stars'") in the Grand Palais in Paris in 2007 and, in the collection of the Pompidou Center, a series of massive paintings of the night sky on which the tattooed numbers of concentration-camp victims are inscribed among the stars, imitating NASA catalog numbers.

**III. Allegorizing**. In our third sense of the term, *allegory* has been applied to works of lit. and art that are imagined to mean something other than they say, even when there is no indication in the work of this alternative meaning. Pedestrian allegorical schemes have thus been imposed on novels by Nathaniel Hawthorne (who denied writing allegory), Herman Melville, Stendhal, George Eliot, and many others. Often referred to in this context as a "mode," allegory becomes a naïve pleonasm for the literary: all lit., all art, is important because it is allegorical and says what we think it ought to say. This is an excuse to make anything an allegory of anything else.

A more coherent, deconstructionist proposal for the meaning of *allegory*—although it is just as arbitrary a use of the term—follows the work of P. de Man (inspired by Benjamin): allegory reveals the temporality in figurative lang. by acknowledging the noncoincidence of the sign with its meaning, thus demystifying the principle of the symbol, which affirms the fusion of the sign with its meaning. Allegory, in this sense, becomes a sort of floating, critical awareness in lit., closely allied with irony. Like irony, it is condemned never to have any rest, repeatedly undoing the ineradicable supposition that figurative lang. is true.

When Benjamin spoke about allegory (which he was polemically opposing to the fetish of the symbol in Ger. romantic crit.), he was referring specifically to 17th-c. *baroque *emblems replete with skulls, dead plants, and the like. Instead of fusing meaning and life, as the symbol purports to do, the baroque emblem sees them off in opposite directions: "Death," as Benjamin put it allegorically, "digs most deeply the jagged line of demarcation between *physis* [in this context, "growth" or "life"] and significance" ("zwischen φύσις und Bedeutung"). In generalizing this powerful insight, de Man did not fully succeed in liberating it from a false concretion of the term *allegory*, which he referred to sometimes as a *"trope" and sometimes as a "mode." Neither term—one is too small, the other too large—is equal to de Man's insight into the opacity of figurative lang.

**IV. Historical Development**. The Gr. word *allegoria* can mean either "saying something other than is meant" or "meaning something other than is said"—or both, where the "other" in question rapidly oscillates between the two positions. *Allegory* often carries the suggestion of prudential encoding. Cicero writes in a letter that, because of the dangerous political situation, he will obscure his meaning with allegories: "ἀλληγορίαις obscurabo." The classic definition is by the Roman rhetorician Quintilian: "continued metaphor"—μεταφορά continuata. His example is a short poem by Horace in which a troubled state is figured by a description of a ship in rough seas. Quintilian's definition is elegant and durable but applies well only to short works such as Horace's poem. Nevertheless, the appearance in late antiquity of the rhetorical term *allegory*, suggesting that a text says something wholly other than it appears to be saying, contributed to the later emergence of the literary form we call *allegory*.

A second factor contributing to the rise of literary allegory is the reduction of minor ancient gods to personifications. Med. personification developed from the widespread tendency to rationalize the gods as abstract universals, on the way to their becoming the traditional virtues and vices and the planetary and zodiacal powers governing our lower world. The cause of everything, including erections and beards, was attributed to some minor god. What we call personifications (the term suggests an actor's mask: *per* "through" + *sonare* "to sound") are more like robotic machines designed to represent abstract universals. There is no independent consciousness behind the face of the machine, only what is necessary for its task to be performed. In Spenser's *The Faerie Queene*, the personification Disdain swings his club at Prince Arthur, who slips under the blow and slashes at Disdain's knee. But because the knee of Disdain would never bend, the entire leg shatters, like a ceramic tube: "But all that leg, which did his body beare, / It crackt throughout, yet did no bloud appeare; / So as it was unable to support / So huge a burden on such broken geare" (6.8.16). Note the word *geare*, telling us Disdain's leg is not part of a body—it does not bleed—but is instead a piece of equipment. When he crashes to the ground, Disdain keeps struggling to rise, with the repetitive action of a broken machine.

A third factor contributing to the emergence of med. allegorical lit. began as far back as the 6th c. BCE, when the poems of Homer began to be interpreted as If they concealed moral, scientific, philosophical, and even spiritual truths. This was called *hermêneia tôn poiêtôn* ("interpretation of the poets," whence our word *hermeneutics*). *Hermêneia* had the advantage of dignifying ideas one favors by associating them, however anachronistically, with the "bible" of the Greeks. It also served to explain away the parts of Homer that were scandalous to a more puritanical age. Such interpretations were called not yet allegories but *hyponoiai*, "undermeanings." Thus, when the artificer god Hephaestus catches his wife Aphrodite with her lover Ares in an invisible net, we are not to suppose this episode from the *Odyssey* is merely for comic relief. It is an encoded *hyponoia*, an "underthought" on the creation of the cosmos from the opposed forces of concord and discord, bound together in the net of the *logos*, which is "reason," or "natural law." Such ideas were entirely foreign to Homer. Similarly fanciful interpretations were put forward in the Middle Ages to rescue pagan lit. for Christian use. For Fulgentius, the struggles of Virgil's Aeneas to get to Italy, the "Lavinian shores," are the Christian soul's strivings for heaven; and in the anonymous *Ovide moralisé,* the bull that rapes Europa, being Jove in disguise, is Christ saving humanity.

Some allegorizations have attained cultural significance in their own right, notably the early Christian interpretation of the erotic Song of Songs as an allegory of Christ's love for his Church and Porphyry's Neoplatonic interpretation of the Cave of the Nymphs in the *Odysssey* as an allegory of souls in the cosmos. In Ren. Florence, Neoplatonic allegorizations of cl. myth had independent aesthetic value, powerfully influencing great artists such as Sandro Botticelli. The elaborate, med. practice of allegorizing the Bible underlay lit., music, painting, and architecture up to the 17th c. Joshua's leading the Israelites across the Jordan River into the Promised Land prefigures Jesus' leading us through death into heaven. For med. churchmen, Joshua's action is a real, historical event, not just an imaginative one, as with cl. tales, meaning that God himself is an allegorist, hiding meaning in history, as he also hides meaning in nature.

The fourth and final condition for literary allegory comes after antiquity and pervades the Christian worldview: the emergence of a logocentric culture of the sign, replacing a polytheistic culture of the *numen* or "indwelling spirit." With the coming of Christianity as the dominant culture, the world is seen as an order of signs, all of them pointing back to their mysterious, transcendent creator. Like gravitation, the effect of this new sense of the signifying character of the world is comparatively weak on the small scale of the textual phenomena we have considered so far: rhetorical figures, fanciful interpretations, and personifications. But when we step back to take in a wider perspective, the large-scale effects of this cause are impressive, drawing vast amounts of iconographical material into galaxy-like structures turning around invisible centers. Under Christianity, people began to sense that everything visible is not quite real, though it points, with everything else, to the invisible real. This feeling created the ideal intellectual climate for the growth of allegorical writing.

Early examples are Martianus Capella's *On the Marriage of Mercury and Philology* (intelligence is the god Mercury, and learning is the maiden Philology, whose bridesmaids are the seven liberal arts) and a poem by Prudentius (ca. 348–405), titled *Psychomachia*, "the battle of virtues and vices in the soul." This work derives from a famous and much-allegorized episode in the *Iliad* called the *theomachia* ("battle of the gods"), in which the gods join in the fighting at Troy. Pious ancient readers had interpreted the episode as a battle of the virtues and the vices in the soul and even as the battle of the different elements in nature. Thus, in the *Psychomachia*, we see gathered together the four ancient factors contributing to the devel. of allegory: continued metaphor (inward moral struggle as an outward battle); personification (Modesty, *Pudicitia*, kills Lust, *Luxuria*); hermeneutics (the gods of the *Iliad* as virtues and vices); and a sense of mystery enveloping the whole and tending to the unity of truth. At the conclusion of the *Psychomachia*, the virtues occupy the city of the purified soul, which resembles the heavenly Jerusalem of Revelation, where the mysterious figure of wisdom (*Sapientia*) is enthroned, the dark center around which everything turns.

*Allegory in the Visual Arts.* Allegory is the only major literary term that is equally applicable to the visual arts, from the complex symbolism of the great cathedrals of the Middle Ages to allegorical imagery on skyscrapers, such as the tower of the *Chicago Sun-Times.* The trad. of pictorial allegory in Christian art of the High Middle Ages began with Abbot Suger's plans for the stained-glass windows of the Abbey of Saint Denis and developed into the comprehensive symbolic system of the great Gothic cathedrals, from Chartres to Rheims.

A chronological selection of secular allegory in the visual arts would include the following: Pietro Lorenzetti's *Allegory of Good and Bad Government*, in the Palazzo Pubblico, Siena (14th c.); Botticelli's *Calumny of Apelles* and his *Primavera*, both in the Uffizi, Florence (15th c.); Francesco del Cossa's decoration of the "Room of the Months," Ferrara (15th c.); Albrecht Dürer's "Triumphal Chariot of Maximilian I" (16th c.); Giulio Romano's frescoes in the Palazzo Te, Mantua (16th c.); Agnolo Bronzino's *Allegory of Felicity* in the Uffizi, Florence, and his stunningly erotic *Allegory of Love* in the National Gallery, London (16th c.); Guido Reni's *Aurora* in the Palazzo Rospigliosi, Rome (17th c.); Rubens's ceiling of the Banqueting House in London, and his *Allegory of War* in the Uffizi (17th c.); Pietro da Cortona's *Apotheosis of the Barberini* in the Barberini Palace, Rome, and his *Medici Ceilings* in the Palazzo Pitti, Florence (17th c.); Pompeo Batoni's *Allegory of Venice*, now in Raleigh, NC (18th c.); Giambattista Tiepolo's stupendous *Allegory of the Continents* in Würzburg (18th c.); Eugène Delacroix's "Greece Expiring on the Ruins of Missolonghi" (1826), his "Liberty Leading the People" (1830), and his allegorical decorations on the ceiling of the "Galerie d'Apollon" in the Louvre (1850–51); Pierre Ducos de la Haille's *France Giving Enlightenment to the Continents of the World*, in the Palais de la Porte Dorée, in Paris (1929–31); and José Clemente Orozco's *Epic of American Civilization* at Dartmouth College in Hanover, NH (1932–34).

**V. Dialectic of the Visible and the Invisible**. The many, powerful examples of allegory in art underline its intensely visual character in lit., where *visibilia* point beyond themselves to *invisibilia* and where *invisibilia*, such as faith, are brought into view. As Machosky (2003) observes, allegory does not merely conceal meaning: it makes visible things that cannot otherwise be perceived. It was noted that, in the transcendentalizing culture of the Middle Ages, to be visible and material was not to be entirely real; but visible, material things can become paths to the real. As Suger put it (in words inscribed on the doors of the Abbey Church of Saint Denis), the weak human mind may rise toward truth only by the assistance of material signs: "mens hebes ad verum per materialia surgit."

But allegory can also bring what is hidden into the light. In this double movement, we may find a solution to Auerbach's rejection of allegory as incompatible with Dante's *irdischen Welt*, his "earthly world." Bunyan's homely and realistic villagers are no less earthly than Dante's hectic Florentines. Spenser's Fairy Land seems not less but more intensely real than our world; his knights champion their respective moral virtues but are not reduced to them. As we read an allegory, the dialectical interaction between sharp, realistic images of things disappearing into universal mysteries and universal mysteries emerging into view as sharp, realistic things is the highest pleasure afforded by the genre. De Man's insight may now be recalled: allegory brings pleasure, not truth.

*See* HERMENEUTICS, IRONY, SYMBOL.

■ Lewis; E. Panofsky, *Studies in Iconology* (1939); J. Seznec, *The Survival of the Pagan Gods*, trans. B. F. Sessions (1953); F. Buffière, *Les Mythes d'Homère et la pensée grecque* (1956); E. Mâle, *The Gothic Image*, trans. D. Nussey ([1913] 1958); E. Wind, *Pagan Mysteries in the Renaissance* (1958); E. Auerbach, "Figura," *Scenes from the Drama of European Literature* (1959); H. de Lubac, *Exégèse médiévale*, 4 v. (1959–64); A. Fletcher, *Allegory* (1964); R. Tuve, *Allegorical Imagery* (1966); A. Henkel and A. Schöne, *Emblemata* (1967; suppl. 1976); H. R. Jauss and U. Ebel, "Entstehung und Strukturwandel der allegorischen Dichtung," *GRLMA* 6.1 (1968); M. Murrin, *The Veil of Allegory* (1969); D. C. Allen, *Mysteriously Meant* (1970); J. MacQueen, *Allegory* (1970); M. R. Jung, *Etudes sur le poème allégorique en France au moyen âge* (1971); P. Dronke, *Fabula* (1974)—med. Platonism; J. Nohrnberg, *The Analogy of "The Faerie Queene"* (1976); J. Pépin, *Mythe et allégorie*, 2d ed. (1976); W. Benjamin, *The Origin of German Tragic Drama*, trans. J. Osborne ([1928] 1977); S. A. Barney, *Allegories of History, Allegories of Love* (1979); M. Quilligan, *The Language of Allegory* (1979); M. Murrin, *The Allegorical Epic* (1980); D. Cast, *The Calumny of Apelles* (1981); *Allegory and Representation*, ed. S. Greenblatt (1981); P. Rollinson

and P. Matsen, *Classical Theories of Allegory and Christian Culture* (1981); J. D. Black, "Allegory Unveiled," *PoT* 4 (1983); de Man, "The Rhetoric of Temporality"; C. Van Dyke, *The Fiction of Truth* (1985); L. Barkan, *The Gods Made Flesh* (1986); R. Lamberton, *Homer the Theologian* (1986); J. Pépin, *La tradition de l'allégorie* (1987); J. Whitman, *Allegory* (1987); D. Evett, "Some Elizabethan Allegorical Paintings," *Journal of the Warburg and Courtauld Institute* 52 (1989); A. Katzenellenbogen, *Allegories of the Virtues and Vices in Medieval Art* (1989); G. Teskey, "Allegory," *The Spenser Encyclopedia*, ed. A. C. Hamilton (1990), and *Allegory and Violence* (1996); S. Greenfield, *The Ends of Allegory* (1998); B. Machosky, "The Phenomenology of the Soul in the Allegory of the *Psychomachia*," *Exemplaria* 15 (2003); N. Conti, *Mythologiae*, trans. J. Mulryan and S. Brown (2006); D. Sanyal, *The Violence of Modernity* (2006); E. Auerbach, *Dante*, trans. R. Manheim ([1929] 2007); N. Guynn, *Allegory and Sexual Ethics in the High Middle Ages* (2007); N. Halmi, *The Genealogy of the Romantic Symbol* (2007); B. Machosky, "Trope and Truth in *The Pilgrim's Progress*," *Studies in English Literature* 47 (2007), and ed., *Thinking Allegory Otherwise* (2009); E. Naginski, *Sculpture and Enlightenment* (2009).

G. TESKEY

**ALLITERATION.** The repetition of the *sound of an initial consonant or consonant cluster in stressed syllables close enough to each other for the ear to be affected. The term is sometimes also used for the repetition of an initial consonant in unstressed syllables, as in E. A. Poe's "lost Lenore," where the weak second *l* affects the ear less than the long *o* followed by *r*, but this less direct patterning is arguably not of the same class as stress-enhanced alliteration. From cl. times up to the 20th c., *alliteration* as a figure in rhet. means the repetition of the initial *letter* of words. Alliteration formerly included the echo of initial vowels, even of initial letters in weak syllables—a fact that explains Charles Churchill's 18th-c. attack on those who unsuccessfully "pray'd / For apt alliteration's Artful aid." In mod. scholarship, *vowel alliteration* usually refers only to the older Germanic langs. It must constantly be borne in mind that, since alliteration is a device of the *sound* stratum of poetry, the vagaries of spelling systems must be discounted: it is sounds, not letters, that count, as in Emily Dickinson's "The cricket sang / And set the sun" ("The Cricket Sang") or John Dryden's "Thy force, infus'd, the fainting Tyrians prop'd; / And haughty Pharoah found his fortune stop'd" (*Absalom and Achitophel*, 842–43), where the *f* phone begins six stressed syllables, one in a medial syllable, one spelled *Ph*.

In the alliterative meters of the older Germanic langs., including *Beowulf* (see ENGLISH PROSODY, Old English; GERMANIC PROSODY), alliteration binds the two *hemistichs, as in "Oft Scyld Scefing sceathena threatum." The alliteration is usually on initial consonants or on certain consonant clusters, but any vowel may alliterate with any other. In Old Saxon, a weakening of phonological stress apparently caused alliterating syllables to be reinforced by a higher proportion of identical vowels, whether the syllable began with the vowel or with a consonant (Suzuki). In poetry after ME, alliteration is neither linear nor structural; in fact, it is often carried through several lines. Today, then, alliteration is one of the four most significant devices of phonic echo in poetry (see ASSONANCE, CONSONANCE, RHYME).

One must remember that unintentional alliteration will occur less often than unintentional assonance, since in IE langs. consonants outnumber vowels. Certain consonant clusters (e.g., *st* and *sp*) alliterate only with themselves in the older Germanic langs. A. E. Housman, aware of this trad., lets his poet in "The Grecian Galley" alliterate seven *st* clusters in three lines.

Almost every major poetry in the world except Hebrew, Persian, and Arabic seems to have made considerable use of alliteration, which has been more popular and persistent than rhyme. Although there is disagreement about the nature or importance of stress in Gr. and Lat. poetry, it is certain that cl. poets understood the uses of alliteration. Aeschylus echoed initials to emphasize key words and phrases, to point up a pun, to aid *onomatopoeia, or simply to please the ear (Stanford). Lucretius reveled in phonic echoes, incl. alliteration, while Virgil, a quieter poet, wrote many lines like these two, heavy with assonance, in which eight important syllables also bear initial *k* or *l*: "cuncta mihi Alpheum linquens locusque Molorchi / cursibus et crudo decernet Graecia caestu."

More than most others, the Romance langs. have neglected alliteration in favor of assonance, the reason perhaps being that It., Sp., and Port. poetry have traditionally preferred short lines with vowel (often followed by consonant) echoes in the final two syllables. Even though it is said that Fr. poetry by the 17th c. considered alliteration "mauvaise" (Thieme), the Fr. cl. *alexandrine did make some use of it, as in Nicolas Boileau's "Des traits d'esprit semés de temps en temps pétillent." But most Fr. poets from Victor Hugo to Saint-John Perse have found other devices more appealing to the ear.

Even the Asian tonal langs. have been as fond of alliteration as of other phonic echoes. Chinese, a monosyllabic lang. with short-line poems based on parallel structure and patterning of rising vs. falling tones, insists on rhyme and plays much with repeated vowels and consonants, as with *ch* in the opening lines of "Fu on Climbing a Tower" by Wang Can (ca. 200 CE; Frankel). Also tonal, but polysyllabic, Japanese poetry has from ancient times employed much alliteration (Brower).

All the Celtic langs., but esp. Ir. and Welsh, have been renowned for their elaborate schemes of phonic ornamentation. Early Welsh and Ir. "cadenced" verse was seldom rhymed but used much alliteration for linking words and lines. By the 6th c., this verse gave way to "rhyming" verse in which each line has stressed word pairs that alliterate or assonate, all to go with the "generic rhyming" that links lines of a stanza (see CELTIC PROSODY). By the 14th c., Welsh bards had evolved the elaborately decorated *cynghanedd* based on exact rhymes in couplets and complex echoes of vowels and consonants, incl. alliteration (Dunn).

Of the poetry in Germanic langs., mod. Ger. has employed alliteration consistently, while Eng. has liked it perhaps even more. J. W. Goethe used alliteration much as Shakespeare did, in conjunction with other phonic devices and normally with restraint. He might, however, open a lyric (e.g., "Hochzeitlied") with heavy alliteration or help elevate Faust's most important speech to Mephistopheles with "Dann will ich gern zu Grunde gehn!" Heinrich Heine preferred rhymed short-line verse and needed alliteration less, but he often tended to heavy ornament (e.g., "Ein Wintermarchen"). Gottfried Benn and R. M. Rilke were perhaps more sound-conscious than most other 20th-c. Ger. poets; and while they too preferred assonance, Benn could write dozens of lines like this one in "Untergrundbahn": "Druch all den Frühling kommt die fremde Frau," a line no more ornate than some by Rilke.

Although alliteration was disparaged by Chaucer's Parson, a southern man, as "rum, ram, ruf," Eng. poets continued to use it widely after the 14th-c. revival of alliterative verse in England and Scotland (see ENGLAND, POETRY OF). The later usage shows no knowledge of the precise rules of meter that have been discovered for alliterative verse of the 14th and early 15th cs. (see ENGLISH PROSODY, Middle English). Edmund Spenser makes use of it in the *Shepheardes Calender*; and in *The Faerie Queene*, the first 36 lines have seven instances of triple alliteration—by some standards very heavy. In *A Midsummer Night's Dream* (5.1.147–48), Shakespeare makes fun of alliteration, but he employs it heavily in the early long poems (e.g., *Lucrece*)—less so in the lyrics, sonnets, and plays—though alliteration is often conspicuous in the plays. John Milton, who loved the sound of words even before his blindness, preferred assonance, but he also liked alliteration, e.g., in "L'Allegro" ("And to the stack, or the barn door, / Stoutly struts his Dames before") and in *Paradise Lost* ("Moping melancholy, / And moonstruck madness" [2.424–25]). Eng. poets from 1660 to 1780 worked hard with phonic echoes in order to vary not only their couplets but their *blank verse and octosyllables. Dryden, Alexander Pope, John Gay, and James Thomson used alliteration best to tie adjectives to nouns, to balance nouns or verbs or adjectives, to stress the *caesura and end rhyme, to join sound to sense, and to decorate their lines. After 1780, poets used alliteration less; still, almost every poet from William Blake to G. M. Hopkins to Housman used it well, sometimes excessively, as with this typical burst in Robert Browning's "The Bishop Orders His Tomb": "And stretch my feet forth straight as stone can point." Alfred, Lord Tennyson is reported to have said, "When I spout my lines first, they come out so alliteratively that I have sometimes no end of trouble to get rid of the alliteration."

In the 20th c., Robert Frost, Ezra Pound, and W. C. Williams are relatively unornamental, though Frost could sometimes alliterate heavily—"Nature's first green is gold, / Her hardest hue to hold" ("Nothing Gold Can Stay"). Others—Wallace Stevens, T. S.

Eliot, W. B. Yeats—are less sparing with alliteration, as Eliot is in the Sweeney poems and "The Love Song of J. Alfred Prufrock," though sometimes they indulge sudden excesses, as with Stevens's "Winding across wide waters." But there is a larger group of more recent poets who, learning from Hopkins and Thomas Hardy, have depended very much on phonic echoes, esp. in unrhymed verse. Among these are Wilfred Owen and Dylan Thomas in Britain and Robinson Jeffers, Marianne Moore, Hart Crane, Theodore Roethke, Robert Lowell, Richard Wilbur, and Mary Oliver in the U.S. Crane, typical of this group, echoes not only initial consonants but important vowels in almost every line—"Sun-silt rippled them / Asunder" ("Repose of Rivers") and "Rail-squatters ranged in nomad raillery" (*The Bridge*). Oliver, whose poems show an awareness of rhetorical figures and prosodical turns, alliterates *s* four times and *f* twice in two lines: "It is the light at the center of every cell. / It is what sent the snake coiling and flowing forward" ("The Black Snake").

All these literary patterns depend for their effectiveness on the salience of alliteration in everyday speech. In the Germanic langs. esp., alliterative formulas have been in common use historically, incl. alliterating names for siblings, e.g., *Heorogar, Hrothgar,* and *Halga* (Minkova). It appears that nonliterary usage both preceded the literary forms and survived them after fashions in verse changed. Recent research using the databases of corpus ling. has revealed the pervasiveness of alliterative formulas in early ME, influenced partly by the alliterative collocations of western Scandinavia (Markus). ME prose with an affinity to the registers of spoken lang. suggests that these collocations were a part of common speech, as they continue to be in present-day Eng.—e.g., *fit as a fiddle, ship-shape, tit for tat, topsy turvy, down in the dumps, worse for wear,* and so on.

■ H. Tennyson, *Alfred, Lord Tennyson: A Memoir By His Son* (1897); R. E. Deutsch, *The Patterns of Sound in Lucretius* (1939); W. B. Stanford, *Aeschylus in His Style* (1942); N. I. Hérescu, *La poésie latine* (1960); L. P. Wilkinson, *Golden Latin Artistry* (1963); W. B. Stanford, *The Sound of Greek* (1967); J. D. Allen, *Quantitative Studies in Prosody* (1968); Wimsatt, esp. essays by Frankel, Brower, Lehmann, and Dunn; P. G. Adams, *Graces of Harmony: Alliteration, Assonance, and Consonance in Eighteenth-Century British Poetry* (1977); J.T.S. Wheelock, "Alliterative Functions in the *Divina Comedia*," *Lingua e Stile* 13 (1978); Brogan, esp. items C111–C170, L65, L406 (Jakobson), L150, L474, L564, L686, and pp. 479–585; D. Minkova, *Alliteration and Sound Change in Early English* (2003); S. Suzuki, *The Metre of Old Saxon Poetry* (2004); M. Markus, "*Bed & Board*: The Role of Alliteration in Twin Formulas of Middle English Prose," *Folia Linguistica Historica* 26 (2005).

P. G. Adams; T. Cable

**ALLUSION.** (Lat., *alludere,* "to joke, jest" [from *ad-* "to" + *ludere* "to play"]), originally meaning "to mock" and later "to make a fanciful reference to." A brief, indirect, and deliberate reference—in a poem or other medium—to a person, place, event (fictitious or actual), or other work of art, allusion may be used by its author to enhance a work's semantic and cultural density, topicality, or timelessness. Despite its etymology, allusion need not be playful but does require that the audience recognize the borrowed reference.

Before describing different kinds of allusion, it may be useful to enumerate what it is not. Allusion differs from *intertextuality because it is purposive; from plagiarism because the poet does not pass off the reference as his or her own; from quotation because it is not cited; and from *topos (e.g., John Milton's "autumnal leaves" simile in *Paradise Lost* 1.303–4 with its antecedents in Isaiah, Homer, Virgil, and Dante) because it has a single source.

Allusion can vary widely in tone, type, degree of obscurity, completion and accuracy, and relation to its precursor. It can be lighthearted, as when, in Tom Stoppard's play *Jumpers,* the protagonist George Moore, brooding on violent acts while holding his tortoise Pat, declares, "Now might I do it, Pat" (alluding to a line of Hamlet's as he considers killing the praying Claudius), or somber, as when, in T. S. Eliot's *The Waste Land,* the narrator (borrowing a line from Dante) declares, "I had not thought death had undone so many." Its context can be historical, as in Gloucester's mention of "These late eclipses of the sun and moon" in Shakespeare's *King Lear* (a possible reference to recent cosmological events) or Sylvia Plath's description of "Daddy" as "Panzer-man" (referring to a German tank used in World War II); artistic, as in W. H. Auden's "Musée des Beaux Arts"(with its debt to the paintings of Peter Brueghel); or autobiographical, as in Milton's references to his blindness throughout *Paradise Lost.* It can be fairly easily noticed, like Eliot's allusions to *Hamlet* in "The Love Song of J. Alfred Prufrock," or more arcane, like his references to Hesiod and Andrew Marvell in the same poem. Allusion, while usually featuring an exact iteration of a prior text, can sometimes paradoxically derive its power from a misquotation or inexact recollection, as when, in Samuel Beckett's *Happy Days,* Winnie tries in vain to remember "that wonderful line" from *Paradise Lost* but can only come up with "oh something lasting woe." Though usually local, it can also inflect an entire work, as when in his sestina "Paysage Moralisé," Auden borrows several end words from Philip Sidney's double sestina. Allusion often derives its power from alteration of a passage or placement in a different context, e.g., the opening clause of *The Waste Land*— "April is the cruelest month"—with its grim new take on Chaucer's "Aprill with his shoures soote."

Broadly speaking, we can classify allusion into the following categories (with much potential for overlap): (1) topical, referring to specific historical events (e.g., John Donne's "the new Philosophy calls all in doubt," a seeming allusion to Nicolaus Copernicus's heliocentric cosmology); (2) personal, referring to circumstances in the author's life (e.g., Shakespeare's punning on his own name in his sonnets); (3) formal, using another poet's techniques such as rhymes or tropes (e.g., Eliot's "But at my back in a cold blast I hear / The rattle of bones, and chuckle spread from ear to ear" (*The Waste Land* 185–86), with its ironic reformulation of "But at my back I always hear / Time's winged chariot hurrying near" from Marvell's "To His Coy Mistress"; (4) metaphorical, referring to earlier works in such a way that they lend the new work added significance and depth (e.g., Milton and the Bible, Auden and Brueghel); (5) imitative, alluding to another work's genre, rhet., mood, or style, whether on a local or larger level (e.g., Alexander Pope's *Rape of the Lock*, with its many send-ups of epic conventions such as invocation, epithet, and simile); (6) structural, recalling the organization of an earlier work (e.g., Auden's sestina).

Allusion tends to assume an intelligent reader, a shared body of knowledge, and the value of previous works or contexts, but its manifestations in hist. and culture are extremely varied. Only a hundred years ago, a poet could assume that a reader would recognize the phrase "through a glass darkly" as a biblical allusion, but few would deny the lesser likelihood of this familiarity today. In the Japanese haiku trad. (see HAIKAI), certain keywords will resonate instantly with readers, lending each instance of the word an immediate depth. Religious allusion is the most common form in many cultures, e.g., Islamic lit.'s overwhelming debt to the Qur'an. As Ricks has written in *Allusion to the Poets*, "allusion is one form that inheritance can take, even while inheritance takes diverse forms in different ages and for individual genius."

Lit. crit. has had much to say about allusion. W. J. Bate described the "burden" that literary trad. places on poets while also allowing them the chance to achieve maturity and originality by wrestling with it; Harold Bloom's theory of the "anxiety of influence" put forth an Oedipal account of poetic borrowing; and Henry Louis Gates used the term *signifying to examine textual interplay within the Af. Am. literary trad. Ricks has also poignantly remarked that allusion can mitigate a writer's loneliness.

Debates about allusion can involve questions of *intention (do authors know they are alluding? Does the alluder display ambition or humility?) and comprehension (is enjoyment of a work predicated on a reader's recognizing the allusion?), but there is no doubt that it is an important technique in lit. and other media, instantly evoking attitudes and beliefs, people and places, communities and trads., and providing a dizzying variety of rich and resonant effects.

*See* IMITATION, INFLUENCE.

■ R. W. Emerson, "Quotation and Originality" (1868); R. D. Havens, *The Influence of Milton on English Poetry* (1922); E. T. Clark, *Hidden Allusions in Shakespeare's Plays* (1931); G. Smith, *T. S. Eliot's Poems and Plays* (1956); S. P. Bovie, "Classical Allusions," *CW* 52 (1958); R. Brower, *Alexander Pope* (1959); R. L. Brower, *Japanese Court Poetry* (1961); D. P. Harding, *The Club of Hercules* (1962); W. J. Bate, *The Burden of the Past and the English Poet* (1972); H. Bloom, *The Anxiety of Influence* (1973); A. Hamori, *On the Art of Medieval Arabic Literature* (1974); H. Bloom, *A Map of Misreading* (1975); Z. Ben-Porat, "The Poetics of Literary Allusion" and A. L. Johnson, "Allusion in Poetry," both in *Poetics and Theory of Literature* 1 (1976); N. Goodman, *Ways of Worldmaking* (1978); C. Perri et al., "Allusion Studies: An International Annotated Bibliography, 1921–1977," *Style* 13 (1979); J. Hollander, *The Figure of Echo* (1981); G. B. Conte, *The Rhetoric of Imitation*, trans. and ed. C. Segal (1986); L. Newlyn, *Coleridge, Wordsworth and the Language of Allusion* (1986); P. Yu, *The Reading of Imagery in the Chinese Poetic Tradition* (1987); E. Cook, *Poetry, Word-Play, and Word-War in Wallace Stevens* (1988); H. L. Gates, *The Signifying Monkey* (1988); E. Stein, *Wordsworth's Art of Allusion* (1988); R. Garner, *From Homer to Tragedy* (1989); *Intertextuality, Allusion, and Quotation,* ed. U. J. Hebel—a bibl. (1989); A. Pasco, *Allusion* (1994); *Literary Influence and African American Writers*, ed. T. Mishkin (1995); E. Gregory, *Quotation and Modern American Poetry* (1996); E. Cook, *Against Coercion* (1998); C. Ricks, *Essays in Appreciation* (1996); E. Kamens, *Utamakura, Allusion, and Intertextuality in Traditional Japanese Poetry* (1997); J. Derrida, *Archive Fever*, trans. E. Prenowitz (1998); S. Hinds, *Allusion and Intertextuality* (1998)—on Roman poetry; D. Kelly, *The Conspiracy of Allusion* (1999); C. Ricks, *Allusion to the Poets* (2002); C. A. Reynolds, *Motives for Allusion* (2003)—19th-c. music; G. Machacek, "Allusion," and P. Yeager, "The Polyphony Issue," *PMLA* 122.2 (2007); S. Harwood, "Poetry in Movies: A Partial List," Poets.org, http://www.poets.org/viewmedia.php/prmMID/19359; R. M. Howard, "Citation, Allusion, Quotation: A Bibliography," http://wrt-howard.syr.edu/Bibs/Citation.htm.

R. WETZSTEON

**AMBIGUITY** (Lat. *ambiguitas*, from *ambigere*, "to dispute about," literally "to wander"). In lit. crit., *ambiguity* is primarily defined as the simultaneous availability of more than one meaning or interpretation. It has been variously identified as a property of verbal structure (lexical, semantic, and syntactic), of literary forms and genres themselves, and of readerly practices. Aristotle regarded ambiguity as a type of fallacious argument that he called *sophistic syllogism*, an argument that defends something false in order to confuse an adversary. For Aristotle, there were only two types of arguments: true and untrue. An ambiguous argument was an argument that appeared to be true and untrue at the same time and was, thus, logically untrue. Aristotle's principle of noncontradiction is at the root of scientific and logical thought. But in a literary context, Virgil's suggestive use of the noun *ambages* in *Aeneid* 6.99 to denote the ambiguous prophecy of the Cumaean Sibyl was noticed by Dante, Boccaccio, Chaucer, and others, who introduce the Lat. term directly into their vernaculars to suggest perniciously doubled meanings ("with double words slye, / Swiche as men clepen a worde with two visages," *Troilus and Criseyde* 5.898–99). By the 16th c., *ambiguity* is established in Eng. (and its counterparts in the other vernaculars) to refer to multiple meanings that may be dangerous, productive, or aporetic (see APORIA), in keeping with the Ren. rupturing of monologic paradigms. For instance, the Rus. theorist Mikhail Bakhtin in the first half of the 20th c. identifies in the works of François Rabelais a socially and historically conditioned use of ambiguity involving multiple meanings in not only words but discourses of all kinds; and in the second half of the century, a train of critics from Leo Spitzer to Claudio Guillén argue that literary works embody contrasting perspectives, the basis of *genres such as the Cervantine novel and the picaresque. The fact that many mod. critics develop theories of ambiguity with reference to Ren. works implies that the concept has a special purchase in the period.

In Anglo-Am. *New Criticism, the broad use of the term *ambiguity* as making available more than one meaning or interpretation became common practice with William Empson's *Seven Types of Ambiguity* (1930), where he defines the term as "any verbal nuance, however slight, which gives room to alternative reactions to the same piece of language." Empson drew attention to ambiguity as constitutive of the lang. of poetry and valued it positively as a source of richness rather than imprecision. Empson offers a taxonomy of ambiguity: *metaphor is the first type of ambiguity; followed by ambiguity as two or more meanings that become another meaning; two concepts inextricably connected via context; two meanings that combine to illuminate the author's state of mind; two opposite meanings that illuminate a division within the author; the lack of apparent meaning and the need for the reader's creation of meaning; and, finally, ambiguity as the act of writing, a channel halfway between the text and the writer.

In the 1960s, literary theorists such as Genette, Barthes, and Wheelwright proposed ambiguity as an intrinsic capacity of poetic lang. Genette theorizes the notion of a nonempty "gap" as the essence of poetry, while Wheelwright and Barthes observe not only the capacity to hold more than one meaning or interpretation but the open state of oscillation between them, which is variously called *plurisignation* (Wheelwright) or *infinite plurality* (Barthes).

In contrast to Barthes' description of an open work that lacks or deliberately eschews centers of orientation, Rimmon considers an ambiguous work to possess marked centers that polarize data and create mutually exclusive systems of meaning. Rimmon distinguishes ambiguity from double meaning, multiple meaning, plurisignation, or infinite plurality, which she refers to as types of *conjunctive ambiguity*. For Rimmon, however, ambiguity is disjunctive, that which both "calls for choice and makes it impossible." According to her, the essential difference between the multiplicity of subjective interpretations given to a work of fiction and ambiguity proper is that, while the subjectivity of reading is conditioned mainly by the psyche of the reader, ambiguity is "a fact in the text—a double system of mutually exclusive clues." While Rimmon emphasizes the function of the reader by offering ambiguity as a plurality of readings from

which we are to determine our own, at the same time she sees such a subjectivity as invited by the text itself and considers each meaning clearly based in a function of the text and context. Rimmon considers Empson's approach too broad, as he analyzes ambiguity by the conjunction or synthesis or fusion or multiplication of meaning, but she ultimately sides with him in locating ambiguity in the verbal structure itself.

For the poststructuralist Kristeva, "communication and that which breaks communication apart" are located not only in the verbal structure but, following Jacques Lacan, in the unconscious. For Kristeva, ambiguity "provides the creative and innovative impulse of modern poetic structure" and is closely related to *significance* or "the eruption of the semiotic within the symbolic." The ambiguity that characterizes *modernism is the unleashing of the semiotic, i.e., the preverbal impulses and bodily drives discharged into signification. Other critics such as Trujillo move even further away from the verbal structure, considering ambiguity not as inherent in lang. but as a performative mechanism used at will by the writing subject.

With its cl. origins and early mod. provenance, ambiguity differs from concepts such as *polysemy or *indeterminacy. Unlike indeterminacy, it refers not to the instability of meaning itself but to the existence of multiple meanings at the same time. And unlike polysemy, it emphasizes not discrete meanings but their simultaneity, thus placing signification in a state of oscillation between meanings but also interpretations, where context and subjectivity play a main role. Ambiguity is an openness to the potentiality of a multiplicity of interpretations, not because all are equally important or relevant at the same time and for the same reader but because they all exist equally within the field and will emerge eventually as actualized—as De Beauvoir puts it, "reinvested with [a particular] human signification."

■ M. Black, "Vagueness: An Exercise in Logical Analysis," *Philosophy of Science* 4 (1937); I. M. Copilowish, "Borderline Cases: Vagueness and Ambiguity," and C. G. Hempel, "Vagueness and Logic," *Philosophy of Science* 6 (1939); W. B. Stanford, *Ambiguity in Greek Literature* (1939); S. de Beauvoir, *The Ethics of Ambiguity*, trans. B. Frechtman (1948); G. W. Cunningham, "On the Meaningfulness of Vague Language," *Philosophy Review* 58 (1949); M. C. Beardsley, *Thinking Straight* (1954); S. Dawson, "Infinite Types of Ambiguity," *BJA* 5 (1965); P. Wheelwright, "On the Semantics of Poetry," *Essays on the Language of Literature*, ed. S. Chatman and S. R. Levin (1967); R. Barthes, *S/Z*, trans. R. Miller (1970); C. Guillén, *Literature as System* (1971); R. Trujillo, *Elementos de semántica lingüística* (1976); R. Barthes, "From Work to Text," *Image, Music, Text*, trans. S. Heath (1977); S. Rimmon, *The Concept of Ambiguity* (1977); G. Pérez Firmat, "Genre as Text," *Comparative Literature Studies* 17 (1980); J. Kristeva, *Desire in Language*, trans. T. Gora et al. (1980); M. M. Bakhtin, *The Dialogic Imagination*, ed. M. Holquist, trans. C. Emerson and M. Holquist (1981); J. Derrida,

*Dissemination*, trans. B. Johnson (1981); M. Perloff, *The Poetics of Indeterminacy* (1981); G. Genette, *Figures of Literary Discourse*, trans. A. Sheridan (1982); D. Wallace, "Chaucer's Ambages," *American Notes and Queries* 23 (1984); J. Ferrater Mora, *Diccionario de la Filosofía* (1988); U. Eco, *The Open Work*, trans. A. Cancogni (1989).

V. Ramos

**AMERICAN INDIAN POETRY.** *See* INDIGENOUS AMERICAS, POETRY OF THE; INUIT POETRY; NAVAJO POETRY.

**AMERICAN POETRY.** *See* UNITED STATES, POETRY OF THE.

**AMERICAN SIGN LANGUAGE POETRY.** American Sign Language (ASL) poetry refers to poetry translated from another lang. into ASL or, more often, originally composed in ASL. Since ASL is one of more than 100 distinct, naturally occurring signed langs. in the world, ASL poetry is not the only signed poetic trad., but it is the most developed. In such works, the poet's body has a strong presence. By skillfully using space, hand shape, movement, facial expressions, and other elements, ASL poets produce three-dimensional poems that express meaning without depending on sound.

The beginnings of ASL poetry are elusive. ASL dates from the early 19th c., when deaf students began to come together at schools in the U.S. However, after the Civil War, some hearing educators started a campaign against sign lang., trying to abolish it from schools. Moreover, because ASL is not a written lang., we have no direct record of it before the advent of motion-picture technology in the 20th c. The first ASL performances are largely lost to us, existing only in what has been passed down through sign of hand.

ASL poets draw on the cultural trads. of the deaf community and on poetry in written langs. Early influences probably included ASL songs, folklore, and deaf literary organizations. Films from the 1930s show deaf Americans signing "The Star Spangled Banner" and "Yankee Doodle." Deaf people also developed original forms like 1-2-3 songs, where crowds rhythmically sign together, and ABC stories, which performers relate using only 26 signs conforming to the hand shapes of the manual alphabet. At the same time, deaf literary groups promoted the trans. of Eng. poems into ASL. In 1939, e.g., Eric Malzkuhn gave a signed version of Lewis Carroll's "Jabberwocky" in which he ingeniously recombined parts of everyday signs to convey Carroll's nonsensical words, making something new.

The greatest effect on ASL poetry came in the 1960s, when linguists recognized ASL as a full human lang. Poets responded with renewed pride, composing more original poems in ASL. Sometimes they took on deaf themes. Thus Clayton Valli, in "Dandelion," implicitly compares ASL to those plants that a gardener can never quite eradicate, and Ella Mae Lentz, in "To a Hearing Mother," invites parents of deaf children to work with the deaf community in raising them. Other poems have less to do with deaf experience. Bernard Bragg's "Flowers and Moonlight on the Spring Water" gracefully evokes the image in the title, while "Need," by Peter Cook and Kenny Lerner, the deaf-hearing team of the Flying Words Project, protests America's dependence on oil.

Like other poets, ASL performers may follow rigid structure or more open-ended forms. Among other techniques, they often use space in symmetrical fashion; choose signs with certain hand shapes to give visual rhyme; use eye gaze, mouth movement, head and body shifts, and other nonmanual indicators to add rhythm and meaning; and employ *simile, *metaphor, and *allusion. By exploiting ASL grammar in multiple ways, they create layers of meaning and poetry that is vividly expressive.

ASL poets tend to be deaf, but not all are. Finally, not all deaf poets sign. Some, like David Wright, publish poetry in the dominant lang. of their nations.

■ C. Padden and T. Humphries, *Deaf in America* (1988); S. Burch, "Deaf Poets' Society: Subverting the Hearing Paradigm," *Literature and Medicine* 16 (1997); B. Brueggemann, *Lend Me Your Ear: Rhetorical Constructions of Deafness* (1999); *Signing the Body Poetic: Essays on American Sign Language Literature*, ed. H. Bauman, J. Nelson, and H. Rose (2006); *Signs and Voices: Deaf Culture, Identity, Language, and Arts*, ed. K. Lindgren, D. DeLuca, and D. Napoli (2008).

C. Krentz

**AMERIND POETRY.** *See* INDIGENOUS AMERICAS, POETRY OF THE.

**AMHARIC POETRY.** *See* ETHIOPIA, POETRY OF.

**AMPHIBRACH** (Gr., "short at both ends"). In *classical prosody, a metrical sequence consisting of a long syllable preceded and followed by a short one. The amphibrach is rare in cl. poetry either as an independent unit or as a continuous meter and equally a rarity in the accentually based prosodies of mod. langs., suggesting it may not exist except as an experiment. Amphibrachic word shapes (a stress flanked by slacks) are easy to finger, esp. polysyllables formed of a monosyllabic prefix + base + suffix (e.g., inspection, romantic); but the amphibrach as a meter risks monotony and is very rare. Lord Byron tried it ("The black bands came over"); J. W. Goethe, Friedrich von Matthisson, and Ernst Moritz Arndt wrote a number of poems in amphibrachs in Ger. In running series with ambiguous ends, amphibrachic lines would be nearly impossible to differentiate from other ternary ones such as dactylic or anapestic.

*See* BINARY AND TERNARY.

T.V.F. Brogan

**AMPLIFICATION.** An ambiguous term, perhaps best avoided in lit. crit., which seeks to distinguish rather than to confuse rhetorical taxonomy. In cl. rhet., amplification is one of the "special" topics used in *epideictic poetry or ceremonial discourse, usually for praise, but it has been used to refer to both the expansion and the diminution of an idea or argument. Its hist. in rhetorical theory and practice helps explain how amplification came to be regarded, at different periods, as a subset of both *inventio* and *dispositio*. Aristotle in the *Poetics* mentions "maximizing and minimizing" as important elements of thought (i.e., rhet.), but in the *Rhetoric* (2.26.1), he contrasts amplification and depreciation, while admitting that both derive from "enthymemes which serve to show how a thing is great or small." It was Cicero (*De oratore* 3.26) who introduced the confusion between amplification and attenuation by saying that the "highest distinction of eloquence consists in amplification by means of ornament, which can be used to make one's speech not only increase the importance of a subject and raise it to a higher level, but also to diminish and disparage it." Quintilian (*Institutio oratoria* 8.4.3) increased the confusion, presenting amplification as a species of inventio, when he spoke of four principal means of amplification: augmentation (*incrementum*), comparison, reasoning, and accumulation (*congeries*). Quoting from Cicero, Quintilian (8.4.4) gives as an example of amplification the following climax: "It is a sin to bind a Roman citizen, a crime to scourge him, little short of the most unnatural murder to put him to death; what then shall I call his crucifixion?" Murphy has shown how the confusion spread in med. rhet., which fused inventio and dispositio, when amplification, referred to variously as a set of eight or ten figures valuable to those writing sermons, speeches, or letters, becomes at the same time a figure and not a figure, a set of figures, and an arrangement of figures. Eng. Ren. rhetoricians perpetuated the confusion, supplying different totals for the rhetorical phenomena grouped under the general heading "amplification" from 17 (Richard Sherry, 1555), to 64 (Henry Peacham, 1577), to 11 (John Hoskins, 1599). Perelman remarks that ancient writers (e.g., Quintilian 3.8.6.73) tended to see both amplification and attenuation as varieties of *hyperbole. Corbett calls amplification "a way of reminding audiences of the importance or cogency or superiority of our points."

Amplification may be obtained by enumeration and *parallelism, as in Othello's speech, when he has just realized that Desdemona is innocent: "Whip me, ye devils, / From the possession of this heavenly sight! / Blow me about in winds! Roast me in sulphur! / Wash me in steep-down gulfs of liquid fire! / O Desdemona! Desdemona! dead!" (5.2.276–80). Or if *amplification* means the devel. of a single principle, idea, or word, an entire poem may be structured by amplification, e.g., Dylan Thomas's "The Hand That Signed the Paper."

The confusion remains to be sorted out. If kept, the term *amplification* should be defined precisely and used with care; its limits become clear only when a text signals by some other means (semantic: change of subject; syntactic: end of stanza or poem; pragmatic: change of *voice, person, or form of *address) a change of direction.

■ W. G. Crane, *Wit and Rhetoric in the Renaissance* (1937); W. Taylor, *A Dictionary of the Tudor Figures of Rhetoric* (1937); C. Perelman and L. Olbrechts-Tytecha,

*The New Rhetoric*, trans. J. Wilkinson and P. Weaver (1969); Murphy; Corbett; Lausberg.

A. W. HALSALL; T.V.F. BROGAN

**ANACLASIS** (Gr., "bending back"). Transposition of short and long positions within a *metron or *colon. The best known anaclast is the *anacreontic, which is an *ionic dimeter with a transposition of the fourth and fifth positions (◡ ◡ – – ◡ ◡ – – becomes ◡ ◡ – ◡ – ◡ – –). West regards this as something like mod. musical *syncopation, in which maintaining the time values is sufficient for keeping the same rhythm.
■ Maas; Koster; Halporn et al.; West.

J. W. HALPORN

**ANACOLUTHON** (Gr., "wanting sequence"). A term of grammar designating a change of construction in the middle of a sentence that leaves its beginning uncompleted. In rhet., however, *anacoluthon* has been treated as a figure, a natural and often effective mode of expression in spoken discourse. Hervey cites Matt. 7:9, which runs, in the Authorized Version, "Or what man is there of you, whom if his son ask bread, will he give him a stone?" Shakespeare sometimes shows depth of feeling in his characters by this means, as at *Henry V* 4.3.34–36, where the king says: "Rather proclaim it, Westmoreland, through my host, / That he which hath no stomach to this fight, / Let him depart." Lausberg finds the commonest form of anacoluthon to be the so-called absolute nominative (as in the Shakespeare above).

Related to anacoluthon is the absence of the second of a pair of correlative expressions, which is known as *particula pendens* when it has to do with correlative particles (e.g., "either . . . or," "both . . . and"), otherwise by the related term *anapodoton* (Gr., "wanting the apodosis," i.e., the main clause in a conditional sentence). Ernesti cites the authority of a Scholiast on Thucydides 3.3; the passage goes, "If the attempt succeeds," the understood but unexpressed apodosis being, "it will be well"; so also Lausberg. Anapodoton includes a subset called *anantapodoton*, in which even the subordinate clause is incomplete.

Group μ classifies anacoluthon among "metataxes" that act on the form of sentences by focusing on syntax. Like *syllepsis, which includes "any rhetorical omission relating to the rules of agreement between morphemes and syntagms, whether it is agreement of gender, number, person, or tense," anacoluthon produces through bifurcation a break in sentence structure. Mod. poetry's frequent suppression of *punctuation removed anacoluthon from the list of taboo figures drawn up by prescriptive rhetoricians. The deletion of punctuation produces rhetorical effects by combining in a single utterance large numbers of agrammatical or potentially incoherent units of discourse. Much poetry after about 1950 draws on anacoluthon for diverse effects, incl. the late poetry of Paul Celan reflecting on human suffering (e.g., *Fadensonnen* [*Threadsuns*], 1968); John Ashbery's plain-lang. meditations on being and becoming; and the verbal artist Kenneth Goldsmith's transcriptive work (e.g., *Fidget*, 2000).
■ C. T. Ernesti, *Lexicon technologiae graecorum rhetoricae* (1795); H. Bahrs, *Die Anacoluthe bei Shake-*

*speare* (1893); G. W. Hervey, *Christian Rhetoric* (1973); Group μ; L. Edelman, *Transmemberment of Song* (1987); N. E. Enkvist, "A Note on the Definition and Description of True Anacolutha," *On Language: Rhetorica, Phonologica, Syntactica*, ed. C. Duncan-Rose, C. Vennemann, T. Vennemann (1988); E. Bloch, "Spoken and Written Syntax: Anacoluthon," *Literary Essays*, trans. A. Joron et al. (1998); Lausberg; Morier.

H. Brown; A.W. Halsall

**ANACREONTIC.** The term *anacreontic* denotes both a *meter and a literary mode. The anacreontic meter (anaclasts: ◡ ◡ – ◡ – ◡ – – or hemiambs: x – ◡ – ◡ – x) is named after the ancient Gr. poet Anacreon of Teos (6th c. BCE), who used it frequently in his verses. The meter was not originally associated with a particular mood: thus, Aeschylus used anacreontics in an emotional graveside speech (*Choephoroi* 327–30), while Euripides included them in his satyr play *Cyclops* (495–500). But by 250 BCE, Anacreon was best known for his sympotic verses, and the meter accordingly was associated with youthful hedonism and a *carpe diem* theme. At about this time, anonymous poets started to write in imitation of Anacreon; these *Anacreontea* were later preserved in one 10th-c. ms. The collection consists of 60 short poems in anacreontic meter on topics of love, wine, and song, composed over a span of 600 years, from the Hellenistic well into the Byzantine era. Lat. poets also experimented with anacreontic meter on different themes (e.g., Hadrian, Boethius); Christian bishops even wrote anacreontic religious *hymns (e.g., Gregory of Nazianzus, Synesius of Cyrene). But it was the Gr. imitative *Anacreontea* that most strongly influenced early mod. and later Eur. poets.

In 1554, Henricus Stephanus (Henri Estienne), convinced that the recently rediscovered collection was genuinely archaic, published the *Anacreontea* to great public acclaim. In Paris, Pierre de Ronsard enthused about the recovery of "du vieil Anacréon perdu / La douce lyre Teienne." In Italy, Torquato Tasso was an early admirer, as were the Eng. poets Robert Herrick and Abraham Cowley. For the next three centuries, the *Anacreontea* were read as archaic artifacts, inspiring trans. and imitators across Europe. J. W. Goethe wrote an elegiac "Anakreons Grab," while Lord Byron teased the Ir. poet Thomas Moore for his devotion to the anacreontic mode. Eur. poets reveal a remarkable consistency in tone and theme, inspired by what Voltaire approvingly called "ces riens naifs et pleins de grace." By the mid-19th c., however, mod. philology had condemned the *Anacreontea* as products of the postclassical age and removed them from the canon of great lit. With this reclassification came a rejection of their poetic quality: the Ger. philologist Ulrich von Wilamowitz-Moellendorff found them tasteless compared to the "pure Hellenic wine" of the archaic period. Only in the late 20th c. was the collection recognized by scholars as a worthy mode of poetry in its own right.

■ H. Zeman, *Die deutsche Anakreontische Dichtung* (1972); M. Baumann, *Die Anakreonteen in englischen Übersetzungen* (1974); G. Braden, *The Classics and English Renaissance Poetry* (1978); M. Brioso-Sánchez, *Anacreónticas* (1981); J. Labarbe, "Un curieux phénomène littéraire, l'anacréontisme," *Bulletin de la Classe des Lettres de l'Académie Royale de Belgique* 68 (1982); M. L. West, *Carmina Anacreontea* (1984) and "The Anacreontea," *Sympotica*, ed. O. Murray (1990); P. A. Rosenmeyer, *The Poetics of Imitation* (1992) and "Greek Lyric Poetry in the French Renaissance," *The Classical Heritage in France*, ed. G. Sandy (2002); F. Budelmann, "Anacreon and the Anacreontea," *Cambridge Companion to Greek Lyric*, ed. F. Budelmann (2009).

P. A. Rosenmeyer

**ANACRUSIS** (Gr., "the striking up of a tune"; Ger. *Auftakt*, "upbeat"). One or more extrametrical syllables at the beginning of a line, normally unstressed. *Procephalous* would be a more accurate and better attested descriptor. *Anacrusis* was adopted by the 18th-c. cl. scholar Richard Bentley in principle and then by Gottfried Hermann in fact, as well as by most of his Ger. successors in the 19th c., who extended the principles they discovered in the quantitative prosodies of cl. verse to the analysis of the accentual prosodies of the mod. vernaculars without due consideration of the systemic differences between the two systems. In mod. times, anacrusis has been posited on the analogy with music, where extra notes can precede the first bar of the melody without objection. Some temporal and musical theories of meter (e.g., Joshua Steele, Andreas Heusler) treat verse lines as if they were set to music, i.e., as if stresses began bars, so that all unstressed syllables that precede the first stress—e.g., the first syllable in the iambic pentameter line—are instances of anacrusis. Outside of such theories, now generally outmoded, and outside of song meters themselves, anacrusis is rare, though indisputable cases do exist, as in Shakespeare. The old belief that anacrusis could alter rising rhythms to falling, or vice versa, is discredited; and seeming instances of anacrusis often disappear under careful attention to measures. In these two lines from William Blake's "The Tyger," for example—"When the stars threw down their spears / And watered heaven with their tears"—one might take "And" to be an anacrusis, noticing that the seven syllables that follow would then be identical in pattern to the seven in the preceding line. But in fact, it is the second line that is regular (an iambic tetrameter); the preceding line is headless (see ACEPHALOUS), and this type of rhythm—called "8s and 7s"—is fairly common in mod. Eng. verse.

OE verse seems to include anacrusis as part of the metrical system—it is a component of the analyses of Sievers, Pope, and Cable—but then poetry in Anglo-Saxon England was perhaps recited to the accompaniment of a harp.

*See* HYPERMETRIC.

■ Schipper 3.950 (index); Sievers; N. A. Bonavia-Hunt, *Horace the Minstrel* (1954); J. C. Pope, *The Rhythm of "Beowulf,"* 2d ed. (1966); Dale; T. Cable, *The Meter and Melody of "Beowulf"* (1974), ch. 3; Morier; P. Bethel, "Notes on the Incidence and Type of Anacrusis in Genesis B: Similarities to and Differences from Anacrusis Elsewhere in OE and OS," *Parergon* 2 (1984), and "Anacrusis in the Psalms of the Paris Psalter," *NM* 89 (1988); S. Suzuki, "Anacrusis in the Meter of *Beowulf*," *SP* 92 (1995), and "Anacrusis in the Meter of *Heliand*," *Interdigitations*, ed. G. F. Carr, W. Harbert, and L. Zhang (1999).

R. J. GETTY; T.V.F. BROGAN

**ANADIPLOSIS**, also *epanadiplosis* (Gr., "doubled back"). In cl. rhet., a figure of word *repetition that links two phrases, clauses, lines, or stanzas by repeating the word at the end of the first one at the beginning of the second: "The crime was common, common be the pain" (Alexander Pope, "Eloisa to Abelard"); "More safe I Sing with mortal voice, unchang'd / To hoarse or mute, though fall'n on evil dayes, / On evil dayes though fall'n, and evil tongues" (John Milton, *Paradise Lost* 7.24–26). Sometimes more than one word repeats: "When I give I give myself" (Walt Whitman, "Song of Myself"). As such, *anadiplosis* is the mechanism of *concatenation and is the usual vehicle for the rhetorical strategy of *climax. It can also be used to link speeches in drama, the second character picking up the train of thought of the first from his or her last word:

> *Othello*: What dost thou think?
> *Iago*: Think, my lord?
> *Othello*: Think, my lord? By heaven he echoes me.
> (3.3.104–07)

Among the Ren. sonneteers, the use of anadiplosis both within the sonnet and to link sonnets together was common practice—visible in Petrarch, Torquato Tasso, Pierre de Ronsard, Joachim du Bellay, Philip Sidney, Samuel Daniel, and many others—Shakespeare showing rather less interest in such effects than most. But Shakespeare's sonnet 129 has "On purpose laid to make the taker mad. / Mad in pursuit and in possession so" (8–9). Anadiplosis fixed at the level of the line and adapted into prosody as a figure of rhyme was practiced by the *rhétoriqueurs, who called it *rime annexée* and *rime fratrisée*.

*See* CHAIN RHYME.

■ Patterson; M. Joseph, *Shakespeare's Use of the Arts of Language* (1947); A. Quinn, *Figures of Speech* (1982); Vickers; Corbett.

T.V.F. BROGAN

**ANAGRAM.** The rearrangement of the letters of a word or phrase to produce another word or phrase. Many critics have denigrated the anagram, often forcefully, along with other forms of graphic play such as the *acrostic, the *palindrome, *paronomasia, *concrete poetry, and the *calligramme. In *Spectator* no. 60 (May 9, 1711), Joseph Addison remarks, "The Acrostick was probably invented about the same Time with the Anagram, tho' it is impossible to decide whether the Inventor of the one or the other were the greater Blockhead." John Dryden banishes Thomas Shadwell to "acrostic land" in "MacFlecknoe." The *Greek Anthology*, which is the *locus classicus* of such types of verse, has often been ridiculed in the same way, esp. by Eng. critics.

The anagram is part of a larger trad. in which writers—esp. poets—play with the graphic elements of alphabetic writing in ways that undermine assumptions about the relationship between writing and speech. It foregrounds semantic functions of writing that cannot be easily explained if writing is viewed merely as a visual substitute for speech. Like other forms of graphic play, the anagram creates an order of signification in a text that frequently cannot be perceived aurally but must be construed on the page. It thus suggests that the relationship between phonetic writing and speech is not mere transcription; anagram and other forms of graphic play create realms of meaning that have a far more complex relationship with speech.

Not all writers have been hostile to the anagrammatic trad. As Vendler, Ricks, Winnick, and others have shown, the golden age of the anagram in Eng. was probably the late 16th and 17th cs., with a particular emphasis on onomastic anagrams. Winnick argues that "English interest in onomastic anagrams, especially in court circles, reached a level of intensity . . . that rivaled and would later surpass sonnet mania." Thus, each text in Mary Fage's *Fame's Roll* (of Brit. royalty and nobility; 1637) is prefaced by the name of its subject and by an anagram of it ("THOMAS HOWARD / ; / ; OH, DRAW MOST, HA!"). Winnick argues that Shakespeare hides the name of the Fair Friend of the sonnets—Henry Wriothesley, third Earl of Southampton and Baron of Titchfield (1573–1624), who was at one time the poet's patron—throughout that work in more than a dozen direct and broken, or dispersed, anagrams.

In the 20th c., ling. and literary theories of the anagram and other elements of graphic play began to take such forms more seriously. Anagrams have been conceived as substantive components of poetic discourse occurring in a number of poetic trads. This view originates with the partial publication in the 1960s of Ferdinand de Saussure's notebooks (for 1906–9) containing his research on anagrams. Saussure studied sound structures in texts of various provenance, incl. IE poetry, Lat. poetry (*Saturnian verse), such authors as Virgil and Lucretius, and Vedic hymns. In the Saussurean model, the functioning of the anagram presupposes both a poet capable of sophisticated operations on verbal material and a reader able to recognize the presence of the anagram and to reconstitute the hidden whole. For a time, Saussure regarded the anagram as a fundamental principle of IE poetry; subsequently, however, he came to question both his methodology and his conclusions, in part because there is no explicit testimony by ancient authors about such widespread use of the anagram.

Saussure's ideas have been further developed by both linguists and literary theorists. From one strand of ling. has come added evidence concerning the principle of word analysis in the IE poetic trad. (e.g., in archaic Ir. verse). In the work of linguists and anthropologists who focus on the devel. of phonetic writing systems, questions of graphic organization have stimulated a deeper look at the nature of the sound-writing-meaning nexus in poetry. This has led some researchers to emphasize the anagram as a phenomenon that semanticizes elements of the lowest levels of the text, i.e., individual syllables and even letters, independent of their placement in particular words or syntactical structures. New evidence concerning the presence of anagrams in the work of mod. poets has been produced by members of the Moscow-Tartu school (see STRUCTURALISM).

Linguists and literary scholars interested in the devel. of writing systems and their use in art have compiled new anthols. of pattern poetry (Higgins) and theories of the physical aspects of texts (Levenston). Of particular note are the collections ed. by Senner and Daniels and Bright, along with books by Houston and esp. the work of the Eng. linguist Harris, who has argued that all writing systems have a wide range of signifying modes in addition to the transcription of speech. In this model, an anagram is a graphic rearrangement that takes advantage of ways that written signs can be manipulated without regard for aurality, let alone syntax. The undeniable existence of such phenomena suggests that the nonsyntactical dimension of graphic systems is powerfully present in all written poetry, even that composed in phonetic systems.

Future research will involve exploring such questions as (1) the conditions under which semantic information overflows onto the lower levels of the text, increasing the interconnections between formally discrete elements; (2) the genres in which anagrams are most likely to arise; and (3) the relation of anagrams and other forms of graphic playfulness to natural speech.

■ H. B. Wheatley, *Of Anagrams* (1862); P. Habermann, "Anagram," *Reallexikon II*; A. Liede, *Dichtung als Spiel*, 2 v. (1963); P. Wunderli, *Ferdinand de Saussure und die Anagramme* (1972); M. Meylakh, "À propos de anagrammes," *L'Homme* 16 (1976); V. V. Ivanov, "Ob anagrammax F. de Sossjura," F. de Saussure, *Trudy po jazykoznaniju* (1977); A. L. Johnson, "Anagrammatism in Poetry," *PTL* 2 (1977); S. Baevskij and A. D. Košelev, "Poetika Bloka: anagrammy," *Blokovskijsbornik* 3 (1979); J. Starobinski, *Words upon Words: The Anagrams of Ferdinand de Saussure*, trans. O. Emmet (1979); S. C. Hunter, *Dictionary of Anagrams* (1982); D. Shepheard, "Saussure's Vedic Anagrams," *MLR* 77 (1982); R. Harris, *The Origin of Writing* (1986); D. Higgins, *Pattern Poetry* (1987); V. N. Toporov, "Kissledovaniju anagrammaticheskix struktur (analizy)," *Issledovanija po structure teksta*, ed. T. V. Civ'jan (1987); *The Origins of Writing*, ed. W. M. Senner (1989); *Ocherki istorii jazyka russkoj poezii XX: Veka. Poeticheskij jazyk I idiostil. Obshchie voprosy, Zvukovaja organizacija teksta*, ed. V. P. Grigorev (1990); E. A. Levenston, *The Stuff of Literature* (1992); R. Harris, *Signs of Writing* (1995); *The World's Writing Systems*, ed. P. T. Daniels and W. Bright (1996); H. Vendler, *The Art of Shakespeare's Sonnets* (1997); R. Harris, *Rethinking Writing* (2000); T. Augarde, *Oxford Guide to Word Games*, 2d ed. (2003); C. Ricks, "Shakespeare and the Anagram," *PBA* 121 (2003); S. D. Houston, *The First Writing* (2004); R. H. Winnick, " 'Loe, here in one line is his name twice writ': Anagrams, Shakespeare's Sonnets and the Identity of the Fair Friend," *Literary Imagination* 11 (2009); F. de Saussure, *Course in General Linguistics*, ed. C. Bally and A. Sechehaye, trans. W. Baskin (1959; rpt. 2011).

H. BARAN; D. J. ROTHMAN

**ANALOGY.** *See* METAPHOR; SIMILE; SYMBOL.

**ANAPEST,** anapaest (Gr.; of uncertain meaning, perhaps "beaten back," i.e., a reversed *dactyl). In the quantitative meters of cl. poetry, a metrical foot of two short syllables followed by one long ( ◡ ◡ –, e.g., *dĕĭtās*), or, in verse-systems based on accent, two unstressed syllables followed by one stressed ( x x /, e.g., *interrupt*). In Gr., the anapest usually appears as a *dipody or *metron with the form ◡ ◡ – ◡ ◡ –. The metron shows total equivalence of single longs and double shorts, unique in Gr.; consequently, in the dimeter (the commonest form), there is usually diaeresis between metra. Anapests were used first as a warlike marching rhythm, then later in Gr. drama as a song meter, both purely, as in the choruses of tragedy and comedy, commonly anapestic *tetrameter catalectic, and in combination with other meters. Runs of anapests are often closed with a catalectic *dimeter or *paroemiac. With the Romans, the single foot replaced the metron as the unit of measure. Plautus made wide use of anapests, esp. in four-foot units (anapestic quaternarii), and acatalectic and catalectic eight-foot units (anapestic septenarii and octonarii). Seneca, however, uses anapests in the Gr. manner (i.e., in metra, not feet) in his tragedies, as anapaestic dimeters, a form used later by Boethius and Prudentius.

In the accentual prosodies of the Ren. and after, the anapest was used in Eng. mainly for popular verse until the beginning of the 18th c.; serious anapestic poems were later written by William Cowper, Walter Scott, Lord Byron, Robert Browning ("How They Brought the Good News"), William Morris, and esp. A. C. Swinburne, who used it in lines of every possible length ("Dolores"). Contemp. poets like Annie Finch have revived interest in anapests and other triple meters as alternatives to canonical iambic meters; they have also challenged common conceptions of anapests as limited to humorous verse (e.g., the *limerick); to depicting mimetic action (typically, hurried motion), e.g., "The Assyrian came down like a wolf on the fold" (Byron, "The Destruction of Sennacherib"); or to conveying excitement, or less frequently, mourning (Matthew Arnold's "Rugby Chapel"). Nonetheless, pure anapests remain comparatively rare in Eng. and can be difficult to distinguish in running series both from other triple meters such as dactylic and *amphibrachic or from some loose duple meters with extensive trisyllabic substitutions, although prosodists have proposed promising solutions to some of these descriptive problems.

*See* CLASSICAL PROSODY.

■ A. Raabe, *De metrorum anapaesticorum apud poetas Graecos usu* (1912); J. W. White, *The Verse of Greek Comedy* (1912); Hardie, chap. 4; Wilamowitz, pt. 2, chap. 11; Koster, chap. 7; Crusius; C. Questa, *Introduzione alle metrica de Plauto* (1967); Dale, chap. 4; D. Korzeniewski, *Griechische Metrik* (1968); D. Hascall, "Triple Meter in English," *Poetics* 12 (1974); Halporn et al.; Snell, 30 ff.; West, passim; J. G. Fitch, *Seneca's Anapaests* (1987); K. Hanson, "English Iambic-Anapestic Meter," "Resolution in Modern Meters" (diss., Stanford University, 1991); A. Finch, "Metrical Diversity," *Meter in English,* ed. D. Baker (1996); T. Steele, *All The Fun's In How You Say a Thing* (1999); C. Hartman, "Anapestics," Finch and Varnes; N. Fabb and M. Halle, *The Meter of a Poem* (2008).

D. S. PARKER; J. W. HALPORN; T.V.F. BROGAN; N. GERBER

**ANAPHORA** (Gr., "a carrying up or back"). *Anaphora* (or *epanaphora*) is the *repetition of the same word or words at the beginning of successive phrases, clauses, sentences, or lines. *Epistrophe* (also *epiphora* or *antistrophe*) reverses the figure, repeating words at the ends of poetic units; anaphora and epistrophe combine in *symploce*. In *epanalepsis*, the same word is repeated at the beginning *and* end of phrases, clauses, or lines. Duplicating the end of one clause or line at the beginning of the next is *anadiplosis*. (In ling., *anaphora* refers to a grammatical system of reference; in musicology, *anaphora* can be used to discuss the rhetorical and poetic effects described above but also names a part of the Christian liturgical service, or music composed to accompany those rites.)

Because it consists of simple repetition, anaphora is a versatile, translatable, and ubiquitous poetic tool: present in the *Epic of Gilgamesh* and the fragments of Sappho; noted by cl. rhetoricians such as Demetrius, Alexander, and Longinus; dominating sections of the Bible and Philip Sidney's *Astrophil and Stella*; and figuring prominently in the work of 20th-c. poets such as H.D., André Breton, Attila József, Allen Ginsberg, and T. S. Eliot, whose "The Love Song of J. Alfred Prufrock" contains anaphora, epistrophe, symploce, and a loose form of epanalepsis.

Anaphora can serve as the main structuring element of *free verse, as in the poetry of Walt Whitman, but it also fits into closed forms (for anaphora in *sonnets, see E. B. Browning's "The Ways of Love" and Bartholomew Griffin's "Most true that I must fair Fidessa love," the latter demonstrating perfect symploce). However, anaphora neither results from nor signifies any poetic stricture; free verse featuring anaphora is still free verse. Anaphora spans generic boundaries as well as formal ones, as it is often used in political and religious rhet. to build cohesion or emphasis (see M. L. King Jr.'s "I have a dream" speech or Winston Churchill's "We shall fight on the beaches"). The natural sound of anaphora—which could plausibly occur spontaneously and unremarkably in speech—may account for its flexibility.

The seemingly straightforward repetitions of anaphora and its related figures can produce contradictory and complicated poetic effects: the devices can both accentuate and undercut a point, can produce both momentum and stasis. W. H. Auden's use of anaphora goes beyond simple adductive emphasis to unpack the contradictory connotations of a repeated word ("Law Like Love") or track a shifting political ideology ("Spain"). In such nuanced uses of anaphora, repetition compels continual reassessment of the repeated terms.

Whereas some poetic devices (meter, slant rhyme) may become apparent only on close or repeated readings, anaphora thrusts itself into the reader's attention: each line begins with an unmistakable reminder of the unfolding pattern. Thus, anaphora highlights poetic lines as discrete units while simultaneously binding those lines together.

Perhaps because of its ubiquity, natural sound, or ostensible simplicity, the definitive critical hist. of anaphora remains to be written; the device is often noted rather than examined.

*See* CHANT, HYPOTAXIS AND PARATAXIS.

■ M. Joseph, *Shakespeare's Use of the Arts of Language* (1947); Vickers, *Defence*; D.A.H. Elworthy, "A Theory of Anaphoric Information," *Linguistics and Philosophy* 18 (1995).

J. WEARE

**ANCEPS** (syllaba, brevis in longo) (Lat., "indeterminate"). A Neo-Lat. term widely used to designate three different metrical phenomena. (1) Syllabic or "prosodic" anceps—i.e., fluctuation in quantity created by the existence of a variable syllable boundary. The word *agro*, e.g., may begin with either a short or a long, depending on whether its initial syllable is open (a-gro) or closed (ag-ro). For anceps in this sense, the preferred term is "common" (Gr. *koiné*; Lat. *communis*). (2) "Final" anceps—at the end of a line or stanza, a syllable that may be either long or short, which the ancients referred to as the *syllaba indifferens* (Gr. *adiáphoros*). The pause that ensues at this point allows or requires lengthening of the syllable immediately preceding; and since almost all verses and stanzas end at a point where the metrical pattern itself either allows or requires a long, the normal quantity of a syllable becomes metrically "indifferent" when it appears in a final position—i.e., it makes no difference whether the poet decides to use a long or a short there. A normally short syllable that has undergone final lengthening in sense 2 may be called final anceps, but it is more frequently and correctly referred to as (*syllaba*) *brevis in* (*elemento*) *longo*, a phrase coined by Maas. (3) Anceps positions—any position in the metrical pattern that permits either a long or a short syllable. This is simply to say that some positions in the meter are not important to perception of the pattern, hence are not regulated strictly. Mod. usage of the term *anceps* tends to be restricted to sense 3 and to insist, correctly, that it is not the syllable that is anceps but the position in the metrical pattern it fills. The ancients sometimes regarded long syllables in these positions as "irrational" (Gr. *alogos*)—shorter than normal longs by some indeterminate amount. Double anceps at the beginning of the line is referred to as "aeolic base."

*See* AEOLIC.

■ Maas; L. E. Rossi, "Anceps: Vocale, Sillaba, Elemento," *Rivista di filologia e di istruzione classica* 91 (1963); A. M. Dale, *Collected Papers* (1969); Snell; M. L. West, "Three Topics in Greek Metre," *CQ* 32 (1982).

A. T. COLE

**ANECDOTE** (Gr. *anekdota*, "unpublished things"). A short narrative of a single incident, usually drawn from everyday life. The word entered the mod. Eur. langs. in the 17th c. with the discovery and publication of Procopius's *Anecdota*, a scandalous hist. of the Justinian court. The word *anecdote* originally referred to an episode in one of the many "secret histories" that were subsequently modeled on the *Anecdota*. These were historical or pseudo-historical works that collected accounts of the private lives of the powerful and famous. Over the 18th c., however, the word *anecdote* began to denote a brief narrative of an inconsequential but interesting event.

In its latter instance, the anecdote was associated with conversational speech and historical, journalistic, and biographical prose. Poets began to make conscious use of the anecdote as neoclassical strictures for writing poetry (see NEOCLASSICAL POETICS) began to break down under *romanticism. Anecdotal poetry was considered to be closer to ordinary lang. and the texture of ordinary life. William Wordsworth published "Anecdote for Fathers" in the first ed. of the highly anecdotal *Lyrical Ballads* (1798) and interpolated many anecdotes throughout *The Prelude* and *The Excursion*.

The anecdote continued to structure much later poetry. In particular, several avant-garde poets have experimented with anecdotal form (see AVANT-GARDE POETICS). Stéphane Mallarmé titled one section of his *Divagations* "Anecdotes ou Poèmes." These *prose poems straddle the boundary between *lyric and *narrative poetry, as well as the boundary between poetry and prose. Wallace Stevens was captivated with the anecdote, making innovative use of the form and using the word *anecdote* itself in the title of several poems, e.g., "Anecdote of the Jar," "Anecdote of Canna," and "Anecdote of the Prince of Peacocks." The anecdote continues to serve as an important template for mod. poetry.

■ K. Burke, *A Grammar of Motives* (1945); H. Grothe, *Anekdote* (1971); R. Schäfer, *Die Anekdote: Theorie, Analyse, Didaktik* (1982); J. Fineman, "History of the Anecdote: Fiction and Fiction," *The New Historicism*, ed. H. A. Veeser (1989); M.-P. Huglo, *Métamorphoses de l'insignifiant: essai sur l'anecdote dans la modernité* (1997); A. Liu, *Local Transcendence: Essays on Postmodern Historicism and the Database* (2008).

J. R. WOOD

**ANTHEM, NATIONAL.** Anthems are songs or other musical compositions that are performed (in most cases, sung) on ceremonial occasions to evoke collective feelings within a population. While many anthems are officially designated by governments, others are recognized by custom, and some nations, such as the U.S., have both a designated ("The Star-Spangled Banner") and an unofficial ("God Bless America") anthem. The official character of most anthems allows that, where they have words, these reflect the langs. of the relevant society: "O Canada" has lyrics in both Fr. and Eng., while the "Schweizerpsalm" (Swiss Psalm) includes versions in the four langs. of Switzerland (Swiss Ger., It., Fr., and Romansh); and South Africa's anthem (based on the Xhosa hymn "Nkosi sikelel' iAfrika" as well as the Afrikaans "Die Stem van Suid-Afrika") is thoroughly macaronic (see MACARONIC VERSE), employing five of the nation's 11 official langs. (besides the aforementioned two, Zulu, Sesotho, and Eng.).

Many national and other political (as opposed to ecclesiastical) anthems appeared between the early mod. period and the 19th c. While the term *anthem*—derived from the Grk. *antiphōna* and the OE *antefn*—had been used for church music (e.g., by the Eng. composers Thomas Tallis [ca. 1505–85] and Henry Purcell [ca. 1569–95]), the dominant mod., international sense of the term involves the use of song as a vehicle for nationalism or other collective ideologies (incl. religion but usually political in some sense). Historically, national anthems were both a product and a mirror of the process through which nation-states were built. The oldest known national anthem, the 1568 Dutch hymn "Het Wilhelmus," was written during the struggle for independence in the Netherlands, establishing a precedent for the adoption of a national song on the achievement of independence (the Turkish "İstiklâl Marşı"), revolution (the Fr. "Marseillaise"), or triumph after political crisis (the Brit. "God Save the King"). Many national anthems were originally written as patriotic poems that were later set to music; others were written by poets commissioned with the specific task of creating a national song.

However unique the national hists. these anthems obliquely celebrate, the poetic results are surprisingly similar; one anthem bears great likeness to the next. Anthems are almost always marches or hymns, although some take the form of folk songs, fanfares, and opera. They sing the praises of the fatherland in quasi-sacred terms and memorialize the mythical battles of forefathers, celebrating the holy connection between nation, hist., and individual. Historical particularities are routinely glossed over by religious connotations; archaic or stylized lang.; and generalized eulogies to people, landscapes, and political symbols (notably the flag).

In most cases, what remains are textual and melodic documents of similar appearance and intent, where names of countries, heroes, and projected qualities are formally interchangeable. Indeed, if countries had not been named, we would have had a hard time guessing the provenance of individual anthems: "O Russia, forever you're a strong and sacred country"; "Our country's God, our country's God / We worship Thy name in its wonder sublime" (Iceland); "O! say does that star-spangled banner yet wave / O'er the land of the free and the home of the brave" (U.S.); "Norse-men, in house and cabin, / Thank your great God! / It was his Will to protect the country / Although things looked dark" (Norway).

Although the poetic text of national anthems is of minimal literary interest, the performative dimension of anthems is noteworthy. Anthems are performed in a variety of contexts: as marching songs for the military; as a form of collective ritualism at sporting events; as the symbolic opening of the school day; as a provider of ambience at political rallies; and in celebration of newly created nation-states or nation-states in the making. Spectators at these events are called on to participate in a national monument through collective song, and singing, unlike many other symbolic representations of nationalism, is participatory—"active" rather than "passive." Thus, as participants engage with the anthem, the imagined national community becomes present in the shape of the choir, the gathering, and the audience. In the harmonious interaction between these groups, they come to represent and embody the unity of the people, galvanizing the gathering in a sense of national identity.

As the symbolic embodiment of the collective past, present, and future of a nation, anthems have become closely tied to the politics of national identity in the changing global sphere. National anthems are, consequently, politically charged and fluid texts: the Brit. anthem "God Save the King" has been variously adopted and then discarded by Commonwealth countries that wished to distance themselves from their colonial pasts; Russia has changed its anthem more times than any country in the world, a direct symptom of that country's tumultuous hist. of political redefinition; and Taiwanese Olympic athletes march to "The Banner Song" of Chinese Taipei, rather than "San Min Chu-I," because of their country's disputed independence. Supranational anthems, such as the instrumental "Anthem of Europe," the African Union's "Let Us All Unite and Celebrate Together," the "Olympic Hymn," and the "Hymn to the United Nations" represent recent devels. in the form. Thus, if the adoption of an anthem is a politically symbolic act, contemp. anthems indicate a global trend toward internationalization.

■ B. Anderson, *Imagined Communities: Reflections on the Origin and Spread of Nationalism,* rev. ed. (1991); *The Invention of Tradition,* ed. E. Hobsbawm and T. Ranger (1983); D. A. Kertzer, *Ritual, Politics and Power* (1988); A. Smith, *National Identity* (1991); M. Billig, *Banal Nationalism* (1995); U. Hedetoft, *Signs of Nations* (1995); *National Anthems of the World,* ed. M. J. Bristow, 11th ed. (2006)—lyrics and scores; *The Cambridge Handbook of Sociocultural Psychology,* ed. J. Valsiner and A. Rosa (2007); S. L. Redmond, "Citizens of Sound: Negotiations of Race and Diaspora in the Anthems of the UNIA and NAACP," *African and Black Diaspora* 4 (2011).

U. HEDETOFT

**ANTHIMERIA** (Gr., "one part for another"). The use of one part of speech for another. William Shakespeare,

who seems to have coined more than a thousand new words, uses anthimeria as one of his chief strategies; examples include "A mile before his tent fall down and knee / The way into his mercy" (*Coriolanus* 5.1.5), "And I come coffin'd home" (*Cor* 2.1.193), and "Lord Angelo dukes it well" (*Measure for Measure* 3.2.100). He esp. develops the use of nouns, pronouns, and adjectives as verbs, securing thereby the greater energy that verb forms convey. But no Eng. poet used this figure more than John Milton, many of whose examples suggest he found it effective for securing compression of meaning (Havens). In *Paradise Lost,* examples include "May serve to better us and worse our foes" (6.440; adjective for verb) and "sea-monsters tempest the ocean" (7.412; noun for verb); chaos is described as "the palpable obscure" and "the vast abrupt," while the sky is "Heaven's azure" (adjective for noun). In mod. poetry, even more transferences have been made by e. e. cummings, many of whose anthimerias are famous, e.g., "he sang his didn't he danced his did" and "anyone lived in a pretty how town." In grammar, the gerund, a verb form serving the syntactic function of a noun, is the same kind of word-class transfer.

■ R. D. Havens, *The Influence of Milton on English Poetry* (1922); M. Joseph, *Shakespeare's Use of the Arts of Language* (1947); A. Quinn, *Figures of Speech* (1982); Corbett, 449.

T.V.F. BROGAN

## ANTHOLOGY

I. Classical
II. Medieval to Contemporary

**I. Classical.** *Anthology* (Gr. *anthologion,* "a gathering of flowers"; Lat. *florilegium*) refers to a collection of short poems or literary passages drawn from multiple authors. It is first attested in the Byzantine lexicon called the *Suda* (10th CE) and is now applied to several literary collections that have reached us in ms. The idea underlying the term is selection of what is useful or beautiful.

The word *anthologion* has a long devel. in Gr. thought. The image of poetry as flowers is as old as Sappho (frag. 55), and Plato (*Ion* 534A–B) compares the poet to a bee collecting honey from the meadows of the Muses. For Isocrates (*Ad Demonicum* 51–52), the bee emblematizes someone who searches for knowledge by gathering the best passages from poets and philosophers. Plutarch (*Moralia* 41E–42A) articulates a distinction common in the imperial age between scholarly collectors, who, like bees, select only what is useful for learning, and literary eds. who, like garland-makers, choose the most beautiful poetic flowers for reading pleasure. Lucian (*Piscator* 6) hints at the coincidence between aesthetic and utilitarian anthols. by explaining that, while readers of philosophical extracts ostensibly praise the beelike collector, they in truth admire the authors who produced brilliantly colored flowers—if the collector knows how to select, intertwine, and harmonize so that no passage is out of tune with another (cf. Lucretius, *De rerum natura* 3.10–12).

Collections of the educational type, called *gnomologia,* began in the cl. period, and examples have been found on papyri of the Ptolemaic era. They typically present extracts on ethical themes, arranged by topic, and were often used in schools. The anthol. of literary passages and short poems made by Johannes Stobaeus to educate his son (5th c. CE) is the best extant example. The title *Anthologiae* for selections made from the astrological writings of Vettius Valens (2d c. CE) indicates that the idea of flower gathering was adapted to edited compilations of works by single authors (cf. Manetho, *Apotelesmatica* 5.6).

Ancient anthols. with aesthetic intentions often involve *epigrams. Our best source for Gr. literary epigrams is the *Greek Anthology*—a mod. designation. The earliest discernible layer in this anthol. is formed by single-authored epigram collections of the early Hellenistic era, both scholarly eds. of such poets as Simonides and Anacreon and poetry books by such epigrammatists as Callimachus, Asclepiades, Anyte, Nossis, and Leonidas of Tarentum. The Milan Papyrus, which contains over 100 epigrams attributed to Posidippus, confirms the existence of epigram books by the late 3d c. BCE; its arrangement by epigram types with subheadings is an early example of the book divisions found in later anthols. The Yale papyrus codex containing about 60 fragmentary epigrams attributed to Palladas preserves a later single-authored collection (late 3d to early 4th c. CE). The first known epigram anthol. was the *Stephanos* (Garland) by Meleager of Gadara (ca. 100 BCE), who added over 100 of his own poems to at least four books of epigrams culled from earlier collections. In the *proem, Meleager presents himself as a garland-maker who has intertwined 48 epigrammatists, each identified with a plant or flower. In his own epigrams, Meleager is fond of mentioning flowers and garlands, which trope his complex arrangement of epigrams by different authors, organized into sequences by theme and often linked sequentially by verbal echoes. His anthol. provided the model for the *Garland* of Philip (late Julio-Claudian period, 1st c. CE), an alphabetically organized selection of early imperial epigrams, and the *Cycle* of Agathias, a thematically organized collection of 6th-c. CE epigrammatists. In the early 10th c., Constantine Cephalas assembled a massive compilation of ancient and Byzantine epigrams, derived not only from Meleager, Philip, and Agathias but from Diogenianus's *Anthology of Epigrams* (Hadrianic; the earliest usage of the title); Strato of Sardis's *Mousa Paidike*, consisting of pederastic epigrams (perhaps Hadrianic); and epigrams by Palladas. The books of Cephalas's anthol. were organized in part by major epigram types—erotic, dedicatory, sepulchral, and epideictic. Within these, the ed. attempted his own rather careless thematic arrangements, to which he added blocks of epigrams taken from earlier collections.

The *Greek Anthology* is based on two major mss. and a few minor sylloges, all derived from Cephalas's anthol. Sometime in the 10th c., the Cephalan collection was redacted into the *Palatine Anthology* of 15 books, which includes *epitaphs by Gregory of Nazianzus (4th c. CE). In 1301, Maximus Planudes produced another, shorter anthol. drawn from Cephalas, rearranged by topics into seven books with subsections. The

*Planudean Anthology*, in Venice, preserves some epigrams lost from the *Palatine Anthology*, incl. ekphrastic epigrams confusingly printed as book 16 in mod. eds. Scholars were unaware of the *Palatine Anthology* until it was rediscovered in Heidelberg in 1606; astonishingly, it was known only in mss. descending from a bad copy made by the youthful Claude Saumaise until published by R.F.P. Brunck in 1772 and more accurately by Friedrich Jacobs from 1813 to 1817. The anthol. of Gr. epigrams that influenced the vernacular lits. of the early mod. era was the reduced version by Planudes.

The *Latin Anthology* (an 18th-c. title) is a mod. compilation of short Lat. poems of the imperial age in various meters. A number of partially overlapping mss. provide the poems for this anthol. The most important is the Codex Salmasianus (ca. 800 CE), which preserves material from Vandal Africa (5th–6th cs. CE), where there was a late flourishing of Lat. literary practice. In numbered sections probably representing different sources, this codex contains a large body of epigrams, incl. a sequence of 100 apparently by an unknown Af. author; Virgilian *centos, incl. a tragic *Medea* by Hosidius Geta (2d c. CE); other long poems, incl. the famed *Pervigilium Veneris* about a spring festival to Venus (perhaps 4th c. CE); epigrams ascribed to Seneca; extracts from Propertius, Ovid, and Martial; the *Aenigmata* of Symphosius (4th–5th c. CE?), consisting of 100 *riddles in three *hexameters supposedly composed at the Saturnalia; and a book of 90 epigrams in various meters by Luxorius of 6th-c. Carthage. The Af. epigrams on such topics as baths and circuses are of interest for the light they shed on Vandal society. Another ms., the Codex Vossianus (ca. 850), contains sequences of epigrams associated with the Neronian circle of Seneca and Petronius.

Early anthols. provide variable contexts for the extracts within them. Epigrams, e.g., may move from fixed inscriptional sites or single-authored collections to anthols., which are subject to repeated reselection and reordering over centuries. Each arrangement produces a different contextual reading and potentially a different understanding. In the right hands, the process of selecting and arranging can be a form of literary composition.

**II. Medieval to Contemporary.** Med. anthols. were created and preserved mainly by the clerical orders and survive in influential ms. collections such as the OE *Proverbs of Alfred* and the Eng. lyric collection called the *Harley Manuscript* (British Museum Ms. Harley 2253; ca. 1330); among other med. *florilegia* esp. notable are the *Carmina Cantabrigiensia* (Cambridge Songs; 11th c.) and the *Carmina Burana* (collected at the Ger. monastery at Benediktbeuren in Bavaria in the 13th c.; see GOLIARDIC VERSE). Ren. collections of *proverbs drew inspiration from Erasmus's *Adagia* (1500, often reprinted and expanded).

Anthols. took on new importance in the Ren. with a vogue inaugurated in England by the collection assembled by Richard Tottel and now called *Tottel's Miscellany* (originally *Songes and Sonettes, written by the ryght honorable Lorde Henry Haward late Earle of Surrey, and other*, 1557; ed. H. R. Rollins, rev. ed., 2 v., 1965). After Tottel, the vogue for the "miscellanies," as they were called (with the accent on the second syllable), grew to a flood in the last quarter of the century, incl. Clement Robinson's *Very Pleasaunt Sonettes and Storyes in Myter* (1566; surviving only as *A Handefull of Pleasant Delites*, 1584; ed. Rollins, 1924); Richard Edwards's *The Paradyse of Daynty Devises* (1576; ed. Rollins, 1927); Thomas Proctor's *A Gorgious Gallery of Gallant Inventions* (1578; ed. Rollins, 1926); *The Phoenix Nest* (1593; ed. Rollins, 1931); and Nicholas Breton's *Brittons Bowre of Delights* (1591; ed. Rollins, 1933) and *The Arbor of Amorous Devices* (1597; ed. Rollins, 1936).

Other significant Eur. anthols. are the massive *Flores poetarum*, compiled early in the 16th c. by Octavianus Mirandula and used throughout Europe until the 18th c.; Jan Gruter's *Delitiae* (1608–14; It., Fr., Belgian, and Ger. poems in Lat.); J. W. Zincgref's *Anhang unterschiedlicher aussgesuchter Gedichten* (1624); Thomas Percy's *Reliques of Ancient English Poetry* (1765), an anthol. of the popular *ballads that proved very influential in the 18th-c. revival of antiquarian interest in primitive poetry; Oliver Goldsmith's *The Beauties of English Poetry* (1767); Thomas Campbell's *Specimens of the British Poets* (1891); and Francis Palgrave's *Golden Treasury of the Best Songs and Lyrical Poems in the English Language* (1861–), the most important Victorian anthol. of lyric poetry.

The popularity of anthols. in the 20th c. only increased, with the expansion of the institutions of higher education, esp. in America. In Eng., important anthols. include the *Oxford Book of English Verse*, successively ed. by Arthur Quiller-Couch (1900, 1939), Helen Gardner (1972), and Christopher Ricks (1999); *The New Poetry* (1917), ed. by Harriet Monroe and Alice C. Henderson, which influenced the high modernists; Herbert Grierson's *Metaphysical Lyrics and Poems* (1921), which inaugurated the vogue for *metaphysical poetry; W. B. Yeats's *Oxford Book of Modern Verse* (1936); Cleanth Brooks and Robert Penn Warren's *Understanding Poetry* (1938; 4th ed. rev. extensively, 1976), which applied to pedagogy the principles of *New Criticism; Donald Allen's *The New American Poetry 1945–1960* (1960), which opened the postmodernist *canon; the Norton anthols. of lit. organized by period in several manifestations (*World, English, American*—often rev.) and anthols. of *Literature by Women* (3d ed., 2007), of *Poetry* (5th ed., 2004), of *Poetic Forms* (2001), of *New Poetry* (2009), and of *Poets Laureate* (2010), among others; the Longman anthols. of *British Literature* (4th ed., 2009) and of *World Literature* (2d ed., 2008), with attention to less studied figures and langs.; and the anthols. of international poetry produced by the poet and critic Jerome Rothenberg, most notably the three volumes of *Poems for the Millennium* (1998–2009), which gathers mod. and postmod. poetry from many langs. and trads.

The appeal of Eng.-lang. anthols. covering international poetic trads. has perhaps never been stronger than in the early 21st c. Among many signal examples, consider *The Columbia Anthology of Traditional Korean Poetry*, ed. P. H. Lee (2002); *Reversible Monuments: Contemporary Mexican Poetry*, ed. M. de la Torre and M. Wiegers (2002); *An Anthology of Modern Urdu Poetry*, ed. and trans. M.A.R. Habib (2003); *The Columbia Anthology of Modern Korean Poetry*, ed. D. McCann (2004); *The New Directions Anthology of Classical Chinese Poetry*, ed. E. Weinberger (2004); *Landscape with Rowers: Poetry from the Netherlands*, ed. and trans. J. M. Coetzee (2004); *Words of the True Peoples*, ed. C. Montemayor, v. 2 (2005)—contemp. indigenous-lang. Mexican poets; *Ottoman Lyric Poetry*, ed. and trans. W. G. Andrews (2006); *The Yale Anthology of Twentieth-Century French Poetry*, ed. M. A. Caws (2008); *Twentieth-Century German Poetry*, ed. M. Hofmann (2008); *The Whole Island: Six Decades of Cuban Poetry*, ed. M. Weiss (2009); *Classical Chinese Poetry*, ed. and trans. D. Hinton (2010); and *The FSG Book of Twentieth-Century Latin American Poetry*, ed. I. Stavans (2011), among many others.

The product of both an intellectual exercise and a market, the contemp. anthol. can be read as a sensitive register—and sometimes, as in the case of Grierson and Allen, an instrument—of canon-making.

*See* BOOK, POETIC; GREEK POETRY; LATIN POETRY; LYRIC SEQUENCE.

■ **I. Classical**: A. Riese, *Anthologia Latina* (1894–96); W. R. Paton, *The Greek Anthology* (1916–18, Gr. and Eng.); J. Hutton, *The Greek Anthology in Italy* (1935), and *The Greek Anthology in France and in the Latin Writers of the Netherlands* (1946); J. Barns, "A New Gnomologium," *CQ* 44 (1950), 45 (1951); *Anthologia Graeca*, ed. H. Beckby, 4 v. (1965); A.S.F. Gow and D. L. Page, *The Greek Anthology: Hellenistic Epigrams* (1965), and *The Greek Anthology: The Garland of Philip* (1968); D. R. Shackleton Bailey, *Anthologia Latina* (1982)—a reediting of Riese v. 1; R. J. Tarrant, "Anthologia Latina," *Texts and Transmission*, ed. L. D. Reynolds (1983); A. Cameron, *The Greek Anthology* (1993); K. J. Gutzwiller, *Poetic Garlands* (1998); *The New Posidippus*, ed. K. J. Gutzwiller (2005); N. M. Kay, *Epigrams from the Anthologia Latina* (2006).

■ **II. Medieval to Contemporary**: J. O. Halliwell-Phillipps, *Early English Miscellanies* (1855); *An Old English Miscellany*, ed. R. Morris (1872); F. Lachère, *Bibliographie des receuils collectifs de poésies publiés de 1597 à 1700* (1901); A. Wifstrand, *Studien zur griechischen Anthologie* (1926); A. E. Case, *A Bibliography of English Poetical Miscellanies, 1521–1750* (1935); *The Harley Lyrics*, ed. G. L. Brook (1948); R. F. Arnold, *Allgemeine Bücherkunde*, 4th ed. (1966); *Die deutschsprachige Anthologie*, ed. J. Bark and D. Pforte, 2 v. (1969–70); "Miscellanies, Anthologies and Collections of Poetry," *New CBEL*, v. 2, ed. G. Watson (1971); E. W. Pomeroy, *The Elizabethan Miscellanies, Their Development and Conventions* (1973); Pearsall 94 ff.; R. McDowell, "The Poetry Anthology," *HudR* 42 (1990); Lucia Re, "(De)Constructing the Canon: The Agon of the Anthologies on the Scene of Modern Italian Poetry," *MLR* 87 (1992); J. Rasula, "The Empire's New Clothes: Anthologizing American Poetry in the 1990s," *American Literary History* 7 (1995); A. Golding, "*The New American Poetry*

*Revisited*, Again," *Contemporary Literature* 39 (1998); P. Yu, "Charting the Landscape of Chinese Poetry," *Chinese Literature* 20 (1998); *Anthologies of British Poetry*, ed. B. Korte et al. (2000); P. Middleton, "The Transitive Poetics of Rothenberg's Transnational Anthologies," *West Coast Line* 34 (2000); A. Ferry, *Tradition and the Individual Poem* (2001); C. Nelson, "Murder in the Cathedral: Editing a Comprehensive Anthology of Modern American Poetry," *American Literary History* 14 (2002); *On Anthologies: Politics and Pedagogy*, ed. J. R. Di Leo (2004); P. Lauter, "Taking Anthologies Seriously," *MELUS* 29 (2004); D. Wojahn, "Shock and Awe: Anthologies and the Nortonization of Poetry," *Shenandoah* 54 (2004); T. Naaijkens, "The World of World Poetry: Anthologies of Translated Poetry as a Subject of Study," *Neophilologus* 90 (2006); J. G. Nichols, "Ezra Pound's Poetic Anthologies and the Architecture of Reading," *PMLA* 121 (2006); J. Spahr, "Numbers Trouble," *Chicago Review* 53 (2007), incl. response by J. Ashton; J. Ashton, "Our Bodies, Our Poems," *MP* 105 (2007), incl. response by J. Scapettone; D. Knechtges, "The Problem with Anthologies: The Case of the 'Bai yi' Poems of Ying Qu (190–252)," *Asia Major* 3d ser. 23 (2010).

T.V.F. Brogan, K. J. Gutzwiller (cl.);
R. Greene (med. to contemp.)

**ANTHROPOLOGY AND POETRY.** From the perspective of the 21st c., the social sciences look as though they have become more scientific, and, with the advance toward an increasingly scientific spirit, the uses of the social sciences for art have shrunk somewhat. All poets are their own amateur social scientists of a low-level sort: historians, psychologists, sociologists, anthropologists, and, all along, folklorists. If nothing else, folklore has provided materials for poetry from the earliest times. Agricultural lore, in particular, has furnished stories, characters, themes, and symbols; and it is easy to find and interpret examples, such as the lore about the finding of a red ear during corn husking that turns up in Joel Barlow's "The Hasty Pudding" (1793), H. W. Longfellow's *Hiawatha* (1855), and elsewhere. As with much rather informal anthropological material of the years before 1860, Longfellow's sources included unsystematic reports by missionaries, traders, explorers, and popularizers.

Geological speculations of the earlier 19th c. and Charles Darwin's *The Origin of Species* (1859) altered the framework of much thought, incl. that based on the age of the earth, which had long been assumed by many Europeans to be only about 6,000 years. Once it was established that the planet had to be much older, speculations about remote origins and gradual devel. were possible not only in the natural sciences but also in ling. and anthropology, and what is generally understood as mod. anthropology began toward the last third of the 19th c. Those devels. were also immediately important for lit.

The period of greatest practical utility for the various studies grouped under the big top of *anthropology* came during the period 1860–1925, when lit. was understood as a continuation of an ancient social practice of human culture practically from its beginnings. (*The Anthropological Review* began in 1863, *The Popular Magazine of Anthropology* in 1866.) Much of early mod. anthropology addressed itself to the study of ritual, *myth, *symbol, and language in ways that provided material for new lit.—drama and poetry more than prose fiction—and also helped to explain the materials presented in lit. that existed already. Particular attention was paid to the primitive origins of mod. practices, either as recorded in antiquity and the Middle Ages or as found in contemp. societies variously classified as "savage," "primitive," "native," "prelogical," "tribal," or "traditional." In most instances, anthropological studies concerned peoples living in territories recently acquired by colonial and commercial empires that flourished in the century between the Napoleonic Wars and World War I. These studies paralleled literary production designed to appeal to an interest in the exotic, such as are obvious in many works by H. Rider Haggard and Rudyard Kipling.

One of the earliest instances of overt collaboration between poetry and anthropology came in 1880 with the publication of Andrew Lang's *XXII Ballades in Blue China*, which includes the "Double Ballade of Primitive Man," annotated to indicate that some stanzas were contributed by "an eminent Anthropologist," elsewhere identified as "the learned doyen of Anthropology, Mr. E. B. Tylor, author of *Primitive Culture*." The stanzas in question are at the end of the poem:

> From a status like that of the Crees,
> Our society's fabric arose,
> Develop'd, evolved, if you please,
> But deluded chronologists chose,
> In a fancied accordance with Mos
> es, 4000 B. C. for the span
> When he rushed on the world and its woes,
> 'Twas the manner of Primitive Man!
>
> But the mild anthropologist, HE'S
> Not RECENT inclined to suppose
> Flints Palaeolithic like these,
> Quaternary bones such as those!
> In Rhinoceros, Mammoth and Co.'s,
> First epoch, the Human began,
> Theologians all to expose,
> 'Tis the MISSION of Primitive Man.
>
> ENVOY
>
> MAX, proudly your Aryans pose,
> But their rigs they undoubtedly ran,
> For, as every Darwinian knows,
> 'Twas the manner of Primitive Man!

The poem was dedicated to J. A. Farrer (1849–1925), author of *Primitive Manners and Customs* (1879), and a member of roughly the same generation as Lang (1844–1912) and Tylor (1832–1917). "Max" is the slightly older philologist Friedrich Max Müller (1823–1900), who opposed Darwinian thought and espoused a theory of "Aryan" origins of much IE lang., religion, and philosophy. Lang, Tylor, Farrer, and Müller were all amateur polymaths who ranged freely over many fields.

For many of these thinkers, the business of anthropology consisted of gathering bits of data from all over—some from long ago or far away or from local folklore—and generalizing them into an all-explaining synthesis that reduced everything to a single principle, such as solar worship, animism, or therapeutic magic. In 1890, J. G. Frazer (1854–1941) published the first version of *The Golden Bough: A Study in Magic and Religion*, which remains the single work of anthropology most influential for lit., if for nothing else. Frazer's approach sought to explain many diverse beliefs and practices by references to ancient fertility cults that periodically sacrificed a priest-king. In some respects, Frazer laid the foundation for what T. S. Eliot called "the mythical method," whereby mod. materials are given shape and depth by reference to an ancient model, usually centered on some such recurrent figure as the trickster or savior. It is one hallmark of many mod. literary works that they offer a complex layering of ancient and mod., so that G. B. Shaw's *Man and Superman* (1903), James Joyce's *Ulysses* (1922), and Thomas Mann's *Doctor Faustus* (1947) track the Don Juan legend, the *Odyssey*, and the Faust legend, respectively. A generation of Eur. and Am. artists born in the 1880s—Pablo Picasso (1881–1973), Igor Stravinsky (1882–1971), Joyce (1882–1941), D. H. Lawrence (1885–1930), Ezra Pound (1885–1972), Eliot (1888–1965)—were in their various ways capable of using anthropological materials to underwrite important innovations that, around 1915, combined the ancient, the primitive, the mod., and the personal in works that could be called both primitivistic and neoclassical. These devels. were contemporaneous with Sigmund Freud's *Totem and Taboo: Resemblances between the Mental Lives of Savages and Neurotics* (1913), which refers to Darwin, Tylor, Lang, and Frazer. (*Totem* comes from Native Am. roots; *taboo* is Polynesian. One of the earliest recorded uses of the latter term is in a book on Hawai'i by the father of G. M. Hopkins.) Freud's adaptation of the mythical method, of which he was one progenitor, leads to the explanation of general cultural practices as well as individual psychic structures by reference to a common obsession with the killing of the same-sex parent and the sexual possession of the opposite-sex parent. There was immense interest and utility for poets in Freud's audacious fusion of the individual materials in dreams and the collective materials in myth, ritual, jokes, and other cultural practices. Eliot was open about his debt to Frazer, as well as to Jessie L. Weston's *From Ritual to Romance* (1920), and he was closely followed and imitated by Archibald MacLeish, whose *Pot of Earth* (1925) takes advantage of lore from Frazer and also of poetic manner from Eliot.

Eliot and Pound were interested in other anthropological generalizations, esp. as they applied to primitive mentality and the abiding functions of poetry. For them, and also for Joyce, Lucien Lévy-Bruhl (1857–1939) contributed the notion of primitive "prelogical" mentality. For primitive humankind, unity trumped dissociation, and concepts that are separate for the civilized are not so for the primitive: individual and group, dream and reality, death and life, child and adult, and other polarities are not distinct but are rather unified. For a poet, such a concept is of capital value. Eliot wrote in 1916, "M. Lévy-Bruhl goes on to insist quite rightly upon a side of the primitive mind which has been neglected by older anthropologists, such as Frazer, and produces a theory which has much in common with the analyses of mythology recently made by disciples of Freud." (That suggests, by the way, that Eliot was less an adherent of Frazer and less an enemy of Freud than many have imagined.)

For Pound, and later for Charles Olson (1910–70) and Guy Davenport (1927–2005), the "culture morphology" of Leo Frobenius (1873–1938) had more impact than Frobenius's anthropological thinking was to have after his death, although he may not have been the racist charlatan that some critics think he was.

Robert Graves (1895–1985) challenged Frazer's standing by publishing a somewhat similar work, *The White Goddess: A Historical Grammar of Poetic Myth* (1948), that, like *The Golden Bough*, uses ancient ritual to explain a good deal of lore and hist. and to provide answers for many riddles. Graves's work, after being rejected by many publishers, was admired by Eliot, who was an influential director of Faber and Faber, the publishers of the book. *The White Goddess* is a bold work of fancy not firmly based on any solid learning in lang., lit., or anthropology, but it makes an entertaining case for the magical powers of authentic poetry against the claims of rather arid secular mod. society. Graves was never himself a great poet, but his style of thinking had influence on certain elders, such as Eliot, and on some younger writers, incl. Dylan Thomas (1914–53), W. S. Merwin (b. 1927), Robert Creeley (1926–2005), and Ted Hughes (1930–98), for whom, in diverse ways, poetry never gave up its ancient bardic involvement with magic and mystery, *charm and spell and curse (see BARD, POET).

Not many poets are anthropologists—although some attention may be given to Pound's *Guide to Kulchur* (1938) and Eliot's *Notes towards the Definition of Culture* (1948), which sound anthropological, and also to some of the prose writings of Nathaniel Tarn (b. 1928) and Gary Snyder (b. 1930), who have long been uncommonly sensitive to the interactions of lang., culture, and ecology.

The experience of anthropology makes people wonder what an anthropologist would make of them, and sometimes poets experiment with what could be called a visiting anthropologist's point of view, which renders the familiar world in unfamiliar terms. At one extreme, the "visitor" is a savage creature, as in Robert Browning's "Caliban upon Setebos" (1864) and Ted Hughes's "Wodwo" (1967). (Caliban, "a salvage and deformed slave" in Shakespeare's *The Tempest*, has a name that seems to be an anagram of *cannibal*, itself a version of *Carib*; Setebos was a demon of the Patagonians, reported by 16th-c. travelers. *Wodwo* is a made-up singular of *woodwose*, a "wild man of the woods.") "Caliban upon Setebos," subtitled "Natural Theology in the Island," represents how Caliban projects his own brutish image upward to imagine a brutish deity. (This is not so different from Émile Durkheim's analysis of religion.) "Wodwo" begins, "What am I? Nosing here, turning leaves over / Following a faint stain on the air to the river's edge . . ." At the opposite extreme is Craig Raine's (b. 1944) celebrated "A Martian Sends a Postcard Home" (1979), which takes a common theme from science fiction and other forms of popular culture. Like Browning's Caliban and Hughes's Wodwo, the Martian pays attention to what he or she interprets as fauna: "Caxtons are mechanical birds with many wings / and some are treasured for their markings." Such poets imagine themselves in the *personae of quasi-anthropologists describing a scene or a landscape as if with new eyes.

Now and then, professional social scientists, often exposed to poetry, write their own, and it is worth noting. Edward Sapir (1884–1939), anthropologist and linguist, and Ruth Benedict (1887–1948) both studied with Franz Boas, and both wrote poems. Some suggest their anthropological studies directly. Benedict's "Myth" (ca. 1941) begins, "A god with tall crow feathers in his hair, / Long-limbed and bronzed, from going down of sun . . ." Sapir's "A Pair of Tricksters" (1919) likewise offers a symbolic black bird:

O one is a raven, glossy black,
He struts on the low-tide beach
And he croaks while the mist drifts over his back,
While the mist lifts out of reach.

A later poem, "Coyote, Reflecting on Just Criticism, Decides to Mend His Ways," by the multitalented Dell Hymes (1927–2009), also involves the figure of a trickster who sounds like Caliban and a Wodwo: "Gee these eels taste good. / It's nice here by the river."

For the future, it is likely that anthropology will grow ever more scientific and ever less fanciful, although it will never completely relinquish fancy as a resource. Information technology has made possible the storage and retrieval of enormous amounts of data, and that, in turn, facilitates a burgeoning of comparative statistical studies. A survey of current interest groups reveals a number of adjectives and adjuncts that have been attached to anthropology: Africanist, archaeological, critical, culinary, cultural, dialectic, ecological, educational, evolutionary, feminist, forensic, humanistic, linguistic, medical, museum, national, pharmacological, physical, psychological, political and legal, queer, sartorial, structural, transnational/global, urban, and visual. There are societies for the "anthropology of" consciousness, food and nutrition, religion, and work. The simple-hearted ethnologists of the 19th c. would be impressed and even appalled at what has become of their science.

Lit., on the other hand, is much harder to sum up. With poetry, esp., when we think things have changed, it is all the likelier that they are essentially staying the same with possibly a superficial change of costume and style. If anything special has happened, it could be that most poets have given up the high modernist ambition of producing art that can operate culturally and communally, comprehending great tracts of historical and social territory, as may have been the case with such poets as Eliot, Pound, W. C. Williams (1883–1963), W. H. Auden (1907–73), Paul Valéry (1871–1945), Saint-John Perse (1887–1975), Pablo Neruda (1904–73), and George Seferis (1900–71). Most of their successors have little interest in writing substantial works of great cultural scope, settling instead for the smaller reach of evanescent psychological and personal expression. Some more recent poets, like Robert Lowell and Snyder, may seem to be exceptions, anomalies, or at least hybrids of some sort, but they are rare.

■ J. G. Frazer, *The Golden Bough*, 3d ed., 12 v. (1905–15); T. S. Eliot, "Review of *Group Theories of Religion and the Religion of the Individual*, by C. C. J. Webb," *International Journal of Ethics* 27 (1916); L. Lévy-Bruhl, *How Natives Think*, trans. L. A. Clare (1926); Frye; J. B. Vickery, "Note on *The Waste Land* and *Totem and Taboo*," *Literature and Psychology* 10 (1960); and *The Literary Impact of the Golden Bough* (1973); *Dialectical Anthropology* 11.2–4 (1986)—spec. iss. on poetry and anthropology; *Modernist Anthropology: From Field Work to Text*, ed. M. Manganaro (1990); P. Rae, "Anthropology," *A Companion to Modernist Literature and Culture*, ed. D. Bradshaw and K.J.H. Dettmar (2006); J. Schuster, "William Carlos Williams, *Spring and All*, and the Anthropological Imaginary," *Journal of Modern Literature* 30 (2007); R. Van Oort, "The Culture of Criticism," *Criticism* 49 (2007); N. Tarn, *The Embattled Lyric: Essays and Conversations in Poetics and Anthropology* (2008); B. Thomas, "The Fictive and the Imaginary: Charting Literary Anthropology, Or, What's Literature Have To Do With It?," *American Literary History* 20 (2008); M. Manganaro, "Mind, Myth, and Culture: Eliot and Anthropology," *A Companion to T. S. Eliot*, ed. D. Chinitz (2009).

W. HARMON

**ANTICLIMAX.** A term apparently first used by Samuel Johnson, quoting Joseph Addison; Johnson defines it as "a sentence in which the last part expresses something lower than the first" (*Dictionary*, 1755). "Lower" in this context concerns the ideas or objects referred to and, as such, restricts the phenomenon to semantic anticlimax, frequently quoted examples of which include Alexander Pope's series of anticlimaxes from *The Rape of the Lock*: "Or stain her Honor, or her new Brocade," "Or lose her heart, or necklace, at a ball." Syntactic anticlimax would include sentences, lines of verse, or propositions that, after a series of elements of increasing length, suddenly introduce in the final position a considerably shorter syntagm, e.g., "Alfred de Musset, charming, likeable, subtle, graceful, delicate, exquisite, small" (Victor Hugo). When used to designate an ineptly expressed idea meant to be superlatively grandiose or pathetic, anticlimax becomes synonymous with the rhetorical figure *bathos. Similarly bathetic is

anticlimax used for a deliberately ironic letdown, as in various absurd similes in Henry Fielding's burlesque of Elizabethan and Restoration tragedy (King Arthur is speaking to his queen Dollalolla): "Whence flow those Tears fast down thy blubber'd Cheeks, / Like a swoln Gutter, gushing through the Streets?" (*The Tragedy of Tragedies* [1731] 1.2.6–7); or Lord Grizzle's impassioned address to the Princess Huncamunca: "Oh! Huncamunca, Huncamunca, Oh! / Thy pouting Breasts, like Kettledrums of Brass, / Beat everlasting loud Alarms of Joy" (2.5.1–3). The effect of anticlimax in all forms is almost invariably comic.
■ C. Perelman and L. Olbrechts-Tyteca, *The New Rhetoric*, trans. J. Wilkinson and P. Weaver (1969), under *gradation*; Group μ.

H. Baran; A. W. Halsall

**ANTIMETABOLE** (Gr., "transposition"). A species of *chiasmus or word repetition in reverse. The term is probably first recorded in Quintilian (*Institutio oratoria* 9.3.85, 1st c. CE), who defines it merely as a figure of words "repeated with variation in case or tense" (others would call this *polyptoton*) but illustrates with examples in which two words are later repeated in reverse order, e.g., "non ut edam vivo, sed ut vivam edo"; it is specifically this symmetrical *abba* pattern of word repetition that the term is most often made to designate by later rhetoricians (e.g., John Smith, *The Mysterie of Rhetorique Unvailed*, 1657). Examples of such manifestly verbal chiasmus in Eng. poetry can be seen in the final line of Shakespeare's sonnet 154, "Love's fire heats water, water cools not love," and in Hamlet's "What's Hecuba to him, or he to Hecuba?" (2.2.559). All in all, it would seem better to use the term *chiasmus* for the genus of figures of reversal, whether of sound, syntax, or meaning, without necessarily involving specific word repetition, and restrict *antimetabole* to the narrower meaning of a single reversed word pair.
■ A. Quinn, *Figures of Speech* (1982); B. Vickers, *In Defence of Rhetoric* (1988); Vickers; Corbett; M. García-Page, "Reflexiones lingüísticas sobre la antimetábole," *Revista de Literatura* 57 (1995); A. Quinn, "Antimetabole," *Encyclopedia of Rhetoric and Composition*, ed. T. Enos and L. Rathbun (1996).

T.V.F. Brogan; A. W. Halsall

**ANTISPAST.** The metrical sequence ◡ – – ◡ used by ancient Gr. metrists (Hephaestion, *Enchiridion* 10) for the analysis of *aeolic meters and viewed by some mod. critics (e.g., Koster) as an authentic foot but largely abandoned by most others except to describe a word shape of that pattern.
■ P. Shorey, "Choriambic Dimeter and the Rehabilitation of the Aeolic," *TAPA* 38 (1907); Koster; West.

T.V.F. Brogan

**ANTISTROPHE** (Gr., "counterturning"). (1) In *classical prosody, the second part of the regular *ode in Gr. choral dance and poetry. The antistrophe follows the first part, the *strophe, and is followed by the third and concluding section, the *epode. The antistrophe corresponds to the strophe exactly in meter, while the epode does not, giving a double-triple *aab* structure that is replicated in several other major verse forms (see CANZONE). (2) In cl. rhet., the repetition of words in reversed order, e.g., "the master of the servant and the servant of the master" (cf. CHIASMUS). *Antistrophe* is also occasionally used as a term for repetition of a word at the end of successive phrases or clauses, but the preferable term is *epistrophe*.

R. A. Hornsby; T.V.F. Brogan

**ANTITHESIS,** *antitheton* (Gr., "opposition"; Lat. *contentio*). The juxtaposition of contraries: the contrast of ideas, sharpened or pointed up by the use of words of opposite or conspicuously different meaning in contiguous or parallel phrases or clauses. Antithesis is a form of expression recommended as satisfying by Aristotle "because contraries are easily understood and even more so when placed side by side, and also because antithesis resembles a syllogism, for it is by putting opposing conclusions side by side that you refute one of them" (*Rhetoric* 3.9.8). The anonymous *Rhetorica ad Alexandrum* (3rd c. BCE, chap. 26) observes that antithesis may oppose words or ideas or both, and later authorities likewise stress the clarity and force that an antithesis may impart to an idea (e.g., *Rhetorica ad Herennium* [86–82 BCE], 4.15.21; Johannes Susenbrotus, *Epitome troporum ac schematum et Grammaticorum* and *Rhetorme arte rhetorica* [1541], under *contentio*). Antithesis is one of the two or three fundamental strategies of biblical *parallelism first defined by Bishop Robert Lowth (1753) and is fairly frequent in OE poetry. In both these trads., as in nearly all others, antithesis achieves heightened effect when confined to the two halves of a *hemistichic line or two lines of a couplet, securing thereby the reinforcement of meter. Antithesis was cultivated by the cl. poets, and while these poets sometimes contrive a strict balance of form (the figure of *parison* [see ISOCOLON] in cl. rhet.) or a complex opposition of idea, e.g., "He aims to fetch not smoke from a flash, but light from smoke" (Horace, *Ars poetica* 142–43), this kind of ingenuity is even more characteristic of the Eng. and Fr. poets of the 17th and 18th cs., e.g., "I would and would not, I am on fire yet dare not" (Pierre Corneille, *Cinna* [1643] 1.2.122). A. Albalat once declared antithesis to be "the generating principle of half of French literature, from Montaigne to Hugo" (192–93); certainly, it is the predominant figure in the romantic poetry of Victor Hugo.

In Eng. poetry, William Shakespeare uses antithesis 209 times in the *Sonnets*, i.e., about once per sonnet, both of content and of form (syntax); he also experiments with double antithesis regularly (e.g., 27.12) and at least once with triple (11.5). He particularly exploits antithesis in series, to develop the (Petrarchan) contrariety of emotional conflict (94, 119, 129, 150): love–hate, truth–falsity, beauty–ugliness, fertility–sterility. But it is the *heroic couplet, which emerged in the course of the 17th c. to become the preferred meter of the Restoration and 18th-c. poets, that offered nearly the ideal medium for that balanced, concise, antithetical expression, serious and witty alike, which is the major characteristic of *neoclassical style. In John Dryden and Alexander Pope, antithesis becomes an inestimable device for the display of satirical wit: "Thus wicked but in will, of means bereft, / He left not faction, but of that was left" (Dryden, *Absalom and Achitophel* 567–68); "It is the slaver kills, and not the bite" (Pope, "Epistle to Dr. Arbuthnot" 1.106); "Be not the first by whom the new are tried, / Nor yet the last to lay the old aside" (*Essay on Criticism* 2.335–36). In contemp. writing, antithesis continues to be used to achieve effects, as, e.g., in T. S. Eliot: "We are the hollow men / We are the stuffed men" ("The Hollow Men").

The antitheses quoted above are among the many forms of expression that exhibit two or more figures of speech as these were defined in cl. rhet. and may be labeled with one term or another according to the particular feature to be distinguished. Thus, the second line of the quotation from Dryden exhibits *chiasmus, *epanalepsis, and isocolon. If the contrastive members of the antithesis are set in adjoining clauses that are not parallel but rather contrastive syntactically, the figure is termed *syncrisis*. Antithesis combined with chiasmus may be seen in the old definition of the scholar: "one who knows something about everything and everything about something." More recently, Group μ describes antithesis as a metalogism of addition, which asserts both "X" and "X is not non-X." Quinn puts this similarly: "rather than saying something and then repeating it in other words, you both deny its contrary and assert it," so that "you have said the thing in two different ways." Antithesis thus offers "the advantage of giving a sense of completeness with only two items."

*See* EPIGRAM, OXYMORON.

■ A. Albalat, *La Formation du style par l'assimilation des auteurs* (1921); M. Joseph, *Shakespeare's Use of the Arts of Language* (1947); P. Beyer, "Antithese," *Reallexikon II*; A. Kibédi-Varga, *Les Constantes du poème* (1963); G. K. Spring, "An Analysis of Antithesis as a Basis of Epic Rhetorical Patterns," *DAI* 26 (1966): 6030; M. Kallich, "Balance and Antithesis in Pope's *Essay on Criticism*," *TSL* 12 (1967); C. Perelman and L. Olbrechts-Tyteca, *The New Rhetoric*, trans. J. Wilkinson and P. Weaver (1969); Lausberg; Sr. M. M. Holloway, "Hopkins' Theory of 'Antithetical Parallelism,'" *HQ* 1 (1974); M. Isnard, "Antithese et oxymoron chez Wordsworth," *Rhétorique et communication* (1979); R. F. Gleckner, "Antithetical Structure in Blake's *Poetical Sketches*," *SIR* 20 (1981); Group μ, 141–42; A. Quinn, *Figures of Speech* (1982); Corbett, 429–30.

T.V.F. BROGAN; A. W. HALSALL

**ANTONOMASIA** (Gr., "naming instead"). A figure in which an epithet or appellative or descriptive phrase is substituted for a proper name (e.g., "The Bard" for Shakespeare; "It was visitors' day at the vinegar works / In Tenderloin Town" [W. H. Auden, *For the Time Being*]) or, conversely, in which a proper name is substituted for an individual, a class, or type ("the English Diana" for Queen Elizabeth; "Some mute, inglorious Milton here may rest" [Thomas Gray, "Elegy Written in a Country Churchyard"]). Similar to the first form above is *periphrasis. Group μ (101–3), however, identifies the two types, respectively, as "particularizing" and "generalizing" varieties of *synecdoche.

Quintilian (*Institutio oratoria* 8.6.29) holds that antonomasia, which is very common in poetry but less so in oratory, may be accomplished in two ways—by substitution of epithets for names (such as "Pelides" [i.e., son of Peleus] for Achilles) and by substitution of the most striking characteristic of an individual for his or her name ("Divum pater atque hominum rex" [Father of gods and king of men; Virgil, *Aeneid* 1.65]). To these he adds a third type, wherein acts may indicate the individual; this, however, may be a spurious emendation. He too points to the relation of antonomasia to synecdoche. George Puttenham (*The Arte of English Poesie*, 1589) distinguishes between epitheton ("fierce Achilles," "wise Nestor"), where name and epithet both appear, and antonomasia, use of one for the other.

■ Group μ; Morier; Lausberg; S. Leroy, "Quels fonctionnements discursifs pour l'antonomase du nom propre?" *Cahiers de praxematique* 35 (2000), and *De l'identification à la catégorisation* (2004).

R. O. EVANS; T.V.F. BROGAN

**ANTROPOFAGIA** (Port. *anthropophagy*, cannibalism). In the Brazilian arts, antropofagia is a critical concept that originates in the writings of poet-essayist Oswald de Andrade (1890–1954), primarily the aggressively toned "Manifesto antropófago" (in *Revista de Antropofagia*, 1928). The term refers to the notion of "cultural cannibalism," a critical appropriation of foreign ideas and aesthetic models and reformulation thereof in new national forms. The aim of antropofagia was to constitute an independent literary discourse immune to sectarian interests and excessive patriotism. The main arms of this effort were *parody, *satire, and provocation via conceptual humor. Andrade did not formulate a platform per se, but there are virtual principles from which one may construct the objectives of an artistic movement involving crit., poetry, and the other literary genres as well as intellectual discourse. Unlike Andrade's previous "Manifesto da Poesia Pau-Brasil" (1924), which is specifically cast as a modernist declaration about poetry (see MODERNISM) and is accompanied by a volume of verse, the manifesto of antropofagia does not have a corresponding book of poems nor does it concern only *lyric. As the first line asserts, antropofagia is a unifying force "socially, economically, philosophically." Discussion of antropofagia necessarily expands into a wide plane of debate involving historical interpretation, national identity, philosophy of culture, and *postcolonial poetics. In the lyric, antropofagia is a generative concept for some of Andrade's own poetry, for select works by other Brazilian modernists, for the articulation of *concrete poetry by the

*Noigandres group in the 1950s, for the poetry of song represented by the Tropicália movement of the late 1960s, and for youth poetry of the late 20th c. Therein one finds direct allusions to the trope of deglutition as well as reworkings of images related to the symbol of cannibalism as an encounter with primitive forces of the unconscious, as an attempt to comprehend an indigenous, totemic sense of eating one's enemies to absorb their forces via magical disposition, and as a figurative form of resistance or new attitude toward cultural relationships with hegemonic powers.

*See* ANTHROPOLOGY AND POETRY; BRAZIL, POETRY OF; MANIFESTO.

■ L. Bary, intro. and trans, "Oswald de Andrade's 'Cannibalist Manifesto,'" *Latin American Literary Review* 19.38 (1991); *Antropofagia hoje / Anthropophagy Today?* spec. iss. of *Nuevo texto crítico* 23–24 (1999); L. Madureira, *Cannibal Modernities* (2005); H. de Campos, "Anthropophagous Reason: Dialogue and Difference in Brazilian Culture" (1981), *Novas*, ed. A. S. Bessa and O. Cisneros (2007).

C. A. PERRONE

**APHAERESIS** (Gr., "a taking away"). In *prosody, the technical term for one form of elision, namely, omission of a word-initial syllable, esp. a vowel, e.g., *'gainst* for *against*, *mid* for *amid*, *'neath* for *beneath*. Aphaeresis of a syllable containing a vowel-consonant or consonant-vowel pairing is also common, e.g., *'zactly* for *exactly*, *'cause* for *because*. In some occurrences of aphaeresis, the following consonant then clusters with the succeeding word, e.g., *'tis* for *it is*, *'twere* for *it were*. Other times, only the vowel is elided, e.g., *supposed* becomes *'pposed* or *s'pposed*. In Eng., the elided syllable carries relatively minimal stress, and the following syllable carries either the primary or secondary stress of the word. An *iambic word or phrase thereby becomes a stressed monosyllable. In Gr. poetry, aphaeresis occurs in the suppression of an initial short *e* following a word ending in a long vowel or diphthong. The Lat. term for this phenomenon is *prodelision*: when a Lat. word ending in a vowel or a vowel followed only by *m* comes before *es* or *est*, the second vowel is "squeezed out," as in Virgil's "Usque adeone mori miserum est? vos a mihi Manes" (*Aeneid* 12.646). Aphaeresis is common in spoken Eng. and can be found in dialect, vernacular, and nation-lang. poetries.

*See* ELISION.

■ L. Kypriotaki, "Aphaeresis in Rapid Speech," *American Speech* 45.1 (1970).

T.V.F. BROGAN; R. A. HORNSBY; D. VERALDI

**APHORISM.** *See* EPIGRAM.

**APOCOPE** (Gr., "a cutting off"). In *prosody, the technical term for one form of elision, namely, loss of a word's final syllable or vowel, e.g., *eve* or *even* for *evening*. Often the apocopated word then fuses with the one following, e.g., "th'Empyrean" for "the Empyrean," "th'army," etc., thereby avoiding *hiatus. Apocope is a common linguistic process.

*See* ELISION.

■ T. Sasaki, "Apocope in Modern English Verse," *SEL* (Tokyo) 13 (1933); M. Joseph, *Shakespeare's Use of the Arts of Language* (1947).

T.V.F. BROGAN

**APORIA.** A logical impasse in which meaning oscillates between two contradictory imperatives. First described in Gr. philosophy as a seemingly insoluble logical conundrum—aporia translates as "without a passage"—it is an important concept in poststructuralist theory, as a term for interpretive undecidability. In deconstructive criticism, an aporia is the site at which a text undermines its own philosophical structure by revealing the rhetorical nature of that structure (de Man). Consider Derrida's deconstruction of the paradox of structure and event in structuralist theories of lang. According to structuralist ling., the structure of a lang. (*langue*) is a product of past speech acts (*parole*), yet every speech act is itself made possible by prior structures (Saussure). Thus, Derrida argues, any account of linguistic origins must oscillate between these two perspectives on lang., each of which shows the error of the other. Instead of discovering a foundational linguistic structure, one finds an irresolvable aporia between structure and event (*Positions*). Because literary texts foreground their own rhetoricity, deconstructive theory often identifies lit. as an exemplary location for identifying and examining such philosophical paradoxes.

In cl. rhet., aporia is a figure of speech that professes doubt or deliberation. Aporia allows a speaker to hesitate on both sides of a question, as when Hamlet asks, "to be or not to be?" The figure, thus, signifies indecision—Plato describes the experience of an aporia as paralysis or numbness (*Meno*)—although in rhetorical practice this uncertainty is often feigned. The philosophical and rhetorical senses of aporia suggest how the term can refer to both a philosophical paradox and to the state of being perplexed by such a paradox.

*See* FIGURATION, PHILOSOPHY AND POETRY, POSTSTRUCTURALISM, RHETORIC AND POETRY.

■ F. Saussure, *Cours de linguistique générale*, ed. C. Bally and A. Sechehaye, 3d ed. (1931); P. de Man, *Allegories of Reading* (1979); J. Derrida, *Positions* (1981); J. Culler, *On Deconstruction* (1982); J. Derrida, "*Ousia and Grammē*: Note on a Note from *Being and Time*" and "Signature Event Context," *Margins of Philosophy*, trans. A. Bass (1986); J. Derrida, *Aporias*, trans. T. Dutoit (1993).

J. C. MANN

**APOSIOPESIS** (Gr., "becoming silent"). A speaker's abrupt halt midway in a sentence, due to being too excited or distraught to give further articulation to his or her thought (Quintilian, *Institutio oratoria* 9.2.54); less commonly, the speaker thinking to impress the addressee with the vague hint of an idea too awesome to be put into words (Demetrius, *On Style* 2.103). These two motives are not always distinguishable, e.g., in

Neptune's threat to the winds (*Aeneid* 1.133–35): "How dare ye, ye winds, to mingle the heavens and the earth and raise such a tumult without my leave? You I will— but first I must quiet the waves"; or Lear's threat of vengeance against his daughters: "I will have such revenges on you both / That all the world shall—I will do such things—" (2.4.282–83). Compare the conclusion of George Herbert's "The Thanksgiving": "Then for thy passion—I will do for that— / Alas, my God, I know not what" (*The Temple*, 1633). If at the point of breaking off, the speaker verbalizes the failure of words to convey the emotion adequately, the figure becomes *adynaton. Related are paraposiopesis, interrupting the sentence with an expression of emotion, and *anacoluthon, ending the sentence with a different construction from that with which it began.

According to the Gr. rhetorician Alexander (*Peri schematon*, 2nd c. CE), aposiopesis is always followed by the speaker's explanation that he or she is passing over in silence matters either already known to the addressee or too sordid to be mentioned; but Quintilian remarks that it is sometimes used as a merely transitional device, where the speaker wishes to introduce a digression or announce an impromptu change in the planned conduct of his or her argument (9.2.55–57).

George Puttenham (*The Arte of English Poesie*, 1589), who calls aposiopesis "the figure of silence, or of interruption," finds it suited to express a range of emotions, incl. fear, shame, distraction, or momentary forgetfulness. Alexander Pope defined aposiopesis as an "excellent figure for the ignorant, as '*What shall I say?*' when one has nothing to say; or '*I can no more*' when one really can no more" (*Peri Bathous*, 1727). Group μ points out that some aposiopeses "have the force of 'etc.,'" while others, "where conjecture is enjoined about the suppressed sequence, may be interpreted as a refusal to proceed"; they "refuse metabole, and precisely for this reason they are metaboles that economize the code . . . as a way of indicating its insufficiencies, of showing that it offers nothing or is, in fact, even a danger" (139). Aposiopesis should not be confused with *paralipsis, the device whereby a speaker pretends not to discuss a subject while actually doing so.

■ Lausberg; Group μ; A. Quinn, *Figures of Speech* (1982); B. Vickers, *In Defence of Rhetoric* (1988); G. Alexander, "Sidney's Interruptions," *SP* 98 (2001).

H. Baran; A. W. Halsall; A. Watson

**APOSTROPHE** (Gr. "turning away"). Poetic address, esp. to unhearing entities, whether these be abstractions, inanimate objects, animals, infants, or absent or dead people. Examples include Petrarch's "Occhi miei lassi, mentre ch'io vi giro . . ." (*Canzoniere* 14); Shakespeare's "thou age unbred" (sonnet 104); Alphonse de Lamartine's "O lac! rochers muets! grottes! Forêt obscure!" ("Le Lac"); William Blake's "Little lamb, who made thee?" ("The Lamb"); or William Wordsworth's "Milton! Thou shouldst be living at this hour" ("London, 1802"). Some poetry critics have treated the term *apostrophe* as interchangeable with the term *address*, so including poetic speech not only to unhearing entities but to the listening beloved, friend, or patron or to contemp. or later readers. The narrower term is more useful, but, as with all varieties of poetic address, it is best to think in terms of prototypes rather than of sharp-edged categories. The term *apostrophe* originates in cl. oratory. An orator was felt to be addressing his audience at all times, such that there is no rhetorical term for address to the audience; *apostrophe* meant instead "turning aside" from the principal audience to address briefly someone or something else (Quintilian, *Institutio oratoria* 4.1.63–70). (The rhetorical trad. does not distinguish between hearing and unhearing addressees; that distinction emerges only in recent poetry crit.) Such side addresses in oratory were said to convey pathos (as in the cry of *Julius Caesar*'s Mark Antony, "O judgment! thou art fled to brutish beasts"), as poetic apostrophe often does too (John Donne's "Full nakedness! All joys are due to thee," *Elegy* 19). Overlap with the figure of exclamation or ecphonesis is frequent. Dupriez suggests that apostrophe "is rhetorical when one of its elements is unexpected" and characterizes the pretense of address to the unhearing as one form this unexpectedness may take.

In mod. poetry crit., Culler's seminal essay "Apostrophe" highlighted the potential embarrassment in apostrophe's excess of pretense or pathos, seeing in this figure of speech the wager that one can pull off this extravagant verbal gesture and so be proven as the poet one claims to be. To cry "O" to something insentient is self-consciously to stage a drama of the self calling. Culler can thus identify apostrophic invocation as a trope of poetic vocation, the self's performance of itself. Positing, moreover, an opposition between narrative temporality and lyric timelessness, he styles *lyric in general as "the triumph of the apostrophic" because poetic hailing seeks to become an event itself rather than to narrate events.

Numerous critics have responded to Culler. Several have built on the suggestion (also found in de Man's essays) that apostrophe is closely linked to *prosopopoeia, making the inanimate speak; others introduce historical considerations, such as different eras' practices of public utterance or familiarity with rhetorical models. It is also important to recognize differences among apostrophes. For the pathos of address to the unhearing may be of a different kind, not embarrassing but moving, when the unhearing addressee is (as in Elizabeth Bishop's "Insomnia" or "One Art") a forsaking lover who will, to the poet's grief, never read her poem, or (as in Catullus's elegy for his brother, poem 101) not a great figure in hist. but the poet's own loved dead.

*See* MONOLOGUE, RHETORIC AND POETRY.

■ P. de Man, "Autobiography as De-Facement," *The Rhetoric of Romanticism* (1984) and "Lyrical Voice in Contemporary Theory: Riffaterre and Jauss," *Lyric Poetry: Beyond New Criticism*, ed. C. Hošek and P. Parker (1985); B. Johnson, "Apostrophe, Animation, and Abortion," *A World of Difference* (1987); J. Hollander, "Poetic Imperatives," *Melodious Guile: Fictive Pattern in Poetic Language* (1988); B. Dupriez, *A Dictionary of Literary Devices*, trans. A. W. Halsall (1991); J. D. Kneale, "Romantic Aversions: Apostrophe Reconsidered," *ELH* 58 (1991); J. Culler, "Apostrophe," *The Pursuit of Signs,* rev. ed. (2002); Lausberg; W. Waters, *Poetry's Touch: On Lyric Address* (2003); H. Dubrow, *The Challenges of Orpheus* (2008).

W. WATERS

**APPRECIATION.** A term widely used in anglophone countries, esp. in the first half of the 20th c. to denote both a cognitive awareness of the aesthetic qualities of a work of fine art or lit. and also the act of interpretation that expresses such awareness. It is a fairly recent addition to the critical lexicon: the word does not appear in Samuel Johnson's *Dictionary,* and its pre-1800 usage, as recorded in the *OED,* is mainly nonartistic (e.g., economic and strategic), referring, as the etymology suggests, to the estimation of true worth. In its new applications to art and lit. in the first half of the 19th c., however, it moves away from evaluation and judgment toward "the perception of delicate impressions or distinctions" and "the sympathetic recognition of excellence." F. D. Maurice, e.g., described the best kind of crit. as that "cordial, genial appreciation" that "delights to draw forth the sense and beauty of a book, and is . . . in sympathy with the heart of the writer." The term thence evolves in tandem with the older concept of *taste, which undergoes a similar shift of meaning from a capacity for correctly judging a work of lit. to a capacity for understanding and enjoying it. Taste and appreciation were explicitly connected by R. G. Moulton, who defined appreciation as the exercise of taste without judgment. In his distinction between "inductive" and "judicial" crit., appreciation is identified with the former and signifies both the cultivation of enjoyment and a practice of holistic interpretation of individual works, esp. appropriate for teaching vernacular lit. in schools and universities. William Henry Hudson embraced and advocated Moulton's positive concept of appreciation but argued that evaluation could not be rigidly excluded.

Appreciation was sometimes used to denote an "aestheticist" crit.—impressionistic, emotional, and digressive, in the style of Walter Pater—hence, a foil for the analytically rigorous or socially engaged critical modes of the early 20th c., though figures like T. S. Eliot, W. K. Wimsatt, and F. R. Leavis still used the term in a neutral or positive sense, and William Empson explicitly distinguished "appreciative" and "analytical" crit. as complementary components of interpretation.

In the 1930s, appreciation was frequently the subject of psychological experiments seeking to establish its characteristics as a mental state or cognitive act (Griffiths). Its main significance for most of the 20th c., however, was as the widely accepted goal of literary pedagogy. Many "guides" and "introductions" to literary appreciation were published in Eng. speaking countries, ca. 1910–70, typically offering a methodical training in understanding, responding to, and interpreting canonical literary works; imputing aesthetic autonomy and unity to the work for the purpose of such analysis; and placing relatively little emphasis on critical evaluation as such. In many cases (e.g., Muel-

ler, Osborne) accounts of literary appreciation were enriched by highlighting its similarities and continuities with the (less contested) practices of appreciation in music and the visual arts.

Since the 1960s, appreciation has fallen foul of the "suspicious hermeneutics" of ideological crit. and poststructuralist theory. There have been indications, however, of a revival of both critical and philosophical interest in literary aesthetics and appreciation (Feagin, Ricks).

*See* AESTHETICISM, CRITICISM, INTERPRETATION, TASTE.

■ F. D. Maurice, "On Critics," *The Friendship of Books and Other Essays* (1874); R. G. Moulton, "Principles of Inductive Criticism," *Shakespeare as a Dramatic Artist* (1885); W. Pater, *Appreciations* (1889); W. H. Hudson, *An Introduction to the Study of Literature* (1910); F. H. Hayward, *The Lesson in Appreciation* (1915); Empson; D. C. Griffiths, *The Psychology of Literary Appreciation* (1932); J. H. Mueller, E. G. Moll, N. B. Zane, and K. Hevner, *Studies in Appreciation of Art* (1934); P. Gurrey, *The Appreciation of Poetry* (1935); H.L.B. Moody, *Literary Appreciation* (1968); H. Osborne, *The Art of Appreciation* (1970); S. L. Feagin, *Reading with Feeling* (1996); C. Ricks, *Essays in Appreciation* (1996).

P. J. BUCKRIDGE

## ARABIC POETICS

I. Classical
II. Modern

**I. Classical.** The first Ar. works on poetics were composed at the end of the 9th and beginning of the 10th c. Four groups of scholars were in varying degrees instrumental in shaping this new literary genre: the experts on ancient poetry, the poets and critics of mod. poetry (for ancient versus mod., see below), the Qur'anic scholars, and the (Aristotelian) logicians. Earlier, the pre-Islamic poets very likely had had a professional lang. for technical features of their poetry, and there are reports about comparative evaluation of poets, but none of this amounts to an explicit *ars poetica.*

In the field of poetry, two devels. are noteworthy. First, ancient, (i.e., pre- and early Islamic) poetry became canonized as a corpus of cl. texts. This meant that ancient poetry was considered a repository of correct and authoritative speech. As such, it became the domain of the philologists, who, around the middle of the 8th c., began to collect the extant poetry into *dīwāns* and anthols.; to these they later added interlinear glosses on lexical and grammatical matters. Once the task of editing and writing commentaries had been mostly achieved, we do find one book that may be called a grammarian's poetics: the *Qawā'id al-shi'r* (Foundations of Poetry) ascribed to the Kufan grammarian Tha'lab (d. 291/904—dates refer to the Muslim and the Common eras, respectively). This is a logically arranged collection of technical terms often provided with definitions and always exemplified with a number of *shawāhid* (evidentiary verses). Significantly, it starts with an enumeration of four basic types of sentences (command, prohibition, report, question) that are introduced as the "foundations of poetry," and it ends with a verse typology based on the syntactic independence or interdependence of the two *hemistichs of the line in which the highest aesthetic value is accorded those lines that have two independently meaningful hemistichs. This atomistic approach to the study and evaluation of poetry prevails in most of the theoretical lit.

The second notable event that had a decisive (indeed, greater) effect on the devel. of poetics and literary theory was the rise, around the middle of the 8th c., of a new school of poetry: the *muḥdathūn* (moderns). By contrasting them with their forebears, the *qudamāʾ* (ancients), critics and theorists became aware of some of the basic dichotomies in poetry. It should be noted, however, that the model of ancient poetry was never seriously challenged, which meant that the innovations of the moderns leaned toward *mannerism and relied heavily on earlier poetry. Critical discussions focused on a phenomenon called *badīʿ*—literally, "new, original, newly invented." The earliest attestations of the word suggest that it was originally used to refer to a special type of *metaphor (imaginary ascriptions such as "the *claws* of death") that played an important role in the poetic technique of the moderns, who created some outrageous—and severely criticized—specimens (e.g., "the eyes of religion were cooled," meaning that the Islamic armies were victorious). However, the term soon spread to other figures of speech. The poet Ibn al-Muʿtazz (d. 296/908), who devoted the first monograph to this topic, *Kitāb al-Badīʿ* (The Book of the Novel [Style]), proposed five figures to be covered by the term—metaphors of the kind just mentioned, *paronomasia, *antithesis, *epanalepsis (or *epanadiplosis*, and playful dialectics imitating theological jargon. The main goal of his book is to demonstrate that the *badīʿ* phenomena are not new but can be found already in ancient poetry as well as in the Qurʾan and in wisdom aphorisms; it is only their exaggerated use that is truly new.

Coming from one of the foremost poets of his time, this line of argument obviously served to legitimize the use of badīʿ. Ibn al-Muʿtazz's book became influential in several ways: (1) the discipline dealing with rhetorical figures was named "the science of badīʿ" after the title of his book; (2) the discovery of legitimizing precedent in ancient texts, esp. the Qurʾan, became commonplace, and as a result, the system of the rhetorical figures came to be considered an integral and static part of the lang.: their proliferation in later rhetorical works was thus thought to be due to closer analysis rather than new invention; (3) the emphasis on figures of speech as the central concern of literary theory originated here; and (4) the difference between poetry and prose in most respects, save the purely formal one, was considered unimportant.

The result of factor (4) in particular meant that, although works on literary theory—mostly rhetorical in outlook—continued to be produced, works on poetics proper tended to become the exception. Two of them were composed by younger contemporaries of Ibn al-Muʿtazz, one by the poet Ibn Ṭabāṭabā (d. 322/934),

titled *ʿIyār al-shiʿr* (The Standard of Poetry), the other by the state scribe and logician Qudāma ibn Jaʿfar (d. after 320/932). Although Ibn Ṭabāṭabā did not use the word *badīʿ* in its technical sense, he is well aware of the predicament of the moderns, who can no longer simply utter truths, as did the ancients, but have to display their wits in a subtle treatment of well-known motifs. He is also remarkable for giving a step-by-step description of the production of a poem; this is quite rare because works on poetics usually offer theories of poetic crit. rather than *artes poeticae* in the strict sense.

This characterization is esp. true of Qudāma's poetics, which the author describes as the first book on the "science of the good and the bad in poetry" and aptly titles *Naqd al-shiʿr* (The Assaying of Poetry). His work is at the same time the first representative of the third approach to literary theory (besides the grammatical and the poetic already mentioned), namely, that of the logician in the Aristotelian trad. This characterization refers, however, less to the content than to the structure and presentation of his work: he starts with a definition ("Poetry is metrical, rhymed utterance pointing to a meaning") that yields the four constitutive elements: meter, rhyme, wording, and meaning. He then discusses first the good qualities of these elements and their combinations, followed by the bad. Although Qudāma was much quoted by later authors, his "foreign" method did not find followers.

The controversies about the mod. poets' use of badīʿ, though reflected in theory, can more accurately be gauged from works of applied crit. such as the books devoted to the controversial "rhetorical" poets Abū Tammām (d. 231/845) and al-Mutanabbī (d. 354/965). The major topics that emerge are the following: (1) The relationship between *ṭabʿ* (natural talent) and *ṣanʿa* (artful or artificial crafting). The latter term came to mean the application of badīʿ to the motif at hand. According to taste and predilection, some considered this *takalluf* (*constraint, artificiality), while others pointed to the element of *taʿjīb* (causing amazement) that it imparted to well-known motifs. Given the general drift toward mannerism, this was a much sought-after effect. (2) The role of *lafẓ* (wording) versus *maʿnā* (meaning) in poetry. Already at the end of the 8th c., a consensus had been reached that poetry was to be judged by its wording, since the meaning was nothing but the material to be shaped. Some authorities are said to have given precedence to the meaning, but on closer inspection, it appears that they intended the *maʿnā al-ṣanʿa* (the special meaning created by the application of a figure of speech; this comes close to the *conceit in Western *mannerist poetry and thus did not undermine the priority of the wording. (3) The relationship between poetry and reality, whether *ṣidq* (truth) or *kadhib* (falsehood). In general, poetry is presumed to depict reality mimetically. Obvious "falsehoods" such as imaginary metaphors and *hyperboles, therefore, tended to provoke objections on the part of the critics. Such figures became so predominant in later Abbasid poetry, however, that some theorists (Ibn Fāris, Ibn Ḥazm) posited falsehood as one of the constituent elements of poetry. (4) Regarding the question of *sariqa* (plagiarism), although this word means "theft" and originally denoted flagrant literary larceny, with the increasing tendency toward mannerism in mod. poetry, sariqa became a way of life, and the disreputable connotation of the term gave way to the more neutral one of "taking over" (an earlier motif); critics even began to talk of "good sariqas." Taking over an earlier poet's motif and improving on it, mostly by the application of badīʿ, constituted an *istiḥqāq* (better claim [to that motif]), for which the poet earned high praise.

Ar. poetics, fostered by the rise of mod. poetry, soon experienced something like arrested growth. The work of the Qurʾanic scholar and grammarian al-Rummānī (d. 384/994), *al-Nukat fī iʿjāz al-Qurʾān* (Thoughtful Remarks on the Inimitability of the Qurʾan), in which he undertook to prove this dogma on the basis of the Qurʾan's *balāgha* (eloquence), soon began to influence works on poetics and rhetorical figures. The first major compilation that resulted, the *Kitāb al-ṣināʿatayn* (Book of the Two Crafts [i.e., poetry and prose]) by Abū Hilāl al-ʿAskarī (d. 395/1004), expressly mentions proving the inimitability of the Qurʾan as its main goal and makes extensive use of al-Rummānī's work. The confluence of the two different technical terminologies, *Qurʾanic* and *poetic*, at first created a notable confusion that was only gradually eliminated, esp. by the greatest of all Ar. literary theorists, ʿAbd al-Qāhir al-Jurjānī (d. 471/1078). In his *Asrār al-balāgha* (The Mysteries of Eloquence), he tried to establish a clear and unambiguous taxonomy for the theory of *imagery (*simile, analogy, metaphor based on simile, metaphor based on analogy); and for the first time, he finds, designates, and describes the phenomenon of *takhyīl* (fantastic interpretation, i.e., inventing imaginary causes, effects, and proofs, often on the basis of metaphors taken literally)—which is so characteristic of later Abbasid poetry. Although not a comprehensive work on poetics, the "Mysteries" certainly is the most sustained effort to reach to the core of Ar. poetry.

Al-Jurjānī's books, the one just mentioned and his *Dalāʾil al-iʿjāz* (Signs for the Inimitability), were later reworked into parts of the scholastic *ʿilm al-balāgha* (science of eloquence) which, from the 13th c. on, dominated the teaching of rhet.—consisting of stylistics, theory of imagery, and figures of speech—in the institutions of higher learning. Poetics was thus incorporated into a discipline that served the religious purpose of demonstrating the inimitability of the Qurʾan, whence it ceased to exist in its own right.

Some theoretical and critical works were produced outside the Qurʾanic trad. One of them, *al-ʿUmda* (The Pillar), by the poet Ibn Rashīq (d. 456/1063 or later), deserves to be cited as a comprehensive handbook for poets that contains well-informed accounts of all the major topics in poetics mentioned above.

A fascinating, though not very influential, sideline of the lit. on poetics was created by Maghribi authors of the late 13th c., who, to various degrees, showed interest in "logical" poetics, i.e., the Aristotelean *Rhetoric* and *Poetics* as part of the *Organon*, a late Alexandrian trad. that was adopted into Ar. logical writings. The most sophisticated among these authors is Ḥāzim al-Qarṭājannī (d. 1285), who adopted the two central terms of logical poetics, "creation of images in the mind of the listener" (*takhyīl*) and "imitating the object of the poem by means of artful description" (*muḥākāt*), in order to identify the cornerstones of the poetic enterprise.

**II. Modern.** From the 13th to the 18th c., Ar. poetics tended to reflect the priorities of the audience for the lit. of the period: the intellectual elite at the various centers of political authority. Elaborating on earlier devels. in poetics, commentators and anthologizers placed primary emphasis on the formalities of rhet. and the compilation of ever-expanding lists of poetic devices and themes. It was the task of pioneers in the 19th c., such as Ḥusayn al-Marṣafī (1815–90), to revive interest in the great cl. works of poetics. However, such exercises in neoclassical revival gradually receded into the background, superseded by the increasing domination of Western literary genres and critical approaches.

From the first intimations of what has been termed *preromanticism* with poets such as Khalīl Muṭrān (1872–1949), Ar. poetry and poetics have undergone what Jabrā has termed a series of "rapid chain explosions of Eur. culture." The poetics of *romanticism are reflected in works such as *Al-Ghurbāl* by Mīkhāʾīl Nuʿayma (1889–1988) and *Al-Dīwān* by two Egyptian critics, Al-ʿAqqād (1889–1964) and al-Māzinī (ca. 1889–1949). The application of Western critical approaches, predominantly Fr. and Eng., to the lit. is also evident in the writings of critics such as Ṭāhā Ḥusayn (1889–1973), Mārūn ʿAbbūd (1886–1962), and Muḥammad Mandūr (1907–65).

Following World War II and the achievement of independence by many Arab nations, lit. of "commitment" (*iltizām*) became *de rigueur* and was much reflected in critical writings. The Lebanese literary periodical *Al-ādāb*, founded by Suhayl Idrīs in Beirut in 1953, had "commitment" as its major guiding force and continues to serve as a major conduit and catalyst for trends in mod. Ar. poetics. In that role, it has since been joined by a number of other jours., most prominent among which is *Fuṣūl*, pub. in Cairo. More recently, growing interest in literary theory, ling., and folklore has led to significant changes in approach to the Ar. literary trad. as a whole. Numerous Western studies in semiotics (see SEMIOTICS AND POETRY), *structuralism, *poststructuralism, *postcolonial poetics, *feminist crit., and reception theory (see READER RESPONSE) have been read by Arab critics either in the original or in the rapidly increasing library of such works in trans. The emergence of these new disciplines and approaches can be seen in the publication of critical and theoretical studies that not only reconsider the nature and precepts of the Ar. literary *canon (e.g., in the realms of popular narrative and prosody) but address genres from all periods of the trad. in entirely new ways. In a number of works, the major poet-critic Adūnis (pseud. of Ali Ahmad Said Asbar, b. 1930?) has devoted himself to a detailed investigation of the issue of modernity itself and the reinterpretation of the past. In his writings and those of many others, this process, at once highly controversial and stimulating, continues to have a profound effect on both the poetic trad. and on attitudes toward the adoption of various modes of interpretation.

In 1972, Adūnis was reflecting a cultural trad. of long standing in titling one of his studies *Zaman al-shi'r* (Poetry's Time). In such a context, it may be seen as a deliberate indication of a shift in that trad. that, in 1999, the Egyptian critic Jābir 'Usfūr (Gaber Asfour) published a work on the novel titled *Zaman al-riwāya* (The Novel's Time). The predominance of visual media in the societies of the Ar.-speaking world has indeed led to a change of balance in the markets for poetic and narrative modes of expression. There has been a concomitant rise of critical interest in the study of narratology, at the hands of scholars such as Sa'īd Yaqṭīn (Morocco), 'Usfūr (Egypt), Yumnā al-'Īd (Lebanon), and Faysal Darrāj (Palestine and Syria), among many others. In the realm of poetry and poetics, a relatively new phenomenon has been a critical concentration on more popular forms of poetic expression and their modes of performance and reception.

■ **I. Classical:** I. Goldziher, "Alte und neue Poesie im Urtheile der arabischen Kritiker," *Abhandlungen zur arabischen Philologie* 1 (1896, rpt. 1982), ch. 2; G. E. von Grunebaum, "Arabic Literary Criticism in the 10th Century A.D.," *JAOS* 61 (1941); and "The Concept of Plagiarism in Arabic Theory," *Journal of Near Eastern Studies* 3 (1944); *A Tenth-Century Document of Arabic Literary Theory and Criticism: The Sections on Poetry of al-Bāqillāni's I'jāz al-Qur'ān*, ed. G. E. von Grunebaum (1950); A. Trabulsi, *La Critique poétique des Arabes jusqu'au Ve siècle de l'Hégire (XIe siècle de J.-C.)* (1955); I. Y. Krachkovsky, "Deux Chapitres inédits de l'oeuvre de Kratchkovsky sur Ibn al-Mu'tazz," *Annales de l'Institut des Études Orientales* (Algiers) 20 (1962); W. Heinrichs, *Arabische Dichtung und griechische Poetik* (1969), and "Literary Theory—the Problem of Its Efficiency," *Arabic Poetics: Theory and Development*, ed. G. E. Von Grunebaum (1973); S. A. Bonebakker, *Materials for the History of Arabic Rhetoric from the Ḥilyat al-muḥāḍara of Ḥātimī* (1975); J. E. Bencheikh, *Poétique arabe* (1975)—additional preface, 1989; V. Cantarino, *Arabic Poetics in the Golden Age* (1975)—anthol. in trans., with introductory essays often ignorant of earlier lit.; W. Heinrichs, *The Hand of the Northwind: Opinions on Metaphor and the Early Meaning of Isti'āra in Arabic Poetics* (1977); K. Abu Deeb, *Al-Jurjānī's Theory of Poetic Imagery* (1979); G. J. van Gelder, *Beyond the Line: Classical Arabic Literary Critics on the Coherence and Unity of the Poem* (1982); A. Arazi, "Une Épître d'Ibrāhīm ben Hilāl alSābī' sur les genres littéraires," *Studies in Islamic History and Civilization in Honour of David Ayalon*, ed. M. Sharon (1986); I. 'Abbās, *Ta'rīkh al-naqd al-adabī 'ind al-'arab*, rev. ed. (1993); W. Heinrichs: "*Takhyīl*: Make-Believe and Image Creation in Arabic Literary Theory," *Takhyīl: The Imaginary in Classical Arabic Poetics*, Part 1: *Texts*, ed. and trans. G. J. van Gelder and M. Hammond; Part 2: *Stud-*

*ies*, ed. G. J. van Gelder and M. Hammond (2008); W. Heinrichs, "Early Ornate Prose and the Rhetorization of Poetry in Arabic Literature," *Literary and Philosophical Rhetoric in the Greek, Roman, Syriac, and Arabic Worlds*, ed. F. Woerther (2009).

■ **II. Modern:** D. Semah, *Four Modern Egyptian Critics* (1974); Adūnis, *Al-Thābit wa-al-mutanawwil*, 3 v. (1974–79); S. al-Jayyusi, *Trends and Movements in Modern Arabic Poetics* (1977); I. J. Boullata, "Adūnis: Revolt in Modern Arabic Poetics," *Edebiyât* 2 (1977); J. Jabrā, "Modern Arabic Literature and the West," *Critical Perspectives on Modern Arabic Literature*, ed. I. J. Boullata (1980); Adūnis, *Introduction to Arabic Poetics*, trans. C. Cobham (1990); I. J. Boullata, *Trends and Issues in Contemporary Arab Thought* (1990); S. Somekh, *Genre and Language in Modern Arabic Literature* (1991); R. Snir, *Modern Arabic Literature: A Functional Dynamic Model* (2001); *Arabischen Literatur postmodern*, ed. A. Neuwirth, A. Pflitsch, B. Winckler (2004).

W. P. HEINRICHS (CL.); R.M.A. ALLEN (MOD.)

## ARABIC POETRY

I. Introduction
II. 6th to 13th Centuries
III. 13th to 18th Centuries
IV. 19th and 20th Centuries

**I. Introduction.** Until relatively recently, poetry has served as the predominant mode of literary expression among those who speak and write in Ar. Poetry was, in the traditional phrase, "*dīwān al-'arab*," the register of the Arabs, and poets had and continue to have a particular status in their own community. The Ar. word for poetry, *shi'r*, is derived from the verb denoting a special kind of knowledge that was believed in the earliest times to have magical or mantic properties. While poetry has afforded poets the opportunity for personal expression, it has been more often than not a *public* phenomenon, whether addressed to the tribe of ancient times, the patron during the predominance of the caliphate and the many dynasties of the med. Islamic world, or the many political causes of the present-day Middle East.

Most hists. of Ar. poetry have adopted a dynastic approach based primarily on political and social devels., concentrating mainly on the poets, their role in society, and their themes. This approach serves to illustrate the close links between poetry and poetics on the one hand and divisions of the Islamic sciences on the other. However, while biblio. sources provide evidence of the richness of the trad. available to us, they also make clear not only that large amounts of poetry are lost to us but that much more poetry remains unpublished and unassessed within the critical canon. Further, the hist. of Ar. poetry has recently been undergoing a reevaluation, based on two interlinked phenomena. First, Ar. poetry itself has been going through a period of transformation and radical experimentation since the beginning of the 1950s: this process has led some critics to attempt a redefinition of what poetry is (or should be) and therefrom to initiate projects aimed at a reassessment of the corpus of cl. Ar. poetry. Second, critics have applied new ideas in analysis and theory—e.g., *structuralism, oral-formulaic and *genre theories, and metrics—to the corpus of Ar. poetry.

## II. 6th to 13th Centuries

**A. *The Beginnings: Oral Tradition*.** What have been recorded as the beginnings of Ar. poetry are versions of a poetic corpus that is already highly developed in the late 5th c. CE. The trad. is an oral one, similar to that of the Homeric poems and Serbo-Croatian songs analyzed by Milman Parry and Albert Lord (see ORAL-FORMULAIC THEORY). Thus, each poem or rather the differing versions of each poem represent a single, isolated yet privileged point in a long process of devel. and transmission from poet to reciter (*rāwī*). Each poem would have been performed before an audience (perhaps accompanied by music or rhythmic beat) and transmitted through generations from one "singer of tales" to another.

**B. *The Poet*.** The ability to improvise was (and often still is) part of the craft of Arab poets. Many occasions would arise at which they would extemporize a poem or recite a work from memory. They were important members of the tribe, in effect propagandists, whose role was to extol the tribal virtues—bravery, loyalty, endurance, swiftness of vengeance—and to lampoon the lack of such virtues in the tribe's enemies. The various thematic "genres" used—eulogy, *elegy, and *satire—all concerned praise or its antithesis (see EPIDEICTIC POETRY). The elegy (*rithā'*) provides some of the most moving examples of the poetic voice, as in the poems of al-Khansā' (d. ca. 644) for her brother, Ṣakhr, killed in tribal combat:

> I was sleepless and I passed the night
>     keeping vigil, as if my eyes had
>     been anointed with pus,
> For I had heard—and it was not news
>     to rejoice me—one making a report,
>     who had come repeating intelligence,
> Saying, "Sakhr is dwelling there in a
>     tomb, struck to the ground beside
>     the grave, between certain stones."
>
> (trans. A. J. Arberry)

The poet used the different genres to depict companionship, the benefits of tribal solidarity, the beauties of women, the qualities of animals, and the joys of wine. Part of this same environment, but from a different social perspective, were several vagabond *ṣuʿlūk* poets such as al-Shanfarā (d. ca. 525), his companion Thābit ibn Jābir (known by his nickname, Taʾabbaṭa Sharran [he who has put evil under his armpit]), and ʿUrwa ibn al-Ward (d. ca. 594). Ostracized from tribal society, they and their peers wrote stirring odes about their ability to withstand prolonged isolation, hunger, and thirst and their feelings of affinity with the wilder

animals of the desert, as in this extract from the poem rhyming on the consonant "l" by al-Shanfarā:

> To me now, in your default, are
>     comrades a wolf untired,
> A sleek leopard, and a fell hyena with
>     shaggy mane.
> True comrades: they ne'er let out the
>     secret in trust with them,
> Nor basely forsake their friend because
>     he brought them bane.
>
> (trans. R. A. Nicholson)

In contrast to this stark vision of life stands that of the courts of the Ghassanids, the tribe that served as a buffer between the Arabs and Byzantium, and the Lakhmids, who fulfilled the same function vis-à-vis Sasanid Iran from their center at al-Ḥīra (in present-day Iraq). To these courts would come not only tribal poets but professional bards like Ṭarafa ibn al-ʿAbd (d. ca. 565) and Maymūn al-Aʿshā (d. 629) in search of patronage and reward for their eulogies.

**C. *The Structure of the Poem*.** The process of oral transmission and the later recording of poetry in written form have not preserved the stages in the early devel. of the Ar. poem. Thus, we find examples of both the short, monothematic poem (*qiṭʿa) and the multi-sectional, polythematic *qaṣīda. Several examples of the latter came to be highly valued, esp. by the early Muslim caliphs and the ruling Arab aristocracy, which regarded these poems as a source and standard for the study and teaching of the cl. Ar. lang. Seven (and later ten) of the longer odes were gathered into what became the most famous collection of early Ar. poetry, the *Muʿallaqāt*. The *Muʿallaqa* of Imruʾ al-Qays (d. ca. 540) is the most famous poem in the collection and indeed probably in all of Ar. lit. Yet each *Muʿallaqa* manages to reflect its poet's vision of life in pre-Islamic Arabia: that of Zuhayr ibn Abī Sulmā is placed within the context of settling a tribal dispute, while the ode of Labīd (d. ca. 662), with its elaborate animal imagery and concluding aphorisms, is virtually a hymn to tribal values.

Recent analyses of some examples of the pre-Islamic *qaṣīda* have challenged the received view that its structure is fragmented, a view canonized in part by the conservative critical trad. of ʿamūd al-shiʿr (the essentials of poetry). It is now suggested that the choice and ordering of the various segments of these poems reflect the poet's desire to illustrate by conjunction and opposition the glaring contrasts in community life, making these elaborate poems a public event of almost liturgical significance. Thus, the *nasīb* (erotic prelude) of many poems will often be placed within the context of the *aṭlāl*, the section describing the poet's arrival at a deserted encampment. The opening lines of the *Muʿallaqa* of Imruʾ al-Qays are esp. famous: "Halt (you two) and let us weep for memory of a beloved and an abode / In the edge of the sand dune between ad-Dakhul and Hawmal." A transitional section describing a departure or desert journey allows the poet to give a description of his riding animal, which is often elaborate and lengthy, and provides some of the most memorable lines from this corpus of poetry. From this interweaving of segments, the poet will then turn—often by means of aphoristic sentiments—to the purpose of the poem: the bolstering of the community through praise of its virtues, criticism of contraventions of them, and sheer self-aggrandizement as a means of fostering tribal pride and solidarity.

D. *The Advent of Islam*. While the advent of Islam brought about radical changes in beliefs and customs in the society of the Arabian Peninsula, the poetic environment changed relatively little. Muhammad himself was not averse to poetry, as sections of *Kitāb al-aghānī* make abundantly clear. Indeed, Ḥassān ibn Thābit (d. 673) is known as "the poet of the Prophet." His contemporary, Kaʿb ibn Zuhayr, the son of the famous pre-Islamic bard Zuhayr ibn Abī Sulmā, composed a famous poem addressed to Muhammad that illustrates the continuation of the poetic trad. into the new social context; the poem is called *al-Burda* (The Cloak), since, upon hearing it, Muhammad is alleged to have placed his cloak around the poet:

> I was told that the Messenger of Allah
> threatened me (with death), but
> with the Messenger of Allah I have
> hope of finding pardon.
> Gently! mayst thou be guided by Him
> who gave thee the gift of the Koran,
> wherein are warnings and a plain
> setting-out (of the matter).
>
> (trans. R. A. Nicholson)

The spirit of defiance in the face of imminent danger and even death that characterizes much pre-Islamic poetry is also to be found in the odes of poets belonging to groups that broke away from the incipient Muslim community on religious grounds and fought vigorously for their conception of Islam. The poetry of the supporters of the Kharijite cause, such as al-Ṭirimmāḥ (d. ca. 723), and of the Shīʿa, such as Al-Kumayt ibn Zayd (d. 743), is esp. noteworthy in this regard. The pre-Islamic penchant for satire of rivals and enemies finds fertile ground in the tribal squabbles that continue well into the period of the Umayyads (660–750). In a series of increasingly ribald satires (gathered into a collection known as *Al-Naqāʾiḍ*), the poets Jarīr (d. 732) and Al-Farazdaq (d. ca. 730), joined among others by the Christian poet Al-Akhṭal (d. 710), followed the pattern of earlier satirical poetry in both form and imagery and adopted rhetorical strategies characteristic of verbal dueling in the Arab world.

E. *The Emergence of New Genres*. The oral transmission of poetry continued into the Islamic period, ensuring that the Arab poet's attachment to many of the themes and images of the desert lingered long after such environments were superseded by the emerging urban centers of the Muslim community. Thus, Dhū al-Rumma (d. 735) was often referred to as "the last of the poets" because he continued to use desert motifs in his poems

a century after the advent of Islam. Inevitably, however, the gradual process of change led to the emergence of new priorities expressed in different ways. On the political level, the changes were far-reaching. During the first century or so of Islam, Muslim armies took the religion to the borders of India in the east and across North Africa to Spain in the west. The center of caliphal authority moved out of the Arabian Peninsula first to Damascus under the Umayyads and then to the newly founded city of Baghdad in 756 under the Abbasids. Under the impetus of this vast exercise in cultural assimilation, authors from different areas of the Islamic world began to adapt the traditional Ar. literary forms and to introduce new themes and genres.

Various segments of the *qaṣīda* gradually evolved into distinct genres. The collected works of poets composed during the first century of Islam begin to contain separate sections devoted to specific categories: hunt poems (*ṭardiyyāt*) and wine poems (*khamriyyāt*)—both of these most notably in the verse of Al-Ḥasan ibn Hāniʾ (d. ca. 810), usually known by his nickname, Abū Nuwās. His wine poetry is noted not only for its disarming lasciviousness but for how he occasionally parodies the desert imagery of the earlier poetry:

> The lovelorn wretch stopped at a
> (deserted) camping-ground to
> question it, and I stopped to enquire
> after the local tavern.
> May Allah not dry the eyes of him that
> wept over stones, and may He not
> ease the pain of him that yearns to
> a tent-peg.
>
> (trans. R. A. Nicholson)

The blind poet Bashshār ibn Burd (d. 784) displayed a similar impatience with Arabian conventions, though in his case it is linked to a desire to express pride in his own Persian ancestry. Another poet of the period, Abū al-Atāhiya (d. 828), is primarily remembered for his moral and ascetic poems (*zuhdiyyāt*).

One of the most remarkable devels. along these lines is that of the love poem (*\*ghazal*). Soon after the advent of Islam, two distinct trends appear in the Arabian Peninsula. The first, emerging from within the tribal poetic trad., placed the aloof and imperious beloved on a pedestal while the poet suffered the pangs of love from a distance, often leading to a love-death. This trad. is termed *ʿUdhrī* after the Banu ʿUdhra tribe, noted for having many such lovers, among whom was Jamīl (d. 701), one of the most illustrious exponents of ʿUdhrī poetry. Each of these love poets also carried the name of his beloved: Jamīl, e.g., is Jamīl Buthayna, the beloved of Buthayna; other poets of this type are Kuthayyir ʿAzza (d. 723) and, most famous of all, Majnūn Laylā. The other trad., sensual and self-centered, developed in the cities of the Ḥijāz; it is usually associated with its most famous exponent ʿUmar ibn Abī Rabīʿa (d. 719). With the gradual devel. of the genre, the two separate strands fused, as can be seen in the works of poets such as ʿAbbās ibn al-Aḥnaf (d. ca. 807) in the east and Ibn

'Abd Rabbihi (d. 940) in al-Andalus (as Islamic Spain was known).

**F. *The Badī' Style: Imagery and Rhetoric*.** During the caliphate of 'Uthmān (d. 644), a generally accepted version of the Qur'ān (Koran) was established in writing, a process that set in motion many intellectual currents later to have a profound effect on poetry. Scholars in Kūfa and Baṣra (both in present-day Iraq) began to prepare the materials needed for authenticating the transmission of the Qur'ān, interpreting its text, and codifying the Ar. lang. in which the sacred text proclaims itself to have been revealed. Anthols. of poetry of different genres and from particular tribes were made, a process that involved the devel. of basic critical terms for the evaluation of literary works. A philologist of Baṣra, Al-Khalīl ibn Aḥmad (d. 791), analyzed the sounds and rhythms of the earliest poetry and set down his results as a set of meters that formed part of a definition of poetry (as "rhymed and metered discourse") that was widely regarded as canonical up to the end of World War II (see ARABIC PROSODY). This philological activity was accompanied by a gradual shift away from the predominantly oral culture of pre-Islamic Arabia toward a society in which verbal art was committed to writing.

Within this environment of compilation, authentification, and analysis, there now emerges in Ar. poetry *badī'*, a term that literally means "innovative" but that involves a greater awareness of the potential uses of poetic imagery. The poet-caliph Ibn al-Mu'tazz (d. 908) wrote a famous analysis of the five most significant tropes (incl. simile and metaphor) entitled *Kitāb al-Badī'*, a work that took many of its examples from early poetry and the text of the Qur'ān. This was to be the first in an increasingly complex series of rhetorical analyses. The discussions that evolved around the subject of badī' were part of a dynamic period in the devel. of Islamic thought on religious, ethnic, ideological, and cultural issues. They also raised questions of literary taste and provoked fierce debate between proponents of the "new" (*muḥdathūn*) poets and the old. Much critical opprobrium was reserved for the poet Abū Tammām (d. 846), who was widely condemned for carrying the use of badī' to excessive lengths. At a later date, the great critic 'Abd al-Qāhir al-Jurjānī (d. 1078) pioneered the analysis of the psychological impact of imagery on the reader and thereby accentuated the originality of many of Abū Tammām's ideas, a verdict gaining increasing credence in modern crit.

With the growth of the bureaucracy at the caliph's court and the expansion of the Islamic dominions—accompanied almost automatically by the emergence of local potentates—plentiful sources of patronage became available to reward poets who would compose occasional poems. During the heyday of cl. Ar. poetry, many such centers existed: the Umayyads and their successors in al-Andalus; the Hamdanids in Aleppo, Syria; the Ikhshidids in Egypt; and the court in Baghdad. To all these centers poets would come in search of favor and reward. The poet who best exemplifies this

patronage system is al-Mutanabbī (d. 965). He composed poems for all kinds of occasions and for a number of rulers and patrons, some of whom are eulogized and later mercilessly lampooned. Developing the use of the badī' style and combining a superb control of the lang. with an innate sense of the gnomic phrase, he was soon widely regarded as the greatest of the cl. Ar. poets. His *Dīwān* (collected poetry) provides us with many splendid examples of the *qaṣīda* as occasional poem; his examples of eulogy (*madīḥ*) are among the most famous contributions to a genre that was a major form of verbal art in Arab civilization:

> Whither do you intend, great prince?
>    We are the herbs of the hills and
>    you are the clouds;
> We are the ones time has been miserly
>    towards respecting you, and the
>    days cheated of your presence.
> Whether at war or peace, you aim at
>    the heights, whether you tarry or
>    hasten.
>
> (trans. A. J. Arberry, 1965)

A great admirer of al-Mutanabbī's poetry was Abū al-'Alā' al-Ma'arrī (d. 1057). This blind poet and philosopher began by imitating his great predecessor, but his collection of poems entitled *Luzūm mā lā yalzam* (Requirement of the Nonrequired), the title of which reflects the fact that he imposes strict formal rules on himself, combines consummate skill in the use of poetic lang. with some of the most pessimistic sentiments to be found in the entire Ar. canon:

> Would that a lad had died in the very
>    hour of birth
> And never sucked, as she lay in child-
>    bed, his mother's breast!
> Her babe, it says to her or ever its
>    tongue can speak,
> "Nothing thou gett'st of me but sorrow
>    and bitter pain."
>
> (trans. R. A. Nicholson)

Three poets of al-Andalus from this period deserve particular mention: Ibn Shuhayd (d. 1035) and Ibn Ḥazm (d. 1063), both of whom contributed to crit. as well as to poetry; and Ibn Zaydūn (d. 1070), who celebrated his great love, the Umayyad Princess Wallāda, and then rued her loss to a rival at court. The Iberian Peninsula was also to contribute to Ar. poetry two strophic genres, the *muwashshaḥ* (see HEBREW PROSODY AND POETICS) and *zajal* (see ZÉJEL). The origins and prosodic features of both genres are the subject of continuing and intense debate. The final strophe or refrain known as the *\*kharja* (envoi) was originally a popular song in Romance or a mixture of Romance and Hispano-Ar. sung by a girl about her beloved:

> My beloved is sick for love of me.
> How can he not be so?

Do you not see that he is not allowed
    near me?

                   (trans. J. T. Monroe)

This refrain provides the rhyme scheme for the other strophes in the poem that are in literary Ar. Interspersed between them are other verses with separate rhymes. In the *zajal* genre, the colloquial lang. sometimes encountered in the *kharja* of the *muwashshaḥ* is used in the body of the poem itself. With its illustrious exponent Ibn Quzmān (d. 1159), the fame of the genre spread to the East.

As the corpus of poetics and rhet. increased in scope and complexity, poetry itself tended to become more stereotyped and convention-bound, e.g., the poetry of Ibn ʿArabī (d. 1240), one of the major figures in Islamic theology; the mystical poet Ibn al-Fāriḍ (d. 1235); and Bahāʾ al-Din Zuhayr, whose death in 1258 coincides with the capture of Baghdad by the Mongols, an event generally acknowledged as signaling the end of the cl. period in Islamic culture.

**III. 13th to 18th Centuries.** The era between the 13th and early 19th cs. has often been characterized as "the period of decadence," a designation that not only reflects the distaste of subsequent critics for poetry in which a penchant for verbal virtuosity and poetic tropes prevailed but serves to conceal a general lack of research that has until recently characterized scholarly interest in this lengthy period. These six centuries have often been subdivided into two subperiods: an earlier Mamluk period (13th–16th cs.) and an Ottoman (16th–early 19th cs.). While the poetic output of the latter period still remains largely unexplored, the example of the poetry of ʿAbd al-Ghanī al-Nābulusī (d. 1731) gives an indication of the riches that further research may reveal. Meanwhile, the poetic production of the Mamluk period clearly runs counter to the "decadent" label. The so-called Burda poem (after that of Kaʿb ibn Zuhayr) composed by al-Būṣīrī (ca. 1212–96) has for centuries found a wide audience within the mystical circles of popular Islam much in evidence throughout the period; concurrently in Spain, Ḥāzim al-Qarṭājannī (d. 1285) was not only a major contributor to the trad. of Ar. poetics but a poet in his own right. The Iraqi poet Ṣafī al-Din al-Ḥillī (d. 1349) not only wrote his own poetry but composed a study of the *muwashshaḥ* and *zajal*. Many of these poets were adept at composing verse full of embellishments, e.g., poems in which each word begins with the same letter or each word starts with the final grapheme of the previous word. This was indeed a period of verbal artifice but also one of compilation (incl. the major Ar. dictionaries) and explication. Ibn Mālik (d. 1274) composed a poem in 1,000 verses on Ar. grammar, a text that was still in use in Egyptian religious schools at the turn of the 20th c.

The limited size of the audience for the elite lit. just outlined may account for the considerable vigor of the popular literary trad. during these centuries. This is most evident in the greatest of all narrative collections, *1001 Nights*, as well as in other popular tales that contain large amounts of poetry in a variety of styles. And, while the trad. of popular poetry is sparsely documented, some intimations of its liveliness and variety can be gauged from the (albeit bawdy) poetry to be found in the shadow plays of the Egyptian oculist Ibn Dāniyāl (d. 1311).

**IV. 19th and 20th Centuries**

**A. *The Beginnings of the Modern Revival.*** The process whereby Ar. poetry enters a new phase is termed *al-nahḍa* (revival). Two principal factors are involved: what one scholar has termed "the Arab Rediscovery of Europe" on the one hand and a reexamination of the cl. trad. of Ar. poetry and poetics on the other. Esp. noteworthy figures in this revival are Rifāʿa al-Ṭahṭāwī (d. 1873) in Egypt, and Buṭrus al-Bustānī (d. 1883), Nāṣīf al-Yāzijī (d. 1871—who was particularly inspired by the poetry of al-Mutanabbī), and Aḥmad Fāris al-Shidyāq (d. 1887) in Lebanon.

**B. *Neoclassicism.*** Al-Mutanabbī was also the inspiration of one of the first major figures in the neoclassical movement, the Egyptian Maḥmūd Sāmī al-Bārūdī (d. 1904), who advocated a return to the directness and purity of cl. Ar. poetry and composed poems to illustrate his ideas. Within the chronology of its own mod. hist., every Arab country fostered neoclassical poets, e.g., the Egyptian Ḥāfez Ibrahim (d. 1932), the Iraqis Jamīl Ṣidqī al-Zahāwī (d. 1936) and Maʿrūf al-Ruṣāfī (d. 1945), and somewhat later, the Palestinian Ibrāhīm Ṭūqān (d. 1941). However, critical opinion is virtually unanimous in judging Aḥmad Shawqī (d. 1932) as the greatest poet of the neoclassical school. Whether in his stirring calls to the Egyptian people, his more personal descriptive verse, or his still-popular operettas, his superbly cadenced poetry seems destined to secure him a place in the pantheon of great Ar. poets. While recent devels. in Ar. poetry produced many changes, several poets continued to compose poetry in the traditional manner, esp. Muḥammad al-Jawāhirī, (d. 1997) Badawī al-Jabal (pseud. of Muḥammad Sulaymān al-Aḥmad, d. 1981), and Al-Akhṭal al-Ṣaghīr (pseud. of Bishāra al-Khūrī, d. 1968).

**C. *Romanticism.*** Signs of a reaction against the occasional nature of much neoclassical verse can be found in the works of the Lebanese poet Khalīl Muṭrān (d. 1949), although not so much in his own poetry as in his writings about poetry and particularly the intro. to his collected poems (1908). Full-blooded romanticism in Ar. poetry comes from the poets of *al-mahjar* (the émigré school), as the Arab poets of the Americas are called. While Amīn al-Rīḥānī (d. 1940) was certainly much admired in the Middle East, the undisputed leader of the northern group was Khalīl Jubrān (Kahlil Gibran; d. 1931), as famous for his works in Eng. as for those in Ar.:

Give me the flute and sing! Forget all
    that you and I have said

Talk is but dust in the air, so tell me of
your deeds.
                    (trans. M. Khouri and H. Algar)

Far removed from their native land, Jubrān and his colleagues, among whom were Mīkhā'īl Nu'ayma (b. 1889), Īliyyā Abū Māḍī (d. 1957), and Nasīb 'Arīḍa (d. 1946), proceeded to experiment with lang., form, and mood and, in so doing, introduced a new voice into Ar. poetry. Jubrān was also in constant touch with his fellow-countrymen in South America, among whom Fawzī Ma'lūf (d. 1930) is the most significant figure.

In the Middle East, the ideals of Eng. *romanticism were vigorously advocated by three Egyptian poets: al-'Aqqād, Ibrāhīm al-Māzinī (d. 1949), and 'Abd al-Raḥmān Shukrī (d. 1958). While all three wrote poetry, the primary function of the group was to criticize the neoclassical school in favor of a new, more individual role for the poet. The 1930s and 1940s were the heyday of romanticism in Ar. poetry. In 1932, Aḥmad Zakī abū-Shādī (d. 1955) founded the Apollo Society in Cairo, which published a magazine to which several poets, incl. Ibrāhīm Nājī (d. 1953), 'Alī Maḥmūd Ṭāhā (d. 1949), and the Tunisian Abū al-Qāsim al-Shābbī (d. 1934) made contributions. Among other important figures in the devel. of romantic Ar. poetry are 'Umar Abū Rīsha in Syria, Yūsuf Tījānī al-Bashīr (d. 1937) in the Sudan, and Ṣalāḥ Labakī (d. 1955) and Ilyās Abū Shabaka (d. 1947) in Lebanon. As a critic Labakī also devoted his attention to the devel. of a symbolist school of poetry, much indebted to Fr. poetic theory (see SYMBOLISM) and associated with the Lebanese poets Yūsuf Ghuṣūb and (esp.) Sa'īd 'Aql.

**D. *The Emergence of "New Poetry": The Role of the Poet.*** The period following World War II was one of political uncertainty, frequent changes of government, and revolution. The creation of the state of Israel in 1948 served as a major psychological catalyst in the Arab world. In the revolutionary atmosphere during the 1950s, the poetry of the late romantics, in particular symbolists such as Sa'īd 'Aql, came to be regarded as elitist, ivory-tower lit. Along with the prevalence of such causes as Palestinian rights, nationalism (whether the Pan-Arab or local variety), revolution, and communism came the rallying cry for "commitment" (*iltizām*). Not surprisingly, among the most prominent contributors to poetry of commitment have been a large group of Palestinian poets; particularly noteworthy are Maḥmūd Darwīsh (d. 2008), Fadwā Ṭūqān (b. 1917), and Samīḥ al-Qāsim (b. 1939). The other overriding topic of political poetry has been life among the poorer classes in both the cities and provinces of the Arab-world nations: the earlier poetry of Badr Shākir al-Sayyāb (d. 1964), 'Abd al-Wahhāb al-Bayyātī (b. 1926), and Ṣalāḥ 'Abd al-Sabūr (d. 1982) shows this concern, as do the works of Aḥmad 'Abd al-Mu'ṭī Ḥijāzī (b. 1935) and Muḥammad Miftāḥ al-Fayṭūrī (b. 1930). The dark visions of Khalīl Ḥāwī (d. 1982) show a more subtle kind of commitment, tinged with bitterness, as in the prescient commentary on the Arab world in the 1960s, "Lazarus 1962":

Deepen the pit, gravedigger,
Deepen it to bottomless depths
beyond the sun's orbit;
night of ashes, remnants of a star
buried in the wheeling abyss.
                    (trans. A. Haydar and M. Beard)

The most widely read poet in the contemp. Middle East in the second half of the 20th c. was undoubtedly Nizār Qabbānī (d. 1998), who earned enormous popularity for his several volumes of sensuous love poetry. During the 1950s, he also wrote poems of social protest, such as his famous "Bread, Hashish and Moonlight"; particularly following the June war of 1967, political and social issues were constant topics in his poetry. Also immensely popular was Darwīsh, who managed for over half a century to encapsulate in his exquisitely crafted poetry the experience of his own Palestinian people.

With Adūnis (pseud. of 'Alī Aḥmad Sa'īd, b. 1930), a different kind of commitment is encountered. After editing with his colleague, the Lebanese Christian poet Yūsuf al-Khāl (d. 1987), the jour. *Shi'r*, which has had immense influence in the devel. of a mod. poetics in the Arab world, Adūnis broke away and in 1968 founded his own jour., *Mawāqif*. He has published numerous poetry collections of startling originality:

To a father who died, green as a cloud
with a sail on his face, I bow.
                    ("*Waṭan*" [Homeland],
                    *Journal of Arabic Literature* 2 [1971])

Using his jour. and its coterie as a conduit for his ideas, he advocates the need for "innovation," viewing the primary purpose of poetry as the use of words in new ways.

**E. *Changes in Form.*** Strophic Ar. poetry has existed from at least the 10th c. The mod. period has also witnessed other experiments, such as *blank and *free verse. Also noteworthy are metrical experiments within folk poetry, particularly in Lebanon where Rashīd Nakhla (d. ca. 1940) and Michel Ṭrād composed poems in strophic form and with mixed meters. In 1947, two Iraqi poets, Nāzik al-Malā'ika (b. 1923) and al-Sayyāb, initiated a break from the concept of the line as poetic unit and thus paved the way for the emergence of *shi'r ḥurr* ("free verse"). In fact, al-Malā'ika's attempt to establish a new set of rules based on the single foot (*taf'īla*) rather than the line (*bayt*) was soon discarded as poets began to experiment with both traditional and new quantitative patterns in their poetry. Other poets have pursued this trend even further by composing prose poetry (*qaṣīdat al-nathr*) in which the sheer conjunction and musicality of words contribute to the poetic moment: *alliteration, *assonance, and *imagery are combined in the works of poets such as Jabrā Ibrāhīm Jabrā (b. 1919), Muḥammad al-Māghūṭ (b. 1934), and Tawfīq Ṣāyigh (d. 1971).

The Arab poet today continues to be influenced and inspired by the great cl. trad., but the stimuli provided by his own time and world are now international and of considerable variety. While poetry continues to hold its traditionally prestigious position and to fulfill an esp. important role in times of crisis, recent cultural trends—particularly the growing prominence of visual media and their markets—have tended to afford a greater cultural priority to narrative genres. One consequence of the increasing role that such media have come to play is the enhancement of the status of more popular forms of poetry (in both standard lang. and colloquial dialects), not least through recordings of their performance modes. The public function of the Arab poet, a permanent feature of the Ar. poetic heritage, is thus being brought to a yet wider audience.

■ **General Reference Works**: C. Brockelmann, *Geschichte der Arabischen Literatur*, 2 v. (1898–1902), *Supplementbanden*, 3 v. (1937–42); A. Fischer, *Schawahid Indices* (1945); *Encyclopedia of Islam*, 2d ed. (1954–), 3d ed. (2007–); J. D. Pearson, *Index Islamicus 1906–1955* (1958), *Supplements* (1956–80); *The Fihrist of al-Nadim*, trans. B. Dodge, 2 v. (1970); M. Alwan, "A Bibliography of Modern Arabic Poetry in English Translation," *Middle East Journal* 27, (Summer 1973); F. Sezgin, *Geschichte des Arabischen Schrifttums*, v. 2 (1975); *Modern Literature in the Near and Middle East 1850–1970*, ed. R. C. Ostle (1991); S. J. Altoma, *Modern Arabic Poetry in English Translation* (1993); R. Allen, *The Arabic Literary Heritage* (1998); *Encyclopedia of Arabic Literature*, 2 v., ed. J. S. Meisami and P. Starkey (1998); H. Toelle and K. Zakharia, *A la découverte de la littérature arabe* (2003); P. G. Starkey, *Modern Arabic Literature* (2006); *Histoire de la littérature arabe moderne*, ed. B. Hallaq and H. Toelle (2007).

■ **Anthologies**: *Arabic Poetry for English Readers*, ed. W. A. Clouston (1881); *Ancient Arabic Poetry*, ed. C. J. Lyall (1885); W. S. Blunt, *Seven Golden Odes of Pagan Arabia* (1903); R. A. Nicholson, *Translations of Eastern Poetry and Prose* (1922); *Modern Arabic Poetry*, ed. and trans. A. J. Arberry (1950); *The Seven Odes*, trans. A. J. Arberry (1957); *Al-Majānī al-Ḥadītha ʿan Majānī al-Ab Shaykhū*, cd. F. Afram al-Bustānī, 3 v. (1960–61); *Dīwān al-Shiʿr al-ʿArabī*, ed. Adūnis (1964–68); *Arabic Poetry* (1965) and *Poems of al-Mutanabbi* (1967), both ed. A. J. Arberry; *Anthologie de la littérature arabe contemporaine*, trans. L. Norin and E. Tarabay (1967); *An Anthology of Modern Arabic Verse*, ed. M. Badawi (1970); *Hispano-Arabic Poetry*, ed. and trans. J. T. Monroe (1974); *Mawsūʿat al-Shiʿr al-ʿArabī*, ed. K. K. Ḥāwī and M. Ṣafadī (1974–); *An Anthology of Modern Arabic Poetry*, trans. M. Khouri and H. Algar (1974); *Modern Arab Poets 1950–1975*, I. Boullata (1976); K. Ḥāwī, *Naked in Exile*, trans. A. Haydar and M. Beard (1984); *Majnun et Layla*, trans. A. Miquel and P. Kemp (1984); *Classical Arabic Poetry*, trans. C. Tuetey (1985); *Modern Arabic Poetry*, ed. S. K. Jayyusi (1987); ʿAbd. al-Wahhāb al-Bayātī, *Love, Death and Exile*, trans. B. K. Frangieh (1990); N. Kabbani, *Arabian Love Poems*, trans. B. K. Frangieh and C. Brown (1993); *Night and Horses and The Desert*, ed. R. Irwin (1999); Adonis, *A Time between Ashes and Roses*, trans. S. M. Toorawa (2004); S. al-Qasim, *Sadder Than Water*, trans. N. Kassis (2006); M. Darwīsh, *The Butterfly's Burden*, trans. Fady Joudah (2007); Mourid Barghouti, *Midnight*, trans. R. Ashour (2008).

■ **Criticism and History**: W. Ahlwardt, *Über Poesie und Poetik der Araber* (1856); I. Goldziher, *Short History of Classical Arabic Literature* (1908), trans. J. Desomogyi (1966); R. A. Nicholson, *Literary History of the Arabs* (1914), *Studies in Islamic Poetry* (1921), *Studies in Islamic Mysticism* (1921); Ṭ. Ḥusayn, *Al-Shiʿr al-Jāhilī* (1926); H.A.R. Gibb, *Arabic Literature* (1926); U. Farrukh, *Das Bild der Frühislam in der arabischen Dichtung* (1937); N. al-Bahbītī, *Tārīkh al-Shiʿr al-ʿArabī* (1950); M. al-Nuwayhī, *Al-Shiʿr al-Jāhilī* (n.d.); R. Serjeant, *South Arabic Poetry* (1951); R. Blachère, *Histoire de la littérature arabe*, 3 v. (1952–66); G. Gomez, *Poesia arabigoandaluza* (1952); G. von Grunebaum, *Kritik und Dichtkunst* (1955); N. al-Asad, *Maṣādir al-Shiʿr al-Jāhilī* (1956); I.ʿAbbas, *Tārīkh al-Adab al-Andalusī* (1959); J. al-Rikābī, *Fi al-Adab al-Andalusī* (1960); N. al-Malāʾika, *Qaḍāyā al-shiʿr al-muʿāṣir* (1962); S. Ḍayf, *Tārīkh al-Adab al-ʿArabī*, 4 v. (1963–73); J. Kamāl al-dīn, *Al-Shiʿr al-ʿArabī al-Ḥadīth wa-rūḥ al-ʿaṣr* (1964); E. Wagner, *Abu Nuwas* (1965); M. Ullmann, *Untersuchungen zur Ragazpoesie* (1966); I. Ismāʿil, *Al-Shiʿr al-ʿArabī al-muʿāṣir* (1967); G. Shukrī, *Shiʿrunā al-Ḥadīth* (1968); J. Vadet, *L'Esprit courtois en Orient dans les premiers siècles de l'Hégire* (1968); W. Heinrichs, *Arabische Dichtung und griechische Poetik* (1969); M. Bateson, *Structural Continuity in Poetry* (1970); M. al-Nuwayhī, *Qaḍiyyat al-shiʿr al-jadīd* (1971); R. Jacobi, *Studien zur Poetik der altarabischen Qaside* (1971); J. T. Monroe, "Oral Composition in Pre-Islamic Poetry," *Journal of Arabic Literature* 3 (1972); M. Ṣubḥi, *Dirāsāt taḥlīliyya fī al-shiʿr al-ʿArabī al-muʿāṣir* (1972); *Arabic Poetry*, ed. G. von Grunebaum (1973); J. ʿAsfūr, *Al-ṣūra al-fanniyya fī al-turāth al-naqdī wa-al-balāghī* (1974); S. Ḍayf, *Al-Taṭawwur wa-al-tajdīd fī al-shiʿr al-Umawī* (1974); A. Hamori, *On the Art of Medieval Arabic Literature* (1974); R. Scheindlin, *Form and Structure in the Poetry of Al-Muʿtamid ibn ʿAbbād* (1974); S. M. Stern, *Hispano-Arabic Strophic Poetry* (1974); M. Badawi, *A Critical Introduction to Modern Arabic Poetry* (1975); J. Bencheikh, *Poétique arabe* (1975); S. A. Bonebakker, *Materials for the History of Arabic Rhetoric from the "Ḥilyat al-muhādara of Hātimīi"* (1975); J. Stetkevych, "The Arabic Lyrical Phenomenon in Context," *Journal of Arabic Literature* 6 (1975); L. F. Compton, *Andalusian Lyrical Poetry and Old Spanish Love Songs* (1976); S. Moreh, *Modern Arabic Poetry 1800–1970* (1976); R. Hitchcock, *The Kharjas* (1977); S. K. Jayyusi, *Trends and Movements in Modern Arabic Poetry* (1977); K. Kheir Beik, *Le Mouvement moderniste de la poésie arabe contemporaine* (1978); M. Zwettler, *The Oral Tradition of Classical Arabic Poetry* (1978); Y. al-Yūsuf, *Al-Shiʿr al-ʿArabī al-muʿāṣir* (1980); M. Abdul-Hai, *Tradition and English and American Influence in Arabic Romantic Poetry* (1982); G. van Gelder, *Beyond the Line* (1982); *Arabic Literature to the End of the Umayyad Period*, ed. A. Beeston et al. (1983); M. Ajami, *The Neckveins of Winter* (1984); S. Stetkevych, "The Ṣuʿlūk and His Poem: A Paradigm of Passage Manqué," *Journal of the American Oriental Society* 104 (1984); Adonis, *Introduction à la poétique arabe* (1985); S. A. Sowayan, *Nabati Po-*

*etry* (1985); M. R. Menocal, *The Arabic Role in Medieval Literary History* (1988); S. Sperl, *Mannerism in Arabic Poetry* (1989); *Abbasid Belles-Letters*, ed. Julia Ashtiany et al. (1990); *Religion, Learning and Science in the Abbasid Period*, ed. M.J.L. Young et al. (1990); C. Bailey, *Bedouin Poetry from Sinai and the Negev* (1991); S. P. Stetkevych, *Abū Tammām and the Poetics of the ʿAbbāsid Age* (1991); A. Hamori, *The Composition of Mutanabbi's Panegyrics to Sayf al-Dawla* (1992); *Modern Arabic Literature*, ed. M. M. Badawi (1992); M. al-Nowaihi, *The Poetry of Ibn Khafajah* (1993); J. Stetkevych, *The Zephyrs of Najd* (1993); K. Abdel-Malek, *Muhammad in the Modern Egyptian Popular Ballad* (1994); T. E. Homerin, *From Arab Poet to Muslim Saint* (1994)—on Ibn al-Fāriḍ; *Reorientations: Arabic and Persian Poetry*, ed. S. Stetkevych (1994); P. M. Kurpershoek, *Oral Poetry and Narratives from Central Arabia*, 3 v. (1994–96); D. F. Reynolds, *Heroic Poets, Poetic Heroes* (1995); *Qasida Poetry in Islamic Asia and Africa*, ed. S. Sperl and C. Shackle, 2 v. (1996); P. F. Kennedy, *The Wine Song in Classical Arabic Poetry* (1997); T. DeYoung, *Placing the Poet* (1998)—on Badr Shākir al-Sayyāb; *The Literature of Al-Andalus,* ed. Maria Rosa Menocal et al. (2000); A. A. Bamia, *The Graying of the Raven* (2001); *The Literature of Al-Andalus*, ed. Maria Rosa Menocal et al. (2000); T. E. Homerin,ʿ*Umar Ibn al-Fāriḍ, Sufi Verse, Saintly Life* (2001); S. Stetkevych, *The Poetics of Islamic Legitimacy* (2002); B. Gruendler, *Medieval Arabic Praise Poetry* (2003); H. Kilpatrick, *Making the Great Book of Songs* (2003); A. Månsson, *Passage to a New World* (2003); A. M. Sumi, *Description in Classical Arabic Poetry* (2004); *Ghazal as World Literature*, ed. T. Bauer and A. Neuwirth, 2 v. (2005–6); M. J. al-Musawi, *Arabic Poetry* (2006); G. Schoeler, *The Oral and the Written in Early Islam*, trans. U. Vagelphol (2006); *Arabic Literature in the Post-Classical Period*, ed. R. Allen and D. S. Richards (2006); Nadia G. Yaqub, *Pens, Swords, and the Springs of Art* (2007); C. Holes, *Poetry and Politics in Contemporary Bedouin Society* (2009).

R.M.A. ALLEN

**ARABIC PROSODY.** Ar. *versification (*al-ʿArūḍ*) is quantitative (see QUANTITY), a unique phenomenon among the Semitic langs., where accent verse systems dominate (see ACCENTUAL VERSE), although in the beginning the ancient Ar. verse was no different from other examples of the archaic Semitic poetry, Akkadian, Ugaritic, or biblical. Ar. poetry starts as the parallelistic verse (see PARALLELISM, at first even unrhymed. From the earliest examples, dating back to the 1st c. CE, it underwent a long evolution until it emerged in the middle of the 6th c. CE as a highly organized metrical system. The intermediate archaic verse forms, found by a researcher as coexisting in time, though they mark stages of devel., are the following:

(1) *Sajʿ*, often translated as "rhymed prose," but for the early oral phase, it is a verse form, based on the parallelistic technique with no concrete meter discernible, attested in the sayings of pre-

Islamic *kāhins* and Bedouins, as well as in the early Meccan sūras of the Qurʾān.

(2) *Rajaz*, later incorporated in the ʿArūḍ system as one of its meters, initially it was a short verse form labeled by the Ar. scholars as "one-hemistich verse" with a rather loose structure where one can already observe the emergence of the alternative rhythm of the quantitative nature, though some of its features, such as the possibility of inner pauses within the verse line, suggest that *accent still played a moderate part in creating the verse rhythm. The adaptation of its loose pattern to the strict (or can we say overstrict) ʿArūḍ rules created difficulties for Ar. scholars starting from the creator of the metrical theory, al-Khalīl ibn Aḥmad (d. ca. 786).

Al-Khalīl noticed that the rhythmic core of Ar. prosody is the alternation of longer and shorter prosodic segments. In other words, it is based solely on quantity or temporal *duration. The very notion of stress is absent from his theory. The notion of *syllable* in its cl. form is also absent, but this is not a symptom of the deficiency of the theory. Al-Khalīl invented another system of concepts for the analysis of the structure of Ar. verse, by far surpassing in that capacity the traditional Eur. notion of *syllable*, as it takes account of the fact—often neglected by Eur. scholars—that the sequence that we call *short syllable* (CV) cannot be pronounced autonomously or is not a syllable at all.

The basis notion is *ḥarf*, which can be either *sākin* (quiescent), i.e., a consonant or a long vowel, or *mutaḥarrik* (moving), i.e., a consonant followed by a short vowel. Both variants (one being structurally identical with the CV) are less than the minimum of pronunciation, as it should always begin with the "moving" ḥarf and end with the "quiescent" one. So, the minimum of Ar. speech is a two-ḥarf segment (structurally identical with a "long syllable"—CVC or CVlong).

The notion has a twofold function in the metrical structure. First, it is used as the means of the segmentation of speech into elementary prosodic units (EPU). The goal is achieved by stops at each unvocalized ḥarf; as a result, each EPU has an identical structural pattern: a number (one or more) of vocalized ḥarfs and a final unvocalized ḥarf. Second, the ḥarf is a unit of measurement of prosodic length, which can be considered a functional equivalent of the universal notion of *mora. So, the length of EPU can be two ḥarfs (this is the minimum), three ḥarfs, four ḥarfs, and so on.

These EPU play the role of metrical syllables in the ʿArūḍ structure, the two-ḥarf unit being the short one and the three-ḥarf unit the long one. The shorter one is called *sabab* (rope or cord) and the longer one *watid* (peg); both terms go back to the image of a Bedouin tent. There is a beautiful legend about an aged shaykh teaching a youth to compose poetry. The master says that all verses are composed of two elements—*naʿam* (yes)—this is watid—and *lā* (no)—this is sabab. So, if we recite, "Naʿam lā naʿam lā lā . . . ," we get one meter, while if we recite, "Lā lā naʿam lā lā naʿam . . . ," we get another meter and so on.

The sababs and watids are the core of the alternative verse rhythm, in which the first EPU functions as *thesis* and the second as *arsis* (see ARSIS AND THESIS), but the actual set of EPU postulated by 'Arūḍ is wider as it comprises four-ḥarf and five-ḥarf segments called *smaller fāṣila* and *larger fāṣila*, which can be treated as prosodic clusters made of a combination of the sababs and watids with the prosodic boundary between them eliminated.

Certain combinations of metrical syllables make 'Arūḍ *feet. The theory postulates eight different types of feet, but only seven of them are real, while the eighth is a purely fictitious foot postulated by al-Khalīl to solve some theoretical difficulties he encountered. They have a uniform structure: one watid that is the arsis of the foot plus one or two sababs (or smaller fāṣila). It follows that the prosodic length of the 'Arūḍ feet is either five or seven ḥarfs (or morae). The seven foot types (presented by mnemonic word patterns taken from Ar. morphology with some modifications that go back to al-Khalīl and by numerical schemes where two stands for sabab, three for watid, and four for smaller fāṣila) are the following:

*fa'ūlun*: 32 (trochaic foot), e.g., *kitābun, dhahabtum*
*fā'ilun*: 23 (iambic foot), e.g., *kātibun, lam yakun*
*mafā'ilun*: 322 (dactylic foot-1), e.g., *hunā shamsun*
*mufā'alatun*: 34 (dactylic foot-2), e.g., *faqad dhahabū*
*fā'ilātun*: 232 (amphibrachic foot), e.g., *min kitābin*
*mustaf 'ilun*: 223 (anapaestic foot-1), e.g., *mustaqbalun, lam yadhhabū*
*mutafā'ilun*: 43 (anapaestic foot-2), e.g., *mutadhāhirun, wahabū lahā*

It can be seen that the Ar. presentation, with the help of ḥarf/mora and EPU/metrical syllables, reveals the structural affinity of Ar. metrics with other systems of versification and gives the firm basis for typological studies.

The system of Ar. meters started to develop from three archaic rhythms, identified with three functional forms (*genres) of ancient poetry that already had names in pre-Islamic vocabulary:

(1) descending, either trochaic (32) or dactylic (322/34), which was initially associated with the trad. of old Ar. singing, now extinct; this form of poetry with short (four-foot) verse lines was called *hazaj*;

(2) ascending, either iambic (23) or anapestic (223/43), which was initially associated with declamation, not singing; this—probably the oldest—form of poetry with extra-short (three-foot) lines was called *rajaz*; see above;

(3) ambivalent, ascending-descending, or amphibrachic (232), which was initially associated with the trad. of Persian singing, imported into Arabia via al-Ḥīra; this form of poetry, the most recent it seems, with short (four-foot) lines was called *ramal*.

The set of meters that constitute the classic system of 'Arūḍ was born out of the three basic rhythms with the help of the processes of elongating verse lines and of introducing strict order in the alternation of inter-watid intervals.

Al-Khalīl himself identified 15 meters, and the 16th meter was added later on. On the basis of their origin and structural affinity, they can be grouped in three metrical families.

**A. Hazaj.** The hazaj family comprises five meters. The rhyme schemes follow each definition:

(1) *ṭawīl* (long): An eight-foot meter of two *hemistichs and the only one that does not have shorter forms. It is the main meter of *qaṣīd* poetry (see QAṢĪDA), almost half of which is written in this meter):

*fa'ūlun / mafā'ilun / fā'ilun / mafā'ilun //*
32      322      32      33
*fā'ilun / mafā'ilun / fā'ilun / mafā'ilun*
32      322      32      322

(2) *wāfir* (abundant, full): A six-foot meter that also has a rare four-foot variation, one of the four main qaṣīd meters:

*mufā'alatun / mufā'alatun / mufā'alatun //*
34           34           34
*mufā'alatun / mufā'alatun / mufā'alatun*
34           34           34

(3) *hazaj* (quick vibration of sound): Theoretically, a six-foot meter but used exclusively as a shorter, four-foot variation. This rare meter, rhythmically close to wāfir, is the direct heir of the archaic hazaj; see above:

*mafā'ilun / mafā'ilun // mafā'ilun / mafā'ilun*
322         322         322         322

(4) *mutaqārib* (contracted or drawn near each other): An eight-foot meter made only of five-ḥarf feet, which is unusual for Ar. verse—hence, its name. Its frequency is 5 to 15 percent, and it is one of the six most popular meters of cl. Ar. poetry. Its short six-foot variation is much less frequent than the long one:

*fa'ūlun / fa'ūlun / fa'ūlun / fa'ūlun //*
32      32      32      32
*fa'ūlun / fa'ūlun / fa'ūlun / fa'ūlun*
32      32      32      32

(5) *muḍāri'* (similar): Theoretically, a four-foot meter but never used by poets. Its scheme is as follows:

*mafā'ilun / fā'ilātun // mafā'ilun / fā'ilātun*
322         232         322         232

**B. Rajaz.** The rajaz family comprises seven meters:

(1) *basīṭ* (outspread, unfolded): An eight-foot meter but with a shorter six-foot variation, one of the four main qaṣīd meters:

*mustaf'ilun / fā'ilun / mustaf'ilun / fā'ilun //*
223         23      223          23
*mustaf'ilun / fā'ilun / mustaf'ilun / fā'ilun*
223         23      223         23

(2) *kāmil* (complete): A six-foot meter that also has a four-foot variation, one of the four main qaṣīd meters:

*mutafāʿilun / mutafāʿilun / mutafāʿilun //*
43         43         43
*mutafāʿilun / mutafāʿilun / mutafāʿilun*
43         43         43

(3) *rajaz* (trembling sound, murmur): One of the oldest meters, rhythmically close to kāmil, used from time immemorial exclusively as a short three-foot (or even a two-foot) variation; in the theory of ʿArūḍ it is presented as a "normal" six-foot meter:

*mustafʿilun / mustafʿilun / mustafʿilun //*
223        223        223
*mustafʿilun / mustafʿilun / mustafʿilun*
223        223        223

(4) *sarīʿ* (quick): A six-foot meter that also has a short, three-foot variation. It definitely shows affinity to rajaz, and if treated according to actual prosodic practice, it becomes a specific variation of rajaz with deformation at the end of each hemistich, nothing more. In the metrical theory, though, it is presented as having at the end the anomalous prosodically incomplete foot, which, in fact, never has the ideal form (its real form can be 222 or 23 but never 223; otherwise, it would turn into rajaz):

*mustafʿilun / mustafʿilun / mafʿūlātu-//*
223        223        2221–
*mustafʿilun / mustafʿilun / mafʿūlātu-*
223        223        2221–

(5) *munsariḥ* (free, easygoing, unbound): A rare six-foot meter that also has a short, two-foot variation. In the metrical theory, it is presented as having the same anomalous foot in the middle of the hemistich, but the prosodically relevant scanning shows that it is another specific variation of rajaz with a watid shifted one step further. Both ways of scanning are shown by numerical indexes in this case:

*mustafʿilun / mafʿūlātu- / mustafʿilun //*
223     2221–     223 (theory)
223     2223       23 (reality)
*mustafʿilun / mafʿūlātu- / mustafʿilun*
223     2221–     223 (theory)
223     2223       23 (reality)

(6) *mujtaṯṯ* (cut or carved off): A very rare four-foot meter:

mustafʿilun / fāʿilātun // mustafʿilun / fāʿilātun
223      232        223      232

(7) *muqtaḍab* (cut or torn off): A four-foot meter that never existed in poetic practice. It is the third meter for which al-Khalīl postulated the occurrence of the same anomalous foot, which is placed in the beginning of each hemistich:

*mafʿūlātu-mustafʿilun // mafʿūlātu-mustafʿilun*
2221–223         2221–223
(theoretical scanning)
2223 23          2223 23
(actual prosodic scanning)

(8) One more meter can be added to this family. It is the 16th meter included in the system after al-Khalīl: *mutadārik*. However, the schema of this meter was never attested in poetic practice:

*fāʿilun / fāʿilun / fāʿilun / fāʿilun // fāʿilun /*
23    23    23    23      23
*fāʿilun / fāʿilun / fāʿilun*
23    23    23

The anomalous foot *mafʿūlātu-*(2221–), which is impossible as it is prosodically incomplete, is the eighth foot of the ʿArūḍ set mentioned above. It was invented by al-Khalīl to overcome a specific theoretical problem that arose in connection with meters that were heirs of the ancient rajaz with its loose structure. The maximum length of the ʿArūḍ foot was postulated as seven ḥarfs, and most of the meters comply with the rule; but in some schemes, we see three sababs in succession between watids, which cannot be divided between adjacent feet. So, a theoretician has an alternative: either to break the rule and postulate the existence of the super-long nine-ḥarf foot or to find another solution, as did al-Khalīl. He postulated the existence of such a foot in three meters: *muqtaḍab, munsariḥ, sarīʿ*, where it occupies the first, the second, and the third position in the hemistich; see above. In order to substantiate the existence of this foot, al-Khalīl had to introduce another conventional notion, that of the abnormal *watid—lātu-*, which has only one location—at the end of this very foot. It carries a significant name—*mafrūq* (disjointed) because, prosodically, it is nothing but a combination of incomplete parts of adjacent EPU. The combination was so successful that many scholars consider these conventionalities to be real and base on them their interpretation of ʿArūḍ.

**C. Ramal.** The *ramal* family consists of three meters:

(1) *khafīf* (light): A six-foot meter that also has a four-foot variation:

*fāʿilātun / mustafʿilun / fāʿilātun // fāʿilātun /*
232     223      232       232
*mustafʿilun / fāʿilātun*
223     232

(2) *ramal* (woven cloth; sound of raindrops): A six-foot meter that also has a four-foot variation:

*fāʿilātun / fāʿilātun / fāʿilātun // fāʿilātun / fāʿilātun*
232    232    232    232    232
*/ fāʿilātun*
232

(3) *madīd* (stretched, extended): Theoretically, an eight-foot meter but used exclusively as a shorter six-foot variation:

*fāʿilātun / fāʿilun / fāʿilātun // fāʿilātun / fāʿilun /*
　 232　　 23　　 232　　　 232　　 23
*fāʿilātun*
　 232

This classification of meters into three families is based on their rhythmical affinity, but the author of ʿArūḍ classified them differently—his famous and mysterious circles, five in number. The system of circles is, in fact, a generative device. It groups meters that can be produced from each other by the shift of the starting point one EPU forward. The generative principle can be shown in the following diagram:

. . . 322 322 322 322 322 322 322 . . . (hazaj rhythm)
. . . 223 223 223 223 223 223 223 . . . (rajaz rhythm)
. . . 232 232 232 232 232 232 232 . . . (ramal rhythm)

So, the first circle is *ṭawīl—madīd—basīṭ*. The second circle is *wāfir—kāmil*. The third circle is *hazaj—rajaz—ramal*. The fourth circle is *sarīʿ—munsariḥ—khafīf—muḍāriʿ—muqtaḍab—mujtaṭṭ*. The fifth circle is *mutaqārib* alone. Later on, *mutadārik* was added.

But the derivational device produces more schemes than are accepted by the theory. The first circle generates five schemes, and only three are recognized as meters. The fourth circle generates nine schemes, and only six are accepted. The rest are labeled as *muhmal* (neglected, unused). The mystery is that, as we have seen, some schemes that were recognized as meters of ʿArūḍ are also unused (*muḍāriʿ–muqtaḍab*), and *mutadārik* was included despite the fact that it was never used by Ar. poets.

The ʿArūḍ system was adopted by Heb., Persian, and Turkish poetry and has undergone serious changes in the process of adaptation to a different prosodic matter. In the 20th c., Ar. poetry witnessed a shift away from the ʿArūḍ metrics to *free verse*.

■ G. W. Freytag, *Darstellung der Arabischen Verskunst* (1830); S. Guyard, "Théorie nouvelle de la métrique Arabe," *Journal Asiatique*, ser. 7, 7, 8, 10 (1877); M. Hartmann, *Metrum und Rhythmus* (1896); J. Vadet, "Contribution a l'histoire de la métrique Arabe," *Arabica* 2 (1955); G. Weil, *Grundriss und System der altarabischen Metren* (1958), and "ʿArūḍ," *Encyclopedia of Islam*, ed. H.A.R. Gibb et al., 2d ed., v. 1 (1960); S. ʿAyyād, *Mūsīqā al-Shiʿr al-ʿArabī* (1968); Ibn ʿAbd Rabbihi, *al-ʿIqd al-Farid*, v. 3 (1968); A. A. Sánchez, "K voprosu o sushchnosti sistemi arabskoy metriki," *Arabskaya Filologiya* (1968); Ibn al-Sarrāj, *al-Miʿyār fī Awzān al-Ashʿār* (1968); I. Anīs, *Mūsīqā al-Shiʿr*, 4th ed. (1972); J. Kuryłowicz, *Studies in Semitic Grammar and Metrics* (1973); K. Abū Deeb, *Fī al-Binya al-Iqāʿiyya li al-Shiʿr al-ʿArabī* (1974); E. G. Gómez, *Métrica de la moaxaja y métrica española* (1975); I. Goldziher, *Abhandlungen zur arabischen Philologie*, v. 1 (1976); J. M. Maling, "The Theory

of Classical Arabic Metrics," *al-Abhāth* 26 (1977); D. Semah, "The Rhythmical Function of the *Watid* and the *Fāsila*," *Journal of Semitic Studies* 28 (1983); and "Quantity and Syllabic Parity in the Hispano-Arabic *Muwashshaḥāt*," *Arabica* 31 (1983); W.F.G.J. Stoetzer, *Theory and Practice in Arabic Metrics* (1989); J. Bellamy, "Arabic Verses from the First/Second Century: The Inscription of ʿEn ʿAvdat," *Journal of Semitic Studies* 35 (1990); G. Bohas and B. Paoli, *Aspects formels de la poésie arabe* (1997); D. Frolov, "The Place of *Rajaz* in the History of Arabic Verse," *Journal of Arabic Literature* 28 (1997); D. Frolov, *Classical Arabic Verse: History and Theory of ʿArūḍ* (2000); D. Frolov, "Meter," *Encyclopedia of Arabic Language and Linguistics*, ed. K. Versteegh et al., v. 3 (2007).

D. FROLOV

**ARAUCANIAN POETRY.** *See* INDIGENOUS AMERICAS, POETRY OF THE.

**ARCHAISM.** Deliberate use of old, old-fashioned, or obsolete words, esp. in poetry, to evoke the mood of an earlier time or to recapture a *connotation or denotation not borne by any mod. word. Archaisms appear in both Virgil and Lucretius; in Fr. poetry of the Ren., archaisms were promoted in the doctrines of the *Pléiade. In Eng. poetry, archaism was once said to have its deepest source in Edmund Spenser's *Faerie Queene* (1590, 1596). But mod. scholarship reveals that archaisms are less common in Spenser than was often thought: there are only about 100 archaic words in *The Faerie Queene*, and half of these are used just once.

The effect of archaism may be achieved by a number of lexical strategies besides resuscitating words found in an older author, as Spenser did with Chaucer. These include the addition of archaic prefixes or suffixes to contemporaneous words, inclusion of words rapidly passing out of fashion, use of rare and unusual (but not obsolete) words, use of dialectal words, and the coining of words that look or sound archaic but are actually neologisms. Syntactic strategies such as *hyperbaton may also give the effect of archaism. Sometimes archaism also serves metrical ends when the older form of a word, having a different number of syllables, more readily fits into the meter than its modern equivalent (e.g., when such words as *loved, wished*, etc., are used in poetry as disyllables—*lovéd, wishéd*).

Archaism was a stylistic landmark of the *School of Spenser in the 17th c., of Spenser's imitators in the 18th, and of the *Pre-Raphaelite Brotherhood in the 19th. It continues to feature in poetry of the mod. and postmod. eras. "Last year's words belong to last year's language," T. S. Eliot remarks in *Four Quartets*, but he also provides a model for poets seeking not only to find new words for new experience but to revive old words for a sense of the past.

*See* AUREATE DICTION, DICTION, EPITHET.

■ G. Wagner, *On Spenser's Use of Archaisms* (1879); R. S. Crane, "Imitation of Spenser and Milton in the Early 18th Century," *SP* 15 (1918); W. L. Renwick,

"The Critical Origins of Spenser's Diction," *MLR* 17 (1922); T. Quayle, *Poetic Diction* (1924); E. F. Pope, "Renaissance Criticism and the Diction of the *Faerie Queene*," *PMLA* 41 (1926); B. R. McElderry Jr., "Archaism and Innovation in Spenser's Poetic Diction," *PMLA* 47 (1932); O. Barfield, *Poetic Diction*, 2d ed. (1952); N. Osselton, "Archaism," and B.M.H. Strang, "Language, General," *The Spenser Encyclopedia*, ed. A. C. Hamilton (1990).

T.V.F. Brogan; M. Weinstein

## ARCHETYPE

I. History
II. Powers and Limitations

Generally speaking, an archetype is an original structure or plan that informs and underlies all copies made from it, so far as they are recognizable as generated from the prototype despite superficial variations in their size, shape, or material. Thus, the archetype of a table would be "a flat horizontal surface upheld by vertical supports for placing things on," and this is the recognizable idea of all tables everywhere.

In poetry, an archetype may be an *image, *symbol, plot, character, or setting that evokes in the reader a sense of its heightened significance because it represents a culturally or psychologically privileged—whether revered or condemned—object, value, or belief. The archetype often expresses essential characteristics of the human condition that are primitive and universal, rather than intellectualized and singular. Some common archetypal subjects are transformative human events, such as birth, childhood, initiation into adulthood, partnering, procreation, senescence, and death; the cycle of the seasons and nature's powers and mysteries; love and all its objects; greed, guilt, and redemption; religion, mutability, and art. Some archetypal themes are crime and punishment, the conflict between reason and imagination, free will and fate, appearance and reality, and the individual and society. Examples of archetypal situations are tensions between family members, a child's search for a father, and the young adult's leaving parents for a new home. Familiar archetypal characters are the hero or heroine of a quest, a person representing the hero's shadow side, the wise old man, femme fatale, scapegoat, trickster, rebel, wanderer, and witch. Some symbolic and archetypal natural images are oceans, rivers, the sun and moon, the bear, birds, serpents, the tree, garden, and mountain. Also used archetypically are colors, such as green, red, blue, and black; and geometric figures, such as the circle, mandala, and labyrinth. When archetypal elements are represented repeatedly in a poem so as to bring forth their underlying, essential, and manifold attributes, then they may be recognized and read as an archetypal pattern or design.

I. History. The hist. of the archetypal approach may be traced through several movements beginning around 1900, with some overlap in both time and focus.

A. *The Anthropological Influence.* Since these studies tend to center on the terms *myth* and *ritual*, a few basic definitions are in order. A myth, strictly speaking, is a sacred story about supernatural beings; it may also include humans with special or supernatural powers who interact with these divine beings. A ritual, on the other hand, is a ceremonial reenactment of a sacred myth, but it has not been definitively established whether the myth was created to explain the ritual or the ritual was invented to dramatize the myth. Either way, the usual anthropological account of ritual is that it provides a way for a culture to express its hopes and fears in those dealings with nature that it believes are basic to its survival.

The earliest anthropological influence on the archetypal approach to lit. was the so-called Cambridge school of comparative anthropology, led by J. G. Frazer, author of *The Golden Bough* (1890), and including fellow scholars Murray, Harrison, and Weston. Their method, often based on armchair research rather than participant-observation in the field, was to collect accounts of myths and rituals from various cultures with a view to tracing their fundamental similarities. The general effect of their approach was to create the impression that myth and ritual the world over and throughout hist. formed certain regular and standard patterns. T. S. Eliot publicly endorsed Weston's and Frazer's sense of the archetype in *The Waste Land*, and his 1923 review of *Ulysses* enthusiastically recommended to modernist writers this new "mythical method," which he said was made possible by the recent discoveries in anthropology and psychology. Several characteristics of an archetypal poetics were cited: the immediacy of symbolic representation, when compared to the traditional narrative method; the intensity of an archetypal symbol, as it simultaneously embodies multiple and even paradoxical meanings; and the implicit authenticity accompanying such a seemingly unplanned creation from the poet's archetypal imagination. Thus, archetypal lit. crit. was launched.

The Am. school of anthropologists, however, represented by such field researchers as Mead and Benedict, took a much more pluralistic stance from 1930 to 1955, pointing out that cultures were fundamentally different from one another, and that if there were "similar" patterns among them, these had differing meanings in their differing contexts. Mead even published her views in the Modern Language Association jour. Nevertheless, from 1960 to 1980, a newer, "structuralist" anthropology, propounded by Lévi-Strauss, along with Eliade's books linking myth, symbols, and the sacred, continued the debate about the universality and importance of the archetype. Certainly, the period 1945 to 1980 saw the flowering of archetypal and mythic crit. in universities.

B. *The Psychological Influence.* One principal reason C. G. Jung broke with Sigmund Freud in 1913 was their disagreement over the archetype. Rather than accept Freud's tenet that only the Oedipus complex/archetype explained every patient's problems, Jung followed what he had observed in his practice. His patients brought in dream symbols that were much more understandable when read in the light of stories and characters found in ancient world myths. To explain how 20th-c. humans could dream in ancient symbols, Jung posited a deeper level of psyche, called the collective unconscious. "Collective" meant shared by every member of the human race, and "unconscious" meant linked to the instinctual level of the brain and, therefore, in some ways beyond the control of the consciousness and reason. The many archetypes that reside there are unconscious patterns of potential emotional and behavioral responses to the many possible stimuli life has presented to the human species during its evolution.

Jacobi explains that Jung made a distinction between the archetype as such and the archetypal image: the former has no material existence but is an informing structure that must be clothed by the conscious mind in material from the external world. It is not clear, however, whether the archetype as such results from the deposit of innumerable experiences on the evolving human psyche or is an a priori condition for human experience itself, or both. Advances in neuroscience's study of connectomics, incl. observing with ever more powerful tools and measuring ever more closely the intensity of the brain's responses to stimuli, coupled with mapping the complex neural pathways linking our inherited genetic brain with our learned, experiential knowledge, continue to bring the answer closer. Post-Jungian analysts—many medical doctors and thus scientists, rather than literary critics—view the psychological archetype as more conditioned by the dreamer's historical context and specific personality than Jung did; they believe that what is important in analytic practice is gauging the intensity of feeling the archetype engenders in the dreamer. Nevertheless, Jung honored both poetry and the poets with his oft-stated belief that the poet who invokes archetypes in her poetry speaks in a voice stronger than her own; using archetypes can lift personal poetry "above the occasional and the transitory into the sphere of the ever-existing . . . and transmute personal destiny into the destiny of humankind. . . . That is the secret of effective art" (1928).

Archetypal lit. crit. takes a number of forms. One practice looks in poetry for resonant echoes and reenactments of ancient and ubiquitous patterns, discovering general types emerging from the specific elements of a given poem and then responding to those types as symbols of human desires, conflicts, and problems; this emerges as a kind of symbolic approach. E.g., one might trace the archetypal image of "The Descent into Hell" from early myth and ritual to Homer, Virgil, *medieval romance, and Dante up to Hart Crane's subway section of *The Bridge* and Eliot's "The Hollow Men," comparing and contrasting the symbols in the various works while also gauging the intensity of the archetypal affect that these pieces carry for readers today. A second critical practice uses the archetypal feminist approach; e.g., Pratt has discovered gender-specific archetypal images and patterns previously unrecognized in women's poetry and fiction. Pratt's work not only challenged the

universality of the most frequently represented myth—the archetypal journey quest plot of the male hero—but refashioned it as a gender-specific pattern, not typical of the patterns followed by heroines in women's lit. Her work has thus helped to revive a buried feminine trad. A third form of archetypal lit. crit. is an interdisciplinary one that brings together different professions—analytical psychologists and teachers of lit.—and illuminates their different practices and goals with regard to the archetype. The analyst Hillman advocated archetypal psychology from the 1970s; his *Healing Fiction* urged psychologists and therapists to envision psychic reality as data not to be interpreted literally but to be understood and dealt with as material "poetic, dramatic, literary in nature." In the 1980s and 1990s, Hillman joined the poet Robert Bly in spreading this interdisciplinary archetypal approach, and it found an enthusiastic audience among the popular Men's Movement. Bly's best-selling book about male psychology, *Iron John: A Book about Men* (1990), is an archetypal meditation on a fairy tale. Bly and Hillman also edited a poetry anthol. whose subtitle is "Poetry for Men." Finally, archetypal crit. has proved better suited than some other crit. approaches for certain kinds of poetry, sometimes termed wisdom lit. or visionary lit.; such art generally aspires to express heightened experiences and relies on an archetypal poetics to achieve its effects. Studying the significance of such heightened experiences is likewise central to archetypal psychologists, and Samuels et al.'s *Dictionary* definition for *numinous*, as possessing a quality of unusually strong *affect, notes that such a heightened state was considered by Jung to be generally "present in all religious experiences." Twentieth-c. poems in Eng. that have consciously reached for the numinous, that exemplify some characteristics of archetypal poetics, include Eliot's *The Waste Land*, esp. "What the Thunder Said"; Crane's *The Bridge*; Allen Ginsberg's *Howl*; Bly's *Sleepers Joining Hands*, esp. "The Teeth Mother Naked at Last"; Galway Kinnell's "When The Towers Fell"; and work from such poets as Denise Levertov, Willam Stafford, Adrienne Rich, W. S. Merwin, Sylvia Plath, and Ted Hughes.

**C. Natural and Universal Symbols.** One may, however, develop an approach to mythological and universal symbols without specifically drawing on the work of either comparative anthropology or psychology. Here one's concern is primarily epistemological—i.e., with the relation between Mind and World and among the various langs. and symbol-systems humanity has devised for bringing them together. Noteworthy in this line is the work of Cassirer, Wheelwright, and Campbell. Notable in this trend of thought are the many correspondences among physical forms and the forms of thought, such as stars for guidance, sun for life, spring for renewal, animals for humanity's physical or emotional side, and mountains for struggle and achievement.

**D. Northrop Frye.** Frye constructed an archetypal symbology based on the parallels between the cycles of human life and those of the natural world and the patterns these parallels have caused to appear in myth, ritual, dream, and poetry. Sidestepping the nature vs. nurture debate over the origin of archetypes, he claimed that it is not very important whether there is any relationship between lit. and reality, nor whether lit. embodies the truths of depth psychology. What *is* more important is that lit., when taken as a whole, reveals inductively the persistence of certain patterns, with the result that lit. is seen to form a highly organized universe of its own. The job of critics, therefore, is to formulate and interpret those patterns—which Frye proceeded to do in *Anatomy of Criticism* (1957) at some length. In the process, he transcended archetypal crit. itself and developed a fourfold set of approaches, of which the archetypal is only one: (1) Historical Criticism: Theory of Modes (fictional, tragic, comic, thematic); (2) Ethical Criticism: Theory of Symbols (literal and descriptive, formal, mythical, anagogic); (3) Archetypal Criticism: Theory of Myths (spring: comedy; summer: romance; autumn: tragedy; winter: irony and satire); and (4) Rhetorical Criticism: Theory of Genres (epos, prose, drama, lyric).

**II. Powers and Limitations**. The archetypal approach to poetry has demonstrated several powers. First, since the early 20th c., general awareness and interest in archetypes and myth have been important in the cultural zeitgeist; many poets and visual artists have turned to them for creative purposes, consciously incorporating them into their work. Since an alert critic will follow where artists lead, a critical approach attuned to the archetypal world may discover significance in works that other approaches might overlook. A second power of archetypal crit. is its usefulness in evaluating and perhaps redirecting mass media culture, whose infinitely reproducible image-products have led to a severe reduction of ancient archetypes into mass culture's comic-book stereotypes. The archetypal critic is well positioned to interrogate these stereotypes and re-present to a contemp. audience the more complex (and more powerful for their visual and psychological complexity) originals found in authentic myth and serious lit. A third strength of the archetypal approach is that it looks beyond the formal limits of the work itself to consider the imaginative impulse of its creator as well as to assess the work's effect and affect for the reader.

There are also limitations to the archetypal approach. First, in practice, archetypal critics themselves can frequently seem reductive, not just in excessive "symbol-hunting," which can lead to ignoring other important aspects of the work, but in overestimating the significance of a symbol whose reach for the archetypal may exceed its grasp. Second, unlike other critical approaches to lit. such as *formalism, *historicism, or *cultural studies, the archetypal approach cannot be applied to every work. But it has proved its worth in evaluating some of the world's most revered lit., e.g., all acknowledged epics, Gr. and Shakespearean tragedies, every culture's holy book (incl. the Bible), and world myths generally.

*See* ANTHROPOLOGY AND POETRY, CRITICISM, MYTH, PSYCHOLOGY AND POETRY.

■ **Anthropological Influence**: J. G. Frazer, *The Golden Bough*, 3d ed., 12 v. (1905–15); J. Harrison, *Themis* (1912); G. Murray, *The Classical Tradition in Poetry* (1927); J. L. Weston, *From Ritual to Romance* (1920); R. Benedict, *Patterns of Culture* (1934); H. M. Block, "Cultural Anthropology and Contemporary Literary Criticism," *JAAC* 11 (1952); M. Mead, "Cultural Bases for Understanding Literature," *PMLA* 68 (1953); C. Lévi-Strauss, *Structural Anthropology*, trans. C. Jacobson and B. Grundfest Schoepf (1963); M. Eliade, *Images and Symbols*, trans. P. Mairet (1969); J. B. Vickery, *The Literary Impact of "The Golden Bough"* (1973); T. S. Eliot, "*Ulysses*, Order, and Myth," *Selected Prose*, ed. F. Kermode (1975); H. Blumenberg, *Work on Myth*, trans. R. M. Wallace (1985); I. Strenski, *Four Theories of Myth in Twentieth-Century History: Cassirer, Eliade, Lévi-Strauss and Malinowski* (1988); R. Ackerman, *The Myth and Ritual School* (1991); J. R. Smith, *Writing Tricksters: Mythic Gambols in American Ethnic Literature* (1997).

■ **Natural Symbols**: E. Cassirer, *Language and Myth*, trans. S. K. Langer (1946); R. Chase, *Quest for Myth* (1949); J. Campbell, *The Hero with a Thousand Faces* (1949); W. H. Auden, *The Enchafèd Flood* (1950); E. Cassirer, *The Philosophy of Symbolic Forms*, trans. R. Manheim, 3 v. (1953–57); R.W.B. Lewis, *The American Adam* (1955); B. Seward, *The Symbolic Rose* (1960); E. Sewell, *The Orphic Voice* (1961); P. Wheelwright, *Metaphor and Reality* (1962); E. Sewell, *The Human Metaphor* (1964); J. B. Vickery, *Myth and Literature* (1966); P. Wheelwright, *The Burning Fountain*, 2d ed. (1968); M. Douglas, *Natural Symbols* (1970); H. Slochower, *Mythopoesis* (1970).

■ **Northrop Frye**: N. Frye, "Archetypes of Literature," *KR* 12 (1954); "Forming Fours," *HudR* 6 (1954); *Northrop Frye in Modern Criticism*, ed. M. Krieger (1966); P. Kogan, *Northrop Frye* (1969); N. Frye, "Expanding Eyes," *CritI* 2 (1975–76); R. D. Denham, *Northrop Frye and Critical Method* (1978); F. Lentricchia, *After the New Critics* (1980); H. Adams, *Philosophy of the Literary Symbolic* (1983); *Centre and Labyrinth*, ed. E. Cook et al. (1983); D. Cook, *Northrop Frye* (1985); I. Balfour, *Northrop Frye* (1988); A. C. Hamilton, *Northrop Frye: Anatomy of His Criticism* (1990).

■ **Psychological Influence**: C. G. Jung, *Psychology of the Unconscious*, trans. B. M. Hinkle (1916); *Psychological Types*, trans. H. G. Baynes (1923); and *Contributions to Analytical Psychology*, trans. C. F. Baynes and H. G. Baynes (1928); M. Bodkin, *Archetypal Patterns in Poetry* (1934); E. Drew, *T. S. Eliot: The Design of His Poetry* (1949); J. S. Jacobi, *Complex/Archetype/Symbol in the Psychology of C. G. Jung* (1959); M. H. Philipson, *Outline of a Jungian Aesthetics* (1963); *Man and his Symbols*, ed. C. G. Jung et al. (1968); J. Hillman, *Re-Visioning Psychology* (1975); J. Olney, *The Perennial Philosophy—Yeats and Jung* (1980); A. V. Pratt, *Archetypal Patterns in Women's Fiction* (1981); J. Hillman, *Healing Fiction* (1983); *Feminist Archetypal Theory*, ed. E. Lauter and C. S. Rupprecht (1985); *Critical Dictionary of Jungian Analysis*, ed. A. Samuels, B. Shorter, and F. Plaut (1986); J. van Meurs and J. Kidd, *Jungian Literary Criticism, 1920–1980* (1988)—annotated bibl.; J. Campbell, *Transformations of Myths through Time* (1990); D. A. Leeming, *The World of Myth* (1990); R. Bly, J. Hillman, and M. Meade, *The Rag and Bone Shop* of the Heart: Poems for Men (1992); Jungian Literary Criticism, ed. Richard P. Sugg (1992); A. V. Pratt, Dancing with Goddesses: Archetypes, Poetry, and Empowerment (1994); Cambridge Companion to Jung, ed., P. Young-Eisendrath (1997); Encyclopedia of Archetypal Symbolism, ed. B. Moon (1997); J. Hillman, Archetypal Psychology, 3rd ed. (2004); Post-Jungian Criticism, Theory and Practice, ed. J. S. Baumlin and T. F. Baumlin (2004).

N. FRIEDMAN; R. P. SUGG

**ARCHILOCHIAN.** The Gr. lyric poet Archilochus of Paros (fl. mid-7th c. BCE) drew on earlier verse forms, esp. dactylic and iambic cola (see COLON), to create a number of complex systems (*asynarteton and *epode), i.e., lines in which different metrical cola are combined. Scholars define the archilochian line variously: (a) xDx + ithyphallic ( x – ‿ ‿ – ‿ ‿ – x | – ‿ – ‿ – – ), where D = *hemiepes; (b) dactylic tetrameter + ithyphallic ( – ‿ ‿ – ‿ ‿ – ‿ ‿ – | – ‿ – ‿ – – ) (Halporn et al.; = Klingner's versus Archilochius); (c) dactylic tetrameter catalectic ( – ‿ ‿ – ‿ ‿ – ‿ ‿ – –; Klingner). Type (a) is found in Archilochus frag. 170 (West; = 109 Diehl); type (b) in frag. 191.1 (West; = 112.1 Diehl); type (c) as the even lines in the first archilochian strophe of Horace (Odes 1.7, 28; Epode 12). Horace has three epodic (strophic) forms named by metrists after Archilochus: first archilochian: dactylic hexameter + type (c); second archilochian: dactylic hexameter + hemiepes (Odes 4.7; Epode 12); and third archilochian: type (b) + iambic trimeter catalectic, i.e., – – ‿ – ‿ – ‿ – ‿ – (Odes 1.4).

■ Horatius: Opera, ed. F. Klingner, 3d ed. (1959); Halporn et al.; Snell; West.

J. W. HALPORN

**AREOPAGUS** (Gr., "Rock of Ares"). Originally referring to a site in which an ancient judicial body met northwest of the Acropolis in Athens, the name has been understood by literary historians to refer to a literary circle of the 1580s established to reform Eng. versification according to cl. models. The name comes from a reference in a letter from Edmund Spenser to Gabriel Harvey pub. in Three proper, and wittie, familiar letters (1580), in which he writes that Philip Sidney and Edward Dyer had recently "proclaimed in their areopagos a generall surceasing and silence of balde Rymers." On the basis of Spenser's comment and Harvey's reply, a trad. arose in the 19th c. that the term referred to a formal literary club similar to the Fr. *Pléiade, incl. Sidney, Dyer, Spenser, Harvey, and Fulke Greville. Although probably not organized in that fashion, those poets were all enthusiastically experimenting with quantitative verse at the time (see QUANTITY), an enterprise that held, for them, serious implications for the value of Eng. as a national and literary lang.

See CLASSICAL METERS IN MODERN LANGUAGES.

R. KAPLAN

**ARGENTINA, POETRY OF.** The Argentine poetic trad. begins with a poem by a soldier on a Sp. expedition, Martín del Barco Centenera's (1535–1602), La Argentina, pub. in 1602 in Lisbon. In its style, verse

form (hendecasyllabic lines with alternating consonant rhyme), and historical description of Indians, the poem echoes the Basque poet Alonso de Ercilla in La Araucana (1569–89), though without the same vitality, which makes del Barco's poem a less auspicious start to this national trad.

Local voices arose in the 19th c., and their styles, like many in Sp. America, featured neoclassicism and patriotic verse (see NEOCLASSICAL POETICS). "Al Paraná" by Manuel José de Lavardén (1754–1809) is a neoclassical *ode published in 1801, a song of praise to the region that predates the Venezuelan Andrés Bello's more famous Silvas americanas (1823). The struggle toward national independence continued and extended patriotic verse, e.g., in the "Marcha patriótica" (1813) by Vicente López y Planes (1785–1856), a nationalistic hymn that would later be revised into the Argentine *anthem. Another locally focused poetic style crucial to this century was *gaucho poetry, and Bartolomé Hidalgo's (1788–1822) work is an early example. His Cielitos y diálogos patrióticos recounted events of the wars for independence and highlighted the perspective of the gauchos, or nomadic cowboys from the plains. Gaucho poetry is based on oral practice, and Hidalgo's cielitos are rhymed quatrains that may come from the Sp. *romance trad. Later gaucho-style poetry was elaborated by Estanislao del Campo (1834–80) and Hilario Ascasubi (1807–75), but it is José Hernández's (1834–86) Martín Fierro that is widely considered to be the culmination of gauchesque lit. The first part of this long narrative poem was published in 1872 and recounts Fierro's marginalization from civilization, while the second chronicles his return (1879). Hernández employs the voice of a gaucho singer or payador to create the effect of improvisation for, as Ludmer has noted, in the gaucho style the lettered elite make use of the popular. Gaucho poetry offers an intriguing link between lit. and politics and highlights certain crucial tensions of the moment: between written and oral cultures and between the rural interior and urbanized center—divisions that are central to 19th-c. cultural production in Argentina.

An important figure in the national political scene, whose presence is felt in the poetry of the decade, is Juan Manuel Rosas. Elected governor of Buenos Aires in 1829, Rosas (a Federalist) later headed a dictatorial regime that lasted from 1835 to 1852. Juan Cruz Varela (1794–1839) was a poet of the opposing Unitarian Party, who composed odes to freedom of the press, commemorated key independence battles, and wrote "El veinticinco de mayo de 1838" (The 25th of May, 1838), attacking Rosas. Varela composed a long love poem, "Elvira" (1831), and odes to national heroes Juan Ramón Balcarce and Manual Belgrano; the critic Menéndez y Pelayo called him the first truly Argentine poet.

During the same period, Esteban Echeverría (1805–51) nationalized romantic poetry and prose. His Rimas (Rhymes, 1837) includes what would become his best-known poem, "La cautiva" (The Captive Woman), a ten-part narrative that recounts the capture of two Argentines by a group of Indians. This poem, in some ways romantic more in sentiment than in form, is an example of a Eur.-influenced aesthetic in an Am. context. It has been read in relation to the struggles for independence and other captivity narratives and creole representations of the Indian and includes references to issues such as miscegenation, gender, the role of nature, and the extension and limits of the nation in Latin America. Later *romanticism (1852–80) is associated with the work of Carlos Guido y Spano (1827–1916), who was not known for Indian or gaucho themes but treated topics that ranged from the intimate to the heroic. He is recognized for adopting romanticism as a way of life, and some of the *Parnassian elements in his poetry link him to early 20th-c. *modernismo.

Leopoldo Lugones (1874–1938) is the Argentine most associated with modernismo and, as Kirkpatrick has observed, his work demonstrates a transformative relationship to this movement. Like other modernists, Lugones attempted to alter or refine lang. and prosody through daring rhymes, verbal skill, and a recherché vocabulary. In Las montañas del oro (The Golden Mountains, 1893), he combined a series of opposing images and linked nature and science; Los crepúsculos del jardín (The Garden's Twilight, 1905) featured excess and exaggeration, and all the irony and tensions of his earlier styles culminate in the parody of Lunario sentimental (Sentimental Moon Journey, 1909). While some qualify Lugones's work as late modernismo, others see it as part of a postmodernist reformulation and critique of that movement. In Sp. America, posmodernismo designates an early 20th-c. transitional period, between approximately 1905 and 1930, in which modernist characteristics expanded and shifted in poetry that largely did not participate in the avant-garde. There is some controversy about whether it exists as a separate movement or as an extension of modernismo; but in any case, it features poetry that is markedly intimate, is often situated in rural rather than urban settings, and involves perspectives regularly marginalized by the dominance of modernismo.

Associated with this early posmodernismo is Evaristo Carriego (1883–1912), whose Misas herejes (Heretical Masses, 1908) describes humble lives with sincerity and emotion, earning him fame as the poet of the arrabal or suburb (a perspective to be elaborated by Jorge Luis Borges). Baldomero Fernández Moreno (1886–1950) is known for capturing urban and rural reality in his poetry, and Las iniciales del misal (The Missal's Initials, 1915) relies on simple musical lyrics. Alfonsina Storni (1892–1938), the best known of this group and one of the now-canonical women poets, demonstrates in much of her poetry a feminist consciousness and anger with prescribed social roles. Her early work, El dulce daño (Sweet Suffering, 1918) has stylistic links to modernismo, while she moves toward the avant-garde in her later, more experimental collection Mascarilla y trébol (Mask and Clover, 1938).

Another Argentine response to modernismo arose in the ultraist movement of the 1920s, which advocated *free verse and sought to condense poetry to its primary element—a revitalized metaphor (see ULTRAISM). The movement, which emphasized aesthetics and cosmopolitanism, is associated with Borges (1899–1986) and the Martín Fierro magazine (1924–27), which featured the work of Borges, Guillermo de Torre, Oliverio Girondo, Norah Lange, Ricardo Molinari, and Leopoldo Marechal. These writers were also associated with the Grupo Florida, an intellectual and aristocratic assemblage concerned with aesthetic renovation, which they defined and put into action; often considered elitist, this group also exhibited some contrasting democratic, urban, and nationalistic traits. Between 1923 and 1930, Borges published three books of poetry, each of which emphasized ultraism through the use of metaphor; formally, the poems combine free verse, hendecasyllables, and the *alexandrine, and many of them are concerned with a mythical space—Buenos Aires and its urban neighborhoods. Later, Borges abandoned ultraism, but he continued to write poetry throughout his life, incl. a variety of themes also present in his fiction: the search for identity, nostalgia, philosophical idealism, and Argentine folklore (e.g., he composed lyrics for tangos and milongas).

Leopoldo Marechal (1900–70) also participated in Martín Fierro in the 1920s, and his first published poetry, Los aguiluchos (The Eaglets, 1922) and Días como flechas (Days like Arrows, 1926), tends toward the avant-garde. His work deals with philosophical preoccupations, order, harmony, and lyrical interpretation of Argentine places and trads. Joining Borges and Marechal was Molinari (1898–1996), whose themes are more existential: lack, the impossibility of communication, the purity of lang. From a metaphysical perspective, he contemplates solitude, death, and time in forms such as the romance, *sonnet, and ode.

Girondo (1891–1967), after Borges and Lugones, is the best known of Argentina's early 20th-c. poets, and his early work is also part of this group. Veinte poemas para ser leídos en el tranvía (Twenty Poems to be Read on the Streetcar, 1922), Calcomanías (Transfers, 1925), and Espantapájaros (Scarecrow, 1932) are all ultraist in style and, although they include some surrealist discontinuities, are more referential than most of his later works (see SURREALISM). En la masmédula (In the Deep Marrow, 1954) features his most radical use of lang., incl. neologisms and phonic relations between terms. Lange (1906–72) was the sole woman in the group, and her personal, dreamlike poetry had surrealist touches within fragmented yet intimate urban landscapes.

The Grupo Boedo, a leftist, socially conscious set opposed to the Florida group's aestheticism, shared a desire for something new and occasionally participated in ultraism and the avant-garde. Raúl González Tuñón (1905–74) was a poet who witnessed the city and its social life instead of producing art for art's sake. Out of El violín del diablo (The Devil's Violin, 1926), his first book, grew marginal figures such as the militant character Juancito Caminador (Johnny Walker). Nicolás Olivari (1900–66), also part of the Boedo group, displayed irony and sarcasm in his portraits of society in La musa de la mala pata (The Bad-Footed Muse, 1926); like some of his compatriots, he composed tango lyrics, notably those of La violeta (The Violet). Both these poets influenced Francisco Urondo (1930–76), who used his idealism and militant poetry to confront the dictatorship of the 1970s. Entering the 1930s and 1940s, previously ultraist poets turned to surrealism or neoromanticism, and the Argentine avant-garde fractured into different elements.

Essays and narrative dominated the 1920s and 1930s, but one transitional poet in this period was both part of the *Martín Fierro* group and different from it: Carlos Mastronardi (1901–76). Called an "anti-vanguard vanguardist," Mastronardi, known for translating Fr. symbolists, was a symbolist himself, whose verse engaged sensibility and landscape, drew on comparison rather than metaphor, and employed traditional musical forms rather than free verse. His poetics make him a precursor to the 1940s generation, whose poets combined avant-garde elements with *symbolism and romanticism to create personal styles that bring them together eclectically as a group.

There is a tendency in mid-century Argentine letters to discuss ten-year generations, loosely affiliating poets who began to publish in the same decade and who share a literary inheritance but not a platform. Some of the 1940s poets, writing during the time that Juan Perón first came to power (1946–55), demonstrate an interest in the irrational, magical, and ritual possibilities of poetry. They tend to see the poem as a way of knowing, while at the same time questioning what it is possible to know or say. Alberto Girri (1919–91) is one of these poets, who counts Ezra Pound and T. S. Eliot among his influences. His early work, such as *Playa sola* (Lone Beach, 1946), is visionary, necromantic, imagistic, and affective. In his later work, the perspective becomes ironic and cerebral in dense, free-verse poems that explore time and space. Enrique Molina's (1910–96) work is more associated with surrealism (he translated André Breton), and in his first book, *Las cosas y el delirio* (Things and Delirium, 1941), he combines reality with hallucination, creating a sense of disintegration and of solitude as a natural experience. His long poetic novel *Una sombra donde sueña Camila O'Gorman* (A Shadow Where Camila O'Gorman Sleeps, 1973) offers its readers a dreamlike approach to a figure from Argentine hist., as well as a genre-crossing postvanguardist experiment. There is a constant tension in the poetry of Olga Orozco (1920–99): a ceaseless motif of desire and lack, a search for a fragmented god or wholeness, amid themes of distance and loss. Poetry is a ritual or an interior journey in her work, which demonstrates a notable coherence of tone, lang., and themes, from *Desde lejos* (From Afar, 1946) to the occult, metaphysical concerns of *Con esta boca en este mundo* (With This Mouth in This World, 1994). Each of these poets turned away from overt engagement with the social world in her or his work to explore other kinds of knowledge through poetry.

In the 1950s and 1960s, a number of younger poets began to publish, some continuing in the postvanguardist mode, such as Alejandra Pizarnik (1936–72), who wrote often-terse, interior-focused poetry on the fringes of surrealism, while others turned to poetry as a means of social transformation. Pizarnik's work is often seen as a self-exile in lang. and away from the poetic values of her generation. She uses a dense, hypercon-

trolled lang. in which solitude and silence play a central role to challenge lit.'s limitations in works such as *El infierno musical* (Musical Hell, 1971). Pizarnik was an inspiration to a series of later poets, and recent readers have begun to explore the full range of her writing.

Liliana Lukin (b. 1951) acknowledges Pizarnik's writing as an inspiration to her own. Her book *Descomposición* (Decomposition, 1986) quotes from Franz Kafka (a source of intertexts favored by Pizarnik as well), whose work reminds us that reading, like writing, is a disturbing and corporeal process. Lukin uses lang. to embody absence, and in both theme and technique, this poetics becomes part of the historical recovery process after the Dirty War (the dictatorship that lasted from 1976 to 1983). Tamara Kamenszain (b. 1947) is another writer who extends Pizarnik's techniques through her concept of lang. as a trope in *Los no* (1977), in which ritualized Japanese *Nō theater exemplifies the renunciation of representation, and in *La casa grande* (The Big House, 1986), a semisurreal evocation of daily life. More recently Anahí Mallol (b. 1968) has explored the impact of Pizanik in her own work and that of others (contemps. Susana Thénon [1937–90] and Orozco, and more recent writers) whose works converse with those of Pizarnik in their intensity and struggle with the liminal zones of lang.

A contemporary of Pizarnik, Juan Gelman (b. 1930), moves through the world and makes his poetry of it, shoring up lang. against dehumanization. His early poetry (*Violín y otras cuestiones* [Violin and Other Questions], 1956) is based on local speech that links experience with imagination in primarily urban settings. Gelman was exiled from Argentina in 1975, and his later books deal with issues such as mourning, politics, and responsibility for the other, employing techniques such as syntactic and linguistic alteration, idiosyncratic punctuation, intertextual references, *heteronyms, and self-translations. During this time of much social and political change, Juana Bignozzi's (b. 1937) poetry joins a personal, confessional tone to social realism. Lucid and conversational, her lang. shares irony and an ethical perspective with that of Gelman; her collected works, *La ley, tu ley* (The Law, Your Law, 2000), demonstrate the scope of her expression. The work of Leónidas Lamborghini (1927–2009) grows out of a social commitment that he expresses in unadorned lang. and short lines. He highlights the construction of a poetic *voice, and this, along with an attention to rhythm, unites his oeuvre. He creates a dialogue or counterpoint by rewriting earlier authors, sometimes with a parodic, ludic tone to remind his readers consistently that art is an artifice—one technique that associates him with the *neobaroque.

After the dictatorship, the floodgates opened, and there was a proliferation of poetry that branched out into new areas, both stylistic and thematic. Néstor Perlongher (1949–92) was a prominent figure of the 1980s whose style is complex, focusing readers' attention on the text's surface and on lit.'s metalinguistic aspects, all elements that situate his work within the neobaroque. Perlongher describes the movement as deterritorialized (departing from the Spaniard Luis de

Góngora), a postcolonial response to inherited paradigms. Although some neobaroque poets may exclude external references, Perlongher insinuates politics and hist. into his early collections (*Austria-Hungría*, 1980), in which orderly syntax and grammatical connections still predominate. In his later work, neobaroque complication reigns: *Parque Lezama* (1990) is a linguistic performance in which any normative identity is destabilized, propelling its readers to ontological questions about what speech and poetry are. Another defiant perspective of the 1980s is that of Diana Bellessi (b. 1946), who established a feminist voice (with a notably lesbian perspective in *Eroíca*, 1988) with which she recreated inherited symbols, images, and words in an erotic intimate tone. Her later work elaborates her ethical interests, often joining popular and high cultural registers. Bellessi's work has been taken in new directions by more recent poets such as Bárbara Belloc (b. 1968), whose *Ambición de las flores* (1997) elaborates the flower as a feminine erotic image, paradoxically loving and carnivorous.

A proliferation of journals in mid- and late 20th-c. Argentina featured poetry: *Poesía Buenos Aires*, *A partir de cero*, and later *Literal*, *Diario de poesía*, *Ultimo reino*, and *\*XUL*, providing venues for local and international poetry and theoretical debate. The economic turmoil of the 1990s, which continued into the next century, heralded more social transformation and a new urban poetry featuring direct communication of experience that some critics have called hyperrealistic. Many younger poets work against alienation and give voice to disillusion through irony and references to the new social margins. Some of this poetry incorporates film, mass media, and popular culture in form and content. Through performance, poetry on the Web, and hypertextual forms, poets find new ways to seek out readers. One example of the many recent writers who challenge the status quo is Washington Cucurto (pseud. of Santiago Vega, b. 1973), whose *Cosa de negros* (Black Folks' Stuff, 2003) has developed a kind of cult following. Cucurto writes from the invisible part of his country and uses *cumbia* and other dance rhythms to express the raw experience of a peripheral world that is denigrated by the dominant culture. Like many of the poets of his generation, he uses lyric conventions to challenge these prejudices—an approach that might characterize much of the poetry of the late 1990s and the early 21st c. in Argentina.

*See* INDIGENOUS AMERICAS, POETRY OF THE; SPANISH AMERICA, POETRY OF.

■ **Anthologies**: *Poesía argentina del siglo XX*, ed. J. C. Ghiano (1957)—also contains hist. and crit.; *Antología lineal de la poesía argentina*, ed. C. Fernández Moreno (1968); *Antología de poesía argentina*, ed. A. del Saz (1969); *La nueva poesía argentina*, ed. N. Salvador (1969); *Antología de la poesía argentina*, ed. R. G. Aguirre (1979); *Antología de la nueva poesía argentina*, ed. H. Alvarez Castillo (1990); *Geografía lírica argentina*, ed. J. Isaacson (2003).
■ **Criticism and History**: M. Menéndez y Pelayo, *Historia de la poesía argentina* (1943); J. Ludmer, *El género gauchesco* (1988); B. Sarlo, *Una modernidad periférica*

(1988); G. Kirkpatrick, *The Dissonant Legacy of Modernismo* (1989); M. González and D. Treece, *The Gathering of Voices* (1992); *Conversaciones con la poesía argentina*, ed. J. Fondebrider (1995); A. Mallol, *El poema y su doble* (2003); M. Prieto, *Breve historia de la literatura argentina* (2006); *Tres décadas de la poesía argentina 1976–2006*, ed. J. Fondebrider (2006); T. Kamenszain, *Boca de testimonio* (2007).

J. KUHNHEIM

**ARGUMENT** has several senses in crit. Loosely used, it can mean \*plot, i.e., a sequence of events; this meaning is authorized by cl. usage (e.g., Terence, *argumentum fabulae*, the plot of the story) and is common during the Ren. It may also refer to a prologue with a prose paraphrase of the verse to follow. But the most common and most important meaning concerns the \*structure of a poem: the framework or design that propels and shapes the sequencing of events. Must every poem have an argument in this sense? Has its argument much—or anything—to do with its value? Ren. poetry was certainly written in a trad. that linked poetry with logic, spoke about the "cause" of a poem, and considered details in relation to their logical function (see RENAISSANCE POETICS). The symbolist view, by contrast, finds the value of poetry in those elements it does not share with prose: the logical or narrative structure of a poem is dispensable (see SYMBOLISM). This seems to be the case in such poems as Stéphane Mallarmé's "L'Après-midi d'un faune" or Paul Valéry's "La jeune parque" (though not in all Valéry): no logical thread links the \*imagery of these poems. The Ezra Pound of \*imagism, Wallace Stevens, and T. S. Eliot stand at least partly in this trad. A rather different antilogical trad. runs from Arthur Rimbaud through \*vorticism to \*surrealism and includes Dylan Thomas: here the brute juxtaposition of imagery is not the result of careful construction but a direct expression of the unconscious.

There seem to be three possible conclusions: that argument is unnecessary; that it is mainly a ploy to attract the reader, relying on the rest of the poem to enable true poetic response; that it is sometimes (always?) part of a poem's true value. It would not be possible to claim that it was the whole of the poem's value without maintaining that the paraphrase was worth as much as the poem. The first view is the symbolist theory. The second is implicit in some romantic crit. and is likely to be held by mod. admirers of romantic poetry. The perfect illustration would be a poem like S. T. Coleridge's "Kubla Khan." The third is the traditional view and, in modified form, is still found among critics for whom structure is a primary consideration. Even in those critics who eschew the term *argument* as old-fashioned, however, it is worth noting what terms they use instead to denote a poem's principle of logic and continuity.
■ J. Kertzer, *Poetic Argument* (1989).

L. D. LERNER

## ARMENIAN POETRY AND POETICS

I. Pre-Christian Origins and Early Epics
II. Ecclesiastic Poetry

**I. Pre-Christian Origins and Early Epics.** The Armenian lang., a branch of the IE ling. family, has an extensive poetic trad. originating in ancient Asia Minor and eventually spanning the globe over more than two millennia. Most historians date the emergence of the Armenians to the 6th c. BCE as a distinct ling. and cultural collective autochthonous to Anatolia in the Republic of Turkey.

Few samples of the earliest Armenian poetry remain. Two reasons account for this scarcity. First, the earliest poetry constituted a segment of the oral trad., thereby leaving no written trace. Second, the Armenians' state conversion to Christianity (ca. 314–15) precipitated the prompt effacement of the Armenian Zoroastrian and pagan pasts, incl. the narratives they inspired.

The remaining fragments, which were partially inscribed following the invention of the Armenian alphabet (ca. 406 CE), suggest rich bardic origins. Armenian historical texts indicate that the first poets were *minstrels, known as *gusans*, who composed a variety of songs, ranging from eulogies for historical personages to festive wedding tunes. Pre-Christian poetry also included two categories of *epics based either on legendary tales or mythologized historical themes. The legendary epic "Vahagn Vishapagagh" (Vahagn the Dragonslayer) found in the *History of the Armenians* by Movses Khorenatsi (Moses of Khoren, "Father of Armenian Historiography") constitutes the oldest surviving Armenian poem and recounts the birth of the divinity Vahagn, god of thunder. Mythologized historical epics appear during the Yervantuni dynasty (ca. 600–200 BCE) and include the popular tale *Tigran and Azhdahak*, relating the struggle between King Tigran I and the king of the Medes, Azhdahak (Astiages). It depicts the first female character to appear in an epic, Tigranuhi, Tigran's sister and Azhdahak's wife. The earliest known post-Christian epic is *Parsits Paterazm* (The Persian War), drawn from folklore and composed between the 3rd and 5th cs. CE and relating the protracted struggle of the Arshakuni (Arsacid) dynasty rulers of Armenia against the Sassanid Empire.

**II. Ecclesiastic Poetry.** The first phase of ecclesiastic poetry commenced following the alphabet's invention by the monk Mesrop Mashtots (ca. 360–440). Though lay poetry continued to appear, verses were primarily restricted to spiritual works, which rendered biblical stories, reproduced ancient Jewish prayers and psalms, and introduced the first specimen of written Armenian *lyric poetry, namely, the spiritual hymn, later known (from the 12th c. CE on) as *sharakan*. Mashtots and one of his patrons, the catholicos Sahak Partev (ca. 345–439), authored the first sharakans, which were performed on Christian feast days and holidays. In addition to Mashtots and Sahak Partev, other noteworthy sharakan writers include Moses of Khoren, renowned for his "Khorhurd metz yev skanjeli"

(Great and Wondrous Mystery) sung on Christmas; Sahak Dzoraporetsi (677–708), who wrote the first sharakans dedicated to the Cross and the Church; Stepanos Siunetsi (d. 735), who turned the canon into the liturgy by organizing hymns and arranging voices and tunes; and Sahakdukht (fl. 8th c.), Siunetsi's sister, who is the first known female Armenian poet.

In addition to sharakans, the Middle Ages also produced one of the most renowned Armenian poets, the monk Grigor Narekatsi (Gregory of Nareg, ca. 950–1003). Narekatsi is acclaimed for his monumental lyric poem *Matyan Voghbergutyun* (Book of Lamentations), known simply as *Narek*, a book of prayers consisting of 95 chapters. Its tone resembles Augustine's *Confessions* with themes of repentance and love of God, heavily imbued with simile and metaphor. After the Psalter and NT, it was the most widely circulated text of med. Armenian lit. and has remained influential.

Another influential early poet is Nerses Shnorhali (Nerses, Full of Grace, ca. 1101–1173). Shnorhali lived and wrote during a trying historical period when the displaced Armenian people were forced to relocate to Syria and Cilicia and had to struggle for autonomy from Byzantine and regional rulers. A pervasive preference for poetry had emerged that led writers and translators to render a wide variety of narratives—historical, didactic, scientific, and literary—into verse in the manner of Homer, David, Solomon, and Jeremiah, and also often converted prose texts into poetry. Shnorhali wrote in this milieu, composing in a vast array of genres. Trained as a priest and later anointed catholicos (1166), Shnorhali was committed to national and ecclesiastic concerns, exemplified in his historical epic *Voghb Yedesio* (Lament for Edessa, ca. 1145), the first of its kind in Armenian lit. The epic recounts the destruction of Edessa (1144) and the massacre of its Christian population by Emir Zangi's troops. It introduced several innovations, incl. *personification and the five-syllable iambic meter, which became the standard for subsequent poets. The work helped reinforce the *lament as a dominant poetic form, inspiring Grigor IV Tgha's (ca. 1133–93) *Voghb Yerusaghemi* (Lament for Jerusalem, 1189); Stepanos Orbelian's (ca. 1250–1305) *Voghb i dimats katoghikein* (Lament on Behalf of the Cathedral); and Arakel Baghishetsi's (ca. 1380–1454) *Voghb Mayrakaghakin Stampolu* (Lament for the Capital Constantinople, 1453), among others.

After Narekatsi and Shnorhali, few noteworthy names or literary devels. appear from the 13th through the 17th cs., a period of protracted political strife for the Armenians embattled by invaders and culminating in the devastating fall of the kingdom of Cilicia (1375) to Mamluk forces. The poets whose names survive from this period lived and wrote chiefly in the 13th c. Hovhannes Yerznkatsi (Pluz, ca. 1230–93) was the era's best-known scholar and philosopher. He was the first to write a secular love poem based on a folk tale about a pair of ill-fated lovers—an Armenian boy and a Muslim girl—divided by their faiths. The spirited Frik (b. ca. 1230) was popular for his bombastic poems condemning corruption and oppression in all spheres.

Kostandin Yerznkatsi (ca. 1304–36) is significant for introducing extensive nature imagery and earned acclaim for his elaborate allegories.

### III. The Rise of Folk Songs and Armenian Classicism.
By the end of the 16th c., a new group of poets emerged consisting of Nerses Mokatsi (ca. 1575–1625), Martiros Ghrimetsi (1620–83), and Simeon Aparanetsi (ca. 1540–1614). At the time, folk songs had a great influence on poetry. Nahapet Kuchak (d. ca. 1592) was a master of the *hairen* variety, an indigenous poetic form written in four lines of *couplets with a single coherent theme.

The 18th c. compensated somewhat for the immediate past's poetic stagnation. Bardic lyricism had developed in the previous century as a branch of folk songs and flourished in the 18th through the works of the two renowned *bards Naghash Hovnatan (1661–1722) and Sayat-Nova (ca. 1712–95). The latter is a dominant figure in the Armenian national imagination, and his songs are still regularly performed. Bardic lyric poems were related to Perso-Arabic lit. and were sung by wandering bards who also performed non-Armenian pieces. They initially expressed historical themes but eventually evolved primarily into love songs. This period also paved the way for formal cl. pieces composed in *grabar* (cl. Armenian) such as those by Paghtasar Dpir (Grigorian, 1683–1768) and Petros Ghapantsi (d. 1784).

The 18th c. also witnessed the rise of the Mkhitarist Congregation (1717) founded by Mkhitar Sebastatsi (Mkhitar of Sivas, 1676–1749) on the island of San Lazzaro in Venice. The Mkhitarist monks were instrumental in reviving the Armenian lang. and lit. Mkhitar was their first author and wrote mainly religious poems with patriotic themes. Arsen Bakratuni (1790–1866) and Ghevont Alishan (1820–1901) succeeded him as the two most prominent Mkhitarist poets. Bakratuni's poem *Hayk Diutzazn* (The Epic Hero Hayk) is one of the longest poems (22,332 lines) in world lit. and represents the height of Armenian classicism. It recounts the heroic exploits of the mythical Armenian forefather Hayk, deriving its influence from ancient Gr. and Lat. sources. Alishan's poems were the first to appear in mod. Armenian and initiated the romantic trad. in Armenian lit., inspiring the patriotic works of such major 19th-c. poets as Raphael Patkanian (1830–92) and Mikayel Nalpantian (1829–66). Alishan's most celebrated poems include "Voghbam Zkez Hayots Ashkharh" (I Weep for You, Armenia) and *Hushigk Hayrenyats Hayots* (Memories of the Armenian Homeland).

The 19th c. inaugurated a culturally fertile epoch, which continued into the early portion of the 20th c. Armenian poetry in particular underwent radical transformation, achieving unprecedented popularity and a central role in facilitating the Armenian national-cultural revival. Interest in the poetic trad. led folklorist Father Karekin Srvandztiantz to the major discovery and inscription in the 1870s of *Sansuntsi Davit* (*David of Sassoun*), part of the cycle *Sasna Tzrer* (Madmen of Sasun) and *Jojants Tun* (House of Giants). It was an epic recounted for the first time in the Middle Ages and had survived in the oral trad. of Mush, one of whose inhabitants, Krpo of Mush, had retained and retold it.

### IV. The National Awakening.
The second half of the 19th c. is known as the era of *Zartonk* (Awakening), which proceeded from various historical, political, and cultural antecedents: the rise of the merchant classes in Armenian global diasporic communities; the creation of Armenian printing presses; the cultural efforts of the Mkhitarist congregation; and the preoccupation of Eur.-educated intellectuals with national concerns. Four poets exemplified the spirit and poetic trends of the Zartonk generation: Mgrdich Beshigtashlian (1828–68) and Bedros Turian (1851–72), both natives of Istanbul, represented the Western Armenian dialect writing in the Ottoman Empire; and Mikayel Nalpantian (1829–66) and Raphael Patkanian (also known as Kamar Katipa, 1830–92), both from Nor Nakhichevan (Rostov-on-Don), wrote in Eastern Armenian in the South Caucasus. Beshigtashlian is renowned for his romantic lyricism, which combined naturalist imagery with nationalist motifs. His poems "Karun" ("Spring") and "Yeghpair Emk Mek . . ." (We Are Brothers . . .) highlight his delicate temperament and profound patriotism. Turian, who died prematurely from tuberculosis at the age of 21, was much beloved by his contemporaries. His poems primarily speak of unrequited love, untimely death, and patriotic struggle. His poems "Ljag" ("Little Lake"), about his imminent death, and "Trkuhin" (The Turkish Woman), about an unattainable beloved, are among his most popular works. Nalpantian was a staunch anti-imperialist activist whose poems reflect his political inclinations, esp. in "Mankutyan Orer" (Childhood Days), "Azatutyun" (Freedom), and "Mer Hayrenik" (Our Fatherland), which became the national anthem of the Republic of Armenia. Similarly, Patkanian considered his work a medium for promoting enlightenment and national consciousness through such poems as "Araxi Artasuke" ("The Tears of the Araxes") and his 1878 collection *Azat Yerger* (Free Songs).

### V. The Rise of the Aesthetes.
In the last decades of the 19th c., as *realism gradually replaced romanticism, preference for poetry waned in favor of prose. The next wave of influential poets emerged afterward, in the first two decades of the 20th c. Taking their cues from the canon of Western lit., some of them demanded and exercised new modes of ling. refinement and aesthetic consciousness, becoming known as the Aesthetes. The outstanding names of this time include, among Western Armenians, Misak Medzarents (1886–1908), Vahan Tekeyan (1878–1945), Tanyel Varujan (1884–1915), Siamanto (Adom Yerjanian, 1878–1915); and among Eastern Armenians, Hovhannes Tumanian (1869–1923), Yeghishé Charents (Soghomonian, 1897–1937), Avetik Issahakian (1875–1957), and Vahan Terian (1885–1920).

Varujan and Charents constitute the apex of these new poetic heights and share similarly tragic fates. Varujan described his perspective as "poetic paganism," which he voiced initially with his rendition of "Vahagn." The poem appeared in his first large collection, *Tzeghin Sirde* (The Heart of the Race, 1909), which was followed by *Hetanos Yerker* (Pagan Songs, 1912), considered two of the most important books of Armenian poetry from the 20th c. On April 24, 1915, the eve of the outbreak of the Catastrophe (the genocide of Ottoman-Armenians, 1915–18), Varujan was captured by Ottoman authorities along with hundreds of his contemporaries and deported to the prison camp of Chankiri, where he was promptly executed. Charents lived across the Ottoman border, in Soviet territory. He was a staunch Communist but soon became disillusioned with the Stalinist regime, which took his life during the 1937 purges. Charents's work expresses a revolutionary spirit that responded with insight and fervor to the harrowing historicopolitical vicissitudes he observed and experienced. His best-known works in his extensive repertoire include *Tandeakan Araspel* (*Dantesque Legend*), a response to the World War I Ottoman atrocities he witnessed as a volunteer soldier; *Ambokhnerë Khelagarvatz* (The Frenzied Masses), which established him as the first major non-Russian Soviet poet; and *Girk Chanaparhi* (Book of the Road), a set of verses dedicated to major Armenian cultural figures alongside religious and love poems.

**VI. Poetry in Diaspora.** Following the Catastrophe and the expansion of the Armenian diaspora, poetry experienced a mixture of decline and experimentation. Surviving and emerging Ottoman-Armenian writers wrote haphazardly and consisted both of traditionalist and avant-garde wings. Among the traditionalists who conformed to the poetic ideals and methods of their predecessors were Mushegh Ishkhan (Mushegh Jerderian, 1913–90), Antranig Dzarugian (1912–90), and Vahé Vahian (Sarkis Abdalian, 1907–98). Among the avant-garde, one finds Nigoghos Sarafian (1902–72), Zahrad (pseud. of Zareh Yaldzjian, 1924–2007), Zareh Khrakhuni (pseud. of Artin Jiumbiushian, b. 1926), and Vahé Oshagan (1922–2000). Dzarugian and Sarafian have left the most indelible marks by vividly expressing their generation's orientation. Dzarugian's controversial poem, "Tught ar Yerevan" (Letter to Yerevan) targeted Soviet Armenian writers' antinationalist propagandist rhet. Sarafian paved a unique and unprecedented path with his long poem *Venseni Andare* (The Forest of Vincennes), which traces the poet's inner journey as the son of a displaced people. During the same years, Soviet Armenian poets were beset by the regime's stringent restrictions. They include Gevork Emin (1919–98), Paruyr Sevak (1924–71), and Silva Kaputikian (1919–2006).

In the wake of the 20th c., Armenian poetry is at a virtual standstill, though several promising voices in the diaspora and the Republic of Armenia remain active. Krikor Beledian (b. 1948), based in France, is author of the groundbreaking works *Yelk: Mantraner B. Shark* (Exit: Mantras B. Series) and *Deghakrutyun Kantvogh Kaghaki Me Hamar* (Diagram for a Collapsing City), which impels Armenian poetry into new uncharted realms of abstraction. Violet Grigorian (b. 1962) is a singular experimental poet whose feminist themes and provocative lang. continue to interrogate and undermine entrenched patriarchal taboos. She has published four collections of poems, incl. *Haremi Vard* (Harem Rose).

■ **Anthologies:** A. Issahakian, *Scent, Smile, and Sorrow: Selected Verse (1891–1957) and Jottings from Notebooks*, ed. and trans. E. B. Chrakian (1975); *Anthology of Armenian Poetry*, ed. and trans. D. Der Hovanessian and M. Margossian (1978); *Armenian Poetry, Old and New: A Bilingual Anthology*, ed. and trans. A. Tolegian (1979); K. Nahapet, *Come Sit Beside Me and Listen to Koutchag: Medieval Armenian Poems of Nahabed Kouchag*, trans. D. Der-Hovanessian (1984); *Bloody News from My Friend: Poems by Siamanto*, trans. P. Balakian and N. Yaghlian (1996); K. Nahapet, *A Hundred and One Hayrens*, trans. E. Osers (1998); *The Heritage of Armenian Literature*, ed. G. Basmajian, E. S. Franchuk, A. J. Hacikyan, and N. Ouzounian, 3 v. (2000–05); *Bosphorus Nights: The Complete Lyric Poems of Bedros Tourian*, trans. J. R. Russell (2005); *Deviation: Anthology of Contemporary Armenian Literature*, ed. V. Grigoryan and V. Ishkhanyan (2008).

■ **Collections:** *Armenian Popular Songs*, trans. G. M. Alishan (1852); V. Komitas, *Armenian Sacred and Folk Music*, trans. E. Gulbekian (1998); G. M. Alishan, *Old Armenian Songs: A Nineteenth-Century Collection*, ed. A. Nercessian (2002); *The Song of the Stork and Other Early and Ancient Armenian Songs*, trans. D. Kherdian (2004).

■ **Histories:** B. S. Hairapetian, *A History of Armenian Literature: From Ancient Times to the 19th Century* (1995); K. B. Bardakjian, *A Reference Guide to Modern Armenian Literature, 1500–1920* (2000); V. Nersessian, "Armenian," *The Oxford Guide to Literature in English Translation*, ed. P. France (2000); S. P. Cowe, "Medieval Armenian Literary and Cultural Trends," *The Armenian People from Ancient to Modern Times, Vol. 1: The Dynastic Periods*, ed. R. G. Hovanissian (2004); V. Oshagan, "Modern Armenian Literature and Intellectual History from 1700 to 1915" and R. W. Thomson, "Armenian Literary Culture through the Eleventh Century," *The Armenian People from Ancient to Modern Times, Vol. 2: Foreign Dominion to Statehood*, ed. R. G. Hovanissian (2004); R. Panossian, *The Armenians: From Kings and Priests to Merchants and Commissars* (2006).

■ **Journals:** *Ararat: A Quarterly* (1960–); *Journal of the Society for Armenian Studies* (1984–); *Raft: Journal of Armenian Poetry and Criticism* (1984–).

■ **Translations and Criticism:** *David of Sassoun: The Armenian Folk Epic in Four Cycles*, trans. A. K. Shalian (1964); Moses of Khoren, *History of the Armenians*, trans. R. W. Thomson (1978); C. Dowsett, *Sayat'-Nova: An Eighteenth-Century Troubadour* (1997); *The Heroes of Kasht: An Armenian Epic*, ed. and trans. J. R. Russell (2000); N. Grigor, *Speaking with God from the Depths of the Heart: The Armenian Prayer Book of St. Gregory of Narek*, trans. T. J. Samuelian (2001); M. Nichanian, *Writers of Disaster, Vol. 1: The National Revolution* (2002); *Yeghishe Charents: Poet of* the Revolution, ed. M. Nichanian (2003); *Divine Liturgy of the Armenian Apostolic Orthodox Church*, trans. A. Aivazian (2005); S. A. Arak'el, *Adamgirk': The Adam Book of Arak'el of Siwnik'*, trans. M. E. Stone (2007); A. Eghiazaryan, *Daredevils of Sasun: Poetics of an Epic*, trans. S. P. Cowe (2008).

N. Kebranian

**ARSIS AND THESIS** (Gr., "raising and lowering"). These terms, and their equivalents, *arsis* and *basis* (step), and *to ano* (the up [time]) and *to kato* (the down), designate the two rhythmical divisions of the *foot in cl. Gr. and Lat. prosody. The thesis always contains a basic *longum* or its resolved equivalent and is the rhythmically prominent portion of the foot; the arsis always contains at least one *breve* or an *anceps and is the nonprominent portion. However, arsis and thesis should not be equated with the up- and downbeats of Western music. In simple feet such as the iamb ($\cup\,-$), trochee ($-\,\cup$), *dactyl ($-\,\cup\,\cup$), and *anapest ($\cup\,\cup\,-$), the arsis is the single or double breve; the thesis is the longum.

**Linguistic Basis.** The two primary attributes of *rhythm are temporal regularity and prominence differentiation. Arsis and thesis pertain to the latter. When subjects in a psychological experiment were presented with a sequence of evenly spaced, identical sounds, they judged alternate sounds to be stronger, i.e., they assigned an alternating arsis and thesis structure to an objectively undifferentiated sequence. In the rhythm of speech, the prominence is commonly stress: strong or thesis syllables have primary or secondary stress, while weak or arsis syllables are unstressed. At least one syllable must be mapped onto thesis, but sometimes no syllable is assigned to arsis. In some langs., a sequence of two syllables within the same word can be mapped onto one thesis (see RESOLUTION).

The terms originally designated the raising and lowering of the foot in walking (Pseudo-Aristotle, *Problemata* 5.41; cf. *Bacchius* 98) and probably entered the technical terminology of music theory from description of the dance. In the later Roman period, *arsis* sometimes refers to the first part of the foot, *thesis* to the second, but their meanings became reversed in the Lat. trad. (e.g., Terentianus Maurus [see Keil 6.366, 1345–46]), probably when the grammarians came to identify arsis and thesis with the lowering and raising of the voice rather than of the foot. The confusion aroused by this reversal of meanings was carried into mod. cl. scholarship by Richard Bentley in the 18th c. and Gottfried Hermann in the 19th. It would be better if both terms were now avoided altogether outside of Gr. metrics. In Old Germanic and OE metrics, the equivalent terms are *lift* and *dip*; mod. metrists speak indifferently of *positions* or else of *ictus* and *nonictus*.

*See* METER.

■ J. Caesar, *Disputatio de verborum "artsis" et "thesis" apud scriptores artis metricae latinos . . . significatione* (1885); E. H. Sturtevant, "The Ictus of Classical Verse," *AJP* 44 (1923); H. Woodrow, "Time Perception," *Handbook of Experimental Psychology*, ed. S. S. Stevens

(1951); R. P. Winnington-Ingram, "Fragments of Unknown Greek Tragic Texts with Musical Notation, II," *Symbolae Osloenses* 31 (1955); Beare, ch. 5; Maas, sect. 8; Dale, 210 ff.; Allen; A. J. Neubecker, *Altgriechische Musik* (1977); Michaelides; West.

L. D. Stephens

**ARTE MAYOR.** As a general Sp. metric term, *arte mayor* may mean any line of nine or more syllables. However, *arte mayor* almost always refers to a line of a certain pattern (*verso de arte mayor*) or to the *strophe composed of such lines (*copla de arte mayor*). The line developed from the late med. Lat. double *adonic modified by an increasingly liberal use of *anacrusis and *catalexis. Late med. poets borrowed the arte mayor directly from the Galician-Port. of the 13th and 14th cs. The form reached the peak of its devel. in 15th-c. Sp. poetry, then gave way to the Italianate *hendecasyllable in the 16th, since which time it has occupied only a minor position in Sp. poetry. Juan de Mena (1411–56) is considered its greatest master. A recitative measure, it was the vehicle for most poetry of weighty or serious subject matter of the 15th c. Unlike most learned Sp. verse, the arte mayor was not restricted by syllable count but depended largely on rhythmic beat. The basic pattern was a 12-beat verse divided into two *hemistichs of six beats each and having triple rhythm ($\cup\,-\,\cup\,\cup\,-\,\cup\,|\,\cup\,-\,\cup\,\cup\,-\,\cup$) with the second syllable in each hemistich receiving secondary stress and the fifth syllable in each primary stress. The primary and secondary stress beats (the latter occasionally lacking) of each hemistich are supplied by accented syllables; the unstressed beats between these two are supplied by two obligatory unaccented syllables; the remaining unstressed beats may each be supplied by one or two unaccented syllables or a rest beat. The pattern was not always strictly followed. The arte mayor was normally arranged in groups of eight lines to form a stanza, the copla de arte mayor, rhyming *abbaacca*, less often *ababbccb* or *abbaacac*. Although the original arte mayor enjoyed great rhythmic and syllabic freedom, the line in later centuries became primarily a 12-syllable or a 6 + 6 syllable verse with marked amphibrachic rhythm.

■ R. Foulché-Delbosc, "Etude sur le *Laberinto* de Juan de Mena," *Revue hispanique* 9 (1902); J. Saavedra Molina, *El verso de arte mayor* (1946); Le Gentil; M. Burger, *Recherches sur la structure et l'origine des vers romans* (1957); D. C. Clarke, *Morphology of Fifteenth-Century Castilian Verse* (1964), and "Line Formation in the Galician-Portuguese Poetry of the Cancioneiro Colocci-Brancuti," *RPh* 35 (1981); J. Lemartinel, "Remarques sur le vers d'arte mayor," *XIV Congresso internazionale di linguistica e filologia romanza*, ed. A. Várvaro (1981); Navarro; G. S. Hutcheson, "Cracks in the Labyrinth: Juan de Mena, *Converso* Experience, and the Rise of the Spanish Nation," *La Corónica* 25 (1996); J. C. Conde, "Praxis ecdótica y teoría métrica: El case del arte mayor castellana," *La Corónica* 30 (2002).

D. C. Clarke

**ARTE MENOR.** Sp. octosyllabic verse (sometimes shorter). The term is used in contrast to *arte mayor,* which has longer lines and is generally applied to the verse characteristic of the *copla de arte mayor*, a late med. stanza having the rhyme scheme of any copla de arte mayor or variation thereof. Both line and *strophe were probably borrowed from 13th- and 14th-c. Galician-Port.

■ D. C. Clarke, "*Redondilla* and *copla de arte menor*," *HR* 9 (1941); Navarro.

D. C. CLARKE

## ARTIFACT, POETRY AS

I. Classical Background
II. Temporalities
III. Contrasts

An artifact is a made thing. The word *artifact* draws on one of the oldest meanings of poetry, from Gr. *poiésis*: fiction, making.

**I. Classical Background.** The three modes of making are creation, transformation, and preservation. In cl. poetics, creation is essentially mimetic. For Plato and his followers, poems imitate nature, and natural objects imitate ideas; even artifacts that are not obviously derived from nature, such as tools and furniture, have ideas behind them at a deeper level of reality. For every artifact, a divine source, such as a *muse, communicates a diminished version of an idea to a human maker. In the Hebraic trad., creation is similarly eidetic insofar as things reproduce the image of their creator.

To transform is to give new qualities to things. In the most influential cl. account of transformation, Ovid's *Metamorphoses*, the mechanism is always a kind of divine action. In the words of Arthur Golding's trans. (1567), the same gods who "wrought" the transformation of "shapes . . . to bodies straunge" will authorize the speaker's voice, directly connecting the origin of the world to the composition and reading of the poem. By imitating nature, artists participate in the transformation of received materials, originally a divine prerogative. On this account, if I am a sculptor working with a piece of stone, I can give the stone qualities that it does not naturally have. I can make it warm, fluid, or transparent; I can make it float. If I am a poet and my material is lang., I should be able to give the words of my lang. the qualities of tears or a fish's scales or an extreme situation such as torture or an emotion such as obsessive love.

To preserve is to maintain something in the given world. The cl. expression of this power is the conventional boast of poetic immortality. Horace seals the third book of his *Odes* with a poem claiming that he has completed "a monument more lasting than bronze and loftier than the pyramid's royal pile." The book extends the life of the speaker's most valuable "part" by sheltering it from the effects of time; because it can be embodied in speech or writing, memorized, recited, copied, quoted, and translated, it achieves a permanence that would be impossible for seemingly durable bronze and stone memorials. The hostility to the other memorials, the confident projection of a future world that would include the *Odes* but not the pyramids, is typical. Given the chance, Roman funeral urns and Egyptian pyramids would proclaim their unique permanence and the unreliability of oral or textual transmission. A surviving fragment of a statue makes this very proclamation in P. B. Shelley's "Ozymandias." It may be that all artifacts privately entertain fantasies of the universal destruction of other artifacts.

**II. Temporalities.** Although secondary, the act of preservation is by no means a weak or diminished species of making. On the contrary, as Heidegger argues, it is deeply involved in the createdness of artifacts. Heidegger is a mod. exponent of a humanist trad. that sees preservation as the artifact's main function. In its most specific meaning, *humanism* is the intellectual movement driving the Eur. Ren.; humanist scholars and artists of the 15th and 16th cs. processed knowledge through cl. poetic models and translated cl. poetry into mod. langs. Wood's study of Ger. Ren. historiography shows that humanists do not periodize artifacts by the time of their manufacture but instead treat them as counters in a "chain of substitutions" across time. As Wood succinctly puts it, humanists use artifacts to "bend time" into a knot tying things in the present to their origins in things from a chronologically distant past. E.g., when John Keats looks into Chapman's Homer, he sees not only the mediator, George Chapman, but Homer and his world; the book might bring Keats closer to Homer than to Chapman. In a broad sense, humanism is a trad., starting with Aristotle if not earlier, of using artifacts to forge links between ancient and mod. epochs, thereby establishing a common world. The maker of an artifact gathers pieces of the past and sends them into the future.

Arendt, an eloquent defender of humanism, explains how artifacts maintain a world. Things promise commonness and objectivity in that several people can encounter the same thing, as well as plurality in that different encounters can be compared and in that the things physically hold persons apart. All things help to separate persons, but Arendt privileges works of art for their claims to permanence. The resistance of works of art to the effects of time and the care that people put into protecting them from decay ensure the continuity of the world. Thus, although J. W. Goethe is not our contemporary, we can look at the same sculptures that he saw and read the poems that he wrote, as well as poems that he read by earlier poets.

Poetry is somewhat exceptional in Arendt's cosmology. Artworks are "the most intensely worldly of tangible things," but poems are less worldly, less "thingly," than other artworks because their medium is lang. and they are not usually object-specific. The indifference of poetry to its particular objectification both guarantees its easy transmissibility and leaves it vulnerable to disappearance from hist. Attempts to locate poetry in unique objects, ranging from Brooks's argument against paraphrase to Howe's argument for the semantic value of Dickinson's pen strokes, inevitably sacrifice the transmissibility without lending poems any additional durability.

Not all made things count as artifacts for Arendt.

Artifacts, which persist in time, belong to the sphere of human activity that she calls work, as opposed to labor, whose ephemeral products only sustain life. A similar division within the category of made things occurs in the aesthetics of the Victorian poet and designer William Morris. According to Morris's lectures on ornament, art enters the artifact as a feeling of joy in working and encountering "resistance in the material." This joy is embodied in the decorative flourishes that covered every surface of the furniture and walls in Morris's home and the pages of the books he printed. The alternative would be a fragmentary or ruined thing, hastily, carelessly, and unhappily thrown together. Morris describes this condition of denuded utility, in which a household object such as a ceramic cup receives only a first impression of form and is good for nothing more than holding a liquid and keeping it at a constant temperature, as one of "useless toil," "slavery," and "death," terms that he uses interchangeably. The aesthetic ideal would be a world of exclusively handmade objects whose every surface displayed legible marks of joy in work. An example of such a mark is the motto that Morris borrows from the early mod. painter Jan Van Eyck and inscribes on many of his artisanal and poetic productions: "Si je puis," meaning "If I can," with the implication "As well as I can." The signature directs attention to the artist's virtuosity while ambiguously calling it into question, suggesting that it has limits or that it is derived from an external, perhaps divine source.

For other theorists, the concept of artifactuality dissolves distinctions between art objects and the tools and products of manual labor. Kubler uses the concept to include ancient Mayan tools in art hist.; Gell uses it to include high art in cultural anthropology, as when he outrageously characterizes Michelangelo's *David* as "a big doll for grownups." Both rely on the artifact's extension in time, its durability as opposed to its unassailable permanence. Kubler defines an artifact as a "fibrous bundle" of durations of varying lengths that facilitate contact between cultures and epochs. E.g., a book is published in the 20th c.; its contents are composed in the 16th c., and they translate an ancient poem that incorporates sources from an untraceable past. Many passages in the book are ignored at the time of their publication, and some will come into view centuries later. The format of the book is worth considering: the font is based on an 18th-c. design; the technology of writing is older than the ancient poem, whereas the printed book, of which the glossy paperback is a recent variation, is a near contemporary of the early mod. trans. To what period does the book belong? What happens when this book is placed on a shelf alongside another book that gives time another shape?

Benjamin, however, would deny an important feature of artifactuality to the printed book. A unique handmade object receives from its maker a spiritual deposit that Benjamin calls its "aura." Objects mass-produced by machine lack this aura; further, the auras of unique objects are compromised merely by the existence of the technology to reproduce them mechani-

cally. The aura is the artifact's historical trace, the footprint that it leaves in time; this mark is erased when it can be replaced by a new copy at any moment. Without aura, there can be no artifact. Through the devel. of technologies of reproduction, all artifacts come to share in the diminished worldliness that Arendt ascribes to poetry.

**III. Contrasts**. In cl. poetics, creativity is not considered a human possibility. Creation in the strong sense of producing something without a precedent in the hist. of forms becomes a value in *romanticism. In *Biographia Literaria* (1817), S. T. Coleridge, e.g., assigns primary creative powers to the faculty of *imagination, which he associates with "the eternal I AM," as opposed to the *fancy, a secondary image-making faculty that can only arrange received materials. The word *creativity*, coined in the early 20th c., reflects the modernist values of novelty and originality. Ezra Pound gives voice to these values in the motto "Make it new." The singularity of modernity is axiomatic in *historicism, a method of historical scholarship that assigns each object in the universe to a single place and time, the context of its moment of origin. Historicist scholars as different as Rosemond Tuve and Stephen Greenblatt agree in positing an absolute division between mod. and premod. epochs and in treating poems and other art objects as symptoms rather than remedies of the division. These devels. present challenges to humanist accounts of artifactuality.

An artifact need not be a product of human civilization, as Paul Valéry demonstrates in an essay on seashells. A seashell is undeniably a made thing; in what he describes as a "naive moment," Valéry writes that the first question in the seashell's catechism is "Who made me?" We live in a world of made things, but we experience the world as given because we do not know how to read the signatures on things or because they naturalize themselves, hiding the signs of their making, or simply because we did not make them. An artifact does not have to be brought into the world through an act of human making or perceiving, but it has to do the more difficult work of maintaining a world for a period of time greater than an instant. It is precisely for this reason that Brooks emphasizes the artifactuality of poetry by appropriating John Donne's image of a "well-wrought urn" as an emblem: he wants a poem to exist in a "history without footnotes" rather than in a single historical context as "the expression of the values of its time." Brooks makes Benjamin's point more strongly: without artifacts, there can be no hist.

The true opposite of artifactuality may be theatricality. A theater is a public space, and the scenes enacted there may be shared among the members of the audience in attendance, but the scenes are impermanent. Theater tends to exhaust the resources of artifice in a single moment of *performance. Historicism privileges theatrical performances because they are specific to cultures and to occasions. An artifact, by contrast, is not specific to a culture; instead, it acts as a portal through which materials pass between cultures. Perhaps no theater of purely improvised performances exists. Theater starts to become artifactual when it shapes actions into things that endure beyond the moment of performance, either through the institutions and conventions of the stage or the repetition of actions, characters, and entire plays or through the memorization and objectification of a script.

Many genres of poetry, including *epic, *ballad, *tragedy, *sound poetry, and spoken word, are theatrical in the sense that they were composed in or for a moment of performance. Some mod. poetry is theatrical in a different but related sense that Fried explores in his hist. of art. The literal assertion of the specific properties of objects that occurs in minimalist art is an unhealthy sort of theatricality, according to Fried, in that the art object solicits the participation of a beholder. *Concrete poetry and conceptual writing are theatrical in Fried's sense by virtue of their redundant thematization of their own appearance, their careful undoing of the tension between figure and ground (see CONCEPTUAL POETRY). *Language poetry is intensely theatrical because, in addition to its orientation toward the materials of lang., it professes to give power to readers. Barbara Guest, a poet of the *New York school, is like Fried in rejecting the typical modernist insistence on the elemental materials of lang. A good poem is no longer made of words, although "it is true that many poems are constructed solely of words. . . . We have all read these poems and know that after we have read them we feel curiously bereft." Guest disagrees with Stéphane Mallarmé's dictum that poems are made of words rather than ideas and with W. C. Williams's definition of a poem as "a small (or large) machine made of words." Instead, a poet gives words the properties of other bodies "even as a painting has flesh."

Most poems have artifactual and theatrical aspects. Robert Herrick deliberately composes the "Argument" of his collection *Hesperides* (1648) out of small unities of each: "I sing of times trans-shifting, and I write / How roses first came red, and lilies white." The acts of the speaker demarcate two ways of thinking about lyric. "I sing" conceives lyric as performance, holding a moment in time to itself. "I write" conceives it as monument, persisting in time, connecting things to their origins in other things. The former approach allows Jackson to consider Emily Dickinson's poems as performances specific to the occasion of their composition; the latter allows Keats to look into Chapman's Homer. Both are valid, demonstrating opposed ways of poetry's participating in hist.

*See* BOOK, POETIC; CLASSICISM; FICTION, POETRY AS; FRANKFURT SCHOOL; INFORMATION, POETRY AS; KNOWLEDGE, POETRY AS; MIMESIS; MODERNISM.

■ Brooks; H. Arendt, *The Human Condition* (1958); G. Kubler, *The Shape of Time* (1962); P. Valéry, *Aesthetics*, trans. R. Manheim (1964); Benjamin; W. Morris, *Unpublished Lectures*, ed. E. Lemire (1969)—esp. "Of the Origins of Ornamental Art"; M. Heidegger, *Poetry, Language, Thought*, trans. D. Hofstadter (1971); R. Greene, *Post-Petrarchism* (1991); A. Grossman, *The Sighted Singer* (1992); S. Howe,

*The Birth-mark* (1993); M. Fried, *Art and Objecthood* (1998); A. Gell, *Art and Agency* (1998); D. Mao, *Solid Objects* (1998); B. Guest, *Forces of Imagination* (2003); V. Jackson, *Dickinson's Misery* (2005); C. Wood, *Forgery, Replica, Fiction* (2008); A. Kunin, "Shakespeare's Preservation Fantasy," *PMLA* 124 (2009).

A. KUNIN

**ARTIFICE, POETIC.** While general definitions of *artifice* link it to contrivance, artistry, and technical skill, *poetic artifice* specifically denotes the densely concentrated sonic, visual, and imagistic properties that mark poetry as distinct from prose. The binaries of poetry/prose and artifice/nature, evident in 20th-c. crit., have characterized theories of poetic artifice since the early mod. period, when artifice was closely tied to artistic invention. In the 1970s, poetic artifice in Eng. came to signify more narrowly those nonsemantic features—such as lineation or overall sonic texture—lost in the attempt to render a poem in prose. Later 20th-c. crit. revised this position to argue that lang. unique to poetry (at the level of device but also above and below it) falls within a continuum of semantic meaning. Despite these marked continuities, the arc of critical conversation on poetic artifice may be seen to modulate from moral debates to formalistic and aesthetic ones, esp. after the 17th c., and from a humanist-derived view of the concept as problematic but necessary to the recent sense that *artifice* is among the terms that best links experimental trads. of the past to those of the present.

Debates over poetic artifice polarized Eng. poetics in the 16th and 17th cs. Denouncers deemed it unnatural, seductive, and morally dangerous; defenders celebrated its demonstrations of human ingenuity and craft. In his *Discourse of English Poetrie*, the 16th-c. critic William Webbe wished some poetic works "bettered, and made more artificiall." Other writers vilified poetry's dissimulations, and their opinions likely colored the strong contemp. association between artifice and rhetorical argumentation: Heinrich Cornelius Agrippa condemned poetry as "the female Architect of falsehood." Indeed, Philip Sidney's *Defence of Poesy* (1595) distances poetry from artifice, as he rejects fixed, "artificial rules" of rhet. in favor of poetry that invents "another nature" more "golden" than that of the world.

Moralistic invectives against artifice peaked at the turn of the 17th c., the age of the *baroque. In his *Worlde of Wordes* (1598), John Florio declared true poetry inimical to "that Art, or rather that Artifice, [which] debauch[es] and corrupt[s] the People." To antibaroque observers, poetry was the Virgin; artifice, the Whore. By the century's end, however, critics alloyed moral judgments with aesthetic ones (e.g., Gilbert Burnet's *Discourse of the Pastoral Care* deemed "artificial poetry" "forced and unnatural . . . in a great measure ridiculous"). By the mid-1700s, discussions of poetic artifice had shifted almost entirely to formal concerns. As the tide turned, many theorists came to view artifice less as corruption of natural lang. and more as elevating play. Robert Lowth, for instance, claimed in *De sacra poesi Hebraeorum* (*Sacred Poetry* *of the Hebrews*) that artifice lent poems, "a certain peculiar colouring, which elevates it above the lang. of the vulgar. Poetry . . . always makes use of . . . artifice." Theorists from the mid-1700s on invoked poetic artifice in ambitious claims about formal structures. Samuel Johnson's preface to *Works of the English Poets* deems the "artifice of rhyme" central to *neoclassical poetic organization; nearly a century later, G. M. Hopkins's "Poetic Diction" theorizes *parallelism as the principle of "all [poetic] artifice." Late 19th- and early 20th-c. poetics, while sensitive to the inherited problem of nature/artifice, continued to approach artifice from a largely technical angle, with new attention to markers of textual self-irony and the artifice of written *"voice."

In the wake of high *modernism and into the postmod. era, formalist critics examined poetic artifice via close textual analysis, in New Criticism, and in ling. theory, such as that of Jakobson (who wrote that "on every level of language the essence of poetic artifice consists in recurrent returns"). In a reconfiguration of Sidney's 16th-c. poetry/rhet. distinction, the New Critic Wimsatt contrasts poetic and rhetorical artifice (see NEW CRITICISM). While rhet. depends on its artifice not being "seen through," poetry is strengthened "by an increase in our understanding of the artifice." He concludes, "In poetry the artifice is art."

An article on the New Critic William Empson's poetry, "Rational Artifice" by Forrest-Thomson, led to her groundbreaking book *Poetic Artifice*. Drawing from Ludwig Wittgenstein, specifically his understanding of poetry as different from the "language-game" of transmitting information, Forrest-Thomson imagines a reading practice that gives more attention to the textures and effects of a poem's lang. than to the "communicable" statements it transmits. While she notes that poetry-specific reading practices are conventionally inscribed in the shape and lineation of a poem, she concentrates on the poem's internal patterns of *sounds, *forms, *tropes, and *images. Concerned with critical praxis, *Poetic Artifice* demonstrates how to study a poem's "nonsemantic" artifice without vulgar "naturalizations" of the poem into prose paraphrase or dilation. It aims to read poetry, in other words, not for its statements or ideas but for the artifice that makes it poetry.

The study of artifice extends well beyond Eng.-lang. crit., to every Eur.-derived lit. that confronts the humanist dichotomy of nature/artifice. Within poetics specifically, Vega Ramos in *El secreto artificio* studies Ren. theories of Sp. vernacular poetry, noting their attention to *fonosimbolismo*, or semantically expressive sounds (*onomatopoeia, alliterated hard consonants, and such). The artifice of emphatic or repeated sounds, Vega Ramos suggests, powerfully shapes meaning. While Forrest-Thomson looks to poems' sounds for nonsemantic art, Vega Ramos regards artful sound as a semantic act of its own.

In "Artifice of Absorption," a verse-essay on Forrest-Thomson's work, Bernstein offers a corrective to her stark distinction between artifice and semantic communication. He writes that, while the test of artifice is its resistance to summary, artifice nonetheless *signifies*; there is no hard line between meaningful and unmeaningful sound. Despite this corrective, Bernstein largely endorses and amplifies Forrest-Thomson's primary claims. Importantly, both critics define *artifice* against *realism. In their view, realism attempts to mimic unmediated transmission, while artifice stresses untransparent materiality. Consequently, though all poems are built of structures defined by poetic artifice, the term in Eng. is most often associated with *Language poetry and other forms of *avant-garde poetry and poetics. In this trad., Perloff's *Radical Artifice* examines how the poetry of media-saturated postmod. culture asserts its artificial constructedness by rejecting principles of "natural language" and syntax, while the 1998 anthology *Artifice and Indeterminacy* generalizes "artifice" to characterize cutting-edge contemp. poetics as a whole.

*See* ABSORPTION, INVENTION, RENAISSANCE POETICS.

■ W. K. Wimsatt, *Hateful Contraries* (1966); V. Forrest-Thomson, *Poetic Artifice* (1978); R. Jakobson, *Language in Literature* (1987); C. Bernstein, *Artifice of Absorption* (1988); M. Perloff, *Radical Artifice* (1991); M. J. Vega Ramos, *El secreto artificio* (1992); *Artifice and Indeterminacy*, ed. C. Beach (1998); F. Masiello, "Oliverio Girondo: Naturaleza y artificio," *Revista de Crítica Literaria Latinoamericana* 24 (1998); B. K. Stefans, "Veronica Forrest-Thomson and High Artifice," *Jacket* 14 (2001), http://jacketmagazine.com/14/stefans-vft.html/.

M. CASTILE

**ARZAMAS**. A Rus. literary circle, active 1815–18 in St. Petersburg. Members (incl. Vasily Zhukovsky, Konstantin Batiushkov, Petr Viazemskii, and Alexander Pushkin) created parodies of the conservative group *Beseda* ("Lovers of the Russian Word") and advanced a more conversational literary lang., following the arguments of the historian and writer Nikolai Karamzin. Arzamas fostered a cult of friendship and lasting bonds among its members. Arzamas dissolved when *Beseda* weakened, but its views triumphed, particularly in the success of Pushkin and others in the 1820s.

*See* RUSSIA, POETRY OF.

■ M. I. Gillel'son, *Molodoi Pushkin i arzamasskoe bratstvo* (1974); W. M. Todd III, *The Familiar Letter as a Literary Genre in the Age of Pushkin* (1976), 38–75; Terras.

S. SANDLER

**ASCLEPIAD**, asclepiadean. An *aeolic line consisting of a *glyconic (x x – ∪ ∪ – ∪ –) internally compounded with a *choriamb, thus: x x – ∪ ∪ – – ∪ ∪ – ∪ –. Though named by later grammarians after the Gr. epigrammatist Asclepiades of Samos (ca. 300 BCE), it is already found in Alcaeus (7th c. BCE) and, in fact, was used long before for both *lyric (monodic and choral) and *tragedy. The asclepiad was used extensively both as a stichic verse and in combination with other aeolic forms to form *strophes. Horace in his *Odes* used the asclepiad frequently, in five different arrangements that have come to be called *first* through *fifth asclepiads*, though mod. scholars do not agree on which types go with which names. The asclepiad line form shown at the end of the first sentence above is known as the *lesser asclepiad*; the *greater asclepiad* (there seems to be no ancient evidence for this term) adds a third choriamb: x x – ◡ ◡ – – ◡ ◡ – – ◡ ◡ – ◡ –. The greater was used by both the aeolic poets and by Horace.

In the Middle Ages, asclepiads (or alcaic hendecasyllables) alternating with glyconics are found in Hilary of Poitiers (4th c. CE), Prudentius (ca. 348–405), and the Carolingian poets; as in Horace, there is usually a break after the sixth position: – – – ◡ ◡ – | – ◡ ◡ – ◡ –. The med. asclepiad strophe kept itself quietly afloat on the steady stream of popularity of the cl. *ode forms— particularly the *sapphic—a stream given its impetus by the authority of Horatian poetics. There are some 40 examples of the asclepiad in the *Analecta hymnica*. In the Ren., accentual imitations and trans. of asclepiadeans were tried by Pierre de Ronsard and the *Pléiade*. Philip Sidney attempts some in the *Old Arcadia* (e.g., "O sweet woods" in the Second Eclogues), and William Collins's "Ode to Evening" is a fourth asclepiadean. The young John Milton essayed an imitation "as near as the Language will permit" of Horace's ode 1.5 (a third asclepiadian), rendering "Quis multa gracilis te puer in rosa" as "What slender youth bedew'd with liquid odours." Ger. examples include F. G. Klopstock's "Der Zürcher See" and Friedrich Hölderlin's "Heidelberg."

■ Wilamowitz; H. Sadej, "De versu Asclepiadeo minore apud Romanos obvio," *Eos* 45 (1951); L. Rotsch, "Zur Form der drei Horaz-Oden im Asclepiadeus maior," *Gymnasium* 64 (1957); A. R. Bellinger, "The Lesser Asclepiadean Line of Horace," *Yale Classical Studies* 15 (1957); Norberg; Maas; W. Bennett, *German Verse in Classical Metres* (1963), ch. 27; L. P. Wilkinson, *Golden Latin Artistry* (1963); Koster; N. A. Bonavia-Hunt, *Horace the Minstrel* (1969); Halporn et al.; Snell; West.

J. W. HALPORN; T.V.F. BROGAN

**ASIAN AMERICAN POETRY.** Asians who migrated to the U.S. beginning in the mid-19th c. quickly established a rich, if ephemeral, literary culture. Chinese migrants detained at Angel Island in San Francisco Bay, the point of entry between 1910 and 1940 for immigrants from China, inscribed poems on the walls of their barracks. Written in the cl. Chinese style, these poems, recovered decades later by Him Mark Lai and others and published in the anthol. *Island* (1980), mix literary and historical allusions with the laments of immigrants detained for weeks or months awaiting admission to the U.S. The community that formed in San Francisco's Chinatown produced a rich body of Cantonese vernacular rhymes of aspiration, struggle, and disillusionment, published in newspapers and anthologies and collected by Marlon K. Hom in *Songs of Gold Mountain* (1987). The overwhelmingly male immigrants, cut off from their families by U.S. policies of Chinese exclusion, often wrote their laments in the voices of wives left behind in China. In Hawai'i, the *hole-hole bushi*, sung by Japanese plantation workers,

set erotic themes and claims to Am. soil to the rhythms of labor.

Writing in Eng. by poets of Asian descent began to appear as early as the 1890s, as cataloged in Juliana Chang's historical anthol. *Quiet Fire* (1996). Sadakichi Hartmann, a writer of Japanese and Ger. ancestry, served for a time as Walt Whitman's secretary and became a pioneering critic of mod. art and photography. Hartmann composed symbolist verse and drama and was among the first to introduce the Japanese forms of tanka and haiku (see HAIKAI) to Am. audiences. The poems of Yone Noguchi, another early advocate of the Eng. lang. *haiku, resonate with techniques of *free verse and *imagism. By the 1920s, poems such as Wen I-to's "The Laundry Song" and H. T. Tsiang's "Chinaman, Laundryman" were offering sharp political commentary on the economic struggles of Chinese immigrants, many of whom had been forced into what had traditionally been "women's work" through restrictive labor laws.

Japanese Am. poetry flourished through the first half of the 20th c. Regional poetry societies devoted themselves to writing in traditional Japanese forms, and poems in Japanese and Eng. appeared widely in community and national publications, launching the careers of poets such as Toyo Suyemoto and Hisaye Yamamoto. During World War II, even as Japanese Americans were forced into internment camps, poetry continued to appear in jours. published in the camps, and the trauma of internment would become a major theme of Asian Am. writing in decades to come. The 1940s also saw the first books of poetry by Filipino authors in the U.S. Jose Garcia Villa, already well known as a pioneering mod. writer in the Philippines, won praise from e. e. cummings and Marianne Moore for his mystical, allusive, modernist lyrics and later gained notoriety for his *"comma poems," visual experiments in which all spaces between words were replaced by commas. Carlos Bulosan, who would later gain fame for his autobiographical novel *America Is in the Heart*, published powerful poems of working-class experience and protest.

In the post–World War II years, Lawson Fusao Inada, who was interned with his family during the war, would become the major Asian Am. poet of his generation. Inada's *Before the War* (1971) was one of the first books of Asian Am. poetry to be published by a major New York publisher, and *Legends from Camp* (1993) established Inada as one of the primary poetic chroniclers of the internment experience. Inada's short, syncopated lines are rooted in jazz rhythms, and his poems are a cool mixture of historical memory, sharp commentary, and imagistic lyricism.

Inada's work featured prominently in the literary flowering of the 1970s, a decade marked by political upheaval and activism, during which the term *Asian American* emerged as a label for a panethnic political and cultural identity. Poetry played a central role in this political awakening, pub. regularly in Asian Am. jours. such as *Gidra* and *Bridge* as a representation of the voice of "the people." The work of poets such as

Fay Chiang, Al Robles, and Ronald Tanaka used direct, colloquial lang., reflecting influences from popular music, oral performance, and the *Beat poets, to offer polemics and reflections on politics, race, and culture. Perhaps the paradigmatic poet of this era was Janice Mirikitani, founder of *Aion*, the first Asian Am. literary magazine. Mirikitani's activist commitments were matched by a populist style, using natural and archetypal imagery to treat topics like internment, sexism, and racial stereotyping, while celebrating Asian Am. community and culture.

In the 1980s, Asian Am. poetry gained increasing recognition from mainstream literary institutions. Cathy Song's *Picture Bride*, which won the Yale Younger Poets prize in 1982, signaled a shift from the politically charged, populist work of the 1970s to what George Uba has called "post-activist" poetry, featuring polished, understated, first-person lyrics and dramatic monologues. Poets such as Song, David Mura, Marilyn Chin, and Li-Young Lee gained wide readerships outside the Asian Am. community with lyrics that explored personal experience, family hist. and sexuality while adopting a skeptical distance from politics. Mura's poems interweave Japanese Am. hist. with reflections on domesticity and addiction; Chin's playful formalism offers ironic takes on identity politics; and Lee's widely taught and anthologized "Persimmons" uses the scene of an Asian Am. boy corrected for his "misuse" of lang. to open up depths of memory and emotion. The definitive statement of this mode is Garrett Hongo's 1993 anthol. *The Open Boat*, which rejects the poetry of "ethnic authenticity" in favor of introspective lyrics on a wide range of subject from a diverse group of writers.

Hongo's anthol. also reflects the increasing ethnic diversity of Asian Am. writers during the 1980s and 1990s. While "Asian American literature" in the 1970s consisted largely of the work of Chinese and Japanese Am. writers, changes in Am. immigration policy after 1965 led to new waves of immigration, esp. from South and Southeast Asia. Indian Am. poets Meena Alexander and Chitra Banerjee Divakaruni have gained wide readerships for their autobiographical and historical poems, while Kashmiri Am. writer Agha Shahid Ali became known for his devel. of the *ghazal* form in Eng.

While Hongo's anthol. celebrated the consonance of Asian Am. poetry with mainstream lyric styles, another anthol. of the 1990s, Walter K. Lew's *Premonitions*, emphasized the role of experimental poetry in Asian Am. writing. Lew's 1995 anthol. coincided with increasing critical interest in poets such as John Yau, Myung Mi Kim, and Mei-mei Berssenbrugge. Some, like Yau and Berssenbrugge, had been publishing since the 1970s, but their work had not been widely discussed among Asian Am. readers, in part because of their more ambiguous approach to autobiography. Berssenbrugge's long, discursive lines structure the page in a manner consonant with her engagement with the visual arts, opening up space for philosophically inflected engagements with consciousness and the body. Kim, a Korean immigrant, employs techniques of *collage and frag-

mentation associated with *Language poetry in poems that grapple with migration, colonialism, and linguistic alienation. The work of Yau, who is also a prolific art critic, has received perhaps the most critical attention in recent years. Yau's poems reflect influences from film, *surrealism, and the *New York school, and in poetic sequences such as "Genghis Chan: Private Eye," he playfully deploys Asian signifiers and stereotypes to create new, hybrid subjectivities.

The catalyst for this new attention to experimental writing was Theresa Hak Kyung Cha's multigenre book *Dictée*, published in 1982 and rediscovered by Asian Am. critics in the early 1990s. Cha's critiques of conventional historical narratives, her investigations of lang., and her focus on imperialism and exile made her a centerpiece of Lisa Lowe's paradigm-shifting critical book *Immigrant Acts* (1996). But experimentalism was not a new devel. in Asian Am. writing. Lew's anthol. which juxtaposes work of the 1970s by Robles, Tanaka, and Luis Syquia with the work of younger writers such as Kim, Tan Lin, and R. Zamora Linmark, suggests that Asian Am. poets have long pursued questions of ethnic identity through explorations of poetic form. *Premonitions* also signals the expansion of the category of Asian Am. writing to include Asian Canadian poets such as Roy Kiyooka, Fred Wah, and Roy Miki.

There has been relatively little critical work on Asian Am. poetry. Despite poetry's central role in Asian Am. political consciousness, Asian Americanist critics have tended to focus on the historical narratives of immigration and identity formation found in memoirs and novels. The pioneering 1974 Asian Am. anthol. *Aiiieeeee!* contained no poetry at all, and essays devoted specifically to Asian Am. poetry did not begin to appear until the late 1980s. Like much early Asian Am. lit. crit., these first forays into Asian Am. poetics sought to establish the cultural and aesthetic distinctiveness of this poetry, as in Shirley Geok-lin Lim's 1987 call for an approach to the subject grounded in *ethnopoetics. George Uba describes a shift from the raw, activist poetry of the 1970s to the more polished "post-activist" writing of the 1980s and 1990s but argues that both subvert "Euro-American" poetics. Uba and Sunn Shelley Wong offer useful historical overviews of Asian Am. poetry and crit. in the 2001 *Resource Guide to Asian American Literature*, focusing on engagements with activism and on contextual reading.

Crit. on Asian Am. poetry has sought to combat the traditional neglect of the topic by emphasizing poetry's ability to challenge and complicate conventional narratives of Asian Am. identity. Juliana Chang's 1995 essay "Reading Asian American Poetry" argues that Asian Am. poetry should be seen as neither personal nor purely social but as a discourse that revises conventional ideas of culture. Essays by poets such as David Mura and Garrett Hongo also highlight the growing diversity of Asian Am. writing. The poetry of Li-Young Lee, which mixes biographical, religious, and erotic themes, has been the subject of numerous articles. More recently, critical attention has focused on experimental writers such as Cha, Yau, and Kim, whose concerns and aesthetics are consonant with current theoretical interests in postcoloniality, hybridity, and diaspora. Brian Kim Stefans's essay "Remote Parsee" proposes such writers as the foundation of an "alternative grammar" for Asian Am. poetry. Dorothy J. Wang suggests that Yau's experimental writing does not reject subjectivity but explores its division and alienation, while Timothy Yu places Yau and other Asian Am. poets in the context of white avant-gardists, such as the Language poets, who have developed their own forms of "ethnicization."

Other critics locate Asian Am. poetry in the context of modernist and Americanist literary studies. Yunte Huang places Asian Am. poetry in a lineage of "transpacific" Am. writing that includes Herman Melville and Henry Adams. Josephine Nock-Hee Park and Steven G. Yao both argue that white Am. poets' engagements with Asia in the 20th c. provide a backdrop for Asian Am. poetry. Yao finds in Ezra Pound's *Cathay* a template for Chinese subjectivity in Eng., while Park sees in Asian Am. poetry a critical response to the orientalism of poets such as Pound and Gary Snyder.

Asian Am. poets continue to work in a variety of trads., from formalist to postconfessional to experimental to spoken word, while further expanding the ethnic diversity of Asian Am. writing. The visceral diction of Vietnamese Am. poet Linh Dinh juxtaposes horror and humor, and Filipino Am. poet Nick Carbó's fluidly structured poems display a hip facility with Filipino and Am. popular culture. Innovative work has also appeared by Hmong and Laotian Am. poets such as Pos Moua and Bryan Thao Worra; Tibetan Am. poet Tsering Wangmo Dhompa; and mixed-race writers such as Sesshu Foster and Christian Langworthy.

■ **Anthologies:** *Roots*, ed. A. Tachiki, E. Wong, and F. Odo (1971); *Counterpoint*, ed. E. Gee (1976); *Breaking Silence*, ed. J. Bruchac (1983); *The Forbidden Stitch*, ed. S. G. Lim and M. Tsutakawa (1989); *Chinese American Poetry*, ed. L. L. Wang and H. Y. Zhao (1991); *The Very Inside*, ed. S. Lim-Hing (1994); *Returning a Borrowed Tongue*, ed. N. Carbó (1995); *Living in America*, ed. R. Rustomji-Kerns (1995); *Contours of the Heart*, ed. S. Maira and R. Srikanth (1996); *Making More Waves*, ed. E. H. Kim, L. V. Villanueva, and Asian Women United of California (1997); *Black Lightning*, ed. E. Tabios (1998); *Watermark*, ed. B. Tran, M. T. D. Truong, and L. T. Khoi (1998); *The NuyorAsian Anthology*, ed. B. A. Realuyo (1999); *Take Out*, ed. Q. Bao and H. Yanagihara (2000); *Tilting the Continent*, ed. S. G. Lim and C. L. Chua (2000); *Bold Words*, ed. R. Srikanth and E. Y. Iwanaga (2001); *Bamboo among the Oaks*, ed. M. N. Moua (2002); *Screaming Monkeys*, ed. M. E. Galang (2003); *Asian American Poetry: The Next Generation*, ed. V. Chang (2004).

■ **Criticism and History:** S. G. Lim, "Reconstructing Asian-American Poetry," *MELUS* 14 (1987); G. Uba, "Versions of Identity in Post-Activist Asian American Poetry," *Reading the Literatures of Asian America*, ed. S. G. Lim and A. Ling (1992); *Reviewing Asian America*, ed. W. L. Ng, S. Chin, J. S. Moy, and

G. Y. Okihiro (1995); C. Altieri, "Images of Form vs. Images of Content in Contemporary Asian-American Poetry," *Qui Parle* 9 (1995); J. Chang, "Reading Asian American Poetry," *MELUS* 21 (1996); B. K. Stefans, "Remote Parsee," *Telling It Slant*, ed. M. Wallace and S. Marks (2002); D. J. Wang, "Undercover Asian," *Asian American Literature in the International Context*, ed. R. G. Davis and S. Ludwig (2002); S. G. Yao, "Toward a Prehistory of Asian American Verse," *Representations* 99 (2007); Y. Huang, *Transpacific Imaginations* (2008); J. N. Park, *Apparitions of Asia* (2008); T. Yu, *Race and the Avant-Garde* (2009).

T. YU

**ASSAMESE POETRY.** Assamese is the lang. of the state of Assam in northeast India. The earliest examples of Assamese poetry are from the 13th c. and are recreations, sometimes trans., of the great Sanskrit epics the *Mahābhārata* and the *Rāmāyaṇa* and the Sanskrit myths in the *Purāṇas*. Assam may have had its own distinctive versions of the *Purāṇas*. This would explain why Hema Saraswati's 13th-c. *Prahlāda Caritra* (The Deeds of Prahlāda) does not conform to any existing Sanskrit text. Other early landmark texts are the 14th-c. *Rāmāyaṇa* of Mādhava Kandalī and the renderings of the *Mahābhārata* (by Kavi Ratna Sarasvatī and Rudra Kandalī). These works attest to a lively trad. of poetry inspired by the Sanskrit classics. Assam has a rich trad. of folk poetry, sung at festivals and weddings, which probably existed alongside these early literary compositions.

With the appearance of the great Vaiṣṇava leader Śaṅkaradeva (1449–1569), Assamese poetry came into its own. Śaṅkaradeva endeavored to spread the teachings of the *Bhāgavata Purāṇa*, which recounts the deeds of the god Kṛṣṇa. His literary output was considerable, incl. trans. into Assamese from the *Bhāgavata Purāṇa*, dramas (*Aṅkīya Naṭa*) on the life of Kṛṣṇa, and short hymns for private and public worship (*Kīrtana Ghoṣā* and *Bargītas*). Some of the *Bargītas* were composed by Śaṅkaradeva's disciple Mādhavadeva (1489–1596). Mādhavadeva also composed devotional and philosophical poems, *Nāma ghoṣā*, and dramas. His *Bhaktiratnāvali* is an Assamese trans. of an anthol. of verses from the *Bhāgavata Purāṇa* compiled by Viṣṇu Pūri (1485).

Roughly contemporary with Śaṅkaradeva, Pītambara Dāsa, Durgāvara, and Manakara composed poetry in a different vein. Drawing on traditional sources, their poetry described the love of the god Śiva for his wife Pārvatī, well known from the *Purāṇas*, and the marriage of the merchant Lakhindār and Behulā. Durgāvara composed the *Gīti Rāmāyaṇa*, based on the Assamese *Rāmāyaṇa* of Mādhava Kandalī. These poets wrote in the style of the oral bardic poetry of Assam, avoiding the ornate figures of speech favored by Sanskrit poets.

The disciples of Śaṅkaradeva continued to compose poems on subjects in the epics and the *Purāṇas* and to translate these Sanskrit texts into Assamese. Rāma Sarasvatī's 16th-c. *Mahābhārata* includes independent poems on the slaying of various demons. These *Vadha kāvyas* are considered a distinctive contribution of Assam to the telling of the *Mahābhārata*.

The Vaiṣṇava movement of Śaṅkaradeva gave rise to a rich biographical lit., often in verse. Daityāri Ṭhākura wrote a biography of Śaṅkaradeva and Mādhavadeva. Nīlakaṇṭha Dāsa composed a biography of Dāmodaradeva (1488–1598), a direct disciple of Śaṅkaradeva and the first schismatic. Bhadra Cāru's poem deals with the life of Ananta and his struggle with the king Gadādhara Siṃha in the 17th c. As the group split, these texts established the lineages of succession. The biographies of Śaṅkaradeva and his followers were not the only historical texts written in verse. A court astrologer, Sūrya Khaḍi Daivajña, born in the late 18th c., wrote a verse hist. of the kings of Daraṅga.

Well into the 19th c., poets continued to draw on Sanskrit sources. Ramākānta Chaudhuri (1846–89) wrote his *Abhimanyuvadha* (The Slaying of Abhimanyu, 1875) based on the story in the *Mahābhārata*. He broke with traditional verse forms and followed the Bengali poet Michael Madhusudan Dutt, whose *blank verse poem on the death of the *Rāmāyaṇa* villain Rāvaṇa had caused a stir in literary circles in Calcutta. The influence of Bengal on Assamese intellectuals remained strong; and new influences, e.g., from Brit. romantic poetry, were apparent in both Bengal and Assam. The periodical *Jonākī*, which published the poems of Chandrakumar Agarwala (1867–1938) and Lakshminath Bezbarua (1868–1938), among others, was begun from Calcutta. *Jonākī* was published for only ten years. It was followed by a period of experimentation with *surrealism, *symbolism, and the thought of Sigmund Freud and Karl Marx. Today, this eclecticism continues; poets from diverse backgrounds continue to seek their inspiration in a variety of sources, in the diverse tribal cultures of Assam, in India's ancient Sanskritic culture, and in poetic movements elsewhere and abroad.

*See* INDIA, POETRY OF; RĀMĀYAṆA POETRY.

■ *Asamiya Sahityar Chaneki or Typical Selections from Assamese Literature*, ed. H. Goswami, 3 v. (1924–27); Birinchi Kumar Barua, *The History of Assamese Literature* (1964); M. Neog, *Śaṅkaradeva and His Times* (1965); M. Neog, *Asamīya Sāhityar Rūparekhā* (1981); *Medieval Indian Literature: An Anthology*, ed. K. Ayyappapaniker, 2d ed. (1997).

P. GRANOFF

**ASSONANCE** (Lat. *assonare*, "to sound to" or "to respond to"; Ir. *amus*). The repetition of a vowel or diphthong in nonrhyming stressed syllables near enough to each other for the echo to be discernible. Examples in Eng. would be *back-cast*, *rose-float*, and *feat-seek*, or the echoes of diphthongs such as *fine-bride* and *proud-cowl*. In some verse forms of *Celtic prosody, the patterning of assonance is strictly governed by elaborate rules; in other prosodies, it may be an occasional *ornament (see, e.g., Gluck or Mariaselvam on assonance in Heb. verse). Between these two extremes fall cases in which assonance substitutes for strict rhyme in a form requiring the latter, as in the case of a poet who ends an Eng.

or Shakespearean *sonnet with a *couplet pairing end words that assonate. In a trad. stemming from OF and Old Sp., and until the 20th c. with its more varied versification, assonance served the same function as rhyme, i.e., formalized closures to lines in the poems of most Romance langs. The OF *Chanson de Roland* (early 12th c.) attempts in each *laisse to have not only the same vowel in the final stressed syllable of each line but the same vowel in the following weak syllable, if there is one. A similar system prevailed in Sp. and Port., as can be seen not only in the great epic *Os Lusíadas* (*The Lusiads*, 1572) by Luís de Camões but also in his lyrics, sonnets, and pastorals. Waley has argued that, because most Chinese syllables end in a vowel or nasal sound, "rhyme" in Chinese poetry is actually assonance, but Liu differentiates assonance from Chinese rhyming compounds, which do require identical final consonants, if there are any. Distinctions between assonance and rhyme are complicated because, as a full taxonomy of rhyme suggests (see RHYME), assonance, like *alliteration and *consonance, falls into the category of sound pairings to which many would assign the larger heading *rhyme*; that *vowel rhyme* or *vocalic rhyme* often appears as a synonym for *assonance* suggests that the latter is a subset of rhyme. But the hist. of the word *assonance* in Eng. suggests that it has served some as the more comprehensive term. According to the *OED*, the word *assonance* first appeared in Eng. in 1727 and meant "resemblance or correspondence of sound between two words or syllables." This definition, which does not limit *assonance* to "the recurrence of syllable-forming vowels" (Gasparov's formulation; see definition 2 in the *OED*), would make assonance the basis not only of all rhyme but of all *prosody.

Along with the complex end echoes in OF, Old Sp., and Port., Romance poets have employed much internal assonance, partly perhaps because their langs., like Lat., are so rich in vowels. Almost any Lat. or Gr. poet can be shown to have loved vowel play (Wilkinson, Stanford). John Dryden quotes this line from the *Aeneid* to demonstrate Virgil's "musical ear"—"Quo fata trahunt retrahuntque, sequamur"—which stresses *a* four times against a background of three unstressed *u* sounds. In mod. times, internal assonance is as marked an acoustic device of the *alexandrine as of later Fr. poetry, as in *Phèdre*, which has a number of lines with assonance of three syllables, this one (1.3.9) with four—"Tout m'afflige et me nuit et conspire a me nuire." Paul Verlaine with his belief in "musique avant toute chose" is often credited with inspiring poets of his day to employ sonorous sounds; assonance was most important in his own versification.

Far less a subject of traditional interest than alliteration but more noticed than consonance, assonance has often been thought a lesser substitute for rhyme. It is true that the Germanic langs. had an early hist. of alliterative poetries—e.g., *Beowulf*—and continue to employ alliteration, often heavily. True, too, the Celtic langs., notably Welsh, developed schemes of sound correspondence, esp. *cynghanedd, that have complex alliterative patterns. But it is equally true that in nearly all langs., incl. Ir. and Welsh, poets have continually employed assonance internally if not as a substitute for end rhyme. The term *assonance* was borrowed by Eng. from Sp. and Fr. to describe the various vocalic substitutes for rhyme in the Romance poetries. But end assonance is only a small part of the total phenomenon called *assonance*.

Since vowels and diphthongs change their pronunciation, sometimes radically, over time and from region to region, while consonants change relatively little, a reader needs to know how the vowels were pronounced by the poet being read. Mod. readers can still hear the alliterations of Germanic poetries, e.g., but they may no longer hear what were originally instances of assonance. In Eng., because the "great vowel shift" was largely completed by Shakespeare's time, the verse of Chaucer and other ME poets sounds different from that of later times. Furthermore, a number of vowels continued to change pronunciation after Shakespeare's day; by the 18th c., Eng. poets were still naturally rhyming *Devil-civil*, *stem-stream*, *pull-dull-fool*, *feast-rest*, *tea-obey*, and *join-fine* (Hanson).

Ger. poets seem to have found assonance even more appealing than alliteration, from Clemens Brentano, who has whole poems with a polysyllabic assonance in nearly every line, to J. W. Goethe, Heinrich Heine, and mod. poets. Goethe, in his lyrics and plays, has more assonance than other phonic echoes, as in Faust's contract with Mephistopheles, which in its last three lines has a six-syllable assonance of *aI* as well as other echoes: "Dann bist du d*ei*nes Dienstes fr*ei*, / Die Ühr mag stehn, der Z*ei*ger fallen, / Es s*ei* die Z*ei*t fur mich vorb*ei*!" And R. M. Rilke, one of the most sonorous of poets, opens "Wendung" with "L*a*nge err*a*ng ers im *A*nschauen."

Rus. poets, too, have employed assonance consistently, esp. Fyodor Tiutchev, Boris Pasternak, Alexander Blok, and Valery Bryusov, the latter two frequently substituting it for end rhyme (Plank, Donchin, Ginzburg).

Finally, the notion that assonance is no longer used for end rhyme must be dispelled. Blok replaced rhyme with assonance in whole series of poems, as did Rilke; Verlaine used assonance instead of rhyme perhaps half the time, and poets such as Dylan Thomas in Britain and Randall Jarrell and Hart Crane in the U.S. have often made such a substitution. It should also be pointed out that poets other than Sp. and It. have dabbled with polysyllabic assonance, the echoes coming only in the weak final syllables. But in Eng. such echoes are rare, difficult, and relatively ineffective. In fact, just as computers would be of little help in finding assonance, any reader should hesitate before including obviously weak syllables in a study of vowel repetitions.

■ *A Hundred and Seventy Chinese Poems*, trans. A. Waley (1919); R. E. Deutsch, *The Pattern of Sound in Lucretius* (1939); W. B. Stanford, *Aeschylus in His Style* (1942); G. Donchin, *The Influence of French Symbolism on Russian Poetry* (1958); N. I. Hérescu, *La poésie latine* (1960); W. Kayser, *Geschichte des deutschen Verses* (1960); P. Delbouille,

*Poésie et sonorités*, 2 v. (1961, 1984); J.J.Y. Liu, *The Art of Chinese Poetry* (1962); W. B. Stanford, *The Sound of Greek* (1967); D. L. Plank, *Pasternak's Lyric* (1966); L. P. Wilkinson, *Golden Latin Artistry* (1963); J. Gluck, "Assonance in Ancient Hebrew Poetry," *De Fructu oris sui*, ed. I. H. Eybers et al. (1971); Wimsatt; P. G. Adams, *Graces of Harmony: Alliteration, Assonance, and Consonance in Eighteenth-Century Britsh Poetry* (1977); R. P. Newton, *Vowel Undersong* (1981); Brogan, esp. items C129–30, C150, C152–53, K2, K116, L233, L322, L406, L518; A. Mariaselvam, *The Song of Songs and Ancient Tamil Love Poems* (1988); Gasparov; K. Hanson, "Vowel Variation in English Rhyme," *Studies in the History of the English Language*, ed. D. Minkova and R. Stockwell (2002); E. Ginzburg, "The Structural Role of Assonance in Poetic Form," *Poetics, Self, Place*, ed. C. O'Neil, N. Boudreau, and S. Krive (2007).

P. G. Adams; S. Cushman

## ASSYRIA AND BABYLONIA, POETRY OF

I. Introduction
II. Narrative Poetry
III. Religious Poetry
IV. Didactic Poetry

**I. Introduction.** Assyrian and Babylonian were the two main dialects of Akkadian, a Semitic lang. Of these, Babylonian and not Assyrian was used for most of the poetry. The earliest surviving poetic texts, preserved on clay tablets written in cuneiform script, date from the end of the third millennium BCE. A very creative period followed in the Old Babylonian period, from ca. 1800 BCE onward. Around and after 1200, again much new poetry was composed. This material is mostly known from copies collected in royal or temple libraries in Assur, Ninive, Sultantepe, Babylon, Uruk, and Sippar in the first millennium.

Most of the texts are anonymous: as exceptions, the author of the *epic poem *Erra and Ishum*, Kabti-ilani-Marduk (who claims to have written it from the gods' dictation); the author of the latest version of the *Epic of Gilgamesh*, Sîn-liqe-unninni; and the poet of the *Theodicy*, Saggil-kinam-ubbib, are known by name. Other names appearing in tablet colophons are generally those of the copying scribes, not of the poets.

With respect to genre, the corpus may summarily be divided into narrative, religious, and didactic poetry, i.e., into epics, *hymns and prayers, and wisdom literature. Purely secular poetry (e.g., the humorous poems discussed below) seems to have been recorded in writing only rarely; traces of it can be found in *charms to avoid scorpions, to remedy toothache, to quiet a crying baby, and so on. As part of an oral trad., the *motifs and stylistic features of such poems can often be traced over long periods in ever-changing new versions. The texts themselves—often embedded in medical or magical prescriptions—resemble *nursery rhymes and suggest a pattern of folk poetry made up of mostly short lines containing similes and wordplay and often con-catenated *repetitions, such as

> Anger advances like a wild bull,
> Jumps at me like a dog.
> Like a lion, it is formidable in progress,
> Like a wolf, it is full of fury.

Some verses whose lyricism would suggest secular *love poetry mostly seem on closer reading to concern divine lovers, as in the Old Babylonian poem

> The women's quarter moans, the bedchamber
>   weeps
> Wherein we were wont to celebrate the wedding;
> The courtyard sighs, the loft laments
> Wherein we were wont to do sweet dalliance.

In an Assyrian elegy, a woman who died in child-birth complains:

> I lived with him who was my lover.
> Death came creeping into my bedroom,
> It drove me from my house,
> It tore me from my husband,
> It set my feet into a land of no return.

The most common formal characteristic of Assyro-Babylonian poetry, shared with *Sumerian and most other Semitic poetry, is syntactic *parallelism, as evidenced in the examples above. It is frequently combined with *chiasmus, while *zeugma is rarely tolerated. A special form of *enjambment, combined with chiasmus, is sometimes used to connect lines in a "Janus construction." *Rhyme (more often internal than final), *alliteration, *onomatopoeia, *anaphora, and epistrophe may be used for special effect. *Rhythm is based on stress, with no strict meter (see ACCENTUAL VERSE); a typical line contains four measures, rarely three or five, with a *caesura in the middle. The verse ending is usually *trochaic, and final syllables that would make the last word a *dactyl are often truncated. *Acrostics and telestics in which the respective syllables spell out a name or a pious wish, as well as poems in which each line of a *strophe begins with the same written sign, are also known.

**II. Narrative Poetry.** Babylonian epics deal with the ex-ploits of gods or mythological beings and are, therefore, often dubbed *myths*. Many of these are already known from the Old Babylonian period, although their first-millennium recensions are usually more elaborate: the story of the bird *Anzû*, who stole the Tablet of Destinies from the supreme god Enlil and was defeated by the god Ninurta; the story of the mythical king *Etana*, who ascended to heaven on the back of an eagle to obtain the herb for childbearing; the story of the sage *Atra-hasis* (Exceedingly Wise), who survived the flood brought about by the gods after they had created hu-mankind; and the *Epic of Gilgamesh* (see below).

Of a slightly later date are the stories of wise *Adapa* and of *Nergal and Ereshkigal*, the latter telling how Nergal came to rule the netherworld together with

its queen Ereshkigal. Only first-millennium sources are known for *Enuma Elish*, the epic of creation in which Marduk defeats the forces of chaos and creates the cosmos out of the body of the primeval monster, thereby being acknowledged as supreme god; *Erra and Ishum*, which describes the calamities that be-fell Babylon when the plague god Erra replaced its tutelary god Marduk; and the *Descent of Ishtar to the Netherworld*.

The 19th-c. discovery of a tablet of the *Epic of Gilgamesh* with an account of the Flood closely par-alleling that in the OT triggered Western interest in this work. It deals with basic human concerns of all times—friendship and the quest for immortality and enduring fame. When Enkidu, a semisavage created by the gods to become Gilgamesh's friend and com-panion, dies, Gilgamesh realizes the same fate awaits him and so begins the quest that eventually leads to an encounter with the sole survivor of the Flood. There, Gilgamesh almost reaches his goal of achieving eternal life but then loses it again in a moment of inattentive-ness. The epic does not end with the death of its hero, however, but as it began, with the description of the ramparts of the city of Uruk, his lasting achievement.

Some narrative poems have historical kings as he-roes, e.g., a cycle about *Sargon and Naram-Sin*, who built the Akkadian empire in the late third millen-nium. An epic about the Assyrian king *Tukulti-Ninurta* (1243–1207 BCE) and his victory over the Babylonian king Kashtiliash reflects Assyrian political ideology, though it is actually written in the Babylonian literary dialect. Other poems are couched as autobiographies, with the king narrating his own hist. Here, the lesson to be drawn from events of the past is held up to the future ruler in a sort of *envoi* at the end, bringing the genre close to that of *didactic poetry.

**III. Religious Poetry.** Most Babylonian hymns ad-dress gods and goddesses, but some are also in praise of cities. These poems are characterized by an elevated style and a vocabulary of rare terms, indicators of their learned origin and sophisticated audience. They are often divided into strophes that are, however, only inconsistently marked on the tablet. The *Hymn to Shamash* (the sun god and god of justice) has exactly 200 lines, divided by rulings into 100 *distichs; other hymns of even greater length were addressed to Ishtar, to Marduk, and to Nabu. Some hymns, such as the 200-line "Hymn to Gula," are styled in the first person, the goddess speaking her own praise. A hymnic-epic poem from the Old Babylonian period addressed to Ishtar, the *Song of Agushaya*, blurs the boundaries of narrative and hymnic poetry.

Like hymns, prayers also address the deity with praise but stress the supplicant's misery and petition. Their poetic virtue lies in their description of mood and feeling. Their plaintive lyricism, in such phrases as "How wet with my tears is my bread!" "Man's sins are more numerous than the hairs on his head," or "What sin have I committed against my god?" reminds us of the *penitential psalms. Prayers are often couched as *incantations and recited during ritual ceremonies to alleviate medical conditions and other misfortunes, while prayers to the gods of divination ask for a favorable answer to the oracle query.

**IV. Didactic Poetry**. This group mostly comprises philosophical dialogues or monologues questioning the fairness of the fate bestowed by the gods, such as the *Theodicy*, an acrostic, and the poem of the *Righteous Sufferer*, with similarities to the biblical book of Job. Animal *fables and *poetic contests in which two rivals—e.g., trees or cereals—extol their own merits and belittle those of their opponent hark back to a well-attested Sumerian genre.

Only relatively few humorous poems are known, and their relationship to didactic poetry remains under discussion. The satirical *Dialogue between Master and Servant* may belong there, while the *Tale of the Poor Man of Nippur*, having close affinities with the *Tale of the First Larrikin* of the *1001 Nights*, seems to be purely secular and has perennial appeal. The *Tale of the Illiterate Doctor*, similarly situated in the Sumerian city of Nippur, draws its humor from the ling. effects of Sumerian interspersed in the Babylonian text.

■ **Anthologies**: M.-J. Seux, *Hymnes et Prières aux Dieux de Babylonie et d'Assyrie* (1976); *Texte aus der Umwelt des Alten Testament*, ed. O. Kaiser, 3 v. and suppl. in 19 fascicles (1982–); S. Dalley, *Myths from Mesopotamia* (1989); B. Foster, *Before the Muses*, 3d ed. (2005)—contains all poems listed below, though sometimes with different titles.
■ **Editions of Individual Works**: *Babylonian Wisdom Literature*, ed. W. G. Lambert (1960)—*Dialogue between Master and Servant, Hymn to Shamash, Righteous Sufferer*, and *Theodicy*; J. Bottéro, "'Le Dialogue Pessimiste' et la Transcendence," *Revue de Théologie et de Philosophie* 99 (1966), and "Rapports sur les Conférences: Histoire et Philologie," *Annuaire: École Pratique des Hautes Études* (1966–67)—*Theodicy*; W. G. Lambert, "The Gula Hymn of Bulluṭsa-rabi," *Orientalia* n.s. 36 (1967); L. Cagni, *L'Epopea di Erra* (1969)—*Erra and Ishum*; W. G. Lambert and A. R. Millard, *Atra-ḫasīs: The Babylonian Story of the Flood* (1969)—incl. trans.; O. R. Gurney, "The Tale of the Poor Man of Nippur and Its Folktale Parallels," *Anatolian Studies* 22 (1972); P. Machinist, "The Epic of Tukulti-Ninurta I," diss. Yale Univ. (1978); E. Reiner, *Your Thwarts in Pieces, Your Mooring Rope Cut* (1985)—*Descent of Ishtar to the Netherworld*; M. E. Vogelzang, *Bin šar dadmē: Edition and Analysis of the Akkadian Anzu Poem* (1988); A. George, "Ninurta-Paqidat's Dog Bite, and Notes on Other Comic Tales," *Iraq* 55 (1993)—*Tale of the Illiterate Doctor*; B. Groneberg, *Lob der Ištar* (1997)—*Song of Agushaya*; J. G. Westenholz, *Legends of the Kings of Akkade* (1997)—*Sargon and Naram-Sin* cycle; M. Haul, *Das Etana-Epos* (2000); G. Pettinato, *Nergal ed Ereškigal* (2000); S. Izre'el, *Adapa and the South Wind* (2001); A. George, *The Babylonian Gilgamesh Epic*, 2 v. (2003); S. Maul, *Das Gilgamesch-Epos* (2005); P. Talon, *The Standard Babylonian Creation Myth* (2005)—*Enuma Elish*.

■ **Criticism and History**: J. Nougayrol, "L'Épopée Babylonienne," *Atti del convegno internazionale sul tema: La poesia epica e la sua formazione* (1970); O. R. Gurney (1972)—see above; E. Reiner (1985)—see above; W. Farber, "Magic at the Cradle: Babylonian and Assyrian Lullabies," *Anthropos* 85 (1990); N. Veldhuis, *A Cow of Sin* (1991); *Mesopotamian Poetic Language: Sumerian and Akkadian*, ed. M. Vogelzang (1996); M. L. West, "Akkadian Poetry: Metre and Performance," *Iraq* 59 (1997); F. d'Agostino, *Testi Umoristici Babilonesi e Assiri* (2000); N. Wasserman, *Style and Form in Old-Babylonian Literary Texts* (2003).

E. REINER; W. FARBER

**ASYNARTETON** (Gr., "disconnected," "disjunct"). A verse composed out of two or more distinct and often dissimilar rhythmical cola, usually in *synapheia but separated from each other by word end and not analyzable as continuous portions of the same rhythm. The genre was invented or first given vogue by Archilochus; and several of the more common examples are linked to his name. Archilochus' asynarteta are always dicola, usually combined with a rhythmically homogeneous line of different length to form a *distich; and their components are, with one exception, identical to the segments normally marked off by recurring word end within the most common stichic meters—*hexameter, *trimeter (full and catalectic), and catalectic *tetrameter (*iambic and *trochaic). The imitations produced by later authors are longer and draw on a more varied repertory of components, and later theoreticians allow for the combination of segments of dissimilar rhythms without intervening word end.

*See* ARCHILOCHIAN, COLON, DACTYLO-EPITRITE, ELEGIAC DISTICH, EPODE.
■ D. Korzeniewski, "Epodische Dichtung," *Griechische Metrik* (1968); L. E. Rossi, "Asynarteta from the Archaic to the Alexandrian Poets," *Arethusa* 9 (1976); B. M. Palumbo Stracca, *La teoria antica degli asinarteti* (1979); Snell; West, "Strophic metres," sec. IIB; B. Gentili and L. Lomiento, *Metrics and Rhythmics: History of Poetic Form in Ancient Greece*, trans. E. C. Kopff (2008).

A. T. COLE

**ASYNDETON** (Gr., "unconnected"). The omission of conjunctions between phrases or clauses; the opposite of *polysyndeton, which is the addition of conjunctions. Omission of conjunctions between words is technically brachylogia—fundamental to all forms of series and *catalogs—but many writers now use asyndeton as the cover term for all types of conjunction deletion. And it is itself, in turn, one species of all the figures of *ellipsis. Asyndeton is used both in rhet. and lit. for the purpose of speed, breathlessness, headlong momentum, and emotional force. Quintilian calls asyndeton *dissolutio* and the Ger. equivalent is *Worthäufung*, "word-piling." Heinrich Lausberg divides forms of asyndeton by two principles of division: according to parts of speech (nominal and verbal asyndeton) and according to length of elements (asyndeton between single words, phrases, and clauses). Also, both Malcolm Hebron and Lausberg organize asyndeton (a.) according to relations of the parts: a. *additivum* (accumulated in list), a. *summativum* (collective sense of list summarized either at beginning or end), a. *disiunctivum* (elements are contradictory or paradoxical), a. *adversativum* (elements are logically antithetical), a. *causale* (reasons following a proposition), a. *explicativum* (elements clarify a preceding proposition), a. *conclusivum* (a series of premises expressed by asyndeton and followed by the logical conclusion). These classifications are neither canonical nor comprehensive. Homer uses it, as does Virgil (e.g., *Aeneid* 4.594), but the classic examples are Aristotle's "I have done; you have heard me. The facts are before you; I ask for your judgment" (*Rhetoric*) and Caesar's *veni, vidi, vici.* Horace and Statius are fond of the device, and their example was followed by many med. Lat. poets. Med. Ger. poets (e.g., Walther von der Vogelweide, Wolfram von Eschenbach) also made much use of asyndeton, but the figure was esp. favored by *baroque poets in Germany (Andreas Gryphius), Spain, and France. In the Latinist John Milton one can find numerous examples as well: "Thrones, Dominations, Princedoms, Vertues, Powers" (*Paradise Lost* 5.601); "The first sort by their own suggestion fell, / Self-tempted, self-depraved; man falls, deceived / By the other first: man therefore shall find grace, / The other none" (3.129–32). In Eng., asyndeton has occurred particularly in mod. poetry—in the work of the imagists, e.g., with their cult of brevity (see IMAGISM)—and in W. H. Auden (e.g., "In Memory of W. B. Yeats"), with his fondness for the pithy and loaded phrase.

■ H. Pliester, *Die Worthäufung im Barock* (1930); Curtius, 285; Group µ; A. Quinn, *Figures of Speech* (1982); E. Blettner, "The Role of Asyndeton in Aristotle's Rhetoric," *P&R* 16 (1983); J. P. Houston, *Shakespearean Sentences* (1988); Corbett; W. G. Müller, "Emotional Asyndeton in the Literature of Feeling," *Anglistentag* (1992); Lausberg; M. Hebron, "Seven Types of Asyndeton in *Paradise Lost*," *English* 52 (2003).

A. PREMINGER; T.V.F. BROGAN;<br>A. W. HALSALL; D. VERALDI

**ATTENTION** (Lat. *ad-tendere,* "to stretch toward"). In 1928, in an introduction to Harry Crosby's book of poetry *Chariot of the Sun,* D. H. Lawrence suggested that "the essential quality of poetry is that it makes a new effort of attention, and 'discovers' a new world within the known world." The idea of a poetic attention has never become a fully theorized concept in literary theory. Yet Lawrence's association of poetry with attention is by no means without precedent; various notions of attention have been operative in rhet. and poetics since antiquity. Indeed, soliciting and manipulating attention are two of rhet.'s main goals. Figures in rhet. and lit. serve to engage the reader's focus, and we might think of literary form as corresponding to the movement of attention.

In cl. Gr. and Roman rhet., discussions of attention appear mainly in the context of the parts of an oration. Engaging the audience is an element of rhetorical persuasion; therefore, many rhetoricians argue that the attention of the audience should be drawn at the introduction (Gr. *prooimion*). Yet already Aristotle warns in the *Rhetoric* against such restrictions: "it is . . . ridiculous to put this kind of thing at the beginning, when every one is listening with most attention. Choose therefore any point in the speech where such an appeal is needed" (bk. 3, ch. 14). In terms of maintaining the attention of the audience, Aristotle perceives a contrast between rhet. and poetic form: "the metrical form destroys the hearer's trust and diverts his attention, making him watch for metrical recurrences" (bk. 3, ch. 8; see FORM). Aristotle also notes, however, that orators may intend to distract their audience: "the appeal to the hearer aims at . . . gaining his serious attention to the case, or even at distracting it—for gaining it [*poiein prosektikon*] is not always an advantage" (bk. 3, ch. 14; trans. W. R. Roberts). While in cl. rhet. attention is a function of public oratory, in Christianity the sense of oration as prayer (or *oratio mentis*) contributes to the emergence of a spiritual notion of attention. In this context, there is a rising interest in poetic form as potentially conducive to focusing attention. In Augustine's *Confessions,* reciting the Psalms appears both as an illustration of the imperfections of human attention and as a way of creating a devotional attention. The Middle Ages and the early mod. period move toward a more methodical focusing of attention, esp. through the practice of meditation. This tendency peaks during the Counter-Reformation with Ignatius Loyola's *Spiritual Exercises* (1548). Loyola's follower, Francis de Sales, defines meditation as "attentive and reiterated thought" in *Traité de l'amour de Dieu* (1630). In the 16th and 17th cs., Catholic and Protestant traditions of meditation influence a number of poets who, like Teresa of Ávila and John Donne, use poetic *artifice to produce a devotional modality of attention.

During the Enlightenment, we see two competing models of attention—moral and cognitive. Sermons continue to invoke 1 Cor. 7:35: "attend upon the Lord without distraction," casting attention as virtue, distraction as vice. In the 17th and 18th cs., however, philosophers such as John Locke, David Hume, and Benjamin Franklin begin to disentangle attention from these religious connotations. They move toward secular models of the mind that naturalize distraction, portraying wandering attention as an aspect of everyday life. 18th-c. poets increasingly describe attention as a limited commodity. While, in his essay "An Account of the Greatest English Poets" (1694), Joseph Addison writes of John Milton that "ev'ry verse . . . my whole attention draws," by 1782, William Cowper resignedly declares in "Retirement," such "habits of close attention" have become "more rare." In his poem, "Conversation," Cowper claims this shift has actually inspired original work: "at least we moderns, our attention less, / Beyond the example of our sires digress." Such comments reflect the period's growing fascination with distraction. Denis Diderot's *Encyclopédie* associates *distraction* with intellectual vivacity: "distraction originates in an excellent quality of understanding, a facility for allowing ideas to re-awaken one another." By the end of the century, romantics such as Jean-Jacques Rousseau, E.T.A. Hoffmann, and Lord Byron (in *Don Juan*) celebrate distraction as a catalyst of poetic invention.

At the turn of the 20th c., interest in attention rises again. Psychologists develop new scientific models of attention; however, the historical friction between attention and distraction persists. In 1890, James defines attention as "the taking possession . . . of one of several possible trains of thought." Attention, for him, is a process of selection and, thus, a "focalization" and "concentration of consciousness." Its opposite is the "confused, dazed, scatterbrained state . . . known as distraction." In 1895, Janet instead emphasizes the "negative effects of attention." He suggests excessive focus narrows "the contents of consciousness" and advocates a more fluid notion of attention.

Poets, artists, and literary critics engage in similar conversations about attention. In "Au sujet d'Adonis" (1921), Paul Valéry describes poetry as "writing down one's dreams" with "the utmost effort of attention." *New Criticism's practice of *close reading models an entire interpretative practice around the value of attention. It is no accident the New Critics are drawn to 16th- and 17th-c. poetry; Brooks, for instance, turns to Donne, emphasizing the discipline one gains by the "perpetual activity of attention" evoked by the "rapid flow . . . and playful nature of thoughts and images" in *metaphysical poetry. In contrast, critics such as Benjamin define mod. perception as "reception in a state of distraction." While Benjamin is nostalgic for an age of attention and "aura," he believes distraction may offer an escape from bourgeois absorption. His contemporary, the Hungarian painter and photographer László Moholy-Nagy, adds that being "forced to simultaneously comprehend and participate in" multiple aesthetic stimuli inspires "moments of vital insight." In this spirit, high modernists such as Gertrude Stein (e.g., *Tender Buttons*) craft a poetics that presents "unfocused" objects from multiple angles simultaneously, modeling an associative yet discontinuous style of thought.

Recent cognitive studies of attention have inspired new interest in the neural dynamics of aesthetic engagement. In *Cognitive Poetics*, Stockwell defines reading as "a dynamic experience . . . of renewing attention" and analyzes poetry's "stylistic patterns [for] focusing attention within textual space." Understanding the neural processes of attention's role in reading poetry may provide a framework for building new cognitive theories of poetic attention. At the same time, the hist. of the relationship between attention and poetry in non-Western and Western trads. alike remains a field calling for further investigation.

*See* COGNITIVE POETICS.

■ W. James, *The Principles of Psychology* (1890); P. Janet, "L'attention," *Dictionnaire de physiologie* (1895); L. Moholy-Nagy, *Painting, Photography, Film* (1925); Benjamin; Brooks; L. Martz, *The Poetry of Meditation* (1954); "Attention," *Dictionnaire de spiritualité ascétique et mystique, doctrine et histoire*, ed. M. Viller, F. Cavallera, J. de Guibert (1937–95); "Attentum parere," *Historisches Wörterbuch der Rhetorik*, ed. G. Ueding (1992–); J. Crary, *Suspensions of Perception* (1999); F. McCormick, "Attention Deficit Disorder," *The English Journal* 88 (1999); M. Riley, *Attentive Listening* (2000); P. Stockwell, *Cognitive Poetics* (2002); M. Hagner, "Toward a History of Attention in Culture and Science," *MLN* 188 (2003); N. Dames, *The Physiology of the Novel* (2007); D. Revell, *The Art of Attention* (2007); G. Starr, "Poetic Subjects and Grecian Urns: Close Reading and the Tools of Cognitive Science," *MP* 105 (2007).

N. PHILLIPS; D. MARNO

**AUDIENCE.** *See* PERFORMANCE; READER; READER RESPONSE; RHETORIC AND POETRY.

**AUREATE DICTION.** Marked density of Latinate-derived words. Aureation in the more general sense has been characteristic of high style or epic *diction since the Middle Ages, as is conspicuous in the works of John Milton. Assimilation of Latinate terms as a process is evident in most of the late med. vernaculars, e.g., MGH (where it is called *gebluemte Rede*) as the natural extension of *macaronic poetry, where Lat. words appear alongside vernacular ones. But in the more restricted and usual sense, *aureate diction* refers to the characteristically overwrought style of ME and Scottish poetry of the 15th c.—that of William Dunbar, John Lydgate, and Stephen Hawes in England and King James I and Robert Henryson in Scotland—as well as of that of the contemporaneous *Grands *Rhétoriqueurs* in France. This style is based on coinages from Lat. copious to the point of excess, as in Dunbar's "Haile, sterne superne Haile, in eterne" (Hail, star on high; hail in eternity), which is followed by the native line "In Godis sicht to shine (In God's sight to shine)." The excess has long been derided by literary historians. If today aureate diction seems less offensive, that is partly because many terms have since been absorbed into the lang. and so do not today strike us as aureate. But they were exotic coinages in their day.

*See* PLAIN STYLE; SCOTLAND, POETRY OF; SCOTTISH CHAUCERIANS OR MAKARS.

■ J. C. Mendenhall, *Aureate Terms* (1919); P. H. Nichols, "Lydgate's Influence on the Aureate Forms of the Scottish Chaucerians," *PMLA* 47 (1932); E. Tilgner, *Die Aureate Terms bei Lydgate* (1936); C. S. Lewis, *English Literature in the Sixteenth Century, Excluding Drama* (1954); J. A. Conley, "Four Studies in Aureate Terms," diss., Stanford (1956); S. Lerer, "The Rhetoric of Fame," *Spenser Studies* 5 (1985)—on Hawes.

T.V.F. BROGAN

**AUSTRALIA, POETRY OF.** Oral poetry among indigenous Aboriginal people in Australia is an ancient trad., reaching back as far as 40,000 years or more. It continues to this day, though much diminished as a result of colonization by the Brit., beginning in 1788. There is no one single Aboriginal trad., as there were hundreds of distinct langs., but they shared common features: the poetry was highly ritualistic and embraced a rich variety of song and narrative, incl. myths, legends, mourning poems, war poems, *satires, *anecdotes, and so on. Performances were usually accompanied by music, and some involved dance and even ground drawings and carvings. Early accounts of this material, starting in the 1830s and 1840s, were recorded by ethnologists, but it took another hundred years before the works of R. M. Berndt and T.G.H. Strehlow brought recognition of Aboriginal poetry as a cultural achievement to the wider world. One of the best-known Aboriginal poems is the 13-part "Song Cycle of the Moon-Bone," of the Wonguri-Mandjigai people of Arnhem Land, which opens with ceremonial preparations (in Berndt's trans.):

> The people are making a camp of branches in that
>     country at Arnhem Bay:
> With the forked stick, the rail for the whole camp,
>     the Mandjigai people are making it. . . .

Although there was Aboriginal writing in Eng. from the early colonial period, it was not until the 1960s and 70s that Aboriginal lit. in Eng. began to be widely disseminated. *We Are Going* (1964) by Oodgeroo Noonuccal (initially known as Kath Walker, 1920–93) was the first poetry collection pub. by an Australian Aborigine, and she was soon followed by Kevin Gilbert (1933–93) and Jack Davis (1917–2000), initiating a new phase of Aboriginal poetry. This recent trad., which has attracted considerable attention, necessarily exhibits a complex relationship to anglophone poetry in Australia generally, simultaneously being a part of it and apart from it. As is the case with other indigenous cultures within postcolonial settler nations (Canada, South Africa, New Zealand, and the U.S., among them), Aboriginal writing is a multilayered and intricate phenomenon, entailing considerations of hist., politics, lang., and identity.

Early colonial poetry also had a strong oral component. Founded as a penal colony, Australia (or New South Wales, as it was called) was populated by convicts who were predominantly poor and urban, with low rates of literacy; subsequently, folk songs, work songs, and ballads flourished alongside the nascent written lit. There are a number of vigorous anonymous ballads from this period (incl. "Van Diemen's Land" and "The Female Transport") and one significant convict poet, Francis MacNamara (or "Frank the Poet," ca. 1810–1861), whose long poem, "A Convict's Tour to Hell" (1839) is a powerful satiric *dream vision in rhyming couplets ("Cook who discovered New South Wales / And he that first invented gaols / Are both tied to a fiery stake / Which stands in yonder boiling lake"). Convict verse marks the beginning of an antiauthoritarian strain

in Australian culture. Australia has a strong trad. of balladry, particularly in what became known as "bush ballads," celebrating outback life and heroic deeds, incl. those of renegade bushrangers, or deploring the trials and failures that attend such hard living. Among the most accomplished and best known of these poets are Adam Lindsay Gordon (1833–70), the only Australian poet to be honored in The Poets' Corner at Westminster Abbey; A. B. ("Banjo") Patterson (1864–1941), the ever-popular author of "Waltzing Matilda" (the unofficial national *anthem) and "The Man from Snowy River"; and Henry Lawson (1867–1922), who, in the pages of the popular and nationalistic jour. the *Bulletin* carried on a famous dispute with Banjo Patterson about the true nature of bush life (Lawson takes a more dour outlook, as in "Up the Country," where the speaker prefers the ease of town life by the coast, "Drinking beer and lemon-squashes, taking baths and cooling down"). It is noteworthy that much of the poetry published in the 19th c. appeared in newspapers and other periodicals, which made poetry—esp. ballads and songs—very much part of a common culture. The high-water mark for these genres was in the 1880s and 1890s, a period of intense nationalism in Australia, prior to federation (1901). But before then, there was already another trad. of "serious" verse that drew on the concerns and forms of Brit., Eur., and even Am. poetry.

The first book of poems published (privately) in Australia was by Barron Field (1786–1846), a magistrate who served in New South Wales for seven years and whose *First Fruits of Australian Poetry* appeared in 1819. His work is informed by an 18th-c. neoclassical taste, as in his wry poem, "The Kangaroo," whereby the first rhyme with "Australia" is "failure." The next significant book, *Thoughts: A Series of Sonnets* (1845), is by Charles Harpur (1813–68), an ambitious and major poet whose work inaugurates a late romantic trad., in the lyrical mode of William Wordsworth and P. B. Shelley. (The intervening quarter of a century between Field's and Harpur's books accounts for the sense of a belated romanticism that marked the devel. of Australian poetry.) In addition to loco-descriptive poems, Harpur wrote narratives, political and satirical verse, a tragedy, and several long visionary works. His most anthologized poems are "A Mid-Summer Noon in the Australian Forest" and "The Creek of the Four Graves," both of which render the Australian landscape in a new and vivid manner. Harpur was an important influence on Henry Kendall (1839–82), who extended Harpur's celebration of the landscape in a more lyrical and lush verse. Like Harpur, Kendall was eager to establish himself as a poet in Australia, but conditions were exceedingly hard financially in the new colony. Kendall did gain a reputation at the time, however, and for a long time was considered Australia's finest poet, with accolades given to "Bell-Birds," "Orara," "Beyond Kerguelen," and "To A Mountain."

Other poets of note writing in the latter half of the 19th c. include Ada Cambridge (1844–1926), whose outspokenness about gender issues was daring for the time; Victor J. Daley (1858–1905), often associated with the Celtic revival; and Bernard O'Dowd (1866–1953), a radical progressive who called for a "Poetry Militant" and initiated a correspondence with Walt Whitman. With O'Dowd, we move into the early 20th c., which featured a number of important poets who straddled both centuries. Mary Gilmore (1865–1962), a colorful and legendary figure, probes Aboriginal subjects, the convict heritage (most notably in "Old Botany Bay"), and many social issues, often from quite radical positions. Christopher Brennan (1870–1932), a scholar of classics and philosophy who studied at the University of Berlin and later taught at Sydney University, turned to poetry after encountering the work of Stéphane Mallarmé, with whom he exchanged letters. Brennan wrote in the mode of the Fr. symbolists (see SYMBOLISM), composing dense, hermetic poems, frequently on magian and visionary themes. An impressive figure, he has more in common with a fin de siècle *romanticism than with literary *modernism. *XXI Poems: Towards the Source* (1897) and *Poems* (1913), which was conceived of as a *livre composé* (or an "architectural and premeditated book," in Mallarmé's phrase) are Brennan's major publications. A contemporary of Brennan, and in many ways his opposite, John Shaw Neilson (1872–1942) is an attractive and engaging poet whose poems are frequently set in rural Australia, where he lived and worked for many years in difficult jobs under difficult circumstances. Despite those conditions, Neilson wrote some of the finest and most delicate lyrics of any Australian poet, as evidenced in his *Collected Poems* of 1934.

Most critics consider Kenneth Slessor (1901–71) the first true modernist in Australian poetry. An early acolyte of the vitalist Norman Lindsay (1879–1969), a bohemian artist whose jour. *Vision* attracted a number of poets in the 1920s, Slessor gradually made his way toward a more experimental and mod. sensibility. A thoroughly urbanized poet, Slessor developed a hard-edged and imagistic verse that assimilated many of the modernist techniques coming out of Britain and the U.S., though never the most radical modes. Slessor's poetic output was not large, but a handful of his poems ranks among the most highly regarded in Australia, esp. the luminous elegy "Five Bells" and the war poem "Beach Burial" (Slessor was a war correspondent in the 1940s). Two other poets associated with the "Vision School" of Norman Lindsay went on to have significant careers: Robert Fitzgerald (1902–87), a discursive and meditative poet; and Douglas Stewart (1913–85), a prolific writer known for his pastoral poems and for his years as lit. ed. of the *Bulletin*. John Blight (1913–95) came to prominence as a poet of the Queensland coast, esp. with his "sea sonnets," but later, in the 1970s, changed his style to a more experimental and idiosyncratic one.

During the 1940s, in the midst of the literary ferment brought on by modernism, there was nonetheless considerable resistance to its more extravagant forms. The infamous Ern Malley hoax is the prime example. Two young (and later prominent) poets, James McAuley (1917–76) and Harold Stewart (1916–95), decided to discredit modernist pretensions by creating a fake

poet, Ern Malley, whose "absurd" work they sent to the avant-garde jour. *Angry Penguins*, which then published it to acclaim in 1944. Exposure of the imposture created a sensation in the press, though "Ern Malley" continues to be regarded by many as genuine poetry of a high order of inventiveness. McAuley went on to become a major figure and write expertly crafted verse marked by fierce intelligence and emotional depth. Stewart, also productive, though more disaffected with postwar Australia, finally moved to Japan, where he devoted himself to Shin Buddhism. Like McAuley and Stewart, A. D. Hope (1907–2000) was critical of modernist excesses and quickly became known for his lashing reviews. But Hope's poetry is regarded as one of the high-water marks of Australian lit., esp. overseas. Cultivated and often epicurean, Hope was a traditionalist in verse and an ardent believer in the orphic power of poetry. Not unlike W. H. Auden, he displays a penchant for the middle style of sophisticated discursive verse but can also write with lyrical grace and distinction.

Prior to the founding of *Angry Penguins* in 1940, another movement began with a more nationalistic purpose: the *Jindyworobaks. Instituted by the poet Rex Ingamells (1913–55), it looked to indigenous Aborigines for inspiration in promoting an original Australian culture, one based on appreciation for the Australian landscape and a belief in its spiritual dimension. The movement was controversial and lasted into the 1950s, attracting a number of artists and writers, most prominently the poet Roland Robinson (1912–92), who frequently incorporates Aboriginal material in his verse. Judith Wright (1915–2000) was also concerned with indigenous issues, though from a different perspective. Known as a fierce environmentalist and a stalwart activist for Aboriginal rights, she writes passionately about Australian landscape and hist. from a deeply personal point of view. A note of despair and bitterness can sound in her work, but it is all the stronger for it. With her inaugural volume of poems, *The Moving Image* (1946), Wright moved immediately to the forefront of Australian poetry and remains one of its most revered figures. Another prolific poet of *pastoral is David Campbell (1915–79), a war hero, a grazier, and a keen observer of the natural world. While many Australian poets at this time engaged thematically with the landscape, others turned to more metropolitan subjects. In Tasmania, Gwen Harwood (1920–95) created not only a series of fascinating personae in her poetry (Professors Eisenbart and Kröte) but *heteronyms under whose names she published (Walter Lehmann, Francis Geyer, and Miriam Stone, among them). Renown for her tart wit and probing intelligence, Harwood, like Elizabeth Bishop in the U.S., has increasingly become prominent in accounts of 20th-c. poetry in Australia. Vincent Buckley (1925–88), one of Harwood's early supporters, was a leading poet and an influential critic in Melbourne. His spare intellectual style could move rapidly between irony and profound emotion. Chris Wallace-Crabbe (b. 1934), also from Melbourne, quickly established himself as a leading poet of his generation and has gone on to solidify that high regard with a prolific output of verse and crit. His poems are often witty and cognitively adventurous, deploying a demotic Australian that counterpoints the sophistication of his work. More overtly sophisticated is the poetry of Peter Porter (1929–2010), an expatriate who lived in London but who maintained close ties with his homeland. Porter is regarded as a major poet in both the U.K. and Australia and is one of the most cultured and skillful of contemporary poets. Bruce Beaver (1928–2004) was influential in the devel. of more experimental poetry. Francis Webb (1925–73) extended the range of mod. Australian poetry with his intensely charged lang., reminiscent at times of Robert Lowell. Like Lowell, Webb spent time in mental asylums, dying in one at an early age, but not before creating a remarkable oeuvre that continues to influence Australian poets for its ling. facility and dynamic emotional power. Whereas Webb can appear to be a poet's poet for his level of difficulty, Bruce Dawe (b. 1930) is unusual for being a genuinely popular poet, much read in schools and widely admired for his ironic humor and colloquial manner. Another popular writer, though primarily for his fiction, is David Malouf (b. 1934), who has compiled a body of verse distinguished by its inwardness and sensitivity. Other notable poets born before World War II include the highly regarded Rosemary Dobson (b. 1920), important in the devel. of Australian women's poetry, as are Fay Zwicky (b. 1933) and Judith Rodriguez (b. 1936); Thomas Shapcott (b. 1935), who helped usher in new devels. in poetry from overseas; Peter Steele (b. 1939), a polished poet with far-ranging and deep interests; and J. S. Harry (b. 1939), an early experimental poet. By far the best-known Australian poet, nationally and internationally, is Les Murray (b. 1938). Frequently mentioned as a candidate for the Nobel Prize, Murray writes a brilliant vernacular that can be astonishing in its thematic range and ling. inventiveness. Looking back to the Jindyworobaks, Murray has woven rural and Aboriginal material together with more urban and urbane matter, creating a poetry that is at once distinctly Australian and cosmopolitan.

By the later 1960s, Australian poetry was undergoing an upheaval similar to the one in the U.S. occasioned by the "war of the anthologies" that attended Donald Allen's *The New American Poetry 1945–1960*. In Australia, the self-styled Generation of '68 or the New Australian Poetry championed an aesthetic associated with the *Black Mountain, *New York school, and *San Francisco Renaissance movements. These Australian poets comprise a lively, talented, and disparate group, a number of whom continue to be important for contemp. poetry, incl. Robert Adamson (b. 1943), a key figure in the movement and often labeled a neoromantic; John Tranter (b. 1943), an early postmodernist; Kris Hemensley (b. 1946), owner of Collected Works, an influential poetry bookshop in Melbourne; John A. Scott (b. 1948), who experimented with poetic sequences; Alan Wearne (b. 1948), author of book-length verse narratives that broke new ground; Laurie Duggan (b. 1949), who used *collage techniques

to good effect; Jennifer Maiden (b. 1949), one of the few women poets in the movement; and John Forbes (1950–1998), a highly gifted seriocomic poet. Out of all of them, Tranter is most active and best known, esp. for his editorship of the online jour. *Jacket*. Two poets who demurred polemically from the aesthetics of the New Australian Poetry were Robert Gray (b. 1945) and Geoffrey Lehmann (b. 1940). Gray writes a finely tuned imagistic poetry, redolent of his interest in Zen Buddhism, while Lehmann is more eclectic. Poets of note that Gray and Lehmann championed include Geoff Page (b. 1940), unusual for his formalist verse; Mark O'Connor (b. 1945); Rhyll McMaster (b. 1947); and Alan Gould (b. 1949), also a fine novelist. As the poetry wars of the 1970s and 1980s faded, other "unaligned" poets came to the fore, incl. those born in the 1940s: Jan Owen (b. 1940); Barry Hill (b. 1943), a novelist and nonfiction writer as well; Diane Fahey (b. 1945); Gary Catalano (1947–2002), an art critic; Alex Skovron (b. 1948); Martin Harrison (b. 1949); and Kate Jennings (b. 1949), an early feminist and novelist. These were followed by other prominent poets, incl. Peter Goldsworthy (b. 1951), also an essayist, novelist, and librettist; Stephen Edgar (b. 1951), a writer of unsurpassed technical facility; Dorothy Porter (1954–2008), whose lesbian detective novel in verse, *The Monkey's Mask*, was a popular sensation; Kevin Hart (b. 1954), a philosopher and theologian, whose rich meditative verse proves haunting and arresting; Peter Rose (b. 1955), a highly cultured and satiric poet; Gig Ryan (b. 1956), a minimalist and feminist; Judith Beveridge (b. 1956), a serene nature poet deeply engaged with Buddhism; Anthony Lawrence (b. 1957), an exuberant storyteller; Sarah Day (b. 1958), a writer of finely wrought lyrics; and Philip Hodgins (1959–1995), whose unflinching exploration of rural life and his own terminal leukemia produced powerful poetry.

As poetry in Australia moves into the 21st c., a sense of capacious pluralism reflects the increasingly multicultural nature of the society. There has been a resurgence of Aboriginal poetry, as seen in Sam Watson (b. 1952), Tony Birch (b. 1957), Lionel Fogarty (b. 1958), Lisa Bellear (1961–2006), and Yvette Holt (b. 1971). Attention to ethnicity has always been a presence in Australia but has become more pronounced since the 1970s. Few, however, would consider themselves "ethnic" writers; indeed, the following poets are seen as mainstream: Dimitris Tsaloumas (b. 1921), Antigone Kefala (b. 1935), Ania Walwicz (1951), Tom Petsinis (b. 1953), Ouyang Yu (b. 1955), Marcella Polain (b. 1958), Dipti Saravanamuttu (b. 1960), and Ali Alizadeh (b. 1976), among others. To a marked degree, poets in Australia remain open to a multitude and plurality of influences. John Kinsella (b. 1963) is an unusually prolific author whose work ranges from the highly experimental (in the *Language poetry manner) to more conventional pastoral and lyrical forms. Kinsella also exemplifies an internationalist impulse that looks beyond national and nationalist borders to embrace a wide variety of poetic modes. The same could be said of John Mateer (b. 1971), of South African heritage, and Alison

Croggon (b. 1962), initially from the Transvaal. There has clearly been an efflorescence of poetry in Australia in the last decades, and it is likely to be furthered by such poets as Jordie Albiston (b. 1961), Craig Sherborne (b. 1962), Brendan Ryan (b. 1963), Tracy Ryan (b. 1964), Michael Farrell (b. 1965), Peter Minter (b. 1967), Bronwyn Lea (b. 1969), Lisa Gorton (b. 1972), Judith Bishop (b. 1972), Michael Brennan (b. 1973), and Petra White (b. 1975), all of whom have published to considerable acclaim. In Australia, poetry continues to be one of the continent's most vibrant arts.

■ **Anthologies**: *Songs of Central Australia*, ed. T. Strehlow (1971); *Three Faces of Love: Traditional Aboriginal Song-Poetry*, ed. R. Berndt (1976); *Penguin Book of Modern Verse*, ed. H. Heseltine (1981); *New Oxford Book of Australian Verse*, ed. L. Murray (1986); *Inside Black Australia*, ed. K. Gilbert (1988); *Penguin Book of Modern Australian Poetry*, ed. J. Tranter and P. Mead (1991); *Australian Poetry in the Twentieth Century*, ed. R. Gray and G. Lehmann (1991); *Penguin Book of Australian Ballads*, ed. P. Butterss and E. Webby (1993); *Oxford Book of Australian Women's Verse*, ed. S. Lever (1995); *Australian Verse*, ed. J. Leonard (1998); *Landbridge*, ed. J. Kinsella (1999); *Calyx 30*, ed. M. Brennan and P. Minter (2000); *Penguin Anthology of Australian Poetry*, ed. J. Kinsella (2008); *Macquarie PEN Anthology of Australian Literature*, ed. N. Jose (2009); *Puncher & Wattmann Anthology of Australian Poetry*, ed. J. Leonard (2009).

■ **Criticism and History**: J. Wright, *Preoccupations in Australian Poetry* (1965); *Oxford History of Australian Literature*, ed. L. Kramer (1981); A. Taylor, *Reading Australian Poetry* (1987); *Penguin New Literary History of Australian Literature*, ed. L. Hergenhan (1988); P. Kane, *Australian Poetry* (1996); *Oxford Literary History of Australia*, ed. B. Bennet and J. Strauss (1998); *Cambridge Companion to Australian Literature*, ed. E. Webby (2000); M. Harrison, *Who Wants to Create Australia?* (2004); P. Mead, *Networked Language* (2008); *A Companion to Australian Literature since 1900*, ed. N. Birns and R. McNeer (2007).

P. KANE

**AUSTRIA, POETRY OF.** Although the langs. of Austrian poetry—Ger. and Germanic dialects—emphasize its closeness to Ger. poetry, the geographical, historical, and political distinctiveness of Austria justify regarding Austrian poetry as a separate entity. This is largely the case throughout the hist. of Austria, whether as duchies, provinces, kingdoms, and empires under the Babenbergs (976–1246) and the Hapsburgs (1278–1918), or as a mod. republic. Nevertheless, it is difficult to speak straightforwardly of an Austrian "national" lit., since from the Middle Ages to the present regional identity has been strong.

Texts of important religious poetry from the early Middle Ages in the Danube valley survive in three ms. collections, the Wiener, Millstätter (or Klagenfurter), and the Vorauer Handschriften (mid-to-late 12th c.). The last of these holds the first surviving poems in Ger. by a woman, Frau Ava or Ava von Melk (ca. 1060–1127), incl. *Das Leben Jesu* (ca. 1125), which shows considerable sophistication. Mariological works include

the *Melker Marienlied* (ca. 1130) and the *Mariensequenz aus St. Lambrecht* (Seckau) from the later 12th c. The *St. Trudperter Hohenlied* (ca. 1160–70), based on the Song of Songs, stems from the Abbey of Admont in Steiermark.

The most celebrated secular work is the MGH *Nibelungenlied* (ca. 1200), probably by someone at the court of Wolfger von Erlau, bishop of Passau. Another secular strand was represented by the poets of *Minnesang*. The Danubian trad. flourished with Der von Kürenberg (fl. mid-12th c.), active in Upper Austria, and Dietmar von Aist (fl. ca. 1160–80), who wrote some of the first love lyrics in Ger. Kürenberg's "Swenne ich stân aleine" is the earliest example of the *Frauenlied* genre. At the same time, the satirical poet Heinrich von Melk (d. after 1150) wrote protests against love songs and a *memento mori*, *Von des tôdes gehugede*. The Minnesänger gradually developed more complex strophic forms and rhyme schemes, and the conventions of the love lyric became modified into the noble form of courtly poetry by poets such as Reinmar the Elder (d. ca. 1205), in whose verses the pain of unrequited love is sublimated into exquisite formal sophistication.

Not until the 13th c. do mss. preserve melodies for Minnesang, but by the time of Oswald von Wolkenstein (ca. 1377–1445), text and setting go hand in hand. He and the Mönch von Salzburg (late 14th c.) wrote for several voices. Many writers of the period had positions at court, incl. Walther von der Vogelweide (ca. 1170–ca. 1230), a Ger. working for Frederick I of Austria in Vienna. The patrons of Frauenlob (Heinrich von Meißen, 1280–1318), a highly original author of the eroticized *Marienleich*, the *Kreuzleich*, and the *Minneleich*, included Wenceslas II of Bohemia. Frauenlob, Walther, Neidhart (ca. 1185–1240), Oswald, and the Styrian Ulrich von Lichtenstein (1198–1275) subvert and redirect the conventions of Minnesang: in his *Vrowen dienst* (1255), e.g., Ulrich wrote perhaps the first extended autobiographical lyric.

The court of Maximilian I was an important literary center, attracting the humanist poet Conrad Celtis (1459–1508), but literary devels. in the Ren. were curtailed by the wars of the Reformation; the success of the Counter-Reformation in Austria restored the hegemony of the Catholic Church and with it Lat. as the lang. of art and learning. The outstanding Ger.-lang. poet of the late 16th c. was the Ren. humanist Christoph von Schallenberg (1561–97). His Lat. verse is formally sophisticated and religious, while the Ger. lieder are simpler and more worldly. He features in anthols. from the early 17th c., such as the *Jaufener Liederbuch*; others, such as the *Raaber Liederbuch* display the influence of Petrarch.

The influence of the It. Ren. continued into the 17th c. Verse *epics such as *Die unvergnügte Proserpina* (1661) and *Der Habspurgische Ottobert* (1664) by Wolf Helmhard von Hohberg (1612–88) were inspired by Ludovico Ariosto. Like other Protestant poets, incl. his friend Catharina Regina von Greiffenberg (1633–94), Hohberg was driven into exile in Germany by the Counter-Reformation. Greiffenberg's first work, the virtuosic *Geistliche Sonnette* (1662), reflects both these political pressures and the psychological tensions of difficult family circumstances and expresses the hope that God will grant in poetry the space for her to unfold personally and spiritually. Catholic writers active in the Austrian lands included the general and statesman Raimundo Graf Montecúccoli (1609–80), author of moving sonnets, as well as members of religious orders, such as the Capuchins Laurentius von Schniflis (1633–1702) and Procopius von Templin (1608–80), whose collection *Hertzen-Freud und Seelen-Trost* (1659) was published in Passau.

The commonplace that, between Abraham a Sancta Clara (1644–1709) and Ferdinand Raimund (1790–1836) or Franz Grillparzer (1791–1872), there is no major Austrian writer of lasting repute masks interesting devels. in poetry. Under Maria Theresa, it moved from the playfully secular *Liederbuch* (songbook) style to works with loftier ambitions. Michael Denis (1729–1800) attempted to familiarize Austria with north Ger. writing in his anthol. *Sammlung kürzerer Gedichte aus den neuern Dichtern Deutschlands* (1762–66), although his own work is more indebted to Jesuit religiosity than to the Ger. Enlightenment. F. G. Klopstock inspired the patriotic odes of Denis's pupil, Lorenz Leopold Haschka (1749–1827), author of the Austrian national *anthem "Gott erhalte Franz den Kaiser!" (1797). Haschka befriended the most prominent woman author of the early 19th c., Caroline Pichler (1769–1843), who, with Joseph Franz Ratschky (1757–1810), represented a contrasting epigrammatic, satirical tone in contemp. verse. In a similar vein, Aloys Blumauer (1755–98) wrote a comic *mock epic parodying Virgil, *Die Abenteuer des frommen Helden Aeneas* (1784–88). Vienna was also the center of a thriving *ballad trad., similarly satirical and often anonymous, although the work of Johann David Hanner (1754–95) stands out for its acute social critique.

While Ger. romantic poetry had its imitators and defenders in Austria, Austria did not imitate Ger. *romanticism. Symptomatic of much early 19th-c. lit. are tones of resignation, *Weltschmerz* (world-weariness), and self-sacrifice that reflect the lives of many authors. Some, such as Michael Enk von der Burg (1788–1843), committed suicide. The most renowned poet, Hungarian-born Nikolaus Lenau (1802–50), died in an asylum, and his work reflects a Byronic searching for meaning and justice. Nature in his poetry (*Gedichte*, 1832) carries the burden of the poet's emotions and experiences, and the lyrical voice seems attenuated and isolated. Lenau's political poetry is also significant, although that of his friend Anastasius Grün (1806–76) is more radical, with *Spaziergänge eines Wiener Poeten* (1831) and *Schutt* (1835) targeting Metternich's reactionary system and the influence of the church on the state. Similar social awareness characterizes the poetry of the otherwise conservative Ferdinand von Saar (1833–1906). The poetry, prose, and drama of Marie von Ebner-Eschenbach (1830–1916) consistently reflect her concern with the poor and the oppressed, as does her correspondence with Josephine von Knorr (1827–1908). Knorr's poetry of melancholy and transience was widely admired by contemporaries but is little known today.

As Austria turned away from Ger. romanticism, a rich trad. of writing celebrating the unique character of the Austrian regions flourished. Anthols. from all periods reflect this: in 1854, e.g., Salomon Mosenthal (1821–77) collected a representative range in his *Museum aus den deutschen Dichtungen österreichischer Lyriker und Epiker*. But Mosenthal excluded *dialect poetry, another important vehicle for the expression of regional identity in the 19th c. Collections of Lower Austrian verse were published by Ignaz Franz Castelli (1781–1862) and Johann Gabriel Seidl (1804–75) in 1828 and 1844, respectively. Others include Karl Stelzhamer (1802–74, Upper Austria), author of *Lieder in obderenns'scher Volksmundart* (1837); Anton von Klesheim (1812–84, Vienna); Peter Rosegger (1843–1918, Styria); and Otto Pflanzl (1865–1943, Salzburg). In the 20th c., the *Heimatkunst* ("regional art") movement lent further impetus to dialect writing, inspiring Joseph Oberkofler (1889–1962, Tirol), Resl Mayr (1891–1980, Lower Austria), and Josef Weinheber (1892–1945, Vienna).

The melancholy and uncertainty of much 19th-c. Austrian poetry are perpetuated at the turn of the century, influenced by Fr. and Ger. *symbolism, *impressionism, *decadence, and *Jugendstil* (the Ger. equivalent of the term *art nouveau*) in lit., and by devels. in psychology. In the 1890s, poetry turned from social crit. to become subjectivized, often to the point of overrefinement, nervousness, and introspection. The group known as Young Vienna cultivated nuances of feeling and subconscious drives in an effort to create a new aesthetic. The precocious Hugo von Hofmannsthal (1874–1929) was the most celebrated: his apparently effortless, expressive verse explores the semimystical power of lang. to convey truth via feeling and atmosphere, the transience of experience, and the fluidity of the boundaries of identity. Before the age of 30, Hofmannsthal ceased writing poetry almost entirely, externalizing the crisis brought about by the intrusion of consciousness between lang. and reality in the so-called Chandos Letter of 1902.

Lesser writers include Felix Dörmann (1870–1928), author of the sensuously solipsistic lyrics of *Neurotica* (1891) and *Sensationen* (1892), and Leopold von Andrian (1875–1951), who published delicate, narcissistic verse in Stefan George's *Blätter für die Kunst*. Tensions between the mannered, impressionistic *Gedichte* (1893) and the euphoric *Eherne Sonette* (1915) greeting World War I characterize the contradictory oeuvre of Richard von Schaukal (1874–1942). The Catholic writer Richard von Kralik (1852–1934) rejected subjectivist writing and turned to Germanic myth, med. mystery plays, and puppet theater to regenerate Ger. culture.

Wholly distinct from these Viennese poets, Rainer Maria Rilke (1875–1926) was among the greatest writers of Eur. *modernism. From the contemplative religious lang. of *Das Stunden-Buch* (1905), via the existential and poetological reflectiveness of the

*Duineser Elegien* (written 1912–22) to the celebratory enthusiasm of *Die Sonette an Orpheus* (written 1922), his poetry explores themes of death, love, and loss, mastering and imaginatively developing a huge variety of poetic forms. He interrogated the relation between his art and the world around him, moving from the neoromantic and the mystical toward the precise craft of expressing the everyday in poetry and the poet's duty to praise the world. During a period in Paris as Auguste Rodin's secretary, he learned to see and look ("Schauen," "Anschauen"), producing two books of *Neue Gedichte* (written 1902–8) that combine observation and precision with inwardness to give new definition to the concept of *\*Dinggedicht*.

Austrian *expressionism was less politically engaged than its Ger. counterpart; it was apocalyptic and emotionally charged and formally experimental. Representatives include Oskar Kokoschka (1886–1980), whose *Die träumenden Knaben* (1908) thematizes art and dream, love and death, the inadequacy of lang. and the attraction of the exotic. His fascination with China was shared by Albert Ehrenstein (1886–1950), who, unlike many Ger. contemporaries, was never caught up by enthusiasm for the war, as *Der Mensch schreit* (1916) demonstrates. The poetry of Hans Kaltneker (1895–1919) expresses visionary intensity and an unquenchable faith in the redemptive power of love with immense ling. sensitivity. The (nondenominational) gospel of love was also propounded by Prague-born Franz Werfel (1890–1945) in his first collection, *Der Weltfreund* (1911).

The most influential Austrian expressionist was Georg Trakl (1887–1914), who, like Werfel, served on the front line. Trakl depicts a world of decay, destruction, and death. He uses lang. radically to express the ruptured universe in free rhythms, fractured syntax, and enigmatic metaphors known as *Chiffren* (ciphers), which establish a relation between the incomparable realms of the referential and the ontological. Guilt and despair are expressed in a sonorous lang. of *alliteration and *assonance that shows the influence of Arthur Rimbaud.

The dual monarchy of Austria-Hungary collapsed in 1918, and the succeeding republic was characterized by economic instability and political polarization. The federal government moved toward "Austro-Fascism" and Austria's annexation by Germany in 1938, while the city of Vienna remained under Social Democrat control until 1934. Contemp. sociopolitical protest was reflected in the writings of the worker-poet Alfons Petzold (1882–1923) and the muted lyricism of Theodor Kramer (1897–1958); Kramer's *Wir lagen in Wolhynien im Morast* (1931) also reflects with restrained intensity on the war. Jura Soyfer (1912–39), a powerful anti-Nazi poet, was murdered in a concentration camp. By contrast, Josef Weinheber (1892–1945) was highly conservative, claiming for the poet in *Adel und Untergang* (1934) the salvation of meaning in a meaningless world. His reputation has not recovered from associations with Nazism. He was a master of complex cl. strophic forms and the *sonnet, and some of

his more experimental ling. effects are recognized as precursors of postwar writing. Similarly indebted to cl. trad. was the grandiose work of the self-styled *poeta doctus* Alexander von Lernet-Holenia (1897–1976). He and Erika Mitterer (1906–2000) were also heavily influenced by Rilke. Both Rilke and the cl. trad. were important to Franz Baermann Steiner (1909–52). Forced into exile during World War II, he, like H. G. Adler (1910–88), has only recently been recognized as a major lyric talent.

The political context of Austria after 1945, in which National Socialism was interpreted as a period of occupation, meant that poetry of this period was frequently conservative, focusing on the values of *Heimat* (homeland or regional identity). Alongside Lernet-Holenia's *Germanien* (1946) and a posthumous collection by Weinheber (*Hier ist das Wort*, 1947), this trend was represented variously by the hugely popular *Heiteres Herbarium* (1950) of Karl Waggerl (1897–1973) and an *Österreichische Trilogie* (1950) by the patriotic Catholic Rudolf Henz (1897–1987). Catholic spirituality was central also to the work of the reclusive poet Christine Lavant (1915–73), whose passionate lyrics hover between poetry and prayer. Like Lavant, Christina Busta (1915–87) progressed toward a more lapidary style, gradually abandoning strict forms. By 1963, the anthol. *Frage und Formel: Gedichte einer jungen österreichischen Generation* makes overt the mod. era's ironic treatment of formal rigor and traditional themes and foregrounds a consciousness of the plasticity of poetic lang.

Excessive density, *hermeticism, even a desire for "absolute metaphors" are accusations unjustly leveled at the work of the towering figure in the postwar poetic landscape, Paul Celan (1920–70), whose relationship to Austria was fatally problematized by Ger. as the lang. spoken by the perpetrators of the Holocaust. Linguistically subtle and innovative, morally uncompromising and poetologically reflexive, his works from *Mohn und Gedächtnis* (1952) to *Die Niemandsrose* (1963) and *Lichtzwang* (1970) are grounded in the belief that meaning finds itself only when it finds lang. Celan lived in Paris; his distinguished contemp. Ingeborg Bachmann (1926–73) settled in Italy. Her poetry engages critically with contemp. Austrian society's blindness to the legacy of the Nazi period using a variety of personas. Rooted in the Austrian trad. (like Celan, she drew inspiration from Hofmannsthal), her lang. is rhythmically restless and her imagery a unique blend of vivid tangibility and intense abstraction. Ilse Aichinger (b. 1921) shared Bachmann's critique of contemp. Austria (cf. *Verschenkter Rat*, 1978).

More politically direct than Celan and Bachmann, Erich Fried (1921–88) was also more formally exploratory; his use of montage and documentary materials paved the way for the explosion of experimental poetry in the 1950s that led to the formation of the Vienna Group around Friedrich Achleitner (b. 1930), Gerhard Rühm (b. 1930), Konrad Bayer (1932–64), and Oswald Wiener (b. 1935), with H. C. Artmann (1921–2000). The group acknowledged the influence of *Dada, Fr. *surrealism, and Ludwig Wittgenstein; and its diverse works, often in dialect or embracing *concrete poetry and multimedia montage, are unified by an interest in games (*Spiel*) and the attempt to free lang. from the primacy of communication. Other avant-garde poets included Andreas Okopenko (1930–2010), exploiting the power of the grotesque and the experimental; and Ernst Jandl (1925–2000). Jandl's humorous but challenging engagement with the reader earned him popular appeal. From 1960, the liberating effects of the Vienna Group served as a springboard for a broader group of avant-garde writers, the Graz Group, which includes a broad spectrum of contemp. authors with ling. and sociopolitical interests, united by a critical stance toward the status quo in art and society. Its jour., *manuskripte*, is edited by the poet Alfred Kolleritsch (b. 1931), whose opaque metaphors examine the content and conditions of consciousness. The Viennese poet Jutta Schutting (b. 1937) also operates in the Wittgensteinian trad., using lang. to question itself.

Avant-garde concerns continue in the work of contemp. poets Ferdinand Schmatz (b. 1953) and Raoul Schrott (b. 1964), whose verse exploits a variety of formal and typographical idiosyncrasies. Schrott is a mod.-day poeta doctus, whose erudition is displayed prominently within and alongside the poetry. The Austrian trad. of reflecting on the nature of lang. continues to be articulated by Peter Waterhouse (b. 1956), who brutally forces lang. to cede to a kaleidoscope of perspectives from the empirical world. After an experimental phase, the later works of Friederike Mayröcker (b. 1924) also mark a return to the real world and recognizable human emotion. This repersonalization of the lyric is reflected, too, in the elegiac poetry of Evelyn Schlag (b. 1952). Like Mayröcker and so many of her contemporaries and predecessors, in volumes such as *Brauchst du den Schlaf dieser Nacht* (2002), Schlag engages in a moving dialogue with the trad. of Austrian poetry.

■ **Anthologies**: *Lyrik aus Deutschösterreich vom Mittelalter bis zur Gegenwart*, ed. S. Hock (1919); *Die Botschaft: Neue Gedichte aus Österreich*, ed. E. A. Rheinhardt (1920); *Dichtungen in niederösterreichischer Mundart*, ed. K. Bacher et al. (1931); *Österreichische Lyrik aus neuen Jahrhunderten*, ed. W. Stratowa (1948); *Dichtung aus Österreich*, v. 2, *Lyrik*, ed. E. Thurnher (1976); *Zwischenbilanz: Eine Anthologie österreichischer Gegenwartsliteratur*, ed. W. Weiss and S. Schmid (1976); *Zeit und Ewigkeit. Tausend Jahre österr. Lyrik*, ed. J. Schondorff (1978); *Verlassener Horizont: Österreichische Lyrik aus vier Jahrzehnten*, ed. H. Huppert and R. Links (1980); *Die Wiener Moderne: Literatur, Kunst und Musik zwischen 1890 und 1910*, ed. G. Wunberg (1981); *Austria in Poetry and History*, ed. F. Ungar (1984); *Austrian Poetry Today*, ed. M. Holton and H. Kuhner (1985); *Contemporary Austrian Poetry*, ed. B. Bjorklund (1986).

■ **Criticism and History**: A. Schmidt, *Dichtung und Dichter Österreichs im 19. und 20. Jahrhundert*, 2 v. (1964); C. Magris, *Der habsburgische Mythos in der österreichischen Literatur* (1966); *Handbook of Austrian Literature*, ed. F. Ungar (1973); *Kindlers Literaturge-schichte der Gegenwart: Die zeitgenössische Literatur Österreichs*, ed. H. Spiel (1976); *Die österreichische Literatur: Eine Dokumentation ihrer literarhistorischen Entwicklung*, ed. H. Zeman, 4 v. (1979–89); A. Best and H. Wolfschütz, *Modern Austrian Writing* (1980); *Formen der Lyrik in der österreichischen Gegenwartsliteratur*, ed. W. Schmidt-Dengler (1981); S. P. Scheichl and G. Stieg, *Österreichische Literatur des 20. Jahrhunderts* (1986); *Geschichte der Literatur in Österreich von den Anfängen bis zur Gegenwart*, ed. H. Zeman, 7 v. (1994–); *Literaturgeschichte Österreichs: von den Anfängen im Mittelalter bis zur Gegenwart*, ed. H. Zeman (1996); *A History of Austrian Literature*, ed. R. Robertson and K. Kohl (2006); A. Bushell, *Poetry in a Provisional State: The Austrian Lyric 1945–1955* (2007).

R. L. VILAIN

**AUTONOMY.** The concept of autonomy is fundamental for poetics because it has been frequently invoked to sustain two claims about works of art—that their foregrounding of internal formal relations affords a distinctive mode of self-consciousness and that the semantic force of these relations cannot be accounted for by the interpretive models we employ in our practical lives.

When we try to apply the term, we find it involving us in tensions basic to any discussion of freedom. *Autonomy* toggles between accounts stressing the negative—what freedom is from—and the positive—what freedom involves for our quality of being.

Concepts of aesthetic disinterest and logical claims that art is irreducible to any other model of value emerged as early as the mid-18th c. Fully celebratory doctrines of autonomy ultimately came to depend on Immanuel Kant's transcendental ontology because that provided systematic parallels between the aesthetic and the moral domains. In Kant's moral philosophy, practical and prudential judgments are "heteronomous" because they submit the subject to empirical and causal factors providing the terms for decisions. The person chooses for various pragmatic reasons rather than a concern for the identity the choice would establish. Autonomous action, in contrast, treats the will as the synthesis of spontaneity and rationality that makes possible self-legislating activity. Moral behavior need not follow rules or pursue prudential policies but can align the self with rational principles to which one lucidly submits one's subjective interests. One wills to be rational and allows rationality to determine how one might be worthy to be happy. Analogously, aesthetic judgment (or the exercise of taste) also "does not find itself subjected to a heteronomy from empirical laws," because it also legislates in accord with "something that is both in the subject and outside him, something that is neither nature nor freedom" (*Critique of Judgment*). This sense of combining intuition and judgment joins "the theoretical and practical power . . . into a unity." *Taste, like moral judgment, depends on refusing mere liking and so cannot be treated in terms borrowed from heteronomous thinking. Rather, agents making judgments of taste that honor the autonomy of art do not act out of "mere liking" but offer approval or disapproval. An aesthetic judgment takes place when agents align their empirical subjectivity with reflective desires to claim "the universal agreement of all men." Aesthetic judgment, however, cannot claim to be a deductive science like morality, because then it could not account for pleasure or honor constant innovation. Its universality, therefore, is a matter not of deduction taking the form of duty but of pleasure being directed toward possible identification with a collective response that the judgment projects.

Aesthetic judgment also provides a model of how artists legislate through their concrete processes of presentation. In the *Critique of Judgment*, Kant envisions the *genius as the maker "who gives the rule to nature." The work of genius is not subject to heteronomy, because there is no pressing desire to achieve something practical by means of the art. Rather, the genius elaborates an intuition into a complex "presentation" (*Darstellung*) that develops an overall purposiveness aimed primarily at establishing internal resonance for how pieces of the work fit together. Neither artists nor critics can fully appreciate how the work forges a distinctive "aesthetic idea" unless they manage to take a disinterested stance, making it possible to overcome the sheer immediacy of purely subjective states. Disinterest toward the practical world (which is not the same thing as ignorance of it) makes it possible to treat the work not only as a thing but as a presentation characterized by a formal density of active internal relationships. The presentation is not a simple object, because those dense internal relationships make their own demands on how we stand toward the work. Realizing this, Kant thought, enabled us to treat the work as "inexponible" intuition that "occasions much thought" without being the stable object of any one thought." Such stability is the goal of the understanding. But the *imagination of the genius resists predicates that would produce unity for the work by assigning it a purpose subjecting it to the understanding. Instead, the work establishes "a purposiveness without purpose" that offers a self-legislating structure that has to be treated as "an aesthetic idea" capable of assuming transcendental powers similar to moral ideas. As we develop the "free play of imagination" provoked by the work, we can experience our own pleasure as producing a possible law for itself that takes the form of a demand for the agreement of other members of the audience.

Both judge and artist, then, make choices that maintain independence from what society offers as rewards for conforming to its preferred roles. Rather than choose prudentially, the work enables a sense that one simultaneously legislates and develops a manifest justification for that legislation. This model of choice echoes an aristocratic ideal of preferring character to calculation, an ideal that will become central to 19th c. writers. For Kant, however, any identification with a particular class would betray the very autonomy asserted because it would submit to social codes rather than transcendental principles. So Kant transforms the core of aristocratic distinction—the capacity for self-legislation—into the fundamental state of binding oneself to the rationality of moral law or binding oneself to intuitions that become symbols of the moral good—not because they provide moral allegories but because they call on legislative powers combining immediacy with self-transcendence. Other thinkers are not so reluctant to identify autonomy with class distinctions.

Kant's conjunction of the aesthetic and the rational did not survive the prevailing cultural dichotomies between the domains of reason and understanding that it intended to resolve. It did open speculative spaces where others could try strategies recasting art as a domain of self-legislation. Friedrich Schiller, e.g., argued that aesthetic experience not merely symbolized moral judgment but provided the conditions of autonomy by producing the psyche's only reliable experience of its own distinctive powers for a nobility not reducible to the practical understanding. Schiller thought that Kant was reductive in his sense of the mind's highest powers involving subordination to fixed universals, so he allied those highest powers with the capacity of the aesthetic spirit to establish its own expressive forms not subject to the understanding but in harmony with the fluid life of the senses. Such forms free sense impressions from the heteronomous causality we attribute to mere perception by providing glimpses of "pure ideal man within himself" (*Letters upon the Aesthetic Education of Man*).

By rejecting Kantian logic, Schiller prepared the way for aestheticist versions of autonomy throughout the 19th c. that would increasingly separate art from any claims to be symbolic of moral action or to be of any use to society (see AESTHETICISM). Thus, Théophile Gautier states in the preface to *Mademoiselle de Maupin* (1825): "There is nothing truly beautiful except what is of no use: everything useful is ugly, for it is the expression of some need, and man's needs are ignoble and disgusting, like his pure infirm nature. The most useful spot in a house is the bathroom." Thus, too, the playwright Auguste Villiers de L'Isle-Adam (*Axël's Castle*, 1890): "As for living, our servants can do that for us." Autonomy now resides in the power of beauty to separate itself from the useful, thereby also generating a distinction between purely aristocratic self-legislation and servitude to bourgeois customs and habits. In "The Painter of Modern Life," Charles Baudelaire celebrated this distinction through the figure of the dandy who pursues "a personal form of originality within the external limits of social conventions." Also noteworthy are Arthur Schopenhauer's and Stéphane Mallarmé's ascetic versions of aristocratic autonomy. All want is cast as submission to heteronomy, so value must reside in humans turning against desire toward contemplative stances that protect ideals from our appropriative instincts.

The 20th c. was more likely to root autonomy in the object rather than in the genius producing the object. Then, readers could pursue contemplative states that set aside practical desires in order to engage the complexity and the elegance of how works established their own purposiveness. There were many theoretical accounts of various aspects of these autonomous objects—incl. Bell on distinctively aesthetic emotion, Adorno on the tension between "beauty" and "truth," and Jakobson on the internal self-sufficiency of the *poetic function. Probably the most radical claims to autonomy were Piet Mondrian's insistence that only an impersonal abstract art could free Western art from the fear of mortality that haunts any representation of subjective interests. In *The Future of the Image*, Rancière offers a summary of these views as prelude to his analysis of how most modernist art came to identify with the synthetic image as a complex synthesis of feeling and thinking. Art becomes the cultivation of "the way in which things themselves speak and are silent." The task of poetics, then, is to articulate the concrete achievement of what images could say, supplemented by accounts of what might matter in their evocative silences that tease the imagination into speculating on its own powers.

Postmodern art and theory have focused on the limitations of claims that art has to be granted a mode of existence distinctive from the states in ordinary life where practical interests prevail and heteronymous causes determine behavior. That version of negative freedom seemed little more than a defensive mechanism for idealizing what had already become art's impotence. After all, as Heumakers observes, to claim that art is free from social influence is tantamount to agreeing with G.W.F. Hegel's thesis about the end of art, since it no longer can compete with the work reason can do. More devastating yet were younger thinkers like Peter Berger and Jay Bernstein formed by immersion in *Frankfurt school writing. Bernstein is esp. eloquent in *Against Voluptuous Bodies*: "Art's autonomy, however, is not the achievement of art's securing for itself a space free from the interference of social or political utility, but a consequence and so an expression of the fragmentation and the reification of modern life. Autonomy is . . . art's expulsion and exclusion from everyday life and the (rationalized and reified) normative ideals, moral and cognitive, governing it."

Such critiques, however, may sell the idea of poetic autonomy short by dwelling only on formulations stressing aestheticist claims to negative freedom and ignoring the conditions of positive agency elaborated in Kant's views of genius and critical response. Can aesthetics do without the distinctions between liking and approving or, for that matter, between art and other modes of engaging experience? At least three modest ways of preserving the positive attributes stressed by autonomy claims could be advanced. The first is essentially historical. One might point out that very few artists and writers with strong claims on us in fact relied on the lang. of autonomy. Rather, they took for granted that art could be different from life in significant ways, and they tried to make those differences into means of giving new articulations to possible states of attention and responsiveness to the world. In the process, modernist artists esp. used that sense of resistance to the categories of the understanding to alter roles traditionally

seen as foundational for the arts (see MODERNISM). Rather than pursue distinctive and fixed concepts of author, work, audience, and world, they treated those conceptual elements as mutually dependent and variable. Each work could in principle define how author, work, audience, and world meshed and, in the process, exemplified potential structures of interrelationship. The simplest example is how noniconic abstract art had to identify artist with audience in order to stage an elemental transpersonality and to merge work and world in order to make good on the desire for an art of pure presentation. T. S. Eliot's poetics, too, makes impersonality a linking of author and audience and treats feeling as the fusion of work and world.

Second, works of art could invite a discourse of autonomy without denying social bonds or responsibilities. The desired freedom can simply be from the modes of blindness or repression driven by specific ideological practices central to that society. Denying the authority of certain instruments typically used in worldly struggles for power certainly need not entail denying other concerns for what seem legitimate social interests. Positively, artists and writers can invoke autonomy without depending on Kant's universal categorical imperatives. As Anscombe has shown, one can claim autonomy as an attribute of expressive agency when one can take overt responsibility for one's actions. Establishing this can be difficult in the case of literary texts. But in principle, autonomy is possible whenever there seem overt intentions capable of accounting for how the purposiveness in the text structures the primary internal relations giving the work its distinctive power. Artists like Gustave Flaubert and James Joyce play on this purposiveness to establish tensions between interest in the world and the disinterest that enables one to reflect on that range of interests.

Third, autonomy extends to the act of critical judgment because there is something symbolic of our sense of moral powers in how readers struggle to give reasons for their investments in seeing the text in a particular way. Probably we have to repudiate Kant's insistence that such acts of approval embody a transcendental demand for universal assent. The effort to establish reasons for one's pleasures suffices, in itself, to distinguish reading from a purely heteronomous cultivation of the empirical ego. Such reading offers a person's considered responses as a potential exemplar for achieving a shared mode of interpretation.

*See* AUTOTELIC.

■ O. Wilde, *The Soul of Man under Socialism* (1891); C. Bell, *Art* (1914); J. P. Sartre, *What Is Literature?*, trans. B. Frechtman (1949); F. W. Schiller, *On the Aesthetic Education of Man*, trans. R. Snell (1954); I. Kant, *Critique of Practical Reason*, trans. L. W. Beck (1956); S. Mallarmé, *Crisis of Poetry*, trans. B. Cook (1956); G.E.M. Anscombe, *Intention* (1957); R. Jakobson, "Closing Statement: Linguistics and Poetics," Sebeok (1960); C. Baudelaire, "The Painter of Modern Life," trans. P. E. Charvet (1964); A. Schopenhauer, *The World as Will and Idea*, trans. R. S. Haldane and J. Kemp (1964); B. Croce, *Aesthetic as Science of Expression and General Linguistic,* trans. D. Ainslie (1978);

J. Derrida, "The Law of Genre," trans. A. Ronell, *Glyph* 7 (1980); M. M. Bakhtin, *The Dialogic Imagination*, ed. M. Holquist, trans. C. Emerson and M. Holquist (1981)—essays from the 1930s; G. Hermerèn, "The Autonomy of Art," *Essays on Aesthetics*, ed. J. Fisher (1983); T. Adorno, *Aesthetic Theory*, trans. C. Lenhardt (1984); P. Bürger, *Theory of the Avant-Garde*, trans. M. Shaw (1984)—important foreword by J. Schulte-Sasse; Ransom, "Poetry: A Note in Ontology"; L. Haworth, *Autonomy* (1986); J. Habermas, *Autonomy and Solidarity*, ed. P. Dews (1986); I. Kant, *Critique of Judgment*, trans. W. Pluhar (1987); B. Croce, *Essays on Literature and Literary Criticism*, ed. and trans. M. E. Moss (1990); *Aesthetic Autonomy: Problems and Perspectives*, ed. B. van Heusden and L. Korthals Altes (2004)—esp. A. Heumakers, "Aesthetic Autonomy and Literary Commitment: A Pattern in Nineteenth-Century Literature"; J. Bernstein, *Against Voluptuous Bodies* (2006); J. Rancière, *The Future of the Image*, trans. G. Elliot (2007); C. Altieri, "Why Modernist Claims for Autonomy Matter," *Journal of Modern Literature* 32 (2009).

C. ALTIERI

**AUTO SACRAMENTAL.** Along with the *comedia*, the *auto sacramental* was shaped during the second half of the 16th c. as one of the two major art forms of Sp. drama. (The word *auto*—i.e., *acto*—had originally been used to refer to any dramatic act or piece but came to refer primarily to a religious play.) The first influential collection of religious autos was that of Diego Sánchez de Badajoz, published posthumously in 1554; in them, he drew on med. antecedents and was able to present theological problems in a dramatic way, using prefiguration and *allegory. The most important playwrights to develop further the genre in the 16th c. were Juan de Timoneda, Félix Lope de Vega, and José de Valdevieso. But the auto sacramental received its definitive form in the 17th c. at the hands of Pedro Calderón de la Barca.

The Calderonian auto sacramental was a paraliturgical, allegorical, one-act play written to celebrate the Eucharist; usually financed by a municipality, it was performed on carts and a special stage constructed in a public square during the feast of Corpus Christi. (In Madrid, from 1649 on, Calderón was the only poet officially commissioned to write autos.) Allegory was used to give concrete literary form to the abstract theological mysteries of Christianity, consisting essentially of the Fall and redemption of humanity; original sin leads to the incarnation of Christ and his crucifixion, commemorated in the Mass, which sums up the entire sequence. The theme, then, was always the same, but many plots were used to retell it allegorically. These plots were taken from a wide range of sources—pagan mythology, the Bible, saints' lives, hist., secular plays. *Emblem lit. and *conceptista* metaphors (see CONCEPTISMO) influenced the structure of these ingenious dramatic texts and their theatrical performances, replete with music and elaborate sets. One of the most typical autos is *El gran teatro del mundo*, based on the *conceit of the *theatrum mundi*, in which God is the Director of the play of human life, distributing costumes and dividing the performance into three acts (under natural law, until the Flood; under the Heb. OT; and under the NT of Grace, ending with Judgment Day); Grace is the prompter. After the show, the Director invites most of the cast to a Eucharistic banquet, excluding only the Rich Man, who is sent to Hell.

One of the few playwrights to compare with Calderón in theological ingenuity and literary brilliance was the Mexican nun Sor Juana Inés de la Cruz, who used both cl. and Aztec mythology for her plots (see MEXICO, POETRY OF). The Calderonian auto sacramental continued to be popular in the Sp. world until, after radical crit. by Fr. neoclassical theorists, it was finally prohibited by the Bourbon government in 1765.

■ M. Bataillon, "Essai d'explication de l'auto sacramental," *Bulletin hispanique* 42 (1940); A. A. Parker, *The Allegorical Drama of Calderón* (1943); E. Frutos Cortés, *La filosofía de Calderón en sus autos sacramentales* (1952); B. W. Wardropper, *Introducción al teatro religioso del Siglo de Oro* (1953); E. M. Wilson and D. Moir, *The Golden Age: Drama 1492–1700* (1971); R. Arias, *The Spanish Sacramental Plays* (1980); B. E. Kurtz, *The Play of Allegory in the Autos Sacramentales of Pedro Calderón de la Barca* (1991); M. Greer, " 'La vida es sueño—¿o risa'? Calderón Parodies the *auto*," *Bulletin of Hispanic Studies* 72 (1995); C. Davis, "Calderón in the Country: Corpus Christi Performances in Towns around Madrid, 1636–60," *BHS* 77 (2000); J. Slater, "Eucharistic Conjunction: Emblems, Illustrations, and Calderón's Autos," *Ekphrasis in the Age of Cervantes*, ed. F. de Armas (2005); B. J. Nelson, "From Hieroglyphic to Representational Sign: An Other Point of View in the Auto Sacramental," *Hispanic Baroques*, ed. N. Spadaccini and L. Martín-Estudillo (2005).

E. L. RIVERS

**AUTOTELIC** (Gr., *auto* [self] and *telos* [end, goal]). Something that is perfect, self-creating, having no meaning or purpose outside of itself. In the realm of aesthetics and crit., it conveys an idea, a structure, or a work of art that derives meaning and justifies its existence through its own resources rather than through external factors such as morality, religion, politics, or the economy (see AUTONOMY). Although the concept derives from cl. philosophy, it became important in modernity, particularly with the work of Immanuel Kant who argued that when we contemplate beauty, we seek nothing other than the pleasure of its formal features. Various Eur. and Am. thinkers, among them Friedrich Schiller, Germaine de Staël, S. T. Coleridge, E. A. Poe, and Oscar Wilde, appropriated this idea and characterized art as autonomous, unique, and self-enclosed (see AESTHETICISM). The term *autotelic* became central to the late 19th-c. movement of art-for-art's sake and to the formalist schools of literary crit. in the 20th c. In the 1980s and 1990s, however, the idea of autotelic art has been put into question by critical schools such as feminism, deconstruction, *new historicism, gay studies, and *postcolonialism, all of which have sought to situate the work of art in its social, cultural, political, and economic contexts.

■ I. Kant, *Critique of Judgment* (1790); F. Schiller, *On the Aesthetic Education of Man* (1795); W. Pater, "Conclusion," *The Renaissance* (1873); T. S. Eliot, "Tradition and the Individual Talent" (1917); Brooks; J. Derrida, "Structure, Sign and Play," *The Structuralist Controversy*, ed. R. Macksey and E. Donato (1972); E. K. Sedgwick, *Epistemology of the Closet* (1990).

C. P. SHEPHERDSON; G. JUSDANIS

**AUXESIS.** The rhetorical strategy by which members are arranged in ascending order or increasing importance, as in Philip Sidney, "I may, I must, I can, I will, I do" (*Astrophil and Stella* 47), and William Shakespeare, "Since brass, nor stone, nor earth, nor boundless sea, / But sad mortality o'ersways their power . . ." (sonnet 65). Auxesis is the opposite of *meiosis. *Climax concatenates the members, as the last element of each member becomes the first of the next; sorites is the logical sequence of members culminating in a conclusion.
■ Vickers.

T.V.F. BROGAN; D. VERALDI

## AVANT-GARDE POETICS

I. Introduction
II. Avant-garde versus Modernism
III. Italian and Russian Futurism
IV. Dada
V. Theory

**I. Introduction.** *Avant-garde* was originally a military term; it designated the front flank of the army—the "advance guard" that leads the way for the rest of the soldiers. In the arts, the first use of the term *avant-garde* is usually attributed to the Fr. historian Étienne Pasquier, who wrote in 1596, "A glorious war was then being waged against ignorance, a war whose avant-garde was constituted by [Maurice] Scève, [Théodore] Bèze, and [Jacques] Peletier; or, to put it another way, these men were the *avantcoureurs* [forerunners] of the other poets." From the first, then, *avant-garde* referred to the members of a cohort who were ahead of their time, who led the way for the less daring soldiers of the ranks. It was only after the Fr. Revolution that avant-garde began to be formulated as a concept, originally with reference to politics. The first periodical to bear the word in its title was the 1794 antiroyalist jour. *L'Avant-garde de l'armée des Pyrenées orientales*, whose watchword was "liberty or death." The subsequent use of *avant-garde* in the literary-artistic context was thus directly derived from the lang. of revolutionary politics. And indeed, in its early utopian phase, the avant-garde was felt to be the arm of political revolution. Although Karl Marx himself did not use the term, the Communist Party was considered the revolutionary avant-garde of the proletariat.

As a movement agitating for political change, the avant-garde was frowned upon by the great Fr. poet of the middle 19th c. Charles Baudelaire, who had contempt for the cult of the new as well as for the avant-garde's subordination of aesthetics to action. By the 1870s, however, the avant-garde had come to designate the small group of advanced writers and artists who transferred the spirit of radical social critique to the domain of artistic forms. Arthur Rimbaud, a great sympathizer of the Paris Commune of 1871, wrote in his famous "Lettre du Voyant" (to Paul Demeny, May 15, 1871) that poetry must be "in advance," providing new ideas and forms. For Rimbaud and other avant-gardists of his time, the artistic and the political went hand in hand: both were simply part of life, which should be lived in an avant-garde manner. Avant-garde thus came to refer to *praxis*, the life lived contra everything bourgeois and conventional.

But the political/aesthetic equation could hardly be sustained. If the Communist Party was to be the inclusive party of the working class, it could not support the restless experimentalism and the drive to "make it new" that characterized the work of avant-garde writers and artists. The central contradiction between the avant-garde's drive to transform the social order and its aesthetic elitism has haunted the avant-garde well into the 21st c. On the one hand, we have those who dismiss all talk of avant-gardes as elitist, aestheticist, and snobbish; on the other, the avant-garde is justified and defended as the manifestation of whatever countercultural drive still exists to oppose the status quo, whether political or artistic. When, e.g., Merce Cunningham died in 2009, having revolutionized the art of mod. dance for decades, he was referred to, in most obituaries, as the "great avant-garde choreographer of the century," the first to have made a clear separation between the dance movements themselves and the music that accompanies them—in Cunningham's case, the music, most frequently, of his fellow avant-gardist John Cage. It is unlikely that the term *avant-garde* will disappear any time soon; on the contrary, it remains the key descriptor of the new, the unfamiliar, the daring, and the provocative. Indeed, in public parlance, accordingly, *avant-garde* means little more than "chic" or "in."

But *avant-garde* also has a much more specific set of meanings. For literary and art historians as well as critics, the term refers to the so-called *historical avant-gardes*, a series of radical movements that took place in the first decades of the 20th c., emanating from continental Europe on the eve of World War I. Indeed, the three preeminent avant-gardes—*futurism, in both its It. and Rus. manifestations (in Russia, various terms like cubo-futurism and suprematism were used for what was most commonly referred to simply as "the Rus. avant-garde"), *Dada, and *surrealism—could not have existed without the war. The futurisms favored "war" as a cleansing of a moribund, hierarchical, stratified society; Dada, by contrast, born during the war in neutral Switzerland, reacted strongly against the killing fields by adopting an absurdist or nihilist stance; and surrealism was deeply opposed to war in all its manifestations. The avant-gardes also positioned themselves vis-à-vis technology. Although only the It. futurists exalted the "new" world of factories and motor cars, all the avant-gardes made use of new technologies in their performance art, their innovative *typography, their modes of instant communication, and esp. their obsession with speed—whether of transport, production, or reception.

The avant-garde was an international if not quite global movement though, paradoxically, it originated in two then marginalized countries: Italy (which became a national state only in 1870) and a still-czarist Russia, whose "new" artists and poets flocked to Moscow and Petersburg from the distant provinces of a backward empire. Paris was the capital of the avant-garde, but few avant-gardists were actually natives: consider Guillaume Apollinaire (Polish-It.), Blaise Cendrars (Swiss), and Tristan Tzara (Romanian). In Germany, again a recently unified nation, an aggressive avant-garde was beginning to flourish, the desire to transform the "moribund" arts finding its outlet in such radical works as Kurt Schwitters's verbal/visual/musical *collages and later the *Merzbau* assemblages (the word *Merz* coined from *merde* [shit], plus *Kommerz*). In Britain, the avant-garde never really took hold: brief eruptions like Wyndham Lewis's *vorticism on the eve of World War I were soon squelched, Eng. poetry, not to mention art, being characterized by its continuity rather than by any appreciable rupture. No doubt, Eng. suspicion of the avant-garde was the natural outcome of its stable political system, its trust in trad. and established conventions as part of its imperialist ethos. But even in postcolonial Britain today, the avant-garde is under suspicion. In the U.S., the same situation obtained at least until World War II, although Marcel Duchamp's presence in the U.S. from 1915 on created a brief spurt of what has been called New York Dada. After the war, esp. thanks to the impact of the Eur. refugees in New York, Los Angeles, and elsewhere, there have been significant "avant-garde" movements like *Black Mountain and *Language poetry.

## II. Avant-garde versus Modernism.
The relation of the avant-garde to *modernism remains a vexed problem. For early theorists of the avant-garde, the two were opposites: a bourgeois status-quo "high" modernism (associated with particular poets like R. M. Rilke, Paul Valéry, and T. S. Eliot) was regularly distinguished from the countercultural avant-garde movements that challenged its status. But increasingly, as the century wore on, the two were seen to be on the same spectrum. For one thing, some of the most prominent writers of the period—Gertrude Stein, James Joyce, Franz Kafka, later Samuel Beckett—emerged as at least as radical and revolutionary in their art as were the futurist F. T. Marinetti or the Dadaist Tzara. Indeed, as Tom Stoppard demonstrates nicely in his play *Travesties* (1974), Lenin, Joyce, and Tzara, all living in Zurich in 1916, had wholly conflicting aesthetic agendas. To label Stein "modernist" and Hugo Ball "avant-gardist" thus makes little sense. We can now see that modernism, far from being monolithic, was itself astonishingly varied. Vladimir Mayakovsky, a central figure in the Rus. avant-garde, was certainly a "modernist" in his

adherence to lyric forms, his indirection and irony, his predilection for organic unity. At the same time, the modernist/avant-garde spectrum has its extremes: no one would call Robert Frost an avant-gardist or label Mina Loy a mainstream modernist. Indeed, the debate about these *isms*, as well as about the relation of modernism and avant-garde to *postmodernism remains a heated one.

## III. Italian and Russian Futurism.
But at least in its origins, the avant-garde was regarded as a definitive rupture. The first notable avant-garde movement was *futurism, inaugurated on February 20, 1909, by the appearance, on the front page of the Paris newspaper *Le Figaro,* of "The Foundation and Manifesto of Futurism" by the It. poet-polemicist F. T. Marinetti. The "First Futurist Manifesto," as this document came to be called, is remarkable for its insistence that the "new" art (hence, the new life) be entirely different from all that preceded it, for its vituperative, aggressive rhetoric, incl. such notorious clauses as "a roaring car that seems to ride on grapeshot is more beautiful than the *Victory of Samothrace*," for its troubling declaration that "War is the hygiene of the people," and for its emphasis on the value of movement rather than individual ethos. Marinetti's *manifesto begins with the word "We" and establishes the first-person plural as the pronoun of choice; from then on, the signatories of futurist manifestos were almost always listed in the plural.

The avant-garde impact of It. futurism came predominantly in the nontraditional genres; its poetry and painting were never as innovative as its manifestos, performance pieces, verbal-visual works on paper (*parole in libertà*), architectural drawings, and musical scores—and its willingness, as a minor lit., to take on the uncontested leadership role of France. Marinetti campaigned for the "destruction of syntax" and for the use of "free words" rather than *"free verse," thus transforming the look (a block of print, usually broken into stanzas) and sound of poetry, eschewing all metrical forms or even an anaphoric free verse à la Walt Whitman (see ANAPHORA). *Parole in libertà* had a profound influence on such Anglo-Am. poets as Ezra Pound and D. H. Lawrence, even as visual poetics looked ahead to such later avant-garde movements as *concrete poetry, esp. that of the Brazilians Augusto and Haroldo de Campos, and the radical poetics of the Vienna Group of the early 1960s.

Although the word *futurism* usually designates the It. movement, its Rus. counterpart can now be seen as even more important and influential. From its first manifesto "A Slap in the Face of Public Taste" (1912), signed by David Burliuk, Aleksei Kruchenykh, Vladimir Mayakovsky, and Velimir Khlebnikov, the Rus. avant-garde produced not only superb manifestos, artist's books, and performance works but also—unlike the Italians—a new *lyric poetry and theater. Unlike It. futurism, the Rus. avant-garde included notable women artists—Natalia Goncharova, Liubov Popova, and Olga Rozanova—and poets like Elena Guro and, more peripherally, Anna Akhmatova. And although the Rus. futurists rejected, as did their It. counterpart, the immediate past of *symbolism and *impressionism, they drew heavily on their indigenous artistic trads. such as the icon and woodblocks called *lubki*. Khlebnikov, who invented, with Kruchenykh, *zaum'* (beyond sense) poetry, stands behind all later *sound poetry, from Schwitters's *Ursonate* to the experiments of Steve McCaffery and Christian Bök. The Rus. Formalist theorist and critic Roman Jakobson considered Khlebnikov to be the greatest 20th-c. poet: the latter's inventions of an etymological poetry, with its puns, coinages, elaborate sound structures, and verbal play, "made new" a world in crisis from the 1905 Rus. Revolution to the Civil War famine of 1921–22, in which Khlebnikov himself met his death. Jakobson also wrote movingly of Mayakovsky's poetry and its avant-garde treatment of *byt*, that untranslatable noun designating the monotony and boredom of everyday routine.

The Rus. avant-garde belonged to the Left even as It. futurism was to shade into Fascism in the 1920s. The Rus. avant-garde poets were strong advocates of the October Revolution and participated in the agit-prop demonstrations of 1916–17. At the same time, their endorsement of war and violence was not unlike Marinetti's: from 1913 on, they wanted war with Germany and praised battle maneuvers and cannon fire in their poetry and prose. Like the It. architectural visionary Antonio Sant'Elia, who was killed on the It. front at age 28, Khlebnikov advocated a new utopian architecture, where pulleys on top of skyscrapers would take passengers from rooftop to rooftop on monorails providing access and travel for all.

**IV. Dada.** In poetry, if not wholly in art where *constructivism was a major movement, the Rus. avant-garde was finished by the early 1920s. But in its symbiosis of politics and poetry, its utopian visionary drive, and its inclusiveness of women and poets of all classes, it was perhaps the greatest of the avant-gardes, even though that pride of place is usually accorded to Dada. This movement was born in 1916 in the Cabaret Voltaire in Zurich in rebellion against the horrors of World War I; its founders were two Romanian poets, Tzara and Marcel Janco, an Alsatian poet-sculptor (Hans [Jean] Arp), and two Ger. sound poet-performers, Hugo Ball and Richard Huelsenbeck. The word *Dada* was baby talk for "yes yes" in Romanian; it means "hobby horse" in Fr. but was mainly coined to sound as nonsensical as possible. Unlike the utopian futurism, Dada was a nihilistic movement that sought to undermine all the conventions, clichés, and ideals of bourgeois lit. and art. Tzara's brilliant manifestos, more individualistic than the futurist proclamations, used complex wordplay, pun, and dislocated syntax, as well as scatological humor and chance operations (like drawing names out of a hat), to create an aura of anarchy and surprise that stands behind a whole trad. of later 20th-c. poetry, musical composition, and art making. But the original Dadas had less than a lifelong commitment to their art: indeed, Hugo Ball soon left the group and entered a monastery, while Huelsenbeck became a psychiatrist.

In the 1920s, Dada split off into Ger. and Fr. wings, the Ger. being more political and biting in its largely visual satire, Fr. Dada soon shading into—and being replaced—by surrealism, one of the longest lasting and most complex of the historical avant-garde movements. In its emphasis on the subconscious and dream states, on the demand for a new "reality," and its strong individualism, surrealism is considered by many, incl. this author, to be, despite its extravagant claims and worldwide influence, less rupture than a return to the concern with identity of the romantics and hence a far cry from the early futurist desire to found a mass movement—a nationalistic movement as was the case in Italy and Russia.

**V. Theory.** To make the proper discriminations among these movements, a theory of the avant-garde is required and such theorizing has now become a growth industry. When Peter Bürger published his influential *Theory of the Avant-garde* in 1980, there had been only one prior attempt at such full-scale theorizing: Renato Poggioli's 1962 book (Eng. trans. 1968) by the same title as Bürger's. Poggioli's aim is to identify the basic principles that characterize the early avant-gardes in Europe: his examples are drawn primarily from It. futurism. He assumes from the outset that the original avant-garde impulse to fuse aesthetics and politics failed after 1880 or so; therefore, he focuses on aesthetic and structural devels. *The Theory of the Avant-garde* begins by distinguishing between the "school" and the "movement": schools presuppose a master, a trad., and a principle of authority, whereas movements are "constituted to obtain a positive result." To this end, avant-garde movements are both activist and agonistic: they are, by definition, *against* the status quo, the prior movement, or the previous generation—hence, the tendency of the avant-garde toward advertisement and propaganda, toward proclamations announcing "the revolution of the word," and the emphasis on youth and the utopian faith in the future.

For Bürger, Poggioli's was much too empiricist a view. His *Theory of the Avant-garde* is a late product of the *Frankfurt school, countering Theodor Adorno and Walter Benjamin's doctrine of aesthetic autonomy—the view that art occupies a special status, detached from the cultural and political system in which it is made. The agonistic aim of the avant-garde, according to Bürger, was not to negate earlier forms of art but to oppose the very institution of art itself "as an institution that is unassociated with the life praxis of men." "Can one make works which are not works of 'art'?" Duchamp had famously written in his notebooks. To which Bürger responds:

> When Duchamp signs mass-produced objects [a urinal, a bottle drier] . . . and sends them to art exhibits, he negates the category of individual production. The signature is inscribed on an arbitrarily chosen mass product because all claims to individual creativity are to be mocked. Duchamp's provocation not only unmasks the art

market . . . it radically questions the very principle of art in bourgeois society, according to which the individual is considered the creator of the work of art. Duchamp's Readymades are not works of art but manifestations. (51–52)

As such, the provocation cannot be repeated: "If an artist today signs a stove pipe and exhibits it, that artist certainly does not denounce the art market but adapts to it." The avant-garde was thus doomed to fail: the capitalist art market remained intact. The so-called neo-avant-gardes of the later 20th c., Bürger posits, could do no more than to imitate the Duchampian gesture, a gesture now empty and meaningless.

Bürger's theory of avant-garde intervention and its inevitable failure to transform the world was fashionable throughout the cold-war years, and it is still, somewhat surprisingly, the starting point for all theorizing on the avant-garde. But its argument is surely flawed. For one thing, it posits a hard and fast line between something called "modernism" and something called the "avant-garde." More important, it bases its entire theory on the work of an artist who insisted throughout his career that he did not belong to Dada or surrealism, that indeed he found "these movements" very "boring." Today Duchamp is seen to be the very "original genius" Bürger was rejecting; he is, by all accounts, sui generis.

Then, too, Bürger and his many successors tend to ignore the Rus. avant-garde, which, for political and historical reasons remained largely inaccessible before 1989. From Andreas Huyssen and T. J. Clark to Paul Mann and Fredric Jameson, the "avant-garde" has been under suspicion as, at best, a one-time manifestation (from Dada to early surrealism) that failed. Given this conclusion, the so called neo-avant-gardes—from Fluxus, Black Mountain, and the Vienna Group to concrete poetry and *lettrisme and culminating in *Flarf today, are negligible. New movements and groups can publish all the manifestos they like, but their shock value and ability to bring about change is gone.

While no manifesto today is going to "matter" as did Marinetti's of 1909, if we go back to the original definition of *avant-garde* as "ahead of its time," its staying power is evident. The poet Ron Silliman regularly distinguishes between the two poles of contemp. po-

etry he calls "post-avant" and "school of quietude." One need not accept these terms to feel that understanding the avant-garde matters. Indeed, given the controversial nature of the avant-garde, it has become, in the 21st c., the very focus of symposia, collections of essays, and monographs. Avant-gardism, it seems, appeals to our continuing belief that, in reconstituting the world of poetry and art, "It must change."

■ H. Richter, *Dada Art and Anti-Art*, trans. D. Britt (1997); R. Poggioli, *The Theory of the Avant-garde*, trans. G. Fitzgerald (1968); M. Duchamp, *The Essential Writings*, ed. M. Sanouillet (1973); *Russian Art of the Avant-garde: Theory and Critics 1902–1934*, ed. J. Bowlt (1976); M. Calinescu, *Five Faces of Modernity*, 2d ed. (1987); C. Russell, *The Avant-Garde Today* (1981); P. Bürger, *Theory of the Avant-garde*, trans. J. Schulte-Sasse (1984); J. Weissberger, "Le Mot et le Concept d'Avant-Garde," in *Les Avant-Gardes Littéraires au XXᵉ Siècle*, ed. J. Weisberger, 2 v. (1984), 18–20; A. Huyssen, *After the Great Divide* (1986); M. Perloff, *The Futurist Moment* (1986); V. Khlebnikov, *Collected Works*, ed. C. Douglas, trans. P. Schmidt, 3 v. (1987); *Russian Futurism through Its Manifestos, 1912–1928*, ed. A. Lawton (1988); M. Ecksteins, *Rites of Spring* (1989); F. Jameson, *Postmodernism* (1991); P. Mann, *The Theory-Death of the Avant-garde* (1991); M. Perloff, *Radical Artifice* (1992); R. Jakobson, *My Futurist Years,* trans. S. Rudy (1997); *European Avant-garde*, ed. D. Scheunemann (2000); R. Sheppard, *Modernism-Dada-Postmodernism* (2000); T. J. Clark, *Farewell to an Idea* (2001); M. Perloff, *21st-Century Modernism* (2002); M. Perloff, "The Avant-garde Phase of American Modernism," *Cambridge Companion to American Modernism*, ed. Walter Kalaidjian (2005); M. Perloff, "Avant-garde Tradition and the Individual Talent: The Case of Language Poetry," *Revue francaise d'études américaines* 103 (2005); D. Scheunemann, *Avant-garde/Neo-avant-garde* (2005); M. Puchner, *Poetry of the Revolution* (2006); S. Bru, J. Baetens, B. Hjartarson, et al., *Europa! Europa?: The Avant-garde, Modernism, and the Fate of a Continent* (2009); *Futurism*, ed. L. Rainey, C. Poggi, and L. Wittman (2009).

M. PERLOFF

**AZTEC POETRY.** *See* INDIGENOUS AMERICAS, POETRY OF THE.

# B

**BACCHIUS,** also bacchiac. In *classical prosody, the metrical sequence ◡ − − , most frequently encountered in Gr. lyric (*monody) and drama as a *clausula to a run of iambs. It may be an instance of *syncopation, i.e., the iambic *metron x − ◡ − with suppression of the third syllable. Bacchii (with *cretics) are among the most common meters in Plautine cantica (see CANTICUM AND DIVERBIUM), appearing mostly as four-foot units (*quaternarii*) or in systems. The Romans felt the bacchius to be esp. suitable for a serious or solemn style. The reverse of a bacchius, i.e., a foot composed of two long syllables and one short one, is known as a palimbacchius (Gr. *palin*, "back") or antibacchius.
■ W. M. Lindsay, *Early Latin Verse* (1922); G. E. Duckworth, *The Nature of Roman Comedy* (1952); Koster; Crusius; Dale; Halporn et al.

J. W. HALPORN

**BALADA.** Occitan dance song with *refrain, akin to the *dansa* but differing from it in having, besides repetition of the full refrain after each stanza, the first line of the refrain repeated after the first and (usually) second line of each stanza. It is a relatively infrequent form.
■ Chambers.

J. H. MARSHALL

**BALAGTASAN.** Named after the 18th-c. poet Francisco Baltazar (Balagtas), the *Balagtasan* is the Philippines's primary debate form, distinctive in its exclusive use of verse. It has served as popular entertainment since its origination in 1924 and lives on today in school contests and town festivals. While intentionally devised by a number of poets, its form is inspired by the *duplo*, an indigenous court drama in verse most often performed at funeral wakes. Traditionally, two poet-debaters compose rhyming and metered passages on opposing sides of a topic, and perform the debate extemporaneously with a moderator. A panel of judges declares the winner. Topics vary widely, from questions of value such as gold versus steel, to domestic issues such as the superiority of a jealous versus a docile husband, to pressing political concerns such as violent versus peaceful revolution during the Am. occupation. On the whole, there is greater emphasis on enduring rather than topical questions. It is more common currently for multiple teams to present scripted debates and for judges to decide a winning team rather than a winner between two competing debaters. Topics continue to reflect Philippine concerns, such as debates between pure and creolized lang. or between traditional and foreign values.

*See* PHILIPPINES, POETRY OF THE; POETIC CONTESTS.
■ **English**: C. G. Quan, "Language Play and Rhetorical Structure in the Tagalog Duplo and Balagtasan," diss., Univ. of Texas, Austin (1990); L. Mercado, *The Filipino Mind* (1994); V. S. Almario, "Art and Politics in the Balagtasan" (2003), http://escholarship.org/uc/item/23b7f9h6.
■ **Filipino**: V. S. Almario, *Balagtasismo versus Modernismo* (1984); P. Libiran, *Balagtasan: Noon at Ngayon* (1985); G. S. Zafra, *Balagtasan: Kasaysayan at Antolohiya* (1999).

M. RAMIREZ TALUSAN

## BALLAD

I. Regional and Linguistic Variation
II. Oral and Written Ballads
III. Scholarship and Influence in Literary History

In scholarly discourse since the 18th c., across the disciplines of lang. and lit., musicology, and folklore, a ballad is a narrative song set to a rounded—i.e., stanzaic—tune or a literary poem modeled on such songs. This stanzaic structure distinguishes the ballad from the sung traditional *epic (a longer narrative set to a chantlike, nonstanzaic tune). Ballads present a series of actions involving protagonists and are thus distinguished from *lyric and other nonnarrative songs or verse. Typically, ballads focus on a single episode where the plot involves a small cast of characters and is directed toward a catastrophe. In all Eur. langs. since the Middle Ages, popular narrative song and *oral poetry have displayed recognizable links and parallels across regions. Moreover, many of the lang. trads. possess cognate forms of particular ballads. With origins in popular idioms, the ballad form represents a collective cultural sensibility, and anonymous popular ballads persist to the present day as folk songs found in diverse variants.

In common parlance, the term *ballad* has been variously employed from the 16th-c. beginnings of its usage in Eng., when the word appeared in connection with danced songs, and considerable ambiguity can still cloud the term. In the 17th and 18th cs., a ballad meant any popular song, and Samuel Johnson's *Dictionary* (1755) applies the term vaguely to any "trifling verse." In the context of jazz or popular music today, the term designates any song in a slow tempo with a sentimental text.

Ballads exist in both polite and popular culture as oral-performance works as well as literary ones, across a range of social registers. Literary ballads are items of individually authored verse that imitate the structure and style of popular ballads. The latter are typically created, performed, learned, and disseminated as songs. These anonymous ballads are best understood as a species of oral poetry that has for centuries intersected with, influenced, and been influenced by writing, while still maintaining widespread oral circulation in the traditional channels documented by folklorists.

The interaction of oral forms with written culture has been pervasive, despite scholarly theories that defined the two expressive realms as entirely in contradistinction to each other. The ballad has commanded literary and scholarly interest across Europe and its colonies, especially beginning in the 18th c. when the form drew attention first as a mode for satire and later as part of a fascination with subaltern expression and sensibility during *romanticism. In Eng., the ballad took on renewed importance in 20th-c. modernist poetry (see MODERNISM) and the poetics of *New Criticism.

**I. Regional and Linguistic Variation.** Ballads are found throughout Europe and in Africa, the Americas, and Australia. Analogous popular narrative songs are found as well in Asia and Oceania. Despite nearly global pervasiveness, regional ballad forms and trads. show as many differences as commonalities. Even among Eur. trads., metrical distinctions are obvious. For example, Eng. and other northern Eur. ballads are stanzaic and set to strophic tunes, the words rendered in *accentual-syllabic verse as quatrains of alternating tetrameter and trimeter lines or, less commonly, as four tetrameter lines (if in *accentual verse, as alternating four- and three-stress lines or as four-stress lines, respectively). Many southern and eastern Eur. ballads are, by contrast, stichic with varying verse structures. Sp. ballads, termed *romances, are for the most part conceived of as octosyllabic with assonant rhyme in the even-numbered lines. However, to underscore their presumed devel. from the earlier epic, these are sometimes typographically rendered in 12 to 16 syllables in *hemistichs linked by rhyme or assonance, as are ballads of Portugal, France, Catalonia, and northern Italy. An octosyllabic line is considered typical of Bulgarian and much Ger. balladry. Romanian ballads, normally in trochaic trimeter or tetrameter, have considerable variation in length as do the Rus. ballads, termed *bylina.

In all trads., the shaping function of the music is crucial to understanding the rhythmic textual patterns. Seeming prosodic irregularities seen in print almost inevitably disappear in oral performance. Indeed, ballad prosody should be understood as a recognizable yet elastic mode governed by the predilections for shaping songs within the collective song-making trad. of a region. Scholars of ballad style typically study the structures, formulas, and conventional patterns of regional and lang. forms as distinct entities, e.g., Eng. and Scottish ballads, Sp. romances, and Rus. bylina.

**II. Oral and Written Ballads.** Popular ballads in Eur. trads. fall into two categories determined by origins, hist., and narrative techniques: (1) the older "traditional" or cl. ballad, usually on a tragic theme, that represents a med. oral poetry reflective of a premod. world; (2) the journalistic or *broadside ballad developed with the advent of popular, commercial printing in urban centers in the late 16th c., often chronicling a newsworthy event such as a sensational crime, natural disaster, military conflict, or love scandal. All Eur. lang. groups with print markets display this division between older, oral ballads and more journalistic ballads shaped by writing and print. However, individual ballads of both types have circulated orally as anonymous songs among singers, and many continue to be learned, sung, and reshaped over time through processes of oral trad. While both types of narratives conform to the ballad genre and relate similar kinds of events, each displays distinct stylistic conventions.

**A. *Oral-Ballad Traditions and Style.*** The older "traditional" or cl. ballads from premod. oral trads. have generated greater literary appreciation and imitation than the later broadside ballads, on the one hand because of their mysterious and almost indefinable artistry and on the other because of their med. archaism. These songs concentrate on two or three characters and develop dramatically and economically through dialogue and action. The plot usually begins in medias res with little attention to settings or circumstantial detail. Cl. ballads present stark and formulaic characters, actions, objects, and scenes. Events are shown with brevity, and *dialogue prevails as protagonists speak to each other, usually without ascription. Individual ballads unfold as a series of gapped paratactic images that Hodgart has likened to the cinematic technique of montage, whereby the narrative develops almost as a series of tableaux. Gummere described this plotting of the traditional ballad style as an abrupt "leaping and lingering" from scene to scene, and Vargyas as a poetry of conventionalized gestures.

In the cl. ballads, repetitive verbal patterns and tight, balancing scenes create a tone of striking objectivity. Repetition and formulaic expression, both marks of oral artistry, are key to traditional ballad style. Commonplace descriptors serve as formulas for what characterization occurs and for construction of the narrative. In Eng. ballads, protagonists typically mount "milk-white steeds" and write "braid letters signed with their hands"; maidens are "taken by their lily-white hands"; characters enter a scene asking "what news, what news"; and so on. Redundancy shapes individual ballads and marks as well the shared nature of the patterned idiom from song to song across a lang. trad. *Incremental repetition is a common strategy in ballad narrative technique, whereby a song unfolds in sequences of repeating lines or stanzas that, with each occurrence, introduce a change of word or phrase that furthers the plot. Thus, "Lord Randall," known across various Eur. langs., unfolds as a question-and-answer dialogue between a mother and son in which details added to each stanza disclose the dying son's report of being poisoned by his lover. The repetition and formulaic structure of the disclosure create the understatement, dramatic irony, and suspense characteristic of oral style.

In all lang. trads., the oral origin and style of cl. ballads is thought to predate the writing-based mode of the broadside ballad, though few individual examples of the oral style are reported before the late 16th and 17th cs. Cl. ballads represent a late-med. world and sensibility. They place their characters in a rural world of feudal objects and settings, med. social roles and practices, and premod. beliefs and mores (castles, knights and ladies, hawks and hounds, herbal potions, supernatural visitants, etc.). Thus, in a typical variant, the eponymous protagonist of the Scottish ballad "Tam Lin" escapes thralldom to the underworld by shape-shifting in the arms of his beloved, who embraces him through a magical rescue as he transforms from one archaic state of being to another: "an esk and adder," "a lion bold," "a burning gleed," and finally, "a naked knight." This counterspell frees him from fairy captivity.

The study of such ballads as representative of oral poetry and of a retrospectively imagined med. past began in the 18th c. with commentary by scholars such as Thomas Percy (1729–1811), the Eng. ed. of *Reliques of Ancient English Poetry* (1765), and the Ger. writer and philosopher J. G. Herder (1744–1803), both influential in Eur. romanticism. For them, ballads posed a collective mythopoetic inheritance for forging a prized national unity. By the 19th c., scholars of the "traditional" ballad—typified by collectors such as the Scottish Walter Scott (1771–1832) and William Motherwell (1795–1835) or the Danish Svend Grundtvig (1824–83)—garnered versions found in mss. and oral variants that they considered purer and more "ancient" for being free from print and commercial associations. The defining collection and cataloging of some 300 narrative songs of this type in Eng. by the Am. medievalist F. J. Child (1825–96) codified the anglophone trad. of these narratives to the extent that scholars refer to them as "Child ballads."

B. *Broadside-Ballad Traditions and Style.* Originating with print production for a popular readership, the broadside or journalistic ballad is a song reproduced on a single sheet of paper (a broadside) and sold on urban streets, in bookshops, and at such gathering places as docks and fairs. From the late 16th c., such marketing of ballads remained a fixture of popular culture in Europe and its colonies for several hundred years. Typically, a woodcut print included the text of one or more ballads, several images and decorative borders, and sometimes the title of a recommended tune. Musical notation almost never appeared. By the 18th c., broadside-ballad presses operated in provincial centers in Europe and its colonies. Frequent literary attacks on the vulgarity of the form and the large numbers of ballad prints from the 16th through the 19th cs. that remain in archives to this day attest to the popularity of broadside ballads.

As a product of urban journalism, the narrative style of the broadside ballad discloses a contrasting worldview to that of the orally based cl. ballad. The broadside ballad narrates in a straightforwardly linear and expository manner, with little repetition, and offers a journalistic rendering of each story with specifically named and particularized places, people, and events. A realistic and moralizing narrative voice portrays a world of more mod. institutions and commerce. As an example, the paratextual heading of the London broad-

side ballad of "The Children in the Wood" (1595) gives details of place and persons as well as the causal outlines of its moralizing plot: "The Norfolk Gentleman, his Will and Testament, and howe he committed the keeping of his children to his own brother whoe delte most wickedly with them, and how god plagued him for it." Not uncommonly, broadside ballads relate first-person stories, identifying precise urban locations, detailed actions, and historical identities. In *The Beggar's Daughter of Bednall Green*, from another Eng. print, the "blind beggar" narrator sings at his daughter's wedding and at the end reveals his true identity as the heir of the rebel earl of Leicester: "And here, noble lordes, is ended the songe / Of one, that once to your owne ranke did belong." These characteristics contrast to the impersonal, third-person narration of orally rooted traditional ballads. Across Eur. and Eur.-colonized regions, song makers and publishers rendered ballad accounts of historical events. Ballads in Eng. from North America exemplify the journalistic specificities of the style: "The Constitution and the Guerrière," an account of an 1812 U.S. sea victory over an Eng. frigate; "Lost Jimmie Whalen," the lamenting story of the death of a 19th-c. lumberman; and murder ballads such as "Charles Guiteau," which tells of the assassination of Pres. James Garfield in 1881, and "Poor Omie," which recounts the 1808 drowning of a North Carolina girl by her former lover.

Many ballads originating in broadsides continued to circulate in oral trads. Typically recomposed through the strategies of repetition and gapped narrative characteristic of oral recall and preservation, some ballads that originated as printed compositions have continued to be passed on for generations—as is the case with the Am. ballads mentioned. Shortened in the process, such orally reformed ballads focus on the central, most patterned, and most emotionally charged points of the story, taking on characteristics of performative orality (repetition, parallel structure, and formulaic expression) not found in the initial broadside version. Conversely, some ballads of the older oral type—"Barbara Allen" and "Lord Beichan" are examples from the Eng. trad.—were sold in printed broadside versions and were refashioned with more details and plot linearity in keeping with the journalistic mode.

Scholars of the printed street ballad amassed collections of ballad broadsides (single-sheet prints) produced by printers from the 16th c. on, a preservation effort that takes on renewed life today with collections made available online. In the 19th c., antiquarian enthusiasm for both traditional and broadside ballads spurred collections of orally disseminated folk songs from live singers, an effort that peaked in the mid-20th c. and amassed an enormous body of ballads and other songs from Europe and Eur.-influenced cultures.

Significant devels. in ballad style have emerged as a result of regional adaptations. Scholars identify in the U.S. the "blues ballad," a narrative song type influenced by Af. Am. oral performance and composition style. With a focus on murder, death, and tragedy typical of all ballads, the blues ballad renders historical events from a contemp. view as did the printed broad-side ballads (see BLUES). However, characteristics of the blues ballad also include the call-and-response techniques of Af. Am. arts, a predilection for antihe-roes and -heroines, a prominent influence of orality in the ballad's creation and dissemination, and a voice more poetic and celebratory than reportorial. In con-trast to the linear, broadside style, such ballads as "John Henry," "Casey Jones," "The Titanic," "Frankie and Al-bert" ("Frankie and Johnny"), and "Stagolee" tell their stories with an oblique, gapped, and sometimes radial rendering of the narrative and an improvisatory style characterized by repetition, parallelism, and a stock of commonplace images ("rubber-tire hearses," guns that are "38s" and "44s," girls "dressed in blue" followed by those "dressed in red"). Ballads in this mode typically celebrate their transgressing protagonists, who emerge from a world of crime. The narrative song trads. brought with the Sp. conquest display a similar devel. in the Americas, with narrative *corridos* emerging, like the blues ballads, from oral trads., even as journalistic *corridos* in reportorial style were sold on broadsides. In Mexico and the southwestern U.S., *corridos* from the 20th and early 21st cs. often feature antihero *bandidos* and stories of narcotics trafficking.

In Germany from the 17th to the 20th c., sellers of the broadside ballad—termed *Bänkelsang* or *Moritat*—used elaborate pictorial representations of the typically sensational and sentimental narratives. Conventionally, the *Bänkelsanger* sang from a platform and displayed scenes from the story on a large poster as passersby pur-chased the song sheets. Nineteenth-c. authors adapted the form to literary ballads and satire, especially after 1848. In the 20th c., such ballads featured in Ger. cabaret culture; the best-known adaptation is Bertolt Brecht and Kurt Weill's "Die Moritat von Mackie Messer" from *Driegroschenoper* (1928), a reworking of the Eng. *Beggar's Opera* (1728) by John Gay.

### III. Scholarship and Influence in Literary History.

Early 20th-c. scholarship divided between theories of the origin of popular ballads in individual or in com-munal creation, eventually reaching consensus that a particular ballad originates with an individual song maker; subsequently, continuing performance across communities recreates the ballad in numerous vari-ants. Scholars applied this model of dynamic creation and re-creation in their study of individual traditional artistry in both the making and the performance of bal-lads (Porter and Gower). Theoretical concern about the reliability of ethnographic records has spurred attention to documenting occasions, modes, and contexts for song performance; the social function and reception of songs; and the interpretive framings of oral hist. (Ives 1978). Studies of contexts reveal in ballads an index for diachronic analysis of sociopolitical hist. and paradigms of gender, class, socioeconomics, power dynamics, etc. (Dugaw 1989, Symonds). Individual ballads afford sites for synchronically examining particular historical mo-ments and events (Ives 1997, C. Brown, Long-Wilgus). The broadside ballad has received renewed scholarly

attention both with analytic studies of prints from dif-ferent eras and regions (Würzbach, Cheesman) and with the availability of online databases (English Broadside Ballad Archive, Roud). Analyses of textual form attend to the aesthetic effects of ballads and to their formulaic and performative mechanisms as examples of oral art-istry (McCarthy, Andersen, Renwick).

The importance of the ballad to Eng.-lang. lit. hist. has received renewed investigation with regard to the 18th-c. literary interest in and emulation of the form and its engendering of a new ethnographic sensibility that gave rise to *ethnopoetics and verse-making be-yond the traditional borders of belles lettres (Groom, Newman). Scholars have examined the ballad in con-nection with the art of particular writers such as John Gay and John Clare (Dugaw 2001, Deacon) as well as the tenets of literary movements such as romanticism (McLane), and in examinations of the historiographi-cal significance of individual ballad scholars (M. E. Brown).

Ballads of every type have influenced lit. in all the lang. trads. E.g., literary poets of early mod. Sp. such as Félix Lope de Vega and Sor Juana Inés de la Cruz wrote *romances* modeled on popular narratives in earlier *can-cionero* collections (see SONGBOOK). The prevalence of poets who wrote ballad-inflected poems in Eng. mirrors the importance of the form in lits. elsewhere. Political satire of the late 17th and early 18th cs. en-listed the ballad form in miscellanies such as *The Cov-ent Garden Drollery* and *Poems on Affairs of State*. Gay's *Beggar's Opera* introduced ballad opera as a burlesque in which pointed songs set to popular ballad tunes forwarded the mood and action of spoken drama. The decades-long popularity of this and imitative bal-lad operas reflected and enhanced interest in ballads. Such antiquarian collections as Percy's *Reliques of An-cient English Poetry* influenced lit. at all levels, shap-ing the poetics of Eng. and continental romanticism. Wordsworth ("Lucy Gray," "Seven Sisters") and S. T. Coleridge (*The Rime of the Ancient Mariner*, "The Three Graves") wrote verse imitative of ballads. The Preface to the 2d ed. of the *Lyrical Ballads* (1800) articulates a theoretical justification for echoing plebeian forms in order to make poetic expression "real lang." without the obfuscations of literary artifice. Ballad-like poems modeled on both oral-traditional and broadside ballads in Britain are among the works of Gay ("Sweet Wil-liam's Farewell"), Thomas Tickell ("Lucy and Colin"), Robert Burns ("The Five Carlins," "Kellyburn Braes"), William Blake ("Mary," "Long John Brown and Little Mary Bell"), John Keats ("La Belle Dame sans Merci"), Christina Rossetti ("Maude Clare," "Lord Thomas and Fair Margaret"), A. C. Swinburne ("The Bloody Son," "May Janet"), Thomas Hardy ("The Second Night," "No Bell-Ringing"), Oscar Wilde ("The Ballad of Reading Gaol"), and others.

The interplay, through collection and study, be-tween the street, workplace, or fireside realm of bal-lads and that of belles lettres is evident in British trads. and throughout Europe. Literary writers—John Clare, e.g., himself a fiddler—participated as well in collecting ballads. In Scotland, 18th-c. ballad collecting by Allan Ramsay and Burns was followed in the 19th c. by James Hogg, in addition to Scott and Motherwell. Ger. poetry through the 19th c. was shaped by Achim von Arnim and Clemens Brentano's *Des Knaben Wunderhorn* (1805–8), a collection prompted by Herder's philosophic championing of popular song.

In the 20th c., the ballad continued as a literary model. In Ireland, modernist writers such as James Joyce, J. M. Synge, and W. B. Yeats identified their work with an Ir. cultural sensibility both ancient and contemp. Yeats collaborated on song and tale collections in Ir. and Eng. with Lady Augusta Gregory and others and also penned ballad-influenced works ("Down by the Salley Gardens," "Moll Magee"). In the U.S., Cleanth Brooks and R. P. Warren formulated a modernist poetics of New Criticism that identified the ballad as a model for an aesthetics of accessibility and collective *voice, echoed in the work of Elizabeth Bishop and others. For Af. Am. modernism and subsequent movements, the blues ballad supplied a model for such poets as Langston Hughes ("Sylvester's Dying Bed," "Ballad of the Landlord") and Gwendolyn Brooks ("of De Witt Williams on his way to Lincoln Cemetery," "The Ballad of Late Annie"). To the present, literary writers from numerous national and ethnic trads. collect and engage ballads in a continuing testimony to the mutually influencing dynamic between literary artistry and the oral and collective realm of popular trads.

■ **Descriptive Catalogs and Research Aids**: G. M. Laws, *American Balladry from British Broadsides* (1957), and *Native American Balladry* (1964); T. P. Coffin, *The British Traditional Ballad in North America*, 2d ed. (1977); B. R. Jonsson et al., *The Types of the Scandinavian Medieval Ballad* (1978); D. Catalán et al., *Catálogo general del romancero*, 3 v. (1984); E. Richmond, *Ballad Scholarship* (1989); L. Syndergaard, *English Translations of the Scandinavian Medieval Ballads* (1995).

■ **Historical Contexts**: A. Paredes, *"With His Pistol in His Hand"* (1958); D. Dugaw, *Warrior Women and Popular Balladry* (1989); M. Herrera-Sobek, *The Mexican Corrido* (1990)—feminist crit.; N. Würzbach, *The Rise of the English Street Ballad 1550–1650*, trans. G. Walls (1990); E. Ives, *The Bonny Earl of Murray* (1997); D. Symonds, *Weep Not for Me* (1997)—ballads in early mod. Scotland; J. McDowell, *Poetry and Violence* (2000)—Mexico's Costa Chica; C. Brown, *Stagolee Shot Billy* (2003); E. Long-Wilgus, *Naomi Wise* (2003).

■ **History of Scholarship**: D. K. Wilgus, *Anglo-American Folksong Scholarship since 1898* (1959); *The Anglo-American Ballad*, ed. D. Dugaw (1995); N. Groom, *The Making of Percy's "Reliques"* (1999); M. E. Brown, *William Motherwell's Cultural Politics* (2001); *Singing the Nations: Herder's Legacy*, ed. D. Bula and S. Rieuwerts (2008).

■ **Literary Contexts**: M. R. Katz, *The Literary Ballad in Early 19th-Century Russian Literature* (1976); D. Dugaw, *"Deep Play"—John Gay and the Invention of Modernity* (2001); G. Deacon, *John Clare and the Folk Tradition* (2004); S. Newman, *Ballad Collection,*

*Lyric, and the Canon* (2007); M. McLane, *Balladeering, Minstrelsy, and the Making of British Romantic Poetry* (2008).

■ **Origins and Style**: F. B. Gummere, *The Popular Ballad* (1907); H. Rollins, "Black-Letter Broadside Ballad," *PMLA* 35 (1919); W. Entwistle, *European Ballad* (1939); G. Gerould, *The Ballad of Tradition* (1939); M.J.C. Hodgart, *The Ballads* (1962); D. Foster, *The Early Spanish Ballad* (1971); E. Ives, *Joe Scott* (1978); O. Holzapfel, *Det balladeske: fortællemåden i den ældre episke folkevise* (1980); C. Slater, *Stories on a String: The Brazilian Literatura de Cordel* (1982); F. Andersen, *Commonplace and Creativity* (1985); D. K. Wilgus and E. Long, "The Blues Ballad and the Genesis of Style," *Narrative Folksong*, ed. C. Edwards and K. Manley (1985); W. McCarthy, *The Ballad Matrix* (1990); C. Harvey, *Contemporary Irish Traditional Narrative* (1992); T. Cheesman, *The Shocking Ballad Picture Show* (1994); J. Porter and H. Gower, *Jeannie Robertson* (1995); R. deV. Renwick, *Recentering Anglo/American Folksong* (2001); D. Atkinson, *The English Traditional Ballad* (2002); V. Gammon, *Desire, Drink and Death in English Folk and Vernacular Song* (2008).

■ **Ballad and Tune Collections**: S. Grundtvig et al., *Danmarks gamle folkeviser*, 12 v. (1853–76); F. J. Child, *The English and Scottish Popular Ballads*, 10 v. (1882–98); G. Doncieux and J. Tiersot, *Le Romancéro populaire de la France* (1904); R. Menéndez Pidal, *Poesía popular y poesía tradicional* (1922); *Deutsche Volkslieder mit ihren Melodien: Balladen*, ed. J. Meier et al., 8 v. (1935–88); *Traditional Tunes of the Child Ballads*, ed. B. Bronson, 4 v. (1959–72); E. Janda and F. Nützhold, *Die Moritat vom Bänkelsang oder Lied von der Strasse* (1959); H. Fromm, ed., *Deutsche Balladen*, 4th ed. (1965); C. Simpson, *The British Broadside Ballad and Its Music* (1966); L. Vargyas, *Hungarian Ballads and the European Ballad Tradition*, trans. I. Gombos 2 v., (1983); J. Jiménez, *Cancionero completo* (2002); *Ballads on Affairs of State*, ed. A. McShane (2009)—17th c. England.

■ **Web Sites**: English Broadside Ballad Archive, University of California, Santa Barbara: http://emc.english.ucsb.edu/ballad_project/index.asp; Roud Folk Song Index: http://library.efdss.org/cgi-bin/home.cgi; Roud Broadside Index: http://library.efdss.org/cgi-bin/textpage.cgi?file-aboutRoudbroadside&access=off.

D. DUGAW

**BALLADE.** The most important of the OF *formes fixes* (fixed forms) and the dominant verse form of OF poetry in the 14th and 15th cs. (Formes fixes are usually three in number: the ballade, the *rondeau, and the *virelai.) The most common type of ballade comprises 28 lines of octosyllables, i.e., three eight-line stanzas rhyming *ababbcbC* and a four-line *envoi rhyming *bcbC*. As the capital letter indicates, the last line of the first stanza serves as the *refrain, repeated as the last line of each stanza and the envoi. In the complexity of its *rhyme scheme, restriction of its rhyme sounds, and use of the refrain, the ballade is perhaps the most exacting of the fixed forms. Some variants of the standard ballade employ ten- or (less often) twelve-line stanzas with, respectively, five- and six-line envois. The envoi, which frequently begins with the address "Prince," derived from the med. *poetic contest (*puy*) at which the presiding judge was so addressed, forms the climatic summation of the poem.

Although the ballade may have developed from an Occitan form, it was standardized in northern Fr. poetry in the 14th c. by Guillaume de Machaut, Eustache Deschamps, and Jean Froissart. It was carried to perfection in the 15th c. by Christine de Pisan, Charles d'Orléans, and, most of all, François Villon, who made the ballade the vehicle for the greatest of early Fr. poetry. Such works as his "Ballade des pendus" and his "Ballade des dames du temps jadis" achieved an unequaled intensity in their use of refrain and envoi. The ballade continued in favor up to the time of Clément Marot (early 16th c.), but the poets of the *Pléiade, followed by their neoclassical successors in the 17th c.—with the exception of Jean de La Fontaine—had little use for the form and regarded it as barbaric. Both Molière and Nicolas Boileau made contemptuous allusions to the ballade.

The ballade of the vintage Fr. period was imitated in England by Chaucer and John Gower, though now in *decasyllables. Chaucer uses it for several of his early complaints and takes the single *octave from it for the *monk's tale stanza. Beyond their practice, it never established itself firmly. In the later 19th c., the so-called Eng. Parnassians (Edmund Gosse, Austin Dobson, Andrew Lang; see PARNASSIANISM) and poets of the 1890s (W. E. Henley, Richard Le Gallienne, Arthur Symons) revived the form with enthusiasm, inspired by the example of Théodore de Banville (*Trente-six Ballades joyeuses à la manière de Villon*, 1873), who gave a new impetus to the ballade equally among fellow Parnassian and decadent poets in France (François Coppée, Paul Verlaine, Jean Richepin, Maurice Rollinat; see DECADENCE). But the mod. ballade, with the possible exception of a few pieces by A. C. Swinburne and Ezra Pound's Villonesque adaptations ("Villonaud for this Yule" and the freely constructed "A Villonaud: Ballad of the Gibbet"), has not aimed at the grandeur and scope of Villon: it has been essentially a vehicle for *light verse, e.g., G. K. Chesterton, Hillaire Belloc, and, more recently, Wendy Cope.

The double ballade is composed of six eight- or ten-line stanzas; the refrain is maintained, but the envoi is optional (e.g., Villon's "Pour ce, amez tant que vouldrez"; Banville's "Pour les bonnes gens" and "Des sottises de Paris"; Swinburne's "A Double Ballad of August" and "A Double Ballad of Good Counsel"). The "ballade à double refrain," which has Marot's "Frère Lubin" as its model, introduces a second refrain at the fourth line of each stanza and again at the second line of the envoi, producing, most characteristically, a rhyme scheme of *abaBbcbC* for the stanzas and *bBcC* for the envoi; Dobson, Lang, and Henley number among the later 19th-c. practitioners of this variant.

*See* FRANCE, POETRY OF.

■ G. White, *Ballades and Rondeaus* (1887); G. M. Hecq, *La Ballade et ses derivées* (1891); Kastner; H. L. Cohen, *The Ballade* (1915), and *Lyric Forms from France* (1922); P. Champion, *Histoire poétique du XVe siècle*, 2 v. (1923); G. Reaney, "Concerning the Origins of the Rondeau, Virelai, and Ballade," *Musica Disciplina* 6 (1952); A. B. Friedman, "The Late Medieval Ballade and the Origin of Broadside Balladry," *Medium Aevum* 27 (1958); J. Fox, *The Poetry of Villon* (1962); G. Reaney, "The Development of the Rondeau, Virelai, and Ballade," *Festschrift Karl Fellerer* (1962); *Christine de Pizan and Medieval French Lyric*, ed. E. J. Richards (1998)—esp. B. K. Altmann, "Last Words: Reflections on a '*Lay mortel*' and the Poetics of Lyric Sequences," C. McWebb, "Lyric Conventions and the Creation of Female Subjectivity in Christine de Pizan's *Cent ballades d'Amant et de dame*," and W. D. Paden, "Christine de Pizan and the Transformation of Late Medieval Lyrical Genres"; Morier; C. Page, "Tradition and Innovation in BN fr. 146: The Background to the Ballades," *Fauvel Studies: Allegory, Chronicle, Music and Image in Paris*, ed. M. Bent and A. Wathey (1998).

A. PREMINGER; T.V.F. BROGAN; C. SCOTT

**BALLAD METER, HYMN METER.** In Eng. poetry, *ballad meter*—or, as it is sometimes termed, *ballad stanza*—refers to the meter of the traditional ballad, a popular narrative song form since the late Middle Ages, and the written literary adaptation of this oral form. Ambiguities abound with regard to the application of the term, which gained importance in literary parlance only with the 18th-c. rise of interest in plebeian poetic forms. Commonly, ballad meter designates quatrains that alternate iambic tetrameter with iambic trimeter and rhyme at the second and fourth lines. For reasons discussed below, the form corresponds to "hymn meter" or "common meter," whose quatrains, however, can rhyme *abab*, as in the well-known instance of Isaac Watts's setting of Psalm 90: "O God, our help in ages past, / Our hope for years to come, / Our shelter from the stormy blast, / And our eternal home." The use of this iambic tetrameter-trimeter form in the two familiar arenas of popular secular ballads and widely sung hymnody is significant, as this structure and its effects over time draw from and represent collectively widespread and recognizable sung utterance. Moreover, in practice, the distinction between the two, ballad meter and hymn meter, is not made consistently, so that a poem in quatrains with either rhyme scheme, whose iambic lines alternate four stresses and three stresses, may be identified as a ballad. Nor is the requirement of the iambic stress pattern rigidly or universally followed in the application of the term. Thus, literary poets may title a work a "ballad" that varies from the quatrain form, the meter, or other aspects of the usual definition. Oscar Wilde's "Ballad of Reading Gaol," e.g., alternates between unrhymed tetrameters and rhymed trimeters but features stanzas of six rather than four lines.

Collective ongoing oral practice, for hundreds of years, constructs a context for understanding the vitality of the ballad meter form, from its origins in sung verse from popular trads. to the uses both hymnodists and literary poets made of it. Both the meter and the quatrain organization derive from the association of the verse with conventional melodic structures and rhythms: Eng. tunes typically follow patterns of four musical phrases. The popular and orally circulating ballads of the anglophone trad.—e.g., such ballads as are found in F. J. Child's *English and Scottish Popular Ballads*—customarily, though not inevitably, follow the accentual 4-3-4-3 pattern of ballad meter, but the words hew less rigorously to metrical form than do the ballads of consciously literary poets such as William Wordsworth, who adhere to metric strategies of poetic formulation. The shaping function of the music allows for greater flexibility in the verbal patterns of orally circulating folk ballads; sung performance inevitably enlivens and smoothes seeming prosodic irregularities in a text.

The origin, devel., and exact nature of ballad meter have prompted considerable scholarly discussion. One point of dispute concerns whether ballad meter is *accentual verse, i.e., isochronous and counting only stresses (see ISOCHRONISM), or *accentual-syllabic, regulating syllable count and not timed. The irregularities of the anonymous popular sung ballads and the importance of *caesura and *dipodism in their isochronic lines have suggested to metrists the application of the concept of accentual meter used for OE verse to ballad meter. However, ballads do not show evidence of such consciously wrought complexities of OE prosody as formulaic hemistichs, structural alliteration, and clear stichic structure. Nineteenth-c. metrists considered ballad meter to be derived from the med. Lat. *septenarius, a line of seven stresses and 14 syllables, and proposed that such long couplets, often with internal rhyme, were formulated into quatrains, perhaps because of exigencies of space on a given codex page. However, no plausible or demonstrable link between Church Lat. hymn verse and the oral vernacular ballads has been found. In the Ren., rhyming iambic heptameter couplets—*fourteeners—function with a syntactic and conceptual coherence that corresponds to the quatrain stanzas of alternating tetrameters and trimeters of ballad meter. The more regular meters and not infrequent heptameter form found in early *broadside ballads suggest a link to this fashion for heptameter couplets; however, no direct lineage between the 16th-c. literary mode and the popular verse quatrains of ballad meter is discernible, and the term *ballad meter* appears only in the romantic period, long after the literary vogue of fourteeners had passed. Rather, the ballad and ballad meter's influencing presence assist the occasional use of iambic-heptameter couplets in mod. poetry in connection with topics from the popular realm, as, e.g., in E. L. Thayer's "Casey at the Bat," whose composed heptameter couplets can be "heard" in recitation as ballad meter.

Another set of pertinent analytic terms attests to the significance of orality and singing traditions with regard to the develop. and study of ballad meter. With the 16th-c. emergence of Eng. Protestantism, such writers of *hymns in the vernacular as Thomas Sternhold and John Hopkins brought Martin Luther's Ger. practice into their hymnody and also made use of the conventional ballad meter and sometimes the actual tunes of Eng. popular ballads for settings of psalm and hymn texts. The widespread collective singing of religious song, thus, formed another context in which the metric predilections of ballad meter influenced the writing of poetry in such authors shaped by hymnody as George Herbert and Emily Dickinson. To this day, metrical designations remain a common feature in the indexes of Protestant hymnals with the following categories typically given (numbers denote the stresses per line): long meter (or measure; abbreviated LM): 4-4-4-4; common meter (or measure; CM): 4-3-4-3; short meter (SM): 3-3-4-3 (see POULTER'S MEASURE); and rarely, half meter (HM): 3-3-3-3. The most common pattern is CM, which conforms metrically to iambic ballad meter and reflects the overlap of the two collective trads. of popular sacred and secular song.

*See* METER, PSALM.

■ F. B. Gummere, *Old English Ballads* (1894); J. W. Hendren, *A Study of Ballad Rhythm* (1936); E. Routley, *The Music of Christian Hymnody* (1957); Saintsbury, *Prosody*; G. W. Boswell, "Reciprocal Controls Exerted by Ballad Texts and Tunes," *JAF* 80 (1967) and "Stanza Form and Music-Imposed Scansion," *Southern Folklore Quarterly* 31 (1967); B. H. Bronson, *The Ballad as Song* (1969); Brogan; J. Hollander, *Rhyme's Reason* (1981); R. Leaver, *"Goostly psalms and spirituall songes"* (1991)—Eng. and Dutch psalms, 16th c.; Attridge, *Poetic Rhythm*; *Meter in English*, ed. D. Baker (1996); J. R. Watson, *The English Hymn* (1997); T. Steele, *All the Fun's in How You Say a Thing* (1999); Carper and Attridge; L. Turco, *The Book of Forms*, 3d ed. (2000).

D. DUGAW

**BARD.** A term borrowed into Eng. from the native Celtic word for "poet," its hist. goes back to Celtic Gaul, where the Gr. ethnographers Strabo and Diodorus Siculus, following Poseidonius, refer to Celtic βάρδοι (pl.). Diodorus says that βάρδοι were poets who sang eulogies and satires accompanied by stringed instruments. The word continued into historical times in the Celtic countries, in Ireland as *bard*, in Gaelic Scotland as *bard*/*baird*, in Wales as *bardd*, in Middle Cornish as *barth*, and in Middle Breton as *barz*. In the same passage, Diodorus mentions δρυίδαι, druids who were philosophers and theologians; and μάντεις, diviners or seers; Strabo calls these latter ουάτεις. These three constituted a privileged, professional class of men who enjoyed high status in early Celtic society. The function of the bard was to support the social order by preserving versified genealogies that affirmed the rights of certain figures to govern, hists. of battles, and other lore; and to create fame for the leaders of that society through eulogy and elegy.

In Ir., in addition to bard (pl. *baird*), the word *fili (pl. *filidh*) was used to signify a poet who also had the power of divination; the word comes from a root that means "see." The word *druid* survived in Ir. as well, but the status of the fili was higher, and he seems to have taken over those magical properties that were associated with the druid in Celtic Gaul. The bard too lost some of his status at the expense of the fili. Like his counterpart on the continent, he continued to be a singer of praise, but his honor-price (a measure of status) was considerably less than that of the fili. The training of the fili was long and included instruction in the various meters, some of which, apparently, were common to the bard as well, but the fili was also trained in divination and the magical arts. In the wake of the Norman invasion, the fili no longer enjoyed his earlier status; rather, he became, like the bard, a singer of praise, and the meters he used were those of the bard. In Wales, *bardd* (pl. *beirdd*) retained the meaning of singer of praise, among other functions such as genealogist, historian, or custodian of lore. Both in Ireland and Wales, the poets were graded according to their training and achievement: the highest grade in Ireland was called *ollamh* (master; professor); in Wales, it was the *pencerdd* (chief of the craft of poetry).

Hence, the trad. of learned craft and proven skill behind the term is far removed from the emotionalism connected with it by the 18th-c. Eng. poets who revived it, such as Thomas Gray and James Beattie. The Eng. romantics were fascinated by the antiquity of the Celtic poets or bards and endowed them with their own ideas concerning "true" poetry, ironically attributing to them the qualities that they least prized, spontaneity and unbridled emotion. That emotionalism is essentially preserved in the mod. Eng. sense of the term, which denotes any poet but often connotes rhapsodic transcendence and is sometimes used as a pejorative; "bardolatry" is the critical term for the idolization of Shakespeare.

*See* CELTIC PROSODY, WELSH POETRY.

■ J. Vendryes, *Lexique Étymologique de L'Irlandais Ancien*, fasc. B, ed. E. Bachellery and P.-Y. Lambert (1981); *Uraicecht na Ríar: The Poetic Grades in Early Irish Law*, ed. Liam Breatnach (1987); Williams and Ford; Dafydd Jenkins, "*Bardd Teulu* and *Pencerdd*," *The Welsh King and His Court*, ed. T. M. Charles-Edwards et al. (2000).

J.E.C. WILLIAMS; T.V.F. BROGAN; P. K. FORD

# BAROQUE

I. History of the Term and Concept
II. Comparative Perspectives
III. National Perspectives

*Baroque* describes a literary style and poetics that flourished in Europe and the Americas between roughly 1575 and 1690, or from Torquato Tasso's *Gerusalemme liberata* to Sor Juana Inés de la Cruz's *Primero sueño*. Prizing wit and difficulty, while variously promoting spectacle and meditation, skepticism and belief, baroque lit. gives expression as well to the causes and effects of sundry epistemological, political, and religious crises riddling early modernity. The baroque thus also designates a period concept and worldview associated with the waning of high Ren. humanist practices and values, the rise of the empirical sciences, Counter-Reformation

theology, and political absolutism. Baroque aesthetic practices circulate from Western Europe to Eastern Europe and follow imperial routes to the Americas, where they combine with indigenous forms. Moreover, the mid-20th c. emergence of *neobaroque aesthetics and discourse in which hybridity, recursivity, perspectivism, and often *parody are paramount, suggests at once the vitality of the baroque style and period concept and that the baroque should continue to play a crucial role in the critique of modernity.

**I. History of the Term and Concept**. The Eng. word *baroque* comes, by way of 19th-c. Fr., from a 13th-c. Port. term for a misshapen, inexpensive pearl, *barroco*, which is ultimately derived from the Lat. *verruca* ("a wart"; "an excrescence on precious stones"; "a slight failing"). A rival, if less plausible etymology, championed esp. by Croce, points to the med. Lat. mnemonic *barroco*, for a logically dubious syllogism. And while the extent to which these two etymologies have contaminated each other over time in various vernaculars is still contested, such confluence neatly emblemizes not only the penchant for semantic ambiguity and wordplay often ascribed to baroque writing, but how the concept is an a posteriori one.

In mid-18th c. France, the term *baroque* was used to decry the perceived excesses and "bizarre" tastes of 17th-c. architecture. Analogously, Jean-Jacques Rousseau in his *Dictionnaire de Musique* (1767) writes: "Une Musique Baroque est celle dont l'Harmonie est confuse, chargée de Modulations & Dissonances. . . ." In the 1860s, Charles Baudelaire was the first to give *baroque* a positive connotation, when, in *Pauvre Belgique*, describing Belgian church architecture, he lauds its "style varié, fin, subtil, baroque." In *Menschliches, Allzumenschliches* (1878), Friedrich Nietzsche views the baroque as an inevitable, overly "rhetorical and dramatical" style that recurs throughout hist. and in all the arts whenever dialectical subtlety is lost.

Wölfflin's *Renaissance und Barock* and *Kunstgeschichtliche Grundbegriffe* first gives the baroque its current meaning designating both a style and a period concept. Wölfflin ascribes three principal "effects" to baroque architecture and visual arts: painterliness, massivity, and mobility. As for mobility, "the baroque never offers us perfection and fulfilment, or the static calm of 'being,' only the unrest of change and the tension of transience" (1888). Michelangelo's funeral sculptures, Caravaggio's swirling angel in *Saint Matthew with the Angel*, Diego Velázquez's *The Weavers*, and Gian Lorenzo Bernini's unrealized plans for the Louvre exemplify this dynamism. Wölfflin is also the first to transfer criteria from the visual arts to lit. when he briefly compares the splendor and "solemnity" of Michelangelo's art and the world-weariness of Tasso to Ariosto's "cheerful playfulness."

In subsequent decades, literary scholars generally concentrate on delineating rhetorical and literary-historical criteria to evaluate the baroque. Still, by the mid-20th c., the term *baroque* acquires so many, often contradictory meanings that it risks losing all methodological and conceptual value. Furthermore, the question of whether and how to delineate a mannerist style or period concept that would precede or be encompassed by the baroque becomes an enormous, often fruitless distraction. While many scholars understandably prefer to dissect late Ren. lit. into mannerist, *précieux*, metaphysical, euphuist, *culturanista*, *conceptista*, and Marinist styles, even so they generally recognize an overarching baroque style and *Weltanschauung*. Wellek (in a 1946 essay that was reprinted with a "Postscript" in 1963), however, helps to clarify the term and save its viability by arguing that the baroque should be interpreted as a period concept containing both stylistic and ideological elements. Wellek contends that the baroque broaches larger issues concerning periodization, the value of historical versus formalist approaches, and the usefulness of stylistic criteria to evaluate lit. "Whatever the defects of the term baroque," he concludes, "it is a term which prepares for synthesis, draws our minds away from the mere accumulation of observations and facts, and paves the way for a future history of literature as a fine art." Accomplishing exactly such a synthesis and spurning the dictates of *bienséance*, Rousset's influential *La littérature de l'âge baroque en France* adduces formal qualities from Bernini's works to establish a multifaceted literary baroque in France and elsewhere. Alternately, in "La curiosidad barroca," Lezama Lima proposes a Lat. Am. baroque exemplified by the neo-Gongorist poetry of Sor Juana in Mexico, but also by Lat. Am. church architecture and the 18th-c. sculptures of the Brazilian O Aleijadinho, with their fusion of indigenous and Eur. elements. Dubbing the Lat. Am. baroque the art of the "contraconquista," Lezama subverts the commonplace of the baroque as the art of the Counter-Reformation.

More recent scholarship on the baroque has sought to deepen and expand analytic, historical, and comparatist perspectives. Genette (1966, 1969), Beverley, and Hampton variously read the baroque as helping to reveal the dynamics of literary imitation. Mining the baroque for its philosophical lessons, Deleuze, (a rediscovered) Benjamin, Buci-Glucksmann, and Lacan (who defines the baroque as "la régulation de l'âme par la scopie corporelle"), find immanence, *aporia*, and transcendence in baroque rhetorical and conceptual excesses. Meanwhile, the emergence of a New World baroque or Lat. Am. baroque as a field of crit. (e.g., Carpentier and Lezama), as well as that of neobaroque crit. (e.g., Sarduy, Calabrese, Buci-Glucksmann, and Moser), have ensured that the baroque remains a vital subject for research and reflection. And if the neobaroque is frequently associated with postcolonialism, Bal and Ndalianis demonstrate that it may also herald, respectively, a broader aesthetics of quotation and spectacle. Recent studies by Zamora (2006) and Davidson confirm just how fruitful the decision can be to view the literary baroque (and New World baroque) through categories borrowed from the visual arts—although in less skilled hands, this panoptic approach sometimes confuses expressive means.

**II. Comparative Perspectives**. Baroque literary style is generally marked by rhetorical sophistication, excess, and play. Self-consciously remaking and thus critiquing the rhet. and poetics of the Petrarchan, pastoral, Senecan, and epic trads., baroque writers challenge conventional notions of *decorum by using and abusing such tropes and figures as *metaphor, *hyperbole, paradox, *anaphora, *hyperbaton, *hypotaxis and parataxis, *paronomasia, and *oxymoron. Producing *copia* and variety (*varietas*) is valued, as is the cultivation of *concordia discors* and *antithesis—strategies often culminating in *allegory or the *conceit. The tendency to amplify greatly a single image or idea is another hallmark. Baroque style typically courts admiration (*admiratio*) as much as assent or pleasure. Writers like Giambattista Marino, Luis de Góngora, Andreas Gryphius, John Donne, and Robert Burton thus trouble the traditional distinction between *invention (*inventio*) and *style (*elocutio*).

Baroque poetics largely continues Ren. debates on how to balance nature and art and how to please, move, and teach audiences and readers. Read directly, or filtered through numerous Neo-Lat. and vernacular poetics, Cicero, Horace, Quintilian, and Aristotle (*Poetics* and *Rhetoric*) still dominate most prescriptive treatises. Eloquence remains the poet's cardinal virtue. Some paratexts and *panegyrics, e.g., Thomas Carew's "An Elegie upon the death . . . of John Donne" (1633) do, however, acclaim baroque innovations in verse. Carew writes, "The Muses garden with Pedantique weedes / O'rspred, was purg'd by thee; The lazie seeds / Of servile imitation throwne away; / And fresh invention planted . . ." A more significant devel. is the handful of encyclopedic treatises on the art and faculty of *wit (*ingenium*). Reacting, respectively, to the stylistic revolutions of Góngora and Marino, Baltasar Gracián's *Agudeza y arte de ingenio* (1648) and Emanuele Tesauro's *Il cannocchiale aristotelico* (1654) offer comprehensive accounts of why wit (*agudeza, argutezza*) should be the writer's highest aim and the conceit (*concepto, concetto*), with its heavy hermeneutic demands and surprising aesthetic, cognitive, and spiritual rewards, poetry and prose's loftiest achievement. By stressing ingenuity in their accounts of invention, Gracián and Tesauro effectively make the imagination a rival to reason, a move that in retrospect nicely epitomizes the baroque.

In baroque lyric, the concision of the *sonnet, *epigram, and *emblem is everywhere cultivated. But Sp. poets also prize the expanded freedom of the *silva*, while John Milton, picking up where Christopher Marlowe and George Chapman leave off, perfects an unrhymed iambic pentameter enabling "things unattempted yet in prose and rhyme." Meanwhile, Gracián and George Herbert refine more direct if still elliptical styles. The myriad genres of baroque prose range from Madame de Sévigné's piquant, sentimental letters to Athanasius Kircher's encyclopedic syncreticism. Baroque novelistic forms—as exemplified by *Don Quixote*, *L'Astrée*, and *Simplicissimus*—may be read, as Lukács suggests, as representing a "degraded" world where God no longer guarantees order. Baroque tragedy and comedy can be distinguished by their willingness to violate Aristotelian "unities," production of spectacle and *affect, and role in promoting absolutism and allegorizing hist. In his influential interpretation of Ger. baroque *Trauerspiele*, Benjamin finds their allegorical representations of tyranny and ruin artistically inferior to the tragedies of Shakespeare and Pedro Calderón de la Barca but more amenable to a "philosophy of art." In *Arte nuevo de hacer comedias* (*New Art of Writing Comedies*, 1609) Félix Lope de Vega underscores the need to satisfy the audience's *gusto* (*taste) and thus of skirting Aristotelian rules forbidding the mixture of genres. His plays may be "monstrous" to the erudite, but their "variety delights." Similarly, concluding that his principal task is "to please" (*plaisanter*), Jean Racine in the preface to *Bérénice* (1670) promotes "simplicité" of plot over any adherence to "régles."

Still, baroque poetics generally cultivates an aesthetics of *difficulty valuing erudition, ingenuity, and rhetorical excess. Rousset (1954) observes that baroque poetics is fueled by "the refusal to simplify by eliminating [and] the accumulation of imagery born from the need to multiply points of view because no one point of view is capable by itself of seizing a fluctuating and fleeting reality." Such perspectivism takes many forms: Jean de Sponde's surprising *pointes*, Milton's epic similes, and Calderón's signature technique of *recolección* (recapitulation). Expressing the horrors of the Thirty Years' War, Gryphius's "Menschliches Elende" (1637) exemplifies baroque paratactic style and preoccupation with transience: "Was sind wir Menschen doch? ein Wohnhaus grimmer Schmerzen, / Ein Ball des falschen Glücks, ein Irrlicht dieser Zeit, / Ein Schauplatz herber Angst, besetzt mit scharfem Leid, / Ein bald verschmelzter Schnee und abgebrannte Kerzen." (But what are we humans? a home of fierce pain, / A ball of false joy, a will-o'-wisp of these times, / A scene of bitter fear, filled with sharp woe, / a quickly melted snowfall and a burned down candle.) By contrast, in his *Polifemo* (1612) and *Soledades* (1612), Góngora creates allusive *pastoral worlds whose greatest violence is that done to conventional poetics.

The motives for the baroque invention and style are quite diverse. From Donne's *Anniversaries* to Calderón's *autos sacramentales*, poets and their patrons proved eager to outdo predecessors and rivals. In Counter-Reformation Spain, Mexico, Italy, and France, in Protestant England and Holland, to say nothing of war-torn, confessionally divided Germany and Bohemia, the consequences of religious strife were as severe as they were heterogeneous. Many writers were tasked with *epideictic or apologetic duties, while others responded with extreme forms of skepticism or mysticism. Baroque documents and monuments typically make more subjective claims than their Ren. predecessors, partly because they are less tied to strictures, respectively, of cl. decorum and linear perspective but also, arguably, because the individual is perceived as increasingly autonomous or monadic, as G. W. Leibniz would have it. Thus, besides their ornamental and ideologi-

cal functions, the resources of baroque style may serve as the heuristic means for representing a world or self that no longer can be credibly represented based on the Ren. system of microcosmic-macrocosmic analogies or other humanist models. *Topoi* such as *life as dream* (Calderón), *world as labyrinth* (Jan Amos Comenius), *world upside-down* (Andrew Marvell), *vanitas mundi* (Quirinus Kuhlmann), and *theatrum mundi* (Gracián) devalorize the world of appearances and point to skeptical or transcendental solutions. Baroque tragedy typically shows how characters' extreme passions are incommensurable with unyielding contingency. This creates astonishment, confusion, and enormous *affectus* and often results in spectacular depictions of death. As with painterly chiaroscuro, thematic and formal ambiguities are produced by devices such as the play within the play or, in lyric, by sonnets about writing sonnets. These *mises-en-abîmes* speak to the more general baroque concern with incommensurable qualities and quantities, whether these refer to the cosmological infinite as championed by Giordano Bruno and decried by Blaise Pascal or express the more palpable mutability and insufficiency of worldly things and pretensions.

While the philosophies of René Descartes and Francis Bacon try to limit the imagination's role, many baroque writers—because of the dynamics of literary imitation, the needs of court, empire, the Church, or, in Protestant countries, in response to iconoclasm—avidly cultivate the marvelous and pathetic in their imagery. "The efficacy . . . in awakening and moving the affections," Maravall affirms, "was the great motive of the baroque." Typical baroque imagery involves alabaster, jewels, bubbles, ruins, corpses, skeletons, flames, tears, dewdrops, mirrors, clouds, rainbows, and fountains. Besides focusing on what pleases or disgusts the senses, baroque writing frequently makes metamorphosis, mutability, disillusionment, melancholy, inexpressibility, and infinity central themes. Mining less "cl." aspects of lit. hist., baroque *imitatio* often turns to early imperial Lat. lit. for models. Francisco de Quevedo borrows directly from Seneca, Juvenal, and Propertius in his devout sequence of poems *Heraclito Cristiano* and his satiric *Sueños*. Marino composes his digressive, 41,000-line epic *L'Adone* on an Ovidian theme, while a sonnet such as "La bella schiava" fashions compact *meraviglie* (wonders) recalling Martial. Echoing Seneca and Plutarch, Donne hyperbolically anatomizes the world's decline in the *Anniversaries*, even as he glimpses its Christian redemption. Imitating Lucan, Théodore-Agrippa d'Aubigné laments the slaughter of his fellow Protestants in *Les Tragiques* but revels in his discovery of the rhetorical means to amplify such violence.

In sum, Spitzer's description of Sp. baroque lit. as riddled by the conflict between *Weltsucht* and *Weltflucht* retains broad explanatory appeal. Baroque play with opposites commonly yields paradoxical imagery, generic instability, tenuous allegories, and irreconcilable spiritual tensions. Bruno's *Candelaio* (1582) and Calderón's *El mágico prodigioso* (1637) try to stage physical and abstract *coincidentia oppositorum*. The ironic sensuality of Marino's amorous verse complements Angelus Silesius's audacious mystical straining. Donne's *Holy Sonnets* fuse the sensual and spiritual in adapting the meditative trad. of Ignatius Loyola for Eng. readers.

**III. National Perspectives.** Baroque lit. is best viewed from a comparatist perspective. Imitation of the same models occurs throughout Europe and the New World, while a vibrant *respublica litteraria* diffuses new stylistic and thematic trends across national boundaries and oceans. Nevertheless, much of the best crit. on the baroque has concentrated first on local occurrences and contexts. Further, just as the literary baroque occurs at different historical moments in different countries, scholarly judgments about the literary baroque have often been shaped by shifting national perspectives. The following adumbrates historical and critical devels. in various vernacular trads.:

**A. Germany.** The Ger. baroque ranges from Martin Optiz's prescriptive *Buch von der Deutschen Poeterey* (1624) to the death of Philipp von Zesen (1689). It includes Gryphius's poetry and drama, Hans Jakob Christoph von Grimmelshausen's picaresques, and Daniel Caspar von Lohenstein's *Trauerspiele*, as well as the lyric poetry of Friedrich Spee, Paul Fleming, Christian Hofmanswaldau, Catharina Regina von Greiffenberg, Silesius, and Kuhlmann. The most sophisticated instance of Ger. baroque poetics is Georg Philipp Harsdörffer's *Poetischer Trichter* (1648–53). As a period concept and name for a literary style, the baroque is first and most fervently embraced by Ger. critics such as Cysarz and Benjamin. This is partly due to the similarities they find between the baroque and Ger. *expressionism, as well as to Wölfflin's vast influence, but also because there was no viable competing term for the baroque to usurp. More recently, while Adorno warns against the misuse of the term *baroque*, Barner, Jaumann, Garber, Althaus, and Kemper (1988, 2006) have greatly deepened the understanding of Ger. baroque rhet., lyric, drama, epigram, and the baroque's reception hist.

**B. *Spain and Latin America.*** Baroque writing may be said to commence with Fernando de Herrera's *Anotaciones* (1578) and Juan Huarte de San Juan's treatise on wit, *Examen de ingenios* (1575); reach full bloom with Miguel de Cervantes's *Don Quixote* (1605, 1615) and *Persiles*, Lope de Vega's dramas, the lyrics of Góngora, Quevedo, and Pedro Espinosa; and then have its magnificent autumn with Calderón's dramas, Gracián's prose, and the poetry of Sor Juana (1648–95). Besides Sor Juana, whose life and work has been the subject of much recent scholarship, other leading Mexican baroque poets include Miguel de Guevara and Luis Sandoval y Zapata. In Brazil, emerging from Luís de Camões's shadow, Gregório de Matos is the most celebrated baroque poet, while António Vieira's ingenious, audacious sermons exemplify baroque prose. As for crit., the untenable duality of the terms *conceptismo* and *culteranismo* has been largely replaced by the rubric

*baroque*, which now is also generally favored over the more traditional *siglo de oro*, esp. when describing 17th-c. lit. Maravall's interpretation of the baroque as a period of "general crisis" and its art as serving "conservative" ends continues to spur new thinking. Following the crit. of Dámaso Alonso and Américo Castro, Orozco Díaz methodically maps the contours of the literary baroque, culminating in his *Introducción al Barroco* (1988). González Echevarría's *Celestina's Brood* (1993) embodies recent efforts to expand the baroque beyond its peninsular, Golden Age confines.

**C. *Italy.*** Some critics have found the baroque already in Michelangelo's poetry and in Tasso's *Aminta*, *Gerusalemme liberata*, and his treatise on poetics, the *Discorsi*; but most prefer a later start, approximately from Marino's *Rime* (1602) and the varied works of Giambattista Basile (d. 1632) to the last edition of *Il cannocchiale aristotelico* (1670) pub. in Tesauro's lifetime. While Croce equated *barroco* with bad taste and aesthetic failure, other scholars gradually adopted the term and gave it more positive connotations. It now competes with the narrower notion of *Marinismo* and the more widely used *seicento*. Raimondi and Getto make perhaps the strongest case for the It. baroque. By focusing mainly on thematic questions, Battistini's *Il barroco* offers a welcome corrective to the tendency to conflate the baroque with Counter-Reformation art, culture, and ideology.

**D. *France.*** The leading Fr. baroque poets are considered to be Agrippa d'Aubigné, Sponde, Marc-Antoine Girard de Saint-Amant, Théophile de Viau, and Jean de La Ceppède. Drama by Molière, Jean Rotrou, Racine, and Pierre Corneille have been convincingly read as baroque; for even when their style heeds François Malherbe's classicizing dicta, often their motifs, metaphors, extreme theatricality, and cultivation of spectacle do not. Nicolas Boileau rings the death-knell for the Fr. baroque with his 1672 *L'Art poétique*: "Evitons ces excès: laissons à l'Italie / De tous ces faux brillans l'eclatante folie . . . Fuyez de ces auteurs l'abondance stérile, / Et ne vous charger point d'un detail inutile" (Let us avoid this excess and leave to Italy, / With all its fake jewels, glittering folly . . . / Flee those authors of sterile abundance, / And do not burden yourself with useless detail). In the 20th c., the pioneering studies of Raymond, Tapié, Buffum, Mourgues, and esp. Rousset, together with more recent scholarship by Lestringant and Mathieu-Castellani, have largely vanquished Fr. reluctance to recognize a period style between the *Pléiade and *classicisme*. Buci-Glucksmann's studies of baroque and neobaroque aesthetics in light of Benjamin, Baudelaire, Lacan, and feminist theory have given new life and theoretical weight to typological readings of the baroque. But introducing a 1980 edition of Tapié's *Baroque et classicisme* (1957), Fumaroli decries the concept of the baroque as a Ger. import and a "délicieux accouplement entre discipline universitaire et imagination romanesque, entre philolettres et rêveries, école des Annales et tourisme sentimental."

E. *England and North America.* Baroque stylistic features and themes characterize verse by Donne, Michael Drayton, Marvell, and Milton; the prose of Donne, Burton, Thomas Browne, and Margaret Cavendish, as well as Shakespeare's poetry and drama (from the *grotesquerie of Troilus,* the perspectivism and wordplay of the *Sonnets,* to the *theatrum mundi* of *The Tempest*). The baroque effectively ends in England with John Dryden's *Essay of Dramatic Poesy* (1668) and his bowdlerization of purple passages in Shakespeare's plays to prepare them for a neoclassical stage. In New England, Jonathan Edwards's sermons and the verse of Edward Taylor, Michael Wigglesworth, and Anne Bradstreet have been read as representing what Warren (1941) calls a "colonial baroque." More generally, though, Anglo-Am. crit.'s attachment to the stylistic terms *metaphysical* and *cavalier,* and the period terms *Elizabethan, Jacobean,* and *Restoration,* as well as the more recent predilection to lump all 16th- and 17th-c. lit. under the rubric "early modern," has forestalled the acceptance of an Eng. baroque. Notable exceptions include Warren (1939) on Crashaw; studies by Daniells, Roston, and Parry on Milton; Croll's reading of Browne's prose; and Kermode pondering the metaphysical poets. T. S. Eliot avoids the word but apprehends the concept: "Seventeenth-century poetry is much like a crucifix ornamented with pearls, except that we are able with some difficulty to perceive the pearls." And while critics writing outside Anglo-Am. circles, esp. Praz (1925, 1958) and Hatzfeld, are less hesitant to apply the term to Eng. lit., within them Bush's 1962 verdict still epitomizes the prevalent attitude: "German exponents of *Geistesgeschichte* have pursued the ramifications of 'Barock' as Browne pursued the quincunx, with a heavier foot and with equally specious and elliptical logic, but for us the simplest definition is 'poetry like Crashaw's.'" Even so, Nelson's (1954, 1961) and Warnke's (1961, 1972) contention that, from a comparatist perspective, the baroque is an ineluctable term to describe the period's style and *Weltanschauung* in England has yet to be been gainsaid.

F. *Holland.* P. C. Hooft's meditative lyrics and Constanijn Huygens's more worldly verse display numerous baroque qualities. Analogies between Dutch lit. and the painterly techniques of Rembrandt and Peter Paul Rubens are also compelling. Yet beginning with Haerten's study (1934) of Joost van den Vondel's dramas, the notion of a Dutch baroque has only been ambivalently embraced. Grootes and Schenkeveld label Daniel Heinsius's Neo-Lat. poetry baroque but are reluctant to apply the term to vernacular lit.

G. *Eastern Europe.* As Segel observes, baroque poetry flourishes later here than in Western Europe. A strong Marinist influence is felt in Croatia, where Ivan Gundulić's psalms and unfinished epic *Osman* (1638) are representative. In Hungary, the lyrics of Miklós Zrínyi stand out, as does his epic *The Siege of Szigetvár* (1651), with its numerous echoes of Tasso. In Poland, where the baroque style waxes around 1700, Jan Andrzej Morsztyn and Daniel Naborowski ingeniously rearrange the ruins of the Petrarchan legacy. Born in Bohemia, Comenius

becomes one of the most celebrated baroque polymaths. In Russia, the baroque may be said to commence with Simeon Polotsky and Avvakum Petrov, and extend into the 18th c. with Vasily Trediakovsky's poetry and theory, Gavrila Derzhavin's odes, and Mikhail Lomonosov's lyrics. Tschiźewskij (1971, 1973) views the "slavic Baroque" as a "synthesis of the Renaissance and the middle ages." Embraced enthusiastically in the 1920s, most recent crit. of Rus. lit. has tended to avoid the period term *baroque,* preferring instead to limit it to descriptions of style. However, Joseph Brodsky's "Great Elegy to John Donne" (1963) makes an extremely compelling, if implicit, case for the centrality of the baroque in the Rus. literary trad.

More generally, imitations like Brodsky's and the emergence of neobaroque critical discourse indicate how the continuing viability of the baroque as a period concept ultimately lies in its heuristic value or how it serves contemp. creative, critical, and theoretical tasks. As Deleuze (1992) observes, "Irregular pearls exist, but the Baroque has no reason to exist without a concept that forms this reason itself. It's easy to render the Baroque non-existent; one only has to stop proposing its concept." Less paradoxically, Zamora (2009) asserts, "The real strength of the neobaroque resides in its engagement of specific historical and cultural contexts." In this respect, Lezama Lima's 1966 novel *Paradiso* is exemplary for its syncretism or *plutonismo* by which the rich textures of contemp. Cuban culture are fused with historical, literary, and metaphysical traits that Lezama elsewhere ascribes to a mythical "señor barroco." Or as Greene more soberly affirms, "The Neobaroque embodies the obligation of early modernists to attend to their period not as a closed episode, like antiquity, but as an uncompleted script for the present."

*See* CONCEPTISMO; MANNERISM; MARINISM; METAPHYSICAL POETRY; RENAISSANCE POETICS; RENAISSANCE POETRY.

■ **Comparative**: H. Wölfflin, *Renaissance und Barock* (1888), and *Kunstgeschichtliche Grundbegriffe* (1915); M. Praz, *Secentismo e marinismo in Inghilterra* (1925); H. Haerten, *Vondel und der deutsche Barock* (1934); E. D'Ors, *Du baroque* (1935); O. de Mourgues, *Metaphysical, Baroque and Précieux Poetry* (1953); L. Nelson Jr., "Góngora and Milton: Toward a Definition of the Baroque," *CL* 6 (1954); M. Praz, *The Flaming Heart* (1958); L. Nelson Jr., *Baroque Lyric Poetry* (1961); *European Metaphysical Poetry,* ed. F. Warnke (1961); J. M. Cohen, *The Baroque Lyric* (1963); R. Wellek, "The Concept of Baroque in Literary Scholarship," *Concepts in Criticism* (1963); M. W. Croll, "The Baroque Style in Prose," *Style, Rhetoric, and Rhythm,* ed. J. M. Patrick and R. O. Evans (1966); G. Lukács, *The Theory of the Novel,* trans. A. Bostock (1971); H. B. Segel, *The Baroque Poem* (1974); J. Lacan, "Du baroque," *Encore, le séminaire XX* (1975); F. Warnke, *Versions of Baroque* (1975); *La Métamorphose dans la poésie baroque française et anglaise,* ed. G. Mathieu-Castellani (1980); V.-L. Tapié, *Baroque et classicisme,* ed. M. Fumaroli (1980); G. Mathieu-Castellani, *Mythes de l'eros baroque* (1981); J. Beverley, "Going Baroque?" *boundary 2* 15 (1988); *Baroque Topographies,* ed. T. Hampton (1991); M. Blanco, *Les rhé-*

*toriques de la pointe* (1992); O. Calabrese, *Neo-Baroque*, trans. C. Lambert (1992); G. Deleuze, *The Fold: Leibniz and the Baroque*, trans. T. Conley (1992); G. Mathieu-Castellani, "Baroque et maniérisme," *Dictionnaire universel des littératures* (1994); É. Glissant, "Concerning a Baroque Abroad in the World," *Poetics of Relation* (1997); W. Moser, "Barock," *Ästhetische Grundbegriffe*, v. 1 (2000); M. Bal, *Quoting Caravaggio* (2001); *Résurgences baroques*, ed. W. Moser and N. Goyer (2001); C. Buci-Glucksmann, *La Folie du voir* (2002); A. Ndalianis, *Neo-Baroque Aesthetics and Contemporary Entertainment* (2004); P. Davidson, *The Universal Baroque* (2008); G. Lambert, *On the (New) Baroque* (2008); R. Greene, "Baroque and Neobaroque: Making This-tory," *PMLA* 124.1 (2009); C. Johnson, *Hyperboles* (2010).

■ **German**: H. Cysarz, *Deutsche Barockdichtung* (1924); W. Benjamin, *Ursprung des deutschen Trauerspiels* (1928); T. W. Adorno, "Der mißbrauchte Barock," *Ohne Leitbild* (1967); W. Barner, *Barockrhetorik* (1970); R. Browning, *German Baroque Poetry, 1618–1723* (1971); H. Jaumann, *Die deutsche Barockliteratur* (1975); H.-G. Kemper, *Barock–Mystik* (1988); *Europäische Barock–Rezeption*, ed. K. Garber, 2 v. (1991)—includes important articles on the Slavic, Dutch, and Scandinavian baroque; T. Althaus, *Epigrammatische Barock* (1996); H.-G. Kemper, *Barock Humanismus: Krisen–Dichtung* and *Barock Humanismus: Liebeslyrik* (both 2006).

■ **Spanish and Latin American**: J. Lezama Lima, *La expresión americana* (1957); H. Hatzfeld, *Estudios sobre el barroco* (1964); S. Sarduy, *Barroco* (1974), and "The Baroque and the Neobaroque," *Latin America and Its Literature*, ed. C. Fernández Moreno (1980); J. A. Maravall, *Culture of the Baroque*, trans. T. Cochran (1986); E. Orozco Díaz, *Introducción al barroco* (1988); L. Spitzer, "The Spanish Baroque," *Representative Essays*, ed. A. K. Forcione, H. Lindenberger, and M. Sutherland (1988); R. González Echevarría, *Celestina's Brood* (1993); A. Carpentier, "The Baroque and the Marvelous Real," *Magic Realism*, ed. L. P. Zamora and W. Faris (1995); L. P. Zamora, *The Inordinate Eye: New World Baroque and Latin American Fiction* (2006), and "New World Baroque, Neobaroque, Brut Barroco: Latin American Postcolonialisms," *PMLA* 124.1 (2009).

■ **Italian**: B. Croce, *Storia dell' età barocca in Italia* (1929); J. V. Mirollo, *The Poet of the Marvelous: Giambattista Marino* (1963); E. Raimondi, *Letteratura barocca* (1982); L. Anceschi, *L'idea del barocco* (1984); *The Sense of Marino*, ed. F. Guardiani (1994); A. Battistini, *Il barocco* (2000); G. Getto, *Il barocco letterario in Italia* (2000); A. M. Pedullà, *Il romanzo barocco e altri scritti* (2001).

■ **French**: I. Buffum, *Agrippa d'Aubigné's "Les tragiques"* (1951); J. Rousset, *La littérature de l'âge baroque en France* (1954); M. Raymond, *Baroque et Renaissance poétique* (1955); I. Buffum, *Studies in the Baroque from Montaigne to Rotrou* (1957); L. Spitzer, "The 'Récit de Théramène,'" *Linguistics and Literary History* (1962); G. Genette, "Hyperboles," *Figures I* (1966); J. Rousset, "Adieu au baroque?" *L'intérieur et l'extérieur* (1968); G. Genette, "D'un récit baroque," *Figures II* (1969); F. Hallyn, *Formes métaphoriques dans la poésie lyr-*

*ique de l'age baroque en France* (1975); F. Lestringant, *La cause des martyrs dans "Les tragiques" d'Agrippa d'Aubigné* (1991); M. Blanchot, "The Baroque Poets of the Seventeenth Century," *Faux pas*, trans. C. Mandell (2001).

■ **English and North American**: A. Warren, *Richard Crashaw* (1939), and "Edward Taylor's Poetry: Colonial Baroque," *KR* 3 (1941); D. Bush, *English Literature in the Early Seventeenth Century* (1962); R. Daniells, *Milton, Mannerism and Baroque* (1963); F. Kermode, *The Metaphysical Poets* (1969); M. Roston, *Milton and the Baroque* (1980); T. S. Eliot, *The Varieties of Metaphysical Poetry*, ed. R. Schuchard (1993); G. Parry, "Literary Baroque and Literary Classicism," *A Companion to Milton*, ed. T. Corns (2003).

■ **Other National or Area Studies**: D. Tschiżewskij, *History of Russian Literature from the Eleventh Century to End of the Baroque* (1960); A. Angyal, *Die slawische Barockwelt* (1961); D. Tschiżewskij, *Comparative History of Slavic Literatures*, trans. R. Porter (1971); J. Bucsela, "The Problems of Baroque in Russian Literature," *Russian Review* 31 (1972); D. Tschiżewskij, *Slavische Barockliteratur I* (1973); *Slavische Barockliteratur II*, ed. R. Lachmann (1983); E. K. Grootes and M. A. Schenkeveld, "The Dutch Revolt and the Golden Age, 1560–1700," *A Literary History of the Low Countries*, ed. T. Hermans (2009).

C. JOHNSON

**BARZELLETTA.** *See* FROTTOLA AND BARZELLETTA.

**BASQUE COUNTRY, POETRY OF THE.** Basque lit. bloomed late because of various sociohistorical circumstances that hindered its devel. and are tightly bound to the ups and downs suffered by Basque, or Euskara, a lang. of pre-IE origin spoken today by some 700,000 people who live on both sides of the Pyrenees, in France and in Spain. The political border that today divides the Basque Country (Euskal Herria) separates two different legislative regions. After the Sp. constitution of 1978 was approved, the Basque lang. was accepted as an official lang., together with Castilian (Sp.), in the provinces in the Sp. Basque region; however, the same is not the case in the Fr. Basque Country, where Basque does not hold the status of an official lang. The consequences of this imbalance are easy to predict: factors such as the establishment of bilingual models of teaching and the existence of grants for publications in the Basque lang. have made the literary system in the Sp. Basque Country much stronger and more dynamic than that on the French side. Within Basque lit., poetry has always been a crucial genre. The first book of any sort published in Basque was a volume of poems by Bernard Etxepare (1493?–1545); moreover, poetry has also held a position of considerable importance in Basque oral lit. Long-established genres such as improvised Basque verse singing, or *bertsolaritza*, are still very popular today.

*Linguae Vasconum Primitiae* (Origins of the Basque Language, 1545) by Etxepare was the first step from an oral to a written lit. It consists of 15 poems dealing with themes such as love and religion; Etxepare expresses his joy at the possibilities created by the invention of the printing press and his hope that it will help disseminate Basque lit. Etxepare had read Erasmus, and his book reveals this influence. Another foundational vol., Arnaut Oihenart's *Atsotitzak eta neurtitzak* (Proverbs and Verses, 1657), is a book not only of proverbs and refrains but of love poems that follow the trad. of *Petrarchism. The dominance of religious texts in this era was almost absolute; Oihenart (1592–1667) was one of the few laic Basque writers of his time.

The last decade of the 19th c. saw the emergence of a new spirit that would transform Basque lit. The dominance of devotional and didactic works began to wane, and the spectrum of literary genres widened. Indalezio Bizkarrondo or "Blintx" (1831–76) and the satiric Pierre Topet or "Etxahun" (1786–1862), e.g., were considered romantic poets.

After the Second Carlist War in 1876, the revocation of foral rights—which had ensured regional autonomy by empowering assemblies of local inhabitants—unleashed a cultural revival, *Pizkundea* (the Basque Renaissance, 1876–1936), the Basque equivalent of the Galician *Rexurdimento* or the Catalan *Renaixença*, in which patriotic renewal would stem from recognition of the Basque lang. The foralist movement gave way to the nationalism of Sabino Arana and from this point on, the fundamental purpose of writing in Basque would be to contribute to the creation of the Basque nation. Nationalism was to influence all Basque lit. of the first third of the 20th c. Poetry was promoted by *poetic contests known as *lorejokoak* (floral games), by Basque festivals, and by the publication of *songbooks containing popular folk songs. During the time of the floral games, the work of Felipe Arrese-Beitia, among others, showed anguish in the face of the potential death of the lang. In the 1930s, two poets, Xabier Lizardi and Esteban Urkiaga (Lauaxeta), explored the expressive possibilities of Basque through postsymbolist poetics. Both nationalists, they participated actively in the *Pizkundea* that took place during the years of the Sp. Second Republic, a time at which nationalist political and cultural activism went hand in hand. Another influential poet and translator of that time was Nicolas Ormaetxea (Orixe), whose love of cl. lit. and knowledge of Scholasticism greatly influenced his writing. *Bide Barrijak* (1931) by Lauaxeta, *Biotz begietan* (1932) by Lizardi, and *Barne muinetan* (1934) by Orixe are considered the premier poetic vols. of the pre–Sp. Civil War period.

The repression and censorship that followed the Sp. Civil War (1936–39) made it impossible to publish in Basque until 1949, when the first mod. book of poetry appeared, but it was not until the 1950s that the dialogue with modernity became more developed through the voices of two poets, Jon Mirande (1925–72) and Gabriel Aresti (1933–75). Mirande, heterodox and nihilist, was the first to transgress the religious spirit latent in Basque poetry. Echoes of his many and varied philosophical and literary readings (such as the Stoics, Friedrich Nietzsche, Oswald Spengler, E. A. Poe, and

Charles Baudelaire) abound in his prose and poetry. Aresti wrote short stories and drama as well as poetry and translated such authors as Giovanni Boccaccio, T. S. Eliot, and Nazim Hikmet. His first collection of poetry was *Maldan behera* (Downhill, 1960), influenced by symbolist poetry and an Eliotian modernism. However, with *Harri eta herri* (Stone and Country, 1964), a landmark in the history of Basque lit., he moved toward a more sociopolitical poetry. Critics praised the book's modernity and innovative spirit, together with its left-wing humanism. It was followed by *Euskal harria* (Basque Stone, 1967) and *Harrizko herri hau* (This Country of Stone, 1971).

In the 1960s, political and cultural activism against the regime of Francisco Franco were closely linked, with the consequence that sociopolitical poetry found its best ally in modern Basque song, esp. in the group *Ez dok amairu*, which was formed by singers like Mikel Laboa (1934–2008) and poets like Xabier Lete (b. 1944), Joxean Arze (b. 1939), and Joxe Anjel Irigarai (b. 1942). Linked to this movement of social commitment, female poets emerged, such as Amaia Lasa (b. 1949) and Arantxa Urretabizkaia (b. 1947). Other authors took a postsymbolist stand, intending for Basque poetry to evolve toward a more concise and synthetic style (e.g., Juan Mari Lekuona, 1927–2005) or to move toward a deeper degree of introspection (e.g., Bittoriano Gandiaga, 1928–2001).

However, things changed radically after Franco's death in 1975; from then on and for the first time in hist., the Basque literary system was supported by a legal framework that allowed the establishment of bilingual education and funding for the publication of books in Basque. In 2005, a total of 1,648 books were published, 247 of which were literary works, including 37 books of poetry. In the 1970s and early 1980s, because of a proliferation of literary magazines, Basque poetry experienced its most avant-garde period. While Joseba Sarrionandia (b. 1958) reminded us that all lit. is metalit., Koldo Izagirre (b. 1953) dabbled in surrealist aesthetics. But the book that truly shook the poetry scene of the time was *Etiopia* (Ethiopia, 1978), by Bernardo Atxaga (b. 1951), the most internationally renowned Basque author. In *Etiopia*, Atxaga addresses the tedium brought about by the end of modernity and declares the impossibility of addressing poetic lang. itself. Freed from the baroque and far removed from the dramatics of his previous work, in *Poemas & Híbridos* (Poems & Hybrids, 1990) Atxaga tries to recover poetry's essence. For this purpose, he tears up the nonneutral, topical lang. that is traditionally used in the modernist poetry and mixes it with Dadaist strategies (see DADA), with the primitive and the infantile, and with humor.

Contemp. Basque poetry can best be described as eclectic. Its primary characteristics include a wide diversity of poetics, the use of various narrative styles, a preference for nonaesthetic poetics rooted in the quotidian, and the emergence of women poets who reclaim other codes based on the female body. Poets such as Felipe Juaristi (b. 1957), Rikardo Arregi (b. 1958), Miren Agur

Meabe (b. 1962), and Kirmen Uribe (b. 1970) seem to be influenced by the *Beat poets and gritty realism. Audiences often enjoy poetic performances that combine poetry with music or other arts. What happened to the other literary genres has also happened to poetry: it has absorbed the characteristics literary critics describe as *postmodern—a denial of transcendental meaning, an assertion that all lit. is metalit. in the end; a nonelitist attitude toward literary creation; the use of *pastiche; a mistrust of lang.; and a hybridization of genres. That is, Basque poetry displays a tendency toward aesthetic populism and a democratizing attitude to the figure of the poet.

■ **Anthologies**: *Antología de la poesía vasca*, ed. I. Aldekoa (1993); *Etzikoak*, ed. and trans. M. Drobnic and M. Prelesnik Drozg (2006); *Montañas en la niebla*, ed. J. Kortazar (2006); *Six Basque Poets*, ed. M. J. Olaziregi (2007); *Cien años de poesía*, coord. J. Sabadell-Nieto (2007).

■ **History and Criticism**: L. Michelena, *Historia de la literatura vasca* (1960); I. Aldekoa, *Historia de la literatura vasca* (2004); *History of Basque Literature*, ed. M. J. Olaziregi (2010).

M. J. Olaziregi

**BATHOS** (Gr., "depth"). Now generally used as an equivalent to the descriptive term *anticlimax, bathos entered literary use with Longinus's treatise *Peri hypsous* (*On the Sublime*), where it was a synonym for *hypsos*, the sublime, and meant either high or deep. To ridicule his poetic contemporaries, however, Alexander Pope wrote the satirical *Peri Bathous: or, Martinus Scriblerus His Treatise of the Art of Sinking in Poetry* (1727), parodying Longinus by converting praise of the sublime into mock-praise of the profound. Pope presents bathos as an attempt at elevated expression that misfires, creating a sudden transition from the sublime to the ridiculous. Pope was responding to Nicolas Boileau's *Treatise of the Sublime* (1674), itself a trans. of Longinus. *Peri Bathous* drew attention to the many deficiencies of the poetry of Pope's rivals: affectation, pertness, needless complexity, confusion, and obfuscation. Since Pope, bathos has been used to suggest an unfortunate or unintended "sinking" or deflation to create a humorously awkward juxtaposition. William Hogarth alluded to Pope with his 1764 engraving *The Bathos: or, the Manner of Sinking in Sublime Paintings*. The similarity to the Gr. *pathos inflects bathos with the sense of sad or pitiable. Bathos is a common technique in *parody, burlesque, and absurdist writing. Pope gives the example, "Ye Gods! Annihilate both Space and Time, / And make two Lovers happy." Elizabeth Barrett Browning produces bathos with "Our Euripides, the human — / With his droppings of warm tears" ("Wine of Cyprus," 89–90) and Alfred, Lord Tennyson with "He suddenly dropt dead of heart-disease" ("Sea Dreams," 64).

■ A. Pope, *The Art of Sinking in Poetry: Martinus Scriblerus' Peri Bathous*, ed. E. Leake Steeves (1952); *'Longinus' On the Sublime*, ed. D. A. Russell (1964); C. Gerrard, "Pope, *Peri Bathous*, and the Whig Sublime," *Cultures of Whiggism*, ed. D. Womersley (2005).

H. Brown; S. Gee

**BEAST EPIC.** Comprising a vast range of global trads., incl. origin myths, wisdom lit., *comedy, and *satire, the term *beast epic* generally designates more or less structurally unified narratives featuring animals as characters rather than as types. A fellow traveler of cosmological and totemic trads. such as the "dreamtime" narratives of aboriginal tribes of Australia or the tales collected by the Roman poet Ovid into the *Metamorphoses*, the beast epic is clearly also related to single-episode forms such as the *fable. Thus, the carefully interwoven structure of the influential Sanskrit *Panchatantra* (The Five Principles), possibly composed in the 3d c. BCE and later translated into Persian and Ar., shows it to be more than a collection of short moral tales. Although the diversity of beast-epic trads. is remarkable, important common points remain, not least how such material maps and describes the contours of human experience, not only charting the world beyond the village but, through the mimicry of human activity and traits imputed to speaking animals, exploring our relations with those strangest of creatures, our human neighbors. In this respect, such sophisticated and subversive materials chart the edges and limits of humankind in their interrogations of social or gender conventions, as well as of the ambition of lang. to describe and tame nature.

This war between weasel words and horse sense is notably reflected in the Eur. trads. of Reynard the Fox, the first surviving tales composed in the mid- to late 12th c. in France, the centerpiece being the fox's rape of the she-wolf and the subsequent trial. These adventures illuminate social, religious, political, and legal institutions and changes, with further episodes as well as trans. and adaptations into Ger., Dutch, and Eng. following over the next three centuries. That the fox did not entirely rule med. Europe's cock-and-bull roost is clear from works featuring God's natural comedian, the ass. Following in the wake of cl. antecedents such as Apuleius's salaciously satirical *Golden Ass* (2d c. CE), med. examples include the *Speculum stultorum* (The Mirror for Fools, ca. 1180) by the Canterbury monk Nigel of Longchamps, and the quasi-apocalyptic Fr. satire *Le Roman de Fauvel* (ca. 1312) by Gervais de Bus, mss. of the latter often lavishly illuminated and featuring musical settings, striking testimony to the prestige accorded this material. There is also a rich trad. of "bird-debate" poems, examples being *The Owl and the Nightingale* (ca. 1190) and Chaucer's *Parliament of Fowls* (ca. 1382). While some trads. feature more or less ontologically stable creatures, such as foxes, wolves, monkeys, and spiders, in others the creature is either less defined in form or capable of transformation (examples here are the Chinese novel *Journey to the West* [ca. 1590] recounting the adventures of Monkey and his companions, the African Ananse stories, or the Japanese tales of magical foxes known as *kitsune*). Accordingly, North Am. Winnebago trickster stories center on a figure proteanly inchoate in form and character, occupying a temporality simultaneously prior to and coextensive with human hist. Thus, although a creator figure who gives rise to the first vegetables, the trickster struggles to integrate into an existing human lifeworld, sending his genitals to marry the daughter of a chief of a neighboring tribe. Lastly, although separate trads. can be identified, beast epics often reflect complex confluences and interactions, stories from *Uncle Remus* and *Br'er Rabbit* reflecting the influences of African Ananse stories as well as of native Am. trads. Taken together, this vast diversity of trads. reflects how humans have harnessed imagined animals as tools for narratives as varied and problematic as the exploitation and commoditization of actual creatures.

*See* INDIGENOUS AMERICAS, POETRY OF THE.

■ **Criticism and History**: C. Lévi-Strauss, *Totemism*, trans. R. Needham (1963); K. Varty, *Reynard the Fox: A Study of the Fox in Medieval English Art* (1967); P. Radin, K. Kerényi, C. G. Jung, *The Trickster: A Study in American Indian Mythology* (1972); D. J. Haraway, *Simians, Cyborgs and Women: The Reinvention of Nature* (1991); M. Green, *Animals in Celtic Life and Myth* (1992); J. Ziolkowski, *Talking Animals: Medieval Latin Beast Poetry, 750–1150* (1993); A. Plaks, "Journey to the West," *Masterworks of Asian Literature in Comparative Perspective*, ed. B. S. Miller (1994); J. E. Salisbury, *The Beast Within: Animals in the Middle Ages* (1994); J. R. Simpson, *Animal Body, Literary Corpus: The Old French "Roman de Renart"* (1996); K. Varty, *Reynard, Renart, Reinœrt and Other Foxes in Medieval England: The Iconographic Evidence* (1999); L. E. Robbins, *Elephant Slaves and Pampered Parrots: Exotic Animals in Eighteenth-Century Paris* (2002); B. Sax, *Crow* (2003); M. Bathgate, *The Fox's Craft in Japanese Religion and Folklore: Shapeshifters, Transformations and Duplicities* (2004); M. Wallen, *Fox* (2006); J. Mann, *From Aesop to Reynard: Beast Literature in Medieval Britain* (2009); S. Carnell, *Hare* (2010); K. Michalska and S. Michalski, *Spider* (2010).

J. SIMPSON

**BEAT.** The recurring pulse in a regular *rhythm. Derived from the motion of the conductor's hand or baton indicating the rhythmic pulse in music, in the analysis of verse it refers to the salient elements of a poetic *meter as experienced by the reader or listener. It is generally agreed that spoken lang. is normally too varied to allow for the emergence of beats (but see Couper-Kuhlen for a different view); metered verse, however, arranges words and sentences in controlled ways that produce a regular movement characterized by the alternation of stronger and weaker beats (or "offbeats"). When beats and offbeats are organized into the patterns enshrined in verse trad., the rhythm created is particularly strong; and once sequences of beats are perceived, the expectation is that they will continue. *Free verse and, more rarely, prose can fall into a sequence of alternating beats and offbeats, but without creating metrical patterns. The equivalent term for the beat in cl. prosody is *ictus.

Analysis of poetry in terms of beats and offbeats—"beat prosody"—emphasizes the relation of verse to music, without attempting to apply musical notation to the rhythms of lang. Both regular verse and cl. Western music are regarded as building on simple, familiar rhythmic forms, the most ubiquitous of which is the four-beat unit (which is produced by doubling a beat, then doubling it again). In the Eng. trad., the four-beat rhythm is the staple of popular verse and song, children's rhymes, advertising *jingles, and *hymns. It is also common in art verse, where, in its most straightforward realization, it becomes *iambic or *trochaic tetrameter. Most commonly, it is found in larger units also created by doubling: four-beat *couplets or, more usually, four groups of four beats. In *dipodic verse, beats alternate between stronger and weaker (an alternation that arises from the hierarchic nature of all regular rhythm).

Once a four-beat rhythm is established, the mind can perceive a beat in certain limited positions even when there is no syllable to manifest it; thus, the common *ballad meter omits the last beat of the second and fourth groups. This perceived but not actual beat is termed an "implied beat," a "virtual beat," or an "empty beat." Most line lengths in the Eng. verse trad. are based on the four-beat group or its variants, the two-beat group or the group of three beats plus an implied beat. A significant exception is the five-beat line, which does not fit easily into the four-beat rhythm, a fact that explains many of its special characteristics: it is rare in popular verse and song, it is often unrhymed, and it almost always takes the form of a strict accentual-syllabic or syllable-stress meter, the *iambic pentameter. It is thus clearly distinct from the trad. of song and closer to the rhythms of the spoken lang. (Some prosodists have argued that five-beat lines have a sixth implied beat, but this is not generally accepted.)

The strong pulse of the four-beat rhythm makes it possible to vary the number of offbeats that occur between the beats. Eng. accentual or stress verse has the greatest freedom in this respect, allowing one or two offbeats and, less frequently, three or none at all. Accentual-syllabic verse, by contrast, controls the number of syllables in the line, and hence the character of the offbeats: before or after a double offbeat, there will usually be a missing offbeat, and vice versa. Offbeats at the beginning and end of the line are less strictly controlled; four-beat verse may begin with a beat or with an offbeat, or it may vary between these, as in these lines from John Milton's "L'Allegro" (where *b* indicates the syllables that take a beat):

And young and old come forth to play
   b        b       b       b

On a sunshine holiday,
 b  b     b  b

Till the livelong daylight fail,
 b    b     b    b

Then to the spicy nut-brown ale.
  b       b   b      b

Verse in a triple or ternary rhythm (almost always in four-beat groups) has more double offbeats than single, but it can begin and end with two, one, or no offbeats. When a duple or binary meter begins regularly with an offbeat, it may be labeled "iambic"; when it begins regularly with a beat and ends with an offbeat, it may be labeled "trochaic." When it begins and ends with a beat, it may be termed both "catalectic trochaic" (see CATALEXIS) and *"acephalous" or "headless iambic"; more simply, it is four-beat verse without initial or final offbeats.

Beats are realized by the most prominent rhythmic feature of the lang.—in Eng., by stress. However, not every stressed syllable is perceived as a beat and not every unstressed syllable as an offbeat. Under certain conditions, such as its occurrence between two stresses carrying beats, a stressed syllable can be felt as the rhythmic equivalent of an offbeat. Conversely, an unstressed syllable can, under certain conditions, such as its occurrence between two unstressed syllables functioning as offbeats, be experienced as rhythmically doing duty for a beat. These processes, *demotion and *promotion, are common in Eng. verse and derive from similar rhythmic processes in spoken Eng. They enable the poet to vary the speed and weight of the verse, the former producing a slower rhythm (since the demoted stress is still given emphasis) and the latter a quicker rhythm (since the promoted nonstress is still uttered lightly).

*Scansion of accentual-syllabic verse in terms of beats and offbeats differs from scansion in terms of cl. feet in that it does not assume the verse line to be divided into units determined by the meter. This difference is particularly evident in their accounts of the patterns / / x x and x x / /, which are frequent in Eng. iambic verse. In foot prosody, the former involves the substitution of a trochaic foot for an iambic foot ($| x / | / x | x / | x / |$), and the latter the substitution of a *pyrrhic and a *spondee for two iambs ($| x / | x x | / / | x / |$). In beat prosody, by contrast, the two successive stressed syllables are understood as two beats, and the two unstressed syllables as realizing a double offbeat. By showing the position of the beats, and the composition of the offbeats in the intervals between beats and at the beginning and end of the line, beat scansion indicates the rhythm as perceived by the reader or listener—who may have no training in cl. prosody.

*See* RHYTHMIC FIGURES.

■ W. B. Ker, *Form and Style in Poetry* (1928); G. R. Stewart, *The Technique of English Verse* (1930); J. Malof, "The Native Rhythm of English Meters," *TSLL* 5 (1964); R. Burling, *Man's Many Voices* (1970); G. D. Allen, "The Location of Rhythmic Stress Beats in English," *L&S* 15 (1972); G. Knowles, "The Rhythm of English Syllables," *Lingua* 34 (1974); Attridge, *Rhythms*; E. Couper-Kuhlen, *English Speech Rhythm* (1993); Attridge, *Poetic Rhythm*; Brendan O'Donnell, *The Passion of Meter* (1995)—Wordsworth's use of rhythm; Carper and Attridge; John Creaser, " 'Service Is Perfect Freedom': Paradox and Prosodic Style in *Paradise Lost*," *RES* 58 (2007).

D. ATTRIDGE

**BEAT POETRY** refers to the work of a group of Am. writers from the late 1940s through the mid-1960s. It rejected as claustrophobic and ethically untenable the formalism of the then-dominant *New Criticism, Southern Agrarians, and other movements that stressed the *autonomy of the work of art; its compressed, intricate, and depersonalized nature; and the "dramatic irony" that arose from its internal and strictly textual contradictions. Beat writing strove to achieve a more romantic, though mod., "marriage of Heaven and Hell" through yoking abject subject matter, often of an autobiographical and socially transgressive nature (homosexuality or other nonnormative relationships, illicit drug use, extreme states of mind, the grittiness of everyday street life, rootlessness, urban squalor, and disillusionment), with exalted spiritual aspiration and insight; the term *beat* invokes both beatitude and despair or destitution, being "beat down to [one's] socks," in the words of Herbert Huncke, the petty criminal, drug addict, and gifted raconteur who befriended some of the writers. (Huncke and some of the other Beat writers, members of the Times Square demimonde, participated as subjects in the Kinsey *Report on Sexual Behavior in the Human Male* [1948].) The term *beat* also refers to Af. Am. expressive culture, esp. bebop jazz, whose argot and "way-out" sound were central to the Beat lexicon and aesthetic, though the movement comprised primarily working-class "white ethnics"—first-generation Italian-, Jewish- and other Americans—whose embrace of what they perceived to be an alternative aesthetic and way of life set them apart from the upwardly mobile, conformist culture of the postwar U.S. After U.S. leftism imploded in the 1950s, the Beats embodied a cultural rather than political revolution, though their work drew on politically informed antecedents such as Am. (esp. Walt Whitman) and Br. (esp. William Blake and P. B. Shelley) *romanticism, *surrealism, and *Dadaism—with an added emphasis on Eastern and Western mysticism, the Eur. *poète maudit* tradition, and French existentialism. Contemporaneous and geographically proximate movements that shared a poetics of open, "organic" form, spontaneity, and personal directness include the *New York and *Black Mountain schools on the East Coast, and the *San Francisco Renaissance poets on the West. Although the poetics of the Beats is best known for phrases like "first thought, best thought," "spontaneous bebop prosody," the invention of the cut-up *collage technique, and obscenity trials (most notably that of Allen Ginsberg's *Howl and Other Poems* [1956]), in later years Ginsberg, who had earlier characterized the Beat generation as a "boy-gang," was careful to counter the widespread impression that the Beats were literary barbarians, naming T. S. Eliot, Marcel Proust, and Herman Melville as additional influences. Recent years have also seen a recuperation of women Beats, notably Joanne Kyger, Bonnie Bremser/ Brenda Frazer, Helen Adam, and Hettie Jones.

Key writers and texts include Ginsberg, *Howl* (1956); Jack Kerouac, *On the Road* (1957) and *Mexico*

*City Blues* (1959); Gregory Corso, *Gasoline* (1958); John Wieners, *The Hotel Wentley Poems* (1958); William Burroughs, *Naked Lunch* (1959); Ted Joans, *The Hipsters* (1961); LeRoi Jones/Amiri Baraka, *Preface to a Twenty-Volume Suicide Note* (1961), *Dutchman* (1964), and *The System of Dante's Hell* (1965); Bob Kaufman, *Solitudes Crowded with Loneliness* (1965); Lawrence Ferlinghetti, *A Coney Island of the Mind* (1968); Bremser, *Troia* (1969); Gary Snyder, *Riprap* (1969); Diane di Prima, *Dinners and Nightmares* (1974); Kyger, *Joanne* (1974); Lew Welsh, *Ring of Bone* (1973); also Ray Bremser, Lucien Carr, John Clellon Holmes, Philip Lamantia, Michael McClure, David Meltzer, Alexander Trocchi, ruth weiss, and Philip Whalen. Important jours. included *Beatitude, The Floating Bear, Measure, City Lights Journal, Big Table/Chicago Review, Evergreen Review,* and *Yugen*; presses included Olympia, Totem, Grove Press, City Lights, Black Sparrow, and New Directions. Institutions with Beat foundations include Naropa University's writing program (The Jack Kerouac School of Disembodied Poetics) in Boulder, CO; and the St. Mark's Poetry Project, at St. Mark's Church in the Bowery, New York City.

■ L. Lipton, *Holy Barbarians* (1959); F. Rigney and D. L. Smith, *The Real Bohemia* (1961); M. McClure, *Scratching the Beat Surface* (1982); M. Davidson, *The San Francisco Renaissance* (1989); J. A. Maynard, *Venice West* (1991); *Beat Culture and the New America: 1950–1965,* ed. L. Philips (1995); D. Cándida-Smith, *Utopia and Dissent* (1996); H. Jones, *How I Became Hettie Jones* (1996); S. Clay and R. Phillips, *A Secret Location on the Lower East Side* (1998); D. Belgrad, *The Culture of Spontaneity* (1999); *Breaking the Rule of Cool,* ed. R. Johnson and N. G. Campbell (2004); P. Whaley, *Blows Like a Horn* (2004); Norman Mailer, "Hipsters," *Advertisements for Myself* (2005).

M. DAMON

**BELARUS, POETRY OF.** *See* RUSSIA, POETRY OF.

## BELGIUM, POETRY OF

**I. Dutch.** *See* LOW COUNTRIES, POETRY OF THE.

**II. French.** Med. Belgian lyric poetry underwent important devels.—as much in religious as in *epic, mystical, or courtly genres—in the feudal principalities that were the foundation of the country. Likewise, during the 16th and 17th cs. under the Burgundian dynasty, Chambers of Rhetoric prospered whose trads. of formal *invention and *irony are undoubtedly similar to certain aspects of mod. poetry in Belgium. The production of original poetry, in Fr. as well as in Dutch, declined when the Netherlands, while retaining its constitution, found itself subservient to Madrid or Vienna (1585–1795).

This section concerns the production of poetry in Fr. that began after the Battle of Waterloo (1815) in the territories of the Catholic Netherlands and the Principality of Liège. The contours of a new Europe were being drawn, a Europe in which nationalist revolutions would break out, incl. the Belgian Revolution of 1830. In this setting, the concept of national lit. was affirmed, and the problem of francophone lits. was worked out; in this, the Belgian literary field was not merely a laboratory but the first great incubator, even if those interested in such questions take into account what was happening at the same time in Haiti and Switzerland. In the romantic period, freed from their imposed union with Holland, Belgian poets such as Théodore Weustenraad (1805–49), André van Hasselt (1806–74), and A.C.G. Mathieu (1804–76) used diverse forms of Fr. verse to celebrate the various industrial realizations of its modernity. As early as the 1820s, poets began to take liberties with dominant Fr. literary models, but it was not until the 1880s and 1890s that a distinctive Belgian Fr. poetry emerged, although one related to larger trends in Europe at the end of the century.

Some of these, in the Fr.-speaking world, arose in a country that hist., through its various means, had better prepared than others to break from the cl. Fr. *canon. This condition brought the generation called the *Jeunes Belgique* (Young Belgium) to take over the mysteries of *symbolism, the stylistic audacity of Arthur Rimbaud and the Comte de Lautréamont (both of them published in Belgium), as well as Stéphane Mallarmé's encouragement. They thus asserted a specific literary identity recognized very quickly—and first of all in other countries—without claiming it as a national possession.

Émile Verhaeren (1855–1916) with *Les Campagnes hallucinées* (The Hallucinated Countryside, 1893) and *Les Villes tentaculaires* (The Tentacular Cities, 1895); Georges Rodenbach (1855–98) with *Le Règne du silence* (The Reign of Silence, 1891); Charles van Lerberghe (1861–1907) with *La Chanson d'Ève* (The Song of Eve, 1904); Max Elskamp (1862–1931) with *Dominical* (Sunday Prayer, 1892); and the Nobel laureate Maurice Maeterlinck (1862–1949) with *Serres chaudes* (Hot Houses, 1899) gave to francophone as well as to world lit. works of note and influence. E.g., Antonin Artaud claimed the six *Hot Houses* in verse as an inspiration (see SURREALISM); the It. *Crepuscolari* (Twilight Poets; see ITALY, POETRY OF) would be incomprehensible without Rodenbach's stimulus, as Ger. *expressionism would be without Verhaeren's poetic upheaval.

These innovators distanced themselves from their peers such as Albert Giraud (1860–1929), Iwan Gilkin (1858–1924), and Valère Gille (1867–1950) who wanted to remain faithful to *Parnassianism and to the Fr. trad. These divisions, which persisted a long time, reached to the very heart of the francophone world. The ruptures of World War I and the Rus. Revolution only served to deepen them.

The flourishing of the avant-garde and a new set of exchanges with Paris followed on these beginnings. *Dadaism found a special radicalism in Clément Pansaers (1885–1922), author of *Le Pan-Pan au cul du nu nègre* (Pan-Pan at the Negro Nude's Ass, 1920), who called very early for the end of the movement by its own logic. In Brussels, a surrealist movement appeared around Paul Nougé (1895–1967) as early as 1924—one that has been both compared to and differentiated from the one led by André Breton in Paris at the same time. The group's mistrust of the literary world, the clear distinction between the rules of political activity and those of writing or painting, and the very Belgian refusal to believe the evidence of lang. engendered production fundamental to the hist. of surrealism.

Of a rare quality and impertinence, as well as an exceptional rigor, this aesthetic and ethical endeavor is inscribed in the titles of the two Nougian *summas* collected by Marcel Mariën (1920–93)—*Histoire de ne pas rire* (A Story of Not Laughing, 1956) and *L'Expérience continue* (The Continuous Experience or The Experience Continues, 1966)—and in this precept: "exégètes, pour y voir clair, rayez le mot surréalisme" (exegetes, to see clearly, scratch out the word *surrealism*). Invented and shared by Marcel Lecomte (1900–66), Louis Scutenaire (1905–87), Camille Goemans (1900–60), André Souris (1899–1970), Paul Colinet (1898–1957), Irène Hamoir (1906–94), Édouard Léon Théodore Mesens (1903–71), and René Magritte (1898–1967), this movement unfolded outside any literary milieu, in a sort of inscribed parenthesis and in a filiation or reinvention between Ger. romanticism and revolution. Entirely coherent, this strand is fundamental to those artistic approaches that exhausted all the methods of the time, incl. advertising.

This inclusivity distinguishes Belgian surrealism from the lyricism that characterizes the work of Achille Chavée (1906–69), of Hainaut, who was faithful to the precepts of Fr. surrealism, and of his follower, Fernand Dumont (1906–45), the post-Nervalian surrealist who wrote *La Région du cœur* (The Region of the Heart, 1939) and *La Dialectique du hasard au service du désir* (Dialectic of Chance in the Service of Desire, 1979). There was lyricism, too, in the work of Charles Plisnier (1896–1952), who was also actively engaged on the Left and who found the means of expressing this engagement—which the followers of Nougé rejected—in the form of the spoken *choruses, such as *Odes pour retrouver les hommes* (Odes to Rediscover Men, 1935) and *Sel de la terre* (Salt of the Earth, 1936).

Close to the modernists whose postulates the surrealists violently contested (among these, Pierre Bourgeois [1898–1976], editor of the *Journal des poètes*), Géo Norge (1898–1990), for his part, aims to plunge to the carnal heart of a *Langue verte* (green language) that he celebrates and puts to work with relish in *Les Oignons* (The Onions, 1953) and *Le Vin profond* (The Deep Wine, 1968).

This trust in the Fr. lang. and trad. likewise declined, though with entirely different connotations, in the works of Marcel Thiry (1897–1977), such as *Toi qui pâlis au nom de Vancouver* (You Who Pale at the Name *Vancouver*, 1924). Thiry expressed this lack of faith in *Le Poème et la langue* (The Poem and the Language, 1967) by opposing his vision to that of Henri Michaux (1899–1984), whose plunges into words and traits sought the instinctual, the irrational, and the irregular—in works such as *La Nuit remue* (Darkness Moves, 1935), *L'Infini turbulent* (Infinite Turbulence,

1957), and *Face à ce qui se dérobe* (Facing the Evasive, 1976). Michaux, whose first works were close to those of Goemans, nevertheless held himself at a distance from the surrealists, even if he did dedicate to Magritte one text strongly expressive of the surrealists' mode of being and of doing: *En Rêvant à partir de peintures énigmatiques* (Dreaming from Enigmatic Paintings, 1972). Furthermore, as early as 1924 in the *Transatlantic Review*, he explained how his poetics aimed to differ from that of his Belgian forefathers.

If Thiry led his reader out of the rural world, notably into the various colonies and trading posts of the planet and into industry, it was to this old harmonized world that Maurice Carême (1899–1978), whose texts such as *Mère* (Mother, 1935) and *Petites Légendes* (Little Legends, 1949) are everywhere in primary schools, preferred to return. The tormented universes of Jean de Boschère (1878–1953) are completely different in *Job le pauvre* (Job the Poor, 1923) and *Derniers poèmes de l'obscur* (Last Poems from the Darkness, 1948), whose wild lyricism is that of the aesthete and the *poète maudit*, as such is equally the case of René Verboom (1891–1955) in *La Courbe ardente* (The Burning Curve, 1922) and of Paul Desmeth (1883–1970), whose dandyism is distilled into a book much rewritten, *Simplifications* (1932).

The period after 1945 yielded a poetic scene even more divided than what had preceded it, but it broadened the already excellent diversity of the interwar years. Under the rubric of *La Belgique sauvage*, one could find the various modulations of the avant-garde, groups such as Les Lèvres nues (The Naked Lips), Phantòmas, Daily-Bul, Temps Mêlés (Mixed Times), and Le Vocatif (The Vocative). Internationally, the most prominent such venture was CoBrA (named for Copenhagen–Brussels–Amsterdam), led by Christian Dotremont (1922–79), who transformed an old house in Brussels into a center for collective innovation in both poetry and sculpture. Dedicated to finding the origin of the corporeal, this team (incl. Asger Jorn [1914–73], Karel Appel [1921–2006], and the painters known as Constant [1920–2005] and Corneille [1922–2010]), which stayed together for three years, took a break from relations with the Communist Party and displaced some key objectives of surrealism.

Next Dotremont became involved in the adventure that would lead him, via his travels to Laponia, to the invention in 1962 of logograms. On a blank sheet of paper of variable dimensions, a dancing line of China ink was traced, in the manner of the most personal of writings, which the writer-sculptor next transcribed to the underside of the page, in small penciled letters. This is how the sensory and cognitive simultaneity that haunts a major segment of Belgian poetry was attained and how the author of *De loin aussi d'ici* (From Afar as from Here, 1973) completed his research.

The years after the war also witnessed the devel. of the work of another writer-artist active from the 1920s, Michel Seuphor (1901–99), whom the publisher Rougerie strove to keep in print even as the artist's word paintings proliferated.

Other works, exceptions to the norm, appeared at the edges of the avant-garde. So it was with François Jacqmin (1929–92), an adolescent whom the hazards of the war took from Fr. to Eng., then from Eng. to Fr. In *Les Saisons* (The Seasons, 1979) and *Le Livre de la neige* (The Book of the Snow, 1990), his lucid lang. creates a relationship (to the natural world as to the self) of dissolution and absorption; he emphasizes the conjunction of mistrust and ineluctability inherent in the literary work. Jacqmin's mix of distance and sensibility is not that of Max Loreau (1928–90), the acute commentator of Dotremont and of Michaux and the high-flying philosopher of *La Genèse du phénomène* (The Origin of Phenomena, 1989), whose radical modernity tries to break lang. in order to reintroduce a lyrical celebration of the world: *Cri* (Scream, 1973), *Chants de perpétuelle venue* (Songs of Perpetual Arrival, 1977), *Florence portée aux nues* (Florence on a Pedestal, 1986).

In the next generation, the Belgian members of the Fr. group TXT, Éric Clemens (b. 1945) and Jean Pierre Verheggen (b. 1942), continued this experimentation with lang. Verheggen—author of *Le Degré zorro de l'écriture* (The Zorro Degree of Writing, 1978), *Divan le terrible* (Divan the Terrible, 1979), and *Sodome et Grammaire* (Sodom and Grammar, 2008)—infused his work with a great Rabelaisian character not unfamiliar to the emblem of Belgian letters in the 19th c., Tyl Eulenspiegel. Finally, in the surrealist circle of influence, Tom Gutt (1941–2002) produced some of the most beautiful love poems in Belgian lit.

Still, the desire to conform to Fr. models had not disappeared. It dominated Belgian poetry institutionally in the years after the war. But if this tendency—exemplified by Serge Vandercam (1924–2005), Robert Vivier (1894–1989), Jean Mogin (1921–86), Charles Bertin (1919–2003), Jean Tordeur (1920–2010), and Arthur Haulot (1913–2005)—wanted to combine the internalization of Fr. ideology (and its universality) with the celebration of humanist values destined to conjure up the ghosts of Nazi abjectness, it also led to works that opened a worldwide dialogue. Thus are the cases of Roger Bodart (1910–73) in *Le Nègre de Chicago* (The Negro from Chicago, 1958) and Fernand Verhesen (1913–2009), the smuggler of Latin Am. lits. There was also some beautiful reshuffling of trad.: Philippe Jones's (b. 1924) filtered restitution of sensory evidence; Liliane Wouters's (b. 1930) fusion with the Flemish trad.; and Henry Bauchau's (b. 1913) return to the very old rhythms of lang. in poetic works that constitute the matrix and the tension point of fiction. A unique and admirable work of this generation was Roger Goossens's (1903–54) *Magie familière* (Familiar Magic, 1956).

Likewise, but in a very different way, for the next generation: Sophie Podolski's (1953–74) *Le pays où tout est permis* (The Country Where Everything Is Allowed, 1974) was charred by the universe of repression. During this period, Claire Lejeune (1926–2008), who plunged next into the essay, destined to facilitate the social birth of the poetic, wrote *Mémoire de rien* (Memory of Nothing, 1972), a masterpiece—along with

Françoise Delcarte's (1936–95) *Sables* (Sands, 1969)—of postwar women's poetry, haunted by modernity. This moment also saw William Cliff (b. 1940) charge onto the literary scene with a return to cl. verse in a narrative sequence of the blessings and misfortunes of a homosexual lifestyle (*Homo sum*, 1973); and Eugène Savitzkaya (b. 1955) in *L'Empire* (1976) and *Mongolie plaine sale* (Mongolia, Dirty Plain, 1976), who pulverizes Fr. phrases to let loose verbal hordes.

Off the beaten paths of the avant-garde and strict classicism but trusting in the strengths of poetry, various strands that evolved in the 1970s nevertheless refer to Heideggerian dogma. In *Promenoir magique* (Magical Promenade, 2009), Jean-Claude Pirotte (b. 1939) made concise Fr. the site of his renewal; in Werner Lambersy's (b. 1941) *Maîtres et maisons de thé* (Masters and Tea Houses, 1979) is a response to Asian culture. In Jacques Izoard (1936–2008), we find baroque sensuality surrounded by harsh metrics. In Christian Hubin's (b. 1941) *La Parole sans lieu* (The Word without Place, 1975), there is the dread of the rift and the threshold, while in Frans De Haes's (b. 1948) *Terrasses et Tableaux* (Terraces and Paintings, 2007), we find the pregnancy of the Bible and post-\**Tel Quel* ling. work. Finally, there is the constant interrogation of the absence of the Other in Yves Namur's (b. 1952) *Le Livre des Sept Portes* (The Book of Seven Doors, 1994).

Rooted in the Walloon soil, certain poets produced works that further escaped the effects of the Franco-centric literary world. In *Les Prodiges ordinaires* (The Ordinary Prodigies, 1991), André Schmitz (b. 1929) worked though contraction and attained the density of a carnal tragedy tamed, while Claude Bauwens (b. 1939) follows his white dream of return to the forgetting of oneself in *L'Avant-Mère* (The Pre-Mother, 1975) and Paul André (1941–2008) returns to the magic of a natural being-in-the-world in *C'est* (It is, 1995). Those who, like Guy Goffette (b. 1947) in *Éloge pour une cuisine de province* (Praise for a Provincial Kitchen, 1988) or Lucien Noullez (b. 1957) in *Comme un pommier* (Like an Apple Tree, 1997), left these rural shores far away from centers of cultural recognition, played, all the same, from a different score, a score that their childhoods continued to nourish deeply. This offers them a foundation that distances them from exaggerated \*modernism and \*postmodernism.

François Muir (1955–97), in *La Tentation du visage* (The Temptation of the Face, 1998), did not find these types of relative balance. Essentially published posthumously and completely iridescent, his life's work is—with Schmitz's—the most enigmatic, most consistent, and most intriguing of the last decades.

■ **Anthologies:** *Poètes français de Belgique de Verhaeren au surréalisme*, ed. R. Guiette (1948); *Lyra Belgica*, trans. C. and F. Stillman, 2 v. (1950–51); *Anthologie du surréalisme en Belgique*, ed. C. Bussy (1972); *Panorama de la poésie française de Belgique*, ed. L. Wouters and J. Antoine (1976); *La poésie francophone de Belgique*, ed. L. Wouters and A. Bosquet, 4 v. (1985–).

■ **Criticism and History**: G. Charlier and J. Hanse, *Histoire illustrée des lettres françaises de Belgique* (1958); R. Frickx and R. Burniaux, *La littérature belge d'expression française* (1980); M. Quaghebeur, *Alphabet des lettres belges de langue française* (1982); R. Frickx and R. Trousson, *Lettres françaises de Belgique, Dictionnaire des œuvres*, v. 2: *La Poésie* (1988); A.-M. Beckers, *Lire les écrivains belges*, 3 v. (1985–); C. Berg and P. Halen, *Littératures belges de langue française* (2000); J. P. Bertrand et al., *Histoire de la littérature belge* (2003).

M. QUAGHEBEUR

## BELIEF AND POETRY

I. Classical to Early Modern
II. Early Modern to the Present

**I. Classical to Early Modern**. The question of belief and poetry was posed as such only in the mod. period, but since virtually every narrative or discursive utterance claims some kind of assent, these claims naturally have received critical attention since cl. antiquity. *Classical poetics, beginning from rhetorical principles, characteristically took conventional beliefs and common sense as normative and sought to avoid conflict with them. Since audiences cannot be instructed or delighted by a poem whose premises or claims they actively reject, the poet must secure their acquiescence as efficiently as possible; to this end, Horace gives the advice to "follow convention, or at least be consistent" (*Ars poetica*). Even Aristotle, who trenchantly distinguished poetry from rhet., took the world of common apprehension to be the object of poetic imitation. Conventional beliefs thus stood as the measure not only of incident but of style, design, and character through Gr. and Roman antiquity.

But as Aristotle recognized, implied in even the most straightforwardly rhetorical address were two claims with a longer reach. First, the very aim of rhetorical persuasion supposes that artful speech can shape and alter those conventional beliefs. Cicero's and Quintilian's insistence that eloquence can turn destructive if wisdom does not steer it affirms its power over the mind; in Longinus, this power becomes an aesthetic value apart from any persuasive end it might serve. Second, rhet.'s status as a form of systematic knowledge supposes that there is something systematic, something enduring and natural, about what sways audiences; conventions may thus disclose the intelligible structures of the real. Aristotle treats the "probable" (*eikos*) as the proper object of imitative composition not merely because audiences accept it but because their acceptance reveals it as the locus of poetry's distinctive truth-claims. By its skillful presentation, poetry could precipitate the universal from its dispersal into particulars and present it to view.

In defending poetry as a kind of knowledge, Aristotle answered the powerful crit. of eloquence and *imitation voiced by Plato, who agreed with the rhetoricians that their enterprise was mortgaged to popular judgment and deplored the fact. Plato's *Republic* says that the artist, bound to flatter his audience's judgment, is like a trainer who has become slave to his animals'

whims. He famously argued that imitative art is illusory art, really distancing and coarsening what it seems to present closely and in detail. Poems conspire with popular error to obscure truth; philosophy must work against both, to clarify truth and reform belief. He thus cast both conventional perception and its artistic representation as forms of what later would be called ideology and cast philosophy as its critique. Plato did not explicitly entertain the possibility that imitative art might itself conduct such critique.

Christianity did. Requiring belief in a truth exigent but nonevident and seeking coherent exposition of that truth in the apparent incoherence of the Bible, it devised an account of literary form and *figuration that found in them resources for conducting the critique Plato sought from philosophy and so for reforming belief. The crucial figure is St. Augustine. From Plato, via Plotinus, he borrowed the thought that the empirical world is a "region of dissimilitude" holding the real at bay; from the exegetical principles exemplified by St. Paul (Gal 4:22–31) and developed by Origen and St. Ambrose, he developed an account of figurative expression as *allegory meant to overcome dissimilitude. His *De doctrina christiana* (*On Christian Doctrine*) describes how the abrupt and enigmatic expressive surface of the biblical text, refusing to supply what the mind finds comfortable, forces it to adapt to meanings more vexing and consequential. In the Middle Ages, these techniques of *interpretation became codified as academic procedure (with its most succinct and profound account in Thomas Aquinas, *Summa Theologica* 1q.1a.10) and as a didactic and homiletic device, offering *medieval poetry a means to make both serious and subversive claims to belief. The letter to Can Grande della Scala, controversially attributed to Dante, illustrates how med. thinkers could treat formal biblical exegesis as a model for composition.

**II. Early Modern to the Present**. The med. emphasis on *hermeneutics and the apprehension of difficult truths in poetry were typically rejected by Ren. humanists, who emphasized instead the persuasive power of poetic fictions. That power was modeled on the force of divine inspiration, but it was attributed to the ability of poetry to move the reader through imaginative constructs rather than appealing to the transcendent ground of belief. Defending poetry against the charge of telling lies, Philip Sidney noted that the poet was not constrained to the "bare was" of the historian but nonetheless was incapable of lying because he never claimed to be telling the truth: "what child is there, coming to a play, and seeing Thebes written in great letters upon an old door, doth believe that it is Thebes?" (*Defence of Poesy*, 1595); instead, as J. C. Scaliger put it succinctly, the poet "imitates the truth by fiction" (*Poetices libri septem* [Seven Books of Poetics], 1561).

The Augustinian emphasis on the revelatory power of metaphorical lang. was countered in the Reformation by an interest in the literal or historical meaning of biblical narrative that characterized much Protestant hermeneutics. This historicism at times challenged

Scholastic claims about the ultimate clarity and significance of mystical signs, esp. as those claims depended on belief or revelation rather than historical corroboration and a close reading of the scriptural text. Literary consequences of the Reformers' interest in hist. and referential lang. were mixed. It clearly reinforced the nascent realism underlying develop. of the early novel, but it also led to the Puritans' iconoclastic rejection of metaphorical signs and imaginative expression of all forms.

Ambivalence about the role of belief in reading and interpretation persisted into the neoclassical era, where it often led to increasingly tenuous and contradictory claims about the centrality of belief to the impact of poetry and drama on their readers and audience. Fr. neoclassicists, e.g., often insisted on strict verisimilitude in drama because they feared audiences would not respond to representations of actions on stage if they could not believe those actions were real, at least temporarily and provisionally. Samuel Johnson, on the other hand, defended Shakespeare against Fr. charges that his work was not credible because it lacked such close correspondence to the world. Shakespeare's work is, in fact, a "mirror of life," Johnson claimed, but qualified that assertion by adding ironically that "it is credited with all the credit due to a drama" ("Preface to Shakespeare," 1765).

Johnson's deliberately paradoxical claim underscores the obvious logical problems of trying to defend lit. on the basis of credibility or belief. At the end of the 18th c., Immanuel Kant avoided those problems by significantly shifting the grounds of the argument. He insisted on the purely subjective basis of aesthetic experience, turning attention from mimetic connections between the work and the world to the effect of the work on the audience. Kant claimed that aesthetic judgments of beauty derived from a purely disinterested sense of pleasure and harmony within the mind of the viewer or reader. Effects of belief associated with those experiences were merely projections of subjective feelings "as if" they were properties of objects in the world or direct manifestations of a transcendent or "supersensible" substratum or spirit or reason, which could only be vaguely intuited in our present condition (*Kritik der Urteilskraft* [*Critique of Judgment*], 1790).

The epistemological skepticism that characterized Kant's aesthetics was quickly abandoned by the Ger. idealists, who replaced Kant's "as if" with a metaphysics of presence that treated poetry as a direct manifestation of spirit in matter. The influence of Ger. idealism on Eng. poetics was felt most directly through the work of S. T. Coleridge and his attribution of "organic form" to poetry, but Coleridge still insisted on the importance of an active, vital *imagination that "struggles to idealize and unify" elements of the poetic symbol in the act of perception. Thus, despite his insistence on the metaphysical union of idea and image, or subject and object, in poetry, Coleridge's emphasis on the role of the imagination in reading recalled the paradoxical claims of Sidney and Johnson. Coleridge argued that, to accomplish its ends, poetry must induce in the reader a "willing suspension of disbelief," a state that

inspired the emotive power of belief without a corollary degree of conviction about the truth or credibility of the work of art as a manifestation or imitation of some transcendent truth (*Biographia Literaria*, 1817).

Karl Marx rejected the claims of Ger. idealism and *romanticism, along with the whole realm of the spirit, as ideological illusions masking the material grounds of lived experience, but the idea of a uniquely poetic form of belief persisted in Anglo-Am. poetics. Matthew Arnold defended poetry as offering the emotional satisfaction of belief without the insistence on a specific doctrine or faith as required by religion and without competing with science for rational commitment and empirical verification ("The Study of Poetry," 1880; "Literature and Science," 1882). Such satisfaction was possible, Richards later claimed, because of differences between poetic and ordinary lang. Although statements made by the poem resemble the truth-claims of science and religion, they are, in fact, *"pseudo-statements" that function as part of the "emotive" discourse of poetry, as opposed to the "referential" discourse of science. Richards distinguished between "intellectual belief" and "emotional belief" (1929), and he said that, rather than asking us to suspend disbelief, a successful poem will evoke emotional beliefs that will be held in balance with other emotional beliefs in terms of the poem rather than tested and resolved in the external world.

Similarly, although T. S. Eliot embraced a much more orthodox notion of belief in his later poetry and religious faith, he claimed that poetry is less about the content of the beliefs than about how it feels for one to hold them. Beliefs are merely the raw material of poetry, Eliot said; the poet is more properly concerned with their "emotional equivalents" as expressed in the poem through their *objective correlatives. Together, Eliot and Richards turned poetics away from the question of belief as doctrine or a state of mind and toward the formalist concerns that occupied Am. crit. in the decades following World War II. New Critics such as Brooks, viewing the poem as an autonomous object, argued that poetic statements of belief existed only as dramatic utterances that functioned solely in the context of the poem. As Brooks argued in "Irony as a Principle of Structure" (1949), a poem should so accurately dramatize a situation that "it is no longer a question of our beliefs, but of our participation in the poetic experience" (see NEW CRITICISM).

In the 1970s, *poststructuralism extended this paradoxical, self-referential, highly qualified status of belief in poetry into a sweeping critique of metaphysical foundations in all forms of discourse. Derrida attributed the claims of belief in philosophy and religion, e.g., to the same self-cancelling properties of lang. traditionally associated with poetic tropes. Foucault and new varieties of Marxian analysis (e.g., Jameson and Louis Althusser) similarly portrayed belief along with more general categories of truth and meaning as mere effects of power produced by the discursive regulation of society. In de Certeau's terms, belief was thus "exhausted" of its content and could best be characterized by the subject's investment in the propositional "act" of making a statement and considering it as true. The result, de Certeau says, is an extension of the constitutive power of narrative beyond the traditional self-referential boundaries of literary fiction to create a *société récitée*, a society of stories in which belief is constituted through an endless citation and recitation of fictional propositions that create a simulacrum of the real. For Bourdieu, one of the most important stories told by society is that of art itself; he argued that the author, the work, and their critics and supporters were inextricably implicated in a field of cultural production that creates and sustains a "circle of belief" in the value and significance of art in society.

Critics of poststructuralism often condemned this rejection of any transcendent content for belief as antihumanist nihilism, but even among the poststructuralists, many theorists remained profoundly interested in the subjective experience of belief as a product of the individual's engagement with lang. and lit. in particular. Derrida argued that, prior to any specific philosophical content, "poetry and literature provide or facilitate 'phenomenological' access to what makes of a thesis *a thesis as such* a nonthetic experience of the thesis, of belief." In his later work, Derrida often focused on a nonfoundational form of "spectral" belief derived from theology and metaphysics but closely resembling the self-conscious illusions of traditional poetics. Similarly, Vattimo (1985) described the experience of belief as what Martin Heidegger called the *Zeigen* or "showing" of poetic lang., an entirely provisional event in time contrary to the constraints and finality of metaphysical certainty. This interest in belief as a dimension of the reader's interaction with lang. could also be found in the reader-oriented analysis of *Rezeptionstheorie* in the work of Iser and Jauss, with its debt to the hermeneutic theory of Friedrich Schleiermacher and other Ger. theologians. It also reflects the more general renewal of religious themes in contemp. phenomenology, esp. in conjunction with lang. as in the work of Ricoeur.

In the latter half of the 20th c., there was a renewed interest (by Abrams, Fraser, and Scott) in poets for whom belief was a central theme. A wide range of theorists revived the traditional poetical question of whether the relation between the poetic work and the world beyond it can best be described as "epiphanic" (Taylor) or "iconic" (Marion). Alternately, Bloom redefined belief in psychoanalytical terms as an agonistic struggle for creative autonomy in which the poet is willing to "ruin the sacred truths to fable and old song," to disbelieve in those truths and so make possible a belief in himself as "a sect of one" (see INFLUENCE). The result would be a form of subjectivity that transcends poststructuralist nihilism and confounds distinctions between literary meaning and religious belief. Arguing that there can be no reasoning or belief without words, the neopragmatist Rorty generalized Bloom's definition of the strong poet as a creator of new langs. to argue that reading poetry makes us more fully human by enriching vocabularies and lang. as a tool for coping with reality. Rorty's claim, in turn, led Poirier to argue that

neopragmatism is "essentially a poetic theory" about how belief is contingent upon poetics.

This attention to the experience of belief among Rorty, Poirier, and other neopragmatists such as West and Mailloux is only one part of the so-called religious or theological turn in critical theory at the beginning of the 21st c. Renewed interest in the efficacy and significance of belief and religion extended well beyond the concerns of traditional poetics and encompassed many different theoretical and philosophical movements. In response to what Vattimo called *pensiero debole* (weak thought) or the general "thinning out" of belief in contemp. society, MacIntyre, Hauerwas, Milbank, and other so-called New Traditionalists attempted to defend traditional beliefs—particularly those of the Aristotelian-Thomistic trad.—against secular liberalism (cf. Stout). According to the New Traditionalists, mod. liberal democracies undermine traditional beliefs and narratives and, as a result, make it impossible to sustain the virtues necessary to confront any major ethical-moral challenge. Conversely, in a book-length debate on belief between the neo-Marxist, Lacanian atheist Slavoj Žižek and the Anglo-Catholic theologian Milbank, Žižek insisted that Milbank's beliefs are illusions; but, following Badiou, Žižek argued that illusions can be useful for militant revolutionary politics if the revolutionaries believe in them. This emphasis on the pragmatic efficacy of belief apart from any transcendent or doctrinal content thus returned the political and philosophical dispute to its literary origins and the "willing suspension of disbelief" that grants tremendous power to poetry but protects literary illusions from the specious certainty of metaphysical delusion.

*See* EXEGESIS, FORMALISM, MIMESIS, NEOCLASSICAL POETICS, PHILOSOPHY AND POETRY, READER, RELIGION AND POETRY, RENAISSANCE POETICS, RHETORIC AND POETRY, ROMANTIC AND POSTROMANTIC POETRY AND POETICS.

■ I. A. Richards, "Poetry and Beliefs," *Science and Poetry* (1926); and *Practical Criticism* (1929); T. S. Eliot, *The Use of Poetry and the Use of Criticism* (1933); H.-I. Marrou, *Saint Augustin et la fin de la culture antique* (1939); Brooks, "The Heresy of Paraphrase," "The Problem of Belief and the Problem of Cognition," "The Well Wrought Urn" (1947); W. J. Rooney, *The Problem of Poetry and Belief in Contemporary Criticism* (1949); Eliot, *Essays*, "Dante"; M. Heidegger, "Der Ursprung des Kunstwerkes" (1935), *Gesamtausgabe*, v. 5 (1950); M. C. Brooks, "Irony as a Principle of Structure," *Literary Opinion in America*, ed. M. D. Zabel (1951); Wellek, v. 1: *The Later Eighteenth Century*; *Literature and Belief*, ed. M. H. Abrams (1958); Heidegger, "Die Sprache" (1950), *Unterwegs zur Sprache* (1959); Weinberg; D. W. Robertson Jr., *A Preface to Chaucer* (1962); P. Courcelle, *Les Confessions de Saint Augustin dans la tradition littéraire: antécédents et postérité* (1963); E. Auerbach, *Literary Language and Its Public in Late Antiquity and in the Middle Ages*, trans. R. Manheim (1965); J. Derrida, *La voix et le phénomène*

(1967); M. Foucault, *L'archéologie du savoir* (1969); W. Iser, *The Implied Reader* (1974); P. Bourdieu, "*La production de la croyance,*" *Actes de la recherche en sciences sociales* 13 (1977); M. De Certeau, *L'invention du quotidien* (1980); F. Jameson, *The Political Unconscious* (1981); H. R. Jauss, *Toward an Aesthetic of Reception*, trans. T. Bahti (1982); R. Rorty, *Consequences of Pragmatism* (1982); A. MacIntyre, *After Virtue* (1984); H. Fraser, *Beauty and Belief* (1985); N. Scott, *The Poetics of Belief* (1985); G. Vattimo, *La fine della modernità* (1985); C. West, *The American Evasion of Philosophy* (1989); H. Bloom, *Ruin the Sacred Truths* (1989); S. Hauerwas and W. Willimon, *Resident Aliens* (1989); C. Taylor, *Sources of the Self* (1989); J. Milbank, *Theology and Social Theory* (1990); P. Ricoeur, "Expérience et langage dans le discours religieux," *Phénoménolgie et théologie*, ed. J.-F. Courtine (1991); R. Poirier, *Poetry and Pragmatism* (1992); J. Derrida, "Foi et savoir: les deux sources de la 'religion' aux limites de la simple raison," *La religion*, ed. J. Derrida and G. Vattimo (1996); G. Vattimo, *Credere di credere* (1996); A. Badiou, *Saint Paul* (1997); J.-L. Marion, *Etant donné* (1997); Henri de Lubac, *Medieval Exegesis: The Four Senses of Scripture*, trans. M. Sebanc, 4 v. (1998); S. Hauerwas, *With the Grain of the Universe* (2001); S. Žižek, *On Belief* (2001); J. Stout, *Democracy and Tradition* (2004); S. Mailloux, *Disciplinary Identities* (2006); S. Žižek and J. Milbank, *The Monstrosity of Christ* (2009).

M. Krieger; S. Justice (Cl. to Early Mod.); M. P. Clark, T. K. Sung (Early Mod. to Present)

**BENGALI POETRY.** The Bengali lang., or Bangla, is a New Indo-Aryan speech of the northeastern part of the Indian subcontinent. The hist. of Bengali lang. and lit. closely links it to the neighboring Assamese, Oriya, and, to a lesser extent in the mod. period, to Maithili. Except for a few commentaries composed in Assam in the 16th c. CE, prose was not used in Bengali lit. before the 18th c.

The first poems in proto-Bengali were preserved in the collection of the *Caryā* songs composed by Buddhist saints in the 11th c. CE. Discovered in 1907 in Nepal, the Caryā songs were not known by later premod. Bengali authors.

Premod. Bengali poetry may be divided into short and long forms. Both forms contained lyrical aspects; performance was a central feature of their composition. The Bengali narrative verse par excellence from the 14th c. is the *payāra*. The payāra is a syllabic meter of 14 feet with a *caesura after the eighth that follows a plain rhyme scheme (*aa, bb, cc* . . . ). Lyrical and descriptive passages are usually composed in *tripadī*, a slightly more complex verse with two caesurae and an internal rhyme. Tripadīs are also arranged in *distichs with the same rhyming pattern as the payāra. Short forms usually use tripadī and other meters borrowed from Sanskrit.

The short forms, or *padas*, heavily drew on the subject of the love between Kṛṣṇa, the incarnation of the Hindu god Viṣṇu, and the cowherd Rādhā. Each poem is a vignette treating one episode of their relationship. Thus, the poem belongs to a wider narra-

tive frame from which it derives its meaning and character. The main themes are love in union (*sambhoga*) and love in separation (*viraha*). The models of this lit. lie in the Sanskrit *Gītagovinda* of Jayadeva (12th c.) and the Maithili poems of Vidyāpati Ṭhākura (14th c.). Caṇḍīdāsa, who composed the *Śrīkṛṣṇakīrtana* (ca. 14th c.), is the first Bengali poet known to have used this theme. The love between Rādhā and Kṛṣṇa illustrated both the mundane ideal of courtly love and the spiritual stages of the devotee. From the 16th c. onward, with the devel. of the sect founded by Caitanya (1486–1533), a rich lit. was composed on this theme. The love between Rādhā and Kṛṣṇa became the archetype of the amatory relationship in Bengali poetry; moreover, Muslim authors also composed poetry in this vein.

Long forms are mainly represented by the *pācāli* tradition. The term *pācāli* refers to a mode of performance combining the declamation of a narrative poem interspersed with more lyrical parts accompanied by music and dance. The first pācālis were adaptations from Sanskrit lit. The *Rāmāyaṇa* of Kṛttivāsa (ca. 15th c.) or Mālādhara Vasu's *Śrīkṛṣṇavijaya* (The Victory of Lord Kṛṣṇa) were pācālis of this kind. Some typical texts of Bengal called *mangalakāvya*s (propitiatory poems) narrate how a goddess imposed her worship among humans in the region. The hagiographic work entitled *Caitanyacaritāmṛta* of Kṛṣṇadāsa Kavirāja (ca. 1517–1615)—about the life and doctrine of Caitanya—pertained to some extent to the poetics of the pācāli. Muslim poets such as Saiyad Sultān (fl. 1584) adapted stories of the prophets of Islam from the Persian and Ar. using the same form. Similarly, other poets like Ālāol (fl. 1651–71) who lived in Arakan, in mod. Myanmar, translated and adapted Hindi and Persian Sufi romances into Bengali. Other important themes of pācāli poetry are the stories of mythic figures like Satyapīra who belong to both Hindu and Islamic cultures in Bengal.

While premod. poetical forms continue today, Bengali poetry underwent major changes during the 18th and early 19th cs. Bhāratacandra (1712–60) was a clerk and a court poet who integrated historical themes in the pācāli trad. In the early 19th c., Michael Madhusudan Dutt (1824–73), a polyglot poet and dramatist familiar with both Indian and Western cl. langs. and lits., introduced *blank verse into Bengali as well as the *sonnet. He composed the *Meghanādavadha kāvya* (The Slaying of Meghanāda, 1861), an *epic poem resorting to the poetics of Gr. tragedy but based on an episode of the Sanskrit *Rāmāyaṇa*.

The versatile author of thousands of poems and songs Rabindranath Tagore (1861–1941), known as the "universal poet" (*viśvakavi*), is a landmark of mod. Bengali poetry. He was awarded the Nobel Prize in 1913 for an Eng. version of his Bengali *Gitanjali* (Song Offerings, 1910). Tagore reshaped traditional topoi through his distinctive genius, thus illustrating the larger dynamics at work in the Bengali literary trad. between the end of the 19th and the first decades of the 20th cs. The Indian and Bangladeshi national *anthems are songs composed by Tagore.

Kazi Nazrul Islam (1899–1976), the "rebel poet" (*vidrohī kavi*), was also a prolific songwriter. The themes of his poetry are variegated. He translated Persian poems of Ḥāfiẓ (1315–89) and composed devotional works dedicated to several Hindu gods and goddesses, as well as powerful nationalist poems. As opposed to that of Tagore, Nazrul's poetry maintains a poetics of chaos and confusion from which a certain creative energy ensues.

Jibananda Das (1899–1954) is the third landmark in the hist. of mod. Bengali poetry. His poems reveal a "complexity" (*jaṭilatā*) in the poet's relation to the world. His conception of poetry as utterly shaped by individual subjectivity—a kind of hermeticism—opposed him to Tagore's universalism and prompted crit. by the followers of an ideologically committed poetry.

In the 1930s, various progressive writers shifted from Tagore's model and engaged in poetic dialogues with his oeuvre. Chief among them is Buddhadeva Bose (1908–74), who devoted several works to the interrogation of Tagore's poetry and composed poems inverting his images. Other poets such as Amiya Chakrabarti (1901–86), Sudhindranath Dutta (1901–60), and Bishnu Dey (1909–82), who did not form a homogenous group, represent different modernist attitudes of the period surrounding World War II.

The independence of India and Pakistan in 1947 marked an important turn in the hist. of Bengali poetry. Dhaka, the capital of East Pakistan, became an alternative to Calcutta as an intellectual center.

Poets of East Bengal expressed a need for a proper identity. During "the language movement" in 1952 up to the independence of Bangladesh in 1971, Bengali poetry became the privileged medium of the nationalist claims of the people of East Pakistan. A variety of voices reflecting the multiple options for the building of a Bangladeshi national identity appear in the poetry of that period. Among them, Shamsur Rahman (1929–2006) was the most influential figure. In his hymn-like poems, his voice melds with the song of freedom and independence of the people of Bangladesh. Jibananda Das's approach to poetry also had a strong influence on the prominent Bangladeshi poet Al-Mahmud (b. 1936). In West Bengal, poetry took a strong ideological turn with the growth of Marxism and the Naxalite movement. Among the noticeable poets of West Bengal of the 1970s and contemp. period are Sunil Gangopadhyay (b. 1934) and Jay Goswami (b. 1954).

■ *A Tagore Reader*, ed. A. Chakrabarti (1961); *The Thief of Love*, trans. E. C. Dimock (1963)—Bengali tales; S. Sen, *History of Bengali Literature* (1979); A. K. Banerjee, *History of Modern Bengali Literature* (1986); C. B. Seely, *A Poet Apart* (1990)—on Jibananda Das; R. Tagore, *Selected Poems*, trans. W. Radice, rev. ed. (1994); "Bengali," *Medieval Indian Literature*, ed. K. A. Paniker, v. 1 (1997); *Voices from Bengal*, trans. and ed. M. Bandyopadhyay et al. (1997); Kṛṣṇadāsa Kavirāja, *The Caitanya Caritāmṛta*, ed. T. K. Stewart, trans. E. C. Dimock, (1999); *Fabulous Women and Peerless Pīrs*, trans. T. K. Stewart (2004); M. M. Dutt, *The Slaying of Meghanada*, trans. C. B. Seely (2004); P. K. Mitra, *The Dissent of Nazrul Islam* (2007).

T. d'Hubert

**BESTIARY.** The bestiary or book of beasts (*liber bestiarum*) is a med. collection of animal stories, written in both Lat. and in the principal vernacular langs. of Western Europe and normally but not always decorated with illustrations. The oldest surviving examples date from the early 10th c., but most of the extant versions were produced in the late 12th and 13th cs. The bestiary is derived from Lat. trans. of the Gr. *Physiologus*, named after its supposed compiler (the Naturalist), and written sometime between the 2d and 4th cs. CE, possibly in Alexandria. Like the bestiary, the *Physiologus* exists in a number of different versions. Purportedly drawn from observation but actually derived from works of natural hist., as well as myth, legend, and fable, the *Physiologus* describes the characteristics of animals, birds, serpents, and insects that are then moralized and used as a vehicle for revealing Christian truths. The bestiary is similar in form to the *Physiologus* but greatly expands the number of both real and imaginary animals that are included and interpolates material from other sources, most notably the *Etymologiae* of Isidore of Seville and the *Hexameron* of St. Ambrose. Like the *Physiologus*, the bestiary assumes that the natural world can be read as a divinely inscribed book and that the characteristics of animals provide a set of lessons for the edification of humanity. Thus, the lion symbolizes the resurrection because it revives its cubs (which are born dead) by blowing into their faces three days after their birth, while the beaver acts as an exhortation to clean living by biting off its own testicles (which are prized for their medicinal qualities) when pursued by a hunter.

Bestiaries provide some of the finest examples of med. ms. illustration, with the most luxurious and expensively produced copies created in England in the early 13th c. While the bestiary reached its apogee at that time, Ren. writers continued to use it as a rich source of images and metaphors (e.g., King Lear condemns his "pelican daughters," a metaphor drawn from the bestiary pelican that brings its young back to life by feeding them with its blood). The bestiary survives in such traditional and proverbial lore as "to lick into shape" (derived from the bear that was said to give form to her cubs by licking them after they are born as shapeless lumps of flesh) and the phoenix that rises from the ashes.

■ *The Bestiary*, ed. M. R. James (1928); F. McCulloch, *Medieval Latin and French Bestiaries*, rev. ed. (1962); B. Rowland, *Animals with Human Faces* (1974); *Physiologus*, trans. M. J. Curley (1979); X. Muratova, *I manoscritti miniati del bestiario medievale* (1985); *Birds and Beasts of the Middle Ages*, ed. W. B. Clark and M. T. McMunn (1989); D. Hassig, *Medieval Bestiaries: Text, Image, Ideology* (1995).

D. Salter

**BHAKTI POETRY.** See India, poetry of.

**BIBLICAL POETRY.** *See* HEBREW POETRY; HEBREW PROSODY AND POETICS; HYMN; PSALM.

**BIEDERMEIER.** A term first used around 1855 to refer ironically to the smug, philistine, and petty-bourgeois mentality and writing style frequently encountered in South Germany and Austria in the period 1815–48. Soon after 1900, *Biedermeier* began to be used descriptively as a period term referring to the style of furniture and fashions of dress prevalent in Central Europe and Scandinavia during the first half of the 19th c.; the painting of Carl Spitzweg and Ferdinand Waldmüller was considered typical of this stylistic mode, as well as the poetic realism and idyllic nostalgia of Ger.-lang. writers such as Eduard Mörike, Adalbert Stifter, Ferdinand Raimund, Johann Nestroy, Franz Grillparzer, and Annette von Droste-Hülshoff (see GERMAN POETRY).

Historical observation shows that features such as resignation and contentedness, idyllic intimacy and domestic peace, conservatism, morality and lack of passion, innocent drollery, and a mixture of dreamy idealism and realistic devotion to detail characterize many writers of the Biedermeier period. However, this poetry is also placed in multiple and complex dialectical relationships with that of writers who emphasized the dynamics of political and social progress, irony, and revolution. Together and in contrast, Mörike and Heinrich Heine express and define a common sociocultural situation. Additionally, the Biedermeier surface of coziness and satisfaction often overlays doubt, oneiric demonism, uncertainty, and ambiguity, which also have to be considered integral parts of Biedermeier writing. Ultimately *romanticism, the Fr. Revolution, and the social upheavals of the Napoleonic age, along with the period of compromise and constriction that succeeded them, created a state of affairs in which a sense of loss, a search for security, individualism, an ironic or tragicomic worldview, and national, political, and social reform could emerge and interact. These features referred back to a common absent center—the idealized heroic age of romanticism and revolution—with the result that Biedermeier writers feel marked by the problematic and the epigonal, a situation to which they respond in a variety of ways, from realistic action to amused or melancholy contemplation.

Ultimately, the background of the cultural events in these decades is not political or economic but informational. The overwhelming increase of available scientific data on the universe, on nature and the human world (in astronomy, in the life sciences, in geography and history, in physics and chemistry, in sociology and psychology), and the multitude of new philosophical and ideological theories obliged writers to devise images, theories, and patterns that would provide synthetic, restful, tranquilizing, and aesthetic solutions for the normality of existence.

The Biedermeier itself as a cultural phenomenon is perhaps limited to Central Europe, but its complex intermeshing with a given intellectual, cultural, and historical situation finds close analogues in the France of Victor Hugo, Alfred de Musset, Alphonse de Lamartine, and Alfred Vigny; and in the Eastern Europe of Adam Mickiewicz, Juliusz Słowacki, and Alexander Pushkin. More than echoes of Biedermeier mentality can be found in the writings of Walter Scott and Jane Austen, of Leigh Hunt and Charles Lamb, and in the ideology of William Cobbett, as well as across the Atlantic in the amiable prose of Washington Irving.

Biedermeier provides a useful if somewhat vague explanatory framework for discussions of poetry in the early 19th c. At the same time, it relates in an interesting way to romanticism, as *rococo does to *baroque or *postmodernism does to *modernism.

■ M. Greiner, *Zwischen Biedermeier und Bourgeoisie* (1953); G. Böhmer, *Die Welt des Biedermeier* (1968); *Zur Literatur der Restaurationsepoche*, ed. J. Hermand and M. Windfuhl (1970); F. Sengle, *Biedermeierzeit*, 3 v. (1971–80); *Begriffsbestimmung des literarischen Biedermeier*, ed. E. Neubuhr (1974); V. Nemoianu, *The Taming of Romanticism* (1984); G. Schildt, *Aufbruch aus der Behaglichkeit: Deutschland im Biedermeier 1815–1847* (1989); C. Herin, "Biedermeier," *Geschichte der deutschen Lyrik*, ed. W. Hinderer, 2d ed. (2001); *Zwischen Goethezeit und Realismus: Wandel und Spezifik in der Phase des Biedermeier*, ed. M. Titzmann (2002); *Biedermeier: Die Erfindung der Einfachheit*, ed. H. Ottomeyer et al. (2006); V. Nemoianu, *The Triumph of Imperfection* (2006).

V. P. NEMOIANU

**BINARY AND TERNARY.** The mod. terms for what used to be called, with considerable inconsistency of usage, "duple" (or "double") and "triple" meter(s). Binary meters have two members per *foot, as in *iambic and *trochaic (also *pyrrhic and spondaic if one recognizes these as admissible meters), while ternary meters have three, as in anapestic and dactylic (or amphibrachic or *cretic). The distinction between two-membered feet and three- is ancient, despite the facts that the basis of cl. Gr. metrics (*quantity) is different from that of the mod. langs. (stress; see ACCENT) and that, despite the retention of cl. names for mod. feet, the generic registers of binary and ternary meters from ancient times to mod. have almost exactly reversed: in Gr., anapestic meter was used for serious and lofty subjects (the *epic), and the iambic for lighter subjects; but in the mod. meters, the opposite is true: iambic is the meter of *heroic verse.

In the quantitative theory of *classical prosody, the members of the intralinear metrical units (feet) have definite durational relations to each other (see DURATION): a long is by convention equivalent to two shorts. Similarly, in mod. "musical" theories of *meter (Sidney Lanier, Morris Croll, J. W. Hendren; see Brogan), stresses are claimed to be double the temporal value of their opposites, and intervals are made isochronous; hence, the iambic foot has three "times" (equal to three shorts) and so is said to be in "triple time," and triple meters are in "duple time" (their three members adding up to four "times," a compound of two). Omond, however, for whom time is the basis of meter but speech syllables are too variable to have definite durations as in music, holds that iambic and trochaic are "duple meters" and in "duple time," i.e., the time required for two average syllables (he lets pauses fill gaps) and that ternary feet are "triple meters" in "triple time." But this contrariety of terms between musical and nonmusical temporal theories of meter seems pointless to those mod. metrists who are not timers: for them, it is only the number of members (syllables) in the foot that matters.

The usefulness if not the necessity of the distinction between binary and ternary arises from the widely acknowledged fact that the distribution of the one class of meters differs from that of the other, even beyond the fact that the former is far more prevalent than the latter: ternary meters are often said to have a different felt cadence, or *rhythm, from binary, hence to be suitable for a different range of subjects—often light-hearted, humorous, rollicking, satirical. What this means is that, in mod. verse, generic constraints are differentially assigned in part by metrical class, hence that this distinction is one valid plane of cleavage in metrical theory.

Further, it is disputed whether the meters within each class are, in fact, distinct meters: iambic and trochaic are said by some to be interchangeable or at least interrelated via rhythms established by word shapes: particularly interesting is the case of iambo-trochaic tetrameters known as *8s and 7s* (see RISING AND FALLING RHYTHM). In Eng., though binary meters appear in early ME, definite ternary meters appear only in the Ren., and even then only sporadically—Ker relates them to *tumbling verse, as in works by Thomas Tusser, and remarks that they are "almost always" the product of a musical tune—effectively, they are not common at all until the later 18th c. (Thomas Gray's "Amatory Lines," John Gay, Oliver Goldsmith) and by far the majority of examples are from the 19th c. (Lord Byron's "Destruction of Sennacherib"; Walter Scott; Alfred, Lord Tennyson's *Maud* and "Charge of the Light Brigade"; Robert Browning's "Saul"; A. C. Swinburne). And ternary meters are notoriously difficult to differentiate in running series, esp. when line ends are irregular and unpredictable: the sequence x / xx / xx / xx / may be felt as anapestic tetrameter with a missing first syllable, but it can also be amphibrachic with a missing final syllable. Schipper indicates the syllabic ambiguities in ternary meters by treating them as "iambic-trochaic" and "trochaic-dactylic," remarking that "the rising and falling rhythms are not strictly separated but frequently intermingle and even supplement one another." Finally, it appears that there may be intermediate stages between these classes, via the admission of extra (unelidable) syllables into binary meters. But this question, which entails the concept of *accentual verse, is too complex to be undertaken here (see Weismiller).

■ Schipper, v. 2, sects. 224–41; T. S. Omond, *A Study of Metre* (1903), esp. 49, 52; Schipper, *History*, ch. 14; W. P. Ker, *Form and Style in Poetry* (1928); K. Taranovski, *Ruski dvodelni ritmovi* (1953); G. Saintsbury, *Prosody*, v. 3, App. 3; A. T. Breen, "A Survey of the Development of Poetry Written in Trisyllabic Metres to 1830,"

diss., Nat. Univ. of Ireland (1965); E. R. Weismiller, "Studies of Verse Form in the Minor English Poems," *A Variorum Commentary on the Poems of John Milton*, ed. M. Y. Hughes, v. 2 (1972); D. L. Hascall, "Triple Meters in English Verse," *Poetics* 12 (1974); M. L. Gasparov, *Sovremennyj russkij stix* (1974); Brogan; M. L. Gasparov, *Ocerk istorii russskogo stixa* (1984); Scherr; M. G. Tarlinskaja, "Meter and Language: Binary and Ternary Meters in English and Russian," *Style* 21 (1987); and "Triple Threats to Duple Meter," *Rhythm and Meter*, ed. P. Kiparsky and G. Youmans (1989); Morier, "Binaire."

T.V.F. BROGAN

## BIOGRAPHY AND POETRY

I. History
II. Value to Readers and Interpreters

**I. History.** Biographies of poets have been written in all major cultures, and literary trads. of detailed lives of poets, located in a specific place, society, and historical moment, emerged independently in Europe, China, and, some centuries later, the Islamic world. In Europe, probably the earliest known biographies of any poet are the imaginative reconstructions of the life of Homer, written in ancient Greece. These were followed by further biographies of poets who wrote in Gr. and Lat., and, in the med. period, in the Romance langs. After around the 17th c., biographies of poets were written in most major Eur. langs.

**A.** *Non-European Traditions.* Ancient Jewish trad. made no effort to write biographies of the authors of the poetry in the Heb. Bible, instead attributing those poems to figures famous for their political and military acts; thus, Solomon was identified as the author of the Song of Songs and David as author of the Psalms. Biographies exist of ancient Chinese and Japanese poets, but the earliest of these biographies tend to focus on the poets' careers as soldiers or courtiers, treating their writings almost incidentally (see CHINA, POETRY OF; JAPAN, POETRY OF). On the Indian subcontinent, ancient trads. often describe as the work of one poet (who may or may not have had a historical existence) a large body of poems that may have been written over many centuries by many anonymous poets but that shared a recognizable set of stylistic and philosophical tendencies (see SANSKRIT POETRY).

In Islamic lit., lives of poets, often in the form of collections, began to be written (usually in verse) around the 10th c. Samarqandi (12th c.) seems to be one of the earliest biographers; having failed to win distinction as a poet, he wrote lives, apparently based on oral trad., of poets he admired. Other Islamic authors wrote collections of saints' lives that included poets who were revered as much for their religious as for their literary merits, e.g., the poet Rūmī. Lives of Islamic poets were sometimes prepared by a later ed. of their poems, e.g., the life of the Persian national poet Firdawsī (10th c.), written perhaps four centuries after his death (see PERSIAN POETRY).

**B.** *European Traditions through the Eighteenth Century.* Ancient biographies of Homer, notably the *Life of Homer*, falsely attributed to Herodotus, seem to be entirely fanciful. The incidents they describe were evidently invented to explain Homer's knowledge of places and events in the Homeric epics or to explain the origin of some verse fragments formerly attributed to Homer. Other biographies of poets in the cl. era tend to be historical or thematic accounts of their work. A life of Virgil, attributed to Suetonius and written perhaps a century after the poet's death, lists and describes Virgil's work, incl. epigrams not otherwise attributed to him, but says little or nothing about his motives for writing them.

In Christian Europe until around the 13th c., an author was understood to be (at least in part) a vessel for divine inspiration. A poet's life, when written about at all, tended to be seen in the same conventionalized terms as med. saints' lives. A more individualizing approach emerged in the *vidas and *razos that appeared in some late 13th- and early 14th-c. *chansonniers*, or collections of poems by *troubadours; and by the mid-14th c., the character of a poet was often understood to shape his work, whether that work was devoted to sacred or amatory themes (see POET). Giovanni Boccaccio's *Trattatello in laude di Dante* (*Life of Dante*, 1351) includes, among a general account of poetry in its relation to cl. mythology and the Bible, an account of Dante's character that emphasizes his unique combination of qualities, incl. his haughtiness, political passions, and lustfulness. When Boccaccio considers alternate interpretations of Dante's *Divina commedia*, he justifies his preferred readings by citing personal characteristics of Dante that tend to confirm those readings. Extending and deepening the interpretative techniques of the razos, this is among the earliest cases in which a critic uses biographical information to interpret the meaning of a vernacular poem, not merely as an explanation of the events that prompted it to be written.

During the next centuries, some national lits. produced far more biographies of poets than others. At two extremes were Spain, which produced almost no poets' biographies until the 19th c., and England, which developed a lively biographical trad. as early as the 17th c. Izaak Walton's *The Lives of Dr. John Donne, Sir Henry Wotton, Mr. Richard Hooker [and] Mr. George Herbert* (1670) contains lengthy accounts of these writers' hists. and characters; their poems are described as incidents in their public lives rather than, as in later trads., the product of their inner thoughts and impulses.

The first systematic set of biographies of a nation's poets was Samuel Johnson's four volumes of *Prefaces, Biographical and Critical, to the Works of the English Poets* (1779–81), which included 52 biographies varying widely in length and depth. These essays were written not as biographies but as prefaces to selections of the poets' works; however, they were marketed as biographies in an early reprint ed., *The Lives of the Most Eminent English Poets* (1781). In telling the life of a poet, Johnson typically described the initial impulses and influences that led the poet to begin writing poems, then described the hist. of the poet's works and his relations with patrons and publishers, and followed this with a critical account of the poet's work. He generally did not attempt to integrate biography and crit. and, except in a few paragraphs in his long life of Milton, seldom explored the inner impulses that prompted a poet to write discrete works.

**C.** *Romantic and Modern Traditions.* Writers in the romantic era and after focused their attention on the inner life of poets in a new way. William Wordsworth, in his posthumously pub. autobiographical work *The Prelude: The Growth of a Poet's Mind* (1805, pub. 1850), recounted, among much else, the devel. of his moral and literary attitudes and their relation to his emotional experiences in childhood and youth. During the romantic period, biographies were written about poets from all earlier periods, ranging far beyond the century and a half covered by Johnson; e.g., in 1822, the Ger. poet and scholar Ludwig Uhland published *Walther von der Vogelweide*, perhaps the first biographical account of a med. poet.

Until the romantic period, eds. and collections of shorter poems by individual poets were generally arranged according to form or genre or in a sequence arranged for aesthetic effect, with the best-known poems placed first or last; rarely, if ever, were such eds. arranged in chronological order of composition. During the 19th c., poets began to encourage biographical readings of their poems by arranging them in chronological sequence. Wordsworth evidently considered but rejected a chronological sequence for his two collected eds., *Poems, in Two Volumes* (1807) and *Poems* (1815); but the 1815 ed. included a chronological listing of his poems that encouraged a biographical understanding of his career. When Mary Shelley edited the first posthumous collection of P. B. Shelley's poems (1839), she arranged many of the poems by year of composition. Alfred, Lord Tennyson's retrospective collection, *Poems* (1842), is divided into two volumes of mostly early and mostly later work, but the contents of each are not arranged in a careful chronological sequence. A more or less strictly chronological arrangement of collected volumes became more common later in the century, although it was by no means a universal practice. Walt Whitman's *Leaves of Grass*, although explicitly autobiographical in content, was not arranged in chronological sequence.

In the 20th c., poets typically published their work in ways that emphasized the larger patterns of their career rather than a closely detailed chronological sequence. Poets tended to arrange their individual volumes of recent poems (written in perhaps the previous half-dozen years) in sequences chosen for aesthetic effect or according to forms or themes; in contrast, the collected eds. chosen by the same poets typically encouraged biographical readings by dividing the ed. into sections each of which corresponded to one of the earlier, smaller volumes, presented in order of publication; a typical example is *The Collected Poems of Robert Frost* (1930).

The many collected eds. prepared by W. B. Yeats are arranged in sequences that represent his earlier volumes, but with the chronology and contents altered for aesthetic effect; e.g., Yeats replaced the contents of his earlier books with newly organized sequences with different titles and contents. In a comparable but less revisionary way, Wallace Stevens organized the final section of his *Collected Poems of Wallace Stevens* (1955) as if it were a book titled "The Rock," which, in fact, had never appeared as a separate volume. When W. H. Auden first collected his poems, for *The Collected Poetry of W. H. Auden* (1945), he arranged the contents by alphabetical order of first lines in the hope of discouraging biographical readings; but in his next collection, *Collected Shorter Poems 1927–1957* (1966), he chose a chronological arrangement, noting in a foreword that he had no objection to his work's being read from a historical perspective.

Many biographies of poets from the romantic period to the present treat poets' inner lives as heroic battles against such enemies as bodily illness, critical philistinism, and public indifference. Examples of such biographies include Richard Monckton Milnes's *Life, Letters and Literary Remains of John Keats* (1848) and G. H. Lewes's *The Life of Goethe* (1855). A countertrad. of reductive, skeptical biographies began in the 20th c., prompted by Lytton Strachey's *Eminent Victorians* (1918). In this trad., the poet's life is typically presented as the product of either neurosis or careerism rather than genius; such books can illuminate aspects of a poet's life and work that are invisible in more idealizing biographies and can add to the understanding of readers who admire the poet more than the biographer does. Examples of such books include Lawrance Thompson's *Robert Frost* (1966–76); Lyndall Gordon's *Eliot's Early Years* (1977) and *Eliot's New Life* (1988); and Humphrey Carpenter's *A Serious Character: The Life of Ezra Pound* (1988). Some esp. illuminating biographies combine idealizing and skeptical approaches, presenting the poet as heroically pursuing a vocation through sometimes unscrupulous means; a notable example is R. F. Foster's *W. B. Yeats: A Life* (1997–2003).

A few 20th-c. poets, notably T. S. Eliot and Auden, actively discouraged biographies, either in last wills and testaments or in comments to friends. They wished that their poems might be read for their literary merits, not explained away as the product of personal or public motives. Such concerns continue to challenge literary biography to expand rather than diminish the pleasure and understanding of critics, historians, and readers.

## II. Value to Readers and Interpreters.
The value of biographical information about poets has been the subject of intense dispute since the mid-20th c. Proponents of critical schools that emphasize the aesthetic or structural aspects of a work of art (e.g., *New Criticism, *structuralism, deconstruction) or that emphasize the public role or public reception of a poem (e.g., *cultural studies, reception hist.) tend to deny that biographical information is relevant in interpreting a poem. In the views held by these critical schools, a poem is the product of inner imaginative acts that are inaccessible to biographers and perhaps unknown even to the poet, generic and aesthetic forces that act independently of a poet's conscious or unconscious intentions, or impersonal cultural forces for which the poet is primarily a medium. Another view holds that the meaning of the poem is created by its readers' interpretations of it, not by any of the personal or impersonal forces that caused it to be written. Among the most influential arguments against biographical reading is "The Intentional Fallacy" (1946) by W. K. Wimsatt and M. C. Beardsley (see INTENTIONAL FALLACY). Earlier arguments against such readings include *The Personal Heresy* (1939) by C. S. Lewis and E.M.W. Tillyard; later ones are implicit or explicit throughout structuralist and poststructuralist crit.

No biography can explain why a poet wrote one poem instead of another in response to the same circumstances and experiences. Biography can, however, offer valid cues to interpretation that would not otherwise be available and can illuminate patterns of implication in a poem that might not otherwise be accessible to readers and critics. These cues, like any other cues to interpretation, may in turn help a reader to find a poem more aesthetically satisfying, intellectually stimulating, and emotionally moving than it would be otherwise.

**A. Biography and Particularity.** Among those readers for whom biographical information is distracting or irrelevant are those who regard individual poems as autonomous objects or as statements of universal themes; a *lyric poem, in such a view, might be one poet's exploration of such universal concerns as love or death. In contrast, readers for whom biographical information can be helpful in interpretation tend to regard poems as responses to unique events in a poet's personal hist., which the reader understands as being analogous to unique events in the reader's own experience; a lyric poem, in such a view, was provoked by one particular love or one particular death, but the reader understands the poem through the analogy of the poet's unique experience with the reader's unique experiences of one particular love or one particular death. To such a reader, the kind of knowledge that is worth having is sympathetic, not objective; the poem is not an object to be understood with the kind of knowledge that gives power over that object but as a subject that is best understood through the kind of knowledge that enables sympathy rather than power.

Readers who benefit from biographical information, thus, tend to regard poems as analogous to individual persons. To such readers, a poem, like a person, is the product of unique circumstances, and its existence was affected and provoked by historical events; it speaks with its own irreplaceable voice, with its own special variations on the grammar and syntax that it shares with other poems written in the same lang. and the same culture. It can enter into a dialogue with the reader and, if the poem is worth reading at all, says different things to the same reader at different stages in the reader's life. In this view, a poem, like a person, can say things that a reader does not wish to hear. Although it is a member of one or more classes or categories of poems (e.g., sonnets, visionary poems, mod. poems), the fact of its membership in a class is less interesting than the ways in which it differs from other members of that class.

This view of poems and other works of art as analogues to expressive, individual persons developed in Western culture in the later 18th c. and became pervasive during the 19th. Its philosophical basis was established by the aesthetic theories of J. G. Herder and Friedrich Schleiermacher, both of whom systematized, but did not originate, similar views already emerging among artists and writers (see ROMANTIC AND POSTROMANTIC POETRY AND POETICS; ROMANTICISM).

**B.** *Readings Made Possible by Biographical Information.* A biography may suggest the extent to which a poem is deliberately artificial or conventional—and, therefore, a response to other poems—and the extent to which it is, in contrast, an expression of a personal passion or belief. Biographies of Yeats, notably Foster's, indicate that his love poems to Maud Gonne were less the expression of passionate feeling than products of his conviction that a romantic poet must suffer from an unhappy and unfulfilled love that provides him with the themes of his poetry and that Yeats consciously elaborated and intensified his feelings for Gonne in something of the same way that he elaborated and intensified his poems from their flat-sounding first drafts to their rhythmic and rhetorical final versions. An alert reader could guess some of these things by reading Yeats's poems without reading a biography, but biography, more than any other mode of crit., makes it possible to detect the depth and pervasiveness of Yeats's artificiality that half-pretends to be passion.

In a similar way, Foster's biography indicates that many of the extreme-sounding attitudes about racial and national matters that Yeats expressed in his later work were deliberately chosen to create controversy and thus generate sales for the pamphlets of his work that were published by his sisters' Cuala Press. Some theoretical arguments against biographical interpretation claim that biography simplifies a poem into a mere statement of personal feeling; but in this and similar instances, biography deepens a poem by pointing toward its complex interplay of performance and authenticity and its complex relation between personal statement and theatrical role-playing.

Biography performs a similar function by identifying experiences that are not explicitly named in a poem but that affect its mood, form, and vocabulary and that may be detected in the poem only by readers who are familiar with the biographical background. Gordon's biography of Eliot points to the erotic renunciations that were part of the experience that prompted the writing of "Burnt Norton"; the religious attitudes expressed in the poem, thus, involve not only an aspiration toward something higher than earthly life but a deliberate refusal of actual earthly and erotic satisfactions that are present in the poem only in the form

of apparently nonspecific metaphors. In a similar way, biography can clarify the private experiences through which a poet writes about public events. Poems in which a poet writes about, e.g., the Irish Civil Wars or the outbreak of World War II, can be more deeply understood if a reader learns from a biography the specific personal and emotional concerns that affected the poet at the same time and that influenced the imagery, vocabulary, and poetic forms that the poet used when describing public events.

Biography can also clarify the ways in which the meaning of one poem is affected by the meaning of an earlier or later one by the same poet. Edward Mendelson's *Early Auden* (1981) describes a sequence of inner psychological events when Auden explored and then rejected a fantasy of himself as a leader figure in the 1930s. This account makes clear that some poems that appear to express simple nationalistic feelings are also statements of personal ambition and that later poems that appear to make general statements about human limitation are also specific renunciations of earlier personal hopes.

The value to readers of any biography varies according to the degree to which the biographer perceives large-scale continuities and trajectories in the poet's life. Carpenter's detailed lives of W. H. Auden and Ezra Pound, e.g., treat these poets' lives as a series of disconnected episodes, so that individual poems are portrayed as more or less immediate responses to recent events, not as events in a life shaped by past events and directed to future ones. Foster's equally detailed life of Yeats, in contrast, treats Yeats's life as a narrative in which memories and intentions are inseparable from daily events, with the effect that Yeats's works are understood both as having value in themselves and as part of a constantly changing but coherent larger whole. As in all other matters in which biographers and critics differ in their approaches, the method that seems most valid to a reader will be the one that more closely corresponds to the reader's own understanding of the nature of a poet's career; but sympathetic and well-informed biographical approaches can expand and intensify the experience of reading in ways that are unavailable through other approaches.

■ L. Lipking, *The Life of the Poet: Beginning and Ending Poetic Careers* (1981); W. Empson, *Using Biography* (1984); S. Fix, "Distant Genius: Johnson and the Art of Milton's Life," *MP* 81 (1984); D. Bromwich, "Some Uses of Biography," *A Choice of Inheritance* (1989); S. Boym, *Death in Quotation Marks: Culural Myths of the Modern Poet* (1991); D. Levertov, "Biography and the Poet," *Ohio Review* 48 (1992); C. Ricks, "Victorian Lives," *Essays in Appreciation* (1996); *Romantic Biography*, ed. A. Bradley and A. Rawes (2002).

E. MENDELSON

**BLACK ARTS MOVEMENT.** BAM is a shorthand term coined by the poet, playwright, critic, and political activist Larry Neal for the outpouring of politically engaged Af. Am. art from the mid-1960s to the late 1970s that was closely joined with the Black

Power movement. BAM encompassed a wide range of ideological and aesthetic stances. Nonetheless, like the Black Power movement, all strains of BAM were generally united by a belief in the need for Af. Ams. to determine their own political and cultural destiny within the international struggle against colonialism, neocolonialism, and racism.

BAM largely emerged out of overlapping circuits of old-left radicalism, artistic bohemianism, and black nationalism. Its early participants were inspired by the revolutions and independence movements of Africa, Asia, and Latin America as well as the civil-rights movement, esp. the student movement that grew out of the Southern sit-ins in 1960 and after. While proto-Black Arts institutions, such as *Liberator*, *Freedomways*, and *Negro Digest* magazines and the Free Southern Theater, were established throughout the early 1960s, it was the murder of Malcolm X and the Watts uprising in 1965 that catalyzed these disparate initiatives into the beginning of a movement. Malcolm X's death pushed Amiri Baraka and other artists living in the downtown bohemia of New York City to join with Harlem activists to form the Black Arts Repertory Theatre and School (BARTS)—an event that many took to signal the arrival of a new movement rooted in black neighborhoods. The spread and increasing frequency of black, urban uprisings and the mass circulation of radical nationalist ideas in the Af. Am. community paradoxically authorized both the repression of black revolutionary organizations and the availability of federal, state, and local public funds to support often radical cultural work and institutions, aiding in the growth of a BAM infrastructure.

BAM poetry had a bifurcated character. Many BAM poets oriented their work toward *performance in public venues from community centers to bars to political rallies. Often these performances were multimedia, multigeneric affairs that mixed spoken word, dance, theater, and music. Even when performing alone, poets like Baraka, Sonia Sanchez, and Haki Madhubuti sang, drummed on microphones or podiums, and employed a range of nonverbal vocalizations to approximate collaborations with musicians. BAM poets also often attempted to represent on the page the rhythms, musical lines, and chordal experimentations of the new jazz, particularly the work of John Coltrane. In this, of course, they were engaging not only the work of Langston Hughes and Sterling A. Brown but the New American Poetry literary counterculture such as Allen Ginsberg's *Howl* and Jack Kerouac's *Mexico City Blues*, where notions of lineation and breath were in part based on the model of bebop soloing.

While there was a tendency to privilege the process of sound performance over textual product, BAM poetry still reached its audience primarily through printed texts. Such journals as *Black World* (originally *Negro Digest*), *Liberator*, and *The Journal of Black Poetry* and black-run publishers, such as Third World Press and Broadside Press, were the vehicles that made this poetry available to an audience beyond the poets' immediate communities. One might argue that BAM was the most successful U.S. small-press and little-magazine literary movement. From 1965 to 1975, Detroit's Broadside Press issued dozens of titles and sold many times the number of books by black poets issued by general publishers in the previous decade; Chicago's still-extant Third World Press published numerous titles and thousands of copies. BAM poets, then, had to think deeply about the textual, the verbal, and the visual on the page as well as the performative.

The end of the movement is hard to date precisely. Certainly by the middle of the 1970s, internal ideological struggles between Marxists and anti-Marxist nationalists took a toll on many Black Power and BAM organizations and institutions. As programs supporting the arts were cut or became increasingly hostile to radical community-arts projects with the presidential election of Ronald Reagan in 1980, BAM largely came to an end.

Black Arts fundamentally changed Am. attitudes toward the arts, demonstrating that "high" art can be popular in form and content while popular culture can be socially and artistically serious. This legacy can be seen perhaps most clearly in hip-hop, where politically conscious artists have long invoked and even worked in collaboration with leading Black Arts activists. At the same time, the Black Arts practice of a socially engaged, formally radical mixture of poetry, theater, music, dance, and visual arts performed for a genuinely popular audience also transformed the cultural field for poetry.

*See* AFRICAN AMERICAN POETRY, HIP-HOP POETICS, JAZZ POETRY, PROTEST POETRY.

■ E. Redmond, *Drumvoices* (1976); K. W. Benston, *Performing Blackness* (2000); L. Thomas, *Extraordinary Measures* (2000)—Afrocentric modernism; C. Clarke, *"After Mecca"* (2005)—women poets and BAM; J. Smethurst, *The Black Arts Movement* (2005); *New Thoughts on the Black Arts Movement*, ed. L. G. Collins and M. Crawford (2006).

J. SMETHURST

**BLACK MOUNTAIN SCHOOL.** The term *Black Mountain school* refers to the nexus of poets associated, directly or indirectly, with Black Mountain College (1933–57), a tiny experimental college in North Carolina that centered its curriculum on the arts. Like many terms for poetic movements, *Black Mountain* is simultaneously social and aesthetic in its reference. Socially, it encompasses poets who attended or taught at Black Mountain between about 1948 and 1956 and extends to associated poets who shared the same networks of correspondence and publication. These personal and poetic connections had so diversified by the late 1960s that the term has little relevance beyond that date.

The movement acquired its name from its poets being grouped together in Donald Allen's germinal anthol. *The New American Poetry 1945–1960*. As Allen introduces them, the Black Mountain poets include Charles Olson, Robert Creeley, Robert Duncan, Ed Dorn, Denise Levertov (the poets most consistently associated with the label), Paul Carroll, Joel Oppenheimer, Larry Eigner, Paul Blackburn, and Jonathan Williams. Some would add John Wieners and the long-neglected Hilda Morley to that group. As with many poetic avant-gardes, a shared geographical location helped spark a self-conscious sense of oppositional community associated with resistance to established conventions in the arts—in this case, to the formally traditional mainstream poetics of the period, which were often derided as "academic." Shared publishing outlets in the form of little magazines (Cid Corman's *Origin*, Creeley's *Black Mountain Review*) and small and independent presses (Creeley's Divers Press, Williams's Jargon Society) were also crucial to the coherence of the Black Mountain school (a "coherence" that some of the participants themselves denied). Through their appearance in these venues, poets like Levertov, Blackburn, and Eigner came to be associated with the Black Mountain school without ever attending the college. The writers were further connected by a common sense of their important poetic predecessors: Ezra Pound, W. C. Williams, the objectivists (see OBJECTIVISM), Gertrude Stein, and H.D.

While appearing differently in the work of the various poets, the central features of Black Mountain poetics reflect the principles of Olson's essay *"Projective Verse" (1950), the movement's unofficial *ars poetica*: *composition by field (the poem as a process of exploration or discovery, historical, spiritual, or emotional); a breath- and speech-based line shaped by the poem's developing content and the poet's physiology, rather than by traditional prosody; the value-laden distinction between experimental "open" forms and "closed" forms inherited from the poetic trad. The Black Mountain poets share a commitment to an organic form that emerges in the writing process—a position articulated in such statements as Levertov's "Notes on Organic Form" (1965), Duncan's "Ideas of the Meaning of Form" (1961) and "Towards an Open Universe" (1964), and Creeley's many short essays and reviews. *Line, *syntax, and page space are taken as key sites of poetic experiment.

Their openness to theorizing their poetics differentiated the Black Mountain poets from contemporaneous movements with which they otherwise had much in common—the *Beats, the *San Francisco Renaissance, the *New York school—and attracted some crit. from proponents of these movements. However, the Black Mountain poets' construction of a literary community via mutual support, correspondence, statements of poetics, publication, and the exchange of sometimes conflicting ideas about the arts became one model for the later practices of the *Language poets, where that construction takes a more politically engaged form.

■ *The New American Poetry 1945–1960*, ed. D. Allen (1960); C. Olson, *Selected Writings* (1966)—"Projective Verse"; M. Duberman, *Black Mountain* (1972); *The Poetics of the New American Poetry*, ed. D. Allen and W. Tallman (1973); S. Paul, *Olson's Push* (1978); P. Christensen, "Olson and the Black Mountain Poets," *Charles Olson* (1979); S. Paul, *The Lost America of Love* (1981); M. E. Harris, *The Arts at Black Mountain College* (1987); E. H. Foster, *Understanding the*

*Black Mountain Poets* (1995); A. Golding, "Little Magazines and Alternative Canons," *From Outlaw to Classic* (1995); A. D. Dewey, *Beyond Maximus* (2007).

A. GOLDING

# BLANK VERSE

  I. Italian
  II. English
  III. Spanish and Portuguese
  IV. German
  V. Scandinavian
  VI. Slavic

**I. Italian**. *Blank verse* is a term for unrhymed lines of poetry, always in lines of a length considered appropriate to serious topics and often in the most elevated, canonical meter in a given national *prosody. The phenomenon first appeared in It. poetry of the 13th c. with "Il Mare Amoroso" (The Sea of Love), an anonymous poem composed of 334 unrhymed *endecasillabo* verses (see ITALIAN PROSODY). In the Ren., this form was transplanted to England as the unrhymed decasyllable or iambic *pentameter. Though these lines are thought to have derived metrically from the cl. iambic *trimeter, they were designed to produce, in the vernaculars, equivalents in tone and weight of the cl. "heroic" line, the *hexameter. The unrhymed endecasillabo, while popular and important for certain writers (e.g., Ugo Foscolo, Giacomo Leopardi, and many 20th-c. poets), did not become a major meter in It. as the unrhymed iambic pentameter did in Eng. Fr. poet-critics noted the work of the It. poets and made experiments of their own, but these never took hold in a lang. where word *accent was weak; hence, Fr. poetry never developed a significant blank-verse trad. The Iberian, Ger., Scandinavian, and Slavic trads. are discussed below.

Luigi Alamanni's *Rime toscane* (1532) and other famous It. works in *versi sciolti* (i.e., *versi sciolti da rima*, verse freed from rhyme), such as Giangiorgio Trissino's tragedy *Sophonisba* (1524) and *epic *L'Italia liberata dai Goti* (1547), were important models for other national poetries such as the Eng.; the first poet to write blank verse in Eng., Henry Howard, the Earl of Surrey (1517–47), surely knew of Alamanni, as well as Niccolò Liburnio's 1534 trans. of Virgil or the 1539 trans. by the de' Medici circle.

**II. English**. Blank verse in England was invented by the Earl of Surrey, who sometime between 1539 and 1546 translated two books of the *Aeneid* (2 and 4) into this "straunge meter." It remains to be shown precisely how the rhythms in Surrey's lines derived from the It. endecasillabo. Rather than the 11 syllables of his It. model, Surrey's lines have 10, in an alternating (*iambic) rhythm, and his more easily identifiable precursors are Eng. writers of rhymed decasyllabic verse such as Thomas Wyatt and (more remotely) Chaucer. Gavin Douglas's Scottish trans. of Virgil's epic (written ca. 1513, pub. 1553), from which Surrey took 40% of his diction, is in rhymed *heroic couplets. Like other pre-Shakespearean blank verse, Surrey's is relatively stiff in rhythm, impeded by end-stops. Dignified in style, it exhibits an extensive network of sound patterning, perhaps to offset absent *rhyme.

As blank verse developed in Eng., generic considerations became important. In Eng., *blank* as used of verse suggests a mere absence of rhyme, not that liberation from a restrictive requirement implied in the It. term. Nevertheless, Eng. defenders of blank verse repeatedly asserted that rhyme acts on poets as a "constraint to express many things otherwise, and for the most part worse than else they would have exprest them" (John Milton). That rhyme has its virtues and beauties needs no argument here. Rhyme does, however, tend to delimit—even to define—metrical structures; it has its clearest effect when the syllables it connects occur at the ends also of syntactic structures, so that *meter and syntax reinforce one another. One associates rhyme with symmetries and closures. Omission of rhyme, by contrast, encourages the use of syntactic structures greater and more various than could be contained strictly within the line and so makes possible an amplitude of discourse, a natural-seeming multiformity, not easily available to rhymed verse. In light of these characteristics, Eng. writers found blank verse a fitting vehicle for long works (for its lack of imposed repetition), drama (for its natural word order), and epic (for its inversion, suspension, and related stylistic devices).

Though blank verse appeared in Eng. first in (trans.) epic, attempts at Eng. *heroic verse after Surrey use, as Hardison remarks, "almost every form *but* blank verse." The form achieved its first great flowering in drama. After Surrey, the dramatic and nondramatic varieties have significantly different hists., suggesting that they differ in nature more than critics once thought (see WRIGHT, HARDISON). In nondramatic verse, the influence of *Petrarchism, manifested in the vogue for the *sonnet sequence, ensured that rhyme held sway in Eng. nondramatic verse up to Milton. The heavy editorial regularization by the editor of *Tottel's Miscellany* (1557) set the trend up to Philip Sidney, who showed that metrical correctness and natural expressiveness were not mutually exclusive (see Thompson), a demonstration extended even further by John Donne—but again, in rhyme.

The first Eng. dramatic blank verse, Thomas Norton's in the first three acts of *Gorboduc* (1571), is smooth but more heavily *end-stopped than Surrey's, giving the impression of contrivance, of a diction shaped—and often padded out—to fit the meter. Thomas Sackville's verse in the last two acts of the play is more alive. But the artificial regularity of Norton's verse came to characterize Eng. *dramatic poetry until Christopher Marlowe came fully into his powers. Marlowe showed what rhetorical and tonal effects blank verse was capable of; his early play *Dido* echoes lines from Surrey's *Aeneid*, and Shakespeare's early works show what he learned from Marlowe.

**A. Shakespeare.** Shakespeare's blank verse, the major verse form of his plays throughout his career, is marked by several features, some of them shared with or derived from earlier Eng. poets (e.g. John Lydgate, Sidney, and Marlowe) but developed with unprecedented coherence. (1) Blank verse is always mixed with other metrical modes (e.g., rhymed verse, songs) and (except for *Richard II* and *King John*) with prose; two plays offer more rhymed verse than blank (*Love's Labour's Lost* and *A Midsummer Night's Dream*), and seven plays (two hists. and five middle-period comedies) are largely or predominantly written in prose. Shifts within a scene from one mode to another are often subtle, gradual, and hard to hear; different metrical registers for different social classes, however, can be heard, and identify sets of characters—as in *MND*. (2) Resourceful use of common Elizabethan conventions of metrical patterning and esp. of metrical variation gives many individual lines great flexibility, variety, melody, and speech-like force. (3) Frequent use of lines deviant in length or pattern (short, long, headless, broken-backed, and epic-caesural) extends the potentialities of expressive variation beyond what was commonly available to Ren. writers of stanzaic verse. (4) Shrewdly deployed syllabic ambiguity, esp. by devices of compression (see ELISION), makes many lines seem packed. (5) Lines become increasingly enjambed: sentences run from midline to midline, and even a speech or a scene may end in midline (see ENJAMBMENT). Conversely, metrically regular lines may comprise several short phrases or sentences and may be shared by characters (*split lines). In the theater, consistently enjambed blank verse, unlike Marlowe's end-stopped "mighty" line, sounds more like speech but also tests the audience's awareness of the meter. Esp. in Shakespeare's later plays, the audience, like the characters it is scrutinizing, follows an uncertain path between comprehension and bafflement. Besides carrying the characters' emotional utterances and conveying (with appropriate intensity) their complex states of mind, Shakespeare's blank verse may figure, through its rich dialectic of pattern and departure-from-pattern, a continuing tension between authority and event, model and story, the measured structures of cosmic order and the wayward motions of erratic individual characters.

**B. After Shakespeare,** and esp. after Donne's (rhymed) *Satyres,* the dramatic blank-verse line grew looser in form. Feminine endings (see MASCULINE AND FEMININE), infrequent in all early blank verse, became common; in John Fletcher, they often carry verbal stress. Later, true feminine endings become common even in nondramatic rhymed verse. Milton uses feminine endings in *Paradise Lost* and *Paradise Regain'd* only with great restraint. They occur rather seldom in the early books of *Paradise Lost*, but much more frequently after Eve and Adam's fall and are thereby appropriated to the speech of fallen mortals.

In dramatic blank verse, extrametrical syllables begin to appear within the line—first, nearly always following a strong stress and at the end of a phrase or clause at the *caesura; later, elsewhere within the line. In some late Jacobean and Caroline dramas (e.g., those of John

Webster) the line has become so flexible that at times the five points of stress seem to become phrase centers, each capable of carrying with it unstressed syllables required by the sense rather than by the metrical count of syllables. But such "Websterian" lines were to call down the wrath of later critics; and the closing of the theaters in 1642 saw the end of a brilliant—if almost too daring—period of experimentation with the structure of the dramatic blank-verse line. When verse drama was written again, after the Restoration and under the impetus of the newly popular Fr. model, the line was once again a strict pentameter but now, and for the next century, rhymed. In any event, after the closing of the theaters, blank verse was never to be of major importance in the drama again. The attempt to renew verse drama (incl. blank verse) in the 20th c. never won either popular or critical acclaim.

**C. *Milton.*** Milton returned blank verse to its earliest use as a vehicle of epic and to strict, though complex, metrical order; his influence was so powerful that the form bore his impress up to the 20th c. He did, of course, write blank-verse drama—*Comus* (*A Mask*) and *Samson Agonistes*, the first much influenced by Shakespeare. In both, blank verse, though it is unquestionably the central form, is intermingled with other forms—lyric in *Comus*, choric in *Samson Agonistes*—to such effect that we think of both works as being in mixed meters. In *Samson Agonistes*, Milton is trying to produce the effect of Gr. tragedy (though with a biblical subject); but the blank verse is similar enough to Milton's nondramatic blank verse that discussion of the two may be merged.

Milton was profoundly familiar with the *Aeneid* in Lat., perhaps in It. trans., and in some Eng. versions; he was equally familiar with It. epic and romance. As a theorist of form, he wanted to make blank verse in Eng. the instrument that the humanist poets had been attempting to forge since Trissino. For his subject in *Paradise Lost*, he needed a dense, packed line, as various as possible in movement within the limits set by broadly understood but absolute metricality; at the same time, he needed a syntax complex and elaborate enough to overflow line form, to subordinate it to larger forms of thought, appropriately varied in the scope of their articulation—"the sense variously drawn out from one verse into another." The idea was not new, yet no one had managed enjambment in Eng. as skillfully as Milton learned to manage it. Before him—except in Shakespeare's later plays—the congruence of syntax with line form had been too nearly predictable.

Even more than Shakespeare's, Milton's blank-verse line differs from his rhymed pentameter in management of rhythm and through constant variation of the placement of pause within the line. In the course of enjambing lines, Milton writes long periodic sentences, making liberal use of inversion, parenthesis, and other delaying and complicating devices. At times, he uses Italianate stress sequences that disturb the double rhythm and in some instances all but break the meter. Also important, given his refusal of rhyme, is a more

extensive (if irregular) deployment of the varied resources of sound patterning. Numerous forms of *in-ternal rhyme occur, as well as final *assonance and half rhyme; and whole passages are woven together by patterns of *alliteration, assonance, and half rhyme.

**D. *After Milton.*** Milton's influence on subsequent nondramatic blank verse in Eng. was, as Havens showed, enormous. Yet, all blank verse after Milton became essentially a romantic form—no longer epic and (the dramatic *monologue excepted) no longer dramatic, but the vehicle of rumination and recollection. The line of descent leads through William Wordsworth ("Michael"; *The Prelude*; *The Excursion*) to Alfred, Lord Tennyson ("Ulysses"; "Tithonus"; *Idylls of the King*) and Robert Browning (*The Ring and the Book*). By the mid-18th c., the forces of metrical regularity had begun to weaken; for the first time, extra syllables that cannot be removed by elision begin to appear in the nondramatic line, producing triple rhythm. The Eng. pentameter, both dramatic and nondramatic, between 1540 and 1780 all but disallowed triple rhythms; strict count of syllables was deemed central to line structure. Real, irreducible triple rhythms before 1780 were associated with music; they occur fairly commonly in song lyrics and *ballads but not in *accentual-syllabic verse. After 1780, however, triple rhythms gradually invade poems in double rhythm, in part because the romantics were devoted to the work of their 16th- and 17th-c. predecessors and often used the diction of Edmund Spenser, Shakespeare, and Milton, though without entirely understanding earlier metrical conventions. There was also a revival of interest in the ballads, which varied the basic double rhythms with irreducible triple rhythms, a practice soon evident in William Blake's *Songs* and even occasionally in Wordsworth. As the 19th c. wore on, rhythmic handling might be restrained (Tennyson) or flamboyant (Browning), but the prevailing stylistic tendency was toward effects of speech (a devel. forecast by S. T. Coleridge's term *conversation poem*).

In the early 20th c., such speech qualities were exploited by E. A. Robinson and esp. Robert Frost in his *North of Boston* (1914). The rise of experimental *modernism severely challenged the form; T. S. Eliot deprecated "the inevitable iambic pentameter." Although with scant critical attention and with diminished prestige, much blank verse continued to be written. The impressive works of the post–World War II generation (e.g., Howard Nemerov, Richard Wilbur, Anthony Hecht, James Merrill) followed in the wake of earlier achievements such as W. B. Yeats's "The Second Coming" and Wallace Stevens's "Sunday Morning." In the later 20th c., some poets, evidently with an eye to *free verse, wrote looser versions of the line with added syllables and with stresses erratically clumped or spaced, so that the standard meter seems a distant paradigm rather than an active presence. More traditionally inclined poets—first the Stanford formalists and later the New Formalists (see NEW FORMALISM)—practiced a stricter adherence to the meter. In the 21st c., blank verse continues in wide use among poets attracted to its generic versatility and its expressive pliancy and power.

**III. Spanish and Portuguese**. In his foundational *Gramática de la lengua castellana* (Grammar of the Castilian Language, 1492), Antonio de Nebrija deplores the use of rhyme for three reasons: the lack of freedom to express the feelings of the poet, the wearisome similarity of sound, and the way the sound distracts from understanding the sense. But the rise of blank verse occurs after Juan Boscán (ca. 1490–1542) wrote a preface to his poems (1543) where he waxed ironic about the readers who felt "nostalgic for the multitude of rhymes" current in traditional courtly poetry. His generation opened the way toward a new Iberian idiom, based on a kind of studied spontaneity, in which rhyme became secondary or nonexistent. Lyric Port. and Sp. rhymed hendecasyllabic poems by Francisco Sá de Miranda (1481–1558) suggest a rhythmical flexibility like that of prose. Boscán himself wrote *Leandro,* a narrative poem of over 2,700 unrhymed lines, and his friend Garcilaso de la Vega (1503–36) composed an epistle in the form. In spite of detractors such as Fernando de Herrera ("Notes on the Poetry of Garcilaso," 1580), blank verse appeared in important *lyric, narrative, and dramatic poetry of the later 16th c. António Ferreira (1528–69) composed the supreme masterwork of 16th-c. Iberian tragedy, *Castro* (first written ca. 1554, pub. 1587, definitive ed. 1598), mostly in blank verse, and expressed elsewhere the same reluctance about rhyme as Nebrija. The first epic poem finished in Port., *Segundo Cerco de Diu* (Second Siege of Diu, ms. ca. 1568, pub. 1574) by Jerónimo Corte-Real (d. 1588), is entirely in unrhymed verse. The Spaniard Francisco de Aldana (1537–75) wrote the mythological *Fábula de Faetonte* and three long epistles in blank *hendecasyllables (pub. 1589–91). There were influential blank verse Sp. trans. of Homer's *Odyssey* in 1550, Virgil's *Aeneid* in 1555, Ovid's *Metamorphoses* in 1580, and of a mod. poem like Corte-Real's in 1597. Corte-Real himself published two other epics mostly in blank verse that received considerable renown, *Victoria de Lepanto* in Sp. (1578) and *Sepúlveda* in Port. (1594, post.), with intertextual links back to Boscán's *Leandro* and not without influence in authors as canonical as Miguel de Cervantes and Milton. In the 17th c., perhaps the only remarkable poem in blank verse was Félix Lope de Vega's *El arte nuevo de hacer comedias* (New Art of Writing Comedies, 1609), and this only for its value as theory of drama (though ironically 17th-c. Sp. drama rejected blank verse). But unrhymed hendecasyllabic verse returned to full effect in some of the best lit. of the 18th c., such as the Brazilian nativist epic *O Uraguai* by Basílio da Gama, the *mock-heroic masterpiece *O Hissope* (The Aspergill) by Antonio Dinis da Cruz e Silva, Leandro Fernández de Moratín's great and moving *Elegía a las Musas* (Elegy to the Muses), and the truculent defense of poetry *Carta a Brito* (Epistle to Brito) by Filinto Elísio. Blank verse was also chosen for the first great work of Port. *romanticism, Almeida Garrett's *Camões* (1825), as well as for mod. long poems by major Iberian figures of the time such as Eugénio de Castro (*Constança,* 1900), Teixeira de Pascoaes (*Regresso ao Paraíso,* 1912) and Miguel de Unamuno (*El Cristo de Velásquez,* 1920).

**IV. German**. The earliest attempt at writing iambic pentameter blank verse in Ger. dates to the beginning of the 17th c., when Johannes Rhenanus wrote a version of Thomas Tomkis's university comedy *Lingua.* In 1682, Rhenanus was followed by E. G. von Berge with a trans. of Milton's *Paradise Lost.* While these attempts were of no further consequence, interest in blank verse was rekindled around the middle of the 18th c., when various writers, incl. J. E. Schlegel and his brother J. H. Schlegel, published trans. of Eng. blank-verse lit. (e.g., James Thomson's *Seasons* and some of his tragedies, William Congreve's *The Mourning Bride*) or wrote their own dramas (J. W. von Brawe, *Brutus*; C. F. Weisse, *Atreus und Thyest*; F. G. Klopstock, *Salomo*). G. A. Bürger applied blank verse to the epic genre in his trans. of passages from Homer's *Iliad*, as did C. M. Wieland in his *Erzählungen* (Tales). The first Ger. blank-verse drama to be performed was Wieland's *Lady Johanna Gray,* staged in Switzerland in 1758. As a translator of Shakespeare's dramatic works into prose, Wieland chose *MND* for a blank-verse trans. (1762). However, it was not until G. E. Lessing's *Nathan der Weise* (1779) that blank verse replaced the *alexandrine as the dominant meter in Ger. cl. and postclassical drama. This change was promoted by K. P. Moritz's handbook on prosody, *Versuch einer deutschen Prosodie* (1786), which J. W. Goethe consulted in rewriting earlier prose versions of his *Iphigenie auf Tauris* (1787) and *Torquato Tasso* (1790). Likewise, Friedrich Schiller rewrote *Don Karlos* (1787) and the second and third parts of his *Wallenstein* trilogy, *Die Piccolomini* and *Wallensteins Tod* (the first part, *Wallensteins Lager*, being in free *knittelvers). Between 1800 and 1804, Schiller wrote *Maria Stuart, Die Jungfrau von Orleans, Die Braut von Messina,* and *Wilhelm Tell,* all (apart from the choruses in *Die Braut von Messina*) in blank verse.

A. W. Schlegel's trans. of Shakespeare's plays (14 plays between 1797 and 1810) helped further establish blank verse as the standard meter of Ger. verse drama. His work was later complemented by Ludwig Tieck, his daughter Dorothea Tieck, and Wolf Graf Baudissin, who even took the liberty of translating Molière's alexandrines into blank verse (1865) because he argued that it had the same dominant position in Ger. drama as the alexandrine had in Fr. Thus, most major and minor dramatists of the 19th c. used blank verse exclusively (as is the case with Heinrich von Kleist, although there are some prose passages in *Das Käthchen von Heilbronn*), extensively (as did Franz Grillparzer, C. D. Grabbe, and C. F. Hebbel), or at least occasionally (Karl Immermann, Karl Gutzkow, and Paul Heyse).

While the earliest attempts at blank verse in Ger. clearly reflected the Eng. models on which they were based (e.g., by the avoidance of feminine endings like Thomson or by construing long periodic sentences over many verse lines like Milton), Lessing, Goethe, and Schiller developed their own metrical styles. Lessing almost disregarded the verse line as a metrical unit by using strong enjambments, by frequently splitting the line into short phrases, often uttered by different speakers, and by splitting lines between speakers 70% of the time (see SPLIT LINES). Thus, Lessing made his verse sound "natural" in the sense of sounding like speech or prose. Goethe went to the other extreme and made his blank verse clearly distinct from speech or prose. His lines are mostly end-stopped, and a change of speakers coincides generally (more than 90%) with the end of a line, at a dramatic climax even in the form of *stichomythia. His syntax is complex but well built, rhythmically balanced, and, stylistic devices such as *sententia* or *genitivus explicativus*, at times highly artificial. Schiller's style lies somewhere between Lessing and Goethe, although he moved toward Goethe in his later plays. However, Goethe's verse always has a smooth, lyrical "ring," whereas Schiller adapts his verse to the dramatic function by, e.g., making Mortimer (*Maria Stuart*, 3.6) utter wildly unmetrical lines in order to convey to the listener or reader that he is out of his mind.

Ger. blank-verse dramas like those of Shakespeare often contain lines that are shorter or longer than the standard ten syllables. Kleist, esp. in his comedies, was less strict than Goethe, but both occasionally loaded an ultrashort or an extra-long line with extra meaning. Insertions of a different meter in Goethe's *Iphigenie* or in Schiller's *Braut von Messina* always have a dramatic function.

Even in late 19th- and 20th-c. drama, blank verse was not entirely abandoned (Ernst von Wildenbruch, Gerhart Hauptmann, Hugo von Hofmannsthal, J. R. Becher, and Walter Hasenclever). After 1945, blank verse experienced a kind of renaissance in the works of some East Ger. dramatists (Heiner Müller, Hartmut Lange, Erwin Strittmatter, and Peter Hacks), who introduced more metrical complexity in their verse dramas by frequently—and even verse-internally—placing trochaic words in weak-strong sequences as in Eng. blank verse.

In Ger. poetry, iambic pentameter verse occurred mostly in its rhymed version. However, after Schiller's early specimen *Das verschleierte Bild zu Sais* (1795), early mod. poets like C. F. Meyer, Stefan George, von Hofmannsthal, and R. M. Rilke (in two of his *Duineser Elegien*) used blank verse for some of their best poetry. Despite the predilection among contemp. poets for free verse, blank verse can still be found, be it in the form of entire poems in blank verse (by Arnfrid Astel and Thomas Rosenlöcher in *Jahrbuch der Lyrik 2001*) or intermingled with shorter lines (Günter Grass) or "hidden" in scattered passages (sometimes incongruent with the printed lines) of free-verse poems (Volker Braun, Norbert Hummelt).

Blank verse in Ger. has at times been criticized as being rhythmically monotonous. Compared to Eng., Ger. blank verse is more "regular" because Ger. lexical words tend to have an unstressed syllable that naturally falls on a weak position, while the lexically stressed syllable falls just as naturally on the strong position (*ictus). However, this view overlooks the rhythmic potential of blank verse in the hands of a poet with a fine ear (such as Goethe or Lessing) and ignores the subtleties of meaning created by an interplay between meter and rhythm.

**V. Scandinavian.** In Scandinavia, blank verse was introduced as an effect of romanticism at the end of the 18th c. It soon replaced the alexandrine in the narrative, philosophical, and dramatic genres. Originally, the Eng. and Ger. varieties were adopted, and trans. of Shakespeare's plays enhanced the reputation of the new meter. The assimilation of blank verse in Scandinavia can be attributed to two factors: the lack of end rhyme in blank verse suited the Scandinavian langs., with their scarcity of rhyme words; and the habit of realizing just four out of five prominence positions brought blank verse close to the med. four-beat line. As it grew in use, the Scandinavian variant of blank verse became distinguished by its alternation between lines of 10 and 11 syllables.

In Denmark, Johannes Ewald initially attempted blank verse in 1768. His music drama *Balders Død* (1773) introduced hendecasyllabic blank verse in Denmark, probably of It. extraction. A. G. Oehlenschläger's first play in blank verse was the comedy *Aladdin* (1805). He used the decasyllable with masculine endings, following the Eng. and the Ger. styles.

The earliest instances of Norwegian blank verse are some farces by Henrik Wergeland, whose versification was probably inspired by Shakespeare. Blank verse in the style of the Danish forerunners dominated Norwegian drama from the middle of the 19th c. Henrik Ibsen tested blank verse in his first play *Catilina* (1850), and Bjønstjerne Bjørnson composed excellent blank verse in his saga dramas *Halte-Hulda* (1858) and *Kong Sverre* (1861).

In Sweden, blank verse was introduced with J. H. Kellgren's narrative fragment *Sigvarth och Hilma* (1788), which was inspired by Ewald's works. The poet F. M. Franzén, influenced by Shakespeare, elaborated blank verse in the 1790s. Since then, blank verse has been a popular Swedish measure in the narrative and philosophical genres, with contributions by poets such as E. J. Stagnelius, Birger Sjöberg, and Gunnar Ekelöf. Most of the space opera *Aniara* (1956) by Harry Martinson is written in blank verse. The versification of Göran Palm's *Sverige—en vintersaga* (1984–2005) is a mod. blank verse that comes close to the rhythm of spoken lang.

**VI. Slavic.** Rus. blank verse emerged in 18th-c. imitations of antiquity, e.g., Vasily Trediakovsky's syllabic blank-verse version of François Fénelon's *Aventures de Télémaque* (1699) and A. D. Kantemir's renderings of Horace. In the 19th c., under the influence of Vasily Zhukovsky's trans. (1817–21) of Schiller's *Die Jungfrau von Orleans* and Alexander Pushkin's *Boris Godunov* (1825), iambic pentameter blank verse became widely associated with drama. Simultaneously, Rus. blank verse appeared in folk stylizations, e.g., Pushkin's "Tale of the Fisherman and the Fish" (1833) and "Songs of the Western Slavs" (1835), inspired by the Serbo-

Croatian epic decasyllable, and Mikhail Lermontov's "Song of the Merchant Kalashnikov" (1837), as well as in lyric monologues such as Pushkin's "Again I visited" (1835), where it acquired a semantic aura later echoed by such 20th-c. poets as Alexander Blok, Vladislav Khodasevich, and Joseph Brodsky.

In Poland, dactylic-hexameter blank verse was employed by Ren. poets writing in Lat. Hendecasyllabic blank verse in Polish-lang. poetry had It. roots; Jan Kochanowski used it in his tragedy *The Dismissal of Greek Envoys* (1578). Polish trans. from antiquity and from Eng., Ger., and It. featured blank verse; however, rhymed verse was the standard for Polish drama. Blank verse plays include Jozef Korzeniowski's *The Monk* (1830) and *Gypsies* (1857), J. C. Słowacki's *Lilla Weneda* (1840, partially rhymed), and Cyprian Norwid's 1880 comedy *Pure Love at a Seaside Spa*.

■ **English**: S. Johnson, *Rambler*, nos. 86–96 (1751); Schipper; J. A. Symonds, *Blank Verse* (1895); J. B. Mayor, *Chapters on English Metre*, 2d ed. (1901); E. Gosse, "Blank Verse," *Encyclopedia Britannica*, 11th ed. (1910–11); Bridges; R. D. Havens, *The Influence of Milton on English Poetry* (1922); A. Oras, *Blank Verse and Chronology in Milton* (1966); R. Beum, "So Much Gravity and Ease," *Language and Style in Milton*, ed. R. D. Emma and J. T. Shawcross (1967); R. Fowler, "Three Blank Verse Textures," *The Languages of Literature* (1971); E. R. Weismiller, "Blank Verse," "Versification," and J. T. Shawcross, "Controversy over Blank Verse," *A Milton Encyclopedia*, ed. W. B. Hunter Jr., 8 v. (1978–80); Brogan, 356 ff.; H. Suhamy, *Le Vers de Shakespeare* (1984); M. Tarlinskaja, *Shakespeare's Verse* (1987); G. T. Wright, *Shakespeare's Metrical Art* (1988); J. Thompson, *The Founding of English Metre*, 2d ed. (1989); O. B. Hardison Jr., *Prosody and Purpose in the English Renaissance* (1989); A. Hecht, "Blank Verse," Finch and Varnes; R. B. Shaw, *Blank Verse* (2007).

■ **Spanish and Portuguese**: I. Navarrete, *Orphans of Petrarch* (1994); *Historia y Crítica de la Literatura Española*, ed. F. Rico, 7 v. (1991–95); *Juán Boscán, Obra Completa*, ed. C. Clavería (1999); *António Ferreira, Poemas Lusitanos*, ed. T. F. Earle (2000); *Fernando de Herrera, Anotaciones a la poesía de Garcilaso*, ed. I. Pepe and J. M. Reyes (2001); H.J.S. Alves, "Milton after Corte-Real," *MP* 106 (2009).

■ **German**: J. G. Herder, *Ueber die neuere deutsche Literatur. Fragmente*, 2d ed. (1768); F. Zarncke, *Über den fünffüssigen Jambus mit besonderer Rücksicht auf seine Behandlung durch Lessing, Schiller und Goethe* (1865); A. Sauer, *Ueber den fünffüssigen Iambus vor Lessing's "Nathan"* (1878); E. Zitelmann, *Der Rhythmus des fünffüßigen Jambus* (1907); W. Rube, *Der fünffüssige Jambus bei Hebbel* (1910); L. Hettich, *Der fünffüssige Jambus in den Dramen Goethes* (1913); R. Haller, "Studie über den deutschen Blankvers," *Deutsche Vierteljahrsschrift für Literaturwissenschaft und Geistesgeschichte* 31 (1957); R. Bräuer, *Tonbewegung und Erscheinungsformen des sprachlichen Rhythmus* (1964); L. Schädle, *Der frühe deutsche Blankvers unter besonderer Berücksichtigung seiner Verwendung durch Chr. M.*

*Wieland* (1972); B. Bjorklund, *A Study in Comparative Prosody* (1978); D. Chisholm, "Prosodische Aspekte des Blankversdramas," *Literaturwissenschaft und empirische Methoden*, ed. H. Kreuzer and R. Viehoff (1981); C. Küper, *Sprache und Metrum* (1988), and "Blankvers," *Reallexikon III*, v. 1 (1997).

■ **Scandinavian**: O. Sylwan, *Den svenska versen från 1600-talets början*, v. 1–3 (1925–34); O. Sylwan, *Svensk verskonst. Från Wivallius till Karlfeldt* (1934); H. Lie, *Norsk verslære* (1967); J. Fafner, *Dansk vershistorie*, v. 1–3 (1994–2000); E. Lilja, *Svensk metrik* (2006).

■ **Slavic**: K. Estreicher, *Bibliografia Polska*, v. 1 (1870); R. Jakobson, "Slavic Epic Verse," v. 4 (1966); M. Gasparov, *Ocherk istori russkogo stikha* (1984); Terras; M. Wachtel, *Development of Russian Verse* (1999); L. Pszolowska, "Dve literatury i dve modeli stikha," *Slavianskii stikh*, ed. M. Gasparov et al. (2001); S. Zurawski, "Wiersz biały," *Literatura polska. Encyklopedia PWN* (2007).

E. R. Weismiller (It.); T.V.F. Brogan, R. B. Shaw, E. R. Weismiller, G. T. Wright (Eng.); H.J.S. Alves (Sp. and Port.); C. Küper (Ger.); E. Lilja (Scand.); N. Friedberg (Slavic)

**BLASON.** A descriptive poem in praise or blame of a single object (Thomas Sébillet, *L'art poétique*, 1548). It gained popularity in mid-16th c. France after Clément Marot's "Blason du beau tétin" (1536) gave rise to the vogue of the *blason anatomique*. However, the term is first used in the late 15th c. with the loose definition of *propos* ("speech") or even "dialogue" in works such as Guillaume Alexis' *Blason des Faulces Amours* (1486) or Guillaume Coquillart's *Blason des armes et des dames* (1484).

The blason received its stricter early mod. definition after Marot's poem, written while in exile in Ferrara and probably influenced by Olimpo da Sassoferrato's love poetry. In response to the poetic competition launched by Marot, dozens of poems celebrating some part of the female body were composed in France and collected in an illustrated anthol., first pub. as a short annex to Leon Battista Alberti's *Hecatomphilia* (1536, 1537, 1539), then as an independent volume, the *Blasons anatomiques du corps femenin: Ensemble les Contreblasons* (1543, 1550, 1554, 1568). In spite of Marot's injunction to avoid offending words or body parts, many blasons from that collection fall under the category of the obscene, in the satirical trad. of the paradoxical eulogy. The genre of the *contreblason*, also initiated by Marot, turns the genre upside down, either by deriding ugly objects or by criticizing the very enterprise of praising the human body (Charles de La Hueterie, *Le Contreblason de la beaulté des membres du corps humain*, 1537).

The poetics of the blason has been connected to its heraldic origin (a description of a coat of arms); to the *emblem, where woodcut, poetic description, and interpretation are similarly linked; to *mannerism (Saunders, Vickers 1997, Giordano); and to *ekphrasis and epideixis (see EPIDEICTIC POETRY). Frequently used devices include *anaphora, *enumeratio*, and *hyperbole.

According to Sébillet, a good blason should be brief, set in octo- or decasyllabic verses, in couplets, and have an epigrammatic conclusion. However, blasons have from the start been of various lengths: they are less defined by a specific format than by their descriptive and epideictic mode. The *Pléiade* expanded the genre with *sonnets-blasons* and *hymnes-blasons*; Paul Éluard, René Étiemble, and Régine Detambel revived it in prose and *free verse in the 20th c.

In studies of early mod. Eur. poetry, the blason has been discussed in the 1980s and 1990s as an instance of appropriation and control. From the perspective of feminist poetics, the blazon is a male inventory of the female body; from that of postcolonial studies, a way of mapping and taking control of the Other.

*See* CATALOG, DESCRIPTIVE POETRY, FEMINIST APPROACHES TO POETRY, PETRARCHISM, SATIRE.

■ J. Vianey, *Le Pétrarquisme en France au XVI^e siècle* (1909); R. E. Pike, "The Blasons in French Literature of the 16th Century," *RR* 27 (1936); K. Kazimierz, "Des Recherches sur l'évolution du blason au XVI^e siècle," *Zagadnienia Rodzajow Literarick* (1967); D. B. Wilson, *Descriptive Poetry in France from Blason to Baroque* (1967); A. Tomarken and E. Tomarken, "The Rise and Fall of the Sixteenth-century French *Blason*," *Symposium* 29 (1975); N. J. Vickers, "Diana Described: Scattered Woman and Scattered Rhyme," *CritI* 8 (1981); A. Saunders, *The Sixteenth-century Blason Poétique* (1982); N. J. Vickers, "'The Blazon of Sweet Beauty's Best': Shakespeare's *Lucrece*," *Shakespeare and the Question of Theory*, ed. P. Parker and G. Hartman (1985); P. Parker, "Rhetorics of Property: Exploration, Inventory, Blazon," *Literary Fat Ladies* (1987); N. J. Vickers, "Members Only: Marot's Anatomical Blazons," *The Body in Parts*, ed. D. Hillman and C. Mazzio (1997); M. J. Giordano, "The *Blason anatomique* and Related Fields: Emblematics, Nominalism, Mannerism, and Descriptive Anatomy as Illustrated by M. Scève's *Blason de la Gorge*," *An Interregnum of the Sign*, ed. D. Graham (2001).

I. SILVER; T.V.F. BROGAN; C. ALDUY

**BLUES.** Originating in Af. Am. folk culture, the blues has developed into a central inspiration for a great deal of Am. poetry. The music is distinguished thematically and philosophically by its posture of direct confrontation with the melancholy psychological state also called *blues* that is produced by unfortunate circumstances of lost love or unjust circumstances of racism and poverty. Ralph Ellison describes this motivation behind the music: "The blues is an impulse to keep the painful details and episodes of a brutal experience alive in one's aching consciousness, to finger its jagged grain, and to transcend it, not by the consolation of philosophy but by squeezing from it a near-tragic, near-comic lyricism." In other words, the blues transcends the pain by keeping it alive in the music itself.

This lyricism took many forms, though it has come to be associated most directly with the 12-bar blues. This form consists of three lines with an *aab* rhyme scheme, with the first line repeated in the second, often with slight variation in syntax or intonation, and with the third providing either ironic commentary or some resolution or both, as in the following lines from "The Backwater Blues": "Backwater blues done call me to pack my things and go / Backwater blues done call me to pack my things and go. / 'Cause my house fell down and I can't live there no more." These lines also convey the typical sense of loss and isolation that permeates the blues and that is reinforced by the repetition, as well as the understatement and ironic humor with which the singer confronts that loss, since her house "fell down" in the third line not of its own volition but because of the dramatic and destructive Mississippi flood of 1927. Indeed, clichés about the blues are sometimes true, as many songs mourn lost loves, castigate two-timing lovers, lament loneliness, and confess melancholy, though occasionally with a similarly understated tongue in cheek, leading Langston Hughes famously to characterize the blues as sometimes laughing to keep from crying. This tone of sadness is also expressed by what is sometimes called the "blue note," notes in the music scale distinctively flattened to melancholic effect. Simultaneously, a call-and-response interaction between voice and instrument, and between singer and audience, expresses at least the hope for unity and sympathy in the isolation. Through this complex leavening of melancholy with ironic humor, the blues exemplifies a defining tragic-comic humor and subtle emotional affirmation of Af. Am. folk culture.

Its own kind of verse, the blues inspired a great number of Af. Am. poets with this formal enactment of its psychological state, its stoic sensibility, and its existential philosophy, allowing the poet to extend into verse the central ideas and practices of black oral trads. First, the blues derives from spirituals, slave work songs and field hollers, cultural forms of communal unity, spiritual renewal, and, at times, political resistance developed by enslaved Afs. and by Af. Ams. enduring segregation. Second, blues singers often adapt folk ballads, using such folk heroes as John Henry, High John the Conqueror, and Stagolee as subjects and even as personae. Also, like those *ballads, blues songs use *rhyme and *repetition to create possibilities for humor, irony, and *lament that would be familiar to the almost exclusively black original audiences for the music. In addition, blues musicians often sing personalized versions of the same songs—called standards—and improvise on several standard *tropes, incl. the train and its whistle as symbols of mobility, moments of decision on the crossroads, and the flood of 1927, as well as the well-known themes of lost or cheating loves. Improvisation itself—the ability to "riff" on common themes and to change songs in every performance—was part of this stoic assertion of self by offering personal versions of common problems. In these ways, the blues fosters the creation of a distinctive Af. Am. communal culture as a bulwark against social oppression and existential angst.

From these common themes and cultural roots emerged varied modes of song that, in their various ways, would come to characterize blues poetry. There is the so-called classic blues like "Backwater Blues" sung in recordings by such well-known artists as Ma Rainey and Bessie Smith, women who complicated the music's traditionally masculine themes with their female perspectives and who helped to establish the 12-bar blues as the music's most identifiable form. There are also several regional subgenres, including the originating, acoustic Mississippi delta blues, which produced Robert Johnson and Muddy Waters, among others; the urban, electric guitar-based Chicago blues; and the later, jazz-influenced Kansas City blues. New Orleans boasts Dr. John, while Eric Clapton is celebrated for his mod. versions of the music.

Langston Hughes initiated the now-prevalent practice of adapting this empowering existential self-assertion of the blues and its variegated musical forms and trads. to literary poetry. In one of his best-known poems, "The Weary Blues," Hughes describes a blues musician whose singing was inspiring and who eased his own pain so that he could sleep. Hughes also included lyrics from an actual song called "The Weary Blues." Moreover, in many other poems, Hughes translated the 12-bar blues into six-line stanzas, both by adapting actual lyrics of the urban blues he heard in Harlem and by creating his own. His contemporary in the 1920s, Sterling A. Brown, likewise adapted rural blues songs from his folklore research into poetry. This turn to folk culture for poetic sources was characteristic of the *Harlem Renaissance, the cultural flourishing of Af. Ams. in and around Harlem in the 1920s in which Hughes and Brown participated. Since then, Gwendolyn Brooks, Melvin B. Tolson, Robert Hayden, Honoree Fannonne Jeffers, and Kevin Young are among the many poets who found in the wit, sarcasm, and existentialism of the music an approach amenable to portraying black people realistically and complexly, eliciting call-and-response relations between poet and poem analogous to that of blues musician and audience. The posture of self-affirmation in the face of a rigid society also appealed to Beat poets (see BEAT POETRY).

Indeed, the blues has come to be understood not only as one of the defining practices and sensibilities of Af. Am. popular and literary culture but as a distinctive Af. Am. contribution to Am. culture, literary and otherwise. E.g., Houston A. Baker suggested that the critic of Af. Am. lit. was much like a blues musician sitting at the crossroads whose imagination constitutes what Baker called a "blues matrix." Tony Bolden went further, implying that even such cultural forms as the *spiritual were actually blues-inflected. Moreover, most scholars of music in poetry acknowledge that jazz not only emerged from the blues but constitutes a musical and thematic continuum from the saddest, most stoic blues to a joyful, improvisational jazz celebration (see JAZZ POETRY). As scholars such as Sascha Feinstein, Meta DuEwa Jones, T. J. Anderson, and Kimberly Benston have pointed out, there is a jazz-blues aesthetic in Am. poetry, ranging from Jack Kerouac to Yusef Komunyakaa. There are also now folk festivals

dedicated to the blues and many of its figures—Robert Johnson, B.B. King, Bessie Smith, Ma Rainey—have become cultural icons, clarifying the powerful influence of the blues.

See MUSIC AND POETRY.

■ P. Oliver, *The Meaning of the Blues* (1963); R. Ellison, *Shadow and Act* (1965); A. Murray, *Stomping the Blues* (1976); H. A. Baker Jr., *Blues, Ideology and Afro-American Literature* (1984); S. Tracy, *Langston Hughes and the Blues* (1988); *The Jazz Poetry Anthology*, ed. S. Feinstein and Y. Komunyakaa (1996); T. Gioia, *The History of Jazz* (1997); A. Davis, *Blues Legacies and Black Feminism: Gertrude "Ma" Rainey, Bessie Smith and Billie Holiday* (1998); K. Benston, *Performing Blackness: Enactments of African American Modernism* (2000); M. Jones, "Jazz Prosodies: Orality and Texuality," *Callaloo* 25 (2002); T. J. Anderson, *Notes to Make the Sound Come Right: Four Innovations of Jazz Poetry* (2004); T. Bolden, *Afro-Blue: Improvisations in African American Poetry and Culture* (2004).

K. D. LEONARD

**BOB AND WHEEL.** A set of *heterometric poetic lines coming at the end of an *isometric stanza. The connecting line, the "bob," is shorter than the others; the following lines, the "wheel," rhyme with themselves and the bob. Both bobs and wheels occur independently of one another in med. poetry as well as together. *Sir Gawain and the Green Knight*, the most celebrated example of the two used together, culminates a series of instances from the 12th c. onward in ME, according to Guest. Following Borroff, both Cable and Duncan emphasize the number of syllables per line over metrical stress, Borroff calling ME rhymed verse "a compromise between native and continental metrical principles" (145). Other examples include the ME poems "Somer Sunday" and "Sir Tristrem," several of the Towneley mystery plays, incl. *The Second Shepherd's Play*, and Chaucer's "Tale of Sir Thopas."

■ E. Guest, *History of English Rhythms* (1838); M. Borroff, *"Sir Gawain and the Green Knight": A Stylistic and Metrical Study* (1962); E. G. Stanley, "The Use of Bob-Lines in *Sir Thopas*," *NM* 73 (1972); T. Turville-Petre, "'Summer Sunday,' 'De Tribus Regibus Mortuis,' and 'The Awntyrs off Arthure': Three Poems in the Thirteen-Line Stanza," *RES* 25 (1974), and *The Alliterative Revival* (1977); T. Cable, *The English Alliterative Tradition* (1991); *A Companion to the Middle English Lyric*, ed. T. G. Duncan (2005).

L. L. HOWES

**BOLIVIA, POETRY OF.** Hists. of Bolivian poetry have regularly struggled to incorporate the poetry created in all the langs. spoken in the nation. Besides Sp., the official lang. and lingua franca, at least three langs. are widely spoken in Bolivia: Aymara, Quechua, and Guaraní. Lit. hists. have been able to describe poetry written in Sp. since the colonial period and have sought to include the poetry written in the indigenous langs., but with limited success. The major impediment is that poetry in native langs. usually is part of an oral trad.

(i.e., none of these cultures had developed advanced writing systems; see ORAL POETRY). Thus, hists. of Bolivian poetry usually start with those texts written in Sp. after the arrival of Francisco Pizarro and Diego de Almagro and the conquest of the Incas (1531–33). Because the major part of the territory of what today is Bolivia (then called Kollasuyo) was part of the Inca Empire, this moment in hist. is considered an origin for the production of Bolivian lit. The present article will follow this conventional route (see also INDIGENOUS AMERICAS, POETRY OF THE).

Bolivian scholars agree that, for the colonial period (1531–1825), the criteria for defining authorship should rely on location more than place of birth for attributing a text to Bolivian lit. hist. Thus Bolivian poetry of the colonial period includes both the poems written by men and women born in the region and those written by colonists of the territory of the Royal Audience of Charcas (1599), an appellate court with jurisdiction over the region that would become Bolivia. *Coplas a la muerte de Don Diego de Almagro* (Songs on the Death of Diego de Almagro, ca. 1540) is recognized as the first poem written in Bolivian territory by an anonymous Sp. poet. Not very skillfully written, this is an epic romance of the execution of Almagro perpetrated by the Pizarro family in 1538. The most important writer of the 16th c. is Diego Dávalos y Figueroa (1552–1608), an Andalusian who lived and died in the city of La Paz. Dávalos wrote a text in prose, the *Miscelánea Austral* (Austral Miscellany), and a book of poems, the *Defensa de damas* (Defense of Ladies), that were published together in Lima in 1602 and received with great admiration by the intellectuals of the Viceroyalty of Peru. Dávalos's writings are considered the best example of *Petrarchism in the Sp. colonies. The life and work of Dávalos are tightly related to the intellectual life of his wife, Francisca de Briviesca y Arellano (ca. 1547–1616). She was a learned woman whose participation in her husband's production seems to have been very significant. In the *Defensa de damas*, she may be the poetess to which the poems refer, as well as the Cilena who signs one of the laudatory poems at the beginning of the book. This exquisite sonnet is the first poem pub. by a woman in the Viceroyalty of Peru. Moreover, the *Defensa de damas* is the first feminist poem in Bolivian—and Latin Am.—lit.

During the 16th and 17th cs., the wealth of the imperial city of Potosí, based in the exploitation of the silver in its famous mountain, attracted adventurers from the New and Old Worlds looking for quick prosperity. Potosí became an exuberant and opulent city typical of the Am. *baroque, drawing numerous writers in the 17th c.

The Port. poet Henrique Garcés (ca. 1522–95), who had an important role in adapting Petrarch's poetry throughout the Viceroyalty of Peru, may have lived in Potosí while he tried to implement a process to separate silver by the use of mercury. His trans. of Petrarch's *Canzoniere* (1591) and his own poetry were so well known that Miguel de Cervantes mentioned him

in a poem. The most important poet of the 17th c. to have dwelled in Potosí is Luis de Ribera (ca. 1555–1623). Born in Seville, he lived in Potosí as well as in La Plata from at least 1621 to 1623. His only book is a collection of religious poetry, *Sagradas poesías* (Sacred Poems), published in Seville in 1612. Ribera worked in a sophisticated baroque style, and despite the devotional orientation, an intense eroticism pervades many of his poems. He had a preference for biblical themes that allowed him to display erotic topics, such as the drunkenness of Lot raped by his daughters or the nakedness of Bathsheba. His poetry is considered not only one of the peaks of Bolivian and Latin Am. colonial production, but among the best of the Sp. Golden Age. Diego Mexía de Fernengil (ca. 1555–after 1617), another important figure born in Seville, resided in Potosí from 1609 to 1617. He was a friend of Ribera, with whom he shared strong religious beliefs. Mexía was a reputed translator of Ovid. In 1608, he published the first part of his *Parnaso Antártico* (Antarctic Parnassus), a trans. of Ovid's *Heroides*. While in Potosí, he probably wrote the second part of the *Parnaso Antártico*, a collection of sonnets, some of them inspired by illustrations of the life of Christ made by the Jesuit Jerónimo Nadal.

José de Antequera (1689–1731) was perhaps the finest poet of the 18th c. He was a judge of the Audience of Charcas, but he rebelled against the Sp. Crown. Sentenced to death in 1731, he wrote several sonnets while in prison, lamenting his fate and the passing of time. The "Testamento de Potosí" (Potosí's Testament, 1800), by an anonymous poet, may well be the closing text of the colonial period. This is a book of satirical poetry that anticipates the character of much 19th-c. poetry.

Bolivia began its independence movement in 1810 and became a nation in 1825. These were long years of war, and few literary texts were produced or survived the armed struggle. In the first decades of the republic, the social and political situation was not much better. Political turmoil engulfed many of the promising writers of this period. *Romanticism, the dominant literary style in Sp. America, did not have large numbers of Bolivian cultivators. However, there were a few poets whose works are recognized as valuable. The outstanding poet of this period is Ricardo José Bustamante (1821–84). He studied in Paris, where he became familiar with Eur. lit.; his best-known poem is "Preludio al Mamoré" (Prelude to the Mamoré). Another important romantic poet is the blind María Josefa Mujía (1812–88), who is considered the first woman writer of the newly independent nation. Her poetry draws on her blindness to convey a dark and tragic perception of life. It is worth mentioning Manuel José Tovar (1831–69), whose poem "La creación" (The Creation), based in the biblical Genesis, is one of the jewels of Bolivian romantic poetry.

The transition to mod. poetry of the 20th c. followed two roads: one opened by the poetry of Adela Zamudio (1854–1928), inclined toward social issues; the other by Ricardo Jaimes Freyre (1866–1933), focused on the renovation of poetic lang., a phenomenon fueled by Sp. Am. *modernismo*. Zamudio's poetry is in some measure romantic, but a profound consciousness of her social situation as a woman generates a radical crit. of the hypocrisy of Bolivian patriarchal society. She is considered the most important feminist writer in Bolivian lit. In her life and works, she was a defender of childhood and women as well as a critic of Bolivian education, in the hands of the Catholic Church at the time. Her best known poem is "Nacer hombre" (To Be Born a Man), a strong crit. of men's privileges. Jaimes Freyre is considered, with Rubén Darío and Leopoldo Lugones, one of the founders of modernismo. He and Darío wrote a *manifesto in 1894 that is considered the beginning of this literary movement. In 1905, Freyre wrote *Leyes de la versificación castellana* (Laws of Castilian Versification), an innovative treatise about the laws of versification in the Sp. lang. His most famous book of poetry is *Castalia bárbara* (Barbarous Castalia), a poetic recreation of some themes of Scandinavian mythology.

It has been argued that the dominant intellect of the first half of the 20th c. in Bolivia was Franz Tamayo (1879–1956). His poetry was fed by the modernist style; however, he took that style to phonetic extremes even as he used cl. Greco-Roman lit. as the foundation of his poetry. He developed a voice so distinctive that it made him the preeminent poet of Bolivia. His erudition allowed him to write poetry heavy with references to antiquity, esp. the cl. trad., as these titles may indicate: *Epigramas griegos* (Greek Epigrams), *Scopas*, and his best-known book, *La Prometheida* (The Promethiad, 1917), a meditation on the Prometheus myth.

The avant-garde movements of the first decades of the 20th c. had some late followers in Bolivia. It is worth mentioning Guillermo Viscarra Fabre (1900–80) and Julio de la Vega (b. 1924). But perhaps the most original poet with avant-garde affinities is Edmundo Camargo (1936–64). These three poets made profuse use of visual images and surrealist topics common in the period's avant-garde movements. Yolanda Bedregal (1916–99), named "Yolanda of Bolivia," was considered an official symbol of Bolivian poetry in the second half of the 20th c. The main topics of her poetry are women as the foundation of the family and God. Although love is central to her writings, it is not always viewed as an easy or pure emotion. Love in her poetry is constantly faced with emotional challenges such as hatred or abuse.

If the first half of the 20th c. was dominated by Tamayo, the second part saw two poets, both his admirers, as the major figures of Bolivian poetry: Oscar Cerruto (1912–81) and Jaime Saenz (1921–86). Cerruto's poetry continues to employ a cl. lang., but without Tamayo's considerable erudition. Impelled by a search for the "precise word" and by his admiration for Sp. Golden Age poetry, Cerruto developed an extremely unadorned poetry to express a disenchanted view of Bolivian society. Among his books, *Patria de sal cautiva* (Fatherland, Captive of Salt, 1958) and *Estrella seg-*

*regada* (Outcast Star, 1975) are considered masterpieces. Saenz's alcoholism and troubling obsession with death became the source of his philosophical and poetic view of life. He experienced his life as a path to transcendental meaning, always bordering on self-destruction. His poetry is born out of this search as a mystical and demonic quest. By the use of nonsense, paradox, and oxymoron, his poetry forces lang. to the limits of signification. Books such as *Aniversario de una visión* (Anniversary of a Vision, 1960), *Recorrer esta distancia* (To Cross this Distance, 1973), and *La noche* (The Night, 1984) are extraordinary examples of a deeply eccentric Bolivian (and Latin Am.) poetics.

The end of the 20th c. and the beginning of the 21st saw at least three important poets: Eduardo Mitre (b. 1943), Humberto Quino (b. 1950), and Blanca Wiethüchter (1947–2004). Mitre writes a celebratory poetry in a highly crafted lang. where words and objects can trade places in the seamless space of the erotic. Quino has produced a no less precise poetry but of an opposite character, by looking at himself with irony, sarcasm, and self-contempt. Wiethüchter wrote a poetry of permanent self-searching that speaks of her womanhood in terms of desire and intellectual aptitude. Her feminism can be seen in the poems of *Itaca* (Ithaca, 2000), where she uses Penelope's voice to recognize how little she needs and wants the return of Odysseus.

*See* COLONIAL POETICS; GUARANÍ POETRY; SPAIN, POETRY OF; SPANISH AMERICA, POETRY OF.

■ A. Cáceres Romero, *Nueva historia de la literatura boliviana*, 3 v. (1987–95); *Cambridge History of Latin American Literature*, ed. R. González Echevarría and E. Pupo-Walker, 3 v. (1996); *Diccionario histórico de Bolivia*, ed. J. M. Barnadas, G. Calvo, and J. Ticlla, 2 v. (2002); *Hacia una historia crítica de la literatura en Bolivia*, ed. B. Wiethüchter and A. M. Paz-Soldán (2002).

L. García-Pabón

## BOOK, POETIC

I. Medieval and Early Modern
II. Modern, Postmodern, and Postbook

**I. Medieval and Early Modern.** *Book* is an inclusive term. Applied to cuneiform tablets, papyrus rolls, bound objects, and electronic devices, it refers both to historically specific literary technologies and to writing in general. This combination drives the book's paradoxical relationship to poetic form and lit. hist. On one hand, books are simply material objects, vehicles for the ostensibly more primary artistic and intellectual works they contain. On the other, their format implies a poetic dimension, a *trope for writing, a shaping force, and a silent collaborator in reading. Similarly, books are at once marked by the time of their construction and transcendent of that time, able to project the human imagination across centuries. The poetics of the book derives from its ability to span these contradictions, to figure paradox as unity and thus to sustain the fragmentary, fissured nature of representation as a coherent whole. In this, the technology of the book asserts a poetic and temporal form at a literary level beneath authorial intention. *Book* is an inclusive term, then, not only because it encompasses multiple technologies of inscription but because it is a jointly material and discursive object of figural representation.

For the med. and early mod. periods, the dominant form of the book is the codex. Derived from the Lat. for "the trunk of a tree," the codex originated as a writing tablet, a wooden board with a carved depression in its center filled with red or black wax and written on with a hard stylus. Homer describes Proteus as using a "folded tablet" in the *Iliad* (6.168), suggesting that, by the 8th or 9th c. BCE, the codex had developed from a slate to two pieces of wood fastened together, a hinged object that protected its internal message. Early examples of the codex feature additional internal leaves of wood, papyrus (a writing surface made from Egyptian reeds), or parchment (animal skin). Throughout the Gr. and Roman world, such codices were used for notational writing—drafts, lessons, calculations, and lists—and were, thus, secondary to the roll. Books are known as a permanent record, yet they originate as a technology for ephemera; and so the hist. of the book, an object that symbolizes depth of learning but is effectively defined by its covers, is cross-cut by contradiction.

This contradictory quality is first articulated by the epigrammist Martial (pseud. of Marcus Valerius Martialis, ca. 40–103), who reflects on the codex in the second poem of his revised *Epigrams* (ca. 103):

Qui tecum cupis esse meos ubicumque libellos
et comites longae quaeris habere viae,
hos eme, quos artat brevibus membrana tabellis:
scrinia da magnis, me manus una capit.
ne tamen ignores ubi sim venalis et erres
urbe vagus tota, me duce certus eris;
libertum docti Lucensis quaere Secundum
limina post Pacis Palladiaeque forum. (1.2)

[You who want to have my books with you wherever you go, and who are looking to have them as companions on a long journey, buy these, which the parchment confines within small covers: give cylinders to the great, one hand can hold me. That you should not be ignorant of where I am on sale and wander aimlessly over the whole city, with me as your guide you will be certain: look for Secundus, the freedman of learned Lucensis, beyond the threshold of the Temple of Peace and the Forum of Minerva.] (Fitzgerald)

In its emphasis on buying and selling, on carrying, covers, and great cylinders, the poem is chiefly about the form of the book. It is also about self-fashioning, about Martial's formulation of his *persona as an urban poet-about-town. Martial highlights a tension between these two forms, book and author, through a metonymic change of name ("I am on sale," "with me as your guide"). This tension is contained in the very word he uses for the codex, *libellus*, which (as Fitzger-

ald remarks) means both a single petition and a complete book of poems. Martial's is a book of petitions twice over: once in that it is a series of fragmentary short poems integrated as a collection by the genre of *epigram and once again in that it is a series of individual sheets constructed into a unity by the codex's binding. Implicitly, Martial asks which is the operative genre that structures his poetry and his poetic self, epigram or codex? From the very start of literary commentary on the book, Martial recognizes that the book-as-codex involves both surface and depth, physical and discursive genres for poetic representation.

Shortly after Martial's observation, the early Christian communities at Antioch and Jerusalem developed the codex from a secondary writing aid to a major textual form. By the 4th c., the codex rivaled the roll, so much so that the term *biblios* became common in Antioch for school texts or Christian books; by the 5th c., 89% of all remaining Gr. books are in the form of the codex. In a quantifiable way, the representative potential inherent in the codex found an audience in Christian readers and writers, and this energized its technological devel. The early Christians' predilection for the codex has no clear explanation beyond the jointly physical and discursive capacities suggested by Martial: codices imply a unified canon even if the actual texts they contain are only fragmentary. In each case—material surface and intellectual depth (substitution), change of name (object for author), and part for whole (a selection of texts representing a total collection)—the codex operates through a singular tropological principle, *metonymy: i.e., technology always includes a figural as well as a material sense. For the book, these two elements coalesce in metonymy. Thus, as much as the book is a material form, it is also a poetic one.

Throughout the Middle Ages, book producers experimented with ways of making the *mise-en-page* (scene of the page) more expressive of this unity. For example, decorative elements such as historiated initials (an introductory capital letter containing a picture, portrait, or scene within it), miniatures (pictures related to the contents), and illuminations (gold or silver decorations that create a sense of light from within the book) transformed the page from a textual to a visual space. Across the 12th and 13th cs., fraternal religious organizations and the Parisian academic book trade developed a visual system to represent the text's internal rhetorical organization, its *ordinatio*, which included numerals, paragraph marks, underlinings, rubrics (the practice of writing titles or marginal glosses in a contrasting color such as red), and tables of contents, all designed to guide the reader's experience. These readers added their own marks to the page. Indeed, the making of books blurs the roles of reader and writer, and this was recognized, in the 13th c. esp., in the compiler, whose task was to reassemble—combine, rearrange, and order by chapter and section—authoritative texts according to a new organizational scheme. Each of these cases—decoration, ordination, and compilation—describes a process by which book makers augmented the texts they copied with design elements unique to the format of the book and in so doing created an increasingly sophisticated and unified object.

Thus, the codex emerges as a powerful trope across the med. and early mod. periods. From Augustine's reading of Paul in his personal Bible in the *Confessions*, to Petrarch's reading of Augustine in his portable copy of the *Confessions* on Mont Ventoux, the intellectual markers of both the med. and the mod. recur on the object of the book. For Eng. poetics, the act of poetic making and book making become almost inseparable. E.g., in the conclusion to book 5 of *Troilus and Criseyde*, Chaucer (ca. 1345–1400) writes:

> Go, litel bok, go, litel myn tragedye,
> Ther God thi makere yet, er that he dye,
> So sende myg64t to make in som comedye!
> But litel book, no making thow n'envie,
> But subgit be to alle poesye;
> And kis the steppes where as thow seest pace
> Virgile, Ovide, Omer, Lucan, and Stace.
> (5.1786–92)

Here, as in Martial, is the notion of book as proxy for the author. Yet Chaucer's book is not simply a metonymic stand-in; possessing its own emotions and engaging in its own activities, it constitutes a metaleptic function in which the book-as-metonym appears within a larger figure of lit. hist. as a pantheon of named authors. This is true for the ms. hist. of *Troilus and Criseyde* as well, for there exists no authorial version of this important text. The remaining mss. of the poem were copied in the 15th c., after Chaucer's death, and not one presents the poem in an authorial form. Rather, most of these versions were created from small booklets or quires, circulated by London lending shops and each possessing variations. The scribes who borrowed these texts were freelance craftsmen, loosely organized by stationers who subcontracted the work, apparently at times out of a tenement that operated as physical hive for the division of labor. Just as Chaucer's "litel bok" appears in a lit. hist. of named authors as a semiautonomous representation, *Troilus and Criseyde* emerges from Eng. literary book culture as an independent construction. The book is a metonymic machine: assembled from parts, it unifies rhetorical and material fragments in the face of contradiction, creating a physical embodiment of a literary imagination that perhaps never existed.

Print technology significantly expands the volume of book production, but it does not revolutionize the fundamental assembly process. Again, the hist. of *Troilus and Criseyde* is instructive. First printed by William Caxton in 1483, it appeared in a series of seemingly separate publications, culminating in William Thynne's famous 1532 ed. of Chaucer's collected works. Thynne's ed. was reprinted and expanded throughout the 16th and 17th cs., finding definitive expression in Francis Thynne's 1602 version. In this progression, the literary *canon appears to develop as a break with the med. past into a mod. sense of authorship and print culture. *Troilus and Criseyde* was complied into exactly such canonical collections from the start, and a number of

early books bind together single-ed. handwritten and printed versions of Chaucer's poetry into composite collections. Ms. producers were, in fact, experimenting with mass-production techniques and woodblock printing from the beginning of the 15th c. Johannes Gutenberg combined these techniques—the division of labor, line assembly, the wooden screw-type press, binding—with moveable metal type and so created a system of textual reproduction that remained essentially unchanged through the 19th c. Yet the format of the codex as a bound object was established by Homer's time, and the inventive plan Gutenberg deployed—the combination of preexisting parts into a new whole—belongs not to mod. print culture but to the governing logic of the book, one that continually figures invention through metonymy.

A book not only creates, as Martial observed, a figure of the self but, as Chaucer suggests, projects this figure across time through a process of assembly both derivative and atemporal: derivative, because it relies on the technologies of the past and hence is always invested in a return, always troping on a preexisting format; atemporal, because it stands outside chronology, able to communicate an imaginative truth in whatever present it is read. Thus, the book not only operates as a *poetic form* but presents a *formal* relationship to hist. The process of lit. hist. often appears a species of naturalism, the settling of literary accounts according to a yearly plan; the book suggests time according to the poetics of the page, one that is fragmentary but nevertheless recoverable, imaginative but still tangible.

**II. Modern, Postmodern, and Postbook.** As the foregoing section argues, the formal and historical character of the book is indivisible. No exception to this statement, the 17th c. in Europe marks a period in which printing and book technology became entwined with the intellectual culture of the day. In Britain, this period opened with the appearance of three books that went on to long lives in different relations to printing: first, in 1611, one of the most often-printed books in Eng., the King James Bible; in 1616, Ben Jonson's *Workes*, the first self-edited collection of a living poet's production and a model for every later collected works; and then, in 1623, a book whose contents have been among the most often reprinted in different ways, the First Folio of Shakespeare's plays. The period then closed with the struggle for freedom of the press and against the legal requirement that all books be approved by an official censor before publication (a struggle evidenced by John Milton's address to Parliament in 1643, pub. in 1644 as *Areopagitica*). For poetry, these two devels. clearly—and for the first time—opened the possibility of the book as a technology of writing not only widely available but adaptable to modification, appropriation, and even "hacking" in many ways to bring format into different alignments with content. Writers in all disciplines became more involved in book technology, sometimes even writing directly to the new adaptability of the medium. By 1669, the Dutch scientist and mathematician Christian Huygens had invented a process to print handwriting and geometrical figures; in the same year, the physician William Petty had developed a method for printing as many copies of a book as the public demanded. Chappell and Bringhurst's *A Short History of the Printed Word* and Finkelstein and McCleery's *An Introduction to Book History* offer a fuller and more nuanced account of the early hist. of the book; but for the purposes of this entry, this authorial involvement with form (the form of the book as much as the material, mechanical limits, and possibilities of the printing press itself), content, medium, and message acted as a catalyst for ever more experiments on the book as a poetic object—very often a poetic object that was as much "content" as the words appearing between the covers. This approach would ultimately give rise to the idea of the artist's book that came to fruition in the latter part of the 20th c.

Insofar as the 17th c. prepared for a new integration of book form and intellectual and artistic content, William Blake's *Songs of Innocence* and *The Book of Thel* are the most obvious 18th-c. outcomes. In 1788, Blake printed *There Is No Natural Religion*, the first instance of illuminated printing. Echoing his concern for how—in opposition to Jean-Jacques Rousseau's notion of natural ideas held by all human beings—each poet and reader had his or her own worldview and system of values, Blake's new method of printing meant that "the metal plates with which he was familiar as an engraver could be etched sufficiently to be printed in relief. . . . [W]hen finished, the etched plate could be used to pull prints as they were needed or ordered, thus allowing him to work with an unlimited edition produced on demand" (Drucker, *Visible Word*). The following year, Blake published his monumental *Songs of Innocence*, a work of painting and poetry; thereafter, he published numerous other works in which the page—a basic unit of composition of the book—is transformed from a neutral, even transparent, surface to a canvas on which margin, border, illustration, and text form a unified whole. With illuminated printing, Blake not only combined the visual arts with the literary but moved away from the expensive process of using a letterpress and thus took back control of the means of production.

If Blake's commitment to expressing independence through the book is one turning point in Brit. letters, then William Morris and his work with the Kelmscott Press—as a counter to rapid industrialization and a demonstration of his growing commitment to socialism—is another. Morris expounded an ethos of craft, function, and respect for materials that made him a pioneer of modern design. While it appears that Morris's notions about book design were rooted in 15th-c. printing practices, his unique innovation was that he extended, not simply imitated, these earlier practices, creating works that were not merely decorative at the level of the page or even at the level of the units of construction on the page but carefully designed wholes. Not surprisingly, then, his highest achievement is generally acknowledged to be his *Works of Geoffrey Chaucer*, which represents his most concerted effort to create

"the ideal book," by which he means "a book not limited by commercial exigencies of price: we can do what we like with it, according to what its nature, as a book, demands of Art" (Morris).

However, it was precisely Morris's dedication to a clean, legible, and harmonious aesthetic of the book, the page, as well as *typography—a dedication he hoped would express a medievalism that took the reader or viewer outside the ugly reality of Victorian England and reflected certain ideas about art, beauty, and the inherent goodness in craftsmanship and simplicity—that led to the early 20th-c. avant-garde embrace of a disruptive, nonlinear, even explosive approach to page design, typography, and the construction of the book. While undoubtedly Stéphane Mallarmé's *Un coup de dés* (*A Throw of the Dice*)—published in the magazine *Cosmopolis* in 1897 but not in book form until after his death in 1914—had a tremendous influence on 20th-c. explorations into words themselves as visual carriers of meaning. Experiments in typography and bookmaking by futurists, Dadaists, and surrealists (see FUTURISM, DADA, SURREALISM) were so far-reaching that their influence is still felt today in online experiments with kinetic typography, animated digital poems, and other digital deconstructions of the page. For instance, in 1913, the It. futurist F. T. Marinetti first proposed the idea of *parole in libertà* (words in freedom) as a call for a typographical revolution that would consist of "Condensed metaphors. Telegraphic images. Maximum vibrations. Nodes of thought. Closed or open fans of movement. Compressed analogies. Color Balances. Dimensions, weights, measures, and the speed of sensations." In an attempt to realize his vision of words-in-freedom, Marinetti published *Zang Tumb Tuuum* (1914)—a typographic tour de force with foldout pages that further unsettled the harmony of the page and the book.

While there are many other instances of influential early 20th-c. experiments on the book and its various units of construction (incl. binding, margin, page, typography, and cover), there seems to be a connection between Marinetti's attempts to turn the space of the page into a nonlinear, painterly canvas on which to explore the shape, dimension, and volume of letters and words and later, even more radical experiments such as Steve McCaffery's monumental typescape *Carnival* (1969–75). A concrete poem (see CONCRETE POETRY) that was originally packaged as a book containing 16 sheets of paper, *Carnival* offered its readers the following instructions: "In order to destroy this book please tear each page carefully along the perforation. The panel is assembled by laying out pages in a square of four." Clearly, the paradox of this work is that to read the book the reader first has to destroy it.

Less obviously related to Marinetti, though no less invested in systematically breaking down conventions of meaning-making and literariness that were tied to the idea of the book, poets and/or artists such as Robert Grenier (in his 1978 *Sentences*) and Carolee Schneemann (in her 1977 *ABC*) took the binding off the book and instead published decks of cards, which utterly undercut any notion of unity as well as clear authorial intent. The Brit. artist Tom Phillips deconstructed the book by constructing five different eds., beginning in 1970, of *A Humument* by "treating" or painting and writing over a copy found by both rule and chance (i.e., the first book Phillips found for three-pence) of the novel *A Human Document* by the Victorian novelist W. H. Mallock. There are countless other examples of 20th-c. artists' books and ostensible books of poetry that have broken down or defamiliarized every conceivable aspect of the book. E.g., the painter Larry Rivers and the poet Frank O'Hara collaborated to create *Stones* (1958)—twelve lithographs made by Douglass Morse Howell by pulling from stones written and drawn on by Rivers and O'Hara; Elisabetta Gut's 1983 *Libro-seme* (*Seed-book*) uses the shell of a seed as the cover of a book inside of which are sheets of music on rice paper that have been cut in the shape of the shells; and Frances L. Swetlund's 1989 *The Messenger* appropriates a Victorian photo album inside of which is a dead bird, a map, bones, shells, and other found objects on which letters and numbers have been stamped (see ALEATORY POETICS, CONSTRAINT).

Thus, having encountered books as everything from decks of cards, fans, accordions, postcards, sculptural objects, and objects made out of cloth to edible works made out of chewing gum, in a sense 21st-c. poets have no choice but to extend this systematic deconstruction (a "hacking" that was anticipated in the early mod. hist. of the medium) to an utter dematerialization of the book through its trans. into the digital. While it is true that certain animated digital poems such as Brian Kim Stefans's "Dreamlife of Letters," as well as his "Suicide in an Airplane," seem to continue, in the digital realm, Marinetti's attempts to bring a sense of dynamism to the page, by and large digital poets are prepared to carry on postbook experiments (*post* in both the sense of looking back on and in the historical sense of coming after). Stephanie Strickland's *V* (2002) and *Zone: Zero* (2008) are postbook works in which poems in book-bound form comment on the same poems in digital form and vice versa, the result of which is a distributed poem such as "slippingglimpse" whose stable text in a two-column form on the page undergoes a radical trans. online where it turns into a ten-part Flash poem that combines the original text with videos of ocean patterns; as Strickland puts it, "In a round robin of reading, the water 'reads' the poem text . . . the poem text 'reads' image/capture technologies . . . and the image-capture video 'reads' the water," thereby utterly destabilizing both the original book-bound text and the conventional notion of what it means to read. Further, a substantial number of digital poems are less about semantic meaning than about a self-reflexive consideration of the materiality of letters and words, as well as about investigating the material limits and possibilities of the computer as a medium for writing. John Cayley's "Translation" exemplifies such poems in that it is often unreadable either because it is constantly algorithmically shifting between Eng., Fr., and Ger. or because the words are, as Cayley puts it, always

either "surfacing, floating, or sinking." It is also likely a matter of time before poets attempt to hack e-readers at least in part to draw attention to how these devices both imitate and undermine the idea and the material reality of the book.

*See* ELECTRONIC POETRY, LANGUAGE POETRY, SONG-BOOK, TECHNOLOGY AND POETRY, VISUAL POETRY.

■ **Medieval and Early Modern**: Curtius; M. B. Parkes, "The Influence of the Concepts of *Ordinatio* and *Compilatio* on the Development of the Book," *Medieval Learning and Literature*, ed. J.J.G. Alexander and M. T. Gibson (1976); E. L. Eisenstein, *The Printing Press as an Agent of Change* (1979); P. Needham, *The Printer and the Pardoner* (1986); C. H. Roberts and T. C. Skeat, *The Birth of the Codex* (1987); *Book Production and Publishing in Britain, 1375–1475*, ed. J. Griffiths and D. Pearsall (1989); D. C. Greetham, *Textual Scholarship* (1994); P. Gaskell, *A New Introduction to Bibliography* (1995); R. Hanna III, *Pursuing History* (1996); C. De Hamel, *A History of Illuminated Manuscripts* (1997); A. Manguel, *A History of Reading* (1997); F. G. Kilgour, *The Evolution of the Book* (1998); *The Cambridge History of the Book in Britain, Vol. III, 1400–1557*, ed. L. Hellinga and J. B. Trapp (1999); *The Cambridge History of the Book in Britain, Vol. IV, 1557–1695*, ed. J. Barnard, D. F. McKenzie, and M. Bell (2002); A. Murphy, *Shakespeare in Print* (2003); S. Füssel, *Gutenberg and the Impact of Printing*, trans. D. Martin (2005); W. Fitzgerald, *Martial* (2007).

■ **Modern, Postmodern, and Postbook**: F. T. Marinetti, *Zang Tumb Tuuum* (1914), http://www.colophon.com/gallery/futurism/2.html/; D. McMurtrie, *The Book* (1973); S. McCaffery, *Carnival* (1969–75), http://archives.chbooks.com/online_books/carnival/; R. Grenier, *Sentences* (1978), http://www.whalecloth.org/grenier/sentences_.htm/; S. McCaffery and bpNichol, *Rational Geomancy: The Kids of the Book-Machine: The Collected Research Reports of the Toronto Research Group, 1973–82* (1992); J. J. McGann, *Black Riders: The Visible Language of Modernism* (1993); W. Morris, *The Ideal Book*, ed. W. S. Peterson (1982); J. Drucker, *The Century of Artists' Books* and *The Visible Word: Experimental Typography and Modern Art, 1909–1923* (both 1994); D. Higgins and C. Alexander, *Talking the Boundless Book* (1996); J. Rothenberg and S. Clay, *A Secret Location on the Lower East Side: Adventures in Writing, 1960–1980* (1998); W. Chappell and R. Bringhurst, *A Short History of the Printed Word* (1999); J. Rothenberg, *A Book of the Book* (2000); B. Bright, *No Longer Innocent: Book Art in America* (2005); D. Finkelstein and A. McCleery, *An Introduction to Book History* (2005); T. Phillips, *A Humument* (1970–2005), http://www.humument.com/; P. Shillingsburg, *From Gutenberg to Google* (2006); S. Strickland, "Slippingglimpse," intro. (2008), http://www.cynthialawson.com/sg/pages/introduction.html; K. Wasserman, *The Book as Art* (2006); *A Companion to the History of the Book*, ed. S. Eliot and J. Rose (2009).

WM. KUSKIN (MED. AND EARLY MOD.);
L. EMERSON (MOD.)

**BOSNIAN POETRY.** The influence of folk genres, in particular *ballad and lyric *songs, is characteristic of both recent and older Bosnian poetry. Traditional Bosnian poetry should be considered part of the broader South Slavic corpus, owing to a shared body of stylistic and thematic features. The first systematic study of folk poetry from this region was undertaken by Milman Parry and Albert Lord in the period 1933–35 (see ORAL-FORMULAIC THEORY) and resulted in Lord's seminal study *The Singer of Tales* (1960). Parry and Lord devoted most of their efforts to long epics, but they also collected over 11,000 women's ballads and lyric songs. It is the shorter folk songs that have left the deepest trace on the lit. of Bosnia-Herzegovina, regardless of the author's ethnic or religious background.

Alongside a lyrical component stemming from traditional lore, in the poetry of Bosnian Muslim authors there is an esoteric-mystical dimension reflecting Islamic spirituality and drawing on poetry that reached Bosnia through the extended presence of the Ottomans in the Balkans. The older generation of authors, such as Safet-beg Bašagić (1870–1934), Musa Ćazim Ćatić (1878–1915), and Ahmed Muradbegović (1898–1972), relied heavily on patterns of folk love poetry but also introduced the refinement and sensibility of a complex multicultural environment.

The next generation of poets introduced elements of the avant-garde, which meant a departure from more traditional forms and the inclusion of the irrational, as well as a more openly erotic dimension saturated with Eastern mysticism and opulent imagery. These characteristics are particularly visible in the poetry of Hamza Humo (1895–1970). Following in this vein is the somewhat younger Skender Kulenović (1910–78), for whom poetry is both an esoteric experience and a voice of social conscience.

Several Serbian poets were active in Herzegovina for all or part of their careers, incl. the symbolist Jovan Dučić (1871–1943) and Aleksa Šantić (1868–1924), who modeled many of his works on traditional love poems. One of the greatest Croatian expressionist poets, Antun Branko Šimić (1898–1925), also spent his youth in Herzegovina before relocating to Zagreb.

Although it draws on a specifically Bosnian heritage, the poetry of Mak (Mehmedalija) Dizdar (1917–71) is stylistically highly accomplished and transcultural. His groundbreaking poem *Plivačica* (The Swimmer, 1954) is a strong statement of individuality, vitality, and formal innovation that reflects elements of surrealism but is also an overt departure from the rigid norms of social realism then prevalent. In his collection *Kameni spavač* (Stone Sleeper, 1966), he takes as his inspiration inscriptions from the *stećak* monuments (med. Bogomil tombstones) and through an ancestral poetic perspective speaks of Bosnia as a country of sorrow and resilience.

The poetry of Abdulah Sidran (b. 1944) is imbued with a sadness resulting from his perception of disharmony in the world. His poems are dialogic and often give the impression of settling accounts with life. Representatives of the younger generation, most notably Semezdin Mehmedinović (b. 1960) and Saša Skenderija (b. 1968), were deeply influenced by the wars of 1990s and often address questions of politics, identity, and everyday life in their poetry, while at the same time experimenting with hybrid genres. Among Bosnian-Herzegovinian women poets, Bisera Alikadić (b. 1939), Mubera Pašić (b. 1945), Josefina Dautbegović (1948–2008), and Ferida Duraković (b. 1957) all have written predominantly introspective, intimate poetry, while the latter two have provided memorable verses on the theme of war.

■ **Anthologies**: B. Bartók and A. Lord, *Serbo-Croatian Folk Songs* (1951); *Serbocroatian Heroic Songs*, ed. and trans. A. Lord et al. (1953–80); *Antologija bošnjačke poezije XX vijeka*, ed. E. Duraković (1995); *Scar on the Stone: Contemporary Poetry from Bosnia*, ed. C. Agee (1998); *Antologija bošnjačkih usmenih lirskonarativnih pjesama*, ed. Đ. Buturović and L. Buturović (2002).

■ **Criticism and History**: M. P. Coote, "Serbocroatian Heroic Songs," *Heroic Epic and Saga*, ed. F. J. Oinas (1978); Lord; C. Hawkesworth, *Voices in the Shadows: Women and Verbal Art in Serbia and Bosnia* (2000); A. Buturović, *Stone Speaker: Medieval Tombs, Landscape, and Bosnian Identity in the Poetry of Mak Dizdar* (2002); E. Duraković, *Bošnjačke i bosanske književne neminovnosti* (2003); A. Vidan, *Embroidered with Gold, Strung with Pearls: The Traditional Ballads of Bosnian Women* (2003).

A. VIDAN

**BOUSTROPHEDON** (Gr., "in the manner of an ox's turning"). A text in which alternate lines or columns are designed to be read in opposite directions is said to be written *boustrophedon*. The term alludes to the alternating direction of the furrows in a ploughed field. Though properly an adverb, it is often used as an adjective or noun. Boustrophedon is a graphic format, not a literary form. Any text that can be written in two or more lines using discrete letter-forms or symbols can be written boustrophedon; a text thus written should not be confused with a *palindrome. The boustrophedon format is found sporadically in the ancient Near East and in Etruscan, early Lat., and runic inscriptions. The best-known examples, however, are in Gr. inscriptions of the 7th and 6th cs. BCE. These include short verse texts as well as law codes, religious dedications, and calendars, inscribed on stone, pottery, or metal. In the Gr. examples, the shapes of the letters, as well as their order, are typically reversed in alternate lines (as if reflected in a mirror); in other cases, alternate lines are not reversed but inverted. Boustrophedon coexisted at this early period with the now-familiar left-to-right format as well as texts with all lines written right to left (probably reflecting the Gr. alphabet's Phoenician roots). It seems to have fallen out of use by the 5th c. BCE. Boustrophedon has been revived on an ad hoc basis by various contemp. writers under the influence of *concrete poetry and *Oulipo. In mod. poems, the retrograde element may involve mirror writing (as in Rosanne Wasserman's "Boustrophedon"), reversal of letters, or reverse ordering of words in alternate lines; the poem's content usually reflects or alludes to the format in some way. Other poets (e.g., John Kinsella) have invoked the term's metaphorical associations (retrograde movement, nonlinear progression, writing-as-ploughing) without using the actual format.

■ L. Jeffery, *The Local Scripts of Archaic Greece* (1961); A. G. Woodhead, *The Study of Greek Inscriptions* (1981).

G. HAYS

**BOUTS-RIMÉS.** A sequence of words rhyming in accordance with a predetermined *rhyme scheme (often that of the *sonnet) and used as the basis of a verse-making game; also (by *metonymy) the game itself. The object of the game, which is said to have been invented by Gilles Ménage (1613–92) and was popular in *précieux* circles of 17th-c. Paris, is to write a poem incorporating the given rhyme words so as to achieve effects as witty as they are seemingly uncontrived. Accordingly, the sequence of rhymes is made as bizarre and incongruous as possible. From the first, *bouts-rimés* tried the ingenuity of even the most considerable poets (Pierre Corneille, Nicolas Boileau), and the diversion spread to England and Scotland and survived as a source of 19th-c. *vers de société*. But any school of poets that regards rhyme as the generative principle of verse composition will favor a method of working essentially by bouts-rimés, as did *Parnassianism, e.g., guided by Théodore de Banville's axiom that "an imaginative gift for rhyme is, of all qualities, the one which makes the poet." Stéphane Mallarmé's enigmatic "ptyx" nonce-sonnet may count as bout-rimés. The rhyming dictionary itself will, when the combinations it offers are severely limited, act as a purveyor of bouts-rimés (see the octave of Charles Baudelaire's "Sed non satiata"). In terms of the materiality of writing, bouts-rimés are the residue *in presentia* of a program that can be imagined by the reader only *in absentia*, while in view of a metaphysics of writing, bouts-rimés are like the cryptic fragments of an oracular utterance that only the priest-poet has the power to reconstitute or construe; the poet is the paleographer of the invisible.

*See* POETIC CONTESTS, PRÉCIOSITÉ.

■ Kastner; T. Augarde, *Oxford Guide to Word Games*, 2d ed. (2003); E. Greber, "Metonymy in Improvisation: Pasternak, Mayakovsky, Jakobson, and Their 1919 *Bouts-Rimés*," *Eternity's Hostage*, ed. L. Fleishman (2006).

C. SCOTT

**BRAZIL, POETRY OF.** Colonial production of verse in Port. America included lyric, drama, and epic. Early composition comprised continuations of med. trads., popular lyrics, and courtly versions of *troubadour ballads. Jesuits used dramatic verse (in Sp., Port., Lat., and Tupi) in their efforts to convert the native population to Christianity. Father José de Anchieta (1534–97) even wrote a modest New World epic in Lat. (printed in Coimbra in 1563). All attempts to write *epic in Port. were penned in the shadow of Luís de Camões and *Os Lusíadas* (*The Lusiads*, 1572), his prodigious

narrative of Portugal's historical achievements. The first local imitation was *Prosopopéia* (1601) by Sp.-born Bento Teixeira (1561–1600), who fled to Brazil as a young man to avoid the Inquisition. His encomiastic heroic octaves exalted the leader of the settlement of the captaincy of Pernambuco. A *baroque phase begins in the mid-17th c. In the 18th c., the principal venues for poetry in large cities were academies where associates met to share work. The outstanding poet of the period was Gregório de Matos (1636–96), nicknamed Boca do Inferno (Mouth from Hell) for his biting satires that prompted authorities in Salvador, Bahia, to exile him to Angola. In a serious vein, he made devotional and amatory poetry. In his sonnets and other poems (all known through codices), Matos practiced the dominant Iberian modes of the day, characterized by conceits, formal dexterity, and imitation, both of Greco-Roman models and of the contemporaneous Sp. masters Luís de Góngora, Francisco de Quevedo, and Baltasar Gracián. While agile in the application of *conceptismo* and *cultismo*, Matos also touched on the mixed nature of Brazilian society, occasionally incorporating indigenous and even Af. elements.

A Brazilian version of arcadianism emerged in the late 18th c. in the gold-rich state of Minas Gerais. Colonial lit. had appeared with little coherence or continuity; now came forth an organized group with shared attitudes and nascent national awareness. Poets adopted pastoral pseuds. To write of bucolic ideals yet managed to constitute the beginnings of "Brazilian personal lyricism" (Coutinho). Their provincial adaptations of neoclassical poetics entailed turning away from perceived baroque excesses, a search for natural simplicity, and preference for graceful rhythmic schemes. While having studied in the Old World, they began to give voice to new feelings of belonging in the New World. As engaged citizens, they read Enlightenment authors, advocated political autonomy, and took part in the first conspiracy against the rule of Portugal (1789). The principal poets were Cláudio Manuel da Costa (1729–89), whose petrous imagery has been seen to reflect emotional attachment to the land; the Port.-born Tomás Antônio Gonzaga (1744–1810), author of the most popular collection of love poems in Port., *Marília de Dirceu* (1792); and Silva Alvarenga (1749–1814), noted for local landscapes. In Lisbon, Brazilian mulatto Domingos Caldas Barbosa (1738–1800) was elected president of the cultivated Nova Arcadia assembly but gained fame in the royal court performing his sometimes sensual songs, lyrics of which were published alongside pastoral poems. His occasional use of an Afro-Brazilian lexicon was a historical milestone.

National spirit was most evident in epic poems. *Caramuru* by José de Santa Rita Durão (1722–84) was composed of ten Camonian cantos about the Port. arrival in Bahia, and *O Uraguai* (1769) by Basílio da Gama (1741–95) narrated the Luso-Hispanic war against the Jesuit missions of southern Brazil. Efforts to relive *epopeia*—epic poetry—continued in Brazil well into the next century. Domingos José Gonçalves de Magalhães (1811–82) with his *A confederação dos tamoios* (1856) celebrated liberty in a crushing military defeat of an Indian tribe, revealing limited sensitivity toward native peoples. The poet's close ally, Manuel Araújo Porto Alegre (1806–79) tried his hand at epic in *Colombo* (1866), extolling Eur. expansionism in the figure of Columbus.

In the mid-1830s, these last two authors had formed a literary association in Paris that in essence launched Brazilian *romanticism, through lyric poetry and the expository essay. The entire period was naturally marked by independence from Portugal (1822), the evolution of the only monarchy (here called an empire) in the Western hemisphere, and the pursuit of Am. forms of identity. In general, the first generation of romantics believed in a historical mission to create lit. of a national character. Led by Antônio Gonçalves Dias (1823–64), they emphasized differences from Europe and autochthonous phenomena. The multigenre movement of Indianism celebrated native peoples, places, sources, and heroism. Among Dias's "American Poems," the most recognized composition was "I-Juca Pirama" (in Tupi, "he who must die"), a classic of Indianist poetry. In this work, Dias employed varied Port. verse forms but, while he assigned narrative voice to Indian personages in some passages, never recovered an indigenous poetics per se. Dias also left an unfinished epic based on a tribal story. Perhaps the most widely known Brazilian poem of all time is his "Canção do exílio" (Song of Exile, 1843), which he wrote while studying in Portugal, where he absorbed myriad romantic influences. The *strophes express the quintessential Lusitanian emotion of *saudade* (longing, homesickness) in relation to the New World homeland. With the former colony now irretrievably the focus of consciousness, the brief piece relates location—Brazil as place of desire—to the romantic emphasis on sentimentality, expressivity, and shared heritage. The poem's importance as a symbol of the country has been compared to those of the flag and the national *anthem. In the second wave of romantic poetry, Manuel Antônio Álvares de Azevedo (1831–52)—a Brazilian parallel to Lord Byron, Alfred de Musset, and some Port. figures—explored intense subjectivity, bohemianism, and pessimistic introspection. In contrast, a third current during romanticism was social poetry, eminently the abolitionist works of Antônio de Castro Alves (1847–71). Influential titles were "Navio negreiro" (The Slave Ship) and "Vozes d'África" (Voice of Africa), impassioned rhetorical verse of ethical purpose known through periodical publication and public declamations. He crafted amatory, bucolic, and patriotic lyric as well. A sui generis figure of the romantic period was Joaquim de Sousa Andrade or Sousândrade (1833–1902), maker of adventurous lines that prefigure *modernism, markedly in the trans-Am. neoepic *O Guesa* (London, 1888), featuring an anthological interlude titled "The Inferno of Wall Street" in its editorial revival of the 1960s.

Following the lead of France, reaction against ultraromanticism and a vogue of "realist" poetry would lead to the devel. of *Parnassian poetry, a school and style based on restraint of feeling, reverence for form

(particularly the *sonnet), and erudition. While in Portugal this practice was relatively modest, the Brazilian applications of Parnassianism were quite extensive in size, thematic variety (from cl. mythology to historical figures of Brazil), and longevity, enduring from 1880 until the 1920s. The depth and reach of the movement are seen in a canonical trinity. Alberto de Oliveira (1857–1937) was the most orthodox Parnassian, as seen in such titles as "Vaso grego" (Grecian urn) and his regular use of *alexandrines. The scrupulous versifier Raimundo Correia (1859–1911) displayed remarkable wealth of vocabulary and expressive variety, incl. pessimism and melancholy. Crowned the Prince of Brazilian Poets (in a 1907 contest sponsored by a leading magazine), Olavo Bilac (1865–1918) cultivated, in addition to amatory themes and art for art's sake, patriotism, progress, and a work ethic. *Symbolism arrived around 1890 and brought forth a major trio of poets. João da Cruz e Sousa (1861–98), son of a slave, witnessed abolition (1888), a cause he supported in print and deed. He produced poetry of pain and suffering alongside typically symbolist verse marked by musicality and spiritual concerns. A mystical poet par excellence was Alphonsus de Guimaraens (1870–1921), preoccupied with death and Catholic faith. Augusto dos Anjos (1884–1914) produced an idiosyncratic verse employing laboratorial lexicon and material philosophical concepts. His single volume, *Eu* (I, 1912), continues to be reprinted regularly. The Parnassian-symbolist phase in Brazil corresponded to *modernismo* in Spanish America, where antiromantic refinement and exaltation of form were similar but New World subject matter was more prominent.

In Port. *modernismo* refers to the complex of antitraditional and avant-garde tendencies beginning around 1920. The Brazilian movement, officially launched with the Modern Art Week of 1922 (the centenary of independence), endeavored to shake the foundations of academic writing, still stilted and Lusitanian, and to liberate poetry from the lingering constraints of obsolete Parnassianism and symbolism. The two fundamental aspects of the new creed were technical renovation of lyric, *free verse above all, and attention to the national, in lang. itself (using the Brazilian vernacular) and themes (folklore, contemp. life). Rioborn Ronald de Carvalho (1893–1935) lived *futurism in Paris; coedited the cutting-edge jour. *Orfeu* (1915) in Lisbon with the multifarious master of mod. Port. poetry Fernando Pessoa (1888–1935); and transported their vanguard cause to Brazil. While having Eur. links, modernismo in Brazil was driven by nationalism. In Carvalho's case such native fervor was tied, in Whitmanian fashion, to a pan-Am. spirit, evident in the neoepic sequence *Toda a América* (All the Americas, 1926). Guilherme de Almeida (1890–1969) celebrated ethnic mixture (Euro-, Afro-, Indo-) in *Raça* (Race, 1926) and essays on "nationalist sentiment." Having written in a panoply of styles, he was elected Prince of Brazilian Poets in 1958 in a poll conducted by a leading São Paulo daily. Mário de Andrade (1893–1945) exemplified an innovative approach attuned to national realities. His *Paulicéia desvairada* (*Hallucinated City*, 1922) advanced a playful musical concept of verse and probed the multicultural cosmopolis of São Paulo, while later collections contemplated the breadth of the country, incl. remote jungles. Oswald de Andrade (1890–1954) incorporated primitivism, *cubism, and various conceptual currents (notably Sigmund Freud) into a clever poetic minimalism and manifestos that clamored, with abstract humor, for aggressive novelty and self-assertiveness. His title *Poesia Pau-Brasil* (1924) takes its name from brazilwood, the first natural resource for export. In a broad civilizational metaphor, the new product of poetry should aspire to reverse the unidirectional influence of the metropolis (Paris, Lisbon) over the (former) colonies. The "Manifesto antropófago" ("Cannibalist Manifesto," 1928)—the declaration of *antropofagia—concerned poetry and intellectual discourse at large. Both *manifestos undermined *sermo nobilis* and sought to expand the restricted literary sense of poetry. A conservative nationalist group under the banner of *verde-amarelismo* (green-yellowism) opposed "alien" influence and favored the symbol of the *anta* (tapir), an animal imagined to embody the primeval power of the land. An enduring poet of this persuasion was Cassiano Ricardo (1895–1974). In Rio de Janeiro, poets attached to the jour. *Festa* were less concerned with *brasilidade* (Brazilianness) than with mod. consciousness and spirituality. Cecília Meirelles (1901–64) wrote neosymbolist collections and a lyrical epic about the capital city itself. Poets from all provinces of Brazil came to embrace their own physical and cultural geographies, natural lang., self-veneration, and differentiation from Europe.

Modernist purposes were wholly fulfilled in the work of Manuel Bandeira (1886–1968) and Carlos Drummond de Andrade (1902–87). The former lived the transition from 19th-c. conventions to mod. flexibility, a change evident in such titles as *O ritmo dissoluto* (Dissolute rhythm, 1924) and *Libertinagem* (Libertineness, 1930). His manipulations of pointedly colloquial lang. and pursuit of popular wisdom endeared him to generations of readers. Drummond exhibited astounding range, over the decades producing *modernista* joke poems, existential reflections, social verse, philosophical meditations, gamesome ling. trials, and even erotic episodes. Among the many other modernist poets, Murilo Mendes (1901–75) composed distinguished surrealistic and metaphysical pieces, and Jorge de Lima (1895–1953) showed striking versatility, from the folk-inspired *Poemas negros* (1946) to the hermetic quasi-epic *Invenção de Orfeu* (Invention of Orpheus, 1952). The iconoclastic "heroic phase" of the modernist movement in Brazil is usually placed in the years 1922–30, while the "constructive" phase extends to at least 1945. The term *modernismo* also encompasses the later works of poets born before 1920.

Chronologically, João Cabral de Melo Neto (1920–99) coincided with the so-called Generation of '45, a mid-century cluster of neo-Parnassian poets who objected to free verse and overtly native topics, instead proposing a return to circumspect versifying and re-

moval from quotidian affairs. A representative name in this cohort was Ledo Ivo (b. 1924). Cabral shared with them an alert regard for formal rigor and discipline, but he opposed their focus on psychic states and insistence on elevated poetic lexicon—in sum, their elitism. Cabral was concerned with tangible reality and the materiality of words rather than romantic or philosophical inspiration. He was a leading exponent of a new objectivity in postwar Latin Am. poetry but commonly connected his lang. of objects to social facts and real-world settings, chiefly his native northeastern region. Cabral never made a concession to sentimental rhet. or confessionalism; his textual geometry and architecture always prevailed.

Brazil was a principal scene in the movement called *concrete poetry, an organized international avant-garde or neovanguard of the 1950s and 1960s. The Brazilian founders were the São Paulo poets Augusto de Campos (b. 1931), Haroldo de Campos (1929–2003), and Décio Pignatari (b. 1927), who formed the *Noigandres group. In the early 1950s, they produced audacious lyrical texts with vehement imagery, fragmentations, and other experimental effects. The spatial minimalism of *poesia concreta* evolved in three phases. In early years (1952–56), the prime procedures were visual—the presentation of words on the page, *typography (esp. the disposition of fonts and colors), the use of empty space—along with a corresponding attention to interrupting or undermining the sentimental dimension of the poem. "Classical" or "orthodox" material arose in a second phase (1956–61) that involved ultrarational principles of composition and extensive theorization, incl. the bilingual manifesto "pilot plan for concrete poetry," built on universal and national planks, such as Stéphane Mallarmé, Ezra Pound, James Joyce, e.e. cummings, Oswald de Andrade, and Cabral. In a third stage of concretism (1962–67), open notions of *invention led to several different behaviors and products, from semantic variations to word *collages and abstract designs with lexical keys. Other groups theorized and practiced vanguardism, concerned with both textual innovation and sociopolitical relevance: *neoconcretismo* (ephemeral splinter of *poesia concreta*, 1959); *Tendência* (centered in Minas Gerais, 1957 and after), led by Affonso Ávila (b. 1928); *Poesia Práxis* (in São Paulo, 1962 and after), conceived by Mário Chamie (b. 1933); and *poema processo* (1967 and after), semaphoric *visual poetry.

After concrete poetry per se, the paths of its principal exponents diverged. From the 1970s to the 2000s, Augusto de Campos continually created forms of lyric that crossed the generic and media borders between literary, visual, and musical arts. In the mid-1980s, his poster-poem "pós-tudo" ("Post All") ignited a landmark debate about *postmodernism. No poet born in the first half of the 20th c. anywhere has better adapted to the digital age than he. Haroldo de Campos proved to be one of the most significant names of Brazilian letters since 1950, inalterably broadening the horizons of textual crit. and theory. His prose-poetry project *Galáxias* (1984) was a paragon of the Latin Am. *neobaroque, and his rethinking of mod. poetry culminated in the notion of the "postutopian poem," informed by the implications of historical transformations. A classically tinged long poem—*Finismundo, a última viagem* (The last voyage, 1990)—brought the cl. Western trad. into the age of computers. *A máquina do mundo repensada* (Rethinking the machine of the world, 2000) exquisitely interrelated Dante, Camões, Drummond, and cosmological theories. The Noigandres group also influenced Brazilian poetry with its many trans. of canonical and experimental world poetry, everything from troubadours and haiku to *metaphysical poetry, Fr. symbolism, and Gertrude Stein.

In the final four decades of the 20th c. and the first decade of the 21st, Brazilian poetry was pluralistic, continually growing in diversity, thematic scope, and sociocultural reach. The poet-critic Mário Faustino (1930–62) was a skilled advocate of Poundian poetics. The widely recognized work of (José Ribamar) Ferreira Gullar (b. 1930) spanned experimentalism, committed poetry (he was the most prominent voice of the socialistic collective *Violão de rua* [Street guitar, 1962–63]), and late-modernist personal lyricism. Of recently active poets, engaging voices from different states and regions include Manoel de Barros (b. 1916), a late discovery who ponders nature and ecology; Thiago de Mello (b. 1926), a noted militant; Roberto Piva (1937–2010), transgressive, exuberant, interested in bodily mysticism; Francisco Alvim (b. 1938), known for brevity, irony, and informality; Carlos Nejar (b. 1939), with his legalistic and mythical tones; Armando Freitas Filho (b. 1940), ever sensitive to evolving modernity; Ruy Espinheira Filho (b. 1942), poet of love and memory; and Marcus Accioly (b. 1943), author of studied lyrical and epic works, incl. the vast *Latinomérica* (2001). Other long, (semi-)narrative titles of neoepic character are Gullar's *Poema sujo* (Dirty poem, 1975), *A grande fala do índio guarani* (The great speech of the Guaraní Indian, 1978) by Affonso Romano de Sant'Anna (b. 1936), *As marinhas* (Seascapes/marines, 1984) by Neide Arcanjo (b. 1940), and *Táxi ou poema de amor passageiro* (*Taxi or Poem of Love in Transit*, 1986) by Adriano Espínola (b. 1952).

In the late 1960s, 1970s, and, to a much more limited extent, beyond, a unique aspect of culture in Brazil has been the recognition of songwriters and lyricists as voices of poetry. The contemp. association of music and lit. was given impetus by Vinícius de Moraes (1913–80), salient modernist poet turned performer and foremost Bossa Nova lyricist. In the eclectic post-Bossa Nova urban popular music of the 1960s generation known as *MPB* (*Música Popular Brasileira*), two names are regularly indicated as having "literary quality": Caetano Veloso (b. 1942) and Chico Buarque (b. 1944), poet-musicians (both with complete lyrics in pub. volumes) who proved the artful complexity of song. Other poetically adept songwriters and numerous poets doubling as composers of song texts participated in this generational phenomenon. In the following decades, Arnaldo Antunes (b. 1960) rose to prominence as a rock singer and lyricist and

achieved recognition as a singular visual and postconcrete poet.

In the 1970s, there was a small-press flourish of informal youth verse (dubbed *poesia marginal*), centered in Rio and São Paulo. This trend shared some traits but mostly contrasted with the rubric of "intersemiotic creation," which comprehended measured verse and nondenominational mixtures of words and sonographic elements. So-called marginal poetry cared little for nationalism or intellectual decorum, preferring casual discursivity and sociability. The concurrent constructivist tendency sought to keep technological advances and literary interrelations in sight. Beginning in the 1980s, poets turned increasingly from spontaneity, on the one hand, and visual exhibitionism, on the other, seeking instead an expressive discourse keen to the rationales of rigor and broadly based creative awareness. Contemp. practice was synthesized in the work of Paulo Leminski (1944–89) for the intensity and variety of his ideas regarding lyric. Another prematurely departed voice of distinct originality was Waly Salomão (1943–2003), whose work spanned antinormative prose poetry, song, and cosmopolitan free verse. In the 1990s and into the new millennium, a reliable taxonomy of Brazilian poetry is hindered by the multiplicity of poets and the sheer diversity of their work. With individualism dominating, ever-expanding scenes have embraced diverse and resourceful stylings by poets born in different decades. Active accomplished poets such as Salgado Maranhão (b. 1953) have already published volumes of their collected work. After Mário de Andrade, Bandeira, Meirelles, Drummond and Cabral, notable mod. and contemp. poets who have been ably rendered into Eng. (in single-author volumes) include Renata Pallotini (b. 1931), Adélia Prado (b. 1935), Astrid Cabral (b. 1936), Paulo Henriques Brito (b. 1951), and Régis Bonvicino (b. 1954). Since 1990, there have been expanded efforts to connect realms of poetry in Brazil (both its hist. and its present-day activity) with international circuits, above all within the Americas and Iberia, notably by poet-professor Horácio Costa (b. 1954). Cooperation at colloquia, writers' meetings, book fairs, and publishing houses has been complemented by articulations achieved through the boundless Internet, which has reinvigorated the past and provided previously unthinkable access to poets and readers of the present.

*See* INDIGENOUS AMERICAS, POETRY OF THE; PORTUGAL, POETRY OF; SPANISH AMERICA, POETRY OF.

■ **Anthologies:** *Antologia dos poetas brasileiros da fase romântica*, 2d ed. (1940); *Antologia dos poetas brasileiros da fase parnasiana*, 2d ed. (1940); *Panorama do movimento simbolista brasileiro*, ed. A. Muricy, 3 v. (1951); *Panorama da poesia brasileira*, 6 v. (1959), *Poesia do modernismo brasileiro* (1968), both ed. M. da Silva Brito; *Poesia barroca* (1967), *Poesia moderna* (1967), both ed. P. E. da Silva Ramos; *An Anthology of Brazilian Modernist Poetry*, ed. G. Pontiero (1969)—texts in Port. with annotations; *An Anthology of Twentieth-Century Brazilian Poetry*, ed. E. Bishop and E. Brasil (1972)—superb team of trans.; *26 poetas hoje,* ed. H. Buarque

(1976); *Brazilian Poetry 1950–1980,* ed. E. Brasil and W. J. Smith (1983)—includes visual poetry; *Nothing the Sun Could Not Explain,* ed. N. Ascher et al. (1997)—late-century voices; *Na virada do século, poesia de invenção no Brasil,* ed. C. Daniel and F. Barbosa (2002); *Poets of Brazil,* trans. F. Williams (2004)—bilingual selection from 1500 on; *Apresentação da poesia brasileira,* 4th ed. (2009), all ed. M. Bandeira.

■ **Criticism and History**: J. Nist, *The Modernist Movement in Brazil* (1967); M. Sarmiento Barata, *Canto melhor* (1969)—intro. and anthol. of social poetry; W. Martins, *The Modernist Idea* (1970); *Poetas do modernismo,* ed. Leodegário A. Azevedo Filho, 6 v. (1972)—selections with crit. by specialists; G. Brotherston, *Latin American Poetry* (1975); *A literatura no Brasil,* ed. A. Coutinho, 5 v. (1986)—sections by scholars on poetry; G. Mendonça Telles, *Retórica do silêncio I,* 2d ed. (1989); D. Treece and M. González, *The Gathering of Voices* (1992)—sociocultural analysis; A. Bosi, *História concisa da literatura brasileira,* 2d ed. (1994)—sections on poetry and epochal styles; *The Cambridge History of Latin American Literature,* ed. R. González Echevarría and E. Pupo-Walker, v. 3 (1996)—chronological blocks since 1830s; C. Perrone, *Seven Faces* (1996); A. C. Secchin, *Poesia e desordem* (1996); A. Bueno, *Uma história da poesia brasileira* (2007)—primarily on premodernists; H. de Campos, *Novas,* ed. A. S. Bessa and O. Cisneros (2007); C. Perrone, *Brazil, Lyric and the Americas* (2010).

C. A. Perrone

**BRETON POETRY.** The independent state of Brittany was formally annexed to France in 1532. Breton writers have produced much Fr. poetry (see FRANCE, POETRY OF), and all educated Bretons since the med. period may be presumed to know Fr. The Breton lang., still spoken in the western half of the region (*Breizh Izel*), belongs to the Brythonic or "P-Celtic" group of Celtic langs., like Welsh and Cornish. It is derived from the speech of settlers from southwest Britain who left their homeland from the 5th to the 7th c. as the Saxons were encroaching from the east. Early Breton poetry would have had much in common with early *Welsh poetry, about which more is known. Marie de France and others indicate that med. Breton poets or *bards sang of love, knightly adventures, and faery and that their compositions were the source of Marie's own form, the *lai;* but the earliest surviving Breton poetry dates from only the 14th c. It consists of fewer than 20 lines of popular verse in an indigenous metrical system whose main feature is obligatory line-internal rhyme similar to *cynghanedd lusg*: "An hegu*en* am lou*en*as / An hegar*at* an lac*at* glas" (Her smile gladdened me, / The blue-eyed love). This native prosody was predominant until the 17th c., when it was superseded by the Fr. system of syllable counting and end rhyme. Traces of it can be found in later works, and some 20th-c. poets (Arzhig, Alan Botrel) have used it deliberately.

Most of the Breton verse from the 15th to the beginning of the 19th c. consists of works of religious edification, *hymns, *carols, a book of hours, and the long and dreary *Mirouer de la mort* (1519). One poem stands out:

*Buhez Mabden,* a powerful meditation on death printed in 1530 but probably written a century earlier. The prophetic *Dialog etre Arzur Roe d'an Bretounet ha Guynglaff* dates back to 1450. There are also numerous plays in verse. A few popular plays, such as the *Pevar Mab Emon,* are based on chivalric romances, but most derive from the Bible and saints' lives. The influence of Fr. models is evident, with a few notable exceptions, mainly mystery plays that recount the lives of Celtic saints.

New stirrings begin with the two mock-epic poems of Al Lae (close of the 18th c.), but the real impetus comes with the rise of 19th-c. *romanticism. The great event is the appearance in 1839 of Théodore Hersart de la Villemarqué's *Barzaz Breiz* (Poetry of Brittany), an anthol. of supposedly ancient oral poetry, which recent scholarship has shown to be more authentic than many 19th-c. critics believed. The effect was profound. A romantic vision of the Breton past was created that stirred the imagination of many and sparked new literary enthusiasm. At the same time, François-Marie Luzel and others undertook more "scientific" collecting of Breton folk poetry, of which there were two main kinds: *gwerzioù,* which are essentially *ballads, and *sonioù,* a broader designation that extends to more lyrical verse, incl. love songs and satires. *Broadside ballads in Breton also circulated. A few of the *gwerzioù* are demonstrably connected to med. Welsh poetry or to med. events in Brittany; some scholars claim that the *gwerzioù* are related to the putative Breton-lang. sources of the *lais* in OF. Songs are still an important form of Breton poetry. Mod. singer-songwriters include Glenmor, Youenn Gwernig, Gilles Servat, Jef Philippe, Louis Bodénès, Nolwenn Korbell, Denez Prigent (who composes *gwerzioù* of his own), and the internationally famous Alan Stivell.

After the Middle Breton literary standard lapsed in the 17th c., four main dialects emerged, associated with the regions of Léon, Trégor, Cornouaille, and Vannes. But following the lead of the grammarian Jean-François Le Gonidec (1775–1838), Breton writers again worked to establish a cultivated literary norm, largely based on the Léon dialect. The dialect of Vannes was used mostly by priests who found inspiration in their faith and in their love for their native land. Esp. popular were Msgr. Yann Vari Joubiouz's *Doue ha mem bro* (1844) and Joakim Gwilhom's imitation of Virgil's *Georgics, Livr el labourer* (1849). From the 1850s to the 1880s, only minor talents emerged. Living uprooted from the Breton countryside, these poets expressed in artificial diction their love of the simple life, of the homeland, and of their inheritance, which was no longer secure. This nostalgic trad. was maintained and reinvigorated in the 1890s by the rich lyricism of François Taldir-Jaffrennou and the more artistic Erwan Berthou, but the outstanding poet of their generation was Yann-Ber Kalloc'h, killed in action in 1917. His poems, written in Vannetais and published posthumously, express strong religious and patriotic convictions enhanced by rich and powerful imagery.

The 20th c. saw the vigorous growth of Breton literary periodicals, each with its coterie. Vannetais writers found expression in *Dihunamb,* ed. by the poet-peasant Loeiz Herrieu. The *Gwalarn* group, founded in 1925 under the leadership of Roparz Hémon, proved by far the most talented and creative. Maodez Glanndour and Hémon stand out from the group, although nearly all were gifted poets. Gwalarn did not survive World War II, but patriotic young writers launched new publications. Most did not last. The single exception was *Al Liamm*: under the guidance of Ronan Huon, it became the leading Breton literary jour. In their poetry, Huon and his contemporaries Youenn Olier, Per Denez, and Per Diolier, later joined by Youenn Gwernig (who also wrote in Fr. and Eng.) and Reun ar C'halan, respected the literary standards set by Gwalarn. Women have also played a significant role in the survival of Breton poetry, esp. Anjela Duval, Vefa de Bellaing, Benead, Naïg Rozmor, Tereza, and, more recently, Maï Jamin and Annaïg Renault. The jour. *Brud* (now *Brud Nevez*), founded in 1957, counted one of the best contemp. poets, Per Jakez Hélias, among its first contributors. The 1960s witnessed a strong resurgence of Breton nationalism. The *Union Démocratique Bretonne*, created in 1964, attracted several young militant poets: Paol Keineg (better known for Fr. poetry), Yann-Ber Piriou, Erwan Evenou, and Sten Kidna. Other poets have since come to the fore: Abanna, Alan Botrel, Yann-Baol an Noalleg, Koulizh Kedez, Padrig an Habask, Gwendal and Herle Denez, Tudual Huon, Bernez Tangi, to name but a few. Many were pub. in *Skrid* (1974–89). New jours. that regularly publish Breton poetry include *Aber*, *An Amzer*, *Al Lanv*, *HOPALA!*, and *Spered Gouez*.

Among the special interests of the 20th and 21st-cs. poets are Breton identity; issues of human rights, cultural autonomy, and lang. survival in Brittany and worldwide; other minority cultures, particularly those of other Celtic lands, an interest sometimes verging on "pan-Celticism" (beginning with the Gwalarn group, many poems have been trans. into Breton); and creative manipulation of the Breton lang. itself. The biggest challenge now facing Breton poetry is to find and maintain a knowledgeable audience outside the ranks of its practitioners.

■ **Anthologies:** *Barzaz Breiz*, ed. T. H. de la Villemarqué (1839); *Gwerziou Breiz Izel*, ed. F. M. Luzel, 2 vols. (1868–74); *Soniou Breiz Izel*, ed. F. M. Luzel and A. Le Braz, 2 vols. (1890); *Les Bardes et poètes nationaux de la Bretagne armoricaine*, ed. C. Le Mercier d'Erm (1918); *Barzhaz: kant barzhoneg berr, 1350–1953*, ed. P. Denez (1953); *Défense de cracher par terre et de parler breton*, ed. Y.-B. Piriou (1971); *Le Livre d'Or de la Bretagne*, ed. P. Durand (1975); *Anthologie de la poésie bretonne, 1880–1980*, ed. C. Le Quintrec (1980); *Du a Gwyn*, ed. D. M. Jones and M. Madeg (1982); *Barzhonegoù*, ed. *Skrid* (1986); *Writing the Wind: A Celtic Resurgence*, ed. T. R. Crowe (1997); *Anthologie de la littérature bretonne au XXème siècle/ Lennegezh ar Brezhoneg en XXvet Kantved*, ed. F. Favereau, 3 vols. (2002–08); *The Turn of the Ermine*, ed. J. Gibson and G. Griffiths (2006).

■ **Surveys:** F. Gourvil, *Langue et Littérature bretonnes* (1952); *Istor Lennegezh Vrezhonek an Amzer-Vremañ*, ed. Abeozen [Y.F.M. Eliès] (1957); Y. Olier, *Istor hol lennegezh "Skol Walarn,"* 2 vols. (1974–75); Y. Bouëssel du Bourg and Y. Brekilien, "La littérature bre-

tonne," *La Bretagne*, ed. Y. Brekilien (1982); J. Gohier and R. Huon, *Dictionnaire des écrivains aujourd'hui en Bretagne* (1984); *Histoire littéraire et culturelle de la Bretagne*, ed. J. Balcou and Y. Le Gallo, 3 vols. (1987); D. Laurent, *Aux sources du Barzaz-Breiz* (1989); F. Favereau, *Littérature et écrivains bretonnants depuis 1945* (1991); M.-A. Constantine, *Breton Ballads* (1996); A. Botrel, "Les chemins de la poésie en langue bretonne," *HOPALA!* 29 (2008).

■ **Prosody:** E. Ernault, *L'Ancien Vers Breton* (1912); R. Hémon, *Trois poèmes en moyen breton* (1962); F. Kervella, *Diazezoù ar sevel gwerzioù* (1965).

D. M. LLOYD; R. GALAND; M. BOYD

**BRIDGE** (Gr. *zeugma*). In metrics, bridges are constraints on word end at certain locations within the line. In *classical prosody, the most important bridges in (1) the iambic *trimeter are the following: (a) Knox's trochee bridge: in the iambographers (Archilochus, Semonides, Solon, Hipponax), a trochaic word shape may not end in third *anceps and is still somewhat constrained in *tragedy; (b) Porson's bridge: after long third anceps outside *comedy, no full word boundary may occur; (c) There is also evidence for a general, if weak, *constraint on word end after short third anceps; (d) Knox's iamb bridge: an iambic word shape may not end in fifth longum in the iambographers; (e) Wilamowitz's bridge: a spondaic word shape may not end in fifth longum in the iambographers; (f) Word boundary should not split a *resolution or *substitution or divide them from the following syllable. Each of the foregoing bridges has its counterpart in the trochaic *tetrameter.

The most important bridges in (2) the dactylic *hexameter are the following: (a) Iterated trochaic division of the first and second feet before a feminine *caesura is avoided in all styles. A line beginning

$$- \cup \cup - \cup \quad \cup - \cup$$

autis epeita pedonde

(*Odyssey* 11.598)

is rare and probably more constrained when all three words are lexical; (b) Meyer's bridge: trochaic division of the second *foot is not permitted before a masculine caesura in Callimachus unless either the word before the division or the word after it is nonlexical; (c) Hermann's bridge: trochaic division of the fourth foot is strongly avoided; (d) Bulloch's bridge: in Callimachus, if a word ends with the third foot, the verse must have a regular caesura and a bucolic *diaeresis, and the syntactic boundary at either or both of the latter positions must be of higher rank than the boundary at the end of the third foot. Callimachus would not permit a line such as

$$- - \quad - - \quad \cup \cup - \cup \cup \quad - \times$$

ede gar deron chronon allelon apechonta

(*Iliad* 14.206)

(e) *Spondee *zeugma: word end after contraction ($-$ for $\cup \cup$) is avoided in the fourth foot, rare in the second, and practically excluded in the fifth. In Callimachus, the zeugma is stricter.

There are also constraints on nonfinal heavy syllables in arsis that are clearly related to some bridges (see ARSIS AND THESIS). E.g., type (1e) above cannot be subsumed along with (1d) under a generalized constraint on disyllables, so that the initial heavy syllable of spondee-shaped words is independently constrained. Furthermore, in the iambographers, words of the shape − − ◡ x are strongly avoided beginning in third anceps. In the hexameter, words of the shape − − x are strongly avoided beginning in the arsis of the fifth foot. These constraints unite with the bridges to form a finely structured hierarchy of strictness according to *genre and style.

The definition of a *bridge* as a point in the verse line where word end is forbidden is adequate for certain descriptive and philological purposes, like identifying corrupt lines; but in offering no explanation, it obscures more than it reveals. Some bridges, such as Knox's (1a, 1d), are apparently simple constraints on patterned iteration of word end. Others, like Bulloch's bridge (2d), are constraints against potential phrase boundary. A third group of bridges (incl. Porson's [1b], which is often regarded as prototypical, and the constraints against "split" resolution [1f]) are not, properly speaking, sensitive to word end at all. What is constrained by these latter is how the syllables of the word are mapped onto arsis and thesis. Word end is simply the right edge of the domain within which syllables are rhythmically organized for speech. Apparent exceptions to bridge rules generally involve function words (e.g., articles, pronouns, prepositions), which coalesce with their head word into a single domain, or fixed phrases. Some styles of verse allow function words at bridges with great freedom, others much less so: this variation reflects the degree to which a verse style allows itself access to fluent speech.

■ R. Porson, *Euripidis Hecuba*, 2d ed. (1802); G. Hermann, *Orphica* (1805); J. Hilberg, *Das Prinzip der Silbenwaegung und die daraus entspringenden Gesetze der Endsilben in der griechischen Poesie* (1879); W. Meyer, "Zur Geschichte des griechischen und lateinischen Hexameters," *Sitzungsberichte der Bayerischen Akademie der Wissenschaften* (1884); L. Havet, *Cours élémentaire de métrique grecque et latine* (1896); Wilamowitz; A. D. Knox, "The Early Iambus," *Philologus* 87 (1932); Maas; A. W. Bulloch, "A Callimachean Refinement of the Greek Hexameter," *CQ* 20 (1970); Allen; A. M. Devine and L. D. Stephens, "Bridges in the Iambographers," *Greek, Roman, Byzantine Studies* 22 (1981); and *Language and Metre* (1984); Snell; West.

A. M. DEVINE; L. D. STEPHENS

**BROADSIDE BALLAD.** A journalistic song printed on a single piece of paper (a broadside) often chronicling a newsworthy event. From the late 16th c., the marketing of broadside ballads was a fixture of popular culture in Europe and its colonies for several hundred years. All Eur. lang. groups with print markets display a division between an older, premod. layer of oral ballads and a more recent body of broadside ballads shaped by writing and print.

■ **History:** H. Rollins, "Black-Letter Broadside Ballad," *PMLA* 35 (1919); G. M. Laws, *American Balladry from British Broadsides* (1957); E. Janda and F. Nützhold, *Die Moritat vom Bänkelsang oder Lied von der Strasse* (1959); C. Simpson, *The British Broadside Ballad and Its Music* (1966); C. Slater, *Stories on a String: The Brazilian Literatura de Cordel* (1982); N. Würzbach, *The Rise of the English Street Ballad 1550–1650*, trans. G. Walls (1990).

*See* BALLAD.

■ **Web Sites:** English Broadside Ballad Archive, University of California, Santa Barbara: http://emc.english.ucsb.edu/ballad_project/index.asp; Roud Broadside Index: http://library.efdss.org/cgi-bin/textpage.cgi?file-aboutRoudbroadside&access=off.

D. DUGAW

**BROKEN RHYME.** *Broken rhyme* usually designates the division by hyphenation of a word at the end of a line in order to isolate the portion of that word that produces a rhyme with a word at the end of a subsequent line: e.g., "As prone to all ill, and of good as for*get-* / ful, as proud, lustfull, and as much in *debt*" (Alexander Pope), or "Winter and summer, night and *morn,* / I languish at this table dark; / My office window has a *corn-* / er looks into St. James's Park" (William Thackeray). In Eng. poetry, poets from Shakespeare to Ogden Nash have used broken rhyme to comic and satiric effect. G. M. Hopkins uses it as a resource for serious poetry, e.g., in "The Windhover" and "To What Serves Mortal Beauty?," going so far as to link the final portion of one line with an isolated phoneme in the next ("at the door / Drowned" rhymes with "reward"); this he called the *rove over* rhyme. Broken rhymes have also been used by John Donne (*Satyres* 3 and 4) and e. e. cummings. Yet broken rhyme is more frequent still in non-Eng. trads.; it was developed extensively in Rus. poetry, particularly in the work of 20th-c. poets Vladimir Mayakovsky, Velimir Khlebnikov, and Joseph Brodsky.

Broken rhyme's counterpart in unrhymed verse is *enjambment. Both rely on visual form: for all the "breaking," the binding of the syllables within the broken word is, in fact, stronger than the line end, generating the tension that characterizes each technique.

In Lord Byron, some instances of broken rhyme also meet the criteria for *mosaic rhyme or split rhyme, in that the rhyme is achieved not by pairing two words but rather by pairing one word with multiple words: "Start not! Still chaster reader—she'll be *nice hence-* / Forward, and there is no great cause to quake; / This liberty is a poetic *licence*"; elsewhere in *Don Juan*, we see pure examples of mosaic rhyme, though this is also now referred to as broken rhyme by numerous sources: "But—Oh! ye lords and ladies intel*lectual,* / Inform us truly, have they not hen-*pecked you all*"?

*See* CHAIN RHYME.

T.V.F. BROGAN; J. CROFT

**BUCOLIC** (Gr. *bu+kol-*, "care of cattle"). The semantic range of *bucolic* stretches from such concrete activities as feeding, grazing, and controlling animals, to tending children or attending to anything the mind can make an object for cognition. As "herdsmanlike," though, *bucolic* commonly connotes "lazy," "thievish," or "distracted," like the mythic herdsman Argos, *panoptes* (all-seeing) with a hundred eyes, said to have been lulled by music and killed by the god Hermes (archetypal trader and cattle rustler). Early and widely too, music and story (*myth) are said to "console" or "sway" with Orphic power, whether in pasture, nursery, school, or political assembly, but contrarily again to "feed" false hopes, so "mislead," "beguile." Thus documented as constitutive for a culture where cattle are the basic capital (McInerney), the encoded contradictions inform and animate the Gr. *Bucolics* by Theocritus (of Syracuse and Alexandria, 3d c. BCE). On the premise that "the herdsman was good to think with," Theocritus first turned the bucolic "figure of analogy" into "the character of focus" (Gutzwiller) creating *idylls, "little scenes," blending *mime with epos, which dramatized and thematized bucolic powers and limits to process the unruly force of love (*eros*). Two centuries later, Virgil redeployed bucolic epos to process the unruly force of revolution at Rome. His *Bucolics* (ten in number, also called *Eclogues*) proclaimed a returning Golden Age (Eclogue 4); transformed the tragic cowherd Daphnis dying of love (idyll 1) into a dead hero and new god (Julius Caesar; eclogue 5); and capped this sequel with a prequel, replacing Daphnis in Sicily (idyll 1) with Roman Gallus dying in Arcadia (eclogue 10). In the aftermath, bucolics, *pastorals, and eclogues get further redeployed from Roman, through Ren. and later moments, viable still for W. H. Auden ("Bucolics—Winds, Woods, Mountains, Lakes, Islands, Plains, Streams," 1955), Sylvia Plath ("Bucolics," 1956; bitter irony and tragic dream), and Maurice Manning (*Bucolics*, 2008; 70 eclogues, mocking "Boss," which recalls bossy [cow], echoing *bous* [Gr.], *bos* [Lat.], and *gwou* [IE]), also divers musical compositions or ensembles, not to mention commonplaces touting real estate as rural and serene.

*See* ALEXANDRIANISM, GREEK POETRY, LATIN POETRY, PASTORAL.

■ D. Halperin, *Before Pastoral: Theocritus and the Tradition of Ancient Bucolic Poetry* (1983); R. Hunter, *Theocritus: A Selection* (1999)—important intro. and commentary; K. Gutzwiller, "The Bucolic Problem," *CP* 101 (2006); and "The Herdsman in Greek Thought," *Brill's Companion to Greek and Latin Pastoral*, ed. M. Fantuzzi and T. Papanghelis (2006); *New Versions of Pastoral: Post-Romantic, Modern, and Contemporary Responses to the Tradition*, ed. D. James and P. Tew (2009); J. McInerney, *The Cattle of the Sun: Cows and Culture in the World of the Ancient Greeks* (2010); J. Van Sickle, *Virgil's "Book of Bucolics": The Ten Eclogues Translated into English Verse* (2011).

J. VAN SICKLE

**BULGARIA, POETRY OF.** Bulgarian poetry began with the adoption of an alphabet newly devised by two learned brothers of Thessaloniki, Cyril and Methodius, and with their trans. of several ecclesiastical books. The brothers devised not the Cyrillic alphabet, as is generally believed, but the Glagolitic alphabet in 855. Its complexity meant that it was quickly replaced by what we now call the Cyrillic alphabet. The Bulgarians converted to Eastern Orthodoxy in 865, under Boris I, who proclaimed it the state religion; this conversion was facilitated by the introduction of literacy in the vernacular.

The lit. in the early med. age was ecclesiastic: it focused on prayers, worship, and church rituals. Its main features fluctuate, but there is an invariant characteristic of poeticism in all eras. Cyril, Methodius, and their disciples translated a large corpus of canonical Christian texts and hymnological texts centered on the lives of the saints. These books contained mostly *troparia* (or *stikhera*) and *kontakia*, short poetical verses of two or three sentences to be sung between biblical psalmody and accepted as parts of vespers and matins. In 9th-c. Byzantium, the 12 volumes of the *Menaion* (Book of Months) were completed, containing proper offices for each day of the calendar year. From Bulgaria this ecclesiastical lit. spread to Serbia, Romania, and Russia, which helped to consolidate Slavdom in the 10th c. In accepting Christianity from Byzantium, along with its ecclesiastical and hymnological texts, Bulgaria accepted its *ars poetica* as well.

The earliest known poetic text of 9th-c. Bulgaria is the *Proglas kâm Evangelieto* (Foreword to the Tetraevangelion); it was most likely authored by Konstantine (Cyril) the Philosopher. It holds 110 verses of high artistic value, ecstatically glorifying the newly received gift the Slavs had received "from God," i.e., literacy in the vernacular. Some scholars, however, believe that this is a slightly later work, meant as a foreword to another artistic piece, *Azbouchna molitva* (Alphabet Prayer) by Konstantin Preslavski, written in 893. This work contains 40 verses with a woven alphabetical *acrostic. Preslavski wrote another poetic pearl, *Ouchitelno evangelie* (Didactic Gospel), thus establishing the role of the capital city of Preslav as the birthplace of Bulgarian poetry.

Two of Cyril and Methodius's followers, Kliment and Naum, established the town of Okhrid as a second cultural center. Mss. from Preslav were written in the Cyrillic alphabet, whereas those from Okhrid were mostly written in Glagolitic. Thanks to the work in both centers, early Slavic became the written lang. of the new culture then developing alongside Byzantium. In the 9th and 10th cs., Bulgaria reached its height as a political and cultural power.

Another cultural surge occurred in 1185, when the state regained its independence from Byzantium after more than a century of subjugation. The new capital, Turnovo, became the next important cultural center. The key figure here was Patriarch Evtimii (?1325–1401), who became famous for his orthographic reform of the Bulgarian literary lang., as well as his hagiographies and eulogies (*zhitija* and *pohvalni slova*) on Bulgarian saints. His name marked the emergence of the author from med. anonymity. He also contributed to the endorsement of the hesychastic norms introduced by another outstanding leader, Teodosiy Turnovski (1300–63). Other renowned figures from the literary school of Turnovo include Kiprian (1336–1406), Grigorii Tsamblak (1330–1406), and Konstantin Kostenechki (1380–1443).

Early in the 14th c., the monasteries of Mount Athos became incubators for saving and developing Slavic letters. Parchment was gradually replaced by paper, which facilitated the spread of lit. The holy mountain with its 20 main monasteries and numerous monastic cells became a natural fortress of Slav–Byzantine culture, which was preserved and transmitted through the following centuries under Ottoman rule (1396–1878).

During this period, Bulgarian lit. withdrew into churches and monasteries. The Ottomans destroyed many churches, and only a few of the remote monasteries survived to become hidden "barrels" where national awareness fermented. The civilization of the Bulgarian Middle Ages had to be conserved and saved within the framework of an alien Islamic doctrine, as the title of Runciman's book suggests.

In the 17th c., the fashion of so-called damaskin lit. began to flourish. It represents adaptations of *slova* (eulogies) and *apocrypha* (branded as "heretical") originally composed by the 16th-c. Gr. preacher Damaskin Studit. Folklore comprising all the oral genres—tales, songs, proverbs, didactic stories, rural beliefs, calendars, and so forth—continued to develop alongside the written trad. under foreign rule.

Secular lit. of modest artistic merit, based on Rus. and later on Fr. models, appeared in the middle of the 19th c. Educated Bulgarians turned first to Russia for secular literary forms. Poetry predominated through the work of writers like Neofit Rilski (1793–1881), Dobri Chintulov (1822–86), Naiden Gerov (1823–1900), and Georgi Rakovski (1821–67), who wrote the famous poem *Gorski Putnik* (A Forest Traveler) in 1857. With the introduction of the printing press in the Ottoman Empire after 1840, new genres emerged: ballads, diaries, travel notes, pamphlets, and short stories. Around 1850, poetic works were produced mainly by teachers, resulting in *daskalska poezija* (school poetry), characterized by patriotic and didactic tendencies.

Several prominent figures who were both poets and revolutionaries spearheaded the cultural resurgence of the 19th c. Vasil Levski (1837–73) was revered by all Bulgarians as the "saint of the revolution." He was hanged by the Turks near Sofia. His life and death inspired other writers such as Hristo Botev (1848–76), who was killed in combat as he led his people against the Turks in the Balkan range. Botev composed his poems using folk motifs and colloquial idioms.

The invariant characteristic of the period's poetry was monosemanticism, in which a limited number of synonyms stand for the poetic word as such. Poets sought a word that fully exhausts its semantic value, signifying a definite meaning. This corresponded to society's sole ideal, national liberation from the Turks. For an example of monosemanticism, we might take the case of Levski; the most celebrated poem extolling his death was written by Ivan Vazov (1850–1921), who exclaimed, "Oh, heroic gallows!" Since then, this expression became a cliché for a heroic death, used to signify the death of a national hero, usually Levski.

The style of these works is most often called realistic, but the events described, witnessed by most of the authors, were so grim and shocking that it might be better termed naturalistic, even dramatic. Another stream of "quiet" poetry emerged at this time; it focused on refining the lang., finding new rhymes and inventing figures. These tales, love songs, and poems did not tell of suffering or pain.

Bulgaria was liberated in the Russo–Turkish War (1877–78). The newly emerging literary star of the time was Vazov, celebrated as the patriarch of modern Bulgarian literature. Vazov worked across the cultural spectrum, writing poems, short stories, lyrics, dramas, and criticism.

The realistic model of lit. slowly began to crumble at this time. Authors sought to reopen a multisemantic fan behind the poetic word (*polysemy as opposed to monosemanticism). Words were given an unusual set of references or paralleled by sudden rhymes that displaced their meaning: unexpected harmony was sought in distant dissonances. E.g., the word *swan* had a whole "fan of meanings," such as the poet's soul, his striving for beauty, his lover, and so forth. The leading figure in this process was Vazov's lifelong rival Pencho Slaveikov (1866–1912), a humanitarian, poet, and philosopher educated in Germany. The playwright Petko Todorov (1879–1916), the poet Peyo Yavorov (1878–1914), the critic Krustyu Krustev (1866–1919), and Slaveikov formed an aesthetic circle around the literary jour. *Misul* (Thought, 1892–1907).

Slaveikov became the first modernist in Bulgarian lit. and the first poet directly connected with international movements. He went his own way, focusing more on great aesthetic questions than on contemp. literary life. A document in the Nobel Prize Committee archive states that Slaveikov was a Nobel Prize nominee in 1912. He died before the committee meeting, however. Slaveikov inherited a rich collection of folkloric work from his father, Petko Slaveikov, and masterfully saturated his own songs with folk motifs. In the epic poems *Ralitsa*, *Boiko*, and *Kurvava pesen* (Song of Blood), he tried to place specific folk sounds within a larger Eur. frame. Slaveikov's attempt to infuse national motifs into foreign models was successfully continued by Todorov, whose refined *Idiliy* (Idylls, 1908) spoke of the deeply symbolic lang. of nature, eluding any fixed literary classifications.

The most cherished figure of the early 20th c. was Yavorov, commonly held as the greatest Bulgarian poet. Although he formally belonged to the so-called *Misul* Circle, his unique talent enabled him to create his own poetic trad. Yavorov reflected the dramatic split of his tormented soul. His personal life seemed to be performed onstage, constantly trailed by a spotlight. His suicide in 1914 seemed a logical finale to his dramatic life.

The high aesthetic criteria of the jour. *Misul* became a lyrical guidepost for many young authors from different movements. From *Misul* to the next important literary circles, *Zlatorog* (Golden Horn, 1920–43) and *Hyperion* (1922–31), the Bulgarian literary trad. remained rooted in an aesthetic *romanticism, which has not ceased. Even later, when poets like Teodor Trayanov (1882–1945), Nikolai Liliev (1885–1960), Dimcho Debelyanov (1887–1916), Emanuil Popdimitrov (1855–1943), and Dimitur Boyadzhiev (1880–1911) brought *symbolism into Bulgarian lit., it still occupied romantic grounds.

This is esp. true of Trayanov, who was considered Yavorov's poetic rival. Trayanov spent 20 years (1901–21) in Vienna where he studied and took a diplomatic position. In this cultural atmosphere, he absorbed the ongoing romantic trad., which remained unbroken in Ger.-speaking countries. Mod. Bulgarian crit. is divided as to who opened the door to symbolism, Yavorov or Trayanov. As the most consistent of the symbolists, Trayanov is the most likely candidate, with his poem "Novijat den" (The New Day, 1905), also pub. in his first collection of 1909, *Regina Mortua*. Although entirely lyrical, his work is also classically symmetrical, divided into cycles, themes, and books. The striving for wholeness that runs throughout Trayanov's verse is typically romantic. His poems resonated deeply with the mood of national resignation during the interwar period, when he wrote his *Bulgarski baladi* (Bulgarian Ballads, 1922). Though Bulgaria had won its chief battles, it lost substantial territories through poor diplomacy and the betrayal of its allies. "The Secret of the Struma" and "Death in the Plains" are his great ballads of that period.

The poetry of Popdimitrov shows the closest relationship to Trayanov. Popdimitrov revived images from the Gothic Middle Ages. Many of his poems are titled with melodious women's names ("Ema," "Iren," "Laura"). The verse of Debelyanov is romantic and elegiac but also warm and lively. It introduced new modes: drinking songs, bacchanalian songs, the confessional genre of short narrative pieces about fashionable bohemian life. Debelyanov was killed in World War I. Similar motifs were to be found in the poetry of Kiril Hristov (1875–1944), whose work is flavored with the unbridled eroticism that was his inspiration. Liliev is considered one of the finest Bulgarian lyricists. His short collections include *Ptitsi v noshta* (Birds at Night, 1918), *Lunni petna* (Moonspots, 1922), and *Stihotvoreniya* (Verse, 1931).

The Fr.-influenced symbolism of Yavorov and the Austrian symbolism of Trayanov clashed with the dominant sociorealistic tendency of Bulgarian lit. During the Communist regime, this tendency continued. But just as Trayanov is more a neoromantic than a symbolist, the "hard" realism of Bulgarian lit. is more a myth than a reality. The term *realist* became the pass, awarded by official critics, that enabled many Bulgarian literary celebrities to enter the rebuilt, low–roofed pantheon of socialist realist writing. Geo Milev (1895–1925) was an expressionist poet among the symbolists. Milev's greatest poem, "Septemvri" (September, 1924), led eventually to his incarceration and death at the hands of the regime. His poetry resumes monosemanticism on a new scale; it demonstratively rejects polysemy for the sake of synonymity, piling up many similar words for one and the same meaning.

A new generation of poets made their debuts through opposing the now old-fashioned symbolism. In his collection *Fragmenti* (Fragments, 1967), Atanas Dalchev (1904–1978) achieved a paradoxical realism based on idiosyncratic imagery. Asen Raztsvetnikov (1897–1951) composed melodious ballads with resigned overtones. Nikola Fournadzhiev's (1903–68) dark and depressive poetry in heavy rhythmic style marked a different pole. The verse of Nikola Rakitin (1886–1934) breathed a quiet and idyllic atmosphere. The poetry of Alexander Voutimski (1919–43) represented an early romantic protest against advancing totalitarianism.

The interwar period also marked the debuts of women poets who began their careers free of any dogmatism. Elisaveta Bagryana (1893–1991) is celebrated for her unrestrained personality and a worship of life, freedom, youth, and travel. Her collections include *Vechnata i svyatata* (The Eternal and the Sacred, 1927), the postwar *Ot bryag do bryag* (From Coast to Coast, 1963), *Kontrapunkti* (Counterpoints, 1972), and *Na brega na vremeto* (At the Shore of Time, 1983). Dora Gabe (1886–1983) imaginatively explored common household objects in bright, optimistic poetry. Her collections include *Zemen put* (Terrestrial Way, 1928), *Pochakai slunce* (Wait Sun, 1967), and *Sgustena tishina* (Condensed Quietude, 1973). Early in the Communist era, an attempt was made to revive a "hard" realistic method. Poets like Nikola Vaptsarov (1909–42), who was shot as a terrorist before the Communist coup, and Penyo Penev (1930–59) were used for this purpose. But resistance won in the long-term conflict. Penev lost his illusions and committed suicide. Many writers were sent to labor camps. The discord between Soviet-style socialist realism and the inventions of contemp. lit. grew rapidly. New trends, masked as experiments, permeated Bulgarian lit. Gifted writers such as Ivan Peichev (1916–76), Andrei Germanov (1932–81), Alexander Gerov (1919–97), Ivan Teofilov (b. 1931), Stefan Tsanev (b. 1936), Nikolai Kunchev (1936–2007), Boris Hristov (b. 1945), and Ivan Tsanev (b. 1941) took advantage of this relative freedom and sent a countermessage to the era's stale ideals. In the late 20th c., the poets Radoi Ralin (1923–2004), Blaga Dimitrova (1922–2003), Konstantin Pavlov (1933–2008), and Vladimir Levchev (b. 1957) became open dissidents.

Even before Communism's collapse in 1989, fresh trends of delicacy and concision could be seen in the poetry of Miriana Basheva (b. 1947), Fedya Filkova (b. 1950), and Georgi Rupchev (1957–2001). Petya Dubarova, born in 1962, was widely recognized as the most gifted younger voice; her suicide in 1979 was believed to be a tragic reaction to the brutality of society. The poetry of Ani Ilkov (b. 1957), Miglena Nikolchina (b. 1955), and Edvin Sougarev (b. 1953) can be described by terms such as *expressionism, *imagism, and *constructivism, as long as *post-* appears before them.

Among a new wave of extremely promising authors, poets such as Georgi Gospodinov (b. 1968), Verginiya Zaharieva (b. 1959), Kristin Dimitrova (b. 1963), Elin Rahnev (b. 1968), and Mirela Ivanova (b. 1962) seek to present the complications and contradictions of the postmod. consciousness in a time of chaos, marked by destructive political events and a radical upheaval of the world picture. Their brilliantly rendered insights and linguistic games have helped to build a warmer and more generous cultural philosophy. Their books of poems have largely appeared either in Eng. or as bilingual editions. Recent names, such as Nadejda Radulova (b. 1975), Dimiter Kenarov (b. 1981), and Kamelia Spasova (b. 1982), mark new experiments, such as living in virtual reality, writing Internet poetry, reflecting on a new femininity, and more.

■ S. Runciman, *The Great Church in Captivity* (1968); *Anthology of Bulgarian Poetry*, trans. P. Tempest (1975); J. Meyendorff, *Byzantine Theology* (1987); *Clay and Star: Contemporary Bulgarian Poets*, trans. and ed. L. Sapinkopf and G. Belev (1992); *An Anthology of Bulgarian Literature*, ed. I. Mladenov and H. R. Cooper Jr. (2007); *Istoria na bulgarskata srednovekovna literatura*, comp. and ed. A. Miltenova (2008).

I. MLADENOV

**BURDEN,** *burthen* (OE *byrthen*; OHG *burdin*—sometimes confused with *bourdon, burdoun*, from Fr. *bourdon*, Sp. *bordin*—there is little or no separation of the two words from the earliest citations in the *OED*). (a) In the Eng. Bible (cf. *onus* in the Vulgate), trans. from Heb. *massa*, a raising of the voice, utterance, oracle; (b) the bass or undersong, accompaniment (the same as *bourdon*): "For burden-wise I'll hum on Tarquin still"—William Shakespeare, *Lucrece*, 1133—cf. Chaucer's obscene pun about the summoner, "General Prologue," 673; (c) the chief theme, the leading sentiment or matter of a song or poem: "The burden or leading idea of every couplet was the same"—Leigh Hunt, *Men, Women, & Books* 1.11.199; (d) the refrain or chorus of a song: "Foot it featly here and there; And, sweet sprites, the burden bear. Hark, hark! *Burden dispersedly.* Bow-wow."—Shakespeare, *Tempest* 1.2.381; in particular, the refrain line in the *carol.

*See* RITORNELLO.

■ R. H. Robbins, "The Burden in Carols," *MLN* 57 (1942); R. L. Greene, *The Early English Carols*, 2d ed. (1977).

T.V.F. BROGAN; R. O. EVANS

**BURLESQUE.** *See* CONTRAFACTUM; PARODY; PASTICHE.

**BURNS STANZA** (also called "Scottish stanza," "standard Habbie"). One variety of *tail rhyme, the Burns stanza is a six-line stanza rhyming *aaabab*, the *a*-lines being tetrameter and the *b*-lines dimeter. Although named for the 18th-c. Scottish poet Robert Burns, the Burns stanza and its close variants are first found in med. *troubadour poetry; the earliest example is found in a poem by William of Poitiers.

Examples in Scots poetry date from the 16th c.; a well-known 17th-c. ballad by Robert Sempill the Younger, "The Life and Death of Habbie Simpson," gave rise to the name "standard Habbie." By the 18th c., Allan Ramsay and Robert Fergusson frequently used it, which influenced Burns; around this point, Scottish writers began to see the form as a distinctively national one. Each stanza typically contains a single sentence; occasionally, two sentences are used. Despite its complexity, the form is an effective one. Following the crescendo of the initial tercet, the short lines lend themselves well to effects of pointing, irony, and closure:

> Ye ugly, creepin, blastit wonner,
> Detested, shunn'd by saunt an' sinner,
> How daur ye set your fit upon her,
> Sae fine a lady!
> Gae somewhere else, and seek your dinner
> On some poor body.
>
> ("To a Louse")

The meter was also used by William Wordsworth, appropriately, for his "At the Grave of Burns."

■ A. H. MacLaine, "New Light on the Genesis of the Burns Stanza," *N&Q* 198 (1953); H. Damico, "Sources of Stanza Forms Used by Burns," *Studies in Scottish Literature* 12 (1975); R. Crawford, *Robert Burns and Cultural Authority* (1997); *The Canongate Burns*, ed. A. Noble and P. S. Hogg (2003).

A. PREMINGER; T.V.F. BROGAN; C. DOAK

**BYLINA** (pl. *byliny*). Scholars use the word *bylina* for the Rus. oral *epic (see ORAL POETRY), but singers employ *starina* (*or starinka*), terms indicating songs about past events. Byliny originated among the princes' retinues in Kyivan Rus' and were produced between the 10th and 15th cs. Ordinarily byliny contain 300–500 lines, are without stanzas or rhyme, are built around typical epic subjects, and employ special ling. and poetic devices. They are performed by a single singer without the accompaniment of a musical instrument. The earliest pub. collection appeared in 1804 and is attributed to Kirsha Danilov, who took down songs in the Ural region in the mid-18th c. Thought extinct by the mid-19th c., byliny were discovered to be a living trad. in the region around Lake Onega by P. N. Rybnikov in 1860. A collecting effort concentrated largely around Lake Onega and the White Sea ensued and continued until about 1950 when the trad. died out.

Scholars divide byliny into three cycles: magical (sometimes "mythological"), Kyivan, and Novgorod. The magical heroes (*bogatyri*) are the earliest. They include the shape-shifter Volkh Vseslavyevich, the villager's son Mikula, and the giant Svyatogor. Kyivan byliny constitute the largest group, and their heroes serve Prince Vladimir, who has been compared to King Arthur. These byliny reflect the struggle of Kyiv with nomadic steppe groups, though after the Mongol conquest, the adversaries appear as Tatars. The low-born Ilya Muromets, who even when snubbed by Vladimir stands up for Rus, the Christian faith, and the downtrodden, is its central hero. Other important heroes include the courteous diplomat Dobrynya Nikitich and the cunning priest's son Alyosha Popovich. The third cycle is connected to the northern city of Novgorod. Its heroes are the rich merchant and gusli player Sadko and the rabble-rouser Vasily Buslayev.

■ A. P. Skaftymov, *Poetika i genezis bylin* (1924); N. Chadwick, *Russian Heroic Poetry* (1932); A. M. Astakhova, *Russkii bylinnyi epos na Severe* (1948), and *Il'ia Muromets* (1958); V. Ia. Propp, *Russkii georicheskii epos* (1958); *Byliny*, ed. A. M. Astkhova (1966); F. J. Oinas, "Russian Byliny," *Heroic Epic and Saga* (1978); B. N. Putilov, *Epicheskoe stazitel'stvo* (1997); *An Anthology of Russian Folk Epics*, ed. J. Bailey and T. Ivanova (1998).

J. O. BAILEY; L. IVANITS

## BYZANTINE POETRY

  I. Hymnography
  II. Songs
  III. Declamatory Poetry
  IV. Epigrams
  V. Religious Poetry
  VI. Satirical Poetry
  VII. Verse Romances and Chronicles
  VIII. Didactic Poetry

The Byzantine millennium is usually divided into three periods: early Byzantine or late antique (330–ca. 600), middle Byzantine (ca. 600–1204), and late Byzantine (1204–1453). Constantinople officially became the capital of the Eastern Roman Empire (now called the Byzantine Empire) in the year 330; around 600, urban civilization and traditional power structures began to collapse, leading to the "dark age" crisis of the 7th and 8th cs. In 1204, Constantinople was conquered by the knights of the Fourth Crusade, and although it was reconquered in 1261, the Byzantine Empire had been reduced to a few territories that were gradually taken by the Ottoman Turks until the city itself fell in 1453. Although the Byzantine Empire was multilingual and produced lit. in Gr., Lat., Coptic, Syriac, Heb., Armenian, and Slavonic, the term *Byzantine literature* stands for med. Gr. lit. Byzantine Gr. is a literary lang. harking back to the ancients (Homeric and Atticistic Gr.) and/or the Bible and the earliest Christian texts (koiné); the first experiments in the vernacular date from the 12th c. Because Byzantine lit. is imitative, it has had a bad press; but *originality is a romantic concept, unknown to the Middle Ages. There are two kinds of Byzantine poetry: poetry set to music, such as *hymns, acclamations, satirical songs, and folk songs; and all other forms of poetry, intended either to be declaimed in public or to be read in private. As most poetry belonging to the first category has come down to us without scores or in later musical adaptations, we are uncertain how Byzantine music, esp. in its early stages, may have sounded. As for meter, all poetry set to music and many of the unsung poems are based on rhythmical patterns regulated by the position of stress accents. Poems in prosodic meters, such as the *iamb, the *hexameter, or the *anacreontic also survive, but these, too, obey certain rhythmical rules.

**I. Hymnography.** Byzantine liturgical poetry falls into three periods: the first (4th–5th c.) characterized by short hymns, the *troparia* and *stichera*; the second (5th–7th c.) by long and elaborate metrical sermons, the *kontakia* (clearly influenced by certain forms of Syriac hymnography); and the third (7th–9th c. and afterward) by a form of hymn-cycle called *kanon*, consisting of eight or nine odes, each set to its own music (*heirmos*). The second is the great period of Byzantine hymnography. The celebrated *Akathistos* hymn, sometimes referred to as the Byzantine *Te Deum*, dates from the 5th c. In the 6th c. lived Romanos, Byzantium's greatest religious poet. Some 85 of his kontakia have been preserved, all metrical sermons for various feasts of the Orthodox Church. Romanos, a conscientious Christian, treated his subject matter exactly as a preacher would. Occasionally, however, he gives rein to his fancy and at such times becomes grandiloquent in the style of epideictic oratorical poetry. His lang. on the whole is pure; he is rich in *metaphor and *imagery and often interweaves in his narrative whole passages from Holy Scripture. Andrew of Crete (around 700), initiates the third period of Byzantine liturgical poetry with his *Great Kanon*, a huge composition, in which elaboration of form results in a magnificent celebration of the Divine. Other representatives are John of Damascus, Kosmas of Maiouma, and Joseph the Hymnographer (8th–9th cs.). Though new hymns continued to be written, by the end of the 9th c., the liturgical calendar had filled up, and only few additions were made, such as a set of hymns written for the feast of the Three Hierarchs by John Mauropous (11th c.).

**II. Songs.** Byzantine chronicles preserve snippets of popular songs, such as the song making fun of Emperor Maurice's sexual prowess. The *Book of Ceremonies* (shortly after 963) contains the lyrics of many acclamations sung by the circus factions, unfortunately, without musical annotation. Some of the Gr. folk songs recorded in the 19th and 20th cs. by anthropologists go back to a centuries-old trad.; but in an oral trad., changes and corruptions are inevitable. There are a few texts in vernacular med. Gr. that clearly rely on an oral substratum. The most famous of these is the *Digenis Akritis* (early 12th c.?), a text of epic proportions that strings together a compilation of earlier ballads into an incoherent and disjointed narrative; the text has come down to us in various mss., the most important of which are the Escorial and the Grottaferrata versions.

**III. Declamatory Poetry.** *Panegyrics, *monodies, and *ekphraseis are just a few of the genres that were intended to be declaimed either at official celebrations, at certain ceremonies, or in so-called *theatra*, literary salons where literati would present their works to each other. The two best representatives of the panegyric (epic encomium) are George Pisides (7th c.) and Theodore Prodromos (12th c.), the former writing iambic verse (called *dodecasyllable* because it consists of 12 syllables) in praise of his patron, Emperor Herakleios, and his victories over the Avars and the Persians; and the latter writing for various patrons, incl. Emperor John Komnenos and other members of the imperial family, whose military feats he celebrated in political verse (a 15-syllable verse with a *caesura in the middle and an iambic rhythm). Monodies are funerary *dirges declaimed at burial ceremonies: the most famous are anonymous monodies on the deaths of Leo VI (912) and Constantine VII (959), the earliest instance of political verse; other monodies mourn the loss of cities, such as the late 12th-c. dirge by Michael Choniates, in which he lamented that ancient Athens was lost forever. Among the many ekphraseis, the detailed descriptions of St. Sophia by Paul the Silentiary (6th c.) and of the Church of the Holy Apostles by Constantine the Rhodian (10th c.) deserve to be mentioned—but *ekphrasis* can take many forms, incl. an anonymous early 11th-c. description of a boat trip on the Bosporus or a detailed account of a day at the races by Christopher Mitylenaios (11th c.).

**IV. Epigrams.** Byzantine *epigrams are either genuine or fictitious verse inscriptions attached to monuments or works of art or inscribed on tombs (*epitaphs). There is not a single Byzantine poet without at least a few epigrams to his name. While Agathias, Paul the Silentiary, and other 6th-c. poets clung to the rules and dictates of Hellenistic epigrammatic poetry, a more Christian and less elaborate form was developed by George Pisides (7th c.), Theodore of Stoudios, and Ignatios the Deacon (both early 9th c.). However, the heyday of the Byzantine epigram spans the 10th to 12th cs.: it was then that John Geometres, Christopher Mitylenaios, John Mauropous, Nicholas Kallikles, and Theodore Prodromos flourished. The anonymous 12th-c. epigrams in the collection of Marcianus Graecus 524 are also quite exceptional. The genre of the Byzantine epigram also comprises the many book epigrams found in Byzantine mss.: epigrams written in honor of the author, the patron who commissioned the ms., or the scribe. Gnomic epigrams (see GNOMIC POETRY), of which there are many, also fall in this category: most of these pithy sayings are anonymous, but some are attributed to Kassia (9th c.), the only known female Byzantine poet.

**V. Religious Poetry.** Apart from hymnography, the singing of which is a communal act of devotion, there are also lyrical effusions of the soul and intimate soliloquies with God; these poems are not sung but either declaimed or read in silence. The poetry of the Church father Gregory of Nazianzus (4th c.) is a brilliant example followed by all Byzantine poets. The greatest of these are John Geometres (10th c.), Symeon the New Theologian (10th–11th c.), and John Mauropous (11th c.). Geometres' masterpiece is a long confession and prayer to the Holy Virgin, in which he tries to come to terms with his human limitations. Symeon the New Theologian was a mystic who wrote inspired poetry relating all his mysti-

cal experiences and divine revelations, such as one in which he recognizes the presence of Christ in his body. Mauropous was an intellectual reluctant to leave his books and step out into the world: when he was forced to become metropolitan of a provincial town, he wrote two poems first praying that this evil might not happen and then, when the imperial decision proved to be irreversible, asking God to teach him how to accept his fate.

**VI. Satirical Poetry.** *Satire is ubiquitous in Byzantine poetry, in both the learned and vernacular trads. A good example of the latter are the *Ptochoprodromic Poems* (12th c.), five satires dealing with different characters who narrate their petty problems and little adventures, posing as a henpecked husband, a hungry *paterfamilias*, a poor grammarian, and a lowly and abused monk. The poems of "Poor Prodromos" are brilliant satires that describe the lives of ordinary citizens in a big city in a vernacular that serves as a vehicle of social crit. and colorful realism. Another good example of satire is the *Entertaining Tale of Quadrupeds* (14th c.), a hilarious poem about an assembly of animals who express their grudges.

**VII. Verse Romances and Chronicles.** In the 12th c., the ancient "novelists" Heliodorus and Achilles Tatius were imitated in a number of verse romances by Niketas Eugenianos, Theodore Prodromos, and Constantine Manasses, all of whom wrote in learned Gr. After 1204, this literary experiment was followed by verse romances in vernacular Gr., most of which also show some familiarity with Western romances of chivalry (see MEDIEVAL ROMANCE), such as the *Livistros and Rodamne, War of Troy, Achilleid,* and *Velthandros and Chrysantza,* all the works of unknown poets. Verse chronicles, too, were composed in learned and vernacular Gr.: the *Synopsis Chronike* by Manasses (12th c.), the *Chronicle of Morea* (14th c.), and the *Chronicle of the Tocco* (early 15th c.). With its emphasis on love, exploring the depths of the human soul, Manasses' chronicle might even be seen as a verse romance.

**VIII. Didactic Poetry.** A few names should suffice for these prose-in-verse creations on all kinds of scientific topics: Pisides' *Hexaemeron,* Leo Choirosphaktes' *Thousand-Line Theology* (early 10th c.), Niketas of Herakleia's grammatical treatises in the form of troparia and kanons (11th c.), and Manuel Philes' *On the Characteristics of Animals* (early 14th c.).

■ **Anthologies:** *Anthologia Graeca Carminum Christianorum,* ed. W. Christ and M. Paranikas (1872); *Poeti byzantini,* ed. R. Cantarella, 2 v. (1948); *Medieval and Modern Greek Poetry,* ed. C. A. Trypanis (1951); *An Anthology of Byzantine Poetry,* ed. B. Baldwin (1985).
■ **Criticism and History:** K. Krumbacher, *Geschichte der byzantinischen Litteratur,* 2d ed. (1897); H.-G. Beck, *Geschichte der byzantinischen Volksliteratur* (1971); H. Hunger, *Die hochsprachliche Profane Literatur,* 2 v. (1978); Trypanis; *Oxford Dictionary of Byzantium,* ed. A. P. Kazhdan (1991); M. D. Lauxtermann, *Byzantine Poetry from Pisides to Geometres* (2003).

M. D. LAUXTERMANN

**CACCIA.** An It. verse form first used in the early 14th c. by Magister Piero, Giovanni da Cascia, and Jacopo da Bologna. Three early *caccia* were cast in the form of the *madrigal. The highly developed caccia consisted of a random number of eleven-, seven-, or five-syllable lines of verse. As in the madrigal, a *refrain might occur as the final section. Other features include *onomatopoeia, elliptical syntax, and exclamatory remarks. As the name indicates, the caccia originated as a hunting song (It. *cacciare*, to hunt); Boccaccio's *Caccia di Diana* (1336), in *terza rima*, is the first. Niccolò Soldanieri created the best examples; later poets such as Giannozzo Manetti, Franco Sacchetti, Ghirardello da Firenze, and Francesco Landini extended the motive and also included battle scenes, fishing scenes, and dancing. Musically, the caccia consists of a canon in two parts for upper voices, which "hunt" each other, normally accompanied by an instrumental tenor. In 1332, Antonio da Tempo wrote the first extensive theoretical treatise of the cacci, the *Summa artis rithmici*. The caccia was particularly popular between 1360 and 1380; after 1400, only a few examples are extant. Forms of the caccia existed in most Eur. countries, such as the Fr. *chace* (*chasse*), the Eng. chase, the Sp. *caça*, and the Ger. *Jagdlied* (Oswald von Wolkenstein). Since the 16th c., the term has generally been applied to hunting songs of various types, e.g., the songs by Nicolas Gombert or Clément Janequin, or the catch in England. Joseph Haydn (Symphony no. 73) and Étienne Méhul (overture of his opera *Le jeune Henri*) applied the term *Chasse* to their works.

■ *Fourteenth-century Italian Cacce*, ed. W. T. Marrocco (1942); N. Pirrotta, "Per l'origine e la storia della caccia e del madrigale trecentesca," *Rivista musicale italiana* 48–49 (1946–47); F. Ghisl, "Caccia," *MGG*; A. da Tempo, *Summa artis rithmici*, ed. R. Andrews (1977); F. A. Gallo, "Caccia," *Handwörterbuch der musical: Terminologie*, ed. H. H. Eggebrecht (1979); K. von Fischer, "Caccia," *New Grove*; A. Classen, "Onomatopoesie in der Lyrik von Jehan Vaillant, Oswald von Wolkenstein und Niccolò Soldaniere," *Zeitschrift für Deutsche Philologie* (1989); *Diana's Hunt*, ed. and trans. A. K. Cassell and V. Kirkham (1991); D. Del Puppo, "Caccia," *Medieval Italy: An Encyclopedia*, ed. C. Kleinhenz (2004).

A. CLASSEN

**CACOPHONY** (Gr., "bad sound"). The opposite of *euphony. Harsh and discordant or dissonant sound, used particularly in dramatic works and poetry to create tension, to express a speaker's rage or indignation, or to evoke other stressful emotions for readers, performers, and their audiences.

In his *Essay on Criticism*, Alexander Pope employs cacophony to show how "The Sound must seem an Eccho to the Sense" when he writes, "But when loud Surges lash the sounding Shore, / The hoarse, rough Verse shou'd like the Torrent roar" (365, 368–69).

It bears noting that what the words are saying may alter one's perceptions of cacophony. Reader/performers are likely to consider the concluding line of G. M. Hopkins's "Felix Randal," with its own insistent *b*'s and *d*'s (and *g*'s), more steadily forceful and admiring (and perhaps suggestive of hammer blows) than cacophonous, as the poet describes how the blacksmith "Didst fettle for the great gray dray horse his bright and battering sandal."

More certain cacophony is evident in Robert Browning's "Soliloquy of the Spanish Cloister." Harsh *g*'s of the opening "Gr-r-r—there go" are followed by the breathy *hea* and *hor* of "my heart's abhorrence"—the physical exhalations accompanying and intensifying the sense of the speaker's hatred of another cloistered monk. After nine stanzas of vituperation, the poem ends with an outburst of harsh sounds such as those that might summon devils, as well as a corruption of the euphonic "Ave Maria, gratia plena": *Hy, Zy, Hine . . .* / 'St, there's Vespers! "*Plena grati* / *Ave, Virgo!* Gr-r-r— you swine!"

*See* DISSONANCE, SOUND.

T. CARPER

**CADENCE.** (1) Technically, the fixed patterning of quantities in the clausula, i.e., the last few syllables of a phrase or clause, in med. Lat. art prose (see PROSE RHYTHM); also, by extension, such prefinal patterning in metrical verse. (2) More generally, the rhythmic pattern or intonational contour of a sentence or line, referring to its accentual pattern, the timing of its delivery, its *pitch contour, or any combination of these. (3) A term often used to describe the rhythmical flow of such nonmetrical prosodies as found in the Bible, in Walt Whitman, in *free verse, and in the *prose poem. Drawn from music, the term used in this third sense implies a looser, more irregular concept of poetic rhythm than that applied to metrical poetry and mainly refers to phrasing, which extends beyond foot-based *scansion. Cadence is here determined by ample and flexible sonic features incl. *assonance and *consonance and is shaped both by stichic concerns and strophic considerations. Most of the poets experimenting in the avant-garde prosodies of the later 19th and early 20th cs. followed injunctions toward cadence-based composition advanced by Ezra Pound and W. C. Williams, esp. per the latter's notion of the *variable foot. Amy Lowell linked cadence not only to music but to breathing, which Charles Olson subsequently theorized in his remarks on *projective verse. Robert Duncan later extended the connection between cadence and breathing to encompass the entire body. In recent years, the continued emphasis on cadence as an alternative to meter is indicative of a more inclusive canon, the revival of *oral poetry, and the ongoing transition from print to digital culture.

*See* COLON, PERIOD, PUNCTUATION.

■ Hardie; A. Lowell, "Some Musical Analogies in Modern Poetry," *The Musical Quarterly* 6, no. 1 (1920); Olson; M. M. Morgan, "A Treatise in Cadence," *MLR* 47 (1952); W. Mohr, "Kadenz," *Reallexikon II*, 1.803–6; Lausberg, 479 ff.; D. Levertov, "Some Notes on Organic Form," *Poetry* 105 (1964); Scott 187 ff.; Morier, see "Clausule"; Norden 2.909 ff.; R. Duncan, "Some Notes on Notation," *Ground Work: Before the War* (1984).

T.V.F. BROGAN; J. M. COCOLA

## CAESURA

I. Caesura vs. Pause
II. Position
III. Extra Syllables

A term that derives from the Lat. verb *caedere*, "to cut off," and refers to the place in a line of verse where the metrical flow is temporarily "cut off." When this "cut" occurs at the beginning of a line, it is called an "initial caesura"; when it occurs in the middle of a line, it is called a "medial caesura"; and when it occurs at the end of a line, it is called a "terminal caesura." In OE poems such as *Beowulf*, caesuras occur predictably between the two half-lines (*hemistich) that are linked by *alliteration. Chaucer used caesuras with greater variety in his *iambic pentameter, and William Shakespeare used them with even more variety in his *blank verse. Poets during and after the Eng. Ren. often placed several caesuras in a line—or no caesuras in a line—to alter the rhythm of the meter, which would otherwise be as monotonous as the ticking of a metronome. 18th-c. poets such as Alexander Pope used caesuras to create a sense of balance or symmetry. In Pope's famous couplet "True wit is nature to advantage dressed, / What oft was thought, but ne'er so well expressed" (*An Essay on Criticism*, 297–98), the caesura in the second line allows the reader to pause before balancing the traditional contraries of wit and nature, thought and speech. 19th- and 20th-c. poets who broke away from metrical verse to write *free verse used caesuras in unexpected places in an attempt to represent more accurately the spontaneous way people thought and spoke. When Ezra Pound and e. e. cummings composed poems by arranging words—or even syllables—in unconventional patterns on the page and when poets such as Charles Olson and Allen Ginsberg declared that poetic lines should be units of breath, caesuras were often indicated by spaces between phrases. In contemp. writing, the poetic term *caesura* is frequently used metaphorically to mean any space, break, or pause in a sequence. Thus, Stephen Melville titles a chapter "Caesura" in *AIDS and the National Body* to refer to a pause in the long "sentence" of dying caused by AIDS. Other contemp.

scholars write of "the caesura of the Holocaust" or "the caesura of religion."

**I. Caesura vs. Pause.** In every sentence, a syntactic juncture or pause between phrases or clauses is usually signaled by punctuation. Traditionally, a caesura is the metrical phenomenon in verse that corresponds to this break in syntax. Often these "breaks" are not carefully distinguished in *prosody and lit. crit. Some critics use *pause*, *rest*, and *caesura* interchangeably. Strict constructionists argue that performative pauses and individual speech tempos have nothing to do with caesuras in a traditional metrical design. Nor do so-called "metrical pauses" (missing syllables in accentual verse and other verse systems whose time is filled by a rest) have anything to do with a caesura. According to the traditional view, a poet deliberately places a caesura in a line to break up the metrical flow of verse and to prevent monotony. By contrast, a reader can break up the flow any way he or she deems appropriate. Although some prosodists have claimed that, strictly speaking, a caesura is not a component of a metrical pattern or is only realized in performance, these are minority views.

**II. Position.** The position and number of caesuras in a line vary from one verse system to another. In cl. prosody, a caesura referred specifically to a pause within a foot of metrical verse. A *diaeresis referred to a pause at the end of a foot. The semantic shift from caesura to diaeresis may have occurred in Pierre de Ronsard's *Abrégé de l'art poétique françois* (1565). During the Ren., the mod. concept of caesura as a pause at the end of a metrical foot first surfaced in the prosody manuals of the *Séconde Rhétorique* of early 16th-c. France. A rule forbidding an extra syllable before the caesura was set forth in the *Pleine rhétorique* (1521) of Pierre Fabri and in the *Art poétique* (1555) of Jacques Peletier du Mans, who seems to have been the first to use the term *césure* in Fr.

In Gr. and Lat. poetry, caesuras were regulated more as to position than as to number, and technical terms have been developed to designate the most common placements in the *hexameter line. The term *penthemimeral* refers to a caesura appearing after the first long syllable of the third foot (i.e., after the fifth half-foot), and *hephthemimeral* refers to a caesura after the seventh half-foot. Cl. poets avoided dividing the hexameter line into two equal halves with a caesura. Fixed caesura placement was a major criterion in romance prosodies, esp. Fr. prosody. Indeed, when Victor Hugo moved the caesura in his Fr. *alexandrine lines to create the *trimètre*, it was considered one of the most revolutionary moments in Fr. romanticism. In Eng. verse, caesura placement varies considerably according to metrical subgenre (dramatic verse vs. narrative and lyric; rhymed couplets vs. blank verse). At the end of the 19th c., Jakob Schipper promoted the doctrine that the caesura was essential to the structure of iambic pentameter (fully half of the 50 pps. devoted to Chaucerian meter in his *Englische Metrik* treated the caesura) and that variation in caesura placement was a deliberate strategy to combat the tedium of perfectly metered lines of verse.

**III. Extra Syllables.** The conventional terminology for line endings, *masculine* and *feminine*, is sometimes still applied to caesuras. Thus, a caesura that follows a stressed syllable is called masculine, and one that follows an unstressed syllable is called feminine. Romance philologists and prosodists of the later 19th c. developed the terms *epic* and *lyric* to refer to two types of feminine caesuras that followed, respectively, an unstressed syllable that is not counted as part of the metrical pattern and an unstressed syllable that is counted. This system of classification arose from speculations about OF epics and lyric poems of *troubadours and *trouvères. In 1903, L. E. Kastner showed that the notion of epic caesuras was "not justified by facts." Unfortunately, these terms were taken up by scholars to describe caesural variation in Chaucer, with the implication that Eng. patterns of syllabic variation around the caesura "strictly correspond to their French models" (Schipper *History*, 133). Further studies have shown that caesura placement in Eng. verse—esp. Chaucer's and Shakespeare's—is not strictly regulated.

■ L. E. Kastner, "The Epic Caesura in the Poetry of the Trouvères and Troubadours," *MLQ* 6 (1903); Schipper, *History* (1910); A. L. F. Snell, *Pause* (1918); A. Oras, *Pause Patterns in Elizabethan and Jacobean Drama* (1960); J. Malof, *A Manual of English Meters* (1970); Allen; J. P. Poe, *Caesurae in the Hexameter Line of Latin Elegiac Verse* (1974); R. Tsur, *A Perception-Oriented Theory of Metre* (1977); G. Wright, *Shakespeare's Metrical Art* (1988); *A Dictionary of Literary Terms and Literary Theory*, ed. J. A. Cuddon (1998); S. Fry, *The Ode Less Travelled* (2006); *A New Handbook of Literary Terms*, ed. D. Mikics (2007).

T.V.F. BROGAN; H. HART

**CALENDRICAL POETRY.** Of poems in the Western trad. that play with calendrical schemes, the first is Hesiod's *Works and Days* (ca. 700 BCE), whose final 64 verses offer an almanac of propitious or unlucky days of any month (but not all days) for various human activities. The miscellaneous topics include agriculture, other practical operations (e.g., shipbuilding), and major life events (birth and marriage). Cl. Lat. didactic poems adapt the Hesiodic movement: Virgil thus briefly advises farmers at *Georgics* 1.276–86, while Ovid in *Art of Love* 1.399–418 parodically itemizes for the wooing lover days of the year when gifts are customary and so when visits to the stereotypically acquisitive girl are to be avoided. The Hellenistic Greek Simias of Rhodes (3rd c. BCE) wrote *Months* (now lost), a poem presumably devoted wholly to the calendar. Ovid continued this devel. at Rome with the *Fasti*, which traces the religious year of the Roman state day by day, with one book devoted to each month; only the first six books survive. The *Fasti* responds to—some would say contests—the emperor Augustus' remaking of the Roman calendar in his own image through the addition of various imperial feast days alongside the traditional festivals. Ovid, moreover, plays civic time off against "natural" temporal schemes by interweaving zodiacal notices and dated weather signs.

In the Middle Ages, the Christian calendar of major liturgical feasts and saints' days occasionally found expression in verse, in both Lat. and the vernacular. The form became popular among humanist poets in Ren. Italy (L. Lazzarelli [c. 1485], L. Bonincontri [1491], B. Mantuan [1516], A. Fracco [1547]), whence it spread to the Protestant north (N. Chytraeus, 1568) and later to France (H. Vaillant, 1674). For all these, Ovid's *Fasti* served as both chief model and polemical pagan foil. In *The Shepheardes Calender* (1579), Edmund Spenser contributes a new form to the pastoral genre by presenting a book of 12 *eclogues as meditations on the individual months. The most conspicuous menological motifs mirror the rustic characters' moods—January's wintry barrenness, a rejected lover's plight; April's showers, the tears for a sad friend. The suggestive Spenserian structure is applied more rigorously by later poets who actually encapsulate the months in ordered sequence: John Clare appropriates Spenser's title for a descriptive survey of village life from January through December (*The Shepherd's Calendar*, 1827), while H. W. Longfellow narrows the focus to a quick progression of summary utterances by the personified months in *The Poet's Calendar* (1882).

In the 20th c., there emerges the genre of verse jours., apparently originated by W. C. Williams in "The Descent of Winter" (1928; actually a mixture of prose and verse). Poetic reflections are arranged according to date, with varying degrees of continuity and calendrical completeness. In personalizing the calendar, the poet either pointedly eschews a day's meaning in public spheres (civic, religious, historical), like William Corbett in *Columbus Square Journal* (1976), or anchors private meditations in larger communal contexts, like Anne Sexton in *Eighteen Days without You* (1969) and Charles Wright in *A Journal of English Days* (1986). Angus MacLise's *Year* (1962), at once minimalist and the fullest poetic calendar, uniquely presents an entire year with a cascade of 366 dated phrases that idiosyncratically characterize the individual days.

■ C. E. Newlands, *Playing with Time* (1995); J. F. Miller, "Ovid's *Fasti* and the Neo-Latin Christian Calendar Poem," *IJCT* 10 (2003); S. Cushman, "'The Descent of Winter' and the Poetry of the Calendar," *Rigor of Beauty*, ed. I. D. Copestake (2004).

J. F. MILLER

**CALLIGRAMME.** The calligramme derives its name from Guillaume Apollinaire's *Calligrammes* (1918) and represents one type of *visual poetry. Its antecedents include Gr. *technopaegnia, Lat. *carmina figurata, med. pattern poetry, Ren. *emblems, and Stéphane Mallarmé's *Un coup de dés* (1897). It thus occupies an intermediary position between older types of visual poetry and more recent forms such as *concrete poetry, hypergraphic poetry, *electronic poetry, and holopoetry. In the context of the early 20th c., the calligramme reflects the influence of cubist painting (see CUBISM), It. *futurism, and the Chinese *ideogram (the first examples were called *idéogrammes lyriques*). Introduced by Apollinaire in 1914, the genre inaugurated a period of radical experimentation by fusing art and poetry to create a complex interdisciplinary genre or intermedium.

Like other forms that dissolve the traditional barriers between visual and verbal, the calligramme mediates between the two fundamental modes of human perception, sight and sound. Whereas the futurists preferred abstract visual poetry, Apollinaire's compositions are largely figurative, portraying objects such as hearts, fountains, mandolins, and the Eiffel Tower, as well as animals, plants, and people. Still, a significant number are abstract, making generalization difficult, though on the whole the abstract calligrammes are later works. Of the 133 works arranged in realistic shapes, the visual image duplicates a verbal image in about half the cases. Some of the poems are autonomous, but most are grouped together to form still lives, landscapes, and portraits, an important innovation in the visual poetry trad. that complicates the interplay of visual and verbal signs. As Apollinaire remarks, "[T]he relations between the juxtaposed figures in one of my poems are just as expressive as the words that compose it." Although some of the calligrammes are solid compositions, most feature an outlined form that emphasizes the genre's connection with drawing. Unlike most of his predecessors, however, Apollinaire adapts visual poetry to lyric themes. Some of the calligrammes are in verse, but many others are in prose. One group, composed in 1917, continues Apollinaire's earlier experiments with *poésie critique* and functions as art crit. Although its critical reception has been mixed, the calligramme was widely imitated in France, Italy, Spain, Mexico, the U.S., and elsewhere.

*See* LETTRISME, TYPOGRAPHY.

■ G. Apollinaire, *Calligrammes*, ed. and trans. A. H. Greet and S. I. Lockerbie (1980); D. Seaman, *Concrete Poetry in France* (1981); W. Bohn, *The Aesthetics of Visual Poetry, 1914–1928* (1986), and *Apollinaire, Visual Poetry, and Art Criticism* (1993); J. Drucker, *The Visible Word* (1994); M. Webster, *Reading Visual Poetry after Futurism* (1995); W. Bohn, *Modern Visual Poetry* (2001) and *Reading Visual Poetry* (2010).

W. BOHN

**CAMBODIA, POETRY OF.** At the beginning of the Common Era, Sanskrit, the sacred lang. of India, spread along the trade routes across most of southern Asia from Afghanistan to Java. This political literary culture, referred to by Pollock as the "Sanskrit cosmopolis," shaped the aesthetics of "Cambodian" or Khmer poetry from the time of Funan, an ancient Indianized kingdom located around the Mekong Delta during the 1st c. CE.

The Khmer lang., an eastern branch of the Mon-Khmer family, which is part of the larger Austro-Asiatic lang. group, is basically monosyllabic, although words may be lengthened to an iambic disyllable by the addition of prefixes or consonants. Old Khmer (7th–12th cs.) was heavily influenced by Sanskrit throughout the Angkor period (9th–13th cs.) and by Pali, the lang. of Theravada Buddhism, from the 13th c. onward. Examples of early lit. are largely found in Sanskrit inscriptions written in verse praising the great deeds of gods and kings. The poetry of six anonymous authors can be identified as written in Sanskrit during the Angkor period.

Jacob (1996) has identified 12 different forms of meter in Cambodian poetry, with certain meters used for specific purposes. "High" vocabulary—i.e., Sanskrit or Pali borrowings—often are combined with a Khmer word as a type of reduplication in Khmer poetics. The linking of one stanza to the next through rhyme is also a feature of this poetry. Since Khmer is replete with alliterative, chiming, and rhyming words, the best poems are melodious, indicating pleasure in *assonance and *alliteration. Such poetry sometimes is recited to the accompaniment of a stringed instrument, reflecting the importance of its musicality. Because of this aesthetic, Jacob (1996) argues that the best representation of Khmer poetry is to be found in *songs. Themes of songs and poems often touch on emotion, such as lost love or separation. Besides songs, *riddles, proverbs, and didactic lit., early Khmer fictions also were written in verse. After attacks by the Siamese, the Angkor period in Cambodia came to a close around 1430. By then, many Khmer writers and books had been relocated to Siam (now Thailand). For the next five centuries, Cambodia suffered predatory attacks on its borders, along with ebbing fortunes. As in Western Europe, where Lat. lit. was largely displaced by vernacular langs. after the fall of the Roman Empire, so too would Sanskrit be displaced by the Khmer lang. during the subsequent Middle Period.

As Cambodia's fortunes declined, its lang. changed. Middle Khmer shows borrowings from Thai, Lao, and, to a lesser extent, Vietnamese. Verse, which was used for all literary texts, was written in Khmer. Because of Cambodia's troubles following the fall of Angkor, no lit. survives that can be precisely dated to the 15th or 16th cs. The earliest written extant lit. consists of the *Rāmakerti I* (Cambodian *Rāmayāna*), and *Cpāp'* (Codes of Conduct; 15th–16th cs.). The earliest stratum of these texts is written in *Pad kākagati* (crow's gait meter). There is a religious element to most of the verse lit. of the Middle Period. The *Rāmaketi* (*Reamker*), Cambodia's version of the *Rāmayāṇa*, was originally a Hindu text. The Cambodian version, filled with allusions to Hindu gods and geography, was influenced by Buddhism, with its hero Ram represented as Buddha. The *Cpāp'*, Buddhist moral poems that teach standards of conduct, also humorously portray details of ordinary lives. Some verses from *Cpāp'* are popularized as proverbs.

Other genres of Middle Period lit. include the *Sātrā lpaeṇ*, verse novels that tell stories of the bodhisattvas, or previous lives of the Buddha, usually portrayed as a prince, and the *jātak*, birth stories of the Buddha in verse, esp. the "ten jātak" (depicting the last ten lives of the Buddha before he entered Nirvana) and the extracanonical "50 jātak." Although originally written in Pali, versions of the 50 jatak are known only in Burma, Laos, Thailand, and Cambodia. Another Buddhist religious text of great importance is the *Trai Bhūm* (The

Three Worlds), whose source is a Siamese ms. written during the reign of the king of Sukhoday.

Historically, the next genre to develop during the Middle Period is the *lyric (*kaṃṇāby*). These are mss. of 18th–19th c. court poets, whose poems express feelings of love and separation. After the fall of Angkor, the Siamese used Cambodian lit. for their own cultural purposes. After many centuries during which changes were made to the texts, the Cambodians gradually recovered much of their lit. in the 19th c. They would also adapt Thai verse forms to Cambodian-lang. poetry, such as the Thai *klong* (seven-syllable meter).

In 1863, Cambodia, along with Vietnam and Laos, became a protectorate of France. The Fr. established public schools in the new capital city of Phnom Penh, where young men were taught solely in Fr. and introduced to Fr. lit. This influence fostered Cambodian novels in prose but did not lead to the devel. of a new mod. poetry. By 1954, when King Sihanouk gained Cambodia's independence from France, Khmer writers were publishing new prose and poetry in literary magazines popular in the larger cities. In 1958, the government stipulated that the verse novel *Tum Teav*, whose authorship is contested, be included as a central text in the Khmer lit. curriculum for secondary schools. Oral versions of this tragic love story are traced to the 19th c., but it might be as old as the Middle Period. Sihanouk, who had abdicated his position as king to become head of state, was overthrown in a 1970 coup as the country gradually devolved into civil war. Poets of the early 1970s, such as Koy Sarun, dealt with the harsh realities of power. On April 17, 1975, the Khmer Rouge took control of Cambodia, emptying its capital city of inhabitants and forcing "new people" from the cities to work in gulag labor camps in remote areas of the country-side. During this period, the majority of Cambodian poets were killed or died from disease, starvation, or exhaustion. Writing was forbidden among the masses under the Khmer Rouge, but poetry reemerged after 1979, when the Vietnamese established a government in Cambodia and drove the Khmer Rouge toward the Thai border. This poetry, in traditional meter, replete with sorrow and loss, would be written by Cambodians in exile, either in refugee camps along the Thai border or in distant lands of the Cambodian diaspora. Poet U Sam Oeur, who moved to the United States, typically uses traditional meter in his poems but sometimes writes in *free verse. Many of his poems describe his experience under the Khmer Rouge:

> There are no more intellectuals, no more
> professors—
> all have departed Phnom Penh, leading children,
> bereft, deceived to the last person,
> from coolie to king.

> ("The Fall of Culture")

Since May 1993, when elections were held in Cambodia under the supervision of the United Nations, Cambodian lit. entered an age of somewhat freer expression. Although poetry was still written in tradi-

tional verse, the use of Pali and Sanskrit to embellish it faded among the younger writers. New poetry often contains mod. themes about the environment or social conditions. Contemp. poets reflect on power and the powerless, along with the transitory quality of the natural world. Yin Luoth's poem "Crippled Soldiers" describes a common scene in Phnom Penh:

> Crippled soldiers
> walking through the market
> missing arm or leg
> hands in supplication
> everyday beg
> even without fingers
> to take the money.

The continuing influence of Buddhism in Cambodian culture, esp. its social concern for the unfortunate and injunction against greed, is also reflected in the poems of Ven. Chin Meas, whose understated symbolism gives his poetry particular poignancy. His poem "Inherited House" traces the happiness of a rural family until the death of the parents unleashes the thoughtless greed of their selfish children:

> They divided up the inherited house
> that had once given them peace
> they can never
> live together again.

Currently in Cambodia, there are very few venues for poets to present their work to the public. Poets typically subsidize the publication of 100 to 200 copies of their chapbooks, which they often give away or try to sell through the book stalls in the various markets in the cities. Phnom Penh, with the largest community of poets in the country, has the Java Café and Monument Books, which support poetry evenings. The government sponsors national literary prizes that are awarded through the National Library in Phnom Penh. The Khmer Writers Association has also sponsored poetry prizes and the publication of chapbooks. Since 1993, the Nou Hach Literary Association has held a yearly conference where prizes for poetry are awarded and then published in its annual jour, *The Nou Hach Literary Journal*, which is distributed for sale in markets. Although poetry books are not a common purchase in Cambodia, the art of poetic expression is still greatly admired by the older generation. There is a resistance to experiment with *free verse, since the melodiousness of poetry—its rhyme, assonance, and alliteration—is what defines it as a genre for Cambodians. Nevertheless, younger poets are branching out to include socially critical themes in their poems and slowly experimenting with freer forms of versification.

■ J. Jacob, "Versification in Cambodian Poetry," *Cambodia's Lament: A Selection of Cambodian Poetry*, ed. and trans. G. Chigas (1991); A. Thompson, "Oh Cambodia! Poems from the Border," *New Literary History* 24 (1993); J. Jacob, *The Traditional Literature of Cambodia: A Preliminary Guide* (1996); *Tum Teav: A Translation and Analysis of a Cambodian Literary Clas-*

*sic*, ed. and trans. G. Chigas (2005); C. Meas, "The Inherited House," *Nou Hach Literary Journal* 4 (2007); S. Pollock, *The Language of the Gods in the World of Men: Sanskrit, Culture, and Power in Premodern India* (2006).

T. S. YAMADA

## CANADA, POETRY OF

I. English
II. French

**I. English.** Prior to the 20th c., Canadian poetry was strung between poles of a colonialism that sought to maintain the aesthetic and social values of the mother country and a nativism that sought to face the particular challenges of a New World exuding both promise and threat. Thus, W. D. Lighthall can, in one of the early anthols. of Canadian poetry—his 1889 *Songs of the Great Dominion*—celebrate Canada as the "Eldest daughter of the Empire" and "the Empire's completest type," while at the same moment the first generation of truly nativist poets—the so-called Confederation poets—were exploring the Canadian landscape and psyche in a lyrical nature poetry that could only have been written in the new country.

Long before this, however, the promise of the new colony sounds in what is probably the first book of poetry written in North America—Robert Hayman's (1575–1629) *Quodlibets Lately Come Over from New Britaniola, Old Newfound-Land* (1628)—in which, as governor of the colony, he advertises Newfoundland as a near-paradise, "Exempt from taxings, ill newes, Lawings, feare." The threat of the New World is given expression in Oliver Goldsmith's (1794–1861) otherwise optimistic "The Rising Village" (1825), a response to his famous great-uncle and namesake's "The Deserted Village":

When, looking round, the lonely settler sees
His home amid a wilderness of trees:
How sinks his heart in those deep solitudes,
Where not a voice upon his ear intrudes.

Nevertheless, one should not be given the impression that Canadian poetry before the 20th c. lacked diversity. Amid narratives of colonization and lyric bursts on nature's fickle blasts, there are poems championing the cause of the laboring classes, as in the ballads of Scottish immigrants James Anderson (1842–1923) and Alexander McLachlan (1818–96), who sounds a republican note in "Young Canada or Jack's as Good as His Master" (1874). With Pauline Johnson (1861–1913), First Nations Canadians, typically subject to their portrayal by settler poets, had their voice heard for the first time—though Johnson (her mother was English, her father Mohawk) tended to perform the archetypal noble savage for the audiences of her popular performances. Her "performance of the hybrid inheritance of Canada and the British Empire," in Gerson's words (1994), can be seen in quintessential Johnson poems such as "The Song My Paddle Sings," with its simultaneous invocations of P. B. Shelley's "Ode to the West Wind" and a solitary native paddling across prairie waters.

As mentioned above, the first generation of poets seen to embody an emergent "Canadian" poetry were the Confederation poets, who, in the decades following the 1867 Confederation, came to be seen as answering D. H. Dewart's call, in *Selections from Canadian Poets* (1864), for a *national poetry as "an essential element in the formation of national character." Born in the 1860s and beginning to publish in the 1880s and early 1890s, William Wilfred Campbell (1860–1918), Charles G. D. Roberts (1860–1943), Bliss Carman (1861–1929), Archibald Lampman (1861–99), and Duncan Campbell Scott (1862–1947) were the dominant voices and driving forces in Canadian poetry for the next three or four decades. Later theories about the "Canadianness" of Canadian poetry, such as Margaret Atwood's notion of "survival" as the national theme, clearly required the bedrock of the Confederation poets' descriptive verse upon which to set their foundations. In this regard, Campbell's "The Winter Lakes" (1889) can stand as a characteristic example:

Lands that loom like specters, whited regions of
winter,
Wastes of desolate woods, deserts of water and
shore;
A world of winter and death, within these regions
who enter,
Lost to summer and life, go to return no more.

With their focus on the particularities of the Canadian landscape and climate, the heavily visual lyrics of these poets could easily give the impression that the lyric mode best characterizes Canadian poetry before World War I. However, the reality is more likely that the long narrative poem and the verse drama, as written by poets such as Charles Sangster (1822–93), Charles Heavysege (1816–76), and Isabella Valancy Crawford (1850–87), were the dominant modes, if measured in terms of their ubiquity and popular success. This trad. continues into the 20th c. in the work of E. J. Pratt (1883–1964), a poet seen either as a throwback to 19th-c. narrative verse or as the "first" modernist (so credited for his realism and use of contemp. themes).

It has sometimes been remarked that Canadian poetry skipped *modernism altogether, moving directly from *romanticism to *postmodernism. Certainly, the "modernization" of Canadian poetry proceeded at a slow pace (if one is to take a poet like Pratt as a transitional figure); however, as early as 1914, Arthur Stringer (1874–1950) was writing in favor of the "formal emancipation" of *free verse, and John Murray Gibbon (1875–1952) commented that "[r]hyme is the natural refuge of the minor poet." W.W.E. Ross (1894–1966) was writing and publishing imagist, free-verse lyrics in the *Dial* and *Poetry* in the 1920s, as was Dorothy Livesay (1909–96), before turning to her politically charged poems during the socialist 1930s and 1940s and then to later "documentary" work.

Canadian modernism had its center in Montreal, where poets A.J.M. Smith (1902–80) and F. R. Scott

(1899–1985) cofounded *The McGill Fortnightly Review* in 1925. "The modern revival began in the twenties," Smith later wrote, as "Canadian poets turned against rhetoric, sought a sharper, more objective imagery, and limited themselves as far as possible to the lang. of everyday and the rhythms of speech." Scott's poetry, though modernizing in terms of "a freer diction and more elastic forms," was, nevertheless, still drawn to what were already well-established "Canadian" tropes and themes. His "Laurentian Shield" is remarkable both for its retrieval of the imagery of the proverbial Canadian "wastes" (the poem can be profitably compared to, and contrasted with, Campbell's "Winter Lakes") and for his updating of such imagery, combining it with a compressed social hist. of an industrializing Canada:

> Hidden in wonder and snow, or sudden with
>     summer,
> This land stares at the sun in a huge silence
> Endlessly repeating something we cannot hear.
> Inarticulate, arctic,
> Not written on by history, empty as paper,
> It leans away from the world with songs in its lakes
> Older than love, and lost in the miles.

The poem goes on to address the "deeper note sounding" from "the mines, / The scattered camps and the mills" as Canada's working classes enter the national dialogue (Scott was for many years associated with the country's first socialist party, the Co-operative Commonwealth Federation). However, the long-established image of the "silent" and "inarticulate" land awaiting (Eur.) inscription unquestioningly recalls the colonial roots of Canadian poetry.

The Montreal circle around Smith and Scott grew in the 1940s to include poets such as A. M. Klein (1909–72) and P. K. Page (1916–2010), as the jours. *Preview* and then *The Northern Review* became the group's main vehicles. Klein, a Ukrainian Jewish immigrant, wrote modernist-inspired lyrics on Jewish culture and hist. Page, similarly influenced by modernists such as T. S. Eliot, pursued a philosophical and introspective imagism over many decades. As Louis Dudek (1918–2001) writes in *The Making of Modern Poetry in Canada*, "By the early 1940s the development of modernism in Canada had reached the point of 'cell divisions,' showing a conflict of generations within the modern movement." Dudek himself, as both poet and ed., played an important role in this "division," as another Montreal circle formed around him to include Irving Layton (1912–2006) and Raymond Souster (b. 1921), and, for a time in the 1950s, Leonard Cohen (b. 1934) and Phyllis Webb (b. 1927). Dudek and Layton joined John Sutherland (1919–56) in editing *First Statement* (later folded, along with *Preview*, into *The Northern Review*), and then, with Souster, *Contact* magazine and press, in the 1950s. If Layton was the flamboyant, outrageous, and sensual *poète maudit* of the new grouping, Dudek was its theorist and propagandist. Dudek was influenced by the Am. modernism of Ezra Pound, as well as the editorial proselytizing of

Cid Corman (and his jour. *Origin*). "Like American lit. in general," he writes in *The Making of Modern Poetry in Canada*, "Canadian poetry divides into two branches: one related through British writing to Eur. literary culture, formal and rooted in traditional sources of the imagination; the other, spontaneous and original in its sources, and relying on the direct report of local experience." Sutherland, in a similar vein, argues in *Other Canadians* that "the American example will become more and more attractive to Canadian writers; that we are approaching a period when we will have 'schools' and 'movements' whose origin will be American. And perhaps it is safe to say that such a period is the inevitable half-way house from which Canadian poetry will pass towards an identity of its own."

Two other poets who provide important bridges between modern and postmodern Canadian poetry need to be mentioned here. Earl Birney (1904–95), who was the first significant modernist poet to be born, live, and write in western Canada (Birney was born in Calgary and lived for many years in Vancouver, where he founded the first creative writing program in the country, at the University of British Columbia), and Al Purdy (1918–2000), who was instrumental in spreading the use of vernacular, conversational (as opposed to overtly "poetic") lang. and everyday themes, influenced a generation of Canadian poets. The work of poets from British Columbia's Patrick Lane (b. 1939) to the East Coast's Milton Acorn (1923–86) and Alden Nowlan (1933–83), from "prairie poets" such as Dennis Cooley (b. 1944) and Andrew Suknaski (b. 1942) to the perennial wanderer John Newlove (1938–2003), is difficult to imagine without the vernacular trad. in part opened by Purdy's work.

In a 1955 study titled "The Poet and the Publisher," Phyllis Webb found only "two or three" presses in the country that regularly published poetry, all located in Toronto. With the 1960s and 1970s, there was an extraordinary expansion of regional presses and little magazines—in part spurred by the founding of the Canada Council for the Arts in 1957—that decidedly decentralized Canadian poetry. "Regional," Atwood noted in 1982, "has changed in recent years from a bad to a good word, in Canada at any rate." Indeed, Canadian poetry since the 1960s has seemed less a national lit. than a cluster of communities divided along regional, aesthetic, class, ethnic, and gender lines. "Canada," as Davey (1994) writes, "is a network of competing canons rather than a single canon."

Postmodernism in many ways enters Canadian poetry through Vancouver: the *TISH poets—George Bowering (b. 1935), Fred Wah (b. 1939), and Daphne Marlatt (b. 1942) among them—and the 1963 Vancouver Poetry Conference, which brought leading lights from the New American poetry (Charles Olson, Robert Duncan, Robert Creeley) together to teach, read, and talk for three weeks of events. Canadian *avant-gardes—in Vancouver, at least—have ever since been deeply influenced by their dialogue with similarly focused Am. poetic movements (TISH and the New American poetry, and then from the 1980s, the *Kootenay School of Writing and *Language poetry)—seeming to fulfill Sutherland's prophetic words cited above. Bowering, Canada's first parliamentary *poet laureate, has, despite that honor, often stood more for a western Canadian sensibility and a transnational poetics that moves more north-south than east-west. Jeff Derksen (b. 1958), one of the founding members of the Kootenay School, has similarly often critiqued the centralizing formation of the nation, writing instead from a position of urban class consciousness that sees the local and global intersect in spaces formed more by late capitalism than by the nation as such.

Since the 1960s, there has been heavy traffic between Vancouver and Toronto avant-gardes, with poets such as bpNichol (1944–88) and bill bissett (b. 1939) moving between the cities. With Steve McCaffery (b. 1947) in Toronto, Nichol's experiments with the Toronto Research Group (TRG) and Four Horsemen led to many innovations in *concrete and *sound poetry. Such work—along with the site-specific projects of Christopher Dewdney (b. 1951)—have cast a long shadow on Toronto poetry, directly leading to the concrete and performance work of Christian Bök (b. 1966), the procedural and digital poetics of Darren Wershler (b. 1966), and—moving out from Toronto—the concrete poetry of derek beaulieu (b. 1973) and Donato Mancini (b. 1974) and sound poetry of a. rawlings (b. 1978) and Jordan Scott (b. 1978). Bök's 2001 Oulipian work *Eunoia* set the standard for, and reanimated work in, *constraint-based poetics, with its five "chapters" each limited to the use of only one vowel. Chapter "A" begins:

> Awkward grammar appals a craftsman. A dada
>     bard
> as daft as Tzara damns stagnant art and scrawls an
> alpha (a slapdash arc and a backward zag) that
>     mars
> all stanzas and jams all ballads (what a scandal).

One could argue that "narrative" reappears in such work, in the form of the quasi-epic conventions and set pieces that structure the prose-poetry of *Eunoia*.

Feminist poetry and poetics in Canada began to find its footing in the 1980s, with notable events such as the Women and Words conference (1983) and the founding of the jour. *Tessera* (in 1984). Lesbian issues and the question of trans. often appeared (as in the case of Marlatt and Fr.-Canadian poet Nicole Brossard [b. 1943] and in the work of Erin Mouré [b. 1955]); established poets such as Webb, Marlatt, and Margaret Atwood (b. 1939) began to interact with newly emerged poets such as Sharon Thesen (b. 1946), Bronwen Wallace (1945–89), and Mouré. This trad. continues in the work of contemp. poets such as Vancouver's Meredith Quartermain (b. 1950), Torontonians Margaret Christakos (b. 1962) and Rachel Zolf (b. 1968), and Manitoba-born Sina Queyras (b. 1963).

Poets writing through an awareness of race, immigrant experience, and the diasporas of globalization often intersect with regional and avant-garde poetries in Canada. George Elliott Clarke (b. 1960) from Canada's East Coast and Wayde Compton (b. 1972) from Canada's West have both explored the hist. of black people in Canada, and Caribbean-born Dionne Brand (b. 1953) writes a similar hist. through feminist and lesbian lenses. Asian Canadian poets have tended to forge links with avant-gardes, as is the case with Roy Kiyooka (1926–94), Wah, and Roy Miki (b. 1942), all born in the prairies and moving to Vancouver to participate in the TISH movement and its aftermath. Both Wah and Miki have, as critics and university professors, influenced the work and thought of the many younger writers drawn to their politicized example. One contemp. poet mining similar territory is Rita Wong (b. 1968), whose 2007 book *Forage* explores the ground upon which race, class, and environmental degradation intersect in a recklessly globalized world:

> the gap between the crying line & electric speech
> is the urbanization of the mouth
> round peasant dialect vowels relocate
> off the fields into city streets
> where sound gets clipped
> like our ability to smell the wet earth.

First Nations poets, such as Marie Annharte Baker (b. 1942) and Gregory Scofield (b. 1966), update traditional themes to new urban environments. Both poets employ an urban-native vernacular and reappropriated stereotypes to question the hist. and policies of government "Indian Acts" and residential schools. The work of Jeannette Armstrong (b. 1948) and Marilyn Dumont (b. 1955) further questions notions of stable identity and literary form.

While the lyric poem, often confessional and anecdotal, has dominated Canadian poetry, Canada has also maintained a vibrant trad. around the long poem. The lyric in contemp. Canadian poetry, whether confessional or imagistic, has tended toward compressed narrative via the epiphanic *anecdote. The dominance of "story" can in part be seen by how frequently Canada's best-known poets have been just as highly regarded as novelists, as in the case of Atwood and Michael Ondaatje (b. 1943). Canadian poets have also often combined fragments into long *lyric sequences, with narrative present in the form of the documentary details of the life and times of the historical subject under investigation, as in Atwood's *The Journals of Susanna Moodie* (1970), Ondaatje's *The Collected Works of Billy the Kid* (1970), and Gwendolyn MacEwen's (1941–87) *The T. E. Lawrence Poems* (1982). Canadian lyric poems often combine astute observation of the external world and condensed expression of internal states with a broadly framed awareness of the social contexts the poet lives and writes through. Hist., it could be said, is the primary "story" haunting Canadian poetry, as in Atwood's "It Is Dangerous to Read Newspapers" (1968):

> While I was building neat
> castles in the sandbox,
> the hasty pits were
> filling with bulldozed corpses

and as I walked to the school
washed and combed, my feet
stepping on the cracks in the cement
detonated red bombs.

It is difficult to underestimate the influence Atwood and Ondaatje have had on the course of Canadian poetry, despite (or because of) their evolution into novelists. Poets such as Don McKay (b. 1942), one of the country's premier ecological poets, and Jan Zwicky (b. 1955), who investigates the philosophical underpinnings of the lyric, continue to be major practitioners of the lyric poem, as Ken Babstock (b. 1970), Karen Solie (b. 1966), and Stephanie Bolster (b. 1969) do among the younger poets.

As narrative has come to dominate the Canadian lyrical anecdote, so the contemp. Canadian *long poem has moved away from narrative as such, toward serial and archival/documentary forms. Phyllis Webb's *Naked Poems* (1965), with its extended minimalism, leads the way to the contemp. long poem in Canada. Moving through a counterpointed sequence of "Suites," *Naked Poems* combines personal, social, and philosophical information into arrestingly compressed ling. spaces:

YOUR BLOUSE
I people
this room
with things, a
chair, a lamp, a
fly, two books by
Marianne Moore.

I have thrown my
blouse on the floor,

Was it only
last night?

"Story" hovers here, but what the story is, the reader is never sure. Just as quickly as narrative appears, it disappears, sinking under a surface of sonic and visual detail:

a curve / broken
of green
moss weed
kelp shells pebbles
lost orange rind
orange crab pale
delicates at peace
on this sand
tracery of last night's
tide

Another early influence on the contemp. long poem in Canada was Robin Blaser's (1925–2009) *The Holy Forest*, the serial components of which were beginning to appear in the 1960s. Blaser, Am.-born but living in Vancouver since 1966, theorized the serial poem in his 1975 afterward to *The Collected Books of Jack Spicer*. With Blaser's work, however, we move beyond the serial or long poem to the lifelong poem, a form so elastic it comes to contain all a poet's work, coming to

a conclusion only with the poet's death. Blaser's *Holy Forest*, along with Robert Kroetsch's (b. 1927) *Complete Field Notes* and Nichol's *The Martyrology* (1967–88) are three highly influential examples of such extended long forms.

More recent practitioners of the long poem tend to trouble the boundary between poem (long or otherwise) and *"book," taking up the writing of a book of poetry as a research project. Anne Carson (b. 1950), Mouré, and Lisa Robertson (b. 1962) have produced some of the most innovative poetry in the country. Recalling the book-length historical projects of Atwood and Ondaatje—but minus the biographical subject and drawing on the broadly philosophical investigations and intertextuality of Blaser and Nichol's long works—these poets have rewritten classical myths (as in Carson's 1998 *Autobiography of Red*), engaged in "translations" with Fernando Pessoa's *heteronyms (as in Mouré's 2002 *Sheep's Vigil by a Fervent Person*), and appropriated the discourse of 18th- and 19th-c. Eng. meteorologists (as in Robertson's 2001 *The Weather*). Both lyrical and formally expansive, philosophically and socially engaged, innovative and yet highly sensitive to cultural heritage on a transnational scale, the work of these poets has reached a wide international audience and is already influencing the next generation of Canadian poets.

**II. French.** In Fr. Canada, a genuine poetic trad. was not established until the 1830s. François-Xavier Garneau (1809–66), the first major Fr.-Canadian author, published a few poems in his youth but devoted most of his efforts to the monumental *Histoire du Canada depuis sa découverte jusqu'à nos jours* (A History of Canada from Its Discovery to the Present Time). Following Garneau, two poets, Octave Crémazie (1827–79) and Louis Fréchette (1839–1908), were known for their patriotic writing. Crémazie, whose poetry published in newspapers venerated nostalgia for France, was celebrated as a national bard, although his romantic "Promenade de trois morts" (The Promenade of the Three Dead) was met with incomprehension. Fréchette, an admirer of Crémazie and a liberal pamphleteer, honored Fr.-Canadian hist. with emphatic poems inspired by Victor Hugo. Less well known than Crémazie and Fréchette, the intimist poets Alfred Garneau (1836–1904) and Eudore Évanturel (1852–1919) are among the few 19th-c. Fr.-Canadian poets who preferred a personal register to a patriotic one.

Émile Nelligan (1879–1941) embodies the ideal of a poet dedicated to his art. Before he was permanently interned in a psychiatric hospital at the age of nineteen, he was involved in the École littéraire de Montréal (Montreal Literary School), where he was celebrated for the quality of his poetry but also criticized for his indifference toward a regionalism promoted by the religious authorities. In 1904, his poems were anthologized by Louis Dantin (1865–1945), one of the period's most accomplished critics and a poet in his own right. Some of Nelligan's poems are purely musical; others seem to foreshadow his fate. His works demonstrate a precocious assimilation of *Parnassianism, *symbolism, and the decadent style (see DECADENCE).

The opposition between the regionalists and those who were known as the "exotics" had a profound impact on the literary scene of the early 20th c. Celebrated by clerical critics, regionalists such as Blanche Lamontagne-Beauregard (1889–1958) sought to render the "Canadian essence." Reacting against this ideal, many poets united in 1918 under the banner of the magazine *Le Nigog* (a Native Am. word meaning "harpoon") to promote the idea of art for art's sake. Typical of the exotic poets, Marcel Dugas (1883–1947) and Paul Morin (1889–1963) lived for many years in Paris. While Dugas practiced prosaic forms of poetry, Morin was dedicated to fixed forms such as the *sonnet. Their inspiration was, first and foremost, contemp. Fr. poetry.

Certain early 20th-c. poets such as Albert Lozeau (1878–1924) found themselves behind entrenched literary positions. Notably, Lozeau's first volume of rhyming poems, *L'âme solitaire* (The Solitary Soul, 1907), can be seen as a continuation of the intimist poetics of the end of the 19th c. Jean-Aubert Loranger (1896–1942), who preferred sober free-verse poetry that expressed the subject's isolation, was influenced by his readings of Fr. poets as well as by his discovery of Asian forms such as the *haiku and the *outa*. As a journalist, he also published numerous tales such as "Le passeur" (The Ferryman), a parable of old age that was included in his initial collection of poems *Les atmosphères* (Atmospheres, 1920), but his poetry was not widely read until the reissue of his work in 1970. The most celebrated poet of the times, and the one who seems to surpass the age's contradictions by invoking Nelligan while addressing regionalist concerns, is Alfred DesRochers (1901–78). His collection *À l'ombre de l'Orford* (In the Shadow of Orford, 1929) includes "Hymne au vent du Nord" (A Hymn to the North Wind), a celebratory epic of the ancestors, as well as his realistic sonnets describing contemporaries: the peasants and the shantymen. Faithful to rhymed and metered verse, DesRochers remained estranged from the new lang. of free verse that became dominant during the 1930s, so much so that his work would be seen as the end of an epoch.

Hector de Saint-Denys Garneau (1912–43) experimented with an unreservedly free verse in *Regards et jeux dans l'espace* (Gazes and Games in Space, 1937), the only volume that he ever published. In a society he found to be a cultural "desert," Garneau found intellectual stimulation in the magazine *La Relève* in 1934 that pushed him to dedicate himself to writing and painting. His enthusiasm, however, would be short-lived. His jour., pub. in 1954, showed that, even though he continued to write poetry and to paint, his profound angst caused him to renounce publishing. After breaking off his formerly abundant correspondence with friends, Garneau was found dead near his family's manor, where he had decided to withdraw. Garneau's poems, jour., and correspondence constitute the most prominent work of a Fr.-Canadian poet since Nelligan; for both, the myth of the poet-martyr would be in-

dissociable from their work. In retrospect, Garneau's despair seems more assumed than endured, as he describes in a famous text from his jour. titled "Le mauvais pauvre va parmi vous avec son regard en dessous" (The bad pauper going among you with his downcast gaze). A few years Garneau's senior, Alain Grandbois (1900–75) established himself in 1944 with *Les îles de la nuit* (The Islands of the Night). While these two poets are often compared, the reclusiveness of Garneau contrasts with the cosmopolitanism of Grandbois, whose travels took him as far as China. Grandbois' poetry is more eloquent than Garneau's and his style, as much as that of Fr. poets of his generation like René Char and Paul Éluard, influenced younger poets. Anne Hébert (1916–2000), Garneau's cousin, published in 1953 *Le tombeau des rois* (The Kings' Tomb), where she explored interior impediments. This book was later published to form a diptych with her next collection of poetry, *Mystère de la parole* (Word's Mystery, 1960), which celebrated a woman's flowering consciousness witnessing the world's regeneration. The same solemn register was also present in the work of Rina Lasnier (1910–97), whose work often evoked the Christian faith, as seen in the biblically inspired *Le chant de la montée* (The Rising's Song, 1947).

During the 1930s and 1940s, a social life shattered by the economic crash dominated the work of several poets, such as Clément Marchand (b. 1912) in *Les soirs rouges* (Red Evenings, 1947). *Surrealism also influenced several poetic works of the postwar era, as exemplified by Claude Gauvreau (1925–71), a signer of the *Refus global* (1948) manifesto. A poet and dramaturge, Gauvreau, along with the painter Paul-Émile Borduas, was a member and principal defender of the "automatist" group, which aimed to replace what it saw as the passivity of Fr. surrealist writing with a state of revolt. For Gauvreau, automatic writing involved accepting an unknown lang. "explorén," something he also integrated into his plays. Several years after his suicide, the publication of his *Œuvres créatices complètes* (Complete Creative Works, 1977) revealed an abundant, sustained level of production, in spite of a marginality accentuated by his mental illness. Also invoking surrealism, Roland Giguère (1929–2003) followed Gauvreau's example, albeit in a more serene fashion. His retrospective collection *L'âge de la parole* (The Word's Age, 1965) reconstituted the author's artistic journey while proclaiming the emancipation of the exploited, as typified in "La main du bourreau finit toujours par pourrir" (The Oppressor's Hand Will Eventually Rot). Giguère's poetry is full of imagery yet always straightforward, embracing both tenderness and violence, and also stresses the idea that, while it is important to map the dreamed world, it is also necessary to reveal "le pouvoir du noir" (the power of darkness).

In the 1960s, Fr.-Canadian nationalism transformed into Quebec nationalism. One of the objectives of this new nationalism was to create a distinctive Quebec lit. This project was nurtured by the publisher Éditions de l'Hexagone, founded in 1953 by a group of young Montreal poets. Resolved to make poetry more socially current, this group organized gatherings and counted on a system of subscriptions to involve potential readers in a genuine communal movement. Although many poets of this generation were devoted to Quebec's political independence, most of them insisted on the *autonomy of poetry. Their writing was often labeled *la poésie du pays* (the poetry of the land), which was, above all, a quest for identity, as in Michel van Schendel's (1929–2005) *Poèmes de l'Amérique étrangère* (Poems from a Foreign America, 1958). More often than not, la poésie du pays celebrated the physical attributes of the land as the pathway to a mythical regeneration, as in Gatien Lapointe's (1931–83) *Ode au Saint-Laurent* (An Ode to the Saint-Laurent, 1963). Moreover, the theme of the land became associated with the devel. of a common lang., one capable of redefining social issues.

At the center of the Hexagone movement was Gaston Miron (1928–96), who defined himself more as its organizer than its poet. Initially, Miron published a collaborative anthol., *Deux sangs* (Two Bloods, 1953), Éditions de l'Hexagone's very first publication. Following this, he published poems in both newspapers and magazines, continually insisting on their provisional character. Miron would redraft his collection *L'homme rapaillé* (Mustered Man, 1970) many times, claiming that each version was fragmentary and incomplete. In each, early poems and political essays frame the poem's cycles in which love, the nation, and commitment are fundamental themes. A call to transform the world is coupled with the testimony of a man who ceaselessly collapses and rises in his "Marche à l'amour" (Walk to Love).

After republishing such poets as Grandbois and Giguère, Éditions de l'Hexagone allowed many young poets to write within an editorial continuity unknown by their elders. This allowed Paul-Marie Lapointe (b. 1929) to republish an anthol. of his youth *Le vierge incendié* (The Burned Virgin), gone unnoticed when it first appeared in 1948 that became, when taken up again in *Le réel absolu* (The Absolute Real, 1971), the first steps of a literary production that never stopped exploring new directions. After the surrealist revelry of his first anthol., Lapointe coupled love with politics in long improvisations, inspired by jazz. The rest of his work was notably comprised of descriptive poems and formalist experimentations, all constituting an illustration of freedom as a "fundamental demand."

Of the same generation as Lapointe, Fernand Ouellette (b. 1930) also elaborated a varied and important body of work. Poet, essayist, and novelist, Ouellette invoked Eur. affinities (Novalis, Pierre-Jean Jouve), linking experience and transcendence by exploring sexuality (*Dans le sombre* [In the Darkness], 1967) and, in what is often cited as his best work, his father's death throes (*Les heures* [The Hours], 1987). Younger than Lapointe and Ouellette, Jacques Brault (b. 1933) also falls clearly within the framework of the poésie du pays movement in his first book, *Mémoire* (Memory, 1965), although he moved away from collective perspectives and expansive writing in his later work. In *L'en dessous l'admirable* (The Underside the Admirable, 1975) and

*Moments fragiles* (Fragile Moments, 1984), the present moment constitutes the only accessible temporality; identity appears increasingly illusory but paradoxically reveals an essential, intimate life.

Paul Chamberland (b. 1939), who is associated with the socialist, separatist magazine *Parti Pris*, published in 1964 *Terre Québec* (Quebec Land), a seminal anthol. of nationalist poetry. Less embarrassed than his elders by a politicized lit., Chamberland put poetry on trial in the name of the "revolution" to be incited. A few years later, after being seduced by Am. counterculture, he invoked a new concept for the revolution. Denis Vanier (1949–2000) proved to be one of the most radical and unswerving poets of the counterculture movement at the end of the 1960s. For certain poets, countercultural references go together with nationalist demands in a quest for fraternity. Such is the case of the prolific Gilbert Langevin (1938–95), who combined the ludic and the tragic in a poetics bordering the spoken word.

Along with counterculture references, two trends influenced the poetics of the young generation of the 1970s: *formalism and feminism. These two orientations came together in the work of Brossard, a leader of an avant-garde that was coming to light, most notably in the magazine *La Barre du jour*. With *Suite logique* (Logical Follow Through, 1970), Brossard opposed textual "mechanics" to literary idealism. Following this, she integrated an explicitly lesbian subject and related fiction and theory in her writing. Another avant-garde magazine founded in 1968, *Les Herbes rouges* (Red Grass), published poets such as Normand de Bellefeuille (b. 1949), Roger Des Roches (b. 1950), and François Charron (b. 1952), all of whom were initially associated with a militant formalism but who gradually diverged from the avant-garde's rhetoric. In the mid-1970s, feminism defined itself in avant-garde terms, and along with the works of Brossard, those of Madeleine Gagnon (b. 1938) and France Théoret (b. 1942) particularly influenced poetry that incorporated a critical and activist perspective.

During the 1980s, esp. with the publication of *Kaléidoscope ou Les aléas du corps grave* (Kaleidoscope or the Unforeseen Solemn Body, 1984), Michel Beaulieu (1941–85) epitomized the expansion of an intimist vein on the margins of a waning avant-garde. Beaulieu, who had experimented with several forms since his debut in the 1960s, achieved an intimist style that subtly plays with ambiguities created by *enjambments. Marie Uguay (1955–81) was also attached to the inner life. Several younger poets inflected feminism with intimism, as in the work of Denise Desautels (b. 1945), or associated intimism with a spiritual quest, as in Hélène Dorion's (b. 1958) work.

With the 1980s, the pluralism of Quebec poetry continued to grow. Publishing houses such as Le Noroît and Les Écrits des Forges published a variety of work, in the trad. of L'Hexagone. The idea of a collective identity was fading, with the exception of emerging "migrant writings." Initially brought forward by Haitian Montrealers such as Anthony Phelps (b. 1928) and Serge Legagneur (b. 1937) and followed by

Montrealers of It. extraction, such as Fulvio Caccia (b. 1952) and Antonio D'Alfonso (b. 1953), this movement not only extended the notion of identity in nationalist poetry but questioned the 1960s definition of the Quebec nation by exposing the cultural diversity of contemp. Quebec society. Often, this was done in a polemical fashion. Marco Micone's (b. 1945) *pastiche "Speak What" (1989), e.g., displaced the perspectives of Michèle Lalonde's (b. 1937) 1960s poem "Speak White," a portrayal of Quebec based on the domination of Francophones by Anglophones. Since the 1970s, poetry has also been linked to the collective question of identity of Canadian Francophones living outside Quebec, notably the Acadians and the Franco-Ontarians (see FRANCOPHONE POETS OF THE U.S.). The poetry of the Acadian Serge-Patrice Thibodeau (b. 1959) is centered on wanderings, while that of the Franco-Ontarian Patrice Desbiens (b. 1948) focuses on the daily alienation of the minority condition. Furthermore, at the beginning of the 21st c., a specifically aboriginal lit. emerged, written in Fr. by such poets as Jean Sioui (b. 1948).

Although the presence of the countryside has played a role in Fr.-Canadian poetry since the 19th c., meditation on physical place has always been marginal when compared to considerations of historical destiny. By the end of the 1970s, in part inspired by Europeans such as Yves Bonnefoy and Philippe Jaccottet, many poets concentrated on place as the focus of their work. Gilles Cyr (b. 1945) with *Sol inapparent* (Inapparent Soil, 1978), Robert Melançon (b. 1947) with *Peinture aveugle* (Blind Painting, 1979), and Pierre Morency (b. 1942) with his series *Histoires naturelles du Nouveau Monde* (Natural Histories of the New World, 1989–96) emerge as the precursors of this movement. An increasing interest in the trans. of poetry, esp. from Eng., also has encouraged diversity.

*See* INDIGENOUS AMERICAS, POETRY OF THE; INUIT POETRY.

■ **Anthologies:** *The Book of Canadian Poetry*, ed. A.J.M. Smith (1943); J. Sutherland, *Other Canadians* (1947); *The New Oxford Book of Canadian Verse in English*, ed. M. Atwood (1982); *The New Canadian Poets*, ed. D. Lee (1985); *The New Long Poem Anthology*, ed. S. Thesen (1991); *Canadian Poetry: From the Beginnings through the First World War*, ed. C. Gerson and G. Davies (1994); *La poésie québécoise contemporaine*, ed. J. Royer (1995); *La poésie québécoise avant Nelligan*, ed. Y. Grisé (1998); *15 Canadian Poets X 3*, ed. G. Geddes (2001); *Anthologie de la littérature québécoise*, ed. G. Marcotte (2004); *Open Field: 30 Contemporary Canadian Poets*, ed. S. Queyras (2005); *La poésie québécoise des origines à nos jours,* ed. L. Mailhot and P. Nepveu (2007).

■ **Criticism and History:** G. Marcotte, *Une littérature qui se fait* (1962); L. Dudek and M. Gnarowski, *The Making of Modern Poetry in Canada* (1967); G. Marcotte, *Le temps des poètes* (1969); M. Atwood, *Survival* (1972); F. Davey, *From Here to There* (1974); P. Nepveu, *L'écologie du réel* (1988)—poetry of Quebec; C. Bayard, *The New Poetics in Canada and Quebec* (1989); R. Kroetsch, *The Lovely Treachery of Words* (1989);

S. Kamboureli, *On the Edge of Genre: The Contemporary Canadian Long Poem* (1991); G. Woodcock, *George Woodcock's Introduction to Canadian Poetry* (1993); A. Brochu, *Tableau du poème* (1994)—poetry of Quebec; F. Davey, *Canadian Literary Power* (1994); C. Filteau, *Poétiques de la modernité: 1895–1948* (1994); L. Mailhot, *La littérature québécoise* (1997); P. Nepveu, *Intérieurs du Nouveau Monde* (1998); F. Dumont, *La poésie québécoise* (1999); J. Blais, *Parmi les hasards* (2001)—poetry of Quebec; P. Butling and S. Rudy, *Writing in Our Time: Canada's Radical Poetries in English, 1957–2003* (2005); M. Biron, F. Dumont, E. Nardout-Lafarge, *Histoire de la littérature québécoise* (2007).

S. COLLIS (ENG.); F. DUMONT (FR.)

**CANCIÓN.** The term is now loosely applied to any Sp. isostrophic poem in Italianate lines (eleven and seven syllables) and in which the poet invents a first *strophe and then models all subsequent strophes on it exactly, in *responsion. *Canciones* of a few lines are often called *liras, canciones aliradas, canciones clásicas,* and *odas.* Many variations have been developed since the Italianate canción (see CANZONE) was introduced by Juan Boscán and Garcilaso de la Vega in the 16th c. The *canción petrarquista* (also called *canción a la italiana, canción extensa,* and *estancias*) is generally considered the purest form of the Italianate type.

In the 15th and early 16th c., before the use of the Italianate form, an entirely different type of canción—an octosyllabic form of *cantiga (see DECIR)—was widely employed. Although some variety in pattern was allowed in the early period, by the end of the 15th c. the form was usually restricted to either a quatrain (*abab* or *abba*) followed by a *copla de arte menor* (eight lines only) whose last four rhymes are identical with those of the initial quatrain, though the order of the rhymes may be changed; or a *quintilla* (two rhymes only, no set order) followed by a *copla real* or a copla de arte menor of nine or ten lines, whose last five rhymes are identical with and follow the same sequence as those of the initial quintilla. Variation in the first type, then, may occur only in the order of rhymes and in the second type only in the length of the second strophe. Vendrell de Millás lists other variations. This canción may be distinguished from the closely related *villancico, according to Le Gentil, by its longer *refrain (four or five lines having *redondilla, serventesio, or quintilla rhyme); its *vuelta, which parallels exactly the initial theme; its shorter length, which rarely exceeds one stanza; and its courtly nature and love theme.

■ *El Cancionero de Palacio,* ed. F. Vendrell de Millás (1945); Le Gentil.

D. C. CLARKE

## CANCIONERO/CANCIONEIRO

I. Introduction
II. Poetry and Poets
III. Manuscripts

**I. Introduction.** The first manifestation of Iberian court poetry of the late Middle Ages is preserved in ms. anthols. that began to be compiled in Galicia and present-day Portugal as early as 1189. Amorous and satirical lyrics composed by Port. and Galician poets from roughly the end of the 12th to the middle of the 14th c., known as *cantigas—cantigas d'amor, cantigas de escarnho e maldizer*, and *cantigas d'amigo*—were collected in these anthols., referred to in Galician-Port. as cancioneiros (*songbooks). Although the *cantigas de escarnho e maldizer* and the *cantigas d'amor* have clear Occitan antecedents in the *sirventes and the *tenso,* the *cantigas d'amigo* of the cancioneiros point to an older trad. of autochthonous oral poetry with roots in rural society, nature, and animism.

Later collections of lyric poetry, known as cancioneros, appeared in Castilian with different types of compositions, marking the change from the Galician-Port. lang. to Castilian as the favored idiom of courtly verse in the western Iberian peninsula. The first Castilian compilation, the *Cancionero de Baena* (ca. 1430), was the work of Juan Alfonso de Baena, secretary to King Juan II of Castile and Leon. With the introduction of the printing press, beginning in the 1480s, the first printed cancioneros began to circulate, culminating in the mammoth, epoch-making *Cancionero general* of 1511. Hernando del Castillo, a book dealer from Segovia who compiled and published the *Cancionero general* in Valencia, spent the years 1489–1509 gathering and selecting the poetry he would include in it, representing all the styles and motifs of the Castilian verse of the second half of the 15th c. The work records some 1,056 poems by 239 known poets, as well as numerous anonymous compositions. Nearly all the verse in the *Cancionero general* belongs to the period encompassing the reign of the Catholic Monarchs (1474 until two years before the *Cancionero's* publication), with the exception of a few earlier compositions that date back to the court of Juan II (1406–54) and Enrique IV of Castile and Leon (1454–74). The *Cancionero general* was republished eight times and became the best and most widely read compilation of poetry in Spain during the 16th c. Clear echoes from its verses may be found among the Sp. poets of the Golden Age—who, according to conventional lit. hist., rejected the older forms of poetry in favor of the new, Italianate styles of composition introduced to the Iberian Peninsula in the 1530s by Juan Boscán and Garcilaso de la Vega.

Three major Galician-Port. cancioneiros came to light in the 19th c. They are the *Cancioneiro da Biblioteca Nacional* (often referred to as Colocci-Brancuti, a name that recalls two of its past owners), the *Cancioneiro da Vaticana*, and the *Cancioneiro da Ajuda*. The latter records the earliest known cancioneiro verse, a *cantiga d'amigo* by Pai Soares de Taverió datable to 1189.

Some 60 cancioneros—literally "collections of *canciones*"—in Castilian survive. They give preference to the *canción, a short lyrical verse with an initial refrain (*estribillo) that is subsequently glossed in the body of the composition. Although the term *cancioneiro/cancionero* derives from OF *cançoner* (precursor of mod. Fr. *chansonnier),* none of the early Iberian mss. of cancioneiros/cancioneros contains musical notation. Contrary to the Fr. and It. trads., where chansonniers and *canzonieri* often appeared with musical notations and exist in multiple copies, in the Iberian peninsula, one generally finds only unmusically annotated, single witnesses of a given anthol. that usually belonged to a royal, monastic, or noble library.

The proliferation of Iberian cancioneros in the 15th c. is generally taken to mark the sudden ascendancy of Castilian court lyric after two centuries of Galician-Port. dominance. However, rather than view the blossoming of Castilian poetry in hegemonic terms, we should probably think of the survival of so much verse as an index of change in courtly values, accompanied by an increase in literacy and the material conditions that favored textual production and preservation. Lyric poetry enjoyed a fashionable revival in 15th-c. Castile and played a significant role in the social and intellectual life of the courts and in the cultural practices of the aristocracy.

**II. Poetry and Poets.** The terms *poesía de cancionero* and *poesía cancioneril* are generally used to refer to the courtly verse preserved in the cancioneros produced in Iberia during the 150-year period from the end of the 14th to the beginning of the 16th c. Several thousand poems survive, composed by over 500 poets whose names have come down to us. Nearly all this verse was written in Castilian, even by poets like the Catalan Pere Torrellas and the Port. Juan Manuel and in transnational settings like the Aragonese court of Naples. Catalan poetry was collected separately; no late med. ms. anthols. of Port. verse survive.

Cancionero poetry embraces numerous types of lyrical verse (love allegories, *dream visions, *serranillas), as well as the short lyric canción and the longer *dezir* or *copla. Although 15th-c. cancionero poetry is considered primarily a form of love lyric, its heterogeneity cannot be overstated. Its repertory includes a large variety of themes and subjects, such as poetic debates (*preguntas y respuestas*—see PREGUNTA), disquisitions on moral or doctrinal issues, personal *invective, political *satire, and misogynist diatribe. The categories of religious verse alone range from solemn Marian hymns to long meditations on the life and passion of Christ, accompanied by daring erotic and risqué *contrafacta* (see CONTRAFACTUM) of the Mass and other liturgical texts. Although burlesque and openly bawdy poetry is notably absent from the early Castilian mss., they play a prominent role in the closing section of the printed *Cancionero general* (under the title *obras de burlas*) and the latter's expanded, independently pub. sequel, the *Cancionero de obras de burlas provocantes a risa* (Valencia, 1519).

Much of cancionero verse was tied to specific events or personalities, recalling incidents or anecdotes at court or commemorating occasions of social or political importance. A great deal of it may as well have been performed in improvised games, competitions, or semitheatrical entertainments (see POETIC CONTESTS). It is difficult to be certain that even the more intimate poems were intended for private reading rather than public *recitation or *performance. Some of the shorter love lyrics must have been sung, but only with the appearance of the musically annotated *songbooks in the closing decades of the century does sure evidence of poems that were intended to be sung or performed appear.

The poets of this verse come from a broad variety of backgrounds, ranging from monarchs, high-ranking nobles, statesmen, diplomats, and knights to bureaucrats, clerics, and entertainers, or latter day *jongleurs. These differences are often reflected in the poetic production of the private person for whom verse served as a social accomplishment implicated in the display of wit and power; the professional dependent on it for a living or social advancement; and the dedicated poet who treated the art as a serious intellectual enterprise. All the major Castilian poets of the 15th c. may be included in this last group: Francisco Imperial, Íñigo López de Mendoza, Fernán Pérez de Guzmán, Juan de Mena, Gómez Manrique, Jorge Manrique, Fray Íñigo de Mendoza, and Garci Sánchez de Badajoz; as well as a number of authors better known for their prose: Juan Rodríguez del Padrón, Diego de Valera, the Bachiller Alfonso de la Torre, and Diego de San Pedro. Archival research has still to uncover biographical data for the majority of the named poets in the cancioneros/cancioneiros, all of whom but a handful were men. The only woman credited with more than one complete poem, Florencia Pinar, is the exception.

**III. Manuscripts.** Brian Dutton's authoritative registry of cancionero poetry (1990–92) records over 200 known mss. However, not all these mss. are strictly cancioneros; some are only fragments of lost collections or prose miscellanies with inscribed verses. Codicological and typological studies of the mss. in light of current methods of ms. study are just beginning. A great deal remains to be examined in terms of the provenance, ownership, production, circulation, readership, and, above all, the criteria and methods of compilation for the verse in cancionero mss., many of which include overlapping compositions.

■ **Anthologies and Translations**: *Medieval Galician-Portuguese Poetry*, ed. and trans. F. Jensen (1992); *Cantigas d'escarnho e de mal dizer*, ed. M. Rodrigues Lapa (1995); *113 Galician-Portuguese Troubadour Poems*, trans. R. Zenith (1995).

■ **Electronic Bibliography**: V. Beltrán, *Bibliografía sobre poesía medieval y Cancioneros*, http://www.cervantesvirtual.com/servlet/SirveObras/p227/12032748817833728098213/index.htm.

■ **Criticism and History**: R. Menéndez Pidal, *Poesía juglaresca y orígenes de las literaturas románicas*, 6th ed. (1957); A. Várvaro, *Premesse ad un' edizione critica delle poesie minori di Juan de Mena* (1964); F. Jensen, *The Earliest Portuguese Lyrics* (1978); M. Rodrigues Lapa, *Lições de literatura portuguesa*, rev. ed. (1981); G. Tavani, *A poesia lírica galego-portuguesa* (1990); *Dicionário da literatura medieval galega e portuguesa*, ed. G. Lanciani and G. Tavani (1993); J. Whetnal, "El *Cancionero*

*general* de 1511: Textos únicos y textos omitidos," *Actas del V Congreso de la Asociación Hispánica de Literatura Medieval* (1995); *La Corónica* 26.2 (1998); *Poetry at Court in Trastamaran Spain*, ed. E. M. Gerli and J. Weiss (1998); J. Weiss, "On the Conventionality of the *Cantigas d'amor*," *Medieval Lyric*, ed. W. D. Paden (2000); B. Liu, *Medieval Joke Poetry* (2004).

■ **Primary Texts and Editions**: *Il canzoniere portoghese della Biblioteca Vaticana,* ed. E. Monaci (1875); *Cancioneiro da Ajuda*, ed. C. Michaëlis de Vasconcellos, 2 v. (1904, 1966), diplomatic ed. by H. H. Carter (1941); *Cancioneiro da Biblioteca Nacional (Colocci-Brancuti)*, ed. E. Paxeco Machado and J. P. Machado, 8 v. (1949–64); *El cancionero del siglo XV, c. 1360–1520*, ed. B. Dutton, 7 v. (1990–92)—includes ms. registry.

E. M. Gerli

**CANON.** *Canon* developed in Eng. as a religious term with two primary designations: ecclesiastical rule, law, or decree; and the collection of books of the Bible validated by the Christian Church, a criterion that excluded other scriptural writings. In literary studies, the term *canon* typically indicates a real or notional list of great works, those discussed in the major studies of lit. hist. and crit. and taught in schools and colleges as elements of proper education. In the last two decades of the 20th c., the idea of the canon moved to the center of Anglo-Am. and other areas of Western literary study and attracted energetic mainstream political debate. At the core of this ferment was the concept of literary value, in particular the question of how and by whom such value has been defined in the past. Scholars began to explore through what historical processes the canon of great books and authors had come into being and through what processes of exclusion other authors and works had been defined as other than "great." Was it the case that the best works, with "best" defined in aesthetic terms, had simply withstood the test of time and been passed from one generation to the next? Or had forces of political and social exclusion, forces whose criteria might now be usefully questioned, elevated some works and diminished others of theoretically equal value? These kinds of questions had a special currency in the Anglo-Am. and postcolonial fields, while they were generally less relevant in many Eur. lits. Scholars debated the content of the current canon, "recovered" unknown writers (often women and people of color), and rewrote literary anthols. They also began to write the hist. of "canon formation," i.e., the hist. of how the canon came into being.

The long hist. of canon-making is inseparable from the hist. of poetics. In Chinese culture of the 6th c. (which saw the appearance of significant comprehensive anthols.) and after, the condition of poetry's being (or becoming) canonical—often called "canonicity"—became an important social and cultural criterion, esp. from the Song dynasty (ca. 960–1279) on. The growth of a class of literati united by their shared education in preparing for the civil-service exams and the spread of inexpensive printed books gave the criterion social force (see CHINA, POETRY OF). Canonicity existed in

Japan as well, though until the Edo period (1600), the concept of the canon was largely limited to a fairly small aristocratic population. Perhaps the more important issue surrounding canonicity in Japan occurs with the Meiji era (1868–1912), when attempts at rapid Westernization and modernization led to the establishment of a "national canon" for largely patriotic and pedagogic purposes (see JAPAN, POETRY OF).

In Eng., as in many langs., poetry was the first canonical genre. The mod. canon was born in the 18th c., at a time when men of letters understood their literary heritage as consisting almost exclusively of poets. While the value of poetry was unquestioned, the relative value of ancient and mod. writings was a subject of heated debate. Used in this context, the word *modern* simply means nonclassical, i.e., written in vernacular or native langs. such as Eng. rather than in the "educated" ancient langs. of Gr. and Lat. While the value of the ancient classics in Gr. and Lat. was assumed, the value of writing in the Eng. lang. had been contested for centuries. Through the middle of the 18th c., common conceptions held that mod. poets like Edmund Waller and John Dryden had improved on writers from the past through their eloquence and smooth, regular verses. They brought the lang. to a stage of devel. superior to where it stood in the poetry of such past figures as Chaucer. In the 1740s and 1750s, the idea that the present improved on the past gave way. Now the idea that ancient texts were valuable was redefined to include not only Gr. and Roman ancients, but the Eng. past and the Eng. lang. as well. The high canonical figures who emerged from this revaluation of the poetic past were the poets Edmund Spenser, Shakespeare, and John Milton. Thus, the Eng. "classics" came into being.

This shift in focus entailed a revision of criteria for judgment. Poetry was now prized not for its smoothness, its regularity, and its ling. improvements over the rough lang. of the past but for its formidable difficulties, historical remoteness, and craggy sublimity. Engaging the Eng. classics was now comparable to interpreting great texts in cl. tongues; only those with special skill would be able to apprehend these texts properly. This new vision of the Eng. past marked it as fundamentally distinct from the realm of the merely popular. Such a distinction was pressing in an era when revolutionary social changes included rising literacy rates; increased access for women to education, reading, and writing; destabilization of class distinctions; and the rise of the novel, all of which created new social and class pressures.

The definitions of both *poetry* and *literature* were thrown into uncertainty by these changes. *Poetry* had once been a more general term for all imaginative lit., incl. verse but not limited to it; now the term *literature* increasingly assumed this more general function, and *poetry* moved to a position more elevated than the prose works that were popular with readers. Shakespeare emerged in the 1750s as *the* national poet, a figure who represented both "literary" qualities antithetical to the market and, simultaneously, enthusiastic popularity.

He represented a resolution to the era's tensions over literary valuation.

A century later, the concept of Eng. "classics" endured, although the terms for defining a classic continued to evolve. In 1879–80, the poet, critic, professor, and literary arbiter Matthew Arnold still identified Shakespeare and Milton as "our poetical classics," ranking the recent poet William Wordsworth in third position. No longer hindered by the need to justify the value of writing in the Eng. lang., Arnold in "The Study of Poetry" saw "the true and right meaning of the word *classic*, *classical*" as "the class of the very best." Our object in studying poetry, according to Arnold, is that of "clearly feeling and of deeply enjoying the really excellent." Arnold's concept of "classics"—works that withstand a test of timeless excellence—would survive well into the 20th c. esp. in popular usage, but in professional settings, it was overtaken by what came to be called "the canon." As Guillory (1993) observes, "The word 'canon' displaces the expressly honorific term 'classic' precisely in order to isolate the 'classics' as the object of critique."

Canon crit. made its first mark in curricula in the wake of the social upheavals of the 1960s. Socially engaged academics carried their politics into the classroom, teaching what came to be called "noncanonical" materials, often by or about people socially disfranchised based on race, class, or gender. Af. Am. poets such as Frances Harper and Paul Laurence Dunbar and women poets such as Alice Cary, Phoebe Cary, Lucy Larcom, and Celia Thaxter, who had been minimized or entirely neglected in 20th-c. textbooks, were now reclaimed by canon-conscious teachers and literary historians. One recurrent question at the core of debate was whether previously noncanonical texts were "as good" as traditionally canonical ones, putting new pressure on the criteria for assessing textual value. Gradually, challenges to the canon began to affect the margins of publishing and scholarship and eventually to alter mainstream publishing and teaching, generating the wide public debate of the 1980s and 1990s in particular. From these interrogations of the idea of the canon (no longer the "classics"), canon scholarship emerged as a new field in its own right, concerned not only with the politics of the current canon but with developing a precise hist. of canon formation at different times and places.

Such scholarship has focused in particular on how canons are formed and disseminated through institutions such as literary anthols. and the school system, esp. the university. The case of one of the most canonical Am. poets, Walt Whitman, provides a useful example of how the poetry canon changes over time. Literary textbooks published since 1919, the centennial of Whitman's birth, vary in how they define his stature. Early textbooks preferred his more conventional verse, such as "O Captain! My Captain!" and did not categorize him as a major poet. By the 1930s, the climate of appreciation for literary *modernism and its radical formal experiments, and the growth of American literature as a professional field and a subject for higher study, had cultivated a new appreciation for Whitman's technical innovations. This change in poetic culture led to a revaluation of Whitman's poetic contributions and to a dramatic change in his stature. By 1950, he had become one of the major Am. writers.

The canon debates of the last two decades of the 20th c. often centered on putatively conservative and liberal positions about whether and how the canon replicated historical exclusions based on race, class, and gender. Guillory redefined the fundamental terms of the debate in 1993, arguing that the actual nature of the problem underlying the canon debates was a crisis in the cultural capital of literary study itself, a form of study "increasingly marginal to the social function of the present educational system." Canon scholarship has dismantled the idea of "the canon" as a single monolithic entity; the term is now more likely to be used in plural or more historically restricted senses.

■ M. Arnold, "The Study of Poetry" and "Wordsworth," *Matthew Arnold's Essays in Criticism*, ed. G.K. Chesterton (1964); E. Miner, "On the Genesis and Development of Literary Systems," *CritI* 5.2–3 (1978–79); B. M. Metzger, *The Canon of the New Testament* (1988); P. Yu, "Poems in Their Place: Collections and Canons in Early Chinese Literature," *HJAS* 50 (1990); P. Lauter, *Canons and Contexts* (1991); J. Guillory, *Cultural Capital* (1993) and "Canon," *Critical Terms for Literary Study,* ed. F. Lentricchia and T. McLaughlin, 2d ed. (1995); A. Golding, *From Outlaw to Classic* (1995); J. Kramnick, *Making the English Canon* (1998); T. Ross, *The Making of the English Literary Canon* (1998); *Inventing the Classics: Modernity, National Identity, and Japanese Literature*, ed. H. Shirane and T. Suzuki (2000); R. Terry, *Poetry and the Making of the English Literary Past* (2001); J. Csicsila, *Canons by Consensus* (2004); W. J. T. Mitchell, "Canon," *New Keywords*, ed. T. Bennett et al. (2005); E. Renker, *The Origins of American Literature Studies: An Institutional History* (2007).

E. RENKER

**CANSO,** *chanso, chanson.* A love song, the literary genre par excellence among the *troubadours. Its distinguishing characteristics are precisely the two great contributions of the troubadours to all subsequent Eur. lit.—a new conception of love involving the exaltation of the lady (see COURTLY LOVE, LOVE POETRY) and a constant striving for perfection and originality of form. It is impossible to draw a sharp line between the *canso* and the older *vers*; but by the time the name *canso* came into common use (toward the end of the 12th c.), the ideals of courtly love had become conventional and the technique of composition more polished, so that the canso is apt to be more artistic, but also more conventional and artificial, than the vers.

The typical canso has five or six stanzas of identical structure, plus a *tornada* (Occitan) or *envoi* (Fr.). Far from following any set metrical pattern, every canso was expected to have a stanzaic structure and a tune that were completely original. This proved too high a hurdle for many poets, but the metrical diversity of the extant cansos is still very impressive. Unfortunately, the same cannot always be said for their contents, which

often ring the changes on a few well-worn themes and situations. The poet's love is almost never named; the proper names used in a canso (commonly secret names, or *senhals*, in the tornada) are for the most part those of friends or patrons to whom the poem is dedicated.

*See* CANZONE, SONG.

■ R. Dragonetti, *La Technique poétique des trouvères dans la chanson courtoise* (1960); M. Lazar, *Amour courtois et fin'amors* (1964); H. van der Werf, *The Chansons of the Troubadours and Trouvères* (1972); L. T. Topsfield, *Troubadours and Love* (1975); Elwert, sect. 194; *Chanter m'estuet*, ed. S. N. Rosenberg and H. Tischler (1981); *A Medieval Songbook*, ed. F. Collins Jr. (1982); Sayce; Chambers; M. L. Switten, *The "Cansos" of Raimon de Miraval* (1985); S. Gaunt and P. France, "Canso," *The New Oxford Companion to Literature in French,* ed. P. France (1995); L. Paterson, "Fin'amor and the Development of the Courtly Canso," *The Troubadours*, ed. S. Gaunt and S. Kay (1999).

F. M. CHAMBERS

**CANTAR.** Throughout Sp. lit., the term *cantar* has been used loosely to mean words for a song. In the 15th c., it was probably the equivalent of *cantiga*. In mod. times, it has come to mean specifically an octosyllabic quatrain having *assonance (occasionally, true *rhyme) in the even-numbered lines and, preferably, unrhymed oxytones in the odd-numbered: "Algún día me verás / cuando no tenga remedio; / me verás y te veré, / pero no nos hablaremos." The composition, also called *copla,* is usually confined to one *strophe. The *seguidilla gitana* (see SEGUIDILLA) is sometimes called *cantar.* The cantar is sometimes defined as an octosyllabic five-line monostrophic poem assonating *ababa.* The *cantar de soledad,* also known as *soledad, soleá, terceto,* and *triada gallega,* is an octosyllabic cantar reduced to three lines. The first and third lines rhyme in either assonance or true rhyme, and the second is left unrhymed. The form is of popular origin. Dance songs, such as the *jota* and the *malagueña,* are also termed *cantar.* The *cantar de gesta,* also called simply *cantar,* is usually a med. *epic poem (see CHANSON DE GESTE). The lines vary in length but are long and divided into *hemistichs. The poem is divided into *laisses of unequal length, each laisse being monorhymed in assonance. The anonymous *Poema del Cid* (ca. 1140) is the most famous example.

■ N. Alonso Cortés, *Elementos de preceptiva literaria,* 7th ed. (1932); S. G. Morley, "Recent Theories about the Meter of the '*Cid*,'" *PMLA* 48 (1933); Navarro; C. Smith, *The Making of the "Poema de mio Cid"* (1983).

D. C. CLARKE

**CANTE JONDO.** A type of primitive Andalusian popular *song or *lament in poetry, music, and dance (*baile flamenco*). The origins of the *cante jondo* have never been completely explained, but it undoubtedly has roots in Christian and Muslim religious chants, which, in turn, were fused with traditional gypsy music and folkloric elements in southern Spain. A Jewish heritage has been claimed on the basis of the chanting nature of cante jondo, which is then taken to mean "deep song"; those favoring a Hebrew source say that it derives from *Jom Tov*, feast day.

The most familiar forms of the cante jondo are the *sequiriya* or *\*seguidilla* (according to Federico García Lorca, the most genuine), the *soleá*, the *saeta*, the *petenera*, the *polo*, and the *martinete*. Among its celebrated interpreters are Pastora Pavón (*La Niña de los Peines*), Juan Breva, Manuel Torres, and Silverio Franconetti. In addition to Sp. musicians such as Manuel de Falla (*El Amor Brujo*) and Isaac Albéniz (*Iberia*), composers of other nationalities, incl. Claude Debussy and Mikhail Glinka, have been influenced by these songs of incantatory rhythm and plaintive tremulos. The classification of the various types of cante jondo is highly complex, but all have in common the expression of deep, dramatic passion and suffering and anguish. The singer uses enharmonism and often slides his or her voice from note to note with minute changes—features thought to be of Byzantine-Oriental origin. Full of pathos and lament, cante jondo's principal themes are love and death, often linked to telluric forces, expressed in solemn ritual. Lorca and Rafael Alberti were esp. successful at integrating these popular motifs into their sophisticated verse, an achievement that gave rise to the trend of neopopularism. The former published his *Poema del cante jondo* in 1931. Twenty years earlier, Manuel Machado had edited *Cante hondo: Cantares, canciones y coplas, compuestas al estilo popular de Andalucía*. In June 1922, the Fiesta del Cante Jondo, organized by de Falla and Lorca, was held in Granada.

■ I. Brown, *Deep Song: Adventures with Gypsy Songs and Singers in Andalusia and Other Lands* (1929); K. Schindler, *Folk Music of Spain and Portugal* (1941); M. de Falla, *Escritos sobre música y músicos* (1950); G. Chase, *The Music of Spain*, 2d ed. (1959); L. F. Compton, *Andalusian Lyrical Poetry and Old Spanish Love Songs* (1976); V. Almáida Mons, "Rito y ritmo: El cante jondo," *Cuadernos Hispanoamericanos* 475 (1990); J. Martínez Hernández, "La cultura de la sangre: Apuntes para una poética del cante jondo," *Cuadernos Hispanoamericanos* 512 (1993).

A. W. PHILLIPS; K. N. MARCH

**CANTICUM AND DIVERBIUM.** In Roman drama, the *canticum* is the part of the play that was declaimed or sung to musical accompaniment, as opposed to the *diverbium* or spoken dialogue. The cantica of Plautus are very numerous, constituting approximately two-thirds of each play, while those of Terence are few. Cantica are chiefly *\*monodies* or duets sung or declaimed by an actor or actors and appear in a great variety of meters. The cantica of Seneca are choral songs written in meters that derive primarily from the metrical system of Horace. The diverbia were written, as a rule, in iambic senarii (see SENARIUS). In some mss. of Plautus, the diverbium is indicated by the marginal notation *DV* and the canticum by *C*.

■ Crusius; H. Drexler, *Einführung in die römische Metrik* (1967); C. Questa, *Introduzione alla metrica di Plauto* (1967); L. Braun, *Die Cantica des Plautus* (1970); A. S. Gratwick, "Drama," *CHCL*, v. 2.

P. S. COSTAS; J. W. HALPORN

**CANTIGA.** The term used to designate poetic compositions that flourished in Iberia from the 13th to the mid-14th cs. in Galician-Port., a lang. of the northwest Iberian Peninsula and the lingua franca of poetry during this time. The general stylistic and thematic cohesion of these compositions make the *cantiga* a "school" of lyric. In their principal mode of dissemination, cantigas were sung or perhaps recited. The anonymous and fragmentary *Arte de trovar* (*AT*) describes genres and the formal attributes of rhyme, syllable count, and rhet. The major genres are *cantiga de amigo*, *cantiga de amor*, and *cantigas de escarnho e mal dizer*. The *cantiga de amigo*, though attributed to male poets, is in the voice of a woman (usually a peasant) lamenting the absence of a lover or "friend." In the *cantiga de amor*, a man sings of love and his lady or *senhor*. The *cantiga de escarnho* and *cantiga de mal dizer* are joke and insult poetry and include a wide range of topics. According to the *AT*, the *cantiga de escarnho* lampoons its target covertly with double entendre (*equivocatio*), while the *cantiga de mal dizer* does so openly, often naming the object of the joke. The generic distinction between the types of joke poetry is often approximate, since many compositions exhibit characteristics of each. A number of minor genres exist such as the *tençáo* (a dialogue in poetic form), the funereal *pranto*, or the satirical *\*sirventes*. Nearly 1700 cantigas are extant, collected in three major *\*cancioneiros* or *\*songbooks*. The numerous cantiga poets include King Denis of Portugal and King Alfonso X *el Sábio* (the Wise) of Castile.

Though the influence of *\*Occitan* poetry is discernible in some compositions, the cantigas are distinct in character and portray the social and natural landscapes of Iberia. The *cantigas de amor* are expressions of the culture of courtly love found in contemporaneous Occitan verse, but unlike the *joi* that typifies the *\*troubadour* poems, these cantigas typically express a *coita d'amor* or amorous suffering. The *cantigas de amigo*, probably inspired by popular and indigenous women's songs, also express a pained affect in the cadences of their highly structured stanzas. These songs are an important testimony to the representation of women's voice and sexuality in med. Eur. lit. Both genres of the love poetry manifest the melancholic yearning or *saudade* that is often held to be characteristic of the Port. literary temperament. The ribald and frequently obscene *cantigas de escarnho e mal dizer* often display cantiga poets at their ling. and semantic best in the joking games of lang. and nuance underlying this genre. These cantigas depict many of the realities of daily life in med. Iberia and are revealing documents of the social and cultural hist. of the peninsula.

*See* CANTAR; PORTUGAL, POETRY OF.

■ **Anthologies and Translations:** *Cantigas d'amor dos trovadores galego-portugueses*, ed. J. J. Nunes (1972); *Medieval Galician-Portuguese Poetry*, ed. and trans. F. Jensen (1992); *Cantigas d'escarnho e de mal dizer*, ed. M. Rodrigues Lapa (1995); *113 Galician-Portuguese Troubadour Poems*, trans. R. Zenith (1995); *500 Cantigas d'Amigo*, ed. R. Cohen (2003).

■ **Criticism and History**: R. Menéndez Pidal, *Poesía juglaresca y orígenes de las literaturas románicas*, 6th ed. (1957); F. Jensen, *The Earliest Portuguese Lyrics* (1978); M. Rodrigues Lapa, *Lições de literatura portuguesa*, rev. ed. (1981); G. Tavani, *A poesia lírica galego-portuguesa* (1990); *Dicionário da literatura medieval galega e portuguesa*, ed. G. Lanciani and G. Tavani (1993); *La Corónica* 26.2 (1998); J. Weiss, "On the Conventionality of the *Cantigas d'amor*," *Medieval Lyric*, ed. W. D. Paden (2000); B. Liu, *Medieval Joke Poetry* (2004).

■ **Primary Texts**: *Il canzoniere portoghese della Biblioteca Vaticana*, ed. E. Monaci (1875); *Cancioneiro da Ajuda*, ed. C. Michëlis de Vasconcellos, 2 v. (1904, 1966), diplomatic ed. by H. H. Carter (1941); *Cancioneiro da Biblioteca Nacional (Colocci-Brancuti)*, ed. E. Paxeco Machado and J. P. Machado, 8 v. (1949–64).

J. BLACKMORE

**CANTO.** A longer subsection of an *epic or *narrative poem, as distinguished from shorter subsections such as *stanzas, and corresponding roughly to chapters in a novel (a series of cantos may form a book in a poem such as *The Faerie Queene*). The term is of It. origin and is synonymous with such designations as *movement* or *fit* in other lits.; it has been used in works by Dante, Ludovico Ariosto, Torquato Tasso, Alonso de Ercilla, Voltaire, Alexander Pope, Lord Byron, and Ezra Pound, among others. In the case of Pound, *Cantos* was from the beginning only a working title for the long poem he envisioned; witness the fact that the titles of the first three installments all began "A Draft of. . . ." But his own life took unexpected turns, and the extent to which the pub. *Cantos* reveal any integrative architecture is uncertain. Pound clearly meant his 800-page "tale of the tribe" to be read as a mod. verse epic, based to some degree on Homeric, Ovidian, and Dantean models, while at the same time, such a title, in foregrounding the poem's units of construction rather than subject matter, emphasized that the poet was still working toward an as yet unseen vision of order that would unify the poem's component parts.

■ R. Sale, "Canto," *The Spenser Encyclopedia*, ed. A. C. Hamilton et al. (1990).

T.V.F. BROGAN; T. GARDNER

**CANZONE.** In *De vulgari eloquentia* (*On Vernacular Eloquence*), Dante defines the *canzone* as the most excellent It. verse form, the one that is the worthy vehicle for those "tragic" compositions that treat the three noblest subjects: martial valor, love, and moral virtue. Noting the intimate link between poetry and music (the term *canzone* comes from *cantio*, a song), Dante remarks that "although all that we put in verse is a 'song' [cantio], only *canzoni* have been given this name" (2.3.4). As a result, the term *canzone* has come to be applied to a number of verse forms with differing metrical patterns. Among the better known types is

the *canzone epico-lirica*, whose center of diffusion was originally the Gallo-It. dialect area: it belongs to the Celtic substratum and is akin to compositions of the same genre in France and Catalonia. More indigenous to the It. soil is the *canzone a ballo* or *ballata* and other popular compositions such as the *frottola and *barzelletta*, the *canto carnascialesco*, and the *lauda sacra*. At various times, these types have been used by the *poeti d'arte*, but the type exclusively employed for refined artistic expression is the so-called *canzone petrarchesca*, which bears strong traces of Occitan influence. The It. *strambotto* and ballata and Ger. *Minnesang* are also said to have conditioned its architectonic structure.

In Italy, the first forms of the canzone are found among the poets of the *Sicilian school. It is employed extensively by Guittone d'Arezzo and his followers and by Dante and the poets of the *Dolce stil nuovo* but acquires a certain elegance and perfection in Petrarch's *Canzoniere*, hence the qualifying adjective *petrarchesca*. Its greatest vogue in Italy occurred during the age of *Petrarchism, which lasted until the death of Torquato Tasso (1595). While the Petrarchan canzone was employed in England by William Drummond of Hawthornden and in Germany by A. W. Schlegel and other Ger. romantic poets, Spain and Portugal were the only countries outside Italy where it was used to a considerable extent.

One structural feature of the canzone proved to be of lasting importance for the subsequent devel. of a number of lyric genres in the Eur. vernaculars, especially Occitan, OF, and Middle High Ger. This is the organization of the poem into a structure that is simultaneously tripartite and bipartite. In the terminology Dante gives in *De vulgari eloquentia* (2.10), the poem is divided into a *fronte* (Lat. *frons*) and a *sirma* (Lat. *cauda*)—head and tail—but the frons itself is further subdivided into two *piedi* (*pedes*, feet) that are metrically and musically identical, making the essential structure *aa/b*. Subsequent Ger. terms for these partitions are the *Aufgesang* divided into *Stollen* and the *Abgesang*. This tripartite structure appears in analogues as late Chaucerian *rhyme royal and the *Venus and Adonis stanza. In some cases, the sirma may be divided into two identical parts called *volte* (Lat. *versus*), thus leading to a quadripartite structure *aa/bb*. In the It. canzone there is, further, usually a single *commiato* (*envoi) at the close of the poem, serving as a valediction. Stanzaic length is indeterminate, varying from 7 to 20 verses. The lines are normally *hendecasyllables with some admixture of *heptasyllables, and this mix of 11- and 7-syllable lines became distinctive of the form. After Tasso, under the strong influence of the Fr. *Pléiade,* this type was supplanted by new forms labeled *canzoni*—the Pindaric and *anacreontic odes, whence the inexact use of *ode as a trans. for *canzone*. Gabriello Chiabrera (sometimes called the It. Pindar) played a leading role in their diffusion. He also revived the *canzonetta* first employed by the poets of the Sicilian school—a form composed entirely of shorter meters, usually heptasyllables. This became the favorite type used by Metastasio and the Arcadian school.

Toward the close of the 17th c., Alessandro Guidi acclimated the *canzone libera*, which reached its highest devel. at the hands of Giacomo Leopardi.

*See* ITALIAN PROSODY, LAUDA.

■ P. E. Guarnerio, *Manuale di versificazione italiana* (1893); O. Floeck, *Die Kanzone in der deutschen Dichtung* (1910); F. Flamini, *Notizia storica dei versi e metri italiani* (1919); R. Murari, *Ritmica e metrica razionale italiana* (1927); V. Pernicone, "Storia e svolgimento della metrica," *Problemi ed orientamenti critici di lingua e di letteratura italiana*, ed. A. Momigliano, v. 2 (1948); E. Segura Covarsí, *La canción petrarquista en la lírica española del Siglo de Oro* (1949); E. H. Wilkins, "The Canzone and the Minnesong," *The Invention of the Sonnet* (1959); I. L. Mumford, "The *Canzone* in 16th-Century English Verse," *English Miscellany* 11 (1960); L. Galdi, "Les origines provençales de la métrique des canzoni de Petrarque," *Actes romanes* 74 (1966); M. Pazzaglia, *Il verso e l'arte della canzone nel "De vulgari eloquentia"* (1967), and *Teoria e analisi metrica* (1974); E. Köhler, " 'Vers' und Kanzone," *GRLMA*, v. 2.1.3; Spongano; Wilkins; M. Fubini, *Metrica e poesia*, 3d ed. (1975); D. Rieger, *Gattungen und Gattungsbezeichnungen der Trobadorlyrik* (1976); J. A. Barber, *Rhyme Scheme Patterns in Petrarch's "Canzoniere,"* *MLN* 92 (1977); C. Hunt, *"Lycidas" and the Italian Critics* (1979); G. Gonfroy, "Le reflet de la canso dans *De vulgari eloquentia* et dans les *Leys d'amors,*" *Cahiers de Civilisation Médiévale* 25 (1982); F. P. Memmo, *Dizionario di metrica italiana* (1983), s.v. "Canzone" et seq.; Elwert, *Italienische*, sect. 79; S. Orlando, *Manuale di metrica italiana* (1994).

J. G. FUCILLA; C. KLEINHENZ

**CANZONIERE** (Fr. *chansonnier*; Sp. *cancionero*, "songbook"). The term is generally used to refer to the early ms. collections of *lyric poetry in the various Romance lit. trads. In Italy, the three major collections of verse dating from the late 13th and early 14th cs.—Vatican, Lat. 3793; Florence, Laurentian Library, Rediano 9; and Florence, National Library, Banco Rari 217—contain the poetry of the *Sicilian school, Guittone d'Arezzo and his followers, the *Dolce stil nuovo*, and others. Many other canzonieri date from the 14th, 15th and 16th cs. and preserve the rich lyric trad. of med. It. poetry. The term *canzoniere* has also been used to designate any collection of poems that appear to have been organized by their author so as to constitute an ordered sequence. This usage has its origin in the title often given to Petrarch's collection of 366 poems, the *Rerum vulgarium fragmenta* or *Rime sparse*, which he wrote, organized, and arranged in various orders from around 1342 until his death in 1374. Divided in two parts—the poems "in vita di Madonna Laura" (1–263) and those "in morte" (264–366)—the *Canzoniere* is primarily concerned with Petrarch's love for Laura and the varied moods it engenders, from ecstatic joy to deep sorrow, as well as with his inner thoughts, desires, and aspirations. Some 30 poems treat literary and political topics. Dante's *Vita nuova* (*New Life*), a combination of poetry and prose that relate the story of the protagonist's love for Beatrice, may have provided the model for Petrarch's *Canzoniere* (which, however, lacks the prose narrative). Retrospectively, critics have applied, perhaps unwisely, the term *canzoniere* to earlier corpora of poetry that they believe were written and organized by the author to tell a story or that could be arbitrarily arranged by mod. eds. so as to accomplish a similar end. It is more prudent, however, to consider *canzoniere* as referring to the numerous ms. songbooks of early It. lyrics and *Canzoniere* as designating Petrarch's verse collection.

*See* CANZONE; ITALY, POETRY OF; PETRARCHISM; SONGBOOK.

■ *Canzonieri della lirica italiana delle origini: I. Il canzoniere vaticano, Biblioteca Apostolica Vaticana, Vat. Lat. 3793; II. Il canzoniere laurenziano, Firenze, Biblioteca Medicea Laurenziana, Redi 9; III. Il canzoniere palatino, Biblioteca Nazionale Centrale di Firenze, Banco Rari 217, ex Palatino 418; IV. Studi critici*, ed. L. Leonardi (2000–01); O. Holmes, *Assembling the Lyric Self: Authorship from Troubadour Song to Italian Poetry Book* (2000).

C. KLEINHENZ

**CAPITOLO** (It., "chapter"). Petrarch's term for the subdivisions of his *Trionfi* (Triumphs, ca. 1340–74). The *capitolo* is an It. verse form based on and identical in structure to Dante's *terza rima, i.e., tercets linked by concatenation (*capitolo ternario—aba bcb cdc*, etc.). Through the 15th c., it was used for didactic subjects—an alternative form, the *capitolo quadernario*, derives from the Occitan *sirventes. The *petrarchisti* of the 16th c. employed the capitolo for ethical meditations, often solemnly allegorized. Ludovico Ariosto in his *Satire* adopted the form to versified memoirs; Francesco Berni transformed it into a vehicle for parody (*capitolo bernesco*). After Ariosto, the form survived into the 18th and 19th cs., to Vittorio Alfieri, Giacomo Leopardi, and Giosuè Carducci, as the chief form for It. verse satire and for quotidian topics treated in a light vein.

*See* PETRARCHISM.

■ M. Pazzaglia, *Teoria e analisi metrica* (1974); Spongano; *La metrica*, ed. R. Cremante and M. Pazzaglia, 2d ed. (1976); F. P. Memmo, *Dizionario di metrica italiana* (1983); Elwert, *Italienische*, sect. 93.2; S. Orlando, *Manuale di metrica italiana* (1994).

T. WLASSICS; C. KLEINHENZ

## CARIBBEAN, POETRY OF THE

  I. Dutch
  II. English
  III. French
  IV. Spanish

### I. Dutch

A. *Language.* The most outstanding character of "Dutch" Caribbean poetry is its ling. diversity. Besides poetry in Dutch, the lang. for administration since the 17th c., poetry is written in Papiamento and Papiamentu in the Leeward Islands (Aruba, Bonaire, Curaçao), whereas Eng. and creole Eng. dominate in Saba, St. Eustatius, and St. Martin, the so-called Windward Islands. Furthermore, in Suriname, the former "Dutch Guiana" on the South Am. continent, the creole lang. Sranan is the most popular, followed by indigenous langs. (Trio, Carib, Arawak), Maroon langs. (Aucan, Saramaccan), Sarnami, Javanese, Chinese, and Hindi. Poets also have a strong affinity for writing in Sp. and Eng.

Critical academic attention to poetry of the Caribbean is fairly recent and began, with a few exceptions, in the 1990s. In the essays included in a special issue of *Callaloo* (1998) and in the second volume of *A History of Literature in the Caribbean* (2001), scholars discuss the different lang. trads. separately. For references to the past, the creole langs. Sranan (Suriname), and Papiamentu (Bonaire, Curaçao) are crucial because they evolved in close relationship with the most intense times of slavery. Both langs. have an impressive record of oral and musical trads. Some written examples have emerged from the second half of the 18th c., but the real outburst came in the 20th c. and runs parallel with the process of decolonization since World War II. Suriname became an independent republic in 1975; Aruba has been an autonomous entity within the Kingdom of the Netherlands since 1986; and Curaçao and St. Martin have had the same status since the end of 2010. In contrast, Saba, St. Eustatius, and Bonaire are now completely incorporated in the Dutch administrative system.

**B.** *Suriname.* When Jahn published his famous anthol. *Schwarzer Orpheus* (Black Orpheus, 1954) with black poets from Africa, the Antilles, and South and North America, he included two poems from Suriname under the heading "Guyana." Jahn indicated that he had translated these poems from the Surinamese lang. (Sranan) in collaboration with A. O. Ehrhardt, a Ger. pastor who worked in Suriname. Sranan was the working lang. for *Creole Drum* (1975), a bilingual (with Eng. trans.) anthol. on creole lit. in Suriname. This ed. includes the same poem "Mama Afrika e krei fu en pikin" (Mama Africa Cries for Her Children) by Julius Koenders (1886–1957) as Jahn did, and the author is praised as the ed. of the first magazine that appeared in Sranan, *Foetoe-Boi* (Foot-Boy, 1946–56). When van Kempen reproduced Koenders's poem again in his 709-page anthol., *Spiegel van de Surinaamse poëzie* (Mirror of Surinamese Poetry, 1995), Sranan is only one of several langs. included. By then, it was no longer an exception to write in Sranan, the lang. that in colonial times was forbidden in schools. The painful process of writing poetry in this lang. is expressed by Trefossa (pseud. of Henri Franz de Ziel, 1916–75), the most outstanding Sranan poet, in a poem dedicated to Koenders from the 1950s: "one true poem is like frightening you. / one true poem is like a struggle against death."

Locally produced literary magazines such as *Tongoni* (1958–59), *Soela* (1962–64), and *Moetete* (1968–69) were catalysts for the overwhelming poetical production in Sranan as well as Dutch. Eddy Bruma (1925–2000), who founded a nationalist movement *Wie Eegie*

*Sanie* (Our Own Things), recalled images from the past and inspired one of the best-known poets in the popular local realm, Dobru (pseud. of Robin Ravales, 1935–83), famous for his performances of the poem "Wan Bon" (One Tree) in the 1970s. February characterizes Dobru's poetry as a "linguistic tour de force" whose effect on the audience obviously was immediate. He further discusses Edgar Cairo (1948–2000), an author who moved to the Netherlands in that same period, together with a considerable part of the Surinamese population in the wake of independence. Cairo also was a performer, and February characterizes him as a "word-workman" or "word-worker," "as a cultural, historical, and literary *obja* [Obeah] man, magically transforming the life of Suriname's Creoles into a completely modern style, and reshaping their reality."

Experimental practices were much more characteristic than nationalism for Cairo as well as for other Surinamese poets living in the Netherlands. Hans Faverey, for instance, born in Paramaribo (1933–90), left an important oeuvre and was even proposed as a Dutch candidate for the Nobel Prize in Literature. For poetic experimentation, the *vijftigers*, a Dutch group of poets closely related to visual art, had prepared the reading audience for provocative metaphoric combinations. Faverey's imagination, however, also extended to memories of his native country. Jones discusses his poem "De vijver in het meer" (The Pond in the Lake), in which the Spider is visited by his son; Jones explains this metaphor of Spider as the "resourceful Anansi of Caribbean legend," judging that Faverey's Dutch has Caribbean modulations. Faverey and other poets, who receive attention in the Netherlands, do not emphasize their "Caribbeanness," as does a poet such as Astrid Roemer (b. 1947), who was at the forefront of women's liberation, ecological awareness, and the struggle against discrimination. She describes the difficulties of being published in her commemorations of Jos Knipscheer (1945–97), the owner of a courageous house for "Dutch" Caribbean authors.

Another important segment of Surinamese poetry comes from the "coolitude"—heritage. Cl. Hindi verse was introduced, and contemp. authors use this lang. together with Sarnami (a Surinamese lang. for people from Indian descent) and Dutch. This poetry also reflects on modernization, such as changing gender role patterns, intimacy and emotions, and lyrical images.

**C.** *Aruba, Curaçao, St. Martin.* Poets in the Netherlands Antilles mostly gather around institutions, libraries, and publishing houses in the three biggest islands of the area. In Curaçao, locally produced literary magazines promoted young talents. Agustin Bethancourt (1826–85), born in the Canary Islands, was the editor of *Notas y Letras,* (1886–88) in Sp. He was surrounded by native Papiamentu speakers, who wrote poetry in Sp. and maintained contacts with other writers in Latin America and Spain. Joseph Sickman Corsen (1853–1911) was an exception, because he also produced poetry in his native creole lang. His poem "Atardi" (Getting Dark, 1905) is still known by most Curaçaoans today, and its melancholic, introverted tone fits perfectly within the contemp. *modernismo* sensibility on the Sp.-Am. continent.

When Chris Engels (pseud. of Luc Tournier, 1907–80)—an immigrant from the Netherlands—founded *De Stoep* (1940–51) 50 years later, writing in Sp. had become marginal, but Papiamentu-writing was quite common already. It was a published lang. since *Civilizadó*, ed. by Bethencourt from 1871 to 1875, as well as thereafter the weekly *La Cruz*—since 1900—in which "Atardi" debuted. Many other publications followed, and Broek defines a prewar period of Papiamentu-lit., supported by the Catholic Mission. Therefore, when *De Stoep* came out with its first issue in Dutch, a group of poets published another magazine, *Simadan* (1940), with contributions in Papiamentu. *Simadan* succeeded in bringing out only two volumes, but it became legendary for writing lit. in Papiamentu. Its initiator was Pierre Lauffer (1920–81), who even founded a musical trio, *Cancionero Papiamento*, in order to make clear in which lang. the feelings of belonging were to be found.

Existential questions were predominantly addressed in poetry written in Dutch. Some works show a strong reminiscence of the contacts with Spain and Sp. America, such as *Bekentenis in Toledo* (Confession in Toledo, 1945), in which Cola Debrot (1902–81) recalls the Sp. 17th c. Other authors who published in *De Stoep* evidence the desperate search for love and the desire to shape the colors and images of the island's landscape. Most of the local contributors were native Papiamentu-speakers. Oversteegen analyzes the poem "Bezoek" (Visit, 1945), with which Tip Marugg (1923–2006) debuted, and interprets its reception as having two different levels of meaning: one for the Dutch reader and one for the Antillean, the native of Papiamentu.

Papiamentu imagination is very strong in Aletta Beaujon's (1933–2001) first work, *Gedichten aan de Baai en elders* (Poems at the Bay and Beyond, 1957), in which the sea is repeatedly placed at the center of the poetical universe. In that same year, Frank Martinus Arion (b. 1936) came out with *Stemmen uit Afrika* (Voices from Africa, 1957), an epos in which he describes the encounter of white tourists with black inhabitants of the rain forest in Africa. Arion also edited the magazine *Ruku* in the 1970s, in which black consciousness is promoted and in which he published poetry in Dutch and Papiamentu.

Poetry written in the creole lang. of Aruba, Papiamento, does not reproduce the same tension between Dutch and Papiamentu in Curaçao. *Cosecha Arubiano* (Aruban Harvest, 1983), the anthol. pub. by Booi and coeditors, reveals that Papiamento, Eng., Sp., and Dutch seem to coexist peacefully together without feeling specifically challenged one by the other. Generally, Papiamento is the most important medium for poetical expression. For others, living abroad, this medium becomes a relative dimension. Henry Habibe (b. 1940), the ed. of the literary magazine *Watapana* (1968–72), which published the poetry of Antillean students in the Netherlands, was highly praised for his exquisite volumes in Papiamento. However, his last poetry vol-

ume came out in Dutch. In contrast, Denis Henriquez (b. 1945), who became a well-known author of novels written in Dutch, produces poetry in Papiamento that to date has not been published.

In St. Martin, creole Eng. is even less involved in a poetical dialogue with Dutch. Wycliffe Smith (b. 1948) published a first survey of poetry in the Dutch Windward Islands, *Windward Island Verse* (1981), in Eng. Thereafter, the activities of Lasana Sekou (b. 1959), who studied in New York, have had far-reaching consequences. His publishing company, House of Nehesi, has attracted local talent and also has attracted other Caribbean writers to St. Martin. In addition, because of in part the Nigerian critic and teacher Fabian Badejo (b. 1950), who lived in St. Martin, the relationship with Africa becomes a concrete point of reference, asserted in performances, theater, and workshops, widely seen but rarely published.

**D. *Traumas, Visions, Rhythms, and Sounds.*** Critical work by Broek, Echteld, van Kempen, van Putte-de Windt, and Wim Rutgers repeatedly addresses the important role of literary magazines in the local settings. Poetry represents historical trauma such as slavery, the search for connections with Africa, the May 1969 rebellion in Curaçao, the December murders in Suriname in 1980, gender roles, or discrimination. The myriad of anthols., (short-lived) magazines, or self-published volumes makes it complicated to distinguish among the different "strategies and stratagems" of "Dutch" Caribbean poetry. Therefore, it might be useful to conclude with some general observations.

First, it is clear that different poetical langs. are not disappearing but are growing stronger, even though Dutch remains the condition for circulating on the literary market. Second, efforts to counter the marginalization of the creole langs. by pushing them forward as written literary langs. have succeeded since the 1940s: their rhythms and rhymes have a strong musical background, and, in this context, Caribbean poetry begins to be increasingly influential. The House of Nehesi has published volumes by Kamau Brathwaite, and his work has also been translated into Sranan in Suriname. Sekou even speaks of the Caribbean as the "universe of sound." Van Mulier, ed. of the anthol. *Nieuwe Oogst* (New Harvest, 2002), belongs to the Surinamese Writers Association in the Netherlands and has recognized this point. He has argued for more attention to musical rhythm in poetry. One of the poets in the volume, the music professor Rudy Bedacht (b. 1932), presents his composition for another melody for the national *anthem, currently based on the 1876 musical composition of a Dutch teacher. The anthem, which has one Dutch and one Sranan *strophe—the latter produced by Trefossa in 1959—was translated into a slightly modified Javanese version in 1998. This detail clearly reveals that the poetical sensibility in this part of America is dealing with different langs. and styles that all refer to the same native intimacy.

**II. English.** Speakers of Eng. begin to inhabit the Caribbean during in the early 17th c., through the colonization of Barbados and then Jamaica. By the end of the 20th c., the region's anglophone poets wrote not only from former Brit. colonies large (Guyana, Jamaica, Trinidad, Barbados, St. Lucia) and small (Belize, the Bahamas, St. Vincent, Grenada, Antigua, St. Kitts, Virgin Islands, Dominica, Montserrat), but from islands that were never Brit., such as Puerto Rico and even St. Martin. In addition, many writers who regard themselves as anglophone Caribbean poets now reside for the most part in North America or the U.K. Such a list is not very helpful for identifying some common ground for all this writing beyond the accident of lang. Another frequent option, "West Indian poetry," is more explicitly grounded in the Eng.-speaking islands themselves but is commonly used more broadly. The most ingenious, and possibly most accurate, attempt at characterization associates this poetry with "the cricket-playing Caribbean."

Venturing to speak of "anglophone Caribbean poetry" turns any traditional notion of national lit. on its head. This is a body of poetry from noncontiguous territories, many of them now sovereign states, some of which once comprised a single political unit, though only fleetingly, as the short-lived Federation of the West Indies (1958–62). This is not the poetry of a nation, nor of a people, nor of a single culture, nor even, strictly speaking, of a single lang. What do we gain by having a catchall phrase for any verse written in some variant of Eng. by someone associated with the Caribbean? Even naming the region itself requires choosing among incommensurate terms: "the Caribbean," "Latin America," "the Antilles," "the West Indies." But if the difficulties of naming this body of work might suggest that it is not really viable as a single object of attention, the repeated efforts to name it seem to belie that suggestion. Indeed, throughout the Caribbean, the issues raised by the very act of naming have been central to cultural self-consciousness (and particularly to poetry) since Europe insisted these islands were "the Indies," gave the slaves ancient Roman names, and described the landscape in the vocabulary of Ren. pastoral. To propose "Caribbean poetry in English" as an object of study is to propose that regarding the poetry through such a frame or optic, rather than as sheaves of separate poems, significantly enhances our experience of the texts. For critics and poets alike, it is inherently intriguing that this body of work is problematic to name.

Thus, e.g., we might start from the common historical narrative/trajectory that these islands share. Then the qualifications must begin at once: at least two of these "islands" (Belize and Guyana) are not islands at all. But the need to make that qualification is not distracting; it sensitizes readers to different roles that topography and geography may play in shaping the local intonation of themes and images common to the experience of the region. Metaphorically speaking, many aspects of Caribbean life are instances of a broad principle, "one language, many accents." This is consistent with Antonio Benítez Rojo's (1931–2005) insight that, in the Caribbean, things are always done "in a certain kind of way." The Tobagonian poet Eric Roach (1915–74) in "Caribbean Calypso" (1965) strikingly envisions the Caribbean as a laboratory, each island a Petri dish in which initially similar cultures, once isolated, evolve quite differently under the influence of what were at first only slightly different conditions, mutations, contaminations. Caribbean writers characteristically bear in mind at once the distinctively local and its regional or international contexts.

Qualifications and variants aside, the common ground for the entire region is archipelagic geography, tropical climate, and a shared hist. Europe intrudes into Amerindian societies, and the rest follows. Emancipation brought an end to plantation slavery on different islands at different times, but in the Brit. colonies, the reach of the empire made it possible to avert the ensuing labor shortage by recruiting indentured workers from India, China, and even West Africa. After extreme economic and political changes and two world wars, Britain moved to dismantle both the plantation and the empire, creating a climate in the Caribbean for the emergence of cultural and political nationalism. Independence came for most of the Brit. Caribbean in the course of the 1960s, unexpectedly inflected by the rise of Black Power movements in the region as well as in North America and the U.K. In the sometimes disappointing aftermath of independence, the salient international pressures on the region were redefined: increasing Am. influence, globalization, and neocolonialism. Such is the grand narrative, though it played out in different terms and on different timetables from island to island.

In the anglophone case, the production of poetry from its beginnings entails decisions about three intertwined questions that have remained perennial for this body of work: Who is the audience? What is the lang. of expression (Standard English [SE] or creole)? What is the envisioned mode of expression (oral or scribal)? Throughout the colonial Caribbean, the various metropolitan langs. isolated territories from one another, while each lang. imported conventions and styles that shaped distinctive literary hists. Almost at once, a variety of creole langs. arise (new spoken langs. developing out of persistent contact between two or more other langs.), and creole becomes an influential part of the ling. experience of writers long before it emerges openly as a lang. of expression in the literary realm. Some societies respond to the emergence of a spoken creole by establishing a barrier between what are perceived as separate and unequal langs. Though the ling. hists. of the Brit. colonies vary considerably, there has been a general tendency to think in terms of a ling. continuum linking rural creole with metropolitan lang. This gives individual speakers considerable control over their self-expression, even within single sentences, and has been an important resource for the distinctive flexibility of anglophone poetry.

In the late 1790s, there appear the first transcriptions of folk songs and stories composed in an Eng.-based creole. These would have been accessible to and used by West Indians of both Af. and Eur. heritage, though it is difficult to date the actual creation of such oral materials. They are recorded in travelogues, hists., and personal jours. published mostly in London and reflect what we would now call an anthropological interest in the region, stimulated at a crucial historical moment: this is the era of the Am., Fr., and Haitian revolutions; of the abolitionist movement; and of the Brit. acquisition of Trinidad.

The first self-consciously literary poems appear somewhat earlier, from about 1750. These are fairly long narrative poems, in *blank verse or *couplets, written according to the conventions of contemporaneous Brit. poetry. Most of the poems of this period are published in London; while a few were printed in Jamaica or Barbados, these authors certainly aspired to reach a Brit. audience. They would also have envisioned a small but interested audience in the Caribbean, made up of planters, government officials, doctors, attorneys, and clergy. It is apparent that West Indian poets have always been aware of the challenges and opportunities entailed by addressing more than one audience at a time.

Individual poets were sporadically active during the 19th c., and it is likely that more of this work will be recovered as research into periodical publications of the era continues. Though there are intriguing exceptions, the dominant themes are predictable: nature, spirituality, moral uplift, and imperial patriotism. Issues of audience and lang. became more prominent at the end of the century with the success of *"dialect poetry"—verse composed in the creole vernacular as a vehicle for comedy or social satire. Intended for newspaper publication, this poetry was written by members of the social elite for a literate readership, but the most popular practitioners reached wide audiences and published reprint collections through local printeries. Soon afterward, in 1912, the young Claude McKay (1890–1948), from a well-to-do black family in rural Jamaica, published two volumes (one in Kingston and the other in London) that are generally regarded as the collections in which poems in an anglophone creole are explicitly presented as lit. The influence of McKay's work was seminal but delayed (perhaps because McKay almost immediately emigrated to the U.S. and never wrote in creole again).

Literary anthols. begin to appear in print in the 1920s and 1930s, but historical perspective is rare in these collections; most include only works of living authors, with few poems from before about 1900. There is one impressive exception, the first anthol. from Guyana (*Guyanese Poetry*, 1931), whose ed., Norman Cameron, unearthed work from as early as 1831. The appearance of anthols. coincides with the devel. in several territories of productive poetry groups, clubs, or salons (such as the Poetry League of Jamaica or the group associated with the *Beacon* magazine in Trinidad), and some tentative printing ventures. In the more developed colonies during this period, we can discern the crucial metamorphosis by which a scattering of writers coalesces

into a lit. There is generally a new interest in local Caribbean geography and hist., and during the late 1930s and the war years, these themes mature into more overt concern with cultural and political nationalism.

From the very beginning of the century, women had taken important initiatives, and during this period, one who learned from McKay's example was Una Marson (1905–65), another Jamaican who published several collections of poetry in the 1930s and so established herself as arguably the first important modernist and the leading female voice of the time. A number of her poems experiment with the poetic resources of vernaculars, drawing on lessons learned not only from Jamaican creole but from her knowledge of *Harlem Renaissance poetry and its exploration of black Am. vernaculars. The greatest exponent of McKay's early mission, however, is Louise Bennett (1919–2006), a collector and performer of folk tales and songs, professionally trained in London at the Royal Academy of Dramatic Art, and the author of several collections of original poems in Jamaican creole, beginning in the 1940s. Her work, however, was not regarded as "literature" until the independence era, despite her jibe in 1944 that, though the Brit. had been trying to stabilize their lang. since the 14th c., "Five hundred years gawn an dem got / More dialect dan we!" ("Bans o' Killing," 1944).

A massive Caribbean migration to Britain occurred between the early 1950s and the restrictive immigration legislation of 1962. As in any migration, there was concern about abandoning home and losing identity, but this turned out to be something different—as Bennett phrased it, a case of "colonization in reverse." Nationalist impulses at home were complemented by the discovery, in London, of both a broader West Indian identity and a black identity. Anglophone migrants from all over the Caribbean were thrown together (Britons tended to call them all *Jamaicans*) and began to sort out not only their common traits but the distinctive differences between local island cultures—in particular (from the perspective of poets) ling. variations in the syntax, lexicon, and accent of their diverse forms of Eng. The formulation of a West Indian identity was facilitated by a number of new institutions. Most powerful in its impact was perhaps the BBC's *Caribbean Voices* program, which featured the voices of West Indian authors resident in London reading current West Indian prose and poetry for listeners in the Caribbean (a number of the early emigrants, incl. novelists Sam Selvon, George Lamming, and V. S. Naipaul, worked for the BBC and wrote their first books on its typewriters). Also significant were the Caribbean Artists Movement (which eventually migrated back to the Caribbean from England), the founding of literary jours. with regional perspective (*Bim* in Barbados [1942], *Kyk-Over-Al* in Guyana [1945], *Caribbean Quarterly* in Jamaica [1949]), and the establishment in 1948 of the University College of the West Indies (soon to become the University of the West Indies). A succeeding generation of writers, building on this thinking about West Indianness, would go on in their own work to formulate what we now call Black British identity. This pattern is repeated when the somewhat later migration to Canada leads to the emergence of yet another "colony" of anglophone Caribbean lit.

Back in the Caribbean, some of the leading poets of this period were Martin Carter (1927–97) and A. J. Seymour (1914–89) in Guyana, and Roach and Harold Telemaque (1910–82) in Trinidad. Between 1962 and 1966, Jamaica, Trinidad and Tobago, Guyana, and Barbados all became independent countries. The timing meant that the process of coming to terms with independence took place in the context of the global emergence of black consciousness. For predominantly black nations like Jamaica and Barbados, this was in the long run a positive influence. For Guyana and Trinidad, with much more diverse populations, the downside was institutionalization of political confrontation along ethnic lines. Among the positive outcomes was (on the one hand) robust growth of both recognizably Afro-Caribbean and recognizably Indo-Caribbean writing and (on the other) a growing confidence among writers about drawing on their multiple cultural trads. Everywhere writers joined in the fundamental debates about "roots"—about whether identity was to be grounded in pristine Af. or Asian heritage or in current creole realities (as in Derek Walcott's view of the archetypal Caribbean man as a "second Adam"). Discussion of the hybrid results of creolization could be framed as biological (what are your parents?), cultural (what do you do, and how do you do it?), even intellectual (what do you talk about and how?). Poets, through the content of their poems, played a vital role in those discussions, but, for the practice of poetry, the leading issues were again lang. and mode of expression.

Among the many rewarding poets of the postindependence era are Edward Baugh (b. 1936), Mervyn Morris (b. 1937), Velma Pollard (b. 1937), and Dennis Scott (1939–91) in Jamaica; Kendel Hippolyte (b. 1952), Jane King (b. 1952), and Robert Lee (b. 1949) in Saint Lucia; Ian McDonald (b. 1933) and David Dabydeen (b. 1955) in Guyana. The single most important poets of the 20th c. were Derek Walcott (b. 1930) and Kamau Brathwaite (b. 1930), both ambitious, prolific poets and highly visible figures on the Caribbean scene. Walcott began publishing in the late 1940s; his poetry has often addressed in complex ways the relation of the Caribbean to its Eur. heritage, while his verse plays have given voice to several West Indian vernaculars. Brathwaite came to prominence in the 1960s with the first volume of what became a trilogy, *The Arrivants* (1967–69), an epic poem of vast scope and resonance, which, among other innovations, set the standard for literary use of anglophone creoles.

Following the magisterial example of Brathwaite's trilogy, many poets joined the project of demonstrating that their anglophone creoles could be literary langs.; some even took the extreme view that SE could not be the lang. of their work. In some cases, the argument for creole was an argument that spoken lang. should be fundamental for poetry (an argument that echoes the likes of William Wordsworth, Chaucer, and Dante). Advocacy of spoken lang. often brought with it an advocacy of spoken *style*, of what Brathwaite called "orature": written poetry that aspired to the condition of oral poetry. This argument invoked several important values of the era: the association of oral verbal arts with the Caribbean "folk" (conceived in various ways) and with ancestral trads. in Africa, and traditional respect for the figure of the Caribbean "man of words." This, in turn, led to a new respect for performers of poetry (such as Bennett), and to the rise, esp. in Jamaica, of composers of "dub poetry" (sometimes called "reggae poetry"): poetry intended for performance that draws heavily on features of Jamaican deejay practice and is often (but not necessarily) accompanied by reggae music. Among the most compelling of these, accessible through commercial recordings, are Linton Kwesi Johnson (b. 1952), Michael Smith (1954–83), Jean "Binta" Breeze (b. 1956), and Mutabaruka (b. 1952).

From a narrowly literary perspective, the *perfor-mance poets no longer dominate the Caribbean scene as they once did. A generation of younger poets has come forward, many of them not esp. interested in performance and often writing rather surprisingly in SE. In particular, women in much greater numbers (and from several generations) began publishing volumes of poetry in the 1980s; they had almost dropped out of the poetry scene during the male-dominated nationalist period. This is a body of work remarkable for diversity and audacity; it is not the exploration of "female subjects" or a narrowly defined "women's style." It addresses a variety of audiences, sometimes in creole, sometimes in SE, sometimes in both. Lorna Goodison (b. 1947) has an international reputation and a clear influence on younger writers. But there are many established figures, such as Pollard and Grace Nichols (b. 1950), while the numerous younger poets often publish locally and are best sought out in anthols.

The current poetry scene has become increasingly diverse in every respect, yet high-profile performance poets like Johnson effectively symbolize the paradox on which anglophone Caribbean poetry stands after the 20th c. Through recordings, concerts, and videos, they reach an enormous global audience, comparable to that of the reggae stars. But what they deliver is a specifically Caribbean (or in some cases Black Brit.) perspective couched in unmediated creole lang. With minimal compromise or homogenization, they do not make their lang. accessible; they successfully invite audiences to make the effort to access it. Increasingly, transnational experience and even transnational identity are marks of most Caribbean poets, yet their work seems ever more interested in the peculiarities of local speech, custom, and behavior. They preserve and celebrate what is distinctively Caribbean but project it globally.

**III. French.** One of the most widely accepted truths of francophone Caribbean lit., and for some readers perhaps Caribbean lit. in its entirety, is that no poetry existed before 1939. Revolutionary ideologies in the francophone Caribbean in the 1930s were constructed around myths of rupture and innovation that condemned the 19th c. as a time of unexamined imitation. This is one of the defining characteristics of the identity politics promoted in such radical jours. as *Légitime Défense, Tropiques*, and *La Revue Indigène*. This yearning for a violent rupture with the past led Frantz Fanon to declare, "Until 1939 the West Indian lived, thought, dreamed . . . composed poems, wrote novels exactly as a white man would have done" (*Toward the African Revolution*, 1964). Indeed, in the case of Haiti, the influential theorist of Haitian *indigenisme* Jean Price-Mars (1876–1969) dismissed his predecessors in 1928 as practicing collective "bovarysme" or "the pathological deviation [of] conceiving of ourselves as other than we are" (*So Spoke the Uncle*, 1928). More recently the promoters of *Créolité* in the Fr. Antilles blindly repeated Price-Mars's term "bovarysme collectif" to describe all the writing done in Haiti between 1804 and 1915.

Before the publication of Aimé Césaire's epic poem *Cahier d'un retour au pays natal* (*Notebook of a Return to the Native Land*, 1939) on the eve of World War II, there was good reason to believe that Fr. Caribbean poetry, at least what was produced in the Fr. colonies, was dominated by sentimental, pastoral, and, most important, apolitical evocations of nature. A local intellectual culture was never encouraged in colonies whose raison d'être was primarily commercial. Education was a fiercely guarded privilege restricted almost exclusively to the white planter elite. This drawback, combined with an inevitable sense of cultural inferiority, meant that, when it did appear, poetry was likely to offer imitative apologies for the economic status quo. For instance, Poirié de Saint-Aurèle (1795–1855), a member of the white planter class from Guadeloupe, fully deserves Fanon's dismissive description, having published a defense of plantation slavery and collections of regionalist verse (*Les Veillées françaises* [French Evenings], 1826; and *Cyprès et palmistes* [Cypresses and Palms], 1833) that defend the plantation hierarchy and display contempt for the black-slave population.

Saint-Aurèle's love for his native land and antipathy to the métropole are a product of reactionary self-interest, as he felt the way of life of the planter class increasingly threatened. This was not always the case, as regionalist verse was also inspired by the ideals of Fr. *romanticism that could allow for the condemnation of racial prejudice and for a healthy interest in representing local flora and fauna. Toward the end of the century in Martinique, René Bonneville (1871–1902) published a regionalist anthol., *Fleurs des Antilles* (1900), to coincide with the Universal Exposition. In Guadeloupe, Oruno Lara (1879–1924) published much regionalist verse in his newspaper *La Guadeloupe Littéraire*. They propagated the exotic image of *les Antilles heureuses* until the outbreak of World War I. Uniform themes and unoriginal styles are the hallmark of this period of Fr. West Indian poetry, typified by such writers as Daniel Thaly (1878–1950), the titles of whose works—*Le Jardin des Tropiques* (The Garden of the Tropics, 1911),

*Nostalgies françaises* (French Nostalgia, 1913)—speak for themselves. Along with this picturesque presentation of local color, there was a more ethnographic trend that insisted on a local identity. Gilbert de Chambertrand (1890–1984) and Gilbert Gratiant (1895–1985) spoke more directly to local concerns, even if in an unoriginal way. The latter experimented with poems in Creole and was even included in Léopold Sédar Senghor's 1948 *Anthologie de la nouvelle poésie nègre et malgache de langue française* (Anthology of the New Negro Poetry in French and Malagasy).

Out of this period of largely white nostalgia and mulatto mystification, there nevertheless emerged the powerful evocation of an Antillean childhood in the early verse of Saint-John Perse (1887–1975), a white Creole native of Guadeloupe. His first book of poems, *Eloges* (Praises, 1911), is as much a love song to Guadeloupe as one of loss motivated by the outlook of a displaced planter class that one finds in Saint Aurèle. Even if the ghost of the planter patriarch haunts the pages of *Eloges*, Perse has become, as much as Césaire, a central figure in Fr. West Indian lit. The Caribbean landscape in Perse's poems is not evoked through the clichés of tropical local color as is the case with the regionalist poets. It is not so much the references to local flora and fauna as the deeply felt personal sense of a lost paradise that make these poems authentically Caribbean. The poet's plantation past becomes an Antillean *lieu de mémoire*, the poetic origin for a trad. of writing Caribbean landscape.

The dismissal of all poetry before the 1930s as Eurocentric seems particularly unjust in the case of Haiti. The themes of early Haitian poetry are drawn from the 1804 Declaration of Independence: pride in Haiti's historic defeat of Napoleon's army, the need to inspire patriotic ideals in the new nation, and the proclamation of Haiti's redemptive mission in a world where plantation slavery still thrived. From very early on, there were calls for a national lit. that would resist cl. forms and references in favor of Haitian hist. and culture. Victor Hugo's robust rhet. and militant politics were a source of inspiration at the time. One of the major exponents of this nationalist verse was Oswald Durand (1840–1906), whose *Rires et Pleurs* (Laughter and Tears, 1896) were an unflagging attempt to celebrate Haitian culture. He is remembered for his poem of unrequited love, "Choucoune" (1884), which was one of the first experiments in Creole-lang. verse. His contemp. Masillon Coicou (1867–1908) was both a military man and a poet and is best known for the tellingly named *Poésies nationales* (1892), which retold Haitian hist. and the independence struggle. At the turn of the 20th c., there was a reaction against what was seen as the excessive nationalism of the patriotic school of Haitian poets. The movement called *La Ronde* felt that, to gain international acclaim, it was necessary to avoid the trap of a narrow parochialism in poetry. Its adherents argued for a literary eclecticism and engaged cosmopolitanism in Haitian verse and felt that regionalist concerns were best left to Haiti's novelists. The works of the poets of

La Ronde—Etzer Vilaire (1872–1951), Edmond Laforest (1876–1915), and Georges Sylvain (1866–1925)—were allusive, impersonal, and reminiscent of the ideals of Fr. *symbolism. This poetic movement was abruptly cut short by the Am. occupation of Haiti in 1915.

Given the radical turn in Haitian poetry after 1915, Césaire's revolutionary poetics was already evident in the wake of the U.S. occupation. Well before the *Negritude movement of the 1930s, the poets of the indigenist movement began to espouse the ideals of a heroic *modernism that valued the poet for his or her visionary power and poetic lang. for its apocalyptic thrust. An antiestablishment iconoclasm was practiced by poets such as Emile Roumer (1903–88), Philippe Thoby-Marcelin (1904–75), and Carl Brouard (1902–65), whose work was published in *La Revue Indigène*. Brouard, in particular, could be seen as an early exponent of the values of Negritude, as he became increasingly preoccupied by Haiti's Af. past and the Vaudou religion. The most outstanding figure of this time is Jacques Roumain (1907–44), who founded the Haitian Communist Party and linked the Haitian Renaissance to similar movements elsewhere in the Caribbean, and North and South America. He was close to the Cuban poet Nicolás Guillén, the Chilean Pablo Neruda, and the Af. Am. Langston Hughes, who were all bound by their ties to Marxism. His fiery book of poems *Bois d'ébène* (Ebony Forest, 1945) favors the grand prophetic manner of the militant utopian rhet. of the 1940s. This epic, militant style would be continued after Roumain's death in 1944 by poets such as Jean Brierre (1909–92), René Bélance (1915–2004), and Roussan Camille (1912–61). Perhaps the most successful of the generation that followed was René Depestre (b. 1926), whose early verse *Etincelles* (Sparks, 1945) and *Gerbe de Sang* (Spray of Blood, 1946) were deeply influenced by the poetry of the Fr. Resistance, esp. that of Paul Éluard and Louis Aragon. Most of Depestre's life would be spent in exile, which would make him an early poet of what would become during the Duvalier dictatorship in the 1960s the Haitian diaspora.

Although he has been eclipsed by Césaire, the Fr. Guyanese poet Léon Gontran Damas (1912–78) was the herald of what came to be known as the Negritude movement. His book of poems *Pigments* (1937) was the first to treat the subject of an international black consciousness and to openly denounce Fr. colonialism. His poetic production was less than that of Césaire and his style less dependent on surrealist techniques, but his direct, spontaneous verse connected him immediately to both the Harlem Renaissance and Haitian indigenisme. He pioneered the use of everyday speech in his verse, drawing on the poetic experiments with spoken Fr. by Raymond Queneau and Jacques Prévert. He found a way of creating *protest poetry that could endure, manipulating pace, humor, and shock to create a number of memorable dramatic *monologues. Damas is as terse and incisive as Césaire is epic and erudite.

Césaire's *Cahier d'un retour au pays natal* inaugurated the heroic modernist verse that would become the hallmark of francophone poetry in the next two decades. In the poetic masterpiece of this period of radical politics, Césaire conceives of the francophone Caribbean in terms of violent images of revolutionary decolonization. The Caribbean past was represented as a sea of running sores, a bloody, open wound with its archipelago of precarious scabs. The Caribbean people eked out a zombified, repressed existence in this putrifying world. The poet proposed a volcanic reordering of space where the tongue of volcanic flame would sweep away the old and found a new utopian order.

The championing of Césaire's apocalyptic poetics had much to do with his meeting with André Breton in 1941 as the latter was heading into exile in the United States. Breton's account of their meeting, which now forms the introduction to *Cahier*, promoted Césaire as a mystical visionary who shared with the leader of the surrealist movement the primitivist dream of an uncontaminated elsewhere beyond the reach of the nightmare imposed by Europe in the colonial past for Césaire and the Nazi present for Breton. Césaire and Breton's visits to Haiti in the coming years would help spread this apocalyptic modernism. However, there is much evidence that Césaire was at least as deeply concerned with the problems of an overly referential verse as he was with a political *prise de conscience*. His high regard for Stéphane Mallarmé, with whom he shared the view that the concrete could short-circuit the poetic, and his siding with Breton in the quarrel with Aragon as to the need for a political poetry are evidence of Césaire's passionate belief in the freedom of the poetic imagination. This is an area of ambiguity that pushes us to rethink the view that Césaire's poetry is exclusively associated with violent militancy.

When the Haitian Marxist Depestre, echoing Aragon, insisted that Caribbean poetry be accessible and nonexperimental, Césaire's response to Depestre, and by extension Aragon and the Communist Party, was indeed entitled "Réponse à Depestre poète haitien, Eléments d'un art poétique" (Response to the Haitian Poet Depestre: Elements of the Art of Poetry, 1955). By giving his reply this subtitle, Césaire invites us to see the poem as prescriptive. With unaccustomed directness, he urged Depestre not to pay heed to Aragon's call for accessible verse but to become a poetic *maroon*, after the early mod. term for escaped slaves who lived independent of colonial society. Depestre was encouraged to learn to conjugate this particular neologism—*marronner*—in the way that the 18th-c. Haitian maroon and Vaudou priest Dutty Boukman understood it. Césaire reminded Depestre that Boukman's rebellious cry incited the rebellions that became the Haitian Revolution and argued that the poetic word should strive for a similar "insane chant" as the ultimate form of marronnage. It is hard to tell whether Depestre heeded Césaire's advice. He was certainly capable of a moving and unpretentious lyricism as in *Journal d'un animal marin* (Journal of a Marine Animal, 1964), arguably the most important poetic work about exile during the Duvalier years, and more relaxed personal pieces in *Minerai noir* (Black Ore, 1957). Nevertheless, he was equally capable of inspiring, accessible verse in response to requests from the Communist Party. His Vaudou ritual poem *Un arc-en-ciel pour l'Occident chrétien* (A Rainbow for the Christian West, 1967) is structured around chants for mobilizing the Vaudou gods to wage war against U.S. imperialism. His *Poète à Cuba* (1976) shows him to be an inveterate producer of poetry for political occasions. His celebration of pagan love as the ultimate catalyst for liberating the self, however, suggests that he has not quite abandoned his early surrealist influences for the rhet. of political activism.

It could be said that Césaire straddles two aspects of literary modernism. On the one hand, he practices a heroic modernism with its notion of the poet's prophetic vision and the poem as a moment of epiphany. On the other, he also espouses a nonutopian poetics based on the values of imaginative freedom and formal experimentation. By the 1950s, however, dreams of revolutionary decolonization had begun and a monolithic racial identity had begun to yield to a poetics that no longer valued marronage and radical difference. The emergence of this new, identifiably postcolonial interest in cultural contact, hybridity, and creolization in the francophone Caribbean is as much linked to the failure of the dream of revolutionary decolonization as to the complex nature of the surrealist movement itself. We should not forget that the poetics of modernism first entered Caribbean lit. not through Césaire but through the group Légitime Défense, among whose members were the now largely forgotten writers René Menil (1907–2004) and Jules Monnerot (1909–95). Their presence has been eclipsed by that of Césaire and the Breton-sponsored idea of revolutionary poetics. However, their ideas often overlapped with members of the surrealist movement who either defected or were expelled by Breton. Here we find the origins of the post-Césairean idea of poetry in the Caribbean. While we tend to associate surrealism with the world of dreams and the unconscious, it also maintained a strong materialist interest in things, in the impossibility of creating abstract formulations from concrete reality. The inscrutable otherness of objects and the inability to systematize the concrete are crucial to the early writings of Monnerot as to such early members of the movement as Roger Caillois (1913–78) and Michel Leiris (1901–90). Subjectivity, in particular artistic subjectivity, depended on *le hasard objectif*, the inscrutable otherness of objects. This interest in the liberating possibilities of otherness is rich in significance for Caribbean writers wrestling with colonial as well as anticolonial constructs of reality. It certainly created a suspicion of the grand ideological formulations of heroic modernism and provoked an interest in the ethnographic mapping of otherness. Some of the surrealist fellow travelers who knew each other and favored this methodology also came to the Caribbean during the 1940s. Pierre Mabille (1904–52) and later the ethnographer Alfred Métraux (1902–63) spent long periods in Haiti in the 1940s. On the invitation of Césaire, Leiris visited Martinique and Haiti in 1948. The importance of travel, the encounter with the other, and self-ethnography were all seen at

this time as the supreme artistic endeavor. Global modernity had turned all places into crossroads where the unpredictable occurred. There could, therefore, be no more ancestral heartlands nor utopian elsewheres.

A prewar apocalyptic poetics now yielded to a poetry based on self-scrutiny catalyzed through interaction with the other. Poets such as Clément Magloire St. Aude (1912–71) of Haiti and Édouard Glissant (1928–2011) of Martinique became major exponents of this mode of poetic expression. The latter's 1955 *Soleil de la conscience* (Sun of Consciousness ) is a perfect example of a poetic self-ethnography as the writer travels not to the native land but to Paris where he is both a stranger to and a product of that reality. The poetics of postwar modernism in the Caribbean is about not new beginnings but a postcolonial errancy that negates, as Glissant has said, "every pole and metropole." It is also not so much about self-expression as about opening poetry to the Caribbean's hemispheric horizons and ultimately to global horizons. This is the central difference between the poetics of Césaire and Glissant. The former projects island space as home, as an unambiguous foundation for the assertion of difference in the face of a deterritorializing incorporation into the transcendent values of the West. The latter replaces the Césairean romance of lost origins with an alternative poetics of location that projects island space as an open yet opaque insularity, a zone of encounter that both acquiesces in yet resists the pressures of global interaction. Consequently, Glissant's poetics was not about idealizing difference in the face of the transcendent will of the West, the reductive force of the Same. He set out, rather, to theorize a "totalizing rootedness," a coming to consciousness of the world in a particular locale. A crucial aspect of Glissant's early assertion of a totalizing vision is the density and tension of locale that underpins this relational model.

In his early book of poems *Les Indes* (1956), Glissant examines the question of place, naming, and the force of the imagination in the Indies—as much dream space as the space of historical nightmare. From the outset, Glissant saw his legacy not so much as that of a Fr. West Indian poet but as that of an Am. modernist. He felt a greater affinity with Perse and William Faulkner than with Roumain and Césaire. Breaking with the demiurgic impulse of heroic modernism, Glissant focuses on the shaping force of landscape. This time it is not the Césairean volcano but Perse's inscrutable marine world that allows Glissant to break with the *poésie de circonstance* that characterized earlier decades. The Manichean combativeness of Negritude is absent from early collections such as *Un champ d'iles* (A Field of Islands, 1953) and *La terre inquiète* (The Anxious Land, 1954). The dense poetic meditations of these early works contain the essence of Glissant's literary project, which is not about providing ideological answers but posing questions "dans la lumière trop diffuse, quand la connaissance est possible et toujours future" (in the too diffuse light when knowing is possible and always to come). Increasingly, Glissant turned from poetry to poetics, from books of poems to poetically derived theory reflecting the larger postcolonial trend in the francophone Caribbean away from poetry that no longer occupies the place it did in the mid-20th c.

Poetry may be overshadowed by prose, but it still retains its prestige because of the need for narrative to reach beyond realistic description. For instance, the novelist Daniel Maximin's *L'invention des desirades* (The Invention of Desirada, 2000) addresses both Caribbean space, as the title suggests, and the need for a verbal inventiveness made possible by poetic lang. Other Antillean writers who attempt to voice the Glissantian ideal of dream space anchored in the real are the prolific Henri Corbin (b. 1934) in works such as *Lieux d'ombre* (Shadow Places, 1991) and *Plongée au gré des deuils* (Descent into the Currents of Loss, 1999) and the densely experimental poet Monchoachi (b. 1946) in *L'Espére-geste* (The Awaited Gesture, 2003). Similar demands on poetic lang. were made by Haitian writers since the 1960s with the short-lived movement Haiti-Littéraire. René Philoctète (1932–90), Anthony Phelps (b. 1928), and Davertige (pseud. of Villard Denis, b. 1940), among others, reacted against the militant Marxist verse of Depestre and saw the early surrealist St. Aude as their literary forebear. The dense elliptical style of George Castera (b. 1936), who returned to Haiti after the fall of Duvalier in 1986, keeps this experimental trad. alive in his prize-winning collection *Le trou du souffleur* (The Prompter's Box, 2006).

**IV. Spanish.** The Hispanic Caribbean is comprised primarily of Cuba, the Dominican Republic, and Puerto Rico. A strong case can be made for incl. in this cultural area the coastal zones of the Circum-Caribbean, i.e., the Gulf Coast of Mexico, the eastern coasts of the Central Am. nations, and the northern coasts of Colombia and Venezuela. However, given the paucity of major poets from these Circum-Caribbean regions, this section focuses on the three Hispanic states of the Greater Antilles. Cuba and the Dominican Republic are independent nations, while Puerto Rico is a "free associated state" of the U.S. Despite the political and economic differences among the three, a common hist. of Sp. colonialism and extractive economies (esp. the plantation), slavery, and racial and ethnic mixing has produced a certain cultural unity (Benítez Rojo).

The most notable features of the poetry of the Hispanic Caribbean are (1) a rich trad. of popular poetry in forms such as *romances*, *décimas*, and *coplas* derived from the Sp. trad., as well as forms such as the *son*, derived from the syncretic Afro-Caribbean trad.; (2) the early introduction of romanticism and modernismo (in Cuba at least) relative to the rest of Latin America; (3) a rich trad. of Afro-Caribbean literary poetry; and (4) the introduction of the *neobaroque strain in Latin Am. letters.

**A. *From the Conquest to the Beginning of the Independence Movements.*** In contrast to Mexico and its archive of Nahuatl poetry from before and during the conquest, there are no examples of Taino poetry. The indigenous peoples of the Hispanic Caribbean were the first to encounter Sp. explorers and did not long survive that encounter. Chroniclers such as Gonzalo

Fernández de Oviedo (*Historia general y natural de las Indias*, 1535) refer to Taino gatherings called *areitos*, dancing and singing rituals in which the recitation of poetry preserved a communal past. However, these poems are lost. The conquistadors were steeped in the poetic trad. of the *romances*. Many anthols. of these *ballads were published in 16th-c. Spain, although the typical method of transmission was oral. Mod. Dominican versions of traditional romances—presumably extant since the early colonial period—were collected in the 20th c. by Pedro Henríquez Ureña and by Edna Garrido.

Hispaniola was the center of Eur. cultural life in the early colonial period, and some of the earliest poems in the New World were written there, often in Lat. The first example of *poesía culta* (learned poetry) in the Hispanic Caribbean is an *ode written in Lat. by Bishop Alessandro Geraldini to celebrate the construction of the cathedral of Santo Domingo in 1523.

Meanwhile, 16th-c. Spain experienced a revolution in poetic form, as the It. *hendecasyllable line, the *terza rima* and *ottava rima* stanza forms, the *sonnet, and other models out of *Petrarchism were imported to Spain by Juan Boscán and Garcilaso de la Vega. These forms—and the courtly ideals and modes of behavior they expressed—quickly became absorbed into the trad. of poesía culta and appeared in the New World. Early examples are the sonnets of the earliest known female poet of the Americas, the nun Sor Leonor de Ovando (fl. 1575).

Most critics would agree that the first major poem of the Hispanic Caribbean trad. is the *Espejo de paciencia* (Mirror of Patience, 1608), a historical *epic written by the Canarian Silvestre de Balboa y Troya de Quesada (1563–1647?), a resident of Puerto Príncipe (mod.-day Camagüey), Cuba. Written in ottava rima, the epic is notable on at least two accounts. First, it is preceded by six laudatory sonnets by local dignitaries, which reflect the existence of an intellectual circle or literary academy in the area of Puerto Príncipe in the early colonial period, surprising given the political marginality of the locale. Second, the poet mixes cl. Gr. mythology with local places and flora (González Echevarría). For Cuban intellectuals, the *Espejo de paciencia* is one of the foundational texts of a transcultural national idiom, of *lo cubano* (Vitier 1958). Inasmuch as hybridity is often seen as a key aspect of the Latin Am. *baroque (*el Barroco de Indias* or "baroque of the Indies"), the *Espejo de paciencia* is viewed as one of the earliest instances.

Of the poets writing in the 17th and 18th cs. in the Hispanic Caribbean, none enjoys the stature of the Mexican nun Sor Juana Inés de la Cruz or even of the Sp. poet in colonial Peru Juan del Valle y Caviedes. Although of little significance outside their country of origin and the search for beginnings, for the 17th c. one can mention the Puerto Rican *criollo* (creole) poet Francisco de Ayerra y Santa María (1630–1708) and the Seville-born Dominican Fernando Díez de Leiva (fl. 1582), and in the 18th c., the Puerto Rican satirist Miguel Cabrera, and the Cuban poets Juan Miguel Castro Palomino (1722–88), José Rodríguez Ucres (known as Capacho, d. before 1788), and Félix Veranés, among others. It is not until the late 18th and early 19th cs. that poets of relevance for the mod. period appear, foremost among them the neoclassical Cuban poet Manuel Zequeira (1764–1846), whose "Oda a la piña" (Ode to the Pineapple, 1808) is a testimony to the growing importance of local landscape and culture.

B. *The Nineteenth Century: Romanticism, Modernismo, and the Struggle for Independence.* While romanticism in Germany and England took root at the end of the 18th c. and the beginning of the 19th, it is a somewhat later phenomenon in France, Italy, and Spain. As a general rule, it appears even later in Latin America, coinciding generally with the end of the wars of independence and the early postwar years but stretching across the 19th c. Yet the major Hispanic Caribbean poet of the romantic period and one of the most important romantic poets in the Sp. lang., the Cuban José María Heredia (1803–39), was a poetic innovator who had already composed many of his major poems by the mid-1820s. Like many other Latin Am. romantics, Heredia was inspired by revolutionary politics; he spent many years in exile for his political activities and commitment to Cuban independence. Heredia's poetry breaks with the balanced tone and measured pace of his neoclassical antecedents. Like many romantics, he represents nature as an overwhelming force that awes him and puts him in contact with the divine. Nature is bound as well to the native country and embodies the desire for independence and autochthony. Other major poets of the first wave of romanticism in Cuba include Gertrudis de Avellaneda (1814–73), better known as a dramatist and novelist (esp. for the antislavery novel *Sab* [1841], 11 years earlier than Harriet Beecher Stowe's *Uncle Tom's Cabin*); the mulatto poet Gabriel de la Concepción Valdés (known as Plácido, 1809–44), author of the romance "Jicotencatl" (1838) and a number of exceptional *letrillas* (incl. "La flor de la caña" [The Flower of the Sugar Cane], 1838), and José Jacinto Milanés (1814–63), a reclusive autodidact who was also a playwright. A second wave of romantic poets in Cuba around midcentury includes Rafael María de Mendive (1821–86), leader of an important *tertulia* (salon) and teacher of José Martí; Joaquín Lorenzo Luaces (1826–67); Juan Clemente Zenea (1832–71); and Luisa Pérez de Zambrana (1837–1922). Of these, Zenea is the most noteworthy, known both for his *love poetry (esp. the elegiac "Fidelia," 1860) and his patriotic verse. His involvement in the movement for Cuban independence resulted in repeated exile and, finally, execution.

The romantic movement in Puerto Rico coincides largely with this second wave of Cuban romantics. The standout is José Gautier Benítez (1851–80), who died young of tuberculosis but managed to produce many of the best-known patriotic verses of 19th-c. Puerto Rico. Having studied in Toledo, he knew Sp. poetry well, esp. that of Gustavo Adolfo Bécquer. The object of his love, however, tends to be the island; nostalgia and longing are the dominant themes of his work. Many Puerto Rican poets of the second half of the century continued in the romantic mode and, like the Cuban romantics, were similarly involved in the island's movement for independence. Lola Rodríguez de Tío (1843–1924) is notable as the first Puerto Rican woman poet with an extensive body of work and a strong believer in independence. Author of the original lyrics to "La Borriqueña" (1868), the national *anthem, she cultivated the stanza form called the *copla*. Francisco Gonzalo Marín (known as Pachín, 1863–97) ended up as a fierce militant for independence, a friend and collaborator of José Martí, after beginning his political life working for a limited autonomy from Spain. His best-known poems (from *Romances* [1892], and *En la arena* [1898]) are clearly in the patriotic mode.

One of the most interesting features of 19th-c. Hispanic Caribbean lit. is the movement toward a local, nativist poetry, emphasizing nature, country folk, the indigenous peoples who lived in the region at the time of the conquest, and popular poetic forms such as the copla and the décima. This autochthonous, *criollista* poetry played a significant role in the construction of national cultures at a time when the islands of the Hispanic Caribbean remained, with the Philippines, Spain's last colonies. In Puerto Rico, Manuel Alonso's (1822–89) book *El gíbaro* (1849) is an early representative of *cuadros de costumbres* (literary sketches of customs) mixed with creolist poetry that adopts the perspective and dialect of the poor *campesinos*, while Daniel de Rivera's (1824–58?) "Agueynaba el bravo" (Agueynaba the Brave, 1854) expressed a fervor for latter-day political independence through the representation of a historical indigenous theme. Indeed, for José Fornaris (1827–90), creator of the *siboneyista* movement in Cuba, the theme of the indigenous inhabitants was appropriate at that moment because the early inhabitants of the island felt the same love of nature and suffered under Sp. oppression as did mod. Cubans. Fornaris's 1855 *Cantos del Siboney* was one of the most popular books of poetry of the time. However, the décimas of Juan Cristóbal Nápoles Fajardo (known as El Cucalambé, 1829–62?), published in his only book of poetry, *Rumores del Hórmigo* (Sounds of Hórmigo, 1856), are the culmination of the movement, inasmuch as they seemed to give voice to country folk (the *guajiros*) and quickly became part of popular culture. In the Dominican Republic, the country's major romantic poet, José Joaquín Pérez (1845–1900), wrote in this indigenous vein in his "Fantasías indígenas" (Indigenous Fantasies, 1877), while Juan Antonio Alix (1833–1918) was a more popular poet who cultivated the décima in the country dialect of the Cibao region.

In the Caribbean, as is often the case in Latin America, schools of poetry that in Europe tended to follow each other in rough succession and in reaction overlapped and coexisted. Thus, in the Dominican Republic, Salomé Ureña (1850–97) followed neoclassical precepts late into the 19th c. and is known for her well-constructed civic verse, incl. the hymn to tropical nature "La llegada del invierno" (The Arrival of Winter) and the elegiac "Ruinas." Influenced by the educator and philosopher Eugenio María de Hostos, she founded the first center of higher education for women on the island.

Associated most often internationally with the name of its most vocal exponent, the Nicaraguan Rubén Darío, the literary movement *modernismo* took the Hispanic world of letters by storm at the end of the 19th c.. Cuba boasts two of the earliest *modernista* writers in Martí (1853–95) and Julián del Casal (1863–93), and the first clearly *modernista* work, Martí's small volume of verse titled *Ismaelillo* (1882), which preceded Darío's *Azul . . .* by six years. Active on political and literary fronts, Martí was the major catalyst of the last Cuban War of Independence from Spain (1895–98) and would likely have become the first president of the Cuban Republic if he had not been killed early in the conflict. A writer in many genres, he published two volumes of poetry in his lifetime (*Ismaelillo* and *Versos sencillos* [Simple Verses], 1892) and left several mss. of poetry at his death (*Versos libres, Flores del destierro*, and uncollected verse), which were published posthumously. Martí also edited magazines such as the literary *La edad de oro*, a magazine for children, and *Patria*, a magazine dedicated to Cuban independence from Spain. Like most of the major modernista poets, Martí observed the important currents of Fr. poetry (*Parnassianism and symbolism, in particular) as well as the classic Sp. trad., but as he argues in the important essay "Nuestra América" (1891), he emphatically rejected servile imitation of foreign models. Thus, while he embraced the Parnassian attention to form and love of color, he yoked it to the symbolist enthusiasm for the image and suggestion, while also underscoring the social involvement of the poet and the social relevance of verse. This unique combination of elements distances his poetry from the elitist *aestheticism of Darío's *Azul . . .* and *Prosas profanas*, as well as from the verse of Casal, José Asunción Silva, Manuel Gutiérrez Nájera, and the other early modernistas.

While *Ismaelillo* consecrated Martí as one of the leading voices of the new poetry, it was the *Versos sencillos* that garnered the respect and adulation of a more general public, with the apparent simplicity of its themes—nature, friendship, sincerity—and a traditional *octosyllable. However, the volume only seems simple. The attention to form results at times in a complex mirroring of signifier and signified, and the book is filled with startling, multivalent images. Between the two, highly polished books that Martí published, he wrote the poems he called his *Versos libres* (Free Verse, 1882), first published posthumously in 1913. These are generally written in what he called "hirsute hendecasyllables," and like most hendecasyllabic poetry in Sp., they seem more sonorous and philosophically weighty than the shorter verse forms. One of Martí's most personal, expressionistic works, the book emphasizes above all a certain disorderly authenticity of emotion and form, heralding the works of 20th-c. poets like Neruda. Martí is clearly the most important poet and writer of the Hispanic Caribbean in the 19th c. and an influence on poets and political thinkers to the present day.

The other major modernista poet of the region is Casal, also Cuban but very different from Martí.

Whereas Martí led a political life from a young age and entered into conflicts with the Sp. colonial authorities that led to prison, exile, and a peripatetic existence, Casal led a literary and sedentary city life, leaving Havana only for one brief trip to Spain. Collaborator in a number of literary and popular magazines (above all, *La Habana Elegante* and the popular *La Caricatura*), Casal published three books of poetry: *Hojas al viento* (Leaves to the Wind, 1890), *Nieve* (Snow, 1891), and *Bustos y rimas* (Busts and Rhymes, 1893). This last work was published after his early death from tuberculosis, just short of his 30th birthday. Influenced greatly by Charles Baudelaire and the Fr. Parnassians, enthralled by the paintings of Gustave Moreau that he recreated in a series of ten sonnets ("Mi museo ideal," My Ideal Museum), Casal echoes these models but transforms them into something new. Firmly within the aestheticist vein of modernismo and apparently distanced from the sociopolitical realities of his time, he has too often been contrasted with a "virile," socially engaged Martí and discounted as artificial, effete, and somehow less Cuban (by Vitier, among many others). Recently critics and younger Cuban poets have analyzed Casal through the lens of queer theory and deconstructed the Martí/Casal dichotomy (Montero, Morán), creating a much richer picture of this fine poet. Bonifacio Byrne (1861–1936) is Cuba's third modernista and author of the immensely popular patriotic poem "Mi bandera" (My Flag, 1901).

Modernismo arrived late in Puerto Rico, in part because of the Sp.-Am. War of 1898 but had strong adherents in José de Diego (1866–1918), Virgilio Dávila (1869–1943), and above all Luis Lloréns Torres (1876–1944). In tune with the patriotic, *mundonovista* strain of the later Darío, these poets adopted the stylistic innovations of the modernistas to exalt their native land (see esp. Lloréns Torres's 1913 poem "Canción de las Antillas"). In reaction to the U.S. invasion of 1898, they show a strong desire to defend what they perceive to be the essences of Puerto Ricanness. Reflecting their generally patrician roots, they cultivate a strong Hispanophilia in their work, and the theme of the *jíbaro* (country dweller supposedly of white, Hispanic ancestry) recurs. In the Dominican Republic, modernismo is also belated and dictates the style of poets such as Fabio Fiallo (1866–1942) and Enrique Henríquez (1859–1940), but the major figure at the turn of the 20th century is Gastón Fernando Deligne (1861–1913), a psychological realist in the mode of the Sp. poet Ramón de Campoamor. His poem "Ololoi" (1907) is a stirring meditation on the conflict between liberty and the oppression of dictatorship.

**C. *The Twentieth Century and Beyond*.** While two important poets, Regino E. Boti (1878–1958) and José Manuel Poveda (1888–1926), were active in the first decades of the First Cuban Republic, these were quiet times for poetry. Boti in particular matures in his style from the modernismo of his first book, *Arabescos mentales* (Mental Arabesques, 1913), through his most coherent collection, *El mar y la montaña* (The Sea and the Mountains, 1921), to the avant-garde verses of *Kodak-Ensueño* (Kodak Daydream, 1928) and *Kindergarten* (1930). The poetic scene gained complexity during the difficult 1920s, with the introduction of the avant-garde at a time of increased political instability, economic troubles, and the ferment of student and workers' movements. The *Grupo Minorista*, incl. the painter Eduardo Abela, the future novelist Alejo Carpentier, the essayists Jorge Mañach and Juan Marinello, and the poets José Zacarías Tallet (1893–1989) and Rubén Martínez Villena (1899–1934), was primarily responsible for the introduction of the avant-garde in Cuba; a number of these figures edited the major avant-garde jour. *Revista de Avance* (1927–30). The experimental avant-garde was short lived, however, and was quickly replaced by two major trends: social poetry with early contributions from Felipe Pichardo Moya (1892–1957), Agustín Acosta (1886–1979), and Regino Pedroso (1896–1983; "Salutación fraterna al taller mecánico" [Fraternal Salutation to the Garage], 1927); and *pure poetry, inspired by the theories of Henri Bremond and exemplified most clearly by the poetry of Mariano Brull (1891–1956; *Poemas en menguante* [Waning Poems], 1928, and *Solo de rosa* [Only Rose], 1941), Eugenio Florit (1903–99; *Trópico*, 1930; and *Doble acento* [Double Accent], 1937), and Emilio Ballagas (1908–54; *Júbilo y fuga* [Joy and Flight], 1931; and *Sabor eterno* [Eternal Taste], 1939). Brull is known for his focus on sound, esp. the *jitanjáfora*, a playful use of nonsemantic sounds to achieve rhythmic effects in poetry, while Ballagas was one of the earliest practitioners of literary *afrocubanismo*.

The avant-garde is poorly represented in the Dominican Republic, although some critics (Gutiérrez) have alleged that Vigil Díaz's (1880–1961) "movement" *vedrinismo*, announced in 1912, preceded Vicente Huidobro's *creationism by a few years. Lacking a true *manifesto and with ultimately only two adherents, vedrinismo is responsible for the introduction of *free verse into Dominican poetry, with Díaz's 1917 poem "Arabesco." The most important Dominican movement of the 1920s—Domingo Moreno Jimenes (1894–1986), Rafael Augusto Zorrilla (1892–1937), and Andrés Aveliño's (1900–74) *Postumismo*—had an ambiguous relationship with the avant-garde. Intent on creating a more mod. and more Dominican poetry (a reaction in part to the U.S. occupation of the island from 1916 to 1924), they consciously broke with what they considered an outmoded, Eurocentric national trad., cultivating free verse and opening poetic lang. to a wider register. In this rupture with trad., they were clearly avant-garde, although they programmatically rejected the *acrobacia azul* (blue acrobatics) of the more experimental "isms" (*Manifiesto postumista*), as well as the masterworks of the Western trad. Moreno Jimenes (1894–1986) was the undisputed leader of the group. His poetry is avowedly colloquial and populist, although his most moving works are profoundly personal poems that address the theme of death ("Poema de la hija reintegrada" [Poem for the Reintegrated Daughter], 1934).

In Puerto Rico, the avant-garde found early adherents in two movements. The first, *Diepalismo*, launched in 1921, was an ephemeral movement led by its only two practitioners, José I. de Diego Padró (1899–1974) and Luis Palés Matos (1898–1959), who privileged *onomatopoeia as the basis for radically new verse. (The name of the group is a combination of the patronymics of the two poets.) The other avant-garde movement, of more lasting consequence, took the bombastic title of *El atalaya de los dioses* (Watchtower of the Gods) and was led from 1928 on by the gifted poet and radical nationalist Clemente Soto Vélez (1905–93). Intent on breaking with a "mummified" trad., these poets rebelled against the remnants of modernismo as well as *realism and academic poetry. Like many of the other *atalayistas*, Soto Vélez was involved early on in the militant nationalist movement led by Pedro Albizu Campos and finally settled in New York. His later works, *Abrazo interno* (Internal Embrace, 1954), *Árboles* (Trees, 1955), *Caballo de palo* (Wooden Horse, 1959), and *La tierra prometida* (Promised Land, 1979), continued to engage in ling. experimentalism and to exploit the surreal images of the avant-garde (see SURREALISM).

Two other poets who came of age poetically among the avant-garde in the 1910s and 1920s deserve mention. Evaristo Ribera Chevremont (1896–1976) was not affiliated with any movement but early on was much influenced by the reigning modernista movement and the Hispanophilia of writers such as Lloréns Torres. After five years in Spain, where he was in direct contact with *ultraism and Huidobro's creationism, he returned to the island as an ardent supporter of the avant-garde. He is widely credited with introducing free verse to the national poetry and, with a career spanning six decades, is one of the most prolific of Puerto Rican poets. Juan Antonio Corretjer (1908–85), a fellow member of the Atalaya group, spent five years in a U.S. prison for his work with Albizu Campos's Nationalist Party. Committed at first to the nationalist project and later to the creation of a socialist state, his poetry is a "telluric *neocriollismo*" that combines the Latin Americanism of the late Darío with the epic ambition of Lloréns Torres (Márquez). The avant-garde is not just a historically delimited movement but a rupturalist, modernizing attitude that can recur at any moment. José María Lima (1934–2009) of the Generation of the 1960s and Joserramón Melendes (b. 1952) of the Generation of the 1970s both exemplify an experimentalist, avant-garde mode.

The Afro-Caribbean poetic movement called *negrismo, poesía negra, poesía afroantillana*, or in Cuba, *afrocubanismo* constitutes one of the most significant devels. in 20th-c. Latin Am. poetry. Incl. poetry both about and by Afro-Caribbeans, it comes into being in the mid-1920s and culminates in the 1930s and 1940s. It is an essential part of a regionalist vein of avant-garde poetry, with analogues in Federico García Lorca's Andalusian gypsy ballads and Jorge Luis Borges's early *ultraísta* verse, and it took energy from parallel movements in the U.S. (the Harlem Renaissance) and Eur. interest in the "primitive" and all things Af. Palés

Matos began publishing his "black" poems in literary magazines in 1925, although they were not collected until the much later publication of his *Tuntún de pasa y griferia: Poesía afroantillana* (Tomtom of Kinky Hair and Black Things: Afro-Antillean Poetry, 1937). Like Ballagas, Ramón Guirao (1908–49), and some of the early cultivators of *afrocubanista* poetry in Cuba, Palés Matos was white and has been criticized by some as creating stereotypical images of Afro-Caribbean peoples. Nevertheless, his poetry has been immensely popular in Puerto Rico and elsewhere; rhythmic and onomatopoeic, it is esp. apt for recitation or declamation. This poetry responds to a vision of the nation as syncretic and transcultural and was daring at the time in light of the racist attitudes of many of the creole elite who saw the essence of Puerto Ricanness in the island's Hispanic—i.e., not Af.—heritage (Pedreira), when that cultural complex was experiencing the disintegrating influence of an overwhelming U.S. economic and political imperialism. Recent critics have done much to clarify Palés's historical specificity and his ludic irony and to give a balanced appreciation of his work beyond the *poesía afroantillana* (López Baralt, Ríos Avila).

In Cuba, Afro-Cuban poets (Plácido and Manzano [1797–1854], in particular) had been publishing since the romantic period, but afrocubanismo begins with the publication of Ramón Guirao's poem "Bailadora de rumba" (Rumba Dancer) in early 1928, followed soon after by Tallet's "La rumba." The next decade saw a flood of poems on Afro-Cuban themes, by both black and white poets. The most important and enduring of these was Nicolás Guillén (1902–89), whose early collections adapted the Afro-Cuban syncretic musical form of the "son" to literary language. His *Motivos de son* (Motifs from the "Son," 1930), *Sóngoro cosongo* (1931), and *West Indies, Ltd.* (1934) are clearly within the afrocubanista vein. By Guillén's second book, he is already proclaiming *mulatez* or the mixing of black and white as the essential process forming Cuban national culture, challenging the widely accepted view of national culture as rooted in the Hispanic and symbolized by the country folk or guajiros. This poetry signals the beginning of a sea change in race relations and notions of national belonging. Although afrocubanismo as a literary movement was largely over by the late 1930s, Guillén continued to publish and evolve as a poet. His poetry shows a sophisticated understanding of the trad. and possibilities of Sp. verse forms, from the Afro-Cuban *son* to the *alexandrine sonnet to *elegies, ballads, and all the way to the postmod. *pastiche. He links this lyrical skill to an authentic concern for social justice, racial equality, and historical analysis, which first alienated him from the dictatorial Batista regime and later made him a favorite of the Cuban Revolution. His poetry, however, has enduring importance, above and beyond any political affiliation.

At this time, the Dominican Republic was suffering under the dictatorship of one of the most brutal and long-lived regimes in Latin America, that of Rafael Leónidas Trujillo (1930–61). Many of the major poets in the post-avant-garde period wrote some of their most important works in exile, incl. two that align with the *poesía negra*, Manuel del Cabral (1907–99) and Tomás Hernández Franco (1904–52). Del Cabral is one of the towering figures of 20th-c. Dominican poetry and has often been compared to the major figures of the Latin Am. avant-garde such as César Vallejo, Neruda, Huidobro, and Guillén. His *Ocho poemas negros* (Eight Black Poems, 1935) and *Trópico negro* (1941) were signal contributions to the devel. of Dominican negrismo, although it is his book centered on the figure of the *campesino* from the Cibao region, *Compadre Mon* (1942), that has garnered the most critical attention. Del Cabral is a protean poet with a plethora of styles and subject matter, incl. the later devel. of a deep metaphysical strain (esp. in *Los huéspedes secretos* [Secret Guests], 1950) and a strong anti-imperialist stance (*La isla ofendida* [The Offended Island], 1965). Franco is known primarily for the mythical epic *Yelidá* (1942), where he insists on the superiority of racial mixing embodied in a sensual *mulata* born of a Norwegian expatriate and a Haitian woman.

In the Cuba of the latter half of the 1930s, as the afrocubanismo movement was losing momentum, a singular poet, José Lezama Lima (1910–76), transformed the poetic scene with the publication of his first poem, *Muerte de Narciso* (Death of Narcissus, 1937). Stimulated by his readings in the Sp. Golden Age poets but forging its own style, Lezama Lima's poetry baffled critics with its *difficulty, its *artifice, and its seeming distance from the sociopolitical realities of the time. He followed this first publication with four more books of poetry over the next four decades: *Enemigo rumor* (Enemy Rumor, 1941), *Aventuras sigilosas* (Stealthy Adventures, 1945), *La fijeza* (Fixity, 1949), and *Dador* (Giver, 1960). His final collection, *Fragmentos a su imán* (Fragments to Their Magnet), was published posthumously in 1977. Lezama Lima often takes other works of art as his starting point; his work in general is densely allusive and assimilative. Some of his best poems ("Rapsodia para el mulo" [Rhapsody for the Mule], "Pensamientos en La Habana" [Thoughts in Havana]) have much to say about Cuban national identity and the neocolonial dynamics of the time. While showing a penchant for expansive free verse, he also exploited a variety of poetic forms (the *prose poem, the sonnet, the décima) over the course of his career, and although he is largely faithful to the neobaroque difficulty he first embraced in *Muerte de Narciso*, the later, posthumous poems are more luminous and personal. Lezama Lima became more known outside Cuba in the 1960s, after the publication of his monumental novel *Paradiso* (1966). In fact, there is no clear line between his poetic production and his prose, and *Paradiso* is considered by many to be the clearest exposition of the poetic system developed in his poetry and his rich body of essays. Lezama Lima's importance to Cuban and Latin Am. lit. is based in part on his own production and in part on his role as ed. of a series of influential literary jours.; the most important of these was *Orígenes* (1944–56). This jour. was the focal point for a group of writers, artists, musicians, and critics, incl. the poets Virgilio Piñera (1912–79), Cintio Vitier (1921–2009), Eliseo Diego (1920–94), Fina García Marruz (b. 1923), and Gastón Baquero (1914–97). Each of these *Origenistas* is an important figure in his or her own right. Of these, Piñera, a reluctant and confrontational member of the group, is best known as a novelist, short-story writer, and dramatist, although his important long poem *La isla en peso* (The Whole Island, 1943) bears comparison to high points of Caribbean poetry such as Césaire's *Cahier d'un retour au pays natal* and Del Cabral's *Compadre Mon* in its negative vision of an asphyxiating island life (Anderson). After Lezama Lima, Diego is perhaps the most gifted poet, deservedly well-known outside Cuba for collections such as *En la Calzada de Jesús del Monte* (On Jesús del Monte Avenue, 1949), *Por los extraños pueblos* (Through Strange Towns, 1958), *Muestrario del mundo o Libro de las maravillas de Boloña* (Showcase of the World or Book of the Wonders of Boloña, 1968), and *Los días de tu vida* (The Days of Your Life, 1977).

In the late 1950s and after the triumph of the Cuban Revolution in 1959, the Origenista poets—esp. Lezama Lima—were roundly criticized for their supposed escapism and lack of social concern. Younger poets gathered around the polemical figure of Piñera and a series of jours. that took the place of *Orígenes* as major venues for Cuban poetry and lit. crit. (*Ciclón, Lunes de Revolución*). The Cuban Revolution in general had a profound impact on the state of poetry. On the one hand, there was initially a widespread enthusiasm for democratization and social justice (incl. educational reform and a literacy campaign), and poetry and art in general were seen by many as tools in this collective project. On the other hand, the cultural politics of the Castro regime favored direct communication with the masses and support of the revolutionary agenda, and this support became more and more compulsory over the course of the first two decades after 1959. As a result, the group of poets known as the Generation of the 1950s, as well as younger poets that came of age in the 1960s and 1970s, shared a colloquial diction and conversational tone. Of this earlier generation, Roberto Fernández Retamar (b. 1930) stands out for his poetry (*Con las mismas manos, 1949–1962* [With These Same Hands] and *Hemos construido una alegría olvidada, 1949–1988* [We Have Built a Forgotten Joy], among many other volumes), influential essays (esp. "Calibán," 1971), and the direction of the important cultural magazine *Casa de las Américas*.

Among poets who began publishing in the 1960s, Heberto Padilla (1932–2000) and Nancy Morejón (b. 1944) have received the most critical attention. Padilla, at first an ardent supporter of the revolution whose early volume *El justo tiempo humano* (A Just Human Time, 1962) has much in common with Retamar's poetry and intellectual stance, arrived at a much more critical attitude in his 1968 *Fuera del juego* (Out of the Game), a complex, ironic collection that won an important prize that year in Cuba but catapulted Padilla into conflict with the regime. Three years later, he was detained for supposedly counterrevolutionary activities,

prompting a firestorm of criticism of the Cuban government by prominent Latin Am. and Eur. intellectuals, many of whom had previously been positive toward the revolution. Ultimately released from prison after a public self-criticism, Padilla was incessantly watched in the years that followed and allowed to leave the island for the U.S. only in 1980. In the U.S., he published two bilingual collections, *Legacies* (1982) and *A Fountain, a House of Stone* (1991), which confirmed his status as a strong poet in the conversational mode. Morejón follows in a line of important Cuban women poets such as García Marruz and Dulce María Loynaz (1902–97), but her closest model is Guillén. Of Afro-Cuban descent, Morejón began publishing after the revolution, and she has remained faithful to its ideals over the years. Author of the much anthologized poems "Mujer negra" (Black Woman) and "Amo a mi amo" (I Love My Owner), she has given women of Afro-Cuban ancestry a critical visibility they lacked in the past. Three other poets of the era 1959–80 deserve mention, although they have published the majority of their work outside the island: Severo Sarduy (1937–93), José Kozer (b. 1940), and Reinaldo Arenas (1943–90). The first two are consummate practitioners of the neobaroque mode initiated by Lezama Lima. Although known primarily as a novelist, Sarduy in his finely crafted poetry adopts the stanzaic forms and the diction of the baroque while referring to novel themes such as homosexual love or the gods of the Cuban syncretic religion, Santería. Kozer's poetry, neobaroque in its complexity, is a moving testimony to his Cuban-Jewish roots. Arenas is also primarily a novelist, but his epic poem "El central" is both daringly experimental in form and radical in its bitter denunciation of oppression.

During the 1940s in the Dominican Republic, a group emerged which shared some characteristics with the Cuban Origenistas, although lacking poets of the stature of Lezama Lima, Piñera, or Diego. This is the *Poesía sorprendida* (Surprised Poetry) group, which coalesced around the jour. of the same name, pub. 1943–47, and which programmatically left behind the traditional Dominican emphasis on autochthony. Openly assimilative, avowedly universalist, these poets embraced a wide range of world lit. The most important members of the group were Franklin Mieses Burgos (1907–76), Aída Cartagena Portalatín (1918–94), Freddy Gatón Arce (1920–94), Manuel Rueda (1921–99), and Antonio Fernández Spencer (1922–95), many of whom were quite prolific (esp. Gatón Arce, the most surrealist of these). Given the repressive nature of the Trujillo government, most of these poets adopted an oblique style and avoided direct criticism of Dominican society or the regime. Several other important Dominican poets active at this time did not affiliate with the sorprendida group, incl. the aforementioned del Cabral and Hernández Franco as well as Héctor Incháustegui Cabral (1912–79) and Pedro Mir (1913–2000). All these are social poets in the best sense of the term. Incháustegui Cabral's best-known collection is *Poemas de una sola angustia* (Poems of a Single Anguish, 1940), in which he took on the cause of the poor and powerless and leveled a rather direct critique at the Trujillo regime. When he was not punished for this by the dictator, he lost faith in the power of poetry to effect political change; he later became one of the few intellectuals who collaborated actively in the government. Mir, on the other hand, was consistent in his critique of Dominican elites and the Trujillo dictatorship, at the price of exile. An identification with poor workers and a spirited denunciation of U.S. imperialism is evident in most of his poetry. Recognized abroad as one of the most important voices of the Hispanic Caribbean, he gains his reputation primarily from *Hay un país en el mundo* (There Is a Country in the World, 1949) and the *Contracanto a Walt Whitman* (1952). The next few generations, the poets of the 1960s and the postwar group, were caught up in the political turmoil of that eventful decade. Their poetry is more often more political than literary. The exceptions are Alexis Gómez Rosa (b. 1950) and Cayo Claudio Espinal (b. 1955), both of whom have matured into exceptional poets unafraid of experimentation.

While Puerto Rico had no group comparable to Cuba's Orígenes or the Dominican Republic's Poesía sorprendida from the late 1930s to the 1950s, it produced two singular poets, Francisco Matos Paoli (1915–2000) and Julia de Burgos (1914–53). Matos Paoli's prolific work extends from the 1930s to the mid-1990s and shows a keen appreciation for Sp. Golden Age poets and the Generation of 1927 (esp. Jorge Guillén), along with Mallarmé and the Fr. symbolists. An ardent nationalist, he was arrested for his support of the 1950 uprising and sentenced to 30 years of prison in San Juan, although he was released in 1955 after a mental breakdown in long periods of solitary confinement. His work is characterized by its adherence to the precepts of pure poetry and its *hermeticism. De Burgos launched her career in 1937 with *Poemas exactos a mí misma* (Exact Poems to Myself), followed by *Poema en veinte surcos* (Poem in Twenty Furrows, 1938) and *Canción de la vida sencilla* (Song of the Simple Life, 1939). In the early 1940s, she completed *El mar y tú* (The Sea and You), although it was not published until 1954, a year after her early death in poverty in New York from alcoholism, depression, and illness. Thoroughly nationalist, De Burgos's most famous poems (such as "Río Grande de Loíza") express a yearning for a fusion with the island landscape, esp. the waters of rivers and sea, a theme that has made her quite popular. Her later verse anticipates the alienation of the Latino immigrant in the impersonal cities of the U.S. and, in its nonconformism, prepares for the feminist poets of the 1960s and 1970s such as Rosario Ferré (b. 1938) and Olga Nolla (1938–2001), as well as the younger Vanessa Droz (b. 1952), all of whom continued to publish important collections into the late 1990s and beyond. Of the same generation as Droz, Manuel Ramos Otero (1948–90) was a complex, iconoclastic writer who deserves to be better known outside the island. Writing from an openly gay perspective, he engages the Sp. baroque trad. in expressionist meditations on death and disease (notably the AIDS epidemic) in his posthumous *Invitación al polvo*

(Invitation to Dust, 1991). José Luis Vega (b. 1948), and Aurea María Sotomayor (b. 1951), also of this generation, are important critics as well as poets. Sotomayor's *Diseño del ala* (Wing Design, 2005) confirms her as a major voice in Caribbean poetry more generally.

Of the younger poets, the Cuban Generation of the 1980s has several standouts, incl. Juan Carlos Flores (b. 1962), Damaris Calderón (b. 1967), Víctor Fowler Calzada (b. 1960), and Antonio José Ponte (b. 1964), among others; several of these are also noted essayists. Reina María Rodríguez (b. 1952) and Francisco Morán (b. 1952), although older than this group, have been close fellow travelers and unifying figures. These writers have not shied away from hermetic lang., eroticism, and philosophical questions and have actively engaged an antihegemonic, less obviously political strand of the Cuban poetic trad. (Julián del Casal, Lezama Lima, and Virgilio Piñera, as opposed to Martí and Guillén). In Puerto Rico, the same generation has resistantly engaged the postmod., recognizing the failure of the dreams of independence and of socialism, while also seeing the pitfalls of neoliberalism (Martínez-Márquez and Cancel). The most important figures here are Rafael Acevedo (b. 1960), Eduardo Lalo (b. 1960), and Mayra Santos Febres (b. 1966). Lalo's postmod. cultural critiques (*Dónde* [Where], 2005), combining photography and essay, add to the interest in this multifaceted artist. The dominant voice of the Generation of the 1980s in the Dominican Republic is José Mármol (b. 1960), poet and essayist, whose training as a philosopher is apparent in prose poems that embrace both ling. and conceptual difficulty.

No review of Hispanic Caribbean poetry would be complete without mention of poetry in Eng. or mixing Eng. and Sp., much of it written by immigrants to the U.S. or their descendants. For more here, see NUYORICAN POETRY.

*See* AFRICA, POETRY OF; AFRICAN AMERICAN POETRY; AVANT-GARDE POETICS; COLONIAL POETICS; FRANCE, POETRY OF; INDIGENOUS AMERICAS, POETRY OF THE; JAZZ POETRY; POSTCOLONIAL POETICS; ROMANTIC AND POSTROMANTIC POETRY AND POETICS; SPAIN, POETRY OF; SPANISH AMERICA, POETRY OF.

■ **Dutch.** *Anthologies*: *Schwarzer Orpheus*, ed. J. Jahn (1954); *Creole Drum*, ed. J. Voorhoeve and U. M. Lichtveld (1975); *Cosecha Arubiano*, ed. F. Booi et al. (1983); *Spiegel van de Surinaamse poezie*, ed. M. van Kempen (1995); "Special Issue: Caribbean Literature from Suriname, the Netherlands Antilles, Aruba, and the Netherlands," *Callaloo* 21.3 (1998); *Literatura en español en Curazao al cambio del siglo: En busca de textos desconocidos de la segunda mitad del siglo XIX y de las primeras décadas del siglo XX*, ed. L. Echteld (1999); *Nieuwe oogst*, ed. L. van Mulier (2002). **Criticism and History**: A. G. Broek, *The Rise of a Caribbean Island's Literature* (1990); F. R. Jones, "A Leak in the Silence: The Poetry of Hans Faverey"; M. van Kempen, "Vernacular Literature in Suriname"; and I. van Putte-de Windt, "Caribbean Poetry in Papiamentu," *Callaloo* 21 (1998); A. J. Arnold, *A History of Literature in the Caribbean*, v. 2 (2001)—esp. T. Damsteegt, "East Indian

Surinamese Poetry and Its Languages"; V. February, "The Surinamese Muse: Reflections on Poetry"; and J. J. Oversteegen, "Strategies and Stratagems of Some Dutch-Antillean Writers"; I. Phaf-Rheinberger, "The Crystalline Essence of 'Dutch' Caribbean Literatures," *Review* 74 (2007).
■ **English**. *Criticism and History*: R. Abrahams *The Man-of-Words in the West Indies* (1983); L. Brown, *West Indian Poetry* (1984); P. A. Roberts, *West Indians and Their Language* (1988); A. Benitez, *The Repeating Island: The Caribbean and the Postmodern Perspective*, trans. J. E. Maranis (1992); E. Chamberlin, *Come Back to Me My Language* (1993); *Dictionary of Caribbean English Usage*, ed. S.R.R. Allsopp (1997); L. Breiner, *An Introduction to West Indian Poetry* (1998); E. A. Williams, *Anglophone Caribbean Poetry, 1970–2001* (2002)—annotated bibl. *Anthologies in English*: E. K. Brathwaite, *The Arrivants* (1973); *Penguin Book of Caribbean Verse in English*, ed. P. Burnett (1986).
■ **French**. M. Condé, *La Poesie Antillaise* (1977); J. M. Dash, *Literature and Ideology in Haiti* (1981); G. Gouraige, *Littérature et société en Haiti* (1987); J. M. Dash, "Engagement, Exile and Errance: Some Trends in Haitian Poetry, 1946–1986," *Callaloo* 15 (1992); *A History of Literature in the Caribbean, Vol. 1: Francophone and Hispanophone Regions*, ed. A. James Arnold (1994); M. Gallagher, "Contemporary French Caribbean Poetry: The Poetics of Reference," *Forum of Modern Language Studies* 45 (2004).
■ **Spanish**. *Anthologies*: *Versiones dominicanas de romances españoles*, ed. E. Garrido (1946); *Antología de la poesía cubana*, ed. J. Lezama Lima, (1965); *Lecturas puertorriqueñas: Poesía*, ed. M. Arce de Vazquez, L. Gallego, L. de Arrigoitia (1968); *Poesía criollista y siboneísta*, ed. J. Orta Ruíz (1976); *La Generación de los años 50*, ed. L. Suardíaz and D. Chericián (1984); *Antología de la literatura dominicana*, ed. J. Alcántara Almánzar (1988); *Publicaciones y opiniones de La Poesía Sorprendida* (1988); *Antología de poesía puertorriqueña*, ed. R. A. Moreira (1992); *Para entendernos: inventario poético puertorriqueño: Siglos XIX y XX*, ed. E. Barradas (1992); *Antología histórica de la poesía dominicana del siglo XX, 1912–1995*, ed. F. Gutiérrez (1998); *El límite volcado: Antología de la Generación de Poetas de los Ochenta*, ed. A. Martínez-Márquez and M. R. Cancel (2000); *La casa se mueve: Antología de la nueva poesía cubana*, ed. A. Luque and J. Aguado (2000); *Poesía cubana de la colonia*, ed. S. Arias (2002); *Poesía cubana del siglo XX*, ed. J. J. Barquet and N. Codina (2002); *Puerto Rican Poetry*, ed. and trans. R. Márquez (2007). *Criticism and History*: M. Menéndez y Pelayo, *Antología de poetas hispano-americanos*, v. 1–4 (1894); A. S. Pedreira, *Insularismo: Ensayos de interpretación puertorriqueña* (1934); C. F. Pérez, *Evolución poética dominicana* (1956); C. Vitier, *Lo cubano en la poesia* (1958); P. Henríquez Ureña, "La cultura y las letras coloniales en Santo Domingo," *Obra Crítica*, ed. E. S. Speratti Piñero (1960); I. A. Schulman and M. P. González, *Martí, Darío y el modernismo* (1969); R. Friol, *Suite para Juan Francisco Manzano* (1977); J. Alcántara Almánzar, *Estudios de poesía dominicana* (1979); E.

Saínz, *Silvestre De Balboa y la literatura cubana* (1982); Instituto de Literatura y Lingüística de la Academia de Ciencias de Cuba, *Diccionario de la literatura cubana* (1984); C. Vitier, *Crítica cubana* (1988); W. Luis, *Literary Bondage: Slavery in Cuban Narrative* (1990); V. Kutzinski, *Against the American Grain: Myth and History in William Carlos Williams, Jay Wright, and Nicolás Guillén* (1987); and *Sugar's Secrets: Race and the Erotics of Cuban Nationalism* (1993); R. González Echevarría, *Celestina's Brood: Continuities of the Baroque in Spanish and Latin American Literatures* (1993); O. Montero, *Erotismo y representación en Julián del Casal* (1993); *The Cambridge History of Latin American Literature*, ed. R. González Echevarría and E. Pupo-Walker, 2 v. (1996)—esp. A. Bush, "Lyric Poetry of the Eighteen and Nineteenth Centuries," v. 1; and J. Quiroga, "Spanish American Poetry from 1922 to 1975," v. 2; B. A. Heller, *Assimilation/Generation/Resurrection: Contrapuntal Readings in the Poetry of José Lezama Lima* (1997); M. López Baralt, *El barco en la botella: La poesía de Luis Palés Matos* (1997); R. Ríos Avila, "Hacia Palés," *La raza cómica del sujeto en Puerto Rico* (2002); E. Bejel, "Poetry," *A History of Literature in the Caribbean: Hispanic and Francophone Regions*, ed. A. J. Arnold, v. 1 (2004); T. F. Anderson, *Everything in Its Place: The Life and Works of Virgilio Piñera* (2006); M. Arnedo-Gómez, *Writing Rumba: The Afrocubanista Movement in Poetry* (2006); F. Morán, *Julián Del Casal o los pliegues del deseo* (2008).

I. Phaf-Rheinberger (Dutch); L. A. Breiner (Eng.); M. Dash (Fr.); B. A. Heller (Sp.)

**CARMEN** (Lat., "song" or "lyric"). Commonly used as in the title of Catullus's *Carmina*; occasionally, it had the broader meaning of "poetry," incl. *epic, drama, and lampoon (see INVECTIVE). Its broadest usage covered *prophetic poetry, *incantation, *hymn, *epitaph, *charm, and even legal formulas. The word seems to connote divine *inspiration, the song of the *poet as the agent of a god or muse, as in Horace's usage in the *Odes*. Ovid wrote cryptically that his banishment to Tomis by the Emperor Augustus was because of "carmen et error" (a poem and a mistake).
■ D. Norberg, "Carmen oder Rhythmus?" *Au seuil du Moyen Âge II*, ed. R. Jacobsson and F. Sandgren (1998).
R. A. Hornsby

**CARMINA FIGURATA.** The Lat. term means "shaped songs" and refers to poems in a figured format. In certain cases, this visual format is used to encode a secondary text within the composition that can be discerned by close reading of the graphical features. The vogue for shaped poetry waxes and wanes, with conspicuous periods of activity in cl. antiquity, the Middle Ages, the late Ren., and the 20th c., separated by long stretches of dormancy. The earliest known examples date back to cl. times where they are referred to as *technopaegnia* among the Greeks and *carmina figurata* among Lat. poets. The Gr. poet Simias of Rhodes (fl. ca. 300 BCE) created handwritten poems in the shape of Eros's wings and other figures that conformed to strict rules of syntax and metrics. The complexity of working with two sets of constraints, visual and verbal, lent an air of virtuosity to these poems. In the early 4th-c. court of Constantine the Great, Publilius Optatianus Porphyrius brought shaped poetry into the Lat. world. Seeking favor from the emperor, Porphyrius wrote (otherwise dreadful) *panegyrics using lines of varying length composed into visual images. In the early 9th c., the Abbot of Fulda, Hrabanus Maurus, composed one of the most renowned collections in carmina figurata format. Hrabanus was a student of Alcuin of York, the advisor to Charlemagne who was responsible for standardization of handwriting and script across the Carolingian empire. Maurus's much copied collection, *In honorem Sanctae Crucis* (In Honor of the Holy Cross), also known as *De laudibus Sanctae Crucis* (In Praise of the Holy Cross), includes 28 poems in which a square grid of text—thirty to forty letters wide and long—contains a poem in metrical Lat. that can be read left to right but like prose, since the lineation is not visible in this format. Certain words and phrases that run against the directionality of the underlying poem (e.g., "divino" spelled vertically, or "arcangeli" in a diagonal, wing-shaped pattern) are foregrounded by means of a graphic line that enclosed them in a shape or, in some presentations such as the influential edition by Jakob Wimpheling published at Pforzheim in 1503, red ink. Hrabanus's works, theologically complex and verbally rich, were ideally suited to this visual format, and lent credibility to the carmen figuratum. Elaborate labyrinths and shaped verse appeared after the invention of moveable type in the 15th c. The most prominent practitioner of later pattern poetry was George Herbert, a 17th-c. Anglican, whose posthumously published poems in the forms of angels' wings and an altar were among the last serious and substantive contributions to this genre. The linear constraints of letterpress meant that these works had to be created within the prevailing grid structure of a typographic form. Though the technology existed for more free-form work, the decision of the 20th-c. avant-garde poet Guillaume Apollinaire to break free of the underlying grid of letterpress technology in his *calligrammes came almost 500 years after the invention of printing.

■ C. Haeberlin, *Carmina Figurata Graeca* (1887); J. Adler and U. Ernst, *Text als Figur* (1987); D. Higgins, *Pattern Poetry* (1987); E. Ulrich, *Carmen figuratum* (1991); R. Maurus, *In honorem Sanctae Crucis*, ed. M. Perrin (1997); C. Chazell, *The Crucified God in the Carolingian Era* (2001).

J. DRUCKER

**CAROL.** Originally referring to a specific formal pattern for sung verse accompanying a dance, *carol* now means a festive or contemplative strophic song. Song and dance intersected in the med. carol: OF *carole* designated singing and dancing in a circle. In England, the carol maintained this identity as a dance song in the 13th and 14th cs.; Chaucer uses it to describe a combination of singing and dancing. The carol was a stanzaic song with a *burden, sometimes called a *fote*: short verses (often a *couplet) that began the song and were repeated as a refrain but that were musically and narratively separate from the stanzas. Stanzas were regular within each carol but varied in form across carols. Performance practice dictated the stanza/burden form. A leader sang stanzas, and a chorus performed the burden as part of a round-dance. Harmonizing Christian feasts with older pagan rituals, the carol always figured in the solstice-associated Christmas and Easter holidays. Its content, however, ranged across religious, political, humorous, and other themes. Parallel devels. existed in the Sp. *villancico* and the It. *lauda*, and Scotland had its own carol trad. The med. Eng. carol blended courtly and popular styles. The earlier carol's lyrics also sometimes drew attention to the singers and the act of performing.

While Scottish carols continued to imply both dancing and singing through the 16th c., the 15th-c. Eng. carol's associations with dance became increasingly attenuated. Even though its form continued to reflect this origin (as in John Audelay's carols), other elements began to contribute to the carol's identity. E.g., liturgy, *hymns, and processional music have been suggested as influences on the late ME carol. Disagreement surrounds the possible use of carols in processions; however, the late med. carol may have had other liturgical functions and certainly displayed other connections with religious culture (see LITURGICAL POETRY). Carols were frequently *macaronic, incorporating accentual Lat. verse. While some of these lines were commonly used phrases or composed for particular carols, others were taken from church services. Because of their similar structures, hymn material was most frequently excerpted in carols; however, the carol generally maintained musical independence from the hymn. In addition, the Franciscan order was instrumental in disseminating carols; both early and late Franciscan carols were probably used in preaching.

Between the 15th and 17th cs., the carol lost its earlier formal definition. The polyphonic carol gained popularity in the mid-15th through the early 16th cs. It may have substituted on feast days for the traditional *Benedicamus* verses sung at the end of the canonical hours. Other carols from this period were courtly rather than liturgical and more uniform in theme, as shown in the ms. of Robert Fayrfax (ca. 1500), which contains musically complex Passion carols. Ultimately, the Elizabethan *madrigal as a polyphonic form replaced the carol. During the 17th c., however, Catholic recusants upheld old trads. of music and dance in celebrating Christmas; a 1650s collection by Thomas Fairfax comprises the largest set of texts labeled as carols from this period. These Christmas songs, marking the period from Christmas to Candlemas, are carols only loosely, most lacking burdens. Over time and in the transmission from England to America, the carol has come to be associated particularly with Christmas. England, however, accommodates a broader range of songs within this definition, incl. Easter carols.

The carol's mod. preservation emphasizes both the evanescence and endurance of its defining features.

Seventeenth–c. carol texts in dramas establish continuity between the carol's earliest performance contexts and its more mod. manifestations. Arrangements by folk musicologists such as Cecil Sharp and Ralph Vaughan Williams have helped preserve the Eng. carol trad., and new carols continued to be written through the 20th c. The Am. folklorist John Jacob Niles collected a North Carolina variant of the Corpus Christi Carol (an unusual nonsecular import). The Eng. carol appears in an early 16th-c. ms. compiled by Richard Hill, in the Dyboski edition:

> Lully, lulley, lully, lulley;
> The fawcon hath born my mak away.
>
> He bare hym up, he bare hym down;
> He bare hym into an orchard brown.
>
> In that orchard ther was an hall,
> That was hangid with purpill and pall.

Despite some glimmering threads of continuity, the following Am. stanza published by Gilchrist reveals the change over time and points to the disappearance of intermediate variants:

> Down in yon forest be a hall,
> Sing May, Queen May, sing Mary.
>
> Its cover-lidded over with purple and pall,
> Sing all good men for the new-born baby.

Thus, while the carol's integration of poetry and performance remains constant, the particularities of its transmission create a hist. of formal vanishings.

■ *Songs, Carols, and Other Miscellaneous Poems, from the Balliol Ms. 354, Richard Hill's Common-place Book*, ed. R. Dyboski (1907); E. K. Chambers, "Fifteenth-Century Carols by John Audelay," *MLR* 5 (1910); R. H. Robbins, "The Earliest English Carols and the Franciscans," *MLR* 53 (1938); A. Gilchrist, "Down in Yon Forest," *Journal of the Folk Song Society* 4 (1942); F. Harrison, *Music in Medieval Britain* (1958); E. Routley, *The English Carol* (1958); R. H. Robbins, "Middle English Carols as Processional Hymns," *SP* 56 (1959); R. L. Greene, "Carols in Tudor Drama," *Chaucer and Middle English Studies*, ed. B. Rowland (1974); *Early Tudor Songs and Carols*, ed. J. Stevens (1975); *The Early English Carols*, ed. R. L. Greene, 2d ed. (1977); F. McKay, "The Survival of the Carol in the Seventeenth Century," *Anglia* 100 (1982); M. Bukofzer, "Polyphonic Carols," *The New Oxford History of Music*, v. 3, ed. D. Hughes (1986); D. Parker, "John Jacob Niles and Revisionist Folklore," *Southern Folklore* 49 (1992); *The New Oxford Book of Carols*, ed. H. Keyte and A. Parrott (1992); K. Reichl, "The Middle English Carol," *A Companion to the Middle English Lyric*, ed. T. Duncan (2005).

S. CHAGANTI

**CARPE DIEM** (Lat., "pluck [enjoy] the day"). A phrase from Horace, *Odes* 1.11, that enjoins full enjoyment of the present time. The hedonistic form of the *motif ("eat, drink, and be merry . . .") is already fully developed in the Egyptian "Song of the Harper"

and in the advice of Siduri to Gilgamesh (Pritchard). Typically, the *carpe diem* injunction is pronounced amid warnings about the transience of life, the uncertainty of the future, and the inevitability and finality of death (". . . for tomorrow we die"). The motif occurs in many genres of Gr. poetry: *lyric (Alcaeus, frag. 38a; *Anacreontea* 32), *elegy (Theognis 973–78), drama (Aeschylus, *Persians* 840–42; Euripides, *Alcestis* 780–802), and *epigrams (*Anthologia Palatina* 5.79, 5.118, 11.38). The advice to enjoy the present can range from eating (*Iliad* 24.618–19) and drinking (Alcaeus, frag. 38a) to love (Catullus 5: "Let us live, my Lesbia, and let us love"). The Roman master of the motif was Horace, many of whose poems urge a refined, Epicurean enjoyment of the day (e.g., *Odes* 1.4, 1.9, 1.11, 2.14, 3.29, 4.7). To stress the urgency of enjoying the present in the face of fleeting time, the speaker often draws analogies from nature; consequently, the subgenre is full of references to rising and setting suns, seasonal changes, and flowers.

The late Lat. poem "De rosis nascentibus" attributed to Ausonius (ca. 400 CE), which describes roses blooming at Paestum and concludes with the advice "Gather, maiden, roses, while the bloom is fresh and youth is fresh," established the rose as one of the emblems of the carpe diem poem (e.g., Pierre de Ronsard, "Mignonne, allons voir si la rose"; Edmund Spenser, *The Faerie Queene* 2.12.74–75; Robert Herrick, "Gather ye rosebuds while ye may"; and Edmund Waller, "Go, lovely Rose"). In Ren. poetry, the carpe diem theme often serves as the basis of "persuasions" to seduce coy young women, as in Samuel Daniel (*Delia* 31), Thomas Carew ("To A. L. Perswasions to love"), and John Milton (*Comus* 736–54); but the best-known example in Eng. is Andrew Marvell's "To His Coy Mistress," which prominently exhibits the syllogistic form implicit in many carpe diem poems. In the 19th c., Edward FitzGerald's versions of *The Rubáiyát of Omar Khayyám* popularized the hedonistic carpe diem theme. Twentieth-c. examples include A. E. Housman's "Loveliest of Trees, the Cherry Now" and John Crowe Ransom's "Blue Girls."

■ F. Bruser, "*Comus* and the Rose Song," *SP* 44 (1947); H. Weber, *La Création poétique au XVIe siècle en France* (1956); J. B. Pritchard, *Ancient Near-Eastern Texts* (1969); R.G.M. Nisbet and M. Hubbard, *A Commentary on Horace, Odes Book I* (1970); C. Yandell, "*Carpe Diem*, Poetic Immortality, and the Gendered Ideology of Time," *Renaissance Women Writers*, ed. A. R. Larsen and C. Winn (1994); and "*Carpe Diem* Revisited: Ronsard's Temporal Ploys," *Sixteenth-Century Journal* 28 (1997); E. H. Sagaser, "Sporting the While: *Carpe Diem* and the Cruel Fair in Samuel Daniel's *Delia* and the *Complaint of Rosamond*," *Exemplaria* 10 (1998).

W. H. RACE

**CATACHRESIS** (Gr., "abuse"). The tidiest definition of this *trope dates back, it has been argued, to the Stoic grammarians: *catachresis* is the use of a borrowed word for something that does not have a name of its own. We speak thus of the "legs" of a table or the "foot" of a bed. Augustine gives the example of *piscina*: the word denotes a swimming pool or tank, despite the complete absence of fish (*piscis*; *De doctrina christiana* 3.29). According to this most straightforward analysis, catachresis functions like a *metaphor, implying the comparison of two objects. However, unlike a metaphor—which enacts a lexical transfer by establishing the equivalence of two terms—catachresis performs its transfers in the face of a *missing* term, thus without anchoring its meaning in the logic of equivalence. For instance, "thunderbolts of eloquence" (*eloquentiae fulmina*)—one of Quintilian's examples of metaphor—describes particularly effective discourse by equating *eloquence* with a *lightning flash* (cf. 8.6.7). In contrast, *piscina* uses the name of fish to describe something that otherwise has no name. A metaphor has, as it were, taken up residence as a proper name. As one mod. theorist explains, "[T]here is no other possible word to denote the 'wings' of a house, or the 'arms' of a chair, and yet 'wings' and 'arms' are *instantly, already* metaphorical" (Barthes). Following this line of thought, writers have often defined *catachresis* as a so-called *dead metaphor: a metaphor so fundamental to expression that no distinction from literal use is possible.

According to this logic, catachresis operates under the pressure of necessity: a catachrestic transfer takes place when a "proper" proper name is lacking. "[I]f for lacke of naturall and proper terme or worde we take another, neither naturall nor proper," writes George Puttenham in his 1589 *Arte of English Poesie*, "and do vntruly applie it to the thing which we would seeme to expresse . . . it is not then spoken by this figure *Metaphore* . . . but by plaine abuse" (3.17). Catachresis borders on *malapropism* (mistaking one word for another) or *paradiastole* (euphemistic redescription); its "abuse" entails a misapplication of terms. But with catachresis, such misapplications are seemingly unavoidable. Impropriety is built into the trope irreducibly, from the ground up.

The figure's irreducible impropriety has led postmod. and poststructuralist observers to privilege catachresis as "the common denominator of rhetoricity as such" (Laclau). For such theorists, *catachresis* becomes the name for the inescapable metaphorical or rhetorical function of lang. The trope then bespeaks our general inability to trace human meaning back to the bedrock, "literal" reality on which it presumably rests. Giving the lie to our handy philological narratives, catachresis instead reveals the ways in which lang. is "always already" figurative. Moreover, thanks to the way it generates new meanings and uses from a semantic void (i.e., the "lack" that Puttenham notes in his definition), catachresis can then be taken to characterize the originary gap at the heart of all systems of meaning. *Catachresis* names the origin of lang.—or indeed of any symbolic system—as "rupture" or "doubling" rather than as singular presence. This general rhetorical analysis of the trope has been deployed in disciplines as diverse as political science, media and cultural studies, anthropology, and psychoanalysis. Some notable examples include Spivak's use of the trope to characterize postcolonial discourse; Laclau's view of social hegemony as catachrestic; Barthes's investigation of the figure of beauty in 19th-c. *realism; and Derrida's critique of metaphoricity in Western philosophy.

The postmod. treatment of the trope is exceptionally powerful and holds great explanatory force. Such readings have tended to focus on only one aspect of the trope's hist., however: namely, the preoccupation with the problem of a primitive semantic lack. It could be argued that another, related thread is equally important: the question of what we might call semantic "place." Here Quintilian's characterization of the trope is paradigmatic. Like many writers before and since, Quintilian defines *catachresis* as a species or version of metaphor. Indeed, his account in many ways anticipates postmod. thought, celebrating catachresis not as the *abuse* of metaphor but rather as metaphor so elemental as to be *necessary*—as when we speak of crops being "thirsty" although they have no throats (8.6.5–6). At the same time, however, the 1st-c. rhetor explains that the trope functions by adapting whatever term is closest at hand: "By [catachresis] . . . is meant the practice of adapting the nearest [*proximo*] available term to describe something for which no actual term exists" (8.6.34).

To privilege catachresis as Quintilian does is to foreground the problem of semantic place. A criterion of proximity—of neighboring place—undergirds his understanding of the trope. Indeed, at stake here is the cl. definition of *trope* itself, with its strongly spatialized conception of ling. property: i.e., the "place" where a word "properly" belongs. Once again, we turn to Quintilian for his influential definition: "[trope is] the transference of words and phrases from the place which is strictly theirs to another to which they do not properly belong" (9.1.4). Thus understood, trope maps out an entire lexical geography, where each word or phrase finds its accepted coordinates in relation not only to a world of things but to the world of other words and phrases. Moreover, as far back as Aristotle, metaphor has been understood to organize these places through the ability "to see the same" (*to homoion therein estin*): i.e., the ability to recognize analogies, resemblances, and hierarchies (*Poetics* 1459a18). Catachresis, however, unsettles our ability to determine such resemblance.

Simply put, a judgment of similarity requires at least two terms for comparison; with catachresis, however, one of these terms is missing. A word is transferred from one place to another—to a place that lacks any name of its own. Where metaphor anchors its transfers on the basis of resemblance, catachresis functions on the basis of sheer proximity. In place of no name, we adapt the nearest available term. We grab what is closest to hand. But what is nearness in lang., proximity of terminology, if it is not a judgment of resemblance? What is semantic place *tout court*? What is a place without a name? Indeed, catachresis raises the uncomfortable notion of an *empty* ling. place: of a place held open *in* lang. but not inhabited *by* lang. Catachresis thus invokes a world whose contours and contents are already shaped, but not yet named, by lang. This is a world that comes to us already articulated and processed by trope, a world chewed up by lang. before we meaning-makers even arrive on the scene.

According to this thread of its hist., the abuse of catachresis is not that it misapplies a name but rather that it violates our sense of place. This violation has lead to a common alternate definition of the trope as a "mixed," "extravagant," or (most tellingly) "far-fetched" metaphor (Lanham). According to this understanding, catachresis disrupts the reassurances and taxonomic ordering of resemblance, offering instead a world where semantics has lost its bearings, where the foreign and far away has collapsed in on the near and the neighborly. It is perhaps the catachrestic oddity of the trope that its hist. reveals two such seemingly opposed interpretations: on the one hand, catachresis as metaphor that is "far-fetched" or "extravagant" (literally: *wandering out of bounds*); on the other hand, catachresis as metaphor so familiar and domesticated as to be considered quite "dead."

■ Augustine, *On Christian Doctrine*, trans. D. W. Robertson (1958); Quintilian, *Institutio oratoria*, trans. H. E. Butler (1958); R. Barthes, *S/Z*, trans. R. Miller (1974); P. de Man, "The Epistemology of Metaphor," *CritI* 5.1 (1978)—spec. iss. on metaphor; D. A. Russell, "Theories of Style," *Criticism in Antiquity* (1981); J. Derrida, "White Mythology: Metaphor in the Text of Philosophy," *Margins of Philosophy*, trans. A. Bass (1982); P. Parker, "Metaphorical Plot," *Literary Fat Ladies* (1987), and "Metaphor and Catachresis," *The Ends of Rhetoric*, ed. J. Bender and D. E. Wellbery (1990); Lanham; E. Laclau, *On Populist Reason* (2005).

L. FREINKEL

**CATALAN POETRY.** *Catalan* is the common name for the lang. spoken in Catalonia, Valencia, and the Balearic Islands. The unique hist. of the region meant that Catalan was not in continuous literary use: Occitan and Catalan were the langs. of poetry in the Middle Ages, Castilian during the phase of Sp. ascendancy, and Catalan again since *romanticism, when Catalan poetry experienced a revival. The *Renaixença* (Rebirth) movement amplified the topics of romanticism and brought about an extraordinary literary period interrupted only by the dictatorship of Francisco Franco in Spain. During the years of political and cultural repression (1939–75), poetry played a prominent role in the preservation of Catalan lang. This role created a unique conflict between ideological and aesthetic objectives, resulting in an unbalanced literary trad. that promoted national survival to the detriment of artistic devel.

The Middle Ages left a rich legacy of poets and texts. *Ensenhamen*, written before 1160 in Occitan by Guerau de Cabrera (d. ca. 1160), contains a full catalog of cl. and Fr. literary topics; such long poetic narratives and brief popular songs were predominant at the time. In the 13th c., amatory and devotional songs were common among preserved texts, such as "Epístola farcida de Sant Esteve," "Plany de Maria Aujats senyors . . . ," and Escolania de Montserrat's "Virolai." When King Alfons I inherited Provença in 1166, he became a strong defender of the poetic use of Occitan, as in Raimon Vidal de Besalú's (1190–1213) *Razos de trobar*, the first poetic grammar and rhetorical treatise in any Romance lang. Thus, the first Catalan poems were written in Occitan, which influenced the subject matter, style, and versification of the genre until the 15th c. Catalan authors contributed to the *troubadour trad., with spectacular poems written according to the *trobar leu* (Guillem de Berguedà, 1138–96) or *trobar ric* (Cerverí de Girona, fl. 1259–85) conventions (see TROBAR CLUS, TROBAR LEU).

In the early 13th c., Ramon Llull (1232–1315), considered the founder of Catalan literary prose, dealt with the diffusion of the Christian faith. His most notable contribution to poetry is *Libre d'Amic e Amat* (The Book of the Friend and His Beloved), a series of 365 mystical prose poems. As in France, this period generated remarkable examples of romances written in verse: works by Raimon Vidal de Besalú; *Blandín de Cornualla* and *Salut d'amor* (both anonymous); and in the 14th c., works by Guillem de Torroella (d. ca. 1348), such as the Arthurian *Faula*. This century also saw narrative poems by Pere (ca. 1336–1413) and Jaume Marc (ca. 1335–1410), and *Fraire de Joi e sor de Plaser*, the anonymous Catalan version of Sleeping Beauty. Francesc de la Via (ca. 1380–1445) wrote several court accounts in the style of *fabliaux, such as *Llibre de Fra Bernat*, and Bernat Serradell (ca. 1375–1445) went beyond this model in *Testament d'En Bernat Serradell*.

In the 14th and 15th cs., Catalan poetry was in full bloom: liberated from their Occitan origins, new writers gained popularity by employing It. Petrarchan models. Nevertheless, the influence of Occitan poetry can still be found in authors from Majorca and northern Catalonia, whose works were collected in a Ripoll *cançoneret* after 1346 (see SONGBOOK). Following the example of the Tolosa poetical school, in 1393 King Joan I created the Consistori de la Gaia Ciència in Barcelona (see GAI SABER). Under the influence of this somewhat remote model, two important books were written in the late 14th c.: *Llibre de concordances* by Jaume March (1336–1410) and *Torsimany* (incl. a rhyme dictionary) by Lluís d'Averçó (1350–1412). The It. Ren. illuminated the verse of minor poets such as Gilabert de Pròxida (d. 1405), Pere de Queralt (d. 1408), and Melcior de Gualbes (d. ca. 1400). Andreu Febrer's (1375–1444) poetry still followed troubadour models, but he was also the author of an excellent verse trans. of Dante's *Divina commedia* into Catalan. Overcoming the durable influence of troubadour poetry, in the 15th c. two major poets started writing. Jordi de Sant Jordi (ca. 1390–1424) expressed personal sorrow while in captivity. After 1425, Ausiàs Marc (or March; 1400?–59), based in Valencia but familiar with It. models, wrote his collection of more than 100 poems. Transcending *Dolce stil nuovo* and Petrarchism, he explored the doubts surrounding love and death. Joan Roíç de Corella (ca. 1430–90) wrote poems of visual and imaginative power about sensual and divine love. He was the first to introduce into Catalan poetics the It. *hendecasyllable. In the midst of civil war (1462–72), poetry became a tool for expressing ideological and political commitments. Joan Berenguer de Masdovelles (d. 1476) wrote long poems in favor of Joan II. Minor poets of the period include Bernat Hug de Rocabertí (ca. 1420–85), Pere de Torroella (d. 1475), and the politician Romeu Llull (1439–96). In prosperous Valencia, among figures such as Bernat Fenollar (1438–1516), an easygoing literary culture of satirical and humorous poems thrived. Also in Valencia, Jaume Roig (ca. 1400–78) wrote *Espill* (Mirror), a prebourgeois fiction in verse with a pessimistic and rude approach to reality and traces of med. misogyny.

Although Catalan poetry was enjoying a healthy life in the early 16th c., a series of historical events related to the political misfortunes of the crown of Catalonia and Aragon subdued literary growth under a newly unified Spain. Catalonia lost two wars with Castile (1640 and 1714), and most of the nobility moved to central Spain to serve Charles V and Philip II. Also, after 1492 the main economic activity shifted from the Mediterranean to the Atlantic Basin. Because of these changes, Catalonia experienced a profound crisis, which may explain why the Ren. and its aftermath (neoclassicism, Enlightenment) were lived with less intensity. Andreu Martí Pineda (d. ca. 1566) and Valeri Fuster (d. ca. 1500) imitated bourgeois Valencian poetry from the late 15th c. *Baroque writing is well represented by authors such as Joan Pujol (1532–ca. 1603), Francesc Vicenç Garcia (1578?–1623), Francesc Fontanella (1622–ca. 1682), and Josep Romaguera (1642–1723), while neoclassicism inspired the Minorcan poets Joan Ramis (1746–1819) and Antoni Febrer i Cardona (1761–1821). From the early 17th c. on, we can easily detect the influence of Golden Age and baroque Sp. writers from Garcilaso de la Vega (whose Italianate poems were first published in a famous volume of 1543 with those of his friend, the Catalan innovator Joan Boscà Almogàver, (Juan Boscán, ca. 1488–1542) to Baltasar Gracián. The lit. of the Counter-Reformation reflected rigidity and asceticism. Vicenç Garcia, also known as Rector de Vallfogona, created a "school" with imitators all the way into the 19th c. The lack of a strong elite lit. is offset by a surge in popular poetry. Some of the most outstanding poems of the time were anonymous. This trend survived until the 19th c., when popular styles were adopted by romantic authors: Pau Piferrer (1818–48), Manuel Milà i Fontanals (1818–84), and Marià Aguiló (1825–97). The myth of Count Arnau was particularly important in popular poetry and became a topic for poets in the 20th c., esp. Josep Maria de Sagarra and Joan Maragall.

During the 19th c., under the auspices of the Industrial Revolution and romanticism, poetry was employed to differentiate Catalonia from Spain. Long considered, together with the *Basque Country, Spain's industrial engine, Catalonia nevertheless carried little political weight in Sp. politics after 1714. Modernization became a means of demanding a distinct political and economic status, as evident in Catalan romantic and modernist lit. Early poetical essays such as Bonaventura Carles Aribau's (1799–1862) "A la pàtria"

(To the Motherland, 1833) have long been considered the starting point of this movement, as is the first book written in Catalan, Miquel Anton Martí's (ca. 1790–1864) *Llàgrimes de viudesa* (Weeping Widowerhood, 1839). That year Rubió i Ors (1818–99), known with his pseud. Lo Gaiter de Llobregat (The Bagpiper from Llobregat), started publishing poems in *Diario de Barcelona;* they were compiled in 1841 under the same *Lo Gaiter de Llobregat*. Tomàs Aguiló (1775–1856) and Tomàs Villarroya (1812–56) followed suit in Majorca and Valencia, respectively, while Milà i Fontanals helped develop an interest in troubadour poetry from a scholarly perspective.

At first, recovery of Catalan lit. began with the Renaixença, a literary movement organized after 1859 around the *Jocs Florals* (*poetic contests), competitions celebrated every first Sunday in May, which aroused new and widespread interest in Catalan lit. This movement included Josep Lluís Pons i Gallarza (1823–94), Víctor Balaguer (1824–1901), Marià Aguiló (1825–97), Teodor Llorente (1836–1911), Francesc Pelagi Briz (1839–89), Jaume Collell (1846–1932), Ramon Picó i Campamar (1848–1916), Francesc Matheu (1851–1938), Josep Anselm Clavé (1824–74), and Joaquim M. Bartrina (1850–80). Jacint Verdaguer (1845–1902), the founder of mod. Catalan literary lang., is the major literary figure of the Renaixença. His two epic poems, *Atlàntida* (1877) and *Canigó* (1885), interpreted Sp. and Catalan hist. in light of mythological and religious references in the style of the Fr. romantic poet Alphonse de Lamartine.

This cultural revival initiated a period of intense literary activity until the Sp. Civil War. Concurrent with major Eur. trends, cultural movements such as *Modernisme* (a version of flamboyant art nouveau style) and *Noucentisme* (a neoclassical revival modeled on Fr. lit.) flowered. In the 1920s and 1930s, there were strong signs of a very active avant-garde, postsymbolist modernity—a moment of splendor that was violently truncated by the onset of the Civil War (1936–39). This period was dominated by the idea of modernization, which was divided along bourgeois and proletarian lines.

At the turn of the century, we detect a second moment of this revival. Under Modernisme, Joan Maragall (1860–1911) masterfully epitomized feelings and obsessions of the time in his poems ("Oda nova a Barcelona," "Oda a Espanya," "Cant espiritual"), painting an accurate portrait of Catalan society incl. anarchism, difficult relations with Spain, and religious doubts. Santiago Rusiñol (1861–1931) wrote the first decadent prose poems in *Oracions* (1893). In Majorca, Miquel Costa i Llobera (1854–1922) and Joan Alcover (1854–1926) wrote poetry with a more classicist penchant. The latter became inspirational for a group of young poets who wrote under Noucentisme. Josep Carner (1884–1970), Guerau de Liost (pseud. of Jaume Bofill i Mates, 1878–1933), and Josep Maria López-Picó (1886–1959) composed formalist poetry. Jours. such as *La Revista* (1915–36) were influential in the introduction of *symbolism and promoted avant-gardism (see AVANT-GARDE

POETICS). Joan Salvat-Papasseit (1894–1924), Josep M. Junoy (1887–1955), and Salvador Dalí (1904–89) adapted *futurism, *cubism, and *surrealism, respectively, with staggering results. This marks a third moment. Josep Vicenç Foix (1893–1987) combined avant-garde (*Gertrudis*, 1927) and cl. models (*Sol i de dol*, 1947). Following a postsymbolist program, Carles Riba (1893–1959), who twice translated *The Odyssey*, wrote in a severe tone (*Estances*, I [1919] and II [1930]). His *Elegies de Bierville* (1943) presents a somber account of exile. Josep Maria de Sagarra (1894–1961) and Ventura Gassol (1893–1980) were the most popular poets before World War II. Other poets drawn toward intimacy and dream include Maria Antònia Salvà (1869–1958), Josep Sebastià Pons (1886–1962), Marià Manent (1898–1988), Tomàs Garcés (1901–93), and Clementina Arderiu (1889–1976). Pere Quart (pseud. of Joan Oliver, 1899–1986) wrote satirical poetry (*Les decapitacions*, 1934), whereas personal experiences of illness and civil war appeared in the poetry of Bartomeu Rosselló-Pòrcel (1913–38) and Màrius Torres (1910–42).

Franco's regime repressed Catalonian culture. For many years, the lang. vanished from public life, with publication in it forbidden. Writers employed poetry as a means of subversion; the genre was easy to distribute illegally, and its inherent abstraction helped keep a rich cultural heritage alive. Riba and Foix presided over literary and political meetings where they inspired writers of the younger generation: Jordi Sarsanedas (1924–2006) and Joan Perucho (1920–2003). Josep Palau i Fabre (1917–2008) and Joan Brossa (1917–2008) maintained an active focus on avant-garde aesthetics. Agustí Bartra (1908–82), a minor poet who lived in exile, represented a revival of *modernista* models. When Riba died in 1959, a radical change occurred under *Realisme Històric* (Socialist Realism), as proposed in Castellet and Molas's influential anthol., *Poesia catalana segle XX*. Quart (*Vacances pagades*, 1960) and Salvador Espriu (1913–85, *La pell de brau*, 1960), created an interest in more realist approaches, particularly evident in Gabriel Ferrater (1922–72, *Les dones i els dies*, 1968). Some authors distantly related to realism are Vicent Andrés Estellés (1924–93), Marià Villangómez (1913–2002), Blai Bonet (1926–97), Josep M. Llompart (1925–93), Màrius Sampere (b. 1928), Montserrat Abelló (b. 1918), and Miquel Martí i Pol (1929–2003).

From the mid-1960s, a remarkable recovery of Catalan poetry began. The arrival of an iconoclastic generation, in dialogue with their Eur. counterparts, provoked a significant shift toward a poetry of universal interest. Characteristically, these poets worried little about the past and were overtly irreverent toward traditional topics, such as the sanctity of lang. Rather than following local literary models, they favored freedom of expression, some adopting a formalistic attitude, others vindicating obscure figures from the past. Pere Gimferrer (b. 1945, *Mirall, espai, aparicions*, 1981) is outstanding among this group, together with Feliu Formosa (b. 1934), Joan Margarit (b. 1938), Narcís Comadira (b. 1942), Francesc Parcerisas (b. 1944), Miquel Bauçà (1940–2005), and Jordi Pàmias (b. 1938). While Catalan poetry today has

lost part of the aura it had during difficult times, nevertheless, poetry is very much alive, and many exceptional poets are worth mentioning: M. Mercè Marçal (1952–98), Salvador Jàfer (b. 1954), Jaume Pont (b. 1947), Josep Piera (b. 1947), Carles Torner (b. 1963), David Castillo (b. 1961), Margalida Pons (b. 1966), Jaume Subirana (b. 1963), Enric Casassas (b. 1951), Arnau Pons (b. 1965), and Lluís Solà (b. 1940).

*See* OCCITAN POETRY; SPAIN, POETRY OF.

■ **Anthologies**: *Anthology of Catalan Lyric Poetry*, ed. J. Triadú and J. Gili (1953); *Ocho siglos de poesía catalana: antología bilingüe*, ed. J. M. Castellet and J. Molas (1976); *Modern Catalan Poetry: An Anthology* (1979), and *Postwar Catalan Poetry* (1991), both ed. and trans. D. H. Rosenthal; *Poesia catalana del barroc*, ed. A. Rossich and P. Valsalobre (2006); *Lights off Water: XXV Catalan Poems 1978–2002*, ed. Anna Crowe (2007); "Made in Catalunya," L. Anderson, L. Reed, and P. Smith reading Catalan, http://www.llull.cat/_cat/_publi/pub.cfm?seccio=publi&subsecci o=25030&CATEGORIA=25030).

■ **Bibliographies**: E. Bou, *Nou diccionari 62 de la literatura catalana* (2000); A. Broch, *Diccionari de la literatura catalana* (2008).

■ **Criticism and History**: M. de Riquer, A. Comas, J. Molas, *Història de la Literatura Catalana*, 11 v. (1964–88); J. Fuster, *Literatura catalana contemporània* (1972); J. Bofill i Ferro and A. Comas, *Un segle de poesia catalana* (1981); J. Marco and J. Pont, *La nova poesia catalana* (1981); A. Terry, *Sobre poesia catalana contemporània* (1985); J. Rubió i Balaguer, *Obres completes: Història de la literatura catalana* (1986); A. Terry, *Quatre poetes catalans* (1991); F Carbó, *La poesia catalana del segle XX* (2007); LletrA: Catalan Literature Online: http://www.lletra.net/; A Rossich, *Panorama crític de la literatura catalana*, 6 v. (2009–11).

E. BOU

**CATALEXIS** (Gr., "coming to an abrupt end"). The process by which a metrical *colon or line is shortened on the end. The adjectival form, *catalectic*, describes omission of one syllable, the final one; the older, technical term for double catalectic forms is *brachycatalectic*. The normal form, where no syllable is lacking, is sometimes called *acatalectic*; and when extra syllables appear at the end, the colon or line is said to be *hypermetric*. Catalexis applies only to ends; shortening at the beginning is normally treated separately since the metrical environment differs (*see* ACEPHALOUS).

Catalexis is evident in both cl. Gr. and Sanskrit prosody and seems to have derived in part from IE prosody, though it would have appeared indigenously as a normal linguistic process. In cl. Gr., all the most common metrical cola (*dactylic, *anapestic, *iambic, *trochaic, *aeolic) have catalectic forms, in which the last two syllables are shortened to one heavy syllable (longum). But the precise mechanism of catalexis in *classical prosody is complex and varies from meter to meter. More important, the catalexis often appears at the end of a metrical period or stanza—esp. in dactylic, trochaic, and anapestic verse—so that the principle of shortening or blunting has double effect.

In the mod. poetries, catalexis is not common at all in iambic verse but is frequent in trochaic and ternary meters (see BINARY AND TERNARY), where the unexpectedly sudden and forceful close (on a stress) gives bite. In Eng., the trochaic *tetrameter of eight syllables is often found together with a catalectic line of seven, both forms meshing smoothly. Why catalexis should operate well in some meters but not others still awaits definitive explanation; temporal metrists would say that in *accentual verse and other meters that retain a close association with music and song, the missing weak syllable at the end is filled by a *pause. In any event, it is manifest that catalexis is one of the fundamental principles of *rhythm, and provision must be made for it in any theory of meter.

■ L.P.E. Parker, "Catalexis," *CQ* 26 (1976); Morier; M. L. West, "Three Topics in Greek Metre," *CQ* 32 (1982).

T.V.F. BROGAN

**CATALOG.** An enumeration of persons, places, things, or ideas in poetry that often displays some common referent or context such as power, heroism, or beauty. The catalog differs from the simple list or inventory by incl. more descriptive information and by affording the writer more opportunity for digression or thematic devel. The catalog is of ancient origin and is found in almost all lits. of the world. In antiquity, the catalog plays a didactic or mnemonic role, e.g., in the Bible (Gen. 10 and Matt. 1). More frequently, however, the catalog has a clearly aesthetic function. In epic lit., e.g., it conveys the size and power of armies, as in Homer's list of ships and heroes in *Iliad* 2, and the technique creates the effect of vastness and panoramic sweep, both in geographical space and in narrative time. Similar effects of epic expansions occur in Virgil's catalog of heroes in *Aeneid* 7 and Milton's catalog of fallen angels in *Paradise Lost* 2.

Med. and Ren. poetry developed catalog techniques based on cl. models to produce an encyclopedic variety of topics and forms. Ovid's catalog of trees drawn to Orpheus in *Metamorphoses* 10 serves that purpose for similar lists in Virgil, Chaucer, and Edmund Spenser. In Spenser's *Faerie Queene* book 1, the catalog of trees places the action of the poem within the epic trad. and marks the poet's position within what Ferry calls a "subliminal catalog of immortal names." A second major form, the *ubi sunt* poem, features a catalog of absences in order to meditate on mortality and the transience of life, asking where the dead are now. Med. Lat. poems feature the phrase itself, as in the hymn "De Brevitate Vitae," and OE poems of the Exeter Book, such as "The Wanderer," call out the individual dead in order to meditate on the common fate of all. A third rich trad. features the catalog of beautiful attributes in order to praise a beloved (see BLASON). The catalog of women is a related type, deriving in the Western trad. from Hesiod and Homer and developing into the catalog of the "good

woman" type in Boccaccio and Chaucer. Although the catalog of feminine beauty may preserve gender stereotypes, it can function in other ways in a poem like Shakespeare's sonnet 130, "My mistress' eyes are nothing like the sun."

In 19th- and 20th-c. Eur. and Am. poetry, other functions of catalog and catalog rhet. have emerged. Writers in antebellum America featured catalog rhet. in both poetry and prose, notably in R. W. Emerson's and H. D. Thoreau's essays, in Herman Melville's encyclopedic fictions, and, most important, in Walt Whitman's long poems. While Whitman's catalog rhet. creates an effect of potentially endless and random multiplicity, it can also combine with effects of thematic or dramatic unity. Whitman's catalog rhet. takes parataxis as a basic organizing principle in order to develop coordinating techniques of syntactic parallelism such as *polysyndeton and asyndeton. Catalog rhet. also features pronounced forms of repetition, such as *anaphora and epistrophe, in order to create effects of nonmetrical rhythm and rhetorical power. Despite formal restrictions of line length, metrical pattern, and generic limitation, catalog enacts a principle of nearly infinite expandability.

■ J. W. Bright, "The 'ubi sunt' Formula," *MLN* 8 (1893); T. W. Allen, "The Homeric Catalogue," *JHS* 30 (1910); D. W. Schumann, "Observations on Enumerative Style in Modern German Poetry," *PMLA* 59 (1944); S. K. Coffman, "'Crossing Brooklyn Ferry': A Note on the Catalogue Technique in Whitman's Poetry," *MP* 51 (1954); L. Spitzer, "La enumeración caótica en la poesía moderna," *Lingüística e historia literaria* (1955); H. E. Wedeck, "The Catalogue in Latin and Medieval Latin Poetry," *M&H* 13 (1960); L. Buell, "Transcendentalist Catalogue Rhetoric: Vision versus Form," *AL* 40 (1968); S. A. Barney, "Chaucer's Lists," *The Wisdom of Poetry*, ed. L. D. Benson and S. Wenzel (1982); N. Howe, *The Old English Catalogue Poems* (1985); M. L. West, *The Hesiodic Catalogue of Women* (1985); A. Ferry, *The Art of Naming* (1988); J. P. Warren, *Walt Whitman's Language Experiment* (1990); G. McLeod, *Virtue and Venom: Catalogues of Women from Antiquity to the Renaissance* (1991); R. E. Belknap, *The List: The Uses and Pleasures of Cataloguing* (2004).

R. A. HORNSBY; T.V.F. BROGAN; J. P. WARREN

**CATHARSIS** (Gr., "purgation," "purification," or "clarification") The use of *catharsis* in connection with the theory of lit. originates in Aristotle's celebrated definition of *tragedy in the *Poetics*. Unfortunately, Aristotle merely uses the term without defining it (though he may have defined it in a putative second book of the *Poetics*), and the question of what he actually meant is a cause célèbre in the hist. of lit. crit. Insofar as there is no universal agreement, all definitions, incl. this one, must be regarded as interpretations only.

The essential function of tragedy, according to Aristotle's definition, is a *representation (*mimesis) of an action that is serious or noble, complete, and of appropriate magnitude; and when such representation is effectively carried out, it will succeed "in arousing pity and fear in such a way as to accomplish a *catharsis* [in one of its fundamental senses] of such emotions." The definition was doubtless framed as an answer to Plato's charge that poetic drama encourages anarchy in the soul by feeding and watering the passions instead of starving them. Aristotle held, to the contrary, that anarchy in the soul is most effectively prevented not by starving and repressing the *emotions but by giving them expression in a wisely regulated manner. Tragedy he regarded as a chief instrument of such regulation, for it works in a twofold way, first exciting the emotions of pity and fear and then allaying them through the cathartic process.

Aristotle's somewhat technical conception of catharsis acquires its particular character from a ling. heritage that is part medical, part religious, and part intellectual. Out of this matrix come several possible meanings of *catharsis* as the key aesthetic term in the *Poetics*. As a medical term, *catharsis* finds early expression in the Hippocratic school of medicine to describe the process of purging the body of humors and impurities that are the cause of disease (Laín Entralgo). The medical view of catharsis, influentially advocated by Bernays, suggests that pity and fear can build up into pathological states that require a therapeutic purgation that is provided by the emotional stimuli of tragedy and that results in pleasurable relief and cure (Lucas). *Catharsis* as a religious term is closely associated with the concept of purification as it applies to rites required for the entry into a holy place, the purification required of believers by certain sects, or the cleansing of guilt by someone who has committed a crime (Laín Entralgo). In the *Phaedo*, Plato uses the term in this religious sense (as well as in an intellectual one) to describe the separation of body from soul, an act that is prerequisite for casting off the illusory world of imitations and shadows and approaching the world of true reality. The interpretation of *catharsis* as purification has been extended to mean purification of any excess or deficiency of pity and fear so that the proper mean of these emotions is achieved (Janko) and to indicate the purification of the tragic deed of the hero from moral pollution so that the audience is able to experience the emotions of pity and fear (Else). The interpretation of *catharsis* as intellectual clarification is based on the use of the term by Plato and others in this sense (Golden and Hardison, Nussbaum), the internal argument of the *Poetics* (Golden and Hardison), and the actual practice of Gr. medicine (Laín Entralgo). Two significant variations on intellectual clarification have also been suggested: emotional (as well as intellectual) clarification (Nussbaum) and ethical clarification (Wagner).

When Aristotle's definition is reconsidered in light of all three of these strands, an important corollary stands forth. Since the new blending that is attained in the cathartic process is psychic and not merely physical, it must involve a new emotional perspective and even, arising from that, a new intellectual vision. A wisdom is distilled from tragic suffering: the person is *pathei mathos* (taught by suffering), as the chorus in the *Agamemnon* sings. The tragic catharsis and the ensuing emotional calm have produced in the spectator a new insight into what the plot of the drama, its action—which is to say, its meaning in motion—most essentially represents. Such insight is what justifies Aristotle's assertions that the essential goal and pleasure of artistic mimesis is *manthanein kai syllogizesthai* (learning and inference) and that "poetry is something more philosophical and more significant than history, for poetry tends to express universals, history particulars" (see HISTORY AND POETRY).

On the whole, later critics have been more inclined to accept than to reject the doctrine of catharsis, although their acceptance has usually involved some degree of reinterpretation. In the It. Ren., Aristotle's definition was revived by such writers as Antonio Minturno (*De poeta*, 1559) and Lodovico Castelvetro (*Poetica d'Aristotele vulgarizzata e sposta*; 1570, 1576), although, in the former, the emphasis is shifted to the "delight and profit" that result to the spectator from his or her cathartic experience. In France a century later, both Pierre Corneille and Jean Racine accept the principle of catharsis in the fairly plain moral sense of regarding the spectator as purified by the tragedy and, thus, as deterred from performing evil acts such as he or she has witnessed. Moreover, Corneille assumes that either pity or fear may operate separately.

In Germany, G. E. Lessing in his influential *Laokoön* (1766) opposed the latter view of Corneille, insisting that the special effect of tragedy must come from the union of the two emotions, from which there emerges the cosmically oriented emotion of awe, as the spectator recognizes through the tragedy the sword of destiny that is suspended above us all. Lessing also emphasizes (*Hamburger Dramaturgie*, 1768) the applicability of Aristotle's ethical standard of "due measure" to the principle of catharsis: tragedy, if it is to transform our pity and fear into virtue, "must be capable of purifying us from both extremes"—from "too little" by its emotional contagion and from "too much" by the restraint that its formal pattern imposes. Friedrich Schiller in his essay "Über das tragische" ("On Tragic Art," 1792) reaffirms the importance of measure, and in "Über das Erhabene" ("On the Sublime," 1801), he draws two corollaries: that the most perfect tragedy is one that produces its cathartic effect not by its subject matter but by its tragic form; and that it has aesthetic worth only insofar as it is *sublime—i.e., as it represents the indifference of the universe to moral ends and so produces in the soul of the spectator an "inoculation against unavoidable fate." J. W. Goethe, in his *Nachlass zu Aristoteles Poetik* (*Supplement to Aristotle's Poetics*, 1827), sees the main importance of the purgatorial or cathartic situation not in reference to the spectator, whose condition is incidental and variable, but in the reconciliation and expiation of the characters in the play. Among later Ger. writers on aesthetics, Arthur Schopenhauer in *Die Welt als Wille und Vorstellung* (*The World as Will and Idea*, 1819) equates the cathartic principle of tragedy with an idealized and universal experience of fellow suffering wholly disproportionate to moral deserts, and Friedrich Nietzsche in

*Die Geburt der Tragödie aus dem Geist der Musik* (*The Birth of Tragedy*, 1872) interprets the matter through the complementary symbols of Dionysus and Apollo, the unresisting plunge into whatever sufferings and joys life may offer and the calm vision that results from this self-surrender.

Of Eng.-speaking writers, John Milton in the preface to *Samson Agonistes* (1671) interprets Aristotle to mean that tragic catharsis operates on the homeopathic principle; he draws an analogy from medicine, wherein "things of melancholic hue and quality are used against melancholy, sour against sour, salt to remove salt humours." William Wordsworth, shifting the reference from dramatic to *lyric poetry, offers a humanitarian interpretation: that readers are to be "humbled and humanized" and to be purged of the prejudices and blindnesses arising from false sophistication and snobbery "in order that they may be purified and exalted" ("Essay, Supplementary to the Preface," 1815). I. A. Richards (*Principles of Literary Criticism*, 1925) interprets the cathartic process as a reconciliation and reequilibration of "Pity, the impulse to approach, and Terror, the impulse to retreat," along with various other groups of discordant impulses, affirming the importance of tragedy on the ground that "there is no other way in which such impulses, once awakened, can be set at rest without suppression." Subsequently, Northrop Frye (*Anatomy of Criticism*, 1957) described *catharsis* as "not the raising of an actual emotion, but the raising and casting out of an actual emotion on a wave of something else." He identifies that "something else" as "exhilaration or exuberance," an experience "as much intellectual as it is emotional." While *catharsis* has long been interpreted as some form of purgation or purification, there has been increasing momentum in recent years toward integrating the concept with ideas from philosophy, psychology, and cognitive science.

*See* CLASSICAL POETICS.

■ J. Bernays, *On Catharsis* (1857); M. T. Herrick, *The Poetics of Aristotle in England* (1903); H. House, *Aristotle's Poetics* (1956); B. Hathaway, *The Age of Criticism* (1962); Aristotle, *Poetics*, trans. D. W. Lucas (1968); *Aristotle's Poetics*, ed. and trans. L. Golden and O. B. Hardison (1968); T. Brunius, "Catharsis," *DHI*; P. Laín Entralgo, *The Therapy of the Word in Classical Antiquity* (1970), ch. 5; D. Keesey, "On Some Recent Interpretations of Catharsis," *Classical World* 72 (1978–79); T. J. Scheff, *Catharsis in Healing, Ritual, and Drama* (1979); F. Sparshott, "The Riddle of *Katharsis*," *Centre and Labyrinth*, ed. E. Cook et al. (1983); R. Janko, *Aristotle on Comedy* (1984); C. Wagner, "'Katharsis' in der aristotelischen Tragödiendefinition," *Grazer Beiträge* 11 (1984); A. K. Abdulla, *Catharsis in Literature* (1985); G. F. Else, *Plato and Aristotle on Poetry* (1986); M. C. Nussbaum, *The Fragility of Goodness* (1986); N. Lukacher, "Anamorphic Stuff: Shakespeare, Catharsis, Lacan," *South Atlantic Quarterly* 88 (1989); C. Willett, "Hegel, Antigone, and the Possibility of Ecstatic Dialogue," *Philosophy and Literature* 14 (1990); B. Rubidge, "Catharsis through Admiration: Corneille, Le Moyne, and the Social Uses of Emotion,"

*MP* 95 (1998); V. C. Sobchack, "The Violent Dance: A Personal Memoir of Death in the Movies," *Screening Violence*, ed. S. Prince (2000); R. W. Rader, "From Richardson to Austen: 'Johnson's Rule' and the Development of the Eighteenth-Century Novel of Moral Action," *The Novel*, ed. D. J. Hale (2006); L. Potter, "Shakespeare, Marlowe, and the Fortunes of Catharsis," *'Rapt in Secret Studies': Emerging Shakespeares*, ed. D. Chalk and L. Johnson (2010).

P. WELLER; L. GOLDEN

**CAUDA,** coda (Lat., "tail"). A short line, or tail, that, in a stanza of longer lines usually rhymes with another, similar line, making the stanza *heterometric. Dante in *De vulgari eloquentia* divides the *canzone into two parts, *frons* and cauda, subdividing the *frons* further into two *pedes*. The form *aabccb* and its derivatives, with *b*-line caudae rhyming, which developed in med. Lat. and was popular in Fr. and ME metrical romances, is known as *tail rhyme. The *sapphic is another caudate form. The *caudate sonnet has a longer, plurilinear tail; cf. the *bob and wheel.

T.V.F. BROGAN

**CAUDATE SONNET.** A sonnet augmented by coda or tail (Lat. *cauda*). Usually the coda following the 14 lines is introduced by a half line and followed by a couplet in pentameters; it may also be followed by additional tails. Established in It. by Francesco Berni (1497–1536), the caudate sonnet was employed by Michelangelo in a poem written while he was painting the Sistine Chapel and was imported by John Milton into Eng. in the satiric "On the New Forcers of Conscience under the Long Parliament." G. M. Hopkins wrote three caudate sonnets, incl. "That Nature is a Heraclitean Fire and of the Comfort of the Resurrection," an especially experimental, expansive sonnet aberration, with its 13-word title, *alexandrine lines, three codas, and extra half line; Feeney writes that "the very form of a caudal sonnet is itself a play on the It. and Miltonic sonnet's traditional form," calling these three sonnets "the climax of Hopkins's poetry and of his play." Other caudate sonnets include those by A. Samain in Fr. and by R. M. Rilke in Ger. The *bob and wheel, though in shorter lines, is analogous, and tailing is another common form of stanzaic variation. The caudate sonnet may be contrasted with shortened sonnet experiments, especially Hopkins's so-called *curtal sonnet.

*See* TAIL RHYME.

■ J. S. Smart, *The Sonnets of Milton* (1921); J. Dubu, "Le Sonetto caudato de Michel-Ange à Milton," *Le Sonnet à la Renaissance*, ed. Y. Bellenger (1988); J. Feeney, *The Playfulness of Gerard Manley Hopkins* (2008); *The Making of a Sonnet*, ed. E. Hirsch and E. Boland (2008).

T.V.F. BROGAN; L. R. SPAAR

**CAVALIER POETS.** A mod. term for poets associated with Charles I's court and cause during the Eng. civil war, also known as Caroline poets (from "Carolus," i.e., Charles). Cavaliers wrote polished *lyrics and *epigrams on love and sex, friendship and convivial drinking, court and country pleasures, and poetry itself. Avoiding the Elizabethan *sonnet, many adopted the aggressive masculinity and bold conceits of John Donne's love lyrics and elegies, as well as Ben Jonson's imitation of cl. models (whence the designation Sons of Ben), particularly *anacreontic celebrations of wine and sex, Roman *carpe diem poems, Horace's convivial and rural *odes, and Martial's epigrams.

Four Cavaliers suggest their range. Thomas Carew (1595–1640) writes an exquisite erotic compliment, "Ask Me No More," and the "Rapture," urging a woman to an "Elysium" of intensely imagined sexual bliss. Amid wars, he celebrates the court and country estates as havens of peace and pleasure; his poems on Jonson and Donne delineate and imitate their achievements. Robert Herrick (1591–1674), whose "Ode to Ben Jonson" commemorates the "lyric feasts" in London taverns with his poetic master before Herrick became a country parson, writes metrically intricate lyrics and epigrams enlivened by surprising diction, both Latinate (e.g., "liquefaction") and colloquial (e.g., "slug-a-bed"). Against Puritan strictures, he celebrates Eng. fairies and spells, country festivities with a blend of cl. and scriptural allusion (most famously in "Corinna's Going A-Maying"), and women's bewitching dress ("Delight in Disorder," "Upon Julia's Clothes"). He urges virgins to marry in a distinctively avuncular carpe diem ("To the Virgins, to Make Much of Time") and writes tender epitaphs on infants (part of his overall celebration of "little things"), earthy comic epigrams, and poems asserting, in Roman accents, poetry's immortalizing power. With psychological acuity regarding male desire and a nonchalant, debunking, intentionally shocking air, the lyrics of John Suckling (1609–41?) expose romance's "couzenage," declare sexual "appetite" the creator of beauty, and prefer sexual titillation to "fruition," i.e., consummation (a theme in several Cavaliers). The Royalist soldier and prisoner Richard Lovelace (1618–57) famously values military "Honor" over love ("To Lucasta, on Going to the Wars") but also indulges in a later poem in explicitly masturbatory fantasy of sexual liberty ("Love Made in the First Age"). Several knotty lyrics draw ethicopolitical lessons from emblematic animals; the best, "The Grasshopper," adapts anacreontic and Horatian motifs to celebrate convivial drinking and endurance after Charles I's defeat.

Other Cavaliers include Edmund Waller (1606–87), whose smooth couplets were a Restoration model but who is now best known for his politely cruel carpe diem, "Go, Lovely Rose"; William Davenant (1606–68), who was unusual in attempting epic, his unfinished *Gondibert*; Richard Corbett (1582–1635); Thomas Randolph (1605–35); Sidney Godolphin (1610–43); William Cartwright (1611–43); and Thomas Stanley (1625–78). Contemporaries who were not primarily Cavaliers sometimes wrote in their vein, incl. Henry Vaughan (1621–95) in his early secular poetry and Andrew Marvell (1621–78), most notably in "To

His Coy Mistress." In his *Poems* (1645) and 1650s convivial sonnets, the ambitious visionary Puritan poet John Milton (1608–74) betrays generic and thematic affinities with Cavalier contemporaries, from whom he self-consciously distinguishes himself.

*See* ENGLAND, POETRY OF.

■ E. Miner, *The Cavalier Mode from Jonson to Cotton* (1971); *Ben Jonson and the Cavalier Poets*, ed. H. Maclean (1974); G. Braden, *The Classics and English Renaissance Poetry* (1979); R. Helgerson, *Self-Crowned Laureates: Spenser, Jonson, Milton, and the Literary System* (1983); L. Marcus, *The Politics of Mirth* (1986); G. Hammond, *Fleeting Things: English Poets and Poems, 1616–1660* (1990); J. Scodel, *Excess and the Mean in Early Modern English Literature* (2001).

J. SCODEL

**CELTIC PROSODY.** Celtic tribes were prominent on the Eur. continent in the middle of the first millennium BCE and by the mid-3rd c. had spread into Asia Minor in the east, the Iberian peninsula in the west, and the Brit. Isles in the north. Celtic warriors sacked Rome in 380 BCE and raided the oracle at Delphi in 260 BCE; they were known as one of the four great barbarian peoples (along with Scythians, Libyans, and Persians). Our information about the nature and customs of these continental Celts comes from Gr. (and later Roman) ethnographers. Their commentaries date from around the 6th c. BCE; but from the Gr. historian Posidonius, by way of Diodorus Siculus (1st c. BCE) and the somewhat later Strabo, we discover important information about the practice of poetry. Diodorus says that the Celts had three classes of learned and privileged men: (1) βάρδοι, *bards who were poets and who sang eulogies and satires accompanied by stringed instruments; (2) δρυίδαι, druids who were philosophers and theologians; and (3) μάντεις, seers (Strabo calls them ουάτεις, Lat. *vates*). Caesar too was probably drawing on the Posidonian trad. when he wrote, concerning the extensive training of the druids, that they commit to memory immense amounts of poetry and that their study may last as long as twenty years. From these and similar accounts, it is clear that poetry was a prestigious occupation among the continental Celts. But it must be emphasized that none of this poetry has survived and that, therefore, nothing is known of its *prosody.

By the time Celtic tribes had migrated into the Brit. Isles, their once-common Celtic lang. had split into two principal branches: Goidelic (whence the Gaelic langs. of Ireland, Scotland, and Isle of Man) and Brittonic (whence Welsh, Breton, and Cornish [see IRELAND, POETRY OF; SCOTLAND, POETRY OF; WELSH POETRY; BRETON POETRY; CORNISH POETRY]). In these langs., and more specifically in Ir. and Welsh, we find the earliest recorded Celtic poetry, though it must be stressed that it is more properly to be regarded as Ir. poetry and Welsh poetry. We must, therefore, speak of Ir. prosody and of Welsh prosody. It is remarkable that the earliest extant vernacular manuals of prosody in Europe are Ir., dating back to the end of the 8th c. (R. Thurneysen [1912], 78–89; G. Calder).

The early Ir. and Welsh poets, like those of their forebears among the continental Celts, exercised an authoritative function in society as members of a professional class (P. Sims-Williams). The earliest Ir. poetry included both rhyming and nonrhyming verse. One type of nonrhyming verse consisted of units with two or three stressed words linked by *alliteration. This type occurs in genealogical poems, poems in secular sagas, and in legal tracts. Another type of nonrhyming verse is syllabic rather than stress, e.g., a seven-syllable line with a trisyllabic cadence at the end (L. Breatnach). Calvert Watkins argued that the most archaic form of versification employed in Old Ir. seems to be a reflex of the IE cadenced verse form that appears in Gr., Sanskrit, and Slavic, if due allowance is made for the fact that IE prosodic patterns were determined by alternation of long and short syllables, whereas Goidelic had adopted alternation of stressed and unstressed syllables as a patterning feature. The earlier term for this nonrhyming verse is *retoiric* (P. Mac Cana), but the favored term now is *rosc(ad)*. While some of the earliest Ir. poetry may well continue an older system derived from IE prosody (in which case we might well call it Celtic prosody), current scholarship argues that the *roscada*, which continued to be composed well into the Old and early Middle Ir. period, are but an elevated form of literary practice and that the influence of late and med. Lat. rhetorical and poetical style on these verse forms cannot be denied (Corthals).

Lat. influence is to be seen also in the syllabic, rhymed verse, which constitutes the bulk of Old and Middle Ir. poetry. Gerard Murphy argued that rhyme and regular syllable count in this poetry derived ultimately from early med. Lat. hymnic poetry. *Dán díreach*, syllabic verse with strict rules about rhyme, alliteration, and so on, characterized the poetry of the middle and early mod. periods in Ireland and in the Gaelic-speaking parts of Scotland as well. *Generic rhyme, whereby consonants were grouped in six phonetic classes, developed early, as did the marking off in the normal four-line stanzas (*rann*). The various metres of *dán díreach* demanded strict employment of *consonance, *assonance, *dissonance, alliteration, and *rhyme; rhyme might be end-line, internal between lines, or end-line with internal of the following line (**aicill* rhyme). The lang. of the poetry was learned in the bardic schools and remained unchanged throughout the period of Ir. cl. poetry, ca. 1200–1650, whether in Ireland or Gaelic Scotland. The intricacy of this poetry is almost unparalleled in Eur. poetry. The complexity of Ir. prosody is paralleled by Welsh prosody, esp. in the period of the Poets of the Princes (*Beirdd y Tywysogion*), 12th to end of the 13th c., and beyond. The following Ir. poem is in a meter called *deibhidhe*, the commonest of the syllabic meters in Ir. bardic poetry and the easiest:

> Dá mbáidhthí an dán, a dhaoine,
> Gan seanchas, gan seanlaoidhe,
> Go bráth, acht athair gach fhir,
> Rachaidh cách gan a chluinsin.
>
> (E. Knott 1966, 78)

(If poetry were suppressed, men, so there was neither history nor old poetry, nothing would be known of any man save only the name of his father.) The unit is the *quatrain. The prosody of *dán díreach* in general involves syllabic count, generic rhyme, internal rhyme, and alliteration. A consonant alliterates either with itself or with the corresponding initial form produced by grammatical mutation; a vowel alliterates with itself or any other. In *deibhidhe*, the meter of the poem quoted, there are seven syllables in each line. Line *a* rhymes with *b*, *c* with *d*. In Ir. rhyme, the stressed vowels must be identical and the consonants of the same generic class and the same quality (i.e., broad or slender). The generic end rhyme is between words of unequal syllabic length (*dhaoine, seanlaoidhe; fhir, chluinsin*). There is alliteration between two words in each line, and the final word of *d* alliterates with the preceding stressed word (*chluinsin, cách*). There must be at least two internal rhymes between *c* and *d* (*bráth, cách; athair, rachaidh*). In every meter, the complete poem should end with the same word or syllable with which it began (*dúnad*, "closure"; see RING COMPOSITION).

Gaelic Scotland shared this trad. of cl. Ir. poetry. Although it was composed and sung in the courts of Scottish chieftains, it remained Ir., both linguistically and culturally (T. Clancy). It is virtually impossible to determine, on purely linguistic or metrical grounds, whether a poem from this period (1200–1650) was composed in Ireland or Scotland or whether it belonged to the beginning or end of that period.

The earliest Welsh poetry, that of Aneirin and Taliesin in the 6th c., seems to have been accentual, although, unlike some of the early Ir. poetry, rhyme as opposed to an unrhymed cadence marked the end of the line. In that early poetry, the syllabic length of lines varies considerably (M. Haycock); however, the number of stresses in each line tended to produce a more or less regular number of syllables. Eventually, syllabic regularity and main rhyme (*prifodl*) characterized all meters in the *awdl*, *englyn*, and *cywydd* categories. An *awdl* is a poem of unregulated length, comprised of various syllabic meters; earlier *awdlau* are monorhymed. The *englyn* forms are stanzaic, the most common being the *englyn unodl union*, comprised of four lines with a single main rhyme. Among the later *awdl* meters are assymetric rhyming couplets (*cywydd* couplets) and, from the 14th c., a *cywydd* is a poem of unregulated length comprised solely of these couplets. The several varieties of these three classes made up the canonical 24 meters. As in Ireland, poets in Wales were trained in bardic schools both orally and with the use of written texts, the bardic grammars (G. J. Williams and E. J. Jones). From the beginning, intricate alliteration and internal rhyme ornamented the lines of the *awdl* and *englyn*; by the end of the 13th c., these features had evolved into the system known as *cynghanedd*. Early in the following century, cynghanedd was introduced into the *cywydd*, and it subsequently became an obligatory feature in every line of strict-meter verse. Dafydd ap Gwilym's *cywydd* address to a seagull (14th c.) is typical:

Yr wylan deg ar lanw dioer,
Unlliw ag eiry neu wenlloer,
Dilwch yw dy degwch di,
Darn fel haul, dyrnfol heli.

(Fair sea gull on the certain tide, of color like snow or the bright moon, spotless is your beauty, a patch like sunlight, gauntlet of the sea.) Each line has seven syllables; the accent in Welsh is usually on the penultimate, so each couplet rhymes a stressed monosyllable with an unstressed polysyllable. Additionally, each line must feature one of the different forms of *cynghanedd*. Lines 1, 2, and 4 of this citation illustrate consonantal *cynghanedd*, i.e., the sequence of consonants around the main stressed vowel before the *caesura is exactly repeated around a different stressed vowel in the second half of the line. Lines 1 and 4 have *cynghanedd groes*; thus, in line 1, the sequence *r l n d* is echoed: yR wyLaN Dég | aR LaNw Díoer. Line 2 has *cynghanedd draws*, with unanswered consonants before the echoed sequence: úNLLiw | [ag eiry neu] wéNLLoer. Line 3 illustrates tripartite *cynghanedd sain*, where the first and second parts of the line rhyme, and the second and third demonstrate consonantal *cynghanedd*: dilwch | yw dy Dégwch | Dí. A further category of *cynghanedd* is *cynghanedd lusg*, where the unstressed penultimate syllable of the line rhymes with the syllable immediately preceding the caesura. A full discussion of *cynghanedd* would require many more pages.

Generally speaking, the Celtic bards, rather like the Ir. illuminators of the *Book of Kells*, chose to fill minute spaces decoratively. At their best, as in the Ir. and Welsh examples just quoted, they were capable of providing not only an intricate phonetic texture but a brilliant network of imagery that illuminated their poems in a manner that is perceptible even in trans.

Traces of one type of Welsh *cynghanedd* may be seen in the few bits of Breton poetry that survive from the late Middle Ages, suggesting that Brittany may have shared in a Brittonic prosodic system. The surviving late med. Cornish verse shows no signs of participating in a Brittonic or Celtic prosodic system.

With the decline of the bardic orders in the Celtic countries, new and simpler meters became increasingly popular. In part, these are the products of amateur versification; in part, they may represent the legitimization of popular and perhaps ancient song meters hitherto unrecorded; and in part, they certainly represent the adaptation of foreign meters. When the secret of generic rhyme was lost, the most appealing device for Ir. and Scottish Gaelic poets seems to have been assonance. Typical is an Ir. song composed by Geoffrey Keating (17th c.), which is in the new Ir. stressed verse known as *amhrán* and begins:

Óm sgeol ar ard-mhagh Fáil ní chodlaim oídhche.

The last stressed vowel of the five stressed syllables in the first line assonates with each of the last stressed syllables in all of the following lines of the stanza, as in the OF *laisse. But, additionally, each of the other four stressed vowels in the first line assonates with its coun-

terparts in all of the following lines, so that the melody of the stanza consists of a sequence of five stressed vowels (here *o-a-a-o-i*).

Scottish Gaelic song poetry begins to appear in mss. and print in the later 18th c., though its roots go back well into the Middle Ages (W. Gillies).

In Wales, *canu rhydd*, free-meter poetry, a poetry depending not upon syllabic regularity but rather upon rhythm and accent, had been around since the time of Aneirin but was not preserved in abundance until the 16th c. (Davies). Some of this is poetry composed in imitation of strict meters but without *cynghanedd* and with less attention to syllable count. The rest consists of stanzas set to existing musical airs, some of which were imported from England. However, strict-meter poetry with *cynghanedd* was not threatened by these popular devels., and its popularity remains strong today.

*See* MASCULINE AND FEMININE.

■ **General:** Parry, *History*; Williams and Ford, *Literacy in Medieval Celtic Societies*, ed. H. Pryce (1998); *The New Companion to the Literature of Wales*, ed. M. Stephens (1998).

■ **Irish:** R. Thurneysen, "Zur irischen Accent-und Verslehre," *Révue Celtique* 6 (1883–85); "Mittelirische Verslehren," *Irische Texte*, ed. W. Stokes and E. Windisch, vol. 3 (1891); "Zu den mittelirischen Verslehren," *Abh. der königl. Akad. der Wiss. zu Gött., philol.-hist. Klasse* 14, no. 2 (1912); "Über die älteste irische Dichtung," *Abh. der königl. Preussische Akad. der Wiss., philos.-hist. Klasse*, nos. 6, 10 (1914); G. Calder, *Auraicept na n-Éces, the Scholars' Primer* (1917); O. Bergin, "The Principles of Alliteration," *Eriu* 9 (1921–23); W. Meyer, "Die Verskunst der Iren in rhythmischen lateinischen Gedichten," Meyer, vol. 3; E. Knott, *Irish Classical Poetry* (1957); G. Murphy, *Early Irish Metrics* (1961); C. Watkins, "Indo-European Metrics and Archaic Irish Verse," *Celtica* 6 (1963); E. Knott, *An Introduction to Irish Syllabic Poetry of the Period 1200–1600*, 2d ed. (1966); P. Mac Cana, "On the Use of the Term *Retoric*," *Celtica* 7 (1966); *Irish Bardic Poetry*, texts and trans. O. Bergin, ed. D. Greene (1970); E. Campanille, "Indogermanische Metrik und altirische Metrik," *ZCP* 37 (1979); L. Breatnach, "Poets and Poetry," *Progress in Medieval Irish Studies* (1996); J. Corthals, "Early Irish *Retoirics* and Their Late Antique Background," *Cambrian Medieval Celtic Studies* 31 (1996); P. K. Ford, *The Celtic Poets: Songs and Tales from Early Ireland and Wales* (1999); P. Sims-Williams, "Medieval Irish Literary Theory and Criticism," *CHLC*, v. 2, ed. A. Minnis and I. Johnson (2005).

■ **Scottish Gaelic:** D. Thomson, *An Introduction to Gaelic Poetry*, 2d ed. (1989); T. Clancy, "The Poetry of the Court: Praise," and W. Gillies, "Gaelic Literature in the Later Middle Ages," *The Edinburgh History of Scottish Literature*, vol. 1 (2007).

■ **Welsh:** G. J. Williams and E. J. Jones, *Gramadegau'r Penceirddiaid* (1934); Jarman and Hughes, esp. E. Rowlands, "Cynghanedd, Metre, Prosody"; Morris-Jones; A. T. E. Matonis, "The Welsh Bardic Grammars and the Western Grammatical Tradition," *MP* 79 (1981); R. Bromwich, *Aspects of the Poetry of Dafydd ap Gwilym* (1986); T. Conran, *Welsh Verse*, 2d ed. (1986); M. Haycock, "Metrical Models for the Poems in The Book of Taliesin," *Early Welsh Poetry*, ed. B. F. Roberts (1988); C. Davies, "Early Free-Metre Poetry," and N. Lloyd, "Late Free-Metre Poetry," *A Guide to Welsh Literature*, v. 3, ed. R. G. Gruffydd (1997).

■ **Breton:** *Histoire Littéraire et Culturelle de la Bretagne*, 3 vols., ed. J. Balcou and Y. Le Gallo (1987).
■ **Cornish:** R. Maber, "Celtic Prosody in Late Cornish: The *englyn* 'an lavar kôth yu lavar guîr'," *Bulletin of the Board of Celtic Studies* (1988); B. Bruch, "Cornish Verse Forms, the Evolution of Cornish Prosody," diss., Harvard University (2005); O. Padel, "Oral and Literary Culture in Medieval Cornwall," *Medieval Celtic Literature and Society*, ed. H. Fulton (2005).

P. K. FORD; A. Ll. JONES

**CENTO** (Lat., "patchwork"). A verse composition made up of lines selected from the work or works of some great poet(s) of the past. Homer largely served this purpose in Gr. lit., ranging from the adaptations by Trygaeus of various lines in the *Iliad* and *Odyssey* reported by Aristophanes (*Peace* 1090–94) to the *Homerokentrones* of the Byzantine period. Similarly, Virgil was the most popular source for *centos* in later Roman times. The oldest of those extant is the tragedy *Medea* by Hosidius Geta (2d c. CE), while the *Cento nuptialis* of Ausonius and the *Cento Vergilianus* of Proba (both 4th c. CE) are among others drawn from his work. Ren. and later works of this kind included the Eng. *Cicero princeps* (1608), a treatise on government compiled from Cicero. Centos are still occasionally published, e.g., the late poem "Antologia" by the Brazilian modernist Manuel Bandeira (1886–1968), a *pastiche of lines from throughout his long career, incl. some of his most widely recognized such as "Vou-me embora pra Pasárgada" (I'm going away to Pasárgada).

*See* ANTHOLOGY, CONTRAFACTUM.
■ J. O. Delepierre, *Tableau de la littérature du centon chez les anciens et chez les modernes*, 2 v. (1874–75); R. Lamacchia, "Dall'arte allusiva al centone," *Atene e Roma* n.s. 3 (1958); "Cento," *Oxford Classical Dictionary*, ed. N.G.L. Hammond and H. H. Scullard, 2d ed. (1970); T. Augarde, *Oxford Guide to Word Games*, 2d ed. (2003); P. K. Saint-Amour, *The Copyrights* (2004).

R. J. GETTY; T.V.F. BROGAN

**CHAIN RHYME** (Ger. *Kettenreim, äusserer Reim, verschr, änkter Reim*). Interlocking or interlaced rhyme that refers to any rhyme scheme in which one line or stanza links to the next line or stanza, forming a pattern of alternating rhymes. *Terza rima is one form: here the medial rhyme in each *tercet becomes the enclosing ones of the next, *aba bcb cdc*, and so on. Robert Frost extends this scheme to the quatrain in "Stopping by Woods on a Snowy Evening." Examples of chain rhyme range widely, from Af. folk forms and Eng. *nursery rhymes to Edmund Spenser's *Amoretti*. According to Myers and Wukasch, the *villanelle also employs chain rhyme, since the first and third lines of the initial tercet alternately recur as the third line of

subsequent tercets, *A1bA2 abA1 abA2*, and so forth. Chain rhyme, like *cross rhyme, has recently been used by scholars to refer to the *abab* pattern. Historically, though, chain rhyme, also identified as linked rhyme by Turco, rhymes the last word of one line to the first word of the next line, creating a chiming effect. In Fr. prosody, the *Grands *Rhétoriqueurs* of the late 15th and early 16th cs. developed the terms *rime fratrisée, entrelacée, enchaînée*, and *annexxée* for a rhyme sound or syllable at line end repeated at the beginning of the next line. The repeated syllable, however, must carry a different meaning. Recent scholars (Alim, Bradley) have noted the abundant use of chain rhyme in Am. rap and hip-hop (see HIP-HOP POETICS), which not only serves to effect a technique of generative improvisation but creates an incantatory effect; the sound repetition is typically amplified by the addition of *internal rhyme. Rapper Talib Kweli, with Pharaoh and Common, employs chain rhyme in "The Truth." Chain rhyme extended to repetition of entire words becomes the rhetorical figure *anadiplosis, a type of *concatenation.
■ Patterson; L. Turco, *The Book of Forms: A Handbook of Poetics,* 3d ed. (2000); H. S. Alim, "On Some Serious Next Millennium Rap Ishhh," *Journal of English Linguistics* 31 (2003); J. Myers and D. Wukasch, *A Dictionary of Poetic Terms* (2003); A. Bradley, *Book of Rhymes: The Poetics of Hip Hop* (2009).

T.V.F. BROGAN; J. CHANG

**CHANSO, CHANSON.** *See* FRANCE, POETRY OF; OCCITAN POETRY; SONGBOOK; TROUBADOUR; TROUVÈRE.

**CHANSON DE GESTE**

  I. Gestes, Continuations, Cycles
  II. Form and Style
  III. Ethics and Politics
  IV. Aesthetics
  V. The Religious, the Exotic, and the Fantastic

An *epic poem recounting the feats of Charlemagne or other kings of the Carolingian era and their barons. The term *geste* originally meant "heroic deeds" but came also to signify the "historical record" provided by the texts relating them and, by extension, the "family" or "lineage" responsible for them. Around 120 poems survive. Early crit. focused on the question of the origins of the corpus: the "traditionalists" argued from the presence of elements of historical fact in the songs that they were the textual remnants of a collective oral trad. going back to the era of the events told (this view was revived in the 1950s by Rychner). But the extant versions, found in some 300 mss., date mainly from the 12th and 13th cs., and their preoccupations are arguably those of this period: hence, the opposing, "individualist" view (pioneered by Bédier) that they are authorial creations with little regard for "tradition." The *chansons de geste* show evidence of interaction with other 12th- and 13th-c. literary genres, principally romance (see MEDIEVAL ROMANCE) but also chronicles, lyric, and hagiography. Some chansons have come down to us in a series of different redactions: e.g., the *Chanson de Roland*, whose Anglo-Norman version is one of the earliest and undoubtedly the best known of all chansons de geste, also survives in three OF and three Franco-It. versions. Carolingian epics were widely diffused: most codices are in OF, but there is an important set of chansons de geste in Anglo-Norman (incl. *Gormont et Isembard* and *La Chanson de Guillaume*, two of the earliest surviving texts), a small group of Occitan epics (*Girart de Roussillon, Daurel et Beton*), and a large corpus of poems in the hybrid literary lang. of Franco-It., mainly locatable to the Veneto (*La Geste Francor, L'Entrée d'Espagne*). Independent It. reworkings of the material grew out of the latter corpus, and chansons de geste were elsewhere translated into MHG, Middle Dutch, ON, and Icelandic, as well as influencing the Castilian epic. The genre was well known and highly popular and continued to be rewritten, compiled, and revived—particularly in prose recasting—into the 16th c.

**I. Gestes, Continuations, Cycles.** Mod. crit. has tended to follow the classification given by the med. author Bertrand de Bar-sur-Aube in the epic *Girart de Vienne* (ca. 1180), which divides the chansons into three gestes: *la geste du roi* (narrating the deeds of Charlemagne and his barons, incl. Roland), *la geste de Garin de Monglane* (concerning the lineage of Garin, ancestor of the great Guillaume d'Orange), and *la geste de Doon de Mayence* (a group of rebel barons and traitors). However, only one of these groupings—*la geste de Garin de Monglane*—appears in mss. as a cycle. The largest cyclical Garin codex unites 18 poems about Guillaume, his ancestors, and his kinsmen the Narbonnais (the Narbonnais poems are also found as a cycle in their own right). Although one codex gathers a selection of texts concerning rebel barons (incl. *Doon de Mayence, La Chevalerie d'Ogier*, and *Renaut de Montauban*), it is perhaps preferable not to give too much priority to Bertrand's categorization but rather to speak of a general tendency of epics to collect themselves into sequences and to recruit additional songs as *proems (such as *Enfances* texts narrating the youthful exploits of well-known heroes) and sequels (incl. *Mort* and *Moniage* texts, telling of a hero's final days). The *Chanson de Roland* inspired a number of continuations and prologues such as *Anseïs de Carthage, Aspremont*, and *Gaydon*. Other groupings are the vast Crusade Cycle (historical poems about the First and Third Crusades, with imaginative continuations); the Franco-It. *Geste Francor* (featuring texts about Pepin and the young Charlemagne and Roland), and sets of poems associated with the heroes Huon de Bordeaux, Jourdain de Blaye, and Renaut de Montauban; and the Loheren, Nanteuil, and Saint-Gille lineages.

**II. Form and Style.** Most chansons de geste are in *decasyllables, although some are in *octosyllables or dodecasyllables, also known as *alexandrines. Lines are grouped into strophes called *laisses, which are united by *assonance in most poems. Rhyme began to feature from the late 12th c., and the use of assonance after this point may be a deliberate archaism signaling the age and trad. of the material. The decasyllabic line normally features a *caesura after four syllables, with the first part of the line often filled by repeated formulas. This can be viewed as evidence of the poems' oral composition (Rychner), but many repetitive, seemingly "oral," elements are, in fact, part of the epics' functioning as written texts. Not only phrases but actions are repeated, such as when a series of laisses retell the same event from different perspectives (*laisses similaires*) or when separate events are made analogous by being described in roughly the same terms (*laisses parallèles*). More broadly, similar characters and plots recur. The overall tendency toward repetition inspired and enabled continuations, many of which feature new generations of warriors who avenge their kinsmen or pursue the grievances of their forefathers. The formulas used to describe characters make them fixed types who act out timeless conflicts: valiant heroes versus their evil opponents, either *Saracens* (a catchall term used interchangeably with the term *pagan* to describe the religious enemies of Christians) or cowardly, underhanded traitors. The entire genre suggests that the past is never dead and buried; the epics are set in a Carolingian past that is always also present, portrayed as having unmistakable similarities with the periods in which the poems were written, reworked, and compiled.

**III. Ethics and Politics.** The dramatic tension animating the chansons de geste comes partly from a clash between a warrior ethos advocating uncompromising, to-the-death violence as the solution to all problems and another ethos that sees violence itself as the problem and seeks to restrain bloodthirsty tendencies. The hero is the privileged site of controversies: he inspires and unifies as the incarnation of the hopes and dreams of a particular community, for victory (e.g., Roland) or for peace and stability (e.g., Guillaume in *Le Couronnement de Louis*); but he also pursues singularity, desiring to stand alone, independent of the rest of humanity (the extreme case is *Raoul de Cambrai*, which describes the unfettered destruction following Raoul's complete alienation from all social structures). There are a number of communal groupings in the epics: families and lineages; crusade identities gathering diverse Western Christian soldiers under the banner of "Franks"; alliances with the emperor or king; and homosocial cohesion on the battlefield, where fellow combatants are frequently mirror images of each other (a logic carried to its culmination in *Ami et Amile*, whose two heroes are practically indistinguishable). Each of these structures creates solidarity but also produces and excludes an opposite: family loyalty leads to vengeful and never-ending feuds against other families; crusade ideology demonizes the Saracen enemy; rebellions ensue when the sovereign favors one party; and restrictive gender politics brings violence against women or their marginalization. Though attempts have been made to incorporate the chansons de geste into a national Fr. literary canon, they generally represent the interests of one narrow social group: powerful regional barons. The "rebel baron" epics argue for the barons' right to attack the king to seek redress for injustice (*Gaydon, Renaut de Montauban*); other poems feature a baron resisting the king in an attempt to preserve the independence of a region not considered to be part of "France," such as Burgundy (*Aspremont*) and Occitania (*Girart de Roussillon*). The baronial perspective explains the tyrannical qualities of the king in many texts, where he is intransigent, omnipotent, and unreasonable. The corpus as a whole is engaged with contemp. politics: the narratives are reflections on concepts such as sovereignty, fealty, and lordship, and they feature ethical debates on the rights and wrongs of war. But such discussions are repeatedly overridden by the prevailing drive to violence, and the society portrayed is subject to self-destructive impulses.

**IV. Aesthetics.** The chansons de geste are thrilling, eventful texts, whose most striking aesthetic feature is the vivid and gory presentation of violence. The sights and sounds of battle are described in horrifying detail: men and horses are chopped in two, limbs are lost, bowels and brains spill out, and blood pours onto grass, producing a contrast of colors that is often remarked on. The recurring phrase "or veïssiez" (now you would have seen) invites readers and listeners to imagine themselves at the scene. There is a repeated movement from an aesthetic of order and beauty, as warriors line up and armor glistens, to one of chaos and destruction. In the thick of battle, critical reflection on the consequences of violence is suspended, and we are encouraged to become emotionally involved in the action. Enemies are often monstrous or devious, whereas heroes are proud, honorable, and muscular. Violence is thereby justified as part of a transcendent struggle between the forces of good and evil.

**V. The Religious, the Exotic, and the Fantastic.** The chansons de geste are ostensibly religious texts: their heroes are the soldiers of God, who pray frequently, devote themselves to war against confessional enemies, and are always ready to sacrifice their lives (martyrs include Vivien in *Aliscans* and Roland). But beneath this lie more earthly considerations: crusade is inspired by the desire for land and power (as witness *Le Charroi de Nîmes*); the East is a place of exotic treasure (*Le Pèlerinage de Charlemagne*), of magic and the fantastic (*Huon de Bordeaux*), or of multilingual diversity (*L'Entrée d'Espagne*); and the Saracen is as much an object of fascination as a religious other. In some texts, an alluring Saracen princess helps the Christian hero conquer territory before converting to Christianity and marrying him (*La Prise d'Orange*). Other Saracens are integrated into Christian society because of their usefulness as warriors and allies, such as the giant Rainouart in *Aliscans*. Elsewhere, the religious aspect of the texts is merely an exit from otherwise intractable narrative problems or a way to transcend violence. In *Girart de Vienne*, God stops a combat between Roland and his future companion Oliver, and the *Chanson de Roland* ends with God's miracle ensuring justice is done. Some texts have saintly endings where the hero becomes a monk or hermit to atone for a life of violent sin (*Girart de Roussillon, Le Moniage Guillaume*).

*See* FRANCE, POETRY OF; HEROIC VERSE; JONGLEUR; NARRATIVE POETRY.

■ J. Bédier, *Les Légendes épiques* (1926–29); J. Rychner, *La Chanson de geste* (1955); W. C. Calin, *The Old French Epic of Revolt* (1962); M. de Combarieu du Grès, *L'Idéal humain et l'expérience morale chez les héros des chansons de geste* (1979); E. Heinemann, *L'art métrique de la chanson de geste* (1993); F. Suard, *La Chanson de geste* (1993); D. Boutet, *La Chanson de geste* (1995); S. Gaunt, *Gender and Genre in Medieval French Literature* (1995); S. Kay, *The "Chansons de geste" in the Age of Romance* (1995); K. Busby, *Codex and Context* (2002); F. E. Sinclair, *Milk and Blood: Gender and Genealogy in the Chanson de geste* (2003); P. Bennett, *Carnaval-héroïque et écriture cyclique dans la geste de Guillaume d'Orange* (2006); S. Kinoshita, *Medieval Boundaries: Rethinking Difference in Old French Literature* (2006); A. Cowell, *The Medieval Warrior Aristocracy* (2007); J. Gilbert, "The *Chanson de Roland*," *The Cambridge Companion to Medieval French Literature*, ed. S. Gaunt and S. Kay (2008); L. Sunderland, *Old French Narrative Cycles* (2010).

L. SUNDERLAND

**CHANSON DE TOILE.** Among the earliest secular Fr. lyric poems are the *chansons de toile* (12th to 13th cs.), short narrative poems with *refrains describing the loves and sorrows of young women. They are mostly anonymous. There is no evidence of female authorship, unlike in the songs attributed to women *trouvères* or *trobairitz*. The chansons de toile are composed in meters and verse schemes similar to early saints' lives or *chansons de geste*. They are said to have accompanied women's textile work, but their surviving melodies are ornate. Their content and use of refrains link them to the OF courtly genres such as the *mal mariée* and the *pastourelle*.

*See* CANSO.

■ E. J. Burns, "Sewing like a Girl: Working Women in the *Chansons de Toile*," in *Medieval Woman's Song*, ed. A. L. Klinck and A. M. Rasmussen (2002); M. O'Neill, *Courtly Love Songs of Medieval France: Transmission and Style in the Trouvère Repertoire* (2006); C. Léglu, "Space and Movement in the Old French *chansons de toile*," *Parergon* 24 (2007).

C. LÉGLU

**CHANT.** A mode of verbal performance between speech and song, chant is, strictly speaking, oral poetry organized rhythmically by the internal rhythms of lang. and the external rhythms of music. Lat. texts of the Roman Catholic liturgy have been sung since the early Middle Ages in monodic, unaccompanied, and metrically flexible Gregorian chant or "plainsong." Oral poetry composed as chant is distinguished by various strong patterns of *repetition: phonetic repetition (e.g., stress, *alliteration, nonsense syllables), lexical and phrasal repetition (key words or stock formulas, *anaphora, *refrains), grammatical and semantic *parallelism and contrast (*catalogs; stichic or hemistichic structures; recurring names, images, or allusions). Such devices may be reinforced with percussive instruments (tapping sticks, drums, rattles, hand claps, foot stamps) and dance steps.

Chant involves a complex thread of associations. Musically, it is an ambiguous term, referring both to the short melody or phrase to which words are sung (as in a *psalm or canticle) and to the psalm or canticle that is chanted. Where chant signifies melody, the emphasis falls squarely on its steady monotonousness. Communally performed chant carries strong symbolic valences. It brings individuals together into a single body of chanters or dancers, in effect creating a society, at least temporarily, through the chant rhythm. This important social function appears in numerous forms of communal chanting: the dance songs of Eskimo villages; the great mythological chants of aboriginal Australian, Polynesian, and southwest Am. Indian ritual; communal prayer, such as the temple chanting of Buddhist monks and the litanies of Christian congregations; work songs of various kinds; the game songs of children (jump-rope rhymes, counting-out verses, taunts).

In written lit., chant appears as far back as the Vedas of India and the Psalms of the Heb. Bible. The oral form has been imitated in various ways by literary poets such as Christopher Smart, William Blake, Walt Whitman, William Morris, W. B. Yeats, Vachel Lindsay, and Allen Ginsberg. Formal admixtures of chant and lyric (as in Smart, Morris, or Yeats) complicate conventional notions of individualist lyric. Written chants also challenge distinctions between the aesthetic and the instrumental and between oral and print modes.

In the past two centuries, chant has often been associated with political activism—Morris's *Chants for Socialists* (1884, 1885, 1891), reprinted in political *songbooks throughout the 20th c., is a case in point. As poetry, chant disturbs conventional high-cultural ideals: subliterate (spoken not written) and subliterary (instrumentalist not aesthetic), chant describes congregational rather than individual experience. Its complex politics are indicated by affiliations with terms such as "enchant" or "incantation," which share etymological origins (Fr. *chanter*, Lat. *cantāre*, Fr. *incantation*, Lat. *incantātiōnem*, Lat. *incantāre*, Fr. *enchanter*). Where these words intersect with *chant* is in the perceived power of musical form: an *incantation* charms a listener by virtue of being chanted; *to enchant* is to captivate, hold in thrall, or influence. These associations suggest opposed political effects. As a protest march derives much of its symbolic power from movement (resistance as a living, mobile force), chant can effect collective action; from another vantage, chant can be seen as inhibiting the individual's critical capacities.

*See* ABSORPTION, POLITICS AND POETRY.

■ M. S. Edmonson, *Lore* (1971); R. Finnegan, *Oral Poetry* (1977); Welsh; C. Waters, *British Socialists and the Politics of Popular Culture, 1884–1914* (1990); P. Zumthor, *Oral Poetry*, trans. K. Murphy-Judy (1990);

A. F. Janowitz, *Lyric and Labour in the Romantic Tradition* (1998).

A. WELSH; C. ROVEE

**CHANTE-FABLE.** A med. Fr. dramatic recitation composed, as the name implies, of sections of verse and prose, the former intended to be sung, the latter spoken, perhaps by two *jongleurs alternately. The verse form is unusual: a seven-syllable line in *assonance, each lyric ending in a four-syllable line without assonance. Alternating verse and prose is not a rare practice in med. Lat. (see PROSIMETRUM), Ar., Celtic, ON, and Occitan writers. But only the anonymous 13th-c. author of *Aucassin et Nicolette* terms his work a *chante-fable*. *Aucassin et Nicolette* is a beautifully constructed, well-unified love story, with distinct dramatic elements, rich in humor and irony; and it skillfully parodies contemporary *epic and romance. But it survives in only a single ms., and the extent to which it represents a vogue is disputed (Holmes). In China, some 10th-c. *bianwen* (narratives) are in a chante-fable form (see CHINA, POPULAR POETRY OF).

■ J. R. Reinhard, "The Literary Background of the *Chante-Fable*," *Speculum* 1 (1926); *CBFL* 1:2127–35; *MGG* 2:1082–84; U. T. Holmes, *History of Old French Literature* (1962); L. Ch'en, "*Pien-wen* Chantefable and *Aucassin et Nicolette*," *CL* 23 (1971); *Aucassin et Nicolette*, ed. J. Dufournet (1973); J. Trotin, "Vers et Prose dans *Aucassin et Nicolette*," *Rom* 97 (1976); P. Menard, "La Composition de *Aucassin et Nicolette*," *Mélanges de philologie et de littératures romanes offerts à Jeanne Wathelet-Willem* (1978); K. Brownlee, "Discourse as *Proueces* in *Aucassin et Nicolette*," *YFS* 70 (1986); W. Godzich and J. Kittay, *The Emergence of Prose* (1987), ch. 5; A. E. Cobby, *Ambivalent Conventions* (1995).

I. SILVER; B. ROWLAND

**CHANT ROYAL.** One of the most complex and difficult of the OF verse forms. Related to the *ballade*, the *chant royal* in its most common form (as described in the 14th c. by Eustache Deschamps) consists of five stanzas of 11 lines each rhyming *ababccddedE* (the capital denotes a *refrain), followed by a five-line *envoi* rhyming *ddedE*. It is further distinguished by the use of the refrain at the end of each stanza and the envoi and by the fact that, except in the envoi, no rhyme words may be used twice. Thus, 60 lines must be rhymed on five rhyme sounds—a formidable technical task. Its most common theme is love, spiritual or human, embodied in the beautiful courtly lady. The name probably derives from its popularity in literary contests in the bourgeois poet guilds of northern France (*puys royaux*). The term first appears in Nicole de Margival's "Dit de la panthère d'amours" (late 13th c.), but the form, not yet fixed, was used by *troubadours and *trouvères in the 12th c. Through Guillaume de Machaut, Jean Froissart, and Deschamps in the 14th c., the chant royal found wide recognition; but by the 15th c., its popularity waned. Clément Marot composed four *chant royaux*, mainly on religious themes. The *Pléiade* banned the form, but in the 19th and 20th cs., attempts were made to revive it by Théodore de Banville and others. Some of these, like Deschamps, used it for satirical commentary as well as for elevated themes; others, e.g., Richard Le Gallienne, reduced it to *vers de société*. Paul Valéry remarked that, by comparison, the *sonnet is child's play.

■ Kastner; Patterson; L. Stewart, "The *Chant Royal*, a Study of the Evolution of a Genre," *Romania* 96 (1975); Morier, "Ballade"; *Revue des langues romans* 108.1 (2004)—spec. issue on chant royal.

A. PREMINGER; B. ROWLAND

**CHARACTER, THEOPHRASTAN.** At the heart of the trad. of the Theophrastan character lies the philosophical question of reference, i.e., the mechanism underlying how words refer either to abstract ideals and generic types or to concrete, particular individuals. At stake is not only the vacillation between abstract and concrete reference but how this vacillation exhibits itself through a parallel tension between definition and description.

The tradition begins in the late 4th c. BCE with the peripatetic philosopher Theophrastus's work Χαρακτῆρες (*Characters*), which expands on the discussions of human nature in his teacher Aristotle's *Nicomachean Ethics* and *Rhetoric*. After briefly defining a vice, such as garrulity or arrogance, each of the work's 30 sketches then illustrates the vice by a list of behaviors typical of Athenians who embody it. These behavioral descriptions are so concrete that they seem to be descriptions of actual Athenian individuals, i.e., to refer to particulars. However concrete they may seem, the descriptions always refer to generic types; therefore, the subjects of both the definitions and the descriptions in Theophrastus's sketches remain abstract.

Although subsumed by Roman rhet. as ornament, after Theophrastus the character sketch as genre remains unimportant until Isaac Casaubon's 1592 trans. of Theophrastus into Latin brings the work back into fashion. In 17th-c. England, Joseph Hall, Sir Thomas Overbury, and John Earle lead the trad. Unlike Theophrastus, their works add sketches of virtues alongside vices to underscore moral purpose. Because they closely imitate Theophrastus's form, however, they preserve the typological character of his definitions and descriptions. Introducing the proper name, Ben Jonson's *Epigrams* (1616) shifts the nature of reference in the trad. While Jonson retains Theophrastus's—and in his case, Martial's—model to exhibit vices through descriptions of anonymous types, he departs from Theophrastus in that certain of his epigrams name actual individuals, such as John Donne or Thomas Overbury, to extol their virtues alongside his own talent for empirical observation. For the first time in the trad.'s hist., concrete descriptions refer to particular individuals.

Further developments take place in 17th-c. Spain and France. In his *Oráculo manual y arte de prudencia* (*The Art of Worldly Wisdom* [1647]), Baltasar Gracián lists behaviors the reader can adopt, according to circumstance, for self-benefit. In turn, his descriptions refer not to types and individuals imbued with defin-

able moral qualities but to virtual conventions. Finally, in his 1688 *Caractères,* Jean de La Bruyère, like Jonson, assigns his characters proper names, seeming to mark again the union between concrete description and particular reference. Unlike Jonson, however, his proper names refer not to actual individuals but to fictional characters, thereby introducing a new referential territory, a virtual space between the particular and the generic. Omitting the traditional opening definition of each sketch's vice, moreover, he forces his reader to induce what vice each fictional individual represents; this reverses the logical procession from abstract definition to concrete description inherited from Theophrastus.

■ J. Bos, "Individuality and Inwardness in the Literary Character Sketches of the Seventeenth Century," *Journal of the Warburg and Courtald Institutes* 61 (1998); M. Escola, "Le statut des définitions dans les *Caractères*: de Théophraste à La Bruyère," *Lalies* 17 (1997); M. Stein, *Definition und Schilderung in Theophrasts Charakteren* (1992).

K. HUME

**CHARM** (Lat. *carmen*, "song" or "lyric poetry"; also "magic formula" or *"incantation"). Now both a physical amulet worn for magical purposes and a verbal formula used for magical effects. In practice, verbal charms accompany ritual actions and are themselves treated as physical actions or "verbal missiles" (Malinowski); they thus can be turned back by a stronger magician. Charms are used worldwide in traditional cultures for healing (medicinal and fertility charms), success (hunting, weather, love charms), and attack and defense (curses and protection charms). They are usually fixed, traditional texts, partly in a "special language" of power marked by thick, irregular patterns of *repetition (sounds, words, phrases) and often involving archaic vocabulary, unusual phonological and grammatical forms, esoteric names and allusions, or other elements of obscure meaning. A dozen metrical charms survive in OE, accompanied by directions in prose for ritual actions, and the power of several (e.g., "For Infertile Land," "Against a Sudden Stitch") can still be felt.

Magical charms have been directly imitated in Eng. lit. from *Beowulf* (the curse laid on the gold, 3069–75) through Shakespeare (the witches' charm in *Macbeth* 4.1.1–38) to Ezra Pound ("The Alchemist"). On a deeper level, the principle of charms lies beneath both *love poetry (words used to attract a beloved) and *satire (words used to wound an enemy). Even deeper connections exist in the belief that power resides in *sound: poetry strongly influenced by thick sound-patterns of *alliteration, *assonance, *internal rhyme, and word repetition (e.g., in Edmund Spenser, E. A. Poe, and G. M. Hopkins) resembles and partakes somewhat of the ethos of lang. selected for magical purposes and is primarily concerned with evoking and transmitting power.

■ H. M. Chadwick and N. K. Chadwick, *The Growth of Literature*, v. 1 (1932), ch. 15; A. Huxley, "Magic," *Texts and Pretexts* (1933); B. Malinowski, *Coral Gardens and Their Magic*, 2 v. (1935)—texts and theory of Trobri-

and charms; *The Anglo-Saxon Minor Poems*, ed. E.V.K. Dobbie (1942)—texts of OE metrical charms; Frye; R. C. Elliott, *The Power of Satire* (1960); H. D. Chickering Jr., "The Literary Magic of 'Wið Færstice,'" *Viator* 2 (1971)—on OE; N. Frye, "Charms and Riddles," *Spiritus Mundi* (1976); Welsh; H. S. Versnel, "The Poetics of the Magical Charm: An Essay in the Power of Words," *Magic and Ritual in the Ancient World*, ed. P. Mirecki and M. Meyer (2002); J. Roper, *English Verbal Charms* (2005); L. K. Arnovick, *Written Reliquaries* (2006)—on med. Eng.

A. WELSH

**CHASTUSHKA.** The miniature Rus. lyric folk song genre called *chastushka* (fast song) emerged in the 1860s and has since, along with the *anekdot* (joke), become one of the most productive forms in Rus. folklore. The chastushka originates in both city and village; mixes literary and folk elements; ranges from "true" (and often bawdy) folk poetry to political slogans; may be sung, recited, accompanied by a musical instrument, or danced to; is highly improvisational and topical; and concerns mainly young people. The most common type consists of four lines, which usually rhyme. A female lead singer and chorus may perform such "ditties" in long thematically related strings. Jarxo connects the chastushka with similar songs in Ger. and Sp.

■ B. Jarxo, "Organische Struktur des russischen Schnaderhüpfles (Častuška)," *Germanoslavica* 3 (1935); S. Lazutin, *Russkaja častuška* (1960); V. Bokov and V. Baxtin, *Častuška* (1966); B. Stephan, *Studien zur russischen Častuška und ihrer Entwicklung* (1969); Y. Sokolov, *Russian Folklore* (1970); Terras; A. Volkov, *Zavetnye chastushki* (1999).

J. O. BAILEY; C. KLAMANN

**CHIASMUS** (Gr., "a placing crosswise," from the Gr. letter X, "chi," and the verb *chiazein*, "to mark with diagonal lines like an X"). The repetition of a pair of sounds, words, phrases, or ideas in the reverse order, producing an *abba* structure, as in Satan's attempt to rally the rebel angels: "The mind is its own place, and in itself / Can make a Heav'n of Hell, a Hell of Heav'n" (*Paradise Lost* 1.254–55). Although the term *chiasmus* appears in Eng. in 1871, its mod. hist. is closely bound up with that of *\*antimetabole*, the Eng. usage of which dates to George Puttenham's *Arte of English Poesie* in 1589 (*OED*). The earliest attestations of *antimetabole* can be found in Cousin, who cites definitions by Quintilian (9.3.85) and Alexander Numenius (3.37.23) and synonymous terms in Phoebammon (3.55.2). Quintilian gives two examples of antimetabole: "Non, ut edam, vivo; sed, ut vivam, edo" (I do not live that I may eat, but eat that I may live) and, from Cicero, "Ut et sine invidia culpa plectatur, et sine culpa invidia ponatur" (That both guilt may be punished without odium, and odium may be laid aside without guilt). While *antimetabole* (and its Lat. term *commutatio*) once covered all such reciprocal exchanges, regardless of alterations in case or tense, *chiasmus* now appears to be the more capacious term and antimetabole a species of chiasmus (Miller and Mermall). In recent literary theory, and esp. work influenced by deconstruction, *chiasmus* has enjoyed wide currency as a critical term. The trope has been esp. important for Derrida, since *chiasmus* lays bare the "natural invertability" of a hierarchy of two terms—a description that could apply just as easily to deconstruction (Beidler). Deconstructionists have employed *chiasmus* in specific instances to describe the tension between "theological thought and its linguistic underthought" in G. M. Hopkins (Miller) and "the reversal of the figural order" in R. M. Rilke (de Man).

Some of the most ancient examples of chiasmus are found in Ugaritic texts (1400–1200 BCE), which may have influenced the composition of the OT. Biblical exegetes have indeed revealed chiasmus in verse (Gen. 9:6: "Whoso sheds the blood of man, / By man his blood shall be shed") and chapter (the Gospels of Matthew and John, the letters of Paul) (Breck, Thomson). Although *chiasmus* frequently describes the repetition of particular phonemes or the inversion of clauses, it is not uncommon to find that an entire poem or novel has a chiastic structure or that several kinds of chiasmus are at work simultaneously. In *Eunoia* (2009), Christian Bök's clever "The scented dessert smells even sweeter when served ere the sweetness melts" features chiasmus of sound and syntax ("smells," "sweeter," "sweetness," "melts"). Affecting both semantics and syntax, Hopkins's line "This seeing the sick endears them to us, us too it endears" ("Felix Randal," 9) concludes with an *\*ellipsis of the grammatical object. If, as Thomson prefers, we construe *chiasmus* more broadly as the bilateral symmetry "of four or more elements around a central axis," the *Epic of Gilgamesh*, Chaucer's *Parliament of Fowls*, John Dryden's "A Song for St. Cecilia's Day," S. T. Coleridge's "Frost at Midnight" (Nänny), Alfred, Lord Tennyson's *In Memoriam*, and Raymond Roussel's *Nouvelles Impressions d'Afrique* might all be considered to have chiastic patterns. E. M. Forster famously attributes the "triumph" of Henry James's *The Ambassadors* to the chiastic, or "hourglass," shape of its plot. Quinn defines *chiasmus* by comparing it to other repetitive figures like *epanodos*, the amplification or expansion of a series, and *\*palindrome*, a sentence that shows the same syntax and meaning forward or backward. The elliptical approach of chiasmus can sometimes be seen as an elegant *\*periphrasis of those emotions for which bald statement is impossible: "Grief has become the pain only pain erases" (Agha Shahid Ali, "Not All, Only a Few Return").

■ C. Walz, *Rhetores Graeci*, 9 v. (1832–36); *Allen and Greenough's New Latin Grammar*, ed. J. B. Greenough et al. (1903); E. M. Forster, *Aspects of the Novel* (1927); J. Cousin, *Études sur Quintilien* (1936); M. Joseph, *Shakespeare's Use of the Arts of Language* (1947); M. M. Mahood, *Shakespeare's Wordplay* (1957); A. Di Marco, "Der Chiasmus in der Bibel," *Linguistica Biblica* 37–39 (1976); P. de Man, *Allegories of Reading* (1979); *Chiasmus in Antiquity*, ed. W. Welch (1981); Group μ; A. Quinn, *Figures of Speech* (1982); H. Hor-vei, *The Chev'ril Glove* (1984); J. Derrida, *Glas*, trans. J. P. Leavey Jr. and R. Rand (1986); J. H. Miller, "The Linguistic Moment," *Gerard Manley Hopkins: Modern Critical Views*, ed. H. Bloom (1986); R. Norman, *Samuel Butler and the Meaning of Chiasmus* (1986); W. Shea, "Chiasmus and the Structure of David's Lament," *Journal of Biblical Literature* 105 (1986); J. Derrida, *The Truth in Painting*, trans. G. Bennington and I. McLeod (1987); M. Nänny, "Chiasmus in Literature: Ornament or Function?" *Word and Image* 4 (1988); T. Mermall, "The Chiasmus: Unamuno's Master Trope," and J. W. Miller and T. Mermall, "Antimetabole and Chiasmus," *PMLA* 105 (1990); J. Veitch, "'Moondust in the Prowling Eye': The History Poems of Robert Lowell," *Contemporary Literature* 33 (1992); J. Breck, *The Shape of Biblical Language* (1994); I. Thomson, *Chiasmus in the Pauline Letters* (1995); Lausberg; E.P.J. Corbett, *Classical Rhetoric for the Modern Student*, 4th ed. (1999); P. G. Beidler, "Chiastic Strands in *The Wreck of the Deutschland*," *VP* 38 (2000); S. Adams, *Poetic Designs* (2003); B. Costello, *Shifting Ground* (2003); H. Vendler, *Poets Thinking* (2006); M. Garber, *Shakespeare and Modern Culture* (2008); W. Engel, *Chiastic Designs in English Literature from Sidney to Shakespeare* (2009).

T.V.F. Brogan; A. W. Halsall; W. Hunter

**CHICAGO SCHOOL.** Originally, the "Chicago critics" were the authors of *Critics and Criticism: Ancient and Modern* (1952) and were so called because of their association with the University of Chicago; the label was later extended to some of their pupils and to others influenced by them. Major figures included R. S. Crane, Richard McKeon, Elder Olson, and Bernard Weinberg in the first generation; and Wayne Booth, Sheldon Sacks, Arthur Heiserman, and Ralph W. Rader in the second. The features of their approach to crit. that distinguished the group most clearly from other 20th-c. schools may be summed up under two heads: (1) what they called their *pluralism* and (2) what has been called by others their *neo-Aristotelianism*, the two terms referring, respectively, to the group's concern, as theorists and historians of crit., with investigating the logical grounds of variation among critical positions, and to its interest, as students of lit., in exploring the possibilities of a particular approach to the analysis and *evaluation of literary works that has seemed to them neglected.

The most explicit statements of their pluralism are contained in McKeon's "The Philosophic Bases of Art and Criticism" (1943), Olson's "An Outline of Poetic Theory" (1952), and Crane's *The Languages of Criticism and the Structure of Poetry* (1953). The basis of the view is the recognition that what any critic says on a literary subject, general or particular, is determined only in part by direct experience with literary works; it is conditioned no less importantly by the tacit assumptions concerning the nature of lit. and the most appropriate method of studying it that are brought to the immediate task: the critic will say different things about a given poem, e.g., or at least mean different things, according as he or she conceives of poetry as a species of artistic

making or as a mental faculty or as a special kind of knowledge, and the results will likewise differ widely according to whether the critic's reasoning about it rests primarily on literal definitions and distinctions within the subject matter or primarily on analogies between it and other things, and so on through a good many other possible variations in principle and method.

In short, the Chicago critics proceeded on the assumption that, while some modes of crit. are more restricted in scope than others, there are and have been many valid critical approaches to lit., each of which exhibits the literary object in a different light and each of which has its characteristic powers and limitations, so that the only rational ground for adhering to any one of them over any of the others is its superior capacity to give the special kind of understanding and evaluation of lit. the reader wants, at least for the time being.

The so-called neo-Aristotelianism of the Chicago school represents a choice of this pragmatic sort. The special interest in the *Poetics* that appears in these critics' earlier work had its origin in their concern, as teachers of lit., with developing a kind of practical crit. of literary texts that (1) would emphasize the specifically *artistic* principles and reasons governing their construction, as distinct from their verbal meanings, their historical and biographical backgrounds, or their general qualitative characteristics, and that (2) would attach more importance to the principles peculiar to different kinds of texts and to individual texts within a given kind than to those common to lit. in general. The appeal of Aristotle to the critics of the Chicago school was that he, more than any other critic they knew, had conceived of literary theory in this a posteriori and differential way and had not only formulated some of its necessary distinctions and principles, in his brief discussions of ancient *tragedy and *epic, but had pointed the way to further inquiries of the same sort in other literary arts still unrealized at the time he wrote, particularly the *lyric, the drama, and the novel.

The Chicago school bequeathed to its students and followers not only its pluralism and neo-Aristotelianism but a general interest in the hist. of crit. By contrast, an intense interest in lang. was more characteristic of the *New Criticism and later *poststructuralism. The second generation of Chicago critics, notably Booth, turned the approach toward narrative and away from poetry, an emphasis that remains visible in the work of Chicago-influenced critics such as James Phelan.

*See* CLASSICAL POETICS.

■ **Criticism and History**: H. Trowbridge, "Aristotle and the New Criticism," *Sewanee Review* 52 (1944); W. K. Wimsatt, "The Chicago Critics," *The Verbal Icon* (1954); M. Krieger, *The New Apologists for Poetry* (1956); H. P. Teesing, "The Chicago School," *OL*, supp. 2 (1958); W. Sutton, *Modern American Criticism* (1963); *Aristotle's Poetics and English Literature*, ed. E. Olson (1965); Wellek, v. 6; M. Sprinker, "What Is Living and What Is Dead in Chicago Criticism," *Boundary 2* 13 (1985); V. B. Leitch, *American Literary Criticism from the Thirties to the Eighties* (1988), ch. 3; A. D. Schneider, *Literaturkritik und Bildungspolitik*

(1994); R. Zorach, "Love, Truth, Orthodoxy, Reticence; or, What Edgar Wind Didn't See in Botticelli's *Primavera*," *CritI* 34 (2007).

■ **Primary Sources**: R. McKeon, "The Philosophic Bases of Art and Criticism," *Critics and Criticism: Ancient and Modern*, ed. R. S. Crane (1952), abridged ed. with new intro. and list of other related writings (1957); N. Friedman and C. A. McLaughlin, *Poetry: An Introduction to Its Form and Art* (1961); R. S. Crane, *The Idea of the Humanities* (1967); E. Olson, *Tragedy and the Theory of Drama* (1961), *The Theory of Comedy* (1968), and *On Value Judgment in the Arts* (1976); W. C. Booth, *Critical Understanding* (1979), and *The Rhetoric of Fiction*, 2d ed. (1983).

R. S. Crane; H. Adams; R. Greene

**CHICANA/O POETRY.** Strictly speaking, Chicana/o poetry begins in the 1960s, with the rise of the Chicano Movement for civil rights and—inseparable from it—a politically engaged poetics. Its emergence and spread was facilitated by the over 60 movement and literary jours., such as *El Grito*, *El Malcriado*, and *De Colores*, that circulated as instruments of communication and politicization, as well as through poetry readings that served to mobilize Chicana/o activists. Most Chicano Movement poetry was committed to the communal struggle of its minority culture, a position reflected in its predominant themes: an identification with the pre-Columbian indigenous past and Mexican revolutionary periods; a revision of U.S. hist.; the glorification of heroic male personages and female icons; the exaltation of communal cohesion in the *barrio* (neighborhood), the centrality of the family, the relations between the sexes, *carnalismo* (brotherhood), and Mexican female strength and endurance; and the channeling of solidarity into political action. Much poetry of this era moved easily between Eng. and Sp. at the level of *diction and *syntax, while the most common rhythms were found in a *free verse adapted to sound like vernacular speech.

Of course, Chicana/o poetry had antecedents as early as the colonial period in the northern provinces of New Spain, now the U.S. Southwest. Gaspar Pérez de Villagrá's (1555–1620) epic *Historia de la Nueva México* (1610) was the first poetic rendering within the present U.S. territory of the racial and cultural conflicts that have plagued the country since the Eur. arrival.

From the mid-19th c. on, the *corrido*—descended from a med. Sp. romance *ballad form—served as the foundation for other literary and artistic genres and constituted a philosophical folklore, a critical vernacular hist. of the region, and a poetic chronicle of the early making of a mod. U.S.-Mexico borderlands culture from out of the Sp. colonial and early republican past. A particular version of the corrido developed along the newly formed U.S.-Mexico border in response to the increasingly violent contact between Anglos and Mexicans along the border after 1848. These "border corridos" expressed a collective adversarial consciousness against oppression and a sense of violated communal social order and told of the actions of a local hero attempting to defend local community values against some outside threat.

"El corrido de Gregorio Cortez" is typical of this genre. An anonymous folk narrative composed in eight-syllable *quatrains with a rhyme pattern of *abcb*, sung in 3/4 or 6/8 time, the ballad narrative is framed with formulaic openings and closings. It sings of a humble workingman who, goaded into violence and unjustly accused, could fight for his rights "with his pistol in his hand." A genre not based on personal experience, the corrido adopts a transpersonal perspective, representing the political and existential values of the community as a whole. Like cl. *epic, it takes a body of symbolically charged, iconically powerful experiences and plunges the audience into the middle of the story. Corridos like "Gregorio Cortez," thus, performed a three-part symbolic function: they served as narratives of political hist., as repositories of the essential facts of social struggle, and as condensed versions of basic knowledge necessary for resistance.

In the 20th c., Eng. appeared more frequently in written poetry produced by Mexican Americans, though community newspapers still published in Sp. poems by leading Latin Am. writers. During the Mexican Revolution and its aftermath (1910–36), a number of Mexican intellectuals immigrated to the U.S. and worked on newspapers; Latin Am. *modernista* poetry was belatedly introduced to Mexican Am. readers during this period. Although the Sp. oral trad. was kept alive through immigration, public schooling in the U.S. was almost exclusively conducted in Eng., affecting both ling. capabilities and the knowledge of a formal poetic trad. in Sp.; this fact, coupled with the dominance of Eng. in the print media, explains the increase in Eng.-lang. poetry written by Mexican Americans in the first half of the 20th c. Fray Angélico Chávez's (1910–96) *Clothed with the Son* (1939) and *Eleven Lady-Lyrics and Other Poems* (1945) were acclaimed by critics.

By the mid-20th c., the twin pressures of Americanization and modernization severely eroded the formerly cohesive qualities of traditional poetic social forms. Américo Paredes's (1915–99) poetry from this period as collected in *Between Two Worlds* (1991) and *Cantos de Adolescencia/Songs of Youth (1932–37)* (2007) points to the multiple and complex reasons for this erosion, incl. attacks by Anglo Am. social institutions on the legitimacy of Mexican cultural forms in a mod. Am. context and the internal stresses, contradictions, and limitations of those traditional forms in themselves. In "Guitarreros" (1935), Paredes directs our attention to the play between langs. and cultures, as sites where modes of consciousness are made and unmade in the space between cultures and trads.:

*Bajaron el toro prieto,*
*que nunca lo habían bajado . . .*
Black against twisted black
The old mesquite
Rears up against the stars
Branch bridle hanging,
While the bull comes down from the mountain
Driven along by your fingers,
Twenty nimble stallions prancing up and down

the *redil* of the guitars.

(*Between Two Worlds*, 1991)

With the end of the historical moment of armed struggle after the sedition of 1915 and the emergence of new historical situations, Paredes laid the groundwork for new formal strategies, a new poetic lang., and a new bilingual aesthetic, to overcome the impasses and contradictions that the values and social structures of a former era could no longer resolve. The invention of these new langs. and forms was Chicana and Chicano *modernism itself.

By mid-century, the vibrant flowering of writings by Chicana writers seeking to raise those articulations of race, class, and gender to the level of critique shows that gender factors, no less than those of class and race, functioned to create a poetry that completely revises the general notion of an undifferentiated Chicano (male) poetic subject. Heirs to the male-centered corrido trad., many male poets of the early Chicano Movement years continued to seek a new spirit of aggressive resistance to assimilation by championing a Chicano cultural nationalism that denied the existence of gender, sexual, racial, or class conflict and diversity.

Rodolfo Gonzales's (1928–2005) *manifesto, *I Am Joaquin/Yo Soy Joaquín: An Epic Poem* (1967), demanded Chicana/os withdraw from U.S. social oppression into their communal trads. to rediscover their identity as survivors and warriors. Abelardo Delgado's (1930–2004) "Stupid america" (1969) proclaimed the nation's future greatness if Chicana/os were allowed to fulfill their creative potential and the self-destruction that was the alternative. Viola Correa's "La Nueva Chicana" (1970) called attention to the multigenerational social roles of Chicanas fighting for revolution. Alurista's (pseud. of Alberto Urista Heredia, b. 1947) *Floricanto en Aztlán* (Flower Song in Aztlán, 1971) proposed a hybrid of pre-Columbian philosophy and third-world anticapitalism as a survival strategy amid U.S. racism and class exploitation. Ricardo Sánchez's (1941–95) *Canto y grito mi liberación* (I Sing and Shout My Liberation, 1971) railed against U.S. life as an alienating prison. In *Perros y antiperros* (Dogs and Anti-dogs, 1972), Sergio Elizondo (b. 1930) toured the hist. and geography of the Southwest to denounce Anglo-Am. encroachment and the dehumanizing character of U.S. society, positing a refuge in the Chicana/o community's love and humanity. In "I Speak an Illusion" (1973), the pinta (prison) poet Judy Lucero articulates the contradictions of her Chicana experience while lamenting the apparently unbreakable bonds that incarcerate her. And while Tino Villanueva's (b. 1941) *Hay Otra Voz Poems* (There is Another Voice Poems, 1972) prefigured the introspective turn and the heightened awareness of lyric craft and *tropes to come in the mid-1970s, it culminated in a declaration of the poet's dedication to communal political struggle in a bilingual idiom that is itself a metaphor of the ideological message.

This poetry's most distinctive stylistic features were the predominance of narrative and mimetic over lyrical and figurative modes of expression and bilingualism, a combination of Sp., Eng., and subdialects. Prime exponents of the latter were José Montoya (b. 1932) and Alurista:

> Hoy enterraron al Louie
> (Today they buried El Louie)
> And San Pedro o sanpinche
> (St. Peter or saintdamned)
> are in for it. And those
> times of the forties
> and the early fifties
> lost un vato de atolle
> (a really down dude)

(Montoya, "El Louie")

> mis ojos hinchados
> (my swollen eyes)
> flooded with lágrimas
> (tears)
> de bronze
> (of bronze)
> melting on the cheek bones
> of my concern

(Alurista, "Mis ojos hinchados")

Many volumes were published with facing trans., e.g. *I Am Joaquin/Yo Soy Joaquín* or *Perros y antiperros*, which opened Chicana/o poetry to a wider readership.

As the Chicano Movement matured into the 1970s, existing tensions within activist communities became more apparent, and the control that Chicano nationalists had exercised over the editorial policies of movement and literary jours. began to ease. Chicanas, many of whom were participants in feminist organizations, increasingly moved onto the editorial boards of existing publications or founded jours. such as *Encuentro Feminil*, *Comadre*, and *Mango* that were dedicated to publishing Chicana writing or editorially controlled by Chicanas. The result was a flowering of poetry by Chicanas that responded to the subordination of women in Chicana/o communities, thematized the act of writing as a strategy for female liberation, explored Chicanas's relationships to each other and to themselves, and celebrated female sexual emancipation. Judy Flores Gonzales's "Canto to My Womanness" (1976) and Lydia Camarillo's "Mi Reflejo" (1980) are just two of the many poems that reconceived the passive female subject in Gonzales's *I Am Joaquin/Yo Soy Joaquín* by linking Chicanas to powerful historical female figures. Lorna Dee Cervantes's (b. 1954) "Declaration on a Day of Little Inspiration" (1976) expressed her struggle to make poetry out of the material available to her as a poor Chicana living in a San Jose barrio. Alma Villanueva's (b. 1944) tender poem "strength" (1978) honors her mother's legacy. Cervantes's "You Cramp My Style, Baby" (1977) uses food imagery and irony to expose the rampant sexism of the more nationalist of the Chicano activists.

The devel. of Chicana/o poetry as a body of lit. brought with it an increased concern with craft. While narrative tendencies, bilingualism, and appeals to an indigenous past remained as significant features, the use of tropes and intertexual references to non-Mexican and Chicana/o source material increased. Bernice Zamora's (b. 1938) *Restless Serpents* (1976) engages the work of Shakespeare, Robinson Jeffers, and Theodore Roethke. Rafael Jesús González's (b. 1935) "The Coin, Ars Poetica" (1977) ends with a cultural juxtaposition that inserts traditional Chicana/o themes into a broader conversation:

> the sky-eagle
> devouring the earth-serpent
> as a sign.
> The Aztec ball player
> losing the game lost his heart
> to keep alive the gods.
> > The wells claim it:
> > Li Po
> > would die
> > needing it
> > for the moon.

("Coin, Ars Poetica")

Lucha Corpi (b. 1945) ends her 1980 tribute to Emily Dickinson with

> We are . . . migrant
> workers in search of
> floating gardens as yet
> unsown, as yet, unharvested.

Cervantes's first book of poetry, *Emplumada* (1981), and Sandra Cisneros's (b. 1954) *Bad Boys* (1980) and *My Wicked Wicked Ways* (1987) treat a wide range of themes even as they set pre-Columbian mythical figures alongside those from the Gr. and Roman pantheons. Luis Omar Salinas (1937–2008), known as a 1960s Movement poet for his "Aztec Angel" poem, has few Chicana/o references in *Darkness under the Tress / Walking behind the Spanish* (1982), yet he remains an influential Chicana/o poet. Gary Soto's (b. 1952) *Black Hair* (1985) is a Chicana/o work, yet readers can easily place it within the broader context of the U.S. experience.

In recent years, Chicana/o poetry has developed in multiple directions, reflecting the values of poets who are perhaps more intellectually and socially diverse than those of the 1960s and 1970s. Juan Felipe Herrera (b. 1948) is best known for a richly lyrical poetry of urban life, often in Los Angeles and San Francisco; his notable books include *Exiles of Desire* (1985); *Akrilica* (1989), a set of 41 poems curated by "color" and topic, like paintings; *Night Train to Tuxtla* (1994), autobiographical poems about the Chicano poet's "continuous trek into himself"; and *Half the World in Light* (2008), a career retrospective with new poems. Cervantes has published two additional volumes of poetry, *From the Cables of Genocide: Poems of Hunger and Love* (1991) and *Drive: The First Quartet* (2006), that combine a developing poetic voice with a concern for social injustice, identity, and women-centered artistic and intellectual activity. The poems in Cisneros's *Loose Woman* (1996) celebrate a fiercely independent woman of Mexican

heritage whose sexuality is a key source of her power. The anthropologist Renato Rosaldo's (b. 1941) *Prayer to Spider Woman/Rezo a la Mujer Araña* (2003) is a collection of 48 poems of enormous cultural range, from the barrio to Mexico to the Philippines. The Chicano and Native Am. poet Jimmy Santiago Baca (b. 1952) began to write in prison, first publishing *Immigrants in Our Own Land* (1979). He maintains a concern with the intersections of work, community, the New Mexican landscape, and myth in such collections as *Martin; And Meditations of the South Valley* (1987) and *Black Mesa Poems* (1989). Ana Castillo (b. 1953), born in Chicago, writes about the complex layers of women's lives in the U.S. and Mexico, as in *My Father Was a Toltec and Selected Poems, 1973–1988* (1995). Cherríe Moraga's (b. 1952) *Loving in the War Years* (1983) is a classic collection of poems, stories, and essays about coming to terms with lesbian sexuality within Chicano culture. Michele Serros (b. 1966) is a spoken-word poet and social commentator; like Moraga's collection, her *Chicana Falsa and Other Stories of Death, Identity and Oxnard* (1993) is multigeneric. Many younger poets deserve notice, among them J. Michael Martinez (b. 1978), whose volume *Heredities* (2009) unsettles the constructions of identity and aesthetics of previous generations to recover a voice estranged from itself ("History gathers in the name we never are"); and the Afro-Chicano John Murillo (b. 1971), whose collection *Up from the Boogie* (2010) displays an array of stanzas and free verse, musical influences from *blues to *hip-hop to reggaeton, and even a parody of Ezra Pound's "In a Station of the Metro" located in the Los Angeles Metro.

*See* INDIGENOUS AMERICAS, POETRY OF THE; MEXICO, POETRY OF; SPAIN, POETRY OF; UNITED STATES, POETRY OF THE.

■ **Anthologies**: *El ombligo de Aztlán*, ed. Alurista (1972); *ENTRANCE: Four Chicano Poets*, ed. L. Adame (1975); *El Quetzal emplumece*, ed. C. Montalvo (1976); *Siete poetas*, ed. M. Bornstein-Somoza (1978); *Fiesta in Aztlán*, ed. T. Empringham (1981); *Contemporary Chicano Poetry*, ed. W. Binder (1986); *Antología de la Poesía Chicana / Anthology of Chicano Poetry*, ed. R. Burk et al. (1997); *La Lunate*, ed. M. D. Pinate (2010)—spoken-word poetry from San Francisco.

■ **Criticism and History**: J. Bruce-Novoa, *Chicano Authors, Inquiry by Interview* (1980), and *Chicano Poetry: A Response to Chaos* (1982); M. Sanchez, *Contemporary Chicano Poetry* (1985); W. Binder, *Partial Autobiographies: Interviews With Twenty Chicano Poets* (1986); C. Candelaria, *Chicano Poetry* (1986); J. E. Limón, *Mexican Ballads, Chicano Poems* (1991); R. Pérez-Torres, *Movements in Chicano Poetry* (1995); A. Arteaga, *Chicano Poetics* (1997); *Formas narrativas de la tradición oral de México*, ed. M. Zavala Gómez de Campo (2009).

J. BRUCE-NOVOA; P.M.L. MOYA; R. SALDÍVAR

**CHILE, POETRY OF.** The Sp.-lang. trad. in Chilean poetry begins with the publication of *La Araucana* (The Araucaniad) by Alonso de Ercilla (1533–94), born in Spain, who wrote about the conquest of Chile. This *epic, which documents the founding of Chile, was published in three parts in 1569, 1578, and 1589; Andrés Bello called it Chile's *Aeneid*. Written in *octavas reales*, it belongs to early mod. trad. in its use of Gr. mythology, cl. references, and themes, incl. the faith and daring of the Spaniards and the heroism and sacrifice of the natives. It inspired later romantics with its vision of the noble savage and also inspired the next well-known colonial Chilean writer Pedro de Oña (1570–1643), who entered into dialogue with Ercilla with his poem *Arauco domado* (1596).

Oña's is a less idealistic portrayal of the indigenous people, written in memory of the poet's father, who was killed by Mapuches. This epic includes 19 *cantos, hendecasyllabic octaves with rhyme schemes that do not follow Ercilla's octavas reales. Oña, born in Chile, received a Sp. education in Lima and has sometimes been regarded as not Chilean; it is clear in his poem that he views the country as a colony. His other notable poems include "El temblor de Lima" (The Earthquake of Lima, 1609), in which he uses a new kind of *ottava rima* and demonstrates the influence of the *culturanismo* of Sp. poets such as Luis de Góngora (see CONCEIT, CONCEPTISMO), and his heroic, religious poems "El Vasauro" (1635) and "El Ignacio de Cantabria" (1639).

Not much poetic production of note was recorded in the 17th and 18th cs.: there are poems of salon life, songs of praise, and popular poetry collected as part of Chilean folklore. Alegría mentions Father López, Father Oteíza, and Captain Lorenzo Mujica but categorizes them as "poets of circumstance." Popular poets wrote in *décimas*, or ten-line stanzas, and popular *quatrains. Corridos (*ballads), *payas* (poetic compositions with improvised verses), and chronicles in verse that use dramatic forms to treat human and divine themes comprise the Chilean version of the Sp. *romancero* (or ballad trad.; see ROMANCE).

Chile gained its independence in 1818, and poets of this period include Camilo Henríquez (1769–1845), a journalist who believed that poetry had a role in the moral and political education of the populace and who was recognized more for his political ideas than his poetry. Bernando Vera y Pintado (1780–1827), though born in Argentina, died in Chile and celebrated Chilean independence in his poems, one of which was transformed into the first national hymn (see ANTHEM, NATIONAL). Mercedes Marín del Solar (1804–66) combined neoclassical and romantic styles. The Venezuelan Bello (1781–1865) and the Argentine Domingo Faustino Sarmiento (1811–88) worked and lived in Chile, and their debates (particularly about *romanticism) were influential in Chilean literary conversations. José Victorino Lastarria (1817–88) wrote noteworthy essays about Chilean lit. and argued that Chile was late in developing its own lit. because of its political autocracy and backward social devel. The literary movement Generation of 1842, an answer to Lastarria, produced a national literary society that emphasized national expression, rejected Sp. romanticism, and championed renovating Chilean lit. by cultivating a progressive attitude.

Romanticism came late to Spain, and still later to Chile, and perhaps for this reason, Alegría argues, it is more distinctive there. Salvador Sanfuentes y Torres (1817–60) follows the indigenist themes of Ercilla and Oña, with *Caupolicán* (1835), a drama in verse in the romantic trad. Other important names in Chilean romanticism include Guillermo Blest Gana (1829–1904), José Antonio Soffia (1843–86), and Eusebio Lillo y Robles (1827–1910), a disciple of José Espronceda and José Zorrilla, who wrote a new Chilean national anthem.

Early 20th-c. Sp. Am. writers experienced a contradictory *modernism, inheriting forms and trads. from Europe usually elaborated by elite writers, who struggled to found their own literary hist. in their poetry. This effort to develop a local perspective in Chile resulted in *Los Diez* (The Ten), a literary group dedicated to independent expression founded by Pedro Prado (1886–1952). Prado was a meditative poet who used *symbolism and *free verse, as well as sonnets and poetic prose, to record the local Chilean landscape and territory. Magallanes Moure (1878–1924) is another member of the group whose first book of poetry, *Facetas* (Facets, 1902), used traditional forms like the sonnet and sought modernist formal perfection in his portraits of country life. Not a member of the group but a notable early avant-garde writer of this time is Rosamel del Valle (pseud. of Moisés Filadelfio Gutiérrez Gutiérrez, 1900–65), who used long lines and a hermetic style in his sometimes visionary poetry; he published seven collections and was admired later by Vicente Huidobro. While some of these writers' styles are grounded in Sp. Am. *modernismo, others move toward the avant-garde, which would prove to be much more fruitful and innovative than earlier poetry in Chile (see AVANT-GARDE POETICS).

Pablo de Rokha (pseud. of Carlos Díaz Loyola, 1894–1968) is an early representative of the Chilean avant-garde. An innovator, he wrote in long lines that often lacked punctuation and chose antipoetic themes. He uses lang. as a weapon and combines many different genres: epic and lyric, popular and surrealist. He attempted to renovate poetry through excess and exaggeration, and his work is an important expression of Chilean identity. Huidobro (1893–1948), who traveled to Buenos Aires, Spain, and France, is perhaps the most recognized proponent of the post-World War II literary avant-garde. He was a modernist in his early work, but his travels led him to found a movement called *creacionismo* (*creationism), complete with its own manifestos that highlighted its poetry's originality and capacity to make things happen with lang. His masterwork is the long poem *Altazor* (1931), which charts the existential and ling. crisis of its namesake.

Gabriela Mistral (pseud. of Lucila Godoy Acayaga, 1889–1957), in 1945 the first Latin Am. to win a Nobel Prize in Literature, addressed in her poetry topics such as Chilean and Am. identity, religion, childhood, love, suffering, maternity, and rebellion. She combines a local, formal lang. with a passionate tone, often speaking as an outsider in her books: *Desolación* (Desolation, 1922), *Ternura* (Tenderness, 1924), *Tala* (Felling, 1938), and *Poema de Chile* (published posthumously in 1967). Writing during the time of multiple avant-gardes, she chose an anachronic *formalism and *tone; for these among other reasons, Concha argues that Mistral's work can be seen as part of an autochthonous vanguard. Mistral is recognized for her prose as well as her poetry, for her stances as an international intellectual and educator, and for her defense of human rights.

Pablo Neruda (pseud. of Ricardo Neftalí Reyes Basoalto, 1904–73) is the major figure in 20th-c. Chilean (and beyond that, Sp. Am.) poetry. In 1924, he published *Veinte poemas de amor y una canción desesperada* (*Twenty Love Poems and a Song of Despair*), his second book of poems with neoromantic roots, which remains popular today. He enters the avant-garde with his *Residencia en la tierra* (*Residence on Earth*), three volumes published in 1935–47, in which the poet uses bold metaphors and rhythmic free verse to communicate surprising experiences of the world. In *Canto general* (1950), Neruda creates a prophetic voice in a long epic poem to sing the social and political hist. of the continent, while his *Odas elementales* (*Elemental Odes*) of the 1950s are direct poems in which he draws on sometimes complex metaphors to catalog everyday objects imbued with unanticipated emotion. Like Mistral, Neruda was a renowned public figure; exiled for his political views and later a senator, he was a supporter of Salvador Allende's Popular Unity presidency, and his death coincided with the coup that brought Augusto Pinochet to power in 1973. Neruda's work has been translated into many langs., and he is the first Chilean figure to enter the *canon of world poetry; perhaps for this reason, contemporaneous poets such as Pablo de Rokha and Nicanor Parra, as well as later poets, reacted against his at times overwhelming influence.

The year 1954 is key in Chilean poetry, when Parra (b. 1914) published his *Poemas y antipoemas* (*Poems and Antipoems*) as a response to Neruda and to the conventional idea of poetry as ritual, elevated expression for elite readers. Parra forged an alternate path through poetry that used colloquial, prosaic lang., self-irony, and ludic qualities to approach everyday life. Parra's relativization of the world was reflected in new attitudes in his poetic speakers, who question and parody trad. and modernity in poems that interrogate both form and content. His ongoing struggle with convention is apparent in *Artefactos* (Artifacts, 1972), a box of picture postcard-poems that challenged the idea of the *book.

Much of mid-20th c. Chilean poetry responds to these canonical figures; it splits or crosses lines of influence from the avant-garde and antipoetry (which has a decisive influence on much of the poetry that follows and is both part of the vanguards and a reaction against them). Gonzalo Rojas (1917–2011) follows Parra's lead with his vigorous social poetry, in themes that extend from the erotic to the existential and ontological. Associated with the surrealist group *La Mandrágora* (The Mandrake), Rojas sought to communicate with a broader audience. Enrique Lihn's (1929–88) work is also more closely linked to Parra's than to Neruda's.

Lihn tackles definitive questions such as the meaning of life, suffering, and death and demonstrates a commitment to social reality, moving toward *poesía situada* (situated poetry), a poetics that speaks from and about the situation of the speaker and that constantly recreates itself. Closer to Neruda, perhaps, is Jorge Teillier (1935–96). He writes of Chile's southern regions in poetry of origins, childhood, nostalgia, and mythic creation; and his speaker is sometimes a visionary witness. He uses simple, direct lines and metaphor to make the region a symbolic zone. Popular poetry in this period may be seen in the work of Violeta Parra (1917–67), who was central to the Chilean New Song movement. Widely recognized as a musician, she also can be considered a popular poet.

The 1960s and 1970s include the pre-Salvador Allende generation and those who first experienced the Pinochet dictatorship following the coup of 1973. Figures of the 1960s include Waldo Rojas (b. 1944), whose work incorporates a reflexive, metapoetic intensity as he writes and rewrites his perceptions of the world. There is a continuity from his early books, such as *Príncipe de naipes* (Prince of Cards, 1966) to the later *Deber de urbanidad* (Urban Obligation, 2001), in which memory and exploration of symbolic space predominate (in the last example, the space is Paris, where Rojas moved in 1974). Jaime Quezada (b. 1942) is another member of this generation, recognized for his contemplation of daily life in an accessible style; Quezada's interest in Chilean poetry is also seen through his work as an editor of authors such as Mistral, Neruda, and Nicanor Parra. The early idealism and political dynamism of the 1960s shifted with the political turmoil in the early 1970s. Topics such as exile, direct repression, and the climate of fear and persecution began to predominate; and for this reason, the 1970s in Chilean letters is called the dispersed or decimated generation. Some of its members are Floridor Pérez (b. 1937), who followed in the footsteps of Teillier but integrated humor and irony more characteristic of Nicanor Parra into his work. Oscar Hahn (b. 1938) uses surrealist elements and imagery in sonnets and free verse with sonorous intensity to speak of mortality, love, and alienation. Gonzalo Millán's (1947–2006) work is a constant rereading of himself. He also examines the relationship between image and text (he was a sculptor and visual artist) with complexity in poems conceived as series. His 1987 book *Virus* reflects on the function of poetry and art confronted with power. Like many members of the 1960s and 1970s generations, both Hahn and Millán spent significant time exiled from Chile.

The 1980s in Chile meant writing within the dictatorship, in a precarious and hostile situation of domination, and writers found different strategies for confronting the role of art in a repressive society. Alejandra Basualto (b. 1944) has discussed the conditions of internal exile for those who remained in the country, the lack of books coming into Chile, and the devel. of workshops to communicate at this time. A community developed among women writers, such as Eugenia Brito (b. 1950), who textualizes physical suffering and combines genres in her more recent *Extraña permanecia* (Strange Permanence, 2004); and Verónica Zondek (b. 1953), who uses her often abstract poetry to reconstruct and learn through pain and memory. Carmen Berenguer (b. 1946) has continued in the avant-garde vein with her radical, experimental, feminist work. She writes hermetic poetry that frequently deals with the situation of marginalized, oppressed, fragmented subjects both during and after the dictatorship. Elvira Hernández (b. 1951) also deals with marginal identities, expressed in ruptured syntax in books like *Santiago Waria* (1992), in which she connects the city to its indigenous past, and *La bandera de Chile* (1991), where she empties and resignifies the national emblem (some of these works circulated clandestinely before they were published in the early 1990s).

Juan Luis Martínez (1942–93) is also in the avant-garde line in his attempt to create a new kind of poetry. *La nueva novela* (1985) is a poetic object or an inter-artistic experiment with a new kind of literary expression that incorporates humor and textual play (he is a clear descendant of Nicanor Parra). Tomás Harris's (b. 1956) mythological and poetic voyages through the city chronicle uneven devel., while Diego Maqueira (b. 1951) combines high cultural and popular registers and alters the conventional depiction of time. Raúl Zurita (b. 1951) extends an avant-garde desire to put poetry into action and uses surrealist images, self-referentiality, and multiple voices in his poetry. He is recognized for conjoining written words with performances via sky and desert writing and photos in his texts, which form a Dantesque chronicle of Chile's suffering: *Purgatorio* (1979), *Anteparaíso* (1982), and *La vida nueva* (1993).

In the 1990s, the transition to democracy opened the doors to increased expression and new voices, many of whom have become known as the shipwrecked generation. The transition also focused attention on multiculturalism and the work of Elicura Chihuailaf (b. 1952), a Mapuche poet (see MAPUCHE POETRY) who publishes in Mapuzungun and Sp.; she became one of a number of poets who undermined the unitary vision of Chile promoted under Pinochet. In some ways, their work can be read as a response to the founding poetry of Ercilla, for they represent their own ethnic and national identity, record trads., and add their voices to political debates and land disputes (Vicuña includes Chihuailaf, Leonel Lienlaf, Jaime Luis Huenun, and Graciela Huinao in her collection). Poets of the 1990s continue the dialogue with precursors such as Lihn, Parra and *anti-poesía*, and Rokha to experiment with *typography and the book (Martínez) and to acknowledge Mistral. Their diversity of topics and styles extends from globalization and mass media to love, loss, and the circumstances of late 20th-c. Chile: material excess and commoditization, visual culture, and shifting social values. One of these, Clemente Riedemann (b. 1953), offers another perspective from the south, using accessible, colloquial lang. in his ironic recording of contemp. society, esp. Chile's role at the turn of the 21st c. The early 21st-c. poets are known as the *novísimos*

(the new ones), and they return to the poets of the 1980s for inspiration. Some names associated with this group are Diego Ramírez (b. 1982), Paula Ilabaca Nuñez (b. 1979), and Héctor Hernández Montecinos (b. 1979), who chose diverse styles to question social and literary convention in work that is not limited to writing but includes music, visual elements, installation, performance, and recordings. Some recent winners of the Neruda Prize in poetry (for writers under 40) include Rafael Rubio (b. 1975), Javier Bello (b. 1972), and Malú Urriola (b. 1967).

■ **Anthologies**: *Antología de la poesía chilena contemporánea*, ed. R. E. Scarpa and H. Montes (1968); *Antología de la poesía chilena (siglos XVI al XX)*, ed. L. Cisternas de Minguez and M. Minguez Sender (1969); *Veinticinco años de poesía chilena (1970–1995)*, ed. T. Calderón, L. Calderón, and T. Harris (1996); *Antología de poesía chilena nueva* (1935), ed. E. Anguita and V. Teitelboim (2001); *20 poetas mapuches contemporaneos*, ed. J. Huenún (2003); *Poesía chilena desclasificada (1973–1990)*, ed. G. Contreras and J. Concha, vol. 1 (2005); *Diecinueve (poetas chilenos de los noventa)*, ed. F. Lange Valdés (2006).

■ **Criticism and History**: F. Alegría, *La poesía chilena* (1954); H. Montes and J. Orlando, *Historia y antología de la literatura chilena* (1965); J. Concha, *Poesía chilena 1907–17* (1971); "La poesía chilena actual," *Literatura chilena en el exilio* 4.1 (1977); and Gabriela Mistral (1987); J. A. Piña, *Conversaciones con la poesía chilena* (1990); *UL: 4 Mapuche poets*, ed. C. Vicuña (1998); F. Schopf, *Del vanguardismo a la antipoesía* (2000).

■ **Web Site**: Escritores y poetas en español, http://www.letras.s5.com.

J. KUHNHEIM

**CHINA, MODERN POETRY OF.** In China, there is not a single standard term for mod. poetry. Before 1949, poetry written in the contemp. vernacular and nontraditional forms was commonly called New Poetry or Vernacular Poetry. After 1949, China was divided into three political entities: the People's Republic of China on the mainland (PRC), the Republic of China on Taiwan (ROC), and Hong Kong under Brit. rule. Whereas New Poetry continued to be used in the PRC, it was gradually replaced by the term *mod. poetry* in Taiwan and Hong Kong as the result of a flourishing modernist movement.

In 1917, Hu Shi (1891–1962), then a PhD student in the U.S., published a short essay titled "A Preliminary Proposal for Literary Reform," in which he envisioned a new poetry written in the "living language" (as opposed to cl. Chinese as a "dead language") and freed from traditional forms. Although certain genres of traditional Chinese poetry, such as folk song, ballad, and *ci* (see CHINA, POPULAR POETRY OF), employ a fair share of the vernacular, the New Poetry that Hu advocated was iconoclastic in its rejection of all poetic conventions, incl. parallelism, stock imagery, allusions, and imitation of ancient masters, as well its lang. and forms.

Understandably, Hu's call for radical reform was met with crit. from conservative scholars, some of whom were his close friends. On the other hand, the poetry reform, newly dubbed Literary Revolution by Chen Duxiu (1879–1942), a mentor of Hu and then dean of humanities at Peking University, triumphed as it converged with the May Fourth movement. Born in the demonstrations against Western imperialism in 1919, the May Fourth movement was spearheaded by progressive intellectuals, some of whom were teaching at Peking University at the time. The movement critiqued all aspects of traditional Chinese culture and introduced mod. Western concepts of science, democracy, and nationalism. Within a few years, New Poetry became a standard bearer of the new "national literature" written in the "national language."

The period 1920–30 witnessed a blossoming of New Poetry. Various foreign trends—such as *romanticism, *symbolism, *realism, Japanese *haikai, and prose poetry (see PROSE POEM)—provided inspirations to a new generation of poets, many of whom had studied abroad and were avid readers and translators of foreign poetry. Poetry societies and jours. also mushroomed. Among the most influential were the Creation Society (1921), the New Crescent Society (1923), and the jour. Les Contemporains (1932). The Creation Society was best represented by Guo Moruo (1892–1978), who had studied in Japan and translated J. W. Goethe before he turned to proletarian lit. The New Crescent was led by Xu Zhimo (1897–1931) and Wen Yiduo (1899–1946). Xu, who had studied in the U.S. and Britain, was dubbed the Chinese Shelley in his pursuit of love, beauty, and freedom. Wen, who had studied art and lit. in the U.S., theorized the ideal poetry as a synthesis of the beauty of painting, music, and architecture. Dai Wangshu (1905–50) was the most influential poet of Les Contemporains; he studied in France and translated symbolist poetry into Chinese. During the 1920s and 1930s, intense debates unfolded along ideological lines, which were often simplified as art for art's sake versus art for life's sake, or *pure poetry versus poetry of social conscience.

The outbreak of the Sino-Japanese War on July 7, 1937, radically changed the poetry scene. Educational and cultural institutions were destroyed or relocated, and poets were scattered across the country. As a result, mod. poetry spread to all corners of the land, from Chongqing, the temporary capital of wartime China, to Shanghai under Japanese occupation, to Kunming and Guilin in the southwest, to the northwest under the Chinese Communist Party based in Yan'an, and to Hong Kong under Brit. rule. Poets joined other writers and artists in mobilizing the masses against the Japanese invasion and promoting patriotism. Poetry was recited and performed in public, often in plain speech and lively dialogue. Whereas before the war the short lyric was the dominant mode, now long narrative poetry flourished. But not all poetry addressed the war. Modernist experiments by younger poets continued; philosophical musings on life and art reached a new height.

The year 1949 was another watershed in the hist. of mod. poetry. Under ironclad ideological control in the PRC, most poets stopped writing and focused on scholarship or trans. Even so, they did not escape persecution in the successive political campaigns throughout the 1950s and 1960s, which culminated in the Cultural Revolution (1966–76). A few weak voices from the underground were silenced. The desolate situation did not change until the late 1970s, when China under Deng Xiaoping opened its door to the free world and embarked on an ambitious program of national modernization.

On the other side of the Taiwan Strait, in contrast, a modernist movement thrived despite censorship and a cultural policy of conservatism under the Nationalist regime (KMT). Led by Ji Xian (b. 1913) and Qin Zihao (1912–63), both of whom had started writing poetry in pre-1949 China, the postwar generation of young poets in Taiwan embraced *avant-garde poetry and art in the West, incl. *surrealism and high *modernism. The most influential poetry societies and jours. were Modernist Poetry Quarterly (1952) and the Modernist School (1954), the Blue Star (1954), and the Epoch (1954). They not only created experimental works of the highest caliber but interacted with young poets in Hong Kong, who shared their enthusiasm for avant-garde art and lit. In the conservative social climate in Taiwan in the 1950s and 1960s, the modernist poetry movement was often derided and attacked. However, it was unstoppable as its influence spread. As a result, Modern Poetry became both a standard term and an institution in Taiwan and Hong Kong.

The next challenge to mod. poetry came in the early 1970s when Taiwan suffered a series of setbacks in the international political arena: the loss of its seat to the PRC in the United Nations and the severance of diplomatic relations with Japan and the U.S. These diplomatic setbacks triggered a legitimacy crisis and an identity crisis among intellectuals and writers, who demanded a "return" to Taiwanese society and Chinese cultural roots. Mod. poetry in Taiwan took a sharp turn toward realism and nativism, with the latter paving the way for the large-scale nativist literature movement (1977–79). Many poets, both old and young, embraced an idealized rural Taiwan, expressed concern for social maladies, and even critiqued the ruling regime. Into the 1980s, as the democracy movement steadily gained momentum, mod. poetry played an important role in raising public awareness of the repressed past and the hopeful future of Taiwan.

A new page also turned in the PRC in the late 1970s and early 1980s. In the liberalizing atmosphere of post-Mao China, commonly referred to as the New Era, underground poetry burst on the scene and enjoyed phenomenal success. The immediate predecessors of underground poetry were poets who wrote during the Cultural Revolution and whose works were hand-copied and circulated among the urban youths who had been sent down to the countryside by Chairman Mao. Chinese trans. of foreign poetry also provided them with an important source of inspiration. The most influential poetry in post-Mao China was represented by Today, founded by a group of young poets and artists in Beijing in 1978. The new generation of poets had recently experienced the Cultural Revolution; their works expressed disillusionment with politics on the one hand and a yearning to return to the private world, romantic love, and nature on the other. The new poetry stirred up a nationwide controversy; critics who condemned its obscurity and individualism called it *Misty Poetry.* As its popularity grew, however, the negative connotations disappeared. In the latter half of the 1980s, the newcomers defined themselves against Misty Poetry, rejecting the latter's lyricism and introspection. Instead, they engaged in a broader range of experiments and developed more radical poetics.

Censorship never ceased to exist in post-Mao China. Throughout the 1980s, Deng Xiaoping authorized several political campaigns against lit. and art that were considered too liberal or "bourgeois." Misty Poetry was constantly targeted. After the violent crackdown on student demonstrations in Tiananmen Square in June 1989, several poets were arrested and imprisoned; more left China in self-imposed exile. In the 21st c., Chinese society has undergone dramatic transformations. Culturally speaking, it has become not only far more diverse but more oriented toward pop commercialism. Poetry has lost the prestige and universal appeal that it once enjoyed. Ironically, while China's economic success has made possible more poetry prizes, jours., readings, and conferences than before, poetry readership has shrunk and the impact of poetry diminished. It is also ironic that despite completely different hists., poetry in 21st-c. mainland China, Taiwan, and Hong Kong faces very similar conditions: commodification of culture, the Information Age, and new technologies. Poets tend to see themselves as poetry makers rather than "poets," and many turn to the Internet as an important venue where free, democratic, and global interactions take place.

The story of mod. Chinese poetry since 1917 is dramatic, to say the least. It arose in reaction against cl. poetry, the most ancient and respected cultural form in traditional China, and successfully established itself as a representative of mod. lit. early on. It has drawn on the rich trads. of world poetry for resources but, in doing so, has repeatedly found itself embroiled in debates that question its cultural identity. What is clear is that mod. poetry represents a new aesthetic paradigm that is simultaneously related to and clearly distinguished from cl. poetry. It has broadened the Chinese lit. trad. in lang. and form and enriched it with a wide range of subject matters and sensibilities that are unique to the mod. era.

■ **Anthologies**: *Twentieth-Century Chinese Poetry,* trans. K. Y. Hsu (1970); *Out of the Howling Storm,* ed. T. Barnstone (1993); *Anthology of Modern Chinese Poetry,* trans. M. Yeh (1994); *Frontier Taiwan,* ed. M. Yeh and N.G.D. Malmqvist (2001); *Sailing to Formosa,* ed. M. Yeh et al. (2006); *Another Kind of Nation,* ed. E. Zhang and D. Chen (2007); *Twentieth-Century Chinese Women's Poetry,* ed. J. C. Lin (2009).

■ **Criticism and History**: J. C. Lin, *Modern Chinese Poetry* (1972); M. Yeh, *Modern Chinese Poetry* (1991); M. Hockx, *A Snowy Morning: Eight Chinese Poets on the Road to Modernity* (1994); M. Van Crevel, *Language Shattered: Contemporary Chinese Poetry and Duoduo* (1996); J. H. Zhang, *The Invention of a Discourse: Women's Poetry from Contemporary China* (2004); M. Van Crevel, *Chinese Poetry in Times of Mind, Mayhem and Money* (2008).

M. YEH

**CHINA, POETRY OF.** Contemp. Chinese poets have a conception of poetry much in common with the view held by their compatriots in other countries, so to use the term *Chinese poetry* may seem at first unproblematic. But before the mod. period, Chinese writers employed no single term that embraced all traditional forms of verse; they referred instead to individual genres. This article reviews major devels.; readers also should examine the detailed articles on genres.

Generally speaking, traditional Chinese poetry consists of forms of writing that employ *rhyme and usually a metric defined by a set number of syllables for each line. Some verse forms also require attention to the tones of the lang., exploiting the effect of rising or falling pitch in certain prescribed patterns. Depending on the lang. register appropriate to various genres, the lang. of traditional poetry may vary from a refined cl. Chinese to a mod. or near-mod. vernacular.

The earliest surviving Chinese poems derive from religious and political rituals; some are preserved in the first significant collection, the *Shijing (Classic of Poetry,* also known as the *Book of Songs),* an anthol. of 305 poems composed during the Zhou dynasty (1046–256 BCE). In most cases, the *Shijing* employs four-syllable lines arranged in *couplets; individual stanzas of four, six, eight, or ten lines are also typical, with the frequent employment of *refrain and repetition. Though mod. readers often detect a "folk" quality in the *Shijing,* traditional commentaries stressed the ethical significance of the poems (and the poems have been read thus throughout Chinese hist.).

Originally, the term *shi referred only to *Shijing* poems (or poems from the same era); but by the 2d c. CE, shi was also applied to contemp. verse composition, both from anonymous popular and folk sources and from educated poets (a significant group of poems with a more explicit connection to song were also termed *yuefu or "music bureau" songs). In both early shi and yuefu, lines of five syllables became increasingly important, though four-syllable line composition continued, usually with archaic associations. Shi poets focused on couplets as the basic poetic unit, and (unlike the poets of the *Shijing*) did not usually construct shi in clear-cut stanza forms. Shi could go on indefinitely but usually lasted from four to thirty lines; long shi stretching for a hundred lines or more do exist but are rare. Themes tended to dwell on autobiographical expression, particularly the public and political experiences of the educated male poet; ethical and spiritual self-cultivation; and the tribulations of private life. Mild erotic content was also common (if frowned on by the educated elite as "unserious"). Since the Ming dynasty (1368–1644), critics have held that traditional shi reached the pinnacle of achievement during the Tang dynasty (618–907); important devels. during this period include the increasing popularity of the seven-syllable line alongside the five-syllable line, as well as quatrain and octet forms with prescribed tonal patterns.

Shi in later ages came to be regarded as the most important form of traditional Chinese verse composition. With the advent of commercial printing in the 11th c., the publication of shi collections (often containing thousands of poems) became widespread, leading to the wholesale preservation of large collections from even minor poets. Shi composition also became common among groups outside the male Chinese elite—e.g., women poets became increasingly visible in later centuries (esp. from the 17th c. onward). Shi also commonly appeared in other contexts; it is not unusual for the author of traditional fiction to insert a shi whenever he needs to express deep emotions, portray combat on the battlefield, or evoke natural scenery. Shi also could become a sort of banal "social glue," appearing not just in literary contexts but in everyday social exchanges and daily rituals and as an inscribed ornament in practically every environment. The prestige and utility of shi resulted in its spread to other countries influenced by Chinese culture (see KOREA, POETRY OF; CHINESE POETRY IN JAPAN; VIETNAM, POETRY OF).

From the 3d to 1st cs. BCE, another form of verse evolved in south China, which achieved finalized form in the anthol. known as the *Chuci or "Songs of Chu" (Chu being a Chinese kingdom located in the central Yangtze Valley). This form involved a more flexible meter, though couplets continued as the main structural unit. Lament was the strongest thematic strain, with erotic and religious elements also present. Chuci-style composition remained popular in the Han dynasty (206 BCE–220 CE) court, though it was gradually replaced by the somewhat similar but more ambitious *fu (rhapsody). Fu were largely courtly or public in origin and became immensely popular from the end of the Han through the Tang. In style, they were rhetorical (evolving in large part from earlier trads. of political and ethical oratorical persuasion). In a broader sense, fu contributed substantially to later descriptive prose style (and, in fact, traditional theorists tended to see it as a form of prose, even though it often employed "poetic" techniques such as *parallelism, couplet structures, rhyme, and tonal regulation).

After shi, the best-known genre of traditional Chinese poetry is the *ci (song lyric), which evolved from Tang dynasty popular songs. Ci are composed to set tune patterns (ci pai) with rigidly prescribed line lengths, stanza divisions, and tonal requirements; in content, they originally emphasized mildly erotic themes, though by the Song dynasty, they broached typical shi topics as well. Though many ci continued to be sung, other ci pai lost their original music, resulting in a strictly spoken poetic form. The Song dynasty is held to be the acme of ci composition, but Qing dynasty (1644–1911) ci are also greatly admired.

In the past millennium, two further significant devels. emerged in traditional Chinese poetry. First, Chinese drama (which became important in the 13th c.) incorporated lyrics to set tunes that function much like the songs in Eng. ballad opera. This form of dramatic lyric became a major outlet for poetic expression both in performance and in print (see CHINESE POETIC DRAMA). Second, numerous popular narrative poetic forms appeared, many of them conveyed through oral performance by a professional storyteller class. While our knowledge of earlier centuries is spotty, from the 18th c. and later a large corpus of texts has been preserved (some produced by women); from the 20th c., we also have eds. based on recordings or oral performance.

With the arrival of the imperial powers in China in the late 19th c. and political and social pressure to use the West as the model for "modernization," traditional Chinese verse forms fell into disfavor among many progressive intellectuals and were continued mostly on the amateur level. "Serious" poetry was influenced considerably by mod. artistic movements in the West and was written in the spoken vernacular lang.; this became known generally as xin shi (new poetry; see CHINA, MODERN POETRY OF). Forms of *free verse have been the most popular, though poets have experimented with other Western poetic forms such as the *sonnet. Interestingly enough, while Chinese poets were experimenting with Westernized forms, mod. Western poets began to employ aspects of traditional Chinese poetry in their own verse experiments (see CHINESE POETRY IN ENGLISH TRANSLATION).

See CHINA, POPULAR POETRY OF; CHINESE POETICS.

■ **Criticism and History**: J.J.Y. Liu, *The Art of Chinese Poetry* (1962); B. Watson, *Early Chinese Literature* (1962); H. Frankel, *The Flowering Plum and the Palace Lady* (1976); *The Indiana Companion to Traditional Chinese Literature*, ed. W. Nienhauser (1986); M. Yeh, *Modern Chinese Poetry* (1991); W. Idema and L. Haft, *A Guide to Chinese Literature* (1997); *The Columbia History of Chinese Literature*, ed. V. Mair (2001); W. Idema and B. Grant, *The Red Brush: Writing Women of Imperial China* (2004)—includes many trans.

■ **Translations**: *Sunflower Splendor*, ed. W. Liu and I. Y. Lo (1975); *Wen Xuan*, ed. and trans. D. Knechtges, 3 v. (1982–96); *The Columbia Book of Chinese Poetry*, ed. and trans. B. Watson (1984); *The Columbia Book of Later Chinese Poetry*, ed. and trans. J. Chaves (1986); *Anthology of Modern Chinese Poetry*, ed. and trans. M. Yeh (1990); *The Red Azalea: Chinese Poetry since the Cultural Revolution*, ed. E. Morin (1990); *The Columbia Anthology of Traditional Chinese Literature*, ed. V. Mair (1994); *An Anthology of Chinese Literature*, ed. and trans. S. Owen (1996); *Women Writers of Traditional China*, ed. K. S. Chang and H. Saussy (1999); *Classical Chinese Literature*, ed. J. Minford and J.S.M. Lau (2002); *How to Read Chinese Poetry*, ed. Z. Cai (2007)—includes critical essays on poems.

P. ROUZER

**CHINA, POPULAR POETRY OF.** China has a long trad. of popular poetry. Alongside a rich and varied trad. of vernacular song, there also exists an equally rich and varied trad. of vernacular narrative verse, often of epic proportions—texts of thousands or even ten thousands of lines are no exception. And alongside this trad. of pure verse narrative, there exists an even richer trad. of prosimetric narrative (see PROSIMETRUM). In these prosimetric narratives, composed in an alternation of prose and verse, the verse sections often are dominant. Because these verse sections were chanted or sung in performance, in contrast to the more colloquial rendition of the prose sections, the mod. Chinese designation of this body of texts is *shuochang wenxue* or "literature for telling and singing," while some Western scholars have used the Fr. term *chante-fable (the term *shuochang wenxue* in practice also includes the many genres of vernacular verse narrative).

While to the 14th c. many forms of popular song eventually were taken up by elite writers and developed into genres of cl. poetry such as *shi*, *ci*, or *qu* (see CHINESE POETIC DRAMA), this did not happen to any of the genres of verse and prosimetric narrative. As a result, our knowledge of the early hist. of these genres is very incomplete; most of our knowledge is based on archaeological discoveries of mss. or printed texts. Texts of verse narratives or chante-fables have only been preserved in greater number from the 17th c. on, and many of them were printed in the 19th c. or later. Other texts were recorded only in the 20th c.

Verse narratives are most often composed in lines of seven-syllable verse, which are called ci or "ballad-verse" (confusingly, this ci is the same term that is also used to designate the genre of the lyric). From the 9th to the 15th c., texts written exclusively in ci are simply called *ciwen* (texts in ci). The basic rhythm of the seven-syllable line is 2-2-3, with a major *caesura following the fourth syllable. Every second line rhymes. From the 15th c. on, one also encounters ten-syllable lines, which are called *zan*. These lines have a basic rhythm of 3-4-3 or of 3-3-4. Initially, the zan was used only for short descriptive passages; but their use became increasingly more common with the progression of time, and in 19th c. and later one find texts only using zan. Many prosimetric genres also rely primarily on the ci (and the zan) for their verse sections, and the element *ci* is often encountered as part of the name of a genre (such as *cihua* or "ballad stories," *tanci* or "string ballads," and *guci* or "drum ballads"). The earliest examples of verse or prosimetric narratives employing ci are the *bianwen* or "transformation texts" of the 9th and 10th cs., discovered at Dunhuang.

Some chante-fable genres, however, rely for their verse sections on songs whose melodies demand lines of unequal length. Whereas in some genres the author may limit himself to a single tune that is repeated as often as required in each verse section, other genres, such as the *zhugongdiao* or "all keys and modes" that flourished from the late 11th to the early 14th c., employ a bewildering variety of tunes, which are organized in suites of varying length. The zhugongdiao acquired its name from the fact that no suite could be followed by another in the same key. The musical sophistication re-

quired in the composition, performance, and appreciation of a genre like the zhugongdiao has ensured that this latter type of genre has always been in a minority.

The preserved texts may derive from oral performances, but in both premod. and mod. times such texts will have been heavily edited before they were printed. Many orally performed texts turn out, on closer observation, to be derived from written texts in some way or another. Other texts were written by performers or aficionados with performance in mind, but some texts in these genres were written primarily for reading. The highly educated women authors of tanci in the 18th and 19th cs. concerning women dressed as men outperforming men in the examinations, at court, and on the battlefield stressed that their works were intended for reading only, but even so some of these works were adapted for performance in later times. Texts from many different parts of China tend to be written in a rather uniform stylized vernacular, but some genres also systematically include the local dialect: tanci produced in Suzhou may include extensive passages in the local Wu dialect; the *muyushu* or "wooden-fish books" from Guangdong make some use of Cantonese; and the *gezaice* or "song books" from southern Fujian and Taiwan became increasingly liberal in their incorporation of Minnanese over the course of the 20th c. The local coloring of genres originating from northern China such as guci and *zidishu* or "youth books" (a genre beloved by Manchu amateurs in 18th- and 19th-c. Beijing) is less obvious because Mandarin became the basis of the mod. standard lang.

The subject matter of verse and prosimetric narrative is extremely broad. It is probably safe to say that the stories of all popular China traditional novels and plays also have been treated in shuochang wenxue. Some genres have an outspoken affinity to a certain class of subject matter. *Baojuan* or "precious scrolls" initially told pious Buddhist tales but as time went by broadened their repertoire. *Daoqing* or "Daoist sentiments" originally focused on tales of Daoist immortals and their conversions. Guci are said to have a greater affinity to tales of warfare and crime, while tanci are said to be more suitable to tales of romance and intrigue. Plots and characters were freely exchanged between the many genres. Some stories that were very popular in shuochang wenxue were rarely or never treated in fiction before the 20th c. One example is the legend of Meng Jiangnü, whose husband was drafted as a corvée laborer for the construction of the Great Wall, soon died of exhaustion, and was buried in the wall. When she came to the construction site to bring him a set of winter clothes and learned of his death, her weeping brought down the section of the wall in which he had been buried. Another example is the romance of Liang Shanbo and Zhu Yingtai. Zhu Yingtai is a girl who in male disguise leaves home and attends an academy. She falls in love with her male roommate Liang Shanbo. When she leaves, she urges him to visit her, but by the time he does so and learns she is a girl, her parents have already engaged her to the son of another family. The now-love-smitten Liang Shanbo soon dies; and when Zhu Yingtai's bridal procession passes by his grave, the grave opens up and she joins him in death, whereupon their souls turn into butterflies. While stories like these are encountered in practically all genres, other stories are more specific to a certain region or genre.

■ *Ballad of the Hidden Dragon*, trans. M. Doleželová-Velingerová and J. I. Crump (1971); *Master Tung's Western Chamber Romance*, trans. L. L. Ch'en (1976); *Tun-huang Popular Narratives*, trans. V. H. Mair (1983); V. Mair, *T'ang Transformation Texts* (1989); *The Story of Hua Guan Suo*, trans. G. O. King (1989); A. E. McLaren, *Chinese Popular Culture and Ming Chantefables* (1998); D. Overmeyer, *Precious Volumes: An Introduction to Chinese Sectarian Scriptures from the Sixteenth and Seventeenth Centuries* (1999); M. Bender, *Plum and Bamboo* (2003) on Suzhou; *Meng Jiangnü Brings Down the Great Wall* (2008), *Personal Salvation and Filial Piety* (2008), *Filial Piety and Its Divine Reward* (2009), *Heroines of Jiangyong* (2009), *Judge Bao and the Rule of Law* (2010), *The White Snake and Her Son* (2009), *The Butterfly Lovers* (2010)—all trans. W. L. Idema; W. L. Idema, "Verse and Prosimetric Narrative," *Cambridge History of Chinese Literature*, ed. K. S. Chang and S. Owen, v. 2 (2010).

W. L. IDEMA

**CHINESE POETIC DRAMA.** *Xiqu*, or "drama," literally means dramatic song, and until the advent of Western-style "spoken drama," all Chinese drama was sung by characters who belonged to role types (e.g., male lead, female lead, clown). Traditional drama encompasses hundreds of regional forms, spanning close to a millennium, from its beginnings around the year 1100 to the present. The vast majority of those forms have left no written trace. Performers rely not on *libretti* but on oral transmission and improvisation. A form as popular as Peking opera (*jingju*) has no scripts to speak of. This entry discusses the few dramatic forms that became important as written lit.: *zaju*, *xiwen* (or *nanxi*), and xiwen's much more important descendant, *chuanqi*. Even in these forms, the vast majority of scripts have been lost. Within the full panoply of Chinese performance trads., these forms—in which the page has been as important as the stage—are anomalous. A 1324 mural of a theatrical troupe that depicts the lead actress in scrupulous detail but never mentions a playwright or a play suggests that, even when it comes to zaju, our contemp. inclination to identify a playwright rather than an actor as the primary creative force might be misplaced.

No written traces of drama predate the 13th c.; however, it is clear from other sources that drama had antecedents in religious ritual and was also closely associated with other forms of poetry meant for paid performance (most particularly prosimetric lit. [see PROSIMETRUM] and *zhugongdiao* [all keys and modes]). From the earliest surviving dramatic texts, two main trads. predominate, one based on northern melodies and rhymes (zaju) and the other based on southern (xiwen). In both cases, melodies were not composed specifically for a play; instead, folk songs and popular ditties circulated as an existing repertoire.

Zaju are closely associated with the performance trads. of the great cities of the 13th c., esp. Hangzhou (then called Lin'an) and Beijing (Dadu, under the Yuan dynasty). The first playwrights whose names are known were largely men of Dadu, Guan Hanqing most famous among them. When the component songs are referred to as *qu* (songs), they relate a narrative as experienced by the individual who sings of it and are considered dramatic verse. Set to the exact same music but unconnected by plot, *sanqu* (or unconnected songs) are considered *lyric poetry.

Whereas the textual integrity of *shi* or *ci* was generally respected by those who transmitted them, these early dramatic texts were clearly regarded as open to modification. We speak of the most famous of zaju, *Xixiang ji* (*The Western Wing*), as if its author were Wang Shifu, but in fact, the play appears in multiple recensions: the most important, a 17th-c. version rewritten by Jin Shengtan, and others, with layers added in the 14th and 15th cs.

Whether they are part of a play or simply a song, qu feature northern slang; a common pattern is to end with an earthy punch line delivered in colloquial northern Chinese. Like ci, qu are characterized by lines of uneven length, dictated by the melody, or *qupai*. Rather than determining the prosodic pattern as strictly as in ci, however, the melody is a signpost. This flexibility has partly to do with performance practice. When these prosodic guidelines were translated to the stage, they made for some of the unusual characteristics of zaju. Usually four acts (with a short additional act or "wedge"), each act is comprised of a single song suite—with one rhyme throughout and only a single singer. Had it not been for the use of *chengzi* (padding syllables) and a flexible understanding of rhyme (with no regard for the tone of the rhyming syllables), zaju would have involved too many prosodic strictures to allow for plot devel.

As it is, plot is secondary in zaju, and many are clearly performance pieces to highlight the skills of a single performer: consider, e.g., the scene in which Dou E is wrongfully executed in Guan Hanqing's *Dou E yuan* (*The Injustice to Dou E*). *Xixiang ji* is a formal exception, a successful romantic comedy only because it is five plays, one after the other, comprising a total of 21 acts; each of the two lovers, as well as a maidservant, takes a turn at singing.

Musically, zaju and xiwen were both governed by rules that are deeply arcane now. Melodies belonged to different modes; an act could contain melodies from a single mode, or it could include melodies from different modes, as long as these followed a prescribed pattern.

The first xiwen to circulate widely as a written text was Gao Ming's *Pipa ji* (*The Lute*), which dates from the mid-14th c. Only recently have scholars been able to collect fragments of a number of nanxi, some from the *Yongle Encyclopedia* and others from various tomb excavations. More than one character could sing within a single act; a solo could turn midstream into a duet or a trio or a chorus. From an early point, xiwen were long, 20 acts or longer and probably intended to be performed over the course of two days.

By the early decades of the Ming dynasty, zaju

had become the favorite form of the imperial court. A number of scripts have survived in the imperial collections, where they were sometimes edited or even rewritten to avoid the appearance of sedition. One of the best known of early Ming dramatists was Zhu Youdun, grandson of the dynasty's founder.

Over the course of the dynasty, zaju ceased to be an important popular form of performance. What took its place was southern drama, whose great heyday was in the last decades of the Ming dynasty, a period that coincided with an explosive growth in the availability of print material. Alone of all genres of Chinese popular drama, *kunqu* (a performance style to sing chuanqi, the written plays) was essentially born in print in the 1570s, its flagship libretto *Huansha ji* (*Washing Silk*) by Liang Chenyu, who had worked closely with the musician Wei Liangfu. Many other plays in the same style began to appear immediately thereafter—and perhaps more strikingly, an entire cultural apparatus for the production and consumption of chuanqi: guidebooks to *prosody, hists. of nanxi, dramatic appreciations. These long plays were probably almost always performed in excerpt. Audiences acquainted themselves with the rest of the play by reading scripts, in which prose dialogue became increasingly important.

Zaju too came under the same pressures and by the late 16th c. was increasingly tied to the world of the imprint. Xu Wei's *Sisheng yuan* (Four Cries of the Gibbon) is four zaju dealing with the same theme, that of theatricality and identity. All the plays toy with the strictures of zaju: e.g., a monk dies midway through and is reincarnated as a woman, each the protagonist and the sole singing role in his or her respective acts. These plays were radical musically as well, mixing northern and southern melodies. After Xu Wei, numerous playwrights wrote plays that were zaju in name only: short, focusing on a single singer, but no longer adhering to the old prosodic regulations.

Much of what in recent centuries has been considered Yuan drama is filtered through a single anthol., *Yuanqu xuan* (Selection of Yuan Drama, 1611), compiled by Zang Maoxun. Comparing extant Yuan and early Ming sources with those in the anthol. reveals that Zang Maoxun had a heavy editorial hand, embellishing prose dialogue and making endings more climactic and moralistic.

Contemp. discussion of drama concerned the place of prosodic rules and of the stage. The most famous chuanqi of all, *Mudan ting* (*The Peony Pavilion*) by Tang Xianzu, originally written in the Yihuang style, was the touchstone for the 17th-c. enthusiasm for romance but almost unsingable. Both Feng Menglong and Zang Maoxun tried their hand at rewriting it according to the stricter prosodic rules advocated by another contemp. playwright, Shen Jing.

Written largely by elite men to be performed by actors, when acting was a despised profession associated with prostitution, chuanqi plays involve men and women from a range of class backgrounds, often masking their true status. Buffoons pretend to be refined scholars; refined scholars disguise themselves as poor men to avoid recognition; girls pretend to be boys—disguise is the norm, and lang. is used to dissimulate as much as reveal. This extreme heteroglossia is important at a thematic and syntactic level: since at least Song ci, one of the most important rhetorical modes of Chinese poetry is an abrupt shift in ling. register. Nowhere are sharp shifts in register more common and central than in chuanqi. The cl. trad. itself becomes the object of commentary. A single aria might include a quotation from the classics, Tang shi, Song ci, and Ming slang. Puns are common.

Chuanqi continued to be popular throughout the 17th c. and into the 18th, although fewer and fewer were written, and under the Manchus increasingly strict rules were imposed both on performance and performers. The 19th c. saw the decline of the form, which essentially was brought to an end by the Taiping Rebellion of the 1860s.

■ **Critical Studies**: W. L. Idema and S. H. West, *Chinese Theater 1100–1450, A Source Book* (1982); S. H. West, "A Study in Appropriation: Zang Maoxun's *Dou E Yuan*," *JAOS* 101 (1991); T. Lu, *Persons, Roles, and Minds* (2001); C. C. Swatek, *Peony Pavilion Onstage* (2002); *Cambridge History of Chinese Literature*, ed. K. S. Chang and S. Owen, 2 vols. (2010).

■ **Translations**: *The Story of the Western Wing*, trans. W. L. Idema and S. H. West (1995); *Scenes for Mandarins*, ed. and trans. C. Birch (1995); *The Peony Pavilion*, trans. C. Birch (2002); *Select Poets and Resources: Monks, Bandits, Lovers, and Immortals: Eleven Early Chinese Plays*, ed. and trans. S. H. West (2010).

T. Lu

**CHINESE POETICS.** A survey of Chinese poetics must keep in view the intimate association between poetry and music in Chinese trad. The following passage from the *Shang shu* (Classic of Documents), in a section of that work that took shape during the Eastern Zhou (8th–3d c. BCE), depicting the moment when music was instituted by a command from the mythic sage-king Shun to his assistant Kui, provides one key reference point for traditional discussions of poetry:

> The divine ruler [Shun] said: "Kui! I command you to preside over music: to instruct the princes of the state, that they be upright, yet affable; tolerant, yet reverent; that they be firm, yet not cruel; and direct, yet not arrogant. The *shi* expresses aims; singing draws out the expression; the musical mode attunes the sounds, so that the eight timbres accord, none usurping another's place. Thus gods and humans are placed in harmony." Kui said, "I strike the stones, stroke the stones; the hundred beasts take up the dance."

The term *shi, in its centrality to traditional Chinese poetic discourse, offers the nearest functional analogue to the Western category "poetry." In the above passage, *shi* means simply "lyrics," the words to a song. The statement that "the *shi* expresses aims" itself also doubles as a definition, since the graphs for "express" ( *yan*) and "aim" (*zhi*) mirror the two halves of the graph *shi*. *Shi* can also designate an ancient musical repertoire overseen by musicians of the Zhou court (1046–256 BCE). This repertoire, seen as descended from the institution of music whose founding is depicted above, became central to the curriculum of traditionalist ritual and musical education. It became fixed over time, and as the old musical settings fell from memory in the Zhou's waning centuries, the remaining written text, an anthol. of 305 poems, was known as the *Shijing* (*Classic of Poetry*, also known as the *Book of Songs*). In med. and later times, the same term referred to "literati *shi*," i.e., poems in a range of newer verse forms, primarily in pentasyllabic or heptasyllabic lines.

For practical purposes, it is important to distinguish which of these disparate meanings applies in a given use of the term *shi*. In Chinese discussions of the fundamental nature and function of poetry, however, its explanatory power often stems precisely from the way one meaning carries resonances from one or more others. Thus, though the word in Shun's speech means "words to a song," for traditional readers the implications of this pronouncement would include its import for their own study and recitation of the *Shijing*; similarly, later critics of literati *shi*, even when discussing technical aspects of those later verse forms, often felt obliged to assert an underlying continuity of their activity with the *Shijing* and the sagely institution of music. Just as fully understanding a given instance of the word *shi* often meant situating the particular use in the broader context of a hist. from high antiquity to the present, skill in reading poetry (or listening to speech or song) meant skill in inferring, from the particular expression, a fullness of what the expressive act revealed, not only the poet's implicit intentions but more generally the world to which the poem responded.

Both these aspects of poetic understanding as contextualization—situating the poem in the context of the legacy of ancient music and understanding its particularity by "hearing" its layers of implication—remain prominent throughout later Chinese critical trad., as in Sima Guang's (1019–86) exegesis of the first half of Du Fu's (712–70) "Chun wang" ("Spring Prospect"):

> The capital shattered, hills and rivers remain;
> city walls in springtime: grass and trees grow
> thickly.
> Stirred by the season—flowers are spattered with
> tears;
> regretting separation—birds startle the heart.

Sima Guang comments: "The poets of antiquity are to be esteemed for the way their conceptions lie beyond the words, leaving the reader to obtain them only upon reflection; thus 'those who spoke were free from blame, and those who heard had ample means of correcting themselves.'" Here Sima Guang cites from the Mao school Great Preface to the *Shijing* the belief that the ancient *shi* had provided a channel for indirect expression of resentments, thus fostering social harmony. The

point of the quotation is less to suggest that Du Fu was expressing a potentially dangerous resentment than to highlight and commend a latent continuity between Du Fu's poem and the ancient trad. Sima Guang next proceeds to an account of the implicit states of the poet and his world, in keeping with this idea of an ancient poetics of indirection: "To say, 'The capital shattered, hills and rivers remain' shows that there is nothing else. To say, 'city walls in springtime: grass and trees grow thickly' shows that there are no human traces. As for 'flowers' and 'birds,' in ordinary times such things are objects of delight. To see them and weep; to hear them and grieve—the sort of time this is may be known."

Though Shun's dictum states "the *shi* expresses aims," the scene in which this statement occurs makes clear that the motivating purpose of the institution was not to express particular aims but rather to shape the personalities of "princes of the state." Scenes in the *Analects* where Confucius (551–479 BCE) discusses the *Shi* (whose meaning, in the *Analects*, we see shifting from the musical repertoire referred to as *shi* toward the fully textual classic *Shi*, or *Shijing*) with his disciples show this *shi jiao* (teaching through poetry) in action. Confucius asserts that having truly studied the *Shi* should entail being competent to act autonomously as the representative of one's ruler in diplomatic exchanges (*Analects* 13.5); indeed, formal performances from the *Shi* were often required at state banquets, demanding not only a command of the repertoire but an acute sensitivity for how contextual meanings might shift with circumstances of performance.

As suggested in the *Shang shu* scene, though, the most immediate purpose of teaching through poetry lay in its shaping effect on the student's personality, instilling a delicate balance between opposed impulses: firmness is desirable but, left unchecked, might turn to cruelty; directness is desirable but, left unchecked, might lead to arrogance. Such harmonizing of opposed tendencies characterizes not only these intended effects of teaching through poetry but the personality of a sage, who is "affable, yet severe; imposing, yet not aggressive; respectful, yet at ease" (*Analects* 7.38, describing Confucius), or the legacy of sagely music itself, which is "joyful, yet not licentious; mournful, yet not grieved to the point of harm" (*Analects* 3.20).

This last comment is uttered by Confucius in response to "Guanju" (Fishhawk), the first poem in the *Shijing*. Evidence within the *Analects* suggests Confucius would have been responding not to a text but to a musical performance. For readers in ages after the musical settings to the *Shi* had been lost, those lost settings became an emblem of the distance separating them from the poems' primordial expressive and transformative power. The Song dynasty scholar Zhu Xi (1130–1200) commented that the reader of the text of "Guanju," by reflection on the poem's words, might gain an understanding of the "rightness of personality" of both the poem's central figure and the poet himself but could never capture the full "harmony of sound and breath" conveyed in the performance as Confucius had heard it. Zhu Xi continues, "[T]hough this seems regrettable, if the student will but attend to the phrases, pondering the inhering principle, so as in this way to nurture the mind, then in this way as well one may attain what is fundamental about studying the *Shi*" (*Shijing jizhuan*). The final aim of the study of the *Shijing* is to recover the efficacy of the musical legacy of the sages through alternate means.

This didactic notion of poetry as an adjunct of the transformative project of sagely music, although it exerted decisive influence over critical statements about poetry's fundamental significance throughout premod. Chinese trad., is far from encompassing the variety of poetry and song as practiced. In ritual contexts, music and song served in communicating with deceased ancestors and other unseen powers. As one human variety of the general cosmic category of *wen*, or patterning, poems were one among many sorts of wen—celestial, terrestrial, and human—that might be fraught with portent based on a dense web of latent interconnections and occult sympathies. We glimpse this element of mystery in the incantatory tone of Kui's response to Shun's charge and in his vision of music as a force to which even animals respond—Kui himself, though euhemerized in the *Shang shu* scene as a human minister, in other contexts appears as a crocodile-like figure, associated with the magical power of drumming via the use of reptile skins for drumheads.

There were always ample instances of poetry and music of ecstatic rapture, divine trance, and sensual abandon to affront traditionalist ideals of harmony and the delicate balancing of opposed impulses, filling scholars with something like the unease Plato felt about allowing poets into his ideal city. Even certain poems and sections within the *Shijing* itself, particularly the "Guo feng" (Airs of the States) sections tied to the states of Zheng and Wei, were deemed symptomatic of a loss of emotional and moral equilibrium, and the significance of their inclusion in the canon (an editorial choice attributed within the trad. to Confucius) was a fraught and productive problem for later crit. The *Chuci*, reflecting a poetics of religious ecstasy and sensual transport, along with the Western Han (206 BCE–8 CE) rise of the poetic genre of *fu*, which drew largely on both the prosody and underlying aesthetic from the Chuci trad., posed further challenges for Han and later scholars striving to accommodate these later poetic modes to the traditionalist paradigm. A typical strategy for accomplishing this involved invoking concepts such as *bian* (mutation) or *liu* (offstream), allowing these poetic modes to be seen as deviations while leaving open the possibility of viewing them as continuations of the legacy of the ancient *shi* by altered means, in response to larger processes of historical change.

The turn of the 3d c. saw the rise of the literati *shi*, along with fu and the full repertoire of genres of belletristic writing. The "Lun wen" (Discourse on Literature) of Cao Pi (186–226), first emperor of the Wei dynasty (220–65), marks a watershed both for its overt assertion that composition in these genres could be a

means to cultural immortality and for its theorization of the system of affinities between particular sorts of talent and particular literary modes. Over subsequent centuries, a view emerged of poetic hist. as a repertoire of styles that could be read in terms both of divergent personalities and of distinct historical eras. Zhong Rong's (ca. 468–516) "Shi pin" (Grades of Poetry) ranked poets in the pentasyllabic *shi* form from its beginnings down to Zhong's own lifetime in "top," "middle," and "lower" grades, giving a précis of each poet's style and in many instances specifying its antecedents. Not surprisingly, among the most praised styles were those affiliated directly to the *Shijing*.

The intermittent inclusion during the Tang dynasty (618–907) of composition in *shi* and fu genres in the requirements for candidates for the prestigious *jin shi* (Presented Scholar) degree is itself unimaginable apart from the ancient conception of music and poetry as tools to mold "princes of the state" into sound administrators. The prestige of these poetic forms, along with increasingly demanding rules for tonal regulation and syntactical *parallelism, created a need for instructional guides for poetic composition. The resulting body of material, largely composed of lists of prohibitions, typologies of parallel couplets, rosters of stylistic subtypes, and so on, came to be viewed as middlebrow at best, since the orthodox view of poetry as stemming organically from the poet's response to events of the world could not admit the validity of fixed rules for poetic composition.

Something of this tension between, on the one hand, the practical need for technical analysis and prescriptive methods and, on the other, reassertions of the organic connection between poetry and the broader project of cl. studies and personal transformation is reflected throughout the proliferating lit. of poetic crit. from the Song dynasty (960–1279) onward. Many of the enduring arguments reprise themes from the early hist. of *shi*, incl. discussions of the relation between inner emotional states and outer scene, calls for *fu gu* (restoration of antiquity), debates about the proper choice of models and about striking the proper balance in studying such models, between careful imitation and the expression of the student's own personality. Analogies to and ideas drawn from Chinese Buddhist trads. became a prominent feature of Song dynasty and later poetic crit., with the critic Yan Yu (late 12th–early 13th c.) often cited as the first to draw an explicit analogy between Zen enlightenment and poetic inspiration and Wang Shizhen (1634–1711) regarded as a highly influential late imperial exemplar.

Just as the fu had been assimilated to the traditionalist view of poetic hist. as a mutated offstream of the ancient *shi*, critical discourses surrounding later lyric genres incl. *ci* (song lyric) or *qu*, the diverse constellation of song forms that from the Yuan dynasty (1271–1368) onward formed the lyrical building blocks of a rich operatic lit. reflect a similar tension between genre-specific technical discussions and the impulse to link the basic expressive and transformative power of these genres back to the ancient *shi* and the mythology of the transformative power of music. Even seemingly remote genres such as narrative fiction and the "eight-legged essay" that was the staple of examination cultures of the Ming and Qing dynasties came to be viewed in their own ways as mutated analogues to the sagely legacy of music.

See CHINA, POETRY OF; CHINA, POPULAR POETRY OF; CHINESE POETIC DRAMA; CHINESE POETRY IN ENGLISH TRANSLATION; CHINESE POETRY IN JAPAN; YUEFU.

■ Liu Xie, *The Literary Mind and the Carving of Dragons*, trans. V.Y.C. Shih (1959)—trans of *Wenxin diaolong*; J.J.Y. Liu, *Chinese Theories of Literature* (1975); R. J. Lynn, "Orthodoxy and Enlightenment—Wang Shih-chen's Theory of Poetry and Its Antecedents," *The Unfolding of Neo-Confucianism*, ed. W. T. de Bary (1975); *Theories of the Arts in China*, ed. S. Bush and C. Murck (1983); S. Owen, *Chinese Poetry and Poetics: Omen of the World* (1985); *The Indiana Companion to Traditional Chinese Literature*, ed. W. Nienhauser (1986); P. Yu, *The Reading of Imagery in the Chinese Poetic Tradition* (1987); S. Van Zoeren, *Poetry and Personality: Reading, Exegesis, and Hermeneutics in Traditional China* (1991); S. Owen, *Readings in Traditional Chinese Literary Thought* (1992); H. Saussy, *The Problem of a Chinese Aesthetic* (1993); R. Ashmore, "The Banquet's Aftermath: Yan Jidao's *Ci* Poetics and the High Tradition," *T'oung Pao* 88 (2002); R. Sterckx, *The Animal and the Daemon in Early China* (2002); M. Kern, "Western Han Aesthetics and the Genesis of the *Fu*," *HJAS* 63 (2003); *Chinese Aesthetics: The Ordering of Literature, the Arts, and the Universe in the Six Dynasties*, ed. Z. Cai (2004).

R. ASHMORE

## CHINESE POETRY IN ENGLISH TRANSLATION.
Chinese poems began to be paraphrased in Western langs. in the 17th c. when Jesuit missionaries, seeking support for their policy of cultural accommodation, reported on the advanced literary, scientific, and philosophical state of China. Efforts at *translation into Fr., Ger., and Eng. were peripheral to lit. and even to scholarship until Ezra Pound published *Cathay* (1915). This book of 14 cl. Chinese poems, rewritten from the word-for-word versions of Ernest Fenollosa and his Japanese tutors, first exhibited the characteristics of the hybrid Chinese-Eng. poetic lang.: *end-stopped, stress-heavy lines, mostly monosyllabic, using coordination rather than subordination and often appearing to have left something out. See the opening lines of Pound's "Poem by the Bridge at Ten-Shin" (from Li Bai, "Gu feng 59 shou," no. 18):

> March has come to the bridge head,
> Peach flowers and apricot boughs hang over a
>    thousand gates,
> At morning there are flowers to cut the heart,
> And evening drives them on the eastward-flowing
>    waters.

Pound's trans. practice foregrounds the "qualities of vivid presentation" he found in Fenollosa's notes

and emulates the way "Chinese poets have been content to set forth their matter without moralizing and without comment" ("Chinese Poetry, I" in *Early Writings*). As if to confirm the imagist call for "direct treatment of the thing, whether objective or subjective" and to "use absolutely no word that does not contribute to the presentation" (Pound, "Imagisme" [1913]), the 8th-c. Chinese poet here ventriloquized uses the present tense, speaks in short bursts of observation, and withholds comment on things not outwardly visible save for the (possibly idiomatic) expression of the flowers' effect on feelings. Weak *personification ("March has come," "evening drives them") serves mainly to give the sentences subjects and verbs. An unobtrusive *allegory (flowers driven on unidirectional currents from morning to evening) supports the elegiac tone.

Contrast the effort of Fenollosa some years earlier to render a different 8th-c. poem (Wang Wei, "Gao yuan") in Eng. verse:

> Crimson the snare of the peaches that catch the
>    dews on the wing.
> Verdant the face of the willows that bathe in winds
>    of the spring.
> Petals have fallen all night, but no dutiful maid is
>    yet sweeping.
> Larks have been up with the dawn, but the guest
>    of the mountain is sleeping.

The end-stopped sentences and the speaker's reticence are all there, but the clockwork meter and banally elaborate diction separate it from the genre of the Eng.-lang. "Chinese poem" initiated by Pound.

"The element in poetry which travels best," as Graham observed, "is of course concrete imagery": Chinese poetry came into fashion in the Eng.-speaking world just when *imagery reigned supreme. Unspoken meanings, another feature of much Chinese poetry, are not the translator's problem. Most translators since Pound, those at any rate whose audience is readers of poetry, have adopted the terse plainness of *Cathay*. The 21 trans. by different hands of a single quatrain by Wang Wei, collected by Weinberger, shows the steady advance of this manner. Wai-lim Yip and Gary Snyder, poets in their own right, contend in theoretical writings and by the example of their trans. that Chinese poetry gives direct access to perception unclouded by lang., a radicalization of the theory of the *ideogram: thus, their versions adapt the Eng. lang. to their purposes, shedding pronouns, tenses, prepositions and other explicative machinery. More recent translators have explored electronic means of staging Chinese poems in some form of Eng. Anthols. of Chinese poetry in trans. permit taking stock of this stream of trad.

The effortless simplicity seen in trans. Chinese poetry is not just a style but an ethos. As ethos, it becomes a mode or manner of mod. Am. poetry, for which knowledge of Chinese is not required. The poets of the Chinese canon become models, ancestors, interlocutors. James Wright addresses an 8th-c. predecessor with an echo of Charles Baudelaire ("As I Step over a Puddle at the End of Winter, I Think of an Ancient Chinese Governor," 1963). Charles Wright paraphrases Du Fu ("China Mail," 1997). Am. poetry of the 20th c. is unimaginable without the Chinese contribution. Chinese poetry since the 1980s has included this Am. poetry in a Chinese manner among its influences, a rhetorical resource separate from the models of cl. Chinese poetry.

*See* IMAGISM.

■ A. C. Graham, *Poems of the Late T'ang* (1977); E. Weinberger, *Nineteen Ways of Looking at Wang Wei* (1987); W. Yip, *Diffusion of Distances: Dialogues between Chinese and Western Poetics* (1993); R. Kern, *Orientalism, Modernism and the American Poem* (1996); S. Yao, *Translation and the Languages of Modernism* (2002); *The New Directions Anthology of Classical Chinese Poetry*, ed. E. Weinberger (2003); E. Pound, *Poems and Translations* (2003); E. Hayot, *Chinese Dreams: Pound, Brecht, "Tel Quel"* (2004); E. Pound, *Early Writings*, ed. I. Nadel (2005); *Classical Chinese Poetry*, trans. D. Hinton (2008); E. Fenollosa and E. Pound, *The Chinese Character as a Medium for Poetry*, ed. H. Saussy et al. (2008).

H. SAUSSY

# CHINESE POETRY IN JAPAN

I. Terminology, Genres, and Characteristics
II. History

## I. Terminology, Genres, and Characteristics

A. *Terminology.* There is no consensus that "Chinese poetry in Japan" is the best way to describe poetry composed by Japanese in a script-lang. often called "Chinese." The disagreement about what to call this poetry indicates how differently these poems are viewed. One not entirely logical trad. among Western scholars uses the Japanese terms *kanshi* and *kanbun* in the sense of, respectively, poems and prose in Chinese composed by Japanese. However, since the late 19th c., these terms, often in the fused form *kanshibun* (poems and prose in Chinese) in Japan refer to any text in Chinese, usually from China; Japanese scholars commonly refer to "Japanese *kanshi*" (*Nihon kanshi*). Alternatively, kanshi from Japan have been often called "Japanese poems in Chinese" and conversely "Sino-Japanese" poetry.

Behind the terminology lurks a lang. question: namely, whether Sino-Japanese poetry is, in fact, "Chinese" or is better understood as a form of Japanese. Choice of terminology has implications for assumptions of "foreignness" of Chinese poetry in Japan. The idea that the lang. of kanshi in Japan is a form Japanese, or at the very least not the same as "Sino-Chinese," is recently gaining some ground and suggests that poems in (some form of) "Chinese" are more and more considered to be an indigenous part of the Japanese literary trad. At the same time, Sino-Japanese poetry is part of a larger East Asian body of poetry in variant forms of Chinese (China, Korea, Vietnam).

B. *Genres and Characteristics.* The poetic trad. of Sino-Japanese poetry is long and diverse, but it is important to understand that these poems are usually seen in contrast with, or even opposition to, poetry in Japanese (*waka). Whereas some of waka's predominant features are its brevity and rather strict adherence to alternating units of five and seven syllables, its stress on ling. purity, and its inclination to limit itself to certain thematic sets (notably love and the nature imagery of the four seasons), Sino-Japanese poetry is free from most such restraints: it can be quite long (several hundreds of lines) and has total thematic freedom—a feature that most appealed to its practitioners. Grounded in a long and varied generic trad. in China, as well as Japan, Chinese poetry in Japan also knows a large variety of formats. Japanese literati of the cl. period already distinguished various literary genres: *bun* (Chinese *wen*, rhyming prose), *hitsu* (Chinese *bi*, rhymeless prose), *shi* (rhyming poem), *fu* (poetic exposition), *ku* (Chinese *ju*, couplet), etc. Rhyming or nonrhyming was perhaps an even more important distinction than poetry or prose.

Nevertheless, from the beginning, one particular form has been preferred by Japanese poets: the shi, usually of eight lines and always with equal lines of either five or seven graphs or characters. In fact, the *shi* in *kanshi* is both a generic term (a poem in Chinese, as opposed to one in Japanese) and a specific genre within the domain of Sino-Japanese poetry (i.e., rhyming poem). "Old style" shi poetry is relatively free of tonal patterns, unlike the "regulated poem" (Chinese *lüshi*, Japanese *risshi*) that became dominant in Tang period (618–907) China and later in Japan as well. Variant forms are the quatrain (Chinese *jueju*, Japanese *zekku*) and the "aligned regulated [poem]" (Chinese *pailü*, Japanese *hairitsu*; a shi of more than eight lines). The shi has a fairly standard structure in which a theme is elaborated and brought to conclusion. The shi also rhymes, which may not be as obvious as it sounds: the Sino-Japanese reading (*on*) of a graph does not lend itself easily to meaningful rhyme, and Japanese poets based their rhyme schemes on classic rhyme dictionaries. For centuries, the same held true for most poets in China.

Sino-Japanese poetry was meant to be read aloud. From at least the cl. period onward, reading, or even singing, was typically performed in *yomikudashi* (var. *kundoku*), a type of pronunciation in which clusters of words are pronounced by their *on* reading (the pronunciation that simulates to some extent Chinese pronunciation) but adjusted to Japanese grammar. This long-standing habit, which continues to this day, is one reason that some scholars feel that Sino-Japanese poetry functions as poetry in Japanese rather than in Chinese.

The composition of Sino-Japanese poetry was almost exclusively a male affair. The existence of a handful of female Sino-Japanese poets at the early cl. court or the uniquely talented Ema Saikō (1787–1861) and a few other contemp. women poets does not detract from the fact that, from the 10th c. on, women were not actively trained in writing Sino-Japanese nor encouraged to express themselves in that lang.

## II. History

A. *Ancient and Classical Periods (to 1185).* By the reign of the emperor (*tennō*) Tenji (r. 661–71), the composition of poetry in Chinese seems to have been a regular activity. Not much is extant from these earliest compositions. The earliest extant anthol. of Sino-Japanese poetry is *Kaifūsō* (Patterned Sea-Grasses of a Cherished Style, 751). *Man'yōshū* (Collection for Ten Thousand Generations, mid- to late 8th c.), Japan's oldest anthol. of waka, also contains several Sino-Japanese poems. Although these early court poems in Sino-Japanese were not much alluded to by later generations, the court continued to be the important locus for the composition of Sino-Japanese poems when the capital was moved from Heijō-kyō (Nara) to Heian-kyō (Kyoto), just as Six Dynasties' (316–589) poetry from China remained a notable touchstone. Many of the poems reflect this court setting, in which congratulatory and banquet poetry formed a central genre. Important are three royal kanshi anthols.: *Ryōunshū* (Cloud Topping Collection, 814), *Bunka shūreishū* (Collection of Beauties among the Literary Flowers, 818), and *Keikokushū* (Collection for Governing the State, 827), as well as the collected poetry of Sugawara no Michizane (845–903). This was also when the Japanese discovered the works of Bai Juyi (772–846), who would remain the best-regarded Chinese poet, and became more enamored of (esp. late) Tang (618–907) poetry. An early and influential text to couple Sino-Japanese couplets (*ku*) to waka is *Wakan rōeishū* (Chinese and Japanese Poems to Sing, early 11th c.), which coincides with the dominance of "verse-topic poetry" (*kudaishi*): poems that were composed to set topics consisting of a line of verse. Later court poets' preference for nature and temple-visiting poetry can be gleaned from *Honchō mudaishi* (Non-Verse Topic Poems from Our Court, 1162–64?).

**B. *Medieval Period (1185–1600).*** With the rise of Zen institutions in Kamakura and Kyoto supported by the new shogunate and collectively known as *gozan* (the five mountains—that is, monasteries), the center of Sino-Japanese composition had by the beginning of the 14th c. shifted to monastic communities. The monasteries were also actively engaged in the printing of Chinese texts and in Chinese scholarship in general, although court scholars continued to be active as well. Unlike court poets before them, several monks visited China. In keeping with the Zen (Chinese Chan) trads. from the mainland, fostered by Chinese priests who came to Japan, such as Yishan Yining (Japanese Issan Ichinei, 1247–1317), lit. and specifically poetry played a central role in the monks' lives. Traditionally, a distinction is made between the Zen Buddhist verse (*geju*) composed by gozan poets and their thematically much freer poetry in the shi format, which shows their readings from Song (960–1279) poets. While most well-known gozan poets such as Kokan Shiren (1278–1346), Sesson Yūbai (1290–1348), Gidō Shūshin (1325–88), or Zekkai Chūshin (1336–1405) emphatically worked within their monastic institutions, the Zen monk Ikkyū Sōjun (1394–1481) operated outside them. From the 15th c., the scholarly

trad. of the gozan monks gained in importance, and here the seeds were sown for the blossoming of neo-Confucian studies in early mod. Japan.

**C. *Early Modern Period (1600–1868).*** Although Sino-Japanese poets existed in the 17th c., notably the former warrior and recluse Ishikawa Jōzan (1583–1672) and the prolific scholar and thinker Hayashi Razan (1583–1657), not many were active. This changed dramatically after the first century of Tokugawa rule (1600–1868): during the early mod. period, Chinese studies became an integral part of literary studies in general, and poetry and prose were composed in numbers that were never equaled before or after. It was the golden age of Sino-Japanese lit. Chinese studies was a natural extension of Confucian studies and esp. the study of the thought of Zhu Xi (1130–1200). The neo-Confucian thinker Ogyū Sorai (1666–1728) and his followers, who emphasized the active composition of Sino-Japanese poetry and prose, played a pivotal role.

In 18th- and early 19th-c. Japan, the obvious centers for Sino-Japanese poets were no longer few in number. Academies (*juku*), both private and operated under the auspices of the lord (*daimyō*) of a domain (*han*), were practically everywhere, and thorough training in the classics could be had throughout the country. Scholars made a living teaching aspiring Sino-Japanese poets. Many Japanese, esp. well-educated city dwellers, both of samurai and merchant descent, were able to compose a Sino-Japanese poem, and many did. Attempts at listing major early mod. poets, therefore, fail by definition; but any list would contain Kan Chazan (1748–1827), the Zen monk Ryōkan (1758–1831), and Ema Saikō's mentor Rai San'yō (1780–1832).

**D. *Modern Period (after 1868).*** The dramatic political and social changes of the mid- through late 19th c. in Japan did nothing to stem the immense outpouring of emotions and ideas in the form of Sino-Japanese poetry. This phenomenon continued even after Japanese had established itself as the new "national language" (*kokugo*), ca. 1890. A symbol of how intertwined Sino-Japanese poetry became with the hist. of Japanese lit. as a whole, Natsume Sōseki (1867–1916), perhaps Japan's most revered novelist, composed a Sino-Japanese poem nearly every day toward the end of his life.

■ **Anthologies:** *Japanese Literature in Chinese*, trans. B. Watson (1975–76); *Poems of the Five Mountains*, trans. M. Ury (1977); *Zen Poems of the Five Mountains*, trans. D. Pollack (1985); *Kanshi: The Poetry of Ishikawa Jōzan and Other Edo-period Poets*, trans. B. Watson (1990); *Great Fool: Zen Master Ryōkan*, trans. R. Abé and P. Haskel (1996); *An Anthology of Kanshi (Chinese Verse) by Japanese Poets of the Edo Period*, trans. J. N. Rabinovitch and T. R. Bradstock (1997); *Breeze through Bamboo*, trans. H. Sato (1997); *Japanese and Chinese Poems to Sing*, trans. J. T. Rimer and J. Chaves (1997); *Early Modern Literature*, ed. H. Shirane (2002); *Dance of the Butterflies: Chinese Poetry from the Japanese Court Tradition*, trans. J. N. Rabinovitch and T. R. Bradstock (2005); *Tradiional Japanese Literature*, ed. H. Shirane (2006).

■ **Criticism:** D. Keene, *World within Walls* (1976);

J. Konishi, *A History of Japanese Literature,* trans. A. Catten and N. Teele (1984–91); H. C. McCullough, *Brocade by Night* (1985); R. Borgen, *Sugawara no Michizane and the Early Heian Court* (1986); D. Pollack, *The Fracture of Meaning* (1986); D. Keene, *Seeds in the Heart* (1993); I. Smits, *The Pursuit of Loneliness* (1995); A. Yiu, "In Quest of an Ending: An Examination of Sōseki's *Kanshi,*" *Studies in Modern Japanese Literature,* ed. D. Washburn and A. Tansman (1997); I. Smits, "Song as Cultural History," *Monumenta Nipponica* 55 (2000); W. Denecke, "Chinese Antiquity and Court Spectacle in Early *Kanshi,*" *Journal of Japanese Studies* (2004); P. Rouzer, "Early Buddhist *Kanshi,*" *Monumenta Nipponica* 59 (2004); W. Denecke, "'Topic Poetry Is All Ours,'" *HJAS* 67 (2007); M. Fraleigh, "Songs of the Righteous Spirit," *HJAS* 69 (2009).

I. Smits

**CHOLIAMBUS** or *scazon* (Gr. "lame iambic," "limping"). Hipponax of Ephesus (ca. 540 BCE) employed this meter for *invective. Its "limping" effect was suggested by the substitution of a long for a short in the penultimate position of the normal iambic trimeter, thus: ∪ – ∪ – | ∪ – ∪ – | ∪ – – x. When the first position in the third *metron was also long, the verse was called *ischiorrhogic* (with broken hips) and was ascribed to Ananius (also 6th c. BCE). The choliambus was used in the Alexandrian period by Herodas for his *mimiambi* and by Callimachus. In Lat. poetry, Catullus uses this meter for eight of his poems (8, 22, 31, 37, 39, 44, 59, 60), all but one of them invectives; the line has a hardened ending that suits a hardened tone. Catullus and his successors apparently imitated Callimachus in altering only the final two syllables. The form is clearly meant as mimetic, a deformed meter for the subject of depravity. Mod. imitations of limping iambics have mainly tried the analogous structure of reversing the fifth foot in the iambic pentameter from an iamb to a trochee: the effect is very distinctive, since the fifth foot is the most highly constrained (least variable) of all in this meter. Examples of choliambic lines or poems include Alfred, Lord Tennyson's "Lucretius" 186, Wallace Stevens's lines "Elations when the forest blooms; gusty / Emotions on wet roads on autumn nights" ("Sunday Morning"), W. H. Auden's "Down There" (in *About the House*), and John Frederick Nims's "Love Poem." W. C. Williams cites a discussion of the choliambus as a kind of epilogue to book 1 of *Paterson,* and, while he does not attempt to recreate the meter, the reference signals an affinity between the poetics of deformity in his own poem and those of the Gr. choliambic poets.

■ Koster; Halporn et al.; West; B. Acosta-Hughes, *Polyeideia: The "Iambi" of Callimachus and the Archaic Iambic Tradition* (2002); M. Payne, *The Animal Part: Human and Other Animals in the Poetic Imagination* (2010).

T.V.F. Brogan; R. J. Getty; M. Payne

**CHORIAMB** (Gr., "consisting of a choree [i.e., a trochee] and an iamb"). A *metron of the structure – ∪ ∪ –, frequently found in Gr. lyric verse—it is used often by Sappho and Alcaeus—and dramatic *choruses, and, in Lat. poetry, by Horace. It is very often found in combination with other cola, esp. *glyconics and *asclepiads (see AEOLIC) but sometimes purely, as in Sophocles, *Oedipus Tyrannus* 484.

*Choriambic dimeter* is a term coined by Wilamowitz to cover a variety of related seven- and eight-syllable cola ending in – ∪ ∪ – ; mod. usage generally restricts it to the *colon o o – x – ∪ ∪ – (where x represents anceps and oo the aeolic base: one of the two must be long). Maas, who treats it as an anaclastic glyconic, uses the honorific but awkward term *wilamowitzianus.* The term *choriambic dimeter* is doubly a misnomer, since the sequence is not a dimeter at all but a single indivisible sequence or colon or, at best, the sequence – x – ∪ ∪ – preceded by an aeolic base, and the sequence – ∪ ∪ – – ∪ ∪ – is actually quite distinct. Choriambic dimeters appear in the "eupolidean" meter of the *parabasis in Old Comedy, but they are most conspicuous in *tragedy. Sophocles uses them occasionally, but they are a favorite of Euripides, being varied more widely later in his career. They are closely related to—and presumably derived from—glyconics, with which they mix and respond.

Accentual imitations of the choriamb are very rare in the mod. vernaculars and usually appear in poems expressly meant as cl. imitations, as in F. G. Klopstock's "Siona," in J. W. Goethe's *Pandora* (choriambic dimeters), and in poems by August von Platen. In Eng., such usage as exists ranges from single lines such as Andrew Marvell's "Lilies without, roses within" ("The Nymph and Her Fawn") to A. C. Swinburne's more extended experiments in his "Choriambics" (*Poems and Ballads, Second Series,* 1878). A few mod. metrists have interpreted the sequence / xx / in the first four syllables of the iambic pentameter, as in lines beginning "Roses have thorns" or "Look in thy Glass," not as an "initial trochaic substitution" but as a choriamb, but this misunderstands both the nature of cl. prosody and the relation of that to the mod. system.

■ Wilamowitz, pt. 2, chs. 3, 7; E. W. Scripture, "The Choriambus in English Verse," *PMLA* 43 (1928)— unsound; Maas; Koster, ch. 10; Dale; K. Itsumi, "The Choriambic Dimeter of Euripides," *CQ* 32 (1982); West.

D. S. Parker; T.V.F. Brogan

**CHORUS** (Gr. *choreuein,* "to dance"). In ancient Greece, a song-and-dance ensemble of performers led by a chorus leader (*choregos*). Choruses played a fundamental role in Gr. life and culture. Participation in choruses contributed to the education and socialization of youths (Plato, *Laws* 653c–55b, 672e–73d) and provided a means of sharing and coming to terms with the joyful and sorrowful highlights of human life. Choruses performed at civic and pan-Hellenic festivals celebrating gods and heroes (Herodotus 5.67), initiatory rituals, funerals, or celebrations of victorious athletes. Specialized genres of choral songs include hymns to the gods Apollo (*paeans) and Dionysus (*dithyrambs), maiden choruses (*partheneia*), *dirges (*threnoi*), and victory odes (*epinikia*). Few precious bits of that intense choral activity have been preserved, incl. maiden songs by Alcman and Sappho (7th c. BCE) and victory *odes by Pindar, Simonides, and Bacchylides (5th c. BCE). Songs initially performed by a solo singer could be reperformed by a chorus in another context, and vice versa.

In Athens, choruses played an important role at the festivals for the wine god Dionysus that provided the context for the devel. of drama, the Dionysia and the Lenaia. According to Aristotle, *tragedy originated from the leaders of the dithyramb and *comedy from the leaders of phallic songs (*Poetics* 4). At the peak of their devel., the Great Dionysia required three choruses of 12 or 15 performers for the tragic contests, five choruses of 24 performers for the comic contests, and 20 choruses of 50 performers for the men's and boys' dithyrambs. Dramatic poets who wished to compete "asked for a chorus" from the magistrate in charge; the expense of dressing and training choruses was assigned by the state to a wealthy citizen (*choregos*). Many surviving tragedies and comedies are named after their chorus (Aeschylus's *Suppliants, Libation Bearers, Eumenides*; Sophocles' *Trachinian Women*; Euripides' *Children of Heracles, Suppliants, Trojan Women, Phoenician Women, Bacchae*; Aristophanes' *Acharnians, Knights, Clouds, Wasps, Birds, Women at the Thesmophoria, Frogs, Assemblywomen*). The competition was as much between rival *choregoi* and their choruses as between poets (Demosthenes, *Against Meidias* 66, [Andocides] 4.21).

Structurally, Athenian drama can be defined as the interplay between actor speech and choral songs, although crossover does occur. In Aristotle's outline, the parts of tragedy include a prologue (the portion preceding the choral entry), episodes (portions between the odes), *exodos* (the part following the last ode), and choral odes, themselves divided in *parodos* (entrance song) and several *stasima* (Aristotle, *Poetics* 12). While actors generally spoke in iambic *trimeters, a meter close to everyday speech, the choral odes were sung in non-Attic dialect and characterized by complex meter, poetic syntax, and rich *imagery. The songs are made of several pairs of metrically identical *strophes and *antistrophes, often followed by an *epode. It is unclear how the dance movements accompanying each strophe and antistrophe corresponded or contrasted with each other.

Chorus members performed in mask and costume and were led by a *coryphaios*. They entered the dramatic space from the side entrances (*parodoi*), took their position in the dancing floor (*orchestra*), and with a few exceptions stayed on stage throughout the drama. Little is known of the movements of choral dancing. It is even unclear whether dramatic choruses performed primarily in rectangular or circular formation. In line with their ritual function elsewhere in Gr. life, choruses often performed rituals integrated in the fiction, incl. libations, hero cult, dancing, wreathing, and curses. Since the plays were performed in the ritual context of the festivals for Dionysus, the interplay between the intra- and extradramatic relevance of ritual utterances could generate powerful effects.

Within the dramatic fiction, choruses often impersonate socially marginal figures such as women, old men, or slaves. Their place in the plot varies over time and from one poet to another. The chorus is central to the plot of Aeschylus's earlier plays (*Persians* and *Suppliants*) but more marginal to the action of Sophoclean drama. In contrast to the individual emotions and heroic isolation of the protagonists, choruses bring in a collective experience drawing on traditional wisdom, collective memory, and inherited stories.

Polyphonic by definition, dramatic choruses could, in turn, take the voice of the poet, the audience, or their own fictional character. The special connection between chorus and audience is esp. clear in the *parabasis of Aristophanic comedy, when the chorus addresses the audience directly and partially or completely abandons its dramatic identity. In tragedy, the chorus's use of traditional lang. and its survivor position at the end of the play facilitated audience identification; by contrast, its marginal identity, withdrawal from the action, and frequent misinterpretations of the action distanced it from the spectators.

After its heyday in the democratic Athens of the 5th c. BCE, the chorus gradually disappears from the stage, a disappearance coinciding with the increasingly private rather than public subject matter of the plays. Choral songs separate acts but are not integral to the action in the late comedies of Aristophanes and Menander (4th c. BCE) and the Roman tragedies of Seneca (1st c. CE). In mod. theater, the use of the chorus was a hotly debated topic that verged on the broader issues of *classicism and the social function of theater. To the skepticism of the Abbé d'Aubignac (*La Pratique du Théâtre*, 1657) and John Dryden (*Essay of Dramatic Poesy*, 1668) contrasted the enthusiasm of André Dacier (*Poétique d'Aristote*, 1692) and later Friedrich Schiller (prologue to *Die Braut von Messina*, 1803), who highlighted the usefulness of the chorus as a means to give coherence to the action and heighten its moral and ethic significance. Notable experiments with the chorus include John Milton's *Samson Agonistes* (1671), Jean Racine's *Esther* (1689) and *Athalie* (1691), P. B. Shelley's *Hellas* (1822), J. W. Goethe's *Faust II* (1832), and T. S. Eliot's *Murder in the Cathedral* (1935).

See CLASSICAL POETICS, DRAMATIC POETRY.

■ C. Calame, *Les choeurs de jeunes filles en Grèce archaïque* (1977); H. Bacon, "The Chorus in Greek Life and Drama," A. Henrichs, "'Why Should I Dance?' Choral Self-Referentiality in Greek Tragedy," and G. Nagy, "Transformations of Choral Lyric Traditions in the Context of Athenian State Theater," all *Arion* 3.1 (1995); J. Gould, "Tragedy and Collective Experience," and S. Goldhill, "Collectivity and Otherness—The Authority of the Tragic Chorus: Response to Gould," *Tragedy and the Tragic*, ed. M. S. Silk (1996); *Der Chor im antiken und modernen Drama*, ed. P. Riemer and B. Zimmermann (1998); D. Mastronarde, "Knowledge and Authority in the Choral Voice of Euripidean Tragedy," *Syllecta Classica* 10 (1999); P. Wilson, *The Athenian Institution of the Khoregia* (2000); H. Foley, "Choral Identity in Greek Tragedy," *CP* 98 (2003); S.

Murnaghan, "Women in Groups: Aeschylus' *Suppliants* and the Female Choruses of Greek Tragedy," *The Soul of Tragedy,* ed. V. Pedrick and S. M. Oberhelman (2005); G. Ley, *The Theatricality of Greek Tragedy* (2007); M. A. Gruber, *Der Chor in den Tragödien des Aischylos* (2008).

M. HOPMAN

**CHRISTABEL METER.** Term for the verse form of S. T. Coleridge's "Christabel" (1797–1800, pub. 1816), believed by Coleridge to be a species of *accentual verse. In the preface to the poem, he writes that "the meter of *Christabel* is not, properly speaking, irregular, though it may seem so from its being founded on . . . counting in each line the accents, not the syllables." The number of syllables in the poem "may vary from seven to twelve," but "in each line the accents will be found to be only four." He calls this a "new principle" in Eng. poetry and claims that variations in syllable count are made intentionally: "occasional variation in number of syllables is not introduced wantonly . . . but in correspondence with some transition in the nature of the imagery or passion." Up to the turn of the 20th c., Coleridge was generally believed in his assertions, and "Christabel" was considered an important example of accentual verse in Eng.

Upon closer inspection, however, numerous scholars have found Coleridge's claims to be false. Robert Bridges showed in 1901 (rev. ed. 1921) that Coleridge is actually writing *accentual-syllabic verse. And Snell showed in 1929 that "four-fifths of the lines of *Christabel* are perfectly regular; that is, they are the conventional four-stress iambic verse usually in couplet form, with only such variations in general as are found in this sort of meter. If [the remaining one-fifth of the poem's lines] is scanned according to the principle that 'light syllables may occasionally be added or subtracted without altering the normal verse meter' . . . the entire poem is iambic with monosyllabic and anapestic substitutions." In short, the poem is heavily iambic and effectively octosyllabic: of the 655 lines of the poem, 523 (80%) are perfectly regular octosyllables, and 92% vary by only one syllable one way or the other. And Coleridge's implication, in the preface, that he is the first to use syllabic *variation for purposes of metrical expressiveness seems an unreasonable slight to earlier poets, such as Shakespeare, John Donne, and John Milton.

■ Bridges; A.L.F. Snell, "The Meter of 'Christabel,'" *Fred Newton Scott Anniversary Papers* (1929); Brogan; B. O'Driscoll, "The 'Invention' of a Meter: 'Christabel' Meter as Fact and Fiction," *JEGP* 100.4 (2001); M. Russett, "Meter, Identity, Voice: Untranslating 'Christabel,'" *SEL* 43.4 (2003).

T.V.F. BROGAN; M. WEINSTEIN

**CHUCI.** Following the earlier *Classic of Poetry* (see SHIJING), the *Lyrics of Chu* (*Chuci*), comprising poetry from the 3d c. BCE through the 2d c. CE, is the second principal source of ancient Chinese poetry. It reflects the distinct literary aesthetics of the southern region of Chu along the mid- and lower Yangzi River. While the songs include words of Chu dialect, their lang. belongs to the literary koiné of ancient China. The anthol. emerged in the 2d c. BCE, was completed in the 2d c. CE, and received its final arrangement in the 12th c. Its principal early commentator Wang Yi (d. 158) attributes more than half of the songs to Qu Yuan (ca. 340–278 BCE) and his shadowy "successors" Song Yu and Jing Cuo; however, many pieces attributed to Qu Yuan are evidently Han dynasty (206 BCE–220 CE) imitations. Wang's readings of the songs as expressions of political frustration, in line with Han interpretations of the *Classic of Poetry*, were challenged only in later imperial times, most prominently by Zhu Xi (1130–1200).

In their mythological imagination, the early parts of the anthol. seem connected to the contemporaneous aristocratic culture of the south such as seen in the funerary banners from the 2d c. BCE burials at Mawangdui (Hunan). Likewise, the songs' lively meter and rhythm must reflect a (lost) southern musical style performed with string and wind instruments. The typical couplet of the "Nine Songs" (*Jiu ge*)—perhaps the earliest section of the anthol.—has two equal lines of four, five, or six syllables, with an additional rhythmic particle *xi* in the middle. "Encountering Sorrow" (*Li sao*), Qu Yuan's lament in 187 couplets and the most celebrated poem of the anthol., further develops the pattern into a more complex meter capable of a narrative style: dum dum-dum *particle* dum-dum *xi* / dum dum-dum *particle* dum-dum. Since Han times, this meter was popular in elegies describing personal misfortune.

Developed as a celestial journey, "Encountering Sorrow" stages an autobiographic narrative of political ambition and frustration; since its earliest reception in Jia Yi's (200–168 BCE) "Lament for Qu Yuan" (*Diao Qu Yuan*), it has been interpreted through the tragic story of its purported author and protagonist, an upright minister at the Chu royal court who was slandered and banished further south where he finally drowned himself. While unknown from any preimperial text, this story existed in several sources, some of which are patched together in Qu Yuan's only surviving biography in Sima Qian's (ca. 145–86 BCE) *Records of the Historian* (*Shiji*). According to trad., "Encountering Sorrow" is the first autobiographic poem in China, and Qu Yuan the first Chinese poet known by name. In reality, he may be the subject but not the author of the texts attributed to him.

The poetic diction of "Encountering Sorrow"—hyperbolic catalogs of natural phenomena in a southern geography, both real and imagined; a large repertoire of rhyming and alliterative binomes; a rapid metric pace—is unlike anything in the *Classic of Poetry*. So are the themes of mystic flight and erotic desire, as well as the fantasies of immortality and command over the cosmic spirits that alternate with complaints about a morally corrupt world. The same rich lang. and melancholic tone also characterizes the "Nine Songs," a set of 11 pieces that Qu Yuan, in Wang Yi's interpretation, developed out of southern religious chants to express his political frustration. Mod. scholars, however, have found in some of the songs—e.g., the delirious fantasies depicting the vain pursuit of alluring water goddesses—the traces of ancient shamanism.

The lang. and themes of "Encountering Sorrow" and the "Nine Songs" reverberate through the remaining parts of the anthol. that include Qu Yuan's despairing lament "Embracing Sand" (*Huai sha*), purportedly composed immediately before his suicide; the incantations "Summoning the Soul" (*Zhao hun*) and "Great Summons" (*Da zhao*) that recall the souls of the dead; "Summoning the Recluse" (*Zhao yin-shi*) where the same theme is transposed to a prince who has fled into the hostile mountains; "Roaming Afar" (*Yuan you*) that turns the celestial journey into an ecstatic experience of magical transcendence; and several cycles of songs, most likely of Han date, that imitate the expression of desolation in "Encountering Sorrow," but in far more constrained terms. While the earliest layers of the *Lyrics of Chu* oscillate between political ambition, extravagant imagination, and sensual desire, the parts by later epigones, up to Wang Yi's own "Nine Yearnings" (*Jiu si*), are tamed by Han Confucian moral thought. Beyond the anthol. proper, however, the quest for the goddess inspired numerous later Chinese poems of love and desire.

Finally, the *Lyrics of Chu* includes "Heavenly Questions" (*Tian wen*), a unique catalog of questions—possibly riddles—that, in 172 tetrasyllabic verses, moves from the origin of the universe to the mythical and historical world of ancient Chu. As much of the underlying mythology is lost, parts of the poem are now cryptic; but even so, "Heavenly Questions" reminds us of the expansive imagination and exuberant cultural vitality of the south at the dawn of the Chinese empire.

■ A. Waley, *The Temple and Other Poems* (1923); J. R. Hightower, "Ch'ü Yüan Studies," *Silver Jubilee Volume of the Zinbun-Kagaku-Kenkyusyo* (1954); A. Waley, *The Nine Songs* (1955); A. C. Graham, "The Prosody of the Sao Poems in the Ch'u Tz'u," *Asia Major* n.s. 10 (1963); D. Hawkes, "The Quest of the Goddess," *Asia Major* n.s. 13 (1967); S.-H. Chen, "On Structural Analysis of the Ch'u Tz'u Nine Songs," *Tamkang Review* 2 (1971), and "The Genesis of Poetic Time," *Tsing Hua Journal of Chinese Studies* n.s. 10 (1973); D. Hawkes, *The Songs of the South* (1985); G. R. Waters, *Three Elegies of Ch'u* (1985); S. Field, *A Chinese Book of Origins* (1986); P. Yu, *The Reading of Imagery in the Chinese Poetic Tradition* (1987); C. H. Wang, *From Ritual to Allegory* (1988); P. W. Kroll, "On 'Far Roaming,'" *Journal of the American Oriental Society* 116 (1996); T. W-K. Chan, "The jing/zhuan Structure of the *Chuci* Anthology," *T'oung Pao* 84 (1998); G. Sukhu, "Monkeys, Shamans, Emperors, and Poets," in *Defining Chu*, ed. C. A. Cook and J. S. Major (1999).

M. KERN

**CI** ("song lyric"). After *\*shi* poetry, the second best-known genre of Chinese poetry was the *ci*, "song lyric," form, which grew out of the popular music of the Tang dynasty (618–907). Song lyrics were composed to set tune patterns (*ci pai*) with fixed metrical structures, rhyme patterns, and tonal euphony. Although the height of the genre is often considered to have occurred in the Song dynasty (960–1279), ci have been composed by elite poets since the Tang, enjoyed an important revival in the hands of many poets in the late Ming (1368–1644) and Qing (1644–1911) dynasties, and are composed even today. The origins of ci in the 9th and 10th cs. are understood only in outline: new music and musical instruments from central Asia, imported along the Silk Road during the med. period, strongly influenced musical composition at both the popular and elite levels of Tang society. In the entertainment quarters of the major Tang cities, musicians and singers composed or adapted new tunes and wrote lyrics to new songs, and these spread to other areas of the empire, to musical composition at the imperial court, and to the musical troupes of Tang officials. In the late 8th and early 9th cs., elite poets became interested in composing lyrics to these new tunes, though relatively few lyrics composed by Tang literati have been preserved. The body of ci discovered in the early 20th c. at Dunhuang, most of which date to the 9th and 10th cs., give us strong evidence of song lyric composition at the popular level.

The birth of ci in the realm of popular music, along with the lyrics' early performance by female entertainers, profoundly shaped the evolution of the genre in the late 9th and early 10th cs., when romantic love was the most common topic and the subjects of the lyrics were predominantly women who were either speaking or were described as objects of a male viewer's gaze. Although elite poets in the late 10th and 11th cs. used ci as a vehicle for masculine voices speaking of romantic love or loss and later Song poets extended the genre into topics once reserved for shi poetry, the genre came to be regarded as the most appropriate form in which to express certain kinds of *qing*, "feeling," in particular, sorrow, longing, and regret. Over the course of the genre's hist., poets who wrote ci frequently experimented with creative tensions that grew out of these early directions. Some examples of these tensions include that between an "elevated" (*ya*) style and a more "vulgar" (*su*) style, indicated by the use of formal lang. punctuated with colloquial phrases, the use of shifting male and female voices in lyrics, the presence or absence of erotic detail, the interplay of memory and the present moment; and the opposition of a highly masculine, hearty style and a suppressed, emotionally suggestive style. Another fundamental feature of ci poetics that emerged from early song lyrics was the intense relationship of the internal emotional world of the speaking subject and the depiction of the external scene. Poets explored this relationship in many ways: the scene could mirror or extend the speaker's feelings or could serve as stark contrast. The stanzaic structure of ci also allowed poets abruptly to juxtapose elements of scene and feeling, implying connections for the reader to complete.

As the genre matured, writers of both shi and ci sought to differentiate the boundaries between the two poetic genres as part of a broader interest in defining the limits of socially acceptable elite composition. However, ci as a genre was always secondary to shi, because of its relative youth, its association with popular entertainment and romantic culture, and its failure to deepen its connections to the elite cl. curriculum. In the eyes of Song and later poets, ci was defined as "not-shi," both topically and formally. The formal features of ci, as defined by individual tune patterns, stabilized over the course of the Song dynasty, when new tune patterns continued to be written and sung. Most but not all tune patterns contained two stanzas of roughly equal length. In some patterns, the stanzas were brief (three or four lines), a form known as "short songs" (*xiaoling*); other patterns contained stanzas of more than a dozen lines each, known as "long" (*man*) lyrics. Two formal features of ci that distinguished it sharply from shi poetry were the use of lines of different length and the unique rhyme and tonal schemes found in individual tune patterns. These features made composing ci technically challenging; they also encouraged poets to experiment with syntax, line length, and line breaks in ways not allowed in shi poetry. Although some poets composed new music for older ci patterns, the general trend of ci from the early Song onward was toward becoming a poetic form that existed independent of music. Anthols. of ci began to be published in the Song dynasty, which gave the genre more prominence in elite culture, even if that prominence remained somewhat suspect.

After the fall of the Tang, the practice of composing ci seems to have become more widespread among the literati of the courts of the 10th-c. Five Dynasties and southern kingdoms. An anthol. from this period, the *Huajian ji* (*Collection from among the Flowers*) was the first extant collection of ci written by elite poets. Its lyrics focus on beautiful women and romantic, mildly erotic scenarios, and it served as a stylistic model for early northern Song writers. Another influential model from the 10th c. was that of the ruler of the southern Tang, Li Yu (937–978), who composed lyrics in a male voice; his works have commonly been read biographically, as expressions of his own despair at the Song conquest.

The growing urban environments of the northern Song and their entertainment quarters increased interaction between literati and female performers and surely inspired more lyrics on that subject. But the social stigma of writing about that world remained powerful in elite society. The poet Liu Yong (987–1053) wrote hundreds of lyrics in a more colloquial style, many of them in the long form, depicting the romantic travails of singing women and literati playboys. Many important Song poets composed both shi and ci, though some, such as the prominent literatus Ouyang Xiu (1007–72), sought to distinguish the two kinds of poetry very clearly, reserving romantic content or melancholy emotional expression for ci. The introduction of cl. literary content into ci by Su Shi (1037–1101), including material such as historical events, reflections on the past, and depictions of the natural world that were

neither romantic nor sentimental, not only broadened the range of ci for later writers but "masculinized" the genre for those uninterested in the excessively feminine style of romantic lyrics. However, he was later criticized for having altered ci in this way. The late northern Song woman poet Li Qingzhao (1084–ca. 1151) was one of the first people to theorize about ci poetics as well as to compose ci herself. Her lyrics stand as an influential early example of a woman writer using a literary form for which there were already "feminine" voices. Her critical assertion that ci, as a genre, had a fundamental nature distinct from shi also gave the form greater legitimacy.

By the southern Song dynasty, writers had a wider range of stylistic models for ci, but these could be roughly divided between a "bold and carefree" (*haofang*) masculine style that avoided romance as a topic and a "delicate and lovely" (*wanyue*) feminine style used more often for expressions of sorrow and longing. Xin Qiji (1140–1207) is best known for his patriotic, energetic version of the masculine style; his best-known lyrics express his distress at the conquest of the northern Song by non-Chinese invaders. Lu You (1125–1210), one of the most important poets of the southern Song, followed in the path laid by Su Shi and incorporated many concerns of shi into his ci. The poet Wu Wenying (ca. 1200–1260) is perhaps the best example of the refined, delicate style that combined elegant craft with romantic subject matter. Notably, few prominent southern Song men were known for their ci composition, an indication of the genre's still dubious reputation.

During the Yuan and Ming dynasties, literati lost interest in ci; with respect to song forms, some writers explored the *qu* or *sanqu* (literally, "detached aria") of the increasingly popular *Chinese poetic drama, which included arias along with spoken text. But the late Ming and early Qing dynasties saw an unexpected revival of ci from two different quarters: from women writers, both courtesans and well-educated elite women, and from Qing scholars who sought to rehabilitate the form. The rising number of women who composed, circulated, and even pub. poetry (in both shi and ci forms) challenged the gender roles of trad. Chinese poetry. Ming and Qing elite women, however, refashioned the genre to downplay its erotic or romantic elements and articulate their experiences in a manner in keeping with their roles as virtuous Confucian daughters, wives, and mothers. Male poets such as Zhu Yizun (1629–1709) also tended to avoid eroticism, and they downplayed colloquial lang., putting a greater emphasis on cl. lang. and allusion. The efforts of both groups helped to revitalize the form, ensuring its continuing popularity into the mod. era.

See CHINA, POETRY OF; CHINA, POPULAR POETRY OF.

■ J.J.Y. Liu, *Major Lyricists of the Northern Sung* (1974); S. Lin, *The Transformation of the Chinese Lyrical Tradition* (1978); K. Chang, *The Evolution of Chinese Tz'u Poetry* (1980); *Lyric Poets of the Southern T'ang*, ed. and trans. D. Bryant (1982); G. Fong, *Wu*

*Wenying and the Art of Southern Song Ci Poetry* (1987); D. McCraw, *Chinese Lyricists of the Seventeenth Century* (1990); P. Rouzer, *Writing One Another's Dream* (1993); *Voices of the Song Lyric in China*, ed. P. Yu (1994); S. Sargent, "Tz'u," *Columbia History of Chinese Literature*, ed. V. H. Mair (2001); S. M. Bell, *Gendered Persona and Poetic Voice* (2004); A. Shields, *Crafting a Collection* (2006).

A. SHIELDS

**CICERONIANISM.** The emulation of Cicero's lang. and application of his rhetorical theory that gained particular currency in 16th-c. Europe. In circulation in the Middle Ages were only Cicero's youthful *De inventione* and his *Topica*; his legacy was already part of the cultural matrix but was limited to narrow stylistic prescription. An emergent rhetorical Ciceronianism, intertwined with the hist. of humanism, can be traced to Petrarch's rediscovery in 1345 of Cicero's letters to Atticus and Gerardo Landriani's unearthing in 1421 of his major works *De oratore*, *Orator*, and *Brutus*. Instrumental to the diffusion of Ciceronianism was the Venetian humanist Pietro Bembo, who established Ciceronian Lat. as the official code of the Roman church in the mid-16th c. The underlying premise for early Ren. emulators was that Cicero's lang. embodied an ideal purity—a paragon of Lat. at its height, still free of the ruggedness of the Silver Age and of med. "barbarisms."

From the start, Ciceronianism was surrounded by contention over the implications of singling out one cl. author for imitation above the rest. Tensions played out repeatedly and across national boundaries between the doctrinaire Ciceronians (e.g., Paolo Cortesi, Bembo, Marco Girolamo Vida, Christophe de Longueil, Sebastian Fox Morcillo) who argued that Cicero should be the exclusive model for rhetoricians and those (e.g., Angelo Poliziano, Giovanni Pico de la Mirandola, Erasmus, Juan Luis Vives, Francisco Sánchez de las Brozas, Philip Sidney, Francis Bacon) who viewed a productive appropriation of antiquity as necessarily drawing from multiple models and adapting to contemp. cultural realities. Among the advocates of the latter position, some denounced Ciceronianism as slavish aping. Exemplary in this respect was Erasmus's *Ciceronianus* (1528), which was at the origin of a robust anti-Ciceronian trad. But beyond the precise divergences among purported friends and enemies of Ciceronianism, its effects on the trajectory of Ren. humanism were wide-ranging. One must be wary of some scholars' view that the Ciceronian model was relevant only to prose composition (i.e., the direct mimicking of sentence structure and vocabulary). Far from being a static mold, as the anti-Ciceronians contended, Ciceronianism evolved along with the complex relationship between Lat. and vernacular letters, generating ideas central to the devel. of poetry in several national trads.

How specifically Ciceronianism permeated the poetic sphere has to do with the encompassing neoclassical agendas of the 16th c. In this context, stylistic guidelines were conceived in tandem with the requirements of a collective *vivere civile*, a vision already embedded in Petrarch's seminal conversation with Cicero. Seduced by the orator's lang. because of its formal beauty and cadence, Petrarch established a personalized rapport with his precursor through letters that he addressed to Cicero (*Epistolae familiares*), setting a tone that would become characteristic of humanism, one distinguishing feature of which was the privileging of individual voice as locus of organic cultural exchange. In contrast with dogmatic manifestations of institutional Ciceronian Lat., Petrarch's dialogic appropriation incorporated Cicero's lang. and teaching to his own milieu as a way of life fostering refined civism, a standard that later informed Baldassare Castiglione's courtly ethos and definition of *sprezzatura*, or naturalized artifice. An important channel of Ciceronian influence, the ideals of courtly self-expression articulated in Castiglione's *Libro del cortegiano* (*Book of the Courtier*, 1528) were pervasive in poetry, as was the related motif of the universally educated poet, well-versed in the liberal arts and social sciences, a notion deriving from Cicero's celebrated wise orator. Cicero's early mod. descendants were, thus, true to his belief that verbal excellence was grounded in intellectual competence. In continuity with these ideals, Bembo's *Prose della volgar lingua* (Writing in the Vernacular, 1525) was another key work in the genealogy of Ciceronianism, providing a lasting paradigm for combining stylistic prescription and social fashioning. Fusing the teachings of *De oratore* with those of Horace's *Ars poetica*, the treatise outlines an aesthetic program for vernacular letters that advanced the public role of poetry by situating it in the framework of oratorical art. Throughout the Ren., the two spheres converged until poetry was largely defined in terms of rhetorical categories: *inventio*, the determination of topic (see INVENTION); *elocutio*, the way in which speech was delivered; and *dispositio*, the organization of matter. The status of poetry as a medium of both beauty and persuasion is reflected in Bembo's lessons on prosody which, proposing Petrarchan lyric as the model for contemp. verse, formulate the mellifluous combination of consonants and vowels as a means of eliciting the requisite emotional register in the listener (see PETRARCHISM). Thus, making use of the civic sensibilities and accompanying formal parameters of Ciceronian rhet.—the careful balance between elocutio and inventio, between gravity and artifice—in the establishment of a Tuscan literary preeminence, Bembo created a blueprint for the construction of a standardized cultural authority that would become pivotal in the consolidation of other literary trads. This process was furthered by theorists and poets such as Bernardino Daniello, Donato Tomitano, Girolamo Muzio, Antonio Minturno, J. C. Scaliger, Étienne Dolet, Joachim du Bellay, and Fernando de Herrera. Through their work, Ciceronianism continued to mix with other antique influences—notably Aristotelian theories of *deco-rum and Quintilianic conceptions of ideal oratory as a measure of moral good—in the devel. of vernacular appropriations of *classicism. The degree to which the Ciceronian mark informed this fluid enterprise is evident in Herrera's commentary on Garcilaso de la Vega's oeuvre (1580). Noting the key role played by Cicero's "divine eloquence" in Lat.'s attainment of "fertility" and "abundance," Herrera upholds these as attributes essential to the cultural legitimacy of Sp. poetry.

The decline of Ciceronianism in the 17th c. can be linked to the crisis of eloquence. In a mounting tide of political skepticism occasioned by protracted territorial and religious wars, humanist belief in consensus was compromised, as was faith in the social powers of the word. The influence of Peter Ramus and his followers brought about a curricular reshuffling, resulting in the separation of rhet. from logic and philosophy, with rhet. relegated to the formal mechanics of style. Another factor contributing to this phenomenon was the increasingly empirical conception of knowledge, manifest in the scientific revolution as well as in the burgeoning notion of politics as a practical science. In relation to these devels., Senecan brevity, with its imperious hyperlucidity, became the preferred standard for communication. If Ciceronianism sought a conciliation between pleasure and usefulness, the *dolce* and the *utile*, laconism stressed mental agility at the expense of formal harmony. Identifiable with this shift is the 17th-c. rise of the poetic *conceit, its exhibition of conceptual prowess often transgressing the principles of decorum (see BAROQUE, CONCEPTISMO). Cicero continued to be hailed, however, among those wishing to rescue aesthetics from excessive formal idiosyncrasy. In this spirit, the orator is celebrated in Baltasar Gracián's formulation (1642) of the conceit as guarantor of civilized subtlety.

*See* RHETORIC AND POETRY.

■ M. W. Croll, *Style, Rhetoric, and Rhythm*, ed. J. M. Patrick et al. (1966)—classic essays on the Ciceronian and anti-Ciceronian trads.; A. Lumsden Kouvel, "La huella ciceroniana en el siglo XVI," *Actas. Asociación Internacional de Hispanistas* 4 (1971); M. Garci-Gómez, "Paráfrasis de Cicerón en la definición de poesía de Santillana," *Hispania* 56 (1973); *The Rhetoric of Renaissance Poetry: From Wyatt to Milton*, ed. T. O. Sloan and R. B. Waddington (1974); T. M. Greene, *The Light in Troy: Imitation and Discovery in Renaissance Poetry* (1982); J. P. Houston, *The Rhetoric of Poetry in the Renaissance and Seventeenth Century* (1983); J. J. Murphy, *Renaissance Eloquence* (1983); K. Meerhoff, *Rhétorique et poétique au XVIe siècle en France* (1986); N. González and J. María, *El ciceronianismo en España* (1993); M. Mora, "El *De oratore* de Cicerón como fuente del *De poeta* de Minturno," *Humanismo y pervivencia del mundo clásico*, ed. J. M. Maestre Maestre, J. Pascual Barea, and L. Charlo Brea (1997); I. Navarrete, *Orphans of Petrarch: Poetry and Theory in the Spanish Renaissance* (1994); R. G. Witt, *In the Footsteps of the Ancients* (2000); J. Dellaneva, *Ciceronian Controversies* (2007).

A. GARCÍA-BRYCE

# CLASSICAL METERS IN MODERN LANGUAGES

I. Introduction
II. Quantitative Imitations
III. Accentual Imitations

**I. Introduction.** Throughout the hist. of Eur. poetry since the Ren., there have been attempts to introduce into the versification of the vernacular languages the metrical principles, the specific meters, and the stanza forms of cl. Gr. and Lat. verse. The most obvious motivation for this endeavor has been the continuing high status of the cl. langs. and esp. of cl. poetry, which for many has represented the epitome of Western literary achievement. In addition, many writers in the mod. Eur. langs., even when not seeking to emulate the achievement of cl. verse, have drawn upon cl. examples to extend the variety of metrical forms in their own literary trads.

These attempts were most frequent in the Ren., esp. in the 15th and 16th cs. Humanism placed a high valuation on cl. lit. at a time when the mod. Eur. langs. were for the most part without a literary trad. of equal stature. The practice of *imitation had long been fundamental to literary art, and the project of enriching the vernacular was encouraged by the growing cultural nationalism of the period. The highly organized nature of *classical prosody also appealed to the Ren. aesthetic sense, which favored the artificial and the complex. By the 17th c., the native verse trads. had established themselves more securely, and there was less incentive to look to ancient Greece and Rome for models. The romantic desire to challenge established verse forms produced a resurgence of interest in cl. meters, esp. in Germany (F. G. Klopstock) and England (S. T. Coleridge, Robert Southey), and the rise of a more historically informed classicism in the late 19th and early 20th cs. resulted in attempts to devise more exact vernacular equivalents to Gr. and Lat. meters (e.g., by Robert Bridges). The experiments of modernism led once more to a free use of cl. verse forms as a quarry for new poetic directions.

Imitations of cl. meters can be broadly divided into two types: those that seek to establish a principle of quantity in the vernacular on which to base *scansion and those that retain the indigenous phonological prominence of the lang. in question (usually stress) as the *marker* of the meter but seek to imitate or reproduce the metrical *patterns* of cl. verse.

**II. Quantitative Imitations,** or "quantitative verse." To appreciate the attempts to write cl. verse in the vernacular langs. based upon a principle of quantity, it is less important to understand what *quantity was in the spoken langs. of ancient Greece and Rome than to understand what the poets of the Ren. and after *believed* it to have been. The terms traditionally used to describe the two types of syllables in quantitative poetry are "long" and "short," and there is a very old claim, inherited from the Gr. *rhythmici*, that long syllables take twice the time of short ones in pronunciation. Regardless of whether this claim accurately described linguistic reality in antiquity (the evidence suggests that quantity was more a structural difference than a temporal one), it bore little relation to the phonetic facts of Lat. as pronounced during the Ren.; in any event, the claim had long since become a convention, accepted without inquiry. This meant that the metrical schemes of Lat. verse were realized only very fitfully in actual reading: the conception of meter that arose was a largely abstract and visual one based on an intellectual classification of syllables according to learned rules.

This accounts for the initially puzzling fact that Ren. cl. imitations frequently have no perceptible rhythmic patterning—or if they do, it is a pattern of accents that cuts across the quantitative scheme. The scheme is there, however, deducible by the rules of cl. prosody, and a Ren. reader trained in Lat. prosody as part of the regular grammar-school education could perceive and enjoy it. Strictly speaking, this verse should be called "pseudoquantitative," since to follow the rules of Lat. quantity in a lang. with a different phonological structure does not produce the same syllabic organization.

The earliest quantitative verse in a mod. vernacular appears to have been written in It. by Leon Battista Alberti and Leonardo Dati in 1441. The extent of the It. quantitative movement can be gauged from the *Versi, et regole de la nuova poesia toscana* of 1539, collected by Claudio Tolomei, which contained verse written on quantitative principles by 24 named poets and several anonymous contributors. Numerous other It. poets attempted quantitative verse in the 15th and 16th cs., many of whom were collected by G. Carducci in 1881.

The Fr. quantitative movement seems to have begun in the late 15th c. with the unpublished work (incl. a treatise) of Michel de Boteauville; in the latter part of the 16th c., many of France's best-known poets attempted *vers mesurés à l'antique.* The link between quantitative meter and music arising from the theoretical basis in strict durations was most productive in the compositions of Jean-Antoine de Baïf's "Académie de Poésie et de Musique." In Germany, the earliest quantitative experiments were made by Conrad Gesner in 1555; other Ren. adherents of the new meters were Johann Clajus, Johann Fischart, Johann Kolross, and Andreas Bachmann. The Ren. also saw quantitative imitations in Dutch and Hungarian and in the Scandinavian and Slavic langs. under the international aegis of humanism.

The quantitative movement in England had its beginnings in discussions by Roger Ascham, Thomas Watson (later bishop of Lincoln), and Sir John Cheke at Cambridge, ca. 1540. Two *hexameters by Watson that survive from these discussions, quoted by Ascham in *The Scholemaster* (1570), will serve as an example of quantitative imitation:

$$- \quad \cup\cup | - \quad - | - \quad \cup\cup | - \quad -$$
All travellers do gladly report great
$$| \quad - \quad \cup \cup | - \, -$$
   prayse of Ulysses
$$- \quad \cup \quad \cup \quad | - \quad \cup \cup \quad | - \quad - | -$$
For that he knew many mens maners

$$- \quad | - \quad - \quad \cup \cup | - \, -$$
and saw many Cities

These lines do not attempt to create aural patterns, either of stresses or of longs and shorts. Stresses may fall in short positions (first syllable of "travelers" and "many"); unstressed syllables may be long and may fall in the *ictus position at the beginning of the foot (last syllable of "travelers" and "maners"). The ear does not perceive the sequence "-ers and" as two long syllables, and the stress on the first syllable of "many" gives it greater length in pronunciation than the second. But Ascham's admiration of these lines is not, in his own terms, misplaced. The lines observe the two most important cl. prosodic rules taught in Tudor grammar schools: the penultimate rule (in words of three or more syllables, a stressed penultimate syllable is long, and an unstressed one is short) and the rule of "position" (a syllable is long if its vowel is followed by more than one consonant in the same or the following words). "Great" is long both by position and because its vowel is a diphthong. (In fact, the rule pertained to digraphs since, like the rule of position, it applied not to pronunciation but to *spelling*; one resource available to many quantitative poets of this period was the variability of orthography.) Where no rules applied, Watson was free to determine quantity himself, provided he was consistent.

Ascham included some quantitative trans. in *Toxophilus* (1545), and James Sandford published specimens in 1576, but the major impetus for the movement in England was Philip Sidney's example in writing quantitative poems for the *Arcadia*, probably between 1577 and 1580, and his discussions with Thomas Drant, Edward Dyer, and Edmund Spenser on the question of cl. imitations. As K. Hanson has shown, Sidney (whose quantitative rules have survived) was extremely alert to the phonological characteristics of Eng. Examples by Spenser and by Gabriel Harvey appear in their correspondence. Numerous poets wrote Eng. quantitative verse over the next 20 years. One of the strictest, technically speaking, was Richard Stanyhurst, who trans. four books of the *Aeneid* (1582); one of the most prolific was Abraham Fraunce, who published several quantitative works between 1587 and 1592; and one of the most skilled was Mary Sidney Herbert, Countess of Pembroke, in her trans. of the Psalms in the 1590s. Several treatises were written in at least partial support of quantitative imitations, notably by William Webbe (1586), George Puttenham (1589), and Thomas Campion (1602). After 1602, the movement virtually came to an end.

The Ren. quantitative movement died when the changing aesthetic climate caused an intellectual notion of meter to give way to a metrical practice based on the experienced rhythms of the lang.—at least partly under the influence of the drama—and when the native verse trads. demonstrated unequivocally that metrical principles arising from the mod. langs. themselves could yield poetry of a grace and power matching that of antiquity. The role of the quantitative experiments in the devel. of the vernacular metrical trads. was, however, significant: they showed the dangers of interpreting the notion of imitation too literally, and they led to other successful innovations such as the introduction of *blank verse. Later attempts to devise a strict quantitative principle for mod. langs. (e.g., by Bridges) succeeded only in showing that quantity is not a phonological feature that can be transferred from the cl. langs.

**III. Accentual Imitations.** Although mod. scholarship has for the most part held the view that Lat. verse should be read with its normal prose stresses, for a long time there existed an alternative mode of reading in which the ictus of each foot is stressed, thereby converting the cl. metrical pattern into a kind of accentual verse. This trad. has sometimes encouraged prosodists (e.g., G. Saintsbury) to use the terminology of cl. prosody (esp. *longs* and *shorts*) in discussing accentual meter. There is evidence of this mode of reading in Ren. schools, and it was firmly entrenched in 19th-c. Eng. and Ger. pedagogy. As a result, the rhythms of these accentual equivalents of cl. meters were familiar to many poets, and it is not surprising that a number attempted to use such meters in their own langs. Two Lat. forms in particular produce distinctive rhythmic patterns when converted into accentual verse: the hexameter and the *sapphic; the latter esp. has had a long hist. in Eur. lit. The influence of accentual versions of cl. meters can be seen in many Ren. imitations, and one of the most significant features of Campion's relatively successful experiments is that they combine a strict pseudoquantitative scansion with an accentual one. In Germany, Martin Opitz argued in 1624 for an equivalence between length and stress, while, in Spain, accentual imitations, esp. sapphics, date from the mid-16th c. However, it was not until the second half of the 18th c. that experiments with accentual imitation became common, and in the 19th c., they are legion. The most influential poet in this movement was F. G. Klopstock, whose accentual hexameters had a profound effect on later Ger. versification and whose example was followed by numerous Ger. and Eng. poets. J. W. Goethe, F. Schiller, A. W. Schlegel, and F. Hölderlin all wrote accentual imitations of cl. schemes, followed by Eduard Mörike, Christian Morgenstern, R. M. Rilke, Thomas Mann, and Bertolt Brecht, while scholars such as A. W. Schlegel, G. Platen, and J. H. Voss attempted a stricter transfer of cl. metrical principles.

Imitations based on Klopstock's principles were introduced into Eng. by William Taylor in the late 18th c., followed by Coleridge and Southey. Alfred, Lord Tennyson made attempts to combine the accentual principle with a quantitative one, while long poems in accentual hexameters by H. W. Longfellow (*Evangeline*), C. Kingsley, and A. H. Clough achieved some success. Numerous hexameter trans. of cl. and Ger. verse were published, many encouraged by Matthew Arnold's advocacy. A. C. Swinburne and George Meredith also experimented with accentual cl. imitations, as have many 20th-c. poets, incl. Ezra Pound, Louis MacNeice, and W. H. Auden. Rus. accentual imitations also date from the latter part of the 18th c.; Vasily Trediakovsky's hexameters were particularly influential, and a number of poets, incl. Alexander Pushkin, used the form in the 19th c., esp. for trans. The accentual pattern that is produced is close to that of the *dol'nik*, a folk meter that became important in the 20th c. It. imitations present a somewhat different picture, since the lang. and verse forms are less strictly based on stress. The most influential naturalizer of cl. versification was Giosuè Carducci, whose *Odi barbare* (Barbarian Odes, 1877–89; 2d ed., 1878, with useful preface by G. Chiarini) made use of the accentual patterns of cl. meters (when read with their normal prose stresses) and ignored the quantitative patterns. He was thus able to bring cl. imitations close to the native trad. of It. verse, though at the cost of the cl. metrical schemes themselves. He added a historical study to his own experiments in 1881. For a different mod. attempt to imitate the meters of an ancient poetry, this one Germanic (see ALLITERATION).

■ K. Elze, *Die englische Hexameter* (1867); *La poesia barbara nei secoli XV e XVI*, ed. G. Carducci (1881); A. H. Baxter, *The Introduction of Classical Metres into Italian Poetry* (1901); R. B. McKerrow, "The Use of So-called Classical Metres in Elizabethan Verse," *MLQ* (London) 4–5 (1901); Kastner; Omond; G. D. Willcock, "Passing Pitefull Hexameters," *MLR* 29 (1934); G. L. Hendrickson, "Elizabethan Quantitative Hexameters," *PQ* 28 (1949); A. Burgi, *History of the Russian Hexameter* (1954); Beare; P. Habermann, "Antike Versmasse und Strophenformen im Deutschen," *Reallexikon II*—extensive bibliographies; A. Kabell, *Metrische Studien II: Antiker Form sich nähernd* (1960)—wide-ranging; *The Poems of Sir Philip Sidney*, ed. W. A. Ringler (1962); W. Bennett, *German Verse in Classical Metres* (1963); Elwert, *Italienische*; D. Attridge, *Well-weighed Syllables* (1974)—Elizabethan imitations; Wilkins; *Die Lehre von der Nachahmung der antike Versmasse im Deutschen*, ed. H.-H. Hellmuth and J. Schröder (1976); S. Schuman, "Sixteenth-Century English Quantitative Verse," *MP* 74 (1977); Brogan; Navarro; Scherr; Gasparov, *History*; R. L. Scott, "The English Hexameter," *CML* 16 (1996); B. E. Bullock, "Quantitative Verse in a Quantitative-Insensitive Language," *JFLS* 7 (1997)—on Baïf; K. Hanson, "Quantitative Meter in English," *ENLL* 5 (2001)—on Sidney; E. Bernhardt-Kabisch, "'When Klopstock England Defied,'" *CL* 55 (2003)—on Ger. and Eng. hexameters; Y. Prins, "Metrical Translation," *Nation, Language, and the Ethics of Translation*, ed. S. Bermann and M. Wood (2005)—Victorian hexameters; H. M. Brown and R. Freedman, "Vers mesurés," *Grove Music Online*, http://www.grovemusic.com/shared/views/article.html?from=az&section=music.29243.

D. ATTRIDGE

**CLASSICAL POETICS**

**I. Early Greek Poetics.** Ancient Gr. poetics at its inception was shaped by two features of archaic culture: the treatment of the Homeric *epics as a source of authoritative knowledge and the nature of early poetry as *song or *recitation performed in social contexts. Accordingly, the concerns of the earliest Western poetics centered on criteria that had little to do with the notion of lyric subjectivity. At issue instead were poetry's ethical and pedagogical value, the poet's relationship to truth, the suitability of a poem to its performative context, and the pleasure and judgment of the audience. These emphases would change with the move away from an oral culture and the rise of formal and aesthetic criteria of judgment.

The term *poetics* itself requires a caveat. Before the 5th c. BCE, there was no single term to mark out poetry as a genre; an early "poetics" can be derived only from the implicit views embedded in early poetry, philosophy, and rhet. Early epideictic prose and poetry were both seen as incantatory (see EPIDEICTIC POETRY); the former displayed *rhythm, figure, and *parallelism, as in the Sophist Gorgias's (ca. 485–380 BCE) *Encomium of Helen*, which itself claims that poetry is merely "*logos* [speech] with meter." Not until the 5th c. is attention directed to the formal study of poetry's properties abstracted from its performance context, perhaps because of the increasing commitment of song to writing (Ford). At this point, the term *poietai* (poets) comes into general use to denote such crafters; in the 4th c., we find, in Aristotle's *Poetics*, a *poietike tekhne*, an art or craft of poetry sustaining formal analysis.

Poetry was held to be the educator of men, esp. early epic, which was seen as a source of ethical and practical knowledge. Homer (ca. 800 BCE) by virtue of his priority, held a cultural authority not unlike that of the Bible later in the Christian West. Yet the epic depiction of the gods as ruled by human passions was a target of crit.: the critic Xenophanes (ca. 570–475 BCE) condemned (in verse) the notion of anthropomorphism and the immoral behavior of the epic Olympians, who engaged in theft, adultery, and deception (fr. B11-16 Diels-Kranz). Similar complaints occur in his near-contemporaries Pythagoras of Samos (570–495 BCE) and Heraclitus of Ephesus (535–475 BCE), while the lyric poets Stesichorus (ca. 640–555 BCE) and Pindar (ca. 522–443 BCE) explicitly correct earlier "tales" (cf. *Olympians* 27–29, *Nemean* 7.20ff.). To take these crits. as evidence for Plato's claim of "an ancient war" between poetry and philosophy (*Republic* 607b), however, is risky. Truth-claims in this period occur in the context of bids for poetic authority, and the genres of philosophy and poetry are not clearly distinct until the cl. period.

From Homer forward, the *Muses, daughters of Memory, were invoked as the source of both the poet's knowledge and his inspiration, a pairing not seen as incompatible until Plato. The *poet represents himself as relying on the Muses in his recreation and memorialization (*aletheia*, bringing out of forgetfulness) of heroic deeds. To listen to this poetic song brings enchantment and forgetfulness of present troubles (*Odyssey* 8.44–45; 17.385, 521; cf. Phemius at *Odyssey* 1.326ff.). Similarly, the Hesiodic Muses, who offer knowledge of the past and future, bring a pleasing forgetfulness of the present (*Theogony* 53–55, 98–105), though Hesiod (writing between 750 and 650 BCE) attributes to them the statement that they can speak true-seeming lies as well as the truth (*Theogony* 27–28).

Aristophanes (ca. 445–385 BCE) devotes several of his comedies to attacks on the tragedian Euripides (ca. 480–406 BCE) and the 5th-c. Sophists, whose newfangled ideas (relativism, skepticism, agnosticism) influenced Euripidean drama. They were pilloried in the *Clouds*, as was Euripides himself in *Acharnians* and *Thesmophoriazusae*. The *Frogs* (405 BCE) stages the first scene of lit. crit., a contest as to whether Euripides or Aeschylus was a better teacher of the Athenians. Aeschylus's view is that the poet should conceal wickedness and speak of honorable things; he sees himself as a latter-day Orpheus or Mousaios, and his old-fashioned morals, martial topics, and larger-than-life heroes carry the day (*Frogs* 1030–36). In contrast, the argumentative and impious characters of Euripides are judged too base to offer ethical models, however realistic his drama may be.

Underlying meanings (*hyponoia*) in Homer and Hesiod were sought by means of etymologized narrative, allegory, and other forms of exegesis. Already in the late 6th c., Theagenes of Rhegium (fl. 6th c. BCE), in the oldest known Gr. treatise on poetry, defended Homer by interpreting the warring divinities of *Iliad* 20 as representing a conflict between physical elements or psychological forces. The Stoics employed a similar approach, reading the Olympian gods as personifications of air, ether, fire, or earth, and relying heavily on etymology in their explications (cf. also the Derveni papyrus; Metrodorus of Lampsacus, 5th c. BCE). The Sophists accepted pay for giving ethical lessons based on Homeric exegesis; Protagoras in Plato's *Protagoras* 316d–317b calls the poets "Sophists in disguise" who conceal their wisdom in verse. This search for underlying meaning was already a familiar procedure in Gr. culture, as evident from interpretations of the Delphic oracle and the fable (*ainos*): Pindar and Theognis (6th c. BCE) claim to speak an "ainos" that will be understood only by the wise. The term *allegoria* (speaking otherly) came into use only in Plutarch's (ca. 46–120) time (*Moralia* 19E; see ALLEGORY).

**II. Plato on Poetry.** With Plato (427–347 BCE), poetry is treated—if only to be condemned—as a field of endeavor with a single object, by analogy to the crafts of painting and sculpture. Plato acknowledges the enormous influence of Homer and the poets as teachers (*Republic* 598d–e, 599a) but criticizes them in the *Ion* and *Republic* esp.; his response to the debate about the ethical and practical uses of poetry is to banish the poets (with a few exceptions) from his ideal state (*Republic* books 3, 10). Their task, he argues, is better achieved by Socratic dialogue (*Protagoras* 347d).

The attack on poetry in *Republic* book 2 focuses on the familiar issue of the poets' representation of the gods: their lying tales are to be rejected, and the gods should be described as unchanging, good, and incapable of violence (2.379a–382e). The vulnerability of the young leads Socrates to reject even poetry sanitized by hyponoia (*Republic* 2.378e)—after all, one poem can lead to many interpretations, nor can the absent poet answer questions about his intent (*Protagoras* 347c–348a). In book 3, we encounter the conceptual tool on which much of Plato's argument rests: *\*mimesis*, i.e., dramatic or expressive representation or a replication of something in material form. Listing three genres—drama, epic, and *\*dithyramb* (a form of choral lyric, though iambic, elegiac, and lyric *\*monody* are omitted)—Plato distinguishes among them based on the difference between "plain narrative" (*diegesis*) and mimetic narrative, i.e., direct speech. Dithyrambs exemplify the former, since there the poet speaks in his own person; in drama, only mimetic narrative is used; a combination of the two occurs in epic (*Republic* 3.392d–394c). The Guardians should not engage in mimetic narrative lest, from enjoying the *\*imitation*, they come to enjoy the reality— or if they do imitate, it should be of courageous, self-controlled, pious, and free people. Thus, they will use Homeric-type narratives, mostly plain narrative and a small amount of mimetic narrative (but only of the ethically appropriate type; *Republic* 3.395d–96d). The lyric modes are excluded except for songs that inspire courage or address the gods (*Republic* 2.299b–c).

For Plato, it is not only the "imitators" but their audience who are at risk. Because the tragic poets mostly portray people suffering and reacting nonphilosophically to their suffering, they strengthen the nonrational part of the audience's souls, throwing into disarray its psychic constitution (*Republic* 10.605b); the same happens in the case of "sex, anger, and all the desires, pleasures, and pains" that accompany our actions. (One might contrast Gorgias's view that "the deceiver is more just than the non-deceiver, and the deceived wiser than the undeceived.") Plato (or his spokesperson Socrates) proposes instead that the citizens be told a "noble lie" justifying the hierarchies in the city (*Republic* 414c). In the *Laws*, however, the Athenian emphasizes the importance of setting up choruses for the city to persuade the citizens that the most philosophical life is the happiest one, harnessing the power of song about which Plato is so cautious in the *Republic* (*Laws* 2.664b–c).

Elsewhere Plato treats poetry under the heading of *\*inspiration* (*enthusiasmos*) rather than mimesis (the two concepts do not appear together until the *Laws*). His treatment of inspiration innovates; in relying on the Muse, the poet does not acquire knowledge so much as enter upon a kind of madness (*mania*) beyond his control (*Ion* passim, *Apology* 22a–c, *Meno* 99c–e,

*Phaedrus* 245, *Laws* 3.682a, 719c–d; see FUROR POETI-CUS). Although the poet does not know what he is saying, he can nonetheless produce beautiful poetry; in the *Phaedrus*, his inspiration is said to be winged by Love (*Eros*) and capable of attaining truth.

**III. Aristotle.** With the *Poetics* of Aristotle (384–322 BCE) comes a shift in emphasis from poetry as a socioreligious activity to poetry as an *\*artifact* with a generic form and *telos*. Aristotle starts his discussion with the "modes of imitation," which differ from each other in their means, objects, or imitative procedures rather than performance context (1447a). Aristotle thus deploys Plato's view of poetry as a mimetic art; even the verse form is a less important criterion than its mimesis of what is fictional. The objects of imitation are the actions of good or bad men; the manner is (as with Plato) plain narrative, mimetic narrative, or a mixture thereof. The bias toward mimesis is also shown in Aristotle's focus on drama rather than *\*lyric*, *\*elegy*, or iambus. But imitation here is not condemned as a poor copy of reality or a corruptive influence; instead, Aristotle points out that imitation is natural to humans from childhood, that it is fundamental to the learning process, and that we delight in realistic works of imitation even if their subject matter is unpleasant: in these traits, he locates the origin of poetry (*Poetics* 1448b). Moreover, since the poet's function is to produce an imitation of what *could* happen rather than what *did* happen, poetry is more serious and more philosophical than hist. (*Poetics* 1451a–b).

*\*Tragedy*, says Aristotle, developed from the improvisations of the leader of choral dithyrambs (1449a). Its "soul" is the *\*plot* (*mythos*). The other elements of tragedy are, in decreasing order of importance, character (*ethos*), thought (*dianoia*, probably the arguments of the characters), poetic expression (*lexis*), the composition of the choral odes (*\*melopoeia*), and spectacle (*opsis*, *Poetics* 1450a). Tragedy is "the imitation of an action that is complete in itself," with a certain order and of a certain magnitude—i.e, long enough for the hero to pass via probable or necessary stages from misfortune to happiness or vice versa (*Poetics* 1452a). It is in the representation of this "action," as constrained by probability and causal necessity (not contiguity), that the famous Aristotelian *\*unity* resides. Aristotle also minimizes the power attributed to rhythmic and melodic discourse by Gorgias and Plato. There is no mention of the dramatist's inspiration; instead, his work is a rational art, a *tekhne*, with a specific goal, the *\*catharsis* of the audience by the evocation of "pity and fear," preferably by the plot rather than the spectacle (*Poetics* 1450b, 1453b). Whether the primary sense of catharsis is medical, ethical, or otherwise is unclear; but the sense is that catharsis improves the human capacity to feel the proper emotions toward the correct objects (Halliwell), and it represents one part of Aristotle's response to Platonic crit.

Plots can be simple or complex. In the former, the protagonist's change of state is linear; in the latter, it is caused by a sudden and unexpected reversal of fortune (*peripeteia*) or a recognition (*anagnorisis*, a change from ignorance to knowledge) or both (*Poetics* 1452a). Two other plot types are the pathetic (where the motive is passion) and the ethical (where the motives derive from character). The best tragedy entails a reversal from happiness to unhappiness; the hero should be a good man but not a perfect one, and the change should be caused not by wickedness but by some *hamartia* (*Poetics* 1453a). The term may mean "moral flaw," "intellectual error," or some intermediate quality; excluding culpability allows for a tragic disparity between a character's intention and its outcome (Halliwell).

Epic (*Poetics* 1459a–60a) is similar to tragedy insofar as it is a representation, in verse, of characters of a higher type. It too must be simple or complex, "ethical" or "pathetic." Tragedy, however, is the superior form; while epic has no limit in time, may portray simultaneous actions, and incorporates elements of the supernatural, tragedy tries to contain its action within a single day and to what can be shown on stage and is thus the more efficient and superior genre (*Poetics* 1462a–b). Aristotle's theory of *comedy may have been contained in a lost second book of the *Poetics* but is probably not represented in the 10th-c. ms. known as the *Tractatus Coislinianus*. Lost are his three books of *On Poets* and six or more of *Homeric Problems*.

**IV. Hellenistic Poetics.** The museum and library founded by Ptolemy I at Alexandria in the early 3rd c. housed not only the ancient world's largest collection of volumes but a community of scholars devoted to *textual criticism, philology, and *exegesis. Zenodotus of Ephesus (ca. 325–260 BCE), the first head of the library, produced authoritative eds. of the Homeric and Hesiodic epics. His successor Eratosthenes (ca. 276–195 BCE) criticized the widespread use of Homer for pedagogy, emphasizing that poetry's goal was enchantment, not instruction (Strabo 1.1.10). Aristophanes of Byzantium (ca. 257–180 BCE) introduced punctuation and chastised Menander (ca. 342–291 BCE) for his borrowings from other poets—an early critique of plagiarism. Aristophanes, and Aristarchus of Samothrace after him (ca. 217–145 BCE), formally evaluated the work of their literary forebears, producing official lists (the *kanones*, or *canons) of those considered best and worthy of preservation; no contemporaries were included. Aristarchus instituted the critical principle that each author is his own best interpreter and that editorial decisions should thus be based on the poet's own usage and thought (as represented by the maxim *Homeron ex Homerou*, Homer from Homer).

A synchronous phenomenon was the rise of *Alexandrianism in poetic composition, a style that emphasized the display of mythological and scientific erudition presented with painstaking poetic craftsmanship. The trend is best represented by Callimachus (ca. 305–240 BCE), whose programmatic statement that "a big book is a big evil" represented the rejection of large-scale Homeric epic in favor of shorter poems on little-known episodes in myth. The introduction to his *Aetia* sets forth a new poetics epitomized by Apollo's

command: "Poet, let your sacrificial victim be fat, but your muse slim."

**V. Poetics and the Hellenistic Philosophers.** Of the three major schools of Hellenistic philosophy—the Epicureans, Stoics, and Cynics—two took distinct positions on the nature and function of poetry. The Stoics detected their own cosmology in Homer and Hesiod; Crates of Mallos (2d c. BCE), e.g., treated Agamemnon's shield in *Iliad* 11 as a representation of the cosmos (Eustathios [ca. 1115–95 or 96 CE] on *Iliad* 11.32–40), while Cornutus (fl. 40 CE), like the Gr. Stoics, used etymological readings of Homer to recover early beliefs about the world. Balbus in Cicero's *De natura deorum* (2.60ff) also invokes *metonymy (Ceres stands for grain) and the deification of virtues and emotions as interpretive techniques. The Stoic emphasis on hyponoia suggests that the Stoics did not feel poetry could lead an audience to virtue without the correct critical reception; the crucial issue was the mental ability of the reader or listener to recognize what was morally commendable and what needed adaptation. The Stoics recognized that poetic form helped the *absorption of content: as reported by Seneca the Younger (ca. 3 BCE–65 CE) in *Epistles* 108.8–11, Cleanthes (331–232 BCE) held that the force of meter and music added greater impact to the thought.

The allegorist Heraclitus (1st c. CE) claims that both Plato and Epicurus (341–270 BCE) were hostile to Homer and that Epicurus himself condemned all poetry "as a destructive lure of fictitious stories" (*Homeric Problems* 4). Sextus Empiricus (ca. 160–210 CE) reports in *Against Mathematicians* (1.296–97) that Epicurus felt that poets pursued falsehood because it naturally moves the soul more than truth and because it inflames the baser human passions. However, Epicurus may have been receptive to poetry as entertainment as long as it made no claims to education. The later Epicurean Philodemus of Gadara (110–40 BCE) wrote that poetry should be beautiful and produce pleasure, not serve any moral or utilitarian purpose; nor did it need to be truthful (*On Poems* 5). Philodemus also argued that style and content are inseparable, with the result that any change in the order of the words (*metathesis*) changes the meaning as well. Epicurean didactic should thus be an *oxymoron, yet Lucretius (ca. 99–55 BCE) composed precisely that in the mid-1st c. BCE. His epic poem *De rerum natura* characterizes itself via the well-known metaphor of the medicinal cup rimmed with honey in order to fool children into taking their medicine; his verse—and perhaps such images as the opening tableau of Mars and Venus sharing a bed—is to be the sweet lure into Epicurean philosophy. His Philodemian view of the inseparability of style and content is reflected in his "atomistic poetics," in which the letters are conceived of as atoms, so that *lignum* (wood) is said to contain *igni(s)* (fire).

We know only a little of the Aristotelian critic Neoptolemus of Parium (3d c. BCE). His division of *poiēma*, *poiēsis*, and *poiētēs* (poem, poetry, poet) linked the first term to style and the second to the mimesis of fictional stories. This division of poetry into (roughly) expression vs. content may be the precursor of a later division between *grammatike* (crit.), philology, and glosses on the one hand and hermeneutics on the other (Walker). Poetic crit. throughout this period thus revolved around the oppositions of form vs. content and pleasure vs. instruction; also at issue was the question of whether poetry was the result more of natural genius or of hard work, with Callimachus naturally the representative of art (cf. Longinus, *On the Sublime* 33.4–5).

**VI. The Romans as Epigones.** The Romans inherited Gr. lit. before they established a lit. of their own. Their earliest recorded poet, the Gr. ex-slave Livius Andronicus (ca. 280–200 BCE), was a translator; he set Homer's *Odyssey* in *Saturnian verse and also translated Gr. comedy and tragedy for staging at the Great Games of 240 BCE. Prose was originally held to be the more authoritative form because of its propriety for forensic oratory and hist., the writing of which occupied the leisure time of the elite classes. Indeed, the first original Roman poetry was the historical epic composed by Naevius (ca. 270–201 BCE) and Ennius (ca. 239–169 BCE). Ennius's treatment, in the *Annales*, of Roman hist. from the fall of Troy to 184 BCE, opened with a description of how Homer's soul was transferred into him by metempsychosis; he also adopted Homer's dactylic hexameter. Despite the temporal priority of Livius Andronicus, later Romans too chose to set Naevius or Ennius at the head of a Roman poetics; Lucretius, e.g., claims that Ennius first brought the poet's crown from Helicon (*De rerum natura* 1.117–18; cf. Horace *Epistles* 2.1.156–59).

These circumstances produced a particular set of anxieties in early Roman poetics: their epigonal status vis-à-vis the Greeks; the tension between imitation of these models and originality; the negative associations that touched on writing poetry; the low social status of the actors of the Roman theater; and, finally the uncomfortable similarity between poetry and political prose in performance. Horace's famous quip, "Greece, though captured, captured in turn her savage victor" (*Epistles* 2.1.156), evokes some of these tensions. This "anxiety of influence" would lead to much discussion of the proper imitation of others both in poetry and in rhet. (cf. Cicero, *De oratore* 2.8–97; the fragments of Dionysius of Halicarnassus, *On Imitation*; Horace *Epistles* 1.19.19 and *Ars poetica* 133ff.; Seneca the Elder, *Suasoriae* 3.7; Seneca the Younger, *Epistles* 84; Quintilian 10.2.27–8; Longinus, *On the Sublime* 13–14). Too literal an imitation of other poetry is to be avoided; instead, the source should be recognized at the same time as the changes (even polemic ones) rung upon it by the poet, a process now termed *intertextuality.

The first Roman dramatic crit. is to be found not in a treatise but in the prologues to the plays of the ex-slave Terence (195 or 185–159 BCE). Like his predecessor Plautus (254–184 BCE), Terence staged trans. of Gr. New Comedy, but his frequent combination of two originals for use in a single Roman drama brought on the accusation of "spoiling" (*contaminatio*) the looted Gr. plays for use by other Roman playwrights (cf. the prologues to the *Andria*, the *Adelphoe*, and the *Self-Tormentor*). These dramas gained in literary stature through the efforts of Aelius Stilo (ca. 154–74 BCE) in the late 2d c. BCE, when they were added to the school curriculum. Stilo is said by Suetonius (ca. 70–135 CE) to have played a key role in the devel. of a literary education at Rome (*Lives of the Grammarians* 3), following the example of Crates of Mallos, who encouraged critical attention to poetry during his visit to Rome in 159 BCE.

The orator and statesman Cicero (106–43 BCE) claims, in his legal defense of the Gr. poet Archias (120–ca. 60 BCE), that the poet's inspiration is divine (*In Defense of Archias* 18). In a more Roman vein, he adds that the poet benefits the state because he celebrates the deeds of Roman heroes and the Roman people and thus provides an incentive to glory (19ff.) In his *Orator*, Cicero suggests that the main distinction between oratory and poetry cannot be great, since Plato and Demosthenes have more in common with poetry than do the writers of comedy (*Orator* 67). Further linking the two, he argues that both orators and poets move the audience by being moved themselves (*De Orator* 2.194; *De divinatione* 1.80; *Orator* 132). As a statesman and advocate, however, he is often careful to affect ignorance about Gr. lit. and to insist on the distance separating the orator from the poet (*Brutus* 191). In his letters, Cicero criticizes the "cantores Euphorionis" (bards of the school of Euphorion), his pejorative term for the poets who adopted the Callimachean program at Rome (*Tusculan Disputations* 3.45). Catullus (ca. 84–54 BCE), Calvus (82–47 BCE) and Cinna (1st c. BCE) are its best-known representatives; they adopted such Alexandrian mannerisms as allowing a *spondee in the fifth foot of their verse (Cicero, *Letters to Atticus* 7.2.1, cf. *Orator* 161). These *Neoteric poets rejected annalistic epic, privileged *ekphrasis* and erudition, used difficult *diction, and produced intricately structured and highly polished verse; Catullus describes his book of poems as a trifle, but an elegant one that has been well polished with dry pumice. He influenced the Roman elegists and Virgil (70–19 BCE), in whose sixth *Eclogue* we find Apollo warning the shepherd Tityrus off martial epic, telling him to keep his sheep fat but his song finely spun.

Roman higher education was based on training in rhet. as well as the reading of poetry, with the result that both were grouped under *litterae* (loosely, the liberal arts) and shared critical terminology and standards of eloquence. Rhetorical handbooks come to include commentary on "criticism," which includes, in the *Art of Grammar* of Dionysius Thrax (170–90 BCE), reading aloud, the explanation of figures, glosses of difficult words, the finding of etymologies, the elucidation of analogies, and judgment of the poetry. The *On Composition* of the Gr. rhetorician Dionysius of Halicarnassus (ca. 60–after 7 BCE) treated the styles of poets, historians, and orators from the cl. period. Focusing on the arrangement of words, Dionysius held that the poetic goal of pleasure and beauty could be created by a particular combination of sounds, variety, and rhythm. These criteria were used to set up three distinct styles: the austere, the elegant, and the mixed (21–24). Demetrius's (b. 350 BCE) *On Style* (possibly 1st c. BCE) treats both poetry and prose under four styles: elevated, elegant, plain, and forcible.

**VII. Horace and the Augustan Age.** The centralization of political power in a single figure after the Augustan victory of 31 BCE oriented contemp. poetics around issues of *patronage, ideology, and the relationship of poet to state. We see accordingly such poetic features as the *recusatio*: originally exemplified by Callimachus's refusal to write grand epic, in the early imperial period it evolved into the poet's statement of his inadequacy to celebrate the deeds of a contemp. military or political "great man" (cf. Horace *Epistles* 2.1, *Odes* 1.6, 2.12, 4.2, 4.15; Propertius *Elegies* 2.1, 3.1, 3.2, 3.3, 3.9; Ovid *Amores* 1.1; Virgil *Georgics* 3.16ff.). Also characteristic of this refusal is the thematic opposition of *amor* (love) to political topics as the subject of poetry.

Horace (65–8 BCE) wrote as both poet and critic. His *Odes* cast him as the Roman heir to Gr. lyric. The *Satires* criticize the unpolished and prolific verse of his predecessor Lucilius (ca. 180–103 BCE) and refuse to imitate his attacks on his peers (*Satires* 1.4, 1.10); instead, his own verse will expose social vice and folly in gentler terms. The *Epistles* make a claim for the moral value of reading poetry; *Epistles* 1.2 finds Homer more useful in this regard than the Stoics, while *Epistles* 2.1 points out the poet's usefulness: he teaches the young, offers moral exempla, and helps the state with hymns and prayers—an echo of Plato's *Republic*. Here Horace also offers a defense of contemp. poets and laments the conservative preference for the past, based on a false analogy, he argues, of the earliest Roman poets to the earliest Gr. poets. A brief hist. of Roman drama gives it a local origin with *fescennine verses at rustic festivals.

The famous *Ars poetica* (*Epistles* 2.3 *to the Pisos*; the name comes from Quintilian) is a Roman variation on Aristotelian poetics combined with Hellenistic concerns. On the evidence of Porphyrio (fl. 2d or 3d c. CE) and Philodemus (ca. 110–ca. 40 or 35 BCE), it seems that Horace took his major precepts here from Neoptolemus, incl. the focus on unity (also Aristotelian), the view of poetry's dual function in delighting and being useful, and his tripartite structure of poiēma, poiēsis, and poiētēs. The focus on unity motivates the famous opening analogy of the bad poem to the painting of a monstrous body with parts from different animals (1–13), a twist on the bodily metaphors used for the coherent poem or speech by Plato (*Phaedrus* 264c), Aristotle (*Poetics* 1450b), and Cicero (*De oratore* 2.325). Horace's demand that the poem be finely crafted recalls the Callimachean program, while his support of the poet's right to coin new words meshes with his critique of conservatism in *Epistles* 2.1. His metaphor of words flourishing

and decaying like leaves and men adapts Homer's original comparison of the generations of men to leaves at *Iliad* 6.14ff., suggesting that lang., too, has a natural life span (*Ars poetica* 46–82).

Horace next addresses what can be represented with propriety in tragedy and comedy (*Ars poetica* 89–98, cf. 180–88) and argues (as in the rhetorical treatises) that the actor must feel what he portrays in order to affect his audience (103–105). From this point onward, it is clear that Horace takes drama, and esp. tragedy, to be his main subject, without particular regard to the contemp. situation at Rome. He includes a number of traditional prescriptions for the dramatist (five acts; three actors; choral odes relevant to the plot, 189–95) but, unlike Aristotle, gives more prominence to character than to plot, a typically Roman concern with ethos also influenced by rhet. (120–24, 156–78). His etiology for Gr. drama differs from that of Aristotle in *Poetics* 1449a, here beginning with poets competing for the prize of a goat (220ff.); one Thespis later invents the mod. version (275–77). Also non-Aristotelian is Horace's attention to the moral role of drama: the chorus should sooth the angry, give good advice, regulate the passionate, praise what is right, and pray to the gods (196–201). The moral role is supported by his claim that Socratic wisdom is the font of good writing (309–10). Avoiding the pleasure/education dichotomy about the role of poetry, he claims that the best poet wishes to do both (342–34). Both *ingenium* (talent) and *ars* (skill) are needed to write good poetry (408–11); Horace does not praise the "divine madness" of the *Ion* and *Phaedrus*, which he associates with a reading of Democritus as requiring poets to be mad (295–308; cf. the mad Eumolpus in Petronius's *Satyricon*).

**VIII. Poetics of the Roman Empire.** Much of the lit. of the 1st c. CE (both poetry and rhet.) identifies itself as in decline from its republican acme. This "poetics of inferiority" could be used as ethical, social, or political commentary; thus, the (supposed) devel. of luxury and sexual deviance, detrimental changes in literary taste, and the end of the political clout of the elite classes were all offered as the causes of deterioration. Lucan's (39–65 CE) epic *Pharsalia* signifies its opposition to the triumphant narrative of the *Aeneid* not only in describing the end of Republican Rome but in describing *itself* as written under conditions of "slavery"—after praising Nero at the poem's start. Similarly, Tacitus's (56–117 CE) *Dialogue on Orators* poses the question of why there are no good orators in the present day but eschews answering it directly in favor of an exploration of three topics: the superiority of oratory or poetry as a career, the superiority of the ancients or the moderns, and the cause of the decline of eloquence. The dialogue itself stages another issue, the danger incurred by one of its three main protagonists, Maternus, for writing drama about historical or mythical tyrants and heroic republicans such as Cato the Younger. Poetry is thus shown to be the site of true political commentary despite Aper's crit. that it is detached from the world of oratory. At the end of the dialogue, Maternus executes a surprising about-face in praise of the quiet times brought on by autocracy; but this very praise from a critic of the regime effectively demonstrates the oppressive force of that autocracy and undermines its own laudatory content. The *Dialogue* thus models the relationship between lit. and politics under the empire and demonstrates the political rather than philosophical uses of allegory.

The Stoic Seneca the Younger devotes several of his letters to poetic issues. Epistle 84 discusses the imitation of our poetic models: we should read as the bees gather and blend the whole into one delicious compound so that it both reveals its source and differs from it (*Epistles* 84.3–5). In Epistle 88, he criticizes the idea that Homer was a philosopher or that the liberal arts can teach us virtue. Poetry can prepare the mind for virtue, but only philosophy can instill it (*Epistles* 88.20, 95.8). His own poetic practice may be seen in the tragedies, which offer an indirect critique of the Aristotelian model by portraying the shocking spectacle of good men coming to a bad end and bad men triumphant. Critics are divided as to whether this dovetails with his philosophical teachings or shows up their idealism, but in any case, it is clear that the dramas require an intellectually engaged audience if they are to provoke more than horror.

The rhetorician Quintilian (ca. 35–100 CE), who held an imperial post under Vespasian, eschews any narrative of decline in his *The Training of an Orator* in favor of describing an educational practice and a theory of rhet. that hearken back to the Ciceronian period. Book 10 contains brief appraisals of Gr. and Roman authors as educators and stylistic models; the reading of these models is necessary for the devel. of true eloquence.

Plutarch's essay on "How the Young Man Should Study Poetry" characterizes epic and tragic verse as an introduction to philosophy. Recapitulating earlier philosophical procedures on negating the force of ethically inappropriate verse, he urges readers to offset apparently immoral passages by recalling other passages from the same author—or another—or even emendation. As such, Plutarch provides an answer to Socrates' demonstration of poetic pliability in the *Protagoras*: here it can always be made to address Zeus's concern for human beings. Augustine (354–430 CE) borrows such techniques from cl. authors in *De doctrina christiana* (*On Christian Doctrine*) when instructing his readers on how to interpret apparent contradictions or immoralities in Holy Scripture.

The mysterious Longinus (1st c. CE?) stands outside the cl. trad. in his *Peri hypsous* (*On the Sublime*), concentrating on forms of expression that "transport us with wonder" and "uplift our souls" (ch. 1). Drawing his examples from oratory, poetry, hist., philosophy, and the OT (the author was most likely a Hellenized Jew), the author known as Longinus argues that both natural genius and skill are required for great writing. The *sublime can be achieved only by writers who have the ability to form "grand conceptions" through their nobility of soul; the other sources of this ability are a spirited treatment of the passions, the use of figures of speech and figures of thought, elegant diction, and an elevated style of composition (ch. 8). *Phantasia*—the power of the imagination—is crucial in both the orator and the poet (ch. 15). The true sublime stands the test of different readerships and different eras and sticks in the memory. Longinus suggests that, when we face a topic that demands grandeur, we should ask ourselves how Homer or Plato or Demosthenes or Thucydides might have given it sublimity. Here, as elsewhere in such cl. lists, we see not so much genre crit. as the establishment of the best writer to emulate in each trad. The final chapter (44) is a brief essay on the decline of eloquence, a common 1st-c. CE topic. Longinus casts this in the form of a dialogue with an unnamed philosopher, who (like Tacitus's Maternus in the *Dialogue on Orators*) claims that the lack of political freedom has suppressed the possibility of sublimity. Longinus in his response plays it safe by citing, traditionally, the moral degeneration of the age and its addiction to luxury and pleasure.

**IX. Neoplatonic Poetics.** The Neoplatonists (3d c. CE onward), a school of philosophy founded by Plotinus (204–70 CE), reiterated the philosophical importance of poetry while allegorizing Homer to show his conformity to Plato's thought. Plotinus protested against the Platonic view that poetry was the imitation of a world that was itself an imitation; the arts, he argued, come from the imagination, not from reality (*Enneads* 5.8.1). In his work "On the Cave of the Nymphs," Plotinus's follower Porphyry (ca. 234–305 CE) offered multiple metaphysical interpretations of the Homeric passage in which Odysseus hides guest-presents in a cave in Ithaca (*Odyssey* 13.102ff): e.g., the cave can stand for our world of matter, being dark, rocky, and damp; or for the cosmos, where the nymphs represent the souls who descend to be reborn. This openness to multiple meanings was unusual in antiquity.

Proclus (ca. 412–85 CE) addresses Plato's crits. of poetry in essays 5 and 6 of his commentary on the *Republic*. Essay 6 in particular takes on Plato's attack on Homer in *Republic* 2 and 3, in which he condemns Homer's depiction of the afterlife in Hades, and of Hera seducing Zeus on Mt. Ida; Plotinus reconciles poet and philosopher by showing that Homer's version is a veiled version of Plato's truth. In his essay on *Republic* 10, Proclus offers a general defense of poetry on metaphysical grounds: not all poetry is at three removes from reality. Inspired poetry allegorizes the union of the soul with the One, didactic poetry offers information about the physical world or about ethics, and mimetic poetry is "eikatic" or "phantastic" and shows things in the sensible world as they appear to the human being; only the last, he argues, is the object of Plato's crit. (6:177.7–196.13).

*See* ALEXANDRIANISM, CLASSICISM, CRITICISM, GENRE, GREEK POETRY, LATIN POETRY, RHETORIC AND POETRY.

■ **General**: G.M.A. Grube, *The Greek and Roman Critics* (1965); R. Pfeiffer, *History of Classical Scholar-*

*ship from the Beginnings to the End of the Hellenistic Age* (1968); *Ancient Literary Criticism,* ed. D. A. Russell and M. Winterbottom (1972)—wide range of ancient sources; D. A. Russell, *Criticism in Antiquity* (1981); *CHCL*; *CHLC*, v. 1, ed. G. A. Kennedy (1989); Y. L. Too, *The Idea of Ancient Literary Criticism* (1998); J. Walker, *Rhetoric and Poetics in Antiquity* (2000); J. Farrell, "Classical Genre in Theory and Practice," *NLH* 34 (2003); *Oxford Readings in Ancient Literary Criticism,* ed. A. Laird (2006).

■ **Aristotle**: G. F. Else, *Aristotle's "Poetics": The Argument* (1957); J. Jones, *On Aristotle and Greek Tragedy* (1962); T.C.W. Stinton, "Hamartia in Aristotle and Greek Tragedy," *CQ* 25 (1975); S. Halliwell, *Aristotle's Poetics* (1986); E. Belfiore, *Tragic Pleasures: Aristotle on Plot and Emotion* (1992); *Essays on Aristotle's Poetics,* ed. A. O. Rorty (1992); *Making Sense of Aristotle: Essays in Poetics,* ed. Ø. Andersen and J. Haarberg (2001).

■ **Augustan Age**: J. K. Newman, *Augustus and the New Poetry* (1967); K. Quinn, "The Poet and His Audience in the Augustan Age," *Aufstieg und Niedergang der römischen Welt* 2 (1982); J.E.G. Zetzel, "Re-creating the Canon: Augustan Poetry and the Alexandrian Poet," *CritI* 10 (1983); D. C. Innes, "Augustan Critics," *CHLC*, v. 1, ed. G. A. Kennedy (1989); R. Tarrant, "Ovid and Ancient Literary History," *The Cambridge Companion to Ovid*, ed. P. Hardie (2002).

■ **Cicero and the Rhetorical Critics**: A. D. Leeman, *Orationis Ratio: The Stylistic Theories and Practice of the Roman Orators, Historians, and Philosophers* (1963); D. M. Schenkeveld, *Studies in Demetrius, "On Style"* (1964); G. A. Kennedy, *The Art of Rhetoric in the Roman World* (1972); L. P. Wilkinson, "Cicero and the Relationship of Oratory to Literature," *CHCL*, v. 2; M. Heath, "Dionysius of Halicarnassus on Imitation," *Hermes* 117 (1989).

■ **Greek Poetics, General and Preplatonic**: C. Segal, "Gorgias and the Psychology of the Logos," *Harvard Studies in Classical Philology* 66 (1962); W. J. Verdenius, "The Principles of Greek Literary Criticism," *Mnemosyne* 36 (1963); R. Harriott, *Poetry and Criticism before Plato* (1969); C. Macleod, "Homer on Poetry and the Poetry of Homer," *Collected Essays* (1983); G. B. Walsh, *The Varieties of Enchantment* (1984); N. Richardson, "Pindar and Later Literary Criticism in Antiquity," *Proceedings of the Liverpool Latin Seminar* 5 (1985); M. Heath, *The Poetics of Greek Tragedy* (1987); and *Unity in Greek Poetics* (1989); S. Goldhill, *The Poet's Voice: Essays on Poetics and Greek Literature* (1991); *Homer's Ancient Readers: The Hermeneutics of Greek Epic's Earliest Exegetes,* ed. R. Lamberton and J. J. Keaney (1992); L. Pratt, *Lying and Poetry from Homer to Pindar* (1993); *Greek Literary Theory after Aristotle,* ed. J.G.J. Abbenes, S. R. Slings, I. Sluiter (1995); M. Detienne, *The Masters of Truth in Archaic Greece*, trans. J. Lloyd (1996); A. Ford, *The Origins of Criticism: Literary Culture and Poetic Theory in Classical Greece* (2002); G. M. Ledbetter, *Poetics before Plato* (2003).

■ **Hellenistic Philosophers and Hellenistic Poetry**: P. De Lacy, "Stoic Views of Poetry," *AJP* 69 (1948); N. A. Greenberg, "The Use of Poiema and Poiesis," *Harvard Studies in Classical Philology* 65 (1961); G. Hutchinson, *Hellenistic Poetry* (1988); G. A. Kennedy and D. C. Innes, "Hellenistic Literary and Philosophical Scholarship," *CHLC*, v. 1, ed. G. A. Kennedy (1989); G. Most, "Cornutus and Stoic Allegoresis: A Preliminary Report," *Aufstieg und Niedergang der römischen Welt* 2 (1989); M. L. Colish, *The Stoic Tradition from Antiquity to the Early Middle Ages,* 2d ed. (1991); E. Asmis, "Neoptolemus and the Classification of Poetry," *CP* 87 (1992); M. C. Nussbaum, "Poetry and the Passions: Two Stoic Views," *Passions and Perceptions,* ed. J. Barnes and M. Nussbaum (1993); J. I. Porter, "Stoic Morals and Poetics in Philodemus," *Cronache Ercolanesi* (1994); E. Asmis, "Epicurean Poetics," *Philodemus and Poetry: Poetic Theory and Practice in Lucretius, Philodemus and Horace,* ed. D. Obbink (1995); *Metaphor, Allegory, and the Classical Tradition,* ed. G. Boys-Stones (2003).

■ **Horace**: C. O. Brink, *Horace on Poetry,* 3 v. (1963–82); K. Reckford, *Horace* (1969); B. Fischer, *Shifting Paradigms: New Approaches to Horace's "Ars Poetica"* (1991); M. Fuhrmann, *Die Dichtungstheorie der Antike: Aristoteles, Horaz, "Longin": eine Einführung* (1992); K. Freudenburg, *The Walking Muse: Horace on the Theory of Satire* (1993); *Philodemus and Poetry: Poetic Theory and Practice in Lucretius, Philodemus and Horace,* ed. D. Obbink (1995).

■ **Neoplatonists**: J. A. Coulter, *The Literary Microcosm: Theories of Interpretation of the Later Neoplatonists* (1976); A.D.R Sheppard, *Studies on the Fifth and Sixth Essays of Proclus' Commentary on the Republic* (1980); R. Lamberton, *Homer the Theologian: Neoplatonist Allegorical Reading and the Growth of the Epic Tradition* (1986).

■ **Plato**: G. F. Else, "'Imitation' in the Fifth Century," *CP* 53 (1958); L. Golden, "Plato's Concept of Mimesis," *BJA* 15 (1975); A. Cameron, *Plato's Affair with Tragedy* (1978); C. Griswold, "The Ideas and Criticism of Poetry in Plato's Republic, Book 10," *Journal of the History of Philosophy* 19 (1981); *Plato on Beauty, Wisdom, and the Arts,* ed. J. Moravscik and P. Temko (1982); J. A. Elias, *Plato's Defence of Poetry* (1984); E. Belfiore, "A Theory of Imitation in Plato's Republic," *TAPA* 114 (1984); G. F. Else, *Plato and Aristotle on Poetry,* ed. P. Burian (1986); G.R.F. Ferrari, *Listening to the Cicadas: A Study of Plato's "Phaedrus"* (1987); S. Rosen, *The Quarrel between Philosophy and Poetry* (1988); G.R.F. Ferrari, "Plato and Poetry," *CHLC*, v. 1, ed. G. A. Kennedy (1989).

■ **Roman Empire**: C. P. Segal, "UYOS and the Problem of Cultural Decline," *Harvard Studies in Classical Philology* 64 (1959); D. A. Russell, "Longinus Revisited," *Mnemosyne* 34 (1981); F. Ahl, "The Art of Safe Criticism in Greece and Rome," *AJP* 105 (1984); E. Fantham, "Latin Criticism of the Early Empire," *CHLC*; S. Bartsch, *Actors in the Audience* (1994); A. Schiesaro, *The Passions in Play: Thyestes and the Dynamics of Senecan Drama* (2003); D. Konstan, "The Birth of the Reader: Plutarch as Literary Critic," *Scholia* 13 (2004); D. S. Levene, "Tacitus' Dialogus as Literary History," *TAPA* 134 (2004); G. A. Staley, *Seneca and the Idea of Tragedy* (2010).

■ **Roman Poetics**: K. Quinn, *Texts and Contexts: The Roman Writers and Their Audience* (1979); C. Martindale, *Redeeming the Text: Latin Poetry and the Hermeneutics of Reception* (1993); S. Hinds, *Allusion and Intertext: Dynamics of Appropriation in Roman Poetry* (1998); L. Edmunds, *Intertextuality and the Reading of Roman Poetry* (2001); S. M. Goldberg, *Constructing Literature in the Roman Republic: Poetry and Its Reception* (2005).

S. Bartsch

# CLASSICAL PROSODY

I. Quantity in Greek and Latin
II. Greek
III. Latin

**I. Quantity in Greek and Latin.** Gr. and Lat. prosody is based on a phonemic distinction between the *durations of syllables and the articulation of that distinction into a conventional system of long and short syllables, called *quantity. Syllables containing a long vowel or a diphthong are long; syllables containing a short vowel not followed by a consonant are short. If a syllable is closed (i.e., ends in a consonant), both Gr. and Lat. also treat it as long. Allen's terms *heavy syllable* and *light syllable* (Allen 1973), although not standard in cl. scholarship, are useful in distinguishing the quantity of syllables from the quantity of vowels.

Gr. and Lat. *meters are quantitative, in that they impose requirements on the sequences of long and short syllables. Though most ancient verse forms show, in addition, some trace of the operation of other principles (syllable counting and accent, discussed below), this condition does not alter the fact that the essential rhythmical nature of a piece of Gr. or Lat. poetry is determined by the ordering of its longs and shorts.

While the syllable is the basic unit of cl. verse, lines can be conceived as sequences of three types of more abstract positions, termed *long* (–) and *short* (◡), which must be filled with long and short syllables, respectively, and *anceps, or "indifferent," position (x), which can be filled by either. Thus, the *iambic *metron schematized as x – ◡ – can be realized as either a long-long-short-long or a short-long-short-long sequence.

Some meters allow *substitutions between two shorts and a single long syllable. While the duration of two shorts was probably not phonetically equal to the duration of a single long, such *equivalence is grounded in the phonologies of the two langs.; the stress/accent systems of both Gr. and Lat. are organized around the same equivalence.

Such substitutions make patterns in two distinct ways. *Resolution allows a long position to be realized with two short syllables, with restrictions (e.g., a word boundary cannot intervene between them; similar restrictions on resolution are found in other langs., incl. Eng.). E.g., the iambic metron x – ◡ – sequence may, under some circumstances, be filled with a long-short-short-short-long sequence, with the first two shorts in resolution. On the other hand, in the dactylic *hex-

ameter and other meters, some ◡◡ sequences, termed *biceps*, may be realized as a single long syllable, by a process called *contraction*. That contraction is distinct from resolution is shown by the fact that the prohibition of a word boundary between two shorts in resolution does not apply to the two shorts of a biceps.

The study of Gr. and Lat. prosody has a long trad. in cl. scholarship. Since the last decades of the 20th c., it has enjoyed a revival of interest in mod. ling., where the devel. of new theoretical models of prosodic structure can be fruitfully tested on the rich empirical material provided by the cl. langs.

Gr. and Lat. versification is by no means unique among the world's poetic systems, even if better known in the Eur. scholarly trad. Quantity plays a role in many other langs. with a phonemic length contrast, e.g., in *Arabic poetry, *Sanskrit poetry, *Turkish poetry, Finnish poetry (see FINLAND, POETRY OF), and others.

**II. Greek.** The complexity of Gr. versification is due to the confluence of several distinct trads. into a heterogeneous whole. The earliest attested Gr. poetry bears witness to at least three distinct systems: *Aeolic, Ionian, and Dorian, each with its own repertoire of meters and genres and each associated with a distinct local dialect of Gr. The three trads. share the close association among poetry and instrumental *performance, *song, and *dance.

The Aeolic trad., represented by the lyrics of Sappho and Alcaeus, is the most conservative. Aeolic meters maintain a constant syllable count, as they recognize no substitutions of a long syllable for two shorts or vice versa. The quantitative requirements are often relaxed at the beginning of the line, in the so-called aeolic base (xx). These features are similar enough to those of Vedic Sanskrit to suggest derivation from a common IE ancestor—essentially a syllable-counting versification based on 8-, 11-, and 12-syllable lines. Quantity in IE was regulated only at line end. While Gr. extended quantitative requirements to the rest of the line, the line-initial aeolic base is an archaism symptomatic of a conservative IE meter.

The eight-syllable pattern most frequently encountered, here and in all subsequent aeolic, is what later came to be called the *glyconic ( x x – ◡ ◡ – ◡ –); seven-syllable patterns combine with iambic or *trochaic to yield the two most famous aeolic forms, the *alcaic and *sapphic hendecasyllable (respectively, x – ◡ – x – ◡ ◡ – ◡ – and – ◡ – x – ◡ ◡ – ◡ – x ). The four- and three-syllable patterns are the familiar iamb ( x – ◡ – ), trochee ( – ◡ – x ), *ionic ( – – ◡ ◡ and ◡ ◡ – –), *choriamb ( – ◡ ◡ –), and *dactyl ( – ◡ ◡). Dactylic and choriambic are inserted rather than prefixed or suffixed to other forms, yielding, e.g., the lesser *asclepiad ( x x – ◡ ◡ – – ◡ ◡ – ◡ –) through combination of choriambic with glyconic. Aeolic poetry may be stichic, or consisting of two or three-line *stanzas repeated in the poem, and recurring from poem to poem. The sapphic stanza, although typically printed in four lines in mod. eds., in fact consists of three lines—two sapphic hendecasyllables followed by an expansion of the same pattern (an *aaA* structure).

In contrast to the Aeolic, the Ionian trad. is characterized by greater regularity and avoidance of non-periodic sequences such as – ◡ ◡ – ◡ –. Resolution and contraction are commonly used. The dactylic hexameter, used in the epics of Homer and in Hesiod, consists of a sequence of five dactyls (– ◡ ◡), followed by a shortened disyllabic *foot (– x). All dactyls can be substituted by *spondees (– –) by contraction; spondees in the fifth foot are rare. *Caesura typically occurs in the third foot, either after the long or the first short position. Other restrictions on the location of word boundaries, such as the avoidance of a word-final spondaic foot, are tendencies in Homer but become strict rules in the Hellenistic poets such as Callimachus. The dactylic hexameter was also used in the *elegiac distich, where it alternates with a so-called *pentameter line consisting of two – ◡ ◡ – ◡ ◡ – sequences.

Iambic and trochaic meters originate in early Ionian poetry of Archilochus and become the standard meters of dramatic verse in *tragedy and *comedy. Iambic trimeter (x – ◡ – x | – ◡ – x – ◡ –) and trochaic tetrameter catalectic (– ◡ – x – ◡ – x | – ◡ – x – ◡ –) were by far the most common meters. Both meters typically require a word break after the anceps position of the second metron, counting from the end of the line (caesura in the trimeter and *diaeresis in the tetrameter), although other locations of the break are possible. The classification of the trimeter as iambic and the tetrameter as trochaic is partly artificial; both meters can be conceived as derived from an undifferentiated periodic sequence (. . . x – ◡ – x . . . —see EPIPLOKE). If the meters are "right-aligned," various constraints on word boundaries, incl. the caesura/diaeresis, are located in the same place in the lines, suggesting that the grouping into iambs and trochees does not reflect their true structure.

Stricter iambic and trochaic meters employ Porson's law, a prohibition of a long syllable preceding a long-short-long word at the end of the line. Some scholars have interpreted this and other such restrictions as due to the presence of stress on word-final long syllables in Gr., in addition to *pitch accent.

Resolution of long positions becomes more common in later drama; plays of Euripides can be dated by the frequency of resolution, which rises in the later plays. Comic meters employ a curious hybrid system, where certain short positions are partial *acipitia*—they can be filled with a short syllable or with two short syllables in resolution, but not a single long.

The use of the meters is typically stichic; where stanzas are used, such as in Archilochus and Hipponax, they consist of no more than three lines.

The Dorian trad., represented by Stesichorus, Alcman, and Ibycus, admits nonperiodic sequences to a far greater extent than Ionian but is also less archaic than Aeolic in allowing resolution and contraction. Dactylic meters such as the tetrameter are the most widely used, usually mixed with iambic cola; *anapests and *cretics are also found. The late archaic poets Pindar, Bacchylides, and Simonides began to integrate the separate trads. of Gr. verse.

The Dorian poets' greatest innovation was in the rich devel. of strophic composition in repeated stanzas. There is a fairly steady tendency for the repeated sequence to become longer and more complicated. The maximum number of identical metra or cola that can be linked together to produce it increases, yielding what ancient metrists called *systems rather than lines; its components may be set off from each other as separate paragraphs or *periods. The latter are sometimes different from each other in their basic rhythmic structure and may be composed of contrasting subcomponents. When the component periods are sufficiently long and exhibit an *aab* pattern, it is customary to regard the larger repeated sequence as a triad divided into *strophe, *antistrophe, and *epode, with metrical *responsion linking the parts. This is esp. true of texts composed to be sung and danced by a *chorus rather than for simpler, monodic performance by a singer accompanied on the lyre or flute. (Stesichorus, the traditional name of the 6th-c. inventor of triadic composition, actually means "chorus master.") The tendency toward increasing length and complexity ends only with the Hellenistic period, by which time poetry and music have begun to go their separate ways.

The specific needs of Attic drama account for most of the 5th-c. innovations in prosodic technique. March anapests are taken over to accompany the entrances and exits of the chorus or, in comedy, formalized debate between protagonists. Musical holds and rests and, in longer stanzas and periods, a regularized colon structure make possible a heightening of dramatic intensity and emphasis. Most pervasively, repeating stanzaic or triadic composition is abandoned. The last devel., which makes lyric composition a series of single poetic sentences or paragraphs, is usually associated with a late 5th-c. BCE innovation, the virtuoso song for a professional soloist, whether in drama or *dithyramb. But even the earliest drama that survives (Aeschylus's *Persae*) has already moved in this direction by limiting itself mainly to single repetitions of a given stanzaic pattern followed, in longer compositions, by further single repetitions of completely different patterns—*aa' bb' cc'*, etc., rather than the *a a' a''* (or, with triads, *aab a'a'b' a''a''b''* of earlier lyric).

The prominence of compositions for professional soloists is symptomatic of how the devel. of music was beginning to outstrip that of poetry, and the resulting separation of the two arts is the main reason for the transformation of Gr. versification that took place in the 4th c. New techniques of vocal and musical embellishment were making the inherited multiplicity of verse forms based on the ordering of long and short syllables irrelevant or even distracting. Poets who wrote for performances by specialists in these techniques tended to confine themselves to a monotonous succession of durationally equivalent metra not unlike the bars of mod. Western music. Other poets, forerunners of the Alexandrians, turned to the task of adapting the hexameters, elegiacs, and trimeters of earlier recited verse to the needs of a reading rather than a listening public. All but the simplest stanzas disappear from such compositions for readers, though occasionally an isolated sequence of syllables will be lifted from an earlier stanzaic context and repeated stichically to form a "new" verse form, often named after its supposed inventor: glyconic, asclepiad, *phalaecean, *sotadean. *visual poetry, written for eye rather than ear, now makes its first appearance.

**III. Latin.** The earliest known Lat. meter, *Saturnian, was probably accentual rather than quantitative, although the small corpus of surviving lines does not allow for definitive analysis. This native trad. was amalgamated with Gr. imports in the late 3d c. BCE, resulting in a complex hybrid system that shared features of both quantitative and *accentual verse. The comedies of Plautus employ the same dramatic meters as their Gr. predecessors—iambic *senarius (corresponding to Gr. trimeter) and trochaic *septenarius (corresponding to Gr. tetrameter), and a complex system of lyric *cantica* or sung verse. The Plautine iambs and trochees relax many of the Gr. restrictions but introduce new ones not found in Gr. meters. Except for the last metron of the line, Plautus allows a long syllable to fill what in Gr. would be a short position, i.e., the Plautine iamb is x – x –, rather than x – ⌣ –. On the other hand, complex restrictions on the location of word boundaries suggest that, in addition to quantity, the meters also regulated word accent. Although the question is vexed and subject to debate, it is clear that the Gr. meters were modified to make their use more natural in a lang. whose phonology differed from that of Gr.

Two such differences are relevant to meter. First, short syllables are much less frequent in Lat. than Gr., making it more difficult to require metrical positions to contain a short syllable, as is evident in Plautus. Contraction in dactylic meters, by necessity, is also far more frequent in Lat. The second difference involves the nature of Gr. and Lat. accent. Gr. accent was most likely solely realized by pitch and played no role in any cl. meter; whether Gr. had stress in addition to accent is subject to debate. Lat. accent, on the other hand, was based not on pitch but on intensity; such accent in other langs. typically is relevant to meter. Whether that was the case in Lat. is the central unresolved question in the field. On the one hand, there are clear statistical tendencies showing alignment between metrically strong positions and accented syllables. On the other hand, Lat. accent is preferentially placed on long syllables, and since the meters are quantitative, the attraction of accent to strong positions might be an illusion. The strongest argument in favor of the role of accent in Lat. verse is that, in quantitatively nondescript sequences of syllables, such as sequences of long syllables in Plautus or in the dactylic hexameter, accent seems to play an organizing role. The result is a system in which stress patterns now reinforce, now supplement, or clash with quantitative ones to such an extent that *rhythm cannot avoid having an added dimension, a counterpoint between the quantitative and accentual properties of the text. One of its essential ingredients is the tension between harmony and dissonance, i.e., expectation fulfilled and expectation frustrated, which is largely foreign to Gr.

The verse that went furthest in this direction is Plautus's favorite line, the trochaic septenarius. Though it corresponds to the Gr. tetrameter, the septenarius is occasionally referred to by a purely Lat. name, *versus quadratus*, and it has the distinction of being the only important cl. form that continues to be important—once suitably modified—in the *accentual-syllabic versification of med. Lat. Some metrists are inclined to see here a "substrate" phenomenon: a partially Hellenized native meter bearing witness to a subliterary type of Lat. versification whose accentual basis made it entirely different from any considered in this article and that was ultimately destined to provide the basis for all med. and mod. Western prosody.

The aliterary, performance-oriented side of the trad. is probably reflected in the cantica of Plautine comedy, though many cantica are considerably more complex than anything in the Gr. texts that survive from the period. After Plautus, the literary side dominates, as the Romans confine themselves to forms already well established in Gr. The metrical constraints become more rigid and more purely quantitative. The variability of the iambic and trochaic meters in Plautus—the large number of various substitutions, liberal use of resolution, and other effects—is unparalleled in later Lat. verse forms. In the lyric forms, only Horace and Seneca go beyond the Hellenistic repertory—either toward a much closer and more extensive reproduction of stanzas found in Alcaeus and Sappho (Horace) or toward entirely new structures produced by excerpting and recombining lines and line sections from those Horatian reproductions (Seneca).

While the meters of the cl. age imitate their Gr. models closely, the native Lat. tendencies still show through. The basic structure of dactylic hexameter is identical to that of Gr.—five dactylic feet with possible contraction, followed by – x. Yet, the meter underwent an evolution in Lat. that suggests an increasing attention to native phonology. The earlier poets (Ennius and Lucretius) imitated the quantitative pattern of Gr., with few other restrictions. Virgil, Propertius, Tibullus, and esp. Ovid impose constraints on the location of word boundaries usually interpreted in terms of word accent: agreement between the accentual and quantitative prominence in the *cadence (last two feet) of the line and clash at the caesura in the third foot—tension between accent and quantity culminates at the caesura and is resolved in the end of the line. This pattern becomes nearly absolute in Ovid and later poets.

The fate of Gr. versification in Lat. is yet another illustration of the truth of Horace's famous dictum on captive Greece as captor, *Graecia capta ferum victorem cepit*. It is only with the radical transformation of both ancient cultures that the captured Muse of the conqueror reasserts her independence.

*See* ALEXANDRIANISM, GREEK POETRY, LATIN POETRY.

■ **Bibliographies**: "Métrique, rythmique, prosodie," *L'Année philologique* 1– (1927–); A. M. Dale, "Greek Metric 1936–57," *Lustrum* 2 (1957); L.P.E. Parker, "Greek Metric, 1957–70," *Lustrum* 15 (1970); D. W. Packard and T. Meyers, *A Bibliography of Homeric*

*Scholarship* (1974); F. Cuppaiolo, *Bibliografia della Metrica Latina* (1995).

■ **General**: A. T. Cole, "Classical Greek and Latin," Wimsatt; Allen.

■ **Greek**: J. W. White, *The Verse of Greek Comedy* (1912); A. Meillet, *Les Origines Indo-Européennes des Mètres Grecques* (1923); Maas,; W. B. Stanford, *The Sound of Greek* (1967); Dale; A. M. Dale, *Collected Papers* (1969); E. Wahlström, *Accentual Responsion in Greek Strophic Poetry* (1970); A. M. Dale, *Metrical Analyses of Tragic Choruses* (1971); G. Nagy, *Comparative Studies in Greek and Indic Meter* (1974); West; A. M. Devine and L. D. Stephens, *Language and Metre: Resolution, Porson's Bridge, and Their Prosodic Basis* (1984); A. Prince, "Metrical Forms," *Phonetics and Phonology I: Rhythm and Meter*, ed. P. Kiparsky and G. Youmans (1989); W. S. Allen, *Vox graeca* (1987); A. T. Cole, *Epiploke* (1988); A. M. Devine and L. D. Stephens, "Stress in Greek?" *TAPA* 115 (1985), and *The Prosody of Greek Speech* (1994); C. Golston, "The Phonology of Classical Greek Meter," *JL* 38 (2000); C. Golston and T. Riad, "The Phonology of Greek Lyric Meter," *JL* 41 (2005).

■ **Latin**: W. M. Lindsay, *Early Latin Verse* (1922); C. G. Cooper, *Introduction to the Latin Hexameter* (1952); L. P. Wilkinson, *Golden Latin Artistry* (1963); D. S. Raven, *Latin Metre* (1965); H. Drexler, *Einführung in die Römische Metrik* (1967); C. Questa, *Introduzione alla Metrica di Plauto* (1967); L. Braun, *Die Cantica des Plautus* (1970); W. S. Allen, *Vox latina* (1978); E. Pulgram, *Latin-Romance Phonology: Prosodics and Metrics* (1975); A. M. Devine and L. D. Stephens, "Latin Prosody and Meter: Brevis Brevians," *CP* 75 (1980); J. Soubiran, *Essai sur la Versification dramatique des Romains* (1988); J. Parsons, "A New Approach to the Saturnian Verse and Its Relation to Latin Prosody," *TAPA* 129 (1999); B. W. Fortson, *Language and Rhythm in Plautus* (2008).

                    T.V.F. BROGAN; A. T. COLE; L. BLUMENFELD

**CLASSICISM.** The term *classicism* carries a cluster of different but interrelated meanings and so presents some challenges of definition. These stem from the varied meanings of the word *classic*, which can mean first class (the word's original, etymological meaning), standard, exemplary, or (in the lang. of consumer culture) obsolete. The description of Greco-Roman antiquity as the cl. period and of the canon of Greco-Roman lit. as the classics was not fully naturalized until the 19th c. and derives from the enormous cultural authority granted to surviving Greco-Roman artifacts. The Eng. word *classicism* is a 19th-c. coinage, used initially in the context of commenting upon culture wars in France and Germany that placed classicism—understood primarily as an aesthetic and political program devoted to the re-creation of an ideal of social harmony and artistic purity associated with cl. Greece—against *romanticism. Of course, romanticism, in Germany and France as in England and elsewhere, likewise featured a robust strain of Hellenism, and it is helpful to think of the opposition between classicism and romanticism in late 18th- and early 19th-c. Europe as a debate within the romantic movement over the importance of formal imitation and restraint that is differently inflected, in each case, by the cultural legacy of prior deployments of the cl. trad. Weimar classicism, the social and aesthetic movement now associated primarily with Friedrich Schiller and J. W. Goethe, is part of the larger movement of Ger. romanticism. But in France, which had a stronger and more culturally authoritative trad. of formal neoclassicism (as represented, for instance, by the tragedies of Jean Racine and codified for poetry in Nicolas Boileau's *L'Art poétique* [1674]), romanticism was received as a challenge to classicism's established sense of *decorum.

By the early 20th c., the binary opposition between classicism and romanticism had hardened, and modernist writers like Ezra Pound and T. S. Eliot created their own form of classicism as a reaction to what they perceived as the excesses of the romantic movement. T. E. Hulme's essay "Romanticism and Classicism" (pub. in 1924, though written more than a decade earlier) distinguishes sharply between two opposed ideas of art, politics, and human nature, arguing that where the romantic sees humans as inherently good, believes in progress, and celebrates subjective creativity, the classicist is conservative, sees humans as flawed, and regards trad. as a useful stay against the debilitating weakness of the individual. Though Hulme refers admiringly to Horace (a perennial favorite of critics and writers who believe in the value of decorum), he is not primarily concerned with cl. antiquity as such. But modernist classicism also involves a reevaluation of artifacts from cl. antiquity as offering artistic alternatives to romanticism. Eliot, whose attitude toward the importance of trad. is broadly cognate with Hulme's classicism, argues for the primary importance of cl. langs. and lits. in his late essay "Modern Education and the Classics" (1932), for instance, and an idealizing fondness for fragments of lyric poetry from the *Greek Anthology*—a poetry stripped of its subjective author and social context by time—is one of the influences behind the *imagism of modernist writers like Pound and H.D.

Because it entered critical discourse framed by its opposition to romanticism, classicism as a term of art in cultural or poetic crit. can still denote formal precision, adherence to trad., artistic conservatism, simplicity, and restraint. And in lit. hists. of France and England, one often encounters the term designating artistic movements (Fr. classicism of the 17th and early 18th cs., and Eng. neoclassicism of the 18th) that put a premium on adherence to formal regularity as well as imitation of cl. antiquity. But classicism also has a larger, second meaning that we can understand by analogy with parallel critical terms like medievalism or Hellenism. In this broader sense, classicism refers to the appropriation and redeployment of cl. antiquity and to ways in which ideas about cl. Greece and Rome have been shaped by and circulated within subsequent cultural milieus. The hundred years' war between classicism and romanticism can be understood as an episode in the long hist. of classicism in this latter sense, since its skirmishes involved both a romantic reaction to earlier, neoclassical ideas of art and a series of competing ideas about the meaning of ancient artifacts as the recovered traces of a primeval, Hellenic Western culture.

If we take the term to refer to the hist. of reception and appropriation pertaining to artifacts and concepts associated with cl. Greece and Rome, then it is obvious that classicism as a category depends on a prior idea of cl. antiquity as a discrete period. Classicism, therefore, depends on a notion of historical period that is usually understood to be a 14th-c. It. innovation and that is often credited, above all, to Petrarch (1304–74). Petrarch had a lifelong interest in recuperating the lit. of cl. Rome, but his essential innovation, for the purposes of understanding classicism as a concept, resides in the role he played in creating and disseminating a new idea of historical period according to which everything from the decline of the Roman Empire through the 14th-c. project of humanist recovery of the classics could be thought of as the dark ages and the period of the humanist project itself could be understood as a renaissance, or rebirth, of cl. learning. This idea of hist., in effect, creates the concept of the classics—Greco-Roman antiquity—with which we are familiar today. Lat. was the lang. of scholars, though, and knowledge of Gr. was comparatively rare, so the focus of Ren. classicism is primarily on Roman antiquity, with the secondary focus on cl. Greece often filtered through the lens of Roman philhellenism.

Petrarch's historiographical innovation is in many ways a flawed characterization of the hist. of cl. reception. Med. Europe was certainly not without its own robust trads. of reading and imitating many of what we today would think of as cl. philosophical and literary texts, often in highly sophisticated ways designed to make sense of the problematic moral status of pagan lit. within a Christian world. One obvious example here is the way Dante imagined Virgil as his guide during the *Inferno* and *Purgatorio* portions of his early 14th-c. *Divine Comedy* but required a suitably Christian guide for the *Paradiso*. Another is the 13th-c. *Ovid Moralisé*, a massive poem and accompanying commentary built on the scaffolding of Ovid's *Metamorphoses*, whose project is to reconcile Ovidian poetry with Christian theology. Moreover, though Petrarch and his followers did make enormous contributions to the philological project of recovering texts from cl. antiquity, they were by no means the first to do so: lit. hists. of Italy often speak of 13th-c. prehumanists, men like Lovato dei Lovati (1240–1309), a Paduan judge sometimes credited with originating the philological project of recovering cl. lit., or his disciple Albertino Mussato (1261–1329), whose Lat., Senecan play *Ecerinis* (1315) is the postclassical era's earliest secular tragedy. Nevertheless, the idea of renaissance evokes the periodization upon which subsequent classicism rests, and so the hist. of classicism properly begins with the invention and spread of ideas concerning hist. and the importance of Rome popularized in 14th-c. Italy.

Though humanists, following Petrarch, were able to conceive of their era optimistically, as a moment of cultural rebirth and recovery, their sense of historical period also put new emphasis on the linked problems of historical loss, ruin, and anachronism. Cl. Rome, understood as a cultural high-water mark, existed for them only in variously decontextualized or fragmented forms: in architectural ruins and in surviving texts and artifacts separated from an original cultural context that was, in turn, impossible to assimilate fully to a Christian, Eur. world. Because Ren. writers operated according to ideas about education and creativity that put a premium on the importance of *imitation, the humanist conception of cl. Rome (as both exemplary and in some sense lost) had an enormous impact on all aspects of the period's intellectual life. We can see this in the ideas and practices governing Ren. poetry and poetics. As Greene has shown in *The Light in Troy*, self-styled Ren. writers from Petrarch onward found themselves attempting to imitate literary models conceptualized, simultaneously, as authoritative classics and as traces of a lost and distant cultural moment; this, in turn, meant that the project of imitating cl. texts shaded into the more complex task of recreating them anew in the context of a strong sense of anachronism. We see in Ren. poetry a good deal of imitation and trans. of authoritative cl. models, periodic vogues for forms like epic and ode associated with writers like Virgil and Horace, and, of course, innumerable allusions to cl. texts. But the project of recreating cl. literary authority for a present understood to be discontinuous with the cl. world also creates space for innovation, resulting in the flourishing of ambitious vernacular lits. and (as Greene suggests) a sophisticated interest in deracinated but endlessly allusive literary self-fashioning that finds its characteristic expression in lyric poetry after Petrarch. Petrarch's own poetic career is illustrative: his *Africa*, a Lat. hexameter epic on the subject of the Second Punic War, exemplifies the period's imitative literary classicism, but he was (and is) better known for his profoundly innovative and influential sonnet sequence, the *Canzoniere*, which is written in the It. vernacular and which is self-consciously preoccupied with the creation of a poetic speaker whose laureate authority is constituted self-referentially by the sequence itself.

The influence of It. humanism spread all over Europe, driven by the international commerce in books and ideas; but they were absorbed at different rates in different places, and, of course, they were inflected differently by confessional, political, and other factors in each locale. It is conventional in literary and intellectual hist. to speak of the Ren. as a 15th-to-16th-c. phenomenon in Fr.-, Sp.-, and Ger.-speaking Europe, e.g., but as a 16th-to-17th-c. phenomenon in England. In all cases, though, the humanist impulse to recover and emulate the classics fused with political or cultural ambitions—the desire to imitate Roman might and the desire to elevate one's own vernacular. The paradigmatic statement of what this means for poetry and poetics may be Joachim du Bellay's 1549 treatise *La Deffence et illustration de la langue françoyse* (*Defense and Enrichment of the French Language*), which argued that Fr. authors should emulate cl. models but should do so not by writing in Lat. or by slavishly replicating cl.

literary forms but rather by fully digesting and so re-creating cl. achievements while writing in Fr. in order to cultivate and ennoble their own native lang. Du Bellay's treatise was meant as a kind of party paper or manifesto for an influential and ambitious group of poets, including most famously Pierre de Ronsard, who have since come to be known as the *Pléiade and who helped to establish an exceptionally strong trad. of classicism in France. But similar ideals and ambitions are also expressed regarding other vernaculars and national trads. throughout the Ren. Ren. classicism, all over Europe, is about emulation in each of its primary senses: both the imitation of and the attempt to compete with cl. attainments.

Local variations notwithstanding, this basic paradigm helps to explain a great deal about the progress and devel. of Eur. classicism through the first half of the 18th c. On the one hand, the canon of the classics provided a shared cultural reference point for cultural and political elites all over western Europe. But, on the other, the goal of matching cl. culture, or of appropriating the mantle of cl. civilization or Roman might for one's own people, continued to be a motor for artistic innovation. Pronounced devels. in Eur. classicism in this period are typically expressions of cultural self-assertion associated with historical moments in which various monarchies or nations experience eras of unusual wealth and power. The brands of classicism they produce are, therefore, often best understood as forms of cultural imperialism designed to make competitive assertions about the attainments of their respective creators. Eras of political consolidation and military expansion in Hapsburg Spain (esp. 16th and early 17th cs.) and the France of Louis xiv (esp. late 17th and early 18th cs.) saw corresponding periods of classically oriented artistic magnificence, as monarchs and other patrons encouraged art, lit., and architecture designed to lay claim upon the cultural centrality and imperial power associated with the cl. world. In England, military success and the wealth associated with colonial expansion and the slave trade helped fuel a cultural self-confidence that found characteristic artistic expression in the neoclassicism of the so-called Augustan Age: the era of John Dryden (1631–1700) and Alexander Pope (1688–1744), each of whom was a notable trans. of cl. lit. into elegant Eng. couplets. Dryden translated, among a great many other cl. texts, Virgil's *Aeneid*; Pope became wealthy from subscription sales of his trans. of Homer.

The characteristic early mod. tension between reverence for the classics and the imperatives of cultural self-assertion is perhaps most perfectly manifested in the late 17th and early 18th c. battle of ancients and moderns that was carried out simultaneously in England and France (see QUERELLE DES ANCIENS ET DES MODERNES). The catalysts for this debate (which readers of Eng. poetry will recognize from Jonathan Swift's satirical treatment in "The Battle of the Books" [1704]) were arguments presented by writers like Bernard le Bovier de Fontenelle (1657–1757) and Sir William Temple (1628–99) about the relative superiority of

mod. thought and culture to those of the ancients. These arguments, self-evidently expressions of early-Enlightenment optimism about the progressive potential of science and reason, were countered by writers like Boileau who reasserted the importance for contemp. culture of imitating cl. models. Strikingly, one can see in these debates early, preromantic intimations of the binary opposition between conservative classicism and progressive romanticism that later finds expression in Fr. literary culture of the 19th c. and in the early 20th-c. writings of Hulme and others (see PREROMANTICISM).

The decisive shift in 18th-c. classicism involved a fundamental reevaluation of the relationship between cl. Greece and Rome championed above all by the Ger. art historian J. J. Winckelmann (1717–68). Before Winckelmann, Eur. classicism operated according to a synoptic view of the classics, one within which mod. writers could draw upon the specific cultural associations of cl. Greece or Rome without jeopardizing an overall conception of cl. excellence shared across the entire period of Greco-Roman antiquity. Winckelmann—and esp. his influential book *Geschichte der Kunst des Alterthums* (The History of the Art of Antiquity), pub. in 1764 and soon trans. into Fr., Eng., and It.—treated Roman art as a pale copy of a more vibrant, original Gr. artistry and thus heralded in a new model of classicism as, primarily, Hellenism. This innovation sparked a Eur. fashion for all things Gr. that lasted well into the 19th c. and undergirded a new model of classicism built upon an idealized picture of the purity and balance of Gr. art and culture with which it became possible to denigrate postclassical art imitative of Roman models as decadent, impure, or *baroque. Indeed, the word *baroque*, from the Port. *barroco*—a jeweler's term for an irregularly shaped pearl—entered the Eng. lang. in tandem with Winckelmann's influence and was used to describe postclassical devels. in art and architecture (esp. in Roman Catholic counties, though also in Germany) that, though they often strove to imitate and better Roman artistic models, had come to be seen as misshapen or overly ornamented from the perspective of the new, Hellenistic ideal of cl. simplicity and balance.

More broadly, the shift in thinking precipitated by Wicklemann set up Greece and Rome as competing cultural models, so that, for the first time, the cultural authority of cl. antiquity could be marshaled against classicism itself. This is part of what we see in the 19th-c. opposition between romanticism and classicism, where romantic writers like John Keats or Lord Byron (who died of a fever fighting for Gr. independence against the Ottoman Empire) could draw upon an idea of Greece as original, natural, and thus eternal, while simultaneously rejecting the formal classicism and restrictive decorum characteristic of proceeding generations of Eng. poets. That the idea of Greece as primeval—as the last true meeting point between nature and civilization—is also of foundational importance within the 19th-c. origins of mod. and postmod. thought is indicated by the importance accorded to Greece in the thinking of Sigmund Freud (whose Oedipus complex is grounded in Sophocles) and Friedrich Nietzsche (who found in the Greece of Aeschylus and Sophocles the last successful balance between the Apollonian and the Dionysian elements of the creative imagination).

As the study of cl. langs., lits., and cultures within Eur. schools has gradually been supplemented and replaced by other forms of humanistic study, the role of classicism as a central mode of cultural self-fashioning has likewise been eroded. Nevertheless, the variety of perspectives built into the hist. of classicism and the eclecticism associated with postmod. artistic praxis combine to ensure that the cultural authority of cl. lit. and art is sampled and reappropriated by late 20th- and 21st-c. writers in innumerable ways. For the poet-as-*bricoleur*, classicism now offers a vast repository of familiar images and personages, freighted with dense layers of meaning accumulated through centuries of recovery, reception, and appropriation. Though the political hist. of the 20th c.—fascism, the Holocaust, postcolonialism, globalization—has made writers leery about idealizing Greece as any kind of original moment of Western purity, associated ideas of Gr. art as exemplifying strong simplicity and the fusion of art and nature or of Greece as the cradle of democracy are still very much part of the lexicon of late 20th- and 21st-c. classicism. However, since the aesthetic idea of classicism remains focused predominantly upon Hellenism of a kind first popularized by Wincklemann, the popular image of Roman antiquity has become more fully and inextricably linked to questions about republic and empire, militarism and governance. These become most acute in the U.S.: from the ostentatious classicism of its federal buildings to the Lat. phrases and emblems incorporated into its money, the national style of the U.S. in the 21st c. is still deeply bound up with an Enlightenment-era ideal of Greco-Roman classicism connoting solid military strength, popular governance, and liberty. But Rome, in 21st-c. art, has also come to connote imperialism, governmental hubris, decadence, and (as exemplified in Cullen Murphy's *Are We Rome?* [2007]) the specter of imperial collapse.

■ E. M. Butler, *The Tyranny of Greece over Germany* (1935); T. E. Mommsen, "Petrarch's Conception of the 'Dark Ages,'" *Speculum* 17 (1942); T. W. Baldwin, *William Shakspere's Small Latine & Lesse Greek*, 2 v. (1944); W. J. Bate, *From Classic to Romantic* (1946); G. Highet, *The Classical Tradition* (1949); Eliot; Curtius; R. M. Ogilvie, *Latin and Greek* (1964)—England, 1600–1918; T. S. Beardsley Jr., *Hispano-Classical Translations Printed between 1482 and 1699* (1970); R. Wellek, "The Term and Concept of Classicism in Literary History," *Discriminations* (1970); F. J. Warnke, *Versions of Baroque* (1972); G. Braden, *The Classics and English Renaissance Poetry* (1978); J. Buxton, *The Grecian Taste* (1978); T. M. Greene, *The Light in Troy: Imitation and Discovery in Renaissance Poetry* (1982); *Latin Influences on English Literature from the Middle Ages to the Eighteenth Century*, ed. C. Kallendorf (1982)—annotated bibl.; *A Dictionary of Classical Reference in English Poetry*, ed. E. Smith (1984); F. M. Turner, *The Greek Heritage in Victorian Britain* (1984); G. Braden, *Renaissance Trag-*

*edy and the Senecan Tradition* (1985); L. D. Reynolds and N. G. Wilson, *Scribes and Scholars* (1991)—med. survival of cl. texts; G. H. Tucker, *The Poet's Odyssey* (1991)—du Bellay and Ren. Fr. classicism; *The Collected Writings of T. E. Hulme*, ed. K. Csengeri (1994); J. M. Levine, *The Battle of the Books* (1994); C. A. Stray, *Classics Transformed* (1998)—educational and curricular reform in mod. England; D. S. Ferris, *Silent Urns* (2000)—romanticism and Hellenism; R. G. Witt, *In the Footsteps of the Ancients* (2000); *The Classical Heritage in France*, ed. G. Sandy (2002); *The Literature of Weimar Classicism*, ed. S. Richter (2005); S. Settis, *The Future of the "Classical,"* trans. A. Cameron (2006); *A Companion to the Classical Tradition*, ed. C. W. Kallendorf (2007).

C. Perry

**CLAVIS** (Lat., "key" or "nail" line). Dante describes clavis as the end of a line of verse that has no matching rhyme within the stanza, though it may rhyme with lines in later stanzas of the poem. Clavis is, therefore, defined as the absence of rhyme where it is expected. Agamben suggests that this deferral of expectation holds a special place in *Occitan poetry and *stilnovismo* poetics (see DOLCE STIL NUOVO) in that it provides the "semblance of coincidence" between sound and sense. Rhyme words in the *sestina can be understood as extensions of the clavis technique. Clavis may also be identified as *rim estramp* (see OCCITAN POETRY), *dissolute*, orphan rhyme, and unrelated rhyme.

■ Dante, *De Vulgari Eloquentia* 2.13.-5; *Las Leys d'Amors*, ed. J. Anglade (1920); G. Agamben, *The End of the Poem*, trans. D. Heller-Roazen (1999).

H. Feinsod

**CLERIHEW.** A form of *light verse consisting of two couplets giving facetious biographical information; the lines are of unequal length and the rhymes often eccentric. Edmund Clerihew Bentley invented the form as a schoolboy (1890) by writing:

> Sir Humphrey Davy
> Detested gravy
> He lived in the odium
> Of having discovered sodium.

The clerihew enjoyed instant popularity with Bentley's fellow students, incl. G. K. Chesterton. Later practitioners are W. H. Auden, Clifton Fadiman, and J.R.R. Tolkien. As the example shows, the clerihew presents the great quirkily. The clerihew differs from other light-verse forms by its roughness: other light verse is polished, but the clerihew is deliberately ragged, burlesquing fixed-form eulogies.

■ E. C. Bentley, *Biography for Beginners* (1905), *The Complete Clerihews* (1951; rpt. 1981), *The First Clerihews* (1982); C. Fadiman, "Cleriheulogy," *Any Number Can Play* (1957); P. Horgan, *Clerihews of Paul Horgan* (1985).

F. Teague

**CLICHÉ** (Fr., *clicher* or *cliquer*, "to click"). The term *cliché* emerged in the early 19th c.: it referred to the stereotype block used in printing and originated in the clicking sound produced when molten lead was struck to make stereotypes. By the second half of the century, the definition was extended to photographic negatives, reflecting the close ties between photography and print as means of mechanical reproduction. As applied to lit., *cliché* was used metaphorically, to connote an overused expression or stock response. In 1887, A.M.V. Barrère defined *cliché* in the dictionary *Argot and Slang* as "a commonplace sentence readymade; commonplace metaphor; well-worn platitude." This figurative meaning was tied to the term's mechanical origin, suggesting a general familiarity with the technology and a sense that conventions of expression had become overused and commercially debased.

Lerner and Barry both connect the distaste for cliché to the romantic emphasis on *originality. Woodmansee and others have explored the complex relations between print culture and understandings of the romantic lyric that espoused qualities opposed to mechanization (e.g., originality, *spontaneity, and *sincerity; see ROMANTICISM). Nonetheless, the romantic emphasis on feeling would strike ensuing generations as mechanical, resulting in new means of resisting cliché: in the early 20th c., modernists associated the cliché (as opposed to the stereotype or *commonplace) with a worn-out romanticism, perpetuated by sentimental poetry (see SENTIMENTALITY) and, according to T.S. Eliot, best countered through strategies of abstraction and impersonality. In surveying the magazine verse of the 1880s, Lowell wrote, "Here are all the old clichés: doves grieving for their lost mates, young lambs at play, swallows who herald the sun, winds that bluster," while Tietjens in her study of the poetic clichés of several langs. concluded that "they pertain . . . in all languages to the tender sentiments." Pound (1918) distinguished *commonplace*, which he defined as "things which we all know and upon which we for the most part agree" from *cliché*, which he defined as "the stock and stilted phraseology of the usual English verse as it has come down to us," arguing that clichés result in "poetry as balderdash—a sort of embroidery for dilettantes and women." Instead, mod. poetry must resist the cliché: "for it is not until poetry lives again 'close to the thing' that it will be a vital part of contemporary life." Critics in this trad. have charged the cliché with impeding the expression of original feeling or thought, threatening an understanding of the poem as a form through which lang., ideas, and feelings can be made or remade anew. Clichés are the opposite of poetry as that which "strikes the reader with the force of a new perception," as Brooks and Warren put it. From this perspective, the cliché puts the human itself at risk of mechanization; for Molnar, it atrophies both intelligence and "the sense of beauty, discrimination, taste, manners." Ricks (1984) sums up this approach thus: "[W]e are in a grim world where if you don't sourly subjugate clichés they will subjugate you. . . . [C]lichés are to be *attacked*."

The power of the cliché to define the human subject and shape culture is implicit in the ideas about lang. of *structuralism and *poststructuralism: as Barthes writes, "inner" expression is "only a ready-formed dictionary," and "the text is a tissue of quotations drawn from the innumerable centres of culture." Riffaterre (1971) sees the cliché as a stable stylistic structure, akin to a quotation, whose discordance from a new textual context generates meaning; what becomes worn is not the cliché but the reader's ability to recognize it as such, because of shifts in ideology and ling. codes. Critics taking a ling., sociological, or anthropological perspective have also emphasized the cliché's constitutive function in culture, regarding it as an "active, structuring, probing feature of our awareness" (McLuhan), as a microinstitution (Zijderveld), and as a species of ordinary lang. that overlaps with the commonplace, idiom, *proverb, stereotype, and slogan.

The cliché as a form of ordinary lang. has similarly interested a number of mod. poets, resulting in a more affirmative response than that of Pound, Eliot, and others. For Sabin, the desire to probe rather than satirize the cliché's ties to common life and lang. is specific to an Anglo-Am. literary trad., while Culler's study of Charles Baudelaire suggests otherwise, demonstrating that Baudelaire does not simply parody but also displays and creates clichés. In turn, the Fr. poetic avant-garde's interest in the mechanization of voice (Noland) has resulted in a sustained interest in cliché. Watson presents Philip Larkin's use of cliché as a means of investigating ordinary speech and habit, while Spargo argues that the cliché articulates a "presumed movement toward assent," enabling Robert Frost to explore the failures and gaps in communication that underlie the "myth of democracy." Inspired by William Empson's observation that clichés are metaphors that "are not dead but sleeping," Ricks and Barry demonstrate Samuel Beckett's interest in the cliché's "tenacity" and "hidden appeals," its expression of "fundamental desires and fears and truths," while Shoptaw, Morse, and Monroe explore a similar use of cliché as a form of "hallowed" lang. in John Ashbery's poetry. Davie and Ricks see the animation of *dead metaphors as one of poetry's fundamental tasks: from this perspective, the deliberate use of cliché in a poem does not debase but purifies or renovates the lang.

*See* CONVENTION, HYPOGRAM.

■ *Dictionnaire de L'Academie Francaise*, 6th ed. (1832–35); *The American Amateur Photographer* (1891); E. Pound, *Pavannes and Divisions* (1918); A. Lowell, *Tendencies in Modern American Poetry* (1921); E. Tietjens, "The Sub-Conscious Cliché," *Poetry 18* (1921); T. S. Eliot, *The Sacred Wood* (1922); E. Pound, *Literary Essays* (1935); E. Partridge, *A Dictionary of Clichés* (1940); Empson; L. Lerner, "Cliché and Commonplace," *Essays in Criticism* 6 (1956); Brooks and Warren; D. Davie, *Purity of Diction in English Verse*, 2d ed. (1967); M. McLuhan, *From Cliché to Archetype* (1970); M. Riffaterre, "Fonction du Cliché dans la Prose Litteraire," *Essais de stylistique structurale* (1971);

E. Pound, *Selected Prose 1909–1965* (1973); R. Barthes, "The Death of the Author," *Image, Music, Text,* trans. S. Heath (1977); M. Riffaterre, *Semiotics of Poetry* (1978); A. C. Zijderveld, *On Clichés* (1979); C. Ricks, "Clichés," *The Force of Poetry* (1984); T. Molnar, "The Anatomy of Clichés," *Chronicles* 10 (1986); M. Sabin, *The Dialect of the Tribe* (1987); W. D. Redfern, *Clichés and Coinages* (1989); J. R. Watson, "Clichés and Common Speech in Philip Larkin's Poetry," *Critical Survey* 1 (1989); J. Monroe, "Idiom and Cliché in T. S. Eliot and John Ashbery," *Contemporary Literature* 31 (1990); C. Ricks, *Beckett's Dying Words* (1993); J. Shoptaw, *On the Outside Looking Out: John Ashbery's Poetry* (1994); J. Morse, "Typical Ashbery," *Tribe of John: Ashbery and Contemporary Poetry,* ed. S. Schultz (1995); M. Woodmansee, *The Author, Art, and the Market* (1996); J. Culler, "Poesie et Cliché Chez Baudelaire," *Le Cliché,* ed. G. Mathis (1998); C. Noland, *Poetry at Stake: Lyric Aesthetics and the Challenge of Technology* (1999); E. Barry, *Beckett and Authority* (2006); R. C. Spargo, "Robert Frost and the Allure of Consensus," *Raritan* 28 (2009).

S. ROSENBAUM

**CLIMAX** (Gr., "ladder"). Loosely refers to any ascending rhetorical figure, whether the rungs are repeated words (*gradatio*), word order (*auxesis*), or logic (*sorites*). Still more commonly, it refers to the highest point of audience interest in a drama or narrative.

In cl. rhet., climax is strictly synonymous with gradatio (Lat., "steps"), in which the last word or phrase of a clause becomes the first of the next, and so on, each repeated word gaining greater importance. Puttenham gives this example: "His virtue made him *wise*, his *wisdom* brought him much *wealth*, / His *wealth* made him many *friends*, his *friends* made him much supply / Of aids in weal and woe." The ladder ascends from virtue, through wisdom, wealth, and friends, to a height of abundant help.

In auxesis (Gr., "increase"), the rungs are not repeated words but words arranged in order from lesser to greater. Puttenham: "He lost, besides his children and his wife, / His realm, renown, liege, liberty, and life." Here each loss is greater than the last until the sequence climaxes in death.

Finally, sorites (Gr., "heap") names a kind of syllogism, not a figure of speech. Hoskyns explains that it concludes gradatio with a clause containing the first and last rungs. Puttenham's example of gradatio would thus end: "therefore, his *virtue* brought him abundant *aid*."

In 1863, Freytag borrowed the term *climax* to describe the apex of the rising action in a drama, the third of a five-part structure called Freytag's pyramid. He made climax, which describes the audience's interest, synonymous with crisis, the structural turning point of the drama, but the term has since been applied more loosely to any peak in audience interest.

The opposite of climax is catacosmesis (Gr., "to set in order"), which describes a descending order. Congeries (Lat., "heap") describes an unordered heaping of words. Puttenham: "how fair, how wise, how good, / How brave, how free, how courteous, and how true / My lady is." Gradatio is sometimes confused with *anadiplosis* (Gr., "double back"), which merely repeats a single word and does not always result in an ascent or descent. Puttenham: "Your beauty was the cause of my first love; / Love while I live." Gradatio must repeat more than one word and must ascend.

Cl. rhetoricians described gradatio as esp. prominent. Quintilian recommended sparing use because it is "produced by art less disguised, or more affected," while Demetrius placed the figure not in the plain, grand, or elegant styles but in the forceful.

Most Ren. rhetoricians placed gradatio among other rhetorical figures, but others created subdivisions. Melanchthon, Susenbrotus, and Peacham characterized gradatio as amplifying, which referred to the goal of rhet., while Puttenham categorized it as sententious or wise.

Conceptually, gradatio was slow to enter Eng. Christian Anglo-Saxon England restricted rhetorical knowledge to elocution. When gradatio finally arrived in the Ren., it was applied to music as well. During the romantic era, cl. education declined, making most subsequent uses of climax either serendipitous or imitative of literary precedents.

*See* RHETORIC AND POETRY, SCHEME, TROPE.

■ G. Freytag, *Die Technik des Drama* (1863); M. Joseph, *Shakespeare's Use of the Arts of Language* (1947); Vickers; D. Bartel, *Musica Poetica* (1997)—rhetorical figures in music; P. McCreless, "Music and Rhetoric," *Cambridge History of Western Music Theory,* ed. T. Christensen (2002); J. Steen, *Verse and Virtuosity* (2008)—med. rhet.

M. L. MANSON

**CLOSE READING.** Close reading is an approach to texts that pays particular attention to their semantic and formal features and often finds in those features a complex coherence and purpose—as one prominent 20th-c. exponent put it, close reading reveals "language so twisted and poised in a form that it not only expresses the matter at hand but adds to the stock of available reality" (R. P. Blackmur, *Poetry* magazine [March 1935]). Attention to poetry's ling. textures has been an activity of critics and readers for centuries, but the term *close reading* is most associated with the *New Criticism. In Ransom's 1941 manifesto for the movement, the term first appears in a discussion of I. A. Richards's psychologically oriented criticism: in *Practical Criticism* (1929), where Richards explores his Cambridge students' skills at reading poetry, "Richards reveals himself as an astute reader. He looks much more closely at the objective poem than his theories require him to do." Developing the procedures of Richards and William Empson (*Seven Types of Ambiguity,* 1930), the New Critics stressed the central role of tension, *paradox, and *ambiguity in poems. They argued that, when read closely, a good poem displays a ling. density and order, both acknowledging the multiple meanings and tones embodied in rhetorical figures and formal patterns and resolving those potentially discordant elements into a unified or balanced whole.

In *The Well Wrought Urn* (1947), for instance, Cleanth Brooks draws attention in poems to what he described as "a pattern of resolutions and balances and harmonizations, developed through a temporal scheme," while Reuben Brower in *In Defense of Reading* (1963) examines poems with an eye for what he calls their "key design." Perhaps the most explicit demonstration of the assumptions and techniques of close reading appears in Brooks and Warren, where poems appear with "exercises" intended to draw the student into a consideration of how various formal and rhetorical features amount to a unity (e.g., on an extract from Alfred, Lord Tennyson's *In Memoriam*: "Is the poem unified?"—see UNITY). Implicit in such work is the sense that poems are "self-contained worlds with their own laws and their own logic" (Dowling), a notion assumed by Riffaterre, a structuralist critic prominent in the 1960s and 1970s, when he argues that poems are generated from a kernel word or *"matrix" and associated "ungrammaticalities" (elements of semantic complexity or *artifice); and by Vendler, one of the most committed contemp. close readers, when she proposes an "aesthetic criticism" able to make visible the "law" or problem that generates and sets in motion a text's "unique configuration" of elements.

Close reading, however, need not necessarily be bound by the expectation that a poem's complications be resolved into a single gesture or tension. Burke made the important claim that a poem is a "symbolic act," the record of a series of attempts, within lang., to identify, analyze, and respond to an initial conflict. A number of critics after Burke—Fish, Poirier, and others—emphasize the processive rather than the teleological nature of close reading; many of these readers concede something to the imperative of coherence and closure but with a heightened sense of the poem's responses to the instability of lang. and the provisionality of form. This approach to close reading has been applied to much mod. and contemp. poetry in Eng. and other langs.; it is a mainstay of recent discourse about *avant-garde poetics from Europe to Asia to the Americas, as in the work of Perloff and others.

Moretti, a scholar of the novel, has argued for a "distant reading" of that genre to take fuller account of the diversity of international fiction: "the trouble with close reading (in all of its incarnations, from the New Criticism to deconstruction) is that it necessarily depends on an extremely small canon. . . . [Y]ou invest so much in individual texts *only* if you think that very few of them really matter." Moretti's view has heralded a reassessment of close reading in poetry, not so much to discard it—the procedure remains an article of faith for nearly all readers and critics—as to place it in historical context and consider its antecedents and alternatives.

*See* EXPLICATION, FORMALISM.

■ J. C. Ransom, *The New Criticism* (1941); Brooks and Warren; R. Brower and R. Poirier, *In Defense of Reading* (1963); S. Fish, *Surprised by Sin: The Reader in "Paradise Lost"* (1967); K. Burke, "Symbolic Action in a Poem by Keats," *A Grammar of Motives* (1969); M. Riffaterre, *Semiotics of Poetry* (1978); H. Vendler, *The Music of What Happens* (1988); R. Poirier, *Poetry and Pragmatism* (1992); W. Dowling, *The Senses of the Text* (1999); F. Moretti, "Conjectures on World Literature," *New Left Review* 1 (2000)—developed in *Graphs, Maps, Trees* (2005); *Close Reading*, ed. F. Lentricchia and A. DuBois (2003); M. Perloff, *Differentials* (2004); J. Gang, "Behaviorism and the Beginnings of Close Reading," *ELH* 78 (2011).

T. GARDNER

**CLOSE RHYME** (Ger. *Schlagreim*, "hammer rhyme"). Two contiguous or close words that rhyme. Common in idioms, proverbs, and formulaic expressions, close rhyme is one of only three modes for forming reduplicatives (binomial word pairs), these modes being identical repetition (e.g., *beep beep*), ablaut change (*zigzag, clip-clop, tick-tock*), and *rhyme (*mumbo jumbo*). Close-rhymed formulas in doublet form are legion: *hobnob, hubbub, humdrum, harum-scarum, hodgepodge, helter-skelter, double trouble, true blue.* They also come in trinomials—*fair and square, wear and tear, near and dear, high and dry, make or break, only the lonely.* Slightly longer formulas—e.g., *put the pedal to the metal*—almost automatically become metrical (this one a trochaic tetrameter) and thus cross into poetry itself, where such figuration was often treated as one or another form of internal rhyme or else that kind of spaced repetition-with-a-difference treated in cl. rhet. as *polyptoton. Wilhelm Grimm maintained that poetic end rhyme itself arose from such rhymed formulas as these. Close rhyming in poetry thus may be seen to cover a small range from tight forms, e.g., T. S. Eliot's "Words after speech reach / Into silence" (one of a dozen examples in *Four Quartets*) or E. A. Poe's "Thrilled me, filled me" ("The Raven") to whole lines. Its compacting effect can also be gained by shortening the lengths of the lines, as in the *Skeltonic and in much *heterometric verse: John Donne has "And swear / Nowhere / Lives a woman true, and fair" ("Song"). In G. M. Hopkins, the technique is all but universal; the effect is that much weight is redistributed from the line ends back into the lines, delivering the maximum amount of force through the entire line. Close rhyme can even be obtained, and concealed, by breaking over line end, as in Louis MacNeice's "The sunlight on the gardens / Hardens and grows cold." The device actuates *echo verse. Close rhyme is also common in popular song lyrics. According to Krims, the dense, close "rhyme complex" is a key feature of rap music: "Notable in many speech-effusive performances are large numbers of syllables rhyming together, so that once a rhyme is established, quite a few rhyming syllables will be produced before the next series of rhymes begins." Krims cites such rap artists as Big Pun(isher), Bone Thugs 'N' Harmony, Nas, Ras Kass, and Raekwon in his *Only Built 4 Cuban Linx* (1995). Close rhyme creates stylistic power in much spoken-word poetry performance, as well (as in Saul Williams's "Scared Money").

See HIP-HOP POETICS, INTERNAL RHYME, NEAR RHYME, POETRY SLAM.

■ A. Krims, *Rap Music and the Poetics of Identity* (2000); S. Williams, *The Inevitable Rise and Liberation of Niggy Tardust* (2008).

T.V.F. BROGAN; L. R. SPAAR

**CLOSET DRAMA.** Drama supposedly intended to be read in the study (closet) or recited to a private audience rather than performed on a public stage. The term is problematic, however, as it originates from the 19th c. and has since been applied retrospectively to earlier times when definitions of "performance" were not as standardized as they now are. In the 1st c. CE, Seneca wrote plays for private declamation at a time when the Neronian stage was dominated by mimes and tumblers; his closet dramas are highly rhetorical and focus far more on lang. than on action—a pattern his successors would imitate. Yet it is difficult to divorce closet drama entirely from the stage: Seneca's works were performed in the Elizabethan period and influenced the stage dramas of Thomas Kyd and Christopher Marlowe. During the same era, literary coteries produced similarly rhetorical plays; the form may be credited for enabling women such as Elizabeth Cary and Mary Sidney, Countess of Pembroke, the opportunity to write drama in an age that banned Englishwomen from acting. Later, though John Milton explicitly stated that his *Samson Agonistes* was never intended for performance, dramatists such as Thomas Killigrew turned to closet drama when the public theaters were closed during the Eng. Civil War and Interregnum.

Several 19th-c. poets hearkened back to the cl. era in writing verse dramas explicitly intended for private reading or recitation. In *Manfred* and *Cain*, Lord Byron set out a "metaphysical drama" intentionally unsuited for stage representation, while P. B. Shelley experimented with both neo-Elizabethan tragedy in *The Cenci* and "lyrical drama" in *Prometheus Unbound*. In 1811, after a number of unsuccessful attempts to write drama, Charles Lamb argued in "On the Tragedies of Shakespeare" that Shakespeare's plays were unsuited for the public stage and best appreciated through reading. In France, Victor Hugo turned from the stage to write for an imagined theater, while Alfred de Musset wrote "armchair" plays. Yet here, too, the difficulty of separating closet drama from the stage becomes apparent: some of de Musset's plays were eventually staged, and J. W. Goethe's *Faust*, now one of the most frequently performed dramas in Ger., was originally composed as a closet drama. Later examples include Robert Browning's *Paracelsus*, Matthew Arnold's *Empedocles upon Etna*, and Thomas Hardy's *The Dynasts*, while 20th-c. poets such as W. B. Yeats, T. S. Eliot, and Christopher Fry wrote verse dramas for the stage that have been far more often read than performed. In 2010, Sylvia Plath's 1962 play *Three Women* was staged in London despite the text's lack of named characters and dialogue. The genre, thus, opens up multiple questions about the nature of dramatic paradigms and conventions.

See DRAMATIC POETRY.

■ F. L. Lucas, *Seneca and Elizabethan Tragedy* (1922); D. Donoghue, *The Third Voice* (1959); C. Affron, *A Stage for Poets* (1971); T. Otten, *The Deserted Stage* (1972); A. Richardson, *A Mental Theater* (1988); J. R. Heller, *Coleridge, Lamb, Hazlitt, and the Reader of Drama* (1990); D.B.J. Randall, *Winter Fruit* (1995); *Readings in Renaissance Women's Drama*, ed. S. P. Cerasano and M. Wynne-Davies (1998); K. Raber, *Dramatic Difference* (2001).

A. G. BENNETT

**CLOSURE.** Refers most broadly to the manner in which texts end or the qualities characterizing their conclusions. More specifically, the term "poetic closure" is used to refer to the achievement of an effect of finality, resolution, and stability at the end of a poem. In the latter sense, closure appears to be a generally valued quality, the achievement of which is not confined to the poetry of any particular period or nation. Its modes and the techniques by which it is secured do, however, vary in accord with stylistic, particularly structural, variables.

Closural effects are primarily a function of the reader's perception of a poem's total structure; i.e., they involve his or her experience of the relation of the concluding portion of a poem to the entire composition. The generating principles that constitute a poem's formal and thematic structure arouse continuously changing sets of expectations, which elicit various hypotheses from a reader concerning the poem's immediate direction and ultimate design. Successful closure occurs when, at the end of a poem, the reader is left without residual expectations: his or her developing hypotheses have been confirmed and validated (or, in the case of "surprise" endings, the unexpected turn has been accommodated and justified retrospectively), and he or she is left with a sense of the poem's completeness, which is to say of the integrity of his or her own experience of it and the appropriateness of its cessation at that point.

Closure may be strengthened by specifically *terminal* features in a poem, i.e., things that happen at the end of it. These include the repetition and balance of formal elements (as in *alliteration and *parallelism), explicit allusions to finality and repose, and the terminal return, after a deviation, to a previously established structural "norm" (e.g., a metrical norm). Closural failures (e.g., *anticlimax) usually involve factors that leave the reader with residual expectations. They may also arise from weak or incompatible structural principles or from a stylistic discrepancy between the structure of the poem and its mode of closure. Weak closure may, however, be deliberately cultivated: much modernist poetry shares with modernist works in other genres and art forms a tendency toward apparent anticlosure, rejecting strong closural effects in favor of irresolution, incompleteness, and a quality of "openness." *Language poet Lyn Hejinian, e.g., advocates a "rejection of closure" and the creation of "open text" that "emphasizes or foregrounds process" and actively engages the reader. One can profitably compare and contrast the self-consciously disruptive rejection of closure as it operates in mod. Western poetry with a long-standing Chinese poetics of incompleteness and suggestiveness.

*See* ORGANICISM.

■ B. H. Smith, *Poetic Closure: A Study of How Poems End* (1968); P. Hamon, "Clausules," *Poétique* 24 (1975); *Concepts of Closure*, spec. iss. of *YFS* 67 (1984); L. Hejinian, "The Rejection of Closure," *Poetics Jour.* 4 (1985); Y. Ye, *Chinese Poetic Closure* (1996); J. E. Vincent, *Queer Lyrics: Difficulty and Closure in American Poetry* (2002).

B. H. SMITH; A. WATSON

**COBLA.** The usual word for "stanza" in Occitan. It is also used, either alone or in the expression *cobla esparsa* (isolated stanza), to designate a poem consisting in its entirety of a single stanza. These *coblas* are fairly common from the end of the 12th c. on. In theme, they are usually like miniature *\*sirventes*, and, in their concision, they represent the troubadours' closest approach to the *\*epigram*. It often happened that a cobla would inspire an answering cobla, and this might well follow the metrical structure of the first, in which case the resultant combination resembles a short *\*tenso*.

*See* OCCITAN POETRY.

■ Jeanroy, v. 1; C. Leube, *GRLMA* 2.1B.67 ff.; E. Poe, "'Cobleiarai, car mi platz': The Role of the *Cobla* in the Occitan Lyric Tradition," *Medieval Lyric*, ed. W. D. Paden (2000).

F. M. CHAMBERS

**COCKNEY SCHOOL OF POETRY.** A derisive epithet applied to a group of writers associated with London, incl. Leigh Hunt, John Keats, and William Hazlitt, in a series of hostile articles signed by "Z" in *Blackwood's Magazine* beginning in October 1817. The attacks are attributed to John Wilson Croker and John Gibson Lockhard, who charge the "school" with "vulgar" diction, "loose, nerveless versification," and "Cockney rhymes," e.g., Keats's rhyming of "thorns" with "fawns" in "Sleep and Poetry" and of "Thalia" with "higher" in "To \* \* \* \*" [Georgiana Augusta Wylie, afterward Mrs. George Keats]. The reviewers' hostility is patently motivated both by the group's association with political and social radicalism and by class bias. The writers are accused of having founded a "Cockney school of versification, morality, and politics," and the humble origins of Keats and Hunt are stressed, while P. B. Shelley, though a "Cockney" in politics, is excused for his "genius" and aristocratic birth. Croker adopted the "Cockney" term in his notorious attack on Keats's *Endymion* in the *Quarterly Review* for April 1818.

*See* DIALECT POETRY, LAKE SCHOOL.

■ W. J. Bate, *John Keats* (1963); J. O. Hayden, *The Romantic Reviewers* (1969); W. Keach, "Cockney Couplets," *SIR* 25 (1986); D. Wu, "Keats and the 'Cockney School,'" *The Cambridge Companion to Keats,* ed. S. Wolfson (2001); J. Cox, *Poetry and Politics in the Cockney School* (2004); D. Gigante, *The Keats Brothers* (2011).

A. RICHARDSON; D. J. ROTHMAN

**CODEWORK.** A term used by new media practitioners and theorists to describe digital writing in which normally invisible lang. addressed to a computer's operating system appears on the screen with lang. addressed to human interpreters. As practiced by such poets as Mez (Mary-Anne Breeze), John Cayley, Talan Memmott, Alan Sondheim, and Ted Warnell and theorized by Cayley, Memmott, Sondheim, and such critics as N. Katherine Hayles and Rita Raley, codework foregrounds for analysis the human-machine interaction, event, or performance that constitutes digital writing.

In a broad sense, all writing draws on semantic or bibliographic codes that prepare information for display. Electronic writing depends on a tower of programming langs. that includes machine code, assembly code, and such higher-level markup codes as BASIC, Perl, and HTML. These langs. share with natural langs. a complex syntax and grammar, a nuanced semantics, and a specific community or culture of address. As Galloway emphasizes, however, code is the only lang. that is executable: programming lang. sets a computing system into motion. For code writers and some critics alike, discussions of \*electronic poetry that fail to account for code miss its most significant feature.

Coined by Sondheim in 2001, the term *codework* has sparked a series of critical discussions that challenge the illusion that the screen is an isolate or isolable entity, situate machine-addressed code as a part of a digital poem's \*"text," position both code and text as artistic compositions, and underscore the temporal unfolding that makes electronic writing an event or \*performance rather than an object or \*artifact.

Extending Sondheim's taxonomy of *codework*, which focused on screenic effects, Cayley (2002, 2004, 2006) distinguishes between code that is operational and has depth and code that is marooned at the interface and thereby rendered inoperable. For Cayley, operational or "strong sense" code exhibits an "aesthetics of compilation"; technically nonreferential or nonperformative code, by contrast, risks becoming at best a "decoration or rhetorical flourish" or at worst new media's equivalent of "baroque euphuism."

For Hayles, by contrast, code or code elements that mingle with natural lang. on the screen construct a creole or pidgin whose semantic, epistemological, and poetic resonances voice the synergy between humans and intelligent machines. As exemplified in Hayles's parsing of compounds such as "cell.f" or "I-terminal" from Memmott's "Lexia to Perplexia" and Raley's reading of "m[ez]ang.elle," the "net.wurked" lang. of Mez's "data][h!][bleeding texts," codework's elaborate and self-confident rhet. layers programming vocabulary and punctuation with poetic and theoretical lang. to capture the hybrid subjectivity, cognitive processes, and textual possibilities of networked culture.

Instead of bringing machine-addressed code to the screen or creating a hybrid human-machine lang., Cayley's new media poems use kinetic programming to capture for the interface the pacing and effects of working code. Representative of a form of writing Cayley calls "literal art," such ambient time-based poems as his "riverIsland," "overboard," and "translation" make coding's active and ongoing modulation of signification visible through algorithms that incrementally replace letters of a stable underlying text with similarly shaped letters from different ling. systems. As it moves the source text into and out of legibility, this "transliteral morphing" generates dynamic tapestries of lang. accompanied, in "riverIsland," by QuickTime movies and, in "overboard" and "translation," by Giles Perring's generative music.

Supplementing Cayley's formal and ling. focus, Mez, Memmott, Sondheim, and others use codework to expose and disrupt the proprietary practices and corporate ethos of contemp. information culture. Like the "hactivism" practiced by the Critical Art Ensemble and theorized by Wark, their tactics envision a utopia of layered, multiple, playful, and often subversive signification, the free circulation of information, and an open, improvisatory future.

In its attention to the materiality of lang., contemp. codework remediates for digitality the process-based writing of *avant-gardes from *Oulipo to *Language poetry. Participating with computational and cybertextual poetics in the invention of textual art for networked and programmable media, it explores the human-machine interface, the nature of code, and the role of the intelligent machine in contemp. constructions of subjectivity. And finally, it generates new strategies for making and new frameworks for understanding lang. in a world that is evolving in conjunction with the code-based operations of intelligent machines.

*See* COMPUTATIONAL POETRY, CYBERTEXT.

■ **Electronic Sources**: T. Memmott, "Lexia to Perplexia" (2000), http://collection.eliterature.org/1/works/memmott__lexia_to_perplexia.html; J. Cayley, "The Code is not the Text (unless it is the Text)," *electronic book review* (2002), http://www.electronicbookreview.com/thread/electropoetics/literal; Mez, "data][h!][bleeding texts" (2002), http://netwurkerz.de/mez/datableed/complete/; R. Raley, "Interferences: [Net.Writing] and the Practice of Codework," *electronic book review* (2002), http://www.electronicbookreview.com/thread/electropoetics/net.writing; J. Cayley, with Giles Perring and Douglas Cape "overboard," (2004), http://homepage.mac.com/shadoof/net/in/overboard.html; J. Cayley, with Giles Perring, "translation" (2004), http://collection.eliterature.org/1/works/cayley__translation.html; and J. Cayley, "riverIsland," version 1.2 (2008), http://homepage.mac.com/shadoof/net/in/riverisland.html.

■ **Printed Sources**: Critical Art Ensemble, *Digital Resistance* (2001); A. Sondheim, "Introduction: Codework," *American Book Review* 22 (2001); A. R. Galloway, *Protocol* (2004); M. Wark, *A Hacker Manifesto* (2004); N. K. Hayles, *My Mother Was a Computer* (2005); J. Cayley, "Time Code Language: New Media Poetics and Programmed Signification," and N. K. Hayles, "The Time of Digital Poetry: From Object to Event," *New Media Poetics*, ed. A. Morris and T. Swiss (2006); N. K. Hayles, *Electronic Literature* (2008).

A. MORRIS

**COGNITIVE POETICS.** One branch of the rapidly growing field of cognitive lit. crit. further divided by Alan Richardson into cognitive rhet., cognitive narratology, cognitive aesthetics of reception, cognitive materialism, and evolutionary literary theory. It grew in the 1970s–80s out of *structuralism, Slavic *formalism (incl. *Russian formalism), generative ling., *New Criticism, and Gestalt theory. Cognitive poetics is an interdisciplinary approach to the study of lit., employing the tools of cognitive psychology, psycholinguistics, artificial intelligence, and certain branches of ling. and philosophy. These investigate information-processing activities during the acquisition, organization, and use of knowledge, incl. perceptual and emotional processes. Cognitive poetics explores how poetic lang. and form are shaped and constrained by cognitive processes.

Cognitive poetics has taken two main directions. Gestalt-oriented cognitive poetics, developed by Barbara Herrnstein Smith and Reuven Tsur, focuses on meaning, *affect, perceived qualities, and *versification. Meaning-oriented cognitive poetics is based on George Lakoff and Mark Johnson's notions of "embodied mind" and conceptual *metaphor, as well as on Mark Turner and Gilles Fauconnier's "blending."

Cognitive poetics can deal with issues traditional poetics is unable to handle. A work of lit. may have emotive content as well as display an emotional quality. Poetic effects may arise from the subtle interaction of versification and elements on the syntactic, figurative, and "world" levels of the poem, combined in a variety of ways. Weak gestalts typically display emotional qualities; strong gestalts generate rational or witty qualities. A special combination of weak gestalts with a more than usually regular *meter may produce a hypnotic quality. Similarly, interacting semantic features in metaphors may yield relatively diffuse or focused gestalts. In synaesthetic metaphors, perceived qualities are governed mainly by direction of transfer and by the presence or absence of stable visual shapes. "Upward" transfer (from less to more differentiated senses) is more frequent (and probably more natural) than "downward" transfer in Western langs. as well as in Chinese, in both colloquial and poetic lang.: "soft color" is more natural than "bright touch." Operating on this principle, John Donne uses "loud perfume" (Elegie 4, "The Perfume") to achieve metaphysical wit. Or we might consider the line:

And taste the music of that vision pale.

(John Keats, "Isabella" 49)

Here, many readers sense an impassioned, uncanny atmosphere. The verse contains a double, upward intersense transfer: the line speaks of "vision" in terms of "music" and "music" in terms of "taste." The word *vision* denotes an abstraction that has no stable visual shape. Unlike *sight*, it suggests not only the thing seen but also an impassioned state of mind with supernatural connotations. The paleness of the vision may be associated with the paleness of the dead, Isabella, or the moonlit scene, but none of these is explicitly mentioned; nor can they usurp each other's place, yielding a diffuse quality of paleness. The interaction of "music" and "vision" deletes the "auditory" feature in "music," which turns the gestalt-free "vision" into a pleasant fusion of percepts, imbued with delicate energy expanding toward the perceiving self. The interaction of "taste" with "music" deletes the "gustatory" feature, foregrounding such meaning components as direct perception of reality, some fine texture or elusive quality. The upward transfer from the less differentiated senses enhances the indistinctness of the fused sensations. Then we have the case of another line by Keats:

The same bright face I tasted in my sleep
(*Endymion* 1.895)

This excerpt also applies the verb *taste* to an object derived from a higher sense and should be perceived as smooth and natural. However, it makes a very different impression: Stephen Ullmann considered it "a strange phrase." Generating an emotional quality requires fusion into a soft focus. Stable, characteristic visual shapes (like the shape of *face*) tend to resist such fusion (or "tasting") and render synaesthetic metaphors less natural and wittier, whereas "thing-free" qualities facilitate fusion.

In considering poetic *rhythm, cognitive poetics assumes three dimensions: versification pattern, linguistic pattern, and *performance. When the first two patterns conflict, they are accommodated in a rhythmical performance such that both are perceptible simultaneously. A deviant linguistic stress intrudes upon meter, generating tension that is relieved at the next point in which the versification and linguistic patterns have a coinciding downbeat; here meter becomes fresh and new. The line is a system that determines the character of its parts. According to *generative metrics, a stress maximum in a weak position violates metricality; according to cognitive poetics, it increases tension, provided that the integrity of the whole is preserved in perception through performance.

Cognitive poetics also pays particular attention to speech sounds. As opposed to impressionistic "chatter," speech research provides systematic arguments concerning phonetic symbolism. Speech sounds are transmitted by rich precategorial auditory information, which is immediately recoded into phonetic categories and excluded from awareness. We perceive only a unitary phonetic category as *i* or *u*. In the poetic mode of speech perception, we can tell that *u* is somehow lower and darker than *i* because recoding has been delayed and some of the lingering precategorical auditory information subliminally reaches awareness: the second formant of *u* is lower than *i* (formants are concentrations of overtones that uniquely determine vowels), and the first two formants of *u* are nearer one another, less easily discernible, than those of *i*. *Rhyme and *alliteration direct attention to the lingering auditory information, which normally serves to preserve verbal material in active memory for efficient processing. Here it serves a differ-

ent—aesthetic—end: when attention is directed to the lingering auditory information, it becomes musicality.

Cognitive poetics as an interdisciplinary endeavor faces the danger of restating in cognitive or neurological lang. what can be stated in traditional critical terms. To avoid reductionism, cognitive or neurological lang. can be justified only when the problems cannot be properly handled without appealing to some cognitive or neurological process or mechanism.

■ **General:** E. D. Snyder, *Hypnotic Poetry* (1930)—an early instance; S. Ullmann, "Panchronistic Tendencies in Synaesthesia," *The Principles of Semantics*, 266–89 (1957); B. Herrnstein Smith, *Poetic Closure* (1968); M. Turner, *Death Is the Mother of Beauty* (1987); R. W. Gibbs, *The Poetics of Mind* (1994); M. Turner, *The Literary Mind* (1996); Y. Shen, "Cognitive Constraints on Poetic Figures," *Cognitive Linguistics* 8 (1997); M. T. Crane and A. Richardson, "Literary Studies and Cognitive Science," *Mosaic* 32 (1999); G. Lakoff and M. Johnson, *Philosophy in the Flesh* (1999); E. Scarry, *Dreaming by the Book* (1999); M. T. Crane, *Shakespeare's Brain* (2001); "Models of Figurative Language, Metaphor and Symbol," *Metaphor and Symbol* 16, ed. R. Giora (2001); G. Fauconnier and M. Turner, *The Way We Think* (2002); "Literature and the Cognitive Revolution," *PoT* 23, ed. A. Richardson and F. F. Steen (2002); *Cognitive Stylistics*, ed. E. Semino and J. Culpepper (2002); P. Stockwell, *Cognitive Poetics: An Introduction* (2002); *Cognitive Poetics in Practice*, ed. J. Gavins and G. Steen (2003); P. C. Hogan, *Cognitive Science, Literature, and the Arts* (2003); "The Cognitive Turn? A Debate on Interdisciplinarity," *PoT* 24, ed. M. Sternberg (2003); N. Yu, "Synaesthetic Metaphor," *Journal of Literary Semantics* 32 (2003); A. Richardson, "Studies in Literature and Cognition," *The Work of Fiction*, ed. A. Richardson and E. Spolsky (2004); R. Tucker, "Consciousness and Literature," *Journal of Consciousness Studies* 11 (2004); M. H. Freeman, "Cognitive Linguistics and Literary Studies," *The Handbook of Cognitive Linguistics*, ed. H. Cuyckens and D. Geeraerts (2005); M. K. Hiraga, *Metaphor and Iconicity* (2005); *European Journal of English Studies* 9, ed. M. Toolan and J. J. Weber (2005); A. Elfenbein, "Cognitive Science and the History of Reading," *PMLA* 121 (2006); D. S. Miall, *Literary Reading* (2006); C. Emmott, A. J. Sanford, E. J. Dawydiak, "Stylistics Meets Cognitive Science," *Style* 41 (2007); P. C. Hogan, "The Brain in Love: A Case Study in Cognitive Neuroscience and Literary Theory," *Journal of Literary Theory* 1 (2007); R. Tsur, *Toward a Theory of Cognitive Poetics* (1992; 2008); *Cognitive Poetics: Goals, Gains and Gaps*, ed. G. Brône and J. Vandaele (2009).

■ **Selected Web Sites:** Cognitive Approaches to Literature, http://www.ucs.louisiana.edu/~cxr1086/coglit/; Coglit, http://coglit.13pirates.org/coglit/; Literature, Cognition, and the Brain, http://www2.bc.edu/~richarad/lcb/home.html; Miall, http://www.ualberta.ca/~dmiall/; Tsur, http://www.tau.ac.il/~tsurxx/index.html; Turner, http://markturner.org/

R. Tsur; T. Sovran

**COLLAGE** (Fr. *coller,* "to glue"). Refers to an abstract visual artwork in which the artist juxtaposes disparate media and various textures, affixing them to a single pictorial surface. *Collage* entered the descriptive vocabulary of art crit. in the second decade of the 20th c. As a compositional technique in painting, collage was among the innovations that distinguished later (synthetic) cubism from earlier (analytic) cubism. Synthetic cubist paintings included, e.g., fragments of newsprint headlines, bits of string, and other materials. (Georges Braque first included pieces of wallpaper in charcoal drawings; later, the Ger. artist Kurt Schwitters began making his famed abstract collage works incorporating found objects and alluding, often, to contemp. events; this work is known as *Merz;* see AVANT-GARDE POETICS.)

*Collage* migrated almost immediately to the lexicon of poetry and poetics, esp. among Fr.- and Eng.-lang. writers: after World War I, poets and critics alike began using the term to describe poems or series of poems built out of abrupt textual juxtapositions, newsprint transcriptions or headlines, direct prose quotations, and so forth. Thus, where the related combinatorial form of *pastiche relies on the imitation of an established voice or style, collage relies on visible textual collocation. For one example in the U.S. context, W. C. Williams's long poem *Paterson* (1946–58) includes transcriptions of historical documents, letters, and anecdotes that maintain the margins of prose and appear in a smaller typeface than the lyric sections.

The quick adoption of *collage* as a poetics term marks a nearly simultaneous instance of how the Horatian analogy *ut pictura poesis* (as in painting, so in poetry) analogy continued to inform poetry and poetry crit. in the 20th c. As with all analogies, however, *collage* ought not to be applied or assumed too easily. While the poetic practices of excerption, juxtaposition, and quotation bear a suggestive formal relationship to the cutting and pasting of a visual collage, the material of a collage poem remains semantic and textual.

■ *Fragments—Incompletion and Discontinuity*, ed. L. D. Kritzman and J. P. Plottel (1981); M. Perloff, "The Invention of Collage," *The Futurist Moment* (1986); E. Adamowicz, *Surrealist Collage in Text and Image* (1998); B. Taylor, *Collage* (2004); P. McBride, "The Game of Meaning: Collage, Montage, and Parody in Kurt Schwitters' *Merz," Modernism/Modernity* 14 (2007).

C. BOWEN

**COLOMBIA, POETRY OF.** While recent studies of Colombian poetry include the voices of pre-Columbian peoples, their legends, *chants, and poems were gathered by scholars in the last 50 years. These chants belong to the U'wa, Cuna, Kogi, Mwiska, Huitoto, Guahibo, and Desana tribes, among others. Despite their ethnographic value, the oral poems of these indigenous peoples have had little effect on the formation of a Colombian poetic trad., which is based on Sp. lang. and culture.

The chronicler Juan de Castellanos (1522–1606) is considered the first Colombian poet. His monumental Ren. *epic *Elegías de Varones Ilustres de Indias* (Elegies of Illustrious Men, 1589, first part), contains 113,609 *hendecasyllabic verses in *octavas reales* (see OTTAVA RIMA), celebrating the heroic deeds of the Sp. conquerors in northern South America and the Caribbean. The later colonial period, from the late 16th to the 18th c., reflects the influence of Sp. *baroque culture. Born in Colombia, Hernando Domínguez Camargo (1606–59) is the best representative of this period. His masterpiece is *San Ignacio de Loyola, Fundador de la Compañía de Jesús: Poema Heroyco* (Saint Ignatius of Loyola, Founder of the Society of Jesus: A Heroic Poem, 1666). Domínguez Camargo brought Gongorist verse (in the vein of the Sp. poet Luis de Góngora), marked by the use of *hyperbaton, elaborate *metaphor, and cl. references. The nun Sor Francisca Josefa del Castillo y Guevara (1671–1742) is one of the most important women writers of the colonial period. She is the author of the Catholic mystical book *Afectos espirituales* (Spiritual Feelings, 1843), which includes prose and verse, and an autobiographical *Vida* (Life, 1817). In the 18th c., the most important Colombian poet was Francisco Vélez Ladrón de Guevara (1721–81?). Mainly a poet of the viceregal court, Ladrón de Guevara wrote an elegant and crafted verse with a *rococo influence, such as *Octavario a la Inmaculada Concepción* (1774).

Across Sp. America, the beginning of the 19th c. was marked by revolutionary movements against the colonial powers. In Colombia, the opposition to Sp. rule united many intellectuals and writers, incl. the poet José Fernández Madrid (1789–1830), who signed the document of Cartagena declaring independence (1811) and was persecuted and exiled by the Spaniards. His *Poesías* (1822) appeared during his exile in Cuba. He is considered a romantic liberal, the link between the neoclassical current of the 18th c. and the romantic movement of the 19th (see NEOCLASSICAL POETICS, ROMANTICISM). Another important poet of this period is Luis Vargas Tejada (1802–29). A precocious intellectual, polyglot, and author of tragedies, comedies, and lyric poetry, he was consumed by the political events of his time. His neoclassical poems were published in the book *Poesías de Caro y Vargas Tejada* (1857).

Although the romantic period in Colombia lacked the resonance that it had in Europe, it represented a change in poetic attitudes and themes. Proof of this is the presence in prose and poetry of certain motifs: nature, freedom, and the faith in the individual as owner of his destiny. José Eusebio Caro (1817–53) is one of the most important Colombian poets of this period. Because of his agitated political life and early death, his poems were published only posthumously in the aforementioned volume with Vargas Tejada (1857) and *Obras escogidas* (Selected Works, 1873). Caro is considered a precursor of fin de siècle *modernismo.

Rafael Pombo (1833–1912) is perhaps the best representative of the romantic period in Colombia. His poetry, highly passionate and obscure, includes two of the best known poems in Colombian lit. hist., "Hora de tinieblas" (Hour of Darkness) and "Noche de diciembre" (December Night). Miguel Antonio Caro (1843–

1909), like Rufino José Cuervo (1844–1911), was an important philologist and grammarian. He is praised as a conservative poet who rejected the advances of Sp. Am. modernismo and looked for an ideal, almost mystical form of poetry. *Horas de amor* (Hours of Love, 1871) and *Poesías* (1896) are his most important books.

In 1886 in Bogotá, José María Rivas Groot (1863–1923) published an extensive anthol. of Colombian poets, *La Lira Nueva* (The New Lyre), seeking to indicate new directions. Thirty-three poets are included, among them Ismael Enrique Arciniegas (1865–1938), Candelario Obeso (1849–84), Carlos Arturo Torres (1867–1911), Julio Flórez (1867–1923), José Asunción Silva (1865–96), and Groot himself.

Silva is one of the leading figures of modernismo. Although his poetry is linked to the romantic period, it represents a breakthrough in Colombian poetry, unifying form, theme, and music. Silva employed an ample variety of poetic forms according to Sp. trad. as well as the resources of the Fr. symbolist movement (see SYMBOLISM). His books were published posthumously.

Two of the poets included in *La Lira Nueva* deserve special attention: Obeso and Flórez. Obeso is among the first Sp. Am. poets to bring Afro-Caribbean diction into Sp. For the Colombian people more than for scholars, Flórez epitomizes the honorific *poet, despite his late romanticism and formalism.

Within modernismo, Guillermo Valencia (1873–1943) epitomizes the highly intellectual poet with a vast knowledge of forms and themes. His books include *Ritos* (Rites, 1899) and *Sus mejores poemas* (His Best Poems, 1926). Porfirio Barba Jacob (1883–1938) represents the *poète maudit. A vagabond, drug addict, and homosexual, Barba Jacob defied Colombian society even as he published some of the better known poems of the period. His work mixed a very personal romantic tendency with modernist forms. Notable volumes are *Rosas negras* (Black Roses, 1933) and *Canciones y elegías* (Songs and Elegies, 1933). Another popular poet of this period is Luis Carlos López (1879–1950). His poetry, sarcastic and humoristic, centers on Cartagena, his native city. López's poetry departs from the main trad. in favor of colloquial and direct lang. that borders on prosaic. His books include *De mi villorio* (From My Town, 1908) and *Por el atajo* (Easy Way Out, 1920).

Best known for his novel *La Vorágine* (*The Vortex*), José Eustacio Rivera (1889–1928) is a modernist poet in the line of *Parnassianism, cl. in form but not completely detached from emotion. His only book was *Tierra de promisión* (Promised Land, 1921). Contemporary with Rivera, Eduardo Castillo (1889–1938) published his books *Duelo lírico* (Lyric Grief, 1918) and *El árbol que canta* (The Singing Tree, 1927) in a symbolist aesthetic.

In 1925, the literary magazine *Los nuevos* (The New Ones) appeared in Bogotá, featuring a large group of young Colombian poets and writers. While it was not aligned with the contemporaneous *avant-garde movements in Europe and Latin America, the jour. sought to bring a change to the literary climate of the country.

León de Greiff (1895–1976) was the most important poet of this group. With a very personal voice and a practice derived from Fr. symbolism and the avant-garde, De Greiff published several important volumes, incl. *Tergiversaciones de Leo Legris, Matías Aldecoa y Gaspar* (Tergiversations on Leo Legris, Matías Aldecoa, and Gaspar, 1923) and *Libro de los signos* (Book of Signs, 1930). In contrast with de Greiff, Rafael Maya (1898–1980), another poet of Los nuevos, dedicated his life to a conservative poetics combining romanticism and modernismo in search of cl. forms.

With his book of poems *Suenan timbres* (Bells Sound, 1926), Luis Vidales (1900–90) introduced the avant-garde into the Colombian trad. The book was to resound in the years to come, esp. for the poets of the 1960s. After *Suenan timbres* Vidales changed his tone and wrote poetry of social commitment. Another poet linked to Los nuevos was Jorge Zalamea (1905–69). Known for his exemplary trans. of Saint-John Perse, his work—esp. *El sueño de las escalinatas* (Dream of the Staircases, 1964)—follows the same discursive and incantatory line, although with a political militancy.

During the 1930s, Sp. Am. poetry developed experimental works and innovative approaches based on *surrealism, *cubism, *creationism, and other movements, both local and imported. Colombian poetry, however, took a more conservative approach, strengthening its relation with traditional Sp. poetry. The product of these ideas was a group called *Piedra y Cielo* (Stone and Sky), which took its name from a book of the Sp. poet Juan Ramón Jiménez. Aurelio Arturo (1906–74) was regularly associated with this group, although his poetry does not greatly resemble the others. In spite of his restrained style, his poetry flows with images, metaphors that illuminate the link between the human and nature (while questioning their existence), and exaltations of love. After the surge of the avant-gardes in the 1960s, Arturo had perhaps the greatest influence on other Colombian poets. He wrote few poems, collected in *Morada al Sur* (Southern Dwelling, 1975).

Eduardo Carranza (1913–85) is the most representative poet of Piedra y Cielo. While conservative and traditional, his verses manifest some traces of the Chilean poet Vicente Huidobro's creationism. The other poets of the school were Arturo Camacho Ramírez (1910–82), Jorge Rojas (1911–95), Tomás Vargas Osorio (1908–41), Darío Samper (1909–84), Gerardo Valencia (1911–94), and Carlos Martín (1914–2008).

With the poets who emerged during the 1940s and 1950s, Colombia's conservative trad. suffered a crushing blow. Although they formed no literary group, these poets have been studied as a generation under the name of the literary jour. *Mito* (Myth), published by Jorge Gaitán Durán (1934–62) in Bogotá after 1955. Gaitán Durán promoted changes in the Colombian intelligentsia, not only with respect to lit. but in the general way of thinking about the nation's problems, esp. the continuous political violence. The poetry of Álvaro Mutis (b. 1923) absorbs the freedom of the avant-garde movements without stridency or obscurity; his important books are *Los elementos del desastre* (Elements of Disaster, 1953) and *Summa de Maqroll el Gaviero* (The Summa of Maqroll el Gaviero, 1973). Fernando Charry Lara (1920–2004), another poet of the Mito generation, condenses several currents of mod. poetry to find a highly particular voice between the obscure and the transparent.

The other poets of this generational cohort are Eduardo Cote Lamus (1928–64), Héctor Rojas Herazo (1921–2002), Fernando Arbeláez (1924–95), and Rogelio Echavarría (b. 1926). Cote Lamus is a conceptual poet, with an introspective and conservative vision of existence. Arbeláez produces a sober poetry with a narrative logic and a universal vision. Rojas Herazo is an exuberant poet, with a strong voice that echoes contemp. colloquialisms. Echavarría's poetry—somber, with a strange beauty—is concentrated in the daily life of the anonymous passersby who populate big cities. His most important book is *El transeunte* (The Transient, 1964).

Close to this group is Carlos Obregón (1929–1963). His life as well as his poetry distanced itself from the Colombian literary world because of his voluntary exile in the United States and Europe. He wrote short, reflective poems with mystical tendencies. His books are *Distancia destruida* (Destroyed Distance, 1957) and *Estuario* (Estuary, 1961).

Before the 1960s, Colombian poetry by women was scarce. Two exceptions are Maruja Vieira (b. 1922) and Dora Castellanos (b. 1924), who wrote often in traditional forms about love.

The convulsive 1960s brought drastic changes in how poets approached poetry, not only from the intellectual but from the existential point of view. The lack of a local avant-garde movement and the continuous political violence made possible the emergence of a group of poets and writers that directly challenged the order and direction of Colombian lit. This group, called *Nadaísmo* (Nothingism), was composed mainly of poets. It had no explicit aesthetic or literary program; its only agenda was complete freedom. The most important poets were Gonzalo Arango (1931–76), Jaime Jaramillo Escobar (b. 1932), Mario Rivero (1935–2009), Jota Mario Arbeláez (b. 1940), Amilkar Osorio (1940–85), Eduardo Escobar (b. 1943), and Armando Romero (b. 1944).

With the slogan "we are geniuses, crazy and dangerous," Arango led the movement. Mainly a prose writer, his scarce poetry was always incendiary, colloquial, and discursive. Arango never collected his poems. A complete selection of them can be seen in the *Antología del Nadaísmo* (2009).

Although he rejected his affiliation with the nadaísta group, Rivero figured in the two main anthols. of this group and was recognized for years as a member. His poetry, colloquial and direct, looks for simplicity in the daily life of the urban dweller. Among his books are *Poemas urbanos* (Urban Poems, 1966) and *Baladas* (1980). Jaramillo Escobar's poems, obscure and transparent at the same time, deal with love, violence, and death, although with a humorous and ironic attitude.

His books include *Los poemas de la ofensa* (Poems of Offense, 1968) and *Poemas de tierra caliente* (Poems of the Hot Land, 1985). Arbeláez's poetry is marked by a colloquial rhythm that borders on the *prose poem. It combines witty humor with surreal metaphors and word plays, dealing with love, sex, and violence. His books include *El profeta en su casa* (Prophet in His House, 1966) and *Mi reino por este mundo* (My Kingdom in This World, 1980). Osorio cultivated a baroque poetry, learned and conceptual, in only one book, *Vana Stanza, diván selecto* (Vain Stanza: Selected Divan, 1984). Escobar's poetry, such as his first books *La invención de la uva* (The Invention of the Grape, 1966) and *Monólogos de Noé* (Monologues of Noah, 1967), is colloquial and irreverent, concerned with love and political topics. Romero's books include *El poeta de vidrio* (The Glass Poet, 1979) and *A vista del tiempo* (A View of Time, 2005).

Contemp. to the nadaístas were three poets who, in spite of a personal voice, followed the moderate character of traditional Colombian poetry. They reinstate its conservative trend. Giovanni Quessep (b. 1939) is a formalist poet who returns to symbolism for musical and verbal elements, which he will transform in incantatory and obscure poems where lyric and narrative become intertwined. José Manuel Arango (1937–2002) was a rigorous poet of brevity and musicality. His first books appeared late in life: *Este lugar de la noche* (This Place of Night, 1973) and *Signos* (Signs, 1978). Jaime García Maffla (b. 1944) is a philosophical and religious poet. His poems, cathedrals of lang., are obscure and liturgical.

During the 1970s, another group of poets, called by critics the *Generación sin nombre* (Generation without a Name), confronted the nadaístas. This challenge was not aesthetic or programmatic, since these poets also espoused freedom of forms and themes, colloquialism, and a questioning of conservative values. Their goal was literary-political, to reshape Colombia's literary world. The critic and poet Juan Gustavo Cobo Borda (b. 1948) was a central figure in remaking the *canon, as in *La tradición de la pobreza* (The Tradition of Poverty, 1980). His poetry, however, followed the line of nadaísmo (sarcasm, humor, colloquialism) with self-confidence. María Mercedes Carranza (1945–2003) continued the trend of colloquial poetry, rejecting sentimentalism in favor of a direct, common speech. Elkin Restrepo (b. 1942) was linked to the nadaísta group at the beginning of his career, although he distanced himself early in the 1970s. His poetry, ranging from the prose poem to conventional verse, deals with urban life and a nostalgic feeling for the past. His books include *Bla, bla, bla* (1967) and *Retrato de artistas* (Portrait of Artists, 1983).

Harold Alvarado Tenorio (b. 1945) is an irreverent poet of love and Colombian society as well as a critic. Among his books are *Pensamientos de un hombre llegado el invierno* (Thoughts of a Man Come to Winter, 1972) and *Recuerda cuerpo* (Remember Body, 1983). Close to the nadaísta group in his first years, Juan Manuel Roca (b. 1946) is an independent poet who combines a deep lyricism and direct, almost surreal images. His themes vary from love and everyday life to social issues, without falling into politics or the colloquialisms of his time. His books include *Memoria del agua* (Memory of Water, 1973) and *Luna de ciegos* (Moon of the Blind, 1990).

Santiago Mutis (b. 1952), Ramón Cote Baraibar (b. 1963), and Orietta Lozano (b. 1956) represent a group that appeared after the turmoil of the 1960s, opening new avenues for contemp. poetry. Mutis's highly lyrical poetry, notably *Tú también eres de lluvia* (You Too Are of the Rain, 1982) and *Soñadores de pájaros* (Dreamers of Birds, 1987), often finds its imagery in paintings. Cote Baraibar is a conservative poet of magisterial craft; his books include *Poemas para una fosa común* (Poems for a Common Grave, 1983) and *El confuso trazado de las fundaciones* (Confused Plan of the Foundations, 1991). Lozano is a very important voice in the emergence of women's poetry. Her poetry is highly sensual and erotic, a drastic change from the cautious poetry written by most women in the Colombian trad. Her books include *Fuego secreto* (Secret Fire, 1980) and *El vampiro esperado* (Expected Vampire, 1987).

*See* SPAIN, POETRY OF; SPANISH AMERICA, POETRY OF.
■ C. A. Caparroso, *Dos ciclos de lirismo colombiano* (1961); R. Maya, *Los orígenes del modernismo en Colombia* (1961); A. Holguín, *Antología crítica de la poesía colombiana (1874–1974)* (1974); J. Arango Ferrer, *Horas de literatura colombiana* (1978); J. Mejía Duque, *Momentos y opciones de la poesía colombiana* (1979); A. Romero, *Las palabras están en situación* (1985); F. Charry Lara, *Poesía y poetas colombianos* (1986); H. Orjuela, *Estudios sobre la literatura indígena y colonial* (1986); *Historia de la poesía colombiana*, ed. M. M. Carranza (1991); R. Echavarría, *Quién es quién en la poesía colombiana* (1998); J. G. Cobo Borda, *Historia de la poesía colombiana* (2006).

A. ROMERO

**COLON** (Gr., "limb, member"). As a metrical term, colon may refer to at least three different things: (1) a metrical or rhythmical unit sometimes divisible into two or three equivalent metra (see METRON) but also capable of functioning alongside cola of a similar or different character as a means of articulating rhythmical sequences that resist division into such metra; (2) a syntactical or rhetorical phrase, usually marked off by punctuation, that combines with comparable phrases to articulate the meaning of a sentence; and (3) the portions of a rhythmical pattern that intervene between any two positions at which word end is significantly more frequent in instantiations of the pattern than its absence. Type 1 cola are *rhythmical*: basic components of a verse design; type 2 cola are *rhetorical*: a way of articulating the text of a given instantiation of the design; type 3 cola are *verbal-rhythmical*: a means of achieving a compromise between the constancy of a given rhythmical design and the large variety of verbal patterns theoretically capable of appearing in its instantiations.

Rhythmical cola are usually what a writer has in mind in discussing those forms in which the colon rather than the metron is felt to be the basic rhythmical unit. Verbal-rhythmical cola appear frequently in discussions of the structure of metric forms such as the Gr. *trimeter, which, in the earliest stages of its devel., is a variable dicolon: either x – ⌣ – x + – ⌣ – x – ⌣ – or x – ⌣ – x – ⌣ + – x – ⌣ –, depending on whether the penthemimeral or hephthemimeral *caesura, one or the other of which was obligatory, appears in the particular line under consideration. It is perfectly possible, however, for this verbal-rhythmical dicolon to be a rhetorical tricolon as well—as in Menander's "*O dystyches! O dystyches! O dystyches!*" ("Woe! Woe! Woe!" [*Dyskolos* 574]). Here the first verbal-rhythmical colon ends after the second "*O*," the first rhetorical one after the first "*dystyches*." (Compare the structure of the *alexandrin ternaire,* which shows a rhetorical 4–4–4 grouping of syllables but usually retains the word end after the sixth syllable that allows it to be, like the cl. *alexandrine, a verbal-rhythmical dicolon).

As the number of attested instances of any given design decreases, it becomes increasingly difficult to distinguish rhetorical from verbal-rhythmical cola, and when regular metric structure is absent, the two tend to merge or become confused with rhythmical cola as well. In such situations, the overall verse design may be so irregular that identification of rhythmical units is possible only if one assumes that rhetorical boundaries or recurring verbal boundaries coincide with the boundaries of basic rhythmical units. Proceeding on this assumption, perfectly justified in many instances, has been standard practice, at least since Aristophanes of Byzantium (ca. 250–185 BCE) established his "measuring into cola" (*colometria)* for the lyric poets and the lyric portions of drama and began the custom of allotting to each colon its separate line of text. It is not valid in all instances, however, and one must reckon with the possibility, first raised by A. M. Dale, that the whole notion of the colon as a basic structural unit analogous to the foot or metron is inappropriate in dealing with certain types of rhythm.

*See* EPIPLOKE, PERIOD, PUNCTUATION.
■ J. Irigoin, *Recherches sur les mètres de la lyrique chorale grecque* (1953), with the review by L.P.E. Parker, *Bulletin of the Institute of Classical Studies* 5 (1958); G. S. Kirk, "The Structure of the Homeric Hexameter," *Yale Classical Studies* 20 (1966); Dale, "Classification and Terminology" (1968), and "The Metrical Units of Greek Lyric Verse," *Collected Papers* (1969); West, "Units of Analysis," sec. IB; L. E. Rossi, "Estensione e valore del *colon* nell' esametro omerico," *Struttura e storia dell'esametro Greco*, ed. M. Fantuzzi and R. Pretagostini (1996); N. Baechle, *Metrical Constraint and the Interpretation of Style in the Tragic Trimeter* (2007).

A. T. COLE

## COLONIAL POETICS

**I. Definition.** The term *colonial poetics* has not been employed systematically in literary and cultural crit. Given this lack of definition, it may be broadly interpreted as any aspect of *poetics that has been affected by conditions of colonialism. Colonialism may be defined as the domination of one political territory over another, whether in the form of settler colonies, unequal trade relations, or any other restrictive political influence. Although *colonialism* is closely related to the term *imperialism*, the two refer to distinct aspects of extraterritorial domination. Imperialism, derived from the Lat. *imperium*, emphasizes the systematic domination of one state over another or many others and often implies an overarching ideological project. Although also derived from a Roman term, in this case for extraterritorial settlements or *coloniae*, colonialism has come to refer to the ground-level practices of imperial domination, with an emphasis on the cultural and social effects upon the colonized territory. Thus, the term has been limited to those imperial projects that actively seek to effect cultural, religious, and political changes in the dominated territories.

A second problem in the definition of colonialism has been whether and how to distinguish it from postcolonialism (see POSTCOLONIAL POETICS). Although the latter suggests a period after political liberation from colonialism, many critics have argued that this temporal division does not recognize the continuity of the cultural effects of colonialism in the postindependence period. It also obscures the possibility of internal colonialism within the postindependence territory and neocolonialism, i.e., analogous forms of colonialism in the territory even after political independence. Given these problems, Ashcroft et al. have argued that the term *postcolonial* should be expanded to describe any resistance to colonialism, regardless of whether this occurs during or after formal colonial rule. Colonialism and postcolonialism have been further confused by the fact that critics who have been labeled "postcolonial" have provided the technical vocabulary for the study of colonialism; thus, studies of colonial history often imply a postcolonial critique. For the purposes of this essay, *colonialism* will be taken in its broadest sense to include cultural manifestations of imperial ideology, colonial practice, and postcolonial critique.

The concept of colonial poetics must be further distinguished from that of colonial discourse, first inaugurated by Said in *Orientalism*. Whereas colonial discourse has often been associated with imperial domination, the term *colonial poetics* suggests a system of figural lang., whether or not this is strictly poetic verse, that can resist as well as further the practice of colonialism. Indeed, poetry and poetics have often served in colonial contexts to draw attention to the limits of imperial reason, whether to unmask its power or to contest it with alternative forms of meaning. Since the concept of colonial poetics ultimately applies a Western notion to situations of domination or competition between Western and non-Western cultural systems, however, the term also calls attention to the cross-cultural tensions around poetry, poetic form, and

nonanalytic meaning inherent in colonial contexts. In order to outline the specific historical ways in which colonialism and poetics have interacted, this essay follows a chronological division that has divided Eur. colonialism into pre- and post-Enlightenment models. It emphasizes points of similarity between these periods, however, and considers the possibilities of applying the term *colonial poetics* to neocolonial, non-Western and premod. forms of political domination.

**II. Classical and Pre-Enlightenment.** Although it could potentially refer to the cultural effects of any large-scale political domination of one state over another, colonialism has most often been associated with Eur. expansion after the 15th c. Initial critiques and theories of colonialism, tied to the post-1945 decolonization of Asia and Africa, were based on post-Enlightenment Brit. and Fr. colonial models. Critics such as Hulme, Dussel, and Mignolo, however, have argued that mod. forms of colonialism began much earlier, with Iberian expansion into Africa, Asia, and, esp., into the Americas. Incl. even earlier empires, such as the Gr., Roman, and Ottoman, within the scope of colonialism has been more contentious, ostensibly because these imperial projects did not involve forced cultural transformation or capitalist economies. Cl. and non-Western philosophy and imperial models, however, have provided Eur. imperialism with many of its framing concepts and practices. Critics have also used theories drawn from later models of colonialism to investigate questions of cultural negotiation and political domination both in med. Europe and in cl. Greece and Rome, without necessarily arguing that these periods were colonialist.

Early mod. Eur. colonialism had its origins in the reconquest of Iberian regions that had been under Islamic rule since 711 and the subsequent economic expansion into Africa. Although the conquest of the Caribbean began in 1492, it was not until after the conquests of the Mexica (Aztec) Empire in 1521 and the Inca Empire in 1532 that the Sp. state began coordinating what until then had been ad hoc colonial practice. One of the strongest models for early mod. imperialist poetics was the cl. *epic. While Luís de Camões's *Os Lusíadas* (*The Lusiads*, 1572), narrating Vasco da Gama's voyage to India, and Alonso de Ercilla's *La Araucana* (*The Araucaniad*, 1569–89), narrating the Sp. conquest of Chile, are the best-known examples of epic poetry on Iberian imperialist themes, numerous lesser-known epic poems were written to celebrate conquests such as those of the Canary Islands and of Ácoma in New Mexico. Vernacular indigenous poetics have to be reconstructed from postconquest documents and include few examples of poetry that react to Sp. colonization. One exception, included in Miguel León-Portilla's anthol. of indigenous sources on the Sp. conquest, is a poem that records the effects of the Sp. siege of Tenochtitlán (Mexico City). Because indigenous systems of education were dismantled under Sp. rule, it is harder to find examples of indigenous poetics that incorporated long-term cultural changes. Critics such as Greene and Dagenais have argued that the Petrarchan lyric trad. provided a poetic model for desire and resistance that anticipated Iberian colonialism and influenced later works such as the *Royal Commentaries* (1609), a history of the Inca empire written by the mestizo author El Inca Garcilaso de la Vega (see PETRARCHISM). In arguments such as these, colonial poetics could be understood to be the shared appropriation of a Western lyric trad. in order to represent the consequences of colonial domination.

Unlike Iberian colonialism, the Brit. colonization of North America was built around closed communities of settlers with little emphasis on widespread indigenous conversion. The rhet. of the 16th-c. Eng. settlement of Ireland, however, holds many similarities to that of Iberian colonization. Edmund Spenser's *A View of the Present State of Ireland* (written 1596), e.g., advocates forced cultural change in order to civilize what he represents as the degenerate peoples of Ireland. Canny has argued that its thematic continuities with Spenser's epic *allegory of the Tudor dynasty, *The Faerie Queene* (1590, 1596), suggest both his initial belief in and later disillusionment with poetry as a medium for moral reform. Although the Petrarchan trad. provides a platform for comparing Brit. and Iberian colonial poetics, the nature of Brit. colonization in the Americas resulted in fewer opportunities for the cross-cultural poetics of Iberian America. Egan has noted that Anne Bradstreet's commendatory poems, e.g., avoided Am. themes altogether in order to escape associations with savagery. Examples of popular *satire, one poetic mode shared by Iberian and Brit. Ams. in the late 17th and 18th cs., also betray the difference between Iberian and Brit. colonialism. In Iberian America, the satiric poetry of Gregório de Matos in Bahia and Juan del Valle y Caviedes in Lima introduced indigenous and Af. lexicon and themes to mock the racial heterogeneity of Am. society. De Matos's poems in particular have led to a pointed debate between de Campos, who considered them to be creative engagements with colonial Brazil's social reality, and Hansen, who argued they are moral correctives in line with colonial governance in Bahia. By contrast, Richards has argued that Brit. Am. satire of the same period included local themes and objects only to highlight the transformation of Brit. settlers in the Americas.

Brooks has shown that in 18th-c. Brit. America a discourse of Christian redemption marked the first pub. works by Af. Am. and Native Am. authors, incl. the poetry of Af.-born Phillis Wheatley and the religious prose and hymnody of Samson Occom, a Mohegan tribal leader. Although transcriptions of Mayan cosmogonic texts such as the *Popol Vuh* and the books of *Chilam Balam* date from the beginning of the 18th c., and could, therefore, be considered under the rubric of a colonial poetics, it was only in the late 20th c. that they were read for their critical perspectives on Sp. colonization.

## III. Post-Enlightenment and Neocolonialism. What is often called "high" Eur. imperialism—the Brit. and Fr. expansion into the Middle East, Asia, and Africa during the 18th and 19th cs.—has been seen to reflect the philosophical and economic changes of the mid-18th c. onward. Young, for instance, distinguishes between the tribute-oriented Iberian imperialism and the market capitalism of 19th-c. imperialism. Enlightenment notions of historical progress also overrode the Iberian emphasis on redemption through conversion to create a Eurocentric evolutionary scale. At the same time, an emphasis on self-expression and representation in both the 18th-c. republican revolutions and in *romanticism created particular paradoxes for 19th-c. imperialism. Romanticism, moreover, established poetry as a field that was morally and cognitively distinct from instrumental reason and thus provided a medium to critique imperial bureaucracy and capitalism. Yet it is important to note that romanticism was also a main source of Orientalism, which, as Said defines it, sought to represent the "other" in collusion with Eur. imperialism.

Despite sharing many Eur. influences, regions that had been subject to pre- and post-Enlightenment colonization developed distinct poetic trads. in the 19th c. In the newly independent Sp. Am. nations, where the creole elite continued a policy of internal colonization even after the end of Sp. rule, indigenous culture also became a source of national identity. The poetic manifestation of this interest in indigenous culture was strongest in imperial Brazil, however, where coastal indigenous people had been ravaged by early settlement. Romantic poetics marked poems such as Antônio Gonçalves Dias's celebration of Tupi warriors in "I-Juca-Pirama" (1851) and prose works such as José de Alencar's *Iracema* (1865), a narrative of the love between a Port. colonizer and an indigenous woman, whose highly poetic style he claimed was inspired by indigenous lang. While in Sp. America and Brazil a marginalized indigenous culture lent itself to the nostalgic invention of national origins, 19th-c. Eur. colonialism was unable to dismantle fully vernacular literary trads. Even so, the survival of vernacular poetics did not indicate a resistance to colonialism, as Pollock has noted in the case of the Sanskrit revival in early 19th-c. Bengal. Instead, Bengali poets such as Michael Madhusudan Dutt sought to assimilate Eur. influences into new vernacular poetic forms such as the Bengali *sonnet and an adaptation of *blank verse in *The Slaying of Meghanada* (1861), an epic poem whose theme is drawn from the Sanskrit epic *Rāmāyaṇa*.

By the end of the 19th c., these regional adaptations of romanticism had led to a more consciously critical anti-imperialist poetics. Both the Cuban José Martí and the Philippine José Rizal, e.g., faced the anomalous transition from Sp. to Am. imperialism by returning to the romantic utopias of Simón Bolívar's pan-Americanism to critique republican nationalism. In Bengal, Rabindranath Tagore's poems blended Bengali metaphysics and Western poetic trads. in a style initially embraced but later critiqued by non-Indian poets such as W. B. Yeats. Chakrabarty has argued that this crit. reflects a lack of understanding of how Tagore's humanist poetics sought a locally rooted idiom for nationalism. The Chinese poet and critic Guo Moruo, whose essay "The National and the Supranational"

(1923) dates from the same period, also selectively appropriated Western influences to find a cosmopolitan idiom beyond nativist nationalism. In the period leading up to and immediately following World War II, anticolonial poetics, such as those of Senagalese Léopold Senghor and Martinican Aimé Césaire, became more strongly drawn to nativist affirmation. Although in the same period, Frantz Fanon critiqued the anticolonial nationalism of the *Negritude movement, of which Sédar Senghor and Césaire were founders, this attack did not indict poetics per se as an instrument of decolonization. Indeed, both Césaire's and Fanon's prose have been called a poetics (Kelley, Bhabha), an application that continues to promote figural lang. as an antidote to colonial reason.

In what has been categorized as the postcolonial period, roughly after 1965, debates on nationalism and decolonization have given way to a divided stance on vernacular lang. and poetic trad. On the one hand, there has been an embrace of the cultural hybridity that has resulted from colonialism. This stance is most evident in Caribbean authors, from the *neobaroque poetics of José Lezama Lima and Alejo Carpentier in the 1940s and 1950s to the later cultural crit. of Édouard Glissant. On the other hand, there has been a movement away from hybridity and toward a recuperation of vernacular poetics and lang. This position is most forcefully argued in Ngũgĩ's *Decolonising the Mind* but may also be seen in the concerted effort to promote indigenous poetics in both North and South America, of which Tedlock's anthropologically informed trans. of the Mayan *Popol Vuh* is representative. A third poetic stance has manifested itself in the critical rewriting of Western and colonial classics, both among poets who embrace cultural hybridity and those who reject it. Examples of the former are Césaire's 1968 rewriting of Shakespeare's *The Tempest*, José Emilio Pacheco's 1969 poetic recreation of Bernal Díaz del Castillo's chronicle of the Sp. conquest of Mexico in "Crónica de Indias," and St. Lucian poet Derek Walcott's 1990 rewriting of Homer's *Odyssey* in his epic poem *Omeros*. An example of the latter is the Mapuche poet Elicura Chihuailaf's 2006 trans. of sections of Ercilla's *La Araucana* into Mapundungun.

Although renewed or continued colonialism during the period of postcolonialism after 1965 has often been referred to as neocolonialism, the distinction between the two is not always easy to make. Arias has called attention to the ways in which Maya intellectuals in Guatemala have become more globally oriented than their political opponents, for instance, even while they continue to suffer from the legacy of internal colonialism. The poetry of Maḥmūd Darwīsh denounces present Israeli politics while taking up the issue of Palestinian memory, a theme closer to those of postcolonial poetics. And Chicano poets such as Gloria Anzaldúa have returned to the memory of indigenous colonization to expose Chicano marginalization in the U.S. These examples challenge the very terms that have limited colonialism to Eur. imperialism from the 15th to the 20th cs. Finally, studies that apply a postcolonial perspective to non-Eur. empires—for instance, to that of the Japanese in Taiwan after 1895—will potentially find relationships between poetics and colonialism that have not been considered by this essay.

*See* ANTHROPOLOGY AND POETRY, CULTURAL STUDIES AND POETRY, ETHNOPOETICS, POLITICS AND POETRY.

■ R.D.G. Kelley, "A Poetics of Anticolonialism," intro. to A. Césaire, *Discourse of Colonialism* (1972); E. Said, *Orientalism* (1979); Ngũgĩ wa Thiong'o, *Decolonising the Mind* (1981); *Popol Vuh*, intro. and trans. D. Tedlock (1985); P. Hulme, *Colonial Encounters* (1986); B. Ashcroft, G. Griffiths, and H. Tiffin, *The Empire Writes Back* (1989); É. Glissant, *Caribbean Discourse* (1989); J. A. Hansen, *A Sátira e o Engenho* [Satire and Wit] (1989); E. Hobsbawm, *The Age of Empire, 1875–1914* (1989); D. Quint, *Epic and Empire* (1993)—on cl. and early mod. imperialist epic; H. Bhabha, *The Location of Culture* (1994); E. Said, *Culture and Imperialism* (1994); E. Dussel, "Eurocentrism and Modernity," in *The Postmodernism Debate in Latin America,* ed. J. Beverley, M. Aronna, and J. Oviedo (1995); F. Lucas, "Brazilian Poetry from the 1830s to the 1880s," *Cambridge History of Latin American Literature*, ed. R. González Echevarría and E. Pupo-Walker, v. 3 (1996); G. Anzaldúa, *Borderlands/ La Frontera* (1999); R. Greene, *Unrequited Conquests* (1999); D. Chakrabarty, *Provincializing Europe* (2000); W. Mignolo, *Local Histories/Global Designs* (2000); L.T.S. Ching, *Becoming Japanese* (2001)—postcolonial perspective on Japanese colonialism in Taiwan; S. Gikandi, *Ngugi wa Thiong'o* (2001); S. Pollock, "The Death of Sanskrit," *Comparative Studies in Society and History* 43 (2001); J. Ramazani, *The Hybrid Muse* (2001); S. Shih, *The Lure of the Modern* (2001)—on modernism in China, 1917–37; R.J.C. Young, *Postcolonialism* (2001); J. Brooks, *American Lazarus* (2003); N. Canny, *Making Ireland British, 1580–1650* (2003); J. D. Blanco, "Bastards of the Unfinished Revolution," *Radical History Review* 89 (2004)—on Rizal and Martí; J. Dagenais, "The Postcolonial Laura," and I. Malkin, "Postcolonial Concepts and Ancient Greek Colonization," *MLQ* 65 (2004); F. Fanon, *The Wretched of the Earth*, trans. R. Philcox ([1961] 2004); C. B. Seely, "Introduction," *The Slaying of Meghanada* (2004); A. Loomba, *Colonialism/Postcolonialism,* 2d ed. (2005); H. de Campos, *Novas*, trans. A. Sergio Bessa and O. Cisneros (2007); *The Broken Spears*, ed. M. León-Portilla, trans. L. Kemp, rev. ed. (2007); A. Arias, "The Maya Movement," *Coloniality at Large,* ed. M. Moraña, E. Dussel, and C. Jáuregui (2008); J. Egan, "Creole Bradstreet," and J. H. Richards, "Barefoot Folks with Tawny Cheeks," in *Creole Subjects in the Colonial Americas,* ed. R. Bauer and J. A. Mazzotti (2009)—Richards on Brit. Am. satire.

A. H. MORE

# COMEDY

I. Definition
II. Ancient Greek
III. Modern Global Comedy

**I. Definition.** To ask what comedy is looses a Pandora's box of wild questions, with slim hope of answers. We can reduce their gamut by acknowledging that the Eng. word's primary meaning is of a stage or film performance involving a course of chiefly humorous and pleasant effects and a fortunate outcome, arousing laughter and joy. Sp. *comedia* can mean *any* stage play, and the best-known It. *commedia* is Dante's epic poem: as having a desired, fortunate end. These last two usages are imprecise, letting us include all drama and *epic, besides Dante, such as the *Rāmāyaṇa*, *Amir Hamza*, the *1001 Nights*, and endlessly more. The Eng. term *comedy* can also name the sort of *theme* apt for comic performance, so that a real-life event, a poem, or a novel is a "comedy," instead of, say, a *"limerick," *"clerihew," or a "comic novel": names implying that the word *comedy* used outside theater or film is derivative. So med. Ar. *maqāmāt* and their likely sequel, the Sp. picaresque, novels such as Amos Tutuola's *Palm-Wine Drinkard*, Ngũgĩ wa Thiong'o's *Wizard of the Crow*, or Samuel Selvon's London series are all "comedies": with a fortunate end and/or humorous episodes. These last, too, can include *satire, burlesque, or fantasy (quite usually in colonial and postcolonial studies of comedy). Such broad usages are not at issue here, where we look at performance, though many of our observations evidently have wider relevance. At the same time, choosing a narrow definition and the specific (Gr.) story enabling it—not least because it was there "paired" with *tragedy as to both performance and later crit.—implies a clarity, even a sort of purity absent from the comic in other world trads. We address this issue further at the start of section III.

Like tragedy, the Western trad. of comedy is taken to have begun with the ancient Greeks. Of comic performance, theirs are the oldest written traces and longest critical trad., going back at least to Plato. The age and clarity of the Gr. trad. make it a good place to seek definitions, even as we agree that the global presence of comedy may confirm (already Gr.) speculations on laughter—like reason and speech—as a defining characteristic of humanity. We need to distinguish between speculative generalizations about the "comic spirit," which can result in the sort of generic elisions already mentioned, and more exact historical description serving to analyze the function of comedy in society. We must also discriminate between such description and efforts to analyze the "psychology" of laughter because the event of comedy and the eruption of mirth are not the same.

The name *comedy* is from Comus, a Gr. fertility god. In ancient Greece, *comedy* named a rite of spring now thought to celebrate cyclical rebirth, resurrection, and rejuvenation. Mod. scholars and critics have thus seen in comedy a universal celebration of life, a joyous outburst of laughter in the face of either an incomprehensible world or a repressive sociopolitical order. Carnival, festival, folly, and a general freedom of action, then, indicate either acceptance of the first or resistance to the second: the latter letting scholars easily explain comedy in colonial and neocolonial conditions (as if its performers had not had comedy for centuries). Scholars have taken such notions further. If tragedy plays a fall from some "sacred irrationality," comedy triumphantly affirms that riotous unreason and humanity's share in the chaotic forces that produce life. The comic protagonist's defeat mirrors the tragic protagonist's failure, both ritual cleansings by way of a scapegoat—in comedy, one representing life-threatening forces. Such speculations have been advanced in various forms by classicists (Cornford, Harrison, Murray), philosophers (Bakhtin, Langer), literary critics (Barber, Frye), anthropologists, and sociologists. Whether such theories help see what *comedies* are is a fair question. They fancy that under any given comedy lies a profound universal "carnival" common to the human world everywhere and always. They remove comedies from their historical time and social context. Yet even so seemingly fantasist a theater as that of Aristophanes is misconstrued by theories neglecting his comedies' basis in the social and political intricacies of their age and place—Athens during the Peloponnesian Wars.

This is not to say that some peoples do not have such a sense of their place in the world. Hopis, writes Stott, see "clowning as fundamental to identity, as they hold that they are descended from an original clown youth and clown maiden. For them [says one ethnographer] 'clowning symbolizes the sacredness of humanity in the strict sense—that there is something sacred in being a finite and mortal being separated from god.' By embracing the identity of their first parents, the Hopi acknowledge the distance between their daily lives and their idea of spiritual perfection, finding religious value in the knowledge that they are flawed." This, besides difficulties in equating clowning with laughter and the comic (the trad. of the sad, even grieving, clown is worldwide), is far from comedy in any familiar Western sense—whatever analogies Stott may perceive with Dante.

Setting aside broad metaphysical speculations, we should look at accounts of laughter as a human reaction to certain kinds of events. We can by and large divide these accounts into three theories. One asserts that laughter is aroused by a sense of superiority (Thomas Hobbes's "sudden glory"); another that it evinces "psychic release" in the face of anxiety, fear, or incomprehension; the third that it is elicited by an abrupt sense of the ludicrous, the incongruous, a dissociation of event and expectation. All three go back to the oldest commentators but with different emphases at different times. The idea of psychic release is analogous to that of emotional purgation popular (esp. apropos of tragedy) in the Eur. Ren. but is nowadays most associated with Freudian and post-Freudian theories of displacement. Too, though the superiority theory goes back to Plato and Aristotle, it was most explored by Hobbes, Henri-Louis Bergson, and George Meredith. It posits our joy in seeing ourselves more fortunate than others or in some way freer. Bergson's idea that one of the causes of laughter is a sudden perception of someone as a kind of automaton or puppet, as though some freedom of action had been lost, is one version of this.

The theory of comedy as the ludicrous or as a dissociation of expectation and event also began with Aristotle and has been evoked by Immanuel Kant, Arthur Schopenhauer, Søren Kierkegaard, Sigmund Freud, and many others. In *Poetics*, ch. 5, Aristotle holds that comedy imitates people "worse than average; worse, however, not as regards any and every sort of fault, but only as regards one particular kind, the Ridiculous, which is a species of the Ugly. The Ridiculous may be defined as a mistake or deformity not productive of pain or harm to others" (trans. Ingram Bywater). Similar remarks exist in his *Rhetoric* and in a med. Gr. ms. known as the *Tractatus Coislinianus*, Aristotelian in argument and possibly even an actual epitome of the otherwise lost work on comedy that Aristotle mentions in the *Poetics* (Janko). Save for suggesting some detail of dissociative word and action, this text adds little to what may be gleaned from extant texts of Aristotle. It does, however, draw a parallel between comedy and tragedy by observing that *catharsis also occurs in comedy: "through pleasure and laughter achieving the purgation of like emotions." The meaning of such a phrase is unclear, though it suggests comedy as an almost Stoic device to clean away extremes of hedonism and root out carnivalesque temptations.

These theories complement each other as explanations of the psychology of laughter, but that of incongruity seems more *particularly* applicable to comedy than the others in seeking also both to indicate *devices* specifically provocative of laughter and to explain their *effect* on a spectator. What unites these devices and effects is the aim to provoke laughter; the use of mockery and satire; the activities of characters who, as to rank, class, or caste, run from low to middle; and plots that begin in uncertainty and uproar and end in the happy reestablishment of calm (symbolized by marriage, banquet, dance, or other ritual of communal bonding). They seem to offer some kind of "lesson," though the political, social, or ethical nature of the lesson may lack clarity. Quite usually, in addition to various degrees of slapstick and other low stage stuff, they incorporate music, song, and dance. The "Aristotelian" analyses are more generally suggestive. First, their sort of laughter requires oddity, distortion, folly, or some such "version of the ugly," without pain. This laughter assumes sympathy. Second, although this theory is kinder than that of superiority, it too has its part of cruelty, lying in that touch of ugliness. Third, all three theories take laughter as *means*, as commentary on or correction of what we may call the real, even local world: unlike metaphysical theories, which make mirth an end in itself and an escape into some "universality." Fourth, these theories (which supplement rather than oppose one another) require the laugher to be aware of some disfiguring of an accepted norm. Comedy and laughter imply a habit of normality, a familiarity of custom, from which the comic is a deviation. It may be the case that comedy, like tragedy, shows the construction of such order, but above all it demonstrates why such order must be conserved.

**II. Ancient Greek.** This fourth trait hints why comic competition began at the Athenian Dionysia in 486 BCE, some 50 years *after* that for tragedy, as a new polity was solidifying. Aristotle tells that the first competition was won by Chionides, who with Magnes represented a first generation of Gr. writers of comedy. Around 455, a comic victory was won by Cratinus, who with Crates formed the second generation. Many titles have survived and some fragments, but these constitute nearly the sum of extant facts about Athenian comedy until Aristophanes' victory with *Acharnians* in 425. We know that in this competition Cratinus was second with *Kheimazomenoi*, and Eupolis third with *Noumeniai*. These names tell us little, but we may assume that Aristophanic comedy was fairly typical of this so-called Gr. Old Comedy: a mixture of dance, poetry, song, and drama, joining fantastic plots to mockery and acid satire of contemp. people, events, and customs. Most of Aristophanes' plays are hardly comprehensible if we know nothing of current social, political, and literary conditions.

Aristophanes did not hesitate to attack education, the law, tragedians, women's situation, and the very nature of Athenian "democracy." Above all, he attacked the demagogue Cleon, the war party he led, and the Peloponnesian War itself. This says much about the nature of Athenian freedoms, for Aristophanes wrote during the struggle with Sparta, when no one doubted that the very future of Athens was at issue. Aristophanes' last surviving play (of 11, 44 being attributed to him) is *Plutus* (388 BCE), a play criticizing myth but whose actual themes are avarice and ambition. Quite different in tone and intent from the preceding openly political plays, *Plutus* is considered the earliest (and only extant) example of Gr. Middle Comedy.

But the situation of comedy differed from that of tragedy, for another strong trad. existed. This was centered in Sicilian Syracuse, a Corinthian colony, and claimed one of the earliest Gr. comic writers, Epicharmus, working at the court of Hieron I in the 470s BCE. We know the titles of some 40 of his plays. Other comic poets writing in this Doric trad. were Phormis and the slightly younger Deinolochus, but the Dorians were supplanted by the Attic writers in the 5th c. and survive only in fragments. Another Sicilian, the late 5th c. Sophron, was the best-known composer of literary versions of the otherwise "para-" or "sub-" literary genre of comic mime, remaining popular for centuries through the Hellenistic period and across its world (Hordern). From the 4th c. exists a series of vase paintings from Sicily and southern Italy, suggesting that comedy still thrived in that area. The initiative had largely passed, however, to the Gr. mainland. *Plutus* is an example of that Middle Comedy, whose volume we know was huge. Plautus's Lat. *Amphitruo* (ca. 230 BCE) seems a version of another one. These imply that a major trait was mockery of myth. (Aristophanes' earlier *Frogs* [405 BCE], attacking Euripides and Aeschylus, tried in the Underworld, may be thought a forerunner.)

By the mid-4th c., so-called New Comedy held

the stage. Among its poets, the most celebrated and influential was unquestionably Menander. His "teacher" was one Alexis of Thurii in southern Italy, so we see how the "colonial" influence continued, though Alexis was based in Athens. Alexis is said to have written 245 plays and to have outlived his pupil. We know of Philemon from Cilicia or Syracuse, of Diphilos from Sinope on the Black Sea, and Apollodorus from Carystos in Euboea: New Comedy's sources were very widespread. Until the 1930s, however, only fragments seemed extant. Then, what can only be considered one of the great literary discoveries turned up a papyrus containing a number of Menander's comedies, complete or almost so. These plays deal not with political matters or crit. of myth but with broadly social matters (sometimes using mythical themes). The situations are domestic, the comedy is of manners, the characters are stock.

The Gr. Mediterranean and beyond knew many comic forms. By the mid-3rd c. at least, itinerant troupes crossed the Hellenistic world. By 240, Livius Andronicus, from Tarentum in southern Italy, had adapted Gr. plays into Lat. for public performance. Like Naevius and later Ennius, this poet composed both tragedy and comedy. From the 3rd c. as well dates Atellan farce (named from Atella in Campania), using stock characters and a small number of set scenes and featuring clowns (called Bucco or Maccus), foolish old men, and greedy buffoons. These farces were partly improvised, on the basis of skeletal scripts, much like the *commedia dell'arte* of almost two millennia later. The influence of Etrurian musical performance, southern It. drama, Gr. mime, New Comedy, and Atellan farce joined in the comedies of Plautus, who wrote in the late 3rd c. (Cicero says he died in 184 BCE). By him, 21 complete or almost complete comedies have survived. A little later Rome was entertained by the much more highbrow Terence, of whom six plays remain extant. These two authors provided themes, characters, and style for much comedy as it was to develop in Europe after the Ren.

**III. Modern Global Comedy.** The definitions and hist. just advanced pose the problem stated at the outset: that other world trads. have not used or relied on such clear generic distinctions as Western trads. imply. They did not do so, at least, until the domination by Western media that began early in the 20th c., perhaps marked in China by aspects of the New Culture (May 4th) Movement (1915–21) and later across colonial Africa and Asia by third-world independence movements (1950s–1970s). But by then Western comic forms were also losing such clarity as they may have had earlier. Let us take two well-known cases. Chinese *zaju* was a kind of drama that matured in the Yuan dynasty (1271–1368), though it grew from a form popular in the preceding Song and Jin dynasties, featuring lowly characters, song, clowns, and slapstick. After the Mongol invasions, the form grew into a more serious genre, with prelude and four acts often dealing with aspects of Mongol oppression, but still incorporating song, clowns, and much comic gesture and interplay. Some

of its plays, Ji Junxiang's *Orphan of the Zhao Family*, e.g., or Li Xingfu's *Chalk Circle*, later found their way into the Western theater, the first as Voltaire's *Orphelin de la Chine*, the second as Bertolt Brecht's *Caucasian Chalk Circle*. Neither would be thought a comedy, and it may be that a category of *comedy* is indeed not useful to describe many other cultures' forms of performance. Elements of *Yuan zaju* subsist in many mod. Chinese dramatic forms, most familiarly, perhaps, in the Beijing Opera.

A similar difficulty of generic distinctions characterizes Japanese *kabuki*, a dramatic form invented early in the 17th c. as a ribald dance theater of everyday life, first performed entirely by women and closely tied to prostitution. Banned in 1629, it revived in mid-century as an all-male performance, though still with its earlier characteristics. Slowly, from the late 17th c., it acquired its mod. form, notably its association with *bunraku*, puppet theater. Kabuki plays are historical, domestic, or dance. The first usually uses samurai characters, the second lowly town or country people. The plays may appeal to serious emotional effect (the most famed of the second kind are those of Chikamatsu Monzaemon, often involving romantic tales of impossible and fatal love) or be happily zany, while all are characterized by highly stylized, even kitsch, costume and makeup and often luridly elaborate staging, sets, and machinery. Here, too, the comic has its place but no separate one. Unlike these 13th–14th- and 17th–18th-c. Asian dramatic forms, Eur. ones continued much in the generic wake of Greco-Lat. antiquity.

While humanist scholars of the 16th c. published and then imitated Plautus and Terence, Eur. vernacular comedy had long been developing in the farces, *sotties*, and comic interludes widely performed in the Middle Ages. So, the early 16th c. saw the publication of much school drama in both Lat. and vernaculars, while, in Italy just a little later, there developed the commedia dell'arte, whose influence was to be enormous. This was improvisational comedy, using sketchy scripts and a small number of stock characters—Harlequin, Columbine, Pantaloon, the Doctor, and others—and situations. Their plots drew on antiquity and med. folk art alike, and the form lived on into the popular *Comédie italienne* of late 17th-c. France, and remained visible in the plays of Pierre de Marivaux and Carlo Goldoni. It survives in our time in performances that often put the old characters or their avatars to work in the service of powerful political satire (as kabuki, esp. the historical, may make sharp commentary on contemp. conditions).

The commedia dell'arte developed in Italy, but other Eur. lands saw their own devel. of comedy, usually from a similar joining of sources. If Spain's late 15th-c. *Celestina* of Fernando de Rojas was a "comedy" in acts and in dialogue but never really intended for performance, by the late 16th c. that country's theater was equal to any in Europe. Félix Lope de Vega, Pedro Calderón de la Barca, and a host of others produced a multitude of romantic and realistic comedies dealing mainly with love and honor. They (and It. writers) provided innumerable plots, themes, and characters for comic writers of France and England, who also benefitted from both indigenous folk trads. and publication of Lat. comedy. In France, humanist comedy gave way in the late 1620s to a romantic form of comedy whose threefold source was the prose romance and novella of Spain, Italy, and France; Sp. comedy; and It. dramatic pastoral. A large group of major writers wrote in this style through mid-century, up to the poet whom many consider the greatest writer of comedy of all times.

Molière (pseud. of Jean-Baptiste Poquelin) wrote an enormous variety, in verse and prose, ranging from slapstick farce to plays approaching bourgeois tragic drama. *Comédie ballet*, comedy of situation, manners, intrigue, and character all flowed from his pen. He readily treated issues that roused the ire of religious *dévots* and professional bigots; nor did he shirk crit. of patriarchy, and much of his work has political overtones. Starting his theatrical career as leader of a traveling troupe, Molière made full use of folk trad., provincial dialect, commedia, and farce, as well as of cl. example. Many of his characters have become familiar types in Fr. trad. (the "misanthrope," "tartuffe," "dom juan"); many of his lines have become proverbial. While his plays do contain the now-familiar young lovers, old men both helpful and obstructive, wily servants both female and male, sensible wives and mothers (whereas husbands and fathers are almost always foolish, headstrong, cuckolded, or obstructive), they bear chiefly upon such matters as avarice, ambition, pride, hypocrisy, misanthropy, and other such extreme traits. What interests Molière is how such excess conflicts directly with the well-regulated and customary process of ordered society.

Following a similar trajectory to that of its southern neighbors in the 16th c., interacting both with them and its own past(s), England created hugely varied and long-lived comic trads. As in much else, Shakespeare's comedy stands out for its diversity: aristocratic romance, bitter and problematic farce, comedy of character, slapstick farce, and the almost tragic *Troilus and Cressida*. If any comedy may be analyzed with some "metaphysical" theory, it is no doubt Shakespeare's, with its concern for madness and wisdom, birth and death, the seasons' cycles, love and animosity. But it stayed unique; he had no direct heir. Ben Jonson's urbane comedy of humors, of types and of character, satirizing manners and morals, social humbug and excess of all kinds, and falling more clearly into the forms already seen, was soon followed by the remarkable flowering of Restoration comedy, with a crowd of authors, not a few copying Molière. They produced a brittle comedy of manners and cynical wit whose major impression is one of decay and an almost unbalanced self-interest. Excepting Shakespeare's, all these forms of Eur. comedy have continued into the present and thrive throughout the Western world. There is no need to detail names here. A late addition to the genre is the so-called dark comedy of the 20th c.'s second half. Perhaps a response to the killing grounds of World Wars I and II and, later, mostly African and Asian colonial wars and their murderous aftermaths, these comedies again portray everyday people; are set in bleak, often highly conflicted situations; and use comic wordplay, gesture, manners, slapstick, and other devices serving plots whose open-endedness is often forlorn, if not desolate, and whose humor figures a kind of defiant resignation before an empty world.

At the same time, one does have to take note of the extraordinary outpouring of drama, incl. comedy, in Africa and the Caribbean since independence. As said earlier, this is all too often interpreted as merely a way to displace varied "postcolonial" anxieties, or indeed an "allegory" of the "postcolonial condition." There is far more to these comedies (and tragedies), however, than this. Wole Soyinka's *Opera Wonyosi*, e.g., a Yoruba-inflected riff on John Gay's *Beggar's Opera* and Brecht's *Threepenny Opera*, whose very ties to these earlier satirical comedies invoke a complex play against a colonizing aesthetics, politics, and the capitalist economics that the earlier plays criticize and satirize at two crucial historical moments, is also a hilariously corrosive attack on the neocolonial Nigerian government that forged the Biafran war and established its military dictatorship. The same may be said of a play such as Efua Sutherland's *The Marriage of Anansewa*, which puts Akan traditional dramatic forms to work not in an attack on the Ghana of its moment (of which she was very optimistic) but in a humorous search to tie somehow together local trad. and a colonial overlay that, however bad, is inescapable. Such diverse concerns are common to comedy across Africa and find their way into the many langs. of Caribbean comedy. In many ways, too, all share interests with contemp. comedy around the world. Its authors sport ironically with the social, moral, political, and metaphysical dimensions of the human condition. Usually such issues are no longer held separate, and all are fair game for an ambiguous, perplexed, and uncertain derision, as if comedy had to dig ever deeper for those social norms referred to at the outset.

*See* DRAMATIC POETRY.

■ G. Meredith, *An Essay on Comedy* (1877); F. Nietzsche, *Die fröhliche Wissenschaft* (*The Gay Science*, 1882); G. Murray, *Greek Comic Verse* (1886); H. L. Bergson, *Le rire* (*Laughter,* 1912); F. M. Cornford, *The Origin of Attic Comedy* (1914); S. Freud, *Wit and Its Relation to the Unconscious* (1916), trans. A. A. Brill (1917); J. Harrison, *Themis* (1927); J. Feibleman, *In Praise of Comedy* (1939); M. T. Herrick, *Comic Theory in the Sixteenth Century* (1950); G. E. Duckworth, *The Nature of Roman Comedy* (1952); W. Sypher, *Comedy* (1956); Frye; S. K. Langer, *Philosophy in a New Key*, 3d ed. (1957); C. L. Barber, *Shakespeare's Festive Comedy* (1959); J. L. Styan, *The Dark Comedy* (1962); A. Nicoll, *The World of Harlequin* (1963); *Theories of Comedy*, ed. P. Lauter (1964); N. Frye, *A Natural Perspective* (1965); W. Kerr, *Tragedy and Comedy* (1967); M. M. Bakhtin, *Rabelais and His World*, trans. H. Iswolsky (1968); E. Olson, *The Theory of Comedy* (1968); W. M. Merchant, *Comedy* (1972); K. J. Dover, *Aristophanic Comedy* (1972); M. C. Bradbrook, *The Growth* and Structure of Elizabethan Comedy, 2d ed. (1973); R. B. Martin, *The Triumph of Wit: A Study of Victorian Comic Theory* (1974); A. Rodway, *English Comedy: Its Role and Nature from Chaucer to the Present Day* (1975); M. Gurewitch, *Comedy: The Irrational Vision* (1975); F. H. Sandbach, *The Comic Theatre of Greece and Rome* (1977); A. Caputi, *Buffo: The Genius of Vulgar Comedy* (1978); E. Kern, *The Absolute Comic* (1980); R. W. Corrigan, *Comedy: Meaning and Form*, 2d ed. (1981); K. H. Bareis, *Comoedia* (1982); D. Konstan, *Roman Comedy* (1983); E. L. Galligan, *The Comic Vision in Literature* (1984); R. Janko, *Aristotle on Comedy* (1984); K. N. Bame, *Come to Laugh: African Traditional Theatre in Ghana* (1985); E. W. Handley, "Comedy," *CHCL*, v. 1; R. L. Hunter, *The New Comedy of Greece and Rome* (1985); W. E. Gruber, *Comic Theaters* (1986); S. C. Shershow, *Laughing Matters: The Paradox of Comedy* (1986); H. Levin, *Playboys and Killjoys* (1987); L. Siegel, *Laughing Matters: Comic Traditions in India* (1987); A. Ziv, *National Styles of Comedy* (1988); P. Gilliatt, *To Wit: Skin and Bones of Comedy* (1990); R. S. Jenkins, *Subversive Laughter: The Liberating Power of Comedy* (1994); R.D.V. Glasgow, *Madness, Masks, and Laughter: An Essay on Comedy* (1995); S. E. Hengen, *Performing Gender and Comedy: Theories, Texts, and Contexts* (1998); E. Segal, *The Death of Comedy* (2001); *Comedy, Fantasy, and Colonialism*, ed. G. Harper (2002); J. H. Hordern, *Sophron's Mimes: Text, Translation and Commentary* (2004); M. Charney, *Comedy: A Geographic and Historical Guide* (2005); A. Stott, *Comedy* (2005); J. Hokenson, *The Idea of Comedy: History, Theory, Critique* (2006); E. Weitz, *The Cambridge Introduction to Comedy* (2009); *The Birth of Comedy*, ed. J. Rusten (2011).

T. J. REISS

**COMMA POEM.** A poem in which every word is followed by a comma. The device was invented by the Filipino poet and critic Jose Garcia Villa (1908–97) to highlight the integrity of each word and emphasize its dual function as both carrier of meaning and aesthetic object. In describing his practice, Garcia Villa wrote that "the method may be compared to Seurat's architectonic and measured pointillism—where the points of color are themselves the medium as well as the technique of expression: therefore functional and valid, as a medium of art and as a medium of personality."

Because the space after each comma is omitted, the commas used in comma poetry effect a different measure of *pause from those operating within a prose context. Since the comma represents the only pause separating words on every line, there ensues both an expansion and a contraction of time at the lineal pace—an expansion due to the excess of commas, a contraction due to the shrinking of space. This procedure ultimately emphasizes the word's primacy as the material of poetry.

*See* TYPOGRAPHY.

■ J. Garcia Villa, "Comma Poems," *The Anchored Angel*, ed. E. Tabios (1999).

J. CRISOSTOMO

**COMMONPLACE** (Gr. *Koinos topos*; Lat. *locus communis*, "common place" or "general theme"). Refers in cl. oratory to a mode of argument. Following the success of Ren. humanist pedagogy, *commonplace* has come to mean a notable passage, poem, or excerpt transmitted via the commonplace book, an important technology of cultural memory. Through association with ideas that are commonly held, it has also come to signify the trivial, hackneyed, or banal. The practice of commonplacing originated with the cl. conception of *topoi, rhetorical strategies designed to increase clarity and enhance authority in philosophical debate. Aristotle's "places" were categories of relationship, such as opposition, adjacency, or the relation of part to whole. Ren. humanists, who placed renewed emphasis on cl. trad., redefined these abstractions as textual fragments suitable for gathering. In two influential treatises of 1512, *De ratione studii* and *De copia*, Erasmus promoted the keeping of commonplace books as the best way of understanding and putting to use the cl. past, promulgating a system for organizing exemplary passages under headings and subheadings. Textualizing the commonplaces—transforming them from places in the mind to places in a text—gave them cultural specificity; they were no longer abstract and portable modes of relation but rather a shorthand for the prevailing cultural code.

Commonplacing is a mode of cultural transmission that allows for the deracination and reframing of authority. In the early mod. period, commonplace books were a primary means for making cl. antiquity accord with mod, Christian consensus. They also helped to elevate vernacular poetry through association with the poetry of the ancients. Echoing the med. trad. of gathering *sententiae* into *florilegia* (books of flowers), Robert Allen's *England's Parnassus* (1600) arranged "[t]he Choysest flowers of Our English Poets" under commonplace headings for future reference and use. Commonplace books were important tools for managing the flood of print that began to emerge from the popular press. Early mod. printed play texts, incl. the first quarto of *Hamlet* (1603), often indicated lines fit for copying by placing commas or inverted commas at the beginning of the line. In the late 17th c., John Locke proposed an alphabetical system for indexing and cross-referencing commonplaces, one that allowed for headings to emerge out of the course of reading (rather than needing to be established beforehand). Locke's scheme was widely reprinted in collected eds. of his work; printed indexes and an explanation of Locke's system were frequently appended to blank books sold to the learned for the purposes of commonplacing.

Commonplace books testify to a long and vibrant trad. of claiming moral authority for verse, pressing whole poems or excerpts into didactic uses. Poetic commonplaces tend to be framed already as quotable, ready to be plucked, favoring brevity, prescriptiveness, and a strong sense of closure. The popularity of commonplace books compiled by major poets, from Ben Jonson's posthumously printed *Timber* (1640) to Robert Southey's *Common-place Book* (1850) and R. W.

Emerson's *Parnassus* (1874), suggests not only readers' curiosity about poetic influence but also the cultural status of poets as moral exemplars.

Ms. and printed commonplace books offer a valuable record of poetic reception. Much women's poetry before the 19th c. survives chiefly in commonplace books and albums, testifying to the lively exchange of women's verse within coteries. The influence of this mode of circulation on canonical poetry is evident from numerous published poems by S. T. Coleridge, E. A. Poe, and others that begin "Lines Written in an Album . . ." Commonplacing thrived as long as printed books were expensive for readers to own; in the late 19th c., they began to give way to scrapbooks and collections that emphasized personal taste, not cultural prescription. Nevertheless, commonplace books remain valuable resources for scholars seeking to understand popular taste in poetry. The decontextualizing and recontextualizing processes at the heart of commonplacing, and its concern with imitation and emulation, can be seen in the Victorian and modernist fascination with *centos or patchwork poems comprised entirely from lines taken from other poems. A commonplace aesthetic can also be seen in the conceptual artist Jenny Holzer's *Truisms* (1977–), which use a wide array of media (incl. light projection, LED feeds, plaques, benches, T-shirts, and the Internet) to map sententious phrases onto public space, putting received wisdom under scrutiny.

*See* CLASSICISM, CLICHÉ, EPIGRAM, RENAISSANCE POETICS.

■ L. D. Lerner, "Cliché and Commonplace," *Essays in Criticism* 6 (1956); A. P. Debicki, "César Vallejo's Speaker and the Poetic Transformation of Commonplace Themes," *Kentucky Romance Quarterly* 17 (1970); J. A. Hiddleston, "*Fusée*, Maxim, and Commonplace in Baudelaire," *MLR* 80 (1985); S. G. Nichols, "Marie de France's Commonplaces," *YFS* (1991); M. T. Crane, *Framing Authority* (1993); A. Moss, *Printed Commonplace-Books* (1996), and "The *Politica* of Justus Lipsius and the Commonplace-Book," *Journal of the History of Ideas* 59 (1998); E. Havens, *Commonplace Books* (2001); T. Cave, "Thinking with Commonplaces: The Example of Rabelais," *(Re)Inventing the Past*, ed. G. Ferguson and C. Hampton (2003); P. Saint-Amour, *The Copywrights* (2003); L. Dacome, "Noting the Mind: Commonplace Books and the Pursuit of the Self in Eighteenth-Century Britain," *Journal of the History of Ideas* 65 (2004); J. Phillips, "'Vox populi, vox dei': Baudelaire's Uncommon Use of Commonplace in the *Salon de 1846*," *French Forum* 31 (2006); Z. Lesser and P. Stallybrass, "The First Literary *Hamlet* and the Commonplacing of Professional Plays," *Shakespeare Quarterly* 59 (2008); D. Allan, *Commonplace Books and Reading in Georgian England* (2010); A. M. Blair, *Too Much to Know* (2010); A. Grafton, "The Humanist and the Commonplace Book: Education in Practice," *Music Education in the Middle Ages and the Renaissance*, ed. R. E. Murray Jr. et al. (2010).

M. McGILL

**COMPANION POEMS.** Two poems designed to be read as complements, opposites, or replies. Truly paired poems are not common in Western poetry. Some of Shakespeare's sonnets are paired, e.g., 44 and 45 (on the four elements) and 46 and 47 (eye and heart), but the best-known companion poems in Eng. poetry are John Milton's "L'Allegro" and "Il Penseroso," which are truly paired, in the manner of rhetorical essays preferring the rival claims of day and night or youth and age. After Milton, there are Abraham Cowley's "Against Hope" and "For Hope," the former of which was also paired with Richard Crashaw's "For Hope"; and John Oldham's "Satyr against Virtue" with the "Counterpart." Such opposed poems were sometimes printed together in alternating stanzas: so Cowley and Crashaw on hope; the 17th-c. Dutch poet Maria Tesselschade Visscher's "Wilde en Tamme Zangster" (Wild and Tame Singer); Robert Burton's "Author's Abstract of Melancholy"; and Edmund Waller's "In Answer of Sir John Suckling's Verses," interwoven with Suckling's "Against Fruition." Some of the poems paired by one author against those by another are answer poems with parodic elements: Christopher Marlowe's "Come live with me and be my love" excited a number of such replies (see CONTRAFACTUM). Thus, Anthony Hecht's "Dover Bitch" may be thought a kind of "answer" to Matthew Arnold's "Dover Beach" a century earlier. John Donne's two "Anniversary" poems—"The Anatomy of the World" and "The Progress of the Soul"—are companion poems more by virtue of relation and contrast in theme, tone, and occasion. William Blake's *Songs of Innocence* and *Songs of Experience* include a number of poems set against each other and understood only by their contrasts. Similarly, Robert Browning's "Meeting at Night" and "Parting at Morning" pair two related experiences (see ECHO VERSE).

In Asian poetry, however, true answer poems, implying social intercourse in verse address, are found in large numbers in collections of Chinese, Korean, and Japanese poetry. The cl. poetic trads. of these countries assumed that the persons addressed were also poets, and, in fact, poetry was often exchanged on occasions that today would call for other forms of contact. Chinese poets often matched a poem received from a friend by writing another in the same form and using the same rhymes. It sometimes happened that Japanese poems not actually paired were brought together editorially with a headnote describing the (imaginary) situation, leading to a genre known as "tales of poems" (*uta-monogatari*), of which *Ise Monogatari* (*The Tales of Ise*) is the best-known example. Another Japanese example that flourished in cl. times was the *utaawase* (poetry match), in which two or more people competed by writing poems on given topics, with a response given by judges (see POETIC CONTESTS).

■ P. Mahony, "The Structure of Donne's *Anniversaries* as Companion Poems," *Genre* 5 (1972); B. K. Lewalski, "Milton, the Nativity Ode, the Companion Poems, and *Lycidas*," *Early Modern English Poetry*, ed. P. Cheney, A. Hadfield, G. A. Sullivan Jr. (2007).

F. J. WARNKE; E. MINER

**COMPLAINT** (Gr. *schetliasmos*, Lat. *plangere*). An established rhetorical term by the time of Aristotle's *Rhetoric* (1395a9), complaint is a varied mode that crosses numerous generic boundaries. Usually, it is a dramatic, highly emotional *lament that reveals the complainant's specific grievances against a public or private injustice. The most influential complaints from antiquity are found in Ovid's *Heroides*, a collection of epistolary complaints in which abandoned lovers narrate their stories in hope of receiving recognition for their suffering (Farrell). The mode also borrows from the Heb. trad. of lamentation in the books of Job and Jeremiah and the med. *planctus* that were central to mourning in the med. church. In the Middle Ages and Ren., three sometimes coinciding strains of complaint are evident: (1) satiric complaints that expose the evil ways of the world (*contemptus mundi*, e.g., Alan of Lille, *De planctu naturae*, and Edmund Spenser's collection *Complaints, Containing Sundrie Small Poems of the Worlds Vanitie* [1591]); (2) didactic complaints that relate the fall of great persons, often called "fall of princes" or "*de casibus*" narratives (e.g., Giovanni Boccaccio, *De casibus virorum illustrium*; Chaucer, "The Monk's Tale"; and the Ren. collection *A Mirror for Magistrates* [1559]); and (3) lover's complaints, including both short poems written in the Petrarchan mode (e.g., by Thomas Wyatt and Henry Howard, the Earl of Surrey, in *Tottel's Miscellany* [1557]; see PETRARCHISM) and more ambitious monologues that are frequently voiced by female speakers but have male complaints embedded within the "female" complaint framework (e.g., Samuel Daniel, *The Complaint of Rosamond* [1592]; and Shakespeare, *A Lover's Complaint* [1609]). Ren. complaints employ legal rhet. in the *ballads and *broadsides of public executions (Craik) and in revenge tragedies (Thomas Kyd, *The Spanish Tragedy* [1592]; and Shakespeare, *Titus Andronicus* [1594]). Other prominent examples of complaint include Chaucer, "A Complaint unto Pity" (Chaucer has many experimental complaints, on the model of Fr. and It., as *ballades or in *ottava rima); Abraham Cowley, "The Complaint" (1663); and Edward Young's long discursive poem *Complaint, or Night Thoughts* (1742–45). In *Occitan poetry, the complaint takes the form of the *enueg, which inspired the 36th of Ezra Pound's *Cantos*. In the 20th and 21st cs., the complaint frequently appears in *blues lyrics and *hip-hop poetics (Berlant).

■ H. Stein, *Studies in Spenser's Complaints* (1934); *The Mirror for Magistrates*, ed. L. B. Campbell (1938); J. Peter, *Complaint and Satire in Early English Literature* (1956); W. A. Davenport, *Chaucer* (1988); L. Berlant, "The Female Complaint," *Social Text* 19–20 (1988); J. Kerrigan, *Motives of Woe* (1991); J. Farrell, "Reading and Writing the *Heroides*," *Harvard Studies in Classical Philology* 98 (1998); K. A. Craik, "Shakespeare's *A Lover's Complaint* and Early Modern Criminal Confession," *ShQ* 53 (2002).

W. H. RACE; J. DIAZ

**COMPOSITION.** *See* ORAL-FORMULAIC THEORY; POET; RHETORIC AND POETRY; VERSIFICATION.

**COMPOSITION BY FIELD** is a phrase by Charles Olson (1910–70) in his seminal essay "Projective Verse" (1950). The phrase evokes at once a poetics (or a philosophy of writing), a mode of practice (or heuristic activity that discovers its own order), and a kind of poem that is recognizable both visually and aurally. In the latter sense, the page space features loosely configured lines, white space in integral relation to the text, interlineal *caesurae, and *fragments following the pulse of thinking and feeling as it occurs. The mode of practice rests on engagement with one's compositional and ontological energies (physical being, breath) in the absolute present of writing. And in the poetics of *projective verse, *form in any particular work emerges from the multiple pressures of content. These verbal constellations relate to several artistic modes of the time, incl. action painting (Jackson Pollock), gestural dance performances using casual movement (Merce Cunningham), and improvisatory modes of jazz (Charlie Parker). Projective verse posits writing as made of existential choices defined by desire and act and as seeing, feeling, and understanding in the present—a kind of phenomenology out of conformity with that of traditional or even *free-verse prosodies. In this lightning-strike poetics, the page (called here *the field*) becomes a zone of "energy transfer." However, there is a tension between two senses of the poet: as the channel of organic energies (*participation mystique*) and as master, constructing the poem.

The polemical feeling of the essay, typical of the rhets. of *manifesto (here featuring a masculinist diction), began in a fervent resistance to the influence of T. S. Eliot. Olson saw the *Four Quartets* in particular as confining, both for its adherence to a traditional religious ideology and for the repetitive architectonics of its "closed" form. Composition by field produced open form and, therefore, resisted conventional poetic markers (such as *rhyme and metrical *repetition) and featured paratactic organization in syntax (see HYPOTAXIS AND PARATAXIS).

In bringing the prosodic and experiential radicalism of the avant-garde into the contemp. period, Olson influenced several poets whose work appeared in Donald Allen's important anthol. of 1960 (e.g., Robert Creeley, Robert Duncan, Robin Blaser, Denise Levertov; see ANTHOLOGY, BLACK MOUNTAIN SCHOOL). While a new phrase in 1950, *composition by field* as concept has analogues to modernist poetic practice, such as the phrasal lobes and white space of Stéphane Mallarmé's *Un coup de dés* (1897; see VISUAL POETRY); the erasure of syntactic connection as a way of freeing words from inherited connotations, described in F. T. Marinetti's 1914 manifesto as *parole in libertà* (words in freedom); and the productive misunderstanding of the *ideogram in Ezra Pound's manifesto-compilation from the notes of Ernest Fenollosa, *The Chinese Written Character as a Medium for Poetry* (1919).

*See* OPEN FORM.

■ M. Perloff, "Charles Olson and the 'Inferior Predecessors': 'Projective Verse' Revisited," *ELH* 40 (1973); G. Hutchinson, "The Pleistocene in the Projective:

Some of Olson's Sources," *AL* 54 (1982); B. Hatlen, "Pound's Pisan Cantos and the Origins of Projective Verse," *Ezra Pound and Poetic Influence*, ed. H. M. Dennis (2000); J. Osborne, "Black Mountain and Projective Verse," *A Companion to Twentieth-Century Poetry*, ed. N. Roberts (2001).

R. B. DuPLESSIS

**COMPUTATIONAL POETRY.** A term used by theorists to describe poems generated by instructions that can be formalized as procedural or algorithmic sequences. Whether executed by hand, in print, or on a computer, the defining features of such poems include a program that precedes and determines the poem, a relation between form and content that distinguishes the poem from concepts of poetry that are either organic or formalist, and a definition of the authorial function that differentiates the poem from conventional romantic notions about poetry.

Generative programs for computational poems include numerical patterning, mathematically driven permutations of ling. elements, schematic transformations of source texts, and an array of alphabetic, syntactic, semantic, or homophonic procedures. As various as the devices that produce them, examples include Ron Silliman's *Tjanting* (1981), in which the number of sentences per unit equals the sum of the number of sentences in the preceding two units (the Fibonacci sequence); Lee Ann Brown's "Pledge" (1999), in which each noun in the Pledge of Allegiance has been replaced by the seventh subsequent noun in a dictionary (N + 7); and Brian Kim Stefans's "Stops and Rebels" (2003), in which texts contained in files on a hard drive have been recombined by a digital algorithm.

Unlike an organic poem, in which form is said to arise from content (see ORGANICISM), or a formalist poem, in which form is said to contain content (see FORMALISM), a computational poem is produced and enacted by a procedure in which the poem's form acts as its intelligence. Having determined the procedure and put it in motion, the poet-programmer steps back to witness, like any other interpreter, the poem's commentary on itself and the world in which it exists.

Although computational poems may generate *affect, their energy is conceptual rather than lyrical. They do not aim to convey a *persona, construct an authentic *voice, capture nuances of *emotion, or put passionate convictions into *form, but rather to engage and probe broad ling. and cultural structures of meaning. In this sense, a computational poem is, to borrow John Cage's definition of experimental music, "not a question of having something to say" but rather a means of attending to flows of information.

Although programmed permutational poetry can be traced back to esoteric practitioners who established models for generative lit. as early as 330 CE, its most influential advocates have been the loose federation of writers and mathematicians who founded the Workshop for Potential Literature or *Ouvroir de littérature potentielle* (*Oulipo) in 1960. In homage, a conference of contemp. writers incl., among others, Christian Bök

(*Eunoia*, 2001), Harryette Mullen (*Sleeping with the Dictionary*, 2002), and Caroline Bergvall (*Via*, 2005) met in 2005 to carry its project forward under the rubric *Noulipo*. Procedural texts such as Lyn Hejinian's *My Life* (1980–87) and projects of "uncreative writing" such as Kenneth Goldsmith's *No. 111. 2.7.93-10.20.96* (1997) and Craig Dworkin's *Parse* (2008) are often regarded as precursors or counterparts of poems composed and performed on computers.

Starting with the earliest mainframes, programmers created algorithms that access, filter, and recombine the contents of databases to generate texts that simulate the ling. structures, promise of interpretability, or cultural capital of poetry. Such combinatory projects as Talan Memmott's *Self Portrait(s) [as Other(s)]* (2003), Millie Niss's *Oulipoems* (2004), and geniwate's *Concatenation* (2004) capture for the screen the experimental energy of the *Beat poet William Burroughs's cut-ups and the Oulipo founder Raymond Queneau's *Hundred Thousand Billion Poems* (1961), a set of *sonnets, originally executed for the page but now remediated for the screen. In a literary milieu incl. texts that migrate among print, electronic, and performed versions, computational projects, data mining, sampling, mixing, and other forms of procedural, combinatory, and computational practice have become an integral part of information culture.

*See* CONCEPTUAL POETRY; CONSTRAINT; ELECTRONIC POETRY; FLARF; INFORMATION, POETRY AS.

■ J. Cage, "Experimental Music: Doctrine," *Silence* (1961); *Oulipo: A Primer of Potential Literature,* ed. and trans. W. F. Motte (1986); F. Cramer, "Combinatory Poetry and Literature in the Internet" (2000), http://ada.lynxlab.com/staff/steve/public/docu/lidia/docu/combinatory_poetry.pdf—mentions earliest examples of generative lit.; C. T. Funkhauser, *Prehistoric Digital Poetry* (2007); *The Noulipian Analects*, ed. M. Viegener and C. Wertheim (2007).

A. MORRIS

**CONCATENATION** (Lat., *concatenare*; "to link together"). Concatenation literally translates as "to connect together like the links of a chain" and describes the act of "chaining" *stanzas together through the use of a word, phrase, or a line at the end of one stanza that is repeated (in its entirety or in a slightly altered version) in the first line of the following stanza.

In verse divided into structural units and particularly in long narrative poems, some means of linking stanzas enhances continuity through the whole since *rhyme schemes tend to emphasize the integrity of the stanza. The simplest means to this end is to carry over a rhyme sound from one stanza to the next, as in *terza rima, or to use *alliteration and other sound echoes. Sometimes the entire line may be repeated or else its sense paraphrased or amplified.

Concatenation makes its earliest appearance in Eng. in popular songs at the end of the 13th c. and is a specific component of northern alliterative verse, where it builds on the unifying principles of alliteration by emphasizing connections between stanzas. In "Song of the Husbandman" (ca. 1300), the end of one stanza and the beginning of the next are connected by an entire line repeated in a modulated form: "that me us honteth ase hound doth the hare. // he us hontethe ase hound hare doth on hulle."

Concatenation also appears in Celtic verse, incl. in six rhyming romances, as well as examples in the late 12th- and 13th-c. northern poems written in Lat. In Eng. poetry, concatenation plays an important part in the most intricately structured poem to be written in ME, *Pearl*. Divided into 101 stanzas and 20 sections, its individual stanzas are linked by the repetition of a single key word, rather than a phrase or line. In addition, the final link word of the entire poem, "pay," also appears in the poem's opening line, as "paye," and so emphasizes the poem's circular structure.

In the Ren., the devel. of *lyric and *sonnet sequences raised the issue of how poems might be linked together—whether (only) thematically or verbally (as the more direct manifestation of the former). George Gascoigne is the first Eng. poet to link his sonnets via repetition of an entire line. Edmund Spenser's practice in *The Faerie Queene* follows Ludovico Ariosto closely. Concatenation has also been a significant resource in some Asian poetries, particularly Japanese *renga*.

*See* JAPAN, POETRY OF; POLYPTOTON.

■ M. P. Medary, "Stanza-Linking in Middle English Verse"; and A.C.L. Brown, "On the Origin of Stanza-Linking in English Alliterative Verse," *RR* 7 (1916); T. Brooke, "Stanza Connection in the *Faerie Queene*," *MLN* 37 (1922); J. M. Bullitt, "The Use of Rhyme Links in the Sonnets of Sidney, Drayton, and Spenser," *JEGP* 49 (1950); J. C. McGalliard, "Links, Language, and Style in *Pearl*," *Studies in Language, Literature, and Culture of the Middle Ages* (1969); E. Miner, *Japanese Linked Poetry* (1979); Morier; *The Poems of Laurence Minot 1333–1352*, ed. R. H. Osberg (1996).

T.V.F. BROGAN; I. D. COPESTAKE

**CONCEIT.** Three meanings are commonly found: (1) the "idea" informing a poem or play (cf. Philip Sidney's *Defence of Poesy*, George Puttenham's *Arte of English Poesie*, and *Hamlet* [2.2.530]); (2) an esp. elaborate metaphor or simile like those in Petrarch's *Canzoniere*; (3) a figure of thought, typical of *baroque and *metaphysical poetry and prose, which ingeniously compares dissimilar things and ideas, cultivating thereby surprise, followed, ideally, by admiration and insight. While all three kinds stress poetic *invention, only the third, rooted largely in 17th-c. theory and practice, ascribes both aesthetic and epistemological value to the conceit. Based on but not limited to *metaphor, the baroque conceit aims wittily to engage both imagination and intellect without acknowledging either's sovereignty. As Gardner writes, "A conceit is a comparison whose ingenuity is more striking than its justness, or, at least, is more immediately striking. . . . [A] comparison becomes a conceit when we are made to concede likeness while being strongly conscious of unlikeness." Such is the case with John Donne's 12-line conceit in "A Valediction: Forbidding Mourning" comparing the souls of separated lovers to the legs of a compass. Cast as a proposition needing proof, the conceit yields images at once more abstract and precise than those typical of Petrarchan conceits.

Often structured like a paralogism or abbreviated syllogism, the baroque or metaphysical conceit exploits literary and cultural commonplaces as well as tropes. Unlike a *simile or strong metaphor, its terms are frequently allusive or qualified by argument, thus its perceived artificiality. When Luis de Góngora in the *Soledades* (1.481–90) compares Ferdinand Magellan's sight of coral islands in the Pacific to Actaeon's gazing on the white limbs of Diana bathing in the Eurotas river, the wit of the *concepto* lies in realizing the common peril for both men; but it also depends on the commonplace of forbidden beauty, as well as the simile that cupidity is like eros. The conceit also typically tries to marry the concrete and abstract, without, though, becoming allegorical. As Donne implores in "A nocturnall upon S. Lucies day":

> Study me then, you, who shall lovers bee
> At the next world, that is, at the next Spring:
> For I am every dead thing,
> In whom love wrought new Alchimie.
> For his art did expresse
> A quintessence even from nothingnesse,
> From dull privations, and leane emptinesse:
> He ruin'd mee, and I am re-begot
> Of absence, darknesse, death; things which are
>     not.

The paradoxical image of the speaker as "every dead thing" is distilled from two premises: first, the notion that alchemy produces "quintessence" from "nothingnesse"; second, the analogy that the "art" of "love" is like alchemy's. Further, the lover's hyperbolic transformation is striking and worth studying, Donne suggests, because his own poetic "art" is able to unite hitherto irreconcilable extremes.

As the finest product of *"wit" (Lat. *ingenium*, It. *ingegno*, Sp. *ingenio*, Fr. *esprit*, Ger. *Witz*), the baroque conceit underscores the subjective aspects of poetic invention. Yet to interpret it, the reader's ingenuity must partly mimic the poet's. As a contemporary, Jasper Mayne, writes of Donne's verse: "[W]e are thought wits, when 'tis understood."

The baroque conceit has various origins. The epigrammatic wit of Martial and the *Greek Anthology*, avidly imitated by J. C. Scaliger, Clément Marot, Ben Jonson, Martin Opitz, and others, encourages its devel. Alternately, Petrarch and his lyric successors refine a sophisticated metaphoric discourse commonly labeled "conceited." In *Canzoniere* 127, Petrarch takes the terms in a simile comparing love's effect on him to the sun melting snow ("come 'l sol neve mi governa Amore") and then elaborates each of them in a complex series of metaphoric images. Pierre de Ronsard's *Amours*, Francisco de Quevedo's *Canta sola a Lisi* (*Poems to Lisi*), and Shakespeare's sonnets exemplify the many ways that the rich array of Petrarchan conceits are later imitated. But Shakespeare's ironic *blason in sonnet 130 ("My mistress' eyes . . .") also indicates how belated Petrarchans seek to find ever more ingenious, extravagant conceits that might still surprise and move. (Such "outdoing" persists into the 19th c.; Charles Baudelaire, e.g., compares his beloved to a rotting carcass in "Une charogne.")

During the mid-17th c., the conceit becomes the focus of a novel, theoretically rich poetics that, borrowing its terms from faculty psychology and scholastic logic, tries to account for the new conceited styles of Giambattista Marino and Góngora, the revival of Senecan and other "pointed" prose styles, and the period's fascination with *emblems, aphorisms, and other forms of wit.

Baltasar Gracián's *Agudeza y arte de ingenio* (1648) defines the concepto as "an act of the understanding" that "consists of an excellent concordance, a harmonic correlation, between two or three knowable extremes." A figure either of "proportion" or "disproportion," the conceit is the chief means by which the ingenio "finds" and then "expresses" the "correspondence" between objects in a manner "that not only is content with the truth, as is judgment, but aspires to the beautiful." The finished product of such invention aims to be more than what is typically called a poetic conceit in Eng. For though Gracián equivocates whether such correspondences exist outside the witty mind, he unambiguously casts the concepto as the most discerning way to express new ideas.

Emanuele Tesauro's *Il cannocchiale aristotelico* (1654) describes the *concetto* as the acme of poetic creation. Comparing its "wonders" (*meraviglie*) to scripture's symbolic, parabolic effects, Tesauro also regards the new science's epistemological novelties as justifying *concetti*. Adapting Aristotle's notion of *asteia* (urbanity), he makes metaphor's "mental flight" and the poet's ingenio the basis for the conceit. Initially compared to an enthymeme, the conceit is later described as a "metaphorical argument" or "caviling fiction." Celebrating how conceits produce new knowledge from old categories of thought, Tesauro dubs them "urbanely fallacious arguments" (*argomenti urbanamente fallici*).

In *Life of Cowley* (1781), however, Samuel Johnson regrets how in metaphysical poetry "the most heterogeneous ideas are yoked by violence together." He blames its overly "analytic" style and "slender conceits and laboured particularities." Yet his perceptive critique of Donne and Abraham Cowley's penchant for *discordia concors*, or "combination of dissimilar images or discovery of occult resemblances in things apparently unlike" neatly defines the conceit. Responding to Johnson and heralding his own poetics, T. S. Eliot (1921, 1926) celebrates the metaphysical conceit as uniquely suited to uniting thought and feeling. Tuve reads conceited imagery as emerging from the dialectics of Peter Ramus and his followers and as a "stylistically very striking" form of judgment. Leaning on Gracián's treatise, 20th-c. Sp. crit. treats the style of Quevedo and Góngora as *conceptista*. Gilman sees similarities between the conceit and anamorphosis. Proctor, Brodsky, and Van Hook analyze the conceit's illogic. Blanco and Vuilleumier regard the

conceit as the culmination of Ren. poetics. Rousset and Hallyn stress how the dissolution of the Ren. analogical worldview encourages the conceit's devel.

Further afield, the surrealist emphasis on startling *imagery recalls the aesthetic claims of the baroque conceit but ignores its epistemological promise (see SURREALISM). Comte de Lautréamont's image of "a boy as beautiful as a chance meeting on a dissecting table of a sewing machine and an umbrella" (from his prose poem *Les Chants de Maldoror*, 1869) is analyzed in André Breton's *Manifesto of Surrealism* (1924): "The value of the image depends upon the beauty of the spark obtained; it is, consequently, a function of the difference of potential between the two conductors. When the difference exists only slightly, as in a comparison, the spark is lacking."

Finally, forms akin to the Petrarchan conceit occur outside the Eur. trad. The *kāvya* (cl.) style of Sanskrit poetry often favors extended, complex metaphors (cf. Kālidāsa's "Cloud Messenger"; see SANSKRIT POETICS). In med. *Persian and *Urdu poetry, the *ghazal* is fueled by elaborate, symbolic comparisons; Ḥāfiẓ's fusion of earthly and divine love yields many strikingly conceited images.

*See* AGUDEZA, CONCEPTISMO.

■ M. Praz, *Studi sul concettismo* (1934); F. Yates, "The Emblematic Conceit in Giordano Bruno's *De Gli Eroici Furori* and in the Elizabethan Sonnet Sequences," *Journal of the Warburg and Courtauld Institutes* 6 (1943); R. Tuve, *Elizabethan and Metaphysical Imagery* (1947); A. Parker, "La 'Agudeza' en algunos sonetos de Quevedo," *Estudios dedicados a Menéndez Pidal*, v. 3 (1952); G. Watson, "Hobbes and the Metaphysical Conceit," *Journal of the History of Ideas* 16 (1955); *The Metaphysical Poets*, ed. H. Gardner (1957); A. Terry, "Quevedo and the Metaphysical Conceit," *BHS* 35 (1958); E. Donato, "Tesauro's Poetics: Through the Looking Glass," *MLN* 78 (1963); J. Rousset, *L'intérieur et l'extérieur* (1968); K.K. Ruthven, *The Conceit* (1969); G. Conte, *La Metafora barocca* (1972); R. E. Proctor, "Emanuele Tesauro: A Theory of the Conceit," *MLN* 88 (1973); E. Gilman, *The Curious Perspective: Literary and Pictorial Wit in the Seventeenth Century* (1978); C. Brodsky, "The Imaging of the Logical Conceit," *ELH* 49 (1982); A. Parker, "'Concept' and 'Conceit': An Aspect of Comparative Literary History," *MLR* 77 (1982); J. W. Van Hook, "'Concupiscence of Witt': The Metaphysical Conceit in Baroque Poetics," *MP* 84 (1986); T. E. May, *Wit of the Golden Age* (1986); J. Tilakasiri, *Kalidasa's Imagery and Theory of Poetics* (1988); M. Blanco, *Les rhétoriques de la pointe: Baltasar Gracián et le conceptisme en Europe* (1992); A. Schimmel, *A Two-Colored Brocade: The Imagery of Persian Poetry* (1992); T. S. Eliot, "The Metaphysical Poets" (1921), "The Conceit in Donne" (1926), *The Varieties of Metaphysical Poetry*, ed. R. Schuchard (1993); T. Althaus, *Epigrammatisches Barock* (1996); A. Zárate Ruiz, *Gracián, Wit, and the Baroque Age* (1996); F. Vuilleumier, "Les conceptismes," *Histoire de la rhétorique dans l'Europe moderne, 1450–1950* (1999); F. Hallyn, "Cosmography and Poetics," *CHLC*, v. 3, ed. G. P. Norton (1999); P. Frare, *"Per istraforo di perspettiva": Il "Can-*

*nocchiale Aristotelico" el a poesia del seicento* (2000); H. Meyer, "Jesuit Concedes Jesuit Conceits: A Hit on Sarbievius' Head," *Gedächtnis und Phantasma*, ed. S. Frank et al. (2001); Y. Hersant, *La métaphore baroque: d'Aristote á Tesauro* (2001); R. Rambuss, "Sacred Subjects and the Aversive Metaphysical Conceit: Crashaw, Serrano, Ofili," *ELH* 71 (2004).

C. JOHNSON

**CONCEPTISMO.** The term *conceptismo* was not coined until the 18th c., when it began to be used to designate the pervasive practice of the *concepto* in 17th-c. Spain. The concepto, or *conceit, is an ingenious trope or ling. device—*metaphor, *metonymy, *paronomasia, *hyperbole, *antithesis—that couples disparate elements. Baltasar Gracián, Spain's foremost theorist of the concepto, celebrated it as a manifestation of heightened cultural achievement, hailing its combination of masterful poetic technique and intellectual acumen. The emergence of conceptismo can be traced back to the 16th c. when salient poets converged in the attempt to equip Sp. with the grandeur of an imperial lang. Upholding Petrarchan verse as a desirable model of refinement, poets such as Garcilaso de la Vega, Juan Boscán, and Fernando de Herrera cultivated a lang. rich in wordplay and syntactic sophistication. Such artifice was amplified by the 17th-c. conceit, which ranged from the logical to the farfetched. The figures classified by Gracián as conceits by virtue of correspondence and proportion pair relatable elements, as in the case of the connection between "puerta" (door) and "alma" (soul) in the following verses by Félix Lope de Vega: "En vano llama a la puerta, / Quien no ha llamado en el alma" (In vain he calls at the door / Who has not called on the soul; quoted in *Agudeza y arte de ingenio*). Meanwhile, those qualified as conceits by disparity and dissimilarity unite terms that are discordant in the extreme: "estuve vivo con la muerte" (I was alive with death; Francisco de Quevedo, poem 337). Not confined to high genres, the concepto figured prominently in satirical poetry. Illustrative in this terrain is Quevedo's parallel, in a poem (826) mocking Luis de Góngora, between "coplas . . . divinas" (divine couplets) and "letrinas" (latrines).

Hispanist scholarship traditionally opposed conceptismo to *culteranismo*, the other preeminent stylistic mode of the *baroque. Where conceptismo is considered an exhibition of *agudeza* or superior cognitive power, culteranismo, also closely linked to aristocratizing Italianate currents, is characterized as an ostentatious mastery of cultural referents. Identified by Collard with the emergence of the *bizarro* (elegant) and the *docto* (highly educated) as prized cultural values, culteranismo presents luxurious ornamentation, abundant mythological and historical references, Latinisms, and labyrinthine syntax. Where conceptismo and culteranismo have distinctive qualities, the idea that they constituted two separate schools, the former headed by Quevedo and the latter by Góngora, has been revised by current scholarship, which notes that they are best approached as stylistic traits that often coexist in the same poetic corpus. The dichotomy, upheld well into the 20th c., was the legacy of Enlightenment critics who, while regarding both tendencies as manifestations of poor taste, took all too seriously the mutual oppositions voiced by Góngora and his enemies.

Culteranismo was famously vilified by doctrinaire figures like Quevedo and the scholar Jáuregui as an affront to moral and social rectitude. Deemed a betrayal of national *gravitas* and a submission to foreign influences, it was tainted by associations with Asiatic effeminacy and *converso* culture. Significantly, the word *culterano*, from which *culteranismo* is derived, was concocted by the anti-Gongorists to echo the word *luterano* (Lutheran), another indicator of heresy. Conceptismo itself was not free of controversy, as Counter-Reformation ideologues denounced the more excessive manifestations of the conceit, arguing that undue emphasis on conceptual ingenuity resulted in the sacrifice of didactic content. Although himself a master of the conceit, Quevedo avoided positive mention of the concepto in his theoretical writings and targeted *conceptista* poets in his social satires. The subversive implications of conceptismo continue to be recognized by contemp. scholars who contend that its more extreme forms (both serious and comic) transgress the balance, harmony, and decorum prescribed by Aristotelian mimetic principles. From this perspective, conceptismo is viewed as a self-conscious subversion of Ren. *classicism, its idiosyncratic tropes approaching a mod. aesthetic awareness in their recognition of the subjective nature of poetic correspondences.

The social and political underpinnings of conceptismo and culteranismo are best understood in relation to early mod. court culture. In its construction of a highly codified lang. requiring discernment and inventiveness on the part of both author and reader, the expression of the new poets was in line with the valorization of supreme prudence and discretion as core virtues of the post-Machiavellian courtier. In an era marked by reason-of-state doctrines and Tacitean skepticism, Ren. paradigms of open civic communication were displaced by an awareness of the need for sinuous craftiness and dissemblance. From a rhetorical perspective, then, the new poetry can be said to depart from Quintilian's standards of eloquence as artful morality and to espouse eloquence as spectacular exhibition. Its links to other art forms that conditioned curial life, such as royal ceremony, theater, and painting, as well as to political lit., are accordingly receiving growing scholarly attention.

*See* RENAISSANCE POETICS, RENAISSANCE POETRY.

■ E. Rivers, "El conceptismo del *Polifemo*," *Atenea* 143 (1961); A. Collard, *Nueva poesía, conceptismo, culteranismo en la crítica española* (1967); J. de Jáuregui y Aguilar, *Discurso poético*, ed. M. Romanos ([1624], 1978); A. García Berrio, "Quevedo y la conciencia léxica del concepto" and J. M. Pozuelo Yvancos, "Sobre la unión de teoría y praxis literaria en el conceptismo: un tópico de Quevedo a la luz de la teoría literaria de Gracián," *Cuadernos hispanoamericanos* 361–62 (1980);

R. Lachman, "'Problematic Similarity': Sarbiewski's Treatise *De Acuto et arguto* in the Context of Concettistic Theories of the 17th Century," *Russian Literature* 26 (1990); M. Blanco, *Les rhétoriques de la pointe: Baltasar Gracián et le conceptisme en Europe* (1992); I. Arellano, "El conceptismo de Góngora: más divagaciones sobre los 'déligos capotuncios' del romance 'Diez años vivió Belerma,'" *Hommage a Robert Jammes*, ed. F. Cerdan (1994); F. de Quevedo y Villegas, "Dedicatoria Al Excelentísimo señor Conde-Duque," *Quevedo y su poética dedicada a Olivares. Estudio y edición*, ed. E. Rivers (1998); E. Marquer, "Conscience baroque et apparences: Le conceptisme de Baltasar Gracián," *Revue de Métaphysique et de Morale* 2 (1999); J. Lieberman, "Estética conceptista y ética mercantilista de *Confusión de confusiones* (Amsterdam 1688)," *BHS* 77 (2000); L. Schwartz, "Linguistic and Pictorial Conceits in the Baroque: Velázquez between Quevedo and Gracián," *Writing for the Eyes in the Spanish Golden Age*, ed. F. de Armas (2004); L. Dolfi, *"Culteranismo" e teatro nella Spagna del seicento* (2006).

A. GARCÍA-BRYCE

**CONCEPTUAL POETRY.** Conceptual poetry (or conceptual writing), usually understood to fall under the rubric of experimental poetry, dates to the late 1990s in Canada and the United States. Works are called *conceptual* when they embody a concept that is more important to their purpose than the actual lang. and ideas they express—the poetic qualities, or even the oddities, of everyday lang., for instance, or the materiality of the signifier or the banality of interpretation. Notable conceptual works include *No. 111 2.7.93-10.20.96* (1997), *Fidget* (2000), and *Soliloquy* (2001) by the artist and archivist Kenneth Goldsmith; *Eunoia* (2001) by Christian Bök; and *Apostrophe* (2006) by Bill Kennedy and Darren Wershler-Henry, based on an earlier poem by Kennedy (1994). In his introduction to *Against Expression*, Craig Dworkin remarks that, before there was conceptual writing, there was conceptual art; yet coeval with the conceptual art of the 1960s, a mode of writing that we can now call "conceptual" was evident in Vito Acconci's early works, such as "READ THIS WORD" (1969), which consists of nothing more than a series of instructions for how to read the very words that constitute the instructions. Likewise, *modernism already exhibited conceptual tendencies, such as in Gertrude Stein's "Five Words in a Line" (1930), which simply reads, "Five Words in a Line."

While poets have arguably been producing conceptual writing for quite some time, conceptualism did not solidify as a literary movement until the digital age and its accelerated procedures for treating lang. as data that can be mined, processed, or generated. Many conceptualists recognize the computer's reduction of all writing to binary code, and the abundance of information through the advent of the Internet significantly changes the ways in which lang. is currently written and understood. Such changes structure a new media environment in which the poet must operate.

Conceptual writing is particularly intent on breaking the widely held belief that writing is a solitary activity characterized by the creative *genius and *originality of an expressive artist, a belief that may have reached its zenith in the late 19th c. but that has persisted into the present. In contrast to expressive models of poetry, conceptualism elevates the concept behind a work and the labor required to produce it over its semantic meaning or emotional content. Goldsmith has explicitly called for an "uncreative writing" in which "all of the planning and decisions are made beforehand and the execution is a perfunctory affair. The idea becomes a machine that makes the text" ("Paragraphs on Conceptual Writing," 2005). Otherwise put, the idea driving the work is a machine that has been programmed to process lang. in some determined way such that the product is not necessarily as important as the production process itself. E.g., *No. 111 2.7.93-10.20.96* is a 600-page collection of phrases ending in *r* sounds, arranged alphabetically and by syllable count until it finally reaches 7,228 syllables by appropriating the entirety of D.H. Lawrence's short story "The Rocking-Horse Winner." However, given the importance of the production process, conceptual writing is also aligned with *Flarf (though conceptual writers such as Goldsmith have pointed out distinctions between the two movements), as well as constraint-based writing (see CONSTRAINT), procedural writing, and appropriative writing. E.g., Bök's *Eunoia* doubles as a constraint-based work insofar as it consists of five chapters, each of which uses only one of the vowels *a, e, i, o,* or *u*. Place and Fitterman write in *Notes on Conceptualisms* that whether a given practice falls under *conceptual writing* depends on whether the poet is trying to "reach for a larger idea outside of the text"; thus, they implicitly argue that the aforementioned writing practices are all modes of conceptual writing.

Certain conceptual writers' attempts to treat lang. as data (exemplified by Goldsmith's work as much as by Bök's recent attempt to inject the DNA of the bacteria *Deinococcus radiodurans* with a string of nucleotides to form a comprehensible poem) is partly driven by a desire to write a poetry that is both reflective of the culture of the digital era and enmeshed in or disruptive of the inner workings of technoscience. Yet other works of conceptual writing, such as Vanessa Place's *Tragodía, 1: Statement of Facts* (2010), elegantly make the argument that conceptual writing in which an idea "becomes a machine" need not necessarily be enabled by the computer; it need only draw attention to (in Goldsmith's words) the "unboring boring" ("Being Boring") or the material practice of writing itself, a practice that—even in the case of the tedious transcription or the rendering into "neutral lang." of court testimonies—cannot help but be inflected by the act of the writer writing. These debates point to the fact that early 21st-c. conceptual writing consists of a rapidly transforming set of speculative practices led by a growing field of innovative poet-theorists.

*See* AVANT-GARDE POETICS, ELECTRONIC POETRY.

■ M. Perloff, *21st-Century Modernism* (2002);

K. Goldsmith, "Being Boring" (2004), http://epc.buf falo.edu/authors/goldsmith/goldsmith_boring.html; "Kenneth Goldsmith and Conceptual Poetics," sp. iss., *Open Letter* 12.7 (2005); M. Perloff, "Conceptualisms, Old and New" (2007), http://marjorieperloff.com/ articles/conceptualisms-old-and-new/; V. Place and R. Fitterman, *Notes on Conceptualisms* (2009); *Against Expression: An Anthology of Conceptual Writing*, ed. C. Dworkin and K. Goldsmith (2011).

L. EMERSON

**CONCISION.** A general term for lexical compression, concentration, and economy, designed to achieve "maximum efficiency of expression" (Pound 1913). Concision is often associated with compact forms— *sonnet, *haiku (see RENGA), and *epigram, among others. Connotations vary considerably in different contexts: concision embodies distinct poetic qualities, e.g., in Chinese *shi, the Augustan *heroic couplet, and *symbolism. It has served as a flashpoint in arguments about metrics, *free verse and poetic *form, didacticism, *difficulty, and *realism.

Concision has been described as "native to the lyric" (Vendler 1995), but poetic media influence its exercise. The terseness of *epitaph is in part conditioned by the need to carve it in stone. Brief forms are suited to the spatial constraints of a print culture in which poems must fit in magazines, on subway walls, and in the pages of anthols. (They are also suited, some would argue, to the pedagogical requirements of academic settings.) Some 21st-c. poetry exhibits the compactness of contemp., character-restricted communications (e.g., text messaging, microblogging).

The privileging of concision is as long as the hist. of poetry and ranges across both Western and non-Western trads. Aristotle's *Rhetoric* gives instructions for achieving concision, such as naming a thing instead of describing it, bracketing two words under one article, and eliminating connectives. Cl. Chinese poetry, in part because of the noninflectional nature of the lang., is distinguished by extreme compression: pronouns are dropped, content words (*shizi*) take precedence, and grammatical connections are minimal. The concluding couplet of Shakespearean sonnets demonstrates the semantic intensities that emerge from verbal concentration. Many forms of *oral poetry, such as the traditional four-line Malay *pantun* and the mod. one- or two-line Somali *balwo*, depend on concision to persist in listeners' auditory memories. The related Japanese forms of *waka, renga, and *hokku*, distinguished by intricate stanzaic patterning and strict sound-unit counts, privilege lexical economy. Comic effects of concision are apparent in the work of the hokku poet Matsuo Bashō, as well as in various Western and non-Western trads. of the epigram, whose "jerk or sting" (John Dryden) is a prominent feature in 18th-c. Eng. verse. In the hands of Augustan poets, heroic couplets show off concision's oratorical and satiric possibilities, and Alexander Pope claimed to write his philosophical essays in verse because he "could express them more shortly this way . . . and . . . the force as well as grace

of arguments or instructions, depends on their conciseness" (*Essay on Man*).

Concision is an arguable feature of romantic poetry. Twentieth-c. New Critics condemned the romantics for an emotionality lacking in concision (see NEW CRITICISM), but this implies a false dichotomy of concision and *affect. The expression of powerful feeling can require concision. In William Blake's *Songs of Innocence and Experience* and the "spots of time" that punctuate William Wordsworth's autobiographical epic *The Prelude*, concision contributes to a mystical quality and to an affective intensity. The romantic argument against poetic *diction associates simplicity with concision, praising a poetry stripped to a threadbare, affective baseline: thus, for Wordsworth, the lines "My lonely anguish melts no heart but mine; / And in my breast the imperfect joys expire," from the middle of Thomas Gray's "Sonnet on the Death of Mr. Richard West," are preferable to its opening: "In vain to me the smiling Mornings shine, / And redd'ning Phoebus lifts his golden fire." The romantic effort was to retrieve the primitive power of expression from the built-up sedimentation of poetic hist. Paradoxically, however, concision can be enabled by shared conventions, be they general (the historical accrual of meaning in specific words or phrases) or particular (intimacy among groups of poets). The importance of brevity in Japanese linked poetry, for instance, has been attributed to the closeness among collaborating poets, which eliminated needless discursiveness and decorousness.

In the Wordsworthian moral trad., plain spokenness could lead to prolixity, but even here, concise expression remains highly valued. Walter Bagehot declared in "Wordsworth, Tennyson, and Browning; or Pure, Ornate and Grotesque Art in English Poetry" (1864) that "poetry should be memorable and emphatic, intense and *soon over*." The question is often, rather, that of what is to be expressed. "What is *not* interesting," Matthew Arnold argued in the Preface to his *Poems* (1853), "is that which does not add to our knowledge of any kind; that which is vaguely conceived and loosely drawn; a representation which is general, indeterminate, and faint, instead of being particular, precise, and firm."

Through the 19th c., the quickened pace of life and the secular apprehension of the transience of experience solicited compact modes of expression. The concentrated aesthetic moment became existentially valuable: "We have an interval, and then our place knows us no more," wrote Walter Pater in *The Renaissance* (1873); "our one chance lies in expanding that interval, in getting as many pulsations as possible into the given time." The movements of *aestheticism and *decadence saw the descriptive compulsions of realism give way to a subjectivist pointillism, and symbolist poetry—more "real" than realism (Stéphane Mallarmé's poetic flower is "l'absente de tous bouquets" (absent from all bouquets)—found its raison d'être not in communicative simplicity or didacticism but in access to a more profound level of existence, expressed in concentrated lyric moments.

*Modernism meant new opportunities for the exercise of concision. What Ezra Pound (1916) called the "one image poem" summoned the sparseness of Japanese and Chinese poetry in recording "the precise instant when a thing outward and objective . . . darts into a thing inward and subjective." The lyric intensity of Pound's "In a Station of the Metro" or of Giuseppe Ungaretti's famously brief "Mattina" captures the profundity of the minute. Such poems anticipate *minimalism, in which diminution and reduction signal authenticity and exemplify the rejection of discursiveness summarized by W. C. Williams's phrase "No ideas but in things." In poems such as "The Red Wheelbarrow" and "As the Cat," Williams uses small structures to force attention to infinitesimal units of meaning within the poem (sounds, stress patterns, line breaks).

The formal openness of these poems points to the centrality of concision in arguments about free verse. Conventional poetic forms are typically seen as demanding compression: Wordsworth's 1806 sonnet "Nuns Fret Not" states the case by linking form with self-denial (" 'twas pastime to be bound / Within the Sonnet's scanty plot of ground"). But for Pound (1918), *vers libre* best facilitates the exercise of concision: "words are shovelled in to fill a metric pattern or to complete the noise of a rhyme-sound. . . . If you are using a symmetrical form, don't put in what you want to say and then fill up the remaining vacuums with slush."

Concision bears political meanings. It can represent an avoidance of a hegemonic discourse or the difficulty of negotiating that discourse or even the outright silencing of voices within it; Adrienne Rich's half-sonnet "An Unsaid Word" uses concision to communicate "a negative experience of power" (Keyes). For Audre Lorde, poetry's concision suits it to the representation of marginalized experience: "of all the art forms, poetry is the most economical. It is . . . the one which can be done between shifts, in the hospital pantry, on the subway, and on scraps of surplus paper." Theodor Adorno's oft-quoted dictum "To write poetry after Auschwitz is barbaric" suggests how a concision evoking silence might be the most appropriate way of describing certain experiences; thus, in Paul Celan's "Chymisch" ("Alchemical"), silence is not only sacramental and memorial but emblematic of lang.'s potential violence: "Schweigen, wie Gold gekocht, in / verkohlten / Händen" (Silence, cooked like gold, in / charred / hands).

■ E. Pound, "The Serious Artist," *The Egoist* (1913); *Gaudier-Brzeska* (1916); and "A Retrospect," *Pavannes and Divisions* (1918); Empson; R. H. Brower and E. R. Miner, *Japanese Court Poetry* (1961); R. Finnegan, *Oral Poetry* (1977); *The Columbia Book of Chinese Poetry: From Early Times to the Thirteenth Century*, ed. B. Watson (1984); A. Lorde, "Age, Race, Sex and Class," *Sister Outsider* (1984); C. Keyes, *The Aesthetics of Power: The Poetry of Adrienne Rich* (1986); H. Vendler, *The Music of What Happens* (1988); P. Zumthor, *Oral Poetry: An Introduction*, trans. K. Murphy-Judy (1990); P. Nicholls, *Modernisms* (1995); H. Vendler, *Soul Says: On Recent Poetry* (1995); *Sources of Japanese Tradition: 1600–2000*, ed. W. T. DeBary et al., 2d ed. (2001); K. Painter, *Flint on a Bright Stone: A Revolution of Precision and Restraint in American, Russian, and German Modernism* (2006); Z. Cai, *How to Read Chinese Poetry* (2007).

C. Rovee

**CONCRETE POETRY.** Although used in a general way to refer to work that has been composed with specific attention to graphic features such as *typography, layout, shape, or distribution on the page, concrete poetry properly understood has a more specific definition created in the mid-1950s by the Swiss-Bolivian poet Eugen Gomringer and the Brazilian poets Décio Pignatari and Haroldo and Augusto de Campos. The original tenets of concrete poetry are clear in the early writings of the group. Their 1958 "Pilot Plan for Concrete Poetry" outlines a distinct approach in which form and meaning (material expression and reference field) would be as close to each other as possible. Thus, *concrete* suggests a unification of the word with its presentation. The poets derived certain ideas from the work of Ezra Pound, in particular his adoption of Ernest Fenollosa's productive misunderstanding of the Chinese ideogram as a self-identical verbal-visual expression. The concrete poets recast this notion into an idea of isomorphism (identity of shape and meaning) that they believed embodied an ideal of structure as content. This attempt to eliminate extraneous associations or ambiguities comports with the aesthetics of "specific objects" expressed by minimalist artists of the 1960s, who sought to strip art objects of all superfluous elements.

Gomringer's poem "silencio" (1953) exemplifies the concretists' aim of creating a total integration of word as image in a single aesthetic expression. By repeating the word "silence" eight times to frame an empty "quiet" space, Gomringer's poem is self-defining and self-referential. Gomringer had been the secretary to Max Bill, a visual artist and graphic designer affiliated with the New Bauhaus, a post–World War II Swiss movement with a highly formalist orientation. Bill used the term *concrete* to identify his own functionalist, analytical methodology, which had an influence on the devel. of Swiss-style graphic design. Though committed to principles of self-identical work, concrete poets were profoundly interested in and attracted by mass culture and the graphic langs. of signage and advertising. Pignatari's famous "beba coca cola" (1957) reworks commercial lang. to critique corporate colonialism.

Concrete poets embraced the concept of intermedia works that could operate simultaneously in verbal-to-visual and acoustic modes. The use of sans serif typefaces, particularly Helvetica and Univers, lent the concrete poets an air of cool modernity that separated their work typographically from trads. of humanist poetry and *lyric voice. Many concrete poets distanced themselves from earlier 20th-c. avant-garde movements by their less explicit political content and absence of inflammatory rhet. But they continued the trad. of writing *manifestos to state their aesthetic positions.

Concrete poetry found many adherents, and the poets who identified themselves with the term quickly expanded to include major figures in Europe, the Brit. Isles, the U.S., Japan, and South America. With increased distance and time, the work of these groups and individuals expanded beyond the strict orthodoxy outlined in the pilot plan. Thus, many poets who experimented with visual forms and typographic features are loosely associated with concrete poetry, even though their work is only pictorial, composed as a field or a score, rather than conforming to the strictly self-referential guidelines of concretism. By the time the first three major anthologies of concrete poetry appeared, ed. by E. Williams (1967), S. Bann (1967) and M. E. Solt (1968), their editorial range included poets from around the globe.

Precedents for concrete poetry can be traced to cl. antiquity and followed into the Middle Ages when poems shaped as religious icons carried theological meaning (see CARMINA FIGURATA). Similar shaped works appeared in printed form in the Ren. and after as part of a contemplative trad. and then in a secular era as novelties and poetic amusements. Few visually shaped works follow the intellectual rigor of concrete poetry's self-identical reduction. Important later 20th-c. devels. brought concrete poetry into dialogue with procedural work, visual arts, installation, film, *sound poetry, typewriter poetry, critical theories of deconstruction and *performance, and later digital works using animation and graphic means.

See TECHNOPAEGNION, VISUAL POETRY.

■ *Concrete Poetry: An International Anthology*, ed. S. Bann (1967); *An Anthology of Concrete Poetry*, ed. E. Williams (1967); *Concrete Poetry: A World View*, ed. M. E. Solt (1968); D. Judd, "Specific Objects," *Donald Judd: Complete Writings 1959–1975* (1975); D. Seaman, *Concrete Poetry in France* (1981); W. Bohn, *The Aesthetics of Visual Poetry 1914–1928* (1986); J. Drucker, *The Visible Word* (1994); *Experimental-Visual-Concrete*, ed. K. D. Jackson, J. Drucker (1996); *Poesure et Peintrie*, ed. B. Blistène, V. Legrand (1998); W. Bohn, *Modern Visual Poetry* (2000).

J. DRUCKER

**CONCRETE UNIVERSAL.** In an essay published in 1947 that was later adapted as a chapter in *The Verbal Icon*, W. K. Wimsatt proposed the term *concrete universal* as a primary concept in "an objective criticism." Wimsatt's term works off the long philosophical and literary preoccupation with similarly opposed terms: *abstract* and *concrete*, *universal* and *individual*, *general* and *particular*. Defining a literary work as a "complex of details" composed and complicated by its "human values," Wimsatt argues that a concrete universal, which may be a character, a figure of speech, or some other formal element of a work, embodies the individual but expresses the universal. In other words, the meaning expressed in the particular way an object or concept is represented becomes inseparable from the meaning expressed by the object or concept itself. For

the *New Criticism, of which Wimsatt was a major exponent, the notion of the concrete universal is a considered approach to the question of how complex formal and structural features produce not only an object that requires a thoroughgoing *explication, but a kind of truth.

Deriving the term from G.W.F. Hegel (*Phenomenology of Spirit*), Wimsatt cites Aristotle, Plotinus, Hegel, and John Crowe Ransom, among others, in tracing the critical legacy surrounding the "concrete" and the "universal" through canonical statements: "Poetry imitates action and that poetry tends to express the universal" (Aristotle); Shakespeare's genius is due to a "union and interpenetration of the universal and particular" (S. T. Coleridge); the artist's "soul reaches straight to the forms that lie behind in the divine intelligence" (Plotinus); "The business of the poet is not to number the streaks of the tulip; it is to give us not the individual, but the species" (Samuel Johnson). Wimsatt believed that New Critics such as William Empson, Allen Tate, R. P. Blackmur, and Cleanth Brooks had "implicitly" elaborated similar assumptions.

Wimsatt's term *concrete universal* is both descriptive and prescriptive, involving both an analysis of rhetorical structure and a judgment of the work's difficulty and sophistication—thus, its use and value; indeed, Wimsatt asserts that "complexity of form is sophistication of content." As a prescriptive concept, the concrete universal is employed as an interpretive tool by the "objective" critic to aid readers to come to a "full realization" on their own and to distinguish the "good" from the "bad." Following the publication of *The Verbal Icon*, Ransom contested the efficacy and clarity of Wimsatt's notion of the concrete universal, finding the concrete and the universal "radically incommensurable," while defending an earlier formulation of his own that emphasized the concrete detail in poetry (*"texture") as central to the knowledge about the world that it makes available (see SCIENCE AND POETRY).

In a substantial critical encounter with the term, Knapp dedicates a chapter in *Literary Interest* to revisiting the concrete universal, finding that Wimsatt's account of the distinctiveness of the literary is troubled by his (unknowing) reliance on notions of *affect such as interest and pleasure. While Knapp finds Wimsatt's use of affect unintentional, he argues that the affectivity of literary representations (and, thus, of *imagination) is endowed with its own type of generality, as well as its own kind of rationality. Knapp does not find the *"unity" of literary works that Wimsatt claims but offers that literary works particularize typical meanings and create new connections and associations short of achieving a complete melding of particularity and typicality. Knapp also interprets the concrete universal in terms of what he calls "literary interest": literary works offer an analogical experience to what it feels like to be an "agent," by reproducing the oscillation between typicality and particularity that characterizes the interiority of human agency.

See AFFECTIVE FALLACY, INTENTIONAL FALLACY.

■ J. C. Ransom, "The Concrete Universal: Observations on the Understanding of Poetry," *KR* 16 (1954); W. K. Wimsatt, "The Concrete Universal," *The Verbal Icon* (1954); S. Knapp, "The Concrete Universal," *Literary Interest: The Limits of Anti-Formalism* (1993); F. Jameson, "The Experiments of Time: Providence and Realism," *The Novel*, ed. Franco Moretti, v. 2 (2006); T. Davis, *Formalism, Experience, and the Making of American Literature in the Eighteenth Century* (2007).

J. K. Mann

**CONFESSIONAL POETRY.** *Confession* in religious, psychoanalytic, criminal, and legal settings refers to the revelation of a shameful secret, as in a sin, crime, moral failing, social transgression, or neurosis. In an Am. literary context, confessional poetry refers to a group of poets writing during the 1950s and 1960s (Robert Lowell, W. D. Snodgrass, John Berryman, Sylvia Plath, Anne Sexton), who often employed the first-person *voice to explore transgressive autobiographical subjects incl. mental illness, familial trauma, gender and sexuality, and moral and political iconoclasm. M. L. Rosenthal originated the term in a review of Robert Lowell's *Life Studies* in 1959: "Because of the way Lowell brought his private humiliations, sufferings, and psychological problems into the poems of *Life Studies*, the word 'confessional' seemed appropriate." Confessional poetry is formally diverse, employing narrative, lyric, and dramatic modes and both free and metrical forms, while stylistically it often follows conventions of 19th-c. realist prose in its presentation of autobiographical material (Perloff). For example, Lowell's *Life Studies* originated in his prose memoir *91 Revere Street*, and he stated in an interview with Ian Hamilton that he wanted the poems to be as "single-surfaced as a photograph." The confessional poets' debts to *modernism are also evident in uses of surrealist imagery (Plath) and multivocality (Berryman).

Confession in postwar Am. poetry can be seen as part of a more general resurgence of neoromantic poetics and a turn to autobiographical practices after World War II. Allen Ginsberg's effort in *Howl* to "stand before you speechless and intelligent and shaking with shame, rejected yet confessing out the soul" spelled an end to poetic impersonality (Eliot) and the New Critical bias against *intention and *affect. A variety of postwar poets sought forms of "naked," honest expression; cultivated spontaneity, immediacy, and a conversational style; privileged process over product; explored the Freudian unconscious and taboo desires; and initiated new methods of conjoining poetry and everyday life. Ginsberg's *Howl*, Frank O'Hara's personism, Amiri Baraka's "Black Art," Adrienne Rich's feminist poetics, and Robert Bly's *Deep Image all share an interest in the poet's person as the ground for varied explorations of self, politics, nation, and aesthetics. Despite the specific connotations of *confessional poetry*, then, it emerges from and converses with trads. of romantic lyric, autobiography, and the poetry of witness. Contemp. poets who explore confession, incl. Sharon Olds, Frank Bidart, and Susan Hahn, indicate its enduring interest.

Judgments of confessional poetry have hinged on interpretations of the poem's relationship to the biographical poet. Detractors have read the poems as naïve autobiographical utterances and often as literal forms of therapeutic catharsis unmediated by aesthetic considerations, or conversely, as exhibitionist, sensationalist, self-serving performances (e.g., Lerner, Bawer, Gullans). Defenders have emphasized the problems with biographical readings, pointing out that judgments of the poetry often rest on moral evaluation of the poet's conduct (Travisano) and that pejorative responses are often feminized. Confessional poets and their sympathetic critics have pointed out the artful, fictive nature of confessional representation and performance, incl. the use of dramatic personae and dramatic *monologue (Lowell, Sexton, Berryman), while feminist scholars have emphasized Sexton's and Plath's performance and interrogation of the gendered self as a critical commentary on cold-war culture and an important influence on feminist poetry and performance art.

Given the pejorative connotations of *confessional poetry*, Travisano has called for its demise as a "critical paradigm," while others argue that the concept of confession can usefully elucidate poetry's truth claims. In that the confessant unveils secrets despite the stigma of shame, this revelation against societal resistance contributes to the expectation of the liberation of truth. As de Man writes, to confess is "to overcome guilt and shame in the name of truth: it is an epistemological use of language in which ethical values . . . are superseded by values of truth and falsehood." Gilmore argues that "as a mode of truth production the confession in both its oral and its written forms grants the autobiographer a kind of authority derived from the confessor's proximity to 'truth.'" Critics influenced by *poststructuralism have found in confessional poetry not liberating, therapeutic expression but complex challenges to ideals of the coherent subject, referential lang., truth, and *sincerity. Foucault's understanding of confession has proven particularly influential. Counter to the belief that confession "unburdens" or "liberates," Foucault argues that confession is "the effect of a power that constrains us." As "a ritual that unfolds within a power relationship," the confession is shaped by the "authority who requires the confession, prescribes and appreciates it, and intervenes in order to judge, punish, forgive, console, and reconcile." Critics have drawn attention to confessional poetry's foregrounding of these power relationships and to the poetry's negotiation of its reader as a potential judge, analyst, jailer, or confessor. From this perspective, confessional poetry reveals the moral problem of judgment and explores the epistemological problems of truth and the relation of life and lit.

If one reads confessional poetry in the context of the longer trad. of confessional lit., Augustine and Jean-Jacques Rousseau provide two important models. For Augustine, self-conscious reflection on and repentance for sin lead to conversion and incorporation within a Christian community, whereas, for Rousseau, confession enacts individual difference rather than moral conformity, permitting the painting of a "portrait in every way true to nature." In Rousseau's text, confession of "sin" allows him to indict an inherently unjust society rather than take responsibility for error; de Man argues that confession-cum-excuse allows Rousseau to take pleasure in the exhibition of shame. Both models are evident in the poetic trad.; as Davie argues, there are poets who confess virtue (William Wordsworth) and those who confess vice (Lord Byron, Charles Baudelaire), poets who seek accommodation within a moral community and others who transgress moral community to critical ends. In mid-20th c. America, although the influence of Augustinian confession persists (New), Rousseau's example dominates; Rosenthal influentially argued that the confessional poet's alienation from society embodies a nation and culture in crisis. Successive critics often treat the confessional poet as "representative victim" (Breslin) and the confessional poem as an instrument that mirrors and critically diagnoses the culture. Hence, Middlebrook argues that "the images of the confessional poem encode the whole culture's shame-making machinery," while others have demonstrated confessional poetry's critical engagements with specific contexts, incl. Freudian psychoanalysis, McCarthyism, surveillance, privacy law, television, commercial culture, and gendered codes.

■ R. Langbaum, *The Poetry of Experience: The Dramatic Monologue in Modern Literary Tradition* (1957); M. L. Rosenthal, *The New Poets: American and British Poetry since World War II* (1967); D. Davie, "On Sincerity: From Wordsworth to Ginsberg," *Encounter* 31 (1968); L. Trilling, *Sincerity and Authenticity* (1972); M. Perloff, *The Poetic Art of Robert Lowell* (1973); M. Foucault, *The History of Sexuality, Volume 1: An Introduction,* trans. R. Hurley (1978); P. de Man, *Allegories of Reading* (1979); P. Breslin, *The Psycho-Political Muse: American Poetry since the 1950s* (1987); L. Lerner, "What Is Confessional Poetry?" *Critical Quarterly* 29 (1987); C. Gullans, "Review of *Live or Die,*" *Anne Sexton: Telling the Tale,* ed. S. E. Colburn (1988); I. Hamilton, "A Conversation with Robert Lowell," *Robert Lowell, Interviews and Memoirs,* ed. J. Meyers (1988); B. Bawer, "Sylvia Plath and the Poetry of Confession," *The New Criterion* 9 (1991); M. Perloff, *Radical Artifice* (1991); J. Rose, *The Haunting of Sylvia Plath* (1991); C. Forché, *Against Forgetting: Twentieth-Century Poetry of Witness* (1993); K. Lant, "The Big Strip Tease: Female Bodies and Male Power in the Poetry of Sylvia Plath," *Contemporary Literature* 34 (1993); D. Middlebrook, "What Was Confessional Poetry?" and G. Orr, "The Postconfessional Lyric," *The Columbia History of American Poetry,* ed. J. Parini (1993); L. Gilmore, "Policing Truth: Confession, Gender, and Autobiographical Authority," *Autobiography and Postmodernism,* ed. K. Ashley, L. Gilmore, G. Peters (1994); R. Felski, "On Confession," *Women, Autobiography, Theory: A Reader,* ed. S. Smith and J. Watson (1998); C. Britzolakis, *Sylvia Plath and the Theatre of Mourning* (1999); I. Gammel, *Confessional Politics: Women's Sexual Self-Representations in Life Writing and Popular Media* (1999); T. Travisano, *Midcentury Quartet: Bishop, Lowell, Jarrell, Berryman, and the Making of a Postmodern Aesthetic* (1999); D. H. Blake, "Public Dreams: Berryman, Celebrity, and the Culture of Confession," *American Literary History* 13 (2001); M. Bryant, "Plath, Domesticity, and the Art of Advertising," *College Literature* 29 (2002); D. Nelson, *Pursuing Privacy in Cold War America* (2002); J. Rose, *On Not Being Able to Sleep: Psychoanalysis and the Modern World* (2003); T. Brain, "Dangerous Confessions: The Problem of Reading Sylvia Plath Biographically," J. Gill, "Introduction," and E. Gregory, "Confessing the Body: Plath, Sexton, Berryman, Lowell, Ginsberg, and the Gendered Poetics of the 'Real,'" *Modern Confessional Writing,* ed. J. Gill (2006); E. New, "Confession, Reformation, and Counter-Reformation in the Career of Robert Lowell," and S. Burt, "My Name Is Henri: Contemporary Poets Discover John Berryman," *Reading the Middle Generation Anew,* ed. E. L. Haralson (2006); S. Rosenbaum, *Professing Sincerity: Modern Lyric Poetry, Commercial Culture, and the Crisis in Reading* (2007); J. Badia, *Sylvia Plath and the Mythology of Women Readers* (2011).

S. ROSENBAUM

**CONNECTICUT WITS.** The Connecticut Wits (or Hartford Wits) were a loose coterie of poets who published numerous poems during the Am. revolutionary and early republic periods. The group originated at Yale College in the early 1770s, when fellow students John Trumbull (1750–1831), Timothy Dwight (1752–1817), David Humphreys (1752–1818), and Joel Barlow (1754–1812) formed a lasting literary friendship around their shared admiration for Alexander Pope, Jonathan Swift, and other Brit. neoclassical writers. This youthful immersion in Augustan poetry would influence the form and content of the Wits' own poetic productions, particularly their emphasis on poetry as a weapon of political or ideological warfare. In general, the Wits supported the patriots in the Am. Revolution and the Federalists during both the constitutional debates of the 1780s and the early partisan political struggles of the 1790s. Their most memorable works include Trumbull's *M'Fingal* (1775); Dwight's *The Triumph of Infidelity* (1788) and *Greenfield Hill* (1794); Barlow's *The Vision of Columbus* (1787) and "The Hasty Pudding" (1793); and the satiric series *The Anarchiad* (1786–87), written in collaboration by Trumbull, Humphreys, Barlow, and fellow Hartford poet Lemuel Hopkins (1750–1801).

By the 1790s, as the original Wits focused their energies on careers in education, law, and diplomacy, they would be succeeded by a second generation of Connecticut Wits (sometimes called the "minor" Wits), which included Hopkins, Richard Alsop (1761–1815), Theodore Dwight (1764–1846), and Elihu Hubbard Smith (1771–98). Writing amid the tumult of the Fr. Revolution and the rise of the Jeffersonian party, the latter group would publish numerous verse *satires both individually and collaboratively, incl. *The Echo* series (1791–98), *The Democratiad* (1795), and *The Political Greenhouse* (1798).

*See* NEOCLASSICAL POETICS.

■ L. Howard, *The Connecticut Wits* (1942); W. C. Dowling, *Poetry and Ideology in Revolutionary Connecticut* (1990); C. Wells, "Revolutionary Verse," *Oxford Handbook of Early American Literature*, ed. K. J. Hayes (2008).

C. WELLS

**CONNOTATION AND DENOTATION.** The distinction between *denotation* and *connotation* was important in lit. crit. and theory from the 1930s to the 1970s. The *denotation* of a word or phrase is its literal or obvious meaning or reference as specified in a dictionary; the *connotations* of a word or phrase are the secondary or associated significances that it commonly suggests or implies. This distinction is complicated in practice because many words have more than one denotation and because dictionaries sometimes include definitions of a word based on connotation as well as denotation. E.g., the first set of definitions of the noun *rose* given by the *OED* tells us that a rose is both "a well-known beautiful and fragrant flower" and "a rose-plant, rose-bush, or rose-tree"; in addition, the *OED* gives a number of "allusive, emblematic, or figurative uses" (e.g., "a bed of roses" or "under the rose") that reveal the huge store of cultural connotations associated with the flower.

The connotations of a word or phrase accrue from the way it is used in a particular lang. community. Our knowledge of connotations comes from our access to the cultural assumptions of the society in which the word or phrase was used. When Robert Burns's speaker declares that his "love is like a red, red rose," we do not read it as a denotative statement of fact but respond to the connotations—of sexual love and passion—that the simile transfers to the woman and/or his feelings for her. These connotations derive from the long association between roses and romantic love in Western culture.

Critics have often suggested that lit., esp. poetry, makes sustained and highly organized uses of connotations. All aspects of poems and poetic lang.—genres, figures, sound patterns, and so on—can evoke connotations through their use in the general culture and in other poetry. Under the influence of early 20th-c. forerunners such as Richards and Empson, Anglo-Am. New Critics assumed that poetry employs the connotations of words and phrases in order to suggest levels of meaning and feeling that embody the subtle nuances of human experience and reveal truths that are unavailable to those nonliterary discourses (such as science) that supposedly employ purely denotative lang. Yet the New Critics also sought to exclude the reader's merely personal associations by insisting that valid connotations are part of the public culture in which the poem was produced. They also argued that the connotations of the poem as a whole make up a coherent, organic pattern—what Ransom called "the tissue, or totality of connotation." For New Critics such as Brooks, a poem's tissue of connotations constitutes an organic complexity that cannot be reduced to denotative statements

without destroying the poem's essence (the "heresy of paraphrase"; see NEW CRITICISM).

Eur. literary theory has attempted to deal with connotation in more rigorous and systematic ways. A concern with the relationship of connotation and denotation was at the core of Barthes's work from the 1950s to the 1970s. Barthes's semiological analysis of everyday cultural phenomena in *Mythologies* (1957) sought to expose how the media and popular culture exploit the connotations of words, phrases, images, or objects to present an ideological view of an aspect of the mod. world as natural and inevitable. In *Elements of Semiology* (1964), influenced by Hjelmslev's "connotative semiotics," Barthes highlights some of the ways that Ferdinand de Saussure's *Course in General Linguistics* (1916) overlooks connotation and then devotes the whole of the final section to a consideration of denotation and connotation. Following Hjelmslev, Barthes suggests that signs on the plane of denotation become signifiers (or "connotators") on the plane of connotation, and he accepts at this point in his career Hjelmslev's assumption that secondary connotations are always anchored by primary denotations. Barthes concludes by anticipating that "the future probably belongs to a linguistics of connotation" (see SEMIOTICS AND POETRY).

The goal of the structuralist analysis of lit. was not to discover the complex meanings or structure of the text being read but to describe the literary system that made it possible in the first place (see STRUCTURALISM). Lit. uses the first-order system of lang. in ways that are made possible by a second-order literary system made up of conventional techniques and codes—narrative techniques, speech situations, genres, and so on—that work through connotation rather than denotation. Barthes's "Introduction to the Structural Analysis of Narratives" (1966) suggests that this second-order system of connotative meaning should become "the object of a second linguistics" and envisages a mode of analysis that would examine individual narratives in terms of what they reveal about the narrative system that made them possible in the first place.

Barthes's almost exclusive focus on narrative texts meant that the devel. of a semiological or structuralist analysis of poetry was left to other theorists. Jakobson's semiotic analysis of E. A. Poe's "The Raven" in *Language in Operation* (1964) highlights how the connotation of the repeated refrain "Nevermore" changes according to its immediate context in the poem. But whereas connotation is fundamentally shaped by context, denotation supposedly remains the same in all contexts. The refrain in "The Raven" thus exemplifies the repetition with α difference that characterizes Jakobson's *po-etic function, and he concludes by announcing that "[t]he tension between this intrinsic unity [of denotation] and the diversity of contextual or situational meanings [connotations] is the pivotal problem of the linguistic discipline labelled *semantics*." Riffaterre's *Semiotics of Poetry* (1978) argues that all aspects of a poem constitute a unified semantic field of denotations and connotations that points to or elaborates its unstated meaning and that a reader of poetry, therefore, needs "to decode connotations as well as denotation." But the challenging aspect of Riffaterre's argument is his proposition that the denotation that we "discover" at the poem's originating kernel is actually an aftereffect produced by the reader's interpretation of its system of connotations. Indeed, he suggests that there is no such thing as a purely denotational lang. that is free of or prior to connotation—lang. is always already "hot with intensified connotations."

One problem with the structuralist analysis of lit. is that the second-order codes and devices that characterize lit. are not like the first-order signs that make up lang. Literary codes and devices exploit and generate connotations, and connotations are provisional and unstable, depend on context, and cannot be organized into a coherent system whose meanings are equally shared by a single interpretive community. And while literary texts exploit the connotative potential of lang. and of literary strategies and forms, they also disrupt and transform those connotations. The realization that literary texts cannot, therefore, be read straightforwardly as products of a system they tend to revise and undermine is one of the motives of the shift from structuralism to *poststructuralism.

In 1970, in *S/Z: An Essay*, Barthes carried out a full-length segmental analysis of Honoré de Balzac's short story "Sarrasine," but by then he had begun to see the problems with the structuralist project. Instead of attempting to constitute the narrative system that makes possible all the world's narratives, Barthes now shows how each arbitrarily divided segment (or "lexia") of the text disseminates plural connotations that cannot be constrained by considerations of *mimesis or by assuming that the text is a coherent structure. Yet although he deconstructs the distinction between denotation and connotation and no longer sees Saussure's *langue* as a primary system of stable denotations against which to measure the "secondary" system of literary connotations, Barthes nonetheless sees a strategic role for attending to connotation in some literary texts; his suggestion that the variety of connotators found in the lexias can be organized into five "codes" indicates that connotations are a fundamental aspect of what Barthes and Julia Kristeva called *intertextuality*—a term that refers to the way literary texts are made up of anonymous "quotations" that have been repeatedly iterated and encountered in the general culture. As we have seen, this is precisely how connotations work.

Connotation, then, was central to the structuralist project and to Barthes's version of poststructuralism. Yet the terms *denotation* and *connotation* hardly figure in subsequent theory and crit. Given that the nuances of meaning and feeling play a key role in the formation and effects of ideology and given that literary texts both exploit and challenge the way connotations make partial views of the world appear natural, it would seem that politically engaged lit. crit. and cultural studies would benefit from the close analysis of connotation. Moreover, the play of connotation remains central to how many nonacademic critics and poets think about

lyric poetry and, indeed, to the way we teach lit. in the classroom.

*See* POLYSEMY, SANSKRIT POETICS, SEMANTICS AND POETRY.

■ Richards; Brooks; W. Empson, *The Structure of Complex Words* (1951); Empson; L. Hjelmslev, *Prolegomena to a Theory of Language*, trans. F. J. Whitfield (1961); R. Barthes, *Elements of Semiology*, trans. A. Lavers and C. Smith (1967); *Mythologies*, trans. A. Lavers (1973); *S/Z*, trans. R. Miller (1974); R. Barthes, *Image, Music, Text*, trans. S. Heath (1977); M. Riffaterre, *Semiotics of Poetry* (1978); R. Jakobson, *Language in Literature*, ed. K. Pomorska and S. Rudy (1987); *Post-Structuralist Readings of English Poetry*, ed. R. Machin and C. Norris (1987); S. Hall, "The Rediscovery of 'Ideology,'" *Literary Theory: An Anthology*, ed. J. Rivkin and M. Ryan (1998)—reprint of extracts; J. C. Ransom, "Criticism, Inc.," *The Norton Anthology of Theory and Criticism*, ed. V. B. Leitch et al. (2001); D. Paterson, "The Lyric Principle" (part one), *The Poetry Review* 97 (2007).

T. FURNISS

**CONSONANCE.** In *prosody, *consonance* refers most strictly to the repetition of the sound of a final consonant or consonant cluster in stressed, unrhymed syllables near enough to be heard together, as in Robert Lowell's "iro*n*ic rai*n*bow" and "Go*bb*ets of blu*bb*er" or Robert Browning's "Rebu*ck*led the chee*k*-strap, chained sla*ck*er the bit," where three final *k* sounds emphasize the stressed syllables bu*ck*-chee*k*-sla*ck*. Consonance parallels the repetitions in *alliteration (initial consonant) and *assonance (vowel) and can be combined either within a syllable to produce other effects, such as *rhyme (assonance + consonance) or pararhyme (alliteration + consonance). Critics have sometimes used the terms *consonance, assonance*, and *alliteration* interchangeably with some loss of precision. *Consonance* also sometimes specifically denotes cases of pararhyme, an effect commonly found in early Celtic, Germanic, and Icelandic poetry, and in W. H. Auden's "*read*er to *rid*er" or in early Ren. verse such as Luigi Pulci's "Stille le stelle ch'a tetto era tutta." This effect has been referred to alternately as *bracket rhyme, bracket alliteration, bracket consonance*, or *rich consonance*, though it may be useful to distinguish this double echo from the single echo of final consonant repetition. This would allow one to say that "rider" both alliterates and consonates with "reader," while in *fur-fair, f* alliterates and *r* consonates. Consonance has often fallen loosely under the terms *half rhyme, near rhyme*, or *slant rhyme*, which may blur the distinction between differing vowel and consonant echoes. Combinations that appear to rhyme to the eye, such as lo*ve*-mo*ve*, may only consonate, though some such pairs are accepted by convention as rhyme. Several critics have identified other instances of "partial" or "semi" consonance when, e.g., one or more echoes involve slightly differing clusters, as in Dylan Thomas's pairing pla*tes*-hea*rts*, which differs by the *r* in hearts but retains the *t-s* echo in both. Likewise, one may find "close" consonance between voiced and unvoiced final consonant echoes, as in the *f* and *v* of wi*f*e-lo*v*e or *s* and *z* of hear*s*e-war*es*. Consonance becomes more subtle, and harder to hear, between complex vowel or glide endings, as in the *y* of da*y*-li*e*, also sometimes called *semiconsonance*, while "zero-consonance" has been used to describe repeating vowels without the final consonant echo. There is little agreement, however, on the use of these more narrowly defined terms. There is no consensus either about how to notate consonantal echoes across stressed and unstressed syllables or in ambiguous rhythms, though most critics take a pragmatic approach to capturing such effects.

Though occasionally criticized as "imperfect" rhyme, consonance has been used with great frequency as ornamentation; as a substitute for or contrast with rhyme; as a device to create *parallelism, to amplify rhythmic effects, or to forestall closure; and as a structuring device in its own right. Lucretius has many lines such as "Cernere adorari licet et sentire sonare," with four final *r*'s in stressed syllables. Though final written consonants are not often pronounced in Fr., Nicolas Boileau echos final *s* and *r* in "Changer Narcisse en fleur, couvrir Daphné d'écorce." Shakespeare normally preferred other phonic echoes, but his couplet from *Romeo and Juliet* (2.3.3–4) is far from unique: "And flecked darkness like a drunkard reels / From forth day's path and Titan's fiery wheels," where six of ten stressed peaks consonate with *k* or *th*. John Dryden used it for parallelism, often with other echoes ("piercing wi*t* and pregnant though*t*); for joining adjective to noun ("*od*ious ai*d*," "exten*d*ed wan*d*"); and for *onomatopoeia ("A buzzing noise of bees his ears alarms," where the *z* of buzz ends every stressed syllable). Emily Dickinson and R. W. Emerson employed consonance often in place of end rhyme, as in Dickinson's "I like to see it lap the miles," with lines ending u*p*-ste*p*, pee*r*-pa*re*, whi*le*-hi*ll*, and sta*re*-doo*r*. G. M. Hopkins is known for a variety of phonic echoes, including pairs such as Gho*st*-brea*st*, ye*ll*ow-sa*ll*ows.

In the 20th c., dozens of poets showed an interest in consonance as an anchor for various formal schema. W. B. Yeats's "Meditations in Time of Civil War" sometimes prefers consonance over end rhyme, as in the *d-r-d-d-r* pattern of woo*d*, wa*r*, roa*d*, bloo*d*, sta*re*. Consonance dominates Dylan Thomas's "And Death Shall Have No Opinion," inverting the usual proportion of end consonance to end rhyme. Ted Hughes combines rhyme and consonance, as in fro*z*en-ey*es*-sno*ws*-ro*ws*-snai*ls*. Wilfred Owen has more consonance by itself (shri*ll*-wai*l*ing-ca*ll*), as do Theodore Roethke and Hart Crane, who lets the consonance of *r* dominate a whole stanza of "Voyages II."

■ K. Burke, "On Musicality in Verse," *The Philosophy of Literary Form* (1941); J. Travis, "Intralinear Rhyme and Consonance in Early Celtic and Early Germanic Poetry," *Germanic Review* 18 (1943); A. Oras, "Surry's Technique of Phonetic Echoes," *JEGP* 50 (1951), and "Lyrical Instrumentation in Marlowe," *Studies in Shakespeare*, ed. A. D. Matthews (1953); D. Masson, "Vowel and Consonant Patterns in Poetry" and "Thematic Analyses of Sounds in Poetry," and A. Oras, "Spenser and Milton: Some Parallels and Contrasts in the Handling of Sound," *Essays on the Language of Literature*, ed. S. Chatman and S. R. Levin (1967); R. Astley, "Stations of the Breath," *PMLA* 84 (1969); G. N. Leech, *A Linguistic Guide to English Poetry* (1969); P. G. Adams, *Graces of Harmony: Alliteration, Assonance, and Consonance in Eighteenth-Century British Poetry* (1977); M. Williams, *Patterns of Poetry* (1986); J. J. Small, *Positive as Sound* (1990); P. G. Adams, "Edward Taylor's Love Affair with Sounding Language," *Order in Variety*, ed. R. W. Crump (1991); D. Robey, *Sound and Structure in the Divine Comedy* (2000); M. W. Edwards, *Sound, Sense, and Rhythm* (2002); S. Heaney, *Finders Keepers* (2002); M. Tyler, *A Singing Contest* (2005); B. Devine, *Yeats, the Master of Sound* (2006); W. Harmon, "A Game of Feet," *SR* 116 (2008); L. Wheeler, *Voicing American Poetry* (2008).

P. G. ADAMS; R. S. STILLING

**CONSTRAINT.** Constrained writing is a literary method in which the writer produces poetic texts through the use of externally derived "constraints." A constraint is a mod. technical term with anticipations but without precise equivalents in the traditional vocabulary of poetics and rhet. It refers to a freely chosen rule added either to the ling. rules of the natural lang. in which the text is written or the traditional rules of a genre to which the text seeks to conform. Systematically applied throughout the entire text, it thus serves as a trigger for *invention and creativity and as an illustration or token of what it is possible to write with the help of such a device. Constraints are usually singular rather than conventional: they often find their origin in the experiments of a particular writer, whereas other poetic features are often collective and anonymous. Moreover, their use is, at least in theory, completely saturated, for in constrained writing, it is compulsory to follow the rule (the only exception allowed is that of the playful or revealing "mistake," in which case the error becomes a unique "clinamen"). As a result, a constrained poem tends to foreground its own constraint as much as the lang. that displays it, which explains why certain readers will discard the result of constrained writing as inauthentic or artificial. Any formal or semantic aspect of a poem can be the locus of a constraint. *Lipograms (the systematic omission of a letter or letters), monosyllabic vocabulary, the graphic alternation of vowels and consonants, the exclusion of all male nouns, or the use of bilingually functioning words are all constraints, provided these devices do not already pertain to the conventional poetic system of the day and they are applied throughout the whole text or a meaningful section of the text.

It may be possible to divide constraints into two types, whose difference owes more to cultural than to technical distinctions. One might call these two types the "anachronisms" and the "neologisms": the former are conventional rules that have fallen into oblivion but are recuperated as constraints; the latter are newly invented constraints. In traditional poetry in Eur. langs., based on the formal difference between poetry and prose, any text is rule-based, at least at the level of *prosody and *rhyme—which used to be compulsory in poetry, but in poetry only. Yet the changes wrought by the *romanticism and *modernism of the 19th and early 20th cs. emphasized the right of the poet to break the rules of prosody and rhyme in the name of personal expression. In the wake, new neologistic forms of constraint emerged, which aimed at taking the place of the now old-fashioned rules. Nevertheless, the rediscovery or reappraisal of old forms continues to form a starting point of constrained writing as well. To use the *sonnet form as it had been canonized by François de Malherbe in the 16th c., and then attenuated and eventually exploded in later centuries, would be an example of constrained writing today.

The literary stakes of constraint are always double. As a negative device, it prevents the writer from freely—yet stereotypically—expressing himself, for writing under constraint is often very difficult and blocks any spontaneous *expression, which defenders of constrained writing dismiss as an outlet for banality and *cliché. As a positive device, constraint forces the writer to invent something new even as he lacks *inspiration in the traditional sense of the word—hence, the praise of constraint as a tool capable of breaking the domination of a sterile *free verse since the gradual blurring of the boundaries between poetry and prose following the end of the 19th c.

In recent Western poetics, the invention of constrained writing is often associated with the Fr. *Oulipo or *Ouvroir de littérature potentielle* (Workshop for Potential Literature, founded in 1960), although the work of John Cage, who tried to merge the apparently incompatible worlds of necessity and chance, is often recognized as well. In the case of the Fr. poet Jacques Roubaud (b. 1932), who has experimented with mathematically inspired forms of rhythm, the use of constraint is a necessary condition of memory in and through lang., for it is the constrained rhythmic backbone of a text that enables poetic and verbal transmission. For Denis Roche (b. 1937), who has worked with new forms of cut-up, constrained writing is a way of exploring the similarities between lit. and photography, i.e., of framing and cropping reality itself. In *Crystallography*, Christian Bök (b. 1966) uses constrained writing as a way of giving shape to the encounter between poetic and scientific lang. Finally, it should be stressed that, for many authors, constraint is a powerful instrument in the democratic and interactive use of literary lang. The reader of a constrained poem is expected to participate in a very active way, not only by discovering the operative constraint (authors do not commonly make the constraints they employ explicit) but most importantly by evaluating how the author proposes a concrete variation of a form that is always open to other and sometimes more interesting occurrences or demonstrations. Constrained writing has, therefore, become an important axis in the new worlds of collective writing and is a common institution of creative writing programs, at least in France and the United States. In anglophone culture, the importance of constrained writing grows along multiple avenues, thanks to the inspiring examples of Cage's mesostichs (a constrained type of cut up) as well as to repeated attempts to restore traditional forms of prosody and verse.

*See* ALEATORY POETICS, FORMALISM.

■ Oulipo, *Atlas de littérature potentielle* (1981); C. Bök, *Crystallography* (1994); D. Roche, *La poésie est inadmissible* (1995); J. Baetens, "Une déclaration d'indépendance," *9e Art* 2 (1998); *Oulipo Compendium*, ed. H. Mathews and A. Brotchie (2005); J. Baetens, "Hergé, auteur à contraintes? Une relecture de L'Affaire Tournesol," *French Forum* 31 (2006); A. S. James, *Constraining Chance: Georges Perec and the Oulipo* (2009); "The State of Constraint: New Work by Oulipo," *McSweeney's Quarterly Concern* 22 (2006), http://www.mcsweeneys.net/quarterly/; Oulipo, http://www.oulipo.net/.

J. BAETENS

**CONSTRUCTIVISM** as a mod. art movement first emerged among Rus. painters around 1913 and included such artists as Vladimir Tatlin and Naum Gabo; the new trend spread to Western Europe in the early 1920s. The constructivists called for the union of art with science and technology. Gradually, the movement's ideas spread to lit. and to poetry in particular. The initiator of this trend was A. N. Čičerin, who drafted the first *manifesto, "Znaem" (We Know, 1923) and was its most radical practitioner, progressing from short, phonetically transcribed poems to more compressed, even wordless visual artifacts in accordance with the principle of maximum expression using a minimum of material. In 1924, a group of Rus. writers organized under the banner of constructivism; these included the poets Il'ja Selvinskij, Eduard Bagritskij, and Vera Inber, as well as the movement's other theoretician, K. L. Zelinskij. The group called for the absorption of the lexicon of science and technology by lit.; it also emphasized what members called "localization" of word pattern and other literary devices, which meant their subordination to subject matter; thus, a poem on war might employ a marching rhythm. But the group's theories were at best hazy and, with the exception of Selvinskij, little more than lip service was paid to them. The movement broke up after 1930.

■ K. L. Zelinskij, *Poèzija kak smysl': kniga o konstruktivizme* (1929); H. Ermolaev, *Soviet Literary Theories, 1917–1934* (1963); G. Weber, "Constructivism and Soviet Literature," *Soviet Union* 3 (1976); E. Mozhejko, "Russian Literary Constructivism: Towards a Theory of Poetic Language," *Canadian Contributions to the VIII International Congress of Slavists*, ed. Z. Folejewski et al. (1978); R. Grübel, *Russischer Konstruktivismus* (1981), and "Russkij literaturnyj konstruktivizm," *Russian Literature* 17 (1985); C. Lodder, *Russian Constructivism* (1985); "Kan-Fun: Konstruktivizm-funkcionalizm," *Russian Literature* 21 (1987); G. Niebuhr, *The Tradition of Constructivism* (1990); C. Cooke, *Russian Avant-Garde: Theories of Art, Architecture and the City* (1995); G. Rickey, *Constructivism* (1995); B. Watten, *The Constructivist Moment* (2003); M. Gough, *The Artist as*

*Producer: Russian Constructivism in Revolution* (2005); C. Kaier, *Imagine No Possessions* (2005); *Rodchenko and Popova: Defining Constructivism*, ed. M. Tupitsyn (2009).

W. E. Harkins; G. J. Janecek

**CONTE DÉVOT.** A type of OF pious tale in prose or verse, popular in the 13th and 14th cs. It is distinct from the saint's legend and the moral tale (see EXEMPLUM). The best-known *conte dévot* is the *Tombeor Nostre Dame*, or *Jongleur de Notre Dame*, in which a *minstrel whose only talent is in dancing performs before the image of Our Lady, to her approval. Such tales were undoubtedly inspired by the great collections known as the *Vitae Patrum* and the *Miracles Nostre Dame*. Many of the contes dévots are miracle tales, though not all. In the *Chevalier au barisel*, a knight is instructed by his confessor to fill a small keg with water but proves unable to do so, despite many attempts, until he sheds one tear of true repentance, which fills the keg miraculously. In the *Conte del'hermite et del jongleour*, a holy hermit is told by an angel that his companion in heaven will be a minstrel. In disgust, the hermit goes to the town marketplace, where he talks with a poor minstrel and listens to his life story. Realizing that the poor man is better than he, the hermit repents, and eventually the two are admitted to heaven together.
■ O. Schultz-Gora, *Zwei altfranzösische Dichtungen*, 4th ed. (1919); E. Lommatzsch, *Del Tumbeor Nostre Dame* (1920); F. Lecoy, *Le chevalier au barisel* (1955).

U. T. Holmes

**CONTESTS, POETIC.** *See* POETIC CONTESTS; POETRY SLAM.

**CONTRAFACTUM** (pl. *contrafacta*; also contrafact[s], contrafacture[s]; Lat., "made against"). The term *contrafactum* refers both to a process of poetic and musical borrowing and to the works that are the result of such a process.

As an imitative form, the contrafactum is typical of the Eur. Middle Ages and Ren., when respect for trad. and authority was often an important factor in poetic composition: whereas later authors increasingly sought *originality, med. and early mod. poets and composers often adapted and recreated existing works. While they are esp. prevalent from the 12th to the 17th c., contrafacta appear in all eras, and the definition of both the process and the genre went through several transformations.

Dating from the 12th c., the earliest identified contrafacta are monophonic. Many *troubadour songs were famous enough to be reused as models throughout the 12th and 13th cs., their melodies or rhymes forming the basis of new songs. Structural analysis of the med. secular lyric has revealed musical and poetic links between the various vernacular Western Eur. trads., esp. the Occitan troubadours, the Fr. *trouvères, the Ger. *Minnesänger, and the Galician-Port. poets of religious *cantigas.

As an example of metrical contrafactum, consider the 18 Occitan contrafacta of "La grans beutatz e.l fis ensenhamens" by the troubadour Arnaut de Maruelh. These all borrow the rhyme scheme of the model song. One advantage of this recycling of verse structure in the same lang. is that the melody can easily be adapted to each new poem. The possibilities of *intertextuality are rich, because the imitative group includes several literary genres: *courtly love songs versus political songs, soliloquies versus dialogic songs. In this network, there is also a poem attributed to a female troubadour or *trobairitz. In fact, recovery of the trobairitz repertoire may be possible only because of research into contrafacta, since women's poetry of the period is often closely responsive to that of male poets; only one song by a woman (the Comtessa de Dia) appears in the manuscript with its music.

A more complex example of the metrical contrafactum is the group of songs apparently based on Bernart de Ventadorn's "Can vei la lauzeta mover," a courtly love song. These imitations include Occitan, Fr., Ger., and Lat. pieces. Here, the melody of each is known, and it is clear that these melodies are not identical. Oral transmission can explain these variations up to a point, but it also seems clear that the basic melody was adapted to each new text. Among these songs are two by Philip the Chancellor of Paris that are loose trans. of each other, one in Fr. and one in Lat. Their melodies are slightly different from one another, which seems to indicate an effort to adapt the melody to the trans.

Networks of contrafacta set the same melody or sound structure in different contexts, among a changing and often expanding set of literary references. E.g., some melodies traveled between secular and religious milieux. One well-known instance is the group of melodic contrafacta apparently built on the short melody of the Gregorian chant "Ave maris stella." From the simple religious piece grew longer, more complex melodies incl. several courtly songs and a Galician-Port. cantiga to the Virgin Mary. Tischler showed links between many religious and secular pieces, among them both monophonic and polyphonic works. Hardy has also shown that some textual contrafacta, while they imitate poetic aspects incl. the verse structure, appear with different melodies for each poem.

In the Middle Ages, Eng. poetry did not participate in the networks of lyric contrafacta. However, some similar borrowings are to be found there, e.g., the Lat. song "Perspice christicola," which is sung to the same music as the Eng.-lang. double canon *Sumer is icumen in*.

In the Ren., the term *contrafactum* came to have a more expansive meaning. In music, the polyphonic masses of the 16th c. were often based on one line or even one word from a secular melody. Taken out of context, this short segment was combined with up to four other voices singing the Gr. and Lat. text of the Roman mass. An example of this type of mass is Josquin des Prez's *Missa L'Homme armé*, which uses as its tenor the melody of a popular song. Often, the line of verse from the short, borrowed song was lost in the mass, and the intertextual allusion had to be understood through familiarity with the original secular song. There are also networks of secular and religious borrowings within the works of the 16th-c. composer Pierre de la Rue: on the same melody, he wrote a five-part *chanson* on the Fr. poem "Incessament mon povre cuer lamente," a contrafactum mass using the same popular melody as its tenor, and a contrafactum motet in Lat., *Sic Deux dilexit*.

In poetry, early mod. contrafacta often involve the reworking of an earlier text through its words, its melody, or both to effect a change in the underlying cultural values: e.g., from sacred to profane or vice versa, from imperialist to critical of the imperial enterprise, from male- to female-voiced. The most common kind of contrafactum in the Ren. is the adaptation of love poetry to sacred purposes. Petrarch's *Canzoniere* was adapted into several contrafacta (e.g., Girolamo Malipiero, *Il Petrarca spirituale*) that rendered the poems into unequivocally Christian statements. (In Eng., this kind of adaptation is sometimes called *sacred parody*, but that term can also refer to the usage of conventions from love poetry for sacred purposes as opposed to the rewriting of actual poems.) Eng., Sp., It., and other langs. witness many instances of contrafactual writing in which the change occurs along an axis other than the spiritual: so one of the most famous intertextual exchanges of the period in Eng. starts from Christopher Marlowe's idealist "The Passionate Shepherd to His Love" ("Come live with me and be my love") and extends to the many adaptations and replies (by Walter Ralegh, John Donne, and others) that criticize the original poem.

There are many later examples of contrafacta. Some of Mozart's operas inspired contrafactum masses, such as the anonymous *Don Giovanni Mass in G major* and *Mass in C major after Cosi fan tutte*, both for four soloists, chorus, and orchestra.

*See* COMPANION POEMS.

■ I. Frank, *Trouveres et Minnesaenger* (1952); L. L. Martz, *The Poetry of Meditation* (1954)—defines *sacred parody*; B. W. Wardropper, *Historia de la poesía lírica a lo divino en la cristiandad occidental* (1958)—classic study with attention to Sp. trad.; F. Gennrich, *Die Kontrafaktur im Liedschaffen des Mittelalters* (1965); F. Noy, record jacket notes to *Cansos de trobairitz*, Hesperion XX, EMI-Réflexe (1978); H. van der Werf, *The Extant Troubadour Melodies* (1984); J. H. Marshall, "Pour l'étude des contrafacta dans la poésie des troubadours," *Romania* 101 (1980); M. L. Switten, "Modèles et variations: St. Martial de Limoges et les troubadours," *Contact de langues, de civilisations et intertextualité. IIIe congrès AIEO* (1990); *Le rayonnement des troubadours, Colloque AIEO*, ed. A. Touber (1990); *Tenso* 16.1 (2001)—sp. iss. on the contrafactum, see esp. I. Hardy, "Stratégies d'emprunt dans l'oeuvre de Raoul de Soissons"; H. Tischler, *Conductus and Contrafacta* (2001); D. Kullmann, *The Church and Vernacular Literature in Medieval France* (2009).

C. PHAN

**CONVENTION.** Any rule that by implicit agreement between a writer and some of his or her readers (or of the audience) allows the writer certain freedoms in, and imposes certain restrictions on, his or her treatment of style, structure, genre, or theme and enables these readers to interpret the work correctly. Combining social and objective functions, literary conventions are intersubjective; they hold (like ling. conventions) the normative force that underlies the possibility of communication at all.

Unlike users of ling. conventions, readers who are party to literary conventions may be very few indeed, else a writer could never create a new convention (e.g., *free verse or *sprung rhythm), revive an old convention (such as *alliterative meters in mod. langs.), or abandon an old convention (the pastoral *elegy). Readers who are ignorant of—or at least out of sympathy with—the convention must to some extent misinterpret a work that exemplifies it; and when the number of such readers becomes large, writers may abandon the convention—though, of course, works that exemplify it remain to be interpreted. Samuel Johnson in his judgment of "Lycidas" is an instance of a reader who misinterprets a work because he is out of sympathy with its conventions (*Life of Milton*).

Conventions govern the relations of matter to form, means to ends, and parts to wholes. Some examples of conventions of style are the rhyme scheme of the *sonnet and the diction of the *ballad; of structure, beginning an *epic *in medias res and the strophic structure of the *ode; of genre, representing the subject of a pastoral elegy as a shepherd; of theme, attitudes toward love in the Cavalier lyric (see CAVALIER POETS) and toward death in the Elizabethan lyric. The function of any particular convention is determined by its relation to the other conventions that together form the literary system. At any point in the hist. of its transmission, this system provides for the finite articulation of infinite literary possibilities.

Conventions both liberate and restrict the writer. Because conventions usually form sets and are motivated by traditional acceptance, a writer's decision to use a certain convention obliges him or her to use certain others or risk misleading the reader. The conventions of the epic, e.g., allow a writer to achieve effects of scale but compel him or her to forgo the conversational idiom of the metaphysical lyric (see METAPHYSICAL POETRY).

To break with conventions (or "rules") is sometimes thought a merit, sometimes a defect; but such a break is never abandonment of all conventions, merely replacement of an old set with a new. William Wordsworth condemns 18th-c. poetry for using poetic diction (Preface to the 1800 *Lyrical Ballads*); Leavis condemns Georgian poetry for adhering to "19th-century conventions of 'the poetical'" (see GEORGIANISM). The institutional character of convention supports theories of literary change based on the dialectic of trad. and innovation. In *New Criticism, "conventional 'materials'" are "rendered dramatic and moving" by the individual work (Brooks), while in *Russian formalism, dominant conventions change in function as they are displaced by the nascent ones they potentially contain.

Innovation results in new conventions. While established conventions may become, like ling. conventions, unconscious and apparently arbitrary, their reliance on implicit social agreement suggests that new conventions arise through nonexplicit cooperation, in the manner of social games of coordination (Lewis, Pavel). Genre theorists hold that when the "traits" of individual works of lit. no longer conform to the "type" specified by an established convention, they may begin to form the "type" of a new convention and thus set a new "horizon of expectation" for writers and readers (Hirsch, Jauss).

The social nature of conventions also distinguishes them from universals; hence, e.g., neo-Aristotelian restrictions of the term *convention* to denote "any characteristic of the matter or technique of a poem the reason for the presence of which cannot be inferred from the necessities of the form envisaged but must be sought in the historical circumstances of its composition" (Crane). *Structuralism concedes the conventionality of all norms but seeks to identify the universal laws of relation by which they are organized. The pervasiveness of convention accounts in *poststructuralism for the absorption of subjectivity and authorial intention into *écriture*, the autonomous productivity of writing as an institution (Barthes 1953), and for the concept of a plural, "writable" text whose meaning is unintelligible in traditional, "readerly" terms and must be written or invented by its readers (Barthes 1970). In *New Historicism, the social basis of literary conventions allows for their resituation in relation to the conventions of nonliterary discourse and of nondiscursive practices and institutions.

Because conventions mediate between *nature and its representation, as well as between authors and readers, different theories of convention (and different historical periods) will lay differing stress on their relation to universals, natural imperatives, trad., society, or the individual.

■ J. L. Lowes, *Convention and Revolt in Poetry* (1922); F. R. Leavis, *New Bearings in English Poetry* (1932); Brooks; R. S. Crane, *The Languages of Criticism and the Structure of Poetry* (1953); R. Barthes, *Writing Degree Zero*, trans. A. Lavers and C. Smith (1968); R. M. Browne, *Theories of Convention in Contemporary American Criticism* (1956); E. D. Hirsch Jr., *Validity in Interpretation* (1967); D. K. Lewis, *Convention* (1969); R. Barthes, *S/Z*, trans. R. Miller (1974); S. R. Levin, "The Conventions of Poetry," *Literary Style: A Symposium*, ed. S. Chatman (1971); V. Forrest-Thomson, "Levels in Poetic Convention," *Journal of European Studies* 2 (1972); J. Culler, *Structuralist Poetics* (1976), and "Convention and Meaning: Derrida and Austin," *NLH* 13 (1981); L. Manley, *Convention, 1500–1750* (1980), and "Concepts of Convention and Models of Critical Discourse," *NLH* 13.1 (1981)—spec. iss. "On Convention: I"; M. Steinmann, "Superordinate Genre Conventions," *Poetics* 10 (1981); H. R. Jauss, *Toward an Aesthetic of Reception*, trans. T. Bahti (1982); *NLH* 14.2 (1983)—spec. iss. "On Convention: II"; C. E. Reeves, "The Languages of Convention," *PoT* 7 (1986), and "'Conveniency to Nature': Literary Art and Arbitrariness," *PMLA* 101 (1986); T. Pavel, "Literary Conventions," in *Rules and Conventions*, ed. M. Hjort (1992); J. Wood, "Truth, Convention, Realism," *How Fiction Works* (2009).

M. STEINMANN; L. MANLEY

**CONVERSATION POEM.** A type of informal, colloquial poem whose tone is meant to echo relaxed conversation. In Eng., the term originates in S. T. Coleridge's subtitle for his *blank-verse meditative lyric "The Nightingale" and has since been applied to other of his poems, incl. "The Eolian Harp," "This Lime-Tree Bower My Prison," and "Frost at Midnight," as well as to William Wordsworth's Tintern Abbey poem ("Lines"). Like the dramatic *monologue, which it anticipates, the conversation poem situates itself between speech and writing, between artifice and spontaneity, and between the subjectivity of the lyric voice and the objectivity of dramatic exchange. Coleridge characterized both "Fears in Solitude" and "Reflections on Having Left a Place of Retirement" (originally subtitled "A Poem which affects not to be Poetry") as *sermoni propriora*, citing Horace's rubric for his *Epistles* and *Satires* ("more appropriate for conversation"). While Horace's epistles (and such Eng. imitations as Alexander Pope's "Epistle to Dr. Arbuthnot") provided models for the conversation poem's informal, intimate, yet serious tone, William Cowper's *The Task* influenced its relaxed, frequently enjambed blank verse, its use of colloquialisms, and its apparent immediacy and spontaneity.

Central to most conversation poems is a "native auditor" (Rajan) who receives the poet's words and helps intensify the sense of immediacy. Wordsworth's *The Prelude*, in which Coleridge functions as auditor, can be read as an epic conversation poem, while Coleridge's "To William Wordsworth," in which the auditor replies to the poet, as an inverted conversation poem. In later 19th- and 20th-c. poetry, the dramatic monologue tends to eclipse the conversation poem, although Robert Pinsky's "An Explanation of America" is a striking late 20th-c. example of the mode.

Another kind of conversation poem was invented by Guillaume Apollinaire shortly before World War I. Although he tried his hand at the genre as early as 1901 (in "Les Femmes"), the final version did not emerge until later, after he had assimilated the lessons of *cubism. In the early version, which was eventually published in *Alcools* (1913), two German women sew and chat before a cozy fire. Neighborhood gossip is interspersed with remarks addressed to various servants. The conversation is accompanied by a poetic narrative that contrasts the comfortable interior with the harsh winter outside. In the best symbolist trad., the poem attempts to create a certain *état d'âme* (mood). The most famous example, titled "Lundi rue Christine" (Monday Christine Street), evokes a visit to a seedy café, juxtaposing random snatches of conversation with random sights and sounds. Conceived as a dynamic verbovisual *collage, the composition describes what the poet sees, hears, and thinks. What distinguishes the *poèmes-conversation* from other works, Apollinaire explained, is that "le poète au centre de la vie enregistre en quelque sorte le lyrisme ambiant" (the poet at the center of life records, as it were, its ambient lyricism). Although he serves primarily as a voice recorder, the poet also functions as a camera. Since conversation poems consist of a series of radical juxtapositions, the reader necessarily participates in their construction.

■ G. M. Harper, "Coleridge's Conversation Poems," *Quarterly Review* 484 (1925); R. H. Fogle, "Coleridge's Conversation Poems," *Tulane Studies in English* 5 (1955); M. H. Abrams, "Structure and Style in the Greater Romantic Lyric," *From Sensibility to Romanticism*, ed. F. W. Hilles and H. Bloom (1965); A. S. Gérard, *English Romantic Poetry* (1968); P. Renaud, *Lecture d'Apollinaire* (1969); T. Rajan, *Dark Interpreter* (1980); T. Mathews, *Reading Apollinaire* (1987); P. Barry, "Coleridge the Revisionary: Surrogacy and Structure in the Conversation Poems," *RES* 51 (2000); J. R. Barth, "The *Biographia Literaria* as Conversation Poem: The Poetry of Coleridge's Prose," *Coleridge Bulletin* 16 (2000); P. Magnuson, "The 'Conversation' Poems," *The Cambridge Companion to Coleridge*, ed. L. Newlyn (2002).

A. RICHARDSON; W. BOHN

**COPLA.** Since the Sp. term *copla* often means simply "stanza," it is necessary to specify the type, such as *copla de arte mayor* (see ARTE MAYOR) or *copla de arte menor* (see ARTE MENOR). The *copla de pie quebrado*, which developed during the 14th and 15th cs., is any variation of the copla de arte menor in which one or more lines have been reduced to half length (four syllables or their equivalent) or half lines have been added or both. The most famous, though not the most common, has the rhyme scheme *ABcABcDEfDEf* (capital letters denote full-length lines) and is often called *copla* (or *estrofa*) *de Jorge Manrique* or *copla manriqueña* after the author of the famous *Coplas por la muerte de su padre*. The *copla real* (also called *décima, décima falsa, estancia real,* or *quintilla doble*) is an important 15th-c. variation of the copla de arte menor. It is a ten-line octosyllabic *strophe, the equivalent of two *quintillas*, the two usually having different rhyme schemes. The copla real was widely used in the 16th c. but in the 17th gradually gave way in popularity to one of its late 16th-c. variations, the *espinela.

*See* CANTAR, JUDEO-SPANISH POETRY.

■ F. Rodríguez Marín, *El alma de Andalucía en sus mejores coplas amorosas* (1929); D. C. Clarke, "The *Copla Real*" and "The 15th-C. *Copla de Pie Quebrado*," *HR* 10 (1942); Navarro; D. H. Darst, "Poetry and Politics in Jorge Manrique's *Coplas por la muerte de su padre*," *M&H* 13 (1985).

D. C. CLARKE

**COQ-À-L'ÂNE** (Fr., "cock and bull"). Name derived from an OF proverbial expression, "C'est bien sauté du cocq a l'asne" (That's a fine spring from cock to ass),

which was, and still is, used to describe an incoherent manner of speaking or writing. The content of the genre is the satiric treatment of the vices, faults, and foibles of persons, social groups, or even institutions. Clément Marot, who created the form in 1530, was the author of four *coq-à-l'âne*, all of them generally in the form of octosyllabic verse epistles of varying length. Joachim du Bellay discusses the coq-à-l'âne in *La Deffence et illustration de la langue françoyse* (1549).

■ C. E. Kinch, *La Poésie satirique de Clément Marot* (1940); Patterson; H. Meylan, *Epîtres du coq-à-l'âne* (1956); P. Zumthor, "Fatrasie et coq-à-l'âne," *Mélanges offerts à R. Guiette* (1961); C. A. Mayer, "Coq-à-l'âne: Définition-Invention-Attributions," *FS* 16 (1962); I. D. McFarlane, *Renaissance France, 1470–1589* (1974); C. Lastraioli, "Deux coq-à-l'âne retrouvés (1554–1561)," *Journal de la Renaissance* 1 (2000).

I. SILVER

**CORNISH POETRY.** The Cornish lang. was spoken in parts of Cornwall until the end of the 18th c. and was revived in the early 20th c. It belongs to the Brythonic or "P-Celtic" branch of the Celtic lang. family and is more closely related to Breton than to Welsh. While Old Cornish (9th–12th cs.) left no literary remains, several works have survived from the Middle Cornish (13th–16th cs.) and Late Cornish (17th–18th cs.) periods. Most Middle Cornish lit. consists of stanzaic verse, incl. a number of plays on religious themes that were performed in a distinctive type of open-air theater in the round known as a "playing place" or *plen-an-guary*. These plays and a closely related poem on the Passion were likely written by the canons of Glasney College in Penryn, a religious foundation dissolved in 1549. The work of Late Cornish poets is more varied, comprising a number of short poems as well as one OT play. Revived Cornish has also produced a significant body of verse lit.

The oldest surviving Middle Cornish verse is a 36-line fragment written on the back of a legal document dated 1340. This "Charter Fragment" may be an actor's part from an unknown play in which an unidentified speaker offers comic advice on marriage to a young couple. Its versification is atypical, since it uses an irregular (possibly accentual) *meter and contains a number of rhymed *couplets, which are otherwise quite rare in Middle Cornish. All other Middle Cornish verse is written in stanzas of four to thirteen lines, using rhyme schemes similar to those found in ME poetry. Unlike Eng., Cornish verse uses a syllabic meter with seven or, occasionally, four syllables to the line. There is no regular pattern of accentuation, and rhymes involving unstressed syllables (like *dá* : *hénna* or *bára* : *hénna*) are commonplace. The lack of a Cornish-speaking nobility during the Middle Cornish period likely prevented Cornwall from developing the complex poetic forms and ornamentation typical of med. Ireland and Wales, since there were no patrons to support a class of professional poets. As a result, Middle Cornish verse does not feature the *alliteration, *internal rhyme, or *cynghanedd found in most Breton, Welsh, or Ir. poetry (see BRETON POETRY; IRELAND, POETRY OF; and WELSH POETRY).

The best-known work of Cornish lit. is the trilogy of biblical plays known as the *Ordinalia*, preserved in a ms. of the mid-15th c. The three plays are *Origo Mundi* (2,846 lines), which presents a series of episodes from the OT; *Passio Christi* (3,242 lines), which depicts Christ's life, persecution, and death; and *Resurrexio Domini* (2,646 lines), which treats Christ's resurrection and ascension and the death of Pontius Pilate. A fourth play on the subject of the Nativity may have existed but has not survived. The principal stanza type in the *Ordinalia* is a six-line verse form rhymed *aabccb* or *aabaab*, sometimes extended to *aaabcccb*. Variants in which the *b* lines have only four syllables predominate in *Resurrexio Domini*, while alternate-rhyme stanzas (*abababab* or *abab*) are common in *Origo Mundi*. The poem *Pascon Agan Arluth*, "The Passion of Our Lord," is also found in a 15th-c. ms. It covers much of the same material as *Passio Christi* and contains some verses that are also found in that play. At 2,074 lines, *Pascon Agan Arluth* is the only lengthy poem from the traditional Cornish period, and it is written almost entirely in stanzas of eight 7-syllable lines rhymed *abababab*.

Two other Middle Cornish dramas are known from 16th c. mss., the only med. plays from Great Britain that deal with saints who are not mentioned in the Bible. *Beunans Meriasek*, "The Life of St. Meriasek" (4,569 lines, dated 1504), features three largely independent storylines concerning St. Sylvester and St. Meriasek (Meriadoc). Meriasek is the patron saint of Camborne, where the play may have been performed. *Bewnans Ke*, "The Life of St. Kea" (3,308 lines), is known from an incomplete ms. of the late 16th c. and tells the story of the patron saint of Kea parish. The second half of *Bewnans Ke* is particularly remarkable, as it comprises the only extant Arthurian material in traditional Cornish: an account largely derived from the 12th-c. *Historia Regum Britanniae* by Geoffrey of Monmouth. The versification of these two plays is substantially similar to that of the *Ordinalia*, although a new stanza form rhymed *ababcddc* with a characteristically short fifth line is prevalent in *Beunans Meriasek* and predominant in *Bewnans Ke*.

The play *Gwreans an Bys*, "The Creation of the World" (2,549 lines, dated 1611), is linguistically Late Cornish but continues the Middle Cornish literary trad., incorporating several passages from *Origo Mundi*. *Gwreans an Bys* has a more mod. feel than the Middle Cornish plays, and there is no clear evidence that it was written for performance in a plen-an-guary. Although the meter is less regular, seven-syllable lines are still the norm in *Gwreans an Bys*, and the verse forms used, while differing from those of the 16th-c. plays, are clearly derived from them. Most other Late Cornish verse dates from the late 17th and early 18th cs. and represents a sharp break from Middle Cornish practice. Late Cornish poems are comparatively short, deal with secular themes, and often use verse forms modeled on those of contemp. Eng. poetry. These works typically have an accentual rather

than a syllabic meter, which may reflect a stronger Eng. influence on the stress patterns of Cornish as well as the bilingualism of the poets, many of whom were not native Cornish speakers.

The Cornish revival of the 20th and 21st cs. has also produced works of significant literary merit. Peggy Pollard's plays imitate Middle Cornish verse forms and offer a satirical reinterpretation of the Middle Cornish dramatic trad. Both N.J.A. Williams and K. J. George have also written verse dramas using stanza forms and stylistic elements found in the Middle Cornish plays. Richard Gendall's work is perhaps best known through the music of Brenda Wootton, who performed many of his songs. While many contemp. poets address themes directly related to the lang. and Cornish identity, the poetry of J.A.N. Snell and Tim Saunders treats a wide range of topics, using verse forms inspired by Eng. and Celtic sources as well as traditional Cornish lit.

▪ *The Ancient Cornish Drama*, ed. and trans. E. Norris, 2 vols. (1859, rpt. 1963); *The Passion: A Middle Cornish Poem* (1860–61), *Gwreans an Bys* (1864), *Beunans Meriasek* (1872)—trans. M. Harris, 1977: all ed. W. Stokes, *Transactions of the Philological Society* (1860–61, 1864); H. Jenner, "The History and Literature of the Ancient Cornish Language," *Journal of the British Archaeological Association* 33 (1877), and *Handbook of the Cornish Language* (1904); D. C. Fowler, "The Date of the Cornish *Ordinalia*," *MS* 23 (1961); R. Longsworth, *The Cornish Ordinalia: Religion and Dramaturgy* (1967); P. B. Ellis, *The Cornish Language and Its Literature* (1974); O. J. Padel, *The Cornish Writings of the Boson Family* (1975); J. A. Bakere, *The Cornish Ordinalia: A Critical Study* (1980); T. D. Crawford, "The Composition of the Cornish *Ordinalia*" and "Stanza Forms and Social Status in *Beunans Meriasek*," *Old Cornwall* 9 (1979–85); *The Creacion of the World*, ed. and trans. P. Neuss (1983); B. Murdoch, *Cornish Literature* (1993); *The Wheel*, ed. T. Saunders (1999); *Looking at the Mermaid*, ed. A. Kent and T. Saunders (2000); *Nothing Broken*, ed. T. Saunders (2006); *Bewnans Ke*, ed. and trans. G. Thomas and N.J.A. Williams (2007); B. Bruch, "Medieval Cornish Versification: An Overview," *Keltische Forschungen* 4 (2009).

B. BRUCH

**CORONA** or Crown of Sonnets. Like the *catena* (chain), the *corona* (crown or garland) is one of several formal devices in It. poetry for joining a series of *sonnets to one another (see SONNET SEQUENCE). In the simple corona, the last line of each of the first six sonnets is used as the first line of the succeeding sonnet, with the last line of the seventh being a repetition of the opening line of the first; a further restriction prohibits the repetition of any given rhyme sound once it has been used in the series. We find the corona appearing early in the hist. of the It. sonnet with Fazio degli Uberti's series on the seven deadly sins. A more complex corona, not unlike the *sestina, consists of a *sonetto magistrale* preceded by 14 dependent sonnets: the first of these begins with the first line of the master sonnet and ends with its second line; the second sonnet begins with its second line and ends with its third, and so on, until the 14th sonnet, which begins with the 14th line of the master sonnet and ends with its first; the master sonnet then closes the interwoven garland. In Eng., the best-known corona is that which serves as the prologue to John Donne's *Holy Sonnets*; it consists of seven sonnets, one on each mythic stage in the life of Christ, beginning and ending with this line: "Deigne at my hands this crown of prayer and praise." Written shortly before 1610 (pub. 1633), Donne's corona draws on both the It. trad. of the *Corona di sonetti* and a specific way of reciting the rosary; he may well have known, too, Annibale Caro's famous corona of 1588 linking nine sonnets and George Chapman's "Coronet for his Mistress Philosophy" of 1595 linking ten. A 20th-c. example is the "Corona de sonetos" (1953) written in blank verse by the Brazilian poet Geir Campos.

*See* CONCATENATION, RING COMPOSITION.

■ L. L. Martz, *The Poetry of Meditation* (1954); W. Mönch, *Das Sonett* (1955); R. Alter, "Saul Tchernikhovsky: To the Sun: A Corona of Sonnets," *Literary Imagination* 3 (2001); B. Spurr, "The Theology of *La Corona*," *John Donne Journal* 20 (2001); A. Patterson, "Donne's Re-Formed *La Corona*," *John Donne Journal* 23 (2004).

E. L. RIVERS; T.V.F. BROGAN

**CORONACH** (Gael.; "wailing together"). A funeral *lament or *dirge originating in Ireland and in the Scottish highlands. The term owes its currency in Eng. lit. hist. to Sir Walter Scott, who refers to the custom in his novels and introduces into his *Lady of the Lake* (3.16) a coronach of his own composition beginning, "He is gone on the mountain. / He is lost to the forest, / Like a summer-dried fountain, / When our need was the sorest. . . ." According to Scott's account, the coronach was usually sung by women.

A. PREMINGER

**CORRELATIVE VERSE** (Lat. *versus rapportati*, Fr. *vers rapportés*). A literary style and subgenre in which lines or stanzas exhibit two (or more) series of elements, each element in the first corresponding to one in the same position in the second, respectively. This structuring device is known as *correlation*. An *epigram in the *Greek Anthology* (3.241) provides an example: "You [wine, are] boldness, youth, strength, wealth, country / To the shy, the old, the weak, the poor, the foreigner." Examples of correlation are found in Gr. poetry from the 3d c. BCE and in Lat. poetry from the 1st c. CE. Med. Lat. poets were very fond of the device, as were the Occitan *troubadours, and early Ren. poets made use of it (Étienne Jodelle, "Des Astres"; Joachim du Bellay, *Amours* 17). A special type of correlative verse, the disseminative-recapitulative type, used by Petrarch, spread, together with *Petrarchism, throughout Italy, France, Spain, and England in the 16th and early 17th cs. Examples include Philip Sidney's "Vertue, beautie, and speeche, did strike, wound, charme / My heart, eyes,

ears, with wonder, love, delight" (*Arcadia*, book 3; see also *Astrophil and Stella* 43, 65, 100; *Certain Sonnets* 18); Shakespeare's "Ho! hearts, tongues, figures, scribes, bards, poets, cannot / Think, speak, cast, write, sing, number—ho!— / His love to Antony" (*Antony and Cleopatra* 3.2.16–18); and John Milton's "Air, Water, Earth / By Fowl, Fish, Beast, was flown, was swum, was walkt" (*Paradise Lost* 7.502).

Correlative verse has been found in Sanskrit, Persian, Ar., and Chinese poetry (Alonso 1944) and thus seems to be one form of structure available to any verse trad.

■ D. Alonso, "Versos plurimembros y poemas correlativos," *Revista de la Biblioteca, Archivo y Museo del Ayuntamiento de Madrid* 13 (1944); D. Alonso and C. Bousoño, *Seis calas en la expresión literaria española* (1951); Curtius 286; D. Alonso, "Antecedentes griegos y latinos de la poesía correlativa moderna," *Estudios dedicados a Menéndez Pidal*, v. 4 (1953); J. G. Fucilla, "A Rhetorical Pattern in Renaissance and Baroque Poetry," *Studies in the Renaissance* 3 (1956); L. P. Wilkinson, *Golden Latin Artistry* (1963); D. Alonso, "Poesía correlativa inglesa en los siglos XVI y XVII," *Filología moderna* 2 (1961); and *Pluralità e correlazione in poesia* (1971); H. Zeman, "Die 'Versus Rapportati' in der deutschen Literatur des XVII. und XVIII. Jahrhunderts," *Arcadia* 9 (1974).

T.V.F. BROGAN; R. MIGNANI

**CORRIDO.** *See* CHICANA/O POETRY; ROMANCE.

**COSSANTE.** A Galician-Port. verse form popular from the 12th to the 14th c. and composed of parallel *couplets, the first ending in *i* sounds and the next ending in *a* sounds. The couplets are separated by a *refrain, with each *a* couplet repeating the thought of the previous *i* couplet. In addition, the second line of the first *i* couplet becomes the first line of the second *i* couplet, and the *a* couplets follow the same pattern. The line pattern can be schematized this way: *abr(i), abr(a), bcr(i), bcr(a), cdr(i), cdr(a)*, where *r* is the refrain. The first half of the following 13th-c. *alba by Nuno Fernandes Torneol provides an example:

> Levad', amigo que dormides as manhanas frias:
> toda-las aves do mundo d'amor dizian.
> Leda m' and' eu.
>
> Levad', amigo que dormides as frias manhanas:
> toda-las aves do mundo d'amor cantavan.
> Leda m' and' eu.
>
> Toda-las aves do mundo d'amor dizian.
> do meu amor e do voss' enmentarian.
> Leda m' and' eu.
>
> Toda-las aves do mundo d'amor cantavan,
> do meu amor e do voss'i enmentavan.
> Leda m' and' eu.

The first and second stanzas urge the friend to arise and listen to the birds sing about love. The third and fourth stanzas repeat the lines about the birds singing but clarify that their song is about the love between the speaker and the listener. This example shows how each *i* or *a* stanza repeats one idea from the previous *i* or *a* stanza before adding new information in the next line.

The use of parallel stanzas and repeated lines creates a weaving pattern known as *leixa-pren*, a dance term signifying two lines of dancers or singers alternating turns. In fact, early *cossantes* were originally accompanied by music. The word itself probably comes from *cosso*, a type of enclosed dance floor. In the *Faerie Queene* 2.12.71, Edmund Spenser provides an Eng. example of leixa-pren:

> The joyous birds, shrouded in cheerful shade,
> Their notes unto the voice attempered sweet;
> Th' angelical soft trembling voices made
> To th' instruments divine respondance meet;
> The silver sounding instruments did meet
> With the base murmur of the water's fall;
> The water's fall with difference discreet,
> Now soft, now loud, unto the wind did call;
> The gentle warbling wind low answeréd to all.

The cossante has its origins in the folk songs of the women from the Galician-Port. region (see GALICIA, POETRY OF; PORTUGAL, POETRY OF). Sp. and Port. *trobadores* and *jograes*, court singers and minstrels (see TROUBADOUR, JONGLEUR) traveled the countryside and noted the *cantigas de amigo* sung by the Galician women as they remembered their absent lovers (see CANTIGA). In turn, these men formalized the cantigas and presented them in the royal courts. Many cossantes, though written by male poets, retain the female speaker as well as the natural imagery that was prevalent in folk songs of the time.

Also, the region was home to the Christian pilgrimage city of Santiago de Compostela, and it is believed that the natives borrowed the form of repeating couplets from the Psalms or from the call and response of two choirs.

Whatever its origins, the cossante was popular for a few centuries until the Castilian lang. began to replace Galician. This occurred after the death of one of the most notable writers of the cossante, the Port. King Diniz, in 1325.

A more recent example of the cossante comes from W. H. Auden, in the "Lauds" section of *Horae Canonicae*. Though criticized by Fuller for dropping the required rhyme scheme, Auden employs a line pattern rather than a rhyme scheme, using *ing* and *l* endings rather than *i* and *a* sounds, and he does not develop the typical theme of the cossante. Also, he connects his last stanza to the first by setting the first line of the first couplet as the second line in the last couplet, a closure usually not found in traditional cossantes.

■ A.F.G. Bell, *Portuguese Literature* (1922); M. Newmark, *Dictionary of Spanish Literature* (1956); G. Brenan, *The Literature of the Spanish People* (1957); *Introduction to Spanish Poetry*, ed. E. Florit (1991); J. Fuller, *W. H. Auden* (1998).

K. V. BROWDER

**COUNTERPOINT.** Since the early 19th c., counterpoint, originally a musical term referring to textures in which multiple melodies sound at the same time, has sometimes been adopted—often very loosely and, more recently, with less of the musical analogy intact—to describe various kinds of tension or interplay between elements in poetry.

G. W. F. Hegel was apparently the first to make the analogy between features of poetry and musical counterpoint, but G. M. Hopkins, in applying the term to a rhythmic effect he admired in John Milton's *Samson Agonistes* and elsewhere, was the first to employ the analogy with any precision. For Hopkins, a contrapuntal effect occurs when, e.g., feet of one kind substitute for two consecutive feet in a regular metrical context, thus "mounting" a secondary rhythmic pattern on the one already established by the meter. The effect can only be local and fleeting, according to Hopkins, because frequent or sustained substitutions "spring" the rhythm, destroying the meter and thereby eliminating the primary rhythmic pattern against which the second one must play. Counterpoint, Hopkins believes, can therefore not exist in "sprung rhythm." Many have criticized Hopkins's notion, viewing the passages he cites from the trad. as mere variations on the meter or as solecisms. Others have pointed out that, because in poetry two rhythms are never actually sounded at the same time, *syncopation, the term for the play of musical rhythms against expectations, would be a more precisely analogous term for the effect Hopkins describes (e.g., Hollander).

Still, Hopkins's implication that meter is merely one pattern of expectation created within a passage, rather than a fixed or abstract constant in the poem, makes him an important precursor for mod. theories about poetry, which tend to see rhythm as a multileveled and dynamic interplay of perceptual groupings, anticipations, trads., and local and global effects. Over the 20th c., Hopkins's term *counterpoint*—now freely redefined and broadly or narrowly applied—became common in descriptions of formal properties in poetry, in spite of continuing complaints about its imprecise and misleading implications (see Attridge, Cureton, Holder). The term has been used for a wide array of poetic interrelationships, incl. those between phrase or word boundary and foot boundary (Fowler, both 1966), between normative and variant stress patterns in phrases (Chomsky and Halle, Gates), and even between the so-called residual "native" strain of four-beat accentual rhythm and the more mod. accentual-syllabic trad. (Malof).

The most common and widely accepted usage since the middle of the 20th c. has referred to the interplay in metrical poetry between the metrical "set" or expectation of regularity and the actual rhythm of the poem, variously called "speech rhythm," "prose rhythm," or the rhythm of the "phonological phrase." This usage is often very loose, without clear definition and with little indication of what kinds of variation—e.g., foot substitutions or changing levels of stress in the strong syllable positions of the metrical scheme—actually count as counterpoint and which are simply acceptable variations within the meter. More recently, the term has been adopted to refer to the interplay between syntactical grouping or juncture and the line end; in that sense, counterpoint has been argued to be the central defining tension of *free verse (Hartman, following Fowler, but see Holder). Loose, imprecise, inconsistent, and ambiguous as current usages of the term are, in the absence of more exact and generally accepted terms for the specific kinds of interplay or tension in poetry, poets and readers from across the poetic spectrum have found the word useful in describing what they think poetry does.

See PROSE RHYTHM, RISING AND FALLING RHYTHM, SPRUNG RHYTHM, SUBSTITUTION.

■ G. M. Hopkins, "Author's Preface" and "To R. W. Dixon (June 13, 1878)," *Poems and Prose,* ed. W. H. Gardner (1953); J. Malof, "The Native Rhythm of English Meters," *TSLL* (1964); R. Fowler, "Structural Metrics," *Linguistics* 27 (1966), and "Prose Rhythm and Meter," *Essays on Style and Language* (1966); Chomsky and Halle; P. Kiparsky, "Stress, Syntax, and Meter," *Lang* 51 (1975); C. O. Hartman, *Free Verse* (1980); Attridge, *Rhythms*; Hollander; R. Gates, "T. S. Eliot's Prosody and the Free Verse Tradition," *PoT* 11 (1990); Cureton; A. Holder, *Rethinking Meter* (1995).

P. WHITE

**COUNTERPOINT RHYTHM.** Often manifest as *syncopation, a rhythmical effect produced by metrical variation, that is, by temporary departure from the dominant metrical base, so that two rhythmic patterns are said to coexist simultaneously. However, it might be truer in perception to say that one rhythm, the underlying meter, is momentarily interrupted, or supplanted, by another. Thus, in these lines from W. B. Yeats's "Leda and the Swan" (x denotes weak syllables, / strong ones):

x  /  x  /  x  /  /  / x  /
A sudden blow: the great wings beating still
x  /  x  / x x  /  x  /  x  /
Above the staggering girl, her thighs caressed
 x  x  /  /  x  /  / x x  /
By the dark webs, her nape caught in his bill

the dominant *iambic is interrupted in the first line by a *spondee in the fourth foot, in the second line by an *anapaest in the third foot—"stagg'ring" would maintain the meter but lose the aptness of the metrical "stagger"—and in the third line by a *pyrrhic substitution in the first foot, a spondaic substitution in the second, and a *trochaic substitution in the fourth. All this counterpointing expresses rhythmically the physical and psychological turmoil generated by Zeus' descent on Leda.

But intermittent single-foot substitutions like these are not sufficient to create counterpoint rhythm as described by G. M. Hopkins ("two or more strains of tune going on together"). If an alternative rhythm is to be mounted on, or heard against, a given metrical base, then (1) it should normally occupy at least two consecutive feet (and particularly, perhaps, what Hopkins calls the "sensitive" second foot), and (2) it should constitute a *reversal* of the dominant meter (trochaic rhythm mounted on iambic, dactylic on anapaestic). Criterion (2) is a necessary qualification both because pyrrhic and spondaic feet can only be substitute *feet*, not substitute *rhythms*, and because any counterpointing of, say, a rising rhythm (iambic) by another rising rhythm (anapaestic) will produce not counterpoint rhythm but what Hopkins calls *logaoedic* or mixed rhythm.

*Counterpoint* is a term designed to capture rhythmic "bifocality," the interweaving of rhythms realized and unrealized, actual and projected. For Hopkins in particular, counterpoint rhythm is a useful, logical bridge between *running rhythm and *sprung rhythm. But we need to be sure that what works well as a notion of rhythmic layering or complexity corresponds to a perceptual reality.

■ G. M. Hopkins, "Author's Preface on Rhythm," *The Poetical Works of Gerard Manley Hopkins*, ed. N. H. Mackenzie (1992).

C. SCOTT

**COUNTRY HOUSE POEM.** A kind of poem, developed esp. in 17th-c. Britain, that celebrates the home of a patron, friend, or model of the poet, treating the house and its landscape as an instance of civility and culture. The original country house poem in Eng. is Aemilia Lanyer's "Description of Cookeham" (1611), which concerns the house of Margaret Clifford, Countess of Cumberland; but the most famous example in the period is Ben Jonson's "To Penshurst" (1616), a tribute to the Sidney family's estate. Such poems commonly rehearse and embellish an aristocratic family's view of its origins and achievements, depict a personified landscape as their paradisiacal setting, and enable the poet her- or himself to show (or imagine) a connection to the family through service, invented *myth, or strategic erudition. The most admired country house poem of the period is probably Andrew Marvell's "Upon Appleton House" (written ca. 1651, pub. 1681).

See CAVALIER POETS; DESCRIPTIVE POETRY; ENGLAND, POETRY OF; LANDSCAPE POEM.

■ G. R. Hibbard, "The Country House Poem in the Seventeenth Century," *Journal of the Warburg and Courtauld Institutes* 19 (1956); R. Williams, *The Country and the City* (1973); D. E. Wayne, *Penshurst: The Semiotics of Place and the Poetics of History* (1984); H. Jenkins, *Feigned Commonwealths* (1998); H. Dubrow, "Guess Who's Coming to Dinner? Reinterpreting Formalism and the Country House Poem," *MLQ* 61 (2000).

R. GREENE

**COUPE.** *Coupes* are the vertical or oblique bar-lines used to separate measures and so indicate the rhythmic segmentation of the Fr. line (cf. Eng. foot divisions), usually according to breaks in the sense. Normally, they fall immediately after each accented (usually word-final) vowel inside the line. In fact, the coupe marks the occurrence of accentuation, and although it is usually accompanied by syntactic juncture in varying degree, it has no necessary connection with juncture;

the *alexandrine traditionally contains four accented vowels—one before the *caesura, i.e., the obligatory, predetermined mid-line coupe (//), one at the rhyme, and two mobile accents (/)—and so in Alphonse de Lamartine's "Ainsi, / toujours poussés // vers de nouveaux / rivages," the measures are 2/4//4/2. The coupe is a tool of analysis, a convenience in *scansion that has little bearing on the enunciation of the line, although it does have some consequences for enunciation where the Fr. *e atone* (or mute *e*) is concerned. In this case, it is possible to identify three types of coupe. First, when a tonic syllable is followed by an articulated (unelided) *e atone*, it is customary to place the coupe immediately after the accented vowel, so that the *e atone* is counted as the first syllable of the following rhythmic measure. This coupe, called the *coupe enjambante*, produces a seamless and supple continuity in the reading of the line, e.g., Jean Racine's "Pour qui / sont ces serpents // qui si / fflent sur vos têtes" (2/4//2/4). There may, however, be syntactic or expressive reasons for choosing to mark a juncture after the *e atone*, esp. if it is followed by punctuation, so that the *e atone* more properly belongs with the accented vowel rather than initiating the measure that follows (*coupe lyrique*, sometimes called *coupe féminine*), e.g., Arthur Rimbaud's "Le Poè / te vous dit: // ô lâches, / soyez fous!" (3/3//3/3). The *coupe lyrique* is fairly exceptional, however, producing rhythmic disruption, fragmentation, and discontinuity, and generally represents a conscious choice on the part of the reader. The *coupe épique*, common in mod. poetry, is used when the reader omits an *e atone*, conforming to natural Fr. speech rather than the artificial, traditional rules of prosody, in order to maintain a regular syllable count, e.g., Michel Houellebecq's "Elle avait / trent(e)-cinq ans // ou peut-ê / tre cinquante" (3/3//3/3), in a poem of 16 alexandrines, where the reader adheres to the strong 6 + 6 metrical context by acknowledging that, in order to observe the caesura correctly and produce 12 syllables rather than 13, the first *hemistich requires a coupe épique and the second a coupe enjambante.

*See* FOOT.

■ Mazaleyrat; C. Scott, *A Question of Syllables* (1986); B. de Cornulier, *Art poëtique* (1995); Morier; M. Gouvard, *La Versification* (1999) and *Critique du vers* (2000); *Le Vers français*, ed. M. Murat (2000).

C. Scott; D. Evans

**COUPLET** (from Lat. *copula*). Two contiguous lines of verse that function as a metrical unit and are so marked either by (usually) rhyme or syntax or both. This two-line unit appears in many poetries, incl. Sanskrit (e.g., the *śloka* of cl. epic; see INDIAN PROSODY; G. Thompson), Chinese (the couplet appeared in the *Shijing*, composed during the Zhou dynasty [1046–256 BCE]; see CHINA, POETRY OF), Ar., and Persian (see GHAZAL). Since the advent of rhymed verse in the Eur. vernaculars in the 12th c., the couplet has counted as one of the principal units of versification in Western poetry, whether as an independent poem of a gnomic or epigrammatic nature (see EPIGRAM), as a

subordinate element in other stanzaic forms—two of the principal stanzaic forms of the later Middle Ages and the Ren., *ottava rima* and *rhyme royal, both conclude with a couplet, as does the Shakespearean *sonnet—or as a stanzaic form for extended verse composition, narrative or philosophical. In each of these modes, the tightness of the couplet and closeness of its rhyme make it esp. suited for purposes of formal conclusion, summation, or epigrammatic comment. In dramatic verse, the couplet occurs in the cl. Fr. drama, the older Ger. and Dutch drama, and the "heroic plays" of Restoration England. It also fills an important function in Elizabethan and Jacobean drama as a variation from the standard *blank verse, its principal use being to mark for the audience, aurally, the conclusion of a scene or a climax in dramatic action. The couplet occupies a unique and interesting position in the typology of verse forms. Standing midway between stichic verse and strophic, it permits the fluidity of the former while also taking advantage of some of the effects of the latter.

In the med. Fr. epic, the older assonanted *laisse* gives way to rhyme in couplets around the 12th c. The earliest examples, such as the *Cantilene de Sainte Eulalie* and the *Vie de Saint Léger*, are in closed couplets (Meyer). Chrétien de Troyes (fl. after 1150) seems to have introduced *enjambement*, which by the 13th c. is common (e.g., Raoul de Houdenc). After the *Chanson de Roland* (early 12th c.), first the decasyllabic, then the *alexandrine couplet is the dominant form of OF narrative and dramatic poetry (see DECASYLLABLE). In the hands of the masters of Fr. classicism——Pierre Corneille, Molière, Jean Racine, Jean de La Fontaine—the couplet is end-stopped and relatively self-contained, but a freer use of enjambment is found among the romantics. Under Fr. influence, the alexandrine couplet became the dominant metrical form of Ger. and Dutch narrative and dramatic verse of the 17th and 18th cs. Subsequently, a more indigenous Ger. couplet, the tetrameter couplet called *Knittelvers*, was revived by J. W. Goethe and Friedrich Schiller. The term *couplet* is sometimes used in Fr. prosody with the meaning of stanza, as in the *couplet carré* (square couplet), an octave composed of octosyllables.

In Eng. poetry, though the octosyllabic or iambic tetrameter couplet has been used well (see OCTOSYLLABLE), by far the most important couplet form has been isometric and composed of two lines of iambic pentameter. As perfected by John Dryden and Alexander Pope, the so-called *heroic couplet is "closed"—syntax and thought fit perfectly into the envelope of rhyme and meter sealed at the end of the couplet—and in this form dominates the poetry of the neoclassical period: "Know then thyself, presume not God to scan," says Pope in the *Essay on Man*, "The proper study of Mankind is Man." When meter and syntax thus conclude together, the couplet is said to be end-stopped.

The couplet is "open" when enjambed, i.e., when the syntactic and metrical frames do not close together at the end of the couplet, the sentence being carried forward into subsequent couplets to any length desired and ending at any point in the line. This form of the couplet is historically older and not much less common than the closed form in Eng. poetry as a whole. It was introduced by Chaucer and continued to be produced (e.g., Edmund Spenser, "Mother Hubberd's Tale" [1591]; Nicholas Breton, *The Uncasing of Machivils Instructions to His Sonne* [1613]) well into the 17th c. during the very time when the closed or "heroical" couplet was being established. George Puttenham and other Ren. critics labeled this older form "riding rhyme." It was further explored in the 19th c. (e.g., Robert Browning), proving then as ever esp. suited for continuous narrative and didactic verse. Long sentences in enjambed couplets constitute the rhymed equivalent of the *"verse paragraph" in blank verse. In a medial form between closed and open, each two-line sentence ends at the end of the *first* line of the couplet, making for systematic counterpointing of syntax against meter.

Not all Eng. couplets are isometric, however. Poets as diverse as George Herbert and Browning have developed couplet forms that rhyme lines of unequal length: "With their triumphs and their glories and the rest. / Love is best!" (Browning, "Love among the Ruins"). A related heterometric form of couplet that developed in Gr. and Lat., a hexameter followed by a pentameter, came to be known for its generic usage as the *elegiac distich*. Passed down through the Middle Ages as a semipopular form (e.g., the *Distichs of Cato*), it survived into mod. times (see DISTICH), often as a vestigial visual format with alternate lines indented, as in W. H. Auden's "In Praise of Limestone" or the first section of "The Sea and the Mirror." In the late 20th and early 21st cs., a two-line, couplet-like stanza established itself as the common visual format of much unrhymed, nonmetrical verse, e.g., A. R. Ammons's *Garbage*.

■ Schipper; P. Meyer, "Le Couplet de deux vers," *Romania* 23 (1894); C.H.G. Helm, *Zur Rhythmik der kurzen Reimpaare des XVI Jahrhunderten* (1895); C. C. Spiker, "The Ten-Syllable Rhyming Couplet," *West Virginia University Philological Papers* 1 (1929); P. Verrier, *Le Vers français*, v. 2 (1931–32); G. Wehowsky, *Schmuckformen und Formbruch in der deutschen Reimpaardichtung des Mittelalters* (1936); E.N.S. Thompson, "The Octosyllabic Couplet," *PQ* 18 (1939); F. W. Ness, *The Use of Rhyme in Shakespeare's Plays* (1941), esp. ch. 5, App. C; B. H. Smith, *Poetic Closure* (1968); J. A. Jones, *Pope's Couplet Art* (1969); W. B. Piper, *The Heroic Couplet* (1969); Brogan, 389 ff.; Gasparov, *History*; J. P. Hunter, "Formalism and History: Binarism and the Anglophone Couplet," *MLQ* 61 (2000); *The Bhagavad Gita*, trans. G. Thompson (2008)—intro. note on the trans.

T.V.F. BROGAN; W. B. PIPER; S. CUSHMAN

**COURTLY LOVE** (Fr. *amour courtois*). A literary and social construct of the Middle Ages that originated in the poetry of the *troubadours in southern France in the late 11th c. As distinguished from other types of love, courtly love is characterized by its ennobling effect on the male lover who assumes a subservient position in relation to the beloved, the idealization of the woman loved, and certain codes of conduct, whether implicit or explicit, that guide the lover in his amorous pursuit.

Although initially a product of the Occitan courts (see OCCITAN POETRY), the influence of courtly love expanded during the Middle Ages to include a variety of langs. and genres. This novel expression of love in the poetry of the troubadours, where it was typically known as *fin'amors*, was soon imitated in the northern Fr. poetry of the *trouvères and esp. in the *romances of Chrétien de Troyes; in Ger. poetry (*Minnesang) and romance of the 12th and 13th cs.; in the It. poetry of the 12th-c. *stil nuovo* poets (see DOLCE STIL NUOVO) and esp. in Dante's *Vita nuova* (1292–93); in Eng. lit. most notably in Chaucer's *Troilus and Criseyde* (composed in the 1380s); and finally, in the poetry and prose of the Iberian peninsula in the 14th and 15th cs. The ling. diversity of courtly love attests to its importance throughout the Middle Ages and into the Ren. The types of works that exemplify courtly love include *lyric poetry, romances both in verse and prose, short narratives such as *lais*, and works of nonfiction, the best known of which is Andreas Capellanus's late 12th-c. treatise *De amore*, also known as *De arte honesti amandi*. The structure of the *De amore* clearly reflects the profound influence of Ovid's *Ars amatoria* and *Remedia amoris* on the topic of love in med. lit. more broadly. While the *De amore* is ostensibly an exhaustive and scientific treatment of love, it is generally considered ironic. Its wry tone somewhat complicates our understanding of the information it provides about love.

Scholars have long contested both the meaning and origins of courtly love, as well as its existence as a historical phenomenon. While there is general agreement that the works of Ovid influenced the *tropes of love in med. lit., the extent of that influence is disputed because courtly love differs in several respects from Ovidian love, most notably in the idealization of women. The meaning of courtly love is often tied to its origins, which are as much concerned with the hist. of the term as an instrument of crit. as they are with the literary and social contexts of the southern and northern Fr. courts in the late 11th and early 12th cs.

Whether this particular expression of love is new to the Middle Ages has been debated, with the polarizing assertions that courtly love inaugurated the Western trad. of romantic love (Lewis, Rougemont), or that it is a universal sentiment with a particular expression in the context of med. feudal and court life. As Dronke has proposed, "'[T]he new feeling' of *amour courtois* is at least as old as Egypt of the second millennium B.C., and might indeed occur at any time and place." In his influential study, Boase summarized the various theories of origins for courtly love as Hispano-Arabic, Chivalric-Matriarchal, Crypto-Cathar, Neoplatonic, Bernardine-Marianist, Spring Folk Ritual, and Feudal-Sociological and concluded that the Hispano-Arabic and Feudal-Sociological theories complement each other by exposing different aspects of the origin of courtly love. The variety of origins advanced for courtly love mirrors the many claims about its meaning and interpretation. The debates have, in large measure, pointed to contradictions inherent in the concept of courtly love, which has been interpreted as simultaneously sexual and spiritual, ennobling and vilifying, in which women are cast as both idols and the passive objects of male desire. The courtly woman is also ambiguous, for she is both lady and master, feminine and masculine. In troubadour poetry, the lady is often referred to as *midons* (my lord). Feminist and gender-oriented approaches to courtly love have also underscored the ambiguities behind the courtly lady, the male lover, and courtly love as a whole. Focusing on these contradictions, Kay (2000) sought to establish courtly love as a mediating discourse between clerical and aristocratic ideologies, which are themselves contradictory in 12th-c. court life. In a similar vein, Jaeger (1994, 1999) has argued that the origins of courtly love lie in the civilizing effect of the clergy on the aristocracy and in the influence of the cathedral schools on the courts. According to Jaeger, the discourse of courtly love derives from the discourse on friendship between noblemen; consequently, the shift in the 12th c. of this notion from men to women created a conflict between a traditionally virtuous love among male public figures and a contradictory erotic discourse about the love of women.

As a critical term, *courtly love* was first introduced in 1883 by Paris as an explanation for the illicit love between Guenevere and Lancelot in Chrétien de Troyes's romance *Le Chevalier de la charrette* (also known as *Lancelot*, ca. 1174–81). The tenets of this love are its ennobling effect on the lover, its idolatrous nature, the primacy of social transgression (usually adultery), and the necessity of secrecy to maintain the adulterous relationship. Lewis posited the relevance of this notion to other med. texts, incl. poetry, and ascribed attributes similar to those proposed by Paris, namely, "Humility, Courtesy, Adultery, and the Religion of Love." The concept of courtly love came under considerable critical scrutiny in the 1960s and 1970s when scholars, notably Robertson (1962), Donaldson, and Benton, opposed the term, arguing that its applicability was, in fact limited, to a single text (Chrétien's *Lancelot*) and suggesting that it was anachronistic on the grounds that the phrase is virtually unknown in the Middle Ages. With the exception of two extant works from the second half of the 13th c., the lyric poem "Gent Es" of the troubadour Peire d'Alvernhe and the Occitan romance *Flamenca*, the Middle Ages left no other traces of the expression *courtly love* (*amor cortes* in Occitan). Robertson further disputed the concept on the grounds that the promotion of adulterous love in Christian culture was implausible. In the same vein, Benton challenged the historical relevance of courtly love since legal and court documents from the period make no mention of it. While the lack of historical documents demonstrates that courtly love was neither a political nor a juridical institution, scholars largely agree that the social dimension of courtly love constituted a form of aristocratic play or diversion. Thus, the "courts of love" mentioned by Andreas are not to be understood in a literal sense. After these attacks on the terminology and the very existence of courtly love as a concept, the majority of studies on the subject have been divided in their support or rejection of courtly love. Most notably, Frappier offered a defense of courtly love as a concept but promoted the use of the Occitan phrase *fin'amors* as a replacement for the controversial term. The debates about the origins and meaning of courtly love, as well as the inherent contradictions in med. love poetry and romance, continue to spur interest in a topic whose exact definition and boundaries may never be precisely known.

*See* GENDER AND POETRY, GHAZAL, LOVE POETRY, MEDIEVAL POETICS, MEDIEVAL POETRY, PERSIAN POETRY, QAṢĪDA.

■ G. Paris, "Lancelot du Lac," *Romania* 12 (1883); Lewis; D. de Rougemont, *Love in the Western World* (1939), trans. M. Belgion (1956); D. W. Robertson Jr., *A Preface to Chaucer* (1962); A. J. Denomy, *The Heresy of Courtly Love* (1965); E. T. Donaldson, "The Myth of Courtly Love," *Ventures* 5 (1965); P. Dronke, *The Medieval Lyric* (1968); *The Meaning of Courtly Love*, ed. F. X. Newman, esp. J. B. Benton, "Clio and Venus" (1968); J. Frappier, "Sur un procès fait à l'amour courtois," *Romania* 93 (1972); R. Boase, *The Origin and Meaning of Courtly Love* (1977); D. W. Robertson Jr., *Essays in Medieval Culture* (1980); C. S. Jaeger, *The Envy of Angels* (1994) and *Ennobling Love* (1999); S. Kay, "Courts, Clerks, and Courtly Love," *Cambridge Companion to Medieval Romance*, ed. R. Krueger (2000); E. J. Burns, "Courtly Love: Who Needs It?" *Signs* 27 (2001); S. Kay, *Courtly Contradictions* (2001); E. J. Burns, *Courtly Love Undressed* (2002); *Discourses on Love, Marriage, and Transgression in Medieval and Early Modern Literature*, ed. A. Classen (2004); D. A. Monson, *Andreas Capellanus, Scholasticism, and the Courtly Tradition* (2005); J. A. Schultz, *Courtly Love, the Love of Courtliness, and the History of Sexuality* (2006).

K. A. BROWN

**COURTLY MAKERS.** A term first used by George Puttenham in *The Arte of English Poesie* (1589) to describe the ideal Eng. poet. Poets were frequently called *makers* in that century; the word *\*poet* is derived from the Gr. *poiein*, "to make." Puttenham's term singles out court poets, and their forms and themes, as part of his defense of Eng. poetry.

Puttenham selects two sets of Tudor courtier-poets as examples of courtly makers. The original set included Thomas Wyatt and Henry Howard, the Earl of Surrey, while the second included a number of Puttenham's Elizabethan contemporaries. Of the first two poets, Puttenham writes that they introduced It. verse to Eng., "polished our . . . vulgar Poesie" and were "the first reformers of our English meetre and stile."

Literary critics since Puttenham have focused on Wyatt and Surrey's formal innovations, esp. Wyatt's trans. and imitations of Petrarch's *\*sonnets and Surrey's *blank verse trans. of books 2 and 4 of Virgil's *Aeneid*. Until recently, both were placed in a teleological account of Eng. verse that saw them as beginning the struggle toward iambic regularity, Wyatt with less success than Surrey.

Beginning in the 1980s, literary critics turned their investigations to the contexts of Henry VIII's and Elizabeth I's courts and their social and material cultures. Rather than using those contexts to dismiss courtly poems as (in Lewis's famous characterization) "a little music after supper," Greenblatt argues that the poems of courtly makers constituted a kind of conduct, produced by the social ambience of the court, with high, sometimes fatal, stakes. Scholars have since shown how themes common to courtly poets—incl. slander, hypocrisy, and the fickleness of fortune, friends, and lovers—relate to the imbalances of power that poets confronted at court. More recently, Greene has pointed out the participation of court poetry in a rhet. of imperialism, while Dolven accounts for courtly poetry as presenting a distinctive kind of style.

■ C. S. Lewis, *English Literature in the Sixteenth Century, Excluding Drama* (1954); J. Stevens, *Music and Poetry in the Early Tudor Court* (1961); R. Southall, *The Courtly Maker* (1964); P. Thomson, *Sir Thomas Wyatt and His Background* (1964); A. Ostriker, "Thomas Wyatt and Henry Surrey: Dissonance and Harmony in Lyric Form," *NLH* 1 (1970); S. Greenblatt, *Renaissance Self-Fashioning* (1980); S. Woods, *Natural Emphasis* (1985); R. Greene, *Unrequited Conquests* (1999), ch. 3; J. Dolven, "Reading Wyatt for the Style," *MP* 105 (2007).

R. KAPLAN

**COWBOY POETRY.** Poetry written for and about the North American ranching culture, often by those involved personally in the way of life. A parallel trad. exists in Australian bush poetry, South Am. *gaucho poetry, and among horseback herding people worldwide. Logsdon has noted that "it is probable that no other industry or occupation continues to produce from its ranks as many poets as does the cattle industry and cowboying." Cowboy poetry descends from *georgic, *pastoral, and romantic *nature poetry (see ROMANTICISM; ROMANTIC AND POSTROMANTIC POETRY AND POETICS). Forms and modes range from unadorned *imagery (similar to *haiku; see RENGA) to *narrative, *lyric, *sonnet, *ode, *ballad, *free verse, and more. All methods of analyzing poetry may be applied to cowboy poetry, incl. narratology and *oral-formulaic theory, as well as postcolonial (the Am. West as "colony" of the East Coast or the rural as "colony" of the urban), feminist, ecofeminist, ecocritical, and Marxist approaches. Folklorists have done extensive investigation of cowboy songs and poetry, but the poetry has escaped serious analysis as lit.

In 1886, Lysius Gough became perhaps the first pub. cowboy poet when he self-published 1,000 copies of his verse composed "on the trail in 1882." Rancher William L. "Larry" Chittendon's *Ranch Verses* was published in New York in 1893. Cowboy songs and poetry were also being published and analyzed in Charles Lummis's *Old West* magazine during the first decade of the 20th c. Several important cowboy poets published single-author books in the second decade: Henry Herbert Knibbs (*Songs of the Outland*, 1914; *Riders of the Stars*, 1916), Charles Badger Clark (*Sun and Saddle Leather*, 1915), Arthur Chapman (*Out Where the West Begins*, 1917), and Carmen William "Curley" Fletcher (*Songs of the Sage*, 1917). Possibly the best craftsman among the classic cowboy poets, Clark seldom used the same rhyme scheme or metrical pattern twice. In June 1918, *Poetry* published a review of three cowboy poets: Arthur Chapman, Knibbs, and Clark.

> Could you turn to a land that was trailless
> And live, as they lived, without salt?
>
> (Chapman, "The Old Trapper Speaks")

> Did you ever wait for daylight when the stars
>     along the river
> Floated thick and white as snowflakes in the water
>     deep and strange, . . . .
>
> (Knibbs, "The Shallows of the Ford")

> The wind was rein and guide to us;
> The world was pasture wide to us . . .
>
> (Clark, "The Tied Maverick")

Important later poets include Frank Linderman (*Bunchgrass and Bluejoint*, 1921), Bruce Kiskaddon (*Rhymes of the Ranges*, 1924), E. A. Brinninstool (*Trail Dust of a Maverick*, 1926), Gail Gardner (*Orejana Bull*, 1935), S. Omar Barker (*Sunlight through the Trees*, 1954; *Rawhide Rhymes*, 1968), and Paul Zarzyski (*All This Way for the Short Ride*, 1996).

Cowboy poetry can be divided into two kinds: written by or for the working class, and written by or for the landowner class. Although analysis of the latter kind has not been done, some critics have commented on the characteristics of working-class poetry. Many favorite poems among the ranching working class come from Kiskaddon, who wrote for a rural audience, who originally composed his poetry for publication by the *Western Livestock Journal* during the 1920s and 1930s, 30 to 40 years after the trail drives ended, and who worked only briefly as a cowboy himself.

> I'll be poor, of course, but astride a horse,
> And breathing the western air.
>
> (Kiskaddon, "The Air That They Breathe Out West")

As in the georgic trad., working-class poetry like Kiskaddon's consistently emphasizes the virtues of living on the edge of wild nature and embracing poverty, work well done, husbandry, and cowboy values. The poetry seems simple, but words and assumptions familiar to readers within the culture contribute depth of experience—for instance, the sense of mutual respect between horse and rider implied in the preposition "astride." An anonymous poem about a stereotyped dude heroically riding "The Zebra Dun," often credited to a black cook, is a favorite of rural audiences because it turns on one word—"thumbed"—into a complex study of friendship, humility, and work. This version was collected by John A. Lomax (*Cowboy Songs, Ballads, and Cattle Calls from Texas*, n.d.):

> He thumbed him in the neck, and he spurred him
>   as he whirled
> To show us flunky punchers he was the wolf of the
>   world.

The "dude" thumbed (not "thumped" as is often printed and heard) the horse he is given to ride: i.e., he scratched his two thumbs up opposite sides of the horse's neck, which causes even the gentlest horse to buck and will increase the effort in one already given to bucking. An audience that understands the word *thumb* realizes that the dude is actually a disguised cowboy, probably hungry, thumbing a horse that could barely buck off a dude, and hoping for a job offer from the boss without either insulting the crew by out-riding them or making his wants too explicit. Horses often play the role of dragons or tricksters, but heroes are hard to find in the best poetry written for the working class. Instead, themes stress humility, equality, and responsibility to encourage the reader or listener to maintain the ideals of conduct.

Narrative cowboy poetry, esp. as used orally within ranching culture, can be analyzed through critical views developed for Native Am. storytelling. E.g., Basso explains how stories are often used for "stalking" in Apache storytelling, meaning to target people listening to reform their conduct. This is similar to the reasons that a poem like "The Zebra Dun" might be recited within cowboy culture: to teach a young person how to apply for a job, to help a newcomer feel welcome, to chastise someone for talking too much, or to remind each other of the finer points of friendship. Just mentioning the name of the poem is often enough, as is mentioning the place where a particular Apache story happened. Allen argues that labeling marginalized lits. as "folklore" is condescending, since much Native Am. lit. is "known only to educated, specialized persons who are privy to the philosophical, mystical, and literary wealth of their own tribe." Rhyming may also help conjure a mythic time and place, similar to the traditional opening of "humma-hah" (long ago) with which, Silko explains, Pueblo storytellers begin their stories in order to provide distancing.

While cowboy poetry has been stereotyped as representing a white male perspective, Hal Cannon, in a preface to his 1968 ed. of Fletcher's *Songs of the Sage*, has observed the mix of ethnic backgrounds among cowboys and argues that "with its own creed, dress, fancy gear, language, poetry and songs, [cowboy identity] often outwardly replaces ethnicity altogether." Within the culture, the word *cowboy* is more often a verb than a noun, referring to the work and carrying no more inherent racial or gender bias than words like *teach* and *teacher* or *poem* and *poet*. As the Arizona poet Sally Bates notes in the unusually named "Generic Titles,"

> if you're gonna call me a cowgirl
> . . . Then you better start callin' them bullboys

When female characters appear in the poetry, they are often admired for possessing greater intelligence, stamina, patience, bravery, and cowboy skills than the men. Wives and daughters inherit ranches as often as do sons. In many small Western towns, the mayors, judges, commissioners, and other governing officials have traditionally been women (Wyoming was the first state to grant women the right to vote). Collections of cowboy poetry written by women have appeared, as well as bawdy poetry written by both genders.

Another misconception is that all cowboy poetry is rhymed. E.g., Rudolph Mellard was writing free verse in the 1920s and published it later (*Along the Way with Horses and Me*, 1975):

> . . . reason is a mighty poor thing to lean on
> When you are in a hurry.

Walter Campbell (writing as Stanley Vestal) was publishing *blank verse in 1927 (*Fandango*):

> The tender naked spider with his rope,
> The cowboy of the grass, who rides the wind.

The contemp. rodeo cowboy poet Zarzyski writes primarily in free verse and challenges the boundaries and definitions of cowboy poetry in many ways. In "The Hand," Zarzyski condemns racism by comparing a white aristocrat's small, "tissue-paper appendage" to a black laborer's large, calloused hand. He combines the cowboy-culture definitions of the words *hand* (a highly skilled cowboy) and *heart* (evoking the capacity for hard work) with landscape imagery to admire the "buttes and mesas" of honest labor eroded into the black man's hand and remarks that the size of the hand determines the size of the fist, which, in turn, indicates the size of the heart. Highly skilled cowboys are called *hands* or *top hands* or *good hands*. Both horses and cowboys are called *handy* and are judged by their hard-working hearts. Cowboy poetry often emphasizes equality based on skill in work, elevating and celebrating working-class skills and values. Although the white aristocrat in the poem wants the world to notice the "difference" between his own hand and that of the black laborer, Zarzyski bestows a cowboy's admiration on the laborer's hand.

Still another popular misconception is that many cowboy poets were illiterate, but examples of the poorest grammar (perhaps rebel or "tawny" grammar, as H. D. Thoreau called it in "Walking," 1861) often comes from the pens of college graduates such as Gardner (Dartmouth) or Lomax (Harvard). One final misconception is that the poetry comes from an oral rather than a written trad. According to one historical publication (strangely titled *Prose and Poetry of the Livestock Industry*, which collects hist. and biographical sketches, no poetry) published by the National Live Stock Association in 1905, cowboys did sing to quiet nervous cattle on the trail but not often to each other. Writing poetry, however, probably did fit their quiet, observational, and introspective lives.

Untangling the hist. of cowboy poetry from cowboy songs and romantic cowboy myth is challenging. Two early folklorists, N. H. "Jack" Thorp (*Songs of the Cowboys*, 1908) and Lomax (*Cowboy Songs and Frontier Ballads*, 1910), created an interest in the performing cowboy with their collections of cowboy songs and probably inspired the singing cowboys of radio and the movies during the 1930s and 1940s. In the mid-1980s, folklorists again revived interest in cowboy poetry and song through the Cowboy Poetry Gathering in Elko, Nevada, which blossomed over time into 150 gatherings in many Western states. Many of the poems recited at the first gatherings were thought to be anonymous and from the trail-driving era, and the performers reciting them were billed as authentic cowboy poets. Cowboy poetry can, of course, be performed by working cowboys, ranchers, or simply performers dressed as cowboys; appropriation and commercialization of the culture are common. The immensely popular, colorful, and entertaining oral performances drew audiences interested in a romantic historical view that evokes campfires, guitars, banjos, harmonicas, and cowboys singing to the longhorns or the moon on the long trails to Montana. These performances, and the poetry now being written esp. for performance, could perhaps be classified as *performance poetry. Quality and authenticity are always contested, and definitions, classifications, and boundaries are still evolving. Most of the poems recited at the early gatherings have since been identified as coming from the poets already mentioned and published after 1890 when the trail drives ended. Many of those poets had brief and sometimes no experience as working cowboys.

More than personal experience, audience seems critical to the cowboy poet's purpose. When the audience changes—esp. in the mind of the poet—the poetry changes. As the gatherings attracted a wider urban audience, the participating poets began composing a different kind of poetry. E.g., some participants used the stage to combat urban stereotypes about ranching, livestock, and cowboys who were being represented as a dying culture: exotic, lawless, uneducated, and exploiting valuable natural resources. The performers and poets also pushed boundaries to include subjects popular with audiences such as the Vietnam War, backyard horses, and politics.

Gioia has praised cowboy-poetry gatherings as one of the "new bohemian" groups reviving poetry outside the "intellectual ghetto" of academia and away from the reach of literary theory and crit., insisting that the revival of cowboy poetry (by the Western Folklife Center) and the publication of several new collections of both old and new poetry have been a boon. Others argue that the performance and entertainment aspects have changed the poetry. Glotfelty (2008) summarizes several controversies: "Experimentation in subject and form has generated lively debates within the field about whether cowboy poetry must rhyme, whether its subject must be ranch life, whether its authors must be cowboys, whether the poetry should be intended for recitation, whether cowboy poetry is folk art or art, and whether cowboy poetry is evolving or has lost its way."

Critics of cowboy poetry often concentrate on the form or mode in which it is presented, but the widespread popular appeal of the poetry may owe something to its philosophical stance—a question that merits further analysis. Much cowboy poetry revisits the ideals of freedoms, rights, and responsibilities that stand behind democratic and religious trads., promoting forgiveness, inclusion, hard work, and the rejection of artifice or possessions. While the details or story line may include livestock, ranch life, tools of the herding trade, or horsemanship skills, the accumulation of those details is about relationships (with land, animals, gods, and one another), identity, instruction, warning, reflection, and all the many topics that poets have been interested in since poetry first sprang from the hoof print of Pegasus.

*See* ENVIRONMENT AND POETRY.

■ **Anthologies**: *Cowboy Poetry*, ed. H. Cannon (1985); *The Whorehouse Bells Were Ringing*, ed. G. Logsdon (1989); *New Cowboy Poetry*, ed. H. Cannon (1990); *Maverick Western Verse*, ed. J. C. Dofflemyer (1994); *Graining the Mare*, ed. T. Jordan (1994); *Leaning into the Wind*, ed. L. Hasselstrom (1997); *Cowgirl Poetry*, ed. V. Bennett (2001); *Open Range*, ed. B. Siems (2004)—all of Kiskaddon's work.

■ **Criticism and History**: A. C. Henderson, "Cowboy Songs and Ballads," *Poetry* 10 (1917); and "Far-Western Verse," *Poetry* 12 (1918); E. W. Said, *Orientalism* (1979)—interpreting the exotic other and cultural appropriation; L. M. Silko, "Landscape, History, and the Pueblo Imagination," *Antaeus* 57 (1986); P. Allen, "The Sacred Hoop: A Contemporary Perspective," *The Sacred Hoop*, 2d ed. (1992); D. Gioia, *Can Poetry Matter?* (1991); b. hooks, "Eating the Other," *Black Looks* (1992); D. Gioia, "Notes toward a New Bohemia," http://www.danagioia.net (1993); A. H. Widman, *Between Earth and Sky* (1995); *The Ecocriticism Reader: Landmarks in Literary Ecology*, ed. C. Glotfelty and H. Fromm (1996); K. Basso, *Wisdom Sits in Places* (1996); *Borrowed Power*, ed. B. Ziff and P. Rao (1997); B. Nelson, "Every Educated Feller Ain't a Plumb Greenhorn," *Heritage of the Great Plains* 33 (2000); *Cowboy Poetry Matters*, ed. R. McDowell (2000); *Cowboy Poets and Cowboy Poetry*, ed. D. Stanley and E. Thatcher (2000); D. Gioia, "Disappearing Ink," *HudR* 56 (2003); B. Nelson, "Dana Gioia Is Wrong about Cowboy Poetry," *Western American Literature* 40 (2006); C. Glotfelty, "A Gathering of Cowboy Poetry," *Literary Nevada*, ed. C. Glotfelty (2008); *A Companion to the Literature and Culture of the American West*, ed. N. Witschi (2011); Western Folklife Center, http://www.westernfolklife.org.

B. B. NELSON

**CREATIONISM** (Sp. *Creacionismo*). An aesthetic movement proposed by the Chilean poet Vicente Huidobro (1893–1948), regarded as both the precursor and the founder of Sp. Am. vanguardism. According to Huidobro's own account, "creationist" was the name given to him when, as a young poet whose work had been steeped in *modernismo*, he delivered a speech in 1916 at the Ateneo Hispano-Americano in Buenos Aires, asserting that "the poet's first condition is to create, the second one, to create, and the third one, to create." Huidobro was perhaps the most productive Lat. Am. writer of manifestos of his generation and cultivated a distinctive theory of poetic creation. Within the proliferation of "isms" in the early 20th c (*futurism, *Dadaism, *ultraism, *surrealism), creationism extolled the virtues of pure, antimimetic, and autonomous art. This autonomous art is to be understood in relation to another vanguardist tenet: the interaction of art with life. For Huidobro, the aesthetic phenomenon should exist like a plant, a star, or a fruit, with its own reason for being. A new reality, the poem imitates the constructive laws of the latter but not its appearances. Thus, in his "Ars poética" (1916, 1918), Huidobro challenged his fellow poets: "Why sing of roses, oh poets? Make them bloom in the poem."

Upon his arrival in Paris at the end of 1916, Huidobro immersed himself in its cultural life and soon participated actively in the Fr. vanguard movement, known as literary *cubism (exemplified by Pierre Reverdy, Guillaume Apollinaire, and Max Jacob). In 1922, Huidobro exhibited *Salle 14*, a series of painted poems, in which he reflected on issues of representation, originality, and referentiality in a manner that evoked cubist practices. His creationist ideas can be viewed as a variation of literary cubism, although Huidobro fashioned himself as a precursor ("contemporary poetry begins in me"). Chronology aside, creationism can be understood as a radical individualization of the idea of the vanguard movement.

Like many vanguardist expressions, Huidobro's poetry also seeks the recreation of lang. itself. *Altazor* (1931), his poetic masterpiece of seven cantos, dramatizes a new era in which the poet's vision is that of a divine game of lang. Falling out into space, Altazor's body is consumed with the old lang. of poetry, and a new lang., progressively more radical, is created. An antipoet and "high-hawk" aeronaut, Altazor travels into the realms of nothingness, the "infiniternity." He asserts, "I speak in the name of a star no one knows / I speak with a tongue moistened by unborn seas." In pursuit of a new poetic lang., Altazor resorts to wordplay: "There is no time to lose / Look here swoops the monochronic swallow / With an antipodal tone of approaching distance / Here swoops the swallowing swallow / At the horislope of the mountizon." The last canto ends in total disintegration toward *glossolalia: "lalalee/ Eeoh eeah/ ee ee ee oh/ Ahee ah ee ahee ah ee ee ee ee oh eeah."

*See* CHILE, POETRY OF; SOUND POETRY.

■ *Vicente Huidobro y el Creacionismo*, ed. R. de Costa (1975); V. Huidobro, *Altazor*, trans. and intro. E. Weinberger (1988); V. Unruh, *Latin American Vanguards* (1994); R. de Costa, *Vicente Huidobro* (1996); *Vicente Huidobro*, ed. C. Goic (2003); J. Read, *Modern Poetics and Hemispheric American Cultural Studies* (2009).

R. SARABIA

**CRETIC** or amphimacer (Gr., "long at both ends"). In cl. prosody, the metrical sequence – ‿ –, sometimes felt as a segment of iambo-trochaic and used alongside iambs and trochees or, like iambic and trochaic, in external compounding with *aeolic units. On other occasions, as is obvious from *resolution of either long syllable, the cretic is really a form of the *paeon, and cretic-paeonic measures, though rare in the choruses of Gr. *tragedy, are not infrequent in *comedy. The cretic meter, different from most other Gr. meters, is thought to have been of foreign origin, from a Cretan poet named Thaletas in the 7th c. BCE. Cretics occur in early Roman drama and are also common in the *clausulae* of Cicero. An example in the former is the song of Phaedromus in Plautus, *Curculio* 147–54:

$$- \; \cup \; - \quad - \; \cup \; - \quad - \; \cup \; - \; - \; \cup \; -$$

pessuli, heus pessuli, vos saluto lubens

$$- \; \cup \; - \quad - \; \cup \; - \quad - \; \cup \; - \quad - \; \cup \; -$$

vos amo, vos volo, vos peto atque obsecro

Duckworth reproduces the meaning and meter of these lines thus: "Bolts and bars, bolts and bars, gladly I greetings bring, / Hear my love, hear my prayer, you I beg and entreat."

Like most other of the more complex Gr. feet, cretics do not exist in the mod. vernaculars except as experiments, but some Ren. songs are in stress-analogue cretics, and the song "Shall I die? Shall I fly?" attributed in 1985 to Shakespeare, is in cretic dimeters. Cretic lines appear in Alfred, Lord Tennyson's "The Oak."

■ G. E. Duckworth, *The Nature of Roman Comedy* (1952); Maas; Koster; Crusius; C. Questa, *Introduzione alla metrica di Plauto* (1967); Snell; West; G. T. Wright, "The Meter of 'Shall I Die,'" *Eidos* 3 (1986).

R. J. GETTY; A. T. COLE; T.V.F. BROGAN

# CRITICISM

  I. Meanings of the Term
 II. History
III. Divisions of Criticism

The most common meaning of the word *criticism* is the expression of disapproval on the basis of perceived faults, and historically, in the domain of lit., much crit. has been the *evaluation of literary productions. Since the 19th c., however, there has been a great expansion of types of writing about lit., and the notion of crit., as determined by the oppositions in which the term figures, has become harder to characterize.

**I. Meanings of the Term.** The capaciousness and variability of the term *criticism*, when connected with lit., as in *literary criticism*, emerge in specific contrasts in which it figures: *criticism* is opposed to *literature*, certainly, as writing about lit. rather than lit. itself, though some of the most elegant and imaginative crit., from Horace's *Ars poetica* and Alexander Pope's *Essay on Criticism* to Jacques Derrida's *Glas*, takes a literary form. Crit. is often opposed to scholarship: the latter produces information, while the former may use such knowledge but offers *interpretation and opinion. Yet this is an opposition that many scholars and critics quite reasonably would contest: scholars cannot produce good scholarship without interpreting and evaluating, and critics must be at least minimally knowledgeable to produce valuable crit. Crit. has been opposed to theory: crit. deals with particular works, while theory discusses general principles of interpretation and method, but the authoritative *Norton Anthology of Theory and Criticism* does not attempt to decide which essays it presents are crit. and which are theory, and Wimsatt and Brooks's earlier *Literary Criticism: A Short History* is a hist. of arguments about conceptions of lit. More narrowly, lit. crit., the discussion of the form and meaning of literary works, is sometimes opposed to lit. hist., an enterprise focused on broad narratives of cultural production rather than on the qualities of works themselves. This contrast, which once seemed decisive—in the era of the *New Criticism it mattered whether one was a literary historian or a literary critic—has faded, and in the 21st c., the different manifestations of lit. hist. are seen as forms of lit. crit.

Despite these functional contrasts, the term *criticism* in its broad sense has come to mean any sort of writing about lit., though its primary meaning today is professional, academic writing about lit. While a drama critic reviews plays and performances and a poetry critic evaluates new volumes of verse, *criticism* today is associated with the academy rather than journalism. Yet, since so many projects in contemp. academic crit. involve discussion of social and cultural topics that literary works help to illuminate, *criticism* has come to seem less and less appropriate as a broad term to describe the writing that professors of lit. produce. A better term has yet to appear, though, and for the purposes of this article, *criticism* is writing about lit., whether evaluative, interpretive, historical, or formal and technical.

**II. History.** What is today called *literary criticism* in the Western trad. can be traced back to various modes of judgment, praise or blame, of archaic *song and its performances. Singing contests and symposia were among the contexts in ancient Greece for the exercise and articulation of critical judgment; but a properly *literary* crit. comes into being only with the emergence of a conception of poetry as a verbal artifact, subject to grammatical and rhetorical analysis, formal classification, and technical evaluation. The classicist Ford writes in *The Origins of Criticism*, "Only when singers became 'poets,' craftsmen of words rather than performers, could a properly 'poetic' literary criticism emerge as the special knowledge that discerns the excellence of poetry so understood." Such crit. depends on a system of *genres that prescribes the correct *telos* or aim of each type of song and what is appropriate to each, making possible judgments of success.

For most of its hist., Western lit. crit. is linked to generic categories based on *mimesis—genres differing according to what is represented. Aristotle's *Poetics* provided a framework of genre theory later developed by Ren. theorists and critics. *Poetics, in the sense of

a general account of literary possibilities and the rules or conventions of each, is central to the Western trad. of crit. Linked with the generic orientation of poetics are writings about poetry, such as the *Ars poetica* and Geoffrey of Vinsauf's *Poetria nova*, which offer advice to poets while discussing poetry's possibilities. The rhetorical analysis of efficacious speech, an important critical trad. of the premod. era, is also linked to a genre-based crit. Writers on *rhetoric, from Quintilian on, are concerned with *invention and *decorum and cite abundant literary examples to illustrate rhetorical techniques.

As early as Plato, whose attack on Homer and on the fables offered by poets illustrates the polemical nature of much of the critical trad., there is discussion of what sort of knowledge poetry offers, whether particular sayings of poets are true and valuable. The Neoplatonic trad. rehabilitates pagan myths and poetic fables by proposing allegorical interpretations. The practice of commenting on sacred texts, in both the Jewish and Christian trads., contributes to the *hermeneutic resources of lit. crit., as in Porphyry's explanation of Homer's episode of the Cave of the Nymphs in book 13 of the *Odyssey* as an *allegory of the soul's fall into the world and Dante's "Letter to Can Grande" describing his *Divine Comedy* in terms of the Christian method of fourfold interpretation of scripture (see EXEGESIS). Crit. of the Ren. explores the possibilities of national, vernacular lits. and their relation to the cl. past and its models. Critical writing of the 17th and 18th cs. continues the evaluative mode but also foregrounds discussions about the relation of lit. to audiences and about concepts of *taste.

The revolution in the concept of lit. that occurs in that generally revolutionary time of the late 18th and early 19th cs. breaks with a conception of lit. linked to generic norms. The shift from a concept of lit. as *mimesis to a concept of lit. as expression disables the primary strain of evaluative crit.: assessment of works in terms of the norms of genres, of verisimilitude, and appropriate expression, specifically the appropriateness of the means of expression to the genre and topic.

This shift in the concept of lit. is ultimately transformative for lit. crit.: no longer is its task to assess the performance of a text in terms of generic norms; a much broader field is open to it. Within this new framework, which gradually comes into play for crit. over the course of the 19th and 20th cs., crit. may still pursue the evaluative project, but since the generic norms are no longer given, it must inquire what the norms should be for the evaluation of a given text. Increasingly, crit., which before 1850 is seldom interpretive, has claimed the task of telling us what works mean. If the work is expressive, then crit. elucidates what it expresses: the *genius of the author, the spirit of the age, the historical conjuncture, the conflicts of the psyche, the functioning of lang. itself. (Such conceptions of what a text might express are the basis of so-called critical schools.) A fundamental paradox of the expressive model of lit. is that the work is mute and the critic must speak for it, unfolding the hidden meaning. What the discourse of the text appears to say is not what the work says: the literary critic must articulate the significance of these mute words. In place of a mimetic crit. that determines the genre and generic perfection of a work based on the action it imitates, there arises an expressive crit. that shows how works express the state of affairs, the lang., or the genius that gave rise to them.

This new expressive poetics opens a vast range of possibilities for lit. crit., ultimately enabling the efflorescence of crit. of the second half of the 20th c. Within the generalized expressive model, where works may express everything from the ideology of a historical situation to the fundamental negativity of lang. or the impossibility of lit. itself, lit. crit. has given itself immense scope, an array of possible "approaches" that may seem to have little to do with each other or to be fundamentally antagonistic, even though they derive from the same principle—the principle that makes lit. crit. fundamentally interpretive yet also hostile to the idea that the work has a message: there is no simple message but a vast range of configurations that the work may express.

The *New Criticism, which became the dominant paradigm for crit. in the mid-20th c., presented itself as antiexpressive: the achieved literary work does not express something; it embodies a complex drama of attitudes, as its formal devices qualify and inflect any direct assertion. But ultimately, for the New Criticism, the work comes to be about lit. itself or about the fusion of form and meaning that lit. seeks to achieve.

It was *structuralism, a major antiexpressive, antiinterpretive project, that sought to account for literary effects by setting forth the codes and conventions of literary and cultural systems that make them possible, that paradoxically spurred the devel. of a wide range of interpretive critical practices. In treating lit. as one cultural practice among others and claiming that wherever there is meaning there is a system that makes that meaning possible, structuralism described multiple discursive practices and cultural codes. Opening up the domain of signification, it in effect encouraged the remarkable exfoliation of critical possibilities that became "approaches" to interpretation, allowing the flourishing of cultural studies, feminism, gender theory, queer studies, ethnic studies, Foucauldian discourse analysis, and postcolonial crit., not to mention various historicisms (see CULTURAL STUDIES AND POETRY, FEMINIST APPROACHES TO POETRY, GENDER AND POETRY, POSTCOLONIAL POETICS, QUEER POETRY). No longer were the expressive possibilities limited to the genius of the author or the spirit of the age. Insofar as all human experience and the imagination of its limits is matter for lit., no realm or conjuncture is too remote or implausible to be something lit. might express in the interpretive paradigm.

**III. Divisions of Criticism.** There are several different ways of conceiving of the domain of crit.: it can be divided (1) according to the aim or purpose of writing about lit., (2) according to the aspect of literary works to which critical writing gives special importance, or (3) according to the theoretical orientation or particular body of knowledge adduced in writing about lit. These different sorts of divisions intersect and overlap, but they provide a sense of the range of crit.

Crit. can be described according to its purposes or functions. There is evaluative crit. that judges whether writers have done well or badly and aims to tell readers which works they should read and value. Such crit. may be focused on new productions, as in journalistic reviewing, or on the critical heritage of the past. When generalized, this sort of crit. becomes prescriptive poetics: advice or rules for writing well, which can be quite formal and technical. As opposed to evaluative crit. in a judicial mode, impressionistic crit. aims to recount a personal response, helping readers to appreciate a given work, author, or literary mode.

Central to the Western trad. have been writings on the general nature of poetry, apologies for poetry, aimed at defending it in a given cultural context and describing its powers and possibilities. Generalized and systematized, this may become descriptive poetics, which aims to account for the general possibilities of poetry or lit.

Much writing about lit. has had an explicit moral, religious, or political purpose: to explore how one should live, to clarify one's place in the world, one's relation to the divine, or more recently, to enlist lit., through its insights or omissions, in advocating political and social change. One version of interpretive crit. that aims as social change is *critique* (of which there are various schools), which seeks to lay bare the political implications of cultural practices and institutions. Much crit. of this sort involves interpretation of literary works, but there is also a broad category of interpretive or hermeneutic crit. that explores the meaning of a work as part of a professional lit. crit. aimed at advancing knowledge in a particular domain (whether of a historical period or a literary form or an author's achievement). Crit. of the late 20th c. often sees itself as advancing understanding of lit. and society while also performing social and cultural critique.

Moreover, crit. can be characterized by the aspect of literary work on which it focuses. Abrams's influential account in *The Mirror and the Lamp* of the four factors in the literary transaction—the "world," the "author," the "audience," and the "work"—distinguishes mimetic, expressive, pragmatic, and objective crit., depending on which factor is the focus. A more refined and specific account would list under "world," historical and sociological crit., cultural studies, and also thematic crit. and archetypal or myth crit.; under "author," biographical crit., some psychoanalytic crit., and genetic crit. (for problems of literary genesis); under "audience," reception theory and reader-response crit., and some rhetorical crit.; and under "work," textual crit. (the establishment of the text), stylistics, linguistic crit., rhetorical crit., and formalist crit. (see LINGUISTICS AND POETICS, FORMALISM).

Finally, there are distinctions among types of critical writing based on the particular bodies of theoretical reflection on which they draw. The list of possible critical schools is potentially large, but some readily identifiable ones are Marxist crit., psychoanalytic crit., deconstructive crit., feminist crit., gay and lesbian crit. (queer theory), the *Geneva school or phenomenological crit., structuralism and semiotics, *Russian formalism, neo-Aristotelian or *Chicago school crit., *Frankfurt school crit., New Criticism, empirical science of lit., *New Historicism, *New Formalism, cultural studies, postcolonial crit., and ecocrit. (see PSYCHOLOGY AND POETRY; SEMIOTICS AND POETRY). Most such modes of crit. can be viewed as operations of contextualization, where literary works are read and interpreted in the context of a body of particular concerns, whether these be accounts of the nature of lang. and meaning (as with deconstruction and structuralism) or a set of social and political concerns (as with feminism, gay and lesbian crit., and ecocrit.).

Professional academic crit., which in the 21st c. dominates the field of lit. crit., frequently takes the form of a contestation of premises or conclusions of other critics, as it seeks to further our understanding of literary works. Much of this crit. enlists literary works in projects that are defined by broad cultural themes: the interpretation of literary works serves as a way to investigate the culture and society that they help to create and that they embody. As lit., in a digital age, transforms itself from the fixed text that originally made lit. crit. possible to a performance whose success and conditions of possibility demand to be evaluated, some more traditional functions of crit.—poetics and evaluation—may become central once again.

*See* CLOSE READING, CULTURAL CRITICISM, POSTSTRUCTURALISM.

■ Abrams; Wellek; Frye; Wimsatt and Brooks; V. B. Leitch, *American Literary Criticism from the Thirties to the Eighties* (1988); *CHLC*; *The Norton Anthology of Theory and Criticism*, ed. V. Leitch et al. (2001); A. Ford, *The Origins of Criticism* (2002); *The Johns Hopkins Guide to Literary Theory and Criticism*, ed. M. Groden et al., 2d ed. (2005).

J. CULLER

**CROATIAN POETRY.** Owing to its firm ties with the Western world and the direct influences of Ren. humanism, Croatia developed a sophisticated lit. as early as the 15th c. The father of Croatian lit., Marko Marulić (pseud. of Marcus Marulus Spalatensis, 1450–1524) was born in Split and was a renowned Eur. humanist. In addition to philosophical and religious treatises in Lat., he wrote poetry in Croatian and is best known for his *Judita* (1501, pub. 1521) about which he explicitly stated that it is written "in Croatian verses," thus officially giving literary status to his native lang. On the matrix of the biblical story of Judith, he vividly describes in doubly rhymed dodecasyllabic lines the perils that his own nation faced before the Ottoman invasion.

Oral traditional poetry, in particular *ballads and lyric *songs, though widely disseminated throughout the region, left deeper traces only on the older layers

of Croatian lit. This is particularly visible during the Ren. when poets in Dubrovnik and along the Dalmatian coast wove elements of Petrarchan and *troubadour style with local traditional poetry to create a unique amalgam (see OCCITAN POETRY, PETRARCHISM). The predominant meter is dodecasyllabic, while the thematic range tilts heavily toward love subjects, with some religious and patriotic verses. A central collection was offered by Nikša Ranjina (1494–1582), who started compiling the works of his contemporaries in 1507. Some of the most prominent names included are those of Sigismund Menčetić (1457–1527), a well-traveled writer of noble background who produced some of the period's most erotic verses, and the cleric Džore Držić (1461–1501), who wrote more restrained, sincere verses. Mavro Vetranović (1483–1576), the most prolific writer of the Dubrovnik circle, was known for his moralizing, metaphysical, and politically colored poetry.

Aside from Dubrovnik, the island of Hvar was the site of important literary activity during this period. It yielded highly respected authors such as Hanibal Lucić (ca. 1485–1553), whose Petrarchan verses are some of the best on this side of the Adriatic and whose dialogic verse narrative *Robinja* (Slave Girl, written before 1530) is the first Croatian secular play. Mikša Pelegrinović (ca. 1500–62) wrote what is likely the most popular piece of the Croatian Ren., *Jeđupka* (The Gypsy), in the vein of Florentine masquerades, with a series of related love poems. Petar Hektorović (1487–1572) is best known for his piscatorial eclogue *Ribanje i ribarsko prigovaranje* (Fishing and Fishermen's Conversation, 1556, pub. 1568), a philosophical meditation on the virtues of a simple life that also includes the earliest recordings of two traditional oral songs, *bugarštice*.

The first Croatian novelistic work combining verse and prose is *Planine* (The Mountains, 1536, pub. 1569) by Petar Zoranić (1508–1569) of Zadar, which provides a patriotic vision of the Croatian Arcadia. Nikola Nalješković (ca. 1500–87) was not only a central figure in Dubrovnik literary circles and left a remarkably diverse corpus of works in terms of genre, incl. a collection of love poetry. From this younger group of Dubrovnik writers, the most renowned today is Marin Držić (1508–67), although mainly for his comedies and pastoral plays (many of them in verse) rather than for the love poetry of his youth. Dinko Ranjina (1536–1607), who like most Croatian writers of this period had close ties with Italy, published his *Pjesni razlike* (Poems of Difference, 1563) in Italy; many of them echo traditional poetry. Dominko Zlatarić (1558–1613), also of Dubrovnik, became known for his own poetry but was perhaps even more renowned for his trans. of cl. and contemp. lit.

The greatest Croatian author of the *baroque period, Ivan Gundulić (1589–1638), also marked the summit of Dubrovnik's literary achievements with his reflexive poem in three *cantos *Suze sina razmetnoga* (Tears of the Prodigal Son, 1621), the pastoral play *Dubravka* (1628), and the *epic *Osman* (1621–38). In the first, Gundulić introduced a longer form, which became particularly popular in this period as a vehicle for pondering the question of sin and the transitory nature of human existence. His unfinished *Osman* (two of the planned 20 octosyllabic rhyming cantos were not completed) focuses on a highly pertinent issue: the precarious balance between the Eur. and Ottoman powers. Gundulić's poem, though structurally influenced by Torquato Tasso's *La Gerusalemme liberata*, does not share the It. author's reliance on events from the distant past but draws his complex narrative line from a contemp. Polish-Turkish battle.

Gundulić's contemp. Ivan Bunić (1591–1658) is a reflexive and sensual writer whose poems are akin to those of metaphysical poets and are often colored with cl. motives. Ignjat Đurđević (1675–1737) was the last great writer of the Dubrovnik Republic; his It. and Lat. poetry is characterized by tight forms and restrained subject matter, while his verses in Croatian are considerably more playful and imbued with the spirit of local traditional poetry. In the continental region, the promising literary career of Fran Krsto Frankopan (1643–71), one of the most erotic and patriotic writers of the time, was cut short by his execution at the hands of the Hapsburgs. One of the most popular Croatian books of all time, *Razgovor ugodni naroda slovinskoga* (Pleasant Conversation of the Slavic People, 1756), was written by a Franciscan monk of Dalmatia, Andrija Kačić-Miošić (1704–60), in the decasyllabic verse of folk poetry and offers a chronicle (albeit fictional) of the Slavs.

Ivan Mažuranić (1814–90), a recognized writer and the governor of Croatia during the period of national awakening, was most famous for his epic *Smrt Smail-Age Čengića* (*Smail-Aga Čengić's Death*, 1846), which describes in the style of traditional epics the Montenegrin rebellion against the Turks. He also completed Gundulić's *Osman*. Patriotic and reflexive, the poetry of Petar Preradović (1818–72) raised awareness of the importance of the national lang. at a time when Croats could not use their mother tongue for official purposes. Silvije Strahimir Kranjčević (1865–1908) was a similarly politically engaged poet whose anguish and calls for social justice were often rendered through the use of cl. motifs.

Antun Gustav Matoš (1873–1914) was a harbinger of *modernism and a great practitioner of the *sonnet form who shifted the focus to introspective themes and insisted on the supremacy of the aesthetic dimension. Other Croatian modernists greatly influenced by Matoš were Vladimir Vidrić (1875–1909) and Ljubo Wiesner (1885–1951), while Vladimir Nazor (1876–1949) remained faithful to Dalmatian motifs. Janko Polić Kamov (1886–1910), known as a Croatian poet-rebel, wrote expressionist verses condemning the hypocrisy of middle-class dogmas (see EXPRESSIONISM). Antun Branko Šimić (1898–1925) was a master of concision and introduced *free verse to Croatian lit. Despite his early death, the expressionistic features of his only published collection had a lasting impact. Augustin Tin Ujević (1891–1955), a disciple of Matoš, likewise holds an important place for his poems of human suffering

and exuberant elation. The musicality of his expression and his ling. opulence, combined with an ability to transcend the realm of the personal and convey universally recognizable mental states, make him unquestionably the most influential Croatian poet.

Miroslav Krleža (1893–1981), the greatest Croatian prose writer, also left a considerable lyric opus, much of it dealing with social themes. Ivan Goran Kovačić (1913–43) is known for his antifascist poem *Jama* (*The Pit*, 1943), while Dobriša Cesarić (1902–80) and Dragutin Tadijanović (1905–2007) have been praised for poetry that celebrates nature and the simple life but also for vignettes of everyday life rendered with seemingly effortless style. Nikola Šop (1904–1982), a Croatian poet from Bosnia, drew the attention of W. H. Auden with his Christian mystic verses and cosmic metaphors. Auden translated some of Šop's poetry into Eng. Jure Kaštelan (1919–90) and Josip Pupačić (1928–71) are both quintessential poets of the south, with the sea permeating their poems, though, in the case of Kaštelan, war also appears as a focal theme of his early period. Along with Pupačić and Kaštelan, Vesna Parun (1922–2010) marked a new postwar generation that introduced a more personal tone in a variety of subjects. Parun is particularly well known for her intimate love poetry.

Ivan Slamnig (1930–2001) gained the status of the most ironic Croatian poet and a ling. innovator whose expression bursts with neologisms, archaisms, and other wordplay. Anxiety, loneliness, and helplessness are central features in the poetry of Slavko Mihalić (1928–2007), who combines the everyday and the sublime with powerful eloquence. Antun Šoljan (1932–93), inspired by the Anglo-Am. school, in particular T. S. Eliot, wrote intellectual poetry, while Daniel Dragojević (b. 1934) shows a philosophical orientation, often employing paradox in order to invert the world and reveal its true meaning. The lexically rich poetry of Drago Štambuk (b. 1950) employs both his native Dalmatian and cosmopolitan imagery, while that of Anka Žagar (b. 1954) plays with the notion of semantic concretization, merging stream of consciousness, syntactic distortions, and neologisms to offer one of the most engaging oeuvres in the contemp. Croatian poetic scene.

■ **Anthologies**: *Hrvatske narodne pjesme*, ed. N. Andrič et al., 10 v. (1896–1942); *Zlatna knjiga hrvatskog pjesništva od početaka do danas*, ed. V. Pavletić (1970); *Leut i truba*, ed. R. Bogišić (1971); *Antologija hrvatskog pjesništva ranog moderniteta*, ed. S. P. Novak (2004); *Utjeha kaosa*, ed. M. Mićanović (2006); *Antologija hrvatskoga pjesništva*, ed. A. Stamać (2007); *Love Lyric and Other Poems of the Croatian Renaissance: A Bilingual Anthology*, ed. and trans. J. S. Miletich (2009).

■ **Criticism and History**: J. Torbarina, *Italian Influence on the Poets of the Ragusan Republic* (1931); A. Kadić, *Contemporary Croatian Literature* (1960); R. Bogišić, *O hrvatskim starim pjesnicima* (1968); I. Slamnig, *Hrvatska versifikacija* (1981); S. P. Novak, *Povijest hrvatske književnosti* (2003).

A. VIDAN

**CROSS RHYME** (Ger. *Kreuzreim, überschlagender Reim*; Fr. *rime brisée, rime croisée*). Also known as envelope rhyme or enclosed rhyme, cross rhyme is now commonly used to refer to the *abab* pattern of end words in a quatrain (Perloff, Scott, Adams). But as Schipper has pointed out, when two long lines of a rhyming *couplet are connected by a rhyme before the *caesura as well as by a rhyme at the end of the line (interlaced rhyme, *rime entrelacée*), they will seem to be broken up into four short lines of cross rhyme, and some overlap between the terms is understandable. Most common in long-line verse, such as the med. Lat. hexameter, cross rhyme also features prominently in certain Ir. stanza forms, such as the *droighneach* and the *rannaigheacht mhor*, both of which have at least two cross rhymes in each couplet (Turco).

■ Schipper, *History*; M. Perloff, *Rhyme and Meaning in the Poetry of Yeats* (1970); C. Scott, *The Riches of Rhyme* (1988); L. Turco, *The Book of Forms* (2000); S. Adams, *Poetic Designs* (2003).

W. HUNTER

**CUADERNA VÍA.** A Sp. meter (also called *alejandrino, mester de clerecía, nueva maestría*) in which syllable counting was used for the first time in Castilian, though the line soon deteriorated or was modified to one of somewhat more flexible length. It was introduced, probably under Fr. influence, in the first part of the 13th c. or earlier by the clergy (hence, the name *mester de clerecía* in contrast to the *mester de juglaría*, or minstrel's meter, typical of the popular *epic and other narrative poetry). This meter, particularly in the work of its earliest known exponent, Gonzalo de Berceo (late 12th–mid-13th c.), is notable for its rigidity of form: syllables are counted carefully; each line consists of two *hemistichs of seven syllables each; the lines are grouped into monorhymed quatrains having true rhyme rather than *assonance. According to Fitz-Gerald, *hiatus was obligatory, though various forms of *elision and metrical contraction were permitted. An example of the *cuaderna vía* from the work of Berceo is the following:

> Yo Maestro Gonzalvo de Berceo nom-
> nado, iendo en romeria, caeci en
> un prado, verde e bien sencido, de
> flores bien poblado; logar cobdi-
> ciaduero pora homne cansado.

The best-known works written largely in cuaderna vía are Juan Ruiz's *Libro de buen amor* and Pero López de Ayala's *Rimado de Palacio*, both from the 14th c. The cuaderna vía was employed for most of the serious poetry written in the 13th and 14th cs., but it was completely supplanted in the 15th by the *arte mayor*.

■ J. D. Fitz-Gerald, *Versification of the Cuaderna Vía as Found in Berceo's "Vida de Santo Domingo de Silos"* (1905); J. Saavedra Molina, "El verso de clerecía," *Boletín de filología* 6 (1950–51); Navarro; C. F. Fraker, "'Cuaderna vía' and Narrative," *Justina: Homenaje a Justina Ruiz de Conde*, ed. E. Gascón-Vera and J. Renjilian-

Burgy (1992); P. Ancos-García, "La forma primaria de difusión y de recepción de la poesía castellana en cuaderna vía del siglo XIII," *DAI* 65 (2005).

D. C. CLARKE

**CUBA, POETRY OF.** *See* CARIBBEAN, POETRY OF THE.

**CUBISM.** A school in the visual arts led by Pablo Picasso and Georges Braque in Paris, ca. 1907–25, which, in part as a reaction against impressionism, stressed the geometrical forms conceived to be inherent in the objects it represented—hence, "les petites cubes," which irritated Henri Matisse but which ironically led to the name of the school. Although three stages have been postulated for this school (Gray), cubism is commonly divided into an "analytic" stage, which dissects the inherent geometrical forms of objects, emphasizing them through a limited palette, and a "synthetic" stage, in which fragments of various objects are reintegrated into a new, self-consciously aesthetic object. At its most sophisticated, synthetic cubism evolved techniques of *collage and *papier collé*, incorporating fragments of real objects into the composition, incl. fragments of verbal texts, thereby challenging a naive acceptance of either visual or verbal representation. Cubism was enthusiastically embraced by the Fr. poet Guillaume Apollinaire, who praised the cubist aesthetic in his *Les Peintres cubistes* (1913), thus encouraging a critical controversy still waged today as to whether there is such a genre as *cubist lit.* in general or *cubist poetry* in particular. In part because Apollinaire (and later Pierre Reverdy and e. e. cummings) denied being a cubist poet, and in part because of a theoretical questioning of the validity of transferring a term from one artistic medium to another, several critics have denied the existence of cubist lit. altogether (Decaudin). However, the term *cubist literature* was accepted as early as 1941 (Lemaître) and has subsequently gained so much acceptance that James Joyce, T. S. Eliot, William Faulkner, Wallace Stevens, cummings, Ford Madox Ford, Gertrude Stein, Max Jacob, and Alain Robbe-Grillet have all been called *cubist writers*. The diversity of these writers has led some critics to conclude that *cubism* best describes the 20th-c. perspective (Sypher) and critical temperament (Steiner).

Despite its increased acceptance, the term *cubist poetry* has very different meanings in the hands of different critics. Since, in contrast to *imagism, *vorticism, or *futurism, there is no poetic cubist *manifesto, it is possible to find cubist poetry defined as a style marked by "new syntax and punctuation, based on typographical dispersion" (Admussen); as a poetic movement between futurism and *expressionism (Hadermann); or as a style characterized by an unusual amount of "punning, contradiction, parody, and word play" in order to create the *ambiguity so characteristic of visual cubism (Steiner). Cubist poetry is variously confined to the writings concurrent with the cubist school, esp. 1912–19 (Carmody) or to the works typically printed in *Nord-Sud*, a jour. ed. by Reverdy (Admussen), or it is extended to works marked by visual fragmentation, such as that of cummings or Louis Zukofsky; works obsessed with perception, such as Stevens's "Thirteen Ways of Looking at a Blackbird"; or works constituted by multiple voices and temporal layers, such as Eliot's *The Waste Land*.

Even within the visual arts, cubism proved to be a highly complex and diffuse movement; and it is reasonable to expect that such diversity would be reflected in the poetry as well, as various poets appropriated different facets of cubism into their work. Thus, W. C. Williams's "The Red Wheelbarrow," with its continually changing in perspectives, and Eliot's *Waste Land*, with *fragments of various langs., disrupted narrative, and multifaceted *allusions, constitute relatively simple and complex versions of the "analytic" pole of poetic cubism. In contrast, Stevens's "Man with the Blue Guitar," which stresses its ambiguous status as a representational *object* by frustrating its own ability to represent, may be described as the poetic embodiment of synthetic cubism. Some poets such as Pound and Eliot incorporate not only multiple allusions but the so-called found poem (see FOUND POETRY) as well, thus approaching the montage or collage that some critics find most characteristic of cubist lit.

In the case of Stein, her *Tender Buttons* in particular has been considered in the context of cubism as a result of its focus on alternative ways of perceiving and evoking objects. Readers have often found Stein's "A Seltzer Bottle" or "A Red Hat" as baffling and unlike their reported objects as Juan Gris' "Violin and Glass" or Braque's "Candlesticks and Playing Cards." In her essay "Portraits," Stein writes of *Tender Buttons*, "the thing that excited me very much at that time and still does is that the words or words that make what I looked at be itself were always words that to me very exactly related themselves to that thing the thing at which I was looking, but as often as not had as I say nothing whatever to do with what any words would do that described that thing."

In a very different way, the attention to visual form inherent in visual cubism invites such *visual poetry as Apollinaire's "Coeur couronne et miroir" or such *concrete poetry as his "Lettre-Océan." The visual impact of the verbal text is further explored in such experimental poetry as Henri Chopin's "il manque toujours l'y" or Eugen Gomringer's "the black mystery is here" (Steiner), both of which stress their status as artistic objects. More radically, the conjunction of visual and verbal texts typical of the later cubist paintings, as well as the tendency toward the fragmentation or "analysis" of form characteristic of all cubist works, may be realized in such complicated pieces as Marius de Zaya's "mental reactions," in which the fragmentation and reassembly of a poem by Agnes Ernst Meyer with visual forms undermines the distinction between the two arts altogether (Bohn). But the most typical visual mark of cubist poetry is the rupture of normal *stanza, *line, and word boundaries, which creates a visual text even less conventional than that of *free verse. The most famous practitioner of this strategy is cummings, whose work includes sentence fragments and open parenthetical phrases, embodying disjunctive forms at the syntactic level.

While it is not possible to devise a list of characteristics that will be present in every "cubist" poem, it is possible to say that, along the spectrum of analytic and synthetic interpretations, cubist poetry is likely to be characterized by a highly self-conscious sense of its own *modernism; attention to visual form (which may move toward the composition of very precise, blocklike stanzas bearing an affinity to imagism or toward a more radical arrangement of the printed page); a rupturing of conventional poetic and semantic forms; and a thematic preoccupation with multiple perspectives, leading to a questioning of the representation itself. Finally, the very fragmentation of form that was ironically so characteristic of a movement preoccupied with form encouraged the blurring of genre and media distinctions, giving rise to the *prose poem of Max Jacob and others or to such intermedia as Zukofsky's epic-length *"A,"* which evolves from poetic to musical composition.

*See* AVANT-GARDE POETICS.

■ G. Lemaître, *From Cubism to Surrealism in French Literature* (1941); C. Gray, *Cubist Aesthetic Theories* (1953); F. Carmody, "L'Esthétique de l'esprit nouveau," *Le Flaneur des deux rives* 2 (1955); W. Sypher, *From Rococo to Cubism in Art and Literature* (1960); F. Steegmuller, *Apollinaire: Poet among the Poets* (1963); G. Stein, *Writings and Lectures 1909–1945* (1967); R. Admussen, "*Nord-Sud* and Cubist Poetry," *JAAC* 27 (1968); J. Golding, *Cubism* (1968); B. Dijkstra, *The Hieroglyphics of a New Speech* (1969); G. Kamber, *Max Jacob and the Poetics of Cubism* (1971); E. Frye, *Cubism* (1978); P. Hadermann, "De Quelques Procédés 'cubistes' en poésie," *Actes du VIIIe Congrès de l'Assoc. Internationale de Littérature Comparée* (1980); F. Igly, *Apollinaire: Poète ami et défenseur des peintres cubistes* (1982); "Cubisme et Littérature," spec. iss. of *Europe: Revue littéraire Mensuelle* 638–39 (1982), esp. Decaudin; W. Marling, *William Carlos Williams and the Painters, 1909–1923* (1982); W. Steiner, *The Colors of Rhetoric* (1982), incl. bibl.; H. Sayre, *The Visual Text of William Carlos Williams* (1983); M. Perloff, *The Dance of the Intellect* (1985); W. Bohn, *The Aesthetics of Visual Poetry, 1914–1928* (1986); J. V. Brogan, *Part of the Climate: American Cubist Poetry* (1991); P. Nicholls, "From Fantasy to Structure: Two Moments of Literary Cubism," *Forum for Modern Language Studies* 28 (1992); J. Pap, "'Entre quatre murs': Reverdy, Cubism, and the Space of Still Life," *Word & Image* 12 (1996); S. Scobie, *Earthquakes and Explorations: Language and Painting from Cubism to Concrete Poetry* (1997); R. Havard, "Jorge Guillén, Picasso, and the Language of Cubism," *Anales de la literatura española contemporánea* 32 (1997).

J. V. BROGAN; B. TATE

**CUECA CHILENA.** A South Am. popular dance song, also called *chilenita*, *zamacueca*, and *zamacueca peruana*, which is an eight-line *seguidilla* in which the basic quatrain is separated from the *estribillo* (refrain) by the insertion of a line that is a repetition of the fourth line plus the word *sí* (yes).

■ F. Hanssen, "La seguidilla," *Anales de la Universidad de Santiago de Chile* 125 (1909).

D. C. CLARKE

**CULTURAL CRITICISM.** During its devel. from the 18th c. onward, cultural crit. in the West has been preoccupied with the social roles of the arts and intellectuals; the uses of education and literacy; the effects of population increase and economic transformations stemming from industrial capitalism; the functions of institutions, esp. the nation state and the media; the relative status and value of popular (low, mass) and canonical (high) culture; and the possibilities for social improvement and political change. Given such concerns, it is not surprising that cultural critics share interests and methods not only with certain anthropologists, communications and media specialists, journalists, historians, and sociologists, but with a wide array of literary critics, incl. nowadays Marxists, myth critics, philologists, semioticians, New Historicists, ethnic critics, feminists, postcolonial critics, and various independents and mavericks. The task of cultural crit., as shaped by contemp. cultural studies, is to analyze and assess the sociohistorical roots, distribution networks, and ethicopolitical impacts of communal artifacts, practices, and organizations. Its methodologies include textual exegesis, historical inquiry, and survey and interview techniques, as well as institutional, ideological, and ethical analyses. Poetry is subject to cultural crit.

One of the perennial preoccupations of cultural crit. is the definition and conceptualization of the term *culture*. In ordinary usage, the word displays a wide range of designations: it names intellectual and artistic practices and works, notably lit., music, visual arts, theater, philosophy, and crit.; it describes processes of intellectual, moral, and aesthetic devel.; it indicates the distinctive way of life of a people, period, or humanity; it signals refinement of *taste, judgment, and intellect; and it includes manners, *conventions, myths, and institutions. Thus, *culture* refers simultaneously to processes and products, to material and symbolic production, to specific and general human devel., to everyday social practices and elite arts, to ethics and aesthetics, to subcultures and civilization. Among cultural critics and theorists, the ambiguity of the word and the continuous contention surrounding the idea reveal less a failure to come to terms or to isolate a discrete object of inquiry than a recurring magnetic pull, a multifaceted quality of attraction, and a struggle, characteristic of both the concept and the enterprise of studying culture. Tylor's still influential definition succinctly suggests the richness of the term: *culture* is "that complex whole which includes knowledge, belief, art, morals, law, custom, and any other capabilities and habits acquired by man as a member of society."

Arnold's formulations on culture in *Culture and An-archy* mark a watershed in the hist. of Western cultural crit. Arnold sums up and transforms a trad. of thought extending from Jonathan Swift and Giambattista Vico through Edmund Burke and J. G. Herder to William Cobbett, S. T. Coleridge, and Thomas Carlyle. Culture is the pursuit of a best self and a general perfection motivated by passion for pure knowledge and for social and moral right action effected by reading, observing, and thinking about the voices of human experience in art, science, poetry, philosophy, hist., and religion. Culture leads people to see things as they are; to increase their sympathy and intelligence; to make right reason and the will of God prevail; to do away with social classes; to render everywhere current the best that has been thought and known in the world; to practice free and spontaneous, disinterested play of thought transcending stock notions and habits; and to attain complete, harmonious perfection. The enemies of culture include confusion, religious zeal, individualism, sectarianism, machinery, industrialism, and anarchy. For Arnold, culture engenders dissatisfaction with, and purgation of, the vulgar philistinism typical of industrial capitalist life. Promoted through education undertaken by the state (a collective apparatus embodying higher reason), culture serves as a principle of authority to counteract tendencies toward social disintegration. The agents of culture are a saving remnant of intellectuals who come from all classes, raise themselves above class spirit, work optimistically and nonviolently, and avoid as much as possible direct political action.

For the poet-critic Arnold and many other cultural critics, poetry is one among a number of arts and sciences that document sociohistorical conditions and, more important, that enlighten the mind and spirit. Poetry serves an ethicopolitical role in society, providing a high ground for personal devel. and social crit., which are linked to a broad project of social reform undertaken by the educational establishment and the state. In the Arnoldian trad., cultural crit. seeks to foster through the free play of consciousness a better social self and a better world. Thus, poetry is valued not primarily for its aesthetic refinement or for its insight into the artist's soul or for its power to entertain us or purge our emotions (as given in formalist, expressive, and affective theories of Western poetics, see AFFECT, FORMALISM), but rather for the efficacy of its agency in social action (the mimetic and didactic functions).

One impulse of cultural crit. is not to place lit. in a hierarchy of aesthetic forms but rather to situate all literary works within a network of other related cultural forms and practices. Yet another impulse is to focus on superior works, on the best that humankind has created, judging most popular and mass forms as degraded and inferior, particularly those produced in the era of mod. industrial capitalism. Arnold is usually taken as representative of the elitist strand of thought, which culminates in various complex ways during the early and mid-20th c. with such politically diverse groups of influential cultural critics as the *Frankfurt school, New Critics (see NEW CRITICISM), New York intellectuals, and *Scrutiny* circle. For these thinkers, lit. and culture constitute superior achievements of human excellence critical of the poor state of mod. civilization. In secularized Western societies, culture also frequently comes to serve displaced religious functions, advocating right action, humility, and harmony.

It is against the tendencies to construe culture as a body of superior works, a standard of excellence, or a repository of ruling-class values that Williams argues in *Culture and Society*, the leading contemp. study of the hist. of cultural crit. For Williams, a culture is "not only a body of intellectual and imaginative works; it is also and essentially a whole way of life." The skilled, intelligent, creative activities that constitute culture include, e.g., gardening, metalwork, carpentry, and active politics, as well as all forms of theater, music, lit., and art. Culture is and should be common not selective, democratic not dominative. Like traditional cultural forms, new modes of cultural practice such as photography, television, cinema, broadcasting, and advertising can be understood and evaluated only by reference to the lived experience of everyday life, to the whole way of existence of a people, incl. its habits, memories, and institutions. Significantly, the productions and processes of numerous class factions and subcultures make it evident that struggle and contradiction characterize culture. Such phenomena discredit static and nostalgic views of culture as a permanent harmonious entity available for an elite minority.

In a representative analysis of Ben Jonson's famous, long *country house poem "To Penshurst" (1616), written in praise of an aristocratic estate, Williams not only appreciates the rural setting and the hospitality figured by lavish meals but assesses what is missing in the sumptuous details: "The actual men and women who rear the animals and drive them to the house and kill them and prepare them for meat; who trap the pheasants and partridges and catch the fish; who plant and manure and prune and harvest the fruit trees: these are not present; their work is all done for them by the natural order." The poem omits the labor, not to mention the property relations, that stands behind the gracious country house. As elaborated in *The Country and the City*, Williams judges this superior aesthetic artifact ultimately a "mystification" when set in the larger context of postmedieval Eng. hist. running up through the 20th c. In his book, Williams both historicizes and demystifies five centuries of pastoral poetry, criticizing the combined ethics of consumption and the obliviousness to labor characteristic of developing capitalist culture and elite poetic trad.

From the 1970s into the 21st c., cultural crit. in the trad. of Williams was transformed into a new discipline—cultural studies—housed in the university. Meanwhile, the Arnoldian trad. continued most noticeably in the nonacademic learned media, particularly cultural reviews like *The New Criterion* (founded in New York in 1982). At this crossroads, cultural studies displayed a liberal left orientation, while cultural crit. exhibited conservative center-right values.

This split flared most dramatically during the culture wars of the 1980s and 1990s. A main point of contention concerned educational priorities assigned great works over popular culture (Shakespeare versus Bob Dylan). Another area of dispute involved the relative importance ascribed to aesthetic quality versus both the socially critical and the compensatory utopian dimensions of the arts. Many other areas of contention continue between left- and right-oriented critics of culture, incl. the roles as well as the relevance of social belonging versus individualism, secularism versus religion, class struggle versus harmony, welfare state versus laissez-faire capitalism, and socially engaged lit. versus art for art's sake.

Much of the poetry crit. and poetics of the late 20th and early 21st cs. reflects the distinctive preoccupations of contemp. cultural crit. and cultural studies locked in culture wars. What cultural critics of all orientations agree on, however, is their long-standing obligation to enter national public spheres in defense of education and literacy focused on the literary *canon (newly expanded for many) for purposes of pleasure, enlightenment, and ethicopolitical uplift.

*See* CULTURAL STUDIES AND POETRY.

■ M. Arnold, *Culture and Anarchy* (1869); E. B. Tylor, *Primitive Culture* (1871); F. R. Leavis, *Mass Civilization and Minority Culture* (1930); T. S. Eliot, *Notes towards the Definition of Culture* (1948); E. Wilson, *The Triple Thinkers*, rev. ed. (1948); A. L. Kroeber and C. Kluckhohn, *Culture* (1952); R. Williams, *Culture and Society: 1780–1950* (1958); T. W. Adorno, "Cultural Criticism and Society," *Prisms*, trans. S. Weber and S. Weber (1967); R. Williams, *The Country and the City* (1973); L. Johnson, *The Cultural Critics* (1979); R. Williams, "Culture," *Keywords*, 2d ed. (1983); *Classics in Cultural Criticism I*, ed. B.-P. Lange (1990); *Classics in Cultural Criticism II*, ed. H. Heuermann (1990); T. W. Adorno, "On Lyric Poetry and Society," *Notes to Literature*, ed. R. Tiedemann, trans. S. W. Nicholsen, v. 1 (1991); *Contemporaries in Cultural Criticism III*, ed. H. Heuermann and B.-P. Lange (1991); F. Mulhern, *Culture/Metaculture* (2000)—leading hist. of cultural crit. and cultural studies; *Counterpoints: Twenty Five Years of "The New Criterion" on Culture and the Arts*, ed. R. Kimball and H. Kramer (2007).

V. B. LEITCH

**CULTURAL STUDIES AND POETRY.** The discipline (or better, interdiscipline) known in the academy today as cultural studies emerged out of several foundational projects of the 1950s, notably Hoggart's *The Uses of Literacy* and Williams's *Culture and Society*, and no less out of a chain of intellectual antecedents such as the morally attuned Eng. literary critic F. R. Leavis, the It. political philosopher Antonio Gramsci, the Fr. Marxist philosopher Louis Althusser, and the Fr. sociologist Pierre Bourdieu, among many others. From this array of influences and models, cultural studies derives certain values that condition its approach to poetry and poetics. To begin with, it focuses on low, mass, and popular culture as opposed to works of high culture. Often emphasizing ideology critique over stylistic analysis or moral evaluation, it tends to study the social forces embedded in artifacts and institutions, sometimes with less concern for, say, artists' lives or aesthetic forms. Moreover, cultural studies often directs its analysis along axes of race, class, and/or gender in the service of multiculturalism. Practitioners of cultural studies renounce the role of the traditional intellectual as disinterested connoisseur and custodian of high culture in favor of the activism and commitment of the public intellectual and engaged field researcher. What usually preoccupies cultural studies is the hegemonic order variously characterized in recent times as postmod. consumer society, postindustrial free-market capitalism, and global empire. The discipline brings attention to resistances to the dominant order at all levels, with a special interest in social margins, micropolitical countercurrents, and creative reappropriations. When it turns to poetry, then, cultural studies often investigates figures, events, and phenomena apart from the main currents as well as socially critical forms and approaches (see MICROPOETRIES).

Gramsci's concept of hegemony has made a decisive contribution to contemp. cultural studies and thus to how cultural studies addresses poetry and poetics. Building on the prior Marxist view that culture is a politicized, subordinating force used by ruling elites to portray their ideas and values as universal, Gramsci distinguishes between coercive domination and negotiated leadership. The success of a controlling group's ideology—which is relative, temporary, and challengeable—depends not only or even primarily on repressive political control through legal, administrative, military, and educational apparatuses, but on freely given civil consensus molded through the family, church, workplace, union, private school, media, and arts—i.e., through civil society. The leadership of the dominant group needs continual renewal and maintenance in order for its values and interests to shape consciousness and to constitute common sense. In this context, revolution requires much more than seizing the economic means of production or securing the various arms of government; it entails changing the hearts and minds of contending groups and cementing them into a unity. In contrast to Arnold's landmark view of culture (see CULTURAL CRITICISM), Gramsci's account shows social harmony, perfection, and order to be strictly relative (if not fictitious); highlights group antagonism and social contradiction; represents civil society as part of the state; stresses everyday activities and negotiations; and presents the state not as a stable embodiment of higher reason but as an agency of dominant-group leadership constantly bargaining with other groups. Where Arnold portrays intellectuals as an elite clerisy above class spirit and direct political action, Gramsci depicts them as a large and active, heterogeneous ensemble of teachers, journalists, clergy, doctors, lawyers, military officers, technicians, managers, policy makers, and writers, who engage in a vast number of organizational functions linking strata of culture into a consensual, historical bloc. So, while poets may solidify, question, or attack the hegemonic order, they cannot elude it.

Among the most cited pioneering works of U.S. cultural studies is Said's critical hist., *Orientalism*. This work fuses, in a now typical blend, critical protocols developed by the social theory of Gramsci, the cultural theories of Arnold and Williams, and the Fr. philosopher Michel Foucault's historiography of discourse. From his postcolonial perspective, the Palestinian-Am. Said construes the long hist. of Franco-Brit.-Am. writing on the Near Eastern Orient as a massive and systematic, disciplinary discourse depicting, structuring, and ruling over the Orient in a consistently racist, sexist, and imperialist manner. Texts scrutinized by Said, a professor of lit., range from scholarly books, political tracts, and journalistic reports to travel narratives, religious and philological studies, and literary works, poetry included. In passing, he cites more than three dozen Eur. poets ranging from Homer and Aeschylus to W. B. Yeats and Paul Valéry, most of whom come in for crit. Among institutions supporting Orientalism are presses, foundations, businesses (esp. oil companies), missions, military and foreign services, intelligence communities, media, and universities. The hegemonic consensus about the East produced and continually reproduced by mod. Orientalism—the institutionalized Western ideological "science" of the Orient—bears little relation to actual human life. On this point Said observes, "Orientalism failed to identify with human experience, failed also to see it as human experience." Another key lesson he draws is that "study, understanding, knowledge, evaluation, masked as blandishments to 'harmony,' are instruments of conquest." Like many scholars of cultural studies, Said, following Foucault, regards knowledge as joined indissolubly to interest and power, all enabled and constrained by interlocking institutions. This view contradicts Arnold's celebrated ideas concerning the attainability of pure knowledge, disinterested thought, harmonious perfection, and the benign rational state. Said ties the knowledge–interest–power nexus to aggressive nation states (where mod. colonial conquest originates), showing the limitations of Arnold's optimistic view of the state. Nevertheless, the Arnoldian legacy of cultural crit. survives in Said's traditional humanistic commitments to see things as they are, to respect actual human experience, to advocate social and moral right, to increase understanding and sympathy, and to struggle against religion, esp. in its most zealous forms.

Cultural studies in the Anglo-Am. academy, like other postmod. interdisciplines such as women's studies and ethnic studies, ranges widely across materials and fields. It concerns itself notably with contemp. popular culture and media, as well as with the institutions of civil and political society. While cultural studies-oriented literary critics typically examine fiction—e.g., working-class novels, romances targeted at women, and science fiction—they turn to poetry, by comparison, more rarely. This lack of attention is esp. true of the Brit. cultural studies pioneered during the 1970s and 80s at the famous University of Birmingham Centre for Contemporary Cultural Studies (CCCS), founded by Hoggart. An interest in poetry, on the other hand, is found somewhat more often in U.S. cultural studies during the 1980s and thereafter.

A primary project of poetry scholars dedicated to cultural studies involves expanding the canon of poetic texts to include more low genres and marginal writers frequently selected from the ranks of ethnic, immigrant, and women poets. This work has led to new anthols., hists., and critical studies of poetry, as in Nelson's *Repression and Recovery* and his *Anthology of Modern American Poetry*. In most such work, the emphasis falls on the documentary, communal, and moral dynamics, as well as the creativity and originality of poets and poetries. This being the case, traditional belletrism is not so much jettisoned as it is repositioned amid social hists., countercultural energies, and ethicopolitical resistances.

In the hands of cultural studies, and particularly in the grip of affiliated contemporaneous postcolonial theory, the Eurocentric core of national lits. has more or less opened to regional, hemispheric, and global transnational formations such as Black Atlantic, Pacific Rim, and inter-Am. poetries. Nevertheless, the devel. of the field of cultural studies, like most academic fields, retains distinctive national frameworks. Specialists of anglophone cultural studies, for instance, distinguish sharply between Australian, Brit., Canadian, and U.S. cultural studies.

From the outset in the 1980s, U.S. cultural studies has criticized contemp. mainstream official verse culture while both defending vanguardist experimental poetry and consecrating minority and popular poetries. (Cultural studies regularly pluralizes formerly unified concepts such as lit. and poetry in line with the promotion of "difference" characteristic of postmod. theory.) For instance, contemp. official verse culture is sometimes represented by the "workshop poem" associated with university programs in creative writing. This so-called MFA poem consists of 20–40 prosaic free-verse lines cast in a confessional, sometimes ironic mode, which is appreciated by magazine editors and classroom teachers for its *concision, approachability, *sincerity, and epiphanic wisdom (see CONFESSIONAL POETRY). In addition to being criticized as a hegemonic genre, a formula, and a commodity, the workshop poem is judged severely by some cultural studies-oriented critics for furthering a notion of the self that is unreflectively suited to consumer society. It may be said to represent such values as possessive individualism, narcissism, and sentimental romantic solitude. Against the cult of the personal poetic voice, cultural studies in the U.S. has sometimes advocated *Language poetry, produced out of a movement of the 1970s and after opposed to the privatized expressive self and the well-made journalistic poetry of bourgeois confessionalism and subjective realism.

Among the opposing poetries of most interest to cultural studies are feminist, ethnic, and diasporic works, as well as experimental ones. But also of interest are popular poetries such as rap or *hip-hop, *poetry slam, spoken-word, and *blues. It is worth noting that these latter forms—oral, nonprint, improvisational, and *performance-based—appeal to nonacademic and antiestablishment audiences in large numbers. They employ conventional forms, notably stanzas, rhymes, and unmistakably rhythmic lines. The speakers of popular poetries often represent the direct vernacular voice of a community rather than the allusive learned script of the solitary elite artist. The venues for these works include bars, bookstores, and festivals rather than classrooms and libraries. Audiences consist of local scenes and subcultures aggregated in national and international networks.

Sometimes remarked by cultural studies, there are noteworthy instances of established poets in the U.S. today, both academic and independent, going beyond the university classroom and the auditorium. Forsaking the workshop poem and engaging with the public, this is unaffiliated grassroots cultural studies. To take the U.S. case again, there is the thriving Poetry in the Schools Program started in the 1970s; the hugely successful Favorite Poem Project initiated in 1997 by the academic and poet laureate Robert Pinsky; and the various high-profile public campaigns undertaken by the conservative poet-critic Dana Gioia since the early 1990s, but esp. during the early 21st c. in his role as chairman of the National Endowment for the Arts. In his provocative essays, in particular, Gioia champions the rise of popular poetry and the new bohemia surrounding it, noting its return to musicality and traditional forms and registering its move beyond obscure vanguardism and the enervated university with its solipsistic guild of Creative Writing.

Scholars of cultural studies have a major complaint against still-dominant accounts and views of poetry as self-expression. According to cultural studies, poetry is discourse. This key proposition underlines the fact that poetry is communal, dialogic, and intertextual. Further, it is embodied and agonistic. Cultural studies stands against the structuralist and poststructuralist idea of lang. as a play of floating signifiers only loosely linked to concepts and things. What is at issue here is the lyric "I" often portrayed as isolated, original, disembodied—a persistent romantic icon and mystification. To the contrary, cultural studies insists on the social foundations of discourse and subjectivity. Neither poetic lang. nor poets are beyond or outside the social order. Theodor W. Adorno, the Ger. cultural critic who is another formative influence on the interdiscipline, put it this way in "On Lyric Poetry and Society" (1957): "the lyric work is always the subjective expression of a social antagonism." As a consequence, the iconic poet of mod. avant-gardism, formerly seen as an isolated generic renegade, is recast as a social figure whose resistance to society is culturally symptomatic despite whatever singular features any one instance might exhibit.

During more recent decades under the sign of neo-liberalism, the postmod. poet has been pictured as a member of the so-called creative class, a historically new social role fashioned esp. by chambers of commerce and city planners. Cultural studies registers this transformation with dismay but not surprise. Social architects today seek to redesign urban downtowns complete with lofts, art galleries, coffee shops, and bookstores fit for bourgeois bohemians (engineers, doctors, and professionals with money). Holders of fine-arts degrees and professors of creative writing belong to the creative class, academic poets included. (Between 2000 and 2009, U.S. colleges and universities awarded more than 40,000 university degrees in creative writing.) The main point here is not simply that the social roles of poets and poetry change through hist. but that today the poet belongs to and is often co-opted by higher education, entertainment, and business interests. This turn of events is unusual within the long historical sequence of poetry's patrons from city-states, churches, monarchies, and aristocracies to book-reading publics, universities, and media conglomerates (see PATRONAGE). Not surprisingly, there is among cultural-studies scholars some nostalgia for earlier times and much glumness about poetry's current incorporation. The poet as social outsider and independent critic survives as an ideal, as in Damon's *The Dark End of the Street*. In this context, popular and minority poetries serve compensatory roles: they keep alive for large audiences not only the socially critical and outsider missions of poetry but also its appeals to emotion, musicality, representation, and ethical judgment.

Cultural studies is often criticized for a set of perceived shortcomings that bear on its treatment of poetry. Despite the vitality of cultural studies as an approach to international lits. and societies (e.g., those of Latin America), the field is too often monolingual, overlooking the multilingual dimensions of national as well as transnational lits. And despite the visibility of scholarly networks of medievalists and early modernists who consider themselves practitioners of cultural studies, too much work in this interdiscipline is presentist, displaying little serious scholarly interest in premod. cultures. Above all, it is sometimes argued that the antielitism and expansion of literary canons characteristic of cultural studies avoid the question of quality. When all is said and done, what are the criteria for great works of lit.? The scholar of cultural studies is said to suffer bad conscience for being both the supposedly independent critic and the hired hand of culture, which is to say he or she is a certified component of the culture industries; such a critic and the field at large operate primarily and profitably inside university and publishing worlds. Each of these charges is partly true and yet easily refuted by reference to the versatility, range, and ambition of contemp. cultural studies. On balance, cultural studies has proven to be a dynamic force in expanding poetic canons and critical protocols, as well as accrediting a wide array of new audiences and poetries.

See CANON, CULTURAL CRITICISM.

■ M. Arnold, *Culture and Anarchy* (1869); R. Hoggart, *The Uses of Literacy* (1957); R. Williams, *Culture and Society: 1780–1950* (1958); A. Gramsci, *Selections from the Prison Notebooks*, ed. and trans. Q. Hoare and G. N. Smith (1971); M. Foucault, *Discipline and Punish*, trans. A. Sheridan (1977); E. Said, *Orientalism* (1978); Centre for Contemporary Cultural Studies, *Culture, Media, Language* (1980); S. Hall, "Cultural Studies: Two Paradigms," *Culture, Ideology, and Social Process*, ed. T. Bennett et al. (1981); R. Johnson, "What is Cultural Studies Anyway?" *Social Text* 16 (1986–87)—landmark conspectus on CCCS methodology; *Marxism and the Interpretation of Culture*, ed. C. Nelson and L. Grossberg (1988); W. Kalaidjian, *Languages of Liberation: The Social Text in Contemporary American Poetry* (1989); C. Nelson, *Repression and Recovery: Modern American Poetry and the Politics of Cultural Memory, 1910–1945* (1989); D. Gioia, *Can Poetry Matter?* (1992); M. Damon, *The Dark End of the Street: Margins in American Vanguard Poetry* (1993); A. A. Berger, *Cultural Criticism* (1995); C. Beach, *Poetic Culture* (1999); *Anthology of Modern American Poetry*, ed. C. Nelson (2000); R. Wilson, *Reimagining the American Pacific* (2000); J. Harrington, *Poetry and the Public* (2002); G. Turner, *British Cultural Studies*, 3d ed. (2002); D. Gioia, *Disappearing Ink: Poetry at the End of Print Culture* (2004); A. Gilbert, *Another Future: Poetry and Art in a Postmodern Twilight* (2006); V. B. Leitch, "Late Contemporary U.S. Poetry," *Living with Theory* (2008); *Poetry and Cultural Studies: A Reader*, ed. M. Damon and I. Livingston (2009); J. Read, *Modern Poetics and Hemispheric American Cultural Studies* (2009); Favorite Poem Project, http://www.favoritepoem.org.

V. B. LEITCH

**CURTAL SONNET.** In the preface to his *Poems*, G. M. Hopkins coins the name "curtal-sonnet" for "Pied Beauty" and "Peace," poems "constructed in proportions resembling those of the sonnet proper, namely 6 + 4 instead of 8 + 6, with however a half-line tailpiece." Feeney calls Hopkins's concern with the mathematical proportions of these sonnets "playful," noting that the word *curtal* not only means curtailed, or shortened, but once referred to animals with their tails cut short. The curtal sonnet is, as Hirsch and Boland point out, "three-fourths of a Petrarchan sonnet shrunk proportionately" and may be contrasted with the expanded *caudate sonnet. Lawler takes issue with Fussell and others who criticized the curtal sonnet for failing to perform "the fundamental Petrarchan action . . . of complication and resolution." Lawler claims that the curtal sonnet allowed Hopkins to prize harmony and praise over the argument of the Petrarchan volta, moving richly by paradoxes "out of unity, through multiplicity, and then back to unity." Ever the innovator, Hopkins inspired contemp. versions of the curtal sonnet (Chad Davidson, Leon Stokesbury, Richard Foerster) and may have led the way for other "contracted" sonnet experiments—the "truly emaciated sonnet" (Anthony Hecht on Arthur Rimbaud's "Drunk Driver"), the short-line sonnets of Elizabeth Bishop, the "curtal double sonnets" of John Poch, the one-syllable-line sonnet of Brad Leithauser, and the "minimalist sonnet" and "extended minimalist sonnet" of Mona Van Duyn.

*See* CAUDA.

■ G. M. Hopkins, "Preface," *Poems* (1876–89); P. Fussell, *Poetic Meter and Poetic Form* (1979); J. Lawler, *Hopkins Re-Constructed* (1998); *The Penguin Book of the Sonnet*, ed. P. Levin (2001); J. Feeney, *The Playfulness of Gerard Manley Hopkins* (2008); *The Making of a Sonnet*, ed. E. Hirsch and E. Boland (2008); J. Poch, "Sonnets, Chad Davidson and Fly Fishing," *32Poems.com* (2008).

L. R. SPAAR

**CYBERTEXT.** A term used by theorists to describe the functioning of dynamic texts in a variety of media. Merging the prefix *cyber-* from Wiener's *cybernetics*, or science of communication and control, with the term *\*text* from poststructuralist literary theory, it identifies a distinctive structure for the production and consumption of verbal meaning.

The defining feature of a cybertext is not an aesthetic, a set of themes, a provenance, or a medium but a particular computational organization. Cybertexts operate through a series of feedback loops that link texts and their users in mutually constitutive exchanges of information. Like all circuits, cybertextual feedback loops consist of a relay of inputs and outputs in which a user's action—a throw of coins in the *I Ching*, a click on a hypertextual link, a swipe of the mouse in an electronic game—reconfigures available interpretive options by altering the material organization of the text.

Cybertexts can be constructed in print, on a computer, or by hand. In addition to printed books (Julio Cortázar's novel *Rayuela* [*Hopscotch*]), electronic hypertexts (Shelley Jackson's *Patchwork Girl*), and digital poems (John Cayley's *riverIsland*), the form could also be said to include ancient divination systems (*I Ching*), early computer programs (Joseph Weizenbaum's *Eliza*), text-based digital games (*Myst*), multiuser domains (MUDs), and real-time virtual worlds (*Second Life*).

The simplest example of a literary cybertext is the digital form known as *hypertext*, anticipated by the post–World War II computer engineers Vannevar Bush and Ted Nelson; elaborated in fiction composed between 1985 and 1995 by writers such as Jackson, Michael Joyce, and Stuart Moulthrop; and disseminated on diskettes by Eastgate Systems. In all genres, hypertext contains three distinct components: links, chunked texts or lexia, and multiple reading paths. By clicking on a succession of links, a user navigates through related sections of a text or between related parts of different texts in the same retrieval system. Each click materially alters the text by closing one set of options and opening another.

In introducing the term *cybertext*, Aarseth paired it with a second coinage to emphasize the "nontrivial" effort this form demands from its users. Like other hermeneutic structures (see HERMENEUTICS), cyber-

texts are *interactive* in the general sense that text and interpreter act on or influence each other; but the effort involved to navigate a cybertext, play a textual game, or interact in a MUD is, in Aarseth's terminology, *ergodic*. From the Gr. *ergon* + *hodos*, or "work" and "path," this term describes the combined actions of individuals and mechanisms that produce sequences of events in computational interactions.

The term emerged with the devel. of second-generation electronic lit. composed after 1995 for presentation on the World Wide Web. Whereas first-generation electronic lit., composed by writers who began to experiment with computers in the late 1950s, remained predominantly text-based, second-generation electronic lit. combines text with graphics, sound, animation, video, and other multimedia components. A more capacious term than *hypertext*, *cybertext* offers a critique of two opposed critical responses to early hypertext: a tendency, on the one hand, to apply poststructuralist literary terms to electronic texts without taking account of the shift in the material apparatus, and a tendency, on the other hand, to treat digital texts as radically different from their mechanical and print precursors. For Aarseth, Hayles, and other digital theorists, cybertexts are textual engines that operate outside conventional author-text-message paradigms and must be understood as computational engines.

As complex systems that evolve unpredictably from an initial set of simple elements, cybertexts of all sorts display emergent or nonlinear behavior that develops in tandem with a user's actions. As a textual category, this term opens the literary canon both to earlier avant-garde projects such as Robert Grenier's *Sentences*, a box containing 500 5-x-8 cards with typewritten phrases a user can lay out in multiple configurations, and to dynamic interactive compositions engineered for the wireless reading devices and mobile platforms of the future.

*See* COMPUTATIONAL POETRY, ELECTRONIC POETRY.

■ N. Wiener, *Cybernetics: Or Control and Communication in the Animal and the Machine* (1948); E. J. Aarseth, *Cybertext: Perspectives on Ergodic Literature* (1997); N. Montfort, "Cybertext Killed the Hypertext Star," *electronic book review* (2000), http://www.electronicbookreview.com/thread/electropoetics/cyberdebates; N. K. Hayles, *Writing Machines* (2002); C. T. Funkhouser, *Prehistoric Digital Poetry* (2007).

A. MORRIS

**CYNGHANEDD.** In \*Welsh poetry, an elaborate system of sound correspondences involving accentuation, \*alliteration, and \*internal rhyme occurring within a single line of verse. G. M. Hopkins described the various types of cynghanedd as "chimes" and admitted that they were a main influence on his own formal experiments. Cynghanedd was well developed in Welsh by the 14th c., although not finally codified until the Caerwys \*Eisteddfod of 1523. Cynghanedd was, and still is, a main feature of Welsh "strict-meter" poetry, but it has often been practiced, with varying degrees of strictness, in the free meters as well and in mod. times even in \*vers libre. There are four basic types of cynghanedd (all examples below are taken from Dafydd ap Gwilym's 14th c. poems *Y Seren* [*YS*, The Star] and *Yr Wylan* [*YW*, The Seagull]):

(1) *C. lusg* (dragging cynghanedd) is the simplest kind of cynghanedd and only occurs in lines with a feminine ending. The sixth syllable of the line is stressed and rhymes with the final syllable of the first stressed word in the line: "mi a g*á*f | heb war*á*fun" (*YS* 15). In the *cywydd* meter, *c. lusg* may only be used in the first line of a rhymed *couplet. *C. lusg* resembles the pattern of internal rhyme found in middle and early mod. *Breton poetry, a case of parallel devel. that is likely related to the penultimate word stress that predominates in Welsh and most dialects of Breton.

(2) In *c. groes* (cross cynghanedd), the line of verse is divided into two parts, and the consonants in the first part of the line are repeated in the same order in the second part, as in "*LL*á*T*ai *DR*úd | i'w *LL*é*T*y *DR*áw" (*YS* 6). Except when the cynghanedd is "uneven" (see below), the consonants at the end of each half line (like the final *d* in *drud*) do not usually participate in the cynghanedd. In a more elaborate variant called *c. groes o gyswllt* (connected *c. groes*), however, one or more consonants at the end of the first half of the line also count as part of the second half line for purposes of repetition, as in "*N*a *TH*a*L*ié*S*i*N* | ei *TH*L*ý*Sach" (*YW* 24), where the *n* of "Taliesin" answers the initial *N* of the line.

(3) *C. draws* (oblique cynghanedd) is similar to *c. groes*; but in this case, the line is divided into three parts, and the consonants of the first part are repeated in the third part of the line: "o*CH* w*ŷR* | [erioed ni] *CH*a*R*awdd" (*YW* 22). Here, the words *erioed ni* do not participate in the cynghanedd.

(4) *C. sain* (sound cynghanedd) combines the internal rhyme of *c. lusg* with the consonantal repetition of *c. groes* and *c. draws*. Here, the line is divided into three parts. The first two parts of the line rhyme, while one or more consonants from the second part are repeated in the same order in the third part: "ei charu'r *wyf* | gwbl *N*wyf | *N*awdd" (*YW* 21).

In addition to this fourfold division, *c. groes*, *c. draws*, and *c. sain* may be further categorized according to whether the two sections with repeated consonants end with stressed vowels (*c. gytbwys acennog*, "even stressed cynghanedd"), unstressed vowels (*c. gytbwys ddiacen*, "even unstressed cynghanedd"), or one of each (normally *c. anghytbwys ddisgynedig*, "uneven descending cynghanedd," where the first half line ends with a stressed vowel and the second half line with an unstressed vowel; the opposite pattern is called *c. anghytbwys ddyrchafedig*, "uneven rising cynghanedd," but is rare except in *c. sain*).

The rules of cynghanedd stated above are only a broad outline, and there are many exceptions and special cases, some of which relate to the phonology of the Welsh lang. Much of the skill and delight of cynghanedd poetry lies in the variation of types in successive lines and in the contrasting of vowel sounds alongside the repetition of consonants. It is an art form capable of a very rich, subtle, melodious, and highly wrought effect that has been extensively exploited by Welsh poets.

*See* CELTIC PROSODY.

■ Morris-Jones; Parry, *History*, chap. 5 (app.); G. Williams, *Introduction to Welsh Poetry* (1953), app. A; E. I. Rowlands, "Introduction" to *Poems of the Cywyddwyr* (1976); A. Lloyd and D. Evans in *Poetry Wales* 14 (1978); R. Bromwich, *Aspects of the Poetry of Dafydd ap Gwilym* (1986); *Welsh Verse*, ed. T. Conran, 2nd ed. (1986)—long intro. and appendix on meter; E. Rowlands, "Cynghanedd, Metre, Prosody," in Jarman and Hughes, vol. 2, rev. D. Johnston (1997); *The New Companion to the Literature of Wales*, ed. M. Stephens (1998); Myrddin ap Dafydd, *Clywed Cynghanedd* (2003); A. Llwyd, *Anghenion y Gynghanedd* (2007).

D. M. LLOYD; T.V.F. BROGAN; B. BRUCH

**CYWYDD** (pl. *cywyddau*). Along with *awdl* and *englyn*, one of the three classes of the 24 strict meters in *Welsh poetry. There are four varieties of cywydd, but normally the term is used to refer only to the *c. deuair hirion* popularized by Dafydd ap Gwilym in the 14th c. This form of cywydd comprises a variable number of heptasyllabic lines grouped in rhyming *couplets. One line of each couplet ends with a stressed syllable and the other with an unstressed syllable, producing asymmetric rhyme pairs of the form *dáncing* : *kíng*, similar to the *rinn agus airdrinn* of the Ir. *deibhidhe* meter. The earliest known examples of the cywydd are without *cynghanedd*. Dafydd, however, embellished most of his lines with cynghanedd, and in the 15th c., it became obligatory to include cynghanedd in every line. Another common ornament in cywyddau is *cymeriad*, whereby two or more adjacent lines are linked by the repetition of a letter, sequence of consonants, word, or phrase at the beginning of each line. The 14th to the early 16th cs. are known as the Cywydd Period in Welsh poetry because cywydd became the staple Welsh meter during this time. It was revived in the 18th c. by Goronwy Owen and Ieuan Fardd and is still popular today.

*See* CELTIC PROSODY.

■ Morris-Jones; T. Parry in *Transactions of the Honourable Society of Cymmrodorion* (1939), 203–31; and Parry, chap. 6; E. Rowlands in *Ysgrifau Beirniadol* 2 (1966); R. Bromwich, *Aspects of the Poetry of Dafydd ap Gwilym* (1986); *Welsh Verse*, ed. T. Conran, 2d. ed. (1986)—long intro. and appendix on meters; Jarman and Hughes, vol. 2, rev. D. Johnston (1997); *The New Companion to the Literature of Wales*, ed. M. Stephens (1998).

D. M. LLOYD; T.V.F. BROGAN; B. BRUCH

**CZECH POETRY.** The first poems to appear in the Czech lands were hymns in Old Church Slavonic that date to the 9th c. The Lat. *Legenda Christiani* (Legend of a Christian), about the lives of St. Ludmila and her grandson Václav (Wenceslaus), is one of the first great poetic compositions to emerge. By the 11th c., religious poetry in Lat. had taken root, while poetry in the vernacular remained scarce.

Widely acknowledged as the first work in the vernacular, the hymn "Hospodine pomiluj ny" (Lord, Have Mercy on Us), ca. 10 or 11th c., echoes the Kyrie Eleison and impresses with its lyricism and melodic sophistication. The Czech hymn "Svatý Václave, vévodo České země" (Saint Wenceslas, Duke of the Bohemian Land), ca. 12th c., is also noteworthy. These hymns derive from 14th-c. mss. The 13th-c. prayer codex of Kunhuta, abbess of the St. George convent in Prague, contains the powerful poem known as the Ostrov Hymn, "Slovo do světa stvořenie" (The Word before the World's Creation) and the hymn "Vítaj kráľu všemohúcí" (Welcome King Omnipotent).

In the early 13th c., the Přemyslid rulers extended their domain and encountered Germanic cultural and poetic trads. The contact resulted in the courtly poetry of the *Minnesang, which dominated Czech poetry in the late 13th c. Among long poems outstanding is the powerful Alexandreis or the Alexandriad (anonymous), composed ca. 1300 and based loosely on Gualtier de Châtillon's Lat. Alexandriad, though it is highly original in its treatment of the exploits and character of the warrior. Another anonymous long poem, Dalimilova kronika (the Dalimil Chronicle, early 14th c.) is marked by its strongly nationalistic bent. The early 14th c. sees Czech verse legends of early Christian figures such as Judas and Pontius Pilate. These were later followed by the brilliant verse legends of St. Procopius and of St. Catherine. The Legend of St. Catherine is outstanding for its use of the erotic lang. of *courtly love poetry and its vivid portrayal of Catherine's passion during her martyrdom.

By the 14th and 15th cs.—the heyday of Czech poetry—the courtly love poetry of the Western Eur. trad. exerts a strong influence. The name of Master Záviš stands out for the high love lyric, filled with the feudal ethos and the sense of impossible love. The almost 9,000-verse Czech version of the story of Tristan and Isolde (Tristan a Izolde), ca. 14th c., is based on the Ger. recension. Satirical poems about university life also emerge, such as "Svár vody s vínem" (The Dispute of Water and Wine), the exceptional "Podkoní a žák" (The Groom and the Scholar), and Czech-Lat. *macaronic verses. Satires not in the "university vein" included the ca. mid-14th c. works "Satiry o řemeslnících a konšelích" (Satires on Tradesmen and Aldermen) and "Desatero kázanie božie" (The Ten Divine Commandments).

The 15th-c. Hussite revolution marked a drastic change in forms and styles. The years of Hussitism saw the rise of poems of moral edification and poetic pamphleteering. Allegorical verse was also popular, the best example being the Hussite dialogue "Hádání Prahy s Kutnou Horou" (Quarrel of Prague with Kutná Hora). Here Kutná Hora is a hag defending Catholicism, while Prague, a beautiful woman, represents the Hussite cause. The Catholics countered with the infamous "Píseň o Viklefici" (Song of the Wycliffite Woman). For the first time, Czech religious songs replaced the Lat. liturgy.

With the election of the Hussite king Jiří z Poděbrad (1420–71), humanism, influenced by It. culture,

emerged as a potent force. Under the influence of Giovanni Boccaccio and others, Jiří's son Hynek z Poděbrad (ca. 1450–92) wrote erotic poems incl. "Májový sen" (May Dream, ca. 1490). Outstanding examples of Lat. verse by Czech Catholics include the Ad sanctum Venceslaum satira (Complaint to St. Wenceslaus, 1489) by the nobleman Bohuslav Hasištejnský z Lobkovic (ca. 1461–1510), the epicurean verses of Šimon Fagellus Villaticus (pseud. of Šimon Bouček, ca. 1473–1549), and the works of Jan Hodějovský z Hodějova (d. 1566). The most important piece to emerge from this circle is the inspired Lat. version of the Song of Songs, composed by David Crinitus z Hlaváčova (1531–86).

The defeat of the Czech Protestants after the Battle of White Mountain (1620, the culmination of the Thirty Years' War) had a decisive and detrimental effect on a literary level. The Catholic victory meant that Lat. verse returned to the fore; education and administration were conducted in Lat. The Czech literary lang. survived among determined émigrés fleeing Catholic Hapsburg rule. Most famously Jan Amos Komenský (or Comenius, 1592–1670) staunchly tried to keep literary Czech intact. From his exile in Amsterdam, Komenský had an agenda for Czech poetry: it should be unrhymed and based on quantitative—i.e., cl.—metrics. His Czech versions of the Psalms and the Song of Songs demonstrate this system's strengths. In Czech lands, Catholic poetry in Lat. enjoyed a phenomenal resurgence, esp. through the work of Bohuslav Balbín (1621–88).

Religious poetry was key during the *baroque period. Brilliant poetry was written by Catholic poets such as Adam Michna z Otradovic (1600–76), composer of several collections of religious songs, and Bedřich Bridel (also known as Fridrich Bridelius, 1619–80), a Jesuit missionary and highly philosophical poet, author of the famed "Co Bůh? Člověk" (What is God? Man? 1658). Of note too is the Jesuit poet Felix Kadlinský (1613–75), who wrote a version of Friedrich von Spee's "Trutz-Nachtigal oder geistliches poetisch Lustwäldlein" (1649) on the love of Christ and of nature: courtly love poetry is reconceived as the soul longs for Christ as her groom. Catholic hymnbooks were compiled to offset the Protestant hymnbooks that had previously dominated: Václav Holan Rovenský's (1644–1718) Capella regia musicalia (1693) is a fine example. Secular poetry of the baroque is usually considered weak, though the work of Václav Jan Rosa (ca. 1620–89) gives examples of well-formed love lyrics. Outstanding among the period's satirical poems is Václav František Kocmánek's (1607–79) "Lamentatio Rusticana" (Lament of the Countrymen, 1644).

By the mid-18th c., religious prose had risen to dominance, though Catholic spiritual verse proved to be a stable force in lyrical poetry. Other verses on topics from sheep farming to gingerbread making also emerged during this time, along with folk songs and popular melodies. These last would exert a great influence over Czech poets of the "Revival" period.

The Národní obrození or Czech National Revival dates to the 1770s and 1780s. At the end of the 18th c., the Czech lands underwent dramatic changes, incl. the introduction of a new religious tolerance and the end of the feudal system under Hapsburg ruler Josef II. The ed. of the verse anthol. *Básně v řeči vázané* (Poems in Metrical Verse, 1785, some of which he composed himself), Václav Thám (1765–1816) is widely considered the father of mod. Czech poetry. The collection included imitations of *anacreontic verse alongside adaptations of Czech baroque poetry. The *ode and the *mock heroic/epic came to prominence, along with a shift, under the influence of Josef Dobrovský (1753–1829), to accentual meters. Antonín Jaroslav Puchmayer (1769–1820) also set out to develop a specifically Czech poetic style at this crucial juncture. Among his anthols. are the five-volume *Sebrání básní a zpěvů* (Collection of Poems and Songs, 1795), and *Nové básně* (New Poems, 1798). His own work includes animal fables (another newly popular genre), "Óda na Jana Žižku z Trocnova (Ode to Jan Žižka, 1802), and "Na jazyk český" (Ode to the Czech Language, 1816). Another giant of the revival, Josef Jungmann (1773–1847) did not write much verse but contributed innovations in *sonnet form and a narrative poem. In 1818, Pavel Josef Šafařík (1795–1861) and František Palacký (1798–1876) wrote the groundbreaking *Počátkové českého básnictví obzvláště prozódie* (Elements of Czech Versification, especially Prosody), which once again promoted cl. (quantitative) meters over accentual ones.

The Slovak poet Jan Kollár (1793–1852), who wrote in Czech, composed the best of the early romantic works, "Slávy dcera" (Daughter of Slavia) in 1824; in this *sonnet sequence, the love of the poetic "I" for a maiden becomes an *allegory for his bond with his native land. Another romantic poet followed James Macpherson's lead in creating an ancient pedigree for his native trad. Václav Hanka (1791–1861) forged two mss. written in quasi-med. Czech: the *Rukopis královédvorský* (Dvůr Králové Ms., 1817) and the *Rukopis zelenohorský* (Zelená Hora Ms., 1817), great poetic works in their own right.

The greatest of the Czech romantics, Karel Hynek Mácha (1810–36), gained notoriety for the scandalous publication of his seminal work *Máj* (May, 1836). Mácha revolutionized *prosody in Czech with this narrative poem by using iambs, a form to which Czech is particularly unsuited. The poem describes the love of a bandit, Vilém, for Jarmila, a young woman who has been seduced by his father. Karel Havlíček Borovský (1821–56) is remembered for his acerbic wit and the satirical poem "Křest sv. Vladimíra" (The Christening of St. Vladimir, 1876), which bucks all regnant institutions and ideologies.

A new generation of Czech writers came to prominence in 1848. Deeply influenced by Mácha, they gathered around the jour. they named *Máj* in his honor. These poets included Jan Neruda (1834–91), the leading member of this group (whose name was later taken as a pseud. by Pablo Neruda); Vítězslav Hálek (1835–74); and Karolina Světlá (1830–99). Another important poet, Karel Jaromír Erben (1811–70), reached his apogee in the balladic collection *Kytice z*

*pověstí národních* (Bouquet of National Legends, 1853).

In the late 19th c., writers split into two factions. The poets who congregated around the jour. *Lumír*, such as Jaroslav Vrchlický (1853–1912), espoused cosmopolitanism in Czech letters, while those who wrote for the jour. *Ruch* were known as the national poets; the dominant figure was Svatopulk Čech (1846–1908). These writers were intent on preserving specifically Czech, or Slavophile, trads.

By the end of the century, the work of poets Otokar Březina and Petr Bezruč marked a turn to *symbolism. Březina's (1868–1929) use of free rhythms influenced poetry in the 20th c. and beyond. The Silesian poet Bezruč (1867–1958) created a mod. prophetic *persona in his *Slezské písně* (Silesian Songs, 1909) and fashioned poems about the oppression of Czechs under Ger., Polish, and native aristocratic powers. *Realism was represented by the poet Josef Svatopluk Machar (1864–1942), who exposed social injustice in his poetry, e.g., the oppression of women in "Zde by měly kvést růže" (Here Should Roses Bloom, 1894). Decadent poets, allied with the jour. *Moderní revue*, included Karel Hlaváček (1874–98), whose poetry follows the typical decadent aesthetics of eroticism and decay; and Jiří Karásek ze Lvovic (1871–1951), whose collections *Sexus necans* (1897) and *Sodoma* (1895) abound in allusions to sadomasochism and necrophilia.

The installation of the First Republic (1918) marked a revolution in Czech lit. *Cubism, *futurism, and civilism emerged as prominent movements in poetry and the arts. Leftism dominated the new schools, and Czech poetry generally found a key influence in Karel Čapek's (1890–1938) groundbreaking trans. of mod. Fr. verse, The poetist movement, influenced by *Dadaism and futurism, called for a poetry that would merge all arts and mod. life together in a playful, populist manner. Poetism had its great theorist in the multitalented Karel Teige (1900–51) and was cultivated by poets such as Vítězslav Nezval (1900–58), Jaroslav Seifert (1901–86), and Konstantin Biebl (1898–1951).

Nezval later passed through a surrealist phase only to turn subsequently to a more socialist realist poetry. Seifert left the Communist Party in the 1930s and abandoned his experimental poetry in favor of a lyrical intimacy. He survived most of his poetist brethren and won the Nobel Prize in Literature in 1984. The poets František Halas (1901–49) and Vladimír Holan (1905–80) also emerge in the interwar period. Halas's highly religious poetry explores mysticism and notions of time. Holan is best known for his postwar works; during communist rule, he went into self-imposed home exile.

The postwar communist regime imposed severe restrictions on writers; socialist realism became the official literary doctrine. Only long after Stalin's death in 1953 did the censorship relax; esp. after 1964, writers were granted greater freedom of expression. The jour. *Květen* (May) published the sui generis poetry of the poet and immunologist Miroslav Holub (1923–98), among others, and long-banned poets began to publish once more. The late 1960s also witnessed a return to extraordinary poetic forms: experimental and surrealist modes were embraced by Emanuel Frynta (1923–75), Josef Hiršal (1920–2003), Ladislav Novák (1925–99), and Vratislav Effenberger (1923–86).

After the Warsaw Pact invasion of 1968, many writers emigrated, while others wrote for the *samizdat* (self-publication) press, "for the drawer," or had their mss. published abroad. By the 1980s, a new generation of poets began to rebel against the so-called normalization. Their work is aggressive and at times purposefully controversial. In samizdat and even in official publishing houses, younger poets like Jáchym Topol (b. 1962), whose collection *Miluju tě k zbláznění* (I Love You to Insanity, 1991) caused an uproar with its intentional vulgarity; Sylva Fischerová (b. 1963); and Zuzana Brabcová (b. 1959) dominated the "subversive" scene.

The fall of Communism in 1989 marked a radical change in Czech lit. Works by many illegal, oppressed, and exiled authors working under the communist regime were published for the first time, and the authors themselves were rehabilitated. The most celebrated poets of recent years include Petr Kabeš (1941–2005), whose poetry draws on *skaz*, direct speech, and colloquialisms; and Petr Borkovec (b. 1970), who combines prosodic virtuosity with precise observations documenting this most recent period of upheaval in Czech culture. He enjoys popularity with readers and critics alike and has earned an international reputation.

■ J. Goll, *Anthologie české lyriky* (1872); *České květy: výbor naší lyriky*, ed. K. Adamec et al. (1890); *Česká poesie XIX věku* (1897–99); *Bělohorské motivy: jubilejní anthologie z české poesie*, ed. J. V. Frič and J. Werstadt (1920); *Modern Czech Poetry*, ed. and trans. P. Selver (1920); *An Anthology of Czechoslovak Poetry*, ed. C. A. Manning, A. V. Čapek, A. B. Koukol (1929); *Anthologie de la poésie tchèque*, ed. H Jelínek (1930); *Lyrika českého obrození (1750–1850)*, ed. V. Jirát (1940); J.Vilikovský, *Staročeská lyrika* (1940); *The Soul of a Century: A Collection of Czech Poetry in English*, ed. R. A. Ginsburg (1942); *Počátky novočeského básnictví: Počátky novočeského básnictví*, ed. K. Polák (1946);

J. Mukařovský, *Kapitoly z české poetiky* (1948); B. Václavek, *Od umení k tvorbe: studie z prítomné ceské poesie* (1949); *Nová česká poesie: výbor z veršů XX. století*, ed. F. Buriánek et al. (1955); J. Jíša, *Česká poesie dvacátých let a básníci sovětského Ruska* (1956); *A Book of Czech Verse*, ed. A. French (1958); *A Handful of Linden Leaves: An Anthology of Czech Poetry*, ed. J. Janu (1960); A. M. Píša, *Stopami poezie: studie a podobizny* (1962); *Versované skladby doby husitské*, ed. F. Svejkovský (1963); F. X. Šalda, *O poezii Uspoř*, ed. M. Petříček and B. Svozil (1970); *Three Czech Poets: Vítězslav Nezval, Antonín Bartusek, Josef Hanzlík*, trans. E. Osers and G. Theiner (1971); *Anthology of Czech Poetry*, ed. A. French (1973); *The Pipe: Recent Czech Concrete Poetry*, ed. and trans. J. Valoch and bpNichol (1973); *Česká poezie 17. a 18. století*, ed. Z. Tichá (1974); *Pohledy: poezie*, ed. J. Balík et al. (1974); *Tisíc let české poezie*, ed. J. Hrabák (1974); V. Kolář, *Mladé zápasy: studie o mladé poezii* (1981); *Vzkazy: výbor ze současné české poezie*, ed. J. Badoučková (1976); R. Jakobson, *Poetry of Grammar and Grammar of Poetry*, ed. S. Rudy (1981); A.M.K. Píša, *Vývoji české lyriky: studie a recenze* (1982); *Zbav mě mé tesknosti*, ed. M. Kopecký, Lat. trans. R. Mertlík (1983); M. Kubínová, *Proměny české poezie dvacátých let* (1984); *Rytířské srdce majíce: česká rytířská epika 14. století*, ed. E. Petrů et al. (1984); Z. Pešat, *Dialogy s poezií* (1985); *The Poet's Lamp: A Czech Anthology*, ed. and trans. A. French (1986); *The New Czech Poetry*, ed. J Cejka et al. (1988); Z. Hrubý, *Na strepech volnosti: almanach české poezie* (1989); M. Červenka, *Slovník básnických knih: díla české poezie od obrození do roku 1945* (1990); *Na strepech volnosti: almanach umlčene české poezie*, ed. J. Horec (1991); M. Červenka, *Styl a význam: studie o básnících* (1991); *Vrh kostek: česká experimentální poezie*, ed. J. Hirsal, B. Grögerová, Z. Barborka (1993); J. Trávníček, *Poezie poslední možnosti* (1996); *Prague 1900: Poetry and Ecstasy*, ed. E. Becker et al. (1999); *Six Czech Poets*, ed. and trans. A. Büchler (2007); *Up the Devil's Back: A Bilingual Anthology of 20th-Century Czech Poetry*, ed. B. Volková and C. Cloutier (2008).

M. STERNSTEIN

# D

**DACTYL** (Gr., "finger"). In *classical prosody, a metrical foot consisting of one long syllable followed by two short ones. In the mod. prosodies based on *accent, an accented syllable followed by two unaccented ones (e.g., *suddenly, ominous*). Dactyl is the metrical basis of much of cl. Gr. and Lat. poetry: in narrative verse, it is used particularly for the *hexameter and *elegiac distich, and in lyric, it is used alone and with other cola, esp. the *epitrite, in various combinations known collectively as *dactylo-epitrite*. These latter did not survive the cl. age, though the dactylic hexameter remained the meter for much Lat. art verse through most of the Middle Ages. In the transition from Lat. to the vernaculars, however, it lost place to iambic—which even in antiquity had been the meter felt to be closest to common (Gr.) speech and had been used for recitation meters such as dialogue in drama—as the staple meter of art verse and *epic. Dactylic verse was, however, revived in Ger. by August Buchner in his opera *Orpheus* (1638), arousing a brief vogue, evidenced in Simon Dach and Friedrich von Logau.

The dactyl is usually mentioned in handbooks of Eng. metrics along with the *anapest and perhaps the *amphibrach as the three mod. ternary meters (see BINARY AND TERNARY), but in running series, these are almost impossible to differentiate, esp. if the line ends are ambiguous. If dactylic meter was suited to Gr., it was less suited to Lat., with its stress accent, and even less suited to the mod. langs. Hence, the status of this metrical foot in mod. times is completely the reverse of its cl. prestige: it is now used mostly for *light verse and humorous subgenres, such as the recent *"double dactyls."

■ A. Köster, "Deutsche Daktylen," *Zeitschrift für Deutsches Altertum und Deutsche Literatur* 46 (1901); Wilamowitz, pt. 2, ch. 10; Koster, ch. 4; Dale, ch. 3; Halporn et al.; Snell; West; C. Golston and T. Riad, "The Phonology of Classical Greek Meter," *Linguistics* 38 (2000).

T.V.F. Brogan

**DACTYLO-EPITRITE.** The name given by the 19th-c. metrists A. Rossbach and J. C. Westphal to a compound rhythm extensively attested in ancient Gr. lyric poetry, esp. Pindar. Its basic components were felt to be – ∪ ∪ – ∪ ∪ – – or – ∪ ∪ – ∪ ∪ – (full or catalectic dactylic tripodies) and – ∪ – – and – – ∪ – (respectively, second and third *epitrite). It is now standard practice to describe the rhythm, more precisely and economically, with a modified version of the symbols introduced by Paul Maas: D (– ∪ ∪ – ∪ ∪ – ), e ( – ∪ – ) and – (a single syllable that may be either long or short but is usually long in the Pindaric examples of the meter—hence, the original use of the term *epitrite* as a label for sequences better described as *iambic and *trochaic metra with long *anceps).

The employing of successive or alternating instances of D and e, usually though not always separated by an anceps, yield forms such as the following:

| | |
|---|---|
| – e – D | iambelegus |
| D – e – (e) | elegiambus |
| D – D | choerilean |
| D – e – D | platonicum |
| – e – D – e – | pindaricum |

D is occasionally extended into – ∪ ∪ – ∪ ∪ – ∪ ∪ – or – ∪ ∪ – ∪ ∪ – ∪ ∪ – ∪ ∪ – and e x occasionally replaced, through a kind of *anaclasis, with – ∪ ∪ –.

Maas's notation brings out clearly the interrelations of the various combinations of D, e, and – —different lengths cut, as it were from the same rhythmical cloth, which begin or end immediately before or after e, D, or –. The sequences attested in Gr. lyric of the 7th and 6th cs. BCE appear alongside much longer ones in later periods, but the character of the earliest attested example, two elegiambi by Alcaeus in which D and – e – are separated by word end, suggest that the rhythm began as a brief, *asynartete combination of the first two and a half feet of a dactylic *hexameter with the corresponding portion of an iambic *trimeter. Subsequent devels. would, on this theory, have allowed expansion of dactylic D into D – D, etc., on the model of iambic or trochaic – e – e and e – e –, as well as the elimination of obligatory word end between line segments containing D and those containing e.

The rhythm is, by lyric standards, a highly regular one; and it was associated, perhaps for that reason, with *encomium, *epitaph, and the poetry of moral reflection. In the Hellenistic period, it seems to have become a preferred metrical vehicle for "educated bourgeois lyric" (West)—most notably in Aristotle's frigidly correct "Hymn to Virtue."

*See* ENHOPLIAN.

■ Maas, sec. 55; A. M. Dale, *Metrical Analyses of Tragic Choruses I. Dactylo-Epitrite* (1971); metrical appendices to the Snell and Snell-Maehler eds. of Pindar (8th ed., 1987–89) and Bacchylides (10th ed., 1970); West, Sec. IIe, III8, and IVa.

A. T. Cole

**DADA.** Dada emerged in Zurich in the midst of World War I from the collaboration of a group of refugee artists united by their intense disdain for the Eur. culture that had brought about the war. Centered at the Cabaret Voltaire from 1916 through 1918, the original Dada artists and writers—Hugo Ball, Tristan Tzara, Richard Huelsenbeck, Marcel Janco, and Hans (Jean) Arp—articulated the most extreme forms of modernist cultural rebellion of the early 20th c. (see MODERNISM). The nature of their assault on political, artistic, and ling. discourse distinguished them from their contemporaries and has posed a constant challenge to generations of artists to confront the essential instability and inauthenticity of all meaning systems. Few artists have been able to meet that challenge, incl. the Dadaists themselves. Thus, while Dada spread widely in the postwar period to other artistic centers (e.g., Berlin, Paris, New York, and cities throughout Europe), it soon proved unsustainable and was succeeded by forms of artistic and political action more aesthetically programmatic and culturally progressive. While these subsequent movements are now solely of historical interest, however, the Dada challenge has continued to spur writers and artists, esp. in the postmod. era.

Like many modernist movements of the late 19th and early 20th cs., Dada questioned bourgeois society and its prevailing aesthetic conventions and sought to establish the bases and practices of a new art appropriate to its time. Dadaist rebellion, however, laid bare the underlying dynamics of modernist and avant-garde innovation: the primacy of negation within all new creation. Janco identified this dynamic as two "speeds" of creativity. The first, the "negative speed," was a "purifying and scandalous force to consume the past and open up a new creative route." That route comprised the second, "positive speed," which Janco saw manifest in "pure, childlike, direct [and] primal" actions. Although he argued that these "speeds" were distinct, in actual Dadaist texts and performances, they seemed simultaneous, at times indistinguishable. The childlike, primal actions could be seen as destructive of existing order as much as constitutive of the new. Caws aptly described Dada "as the place where the 'yes' and the 'no' meet." Because Dada expressed so adamantly the absoluteness of that "no," every "yes" Dadaists asserted was haunted by the potency of negation. "Let each man proclaim: there is a great negative work of destruction to be accomplished," Tzara wrote; and Georg Grosz, looking back at Berlin Dada, admitted that the artists and their art could not escape that destruction: "ours was completely nihilistic. We spat on everything, including ourselves."

Most significantly, Dada poets spat on the tools of their creative work: their words, and more broadly, on lang. itself. To the Dadaists, lang., as an essential organ of the cultural order, had been debased, indeed defiled by the bourgeois world. Its complicity in constraining how human beings saw, understood, and judged their lives had to be revealed and reviled. Consequently, all Dadaist writing entailed a radical critique of the nature, power, and authority of lang. The "negative speed" of Dadaist poetic production was manifest in the movement's efforts to subvert all lang. systems through transgression of the most basic components of meaning: its sonic, semiotic, and semantic operations. Dadaist works and performances disrupted grammar and syntax, manipulated semantic associations of words and phonemes, and dissected lang. into its elements, such as syllables, letters, and brute sounds.

The Dadaist disruption of lang. should be seen in relation to the wider modernist investigation of lings.

and aesthetics, such as that evident in It. and Rus. *futurism. For instance, F. T. Marinetti's *immaginazione senza fila e le parole in libertà* (wireless imagination and words in freedom) texts also disrupted syntax, largely by reducing poetic lines to strings of conjoined nouns and verb infinitives. Such experiments were not intended, however, to challenge the foundations of basic discourse but rather to make it more efficient and powerful by quickening and intensifying direct, intuitive communication between poet and audience. Alternatively, Rus. futurists, such as Aleksei Kruchenykh and Velimir Khlebnikov, deconstructed poetic lang. to focus on its semantic and phonetic components in the hope of "scientifically" establishing new ling. combinations leading to a new literary lang.

The Dadaists' disruptions of conventional ling. behavior signaled a far more aggressive, even nihilistic assault on the role of lang. than either group of futurists envisioned. Dada poetry and esp. its public performances, whether at the Cabaret Voltaire or in postwar political demonstrations in Berlin and literary events in Paris, mocked society, lang., and the aesthetic realm. Dadaists demonstrated an intense delight in smashing idols, and they reveled in the liberating and purifying spirit of their nonsensical creations. Rebellion was at once angry, sardonic, naughty, and playful. Dismantling of lang. proved both a demystifying and purifying activity through which the "second speed" of Dada might announce new forms of expression and new contents.

The poet's incantation of raw sounds or chance play with semantically rich if surprising images resulted for many in a sense of being attendant at the recovery of a primal state of creativity. Negation unleashed creation. Although it is often difficult to distinguish the two in any particular Dadaist work, within the *cacophony produced by simultaneous readings of poetic declamations in three langs.; the incantation of onomatopoeic constructed "words"; the conjoining of widely disparate words through *aleatory methods to create nonsensical, paradoxical, or at best semantically ambiguous images; and the fragmentation of words into deracinated syllables or manipulated alphabetic images, the Dada poets simultaneously destroyed literary values, reduced meaning to levels of blatant absurdity, and also uncovered an immediately experienced realm of imaginative freedom. While chanting his "sound poems," such as "gadji beri bimba" and "elefantenkarawane," Ball believed himself to be entering a primitive, subconscious state that connected him both to a child's trembling encounter with sacred and mystical being and to the sources of a new spiritual awakening.

Like many modernist writers and artists, Dadaists were fascinated by the idea of the primitive and the instinctual presumed to have been repressed by the strictures of civilization but potentially accessible within everyone who could break down the internalized operations of the social order. And like the expressionists and later the surrealists (see EXPRESSIONISM, SURREALISM), in their idealization of the unsocialized drawings of children, the schizophrenic's supposedly direct access to unconscious processes, and the seemingly irrational rituals of non-Western "primitives," Dadaists shared both a nostalgia for a lost state of primal connection with self and the world and a romantic hope that it could be recovered through the revitalized powers of a purified imagination.

Even as their inherently nihilist transgressions threatened to undermine any work they composed, Dada poets and artists created artworks in an effort to transform the human order. Thus, as much as the intensity of Dadaist negativity encompassed not only bourgeois academic conventions but modernist innovations as well, Dadaists never completely denied an inherently modernist utopian faith that a new lang., hence a new imaginative vision, and ultimately a new way of being in the world could result from their art.

To sustain that hope, that "positive speed," every Dada poet and artist eventually moved away from the radical "no" within the Dadaist moment toward a more sustainable and collective "yes." Some, like Janco and Arp, imagined an art more attuned to the spiritual longing of mod. life while others, like Marcel Duchamp, consigned themselves to ironic games of aesthetic self-reflection, and others allied themselves with more programmatic avant-garde art movements, such as surrealism (Tzara), or threw themselves into political activism (Huelsenbeck, Raoul Hausmann). Some simply left art altogether and pursued another vocation (Janco). In the process, Dada died as a literary and artistic movement.

Nonetheless, the Dadaist challenge to the authority of all forms of discourse has remained and has been recalled whenever the bases of cultural and artistic meaning are questioned. Dada's critique of the cultural and ling. order has found resonance in poststructuralist thought and in the neo-avant-garde of the postmod. era. Dada poetry's strategies of ling. dismantling inform the ironic games of appropriation and *pastiche in recent poetry, e.g., *visual or *concrete poetry, sound or "noise" creations, or *Language poetry. Absent from much of contemp. Dada-inflected work, however, is the sense of rage and rebellion that motivated the original Dadaists and that linked them to the spirit of modernist despair and utopianism. In its place, contemp. cultural critique has assumed increasingly academic forms of ironic manipulation of discourse systems with little hope of—or desire for—an art of purifying scandal.

*See* AVANT-GARDE POETICS, POSTMODERNISM, POSTSTRUCTURALISM, PRIMITIVISM, RUSSIAN FORMALISM, SOUND POETRY.

■ *The Dada Painters and Poets*, ed. R Motherwell (1951); *Als Dada Begann*, ed. P. Schifferli (1957); M. Sanouillet, *Dada á Paris* (1965); M. A. Caws, *The Poetry of Dada and Surrealism* (1970); M. Grossman, *Dada* (1971); M. Janco, "Dada at Two Speeds"; T. Tzara, "Dada Manifesto"; and G. Grosz and W. Herzfelde, "Art Is in Danger," all in *Dadas on Art*, ed. L. Lippard (1971); *Dada et le surréalisme*, ed. M. Tison-Braun (1973); *Dada*, ed. G. Ribemont-Dessaignes (1974); S. Foster and R. Kuenzli, *Dada Spectrum* (1979); *Dada/Dimensions*, ed. S. Foster (1985); J. Freeman, *The Dada and Surrealist Word-Image* (1989); R. Meyer, *Dada Global* (1994); *Crisis and the Arts: The History of Dada*, ed. S. Foster, 10 v. (1996–2005); M. Pegrum, *Challenging Modernity* (2000); R. Sheppard, *Modernism—Dada—Postmodernism* (2000); *The Dada Reader*, ed. D. Ades (2006); R. Kuenzli, *Dada: Themes and Movements* (2006); L. Dickerman et al., *Dada: Zurich, Berlin, Hannover, Cologne, New York, Paris* (2008).

C. RUSSELL

# DANCE AND POETRY

I. Historical Convergences
II. Poetry on Dance

**I. Historical Convergences.** In the cultures of Crete and ancient Greece, dancing and poetry were linked in ritual and religious practice. A wide variety of dances dedicated to deities were performed with song and music; worship of Apollo included the *hyporchema*, a mimetic dance accompanied by song. In the late 6th c. BCE, the City Dionysia competition generated the *dithyramb, composed of *choruses of citizens circling within the space of the orchestra while intoning poetry, directed by a poet who often led the movements; singing and dancing choruses also punctuated performances of *tragedies and *comedies. In cl. Gr. civilization, the interweaving of voice, movement, and music—the concept of *mousikē*—was central to cultural practice in state functions and private gatherings alike (see MUSIC AND POETRY). Poetry and dance were important components of entertainments and celebrations and frequently appeared together on the after-dinner menu of symposia, providing material—as recorded by Xenophon—for philosophical debate. Plato emphasized the role of dance in the education of a well-rounded citizen, and Socrates famously expounded on the benefits to the mind of a body kept healthy by dancing, foreshadowing Friedrich Nietzsche's dancing philosopher.

The early Christian era saw various polemics and prohibitions against dance, although Eur. med. texts and paintings carry descriptions of round dances accompanied by song. The late med. *danse macabre* genre in woodcuts and paintings features an early instance of dialogue between dance and *dramatic poetry, frequently consisting of images glossed by exchanges between Death and his victims. Dance took on a more positive allegorical cast in the Ren., as scholars and artists, reemphasizing the ancient concept of the music of the spheres, developed the image of celestial bodies participating in a cosmic dance, as in John Davies's "Orchestra, or a Poem of Dancing" (1596). This metaphysical *trope provided the ground for the court ballets and *masques of 16th- and 17th-c. Italy, France, Spain, and England: large-scale spectacles featuring music, poetry, dance, drama, and extravagant stage designs, they offered images of a universal harmony that carefully mirrored the harmonious social order presided over by the monarch. Poets such as Ben Jonson composed masques whose descriptive verses give some idea of their choreography and whose meter is carefully calibrated to the rhythm of the dance steps, being particularly marked at certain points to guide dancers through complicated moves. The It. *ballo* choreographer Fabritio Caroso explicitly underlined the homology between steps in dance and poetry—both measured, as he noted, in *feet (see METER)—and even invented steps based on lyric (particularly Ovidian) meter, e.g., the *spondeo*. (Some mod. scholars have made the controversial suggestion that Homeric *epic was itself structured by dance rhythm.) The Ren. also saw the appearance of dance manuals and treatises that argued for the significance of dance as an art form, an argument buttressed in poetry by Soame Jenyns's *The Art of Dancing* (1727).

During the Enlightenment, in opera and *ballets d'action*, dance gravitated increasingly in the direction of narrative: telling a story rather than merely serving as decoration or diversion. The early 20th c. would see a revolt, however, against cl. ballet's subordination to the machinery of plot and what were seen as constricting techniques of expression. Inspired in part by Nietzsche's writings on Gr. tragedy and the chorus, a variety of dancers across Europe and North America turned once more toward the ideal of mousikē, forging close links with poetry and music, as well as painting. In freeing dance from the demands of narrative or drama, the first generation of mod. dancers were seen as bringing it closer to poetry—or as Rudolf Laban wrote of Isadora Duncan, "[She] reawakened a form of dance-expression, which could be called dance-lyrics, in contrast to the mainly dramatic dance forms of ballet."

Several of these dancers experimented with combining the two art forms, claiming inspiration by poems or having their performances accompanied by poetry. Duncan performed the *Idylls* of Theocritus and the Homeric *Hymn to Demeter* alongside readings of poetry. The Fr. futurist Valentine de Saint Point combined dance and poetry of her own composition in what she termed "metachoric" performances (see FUTURISM). Even the dissonant *Dada dances of the Germans Mary Wigman and Sophie Taeuber-Arp, set to readings of Nietzsche or of *nonsense verse, might be seen as probing the possibility of mousikē in war-torn modernity. Others turned to recent reworkings of Gr. culture in their experiments with fusing ancient and mod., poetry and dance. Vaslav Nijinsky's *Afternoon of a Faun*, for instance, is an interpretation of a Gr.-styled poem by Stéphane Mallarmé, "L'Après-midi d'un faune." In 1934, Kurt Jooss choreographed a full-length *Persephone*, with text by André Gide based on the Homeric *Hymn to Demeter,* and music by Igor Stravinsky. Martha Graham frequently experimented with poetry as source and structure: in the solo *Dithyrambic* in 1931, the 1940 *Letter to the World* (an homage to Emily Dickinson), and *Hérodiade* (1944), a piece for two female dancers inspired by an unfinished poem by Mallarmé. The choreographer Merce Cunningham, known for his collaborations with artists in other media (see

AVANT-GARDE POETICS), prepared two pieces with the Canadian poet Anne Carson, *Nox* and *Stacks* (2011).

This narrative of harmonies between the two art forms might also be written in a more dissonant key, taking into account meditations on the hierarchical or historical precedence of one or other mode of discourse. Gr. and Roman treatises on oratory mapped out repertoires of effective gestures to accompany speech yet cautioned against excessive mimeticism; Quintilian pointedly distinguished between orator and dancer (although later dancers would themselves proscribe pantomimic gesture; see MIME). Enlightenment debates over the origin of lang. pressed particularly on its relation to the body, seeking to determine whether speech or gesture took historical precedence. Jean-Jacques Rousseau meditated on the enduring question of dance's universality of gesture, its capacity to communicate more easily across cultures than lang. because of a transnational and transhistorical human grammar of movement. And at the turn of the 20th c., the Cambridge Ritualists confidently placed dance at the origin of human expression.

**II. Poetry on Dance.** Poems about dance, rather than constituting a genre unto themselves, appear intermittently in the corpus of established poets; they may present dance as a narrative, as a lyrical expression of feeling, as an interpersonal duet (frequently between the speaker and a desired other), or, very occasionally, from the point of view of the performer. Considered broadly, poems tend to align dance with either the social or the artistic, ethics or aesthetics. In the former camp, dance is conceived as a pattern of social organization, from the utopian (social ritual, e.g., Luis Palés Matos's "Black Dance") through the practical (court and civil society, e.g., Friedrich Schiller's "The Dance") to the dystopian (the "sudden mobs of men" of Wallace Stevens's "Sad Strains of a Gay Waltz"); movement in these poems is often carefully choreographed within a fixed structure, as in the image on Achilles' shield in the *Iliad*, whose lines trace the to-and-fro movements of a chain dance. The second camp, which treats dance as an art form in its own right, tends toward more mimetic patterning, straining to capture the movements of the performer in its own rhythms and syntax (Gertrude Stein's "Susie Asado," R. M. Rilke's "Spanish Dancer"). These latter poems insist that dance fully activates the body of the artist (whether performer or choreographer—the two are usually merged), with a complementary kinesthetic effect on the viewer; by inscribing dance in their poems, poets seek to harness some of this power of movement.

In the symbolist period (see SYMBOLISM), dance's seeming evanescence as an art form was recast as a moment of full *presence, an ideal integration of signifier and signified (see SIGN, SIGNIFIED, SIGNIFIER): W. B. Yeats's dancer in "Among School Children" fused with the dance itself, coinciding wholly with a meaning or expressive intention pursued in vain by the writer. In Mallarmé's famous dictum ("Ballets"), "*the dancer is not *a woman dancing,* for these juxtaposed reasons: that *she is not a woman,* but a metaphor summing up one of the elementary aspects of our form: knife, goblet, flower, etc.; and that *she is not dancing,* but suggesting, through the miracle of bends and leaps, a kind of corporal writing, what it would take pages of prose, dialogue, and description to express, if it were transcribed: a poem independent of any scribal apparatus." Symbolist poets were indeed some of the first professional dance critics: Théophile Gautier, Mallarmé, Paul Valéry. From the latter half of the 19th c. through the early decades of the 20th, they and their followers watched an eclectic mix of solo dancers and troupes—from La Cornalba and the Tiller Girls to Anna Pavlova and the Ballets Russes—perform a range of cl., expressivist, "ethnic," and machine-inspired dances, and produced an abundance of poetry in response. Dance became the focal point for intermedial artworks, interwoven with music, scenery, costumes, and lighting effects by well-known avant-garde contemporaries. But intermediality has in many ways always characterized the encounter between dance and poetry, with appeals to a third or fourth art form (music, painting, sculpture) to heighten the multisensory kinesthesia promised by their meeting. This phenomenon is encapsulated in W. C. Williams's 1944 poem "The Dance," inspired by a Ren. painting of a village dance: its identical opening and closing lines provide a static frame for the whole, but what comes between them ramps up visual, tactile, and sonorous effects to gather dance into the embrace of poetry.

■ *Poems of the Dance,* ed. E. Dickson (1921); R. von Laban, *Modern Educational Dance* (1948); *Dance in Poetry,* ed. A. Raftis (1991); G. Brandstetter, *Tanzlektüren* (1995); E. Goellner and J. Shea Murphy, *Bodies of the Text* (1995); A. Koritz, *Gendered Bodies/Performing Art* (1995); *The Dance,* ed. E. Fragos (2006); S. Mallarmé, *Divagations,* trans. B. Johnson (2007); *The Ancient Dancer in the Modern World,* ed. F. Macintosh (2010); J. Townsend, *The Choreography of Modernism* (2010); C. Preston, *Modernism's Mythic Pose* (2011).

M. CLAYTON

**DANISH POETRY.** *See* DENMARK, POETRY OF.

**DANSA.** Occitan lyric genre, commonly of three stanzas, set to a lively tune of popular cast. An opening *respos* or *refrain* (A) was perhaps repeated after each stanza, of which the second part matched the form and tune of the respos, while the two symmetrical halves of the first part were independent of it: schematically, *A bba(A) bba(A) bba(A)* for a three-stanza piece. The OF *balete* shows the same structure.

■ *GRLMA* 2.1B; Bec; Chambers; G. Avenoza, "La *dansa*: Corpus d'un genre lyrique roman," *Revue des langues romanes* 107 (2003).

J. H. MARSHALL

**DARK ROOM COLLECTIVE.** As Harvard undergraduates, the poets Thomas Sayers Ellis and Sharan Strange founded the Dark Room Reading Series in

Cambridge, Massachusetts, in 1987. The series became known as the Dark Room Collective and supported burgeoning and established Af. Am. writers through a communal network free of particular aesthetic or political ideologies. Among others, the collective launched Kevin Young, Natasha Trethewey, John Keene, Major Jackson, and Carl Phillips. Young's renewal of elegiac and *blues poetry; Trethewey's lyrical explorations of Southern hist. and Af. Am. culture; and Jackson's urbane, formal sophistication are illustrations of the Dark Room Collective's influence on contemp. Am. poetry.

*See* AFRICAN AMERICAN POETRY; UNITED STATES, POETRY OF THE.

■ **Anthologies and Criticism:** *Giant Steps: The New Generation of African-American Writers,* ed. K. Young (2000); E. Alexander, *The Black Interior: Essays* (2007); B. Reed, "The Dark Room Collective and Post-Soul Poetics," *African American Review* 41.4 (2007).
■ **Novels and Poetry Collections:** J. Keene, *Annotations* (1995); C. Phillips, *The Rest of Love: Poems* (2004); N. Tretheway, *Native Guard* (2007).

W. MUYUMBA

**DEAD METAPHOR.** An expression that was originally metaphorical but no longer functions as a *trope and is now understood literally, e. g., "tail light," "foot of the mountain," "head of state." Scholars differ as to how and why a metaphor becomes "dead." The common theory holds that the cause is repeated use over time. If the meaning generated by a metaphor is based on the tension it establishes between two things—subject and analogue, *tenor and vehicle, target and source—normally perceived to be different, then a dead metaphor has lost that tension. Thus, while we may refer to the base of a mountain (tenor) as its "foot" (vehicle), we no longer see it as involving a reference to an object in nature in terms of a human body part.

To conflate dead metaphor with either *cliché or idiom is a mistake, since metaphors can be conventional without being literal (e.g., "the eyes are windows on the soul," "Juliet is the sun") and since some etymological dead metaphors can be unexpectedly fascinating (e.g., "pedigree" from the Fr. for "foot of a crane," "magazine" from the word for "storehouse"). Cognitive linguists and philosophers of lang. point out that the very terms "literal" and "metaphorical" are historically and socially dependent and that dead metaphors can indicate interesting conceptual frameworks (e.g., "a car is an animal") that may be very much alive.

*See* METAPHOR.

■ W. K. Wimsatt, *The Verbal Icon* (1954); O. Thomas, *Metaphor and Related Subjects* (1969); M. C. Beardsley, "The Metaphorical Twist," *Essays on Metaphor,* ed. W. Shibles (1972); D. Davidson, "What Metaphors Mean," *On Metaphor,* ed. S. Sacks (1979); E. C. Traugott, "'Conventional' and 'Dead' Metaphors Revisited," *The Ubiquity of Metaphor,* ed. W. Paprotté and R. Dirven (1985); D. E. Cooper, *Metaphor* (1986); G. Lakoff, "The Death of Dead Metaphor," *Metaphor and Symbol* 2.2 (1987); R. W. Gibbs, *The Poetics of Mind* (1994); Z. Radman, "Difficulties with Diagnosing the Death of a Metaphor," *Metaphor and Symbol* 12.2 (1997); R. Claiborne, *Loose Cannons, Red Herrings, and Other Lost Metaphors* (2001).

N. Friedman; A. L. French

**DECADENCE** (Lat., *de-cadere*, "falling away"). A term used ostensibly in reference to periods or works whose qualities are held to mark a "falling away" from previously recognized conditions or standards of excellence. The term is often applied to the Alexandrian (or Hellenistic) period in Gr. lit. (ca. 300–230 BCE—see ALEXANDRIANISM) and to the period in Lat. lit. after the death of Augustus (14 CE—see LATIN POETRY). In mod. poetry, decadence has been identified most persistently in the works of the Fr. symbolist-decadent movement of the late 19th c. (coinciding with a sense of national decline after the Franco-Prussian War of 1870), whose influence in the British isles encouraged native tendencies already nurtured by the ideas of Walter Pater, the poetry of D. G. Rossetti and A. C. Swinburne, and the general ambience of *Pre-Raphaelitism (see SYMBOLISM). Symbolist influence was widespread also among the poets of fin de siècle Europe outside France, incl. Russia, where there was a vital symbolist movement. It did not significantly affect the poetry of the United States until the 20th c., although E. A. Poe was himself a progenitor of important ideas and practices of the Fr. symbolists.

In a limited sense, decadence may be seen as exemplified in the tastes and habits of such fictional characters as Petrus Borel's Passereau l'Ecolier, Gabriele D'Annunzio's Count Andrea Sperelli-Fieschi d'Ugenta, J.-K. Huysmans's Des Esseintes, Poe's Roderick Usher, Thomas Mann's Gustav von Aschenbach, Auguste Villiers de l'Isle-Adam's Axël d'Auersperg, and Oscar Wilde's Dorian Gray and Lord Henry Wotton; in passages like those on the lang. of decaying civilizations by Charles Baudelaire and Théophile Gautier; in the apostrophe of Stéphane Mallarmé's Hérodiade to her mirror; in Paul Verlaine's verses beginning "Je suis l'Empire à la fin de la décadence"; in Valery Bryusov's scandalous one-line poem, "Oh, cover your pale legs"; in Aubrey Beardsley's self-described "strange hermaphroditic creatures wandering about in Pierrot costumes or modern dress; quite a new world of my own creation"; in the sumptuous paintings and illustrations of Léon Bakst, Alexandre Benois, Konstantin Somov, and the other artists associated with the jour. *The World of Art*; in Wilde's *Salomé* and Ernest Dowson's famous poem to Cynara; in the affectations of Count Robert de Montesquiou-Fezensac; and in the remarkable production in 1891 of Paul-Napoléon Roinard's *Cantique des cantiques* in the perfumed atmosphere of Paul Fort's Théâtre d'Art. Decadence in this sense was often a mannerism of the sort prevalent in the England of the Yellow Nineties, with its brilliant and superficial fin de siècle aesthetic pose that played perhaps a more significant role than is generally recognized in opposing the crushing force of the current materialism. But the word *decadence* has come to be used by hostile critics in a larger sense than this.

If there was a single figure that captivated the decadent imagination and served as decadence's unofficial muse, it was the biblical character of Salome, whose image circulated among the male writers and artists who dominated literary and artistic circles throughout fin de siècle Europe. Salome figured prominently in Mallarmé's *Hérodiade*; in Gustave Flaubert's short story "Hérodias," which directly influenced Jules Massenet's opera *Hérodiade*; in numerous paintings and illustrations by Gustave Moreau, incl. *Salome Dancing before Herod* and *The Apparition*, which are discussed at length in Huysmans's so-called breviary of decadence, *À rebours*; in Wilde's play *Salomé*, which inspired Beardsley's illustrations to the play, as well as Richard Strauss's opera *Salome*; and in Alexander Blok's poem "Venice II," where "Salome stealthily walks by / With [the poet's] bloody head." With her extravagant jewels and veils and seductive dance in exchange for the head of John the Baptist, Salome responded not only to the decadent fascination with aestheticism, exoticism, and eroticism but to male anxieties at the fin de siècle in the face of the rise of the new woman and the dance-hall girl. Although Salome was the subject of intense fascination among male writers and artists, who identified with the symbolically "castrated" John the Baptist as well as with the femme fatale Salome, the Jewish princess also became the source of inspiration for women writers and artists associated with symbolists and decadent circles. Thus, Mirra Lokhvitskaya drew on the attributes of Salome in fashioning her unabashedly feminine poetic persona, while Zinaida Gippius, who adopted an unmarked, masculine voice for her highly restrained metaphysical poetry, was known to appear in literary circles *à la Salomé* in ultrafeminine attire and with a jewel suspended from her forehead.

In addition to gender ambiguity and anxiety, which were reflected in, among other things, the decadents' complex attraction to and identification with the femme fatale Salome, a basic characteristic of decadence has been a failure to recognize objective or timeless values that transcend and give form and direction to individual experience and effort. In these terms, the decadent poet is seen living in a state of Heraclitian or Bergsonian flux, with his values confined within narrowly egocentric limits and unlikely to satisfy his desires. Here the poet tends to be concerned not with "the fruit of experience" but with "experience itself" and with private sensations; and his poems are likely to reveal a number of the following "decadent" characteristics: ennui; a search for novelty, with attendant artificiality and interest in the unnatural; excessive self-analysis; feverish hedonism, with poetic interest in corruption and morbidity; abulia, neurosis, and exaggerated erotic sensibility; aestheticism, with a stress on "art for art's sake" in the evocation of exquisite sensations and emotions; dandyism; scorn of contemp. society and mores;

restless curiosity, perversity, or eccentricity in subject matter; overemphasis on form, with a resultant loss of balance between form and content—or interest in lapidary ornamentation, resulting at times in disintegration of artistic unity; bookishness; erudite or exotic vocabulary; frequent employment of *synaesthesia or *transpositions d'art*; complex and difficult syntax; experiments in the use of new rhythms, rich in evocative and sensuous effects alien to those of trad. and often departing from the mathematical principles of control in established prosody; substitution of coherence in mood for coherence and synthesis in thought; "postromantic" irony in the manner of Tristan Corbière, Jules Laforgue, and the early T. S. Eliot; *obscurity, arising from remote, private, or complicated imagery; and a pervasive sense of something lost—a nostalgic semimysticism without clear direction or spiritual commitment, but with frequent reference to exotic religions and rituals, e.g., to tarot cards, magic, alchemy, Rosicrucianism, Theosophy, the Kabbalah, Satanism, and the like.

From the foregoing summary emerge certain fundamental distinctions between the symbolist and the decadent, distinctions that derive from the decadent's essential condition, that of an artist whose symbolist aspirations are constantly thwarted by a persistent *naturalism. For all his efforts to create for himself an existence of infinitely renewed moments, to concentrate life into a sequence of sensations, the decadent is fatally bound to hist., and a Darwinian hist. at that. While the symbolist inhabits a world of seamless and cumulative duration, a world of temporal synthesis, which accounts for his peculiar equanimity in the face of external events, the decadent endures the forces of heredity, which characteristically produce an oscillation between febrility and neurasthenia, culminating in psychological exhaustion. Untouched by disorders of the nerves, the symbolist can submerge personality in the play of universal analogy, can "yield the initiative to words" (Mallarmé); the decadent, on the other hand, feels bound to protect and promote personality, to isolate the self, by the exercise of irony and a vigilant self-consciousness. Consequently, the mask of the decadent is not the symbolist's mask of self-transcendence or self-surrender but the dandy's mask of self-defense, of noncommitment. Paradoxically, then, the decadent needs the very society he rejects as an audience against which he can measure his superiority; his art is thus more aggressive than the symbolist's, more intent on strategies of outrage and shock. For this reason, perhaps, the decadent's rebellion by blasphemy and sacrilege often takes place within the framework of Catholic orthodoxy, while the symbolist's "religion" is either atheistic or syncretic.

But the decadent's ineradicable naturalism is most evident in a stubborn materialism, both in taste and style. The decadent is a collector and connoisseur of aesthetic objects with which he can fill his spiritual vacuum and dissociate himself from grosser forms of materialism. Unlike the symbolist, therefore, the decadent aims to aestheticize or refine the object, rather than transform it. And his style is equally materialist; it collects words like aesthetic objects, like possessions, whether they be archaisms, neologisms, technical terms, or exotic images, and sets them, like jewels, in a finely wrought syntax designed to show them off. For all his ostensible rejection of Parnassian (see PARNASSIANISM) and naturalist principles, the decadent remains a descriptive rather than transmutative writer; he can name only words or objects that already have an inherent value for him. In his falling short of symbolist ideals, in the paradoxes of his existence, in his exasperated failure to break free from naturalism, the decadent assumes a certain tragic grandeur.

In keeping with this naturalistic coloring, Laurent thought he could identify certain characteristics of a *physiognomie décadente*: a lack of forehead; prognathous features; oddly shaped heads ("plagiocéphales, oxycéphales, acrocéphales"); deformed noses; glabrous, asymmetrical faces; wide ears; enormous cheek bones, and so on. All this was a continuation of the thesis of Max Nordau's *Entartung* (*Degeneration*, 1892), which found that the Fr. symbolists "had in common all the signs of degeneracy and imbecility." G. B. Shaw's *The Sanity of Art* (1895) was an effective reply to this sort of nonsense.

See AESTHETICISM, GEORGIANISM, HERMETICISM.

■ T. Gautier, "Charles Baudelaire" (1868); D. Nisard, *Études de moeurs et de critique sur les poètes latins de la décadence*, 4th ed. (1878); A. Symons, "The Decadent Movement in Literature," *Harper's Magazine* 87 (1893); E. Laurent, *La poésie décadente devant la science psychiatrique* (1897); A. J. Farmer, *Le Mouvement esthétique et "décadent" en Angleterre (1873–1900)* (1931); W. Binni, *La poetica del decadentismo* (1949); M. Praz, *The Romantic Agony*, 2d ed. (1951); J. M. Smith, "Concepts of Decadence in 19th-Century French Literature," *SP* 50 (1953); A. E. Carter, *The Idea of Decadence in French Literature, 1830–1900* (1958); K. W. Swart, *The Sense of Decadence in Nineteenth-Century France* (1964); P. Jullian, *Esthètes et magiciens* (1969); P. Stephan, *Paul Verlaine and the Decadence, 1882–90* (1974); *Pascoli, D'Annunzio, Fogazzaro e il decadentismo italiano*, ed. R. Tessari (1976); M. Calinescu, *Faces of Modernity* (1977); L. C. Dowling, *Aestheticism and Decadence* (1977)—annotated bibl.; J. Pierrot, *L'Imaginaire décadent, 1880–1900* (1977); M. Lemaire, *Le Dandysme de Baudelaire á Mallarmé* (1978); R. Gilman, *Decadence* (1979); Terras, "Decadence"; *Degeneration*, ed. J. E. Chamberlain (1985); J. D. Grossman, *Valery Bryusov and the Riddle of Russian Decadence* (1985); J. R. Reed, *Decadent Style* (1985); J. Birkett, *Sins of the Fathers* (1986); B. Dijkstra, *Idols of Perversity* (1986); L. C. Dowling, *Language and Decadence in the Victorian fin de siècle* (1986); D. Pick, *Faces of Degeneration* (1989); B. Spackman, *Decadent Genealogies* (1989); G. A. Cevasco, *Three Decadent Poets* (1990)—annotated bibl.; C. Paglia, *Sexual Personae* (1990); E. Showalter, *Sexual Anarchy* (1990); E. Donato, *The Script of Decadence* (1993); M. H. Pittock, *Spectrum of Decadence* (1993); A. Sinfield, *The Wilde Century* (1994); D. Weir, *Decadence and the Making of Modernism* (1995); E. Hanson, *Decadence and Catholicism* (1997); R. K. Garelick,

*Rising Star* (1998); *Perennial Decay*, ed. L. Constable, D. Denisoff and M. Potolsky (1999); C. Bernheimer, *Decadent Subjects*, ed. T. J. Klein and N. Schor (2002); G. C. Schoolfield, *A Baedeker of Decadence* (2003); O. Matich, *Erotic Utopia* (2005); K. MacLeod, *Fictions of British Decadence* (2006); *The Cambridge Companion to the Fin de Siècle*, ed. G. Marshall (2007).

A. G. Engstrom; C. Scott; J. Presto

**DECASYLLABLE.** A line of ten syllables; metrical structures built on it vary, but normally the term refers to the Fr. *décasyllabe* and the Eng. *iambic pentameter. In Fr. verse, the decasyllable appeared about the middle of the 11th c., in *La Vie de St. Alexis* and *Le Boèce*, with a *caesura after the fourth syllable and two fixed accents on the fourth and tenth syllables: so 4//6, with 6//4 as a possible variant form; 5//5, perhaps the oldest version of the decasyllable, also occurs both in the med. period and among poets of the 19th c. The classic 4//6 form leads one to expect a line of three rhythmic measures, one in the 4 and two in the 6; the description of the 5//5 alternative by Bonaventure des Périers (early 16th c.) as "taratantara" (2 + 3) suggests the expectation of two measures in each *hemistich of 5. With the appearance of the *Chanson de Roland* (early 12th c.), the decasyllable became the standard line of Fr. epic and narrative verse, i.e. the *chansons de geste*, until the appearance of the *alexandrine at the beginning of the 12th c., which gradually supplanted it. In OF lyric verse, it is more common than the *octosyllable, making it the principal Fr. meter from the 14th c. to the mid-16th c., when the poets of the *Pléiade appropriated the alexandrine for the lyric, too (Joachim du Bellay referred to the decasyllable as the *vers héroïque*; Pierre de Ronsard dubbed it the *vers commun* and employed it in his *Franciade* [1572], albeit against his better judgment). Thereafter, the alexandrine became the standard line for most serious poetry in Fr., though the decasyllable continued to play an important role: in the 17th and 18th cs., it served the *ballade, the *epigram, the *ode, the *mock epic, (e.g., Jean-Baptiste-Louis Gresset's *Ver-Vert* [1734]), the *verse epistle (Jean-Baptiste Rousseau), and comedy (Voltaire) and appeared among the *vers mêlés* of the fable; the intermittent use of the 5//5 version, alongside 4//6, in the 19th c. (Pierre de Béranger, Alfred de Musset, Marceline Desbordes-Valmore, Victor Hugo, Théophile Gautier, Charles Baudelaire, Théodore de Banville, Charles-Marie Leconte de Lisle) often harked back to its med. origins in song (e.g., *chansons de toile*) but was susceptible to other modalities, while in the hands of Paul Verlaine, Arthur Rimbaud, and Jules Laforgue, the line also became a site of metrico-rhythmic polymorphousness; in the 20th c., Paul Valéry was prompted by the decasyllable's insistent rhythmic shape to adopt it for "Le Cimetière marin" (1922), although he acknowledged its lack of popularity, characterized it as "poor and monotonous," and recognized the need to "raise this *Ten* to the power of *Twelve*." Ironically, it is in *vers libre* that the decasyllabic line

recovered much of its lost status, whether as an "authentic" decasyllable, metrically constituted, or as a nonce string of ten syllables.

In Italy, the *endecasillabo* (11 syllables but with a feminine ending) appeared early in the 12th c. and was used by Dante, Petrarch, and Boccaccio. Chaucer may have discovered the line in their work (the last syllable would have been dropped in Eng. pronunciation), if he had not already become acquainted with the corresponding Fr. meter. In any case, the decasyllabic line in Chaucer's hands took on the five-stress alternating pattern later to be called *iambic*, a form that, regardless of whether one counts syllables or stresses or both, and despite the considerable variation it enjoyed in the 15th c., as Chaucer's successors tried to imitate a meter they imperfectly understood, was secured by the authority of Chaucer's reputation until "rediscovered"—i.e., reconstructed—by Thomas Wyatt and Henry Howard, the Earl of Surrey, in the early 16th c. In the hands of Philip Sidney, Edmund Spenser, and William Shakespeare, the Eng. decasyllable—given the Latinate name *pentameter* by the classicizing Ren.—became the great staple meter of Eng. poetry and the foundation of *blank verse, the *heroic couplet, the *sonnet, and many other stanzaic forms; it has been estimated that some 70 percent of Eng. poetry of the high art-verse trad. has been written in the iambic pentameter line.

■ Bridges; P. Valéry, "Au sujet du *Cimetière marin*," *Oeuvres I*, ed. J. Hytier (1957); G. T. Wright, *Shakespeare's Metrical Art* (1988); J.-P. Bobillot, "Entre mètre et non-mètre: le « décasyllabe » chez Rimbaud," *Parade Sauvage* 10 (1994); B. de Cornulier, *Art poétique* (1995); M. J. Duffell, "'The Craft So Long to Lerne': Chaucer's Invention of Iambic Pentameter," *Chaucer Review* 34 (2000); A. English, *Verlaine, poète de l'indécidable* (2005).

T.V.F. Brogan; C. Scott

**DÉCIMA.** Sp. metrical term used loosely to denote any ten-line stanza but now usually used as the equivalent of *espinela, occasionally of *copla real*. The first *décimas* approximating the final form were the 14th- and 15th-c. ten-line variations of the *copla de arte menor*. The *décima italiana*, probably first used in the 18th c., is an octosyllabic *strophe rhyming *ababc:dedec*, the *c* rhymes being oxytones and the *colon denoting a pause. Other meters, particularly the *hendecasyllable with *heptasyllable, may be used, and the rhyme scheme and the position of the pause may vary, or lines may be unrhymed, provided that the two oxytones rhyme and are found one at the end of the strophe and the other at the pause. This strophe is related to the It. ten-line stanza, *decima rima*.

*See* lauda.

■ A. Paredes, *The Décima on the Texas-Mexico Border* (1968); Navarro; A. Paredes and G. Foss, *The Décima on the Texas-Mexican Border* (1968); *Formas narrativas de la tradición oral de México*, ed. M. Zavala Gómez de Campo (2009).

D. C. Clarke

**DECIR** (Sp., "to say" or "to compose," often used with the adverb *bien* [well] to denote the act of writing poetry; also spelled *dezir*). The act of writing or a poetic composition, used primarily in rubrics of the 15th-c. *cancioneros* and by their poets. Although scholarship has opposed *cantiga canción* (see CANTIGA) and *decir* by designating one as a fixed form set to music and sung and the other as read, recent studies indicate that the terms coincided, as music was not a consistent designator of genre, and most cancionero poetry appears to have been recited or silently read (Gómez-Bravo). The decir typically treats didactic or political rather than amatory matters and consists of an indeterminate number of octosyllabic *arte menor*, dodecasyllabic *arte mayor*, or mixed-verse *coplas*. Related to other terms of med. rhet. such as *dictar* (to compose) and the *ars dictaminis* (the art of writing pleasingly), the term *decir* was used to indicate competence in poetic composition related to the arts of rhet. and grammar (*ars poetriae*) and *ars dicendi* following Quintilian's definition in *Institutio oratoria*: "rhetoric ars est bene dicendi" (rhetoric is the art of speaking well, 2.17.37). Although the terms could be used interchangeably, *decir* became the favored term for a poetic composition and for the act of writing poetry, replacing *dictado* and dictar, from the mid-14th to mid-15th c.: "salve en la manera del trobar e del dezir" (save in the manner of invention and of proper composition; *Libro de buen amor*, S45–4, 14th c.); "dezires muy limados e bien escandidos" (very refined and well measured poetic compositions; *Cancionero de Baena*, PN1, Prologue, 15th c.).

■ Le Gentil; F. López Estrada, *Introducción a la literatura medieval española* (1952); T. Navarro Tomás, *Metrica española* (1956); *Cancionero de Juan Alfonso de Baena*, ed. B. Dutton and J. González Cuenca (1993); A. M. Gómez-Bravo, "*Decir canciones*: The Question of Genre in *Cancionero* Poetry," *Medieval Lyric*, ed. W. D. Paden (2000).

M. GALVEZ

**DECORUM** (Gr. *to prepon*, "what is decorous"). The cl. term *decorum* refers to one of the criteria for judging those things whose excellence lends itself more appropriately to qualitative than to quantitative measurement. This definition depends on the ancient distinction between two types of measure posited by Plato in *The Statesman* (283d–85a) and adopted by Aristotle in his ethical, political, rhetorical, and literary treatises. Excess and deficiency, Plato says, are measurable in terms of not only the quantitative largeness or smallness of objects in relation to each other but each object's approximation to a norm of "due measure." All the arts owe the effectiveness and beauty of their products to this norm, *to metron*, whose criteria of what is commensurate (*to metrion*), decorous (*to prepon*), timely (*to kairon*), and needful (*to deon*), all address themselves to the "mean" (*to meson*) rather than to the fixed, arithmetically defined extremes. This distinction is central to literary decorum, because lit. shares its subject matter and certain principles of stylistic representation

with the disciplines of law, ethics, and rhet., which also are concerned with the qualitative analysis and judgment of human experience.

With respect to subject matter, Aristotle says that poetry treats human actions (*Poetics* 2, 4, 6–9) by revealing their universal significance in terms of the "kinds of things a certain kind of person will say or do in accordance with probability or necessity" (Else trans., 9.4). The kinds of things said or done will indicate certain moral qualities (*poious*) of character that, in turn, confer certain qualities (*poias*) on the actions themselves (6.5–6). Extending the terms of Plato's *Statesman* (283d–85b, 294a–97e) to ethics, law, and rhet., Aristotle defines the concept of virtue necessary to evaluate such qualities of character as a balanced "disposition" (*hexis*) of the emotions achieved by the observation of the "mean" (*mesotes*) relative to each situation (*Nicomachean Ethics* [*EN*] 2.6). Likewise in law, equity is a "disposition" achieved through the individual application of a "quantitatively" invariable code of statutes for (amounts of) rewards and penalties to "qualitatively" variable and unpredictable human actions. As the builder of Lesbos bent his leaden ruler to a particular stone, so the judge, in drawing upon the universal law of nature (*to katholou*), might rectify the particular application of civil law by making a special ordinance to fit the discrete case (*EN* 5.7, 10). Equity brings these universal considerations to bear by looking to the qualitative questions of the legislator's intentions and of the kind (*poios*) of person the accused has generally or always been in order to mitigate his present act (*Rhetoric* 1.13.13–19).

With respect to stylistic representation, all verbal (as opposed to arithmetical) expression is qualitative and rests content if it can establish a likely similarity (rather than an exact equivalence) between things (Plato, *Cratylus* 432ab, *Timaeus* 29cd). *Diction achieves decorum by a proper balance between "distinctive" words, which contribute dignity while avoiding obtrusiveness, and "familiar" words, which, while avoiding meanness, contribute clarity (Aristotle, *Rhetoric* 3.2–3, *Poetics* 21–22). Lang. in general achieves decorum if the style expresses the degree of emotion proper to the importance of the subject and makes the speaker appear to have the kind of character proper to the occasion and audience. The greater the subject, the more powerful the emotions the speaker or writer may decorously solicit. The more shrewdly he estimates the "disposition" that informs the character of his listeners, the more he can achieve the "timely" (*eukairos*) degree of sophistication appropriate to the occasion (*Rhetoric* 3.7; cf. Plato, *Phaedrus* 277bc).

Influenced by the Middle Stoicism of Panaetius and Posidonius, Cicero did most to define and transmit the relation of literary decorum to ethics and law, suggested by such words as *decor* and *decet*, in his philosophical and rhetorical treatises (*De officiis* 1.14, 93–161; *De oratore* 69–74, 123–25). From his reformulation of Platonic, Aristotelian, and Isocratean attitudes, there flowed an immense variety of literary and artistic applications of the concept by grammarians, poets, rhetoricians, historians, philosophers, theologians, and encyclopedic writers on specialized disciplines. Most exemplary, perhaps, of the vitality and versatility of this trad. is Augustine's adaptation of it to Christian oratory and exegesis in *De doctrina christiana*, where, while virtually rejecting the cl. *doctrine* of "levels of style"—to which decorum was often reduced—he gave the cl. *principle* of decorum new life and applications (see Auerbach).

Like the "mean" and "disposition" of ethics and equity, decorum is an activity rather than a set of specific characteristics of style or content to be discovered, preserved, and reproduced. It is a fluid corrective process that must achieve and maintain, instant by instant, the delicate balance among the formal, cognitive, and judicative intentions of literary discourse. Its constant resistance to imbalance, taking different forms in different periods, never offers a "solution" to be found or expressed by literary "rules" with which later neoclassical theorists often try to identify it. As soon as they reduce it to a doctrine concerning either a given kind of subject or a given kind of style or a fixed relation of the one to the other, decorum ceases to exist, because its activity is a continuous negotiation between the two. For the forms that particular reductions or recoveries have taken, the reader must look to those literary controversies endemic to the period, genre, or issue of interest.

■ E. M. Cope and J. E. Sandys, *The Rhetoric of Aristotle*, 3 v. (1877); G. L. Hendrickson, "The Peripatetic Mean of Style and the Three Stylistic Characters," *AJP* 25 (1904); and "The Origin and Meaning of the Ancient Characters of Style," *AJP* 26 (1905); J.W.H. Atkins, *Literary Criticism in Antiquity*, 2 v. (1934); W. Jaeger, *Paideia*, 3 v. (1943)—cultural background; E. De Bruyne, *Études d'esthétique médiévale*, 3 v. (1946)—med. background; M. T. Herrick, *The Fusion of Horatian and Aristotelian Literary Criticism, 1531–1555* (1946); Curtius, ch. 10; Norden; H. I. Marrou, *Histoire de l'éducation dans l'antiquité*, 5th ed. (1960)—cultural background; Weinberg; F. Quadlbauer, *Die antike Theorie der Genera Dicendi im lateinischen Mittelalter* (1962); C. O. Brink, *Horace on Poetry*, 3 v. (1963–82); G. F. Else, *Aristotle's Poetics: The Argument* (1963); E. Auerbach, *Literary Language and Its Public in Late Latin Antiquity and in the Middle Ages*, trans. R. Manheim (1965), ch. 1; T. A. Kranidas, *The Fierce Equation* (1965); M. Pohlenz, "*To prepon*," *Kleine Schriften*, ed. H. Dorrie (1965); A. Patterson, *Hermogenes and the Renaissance* (1970); T. McAlindon, *Shakespeare and Decorum* (1973); Murphy; W. Edinger, *Samuel Johnson and Poetic Style* (1977)—18th-c. background; W. Trimpi, *Muses of One Mind* (1983)—see index; K. Eden, *Poetic and Legal Fiction in the Aristotelian Tradition* (1986); J. Mueller, "The Mastery of Decorum: Politics as Poetry in Milton's Sonnets," *CritI* 3 (1987); T. Krier, *Gazing on Secret Sights: Spenser, Classical Imitation and the Decorum of Vision* (1990), chs. 3–5; S. D. Troyan, *Textual Decorum: A Rhetoric of Attitudes*

*in Medieval Literature* (1994); W. V. Clausen, *Virgil's "Aeneid": Decorum, Allusion, and Ideology* (2002); R. Sowerby, "The Decorum of Pope's *Iliad*," *Translation and Literature* 13 (2004); A. Paternoster, "Decorum and Indecorum in the '*Seconda redazione*' of B. Castiglione's '*Libro del Cortegiano*,'" *MLR* 99 (2004); L. Kurke, *Aesopic Conversations* (2011).

W. Trimpi; F. L. Blumberg

**DEEP IMAGE.** The Deep Image school of poetry, more than any other movement of the time, proved to be both a watershed and a catalyst for the diverse energies suddenly appearing in Am. lit. and culture throughout the 1960s. It gave rise to a poetry whose characteristics recombined elements of other groups (esp. the *Black Mountain school) with a new energy source, Sp. *surrealism, to produce what two of its central apologists, George Lensing and Ronald Moran, define as a poetry of "the emotive imagination." The base element of this poetry is the *image, and its "form" is a dreamlike, rather than objectively recognizable, progression of images, whose aim is not to dismantle the reader's sense of self and the world but to startle her into quiet, unwilled acts of recognition. In this poetry, also known as *deep-image poetry* (the term was first used by Robert Kelly in his essay "Notes on the Poetry of Deep Image"), the poet's inner self and the outer world become landscapes described and fused by images that treat both as physical yet highly charged phenomena. In the best of these poems, the poet brings self and reader into a shared, exploratory state of mind that involves both in an associational journey to an open-ended sort of closure—a final image that feels like revelation yet leaves the participants feeling suspended and pleasantly provoked.

The Deep Image movement, although it arose partly in response to the spirit of the decade, nevertheless came about largely through the singular energy of Robert Bly, who promoted it as an antidote to modernist aesthetics (see MODERNISM). His and William Duffy's magazine, *The Fifties*, which began in 1958 and soon became *The Sixties*, flourished throughout the decade as the showcase for writers they felt would steer contemp. Am. poetry in the direction it needed to go: inward, toward the underexplored regions of the psyche, by means of startling but rightly intuited images. The magazine also provided Bly with an arena for the impassioned, reductive, provocative lit. crit. for which he became famous, a crit. that ranks intuition over rationalism and *imagery over discourse as a means of penetrating, for a moment, the reader's subconscious.

If Bly's sense of mission inspired him to dismiss Shakespeare and the entire formal Eng. trad. with a theatrical sweep of his pen, it also made him recognize and offer to the public North Am. poets for whom images were a mode of thought rather than skillfully crafted decoration—poets such as James Wright, Galway Kinnell, W. S. Merwin, David Ignatow, Donald Hall, William Stafford, and Louis Simpson. Bly also produced and published trans. of Eur. and Latin Am.

poets whose work, more than any other single factor, startled a younger generation of poets into seeing new possibilities for their own energies. Esp. influential were Bly's trans. of the Ger. writers Gottfried Benn and Georg Trakl, Sp. writers Federico García Lorca and Antonio Machado, Peruvian writer César Vallejo, Chilean writer Pablo Neruda, Fr. writers René Char and Paul Éluard, and numerous other 19th- and 20th-c. poets from Norway, Latin America, and other parts of Europe. All of them, Bly maintained, had "passed through surrealism" and, as a result, spoke from that fecund area of the subconscious where spirituality resides. This spirituality, as Bly demonstrated both in his crit. and his own poetry, derives its force from the natural world, from silence and solitude, and equips the writer to confront the complexities of mod. life.

Like the Black Mountain poets, Bly sought to explore the self in an area beyond that of ego, an area that might offer "organic" truth of its own. He mapped this area via the psyche, using ground broken by Sigmund Freud and Carl Jung to highlight the associative powers of the mind as it responds to resonant imagery and opens the self to depths that must be acknowledged despite pressures from the culture and the individual's self-protective efforts to avoid them. Although the Black Mountain poets concerned themselves more with the physical body than with the image as a basis for their "organic poetry," much of the work they produced in the 1960s, esp. that of Denise Levertov, Gary Snyder, and Robert Creeley, explored and revealed new depths of interaction between the self and the physical world; in the process, it addressed itself to nature and to perception in resonant new ways. Bly recognized this achievement by publishing and discussing their poetry at length in his magazine. Indeed, another of the many repercussions of Bly's energetic revamping of the poetic imagination in America was the melting of boundaries between these two important movements, one of which was legitimately avant-garde in the 1950s and one of which seemed an inevitable condensation of the energies burgeoning anyway, throughout the culture, in the 1960s.

*See,* UNITED STATES, POETRY OF THE.

■ R. Kelly, "Notes on the Poetry of Deep Image," *Trobar* 2 (1961); "Introduction," *Contemporary American Poetry*, ed. D. Hall (1962); R. Bly, *Leaping Poetry* (1972); P. Zweig, "The New Surrealism," *Contemporary Poetry in America*, ed. R. Boyers (1974); C. Altieri, *Enlarging the Temple* (1979); R. Bly, "A Wrong Turning in American Poetry" and "What the Image Can Do," *Claims for Poetry*, ed. D. Hall (1982).

■ Poetry: R. Bly, *Silence in the Snowy Fields* (1962); W. S. Merwin, *The Moving Target* (1963); L. Simpson, *At the End of the Open Road* (1963); W. Stafford, *Traveling through the Dark* (1963); J. Wright, *The Branch Will Not Break* (1963); G. Kinnell, *Flower Herding on Mount Monadnock* (1964); R. Bly, *Light around the Body* (1967); W. S. Merwin, *The Lice* (1967); G. Kinnell, *Body Rags* (1968); M. Strand, *Reasons for Moving* (1968); J. Wright, *Shall We Gather at the River*

(1968); W. S. Merwin, *The Carrier of Ladders* (1970); M. Strand, *Darker* (1970).

L. ULLMAN

**DEFAMILIARIZATION.** "The technique of art is to make objects 'unfamiliar,' to make forms difficult, to increase the difficulty and length of perception because the process of perception is an aesthetic end in itself and must be prolonged. Art is a way of experiencing the artfulness of an object; the object is not important." In this famous passage from "Iskusstvo kak priem" ("On the Newest Russian Poetry," 1917), the Rus. formalist Viktor Shklovsky coined the term *ostranenie*, a neologism often trans. into Eng. as "defamiliarization" or, less commonly, "estrangement" or "alienation." Defamiliarization refers to the artist's and critic's attention to the "devices" and formal elements of literary creation. The purpose of art, in this view, is to impart the sensation of things as they are perceived, not as they are known. Perception, moreover, becomes an aesthetic end in itself, with a focus on the reading process.

The idea of defamiliarization grew from the formalists' analysis of futurist *manifestos and poetry (see FUTURISM). The manifestos play with the form by incorporating poetry, artwork, and creative prose. The term the futurists use for this aesthetic instigation is *sdvig* or shift in perception. The focus lies in making the lang. and the form in which it is presented strange and uncomfortable so that the process of perception slows down and alters.

In Roman Jakobson's theory of poetics, the poet strives to liberate the word from the signified, from communicative meaning, thereby restoring it to the level of aesthetics. For Jakobson, formal defamiliarization connotes that which separates poetic lang. from the mundane (*bytovoj iazyk*). He characterizes Velimir Khlebnikov's writing as laying the device bare ("*obnazhennost',—otsutstvie opravdatel'noj provolki*" ["Iskusstvo kak priem"]).

The notion of defamiliarization in poetry predates the Rus. formalists. E.g., in *De vulgari eloquentia* (*On Vernacular Eloquence*, 1304), Dante sets out to prove that there is an "illustrious vernacular," which should be venerated as a lang. suitable for poetry the same as the "sacred, solemn and eternal Latin language." He seeks to prove that the vernacular can be poetic, that the poetic exists in the mundane.

The idea of using the familiar lang. because it has paradoxically become unfamiliar prompts William Wordsworth in his Preface to *Lyrical Ballads* (1800) to propose the use of "the real language of men" to replace the "gaudiness and inane phraseology" of the erudite, neoclassical style that dominated contemp. writing at the time. Wordsworth exceeds even Dante in his critique of elevated poetic speech in favor of ordinary lang. Wordsworth complicates the discussion, though, when he seeks to rediscover the "language really used by men" yet sees the need to "throw over them a certain coloring of imagination, whereby ordinary things should be presented to the mind in an unusual aspect."

Defamiliarization is the basis of Yuri Tynianov's claims regarding literary evolution. Tynianov's thesis revolves around the idea that the defamiliarized itself, at some point, must become automatized. Literary evolution is, thus, both motivated by and results from defamiliarization. The Rus. formalist theory of defamiliarization was influential in 20th-c. critical theory, possibly, most significantly in Bertolt Brecht's *Verfremdung* theory of alienation in theater.

■ *Russian Formalist Criticism: Four Essays*, ed. L. Lemon and M. J. Reis (1965); A. Kruchenykh and V. Khlebnikov, *Slovo Kak Takovoe* (1969); *Texte Der Russischen Formalisten Band I-IV: Texte zur Theorie des Verses und der poetischen Sprache*, ed. M. Imdahl et al. (1972); D. Laferriere, "Potebnya, Shklovskij and the Familiarity: Strangeness Paradox," *Russian Literature* 4 (1976); R. H. Stacy, *Defamiliarization in Language and Literature* (1977); V. Erlich, *Russian Formalism: History—Doctrine*, 4th ed. (1981); *Russian Formalism: A Retrospective Glance*, ed. R. L. Jackson and S. Rudy (1985); R. Jakobson, *Language in Literature*, ed. K. Pomorska and S. Rudy (1987); J. Striedter, *Literary Structure, Evolution, and Value: Russian Formalism and Czech Structuralism Reconsidered* (1989); V. Shklovsky, *Theory of Prose*, trans. B. Sher (1990); I. Gregson, *Contemporary Poetry and Postmodernism: Dialogue and Estrangement* (1996); L. Trotsky, *Literature and Revolution*, ed. W. Keach, trans. R. Strunsky (2005); "Estrangement Revisited (II)," *PoT* 27.1 (spec. iss., 2006); S. Jestrovic, *Theatre of Estrangement: Theory, Practice, Ideology* (2006); D. Robinson, *Estrangement and the Somatics of Literature: Tolstoy, Shklovsky, Brecht* (2008); *Ostranenie*, ed. A. Van Den Oever (2010).

Y. LORMAN

**DEIXIS.** *Deictics* (or shifters, *embrayeurs*) are features of lang. involving a reference to a specific act of communication in which they are used; *deixis* is the process of deictic speech. Deictic terms refer to a present situation of utterance and its speaker rather than to a fixed object, concept, or reality. Common deictics are those of time (e.g., *now, today*), space (e.g., *here, this town*), person (*I, you*), and social position (e.g., formal and informal address); but many ling. elements such as demonstratives, verb tenses, and anaphoric articles are potentially deictics, depending on how they refer to the situation of utterance. In each case, the reality to which the deictic term refers is solely a "reality of discourse" (Benveniste): the instance of deixis can be identified only within the discourse that contains it and, therefore, has no meaning except in the context in which it is produced. In lit., and esp. in poetic lang., deictics function as important interpretive devices. By alluding to a real or hypothetical situation of utterance (such as the present moment from which a poem is spoken within its fiction) and relating it to other situations (e.g., a past event that informs that present) or by collapsing such distinctions (as Walt Whitman and *Language poetry often do), deictics are factors in the establishment of a poetic *persona, temporality, and relation to hist.

*See* LINGUISTICS AND POETICS.

■ U. Weinreich, "On the Semantic Structure of Language," *Universals of Language*, ed. J. Greenberg (1966); E. Benveniste, *Problems in General Linguistics*, trans. M. E. Meek (1971); R. Jakobson, "Shifters and Verbal Categories," Jakobson, v. 2; Culler; O. Ducrot and T. Todorov, *Encyclopedic Dictionary of the Sciences of Language*, trans. C. Porter (1979); R. Greene, *Post-Petrarchism* (1991).

N. PINES

**DEMOTION.** In Eng. versification, when three consecutive syllables or single-syllable words are stressed in a line whose metrical pattern has been securely established—by preceding lines or by a reader/performer's sense of its trad. ("this is a tetrameter stanza"; "these are pentameter lines")—the middle syllable is experienced as "demoted," although it may have exactly the same stress, emphasis, or loudness as the adjacent words or syllables. Derek Attridge states a rule for this demotion thus: "A stressed syllable may realise an offbeat when it occurs between two stressed syllables." The reader/performer recognizes that to maintain the metricality of the work, only the first and third emphasized syllables will "carry the *beat."

E.g., when Thomas Hardy speaks about being undistressed "By hearts grown cold to me," an established expectation of a *trimeter line will demote "grown" between "hearts" and "cold." When Emily Dickinson, writing of agony, says that "The eyes glaze once, and that is Death," the four-beat expectation is realized by the demotion of "glaze."

Demotion can also occur in a second metrical circumstance that Attridge defines as being "after a line-boundary and before a stressed syllable." In Shakespeare's song beginning with the tetrameters "Full fathom five thy father lies; / Of his bones are coral made," the initial stressed word, "Full," is demoted.

Both "after a line-boundary" and "between two stressed syllables" conditions are in play when Alexander Pope's pentameter states that "True ease in writing comes from art, not chance," where a performer can experience demotions of both "True" and "not."

Demotion thus allows these additionally stressed lines better to convey, within the alternations of familiar patterns, Hardy's and Dickinson's heightened emotions, the depth of a father's drowning, and the strength of Pope's conviction about artful writing.

■ Attridge, *Rhythms*; Carper and Attridge.

T. CARPER

**DENMARK, POETRY OF.** *Rune inscriptions prove the existence of a lost heroic poetry in Denmark, known only from Saxo Grammaticus's Lat. prose and hexameter rendering in *Gesta Danorum* (ca. 1200). *Bjarkamál* (The Lay of Bjarke)—whose heroes also appear in the OE poems *Widsith* and *Beowulf*—and the so-called Lay of Ingjald celebrate courage and loyalty, reflecting an aristocratic ethos that epitomizes the ideals of the Viking age.

During the Middle Ages (1100–1500), Danish poetry follows the Eur. models of courtly and sacred poetry. In the five lyric poems to the Virgin Mary attributed to Per Räff Lille (ca. 1450–1500), *troubadour influences blend with imagery from the biblical Song of Songs. The anonymous *Den danske Rimkrønike* (The Danish Rhymed Chronicle), a hist. of the Danish kings, is an important work in *Knittelvers*. The dominant genre of the Middle Ages, however, is the folk *ballad, which reached Denmark from France in the early 12th c. In the 16th c., poetry in the vernacular was still med. in spirit and form, notably subject to a growing Ger. influence in the wake of the Lutheran Reformation.

In the 17th c., as the Ren. reached Denmark, efforts were made to create a Danish *national poetry on cl. models. Anders Arrebo (1587–1637) produced a religious epic, *Hexaëmeron* (ca. 1622, pub. 1661), describing the six days of Creation. Based on Guillaume de Salluste du Bartas's *La Sepmaine*, it is composed partly in twice-rhymed *hexameter, partly in *alexandrines. The artificiality of the poem's cl.-mythological diction is offset by descriptive details from Scandinavian nature and folk life. Following Martin Opitz's *Das Buch der Deutschen Poeterey* (The Book of German Poetics, 1624), Hans Mikkelsen Ravn (1610–63) in 1649 published a manual of prosody with illustrations, making available to future poets a varied formal repertoire. Anders Bording (1619–77) is noted for his *anacreontic verse, but he also single-handedly published a rhymed monthly newspaper, *Den Danske Mercurius* (The Danish Mercury, 1666–77), composed in stately alexandrines. Thomas Kingo (1634–1703), a much greater poet, was able to exploit fully the new formal variety. His principal achievement is his two volumes of church hymns, still sung today, *Aandelige Siunge-Koor* (Spiritual Choirs, 1674–81). With their thematic counterpoints, sensuous imagery, and often high-strung metaphors, Kingo's hymns are unmistakably *baroque in style, the highlights being his Easter hymns.

In the early 18th c., Fr. neoclassicism entered Danish lit., mainly because of the activity of the Dano-Norwegian Ludvig Holberg (1684–1754). Best known for his bourgeois prose comedies, Holberg in his verse *mock epic *Peder Paars* (1719–20) showed himself to be a brilliant satirist. The rationalism of Holberg, and of the period, is counterbalanced, however, by a sentimental undercurrent, represented by Ambrosius Stub (1705–58) and Hans Adolf Brorson (1694–1764). Stub practiced a wide variety of genres, from religious lyrics to drinking songs. His concise, graceful form and light, melodious rhythms are influenced by the It. operatic aria, and his delicately picturesque style reveals *rococo features. Brorson, a religious Pietist, also composed hymns in complex meters derived from the elegant rococo aria, with its dialogue and echo effects.

Danish neoclassicism was continued by a group of Norwegian authors living in Copenhagen, members of *Det norske Selskab* (The Norwegian Society; see NORSKE SELSKAB), while Johannes Ewald (1743–81), a preromantic deeply influenced by the Ger. poet F. G. Klopstock, championed the claims of subjectivity. Ewald's mythological dramas on ON themes are largely forgotten, but his pietistically inspired lyric verse is very much alive. He excelled in the religious ode, exemplified by *Rungsteds Lyksaligheder* (The Joys of Rungsted, 1773), where nature description is a vehicle for the glorification of God. The only noteworthy poet of the last 20 years of the century was Jens Baggesen (1764–1826), a mercurial spirit who alternated between cl. and romantic sensibility in accordance with the tenor of his personal experience.

Adam Oehlenschläger (1779–1850) achieved the breakthrough of *romanticism in Danish poetry; his first collection, *Digte* (Poems, 1803), was inspired by the aesthetics of the Jena school of Friedrich Schelling, A. W. Schlegel, and K.W.F Schlegel as mediated by the Copenhagen lectures of Henrich Steffens (1802). These poems signified a fierce rejection of the rationalist spirit of the 18th c., together with a rediscovery of Nordic hist. and mythology and a glorification of the creative genius who alone is capable of a unified view of nature and hist. Oehlenschläger increased his range in *Poetiske Skrifter* (Poetic Writings, 1805), which contained prose and poetry, narrative cycles, drama, lyric, and ballads and romances in varying meters. After 1806, Oehlenschläger's subjectivism is tempered by the growing influence of J. W. Goethe's and Friedrich Schiller's objective poetry and the Heidelberg romantic school, reorienting his work—as well as Danish lit. generally—toward national and patriotic themes. *Nordiske Digte* (Nordic Poems, 1807) included several dramas based on ON figures and themes. The narrative cycle *Helge* (1814), with its impressive array of metrical forms and styles marking subtle shifts of moods, rises to Sophoclean heights in the concluding dramatic episode. Prompted by Oehlenschläger's publication of *Digte* (1803), A. W. Schack von Staffeldt (1769–1826) published his own collection titled *Digte* (1804), and later *Nye Digte* (New Poems, 1808). Staffeldt's poetry, with its emphasis on the poet's longing to bridge the separation between this world and a divine, Platonic world of Ideas, received little attention during his lifetime but is now considered an important contribution to Danish romanticism. The work of another romantic, N.F.S. Grundtvig (1783–1872) was more national in inspiration. Grundtvig, while more a cultural leader than a poet, created an enduring literary monument in his hymns. With their union of humanism and Christianity and their pervasive imagery taken from the Danish landscape and Nordic mythology, they represent a unique poetic achievement.

Around 1830, Danish poetry moved toward greater realism and psychological diversity, its focus shifting from an idealized past to a more complex present. Johan Ludvig Heiberg (1791–1860), the theorist of *romantisme*, as this movement has been called, managed to shuttle elegantly between actuality and the dream world in his romantic plays. Christian Winther (1796–1876) blended lyric and narrative elements in the *idyll, as in *Træsnit* (Woodcuts, 1828). Winther's formal virtuosity is demonstrated in the romance *Hjortens Flugt* (The Flight of the Hart, 1855), set in med. times and employing a modified *Nibelungenstrophe. The cycle of love poems *Til Een* (To Someone, 1843, 1849), in which eros is worshipped as a divine force, is notable for its poignant lyricism. The brief lyrics of the Heinrich Heine–inspired *Erotiske Situationer* (Erotic Situations, 1838) by Emil Aarestrup (1806–56), with their picturesque detail, psychological complexity, and emotional dissonance, express a distinctly mod. sensibility—sophisticated and sensual—and represent a high point in Danish love poetry. While the early work of Frederik Paludan-Müller (1809–76) is fraught with aestheticism, *Adam Homo* (1841–48), a three-volume novel in verse, embodies a rigorous ethical philosophy. Through its portrait of a gifted, opportunistic antihero who pays for worldly success with the loss of his soul, the book presents a satirical picture of contemp. Danish culture.

After *naturalism was introduced by the critic Georg Brandes (1842–1927) around 1870, writers turned their attention to political, social, and sexual problems—fitter subjects for prose than poetry. Yet Brandes was important to both Jens Peter Jacobsen (1847–85) and Holger Drachmann (1846–1908), each with a distinctive profile as a poet. The sparse but first-rate lyrical production of Jacobsen, known chiefly as a novelist, was published posthumously as *Digte og Udkast* (Poems and Sketches) in 1886. Unique are his "arabesques," capriciously winding free-verse *monologues—the first modernist poetry in Denmark—whose intellectual probing is veiled in colorful ornamental lang. and evocative moods. The youthful *Digte* (1872) of Drachmann more directly echoed the radical ideas of Brandes, as in the poem "Engelske Socialister" (English Socialists). But soon Drachmann abandoned ideology for personal lyricism. In *Sange ved Havet* (Songs by the Sea, 1877), his best collection, the sea is perceived as an image of his own protean spirit. With *Sangenes Bog* (Book of Songs, 1889) radicalism reappeared, though now tempered by an awareness of age and mutability that lends a poignant existential resonance to the texts. Through his free rhythms and melodiousness, formal inventiveness, and unprecedented range of moods and attitudes, Drachmann renewed the style of romantic verse and made an extraordinary impact on subsequent Danish poetry.

Both Drachmann and Jacobsen, as well as Charles Baudelaire and Paul Verlaine, influenced the neoromantic movement of the 1890s in Danish poetry, which rejected naturalism in favor of an aesthetic demand for beauty and a mystically colored religiosity. Its program was formulated in *Taarnet* (The Tower, 1893–94), edited by Johannes Jørgensen (1866–1956), who with *Stemninger* (Moods, 1892) had introduced the dreams and visions of *symbolism into Danish poetry. Jørgensen's later poetry is marked by his 1896 conversion to Catholicism. After 1900, he further refined his condensed mode of expression, employing simple meters and rhythms to express a fervent religiosity. A more consistent follower of Fr. symbolism, as both a metaphysical and an aes-

thetic theory, was Sophus Claussen (1865–1931). This outlook is evident in his erotic poetry, where the surface sexual theme masks an underlying ontology, one of irreducible opposites. Claussen was deeply concerned with the nature of the creative process and with the poet's role. In his last major collection, *Heroica* (1925), a highlight of Danish poetry, art and beauty are invoked as the only means of spiritual survival in a materialistic world. Notable is the poem "Atomernes Oprør" (Revolt of the Atoms), a dystopian fantasy in which Claussen shows himself to be the last great master of the hexameter in Danish poetry. Other major neoromantics were Viggo Stuckenberg (1863–1905), Helge Rode (1870–1937), and Ludvig Holstein (1864–1943). While Stuckenberg's melancholy meditations on love's tragedy are executed with an exquisite sense of style, Rode's ethereal poems verge on the ecstatic. The best of Holstein's unadorned lyrics derive from his pantheistic vision of the unity of the human being and nature.

Danish poetry of the 20th c. encompasses diverse currents and styles, determined partly by international vogues, partly by sociopolitical events. The period before World War I replaced the introverted neoromanticism of the 1890s with *realism. A Jutland regional lit. emerged, dominated by Jeppe Aakjær (1866–1930). The central poet of the period, and one of Denmark's greatest writers, was the Nobel Prize winner Johannes V. Jensen (1873–1950). His first collection, *Digte* (Poems, 1906), a milestone in mod. Danish poetry, centers on a conflict between longing and a zest for life, alternating with *Weltschmerz*. Characteristic are a number of prose poems in which Jensen voices his worship of 20th-c. technology, together with a yearning for distant places and periods rendered in timeless, mythic images. After 1920, he used more traditional meters as well as alliterative ON forms. Jensen's poetry constitutes a unique blend of precise observation, philosophical reflection, and romantic vision. His innovative poetic *diction, with its incongruous mixture of crass realism and refined sensuousness, bold visionary imagery and muted lyricism, has been enormously influential.

During and after World War I, a generation of poets emerged who, inspired by Jensen and by *expressionism in painting and in Ger. poetry, endeavored to create new forms of beauty. Most sensational was Emil Bønnelycke (1893–1953), whose exuberant zest for life and glorification of technology were expressed in hymnlike prose poems, but Tom Kristensen (1893–1974) was artistically more accomplished. In *Fribytterdrømme* (Buccaneer Dreams, 1920), Kristensen conveyed the restless spirit and explosive primitivism of the Jazz Age in an orgiastic display of color and sound. In the poem "Reklameskibet" (The Show Boat, 1923), Otto Gelsted (1888–1968) charged expressionist art with pandering to commercialism and neglecting fundamental human concerns from a Marxist point of view.

The poetry of Nis Petersen (1897–1943) and Paul la Cour (1902–56), the dominant figures of the 1930s, is also informed by humanist concerns. Petersen's anguished verse voices concern for the predicament of Western culture. La Cour, whose sensibility was formed by Claussen and mod. Fr. poets, stressed the redemptive nature of poetry. His *Fragmenter af en Dagbog* (Fragments of a Diary, 1948), which mingles philosophy, poetic theory, and verse, profoundly influenced the poets who came to maturity during the war. The surrealist Jens August Schade (1903–78) defined his attitude to the times by espousing a Lawrencian *primitivism. His *Hjertebogen* (The Heart Book, 1930) contains sexually explicit love poems, along with nature impressions transformed by erotic feeling and a cosmic imagination.

Under the pressure of war and Nazi occupation, the 1940s instilled new vigor and urgency into Danish poetry. Two distinct responses to the brutality and destructiveness of World War II were evident: an activation of political consciousness, on the one hand, and an intensive quest for a meaningful, often metaphysical worldview, on the other. Inspirational was the work of Gustaf Munch-Petersen (1912–38), a literary existentialist who foreshadowed postwar *modernism; through his death in Spain fighting Fascism, he became the prototype of the committed writer. Possessed by a vision of total union between conscious and subconscious, dream and reality, and stimulated by the *imagism and *surrealism of the Swedish and *Finland-Swedish modernists, Munch-Petersen created a remarkable poetry that expressed a personal myth of self-making and self-liberation. Another paradigmatic poet was Morten Nielsen (1922–44), whose hard, weighty, unfinished verse oscillates between an existentialist affirmation of self and renunciation and death. Closely related to these two figures was Erik Knudsen (1922–2007), who, torn between beauty and politics, increasingly used poetry as the vehicle for a Marxist critique of society.

The central poets of the 1940s, following la Cour, saw poetry as a means of personal and cultural redemption. Striving for a form that would mirror their perception of a fragmented reality, they shaped a richly symbolic style inspired by T. S. Eliot and R. M. Rilke. The absence of a shared cultural and spiritual heritage, together with messianic longings, was most convincingly expressed by a group of poets whose original forum was the jour. *Heretica* (1948–53). Ole Sarvig (1921–81) and Ole Wivel (1921–2004) both embodied the pattern of rebirth after cultural catastrophe in their poetry, utilizing essentially Christian symbolism. Thorkild Bjørnvig (1918–2004) saw poetry itself as a liberating force. In his first, Rilke-inspired collection, *Stjærnen bag Gavlen* (The Star behind the Gable, 1947), eros is the predominant theme, treated with classic discipline in stanzas of great musicality and substance. In the 1970s, Bjørnvig changed the focus of his poetry to deal with ecological issues.

Others pursued different paths, unaffected by ideology or metaphysical probing. Tove Ditlevsen (1918–76) followed trad. and wrote rhymed verse in a neoromantic style. Piet Hein (1905–96) in his 20 volumes of *Gruk* (*Grooks*, 1940–63) combined scientific insights with a skillful, epigrammatic play of words and ideas. And Frank Jæger (1926–77), an elusive successor to

Schade, noted for his verbal wizardry, cultivated the *idyll, though in a broken form with an ominous undertone.

During the 1960s, an extroverted poetic experimentalism emerged, directed both against the materialism of the mod. welfare state and against prevailing ivory-tower literary attitudes. This change was largely due to Klaus Rifbjerg (b. 1931), the most versatile Danish postwar writer. Rifbjerg's verse registers the chaotic plenitude of experience in technological society by means of a fractured syntax and a vast, often technical-scientific vocabulary. Rifbjerg's two early collections *Konfrontation* (1960), with its photographically precise observations of the mod., technical world, and *Camouflage* (1961), which draws on cinematic montage and free association in a surrealist search for origins and a liberated self, profoundly affected Danish modernism. The themes of Rifbjerg's many subsequent collections of poetry are diverse and include everyday life, politics, and mythology.

A continuation of the introspective approach of the 1940s is evident in the poetry of Jørgen Sonne (b. 1925), which is marked by intellectual complexity and formal rigor, and Jørgen Gustava Brandt (1929–2006), who used myths and religious symbols to express a longing for epiphany.

In the mid-1960s, a tendency emerged toward ling. experimentation and concretism (see CONCRETE POETRY), the use of words as building blocks possessing intrinsic value, without reference to any other reality. This structuralist approach is present in *Romerske Bassiner* (Roman Pools, 1963) by the Marxist poet Ivan Malinowski (1926–1989). In the esoteric, systemic texts of Per Højholt (1928–2004), a major figure in Danish poetic modernism, lang. is transformed into intellectually challenging signs and closed symbols. Characteristic for Højholt's experimental and often humorous approach are *Poetens hoved* (The Poet's Head, 1963), *Turbo* (1968) and the 12 volumes of his *Praksis* (Practice, 1977–96) series. In his similarly untraditional and experimental poetry, the very productive Peter Laugesen (b. 1942) uses a genre-defying and self-reflective poetic lang. inspired by *Beat poetry, surrealism, and Zen Buddhism to expose and confront the ideological lang. of power and society. Wordplay and verbal *ambiguity also characterize the popular, witty, and thought-provoking verse of Benny Andersen (b. 1929). Klaus Høeck (b. 1938) uses systematic compositional principles inspired by mathematics, ling., and other forms in his often monumental poetry collections, as in *Hjem* (Home, 1985), where lang. is recast into complex structures in an attempt to illustrate the poet's striving to define God. Poul Borum (1934–96) connected visual perception with existential reflection. The poetry of Henrik Nordbrandt (b. 1945) often displays a sense of melancholia expressed in paradoxical metaphorical descriptions of an existential interplay between presence and absence.

Inger Christensen (1935–2009) used complex systems and principles to shape her poetry. An important work in Danish modernism, *det* (*it*, 1969), incorporates terms from the work of the linguist Viggo Brøndal and is structured according to mathematical systems. In *Alfabet* (*Alphabet*, 1981), the alphabet and the Fibonacci sequence (1-2-3-5-8-13-etc.) are used to create a compositional structure. A classic in Danish literature, *Sommerfugledalen—et requiem* (*Butterfly Valley: A Requiem*, 1991) combines a received poetic structure, the *sonnet sequence, with mod. and existential themes: life, death, memory, lang.

Following the political and social changes of the late 1960s and early 1970s, Danish poetry became more realistic. The poems of Vita Andersen (b. 1942) revolve around childhood experiences and the workplace, and the collections of Marianne Larsen (b. 1951) analyze sexual repression, class struggle, and imperialism from a feminist perspective.

By the end of the 1970s, a new poetry, frequently referred to as *body modernism*, began to emerge, building on the ling. experiments of the 1960s but with a focus on the body, city life, and a sense of alienation. F. P. Jac (1955–2008) created a unique poetic lang., breaking up grammatical categories and constructing new words and expressions. Jac's *Misfat* (1980) is typical for the period with its insistence on erotic and bodily ecstasy as a liberating force and its fascination with the nightlife of the city, themes that also characterize the poetry, both desperate and ecstatic, of Michael Strunge (1958–86). City life is also the preferred environment in *City Slang* (1981) by Søren Ulrik Thomsen (b. 1956). In *Hjemfalden* (Reverted, 1991) and *Det skabtes vaklen* (The Wavering of Creation, 1996), Thomsen reflects on death, loneliness, and aging, using intricate poetic lines. The poetry of Pia Tafdrup (b. 1952) combines the erotic with images of nature in rhythmic, sensuous lang. *Dronningeporten* (*Queen's Gate*, 1999) interweaves images of water in nature (sea, river, rain) with an inner emotional landscape.

Danish poetry of the 1990s incorporated ling. and postmod. awareness with an interest in everyday life. In *Mellem tænderne* (Between the Teeth, 1992), Kirsten Hammann (b. 1965) dismissively describes the body in playful, ironic, and colloquial lang. Pia Juul (b. 1962) experiments with the poetic voice, creating a fragmented, dialogical poetry that mirrors everyday spoken lang. in *sagde jeg, siger jeg* (I said, I say, 1999). The emotionally charged poetry of Naja Marie Aidt (b. 1963) is centered on everyday life. The complex, hermetic poetry of Simon Grotrian (b. 1961), inspired by surrealism, concretism, and baroque poetry, combines striking poetic images with religious elements.

A multidimensional mix of poetic styles, genres, topics, and influences characterizes the poetry of young Danish poets after 2000. Ursula Andkjær Olsen (b. 1970) plays with lang. by breaking up and reassembling colloquial phrases and *dead metaphors in a combination of styles, commenting on daily life, ideology, politics, commercials, and other topics. Similarly multifaceted and unconventional, in style and content, is *kingsize* (2006) by Mette Moestrup (b. 1969).

■ **Anthologies and Primary Texts**: *Oxford Book of Scandinavian Verse*, ed. E. W. Gosse and W. A. Craigie (1925); *The Jutland Wind*, ed. R. P. Keigwin (1944); *In Denmark I Was Born*, ed. R. P. Keigwin, 2d ed. (1950); *Twentieth-Century Scandinavian Poetry*, ed. M. S. Allwood (1950); *Modern Danish Poems*, ed. K. K. Mogensen, 2d ed. (1951); *Danske lyriske digte*, ed. M. Brøndsted and M. Paludan (1953); *A Harvest of Song*, ed. S. D. Rodholm (1953); *Den danske Lyrik 1800–1870*, ed. F.J.B. Jansen, 2 v. (1961); P. Hein, with J. Arup, *Grooks* (1966–78); *Danish Ballads and Folk Songs*, ed. E. Dal (1967); *A Book of Danish Ballads*, ed. A. Olrik (1968); *A Second Book of Danish Verse*, ed. C. W. Stork (1968); *Anthology of Danish Literature*, ed. F.J.B. Jansen and P. M. Mitchell (1971); *A Book of Danish Verse*, ed. O. Friis (1976); *Contemporary Danish Poetry*, ed. L. Jensen et al. (1977); F. Paludan-Müller, *Adam Homo*, trans. S. I. Klass (1980); *Seventeen Danish Poets*, ed. N. Ingwersen (1981); *Scandinavian Ballads*, ed. S. H. Rossel (1982); *Digte fra 1990'erne*, ed. N. Lyngsø (2000); *Danske forfatterskaber*, ed. S. Mose, P. Nyord, O. Ravn, 4 v. (2005–6); I. Christensen, *Alphabet*, trans. S. Nied (2001); P. Tafdrup, *Queen's Gate*, trans. D. McDuff (2001); I. Christensen, *Butterfly Valley: A Requiem*, trans. S. Nied (2004), and *it*, trans. S. Nied (2006).

■ **Criticism and History**: A. Olrik, *The Heroic Legends of Denmark* (1919); C. S. Petersen and V. Andersen, *Illustreret dansk Litteraturhistorie*, 4 v. (1924–34); H. G. Topsøe-Jensen, *Scandinavian Literature from Brandes to Our Own Day* (1929); E. Bredsdorff et al., *Introduction to Scandinavian Literature* (1951); P. M. Mitchell, *A Bibliographical Guide to Danish Literature* (1951); J. Claudi, *Contemporary Danish Authors* (1952); F.J.B. Jansen, "Romantisme européen et romantisme scandinave," *L'Âge d'Or* (1953); *Danske metrikere*, ed. A. Arnoltz et al., 2 v. (1953–54); S. M. Kristensen, *Dansk litteratur 1918–1952*, 7th ed. (1965); and *Den dobbelte Eros* (1966)—on Danish romanticism; F.J.B. Jansen, *Danmarks Digtekunst*, 2d ed., 3 v. (1969); *Modernismen i dansk litteratur*, ed. J. Vosmar, 2d ed. (1969); S. H. Larsen, *Systemdigtningen* (1971); P. M. Mitchel, *History of Danish Literature*, 2d ed. (1971); *Nordens litteratur*, ed. M. Brøndsted, 2 v. (1972); *Opgøret med modernismen*, ed. T. Brostrøm (1974); *Dansk litteraturhistorie*, ed. P. H. Traustedt, 2d ed., 6 v. (1976–77); P. Borum, *Danish Literature* (1979); S. H. Rossel, *History of Scandinavian Literature 1870–1980* (1982); *Digtning fra 80'erne til 90'erne*, ed. A.-M. Mai (1993); P. Stein Larsen, *Digtets krystal* (1997); and *Modernistiske outsidere* (1998); *Danske digtere i det 20. århundrede*, ed. A.-M. Mai, 4th ed., 3 v. (2000); E. Skyum-Nielsen, *Engle i sneen* (2000); *Læsninger i dansk litteratur*, ed. P. Schmidt et al., 2d ed., 5 v. (2001); J. Rosiek, *Andre spor* (2003); E. Skyum-Nielsen, *Dansk litteraturhistorie, 1978–2003* (2004); *Dansk litteraturs historie*, ed. K. P. Mortensen and M. Schack, 5 v. (2006–9).

S. Lyngstad; S. H. Rossel; J. K. Nielsen

**DESCORT** (Occitan, "discord"). Occitan and OF lyric genre, courtly in substance, heterostrophic in versification. The *descort*, like the lyric *lai*, was constructed from stanzas or versicles, each different from the others but each showing twofold (sometimes three- or fourfold) metrical and musical symmetry. The title referred to this irregularity, to the contrast between lively tunes and melancholy words, and, in one exceptional case, to the five different langs. used in the five stanzas.

■ H. R. Lang, "The Descort in Old Portuguese and Spanish Poetry," *Beiträge zur romanischen Philologie: Festschrift Gustav Gröber* (1899); I. Frank, *Répertoire métrique de la poésie des troubadours*, 2 v. (1953–57); J. Maillard, "Problèmes musicaux et littéraires du descort," *Mélanges . . . à la mémoire d'István Frank* (1957), and *Évolution et esthétique du lai lyrique* (1963); E. Köhler, *GRLMA* 2.1B; R. Baum, "Le Descort ou l'anti-chanson," *Mélanges de philologie romane . . . Jean Boutière* (1971); J. H. Marshall, "The Isostrophic Descort in the Poetry of the Troubadours," *RPh* 35 (1981); D. Billy, "Le Descort occitan: Réexamen critique du corpus," *Revue des langues romanes* 87 (1983); Chambers; E. W. Poe, "Lai-descort," *Medieval France: An Encyclopedia*, ed. W. W. Kibler et al. (1995).

J. H. Marshall

## DESCRIPTIVE POETRY

I. Classical and Late Antiquity
II. The Modern Period

**I. Classical and Late Antiquity.** Descriptive poetry in the West concerns the theory and practice of description in versified texts. Descriptive poetry is not a genre in itself, but descriptive portrayal has always played an important role in verse art, in a trad. reaching back to the oldest surviving poetic texts. Its tenacity is epitomized in Horace's well-known phrase *ut pictura poesis* (*Ars poetica* 361), which, divorced from its context, became a Ren. dictum encapsulating the aspiration of poetry to portray its subject matter quasi-visually. Ultimately, description should be considered as a strategy and an instancing of the doctrine of *imitation (see MIMESIS). Plato's condemnation (*Republic* 10) of the powerful mimetic arts of epic and tragic poetry as dangerously misleading "copies of copies" was historically superseded by Aristotle's defense of imitation as satisfying a natural instinct for knowledge and instruction, hence, an effective means of learning. This article aims to point out some of the diverse functions of description in Western poetry, recognizing that its presence in Eastern lits. is equally widespread and profound.

In practice, descriptive technique has been applied mainly (1) to the female body, as in the biblical Song of Solomon (1.5, 10, 15; 4.1–7, 10–15; 6.4–7, 10; 7.1–9; but at 1.13–14 and 5.10–16 the man's body is eulogized) and the Fr. *blason*; (2) to human surroundings and habitat, whether natural or cultivated landscape or crafted architecture; and (3) to isolated objects, whether utensils or representational works of art.

Cl. rhetoricians elaborated a theory of description (*ekphrasis, descriptio*) for practical use, but it was equally applicable, with certain modifications, to poetry. Gr. and Lat. rhetorical handbooks frequently cited poetic examples, esp. *epic, to illustrate their points. *Ekphrasis*, one of the elementary rhetorical exercises (*progymnasmata*), was intended to train pupils in the art of "bringing a subject before the eyes [of the audience]." Events and actions unfolding in time were as appropriate to *ekphrasis* as static entities such as cities, landscapes, and buildings. The mod. distinction between the narrative thread and interpolated descriptive "digressions" does not apply in antiquity. Quintilian (8.3.68–70, quoted by Erasmus, *De copia* 2.5) shows how the summary phrase "a sacked city" can be expanded to show in action the unfolding process of its devastation in pictorial detail. This example would apply not only to prose oratory but to versified poetry, as can be seen from the fact that the quotations in 6.2.32–33 are all from the *Aeneid*.

Vividness or *enargeia* is the effective quality deriving from poetic description. Both rhetorical and poetic arts connect the subjective faculties of the performer (poet, actor, or orator) who delivers the text to those of the audience. The stimulation of inward vision in the *imagination and the arousal of concomitant feelings are closely linked. The practical aim is to evoke the scene of an action or the situation of an object. Longinus praises passages in tragedy where the poet seems to have been actually present at the scene (*De sublimitate* 15). The immediacy of the effect of subjective representation is more important than the strict truth of its contents. In poetry, the intended effect was the qualitatively more striking one of *ekplexis*— astonishment, amazement—which permitted, even encouraged, the depiction of fantastic, supernatural, and mythological creatures such as the Furies, allegorical personifications (e.g., the figure of Discord in *Iliad* 4.442, which is praised at the expense of the description of Strife in the pseudo-Hesiodic *Shield of Herakles* in *De sublimitate* 9), and powerful events such as the battle of the Titans in the *Gigantomachia*.

Aristotle (*Rhetoric* 1411b–1412a) always uses the adverbial phrase "before the eyes" (*pro ommathon*) as a concrete synonym for the abstract notion of "vivid(ness)." And he goes further in asserting that this quality produces an effect of "actuality": the Gr. term is *energeia*; and lexical confusion with *enargeia* may stem from this source. The aim of such representation remains that of vitality. Aristotle recommends the use of adjectives of visual or tactile qualities and even more of verbs of motion (esp. present participles) and adverbial phrases representing active movement. He draws his examples from Euripides and Homer.

The Homeric poems were composed long before any extant rhetorical handbook, yet they are full of vividly described events and places. The most famous descriptive passage in Homer is indubitably the ekphrasis of the shield of Achilles in *Iliad* 18. The account of the object is presented in a narrative form: Homer depicts Hephaestus actually making the object and describes the scenes on the shield as if they were unfolding in time. Poetry, thus, invests static spatial objects with vitality by transfusing into them its own rhythmic, temporal succession.

Such use of description for vividly heightened narrative and for pictorial set pieces can be found throughout the hist. of epic in authors such as Apollonius of Rhodes, Nonnus, and Virgil. Virgil adopts Homer's device of the shield (*Aeneid* 8) but takes the finished object as the point of departure for his description. He takes each scene portrayed as the occasion for a prophetic excursus on the future glory of Rome. Different kinds of allegorical exegesis were applied to Homer's descriptions by late antique interpreters (e.g. Porphyry, *On the Cave of the Nymphs*). Allegorical significance was detected in Virgil's (descriptive) *pastoral poetry by Servius and others.

The highly polished, smaller-scale genres such as the *epigram, pastoral, and *epyllion developed in the Hellenistic age also made use of concentrated description, usually of places and scenes, as in Theocritus's *Idylls*. The physical characteristics and attributes of the pastoral context are explicitly described either by the author or in the speech of the characters (see ECLOGUE; IDYLL). Here, descriptions constitute a nostalgic evocation of a state of rustic innocence remote from urban life, mores, and lit. But the bucolic *locus amoenus* might equally stand for quiet leisure, necessary for sophisticated poetic learning, a simple, agreeable metaphor for *otium* (see BUCOLIC, GEORGIC). In Roman poetry, this theme is developed in accounts of the Golden Age such as in Virgil's fourth *Eclogue*, Horace's 16th *Epode*, and, with irony, in Catullus 64.

Isolated objects such as a rustic cup (Theocritus, *Idylls* 1.27–56), a ship ("Phaselus ille," Catullus 4; Horace, *Odes* 1.3) or a water droplet caught in a crystal (Claudian, *Epigrams* 4.2.12, a set of nine different descriptions of the same thing) can be found alongside poems addressed to (and evocative of) real places ("O funde noster," Catullus 44; "O Colonia," Catullus 17) or imagined locations, like the Palace of the Sun and the dwellings of Sleep and Fame in Ovid's *Metamorphoses*.

In descriptions of weather, meteorological eulogy (e.g., of spring, Horace, *Odes* 1.4) may be developed as political allegory (e.g., storms as a metaphor for civic turbulence: Horace, *Odes* 1.2), as observations on the social economics of agriculture (*Odes* 2.15), or as a parable of Fortune and her consolations (*Odes* 1.9); this practice is still evident in the 19th c.

The use of description in dramatic action finds its natural function in evoking absent scenes (remote in time and space), and esp. in messenger speeches that describe a (usually violent) action that has taken place offstage. Where this device includes reported speech, it is related to the *progymnasma* called *prosopopoeia or ethopoeia*, which consists of a re-creation of the words of an individual in a certain situation (see ETHOS), an exercise that would have trained an author in the composition of pithy, highly characteristic, direct speech. Longinus cites passages from tragedy to illustrate the dramatic effect of description and to underline the need for the poet to use the visual imagination in the composition process (*De sublimitate* 15). In Euripides' *Hecuba* (444–83), the chorus of captive Trojan women contrasts the beautiful images of their memories of the sea, the sun, and the winds with the misery of their present plight and surroundings. Talthybius then enters to relate (518–82) the sacrifice—or murder—of Polyxena by Neoptolemos, son of Achilles. His speech is full of vivid descriptive

detail; and his representation of Polyxena's physical beauty, her decorous *pudeur*, and radiant nobility (557–70) evokes *pathos by the intensity of its contrast with the barbarity of the act.

The importance of description in intensifying the rhetorical effect and dramatic impact of messenger speeches is attested by Erasmus (*De copia* 2.5; rev. 1532 ed.) as part of his analysis of description as a powerful device of oratory in all prose and verse genres. Erasmus's treatment includes four divisions: *descriptio rei, personae, loci*, and *temporis*. He cites examples from lyric, dramatic, and epic poetry, as well as from prose speeches, historiography, and "natural science." It remains the most comprehensive classicizing Ren. survey.

*Didactic poetry such as Hesiod's *Works and Days*, Lucretius' *De rerum natura*, and Virgil's *Georgics* uses descriptive passages and *personification to invest the subject matter with immediacy and vitality. Such appeals to the visual imagination may also have reinforced the poets' didactic intentions since ancient memory techniques relied on visualization to store information in the form of images.

In the early centuries CE, parallel devels. can be seen in the use of description in poetry and rhet. Under the Roman Empire, rhet. changed from a practical instrument used in courtrooms—and, thus, directly concerned with real human actions—to a highly sophisticated art form, a display of the orator's skill and ingenuity. Judicial rhet. is replaced by epideictic. School exercises such as *ekphrasis* became an end in themselves rather than a means. Speeches were often composed for particular occasions to praise objects such as cities, temples, or civic landmarks. Statius's *Silvae*—a collection of poems describing villas, statues, society weddings—illustrates the use of description in poetry for similar ends (see EPIDEICTIC POETRY).

In Byzantium, which continued the trad. of ancient epideictic, versified poetry often replaced prose rhet.: long *ekphraseis* were composed in poetic meter using a literary, quasi-Homeric lang. Paul the Silentiary's verse *ekphrasis* of Hagia Sophia was publicly recited, like an epideictic speech, at the second consecration of the church in 563. Like prose *ekphraseis*, these metrical works reproduce a viewer's sense impressions of the building (glittering gold, variegated marble) and expound its spiritual significance, thus translating the inner response to the subject matter or its figural decoration of biblical scenes. These inward reactions are described in a radically subjective manner: they do not normally provide accurate information as to the exact appearance of the object. Nor are they exact in the archaeological sense, permitting the detailed and precise reconstruction of an original. This is a legacy of the emotive function of description in rhet., where *vraisemblance* is more important than truth to nature.

**II. The Modern Period.** Descriptive technique is crucial to the effect of Ren. epic. In Torquato Tasso's *Gerusalemme liberata*, the interpenetration of vivid imagery, pictorial intensity, and psychological discernment powerfully emphasizes the seriousness of Rinaldo's desertion and reconversion. The fantastic, mythic-encyclopedic vision of the "Mediterranean" (canto 15), the enchanted palace and gardens of Armida (15, 16), and the picturesque review of the Egyptian armies (17) are all resolved into the transfiguration of Rinaldo (canto 18).

Ancient pastoral was revived in Ren. Neo-Lat. eclogues (Petrarch, Boccaccio) and in long poems such as Jacopo Sannazaro's *Arcadia*. In England, Philip Sidney also wrote an *Arcadia*, and Edmund Spenser used descriptive technique in evoking the surroundings of the "Bower of Bliss" episode in *The Faerie Queene*. John Milton composed pastoral poems in both Lat. ("Damon") and Eng. ("Lycidas") and used the pastoral setting for his depiction of Eden in *Paradise Lost* (4.689 ff.). But the whole epic is permeated by startling descriptive and visual style: Satan's call-to-arms ("Pandaemonium," 1.283 ff.) of his legions and their terrestrial advance (4.205 ff.), the portrayal of Raphael (5.246 ff.), and Michael's representation to Adam of a vision of the future course of hist. down to the Flood (bks. 11, 12) are all splendid examples, as is Satan's temptation of Christ in *Paradise Regain'd* (4.25 ff.).

In the 17th c., Nicolas Boileau (*L'Art poétique* 3.258 ff.) recommended a rich and sensuous elegance in description so as to avoid tedium, inertia, and cold melancholy and to relieve the austerity of the severe high style in epic and romance. Here too, description should enliven narrative. Boileau's acknowledged master is Homer. Jean Racine's messenger speeches (*récits*) are also animated through description (*Phèdre* 5.6.1498–1592; *Andromaque* 5.3.1496–1524; *Iphigénie* 5.6.1734–90).

Perhaps the finest example, in this period, of description functioning as laudatory rhet. is Jean de La Fontaine's long (though incomplete) *Le Songe de Vaux* (1659–61), which describes the architecture and gardens of Nicolas Fouquet's Château of Vaux-le-Vicomte and the spectacular celebrations prepared there for Louis XIV in 1661. The poem was intended as a monument in verse to Fouquet's worldly glory and munificence. The close relation in antiquity between *ekphrasis/descriptio* and *encomion/laus* is preserved in Fr. 17th-c. *classicism. Of equal interest is the cycle of odes by Racine, *Le Paysage*, which describes a journey on foot to a Jansenist convent. It is a eulogy of the retired, contemplative religious life, couched in the pastoral terms of the idyll.

In Germany, the most significant text on poetic description to appear is G. E. Lessing's *Laokoön* (1766), which, although it had immediate polemical intent in a dispute with Johann Winckelmann, presents a pivotal analysis of the effects of poetry in comparison with painting and sculpture. Lessing quotes the epigrammatic statement attributed by Plutarch to Simonides, "painting is dumb poetry and poetry speaking painting," to show that, although there may be similarity or even identity of mental and spiritual effect ("vollkommene Ähnlichkeit der Wirkung") between two different arts, their technical systems of construction and expression remain irreducibly different. Less-

ing exemplifies his theoretical exposition by citing examples from Virgil and Homer, but he draws on a formidable range of cl. sources, as well as citing Ludovico Ariosto, Milton, and Alexander Pope. The *Laokoön* is arguably the fundamental Western text for any appraisal of poetic description.

J. W. Goethe rarely presents such full description as can be found in *Ilmenau* (which like *Zueignung* continues a moral allegory) or *Ein zärtlich jugendlicher Kunimer*; but *Harzreise im Winter* shows more typically how vivid sense perception, subjective emotion, and moral reflection are everywhere interwoven in the fabric of Goethe's poetry. A couplet from the seventh *Roman Elegy* ("Now the sheen of the brighter ether illumines the stars; Phoebus the god calls forth forms and colors") shows how closely his poetic eye informs the "Theory of Colors" (*Farbenlehre*). And the light-hearted parable *Amor als Landschaftsmaler* puts in a humorous light Goethe's intuitive sense that Eros is the motivating force in art as well as in nature.

In the Eng. 18th c., James Thomson's *The Seasons* (1730) initiated a literary fashion for poems describing the working conditions and settings of agricultural life, the pictorial elements of landscape, anecdotal details of rustic existence, and humanity's relation to nature. But the specific genre of topographical poetry was not recognized until 1779, when Samuel Johnson characterized it as "local poetry, of which the fundamental subject is some particular landscape . . . with the addition of such embellishments as may be supplied by historical retrospection, or incidental meditation" (*Life of Denham*); this prescription of landscape as subject matter restricts the wide historical application of the inherent power of vivid description of all kinds of objects. Hence, the genre needed to be sustained by strength of style. Dr. Johnson's observations were made in regard to John Denham's "Cooper's Hill" (1642); and indeed, he found Denham's style to possess compact strength and concision. Denham had made paraphrastic trans. of Virgil in 1636, and some bucolic fragments of these found their way into "Cooper's Hill" (Bush).

In the hands of William Wordsworth, the technical limits and psychological distinctions of sense perception respected by earlier writers are dissolved. The early poems *An Evening Walk* and *Descriptive Sketches* (1793) show an attention to natural detail close to 18th-c. practice. But the tendency in "Tintern Abbey," the "Intimations" ode, and *The Prelude* (e.g., the opening of bks. 6 and 12) is to dissolve the separate boundaries of sense and cognition so as to achieve an utterly subjective union with an undifferentiated pantheistic nature. This utterly inward response to nature took to an extreme Johnson's recommendation to include in descriptive poetry the fruits of "incidental meditation"; and in so doing, it spelled the end of the topographical poem as such. Wordsworth's response is rapturous and utterly involving, but he rarely provides the common natural details of description for the reader to absorb and process mentally and so to translate into congruent images.

In Germany, Heinrich Heine's *Die Harzreise* (1824) and *Die Nordsee* (1825–26) show that the confrontation of a traveler on foot with the natural landscape in the hills or on the coast could still form the basis for an extended cyclical poem. But the concrete representation of landscape tends to fragment into a series of vignettes that cohere only by virtue of the underlying current of the poet's subjective response. The telling descriptive detail used by Friedrich Hölderlin and Eduard Mörike always serves the ends of emotion or of metaphysical speculation. Mörike's fantasy island landscape of Orphid and Hölderlin's baffling *Hälfte des Lebens* are two instances of descriptive evocation utterly dissimilar in approach.

For various mod. poets (Charles Baudelaire, Stéphane Mallarmé, T. S. Eliot, George Seferis, W. H. Auden, R. M. Rilke, Yves Bonnefoy), the descriptive values of image and *metaphor can be seen as an essential quality in poetic perception. Trace elements of sensation, drawn from experience and recombined to form images, are presented so as to stimulate vivid awareness of the external world or to express particular, sometimes extreme inner states. The result is a kind of "psychological description" (as detected by De Robertis in Giacomo Leopardi's *Canti*) that portrays an "interior landscape," the *Weltinnenraum* of Rilke, or the spiritual pilgrimage toward Bonnefoy's *arrière-pays*. Even the ekphrastic poems-about-paintings of Bruno Tolentino ("About the Hunt," "Those Strange Hunters") contain more of the reflective "embellishments . . . of incidental meditation," i.e., of imaginative appraisal of the subject matter, than an accurate verbal reconstitution of their subjects' physical construction. For C. P. Cavafy, too, the act of radically subjective appropriation is the kernel of vivid poetic narrative: "You won't encounter [Odysseus' adventures] unless you carry them within your soul, unless your soul sets them up in front of you" (*Ithaka*). And Giuseppe Ungaretti's "Choruses Descriptive of Dido's States of Mind" (*La Terra promessa*) attempt a direct physiognomy of the soul rather than of the external symptoms of emotion.

The mod. rural descriptions and nature poems of R. S. Thomas, Seamus Heaney, Ted Hughes, and Charles Tomlinson show neither the sophisticated pastoral ease of the urbanite at leisure nor the pantheist fervor of an idealizing imagination such as Wordsworth's, but rather a grim confrontation with the pitiless harshness, even brutality, of the natural world they observe. They describe unsentimentally the struggle for survival within the animal kingdom and the dogged, heroic resistance of real farmers to nature's destructive power.

Altogether, description on a broad canvas, elaborate, explicit, and comprehensive in scope, was probably less common in 19th- and 20th-c. poetry than concentration on intensity of descriptive detail in the imagery of lyric. And while the persistence of certain conventional themes, which create the fictional assumption of a travel jour. or pilgrimage, or of a poetic monument to a piece of architecture or sculpture or of a versified record of a geographical or topographical survey may give the initial impression that there is a specifically descriptive

genre, there is, in fact, always another governing intention (moralizing, didactic, persuasive, emotive) that is served, rather than conditioned, by the technique of description, which is rather to be considered as a rhetorical-poetic strategy to be applied in genres established on other grounds, as occasion demands.

*See* ICONOLOGY, IMAGE, IMAGERY, NATURE, PAINTING AND POETRY, SCULPTURE AND POETRY.

■ E. W. Manwaring, *Italian Landscape in 18th-Century England* (1925); M. Cameron, *L'Influence des 'Saisons' de Thomson sur la poésie descriptive en France (1759–1810)* (1927); R. A. Aubin, *Topographical Poetry in 18th-Century England* (1936); D. Bush, *English Literature in the Earlier 17th Century* (1945); G. De Robertis, *Saggio sul Leopardi* (1960); R. L. Renwick, *English Literature 1789–1815* (1963); J. Arthos, *The Language of Description in 18th-Century Poetry* (1966); A. Roper, *Arnold's Poetic Landscapes* (1969); J. W. Foster, "A Redefinition of Topographical Poetry," *JEGP* 69 (1970); G. Genette, *Figures III* (1972); P. Hamon, "Qu'est-ce qu'une description?" *Poétique* 2 (1972); H. H. Richmond, *Renaissance Landscapes: English Lyrics in a European Tradition* (1973); J. B. Spencer, *Heroic Nature: Ideal Landscape in English Poetry from Marvell to Thomson* (1973); R. Williams, *The Country and the City* (1973); J. Gitzon, "British Nature Poetry Now," *MidwestQ* 15 (1974); E. Guitton, *Jacques Delille (1738–1813) et le Poème de la nature en France de 1750 à 1820* (1974); D. Lodge, "Types of Description," *The Modes of Modern Writing* (1977); J. G. Turner, *The Politics of Landscape: Rural Scenery and Society in English Poetry, 1630–1660* (1979); B. Peucker, "The Poem as Place," *PMLA* 96 (1981)—the lyric; "Towards a Theory of Description," ed. J. Kittay, *YFS* 62, spec. iss. (1981); R. Barthes et al., *Littérature et réalité* (1982); A. Reed, *Romantic Weather* (1983); C.-G. Dubois, "Itinéraires et impasses dans la vive représentation au XVIe siècle," *Litt. de la Ren.* (1984); J.A.W. Heffernan, *The Re-Creation of Landscape* (1984); D. E. Wellerby, *Lessing's "Laocöon": Semiotics and Aesthetics in the Age of Reason* (1984); J. Applewhite, *Seas and Inland Journeys: Landscape and Consciousness from Wordsworth to Roethke* (1986); J. Holden, "Landscape Poems," *Denver Quarterly* 20–21 (1986); E. W. Leach, *The Rhetoric of Space: Literary and Artistic Representations of Landscape in Republican and Augustan Rome* (1988); B. Costello, *Shifting Ground: Reinventing Landscape in Modern American Poetry* (2003); A. Fletcher, *New Theory for American Poetry* (2004); K. Goodman, *Georgic Modernity and British Romanticism* (2004); W. Spiegelman, *How Poets See the World: The Art of Description in Contemporary Poetry* (2005); J. Koelb, *The Poetics of Description* (2006); B. Costello, *Planets on Tables: Poetry, Still Life, and the Turning World* (2008).

R. H. WEBB; P. WELLER

**DEVOTIONAL POETRY.** Although the distinction between religious poetry in general and devotional poetry in particular is never absolute, devotional poetry is often recognizable for its tendency to address a divinity, a sacred thing, or a religious figure. Poetic addresses with religious meaning constitute part of the sacred lit. of many religions, and they often influence later trads. in devotional poetry. Because of its reliance on poetic *address, devotional poetry shows a close kinship with *lyric poetry, and it often uses an intimate, first-person voice. Yet this first person may stand for a community rather than an individual, and devotional poetry, esp. when sung or chanted, may serve liturgical functions. This article concentrates on devotional poetry in Hinduism, Judaism, Christianity, and Islam. In general and in this article, the term excludes polemical and homiletic poetry, as well as *epics and other long narrative forms, though these may include devotional forms and serve devotional purposes.

Much devotional poetry portrays the relation to the divine in terms of wonder and praise, but some concerns painful experiences of affliction, guilt, unfulfilled longing, estrangement, and doubt. Its most common forms are prayer, meditation, and *hymn; and its purposes include praise (see EPIDEICTIC POETRY), supplication, *complaint, *lament, consolation, self-examination, and confession. How the divine is experienced and understood—whether as master, parent, lover, judge, king, confessor, creator, teacher, savior, or friend—often determines the poetic mode by which it is addressed, and this mode in turn determines the classes of thoughts and feelings that the poetry expresses.

Many devotional trads. employ a highly metaphorical lang. to describe experiences of the unseen. In general, such lang. reflects the representational challenge posed by devotional poetry's central concern with the relationship between human and divine, body and soul. Specific metaphors, esp. those drawn from erotic experience and from human governmental and disciplinary structures, suggest links between devotion and these areas of experience, though the significance of these links varies.

The Hindu devotional trad. begins with the *Rig Veda*, a collection of Sanskrit hymns, prayers, and supplications possibly dating to the 15th c. BCE. The *Rig Veda* is one of the four Vedas, the most sacred texts of the Hindu religion, and it is thought that its verses were recited by Vedic priests during ritual sacrifices. The most important influence on Indian devotional poetry since antiquity was the *Bhakti* movement, which began around the 6th c. CE in the Tamil-speaking south and spread through northern India over the next thousand years, enriching lit. in many langs (see INDIA, POETRY OF). The movement emphasized inner experience over external forms, and universal access to God over control by a priestly hierarchy. Bhakti poet-saints incl. Kabīr (15th c.) and Sūrdās (16th c.) have influenced such mod. writers as Rabindranath Tagore and Robert Bly.

The Heb. Bible also contains important poetic texts, incl. the Song of Solomon, which trad. has taken to license the erotic expression of devotional feeling; the book of Job, an important source for later poetry of affliction; and, above all, the Psalms, which mix confession with praise, supplication with thanksgiving, and fear

with love, sometimes in a tone of bold familiarity (see PSALM; PSALMS, METRICAL). Later Heb. devotional poetry, such as that of Solomon Ibn Gabirol (ca. 1021–55) and Jehudah Halevi (ca. 1074–1141), the two greatest poets of the Heb. Golden Age in Spain, remains deeply biblical. Gabirol's *Keter Malkhut* (Kingly Crown) combines numerous themes of the Psalms: praise for God's attributes and the work of creation, the contrast between God's magnificence and the speaker's sin and insignificance, the hope of mercy, the recognition of God's wrath, and gratitude for God's goodness in saving the speaker.

Christian devotional poetry is also greatly indebted to biblical models such as the Psalms, esp. the seven *penitential psalms, as well as to early Christian hymns such as those of Prudentius and Ambrose (both 4th c.). To the themes of the psalter, Christian poetry adds an emphasis on absolution and redemption through the Incarnation, Passion, and Resurrection of Jesus Christ; Roman Catholic poetry also meditates on the lives of the saints and the Virgin Mary. The doctrinal controversies and spiritual intensity of the Reformation and Counter-Reformation reinvigorated Christian verse. Biblical forms and themes mixed with new devotional practices and with courtly forms such as the *sonnet and the Ren. lyric to produce, in the vernacular lits. of Europe, many of Christian poetry's highest achievements. These include the stirring hymns of Martin Luther in Germany; the mystic journey of St. John of the Cross's *Noche oscura del alma* (*Dark Night of the Soul*) in Spain; the metrical psalters composed by Clément Marot and Théodore de Beza in France and by Philip Sidney and Mary Sidney in England; the spiritual sonnets and religious lyrics of John Donne, George Herbert, and many others in England; and the late *metaphysical poetry of Edward Taylor's *Preparatory Meditations* in colonial New England. Victorian poets such as G. M. Hopkins also wrote distinguished devotional verse.

Although several verses in the Qur'an criticize poets (26:224–26), the following verse (26:227) allows for exceptions; and in the 9th and again in the 13th c., Sufi mystics developed an exceptional body of poetry expressing a personal, loving relationship to Allah. Thirteenth-c. Sufi poets include Ibn al-Arabī, Ibn al-Fāriḍ (both Arabic), and Rūmī (Persian), whose central theme is perhaps the power of divine love to transcend cultural and religious differences. Also important in Islam is the *qaṣīda, or praise poem, which was adapted to express devotion to the Prophet Muhammad, typically celebrating his birth, attributes, exploits, and powers. The most famous example is the "Qaṣīdat al-Burdah" (The Mantle) of the Egyptian Sufi poet al-Būṣīrī (ca. 1212–96), itself modeled on the 7th-c. poem of the same name said to have been presented to Muhammad by Ka'b ibn Zuhayr.

Devotional poetry has traditionally been one of the literary forms most available to women, and female poets have made important contributions to most of its trads. Rābi'ah al-'Adawīyah (d. 801) profoundly influenced the devel. of Sufi devotional poetry by introducing its emphasis on love and mystic union.

Kāraikkāl Ammaiyār (6th c.), a devotee of Śiva, was an early Tamil *Bhakti* poet-saint. Mīrābāī (15th c.) remains one of the most beloved poet-saints of the later Bhakti trad.; her emphasis on Krishna's physical beauty and her desire to share her bridal bed with him raise questions about the gender of devotion. The Christian devotional revival of the 16th and 17th cs. drew notable contributions from St. Teresa of Ávila in Spain; Gabrielle de Coignard and Anne de Marquets in France; Sor Juana Inés de la Cruz in Mexico; and Aemilia Lanyer, An Collins, and Hester Pulter in England. Christina Rossetti is second in reputation only to Hopkins among practitioners of the Victorian devotional lyric. Emily Dickinson treats many devotional themes while tending more toward uncertainty than to the comforts of faith.

Dickinson anticipates an important trend in 20th-c. devotional poetry. Some poets have reacted to the modernist themes of the crisis of civilization and the death of God by amplifying the elements of complaint and doubt already present in many devotional trads. Wallace Stevens's "Sunday Morning," T. S. Eliot's *Four Quartets,* Anthony Hecht's "Rites and Ceremonies," and Louise Glück's *The Wild Iris* ask more questions than they answer, showing that devotional poetry can be written in the interrogative mood.

*See* LITURGICAL POETRY, RELIGION AND POETRY.

■ H. Brémond, *Prière et Poésie* (1926); L. Martz, *The Poetry of Meditation* (1954); W. T. Noon, *Poetry and Prayer* (1967); R. Woolf, *The English Religious Lyric in the Middle Ages* (1968); T. Cave, *Devotional Poetry in France, c. 1570–1613* (1969); B. K. Lewalski, *Protestant Poetics and the Seventeenth-Century Religious Lyric* (1979); G. B. Tennyson, *Victorian Devotional Poetry* (1981); A. Schimmel, *Mystical Poetry in Islam* (1982); R. Strier, *Love Known* (1983); R. Alter, *The Art of Biblical Poetry* (1985); P. S. Diehl, *The Medieval European Religious Lyric: An Ars Poetica* (1985); N. Cutler, *The Poetics of Tamil Devotion* (1987); J. N. Wall, *Transformations of the Word: Spenser, Herbert, Vaughan* (1988); M. Schoenfeldt, *Prayer and Power* (1991); R. Rambuss, *Closet Devotions* (1998); R. Targoff, *Common Prayer: The Language of Public Devotion in Early Modern England* (2001); F. B. Brown et al., "Poetry," *The Encyclopedia of Religion,* ed. L. Jones, 2d ed. (2005); J. S. Hawley, *Three Bhakti Voices* (2005).

K.J.E. GRAHAM

**DHVANI** (Sanskrit, "suggestion," "sound"). The origin of the dhvani school in Sanskrit poetry is lost in obscurity. But it is Ānandavardhana (820–90) who developed the theory of *dhvani* into an elaborate system, assimilating in the process all the earlier theories of poetry such as *rasa* (flavor), *alaṃkāra* (*ornament), and *rīti* (a theory of the lang. of lit.), and propounded that dhvani or suggestion is the soul of poetry: *kāvyasyātmā dhvani.* The doctrine is based on the threefold power of the word, *abhidhā, lakṣaṇā,* and *vyañjanā,* producing, respectively, three kinds of meaning: *vācyārtha* (the literal meaning), *lakṣaṇārtha* (the figurative meaning, developed through a *trope), and *vyañjanārtha* (the suggested meaning, which subsumes and replaces the

earlier two meanings). The *vyañjanā* consists not in the utterance of something new but in suddenly revealing, almost in a flash, what is already there, as a jar is revealed when a lamp is lit. According to Ānandavardhana, dhvani is not something mystical but is grasped by disciplined readers of poetry. It is an all-embracing principle that explains the structure and functions of all the other schools—alaṃkāra, rīti, rasa, etc. Rasa, e.g., is only the effect of dhvani. The poetry of suggestion is regarded by many Sanskrit poetic theorists, anticipating the poetics of *symbolism in 19th-c. France, as more powerful than the poetry of description.

*See* SANSKRIT POETICS, SANSKRIT POETRY.

■ Daṇḍin, *Kāvyādarśa* (1924); Vāmana, *Kāvyālaṃkāra-sūtra* (1928); Bharata, *Nāṭyaśāstra* (1950); P. V. Kane, *Sāhityadarpaṇa: Paricchedas* I, II, X *Arthālaṃkāra with Exhaustive Notes* (1965); Rudraṭa, *Kāvyālaṃkāra* (1965); Ruyyaka, *Alaṃkārasarvasva* (1965); R. Mukherji, *Literary Criticism in Ancient India* (1966); Bhāmaha, *Kāvyālaṃkāra* (1970); *Dhvanyāloka of Ānandavardhana,* ed. K. Krishnamoorthy (1974); S. K. De, *History of Sanskrit Poetics* (1976); K. Kapoor, *Literary Theory: Indian Conceptual Framework* (1998); B. Pal, *Alamkāra-Vicintā* (2007).

M. K. RAY

**DIAERESIS,** also spelled "dieresis" (Gr., "division"). Refers either to the division between successive vowels within a word or, in cl. prosody, to the coincidence of word end with the end of a metrical foot. In the former meaning, the term denotes both the phenomenon itself and the accent once used commonly to mark it: e.g., "naïve." In the latter meaning, it is used to distinguish a metrical pause between two feet from a pause within a foot, known as a *caesura. West has pointed out that this is a mod. extension of Quintilian's use of the term, but it is valuable nonetheless, particularly in analyzing dactylic hexameters. The diaeresis at the end of the fourth foot is commonly referred to as "bucolic" by virtue of its frequency in Hellenistic *bucolic poetry. However, the major precedent for this diaeresis is to be found in Homer's epic, where it occurs in more than 60% of his verse. A syntactic pause at the bucolic diaeresis can often lead to various poetic effects, such as *enjambment. David has suggested that the bucolic diaeresis reflects a continuation between epic and mod. Gr. dance, but this remains controversial. This diaeresis, in its function as a secondary or "late" caesura often leading to enjambment, can also be seen as an influence on mod. poetry, such as the opening lines of T. S. Eliot's *The Waste Land.*

■ J. Halporn et al.; M. L. West, "Three Topics in Greek Metre," *CQ* 32 (1982); M. Clark, *Out of Line* (1997); A. P. David, *The Dance of the Muses* (2006).

R. A. HORNSBY; T.V.F. BROGAN; D. KUTZKO

**DIALECT POETRY.** A dialect is a particular way of speaking and writing a lang. Although there is no test to determine precisely when a set of conventions becomes a dialect or when a dialect becomes a discrete lang., a dialect is generally understood to possess a distinctive grammar, vocabulary, and pronunciation that may or may not be intelligible to other speakers of the lang. Dialects are often identified with ethnic groups, social classes, or geographic regions within cultures or nation-states, and they are thought to emerge historically from social or territorial separation. Several dialects may coexist on relatively equal footing within a lang., but, more often, one set of conventions (usually that of the ruling class or the most powerful region or ethnic group) predominates and is institutionalized as the standard lang. Consequently, dialects may be stigmatized as uneducated or provincial ways of speaking, although they may also be praised for possessing a vigor and authenticity that the standard lang. lacks.

Although every lang. has dialects, dialect lits. have developed only in certain langs. (diglossic langs. such as Chinese or Ar., for instance, tend not to have dialect lits., despite having a huge range of dialects). A dialect poem is a composition in a poetic genre that uses ling. conventions different from the conventions of the standard lang. and specific to an identifiable region, class, or ethnic group. Because dialects may possess idiosyncratic vocabularies and also variant pronunciations, dialect poems may be recognized by their use of characteristic words and expressions, as well as by unconventional orthography. The orthographic variations take two forms: cacography, or "eye-dialect," which provides nonstandard spellings without fundamental changes to pronunciation (such as "sez" for "says") and is thus a phenomenon of print; and phonetic spelling, which denotes a distinct pronunciation (such as "gwine" for "going"). The orthographic conventions that often strikingly identify a dialect poem also raise the question of whether dialect poetry is best understood as an oral- or print-mediated lit. Although dialect poetry may use phonetic spellings to convey distinctive speech accents, the print materiality that creates dialect poetry's aural significations indicates that dialect poems should not be understood as exclusively, or even originally, orally mediated forms of expression. It may be more helpful to think of dialect poems *generically*, as recognizable *kinds of writing* meant to signal identifiable modes of speaking.

Early instances of dialect poetry come from cl. Gr., which was composed in four dialects—Ionic, Attic, Aeolic, and Doric—each of which became so strongly associated with specific genres that poets used the dialect appropriate to the genre, not necessarily their native dialect. The Homeric epics were composed in Ionic, the dialect of western Asia Minor; Ionic Gr. became associated with *epic poetry and the *dactylic hexameter line. By the cl. period, Ionic had merged with Attic Gr., spoken in Athens. Attic, the prestige lang. of Hellenism after the Alexandrian conquests, was the lang. of the tragedians, and it became identified with the drama and a refined purity and elegance of style. Aeolic, described as "barbarous" in Plato's *Protagoras*, was spoken around Lesbos and was used by Sappho and Alcaeus. Aeolic became associated with *lyric and *melic poetry, with *glyconic meter, the hendecasyllabic line, and the *sapphic and *alcaic stanzas. The choral *ode

developed out of Doric Gr., the dialect of the western and southern Aegean, which was considered a broad and rustic style of speaking. The most celebrated Doric poet was Theocritus, the founder of *pastoral poetry. A rougher "Doric" style would henceforth characterize the bucolic poetry of later centuries.

Although the speaking of Lat. differed widely across the Roman imperium, no dialect lits. developed. The growth of the Lat.-derived Romance langs. slowly gave rise to vernacular lits.: though written in Lat., Dante's *De vulgari eloquentia* (ca. 1304) defended vernacular langs. as appropriate vehicles for poetry and song. Strictly speaking, all med. Eur. lit. in the vernacular was composed in dialect, since ling. standardizations did not begin in earnest until the 17th c.

Since the 18th c., lang. has been closely affiliated with social and national identity, and lit. has accrued significance as the carrier of a community's sense of itself. In consequence, ling. policies often oscillate between efforts to maintain "pure" literary standards through centralized institutions (such as the Académie Française or the Turkish Lang. Assoc.) and efforts to protect local and distinctive ways of speaking (as in the UNESCO initiative on endangered langs.). Within the framework of mod. literary and ling. nationalism, dialect lit. has held varied political and social meanings, at times celebrated for embodying an authenticity or identity specific to a nation's imagined trads., at other times, particularly moments of crisis, boding the danger of corruption or fragmentation within the communal order.

Fr. is one case of sharp distinction between the centralized regulation of lang. and a profusion of dialects at the peripheries. OF grew from a combination of Lat. and Celtic langs. and was split between the *langues d'öil* of northern France and the *langues d'oc* of the south. Lyric poetry came primarily from the southern *troubadours, who composed songs on courtly love in the Occitan dialects, and the northern *trouvères, who used the Norman dialects. The *chansons de geste* and the romans, epic song cycles like the Arthurian romances, also came from the northern dialects, which became the primary dialect of med. Fr. poetry in forms like the *ballade, *rondeau, aubade, and *lai. In 1539, Francis I decreed that a composite version of the northern dialects would be the monarchy's administrative lang., and efforts to reform and standardize spelling and grammar began. The centralization of ling. and literary authority continued through the cl. Fr. period, culminating in the establishment of the Académie Française in 1635. However, Fr. imperialism proliferated Fr. dialects around the world, and in many places—such as Québec—poetry in Fr. dialect has fostered a local identity opposed to reigning structures of power, as in the work of Gaston Miron. In Haiti, the dialect poetry of Félix Morisseau-Leroy inspired the Créole Renaissance, and movements like *Créolité* use Fr. Creole poetry in anticolonial cultural politics.

Italy is different in that for centuries the standard literary lang. did not subordinate dialect poetries to provincial or minor status. The political fragmentation of the It. peninsula after the fall of Rome allowed many regional dialects to emerge. Largely because of the prestige of Dante and Petrarch, Tuscan It. assumed preeminence as the written standard among educated Italians after its endorsement by Pietro Bembo during the Cinquecento. However, Italy remained polyglot; at the time of national unification in the 19th c., only a small minority was familiar with the literary standard, and dialect poetries have been a continuous trad. since the 17th c., with major poets writing in dialect. These have included Giovanni Meli (Sicilian), Salvatore di Giacomo (Neapolitan), and Giuseppe Belli (Romanesco), among many others.

The literary and ling. hist. of Ger. offers a third case: like Italy, the Ger.-speaking zone was divided geographically and politically, and the written standard that emerged in the 17th and 18th cs. was remote from all spoken forms. In the late 18th c., romantic philologists like J. G. Herder championed the use of spoken Ger. as a literary lang., arguing that lit., esp. folklore and folk songs, formed the national spirit. This turn to *Volkspoesie* reached high points in the *Märchen* of the Brothers Grimm and the Alemannic poetry of J. P. Hebel. At the same time, however, the High Ger. of central Germany—the poetic lang. of J. W. Goethe and Friedrich Schiller, among others—was promulgated as the spoken standard, displacing other dialects and making later dialect poetry, such as that of Klaus Groth, self-consciously provincial.

Eng. has an esp. complex hist.: OE, or Anglo-Saxon, was a loose collection of Germanic dialects (influenced by Lat. and Celtic langs.) spoken and written in portions of Britain after the Saxon invasions of the 5th c. OE survives in an assemblage of writings, the most famous being *Beowulf*, an epic poem in the West Saxon dialect composed sometime before 1000 CE. Britain's ling. order changed profoundly after the Norman invasion in 1066, which made Lat. and the Norman dialect of OF the official langs. of church and state. ME developed out of the fusion of Anglo-Saxon and Norman and became a literary lang. sometime after 1200. Though ME lacked a written standard, in the 14th c. the London dialect gained hegemony as the city's cultural and political power increased. This dialect achieved literary distinction in Chaucer's poetry, which combined it with five-stress, decasyllabic lines and rhyming *couplets, both Fr. importations. While Enlightenment projects like Samuel Johnson's *Dictionary of the English Language* (1755) promoted a Latinate literary standard, the mid-18th-c. Ballad Revival and *graveyard poetry popularized a rural, archaic "Saxon" sensibility that contrasted with the metropolitan polish of the Augustan poets. Many different dialect poetries subsequently became popular, incl. the Ayrshire Scots poems of Robert Burns and the Northamptonshire poems of John Clare. William Barnes's poems in Dorset inspired Alfred, Lord Tennyson and Thomas Hardy to compose poems in the dialects of Lincolnshire and Wessex, while Samuel Laycock wrote well-received poems in a Lancashire working-class dialect. The British Empire, meanwhile, created anglophone dialects around the world, which exist in strong tension with other local langs. and the normative, Oxbridge-derived "BBC English." Dub poetry, which originated in Jamaica in the work of Linton Kwesi Johnson and others, is one example of a creole Eng. poetry that has attained a global audience.

Eur. colonial enterprises in the Americas, along with Af. slavery, brought dozens of Atlantic langs. into contact with thousands of indigenous langs. Across Latin America the collision of colonial, Af., and Amerindian langs. and cultures created Afro-Creole dialects that became the basis for literary movements like *poesía negra*, which blended Caribbean vernaculars with Af.-derived song forms into expressions of the black underclass, as in the poetry of Nicolás Guillén. Other trads. derive from rural work cultures of the postindependence era. The most prominent of these is probably *gauchesco*, the cowboy poetry of the Southern Cone most famously embodied in José Hernández's epic *Martín Fierro*. *Gaucho poetry employed traditional song forms, colloquial idioms, and phonetic spellings to evoke an idealized, rural way of life that was ideologically central to emergent national identities in Argentina and elsewhere.

Although Britain dominated colonial North America after the Seven Years' War, Eng. competed with many Eur., Af., and indigenous langs. Combined with the continent's geographic spread, this multilingualism created highly distinct regional and ethnic dialects. The first prominent dialect poetry emerged early in the 19th-c. U.S. with the minstrel songs composed in imitation of Af. Am. speech patterns. In the antebellum era, Am. dialect writing was primarily a satiric form of critique, heavily dependent on cacography, while after the Am. Civil War the use of dialect became ethnographic, valuing representational precision to portray the "local color" of regions across the country. Though the comic use of ethnic dialects continued into the 20th c. in the songs of vaudeville, *Harlem Renaissance authors legitimized a vernacular dialect poetry ideologically linked to *blues and jazz (see JAZZ POETRY). More recently, Nuyorican Eng., a Latino dialect of New York City, has had a distinguished poetic trad. centered on the *Nuyorican Poets Café.

*See* AFRICAN AMERICAN POETRY; CANADA, POETRY OF; CARIBBEAN, POETRY OF THE; ENGLAND, POETRY OF; UNITED STATES, POETRY OF THE; YIDDISH POETRY.

■ P. Bembo, *Prose della volgar lingua* (1525); W. Barnes, *Poems of Rural Life, in the Dorset Dialect* (1844); S. Laycock, *Lancashire Rhymes* (1864); G. Milner, "The Dialect of Lancashire Considered as a Vehicle for Poetry," *Papers of the Manchester Literary Club* 1 (1875); B. Croce, *Poesia Popolare e Poesia d'Arte* (1933); C. D. Buck, *The Greek Dialects* (1955); J. P. Hebel, *Gesammelte Werke*, v. 1 (1958); *Poesía Gauchesca*, ed. J. B. Rivera (1977); L. R. Palmer, *The Greek Language* (1980); *The Invention of Tradition*, ed. E. Hobsbawm and T. Ranger (1983); K. Brathwaite, *History of the Voice* (1984); J. DeFrancis, *The Chinese Language* (1984); *The Hidden Italy*, ed. and trans. H. W. Haller (1986); G. Miron, *The March to Love*, ed. and trans. D. G. Jones (1986);

H. L. Gates Jr., *Figures in Black* (1987); R. D. Grillo, *Dominant Languages* (1989); F. Brevini, *Le parole perdute* (1990); B. Anderson, *Imagined Communities* (1991); P. Bourdieu, *Language and Symbolic Power*, trans. G. Raymond and M. Adamson (1991); *A Handbook of the Troubadours*, ed. F.R.P. Akehurst and J. M. Davis (1995); *Twentieth-Century Latin American Poetry*, ed. S. Tapscott (1996); L. Bonaffini, "Translating Dialect Literature," *World Literature Today* 71 (1997); G. Jones, *Strange Talk* (1999); L. McCauley, "'Eawr Folk,'" *Victorian Poetry* 39 (2001); G. Lewis, *The Turkish Language Reform* (2002); *The Cambridge Encyclopedia of the World's Ancient Languages*, ed. R. D. Woodard (2004); L. K. Johnson, *Mi Revalueshanary Fren* (2006); S. K. Lewis, *Race, Culture, and Identity* (2006); D. Ahmad, *Rotten English* (2007); M. Cohen, "Paul Laurence Dunbar and the Genres of Dialect," *African American Review* 41 (2007); A. Dawson, *Mongrel Nation* (2007); R. Epstein, "'Fer in the north; I kan nat telle where,'" *Studies in the Age of Chaucer* 30 (2008); T. L. Burton and K. K. Ruthven, "Dialect Poetry, William Barnes and the Literary Canon," *ELH* 76 (2009).

M. C. Cohen

**DIALOGUE.** Denotes an exchange of words between or among dramatized speakers in lit., whether or not their speeches are written with a view to theatrical representation. Dialogue has characterized writing for the stage at least since the first actor stepped out from a chorus, although there are also important uses of *monologue in the drama. In poetic as in theatrical dialogue, a responsive conversation expresses diverse viewpoints, which are thereby opened to possible change. The device allows a wider range of ideas, emotions, and perspectives than is readily available to a single voice and reliably generates dramatic conflict of a kind that a collection of discrepant monologues, such as Edgar Lee Masters's *Spoon River Anthology* or even Robert Browning's *The Ring and the Book*, does not. Monologues tacitly interrupted and poems in which one framing voice introduces another main voice are not legitimate examples of dialogue, which demands interactive response. Dialogue impels all forms in which it appears toward dramatic confrontation, even as it tends to favor the rhythms and nuances of speech.

The best known cl. examples are the Socratic dialogues of Plato, written in prose but apparently based on 5th-c. BCE dramatic mimes by Sophron and Epicharmus. Cl. authors included verse dialogue in satiric, *pastoral, and philosophical poems. Lucian modeled his prose *Dialogues of the Dead* on Plato but used the form primarily for satiric and comic purposes. Numerous satires of Horace became models of vivid colloquial exchange between poetic speakers. Virgil's *eclogues presented short pastoral dialogues in verse. Dialogue in poetry often remained purely literary, although it also encouraged *recitation, as in formal philosophical disputation and such musical developments as the love duet, liturgical antiphony, and oratorio.

Verse dialogue flourished in the Middle Ages in debates and *flyting. The dualistic philosophical temper of the age fostered dialogue, as in *The Owl and the Nightingale*. A typical subject was the debate between the soul and the body. *Med. romances and *allegories used dialogue in ways that raise a doubt as to whether they were solely for reading or were also meant to be staged. Many Asian poems fit this description as well. The 13th-c. *Roman de la Rose* employed multiple speakers for satiric and dramatic purposes, while the Fr. *débat* and *parlement* were forms of *poetic contest that influenced the med. devel. of the drama, François Villon's dialogue between heart and body being a notable example. Popular ballads often included more than one speaker to heighten dramatic tension or suspense, as in "Lord Randall" and "Edward."

The Ren. revived specifically philosophical dialogue in verse, related to the devel. of prose dialogues by Thomas Elyot, Thomas More, and Roger Ascham. Torquato Tasso called the dialogue *imitazione di ragionamento* (imitation of reasoning), claiming that it reconciled drama and (its cognate and companion since Plato) dialectic. In the 16th and 17th cs., John Heywood's "Dialogue of Proverbs" and Margaret Cavendish's dialogue poems were effective examples of the form. Songs in question-and-answer format by Shakespeare and Philip Sidney emphasized the link between dialogue and the interrogative mode. Multiple voices in Edmund Spenser's *Shepheardes Calender* recalled the dialogue trad. of Virgil's *Eclogues*. Notable Ren. examples of dialogue poems include Samuel Daniel's "Ulysses and the Siren" and Andrew Marvell's "Dialogue between the Soul and the Body." Courtly *masques (Ben Jonson, John Milton) prominently combined dialogue with music and lyrics, a combination that was also adapted for interludes within stage comedy and romance. Allegorical poems like John Dryden's *The Hind and the Panther* provided an occasion for dialogue, as did 18th-c. direct-speech poems like Alexander Pope's "Epilogue to the *Satires*." The adoption of multiple speakers in the Scots ballads of Robert Burns and the Dorset eclogues of William Barnes suggests some affinity between dialogue and dialect.

The romantic predilection for lyrical solo did not prevent the deployment of dialogue in poetic experiments by Lord Byron, John Keats, and esp. P. B. Shelley. Ger. and Scandinavian writers of songs and ballads made widespread use of the device. Victorian efforts to contextualize the romantic lyric chiefly took form in the dramatic monologue, but Alfred, Lord Tennyson; Browning; Matthew Arnold; and Thomas Hardy all used dialogue in poems as well as verse dramas. Revived interest in prose dialogue appears in Oscar Wilde and later, in France, in the dialogue experiments of Paul Valéry.

Twentieth-c. poetry exhibits further blurring of generic distinctions pertinent to this topic. "A Dialogue of Self and Soul" is only the clearest example of W. B. Yeats's frequent reliance on traditional verse dialogue. Writings by Samuel Beckett, Dylan Thomas, and Robert Frost suggest the role of poetic dialogue in a wider variety of dramatic and nondramatic forms. Polyphonic, juxtapositive, and commentatorial modes in T. S. Eliot and esp. Ezra Pound often read like dialogue by other means. Call-and-response conventions have revitalized dialogue in poetry from the Af. diaspora. Implied dialogue in lyrics by Geoffrey Hill and Ted Hughes objectifies the subject and produces heightened dramatic tension. In all these ways, as in the Victorian dramatization of the monologue, dialogue poems deemphasize the autonomy of the poetic word, stressing instead the conditional aspects of utterance. Dialogue thus retains an important place, even as traditional distinctions between verse and poetry, lit. and performance, are questioned and explored.

The historically recurrent overlap among dialogue, dialectics, and dialect finds its major mod. theorist in the Rus. critic Mikhail Bakhtin. Although Bakhtin's writings emphasize the novel, his analysis of the role of the "dialogic" has implications for understanding all literary meaning. On Bakhtin's showing, even ostensible monologues always harbor a conditioning dialogic element. This view implicitly decenters the authority often claimed for first-person lyric or poetic narrative. For Bakhtin, the unsaid, the partially said, and the equivocally said are as potentially meaningful as the clearly said; and these moreover, like all lang. uses, result from social forces, whose contending interplay it remains the privilege, and accordingly the ethical duty, of dialogue to play out.

*See* PREGUNTA.

■ E. Merrill, *The Dialogue in English Literature* (1911); E. R. Purpus, "The Dialogue in English Literature, 1660–1725," *ELH* 17 (1950); W. J. Ong, *Ramus, Method, and the Decay of Dialogue* (1958); F. M. Keener, *English Dialogues of the Dead* (1973); J. Mukarovskij, *The Word and Verbal Art*, trans. and ed. J. Burbank and T. Steiner (1977), ch. 2; M. E. Brown, *Double Lyric* (1980); D. Marsh, *The Quattrocento Dialogue* (1980); M. M. Bakhtin, *The Dialogic Imagination*, ed. M. Holquist, trans. C. Emerson and M. Holquist (1981); A. K. Kennedy, *Dramatic Dialogue* (1983); T. Todorov and M. M. Bakhtin, *The Dialogical Principle*, trans. W. Godzich (1984); *Bakhtin*, ed. G. S. Morson (1986); J. R. Snyder, *Writing the Scene of Speaking* (1989); *The Interpretation of Dialogue*, ed. T. Maranhão (1989); G. S. Morson and C. Emerson, *Mikhail Bakhtin* (1990); D. H. Bialostosky, *Wordsworth, Dialogics, and the Practice of Criticism* (1992); M. S. Macovski, *Dialogue and Literature* (1992); M. Eskin, *Ethics and Dialogue* (2000); K. Njogu, *Reading Poetry as Dialogue* (2004).

B. A. NICHOLS; H. F. TUCKER

**DICTION.** Diction signifies the words or phrases chosen for a piece of writing. It is the Latinate equivalent of Gr. *lexis*, which was accepted as Eng. usage by the *OED* in the second ed. (first citations in 1950 [citing *MP*]; Frye [1957]). *Lexis* is a more useful term than *diction* because more neutral, but it is still chiefly used in ling. (*OED*, sense 1.2), not in poetics. It is important to distinguish "the diction of poetry" from "poetic diction" (esp. in the 18th-c. sense). "Poetic diction" or even just "diction" may elicit only the question of unusual lang. rather than questions concerning all the lang. of poetry.

The primary rule for thinking about diction is that words in a poem always exist in relation, never in isolation: "there are no bad words or good words; there are only words in bad or good places" (Nowottny). Otherwise, classifying diction can be a barren exercise, just as concentrating on isolated words can be barren for a beginning poet. Consistency within the chosen area of diction is necessary for a well-made poem, and consistency is not always easy to achieve. Listening for a poem's range of diction enables the reader to hear moves outside that range. Great skill in diction implies that a poet knows words as he or she knows people (Hollander 1988), knows how "words have a stubborn life of their own" (Elton), and knows that words need to be "at home" (Eliot, *Little Gidding*, the best mod. poetic description of diction "that is right").

Some useful categories for studying diction may be drawn from the *OED*'s introductory matter (now also online), where vocabulary may be examined as follows: (1) *identification*, incl. usual spelling, pronunciation, grammatical part of speech, whether specialized, and status (e.g., rare, obsolete, archaic, colloquial, dialectal); (2) *etymology*, incl. subsequent word formation and cognates in other langs.; (3) *signification*, which builds on other dictionaries and on quotations; and (4) *illustrative quotations*, which show forms and uses, particular senses, earliest use (or, for obsolete words, latest use), and connotations. Studies of diction might test these categories for any given poem. In common usage, *meaning* refers to definition under category (3), but *meaning* as defined by the *OED* incl. all four categories. And *meaning* in poetry, fully defined, includes all functions of a word.

Diction includes all parts of speech, not simply nouns, adjectives, and verbs. Emphasis on what is striking tends to isolate main parts of speech and imposes a dubious standard of vividness (though see ENARGEIA). Even articles matter (cf. Walt Whitman and E. M. Forster on passages to India). Verb forms matter (see Merrill, 21, on first-person present active indicative). Prepositions can have metaphorical force or double possibilities (e.g., "of," a favorite device of Wallace Stevens; see Hollander 1997). The grammatical structures of different langs. offer other possibilities for plurisignation and ambiguity (see SYNTAX, POETIC).

Discussions of diction often pull more toward polemics than poetics. It may be impossible to separate the two, but the effort is essential (Nowottny is exemplary). S. T. Coleridge's dictum should be remembered: every great and original author "has had the task of creating the taste by which he is to be enjoyed" (cited by Wordsworth 1815), a task that perforce includes polemics. Thus, T. S. Eliot's attacks on the Keats–Tennyson line of diction, esp. as developed by A. C. Swinburne, are better read generically in terms of *charm and *riddle, as Frye does (1976). Similarly, it is important not to read mod. assumptions about diction back into older poetry. (See Strang, on reading Edmund Spenser's work in Spenser's lang., not "as if he were writing mod. Eng. with intermittent lapses into strange expressions.") Critics need to pay attention to historical scholarship on the contemporaneity or *archaism of words—often difficult to assess.

There are only a few general questions concerning diction, and they have remained for centuries. The most fruitful may be the more particular ones. One long-standing general issue is whether a special diction for poetry exists or should exist. This, in turn, depends on how poetry is defined or what type of poetry is in question. Of discussions in antiquity, those by Aristotle, Dionysius of Halicarnassus, Horace, and Longinus are the most important. Aristotle's few remarks remain pertinent: poetic diction should be both clear and striking: "ordinary words" give clarity; "strange words, metaphors" should be judiciously used to give surprising effects, to make diction shine and to avoid diction that is inappropriately "mean." In the Middle Ages and early Ren., the issue of diction became important as med. Lat. gave way to the vernaculars. Dante's *De vulgari eloquentia* (*On Vernacular Eloquence*, ca. 1304) is the central text in the *questione della lingua*. Dante classifies diction according to various contexts. E.g., in *DVE* 2.7, he gives detailed criteria for words suitable for "the highest style." Some are as specific as in Paul Valéry's well-known search for "a word that is feminine, disyllabic, includes P or F, ends in a mute syllable, and is a synonym for break or disintegration, and not learned, not rare. Six conditions—at least!" (Nowottny). Dante sees that the main question, as so often, is appropriateness or *decorum. He also stresses appropriateness for the person using a given lexis (e.g., sufficient natural talent, art, and learning), a criterion largely unfamiliar today.

The term *poetic diction* is strongly associated with 18th-c. poetry, largely because of William Wordsworth's attacks on it in the Preface to *Lyrical Ballads*. Wordsworth notes that *Lyrical Ballads* includes "little of what is usually called poetic diction," by which he means the *epithets, *periphrases, *personifications, archaisms, and other conventionalized phrases too often used unthinkingly in Augustan poetry. As against Thomas Gray, e.g., who wrote that "the language of the age is never the language of poetry" (letter to R. West, April 1742), Wordsworth advocated using the "real language of men," esp. those in humble circumstances and rustic life. But Wordsworth laid down many conditions governing such "real language" in poetry (e.g., men "in a state of vivid sensation," the lang. adapted and purified, a selection only).

Coleridge (1817), with his superior critical mind, saw that "the language of real life" was an "equivocal expression" applying only to some poetry, and there in ways never denied (chaps. 14–22). He rejected the argument of rusticity, asserting that the lang. of Wordsworth's rustics derives from a strong grounding in the lang. of the Eng. Bible (authorized version, 1611) and the liturgy or hymn-book. In any case, the best part of lang., says Coleridge, is derived not from objects but from "reflection on the acts of the mind itself." By "real," Wordsworth actually means "ordinary" lang., the *lingua communis* (cf. *OED*, Pref., 2d ed.), and even this needs cultivation to become truly *communis* (Coleridge cites Dante). Wordsworth's real object, Coleridge saw,

was to attack assumptions about a supposedly necessary poetic diction. The debate is of great importance for diction. It marks the shift from what Frye calls a high mimetic mode to a low mimetic one, a shift still governing the diction of poetry today. (In Fr. poetry, the shift comes a little later and is associated with Victor Hugo [Preface to *Cromwell*, 1827].)

Coleridge disagreed with Wordsworth's contention that "there neither is, nor can be any *essential* difference between the lang. of prose and metrical composition." Though there is a "neutral style" common to prose and poetry, Coleridge finds it notable that such a theory "should have proceeded from a poet, whose diction, next to that of Shakespeare and Milton, appears to me of all others the most *individualized* and characteristic." Some words in a poem may well be in everyday use; but "are those words *in those places* commonly employed in real life to express the same thought or outward thing? . . . No! nor are the modes of connections; and still less the breaks and transitions" (chap. 20). In Coleridge's modification of Wordsworth's well-intentioned arguments, readers may still find essential principles applicable to questions of poetic diction.

The 20th c., in one sense, took up Wordsworth's argument, steadily removing virtually every restriction on diction. The 21st c. now generally bars no word whatever from the diction of poetry, at least in the Germanic and Romance langs. Struggles over appropriate diction in the 19th c. included attacks on the romantics, Robert Browning, and Whitman. Attempts by Robert Bridges and others to domesticate G. M. Hopkins's extraordinary diction are well known. In the early 20th c., Edwardian critics with genteel notions of poetry objected to Rupert Brooke's writing about seasickness and to Wilfred Owen's disgust at the horrors of World War I (Stead). Wordsworth's "real language of men" was twisted by some into attacks on any unusual diction whatsoever—difficult, local, learned—a problem to this day, though now less from genteel notions than egalitarian ones inappropriately extended to the diction of all poetry. Yet the diction of poetry may still be associated with the lang. of a certain class—see Tony Harrison's poems playing standard Eng. against working-class Eng. But if poetry now generally admits all types of diction, it remains true that the diction of poetry—of the Bible, Shakespeare, and the ballads, e.g.—needs to be learned. Otherwise, most older poetry, as well as much contemp., cannot be well read at all (Vendler). The diction of the authorized version of the Bible and of the Gr. and Lat. classics has influenced Eng. poetry for centuries. Virgil's diction in *eclogue, *georgic, and *epic was admired and imitated well past the Ren. (see IMITATION, INFLUENCE). The strategies and effects of *allusion should not be overlooked.

Historical changes in the lang. make the use of good dictionaries mandatory. In Eng., the *OED* is the most generous and its quotations invaluable, but other dictionaries are also needed (e.g., of U.S. Eng., for etymology). The elementary philological categories of widening and narrowing and raising and lowering in meaning are useful. (Cf. *wanton*, where solely mod.

senses must not be applied to John Milton's use, or even as late as Bridges's "Wanton with long delay the gay spring leaping cometh" ["April, 1885"]; *gay* is well known.) Hidden semantic and connotative changes must be esp. watched, along with favorite words in a given time (Miles). The diction of some mod. poets pays attention to historical ling., while that of others is largely synchronic; readers should test.

Etymologies are stories of origins. The etymologist cares whether they are true or false, but a poet need not (Ruthven); mythologies are for the poet as useful as hists. Philology may include certain assumptions about poetic diction (see Barfield against Max Müller). Etymologies may include hists. of war and struggle (for nationalism involves lang. just as class does). Poets may exploit the riches of etymology (see Geoffrey Hill's *Mystery of the Charity of Charles Péguy* on Eng. and Fr. diction). Etymology may function as a "mode of thought" (Curtius) or as a specific "frame for trope" (see Hollander 1988, on Hopkins) or both. Invented or implied etymologies can also be useful (*silva* through Dante's well-known *selva* links by sound and sense with *salveo, salvatio*, etc.). Milton plays earlier etymological meaning against later meaning, such play functioning as a trope for the fallen state of lang. (Cook). Eng. is unusually accommodating, combining as it does both Latinate and Germanic words. Other important word roots should also be noted (cf. the etymological appropriateness of *sherbet* in Eliot's "Journey of the Magi").

Diction may be considered along an axis of old to new, with archaism at one end and innovation (incl. neologism) at the other. Archaism may be introduced to enlarge the diction of poetry, sometimes through native terms (Spenser, Hopkins). Or it may be used for certain genres (e.g., literary imitations of oral ballads) or for specific effects, ironic, allusive, or other. Innovation may remain peculiar to one poet or may enlarge the poetic lexicon. Neologisms (new-coined words) tend now to be associated with novelty more than freshness and sometimes with strained effects. The very word indicates they are not common currency. Some periods are conducive to expanding diction in general (the mid-14th c., the late 16th c.) or to expanding diction in some areas (the lang. of digital technology, nowadays, though not yet in general poetic diction). Where poets do not invent or resuscitate terms, they draw on vocabulary from different contemporaneous sources (see the *OED* categories). Foreign, local, and dialectal words, as well as slang, are noted below. The precision of terms drawn from such areas as theology, philosophy, or the Bible must not be underestimated, for controversy can center on one word. Studies working outward from single words (e.g. Empson; Lewis; Barfield on *ruin*) are valuable reminders of historical and conceptual significance in diction.

Shakespeare has contributed most to the enlargement of our stock of words; critics regularly note how often he provides the first example of a given word in the *OED*. He adapts words from the stock of both Eng. (e.g., *lonely*, presumably from Sidney's *loneliness*) and other langs. (*monumental*, from Lat.); he apparently invents words (*bump*); he shifts their grammatical function (*control* as a verb rather than a noun), and more. He possesses the largest known vocabulary of any poet, but it is his extraordinary *use* of so large a word hoard (as against ordinary recognition) that is so remarkable.

Most new words are now generally drawn from scientific or technical sources, though poetry makes comparatively little use of them. In the 18th c., poets could say that "Newton demands the Muse" (see M. H. Nicholson's title), but poets today do not generally say that "Einstein demands the Muse." A. R. Ammons is one of the few mod. poets exploiting the possibilities of new scientific diction: e.g., *zygote* (1891, *OED*) rhymed with *goat*; *white dwarf* (1924, *OED* 2d ed.); and *black hole* (1969). Of the large stock of colloquial and slang expressions, many are evanescent or inert, though special uses may be effective. Shakespeare's gift for introducing colloquial diction is a salutary reminder not to reject colloquialisms per se. Or see Stevens (*Shucks, Pfff* in "Add This to Rhetoric") or Merrill (*slush* [funds] in "Snow Jobs"). The same may be said of slang, a vernacular speech below colloquial on a three-part scale of (1) standard or formal Eng., (2) colloquial Eng., and (3) slang. (See *The New Partridge Dictionary of Slang and Unconventional English*, 8th ed. rev. [2006].) Slang may come from the lingo of specialized trades or professions, schools, sports, etc., and may move up through colloquial to standard Eng. It appears more often in prose than in poetry. But poetry can make effective use of it from François Villon's underworld slang of the 15th c. to T. S. Eliot's *demobbed* in *The Waste Land*. For a brief telling discussion of the question, see George Eliot, *Middlemarch*, chap. 11.

Along the axis of old to new, the most interesting question is why and how some diction begins to sound dated. Archaisms and innovations alike are easy to hear. So also is the diction we designate as, say, 18th-c. or Tennysonian or Whitmanian. But what is it that distinguishes the poetic diction of a generation ago, and why do amateur poets tend to use the diction of their poetic grandparents? The aging of words or the passing of their claim on our allegiance is of continuing interest to poets as part of the diachronic aspect of their art.

Different types of poetry require different lexical practice, though such requirements vary according to time and place. *Oral poetry makes use of stock phrases or epithets cast into formulas (see FORMULA). Some of Homer's epithets became renowned, e.g., *poluphloisbos* (loud-roaring) for the sea (see Amy Clampitt's echo of this). Compound epithets in OE poetry are known by the ON term *kenning* and sometimes take the form of a riddle. Different genres also require different practice (Fowler), a requirement much relaxed today. Epic required a high-style diction, as did the *sublime (see Monk). Genres of the middle and low style drew from a different register. *Satire usually works in the middle style but allows much leeway, esp. in Juvenalian as against Horatian satire. Any diction may become banal—e.g., that of the 16th-c. sonnetteers or that of some *pastoral writers (cf. Coleridge, *Letters,* 9 Oct. 1794: "The word 'swain' . . . conveys too much of the Cant of Pastoral"). *Connotation or association is governed partly by genre and is all-important for diction.

Diction also depends partly on place. The largest division in Eng. is between Great Britain and the U.S., but poetry from elsewhere (Africa, Asia, Australasia, Canada, the Caribbean, Ireland) also shows important differences. Establishing a distinctive poetic style in a new country with an old lang. presents peculiar problems that novelty in itself will not solve. Within a country, diction will vary locally, and poets can make memorable uses of local terms (Yeats of *perne* in "Sailing to Byzantium," Eliot of *rote* in *The Dry Salvages*; Whitman uses native Amerindian terms). The question of dialect shades into this. Robert Burns and Thomas Hardy draw on local and dialectal words. Hopkins's remarkable diction derives from current lang., dialectal and other, as well as older words; some (e.g., *pitch*) have specific usage for Hopkins (see Milroy). The use of Af. Am. vernacular Eng. is familiar (Paul Laurence Dunbar, Langston Hughes, James Weldon Johnson; see AFRICAN AMERICAN POETRY); Derek Walcott includes the Creole of St. Lucia. Foreign diction or *xenoglossia, a special case, works along a scale of assimilation, for standard diction includes many words originally considered foreign. Considerable use of foreign diction (apart from novelties like *macaronic verse) implies a special contract with the reader, at least in societies unaccustomed to hearing more than one lang. Diction may also vary according to class (see above). It is doubtful if it varies in a general way according to gender.

Interpretive categories are numerous, and readers should be aware of them as such; even taxonomies are interpretive. Beyond the categories already mentioned, diction may be judged according to the degree of "smoothness" (Tennyson as against Browning is a standard example; see Frye 1957), centering on the large and important question of sound in lexis (cf. Seamus Heaney on W. H. Auden: "the gnomic clunk of Anglo-Saxon phrasing . . ." [*The Government of the Tongue* (1989), 124]). Or diction may be judged by the degree of difficulty (Browning, Hopkins, Eliot, Stevens), though once-difficult diction can become familiar. Strangeness in diction can contribute to the strangeness sometimes thought necessary for aesthetic effect (Barfield) or for poetry itself (Genette, arguing with Jean Cohen, also compares the *ostranenie* [*defamiliarization] of the Rus. formalists and the lang. of a state of dreaming). Some poets are known for difficult or strange diction (e.g., Spenser, the metaphysical poets, Whitman, Browning), but readers should also note consummate skill in quieter effects of diction (e.g., Robert Frost, Philip Larkin, Elizabeth Bishop).

Distinctive diction is part of what makes a poet familiar, and the diction of a poet may be studied in itself (see Fowler). The discipline of the art of diction is still best understood by studying the comments and revisions of good poets.

■ **General Studies:** W. Wordsworth, "Preface, *Lyrical Ballads,* 3d ed. (1802), incl. "Appendix on . . . Poetic Diction"; and Wordsworth, "Essay, Supplementary to the Preface" (1815); S. T. Coleridge, *Biographia Literaria* (1817); Aristotle, *Poetics,* trans. I. Bywater (1909); O. Elton, "The Poet's Dictionary," *E&S* 14 (1929); W. Empson, *The Structure of Complex Words* (1951); D. Davie, *Purity of Diction in English Verse* (1952); Curtius; Frye; C. S. Lewis, *Studies in Words* (1960); W. Nowottny, *The Language Poets Use* (1962)—essential reading; J. Miles, *Eras and Modes in English Poetry,* 2d ed. (1964); K. K. Ruthven, "The Poet as Etymologist," *CQ* 11 (1969); O. Barfield, *Poetic Diction,* 3d ed. (1973)—important reading; F. W. Bateson, *English Poetry and the English Language,* 3d ed. (1973); A. Sherbo, *English Poetic Diction from Chaucer to Wordsworth* (1975); N. Frye, "Charms and Riddles," *Spiritus Mundi* (1976); Fowler—excellent on diction and genre; G. Genette, *Figures of Literary Discourse* (trans. 1982), esp. 75–102; J. Merrill, *Recitative: Prose* (1986); J. Boase-Beier, *Poetic Compounds* (1987); C. Ricks, *The Force of Poetry* (1987); A. Ferry, *The Art of Naming* (1988); J. Hollander, *Melodious Guile* (1988); H. Vendler, *The Music of What Happens* (1988); S. Adamson, "Literary Language," *CHEL* (1992), v. 3, 539–653; v. 4, 589–692; J. Hollander, *The Work of Poetry* (1997).

■ **Specialized Studies:** S. H. Monk, *The Sublime* (1935); V. L. Rubel, *Poetic Diction in the English Renaissance* (1941); J. Arthos, *The Language of Natural Description in 18th-Century Poetry* (1949); M. M. Mahood, *Shakespeare's Wordplay* (1957); Wimsatt and Brooks, ch. 16; A. Ewert, "Dante's Theory of Diction," *MHRA* 31 (1959); C. K. Stead, *The New Poetic* (1964); G. Tillotson, *Augustan Poetic Diction* (1964); W.J.B. Owen, *Wordsworth as Critic* (1969); H. Kenner, *The Pound Era* (1971), esp. 94–191; D. Alighieri, *Literary Criticism of Dante Alighieri,* ed. and trans. R. S. Haller (1973); J. Milroy, *The Language of G. M. Hopkins* (1977); N. Hilton, *Literal Imagination: Blake's Vision of Words* (1983); M. H. Abrams, "Wordsworth and Coleridge on Diction and Figures," *The Correspondent Breeze* (1984); R.W.V. Elliott, *Thomas Hardy's English* (1984); C. Ricks, *T. S. Eliot and Prejudice* (1988); R.O.A.M. Lyne, *Words and the Poet* (1989)—Virgil; B.M.H. Strang, "Language," *Spenser Encyclopedia,* ed. A. C. Hamilton et al. (1990); E. Cook, *Against Coercion: Games Poets Play* (1998); C. Miller, *The Invention of Evening* (2006).

E. COOK

## DIDACTIC POETRY

  I. Concept and History
  II. Antiquity
  III. Medieval, Renaissance, Enlightenment
  IV. 19th and 20th Centuries

**I. Concept and History.** *Didaktikos* in Gr. relates to teaching and implies its counterpart: learning. "All men by nature desire knowledge" (Aristotle) and all experience (embodied in lang., says Benedetto Croce); hence, all lit. (in the broadest sense) can be seen as "instructive."

Given such interacting complexities, our problem becomes one of "historical semantics" (Spitzer): of modulations and transformations (Fowler) of the didactic concept, and of attempts to distinguish it from near neighbors such as *allegory, *archetype, *myth, *symbol, *fable, and *satire. The category of unconscious or unintended teaching could lead us astray into infinite mists and abysses. (What do we learn from "Jabberwocky"? That "nonsense" can make an attractive poem.) Aware of such proliferating contexts, we try to focus here chiefly on poetry that clearly intends "useful teaching," embodying Horace's "instruction *and* delight" in the genre of didactic poems.

Basic categories relate to the contents of poems, inseparable from their forms. In *De vulgari eloquentia*, Dante specified the worthiest objects as safety, love, and virtue—his corresponding poetic themes being war, love, and salvation (or morality: "direction of the will"). To these we add *knowledge (science and philosophy), beauty (aesthetics), efficiency (e.g., "How to" run a farm or write a poem), and *information ("Thirty days hath September"). Mod. discussions have tended to emphasize the problematics of knowledge and morality. M. C. Beardsley treated "the Didactic Theory of literature" as seeing "a close connection between truth and value." He mentions *De rerum natura*, but no one reads Lucretius' poem today for information on materialism and atomic theory; Beardsley wants rather to clarify the relations among "predications," cognition, and how readers submit poems to experiential "testing"—with reference to "philosophical, economic, social, or religious" doctrines. Arnold Isenberg confronted the "strong case" of "the didactic poem or essay" in an intricate analysis.

Another necessary preliminary is Alastair Fowler's concept of "mode," illuminating the continuing life of genres. Fowler writes that "modal terms never imply a complete external form" and "tend to be adjectival"— as in "didactic essay" or "didactic lyric." He finds it remarkable that "several important literary kinds, notably georgic, essay, and novel, are not supposed to have corresponding modes. Can it be that these modal options have never been taken up? By no means." Once we accept modal extensions of didacticism, its presence and power throughout the hist. of poetry become obvious.

**II. Antiquity.** Didactic modes probably preceded the invention of alphabets and writing. Indeed, for oral trads. (religious and secular), rhythm and *metaphor have always been used to aid memory and enliven ritual; such speculations about prehistoric poetry are confirmed by surviving fragments and mod. anthropology. Religious scriptures in all langs. tend to be "poetic," mingling freely epic hist. (narrative), *hymn and *psalm, and prophetic vision and preaching. In the Judeo-Christian Bible, e.g., there are elements of poetic drama, philosophy, practical wisdom (*proverbs), and parable in didactic modes.

The Greeks first, in Europe, distinguished clearly between poetry of *imitation (Homer) and versified science (e.g., the lost poem by Empedocles); within mimetic uses of melodious lang., between "manners" of narration and drama; and within the latter, analyzed the tragic *catharsis (Aristotle) with comedy, *epic, and other "kinds" in the background. Plato banished the poets from his ideal republic because they taught lies about the gods and aroused and confused men's passions. Two main tendencies of the didactic in verse were created by Hesiod (8th c. BCE): in *Theogony*, knowledge about the gods, their origins and stories, problems of culture—moving toward philosophic abstractions; and in *Works and Days*, "how to" farm and the like—toward practical and specific information. Each kind (details are fragmentary) leaned toward a different style and *meter (e.g., Aratus' "Phainomena" used hexameters); and in later Alexandria, the latter emphasis (erudition, technical information) became popular (e.g., Nicander of Colophon).

The Romans derived from the Greeks not only gods and ideas but most of their poetic genres (translating and adapting Empedocles and Aratus, e.g.). Four major Lat. poets wrote masterpieces that transformed didactic poetry creatively: (a) Lucretius' *De rerum natura* became the prototypical "philosophic" poem (Santayana) in the Empedocles and *Theogony* line, invoking the values of sense-experience and materialistic metaphysics. (b) Virgil's *Georgics*, derived from Hesiod, became the popular "how to" poem: running a farm, living with the seasons, keeping bees, and so forth (see GEORGIC). (c) Horace, on his Sabine farm, wrote not only *odes, satires, and epistles but letters of practical advice to poets (*Epistulae ad Pisones*, i.e., the *Ars poetica*), some of his ideas and phrases becoming proverbial: e.g., "the labor of the file," "in the midst of things," "from the egg," and "make Greece your model." Finally, (d) Ovid's versified advice related chiefly to "sex and society" (*Ars amatoria*), a Lat. primer in matters of love. Manilius wrote a five-book poem on astrology (ed. A. E. Housman); and there were others.

Lat. poets gave priority to instructing citizens and artists in a variety of subjects. Satire developed beyond light-hearted Horace to bitter Juvenal (*The Vanity of Human Wishes*). And in Asia, esp., poetry was central to Confucian teaching. Hindu philosophy is embodied in Vedic hymns (with the *Upaniṣads*); Buddhism, in epic poems (*Mahābhārata* and *Rāmāyaṇa*); and Persian "teaching" is embodied for Westerners in ʿUmar Khayyām's *Rubáiyát* (*quatrains) and the *Avesta* of Zoroaster. The scripture of Islam, the Qurʾan, is quintessential *Arabic poetry.

**III. Medieval, Renaissance, Enlightenment.** Christian lit. in Europe was almost entirely didactic. Even in mimetic (narrative and dramatic) modes, its central purpose was to impart religious doctrines and values (see Curtius, chap. 3 and passim). E.g., Martianus Capella, *On the Marriage of Mercury and Philology* (Menippean satire), *Roman de la Rose*, and Edmund Spenser's *Faerie Queene* (allegory), Dante, Chaucer— didactic elements are everywhere. Vagabond scholars mixed orthodox doctrine and symbols with irreverent satire and "pagan" feeling (see GOLIARDIC VERSE). Med. lit. is dense with rhymed chronicles, encyclopedias, devotional manuals and saints' lives, popularized excerpts from church doctrine, and collections of aphorisms. Early modes of theater in western Europe—mysteries and moralities, passion plays—aimed to combine indoctrination with celebration and entertainment. This is also true of the late *masque, where the allegorical teaching is increasingly subordinated to spectacle and dance. John Milton's *Comus* (1637), e.g., ends with a moral: "Love Virtue."

The emerging Ren. and Reformation saw Lat. poetry enriched by the vernacular langs. In Germany, e.g., didactic works included Luther's Bible, *Bescheidenheit* by "Freidank" (1215–16), *Der Renner* by Hugo von Trimberg (ca. 1300), *Narrenschiff* by Sebastian Brant (1494), *Narrensbeschwörung* and *Gauchmatt* by Thomas Murner (1514, 1519). In Spain, such authors as Francisco Pacheco, Lope de Vega, and Miguel de Cervantes wrote didactically at times. In Italy, literary theory flourished, reaffirming cl. ideals and finding Virgil a "better teacher" than Cato (but Girolamo Fracastoro wrote that "teaching is *in a measure* the concern of the poet, but *not* in his peculiar capacity" [1555; emphases added]). Such satires as those of Giuseppe Parini and Ludovico Ariosto mingled didactic elements with satire and autobiography; and the *Georgics* were imitated. In France, François Rabelais and Michel de Montaigne virtually created a lit. that excelled in *raison* as well as *esprit*; masterpieces by Jean Racine and Molière shaped the nation's emerging trad. and education; Denis Diderot preferred the *Georgics* to Virgil's other poetry; A. Chenier's enthusiasm for "modern" science parallels that of J. W. Goethe and the Eng. romantics; and Jacques de Lille trans. Virgil and wrote *Les Jardins*.

But the didactic line (and problem) was most clearly developed, perhaps, in England, as in Philip Sidney's *Defence of Poesy* (1595, passim—but, despite Plato, the poet is for Sidney not a liar: "he nothing affirms and therefore never lieth"). Milton's great epic attempt was "to justify the ways of God to men." The Restoration in England (one of whose classics is John Dryden's *Virgil*), like the neoclassic century that followed, was a long period of transitions leading to *romanticism. Dryden wrote political, historical, satiric, religious, and theological poems and trans. all four of the great Lat. didactic poets; Alexander Pope wrote *An Essay on Criticism* (1711) and other imitations of Horace, philosophical and "moral" essays in verse, and *The Dunciad* (1742–43), a didactic and *mock-epic satiric masterpiece; and it is hardly necessary to insist on the didacticism of Jonathan Swift and Samuel Johnson. As Chalker puts it, important poems in the georgic trad. "were often remote from any practical purpose, although others were didactic *in intention*" (emphasis added).

The emergence of Newtonian science (see Nicolson) and the Royal Society (Abraham Cowley's poems) bore poetic fruit. New concepts of *nature and light (optics) mingled with the descriptive *paysage moralisé*

in complex ways, transforming georgic trad. most effectively in James Thomson's *The Seasons* (1730; see Cohen). We recall Dr. Johnson's distinction: the poet "does not number the streaks of the tulip." Grierson and Smith's hist. (1944) shows the dominance of didactic and satiric modes, as well as the representative "timid revolt" of Thomas Gray in his odes, yet few poems are more blatantly moralistic than Gray's "Elegy Written in a Country Churchyard." The scientific (informative and theoretic) tendencies bore strange and influential fruit in Erasmus Darwin's poems (e.g., *The Botanic Garden*, 1791). And we recall the variety of didactic elements in George Crabbe, Oliver Goldsmith, and Robert Burns: the Am. and Fr. Revolutions did make a difference.

**IV. 19th and 20th Centuries.** After 1800, didactic aims and methods underwent radical transformations. The main shift was one from a *neoclassical use of models to a growing variety of philosophies and ideologies, followed by later compromises that made the term *Victorian* almost synonymous with moralizing in prose and verse—as in Thomas Carlyle, R. W. Emerson, Alfred, Lord Tennyson, John Ruskin, some pre-Raphaelites, and Matthew Arnold. Few poets are more obviously didactic than William Blake, e.g., but his mode became one of vision and prophecy, of what we now see as "myth-making." William Wordsworth and S. T. Coleridge wrestled with didacticism, esp. in odes and poems of meditation ("The Growth of a Poet's Mind"); and though Coleridge lived to regret it mildly, he did conclude *The Rime of the Ancient Mariner* with a moral.

In P. B. Shelley's *Defense*, Milton's "bold neglect of a *direct* moral purpose" (emphasis added) is seen as proof of that poet's genius; but neither Blake nor Shelley was unaware that to seek "to justify the ways of God to men" was to be essentially didactic. True, Shelley wrote in the preface to *Prometheus Unbound* that "didactic poetry is my abhorrence"—meaning poetry whose teaching "can be equally well expressed in prose" (I. A. Richards' "separable content"—implying superficial moralizing); but surely in *Prometheus* and elsewhere, Shelley was, and understood himself to be, a prophet-teacher, one of the "unacknowledged legislators" of the world. Thus, Wimsatt and Brooks characterize his critical position correctly as a "rhapsodic didacticism" and "a didacticism of revolution."

The opposites of the Horatian pleasure–use polarity often tend to meet. A strong antididacticism usually emerges in opposition to a boringly conservative culture (cf. Blackmur's "intolerable dogma"). When E. A. Poe attacked "the heresy of the Didactic" (a position later adopted by the Fr. symbolists and others), it was because, like Shelley, he was surrounded by inept poetasters spouting clichés; and Walt Whitman (whose didacticism has been compared to that of Blake and Wordsworth) picked up Poe's (and Emerson's) idea of working "indirectly" and symbolically. Even the fin de siècle proponents of art for art's sake were themselves moralists in rebellion against Arnold's "Barbarians" and "Philistines." But the older, moralizing trad. of W. C. Bryant, H. W. Longfellow, J. G. Whittier, and others in America and England had a strength of its own. In the 20th c., the best poets (e.g. W. B. Yeats, W. H. Auden) were ardently "engaged" in various social, political, philosophical, and religious controversies.

Mod. didacticism assumed protean forms that could no longer be forced into the genre classifications of the Ren. and Enlightenment. We can follow this process clearly through Wellek's *History of Modern Criticism*: when A. W. Schlegel discusses "the didactic philosophical poem," he falls into the trap (for Wellek) of defining all poetry as "esoteric philosophy"—excusable, however, when one means, as the romantics did, "a poetic philosophy, a thinking in symbols as it was practiced by Schelling or Jakob Boehme." In this, Wellek is disparaging inferior poems "held together *merely* by logic." Similarly, Wellek remarks that "with the years Wordsworth's point of view became . . . more and more *simply* didactic and instructive" (emphases added). Still, Wellek quotes Wordsworth (1808): "every great poet is a teacher: I wish either to be understood as a teacher, or as nothing." This debate about the changing nature of didacticism took a variety of shapes in England, America, and Europe. Yet what long poem in Eng. had a more clearly didactic intent (i.e., interpretation of hist., fate) than *The Dynasts*—Thomas Hardy's *War and Peace*? Since the substance of such teachings has become increasingly complex, fragmented, and problematic, we find the emphasis now falling on conflict, dialectics, quest, doubt, psychology, existential immediacy, and pluralism rather than on any fixed doctrine.

For instance, in a poem such as Karl Shapiro's *Essay on Rime*, in much of T. S. Eliot, in the Ezra Pound of *The Cantos*, and in Wallace Stevens's "meditations," we witness modal transformations of the didactic. Robert Frost's inveterate didacticism finds expression by transformations of cl. eclogue and pastoral (e.g., "Build Soil," "The Lesson for Today"; see Empson; and see ECLOGUE and PASTORAL). Mod. degradations of didacticism, of course, occur in the use of poetry for propaganda or even advertising. Anglo-Am. poetry is esp. rich in works with historical, regional, geographic, philosophic, and political substance. The "how to" motif is still evident when Pound writes an *ABC of Reading* or John Hollander a versified textbook on prosody. One thinks of such old-new genres as utopian (and dystopian) narrative and science fiction; and there is a strong didactic element in mod. satire (R. Campbell, A. M. Klein). A recent study by H. J. Blackham devotes a chapter to "Modern Instances" and concludes with "The Message" (cf. Scholes).

The didactic *mode* is very much alive in mod. lit. (possibly more in prose than in verse); and many of the traditional didactic genres have undergone complex transformations and modulations. We find not only "modern georgics" (Frost, Louis MacNeice), but *epigrams (Ogden Nash), parodies without number, parables (Franz Kafka), and other genres aiming at some sort of didacticism. Critical theory, however, has

tended either to skirt the issues or to convert the didactic mode into related categories.

*See* BEAST EPIC, BESTIARY, CRITICISM, EXEMPLUM, FABLIAU, SPRUCHDICHTUNG.

■ R. Eckart, *Die Lehrdichtung: ihr Wesen und ihre Vertreter*, 2d ed. (1909); G. Santayana, *Three Philosophical Poets* (1910); W. Kroll, "Lehrgedicht," Pauly-Wissowa; I. A. Richards, "Doctrine in Poetry," *Practical Criticism* (1929); H. M. and N. K. Chadwick, *The Growth of Literature*, 3 v. (1932–40); T. S. Eliot, *The Uses of Poetry and the Uses of Criticism* (1933); W. Empson, *Some Versions of Pastoral* (1935); G. Solbach, *Beitrag zur Beziehung zwischen deutschen und italienischen Lehrdichtung im Mittelalter* (1937); H.J.C. Grierson and J. C. Smith, *A Critical History of English Poetry* (1944); M. H. Nicolson, *Newton Demands the Muse* (1946); R.A.B. Mynors, "Didactic Poetry," *Oxford Classical Dictionary* (1949); Curtius; Wellek; D. Daiches, *Critical Approaches to Literature* (1956), chaps. 3–4; T. S. Eliot, *On Poetry and Poets* (1957), esp. "The Social Function of Poetry"; Wimsatt and Brooks; M. C. Beardsley, *Aesthetics* (1958); G. Pellegrini, *La Poesia didascalia inglese nel settecento italiano* (1958); E. Neumann, "Bispêl," W. Richter, "Lehrhafte Dichtung," and H. Zeltner, "Philosophie und Dichtung," *Reallexikon II*; B. F. Huppé, *Doctrine and Poetry* (1959); W. G. Lambert, *Babylonian Wisdom Literature* (1960); R. Cohen, *The Art of Discrimination: Thomson's "The Seasons" and the Language of Criticism* (1964); H. de Boor, *Fabel und Bispêl* (1966); L. L. Albertsen, *Das Lehrgedicht* (1967); L. Lerner, *The Truthtellers* (1967); R. Scholes, *The Fabulators* (1967); J. Chalker, *The English Georgic* (1969)—good bibl.; C. S. Lewis, *Selective Literary Essays* (1969); B. Sowinski, *Lehrhafte Dichtung im Mittelalter* (1971); A. Isenberg, "Ethical and Aesthetic Criticism," *Aesthetics and the Theory of Criticism* (1973); C. Siegrist, *Das Lehrgedicht der Aufklarung* (1974); B. Boesch, *Lehrhafte Literatur* (1977); B. Effe, *Dichtung und Lehre* (1977)—typology of cl. didactic genres; Hesiod, *Works and Days*, ed. M. L. West (1978), "Prolegomena"—excellent comp. survey; R. L. Montgomery, *The Reader's Eye* (1979); *GRLMA*, v. 6, *La Littérature didactique, allegorique et satirique*; *Europäische Lehrdichtung*, ed. H. G. Rötzer and H. Walz (1981); Fowler; R. Wellek, "Criticism as Evaluation," *The Attack on Literature and Other Essays* (1982); M. B. Ross, *The Poetics of Moral Transformation: Forms of Didacticism in the Poetry of Shelley* (1983); "Literature and/as Moral Philosophy," *NLH* 15, spec. iss. (1983); K. Muir, *Shakespeare's Didactic Art* (1984); L. Sternbach, *Subhasida: Gnomic and Didactic Literature* (1984)—Indian; H. J. Blackham, *The Fable as Literature* (1985); W. Spiegelman, *The Didactic Muse* (1990).

T.V.F. BROGAN; S. J. KAHN

**DIFFICULTY.** Resistance to swift and confident interpretation. While the term more accurately denotes an interpretive experience in affective terms—as "the subjective counterpart to resistance" (Prynne)—difficulty is a quality conventionally attributed to poems themselves. By putting the communicative efficacy of lang. at risk, poetic difficulty prompts readers to question their normative reading practices, reconsider what may count as understanding or the proper end of reception, and seek alternative methods of achieving that end. Difficulty may serve also as an index of lyric privacy, suggesting that the speaker's very intent—not just the voiced address—is turned away from the poem's audience, availing an aura of overheard authenticity (Mill). Whereas *obscurity is a specifically visual metaphor and may result from neglect, difficulty may be experienced, as Diepeveen suggests, according to any of the three primary conceptual metaphors for understanding: as obstacles to seeing, grasping, or following.

When Dante warns that those "in piccioletta barca" (in your little bark) may not be able to follow his poetic navigations through the *Paradiso* (2.1) and John Milton invokes Urania to "fit audience find, though few," for the second half of *Paradise Lost* (7.31), each poet acknowledges that most readers will encounter difficulty. William Wordsworth, whose prefatory manifestos anticipate readerly anxiety and exemplify a growing concern to manage it, likens the poet of taste-making *genius to "Hannibal among the Alps, . . . called upon to clear and often to shape his own road" and suggests that readers should not expect to travel the same road with ease ("Essay, Supplementary," 1815). Latané argues that Robert Browning's *Sordello* helped sponsor an "aesthetics of difficulty."

But the currency of *difficulty* as a critical term rose dramatically with *modernism's characteristic challenges to the legitimacy of traditional forms, aesthetic criteria, and hermeneutic methods. Bernstein jocularly refers to "the outbreak of 1912" as "one of the best-known epidemics of difficult poetry." T. S. Eliot, pairing his expectation that "refined sensibilit[ies]" would represent the culture's "variety and complexity" with the symbolist poet's inclination "to force, to dislocate if necessary, language into his meaning" speculated in a 1921 review "that poets in our civilization, as it exists at present, must be *difficult*." The imperative core of this multiply hedged aside has been credited broadly for difficulty's revaluation as a potential poetic good. Wallace Stevens's later dictum "The poem must resist the intelligence / Almost successfully" and his call for "venerable complication" are also frequently cited promotions of difficulty. Poirier faulted Eliot and his champions for conceiving a "compendiously learned and disjointed" difficulty as a form of "cultural heroism."

Critical controversy about modernist difficulty often has grouped around such poetic features as esoteric *symbolism, imagist *concision, intertextual and polyvocalic montage, disjunctive *syntax and alogical sequencing, typographical play, and techniques of *defamiliarization (Viktor Shklovsky's *ostranenie*). In *A Survey of Modernist Poetry*, the earliest ostensibly retrospective study of the literary period, Riding and Graves present the difficulty for "the plain reader" of poems by Eliot and e. e. cummings as characteristic, and they distinguish G. M. Hopkins as a modernist because his "unconventional" diction, *prosody, and notation ensured that his poems "*had to be understood as he meant them to be, or understood not at all.*" Eastman's popular

critique of "the cult of unintelligibility" exemplified by cummings and Gertrude Stein was typical of detractors who suspected difficulty to be symptomatic of decadent freedoms, indistinct forms, and elitist exclusivity. Defenders argued that many canonical poems were intrinsically difficult, and that time has not always dispelled their difficulty. The critical reputation of the *metaphysical poets, esp. John Donne, was resurrected by the New Critics with the aid of such arguments. They defended the difficulty of certain contemp. poems as similarly integral. Blackmur wrote of Stevens's "The Comedian as the Letter C," e.g., as having "the merit of difficulty—difficulty which when solved rewards the reader beyond his hopes of clarity," a species, moreover, that he assiduously distinguished from Ezra Pound's and Eliot's, respectively (see NEW CRITICISM).

In the pursuit of professional objectivity, however, modernist critics who defended difficulty as a poetic attribute tended to discount as irrelevant to interpretation even predictable affective responses (see AFFECTIVE FALLACY). Ostensibly countering such formalist biases, Stanley Fish argued in *Surprised by Sin* (1967) that, as he later put it, "the difficulties one experiences in reading [*Paradise Lost*] are not to be lamented or discounted but . . . seen as manifestations of the legacy left to us by Adam when he fell"; Fish then extended his claims regarding "Milton's strategy . . . to make the reader self-conscious about his own performance" to other historically disparate works. On this view, difficulty itself may be read—not just overcome in preparation for a reading—much as, according to Grice's coeval theory of conversational implicature, an expression that flouts one or more maxims of manner may alert listeners to circumstances that preclude greater perspicuity even as they discern the expression's sense. In *Reading the Illegible*, Dworkin similarly attributes significance to difficulty at the materialized extreme where interpretive resistance results from a visually prosodic or paragrammatic poem's "erasures, overprintings, excisions, cancellations, [or] rearrangements" of a source text thus rendered at least partially unreadable. Relying on the redemptive logic of such systems as information theory (with its positive valuation of noise), various conceptions of the sublime, and George Bataille's general economy, Dworkin accounts for the salvaging of apparently forfeited textual meaning—in Rosmarie Waldrop's *Camp Printing* and Jackson Mac Low's *Words nd Ends from Ez*, e.g.—as insight regarding political and material situation or as affect.

Stein, for whom the syntactical ambiguity occasioned by her omission of commas manifested an attractive inner vitality, had long since broached an erotics of difficulty: "Why if you want the pleasure of concentrating on the final simplicity of excessive complication would you want any artificial aid to bring about that simplicity. . . . When it gets really difficult you want to disentangle rather than to cut the knot." Vincent likens negotiating the difficulty of certain "queer" lyrics (e.g., John Ashbery's or Hart Crane's) to homosexual cruising, claiming that, in both cases, "boredom, disenchantment, fear, shame, and even disgust are likely components of desire and excitement." Presenting difficulty as a "poetic device," Hejinian borrows lang. from Peter Nicholls to ally it with a sense of sincerity shared by philosopher Emmanuel Levinas and objectivist poets Louis Zukofsky and George Oppen that "involves 'exposure to the claims of others . . . [,] an acceptance of what *exceeds* the self' . . . in unassimilable surpluses of meaning, in impossible games, in rage, in disruptive and disordering pleasure, in laughter" (see OBJECTIVISM). As difficulty is experienced at the juncture of thought and feeling, its appreciation would seem to hold out opportunities for a reversal of what Eliot identified as a *"dissociation of sensibility" prevailing since Donne.

Of the four sources of difficulty Eliot addressed in his 1932–33 Harvard lectures, two correspond to receptive attitudes: anxious overpreparedness, cleverly dubbed "gallery fright," and "novelty" (readerly underpreparedness). His remaining two sources originate, intentionally or unintentionally, with the author. Steiner's more sophisticated, influential taxonomy also distinguished four types. "Contingent" difficulty is referential, allusive; archaic and foreign diction, proper nouns, slang, and other idiolects may need to be looked up. "Modal" difficulty, in contrast, is elusive and manifests itself as an empathic impasse with respect to a poem's apparent nexus of values. While Steiner focused on temporal changes in expectation as the cause, Shetley notes that such difficulty results as readily from crossing between contemporaneous interpretive communities. Steiner's third type, "tactical" difficulty, with "its source in the writer's will or in the failure of adequacy between his intention and his performative means," recalls Aesopian responses to censorship and parabolic restrictions of understanding to initiates; here Steiner echoes Eliot's call on the poet "to dislocate . . . language into his meaning," and, as Shetley observes, such difficulty is essential to lyric's "project . . . of embodying subjectivity in the impersonal and resistant medium of language." Finally, "ontological" difficulty, as Steiner defines it, breaches "the contract of ultimate or preponderant intelligibility between poet and reader, between text and meaning."

Steiner's four types seem, like Eliot's, to fall into two pairs—difficulty for which the reader or the poet is responsible, respectively. Yet, intentional, implicative versions of Steiner's first two types exist. For instance, Brooks and Warren's midcentury approach to *The Waste Land*—that Eliot situates the mod., secular reader in "the position of the knight in the Grail legends," bewildered among thickets of *allusion, forced to feel and question the apparent meaninglessness of his or her condition—ascribes a tactical use to referential and modal difficulty alike. Paul Celan's obliquely allusive, semantically and syntactically fractured, neologistic, elliptical poetry is the most cited exemplar of ontological difficulty, yet the proliferation of compelling readings suggests that this type, too, is not securely distinct from the tactical. Even highly competent readers are liable to experience difficulty not as any one recognizable type but as a threat to expected cooperation between the poet and themselves, uncertainty about how to proceed, and doubt regarding whether the apparent obstacles are significant guides or the result of authorial exclusivity or incompetence. The terminological vagueness of *difficulty* significantly corresponds to the vagueness of a reader's perplexity; to classify the source of difficulty is to begin to dispel it.

Ashbery and Jorie Graham are the two Eng.-lang. poets whose work has most provoked continued disputation regarding difficulty in the second half of the 20th c. and since. A 1976 *New York Times Magazine* profile titled "How to Be a Difficult Poet" secured the adjective to Ashbery. Shetley encapsulates numerous attempts to account since then for Ashbery's difficulty, arguing that the poet sought "to make reading difficult again" by systematically flouting the New Criticism's dramatistic techniques of making difficult poems accessible. Ashbery's selection of Graham's "On Difficulty" for *The Best American Poetry of 1988* coincided with her establishment as an importantly difficult poet, a reputation she has earned with her syntactically sustained errancies—part wandering inquiry, part tactical "wrong"-doing—and sophisticated extrapoetic defenses of difficulty's value in her own and others' poetry. The Language movement has influentially framed difficulty as a marker and medium of social critique in its collaborative efforts to expose, in Hejinian's words, "the world view (and ideology) secreted not only in our vocabulary but at every linguistic level incl. the ways in which sentences are put together" and to explore "new ways of thinking by putting language (and hence perception) together in new ways" (see LANGUAGE POETRY).

*See* OBSCURITY.

■ J. S. Mill, "Thoughts on Poetry and Its Varieties" [1833], *Dissertations and Discussions* (1859); T. S. Eliot, "The Metaphysical Poets," *Times Literary Supplement* (1921); L. Riding and R. Graves, *A Survey of Modernist Poetry* (1928); M. Eastman, *The Literary Mind* (1931); R. P. Blackmur, "Examples of Wallace Stevens," *The Double Agent* (1935); G. Stein, "Poetry and Grammar," *Lectures in America* (1935); W. Stevens, "Man Carrying Thing" and "The Creations of Sound," *Transport to Summer* (1947); Brooks and Warren; Frye; J. H. Prynne, "Resistance and Difficulty," *Prospect* 5 (1961); G. Steiner, "On Difficulty," *On Difficulty and Other Essays* (1978); S. Fish, "Literature in the Reader: Affective Stylistics," *Is There a Text in This Class?* (1980); D. E. Latané Jr., *Browning's "Sordello" and the Aesthetics of Difficulty* (1987); R. Poirier, *The Renewal of Literature* (1987); H. P. Grice, "Logic and Conversation," *Studies in the Way of Words* (1989); V. Shetley, *After the Death of Poetry* (1993); L. Hejinian, "Barbarism," *Language of Inquiry* (2000); J. E. Vincent, *Queer Lyrics* (2002); L. Diepeveen, *The Difficulties of Modernism* (2003); R. Kaufman, "Difficulty in Modern Poetry and Aesthetics," *Just Being Difficult?*, ed. J. Culler and K. Lamb (2003); C. Dworkin, *Reading the Illegible* (2003); I. Yaron, "What Is a 'Difficult Poem'? Towards a Definition," *Journal of Literary Semantics* 37 (2008); C. Bernstein, *Attack of the Difficult Poems* (2011).

A. L. OSBORN

**DIMETER** (Gr., "of two measures"). A line consisting of two measures. In *classical prosody, the *metron in *iambic, *trochaic, and *anapestic verse is a dipody (pair of feet); hence, the cl. iambic dimeter contains two metra or four feet. But in mod. prosodies, the concept of the metron was never established: here -*meter* is synonymous with foot. The Eng. iambic dimeter, therefore, consists of two feet, the trimeter of three feet, etc. This terminology applies only to *accentual-syllabic verse, which is regular: *accentual verse—e.g., a line of two stresses but a variable number of syllables—is not, properly speaking, a dimeter. Short-lined verse in Eng., such as the *Skeltonic, is rarely regular enough to be called dimeter, though dimeter lines feature in the *Burns stanza and the *limerick. More regular examples do occur, particularly in the 16th- and 17th-c. lyric, e.g., Michael Drayton's "An Amouret Anacreontic" and Robert Herrick's "To a Lark." More recent approximations include W. H. Auden's "This Lunar Beauty" and Donald Justice's "Dreams of Water."

T.V.F. Brogan; J. M. Cocola

**DINDSHENCHAS** (Gael., *Dind*, "eminent, notable place"; *senchas*, "ancient, traditional lore"). Collections of med. Ir. didactic material. The Ir. poet, the *fili*, was expected to know the meaning and historical significance of every place name, every geographical and topographical feature in Ireland, and that knowledge is what *dindshenchas* represents. The earliest extant collection of *dindshenchas* material is in the Book of Leinster (mid-12th c.). Two types of collection occur there, one consisting entirely of verse and the other of prose accounts, each with a single *quatrain that occurs at or near the end. This prose type occurs in several later mss. as well. A third type consists of a prose account followed by verse, and this type is represented in many mss. from the 14th to 16th cs. The poetry is of the *dán díreach* type, and the number of quatrains ranges from only a few to 80. The majority of the poems are without attribution, but a few are attributed to poets and monastic literati of the 9th to 11th cs. Thurneysen and Gwynn argued that the prose and poetry accounts of individual articles were originally separate and that they were integrated by around the beginning of the 13th c. However, Tomás Ó Concheanainn has argued that the full and original form of the *dindshenchas* is that in which each place-name legend is given first in prose and then in verse and that the so-called "metrical *dindshenchas*," that is, the verse-only versions, were abstracted from the underlying original, the prose with single quatrain versions being abridged forms of the original.

See CELTIC PROSODY, FILI.

■ W. Stokes, "The Bodleian Dinnshenchas," *Folklore* 3 (1892); "The Edinburgh Dinnshenchas," *Folklore* 4 (1893); "The Prose Tales in the Rennes Dinnshenchas," *Revue Celtique* 15 (1894), 16 (1895); R. Thurneysen, *Die irische Helden- und Königsage bis zum siebzehnten jahrhundert* (1921); *The Metrical Dindshenchas*, 5 vols., text and trans. by E. Gwynn (1903–35; rpt. 1991); M. O Daly, "The Metrical Dindshenchas," *Early Irish Poetry*, ed.

J. Carney (1965); C. Bowen, "A Historical Inventory of the *Dindshenchas*," *Studia Celtica* 10/11 (1975/76); T. Ó Concheanainn, "The Three Forms of *Dinnshenchas Érenn*," pt. 1, *The Journal of Celtic Studies* 3, no. 1 (1981); pt. 2, 3, no. 2 (1982); Williams and Ford.

P. K. Ford

**DINGGEDICHT.** (Ger., "thing-poem"). A form of poetry exemplified most copiously by the *Neue Gedichte* that R. M. Rilke (1875–1926) wrote during his middle period, 1902–8, which he spent mostly in Paris. These poems represent concrete objects and situations (as well as a pictorially perceived constellation of things or actions) in a style of factual precision and semantic concentration. Their exactitude results from intense observation, which promises, usually in a concluding epiphany, to yield insights into the essential, though often ineffable, nature of things. A poem written as a *Kunst-Ding* is the complete opposite of an inspirational *poésie du coeur* (poem of the heart) and may be said to be the ideal symbolist poem (see SYMBOLISM). Its detached concern with objective facticity abstains from evoking moments of emotive proximity between the reader, the (implicit) lyrical persona, and the artistic "counterworld" into which they enter. The evocation of "inner" experiences, when not altogether limited to epiphanic instances, opens an interior space that is a sacral nowhere, an imaginary locus (*das Imaginäre*). This is to say that the *Dinggedicht*, strictly defined, enacts a process of transformation in which select forms and objects (delicate animals and flowers, exceptional human beings, artful constructs) are turned into aesthetic entities. In other words, a select item of factual reality is made into an aesthetic object (*Ding*) that exists, fully self-contained and self-sufficient, only as lang.; it is insubstantial. Paradoxically, it is the unattainable intent of this lang. to fill this void by transmuting itself into the real, incarnate presence of the "thing" or "image" invoked.

Historically, Rilke's perfection of thing-poetry after 1900 reflects a pervasive notion that quotidian life had become aggressively inimical to poetic sensibilities. The most influential response to this traumatic realization was Friedrich Nietzsche's defiant claim (made first in *The Birth of Tragedy*, 1871) that art, not morality, is "the true metaphysical activity of this life" and "that the existence of the world is *justified* only as an aesthetic phenomenon." Rilke's own reorientation was guided primarily by his perception of Auguste Rodin and Charles Baudelaire (as mediated by the exemplary sculptor) and, after 1907, by the equilibrium of colors achieved in the paintings of Paul Cézanne. Though he must have been familiar with some examples of the Dinggedicht—the term was not introduced into scholarly discussions until 1926— in Ger. postromantic verse (Eduard Mörike, Friedrich Hebbel, C. F. Meyer), the *poésie objective* of *Parnassianism (Théodore de Banville, Théophile Gautier, Charles-Marie Leconte de Lisle, J.-M. de Heredia, and others) left no traces in his aesthetic reflections.

Convincing evidence for the general (and individually modified) relevance of the Dinggedicht can be found in the poetics of *imagism (i.e., in Ezra Pound's definition of image as "that which presents an intellectual and emotional complex in an instant of time"), in T. S. Eliot's concept of the *objective correlative, and in the early poetry of W. C. Williams ("no ideas but in things"), Marianne Moore, Gertrude Stein, Vicente Huidobro, and Wallace Stevens that gives priority to the objective status of physical phenomena over the perceiving mind. Hence, "object-poem" (Sandbank) has established itself as the term's most felicitous Eng. equivalent.

*See* CREATIONISM, OBJECTIVISM.

■ W. G. Müller, "Der Weg vom Symbolismus . . . zum Dinggedicht . . . ," *Neophilologus* 58 (1974); D. Wellbery, "Zur Poetik der Figuration . . . ," *Zu R. M. Rilke*, ed. E. Schwarz (1983); S. Sandbank, "The Object-Poem: In Defense of Referentiality," *PoT* 6 (1985); L. Ryan, "Rilke's *Dinggedichte*: The 'Thing' as 'Poem in Itself,'" *Rilke-Rezeptionen—Rilke Reconsidered*, ed. S. Bauschinger and S. L. Cocalis (1995); L. Powell, *The Technological Unconscious in German Modernist Literature* (2000).

M. WINKLER

**DIPODISM, DIPODIC VERSE.** Dipody (literally, two-footed) has been used to describe (1) a metrical unit larger than the *foot, (2) a kind of *meter, and (3) a rhythmic tendency. This line by John Masefield ("A Ballad of John Silver") can be described as eight trochees, the final foot catalectic, lacking a final syllable: "Shé was bóarded, shé was lóoted, shé was scúttled tíll she sánk." More sensitive ears, however, will hear four primary stresses (´) and four secondary stresses (`): "Shè was bóarded, shè was lóoted, shè was scúttled tìll she sánk." Moreover, there is a regular pattern pairing each primary stress with a secondary stress, creating four dipodes, each consisting of two trochees, the second trochee more emphatic than the first. Thus, a dipodic meter describes a regular pattern of primary and secondary stresses combining feet hierarchically into the larger metrical unit of the dipode.

The term *dipody* was first applied to Eng. verse in 1857 by Coventry Patmore, who borrowed it from *classical prosody. In cl. prosody, iambic, trochaic, and anapestic meters are usually counted dipodically rather than as feet. Iambic *trimeter, e.g., describes not three iambs as it would in Eng. but three dipodes, each having two feet. In each dipode, the first foot can be either iambic or spondaic, but the second foot must be iambic.

Patmore argued that dipody formed the foundation of all Eng. verse, incl. *iambic pentameter, making dipody a rhythmic principle as well as a meter. During the metrical experimentation of the late 19th c., many—incl. Masefield—wrote in dipodic meters. These poems have also been described as tetrasyllabic, quadruple, or paeonic verse (a *paeon is a four-syllable foot). Masefield's line can be described as "third paeons," the third syllable receiving the strong stress: "She was bóarded."

A perceptual basis for dipodism was established when Woodrow's experiments in 1909 indicated that primary stress on the first member of a subjective group of four usually produces secondary stress on the third. In 1930, Stewart first articulated a comprehensive theory of dipody in Eng. In 1959, Wimsatt and Beardsley argued that their theory of meter explains why "no *great* English poems" have been written in dipodic meters. Since then, dipodic meters have been left out of many practical handbooks.

In 1982, Attridge revised key portions of Stewart's argument. For Attridge, dipody does not underlie all verse but is one of several linguistic resources available: dipody usually plays a role in the most rhythmically insistent poetic forms, but iambic pentameter structurally resists dipody. Citing data gathered by Tarlinskaja in 1976, Attridge explains that folk poetry typically places the primary stress first, while literary poetry tends to place the secondary stress first. While the pattern in Masefield is secondary-primary, Attridge hears a primary-secondary pattern in the F. J. Child ballad "Thomas Rhymer": "Her skírt was òf the gráss-green sìlk, / Her mántel òf the vélvet fìne." Scholars of OE and of ME have argued whether these prosodies were dipodic, and scholars such as Turco use dipodic to refer to any group of feet, requiring no hierarchy of primary and secondary stresses.

*See* MEDIEVAL POETICS, METRON, RELATIVE STRESS PRINCIPLE.

■ C. Patmore, *Essay on English Metrical Law* (1857); H. Woodrow, "A Quantitative Study of Rhythm," *Archives of Psychology* 14 (1909); G. R. Stewart, *The Technique of English Verse* (1930); Wimsatt and Beardsley; Tarlinskaja; Attridge, *Rhythms*; L. Turco, *The New Book of Forms* (1986); D. Taylor, *Hardy's Meters and Victorian Prosody* (1988)—19th-c. experiments; T. Cable, *The English Alliterative Tradition* (1991); Gasparov, *History*.

M. L. MANSON

**DIRGE.** A song for the dead, sung at the funeral ceremony, at the procession, or afterward; the ancients made some generic distinctions. The Eng. term derives from the beginning of the antiphon in Lat. of the Office of the Dead ("Dirige, Domine . . .") adapted from Psalms 5:9. As a literary genre, the dirge developed out of Gr. funerary songs, particularly the *epicedium, the song sung over the dead, and the *threnos*, sung in memory of the dead. The Gr. dirge influenced the Lat. *nenia*, laments sung by hired professional poets, but these never became a literary genre, nor did the *laudatio funebris*, the public funeral oration. Originally a choral *ode, the threnody evolved into a *monody that was strophic in form and employed various metrical systems; it is common in Gr. poetry after the 6th c. BCE, and the distinction between epicedium and monody was still recognized in the Ren. (Puttenham).

Although in ancient lit. the dirge was sometimes influenced by the *consolatio* and closely connected with the *elegy, its chief aim was to lament the dead, not to console survivors—cf. the *lament for Hector at *Odyssey* 24.746 ff. But the subject matter included lamentation and eulogy, often with consolatory reflections, *apostrophes, and invocations. Not only human beings but animals might be mourned (cf. Catullus 3). In Gr., Simonides, Pindar, and the Alexandrian poets used the genre; in Lat., Calvus and Catullus used it first, and

Propertius brought it to its greatest perfection (4.11). The meter in Lat. was the *hexameter or the *elegiac distich. The med. writers combined the Lat. form with the Church's lamentation for the dead, employing in the process Christian themes. Eng. examples of dirges include Henry King's "Exequy" on his young wife, R. W. Emerson's "Threnody on His Young Son," and George Meredith's "Dirge in Woods."

*See* ENDECHA.

■ R. Leicher, *Die Totenklage in der deutschen Epik vom der Ältesten Zeit bis zur Nibelungen-Klage* (1927); G. Herrlinger, *Totenklage um Tiere in der antiken Dichtung* (1930); E. Reiner, *Die rituelle Totenklage der Griechen* (1938); V. B. Richmond, *Laments for the Dead in Medieval Narrative* (1966); M. Alexiou, *The Ritual Lament in Greek Tradition* (1974); E. Vermeule, *Aspects of Death in Early Greek Art and Poetry* (1979); *Poèmes de la mort de Turold à Villon*, ed. and trans. J.-M. Paquette (1979); *Do Not Go Gentle: Poems on Death*, ed. W. Packard (1981); *Japanese Death Poems*, ed. and trans. Y. Hoffmann (1986); R. J. Cutter, "Saying Goodbye: The Transformation of the Dirge in Early Medieval China," *Early Medieval China* 10–11 (2004); Puttenham.

R. A. HORNSBY; T.V.F. BROGAN

**DISCORDIA CONCORS.** Derived through the reception of Pythagorean thought during the Ren., the phrase *discordia concors* received its canonical formulation in Franchino Gafurio's *De harmonia musicorum instrumentorum* (1518), which adapted Philolaus's definition of *harmony* into the maxim *harmonia est discordia concors* (harmony is discord concordant). The expression is an inversion of *concordia discors*, a doctrine common to the Empedoclean theory of elements (see Horace, *Epistles* 1.12). Significant for Ren. mathematics, music, and poetics, the legacy of discordia concors as a concept for lit. crit. was secured by Samuel Johnson's use of the phrase to critique the unnatural imagery of *metaphysical poetry.

*See* CONCEIT, MUSIC AND POETRY, NEOCLASSICAL POETICS, RENAISSANCE POETICS.

■ S. Johnson, "Life of Cowley," *Lives of the English Poets* (1781); H. Diels, *Die Fragmente der Vorsokratiker* (1934); R. Wittkower, *Architectural Principles in the Age of Humanism*, 5th ed. (1998).

C. DONALDSON

**DISSOCIATION OF SENSIBILITY.** The phrase appeared in T. S. Eliot's "The Metaphysical Poets" (1921), where Eliot proposed that "something . . . happened to the mind of England between the time of Donne or Lord Herbert of Cherbury and the time of Tennyson and Browning. . . . Tennyson and Browning are poets, and they think; but they do not feel their thought as immediately as the odour of a rose. A thought to Donne was an experience; it modified his sensibility." To explain the change, Eliot proposed a "theory": "the poets of the 17th century, the successors of the dramatists of the 16th, possessed a mechanism of sensibility which could devour any kind of experience. . . . In the

17th century a dissociation of sensibility set in, from which we have never recovered; and this dissociation . . . was aggravated by the influence of the two most powerful poets of the century, Milton and Dryden." The first consequence was that "while the language became more refined, the feeling became more crude"; the second was the "sentimental age," which "began early in the 18th century, and continued. The poets . . . thought and felt by fits, unbalanced; they reflected."

What caused the dissociation of sensibility? In "Milton II" (1947), Eliot suggested that it involved issues at stake in the Eng. Civil War. The breakup of the Christian Eur. order, with which the dissociation of sensibility coincides, was in Eliot's view the central event of Eur. cultural hist., as it was for some of his New Critical followers. Those adopting the term have assigned responsibility variously to Thomas Hobbes (Brooks), Francis Bacon (Knights), Cartesian dualism (Willey), and the rise of capitalism (Kramer). It has also been suggested that a dissociation of sensibility is a permanent cultural condition that poetry specifically addresses (Altieri).

Eliot may have adapted the phrase from a sentence in Remy de Gourmont's essay on Jules Laforgue, but the "sensuous apprehension of thought" is one of the ideals of romantic poetics (Kermode). Eliot later backtracked and denounced both Donne and Laforgue for dissociating thought and feeling; in 1931 he argued that "in Donne, there is a manifest fissure between thought and sensibility." Still, a hypothetical "dissociation" and the identification of two distinct lines in the hist. of Eng. poetry inform modernist lit. hists. such as F. R. Leavis's *Revaluation* (1936) and C. Brooks's *Modern Poetry and the Tradition* (1939). The view that 19th-c. Eng. and Am. poetry suffers from sentimentalism and makeshift philosophizing was for a time crucial to claims for the significance of modernist poetry.

*See* SENSIBILITY.

■ R. de Gourmont, "La Sensibilité de Jules Laforgue," *Promenades littéraires* 1 (1904); T. S. Eliot, "The Metaphysical Poets" (1921, rpt. *Essays*); "Donne in Our Time," in *A Garland for John Donne*, ed. T. Spencer (1931), and "Milton II" (1947, rpt. *On Poetry and Poets*, 1957); B. Willey, *The Seventeenth-Century Background* (1934), ch. 5; L. C. Knights, "Bacon and the Seventeenth-Century Dissociation of Sensibility," *Scrutiny* 11 (1943); R. Tuve, *Elizabethan and Metaphysical Imagery* (1947), ch. 7; F. W. Bateson, "Dissociation of Sensibility," *Essays in Criticism* 1–2 (1951–52); F. Kermode, *Romantic Image* (1957), ch. 8; J. E. Duncan, *The Revival of Metaphysical Poetry* (1959); J. Kramer, "T. S. Eliot's Concept of Tradition," *New German Critique* 6 (1975); E. Lobb, *T. S. Eliot and the Romantic Critical Tradition* (1981); P. Meisel, *The Myth of the Modern* (1987); L. Menand, *Discovering Modernism* (1987); C. Altieri, "Theorizing Emotions in Eliot's Poetry and Poetics," in *Gender, Desire, and Sexuality in T. S. Eliot*, ed. C. Laity and N. Gish (2004).

L. MENAND

**DISSONANCE.** The quality of being harsh or inharmonious in rhythm or sound; akin to *cacophony. Insofar as the terms may be distinguished, cacophony is that which is harsh-sounding in itself, while dissonance is that which is discordant or inharmonious with what surrounds it. Dissonance, rather than cacophony, is invoked in discussions of *rhythm; and while cacophony is sometimes unintentional, dissonance usually implies deliberate choice. By extension, the term may also refer to other elements in a poem that are discordant in their immediate context: tonality, theme, imagery (*catachresis), or syntax (*anacoluthon). Just as there is frequent confusion between the euphonious and the musical, so too there is a tendency among critics and readers to identify dissonance with the unmusical. But as Northrop Frye reminds us, music is concerned not with the beauty but with the organization of sound. A musical discord is not an unpleasant sound but an energetic one. Applying this principle to poetry, we can say, with Frye, that when we find harsh, barking accents, crabbed lang., mouthfuls of consonants, and the like, we are likely to be reading a poet influenced by music. Robert Browning ("Not a plenteous cork-crop: scarcely") and G. M. Hopkins ("sheer plod makes plough down sillion / Shine") made notable use of dissonance. It is also frequently found in Fr. *baroque, Eng. *metaphysical, and Sp. mannerist poetry.

*See* EUPHONY, MANNERISM, SOUND.

■ J. B. Douds, "Donne's Technique of Dissonance," *PMLA* 52 (1937); A. Stein, "Donne's Harshness and the Elizabethan Tradition," *SP* 41 (1944); N. Frye, "The Rhythm of Recurrence: Epos," *Anatomy of Criticism*, and "Lexis and Melos," *Sound and Poetry*, ed. Frye (both 1957); A. Ostriker, "Thomas Wyatt and Henry Surrey," *NLH* 1 (1970); M. Gibson, "The Poetry of Struggle: Browning's Style," *VP* 19 (1981); S. F. Walker, "The Wrong Word at the Right Time," *Proceedings of the Tenth Congress of the International Comparative Literature Association*, ed. A. Balakian et al., vol. 2 (1982); E. DeLamotte, "Dissonance and Resolution in *Four Quartets*," *MLQ* 49 (1988); M. A. Evans, "*Soubresaut* or Dissonance? An Aspect of the Musicality of Baudelaire's 'Petits Poèmes en prose,'" *MLR* 83 (1988).

L. BISHOP; A. WATSON

**DISTICH.** A pair of metrical lines, a *couplet, *heterometric in cl. poetry but usually *isometric in mod. In cl. poetry, the most common type is the *elegiac distich, consisting of a dactylic *hexameter followed by a dactylic *pentameter and often used for *epigram. The widely known *Distichs of Cato* carried the form of the distich from Lat. into the Middle Ages; it is still common in mod. Gr. poetry. But with the emergence of the romance vernaculars, the couplet (most often octosyllabic) was normally isometric and rhymed. Thomas Sébillet was the first to use the term *distique* in *French prosody, where it retained more currency than in Eng.

■ G. Soyter, "Das volkstümliche Distichon bei den Neugriechen," *Laographia* 8 (1925); *Disticha Cantonis*, ed. M. Boas (1952); Koster.

T.V.F. BROGAN

**DIT.** A type of med. Fr. composition of notorious nebulousness, the generic specificity of which is often called into question by mod. critics (indeed, many scholars would consider the *Roman de la Rose* a self-proclaimed *roman*, to be the most important med. *dit*). The designation first appeared around 1200 and continued to be used frequently through the 14th c. The only constants of the dit are its relatively brief length (at least before the mid- to late 14th c.), verse form, and the fact that it was usually spoken (or read) rather than sung. With the exception of drama, it was the only major nonlyric verse genre in Fr. of the later Middle Ages and often served as a site for *lyric insertion. Its verse form is usually nonstanzaic (rhyming octosyllabic couplets are esp. common), but two stanzaic forms—rhymed quatrains of *alexandrines and *strophes d'Hélinand* (12 octosyllabic lines, *aabaabbbabba*)—are not uncommon. Critics often remark on the didactic aspirations of the dit (see DIDACTIC POETRY)—particularly when didacticism is taken to include the religious, satirical, moral, and courtly—and on the strong presence of a first-person speaker throughout the entire poem (in contradistinction to the romance). In the later Middle Ages in particular, the dit was the privileged form for ambitious explorations of the relationship between personal experience and knowledge. Famous practitioners include Rutebeuf, Guillaume Le Clerc de Normandie, Huon Le Roi, Henri d'Andeli, Beaudouin de Condé, Jean de Condé, Guillaume de Machaut, Jean Froissart, and Christine de Pizan. Texts described as dits by authors or rubricators often receive another generic label, such as *conte*, *fabliau*, *traité*, *complainte*, *lai*, and sermon. The term's fluidity may result from its ability to denote a text conceived of as the result of poetic composition; early on it often appears paired with the term *trouver* (to compose).

■ J. Cerquiglini, "Le Clerc et l'écriture: Le 'Voir dit' de Guillaume de Machaut et la définition du 'dit,'" *Literatur in der Gesellschaft des Spätmittelalters*, ed. H. U. Gumbrecht (1980); M. Zink, *La subjectivité littéraire: autour du siècle de saint Louis* (1985); J. Cerquiglini, "Le Dit," *La littérature française aux XIVe et XVe siècles*, ed. D. Poirion (1988); M. Léonard, *Le dit et sa technique littéraire des origines à 1340* (1996); A. Armstrong and S. Kay, *Knowing Poetry: Verse in Medieval France from the "Rose" to the "Rhétoriqueurs"* (2011).

E. ZINGESSER

**DITHYRAMB.** A genre of Gr. choral *lyric or *melic poetry performed in honor of Dionysus. The earliest reference (Archilochus, frag. 77) associates the dithyramb with drunken revelry: "I know how to lead the beautiful dithyramb-song of Lord Dionysus when my mind is thunder-struck with wine." The genre's origins are obscure, but Arion is credited with introducing formal improvements and a circular *chorus in Corinth at the beginning of the 6th c. BCE, while, at the end of the same century, Lasus of Hermione improved the music and dance and helped establish dithyrambic contests at Athens. Dithyrambs were also performed at Delos during the winter months when they replaced *paeans to Apollo. Judging from extant 5th-c. examples and from the names given by Alexandrian editors (e.g., Bacchylides, the Sons of Antenor, the Youths, or Theseus), heroic narratives, often unconnected with Dionysus, later became a prominent feature of the genre. Although Simonides was a leading composer of dithyrambs (credited with 56 victories in contests), not a verse remains. We possess only fragments of Pindar's two books of dithyrambs but have substantial portions of five dithyrambs and the beginning of a sixth by Bacchylides (Jebb, Burnett). In the 4th c., the dithyramb underwent considerable modification—and evident decline—at the hands of Philoxenus and Timotheus, who originated what is sometimes called the New Dithyramb (Smyth) by abolishing the strophic structure and introducing solo singing along with musical and verbal virtuosity (Pickard-Cambridge). Since there is no appreciable difference between the style of Pindar's and Bacchylides' surviving dithyrambs and that of their other poems, the later reputation of the dithyramb for extreme license (cf. Horace, *Odes* 4.2) must stem from its later stages of devel. Although *hymns to Bacchus continued to be written (e.g., Horace, *Odes* 2.19, 3.25), the genre of dithyramb was moribund by the 2d c. BCE. In mod. usage, *dithyrambic* characterizes a style that is ecstatic, vehement, or unpredictable; probably the best-known mod. example in this mode is John Dryden's "Alexander's Feast."

*See* GREEK POETRY.

■ O. Crusius, "*Dithyramb*," Pauly-Wissowa; H. W. Smyth, *Greek Melic Poets* (1900); R. C. Jebb, *Bacchylides* (1905); H. Färber, *Die Lyrik in der Kunsttheorie der Antike* (1936); A. E. Harvey, "The Classification of Greek Lyric Poetry," *CQ* 5 (1955); A. W. Pickard-Cambridge, *Dithyramb, Tragedy and Comedy*, 2d ed. (1962); A. P. Burnett, *The Art of Bacchylides* (1985); R. Hamilton, "The Pindaric Dithyramb," *Harvard Studies in Classical Philology* 93 (1990); A. D'Angour, "How the Dithyramb Got Its Shape," *CQ* 47 (1997).

W. H. RACE

**DITTY,** dittie, dictie, etc. (Lat. *dictum, dict,* a saying). In ME, *ditty* denoted a composition or treatise and then a piece of verse; by the 16th c., it had come to mean the words of a song. As a verb, *ditty* could mean to sing a song or to set words to music—now obsolete. In Thomas Morley's *Plaine and Easie Introduction to Practical Musicke* (1597), the section on how to fit music to a text is titled "Rules to be Observed in Dittying," and Samuel Daniel in *A Defence of Ryme* (1603) remarks that feminine rhymes are "fittest for Ditties." But in its mod. sense a song or tune, esp. a light or simple one, *ditty* has almost lost its association with words.

■ L. E. Auld, "Text as Pre-text: French Court Airs and Their Ditties," *Literature and the Other Arts*, ed. D. L. Rubin (1993).

E. DOUGHTIE

**DIVAN.** A Middle Persian word (also spelled as *diwan*) borrowed in Ar., Armenian, Pashto, mod. Persian, Turkish, and Urdu to refer to a collection of poems or the corpus of a single poet. The same word exists in several langs. for a list or register, the state or legal council, chancery, administrative and bureaucratic branches of the government, state records, written scrolls, bureaucrats, a site for governmental records, and a hall for official meetings in Islamic states. The usage of *divan* in poetics—not for a genre but for a form of traditional publication since the Abbasid period (750–1258) by Ar. philologists (many of them of Persian origin) to assemble the works of pre-Islamic Arab poets—is likely related to the other usages, associated with words, letters, records, and a particular kind of seat associated with high rank, contemplation, conversation, and leisure culture.

Typically, the divan of a poet contains all of his or her poetic works without the long poems (*masnavīs*). Most mss. (or mod. eds.) are organized according to (Asian) poetic forms, usually with *qasīdas* first, then *ghazals*, *qiṭas*, and *rubā'ī* last. The order of these forms within a section follows the logic not of chronology but of the alphabet. The rhyming word in combination with the first word of the first line of each poem nearly always determines its place among other poems of its kind. However, early Arab and Persian mss. are generally not arranged alphabetically but often grouped by subject.

The Ger. trans. of the divan of the 14th-c. Persian poet Ḥāfiẓ in the early 19th c. inspired the first collection of poems in Europe that used the word *divan* in its title: J. W. Goethe's *West-östlicher Divan* (*West-Eastern Divan*, 1819), his largest collection of lyric poems and one of the first mod. examples of cross-cultural and transnational poetics. While adopting Islamic and Persian themes (such as Suleika, the wife of Potiphar in the Joseph story in the book of Genesis, and *saqi* the cupbearer) as well as incorporating various metaphors of cl. Persian poetry (e.g., moth, candle light, pearl), Goethe does not arrange the poems according to the received model. Following the organizational logic of Joseph Hammer-Purgstall's Ger. trans. (1812) of Ḥāfiẓ's *Divan*, Goethe structures his *Divan* thematically in books: "The Book of the Singer," "The Book of Love," "The Book of Paradise," and so on.

While a collection of cl. poems in traditional forms is still often published as a divan or complete works, the poems of 20th-c. and contemp. poets are less frequently published under the rubric but are simply designated as a collection or collected works.

*See* ARABIC POETRY, GERMAN POETRY, PERSIAN POETRY, TURKISH POETRY.

■ E. G. Browne, *A Literary History of Persia*, 4 v. (1902–28); J. Rypka, *History of Iranian Literature*, trans. K. Jahn (1968); *Der Diwan von Mohammed Schemsed-din Hafis*, trans. J. F. Hammer (1973); *Divan-i Hafiz*, ed. P. N. Khānlarī (1982); J. Rūmī, *Divan-i Shams-e*

*Tabrizi*, trans. R. A. Nicholson (2001)—selected trans.; Z. Safa, *Tarikh-i Adabiyat dar Iran*, 16th ed., 8 v. (2001)—hist. of lit. in Iran; *Le Divan: Oeuvre lyrique d'un spiritual en Perse au XIVe siècle*, trans. C.-H. de Fouchécour (2006)—Fr. trans. of Ḥāfiẓ; *The Collected Lyrics of Ḥāfiẓ of Shíráz*, trans. P. Avery (2007)—Eng. trans.; *General Introduction to Persian Literature*, ed. J.T.P. de Bruijn (2009).

S. SHAMEL

**DIZAIN.** In Fr. poetry, the *dizain* is either a short poem of ten lines or a ten-line stanza within a longer form, such as the *ode, the *ballade, the chanson, or the *chant royal*. As a separate poem, it was popular in the 15th and 16th cs. as a composition of octosyllabic or decasyllabic lines that, in the work of Clément Marot and Mellin de Saint-Gelais, had the rhyme scheme *ababbccdcd*. Maurice Scève composed the first Fr. *canzoniere*, *Délie* (1544), with 449 decasyllabic dizains, all but 15 following this scheme. Used uniformly as the sole building unit for an entire Petrarchan sequence, the *dizain scévien* thus marks the transition between med. lyric forms such as the *rondeau or the chanson and the *sonnet. Thomas Sébillet in his *Art poétique françoys* of 1548 associates both dizain and sonnet with the *epigram: for him, the dizain is "l'épigramme aujourd'hui estimé premier," while the "sonnet n'est autre chose que le parfait épigramme de l'Ita. comme le dizain du Français" (the sonnet is nothing but the perfect epigrammatic form in It. as the dizain is in French). As employed later by the *Pléiade, the dizain has the rhyme scheme *ababccdeed*, is less often found as a separate poem, and may be composed of verses of different lengths. Three or five dizains, each group with an *envoi, form together a ballade or a chant royal, respectively. Those med. forms are banished by the Pléiade; but in the wake of François de Malherbe, the dizain continues to be the most widely used stanza in the cl. ode. With the scheme *ababccdeed* and in octosyllables, it is taken over into Rus. versification in the 18th c. by Mikhail Lomonosov and Gavrila Derzhavin. Several dizains appear in Philip Sidney's *Old Arcadia* and *New Arcadia* (e.g., the dialogue between Strephon and Claius after book 4 in the *Old*, book 2 in the *New*): they do not, however, keep the double internal *couplets and mirror-image rhyme scheming of Scève's model. As a separate poem, the dizain is revived in the 19th c. by François Coppée and Paul Verlaine.

*See* FRANCE, POETRY OF; PETRARCHISM; SONNET SEQUENCE.

■ P. Martinon, *Les Strophes* (1912); H. Chamard, *Histoire de la Pléiade*, v. 4 (1941); T. Sébillet, *Art poëtique françoys*, ed. F. Goyet (1990); E. M. Duval, "From the *Chanson parisienne* to Scève's French *Canzoniere:* Lyric Form and Logical Structure of the Dizain," *A Scève Celebration: Délie 1544–1994*, ed. J. C. Nash (1994); B. de Cornulier, *Art poétique: Notions et problèmes de métrique* (1995); C. Alduy, *Politique des "Amours"* (2007).

I. SILVER; T. V. F. BROGAN; C. ALDUY

**DIZER** (Galician-Port., "to say"). A satirical song in Galician-Port. during the 13th and 14th cs. composed to speak ill (*mal dizer*) of someone, often in the form of obscenities. In the corpus of *Cantigas d'Escarnho e de Mal Dizer* (Songs of Mockery and Insult), authors sometimes use the terms *dizer* and *razões* to indicate words as opposed to tunes (*sões*).

*See* CANCIONERO/CANCIONEIRO, CANTIGA.

M. GALVEZ

**DOCHMIAC** or dochmius (Gr., "slanted"). A metrical sequence found almost exclusively in Gr. tragedy, chiefly in passages expressing intense emotion, agitation, or grief. The basic form is x – – ◡ – (the commonest form x ◡ ◡ – ◡ – ), but there are about 30 varieties, and they also appear combined with iambs. Some metrists (e.g., Snell) do not acknowledge the existence of dochmiacs outside of Gr. drama; others find them in Pindar and Bacchylides. Lat. metrists sometimes group such structures among bacchiac cola (see BACCHIUS) or catalectic bacchiac dimeters (Crusius). The anaclastic (see ANACLASIS) form is called the hypodochmiac (– ◡ – ◡ – ).

■ Maas; N. C. Conomis, "The Dochmiacs of Greek Drama," *Hermes* 92 (1964)—the fundamental collection of material and statistics; Koster, chap. 12; Crusius; Dale, chap. 7; Halporn et al.; Snell; West.

J. W. HALPORN

**DOCUMENTARY POETICS** is less a systematic theory or doctrine of a kind of poetry than an array of strategies and techniques that position a poem to participate in discourses of reportage for political and ethical purposes. In this, it is *documentary* in two potentially conflicting senses: it consists of, concerns, or is based on purportedly objective records of facts or events but uses those records to support, elaborate, or advance an often passionately held partisan position. At once factual and ideological, documentary poetics engages both the empirical world in which we live and the political or ethical ideals through which we navigate that world.

Most fully elaborated in film crit. and theory, the term *documentary* was coined in 1926 by the filmmaker John Grierson to describe Robert J. Flaherty's account of Polynesian island life in the film *Moana*. Three variants of the *genre emerged in the 1920s and early 1930s: Flaherty's romanticized documentaries portraying native cultures, Grierson's sponsored documentaries promoting governmental or corporate solutions to contemp. social problems, and Dziga Vertov's avant-garde documentaries foregrounding the camera as a "mechanical I . . . showing the world as it is" in service of a revolutionary Marxist analysis. Each of these iterations of the form positioned itself against the burgeoning Hollywood entertainment industry, established a relationship with viewers based on a claim to objective representation of actuality, and insisted on the truth-value and social consequence of its findings.

Like Walt Whitman, who held that "the true use for the imaginative faculty of modern times is to give ultimate vivification to facts, to science, and to common lives," the poets of *imagism and *objectivism who laid the groundwork for documentary poetics pushed aside scholastic logic, romantic introspection, and Victorian didacticism to think with or through things. "Thinking," Ernest Fenollosa declared, "is *thinging.*" "Consider the way of the scientists," Ezra Pound exhorted aspiring imagists in 1913: begin by learning what has already been established, scrutinize the data, and persuade not by force of personality but through discovery of facts. While imagism led to such brief, intense poems as Pound's "In a Station of the Metro" (1913) or H.D.'s "Oread" (1914), the turmoil following World War I drew modernists toward longer hybrid forms that could include historical, civic, scientific, legislative, or journalistic information. The public records embedded in such works as Pound's Malatesta, Jefferson, and Confucian *Cantos* (1925, 1934, 1940); W. C. Williams's *Paterson* (1946–58); Charles Olson's *Maximus Poems* (1960–75); Susan Howe's *Articulation of Sound Forms in Time* (1987); Rosmarie Waldrop's *Shorter American Memory* (1988); and Mark Nowak's *Shut Up Shut Down* (2004) are documentary in both senses of the word: they turn, i.e., empirical, historical fact to passionate political use.

The most distilled iteration of facts in documentary poetics emerges in the Am. 1930s. Mike Gold's and Tillie Olsen's excerpts from workers' correspondence; Muriel Rukeyser's citations of congressional hearings, medical reports, and stock ticker readouts in *Book of the Dead*; and Charles Reznikoff's condensations of legal documents in *Testimony* coincided with the rise of documentary photography and photojournalism, newsreels, and documentaries, the Federal Theater Project's living newspapers, and on-the-spot radio broadcasts by such reporters as Edward R. Murrow and William Shirer. Poets aimed, in Whitman's words, "to give ultimate vivification to facts" or, in Rukeyser's words, "extend the document" by lineating instances of violence, hatred, suffering, and injustice.

The social, political, and epistemological crises of the 1960s put terms like *objective, factual,* or *truthful* under withering scrutiny. In response to the demystification of the ideal of transparency, documentarians in all the arts turned to notions of spontaneity and authenticity as guarantors of the real: just as *cinema verité* filmmakers such as Frederick Wiseman foreswore scripting, lighting, and staging, jazz musicians such as Dizzy Gillespie and Charlie Parker composed in the moment of performance, Jack Kerouac developed a freeform "spontaneous bop prosody," and Allen Ginsberg documented his generation and attacked the military-industrial establishment in the explosive breath units of such poems as *Howl* and "Wichita Vortex Sutra" (see BEAT POETRY).

Skeptical of the romantic interiority that accompanies improvisatory composition, such 21st-c. poets as Mark Nowak and Claudia Rankine sample the journalistic, corporate, and governmental records of a media-driven globalized economy. Resistant to unified perspective, their poems participate in a broad culture that operates through the sharing and recombining of data. Often but not necessarily digitized, this information-age database poetics, like the documentary poetics of the 1930s and 1960s, makes empirical and ethical use of archival materials.

As Nichols emphasizes, the term *documentary* is relational or comparative. Just as documentary filmmakers position themselves against mainstream cinema, documentary poets position themselves against the late romantic lyric. The flexible inventory of strategies and techniques that constitute documentary poetics, however, rests on shared assumptions about the purpose of poetry, the poet's responsibility to objective or empirical knowledge, and the imperative of ethical action in the face of social crisis and catastrophe.

*See* ELECTRONIC POETRY; INFORMATION, POETRY AS; MODERNISM.

■ W. Whitman, "A Backward Glance O'er Travel'd Roads," *Leaves of Grass* (1891–92); E. Pound, "A Few Don'ts," *Poetry* 1 (1913); L. Zukofsky, "An Objective," *Poetry* 37 (1931); M. Rukeyser, *U.S. 1* (1938); L. Chisolm, *Fenollosa* (1963); W. Stott, *Documentary Expression and Thirties America* (1973); D. Vertov, "Kino-eye" (1926), *Kino-Eye*, ed. A. Michelson (1984); *Theorizing Documentary*, ed. M. Renov (1993); B. Nichols, *Introduction to Documentary* (2001); M. Vescia, *Depression Glass* (2006); P. Aufderheide, *Documentary Film* (2007).

A. MORRIS

**DOGGEREL** (origin unknown). Rough, poorly constructed verse, characterized by either (1) extreme metrical irregularity or (2) easy rhyme and monotonous rhythm, cheap sentiment, and triviality. George Saintsbury and others formerly used the term as a pejorative for stress verse. Chaucer refers to his burlesque "Tale of Sir Thopas" as *rym dogerel*, and Samuel Johnson stigmatized its vices with a famous parody:

As with my hat upon my head
I walk'd along the Strand,
I there did meet another man
With his hat in his hand.

(G. Steevens in *Johnsonian Miscellanies*,
ed. G. B. Hill, v. 2 [1897])

Northrop Frye has characterized doggerel as the result of an unfinished creative process, in which a "prose initiative" never assumes the associative qualities of true poetry, revealing its failure in an attempt to resolve technical difficulties through any means available (Hinsey). There are, however, some works of real poetic value in which features of doggerel are deliberately used for comic or satiric effect. John Skelton, Samuel Butler, and Jonathan Swift are all masters of artistic doggerel, and much Ger. *knittelvers* also achieves a brilliant parodic effect.

*See* ACCENTUAL VERSE.

■ P. Reyher, *Essai sur le doggerel* (1909); Frye; E. Hinsey, "The Rise of Modern Doggerel," *NER/BLQ* 19, no. 2 (Spring 1998); N. Page, *In Search of the World's Worst Writers* (2001).

L. B. PALACHE

**DOLCE STIL NUOVO** (It. "Sweet new style"). Term commonly used to designate a group of late 13th-c. It. love poets and to describe the special character of their *lyric production. The term first appears in Dante's *Purgatorio* (24.57), where it defines his poetic style (*stil*), separating it from that of the earlier Sicilian and Guittonian poets and describing its characteristics as audibly and intellectually pleasing (*dolce*) and new in concept (*nuovo*). Generally speaking, Dante's term has considerable validity: the "sweetness" of his style is attained, analysts have discovered, through a careful selection and ordering of words of pleasurable sound. The "newness" most probably refers to the poet's inventive variations on traditional poetic themes.

The literary background from which the *Dolce stil nuovo* emerged was chiefly Occitan *troubadour poetry, a trad. two centuries old and still vital in Italy at the time of Dante's birth. From *Occitan poetry, the *stilnovisti* learned the conventions of *courtly love with its religious overtones, its idealization of women, its emphasis on nobility (*gentilezza*), and its faith in the ennobling effect of love on the lover. A second influence important for the *stil nuovo* is the Franciscan revival, which stressed sincerity, simplicity, and a feeling for the unity of the human being with nature. For their poetry that transcends the secular adoration of woman, the stilnovisti adapted the lang. and imagery employed for the mystical adoration of the Virgin by the Marian cults. Philosophy, too, had an important influence on the *stil nuovo*. From Guido Guinizzelli to Guido Cavalcanti and even Petrarch, all the important stilnovisti had contact with the University of Bologna, where Thomistic theology and medicine were taught, both of which were allied to the great 13th-c. revival of Aristotelianism. Avicenna on medicine and Averroës on Aristotle were also influential. The joint result of these several influences was to deepen the analysis of love found in the poetry of the Dolce stil nuovo. In fact, it has been suggested that the philosophical and often metaphysical bent of stil nuovo poetry is its most distinctive characteristic (Vossler). Another important influence is that of the *Sicilian school of poets, which flourished in the first half of the 13th c. and whose most prominent figure is the notary Giacomo da Lentini, the probable inventor of the *sonnet.

The first poet in the so-called school of the Dolce stil nuovo is the jurisconsult Guido Guinizzelli, who composed the important doctrinal *canzone* "Al cor gentil rempaira sempre amore." His emphasis on the poetics and thematics of praise was imitated by Dante in many poems, most notably in his well-known sonnet in the *Vita nuova*, "Tanto gentile e tanto onesta pare." Guinizzelli repeats the troubadour commonplaces but seems to expand on the basis of Platonic doctrine: the eyes (as in Plato's *Republic*, book 4) are the most beautiful part of the body—the windows of the soul. The *saluto* (greeting) ranks second (in accordance with Aristotle's teaching of the "smile"). Love and the noble heart are one and the same; love cannot exist anywhere save in a noble heart, and a noble heart cannot exist without love. This nobility is of the spirit, not of heredity

through blood or worldly riches; it derives from one's innate virtue. In Guido's conception, the beloved activates the lover's inborn disposition toward good and is instrumental in raising the lover's soul to the Highest Good, making for communion with the Absolute and the Eternal. Guinizzelli's method is Scholastic, but his manner is distinguished by use of scientific observation of natural phenomena in images and similes to objectify the internal sensations of love.

Guido Cavalcanti, Dante's "first friend" (*primo amico*), devoted his doctrinal canzone "Donna me prega per ch'eo voglio dire" to his Christian, neo-Aristotelian understanding of love. His treatment of love's origins and nature may show some Averroistic influence, but in the main, his work consists of profoundly intimate reveries on feminine beauty. Amid the agitation and anguish caused by his state, he is haunted by the phantom of love and the specter of death.

In the *Vita nuova*, Dante discloses his personal poetic and amorous *iter* through a combination of poems and prose narratives or glosses that, by recounting his love for Beatrice, summarizes in a specific way the general outline of the evolution of the love-lyric trad. The early poems in the *Vita nuova* are pervaded by morbid introspection, anguish, and self-pity that derive from Cavalcantian models. The first canzone of the *Vita nuova* ("Donne ch'avete intelletto d'amore") marks the break with these attitudes and embraces Guinizzelli's view of love; from this point, the poems of this work adhere to the theme of praise and contain elements of the Platonic outlook, particularly seeing the beloved as angelic. The death of the lady in the case of Dante's Beatrice (as well as of Petrarch's Laura) is a supreme milestone in the pilgrim's progress in love. Having died, she becomes an angelic form who, through the light of the eyes and radiance of the smile, leads the lover, as true guide and symbol of virtue, to God in his goodness, the ideal of perfection. In Dante's *Convivio* (1304–7), we learn (2.15.10, 3.12.2–3, 4.2) that he reserved a special manner of sweetness of expression for rhymes of love and that his conception of *amore* included the eager pursuit of knowledge. In his unfinished Lat. treatise *De vulgari eloquentia* (ca. 1304), Dante elaborates (2.8, 12) on his ideas on style (the tragic being the highest), lang. (the illustrious vernacular being the sweetest), form (the canzone being the noblest), and meter (the *hendecasyllable being the most excellent). In the same work, he names Cavalcanti, Lapo Gianni, himself, and Cino da Pistoia, whom he favors esp. for his subtlety and sweetness, as those poets who composed lyrics in the high style. Dante's remarks have led some critics to believe in the existence of a more or less self-conscious "school" of the Dolce stil nuovo. More likely, it was simply a loosely organized group of friends with more or less common poetic interests. Critics have added to the supposed group Gianni Alfani and Dino Frescobaldi. Later poets such as Guido Novello da Polenta (Dante's host in Ravenna during his exile) and Giovanni Quirini imitate the essential traits of the Dolce stil nuovo.

Petrarch throughout his several reworkings of the *Canzoniere* shows much influence of the Dolce stil nuovo. However, he was not altogether successful in his attempt to subjugate his great passion to the Dantean ideal. His awareness of this dilemma is expressed in the crescendo and diminuendo, the ebb and flow, throughout his carefully contrived poetic collection. Later followers of the stilnovisti include Matteo Frescobaldi, Franceschino degli Albizzi, Sennuccio del Bene, Giovanni Boccaccio (the last two, poetic correspondents of Petrarch), Cino Rinuccini, and Giovanni Gherardi da Prato.

Through the influence of Petrarch, the conventions of the stil nuovo were spread throughout Europe, profoundly affecting the develop. of lyric poetry in France, Spain, England, and elsewhere. Lorenzo de' Medici, the reviver of *Petrarchism for the It. Quattrocento, consciously imitated the stil nuovo. He also appreciated the minor stilnovisti, as evidenced by his letter to Frederick of Aragon accompanying the anthol. of early It. poetry he compiled for Frederick.

*See* ITALY, POETRY OF.

■ **Criticism**: K. Vossler, *Mediaeval Culture*, trans. W. C. Lawton (1929); A. Figurelli, *Il Dolce stil nuovo* (1933); A. Lipari, *The Dolce Stil Nuovo according to Lorenzo de' Medici* (1936); J. E. Shaw, *Guido Cavalcanti's Theory of Love* (1949); E. Bigi, "Genesi di un concetto storiografico: 'dolce stil nuovo,'" *Giornale Storico della Letteratura Italiana* 132 (1955); M. Valency, *In Praise of Love* (1958); Fisher; G. Petrocchi, "Il Dolce stil nuovo," *Storia della letteratura italiana*, ed. E. Cecchi and N. Sapegno (1965); P. Boyde, *Dante's Style in His Lyric Poetry* (1971); E. Pasquini and A. E. Quaglio, *Lo Stilnovo e la poesia religiosa* (1971); M. Marti, *Storia dello stil nuovo*, 2 v. (1973); R. Russell, *Tre versanti della poesia stilnovistica* (1973); E. Savona, *Repertorio tematico del dolce stil nuovo* (1973); Wilkins; G. Favati, *Inchiesta sul dolce stil nuovo* (1975); F. Suitner, *Petrarca e la tradizione stilnovistica* (1977); M. Marti, "Stil nuovo," *Enciclopedia dantesca*, v. 5 (1978); V. Moleta, *Guinizzelli in Dante* (1980); A. Solimena, *Repertorio metrico dello Stil nuovo*, 1980—metrical index; G. Gorni, *Il nodo della lingua e il verbo d'amore* (1981); I. Bertelli, *La Poesia di Guido Guinizzelli e la poetica del "dolce stil nuovo"* (1983); I. Bertelli, *I fondamenti artistici e culturali del "dolce stil nuovo"* (1987); L. Pertile, "Il nodo di Bonagiunta, le penne di Dante e il Dolce Stil Novo," *Lettere Italiane* 46 (1994).

■ **Primary Texts**: *Rimatori del Dolce Stil Nuovo*, ed. L. di Benedetto, 2d ed. (1939); Guido Cavalcanti, *Rime*, ed. G. Favati (1957); *Poeti del Duecento*, ed. G. Contini, 2 v. (1960); *Dante's Lyric Poetry*, ed. and trans. K. Foster and P. Boyde, 2 v. (1967); *Poeti del Dolce stil nuovo*, ed. M. Marti (1969); *The Poetry of Guido Cavalcanti*, ed. and trans. L. Nelson Jr. (1986); *The Poetry of Guido Guinizzelli*, ed. and trans. R. Edwards (1987).

L. H. GORDON; C. KLEINHENZ

**DOL'NIK** (pl. *dol'niki*). Rus. accentual meter. Unlike Rus. syllabotonic (or *accentual-syllabic) meters,

which have a constant syllabic interval between ictuses, the *dol'nik* has a variable interval of one or two syllables. The dol'nik remained an oddity in late 18th- and 19th-c. Rus. poetry, in which syllabotonic meters predominated; it appeared only in poems stylized after folk songs or trans. In Ger. and Eng., the equivalent of the dol'nik appeared toward the end of the 18th c. and was based on native folk verse, but the popular 19th-c. Rus. trans. of Ger. and Eng. accentual ballads used mostly syllabotonic verse. Thus, the dol'nik does not carry folkloric connotations in Rus. poetry, unlike its equivalent in Eng. and Ger. Only in 20th-c. Rus. verse does the dol'nik become widespread, esp. in the work of the symbolist Alexander Blok. By 1930, the three-stress dol'nik had become one of the staple meters of Rus. poetry; Joseph Brodsky often made use of the meter.

Although the dol'nik exists in three-, four-, and variable-stress lines, that with three ictuses prevails. The *anacrusis, the number of syllables before the first stress, may be fixed or may vary; the line end is usually rhymed. The line tends to consist of eight syllables (excluding syllables after the last stress); the first *ictus coincides with the third syllable, the second ictus with the fifth or sixth, and the third with the eighth. Some poets use an isosyllabic line in which the second ictus is fixed on the sixth syllable, a variant sometimes called *logaoedic verse.

■ A. Kolmogorov and A. Proxorov, "O dol'nike sovremennoj russkoj poézii," *Voprosy iazykoznaniia* (1963, 1964); J. Bailey, "Some Recent Developments in the Study of Russian Versification," *Lang&S* 5 (1972); Gasparov; G. S. Smith, "Logaoedic Metres in the Lyric Poetry of Marina Tsvetayeva," *Slavonic and East European Review* 53 (1975); Tarlinskaja; Terras; Scherr; M. Wachtel, *The Development of Russian Verse* (1998); G. S. Smith, "The Development of Joseph Brodsky's Dol'nik Verse, 1972–1976," *Russian, Croatian and Serbian, Czech and Slovak, Polish Literature* 52.4 (2002).

J. O. BAILEY; C. DOAK

**DOUBLE DACTYL.** A *light verse form in two quatrains. The last lines of the quatrains must rhyme, using a dactylic foot followed by a stress. The other six lines are all hexasyllables of two dactylic feet, hence the name. The first line is a nonsense phrase, usually "Higgledy piggledy," the second line a proper name, and the second line of the second quatrain a polysyllable, the more recondite the better.

Blosody-frosody
Ralph Waldo Emerson
Thought transcendentally
Far beyond form.
Often he suffered from
Humdrumophobia
Probably worsened by
Some Harvard dorm.

The form is notoriously flippant. Paul and Naomi Pascal and Anthony Hecht invented double dactyls in the early 1950s; in the 1960s, Hecht and John Hollander published the first collection.

■ A. Hecht and J. Hollander, *Jiggery Pokery* (1966); W. Espy, *Almanac of Words at Play* (1980); A. Harrington, *Tersery Versery* (1982).

F. TEAGUE; S. CUSHMAN

**DOZENS**. A game of exchanging, in contest form, ritualized verbal insults, which are usually in rhymed *couplets and often profane. The term is probably a literate corruption of the vernacular *doesn'ts*, relating to forbidden lang. activity. The game is practiced now mostly among adolescent Af. Am. males, though its origin is thought to lie in the verbal insult contests of West Africa. The dozens is a subcategory of *signifying. Sometimes referred to as *woofing, sounding, cutting, capping,* or *chopping,* the ritual is most often called *playing the dozens.* The subjects of the insults are frequently the relatives of the verbal opponent, esp. his mother, and the insults are frequently sexual. A mildly phrased example of the dozens technique and style would be "I don't play the dozens, the dozens ain't my game, / But the way I loved your mama is a crying shame."

The players of the dozens must display great skill with *rhyme, *wit, and *rhythm to win the approval of their audience. The dozens is partly an initiation ritual that teaches a player how to hold his equilibrium by learning to master the power of words and humor. The exchange takes place as a verbal duel in which words and humor are chosen to sting, so that the opponent will be goaded to either greater lexical creativity or defeat. Langston Hughes draws on the trad. of the dozens, particularly in his long poetic work *Ask Your Mama* (1961), as do Richard Wright and Ralph Ellison. Several genres of popular music, most recently *hip-hop, have maintained the visibility of the dozens in mass culture.

*See* FLYTING, INVECTIVE, POETIC CONTESTS.

■ R. D. Abrahams, *Deep Down in the Jungle* (1970); *Rappin' and Stylin' Out,* ed. T. Kochman (1972); W. Labov, *Language in the Inner City* (1972); L. W. Levine, *Black Culture and Black Consciousness* (1977); G. Smitherman, *Talkin and Testifyin* (1977); H. L. Gates Jr., *The Signifying Monkey* (1988); M. Morgan, "The Africanness of Counterlanguage among Afro-Americans," *Africanisms in Afro-American Language Varieties,* ed. S. Mufwene (1993); J. R. Rickford and R. J. Rickford, *Spoken Soul* (2000); E. Wald, *The Dozens* (2012).

E. A. PETERS

**DRAMATIC MONOLOGUE.** *See* MONOLOGUE.

**DRAMATIC POETRY**

  I. Definition
  II. Dramatic Poetry and Drama in Verse
  III. Dramatic Poetry and Performance Theory
  IV. Dramatic Poetry in the Theater

**I. Definition.** Dramatic poetry is at best an intrinsically contestable critical category and at worst a violent oxymoron, sparking the theoretical and historical friction

between performance and poetry, theater and writing, action and lang. For Aristotle, drama is one kind of *poesis,* but within his analysis of drama, lang.—the verbal, *poetic* dimension of plays—is subordinate to plot, character, and thought. In the context of the *Poetics,* this hierarchy makes sense because dramatic *mimesis is composed not of words but of deeds (the "imitation of action"). Dramatic poetry implies that words are defined in relation to the work of the theater's other instruments of mimesis—the temporal structure of the event, its plot; the practices of acting and the projection of character, or *ethos*; the design of music and spectacle—principally conveyed not by lang. but by actors, "with all the people engaged in the *mimesis* actually doing things" (*Poetics* 1448a). Nonetheless, drama has a persistent association with formally inventive lang., from the range of verse forms encompassed by tragedy and comedy in Aristotle's era to the verbal richness of much contemp. drama, even when that drama is written in prose. Cohn pointed out in the previous edition, "Western critics have interpreted the phrase dramatic poetry in three main ways: (1) lyrics or short poems that imply a scene; (2) plays that are valorized with the adjective 'poetic'; and (3) dramas whose dialogue is calculatingly rhythmed—in rhythms that are often regularized into meters and are usually presented as discrete lines on the page." As Cohn recognized, resigned to treat dramatic poetry as synonymous with "verse drama," these definitions are inadequate. The first embraces lyric poems written from the perspective of individual characters and so understands *drama*—as a mode of cultural production involving *performance as well as scripted lang.—in metaphorical terms: for all their "drama," Robert Browning's "My Last Duchess" or T. S. Eliot's "The Love Song of J. Alfred Prufrock" are not conceived for embodied mimesis. The second turns the word *poetic* into a term of approbation, without critical purchase on the function or purpose of lang. in performance. The third—verse drama—segregates a class of drama according to the accidents of culture and hist.: emphasizing the use of verse rather than the distinctive contribution that verbal design makes to the conception of dramatic action. Although verse has had a complex impact on drama and its performance, "dramatic poetry" points toward a more searching problem, having to do with the functioning of writing in the making of drama, a form of *poesis* extending beyond words, in which—to recall Austin's discussion of *performative* speech—scripted words are expected to *do things* well beyond what the words themselves *say.* More than verse drama, dramatic poetry is a term of theoretical inquiry, pointing to the troubled interface where writing meets performance in the definition of drama.

**II. Dramatic Poetry and Drama in Verse.** Dramatic writing has a longstanding historical connection with verse. The reciprocity between drama and ritual is often marked in the ceremonial character of dramatic performances staged in connection with religious or civic events or with the formalities of an aristocratic court reflected by patterned and often elevated lang. In Eur. drama, the lineage of scripted dramatic performance originates in the 6th- and 5th-c. BCE Gr. civic festivals sponsoring competitions in the performance of *dithyrambs (large choruses of men or boys), tragedy (a trilogy of three tragedies composed by a single playwright, followed by a satyr play), and eventually comedy; the major festival, which sponsored the plays of the surviving dramatists Aeschylus, Sophocles, Euripides, and Aristophanes, was the Athenian City Dionysia, held annually in March–April. Cl. Gr. tragedy used a variety of verse meters for the *chorus, while individual roles (like the chorus, all played by men) were assigned iambic trimeter and developed a characteristic structure: a *prologue*, in which a single character—the Watchman in Aeschylus's *Agamemnon*, Dionysus in Euripides' *Bacchae*—opens the play; the *parodos*, or singing/dancing entrance of the chorus; a series of *episodes* in *dialogue between individual characters, punctuated by choral *odes*, with their characteristic verbal (and, logically, physical) movements of *strophe*, *antistrophe*, and *epode*; and, after the stunning *catastrophe*, the *exodos* of the chorus. In comedy, Aristophanes deployed a wider range of metrical forms both for choruses and for individual speeches. Roman drama, initially based on Gr. models, was first performed in the 3rd c. BCE and quickly developed its own formal and thematic identity; the verse meter of Plautus's comedies was generally based on the trochaic *septenarius, though with considerable latitude, while Terence consistently favored the iambic *senarius and Seneca scrupulously employed the iambic trimeter.

The decline of the Roman Empire brought the decline of its institutions, incl. theater; while popular performance surely persisted, formal, written drama emerges—uneasily—as an instrument of the Church, in the versified *tropes that minimally illustrated and enacted portions of the Roman Catholic Mass, beginning in the 9th or 10th c. CE. The Lat. tropes were very occasionally adapted into vernacular langs.—as in the 12th-c. Anglo-Norman *Jeu d'Adam*—but the energetic vernacular drama of 14th- and 15th-c. Europe was also typically based on religious themes, either in the scriptural narratives of the great Corpus Christi cycles or the theological debate of the morality plays, and developed indigenous verse forms as well. Though the verse of the anonymous Wakefield Master, involving the deft balance of assonance and rhyme in a complex nine-line stanza form, is best known, the Eng. cycles (Wakefield, York, Chester, and N-Town) generally make fine use of the metrical trads. and alliterative verse of the period, echoed in the surprisingly fluid use of a basic octosyllabic line in the 15th-c. Fr. farce *Master Pathelin*.

In Europe, then, verse plays an important role at the origin and devel. of dramatic writing from Athenian tragedy through both the Lat. and vernacular forms of med. drama to the two principal venues of dramatic performance in the early mod. period: the commercial public theater and the more stylized theater of the aristocratic courts. Verse coordinates with elevated subject matter and the elite social world of a specific audience

in other early dramatic trads., linking aesthetic to social functions in cl. Sanskrit drama and in the *Nō theater of the med. Japanese court, much as in the Stuart court *masque and the neoclassical Fr. drama of the 17th c. In some theatrical genres, however, the elaborate verbal script is held apart from the sphere of enactment. In the South Asian dance drama Kathakali, the performers are accompanied by song and narration, but they do not speak themselves; in the *Ramlila*—a ten-day enactment of Ram's battle with Ravan in the *Rāmāyaṇa*—the actors improvise their performance, coordinating it with the simultaneous recitation of the Hindu epic.

The pervasive devel. of two institutions—print publishing and the secular commercial theater—redefined the practices of dramatic writing and performance in 16th- and 17th-c. Europe. Though most of the printed drama in the period was propelled by the theater's need for new material, a developing notion of "lit." as a distinct, valuable genre of writing coordinated with the perception of dramatic poetry's signifying a special class of drama, in which an elaborate verbal structure has a value independent from its utility in instigating or sustaining stage performance. And yet, segregating the complexities of dramatic composition in verse from the intricacies of dramatic writing in prose miscasts the literary and theatrical hist. of Western drama. Many of the early mod. masters of dramatic verse—Shakespeare and Ben Jonson among them—were masters of dramatic prose and masters of stagecraft as well, shaping verse or prose and various dramatic genres to meet the demand of specific theaters and their audiences. A richly pointed prose sustains the hist. of comic drama, from Niccolò Machiavelli's satiric *Mandragola* (1518) through Jonson's *Bartholomew Fair* (1614) to the plays of William Wycherley, George Etherege, William Congreve, George Farquhar, Oliver Goldsmith, and R. B. Sheridan in the 17th and 18th cs.; and to mods. like Oscar Wilde, G. B. Shaw, and Tom Stoppard, much as comedy from Shakespeare to Molière to Caryl Churchill has also been written in a fluent and supple verse.

Verse is undeniably associated with social class in Eur. drama, the privileged mode of courtly works like the masque and the plays of Fr. neoclassicism; it is also associated with aristocratic characters in the plays of the early mod. Eng. commercial theater and sustains related notions of dramatic *decorum. In his *Defence of Poesy* (written ca. 1580, pub. 1595), Philip Sidney complains about the mingling of verse and prose, which implies a "mongrel" blending of tragedy and comedy (see VERSE AND PROSE); and Félix Lope de Vega's *El arte nuevo de hacer comedias* (1609) similarly encourages Sp. poets to avoid blending high and low subjects, suggesting different verse forms as appropriate to different events: *décimas for complaints, *sonnets for those waiting in expectation, *tercets for serious matters, and *redondillas for love. Expanding Lope's principles, a typical role in one of Pedro Calderón de la Barca's plays moves through a range of verse forms, each appropriate to the ethical and dramatic situation of the moment. Rather than multiplying verse forms, 17th-c. Fr. theater relies on the poet's mastery of the *alexandrine couplet, the vehicle of heroic clamor in Pierre Corneille, of balanced wit in Molière, and of probing ethical dilemma in Jean Racine, while Eng.-lang. verse drama typically relies on the more fluid informality of *blank verse.

The association between verse and high, serious, "tragic" drama in early mod. Europe is a matter of convention, regardless of whether writers like Christopher Marlowe, Shakespeare, Jonson, or Racine considered themselves part of a "poetic" heritage. The rising prestige of Shakespeare as a poet in the later 18th and 19th cs., alongside the democratization of literacy and lit., lends dramatic poetry its mod. inflection, the sense that the value of a play's verbal composition, its *poetry*, is independent of its functioning in theatrical representation. The great Eur. poets of the romantic period succeeded in some measure in writing a theatrically ambitious verse drama, notably G. E. Lessing's *Nathan der Weise* (1779), Friedrich Schiller's *Maria Stuart* (1800), Heinrich von Kleist's durable comedy *The Broken Jug* (1808) and his scarifying tragedy *Penthesilea* (1808), S. T. Coleridge's *Remorse* (1813), Lord Byron's *Manfred* (1819), P. B. Shelley's *The Cenci* (1819, staged at the Thèâtre Alfred Jarry by Antonin Artaud in 1935), Alexander Pushkin's *Boris Godunov* (1825), Alfred de Musset's *Lorenzaccio* (1834), Robert Browning's *A Blot in the 'Scutcheon* (1843), and Alfred, Lord Tennyson's *Becket* (1895).

In 1881, Émile Zola called for poets to recognize "that poetry is everywhere, in everything": poetic lang. appeared, by the late 19th c., incapable of addressing the dramatic situations of mod. life. After a brilliant and theatrically successful career as a verse dramatist culminating in *Brand* (1866) and *Peer Gynt* (1867), Henrik Ibsen, e.g., decided to address a broader contemp. audience about mod. social life with plays written in prose. And yet, while some contemporaries complained about the unpoetic superficiality of Ibsen's lang., his prose— rigorously impoverished of decoration—enables the slightest nuance to gain richly "poetic" depth: the icy, black water of Nora's imagined suicide, Hedda's "vine leaves in his hair," the secret demons of will and desire that flay Solness's flesh. Indeed, the attraction of verse remained strong: Ibsen's great rival August Strindberg wrote prose and verse dramas throughout his career, as did other playwrights now sometimes remembered for their naturalistic plays, such as Gerhart Hauptmann. Maurice Maeterlinck wrote symbolic dramas in an image-laden prose; and, without resorting directly to verse, Frank Wedekind frequently experimented with lang. in ways that resisted a strict division between naturalistic prose and more evocative poetry.

Foregrounding the artifice of the play's verbal dimension, mod. verse drama resists the subordination of its lang. to the representational "surface" characteristic of naturalism's attention to everyday life. For this reason, in the 20th c. dramatic poetry becomes increasingly cognate with a deeply antitheatrical impulse visible in the work of a range of playwrights largely continuing the trad. linking verse to elevated subject matter and philosophical introspection: Edmond Rostand's durable *Cyrano de Bergerac* (1897) and the plays of Stephen Phillips, Maxwell Anderson, Christopher Fry, and Paul Claudel, among many others. Dramatic poetry, though, also provided an alternative means of using lang. to impel the potential innovation of theatrical experience; here, the varied use of verse and prose in the plays of W. B. Yeats, Eliot, W. H. Auden, and Auden's collaborations with Christopher Isherwood, as well as the more experimental work of Gertrude Stein and Samuel Beckett, charts an effort not to withdraw dramatic poetry from theatricality but to use lang. to explore new means of articulating writing with stage action. The intercalation of different verse forms, or of verse with prose, also jibes with the critical disorientation at the heart of Bertolt Brecht's *Verfremdungseffekt* (usually translated as "alienation effect" or "distancing effect"), visible in his own plays like *Saint Joan of the Stockyards* (1931) and *The Resistible Rise of Arturo Ui* (1941) and in the function of *song throughout his plays. The use of verse as a means of emphasizing the theatrical work of dramatic lang. sustains much of Peter Weiss's work (incl. his best known play, *The Persecution and Assassination of Jean-Paul Marat as Performed by the Inmates of the Asylum of Charenton under the Direction of the Marquis de Sade,* widely known as *Marat/Sade* [1963]), as well as embodying a postcolonial concern for the politics of lang. and performance genres in several of Wole Soyinka's plays, notably *The Lion and the Jewel* (1963); in Aimé Césaire's adaptation of Shakespeare, *A Tempest* (1969); and often in the plays of Derek Walcott. Verbal experiment sustains much contemp. dramatic writing, often writing conceived to generate political or social friction in performance: Caryl Churchill's satiric *Serious Money* (1987), John Arden's drama, the brilliant use of verse and song alongside the prose of Edward Bond's plays. Several playwrights whose lang. is formally inventive yet not restricted either to formal or *free verse—Thomas Bernhard, Heiner Müller, María Irene Fornes, Suzan-Lori Parks—are precisely engaged in the problem of dramatic poetry.

**III. Dramatic Poetry and Performance Theory.** Given that different performance conventions construct the force of lang. in and as performance, what does *poetic* writing contribute to drama? In one sense, poetry lends its distinctive verbal density to the dramatic event, creating an opportunity for form, imagery, and meter to be woven into the conceptual practices of performance. Yet while mod. poets sometimes assume that poetry should govern the practices of the stage, the most enduring experiments in dramatic poetry tend in a different direction. Yeats's *Plays for Dancers* coordinates an imagistic moment of intense, verbalized perception against the parallel, speechless, physical expression of dance to music. Rather than taking the physical expression of theater merely to illustrate the verbal "meanings" of the poetry, Yeats's plays provoke a rich reciprocity between the ultimately incompatible discourses of lang. and movement, poetry and embodiment in the theater.

Among playwrights, Eliot most searchingly attempted to chart the extent to which it was possible for dramatic composition to alter, even revivify, the circumstances of performance. Although Eliot's writing about dramatic poetry spans his career—from "The Possibility of a Poetic Drama" and "Rhetoric and Poetic Drama," both of which appeared in *The Sacred Wood* (1920), to *Poetry and Drama* (1951)—his obituary for the music-hall star Marie Lloyd expresses his canniest vision of theater, the sense that the "working man" who saw Lloyd in the music hall and "joined in the chorus was himself performing part of the act; he was engaged in that collaboration of the audience with the artist which is necessary in all art and most obviously in dramatic art" (*Selected Essays*). From his early dramatic monologues onward, Eliot's poetic imagination engaged with drama; turning to the writing of plays, he explored how writing might galvanize the social ritual of theatrical performance, might provide a means to shape that collaboration among poet, performers, and participating audience through the process of playing.

But while Eliot typically takes dramatic poetry as synonymous with verse drama, his most experimental play, *Murder in the Cathedral* (1935), demonstrates that it is not the difference between verse and prose that identifies the force of poetic drama but the ways lang. engages with the means of theater. *Murder in the Cathedral* is largely written in prose, using different modes of written discourse—the Chorus's rhythmically chanted verse, Thomas's prose sermon, the Knights' Shavian apology—to afford different opportunities for collaboration in the dramatic event. In *Poetry and Drama*, Eliot confessed that he may have been chasing a "mirage," a verse drama at once composed "of human action and of words, such as to present at once the two aspects of dramatic and of musical order." New forms of verbal composition (here limited to verse drama) might afford powerful, innovative forms of human action, which would—taking up the distinction between drama and music—use representation, the dramatic fiction, to render the present, transitory harmonies of the performance itself significant. Eliot imagined that this design of theatrical experience could take shape only through verse, rather than through a systematic use of verbal/oral genres to reposition the work of lang. on the stage. Perhaps he was looking in the wrong direction: the play that would transform the Western theater's sense of the overlapping of lang. and event, dramatic poetry and the music of experience, the represented fiction and the ephemeral *thereness* of performance, took the stage the following 1952–53 season, at an obscure Parisian theater, written in Fr. by an Ir. expatriate named Samuel Beckett, its lyrical prose betrayed by its prosaic title, *En Attendant Godot*.

That is, as opposed to verse drama, dramatic poetry seizes the theoretical function of lang. in theatrical performance. In the middle decades of the 20th c., dramatic poetry provided a critical code for imagining the work of dramatic writing as instigating new forms of performance, action not subordinated to the rhet., politics, or sociology of theatrical verisimilitude (see Bent-ley, Fergusson, R. Williams). In the U.S., the Living Theatre—which would become notorious for its participatory spectacles in the late 1960s and 70s—charted the consequences of using poetry to instigate new performance, staging Paul Goodman's plays, Gertrude Stein's *Doctor Faustus Lights the Lights* (1938), Eliot's *Sweeney Agonistes* (1932), John Ashbery's *The Heroes* (1950), W. H. Auden's *The Age of Anxiety* (1947), W. C. Williams's *Many Loves* (1961), and Jackson Mac Low's *The Marrying Maiden* (1961). What this drama and many of the most innovative plays since Beckett—Sam Shepard's *Tooth of Crime* (1972), Peter Barnes's *The Bewitched* (1974), Müller's *Hamletmachine* (1977), Parks's *The Death of the Last Black Man in the Whole Entire World* (1990), Sarah Kane's *4.48 Psychosis* (1999)—suggest is that, while some forms of dramatic innovation arise in theatrical practice (the opportunities afforded by the box set, electric lighting, simultaneous video, V. E. Meyerhold's biomechanics, Artaud's theater of cruelty, Brecht's epic theater), others are summoned by new forms of writing, writing that demands a different accommodation to, and often the invention of, new performance practices. And while that writing is not always in verse, what defines it as dramatic poetry is an original imagination both for the interplay between words and for the interplay among words and the material signification they will inevitably impel, mediate, and be absorbed into in the process of dramatic performance.

How should we understand the function of scripted lang. in the Western trads. of drama and its performance? Dramatic poetry imagines a recalibration of the *agency* of writing in the process of theater; it implies a significant role in dramatic *poesis* for its verbal element, lang. In Western theater—esp. since the rise of print and the incorporation of printed plays into lit. as books—this role has sometimes been imagined as determinative, as though the poet created the play in lang. and theatrical performance has a secondary ministerial function merely to execute the poet's completed work in the medium of performance. But the words on the page cannot determine their performance. As Austin discovered, in "performative" speech, words do not make statements; sometimes—as in the sentence "I promise" or the "I do" of a marriage ceremony—they "do things": to speak the words is to act within a sustaining context of performance *convention, convention that limits what, how, and whether the performance *performs*. In this sense, the notion of theater as executing the text's direction might form one paradigm of performance but is hardly essential to dramatic performance, nor is it illustrated by the hist. of theatrical practice, the unfolding narrative of changing ways to make writing do work as theater in the changing performative conventions of the stage.

While one line of critique has attempted to restrict dramatic performance to the appropriate "stage presentation" of a literary work fixed and complete as dramatic poetry (see Brooks and Heilman; see also Lehmann), the real challenge of understanding dramatic poetry is to model its contribution to the performance process, a process that arises outside and beyond the control of the text. Dramatic poetry animates the dual scene of performance, the fictive play and its theatrical playing, where lang. is the instrument of the actor's work, what he or she has to work with in the creation of something that is *not* poetry, not even principally verbal: theatrical and dramatic action. Recalling Burke's "dramatistic" model for the analysis of actions—any action can be conceived in terms of the ratio between the *act*, *agent*, *agency*, *purpose*, and *scene* of performance—dramatic performance foregrounds an inherently duplicitous event, in which the represented acts, agents, purposes, and scene of the dramatic fiction can be created (and known to the audience) only through their implication by the material grammar of theatrical practice, the *acts* we understand as theatrical performance, the actors as *agents* of stage action, the leading *purposes* of the production, the *scene* of the theater itself. Dramatic poetry occupies a dual *agency*, at once the fictive dialogue between characters—the *agency* of their actions—and the actor's *agency*, i.e., his or her instrument for embodied mimesis, for making play. In performance, dramatic poetry may or may not be privileged among a given theater's various *agencies*—visual design, movement vocabulary, vocal production—for articulating dramatic action through the theatrical event. Although Yeats based his *Plays for Dancers* on an understanding of the Japanese Nō, Nō performance clearly situates its writing within a highly conventionalized performance trad.: the actors are masked, follow a generally prescribed trajectory around the stage, adopt patterned gestures, and give voice to the text (singing it) in largely determined ways (some of the characters' lines are spoken by the seated musicians as well). Rather than seeming subordinate to the structure and meaning of the script, performance seems to govern how the densely ornate, "literary" script will be incorporated as an event.

**IV. Dramatic Poetry in the Theater.** The study of dramatic poetry is often undertaken in purely literary terms, considering *prosody and *meter, *imagery and *metaphor, structure and theme. These elements are important and may well bear on performance. The meter of Shakespeare's plays creates a range of opportunities for actors: Romeo's sudden monosyllables when he first sees Juliet; the tension between the intensification and evacuation of meaning in King Lear's "Never, never, never, never, never." But while purely verbal structures may provide opportunities, how or whether they are seized and transformed into action, depends on the behavioral conventions of contemp. performance. Dramatic poetry is always altered by its theatrical use, even when those uses are seen as scrupulously "faithful" to the play: the heavily built "realistic" Shakespeare of the 19th c. necessitated the reordering of scenes and extensive cutting of the text for the play to be staged in a reasonable duration; despite his elegant delivery of Hamlet's verse, Laurence Olivier cut roughly half the text and the roles of Rosencrantz, Guildenstern, and Fortinbras from his 1948 Oscar-winning film; most Eng.-lang. productions of Molière's plays today substitute blank verse or heroic couplets for the Fr. alexandrines.

While dramatic poetry is changed by performance, it also makes demands on performance that the contemp. theater struggles to engage: in the 1880s and 1890s, Ibsen's leading female roles—Nora Helmer in *A Doll's House* or Hedda Gabler—were difficult for actors to perform because they violated generic (and gender) performance conventions; Master Builder Solness, with his deeply disorienting discourse of demonic wish fulfillment, seemed nearly impossible to accommodate to the demands of the contemp. framing of dramatic character. Ibsen's lang. required a new approach to making dramatic poetry signify in the register of stage "character." Later, the inaction of Beckett's *Waiting for Godot* seemed, perhaps purposely, both undramatic and untheatrical, at least until Beckett's peculiar poetry was seen to invoke and transform a familiar performance discourse: the fractured coupling of vaudevillians, Gogo and Didi, as an eternal, poignant, even allegorical Laurel and Hardy. Some plays—Djuna Barnes's *Antiphon* (1958); nearly all of Stein's drama; Adrienne Kennedy's *Funnyhouse of a Negro* (1962); the "synthetic fragments" of Müller's *Germania Death in Berlin* (1978), *Despoiled Shore Medea-material Landscape with Argonauts* (1982), and various "performance texts"; Parks's *America Play* (1994), *Venus* (1996), *Fucking A* (2000), with their strikingly idiosyncratic typographic design on the page—illustrate how dramatic poetry puts pressure on theatrical practice, enforcing a search for new modes of articulation, enunciation, and embodiment.

Perhaps the most familiar example of this problem is the notion of the animating "subtext" of desire, a through-line of psychological action trending toward a distinctive "objective" that the director Konstantin Stanislavski devised in his work on Anton Chekhov's refractory plays. Chekhov's poetry is elusive and indirect; the writing did not conform to conventional notions of dramatic action at the turn of the 20th c. and so seemed not to provide an appropriate agency for acting. Harmonizing each actor/character's objective into the overall purpose of the production, Stanislavski developed the notion of the emotional subtext, the act that the actor/character was attempting to perform *through* the often-elliptical script. The subtext implies the essential fungibility of the words on the page: the words may say one thing, but they enable the actors to do something else with them, to seduce, challenge, insult, rebuke, flatter. As Eliot knew, words fail; for Stanislavski, dramatic action is falsified by what the words say, even as it is enabled by what the words can be made to do (the script's "I love you" might be sustained in performance as "I really dislike you" or "I am trying to hurt you by telling you 'I love you'" or "I hate myself"). Stanislavski found a means to transform Chekhov's dramatic poetry into dramatic performance by framing lang. as agency, a means to use the poetry to perform a legible, significant act. It is a measure of Stanislavski's theatrical imagination—and, perhaps, of the compromised place of poetry in mod. theater—that his terms are now essential to any discussion of Chekhov, of mod. drama, and of a significant range of mod. performance training.

Although Stanislavski's invention of the theatrical means for Chekhov in the theater is a specific case, it suggests that drama is always performed in cultural and theatrical circumstances redefining its poetry (it is notable, but not surprising, that Chekhov was not impressed with all of Stanislavski's decisions as a director). Classic drama, now incl. Chekhov, of course, inevitably provides the agency for performances unimaginable to the poet. *The Taming of the Shrew*, *The Merchant of Venice*, *Othello* today are animated by contemp. attitudes about gender, religion, race; words such as *woman*, *Jew*, *black* signify differently from the way they did on the early mod. stage, implicating the speaker (both actor and character) in different ethical terms, as a different kind of agent; and their performance also implicates us, as agents of contemp. theater and society. Even lines that seem to describe the action they perform—Herod's "I stamp! I stare! I look all about!" from the Coventry nativity play—clearly provide the actor with the instigation to action, an action that will gain its specific force and meaning from the way the actor uses the lines (esp. given the ms.'s stage direction that Herod "rages in the street").

Dramatic writing is writing for use, and even writing that seems to direct its performance evinces this truth: Beckett's *Quad* (1981)—a play that exists entirely in stage directions, which command actors to circumnavigate and bisect a square-shaped pattern in a specific sequence—has given rise to an arresting range of productions. Indeed, one of the most surprising turns of mod. literary and theater hist. has to do with Beckett's plays in the theater. Although dramatic poetry has generally been equated with the dialogue, taking stage directions as merely theatrical instruments extrinsic to the play's literary identity, in the 1980s Beckett's stage directions became the center of an important critical controversy, as several productions—JoAnne Akalaitis's *Endgame* at the American Repertory Theatre in 1984, Gildas Bourget's pink-set *Fin de partie* at the Comédie Française in 1988, an all-women *Waiting for Godot* by De Haarlemse Toneelschuur the same year, Deborah Warner's environmental *Footfalls* in London in 1994, the casting of twin sisters as Didi and Gogo in a 2006 *Godot* in Pontadera, Italy—drew legal attention for changing the theatrical scene imaged in the text. What this controversy illustrates is the fact that the propriety of dramatic poetry is determined not on the page but by the social, theatrical, and (here) legal structures through which poetry and performance are defined.

Indeed, George Tabori's idiosyncratic productions of *Waiting for Godot* usefully refract this question. In his 1984 *Godot* at the Munich Kammerspiele, the actors playing Didi and Gogo sat at a table, text in hand, apparently rehearsing the play, reading stage directions aloud, working themselves deeply into "performance," and then pulling back to examine the script: the production allegorized the ways writing, rather than governing stage practice, is an instrument in the actors' hands, used to create something else, a performance. In Tabori's 2006 *Godot* at the Berliner Ensemble, the actors frequently extemporized with the audience and—more to the point—had an ongoing conversation with the prompter, seated at her table just outside the circular playing area. Rather than staging the "performance" as an objectified image, derived from the text and situated frontally before the audience, this production conceived dramatic performance as transactional, dramatic poetry sustaining a collaboration between the institutionalized conventions of performance (the prompter) and the individual temperament of the actors, and between the actors—who, in any production, are always available to us, speaking for themselves as well as "in character"—and the audience, collaboration sustained by the actors' ongoing ironic byplay about the play and their performance of it. For some audiences, no doubt, Tabori's *Godot* approached travesty, epitomized by the moment when Didi and Gogo knocked over the tree in Act 2, perhaps confirming Beckett's withering remark to his biographer Deirdre Bair that, in his ideal drama, there would be "no actors, only the text." And yet, as Tabori's productions suggest, dramatic poetry is an important but not necessarily *the* governing instrument of theater: dramatic performance will locate dramatic poetry as poetry in a Burkean ratio to the other elements of theatrical action, an event in which the poetry is recomposed in the immediate bodily and spatial discourse devised by actors and audiences.

Dramatic poetry summons a poetics of duplicity, suggesting that while lang. might have a range of function in the dramatic fiction, it will be remade by the process of production into specific actions that cannot be anticipated from the words alone. What does the actor do on Othello's line "And smote him, thus," the line in which he executes the terrible justice of Venice—the justice he once exercised on the turbaned Turk who "traduced the state"—on himself? In the late 19th c., the It. actor Tommaso Salvini created a sensation by seeming to hack away at his sinewy throat with a small knife. Other actors have opted for different gestures: Anthony Hopkins grinning ironically as he plunges a silver poniard into his abdomen; Laurence Fishburne, strangling himself with his necklace as he takes the "circumcised dog" by the "throat," before finishing his work with a knife to the heart. If how this gesture is performed frames our sense of the event—how Othello acts shaping what Othello means, what the experience and so the content of this justice is—then how much more significant is every nuance and shading of the actor's transformation of words into deeds. What does the actress perform with Cordelia's "Nothing": a repudiation of Lear's inappropriate question? Insolence directed toward her sisters? Fearful self-protection? Punctilious coolness? Posture and movement, vocal tone, the production's general conventions of address, the entire corporeal armature of social behavior—rendered esp. significant through the marked conventions of stage acting—will operate with this single word to make it work, do significant work here, work that must say and do much more than "Nothing."

Finally, dramatic poetry is both material to be reshaped (words made into acts) and an instrument, an agency of theatrical labor, something the agents of the production both work on and work with to fashion the performance. A specific performance is neither implicit in nor derivable from the text alone. Since poetry is the dual agency of both dramatic (fictional) and theatrical (actual) activity onstage, can we finally distinguish meaningfully between presence and representation in performance? In any fully dramatic performance, even those most insistent on a scrupulous "fidelity" to "the text," presentational immediacy is the principal node of our engagement in the play. Echoing S. T. Coleridge, this effect has been seized as a "willing suspension of disbelief," but the reference to "belief" is a distraction: belief in the dramatic fiction is never significantly in play in the theater—we are always aware that Olivier is not murdering anyone, even though Othello is. Yet Othello cannot be distinguished from Olivier; Othello is what Olivier is doing, making there with us, an enacted poetry that disappears the moment the actor loses his bearings or we our concentration. To swing into action, leap to the stage, and save Desdemona is not merely to mistake the role of the audience but to mistake the event entirely and so destroy it: Desdemona will not be saved; she will simply stop being there as the actress stops working and calls for the police.

Dramatic performance refuses a strict opposition between word and deed, speech and action, representation and presentation, the drama and its performance. Although the poet's work is completed with the framing of the dramatic poem, we may well feel that *Antigone* or *Phèdre* or *Hamletmachine* have a semantic identity richer than the other tools and materials of theatrical performance. While dramatic poetry will be actualized in means that lie outside the script, specific opportunities for using dramatic poetry emerge in clearer outline when the text is conceived in relation to the performance practices of its original theater, esp. when—as is the case with Shakespeare or Chekhov—the playwright worked within a specific stage architecture, system of production conventions, and with a given acting company. For all the character's famous seductiveness, the Cleopatra of Shakespeare's *Antony and Cleopatra* is a considerably ironic role, availing itself of the verbal japes typical of the cross-dressing boy actor and drawing our attention to the convention as well: Cleopatra, after all, commits suicide in order to avoid seeing "some squeaking Cleopatra boy my greatness," exactly what Shakespeare's original audiences saw. Chekhov wanted Stanislavski—drawn to serious, sentimental roles—to play the part of Lopakhin in *The Cherry Orchard*; though Stanislavski chose to play Gaev, perhaps Chekhov wanted the performance to resist framing Lopakhin as a stereotypically comic peasant. So, too, some playwrights have been closely involved in staging their work, leaving a record of

their intentions with regard to theatrical production. Beckett came to direct many of his plays and (perhaps surprisingly) often revised his own texts to accommodate an altered sense of the work the text could do as performance. For stage productions of *Not I* (1972), he came to prefer dropping the silent Auditor, nonetheless insisting that this role be retained in published scripts of the play.

Beyond that, dramatic poetry sometimes appears to allegorize thematic aspects of the animating ethical dynamics of its originating theater, particularly if we seize the role as an instrument for doing, rather than as the representation of a fixed character. The potentially incoherent seriality of the role of Hamlet, demanding a strikingly distinct temperament in every scene, speaks to an early mod. anxiety about the stability of the ethical subject, one perhaps recorded in the poetry, too, in Hamlet's *or*, his tendency to multiply adjectives—"Remorseless, treacherous, lecherous, kindless villain!"—in an ultimately vain attempt to fix the nature of human character (and much else) in words. The harrowing exploration of a tormented psychological inscape in Ibsen's Rosmer similarly engages with the instability of the mod. "self"; the repetitive expressionless movement of Parks's Black Man with Watermelon in *Death of the Last Black Man in the Whole Entire World* signifies within an embodied, and alienated, historical discourse for the evocation "race" in performance.

And yet plays are limited neither to their original theaters nor to their original circumstances of production. One of the lessons of the reconstructed Globe Theatre in London is that its productions articulate a complex historical ambivalence, enabling us to see some of the working elements of Shakespeare's poetry in an open-air platform theater, but with the constant recognition that, despite the authentic timbers, hand-made costumes, and even reconstructed accents and performance techniques, we are participating in a specific form of *mod.* performance—the living-hist. historical reconstruction—taking its place along other mod. performance genres, the living-hist. museum, the theme park, performance art, and contemp. Shakespeare production, for that matter.

Along similar lines, critics sometimes imply that dramatic performance is a special genre of performance, one in which theatrical meaning *should* be determined by the aims of the poet, that the rhetorical purpose of dramatic performance is precisely to evince the *poet's* work. Some dramatic trads. have been notably conservative in this regard, often by massively restricting the repertoire, and strictly codifying legitimate training and performance practice so as to establish a relatively unchanging relation between poetry and its performance: Japanese Nō is a familiar case in point, as is the Comédie Française. Yet while this understanding appears to subordinate stage to page, it actually suggests just the opposite. It is the practice of the stage that encodes the signs of proper "fidelity" to the poetry: rhythmic utterance, for instance, or a pause at line endings. Whether it is speaking the verse emphatically without motion or gesture (Yeats rehearsed his actors in barrels), wearing doublet and hose for mod. Shakespeare, or adopting the Method "crouch" to express an emotional volatility ready to spring into being: to the extent that these behaviors signify fidelity to a specific play, they do so by encoding the poetry in a specific regime of performance, one both outside and beyond the imagination of the text.

The hist. of Western theater is a hist. of change: the workable practices for transforming dramatic poetry into theatrical play dynamically reciprocate with forms of social behavior, with ideas about identity and society, with notions of the purposes of art. To see Shakespeare's *The Winter's Tale* in a regional summer Shakespeare festival in the U.S. or directed by Sam Mendes at the Old Vic in London or directed by Robert Wilson at the Berliner Ensemble is more than seeing three "versions" of one "play" (let alone an event directly cognate with the play that might have taken place in Shakespeare's London). It is to see three distinct articulations of the purpose and agency of dramatic poetry, the materialization—with all that the word implies for the resources of time, talent, space, audience—of three distinct ideas of what dramatic performance is and is for and how its poetry might be forcefully configured as something else, dramatic action. Much as the self-evident "meanings" of poems change as they are read in new locations, with new purposes, and as part of changing systems of social and cultural understanding, so dramatic poetry—performed in a more extraverted, embodied, public fashion, through articulate but changing conventions of signification—will inevitably provide the instrument for new, unanticipated action and experience in the theater. Lang. and narrative are embedded in the world as well as in lit., and plays—whether classics like *Medea* and *King Lear* or more recent work like Kane's *Blasted* (1995) or Gao Xingjian's *The Other Shore* (1986)—seem, in a given time and place, to afford certain possibilities of performance, some familiar and conventional, some surprising and unexpectedly effective, some so controversial as to raise the question of whether they work, perform theatrical *work* with the poetry at all. While it may appear to compromise the poetic integrity of the text, the transformation of words into legibly embodied acts—acts that necessarily exceed, qualify, remake the text as our understanding of its theatrical agency changes—is what enables the continued vitality, the performative force, of dramatic poetry and dramatic performance.

*See* AUTO SACRAMENTAL, CLASSICAL PROSODY, CLOSET DRAMA, COMEDY, GENRE, HUMORS, MIME, MONOLOGUE, POETICS, REALISM, TRAGEDY.

■ **Literary Criticism and History**: L. Abercrombie, "The Function of Poetry in the Drama," *Poetry Review* 1 (1912); M. E. Prior, *The Language of Tragedy* (1947); C. Brooks and R. B. Heilman, *Understanding Drama* (1948); G. F. Else, *Aristotle's Poetics* (1957); R. Lattimore, *Poetry of Greek Tragedy* (1958); D. Donoghue, *The Third Voice* (1959); M. Bieber, *History of the Greek and Roman Theater*, 2d ed. (1961); M. C. Bradbrook, *English Dramatic Form* (1965); V. A. Kolve, *The Play Called Corpus Christi* (1966); J. Scherer, *La Dramaturgie classique en France* (1968); J. Barish, *Ben Jonson and the Language of Prose Comedy* (1970); R. Williams, *Drama from Ibsen to Genet* (1971); H.H.A. Gowda, *Dramatic Poetry from Medieval to Modern Times* (1972); K. J. Worth, *Revolutions in Modern English Drama* (1972); A. P. Hinchcliffe, *Modern Verse Drama* (1977); O. Taplin, *Greek Tragedy in Action* (1978); J. Baxter, *Shakespeare's Poetic Styles* (1980); D. Breuer, *Deutsche Metrik und Vergeschichte* (1981); C. Freer, *The Poetics of Jacobean Drama* (1981); G. R. Hibbard, *The Making of Shakespeare's Dramatic Poetry* (1981); E. Havelock, *Preface to Plato* (1982); T. Rosenmeyer, *The Art of Aeschylus* (1982); A. Brown, *A New Companion to Greek Tragedy* (1983); G. Hoffmanm, "Das moderne amerikanische Versdrama," *Das amerikanische Drama*, ed. G. Hoffman (1984); G. T. Wright, *Shakespeare's Metrical Art* (1988); J. W. Flannery, *W. B. Yeats and the Idea of a Theatre* (1989); D. Bair, *Samuel Beckett* (1990); W. B. Worthen, *Modern Drama and the Rhetoric of Theater* (1992); R. Cohn, "Dramatic Poetry," *New Princeton Encyclopedia of Poetry and Poetics,* ed. A. Preminger et al. (1993); M. Bristol, *Big-Time Shakespeare* (1996); F. Zeitlin, *Playing the Other* (1996); Aristotle, *Poetics*, trans. M. E. Hubbard (1998); J. S. Peters, *Theatre of the Book* (2000); R. McDonald, *Shakespeare and the Arts of Language* (2001); T. Eagleton, *Sweet Violence* (2002); J. Enders, *The Medieval Theater of Cruelty* (2002); S. Orgel, *The Authentic Shakespeare* (2002); N. Slater, *Spectator Politics* (2002); J. Enders, *Death by Drama and Other Medieval Urban Legends* (2005).

■ **Theater History**: N. Díaz de Escovar and F. de P. Lasso de la Vega, *Historia del teatro español*, 2 v. (1924); H. C. Lancaster, *History of French Dramatic Literature in the 17th Century*, 9 v. (1929–42); A. Nicoll, *A History of English Drama, 1660–1900*, 6 v. (1952–59); A. Nicoll, *English Drama 1900–1930* (1973); F. H. Sandbach, *The Comic Theatre of Greece and Rome* (1977); J. Barish, *The Antitheatrical Prejudice* (1981); W. B. Worthen, *The Idea of the Actor* (1984); J. R. Roach, *The Player's Passion* (1985); A. W. Pickard-Cambridge, *The Dramatic Festivals of Athens*, 2d ed. (1989); *Nothing to Do with Dionysos?*, ed. J. Winkler and F. Zeitlin (1990); M. McKendrick, *Theatre in Spain, 1490–1700* (1992); *A New History of Early English Drama*, ed. J. D. Cox and D. S. Kastan (1997); T. Hauptfleisch, *Theatre and Society in South Africa* (1997); *Cambridge History of American Theatre*, ed. D. Wilmeth et al., 3 v. (1998); S. Chatterjee, *The Colonial Staged* (1998); *World Encyclopedia of Contemporary Theatre,* ed. D. Rubin et al., 5 v. (2000); *Encyclopedia of Latin American Theater*, ed. E. Cortés and M. Barrea-Marlys (2003); M. Banham, *A History of Theatre in Africa* (2004); N. Bhathia, *Acts of Authority/Acts of Resistance* (2004); *Cambridge History of British Theatre*, ed. P. Thomson et al. (2004); *Contemporary Theatres in Europe*, ed. J. Kelleher and N. Ridout (2006); P. Zarrilli, B. McConachie, G. J. Williams, C. F. Sorgenfrei, *Theatre Histories* (2006); J. Hollander, *Indian Folk Theatres* (2007); O. Okagbue, *African*

*Theatres and Performance* (2007); A. Versenyi, *Theatre in Latin America* (2009).

■ **Theory and Performance Studies**: S. T. Coleridge, *Biographia Literaria* (1817); É. Zola, *Le naturalisme au théâtre* (1881); T. S. Eliot, *The Sacred Wood* (1920); W. B. Yeats, *Essays* (1924); H. Granville-Barker, *On Poetry in Drama* (1937); K. Burke, *A Grammar of Motives* (1945); E. Bentley, *The Playwright as Thinker* (1946); Eliot, *Essays*; J. L. Barrault, *Reflections on the Theatre* (1951); T. S. Eliot, *Poetry and Drama* (1951); F. Fergusson, *Idea of a Theater* (1953); A. Artaud, *The Theater and Its Double*, trans. M. C. Richards (1958); W. H. Auden, *The Dyer's Hand* (1962); R. Barthes, *On Racine*, trans. R. Howard (1963); P. Brook, *The Empty Space* (1968); J. Cocteau, "Préface de 1922," *Les Mariés de la Tour Eiffel* (1969); M. Goldman, *Shakespeare and the Energies of Drama* (1972), and *The Actor's Freedom* (1975); B. Brecht, *Brecht on Theatre*, ed. and trans. John Willett (1977); J. L. Styan, *The Shakespeare Revolution* (1977); B. Beckerman, *Dynamics of Drama* (1979); H. Blau, *Take up the Bodies* (1982); O. Mandel, "Poetry and Excessive Poetry in the Theatre," *Centennial Review* 26 (1982); M. Carlson, *Theories of the Theatre* (1984); C. J. Herington, *Poetry into Drama* (1985); C. W. Meister, *Dramatic Criticism* (1985); B. O. States, *Great Reckonings in Little Rooms* (1985); M. Esslin, *The Field of Drama* (1987); H. Berger Jr., *Imaginary Audition* (1989); E. Fischer-Lichte, *Semiotics of Theatre* (1992); S. B. Garner Jr., *Bodied Spaces* (1994); U. Chaudhuri, *Staging Place* (1995); S-L. Parks, "From Elements of Style," *The America Play and Other Works* (1995); J. L. Austin, *How to Do Things with Words*, 2d ed., ed. J. O. Urmson and M. Sbisá (1997); J. Wise, *Dionysus Writes* (1999); M. Puchner, *Stage Fright* (2002); B. Bennett, *All Theater Is Revolutionary Theater* (2005); H.-T. Lehmann, *Postdramatic Theatre* (2006); W. B. Worthen, *Print and the Poetics of Modern Drama* (2006); R. Weimann and D. Bruster, *Shakespeare and the Power of Performance* (2008); E. Fischer-Lichte, *Transformative Power of Performance* (2008); *Companion to Shakespeare and Performance*, ed. B. Hodgdon and W. B. Worthen (2008); K. Stanislavski, *An Actor's Work*, ed. and trans. J. Benedetti (2008); W. B. Worthen, *Drama: Between Poetry and Performance* (2010).

W. B. Worthen

**DREAM VISION.** A literary work describing the dream(s) of a first-person narrator identified with the author. Although religious and apocalyptic visions were composed from late antiquity on, the literary genre flourished in Europe from the 12th through the early 16th c. Its major antecedents included biblical dreams and revelations, Macrobius's commentary on Cicero's *Somnium Scipionis* (ca. 5th c.), and Boethius's *De consolatione philosophiae* (early 6th c.). Significant themes included erotic desire, religious or philosophical questions, and social critique, subgenres that could be combined in a single work. The genre is defined by a frame that sets the narrator's actual circumstances against the dream, but many influential works borrowed its conventions for waking visions (as in *De consolatione philosophiae,* Alain de Lille's *De planctu naturae,* Dante's *Divina commedia,* John Gower's *Confessio amantis,* and Christine de Pizan's *Livre de la cité des dames*). Dream visions were frequently allegorical (see ALLEGORY) and had close ties to debate lit., emphasizing a sequence of reported speeches. The narrator often wanders in a field or garden on a spring morning before falling asleep and dreams of a densely symbolic landscape in which he converses with various *personifications, is instructed by an otherworldly mentor, or overhears debates among nonhuman interlocutors such as birds or the body and soul. The dreamer is typically distressed by love or melancholy in waking life and is characterized as isolated, naïve, or awkward; the vision develops the tension between his ignorance at the time of the dream and the wisdom of the poet writing with the benefit of experience. This double consciousness underscores the self-conscious quality of the dream vision, calling attention to the author and the artifice of his *persona. Debates over the interpretation of dreams and their supernatural, psychological, or somatic origins inform the genre's epistemological and hermeneutic concerns, allowing it to explore the truthfulness of literary fictions, the relationship between natural and divine knowledge, and the limits of human reason. Many visions associate the ephemeral and multivalent dream form with irresolvable debates and unanswered questions rather than with fully revealed truth, and the vision may or may not provide a remedy for the dreamer's initial suffering.

The dream vision first attained popularity in France with the genre-defining *Roman de la Rose* (ca. 1230, ca. 1270–80) and the philosophical *De planctu naturae* (composed mid-12th c.), which were followed by the courtly amatory poems of Guillaume de Machaut and Jean Froissart. The form was embraced by the major poets of late 14th c. England, notably in Chaucer's four long dream-vision poems, which inspired many imitations, and in the alliterative trad. best exemplified by *Pearl* and by William Langland's *Piers Plowman*. Dream visions maintained their popularity throughout the 15th c. in works by John Lydgate, John Skelton, and several Scottish poets but declined ca. 1500, esp. with the resurgence of *lyric as a vehicle for poetic introspection. Dreams remained a popular literary device, however, and later analogues to the framed narrative vision appear in John Bunyan's *Pilgrim's Progress* and in works by John Keats and James Joyce.

*See* MEDIEVAL POETICS, MEDIEVAL POETRY.

■ H. R. Jauss, *La Génèse de la poésie allégorique française au moyen âge* (1962); C. Hieatt, *The Realism of Dream Visions* (1967); E. Kirk, *The Dream Thought of "Piers Plowman"* (1972); A. C. Spearing, *Medieval Dream Poetry* (1976); K. L. Lynch, *The High Medieval Dream Vision* (1988); J. S. Russell, *The English Dream Vision* (1988); S. F. Kruger, *Dreaming in the Middle Ages* (1992); *Reading Dreams*, ed. P. Brown (1999); K. L. Lynch, *Chaucer's Philosophical Visions* (2000).

A. Walling

**DUB POETRY.** *See* CARIBBEAN, POETRY OF THE.

**DURATION.** One of the three intonational characteristics of spoken sound, the other two being stress (see ACCENT) and *pitch. In poetry, duration concerns the timing of syllables, words, and lines, such timing being either actual or conventional—much more so the latter than the former. Actual duration falls under the category of *performance or *recitation. Adjustment of the duration of syllables in utterance, i.e., in the reading of the line, is a matter of delivery speed or tempo: this is not a part of the poem itself—i.e., of meter—but of personal choice and style in delivery. Some readers will read more slowly, deliberately, or expressively than others. Still, some ling. features of the line obviously affect tempo, the chief among these being morphology. It has long been known to poets in England that large numbers of monosyllables slow down delivery of the line, while polysyllables, by contrast, speed it up: Alexander Pope makes much use of monosyllables in his mimetic lines in the *Essay on Criticism*, particularly "Though ten low words oft creep in one dull line" (2.347)—to which compare the speed of "A needless Alexandrine ends the song"—; and the contrast is pointed up starkly in Shakespeare's "The multitudinous seas incarnadine, / Making the green one red" (*Macbeth* 2.2.59–60). To some degree, this is simply a function of the fact that heavily monosyllabic lines contain more junctures (pauses). Because of the limitations of the human vocal apparatus, the maximum delivery rate is about eight syllables per second (Lehiste). Langs. control change of duration for semantic and signaling purposes: one of the most important is final lengthening before terminal juncture. Syllables may be lengthened to signal the end of a syntagm, in speech or line, in poetry: this phenomenon is well attested in IE and Gr.

But more important than actual durations in verse are conventional ones, and by far the most important of these is the opposition of *long* and *short*, known as *quantity. This much-disputed contrast holds perhaps the central position in the hist. of Western prosody from archaic Gr. down to the 19th c. At least some ancient grammarians held that certain *vowels* were long, others short; the ancient metrists (*metrici*; see METRICI AND RHYTHMICI) held that the former were twice the length of the latter; they then devised a set of rules (incl. other criteria) for classifying *syllables* as "long" versus "short" and on this basis constructed a quantitative prosody (see CLASSICAL PROSODY). The ancient musical theorists (*rhythmici*), however, held that there were more distinctions than 2:1 and that some syllables were indeterminate. But over time, actual vowel (or even syllable) length quickly lost ground to conventional classification. Length was indeed phonemic in cl. Gr., but in the subsequent evolution of the cl. langs., it was lost, so that auditors no longer heard a long/short distinction at all. Nevertheless, the notion that syllables could be grouped into long versus short persisted among grammarians and prosodists literally for millennia. Mod. linguists distinguish between "tense" and "lax" vowels (Jakobson and Halle; see Jakobson, 1.550 ff., and Chomsky and Halle, 68–69, 324–26).

The time value of one short syllable was called a *mora by some of the ancient grammarians and has been used by mod. prosodists from time to time (see METER). The temporality or duration of syllables is a phenomenon of interest to performance theory in regard to tempo and the semantic cues tempo changes can deliver; it is of interest to metrical theory in that some verse systems use length, as others do stress or pitch, as the marker of the meter—but only when that intonational feature is phonemic.

*See* BINARY AND TERNARY, FOOT, MEASURE.

■ P. Barkas, *Critique of Modern English Prosody* (1934); Jakobson; Jakobson and Halle; Chomsky and Halle; I. Lehiste, *Suprasegmentals* (1970), ch. 2; Allen, esp. ch. 4; Brogan; West; R. P. Newton, *Vowel Undersong* (1981); I. Lehiste, "The Many Linguistic Functions of Duration," *New Directions in Linguistics and Semiotics*, ed. J. E. Copeland (1984); J. Clark, C. Yallop, J. Fletcher, *An Introduction to Phonetics and Phonology*, 3d ed. (2007); B. de Cornulier, "Minimal Chronometric Forms: On the Durational Metrics of 2-2 Stroke Groups," *Towards a Typology of Poetic Forms*, ed. J.-L. Aroui and A. Arleo (2009); X. Zheng, "The Effects of Prosodic Prominence and Serial Position on Duration Perception," *Journal of the Acoustical Society of America* 128 (2010).

T.V.F. BROGAN

**DUTCH POETRY.** *See* LOW COUNTRIES, POETRY OF THE.

**DYFALU.** A poetic technique in *Welsh poetry that reaches its highest excellence in the work of Dafydd ap Gwilym (14th c.) but that long remained current practice and, after its degeneration, was ridiculed by Ellis Wynne in his *Visions of the Sleeping Bard* (1703). The term also means "to guess" and has affinities with the *riddle and the *kenning. Dyfalu at its best is an animated play of fancy, whereby the object on which the poet's mind dwells—be it the stars or mist or a bird, a girl's yellow hair or her white arms—is rapidly compared in a concatenation of *metaphors of strong visual imagery with other objects in nature. The stars are the sparks of a conflagration lit by the saints, berries belonging to the frozen moon, the reflection of hail on the sun's bright floor. This onrush of metaphors is well suited by its exuberance to convey Dafydd ap Gwilym's exciting vision of the ever-renewed miracle of creation. Other poets, such as Dafydd Nanmor in the 15th c., employ the same device with fine effect, but later it became mechanical and stereotyped.

■ J. Vendryes, *La Poésie galloise des XIIe–XIIIe siècles dans ses rapports avec la langue* (1930); Parry, *History*, chap. 6; R. Loomis, *Dafydd ap Gwilym: The Poems* (1982); R. Bromwich, *Aspects of the Poetry of Dafydd ap Gwilym* (1986); Jarman and Hughes, vol. 2, rev. D. Johnston (1997), esp. chap. 5; *The New Companion to the Literature of Wales*, ed. M. Stephens (1998).

D. M. LLOYD

**ECHO VERSE.** A poem of which the final syllables of the lines are repeated, as by an echo, with the effect of making a reply to a question or a comment, often contrastive, punning, or ironic. A critic of 1665 calls it a "kind of Poem imitating the resounding Rocks, wherein the last Syllables of a sentence repeated, give answer to a question in the same, or divers, and sometime a contrary sence." The poem is sometimes set in *couplets, the echo words alone forming the even lines, as in the following examples: "Qu'est-ça du monde la chose la plus infame? / Femme!" (Gracien du Pont, 1539); "Echo! What shall I do to my Nymph when I go to behold her? / Hold her!" (Barnabe Barnes, 1593). Postclassical echo verse is found in Fr. as early as the 13th c. (Kastner) and was known to the *troubadours but was given its name only in the 16th c. by du Pont. The examples in the *Greek Anthology inspired a vogue for echo poems in Fr., It., and Eng. verse of the 16th and 17th cs., which are also associated with the *eclogue on account of *stichomythia. Well-known examples are by Johannes Secundus, Joachim du Bellay, Martin Opitz, George Herbert ("Heaven"), Jonathan Swift ("A Gentle Echo on Woman"), A. W. Schlegel ("Waldgespräch"), and G. M. Hopkins ("The Leaden Echo and the Golden Echo"). Found most often in *pastoral poetry and drama, echo verse has unrequited love as its commonest subject but has also been used for religious poetry, political satire, and society verse. In structure, echo verse would seem to be one (particularly effective) species of *close rhyme or else *rich rhyme. Hollander takes the return of the sound in echo as a *trope for the mode of *allusion itself.

■ Kastner, 62–63; E. Colby, *The Echo-Device in Literature* (1920); J. Bolte, *Die Echo in Volksglauben und Dichtung* (1935); A. Langen, *Dialogisches Spiel* (1966); J. Hollander, *The Figure of Echo* (1981); T. Augarde, *Oxford Guide to Word Games*, 2d ed. (2003).

T.V.F. Brogan; L. Perrine

**ECLOGUE** (Gr. *ek* + *leg-*, "to pick from"). As a noun, *ekloge* was used to describe harvesting crops, drafting soldiers, electing leaders, reckoning accounts, and sampling texts; then in Lat. as *ecloga*, its meaning was specialized to, e.g., part of a poetry book (Statius, *Silvae*, 3 Pref. 20: *summa est ecloga*, "is the last component"). The term was similarly used by commentators for Horace's *Epistles* 2.1 and book of *Epodes*, also for the ten components of Virgil's *Bucolics* (or *Eclogues*), perhaps by the poet himself defining them as parts of a designed book (Hutchinson, Van Sickle). The Virgilian example focused *eclogue* to mean short dialogue or monologue with more or less oblique *allegory of politics, erotics, and poetics, all presented in dramatic form (enabling their early and recurrent theatrical success) as speech by herdsmen (*pastores*), from which later came the name *pastoral for a *genre featuring shepherds.

At his book's climax, Virgil also invented the mytheme of Arcadia as song's origin and ideal, challenging the Sicily of Gr. Theocritus, whose *idylls (little forms), were collected as *Boukolika* (about cowherds). They featured herders of cattle, sheep, and goats, dramatizing an old Gr. cognitive *metaphor, to herd thoughts (*boukolein*; Gutzwiller). Deploying herdsmen in heroic meter (epos), Theocritus prefigured the tension between *bucolic and heroic themes, characters and plots that was to animate Virgil and later trad., with recurrent contrasts between slight and great.

Eclogue as pastoral allegory in the manner inaugurated by Virgil recurs in subsequent Lat. *Bucolics* (Calpurnius, Nemesianus) and served Dante to defend his *Divine Comedy* in a programmatic eclogue to Giovanni di Virgilio. Outdoing Virgil's ten, Petrarch assembles 12 eclogues into a bucolic book, declaring himself moved by "lonely woods" to write something "pastoral" (*Epistolae familiares* 10.4). Emulative eclogue books proliferate, among them Giovanni Boccaccio's miscellany of 16 (*Bucolicum carmen . . . distinctum eglogis*, following Petrarch with allegorical meaning "beneath the bark"); 12 Christian eclogues of Antonio Geraldini; six of Jacopo Sannazaro featuring fishermen (*piscatores*); ten of Mantuan's pious *Adulescentia* (mentioned with affection by Shakespeare); and 12 in Edmund Spenser's *Shepheardes Calender* (1579), programmatically mingling erotics and metapoetics with court flattery and religious satire, also turning *ekloge*, *ecloga* (Gr., Lat.), *egloga* (Italianate Lat., It.), *égloga* (Sp.), *eclog* (Eng.), and *eclogue* (Fr., Eng.) into "aeglogue," explained as "Goteheards tales" by Spenser in the appended commentary he attributes to the otherwise unidentified E. K. (cf. Gr. *aiges* + *logos*). Affirming the allegorical and cognitive heritage of eclogues, George Puttenham's *Arte of English Poesie* (1589) says that an eclogue is written "not of purpose to counterfeit or represent the rusticall manner of loves and communication, but under the vaile of homely persons and in rude speeches to insinuate and glaunce at greater matters."

As such, the eclogue prompted remarkable diversity of cognitive applications apart from books, e.g., in Fr., Pierre de Ronsard's *Bergeries, eclogues et mascarades* (which was acted at court); in Sp., Garcilaso de la Vega's *Églogas*; and in Eng., Alexander Barclay's *Eclogues* and Barnabe Googe's *Eglogs*. The cognitive outreach spread to produce, e.g., town eclogues (John Gay, Jonathan Swift, Mary Wortley Montagu, Royall Tyler) and still prompts scattered pieces, e.g., from W. H. Auden and Seamus Heaney; and sequences or books, e.g., from W. Antony, Derek Walcott, and David Baker, extending too the pastoral realm of "green thought" (Andrew Marvell) to mod. ecology in the widespread coinage *ecologue*.

■ W. W. Greg, *Pastoral Poetry and Pastoral Drama* (1906); R. F. Jones, "Eclogue Types in English Poetry of the Eighteenth Century," *Journal of English and Germanic Philology* 24 (1925); A. Hulubei, *L'Églogue en France au XVIe Siècle, Époque Des Valois (1515–1589)* (1938); D. Lessig, *Ursprung und Entwicklung der Spanischen Ekloge Bis 1650; mit Anhang Eines Eklogenkataloges* (1962); E. Bolisani and M. Valgimigli, *La Corrispondenza Poetica di Dante Alighieri e Giovanni di Virgilio* (1963); W. L. Grant, *Neo-Latin Literature and the Pastoral* (1965); W. Antony, *The Arminarm Eclogues* (1971); G. Otto, *Ode, Ekloge und Elegie Im 18. Jahrhundert Zur Theorie und Praxis Französischer Lyrik Nach Boileau* (1973); D. Walcott, "Italian Eclogues [for Joseph Brodsky]," *The Bounty* (1997); D. Baker, *Midwest Eclogue* (2005); K. Belford, *Ecologue* (2005); K. Gutzwiller, "The Herdsman in Greek Thought," *Brill's Companion to Greek and Latin Pastoral*, ed. M. Fantuzzi and T. Papanghelis (2006); P. McDonald, *Pastorals* (2006); I. Twiddy, "Seamus Heaney's Versions of Pastoral," *Essays in Criticism* 56 (2006); G. O. Hutchinson, *Talking Books: Readings in Hellenistic and Roman Books of Poetry* (2008); J. Van Sickle, *Virgil's "Book of Bucolics": The Ten Eclogues Translated into English Verse* (2011).

J. Van Sickle

**ECOPOETRY.** *See* ENVIRONMENT AND POETRY.

**ÉCRITURE.** In his lit. crit. from the early 1950s on, the Fr. scholar Roland Barthes elaborated on an intransitive use of the verb *to write* (*écrire*) by which he meant to shift emphasis from the something written to writing (*écriture*) itself. Writing, in Barthes's work, becomes a free activity from which the writer derives a gratuitous pleasure (*jouissance*). Contra Jean-Paul Sartre, the political charge of writing would be carried not in the content or communicated meaning but in the act of writing, as lit. itself becomes a subversive practice.

In the 1960s, Barthes's work was important for the contributors to the literary review *Tel Quel (such as Philippe Sollers and Julia Kristeva) for whom formal experimentation in literary works was a political gesture worked on and through lang., the medium of the political. The critical work of *Tel Quel* tended to valorize writers and poets who produced what they called *limit texts*, writings that could be read as presenting a radical challenge to conventional notions of lit. A *canon of authors developed incl. figures such as Stéphane Mallarmé, the Comte de Lautréamont, James Joyce, Antonin Artaud, and Georges Bataille.

In the second half of the 1960s, Jacques Derrida contributed often to *Tel Quel*, and in his work, the notion of écriture underwent a further transformation. For Derrida, following Martin Heidegger, Western thought is metaphysical in its entirety and has never placed in question the privilege accorded to presence. It is only with the historical closure of this metaphysical project in the 19th c., a moment most often associated in Derrida's work with G.W.F. Hegel's system of philosophy, that it becomes possible to read in the trad. the mechanism of exclusion through which it was able to constitute itself. For Derrida, metaphysics is "logocentric," meaning that it has privileged speech (because of the presumed proximity of the speaking subject to the word spoken) over writing (characterized through the "dangerous" traits of loss and absence from the subject), which it has tended to marginalize. Through his reading of the phenomenologist Edmund Husserl and engaging with the broader structuralist and psychoanalytic context of postwar Fr. thought, Derrida developed a generalized conception of writing that radically questioned the metaphysical notion of presence. In work published in 1967 (*Of Grammatology; Writing and Difference*; and *Voice and Phenomenon*), he argued that the present does not exist as the purity of an origin but is constituted as an effect of writing (*écriture*). No longer understood as secondary and representational, écriture in Derrida's work is a subversive notion calculated to disrupt the trad. of Western thought.

Derrida's further qualification of the metaphysical trad. as "phallogocentric" was taken up and developed by feminist critics and authors in the 1970s. In "Le Rire de la Méduse" ("The Laugh of the Medusa," 1975), Hélène Cixous first used the term *écriture feminine* to designate a writing practice that attempts a break with a trad. in which the feminine has been excluded. In Cixous's discourse, écriture feminine is not simply writing produced by women, nor does it imply a female author. It refers, rather, to a writing that seeks to undo a trad. understood to be profoundly aligned with masculinity, creating the space for a previously impossible discourse and creative practice.

*See* POSTSTRUCTURALISM, TEXT.

■ R. Barthes, *Writing Degree Zero*, trans. A. Levers and C. Smith (1967); J. Kristeva, *Revolution in Poetic Language*, trans. M. Waller (1984); R. Barthes, *A Barthes Reader*, ed. S. Sontag (1993); P. ffrench, *The Time of Theory: A History of Tel Quel (1960–1983)* (1995); J. Derrida, *Of Grammatology* (1974), trans. G. Spivak, rev. ed. (1997); J. Derrida, *Writing and Difference*, trans. A. Bass, 2d ed. (2001); H. Cixous, *White Ink: Interviews on Sex, Text and Politics*, ed. S. Sellers (2008).

B. Norman

**ECSTATIC POETRY.** Ecstasy, associated by many with rapture, vision, mysticism, alcohol, drugs, or sex, derives from the Gr. *ekstasis* (*ex* [out of] + *histanai* [to stand, to place]) and signifies a motion away from stasis, of being "beside the self." It implies a foray from an ordinary to an extraordinary situation, from a normal or contained to an altered or unusual state, from one condition or knowledge to another.

Little wonder that poetry is closely allied with ecstasy. Ecstasy as phenomenon and poetic act preoccupied the earliest writers, finding expression in ancient Heb., Gr., Asian, Persian, Tamil, and Bhakti poetry, as well as in the work of thinkers like Plato, who in the *Ion* refers to the Bacchic frenzy of poets and in the *Republic* insists on exiling them because of their imaginative threat to civil order. Plotinus, Longinus, and others related ecstatic states to the condition of the poet and poetry.

Ecstatic poetry may seem a tautology. But is the poetic effort of every delirious lover or religious zealot an ecstatic poem? Mordell considers ecstasy the first condition of all poetry, arguing that traditional classifications—epic, dramatic, pastoral, didactic, and elegiac—are artificial and that only ecstatic utterances are genuine. By contrast, Valéry points out that "a poet's function . . . is not to experience the poetic state: that is a private affair. His function is to create it in others." The carnal twitch of verses like "There once was a girl from Nantucket" and wooings of the "Roses are red / Violets are blue" ilk cannot compare with the pent erotic lyricism of Emily Dickinson in the "Master" letters ("No rose, yet felt myself a' bloom, / No bird—yet rode in Ether") or the desire-whetted declarations of the Shulamite in the Song of Songs: "Let me lie among vine blossoms, / in a bed of apricots! / I am in the fever of love" (trans. A. and C. Bloch).

Barnstone posits five precincts of poetic ecstasy: rage and anger; madness; felicity and enthusiasm; secular love and physical union; and the rapture of mystical union, religious and profane. The poet's task, he writes, "is to note the [ecstatic] experience, describe it as best one can, note the specific physical and spiritual manifestations, and then hope that the reader . . . will be convinced at least of the authentic occurrence of the experience itself."

An ecstatic poem, then, must not only, or even necessarily, concern itself with an ecstatic subject but itself enact an ecstatic experience, whether through strategies of figuration and displacement, as in 9th-c. Chinese poet Yuan Chen's lines, "I cannot bear to put away / the bamboo sleeping-mat: / / / that night I brought you home, / I watched you roll it out" ("The Bamboo Mat," trans. D. Young); the incantatory effects of music and rhythm, exemplified by G. M. Hopkins's "My cries heave, herds-long; huddle in a main, a chief- / woe, world-sorrow; on an age-old anvil wince and sing—"; paradox and juxtaposition, prominent in Sappho's address to Aphrodite: "But you, O blessed one, / smiled in your deathless face / and asked what (now again) I have suffered and why / (now again) I am calling out" (fragment 1, trans. A. Carson); and other syntactic manipulations, such as Pablo Neruda's "Body of skin, of moss, of eager and firm milk. / Oh the goblets of the breast! Oh the eyes of absence!" ("Body of a Woman," trans. W. S. Merwin).

Formally and temperamentally, there appear to be "yes" ecstatics, whose method and subject involve affirmation, an overflow of feeling (St. Teresa of Ávila, Walt Whitman, Hart Crane) and "no" ecstatics, for whom denial, distance, negation, even death, blur boundaries of self (Sappho, Dickinson, St. John of the Cross, Paul Celan). When the Sufi poet Rūmī calls love an ocean and the Milky Way a flake of foam floating in it, or the Bhakti mendicant Mīrabāī says, "Friends, I am mad / with love and no one sees" (trans. J. Hirschfield), one feels the powerful transgression by which words of ardor and of the romance of oblivion are made holy, and vice versa. Such ecstatic utterance suggests, as Barthes argues, that "the brio of a text is its will to bliss."

*See* CHARM, EROTIC POETRY, INCANTATION, INSPIRATION, INTENSITY, RELIGION AND POETRY, SUBLIME.

■ A. Mordell, *The Literature of Ecstasy* (1921); P. Valéry, "Poetry and Abstract Thought" [1939], *The Art of Poetry*, trans. D. Folliot (1958); R. Barthes, *A Lover's Discourse*, trans. R. Howard (1978); W. Barnstone, *The Poetics of Ecstasy* (1983); A. Carson, *Eros the Bittersweet* (1986); *Holy Fire*, ed. D. Halpern (1994); *Burning Bright*, ed. P. Hampl (1995); *Women in Praise of the Sacred*, ed. J. Hirschfield (1995); *The Erotic Spirit*, ed. S. Hamill (1996).

L. R. SPAAR

**ECUADOR, POETRY OF.** The hist. of Ecuadorian poetry has been divided into common Latin Am. periods: pre-Hispanic, colonial, 19th c., and contemp. But it also has been divided in accordance with international literary movements—*baroque, *neoclassical, romantic, modernist, postmodernist, realist, and so forth. While pre-Hispanic poetry remains to be reconstructed to enter the Ecuadorian *canon and the making of a list of nationally recognized poets has largely depended on literary critics' predilections and their relations to power, it is commonly accepted that the Jesuits Jacinto de Evia (b. 1629) and Juan Bautista Aguirre (1725–86), whose work shows the influence of Sp. poets of their times such as Luis de Góngora and Francisco de Quevedo, are the first poets of Ecuador. Aguirre's poetry is baroque and satirical and reflects the political dilemmas of the period, namely, the dominance of regionalism and the conflict between Ecuadorians from the coast and those from the Andean highland. During the 19th c., José Joaquín de Olmedo (1780–1847) wrote the epic poem "La victoria de Junín: Canto a Bolívar," and his poetic contributions have been widely celebrated in literary anthols. (Franco, Anderson Imbert and Florit).

Dolores Veintimilla de Galindo (1829–57), the only 19th-c. female poet to be studied in Ecuador at present, combines in her work a romantic style with a questioning of the limits imposed on women during the independence period. Her poem *Quejas* (Complaints), usually cited as a testimony of personal suffering and the social misunderstanding of women, also foretells the poet's suicide. Luis Cordero (1833–1912), a former president of Ecuador (1892–95), wrote epigrammatic and satirical poems in Quechua and in Sp. (Echeverría, Mera, Molestina).

At the beginning of the 20th c., the young poet Medardo Angel Silva (1898–1919) embraced in his life and work the transition between late *romanticism and *modernismo. He played the piano, read several langs., and wrote poetry and urban chronicles in a local newspaper. He also disdained money, fame, and power, displaying a belated, decadent Baudelairean style as a *flâneur* in Guayaquil. His hidden Af.-Ecuadorian ancestry and his early, tragic death are topics of gossip as well as scholarship (Benavides).

Equally important is the contribution of the avant-garde Hugo Mayo (1897–1988). Mayo's style was mainly abstract, hermetic, and humorous; and he was one of the most influential figures of the 20th c., providing new ling. and imaginative avenues to be rediscovered by later poets.

During the first half of the 20th c., Ecuadorean and international scholars agree, the work of Alfredo Gangotena (1904–44), Jorge Carrera (1902–78), and Gonzalo Escudero (1903–72) represents the most challenging poetry of Ecuador. Partly because of their family influences and economic positions, these three poets were in constant literary exchange with other poets around the world, and much of their work was translated into Fr., Eng., and Ger. Their poetry is mainly personal, metaphysical, and religious. But social issues also emerge in their works and remind us of their shared convictions about justice and freedom. César Dávila (1919–67) followed the steps of his three predecessors but embraced a more fantastic and abstract lang. in his work. His preference for obscuring the meaning of his poems became more relevant to poets such as Efraín Jara (b. 1926); Oswaldo Calisto Rivera (1979–2000, also known as Cachivache); and others who promote an obscure, bookish, and pedantic style as fundamental literary values of the late 20th c. Dávila also wrote short stories and, to the surprise of many, a long poem titled *Boletín y Elegía de las Mitas* to protest the inhumane conditions endured by Indians since the Sp. conquest. His tragic end occurred in Caracas, and his poetry immediately became *razón de culto* for young readers.

Jorge Enrique Adoum (1926–2009) and Hugo Salazar Tamariz (1923–99) were friends and contemporaries of Dávila. Their poetry is clearly marked by Marxist political convictions and, thus, by socialist realism and the style of the Rus. poet Vladimir Mayakovsky. The volumes of their collected poems, recently released in Ecuador, provide examples of social concerns and give us a clear idea of hegemonic literary discourses in the context of the cold war.

During the last half of the 20th c., Ecuadorian poetry matured and slowly became more international and ambitious. Hence, it reflects varied personal views shaped by global and national events, as well as inevitable literary influences from Europe and the U.S., while presenting a wide range of contemp. styles, voices, and themes. Ecuadorian poetry from the second half of the 20th c. includes the work of Carlos E. Jaramillo (b. 1932), David Ledesma (1934–61), Fernando Cazón (b. 1931), and other members of the *Grupo Madrugada* (Group of the Dawn) and the *Generación Huracanada* (Wrecked Generation) of the late 1950s and 1960s. The poets of these groups were united in revolt against governmental violence, repression, and social injustice, both domestic and worldwide. During the 1970s, the decade of the last Ecuadorian military

dictatorship, Hipólito Alvarado (b. 1934), Agustín Vulgarín (1938–86), Euler Granda (b. 1935), Antonio Preciado (b. 1941), Humberto Vinueza (b. 1942), Julio Pazos (b. 1944), Sonia Manzano (b. 1947), Fernando Nieto (b. 1947), Javier Ponce (b. 1948), and Hernán Zúñiga (b. 1950, best known as a painter) were actively involved in developing and experimenting with new forms of poetry. The voice of the poor, represented through the use of urban colloquial lang. such as that of Guayaquil, was a special concern of the group *Sicoseo*, with Nieto as its mentor and leading figure.

The poetry of two members of Sicoseo—Fernando Balseca (b. 1959) and Jorge Martillo (b. 1957)—as well as that of Maritza Cino (b. 1957), Edwin Madrid (b. 1961), Eduardo Morán (b. 1957), Roy Sigüenza (b. 1958), and Diego Velasco (b. 1958) belongs to the 1980s. These poets were highly influenced by Ecuadorian predecessors but also by their times: the return of democracy to Ecuador, the end of national and international communist aspirations, and the impact of postmod. culture.

Among the dozens of new poets whose work has appeared in recent years are Siomara España (b. 1976), Luis Alberto Bravo (b. 1979), Augusto Rodríguez (b. 1979), Alex Tupiza (b. 1979), Victor Vimos (b. 1985), Ana Minga (b. 1983), and Dina Bellrham (1984–2011). They have been actively involved in public literary events and exchanges with poets from other countries and are the most innovative voices of their groups (*Buseta de papel, Reverso*), making extensive use of blog writing and integration of poetry with the visual arts (Iturburu and Levitin).

*See* COLONIAL POETICS; INDIGENOUS AMERICAS, POETRY OF THE; SPANISH AMERICA, POETRY OF.

■ V. E. Molestina, *Lira Ecuatoriana* (1866); J. A. Echeverría, *Nueva lira ecuatoriana* (1879); J. L. Mera, *Ojeada histórico-crítica sobre la poesía ecuatoriana* (1893); E. Anderson Imbert and E. Florit, *Literatura hispanoamericana* (1970); O. H. Benavides, *The Politics of Sentiment: Imagining and Remembering Guayaquil* (1970); J. Franco, *An Introduction to Spanish-American Literature* (1975); *Tapestry of the Sun: An Anthology of Ecuadorian Poetry*, ed. F. Iturburu and A. Levitin (2009).

F. ITURBURU

**EDDA.** The two 13th-c. Icelandic eddas share a backward-looking, collecting aspect, ancient pagan mythic contents, and a literary-historical relationship; yet the *Prose Edda* and the *Poetic Edda* contrast sharply as literary works and often constitute different fields of research.

The appellation derives from a single sentence in an early 14th-c. Uppsala ms.: "This book is called Edda; Snorri Sturluson composed it. . . ." *Edda* is indistinguishable from the common noun meaning "great grandmother" and so may refer to the hoary age of the tales. But the purpose of the *Prose Edda* (also called *Younger Edda* or *Snorri's Edda*) is cultural renewal. Snorri (ca. 1178–1241), the best-known author from the most vital period of Icelandic lit., aimed to teach younger generations the poetics of the intricate traditional verse, chiefly the type now known as *skaldic*. Despite its cultural specificity, the *Prose Edda* resembles other Icelandic treatises on *grammatica,* and continental impulses have been convincingly asserted. Finished 1220–23 and structured in four parts, it teaches metrics (102 different named stanzas), poetic diction (esp. *kennings), and most famously mythological background; this is couched in a brilliant narrative dialogue that distances pagan stories from the contemp. Christian audience. The Prologue further sets a euhemerizing Christian scene for the whole; but Snorri's authorship is disputed.

When the main ms. of the *Poetic Edda* (Codex Regius 2365 4to; c. 1270) was rediscovered in the 17th c., scholars deemed it the probable chief source of the *Prose Edda* and transferred the name *Edda*; thus, the *Poetic Edda* is also called *The Elder Edda* (or, following an early misattribution, *Sæmund's Edda*). The *Poetic Edda* is an anthol. of some 29 poems (several composite) and prose transitions; the first 11, telling *myths, are ordered by the principal god concerned—Odin, Freyr, Thor, and minor divinities. The manuscript's second section arranges *heroic poems according to supposed chronology of events. A fragmentary second ms. (AM 748 4to; 14th c.) is unordered. Besides mythological and heroic narrative, *gnomic material occurs in both sections of the *Poetic Edda*. Of the four meters used, one, "old lore meter" (*fornyrðislag*), is closely matched in OE, OHG, and Old Saxon and so stems from Germanic antiquity. The poems are variously dated 9th to 13th cs., but as products of an oral period and oral transmission, they are not dateable with precision. The ms. opens with a poem of great beauty, mystery, and cultural importance, *Völuspá* (The Sybil's Prophecy), a sweeping survey of the origin and end of the universe, perhaps composed toward the end of the pagan era (late 10th c.). As a whole the mythic and heroic material of the *Poetic Edda* belongs to the most precious intellectual heritage of early Europe; the *Prose Edda* overlays such cultural-historical value with superb self-conscious artistry of a fully literate Christianity.

*See* GERMANIC PROSODY, NORSE POETRY, ORAL POETRY.

■ S. Sturluson, *Edda*, trans. A. Faulkes (1987); J. Kristjánsson, *Edda and Saga* (1988) and *The Poetic Edda*, trans. C. Larrington (1996); T. Gunnell, "Eddic Poetry," *A Companion to Old Norse-Icelandic Literature and Culture*, ed. R. McTurk (2005)—*see also* other relevant chapters.

J. HARRIS

## EGYPT, POETRY OF

I. The Old Kingdom (ca. 2750–2260 BCE)
II. The Middle Kingdom (ca. 2134–1782 BCE)
III. The New Kingdom (ca. 1570–1070 BCE)
IV. The Coptic Period (284–640 CE)
V. Poetry in Arabic (640–present)

Poetry in Egypt passed through epochal changes in langs.: the ancient Egyptian, the Coptic, and the Ar. Whatever continuity there may be has less to do with any constant poetic heritage than with the common history and psychology of the Egyptian people.

The ancient Egyptian era is subdivided into three periods.

**I. The Old Kingdom (ca. 2750–2260 BCE).** We can suppose that, in addition to the poetry written in heightened lang. by educated scribes, there existed a less sophisticated "poetry," which was simple and humble, represented in the singing of the working people in accompaniment to their work.

The poetry in elevated langs. can hold place beside the achievements of the Egyptians in the artistic and technical spheres. They took pleasure in giving artistic shape to their songs, tales, and a world of contemplation extending beyond the quotidian routine and religion (Erman).

All that scribes wrote falls into short lines of equal length. Knowing nothing about their sound, we can regard them as verse, but their *meter remains unknown. It is generally supposed, however, that there are verses esp. characterized by the free *rhythm. In the early 1970s, Assmann argued that it was necessary to view Egyptian lit. (esp. poetry) not only as an instrument for the systematizations of religious or social rules but also as autonomous cultural discourse. Lichtheim (1973) based her literary classification on three categories: free prose; poetry (esp. characterized by the use of *parallelism or a mixed genre she calls "systematically structured speech"); and orational style. Egyptian literary texts were not read silently by individuals but were recited on special occasions.

Of the old poetry, little survived. What remains is only formulas and religious *hymns (songs of praise, chorales, *carols, *psalms). They are spirited and suggestive. The pyramid texts contain a collection of ancient formulas concerned with the destiny of the blessed dead kings, hymns, and banquet songs glorifying the deceased (Hassan).

During the fifth dynasty (2750–2625 BCE), the autobiography acquired its characteristics: a self-portrait in words mingling the real and the ideal, and emphatically eulogistic. The instructions in wisdom are a major literary genre created in the Old Kingdom (Lichtheim 1973).

**II. The Middle Kingdom (ca. 2134–1782 BCE).** Egypt's cl. age introduced extensive literary works in a variety of genres with accomplished command of forms. In the composition known as *The Eloquent Peasant*, rich in *metaphors and other poetic *imagery, the art of fine speaking was made to serve the defense of justice. Hymns to the gods are a close relation to the biblical psalms, and hymns to the kings were expressed in emotionally charged poems. *The Story of Sinuhe*, the crown jewel of Middle Kingdom lit., employs three styles: prose, poetry, and oration. The narration is interspersed with three poems, each being an example of a genre. Other genres include coffin texts and didactic writing. The so-called coffin texts were written in the intermediate period between the Old and Middle Kingdoms. Coffins of nonroyal well-to-do persons were inscribed with spells designed to protect the dead against the perils of the netherworld. Didactic lit. (wisdom and the genre of instruction) was not just the guidelines of a father to his son but the contemplation of profound problems of the human condition.

The theme of national distress or even human torment was only a literary topos that required no basis in society ("The Complaints of Khakheperr-Sonb"). The author addresses his complaints to his heart, and poetic elaboration uses overstatements.

In the "Satire of the Trades," a father instructs his son in the duties and rewards of the scribal profession, ridiculing the other trades. The composition is in the orational style.

**III. The New Kingdom (ca. 1570–1070 BCE).** One characteristic of ancient Egyptian poetry in general is the integrating of elements from different genres such as teachings, laments, eulogies, and oral compositions. But the *epic form appears for the first time in the Kadesh Battle inscriptions of Ramses II in the long section known as the *Poem*. Hymns to the gods are another genre in which the New Kingdom went beyond the Middle, depicting new trends of religiosity: the god of all who is accessible to the pious individual. A large number of hymns are addressed to the sun god. A qualitative change, the doctrine of the sole god worked out by Amonhotep IV, Akhenaten's monotheistic teachings, followed.

*The Book of the Dead* is the continuation of the coffin texts. Instead of being inscribed on coffins, the spells are now written on papyrus scrolls, grouped into chapters and accompanied by vignettes (Lichtheim 1976).

Although *lyric poetry was well developed in the Middle Kingdom, love lyrics seem to be a creation of the New Kingdom. Love poems are rich in elaborate puns, metaphors, and rare words. Calling them *love poems*, rather than *love songs*, emphasizes their literary origin. The lovers referred to each other as brothers and sisters. The poems have the conceptual accessibility and the pithiness of lang.

**IV. The Coptic Period (ca. 284–640 CE).** In the earliest stage of Christianity, poetry and religion were rather coextensive, but at a later stage, poetry separated itself to some extent from religion. Drama also separated itself from liturgy. The relation between religion and poetry, however, was closest in the lyric. The lyric expressed the individual's sense of awe, wonder, or guilt in the presence of the sacred. Mystic poets used erotic metaphors to express their epiphanies.

The Coptic lang. and literary trad. use familiar, simple, and direct expressions inspired by the Bible. The influence of the NT can be found not only in the ideas but also in symbols and *diction.

**V. Poetry in Arabic (640–present).** In 640 CE, the forces of Islam conquered Egypt, and some Arab tribes settled in Egypt. Their poets produced mainly vainglorious poems in meter and rhyme, part of the collective trad. However, Egyptian poetry developed historically under political and social conditions different from those in many Arab countries, and it changed in isolation. Egypt attracted many Arab poets in pursuit of rewards and settlement. Many remarkable Arab poets visited Egypt, among whom were Jameel Bothaaina (d. 701) and Kothayer Azza (ca. 660–723), two poets of platonic love; and Abū Nuwās (756–814) and Abū Tammām (788–845). Under the reign of Tulunides (868–905), Egypt had many poets, e.g., al-Kassem ben Yehia Almaryamy (d. 928) and al-Hussain Ibn Abel-Salam (d. 871). The great poet al-Bohtory (b. ca. 821) praised Ahmed Ibn Tulun and his successor. After ending his relation with his patron Saif Al-Dawlah in 951, the great Ar. poet al-Mutanabbī (915–65) came to Cairo and lavishly praised the ruler Kafur. When the latter did not respond to the poet's political ambitions, al-Mutanabbī fled at night and cruelly satirized him.

In later centuries, Ibn Maṭrouh (1196–1251), Bahāʾ al-dīn Zuhayr (1186–1258), Ibn Nubatah al Misri (1287–1366) and Ṣafī al-Din al-Ḥillī (d. 1349) made Cairo an important cultural center.

The poetic genre that had dominated poetry was *eulogy, which was initially meant to depict the ideal image of the perfect man. Soon the *panegyric lost much of its credibility, and the genre became imitative, repetitious, and tedious.

After the caliphate disintegrated, small regions were governed by many minor rulers, many of whom did not speak Ar. and had no interest in poetry. Over long periods, poetry stagnated; artificial embellishments and wordplay took the place of serious concerns. This kind of poetry was contemporaneous with enduring experiments in Sufi and religious poetry, a prominent representative of which was Ibn al-Fārid (ca. 1181–1235). His mystical poetry was characterized by its rich imagery of symbolic wine and love. Al-Būṣīrī (ca. 1212–96) wrote the "Qaṣīdat al-Burdah" (Mantle Ode), a luminous *ode in praise of the Prophet.

Bahāʾ al-dīn Zuhayr, born in Mecca, spent most of his life in Egypt. He was a favorite of the Ayyubid ruler al-Malek al-Ṣaleh. His poems were lucid, simple, and very close to spoken lang.

Egyptian cultural life was roused from its lethargy by Napoleon's expedition of 1798, with little immediate effect on poetry. Mohamed Ali's cultural innovations were in the sphere of education. Egyptian students were sent to study in France; the Bulaq printing press was founded; and Enlightenment books were ordered to be trans. leading to an important trans. movement and a shift in readership, which was confined earlier to the traditional Islamic scholars (Starkey). A major role in the devel. of the literary revival was played by the press.

A great part of Ar. poetry had declined from the fall of Baghdad in 1258 to the Fr. occupation of Egypt in 1798. Mahmoud Sami al-Barudi (1835–1904) tried to restore the style, spirit, and trads. of the great Ar. poets. This was possible only through the availability of eds. of their collections of poems by the printing press. The Eur. concept of *neoclassicism*, however, does not apply to al-Barudi and his successors, Ahmad Shawqī (1869–1932) and Ḥāfez Ibrāhīm (1871–1932). Al-Barudi wrote mainly in the manner of pre-Islamic poets about love, war, and desert life in a tribal heroic society. At his best, he was a conscious innovator with an ability to express vividly his subjective experiences through traditional idioms.

After Al-Barudi, it is possible to speak of a school that included Shawqī, Ḥāfez, Ismail Sabri (1854–1923), Ali al-Jarem (1881–1949), and others, although it was a school without theoretical foundations. The trad. considered the poet as the spokesman of his nation, the enlargement of his tribe, which was a function long lost (Badawi). Shawqī, the *poet laureate, initially composed panegyrical poems on official occasions. The Brit. authorities exiled him; he went to Spain, where he reflected his deep nostalgia for Egypt. After his return, he expressed the popular attitude toward national and social subjects and refused to be the mouthpiece of the court. During this period, he wrote most of his poetic dramas. He used the idioms and imagery of traditional Ar. poetry to address contemp. social, cultural, and political concerns. The critic Taha Hussain described him and comparable poets as mere revivalists, but in 1927 he was called the Prince of Poets by fellow Arab poets.

A great Lebanese poet, Khalīl Muṭrān (1872–1949), who settled in Egypt, was one of the first Arab romantic poets to create new themes and imagery, in addition to his full mastery of conventional poetic diction. In Egypt, he had many admirers, among them many prominent romantic poets such as Ibrāhīm Nājī (1898–1953), 'Alī Maḥmūd Ṭāhā (1901–49), and Saleh Jawdat (1912–76), who all joined the Apollo group founded by Aḥmad Zakī abu-Shādī (1892–1955) in 1932. The group included members writing in different styles, but all worked for "lofty poetical ideals," as the group stated in its *manifesto. Abu-Shādī was not considered a great poet, but he was a versatile experimenter with *muwashshaḥ* forms (a postclassical form of Ar. poetry arranged in stanzas), Eng. *free verse and *sonnets, but with no followers.

The movement called *al-Dīwān* (The Register) appeared at the turn of the 20th c. in opposition to Shawqī and Ḥāfez. It aspired to be a new direction that endeavored to establish a genuine Egyptian lit. under the influence and guidance of Western literary romantic ideas. This trend was defended by Mahmoud Abbas al-'Aqqād (1889–1964), Abdel-Raḥmān Shukrī (1886–1958), and Ibrāhīm Abdel-Kader al-Māzinī (1889–1949). Their so-called revolution tried to find the appropriate form to express the Egyptian national spirit, but it did not lead to new forms: the Ar. literary trad. dominated the poetry of this movement.

After World War II, there were attempts to formulate new forms of poetic discourse to express new national and popular requirements. Sometimes, these attempts were under the banner of what was called "commitment," i.e., commitment to revolutionary subjects of independence and social justice, whose prominent contributors were the leftist poets Kamal Abdel-Halim

(1926–2004) and Abdel-Rahman al-Sharqawi (1920–87). A leading figure in that movement was Fouad Haddad (1927–85), who wrote in colloquial Ar. Those poets published in leftist magazines, e.g., *Almalayeen* (Millions) and *Al Kateb* (The Writer), as well as in other cultural reviews of daily newspapers. The movement for what was called *modern poetry* was wider than the commitment in themes, incl. quotidian and existential experiences. It included among many poets Ṣalāḥ 'Abd al-Sabūr (1931–81), Ahmad Ā. Hijazy (b. 1935), and Muḥammad Miftāḥ al-Faytūrī (b. 1936?). Abd-Alsabour wrote dramatic pieces on the theme of cosmic distress. Hijazy was the poet of the Arab revolution, though his views radically changed later. What was known as mod. poetry in Egypt was mainly based on the single foot (*taf'ela*) rather than the complete meter (*baḥr*) and on a variety of rhymes.

The generation that followed in the 1960s included Amal Dunqul (1940–83), Mohamad Afifi Matar (1935–2010), and Mohamad Ibrahim Abu-Sinna (b. 1937), who were of different orientations. Dunqul was popular for his poems against the official politics. Abu-Sinna is known for his revolutionary romantic verses. Afifi Matar was known for his significant contribution to experimental poetry and his influence on the next generation of poets.

The 1970s were the years of the defeat of the Arab national project after the war with Israel and the occupation of Arab territories in 1967. Two groups of poets issued collective manifestos in Egypt: *Idạ̄'a 77* (Illumination) and *Aswât* (Voices). These groups were similar in experimental orientation and their rejection of the traditional canon. They set themselves apart from the poets of the 1950s and 1960s and opposed the status quo. Among the Idạ̄'a group were Helmy Salem (b. 1951), Hassan Tilib (b. 1944), Ref'ât Sallam (b. 1951), Mahmoud Nasim (b. 1955) and Sha'ban Youssef (b. 1955). The Aswât group included Abdul-Mon'im Ramadan (b. 1951), Ahmad Taha (b. 1948), Âbdul Maqsud Âbdul-Karim (b. 1956), Mohamed Eid Ibrahim (b. 1955), and Mohamed Sulaiman (b. 1946), who also experimented with *prose poems in the 1990s. Their poetry abandoned ideology and nationalism, focusing on personal and relative truth. Other Egyptian poets, such as Mohamed Salih (1940–2009), Fathy Abdulla (b. 1957), Fatma Qandil (b. 1958), and Ali Mansour (b. 1956), did not belong to either of the two groups but became prominent for their prose poems (Mehrez). Since the 1990s, the poetry scene has been characterized by the predominance of the prose poem.

■ M. Lichtheim, *Ancient Egyptian Literature*, v. 1: *The Old and Middle Kingdoms* (1973), foreword by A. Loprieno (2006); M. Badawi, *A Critical Introduction to Modern Arabic Poetry* (1975); S. Mureh, *Modern Arabic Poetry, 1800–1970* (1976)—devel. of its forms and themes; J. Brugman, *An Introduction to the History of Modern Arabic Literature in Egypt* (1984); S. Mehrez, "Experimentation and the Institution, The Case of Idạ̄'a 77 and Aswât," *Alif* 11 (1991); A. Erman, *Ancient Egyptian Poetry and Prose*, trans. A. Blackman (1995); S. Hassan, *Encyclopedia of Ancient Egypt*, v. 17 and 18:

*Ancient Egyptian Literature* (2000)—in Ar.; J. Assman, *The Mind of Egypt: History and Meaning in the Time of the Pharaohs*, trans. A. Jenkins (2002); S. Deif, *History of Arabic Literature*, v. 7: *Epoch of States and Emirates, Egypt* (2003)—in Ar.; R. Allen, "The Post-classical Period: Parameters and Preliminaries," *Cambridge History of Arabic Literature: Arabic Literature in the Post-Classical Period*, ed. R. Allen and D. S. Richards (2006); M. Lichtheim, *Ancient Egyptian Literature*, v. 2: *The New Kingdom*, 2d. ed., foreword by H. Fischer-Elfert (2006); P. Starkey, *Modern Arabic Literature* (2006).

I. FATHY

**EISTEDDFOD** (bardic session or assembly; pl. *eisteddfodau*). A main feature of Welsh literary activity that can be traced back with certainty to the 15th c. and perhaps to the bardic festival held by Lord Rhys in 1176 at Cardigan. The early eisteddfod was an assembly of the guild or order of bards, convened under the aegis of a distinguished patron, and in the 16th c. even under royal commission. Its chief function was to regulate the affairs of the profession, such as the establishment of metrical rules and the issuance of licenses to those who had completed the prescribed stages of their apprenticeship. Awards were also granted for outstanding achievements in poetry and music. The most important of these eisteddfodau were Carmarthen (ca. 1450) and Caerwys (1523 and 1567). Decay then set in, and the institution degenerated to the tavern eisteddfodau of the 18th c. After a period of decline, the eisteddfod was revived during the 19th c., and Welsh immigrants brought the trad. with them to North America, Argentina, and Australia. Today, the National Eisteddfod of Wales is a cultural festival of wide range and influence that provides for poetry, prose, drama, massed choirs, and other vocal and instrumental music. It has given much-needed patronage and publicity to poetry and has enabled several important literary critics to impose standards and to mold literary taste. Since the 20th c., eisteddfodau promoting indigenous linguistic, musical, and literary trads. have been held in Cornwall, the Channel Islands, and other countries. While not directly related to the Welsh eisteddfod trad., the Scottish Royal National Mod fulfills a similar function in Scotland.

*See* WELSH POETRY.

■ E. J. Evans, *The History of the Eisteddfod*, diss., University of Wales (1913); T. Parry, *Eisteddfod y Cymry: The Eisteddfod of Wales*, trans. R. T. Jenkins (1943); Stephens.

D. M. LLOYD; B. BRUCH

**EKPHRASIS** (pl. *ekphraseis*). Detailed description of an image, primarily visual; in specialized form, limited to description of a work of visual art. *Ekphrasis* is a term proper first to cl. rhet. but becomes a key part of the art of description in poetry, historiography, romance, and novels. As Hagstrum contends, ekphrasis probably entered mod. poetry from Gr. romance. While mod. ekphrasis has never belonged exclusively to a single genre, certain kinds of ekphraseis have become associated with particular styles and forms—the *blason and the Petrarchan lyric, e.g.

Ekphrasis in rhet. was used to focus and amplify emotions, with the rhetor lingering over key aspects of an image in order to persuade his audience (Cicero, *De oratore*; Quintilian, *Institutio oratoria*). *Ekphrasis* in this regard is often conflated with *enargeia, Aristotle's term not just for visual detail, but for *tropes of animation (*Rhetoric* 3.11.2). Ekphraseis were also a crucial part of the rhetor's method for memorizing a speech. All a rhetor's examples or major points of argument could be "placed" in imagination in a particular part of a mental image—the 12 houses of the zodiac, imagined in a wheel, were often used for this purpose. The rhetor then needed to recall only the image to have access to the items stored there. Detailed mental images were a crucial part of this art of memory from Gorgias (*Encomium of Helen*) forward, and in this context, emotionally powerful images were particularly important. The formative example here is of the poet Simonides of Ceos, who was able to identify the victims of a building collapse by remembering exactly where they had been seated during dinner (Cicero, *De oratore*). In the med. period, the *ars memoria* have a rich hist., with several texts devoted to describing and understanding the *imagery deemed necessary to remembering (Thomas Bradwardine, *De memoria artificial adquirenda*, among others).

The poetic representation of works of visual art was promoted by the trad. most often identified with Horace of *ut pictura poesis* (as is painting, so is poetry). Theories of the sister arts held not only that poetry and painting (as well as music) would present the same subject matter but that their moral content, instructional value, and affective potential were parallel. While the sister-arts trad. has never disappeared, the status of the poetic image has undergone significant shifts. During the Reformation, as Gilman shows, iconoclastic approaches to worship made ekphraseis both dangerous and desirable. Poetic ekphraseis took a reader's attention from exterior, potentially idolatrous imagery and pointed inward to the mind and soul; however, the images of poetry were understood to be deeply powerful and thus required great care in their use. In the 20th c., the imagist poets sought to renew the power of poetry to set objects before the reader's eyes and used stripped-down forms of description to attempt to create a sense of visual immediacy (see IMAGISM).

The most famous ancient examples of ekphrastic descriptions of art were frequently imitated in med. and Ren. writing and include Homer's description of Achilles' shield in the *Iliad*, the shield of Aeneas in Virgil's *Aeneid*, and the tapestries of Arachne and Minerva in Ovid's *Metamorphoses*. Buildings have also been important subjects, as with John Milton's description of Pandaemonium in *Paradise Lost* or with the Ren. trad. of the *country house poem. More rarely, ekphraseis may also represent music, as in Thomas Mann's *Magic Mountain* or John Dryden's "Alexander's Feast."

There is a rich variety of ekphrastic description beyond those of works of art, as may be seen in the med.

*dream vision, the Petrarchan blason of a woman's beauty, or in *emblem poems. Landscape description is one of the more common forms of ekphrasis, and gardens are also a rich subject (Andrew Marvell's "The Garden" is a particularly powerful example, where the last stanza pictures a parterre with a sundial and zodiac). *Georgic poetry, with its representations of labor, is also home to ekphrastic description of landscape and its alterations.

Ekphraseis serve many (nonexclusive) purposes. Some are virtuoso displays of poetic skill intended to align the author with the cl. trad., esp. with Virgil (as part of the poetic apprenticeship identified with Virgil's movement from *pastoral to georgic and then *epic). With the med. *ars memoria*, images were understood to have mental power, allowing vast amounts of information to be collated and stored in the mind; detailed description was essential to this function. Some images have almost magical meanings, as with elements of dream visions or with Gnostic writings. Other ekphraseis, as with emblem poems, are offered as subjects of religious meditation (George Herbert, Richard Crashaw, John Donne). Religious iconography may also determine which visual elements in a poem receive detailed description (as with the pentangle in *Sir Gawain and the Green Knight*); other objects or places may be carefully drawn in order to emphasize allegorical meaning (Gawain's armor) or ritual (Gawain's hunt—some ekphraseis in *Gawain* serve multiple purposes). Some ekphraseis are used to emphasize cultural norms or exemplary kinds of virtue; in the country house poem, e.g., the landowner's hospitality, power, taste, and lineage are made manifest by descriptions of his property (Andrew Marvell's "Appleton House" or Ben Jonson's "To Penshurst"). At times, ekphraseis are hidden, used as puzzles or to indicate esoteric knowledge, as in Donne's "A Valediction: Forbidding Mourning," where a compass sketches out a circle with a pinpoint at its center—the alchemical symbol for gold—while the poem evokes gold "to airy thinness beat." While ekphraseis perhaps most often are of objects of beauty, the grotesque and ugly are represented as well (the contents of London's gutters in Jonathan Swift's "A Description of a City Shower" or the decayed face of the prostitute in his "A Beautiful Young Nymph Going to Bed").

Ekphraseis play important roles in novels, too. They may be used in many of the ways listed above, but they also come into new prominence with the realist novel. The proliferating objects of the mod. world populate the 19th-c. novel, and the details of 19th-c. interiors or the clutter of the city form the backbone of realism. In novels as well as in poetry, ekphrastic descriptions also may be used to create foci that bring subjective experience into play, so that the emotions of a character emerge through description of the external world. This is often the case in epistolary fiction, as with Belford's description of Clarissa's prison in Samuel Richardson's *Clarissa* or the landscapes of Charlotte Smith's *Desmond*.

The psychological and neurological mechanisms underlying ekphraseis are becoming better understood, as cognitive science has begun to explore imagery across the senses. While most investigations have focused on visual imagery, there have also been investigations of the imagery of sound, taste, touch, and smell, as well as on effects, like those of motion, that involve combinations of imagery from across the five senses (Scarry, Starr).

*See* AFFECTIVE FALLACY, COGNITIVE POETICS, DESCRIPTIVE POETRY, ICONOLOGY, IMAGERY, LANDSCAPE POEM, PAINTING AND POETRY.

■ Curtius; F. Yates, *The Art of Memory* (1965); M. Krieger, "Ekphrasis and the Still Movement of Poetry; or *Laokoön* Revisited," *The Poet as Critic*, ed. F. McDowell (1967); E. Gilman, *Iconoclasm and Poetry in the English Reformation* (1986); J. Hagstrum, *The Sister Arts* (1987); W.J.T. Mitchell, *Iconology* (1987); J. Hollander "The Poetics of Ekphrasis," *Word and Image* 4 (1988); M. Carruthers, *The Book of Memory* (1990); J.A.W. Heffernan, *Museum of Words: The Poetics of Ekphrasis from Homer to Ashbery* (1993); M. Doody, *The True Story of the Novel* (1996); M. Carruthers, *The Craft of Thought* (1998); E. Scarry, *Dreaming by the Book* (1999); *The Medieval Craft of Memory*, ed. M. Carruthers and J. Ziolkowski (2002); E. Freedgood, *The Ideas in Things* (2006); C. Wall, *The Prose of Things* (2006); G. G. Starr, "Multisensory Imagery," *The Johns Hopkins Handbook of Cognitive Cultural Studies*, ed. L. Zunshine (2010).

G. G. STARR

**ELECTRONIC POETRY.** Also known as e-poetry, digital poetry, new-media poetry, hypertext poetry, and computer poetry, all but the last of which have been used more or less interchangeably. Whereas once computer poetry might have been assumed to denote combinatory texts automatically generated from the formal rules and logic of a computer program (a practice dating back to the 1950s), the shift to electronic poetry is indicative of the much wider spectrum of creative activity now taking place, with poets using personal computers as platforms for compositions intended to be encountered and experienced in native digital format. Electronic poetry as it is discussed here should, therefore, not be confused with poetry that is only incidentally distributed through electronic media, such as a poem reproduced in the online ed. of a magazine or review; rather, electronic poetry seeks to exploit the unique capabilities of computers and networks to provide a text whose elements and behaviors would not "translate" to the printed page.

Electronic poems typically include one or more of the following: multimedia, animation, sound effects or soundtracks, reader interaction in the form of choices or other participatory features, and automated behaviors. Electronic poetry can exist in a networked environment such as the World Wide Web where it is accessed via a browser, or it can take the form of standalone works that are installed either as software or (even) as room-sized immersive environments. There are hundreds if not thousands of e-poets working today, there are workshops and conferences devoted to the practice, and there are (electronic) jours. and collections as well as dedicated competitions to promote and disseminate the work. Public readings and "open-mouse" events are increasingly common. Some poets identify themselves exclusively as e-poets, while others see electronic experimentation as merely one element of their writing practice. Electronic poetry has been written in Eng., Fr., Sp., Ger., It., Rus., Chinese, Korean, and undoubtedly other langs. Among non-Eng. writers, there has been a particularly important trad. in France, notably the work of Philippe Bootz and the L.A.I.R.E. group that founded the electronic jour. *Alire: A Relentless Literary Investigation* in 1989. The Writing Machine Collective is a more recent Hong Kong-based group that has produced innovative and dynamic work.

There is no way to unify or summarize the diversity of electronic poetry under a common method or theme; some of it is whimsical, some of it serious with high-literary pretensions; some of it is narrative, some of it is confessional, and some of it is self-referential and stochastic in the trad. of the 20th-c. avant garde. All electronic poets, however, would surely admit to some level of fascination with digital technology and the way in which its formal logics can be superimposed upon that other formal system par excellence, lang. John Cayley's *windsound* (1999), which introduced his technique of transliteral morphing, is exemplary here. Cayley's poem supposes grids of legible texts, one atop the other, and exposes the process of transformation by which one morphs into another through looping letter replacements. Visually and aurally, the experience of *windsound* is that of watching constellations of letters appear on a black canvas, coalescing into individual words and complete lines. A computer-generated voice (actually multiple voices) reads the generated text over the sound of wind and other effects; as the voice reads, the text is subtlety shifting, creating the illusion of constant motion, like wind (perhaps) over water. The piece is approximately 25 minutes in length.

The ability to incorporate time as an element of textual composition is, in fact, one of the most pronounced features of electronic poetry, since, unlike poetry printed on the page, the author can maintain some control over the pace of a reader's progress through the text. Brian Kim Stefans's "The Dreamlife of Letters" (2000), a remix of an e-mail message originally authored by Rachel Blau DuPlessis, thus uses the popular animation tool Flash to create a series of kinetic and concrete texts that follow an alphabetical progression. The reader is merely a spectator. David Knoebel's "click poetry," as he calls it, employs somewhat different conventions. In "A Fine View," the reader follows a brief narrative of roofers taking a smoke break amid the rafters of a half-completed job; the text scrolls toward the viewer, who must read more rapidly than is perhaps comfortable in order to take it all in before it disappears off the edges of the screen—there is no

way to pause or rewind. We then see that the "reader," in fact, occupies the position of a cigarette butt, falling through the rafters (like the absent compatriot whose story they tell) toward a concrete foundation below. The rafters, we recognize, are the lines of text themselves.

Electronic poetry is no less material or embodied than other forms of poetry; indeed, it is arguably more so, since any electronic poem will be embedded amid complex layers of technologies and producers. Just as poets have repeatedly responded to the intro. of new writing technologies—such as the typewriter—so too do electronic poets engage with new and emerging software tools and data formats, often bending or breaking the technology as they seek to exploit its capabilities for maximum effect while simultaneously commenting—self-reflexively—on the properties of the medium. Jim Rosenberg's ongoing series of experiments with diagrammatic texts (since the late 1960s) have explored a variety of electronic media and formats, incl. HyperCard, HTML, and Java. Daniel C. Howe and Aya Karpinska's "open.ended" (2004) uses the Java programming lang. to present the reader with two graphical cubes rendered one inside the other; the reader is able to rotate and spin the faces of the cubes to reveal layers of shifting text written on each, yielding compositions of indeterminate scope—one may choose to restrict one's reading to the text of a single face or explore the cubes, whose content is constantly changing, at greater depth.

While electronic poetry's native habitat is the computer, occasionally poets also seek to create a fuller or more immersive environment for their work. William Gibson's "Agrippa" (1992) was originally included on a diskette embedded at the back of an artist's book of the same name published by Kevin Begos Jr. with etchings by the artist Dennis Ashbaugh; famously, Gibson's text was programmed to encrypt itself after a single reading, although the poem has long since been transcribed and posted to the Internet. Stephanie Strickland's *V: WaveSon.nets / Losing L'una* is an "invertible book" published in 2002, with a URL at its center leading to the third leg of the composition, *V: Vniverse*, available only online as an interactive work. Oni Buchanan's *Spring* (2008) includes a CD-ROM that features Flash-animated versions of "The Mandrake Vehicles," a sequence whose print form in the volume explores processes of poetic formation and deformation. Noah Wardrip-Fruin's *Screen* (2002) was designed for a CAVE, a room-sized virtual-reality environment. Texts appear on the walls of the CAVE and appear to approach and recede; the reader can interact with them through gesture and motion, batting them back and forth. *Screen* is, in fact, a collaborative work, involving a small group of poets and programmers, a common occurrence for electronic poetry. As one might imagine, preserving and archiving electronic poetry for posterity is already presenting daunting challenges for librarians and collectors.

Meanwhile, the older practice of computer poetry,

where computers are programmed to generate poetic compositions, is still practiced. Such work tends to be playful, focused more on the pleasures of found or chance texts, rather than on overly earnest attempts to have the machine script poetry that might conceivably pass for human-authored (see FOUND POETRY). This activity also now finds an added dimension in so-called *codework, which appropriates the actual langs. of computer programming for poetic expression. Perl poems, e.g., use the lang. Perl to create texts that are both computationally executable (they can be "run" as valid Perl code) but also lyrically compelling. Writing Perl poetry is popular with professional coders because they find the constraints of the form challenging. "Listen" (1995) by Sharon Hopkins is among the best known and has been published in the *Economist* and the *Guardian*. It begins

```
#!/usr/bin/perl
APPEAL:
listen (please, please);
```

More experimental practitioners of codework, such as Alan Sondheim and Mary-Anne Breeze (Mez), are less interested in producing executable texts than in using code as a vehicle to explore the semantic boundaries of lang. and textuality.

As for the future of electronic poetry, there is no way to predict except to say that it will surely embrace multiple futures. Mobile platforms such as cell phones and iPods are becoming venues for literary experimentation via their texting features. The links, feeds, and tags of "Web 2.0" engage even conventional writers in some highly unorthodox writing practices; poets have even experimented with using the game engines from multiplayer worlds like DOOM and Second Life to provide a repurposed writing environment. What electronic poetry demonstrates above all is perhaps a constant human appetite to make over space, virtual and otherwise, into surfaces suitable for inscription.

*See* COMPUTATIONAL POETICS, CONCRETE POETRY, CYBERTEXT, VISUAL POETRY.

■ **Select Critical Studies:** C. O. Hartman, *Virtual Muse* (1996); L. Pequeño Glazier, *Digital Poetics* (2002); *New Media Poetics,* ed. A. Morris and T. Swiss (2006); C. T. Funkhouser, *Prehistoric Digital Poetry* (2007); N. K. Hayles, *Electronic Literature* (2008); M. G. Kirschenbaum, *Mechanisms* (2008).

■ **Select Poets and Resources:** Alire: http://motsvoir.free.fr/; J. Andrews: http://www.vispo.com/; BeeHive: http://beehive.temporalimage.com/; O. Buchanan, *Spring* (2008); J. Cayley: http://www.shadoof.net/in/; Eastgate Systems: http://www.eastgate.com/; The Electronic Literature Collection, vol. 1 (2006), http://collection.eliterature.org/1/; The Electronic Literature Organization: http://www.eliterature.org; The Electronic Poetry Center: http://epc.buffalo.edu/; The Iowa Review Web: http://research-intermedia.art.uiowa.edu/tirw/; D. Knoebel: http://home.ptd.net/~clkpoet/; J. Nelson: http://www.secrettechnology.com/; Poems That Go: http://www.poemsthatgo.com/; J. Rosenberg: http://

www.well.com/user/jer/; The Writing Machine Collective: http://www.writingmachine-collective.net/.

M. G. KIRSCHENBAUM

**ELEGIAC DISTICH,** elegiac couplet (Gr., *elegeion*). In Gr. poetry, a distinctive meter consisting of a *hexameter followed by an *asynartete combination of two end-shortened dactylic tripodies ( $- \cup \cup - \cup \cup - + - \cup \cup - \cup \cup -$ ). It is, thus, a species of *epode (sense 2), in which the second line (later analyzed as a *pentameter consisting of a central *spondee between pairs of *dactyls and *anapests) gives the distinctive and satisfying effect of medial and final shortening (*catalexis). Originally used by the 6th- and 7th-c. BCE writers Archilochus, Callinus, Tyrtaeus, Theognis, and Mimnermus for a variety of topics and occasions—flute songs, symposiastic and poetic competitions, war songs, dedications, *epitaphs, inscriptions, *laments on love or death—it came to be associated thereafter with only one, i.e., loss or mourning—hence, *elegy in the mod. sense. It seems to embody reflection, advice, and exhortation—essentially "sharing one's thoughts." Threnodies, ritual laments, or cries uttered by professional poets at funerals may also have used the meter.

Outside the "elegiac" context, whether on love or death, the *distich was specifically the meter of *epigrams, esp. after the 4th c., when literary imitations of verse inscriptions were cultivated by the Alexandrian poets. This fixation of meter to genre lasts the longest. Ennius introduced it into Lat. and later the skill of Martial ensured its passage into the Middle Ages. In Lat., the love elegy emerges as a major genre, characterized in the Augustans (Tibullus, Propertius, Ovid) by a preference, not noticeable in Catullus and his Gr. predecessors, for sense pause at the end of each couplet. A further refinement, esp. evident in Ovid and his successors, was the requirement that the final word in the pentameter be disyllabic. In the opening lines of the *Amores*, Ovid jokes that, though he intended to write of things epic—hence, in *hexameters—Cupid first stole a foot from his second line, then supplied the poet with suitable subject matter for the resulting combination of hexameter and pentameter by shooting him with one of his arrows.

In the Middle Ages, the elegiac distich was associated with *leonine verse, where it acquired rhyme. In the Ren., it was imitated, along with other Gr. quantitative meters, and such efforts were revived in the 18th and 19th cs. Examples are found in Eng. in works by Edmund Spenser, Philip Sidney, S. T. Coleridge, Arthur Clough, Charles Kingsley, and A. C. Swinburne; in Ger., by F. G. Klopstock, Friedrich Schiller, J. W. Goethe, and Friedrich Hölderlin; and in It., by Gabriele D'Annunzio. Coleridge's trans. of Schiller's elegiac distich is well known: "In the hexameter rises the fountain's silvery column, / In the pentameter aye falling in melody back." Naturalized into the accentually based prosodies of the vernacular meters, it was imitated in isometric couplets, as in Christopher Marlowe's Ovid, whence it exerted influence on the devel. of the *heroic couplet.

■ R. Reitzenstein, "Epigramm," Pauly-Wissowa, 6.1

(1907); K. Strecker, "Leoninische Hexameter und Pentameter in 9. Jahrhundert," *Neues Archiv für ältere deutsche Geschichtskunde* 44 (1922); C. M. Bowra, *Early Greek Elegists,* 2d ed. (1938); P. Friedländer, *Epigrammata: Greek Inscriptions in Verse from the Beginnings to the Persian Wars* (1948); M. Platnauer, *Latin Elegiac Verse* (1951); L. P. Wilkinson, *Golden Latin Artistry* (1963); T. G. Rosenmeyer, "Elegiac and Elegos," *California Studies in Classical Antiquity* 1 (1968); D. Ross, *Style and Tradition in Catullus* (1969); M. L. West, *Studies in Greek Elegy and Iambus* (1974); A.W.H. Adkins, *Poetic Craft in the Early Greek Elegists* (1984); R. M. Marina Sáez, *La métrica de los epigramas de Marcial* (1998).

T.V.F. Brogan; A. T. Cole

**ELEGIAC STANZA,** elegiac quatrain, heroic quatrain. In Eng., the iambic pentameter quatrain rhymed *abab*. While it had been frequently employed without elegiac feeling or intention by other poets, e.g., Shakespeare in his sonnets and John Dryden in his *Annus Mirabilis,* the term *elegiac stanza* was apparently made popular by its use in Thomas Gray's "Elegy Written in a Country Churchyard" (1750), though, in fact, the association of the *quatrain with *elegy in Eng. appears at least as early as James Hammond's *Love Elegies* (1743) and was employed "almost invariably" for elegiac verse for about a century thereafter (Bate)—cf. William Wordsworth's "Elegiac Stanzas Suggested by Peele Castle."

■ W. J. Bate, *The Stylistic Development of Keats* (1945).

T.V.F. Brogan; S. F. Fogle

# ELEGY

I. History
II. Criticism

**I. History.** In mod. usage, an *elegy* is a poem of loss or mourning. The term is Gr., its initial significance metrical: *elegeia* designates a poem in elegiac *couplets. In antiquity, the meter is used for a range of subjects and styles, incl. the kind of combative, promiscuous love presented in the poetry of Propertius, Tibullus, and Ovid. The popularity and prestige of what is still called Roman love elegy make *elegy* a loose synonym for "love poem" in early mod. usage, though the cl. exemplars are not generally "elegiac" in what becomes the dominant sense of the term. The meter, however, was also popular for *epitaphs, both literal and literary; all the Roman elegists also wrote elegies in the mod. sense, and in antiquity, the metrical term also becomes a synonym for *"lament." Neo-Lat. poets from the 15th-c. on compose new works in elegiac couplets, and attempts are made to transfer the meter to the vernaculars. Among the most successful is J. W. Goethe's, incl. a collection of *Römische Elegien* (1795), scandalously sensual love poems, defiantly unmournful. Some critics (such as J. C. Scaliger in the 16th c.) try to theorize a common ground between Roman love elegy and lament for the dead (both involve *complaints); the popularity of *Petrarchism in the Ren. strengthens a feeling that absence and frustration are central themes in *love poetry; and along these lines, "dire-lamenting elegies" (Shake-speare, *Two Gentlemen of Verona*) can be recommended to a would-be seducer. This composite understanding of the genre, however, is never fully worked out and gradually fades.

The most important cl. models for the later devel. of elegy are *pastoral: the lament for Daphnis (who died of love) by Theocritus, the elegy for Adonis attributed to Bion, the elegy on Bion attributed to Moschus, and another lament for Daphnis in the fifth *eclogue of Virgil. All are stylized and mythic, with hints of ritual; the first three are punctuated by incantatory *refrains. The elegies on Daphnis are staged performances within an otherwise casual setting. Nonhuman elements of the pastoral world are enlisted in the mourning: nymphs, satyrs, the landscape itself. In Virgil, the song of grief is paired with one celebrating the dead man's apotheosis; the poem is usually read as an *allegory on the death and deification of Julius Caesar. Virgil's poem becomes particularly influential and adaptable. In the 9th c., Paschasius Radbertus composes an imitation in which the nuns Galathea and Phyllis sing of a deceased shepherd monk as a figure for Christ. At the prompting of humanism, Ren. poets experiment with the pastoral elegy and use it for a range of personal, political, and symbolic reference. Few collections of pastorals in the Ren. are without at least one elegy, and there are important stand-alone examples, such as Clément Marot's "Eglogue" on the death of Louise of Savoy (1531). John Milton composes two full-fledged pastoral elegies: *Epitaphium Damonis* in Lat., on a close friend (1639), and "Lycidas" in Eng., on a schoolmate (1637). The latter is widely regarded as Milton's first major poetic achievement and the most successful vernacular instance of the genre. It was, nevertheless, sharply criticized in the next century by Samuel Johnson for its artificiality; he speaks for a growing disenchantment with the genre. Major poets, however, can return to it in full dress: P. B. Shelley in "Adonais" (1821) on the shockingly early death of John Keats, W. B. Yeats in "Shepherd and Goatherd" (1918) on an unnamed shepherd who "died in the great war beyond the sea." The presence of the genre can also be felt in less-adorned poems, in the general sense that the countryside is the right place for elegiac feeling (Thomas Gray's "Elegy Written in a Country Churchyard," 1750) or in the arch affirmation of natural sympathy with which W. H. Auden opens his elegy on Yeats (1939).

Pastoral, however, is only a specialized trad. within the wider field of poetic treatments of death and loss. Such poems (which may or may not call themselves elegies) show an immense diversity, within which filiations can be complex. Some important examples are really *sui generis*; among the few unforgettable Eng. poems of the first decade of the 16th c. is John Skelton's *Philip Sparrow,* 1,400 unpredictable lines on the death of a young girl's pet bird. The object in question is usually another person, often specifically identified: an important public figure or someone with a close personal connection to the poet, such as a spouse, lover, parent, child, or friend. Elegies on other poets are particularly common; elegies for oneself are at least as old as Ovid's exile poems. Elegies for groups or classes of people (esp.

those killed in war) date back to the Greeks but become a particular feature of the 20th c. (such as Anna Akhmatova's *Requiem* (1935, pub. 1963) on the "nameless friends" lost in the Stalinist terror of 1935–40). Poems can present themselves as epitaphs or as containing epitaphs, sometimes addressing a visitor to the cemetery (*siste viator*). Even in times that value poetic artifice at its most elaborate, poems of personal grief—such as Henry King's "Exequy" on the dead wife he calls "his matchless never to be forgotten friend" (1634)—can be strikingly direct in their effect. In 20th-c. writing, the appetite for directness becomes conspicuous, at times brutal ("he's dead / the old bastard"; W. C. Williams, "Death" [1930]). It is, however, an equally famous resource of elegies to proceed by complicated indirection. In Chaucer's *The Book of the Duchess* (ca. 1368), occasioned by the death of his patron's wife, the dreaming narrator cannot acknowledge that occasion until the last of the poem's 1,300 lines, long after the reader has divined it. The mourning in Keats's ode "To Autumn" (1819) is almost entirely subliminal and inexplicit, but strong enough to make three stanzas of seasonal description one of the touchstone lyrics in the lang.

Some important elegies are expansive in their reach. In Walt Whitman's "Out of the Cradle Endlessly Rocking" (1860), a child (as in *Philip Sparrow* reacting to the death of a bird) hears from the sea a message of "Death, death, death, death, death" that is also the start of a visionary poetic calling. Paul Valéry's "Le Cimitière marin" (1922) sets an individual attempt at spiritual and intellectual transcendence amid the felt presence of the dead in a seaside graveyard at noon (its text is appropriated by Krzysztof Penderecki for "Dies irae" [1967], an oratorio on Auschwitz). Perhaps the most distinguished 20th-c. poems to call themselves elegies are R. M. Rilke's *Duineser Elegien* (written 1912–22), which move between a sense of insufficiency and loss basic to human consciousness—"And so we live, and are always taking leave"—and a higher order of awareness among beings whom the poet calls "Angels."

**II. Criticism.** Critical thought about elegy has been an attempt to come to grips with this diversity, sometimes inadvertently amplifying it. Despite, e.g., current acknowledgment that they have little claim to the term, a number of poignant OE poems have for 200 years been called *elegies* in a move so closely associated with a sense of their value that the designation is unlikely to change. The prestige and longevity of the genre have increased its variety, and it has often splintered and become unrecognizable to itself; an important "school of elegy," for instance, in early 19th-c. Rus. poetry produced poems that share emotional intimacy and style but little topical focus. A mountain setting is required by the trad. of cl. Ger. elegy identified in Ziolkowski's study of Friedrich Schiller's originary "Der Spaziergang" (1795). Yet wherever we draw the boundaries of kind, some version of elegy is pervasively written about in every lang.

Critics writing in Eng. seem to agree that the topics of loss and death and the speech act of lament char-

acterize the genre; that its mode is primarily *lyric, with certain characteristic generic markers (*apostrophe, exclamation, *pathetic fallacy, epideixis, pastoral topoi, *allusion, *epitaph); and that its indigenous moods are sorrow, shock, rage, longing, melancholy, and resolution—often in quick succession. Most literary historians have understood elegy as closely linked to the hist., theory, and decorum of cultural practices of mourning. Pigman's *Grief and Renaissance Elegy* and Sacks's *The English Elegy* are two particularly influential studies, both pub. in 1985, that continue to set questions and topics for later scholars. While studies vary in the extent of their embrace of psychoanalysis or cultural hist., they concur in describing the elegy as, in Pigman's phrase, "a process of mourning." Pigman identifies a shift in Reformation views and practices of mourning with consequences for elegy; Sacks sees the conventions of the genre from Edmund Spenser to Yeats as answerable to psychological needs. Later critics weigh in with some mix of social hist., psychology, and aesthetic analysis. Ramazani registers a protest by mod. elegy against normative cultural models of mourning; Zeiger, Kennedy, and others explore the importance of elegy as a resource for traumatic collective grief over breast cancer, AIDS, and the events of September 11, 2001; Spargo explores the psychological dimension of the form with philosophical attention.

Other puzzles invite attention. Why, if elegy is "a process of mourning," are so many elegies lyrics with little narrative or processional content? Standard definitions of *elegy* can strain against the temporality of lyric. Elegy's recourse to emotion seems incompletely explained by psychological or social models of grief or even by a notion of the poem as expressive. The emotions represented by the poem and the emotional experience that the poem offers to the reader are distinct; their trajectories need not coincide. They can, of course—as when, in a practice shared by other contemp. readers, Queen Victoria and George Eliot annotated the text of Alfred, Lord Tennyson's *In Memoriam* (1850) so that it referred to their own lost loves. Such evidence suggests that elegy is a kind of manual or liturgy for personal use; this function of the genre encouraged criteria such as *sincerity or Johnson's "passion" to dominate critical evaluation of it. Yet such criteria seem ill suited to the power of poems such as "Lycidas," Spenser's "Daphnaida," Whitman's "When Lilacs Last in the Dooryard Bloom'd," and Auden's "In Memory of Sigmund Freud," which lament the deaths of persons who were not, in the standard sense of the term, "mourned" by the authors. Neither do current theories about the genre's purposes, collective or private, account for the numerous elegies of animals, objects, and so forth or for the peculiar ludic uses of the form by poets like Skelton, Emily Dickinson, Robert Burns, and the anonymous author of "Groanes from Newgate, or, An elegy upon Edvvard Dun, Esq. the cities common hangman, who dyed naturally in his bed the 11th of September, 1663."

The publication of elegy awaits further study. Chaucer's ms. *Book of the Duchess* is thought to have been produced for and performed at anniversary memorial events continuing long after the death of the duchess. With the advent of print, volumes of elegy were collected and printed to honor particular deaths (such as the famous volumes for Philip Sidney and the one containing "Lycidas"). Print also facilitated the voluminous appearance of elegy in broadside, and in the 17th c., the form developed what now seems like an incongruous affinity for *acrostics and *anagrams. Cavitch (2002) describes the publication of elegy in early New England with a traveler's report that there was not "one Country House in fifty which has not its Walls garnished with half a Score of these Sort of Poems." The changing forms of publication suggest a different hist. of elegy from what crit. might lead us to expect and also disabuse us of the sense that that hist. has reached any kind of conclusion.

See BLUES, CORONACH, DIRGE, ELEGIAC DISTICH, ELEGIAC STANZA, ENDECHA, EPICEDIUM, GRAVEYARD POETRY, MONODY.

■ E. Z. Lambert, *Placing Sorrow: A Study of the Pastoral Elegy Convention from Theocritus to Milton* (1976); T. Ziolkowski, *The Classical German Elegy 1795–1950* (1980); G. W. Pigman III, *Grief and English Renaissance Elegy* (1985); P. Sacks, *The English Elegy* (1985); C. M. Schenck, *Mourning and Panegyric* (1988); D. Kay, *Melodious Tears: The English Funeral Elegy from Spenser to Milton* (1990); J. Ramazani, *Poetry of Mourning: The Modern Elegy from Hardy to Heaney* (1994); E. Schor, *Bearing the Dead: The British Culture of Mourning from the Enlightenment to Victoria* (1994); W. D. Shaw, *Elegy and Paradox* (1994); M. F. Zeiger, *Beyond Consolation: Death, Sexuality, and the Changing Shapes of Elegy* (1997); M. Homans, *Royal Representations: Queen Victoria and British Culture 1837–1876* (1998); J. Hammond, *The American Puritan Elegy* (2000); M. Cavitch, "Interiority and Artifact: Death and Self-Inscription in Thomas Smith's *Self-Portrait*," *Early American Literature* 37 (2002); R. C. Spargo, *The Ethics of Mourning* (2004); M. Cavitch, *American Elegy* (2007); D. Kennedy, *Elegy* (2007); *The Oxford Handbook of the Elegy*, ed. K. A. Weisman (2010).

G. BRADEN; E. FOWLER

**ELISION** (Lat., "striking out"; Gr., *synaloepha*). In *prosody, the general term for several devices of contraction whereby two syllables are reduced to one. The Gr. term *synaloepha* nowadays tends to be restricted to only one form; other terms formerly used for elision in cl. prosody include *crasis* and *synizesis*. The forms of elision are: (1) *aphaeresis: dropping of a word-initial syllable (vowel); (2) *syncope: dropping of a word-internal syllable; (3) *apocope: dropping of a word-final syllable (vowel); (4) *synaeresis: coalescing of two vowels within a word; and (5) *synaloepha*: coalescing of two vowels across a word boundary, i.e., ending one word and beginning the next. (The corresponding terms for addition of a syllable to the beginning, middle, or end of a word are *prosthesis*, *epenthesis*, and *proparalepsis*, respectively.)

Collectively, these are sometimes called, on the analogy of rhet., the "metric figures" (Elwert); Johann Susenbrotus, e.g., gives a taxonomy, calling the types of elision *metaplasms*, i.e., the class of figures for adding or subtracting a letter or syllable. Elision of whole words or phrases is *ellipsis. Probably at least some of the older terminology is confused, and certainly many prosodists over the centuries have failed to grasp that the reductive processes at work here are normal linguistic ones, not "poetical" devices peculiar to metrical verse. The shortening of words and smoothing out of the alternation of vowels and consonants are both common processes in speech. The opposite of elision is *hiatus.

In Gr., elision, variable in prose but more regular in poetry, is indicated by an apostrophe (') to mark the disappearance of the elided vowel (generally short *alpha*, *epsilon*, and *omikron* as well as the diphthong *ai* occasionally in Homer and in comedy); but when elision occurs in Gr. compound words, the apostrophe is not used. In Lat., a final vowel or a vowel followed by final *m* was not omitted from the written lang.; but as a rule, it was ignored metrically when the next word in the same measure began with a vowel, diphthong, or the aspirate *h*. In the mod. vernaculars, the apostrophe was retained to indicate graphically certain types of elision, but outside these, there is a larger case of words that have syllabically alternate forms in ordinary speech, e.g., *heaven*, which some speakers pronounce as a disyllable, some as a monosyllable. This syllabic variance is, of course, useful to poets who write in syllable-counting meters; thus, Sipe shows that in the overwhelming number of cases, Shakespeare chooses the one or other form of such words, which she terms "doublets," so as to conform to the meter.

There is some presumption that the number of syllables in the word that fits the *scansion of the line will be the number uttered in *performance (reading aloud) of the line. Robert Bridges, however, who has one of the seminal mod. discussions, uses the term *elision* in a special sense, to denote syllables that should be elided for purposes of scansion but not in pronunciation, a theory that divides scansion from performance. Ramsey has termed this "semi-elision," in his crit. of Bridges's position. The problem of poets' alteration of the syllabic structure of their lang. for metrical purposes is far more complex than is usually assumed; indeed, the very problem of determining what was ordinary speech practice at various times in the past itself is very difficult. Most of the hist. of Eng. metrical theory from ca. 1650 to 1925 could be framed in terms of dispute about elision, i.e., syllabic regularity.

■ T. S. Omond and W. Thomas, "Milton and Syllabism," *MLR* 4–5 (1909–10); Bridges; Omond; W. J. Bate, *The Stylistic Development of Keats* (1945); P. Fussell Jr., "The Theory of Poetic Contractions," *Theory of Prosody in 18th-Century England* (1954); A. C. Partridge, *Orthography in Shakespeare and Elizabethan Drama* (1964); Chatman; R. O. Evans, *Milton's Elisions* (1966); J. Soubiran, *L'elision dans la poésie latine* (1966); D. L. Sipe, *Shakespeare's Metrics* (1968); Allen;

P. Ramsey, *The Fickle Glass* (1979), appendix; West; El-
wert, *Italienische.*

T.V.F. BROGAN

**ELLIPSIS** (or *eclipsis*; Gr., "leaving out," "defect";
Lat. *detractio*). The most common term for the class
of figures of syntactic omission (deletion). (Omission
or deletion of syllables for metrical purposes is treated
as *elision). Ellipsis as a genus includes several species:
ellipsis of conjunctions between words is brachylogia,
between clauses, *asyndeton; ellipsis of a verb (in a dif-
ferent sense) is *zeugma; ellipsis of a clause, particularly
the main clause (B) after a subordinate (Y) in a con-
struction such as "If X, then A; if Y then B"—e.g. "If
you will do it, all will be well; if not, . . ."—is anapodo-
ton. These differ from figures such as *aposiopesis, the
dropping of the end of a sentence, leaving it incom-
plete, in that, in ellipsis, the thought is complete; it is
only that a word or words ordinarily called for in the
full construction but not strictly necessary are omitted
(since obvious). This obviousness that makes the omis-
sion possible is, therefore, much facilitated by the use
of *parallelism of syntactic members in the construc-
tion, which explains the importance of such parallelism
for achieving that effect of compression, the hallmark
of the closed *heroic couplet. So Alexander Pope has
"Where wigs [strive] with wigs, // [where] with sword-
knots sword-knots strive" (*The Rape of the Lock* 1.101).

Gr. rhetoricians permitted omission of substan-
tives, pronouns, objects, finite verbs, main clauses, and
(more rarely) clauses; poets since the Ren. have allowed
omission of almost any member so long as the meaning
remains clear (Quintilian, *Institutio oratoria* 9.3.58).
Shakespeare has "And he to England shall along with
you" (*Hamlet* 3.3.4) and "when he's old, cashiered"
(*Othello* 1.1.48). Mod. poets (e.g., Ezra Pound, T. S.
Eliot, W. H. Auden, W. C. Williams) have found el-
lipsis esp. useful for conveying the speed and clipped
form of colloquial speech and for expressing emotion.

*See* SYNTAX, POETIC.

■ E. A. Abbott, *A Shakespearean Grammar* (1886),
279–94—extensive lists of examples; Group μ, 69 ff.;
Corbett—prose examples; E. Rozik, "Ellipsis and the
Surface Structures of Verbal and Nonverbal Metaphor,"
*Semiotica* 119 (1998); J. Merchant, "Fragments and El-
lipsis," *Linguistics and Philosophy* 27 (2004); *The Syntax
of Nonsententials*, ed. L. Progovac et al. (2006).

T.V.F. BROGAN

**EL SALVADOR, POETRY OF.** According to the Sp.
scholar Marcelino Menéndez y Pelayo, no country
as small as El Salvador should be able to lay claim to
so many fine poets. The hist. of Salvadoran poetry is
characterized by two salient features: individuals who
shine like beacons among their contemporaries and the
tragic nexus between lit. and politics.

The Salvadoran poetic trad. dates to before 1524,
when Pedro de Alvarado conquered the pre-Columbian
kingdom of Cuscatlán. Its principal inhabitants, the
Pipiles, spoke Nahuatl, an Aztec lang. Although no rec-
ord remains of Nahuatl lit., echoes of its sung poetry
have survived in oral trads. Oswaldo Escobar Velado
(1919–61) and Salarrué (pseud. of Salvador Salazar
Arrué, 1899–1979) employed features of Nahuatl po-
etry, incl. formulaic repetitions, *parallelisms, a fond-
ness for diminutives, a profusion of *metaphors, and
creation myths.

Some poetry of note was produced during the co-
lonial era, mainly by Sp. administrators or clerics. The
colonial poet Juan de Mestanza (b. 1534) lord mayor
of Sonsonate between 1585 and 1589, was praised by
Miguel de Cervantes for his witty *sonnets. A national
lit. arose during the Salvadoran struggle for inde-
pendence (1811–59). The first national poet, Miguel
Alvarez Castro (1795–1856), wrote neoclassical patri-
otic verses, such as "A la muerte del Coronel Pierzon"
(Upon the Death of Colonel Pierzon, 1827).

*Romanticism prevailed from mid-century to the
first decade of the 20th. Significant poets in this mode
were Juan J. Cañas (1826–1918), who composed the
national *anthem, and Antonia Galindo (1858–93),
the first major woman poet. Two talented romantics
whose careers were cut short by suicide were José Ca-
lixto Mixco (1880–1901) and Armando Rodríguez Por-
tillo (1880–1915). The multifaceted work of Vicente
Acosta (1867–1908) reflects a shift from romanticism
to the novel aesthetic of *modernismo.

The high priest of Salvadoran modernismo was
Francisco Gavidia (1864–1955), a pioneer in the ap-
plication of Fr. forms to Sp. poetry. In such poems
as "Stella," "La ofrenda del bramán" (The Brahman's
Offering), "Sóter o tierra de preseas" (The Savior or
Land of Precious Things), and "La defensa de Pan" (In
Defense of Pan), Gavidia addressed national themes in
many forms, incl. *romances (*ballads) and *redondillas
(Sp. quatrains). The next poetic movement in El Sal-
vador was *costumbrismo* (lit. of customs and manners),
represented by Alfredo Espino (1900–28). Espino's
posthumous collection, *Jícaras tristes* (Gourds of Sad-
ness, 1930), celebrated El Salvador's natural wonders
and indigenous heritage.

*La Matanza* (the Great Slaughter) in 1932 of more
than 30,000 peasants ushered in six decades of turmoil
until the brutal civil war between 1980 and 1992. Dur-
ing this time, writing became a medium for evading
or confronting political horror. Claudia Lars (pseud.
of Carmen Brannon, 1899–1974) became known as
"the divine Claudia" for her mastery of cl. meters to
treat spiritual, mystical, and erotic themes. Mean-
while, some poets strove to preserve truth and beauty
from the contamination of politics, among them Vi-
cente Rosales y Rosales (1894–1980), Serafín Quiteño
(1899–1952), and Hugo Lindo (1917–85). Raúl Con-
treras (1896–1973) wrote a series of haunting sonnets
under the pseud. Lydia Nogales.

During these decades, a constellation of women
poets cultivated cl. forms (particularly the sonnet) and
a lyrical idiom to explore a gamut of themes. Note-
worthy names include Alice Lardé (1896–1983), María
Loucel (1899–1957), Lilian Serpas (1905–85), Berta

Funes Peraza (1911–98), Matilde Elena López (1922–2010), and Mercedes Durand (1933–99). Hypnotic images and *surrealism were the hallmarks of Emma Posada (1912–97). Lydia Valiente's (1900–76) book *Raíces amargas* (Bitter Roots, 1952) employed choral verse in a proletarian voice to denounce injustice.

Defiance and rebellion motivated successive poetic generations, the first of which included Pedro Geoffroy Rivas (1908–79) and Antonio Gamero (1917–74). Escobar Velado's *10 sonetos para mil y más obreros* (10 Sonnets for a Thousand Workers and More, 1950) inspired the Committed Generation, represented by Italo López Vallecillos (1932–86), Tirso Canales (b. 1930), and Manlio Argueta (b. 1935), who in turn influenced "the poetry of combat and resistance" by José María Cuéllar (1942–80) and Miguel Huezo Mixco (b. 1954). Marxist fervor infuses the work of guerrilla-poet Roque Dalton (1935–75), a master of *collage who blended verse with songs, letters, reportage, and historical chronicles. Claribel Alegría (b. 1924), a Salvadoran-Nicaraguan, combined revolutionary commitment with aesthetic refinement in such collections as *Sobrevivo* (I Survive, 1978) and *La mujer del río Sumpul* (The Woman of the Sumpul River, 1987). Alegría also excels at poetry of sensuous lyricism, incl. love poems for her deceased husband and translator Bud Flakoll (*Thresholds/Umbrales*, 1996).

Among the poets straddling the civil war are Roberto Armijo (1937–97), Roberto Cea (b. 1939), and Alfonso Kijadurías (b. 1940). Undoubtedly, the most talented nonpartisan poet is David Escobar Galindo (b. 1943). From his first collection, *Las manos en el fuego* (Hands in the Fire, 1967), to his most recent, *El poema de David* (David's Poem, 2007), he displays mastery of versification.

Since the civil war, Salvadoran poets at home and among the diaspora in North America, Australia, and Europe, incl. Ricardo Lindo (b. 1947), Javier Alas (b. 1964), Álvaro Darío Lara (b. 1966), and Luis Alvarenga (b. 1969), have eschewed partisan ideologies to probe the paradoxes of identity and existence. Liberated women poets, incl. Claudia Herodier (b. 1950), Silvia Elena Regalado (b. 1961), Brenda Gallegos (b. 1972), and Claudia Meyer (b. 1980), explore sex and desire in a range of registers, from the controlled passion of Carmen González Huguet (b. 1958) to the graphic eroticism of Dina Posada (b. 1946) in "Plegaria al orgasmo" (Prayer to Orgasm, 1996). In conclusion, as anthologies by Poumier (2002) and Amaya (2010) attest, poets of different generations, genders, and styles continue to build upon El Salvador's vibrant literary trad.

*See* COLONIAL POETICS; INDIGENOUS AMERICAS, POETRY OF THE; SPANISH AMERICA, POETRY OF.

■ *La margarita emocionante*, ed. H. Castellanos Moya (1979); L. Gallegos Valdés, *Panorama de la literatura salvadoreña* (1981); *Poesía de El Salvador*, ed. M. Argueta (1983); *Indice antológico de la poesía salvadoreña*, ed. D. Escobar Galindo (1988); *Piedras en el huracán*, ed. J. Alas (1993); *Alba de otro milenio*, ed. R. Lindo (2000); R. C. Boland, "A Short History of the Literature of El Salvador," *Antípodas* 18.19 (2002); *Poésie Salvadorienne du XX Siècle*, ed. M. Poumier (2002); *Una madrugada del siglo XXI*, ed. V. Amaya (2010).

R. C. BOLAND

**EMBLEM.** The printed emblem typically consists of three parts: motto (*inscriptio*), image (*pictura*), and *epigram (*subscriptio*). Applied emblems frequently consist of only a motto and an image. So-called nude emblems are not illustrated but contain descriptions of the image. The emblem presents an argument composed of words and pictures. It is too simplistic to say that the pictura illustrates the texts or that the epigram explains the meaning of the motto and the image. Emblems are more than the sum of their parts, and this innovative practice of reading combinations of words and images reorients readers' thinking and understanding. The genre began with the publication of *Emblematum Liber* (1531) by the It. jurist Andrea Alciato (Alciati, Alciatus); many of the early emblematists were lawyers (Hayaert). In the following centuries, the emblem often expanded from a single page or opening of the book to lengthy, often multilingual text-image constructions consisting of several mottos and numerous paratexts that could include poetry, prose commentaries, marginalia, sermons, references to the liturgical year, and other literary and devotional materials.

During the 16th and 17th cs., emblems emerged as a culturally significant innovation whose presentation of texts and images often introduced new meaning into traditional modes of expression. Authors and artists worked with printers and publishers to produce emblem books on topics ranging from natural hist. and politics to love and religion. Emblems were integral to the print and material culture of Ren. and baroque Europe. Emblem production was not limited to the printed page, and applied emblems were painted, carved, and etched both onto decorative objects, such as tankards and furniture, and in architectural spaces, incl. churches, town halls, manor houses, and hospitals (Bath 1994, 2003; McKeown). Emblems were enacted in the theater (Schöne 1993) and embellished court pageants and funerals (Bøggild-Johannsen, Choné, Young 1988, Wade 1996). Emblematics formed a pan-Eur. genre in Lat. and thousands of books were produced in all vernacular langs. (Daly 2008, Russell 1999). At a time when national langs. were developing their discrete lits. in the wake of humanism, emblems became one of the primary vehicles of cultural knowledge, expressing highly complex ideas in compact and compelling forms.

Emblems emerged from several trads., the most important of which is the *impresa*. Ren. iconologies (such as the foundational *Iconologia* of Cesare Ripa) provided encyclopedias of pictorial and allegorical meanings, while collections of proverbs and adages (such as Erasmus's *Adagia* and the *Greek Anthology*), together with heraldry and hieroglyphics (a famous treatise on the latter by Horapollo was published by Aldus Manutius in 1505), contributed to the making of the emblem. The

Fr. trad. of portraying the emblem as a cohesive graphic unit, often within an elaborate decorative frame, was esp. important to the early devel. of the printed genre.

Several early mod. print genres might be considered emblematic, while not portraying emblems in the strict sense. Such highly allegorical arts require what might be termed an emblematic cast of mind, i.e., the mental agility to follow and (re-)create analogues, to make intellectual parallels, and to parse words and texts according to new visual contexts. These genres can include broadsheets, illustrated fables (such as eds. of Ovid and Aesop), paupers' bibles, dances of death, and other dual-media literary phenomena. Printer's marks and title pages from this period are often emblematic as well (Wolkenhauer). All these examples require new readings of words and pictures that created the practice of thinking and reading emblematically.

The emblem revival of the 19th c. gave impetus to mod. emblem studies and the appearance of new, innovative emblem books. Emblem books continue to be printed in mod. times, as evidenced by Lucie-Smith's *Borrowed Emblems*, Finlay's *Heroic Emblems*, Davidson and Buchanan's *The Eloquence of Shadows*, and the leaf book on Alciato by Bregman.

Important bibls. of emblem books have been published for national trads.: Sp. (Campa) and Fr. (Adams, Rawles, and Saunders); for religious trads. (Daly and Dimler); and for important individual collections (McGeary and Nash; Heckscher and Sherman; Visser and Westerweel). The scholarly journal *Emblematica* and the series *Glasgow Emblem Studies* are devoted entirely to the genre.

*See* BAROQUE, HIEROGLYPH, RENAISSANCE POETICS, VISUAL POETRY.

■ J. Landwehr, *Dutch Emblem Books* (1962); M. Praz, *Studies in Seventeenth-Century Imagery*, 2d ed. (1964); E. Lucie-Smith, *Borrowed Emblems* (1967); J. Landwehr, *German Emblem Books 1531–1888* (1972); and *French, Italian, Spanish, and Portuguese Books of Devices and Emblems 1534–1827* (1976); I. H. Finlay, *Heroic Emblems* (1977); A. Young, *Henry Peacham* (1979); P. Daly, *Literature in the Light of the Emblem* (1979); and *Emblem Theory* (1979); D. S. Russell, *The Emblem and Device in France* (1985); P. Daly, *The English Emblem and the Continental Tradition* (1988); *The English Emblem Tradition*, ed. P. Daly et al., v. 1 (1988); J. Landwehr, *Emblem and Fable Books Printed in the Low Countries* (1988); A. Young, *The English Tournament Imprese* (1988); *Andrea Alciato and the Emblem Tradition* (1989), ed. P. Daly; P. Campa, *Emblemata Hispanica: An Annotated Bibliography of Spanish Emblem Literature to the Year 1700* (1990); P. Choné, *Emblèmes et pensée symbolique en Lorraine, 1525–1633* (1991); A. Schöne, *Emblematik und Drama im Zeitalter des Barock*, 3d ed. (1993); M. Bath, *Speaking Pictures: English Emblem Books and Renaissance Culture* (1994); P. Davidson and H. Buchanan, *The Eloquence of Shadows: A Book of Emblems* (1994); *Emblemata: Handbuch zur Sinnbildkunst des XVI. und XVII. Jahrhunderts*, ed. A. Henkel

and A. Schöne, 3d ed. (1996); M. R. Wade, *Triumphus Nuptialis Danicus: German Court Culture and Denmark* (1996); P. Daly and R. Dimler, *The Jesuit Series* (1997–); *A Bibliography of French Emblem Books of the Sixteenth and Seventeenth Centuries*, ed. A. Adams, S. Rawles, A. Saunders, 2 v. (1999, 2002); P. Daly, "Emblem," *Encyclopedia of the Renaissance*, ed. P. F. Grendler (1999); D. Russell, "The Genres of Epigram and Emblem," *CHLC*, v. 3, ed. G. P. Norton (1999); J. Manning, *The Emblem* (2002); M. Bath, *Renaissance Decorative Painting in Scotland* (2003); *Digital Collections and the Management of Knowledge: Renaissance Emblem Literature as a Case Study for the Digitization of Rare Texts and Images*, ed. M. R. Wade (2004); C.-P. Warncke, *Symbol, Emblem, Allegorie* (2005); B. Bøggild-Johannsen, "Ritual and Representational Aspects of the Royal Funeral Ceremonial in Early Modern Denmark," *Tod und Trauer*, ed. T. Fischer and T. Riis (2006); S. McKeown, *Emblematic Paintings from Sweden's Age of Greatness: Nils Bielke and the Neo-Stoic Gallery at Skokloster* (2006); A. Bregman, *Emblemata: The Emblem Books of Andrea Alciato* (2007); *Companion to Emblem Studies*, ed. P. Daly (2008); V. Hayaert, *Mens Emblematica et Humanisme Juridique: Le Cas du Pegma cum Narrationibus Philosophicis de Pierre Coustau, 1555* (2008); P. Boot, *Mesotext Digitised Emblems, Modelled Annotations and Humanities Scholarship* (2009).

M. R. WADE

# EMOTION

I. Reader's Emotion
II. Poet's Emotion
III. Recent Developments

A poem involves two people, writer and reader; and a discussion of the place of emotion in poetics from cl. antiquity to the 21st c. can be divided accordingly. The division is chronological as well as logical: until the end of the 18th c., emphasis fell on the reader's emotion; after *romanticism, it tended to shift to the poet's, and then in the 20th c., emotion itself became an esp. problematic topic. Recent scholarship on the emotions, which this article will review by way of conclusion, has considered both standpoints.

**I. Reader's Emotion.** A good poem moves the reader: this has been a critical truism (perhaps even *the* critical truism) since lit. crit. as we know it began, though the reading of a poem as an emotional experience has moved from the center of attention, replaced by reading as an interpretive activity. The emotion may be aroused for purely aesthetic purposes—for "delight"—or else as an indirect means of inciting to virtue (see DIDACTIC POETRY). This latter is the Horatian view that poetry is both *dulce et utile*—that it "teaches delightfully"—and it is by far the more common in the Ren.: it can be illustrated from almost any early mod. poet who discusses his or her craft:

> O what an honor is it, to restraine
> The lust of lawlesse youth with good advice . . .

Soone as thou gynst to sette thy notes in frame,
O, how the rurall routes to thee doe cleave:
Seemeth thou dost their soule of sence bereave . . .

(Edmund Spenser, *The Shepheardes Calender*,
"October" 21–22, 25–27)

Is the emotional effect normative—i.e., can we say that a good poem arouses strong emotions and a bad poem does not? Aristotle probably thought not: he admits in the *Poetics* that terror and pity can be aroused by the spectacle (a lesser element of poetics), though it is preferable to raise them by the words; and he does not indicate that the less preferable method arouses a weaker or even a different emotion. The usual answer, however, has been "yes." When Philip Sidney confesses in the *Defence of Poesy*, "I never heard the olde song of *Percy* and *Duglas*, that I found not my heart mooved more then with a Trumpet," he clearly assumes that this is a testimony to the poem's excellence. This normative view was carried much further in the 18th c., when it was claimed explicitly and at length (notably by Denis Diderot) that the good poet must be judged by his power to arouse our emotions. This tenet of neoclassical doctrine passed unchanged and naturally into romantic poetics.

One common objection to using one's emotional reaction as a touchstone is that it is completely subjective: a poem has many readers, and they cannot compare their private emotions. One theoretical reply to this is contained in the doctrine of intersubjectivity (as formulated, e.g., by Morris): the use of lang. as a means for comparing purely private experiences. Nonetheless, the objection is useful if taken as a warning to the practical critic to talk about the matter of the poem rather than the emotion it arouses; for the latter will result either in vagueness, as in most impressionistic or rhapsodic crit., or in such physiological descriptions as A. E. Housman's account of his skin bristling, or Emily Dickinson's "If I feel physically as if the top of my head were taken off, I know that is poetry."

A poem, then, arouses in the reader an emotional response that can be intersubjective. What is this emotion like? The first question here is whether there is such a thing as a purely aesthetic emotion. The experience of reading, say, a satire of Alexander Pope is not the same as being angry, but critics are divided on whether the difference can profitably be described by postulating a specifically poetic or aesthetic emotion, which is distinct from anger and all the other "life" emotions, such as fear and love.

For the Horatian, the emotion induced by reading good poetry was usually called, quite simply, *pleasure*; but it was clearly thought of as a special kind of pleasure, and there was some discussion in the 18th c. of its exact nature (e.g., by David Hume in his essays on tragedy and "the standard of taste" and by Immanuel Kant in the *Critique of Judgment*). Early 20th-c. critics who believed in a special aesthetic emotion include Clive Bell ("The starting point for all systems of aesthetics must be the personal experience of a particular emotion. . . . All sensitive people agree that there is a peculiar emotion provoked by works of art") and T. E. Hulme ("You could define art as a passionate desire for accuracy, and the essentially aesthetic emotion as the excitement which is generated by direct communication"). One can also mention Sigmund Freud, who believed that there was a "purely formal, that is, aesthetic pleasure" offered by poetry, and who also (not surprisingly) believed that it was unimportant: an "increment," a "bribe," to release a greater pleasure arising from deeper sources in the mind. Freud held exactly the opposite view to Hume (and William Wordsworth) on this point: for him, the aesthetic pleasure, or fore-pleasure, is a trigger that releases a discharge of emotion that provides the true enjoyment of lit. On the other hand, for Hume the aesthetic pleasure "softens," while for Wordsworth it "tempers" the passions.

Up to the 18th c., the two main views of the reader's emotion were the Horatian (that it was a pleasure) and the Aristotelian (that it was a *catharsis). There is a potential contradiction between these two in that the latter view would tend, implicitly, to deny the aesthetic emotion: it is real pity and real terror that are to be felt. In mod. times, the aesthetic emotion is denied by those who repudiate an ivory-tower or esoteric view of lit.: by Marxists; by Richards (who says curtly that "psychology has no place for such an entity" in *Principles of Literary Criticism*); and, in effect, by Dewey, who, though he uses the term "aesthetic emotion," complains that those who believe in "an emotion that is aboriginally aesthetic . . . relegate fine art to a realm separated by a gulf from everyday experiences."

In speaking of the reader's emotions, one must mention those critics who deny that emotion has any place at all in reading. This denial can reflect mainly theoretical motives, as in the case of Vivas, who wishes to substitute *"attention" as the key concept; or as part of a specific literary program, as in the case of T. S. Eliot. Not always consistent, Eliot suggested that the emotions provoked by a work of art "are, when valid, perhaps not to be called emotions at all." This can be linked with his doctrine of impersonality (he tends to think of an emotion as something personal, even self-regarding); sometimes he prefers the term *feeling*. The "calm" or "cold" that these writers find in the poetic response might by others be considered a kind of emotion, but there is a real cleavage here. What no one (presumably) denies is that, even if the poem kills the emotion, it must deal with a situation that would have aroused emotion in the first place.

Richards maintained that a response to poetry is highly complex, and reading a poem a matter of emotional accommodation and adjustment. He prefers, however, to speak of the attitudes ("imaginal and incipient activities or tendencies to action") that poetry organizes in the reader "for freedom and fullness of life." This organization is the function of emotive lang., sharply distinguished by Richards from referential lang., which makes statements (see PSEUDO-STATEMENT).

Empson, whose view of lang. was influenced by Richards's, goes even further in *The Structure of Complex Words* in not wishing to discuss the emotions aroused by words: "Normally they are dependent on a Sense which is believed to deserve them"; the way to discuss the emotional impact of a poem is to analyze the structure of sense and implication in its key words.

Other 20th-c. formalist critics, such as the New Critic Wimsatt and the philosopher Beardsley (see AFFECTIVE FALLACY), argued that lit. crit. should focus on "the poem itself" rather than its effects, incl. emotional effects, on the reader. By and large, structuralist and poststructuralist critics also minimized the importance of emotion to either the creation or the interpretation of poetry. Deconstructing a text, as described by Derrida and his followers, is primarily a matter of intellect rather than feeling; similarly, for Barthes, interpretations are constructed through manipulating various "codes" of reading, although Barthes does acknowledge the quasi-sexual pleasure of engaging with a "writerly" text in new and playful ways. Much *cultural criticism, incl. feminist crit., has marginalized emotion because it emphasizes the political rather than the individual, but since 2000 that distinction has been challenged by several critics (see esp. Ngai). There has been some attention to feminist emotional responses in reader-response crit., but most of the attention (e.g., Fetterley) has been focused on prose fiction.

**II. Poet's Emotion.** Most of the remaining problems are best discussed under this heading. The first point to note is that consideration of the emotion of the poet must be a descriptive and not a normative inquiry. A poem in itself can never offer conclusive evidence that the poet did not feel a certain emotion, nor (except on certain rather naïve theories) that he or she did; this external, biographical fact can only be established separately and has no critical relevance. Ruskin tried to classify certain forms of poetry as worse than others according to whether the poet was insincere or—worse still—deliberately, in hardness of heart, weaving intricate metaphors "with chill and studied fancy" (see SINCERITY). Here we have left lit. crit. for moralizing. As a reaction against this sort of thing, some aestheticians (notably Beardsley and Osborne) have tried to make logical mincemeat of the very concept of artistic expression. It is much easier for them to do this when they are considering it as a normative concept than when treating it as part of literary psychology.

As part of such a descriptive inquiry, there is a great deal to say about the poet's emotion. First, does a poet need to feel any? The view that he does not—that Shakespeare's sonnets, say, are literary exercises—repels most readers; however, it is a view that seems to be supported by the pronouncements of some poets, very conscious of the impersonality and labor involved in composition. The Horatian-Ren. critical trad., with its manuals of instruction and its advice on *decorum, has little to say on the poet's feelings but a great deal to say on craft. Even the famous line in the *Ars poetica*, "si vis me flere, dolendum est primum ipsi tibi"

(if you wish to make me weep, you must first feel grief yourself), is addressed to characters in a play and refers simply to the need for good writing or good acting. It might be thought that the Platonic doctrine of *inspiration runs counter to this trad., but as expressed by Plato (and, generally, by everyone else) this has nothing to do with the poet's emotions: inspiration comes to the poet from without and enables him, with the Muse's help, to solve problems in his craft that would defy his unaided wit—but they remain problems of craft. The doctrine that art is the expression of emotion is one we owe to the romantic movement; earlier statements of it are very hard to find.

Is the emotion expressed in a poem the same as that originally experienced by the poet? Most of the difficulties here vanish if we reject too naïve a view of the temporal priority of this original emotion. What a poem expresses is clearly not the emotion of the poet *before* he began writing it, but it may be his original emotion insofar as the writing of the poem helped him to discover, even to feel it: "Expression is the clarification of turbid emotion," says Dewey. Alexander, however, prefers to postulate two emotions, the material passion ("the passions appropriate to the subject") and the formal passion (the "passion proper to the artist" that guides him "more surely than conscious ideas . . . unifying his choice of words . . . into an expressive whole"). This formal passion is clearly the equivalent for the poet of the aesthetic emotion of the reader; Alexander suggests that the material passion need not be present, citing the example of dramatic poetry: "It is not necessary to suppose that Meredith or Shakespeare actually felt the emotions of his characters, but only that he understood them." Murry, however, who advances an extreme version of the expression theory, would prefer to say that the material passion is not the emotion of Macbeth but that of Shakespeare about the *Macbeth* situation, which is expressed by the play as a whole and which Shakespeare presumably felt as well as understood.

The central difficulty in any view of art as the expression of emotion is to find a way of indicating that the poet, though in the grip of an emotion, is also in control of it: that he or she is possessed by emotion but also possesses it. A critic's way of resolving this paradox may often show the heart of his doctrine. A typical Victorian answer is that of Ruskin, for whom the second-order poet is in the grip of his feelings (or chooses to write as if he were), whereas the first-order poet has command over himself and can look around calmly. When it comes to applying this distinction to poems, Ruskin shows a naïveté that is almost ludicrous: the great poet's "control of emotion" consists mainly in avoiding *metaphor and factually untrue statements, even in preferring *similes to metaphors.

Since genuine emotion, in real life, may well be accompanied by complete inarticulateness, we need to distinguish between its expression in a poem and the symptoms in which it issues in actual situations. Croce views expression as either aesthetic or naturalistic: "there is . . . an abyss . . . between the appearance, the cries and contortions of some one grieving at the loss of a dear one and the words or song with which the same individual portrays his suffering at another time." Dewey makes a distinction between giving way to, and expressing, an impulse: raging is not the same as expressing rage, and he links it with his more general theory that the arresting of the physiologically normal outlet of an impulse is the necessary precondition of its transformation into a higher level of experience. Perhaps the most valuable formulation of the difference is that of Collingwood, who distinguishes between expressing and betraying an emotion, linking this with his view of art as an enlarging and clarifying of consciousness.

These are philosophical formulations; to the poet and practical critic, what matters is the application of the distinction to the actual lang. of poetry. The classic instance of failure to draw this distinction is Samuel Johnson's attack on John Milton's "Lycidas" on the grounds that "where there is leisure for fiction, there is little grief." The naturalistic discharge of grief may have no such leisure, but its expression has. This element of control in expression was no doubt one of the things S. T. Coleridge wished to indicate by attributing to imagination "a more than usual state of emotion, with more than usual order" and that Eliot was thinking of when he described poetry as "an escape from emotion." Eliot's objections to *Hamlet* spring from a feeling that loose emotion, inadequately expressed, is betrayed in the play, though he shows some uncertainty whether the emotion is Shakespeare's or also Hamlet's.

Wordsworth's account of poetry as originating in "the spontaneous overflow of powerful feelings" looks like a discharge theory, but he goes on to add that, as well as having "more than usual organic sensibility," the poet must be someone who has "thought long and deeply." Wordsworth was, in fact, usually aware (though he is inconsistent) that the emotion as expressed is not the same as that originally felt: in his account of emotion recollected in tranquillity, he remarks that the recollected emotion, that which issues in the poem, is "kindred" to the original one.

Of all mod. theorists, the one who perhaps comes closest to a view of art as the mere discharge of emotion is Freud. He happens to be talking of the reader's emotions, but his view (already mentioned) seems relevant here. He recognizes no element of control in the "release of tension" provided by lit. and sometimes indicates a view of art that equates it with indulgence in wish fulfillment. (At other times he holds what amounts to a cognitive view.) Carl Jung, though his interpretation is different, holds the same view of what the poetic emotion is like and describes it with the same metaphors: "the moment when the mythological situation appears is . . . as though forces were unloosed of the existence of which we had never even dreamed; . . . we feel suddenly aware of an extraordinary release." There can be no doubt that the distinction between expressing and betraying is invaluable in the actual crit. of lit. Collingwood applies it, briefly but brilliantly, to Thomas Hardy's *Tess of the D'Urbervilles* and to Ludwig van Beethoven; it provides the best terminology for sorting good from bad in writers such as P. B. Shelley, Thomas Carlyle, and D. H. Lawrence.

How does emotion work in the creative process? If writing a poem is like driving a car, the emotions can be thought of either as the destination or the gasoline—the subject of literary creation or the force that makes it possible. Eliot holds the first view: "What every poet starts from is his own emotions," he says in contrasting Shakespeare to Dante, and he suggests that Dante expresses not belief but certain emotions of believing. Alexander, on the other hand, holds the second view: "The artist aims to express the subject which occupies his mind in the means which he uses. His purpose may be dictated by passion but is still a passionate *purpose*." The resolution of this dispute (which seems at least partly terminological) lies outside literary theory, but the dangers and implications of each view are worth noting. If you believe that the poet's emotions are the subject of a poem, you are likely to emphasize, even overemphasize, the typicality of poems dealing explicitly with emotions, such as Shakespeare's sonnets, Coleridge's "Dejection: An Ode" and even (as in the case of many romantic critics) lyric poetry in general. If, on the other hand, you regard emotion as merely the fuel, you have to deal with the fact that the writing of philosophy, psychology, even mathematics may often be fueled by emotion. The romantic doctrine of the presence of the writer's emotion as not merely external cause but in some way intrinsic to the product at least had the advantage that it provided a criterion for distinguishing poetry (more generally, imaginative lit.) from other forms of writing.

**III. Recent Developments.** The decline of romantic theories and the rise of critical positions such as *formalism and *structuralism in the 20th c. tended to direct attention away from the question of emotion. Structuralist theories, which treat lit. by the methods of ling., often assimilated poetry to other forms of lang., and their emphasis on codes led to a concentration on the activity of the lang. rather than on the resulting experience. Even the influential school of reader-response crit. has tended to concentrate on responses that, in Culler's words, "are generally cognitive rather than affective: not feeling shivers along the spine, or weeping, but having one's expectations proved false, or struggling with an unresolvable ambiguity."

Theories of the dispersed or decentered subject, deriving from Louis Althusser, Jacques Lacan, and Roland Barthes, which eliminate or at least minimize the autonomous creative act, naturally also minimized the importance of emotion: if there is no autonomous subject, then there is no originating emotion. Kristeva sees poetic lang. (by which she means the lang. of *modernism) as a struggle against oppression by the social order and an attempt to express the subversiveness of immediate experience, which she calls desire, but it is an impersonal desire, not an individual experience of desiring.

Beginning in the 1960s and 1970s, however, anti-emotion theories have been challenged by literary theorists influenced by the recent explosion of research into the emotions by psychologists (Lazarus, Ekman, Scherer, Frijda, Zajonc), philosophers (Solomon, Nussbaum, de Sousa, Wollheim, Prinz), neuroscientists (LeDoux, Damasio), anthropologists (Harré, Lutz), and others. The result has been a clearer understanding of what emotions are and why we have them. In turn, this has enabled critics to examine the relationships between emotion and poetry from an empirical perspective. Despite continuing disputes about more specific issues, a consensus has emerged about the most important components of emotion:

1. Emotions appraise or evaluate the environment in terms of their significance to my survival or well-being or that of "my group." Emotions make salient or pick out for special attention the threatening, the offensive, the admirable, and so forth.

2. Some (Solomon, Nussbaum, Gordon) have argued that these appraisals are evaluative *judgments*, such as the judgment that I have been insulted or that I am in danger. Others think of these appraisals as more like *perceptions* of value: for the psychologist Frijda emotional experience is "the perception of horrible objects, insupportable people, oppressive events." The philosopher Wollheim has a similar view: emotions provide us "with an orientation, or an attitude to the world—emotion tints or colours" the world.

3. It is widely agreed that bodily changes are important in emotion. James famously argued that, without an awareness of bodily changes, there would be nothing emotional about an emotion; it would simply be a "cold and neutral . . . intellectual perception" that, e.g., an offense has occurred. Frijda stresses that among the relevant bodily changes are "changes in action readiness," evoked by the appraisal of situations or events that impinge on a person's concerns. Emotions not only appraise the world as dangerous or offensive; they ready us to deal with the world as so appraised.

4. These various bodily changes are often consciously experienced as *feelings*, such as a feeling of flushed cheeks and racing heart. The neuroscientist Damasio makes a slightly different distinction. In his terminology, *emotions* are patterns of bodily response: *primary* emotions are responses that are preprogrammed, such as fear of a sudden loud sound, and *secondary* emotions are responses to mental images of more complex stimuli, involving some kind of evaluation. A *feeling* of emotion, on the other hand, is the brain's registration of these patterns of bodily response. (Paradoxically, this means that Damasio's "feelings" are not always consciously felt.)

5. Many theorists think of emotions as *processes*, initiated by an appraisal, resulting in bodily changes of various sorts that prepare for action and that may be registered in consciousness as feelings. On this view, the function of emotion is to get us to respond rapidly to important "adaptational encounters" with the environment. However, although the initial emotional response seems to be urgent and automatic, human beings typically monitor their responses for their appropriateness and try to "regulate" or "manage" them as the emotional process unfolds.

How can the theory of emotion contribute to poetics? Recent emotion theory can throw light on both the nature of poetic *expression* and readers' emotional responses as well as their interaction. Understanding the emotions expressed by a romantic lyric poem typically involves understanding the emotional perspective from which the poem is written. Thus, the dramatic speaker in John Keats's "Ode to a Nightingale" expresses his *appraisal* of the mundane world as dominated by "the weariness, the fever and the fret" and his *perception* of the nightingale as the creator of a song that transports him into a timeless world of art and beauty. Moreover, Keats is not simply betraying his emotions but articulating and elucidating them as a result of cognitively monitoring the emotional experience after the fact: as Wordsworth put it, he is "recollecting" an emotional experience "in tranquility."

Ribeiro has noted that by far the majority of poems are lyric poems written from the first-person perspective, in which we are invited to "identify" with the poetic speaker and "appropriate" the viewpoint expressed as our own. The discovery of "mirror neurons" in macaque monkeys has fueled speculation that humans can empathize with the feelings of others by "simulating" their emotional experiences. Some theorists (Currie, Feagin, Goldman) have adopted the idea that "identification" with a narrator or dramatic speaker amounts to "simulation" or adoption "off-line" of the speaker's emotional states. Thus, when we respond emotionally to Shelley's dramatic speaker who cries "I fall upon the thorns of life! I bleed!" we may be adopting "off-line" the anguish and despair expressed by this speaker and thereby coming to empathize with him. In such cases, my emotions may guide me to a better understanding of the poetic speaker and what he or she is expressing in the poem. Something similar may happen in narrative poetry if the narrator is also the main protagonist, as in Coleridge's *The Rime of the Ancient Mariner*. Readers are encouraged to take the perspective of the mariner and to experience the events described as he describes them (see ABSORPTION), although we might spare an occasional thought for the importuned wedding guest.

One question about this idea is whether poetry or lit. in general is capable of arousing emotions in its readers at all. Philosophers of lit. have debated (e.g., in *Emotion and the Arts*) the so-called paradox of fiction, i.e., the question whether actual emotions are aroused by characters in lit. or whether it is only make-believe that we feel such emotions. The paradox arises out of the "appraisal" theory of emotion: if sadness, say, requires that we judge that we have suffered a loss, then why should we respond with horrified sadness to Keats's story of Isabella, if the story is entirely fictional and no one's head has actually been buried in a pot of basil? Some (Walton) say that the emotions aroused are "quasi-emotions," having the physiological components of emotion without the requisite evaluative judgment, whereas others think that emotion systems respond as reliably to thoughts or imaginings about a loss as they do to an actual loss and that we feel genuine emotion for fictional characters (Robinson).

A related "paradox of tragedy" considers why we should respond with pleasure or positive emotions to *Oedipus Rex* or *King Lear*, which depict events that are painful. One response that goes back to Hume is that the formal features of a well-written tragedy distract us from the unpleasant content. In terms of recent emotion theory, the formal devices that shape a great tragedy can act as psychological defenses or coping mechanisms, helping us to deal with or manage the powerful emotions evoked by the story (Robinson).

More generally, Fish's early essay "Affective Stylistics" describes how a good poem controls the individual reader's emotional responses to subject matter by formal manipulations. In that essay, he seems to assume an ideal reader who will respond as the poem—or the poet—wants us to respond. Later versions of affective reader-response theory, such as Holland's, recognize that individual readers bring their own experiences and temperaments to bear on their readings. In later essays, Fish argues that different readings are associated with different "interpretive communities," but he no longer emphasizes readers' *emotional* responses. Nevertheless, readers' emotional responses are often important in interpretation and evaluation not only for grasping what emotions the poem expresses but also more generally for bringing *salient* features of the poem to attention. Of course, different readers from different interpretive communities and with different background assumptions will tend to find salience in different places, nor are all readers' emotional responses appropriate to the poem (despite what Fish and others sometimes seem to claim). However, interpretation requires not just emoting but reflecting on our emotional responses. The reflective critic will deem some of his or her responses inappropriate and idiosyncratic and hence irrelevant to understanding.

Recently there have been a few attempts (Gerrig, van Peer, Harris) to study empirically how readers respond emotionally to lit., incl. poetry. Several studies focus on the perspective readers take on what is happening in a literary work. Empirical evidence suggests that readers do indeed "mentally situate themselves at a particular locus within the scene being described," typically one that is the same as or close to the main protagonist. This has implications for the reader's emotional responses: e.g., readers find a probe term faster if it coincides with the protagonist's emotional state. In general, it seems as though emotion theory and empirical research into the reception of poetry will continue to further our understanding of poetry and its emotional effects.

*See* ETHOS, JAPANESE POETICS, NEOCLASSICAL POETICS, PATHOS, RHETORIC AND POETRY, ROMANTIC AND POSTROMANTIC POETRY AND POETICS.

■ J. Ruskin, "The Pathetic Fallacy," *Modern Painters* (1856), 3.4; B. Croce, *Aesthetic*, trans. D. Ainslie (1909); T. S. Eliot, "The Perfect Critic," *The Sacred Wood* (1920); S. Freud, "The Relation of the Poet to Day-Dreaming," *Collected Papers*, trans. G. Duff, v. 4 (1925); J. M. Murry, *The Problem of Style* (1925); C. G. Jung, "On the Relation of Analytical Psychology to Poetic Art," *Contributions to Analytical Psychology*, trans. H. G. Baynes and C. F. Baynes (1928); I. A. Richards, *Practical Criticism* (1929); S. Alexander, *Beauty and Other Forms of Value* (1933); J. Dewey, *Art as Experience* (1934); E. Vivas, "A Definition of the Aesthetic Experience," *Journal of Philosophy* 34 (1937); R. G. Collingwood, *Principles of Art* (1938); C. W. Morris, *Foundations of the Theory of Signs* (1938); Eliot, *Essays*, esp. "Tradition and the Individual Talent," "Shakespeare and the Stoicism of Seneca," and "Dante"; W. K. Wimsatt and M. C. Beardsley, "The Affective Fallacy," *The Verbal Icon* (1954); W. Empson, *The Structure of Complex Words* (1951); E. Kris, *Psycho-analytic Explorations in Art* (1952); H. Osborne, *Aesthetics and Criticism* (1955)—ch. 7 attacks the expression theory; Wimsatt and Brooks, ch. 14; S. O. Lesser, *Fiction and the Unconscious* (1957); H. Osborne, "The Quality of Feeling in Art," *British Journal of Aesthetics* 3 (1963); N. N. Holland, *The Dynamics of Literary Response* (1968), and "The 'Unconscious' of Literature," *Contemporary Criticism*, ed. M. Bradbury and D. Palmer (1970); S. Fish, "Literature in the Reader: Affective Stylistics," *NLH* 2 (1970); R. Barthes, *S/Z*, trans. R. Miller (1974); and *The Pleasure of the Text*, trans. R. Miller (1975); N. N. Holland, *5 Readers Reading* (1975); and "Unity Identity Text Self," *PMLA* 90 (1975); J. Derrida, *Of Grammatology*, trans. G. C. Spivak (1976); R. C. Solomon, *The Passions* (1976); S. Fish, *Is There a Text in This Class?* (1980); J. Kristeva, *Desire in Language*, trans. T. Gora et al. (1980); R. Zajonc, "Feeling and Thinking: Preferences Need No Inferences," *American Psychologist* 35 (1980); J. Fetterley, *The Resisting Reader* (1981); W. James, *The Works of William James*, ed. F. H. Burkhardt, 3 vols. (1981); J. Culler, *On Deconstruction* (1982); R. Zajonc, "On the Primacy of Affect," *American Psychologist* 39 (1984); N. Frijda, *The Emotions* (1986); R. Harré, *The Social Construction of Emotions* (1986); R. de Sousa, *The Rationality of Emotion* (1987); R. M. Gordon, *The Structure of Emotions* (1987); C. Lutz, *Unnatural Emotions: Everyday Sentiments on a Micronesian Atoll and Their Challenge to Western Theory* (1988); K. Walton, *Mimesis as Make-Believe* (1990); R. Lazarus, *Emotion and Adaptation* (1991); C. Bell, "The Aesthetic Hypothesis," *Art in Theory, 1900–1990*, ed. C. Harrison and P. Wood (1992); R. Gerrig, *Experiencing Narrative Worlds* (1993); A. Damasio, *Descartes' Error: Emotion, Reason, and the Human Brain* (1994); G. Currie, "Imagination and Simulation: Aesthetics Meets Cognitive Science," *Mental Simulation*, ed. M. Davies and T. Stone (1995); P. L. Harris, *The Work of the Imagination* (1995)—on experiment by M. Rinck and G. H. Bower; *Collected Writings of T. E. Hulme*, ed. K. Csengeri (1996); S. Feagin, *Reading with Feeling: The Aesthetics of Appreciation* (1996); J. LeDoux, *The Emotional Brain* (1996); *Emotion and the Arts*, ed. M. Hjort and S. Laver (1997), esp. J. Levinson, K. Walton, G. Currie, D. Matravers, and N. Carroll; R. Wollheim, *On the Emotions* (1999); M. Nussbaum, *Upheavals of Thought: The Intelligence of Emotions* (2001); K. Scherer, "The Nature and Study of Appraisal: A Review of the Issues," *Appraisal Processes in Emotion*, ed. K. Scherer et al. (2001); W. van Peer and S. Chatman, *New Perspectives on Narrative Perspective* (2001); G. Currie and I. Ravenscroft, *Recreative Minds* (2002); A. Damasio, *Looking for Spinoza: Joy, Sorrow, and the Feeling Brain* (2003); P. Ekman, *Emotions Revealed* (2003); R. C. Solomon, *Not Passion's Slave* (2003); J. Prinz, *Gut Reactions: A Perceptual Theory of Emotion* (2004); J. Robinson, *Deeper Than Reason: Emotion and Its Role in Literature, Music and Art* (2005); A. Goldman, *Simulating Minds* (2006); N. Frijda, *The Laws of Emotion* (2007); S. Ngai, *Ugly Feelings* (2007); R. C. Solomon, *True to Our Feelings* (2007); A. C. Ribeiro, "Toward a Philosophy of Poetry," *Midwest Studies in Philosophy* 33 (2009); P. C. Hogan, *What Literature Teaches Us About Emotion* (2011).

L. D. Lerner; J. Robinson

**EMPATHY AND SYMPATHY.** *Empathy* is usually defined as projection of oneself into the other or identification with the other, but the term, in fact, has referred to many divergent phenomena in both psychology and aesthetics. Coined by E. B. Titchener to translate a technical term, *Einfühlung*, and first used by Theodor Lipps in 1897 in a psychological analysis of aesthetic appreciation, *empathy* originally meant a fusing of self with (or loss of self-awareness in) the object of one's attention. The conception (if not the term) was developed by both R. H. Lotze and F. T. Vischer in elaboration of Hegelian aesthetics, which made empathy constitutive of beauty. In the social sciences, its meaning shifted to the ability to put oneself in the place of another, imaginatively, or to experience what the other's feelings must be like. Sigmund Freud saw empathy as emerging from identification by way of imitation, a third stage in our taking on the attitudes of others. Some theorists of *interpretation* have made empathy in a broad sense basic to hermeneutic understanding, but not Wilhelm Dilthey, whose *Nacherleben* (mistranslated as "empathy") is quite different from *Einfühlen*.

Significant contributions to the conception of empathy have also been made by Max Scheler and Martin Buber. Buber's characterization of empathy allows us to see how the term could be put to use in readings of romantic poetry (see Fogle, Bate, Bloom): "Empathy means, if anything, to glide with one's own feeling into the dynamic structure of an object, a pillar, or a crystal or the branch of a tree, or even of an animal or a man, and as it were to trace it from within, understanding the formation and motoriality of the object with the perceptions of one's own muscles." Though other theorists do not share this emphasis on the visceral, most agree in contrasting the term *empathy* with *sympathy*, which is seen as more reflective, comparative, and cognizant of one's own feelings. This sense of *empathy* has been predominantly applied in studies of poetry. More recently, empathy and sympathy, distinguished in a different way, have been the focus of studies of the novel, its social content and context, as well as the dynamics of the reader's participation (identification, imitation).

Fogle saw empathy as the source of *personification in poetry and the basis for all *metaphor that endows the natural world with features of mind or human feeling. As such, he identified it with "what modern critics have termed the mythical view" and thus with "the essential attitude of poetry and art." In a narrower sense, *empathy* refers to metaphors that convey the meaning of an object by evoking a physical (kinesthetic) response to it. John Keats's lines in *Hyperion*, "crag jutting forth to crag, and rocks that seem'd / Ever as if just rising from a sleep, / Forehead to forehead held their monstrous horns," aptly illustrate the empathic interpretation of objects by physical suggestion. However, there is a paradox in such usage insofar as it implies projection of features not actually to be found in the object (see PATHETIC FALLACY), since empathy is otherwise taken as a form of knowledge or insight.

In its projection into or identification with the object (the metaphysical crux of romantic nature poetry), empathy is distinguishable from sympathy by its element of sensation and its more intimate union with its object—sympathy runs parallel, while empathy unites. The importance of sympathy to poetics lies in its relation to extrapoetic issues. The sympathetic imagination, e.g., makes possible organized social action by awakening us to the kinship of all things. In S. T. Coleridge's *The Rime of the Ancient Mariner*, the Ancient Mariner's crime is a failure of sympathy toward a creature that has already been associated with humanity: "As if it had been a Christian soul, / We hailed it in God's name" (see also NEGATIVE CAPABILITY).

In *A Treatise of Human Nature*, David Hume found no human quality "more remarkable, both in itself and in its consequences, than that propensity we have to sympathize with others, and to receive by communication their inclinations and sentiments, however different from, or even contrary to our own." Hume saw sympathy as essential to the spread of attitudes and manners, as well as the intersubjective communication of feelings. In both cases, sympathy was a sort of contagion that seemed unreflective to the subject, although a philosopher could trace the swift conversion of idea into impression. In *The Theory of Moral Sentiments*, Adam Smith made sympathy more reflective and deliberate, depending on our imagining what we would feel in the other's place. He stressed its affinity to compassion and pity but used it "to denote our fellow-feeling with any passion whatever." Smith drew on Stoic self-command and *sympatheia* (a cosmic as well as social bond).

Starting with Marshall, and then Roberts and Hinton in parallel, sympathy became central to studies of the novel, with persistent attention to its problematic or ambivalent nature, as the reader enters into—and derives pleasure from—the fictional sufferings of the hero or, more often, heroine. Both Roberts and Hinton focus not only on Samuel Richardson's *Clarissa* but on Henry James's *The Portrait of a Lady*; Boudreau has chapters on Henry and William James, and (like Roberts) on Nathaniel Hawthorne. Focusing on relations between men, Crain devotes two chapters each to Charles Brockden Brown and R. W. Emerson. "The spectator" of Smith's moral theory and the affinity of sympathy and theatricality or spectacle (representation) seen by Marshall in Anthony Ashley Cooper, the third Earl of Shaftesbury, resurface in the "scenes of sympathy" discussed by Jaffe. Miranda's speech in *The Tempest* 2.2, cited by Marshall, provides the link for Ratcliffe's readings of dramatic *monologues by Robert Browning, W. H. Auden, and Samuel Beckett that allude to the passage. Keen's wide-ranging study of "narrative empathy" identifies empathy with the sympathy of Hume and Smith and explores it in readers, the market, authors, and academic opponents of empathy.

*See* ABSORPTION, AFFECT, EMOTION.

■ H. Lotze, *Microcosmos*, trans. E. Hamilton and E.E.C. Jones (1886); T. Lipps, *Ästhetik* (1903), *Leitfaden der Psychologie* (1906), and *Psychologische Untersuchungen* (1907–13); V. Lee, *The Beautiful* (1913); M. Scheler, *The Nature of Sympathy* (1913); H. S. Langfeld, *The Aesthetic Attitude* (1920); I. A. Richards et al., *Foundation of Aesthetics* (1925); G. H. Mead, *Mind, Self and Society* (1934); W. J. Bate, *From Classic to Romantic* (1946), ch. 5; R. H. Fogle, *The Imagery of Keats and Shelley* (1949), ch. 4; M. Buber, *Between Man and Man*, trans. R. G. Smith (1955); R. L. Katz, *Empathy, Its Nature and Uses* (1963); H. Bloom, *Shelley's Mythmaking* (1969); W. Perpeet, "Einfühlungsästhetik," *Historisches Wörterbuch der Philosophie*, ed. J. Ritter (1971–2007); M. F. Basch, "Empathic Understanding: A Review of the Concept," *Journal of the American Psychoanalytic Association* 31 (1983); D. Marshall, *The Figure of Theatre* (1986), and *The Surprising Effects of Sympathy: Marivaux, Diderot, Rousseau, and Mary Shelley* (1988); N. Roberts, *Schools of Sympathy, Gender and Identification through the Novel* (1997); L. Hinton, *The Perverse Gaze of Sympathy* (1999); A. Jaffe, *Scenes of Sympathy: Identity and Representation in Victorian Fiction* (2000); C. Crain, *American Sympathy: Men, Friendship and Literature in the New Nation* (2001); K. Boudreau, *Sympathy in American Literature* (2002); B. Lowe, *Victorian Fiction and the Insights of Sympathy* (2007); S. Keen, *Empathy and the Novel* (2007); S. Ratcliffe, *On Sympathy* (2008).

R. H. FOGLE; J. BARNOUW

**ENARGEIA** (Gr. *arges*, "bright"; Lat. *evidentia, inlustratio, repraesentatio*). *Enargeia* or vividness is defined in cl. rhetorical treatises as a quality that appeals to the listener's senses, principally that of sight. In the *Progymnasmata* (School Exercises), enargeia is, with *sapheneia*, or clarity, one of the defining characteristics of *ekphrasis*, the description in poetry of pictorial scenes on objects (a shield, a vase). Aristotle mentions enargeia in the *Rhetoric* (1410b36), but it is Quintilian who gives the most detailed treatment of the property in cl. rhet.: by penetrating the visual imagination of the listener and involving him in the subject of the speech, the orator can persuade more effectively than through logical argument alone (8.3.62). To achieve enargeia, the orator must use his visual imagination (*phantasia*) to evoke the scene mentally (10.7.15). He then represents this vision in the delivery of the speech, producing an analogous image, and the concomitant feelings, in the minds of the audience (6.2.29–32). One important descriptive technique for vivid portrayal is the selection and disposition of significant detail (8.3.66, 9.2.40). The theory of enargeia supposes a close reciprocal relation between mental images and the arousal of *emotion (see PATHOS) and is thus linked to the notion of *psychagogia*—leading or enchanting the mind.

Outside practical rhet., enargeia was also felt to be a desirable quality in historiography and, esp., poetry. The Lat. rhetoricians often drew their examples of enargeia from Virgil, as the Greeks did from Homer. Ancient commentaries on Homer and on Attic *tragedy frequently draw attention to vividly pictorial passages and phrases. For Longinus (*On the Sublime* 15), vivid *imagery (which he usually refers to as "phantasia") is one means of attaining the *sublime. But he makes an important distinction between the use of such imagery by the orator, who must keep within the bounds of credibility, and by the poets, who are free to invent and elaborate fabulous subjects.

The psychological mechanism linking mental imagery and emotion was known to Aristotle (*Rhetoric* 1411b–1412a), who used the concrete adverbial phrase "before the eyes" rather than the abstract term *vividness* to signify the effect of such vision. For Aristotle, mental picturing produces the semblance of vitality and actuality: the Gr. for this is *energeia*, a term that has often been confused with enargeia.

■ J. H. Hagstrum, *The Sister Arts* (1958); T. Cave, "*Enargeia*: Erasmus and the Rhetoric of Presence in the Sixteenth Century," *L'Esprit Créateur* 16 (1976); L. Galyon, "Puttenham's *Enargeia* and *Energeia*: New Twists for Old Terms," *PQ* 60 (1981); G. Zanker, "*Enargeia* in the Ancient Criticism of Poetry," *Rheinisches Museum für Philologie* 124 (1981); S. K. Heninger Jr., "A World of Figures: Enargeiac Speech in Shakespeare," *Fanned and Winnowed Opinions: Shakespearean Essays*, ed. J. W. Mahon and T. A. Pendleton (1987); R. Meijering, *Literary and Rhetorical Theories in Greek Scholia* (1987); Corbett; F. Dumora-Mabille, "Entre clarté et illusion: l'*enargeia* au XVIIe siècle," *Littératures classiques* 28 (1996); R. Cockcroft, "Fine-Tuning Quintilian's Doctrine of Rhetorical Emotion: Seven Types of *Enargeia*," *Colección Quintiliano de Retórica y Comunicación* 2 (1998); Lausberg; I. Lunde, "Rhetorical *Enargeia* and Linguistic Pragmatics: On Speech-Reporting Strategies in East Slavic Medieval Hagiography and Homiletics," *Journal of Historical Pragmatics* 5 (2004).

R. H. WEBB; P. WELLER

**ENCOMIUM.** Strictly, a Gr. choral lyric performed "in the revel" (*komos*) to celebrate a person's achievements. More generally, the name is applied to any poem praising a human rather than a god (Plato, *Republic* 607a; Aristotle, *Poetics* 4), and it coincides with other designations such as *panegyric and *epinikion.

In the generic categories devised by the Alexandrian librarians to classify Gr. choral lyric, *encomium* referred to poems that were less formal than epinikia and that were probably, like the *skolion, performed at banquets. Simonides brought the genre to its maturity, but no examples of his encomia are extant; only fragments remain of the encomia of the two most important subsequent authors, Pindar (fr. 118–28) and Bacchylides (fr. 20Aa–g). In its broadest application, *encomium* becomes indistinguishable from *praise* as a subdivision of epideictic oratory (Aristotle, *Rhetoric* 1358b18 ff.). Both the first Sophistic movement (5th c. BCE) and the second (2d c. CE) produced prose encomia of frivolous and paradoxical subjects (Pease), forerunners of Erasmus's *Moriae encomium* (*The Praise of Folly*).

Although encomiastic passages can be found throughout Greco-Roman poetry (Burgess), salient examples include Theocritus, *Idylls* 16 and 17; Horace, *Odes* 4.4 and 4.14; (Tibullus) 3.7; and the anonymous *Laus pisonis*. Encomia continue to be written in the Byzantine period (Viljamaa), the Middle Ages (Baldwin), and the Ren. (Hardison, Garrison).

*See* EPIDEICTIC POETRY.

■ Pauly-Wissowa; T. Burgess, *Epideictic Literature* (1902); G. Fraustadt, *Encomiorum in litteris Graecis usque ad Romanam aetatem historia* (1909); A. S. Pease, "Things without Honor," *CP* 21 (1926); C. S. Baldwin, *Medieval Rhetoric and Poetic* (1928); A. E. Harvey, "The Classification of Greek Lyric Poetry," *CQ* 5 (1955); H. K. Miller, "The Paradoxical Encomium with Special Reference to Its Vogue in England, 1600–1800" *MP* 53 (1956); O. B. Hardison Jr., *The Enduring Monument* (1962); W. Meinke, *Untersuchungen zu den Enkomiastischen Gedichten Theokrits* (1965); T. Viljamaa, *Studies in Greek Encomiastic Poetry of the Early Byzantine Period* (1968); J. D. Garrison, *Dryden and the Tradition of Panegyric* (1975); A. W. Nightingale, "The Folly of Praise: Plato's Critique of Encomiastic Discourse in the *Lysis* and *Symposium*," *CQ* n.s. 43 (1993).

W. H. RACE

**ENDECHA.** A Sp. *dirge or *lament, usually written in five-, six-, or seven-syllable lines; the even-numbered lines have *assonance, though any simple rhyme scheme in true rhyme and any type of verse may be used, since the name refers primarily to subject matter. The *strophe employed in the *endecha real*, however, introduced in the 16th c., is usually limited to four lines, generally three *heptasyllables plus one *hendecasyllable, the second and fourth lines assonating and the others left unrhymed. The position of the hendecasyllables may vary, or the strophe may alternate hendecasyllables with heptasyllables. Alternating rhyme (*serventesio*) may also be used. The short-line forms, according to Le Gentil, are found as early as the 15th c., although the typical assonance of the learned poetry is a devel. of the 16th. The endecha is sometimes called *romancillo*. A famous example is Félix Lope de Vega's *Pobre barquilla mia*.

■ Le Gentil; M. Alvar, *Endechas judeo-españoles* (1968); Navarro; E. Gutwirth, "A Judeo-Spanish ende-*cha* from the Cairo Geniza," *Mediterranean Language Review* 6–7 (1993).

D. C. CLARKE

**END-STOPPED** lines are those in which meter, syntax, and sense come to a conclusion at line end. "Conclusion" is, however, not an unequivocal absolute: syntactically, the end of a phrase is the minimum requirement, but end of clause or sentence is normal: "Hope springs eternal in the human breast; / Man never is, but always to be, blest," Alexander Pope says (*Essay on Criticism*). A single *line may be said to be end-stopped, but the term normally applies to the *couplet, and particularly the closed *heroic couplet of 18th-c. Eng. poetry, as well as to the *alexandrine of Fr. classicism. The term *end-stopped* is opposed to *run-on* or *enjambé* (see ENJAMBMENT), terms used to describe the free and uninterrupted carry over of syntax from one line to the other, as in most Eng. *blank verse and most *romantic poetry.

A. PREMINGER; T.V.F. BROGAN

## ENGLAND, POETRY OF

I. Old English, 650–1066 CE
II. Middle English, 1066–1500
III. The Renaissance, 1500–1660
IV. The Restoration and the Eighteenth Century, 1660–1789
V. The Romantic Period, 1789–1830
VI. The Victorian Period, 1830–1900
VII. Modernism to the Present, from 1901

**I. Old English, 650–1066 CE.** When Lat. literary culture took hold in early med. England, one surprising result was a flourishing of vernacular verse in a wealth of *genres, from sophisticated *riddles and emotionally intense *lyrics, to long biblical narratives and *epics such as *Beowulf*. Although writing occurred almost exclusively in monastic scriptoria where Lat. predominated, OE poetry developed alongside Anglo-Lat. lit. Nearly all OE poems survive as copies in four codices dating from the late 10th or early 11th c.: the Exeter Book, the Vercelli Book, the *Beowulf* or Nowell Codex, and the Junius ms. It is, therefore, extremely difficult to establish dates of composition or to track changing metrical patterns. Nonetheless, we know that OE poetry was composed at least from the late 7th through the 11th c. In his *Ecclesiastical History of the English People* (completed 731 CE), Bede (673–736) describes a body of written vernacular biblical verse, which he attributes to the miracle of an illiterate lay worker named Cædmon (fl. 657–79) whose divinely inspired songs were transcribed by the brothers at Whitby. The illustrated Junius ms., clearly the work of multiple authors, contains the long biblical verse narratives *Genesis*, *Exodus*, *Daniel*, and *Christ and Satan*, although its hist. is obscure. A few OE poems, such as "The Battle of Brunanburh," "The Battle of Maldon," and "Durham," can be securely dated to the late 10th and 11th cs. because they refer to contemp. events.

OE poetry's stress-based, *alliterative verse was cultivated from traditional, probably oral, forms in the context of Lat. versification and Saxon poetry written on the continent (see GERMANIC PROSODY). This verse bears affinities to *accentual verse, which is organized by count of stresses rather than syllables, but its emphasis is on patterns of alliterating stresses that bind half lines across a *caesura; the total number of stressed syllables in a line can vary, although syllabic count, a feature of Romance prosodies (see SYLLABIC VERSE), may have been a consideration for some OE poets. Literary interchange, particularly with Carolingian courts and with Rome, was rich and complex. Some Anglo-Saxon authors knew an array of cl. and early med. *Latin poetry, incl. Virgil's *Aeneid*, and Lat. meter was among the topics taught at Canterbury in the 7th c. by Archbishop Theodore and Abbot Hadrian, both from the Gr.-speaking Mediterranean. This confluence of langs. and poetic *conventions generated a robust verse suitable for lyric, martial, or religious poetry. *Kennings and other metaphoric compounds (such as *hran-rad*, "whale-road," for "sea" and *ban-hus*, "bone-house," for "body"), *litotes, strings of appositional modifiers, and a heroic, aristocratic tenor feature prominently. OE poets experimented with *rhyme, and occasionally with stanzaic form and *macaronic verse. Poets who composed in OE probably also composed Anglo-Lat. poetry, which shares some characteristics with OE poetry. A good deal of alliterative, rhythmic OE prose survives, and the line between prose and poetry is sometimes unclear.

OE poets experimented with first-person *voice, using it to realize emotional intensity and to sustain *unity, often with self-conscious reference to poetic composition. The speakers of lyrics such as "The Wanderer," "The Seafarer," "The Riming Poem," and "The Order of the World" meditate poignantly on the transience of worldly joy, offering poetic imagination and their own experience as a bridge to wisdom and theological understanding. The poet Cynewulf, whose dates are uncertain, muses on his own artistry and on salvation as he disperses the letters of his name, encoded in *runes, across each of the lyric epilogues to "Fates of the Apostles," *Christ II*, *Elene*, and *Juliana*. The speaker of *Widsith* (far-traveler) seems the voice of poetry itself, cataloguing his successes as a court poet for kings whose historical existence far exceeds a single lifespan. Objects often speak, particularly in riddles, which share qualities with both lyric and *gnomic poetry. In Riddle 26, the first-person voice speaks of itself as both a living animal and an ornamented gospel book made from the animal's skin, and vaunts its salvific qualities. In "The Dream of the Rood," the first *dream vision in Eng., the rood describes itself as a living tree and a jeweled cross and commands the dreamer to compose its story. OE poetry maintains strong ties to material culture, and some objects, such as the Alfred Jewel, also bear first-person inscriptions. Most notably, a runic poem

corresponding to a portion of "The Dream of the Rood" is carved into the stone shaft of the 8th-c. Northumbrian Ruthwell Cross. First-person lyric also punctuates long historical poems such as *Beowulf*, particularly at points of transition, where it links narrative segments and distant times.

In many poems of different genres, this dramatic voice turns dialogic. In the saints' lives *Andreas, Juliana, Guthlac A*, and *Elene*, and in the epic *Christ and Satan*, rhetorically heightened episodes—such as Andrew's probing interrogation of Christ, Juliana's and Guthlac's verbal duels with demons, Elene's interchange with the Jewish priest Judas, and the fallen Satan's dialogue with his inferiors—anchor the narrative structures and dramatize didactic lessons. Different in tone but no less dramatic are the *Advent Lyrics* (also known as *Christ I*), a series of *apostrophes inspired by the Advent antiphons and addressed mainly to God, Christ, or Mary, with the exception of *Lyric VII*'s cagey dialogue between Joseph and Mary regarding her pregnancy.

Many OE poems are considered trans., although their inventive reworkings of sources attest to a process that brought extensive study, bold interpretation, and poetic imagination to bear on even the most sacred texts. The epic *Genesis*, a portion of which translates an Old Saxon poem, begins with the apocryphal fall of the angels and includes an unusual version of the temptation. Hagiographical poems such as *Andreas* (on the Apostle Andrew's conversion of the cannibal Mermedonians), *Juliana* (an early Christian virgin-martyr tale), and *Elene* (a version of St. Helen's discovery of the true cross) work freely with multiple Lat. versions, adapting them to the heroic style characteristic of OE poetry. Although most trans. are biblical or hagiographical, the Exeter Book, a diverse *anthology of poetry, contains three trans. from *Physiologus* ("The Panther," "The Whale," and "The Partridge") and "The Phoenix," which translates and then interprets the "De Ave Phoenice" attributed to Lactantius.

All long narrative OE poems except *Beowulf* are biblical or hagiographical. What these poems have in common, however, is historiography. Anglo-Saxon authors, beginning with Bede, worked assiduously to weave northern Eur. hist. into the strands of universal hist., dominated by biblical Heb. genealogy and the ascendance of the Roman Empire. Despite its many fantastical elements, *Beowulf* is deeply grounded in hist.: it documents the military and territorial campaigns of the Danes, Swedes, and Geats; it describes Grendel as "kin of Cain," thus incorporating its narrative into the sweep of biblical hist.; and it features ancestors who also appear in genealogies of the *Anglo-Saxon Chronicle* and other historiographical texts. Together with more localized martial poems such as "The Battle of Maldon" and native saints' lives like the *Guthlac* poems, this epic stakes a claim for Eng. in literary hist.

**II. Middle English, 1066–1500.** The later Eng. Middle Ages bear witness to an intense period of literary experimentation. Almost all of this experimentation is in poetry; nonrhythmic prose is not a coherent medium (with cultural prestige, genres, and so on) in literary Eng. composition until after the invention of the printing press in about 1450. The experimental impulse originates from a fundamental ling. change: in the aftermath of the Norman Conquest (1066), which roughly divides the two phases of the Middle Ages in England, Norman poetic practices collide with OE practices to produce the first flowering of ME poetry, incl. *The Owl and the Nightingale* (late 12th c.). It deploys debate conventions that appear in both OE and Fr. but also uses a continental octosyllabic line and mixes courtly Fr. vocabulary into its largely Eng. lexicon. The synergy between Fr. and insular lang. and literary convention yields new literary forms from the 12th through the 14th c. These new forms arise both in *narrative and lyric poetry and in both religious and secular contexts, though one upshot of the experimental energy of the period is that both of these oppositions—narrative versus lyric, religious versus secular—are examined and reinvented by the end of the Middle Ages, particularly in the large-scale narrative fictions of the major poets of Edwardian, Ricardian, and Lancastrian England.

In the first phase of ME narrative poetry, the literary landscape is dominated by biblical paraphrase, hagiography, and homily. Incl. *Genesis and Exodus* (1250), the *South English Legendary* (late 13th c.), the *Gospel of Nicodemus* (1325), the *Poema morale* (ca. 1170), and the *Ormulum* (ca. 1200), these religious narratives announce their primary cultural purpose as didactic, though many (the *Ormulum* in particular) have a clear and sustained interest in lang., *rhythm, and the aesthetic field in which didacticism is produced.

Early lyrical poetry, too, is often religious in theme. Many early religious lyrics are structured as apostrophes to the Virgin Mary, while others are prayers to Jesus. As in OE poetry, some of the most interesting religious lyrics are dialogic, for instance containing an exchange between Mary and Jesus. There is no single unifying or typically "Eng." lyrical form for religious verse in the period; instead, a wide variety of Fr. and Lat. verse forms and meters are adapted to the exigencies of Eng. stress patterns. Line lengths and *rhyme schemes in lyric poetry are variable, as are the lengths of stanzas and the prosodic patterns within lines.

Contemporaneous with biblical narratives and *devotional poetry, more secular poetic works appear in early ME as well. Early secular lyrics are deeply indebted to Fr. and Norman amatory lyric forms; again, as poets adapt these forms to ME, a great deal of formal innovation results. These early experiments with lyrical form, *meter, and *syntax prove a crucial resource for later makers of large-scale fictional narrative, who interpolate short lyrical passages into their larger works.

Extensive, nonbiblical narrative poetry has often been categorized either as fact-based historical chronicle or as fictional *romance, though recent scholarship suggests that the boundary demarcating "fact-based" hist. from "fictional" romance may have been far blurrier in the Middle Ages than it seems to mod. readers, since many of the "romance" narratives clearly under-

stand themselves as historical, pertaining either to Brit. prehist. (Lawman/Layamon's *Brut*, ca. 1205; *King Horn*, ca. 1225; *Havelock the Dane*, ca. 1280), Lat. prehist. (the Alexander romances *Alisaunder*, *Alexander and Dindimus*, and *Wars of Alexander*; and the Trojan hists. *Gest Historiale of the Destruction of Troy*, ca. 1350–1400, and the *Seege of Troye*, ca. 1300–25), or, more rarely, Fr. hist. Toward the 14th and 15th cs., the Arthurian romances flourish, incl. the alliterative *Morte Arthure*, the ballad *Legend of King Arthur*, and the justly famous *Sir Gawain and the Green Knight*, which synthesizes insular and Fr. verse forms (*alliteration with rhyme; long verses with stanzaic organization), narrative and lyrical formal strategies (large-scale chronological story told through an intricately versified stanzaic form), and historical and fantastic material (Trojan backstory and supernatural contemp. events). Largely through its formal complexity, *Gawain* constitutes what many scholars see as the pinnacle of romance invention in ME.

Another reason for the critical accolades to *Sir Gawain and the Green Knight*, however, is its larger context, both in the ms. in which it appears (Cotton Nero A.x) and the literary movement to which it bears witness, the Alliterative Revival. The Cotton Nero ms. contains *Gawain* and three other poems: *Cleanness*, *Patience*, and *Pearl*, all of which seem to have been composed by the *Gawain* poet. *Patience* is a dramatic and animated paraphrase of the book of Jonah, and it thus represents a late and unusually artful instance of biblical paraphrase narrative. *Cleanness* ranges more widely in its plot, covering stories of the Flood, the destruction of Sodom, and Belshazzar's feast. In *Pearl*, courtly lang. blends with theological content to create an elegant meditation on the nature of loss: the dreamer-poet mourns the loss of his "precious pearl," a daughter who has died in infancy. The poem's elaborate artistry and profound rendering of human emotion find no parallel in ME poetry. Though *Pearl* is unique in having end rhyme, alliterative patterning, and stanzaic structure, the rest of the Cotton Nero poems are also formally intricate, written in an alliterative meter, which is the staple meter of all those poems that have come to be loosely denominated as the Alliterative Revival. The generic multiplicity and stylistic variation of Cotton Nero A.x suggest that its poet was very much part of his or her cultural moment: the corpus of works composed in this late phase of ME lit. by the major authors is likewise characterized both by synthesis and revision of extant and authoritative literary forms and genres.

Of late med. writers, William Langland (ca. 1330–1400) is the first and arguably the most influential. Of the over 50 surviving copies of his *Piers Plowman* (written ca. 1360–87), there are three authorial versions, A, B, and C. These three revisions, though unquestionably motivated in part by aesthetic concerns, are likely also responses to the sociopolitical and theological controversies that wracked England in the middle and late 14th c., incl. the culmination and end of King Edward III's tumultuous reign and the increasing theological threat posed by the reform-minded

Wycliffites and Lollards. Responding to these sociopolitical pressures, in each of Langland's revisions the poem changes its theological shape and political tenor, though, in all cases, it is rubricated into a *visio*, which recounts the dreaming narrator's vision of the social ills of 14th-c. England, and a *vita*, which recounts his pilgrimage to Truth. Langland's poem is notoriously slippery of genre, encompassing not only dream vision and pilgrimage narrative but consolation, autobiography, *personification allegory, debate, philosophy, trial drama, and apocalypse. Moreover, its episodic construction and its three distinct versions make the basic plot of the poem very difficult to tease out, though this resistance to interpretation may have been what made the poem wildly successful and influential in its own time, by inspiring readers to engage actively with the strangeness and complexity of its ideation and its self-conscious positioning both as a literary work and a sociopolitical and theological treatise.

Whether Chaucer (ca. 1345–1400) read Langland's marvelously complex poem remains an open issue, although the thematic and formal consonances in their major works (both tell pilgrimage narratives; both are interested in the interplay between *allegory and autobiography; both work with the Boethian *consolatio* genre; both stitch together a series of shorter vignettes into a more expansive fictional narrative; both are profoundly interested in the social fabric of 14th-c. England) make it seem likely that Chaucer was at least somewhat influenced by *Piers Plowman*, particularly later in his career. The precise chronology of Chaucer's poetry is unknown, although it is usually divided into an earlier "French" period (influenced by Jean de Meun, Guillaume de Machaut, and Jean Froissart) and a later "Italian" period (influenced by Dante and Boccaccio). Many of Chaucer's early works are either trans. (*Roman de la Rose*) or dream-vision narratives that work within and reinvent the conventions of the debate genre, while also being written for particular occasions (*Book of the Duchess* commemorates the death of Blanche of Lancaster; *Parliament of Fowls* is a Valentine's Day poem). By the mid-1380s, Chaucer's poetry took a significant turn. He translated Boethius's *De Consolatione philosophiae* into prose, and spent much of the rest of his life revisiting its themes in his poetry. Based on Giovanni Boccaccio's *Il Filostrato,* Chaucer's *Troilus and Criseyde,* for instance, sets a star-crossed love affair against the historical events of the Trojan War as a pre-Christian test case for Boethian philosophy. In particular, in this poem, Chaucer stages the inevitable tragedy of the Trojan War as an occasion for meditating on the Boethian notions of fate versus free will, the nature of fortune, and the emptiness of worldly desire.

Having completed his antiquarian and philosophical romance, Chaucer turned his energies toward the contemp. reality of late med. England as his primary subject matter: by the late 1380s, he was working on the unfinished collection of ten extant fragments that are now known as the *Canterbury Tales*. The "General Prologue" that opens the poem describes the 29 characters on a pilgrimage to Canterbury both as oc-cupational types (e.g., a lawyer, a parson, a wife) and as unique individuals. Throughout the *Tales*, to fulfill the terms of a tale-telling contest, each pilgrim tells a prologue and then a tale to the rest of the pilgrims. Chaucer likely derived his inspiration for this narrative invention from Boccaccio's *Decameron* (see ITALY, POETRY OF) and, in all likelihood, from the Ar. frame tale (see ARABIC POETRY). In the *Canterbury Tales*, however, Chaucer experiments with the templates he inherits. First, he devises a dynamic interplay between the prologue and the tale, which complicates each speaker's character and his or her place in the larger social world. Second, he develops distinct and socially situated voices for all his pilgrims; in doing so, he engages with and undercuts the genre of estates' satire, which depicts the world as comprised of only three basic social groups, clergy, warriors, and workers. Third, each pilgrim tells a tale that fits into and often reinvents an available literary genre: romances, *fabliaux, *fables, sermons, saints' lives, allegories, *tragedies, and exempla all appear in the *Tales*. In its use of dialectic structure to devise characters who are at once types and individuals, in its exploding of social ideology, and in its relentless will to integrate a polyphony of different literary modes, voices, and genres into a single, unified, and remarkably realistic composition, the *Canterbury Tales* remains one of the most innovative compositions of the Middle Ages in any lang.

Where Langland's career was influenced by Edwardian politics and Chaucer's by Ricardian, John Gower's (ca. 1330–1408) poetic career straddles the late Ricardian and early Lancastrian positions, and his poetry reflects that historical positioning—indeed, his magnum opus the ME *Confessio amantis* (written ca. 1386–90) has two prologues, one written in dedication to Richard II, the other to Henry IV. After the prologue follow eight books, each of which comprises a series of moral tales organized around the central theme of sin and right behavior. Seven sections draw from penitential manuals in the period; the outlier responds to the emerging vernacular *Fürstenspiegel* genre, also known as *mirror for princes*. This genre (which also includes Chaucer's "Tale of Melibee" in the *Canterbury Tales*, as well as certain passages from *Piers Plowman*) seems to gain power in the literary imagination of the late Ricardian and early Lancastrian periods, perhaps in response to the political turmoil of the period, as Richard II is forcibly deposed and Henry IV comes to power. Couching what could be incendiary political content carefully in literary form, Gower enfolds his gargantuan compilation of didactic exempla into a tidy fictive frame, adapted from the dream-vision narratives of Boethius, Jean de Meun, and Alan of Lille, in which a lover (Amans, later revealed to be Gower himself) seeks amatory counsel from a beneficent teacher (the Confessor). Perhaps because of the political bent of his writings or the overtly moralizing thrust of his composition and certainly because of Chaucer's famous dedication of his *Troilus* to "moral Gower," Gower was absorbed into lit. hist. as a "moral" writer, more concerned with didacticism than pleasure or entertainment.

The two most significant poets of the 15th c. are John Lydgate (ca. 1370–1449) and Thomas Hoccleve (ca. 1370–1430), both of whom read Chaucer extensively, and at least Hoccleve likely also read Langland and Gower. Lydgate is esp. well known for his *aureate diction, his assembly of extensive works of hist., and his interest in the mirror-for-princes genre. Over the course of his long poetic career, however, he composed in nearly every important med. genre and, thus, represents a synthesis and culmination of ME poetic hist. Like Lydgate, Hoccleve experiments with a variety of poetic genres and modes, ranging from religious lyric to autobiography, from political poems to a voluminous mirror for princes. But Hoccleve also picks up from his Ricardian and Lancastrian forebears an ironic fluency and self-mocking tone, which make him seem startlingly "mod." and his works a bridge between the Middle Ages and the early poetry of the Ren.

### III. The Renaissance, 1500–1660.
When William Caxton opened England's first printing press in Westminster in 1476, he not only disseminated a standard early mod. Eng. but also helped establish Eng. as a literary lang. Caxton printed Eng. poetry—Gower, Lydgate, and Chaucer—for the first time. He also published trans. of cl. and continental poetry, making available various literary models for future generations. As the 16th c. unfolded, printing and literacy increased, and Eng. education was transformed by humanism—"the new learning" imported from continental Europe with its cornerstone disciplines of rhet. and eloquence. Particularly in the second half of the century, inventive, well-made poetry was useful and often esteemed; it elevated the lang. and thereby England itself, as well as the poet's own status. The Reformation also thrust poetic lang. into the forefront of culture. Distrustful of the ecclesiastical hierarchies of the established church, Protestants sought truth in scripture itself (trans. now into the vernacular) and embraced devotional verse as a pathway to God.

Usually considered England's first Ren. poet, John Skelton (ca. 1460–1529) was on the cusp of this new momentum. Learned and versatile, Skelton tutored the young Prince Henry (later Henry VIII) in the court of Henry VII, and he wrote *occasional poetry celebrating the reign of the Tudors. Most of his poems, however, exhibit an independent mind, by turns reflective, playful, and satiric. He draws on ME forms and conventions, esp. alliteration, but develops his own contemp. voice, particularly when he writes in the style later dubbed *Skeltonics—short, rhyme-rich lines featuring colloquial diction and rhythms. Skelton's major poems include *The Bouge of Court* (1499), an allegorical dream vision warning of court corruption; "Speak, Parrot," "Colin Clout," and "Why Come Ye Not to Court?" (written ca. 1522), fierce *satires lambasting the powerful Cardinal Thomas Wolsey; and *Philip Sparrow* (written ca. 1509), an exaggerated *elegy for a young girl's pet, replete with liturgical *allusion and structure, spiritual instruction, social satire, erotic suggestion, everyday emotion, and reflections on cl. and Eng. poetry.

Thomas Wyatt (1503–42) is widely considered the first great Eng. poet of the Ren. Rigorously educated in the humanist trad. and a diplomat for Henry VIII, Wyatt was well prepared to represent the complexities of the Tudor court, particularly the intermeshing of political and personal desires. Wyatt's verse letters and satires warn of court corruption, and his dozens of poems about love recount and enact disillusionment, incl. his much-anthologized *rhyme-royal masterpiece "They Flee from Me" (ms. ca. 1530s); his lyrics for musical accompaniment, such as "My Lute, Awake" (ms. ca. 1530s); and the *sonnets he adapts from Petrarch's *Canzoniere*, such as "Whoso list to hunt" (ms. ca. 1526–27) based on *Canzoniere* 190 "Una candida cerva" (see PETRARCHISM). Wyatt's Petrarchan sonnets are the first known sonnets in Eng. excepting Chaucer's trans. of *Canzoniere* 132 in *Troilus and Criseyde*. Wyatt also translated the seven *penitential psalms, introducing *terza rima to Eng. and representing David as a prototype of the reformed Protestant seeking his own intimate connection to God.

Wyatt's poems were not printed during his lifetime but circulated in ms., the expected mode of publication for the courtly elite through the 16th c. Such mss. often found their way into print after an author's death and sometimes before. In 1549, Wyatt's penitential psalms appeared in print, and eight years later, 97 of his secular poems were published by an enterprising printer, Richard Tottel, in a popular collection of poems titled *Songes and Sonettes* and later known as *Tottel's Miscellany*.

Tottel's collection also featured the poetry of Henry Howard, the Earl of Surrey (1517–47), a fact noted prominently on the title page. High-born, polished, and ambitious, Surrey was still famous a dozen years after he had lost his head to an aging, suspicious Henry VIII. Surrey adapted sonnets from the *Canzoniere* into Eng. as his friend Wyatt also did, but Surrey is credited with inventing the Eng. sonnet (later called the Shakespearean sonnet), by organizing the 14 lines into three quatrains and a couplet (*ababcdcdefefgg*) instead of the It. sonnet's *octave (*abbaabba*) and *sestet (rhyming in several ways, incl. *cdcdcd* or *cdecde*). Surrey also developed *blank verse in Eng. for the first time, translating books 2 and 4 of Virgil's *Aeneid* into lines of unrhymed iambic pentameter.

Another popular book in the second half of the 16th c. was *A Mirror for Magistrates* (1559), a collection of poems by various authors recounting the downfall of princes and other powerful figures in Eng. hist. With various additions and deletions, the collection was reprinted eight times between 1559 and the end of the century and has engaged students of early mod. political culture since then. Poetically, it is not generally distinctive, but there are exceptions, incl. the chilling "Induction" and "Complaint of Henry, Duke of Buckingham" by Thomas Sackville (1536–1608).

Queen Elizabeth I began her long reign in 1558. Exceptionally intelligent, fluent in several ancient and mod. langs., and educated by leading humanists of the day, Elizabeth I wrote her own famous speeches, volumes of official and personal correspondence, and a handful of poems. She understood the theatrical nature of monarchy and the myriad ways political and poetic lang. inform each other, and she expected her courtiers to understand these subtleties as well. She also undersood the capacity of poetry (in a popular play or in love poems circulating at court) to engage, instruct, unite, or distract people. Moreover, her reinstatement of "the reformed religion," Anglican Protestantism, fostered the translating into Eng. of biblical verse, as well as the composing of original devotional poetry.

In 1560, having returned to England from exile during Mary's reign, Anne Lock (1530–after 1590) published the first known *sonnet sequence in Eng., *A Meditation of a Penitent Sinner* (1560), appended to a trans. of four sermons by John Calvin. The sequence includes five prefatory sonnets followed by 21 sonnets dilating on a passage in Psalm 51. From a family of moderate means and personally acquainted with the Scottish Calvinist John Knox, Lock received an excellent education for a woman of the period. While many intellectual leaders of the later 16th c. advocated literacy in women, few encouraged them to study rhet., the lifeblood of humanism and poetics.

Isabella Whitney (fl. 1567–73), a servant through at least part of her life, was thus unusual in her publishing of a love *complaint (ca. 1567) and a collection of poems and prose, *A Sweet Nosgay, or Pleasant Posye* (1573). The latter is based on Hugh Plat's anthol. *The Flowers of Philosophy* (1572) but evidences Whitney's female experience, colloquial voice, and sense of purpose. In some poems, such as "The Will and Testament," an elegy for the London her impoverishment required her to leave, we find her appropriating conventional male genres with wit and self-assurance.

George Turberville (1544–97), Barnabe Googe (1540–94), and George Gascoigne (1534–77) also wrote compendiums of verse and prose in the 1560s and 1570s. All favored a mostly straightforward *plain style. The numerous engaging poems in Gascoigne's *A Hundred Sundry Flowers* (1573), include "Gascoigne's Lullaby," in which the poet offers subtle wisdom in direct speech, blending melancholy and humor, self-mockery and self-acceptance.

Known to later times as "the poet's poet," Spenser (1552–99) appeared in the late 1570s with a very different poetic sensibility. Spenser embraced Eng. on every level—semantic, syntactic, etymological, and musical. He reveled in abstract metrical and aural patterns while simultaneously immersing readers in a unique lexicon, one that included OE terms, Chaucerian words, ornate phrases, and original coinages in which spelling itself was a medium of expression, able to make a pun, recall an etymology, or sound a chord. Spenser launched his career with *The Shepheardes Calender* (1579), a collection of 12 *eclogues, one for each month, in various forms and meters, some *monologues, some dialogues. Published with fine woodcut illustrations and scholarly notes like those accompanying cl. lit., the printed text insisted on its own importance. Furthermore, by making his debut in the *pastoral mode as Virgil had done with his *Eclogues*, Spenser placed himself in the most august literary *canon, and he put the Eng. lang. in the prestigious company of Lat. and Gr. as one of the world's great literary langs. He continued these associations in "Astrophel" (1595), a pastoral elegy for his friend and fellow poet Philip Sidney based on Virgil's fifth eclogue. In 1595, Spenser also published his *Amoretti,* an elaborate Petrarchan sonnet sequence, and in the same volume, his *Epithalamion,* a wedding-day gift for his bride (see EPITHALAMIUM).

Spenser's greatest work is *The Faerie Queene*, an allegorical epic that aims to "fashion a gentleman or noble person in vertuous and gentle discipline," as Spenser explains in a letter to Walter Ralegh, arguing that "delight" and "doctrine by ensample" are better teachers than "good discipline . . . sermoned at large" and "doctrine . . . by rule." Elizabeth I is the Faerie Queene, he explains, who "in a dream of vision" has inspired Arthur (not yet king) to find her. Arthur possesses Aristotle's 12 moral virtues, and each of 12 books of the epic will follow the adventures of a knight representing one of these virtues. Spenser ultimately wrote six books of 12 cantos each, and two cantos of a seventh book. These last two cantos, later known as the "Mutability Cantos," recount the goddess Mutability's attempt to reign over all other forces and her compelling but unsuccessful trial in Nature's court. *Faerie Queene* books 1–3 were published in 1590, books 1–6 with the "Mutability Cantos" in 1596. Cl. allusion abounds in the *Faerie Queene*, but Eng. hist. and legend are also pervasive. In many obvious ways, the epic celebrates Elizabeth I and Tudor rule, but it is also a complexly satiric, richly suggestive text, full of surprises and contradictions. Spenser created a new stanza for his masterpiece, nine iambic lines—eight pentameter, the ninth hexameter—rhyming ababbcbcc. The *Spenserian stanza feels like an expansion and intensification of rhyme royal and makes the *Faerie Queene* all the more suspenseful, thought-provoking, musical, and even mesmerizing.

Born the same year as Spenser, Walter Ralegh (1552–1618) was an ambitious courtier and explorer as well as a poet. Although Ralegh perfected that meshing of poetic and political rhet. so valued by Elizabeth I, particularly in "The Ocean to Cynthia," his long poem of praise for the queen who (for a while) raised him to great status, he is better known for his cynical and world-weary *lyric poems recounting human vanity and the futility of life, e.g. "On the Life of Man," "The Lie," "Nature that washed her hands in milk," and "Even such is time." A more playful poem is "The Nymph's Reply to the Shepherd," a shrewd response to Christopher Marlowe's seductive "The Passionate Shepherd to His Love." Ralegh's poems circulated in ms. and also appeared in various miscellanies of the late 16th and early 17th cs., most notably the popular *The Phoenix Nest* (1593).

In Thomas Hoby's 1561 trans. of Baldassare Castiglione's *Il Cortegiano* (*The Courtier*), the premier handbook for Ren. courtiers, Castiglione advises courtiers "to practice in all things a certain *sprezzatura* [nonchalance], so as to conceal all art and make whatever is done or said appear to be without effort and almost without any thought about it." It is this quality exactly that describes the poetry and prose—and indeed, the person—of Philip Sidney (1554–86). Born to enormous power and privilege, Sidney was politically ambitious as well as a champion of the Eng. lang. and a great patron of fellow poets. His own poetry and prose circulated in ms. in the 1570s and 1580s, entertaining and inspiring an elite circle of readers, incl. his younger sister, Mary Sidney Herbert, Countess of Pembroke, who soon became a poet in her own right. Sidney dedicated to Mary the *Old Arcadia* (also known as *The Countess of Pembroke's Arcadia*), a prose romance bejeweled with 78 lyric poems, incl. the beautiful double *sestina "Ye Goteherd Gods." In 1579, Sidney circulated his rhetorically dashing *Defence of Poesy* (1595; also called *An Apology for Poetry*) in which he refutes charges against poetry (and lit. in general) with sparkling logic, learning, and wit.

Sidney's most influential work is his sequence of sonnets and songs *Astrophil and Stella*, consisting of 108 mostly Petrarchan sonnets and 11 songs in various forms. Astrophil (lover of stars) woos and muses on Stella (star), representing ever-changing states of mind and a sophisticated literary self-consciousness. Petrarch's *Canzoniere* is the prototype for Sidney's sequence, but Astrophil's passion takes place in the present-day Elizabethan court, and Stella is well aware that she is being pursued. Astrophil's voice is youthful, energetic, ironic, playful, defiant, self-mocking—and ultimately dejected. *Astrophil and Stella* caused a stir when it appeared in print in 1591 after Sidney's premature death, prompting the publication of numerous sonnet sequences during that last decade of the century, incl. Samuel Daniel's *Delia* (1592), Michael Drayton's *Idea's Mirror* (1594), and Spenser's aforementioned *Amoretti* (1595).

It was most likely within this decade as well that William Shakespeare (1564–1616) wrote most or all of the sonnets that would be published in 1609, probably surreptitiously, under the title *Shakespeare's Sonnets*. This text is not only the most innovative and psychologically complex of all the sonnet sequences but also arguably one of the greatest collections of lyric poems in Eng. Developing further the Eng. sonnet first established by Surrey, Shakespeare represents the mind in many moods and patterns of thought. His sonnets do not sound like imitations of other sonnets but instead seem driven by lived—and living—experience. Vulnerability, anxiety, longing, rejection, confidence, disgust, worldliness, anger, regret, hope, jealousy, and depression are all palpable at various points in the sequence. In many of the poems, the speaker tries to meet his most profound challenge, confronting the ravages of time and the facts of mortality; as he says succinctly in sonnet 64, "Ruin has taught me thus to ruminate, / That time will come and take my love away." These confrontations are esp. moving because Shakespeare's speaker does not seek conventional consolations nor defer to religious views. He is not dismissively cynical but unrelentingly analytical and self-scrutinizing. His sonnets revise and explore themselves before our eyes,

and repeatedly they implicate us, the readers of the future, for the beloved can only live on in the poem's lines "as long as men can breathe, and eyes can see."

Shakespeare's sonnets are also unconventional because the poet-lover addresses not a lady but a beloved young man (in sonnets 1–126), and when he does address a lady (in sonnets 127–52), we learn quickly that she is neither ideal nor unattainable; to the contrary, she and the poet-lover are sexual partners. With pleas, praise, questions, accusations, confessions, and hard-won yet unresolved insight, the speaker represents the crises of intimacy and identity provoked by these relationships.

The sonnet sequence was not the only popular genre of the 1590s. Also popular were long narrative poems based on erotic tales in cl. (usually Ovidian) mythology, called *epyllia by 19th-c. scholars. The best of these are Shakespeare's *Venus and Adonis* (1593) and *The Rape of Lucrece* (1594), and Christopher Marlowe's unfinished *Hero and Leander* (1598). *Venus* (99 stanzas of *ababcc* iambic pentameter) and *Hero* (409 *heroic couplets) are masterpieces of lush, seductive storytelling, dazzling rhet., erotic tension, and comedic use of syntax, meter, and rhyme. *Lucrece*, 265 stanzas of rhyme royal, is all these things but in a darker key.

Mary Sidney Herbert, Countess of Pembroke (1561–1621), was the most accomplished female writer of the 16th c. She translated Petrarch's *Trionfo della Morte* (*Triumph of Death*) into Eng. terza rima and Robert Garnier's *Antonius, A Tragœdie* (1592) into Eng. blank verse. *Antonius* probably influenced Elizabeth Cary, Lady Faulkland (1585–1639) in her writing of the *closet drama, *The Tragedy of Mariam* (1613), the first original blank-verse play by an Englishwoman. Pembroke's greatest achievement was her completion of a trans. of the Psalms begun by her brother Philip Sidney, who had translated 43 of the psalms by the time of his death. Pembroke translated the remaining 107 psalms, incl. the 22 poems that make up Psalm 119. She was meticulous in her consultation of sources in Eng., Fr., and Lat., but she artfully cast the psalms into varying Eng. forms and meters and wove into the poems her own sensibility and arguably female perspective. Her psalms, thus, convey both deference and boldness, scholarship and innovation. Particularly interesting are the two original dedicatory poems that survive with one ms. copy of the sequence. In "Even now that care," the more formal of the two, Pembroke addresses Queen Elizabeth. In "To the Angell Spirit of the most excellent Sir Philip Sidney," she addresses her late brother's spirit—at least, she begins to, but images of his death interrupt her, and she finds herself conjuring not Philip's spirit but her own memory. She struggles to resume her dedication, succeeds somewhat, but again is distracted by grief and self-doubt. Throughout the poem, Pembroke's anguished longing flares up as she strives to maintain the dedication's lofty diction and apparent purpose. The result is a compelling poetic voice. Although not published until the 19th c., the Sidney Psalter circulated widely in its own time. John Donne, among many poets influenced by the text, praised the siblings' collaboration in his poem, "Upon the Translation of the Psalms by Sir Philip Sidney, and The Countess of Pembroke" (1621). Other important poets influenced by the psalter include Aemilia Lanyer, George Herbert, Henry Vaughan, and John Milton.

Among the poets Pembroke invited into her circle of *patronage was Daniel (1562–1619), who addressed his sonnet sequence *Delia* (1592) to Pembroke herself. Daniel also wrote *A Defence of Ryme* (1603) in which he celebrates the Eng. lang. and the poetic forms it generates, not only praising the sensual pleasures of lang. but associating these pleasures with reason, judgment, and memory. Daniel's essay is an answer to the somber tract *Observations in the Arte of English Poesie* (1602) by a young and temporarily didactic Thomas Campion (1567–1620), who, at that point in his career, advocated writing Eng. poetry in "numbers"— quantitative meter, as in Lat. (see CLASSICAL PROSODY, QUANTITY). Happily for readers and listeners, Campion did not spend much more time in theoretical arguments. He wrote instead some of the most beautiful unrhyming and rhyming Eng. lyrics in his age, many of which he set to music.

In the rapidly growing city of London in the last decades of the 16th c., the art and business of theater took root and flourished. Each week, thousands of Londoners (up to 15,000 by one estimate) visited worlds beyond their own, witnessed human character and conflict on a grand scale, and listened to thousands of lines of poetry. Some plays were written in prose, but predominantly, they were written in iambic pentameter, usually in blank verse. Able to represent a person thinking or speaking in a fairly natural yet elevated way, iambic pentameter developed in lyric, narrative, and dramatic genres at once.

In 1587, the tempestuous university wit Marlowe (1564–93) transfixed audiences with the blank verse of his two-part tragedy *Tamburlaine the Great*. In the next few years, until his death in a tavern brawl at age 29, Marlowe confirmed his place as the Elizabethans' most exciting dramatist with a series of highly successful plays: *Doctor Faustus* (written ca. 1588), *The Jew of Malta* (written 1589), and *Edward II* (written ca. 1593). Marlowe's protagonists compelled audiences with their self-aggrandizing speeches replete with Latinate polysyllabic words and sweeping metaphors, all in thundering *end-stopped iambic pentameter. Marlowe was the star poet-playwright when Shakespeare arrived on the scene in the late 1580s or early 1590s. The rivalry that ensued benefited both dramatists and, of course, their audiences. At Marlowe's death, Shakespeare had written seven plays. He would write almost 30 more.

In the early plays, Shakespeare's lines are frequently end-stopped like Marlowe's. Unlike Marlowe's, Shakespeare's lines also sometimes rhyme, particularly when love-struck characters strive to woo—in *Love's Labour's Lost* (written 1594–95), *A Midsummer Night's Dream* (written 1595–96), *As You Like It* (written 1599–1600), and *Much Ado About Nothing* (written 1598–99), e.g. In *Romeo and Juliet* (written 1594–95), the star-crossed lovers create a sonnet when they first speak with each other (1.5.93–106). Dialogue in later plays rarely rhymes, but magic spells, riddles, and *chants surely do (witness *Macbeth* [written 1605–6], or *The Tempest* [written 1611]), and rhyming songs can be found in nearly every play, from *lullabies to drinking songs to country ballads at sheep-shearing festivals.

As his career progressed, Shakespeare explored with increasing nuance the expressive possibilities of blank verse, esp. *enjambment. The result is a poetry that highlights the stops and starts of troubled thought, the momentum of suspicion, ambition, or anger, the questions and obsessions of grief or love, and subtle degrees of understanding, cooperation, curiosity, tension, or antagonism between characters. Esp. in later plays— *King Lear* (written 1606), *Antony and Cleopatra* (written 1606–7), *The Tempest*, *The Winter's Tale* (written 1611–12), and others, Shakespeare's enjambments are as powerful as John Milton's will be in *Paradise Lost*.

In his plays as in his sonnets, Shakespeare demonstrates fluency in the *diction, idioms, and rhetorical styles heard in many venues of the day, from street to court, village to university, craftsman's shop to merchant's office—and with these, a heightened perception of political, social, and esp. interpersonal contexts for lang. This fluency and perception yield a wide range of complex, credible characters and perpetual metaphoric richness.

In the late 1590s, the brilliant and irascible Ben Jonson (1572–1637) established himself as a superb writer of satiric comedy with *Every Man in his Humour* (written 1598) and *Every Man out of his Humour* (written 1599). His numerous plays include the masterpieces *Volpone* (written 1605–6), *Epicoene or the Silent Woman* (written 1609–10), *The Alchemist* (written 1610), and *Bartholomew Fair* (written 1614). Jonson constructed his plays according to cl. rules for drama, but they are as urban and contemp. as can be in lang., plot, and reference.

Until the Puritans closed the theaters in 1642, many playwrights succeeded in entertaining London audiences with rousing and sometimes innovative dramatic verse, incl. John Webster (ca. 1578–1625), John Fletcher (1579–1625), Thomas Middleton (1580–1627), Philip Massinger (1583–1649), and Francis Beaumont (1584–1616). However, no plays engaged and influenced poetry as much as Shakespeare's did, and no poets beyond Shakespeare, Jonson, and, to a lesser extent, Marlowe achieved greatness as narrative or lyric poets.

As a conventional period of literary study, the 17th c. begins in 1603, the year of Queen Elizabeth I's death and King James I's accession, and runs to the Restoration in 1660, though anthols. and academic courses often follow Milton's career through the writing and publication of *Paradise Lost*, which closes this signal episode in Eng. lit. hist. James I was an advocate not only of plays but of *masques—lavish, symbolic court theatricals in which the nobility themselves performed. Jonson tried his hand at this genre early on in the new reign and triumphed so thoroughly that he quickly became the court's premier writer of masques, a position he held for more than two decades. With their seductive musical verse, nuanced allegory, and carefully calibrated timing and proportions, Jonson's masques established a new standard in the genre.

As a lyric poet, Jonson modeled himself on his beloved Gr. and Roman poets, favoring their genres of *epigram and satire and alluding to them frequently. His poems evoke ease and polish whether reflecting on personal struggles or making social overtures. In elegies for his children, "On My First Son" (1616) and "On My First Daughter" (1616), he is earnest and vulnerable. In his epigrams, he is ironic and amused. We hear an affable, epicurean, and intermittently self-effacing voice in "Inviting a Friend to Supper" (1616) and a polished witty tone in his flattering poems to patrons, most notably his famous *country house poem "To Penshurst" (1616). In 1616, Jonson published grandly his own collected works in folio ed., making sure as Spenser always had that the importance of his work was evident in its very presentation. Seven years later, Jonson wrote a tribute to the contemporary he envied and admired most. "To the Memory of My Beloved, Master William Shakespeare, and What He Hath Left Us" appeared in the First Folio of Shakespeare's plays (1623). Aptly, he addresses Shakespeare as "Soul of the age!" *and* asserts, "He was not of an age, but for all time!"

John Donne (1572–1631), considered by many to be one of England's greatest poets, was born the same year as Jonson and, like Jonson, was prolific, ambitious, and often keenly satirical. Both poets were fluent in colloquial and dramatic speech. However, where Jonson's voice is measured and cultivated, Donne's is passionate, argumentative, and immediate: "For God's sake hold your tongue, and let me love!" the speaker begins in one poem; "Busy old fool, unruly Sun!" in another. Donne foregrounds colloquial diction and syntax, enjambment, exclamations, imperatives, and references to the speaker's immediate surroundings. His unexpected metaphors yoke specific and abstract phenomena in contemp. science, travel and exploration, recent political and social events, and everyday objects and happenings. Critiquing the presence of these *conceits and arguments in love poetry, John Dryden accused Donne of "affecting the *metaphysics*." The term stuck, but not in the pejorative sense Dryden had intended (see METAPHYSICAL POETRY). In some poems, Donne's speaker swaggers and brags about sexual conquests; in some, he unleashes all his rhetorical cleverness to seduce a desired other. In many other *Songs and Sonnets*, his speaker attests to loving one woman profoundly and rejects the conventional dichotomies of body and soul to represent the completeness of that love. "Nothing else is," he argues in "The Sun Rising."

For practical as well as philosophical reasons, Donne converted to Anglicanism as a young man. He saw no benefit in dying for Catholicism as his uncles and brother had done. He was not eager to be an Anglican priest, but after years of struggling to support a large family (ten children at the final count) and believing, as he writes in one of his famous sermons, that "No man is an Island, entire of it self," he responded to King James I's urging that he take orders. Donne rose quickly in the church, becoming Dr. Donne, dean of St. Paul's Cathedral, in his early forties and writing sermons of arresting eloquence and imagination. He also wrote some of England's greatest religious poetry, incl. the famous *Holy Sonnets* (1633). Petrarchan instead of Eng. in form, the octave-sestet structure of these poems dovetails with Donne's dramatic sentences: dependent clauses build in intensity; then at line nine, there is a shift to a simpler lexicon and syntax.

Although religious verse was the most conventionally acceptable kind of poetry for women to write, Aemilia Lanyer's (1569–1645) *Salve Deus Rex Judaeorum* (1611), a retelling of Christ's passion in stately rhyme royal with a protofeminist agenda, was anything but conventional. Appended to *Salve Deus* was "Description of Cookeham," a country house poem published before (and possibly written before) Jonson's "To Penshurst." In heroic couplets, Lanyer honors and mourns the house in which she spent her formative years under the guardianship of a noble family.

While the middle-class Lanyer dared enter the realm of patriarchal theology, the aristocratic Lady Mary Wroth (ca. 1587–1651) braved the male-dominated sphere of secular lit., particularly the genres popularized by her uncle Philip Sidney. Wroth wrote both the first pastoral romance and the first secular sonnet sequence to be published by a woman: *The Countess of Montgomery's Urania* (1621), an epic-length romance incl. more than 50 poems; and *Pamphilia to Amphilanthus* (1621), a Petrarchan lyric sequence of 103 sonnets and songs. Wroth also composed the unfinished but already epic-length pastoral romance *Love's Victory*, a sequel to *Urania*.

At his death, George Herbert (1593–1633) left to a friend the fate of his unknown collection of sacred poems *The Temple*. The volume appeared in print soon after and became so popular it was reprinted at least seven times before the end of the century. To dazzling and often haunting effect, Herbert juxtaposes ideas, events, and imagery in unexpected ways; he is as metaphysical as Donne. However, where Donne exhibits a rhetorician's persuasive intensity, Herbert gives us a storyteller's quiet magnetism, using original stanza forms, enjambment, shifting verb tenses, and other techniques to involve our attention. And while Donne speaks to and about God in urgent, sometimes violent lang., Herbert's addressing of God evokes the trust between a child and a loving parent. At the same time, Herbert conveys a profound awareness of the paradoxes involved in his project, incl. the central fact that the very medium of his relationship to God, poetry, could be merely "pretense" and "fine invention." Among Herbert's most admired poems are "The Pulley," "The Collar," "Love III," and the *technopaegnion "Easter Wings." A few of the many poets who emulated Herbert did so with skill and independence enough to forge distinctive voices of their own, particularly Henry Vaughan (1621–95), Richard Crashaw (ca. 1613–49), and Thomas Traherne (1637–74).

In contrast to Herbert, *Cavalier poets were libertines who admired the bawdy *classicism and elegant metrical verse of Jonson and, of course, were influenced by the sexual frankness of Donne's *Songs and Sonnets*. In general, they supported the institutions of King Charles I and the Anglican Church; some even fought for the king in the Civil War and fled the country during Oliver Cromwell's government. Among the best-known Cavaliers are those followers of Jonson known as the Tribe of Ben (also called Sons of Ben), incl. Robert Herrick (1591–1674), Thomas Carew (1595–1640), and John Suckling (1609–42).

Herrick was the foremost member of the tribe and wrote two spirited tributes to the elder poet. Though an Anglican preacher and author of *Noble Numbers*, a collection of sacred verse, Herrick was a secular poet above all. His *Hesperides*, the volume of poems pub. with *Noble Numbers* in 1648, includes some of the most joyful poetry of the century or any century—fine-tuned, playful, erotic poems often in iambic trimeter or tetrameter about the small wonders and sensual pleasures of country life, friendship, and love. The flip side of Herrick's focus on beauty and pleasure is his keen awareness of mortality, and he makes this awareness plain in numerous poems, particularly his much-anthologized "To the Virgins, to Make Much of Time" ("Gather ye rosebuds while ye may").

Katherine Philips (1632–64) was the most accomplished and admired female poet of her generation. In her poems for close female friends—e.g., "Friendship's Mystery, To my Dearest *Lucasia*," and "To Mrs. M.A. at Parting"—she argues in elegant metaphors that friendship between women is greater than military conquest, political power, or other measures of success in a patriarchal world. In "A Married State" she warns women about the unending the burdens that follow "love's levity." She is also known for the explicitly political "Upon the Double Murder of King Charles" and the intensely personal elegies for her infant son Hector, in which she struggles to reconcile hard facts with conventional consolation. Philips circulated her work but seems to have agreed with other intellectual women of her day, incl. her close friend, the brilliant letter writer Dorothy Osborne (1627–95), that it was unseemly for a woman to display her feelings and opinions publicly. Most likely the 1664 volume of Philips's poems was published without her knowledge.

Milton (1608–74) is universally considered one of England's greatest poets. His far-reaching imagination, tremendous ambition, profoundly sensitive ear for the music and rhythms of lang. (with echoes of Spenser and Shakespeare, yet his own synthesis and subsuming of these), and deeply considered knowledge of the Western world, particularly of biblical hist. and ancient langs. and lits., are evident already in "On the Morning of Christ's Nativity," written when Milton was 21 (see NATIVITY POEM). Other early work includes "On Shakespeare" (1632), pub. in the second folio, and "L'Allegro" and "Il Penseroso," companion poems in iambic tetrameter couplets addressed to Mirth and Melancholy, respectively, that reenact contrasting states of mind and ways of being. *Comus, a masque*

*performed at Ludlow Castle in 1634*, anticipates major themes of *Paradise Lost*, incl. seduction. In "Lycidas," a pastoral elegy pub. in a 1637 volume of commemorative verses on his classmate and fellow poet Edward King, Milton questions the meaning and possibilities of life, death, poetry, pleasure, faith, fame, and authority of all kinds—literary, religious, and political. These are questions and anxieties he confronts in all his work, but always anew, with added complexity, self-consciousness, or vision. Milton makes every form he uses his own. In his sonnets, enjambment and nimble syntax sometimes double the power of words and lines, and sentences of multiple dependent clauses and interweaving rhymes draw the reader to an intense experience of thought.

Through the Civil War and Interregnum, Milton turned from poetry to political writing and action, publishing radical, influential arguments for freedom of the press, divorce, and republican government. In the first decade of the Restoration, having endured one severe loss after another (the death of both his first and second wives and an infant daughter, the loss of his eyesight, and the failure of his hopes for the revolution and republic), he wrote his first and greatest epic poem *Paradise Lost*. His purpose was no less than to "justify the ways of God to men," and his attempt yields a hybrid of cl. epic, Christian prophecy, and recent Brit. revolutionary hist. Since it was first printed in ten books in 1667 and then in its final form of 12 books in 1674, the epic has not failed to engage, provoke, inspire, anger, vex, and dazzle its readers. *Paradise Lost* gives us a Satan who says, "the mind is its own place, / And in itself can make a hell of heaven, / A heaven of hell"; a God who resembles at times King Charles I and at times Cromwell; an Adam and Eve who love each other more humanly than any god could have imagined; vivid scenes of hell, heaven, paradise, and chaos; suspenseful, persuasive dialogue, and soliloquies that expose the contradictory inner travails of the mind. In his invocations to books 1, 3, 7, and 9, Milton reflects on the project with varying degrees of confidence, ambition, humility, and doubt.

The poetic career of Milton's friend Andrew Marvell (1621–78) spanned the Civil War, Interregnum, and first two decades of the restored monarchy. Like Milton, Marvell was a worldly, multilingual scholar, poet, and statesman deeply involved in the political complexities of his day. Unlike Milton, Marvell exuded flexibility and ironic detachment in both his life and work. His sophisticated rhyming couplets, often in iambic tetrameter, contrast strikingly with Milton's late style of boldly enjambed blank verse. During the Protectorate, Milton served as Cromwell's secretary for foreign tongues and Marvell as Milton's assistant. When the Protectorate crumbled, Marvell not only evaded reprisal but became a member of Parliament and probably facilitated Milton's release from prison in 1660. Marvell's political poems—incl. commendatory verses on both Cromwell and Charles II—are polished and canny, imparting irony only to those who are looking for it. His pastoral poems—"The Garden," the group of "mower" poems, and many more—simultaneously embrace and interrogate the idea of pastoral. Marvell's love poems are frequently grouped with Donne's and described as metaphysical, a particularly apt description of Marvell's "The Definition of Love" and his tour de force, "To His Coy Mistress." In this widely anthologized poem, Marvell's speaker concludes: "though we cannot make our sun / Stand still, yet we will make him run."

### IV. The Restoration and the Eighteenth Century, 1660–1789.

The variety of topics and tones achieved in Restoration and 18th-c. poetry reminds us of the now-lost status of poetry in society: not only was it considered the most important genre for treating weighty matters—political, social, or religious—but it could touch the smallest events of daily life. To teach and be taught are desires that animate much Restoration and 18th-c. poetry. Many poems teach their readers how to live morally, where such instruction is often inseparable from 18th-c. readers' growing preoccupation with the search for happiness. Such guidance is heard in Samuel Johnson's (1709–1784) counsel to "raise for Good the supplicating Voice, / But leave to Heav'n the Measure and the Choice" (*The Vanity of Human Wishes*, 351–52 [1749]). The expanding presence of poetry coincides with a time in which poets and readers came from a wider range of social and educational backgrounds than ever before in Eng. lit. While many writers and readers knew poetry by exchanging it in ms., the availability of relatively inexpensive print materials, incl. broadsides, chapbooks, and periodicals, significantly increased poetry's accessibility to new readers eager for its pleasures and wisdom.

With Janus-faced vision, Restoration and 18th-c. writers transformed poetic practices and criteria. On the one hand, many poets attended to cl. models, as did their immediate predecessors in the Ren., and through trans. made the classics available to readers untrained in Lat. or Gr. Trans., however, was often an exercise of modernization, where the poet "imitated" the old text to make it new, renovating it to the concerns, tastes, and langs. of the present. Restoration and 18th-c. poets changed the landscape of poetry in Eng. by their experiments not only with the classics but with *kinds (e.g., the *georgic) and modes (e.g., satire). At the beginning of the period, the traditional hierarchy of kinds tied poetic achievement to difficulty: thus, an excellent pastoral, nearer the bottom of the hierarchy, could never equal an excellent epic, at the top. An easy crit. of this era's poetry is that it produced no great epic, yet this judgment resuscitates the hierarchy of poetic kinds that many poets worked to dismantle. Many of the cultural functions of epic were supplanted by the works of John Dryden (1631–1700) and Alexander Pope (1688–1744), who translated into Eng. Virgil and Homer, respectively. Numerous writers in this era revised the functions of epic by developing the range of *mock epics, satire, and the encyclopedic quality of the long *descriptive poem in blank verse. With various genres and modes often used and modified by a single poet, this period saw the proliferation of hybrids and new kinds of poems that cumulatively reorganized and redefined poetic voice and values. The wit of Dryden's *Absalom and Achitophel* (1681) lies as much in its verbal inventiveness as in its mixture of biblical prophecy, satire, and hist. to create didactic political allegory. The revisions of the lyric by John Wilmot, the Earl of Rochester (1647–80), turned this "lower" kind into a scathing critique of power relations, desire, and hypocrisy. Anne Finch (1661–1720) blended pastoral, "retirement" poetry, autobiography, and religious confession in "The Petition for an Absolute Retreat" (1713). Among the new generic achievements was the congregational *hymn, associated esp. with Charles Wesley (1707–88). Variations on the hymn and other religious verse are among the major accomplishments of Christopher Smart (1722–71; *Jubilate Agno* [written ca. 1758–63] and *A Song to David* [1763]) and William Cowper (1731–1800) in the *Olney Hymns* (1779).

Restoration and 18th-c. poets' experiments with the lyric often mix private matters with public ones. In the Restoration, the *song is the dominant kind of lyric poem and partakes of a social setting (even if on an intimate scale) in its framework of a musical performance. Similarly, the era's revisions of the *ode, originally an elevated form of the lyric intended for public occasions, rapidly expanded this kind to treat a range of more personal topics and experiences far from its traditional uses. Anne Finch's ode "The Spleen" (1701) addresses this condition, known today as depression, to pursue its "still varying" and "perplexing form." Never abandoned in the Restoration and earlier 18th c., the sonnet reemerged as an important shape for the lyric in the second half of the century. But by this time, poets were using the brevity of the form to focus less on the qualities of Petrarchan love and more on the speaker's sensitive perceptions of the landscape. In the last decades of the 18th c., Anna Seward (1742–1809) and Charlotte Smith (1749–1806) would develop the sonnet to treat a new range of topics, such as Smith's meditations on the speaker's suffering in contexts that replace Petrarchan frames with material exigencies.

Such changes in poetic kinds combined with other forces to further the inclusiveness of poetry. One of the era's most transformative values is its fascination with occasions. Tuned to large and small events, occasional poetry articulates affairs of state (e.g., Dryden's *Annus Mirabilis*, 1667) or affairs of the day (e.g., John Winstanley's "To the Revd. Mr— on his Drinking Sea-Water," 1751). Poetry's role in affairs of state did not deter women writers from engaging in the same, as seen in Anna Letitia Barbauld's (1743–1825) "Corsica" (1773). Critiques of gender norms and patriarchy invoked poetry's role as a vehicle of political and social intervention (e.g., Mary Collier's *The Woman's Labour* [1739]). Concern with social and political issues informed the extraordinary satires of this era. Even an incomplete roll call reminds us of the heterogeneity in topic and tone of these works: Rochester's "Upon Nothing" (1679), Aphra Behn's "The Disappointment" (1680), Dryden's "MacFlecknoe" (1682), Jonathan Swift's "Verses on the Death of Dr. Swift" (1739), Pope's *Dunciad* (final version, 1743), Lady Mary Wortley Montagu's *Six Town Eclogues* (printed in part 1716, in full 1747), Mary Leapor's "Man the Monarch" (1751), and Charles Churchill's *Night* (1761).

Writers changed the practice and values of poetry by experimenting with kinds as well as with the *couplet and blank verse. Couplets could continue for short or long *verse paragraphs, conveying complex arguments where structures within the couplet enabled *amplification, example, *antithesis, and *parallelism. With couplets, writers could achieve the clarity, formality, and lapidary compression that suited the poet's public voice and role in affairs of state. Just as effectively, couplets evoked the cadences of conversation or jaunty humor that made poetry and daily life inseparable for those who could write or read it. In his extraordinary dexterity with the couplet, Pope reveals the invisible sylphs: "Transparent forms, too fine for mortal sight, / Their fluid bodies half dissolv'd in light" (*The Rape of the Lock* 2.59–62 [1714]). In "Eloisa to Abelard" (printed in different versions 1712–17), his couplets express the force of Eloisa's desperate command to Abelard: "Come, if thou dar'st, all charming as thou art! / Oppose thy self to heav'n; dispute my heart; / Come, with one glance of those deluding eyes, / Blot out each bright Idea of the skies" (281–84).

Blank verse offered a flexible form different from the couplet but also allowed for any number and size of verse paragraphs. James Thomson's (1700–48) expansive blank verse and richly descriptive diction in *The Seasons* (first printed in its entirety in 1730) demonstrated that the seriousness and beauty of the form was not confined to Milton's achievement in his major poems. In *The Task* (1785), Cowper's blank verse is as various as the kinds and modes from which he borrows. He layers the tones of stately pronouncement, compassion, satiric attack, and prophetic warning in this description of urban poverty: "'Tis the cruel gripe / That lean hard-handed poverty inflicts, / The hope of better things, the chance to win, / The wish to shine, the thirst to be amused, / That at the sound of Winter's hoary wing, / Unpeople all our counties, of such herds / Of flutt'ring, loit'ring, cringing, begging, loose / And wanton vagrants, as make London, vast / And boundless as it is, a crowded coop" (3.826–34).

Elastic forms and genres for varied subjects complemented the era's changing aesthetic values. The *verse epistle is an important case where genre and relation— the letter—are also an aesthetic value that was for the first time fully developed in Eng. by poets in this era. Unrestricted by "high" or "low" subject matter, the verse epistle values sociable exchange, but it esp. explores how the "private" can be read by the "public" to assert the relations between these domains (e.g., "Epistle to Dr. Arbuthnot," 1735). The epistolary poet expects, or imagines, that the reader can write back, and although such a sense of conversation and participation is often elite, it epitomizes how so many poems were written and read as social actions. The verse epistle's compelling paradox of privacy and exposure was one of several means used by Restoration and 18th-c. writers to shape an aesthetics of intimacy that was also social.

Aesthetic values such as *wit, the *sublime, the *imagination, *taste, and *sensibility drove shifts in the topics, forms, and langs. of poetry. Empiricism opened worlds of sensory perceptions with widely divergent literary results, from the philosophical and sexual libertinism of the Restoration to the cult of sensibility associated esp. with the middle and end of the 18th c. The lang. of the senses draws much into its orbit in the era's poems of natural description. In Finch's "A Nocturnal Reverie" (1713), the senses work with animating imagination to describe the moment "When in some River, overhung with Green, / The waving Moon and trembling Leaves are seen" (9–10). Thomson's *The Seasons* explores the processes of *nature that include the human and divine but could not have been so expressed without empirical attention to detail: "Th' uncurling Floods, diffus'd / In glassy Breadth, seem thro' delusive Lapse / Forgetful of their Course. 'Tis Silence all, / And pleasing Expectation" (*Spring*, 159–62). In "Elegy Written in a Country Churchyard" (1750) by Thomas Gray (1716–71), the fading of "the glimmering landscape on the sight" turns the speaker toward the air, which "a solemn stillness holds," and the sounds of twilight "where the beetle wheels his droning flight" (5, 6, 7). As poets looked at and listened to the world around them, they also saw and heard themselves: a heightened self-consciousness about perception and creative processes gives the faculty of *imagination supreme power in Mark Akenside's (1721–70) *The Pleasures of Imagination* (1744), Joseph Warton's (1722–1800) *The Enthusiast: Or, the Lover of Nature* (1744), and Thomas Warton's (1728–90) *The Pleasures of Melancholy* (1747). *Imagination* shifts from its earlier sense (the common human capacity for image making) to a rarified individual talent; and *genius*, long understood as something one could have or participate in, becomes a term limited to and originating in the rare artist-figure. The increasing attention to taste, often seen as an attempt to instate another form of cultural and social hierarchy on literary value in the growing print culture, likewise turned the hierarchy of poetic kinds into an inward scale where tasteful aesthetic judgment defined new poetic values.

The cult of sensibility, with its pendulum of self-absorption and social consciousness, privileged an individual's perceptions and feelings that could also extend to sympathy with the sufferings of those oppressed by patriarchy, poverty, or slavery (e.g., George Crabbe's [1754–1832] *The Village*, 1783, and Cowper's "The Negro's Complaint," 1789; see EMPATHY AND SYMPATHY). Sensibility privileged *intensity of feeling as an index of aesthetic merit—in poet and reader—and as a moral good. Readers looked anew at *oral poetry, esp. the *ballad. A fascination with "untutored" poets who possessed "natural" genius extended the langs. of and criteria for poetry. Thomas Percy's (1729–1811) *Reliques of Ancient English Poetry* (1765) heightened the interest in indigenous trads. and langs. (whether real or imagined, as in James Macpherson's [1736–96] *The Works of Ossian*, 1765, and Thomas Chatterton's [1752–70]

Rowley poems, posthumously collected in 1777) and prepared for a growing appreciation of *dialect poetry, incl. that of Robert Burns (1759–96).

**V. The Romantic Period, 1789–1830.** The romantic period in Eng. poetry is traditionally considered to date from 1789, the beginning of the Fr. Revolution.

While the poetry of William Blake (1757–1827) had a modest impact when first published, Blake is now regarded as one of the most original Eng. poets and a major figure in the romantic movement. His early *Songs of Innocence and of Experience* (1794) foreshadowed the interest in simple lang., as well as the fascination with the imaginative world of childhood, that would later characterize the work of William Wordsworth (1770–1850) and S. T. Coleridge (1772–1834). Blake's prophetic poems, meanwhile, incl. *The Marriage of Heaven and Hell* (1790), *The Four Zoas* (1797), and *Milton* (1804), display in extreme form the political radicalism and the visionary imagination that typify much romantic writing. The form of these later poems is also significant: written predominantly in long, unrhymed lines that resist regular meter, they anticipate the innovations of Walt Whitman.

Nearly as radical as Blake's work, and more directly influential, was Wordsworth and Coleridge's *Lyrical Ballads* (1798), probably the most important single volume of poetry of the romantic period. Its protagonists are rustic, often marginalized figures—vagrants, madwomen, a mentally retarded child—but they are not sentimentalized and are always treated as individuals. The poems are written, for the most part, in deliberately simple lang., avoiding the elaborate diction of much 18th-c. poetry. Wordsworth, who wrote the great majority of the volume, defended these choices in his famous Preface to the 2d ed. (1800). Perhaps the chief claim of the preface, however, is that the true importance of any situation (and of any poem) is wholly subjective, deriving from the feeling it engenders in the perceiver; poetry, then, ultimately reflects not the world but the self. This notion is exemplified by the poem commonly known as "Tintern Abbey," the last in the 1798 *Lyrical Ballads*, in which Wordsworth's speaker surveys a landscape, not to reveal its inherent or universal significance, but to explore its personal meanings and associations.

Most of Wordsworth's greatest poetic accomplishments are concentrated in the years immediately after *Lyrical Ballads*, yet they cover a wide variety of genres. His "Ode: Intimations of Immortality" (1804), like "Tintern Abbey," regrets the loss of youthful immediacy and seeks recompense in a greater sense of human sympathy. Wordsworth's masterpiece, *The Prelude*, was largely complete by 1805, though not pub. until after his death (1850). A blank-verse autobiographical epic, *The Prelude* traces the growth of the poet's mind and sensibility, exploring how his "love of nature" led to a "love of mankind." Although it follows a roughly chronological organization, the poem focuses not on what would usually be considered major life events but on what Wordsworth calls "spots of time"—moments

of sudden, often fearful perception, which are not fully understood at the time and which for that very reason continue to haunt and shape the poet's imagination. Beginning in 1802, Wordsworth also began composing sonnets, a form that had been revived toward the end of the 18th c. Wordsworth's sonnets, which in their mingling of public and personal concerns harken back to those of Milton, contributed to the popularity of the form through the rest of the 19th c.

Wordsworth developed many of his theories and practices in collaboration with Coleridge. The latter's poetic output was relatively small, but his three vivid and often psychologically harrowing supernatural poems—*The Rime of the Ancient Mariner* (1798), "Kubla Khan" (1816), and "Christabel" (1816)—have bewitched generations of readers. "Christabel" also reintroduced into Eng. poetry (outside the ballad) the widespread use of *accentual verse (see CHRISTABEL METER). But Coleridge's most important contribution to Eng. poetic hist. was his devel., in such pieces as "The Eolian Harp" (1795) and "Frost at Midnight" (1798), of the *conversation poem—short, blank-verse lyrics characterized by their colloquial style, which prefigure the dramatic monologues of the Victorians.

The next generation of romantic poets appealed to their readers' emotions even more directly than Wordsworth and Coleridge had, while at the same time exhibiting a keener sense of irony and skepticism. Felicia Hemans (1793–1835), for instance, won tremendous popularity with her early poems of passion and patriotism, but her most important work, *Records of Woman* (1828), mingles these themes with a more critical view of the trials faced by women throughout hist. Lord Byron (1788–1824), meanwhile, first achieved fame with the publication of *Childe Harold's Pilgrimage* (1812), the eponymous hero of which is brooding and passionate, yet at the same time world-weary and cynical. This figure of the so-called Byronic hero, who was quickly identified with the poet himself, reappears under various names in a series of Orientalist romances (*The Giaour*, 1813; *The Corsair*, 1814) that won Byron adulation throughout Europe. But Byron's greatest work by far was his last, the sprawling comic picaresque *Don Juan* (1819–24), left unfinished at his death. Irreverent (even blasphemous) and sentimental at once, *Don Juan* set new standards both for satire and for narrative in Eng. poetry.

Byron's friend P. B. Shelley (1792–1822) was, with Blake, the most radical and politically engaged of the romantic poets, although his poetry, like Blake's, tends toward metaphysical abstraction, even in such an explicitly topical work as the populist *Mask of Anarchy* (1832). Much of Shelley's best poetry (incl. the *Mask*) went unpublished in his lifetime, as did his brilliant critical treatise *A Defence of Poetry* (1840), which defines the act of poetic composition as a noble but ultimately futile attempt to recapture an original moment of fleeting inspiration. The same theme, of the idealistic pursuit of evanescent beauty, informs Shelley's finest lyric poems, incl. "Hymn to Intellectual Beauty" (1817) and "To a Skylark" (1820), as well as his great allegorical narratives, such as "Alastor" (1816). Shelley's full powers are on display in "Adonais" (1821), his elegy for John Keats, which while eschewing religious consolation (Shelley being a self-proclaimed atheist) expresses a deep faith in the ability of the human imagination to transcend all things, incl. death.

Keats (1795–1821), the latest born as well as the shortest lived of the major Eng. romantics, developed with astonishing rapidity over the course of his brief career. The lushly sensuous lyrics of his first volume of poems (1817) and his extended cl. reverie *Endymion* (1818) display enormous promise, often self-consciously: many of Keats's early sonnets, such as "On First Looking into Chapman's Homer" (1817), candidly describe his eager poetic ambition. That promise found fulfillment in the handful of masterpieces Keats went on to compose before tuberculosis rendered him too weak to write, most of which were published in his final volume of verse (1820). These include two romances, "Lamia" and "The Eve of St. Agnes," both rich in brilliant description, which explore the troubled interaction between the world as we know it and the immortal world of dreams; and *Hyperion*, a powerful epic fragment in Miltonic style. The most enduring works of Keats's final period are his great odes—incl. "Ode to Psyche," "Ode on a Grecian Urn," "Ode to a Nightingale," and "To Autumn"—which in controlled yet richly textured lang. explore the pains and challenges of mortal life and the ability of art to redeem or overcome them. Although he died in relative obscurity, Keats gained a devoted following, which has increased ever since, through the sheer beauty of his poetry; and his unstinting commitment to (in his words) "a life of sensations rather than of thoughts" has earned him a place beside Wordsworth as an archetype of the romantic poet.

**VI. The Victorian Period, 1830–1900.** By the time Queen Victoria came to the throne in 1837, almost all the major romantic poets had either died or ceased writing their best poetry. The traditional division of 19th-c. Eng. poetry into "romantic" and "Victorian" (Victoria reigned until 1901) is therefore sensible, although the new generation of poets that began publishing in the 1830s remained deeply influenced by their immediate predecessors. One significant difference lay in their avoidance of the directly personal, confessional style of poetry popularized by Byron and Shelley—a reticence reflected in the early work of Alfred, Lord Tennyson (1809–92), who went on to become *poet laureate and a dominant figure of the period. The finest poems of his first two volumes (1830, 1833), incl. "Mariana" and "The Lady of Shalott," focus, like many romantic poems, on an isolated, introverted consciousness, but that consciousness is explicitly not the poet's own. This preference for displaced self-consciousness led Tennyson shortly afterward to develop (at the same time as Robert Browning, but independently) the classic Victorian form of the dramatic monologue; his paired monologues "Ulysses" and "Tithonus" are exemplary of the genre.

Tennyson's greatest work was *In Memoriam* (1850), his hauntingly beautiful book-length elegy for his friend Arthur Hallam. In contrast to the earlier lyrics, *In Memoriam* is avowedly a deeply personal poem. Yet its widespread appeal—it was a best seller and quickly made Tennyson a household name—derives from its extraordinary ability to connect private grief to issues of major public concern, incl., most notably, the contemp. struggle between traditional religious faith and mod. scientific discoveries. Tennyson's later achievements include *Maud* (1855), a sensational narrative in the spasmodic mode conveyed entirely through lyrics (see SPASMODIC SCHOOL), and *Idylls of the King* (1859–85), a 12-book, blank-verse epic recounting the rise and (more successfully) decline of King Arthur's Camelot.

Robert Browning (1812–89) is often paired with Tennyson as the representative Victorian poet, but his reputation came late because of the frequent obscurity of his poetry. Browning's reputation today rests almost entirely on his dramatic monologues, of which he is the acknowledged master. His early monologues ("My Last Duchess," 1842; "The Bishop Orders His Tomb," 1845) tend to feature vivid, often grotesque speakers who reveal more about themselves than they intend and frequently undermine their own purpose in speaking. The *irony is gentler in the mature monologues of his two most important collections, *Men and Women* (1855) and *Dramatis Personae* (1864), which include such psychologically nuanced portraits as "Andrea del Sarto" and "Rabbi Ben Ezra." Browning's experiments with the dramatic monologue culminate in his most ambitious work, the epic-length *The Ring and the Book* (1868–69), in which the story of an obscure 17th-c. murder case is retold from nine viewpoints. In its characterization of the speakers and protagonists, the poem, which finally won Browning his overdue recognition, reaches a Shakespearean pitch of complexity and profundity.

When Elizabeth Barrett Browning (1806–61) married Robert Browning in 1846, her reputation far exceeded his, and it grew even greater with the publication of her *Sonnets from the Portuguese* (1850), which was written during their courtship. *Sonnets from the Portuguese* (the title is deliberately misleading: the poems are not trans.) is the first amatory sonnet sequence in Eng. since the Ren. and represents a brilliant contribution to, and revision of, the genre. Just as impressive is Browning's experimental verse novel about a professional woman writer, *Aurora Leigh* (1856). Alongside these longer works, Browning produced lyric poems on a wide range of social and political issues, incl. child labor, the It. struggle for independence, and most movingly abolition ("The Runaway Slave at Pilgrim's Point"). Her poetry was a major source of inspiration for a younger generation of women, incl. Christina Rossetti, Augusta Webster, and, in the U.S., Emily Dickinson.

Religious faith and its mod. vicissitudes form a recurrent concern of mid-Victorian poetry. Much of Matthew Arnold's (1822–88) best poetry, such as "The Scholar-Gipsy," laments the aimlessness of mod. life, esp. the loss of a simple, reliable religious faith (notably in "Stanzas from the Grande Chartreuse" and "Dover Beach"). Arnold's friend A. H. Clough (1819–61) also wrote extensively about a rapidly secularizing world—although his most accomplished poem, the urbane epistolary romance *Amours de Voyage* (1855), is in a very different vein. Christina Rossetti (1830–94), by contrast, maintained a devout Anglo-Catholic faith, which is reflected in her large body of typically brief, breathtakingly understated religious lyrics. Her best-known and most original poem, however, *Goblin Market* (1862), though it has religious overtones, differs sharply from the majority of her work. Cast as a children's fairy tale, yet filled with surprisingly graphic violence and sexuality, it remains one of the era's most fascinating works. Similarly devout but of a very different texture are the poems of the Jesuit G. M. Hopkins (1844–89), which, when finally pub. in 1918, had a profound impact on modernist poetics. Hopkins's highly original experiments with what he called *sprung rhythm, together with his heavy use of alliteration, neologism, and knotty syntax, lend his poems of religious praise and occasional religious despair (the so-called terrible sonnets) extraordinary force and conviction.

Some Victorian poetry aimed at realism, incl. E. B. Browning's *Aurora Leigh* and George Meredith's (1828–1909) *Modern Love* (1862), a subversive sonnet sequence (the "sonnets" have 16 lines) detailing the breakdown of a marriage. But realism was mostly ceded to the increasingly dominant genre of the novel, while poetry moved in an opposite direction. Dante Gabriel Rossetti (1828–82), for instance, the brother of Christina and one of the founders of the *Pre-Raphaelite Brotherhood of painters (see PRE-RAPHAELITISM), extended the often ornate, medievalizing style of his painting to his poetry as well; his sonnet sequence *The House of Life* (1881) contrasts with Meredith's in its heavy use of allegory. William Morris (1834–96), another member of the Pre-Raphaelite circle, wrote primarily on legendary themes, recounting stories from the Arthurian trad. and, more unusually, from Norse sagas. Perhaps the most significant poet of this group was the spectacularly talented A. C. Swinburne (1837–1909), whose celebrations of pagan sensuality were partly inspired by the work of the Fr. poet Charles Baudelaire (see FRANCE, POETRY OF; SYMBOLISM), but whose style of fluid verbal and imagistic profusion is all his own.

Influenced by these precedents, as well as by the theories of Walter Pater, poets of the aesthetic movement of the 1880s and 1890s (incl. Oscar Wilde, Ernest Dowson, Michael Field, and the young William Butler Yeats) turned away from the moral and social concerns of much mid-Victorian verse to concentrate on the cultivation of beauty for its own sake (see AESTHETICISM). The most enduring work from the end of the century, however, is A. E. Housman's (1859–1936) *A Shropshire Lad* (1896), a collection of deceptively simple, deeply melancholic lyrics of pastoral nostalgia. A similarly melancholy pessimism, though

more ironic, marks the poetry of Thomas Hardy (1840–1928), who is usually classed (and who classed himself) as a Victorian poet, even though the majority of his poems were written in the 20th c. Hardy's verse is characterized by idiosyncratic vocabulary and often contorted syntax reminiscent of Robert Browning. His finest work, a series of elegies for his late wife titled *Poems of 1912–13*, looks back even more to *In Memoriam*—but, crucially, without the ultimately consolatory faith and resolution displayed by Tennyson's poem 60 years earlier. The fracturing of faith and form, which had been foreshadowed by Tennyson and which grew more pronounced across the Victorian period, prepared the way for the major poetic devels. of the 20th c.

**VII. Modernism to the Present, from 1901.** From Hardy's pessimistic belated romanticism to the aestheticism (tinged with Ir. cultural nationalism) of the early Yeats (1865–1939), the voices of the early 20th c. remained rooted in 19th-c. styles and concerns, accommodating changing historical circumstances in contradictory ways. Rudyard Kipling (1865–1936) projected an expansive view of Eng. imperial culture, while others reconsidered the domestic fate of received forms. Robert Bridges (1844–1930) explored the syllabic resources of traditional prosodies and introduced sprung rhythm through the posthumous publication of Hopkins. Anthologized between 1911 and 1922, Georgian poets included such popular figures as Walter de la Mare (1873–1956) and John Masefield (1878–1967), as well as D. H. Lawrence (1885–1930; see GEORGIANISM). Georgian anthols. also introduced a generation of writers best known for increasingly bitter depictions of World War I (1914–18). Moving from Rupert Brooke's (1887–1915) patriotic sonnets and Edward Thomas's (1878–1917) ambivalent *bucolics to the pointed ironies of Siegfried Sassoon (1886–1967) and Wilfred Owen (1893–1918), *war poetry progressively deployed the resources of 19th-c. lyricism to call its underlying values into question, systematically turning experience against inherited notions of beauty.

Gathering force before the war and consolidating an ambitious aesthetic program after it, *modernism assailed such values comprehensively, introducing new forms and subjects, often challenging conventional distinctions between verse and prose. Fusing the influence of Fr. symbolism after Baudelaire and Gustave Flaubert with the iconoclasm of later *avant-gardes such as F. T. Marinetti's It. *futurism, early modernists such as T. E. Hulme (1883–1917) and F. S. Flint (1885–1960) rejected expressive rhetorical modes in favor of a spare *free verse predicated on the image (see IMAGISM). Codified in the manifestos and prosodic experiments of the Am. Ezra Pound (1885–1972), early modernism absorbed the influence of historically distant forms (such as the Occitan *trobar clus and the Chinese *ideogram) and registered shifts under way in other arts, from painting and sculpture to architecture and music. The Poundian avant-garde (captured in Wyndham Lewis's journal *Blast* (1914; see VORTICISM) traded insular frames of reference for the expatriate's cosmopolitan London, attuned to multiple trads. and langs. and populated by artists from Ireland, North America, and Europe, working in every medium. Before memorializing his departure from London with *Hugh Selwyn Mauberley* (1920) and embarking on *The Cantos*, Pound consolidated extensive networks of literary magazines significantly dedicated to new poetry. The open forms most identified with a modernist style have never been uncontroversial, often associated with Am. rather than Brit. idioms, but may nonetheless be found in figures as various as Edith Sitwell (1887–1964) and Mina Loy (1882–1966).

Pound also impressed his influence on the work of Yeats and of contemporaries such as James Joyce (1882–1941) and T. S. Eliot (1888–1965). High modernism of the early interwar years aspired to more monumental forms, culminating in the publication (in Paris) of Joyce's *Ulysses* (1922). Poetically, the period is galvanized by the austere turn of Yeats's most anthologized work, driven to explicitly political and philosophical themes from *The Wild Swans at Coole* (1919) to *The Tower* (1928). The pressures of Ir. politics and the emergent Free State pervade "Easter, 1916" and "Meditations in Time of Civil War" (1923) while "Leda and the Swan" (1928) and "The Second Coming" (1920) link social turbulence to the esoteric historical views propounded in *A Vision* (1925) and adduced as artistic models in "Among School Children" (1926) and "Sailing to Byzantium" (1927). Uniting private mythology with an insistently public and prophetic voice, the stark verse of Yeats's late serial epitaphs such as "Under Ben Bulben" (1939) and "The Circus Animals' Desertion" (1939) projects an oracular shadow over later Eng. and Ir. poets alike.

It was Eliot, however, who most decisively shaped the period's aesthetic as poet, critic, and later ed. at Faber and Faber, still England's premier poetic imprint. *Prufrock and Other Observations* (1917) decomposed the form of the dramatic monologue in a fragmented arrangement of densely orchestrated figures and rhythms, stylistically derived from Stéphane Mallarmé, Jules Laforgue, and Eng. metaphysical poetry but set against the mundane scenes of the mod. city. This effect was heightened in "Gerontion" (1920), which maintained the monologue's shape but abandoned any single identifiable voice, while other poems from *Ara Vos Prec* (1919) explored the satiric possibilities of stricter forms, inspired by Théophile Gautier's quatrains (see PARNASSIANISM). Eliot's resonant musical conception of free verse, designed not to displace meter and rhyme but rather to restore their harmonic variety and intensity, sought to create an impersonal classicism capable of rendering the "simultaneous existence" and "simultaneous order" of "the whole of the literature of Europe from Homer," as he writes in "Tradition and the Individual Talent" (1919). For Eliot, "poets in our civilization, as it exists at present, must be *difficult*. . . . The poet must become more and more comprehensive, more allusive, more indirect, in order to force, to dislocate if necessary, lang. into his meaning" ("The Metaphysical Poets,"

1921). *The Waste Land* (1922) enacted this argument poetically. Compressed to 434 lines by Pound's severe editing, Eliot's masterpiece discarded unities of narrative and voice, compiling allusive fragments of other texts into an intricate depiction of London and interwar Europe. Setting refrains from Dante, Baudelaire, and Richard Wagner alongside an array of mythic elements and demotic passages, the poem paradoxically shored fragments against ruins, juxtaposing haunting signs of cultural sterility with a rich archive of elusive critical meanings, buttressed by Eliot's own (often ironic) annotations. Eliot's Anglican conversion is reflected in *Ash Wednesday* (1930) and in the looser meditative tone of *Four Quartets* (1936–42), concerned with theological problems of time and hist. and, in "Little Gidding" (1942), with the searing experience of the second war.

The 1930s witnessed ambivalent reactions to modernism's recondite styles, most notably in the work of W. H. Auden (1907–73) and the poets around him: Cecil Day-Lewis (1904–72), Stephen Spender (1909–95), and Louis MacNeice (1907–63). Radicalized to varying degrees by the influence of Karl Marx and Sigmund Freud and by the decade's political and economic crises, Auden's generation balanced traditional forms against contemp. subject matter. The terse lyricism of Auden's (usually untitled) early poems and the political urgency of longer works such as *The Orators* (1932) gave way to more resigned tones by the decade's end. MacNeice's *Autumn Journal* (1939) and Auden's *Another Time* (1940) record the turn of the Spanish Civil War and the more general Eur. collapse before an ascendant Fascism. Auden's emigration to the United States prompted a series of more meditative volumes, often preoccupied with religious and philosophical matters: *New Year Letter* (1941), *For the Time Being* (1945), *The Age of Anxiety* (1947). Elsewhere, the 1930s saw the devel. of modernist tendencies in other directions. Hugh MacDiarmid (pseud. of Christopher Grieve, 1892–1978), the leading voice of the Scottish renaissance, adapted *collage forms into Scots with *A Drunk Man Looks at the Thistle* (1926) and mingled nationalist and communist programs through *In Memoriam James Joyce* (1955). David Jones (1895–1974) probed Welsh lang. and culture to explore the memory of war with *In Parenthesis* (1937) and Catholic liturgy in *The Anathémata* (1952).

With Yeats's death, Eliot's increasing reticence, and Auden's departure, mid-century poetry lost its guiding authorities. The light verse of John Betjeman (1906–84) and exuberant neoromanticism of Dylan Thomas (1914–53) gathered popular followings but never defined durable trajectories, while singular figures such as R. S. Thomas (1913–2000) in Wales and Norman MacCaig (1910–1996) and W. S. Graham (1918–1986) in Scotland received less popular attention. The definition of a recognizable postwar style instead fell to the *Movement, comprising the poets grouped around Philip Larkin (1922–84) in anthols. of the 1950s, incl. Donald Davie (1922–95), Kingsley Amis (1922–95), Elizabeth Jennings (1926–2001), and Thom Gunn (1929–2004). Explicitly rejecting both modernist obscurantism and neoromanticism in favor of accessible plain speech, the Movement sought to restore insular trads. (championing Hardy, e.g.). The wry postimperial sensibility of the Movement lyric as perfected by Larkin uses insistently regular stanzas and meters to measure the ironic distance between a rich cultural heritage and the diminished realities of postwar social life. Poems such as "Church Going" (1954) and "The Whitsun Weddings" (1958) adopt a detached but elegiac attitude toward increasingly anachronistic rituals, while later pieces like "High Windows" (1967) exploit and preserve a tension between apparently degraded everyday speech and scattered moments of vision that it fails to eclipse.

Resistance to the Movement's perceived gentility, polemically intimated in *The New Poetry* (1962, 1966), catalyzed more expansive styles in succeeding generations, often receptive to both traditional and modernist formal practices. Ted Hughes (1930–98) developed a distinctively bardic voice, grounded in the immediacy of an often ruthless nature. Volumes from *The Hawk in the Rain* (1957) to *Crow* (1970) use animals to conjure scenes of primal violence and transformation, while later sequences concentrate on the slower rhythms of rural life at the fringe of mod. devel. Hughes's extremity is perhaps matched only by that of Sylvia Plath (1932–63), whose posthumous *Ariel* (1965) fuses confessional and naturalist elements with nightmarish visions of 20th-c. hist. Jon Silkin (1930–97) and Charles Tomlinson (b. 1927) have suffused a deep awareness of Eng. lit. hist. with the influence of other cultural and poetic trads. Roy Fisher (b. 1930) has adapted collage techniques to an ongoing excavation of his native Birmingham. The densely textured lang. of Geoffrey Hill (b. 1932), developed in *King Log* (1968) and *Mercian Hymns* (1971), turns Eliotic difficulty to the work of historical meditation and recovery, mixed in later volumes with implacable strains of religious and political prophecy. Tony Harrison (b. 1937) has infused the precision of modernist classicism with an unsparing political urgency, anchored in the perspective of working-class Leeds.

The Brit. Poetry Revival of the late 1960s and early 1970s saw the resurgence of more distinctly experimental strains, resistant to mainstream conventions and enabled by the proliferation of loosely affiliated networks of small presses. With the appearance of his late masterpiece *Briggflatts* (1966), the spare but sonorous musicality of Northumbrian modernist Basil Bunting (1900–85) inspired an eclectic array of younger poets, as did a host of postwar Am. and Eur. avant-gardes. Though short-lived, the revival left behind vibrant artistic scenes in northern England, in London, and in Scotland, with Edwin Morgan (1920–2010) and Ian Hamilton Finlay (1925–2006). In the work of figures from Tom Raworth (b. 1938) and Allen Fisher (b. 1944) to Maggie O'Sullivan (b. 1951), it also systematically integrated other arts and media. Elsewhere, the intensely wrought manner of J. H. Prynne (b. 1936) has fostered a range of more academic and self-consciously critical styles, garnering international interest even when resisted by the Brit. mainstream. The same synthesis of formal and conceptual rigor marks the work of younger figures from Veronica Forrest-Thomson (1947–75) to Denise Riley (b. 1948).

More general notice has gathered to poets emerging from Northern Ireland, from John Montague (b. 1929) to the group originally centered in Belfast, incl. Michael Longley (b. 1939), Derek Mahon (b. 1941), and Seamus Heaney (b. 1939), perhaps the most widely read Eng.-lang. poet of the era. Like Yeats, Heaney has synthesized and reworked Eng. and Ir. trads. alike, crafting a lyricism that simultaneously imbibes and seeks to transcend place and historical circumstance. More recently, the intricate verbal dexterity of Paul Muldoon (b. 1951), elusive syntax of Medbh McGuckian (b. 1950), and adventurous long lines of Ciaran Carson (b. 1948) have united an expansive sense of postmodern play with an often fraught sense of Ir. hist.

Recent laureates Andrew Motion (b. 1952) and Carol Ann Duffy (b. 1955) have emphasized accessibility in mainstream poetic culture, respectively recovering elements of the Movement's legacy and developing an inclusive dramatic populism alert to larger social issues. Often sustained by an expanding economy of prizes and writing programs, the New Generation of the 1990s includes Simon Armitage (b. 1963), Lavinia Greenlaw (b. 1962), Kathleen Jamie (b. 1962), and Glyn Maxwell (b. 1962), among numerous others. Furthermore, the poetic culture of the late 20th and early 21st cs. has expanded to new sites and incorporated accents from beyond the Brit. archipelago, ranging from the dub rhythms of Linton Kwesi Johnson (b. 1952) to the diasporic hists. underlying the work of David Dabydeen (b. 1955) and Grace Nichols (b. 1950).

*See* CARIBBEAN, POETRY OF THE; ENGLISH PROSODY; IRELAND, POETRY OF; LATIN POETRY; MEDIEVAL POETICS; MEDIEVAL POETRY; NEOCLASSICAL POETICS; POSTCOLONIAL POETICS; PREROMANTICISM; RENAISSANCE POETICS; RENAISSANCE POETRY; ROMANTIC AND POSTROMANTIC POETRY AND POETICS; SCOTLAND, POETRY OF; WELSH POETRY.

■ **General**: T. Warton, *History of English Poetry* (1774–81); S. Johnson, *Lives of the English Poets* (1781); Brooks; S. Fish, *Surprised by Sin: The Reader in "Paradise Lost"* (1967); B. H. Smith, *Poetic Closure* (1968); H. Bloom, *The Anxiety of Influence* (1973); R. L. Colie, *The Resources of Kind* (1973); P. H. Fry, *The Poet's Calling in the English Ode* (1980); Attridge, *Rhythms*; J. A. Winn, *Unsuspected Eloquence: A History of the Relations between Poetry and Music* (1981); C. Ricks, *The Force of Poetry* (1984); Hollander; H. Vendler, *Voices and Visions* (1987); J. Hollander, *Melodious Guile* (1988); H. Vendler, *The Music of What Happens* (1988); C. Ricks, *Essays in Appreciation* (1996); S. Stewart, *Poetry and the Fate of the Senses* (2002); T. Eagleton, *How to Read a Poem* (2007); *The Oxford Handbook of the Elegy*, ed. K. A. Weisman (2010). **Digital Resources**: Early English Books Online, http://eebo.chadwyck.com/home; Eighteenth-Century Collections Online, http://gale.cengage.co.

uk/product-highlights/history/eighteenth-century-collections-online.aspx; Orlando: Women's Writing in the British Isles from the Beginnings to the Present, http://library.mcmaster.ca/articles/orlando-womens-writing-british-isles-from-beginning-present; Perdita Manuscripts: Women Writers, 1500–1700, http://www.amdigital.co.uk/Collections/Perdita.aspx; Literature Online, http://lion.chadwyck.com; Representative Poetry Online, http://rpo.library.utoronto.ca.

■ **Old English.** *Anthologies*: *Anglo-Saxon Poetic Records*, ed. G. Krapp and E. Dobbie, 6 v. (1931–53); *An Anthology of Old English Poetry*, trans. C. W. Kennedy (1960); *Poems of Wisdom and Learning in Old English*, ed. and trans. T. A. Shippey (1976); *The Old English Riddles of the Exeter Book*, ed. C. Williamson (1977); *A Choice of Anglo-Saxon Verse*, ed. and trans. Richard Hamer (1981); *Anglo-Saxon Poetry*, trans. S.A.J. Bradley (1982); *Old English Minor Heroic Poems*, ed. Joyce Hill (1983); *The Earliest English Poems*, trans. M. Alexander (1991); *The Old English Elegies*, ed. A. L. Klinck (1992); *Sixty-Five Anglo-Saxon Riddles*, ed. and trans. L. J. Rodrigues (1998); *Old and Middle English*, ed. E. Treharne (2000); *Eight Old English Poems*, ed. J. C. Pope, rev. R. D. Fulk (2001); *The Word Exchange: Anglo-Saxon Poems in Translation*, ed. G. Delanty and M. Matto (2010). **Criticism and History**: *Essential Articles for the Study of Old English Poetry*, ed. J. B. Bessinger and S. J. Kahrl (1968); S. B. Greenfield, *The Interpretation of Old English Poems* (1972); F. C. Robinson, *Beowulf and the Appositive Style* (1985); S. B. Greenfield and D. G. Calder, *A New Critical History of Old English Literature* (1986); N. Howe, *Migration and Mythmaking in Anglo-Saxon England* (1989); G. R. Overing, *Language, Sign, and Gender in Beowulf* (1990); K. O'Brien O'Keeffe, *Visible Song* (1990); *Old English Shorter Poems: Basic Readings*, ed. K. O'Brien O'Keeffe (1994); *Beowulf: Basic Readings*, ed. P. S. Baker (1995); *Cynewulf: Basic Readings*, ed. R. E. Bjork (1996); *Beowulf: A Verse Translation*, ed. D. Donoghue, trans. S. Heaney (2002); *The Poems of MS Junius 11*, ed. R. M. Liuzza (2002); T. A. Bredehoft, *Early English Metre* (2005); E. M. Tyler, *Old English Poetics: The Aesthetics of the Familiar* (2006); J. D. Niles, *Old English Heroic Poems and the Social Life of Texts* (2007); R. R. Trilling, *The Aesthetics of Nostalgia* (2009). **Digital Resources**: *Labyrinth: Resources for Medieval Studies*, http://www8.georgetown.edu/departments/medieval/labyrinth/; *Internet Medieval Sourcebook*, http://www.fordham.edu/halsall/sbook.html; *The Electronic Exeter Anthology of Old English Poetry: An Edition of Exeter, Dean and Chapter MS 3501* (DVD-ROM), ed. B. J. Muir (2006); *Dictionary of Old English: A to G online*, http://tapor.library.utoronto.ca/doe/; *The Electronic Beowulf*, ed. Kevin Kiernan, http://www.uky.edu/~kiernan/eBeowulf/guide.htm.; *Old English Newsletter Bibliography Database*, http://www.oenewsletter.org/OENDB/index.php; *Norton Anthology of English Literature: Middle Ages*, http://www.wwnorton.com/college/english/nael/middleages/topic_4/welcome.htm.

■ **Middle English.** *Anthologies*: *Secular Lyrics of the Fourteenth and Fifteenth Centuries*, ed. R. H. Robbins, 2d ed. (1955); *Historical Poems of the Fourteenth and Fifteenth Centuries*, ed. R. H. Robbins (1959); *Early Middle English Verse and Prose*, ed. J. A. W. Bennett and G. V. Smithers (1968); A. C. Spearing, *Readings in Medieval Poetry* (1987); *Alliterative Poetry of the Later Middle Ages*, ed. T. Turville-Petre (1989); *A Book of Middle English*, ed. T. Turville-Petre and J. A. Burrow (1996). **Criticism and History**: P. Dronke, *The Medieval Lyric* (1968); J. A. Burrow, *Ricardian Poetry* (1974); *Middle English Alliterative Poetry and Its Literary Background*, ed. D. A. Lawton (1982); A. C. Spearing, *Medieval to Renaissance in English Poetry* (1984); J.A.W. Bennett and D. Gray, *Middle English Literature* (1986); *Medieval Literary Theory and Criticism, c. 1100–c. 1375*, ed. A. J. Minnis and A. B. Scott (1988); P. Zumthor, *Toward a Medieval Poetics*, trans. P. Bennett (1992); *Medieval Lyric: Genres in Historical Context*, ed. W. Paden (2000); C. Chism, *Alliterative Revivals* (2002); *The Cambridge History of Medieval English Literature*, ed. D. Wallace (2002). **Chaucer**: C. Muscatine, *Chaucer and the French Tradition* (1957); D. W. Robertson, Jr., *A Preface to Chaucer* (1962); B. F. Huppé, *A Reading of the "Canterbury Tales"* (1964); E. T. Donaldson, *Speaking of Chaucer* (1970); P. M. Kean, *Chaucer and the Making of English Poetry* (1972); J. Mann, *Chaucer and Medieval Estates Satire* (1973); D. R. Howard, *The Idea of the "Canterbury Tales"* (1976); V. A. Kolve, *Chaucer and the Imagery of Narrative* (1984); C. Dinshaw, *Chaucer's Sexual Poetics* (1989); P. Strohm, *Social Chaucer* (1989); J. Fleming, *Classical Imitation and Interpretation in Chaucer's "Troilus"* (1990); H. Marshall Leicester, *The Disenchanted Self* (1990); L. Patterson, *Chaucer and the Subject of History* (1991); S. Lerer, *Chaucer and His Readers* (1993); D. Wallace, *Chaucerian Polity* (1997); C. Cannon, *The Making of Chaucer's English* (1998); K. L. Lynch, *Chaucer's Philosophical Visions* (2000); M. Miller, *Philosophical Chaucer* (2004); L. Scanlon, *Narrative, Authority, and Power* (2004). **Fifteenth-Century Poets**: A. Renoir, *The Poetry of John Lydgate* (1967); D. Lawton, "Dullness and the Fifteenth Century," *ELH* 54 (1987); D. Pearsall, "Hoccleve's *Regement of Princes*: The Poetics of Royal Self-Representation," *Speculum* 69 (1994); P. Strohm, *England's Empty Throne* (1998); E. Knapp, *The Bureaucratic Muse* (2001); J. Simpson, *The Oxford English Literary History, Vol. 2: Reform and Cultural Revolution, 1350–1547* (2002); M. Nolan, *John Lydgate and the Making of Public Culture* (2005). **Gawain-/Pearl Poet**: M. Borroff, *Sir Gawain and the Green Knight* (1962); J. A. Burrow, *A Reading of "Sir Gawain and the Green Knight"* (1965); L. D. Benson, *Art and Tradition in "Sir Gawain and the Green Knight"* (1965); L. M. Clopper, "Pearl and the Consolation of Scripture," *Viator* 23 (1992); A. Putter, *An Introduction to the Gawain-Poet* (1996); *A Companion to the Gawain-Poet*, ed. D. Brewer and J. Gibson (1997); M. Borroff, *Traditions and Renewals* (2003). **Gower**: R. Peck, *Kingship and Common Profit in Gower's "Confessio amantis"* (1987); R. F. Yeager, *John Gower's Poetic* (1990); J. Simpson, *Sciences and the Self in Medieval Poetry* (1995); D. Aers,

*Faith, Ethics and Church* (2000); L. Staley, "Gower, Richard II, Henry of Derby, and the Business of Making Culture," *Speculum* 75 (2000); D. Watt, *Amoral Gower: Language, Sex, and Politics* (2003); P. Nicholson, *Love and Ethics in Gower's "Confessio amantis"* (2005). **Piers Plowman**: M. Bloomfield, *"Piers Plowman" as a 14th-C. Apocalypse* (1962); K. Kerby-Fulton, *Reformist Apocalypticism and "Piers Plowman"* (1990); S. Justice, *Writing and Rebellion: England in 1381* (1996); E. Steiner, *Documentary Culture and the Making of Medieval English Literature* (2003); N. Zeeman, *"Piers Plowman" and the Medieval Discourse of Desire* (2006).

■ **Renaissance.** *Anthologies*: *English Poetry of the Seventeenth Century*, ed. G. Parfitt (1992); *English Poetry of the Sixteenth Century*, ed. G. Waller (1993); *The Penguin Book of Renaissance Verse*, ed. D. Norbrook and H. Woudhuysen (1993); *Women Poets of the Renaissance*, ed. M. Wynne-Davies (1999); *Early Modern Women Poets*, ed. J. Stevenson and P. Davidson (2001); *Poetry and Revolution: An Anthology of British and Irish Verse, 1625–1660*, ed. P. Davidson (2001); *Sixteenth-Century Poetry*, ed. G. Braden (2005); *Seventeenth-Century British Poetry, 1603–1660*, ed. J. Rumrich and G. Chaplin (2005); *Metaphysical Poetry*, ed. C. Ricks and C. Burrow (2006); *The New Oxford Book of Seventeenth-Century Verse*, ed. A. Fowler (2008); *New Oxford Book of Sixteenth-Century Verse*, ed. E. Jones (2009); *Elizabeth I and Her Age*, ed. S. Felch and D. Stump (2009); *Women Writers in Renaissance England: An Annotated Anthology*, ed. R. Martin (2010); *The Broadview Anthology of British Literature: v. 2: The Renaissance and the Early Seventeenth Century*, ed. J. Black et al., 2d ed. (2010). **Criticism and History**: S. Greenblatt, *Renaissance Self-Fashioning* (1980); J. Guillory, *Poetic Authority* (1982); *Re-membering Milton: Essays on the Texts and Traditions*, ed. M. Ferguson and M. Nyquist (1988); *The Spenser Encyclopedia*, ed. A. C. Hamilton (1990); A. R. Jones, *The Currency of Eros: Women's Love Lyric in Europe, 1540–1620* (1990); *The Cambridge Companion to English Poetry, Donne to Marvell*, ed. T. Corns (1993); A. Marotti, *Manuscript, Print, and the English Renaissance Lyric* (1995); D. K. Shuger, *Habits of Thought in the English Renaissance: Religion, Politics and the Dominant Culture* (1997); *Worldmaking Spenser: Explorations in the Early Modern Age*, ed. P. Cheney and L. Silberman (1999); A. Hadfield, *The English Renaissance, 1500–1620* (2000); *A Companion to Early Modern Women's Writing*, ed. A. Pacheco (2002); *A Companion to English Renaissance Literature and Culture*, ed. M. Hattaway (2002); D. Norbrook, *Poetry and Politics in the English Renaissance* (2002); *Reading Early Modern Women*, ed. H. Ostovich and E. Sauer (2002); *Renaissance Poetry and Its Formal Engagements*, ed. M. Rasmussen (2002); R. Smith, *Sonnets and the English Woman Writer, 1560–1621* (2005); *Early Modern Poetry: A Critical Companion*, ed. P. Cheney, A. Hadfield, G. Sullivan (2006); J. Griffiths, *John Skelton and Poetic Authority* (2006); *John Donne's Poetry*, ed. D. Dickson (2007); A. Nicolson, *Quarrel with the King:*

*The Story of an English Family on the High Road to Civil War* (2008); *Aemilia Lanyer: Gender, Genre, and the Canon*, ed. M. Grossman (2009); *The Cambridge Companion to Early Modern Women's Writing*, ed. L. Knoppers (2009); H. Dubrow, *The Challenges of Orpheus: Lyric Poetry and Early Modern England* (2011). **Digital Resources**: Voice of the Shuttle: Renaissance and Seventeenth Century, http://vos.ucsb.edu/browse. asp?id=2749; *Luminarium: Renaissance and Seventeenth Century*, http://www.luminarium.org; Mr. William Shakespeare and the Internet, http://shakespeare.palomar.edu/; CERES Cambridge English Renaissance Electronic Service, http://www.english.cam.ac.uk/ceres/; *Norton Anthology of English Literature—16th Century and Early 17th Century*, http://www.wwnorton.com/college/english/nael/welcome.htm; CRRS Centre for Reformation and Renaissance Studies, http://crrs.ca/; The Folger Shakespeare Library, http://www.folger.edu/; The English Renaissance in Context (ERIC), http://sceti.library.upenn.edu/sceti/furness/eric/index.cfm; Representative Poetry Online, http://rpo.library.utoronto.ca/display/index.cfm; John Milton—The Milton-L Home Page, https://facultystaff.richmond.edu/~creamer/milton/; The Milton Reading Room, http://www.dartmouth.edu/~milton/reading_room/contents/index.shtml; Christ's College Cambridge—400th Anniversary Celebration of Milton, http://www.christs.cam.ac.uk/milton400/index.htm; The Edmund Spenser Homepage, http://www.english.cam.ac.uk/spenser/; The Sidney Homepage, http://www.english.cam.ac.uk/sidney/index.htm.

■ **Restoration and the Eighteenth Century.** *Anthologies*: *Kissing the Rod: An Anthology of Seventeenth-Century Women's Verse*, ed. G. Greer et al. (1989); *Eighteenth-Century Women Poets*, ed. R. Lonsdale (1989); *Amazing Grace: An Anthology of Poems about Slavery, 1660–1810*, ed. J. G. Basker (2002); *Poetry from 1660 to 1780: Civil War, Restoration, Revolution*, ed. D. Wu and R. DeMaria (2002); *Eighteenth-Century English Labouring Class Poets*, ed. J. Goodridge et al., 3 v. (2003); *The Poetry of Slavery: An Anglo-American Anthology, 1764–1865*, ed. M. Wood (2003); *Eighteenth-Century Poetry*, ed. D. Fairer and D. Gerrard (2004); *British Women Poets of the Long Eighteenth Century*, ed. P. R. Backscheider and C. Ingrassia (2009); *Restoration Literature*, ed. P. Hammond (2009); *The New Oxford Book of Eighteenth-Century Verse*, ed. R. Lonsdale (2009). **Criticism and History**: E. Rothstein, *Restoration and Eighteenth-Century Poetry, 1660–1780* (1981); J. Sitter, *Literary Loneliness in Mid-Eighteenth-Century England* (1982); D. B. Morris, *Alexander Pope: The Genius of Sense* (1984); A. Williams, *Prophetic Strain: The Greater Lyric in the Eighteenth Century* (1984); M. A. Doody, *The Daring Muse: Augustan Poetry Reconsidered* (1985); C. Gerrard, *The Patriot Opposition to Walpole* (1994); B. Parker, *The Triumph of Augustan Poetics* (1998); S. Kaul, *Poems of Nation, Anthems of Empire* (2000); W. J. Christmas, *The Lab'ring Muses* (2001); D. H. Griffin, *Patriotism and Poetry in Eighteenth-Century Britain* (2002); D. Fairer, *English Poetry of the Eighteenth*

*Century* (2003); P. R. Backscheider, *Eighteenth-Century Women Poets and Their Poetry* (2005); P. Hammond, *The Making of Restoration Poetry* (2006); W. Overton, *The Eighteenth-Century British Verse Epistle* (2007); P. M. Spacks, *Reading Eighteenth-Century Poetry* (2009); J. Sitter, *The Cambridge Introduction to Eighteenth-Century Poetry* (2011). **Digital Resources**: Eighteenth-Century Resources, http://ethnicity.rutgers.edu/~jlynch/18th/index.html; *18thConnect*, http://www.18thconnect.org; Literary Resources on the Net, http://ethnicity.rutgers.edu/~jlynch/Lit; Voice of the Shuttle, http://vos.ucsb.edu.

■ **Romantic Period**. *Anthologies*: *New Oxford Book of Romantic Period Verse*, ed. J. McGann (1993); *English Romantic Writers,* ed. D. Perkins (1995); *British Literature, 1780–1830,* ed. A. Mellor and R. Matlak (1996); *British Women Poets of the Romantic Era,* ed. P. Feldman (1997); *Romantic Women Poets,* ed. A. Ashfield (1998); *Longman Anthology of British Literature: The Romantics and Their Contemporaries,* ed. S. Wolfson and P. Manning (1999); *New Penguin Book of Romantic Poetry,* ed. J. and J. Wordsworth (2001); *Romanticism,* ed. D. Wu (2006); *Romantic Poetry,* ed. M. O'Neill and C. Mahoney (2008). **Criticism and History**: Abrams; H. Bloom, *The Visionary Company* (1961); G. Hartman, *Wordsworth's Poetry, 1787–1814* (1964); M. H. Abrams, *Natural Supernaturalism* (1971); K. Kroeber, *Romantic Landscape Vision* (1975); M. Jacobus, *Tradition and Experiment in Wordsworth's Lyrical Ballads* (1976); A. Mellor, *English Romantic Irony* (1980); J. McGann, *The Romantic Ideology* (1983); H. Vendler, *The Odes of John Keats* (1983); S. Curran, *Poetic Form and British Romanticism* (1986); M. Levinson, *Wordsworth's Great Period Poems* (1986), *Keats's Life of Allegory* (1988); J. Watson, *English Poetry of the Romantic Period, 1789–1830* (1992); K. Kroeber, *Ecological Literary Criticism* (1994); J. J. McGann, *The Poetics of Sensibility* (1996); M. O'Neill, *Romanticism and the Self-Conscious Poem* (1997); S. Wolfson, *Formal Charges* (1997); J. Chandler, *England in 1819* (1998); S. Wolfson, *Borderlines: The Shiftings of Gender in British Romanticism* (2006); *Cambridge Companion to British Romantic Poetry,* ed. J. Chandler and M. McClane (2008); D. Gigante, *Life: Organic Form and Romanticism* (2009).

■ **Victorian Period**. *Anthologies*: *Victorian Poetry and Poetics,* ed. W. Houghton and G. R. Stange (1968); *New Oxford Book of Victorian Verse,* ed. C. Ricks (1987); *Victorian Women Poets,* ed. A. Leighton and M. Reynolds (1995); *Nineteenth-Century Women Poets,* ed. I. Armstrong and J. Bristow (1996); *Penguin Book of Victorian Verse,* ed. D. Karlin (1997); *Broadview Anthology of Victorian Poetry and Poetic Theory,* ed. T. Collins and V. J. Rundle (1999); *The Victorians,* ed. V. Cunningham (2000); *Victorian Poetry,* ed. F. O'Gorman (2004); *Decadent Poetry,* ed. L. Rodensky (2007); *Victorian Women Poets,* ed. V. Blain (2009). **Criticism and History**: E.D.H. Johnson, *The Alien Vision of Victorian Poetry* (1952); R. Langbaum, *The Poetry of Experience* (1957)—dramatic monologue; C. Ricks, *Tennyson* (1972); D. Mermin, *The Audience in the Poem* (1983);

H. F. Tucker, *Tennyson and the Doom of Romanticism* (1988); E. Griffiths, *The Printed Voice of Victorian Poetry* (1989); A. Leighton, *Victorian Women Poets* (1992); I. Armstrong, *Victorian Poetry* (1993); Y. Prins, *Victorian Sappho* (1999); M. Reynolds, *The Realms of Verse, 1830–1870* (2001); B. Richards, *English Poetry of the Victorian Period, 1830–1890* (2001); *Companion to Victorian Poetry,* ed. R. Cronin, A. Chapman, A. Harrison (2002); R. Cronin, *Romantic Victorians* (2002); *The Fin-de-Siècle Poem,* ed. J. Bristow (2005); H. F. Tucker, *Epic: Britain's Heroic Muse* (2008); L. K. Hughes, *Cambridge Introduction to Victorian Poetry* (2010); V. Cunningham, *Victorian Poetry Now* (2011). **Digital Resources**: *Nineteenth-century Scholarship Online,* http://www.nines.org/; Romantic Circles, http://www.rc.umd.edu/; William Blake Archive, http://www.blakearchive.org/blake/; British Women Romantic Poets, http://digital.lib.ucdavis.edu/projects/bwrp/; Poetess Archive, http://unixgen.muohio.edu/~poetess/; Rossetti Archive, http://www.rossettiarchive.org/; Morris Online, http://morrisedition.lib.uiowa.edu/; Swinburne Project, http://swinburnearchive.indiana.edu/swinburne/www/swinburne/.

■ **Modernism to the Present**. *Anthologies*: *Georgian Poetry,* ed. E. Marsh (1911–22); *Des Imagistes* (1914) and *Catholic Anthology* (1915), both ed. E. Pound; *Some Imagist Poets* (1915); *New Signatures* (1932), *New Country* (1933), and *Faber Book of Modern Verse* (1936), all ed. M. Roberts; *Oxford Book of Modern Verse,* ed. W. B. Yeats (1936); *The New Apocalypse,* ed. J. F. Hendry (1939); *New Verse,* ed. G. Grigson (1942); *Faber Book of 20th-Century Verse,* ed. J. Heath-Stubbs and D. Wright (1953); *Poetry of the 1950s,* ed. D. J. Enright (1955); *New Lines,* ed. R. Conquest (1956); *The New Poetry* (1962), ed. A. Alvarez, rev. ed. (1966); *Children of Albion,* ed. M. Horovitz (1968); *British Poetry since 1945,* ed. E. Lucie-Smith (1970); *Oxford Book of Twentieth-Century English Verse,* ed. P. Larkin (1973); *Oxford Book of Contemporary Verse,* ed. D. J. Enright (1980); *Penguin Book of Contemporary British Poetry,* ed. B. Morrison and A. Motion (1982); *A Various Art,* ed. A. Crozier and T. Longville (1987); *The New British Poetry,* ed. G. Allnutt et al. (1988); *Conductors of Chaos,* ed. I. Sinclair (1996); *Penguin Book of First World War Poetry* [1979], ed. J. Silkin, rev. ed. (1996); *Out of Everywhere,* ed. M. O'Sullivan (1996); *Penguin Book of Poetry from Britain and Ireland since 1945,* ed. S. Armitage and R. Crawford (1998); *Harvill Book of Twentieth-Century Poetry in English,* ed. M. Schmidt (1999); *Other: British and Irish Poetry since 1970,* ed. R. Caddel and P. Quartermain (1999); *Bloodaxe Book of 20th Century Poetry from Britain and Ireland,* ed. E. Longley (2001); *Anthology of Twentieth-Century British and Irish Poetry,* ed. K. Tuma (2001); *Norton Anthology of Modern and Contemporary Poetry,* ed. J. Ramazani, R. Ellmann, R. O'Clair (2003); *New British Poetry,* ed. D. Paterson and C. Simic (2004). **Criticism and History**: A. Symons, *The Symbolist Movement in Literature* (1899), rev. ed. (1919); I. A. Richards, *Science and Poetry* (1926); F. R. Leavis, *New Bearings in English Poetry* (1932); C. Brooks, *Modern Poetry and the Tradi-*

*tion* (1939); Eliot, *Essays*; D. Davie, *Purity of Diction in English Verse* (1952); and *Articulate Energy* (1955); H. Kenner, *The Pound Era* (1971); D. Davie, *Thomas Hardy and British Poetry* (1972); S. Hynes, *The Auden Generation* (1975); D. Perkins, *A History of Modern Poetry,* 2 v. (1976, 1987); B. Morrison, *The Movement* (1980); V. Cunningham, *British Writers of the Thirties* (1988); D. Davie, *Under Briggflatts: A History of Poetry in Great Britain, 1960–1988* (1989); N. Corcoran, *English and Irish Poetry since 1940* (1993); A. Duncan, *The Failure of Conservatism in Modern British Poetry* (2003); R. Stevenson, *The Last of England?* (2004); P. Middleton, *Distant Reading* (2005); P. Barry, *Poetry Wars* (2006); S. Broom, *Contemporary British and Irish Poetry* (2006); J. Ramazani, *A Transnational Poetics* (2009). **Digital Resources**: *The First World War Poetry Digital Archive*, http://www.oucs.ox.ac.uk/ww1lit/; The Modernist Journals Project, http://dl.lib.brown.edu/mjp/.

> K. Davis (OE); E. Johnson (ME); E. H. Sagaser (Ren.); J. Keith (Restoration and 18th C.); E. Gray (Romantic and Victorian); C. D. Blanton (Mod. to Present)

## ENGLISH PROSODY

I. Old English
II. Middle English
III. Modern English

**I. Old English** (ca. 500–1100 CE). OE verse, like that of the other early Germanic langs. (Old Saxon, OHG, ON), is composed in hemistichs or verses linked by *alliteration into long lines. Despite some technical differences between the strict metrical style of *Beowulf* or *Exodus* and the freer style of the late poem "The Battle of Maldon" (ca. 991), the extant trad. during the four centuries from Cædmon's "Hymn" (ca. 670) to the Norman Conquest (1066) is remarkably homogeneous. The main variation from this normal *meter is the infrequent *hypermetric verse (Ger. *Schwellvers*). Of the 30,000 lines of OE poetry, there are fewer than 950 hypermetric verses, which usually occur in clusters and exceed the normal metrical limit by several heavy syllables.

It has sometimes been said that OE poetry is in the "strong-stress" trad. along with mod. *accentual verse on the assumption that each hemistich contains two main stresses and an indeterminate number of unstressed syllables. Although it is obvious that word stress is an important element of OE meter (alliteration depends on it), it has also become clear in studies of the past four decades that OE meter is a complex mix of at least three elements that are usually assigned to different metrical typologies: stress, quantity, and syllable count. At present, there is no agreement on which element is most basic and which two are derivative. In addition to these phonological determinants, some studies posit word shape as a prime (Russom, Bredehoft).

It has always been known that quantity was an element of OE meter, although its position was considered secondary: in summaries of OE meter for handbooks and anthols., it was often omitted altogether. The tech-

nicalities involve *resolution (whereby a short stressed syllable is grouped with the following syllable into a unit) and suspension of resolution. Renewed attention to Kaluza's Law has highlighted the importance of syllable quantity in the formulation of an adequate theory (Fulk).

Syllable counting is the least obvious of the elements to figure into a statement of OE meter. A glance down a page of OE poetry in a mod. ed. confirms the variable length of lines that seem far from being "syllabic." However, the accordion-like expansion of the OE line is permitted only in certain specified parts of the verse. Elsewhere, there is a close matching of syllable or "syllable equivalent" with the abstract metrical unit, the "position" or "member." Because a pattern of four members was posited in the most influential study of OE meter (Sievers), there is nothing radical in beginning with a one-to-one mapping of syllable (or syllable equivalent) and metrical unit. A syllable-count pattern is generally accepted for a reconstructed IE meter (manifested in Avestan and, with secondary quantitative patterns, in Vedic). Just as Gr. meter seems to have developed by expanding the syllable count through quantitative equivalences, esp. in the dactylic hexameter, so possibly did Germanic meter (although distinguishing historical derivation from convergent innovation within a limited repertoire of possible elements is beyond reach). ON meter reflects syllable count even better than OE, the meters of Old Saxon and OHG much less so.

If Sievers's system invites these speculations in its "four members," this aspect has been completely displaced by his simultaneous but more tangible reification of the "five types," the most common patterns of syllables bearing full stress, secondary stress, and weak stress. The five types (labeled A through E) appear in every intro. to OE poetry of the past century, and the scheme serves as a convenient taxonomy for mnemonic, pedagogical, and classificatory purposes:

| A | / x / x | gomban gyldan |
| B | x / x / | þenden wordum wēold |
| C | x / / x | ofer hronrāde |
| D | / / \ x | cwēn Hrōðgāres |
| E | / \ x / | flōdȳþum feor |

Still, one may question whether Sievers's types are the cause (the paradigm) or the effect (epiphenomena of a more basic pattern) and in any event whether the types are compatible with the two-stress idea. Types D and E regularly have three stresses (with the lightest falling on a syllable that elsewhere counts as a full *ictus), and many types A and C appear to have only one stress.

The most obvious feature of the earliest poetry in the Germanic langs. is alliteration. As with *rhyme in later accentual-syllabic verse, alliteration does not determine metrical structure, which is easily discoverable without this cue. This superficial feature survived the rupture in the trad. caused by the Norman Conquest.

**II. Middle English.** ME prosody, a highly controverted field, has achieved little consensus as to the exact nature and origin of forms or even basic terminology. What is beyond dispute is that between the late tenth and late 14th cs., metrical innovation in ME verse flourished, encouraged by complex influences both foreign and native.

**A. *Evolution of the Native Tradition.*** Alliterative poetry of the cl. OE type continued to be written up to the Norman Conquest, the last poem in the strict meter arguably being *The Death of Edward* in 1066, on the event that brought about William's invasion. By the time of *The Description of Durham*, ca. 1104–9, only superficial elements of the meter remain, and the early ME verse that followed (e.g., *The Departing Soul's Address to the Body*, *The First Worcester Fragment*, Layamon's *Brut*) is clearly "looser" than OE alliterative verse. Whether it was modernized in lang. and meter from the cl. OE trad. or descended from a "popular" oral trad. or developed from the "rhythmical alliteration" of Wulfstan's and Ælfric's prose, early ME verse does share some features of OE verse. Lines are composed of two half lines usually linked by alliteration. However, half lines carry a greater number of unstressed syllables than in OE meter, and the rising and falling rhythm (x / x / x) predominates. Rhythmic patterns are irregular and cannot usefully be categorized on the basis of Sievers's five types (see sect. I above). Both alliteration and *leonine rhyme are treated as ornaments, but often neither alliteration nor rhyme occurs.

**B. *Middle English Accentual-Syllabic Verse.*** By the early 12th c., rhyme comes into use as a structural principle, borrowed probably from med. Lat. (e.g., Godric's *Hymns*, ca. 1170) but also under the influence of Fr., particularly the Anglo-Norman *vers décasyllabe*. Finally, it supplants alliteration altogether. The adaptation of Anglo-Norman and Fr. models to Eng. phonology leads to the octosyllabic couplet in contours of alternating stress, a staple of ME verse, as in John Gower's *Confessio amantis* and Chaucer's *House of Fame*. Octosyllabic verse in a variety of forms—couplets, the ballade stanza, cross-rhymed quatrains, and octaves—continues through the 15th c. (see OCTOSYLLABLE).

A number of other forms indebted to both med. Lat. and Anglo-Norman models come into play at the end of the 12th c.: a long line in mixed lengths of 12 and 14 syllables rhyming in couplets, quatrains, or octaves; the *Burns stanza; and the ballade. It is believed that couplets of the 14-syllable line, by adding internal rhyme and breaking at the half lines into short-line quatrains, produced "8s and 6s," a form isomorphic to *ballad meter. The same internal rhyme breaks the alliterative long line into a short alliterative complex that persists from Layamon through the late *tail-rhyme stanzas (e.g., *Sir Degrevaunt*). Tail rhyme, also derived from med. Lat. and Anglo-Norman exemplars, becomes the characteristic stanza of the Eng. metrical romances, usually in six- or 12-line stanzas. The addition of rhyme to the ornamental alliterative line produces a wide range of stanzas, as in the celebrated Harley lyrics. Generally speaking, the addition of rhyme coincides with a shift from accentual to accentual-syllabic verse, so that the number of syllables and the number and position of stresses in the line become relatively fixed. ME verse normally imitates the simple binary meters characteristic of med. Lat. verse, e.g., the *Poema morale* (ca. 1170), which imitates the Lat. septenarius.

**C. *The Alliterative Long Line.*** Alliterative composition in prose and rhymed verse continues throughout the 13th and 14th cs. in a broad continuum of styles derived from both the native trad. and from Lat. and Fr. The Harley lyrics (ms. composed ca. 1340–50) beautifully illustrate the difficulty of sorting out the separate strands. Of the 18 alliterative lyrics, 15 are arguably in a mixed iambic-anapestic meter more akin to meters found in Alfred, Lord Tennyson; Robert Browning; A. C. Swinburne; and Robert Frost than to anything in OE or early ME (hence, the apparent familiarity of the rhythms of these poems). For the rhythm of early 14th-c. lyrics, studies of "strict stress-meter" in Eng. by Tarlinskaja (cf. Rus. *dol'nik) are more revealing than comparisons with OE meter.

For the so-called Alliterative Revival of the mid-14th c., no substantial recent scholarship has examined the old problem of the external reasons for this remarkable flowering in the West Midlands. However, much progress has been made in understanding the metrical structure. These discoveries make it more difficult to trace a natural evolution, as Oakden did, from late OE through Layamon at the turn of the 13th c. to the Alliterative Revival of the late 14th and early 15th cs. Meanwhile, the term Alliterative Revival has been questioned in recent scholarship for ignoring much poetry of the 13th and 14th cs. that would show a more continuous trad. if our records were more complete.

It is not clear that our fuller understanding of the metrical structure can be tied to datable cultural and intellectual trends or the influence of other langs. It is equally unclear how the similarities with OE meter can be established as derivative from the earlier stage: e.g., both trads. have a highly specified element of syllable count, but it is hard to know whether this element was handed down as a metrical artifice or if the syllable count and departures from it in extra unstressed syllables are to be expected in a *stress-timed* language: in both OE and ME, the intervals between stresses appear to be regulated, as opposed to a *syllable-timed* language like Fr., in which the intervals between syllables are (see ISOCHRONISM OR ISOCHRONY).

What can be specified precisely for poems like *Sir Gawain and the Green Knight* is the metrical structure of the second half of the long line (the b-verse) in terms of syllables that receive a metrical beat and syllables that do not. For the most part, the syllables that receive a beat are the stressed syllables of lexical words (esp. nouns and adjectives) and syllables that do not receive a metrical beat (thus forming an offbeat) are syllables of function words and unstressed syllables of lexical words. The requirements are technical but crucial for any generalization about Eng. metrical typology in the Middle Ages: the b-verse must contain two beats and exactly one "strong dip" or "long dip" (two or more metrically unstressed syllables—Duggan, Cable); furthermore, the verse must end with exactly one unstressed syllable

(Putter et al.), and the vowel of that syllable must be a schwa (Yakovlev). Having stated all these prescriptions for the b-verse, one can hypothesize that the a-verse is "otherwise, anything," i.e., any combination of long and short dips and of schwa and nonschwa vowels that does not meet the requirements for the b-verse. The two halves of the long line would then be "heteromorphic" (a term introduced by McIntosh but used only at the level of the foot); efforts to confirm or falsify this hypothesis are part of the ongoing scholarship in ME metrics. Meanwhile, there are exceptions to all the "rules" stated above (and resulting disagreements among metrists), and William Langland's *Piers Plowman* has more exceptions than most.

**D.** *Chaucer and the 15th Century.* The declining fortunes of Anglo-Norman in the mid-14th c. seem to have encouraged a shifting of attention to strict Fr. forms, and Chaucer's indebtedness to native ME prosody has proved increasingly difficult to demonstrate. Chaucer can certainly use ornamental alliteration, particularly in battle scenes (e.g., "The Knight's Tale," 2601 ff.), but his clearest adaptation of native ME prosody, in the tail rhyme and bob lines of "Tale of Sir Thopas," is satiric. In *The Parliament of Fowls*, Chaucer abandons the octosyllabic couplet for *rhyme royal, his staple stanza for formal poems (*Troilus and Criseyde*), and a form related to the *monk's tale stanza. Chaucer also imitates the Fr. triple ballade ("Complaint of Venus") and *rondel and the It. *terza rima ("A Complaint to His Lady"); *Anelida and Arcite* contains much prosodic experimentation.

But Chaucer's most significant technical achievement is the heroic or decasyllabic line (see DECASYLLABLE) in couplets, derived perhaps by expanding the octosyllabic couplet, perhaps from the rhyme royal stanza; its origin is disputed, so the very terms used to refer to it have never been settled. Chaucer is the first to use the five-beat or iambic pentameter couplet in Eng. (either in the prologue to the *Legend of Good Women* or in an early version of the "Knight's Tale"). Most prosodists agree that Chaucer's line has a predominantly "iambic" rhythm with variations: line-initial trochaic substitution (occasionally after the caesura), secondary stress on polysyllables, elision, and occasional weak stresses. Chaucer's greatness as a metrical artist lies in his skill at tensing rhetorical and syntactic accent against the basic metrical pattern.

Chaucer's enormous influence after his death in 1400 preserved his verse forms through the 15th c. It is not clear that his disciples understood what they imitated, although part of the problem may be gaps in our mod. understanding analogous to faulty readings of Chaucer before mod. texts were edited and the phonology of final *e* was established. John Lydgate's prosody, which influenced nearly every 15th-c. poet, is known especially for the "broken-backed" line, in which only a caesura appears to separate two strong stresses. However, an assumption of Chaucerian phonology will often justify a final *e* even if it is not written in the ms., and many lines become smoother. In fact, some of the undeniable badness of Lydgate's verse may result from an insistent, artificial regularity rather than from the stumbling rhythms that have usually been perceived. The 15th c.'s main contribution is the *carol, though the pentameter couplet and rhyme royal are its staple forms.

**III. Modern** (after 1500)

**A.** *16th and Early 17th Centuries.* Early mod. Eng. verse represents competing trads.: (1) cl. quantitative verse, from Gr. and Lat. models (both strophic and hexameter lines), which proved incompatible with the accentual structure of Eng.; (2) "old-fashioned" accentual and alliterative poetry favored by John Skelton and others, a native form surviving until midcentury in the *tumbling verse of the popular stage; and (3) the decasyllabic line, originating with Chaucer, sustained by his successors, and modified by the Eng. imitators of Petrarch and his It. and Fr. followers. Losing interest in quantitative schemes, Tudor poets and dramatists taught themselves to convert the *patterns* of cl. meters, especially iambic, to an accentual verse system in which accent or stress, not length, determines the measure. Early forms employed until almost the 17th c. include *fourteeners and *poulter's measure, but the iambic pentameter line soon began to show its flexibility and expressive powers in various tonal registers. Favored by Thomas Wyatt in some of his most successful sonnets, the form was taken up without rhyme by Henry Howard, the Earl of Surrey, for his trans. of part of the *Aeneid* and then used by Thomas Sackville and Thomas Norton for their political tragedy *Gorboduc* (1571). In the hands of Philip Sidney, Christopher Marlowe, Edmund Spenser, Shakespeare, and Ben Jonson, the iambic pentameter line revealed qualities that transformed lyric verse, helped usher in the greatest period of Brit. drama, and determined the future of Eng. poetry.

The virtues of the blank verse line derive from its moderate length, the ten syllables avoiding the liability of the longer line to split in half and of the short line to sound childish. The particular dynamic of *blank verse, especially for drama, dwells in the tension between, on the one hand, the semantic energies and grammatical claims of the sentence and, on the other, the rhythmic regularity of sequential pentameter lines (Wright). Poets exploited the variety of blank verse by finding that (1) the midline phrasal break could be variously located, (2) stressed syllables might be unequal in strength (and unstressed ones, too), (3) variations in the placement of stressing in the line could confer grace and energy, and (4) with occasional, even frequent, *enjambment, a passage could flow smoothly through unequal grammatical segments and seem as much speech as verse.

Discovering the malleability of the line, some poets developed its capacity for variation so thoroughly as to threaten the security of the pentameter frame. The later Shakespeare, John Webster, Thomas Middleton (in dramatic verse), and especially John Donne (in his *Satyres, Elegies,* and letters) exaggerate such features as enjambment, elision, inversion and other accentual variations, line length (both abbreviated and extended), and multiple pauses within the line. In achieving a speech-like immediacy, they vastly expanded the tonal possibilities of the form. Donne also pursued such variety in his *Songs and Sonnets*, leading Jonson to complain that he should be hanged for not keeping the accent. This vigorous period of innovation was contemporaneous with the less extreme prosodic experiments of Jonson and his followers. Their commitment to cl. forms and balanced lines gave rise to less radical but equally significant creativity with rhythm, rhyme, and length of line.

**B.** *Later 17th and 18th Centuries.* Spenser, Jonson, and George Herbert became the models for much lyric verse of the 17th c., with most poets endorsing Samuel Daniel's conservative view about the value of rhyme (*A Defence of Ryme*, 1603). Donne's successors (see METAPHYSICAL POETRY), down through Andrew Marvell, John Milton, and Jonathan Swift, employ the tetrameter couplet as a balanced form for conveying subtle and sometimes ironic argument. The multiplicity of the blank verse line attracted an unparalleled voice in Milton, who chose it for *Paradise Lost* and explicitly defended it in a prefatory note to the poem. Prosodically correct (though in accordance with rules that are apparently his own—see Bridges, Sprott, and Weismiller) and extraordinarily resourceful, his epic verse, audaciously blank, keeps the grand grammatical sentence boldly diverging from yet counterpoised with the equally heroic line.

But it is the *heroic couplet, deriving from the decasyllables of Chaucer and Jonson and usurping the rhythmic possibilities of the blank-verse line, that becomes the sovereign form in Eng. poetry for over a century. It invited Edmund Waller, John Denham, John Dryden, and eventually Alexander Pope to exploit its hospitality to antithetical words and phrases: they built oppositions into the line or set line against line in a seemingly inexhaustible display of verbal balance, polish, ingenuity, and "bite." *Odes, Pindaric or Horatian, afforded the resourceful poet a different variety of challenging formal (and cl.) structures. Augustan prosodists (Edward Bysshe, Richard Bentley, and Henry Pemberton) and critics (Samuel Johnson) condemn departures from metrical norms, but toward the end of the century, monotony and desire for change eventually hastened the return of blank verse, esp. as a medium for reflection. At the same time, the rediscovery of the ballad stimulated the writing of lyric poems in looser forms and encouraged other variation in poems with an iambic base.

**C.** *19th Century.* Liberated from the couplet, romantic poetry explores rich veins of blank and stanzaic verse of various shapes and dimensions (Curran). But the century's poets soon divide into opposing distinct prosodic camps: one moves toward accentual verse, with its strong recurrent pattern of regular beats, the other toward free verse and its highlighting of the rhythmical phrase. The first group tries on various modes: triple meters (E. A. Poe and H. W. Longfellow), anapestic variation in iambic verse (Browning, Swinburne, Thomas Hardy), the accentually *sprung rhythm of the *"Christabel" meter and G. M. Hopkins, and *dipodic rhythms (Browning, George Meredith, Rudyard Kipling), all of which, as they strengthen both the equality and the isochronism of the beat, diminish the role of expressive variation within the line. Tennyson and Browning are exceptional in their ability still to write compelling blank verse. The second party prefers early types of free verse, expressive (as in Walt Whitman) of loosely measured sequences of self-reliant perceptions. The ordered lines of Ren. and Augustan verse, apparently representing some combination of natural order, the forces of authority, and social and political hierarchies, begin increasingly to lose their appeal as the century proceeds. They yield to the romantic and postromantic quest for a vehicle appropriate to the inner experience of a human subject deprived of religious and social certainty.

**D.** *20th Century.* The most influential voices soon make free verse the chief metrical mode. Ezra Pound and W. C. Williams embrace Whitman's elevation of the rhythmic phrase, apparently imitating ordinary speech but often introducing such effects as unexpected rhyme and audacious rhythmic play. Certain modernist poets mix familiar forms, including blank verse, with a freer prosody, as in T. S. Eliot's *The Waste Land*, where disintegration is a principal motif. Some of Whitman's self-proclaimed followers (e.g., Allen Ginsberg and the Beat poets) eschew conventional forms almost entirely. Poets who often retain traditional meters (e.g., Wallace Stevens, Robert Lowell, John Berryman) adapt them freely, as if they represented some order of reality, sanity, or conduct only dimly and intermittently descried; and in many major poets, traditional forms recur, sometimes brilliantly redeemed (W. B. Yeats, Robert Frost, W. H. Auden, Richard Wilbur, Philip Larkin, Anthony Hecht, and several contemp. Eng. poets). Other forms explored by 20th-c. poets (esp. Marianne Moore and Auden) include *syllabic verse, which furnishes a concealed formal structure, and *concrete poetry. Late in the century, many *Language poets consciously represent their subversion of form as an attack on the social conventions and practices of capitalism; and Af. Am., Caribbean, and postcolonial writers, grown increasingly accomplished and prominent, promote their own cultural forms, often in combination with the conventions of the Eng. trad. Fed by all these strains, Eng. poetry at the beginning of the 21st-c. has contrived a truce between the surety of familiar forms and the liberty of the individual voice, with poets adjusting the emphasis according to their bent.

Analysis of poetic modes comes generally after the fact, but in every period, prosodic crit. has a moralistic flavor, with many critics and poets disdaining their predecessors: e.g., 19th-c. poets, such as John Keats and Matthew Arnold, sometimes dismissed their Augustan precursors as writers of mere prose. Inconclusive debate has always attended the effort to relate prosody to meaning. Pope's famous dictum that "the sound should seem an echo to the sense," illustrated with his lines about "swift Camilla," represents one side of the case; the other is taken by Johnson, who (also famously) dismisses the general applicability of the contention. In various periods, poets, critics, and readers have sensed a semiotic function of prosody without being able to generalize persuasively about it. The regular pentameter line and the internal aural challenges to it represent a wider contest between order and individuality, and in the 20th c., the failure of traditional forms often signifies personal and social collapse. Some feminist critics have identified traditional meter with the restrictions of patriarchal control: Emily Dickinson, e.g., is said to have mostly avoided iambic pentameter as connoting the forces of Father and Christianity. But there is little agreement on such an iconic function of prosody.

*See* ALLITERATION; ENGLAND, POETRY OF; FREE VERSE; HEROIC VERSE; RHYTHM; SOUND; STANZA; VERSIFICATION.

■ **Old English:** Sievers; M. Kaluza, *A Short History of English Versification* (1911); J. C. Pope, *The Rhythm of "Beowulf,"* 2d ed. (1966); A. J. Bliss, *The Metre of "Beowulf,"* 2d ed. (1967); T. Cable, *The Meter and Melody of "Beowulf"* (1974); Brogan, sect. K; G. Russom, *Old English Meter and Linguistic Theory* (1987); W. Obst, *Der Rhythmus des "Beowulf"* (1987); R. D. Fulk, *A History of Old English Meter* (1992); B. R. Hutcheson, *Old English Poetic Metre* (1995); S. Suzuki, *The Metrical Organization of "Beowulf"* (1996); T. A. Bredehoft, *Early English Metre* (2005).

■ **Middle English:** *General:* Schipper; K. Luick *Englische Metrik* (1893); B. Ten Brink, *The Language and Metre of Chaucer* (1920); J. P. Oakden, *Alliterative Poetry in Middle English*, 2 v. (1930–35); A. McI. Trounce, "The English Tail-Rhyme Romances," *Medium Ævum* 1–2 (1932–34); F. Pyle, "The Place of Anglo-Norman in the History of English Versification," *Hermathena* 49 (1935); P. F. Baum, *Chaucer's Verse* (1961); M. Borroff, *"Sir Gawain and the Green Knight": A Metrical and Stylistic Study* (1962); M. D. Legge, *Anglo-Norman Literature and Its Background* (1963); Pearsall; Brogan, sect. K; U. Fries, *Einführung in die Sprache Chaucers* (1985); A.V.C. Schmidt, *The Clerkly Maker* (1987); M. Tarlinskaja, *Strict Stress-Meter in English Poetry* (1993). *Alliterative Revival:* J. R. Hulbert, "A Hypothesis Concerning the Alliterative Revival," *MP* 28 (1930); R. A. Waldron, "Oral-Formulaic Technique and Middle English Alliterative Poetry," *Speculum* 32 (1957); E. Salter, "The Alliterative Revival," *MP* 64 (1966–67); T. Turville-Petre, *The Alliterative Revival* (1977); A. McIntosh, "Early Middle English Alliterative Verse," and D. Pearsall, "The Alliterative Revival," *Middle English Alliterative Poetry*, ed. D. A. Lawton (1982); H. Duggan, "The Shape of the B-Verse in Middle English Alliterative Poetry," *Speculum* 61 (1986); T. Cable, *The English Alliterative Tradition* (1991); R. Hanna, "Alliterative Poetry," *Cambridge History of Medieval English Literature*, ed. D. Wallace (1999); C. Chism, *Alliterative Revivals* (2002); H. Zimmerman, "Continuity and Innovation: Scholarship on the Middle English Alliterative Revival," *Jahrbuch für Internationale Germanistik* 35 (2003); A. Putter, J. Jefferson, and M. Stokes, *Studies in the Metre of Alliterative Verse* (2007); N. Yakovlev, "Prosodic Restrictions on the Short Dip in Late Middle English Alliterative Verse," *YLS* 23 (2009).

■ **Modern:** Schipper; Smith—texts of Ren. prosodists; Schipper, *History*; Bridges; Omond; O. Jespersen, "Notes on Metre," rpt. in his *Linguistica* (1933); G. W. Allen, *American Prosody* (1934)—dated but not yet replaced; S. E. Sprott, *Milton's Art of Prosody* (1953); P. Fussell, *Theory of Prosody in Eighteenth-Century England* (1954); Wimsatt and Beardsley; Saintsbury, *Prosody*—eccentric theoretically; J. Thompson, *The Founding of English Metre* (1961); M. Halpern, "On the Two Chief Metrical Modes in English," *PMLA* 77 (1962)—fundamental; Chatman; K. Shapiro and R. Beum, *A Prosody Handbook* (1965); W. B. Piper, *The Heroic Couplet* (1969); J. Malof, *A Manual of English Meters* (1970); D. Attridge, *Well-Weighed Syllables* (1974); D. Crystal, "Intonation and Metrical Theory," *The English Tone of Voice* (1975); Tarlinskaja; E. Weismiller, "Blank Verse," *A Milton Encyclopedia*, ed. W. B. Hunter et al. (1978); H. Gross, ed., *The Structure of Verse*, 2d ed. (1979); C. O. Hartman, *Free Verse* (1980); Brogan—full list of references with annotations; Hollander; D. Wesling, *The New Poetries* (1985); S. Woods, *Natural Emphasis* (1985); S. Curran, *Poetic Form and British Romanticism* (1986); G. T. Wright, *Shakespeare's Metrical Art* (1988); O. B. Hardison Jr., *Prosody and Purpose in the English Renaissance* (1989); A. Finch, *The Ghost of Meter* (1993); H. Gross and R. McDowell, *Sound and Form in Modern Poetry*, 2d ed. (1996); R. McDonald, *Shakespeare's Late Style* (2006); J. Longenbach, *The Art of the Poetic Line* (2007).

T. CABLE (OE); R. H. OSBERG AND T. CABLE (ME); G. T. WRIGHT AND R. McDONALD (MOD.)

**ENGLYN** (pl. *englynion*). Along with *awdl* and *\*cywydd*, one of the three classes of the 24 strict meters of *\**Welsh poetry. Six of the eight varieties of englynion are quatrains, and the most common line length is the heptasyllable. The earliest forms are *\**tercets, like the *e. milwr* (warrior's englyn) that consists of three lines linked by end rhyme, or the *e. penfyr* (truncated englyn) that resembles the first three lines of an *e. unodl union* (see below). The famous early Welsh poems of the Llywarch Hen and Heledd cycles are series of such englynion, often joined to one another by *cymeriad*, the repetition of a word or phrase at the beginning of each englyn. After the 12th c., tercets gave way to *\**quatrains with lines linked by *\**rhyme or *proest* (see ODL). Since the 12th c., the most popular variety has been the *e. unodl union* (direct monorhyme englyn), a quatrain of lines of ten, six, seven, and seven syllables. The main rhyme in the first line appears one to three syllables before the end of the line and rhymes with the ends of the other three lines. The final one to three syllables of the first line are known as the *cyrch* or *gair cyrch* (reaching-out word; cf. G. M. Hopkins's "outriders") and must echo or alliterate with the first few syllables of line two. While the *gair cyrch* need only be related to what follows by means of light alliteration, strict *cynghanedd* has been observed in all other parts of the englyn since the 15th c. The end rhyme in the last two lines is always between a stressed and an unstressed syllable (as in Eng. *kíng* : *dáncing* or *hónest* : *bést*), a rule preserved since the 13th c. and also found in the Welsh cywydd meter. If the second couplet (*esgyll*, "wings") precedes the first two lines (*paladr*, "shaft"), the form is called *e. unodl crwca* ("crooked" monorhyme englyn).

*See* CELTIC PROSODY.

■ Morris-Jones; *Early Welsh Gnomic Poems*, ed. K. Jackson (1935); K. Jackson, "Incremental Repetition in the Early Welsh Englyn," *Speculum* 16 (1942); Parry, *History*; *Welsh Verse*, ed. T. Conran, 2nd ed. (1986); *Early Welsh Saga Poetry*, ed. J. Rowland (1990); *The New Companion to the Literature of Wales*, ed. M. Stephens (1998); A. Llwyd, *Anghenion y Gynghanedd* (2007).

T.V.F. BROGAN; D. M. LLOYD; B. BRUCH

**EN(H)OPLIAN**, *en(h)oplios, en(ho)plion* (Gr., "in arms," "martial"). A metrical term first attested in Aristophanes (*Clouds* 638) where, however, its exact reference is unclear. Later writers use it more or less interchangeably with *prosodion* or *prosodiakos* to designate various forms, all of which contain the sequence – ∪ ∪ – – ∪ ∪ – preceded and/or followed by some additional element. When it follows, this element is a single syllable, long or short; when it precedes, it may also be a double short. One form of enoplian ( ∪ ∪ – ∪ ∪ – – ∪ ∪ – – ) is thus identical with the *paroemiac*, others with sequences frequently found in *dactylo-epitritic*. Some mod. metrists have argued for the existence of a free version of the rhythm as well, similar to the paroemiac but allowing some substitution of single for double shorts. Such "single-short" enoplians are more usually and more correctly analyzed as *aeolic*.

■ A. M. Dale, "Aeolic: (2) Prosodiac-Enoplian"; K. Itsumi, "Enoplion in Tragedy," *CQ* 34 (1984); B. Gentili and L. Lomiento, "Kat' enoplion Meters," *Metrics and Rhythmics: History of Poetic Forms in Ancient Greece*, trans. E. C. Kopff (2008).

A. T. COLE

**ENJAMBMENT** (Fr., *enjamber*, "to straddle or encroach"). The continuation of a syntactic unit from one line to the next without a major juncture or pause; the opposite of an *end-stopped* line. While enjambment can refer to any verse that is not end-stopped, it is generally reserved for instances in which the "not stopping" of the verse is felt as overflow, esp. in relation to some poetic effect, as in the opening lines of Shakespeare's sonnet 116: "Let me not to the marriage of true minds / Admit impediments." In these lines, the desire not to admit impediments to the marriage of true minds is enacted poetically because the sentence "refuses" to stop at the line's end. One way to emphasize enjambment is to combine the use of enjambment with *caesura* (mid-line pause), as demonstrated in the following passage from *Hamlet*: "[The world is] an un-

weeded garden / That goes to seed; things rank and gross in nature / Possess it merely. That it should come to this!" (1.2.135–7). The enjambments and caesuras in these lines reinforce the image of a weedy garden outgrowing its proper boundaries, as well as the jumps in Hamlet's thoughts.

Enjambment can give the reader mixed messages: the closure of the metrical pattern at line end implies a pause, while the incompletion of the phrase says to go on. These conflicting signals can heighten tension or temporarily suggest one meaning only to adjust that meaning when the phrase is completed. To some degree, enjambment has been associated with freedom and transgression since *romanticism*; such associations are predicated on a norm of end-stopped verse and sparing use of enjambment, in relation to which the enjambment appears liberating. Enjambment ultimately depends on expectation of a pause at line's end; if verses are enjambed routinely, readers may perceive the text as something like prose.

Cl. *hexameter* is mainly end-stopped, as is Sanskrit verse. Though Homer's hexameters are more frequently enjambed than, say, those of the Hellenistic writers, it is often hard to discern poetic motivation behind the enjambments (the effect of enjambment in *oral poetry* and in *song* may be different from that of written verse). Virgil uses enjambment in ways that sometimes seem poetically motivated and sometimes not. Enjambment can be found in biblical Heb. and cl. Ar. verse, but it is not the norm. Enjambment is the norm in Old Germanic alliterative verse, incl. OE, where rhyme is unknown and lines are bound together by *alliteration* used to mark the meter. Prior to the 12th c., enjambment is rare in OF poetry: the *trouvère* Chrétien de Troyes (fl. after 1150) seems to have been the first poet in the Eur. vernaculars to break his verses systematically. By the 15th c., enjambment is widely used, and even more so in the 16th, esp. by Pierre de Ronsard (who coined the term) and the poets of the *Pléiade*. In the 17th c., enjambment was impugned by François de Malherbe and later Nicolas Boileau. These neoclassical authorities, however, allowed its use in certain circumstances—in *decasyllabic* poetry and in the less "noble" genres such as comedy and *fable*. Occasionally, enjambment occurs even in tragedy.

Since André Chénier (1762–94), enjambment has been accepted in all genres in Fr. The device was exploited to the full by Victor Hugo, whose famous enjambment at the beginning of *Hernani*—"Serait-ce déjà lui? C'est bien à l'escalier / Dérobé" (Is he already here? It must be by the secret staircase)—had the force of a manifesto (because adjectives generally follow nouns in Fr., Hugo is able to place *dérobé* [secret] on the other side of the line break). Enjambment was a fundamental characteristic of the *vers libéré* of the later 19th c. and the *vers libre* that emerged from it. In *French prosody*, enjambment has been a subject of controversy: since Fr. rhythms are in essence phrasal, line-terminal accents tend to coincide with significant syntactic junctures. Consequently, the terminology for analyzing types of constructions in enjambment is more developed in Fr. prosody than in Eng.

In Eng., enjambment was used widely by the Elizabethans for dramatic and narrative verse. The neoclassical *couplet drove most enjambment from the scene in the 18th c., but the example of John Milton revived it for the romantics, who saw it as the metrical emblem for liberation from neoclassical rules. (In Milton, enjambment is sometimes used to thwart readers' expectations—to provide a momentary shock of error that may be likened to a recognition of living in a fallen world.) William Wordsworth makes frequent use of enjambment in his *blank verse poems ("Tintern Abbey," *The Prelude*), as does John Keats (*Endymion*). G. M. Hopkins's *"sprung rhythm" introduces "roving over" (metrical and syntactic enjambment) so that "the scanning runs on without a break from the beginning . . . of a stanza to the end." 20th-c. poets like W. C. Williams and e. e. cummings use enjambment so frequently that it is the rule rather than the exception in many of their poems.

Since at least the mid-19th c., poets have made increased use of what is sometimes called "hard enjambment"—enjambment so striking it cannot help but be felt. Enjambment of this sort might include enjambment across stanzas (as when Charles Baudelaire, speaking of how the "belly and breasts" of his mistress "advanced" toward him in "Les Bijoux" ["Jewels"], places the verb *advanced* at the beginning of a stanza); enjambment separating articles or adjectives from their nouns (as in Williams's *Spring and All*: "under the surge of the blue / mottled clouds driven from the / northeast—a cold wind."); and enjambment that splits a word across a line (as in Hopkins's opening to "The Windhover": "I caught this morning morning's minion, king- / dom of daylight's dauphin"). Perception of hard enjambment, like the perception of enjambment in general, depends on such factors as the reader's experience and literary-historical context. No comprehensive taxonomy of types or effects of enjambment exists.

*See* LINE, VERSE AND PROSE, VERS, REJET.

■ M. Parry, "The Distinctive Character of Enjambment in Homeric Verse" (1929), rpt. in Parry (1971); J. Hollander, "'Sense Variously Drawn Out: Some Observations on English Enjambment," *Vision and Resonance* (1973); H. Golomb, *Enjambment in Poetry* (1979); S. Cushman, *William Carlos Williams and the Meanings of Measure*, chap. 1 (1985); R. Silliman, "Terms of Enjambment," *The Line in Postmodern Poetry*, ed. R. Frank and H. Sayre (1988); A. Sanni, "On *tadmin* (Enjambment) and Structural Coherence in Classical Arabic Poetry," *Bulletin of the School of Oriental and African Studies* 52, no. 3 (1989); C. Higbie, *Measure and Music: Enjambment and Sentence Structure in the "Iliad"* (1991); M. E. Clark, "Enjambment and Binding in Homeric Hexameter," *Phoenix* 48 (1994); M. L. Shaw, "Verse and Prose," *The Cambridge Introduction to French Poetry* (2003).

T.V.F. BROGAN; C. SCOTT; S. MONTE

**ENSALADA.** A Sp. poem consisting of lines and *strophes of varying lengths and rhyme schemes, generally depending on the music to which the poem is sung. According to Henríquez Ureña, the earliest known *ensalada* is one by Fray Ambrosio Montesinos (d. ca. 1512) found in Francisco Asenjo Barbieri's *Cancionero musical de los siglos XV y XVI* (no. 438). The ensalada apparently was never very popular.

■ P. Henríquez Ureña, *La versificación irregular en la poesia castellana*, 2d ed. (1933); Le Gentil; Navarro; M. Gómez, "The *Ensalada* and the Origins of the Lyric Theater in Spain," *Comparative Drama* 28 (1994).

D. C. CLARKE

**ENSENHAMEN.** A didactic poem in Occitan, ordinarily composed in a nonlyric meter, such as rhymed *couplets, and designed to give advice or instruction to a person or a class. Some of the poems are like books of etiquette. Others are addressed to the *jongleurs who sang the poets' compositions, telling them the things they should know and how they should perform their task. The knowledge expected is doubtless exaggerated, but the poems have a certain interest for what they reveal about contemp. taste in literary and other matters.

■ G. E. Sansone, *Testi didattico-cortesi di Provenza* (1977); D. A. Monson, *Les "ensenhamens" occitans* (1981).

F. M. CHAMBERS

**ENVELOPE.** The envelope pattern is that form of repetition in which a rhyme (sound), phrase, line, or stanza recurs so as to enclose other material, giving the structural pattern *abba*; *chiasmus*, derived from rhet., is another term for the same structure. Most often, a phrase or line will bracket a stanza or whole poem; a complete stanza may also enclose a poem or section of a poem. Envelope has the effect of framing the enclosed material, giving it unity and closure: the reader recognizes the return to the original pattern after movement away in the interim. Related but less specific effects include those of the *burden in the *carol, the *refrain, and *incremental repetition; in these, the reiterated line gains meaning or force from the new material preceding each occurrence of it, but there is no sense of bracketing or framing. The single-line envelope, as it applies to a stanza, may be seen in James Joyce's "I Would in That Sweet Bosom Be" and, as it applies to an entire poem, in Robert Frost's "Acquainted with the Night." A stanza used as an envelope for an entire poem may be seen in William Blake's "The Tyger" and in John Keats's "The Mermaid Tavern." Envelope rhyme (Ger. *umarmender Reim*, Fr. *rime embrassée*) is the rhyme scheme *abba* or any expanded version thereof; a quatrain having such rhyme is sometimes called the envelope stanza: the *In Memoriam stanza is an iambic tetrameter envelope stanza.

*See* RING COMPOSITION.

■ C. B. Hieatt, "On Envelope Patterns and Nonce Formulas," *Comparative Research on Oral Traditions*, ed. J. M. Foley (1987); C.A.M. Clarke, "Envelope Pattern and the 'Locus Amoenus' in Old English Verse," *N&Q* 50 (2003).

S. F. FOGLE; T.V.F. BROGAN

**ENVIRONMENT AND POETRY.** Environmental poetry, or ecopoetry, is related to the broader genre of nature poetry but can be distinguished from it by its portrayal of nature as threatened by human activities (see NATURE). Scattered examples of such concerns appear throughout the hist. of poetry, but clusters of poems about the natural world endangered by humans are apparent above all in Eur. romanticism and in poetry connected to the rise of the mod. environmentalist movement since the 1960s. The emergence of environmentally oriented literary and cultural crit.—or ecocriticism, for short—since the early 1990s has substantially contributed not only to the study of such poetry but also to a new look at nature poetry more broadly conceived.

Environmentally oriented studies of poetry have focused above all on Brit. romanticism and contemp. Am. poetry, with some additional work on Ger., Japanese, and Lat. Am. devels. While the natural world in Eur. romantic poems has often been understood as a metaphor for the poet's mind, ecocritics such as Jonathan Bate and Karl Kroeber tend to place a new emphasis on the romantics' engagement with the materiality of nature and their acute sense of the deterioration of wild and rural landscapes during processes of enclosure and industrialization. Such motifs can be traced in the works of major poets such as William Blake, William Wordsworth, S. T. Coleridge, and P. B. Shelley; but they have also led to the critical revaluation of the work of John Clare, whose poetry had played a more marginal role in the romantic canon. Clare's sharp eye for the details of the natural world and his anguish over the transformation of the landscape around him make his poetry a model for later forms of ecologically oriented poetic expression.

Poetry influenced by mod. environmentalist thought emerged in a variety of countries between the late 1950s and the early 1970s. In spite of certain shared themes—fears over deforestation, soil erosion, air and water pollution, urban sprawl, mechanization and commodification of nature, resistance to nuclear plants and weapons, and the decline of indigenous, sustainable ways of life, e.g.—this kind of poetry took shape under different cultural circumstances and with different emphases. In the U.S., ecopoetry connected not only with the desire to return to nature expressed in some parts of the 1960s counterculture but also with a long trad. of nature writing extending back to R. W. Emerson, H. D. Thoreau, Walt Whitman, Mary Austin, Willa Cather, and Aldo Leopold. In addition, poets such as Wallace Stevens, W. C. Williams, and Charles Olson, whom one would be reluctant to call "nature poets," had nevertheless explored local places with close attention to both nature and culture. The ecological poetry of Gary Snyder, Wendell Berry, Robinson Jeffers, A. R. Ammons, W. S. Merwin, Mary Oliver, and Joy Harjo, to name a few of the most prominent writers, could therefore situate itself in a long trad. of lyrical descriptions and celebrations of the natural world, as well as in a trad. of poetic critiques of mod. society that highlighted its alienation from nature, its scientific and instrumental rationalism, its capitalist drive to commodification, and its large-scale and anonymous institutions. Some of these critiques draw on older models of Am. society, as is obvious in the Jeffersonian agrarianism of Berry's poetry; on Native Am. ways of life, as in Harjo's poems; or on other cultures with what are understood to be their different perspectives on the natural world. Snyder's poetry, e.g., which has commanded by far the greatest amount of ecocritical attention, combines references to Native Am. models of knowledge and inhabitation with allusions to Chinese and Japanese trads. of thought about humans' connection to the environment. While formally most of this poetry follows fairly well-established high modernist models of *free verse, the jour. *Ecopoetics,* first published in 2001, has dedicated itself to connections between environmentalist thought and more experimental, lang.-oriented forms of poetic expression. In this vein, ecocritics have also begun to reexamine the work of poets such as Charles Olson, Larry Eigner, and Lorine Niedecker.

Lat. Am. poets have also increasingly made environmental concerns part of their poetic works. As critics such as Niall Binns, Roberto Forns-Broggi, and George Handley have pointed out, reverence for Mother Earth, the celebration of natural landscapes, and the reflection on precolonial, indigenous ways of life have a long trad. in various Lat. Am. lits.; such elements are visible in some of the works of the best-known 20th-c. poets, such as the Chileans Pablo Neruda and Gabriela Mistral and the Nicaraguan Ernesto Cardenal, but also in those of indigenous poets who have only more recently been integrated into the poetic canon—partly as a consequence of increased environmental awareness and the questioning of rapid modernization processes—e.g., the Mapuche poets Elicura Chihuailaf and Leonel Lienlaf. If some of Neruda's and Cardenal's later works take a clear ecological turn, the intensifying awareness of an ecological crisis is even more obvious in the work of others, such as the Chilean Nicanor Parra and the Mexicans José Emilio Pacheco, Homero Aridjis, and Alberto Blanco, in which pollution, species extinction, and devastated urban landscapes figure prominently. Aridjis, in particular, has become well known in Mexico and abroad for his environmentalist activism as director of the organization Grupo de los Cien (Group of 100), which has, in turn, popularized his ecologically engaged poetry inside and outside Mexico.

In Germany, a country with one of the most politically successful environmentalist movements, environmental poetry in the 1960s and 1970s emerged from a different literary and political background. Poetic engagements with nature had featured prominently in Ger. poetry at least as far back as the romantic age, but National Socialism had appropriated many of the crucial elements of this trad.—symbols such as the Ger. oak, the forest, and the attachment to one's home soil—in such a way that they became exceedingly difficult for poets interested in the emergent Green movement, many of whom were politically engaged and left-oriented, to use. In addition, nature poetry in the 1930s and 1940s had mostly been written by writers intent on evading direct engagement with the political realities of the time, so that "conversations about trees," famously denounced in Bertolt Brecht's 1939 poem "An die Nachgeborenen" as "almost a crime" because they evaded ongoing atrocities, smacked of political escapism. It was, therefore, against the thrust of recent hist. that poets such as Nicolas Born, Heinz Czechowski, Hans Magnus Enzensberger, Erich Fried, Sarah Kirsch, Günter Kunert, Richard Pietraß, and many others had to reintroduce nature as a prominent lyrical theme. Some Ger. ecopoetry emerged during and around demonstrations against nuclear plants and airport-runway projects and therefore took the shape of militant songs and chants. But the more properly lyrical ecopoems, too, stand out by an overall more pessimistic and combative tone than those of Am. ecopoets, who denounce contemp. society angrily but also celebrate landscapes, views, and hikes in a manner only rarely found in the works of their Ger. counterparts.

Studies of environmentally oriented poetry have so far been mostly carried out for individual countries and poets. Comparative studies that consider the genre in the context of culturally divergent attitudes toward modernization, technology, and urban landscapes, as well as against the context of different political and literary trads., are only beginning to emerge.

■ W. Emmerich, "Kein Gespräch über Bäume: Naturlyrik unterm Faschismus und im Exil," *Exilliteratur 1933–1945,* ed. W. Koepke and M. Winkler (1989); J. Bate, *Romantic Ecology* (1991); A. Goodbody, "Deutsche Ökolyrik: Comparative Observations on the Emergence and Expression of Environmental Consciousness in West and East German Poetry," *German Literature at a Time of Change 1989–1990,* ed. A. Williams, S. Parkes, and R. Smith (1991); K. Kroeber, *Ecological Literary Criticism* (1994); J. Elder, *Imagining the Earth,* 2d ed. (1996); J. Egyptien, "Die Naturlyrik im Zeichen der Krise: Themen und Formen des ökologischen Gedichts seit 1970," *Ökologie und Literatur,* ed. A. Goodbody (1998); R. Forns-Broggi, "¿Cuáles son los dones que la naturaleza regala a la poesía latinoamericana?," *Hispanic Journal* (1998); and "Ecology and Latin American Poetry," *The Literature of Nature,* ed. P. D. Murphy (1998); L. M. Scigaj, *Sustainable Poetry* (1999); J. Bate, *The Song of the Earth* (2000); J. S. Bryson, ed., *Ecopoetry* (2002); N. Binns, "Landscapes of Hope and Destruction: Ecological Poetry in Spanish America," *The ISLE Reader: Ecocriticism, 1993–2003,* ed. M. P. Branch and S. Slovic (2003); *The West Side of Any Mountain,* ed. J. S. Bryson (2005); G. B. Handley, *New World Poetics* (2007).

U. K. HEISE

**ENVOI,** envoy (Fr., "a sending on the way"). A short concluding stanza, often addressed to a noble patron (frequently "Prince") and summarizing the argument of a lyric. In the *sestina, the envoi normally consists of three lines, in the *ballade of four, and in the *chant royal of either five or seven, thus repeating the metrical pattern as well as the *rhyme scheme of the half stanza that precedes it. During the great period of the OF fixed forms, it restates the poem's major theme, serving as an interpretive gloss within the poem itself. For this reason, the Occitan *troubadours called their envois *tornadas* (returns).

Among the Eng. poets, Walter Scott, Robert Southey, and A. C. Swinburne employed envois. Chaucer wrote a number of ballades in which he departs from the customary form by closing with an envoi that is equal in length to a regular stanza of the poem, usually his favorite *rhyme royal. In mod. imitations, the envoi is often ironic or satirical and may be addressed to any entity related to the poem, e.g., "birds" (N. E. Tyerman's "Ballad: Before My Bookshelves"), "bookmen" (Lionel Johnson's "Ballade of the *Caxton Head*"), "moralists" (Brander Matthews's still humorous "The Ballade of Fact and Fiction"), and so on.

■ H. L. Cohen, *Lyric Forms from France* (1922); R. Dragonetti, *La Technique poétique des trouvères dans la chanson courtoise* (1960), pt. 1, ch. 4; Tarlinskaja, ch. 7; Gasparov, *History.*

A. PREMINGER; D. J. ROTHMAN

**EPANALEPSIS** (Gr., "a taking up again"; Lat. *resumptio,* "a resumption"). In cl. rhet., a figure most often defined as the repetition of a word or words after intervening words, either for emphasis (e.g., "Hell at last / Yawning receiv'd them whole, and on them clos'd, / Hell their fit habitation" [Milton, *Paradise Lost* 6.874–76]) or for clarity, as to resume a construction after a lengthy parenthesis (Demetrius, *On Style* 196; e.g., "Say first, for Heav'n hides nothing from thy view, / Nor the deep Tract of Hell, say first what cause / Mov'd our Grand Parents" [*Paradise Lost* 1.27–29; cf. Milton's "Lycidas" 1.165]).

In Ren. and modern rhet., epanalepsis is more specifically defined as the practice of ending a clause or sentence or line or stanza with the word at its beginning. In verse, the repeated words most often begin and end a line, as in Philip Sidney's "They love indeed who quake to say they love" (*Astrophil and Stella* 54), but they may also be internal, as in Shakespeare's "Blood hath bought blood, and blows have answered blows; / Strength match'd with strength, and power confronted power" (*King John* 2.1.329). John Donne brackets each stanza with an epanaleptic line in "The Prohibition." Peacham says epanalepsis is used "to place a word of importance in the beginning of the sentence to be considered, and in the end to be remembered." Various types have been distinguished in Walt Whitman's poetry: more than 40% of the lines of *Leaves of Grass* employ epanalepsis of one sort or another. It is one of T. S. Eliot's most conspicuous and effective devices in *Four Quartets.* Like *anadiplosis, where the repeated word ends one line and begins the next, epanalepsis strikingly marks the limits of signifying syntagms: "Possessing what we still were unpossessed by, / Possessed by what we now no more possessed" (Robert Frost, "The Gift Outright"). Epanalepsis also appears in prose: Zimmerman identifies it in E. A. Poe's story "The Black Cat" in the sentence "Evil thoughts became my sole intimates—the darkest and most evil of thoughts"; he opines that the device creates a gloomy effect of enclosure, immurement. Vickers, by contrast, sees a playful use of epanalepsis in the sentence "Cemetery put in of course on account of the symmetry" from James Joyce's *Ulysses*.

■ A. N. Wiley, "Reiterative Devices in *Leaves of Grass*," *American Literature* 1 (1929); Lanham; A. Quinn, *Figures of Speech* (1982); B. Vickers, *In Defence of Rhetoric* (1988); Vickers; Corbett; B. Zimmerman, *Edgar Allan Poe* (2005).

R. O. Evans; T.V.F. Brogan;
A. W. Halsall; A. L. French

**EPENTHESIS** (Gr., "putting in"). The addition of a syllable within a word, usually for metrical *equivalence or rhetorical emphasis (*puh-leeze* for *please*). Epenthesis includes *anaptyxis* (the addition of a vowel) and *excrescence* (the addition of a consonant); the most common epenthetic vowel in Eng. is the schwa, the toneless and neutral vowel added to *please* in the example above. Metrical or rhythmic epenthesis often establishes ironic parallelism (as in Irving Berlin's rhyming of "Rockefellers" with "umbrellas" in "Puttin' on the Ritz"). The Brazilian poet Haroldo de Campos's "circuladô de fulô" (written 1965; pub. in *Galáxias*, 1984) takes its first lines (incl. those three opening words) from a minstrel song descended from the Galician-Port. *cantiga* overheard by Campos in northeast Brazil: the minstrel's original words were probably "circulado de flores," which A. S. Bessa translates as "'rounded by flowers." A deformation of *flores*, "fulô" would then be perhaps a mimetic epenthesis (in which Campos imitates a local pronunciation) or a case of epenthetic *defamiliarization.

*See* ELISION, TMESIS.

R. Greene

# EPIC

 I. History
 II. Theory

## I. History

A. *Definitions.* An epic is a long narrative poem of heroic action: "narrative," in that it tells a story; "poem," in that it is written in verse rather than prose; "heroic action," while reinterpreted by each major epic poet, in that, broadly defined, it recounts deeds of great valor that bear consequence for the community to which the hero belongs. An epic plot is typically focused on the deeds of a single person or hero, mortal though exceptionally strong, intelligent, or brave, and often assisted or opposed by gods. Epic is set in a remote or legendary past represented as an age of greater heroism than the present. Its style is elevated and rhetorical. To compose an epic has often been viewed as the foremost challenge a poet can undertake, and the enduringly successful epics are a small and select group.

A distinction is commonly drawn between oral or "primary" epic, which has its origins in oral *performance, and literary or "secondary" epic, composed as a written text. Oral poetry is performed by a skilled singer who improvises on familiar material, drawing on a stock of *formulas, fixed phrases in particular metrical patterns, like an improvising musician's repertory of riffs. The oral poet also employs formulaic type-scenes, such as the feast, assembly, arming of the hero, or single combat, which can be varied as the context requires. In the 1920s, a young Am. scholar, Milman Parry, demonstrated that the *Iliad* and the *Odyssey* bear traces of oral composition. The Homeric epithets, or characterizing phrases—"strong-greaved Achaians," "Agamemnon, lord of men"—vary, Parry noted, according to grammatical case and position in the line, a phenomenon best accounted for by origins in oral performance. Parry subsequently tested his hypothesis by recording living oral poets in the Balkans, who improvised using formulaic lines, phrases, and scenes in similar fashion. Trads. of oral heroic poetry exist in Egypt, Arabia, Kirghistan, Mali, and elsewhere (see ORAL-FORMULAIC THEORY).

The distinction between oral and literary epic is not absolute and can mislead if treated too rigidly. Poems that have been passed down unwritten into recent times can be considered oral in a straightforward sense, but, in cases such as the *Iliad*, we are necessarily dealing with written texts, whose proximity to a prior oral trad. is a matter of conjecture. The *Iliad* contains traces of oral composition, but the text we have is not itself an oral poem, nor should we assume that it was the first version to be transcribed. Primary epic is sometimes described as "traditional," but, in fact, both primary and secondary epic are traditional forms of art; the process of *traditio* or handing down takes place directly in primary epic, at a distance in secondary epic. In oral poetry, the matter of the song and the art of recitation are handed down from *bard to bard, presumably through sustained personal contact. In literary epic, the new poet signals participation in the epic trad. by imitating formal, thematic, and stylistic elements of previous epics, so that an informed reader may readily sense the relation between old and new. While all genres contain such imitative gestures, they are esp. prominent in epic, where the presence of the old in the new is strongly felt.

To define *epic* broadly as any long narrative poem of heroic action has the advantage of inclusiveness. It recognizes the artistry of heroic narrative poems around the world and allows for cross-cultural comparisons such as the studies carried out by Parry and his student Albert Lord. The disadvantage of applying the term *epic* to poems around the world is that to do so effaces the trads. to which each poem belongs. The Babylonian *Epic of Gilgamesh*, the Sanskrit *Mahābhārata*, the OF *Chanson de Roland*, the OE *Beowulf*, and the South Slavic oral poems recorded by Parry and Lord in the 1930s—not to mention the *Odyssey* and the *Iliad*—all qualify as narrative poems of heroic action, but to call them all epics is to subsume them within a category that would have been unrecognizable to their authors and first audiences. They are most accurately understood within their own cultural contexts, on their own generic terms.

The term *epic* has a long hist. of usage in a narrower sense, to refer to the trad. of heroic narrative poetry written in conscious descent from the *Iliad* and the *Odyssey* by way of Virgil's *Aeneid*. That the two Homeric poems were the source of this trad. was taken as fact in antiquity and never forgotten; but while the prestige of Homer's name endured, the texts themselves became, in most of Europe, lost poems in a lost lang. from late antiquity into the Ren., known only in *fragments and redactions. The *Aeneid* was received as a classic virtually from the moment of its appearance; since it was written in Lat., it never lost its familiarity, and it retained its status as the paradigmatic epic even after the 16th c. when the Homeric poems became more widely known in Europe. More than any other poem, the *Aeneid* established the conventions of epic as they were understood by later poets; while many of these conventions originate in Homer, their Virgilian versions would become the most widely imitated. These conventions, described in greater detail below, include stylistic elements such as extended *similes, elevated *diction, and *epithets; formal elements such as the *proem, bringing the audience *in medias res*, digression, and prophecy (see PROPHETIC POETRY); recurrent scenes such as the celestial descent, the earthly paradise, the *catalog, the *locus amoenus*, *ekphrasis, and *katabasis*. No epic poem contains every conventional feature, and no feature is present in every poem. The unity of the genre is best understood in terms of Ludwig Wittgenstein's concept of family resemblance, "a complicated network of similarities overlapping and criss-crossing: sometimes overall similarities, sometimes similarities of detail" (*Philosophical Investigations*). Thinking of generic unity in this way releases the critic from the fruitless task of distinguishing between essential and accidental features of epic and from the equally fruitless task of determining which poems deserve inclusion; as Greene saw it, poems participate in the epic mode to different degrees.

**B. Conventions.** (i) Proem. An epic poem conventionally begins with an introductory passage or *proem (Lat. *proemium*, "preface" or "introduction"). The proem includes a proposition or brief statement of the poem's subject. The choice of words in the proposition is of special significance since it indicates the poem's major themes and emphases, frequently with a revisionary gesture toward previous epics. As so often, the paradigmatic instance is Virgilian. The first words of the *Aeneid*, "arma virumque cano" (I sing of arms and a man) allude, in "arms," to the martial subject matter of the *Iliad* and, in "man," to the lone voyaging hero of the *Odyssey*, thus indicating Virgil's aim to encompass the subjects of both Homeric poems within his own. The proem also includes an invocation, where the poet invokes the assistance of the *Muse to inspire his song. In Gr. mythology, the Muses are the nine daughters of Zeus and Mnemosyne, goddess of memory; the Muse associated with epic poetry is named Calliope. The convention of invoking the Muse derives from epic's origins in oral performance. In Gr. oral trad., the invocation was a prayer, overheard by the audience, of-

fered at the start of each performance to the Muse or Muses, patron deities of the professional singer. The convention was retained in literary epic, with postclassical poets understanding it in symbolic or Christian terms. A third element commonly found within the epic proem is a dedication, or expression of homage by the poet toward an earthly patron or head of state. Thus, e.g., Statius addresses the Roman emperor Domitian at the beginning of the *Thebiad*: "And you, glory added to Latium's fame, whom, as you take on your aged / father's enterprises anew, Rome wishes hers for eternity . . ." (1.22–4).

Secondary proems and invocations are sometimes to be found within a poem, typically preceding heightened moments or major changes of scene.

(ii) In medias res. The Lat. phrase *in medias res* means "into the midst of things" and refers to the epic convention of beginning not at the earliest point of the story but with the action already under way. The phrase derives from Horace's *Ars poetica*. A poet telling of the Trojan War, Horace writes, should not begin with Helen's birth from an egg:

> He gets right to the point and carries the reader
> Into the midst of things, as if known already . . .
>
> ("To the Pisos," 147–49)

In this passage, Horace is discussing the skill, necessary to all narrative poets, of capturing the interest of the audience from the outset. It is the reader or listener (Lat. *auditor*), not the poem, who is to be carried into the middle of events. While Horace's example is taken from the epic subject of Troy, he is not making a point about epic specifically. The phrase *in medias res* came to be understood and applied, however, as prescribing a particular nonlinear shape for epic narrative: the poem was to start at the heart of the story, usually with a burst of action, and fill in the chronologically prior events at a later point. This understanding probably came about through the combination of Horatian precept with Virgilian example. The *Aeneid* begins not with the fall of Troy but with the Trojan exiles approaching their destination, when the goddess Juno drives them off course with a violent storm; once on shore, Aeneas recounts earlier events in a flashback. Among numerous later examples, Marco Girolamo Vida's *Christiad* (1535), a Neo-Lat. epic on the passion of Christ, begins not with Christ's birth but with his entry into Jerusalem; Luís de Camões's *Lusiads* (1572), which tells of Vasco da Gama's voyage from Portugal to India, begins with the Port. mariners already past the Cape of Good Hope and approaching Mozambique.

(iii) Forms of digression. The nonlinear shape of epic narrative has other conventional features. If the poem begins by bringing the reader in medias res, prior events must be filled in subsequently. One standard way of doing so is through an embedded narrative told by a guest to a host after a meal, when the host, having fulfilled the first obligations of hospitality, may with courtesy put questions, and the refreshed guest may answer at leisure. Thus, Odysseus relates his famous "wanderings" to the Phaeacian king Alcinous and his court; Aeneas tells of the fall of Troy and the Trojans' subsequent journey to Dido and her court at Carthage; and in John Milton's *Paradise Lost*, the angel Raphael descends to Adam and Eve, is welcomed as their guest, and thereafter tells them of the war in heaven and the creation of the world.

Another form of digression is the epic prophecy, in which a seer furnishes the hero with an account or vision of future events. Through prophecy, the legendary past in which the epic is set can be linked to the historical present from which it is told. Typically, the prophet is a supernatural character or prophesies by supernatural means. The prophecy takes place in a special setting reached by a guided journey: in the underworld (see katabasis, below) or the heavens or during a sea voyage. A distinctive subcategory is the dynastic prophecy, in which the seer tells or shows the hero a genealogy of glorious descendants. Prophetic digression can also be expressed by the narrative voice, as in this succinct Miltonic example: "So clomb this first grand thief into God's fold: / So since into his church lewd hirelings climb" (*Paradise Lost* 4.192–93).

A third form of epic digression is the episode or incident loosely connected to the primary epic plot. The tale of Olindo and Sofronia in Torquato Tasso's *Gerusalemme liberata*, book 2, is an example. Heroic poems in the chivalric *romance trad., such as Ludovico Ariosto's *Orlando furioso* and Alonso de Ercilla's *La Araucana*, are highly episodic. In the *Poetics*, book 9, Aristotle deprecates episodic plot, which he defines as a structure in which "the episodes or acts succeed one another without probable or necessary sequence"; the *Odyssey*, he felt, was properly unified, because Odysseus's various adventures were sufficiently connected to one another. In the early mod. period, after Aristotle's *Poetics* gained renewed influence in the 16th c., the subject of episodes received considerable attention from literary critics. Some authors criticized *Orlando furioso* and other romances for violating Aristotelian unity of action; others praised their episodic plots for their variety; others such as Torquado Tasso sought a middle way, attempting to reconcile the pleasures of romance with Aristotelian principles.

(iv) Katabasis. Among the most distinctive of epic conventions is the katabasis (Gr., "descent") or descent to the underworld. As so often, Virgil's treatment is inspired by Homer, and it is Virgil's that becomes paradigmatic. Odysseus's visit to the land of the dead in the *Odyssey*, book 11, is not, strictly speaking, a katabasis but a *nekuia*, or summoning of ghosts, though the place's location is indistinct, Odysseus reaches it by ship. The journey of Aeneas to the underworld in the *Aeneid*, book 6, is a heightened supernatural episode rich in symbolic detail, through which Aeneas gains a fuller understanding of his mission and its fated consequences. Aeneas's journey involves several parts: first, elaborate ritual preparation for the descent, guided by the Cumaean Sibyl, priestess of Apollo; second, passage through the various regions of the underworld, encountering familiar ghosts; last, Aeneas's meeting with his father Anchises in Elysium, abode of the blessed.

Anchises explains to his son the progress of the soul from death to rebirth and shows him a spiritual pageant of famous Romans culminating in Virgil's own time. The episode has proven among the most influential in Western lit. The whole of Dante's *Divine Comedy* could be described as a Christianized expansion of the *Aeneid*, book 6. In *Orlando furioso*, Ariosto includes a katabasis touched with travesty; the dynastic heroine Bradamante is treacherously dropped down a hole and happens to land at the tomb of Merlin, who shows her a dynastic pageant of her glorious descendants, enacted by conjured demons. The Mammon episode in Edmund Spenser's *Faerie Queene* is a form of katabasis.

(v) Celestial vision. Epic narrative moves between heaven and earth, juxtaposing the earth-bound perspectives of mortal characters with the exalted viewpoint of gods. On rare occasions, a mortal hero is allowed to see from a higher perspective, either by means of a vision or a literal ascent. Like the katabasis, such episodes involve a supernatural guide and show exceptional divine favor to the recipient; they provide the hero with higher knowledge, often prophetic or metaphysical, with which he returns enlightened to his earthly endeavor. Where the katabasis provides knowledge from below, the celestial vision provides knowledge from above. In ancient epic, certain heroes are granted brief moments of privileged sight, in which a god removes the film from their vision (Diomedes at *Iliad* 5.127–28, Aeneas at *Aeneid* 2.604–6). The more sustained form of celestial vision, however, is a postclassical convention, incorporating elements of the *dream vision and the genre of apocalypse or revelation, whose best-known instance is the last book of the NT. Dante's *Paradiso* is the most extended example of an epic celestial vision; others include Astolfo's voyage to the moon in *Orlando furioso*; Goffredo's dream vision in *Gerusalemme liberata*, book 14; Redcrosse Knight's vision of the New Jerusalem in *The Faerie Queene*; and Michael's instruction of Adam in the last two books of *Paradise Lost*.

(vi) Ekphrasis. An ekphrasis (Gr., "description") is a verbal account of a work of visual art. The description of Achilles' shield in the *Iliad*, book 18, is the epic prototype. Made for the hero by the god Hephaestus, the shield is decorated with images of the heavenly bodies, scenes of a city at peace, and scenes of a city at war; its imagery has been subject to a wide range of interpretation. Virgil uses ekphrasis to describe legendary events prior to the poem's main narrative and historical events posterior to it: the doors of Juno's temple in Carthage are decorated with scenes from the Trojan War, and Aeneas's divinely wrought shield is decorated with scenes of future Roman triumphs. Later poets would follow Virgil in using ekphrasis to link epic past with historical present. Thus, in *Orlando furioso*, the walls of Tristan's castle show the deeds of Frankish kings from Sigibert to Francis I, while in *The Lusiads*, the painted flags of Vasco da Gama's ship depict Port. heroes from the legendary founding of the nation to the 15th c.

(vii) *Aristeia*. The aristeia (Gr., "prowess") is an episode in which a warrior performs great exploits on the battlefield. The model here is the *Iliad*, which contains five major *aristeiai* whose characteristic elements were widely imitated by later poets. These elements include the arming of the hero; his killing of enemy champions; his driving the enemy before him in a rout; an initial setback (a wound or removal from battle), followed by prayer to the gods, reinvigoration, and return to combat. An aristeia does not necessarily end in victory, even in the short term; often the episode concludes with the hero driven back, wounded, or even killed. The aristeia provides one means of introducing variety into battle scenes. By exalting secondary warriors earlier in the poem with their own aristeiai, the poet can amplify the deeds of the primary hero; to do so, however, requires of the poet sufficient skill to describe gradations of extraordinary valor. In the *Iliad*, the first four aristeiai of Diomedes, Agamemnon, Hector, and Patroclus are genuinely impressive; when Achilles finally enters the fighting, however, his irresistible accomplishment in killing exceeds anything that has come before.

(viii) *Locus amoenus*. The locus amoenus (Lat., "delightful place") is an earthly paradise, a place of bliss and repose. It features lush gardens, splashing fountains, tame creatures, clement weather, fruit-bearing trees, and often the promise of sexual pleasures. Its mythological antecedents include the Elysian fields of cl. trad. and the Garden of Eden in Genesis; its representation in epic owes much to the *pastoral trad. In Ren. epics such as *The Faerie Queene* and *Gerusalemme liberata*, earthly paradises frequently prove false; their pleasures are created by enchantment, and they are inhabited by temptresses who would lure the hero from his duties. Benign versions include Dante's earthly paradise atop Mt. Purgatory, Venus's isle of love in the *Lusiads*, and, above all, Milton's Paradise, a representation of the Garden of Eden itself.

**C. *Style*.** Epic is written in an elevated *style, befitting its subject matter. *Archaisms and poetic diction are accepted in epic to a greater extent than in genres dealing with subjects closer to their readers' quotidian experience. In poems written in Eng. or mod. Romance langs., Latinisms and Latinate forms are common. Stylistic features include the epithet or characterizing phrase, such as "swift-footed Achilles" or "Hector, breaker of horses." Also common is *periphrasis, an indirect expression used in place of a direct one, as in "Cytherea's son" for Aeneas (*Paradise Lost* 9.19). Of special note is the epic simile, an extended comparison in which the vehicle (the term used to describe) is developed beyond its ground of analogy with the tenor (the term described), so that the simile becomes a miniature tale unto itself (see TENOR AND VEHICLE). Here, for instance, Milton's Satan is described lying on the fiery lake of hell:

> . . . in bulk as huge
> As whom the Fables name of monstrous size,
> Titanian, or Earth-born, that warr'd on Jove,
> Briareos or Typhon, whom the Den
> By ancient Tarsus held, or that Sea-beast

> Leviathan, which God of all his works
> Created hugest that swim th' Ocean stream:
> Him haply slumbring on the Norway foam
> The Pilot of some small night-founder'd Skiff,
> Deeming some Island, oft, as Sea-men tell,
> With fixed Anchor in his skaly rind
> Moors by his side under the Lee, while Night
> Invests the Sea, and wished Morn delayes:
> So stretcht out huge in length the Arch-fiend lay
> Chain'd on the burning Lake.

The difficulty of maintaining an appropriately high style over the course of a long poem, without lapses into grandiosity on the one hand or *bathos on the other, is one reason that successful epics have been rare.

Epic's marriage of high style and heroic matter makes possible the parodic subgenre of *mock epic, where the high epic style is applied to low, everyday, or absurd subject matter, creating a humorous mismatch.

**D. *Women in Epic*.** There is a long trad. of women warriors in epic. A lost epic, the *Aethiopis* of Arctinus of Miletus, recounted the story of Penthesileia the Amazon queen, who was an ally of the Trojans. The most influential example of the type is Virgil's Camilla, leader of the Volscians, who fights against the Trojans in an impressive aristeia until she is killed by a javelin. Her successors include Bradamante and Marfisa in *Orlando furioso*, Clorinda in *Gerusalemme liberata*, and Britomart in *The Faerie Queene*. Ariosto's Bradamante combines the figures of woman warrior and dynastic spouse; formidable with sword or lance, she is also the legendary progenitrix of the House of Este, Dukes of Ferrara and Ariosto's patrons. Spenser follows Ariosto in this combination; his Britomart is a female knight who allegorically embodies the virtue of chastity and the mythical ancestor of Queen Elizabeth. Tasso's Clorinda is both warrior and tragic lover. Raised a Muslim, she is beloved of the Christian knight Tancredi, who mortally wounds her in an eroticized duel and baptizes her as she dies.

Another recurrent female character type impedes the hero's progress, keeping him from his path through seduction or constraint until he breaks free and abandons her. The prototypes here are Calypso and Circe in the *Odyssey*. Calypso is an immortal nymph who keeps Odysseus for herself on her island until commanded by the Olympian gods to let him go. Circe, also an island nymph, lures men into her house and, by witchcraft, transforms them into beasts; once Odysseus, with divine assistance, breaks her spell, she becomes his lover and assists him. In the *Aeneid*, the woman with whom the hero dallies and delays becomes a tragic figure. Virgil's Dido is a mortal woman, the widowed queen of Carthage; when Aeneas and his Trojans are shipwrecked on her shores, she falls in love with him, and they live as a couple until the gods intervene, commanding Aeneas to depart—whereupon she kills herself. Virgil leaves no doubt that Aeneas must leave Dido to fulfill his destiny, and Roman readers would note her association with Carthage, Rome's old enemy; but the queen is portrayed sympathetically as a victim of circumstance, an unfortunate (*infelix*) casualty in the founding of Rome. Many readers have shared the reaction of the young Augustine, who shed tears for Dido's death. Ren. versions of these figures include Alcina in the *Orlando furioso*, Armida in the *Gerusalemme liberata*, and Acrasia in *The Faerie Queene*; these similarly named characters are ill-intentioned temptresses from whose clutches seduced knights must be rescued. Although the epic trad. generally represents such female characters as a temptation that the male hero must overcome to carry out his mission, they appeal powerfully to hero and readers alike; these episodes have often been recognized as among the most memorable in their respective poems. An intriguing version of Dido appears in *La Araucana* and belongs to a robust "Defense of Dido" trad. that was esp. popular in Spain.

Discussion of the right relation between the sexes becomes a major theme in at least two epics of the Ren. The marriage of Adam and Eve, companionate yet hierarchical, is an important focus of *Paradise Lost*. *Orlando furioso* carries on a running discussion about women's virtue, sometimes ironically and sometimes in earnest, with Ariosto frequently giving voice to what in 16th-c. terms would have been a profeminist position.

Epics written by women include *Enrico ouvero Bisancio acquistato* (*Enrico, or Byzantium Conquered*, 1635), by the Venetian Lucrezia Marinella; the biblical epic *Iudith* by the Fr. woman of letters Marie de Calages (1660); and the creation poem *Order and Disorder* (1679; first complete ed. 2001), identified in 2001 as the work of Lucy Hutchinson.

**E. Divine Action.** Epic is primarily concerned with the deeds of mortals, but its most powerful characters are gods. In the *Iliad,* the *Odyssey,* and the *Aeneid* the Olympian gods intervene frequently in human affairs, assisting some and destroying others. Sometimes the gods act in the interest of justice as they see it; sometimes they act on their own prerogative or even whim. Their enormous power is neither good nor evil; it simply is. The supreme Olympian god (Zeus in Gr., Jupiter in Lat.) holds final authority, but he allows wide latitude to his fellow Olympians to act as they see fit, and so they do. This latitude allows for factions or competing interests among the gods, which play a major structural role in cl. epic plot. The quarrelsome, anthropomorphized gods of epic scandalized some readers even in antiquity, Plato among them, but since they figured so prominently in the most prestigious poems of the age, they were too important to ignore.

How to Christianize divine action was one of the enduring problems of postclassical epic. Christian poets who sought to imitate Homer and Virgil assumed that a mod. epic that would rival the ancients required a supernatural element of some kind; they also knew that, in this respect, their cl. models could not be followed too closely. The pagan gods were no longer acceptable, but what could be put in their place? One approach, derived from the long hermeneutic trad. of reading the gods of cl. epic allegorically, was to introduce allegorized divine characters. These might be *personifications, like Milton's Sin and Death; they might be the Olympian gods themselves in allegorical guise, as in the *Lusiads*, Petrarch's *Africa*, or Spenser's "Mutability Cantos." Another approach, derived from the chivalric trad., was to replace intervening gods with magic: enchanted woods, mythical beasts, sorcerers, demons, and the like. A third approach, the most distinctively Christian, was to substitute God and Satan for the community of Olympian gods, as in Vida, Tasso, or Milton. None of these approaches was without its difficulties.

## II. Theory

**A. Classical and Alexandrian Greek.** The rich epic trad. of the Greeks (Homer, Hesiod, Arctinus, Antimachus) was at first criticized more from an ethical than a literary standpoint. Xenophanes (frag. 11, Diels-Kranz), e.g., objected to Homer and Hesiod's depiction of gods as thieves, adulterers, and deceivers. In the *Republic*, Plato combines the ethical and literary when he attacks Homer for teaching the young morally pernicious ideas by the method of *imitation. Since, for Plato, Homer is also the founder of *tragedy, both genres stand condemned.

For Aristotle, too, poetry is imitation, but from this, he draws a radically different conclusion. Not only is imitation natural to humans, but, as intensified by tragedy, it can produce, by means of pity and fear, a *katharsis ton pathematon* (see CATHARSIS). That for Aristotle this puzzling but evidently drastic effect is also valid for epic follows from his acceptance of another Platonic insight, that epic is inherently dramatic. Since, unlike Plato, Aristotle argues that drama is the superior genre, the best epic must be Homer's because it is already "dramatic" (an adjective that Aristotle may have coined). Since Aristotle believes that drama (Gr., "that which is done") is important, it follows that the action has primacy. Not the soul of the hero but the mythic interaction of personae is the soul of the play, and indeed Aristotle criticizes epics that assert their unity merely by hanging a collection of disparate adventures onto a well-known name. Aristotle demands organic unity from the epic and requires that it be *eusynopton* (easily grasped in its totality) and that it not exceed the length of dramas shown at one sitting, a period of time usually calculated at 6,000 or 7,000 lines. Apollonius of Rhodes's *Argonautica*, written in Alexandria (3d c. BCE), exactly meets the criterion.

Aristotle objects to the confusion of epic and historical narrative, perhaps because he has a strict notion of the historian's duty to record. He ignores the fact that already Thucydides, e.g., had used mythical models to interpret events. He disapproves of the versification of Herodotus, but in allowing for "poetic" or imaginative prose, Aristotle opened the door to the mod. epic novel. The definition of *epic* attributed to his pupil and successor as head of the Lyceum in Athens, Theophrastus, as "that which embraces divine, heroic, and human affairs," shifts the emphasis from form to content. Aristotle's modification in the *Rhetoric* of his views on vocabulary is related. The *Poetics* had laid down that epic vocabulary should be clear but elevated, marked by the use of poetic words or "glosses." The later *Rhetoric*, however, under the impulse of Euripides, permits the use of words from the lang. of everyday life. He accepts as Homeric the comic *Margites* (The Crazy Man; cf. *Orlando furioso*), now lost, a silly account in mixed meters of a bumpkin who is not even sure how to proceed on his wedding night. Such openness contradicts Plato's severity and that of many later "Aristotelians."

The scholia or interpretive comments written in the margins of Homeric mss. prove that, after Aristotle, a practical crit. was worked out that preserved and extended his insights. Here, the *Iliad* and the *Odyssey* are regarded as tragedies, though the notion was not lost that Homer was also the founder of comedy. The contrast between epic and hist. is maintained. "Fantasy" is praised (cf. Dante, *Paradiso* 33.142) both as pure imagination and as graphic visualization of detail. Nonlinear presentation of the story may be made and at a variety of ling. levels.

The *Certamen*, also called the *Contest of Homer and Hesiod*, is extant in a text from the 2d c. CE but is believed to stem from an earlier work by Alcidamas (4th c. BCE). From antiquity, the question of which poet wrote first, and therefore had greater claim to legitimacy, existed, as did the idea that a *poetic contest had taken place between the two. In the *Certamen*, which expands on a brief mention of a competition in the *Works and Days* (8th c. BCE), Hesiod wins because his works deal with the domestic and agricultural, rather than the martial. This issue of the domestic as an appropriate focus for epic will appear again in Milton's *Paradise Lost* and in later explorations of the relationship between novel and epic.

Callimachus in Alexandria (3d c. BCE) shared Aristotle's objections to the versification of Herodotus. In rejecting the eulogistic epic, he worked out, in his own epic *Hecale*, a different kind of Homer-*imitatio* from the straight comparison of the mod. champion to a Homeric counterpart, a type apparently sought by Alexander the Great from the poetaster Choirilos of Iasos. Too little of Callimachus's epic *Galateia* now survives to make judgment possible, but his *Deification of Arsinoe* in lyric meter set the precedent for the appeal by a junior deity to a senior for elucidation that would become a *topos* of the Lat. eulogy (e.g., in Claudian and Sidonius Apollinaris) and even be adapted by Dante in the first canzone of the *Vita nuova*. Since this topos had Homeric precedent (*Iliad* 1.493 ff.), Callimachus was indicating which parts of the Homeric legacy were imitable and how. In his elegiac *Aetia*, Callimachus advanced Hesiod as the figurehead of his new approach to epic.

The *Argonautica* is a further demonstration of the Alexandrian theory of epic. Out of their element in the heroic ambience, the characters collectively and Jason individually are often gripped by *amekhanie* (helplessness). Unified by verbal echoes of the red-gold icon of the fleece, the poem underplays the conventionally heroic in showing both the futility of war and the degradation of the hero who, dependent on a witch's

Promethean magic, eventually becomes the cowardly murderer of Apsyrtus. Homeric allusions point the lesson, and the reader knows from Euripides that eventually the marriage of Jason and Medea will end not in triumph but in disaster (see ALEXANDRIANISM).

**B. Classical and Medieval Latin.** The Callimachean and Apollonian epic, i.e., the kind written by scholar-poets, treated the lit. of the past by *allusion and reminiscence in a polyphonic way. Catullus, the bitter foe of historical epic, also uses this technique in his poem 64. Similarly, in the *Aeneid*, Virgil uses Homer as a sounding board rarely for simple harmony but to secure extra and discordant resonance for his mod. symphony. Thus, Dido is at once the *Odyssey's* Calypso, Circe, Nausicaa, and Arete, and the *Iliad's* Helen and Andromache. Aeneas is Odysseus, Ajax, Paris, Agamemnon, Hector, and Achilles. There is no end to the sliding identities and exchanges (*metamorphoses*) of the characters. The poet who had quoted from Callimachus in *Eclogue* 6 in order to introduce an Ovidian poetic program and had progressed to epic through the Hesiodic *Georgics*, may, therefore, be properly regarded as Callimachean. But he is also Aristotelian, both in the dramatic nature of his poem and in its tragic affinities. In Italy, Aeneas gropes toward victory over the bodies of friend and foe alike. Vengeful Dido, by the technique of verbal reminiscence and recurrent imagery, is never absent from the poem. And although the epic exalts the origins of Rome, "umbrae" (shadows) is characteristically its last word.

The first Alexandrians were scholar-poets, and the third head of the library, Eratosthenes, still exemplified this ideal. But the early divergence of the two vocations led to a split between creative and critical sensibilities. Horace's *Ars poetica* (1st c. BCE), described by an ancient commentator as a versification of the prose treatise of the Alexandrian scholar Neoptolemus of Parium, though clearly in its emphasis on the *vates* more than this, recommends by its form a musicality in which arrangement and correspondence, interlace and arabesque, will replace the pedestrian logic of prose. A Roman and an Augustan, Horace moves beyond Callimachus when he urges that the poet, without in any way betraying Gr. refinement, must also be a *vates*, engaged with his society and with the reform of public morals. This is an aspect of cl. epic subsumed by Dante in his allusion to *Orazio satiro* (*Inferno* 4.89).

Finally, Horace, who spoke of Homer's "auditor" (listener), took for granted a feature of ancient epic theory now often overlooked. Epic did not cease to be oral with Homer. The power of Virgil's "hypocrisis" (acting ability), the "sweetness and marvelous harlotries" of his voice, are attested in the *Life* written by Donatus (4th c. CE). This Aristotelian closeness to drama again implies polyphonic composition. According to this understanding of Virgil, there cannot be a single, univocal, "right" interpretation of the action.

However, with Virgil, epic, generally concerned with reflecting and establishing the self-identity of the culture that produces it, becomes heavily invested in the political. Virgil casts Aeneas as the first of a line of rulers culminating in the emperor Augustus, thus tying the foundation of Rome to the Trojan War and rewriting Aeneas's adventures as a myth of imperial foundation. He reinvents the crafty hero of the *Odyssey* as the ideal Roman character: Aeneas is an extraordinary warrior, but he is *pius* and obedient, qualities that were more valued by imperial Rome, and are, in the *Aeneid*, responsible for its founding. If Virgil's dramatic qualities are polyphonic, his narrative is nonetheless what M. Bakhtin, writing about epic in the mid-20th c., would term "monologic": the *Aeneid*'s story is told in the inimitable and defined voice of a national identity that, as Quint argues, accepts its own version of events as absolute and ignores the possibility of another, outside voice. While the voices of marginalized figures—the abandoned Dido, the defeated Rutulians—continually intrude, Virgil's epic is nonetheless the act of a civilization writing its own self-contained and victorious hist.

The crit. by Agrippa of the *Aeneid* for its *communia verba*, recorded by Donatus in his *Life of Virgil*, shows that there had developed even under Augustus the theory that epic, as the most sublime of genres, demanded the most sublime lang. Petronius's implied crits. of Lucan in the *Satyricon* prove the persistence of this notion. At the end of cl. antiquity, the same theory received a fatally deceptive application. *Rhetorica ad Herennium* (ca. 86–82 BCE), influential in the Middle Ages, distinguished three styles, high, middle, and low; and, conveniently, Virgil had written three major poems: obviously, the *Eclogues* must exemplify the low style, the *Georgics* the middle, and the *Aeneid* the high. This was the doctrine that eventually found its med. canonization in the *\*rota virgiliana* (Virgilian wheel) devised by John of Garland. By this, names, weapons, even trees that could be mentioned in the different styles were carefully prescribed. One part of the deadly consequences of this doctrine was that the opening toward comedy in the epic (the *Margites*) was lost. Yet even the late antique commentator Servius had remarked of the *Aeneid*, book 4, "paene comicus stilus est: nec mirum, ubi de amore tractatur" (the style is almost comic, and no surprise, considering the theme is love), and the trad. of Virgilian epic practice does not reject the comic.

Stung by Platonic crit. of Homer's "lying," Gr. Stoic philosophers in particular had developed a method of interpreting the Homeric narrative in symbolic terms intended to rescue its moral and theological credibility. In his efforts to reclaim all the genres for the new religion, the Christian Lat. poet Prudentius (ca. 348–405) wrote the epic *Psychomachia*, in which the contending champions were no longer flesh-and-blood heroes but abstract qualities of the soul. It was only a short step from this to allegorizing Virgil's *Aeneid*, the most important example of this being Fulgentius (late 5th–early 6th c.). Highly praised allegorical epics have been written, of which the most important is probably Spenser's incomplete *Faerie Queene* (1590, 1596; see ALLEGORY).

The critical failure of later antiquity meant, in effect, that any epic theory that was to make sense had to be recoverable from the practice of major poets. This fact lent even greater significance to the already towering figure of Dante, since it was he who, as the author of the epic *Divine Comedy* in the vernacular, broke decisively with both med. prescription and practice. He acknowledges the influence of Virgil's style (*Inferno* 1.85–87), and invokes in reference to his own journey that of Aeneas to the underworld, during which the future hist. of Rome is revealed to him (2.13–27). However, even as Dante is influenced by Virgil's political vision of epic, the epic journey is here recast as a personal and internal process, the struggle of the Christian soul to find God; the grandeur of conquest becomes the humility of spiritual seeking.

*C. Renaissance to Modern.* The Ren. critics (Marco Girolamo Vida, *De arte poetica*, 1527; Francesco Robortello, *In librum Aristotelis de arte poetica explicationes*, 1548; Antonio Minturno, *De poeta*, 1559; *L'arte poetica*, 1563) were often prescriptive rather than descriptive. Armed with the *Poetics* (trans. into Lat. by Giorgio Valla in 1498, 1536; Gr. text 1508; It. trans. 1549) and eventually with an amalgam of Aristotle and Horace, they advanced to war down the "unclassical" in epic but were largely the unconscious victims of old ideas. J. C. Scaliger, the most gifted scholar among them (*Poetices libri septem*, 1561), uses the evidence of lang. to decry Homer and exalt Virgil: the display by Homer of *humilitas, simplicitas, loquacitas*, and *ruditas* in his style must make him inferior to the Roman. If Virgil echoes Homer's description of Strife in his picture of Fama in book 4 of the *Aeneid*, that is an excuse for loading Homer with abuse. And just as ruthlessly as Agrippa with Virgil, these critics set about Dante, Ariosto, and Tasso for their unclassical backsliding.

In particular, because of the runaway popularity of Ariosto's *Orlando furioso* (1516), the issue of what kinds of subject matter, lang., and formal structure could be considered legitimately epic was of great interest in Italy in the mid-16th c. A number of critics objected to Ariosto (often in the strongest terms) because of his lack of moral purpose and, more significant, his failure to adhere to Aristotle's requirements for both a single, unified story and "probability" (which for Aristotle meant persuasiveness rather than, as for these critics, the absence of the fantastic). Attempting to rescue Ariosto from his detractors, Giambattista Giraldi Cinthio (*Discorso intorno al comporre dei romanzi*, 1554) and Giambattista Pigna (*I romanzi*, 1554) wrote that Ariosto's text was not a bad epic, but of a distinct genre with its own narrative conventions and subject matter: the romance. Cinthio argued against the stultifying *\*classicism of his contemporaries, suggesting that, as cultures and tastes develop, so too do literary forms, which should be judged by practical example rather than by abstract theory. According to the precept set by Ariosto and his predecessor Matteo Maria Boiardo, epic tells the story of one man, romance the story of many; thus, the latter has a more episodic, less unified structure than epic. The publication of Tasso's *Gerusalemme liberata* (1581) brought the discussion to near-fever pitch: his work was frequently pitted against Ariosto's, and both were praised as an example of Aristotelian unity (Camillo Pellegrino, *Il Carrafa*, 1584) and dismissed as a work of inferior artistry. Tasso, responding to the debate (*Discorsi dell'arte poetica*, 1587, although composed 1567–70), takes the part of the Aristotelians, insisting that romance and epic are not discrete genres and that, instead, Ariosto's loose structure and multiplicity of action make for a highly flawed epic.

The political nature of Virgilian epic continues in the Ren. Camões's *Lusiads* builds on an ostensibly prosaic story—the trading expedition of da Gama—to write a glorious and elaborate Port. hist. Tasso's portrayal of the First Crusade as the rightful liberation of Jerusalem by an army of virtuous Christians is intended to stir up support for the Catholic ambition, during the Counter-Reformation, of capturing Jerusalem from Ottoman control. Spenser's layered allegory is a celebration of Queen Elizabeth I in the figure of the "Faerie Queene" Gloriana, while it simultaneously casts her as the direct descendant of Gloriana and King Arthur. The poem, moreover, deals with a number of contemp. political issues, incl. the trial of Mary, Queen of Scots; anxieties about Catholicism and the empire of Philip II; and England's colonial interest in Ireland.

In Eng., Milton (*Paradise Lost*, 1667, 1674; *Paradise Regain'd*, 1671) was greatly influenced by both It. example and precept. He knew Giacopo Mazzoni's *Difesa della Commedia di Dante* (1587) and the theoretical work of Tasso, whose old patron, Count Manso, he had met during his travels in Italy (1637–39). He quotes from the *Orlando furioso* at the beginning of *Paradise Lost* (1.16, cf. *Orlando furioso* 1.2.2). And yet *Paradise Lost* is a self-consciously Eng. work, employing a traditionally Eng. meter and thoroughly Protestant in its theology. Milton's *Epitaphium Damonis* (1639) toys with the idea of a historical epic on Arthurian legends, and his notebooks, preserved in Cambridge, show that he considered a dramatic treatment of the same topics and of the story of Adam. In returning to epic, he fixed on this theological theme, to which the closest cl. parallel would be Hesiod's *Theogony*. It enabled him to set out his profoundest beliefs in the origin of the moral order of the universe, the human condition, and the Christian promise of atonement. Like Hesiod, moreover, Milton moves away from the subject matter of the Virgilian trad., the "Warrs, hitherto the onely Argument / Heroic deem'd" (*Paradise Lost* 9.28–29). His epic contains an extended martial episode—the war in heaven, in which Satan's followers rebel against divine authority—but the work is largely domestic in its focus, portraying the relationship between Adam and Eve as one of shared work, untainted sexuality, and great mutual love, thus prefiguring the domestic focus of the novel. Milton's assumption in the poem of a difficult lang., criticized by Samuel Johnson, is part of the struggle to convey truths larger than life. His *Paradise Regain'd* uses a simpler style to depict Christ's rebuttal of the temptations of Satan, emphasizing his human-

ity rather than divinity and, in Dantean fashion, his humility rather than glory.

In the 17th c., Fr. critics adapted and propagated the It. recension of Aristotle's rules, emphasizing *unity, *decorum, and verisimilitude, although the first trans. of the *Poetics* into Fr. did not appear until 1671. André Dacier's ed. and commentary (*La Poétique d'Aristote contenant les règles les plus exactes pour juger du poème héroique et des pièces de théâtre, la tragédie et la comédie*, 1692) became standard. This and other critical works (René Rapin, *Réflexions sur la poétique d'Aristote*, 1674; René le Bossu, *Traité du poème épique*, 1675) were regarded as normative throughout Europe. The epics they inspired have been universally regarded as failures.

By the late 17th. c., in Eng., epic was both a major influence and a source of anxiety. It was impossible to write epic in the straightforward manner of the Ren. poets; the genre was no longer part of current literary practice, and any attempt to produce it was to self-consciously and artificially to delve backward into the archaic. The poets of the Restoration and 18th c. wrote mock epic, which both parodied, portraying the trivial or the ridiculous in lofty style (John Dryden, "MacFlecknoe," 1682; Alexander Pope, *The Rape of the Lock*, 1714; and *The Dunciad*, 1743) or mocking lofty lang. (Samuel Butler, *Hudibras*, 1663–78), and reverenced the original epic form. Both Dryden and Pope produced trans. of cl. epics. The continued public interest in early epic is likewise reflected in James Macpherson's 1760–62 publication of *Ossian*, which he claimed to have translated from an ancient Gaelic text and which sparked controversy between those who insisted on its inauthenticity (Samuel Johnson among them) and those who argued for its antiquity and formal unity. In an argument that proved enormously influential even into the 20th c., G.W.F. Hegel theorized that epic, as a primitive form, was the expression of a nation's unified character, system of values, and worldview; the age of technological modernity cannot produce epic because people no longer engage vitally with the world around them (*Lectures on Aesthetics*, compiled 1835–38).

Conflict with France and increasing status as an imperial power helped to spur a resurgence of epics or works with significant epic characteristics in 19th c. Eng. (Dentith, Tucker). The romantics admired the vast cultural and poetic scope of the epic but were less intimidated by it than their predecessors: P. B. Shelley is as quick to criticize what he sees as the derivative efforts of Virgil as he is to praise Homer, Dante, and Milton (*Defence of Poetry*, 1821). However, poets who addressed martial, political, or national themes confronted the same potential archaism that had troubled writers in the previous century and a half, with widely varying results (Walter Scott, *Marmion*, 1808; Alfred, Lord Tennyson, *Idylls of the King*, 1859–85; William Morris, *Sigurd the Volsung*, 1876). At the same time, another kind of epic emerged, which dealt with nonmartial, contemp. subject matter and which was largely unhampered by issues of archaism because it addressed directly the values and concerns—here, primarily issues of selfhood and individual experience—of the age that produced it. In *The Prelude* (1805, pub. 1850), William Wordsworth adapts the traditional proem to declare human intellect and emotion, as well as a few intangibles (e.g. Truth, Beauty, Love) his epic subjects; Lord Byron's worldly and satirical *Don Juan* (1819–24), through the adventures of an oft-seduced innocent, reinscribes the epic conventions into a world-weary and ironic voice; Elizabeth Barrett Browning's *Aurora Leigh* (1856) uses a lofty and heroic style to narrate the adventures of an intellectually gifted young woman, who, in turn, insists that epic heroism is possible in any age.

But it is the novel that has proven the most resilient and productive descendant of the epic trad. Two 20th.-c. studies, Georg Lukács's *Theory of the Novel* (1916) and Bakhtin's essay "Epic and Novel" (written 1941, pub. 1970), have been influential in examining the relation between the two genres, which, following Hegel, they see as an issue of antiquity versus modernity. For Lukács, epic expresses a "totality" of collective experience that precludes individualism because the society that produces epic is utterly unified; the novel is the mod. attempt to recover that sense of totality, now lost, by reshaping the world through a process of individual experience. Bakhtin argues that epic deals with a founding hist. that exists before any sense of a transitory present and that, therefore, its perspective is absolute: there is no possibility of reinterpretation because there are no outside voices. The novel, by contrast, consists of many voices in a world of mutable time. For both, epic is the product of an absolute totality: Lukács sees the novel as heralding the loss of this totality, while for Bakhtin, it signals its triumphant overthrow. In addition, novels frequently address similar questions of modernity, often casting themselves as a derivation of or departure from antiquity (Scott, *Ivanhoe*, 1819; Gustave Flaubert, *Madame Bovary*, 1856–57]). Perhaps most famously, George Eliot's *Middlemarch* (1871–72) draws on St. Theresa's "epic life" as a symbol to explore the frustration that passionate and inspired young women encounter in an age that allows them few opportunities for greatness. The novel ends on a domestic note, as its heroine redirects her potentially epic nature to marriage and private life.

This is not to say that the cl. epic was effaced by modernity or the birth of the novel. On the contrary, literary *modernism of the early 20th c., which was deeply influenced by the unprecedented violence of World War I, brought with it an interest in reviving and reincorporating the trad. T. S. Eliot's *The Waste Land* (1922), Ezra Pound's many publications of the *Cantos* (1925–72), and James Joyce's *Ulysses* (1922) reinvent the stories and themes of cl. epic to reflect a new kind of consciousness, marked by disillusionment, fragmentation, and discontinuity. *Ulysses* translates the vast scope of the Homeric epic to a novel spanning only one day and dealing with ordinary, middle-class characters and concerns; far from the monologic epic spirit or the polyphony of Virgil's style, Joyce's novel is a cacophony of voices and thoughts, and it is often impossible to distinguish the thoughts of one character from the voice of another or from the narrator.

The creation of epic continues in recent years; the most prominent example is Derek Walcott's *Omeros* (1990), which translates Homeric elements into a story dealing with African hist. and working-class protagonists on a Caribbean island. *Omeros* is, like the epics of the Virgilian trad., explicitly political, bringing to light the effects of colonialism and slavery and imbuing the lives of its disenfranchised characters, as Dentith observes, with epic importance and dignity.

*See* NARRATIVE POETRY, ORAL POETRY.

■ **Criticism and History**: H. T. Swedenberg, *The Theory of the Epic in England, 1650–1800* (1944); C. M. Bowra, *From Virgil to Milton* (1945), and *Heroic Poetry* (1952); E.M.W. Tillyard, *The English Epic and Its Background* (1954); R. A. Sayce, *The French Biblical Epic in the Seventeenth Century* (1955); T. M. Greene, *The Descent from Heaven: A Study in Epic Continuity* (1963); R. Durling, *The Figure of the Poet in Renaissance Epic* (1965); J. M. Steadman, *Milton and the Renaissance Hero* (1967); A. B. Giamatti, *The Earthly Paradise and the Renaissance Epic* (1966); M. R. Lida de Malkiel, *Dido en la literatura española* (1974)–on the *Defense of Dido*; L. Ariosto, *Orlando Furioso*, trans. B. Reynolds (1977); Parry; F. Blessington, *"Paradise Lost" and the Classical Epic* (1979); G. Nagy, *The Best of the Achaeans* (1979); M. Murrin, *The Allegorical Epic* (1980); M. M. Bahktin, "Epic and the Novel," *The Dialogic Imagination*, ed. M. Holquist, trans. C. Emerson and M. Holquist (1981); S. Revard, *The War in Heaven* (1980); A. Fichter, *Poets Historical: Dynastic Epic in the Renaissance* (1982); J. Kates, *Tasso and Milton: The Problem of Christian Epic* (1983); L. Robinson, *Monstrous Regiment: The Lady Knight in Sixteenth-century Epic* (1985); C. Martindale, *John Milton and the Transformation of Ancient Epic* (1986); R. Martin, *The Language of Heroes* (1989); A. Parry, *The Language of Achilles and Other Papers* (1989); D. C. Feeney, *The Gods in Epic* (1991); J. B. Hainsworth, *The Idea of Epic* (1991); A. Lord, *Epic Singers and Oral Tradition* (1991); A. Ford, *Homer: The Poetry of the Past* (1992); S. Wofford, *The Choice of Achilles: The Ideology of Figure in the Epic* (1992); C. Burrow, *Epic Romance: Homer to Milton* (1993); P. Hardie, *The Epic Successors of Virgil* (1993); D. Quint, *Epic and Empire* (1993); M. Desmond, *Reading Dido* (1994); M. Murrin, *History and Warfare in Renaissance Epic* (1994); J. Watkins, *The Specter of Dido: Spenser and Virgilian Epic* (1995); F. Moretti, *Modern Epic* (1996); G. Teskey, *Allegory and Violence* (1996); *Epic Traditions in the Contemporary World: The Poetics of Community*, ed. M. Beissinger, J. Tylus, S. Wofford (1999); Lord; J. Everson, *The Italian Romance Epic in the Age of Humanism* (2001); Horace, *The Epistles of Horace*, trans. D. Ferry (2001); Statius, *Silvae*, ed. and trans. D. R. Shackleton Bailey (2003); R. Padrón, *The Spacious Word: Cartography, Literature, and Empire in Early Modern Spain* (2004); *A Companion to Ancient Epic, ed.* J. M. Foley (2005); J. C. Warner, *The Augustinian Epic, Petrarch to Milton* (2005); T. Gregory, *From Many Gods to One: Divine Action in Renaissance Epic* (2006); S. Zatti, *The Quest for Epic: From Ariosto to Tasso* (2006).

■ **Theory**: D. Comparetti, *Vergil in the Middle Ages*, trans. E.F.M. Benecke (1895); Faral; J. E. Spingarn, *History of Literary Criticism in the Renaissance*, 2d ed. (1925); H. Strecker, "Theorie des Epos," *Reallexikon I* 4.28–38; E. Reitzenstein, "Zur Stiltheorie des Kallimachos," *Festschrift Richard Reitzenstein* (1931); Lewis; M.-L. von Franz, *Die aesthetischen Anschauungen der Iliasscholien* (1943); M. T. Herrick, *The Fusion of Horatian and Aristotelian Literary Criticism, 1531–1555* (1946); Auerbach; Curtius; Frye; Weinberg; D. M. Foerster, *The Fortunes of Epic Poetry: A Study in English and American Criticism 1750–1950* (1962); F. J. Worstbrock, *Elemente einer Poetik der Aeneis* (1963); G. N. Knauer, *Die Aeneis und Homer* (1964); A. Lesky, *A History of Greek Literature*, trans. J. Willis and C. de Heer (1966); K. Ziegler, *Das hellenistische Epos*, 2d ed. (1966); J. K. Newman, *Augustus and the New Poetry* (1967); E. Fränkel, *Noten zu den Argonautika des Apollonios* (1968); S. Koster, *Antike Epostheorien* (1970); *Classical and Medieval Literary Criticism*, ed. A. Preminger et al. (1974); *Homer to Brecht: The European Epic and Dramatic Tradition*, ed. M. Seidel and E. Mendelson (1976); R. Häussler, *Das historische Epos der Griechen und Römer bis Vergil* (1976); G. S. Kirk, *Homer and the Oral Tradition* (1976); R. Häussler, *Das historische Epos von Lucan bis Silius und seine Theorie* (1978); J. K. Newman, *The Classical Epic Tradition* (1986); S. M. Eisenstein, *Nonindifferent Nature* [1964], trans. H. Marshall (1987); R.O.A.M. Lyne, *Further Voices in Vergil's "Aeneid"* (1987); D. Shive, *Naming Achilles* (1987); B. Graziosi, *Inventing Homer: The Early Reception of Epic* (2002); S. Dentith, *Epic and Empire in Nineteenth-Century Britain* (2006); H. F. Tucker, *Epic, Britain's Historic Muse 1790–1910* (2008).

T. B. Gregory (hist.); J. K. Newman; T. Meyers (theory)

**EPICEDIUM** (Lat.; Gr. *epikedeion*, "funeral song"). A song of mourning in praise of the dead, sung in the presence of the corpse and distinguished from *threnos*, a \*dirge, which was not limited by time or place. The word does not occur before the Alexandrian period, or in Lat. before Statius (1st c. CE), although the lamentations over the bodies of Hector and Achilles in Homer are, properly speaking, *epicedia*. The epicedium became very popular in the Hellenistic period and was widely imitated in Lat. lit. It was accompanied by a solemn dance with music provided by a flute in the Lydian mode. Written originally in a variety of meters, it was confined after the cl. period entirely to elegiac \*distichs and \*hexameters. Epicedia also included lamentations in verse for pet animals and birds (e.g., Catullus 3; Ovid, *Amores* 2.6; Statius, *Silvae* 2.4 and 5).

*See* ELEGY, LAMENT.

■ Pauly-Wissowa; G. Herrlinger, *Totenklage um Tiere in der antiken Dichtung* (1930); W. Kese, *Untersuchungen zu Epikedion wid Consolatio in der rümischen Dichtung* (1950); D. C. Allen, "Marvell's 'Nymph,'" *ELH* 23 (1956); M. Alexiou, *The Ritual Lament in Greek Tradition* (1974); H. H. Krummacher, "Deutsche barocke Epikedeion," *Jahrbuch der Deutschen Schillergesellschaft* 18 (1974); Michaelides.

P. S. Costas; T.V.F. Brogan

**EPIDEICTIC POETRY.** In the strict sense, poetry that follows the model of epideictic (or demonstrative) oratory, one of the three kinds of eloquence according to Aristotle's *Rhetoric*—the others being deliberative or political and forensic or legal—and the one in which, absent any urgent need to persuade, the speech can be appreciated for its own sake along with the object praised or blamed. The term can be used in a looser sense to designate any poetry that eulogizes someone or something, but it is usually employed in cases in which the praise feels "oratorical," whether or not it can be traced back to rhetorical models also used in prose. In ancient Greece, lyric forms dedicated to the act and function of extolling the gods, rulers, or victors at the national games (as in Pindar's *epinicia*) predated the formalization of epideictic eloquence in prose; poets of later eras, on the other hand, could follow such lyric templates while also borrowing from rhetorical ones. The fullest ancient presentation of the formulas is the *Peri epideiktikon* ("On Epideictic Oratory") of Menander (3d c. CE). Among the types are \*encomium, \*panegyric, \*elegy, and \*epithalamium, but places and objects can be praised as well as human subjects—whence formulas for praise of births, deaths, weddings, or victories, but also cities, monuments, public holidays, personal gifts, landscapes, and works of art.

While an important aspect of poetry (and a justification for it as well), the epideictic function was not always allowed to govern poetry rhetorically. An epic such as Virgil's *Aeneid* praised the emperor Augustus but found indirect ways to do so while developing the poem's fiction. In the lyric genre, Horace's *Carmina* imitated Sappho as well as Pindar: cl. lyric poetry, which "sang" of various objects, did not necessarily praise or blame them. Later in Rome's imperial period, however, as epideixis tended to overtake other forms of oratory, it also came to dominate poetry: many of the subjects treated, great or small, were posited as objects of praise and developed along recognized patterns. This remained the norm during much of the Middle Ages, esp. in Lat. Epideixis in poetry often came with an aestheticizing effect, which increased as the object of praise moved from the public sphere to more private domains; the mode that best encapsulated this trend was \*ekphrasis or description of a beautiful object, often a work of art. Thus, the epideictic established a rhetorical niche for poetry, an area in which the aesthetic of praise fostered the praise of the aesthetic, within a larger culture of eloquence.

The poets of the Ren., who inherited much of antiquity's poetic trad., remained tempted by this arrangement, in which specialized forms of praise could deal with a wide variety of objects and circumstances and fulfill numerous social or political duties under an aesthetic patina. But they were just as likely to question or overturn it: on the one hand, they pushed their rhet. of praise toward *paradox and *satire; on the other, rather than contenting themselves with the regulated aestheticization of the praiseworthy, many of these poets went back to the original models of the *epic and *lyric genres, which practiced praise in different, less codified terms. Thus, while someone like Pierre de Ronsard was fully versed in the motifs of epideictic rhet., he also thought that poetry alone, in its unruly way, could deliver the highest, most powerful, and most civic form of eulogy (as Pindar had shown); *and* he refused at the same time to be constrained (any more than Horace had been) by such a lofty mission. Praising himself and his calling above all, he reserved the right to "immortalize" whatever he wanted, from the king of France to a wine glass; but he could also denounce praise as courtly flattery, unworthy of a true poet. He often praised or blamed his targets according to the degree of their support for poetry, subtly wove compliments into the veils of fabulous narratives, and put epideictic hyperboles to work in a different field—notably love poetry, as Petrarch had done in his *Canzoniere* by claiming that his beloved Laura was worthier than even Aeneas or Scipio.

In this way epideictic poems became rife with ambiguities, suggesting at once how poetry could find its proper place within a rhetorical frame and how it could escape from that place or adapt that frame to its own purposes. Something of the range of these possibilities appears in the following Eng. examples, which find distinctive ways to practice and inflect epideixis: Philip Sidney's *Astrophil and Stella* (praise as well as blame of a desired woman), Edmund Spenser's *Epithalamion* (a celebration of the poet's wedding), John Donne's *Anniversaries on the Death of Elizabeth Drury* (a funeral elegy), and Ben Jonson's "To Penshurst" (praise of a country house).

■ O. B. Hardison Jr., *The Enduring Monument* (1962); D. Ménager, *Ronsard* (1979); J. B. Allen, *The Ethical Poetic of the Later Middle Ages* (1982); C. Kallendorf, *In Praise of Aeneas* (1989); L. Pernot, *La rhétorique de l'éloge dans le monde gréco-romain* (1993); R. D. Lockwood, *The Reader's Figure* (1996); *Poétiques de la Renaissance*, ed. P. Galand-Hallyn and F. Hallyn (2001); *L'éloge du prince*, ed. I. Cogitore and F. Goyet (2003); J. A. Burrow, *The Poetry of Praise* (2008).

F. CORNILLIAT

**EPIGRAM** (Gr. *epigramma*, "inscription"). An ancient form, first carved on gravestones, statuary, and buildings. Epigrams encompass an almost infinite variety of tone and subject, but they are defined by *concision (relatively speaking: while many epigrams are two to four lines long, others are considerably longer). Many but certainly not all epigrams aim for a point or turn. Alone and as part of other forms, the epigram has many formal affiliations. Longer epigrams can shade into *elegy or *verse epistle. Poetic *epitaphs are a subgenre of epigram, and *emblems, *proverbs, aphorisms, maxims, and adages have often been shaped into epigrams. The *sonnet, particularly the Eng. sonnet, with its structure of three *quatrains and a concluding *couplet, has strong roots in the epigram.

Epigrams influenced Western poetry through two cl. sources: the *Greek Anthology* and Roman epigrammatists, esp. Catullus and Martial. The *Greek Anthology* is additive, incl. poems written over the course of more than a thousand years, a gathering first begun by Meleager around 90 BCE. It originates the concept of *anthology itself (literally, "garland or gathering of flowers"), a collection arranged by some kind of ordering principle. *Greek Anthology* epigrams range from epitaphic to erotic, from invitations to thank-you notes, from satiric to polemical to moral; most are in *elegiac distichs. In the 10th c. CE, Constantine Cephalas, a Byzantine Greek, compiled a 15-part anthol., combining and rearranging earlier collections. In 1301, Maximus Planudes compiled an expurgated version, the first to appear in print (in 1494; called the *Planudean Anthology*). It had a profound effect on subsequent Neo-Lat. and developing vernacular poetry. In 1606, Claudius Salmasius (Claude Saumaise) discovered a copy of Cephalas's version of the anthol. in the Elector Palatine's library in Heidelberg. This full version, known as the *Palatine Anthology*, was finally published between 1794 and 1814 in 13 volumes.

Roman devels. of the epigram trad. bear the stamp of particular authors. Especially influential are Catullus and Martial, who arranged epigrams in groups unified by the presence of a witty, observant persona. Catullus's epigrams of everyday life and intimate social relationships demonstrate the form's lyric potential. Martial explicitly modeled his epigrams on Catullus's but developed a much sharper degree of social *satire, underscored by the strong closure effected by a point or turn.

Ren. poetry embraced the epigram: from anthol.-influenced collections incl. sonnet sequences (e.g., Clément Marot in France), to incisive satiric epigrams influenced by Martial (e.g., Baltasar Alcázar and Juan de Mal Lara in Spain), to aphoristic commonplaces. The extensive treatment of the epigram by important theorists such as J. C. Scaliger (*Poetices libri septem* [Seven Books of Poetics], 1561) and George Puttenham (*The Arte of English Poesie*, 1589) established it as a core cl. genre. Because of its antiquity and brevity, the epigram was central to humanist education, trans. and imitated by pupils throughout Europe. Thomas More's and Étienne Pasquier's Neo-Lat. epigrams exemplify the international humanist culture that remained vibrant through the 17th c.

In Eng., notable 16th-c. epigrammatists include John Heywood, John Harington, and John Davies. The mature flowering of the Eng. epigram came in the 17th c. with Ben Jonson, Martial's most influential Eng. imitator. His epigrams combine cl. learning with dramatic accuracy; they range from miniature portraits of city and court denizens ("To My Lord Ignorant": "Thou call'st me Poet, as a terme of shame: / But I have my revenge made, in thy name"), to *epideictic epigrams of named personages and touching epitaphs such as "On My First Son." Emblems, most famously Francis Quarles's, yoked epigrams with images. George Herbert wrote Lat. epigrams, and not only his

Eng. poetry but his very conception of *The Temple* as a linked poetic book is indebted to the epigram trad. Richard Crashaw's divine epigrams are shockingly physical performances of baroque compression. Robert Herrick experimented with *tone and subject; *Hesperides* includes hundreds of epigrams ranging from versified maxims to social satire, Catullan love lyrics, and epitaphs for flowers, pets, and himself. While Andrew Marvell also wrote discrete epigrams, "Upon Appleton House," with its tight, allusive stanzas, is one of the great achievements of the epigram trad.

At different historical moments, the two epigrammatic strains (brief lyrics, on the one hand, pointed aphorisms or satires, on the other) can coexist, or one can dominate. In a sense, the epigram was most pervasive in the long 18th c. John Dryden, Nicolas Boileau, Alexander Pope, Voltaire, J. W. Goethe, and Friedrich Schiller wrote epigrams; and, more generally, the centrality of the couplet to *neoclassical poetics is an epigrammatic devel. By the late 18th c., however, many poets reacted against pointed wit and turned to epigram's lyric potential. Thomas Gray's "Elegy Written in a Country Churchyard" combines aphoristic formulations with elegiac reverie; and William Wordsworth, while explicitly rejecting epigrammatic wit, worked extensively with epigram's subgenre, epitaph. Nevertheless, the pointed epigram remained important. William Blake returned to epigram's origins, engraving poetry with image. The proverbs embedded in Blake's *Marriage of Heaven and Hell* ("The road of excess leads to the palace of wisdom") foreshadow the strongly turned, witty aphorisms of Oscar Wilde, Mark Twain, and Dorothy Parker. W. S. Landor is a notable epigrammatist, and epigram is the building block of Lord Byron's mock epic *Don Juan*. Antonio Machado and Fernando Pessoa make an epigrammatic mode available as a stance or perspective.

American poetry has fostered a brilliant epigram trad. Emily Dickinson's aphoristic, gathered poems are epigrams. Ezra Pound's imagistic "In a Station of the Metro" attempts to fuse epigram and *haiku (see JAPAN, MODERN POETRY OF); H.D., Wallace Stevens, and W. C. Williams used the epigrammatic mode to capture direct address and strong imagery; J. V. Cunningham's epigrams are explicitly cl. Because of its ling. compression, strong turn, and use of rhyme for point, epigram continues to be a dominant form in contemp. lyric poetry.

■ T. K. Whipple, *Martial and the English Epigram from Sir Thomas Wyatt to Ben Jonson* (1925); J. Hutton, *The Greek Anthology in Italy* (1935) and *The Greek Anthology in France and the Latin Writers in the Netherlands* (1946); H. H. Hudson, *The Epigram in the English Renaissance* (1947); I. P. Rothberg, "Hurtado de Mendoza and the Greek Epigrams," *Hispanic Review* 26 (1958); B. H. Smith, *Poetic Closure* (1968); G. Hartman, *Beyond Formalism* (1970); R. L. Colie, *The Resources of Kind: Genre-Theory in the Renaissance* (1973); A. Fowler, *Kinds of Literature* (1982); A. Cameron, *The Greek Anthology: From Meleager to Planudes* (1993); D. Russell, "The Genres of Epigram and Emblem," *CHLC*, v. 3, ed. G. P. Norton (1999); *Oxford Classical Dictionary*, ed.

S. Hornblower and A. Spawforth, 3d ed. (2003); A. W. Taylor, "Between Surrey and Marot: Nicolas Bourbon and the Artful Translation of the Epigram," *Translation and Literature* 15 (2006); W. Fitzgerald, *Martial: The World of the Epigram* (2007); *Brill's Companion to Hellenistic Epigram*, ed. P. Bing and J. Bruss (2007).

A. B. COIRO

**EPINIKION,** also *epinicion, epinician*. A triumphal song, an *ode commemorating a victory at one of the four great Gr. national games. It was sung either on the victor's arrival at his native town, during the solemn procession to the temple, or at the banquet held to celebrate his victory. The ordinary *epinikion* consisted of a number of groups, each of three stanzas (*strophe, *antistrophe, *epode), and contained an account of the victory of the hero, a myth (the most important part of the poem, relating the victor's deed to the glorious past of his family), and the conclusion, which returned to the praise of the victor and ended with reflective admonitions or even a prayer. The most eminent representatives of this type of composition are Simonides, Pindar, and Bacchylides. One of the latest *epinikia* on record is that composed by Euripides for Alcibiades on the occasion of the latter's victory in three chariot races at Olympia (420 BCE).

■ Schmid and Stählin; M. R. Lefkowitz, *The Victory Ode* (1976); Michaelides; *Pindar's Victory Songs*, ed. and trans. F. J. Nisetich (1980); K. Crotty, *Song and Action* (1982); W. Mullen, *Choreia* (1982); A. P. Burnett, *The Art of Bacchylides* (1985); L. Kurke, *The Traffic in Praise* (1991); H. W. Smyth, *Greek Melic Poets* (1900, rpt. 2006).

T.V.F. BROGAN; P. S. COSTAS

**EPIPLOKE** (Gr., "plaiting" or "weaving together"). A term occasionally applied by ancient metrists to metrical sequences capable of alternative *scansion depending on where the *colon or *metron boundary is located—e.g., x – ᴗ – x – ᴗ – x, which will be *iambic if a boundary precedes each *anceps, and *trochaic if it follows. Such sequences were seen as composed of an "interweaving" of the alternative forms involved—iambic with trochaic, *ionic ( ᴗ ᴗ – – ) with choriambic ( – ᴗ ᴗ – ), bacchiac ( ᴗ – – ) with *cretic ( – ᴗ – ) (see CHORIAMB, BACCHIUS). With the exception of *dochmiacs and dipodic *anapests, all Gr. rhythmical types are subject to interweavings of this sort, and certain verse structures are better described as *epiploke* than as a succession of discrete cola and metra, division into units of this latter sort becoming possible, if at all, only once the verse design is instantiated in a particular line, *strophe, or antistrophe. There is, however, no agreement as to the frequency of such structures or their general importance in the Gr. prosodic system.

■ Hephaestion, *Enchiridion*, ed. M. Consbruch (1906), 110–11, 120–21, 127; A. M. Dale, *Collected Papers* (1969); T. Cole, *Epiploke* (1988), ch. 1.

A. T. COLE

**EPITAPH** (Gr., "writing on a tomb"). A funerary inscription or a literary composition imitating such an inscription. Literate cultures have often commemorated the dead in artful epitaphs: e.g., laudatory epitaphs combining ornate prose and verse were an important premod. Chinese literary genre, while cl. Ar. inscriptions combined prose biography with verse warnings of divine judgment.

In the West, pithy Gr. verse grave inscriptions, most influentially in elegiac couplets, arose in the 7th c. BCE. Epigrammatists through the Hellenistic period composed both inscriptional and pseudoinscriptional epitaphs, some ribald and satiric. Many appear in book 7 of the *Greek Anthology*. With expressive brevity epitaphs lament, beg remembrance, proclaim fame, warn of death's inevitability, and bid the passerby enjoy life or imitate the deceased. The dead sometimes "speak" (imperiously or imploringly) to the visitor, as in Simonides' famous elegiac distich on the Spartans at Thermopylae ("Go, stranger, tell the Spartans / That here obedient to their laws we lie").

Poets of Augustan Rome adapt the epitaphic voice of the dead for highly original fictional epitaphs (e.g., Horace's *Odes* 1.28, Propertius's *Elegies* 1.21). They also influentially provide pithy epitaphic self-descriptions: an elegiac *distich ancient biographers ascribe to Virgil encapsulates his life and achievement, Propertius and Tibullus incorporate two-line epitaphs on themselves in their love elegies, and Ovid provides a two-couplet epitaph imploring fellow lovers to wish his bones lie soft (a traditional formula) in *Tristia* 3.3. Virgil's *Eclogues* 5 and Ovid's *Amores* 2.6 also influentially conclude lengthy *laments with brief *panegyric epitaphs providing forceful closure and the consolation of fame. The Silver Lat. epigrammatist Martial writes muchadmired satiric epitaphs and tender ones on beloved slave boys and pets.

Early Christian and med. epitaphs combined commemoration with *memento mori* verses, proclamations of the afterlife, and requests for prayers. Lat. and then vernacular formulas like the grimly chiastic "As you are now, so once was I, / As I am now, soon you must be" appear on med. to 19th-c. gravestones. Numerous Ren. epigrammatists, by contrast, recall cl. accents of restrained grief or praise of individual achievement, such as the 15th-c. Neo-Lat. poet Michele Marullo: "Here I, Alcino, lie: my mourning parents buried me. / That is life's and childbirth's reward"; "His ancestry if you are told, you will feel contempt, but you will admire his deeds. / The former derives from fortune, the latter from character." Giovanni Pontano's *De tumulis* (Of Grave Mounds, 1505) combines cl. and Christian motifs in epitaphs on family and friends. Seventeenth-c. Eng. epigrammatists produce memorable epitaphs. Ben Jonson's "On My First Daughter" describes the mourning parents with third-person restraint; depicts the daughter Mary in a feminized heaven; tenderly plays (as is common in epitaphs) with her name; and closes with Roman solicitude for her earthly remains. "On My First Son" laments before deploying epitaphic formulas and a Martial echo to express Jonson's paternal pride tempered by a wish henceforth not to be attached "too much" to what he loves. Jonson's disciple Robert Herrick writes self-consciously modest epitaphic tributes to humble creatures (infants, his maid, his dog) as well as to himself.

Eighteenth- and 19th-c. inscriptions for the social elite were often verbose, bombastic panegyrics; critics lambasted "sepulchral lies" (Alexander Pope). In his essay on epitaphs, Samuel Johnson warned against falsehood but approved omitting faults. Yet poets continued to write epigrammatic epitaphs both for panegyric, as in Pope's heroic couplet on Isaac Newton ("Nature, and Nature's Laws lay hid in Night. / God said, *Let Newton be*! And all was *Light*"), and *satire. Alexis Piron mocked the Fr. Academy that had rejected him: "Ci-gît Piron, qui ne fut rien, / Pas même académicien" (Here lies Piron, who was nothing, / Not even a member of the Academy). With a terse somberness recalling Gr. epitaphs, by contrast, Herman Melville's Civil War epitaphs commemorate unnamed soldiers' tragic honor.

Late 18th- and 19th-c. poets also treat the epitaph as spur to *lyric. Thomas Gray's "Elegy Written in a Country Churchyard" influentially meditates on people's desire for remembrance, exemplified by humble churchyard epitaphs, before concluding with the poet's own epitaph. William Wordsworth, the author of three essays on the genre, composed epitaphs, lyrical responses to epitaphs, and poems such as "The Solitary Reaper" adapting motifs such as the address to the passerby. Walt Whitman's "As Toilsome I Wander'd Virginia's Woods" incorporates a "rude" one-line Civil War inscription as its insistent refrain.

In the 20th-c. West, grave inscriptions largely disappeared as a serious poetic form with the decline of the living's contact with the buried dead. Poets have continued to write comic, satiric, and fictional epitaphs (such as Thomas Hardy's Gr.-indebted epitaphs on cynics and pessimists and those on an imaginary Midwestern town's inhabitants in Edgar Lee Masters's *Spoon River Anthology*, 1915). Poetic epitaphs on soldiers and victims of war have been the most common type of serious epitaph, such as Rudyard Kipling's and A. E. Housman's World War I compositions. Otherwise, poets composing epitaphs have self-consciously revised the tropes of a genre whose anachronism is part of the point. R. M. Rilke's epitaph on himself, "Rose, oh pure contradiction, delight / in being nobody's sleep under so many / eyelids," hermetically addresses the rose, a symbol of poetry itself, rather than the reader. W. B. Yeats's self-epitaph from "Under Ben Bulben," "Cast a cold eye / On life, on death. / Horseman, pass by," substitutes for the cl. pedestrian wayfarer an equestrian evoking antiquated Ir. nobility and deploys cl. pithiness to demand not respect or pity for the dead but heroic disdain for the mortal. Anne Carson's *Men in the Off Hours* (2000) contains pithy, highly enigmatic "Epitaphs" on "Evil," "Europe," and "Thaw," evoking cl. epitaphs' elegiac couplets but written as if they were partially comprehensible fragments from bygone civilizations. Carson also discovers in ms. crossouts a new form of epitaph, where "all is lost, yet still there."

*See* ELEGY, EPIGRAM.

■ P. Friedländer, *Epigrammata: Greek Inscriptions in Verse from the Beginnings to the Persian War* (1948);

W. Peek, *Griechische Grabgedichte* (1960); R. Lattimore, *Themes in Greek and Latin Epitaphs* (1962); E. Bernhardt-Kabisch, "Wordsworth: The Monumental Poet," *PQ* 44 (1965); G. Hartman, "Wordsworth, Inscriptions, and Romantic Nature Poetry," *From Sensibility to Romanticism*, ed. F. W. Hilles and H. Bloom (1965); *L'Epigramme Grecque*, ed. A. E. Raubitschek (1968); G. Grigson, *The Faber Book of Epigrams and Epitaphs* (1977); E. Bernhardt-Kabisch, "The Epitaph and the Romantic Poets: A Survey," *Huntington Library Quarterly* 30 (1978); P. Ariès, *The Hour of Our Death*, trans. H. Weaver (1981); D. Fried, "Repetition, Refrain, and Epitaph," *ELH* 53 (1986); K. Mills-Court, *Poetry as Epitaph: Representation and Poetic Language* (1990); J. Scodel, *The English Poetic Epitaph: Commemoration and Conflict from Jonson to Wordsworth* (1991); A. Schottenhammer, "Characteristics of Song Epitaphs," *Burial in Song China*, ed. D. Kuhn (1994); A. Petrucci, *Writing the Dead: Death and Writing Strategies in the Western Tradition*, trans. M. Sullivan (1998); K. S. Guthke, *Epitaph Culture in the West* (2003); W. Waters, *Poetry's Touch: On Lyric Address* (2003); W. Diem and M. Schöller, *The Living and the Dead in Islam: Studies in Arabic Epitaphs*, 3 v. (2004).

J. SCODEL

**EPITHALAMIUM** (Gr., "in front of the wedding chamber"). The term *epithalamion* (Lat. *epithalamium*) categorizes texts concerning marriage, but epithalamia are as varied in their structures and tonalities as the occasions they commemorate. They range from poems that sedulously engage with norms established by earlier participants in the genre to ones linked to their predecessors merely by their subject matter. Some are unambiguously and joyously celebratory; others, such as John Suckling's "Ballade, Upon a Wedding," parody the participants, the event, and the convention, while yet other texts uneasily occupy shifting positions on that spectrum. Similarly, the genre encompasses everything from poems erotic enough to court the label of pornography, notably the work of the Neo-Lat. writer Johannes Secundus, to some that virtually ignore sex. Different though epithalamia are in these and other ways, they typically offer a particularly valuable occasion for studying the interaction of literary conventions and social practices and pressures on issues ranging from gender to politics to spatiality.

Reflected in the name of the genre, the folk practice of singing outside the room where the marriage is consummated lies behind later versions of the epithalamium. The Song of Solomon and Psalm 45 offer scriptural antecedents. Many Gr. and Lat. poems, notably Theocritus's *Idyll* 18, describe weddings; but by far the most influential cl. contributions are three poems by the Roman poet Catullus: 61, 62, and 64. The imitation of these earlier models common in later poems mirrors the concern for lineage thematized in the poems themselves.

Although the Middle Ages witnessed the use of epithalamic lang. in descriptions of mystical spiritual marriages, the genre did not enjoy a vogue until the Ren. That period saw numerous Neo-Lat. epithalamia, as well as an extensive discussion of both literary and folk versions of this mode in the monumental Lat. text by J. C. Scaliger, *Poetices libri septem* (Seven Books of Poetics, 1561). The Fr. poets participating in the genre include Clément Marot and Pierre de Ronsard. Contributions from the Sp. Golden Age often incorporate the allegorical figure of Fame; indeed, many epithalamia in the early mod. era, incl. Edmund Spenser's *Prothalamion* (1596), court *patronage through eulogistic tributes to the participants in a royal or aristocratic wedding. By far the most influential Eng. instance, however, is Spenser's *Epithalamion* (1595), written for his own wedding. The popularity of the genre soared in the 17th c., with John Donne, Ben Jonson, and Robert Herrick, among others, writing such lyrics. Epithalamia also appeared in 16th- and 17th-c. plays and in *masques.

Versions arise in many other cultures and eras as well. Asian trads., e.g., include ancient poems praising members of the couple. Alfred, Lord Tennyson's *In Memoriam* (1850) ends on verses about a wedding, an example of the elegiac elements so common in wedding poetry (perhaps encouraged by the tale of the fatal events at the marriage of the mythological poet Orpheus). Among the many 20th-c. epithalamia are wedding poetry by W. H. Auden, James Merrill, and Gertrude Stein.

Common conventions of the Eng. and continental trads. include praise of the couple; invocations of the mythological figure associated with marriages, Hymen; prayers for children; allusions to dangers that must be avoided; and references to houses and thresholds. Often the poet assumes the role of master of ceremonies. *Refrains frequently appear, as do images of nature and warfare, as well as references to political events, the latter exemplifying the social and public orientation of many epithalamia. Critics often divide the genre into two types: the so-called lyric epithalamium, which generally describes the events of the wedding day in chronological form, as Catullus 61 does; and the epic epithalamium, exemplified by Catullus 64, which recounts a mythological story connected with a marriage. Other scholars have, however, challenged this binary categorization, stressing that some poems fit imperfectly and many others not at all.

In addition to the elegiac propensities exemplified by the work of Tennyson and many other poets, the genre of marriage often effects its own flirtations or marriages with and divorces from many other poetic genres. *Pastoral elements are common. The epithalamium borrows from Petrarchan love poetry and often also offers a countervailing vision in which conjugal happiness replaces the frustrations often though not invariably associated with *Petrarchism. Epithalamia within masques, a number of which celebrate weddings, gesture toward an affinity between those modes that encapsulate recurrent characteristics of wedding poetry: both that genre and masques are concerned to acknowledge but contain threats, esp. to communal order, and both emphasize the relationship between individuals and the community. Esp. intriguing is the link between the *paraclausithyron*, a convention that portrays a lover attempting to gain admission to the house of the beloved, and the epithalamium: on one level, the wedding poem is a potential sequel or alternative to this sort of "closed-door poem," while spatially it reverses positions, placing the lover within an enclosed space suggested by its title and the rest of the community outside.

*See* BLASON, EPIDEICTIC POETRY.

■ *English Epithalamies*, ed. R. Case (1896); J. McPeek, *Catullus in Strange and Distant Britain* (1939); T. M. Greene, "Spenser and the Epithalamic Convention," *CL* 9 (1957); A. Hieatt, *Short Time's Endless Monument* (1960); V. Tufte, *The Poetry of Marriage* (1970); *High Wedlock Then Be Honored,* ed. V. Tufte (1970); J. Loewenstein, "Echo's Ring: Orpheus and Spenser's Career," *English Literary Renaissance* 16 (1986); C. Schenck, *Mourning and Panegyric* (1988); T. Deveny, "Poets and Patrons: Literary Adulation in the Epithalamium of the Spanish Golden Age," *South Atlantic Review* 53 (1988); H. Dubrow, *A Happier Eden* (1990); J. Owens, "The Poetics of Accommodation in Spenser's 'Epithalamion,'" *SEL* 40 (2000); B. Boehrer, "'Lycidas': The Pastoral Elegy as Same-Sex Epithalamium," *PMLA* 117 (2002).

H. DUBROW

**EPITHET.** A modifier specifying an essential characteristic and appearing with a noun or a proper name to form a phrase. The word derives from the Gr. *epitheton* (attributed, added), which Lat. grammarians considered to be equivalent to "adjective." Isidore of Seville writes that epithets "are called either adjectives (*adiectivus*) or additions, because they are 'added to' (*adicere,* ppl. *adiectus*) nouns to complete the meaning." In mod. scholarship, the term designates a rhetorical device whose best known examples come from Homer, such as the first elements of "wine-dark sea" and "swift-footed Achilles." They appear in formulaic constructions, i.e., each phrase follows a metrical pattern and conveys an essential idea. In this rhetorical sense, epithets are not restricted to single adjectives; they may include nouns or phrases. Conveying what is essential to the noun continues to characterize epithet even in later centuries when the phrase is not formulaic. George Herbert's "quick ey'd love," which resembles the Homeric "gray-eyed Athena," and John Milton's "all-ruling heaven," which William Wordsworth later adopted, illustrate this defining characteristic. The distinction between epithet and adjective, however, is not always clear.

The formulaic nature of older epithets is not limited to Gr. and Lat., which inherited them as a feature indigenous to IE verse, as with the Homeric phrase for "imperishable fame" (κλέος ἄφθιτον), which has an exact analog in the ancient *Rig Veda* (*śrávas ákṣitam*). Still other formulaic epithets find parallels among various IE poetic trads. However, the device extends beyond IE languages. Epithets or constructions very like them can be found, e.g., in med. Ar. love poetry, Twi literature of Ghana, and early Japanese court poetry known as *\*waka*, which calls them *makura-kotoba* (pillow words).

In Eng. lit., the device has an older hist. than, for instance, the Homeric imitation in Edmund Spenser's "rosy-fingred Morning." *Beowulf* and other OE poems made frequent use of formulas like *æþeling ær-god*, "preeminent prince," and kennings like *lyft-floga*, "air-flier, dragon" and *freoðu-webbe*, "peace-weaver, lady." The appositive syntax allowed multiple epithets in lines like *he on ræste geseah / guð-werigne Grendel licgan, / aldorleasne*, "he saw Grendel lying in rest, battle-weary, lifeless." Another influence in Eng. and elsewhere, though difficult to measure, may be the litanies in Christian liturgy, which include sequences such as *Jesu potentissime, Jesu patientissime, Jesu obedientissime, Jesu mitis et humilis corde*. Not limited to Christianity, the repetition of epithet-like names for the divine is a feature of religious trads. throughout history.

The device can be extended. Once it becomes well established, an epithet can stand alone, such as "The Philosopher," meaning "The Philosopher Aristotle." This omission of the noun was known in cl. rhet. as *\*antonomasia*. In a "transferred epithet," the modifier typically specifies a human attribute and applies it to an inanimate noun (e.g., "angry crown," "condemned cell"). A colloquial use since the 19th c., which owes little to the rhetorical device, applies to any offensive or abusive term, e.g., "racial epithet."

■ B. Groom, *The Formation and Use of Compound Epithets in English Poetry from 1579* (1937); L. H. Ofosu-Appiah, "On Translating the Homeric Epithet and Simile into Twi," *Africa* 30 (1960); F. C. Robinson, *"Beowulf" and the Appositive Style* (1985); *A Waka Anthology*, trans. E. A. Cranston (1993); *The Etymologies of Isidore of Seville*, trans. S. A. Barney et al. (2006); M. L. West, *Indo-European Poetry and Myth* (2007).

D. G. DONOGHUE

**EPITRITE,** epitritic (Gr., "one-third as much again"). One of the four categories of rhythm, in Gr. prosody, for any foot containing one short and three long syllables: so described because the ratio of two longs to a long and a short is, in temporal units, 4:3. The position of the short syllable determines the description of the epitrite as first, second, third, or fourth (respectively, ∪ – – – , – ∪ – – , – – ∪ – , – – – ∪ ), but the first and fourth were avoided by Gr. poets as unrhythmical.

*See* DACTYLO-EPITRITE.

■ Koster; West; J. M. v. Ophuijsen, *Hephaestion on Metre* (1987).

R. J. GETTY; T.V.F. BROGAN

**EPODE** (Gr., "after-song"). (1) Gr. lyric *\*odes of the archaic and cl. periods often consisted of three parts: the *\*strophe and *\*antistrophe, which were metrically identical, i.e., in *\*responsion, and the concluding epode, which differed in meter. Ben Jonson called them, usefully, "turn," "counter-turn," and "stand." Collectively, they are called a "triad." Stesichorus used extended sets of such triads for lyric narrative, Pindar and Bacchylides composed *\*epinikion odes in triads, and the choral songs of Attic drama often contain an epode after one or more sets of responding strophes and antistrophes. The Gr. noun *epōidos* (Lat., *epodos*), which was originally an adjective, was feminine in gender when used to designate the last part of a triad (*epōidos strophē*). (2) When masculine (*epōidos stichos*), it denoted the second (and occasionally third), shorter *colon of a brief strophe, consisting in most cases of a *hexameter or an *iambic *trimeter followed by a colon in *dactylic or iambic meter. The poems composed of strophes with such alternating meters in their two (or three) cola are also called epodes. The archaic poets Archilochus and Hipponax used this kind of composition, often for personal *invective, e.g., Archilochus' "Cologne Epode," recounting a seduction. In the Hellenistic age, epodic composition was adapted to book poetry, as in Callimachus' *Iambi* 5, 6, and 7 and in some *epigrams. Horace introduced the form into Lat. in his epodes, which he called *Iambi*.

■ Dale; Maas; West.

R. J. Getty; J. W. Halporn; K. J. Gutzwiller

**EPYLLION.** The Gr. word *epyllion* (a diminutive of *epos*, "word," "hexameter verse," "hexameter poem") meant "versicle" or "short poem," often in a pejorative sense. From the first half of the 19th c., it has been used in the sense "little epic" to refer to short narrative poems in *dactylic hexameters. The Gr. *epic trad. has provided one early example in the pseudo-Hesiodic *Shield*, which describes a shield used by Heracles in combat. The epyllion was particularly cultivated in the Hellenistic era, in correlation with a new critical distinction between *poiēma*, "short poem," emphasizing word choice and stylistic arrangement, and *poiēsis*, "long poem," conceived as a complex weaving of plot and characterization. Hellenistic epyllia, which ran from about 100 to more than 1,000 lines in length, i.e., short enough to fit on one papyrus bookroll, presented mythical narratives that subverted the heroic trad. by shifting the focus to previously marginalized characters, such as the elderly, the poor, women, herdsmen, and even animals. The poem presented a single episode, often illuminated by a digressive secondary story, sometimes in the form of an *ekphrasis*. The interest was placed on personal relationships, involving romance or emotional bonds between persons of different status. Early epic, the Homeric *hymns, and narrative *lyric provided models, reworked by humanization and humor. The style was highly polished, with choice vocabulary and learned allusions. The most famous epyllion was Callimachus' now fragmentary *Hecale*, recounting the modest entertainment of Theseus by the elderly Hecale; other Hellenistic examples include Theocritus's *Hylas* and *Baby Heracles*, the Theocritean *Heracles the Lionslayer*, and Moschus' *Europa*. Epic *parodies, such as the *Battle of the Frogs and Mice*, also fit the category. Epyllia were favored by the Lat. *neoterics, as exemplified by Catullus 64 on the marriage of Peleus and Thetis inset with an ekphrastic digression on the abandonment of Ariadne. Other Lat. examples are the pseudo-Virgilian *Culex*, *Moretum*, and *Ciris*. In the Augustan Age, the epyllion form began to appear within other genres: Virgil's *didactic *Georgics* ends with the Aristaeus epyllion featuring a digressive account of Orpheus and Eurydice, and Ovid's *Metamorphoses* was constructed as a series of epyllia, which heavily influenced early mod. examples. Epyllia were again composed in late antiquity, in both Gr. (Triphiodorus' *Sack of Ilion*, Colluthus' *Rape of Helen*, and Musaeus' *Hero and Leander*) and in Lat. (Dracontius). The term *epyllion* has been applied to certain Eng. Ren. poems (e.g., Christopher Marlowe's *Hero and Leander*, William Shakespeare's *Venus and Adonis*), Fr. poems of the *Pléiade* school (e.g., Pierre de Ronsard's *Hymnes*, Jean-Antoine de Baïf's *Ravissement d'Europe*), and Ger. *rococo poems.

■ M. M. Crump, *The Epyllion from Theocritus to Ovid* (1931); W. Allen Jr., "The Epyllion," *TAPA* 71 (1940); J. F. Reilly, "Origins of the Word 'Epyllion'," *CJ* 49 (1953–54); W. Allen Jr., "The Non-Existent Classical Epyllion," *SP* 55 (1958); *Elizabethan Minor Epics*, ed. E. S. Donno (1963); A. Maler, *Der Held im Salon* (1973); W. Keach, *Elizabethan Erotic Narratives* (1977); K. J. Gutzwiller, *Studies in the Hellenistic Epyllion* (1981); G. W. Most, "Neues zur Geschichte des Terminus 'Epyllion'," *Philologus* 126 (1982); É. Wolff, "Quelques précisions sur le mot 'epyllion'," *RPh* 62 (1988); D. F. Bright, *The Miniature Epic in Vandal Africa* (1987); C. U. Merriam, *The Development of the Epyllion Genre* (2001); A. Bartels, *Vergleichende Studien zur Erzählkunst des römischen Epyllion* (2004); R. Hunter, "Epic in a Minor Key," *Tradition and Innovation in Hellenistic Poetry*, ed. M. Fantuzzi and R. Hunter (2004); A. Hollis, "The Hellenistic Epyllion and Its Descendants," *Greek Literature in Late Antiquity*, ed. S. F. Johnson (2006); *Callimachus: Hecale*, ed. A. Hollis (2009).

K. J. Gutzwiller

**EQUIVALENCE.** In its strict metrical sense, equivalence is key for understanding both cl. and mod. *versification in Eur. langs.; in its more recent meaning, equivalence is one of the foundational principles of metrical theory.

In *classical prosody, *equivalence* is sometimes used to denote *resolution, the metrical principle whereby one *longum* may replace two *brevia*. Thus, in the epic hexameter, *spondees may replace certain *dactyls, typically in the sixth foot, as Homer does in the first line of the *Odyssey*, or in the sixth and third feet, as in the first line of the *Iliad*. The principle or system of metrical equivalence (based on orthography) justifies such substitution of feet, not any actual temporal ratio of one long being equal to two shorts, though that belief has persisted since ancient times. The rules of syllable equivalence, thus, allow metrical variety in successive lines while ensuring identity in their *measure, i.e., conformity to the *meter.

In the older Eng. metrists, the sense of equivalence is less clear than in the cl. langs. Some, even up to the 20th c., argued that Eng. could be scanned just like Gr. or Lat.; others argued these durational values could be heard and felt, still others that they were a useful convention of lesser temporal accuracy. The stress-based concept of foot equivalence came to dominate over time, in the sense that George Saintsbury gives it: the metrical "foot or group-system requires *correspondence* of feet or groups, and this . . . at once enjoins and explains . . . the main charm of English poetry," even though such correspondence is "not mathematically" exact: "the elasticity of the system" ensures "its suitableness to the corresponding elasticity of English verse."

The mod. theoretical sense of equivalence is fundamental to all contemp. ling. understanding of meter. This understanding derives from the realization that the equivalence between syllables and stresses is generalizable to all notions of ling. measurement and, hence, central to the very conception of a verse system itself. One of the most influential formulations is Roman Jakobson's classic dictum of 1958 (originally in Sebeok): "the poetic function projects the principle of equivalence from the axis of selection into the axis of combination" (see POETIC FUNCTION). According to Jakobson, lang. has multiple functions and becomes poetic in function whenever equivalence becomes not merely ornament but "the constitutive device of the sequence." Thus, any given sentence, such as "the child sleeps," is arrayed on two principal axes, one lexical, simultaneous, vertical (the paradigm); the other syntactic, sequential, horizontal (the syntagm). A speaker selects "child" from the lexicon's register of equivalent nouns (*infant, baby*), as she does with the verb "sleeps," then combines them serially in the syntagm to complete the utterance. Items in the paradigm are related by equivalence (similarity-dissimilarity), items in the syntagm by contiguity; cf. the factors of similarity and proximity in Gestalt psychology. In ordinary speech and prose, the principle controlling both the selection and arrangement of words is essentially semantic (referential), but in poetry, the "principle of equivalence" is foregrounded and words with different syntagmatic functions are also presented as potentially equivalent. Poetic lang. heightens its substantiality and memorability by increasing the degree of its orders through selection and *repetition of an element so as to effect a pattern. The principle of equivalence, which equates words in the vertical register of lang., can equate other features in poetry and thus become superimposed on the horizontal sequence as well (see RESPONSION). Rhyme is a good example of this, but so are words or syllables in similar metrical positions, entire lines, stanzas, and so on.

Equivalence is esp. prominent in metrical verse, where multiple ling. features are deployed systematically. Equivalence, however, is not the meter but the system that *makes the meter possible*. The particular features the meter employs (stress, length, pitch, syllable count) are determined by the lang. and by the poet, and the specific pattern the meter will assume is mainly a convention. *Meter*, then, is a *synecdoche for *equivalence*, but *equivalence* is a *metonym for *parallelism*; indeed, Jakobson identifies parallelism as "the fundamental problem of poetry." As with the meter, so with all the other formal elements in the poem—

sound patterning, rhetorical figures, lexical echo and allusion, syntactic metaplasm, stanza forms, and even generic conventions: in every case "equation is used to build up a sequence." Equivalence is, thus, "the indispensable feature inherent in any piece of poetry." The great difficulty in discussing it has to do with the fact that equivalence is a nonreferential function of lang. and, therefore, quite challenging to construe as if it were syntagmatic. It is perhaps best thought of not as propositional but rather as a kind of speech act, a transreferential ordering of lang.

In sum, when similarity (equivalence) processes are superimposed on contiguity processes, the superimposition compounds the degree of organization—the amount of order—in the words, thereby increasing the meaningfulness of the words without increasing their number, raising the amount of readerly attention necessary for comprehension, and marking the text aesthetically. Equivalence increases meaningfulness by adding new levels of functionality to semantics and brings into play every numerable or patterned function of lang., from rhythm to stanza to the full range of poetic effects, all the way up to the largest possible generic concerns.

*See* VERSE AND PROSE.

■ Bridges, App. F; A. W. de Groot, *Algemene Versleer* (1946); R. Jakobson, "Closing Statement: Linguistics and Poetics," Sebeok, rpt. in Jakobson, v. 3; Saintsbury, *Prosody*, v. 1, App. 1; S. R. Levin, *Linguistic Structures in Poetry* (1962); *Versification: Major Language Types*, ed. W. K. Wimsatt (1972)—see M. Halle and S. J. Keyser, "The Iambic Pentameter"; D. Attridge, *Well-Weighed Syllables: Elizabethan Verse in Classical Metres* (1974); Hollander, esp. "The Metrical Frame"; O. Jespersen, "Notes on Metre" (1901), *The Structure of Verse*, ed. H. Gross, rev. ed. (1979); R. Bradford, *A Linguistic History of English Poetry* (1993).

T.V.F. BROGAN; D. J. ROTHMAN

**EROTIC POETRY.** Whereas *love poetry necessarily involves feelings of affection, erotic poetry deals with sexual passion or desire. This simple theoretical distinction becomes impossibly complex to maintain in practice. There are love poems, such as Thomas Hardy's "Neutral Tones," that are not particularly erotic, and erotic poems, such as Pietro Aretino's *Sonetti Lussuriosi* (Lust Sonnets), that have nothing to do with love. But, obviously, the two categories often overlap: many love poems are erotic, and many erotic poems deal with affection or strong feeling.

Part of the difficulty with categorization is that "eroticism" is in many ways a subjective quality that is ultimately judged by the reaction of the reader rather than the content of the text itself. Judgments about what is erotic, like judgments about what is funny, are extremely personal and seldom swayed by external opinion. Nonetheless, one might define an erotic poem as any poem that clearly (if not necessarily explicitly) has sexual desire or passion for its subject. Like all poetry, erotic poetry is a literary artifact, shaped by cultural and generic expectations. It should not generally be taken as hard evidence for either the personal sexual practices of the poet or of the normative sexual practices of the poet's culture and society. Erotic poetry can, however, give valuable insight into how certain practices were culturally imagined in different places and times. It can also be revelatory about cultural fears and fantasies regarding various forms of sexual activity.

Erotic poetry in the form of marriage songs from Mesopotamia survives from as early as the second millennium BCE. Egyptian poems from the 13th and 12th cs. BCE describe the attractions of the beloved's body and the torment of unfulfilled sexual desire, as well as boasting of the joys of consummation and possession of the beloved. The OT Song of Solomon (3d or 4th c. BCE) draws strongly on these earlier trads. Despite (or because of) its powerful erotic imagery, the Song of Solomon was interpreted allegorically from a very early date as an expression of God's love for Israel, or in the Christian trad., Christ's love for the Church (see ALLEGORY). This allegorization of eroticism was to prove a powerful model for passionate religious poetry in Judaism, Christianity, and Islam. In the Song of Solomon, as in earlier Egyptian and Mesopotamian erotic poetry, the speakers are both male and female, whatever the gender of the author may have been.

Some of the earliest surviving erotic poems in the Western trad. are the homoerotic Gr. lyrics of Sappho (7th c. BCE), which describe the sensations of unfulfilled sexual yearning in exquisite detail: speechlessness, hot flashes, sweating, trembling, paleness. Although Sappho's poems describe a woman's desire for another woman, the symptoms she lists would become canonical for lovesick men and women, whatever their object of desire, in both medical texts and imaginative lit. until the mod. period.

Though the Homeric poems have relatively little to say in detail about sexual passion, eroticism firmly enters the *epic trad. with the story of Dido and Aeneas in Virgil's Aeneid. Michel de Montaigne was famously impressed with the erotic intensity of Virgil's description of Venus making love to her husband Vulcan in book 8 of the Aeneid. Eroticism continued to play a large role in Ren. epics such as Ludovico Ariosto's Orlando fursioso, Torquato Tasso's Gerusalemme liberata, and Edmund Spenser's Faerie Queene. John Milton's Paradise Lost is more restrained in this regard, though he does emphatically praise sexual pleasure in the prelapsarian marriage of Adam and Eve and suggests that angels also enjoy some form of pleasurable conjunction.

Catullus introduced Gr. models of erotic lyric into Lat. poetry, but the most influential Lat. writer of erotic poetry is Ovid. His Amores describes a young man's passionate affair with a young woman. His Ars amatoria offers tongue-in-cheek advice on how to seduce women successfully, and his Metamorphoses is a catalog of sexual encounters between humans and gods that explores all forms of sexual relations, incl. rape, incest, lesbianism, male homoeroticism, fetishism, and narcissism. Ovidian poetry too was revived during the

Ren., notably in the Eng. narrative poems of Christopher Marlowe and Shakespeare.

Little erotic poetry survives from the early med. period, but by the late Middle Ages, Fr. *fabliaux (later adapted by Chaucer in the Canterbury Tales), the Carmina Burana, and the verse of François Villon all foreground a rough bawdiness set in opposition to the developing trads. of *courtly love. In the early 16th c., Aretino took a similarly parodic stance in writing his Sonetti Lussuriosi—poems that used the Petrarchan *sonnet form for the explicit and rude depiction of sex, rather than elegantly composed expressions of love.

In 17th-c. England, John Donne's poetry combined overt eroticism with a wide range of passionate and tender emotion to create some of the most resonant and complex love poetry in Eng. But in general, early mod. Eng. poetry reserved explicit eroticism for satirical, comic, or parodic poems. Some texts, like Thomas Nashe's narrative known both as "Nashe's Dildo" or "Choice of Valentines," mocked the fragility of male sexual prowess. This theme was taken up in Restoration poetry by both John Wilmot, the Earl of Rochester, and Aphra Behn. Michelangelo, Shakespeare, and Richard Barnfield all wrote love poetry to beautiful young men, but there is little explicitly homoerotic or lesbian verse extant from the early mod. period.

The romantic poets' valorization of strong passion was generally accompanied by a decorousness in lang., even when, as in S. T. Coleridge's "Christabel," the subject was lesbian vampires. In the mid-19th c., Charles Baudelaire depicted the horrors of diseased sexuality with shocking explicitness. Paul Verlaine and Arthur Rimbaud wrote openly of homosexual desire, as did Walt Whitman, albeit more politely.

Erotic poetry in the 20th c. was both more explicit and more varied in its themes than at any time since the cl. period. From the ecstatic celebrations of sexuality in Pablo Neruda to the openly gay poetry of Allen Ginsberg and Adrienne Rich, eroticism was explored, expressed, and celebrated with a frankness that would have been astonishing in earlier periods.

See GAY POETRY, LESBIAN POETRY, LOVE POETRY, PETRARCHISM, PRIAPEA.

■ G. E. Enscoe, Eros and the Romantics (1967); Dronke; S. Minta, Love Poetry in Sixteenth-Century France (1977); J. H. Hagstrum, Sex and Sensibility: Ideal and Erotic Love from Milton to Mozart (1980); T. A. Perry, Erotic Spirituality: The Integrative Tradition from Leone Ebreo to John Donne (1980); R.O.A.M. Lyne, The Latin Love Poets from Catullus to Horace (1981); P. J. Kearney, A History of Erotic Literature (1982); A. Richlin, The Garden of Priapus: Sexuality and Aggression in Roman Humor (1983); J. H. Hagstrum, The Romantic Body: Love and Sexuality in Keats, Wordsworth, and Blake (1985); G. Woods, Articulate Flesh: Male Homoeroticism and Modern Poetry (1987); P. Veyne, Roman Erotic Elegy: Love, Poetry, and the West (1983), trans. D. Pellaur (1988); D. O. Frantz, Festum Voluptatis: A Study of Renaissance Erotica (1989); A. R. Jones, The Currency of Eros: Women's Love Lyric in Europe, 1540–1620

(1990); C. Paglia, *Sexual Personae: Art and Decadence from Nefertiti to Emily Dickinson* (1990); B. Talvacchia, *Taking Positions: On the Erotic in Renaissance Culture* (1999); I. Moulton, *Before Pornography: Erotic Writing in Early Modern England* (2000); J.C.B. Petropoulos, *Eroticism in Ancient and Medieval Greek Poetry* (2003); S. Guy-Bray, *Loving in Verse: Poetic Influence as Erotic* (2006); S. Fredman, *Contextual Practice: Assemblage and the Erotic in Postwar Poetry and Art* (2010).

I. F. MOULTON

**ESPERANTO POETRY** began with the booklet *International Language Esperanto*, pub. in Warsaw in 1887 by Lazar Ludvik (Markovich) Zamenhof (1859–1917) under the pseud. Dr. Esperanto (one who hopes). The booklet included three poems—one trans. and two original—to demonstrate that this proposed second lang. for international use was no lifeless project but a potential living lang. Zamenhof also produced numerous Esperanto trans., incl. *Hamlet* (1894) and the entire OT. The earliest Esperanto magazines published poetry, early poets drawing on their native trads. to establish poetic norms for Esperanto. Numerous periodicals now publish trans. and original Esperanto poetry. Esperanto lit. runs to several thousand volumes, and the Esperanto lang. is used or understood by several million speakers in the world. Esperanto is a planned, Eur.-based language with simplified grammar and pronunciation but a large vocabulary of fresh and interesting word forms and grammatical combinations unknown in Eur. langs., e.g., Eugen Michalski's poetic coinage *chielenas* (goes upward to the sky), in which *-as* denotes the present tense, *-n* direction toward, and *-e* the adverbial ending, while *chiel-* is the root associated with sky or heaven, *chielo*. Thus, *chiele* = in the sky; *chielen* = toward in-the-sky; and *chielenas* = is toward in-the-sky.

Serious projects for universal langs. began in the 17th c. with George Dalgarno (1661) and John Wilkins (1668) and engaged the attention of René Descartes, G. W. Leibniz, and Isaac Newton. Apart from Esperanto, only Volapük (1880) and Ido ("offspring"; 1908), a modification of Esperanto, developed any significant following, now dissipated. By 1900, Esperanto spread beyond Poland, Russia, and Germany to Western Europe. Collections of poems appeared, incl. three by the Czech Stanislav Schulhof (1864–1919) and the polished and musical *Tra l'silento* (Through the Silence, 1912) of Edmond Privat (1889–1962). Antoni Grabowski (1857–1921), friend of Zamenhof and skilled linguist, published an international anthol., *El parnaso de popoloj* (From the People's Parnassus, 1913), and a brilliant trans. of the *Pan Tadeusz* of Mickiewicz (1918). His audacious ling. experiments prepared for the flowering of Esperanto poetry. The Hungarians Kálmán Kalocsay (1891–1976), in *Mondo kaj koro* (World and Heart, 1921), and Gyula Baghy (1891–1967), in *Preter la vivo* (Beyond Life, 1922), led the way. They founded the influential magazine and publishing company *Literatura Mondo* (Literary World) in 1922.

Zamenhof's interest in Esperanto lit. aimed to create an Esperanto literary and cultural trad., to expand and test the lang. by stretching it to its limits, and to demonstrate that it was as capable of expression as any ethnic lang. Unlike some other projects for an international lang. (none of which withstood the test of time), Esperanto did not spring fully armed from its creator's head. Zamenhof's 1887 booklet contained only the basis of Esperanto; others expanded its lexicon and discovered latent syntactic and morphological possibilities. Kalocsay, in numerous trans. and original poetry (esp. *Strechita kordo* [Tightened String], 1931), sought diversity: his work includes lyrics, *free verse, and strict verse forms. The Rus. Eugen Michalski (1897–1937) wrote introspective poems of startling *imagery and ling. experiment. While Privat and Kalocsay demonstrated Esperanto's affinities with the Eur. trad., Michalski sought originality. But Stalinism claimed Michalski's life and silenced the talented Nikolai Hohlov (1891–1953). Kalocsay dominated the interwar years as mentor, ed., and publisher. Kalocsay and Gaston Waringhien's *Parnasa gvidlibro* (Guidebook to Parnassus, 1932) with its *Arto poetika* and glossary of literary terms and neologisms helped establish an Esperanto trad.; in 1952, *Kvaropo* (Quartet) extended this trad. This work, by four Brit. poets incl. William Auld (1924–2006), began a new era. Auld's *La infana raso* (The Child Race, 1956), a modernist poem of great variety and technical virtuosity, is widely regarded as the most impressive achievement of Esperanto poetry to date, though rivaled by the epic breadth of *Poemo de Utnoa* (Utnoa's Poem, 1993) by the Catalan Abel Montagut (b. 1953). Poets of Auld's generation include the Icelander Baldur Ragnarsson (b. 1930), whose collected works *La Lingvo Serena* (The Serene Language, 2007) established him as the leading poetic voice of the day. Other major contributors to Esperanto poetry in the latter years of the 20th c. include the Brit. scholar Marjorie Boulton (b. 1924), the Czech Eli Urbanová (b. 1922), the Japanese Miyamoto Masao (1913–1989), the Brazilians Geraldo Mattos (b. 1931) and Roberto Passos Nogueira (b. 1949), the South African Edwin de Kock (b. 1930), and the Rus.-Israeli Michael Gishpling (b. 1924).

The poetic trad. has been enriched by numbers of East Asian poets, among them Ueyama Masao (1910–1988) of Japan and Armand Su (1936–1990) and Mao Zifu (b. 1963; *Kantoj de Anteo* [Songs of Anteo], 2006) of China, representative of a long history of Esperanto in China and Japan, where the lang. was associated with anarchist and left-wing causes and with efforts at romanization. The task of codifying and establishing this poetic trad. has fallen in part on a succession of writers on the ling., prosodic, and cultural issues involved in writing Esperanto poetry, among them Auld, Ragnarsson, and Gaston Waringhien (1901–91) of France, who also wrote exquisitely crafted poetry under the pseud. Georges Maura.

In the Esperanto poetic trad., trans. and original work are closely linked. Trans. incl. many of Shakespeare's plays (some by Kalocsay and Auld), his *Sonnets* (trans. Auld), Luís de Camões's *Lusiads*, Dante's

*Divine Comedy*, the *Kalevala*, the Qur'an, and works by J. W. Goethe, Charles Baudelaire, Sophocles, Antônio de Castro Alves, Federico García Lorca,ʿUmar Khayyām, Rabindranath Tagore, and many others. Anthols. of national lits. (Eng., Scottish, It., Catalan, Chinese, Estonian, Swedish, Australian, Hungarian, and others) are frequently pub., with trans. of poetry.

With its concision and suitability for ling. experiment, Esperanto poetry has developed faster than the novel or drama, though in recent years many original novels have appeared. Esperanto's lexicon has expanded: Zamenhof's initial vocabulary comprised fewer than 1000 roots, from which perhaps 10,000 words could be formed. The largest contemp. dicts. now contain 20 times that number. The lexicon remains largely Eur., but Esperanto grammar and syntax resemble isolating langs., like Chinese, and agglutinative langs., like Swahili and Japanese. The future of Esperanto poetry is promising. Poets such as Zifu and Montagut, Mauro Nervi (b. 1959) of Italy, Krys Ungar (b. 1954) of Britain, Jorge Camacho (b. 1966) of Spain, and Gonçalo Neves (b. 1964) of Brazil live in an era of increased scholarly attention to Esperanto. Esperanto appears to have established itself as a ling. and cultural community with its own critical norms and standards.

■ W. Auld, *The Development of Poetic Language in Esperanto* (1976), and *Enkonduko en la originalan literaturon de Esperanto* (1979); P. Ullman, "Schizoschematic Rhyme in Esperanto," *Papers on Language and Literature* 16 (1980); *Esperanta antologio*, ed. W. Auld (1984); H. Tonkin, "One Hundred Years of Esperanto: A Survey," *Language Problems and Language Planning* 11 (1987); D. Richardson, *Esperanto: Learning and Using the International Language* (1988)—learning the lang.; P. Janton, *Esperanto: Language, Literature, and Community* (1993)—lang., lit., and community; H. Tonkin, "The Role of Literary Language in Esperanto," *Planned Languages,* ed. K. Schubert; J. Pleadin, *Ordeno de verda plumo* (2006)—encyclopedia; H. Tonkin, "Recent Studies in Esperanto and Interlinguistics," *Language Problems and Language Planning* 31 (2006); G. Sutton, *Concise Encyclopedia of the Original Literature of Esperanto* (2008).

H. TONKIN

**ESPINELA.** An octosyllabic ten-line Sp. stanza form having the rhyme scheme *abba:accddc*. There is a pause after the fourth line as indicated by the colon. The *strophe was supposedly invented by Vicente Espinel (1550–1624) and so named after him, though the form is found as early as ca. 1510, in the *Juyzio hallado y trobado*. The *espinela* is occasionally augmented by two lines rhyming *ed*. Also called *décima* or *décima espinela*, the espinela has been termed "the little sonnet," and justly so since some of the most beautiful lines in Sp. poetry (e.g., in Pedro Calderón's *La vida es sueño*) have taken this form. Since the late 16th c., the espinela has been widely employed. One of the most self-reflexive instances is the Peruvian modernist Martín Adán's *La rosa de la espinela* (1939), a collec-

tion of espinelas in which the rose as an emblem of transcendent vision and the stanza form are yoked in reciprocal relation.

■ D. C. Clarke, "Sobre la espinela," *Revista de Filología Española* 23 (1936); J. Millé y Giménez, "Sobre la fecha de la invención de la décima o espinela," *HR* 5 (1937); J. M. de Cossío, "La décima antes de Espinel," *Revista de Filología Española* 28 (1944); J. Milléy Giménez, "Espinelas in the *Juyzio hallado y trobado* (c. 1510)," *Romance Notes* 13 (1971); Navarro; J. M. Micó, "En la orígenes de la espinela: Vida y muerte de una estrofa olvidada: La novena," *Romanistisches Jahrbuch* 56 (2005).

D. C. CLARKE

**ESTAMPIDA** (Occitan; OF, *estampie*). Lyric genre of pseudopopular type, its music closely related to instrumental dance tunes. The structure of the latter (schematically *az1az2 bz1bz2 cz1cz2*, in which *z1* and *z2* are differently cadenced versions of a recurring musical tail piece) is reflected in the heterostrophic form of most OF examples. In the few Occitan pieces, a similarly structured but shorter tune matched a single stanza of text and was then repeated for following stanzas, giving a regular isostrophic verse form.

■ F. Gennrich, *Grundriss einer Formenlehre des mittelalterlichen Liedes* (1932); Bec; P. M. Cummins, "Le Problème de la musique et de la poésie dans l'estampie," *Romania* 103 (1982); Sayce, ch. 9; Chambers; D. Billy, "Les Empreintes métriques de la musique dans l'estampie lyrique," *Romania* 108 (1987); T. J. McGee, "Estampie," *Medieval France*, ed. W. W. Kibler (1995).

J. H. MARSHALL

**ESTILÍSTICA** (Sp., "stylistics"). Sp. philology of the early 20th c. was concerned with the hist. of lang. and the philological and historicist study of lit. according to the principles of the *Escuela Española de Filología* (Sp. School of Philology), headed by Ramón Menéndez Pidal. From the 1930s onward, a branch of scholarship called *estilística* emerged from this school and would go on to occupy a prominent place in the panorama of the discipline, not only in Spain but internationally—for instance, in Am. comparative lit. Its initiator was the scholar Amado Alonso, and its most famous exponent (who by coincidence had the same surname) was the writer Dámaso Alonso.

Amado Alonso's approach to *stylistics stands eclectically between two schools of thought, the positivist *Stylistique* of Charles Bally, a disciple of Ferdinand de Saussure, and the idealist *Stilforschung* of Leo Spitzer, a follower of the philosophy of Benedetto Croce and the ling. theory of Karl Vossler. In two essays collected in the posthumous volume *Materia y forma en poesía*, Alonso proposes "the intimate knowledge of the literary work" (a Vossler–Spitzer axiom) and the study of the "expressive values of the language" (Bally's axiom) as the means to achieve it. Faced with the challenge of identifying the historical and social forces that gather and resolve in the work of a particular author, stylistics will put this resolution in question: "all artistic endeavor is the result of the union of the individual with the social, of liberty with establishment; admitting both extremes, traditional criticism has focused on the social; stylistics, on the individual." However, ling. inquiry into *style is not in any way isolationist but requires a historical or cultural dimension to complete it. If any stylistic account that does not consider lang. is incomplete, then any account that relies solely on lang. is inadmissible.

Dámaso Alonso's doctrine of stylistics can be characterized as following Bally in form and Spitzer in substance. While he accepts structuralist categories, he reinterprets them, as in his new reading of the influential dichotomies put forward by Saussure, *langue/parole* and *signifier/signified* (see SIGN, SIGNIFIED, SIGNIFIER).

As an idealist, D. Alonso refuses to begin from an abstraction like *langue* (lang. as system), arguing that all we have is *parole* (lang. in use) in two senses: that which is common to all langs. and that which is peculiar or unique to one lang. The first is the object of grammar, the second, of stylistics, which may examine ordinary or literary uses of lang., since, between the two, the only real difference is one of "nuance or degree."

This statement, in opposition to Bally's doctrine, was defended later by Eugenio Coseriu and others. Although one may refer to literary stylistics, the view of lit. as merely a form of potentiated common speech cannot be sustained without qualification, since words signify only within a system and in context. The same words, when inserted in a different system, become other words.

The opposition *signifier/signified* is also reinterpreted by D. Alonso from an idealist position. The *signifier* is not only an acoustic image but its exteriorization, "anything in speech that modifies, on any scale, our psyche." For this reason, Alonso considers the signifier of the work the sum of partial signifiers.

*Signified* does not mean *concept*, according to D. Alonso, but implies instead a complex inner world of objective and subjective aspects that represent reality and includes the individualizing characteristics of this reality received through the senses; the assignment to a certain genre, through the operation of the intellect; and the attitude of the speaker facing this reality, expressed emotionally. Alonso sees the work of lit. as an entity, a complete sign, composed of a total signifier (A) and a total signified (B), each of which contains its respective complex of partial signifiers ($a^1$, $a^2$, $a^3$, . . . , $a^n$) and partial signifieds ($b^1$, $b^2$, $b^3$, . . . , $b^n$). Because of the linear aspect of lang., the sign has to be formed from successive pairs of a–b and "any other motivational ties that may exist between them, according to how successful the poetic organism is." Given this background, Alonso proposes two paths of critical approach, one "external," the other "internal." The external proceeds from signifier to signified, justifying the choice of signifiers in light of the signifieds available. Inversely, the internal route tries to assess "how creative feeling, thinking and will are impelled toward their own shaping, just as matter, unfashioned, seeks out its mold."

In fact, there are numerous examples of the "external" route, but it is more difficult to find specific cases of the "internal"—following the successive corrections of a poem, e.g. In the end, the attempt to reproduce the creative itinerary, to bridle the uncontrollable and ineffable from the interior, is a chimera, but an inevitable preoccupation of the poet-critic.

The Sp. school of stylistics developed initially in Argentina, after A. Alonso emigrated there in 1927. Later, inspired by D. Alonso, the school extended to several Latin Am. countries such as Brazil, Colombia, Chile, and Cuba, notably in the work of the critic Roberto Fernández Retamar. In Spain, stylistics continues as a critical approach, but ultimately, as in the case of the *Stylistique* and the *Stilforschung*, it has become a focus or an antecedent to the mod. critical fields of *semiotics, pragmatics, neorhet., and literary discourse analysis.

*See* LINGUISTICS AND POETICS.

■ L. Spitzer, *Linguistics and Literary History* (1948); D. Alonso, *Poesía española: ensayos de métodos y límites estilísticos* (1950); C. Bally, *Traité de stylistique française*, 3d ed. (1951); A. Alonso, *Materia y forma en poesía* (1954); M. A. Garrido Gallardo, *La musa de la retórica: problemas y métodos de la ciencia de la literatura* (1994); *El Lenguaje literario: Vocabulario crítico*, ed. M. A. Garrido Gallardo (2009), esp. chs. 1.3 and 4.3.

M. A. GARRIDO GALLARDO

**ESTONIA, POETRY OF.** The Estonian lang., like Finnish, has the word accent on the first syllable, is highly inflected, and tends toward polysyllabism. Its relatively small number of initial consonants favors *alliteration, which, however, is unobtrusive because of the unemphatic articulation. Oral folk poetry, recorded in hundreds of thousands of texts, features an octosyllabic, trochaic meter that is shared with the other Balto-Finnic peoples. Alliteration within lines and semantic *parallelism between lines are characteristic:

> Igav on olla iluta,
> hale olla laulemata,
> kole käo kukkumata,
> raske rõõmuta elada!
>
> (Boring to be without beauty,
> sad to be without song,
> terrible without a bird's twitter,
> hard to live without happiness!)

Written poetry and metrical trads. began with trans. Lutheran hymns; Reiner Brockmann (1609–47) also wrote dedicatory verses in Estonian. The first known example of a poem written by a native Estonian is "Lament about the Destruction of Tartu" (1708) by Käsu Hans. Serfdom and Baltic-Ger. social, economic, and political domination harnessed the intellectual life of the Estonians until the early 19th c. Poets of the Estonian national renaissance drew inspiration from folklore, cl. antiquity, and Finnish and Ger. romantic and preromantic poetry. The first notable poet, the short-lived Kristjan Jaak Peterson (1801–22), wrote inspired Pindarics. F. R. Kreutzwald's epic *Kalevipoeg* (1857–61), based on runic folk ballads and meter, owed much to Elias Lönnrot's Finnish *Kalevala*. The powerful patriotic lyrics of Lydia Koidula (1843–86) developed the romantic *lied* genre. A more intimate poetry emerged later in the century, exemplified in the profoundly personal, tragic symbolism of seemingly simple lyrics by Juhan Liiv (1864–1913). *Symbolism in its Western form, intellectually searching, emphasizing individualized, sophisticated style, appears in the verse of the *Noor-Eesti* (Young Estonia) group; its leader Gustav Suits (1883–1956) was torn between high flights of emotion and bitter, satirical skepticism. The quiet, introspective mysticism of Ernst Enno (1875–1934) and the sensitive island landscapes of Villem Grünthal-Ridala (1885–1942) added new wealth of lang., imagery, and versification to a rapidly expanding lit.

Toward the end of the World War I, shortly before the Estonian declaration of independence in 1918, a new group, named after a mythological bird, *Siuru*, inaugurated an era of lyrical exuberance and extreme individualism in both form and content. Its leaders, Marie Under (1883–1980) and Henrik Visnapuu (1889–1951), later abandoned subjectivism for strenuous thought, universal themes, and firmly crystallized form. Under, the greatest master of lyrical intensity, passed through psychological and metaphysical crises culminating in a poetry of extraordinary translucency and human insight, expanded by the eclectic but keenly picturesque aestheticism of Johannes Semper (1892–1970). The deeply rooted native tendency toward symbolism reasserted itself in a disciplined new form among the *Arbujad* (Magicians) group, including Uku Masing (1909–85), Bernard Kangro (1910–94), Heiti Talvik (1904–47), and Betti Alver (1906–89). Keenly aware of the great trad. of Eur. poetry and thought, these poets sought "to enclose in slim stanzas the blind rage of the elements" (Talvik, "Dies irae," pt. 12 [1934]), imposing the finality of perfect expression on the emotional turbulence of a world heading toward chaos.

After World War II, during Stalinist rule in Estonia, socialist realism was compulsory. Only those who left Estonia could write freely; among them were Under, Kangro, and Suits, succeeded by Kalju Lepik (1920–99), the surrealist Ilmar Laaban (1921–2000), the lyrical dialect poet Raimond Kolk (1924–92), and Ivar Grünthal (1924–96). Ivar Ivask (1927–92), ed. of *Books Abroad*, wrote *Baltic Elegies* in Eng., concluding the rich, tragic hist. of Estonian poetry in exile.

In Soviet Estonia, the Stalinist poetry of Juhan Smuul (1922–71) demonstrated professionally crafted eloquence. Other pre-Soviet poets were persecuted: Talvik died in a Siberian labor camp, his gravesite unknown. Alver refused to cooperate with the Soviets, earning the label of "formalist," which barred publications until the 1960s; she was a moral compass for emerging poets. Debora Vaarandi (1916–2007) broke from her earlier Stalinist praise poetry in 1957, reviving lyrical attention to "simple things." Alver and other

Arbujad expelled from the Writers Union in the 1940s were rehabilitated; among them was August Sang (1914–69), whose humane, self-deprecating poetry signaled a "new beginning."

After Stalinism, a revival of poetry was spearheaded by Jaan Kross (1920–2007), writing in an Aesopian style, and by Artur Alliksaar's (1923–66) surrealist-absurdist wordplay. From 1959 to 1961, Ain Kaalep (b. 1926), notable for creating Estonian equivalents of cl. Gr. and Lat. meters, precipitated a public debate over *free verse; the poetry of Kross and of Ellen Niit (b. 1928) was also accused of displaying "decadent tendencies." The mid-1960s witnessed existential despair and the mysticism of nature, followed by a return to formal verse, *irony, and *surrealism in the 1970s. Hando Runnel (b. 1938) confronted the imminent destruction of the Estonian nation through Sovietization. Jaan Kaplinski's (b. 1941) austere, epiphanic free verse opened windows to Buddhism and ecological harmony. Viivi Luik's (b. 1946) mystical nature poetry shifted in the 1970s to express muted rage bordering on despair. The polyphonic lyricism of Paul-Eerik Rummo (b. 1942), the ironical personae employed by actor Jüri Üdi (Juhan Viiding, 1948–95), and the masterfully crafted, reserved love poetry of Doris Kareva (b. 1958) still hold their power. New works by these authors who emerged during the Soviet "thaw" are major cultural events today. In the Soviet period, an explicit distance between poet and lyric first person protected authors from accusations of disloyalty if their works contained subversive ideas; Kaplinski's intensely personal poems reconnected author and works. Poetry's status as semi-sacred ritual dissolved with the end of censorship in the late 1980s, and metaphorical lang. of tragic intonations gave way to antipoetry or metapoetry, with the occasional comic twist.

Under the Soviets, Runnel's and Rummo's censored poetry circulated in ms.; a more radical underground poetry appeared in the mid-1980s, when Matti Moguči (pseud. of Priidu Beier, b. 1957), produced three volumes of obscene and offensive poems, among them the ironic "Hymn to the KGB." In the 1990s, Sven Kivisildnik's (b. 1963) "politically incorrect" parodies desacralized Rummo and other prophets of the Soviet period. Pronouncing himself a "national poet," he wrote aggressive, sarcastic, and innovative haiku that rails against the market economy and commercialism. The mercilessly honest fs (pseud. of Indrek Mesikapp, b. 1971) continues trads. of social crit., but he is above ground, a recipient of national poetry awards.

In recent decades, a new generation has stretched the limits of physical form, publishing in virtual hypertext, on beer-bottle labels, and even in a deck of playing cards doubling as an anthol. of new poetry. Valdur Mikita's (b. 1970) ironic poems force a reader to interpret pictograms. Poetry has merged with song in punk, rap, slam, and improvised *regilaul* performances; some argue that performers such as Tõnu Trubetsky (b. 1963) belong to pop culture, not poetry. Poets today play with a mixture of langs. and orthographies, melding together high and low style, folk poetry and mod. slang. *Ethnofuturism*, a fluid term invented by Karl Martin Sinijärv (b. 1971), embraces a new current that joins archaic, uniquely Estonian form or content with futuristic content or form. Kauksi Ülle's (b. 1962) poems in Võro, the lang. or dialect of southern Estonia, are emblematic. On the other hand, Margus Konnula (b. 1974) in *Tarczan* (1998) presents the mass-culture, cosmopolitan Tarzan in the national, archaic form of the 19th-c. epic *Kalevipoeg*; neither hero nor form offers a satisfactory frame for Estonian poets gazing into their lit.'s future. The future foundations, however, are clearly intertextual. Hasso Krull's (b. 1964) "Meter and Demeter: An Epic" (2004) experiences in 100 stanzas the destruction of the world by deluge and the creation of the world that follows or precedes, in the myths of many nations and epochs. Its untranslatable medium contains multiple allusions to Estonian literary trad., from *regilaul* to Kaplinski, connected by rhythms, sounds, and grammatical concepts available only in the Estonian lang., at times merging future, present, and past tense:

> kui lõpeb vihm
> siis on lõppenud kõik
> nii lõppenud et ainult vesi on
> alguses ikka veel olemas
>
> (When the rain ends
> then all has/will have ended
> so ended that only water is/will be
> remaining in the beginning)

■ **Anthologies**: *An Anthology of Modern Estonian Poetry*, ed. W. K. Matthews (1953); *Kalevipoeg*, ed. J. Kurman (1982); *Contemporary East European Poetry*, ed. E. George (1985); *Ilomaile*, ed. J. Kurrik (1985); *Sõnarine*, ed. K. Muru, 4 v. (1989–95); *Varjatud ilus haigus*, ed. K. Pruul (2000); *Windship with Oars of Light*, ed. D. Kareva (2001), and *Six Estonian Poets in Translations of Ants Oras* (2002); *Anthology of Estonian Traditional Music*, ed. H. Tampere et al. (2003)—field recordings of folk songs with Eng. trans.; *A Sharp Cut*, ed. H. Krull (2005), http://www.estlit.ee/public/A_Sharp_Cut.pdf.
■ **Criticism and History**: W. F. Kirby, *The Hero of Esthonia*, 2 v. (1895)—on *Kalevipoeg*; W. K. Matthews, "The Estonian Sonnet," *Slavonic and East European Review* 25 (1946–47); E. Nirk, *Estonian Literature* (1987); E. Annus et al., *Eesti kirjanduslugu* (2001); I. Tart, *Eestikeelne luuleraamat 1638–2000* (2002)—statistical poetic analysis of 4,887 books by 933 authors; M. Väljataga, "Vee uputuste vahel," *Eesti Express* (Feb. 9, 2004); A. Annist, *Friedrich Reinhold Kreutzwaldi Kalevipoeg* (2005); *Estonian Literary Magazine*, http://elm.einst.ee; *Looming*—annual poetry surveys in March issue; Estonian Literature Centre, http://www.estlit.ee.

A. ORAS; I. IVASK; G. ŠMIDCHENS

**ESTRIBILLO.** A *refrain in Sp. lyrics and ballads that apparently originated in the *zéjel*, of Ar. origin. The zéjel came through the Galician-Port. to the Sp. court lyric in the 14th c., where it developed into the *cantiga*, which, in turn, produced various types of poems during the pre-Ren. period. In the early period, the *estribillo* was the introductory stanza—stating the theme and often called *cabeza* or *texto*—of a poem and was repeated at the end of each stanza of the poem; cf. the Eng. *burden. Later, it is sometimes found only at the end of each stanza.
■ Le Gentil; Y. Malkiel, "Spanish *estribillo* 'refrain': Its Proximal and Distal Etymologies," *Florilegium Hispanicum*, ed. J. S. Geary et al. (1983); Navarro.

D. C. CLARKE

## ETHIOPIA, POETRY OF

I. Folk Poetry
II. Church-inspired Poetry
III. Modern Poetry

Ethiopian poetry can be divided into three groups: traditional folk songs and poetry; church-inspired poetry; and mod. poetry. After Ethiopia became officially Christian in the early 4th c., it established educational institutions that standardized rules for poetic creation and influenced both traditional and mod. poetry.

**I. Folk Poetry.** Folk poetry is found in all of Ethiopia's approximately 80 cultural groups and langs., although most of what exists in print is in the national lang., Amharic, and the northern lang. Tigrinnya. Professional singer-poets (*azmari*) are admired for their ability to compose songs on the spur of the moment, commenting on day-to-day matters. *Ballads are rare; short, pithy poems are more common and popular. The most common kinds of folk poetry are the following:

(a) love songs, often expressing nostalgia for a desired girl or woman, such as a *lament written by a local governor when he received news that his wife had taken a lover;

(b) *dirges, mostly performed in standardized form by professional wailing women, although specific poems about the dead person are often composed by members of the bereaved family;

(c) songs celebrating important historical events. These are plentiful in so-called royal chronicles, which have been written since the 13th c.;

(d) imperial praise songs; sometimes also songs mocking an unpopular emperor, e.g., Téwodros II;

(e) martial songs (*shillela* and *fukkera*), which are performed either by warriors or by hired minstrels and which consist of boasts about heroic deeds;

(f) litigation in poetic form. There was a time when plaintiff and defendant conducted their own cases in court in poetic form, and the one who impressed and pleased the listeners most won the case, irrespective of right or wrong;

(g) *occasional verse by professional singers, who compose songs and also sing and play an instrument (mostly the one-stringed violin, *krar*). They often improvise and comment on a situation as it occurs, in some cases composing songs on behalf of competing groups, e.g., of two men who both want the same woman; but political messages may also be passed on in this way, often in cryptic form. The cryptic form in such contexts is usually a vulgarized application of what is called the "wax and gold" (*sem-inna-werq*) method of writing poetry developed in ecclesiastical institutions of learning (see below), based on puns and double meanings. Ambiguity has served the need for secrecy often associated with political power in Ethiopia, where too-open expressions of opinions and sentiments could be risky.

**II. Church-inspired Poetry.** *Qiné*, or church-inspired poetry, is both religious and secular, distinguished by form rather than content. It is primarily written in Geez (old Ethiopic) and Amharic. Such poems are named after their forms (depending on the number of syllables in a line and the number of lines in the poem). The originator of this poetic form is commonly believed to be St. Yaréd, who lived in the holy city of Aksum in the 6th c.; but some of the religious poetry beloved in Ethiopia is ascribed to St. Efrem of Edessa, who lived in the 4th c. and translated into Geez. Qiné was further developed in the Amhara culture from the 16th c. or somewhat earlier. Prominent qiné poets include Yohannis Geblawî (15th c.), Tewaney (16th c.), and Kifle-Yohannis (17th c.).

Before Western models of mod. education became common in Ethiopia (primarily during the reign of Emperor Haile Selassie, 1930–74), most Ethiopians who sought an education went to religious institutions called "church" or "priest schools" or to monastic schools for higher learning, where they could learn to appreciate and create qiné. A prominent feature of this poetry is the use of "wax and gold." Its basis is the Monophysite conception of Christ professed by the Ethiopian national church. In this belief, Christ was God and man, but his manhood was only a shell that hid his real, divine essence. The poetry framed on this model is not only ambiguous but also contains a superficial meaning (the wax) that "hides" the genuine message (the gold). The rules of this poetry are complicated and take years to master. Main centers for teaching this type of poetry are found in the provinces of Gojjam (at Gonj, Weshira, and Méch'a), Begémdir (at Ch'ereqa in Dawint, and in the town of Gonder), Wello (at Tabor in Sayint), and Lasta (at Abdiqom in Wadla). The main forms of qiné have names according to how many syllables there are in a line (e.g., Gubaé Qana, 4+4; Ze-Amlakîyyé, 4+4+4; Wazéma, 6+4+4+3+3; Meweddis, 9+4+5+3+3, etc.; there are 13 main forms). There are two different main styles of qiné, taught in the schools of Gonj and Wadla, respectively.

Religious poetry is found, e.g., in parts of the *Diggwa*, which contains songs for Lent, ascribed to St. Yaréd; *Zimmaré*, sung after Mass; *Mewasît*, which are prayers for the dead; *Qiddasé*, sung during Mass but containing also the Hourly Prayers, the Horologium (*satat/seatat*); *Selamta*, songs of praise to God and hom-

age to saints. There is no congregational singing in this church, and the songs/hymns are mostly performed by church-educated but unordained persons known as *debtera*; but there are also occasions (mainly on public religious holidays) when priests perform songs accompanied by drums and sistra, and the rhythm is beaten with prayer-staffs, while the priests dance on the pattern of OT Levites.

St. Yaréd is believed to have both composed hymns and set them to music. The Ethiopian church is conservative and has preserved old songs with little innovation in its liturgies or *anaphoras (of which the church has 14); but new poetry is constantly being made in other contexts. Here the secular use of the poetic styles developed in monastic institutions is marked. A well-known name among church-trained people who used the "wax and gold" model both for serious poetry and in other contexts was *Aleqa* (scholar) Gebre-Hanna Gebre-Mariyam, who was in the service of several emperors in the 19th c. Many of Ethiopia's foremost mod. poets have also been exposed to this kind of poetry and use it (sometimes somewhat freely) in their modernized poetry.

**III. Modern Poetry.** Ethiopia was only marginally influenced by the colonial movement and, thus, has kept much more of its traditional culture than the rest of Africa. Mod. Ethiopian poetry has received significant influences from outside, esp. the West and mostly from poetry written in Eng. but also to some extent Fr. and It. However, even the most Westernized poets have retained strong traditional elements, not least as this was passed on by church institutions. Among the foremost mod. poets is Kebbede Mikaél (1914–98), whose first foreign lang. was Fr. and who did not attend Ethiopian church schools. He wrote nationalistic poems (and may be regarded as a forerunner of *Negritude poetry) in opposition to the It. invasion and occupation of Ethiopia (1935–41). Mengistu Lemma (1928–88) was educated in both church and mod. schools and became an advocate of the socialist revolution of 1974. He has more humor in his poems than is common in Ethiopian writers. One of the foremost mod. poets, more experimental and more influenced by foreign models than those mentioned above, was S'eggayé (Tseggaye) Gebre-Medhin (1936–2006). Because he coined new Amharic words based on old Ethiopic as well as Eng. roots or ideas, his poetry is often considered difficult but of a high artistic order. Debbebe Seyfu (1950–2000), often inspired by visions of a more prosperous Ethiopia, also often played on words in keeping with the "wax and gold" device. A poet of a lighter kind was Afeqerq Yohannîs (1927–80), whose poems were much read and sung by Ethiopia's most popular singers. Almost all poets, and writers generally, in Ethiopia are men, but a few women authors are coming up, incl. the pioneer Siniddu Gebru (1916–2009), though she published only one book of poetry.

Poetry is popular in Ethiopia, and many try their hands at it, often in praise of the ruler or prevailing ideologies. Western churches have put down roots in Ethiopia and introduced congregational singing. The quality often shows more enthusiasm than talent, but dedicated and capable poets are not lacking, even with limited opportunities to express rebellious ideas. Ethiopian poetry is usually idealistic, expressing hope for the country and encouraging fellow Ethiopians to promote the best interests of their native land. Poets of note in more recent years include Aseffa Gebre-Mariyam Tesemma (b. 1935), the author of the national *anthem, and Aberra Lemma (b. 1953).

■ E. Littmann, *Die altamharischen Kaiserlieder* (1914); Hiruy Welde-Sillasé, *Mis'hafe qiné* (1926), and *Iné-nna wedajocché* (1935); Mahteme-Sillasé Welde-Mesqel, *Amarinnya qiné* (1955); M. Kamil, *Amharische Kaiserlieder* (1957); Haddis Alemayyehu, *Fiqr iske meqabir* (1965); Habte-Mariyam Werqineh, *T'intawî ye-Îtyopiya timhirt* (1970); R. K. Molvaer, *Tradition and Change in Ethiopia: Social and Cultural Life as Reflected in Amharic Fictional Literature ca. 1930–1974* (1980); Mengistu Lemma, *Yegi'iz qinéyat, yenne t'ibeb qirs* (1987); Gebre-Igziabiher Elyas and R. K. Molvaer, *Prowess, Piety and Politics: The Chronicle of Abeto Iyasu and Empress Zewditu of Ethiopia (1909–1930)* (1994); R. K. Molvaer, *Socialization and Social Control in Ethiopia* (1995); "About the Abortive Coup Attempt in Addis Abeba from 5 Tahsas to 8 Tahsas 1953 (14–17 December 1960)," *Northeast African Studies* 3 (1996); *Black Lions: The Creative Lives of Modern Ethiopia's Literary Giants and Pioneers* (1997); and "Siniddu Gebru: Pioneer Woman Writer, Feminist, Patriot, Educator, and Politician," *Northeast African Studies* 4 (1997); Ayele Bekerie, *Ethiopic: An African Writing System: Its History and Principles* (1997); R. K. Molvaer, "The Achievement of Emperor Téwodros II of Ethiopia (1855–1868): From an Unpublished Manuscript by *Aleqa* Tekle-Îyesus ('*Aleqa* Tekle') of Gojjam," *Northeast African Studies* 3 (1998); "Afewerq Yohannis and Debbebe Seyfu: Notes on Ethiopian Writers of the Late Twentieth Century," *Northeast African Studies* 6 (1999); and "Some Ethiopian Historical Poems," *Aethiopica* 9 (2006).

R. K. Molvaer

**ETHNOPOETICS** Gr. *ethnos*, "nation"; and *poiēsis*, "creation, a making-process." The term was coined in 1968 by the poet and anthologist Jerome Rothenberg in collaboration with George Quasha as a parallel term to "ethnomusicology." Thus, to paraphrase a cl. definition of the latter, ethnopoetics could be said to comprise "the study of social and cultural aspects of [poetry] in local and global contexts" (Pegg). Ethnopoetics, which emerged in the 1960s and 1970s, generally refers to the develop. of an interest among poets and scholars, esp. anthropologists, in (1) a hypothetical worldwide body of poetry, equivalent in value, that included materials heretofore deemed crude, "primitive," or "uncivilized," such as folk poetry and oral trads., shamanistic incantations, anonymously or collectively composed works, and other nonliterary verbal events saturated with meaning for their particular cultures; (2) the humanistic and expressive value of alternative (poetic, e.g.) ethnographic writing; and, in response to the decentralization of "highbrow" art in the post-1968 academic curriculum, (3) the study of and/or

participation in poetry movements, poetic practices and activities, and bodies of work that reflected the lives and aspirations of politically or socioeconomically underrepresented members of the world's many communities, as well as in underrepresented aspects (hidden social hurts and hists., collective origins, and so forth) of more traditionally canonical verse. Most broadly, the movement sought to locate poetry and the poetic in a global range of utterances and local expressive practices, focusing initially on the collection, trans., and sometimes emulation by Western (esp. U.S.) scholars and poets of indigenous verbal artifacts as "poetry." The intentions were to acknowledge the cultural and aesthetic sophistication of these expressions, to introduce the Western literary establishment to these powerful cultural writings, and to declare them equal in significance and achievement to the canon of poetic masterpieces by individuated and revered poets. Major participants in the movement have included Rothenberg and Quasha; anthropologists Dell Hymes, Barbara Tedlock, and Dennis Tedlock (also a poet and literary trans., of, among other texts, the Mayan *Popol Vuh*); linguistics scholar Ulli Beier; poets Armand Schwerner, Charles Stein, and Nathaniel Tarn (who also holds a doctorate in anthropology); and others who translated, wrote, anthologized, or otherwise edited jours. and books showcasing the traditional praise songs, incantations, verbal ceremonies, or individual poems of indigenous people and poets writing with an awareness of their ethnic trads. One of the major tenets of the movement, stated in the first issue of the jour. *Alcheringa*, a key publication, was "to combat cultural genocide in all of its manifestations" (Rothenberg and Tedlock, 1975); emphasis on the "tribal" as a concept and a specific social formation and of a vatic or bardic understanding of poetics permeates much of the movement's discourse.

Critiques of ethnopoetics have arisen in response to theoretical revisions of both "nationalism/ethnicity" and "poetry"—the two primary components of the neologism. "Nation" has been complicated by "postnationalism," "ethnicity" by "hybridity," and "poetry" by "poetries" and by critical approaches that do not attend to distinctions in genre. Until the late 1980s and 1990s, ethnopoetics primarily consisted of efforts by Western, majority-culture poets and scholars to bring globally underrepresented poetries to the attention of other Western, majority-culture poets and scholars under the banner of an avant-garde modernist universalism (ethnopoetics claims kinship with the Western avant-garde's attraction to "primitivism"), coupled with a desire to heal cultural damage. However, some postcolonial critics later faulted ethnopoetics for cultural imperialism and a failure to put such works in their appropriate historical and political context. The tendency of ethnopoetics to find similarities across cultures conflicted with the poststructuralist emphasis on difference and incommensurability, as well as skepticism about the distinction between oral and written trads.

A wider understanding of ethnopoetics might consider the historical and intellectual relationship between ethnography and poetry/poetics, incl. (1) poetry or poetic writing by ethnographers (incl. Ruth Benedict, Renato Rosaldo, Edward Sapir, Michael Taussig, Ruth Behar, Susan Stewart, and others) that embodies or thematizes elements common to both ethnographic and literary inquiry, such as the experience of ling. and cultural defamiliarization, the participant-observation method of fieldwork, cultural documentation, the problem of "self"-positioning, and the ethics and violence of representation; (2) repoliticized scholarship and creative work by indigenous or ethnic subjects and communities about themselves that portray their own complexity as not merely tribal or ethnic but also as cosmopolitan, hybrid, or multi-influenced aesthetic and social agents; and (3) continued exploration of "cultural poetics" as a valid mode of scholarly inquiry, and the need for social engagement in poetic praxis.

■ **Critical Studies**: *Modern Poetry from Africa*, ed. U. Beier and G. Moore (1962); *Technicians of the Sacred*, ed. J. Rothenberg, 2d ed. (1985), and *Shaking the Pumpkin* (1972); J. Rothenberg and D. Tedlock, "Statement of Intention," *Alcheringa* 1 (1975); R. Finnegan, *Oral Poetry* (1980); D. Tedlock, *The Spoken Word and the Work of Interpretation* (1983); *Symposium of the Whole*, ed. J. Rothenberg (with D. Rothenberg) (1985); M. Taussig, *Mimesis and Alterity* (1992); B. Tedlock, *The Beautiful and the Dangerous* (1992); S. Stewart, *On Longing* (1993); *Poems for the Millennium*, ed. J. Rothenberg and P. Joris, 3 v. (1995–2008); S. Hartnett and J. Engels, "'Aria in Time of War': Investigative Poetics and the Politics of Witnessing," in *The SAGE Handbook of Qualitative Research*, ed. N. Denzin and Y. Lincoln (2005); M. Taussig, *Walter Benjamin's Grave* (2006); K. Stewart, *Ordinary Affects* (2007).

■ **Journals**: *Alcheringa*; *A Gathering of the Tribes*; *Cultural Anthropology*; *XCP: Cross-cultural Poetics*; *Tropiques*.

■ **Web Sites**: C. Pegg, "Ethnomusicology," *Grove Music Online*, ed. L. Macy, http://www.grovemusic.com; UbuWeb: Ethnopoetics, http://www.ubu.com/ethno.

M. Damon

**ETHOS** (Gr., "custom," "character"). In cl. rhet., one means of persuasion: an audience's assessment of a speaker's moral character (e.g., honesty, benevolence, intelligence) primarily as reflected in the discourse, although at least secondarily dependent on the speaker's prior reputation. In the *Rhetoric* 1:1356a, Aristotle distinguishes three ways of achieving persuasion: ethical (*ethos*), emotional (*pathos*), and logical (*logos*); and although he comes close to affirming ethos as the most potent means of persuasion, he gives it the least theoretical devel.; that devel. must for the most part be traced outside rhet., in the works of moral philosophers on virtue. From the standpoint of education, however, ethos became historically the most widely addressed principle of rhet., as theorists from the Sophists through the Ren. humanists made the study of ethics a central means of preparing students for civic responsibilities. Along with pathos, ethos serves to distinguish rhet.'s inclusive concerns from dialectic's more exclusive concentration on formal validity in logos. Although ethos centers in the speaker and pathos in the audience, the force of ethos consists in arousing *emotions; and the nature of pathos, or what emotions can be aroused, depends on the character of their host.

This conceptually close relation between ethos and pathos is evident not only in cl. rhetorical treatises but in the long trad. of writing *"characters." This literary genre, comprised of short disquisitions on personality types and behaviors, originated with Aristotle's pupil Theophrastus and achieved high popularity in the Ren. The devel. of "humoral psychology" and such works as Ben Jonson's *Every Man in His Humour* further reveal the traditionally close union of ethos and pathos (see HUMORS). From the standpoint of rhet., ethos in poetry bears obvious relations to *persona and authorial identity: ethos is, in sum, the strategic rationale of both, a determinant of the audience's response to the speaker or speakers in a text as well as to the artist as speaker of a text, investing the latter speaking role with something of the ethos-driven quality of *auctoritas*, famously described by Virgil as belonging to that orator who, "influential in piety and deeds," can rule the ignoble mob with words (*Aeneid* 1.148–53). Among mod. critics, ethos has figured in the discussion of such subjects as the distinction between dramatized and undramatized speakers, or between dramatic *monologues and *lyric poems, as well as in discussions of the morality of impersonal narration and the character of implied authors.

*See* RHETORIC AND POETRY.

■ M. Joseph, *Shakespeare's Use of the Arts of Language* (1947), ch. 5, 9; G. T. Wright, *The Poet in the Poem* (1962); E. Schütrümpf, *Die Bedeutung des Wortes éthos in der Poetik des Aristoteles* (1970); Group μ, ch. 6; S. Greenblatt, *Renaissance Self-Fashioning* (1980); W. Booth, *The Rhetoric of Fiction*, 2d ed. (1983); C. Gill, "The *Ethos*/Pathos Distinction in Rhetorical and Literary Criticism," *CQ* 34 (1984); W. Booth, *The Company We Keep* (1988); J. M. May, *Trials of Character: The Eloquence of Ciceronian Ethos* (1988); Corbett, esp. 80–86; E. Schütrumpf, "The Model for the Concept of *Ethos* in Aristotle's *Rhetoric*," *Philologus* 137 (1993); Lausberg; *Ethos et pathos: Le statut du sujet rhétorique*, ed. F. Cornilliat and R. Lockwood (2000); R. Amossy, "*Ethos* at the Crossroads of Disciplines: Rhetoric, Pragmatics, Sociology," *PoT* 22 (2001); F. Woerther, "Aux origines de la notion rhétorique d' 'èthos,'" *Revue des Études Greques* 118 (2005); D. Randall, "*Ethos*, Poetics, and the Literary Public Sphere," *MLQ* 69 (2008).

T. O. Sloane

**EUPHONY** (Gr., "good sound"). Euphony, particularly in dramatic works and poetry, is a smoothness and harmony of sounds that are agreeable to the ear and pleasing in the physical act of pronouncing them or in the mental act of their unvoiced performance.

John Milton begins his elegiac "Lycidas" with euphony's engaging calmness, "Yet once more, O ye Laurels, and once more, / Ye Myrtles brown, with ivy never sere," before turning to the more rugged sounds of *cacophony, the opposite of euphony, as he speaks of his own poetry's unmellowed maturity: "I come to pluck your berries harsh and crude."

Sometimes it is difficult to determine the part played by such sound effects. Reader/performers of the final line of Elizabeth Barrett Browning's sonnet that begins "How do I love thee? Let me count the ways" are unlikely to experience cacophony in "I shall but love thee better after death"—even though the line contains the same *sh, b, d,* and *r* sounds as Milton's dissonant line about plucking "berries harsh and crude." What the line says is likely to suppress possible perceptions of discordance.

Euphony is evident in W. B. Yeats's poem "Adam's Curse" when the poet praises labor "to articulate sweet sounds together," bringing the result of his own effort to our attention by means of euphonious harmonies of sound and meaning in a memorable phrase. His concluding line for "The Lake Isle of Innisfree," about "lake water lapping," is a study in the soothing lowering of vowel sounds from *e* to *a* to *o*: "I hear it in the deep heart's core."

Alexander Pope, in his *Essay on Criticism*, demonstrates that "The Sound must seem an Eccho to the Sense" with his own euphonious lines: "Soft is the Strain when Zephyr gently blows, / And the smooth Stream in smoother numbers flows" (365–67). However, Pope also notes that euphony can be overdone by "tuneful Fools," who "Equal syllables alone require, / Tho' oft the Ear the open Vowels tire" (340, 344–45).

*See* SOUND.

■ L. Bishop, "Euphony," *Lang&S* 18 (1986).

T. CARPER

## EVALUATION

  I. Authorial Intention
  II. Morality
  III. Aesthetics
  IV. Historical Representativeness
  V. Critiques of Evaluation in Criticism

*Evaluation* refers to an appraisal of the worth or goodness of a poem or of a part or aspect of a poem (an image, metaphor, theme, metrical scheme, etc.) or of a larger work or oeuvre. Debates about evaluation are often closely tied to questions of *canon. Evaluation was once considered a central task of *criticism, but its place in crit. is now contested, having been supplanted to a large degree by *interpretation. The criteria for evaluation implicitly depend on specific theories of poetry and of authorship and thus vary widely. Indeed, von Hallberg (2003) has argued that a great poem is by definition *sui generis*; thus, evaluative criteria cannot even be established in advance of the poems themselves.

Poetic values are often divided into "intrinsic" and "extrinsic" categories. Intrinsic values are used to measure the worth of a poem "in itself," i.e., in its capacity as a poem. Extrinsic (or instrumental) values are used to measure the success with which poems meet aims that do not depend on their status as poetry. Intrinsic values are usually seen as "in bounds," whereas extrinsic values are often regarded as representing an illegitimate attempt to marshal poetry to other nonpoetic, interested ends. Yet to designate a value "intrinsic" or "extrinsic" is already to make an argument about what constitutes the art of poetry, making the categories themselves subject to debate.

This article will review some major evaluative criteria and then describe critical challenges to the project of evaluation.

**I. Authorial Intention.** In "The Intentional Fallacy," Wimsatt and Beardsley lambaste the pervasive practice (by Longinus, J. W. Goethe, Benedetto Croce, and others) of evaluating poems on the basis of the success with which they fulfill the author's intentions—to express a particular sentiment, to create a particular effect, to display mastery of a form, and so on (see INTENTIONAL FALLACY). A critic evaluating a poem by the criterion of *intention judges the craft or skill with which the poet has executed a preexisting vision. Wimsatt and Beardsley assert that authorial intention is an extrinsic criterion, having no bearing on the poetic quality of a poem, and is therefore out of bounds for evaluating poetry. While intention has remained a point of critical debate, it has lost the association with evaluation maintained by Wimsatt and Beardsley and taken on interpretive associations, as the title of a key contribution to the intentionality debate, Hirsch's *Aims of Interpretation*, indicates.

**II. Morality.** By the criterion of morality, the critic examines the moral goodness of a poem's intended or expressed sentiments or its capacity to produce moral sentiments or behaviors in a reader. This criticism assumes that a central aim of poetry is to exert a moral and humanizing influence on society and is often associated with earlier critics, such as Matthew Arnold and F. R. Leavis. In later decades, however, moral crit. has also played a role in postcolonial, feminist, and ethnic studies, as well as other projects. In a famous critique of *Heart of Darkness*, Achebe asserted, "The question is whether a novel which celebrates this dehumanization [of Africans] . . . can be called a great work of art. My answer is: No, it cannot." Likewise, Rainey argues that feminist critics have rehabilitated the poet H.D. on the basis of "current moral concerns," which he considers illegitimate.

**III. Aesthetics.** Immanuel Kant's *Critique of Judgment* has powerfully influenced the study of aesthetics; following Kant's description of beauty, many critics implicitly or explicitly consider aesthetic qualities to be simultaneously subjective (located in an individual experience or encounter) and universal (apprehensible by all who encounter the aesthetic object). Aesthetic evaluation measures any number of values, incl. beauty, sublimity, aesthetic distance, *wit, sense of play, or a feeling of transcendence.

An aesthetic consideration that deserves special mention is novelty. In the 20th c. in particular, we begin to see a tendency to speak of poetry as a form of invention analogous to the inventions of science and industry. Thus, Winters writes that "a poem in the first place should offer us new perceptions, not only of the exterior universe, but of human experience as well; it should add . . . to what we have already seen." Pound goes so far as to propose the hist. of poetry as "a twelve-volume anthology in which each poem was chosen . . . because it contained an invention, a definite contribution to the art of verbal expression." Von Hallberg (2003) cites Pound and other poets as precursors to his own implication of novelty in aesthetic evaluation: "The fully realized poem in one sense sets its own terms for success. . . . Each poem [is] an isolato or wonder." As Vendler puts it, the good poem is "strenuous, imaginative, vivid, new."

**IV. Historical Representativeness.** Representativeness is widely agreed to be an extrinsic value, incl. by those who argue for its importance. It values knowledge of a particular time period, oeuvre, *genre, or other category. It is often adduced as the rationale for revising canons through syllabi, anthols., etc., to include popular lit. or work by less traditionally visible authors. E.g., Packer concedes that most popular 19th-c. Am. poetry is not "fully achieved" but argues that "[t]o study these different species of poetry . . . gives us access to nineteenth-century culture in a way that nothing else can." Such criteria may be aesthetic (representative of a popular style) or social (representative of a social or political zeitgeist).

**V. Critiques of Evaluation in Criticism.** In the second half of the 20th c., newer critical approaches presented a powerful challenge to evaluation's legitimacy as a scholarly enterprise. This was not an appeal to extrinsic values but rather a challenge to the objectivity and historical responsibility of evaluation itself. Historicist, feminist, and Marxist scholars, among others, questioned whether evaluative criteria were portable across historical periods and the human populations. Many such critics, influenced by the sociology of Pierre Bourdieu and the hist. of Michel Foucault, have emphasized the role of institutions, power, and wealth in creating social value. The historicist critic Wolosky argues that the ability to maintain dialogue with contemp. political discourses is an intrinsic feature of 19th-c. Am. poetry, implying that poetry of different periods and trads. must be evaluated each on its own terms. Likewise, the feminist critics Gilbert and Gubar have pointed out the often all too literal ways in which poetic creativity was defined as a manifestation of the author's masculine vigor. Such critics have argued that evaluation too often relies on circular reasoning, in which unexamined preexisting values are taken to confirm the greatness of certain poems, which is, in turn, used to confirm the values with which we began.

*See* AESTHETICISM, HISTORICISM, HISTORY AND POETRY.

■ I. A. Richards, *Practical Criticism* (1929); J. Dewey, *Theory of Valuation* (1939); Y. Winters, *In Defense of Reason* (1947); W. K. Wimsatt and M. C. Beardsley,

"The Intentional Fallacy," *The Verbal Icon* (1954); G. Hough, *An Essay on Criticism* (1966); W. K. Frankena, "Value and Valuation," *Encyclopedia of Philosophy* (1967); E. Pound, "How to Read," *Literary Essays of Ezra Pound*, ed. T. S. Eliot (1968); N. Frye, "On Value-Judgments," *The Stubborn Structure* (1970); R. Barthes, *S/Z*, trans. R. Miller (1974); E. Olson, *On Value Judgments in the Arts* (1976); E. D. Hirsch Jr., *The Aims of Interpretation* (1976); C. Achebe, "An Image of Africa: Racism in Conrad's *Heart of Darkness*," *Massachusetts Review* 18 (1977); M. Foucault, *Discipline and Punish*, trans. A. Sheridan (1977); S. M. Gilbert and S. Gubar, *The Madwoman in the Attic: The Woman Writer and the Nineteenth-Century Literary Imagination* (1979); P. Bourdieu, *Distinction: A Social Critique of the Judgement of Taste*, trans. R. Nice (1984); F. R. Leavis, *Valuation in Criticism*, ed. G. Singh (1986); W. C. Booth, *The Company We Keep* (1988); B. H. Smith, *Contingencies of Value* (1988); H. Vendler, *The Music of What Happens* (1988); L. Rainey, "Canon, Gender, and Text: The Case of H.D.," *College Literature* 18 (1991); R. von Hallberg, "Literature and History: Neat Fits," *Modernism/Modernity* 33 (1996); P. C. Hogan, "Poetic Universals," *PoT* 18 (1997); "A *Cambridge Literary History of the U.S.* Forum," spec. iss., *American Literary History* 15.1 (2003): see A. DuBois, "Historical Impasse and the Modern Lyric Poem"; A. Filreis, "Tests of Poetry"; B. L. Packer, "Two Histories Contending"; R. von Hallberg, "Literary History and the Evaluation of Poetry"; S. Wolosky, "The Claims of Rhetoric: Toward a Historical Poetics (1820–1900)."

N. Cecire

**ÉVORA CRITICS.** The label is attributed to 17th-c. Port. intellectuals whose activity as critics and theorists of poetry centered on Manuel Severim de Faria (1583–1655), choir director of Évora cathedral. Their activity probably began in 1615, when Luís da Silva de Brito (d. 1632) gave a lecture on poetry and poetics in Évora's Academia Sertória. But it was after Severim published a *panegyric of Luís de Camões and an analysis of his *The Lusiads* (*Discursos Vários Políticos*, 1624) that the polemical nature of the Évora critics came through in full. Manuel Pires de Almeida (1597–1655), who was born in Évora and studied at its university, soon opposed Severim's views. Writing and controversy on *epic poetics followed during the 1630s and 1640s, involving also João Franco Barreto (1600?–74), João Soares de Brito (1611–64), and Manuel de Galhegos (1597–1665). Issues included *imitation, mythology, verisimilitude, the beginning *in medias res, and the comparison of *The Lusiads* with other poems (esp. with Torquato Tasso's *Gerusalemme liberata*, 1581, and Gabriel Pereira de Castro's *Ulisseia*, 1636). The most intense polemic revolved around the interpretation of King Manuel's dream in Canto 4 of Camões's poem. The massive and very influential commentary on *The Lusiads* by Manuel de Faria e Sousa (1590–1649), published in Madrid in 1639, reflects the author's ongoing polemic with Almeida, esp. in issues such as the hero, epic form, and allegorical interpretation. All the critics named above exchanged correspondence assiduously on matters of poetry and poetics. Generally speaking, all of them praised Camões highly, but Almeida and Galhegos pointed out vehemently what they thought to be the poet's errors. The most important contributions of the Évora critics to Western poetics occur esp. when the poetry (mostly that of Camões) leads them to lively discussions of theory and impels them toward rethinking anew the inherited rules of *neoclassical poetics.

*See* PORTUGAL, POETRY OF.

■ A. S. Amora, *Manuel Pires de Almeida* (1955); H. Martins, *Manuel de Galhegos* (1964); M. L. Gonçalves Pires, *A Crítica Camoniana no Século XVII* (1982); J. C. Miranda, "Camões/Tasso: um confronto," *Revista da Universidade de Coimbra* 33 (1985); M. Severim de Faria, *Discursos Vários Políticos*, 4th ed. (1999); T. Cochran, *Twilight of the Literary* (2001); *Ulisseia*, v. 2, ed. J.A.S. Campos (2004)—for texts by Severim and Galhegos about this epic; M. C. Ferreira Pires, *Os Académicos Eborenses na Primeira Metade de Seiscentos* (2006).

H.J.S. ALVES

**EXEGESIS.** One of a family of terms belonging to the art and science of *hermeneutics, the word is used for the explanatory and critical *interpretation and elucidation and application of a text, originally an authoritative or canonic text (e.g., scripture), for the understanding of a secondary audience. A root of the word appears in Acts 15:12: "Then all the multitude kept silent, and gave audience to Barnabas and Paul, declaring [*exegeomai*] what miracles and wonders God had wrought among the Gentiles by them." But the term has often implied an esp. detailed interpretation; also built into this is the assumption that exegesis is directed to passages that are not obviously self-explanatory and need supplementary exposition or unfolding to be comprehended properly.

Historically speaking, exegesis is almost inevitably associated with the expounding of the Bible, in part because of the long-term devel. of exegesis in the West, from Hellenistic times, and incl. rabbinic commentaries as found in collections of Midrash and the Talmud. Observance of the Jewish law required halakic exegesis or guidance as to *how* the law was to be observed and applied and how transgressions were to be avoided. Exegetical operations, both past and present, include glosses and running commentary on a text—keyed to it, annotating it, and placed beside or below it on the same or a facing page —to function somewhat like a Targum or trans.

From Augustine on, it is axiomatic for figural interpretation that "In the Old Testament the New is concealed, in the New the Old is revealed" (*Quaestionum in Heptateuchum libri septem*). Augustine also theorized exegetical practice in book 3 of his *De doctrina christiana*, from a rhetorician's point of view. Thomas Aquinas cites Gregory of Nyssa on biblical rhetoric: "in one and the same sentence, while it describes a fact, it reveals a mystery" (*Summa Theologica* 1q.1a.10). The

systematic exposition of scripture in these lights culminated in the medievals' "fourfold method" of treating any given text from the Bible as having a quadruple sense—a literal (or historical) sense (*sensus historicus*) and three less literal senses: an allegorical (or Christological or typological or figural or figurative) sense, a moral (or tropological) sense, and an "anagogic" or ultimate sense.

The audience was informed, in the proper exposition of the four possible senses of scripture, of what it must know, believe, do, and expect, according to the following popular formulation (apparently by Augustine of Dacia):

Littera gesta docet, quid credas allegoria,
Moralis quid agas, quo tendas anagogia

(The literal teaches what happened, the allegorical what you should believe, the moral what you should do, the anagogic where you are going.)

Aquinas made refinements on the literal sense—in relation to what is primarily or directly meant by obviously figurative speech in the scriptures (where the vehicle is *not* the tenor, as when God's arm means not a limb but his "operative power"; see TENOR AND VEHICLE).

In the writings of the early med. theologians known as the church fathers, the three allegorical senses found from Cassian on (*Collations* 14:8) have a temporal aspect. The Christological or typological sense pertains to the "historical" Jesus, in the past; the moral sense to a Christian's moral conduct, in the present; and the anagogic sense (a second typological sense) to the destinies of the creation and the church, in the future. Insofar as events recorded in the OT are understood as signs and "types" of things to come in the NT, they are both "allegorical" and future-oriented already—and insofar as events in the NT are oriented on the *eschaton* (endtime), they can be deemed allegorical foreshadowing as well.

The Christological or second sense develops out of readings of the OT already found in the NT, i.e., whenever matters from the former are treated as adumbrating or betokening the mysteries and revelations of the latter. An obvious model here was the existence of such prophetic motifs and "prooftexts" as a New Law and New Covenant as found in Jer. 31–32, a New Jerusalem as found in Isa. 52, a New Temple as in Ezek. 40, a second Moses in Deut. 18:18, and a new Davidic king and a new Exodus in Isa. 11. The Israelite prophets promised that the God who had acted in the past would do so again. Thus, his past actions became readable as "types" of his future ones, esp. in the life, ministry, death, and resurrection of Jesus Christ and in his church and in the lives of his followers—esp. the lives of the saints and martyrs but also in the life of any Christian who had been baptized into Christ's death, died unto sin, and expected to be raised from the dead to share in his glory. Noah's passage through the Flood, the Israelites' through the Red Sea, the Israelites' and Joshua's and Elijah's over the Jordan River, e.g., could all be read by the Christian expositor as types of an initiation procedure whereby the initiate is "born again" through the application of water or immersion in it: namely, the sacrament of Baptism, which exegetes also read into the waters of Siloe (John 9).

The third or moral sense figures heavily in *parenesis*, or preaching from scripture, and in homilies. In his report of the fourfold method in the *Convivio*, Dante says this sense "is the one that lecturers should go intently noting throughout the scriptures for their own behoof and that of their disciples": that is, this sense was the basis for sermons and homilies instructing congregations and communicants in how to conduct their lives. It necessarily read scripture as applying parabolically, in the way Luke's Jesus asked his audience to read his story of the Good Samaritan: "go thou and do likewise."

The fourth or anagogic sense, which reveals a mystic or ultimate or eschatological meaning or purpose, gets added to the other three, in conjunction with the lengthening of Christian hist. and the delaying of the *parousia*, or second coming of Christ, but also in concert with a tendency in Christianity to become a form of *gnosis* or initiation into an esoteric form of knowledge—a knowledge of "mysteries." Thus, Paul at Gal. 4:24, on Sarah and Hagar: "Now these are things spoken allegorically [*allegourmena*]: these women are the two covenants," where the election of Sarah is reassigned to the church, and the diselection of Hagar (and, thus, the Hagarenes) is now applied to the synagogue or the Jews—all of whom were descended from Sarah—and *not* Hagar.

The Neoplatonic biblical commentaries of Philo and Origen had distinguished between a literal or physical sense and psychical and/or spiritual senses, where Paul distinguished between the letter and spirit of the Old Law and where apologists for Christianity discovered New Covenant fulfillments of Old Covenant promises and prefigurations. Influential in the devel. of such a fourfold scheme may have been the four levels of knowledge in Plato (illusion of appearances, opinion of impressions, deductions of reason, and participation in the Forms), and the four senses of causation in Aristotle (material, instrumental or efficient, formal, and final). Thus, the Platonic kind of knowledge goes behind the veil of initial impressions, while the Aristotelian kind of causal explanation (for the existence or occurrence of anything) is teleological. It also seems possible that the somewhat parallel rabbinic division of scriptural interpretation into simple interpretation (*Peshat*, as in paraphrase and literal trans.), allusion or implied meaning (*Remez*), interpretive and homiletic (*Derash*), and secret, esoteric, allegorical, or mystical (*Sod*) influenced the Christian fathers. Derash, e.g., "is a subjective method which attempts to make the text applicable to the time of the exegete" (*Encyclopedia Judaica*) and so accommodates itself to the secondary audience also implied for the moral sense.

In the term *intratextual exegesis*, a contemp. biblical scholar refers to a feature internal to the scriptures themselves, for no responsible commentator can fail to recognize the echoes of scripture in scripture and indeed to hear one scripture actively interpreting another, as Luther's commentaries regularly report. But where Christian medievals and their heirs understood the OT to prophesy Christ, mod., scientific exegetes are generally concerned to keep the historical Jesus out of the immediate range of the OT's implication or intention.

By the time of Dante, examples of one or another of the four senses were more than available to interpreters and exegetes as a predictable matrix for commentary on scripture, owing to synoptic annotations and previous commentaries, assembled from and depending on patristic authorities, such as the *Glossa Ordinaria* (once attributed to Walafrid Strabo), the interlineal gloss attributed to Nicholas of Lyra, and the *Distinctiones* or encyclopedic compilations of figurative explanations of specific words. (The plurality and nominal integration of interpretations of the words in the Gospels can be most readily sampled in Aquinas's *Catena Aurea* in the 13th c. and Cornelius à Lapide's *Great Commentary* in the 17th.)

The two most common stock examples of the fourfold method are the interpretation of the Exodus and Jerusalem, and Dante avails himself of both: the Exodus in his famous letter to his patron Can Grande and Jerusalem in a long passage in his *Convivio*. For the fourth sense, Dante says, regarding the anagogy of the Exodus, "When the soul goeth forth out of sin, it is made holy and free," which really seems to be a version of the moral sense (with the old typology of Pharaoh as the devil). The anagogic sense of Jerusalem can be Cassian's "city of God which is the mother of us all" or, later, in Guibert of Nogent's variation, "the life of the celestial citizen who sees the face of God revealed in Zion" (*Commentary on Genesis*). The first sounds appropriate to a monastery under the rule of an abbot or abbess, the second more likely to have been affected by the emergence of a med. citizenry living in urban centers (Morris). But the readings agree that the anagogic Jerusalem is not Zion in Palestine but the Kingdom of God at the end of hist.

Exegetes expounding the allegoric sense, in practice, are not necessarily univocal, yet exegesis tends to refer itself to interpretations preauthorized by trad. or scriptural indications themselves. Ambrose's commentary on—or exegesis of—Jesus' refusal to rebuke his disciples' exaltation of him, where he says that, if they were silent, the very stones should cry out, insists on Jewish obduracy and hardheartedness: "Nor is it wonderful that the stones against their nature should chant forth the praises of the Lord, whom His murderers, harder than the rocks, proclaim aloud, that is, the multitude, in a little while about to crucify their God, denying Him in their hearts whom with their mouths they confess." But Origen's exegesis of the same text makes *us* the hardhearted party, while also implying a new election to the Jews' place: "When we also are silent, (that is, when the love of many waxeth cold), the stones cry out, for God can from stones [Heb. *baneh*] raise up children [Heb. *ben*] to Abraham" (Aquinas, *Catena Aurea, In Lukam*). Origen has leapt across the gap between different sayings of Jesus to suggest that the stones have a symbolic life of their own and that this needs to be brought to bear by the exegete.

Dante might have known both the above readings, when he extends the fourfold exegetical method to the reading of poetry:

> This exposition [of poetry] must be both literal and allegorical; and that this may be understood it should be known that writings may be taken and should be expounded chiefly in four senses. The first is called the literal, and it is the one that extends no further than the letter as it stands; the second is called the allegorical, and is the one that hides itself under the mantle [or *veil*] of these tales, and is a truth hidden under beauteous fiction [*or*: "under a beautiful lie"]. As when Ovid says that Orpheus with his lyre made wild beasts tame and made trees and rocks approach him; which would say that the wise man with the instrument of his voice maketh cruel hearts tender and humble; and moveth his will such as have the life of science and of art; for they that have not the rational life are as good as stones. (*Convivio*, trans. Wicksteed)

Was Orpheus a spell caster like the Pied Piper or a rhetor and persuader like Jesus addressing the potentially hard of hearing and hardhearted or the uneducated (or ineducable)? Knowing the degree of such an interpretation's preestablishment in the exegete's own culture is the main index as to whether such deductions are to be seen as an appliqué or as intrinsic—or as conventional or deviant. When interpretation has gone inside the text, as may happen editorially or in the practice and mode of allegory, the resulting internal or intratextual exegesis can oblige external commentary to become somewhat echoic—as if carrying coals to Newcastle by moralizing a song that (as Spenser's *Faerie Queene* initially announces) has already been moralized.

A contrasting term is *eisegesis*, or discovering in a text significances that are not there and cannot be justified by an honest—as opposed to a facetious—appeal to that text. When Chaucer's Friar (in the "Summoner's Tale") says "Glosynge is a glorious thyng," the preaching trad.—or exegesis as a performative art—is mocked for its abuses, as a self-indulgent, exhibitionistic, vainglorious, sterile, tangential, and shadow-chasing exercise without any genuine catechetical or homiletic effectiveness. Dante's (or Beatrice's) animadversions on fantastical and meretricious spiels by loquacious preachers or teachers as vulgar showmen imply the same censure of exegetical licentiousness and excess (*Paradiso* 29, 109–11). The partisan reading of a text to extract an ideologically, politically, or socially acceptable sense from it is also reprehended in the Qur'an: "He it is Who hath revealed unto thee the Scripture wherein are clear revelations—They are the substance of the Book—and others allegorical. But those, in whose hearts is doubt, pursue, forsooth, that which is allegorical, seeking dissension by seeking to explain it" (Surah III, 6f., after Pickthall trans.) But mod. interpretive techniques thrive on ambiguities, anomalies, *aporia, disconnects, misreadings, mistrans., lapses, gaps, suppressed information, and self-contradictions in texts; and have developed an almost neorabbinic exegetical armamentarium on their basis. Traces of the quadrivial method survive in Northrop Frye's "Theory of Symbols" ("literal," "formal," "mythical," "anagogic") in his *Anatomy of Criticism* (1957), which is indebted to Ernst Cassirer's hist. of spiritual signs and the footsteps of God in Christian thought, in v. 2 of his *Philosophy of Symbolic Forms: Mythical Thought* (1955).

In conclusion, *exegesis* is a term for the methodical interpretation (and interrogation) of texts, originally a theological kind of exposition practiced by the rabbis and the church fathers on the polysemous sacred page (as above); it has since been more widely used for the sustained application of critical and interpretive technique to any text being studied or searched for its less than wholly manifest or obvious meaning or implication, in order to give—or construct—a more exploded or unveiled or fuller view of it. The text in question is most often a more complex one, a literary or philosophic one, or one figuring in the study of the humanities and/or the social sciences.

When James Joyce says in *Finnegans Wake*, "Wipe your glosses with what you know," he may imply that the exegete needs to appeal to context to determine what a text means (or is really saying), or he may suggest that philological study of cognates, etymologies, etc., allows one to translate or understand what one is reading. But he may also come close to Frye's suggestion that not only the works of Jakob Boehme but all other texts as well are picnics to which the author brings the words and the reader the meanings. In the hist. of interpretation, the interpreter has often brought with him or her some version of the fourfold method. But where once they were Pauline, Alexandrine, patristic, rabbinic, or kabbalistic, in the latter day the lenses focused on a text can be those of the Marxist, Freudian, Jungian, Straussian, Lacanian, feminist, deconstructionist, New Historicist, etc., depending on the training, the school, and the prehensions and preconditioning of the exegete but also on his or her own convictions and experience.

■ Migne, *PL*, v. 112; H. Caplan, "Four Senses of Scriptural Interpretation and the Mediaeval Theory of Preaching," *Speculum* 4 (1929); C. Spicq, *Esquisse d'une histoire de l'exégèse latine au moyen âge* (1944); H. A. Wolfson, *Philo*, 2 v. (1947); F. Stegmüller et al., *Repertorium biblicum medii aevi*, 11 v. (1950–80); J. Daniélou, *Bible et Liturgie, la théologie biblique des sacrements and des fêtes d'après les Pères de l'Église* (1951); D. W. Robertson Jr., and B. F. Huppé, *"Piers Plowman" and Scriptural Tradition* (1951); Empson; G.W.H. Lampe and K. J. Woolcombe, *Essays on Typology* (1957); J. Chydenius, *The Typological Problem in Dante* (1958); R.P.C. Hanson, *Allegory and Event* (1959); H. de Lubac, *Exégèse medieval*, 4 v. (1959); B. M. Casper, *An Introduction to Jewish Bible Commentary* (1960); S. Mowinckel, *He That Cometh*, trans. G. W. Anderson (1954);

J. Daniélou, *From Shadows to Reality: Studies in the Biblical Typology of the Fathers* (1950), trans. W. Hibberd (1960); T. F. Glasson, *Moses in the Fourth Gospel* (1963); *The Cambridge History of the Bible*, ed. P. R. Ackroyd et al., 3 v. (1963–70); A. C. Charity, *Events and Their Afterlife: The Dialectics of Christian Typology in the Bible and Dante* (1966); J. S. Preuss, *From Shadow to Promise: Old Testament Interpretation from Augustine to the Young Luther* (1969); J. Pelikan, *The Emergence of the Catholic Tradition (100–600)* (1971); C. Morris, *The Discovery of the Individual, 1050–1200* (1972); *Biblical Studies: The Mediaeval Irish Contribution*, ed. M. McNamara (1976); M.-D. Chenu, *La théologie au douzième siècle*, 3d ed. (1976); J. Pelikan, *The Growth of Mediaeval Theology (600–1300)* (1978); P. Ricoeur, *Essays on Biblical Interpretation*, ed. L. S. Mudge (1980); J. Marenbon, *From the Circle of Alcuin to the School of Auxerre: Logic, Theology, and Philosophy in the Early Middle Ages* (1981); L. Goppelt, *Typos* (1939), trans. D. H. Madvig (1982); F. Kermode, *The Genesis of Secrecy* (1979); de Man; B. Smalley, *The Study of the Bible in the Middle Ages*, rev. ed. (1983); G. Evans, *The Language and Logic of the Bible: The Earlier Middle Ages* (1984); J. Freccero, *Dante: The Poetics of Conversion*, ed. R. Jacoff (1986); J. L. Kugel and R. A. Greer, *Early Biblical Interpretation* (1986); *A Guide to Contemporary Hermeneutics*, ed. D. K. McKim (1986); H. Fisch, *Poetry with a Purpose: Biblical Poetics and Interpretation* (1988); R. E. Kaske et al., "Biblical Exegesis," *Medieval Christian Literary Imagery* (1988); G. D. Fee, *Garments of Torah: Essays in Biblical Hermeneutics* (1989); M. Fishbane, *Biblical Interpretation in Ancient Israel* (1989); H.-G. Gadamer, *Truth and Method*, trans. J. Weinsheimer and D. G. Marshall, 2d rev. ed. (1989); *Annotation and Its Texts*, ed. S. Barney (1990)—esp. J. C. Nohrnberg, "Justifying Narrative: Commentary in Biblical Storytelling"; *Medieval Literary Theory and Criticism c. 1100–c. 1375: The Commentary Tradition*, ed. A. J. Minnis, A. B. Scott, and D. Wallace (1991); K. Hagen, *Luther's Approach to Scripture as Seen in His "Commentaries" on Galatians: 1519–1538* (1993); H. Bornkamm, *Luther and the Old Testament*, trans. E. W. and R. C. Gritsch, 2d ed. (1997); A. Grafton, *The Footnote* (1997); *The Margins of the Text*, ed. D. C. Greetham (1997); G. D. Fee, *The Exegetical Imagination: On Jewish Thought and Theology* (1998); P. M. van Buren, *According to the Scriptures: The Origins of the Gospel and of the Church's Old Testament* (1998); P. S. Hawkins, *Dante's Testaments: Essays in Scriptural Imagination* (1999); C. V. Kaske, *Spenser and Biblical Poetics* (1999); R. N. Longenecker, *Biblical Exegesis in the Apostolic Period*, 2d ed. (1999); R. Hollander, "Dante *Theologus-Poetam*," *Dante Studies* 118 (2000); G. D. Fee, *To What End Exegesis?* (2001); H. Bloom, *A Map of Misreading*, 2d ed. (2003); B. Van Name Edwards, "The Manuscript Transmission of Carolingian Biblical Commentaries," Carolingian Biblical Exegesis homepage (2005), http://www.tcnj.edu/~chazelle/carindex.htm; "Exegesis and Study" and "The Third Period" *sub* "History of the Text," both *sub* "Bible," *Encyclopedica Judaica*, ed. F. Skolnik and M. Berenbaum, 2d ed., v. 3 (2007).

J. Nohrnberg

**EXEMPLUM.** A short, embedded narrative used to illustrate a moral point. The term is applied chiefly to the stories used in med. sermons, first in Lat., then in the vernaculars, and derived from both cl. rhet. and the parables of the NT; the illustrative *anecdote is still, perhaps, the commonest feature of public speaking. The most famous source of such stories was the Lat. prose *Gesta Romanorum* (late 13th c.), but collections for the use of preachers were also made in verse, e.g., *Handlyng Synne* (begun 1303) by Robert Mannyng of Brunne, a treatise on the Seven Deadly Sins with illustrative stories, adapted from the Fr. *Somme le Roy*. A secular use is shown in John Gower's *Confessio amantis* (written ca. 1386–90), where the *exempla* illustrate sins against Venus. Chaucer's "Pardoner's Tale" furnishes the best Eng. example; not only the main story but many lesser narratives too are used as exempla of the Pardoner's text. The ME *Alphabet of Tales* (trans. late 15th c.) lists exempla under rubrics such as Abstinence, Adulation, etc. The MHG form is the *Bîspel*.

*See* DIDACTIC POETRY.

■ J.-T. Welter, *L'Exemplum dans la littératur religieuse et didactique du moyen âge* (1927); Curtius; E. Neumann, "Bîspel," and J. Klapper, "Exempel," *Reallexikon II*; G. R. Owst, *Literature and Pulpit in Medieval England*, 2d ed. (1961); H. de Boor, *Fabel und Bîspel* (1966); F. C. Tubach, *Index exemplorum: A Handlist of Medieval Religious Tales* (1969); J. D. Lyons, *Exemplum* (1990); D. Roth, "Das Exemplum zwischen illustratio und argumentatio. Zum Exempla-Gebrauch in der 'Disciplina clericalis,'" *Mittellateinisches Jahrbuch* 29 (1994); *Unruly Examples*, ed. A. Gelley (1995); *Les Exempla médiévaux*, ed. J. Berlioz (1998); J. Aragüés Aldaz, "*Deus Concionator*": Mundo predicado y retórica del "exemplum" en los Siglos de Oro (1999); H. E. Keller, "Zorn-Prüfstein der Exemplarität? Eine Fallstudie zum Exemplar und seinen Paratexten," *Anima und sêle: Darstellungen und Systematisierungen von Seele im Mittelalter*, ed. K. Philipowski and A. Prior (2006); E. Palafox, "Medieval Spanish Exempla Literature," *Castilian Writers, 1200–1400*, ed. G. Greenia and F. A. Domínguez (2008).

R. P. apRoberts; T.V.F. Brogan

**EXOTICISM.** In a narrow sense (sometimes called "pure" exoticism), the depiction of the distantly foreign or strange for the sake of novelty or picturesque effect, without concern for accuracy or comprehension. More broadly, however, *exoticism* describes any extended use in Western lit. of non-Western, esp. "Oriental," settings, motifs, or cultural references, whether for merely decorative or more serious purposes.

*Exotic* implies "outside"; hence, in Occidental poetry, it refers to what is "outside" the Western trad. In Homer, parts of Asia are presented as alien and bizarre; Aeschylus in *The Persians* and Euripides in *The Bacchae* portray Asia as (respectively) despotic and sensual, irrational and effeminate, connotations that persisted throughout later Western lit. hist. With Roman ascendancy, *Orient* emerges as a term for Asia and North Africa, associated by Virgil, Propertius, Juvenal, and other Roman poets with luxury, barbarous customs, magic, and colorful dress. In med. and early mod. Eur. poetry, the Orient is identified with Islam, appearing as Christendom's political and religious antagonist in the *Chanson de Roland*, the *Poema del Cid*, in Ludovico Ariosto, in Torquato Tasso, and in Luís de Camões's *The Lusiads*. This Orient is at once exotic and familiar, with Islam a parodic distortion of Christianity and Muslims sometimes chivalrous and sometimes treacherous, colorful, fierce, and inclined to sorcery and sensuality. In Ren. and neoclassical poetic drama, from Christopher Marlowe and Shakespeare through Pierre Corneille, William Davenant, and John Dryden to Joseph Addison and Samuel Johnson, Oriental settings—esp. such border areas as Islamic Spain and the Mediterranean—underscore divided religious and political loyalties socially and, psychologically, characters' internal conflicts between (Oriental) irrationality and eroticism and (Occidental) rationality and duty.

Several devels. foster the prominence of literary Orientalism in the 18th and early 19th cs.: the cult of *chinoiserie* in gardening and the decorative arts; Antoine Galland's trans. of the *1001 Nights* (1704–08) and its many imitations; the new interpretation of the Bible, advanced by Robert Lowth, J. G. Eichhorn, and J. G. Herder, as essentially Oriental; and the rise of Oriental studies with such important trans. as Sir William ("Oriental") Jones's *A Persian Song of Hafiz* (1771) and *Shakuntala* (1789)—all associated with (if not implicated in) the establishment of Eur. hegemony over the East, esp. the Brit. Empire over India. Picturesque exoticism becomes prominent in such works as William Collins's *Persian Eclogues* (1742) and William Beckford's *Vathek* (1786), a prose Oriental fantasy that influenced Eng. and Fr. romantic poets. At the same time, a measure of cultural relativism, enabled by the new historicism of Giambattista Vico and Herder, can be seen in Lowth's use of "Oriental" poetry to criticize neoclassical standards of taste (*De sacra poesi Hebraeorum*, 1753) and in the fabrication of an Oriental perspective for the social satire of Montesquieu, Oliver Goldsmith, and Voltaire, strategies closely related to *primitivism.

Orientalism in romantic poetry is marked simultaneously by exoticism and by the more profound cultural interest in Asia exemplified by Friedrich Schlegel's *Über die Sprache und Weisheit der Indier* (1808). In works such as J. W. Goethe's *West-östlicher Divan* (1819) and Victor Hugo's *Les Orientales* (1829), the Orient provides both a picturesque locale (as in paintings by Eugène Delacroix and Jean-Auguste Ingres) and a cultural alternative. Although the Eng. romantics were deeply interested in Asian mythologies, picturesque exoticism lay behind the popularity of such poems as W. S. Landor's *Gebir* (1798), Robert Southey's *Thalaba* (1800), Lord Byron's *Giaour* (1813), and Thomas Moore's *Lallah Rookh* (1816). François René de Chateaubriand, Alphonse de Lamartine, and Gérard de Nerval wrote poetry that reflected their literary pilgrimages to the Near East. Edward FitzGerald's trans. of *The Rubáiyát of Omar Khayyám* (1859), one of the most popular poems of the Victorian period, reflected a renewed Brit. interest in *Persian poetry, shared by FitzGerald's friend Alfred, Lord Tennyson and by Matthew Arnold, whose *Sohrab

*and Rustum* (1853) is based on the *Shāhnama*, the Persian national epic.

Thereafter, as Europe comes to be seen as increasingly dull, colorless, and mechanized, a purer exoticism, emphasizing the new, the strange, and the sensuous and associated more with China and Japan than with India and the Near East, develops in the poetry of Théophile Gautier and Judith Gautier, whose *Livre de jade* (1867) esp. inspired such poets of the exotic as J.-M. de Heredia and Charles Cros, with a later Ger. analogue in Hans Bethge. Similarly, in America the cultural interest in India evidenced in R. W. Emerson and Walt Whitman eventually yields to the exoticism of the imagist poets John Gould Fletcher and Amy Lowell (see IMAGISM), although Ezra Pound's engagement with Chinese thought and poetics through Ernest Fenollosa runs much deeper. Late 20th-c. poet-travelers like James Merrill manifest a relation to the exotic at once nostalgic and ironic, as technological advances in transportation and communications make the distant near and its strangeness familiar.

■ W. L. Schwartz, *The Imaginative Interpretation of the Far East in Modern French Literature, 1800–1925* (1927); P. Jourda, *L'Exotisme dans la littérature française depuis Chateaubriand* (1938); R. Schwab, *La Renaissance orientale* (1950); E. S. Shaffer, *"Kubla Khan" and The Fall of Jerusalem* (1975); C. Le Yaouanc, *L'Orient dans la poésie anglaise de l'époque romantique, 1798–1824* (1975); E. Said, *Orientalism* (1978); B. Yu, *The Great Circle* (1983); C. Daileader, "Back Door Sex: Renaissance Gynosodomy, Aretino, and the Exotic," *ELH* 69 (2000); T. Morton, *The Poetics of Spice* (2000); G. Huggan, *The Postcolonial Exotic* (2001); V. Bazin, "'Just Looking' at the Everyday: Marianne Moore's Exotic Modernism," *Modernist Cultures* 2 (2006); L. Morton, *The Alien Within* (2009)—on 20th-c. Japanese lit.

A. RICHARDSON

**EXPLICATION.** A procedure for interpreting poetry that was conceived and developed in the 20th c. under several auspices: in France as *explication de texte* according to principles articulated by the literary critic Gustave Lanson, director of the École Normale Supérieure, and others; and in the U.S., the U.K., and other Eng.-speaking countries under the influence of I. A. Richards, William Empson, Cleanth Brooks, and other critics whose work was identified sympathetically by John Crowe Ransom in the book *The New Criticism* (1941). Explication typically involves a statement of the argument or theme of the poem, an inventory of formal and rhetorical elements, and a running annotation of difficult or opaque items. In this sense, explication is often closer to commentary, glossing, or exposition than to a thorough *interpretation, or what is known idiomatically in Eng. as a *reading*. The Fr. explication de texte is more formalized and more attentive to authorial *intention and the social milieu of a poem than Anglo-Am. explication: a directive from the Fr. Ministry of Education in 1938 stipulates a set of practices that must be observed in "l'explication française," incl. putting "ourselves in the author's place," and concludes that "it would be illogical and arbitrary to separate, in the interpretation of a text, form from content, thought from language." The same year, Brooks and Robert Penn Warren published *Understanding Poetry*, the most influential handbook of the *New Criticism, which poses questions and demonstrates methods far more than it gives directives. Professional readers with intellectual origins in other trads. such as the Am. literary historian Harry Levin, the Czech critic René Wellek, and the Rus. linguist Roman Jakobson sometimes performed explications in the course of their historical or theoretical investigations. Closely associated with pedagogy but also a staple of sophisticated analysis, the procedure became a common currency across methodological and other divisions throughout the 20th c.

In the New Criticism, "explication is often a process of 'explicitating' the implied cognitive content of metaphors or other figures in a poem" (Strier). Working toward rendering poems intelligible, explication as decipherment attends to detail; it is perhaps a paradox that, by explaining *diction, unbraiding *syntax, observing *connotations, and confronting *difficulty in all its manifestations, teachers work to move novices away from "single-layered readings" and toward appreciation of poetic complexity (in the economy of explication, always an honorific concept). Explication's glosses are preliminary to the work of "reading for complexity," first steps before the student or reader is ready to recognize a poem's "competing patterns." Some ages in lit. hist. are nearly constituted by explication: confronted with the obliquities of *modernism, e.g., a poetry rendered almost "inarticulate" by its difficulty, readers found that "poetry must be explicated to speak" (Strier). Even so, apologists for avant-garde poetries may resist what is most characteristic of explication, the preliminary acts of recasting nodes of poetic obscurity and novelty into more familiar terms. For the Fr. philosopher Jacques Rancière, "explication is not necessary to remedy an incapacity to understand"; rather, "that very incapacity provides the structuring function of the explicative conception of the world." By this logic, explicators make themselves necessary by inventing a self-serving world split between the knowing and ignorant; "explication is the myth of pedagogy."

Today, the term *explication* is less a drawing of battle lines than it was in the heyday of the New Criticism from about 1940 to 1960. To claim to explicate a poem now is not necessarily to align oneself with a particular method or theory. If explication implies untangling syntactic knots, annotating arcane or archaic words, and identifying historical or local references, this work is in the service of interpretation, a search for complexity and richness. In its current workaday sense, *explication* is an alternative term for *close reading. Others locate the essence of explication in the explanatory addenda that scholarly editors supply in annotated eds., responses to Steiner's first kind of difficulty, "something that 'we need to look up.'" Procedures of "practical criticism" can claim a venerable, mixed parentage (incl. biblical *exegesis, *textual criticism of Shakespeare,

and pedagogical expedients for students unversed in poetic trads.). But the familiar kind of leisurely but detailed stroll through a poem that follows the usual sense of *explication*, a process of unhurried clarification and making salient, where care is taken to identify and comment on all cruxes, landmarks, or shifts of tone or figure, is difficult to find in print before the 20th c.— and is becoming scarcer in the 21st. Of course, explication will survive as long as there are readers. But as the procedure (in its guise as close reading) is now called into question by digital humanists who argue for computer-driven modes of reading, as textual crit. becomes increasingly skeptical of the possibility of a definitive ed., and as annotators are less interested in fixing than in multiplying meanings, it might be wondered whether the practice of explication that was ubiquitous and inevitable in the past century will remain so in the current one.

*See* FORMALISM.

■ **Criticism and History**: W. K. Wimsatt, "Explication as Criticism," *The Verbal Icon* (1954); Brooks and Warren; H. Kenner, "The Pedagogue as Critic," *The New Criticism and After*, ed. T. D. Young (1975); R. Strier, "The Poetics of Surrender: An Exposition and Critique of New Critical Poetics," *CritI* 2 (1975); G. Steiner, "On Difficulty," *On Difficulty and Other Essays* (1978); F. Lentricchia, *After the New Criticism* (1980); J. Stout, "What Is the Meaning of a Text?" *NLH* 14 (1982); H. Levin, "The Implication of Explication," *PoT* 5 (1984); J. Rancière, *The Ignorant Schoolmaster: Five Lessons in Intellectual Emancipation*, ed. K. Ross (1991); D. Mao, "The New Critics and the Text-Object," *ELH* 63 (1996); D. P. Britzman, "On Refusing Explication: Toward a Non-Narrative Narrativity," *Resources for Feminist Research* 25 (1997); M. Welsh, "Hypotheses, Evidence, Editing, and Explication," *Yearbook of English Studies* 29 (1999); N. L. Chick, H. Hassel, A. Haynie, "Pressing an Ear against the Hive: Reading Literature for Complexity," *Pedagogy* 9 (2009).
■ **Collections of Brief Explications**: C. Paglia, *Break, Blow, Burn* (2005); H. Vendler, *Dickinson: Selected Poems and Commentaries* (2010); S. Burt and D. Mikics, *The Art of the Sonnet* (2010).

D. FRIED

**EXPLICATION DE TEXTE**. In literary analysis, *explication de texte* may be considered similar to *close reading. It originated as a mode of analysis typical to the Fr. educational system, in which the student provides a commentary on a short literary work or an extract from a longer work. The term may also be applied to the analysis of an extract from a philosophical text.

When explication de texte was established as a way of approaching Fr. lang. texts in the 18th and 19th cs., it was, to a large degree, modeled on *prælectio* as practiced in the schools of ancient rhet., where the reading and interpretation of poetic works would furnish future orators with suitable embellishments for their speeches. Explication de texte became an official element of the baccalaureate examinations in 1840, at which time the cl. heritage and the norms established in the previous century resulted in an emphasis on rhet. The devel. of good *taste and the moral well-being of the pupil were also important considerations in *interpretation. Through the work of Gustave Lanson (1857–1934), the consideration of broader social and historical forces was integrated into the commentary of texts. The tools of neoclassical rhet. and sociohistorical analysis were, however, inadequate to the task of explicating the poetry of the late 19th c., esp. the highly self-reflexive work of some of the leading symbolists, whose practice tended to draw attention to the "material" and sonorous qualities of lang. In the 20th c., analysis of texts from this period led to a reconsideration of the practice of explication de texte.

During the latter half of the 20th c., the two terms of the practice, *explication* and *texte*, were persistently questioned, and this self-consciousness has become a significant aspect of the reading of a work. The writings of Roland Barthes (1915–80) were particularly influential in drawing attention to the problems of presuming knowledge of what a *"text" is and what is entailed by *"explication." Poststructuralist analysis (see POSTSTRUCTURALISM) tended to emphasize the "openness" as opposed to the *"closure" of the text. An open text refuses the allocation of a determinate meaning, which, in turn, engages readers, involving them in the processes of the production of meaning. In Barthes's terminology this would be a "writerly" text (*texte scriptable*) and the closed text a "readerly" text (*texte lisible*). The writers and theorists associated with the jour. *Tel Quel*, which represented an important intervention in the field of lit. crit. in 1960s France, recognized the political implications of the open text, which they understood as presenting a radical challenge to explication de texte, institutionalized as reading practice by the bourgeoisie. In the late 1960s and early 1970s, Jacques Derrida (1930–2004) worked closely with the *Tel Quel* group, and in his work, he associated the closed text with the metaphysical concept of the "book," which he argued had been superseded.

These critiques have unseated the notion that there could be a "correct" reading of any text and led to a recasting of explication de texte as an interminable, open-ended process. Explication de texte went from being the close analysis of the text in itself to the self-critical analysis of the literary object and the presuppositions of that analysis.

◼ P. Sollers, *L'écriture et l'expérience des limites* (1968); R. Barthes, "The Death of the Author," *Image-Music-Text*, trans. S. Heath (1977); J. Derrida, *Dissemination*, trans. B. Johnson (1981).

B. NORMAN

**EXPRESSION.** In "What Is Poetry?" (1833), John Stuart Mill proposes that "[p]oetry and eloquence are both alike the expression or utterance of feeling." Mill's proposition draws on a theory of expression developed in antiquity. By the time of Cicero, *elocutio* (the attunement of expression to subject matter) had long been considered indispensable to an orator in "conciliating, informing, and moving the feelings of the audience" (*De oratore*

2.28, 3.5–6). Cicero followed Aristotle (*Rhetoric* 1356a, *Poetics* 1455a) in declaring the eloquent expression of feeling essential to both rhet. and poetry, but it was Horace who first transformed this notion of expression into an aesthetic imperative: "if you would have me weep, you must first feel grief yourself" (*Ars poetica*, 102–3).

In *The Mirror and the Lamp* (1953), M. H. Abrams identifies Horace's injunction as a precursor to the expressive theory of poetry that emerged during the decades following the Enlightenment. This "radical shift . . . in the alignment of aesthetic thinking" gained momentum with the decline of cl. and neoclassical aesthetics in the late 18th c. (see CLASSICISM, NEOCLASSICAL POETICS). During this period, the Aristotelian classification of poetry as a species of *mimesis* (*Poetics* 1447a) was superseded by an aesthetic theory that stressed the primacy of the expression of the poet's *emotions and *imagination. "Aristotle . . . considered the essence of poetry to be *Imitation*," wrote J. Keble in his review of J. G. Lockhart's *Life of Scott* (1838): "*Expression* we say, rather than *imitation*; for the latter word clearly conveys a cold and inadequate notion, of the writer's meaning."

This revolution in aesthetics began on the Continent, where, in the early 18th c., Giambattista Vico's *Scienza nuova* (1725) defined poetry as a spontaneous, natural lang. "formed by feelings of passion and affection." A decade later, in his *Enquiry into the Life and Writings of Homer* (1735), Thomas Blackwell claimed the lang. of poetry to be "Words taken wholly from rough Nature, and invented under some Passion." This hypothesis was adapted and expanded throughout the century in works such as Charles Batteux's *Les beaux arts réduits à un même principe* (1747), J. G. Herder's *Abhandlung über den Ursprung der Sprache* (1772), and Hugh Blair's *Lectures on Rhetoric and Belles Lettres* (1783), but it received its most canonical formulation in William Wordsworth's Preface to the second ed. of *Lyrical Ballads* (1800): "all good poetry is the spontaneous overflow of powerful feelings." Wordsworth's declaration, which assumes *spontaneity and subjectivity to be integral to expression, became a central tenet of romantic poetics and has been invoked repeatedly in analyses of the post-Ren. lyric trad.

The lyrical mode of expression advocated by Wordsworth prevailed throughout the 19th c. In his book *Esthétique* (1878), Eugene Véron elaborated on Wordsworth's ideas by claiming that "art is the manifestation of emotion, obtaining external interpretation either by the expressive arrangement of lines, forms, or colors, or by a series of gestures, sounds and words brought under a particular rhythm." In his *Essay on Style* (1888), Walter Pater pushed this claim even further: "all beauty is in the long run only fineness of truth, or what we call expression, the finer accommodation of speech to that vision within." A generation later, Benedetto Croce's *Estetica come scienza dell'espressione e linguistica generale* (1902) adapted these ideas to advance one of the most significant postromantic theories of expression.

All poetry, asserts Croce, is lyrical inasmuch as it constitutes an act of expression; however, rather than directly representing emotion, expression manifests as an idea, or composite mental image, derived from the poet's intuition. The aesthetic value of expression is, therefore, determined by the accordance of the idea to the emotion it expresses. In this respect, Croce's theory approaches T. S. Eliot's notion of the *objective correlative as the "only way of expressing emotion in the form of art." Ernst Cassirer, one of the foremost critics of Croce's aesthetics, has disputed elements of this theory, challenging its reduction of art to expression and its failure to differentiate between expression as an act and as a mode. In *Philosophie der symbolischen Formen*, v. 3 (1929), Cassirer proposes an alternative theory of expression that extends beyond the boundaries of art to encompass the "expressive function" of consciousness.

In the mid-20th c., the lyricist and idealist poetics of critics like Croce and Cassirer were largely supplanted by *structuralism and *semiotics. An example of this can be found in Louis Hjelmslev's *Prolegomena to a Theory of Language* (1943), which adapted Saussurean ling. to advance a theory of expression based on the concept of "sign function" (the interdependence between the expression and content of a sign; see SIGN, SIGNIFIED, SIGNIFIER). The sign, according to Hjelmslev, is never simply an expression pointing to content outside itself; rather, it is a matrix of intersecting planes of expression and content, which are "coordinate and equal entities in every respect." Adopting elements of Hjelmslev's model, Umberto Eco's *Trattato di semiotica generale* (1975) characterized aesthetic expression as a type of communication. "[T]he aesthetic text," writes Eco, "represents a sort of summary and laboratory model of all the aspects of sign function"; i.e., a semiotic sequence constituted by the combination of signs and codes in a "system of mutual correlations"; these "correlations," argues Eco, structure the "aesthetic idiolect" (or "key") of the text.

*See* LYRIC; ROMANTIC AND POSTROMANTIC POETRY AND POETICS.

■ T. S. Eliot, *The Sacred Wood* (1920); W. R. Roberts, *Greek Rhetoric and Literary Criticism* (1928); G.N.G. Orsini, *Benedetto Croce* (1961); J. Hospers, *Artistic Expression* (1971); T. I. Bayer, "Art as Symbolic Form: Cassirer on the Educational Value of Art," *Journal of Aesthetic Education* 40 (2006).

G. COSTA; C. DONALDSON

**EXPRESSIONISM.** *Expressionism* refers to an avant-garde movement in the arts in Germany from approximately 1910 to 1920 that developed first and most prominently in the visual arts (painting, sculpture, lithographs, and woodcuts) before spreading into the verbal arts (drama, poetry, and prose fiction), as well as into music and film. In any medium or genre, the term has always encompassed a broad range of very different works, which has made attempts at a narrow definition of *expressionism* problematic and contradictory, esp. in the case of literary expressionism. Nonetheless, early scholarship, esp. after the hiatus of World War II, contributed greatly to recovering the works, defining

their significance, and establishing principal lines of interpretation, though expressionism was often viewed as a separate and singular phenomenon apart from Ger. *modernism, as exemplified by the figures of R. M. Rilke (poetry), Thomas Mann (fiction), and Bertolt Brecht (drama). Scholarship has since sidestepped the question of a specific definition of *expressionism* by emphasizing the affiliations and affinities of a heterogeneous expressionism with Ger. and Eur. modernism as well as other *avant-garde poetics (*futurism, *vorticism, *surrealism, and *Dada). This approach allows broad synthetic and theoretical perspectives that bring literary expressionism into the mainstream of Ger. and Eur. modernity and allow greater attention to individual, often highly idiosyncratic, writers of significance who did not fit easily into prior discussions of expressionism. The greater degrees of generality and specificity highlight the role of expressionism in Ger. modernism.

Both artists and writers of expressionism share common influences such as, above all, Friedrich Nietzsche, whether the ecstatic life-affirming side or the analytical-nihilistic side; and the art historian Wilhelm Worringer, whose works *Abstraktion und Einfühlung* (*Abstraction and Empathy*, 1908) and *Formprobleme der Gotik* (*Form in Gothic*, 1911) were read as scholarly *manifestos for contemp. expressionism, providing it with aesthetic justification and an artistic lineage. In comparison to the preceding generation of impressionism in painting, realism-naturalism in lit., and esp. academic classicism, expressionism aims for concentrated and provocative intensity of expression in each medium, which means departure from the inherited norms of composition and an embrace of nonnaturalistic representation on multiple levels. Painters such as Erich Heckel, Ernst Ludwig Kirchner, Otto Mueller, Emil Nolde, Max Pechstein, Karl Schmidt-Rottluff of the Bridge group in Dresden (*Die Brücke*, 1905–11); Wassily Kandinsky, August Macke, Franz Marc, Gabriele Münter, Alexej von Jawlensky, and others of the Blue Rider group in Munich (*Der Blaue Reiter*, 1909–12); and others such as Max Beckmann, Otto Dix, Georg Grosz, Oskar Kokoschka, Paul Klee, Ludwig Meidner, and Egon Schiele used vivid, even garish colors, large color fields, tilted perspectives, heavy brushstrokes, edgy lines, and little modeling, proportion, or draftsmanship to create magical or unsettling, satirical or apocalyptic landscapes and figures. Both painters and writers borrowed from non-Western sources, particularly Af. art (see PRIMITIVISM), and rejected cl. ideals of harmonious beauty: indeed, the opposite would lead toward truth. These artists shared cafés and jours. with the writers of expressionism (many were dual talents), as well as influences, ideals, and themes, such as alienation from society (the outsider), rejection of bourgeois norms, return to nature, and antirationalism (madness or exaltation, physical vitality or sickness, instinct and animality, sexuality). Writers added a rhetorical dimension of apocalyptic pathos and messianic fervor even before World War I.

The lit. of expressionism divides into three phases

before, during, and after World War I. Poetry, the most concentrated form, is also the most representative of the poetics: in the anthology *Menschheitsdämmerung* (Twilight/Dawn of Humanity, 1920) the poems (by Gottfried Benn, Georg Heym, Jakob van Hoddis, Else Lasker-Schüler, Alfred Lichtenstein, Ernst Stadler, August Stramm, Georg Trakl, and Franz Werfel, among others) range from rhetorical pathos, often evoking the brotherhood of humankind, to a truncated "telegram" style—the longest and shortest lines of poetry in Ger.; from darkly lyrical symbolism to brutal cynicism and rhapsodic "absolute ciphers"; from apocalyptic visions of death and destruction to grotesque satire. The principal poetic features are stark imagery and contrasts, staccato rhythms, elevated rhetorical apostrophes, and abrupt discontinuities (see HYPOTAXIS AND PARATAXIS), shared by the prose of expressionism (by writers such as such as Benn, Alfred Döblin, Carl Einstein, Kasimir Edschmid, Albert Ehrenstein, Heym, Franz Jung, Gustav Sack, Carl Sternheim, and Werfel, among others). The drama of expressionism, whether by painters (Kokoschka), by poets (Benn, Stramm), or by dramatists (Walter Hasenclever, Georg Kaiser, Reinhard Sorge, and Ernst Toller) stripped down the naturalist stage to bare essentials of decor, plot, and dialogue in order to convey anguish (the *Schrei* or scream) or mystical spirituality (*Geist* or mind/spirit) in allegorical fashion. Highly stylized and abstract stage compositions with heightened contrasts in paint, sound, and lighting emphasize the stark oppositions of characters and the importance of physical (or verbal) gesture, much of which carried over into early film in the Weimar period, as in the prototypical *Cabinet of Dr. Caligari* (1920). The politics of expressionism (both social critique and utopianism) emerged fully and forcefully during and after World War I, though expressionism influenced artists and writers on both ends of the political spectrum (Communism and Fascism). In 1934, Georg Lukács's condemnation of expressionism for its escapism in his essay "Größe und Verfall des Expressionismus" (Greatness and Decline of Expressionism), like Klaus Mann's denunciation of Benn in his essay "Gottfried Benn: Geschichte einer Verwirrung" ("Gottfried Benn: The Story of a Confusion," 1937), led to a debate over expressionism among exiles. Nazism condemned the movement as "degenerate." Nonetheless, expressionism exerted a strong influence in the arts after World War II, in Germany and beyond.

■ *Menschheitsdämmerung*, ed. K. Pinthus (1920); W. Sokel, *The Writer in Extremis* (1959); W. Rothe, *Expressionismus als Literatur* (1969); R. P. Newton, *Form in the "Menschheitsdämmerung"* (1971)—study of prosody; G. Perkins, *Contemporary Theory of Expressionism* (1974); R. F. Allen, *German Expressionist Poetry* (1979); *Begriffsbestimmung des literarischen Expressionismus*, ed. H. G. Rötzer (1976); *Expressionism Reconsidered*, ed. G. Pickar and E. Webb (1979); R. Brinkmann, *Expressionismus* (1980)—international research report; *Expressionismus: Manifeste und Dokumente zur deutsche Literatur, 1910–1920*, ed. T. Anz and M. Stark (1982); R. F. Allen, *Literary Life in German Expressionism* (1983); *Die Autoren und Bücher des literarischen Expressionismus*, ed. P. Raabe (1985); N. H. Donahue, *Forms of Disruption* (1993); *German Expressionism: Documents*, ed. R.-C. Washton-Long (1993); *Dawn of Humanity: A Document of Expressionism*, ed. J. Ratych, R. Ley, R. C. Conard (1994); R. Rumold, *The Janus Face of the German Avant-Garde* (2002); *A Companion to the Literature of German Expressionism*, ed. N. H. Donahue (2005).

N. H. DONAHUE

**EYE RHYME** (sight rhyme, visual rhyme). Two or more words that seem to rhyme visually, in that their spelling is nearly identical (they begin differently but end alike), but in pronunciation do not. Example: *rough/cough/through/though/plough*. Eye rhymes must be discriminated with care, for, although their quantity is greater than is often thought, they are a relative rarity. Many words that are spelled similarly but do not now seem to rhyme in the aural sense did rhyme in earlier stages of the lang. or do or did so in other dialects than our own; none of these is a genuine eye rhyme.

Still, poets have always been conscious of the visual dimension of poetry (Hollander's "poem in the eye"). This consciousness extends from larger effects—e.g., conceiving of the poem as a purely visual entity, in forms of *visual poetry such as pattern poetry and *concrete poetry—to smaller—e.g., playing with the visual shapes of words, chiefly in eye rhyme. Though eye rhymes certainly exist in cl. and med. Lat., the invention of printing in the West intensified interest. Poets of the past two centuries particularly have seen the correspondence of visual forms as an important strategy for expanding the domains and resources of poetry beyond those of traditional prosody.

Strictly speaking, eye rhyme is not a rhyme at all. But genuine instances of eye rhyme address the relations of sound to spelling in lang. and poetry. E.g., spelling differences in aural rhyme are invisible, whereas spelling similarities in eye rhyme are opaque: they are the marked form. *Rhyme is by definition sound correspondence, but insofar as spelling is meant to denote sound, we must both ignore it and, when necessary, pay attention to it. Hence, accurate knowledge not only of historical phonology and dialectology but of the spelling conventions of the lang. (the idea of a "correct" spelling scarcely exists before the 19th c.) is key to understanding rhyme in both the aural and visual senses. Eye rhyme thus raises the very question of the aural and (or versus) the visual modes of poetry.

■ Schipper, *History*; H. C. Wyld, *Studies in English Rhymes from Surrey to Pope* (1923); Hollander; K. Hanson, "Vowel Variation in English Rhyme," *Studies in the History of the English Language*, ed. D. Minkova and R. Stockwell (2002).

T.V.F. BROGAN; S. S. BILL

# F

**FABLE.** A brief verse or prose narrative or description, whose characters may be animals ("The Cicada and the Ant") or inanimate objects ("The Iron Pot and the Clay Pot") acting like humans; or, less frequently, personified abstractions ("Love and Madness") or human types, whether literal ("The Old Man and the Three Young Men") or metaphorical ("The Danube Peasant"). The narrative or description may be preceded, followed, or interrupted by a separate, relatively abstract statement of the fable's theme or thesis.

**I. History.** Despite suggestions that the *Panchatantra* (transcribed ca. 3rd c. BCE) is the fountainhead of the Eur. fable, the genre probably arose spontaneously in Greece with Hesiod's poem of the hawk and the nightingale (8th c. BCE), followed by Archilochus's fragments on the fox and the eagle (7th c. BCE). The first collection of Gr. fables is attributed to Aesop (6th c. BCE) and is known to us through Maximus Planudes' 14th-c. ed. of a prose text transcribed by Demetrius of Phalerum (4th c. BCE). Phaedrus and Babrius were the first to cast the fable into verse, and their works attained such popularity that fables became part of school exercises.

Phaedrus (1st c. CE), the first fabulist we may reckon a poet, imitated Aesop in Lat. iambic senarii (see SENARIUS) but also invented many new fables, recounted contemp. anecdotes, and introduced political allusions. Babrius, writing in Gr. (2nd c. CE), went further by inventing racy epithets and picturesque expressions while enlarging the formula of the genre in the direction of *satire and the *bucolic; his *Muthiamboi Aisopeioi*, originally in ten books, is in choliambics (see CHOLIAMBUS), the meter of the lampoon. A famous collection by Nicostratus, also of the 2nd c., is now lost. Avianus (4th c. CE) paraphrased and expanded Babrian models, which he enriched with Virgilian and Ovidian phraseology for *mock-heroic effect. *Romulus*, a 10th-c. prose trans. of Phaedrus and Babrius, was later versified and enjoyed celebrity into the 17th c. But the best med. fabulist was Marie de France, who composed 102 octosyllabic fables (ca. 1200) combining Gr. and Lat. themes with insight into feudal society, fresh observation of man and nature, and Gallic irony. The *Ysopets* (13th and 14th c.) were Fr. verse trans. of older Lat. fables.

The Eur. *beast epic, in particular the *Roman de Renart*, owes much to many fables as told in antiquity and in their med. Lat. forms (notably Babrius and Avianus) and to Marie. It, in turn, influenced many fables, esp. those in the *Ysopets* and in Robert Henryson's late 15th-c. *Moral Fabillis of Esope*—an innovative version in lowland Scots Eng. Beast epic differs from fable not only in magnitude and in its exclusively animal cast of characters but also in its single, mock-heroic modality.

*Bestiary differs from fable in its emphasis on the symbolic and allegorical meanings of the features or traits attributed to its subjects, animals both legendary and real.

The *Fables choisies et mises en vers* of Jean de La Fontaine (1621–95) are both summative and innovative. In the first two collections (1668), the Fr. poet adapted subjects and techniques from trans. of Phaedrus, Babrius, and Avianus, incl. Gilles Corrozet's *Fables du très ancien Esope Phrygien* (1542), which anticipated La Fontaine's use, in the same poem, of *vers mêlés*. The second collection and subsequent additions (1678–79; 1693) contained materials from Indic sources, incl. *Le Livre des Lumières*, a 1644 trans. of fables based on an 8th-c. Ar. version of the *Panchatantra*. Two features distinguish La Fontaine's *Fables* from their forerunners: first, they make thematically significant use of *pastiche and *parody across a wide spectrum of modes and genres; and second, they are systematically philosophical, setting forth, extending, and revising an Epicureanism derived from Lucretius and Pierre Gassendi.

La Fontaine was widely imitated during the 17th and 18th cs.: in France, by Eustache le Noble (1643–1711) and J.-P.-C. de Florian (1755–94); in England, by John Gay (1685–1732); in Spain, by Tomás de Iriarte (1750–91); and in Germany, by C. F. Gellert (1715–69). G. E. Lessing (1729–81) modeled his fables on Aesop.

In the first two decades of the 19th c., the Rus. Ivan Adreyevich Krylov (1768–1844) won wide acclaim for his trans. of La Fontaine and his original fables, still read for their satire and realism of matter and lang. The verse fable trad. was carried on in America by Joel Chandler Harris, who drew on Af. Am. trads. in his Uncle Remus collections (1881–1906).

**II. Types.** All fables are didactic in purpose but may be subdivided by technique into three categories: the assertional, the dialectical, and the problematic. Assertional fables plainly and directly expound simple ideas through a harmonious union of precept and example. The Aesopic trad.—ancient and mod.—is in the main assertional. Certain versions of the *Panchatantra* and other Indian collections are dialectical. They present assertional fables in a sequence where each is clarified, nuanced, or even corrected by those that follow. Problematic fables feature moral dilemmas or enigmatic presentation. Among the devices used to "problematize" a fable are omission of the thesis statement, unreliable or playful narration, subtle allusion to other literary works, verbal ambiguity, abstruse metaphors, and symbolism. Many fables by La Fontaine, Ambrose Bierce, and James Thurber are problematic because of one or more of these devices.

*See* FABLIAU, NARRATIVE POETRY.

■ L. Hervieux, *Les Fabulistes latins depuis le siècle d'Auguste jusqu'à la fin du moyen-âge*, 2d ed., 5 v. (1893–99); A. Hausrath, "Fabel," Pauly-Wissowa 6.1704–36; *Krylov's Fables*, trans. B. Pares (1921); F. Edgerton, *The "Panchatantra" Reconstructed* (1924); M. Staege, *Die Geschichte der deutschen Fabeltheorie* (1929); "Avianus—*Fabulae*," *Minor Latin Poets*, trans. and ed. J. W. Duff and A. M. Duff (1934); Marie de France, *Fables*, ed. A. Ewert and R. C. Johnston (1942); C. Filosa, *La favola e la letteratura esopiana in Italia . . .* (1952); *Fables of Aesop*, trans. S. A. Handford (1954); M. Guiton, *La Fontaine: Poet and Counter-Poet* (1961); M. Noejgaard, *La Fable antique*, 2 v. (1964–67); *Babrius and Phaedrus*, trans. B. E. Perry (1965)—invaluable intro. and appendices; H. de Boor, *Fabel und Bîspel* (1966); T. Noel, *Theories of the Fable in the 18th Century* (1975); H. J. Blackham, *The Fable as Literature* (1985); P. Carnes, *Fable Scholarship* (1985); R. Danner, *Patterns of Irony in La Fontaine's Fables* (1985); *La Fontaine: Fables*, ed. M. Fumaroli (1985)—excellent intros., bibl., commentary; G. Dicke and K. Grubmüller, *Die Fabeln des Mittelalters und der frühen Neuzeit, ein Katalog der deutschen Versionen und ihrer lateinischen Entsprechungen* (1987); M.-O. Sweetser, *La Fontaine* (1987)—commentaries and bibl.; C. D. Reverand, *Dryden's Final Poetic Mode: The Fables* (1988); P. Dandrey, *La Fabrique des Fables* (1991); A. Patterson, *Fables of Power* (1991); D. L. Rubin, *A Pact with Silence* (1991); J. Brody, *Lectures de La Fontaine* (1995); A. L. Birberick, *Reading under Cover* (1998); R. P. Runyon, *In La Fontaine's Labyrinth* (2000); *The Complete Fables of Jean de La Fontaine*, trans. N. Shapiro (2007).

D. L. RUBIN; A. L. SELLS

**FABLIAU.** A comic tale in verse that flourished in the 12th and 13th cs., principally in the north of France. While the name, which means "little fable" in the Picard dialect, suggests a short story, some fabliaux run over a thousand lines. Most are short, however, and share an unabashedly bawdy humor, focusing mainly on the body and its functions. From sexual excitation to excretory humiliation to gastronomic satisfaction, fabliaux focus on the materiality of everyday embodment. Although cartoonish violence separates the fabliau from *realism, the attention to food, sex, and feces presents an unadorned view of bodily experience. Nearly all of the approximately 150 tales that can be called fabliaux were written in octosyllabic couplets, and although a few names, such as Rutebeuf, Philippe de Beaumanoir, Jean Bodel, and Gautier le Leu, have been associated with the fabliau, most examples remain anonymous.

Much debate surrounds the criteria for defining the genre itself, incl. audience and purpose of the fabliau. First proposed in 1883, Bédier's argument for the genre's bourgeois origins remained unquestioned until Nykrog's analysis, which pointed to the predominance of noble and lyrical sentiments in the fabliaux as proof of their courtly aims. Mod. scholars tend to favor the view that authors as well as audiences were not limited to any one social class, which means that fabliaux are not united by a single thematic purpose. Despite acknowledging greater thematic diversity, Noomen and Boogaard posit a more limited stylistic range for the fabliau (they accept only 127 tales, as opposed to Nykrog's 160).

More recent crit. has focused on the fabliau's challenge to systems of bodily order, incl. gender, status, and religion. Though many tales are antifeminist in their association of women with voracious sexual desire, the same narratives illustrate female ingenuity and superiority, often over foolish or arrogant husbands. If there is a prevailing theme in the plots of the fabliaux, it is that of "the trickster tricked." Besides gender, hierarchies of social status and religious authority are frequently subject to upheaval. Priests are humiliated, merchants are bilked, and husbands are fooled. Yet this emphasis on instability extends even further: scholarship of late has investigated the impact of fabliaux on the med. written lang., with some critics arguing that the vulgar lang. of the genre called for a new literary vocabulary. Other scholars have examined narrative presence in the poems, which is often marked by idiosyncratic asides suggesting an improvised oral performance. Since many of the tale's tellers are identified with the shiftless, scheming characters of the tales, poetic production is also associated with bodily disorder, primarily through the tales' impetus to laughter.

In the 14th c., the vogue of the fabliau spread to Italy and England, where Chaucer borrowed freely from the genre for several of his *Canterbury Tales*, most notably "The Miller's Tale" and "The Reeve's Tale." Fabliau trad. continued in the prose *nouvelle*, but the influence of the older form may be seen centuries later in the poetry of Jean de La Fontaine in France, C. F. Gellert in Germany, and I. A. Krylov in Russia.

*See* FABLE.

■ W. M. Hart, "The Fabliau and Popular Literature," *PMLA* 23 (1908), and "The Narrative Art of the Old French Fabliau," *Kittredge Anniversary Papers* (1913); J. Bédier, *Les Fabliaux*, 5th ed. (1925); J. Rychner, *Contribution à l'étude des fabliaux*, 2 v. (1960); *The Literary Context of Chaucer's Fabliaux*, ed. L. D. Benson and T. M. Andersson (1971); P. Dronke, "The Rise of the Medieval Fabliau," *Romanische Forschungen* 85 (1973); P. Nykrog, *Les Fabliaux*, rpt. with a "Post-scriptum 1973" (1973); *Gallic Salt*, trans. R. L. Harrison (1974); *The Humor of the Fabliaux*, ed. T. D. Cooke and B. L. Honeycutt (1974); T. Cooke, *The Old French and Chaucerian Fabliaux* (1978); *Cuckolds, Clerics, and Countrymen*, trans. J. Duval (1982); R. E. Lewis, "The English Fabliau Tradition and Chaucer's 'Miller's Tale,'" *MP* 79 (1982); P. Ménard, *Les Fabliaux* (1983); *Nouveau recueil complet des fabliaux*, ed. W. Noomen and N. van den Boogaard, 10 v. (1983–); R. H. Bloch, *The Scandal of the Fabliaux* (1986); C. Muscatine, *The Old French Fabliaux* (1986); J. Hines, *The Fabliau in English* (1993); L. Rossi, *Fabliaux Érotiques* (1993); S. Gaunt, *Gender and Genre in Medieval French Literature* (1995); N. J. Lacy, *Reading Fabliaux* (1999); B. J. Levy, *The Comic Text* (2000); J. A. Dane, "The Wife of

Bath's Shipman's Tale and the Invention of Chaucerian Fabliaux," *MLR* 99 (2004); H. A. Crocker, *Comic Provocations* (2006).

A. Preminger; R. L. Harrison; H. Crocker

**FANCY.** The short form, common since the Ren., of *fantasy* (Lat. *phantasia*, transliterated from Gr. *phanos*, "image," and later replaced by *imaginatio*). In Western poetics, the hist., definition, and use of fancy in crit. and psychology are inseparably linked to that of *imagination, the two terms being sometimes distinguished but more often used similarly if not identically. *Phantasia* originally carried suggestions of creativity and free play of mind, a power generating images and combinations of images not previously found in nature or sense experience. Albertus Magnus uses the term this way, with *imaginatio* reserved for the static mental recording of perceived images. However, even in the Middle Ages, distinctions or inversions of the two terms occur. Thomas Aquinas uses them synonymously; in a later (failed) attempt to fix them, Joseph Addison does, too: usage did not stabilize in Eng. until the later 18th c. In Ger., a variety of terms (*Phantasie*, *Einbildungskraft*, *Dichtungskraft*, *Perceptionsvermügen*) are employed throughout the 18th and 19th cs. without consistency. In Italy, *fantasia* generally retains its "higher" stature as a creative and altering power, while *immaginazione* pertains more to a form of memory, the retention and reproduction of sense impressions. However, even here there is no rule; Giambattista Vico uses *fantasia* for both recollective and original productive functions.

In the period 1660–1820, Eur. crit. self-consciously turns to the issue of discriminating fancy from imagination. In England, despite early confusion, something of a norm is reached by the 1780s and 1790s. Thomas Hobbes employed fancy for the greatest creative range of mind, but John Dryden at least once subordinates fancy to imagination. Anticipating later devels., Dryden makes fancy responsible only for manipulation, rearrangement, and juxtaposition of images already created or experienced; in poetic composition, fancy is the power that distributes and arranges images already invented. Imagination encompasses both powers, as well as their formulation in words and figures of speech. Addison claims no difference between fancy and imagination but in practice tends to elevate imagination to a higher creative plane. As early as Lord Shaftesbury's *Characteristics* (1711), imagination is the stronger term, while fancy suggests "mental abandon," which Shaftesbury exemplifies by the same passage from Thomas Otway's *Venice Preserved* that S. T. Coleridge later quotes in the *Biographia Literaria* to illustrate fancy: "Lutes, lobsters, seas of milk, ships of amber."

In poetry, the elevation of the term *imagination* at the expense of *fancy* occurs a little later; until the romantic period, fancy is generally used in poetic diction. John Keats uses imagination heavily in his letters and in the late *Fall of Hyperion*; elsewhere, fancy may be a fickle power of pleasure ("Fancy"), a power of end-lessly novel and procreative embellishment ("Ode to Psyche"), or potentially synonymous with imagination ("Ode to a Nightingale"). It is significant that William Wordsworth consciously chooses imagination as the key term in *The Prelude*; unlike Coleridge, he generally views fancy and imagination as differing in degree, not kind.

For Coleridge, fancy "has no other counters to play with, but fixities and definites. The Fancy is indeed no other than a mode of Memory emancipated from the order of time and space; and blended with, and modified by that empirical phenomenon of the will, which we express by the word choice. But equally with the ordinary memory it must receive all its materials ready made from the law of association" (*Biographia Literaria*, chap. 13). His definition has become a touchstone in part because it captures the essence of a set of emergent Eng. and Ger. distinctions. Fancy operates without a unifying design and does not meld, transform, or newly create images or ideas. Rather, it juxtaposes or connects them in a more mechanical fashion, appealing to novelty of sense impression instead of strength or grandeur of intellectual conception and power. Often described as "aimless" or "sportive," fancy suggests a phantasmagoria of passing, fixed images, whose mingling does not mutually transform or resolve or unify them into larger patterns. John Ruskin continues to distinguish the two terms in *Modern Painters*.

In Germany, Christian Wolff, Immanuel Kant, Jean-Paul, Friedrich Schelling, G.W.F. Hegel, Friedrich Schiller, J. G. Fichte, I. G. Fichte, J. N. Tetens, and J. W. Goethe all make distinctions between fancy and imagination, some elaborate, others casual. Schelling and at times Kant parallel the Eng. elevation of imagination (*Einbildungskraft*), while others, such as Jean-Paul, echo the It. supremacy of fancy (*Phantasie*) as the highest creative power. Benedetto Croce in the earlier 20th c. retains the It. primacy of *fantasia*, the equivalent of the Eng. *imagination*, while *immaginazione* corresponds roughly to fancy as Coleridge defines it. Aside from studies grounded in historical uses of the term, fancy has become increasingly rare as a serious concept in poetics and crit.

■ *See* bibliography for imagination.

J. Engell

**FATRAS** (also called *fatrasie*, *fratrasie*, *resverie*). An irrational and deliberately obscure piece of verse that, originating in the Middle Ages, constituted a mode of licensed regression into unreason, absurdity, and nonsense in which pleasure is taken in the creative and willful defiance of sense that the verse form celebrates. It is generally lively and joyous in style, full of word play, ridiculous associations of ideas, and deliberate nonsense. Charles-Victor Langlois defines two forms: the *fatras possible,* which offers a coherent text, and the *fatras impossible*, which, like the later *coq-á-l'âne*, seems to make no sense at all. Qua genre, however, it is not the incoherence of content that constitutes the fatras but its special form: a *strophe of 11 lines, the first and last of which form a *distich placed at the beginning as the theme of the composition. This is known as the *fatras simple*. The *fatras double* is formed from this by "restating the initial [distich] in reverse order, and adding a second strophe of ten lines ending with an 11th, a restatement of line one of the [distich]" (Porter). Porter distinguishes between the *fratrasie* and the fatras, a later devel. The former is invariably composed of a single strophe of 11 lines, and its content is always irrational; in the fatras, the opening distich introduces the next 11 lines, serving as their first and last line and imparting a uniform rhythm to the whole poem.

*See* ADYNATON, FROTTOLA AND BARZELLETTA, NONSENSE VERSE.

■ C.-V. Langlois, "Watriquet, ménestrel et poète français," *Histoire littéraire de la France*, t. 35 (1921), 393–421 ; A.-M. Schmidt, "La Trésor des Fatras," *Les Cahiers de la Pléiade* 11–12 (1950–51); P. Zumthor, *Histoire littéraire de la France médiévale* (1954); L. C. Porter, *La Fatrasie et le Fatras* (1960); P. Zumthor, "Fatrasie et coq-à-l'âne," *Fin du Moyen Âge et Renaissance* (1961); E. G. Hessing and R. Viglbrief, "Essai d'analyse des procédés fatrasiques," *Romania* 94 (1963); *Fatrasies*, ed. J. P. Foucher (1964); W. Kellermann, "Über die altfranzösischen Gedichte des uneingeschränkten Unsinns," *Archiv* 205 (1968); *Poésie et rhétorique du non-sens. Littérature médiévale, littérature orale*, ed. S. Mougin and M. G. Grossel (2004).

I. SILVER; T.V.F. BROGAN; I. D. COPESTAKE

**FEIGNING** (also feynynge, faining, fayning; Lat. *fingere*, "to form" or "to make," "to mold" or "to sculpt" dough or clay; Gr. *poiēsis*). The verb *feign* derives from the same Lat. root as *fiction*, its nominal counterpart, to which it was closely related in the Ren. imagination. In Ren. Eng. poetry and poetic treatises, *feigning* denotes imaginative lit. (verse or prose) and its composition, and *to feign* means the act or art of fiction-making. *Feigning* also signified pretense or deception and, thus, supported moral arguments against poetry as falsehood. Both meanings of *feigning* are grounded in antiquity, notably Plato's indictment in the *Republic* of poetry as lies, opposed to philosophy's claims to truth. Artifice and dissembling were integral to Ren. court life; therefore, the semblance of *sincerity in the 16th-c. poet Thomas Wyatt's "hert unfayned" carried political as well as poetic import.

Chaucer represented the medieval distinction between feigning or fabling and truthful chronicle in *The House of Fame* (written ca. 1379–80), where Dares Phrygius, a Trojan mentioned in Homer's *Iliad* who supposedly wrote an eyewitness account of the war, criticizes Homer's epics as "feynynge" and "lyes." Common in Ren. poetics was the "apology," or defense of poetry's moral value, which sought to distinguish poetry from associations of *medieval romance. Arguing for the moral value of *dramatic and *epic poetry in the *Defence of Poesy* (written ca. 1580, pub. 1595), Philip Sidney positively values feigning as imaginative lit. in contradistinction to counterfeiting. For Sidney, the principles that poetry teaches extend into the public domain, where the exemplary knowledge that poetry promotes—surpassing that of hist. or philosophy—translates into virtuous action. Thus, Sidney's political imagination is structured by principles of poetic *imagination. Similarly, George Puttenham in *The Art of English Poesie* (written ca. 1579, pub. 1589) commends the poet's ability "to faine a thing that never was nor is like to be," where *feigning* denotes the superior products of *"wit" and *"invention" that allow a poet to describe things he never witnessed. *Pastoral poetry, notably Edmund Spenser's *The Shepheardes Calender* (1579), presents a fiction conscious of itself as such. Its numerous marginal glosses and the invented narrator, E. K., foreground questions of authority and authenticity that preoccupied *Renaissance poetics.

The several poetic connotations of *feigning*—faithful imitation, imaginative invention, and falsehood—demonstrate tensions in the historical debate over poetry's moral value. Moreover, in Ren. Eng., the variable spelling of *feign* (often as *fain*) and the homonymy of *feign* and *fain* (the latter as adjective or adverb meaning "glad" or "gladly, willingly") occasion considerable wordplay suggesting poetry's effects on the will (see Shakespeare's *As You Like It*, 3.3, and the first *sonnet of Sidney's *Astrophil and Stella*). *Faining* or *feigning* often connoted poetry's power of enchantment, appearing ambiguously in *A Midsummer Night's Dream* in an accusation against a designing lover who speaks "with faining voice verses of faining love" (1.1.31), inviting interplay between meanings of falsehood and seduction.

The primary meaning of *feigning* changed from the 17th c., when Ben Jonson glossed the poet's craft as "an art of imitation, or faining," demonstrating *feigning* as synonymous with poetic composition that produces "things *like* truths" but more valuable for their fabrication. John Dryden describes dramatic poetry as "feigned action," and John Milton treats *feigned* and *fabled* as literary synonyms. Samuel Johnson defines *feigning* in the *Dictionary* (1755) as both falsehood and fictionality: "to relate falsely; to image from the invention," although his primary definition cites Jonson on poetic invention. By the 19th c., *feigning* primarily referred to false conduct or forgery. The moral value of poetry became detached from the question of poetic value, and concerns about *feigning* were voiced primarily in discourses of public law and private self. Along with *invention*, *feigning* lost poetic meaning by the early 19th c.: revised eds. of the *Dictionary* omit poetic meaning in the definition for *feigning* but still include *feigning* in the definition of *fable*.

Levao theorizes the importance of *feigning* in the vocabulary and intellectual consciousness of Ren. England. Levao identifies the "joint development[s] of historical consciousness, new-world exploration, astronomical speculation, and skeptical thought" as key factors in a culture of instability preoccupied "with the nature of poetic fictions," ultimately shaping a "vision of culture . . . not as structured by eternal categories, but as a distinctly human artifact." Since the Ren., critical intervention has reframed *fiction* and *reality* not as independent categories but as interactive modes producing the "imagined" text (Iser). Twentieth-c. studies of *feigning* often sought to deconstruct binary conceptions of *philosophy and poetry (Norris).

See ARTIFACT, POETRY AS; FICTION, POETRY AS; MIMESIS.
■ A. H. Shutz, "Did the Poets 'Feign' or 'Fashion'? *Symposium* 11 (1957); W. Nelson, *Fact or Fiction* (1973); C. Norris, "'That the Truest Philosophy is the Most Feigning': Austin on the Margins of Literature," *Renaissance and Modern Studies* 27 (1983); W. Iser, "Feigning in Fiction," *Identity of the Literary Text*, ed. M. J. Valdés and O. Miller (1985); R. Levao, *Renaissance Minds and Their Fictions* (1985); C. R. Kinney, "Feigning Female Faining: Spenser, Lodge, Shakespeare, and Rosalind," *MP* 95 (1998); R. E. Stillman, *Philip Sidney and the Poetics of Renaissance Cosmopolitanism* (2008).

R. LEWIS

**FÉLIBRIGE.** A Fr. literary assoc. founded in 1854 by seven Occitan poets who called themselves *félibres*, perhaps meaning "nurslings," as their leader Frédéric Mistral explained, because they intended to nurse at the bosom of wisdom. Through the annual publication of the *Armana prouvençau* (Provençal Almanac) and later *L'Aiòli*, they strove to reform Occitan spelling, to renew the lang., to compose great poetry, and to revive Occitan culture. Although they described their movement as a renaissance, they did not seek to revive poetry in the manner of the med. *troubadours. Joseph Roumanille organized the movement, which triumphed with the publication in 1859 of Mistral's romantic epic *Mirèio* (Mireille), and again in 1860 with Théodore Aubanel's collection of love poems, *La Mióugrano entre-duberto* (The Split Pomegranate). Originally limited to Provence in the narrow sense (east of the Rhône), *Félibrige* was reorganized in 1876 to include all the Occitan dialects and regions from the Atlantic to the Alps. In 1904, Mistral shared the Nobel Prize for poetry and philology. Perhaps the most lasting achievement of Félibrige was the impetus it gave to regional lit. in France, an impetus that continues into the 21st c.

See OCCITAN POETRY.
■ *L'Anthologie du félibrige*, ed. A. Praviel and J.-R. de Brousse (1909); E. Ripert, *Le Félibrige*, 3d ed. (1948); C. Camproux, *Histoire de la littérature occitane* (1953); *Morceaux choisis des auteurs provençaux de la fondation du félibrige à nos jours*, ed. L. Bayle, 2 v. (1969–71); R. Lafont and C. Anatole, *Nouvelle Histoire de la littérature occitane*, 2 v. (1970); T. R. Hart, "La Reneissènço Felibrenco," *Journal of European Studies* 25 (1995).

W. D. PADEN

## FEMINIST APPROACHES TO POETRY

I. Early 20th-century Poetry and First-wave Feminism
II. Mid-20th-century Poetry and Second-wave Feminism
III. Late 20th- and Early 21st-century Poetry and Third-wave Feminism

Feminism has never been monolithic. Worldwide, feminism is articulated differently in different times and places and emphasizes those aspects of gender and sexual inequality characteristic of its local or national contexts. Even within a single time and location, feminists of different classes, races, sexualities, and religions have proposed conflicting analyses of patriarchal dynamics and institutions. Self-consciously articulated feminism—i.e., an analytical perspective that understands gender-based discrimination as systemic and as pervasive in private and public life—first became significant to a wide range of poets and to poetic analysis at the turn of the 20th c. in Europe and North America. Much pre-20th-c. poetry celebrates aspects of female intelligence and agency or protests misogynistic and patriarchal practices; poets such as Christine de Pizan (1365–ca. 1434) and Elizabeth Barrett Browning (1806–61) also protested gender-based oppression. These antecedents were crucial to the development of both feminism and deliberately feminist poetics. This entry focuses on the intersections of feminist critical thought with the writing and reception of poetry, particularly in the U.S. and Europe, in rough alignment with what have been identified as the three major waves of Western feminism.

**I. Early 20th-century Poetry and First-wave Feminism.** *Modernism is notable as the first literary and artistic movement in which women played major roles internationally, not just by their writing but in developing its foundational ideas—incl. feminism—and in shaping literary production through editing and publishing. While feminist poetry was not always formally innovative, feminist approaches to poetry at the beginning of the century were strongly associated with experimental modernism. This period coined the words *homosexuality* (first used in Eng. in 1883) and *feminism* (perhaps as early as 1837 in France, 1894 in Britain, and 1910 in the U.S.). By the early 20th c., women's movements were rejecting the essentialized definitions of gender that had dominated 18th- and 19th-c. thought, advocating for social change and asserting women's equality with men across a wide spectrum of intellectual and creative fields. The goal was often to degender both women and men rather than to redraw the lines of gender distinction. Early Ger. and Rus. feminisms were more socialist in their understanding of labor and more influenced by notions of essential difference than Brit. or Am. feminisms, but all claimed membership in a "human sex" and demanded greater economic, legal, and social rights for women.

Theorizing women's writing in *A Room of One's Own* (1929), Virginia Woolf (1882–1941) proposes that "a woman must have money and a room of her own if she is to write fiction"; for women to write poetry, however, requires in addition the "habit of freedom and the courage to write exactly what we think." Woolf sees women's writing of poetry as particularly difficult because she assumes that poetry is the most prestigious literary genre, the genre most closely associated with the category of "*genius," defined as exclusively masculine, and the one demanding the strongest affirmation of the writer's self, given the assoc. of lyric with a speaking voice. Yet by 1929, significant numbers of women were writing explicitly feminist poetry.

As Woolf anticipated, women were most active as poets in countries where they enjoyed access to higher education and extensive economic and legal rights and in langs. where there was a long trad. of women writing poetry. At the turn of the 20th c., the countries most supportive of women's active involvement in literary movements were Russia, Germany, England, and the U.S. Female poets in the Rus. avant-garde who wrote from a feminist perspective about gender and women's lives included Anna Akhmatova (1889–1966), Zinaida Gippius (1869–1945), and Marina Tsvetaeva (1892–1941). This surge of gender-oriented poetry was relatively short lived. Following Josef Stalin's rise to power, Tsvetaeva and Gippius left Russia; Akhmatova remained, but publication of her work was banned from 1925 until shortly before her death (see RUSSIA, POETRY OF). In Germany, the "question" or figure of "woman" was fiercely debated in literary circles at the turn of the century, both because of the philosophical trad. of an idealized "eternal feminine" seen as most significantly manifest in creative men and because of Germany's powerful women's movements. The most significant feminist poet of these decades was Else Lasker-Schüler (1869–1945), whose poetry questioned categories of religion, sexuality, gender, and race. Surprisingly, although France was hospitable to lesbian and feminist expatriate writers, its own literary scene was inhospitable to feminism and strongly dominated by men; there were no prominent Fr. female poets in the first half of the 20th c. In Central and South America, Fr. *symbolism influenced *modernismo; its poets who explicitly challenged the social treatment of women and patriarchal domination include Delmira Agustini (Uruguay, 1886–1914), Dulce María Loynaz (Cuba, 1902–1997), and Gabriela Mistral (Chile, 1889–1957). Because It. *futurism defined itself in part around the celebration of masculinity and excoriation of femininity, women and feminism played a minor role in this movement. In Portugal, Irene Lisboa (1892–1958) and Judith Teixeira (1880–1959) were among those who challenged masculinist stances in poetry and crit. during the modernist period.

With the exception of Mina Loy (who was born in London), writers born in the U.S. dominated the production of modernist Anglo-Am. feminist poetry. Gertrude Stein's publication of *Tender Buttons* and Loy's first publication of poems in 1914, along with Loy's composition of a (posthumously pub.) "Feminist Manifesto" in the same year, usher self-consciously feminist analysis into Eng.-lang. poetry. Both Stein (1874–1946) and Loy (1882–1966) understand patriarchal psychological, economic, and sexual practices as impinging directly on women's creativity, as Stein articulates in her 1927 composition "Patriarchal Poetry." During the 1910s, H.D. (Hilda Doolittle, 1886–1961), Amy Lowell (1874–1925), Edna St. Vincent Millay (1892–1950), and Marianne Moore (1887–1972) were also publishing poetry that challenged traditional gender conventions, demanded or predicted greater rights for women, protested patriarchal oppression, and asserted women's empowerment in ways for the most part implicit or understated, following the modernist preference for conveying ideas in poetry without stating them directly. E.g., Stein's *Tender Buttons* describes food, rooms, and objects of domestic apparel or use in a series of cubist prose poems eschewing standard grammar and logic. Feminist readers have found these poems to celebrate the domestic and women's sexuality, through puns and *synecdoche involving suggestive words like *petticoat*, *pink*, and *roast beef*. In her poem "Marriage," Moore represents that "institution / perhaps one should say enterprise" as part of a patriarchal system in which "men have power and sometimes one is made to feel it" and as "requiring all one's criminal ingenuity / to avoid!" H.D. turns to Gr. and Egyptian mythologies to reenvision women's agency. Stein, H.D., and Moore all redefine aesthetics from a feminist perspective, understanding beauty as complex, "wind-tortured" (H.D.), embodied best in "thorns" rather than petals (Moore). The 1920s saw an increase in attention to sexuality, due in part to psychoanalytic conceptions of the sex drive and desire, accompanied by more frank and open avowal of desire in poetry by women. H.D. underwent analysis with Sigmund Freud, and some feminist critics regard Stein's sexual punning as influenced by Freud's theories of the unconscious. Lowell, H.D., and Stein wrote *lesbian poetry or fiction, although both Stein's and H.D.'s frankly lesbian work was published only much later.

Af. Am. women of the period articulated feminism within the context of a struggle for racial equality. Gwendolyn Bennett (1902–81) and Helene Johnson (1906–95) wrestled with the contradiction of embracing both the antibourgeois aesthetic of the new arts and affirming broad-based respect for middle-class black women, countering the prevalent "mammy" and "Jezebel" stereotypes. Female *blues singers Ida Cox (1896–1967), Ma Rainey (1886–1939), and Bessie Smith (1894?–1937) wrote and sang lyrics supporting black women's economic and psychological independence and celebrating female sexuality. Through experiment in figurative lang., poetic form, and topic, these and other poets mapped a feminist understanding of the links among economic, legal, and artistic systems of hierarchy and anticipated later theorizing of gender as both constructed and performed.

**II. Mid-20th-century Poetry and Second-wave Feminism.** With the gains in women's rights occurring in many countries following World War I, the international women's movement lost some of its impetus, and feminism as such waned in cultural force until the 1960s. During the 1930s, writers concerned with social justice were most apt to express those concerns in relation to Marxism or other socialist movements or in relation to racial and religious persecution. Muriel Rukeyser (1913–1980), who later turned to feminist themes, wrote poetry primarily about labor injustice. With World War II, women temporarily gained social and economic power as men were called into the military. This trend was sharply reversed in a postwar reaction that sent middle-class women back to domestic roles. The retreat from a bold vision of women's powers that began in the 1920s and that Betty Friedan

(1921–2006) famously traces in magazine writing from the 1940s to the 1950s was evident in poetry as well; by mid-century, feminist perspectives were hardly visible. Gwendolyn Brooks (1917–2000) was exceptional for this period in publishing her Pulitzer Prize-winning *Annie Allen* (1949), with its "Anniad" rewriting the conventions of the masculinist epic. Puerto Rican Julia de Burgos (1914–53), too, continued writing feminist poetry from the 1930s to the 1950s—incl. her influential "Yo misma fui mi ruta" (I was my own path)—and Rosario Castellanos (Mexico, 1925–74) was advocating indigenous as well as women's rights by the late 1950s. The civil-rights and antiwar activism of the 1960s brought young women of the U.S. back into the public sphere and encouraged battles for social justice, incl. "women's liberation," in which feminist presses and jours., feminist poetry, and the feminist bookstores where it was sold played an important role.

The early career of Adrienne Rich (1929–2012) exemplifies the changes wrought by this second wave of feminism: having gained recognition from the male literary establishment in the 1950s, Rich struggled to perform as wife and mother of three while also producing as a poet. In the 1960s, she became involved in antiwar activism and the New Left, and her poetry began to reflect the feminist conviction that "the personal is the political" and to examine personal experience in terms of women's oppression within patriarchal society, albeit within the terms of humanism and a Jungian androgyny. For Rich, this new direction in her work required casting off the "asbestos gloves" of traditional formalism. By this time, she was directly representing her own life experiences, and by 1976 she identified publicly as a lesbian; by 1978, when she published *The Dream of a Common Language*, Rich was writing exclusively about and for women, offering forceful critiques of patriarchal society as she extended her influential self-debates about gender and sexuality.

In the early 1960s, new experimental movements had already proposed alternatives to the neatly contained aesthetics of late modernism and *New Criticism, but these New American poetries remained male-dominated. The gender-oriented perspectives of the women writing within these movements—Barbara Guest (1920–2006) in the *New York school, Diane di Prima (b. 1934) and Diane Wakoski (b. 1937) among the *Beat poets, Denise Levertov (1923–97) among the *Black Mountain writers, or slightly later, Sonia Sanchez (b. 1934) among the *Black Arts writers—often went unrecognized or were disparaged within the larger movements. The *confessional movement, in which Sylvia Plath (1932–63) and Anne Sexton (1928–74) were prominent, helped open a space for feminist writing that could address formerly taboo subjects and emotions. Those poets who were widely recognized as feminist in the 1970s typically wrote in a relatively accessible *free verse and offered bold first-person testimony to such female experiences as childbirth, menstruation, and female sexuality, along with celebrations of under-recognized female achievement in the past. Rather than seeing themselves as carrying on the work

of first-wave women, their second-wave emphasis on gender difference limited their appreciation of earlier versions of feminism that focused on gender equality. Lucille Clifton (1936–2010), Nikki Giovanni (b. 1943), Judy Grahn (b. 1940), Carolyn Kizer (b. 1925), Irena Klepfisz (b. 1941), Alicia Ostriker (b. 1937), Marge Piercy (b. 1936), and Alice Walker (b. 1944) were among the many explicitly feminist poets of these decades. Such older poets as Elizabeth Bishop (1911–79) and Lorine Niedecker (1903–70) shared feminist concerns, even when they resisted that classification.

In the U.S. in the 1970s and early 1980s, some female poets who considered themselves feminists but were interested in experimental aesthetics rather than more straightforward personal statement found themselves marginalized in relation to both those recognized as feminist poets and the experimental Language group (see LANGUAGE POETRY). For, while the Language community was receptive to feminist thought and included such feminists as Rae Armantrout (b. 1947), Carla Harryman (b. 1952), and Lyn Hejinian (b. 1941), its major spokespersons were male, and its theorizing was not focused around gender. *HOW(ever)*, a jour. founded in 1983 that looked to the achievements of experimental female modernists for models of feminist poetics, was a crucial outlet for such experimentalists as founding ed. Kathleen Fraser (b. 1937) and Rachel Blau DuPlessis (b. 1941). By this time, women of color, who had often felt their concerns ignored by both men of their own race and white women, were also disenchanted with the largely white middle-class feminist movement, which they saw as having overlooked its own racial and class privilege. Audre Lorde (1934–92) was among the most significant poets articulating the intersections of feminism and race, in both her poetry and nonfictional writing, incl. the influential 1984 essay collection *Sister Outsider*. As U.S. literary crit. moved toward "multiculturalism," white feminist writers attended more to the experience and perspectives of women of color, while poets of color with feminist commitments such as Paula Gunn Allen (1939–2008), June Jordan (1936–2002), and Gloria Anzaldúa (1942–2004) gained greater visibility.

In other places and poetic trads., feminism also lost prominence in the 1930s relative to other social justice concerns before returning to high visibility in the 1960s or later. In Germany, e.g., 1966 Nobel Prize-winning poet Nelly Sachs (1891–1970) focused her work more on personal stories of suffering (specifically of Jewish loss) than on feminist issues, as was typical of Ger. feminist poets until the 1970s. Ingeborg Bachmann (1926–73), who was among the most influential mid-century Ger.-lang. poets, turned to feminist analysis of human relationship only in the 1960s and in prose. Poets of later generations have been more likely to write from distinctly feminist perspectives throughout their careers, as Ursula Krechel (b. 1947) has done. In Britain, many feminist poets were also leftist activists or influenced by Marxism. By the 1970s, female poets such as Alison Fell (b. 1944), Michele Roberts (b. 1944), Michelene Wandor (b. 1940), and Carol

Ann Duffy (b. 1955), Britain's first openly gay *poet laureate, were publishing in identifiably feminist contexts. Black Brit. poets such as Grace Nichols (b. 1950 in Guyana) and Jackie Kay (Scotch-Nigerian, b. 1961) combine feminist concerns with issues of immigration, diaspora, postcolonialism, and race. Similarly, feminist poets in Wales (e.g., Gillian Clark, b. 1937), Scotland (Liz Lochhead, b. 1947), and Ireland (Eavan Boland, b. 1944) reconsider national identity and hist. in terms of gender. In Britain, as in the U.S., feminism was associated with a transparent and personal mode of writing for several decades, generating a tension between the experimental aesthetic of writers such as Wendy Mulford (b. 1941) and Denise Riley (b. 1948) or, later, Maggie O'Sullivan (b. 1951) or Caroline Bergvall (b. 1962) and the dominant, plain-spoken, consciousness-raising aesthetic. Canadian feminist poets, whether more formally conventional such as Margaret Atwood (b. 1939), Joy Kogawa (b. 1935), and Dionne Brand (b. 1953 in Trinidad), or more formally innovative such as Daphne Marlatt (b. 1942 in Australia) or M. NourbeSe Philip (b. 1947 in Tobago), have tended to receive more acknowledgment, particularly in academic contexts, than their Brit. counterparts.

### III. Late 20th- and Early 21st-century Poetry and Third-wave Feminism.
In the 1980s, the rise of poststructuralism and particularly the devel. of poststructuralist Fr. feminism by Luce Irigaray (b. 1932), Hélène Cixous (b. 1937), Julia Kristeva (b. 1941), Monique Wittig (1935–2003), and others profoundly shifted the directions of feminist thinking and writing throughout Europe and North America. This kind of theory, formulated partly in response to Freudian thinking about sexual devel. and identity and to Jacques Lacan's revisions of Freud, turned away from attempts to define "woman," emphasizing instead the role of lang. in the construction of subjectivity, itself something always in process, and exploring the relation between sexuality and lang. Irigaray theorizes a disruptive, nonlinear feminine form of writing (*écriture féminine*) from the female body that would challenge existing ling. structures, which were seen as phallocentric. Kristeva opposes the semiotic—a bodily drive within signification that is associated with the pre-Oedipal—to the symbolic and explicitly links the semiotic to the poetic. While some more experimental poets attempted to write the body and to inscribe the "polymorphous perversity" or "jouissance" thought to characterize female sexuality or, as Fr. poet Anne-Marie Albiach (b. 1937) does, to use typographical space to explore the position of the body, others who were less formally experimental explored the pre-Oedipal bond between mother and daughter. As varied in form as in its understandings of feminism, feminist poetry in the U.S. in the 1980s encompasses approaches to free verse as different as those of Alice Fulton (b. 1952) and Olga Broumas (b. 1949 in Greece), strict formalism like that of Marilyn Hacker (b. 1942), and multigeneric innovations such as those of Theresa Hak Kyung Cha (1951–82) or Susan Howe (b. 1937).

By the mid-1990s when young feminists—assertive, globally conscious, often more individualistic than collective in their orientation—began labeling themselves the "third wave," both feminist theory and feminist poetics had diversified. Poetry written to identify or celebrate distinctively female experience and to honor the courage of individuals suffering patriarchal persecution or oppression has continued to thrive. Additionally, as the influence of Language writing and its radically experimental analogues has spread, feminist experimentalism and the idea that profound ling. change may be a necessary foundation for social change have gained wider credence. Feminist theory increasingly informs or complements other critical discourses, particularly those concerned with marginality or oppression in an increasingly international context. Thus, postcolonial studies has heightened awareness of international feminist writing, such as that by Jamaican-born Louise Bennett (1919–2006) and Lorna Goodison (b. 1947), Indian Kamala Das (b. 1934), Afro-Cuban Nancy Morejón (b. 1944), and Bangladeshi Taslima Nasrin (b. 1962). This attention has increased awareness of many poets' marginalization by empire as well as gender and their consequently vexed poetic relations to the Eur. langs. that dominate international publication. As the field of queer studies has become more established, gender studies have often subsumed feminist studies as the academic field examining work that explores feminist concerns; e.g., Judith Butler has influentially theorized gender as a performed behavior, understanding lang. use as an aspect of this performance. Another subset of feminist theory has turned away from a lang.-based psychoanalytic focus and other stances obviously conducive to text-based analysis toward the economic and global concerns of transnational feminism. While there is no longer a widely recognized community of self-identified feminist writers or a predominant focus or style associated with openly feminist poetry in most Western nations, a vast number of writers throughout the globe, male and female, continue to register feminism's international transformation of understandings of identity, relationships, institutions, hist., and power in their poetry.

*See* GENDER AND POETRY, POLITICS AND POETRY.

■ *One Foot on the Mountain*, ed. L. Mohin (1979)—Brit. feminist poetry, 1969–79; *Shakespeare's Sisters*, ed. S. Gilbert and S. Gubar (1979); M. Homans, *Women Writers and Poetic Identity* (1980); A. Rich, *On Lies, Secrets, and Silence* (1980); *This Bridge Called My Back*, ed. C. Moraga and G. Anzaldúa (1981)—radical women of color; L. Bernikow, *The World Split Open* (1984); A. S. Ostriker, *Thieves of Language* (1986); A. Rich, *Blood, Bread, and Poetry* (1986); *Making Waves*, ed. Asian Women United of California (1989); R. B. DuPlessis, *The Pink Guitar: Writing as Feminist Practice* (1990); J. Butler, *Gender Trouble* (1990); P. G. Allen, *The Sacred Hoop* (1992)—Am. Indian trads.; *No More Masks!*, ed. F. Howe, rev. ed. (1993); *Feminist Measures*, ed. L. Keller and C. Miller (1994); C. Hogue, *Scheming Women* (1995); E. Boland, *Object Lessons* (1996); M. O'Sullivan, *Out of Everywhere* (1996); K. Whitehead, *The Feminist Poetry Movement* (1996); T. Threadgold, *Feminist Poetics* (1997); S. F. Friedman, *Mappings*

(1998)—feminism and cultural geography; *Women Poets of the Americas*, ed. J. V. Brogan and C. C. Candelaria (1999); A. Vickery, *Leaving Lines of Gender* (2000); L. Hinton and C. Hogue, *We Who Love to Be Astonished* (2001)—experimental writing and performance poetics; *American Women Poets in the 21st Century*, ed. C. Rankine and J. Spahr (2002); J. Dowson, *Women, Modernism, and British Poetry 1910–1939* (2002); L. Kinnahan, *Lyric Interventions* (2004—Br. and Am. experimentalism); J. Dowson and A. Entwistle, *A History of Twentieth-Century British Women's Poetry* (2005); K. Fraser, *Translating the Unspeakable* (2005); E. Frost, *The Feminist Avant-Garde in American Poetry* (2005); J. Ramazani, *A Transnational Poetics* (2009).

L. KELLER AND C. MILLER

**FESCENNINE VERSES** (*versus Fescennini*). A form of Lat. *occasional verse, chiefly lascivious wedding songs, of great antiquity, which perhaps originated as ribald or abusive songs sung at harvest festivals: Claudian's Fescennine verses for the wedding of Emperor Honorius are extant (cf. Catullus 61.126–55). Fescennine verses were roughly dramatic, taking the form of a dialogue between peasants, and were probably first composed in the *Saturnian meter. In antiquity, the name was derived either from *fascinum*, a phallic emblem worn as a charm, or, as is more likely, from the town of Fescennium in Etruria. In the period of the empire, Fescennine verses were so popular for personal invective that they were outlawed. Livy (7.2) implies that Fescennine verses developed into Roman satire and comedy, but this is disputed.

*See* EPITHALAMIUM.

■ Pauly-Wissowa, "Fescennini"; W. Beare, *The Roman Stage*, 3d ed. (1968); G. E. Duckworth, *The Nature of Roman Comedy*, 2d ed. (1994).

R. J. GETTY

**FICTION, POETRY AS.** In Eng., the term *fiction* is apposite to the novel and the short story, but not necessarily to poetry. Readers assume that novelists draw loosely on facts and freely on the *imagination to create characters, stories, and objects; but they know that poems can be—but do not have to be—fictional. The fictional status of a work of lit. depends not on ling. or formal considerations but on cultural conventions such as the suspension of disbelief or the willingness to entertain possibilities and impossibilities. In a work of fiction, the audience is willing to approach what it is being told in a spirit of make-believe and to allow that the pronouncements of a narrator or a lyrical *voice may not correspond to the beliefs of an author. Moreover, the relation between a writer and his or her audience is a social one based on the understanding that the imagination does not have to adhere to facts. The social, almost contractual nature of this relationship is underscored by the sense of betrayal some feel when a work they thought was autobiographical or historical turns out to be grounded on the kind of fabrication that would have been readily accepted in a work of fiction.

Poems can be fictional if they are primarily about imagined characters, events, places, or objects; but

poets do not have to accommodate fictionality when exploring feelings, ideas, or emotions—for instance when their poems are prayers, exhortations, or meditations on particular subjects. Poets can be deliberately indeterminate about the connections between their work and any external reality, as Federico García Lorca was in some of his Andalusian poems. And where it is openly nonfictional, poetry can range from the *occasional verse—as in funeral orations or commemorations of sporting events—to the autobiographical. William Wordsworth's *The Prelude* (1805, pub. 1850), which bears the subtitle *The Growth of a Poet's Mind*, registers the accidents and experiences that informed his inner world. Poetry can also bear witness to political or historical events, as in the Spanish Civil War poems of Pablo Neruda and César Vallejo. The religious *hymns and *panegyrics in praise of leaders and warriors that Plato would have countenanced for his republic would not count as fictional for a public expected to worship their gods and to venerate the deeds of real men.

The demarcation between the fictional and the nonfictional ought not to be confused with that between the figurative and the literal. A poem can be fictional without the use of a single *trope, but it can be nonfictional even when grammar appears to fail (see ANACOLUTHON), as in the later poems of Paul Celan (in *Fadennsoen* and *Eigedunkelt*, whose titles are neologisms) that address human suffering in the wake of the Holocaust. In the early mod. period, *epic poems such as *La Araucana* (1569–89) by Alonso de Ercilla or *The Lusiads* (1572) by Luís de Camões were considered to be historical works of the highest rank, notwithstanding the interventions of mythological characters from the pagan world, which a Christian audience would have understood as true in a deeper sense than the merely literal. No reader in Elizabethan England would countenance the possibility that the heroine of Edmund Spenser's *The Faerie Queene* (1590, 1596) is a fictional character in the mod. sense. On the contrary, the poem's *allegory and *artifice were intended to honor the attributes of an exalted monarch. Since the devel. of mod. historiography in the 18th c., readers have had scruples about reading epic poems as historical documents. Nonetheless, there is a line of research, from Heinrich Schliemann's scholarship on the Homeric epics to Jesse Byock's recent studies of Nordic sagas, that has led to archaeological and historical discoveries based on what a contemp. sensibility could dismiss as pure invention.

Fictions are often inspired by personal experiences, historical or current events, moral dilemmas, philosophical conundrums, or other works of fiction. Since poems do not have to be fictional, they can simply be concerned with personal experiences, historical events, and the like. In both fictional and nonfictional modes, philosophers from Lucretius to Friedrich Nietzsche have expressed some of their fundamental insights in poems. For a poem to be considered fictional, it is not necessary to determine which of its elements are fabrications; nor does a poem have to be fictional to the exclusion of other orientations to reality (such as the historical, the intellectual, or the ritual). It is enough for

FIGURA    485

the reader to recognize that central characters, places, objects, or events are likely to be imaginary. Fiction affords writers and readers the possibility of distancing themselves from the real, and this allows for difficult or controversial topics to be addressed with a measure of emotional, moral, legal, or political cover, although the rawness of a personal emotion can be intensified, as in Arthur Rimbaud's "Le Bateau ivre" (The Drunken Boat, 1871), by the liberties a poet can take through fiction. At most, fictionality allows writers and readers to explore alternative realities, to escape into worlds of fantasy different in kind from the actual world. But at the least and in poems of many sorts, fictionality allows writers to project their musings about *what if, what might have been* and *what could be* onto facts and images that come to life in the mind, producing a world different from actuality in degree rather than kind.

Some theorists of fiction place the emphasis on the notion of make-believe (Walton, Currie), others on the nonreferential (Cohn), on possible worlds (Pavel, Doležel), on suspension of disbelief (Lamarque and Haugum Olsen), or on pretense (Searle, Genette). There are important insights to be gained from each of these positions even if, as Davies and others have underscored, the recent scholarship on fiction abounds with unresolved polemics and gray areas. Some contend that the distortions of fiction are always in the offing of a poem because, in principle, any work of lit. may be read as if it were fictional. Others make the stronger claim that the lines between fiction and nonfiction are always blurred in both fictional and nonfictional works. The views of Richard Rorty, Jacques Derrida, Barbara Cassin, and other influential postmodernist theorists go in this direction.

There is no consensus among theorists of fiction regarding answers to searching questions such as what kind of emotional response a reader experiences when considering the fate of a fictional character (see EMOTION) or how and to what degree readers supplement the information they gather from their reading to engage with a fiction imaginatively or cognitively. At the same time, there are some fascinating convergences among theorists who approach fiction from diametrically opposed perspectives. Schaeffer, e.g., argues that *mimesis is at the heart of poetry in one way or another. Doležel, on the other hand, argues that the poetic imagination generates alternative realities as opposed to imitating reality. Notwithstanding their differences, Doležel and Schaeffer coincide in their assessment that fiction is a move away from reality that allows for a return to it with added perspective and value.

*See* ARTIFACT, POETRY AS; INFORMATION, POETRY AS; KNOWLEDGE, POETRY AS.

■ J. Searle, "The Logical Status of Fictional Discourse," *NLH* 6 (1974); T. Pavel, *Fictional Worlds* (1986); G. Currie, *The Nature of Fiction* (1990); K. Walton, *Mimesis as Make-Believe* (1990); R. Greene, *Post-Petrarchism* (1991)—intro.; G. Genette, *Fiction and Diction*, trans. C. Porter (1993); J.-M. Schaeffer, *Pourquoi la Fiction?* (1999); P. Lamarque and S. Haugom Olsen, *Truth, Fiction and Literature* (1994); L. Doležel, *Heterocosmica: Fiction*

*and Possible Worlds* (1998); D. Cohn, *The Distinction of Fiction* (1999); D. Davies, *Aesthetics and Literature* (2007).

E. KRISTAL

**FIGURA** (Lat., "form," "kind," "figure"). First attested in Terence (*Eunuchus* 317), *figura* originally meant "plastic composition." Gr. philosophy distinguished between a sense of form that "informed" entities from within, akin to a structural principle (*morphe* or *eidos*) and a sense of phenomenal, perceptible form (*schema* or *typos*). In order to understand the devel. and significance of the term *figura* for lit., it is crucial to note that the word translated primarily the second, phenomenal sense of *form*. Accordingly, the word soon acquired additional meanings of perceptible, external, superimposed, and potentially transient form, incl. the imprint of a seal, shadow, ghost, and deceptive semblance.

In the 1st c. BCE, *figura* was also used to refer to ling. phenomena. Its first application for lang. was in the field of grammar, where it was used in the sense of "forms" or inflections of a word (Varro). Cicero uses the term in the context of rhet.; however, the *figurae orationis* in *De oratore* are not yet the rhetorical figures of speech (to which Cicero refers as *formae*) but the three levels of style and in a more general sense the various modes of eloquence.

With Quintilian, the rhetorical sense of *figurae* as figures of speech was established. The *Institutio oratoria* makes a distinction not only between figurative and "plain" modes of speech but between figures of speech and *tropes. While tropes substitute words for other words, figures constitute a larger category of lang. used in a rhetorical or poetic way (and at times they seem to include tropes as well). Quintilian's treatment of the topic became the dominant influence on med. and early mod. rhet., which also inherited the complications of the concept of rhetorical figures.

During the early centuries of Christianity, a new sense of *figura* emerged as a result of the church's attempts to build a correspondence between the Heb. Bible and the Christian NT. The Christian apologist Tertullian referred to the biblical character Hosea as *figura futurorum* (a prefiguration of future events), in which an image of Jesus can be identified prospectively (*Adversus Marcionem* 3, 16). Not rejecting the historical authenticity of characters and events in the Heb. Bible, Tertullian read them as figurae, i.e. real prophecies, of characters and events in the NT. In his retrospective interpretation, persons and episodes in both the Heb. Bible and the Christian NT are considered real (i.e., historical), but in the latter they are conceived of as realizations and fulfillments of their corresponding figurae in the former.

Tertullian's main source is Paul's First Letter to the Corinthians; but by the time of the Vulgate, the Lat. trans. of Paul's Gr. letters reflects the patristic notion of *figura*. When Paul refers to the Jews as "typoi" (examples) for the Christians in 1 Cor. 10:6, the Vulgate translates the Gr. by using the Lat. "figura." But when in the apocalyptic 1 Cor. 7:31, Paul refers to the "schema" (present form) of the world passing away, the Vulgate uses "figura" again. Thus, following the exegetical method developed by Tertullian and other early church fathers, *figura* emerges as the central concept of typological interpretations of both the scriptures and hist. itself. In this typological conception, *hermeneutics and ontology are closely related. The unfolding of hist. follows a textual pattern in which earlier events and characters signify not only themselves but later ones as well; at the same time, this unfolding of hist. also implies an ontological progression from the figura or semblance of things toward an apocalyptic *veritas* or truth. Hist. in this view is a process of revealing that which hides under the imprint or figura.

How the rhetorical and the Christian exegetical meanings of *figura* are related to each other is a vexed question. Originally, the rhetorical sense of *figura* referred to modes of speaking, while the Christian exegetical sense focuses on hermeneutical strategies. But the rhetorical and the exegetical senses soon merged, particularly in Christian authors who set out to produce texts that could be read in a Christian figural way. Dante, for instance, was both a theorist of the so-called fourfold *exegesis of the scriptures ("Letter to Can Grande") and a practitioner of the figural method in the *Divina commedia*, where historical "pagan" characters such as Virgil appear as figures or types whose fulfillments Dante encounters in the afterlife. While med. and early mod. Catholic readers and authors tended to use figurative exegesis to integrate Gr. and Roman events and characters into a Christian hist., post-Reformation Protestant authors returned to emphasizing the figurative interpretation of the Heb. Bible. Thus, John Milton's *Paradise Lost* is a comprehensive attempt to retell the story of the biblical fall as a figura of both the Christian Messiah and the contemp. events of his own times ("shadowy types to truth, from flesh to spirit" [12.303]). Better known in Eng. as *typology*, this sense of figuralism remains influential in certain trends of Protestant lit., particularly in America from the metaphysical poet Edward Taylor to R. W. Emerson.

In the 20th c., *figura* became an important term in literary studies following the work of the philologist and comparatist Erich Auerbach. His essay "Figura" (1944) remains the most influential treatment of the subject. Rather than a mere philological subject, however, for Auerbach the word *figura* held the key to the hist. of Western literary representation, which he expounded in his 1946 *Mimesis*. In order to uncover the significance of *figura*, Auerbach insisted on distinguishing it from *allegory: while allegory is a "spiritual" mode of *interpretation in that it denies reality from the sign itself, figura is a sign that signifies both itself and its own fulfillment. Auerbach admits that such a distinction is not always clear and, therefore, warns against oversimplifying the matter. The contrast between an allegory and a figura nevertheless emerges in his work as a contrast between Greco-Roman and Judeo-Christian modes of representing (and indeed perceiving) reality, with figura and figural modes of representation corresponding to the Judeo-Christian historical view of reality. While Auerbach's theory of figural mimesis is heavily indebted to 19th-c. *histori-

cism and its emphasis on the historical nature of reality and while his preference for what he saw as the Judeo-Christian mode of figural representation must be understood in the context of Nazi Germany's penchant for Greco-Roman mythology, White has argued that *Mimesis* contains a particularly modernist concept of lit. hist., one that sees "Western literary history as a story of the fulfillment of the idea of figurality."

*See* FIGURATION, SYMBOL.

■ E. Auerbach, "Typological Symbolism in Medieval Literature," *YFS* 9 (1952); and "Figura," trans. R. Manheim, *Scenes from the Drama of European Literature* (1959); *Typology and Early American Literature*, ed. S. Bercovitch (1972); *Reading the Text: Biblical Criticism and Literary Theory*, ed. S. Prickett (1991); R. K. Emmerson, "Figura and the Medieval Typological Imagination," *Typology and English Medieval Literature*, ed. H. T. Keenan (1992); J. M. Gellrich, "*Figura*, Allegory, and the Question of History," *Literary History and the Challenge of Philology*, ed. S. Lerer (1996); J. Knape, "Figurenlehre," *Historisches Wörterbuch der Rhetorik*, ed. G. Kalivoda et al. (1996); J. T. Shawcross, "The Christ *Figura* in Some Literary Texts: Image and Theme," *Cithara* 35 (1996); H. White, "Auerbach's Literary History," *Figural Realism* (1999); L. Costa Lima, "*Figura* as a Kernel of Auerbach's Literary History," *Literary Research/Recherche Littéraire* 17 (2000); L. Freinkel, *Reading Shakespeare's Will: The Theology of Figure from Augustine to the Sonnets* (2002); J. I. Porter, "Erich Auerbach and the Judaizing of Philology," *CritI* 35 (2008).

F. M. Aresu; D. Marno

**FIGURATION.** The transmutation of ideas into images, figuration is the product of the formative power of human cognition and is realized in all the ways in which verbal, mental, perceptual, optical, and graphic images interact. Figuration punctuates the complexity of time and space with interpretable forms, incl. all kinds of signs; the very idea of an "idea" is linked to seeing and hence to the *eidolon* or "visible image." Platonic trad. distinguishes between idea and image by conceiving of the former as a suprasensible realm of forms, types, or species and the latter as a sensory impression that provides a mere likeness (*eikon*). Mental imagery or figuration has been a central concern of theories of mind since Plato's cave allegory in the *Republic* and Aristotle's *On Interpretation* and continues to be a cornerstone of psychology, as in Gestalt construction of images. And at least since Macrobius's commentary on the dream of Scipio in Cicero's *Orator*, dreams and esp. visions have been understood as interpretable in various figural senses.

While it is a function of *allegory to personify abstractions, figuration works in the reverse direction, treating real persons or things in a formulaic way so that they become concrete or living ideas grounded in a shared quality. In med. literary fiction and interpretation, when the things treated are historical persons taking part in God's providential structuring of time (as in Dante's *Divine Comedy*), imbuing them with the power to delineate events, the resulting narrative is called *figura (Auerbach). Yet figura need not treat only Christian events; in the *Aeneid*, e.g., the hero arrives at the site of Pallanteum just when the rites of Hercules are being performed. The day is to be interpreted as significant because this arrival refers back to Hercules' own rescuing mission at the same site and at the same time prefigures the advent of the emperor Augustus, Virgil's patron, at the same site again, fresh from his triumph over Antony and Cleopatra at Actium. For Dante, in turn, Aeneas' founding of Roman civilization not only facilitates but prefigures the birth of Christ within the bounds of the empire and the resulting renovation of humanity. *Figura*, or narrative typology, is thus but one specialized instance of figuration, which is essential to all interpretive strategies.

In the constitution of literary works, figuration is the means whereby a system of beliefs and ideas is rendered palpable. A large quotient of figurative expression accounts for much of the traditional distrust of poetry among philosophers. Literary discourse provides authors with a great deal of latitude, whereas figures (taken in the sense of rhetorical strategies) that become part of ordinary lang. tend to lose their figural status. E.g., Lat. *pastor*, "shepherd," was augmented by a Christian figurative meaning, "head of the congregation," an idea that has survived, defiguralized, in mod. Eng. In texts, figuration retains a strong visual connotation: when Walter Pater uses the term *figure* to represent the It. Ren., the model for the figure is always visual.

The hist. and theory of figuration is, therefore, bound up with the status of images. David Hume follows John Locke and Thomas Hobbes in the use of pictorial figures to describe the chains of cognition and signification: ideas are "faint images" or "decayed sensations" that eventually become linked by conventional associations with words. The ensuing conception of meaning traces it back to its origin in an impression, with the consequent understanding of lang. as the means of retrieving that original impression. The view of poetry and of lang. in general as a process of pictorial reproduction exemplifies one idea of figuration. In *romantic poetics, verbal, mental, and pictorial imagery were assimilated to the process of *imagination as redefined in opposition to the mere "recall" of mental pictures. Abrams finds that figures of *expression come to replace figures of *mimesis in the course of the 19th c. Indeed, an abstract figure such as the Coleridgean symbol displaces or subsumes the notion of the figure as a representation of material reality.

A progressive elevation or sublimation of the figure reaches its logical culmination when an entire poem is regarded as a figure, as in the "verbal icon" of Wimsatt, a synchronic structure embodying a complex figure. Poetic *iconicity ranges from a literal basis in shaped and concrete poems (see CONCRETE POETRY, CALLIGRAMME), in which the text is charged with pictorial features, to forms such as the *sestina, in which figuration is implicit, to ekphrastic poetry (see EKPHRASIS), where the text represents a work of visual art, to *dialogue forms, which appropriately figure the dialectical method of argumentation.

Formalist crit. programmatically demonstrates the congruence or lack of congruence among a poem's propositional content, its architectonics, and its figurative energies so as to display the many dynamic patterns cohering within the whole. The concept of the entire poem as figure notwithstanding, the main direction of figurative interpretation in the mod. era has been to proceed from the manifest or surface content to the word conceived as latent meaning, lying beneath the aesthetic surface. Freud's *Interpretation of Dreams*, while not a text of lit. crit., articulates a poetics of dreaming that assimilates the psychic material of which dreams are made to the material of visual art. Dream analysis provides strategies for extracting the hidden verbal message from a possibly misleading and certainly inarticulate pictorial surface, namely, the four figurative processes of condensation, displacement, identification, and *symbolism.

The symbolic connection of dreams to experience is thus one of figuration, wherein symbols and the things symbolized are integrated in a speculative reality in which they participate mutually. The establishment of such invisible bonds is characteristic of poetic conceptions of the universe, which may, e.g., produce descriptions that intertwine physical setting and human emotion where connections of a causal type might otherwise have been invoked. Yet often a setting presented as figurative by a description, without overt justification, does the work of postulating so strong a participation between persons and environment that the smallest occurrence can assume permanent symbolic value.

*See* EXEGESIS, ICONOLOGY, IMAGE, IMAGERY, METAPHOR, PSYCHOLOGY AND POETRY, RHETORIC AND POETRY, SCHEME, TROPE.

■ Abrams; W. K. Wimsatt, *The Verbal Icon* (1954); S. Freud, *The Interpretation of Dreams* (1955); E. Auerbach, "Figura," trans. R. Manheim, *Scenes from the Drama of European Literature* (1959); Jakobson, "Linguistics and Poetics," *Selected Writings*, v. 3; A. Fletcher, *Allegory* (1964); F. E. Peters, *Greek Philosophical Terms* (1967); E. Panofsky, *Idea* (1968); W.J.T. Mitchell, *Iconology* (1986); M. and M. Shapiro, *Figuration in Verbal Art* (1988); N. C. Burbules, G. Schraw, and W. Trathen, "Metaphor, Idiom, and Figuration," *Metaphor and Symbolic Activity* 4 (1989); S. Lattig, "The Perception of Metaphor and the Metaphor of Perception: The Neurodynamics of Figuration," *Intertexts* 9 (2005).
M. SHAPIRO

**FILI** (pl. *filid[h]*, mod. Ir. *file*, pl. *filí*). *Fili* has always been the Ir. word for poet, and it is unfortunate that a considerable body of Ir. poetry (*filidheacht, filíocht*) is called in Eng. "bardic" poetry, with the misleading suggestion that it is the work of the Ir. bard (pl. *baird*; see BARD). The word *fili* is cognate with the Welsh *gwel(-ed)* (to see), and originally the fili was the "seer," the "diviner"; hence, it does not occasion surprise that *fili* and *druí* (druid) were at one time interchangeable words and that some of the knowledge of the fili was then regarded as knowledge gained by means of occult practices. However, the fili gained most of his knowledge by the more usual process of learning at school—there were special schools for *filid*—and the knowledge thus gained was always regarded as an important part of his qualifications. The fili in earlier times was not sharply distinguished from the *breithem*, "judge" (literally, the maker of judgments) and the *senchaid*, "historian," "reciter of lore"; indeed, it is possible that at one time he combined their functions with his own and that their emergence as separate classes is the result of specialization. The fili was from the beginning a member of an important and highly organized corporation classed among the *saer-nemed* (privileged classes). There were seven grades of *filid*, the highest being the *ollam filed*, a fully qualified fili appointed to the service of a king. A fili was usually attached to the household of a chief, his calling was hereditary, and the office of fili to the head of a clan was, in later times at any rate, often the prerogative of a particular family. He was at all times distinguished from the bard, whose qualifications and status were inferior. The word *bard* is derived from the Celtic *bardos*, who, among the Gauls, was predominantly the "singer of praise." It is sometimes assumed that the fili arrogated to himself the function of the bard as a singer of praise (as well as a proclaimer of satire) and that his function as such was overshadowed by those that he must have undertaken in part from the druid at the advent of Christianity. However that may be, singing the praise of his chief was the foremost function of the fili in the Middle Ages.

■ G. Murphy, "Bards and Filidh," *Éigse* 2 (1940); J.E.C. Williams, "The Court Poet in Medieval Ireland," *PBA* 57 (1971); Williams and Ford; L. Breatnach, *Uraicecht na Ríar: The Poetic Grades in Early Irish Law* (1987); P. A. Breatnach, "The Chief's Poet," *Proceedings of the Irish Royal Academy* (1983).

J.E.C. WILLIAMS

**FINIDA.** In 14th- to early 16th-c. Sp. poetry, the *finida* is the approximate equivalent of the *\*remate* of the later *canción petrarquista*. Lang writes,

> Like the [Occitan] *tornada*, the *finida* serves as a conclusion to a poem, and with the *tornada* and kindred forms, such as the *envoi*, the *desfecha*, the *estribote* and others, this stanza was originally, in all probability, a sequence to a musical composition. According to the *Leys d'Amors*, the *tornada* repeats in its rhyme-order the second part of the last stanza in case this has the same number of verses; otherwise it may have one verse more or less than the last half-stanza. In the Portuguese . . . the *finida*, which is regarded as essential to a perfect composition, may have from one to four verses, and must rhyme with the last stanza or, if the poem be a *cantiga de refram*, with the refrain. The practitioners of the *Cancionero de Baena* (ca. 1450) appear to have followed the example of the Provençals and Catalans.

■ H. R. Lang, "Las formas estróficas y términos métricos del *Cancionero de Baena*," *Estudios eruditos "in memoriam" de Adolfo Bonilla y San Martín*, v. 1 (1927); Le Gentil; Navarro.

D. C. CLARKE

## FINLAND, POETRY OF

I. The Beginnings
II. The Rise of Finnish Poetic Language
III. The Modern Period

Finnish poetry has developed over a long hist., though the oldest extant texts written in Finnish date only from the early 19th c. and though some of its classics were initially written in Swedish. It presents a complex hist. of cultural and literary influences, but thematically and taken as a whole, it shows a remarkably unified inspiration from early oral trad. to contemp. *modernism. The Finnish lang. belongs to the non-IE, Finno-Ugrian group of langs. like Hungarian and Estonian. Finnish poetry has developed at the periphery of the IE family of langs. but has had close cultural contacts with the major movements of Eur. civilization.

**I. The Beginnings.** A rich treasury of traditional oral songs and tales, representing both the lyric and the epic genres, is extant, incl. about 1,270,000 lines and 85,000 variants of the poetry composed in the so-called Kalevala meter (trochaic tetrameter in its simplest form). These works are traditionally that of anonymous singers, men and women, but some of the principal singers are known by name, such as Arhippa Perttunen and Ontrei Malinen, both of whom were important sources for Elias Lönnrot's compilations, the epic *Kalevala* (1835, 1849), and the *Kanteletar*, a collection of lyrics and short narrative poems (1840–41). Finnish folk poetry consists of elements dating from different periods and deriving from various cultural strata. There is evidence of the existence of a vital oral poetry before the Swedish cultural and political expansion during the 12th c. that brought Christianity via Sweden to Finland. Finno-Ugric mythology, based on animistic and shamanistic religion, is an intrinsic part of the early cosmogonic poems, magic songs, and ritual incantations of this trad. Med. Christianity introduced new elements to Finnish folk poetry. *Ballads, legends, and *laments expressed both religious and secular themes, and poems sung at weddings or at burials reflected their function for the life of the community. In an exquisite cycle about the birth of Christ, a Finnish maiden, Marjatta, a variant of the Virgin Mary, becomes pregnant by eating cranberries (Finnish *marja*). The religious basis of these poems, which were composed by individual singers according to their poetic skill, derives from a fusion of native rituals, Catholic, and Gr. Orthodox beliefs.

While oral poetry survived in the agrarian parts mostly of eastern Finland, its importance decreased as other attempts were made to forge the Finnish lang. into a literary medium. Most important of these is

Mikael Agricola's (1510?–57) trans. of the NT (1548), a decisive ling. landmark, as well as one of the first literary monuments of the Protestant era. At the end of the 17th c., Lat. and Swedish-lang. poems were composed, but the verse remained conventional and derivative, with the exception of a few names such as Juhana Cajanus (1655–81) and Jakob Frese (1691–1729). It was not until the rediscovery of the oral trads. in the 18th c., inaugurated by the study of Finnish folk poetry such as Henrik Gabriel Porthan's (1739–1804) *De poesi fennica* (1766–78), that Finnish-lang. poetry began to emerge from obscurity. The realization that the Finnish people had created poetry worthy of comparison with the *Iliad* and the *Odyssey* had an enormous impact in Finland. The lines by Arhippa Perttunen illustrate the proud self-assertion of a native poet:

My own finding are my words
my own snatching from the road.

(*Finnish Folk Poetry*, trans. K. Bosley)

**II. The Rise of Finnish Poetic Language.** While Swedish-lang. poetry of Eur. orientation dominated literary production in Finland, examples of early Finnish-lang. poetry belong to the didactic and exhortatory trad. of the Enlightenment. The termination of Swedish rule in 1809 brought about an altogether new situation. A few Swedish-lang. poets, such as Frans Michael Franzén (1772–1847), whose poetry expressed a strong pre-romantic conception of nature and of humanity as divine creation, were also influential in the devel. of Finnish poetry. As the Napoleonic wars resulted in a redistribution of the northern territories of Europe, Finland fell under Rus. rule as a virtually autonomous Grand Duchy in 1809. This situation compelled the Finns, incl. the Swedish Finns, to turn their philosophical and literary attention to questions of Finnish national identity. It was an original moment in Finnish lit. hist. Helsinki became the center of Finnish cultural and literary life. The university was moved there from Turku in 1827, the Finnish Literary Society was founded in 1831, and the newspaper *Helsingfors Tidningar* (Helsinki News) began to appear in 1829. J. L. Runeberg (1804–77) became the foremost Swedish-lang. poet of that time with his *Dikter* (Poems, 1830). Combining a deep feeling for simple country folk with expert knowledge of both cl. lit. and Finnish oral trad., Runeberg renewed lyrical lang. with his mastery of technique. His epic poems in hexameters, e.g., the *Elgskyttarne* (Elkhunters, 1832), a narrative about love and hunting, demonstrate how cl. style can be effectively used to describe humble country life. His romanticism, both lyrical and patriotic, may be seen as an important precursor of the Finnish-lang. poetry that emerged in the 1860s.

Runeberg, the philosopher and writer J. W. Snellman (1806–81), Lönnrot (1802–84), and the writer and poet Zachris Topelius (1818–98) all shaped the Finnish national consciousness and cultural identity, but the conditions were not yet ripe for the production of Finnish poetry of merit. Lönnrot showed some genuine poetic talent in assembling the epic *Kalevala* by introducing lyric material into the narratives, adding songs, and replacing missing lines according to his vision. But the preeminent figure at the time was Aleksis Kivi (pseud. of Alexis Stenvall, 1834–72), primarily a playwright and novelist whose poetic achievement was not fully recognized until the 20th c. Kivi's contemporaries considered his poetry unfinished: it was more daring and personal than anything written at the time. Many of his poems were lyrical narratives that broke away from rhyming verse and used free rhythms, creating an intensity familiar from the folk lyric. From the mod. perspective, Kivi is recognized as one of the greatest Finnish poets.

After Kivi, there were no major poets until the end of the 19th c., though Kaarlo Kramsu (1855–95) and J. H. Erkko (1849–1906) played important roles in forging Finnish poetic lang. that could effectively express new social and historical themes. Industrialization, educational reforms, and new scientific thought were reflected in the work of Finnish novelists and dramatists, who explored the forms of Eur. *realism in the 1880s. Swedish-lang. poetry was mainly represented by J. J. Wecksell (1838–1907) and Karl August Tavaststjerna (1860–98), who reflects the new sense of alienation felt by the Swedish-speaking writers.

*National neoromanticism* was the term coined by the poet Eino Leino (1878–1926) to characterize certain currents in Finnish lit. and in the fine arts influenced by Eur. *symbolism. It combined enthusiasm, determination, and outstanding talent in all fields: the composer Jean Sibelius, the painter Akseli Gallen-Kallela, and the architect Eliel Saarinen were all representatives of Young Finland. A prolific poet, Leino developed an innovative technique that radically changed the Finnish poetic idiom. Leino put the stamp of originality on everything he wrote. While drawing on traditional sources such as myth and folk poetry for themes and motifs, he was fully versed in Eur. and Scandinavian lit., and translated Dante, Pierre Corneille, Jean Racine, J. W. Goethe, and Friedrich Schiller. His *Helkavirsiä* (Whitsongs, 1903, 1916) recreate the most ancient folk trads. in narrative lyrics of visionary character having a symbolic resonance that transcends the national sphere. Leino's lyrical lang. is supple and resourceful: in "Nocturne" (from *Talvi-yö* [Winter Night], 1905), the melodious lines evoke the infinite in a clearly defined space:

The corncrake's song rings in my ears,
above the rye a full moon sails; . . .

(trans. K. Bosley)

The inner dynamics of Leino's poetry spring from a fruitful tension between an ultraindividualistic, egocentric, amoral hero and a prophet-seer who could capture and articulate the complex spirit of his epoch.

Several of his contemporaries added other elements to the vigorously developing Finnish poetic lang. Leino's companion L. Onerva (1882–1972) provided a free spirit to explorations of femininity in sensual lyric verse, while Otto Manninen (1872–1950) and V. A. Koskenniemi (1885–1962) wrote in the Eur. classic mode. Manninen, a virtuoso poet, wrote clear, concise verse on symbolist themes and translated Homer, Gr. tragedy, and Molière. Koskenniemi expressed his pessimistic philosophy in tightly controlled verse inspired by ancient poetry. With Finland's independence in 1917, poetry reconfirmed its central role in the expression of both individual and social sentiments. And by 1920, Finnish poetic lang. had attained a variety and depth that guaranteed it a worthy place among Eur. lits.

**III. The Modern Period.** While Leino has a strikingly mod. timbre at times, modernism appeared in Finnish poetry only after World War I. This was in the unique work of the Finnish modernists writing in Swedish, such as Edith Södergran (1892–1923) and Elmer Diktonius (1896–1961). Literary modernism coincided with antipositivism in philosophy and was a reaction against 19th-c. empiricism and realism. In the 1920s, Eur. movements such as *futurism, *cubism, *constructivism, *expressionism, and *surrealism arrived in Finnish art and poetry almost simultaneously. Denying the ability of art to describe reality, the new poets increasingly turned away from mimetic art, even as they rejected the past and everything connected with it. This was first seen in lang. experiments, e.g., in *Jääpeili* (Ice Mirror, 1928) by Aaro Hellaakoski (1893–1952), in the poetry of Katri Vala (1901–44), in the prose of Olavi Paavolainen (1903–64), and in the early work of P. Musttapää (1899–1973). The new generation that brought modernism to Finland formed a group called the Firebearers, publishing albums and a jour. of that name, *Tulenkantajat*. The Firebearers issued a *manifesto in 1928, declaring the sacredness of art and life in tones reminiscent of the writings of the *Finland-Swedish modernists, but with an even greater fervor and passion. Vala and Uuno Kailas (1901–33) expressed these ideals, and by this time, all important literary movements had arrived in Finnish poetry. Another literary group, *Kiila* (The Wedge), devoted itself to radical socialism after 1936. Arvo Turtiainen (1904–80) and the novelist Elvi Sinervo (1912–86) were among its most important members, many of whom were imprisoned during World War II. The nation, divided by the Civil War (1918–19) following Finnish independence, unified again for the effort of the Winter War, but the schism was not closed until the postwar era, as is described by Väinö Linna (1920–92) in his epic trilogy *Täällä Pohjantähden alla* (Here under the North Star, 1959–62).

In the 1950s, poetic modernism in Finland turned antitraditionalist, dissociating itself from ordinary lang. While drawing inspiration from East and West, America and the Far East, its lang. became more hermetic. Paavo Haavikko (1931–2008), Eeva-Liisa Manner (1921–95), Helvi Juvonen (1919–59), and Marja-Liisa Vartio (1924–66) were among the most important poets, followed by other original talents such as Mirkka Rekola (b. 1931), Tyyne Saastamoinen (1924–1998), Lassi Nummi (b. 1928), and Pentti Holappa (b. 1927). Pentti Saarikoski (1937–83), whose first collection, *Runoja* (Poems), appeared in 1958, is not tied to any movement or decade. Saarikoski, a maverick genius and iconoclast, was one of the most learned of mod. Finnish poets, as well as a translator of Homer, Euripides, James Joyce, and others. With his *Mitä tapahtuu todella?* (What Is Going On, Really?, 1962) Finnish poetic lang. was taken to a new level where everything had to start from point zero in order to go on: the split word, the word mobile, the *collage, and the explicit rejection of poetic structure all conveyed a sense of both freedom and despair. Saarikoski's work culminated in a long, free-floating philosophical poem *Hämärän tanssit* (The Dances of the Obscure, 1983), written during the period when the poet lived in Sweden. It expresses the poet's yearning for beauty and the unification of all living things.

Rekola, Haavikko, and Manner, in their different ways, have been regarded as the leading Finnish modernists. Haavikko uses compelling rhythmic sequences and incantations to express, through a series of negatives, abstractions, and ironies, his skepticism about the relationship of lang. to the external world. It is an original vision, and in 1984, Haavikko received the Neustadt Prize for his achievement. Rekola, who was a candidate for the Neustadt Prize in 2000, studies lang. and perception in a universal trad. Manner has explored the conflict between magical order and logical disorder, as she calls it, and has brought to Finnish poetry, since her breakthrough collection *Tämä matka* (This Journey, 1956) a mythical dimension, a lang. suggestive of another reality.

Finnish poetry in recent times and since Finland's entry in the European Union in 1994 shows an unprecedented diversity; all directions seem possible. As the motto of the Firebearers once indicated, Finnish poetry has become receptive to world literary currents. Among the poets writing in contemp. Finland are Sirkka Turkka (b. 1939), Kari Aronpuro (b. 1940), Pentti Saaritsa (b. 1941), Kirsti Simonsuuri (b. 1945), Caj Westerberg (b. 1946), and Arja Tiainen (b. 1947). Saaritsa, Westerberg, and Simonsuuri are also major translators of world poetry into Finnish. The new generation is represented by Olli Heikkonen (b. 1965), Sanna Karlström (b. 1975), Teemu Manninen (b. 1977), Katariina Vuorinen (b. 1976), and numerous other poets born in the 1980s, and there is a new intellectual current in Finnish lit. Both poetry and prose continue occupying an important place in contemp. cultural life. Finnish-Swedish modernists like Bo Carpelan (b. 1926) and Solveig von Schoulz (1907–95) have carried on the earlier modernist trad. while adding new elements. In the present day, one is justified in speaking of Finnish poetry as including all verse written by Finns, whether in Swedish or in Finnish, and whether in or outside Finland.

■ **Anthologies and Translations:** *Moderne Finnische Lyrik*, ed. and trans. M. P. Hein (1962); *Suomen kirjallisuuden antologia I–VIII*, ed. K. Laitinen and

M. Suurpää (1963–75); P. Haavikko, *Selected Poems*, trans. A. Hollo (1974); *Finnish Folk Poetry: Epic*, ed. and trans. M. Kuusi et al., trans. K. Bosley (1977); E. Leino, *Whitsongs*, trans. K. Bosley (1978); *Snow in May*, ed. R. Dauenhauer and P. Binham (1978); *Territorial Song: Finnish Poetry and Prose*, trans. H. Lomas (1981); P. Saarikoski, *Selected Poems*, trans. A. Hollo (1983); *Salt of Pleasure: 20th-Century Finnish Poetry*, ed. and trans. A. Jarvenpa and K. B. Vähämäki (1983); E. Södergran, *Complete Poems*, trans. D. McDuff (1983); P. Saarikoski, *Love and Solitude*, trans. S. Katchadourian (1985); *Modern finlandssvensk Lyrik*, ed. C. Andersson and B. Carpelan (1986); B. Carpelan, *Room without Walls: Selected Poems*, trans. A. Born (1987); P. Saarikoski, *Dances of the Obscure*, trans. M. Cole and K. Kimball (1987); *Ice around Our Lips:. Finland-Swedish Poetry*, ed. and trans. D. McDuff (1989); *The Kalevala*, trans. K. Bosley (1989); *Poésie et prose de Finlande*, ed. M. Bargum (1989); *Enchanting Beasts: An Anthology of Modern Women Poets in Finland*, ed. and trans. K. Simonsuuri (1990); *Contemporary Finnish Poetry*, ed. and trans. H. Lomas (1991).
■ **Criticism and History:** E. Enäjärvi-Haavio, "On the Performance of Finnish Folk Runes," *Folkliv* (1951); J. Ahokas, *History of Finnish Literature* (1974); *Modern Nordic Plays: Finland*, ed. E. J. Friis (1974); T. Wretö, *Johan Ludvig Runeberg* (1980); *The Two Literatures of Finland*, spec. iss. of *World Literature Today* 54 (1980); M. Kuusi and L. Honko, *Sejd och Saga* (1983); T. Warburton, *Åttio år finlandssvensk litteratur* (1984); G. Schoolfield, *Edith Södergran* (1984); K. Simonsuuri, "The Lyrical Space: the Poetry of Paavo Haavikko," *World Literature Today* 58 (1984); *Europe: Littérature de Finlande* (June–July 1985); K. Laitinen, *Literature of Finland: An Outline* (1985); P. Leino, *Language and Metre: Metrics and the Metrical System of Finland*, trans. A. Chesterman (1986); K. Laitinen, *Finlands Litteratur* (1988); *A History of Finnish Literature*, ed. G. C. Schoolfield (1998); "Finnish and Finland-Swedish," *The Oxford Guide to Literature in English Translation*, ed. P. France (2000).

K. K. SIMONSUURI

**FINLAND-SWEDISH MODERNISTS.** A group of path-breaking poets in Finland writing in Swedish during and shortly after World War I. Chief among these were Edith Södergran (1892–1923), Hagar Olsson (1893–1978), Elmer Diktonius (1896–1961), Gunnar Björling (1887–1960), Rabbe Enckell (1903–74), and Henry Parland (1908–30). They were influenced by Ger. *expressionism, Rus. *futurism, and Anglo-Am. *imagism, as well as other Eur. movements in philosophy, poetry, painting, and music, but cannot be defined as a separate school. Nor were they imitators; their work was a unique creation—a response to a turbulent period in Finnish hist. and culture—whose form varied according to their distinctive talents. Södergran was the clear pioneer: she published Scandinavia's first avant-gardist *manifesto, titled "Individual Art," in a Helsinki newspaper in 1918. She died in 1923 at age 31, but her radical poetry inspired an entire genera-

tion of Finland-Swedish modernists. Their poetic program, presented in two avant-garde periodicals, *Ultra* (1922) and *Quosego* (1928–29), represents the birth of *modernism in Scandinavian poetry; elsewhere in the region, modernism did not emerge fully until the 1940s. Their program's revolutionary aesthetic defines poetry as a dynamic process whose forms give direct expression to instinctual and subconscious life while reflecting philosophical shifts in sensibility, intellectual and moral values, and sexual attitudes. Their work included many new poetic techniques, such as *vers libre*, unrhymed lines with free rhythms, a strong emphasis on associative imagery, and startling, spontaneous lang. Nature and animals are frequent tropes. They expanded the topics of poetry, dealing with the inner life of the individual as well as with contemp. society. Their strong influence can be seen in Sweden, particularly in the *Fyrtiotalisterna* (the Poets of the 1940s), and throughout Scandinavia. They also influenced the Finnish modernist poets, the Firebearers.
*See* FINLAND, POETRY OF.
■ B. Carpelan, *Studier i Gunnar Björlings diktning* (1960); J. Wrede, *Tidskriften Ultra* (1970); E. Södergran, *Love and Solitude: Selected Poems*, trans. S. Katchadourian (1992); C. Zilliacus, *Finlands svenska litteraturhistoria Andra delen* (2000); U. Lindqvist, "The Paradoxical Poetics of Edith Södergran," *Modernism/Modernity* 13 (2006).

S. LYNGSTAD; K. K. SIMONSUURI; U. LINDQVIST

**FIRESIDE POETS.** The 19th-c. Am. poets H. W. Longfellow (1807–82), W. C. Bryant (1794–1878), J. G. Whittier (1807–92), J. R. Lowell (1819–91), and O. W. Holmes (1809–94) were known collectively as the Fireside poets; they were also sometimes called the Household or Schoolroom Poets. They did not self-identify as a literary circle: Bryant was involved in New York's Knickerbocker Club; Whittier was a farmer's son and a Quaker activist; and Longfellow, Holmes, and Lowell were Boston brahmins. Rather, these poets were linked and named by others for the prominence of their work in domestic (fireside) and pedagogical (schoolroom) settings. Their poems were disseminated through "Household Editions" meant to ornament middle-class parlors, and through textbooks such as the multimillion-selling *McGuffey's Reader* series. Regular meters, full rhymes, and accessible sentiments made a typical fireside poem easy to read, recall, and repeat. By the 1880s, a canon of "standards" emerged, incl., e. g., Holmes's "Old Ironsides" ("Ay, tear her battered ensign down!"); Longfellow's "Paul Revere's Ride" ("Listen, my children, and you shall hear . . ."); Whittier's "Barefoot Boy" ("Blessings on thee, little man!"); and Lowell's "The Vision of Sir Launfal" ("And what is so rare as a day in June?").

Children memorized such poems in school, and adults remembered them with nostalgia because—in recalling lines of poetry—they were recalling their own youth. In this way, fireside poems functioned much like later 20th-c. popular songs: they worked as repositories for personal and cultural memories. As they were canonized, the poems of the Fireside poets also served an ideological agenda, helping or pushing immigrants to assimilate, North and South to reconcile, and ethnic minorities to identify with the dominant group. Longfellow, esp., became an icon in Am. schoolrooms, representing not just literary virtues but white, middle class, New England values as well. At the same time, however, the Fireside poets were democratic in the sense that they were appreciated by a large section of the Am. public. Readers who knew fireside poems by heart tended to take ownership of them, quoting or parodying them in a range of contexts from sermons to scrapbooks. By the turn of the 20th c., the Fireside poets were an entrenched part of Am. popular culture; as one playground rhyme put it, "You're a poet / and don't know it, / your feet show it / they're long-fellows."

The Fireside poets fell from fashion in the early 20th c. Literary modernists promoted more esoteric and diverse (though often less accessible) forms of poetry, rebelling against what they saw as ossified Victorian conventions. In public schools, new pedagogies deemphasized memorization. Meanwhile, in the domestic sphere, recorded music and radios replaced recitation and parlor theatricals. In the later 20th c., after years of neglect, scholars renewed their interest in the Fireside poets, reading their work as expressions of literary sentimentalism and nationalism or as part of the hist. of childhood. The Fireside poets remain significant, however, mainly because they achieved a level of popularity and familiarity unmatched (thus far) by any other group of Am. poets.

*See* PERFORMANCE; RECITATION; UNITED STATES, POETRY OF THE.

■ J. Justus, "The Fireside Poets," *Nineteenth-Century American Poetry,* ed. A. R. Lee (1985); K. Gruesz, "Feeling for the Fireside," *Sentimental Men,* ed. M. Chapman and G. Hendler (1999); A. Sorby, *Schoolroom Poets* (2005).

A. SORBY

**FLARF.** A 21st-c. school of experimental poetry in the U.S., initiated in 2001 when the Brooklyn poet Gary Sullivan and several friends attempted to write poems so execrable they would be rejected by an online vanity press. The group soon formed an e-mail collective in which they shared their work, collaborated, and developed various signature methods, incl. (but not limited to) the technique of using the Google search engine to mine the Web for verbal material.

Flarf is partly influenced by aspects of earlier avant-garde movements, incl. *futurism's strident trumpeting of new technology, *Dada's antiart ungainliness, *Oulipo's use of game-based *constraints, and *Language poetry's decentering of syntax and reference. Flarf shares with *conceptual poetry the habit of appropriating demotic and commercial discourse, but whereas conceptualist appropriation typically operates at the level of pure citation and transcription, Flarfists often take considerable liberties with their source materials, sculpting and reframing at will.

Increasingly, *flarf* has entered common usage to denote any form of Web-based verbal *collage or any purposely frivolous or incoherent poetry (e.g., "this is just some flarfy drivel I wrote when I was drunk"). It is also sometimes used as a verb (e.g., "she flarfed the senator's speech by replacing all the nouns with *asshat*").

■ *Flarf: An Anthology of Flarf,* ed. K. Mohammad, G. Sullivan, N. Gordon, and S. Mesmer (2013).

K. S. MOHAMMAD

**FLEMISH POETRY.** *See* LOW COUNTRIES, POETRY OF THE.

**FLESHLY SCHOOL OF POETRY.** The name given by Robert Buchanan to D. G. Rossetti, A. C. Swinburne, and William Morris, together with the lesser-known poets Arthur O'Shaughnessy, John Payne, and Philip Bourke Marston. Buchanan coined the term in a review of Rossetti's *Poems* (1870) pub. in the *Contemporary Review* in 1871 under the pseud. Thomas Maitland. Rossetti replied in a letter to the *Athenaeum.* Buchanan then expanded his article into a pamphlet, pub. under his own name, incl. an answer to Rossetti and further attacks on Swinburne. Under the pressure of Buchanan's ad hominem attacks, Rossetti's mental and physical health collapsed. Swinburne counterattacked in his scathing pamphlet *Under the Microscope* (1872), continuing to taunt Buchanan in print until he sued Swinburne's publisher for libel in 1876. Buchanan retracted his crits. of Rossetti in the dedication to his novel *God and the Man* in 1881 and again more explicitly after Rossetti's death, but Rossetti's friends and family never forgave him.

The origins of the fleshly school controversy lay partly in the culture of Victorian literary journalism. Buchanan had published a hostile review of Swinburne's *Poems and Ballads* (1866) in the *Athenaeum,* which led to dismissive remarks about Buchanan's own poetry and that of his dead friend David Gray in articles by Swinburne and his friend W. M. Rossetti. In the late 1860s, Buchanan was supplanted by Swinburne and his circle as the in-house poets of the *Fortnightly Review.* When Buchanan published his ambitious poem *The Book of Orm* in 1870, it received poor reviews, while Rossetti's *Poems* were highly praised in a carefully orchestrated series of reviews written by his friends, incl. Swinburne and Morris.

There were also important aesthetic and ideological differences between Buchanan and his opponents. Buchanan disliked what he considered to be their affected poetic diction and forms, which he exposed through selective quotation and parody. More crucially, he objected to the sensuality of their poetry. Buchanan protested that he was not opposed to the representation of bodily desire itself, only to its elevation into the sole preoccupation of poetry without any spiritual or moral purpose. For all Buchanan's self-justifications, however, the real point at issue was how far it was appropriate to articulate the private realm of sexuality and desire in poetry. The fleshly school controversy thus represents a revealing and important moment in the continuing debate over, in Rossetti's words, "how much . . . is admissible within the limits of Art."

*See* AESTHETICISM, PRE-RAPHAELITISM.

■ T. Maitland [R. Buchanan], "The Fleshly School of Poetry: Mr. D. G. Rossetti," *Contemporary Review* 18 (1871); D. G. Rossetti, "The Stealthy School of Criticism," *Athenaeum* (Dec. 16, 1871); R. Buchanan, *The Fleshly School of Poetry and Other Phenomena of the Day* (1872); A. C. Swinburne, *Under the Microscope* (1872); R. Buchanan, "To an Old Enemy," *God and the Man* (1881)—expanded in 2d ed. (1882) and "A Note on Dante Rossetti," *A Look Round Literature* (1887); J. A. Cassidy, "Robert Buchanan and the Fleshly Controversy," *PMLA* 67 (1952); C. D. Murray, "The Fleshly School Revisited," *Bulletin of John Rylands Library* 65 (1982–83); J. Marsh, *Dante Gabriel Rossetti* (1999); G. Budge, "The Aesthetics of Morbidity: D. G. Rossetti and Buchanan's *The Fleshly School of Poetry*," *Outsiders Looking In*, ed. D. Clifford and L. Roussillon (2004); J. Holmes, *Dante Gabriel Rossetti and the Late Victorian Sonnet Sequence* (2005).

J. HOLMES

**FLYTING.** A Middle Scots word from the verb *to flyte*, "to scold, quarrel, vituperate." At the Stuart courts, it came to mean a contest in verse between two poets in which they insulted each other employing as much metrical expertise, wit, and outrageous invention as they could muster. The earliest surviving flyting is between William Dunbar and Walter Kennedy for the court of James IV. The best is between Alexander Montgomerie and Polwart, presumably Sir Patrick Hume of Polwarth, composed for James VI. These court entertainments are related to the Occitan *tenso and the Welsh *ymryson. Most probably, other flytings were composed that have not survived, but evidence for flytings earlier than Dunbar and Kennedy is lacking. The antiquity of such contests in Scotland is presumed. In England, although they are not called *flytings* as such, we have examples of similar contests: John Skelton's "Against Garnishe" (lacking Garnishe's responses) and "The Contention betwixt [Thomas] Churchyard and Camel" (1560).

The term *flyting* has been extended by scholars to apply to boasting and slanging matches between speakers in literary works. It is often applied to the scene in *Beowulf* between the hero and Unferth. This scene and others like it in *epic and *saga should properly be called *vaunts*. They are often in the context of a court, but they are not ludic contests between poets as in the genuine flyting. There is a close contender, however, in the ON *Lokasenna*.

Invective matches are found in other langs. as well, Ar., Gr., and It. A kind of folk flyting is represented by the *dozens and boys' verbal dueling documented in Turkey.

■ H. M. Shire, *Song, Dance and Poetry of the Court of Scotland under King James VI* (1969); A. Dundes, J. W. Leach, and B. Özkök, "The Strategy of Turkish Boys'

Dueling Rhymes, *JAF* 83 (1970); W. Parks, "Flyting, Sounding, Debate: Three Verbal Contest Genres," *PoT* 7:3 (1986); R. D. Abrahams, "Playing the Dozens," *Mother Wit*, ed. A. Dundes (1990); W. Parks, *Verbal Dueling in Heroic Narrative* (1990); *The Edinburgh History of Scottish Literature*, ed. I. Brown, T. Owen, S. Manning, and M. Pittock, vol. 1 (2006).

E. SLOTKIN

**FOLIA.** Sp. stanza form. A popular four-line variation of the *seguidilla probably related to a Port. dance-song form and normally expressing a nonsensical or ridiculous thought. The lines may be octosyllabic or shorter; if the lines are not of equal length, the even-numbered are generally the shorter and very often—some think properly so—oxytonic. Its origin is unknown, but *folías* antedating 1600 are extant. The following example is from Miguel de Cervantes's *Rinconete y Cortadillo*:

> Por un sevillano
> rufo a lo valón
> tengo socarrado
> todo el corazón.

D. C. CLARKE

**FOLK POETRY.** *See* ORAL POETRY.

**FOOT**

I. Classical
II. Modern

**I. Classical.** The foot (Gr. *pous*, Lat. *pes*, Sanskrit *mātrā* ["measure"], Fr. *pied*, Ger. *Takt* or *Versfuss*) was a basic analytical unit for the prosodic analysis of verse in both the metrical and the musical theories of the ancient Greeks and Romans, consisting in metrical theory of *syllables and in musical theory of abstract temporal units (*morae*) measured in terms of the *chronos prōtos* (primary time). (See MORA; METRICI AND RHYTHMICI.) These fundamental elements—syllables or times—were organized at one higher level into *arsis and thesis, the two components, in most ancient accounts, of every metrical foot. (In Gr. theory, *thesis* refers to the metrically prominent part of the foot, *arsis* to the less prominent part.) Thus, combining two definitions given separately in the scholia to Hephaestion (2d c. CE), Marius Victorinus writes, "The foot is a definite measure of syllables, consisting of arsis and thesis, by which we recognize the form of the entire meter" (6.43, in Keil). Ancient theory classified feet according to (a) the ratio of the duration of arsis to thesis—musically in terms of primary times, metrically in terms of the values *breve* ($\cup$) = 1, *longum* (–) = 2; and (b) the overall duration of the foot. A long syllable (*longum*) was one that ended with a long vowel, a diphthong, or a consonant; a short syllable (*breve*) ended with a short vowel. Although the duration of long syllables in speech was probably not exactly twice that of short syllables, this ratio was assumed for formal purposes, so that a *dactyl (– $\cup$ $\cup$), e.g., could be considered temporally equivalent to a *spondee (– –). The scheme for the simple feet of Gr. verse is as follows:

*genos ison* (1:1):
  tetrasemic:  anapaest  (∪ ∪ –)
                  dactyl    (– ∪ ∪)
*genos diplasion* (2:1, 1:2):
  trisemic:    iamb      (∪ –)
                trochee  (– ∪)
  hexasemic:  ionic a *minore*
                        (∪ ∪ – –)
              ionic a *maiore*
                        (– – ∪ ∪)
*genos hēmiolion* (3:2, 2:3):
  pentasemic: first paeon
                        (– ∪ ∪ ∪)
              cretic    (– ∪ –)
              bacchiac  (∪ – –)

Other ratios are also found, and an *alogos* (Gr., "irrational") ratio, not expressible in terms of the lower integers, was also asserted by some.

Unfortunately, we do not have extant any complete exposition of ancient theory with illustrative analyses of extended passages of *lyric verse; even in antiquity, there were various not completely compatible accounts. Attempts in the 19th c. to interpret ancient theory and apply it to lyric verse, particularly to *aeolic meters, did not achieve satisfactory results. In the 20th c., cl. prosodists have generally rejected both the reality and the descriptive utility of the foot in favor of units defined strictly in terms of *responsion such as the *metron (double the length of the simple feet in some meters and indistinguishable in others) and the *colon (a longer metrical sequence having continuity). Cola, in particular, have been argued for both on metrical grounds and on grounds beyond the strictly metrical, such as their correspondence to repeated lexical/syntactic formulas.

There are good structural and historical reasons to pay attention to metra and cola. The rejection of the foot, however, has tended to sever metrical theory from its linguistic basis. The foot has become more established in phonological theory and cognitive psychology even as it has been called into question in literary studies of ancient and mod. versification. The foot, or something like it, is a principal unit of rhythmic organization in human behavior and perception (see discussion below). Verse achieves greater regularity than speech by constraining the number and sequence of permissible feet.

**II. Modern.** Ren. prosodists and critics, in reaction against medievalism, looked back to cl. antiquity for doctrine on the making of poetry. Many speak of verse's being organized only by syllable count "with some regard of the accent" (Philip Sidney, *Defence of Poesy*), but Brit. schoolchildren from Shakespeare through S. T. Coleridge learned to scan and write the forms of the Lat. feet at school, and John Donne in "A Litanie" speaks of "rhythmique Feete." As

George T. Wright shows, in the early Tudor poets, one finds lines that are clearly composed by feet: they have disyllabic segmentation to excess. But the better poets soon discovered that the verse paradigms they learned at school could be manipulated at a higher level of sophistication; gradually, they began to write lines that could be composed, and understood, without such mechanistic rules yet that could still be scanned—though less simply—by such rules. Scholarly treatises on prosody continued for centuries to teach the doctrine of feet.

Further, from about 1550 to at least 1900, most Western metrical theories derived from *classical prosody, as that was reinterpreted in successive eras–particularly in the 19th c., which saw the rise of cl. philology in Germany. Common to all these theories was the presumption that, in metrical lines, syllables are to be taken together in groups, as metrical units; such units occupy a position in the theory midway between the metrical position (or syllable) and the *line. Both the concept of the metrical foot itself and the particular names and forms of the feet were taken directly from Gr., all of them being redefined as the accentual equivalents of the identical patterns in the quantitative prosody of cl. Gr. Thus, the Gr. *iamb, short + long (∪ –), was reformulated as unstressed + stressed (x /). The Gr. notion of the metron in certain meters was ignored (as were, by and large, other cl. concepts such as the colon, the *anceps syllable, and *brevis in longo). Many prosodists continued to talk of longs and shorts—indeed, for centuries—but, in fact, stress and/or syllable count was the basis for most Western meters by about the 4th c. CE. Whether the foot was an element of poetic composition or merely of analysis—i.e., *scansion—remained an issue of dispute.

Classicizing prosodists in the 19th and early 20th cs., such as J. M. Schipper and G. Saintsbury, tried to map the forms and rules of cl. prosody directly onto Eng., resulting in the foot-substitution model, in which variations from a basic meter are described as substitutions of alternative feet, such as *"trochaic substitutions" in the *iambic line. Thus, highly complex patterns can be made by stringing together various feet. It is apparently this model that T. S. Eliot refers to in "Reflections on Vers Libre" (1917) when he writes, "Any line can be divided into feet and accents. The simpler metres are a repetition of one combination, perhaps a long and a short, or a short and a long syllable, five times repeated. There is, however, no reason why, within the single line, there should be any repetition; why there should not be lines (as there are) divisible only into feet of different types." Versions of this model—sometimes more linguistically sophisticated—are still widely used in poetry handbooks and textbooks.

**A. *Arguments for the Foot.*** After 1920, in the general repudiation by theorists of classicizing theories, a reaction abetted by the rising influence of *free verse and other footloose prosodies, the concept of the metrical foot was called into question. Given the grounds on which it had been justified, such suspicion was deserved. Nevertheless, there are several grounds on which one might yet argue that the foot is a useful component of a theory of *meter, and of Eng. meters in particular:

(1) Lit. hist. As mentioned above, the majority of poets in Eng. for several centuries were schooled in foot-based theories. Some knowledge of the concepts they were taught might help readers to understand these poets' practice and certainly would help to understand their prose writing about poetics.

(2) The very concept of meter as *measure, the measuring out of the flow of words in the line. Measuring requires a unit by which the measuring is done, like the bar lines on a musical score, the dividing lines of which are fictitious but useful. An analogy: the wall of a natural-log house may be 14 feet high and composed of 12 logs, no two of which are the same diameter. If the wall is taken apart, the logs will still have some kind of meaningful existence, but the feet will not. Yet it may still be useful to refer to 14 feet rather than 12 logs. Similarly, words, morphemes, and (to some extent) syllables are recognizable units independent of metrical context, while feet are not. Yet many have found the terminology of feet useful in describing poetic lines.

(3) Comparative metrics. There is at least one metrical unit between the levels of syllable and line in many of the verse systems of the world. These units, naturally, vary in positioning and scope. In the romance prosodies, such as Fr., the units are formed at the phrasal level rather than the word level. In Gr. and Sanskrit prosody, even theorists who do not use feet typically refer to some units, such as metra or cola, that can be combined into lines. In recent years, foot theory has even been applied to "accentual" OE prosody (e.g., by Geoffrey Russom) and to putatively syllabic verse forms such as Welsh *englyn penfyr (by Nigel Fabb).

(4) The structure of lang. itself. Several 20th- and 21st-c. linguists have developed the concept of a foot (or "stress group") as a basic unit of *rhythm, as a domain in which certain phonological rules apply and, in some cases, as a unit of information, in nonpoetic as well as poetic lang. In Great Britain, David Abercrombie, followed by M.A.K. Halliday, designated the foot as a stress followed by one or more optional unstressed syllables, one or more feet then comprising a "tone group," the last of which (usually) bears the sentence accent. In the U.S., Mark Liberman and Alan Prince, Elisabeth Selkirk, and many others developed a similar concept of the foot in phonology, only over a slightly smaller domain: Selkirk also distinguishes a "prosodic word." Indeed, much of the terminology of traditional verse theory, incl. the foot, has been adopted and adapted, from the 1970s onward, by the theories of autosegmental and metrical phonology and more recently by optimality theory. Researchers point out that many unrelated langs. tend to have stress on alternating syllables, so that one stressed and one unstressed syllable form a binary foot; ternary systems are rarer (although these claims are shored up by classifying some unstressed syllables as "extrametrical"). This phonological foot, though defined quite differently from Saintsbury's foot (e.g., it is frequently defined in terms of morae instead of or in addition to syllables), is now widely accepted as a unit in phonological theory—though how it applies to domains as large as a long line of verse is less well agreed upon.

(5) Perceptual psychology and cognitive science. There is evidence suggesting that segmentation or grouping is a natural process manifested in the perception of any rhythmic series. When subjects in experiments are presented with a sequence of identical or different stimuli ranging from roughly 0.5 to 8 times per second, they rapidly (and involuntarily) perceive and learn a rhythmic pattern. The most favored foot structure in such patterns has two differentiated elements. Acoustic stimuli that are differentiated are perceived as strong and weak on the basis of their differences in intensity, duration, and frequency. Trochaic feet are perceived if the strong element is louder and iambic feet if it is (significantly) longer. Linguistic feet also have some degree of temporal regularity; though they are not truly isochronous, they may seem so to listeners (see ISOCHRONISM OR ISOCHRONY). Thus, verse, like lang. and all information-delivery processes, segments the sound stream into units that are set in a relation of correspondence or equivalence with one another. Segmentation and repetition have come to seem fundamental cognitive and aesthetic processes.

Such segmentation does not have to be defined in terms of feet; e.g., some theorists prefer to use the musical terminology of *beats and offbeats, while others have seen the verse line as a string of weak and strong positions or as a "grid" of more and less strongly stressed syllables. However, such theories often wind up indirectly incl. similar kinds of principles, units, and rules (sometimes under different names); e.g., grid theory has evolved to include "bracketing" of feet and larger units. Without some form of segmentation, it would be impossible to distinguish regular or periodic metrical sequences (those that consistently repeat similar units) from irregular ones (those that do not).

**B. Types.** Assuming we call our units feet, the next question is how many types of feet there are, which entails the question of what principles are used to construct the foot. Even well into the 20th c., classicizing prosodists were inclined to admit nearly as many feet in Eng. poetry as in Gr.: Saintsbury lists 21 feet; as late as 1979, Paul Fussell admits six but thinks "it does no harm to be acquainted with" 11 others. But the great majority recognized, by the late 19th c., only four to six types: these included the two commonest binary feet—iambs (x/) and trochees (/x)—and ternary feet—dactyls (/xx) and anapests (xx/)—with the ternary feet far less common than the binary; and some metrists added spondees (//) and *pyrrhics (xx). The nature of Eng. phonology makes verse forms based primarily on spondees and pyrrhics impossible, but these units sometimes play a role in foot-substitution approaches to meter. A few other feet, such as *amphibrachs (x/x), have been used as the basis of metrical composition, but more rarely. Some mid-20th-c. structural linguists admitted dozens or even thousands more types of feet by making distinctions on the basis of linguistic features such as whether the stresses fall in mono- or polysyllables, whether the stresses are natural or promoted-demoted, or other features (see DEMOTION, PROMOTION). But these schemes complicated the analysis unnecessarily by mixing various levels of structure. E.g., there is good evidence that metrical rules distinguish between stress in polysyllables and in monosyllables (lexical stress in polysyllables is often more strictly constrained in what positions in the line it can occupy), but this fact can be handled more elegantly by keeping the levels separate and adding simple rules stating where each type of stress can go or at what level of stress particular rules apply. Most current theories number the foot types in Eng. poetry somewhere between two and five, depending on the principles and criteria applied.

Many prosodists would argue that a foot must contain at least two elements that differ from one another. These arguments posit *alternation* as a fundamental feature of rhythm that operates at every level of the linguistic hierarchy and is, hence, a fundamental process in verse design at several levels of metrical organization. As W. S. Allen puts it, the "principle of alternation is crucial to the manifestation of prosodic pattern, since without it there is only formless succession." The two elements of the foot have been variously termed *arsis* and *thesis* in cl. metrics, *lift* and *dip* in Old Germanic and OE metrics, and *strong* and *weak positions* or else *ictus* and *nonictus* in mod. metrics. These positions in the metrical pattern are typically filled by syllables in the actual line—usually one syllable each, but sometimes more, as specified by the rules of the particular meter.

Some early 20th-c. metrists proposed the "monosyllabic foot"—i.e., a stressed syllable alone without any attached unstressed syllables (or stress plus a hypothesized pause)—to account for irregularities such as extra syllables, missing syllables, or displaced stresses in lines. In this view, sequences such as /xx/ in the first four syllables of the Eng. iambic *pentameter are seen not as a trochaic substitution or inverted foot followed by an iamb, but as a monosyllabic foot followed by a trisyllabic substitution—or, if stress always comes first, as a dactyl followed by a monosyllabic foot. But on the principle of alternation or opposition of heterogeneous members, monosyllabic feet are apparently not legitimate feet at all, but a contradiction in terms (a point made as early as Aristoxenus: "one *chronos* cannot make a foot"). Equally inadmissible would be all feet with homogeneous members such as the spondee, pyrrhic, *molossus, and *tribrach.

However, other metrists have suggested ways in which monosyllabic feet could play a role. First, if feet are based on morae rather than syllables (as they frequently are in metrical phonology), a two-mora (heavy) syllable can be a foot without violating the

alternation principle. Second, temporalist poetic theorists such as George Stewart and Derek Attridge have argued that pauses corresponding to "implied offbeats," somewhat like musical rests, may follow a stress or beat to maintain rhythm in some circumstances, notably that of stress clash (roughly speaking, adjacent stressed syllables). Although Attridge's analysis avoids using feet, there is no a priori reason stress plus lengthening or silence could not form a two-part, strongweak foot. This view is consistent with phonological theories claiming extra time added in such positions (even if the pause is much shorter than an actual unstressed syllable) and with poetic lines in which an unstressed syllable seems to be missing. E.g., in Shakespeare's "Blow, winds, and crack your cheeks! Rage! Blow!" (*King Lear*), the expectation of iambic pentameter can only be met if we allow "Rage!" and "Blow!" to be feet by themselves. In P. B. Shelley's "To The Night," the line "Thy brother death came, and cried" (cited by Attridge) occurs in an iambic *tetrameter context; the line that rhymes with it is the regular eight-syllable "Thy sweet child Sleep, the filmy-eyed." These lines are congruent if we alleviate stress clash by hearing an "implied offbeat" (x) between "death" and "came:"

Thy bro | ther death | (x) came, | and cried

Thy sweet | child Sleep, | the fil | my-eyed

Foot-substitution theory deals with such lines only awkwardly. Popular verse such as *ballads, *nursery rhymes, and advertising *jingles provides many similar examples, as (less obviously) does literary iambic verse. Even where the syllable count is regular, as in Alexander Pope's pentameter line "And the pressed watch return'd a silver sound," Stewart argues that scanning the first four syllables as a trisyllabic foot (*anapest) followed by a monosyllabic foot corresponds better to readers' actual experience of the line than calling them two iambs (one stressed weakly, one strongly).

Monosyllabic feet aside, if every foot must contain just one stress along with its contiguous unstressed syllables, there can be only five types of binary and ternary feet: iamb, trochee, dactyl, anapest, amphibrach. But the latter three are very difficult to differentiate in running series, esp. when line ends are irregular and unpredictable: in mod. verse, the sequence x/xx/xx/xx/ may be felt as anapestic tetrameter with a missing first syllable, but it can also be amphibrachic with a missing final syllable—that perception depends on the larger context and on word and phrase boundaries in the line. In practice, all ternaries are effectively one meter, esp. in relatively long lines. The same argument has been made about the two binary meters, and the frequency of lines such as /x/x/x/ or /x/x/x/x/ in both iambic and trochaic contexts lends this claim some support. In that case, there are basically two types of meter in Eng.: *binary and ternary. However, Halpern (followed by others) has suggested that iambic differs from all trochaic, ternary, and accentual meters in that these latter do not admit of modulation. For him, there are only two classes of mod. meters, iambic and accentual. (See ACCENTUAL VERSE.)

C. *Applicability.* We have seen evidence that the foot can be more than a mere device for scansion, that it is a principle of structure. If, in fact, the foot is a fundamental element of rhythm, then it must play a role in both the composition and performance of rhythmic poetry. However, this does not necessarily mean that poets consciously think of feet as they compose, much less that readers think of feet as they perform aloud. One difficulty is that traditional foot-substitution scansion works only on regular verse. If irregularity exceeds a certain threshold, the idea of substitution becomes nonsensical, and we must turn to other ways of describing the rhythm. Another problem is that this device naturally tends to become reified, so that readers (and even poets) may come to believe that poets actually make verse foot by foot, laboring to find a dactyl or a molossus rather than to write rhythmic lines and sequences of lines. (Eliot remarks, in "The Music of Poetry," that "a study of anatomy will not teach you how to make a hen lay eggs.") The fact that feet are, arguably, one component of the verse structure does not tell us whether the poet composed, or the performer should recite, with feet in mind.

See ACCENT, COUPE, EQUIVALENCE, PERIOD, QUANTITY, RELATIVE STRESS PRINCIPLE, RISING AND FALLING RHYTHM, SYNAPHEIA, VARIABLE FOOT.

■ **Classical:** Keil; Wilamowitz; L. Nougaret, *Traité de métrique latine classique* (1948); L. P. Wilkinson, *Golden Latin Artistry* (1963); Koster; Dale; W. S. Allen, *Accent and Rhythm* (1973); J. Halporn, M. Ostwald, and T. G. Rosenmeyer, *The Meters of Greek and Latin Poetry*, rev. ed. (1980); West; A. M. Devine and L. D. Stephens, *Language and Metre* (1984); A. S. Gratwick, *Plautus: Menaechmi* (1993); A. M. Devine and L. D. Stephens, *The Prosody of Greek Speech* (1994); Gasparov, *History*; L.P.E. Parker, *The Songs of Aristophanes* (1997); J. Parsons, "A New Approach to the Saturnian Verse," *TAPA* 129 (1999); G. Nagy, *Homer's Text and Language* (2004); C. Golston and T. Riad, "The Phonology of Greek Lyric Meter," *JL* 41.1 (2005); C. Questa, *La Metrica di Plauto e Terenzio* (2007).

■ **Modern:** G. Saintsbury, *A History of English Prosody* (1906–10), and *Historical Manual of English Prosody* (1910); Schipper, *History*; G. Stewart, *The Technique of English Verse* (1958); M. Halpern, "On the Two Chief Metrical Modes in English," *PMLA* 77 (1962); Chatman; C. L. Stevenson, "The Rhythm of English Verse," *JAAC* 28 (1970); W. S. Allen, *Accent and Rhythm* (1973); M. Shapiro, *Asymmetry* (1976); R. Jakobson, "Linguistics and Poetics" (1960), rpt. in *Selected Writings*, vol. 5 (1988); P. Fussell, *Poetic Meter and Poetic Form* (1979); Scott; Brogan, sect. E; D. Attridge, *The Rhythms of English Poetry* (1982); G. T. Wright, *Shakespeare's Metrical Art* (1988); J. A. Goldsmith, *Autosegmental and Metrical Phonology* (1990); Cureton; B. Hayes, *Metrical Stress Theory* (1995); K. Hanson and P. Kiparsky, "A Parametric Theory of Poetic Meter," *Language* 72.2 (1996); G. Russom,

*"Beowulf" and Old Germanic Meter* (1998); M. Kinzie, *A Poet's Guide to Poetry* (1999); T. Steele, *All the Fun's in How You Say a Thing* (1999); N. Fabb, *Language and Literary Structure* (2002); N. Fabb and M. Halle, *Meter in Poetry* (2008).

A. M. DEVINE; L. D. STEPHENS;
T.V.F. BROGAN; G. B. COOPER

**FORM.** As a term for the multiple systems that shape as well as convey information, *form* is a dynamic subject in philosophy and metaphysics, linguistic theory, literary analysis, visual and material arts, and culture at large. The *OED* gives 22 definitions, with subcategory refinements and variations. Even with a focus on poetry and poetics, coherent definition is difficult. Poetic form used to be binary: what was not content or context; the shape rather than the substance; any element or event of lang. not translatable, paraphrasable, or reducible to information. The binary entails a distinction between preexisting origin and material result, between determination and effect, between idea or feeling and its realization. Yet lang. theory from the 18th c. on (and poetic practice well before) has been challenging these binaries, most forcefully with the notion of constitutive form—form as active producer, not just passive register, of meaning.

To appeal to the Lat. root *forma* is suggestive but inconclusive, for it reproduces the question, indicating both an ideal abstraction (correlative to the Gr. *eidos*, "primary idea") and a material appearance or shape. Plato and Aristotle often stand for this difference: form as the unchanging, structuring principle; form as the structure of a particular instance. In the Platonic view, famously articulated in *The Republic*, bk. 10, form is a transcendent idea and essential ideal, distinct from merely suggestive material instantiations. For Aristotle, form is immanent, emergent, and coactive with its expressive materials—the several cases from which a general typology may be deduced. Platonic form is authorized by transcendent origin; Aristotelian form is realized in process, devel., and achievement.

Prose form may refer to macrostructures of argument, narrative, plot, or schemes of fictive organization; to the length and array of its composite units (chapters, paragraphs, sentences); or to the formation of the sentence by patterns of syntax, rhythm and sound, image and figure. Prose can be "poetic" in these aspects (and there is a genre of *prose poem); conversely, poetry may sound prosaic (as some complain about *blank verse), relaxing formal definition to evoke conversation or a pre-formal flux of consciousness. There are, moreover, composite forms: interplays of prose and verse, of visual and verbal forms. William Blake's pages show all this, as well as a visual poetics of verbal forms: the sublime walls of words, the semiotics of block letters and free-flowing script. Another form is the shaped poem (see VISUAL POETRY), such as George Herbert's "Altar" and "Easter Wings," with the poetic lines organized into a visual shape, to signify a close connection of informing subject and expressive form.

What distinguishes *poetic* form is the *line that

is a poet's determination, not a compositor's. Line-forms may involve the suspense of *enjambment and the punctuation of blank space at the line's end—as in William Wordsworth's "There was a Boy": "in that silence, while he hung / Listening." While the compositor of the second ed. of *Lyrical Ballads* (in which this verse was first published) set the lines of its new Preface, the poet shaped this line and decided where to end it (here, to recruit the pause and cut to the suspense of "hung."). Blake is among those poets for whom even hyphenation can be poetic form, springing semantically pertinent syllables at a line's end, sometimes flouting standard practice ("Here alone I in books formd of me-/-tals")—this cut set to spring "me" from the medium. The form of a poetic line can follow, press against, or overturn metrical forms and trads.; it can be arranged in stanzas (regular or not, traditional or innovative), and play across end-rhyme patterns and rhyme fields. In all its events, poetic form signals a relation to trad.—whether using or refusing it, whether honoring or violating decorum, whether endorsing standards or applying a new signature. There is a trad. of auto-referential poetic forms, such as sonnets on the *sonnet.

Mindful of cl. theories, and with immediate debts to A. W. Schlegel, S. T. Coleridge distinguishes "mechanic form" from "organic form" (see ORGANICISM): "mechanic form" is the impression of "a pre-determined form, not necessarily arising out of the properties of the material," while "organic form" is "innate; it shapes, as it develops itself from within, and the fullness of its devel. is one and the same with the perfection of its outward form. Such as the life is, such is the form" (*Lectures on Shakespeare*). G. M. Hopkins's poetics of *inscape and instress evolve from this distinction. Like Hopkins, Coleridge reflects, even dramatizes, organic poetics in his practice. He may work a received form against the emotional and dramatic demands of the event at hand (his sonnet "To Asra" plays its "overflowing" passion across enjambments that challenge the orders of rhyme); or he may make the mechanics part of the meaning: the poetic forms of repetition that plague *The Rime of the Ancient Mariner* correlate the endless repetitions of the mariner's existential fate. Or he may use shifts in meter for dramatic effects, as in the leveling of a curse in "Christabel" (see CHRISTABEL METER).

Lang. itself is both a received form and material for transformation. Invoking the complexities of *forma*, Coleridge correlates outward shape with shaping principle, contingency with determinate forces, to theorize a living process materially realizing itself: "'*Forma formans per formam formatam translucens*' [forming form through formed form shining] is the definition and perfection of *ideal* art" (*Biographia Literaria*); "Something there must be to realize the form, something in and by which the *forma informans* reveals itself" ("Principles of Genial Criticism"). Formal practices are also contextually charged. In the era of the French Revolution, a discourse of "organic form"—seemingly liberated from

prescription to follow the pulse of nature—could be invoked for principles of liberal education or could be harnessed to conservative ideology, to defend a system of unequal but complementary subjects on the model of nature. Thus, Edmund Burke on the hierarchy of classes, of rank and servitude stated in *Reflections on the Revolution in France* (1790): "Our political system is placed in a just correspondence and symmetry with the order of the world . . . moulding together the great mysterious incorporation of the human race . . . preserving the method of nature in the conduct of the state"; "The characteristic essence of property, formed out of the combined principles of its acquisition and conservation, is to be *unequal*."

Choices of poetic form signify, too. To write in *ballad form is to evoke an alliance, desired or ironized, with oral and popular culture; a *Spenserian stanza conjures Spenserian "romance." The difficulty of this last form, moreover, flaunts a poet's skill, as do other famously intricate forms, such as *terza rima or the *sestina and its multiples. A first-person blank-verse lyric recalls the soliloquies of William Shakespeare's tragic heroes, as John Milton knew when he dictated the great, anguished meditation on his blindness at the head of *Paradise Lost*, bk. 3. Milton's epic blank verse also bears a politics of form, which he advertised in 1674 as a recovery of "ancient liberty" from "the troublesom and modern bondage of Rimeing" for the sake of "apt Numbers, fit quantity of Syllables, and the sense variously drawn out from one Verse into another." To write a blank-verse *epic in the 19th c. is to declare not only a release from the regime of 18th-c. *couplets but an affection (with aesthetic or political prestige) for Miltonic poetics. When Wordsworth wrote about shepherd Michael in epic blank verse (rather than in a ballad), his challenge to decorum struck some contemporaries as unpoetic, ludicrous, or worse: the poetic wing of the French Revolution in advancing the lower classes to higher forms. But the quiet dignity brought tears to Matthew Arnold's Victorian eyes.

In 1818, William Hazlitt took a satiric perspective on the patent politics of mod. poetics: "rhyme was looked upon as a relic of the feudal system, and regular metre was abolished along with regular government" ("Living Poets"). Even so, such allegories are slippery. By 1814, Tory Wordsworth was writing a blank-verse epic (*The Excursion*), and Liberal Lord Byron was hewing to rhyme: "Prose poets like blank-verse, I'm fond of rhyme, / Good workmen never quarrel with their tools," he wrote in *ottava rima (*Don Juan*, 1819). In 1816, political liberals such as Leigh Hunt were wielding couplets with cheeky avant-garde flash. Even the affection in the 18th c. for orderly heroic couplets is no clear signifier: it may convey a neoclassical ethos (aesthetic, political, social) of balance and symmetry; or it may pose a highly wrought artificial contrast to the messiness of material life in its economic turmoil, political intrigues and perils, and unrelenting urban filth. A dramatic *monologue arrayed in *pentameter couplets, yet with rhythms and enjambments that mute meter and rhyme, stages an artifice of subtly crafted casual conversation—the canny form that Robert Browning devised for a duke speaking with affable condescension to a count's envoy about his last and (he hopes) next duchess.

When, in 1951, Cleanth Brooks contended that "form is meaning," he was holding faith with "the primary concern of criticism": "the problem of unity—the kind of whole which the literary work forms or fails to form, and the relation of the various parts to each other in building up this whole" ("Formalist Critic"). Yet Paul de Man saw in this "problem" a blind but incipient theorizing of form as indeterminacy, a "rhetoric of temporality" in which form can never achieve organic completion or totality ("Temporality"). As the dynamic register and producer of tensions, ironies, and contradictions, form, to de Man, necessarily subverts the "totalizing principle" in the mind of the poet and reader to open into a field of active, ceaseless negotiation ("Form and Intent").

Even critics such as Terry Eagleton in 1976, who tended to indict the stabilizing allure of literary forms for recasting "historical contradictions into ideologically resolvable form," have been rethinking the charge. By 1986, Eagleton was admitting that while a literary text is "constrained" by formal principles, it can also put these into question—a dynamic "most evident in a poem, which deploys words usually to be found in the lexicon, but by combining and condensing them generates an irreducible specificity of force and meaning." By 2007, he was writing about poetic form in terms with which Brooks (though with different social poetics) might concur:

> Form and content are inseparable in this sense—that literary criticism typically involves grasping *what* is said in terms of *how* it is said . . . . this seems true above all in poetry—a literary genre which could almost be defined as one in which form and content are intimately interwoven. It is as though poetry above all discloses the secret truth of literary writing: that form is *constitutive* of content and not just a reflection of it. Tone, rhythm, rhyme, syntax, assonance, grammar, punctuation, and so on, are actually generators of meaning, not just containers of it. To modify any of them is to modify meaning itself.

In theory, crit., and poetic practice, distillations of form from contexts, contents, and contingencies of event are difficult to manage because form is meaningful and meanings are formed. Lang. shaped in poetic form resists conscription as information for other frameworks of analysis; the forms are performative, informative, a context, a content, and an activity in reading. Our bibliographies are rife with titles that begin "*Form and* . . ." or "*Forms of* . . ." (often with the deconstructive pressure of a sequel, ". . . *of Forms*") or that pun into cognates of *reform, deform, perform, inform, formal*. Far from supplying a stable referent, form shapes the question, restlessly in play as a barometer of critical and theoretical investments. Form, poetry, and poetics seem destined to versatile, volatile, unpredictable transformations.

*See* FORMALISM, METER, NEW CRITICISM, RHYME, RUSSIAN FORMALISM, STANZA.

■ C. Brooks, *The Well Wrought Urn* (1947), and "The Formalist Critic," *KR* (1951); E. Cassirer, *Philosophy of Symbolic Forms*, trans. R. Manheim (1953); S. Langer, *Feeling and Form* (1953); K. Burke, *Philosophy of Literary Form* (1957); G. Hartman, *Beyond Formalism* (1970); P. de Man, "The Rhetoric of Temporality" (1969) and essays in *Blindness and Insight* (1971); C. Ricks, "A pure organic pleasure from the lines," *Essays in Criticism* (1971); Hollander; T. Eagleton, *Criticism and Ideology* (1976); P. Fussell, *Poetic Meter and Poetic Form* (1979); M. Perloff, *The Poetics of Indeterminacy* (1981); R. Barthes, *The Responsibility of Forms*, trans. R. Howard (1982); W. Keach, *Shelley's Style* (1984); J. H. Miller, *The Linguistic Moment* (1985); T. Eagleton, *William Shakespeare* (1986); D. Attridge, *Peculiar Language* (1988); J. Hollander, *Melodious Guile* (1988), and *Rhyme's Reason* (1989); *The Politics of Poetic Form,* ed. C. Bernstein (1990); M. Jay, *Force Fields* (1993); D. Attridge, "Literary Form and the Demands of Politics," in *Aesthetics and Ideology*, ed. G. Levine (1994)—also essays therein by Keach and Wolfson; P. Hobsbaum, *Metre, Rhythm and Verse Form* (1996); S. Wolfson, *Formal Charges* (1997); I. Armstrong, *The Radical Aesthetic* (2000); R. Strier, "How Formalism Became a Dirty Word, and Why We Can't Do without It," in *Renaissance Literature and Its Formal Engagements* (2002); D. Donoghue, *Speaking of Beauty* (2003); W. Keach, *Arbitrary Power* (2004); C. Levine, "Strategic Formalism," and H. Tucker, "Tactical Formalism," *Victorian Studies* (2006); P. Alpers, "Renaissance Lyrics and Their Situations," *NLH* 38 (2007); T. Eagleton, *How to Read a Poem* (2007); A. Leighton, *On Form: Poetry, Aestheticism, and the Legacy of a Word* (2007); M. Levinson, "What is New Formalism?" *PMLA* 122 (2007); *Reading for Form*, ed. S. Wolfson and M. Brown (2007).

S. J. WOLFSON

# FORMALISM

**I. Theory and Criticism**
**II. Poetry**

**I. Theory and Criticism.** In crit. and theory, as in aesthetics, *formalism* signifies a concern with a work's formal features, not only its representational or thematic elements. For Brooks, "a good poem is an object in which form and content can be distinguished but cannot really be separated" (*The Well Wrought Urn*, "Afterword"). In the extreme formalism of the Eng. artist and critic Roger Fry, attention to form is indeed separated from and may even displace issues of content and meaning (Fried); Fry's elder contemporary, J.A.M. Whistler, titled his portrait of his mother *Arrangement* *in Grey and Black*. But for most formalist critics, the isolation of formal properties is only a necessary first step; the second step is to interpret those properties so as to connect their signifying power with the meanings produced by semantic and thematic elements. A work's form cannot finally be separated from its meaning because form itself, when interpreted, is an essential source of meaning.

Not confined to a single critical school, formalism is most closely associated with the linguistically oriented Rus. formalists and their efforts to define features and effects of poetic lang. (see RUSSIAN FORMALISM); with Am. New Critics' concern to eschew paraphrase and disclose the distinctive lang., structure, and organic unity of poems (see NEW CRITICISM); and with the Fr. pedagogical trad. of *explication de texte*. Formalism's technique of detailed textual attention—*close reading—also links it with the philologically based crit. of E. R. Curtius and esp. Erich Auerbach and Leo Spitzer (who place little emphasis on works as artistic wholes) and, more loosely still, with the trad. of Ger. stylistics (Karl Vossler and Emil Staiger, among others). Close reading is also a feature of deconstruction, which rejects the New Critics' quest for textual unity in favor of the complex, often dissonant processes of signification, and of *New Historicism, which applies close reading to literary texts but also to nonliterary documents and cultural beliefs, practices, and objects—incl. material objects. While most of these modes of analysis employ techniques of close reading, however, New Criticism and contemp. neoformalism focus intently on the lang. and meaning of texts understood as formally unified wholes and complex organizations of meaning.

The New Critics, building on T. S. Eliot, I. A. Richards, and William Empson (preceded by S. T. Coleridge and, at a great distance, Aristotle), put formalist attention to lang. in the service of literary interpretation according to the following assumptions. The sources of a poem and the responses of its readers should be subordinated to examination of the literary object itself. Poetic lang. is rich, complex, and paradoxical, and poems are organic—but tensional—unities, "ironic" in Brooks's special sense of acknowledging contradictory alternatives to their formulations or attitudes, much as Andrew Marvell's poetry "involves . . . a recognition, implicit in the expression of every experience, of other kinds of experience which are possible" (Eliot). These verbal and thematic tensions intimate a view of experience that is "mature": it is complex, it refuses simplifications or slogans, and its affirmations fully acknowledge contrary experience and counteraffirmations. The poem, moreover, participates in the experience it represents, and as Wimsatt and others argue, is a verbal analogue of that experience rather than a mere reference to it.

Brooks and Ransom differ significantly on the concept of unity and on the poem's relation to the world. For Brooks, the poem's details, however recalcitrant, are finally absorbed into its overarching structure; the poet's task "is finally to unify experience." And the poem—"a simulacrum" of that unified reality—is "an

experience rather than any mere statement about experience" (Brooks). In contrast, Ransom imagines a poem as "a loose logical structure with an irrelevant texture," a texture consisting of particulars that "the poem's logical argument or prose sense cannot fully absorb" (Ransom). The refractoriness of these textural elements mirrors the resistance of concrete, worldly particulars to modes of instrumental discourse (abstract, generalizing, scientific) that would assimilate and ontologically tyrannize over those particulars rather than know them for their own sake (Ransom 1938).

Starting in the last decades of the 20th c., formalist crit. has seen a resurgence, chiefly in the Am. academy and concerning Eng.-lang. poetry. While they are not organized as a school or movement, and some would resist labeling their work at all, recent neoformalists generally agree to reject or revise a number of New Critical assumptions, particularly the belief in organic unity, in a distinctively literary or poetic lang., in the intrinsic character of textual meaning, and in the text as a "given" object. Instead, they pursue close reading without the assumption of organic form or explore deconstructive and other models of textual heterogeneity and disunity or posit unity as an enabling fiction rather than an empirically verifiable quality—creating "makeshift, contingent wholes in order to study [literary and] cultural events and patterns" (Levine).

A similar move—positing a text's literariness or assuming that critical attention itself confers literariness—replaces the New Critical belief in intrinsic differences between literary and nonliterary texts; literary meaning, too, is the product of framing a text in a way that generates such meaning. Poetic speaker or *persona, *intention, and reference are similarly reconceived by neoformalists. In contrast to once-controversial arguments that a text's meaning can be only its author's *intended* meaning, some neoformalists extend the New Critical argument that speaker and intention (like audience) are internal rather than external phenomena. Others view intention, and even reference, as generated by a text on the model of back formation, a ling. process analogous to the narrative "prequel": *enthuse* produced by back formation from *enthusiasm*, e.g., or (comically) *gruntled* from *disgruntled* (Štekauer; Bogel). On this model, speaker, intention, and referent do not preexist—but are generated by—the text itself.

Addressing the reiterated charge that formalism ignores historical and social reality and retreats into an aestheticism the politics of which is quietist or worse, one strand of neoformalism explicitly links the study of literary form with hist., politics, and culture. Wolfson argues that "the articulation of form" should be understood "not merely as a product of social evaluations, but as a social evaluation itself, one of the texts in which culture is written." For Wolfson, "Romanticism's involvement with poetic form . . . participates in central discussions of its historical moment" (Wolfson). But if some critics view contemp. formalism as capable of revitalizing critical modes traditionally opposed—or immune—to formalist inquiry, they often refuse to assume that formalism is ancillary to historical crit. Instead, many contemp. practitioners see formal reading as a mode of historical or political crit. or vice versa and explore the convergence among these critical modes in ways that would have been unheard of in earlier formalisms.

Neoformalism has also fostered a rethinking of Kantian and post-Kantian aesthetics. One version of this rethinking concerns feeling, particularly pleasure—e.g., the possibility of staging affective identificatory moments between reader and text (Altieri). Another version moves toward the cognitive, the moral, and the constitution of human agency. It contends that "aesthetic experience is 'formal' because it provides *the form for* conceptual, 'objective' thought or cognition" and that "aesthetic form" contributes to "the possibilities of critical thought and agency," incl. moral agency (Kaufman; see also Knapp and Levinson).

If neoformalists share a single, fundamental belief, it is that there can be no meaning without form, that "formalism is a matter . . . of refusing to reduce reading entirely to the elucidation, essentially the paraphrase, of themes—theoretical, ideological, or humanistic" (Rooney).

**II. Poetry.** In virtually all eras and langs. until the 20th c., verse has been distinguished from prose by formal patterns of *meter, *rhyme, and other audible repeating structures of lang. (see VERSE AND PROSE). Perhaps because these repeating structures were previously so ubiquitous as to seem inseparable from verse, in the West it was only with the romantic period and the growth of *free verse that strict adherence to certain kinds of repeating structures became a conscious strategy and *formalism* (the *OED* documents the first usage of the word in 1840) a manifest poetic attitude.

After a century dominated by free verse, the role of form in poetry has become more evident. Formal devices, esp. meter, help cultures pass on poetic trads. through generations, even without writing, by making poems easier to memorize (see ORAL POETRY). Furthermore, meter sensitizes readers to lang. because its repeating elements are meaningful in their lang. (Kiparsky). Thus, *accent, carrying lexical meaning in Ger. but not in Fr., is a prosodic element in Ger. poetry (not in Fr. poetry), while *tone, carrying lexical meaning in Chinese but not in Eng., is a prosodic element in Chinese poetry (not in Eng. poetry). While these mnemonic and educational functions are less essential in the age of contemp. technologies, they still contribute to the value and importance of form. A third function of form is neurological and may have therapeutic as well as aesthetic implications: the repetitions of poetic structure appeal to the right hemisphere—the part of the brain that processes music. In this context, formal poetry is closer to music than to free verse and prose, both of which appeal to the part of the brain that processes logical thought (Jaynes). The hypnotic effect of formal poetry has been recognized by writers on poetics from Plato to Coleridge, and contemp. science may

prove it to have pragmatic value: research in progress indicates that autistic people learn meter and strict poetic forms such as the *villanelle readily and suggests that poetic forms have a calming effect on the right hemisphere of the brain (Savarese).

Today, the term *formalism* refers both to the writing and reading of poetry in a way that foregrounds the unique role of ling. structures. Recent proponents of form in poetry, incl. the group known as the New Formalists, who achieved prominence in the 1980s and 1990s, cite its unifying and pleasurable (whether lulling or stimulating) effects and its potential appeal to a wide circle of readers (see NEW FORMALISM). Some cite the emergence of audio technologies and performance poetry as a major factor in the resurgence of form (see PERFORMANCE). Whatever the reasons, while formal poems have been a small minority of those published in the U.S. in the late 20th and early 21st cs., interest in form began to accelerate in the late 1980s and early 1990s, with handbooks, anthols., special issues of jours., and conference panels devoted to poetic form burgeoning.

At the same time that poetics of the late 20th c. was ostensibly dominated by conflict between the stereotypes of progressive "free" and hidebound "formal" verse, avant-garde exploratory poetry, particularly the procedural poets influenced by the *Oulipo movement through Jackson Mac Low, became increasingly concerned with questions of form. As Cushman remarks, *formalism* in the poetry of the U.S. "implies a profound engagement with various aspects of poetic form, regardless of whether they are traditional or avant-garde." After all, the Language poets' emphasis on "opacity" had been anticipated by the Rus. formalist emphasis on the "defamiliarization" of lang. (see LANGUAGE POETRY).

While form in Eng.-lang. poetry before the 20th c. was dominated by rhymed or unrhymed *iambic poetry, contemp. poetic form is radically altered because of the influence of avant-garde movements and trads., the intervening century of free verse, and the borrowing of forms from many cultures. Fr. and Japanese forms in the early 20th c., followed by the *blues, *décima, *ghazal, and *pantun in the later 20th c., have all broken open and widened the idea of form. Nonetheless, a basic inclusive definition of form still suffices. Simply put, a formal poem is a poem structured by the predictable repetition of a lang. element or elements. Any lang. element can be repeated to structure a poem. The more conspicuous the repeated lang. element, such as accent in *accentual verse, the more "formal" the poem feels to us. (It is important to distinguish between structure and decoration; any poem can be decorated by *alliteration, but only a poem in which alliteration forms a predictable skeleton, such as OE alliterative verse, is structured by it).

The same definition of form and formal devices also largely applies to langs. other than Eng., in most of which the mod. Western trend of free verse displaced traditional forms during the 20th c.—e.g., Ar., Chinese, Farsi, Fr., Ger., Japanese, It., Nepalese, Norwegian, Port., Rus., and Swedish. In some of these langs., formalism subsequently made a slight resurgence, though the New Formalist movement in the U.S. has remained more organized and widespread than its counterparts in other countries. Organized resurgences of poetic formalism outside the U.S. today include the Swedish-Norwegian retrogardist movement, centered on the jour. *Aorta* pub. in Gothenburg, Sweden, and similar movements in Belgium, Estonia, and Slovenia. Where there is no organized movement, there are often individual scholars or poets with strong interests in formalism who are aware of Am. New Formalism (Amaral, Fricker). In an era when consumer novelty and incessant growth are giving way globally to the need for more sustainable structures, formalism may soon uncover new analogues for poetic form.

*See* ESTILISTICA, FOOT, PROSODY, REFRAIN, RHYTHM, SCANSION, SOUND, VERSIFICATION.

■ **Theory and Criticism:** J. C. Ransom, *The World's Body* (1938), and *The New Criticism* (1941); Brooks; W. K. Wimsatt, *The Verbal Icon* (1954); Brooks and Warren; Wellek and A. Warren; G. Hartman, "Beyond Formalism," *Beyond Formalism* (1970); T. S. Eliot, "Andrew Marvell," *Selected Prose of T. S. Eliot*, ed. F. Kermode (1975); V. Erlich, *Russian Formalism*, 3d ed. (1981); A. Liu, "The Power of Formalism: The New Historicism," *ELH* 56.4 (1989); S. Knapp, *Literary Interest: The Limits of Anti-Formalism* (1993); W. J. Spurlin, "Afterword: An Interview with Cleanth Brooks," *The New Criticism and Contemporary Literary Theory*, ed. W. J. Spurlin and M. Fischer (1995); S. J. Wolfson, *Formal Charges: The Shaping of Poetry in British Romanticism* (1997); R. Kaufman, "Everybody Hates Kant: Blakean Formalism and the Symmetries of Laura Moriarty," *MLQ* 61.1 (2000); P. Štekauer, *English Word-Formation* (2000); *Renaissance Literature and its Formal Engagements*, ed. M. D. Rasmussen (2002); C. Altieri, *The Particulars of Rapture* (2003); D. Donoghue, *Speaking of Beauty* (2003); M. Fried, *Roger Fry's Formalism* (2004); C. Levine, "Strategic Formalism: Toward a New Method in Cultural Studies," *Victorian Studies* 48.4 (2006); E. Rooney, "Form and Contentment," *Reading for Form*, ed. S. J. Wolfson and M. Brown (2006); M. Levinson, "What Is New Formalism?" *PMLA* 122 (2007), http://sitemaker.umich.edu/pmla_article/home/.

■ **Poetry:** V. Nabokov, *Notes on Prosody* (1965); *Readings in Russian Poetics*, ed. L. Matejka and K. Pomorska (1971); P. Kiparsky, "The Role of Linguistics in a Theory of Poetry," *Daedalus* (Summer 1973); P. Fussell, *Poetic Meter and Poetic Form* (1975); J. Jaynes, *The Origin of Consciousness in the Breakdown of the Bicameral Mind* (1976); *The Structure of Verse*, ed. H. Gross (1979); G. Doczi, *The Power of Limits* (1981); P. Steiner, *Russian Formalism* (1984); P. Oppenheimer, *The Birth of the Modern Mind* (1989); S. Cushman, *Fictions of Form in American Poetry* (1993); F. Capra, *Web of Life* (1996); *Meter in English*, ed. D. Baker (1996); *After New Formalism*, ed. A. Finch (1999); V. Amaral, "Poesia contemporânea nos Estados Unidos," *Revista Garrafa* (2005), http://www.ciencialit.letras.ufrj.br/

garrafa7/9.html; C. Fricker, *Living Together* (2006); J. Tuo, "Origin and Evolution of New Formalism in American Poetry," *Journal of Tianjin Foreign Studies University* 5 (2007); *Multiformalisms*, ed. A. Finch and S. Schultz (2008); R. Savarese, "The Lobes of Autobiography: Poetry and Autism," *Stone Canoe* 2 (2008).

F. BOGEL (THEORY AND CRITICISM);
A. FINCH (FORM)

**FORMULA.** Formula, theme, and story pattern are the structural units of oral composition delineated by the *oral-formulaic theory. Originally defined by Milman Parry in *The Traditional Epithet in Homer* (1928) as "a group of words which is regularly employed under the same metrical conditions to express a given essential idea," the formula has since been identified as the "atom" of oral-traditional phraseology in dozens of trads. South Slavic oral epic singers (*guslari*; see GUSLAR), e.g., identify their *reči* (words) as no smaller than a whole or partial poetic line (Foley 2002), a composite formula unit. The formula is to be distinguished from simple repetition on the basis of its consummate usefulness to the composing oral poet, who employs it not because of its rhetorical effect but because it is part of the traditional poetic idiom bequeathed to him by generations of *bards, an idiom that combines the practical and immediate value of ready-made phraseology with the aesthetic advantage of enormous connotative force.

Although earlier scholars, chiefly the Ger. philologists of the 19th c., had referred in general terms to formulaic diction (esp. Sievers's *Formelverzeichnis* and the ling. analyses of Düntzer), Parry was the first to describe the existence and morphology of this phraseological element with precision, to demonstrate its tectonic function, and to link the traditional phrase with composition in oral performance. His studies of Homeric epic (1928–32) showed how traditional composition was made possible by the bard's ability to draw on an inherited repertoire of poetic *diction consisting of formulas and formulaic systems, each system comprising a set of formulas that share a common pattern of phraseology. Thus, he was able to illustrate, e.g., how *prosêuda* (addressed) could combine with 11 different nominal subjects to constitute a metrically correct measure in the hexameter line (selections below):

| *prosêuda* + | |
| --- | --- |
| *dia theaôn* | (divine of goddesses) |
| *mantis amumôn* | (blameless seer) |
| *dios Achilleus* | (divine Achilles) |
| *dios Odusseus* | (divine Odysseus) |

Parry understood the poet's task not as a search for original diction but as a fluency in this traditional idiom—i.e., as the talent and learned ability to weave together the ready-made diction and, occasionally, new phraseology invented by analogy to existing formulas and systems to produce metrically correct hexameters in ancient Gr. epic. Having concentrated in his 1928 thesis principally on the noun-epithet formulas so typical of Homeric style, Parry then broadened his examination in 1930 and 1932 to consider all of Homer's diction. His analysis of the first 25 lines of the *Iliad* and the *Odyssey*, which show graphically how Homer depended on formulas and systems to make his poems, remains a *locus classicus* for the interpretation of ancient Gr. epic lang.

These deductions were augmented as a result of fieldwork in the former Yugoslavia carried out by Parry and Albert Lord. Lord demonstrated that the Yugoslav guslar employed a similar formulaic idiom in the making of South Slavic epic, using stock phrases like *lički Mustajbeže* (Mustajbeg of the Lika), as well as more flexible formulaic systems, to compose his poem in oral *performance. With the benefit of a large corpus of unambiguously oral performances, incl. songs from the same guslar, Lord was able to show that virtually every line of South Slavic oral epic could be understood as a formula or member of a formulaic system.

During the period 1950–90, other scholars erected a series of comparative studies of the formula based on the Parry-Lord foundation, some treating ancient, med., and other ms. trads., others focusing on recoverable mod. trads.—e.g., Webber on formulaic frequency in the Sp. ballad; Magoun on the first 25 lines of *Beowulf*; Duggan on the OF *chanson de geste*; Lord (1986) on comparative studies; Culley on the Bible; Edwards (1986, 1987) on ancient Gr.; Olsen (1986, 1987) on OE; Parks on ME; and Zwettler on Ar. Foley provides bibl. (1985) and detailed hist. (1988) of this 40-year period and its interdisciplinary roots.

Since the 1990s, scholars have shifted their attention to two linked problems. One concerns the discovery of ling. and metrical rules underlying the generation of formulas, which vary in structure and texture across different trads. (Foley 1990). Of special significance has been the question of whether the idiom is so predetermined and mechanical as to preclude verbal art as we know it, whether the oral poet can select esp. meaningful formulas appropriate to certain narrative situations and thus place his individual stamp on the composition, or whether some other aesthetic must be applicable. Increased emphasis has been placed on the contrasts as well as similarities among formulas, with attention to different trads., genres, and witnesses (e.g., mss. vs. acoustic recordings). Similarly, the referential fields of meaning commanded by formulas have been probed more deeply, a crucial direction of research because formulas and other structural units convey meaning not by abstract denotation but by idiomatic and metonymic reference to the trad. as a whole (Foley 1991 et seq.).

*See* ORAL POETRY.

■ H. Düntzer, *Homerische Abhandlungen* (1872); E. Sievers, "Formelverzeichnis," *Heliand* (1878); R. Webber, *Formulistic Diction in the Spanish Ballad* (1951); F. P. Magoun, "The Oral-Formulaic Character of Anglo-Saxon Narrative Poetry," *Speculum* 28 (1953); Parry; J. Duggan, *The Song of Roland: Formulaic Style and Poetic Craft* (1973); M. Nagler, *Spontaneity and Tradition* (1974); M. Zwettler, *The Oral Tradition of Classical Arabic Poetry* (1978); J. Foley, *Oral-Formulaic Theory and Research* (1985)—updates in *Oral Tradition* 3 (1988) and 12 (1997); R. Culley, "Oral Tradition and Biblical Studies," *Oral Tradition* 1 (1986); A. B. Lord, "Perspectives on Recent Work on the Oral Traditional Formula," *Oral Tradition* 1 (1986); W. Parks, "The Oral-Formulaic Theory in Middle English Studies," *Oral Tradition* 1 (1986); M. Edwards, "Homer and Oral Tradition: The Formula," *Oral Tradition* 1–2 (1986–87); A. Olsen, "Oral-Formulaic Research in Old English Studies," *Oral Tradition* 1–2 (1986–87); J. Foley, *The Theory of Oral Composition* (1988); *Traditional Oral Epic* (1990); *Immanent Art* (1991); *The Singer of Tales in Performance* (1995); and *Homer's Traditional Art* (1999); Lord; J. Foley, *How to Read an Oral Poem* (2002), and *The Wedding of Mustajbey's Son Bećirbey as Performed by Halil Bajgorić* (2004); *Oral Tradition*, http://journal.oraltradition.org.

J. M. FOLEY

**FOUND POETRY.** Found poetry, also called the poetry of citation or appropriation, is created by taking words, phrases, and, even more commonly, entire passages from other sources and reframing them as "poetry" by altering the context, frame, and format in which the source text appears. Found poetry is always intertextual: the intertext may be a recipe, a newspaper article, a personal letter, a document, an earlier poem, or—as is most common today—a text appropriated from the Internet (see INTERTEXTUALITY). The contemp. movement called *Flarf is essentially found poetry: its members "write through" Web sites or blogs, usually by following particular mathematical rules. Another contemp. movement using found text is the Fr. *Oulipo, which began its "researches" in the 1960s. Indeed, in the 21st c., it is difficult to find poetry that does not have some "found" component, the *ne plus ultra* exemplified by Kenneth Goldsmith's *Day* (2003), which is the transcription of the entire text of a single day's—September 1, 2000—*New York Times* from beginning to end, consolidating headlines, columns, and ads, so as to make one seamless and surprisingly novel text. Goldsmith himself calls such works "uncreative writing." His New York Trilogy of 2003–5 (*Weather*; *Traffic*; and *Sports*) is entirely found text: its transcription of the specific radio broadcasts in a given time period does not include a single word that the poet can call his own.

Found poetry originated in the early 20th c. in response to the new media and print technologies; it is often linked to *collage in the visual arts, although cubist collage still involves a blend of individual brushstroke and found text (see CUBISM). A more significant visual counterpart is the Duchampian Readymade—an "ordinary" object like a clothes hanger or comb that is recontextualized by its placement, framing, title, or caption. In France, the found poem or *objet trouvé* was popular with the pre–World War I avant-garde: an early example is Blaise Cendrars's "Me Too Boogie" (1914), which is a lineated version of a passage from a 19th-c. travel book about the natives of Tonga.

Cendrars's earlier "Le Panama ou les aventures de mes sept oncles" (Panama or the Adventures of My Seven Uncles) incorporates a train schedule from the Union Pacific Railroad and a prospectus for "Denver, the Residence City and Commercial Center."

Both *Dada and surrealist poets (e.g., Kurt Schwitters, Francis Picabia, André Breton) exploited found poetry, as did the great Viennese satirist Karl Kraus, whose long, unfinished poetic drama of the 1920s *Die letzten Tage der Menschheit* (*The Last Days of Mankind*), contains a wealth of documentary fragments, newsflashes, placards, and political speeches (see SUR-REALISM). The most prominent example for the Eng.-speaking reader is surely Ezra Pound's *Cantos*, which incorporates "real" letters by Thomas Jefferson and John Adams, papal documents, poems by Guido Cavalcanti, government and bank documents, extracts from Confucius, and so on. Pound's strategy was taken over by W. C. Williams in *Paterson*, by Charles Olson in the *Maximus Poems*, and by Louis Zukofsky in "Poem beginning 'The'" and "A." Another objectivist, Charles Reznikoff inserted lineated sections of law reports and similar documents into the fabric of his long poem *Testimony* (1979; see OBJECTIVISM).

But it is only in the information age that entire poems have been made from found text. In "Poem beginning 'The',," Zukofsky acknowledged his sources, as did Walter Benjamin in his monumental *Arcades Project*, made almost entirely of citations. In the case of contemp. poetry, however, the reader cannot be sure whether he or she is reading an "original" text or a found one. Susan Howe's *The Midnight* (2003), e.g., draws on biography, document, anthol., and letters, to create a poetic form where "original" and "found text" overlap and interact. Craig Dworkin's "Legion" (2003) is a rearrangement of the true/false questions of the first ed. of a 1942 psychological questionnaire, *The Minnesota Multiphasic Personality Inventory*. And Caroline Bergvall's poem *Via* (2005) alphabetizes a series of Eng. trans. of the first tercet of Dante's *Inferno*, so as to create an entirely new and strange poem. In all these instances, found poetry confronts the media world of our moment and transforms its debris into complex verbal artifacts.

See AVANT-GARDE POETICS, CONCEPTUAL POETRY.

■ M. Duchamp, *The Writings of Marcel Duchamp*, ed. M. Sanouillet and E. Peterson (1973); J. Bochner, *Blaise Cendrars: Discovery and Re-Creation* (1978); A. Compagnon, *La Seconde Main* (1979); M. Perloff, *Radical Artifice: Writing Poetry in the Age of Media* (1992); S. McCaffery, *North of Intention* (2000); C. Dworkin, *Reading the Illegible* (2003); M. Perloff, *Differentials* (2004); K. Goldsmith, *On Conceptual Writing* (2007); M. Perloff, *Unoriginal Genius: Poetry by Other Means in the New Century* (2010); *Against Expression: An Anthology of Conceptual Writing*, ed. C. Dworkin and K. Goldsmith (2011); K. Goldsmith, *Uncreative Writing* (2011).

M. PERLOFF

**FOURTEENER.** In Eng., a metrical line of 14 syllables, usually comprising seven *iambs, which since the Middle Ages has taken two distinct forms used for vari-

ous kinds of poetry and thus exhibiting widely differing characteristics. When a pair of fourteeners are broken by *hemistichs to form a quatrain of lines stressed 4-3-4-3 and rhyming *abab*, they become the familiar "eight-and-six" form of *ballad meter called common meter or common measure. S. T. Coleridge imitated the looser form of this meter in "Kubla Khan," as did many other 19th-c. poets attempting literary imitations of "folk poetry." William Blake often used an unbroken fourteener in his "prophetic books," possibly in imitation of the biblical style from various Eng. trans.

The eight-and-six pattern was used widely in the 16th c. for hymns; indeed, Thomas Sternhold and John Hopkins adapted it from contemp. song specifically to take advantage of its popularity and energy for their metrical *psalter. It was also used for polished lyrics such as Robert Herrick's "Gather ye rosebuds while ye may." Shakespeare uses it for comic effect in the "Pyramus and Thisbe" play performed by the "rude mechanicals" in *A Midsummer Night's Dream*. Closely related is *poulter's measure, a line of 12 syllables followed by a fourteener, which when broken into a quatrain gives the 3-3-4-3 pattern of short meter. But the fourteener was also used extensively in the 16th c. for the elevated genres, in particular for translating Lat. tragedy and epic. It is used for trans. of Seneca's tragedies by Jasper Heywood and others published by Thomas Newton in the *Tenne Tragedies* (1581) and by Arthur Golding for his trans. of Ovid's *Metamorphoses* (1567). The most famous and impressive use of fourteeners in Eng. is probably George Chapman's trans. of Homer's *Iliad* (1616). The contrast between the effect of fourteeners in popular and learned genres is striking:

> The king sits in Dumferline town
> Drinking the blood-red wine;
> "O whare will I get a skeely skipper
> To sail this new ship of mine?"
>
> ("Sir Patrick Spens")

> Achilles' banefull wrath resound, O Goddesse, that
>   impos'd
> Infinite sorrowes on the Greekes, and many brave
>   soules los'd
> From breasts Heroique—sent them farre, to that
>   invisible cave
> That no light comforts; and their lims to dogs and
>   vultures gave.
>
> (Chapman's Homer)

Opinions differ about the origins of the fourteener. Schipper calls it a *septenarius—more precisely, the trochaic tetrameter brachycatalectic—implying that it was derived from imitation of med. Lat. poems in that meter. The native influence of ballad meter is also obvious. But another explanation is equally likely: the great cl. epic meter, the dactylic hexameter, contains on average about 16 "times," and it may be that early Eng. translators thought the fourteener was the closest vernacular equivalent.

■ Schipper, *History*; P. Verrier, *Le Vers français*, v. 2–3 (1931–32); J. Thompson, *The Founding of English Metre*, 2d ed. (1989); O. B. Hardison Jr., *Prosody and Purpose in the English Renaissance* (1988); M. Hunt, "Fourteeners in Shakespeare's *Cymbeline*," *N & Q* 47 (2000).

O. B. HARDISON; T.V.F. BROGAN; S. S. BILL

**FRACTAL VERSE.** Fractal verse provides a way to conceptualize irregular poetic forms by drawing upon fractal geometry, a branch of chaos theory developed in the 1970s and subsequently popularized by the mathematician Benoît Mandelbrot. While Euclidean geometry describes smooth and regular forms, fractal geometry accounts for the irregular forms now recognized to predominate in nature, e.g., in the shapes of clouds or coastlines. Mandelbrot's coinage, *fractal*, emphasizes the fractured character of these complex forms as well as their fractional dimensions; their corrugated surface (made, for instance, from an infinitely long line within a finite area) gives fractals an added fraction of a dimension. Fractals are characterized by self-similarity across different scales. They are attractive to contemporary poets and critics because they mediate between chaos and order, allowing recognition of complex pattern where formerly only randomness or disorder had been observed. As Hayles insists, writing readily analyzed in terms of fractal geometry is not necessarily influenced by science. Rather, both lit. and science reflect culture; in the late decades of the 20th c., a cultural shift was evident as many disciplines moved toward challenging rigid binaries and attending to nonlinear dynamics. Like some who theorize fractal verse, Hayles notes commonalities between the science of chaos and *postmodernism, particularly poststructuralist thought.

The term *fractal verse* was introduced by the poet Alice Fulton in her essay "Of Formal, Free, and Fractal Verse: Singing the Body Eclectic" (1986) and further developed in "Fractal Amplifications" (1997). "Of Formal, Free, and Fractal Verse" stresses the need for ways to discern and discuss the orders found in irregular (*free verse) forms and offers fractal form as a promising analog. Among the "fractal precepts" Fulton proposes are that individual lines will be as richly detailed as the larger poem containing them; the poem will contain an infinite regression of details, "a nesting of pattern within pattern"; "digression, interruption, fragmentation and lack of continuity will be regarded as formal functions rather than lapses into formlessness"; and the occurrence of metrical patterns or rhythms in a poem will not predict the poem's subsequent metrical or rhythmic behavior. "Fractal Amplifications" engages more directly with complexity theory and postmodernism. Emphasizing that fractal verse is not based on a conventional usage of *voice, Fulton claims the form itself dismantles assumptions of the "natural" by breaking the "poem plane" as modernist free verse, according to Ezra Pound, broke the pentameter.

Other poets who have also seen potential in fractal geometry for appropriately current thinking about poetry have interpreted the relevance of fractals differently. Swensen, using fractal geometry to analyze poetry that makes innovative use of the visual page, emphasizes a multidirectional fractal motion that "infinitely complicates itself along a pattern of self-similarity." Retallack invokes fractals as models of "pattern-bounded unpredictability" that provide new ways of thinking about poetry's relation to extratextual reality, "redefining relationships between order and disorder, pattern and unpredictability, the finite and the infinite."

Critics have sometimes claimed for earlier poets, such as Gertrude Stein, Pound, or H.D., an intuition of fractal geometry before it was modeled by scientists. More often, critics have used the characteristics of fractals as analogs that illuminate previously underappreciated aspects of particular poets' writing, esp. their handling of *repetition (self-similarity) on varied scales.

*See* FORM, POSTSTRUCTURALISM, SCIENCE AND POETRY.

■ B. Mandelbrot, *The Fractal Geometry of Nature* (1983); N. K. Hayles, "Introduction: Complex Dynamics in Literature and Science," *Chaos and Order* (1991); C. Swensen, "Against the Limits of Language," *Moving Borders*, ed. M. M. Sloan (1998); A. Fulton, *Feeling as a Foreign Language* (1999); J. Retallack, *The Poethical Wager* (2003); N. Sala, "Fractal Geometry in the Arts: An Overview across the Different Cultures," *Thinking in Patterns*, ed. M. M. Novak (2004).

L. KELLER

**FRAGMENT** (Lat. *frangere*, "to break"). In poetry, *fragment* connotes a broken part or detached piece of a complete and integral poem—either a whole that once existed or one that was never written and can only be imagined. The hist. of poetry witnesses a shift from the fragment made by time and circumstances (that which was once complete) to the intentional fragment (that which is written incomplete). In the Western trad., this shift occurs most prominently in the romantic period. Twentieth- and 21st-c. inheritors of the fragment form increasingly employed internal fragmentation within their works.

The fragment is as old and universal as the written poetic word. The lyric poet Sappho (fl. ca. 600 BCE) has garnered particular attention for her 213 extant poems, only one of which survives in entirety. These fragments—and most incomplete ancient work—present a challenge to translators and interpreters alike. While some (Mary Barnard, Guy Davenport, Willis Barnstone) have approached Sappho's fragments as a venue for creation, transforming a few words into multistanza poems, others have strived for complete fidelity to Sappho's original text; Carson inserts brackets wherever the original papyrus was lost, thus implying "a free space of imaginal adventure."

It was largely the aesthetic behind cl. fragments that inspired the romantic vogue for the intentionally fragmentary poem in England and Germany. Even before the romantic era, Eng. poetry was read in unfinished form, often with biographical causes (such as death or a shift in creative interest) behind its incompletion; two significant examples are Chaucer's *Canterbury Tales* (late 14th c.) and Edmund Spenser's *Faerie Queene* (1590, 1596). These never-finished works may have acclimated readerships to the more stylized fragments to come. However, it was the Ossianists that launched the romantic fragment genre in England. Drawing on the neoclassical fervor of his era, the Scottish poet James Macpherson published *Fragments of Ancient Poetry, Collected in the Highlands of Scotland, and Translated from the Gaelic or Erse Language* (1760) as his first "translations" of the fictional writer Ossian, inspiring a wave of "Hoax Poets" (see PREROMANTICISM).

During the romantic period, there are few major Eng. poets who did *not* produce fragment poems. S. T. Coleridge composed two for *Lyrical Ballads* (1798) and later wrote the significant fragments "Christabel" (1816) and "Kubla Khan" (1816), which resembles an opium dream in its intentional fragmentation. Lord Byron's *Giaour* (1813) is "three disjointed fragments" expanded piece by piece. John Keats's *Hyperion* (1820), which ends mid-line with the word "celestial," and *The Fall of Hyperion* (written 1819, pub. 1856) were both left unfinished. P. B. Shelley's corpus contains more fragments than that of any other romantic poet; notable among them are *Posthumous Fragments of Margaret Nicholson* (1810) and "The Triumph of Life" (1822). The popularity of these fragments can be contextualized in romantic aesthetic discourse. Espousers of the *sublime admired fragment poetry for its suggestion of nature's triumph over civilization, and the ruined aesthetic of the fragment appealed to the Eng. picturesque imagination. Meanwhile, the fragment's implication of the passage of time and its lack of temporal context aligned with the *sic transit gloria mundi* meditation.

While Eng. poets produced a body of work that can be called fragmentary in retrospect, Ger. romantic poets actively cultivated a fragmentary aesthetic. The Jena circle, founded by K.W.F. Schlegel and A. W. Schlegel, published a series of philosophical fragmentary epigrams in *The Athenaeum* (1798–1800). These short pieces, inspired by cl. fragments, often commented on the nature of the fragment form: as K.W.F. Schlegel writes, "Many of the works of the ancients have become fragments. Many modern works are fragments as soon as they are written." The *Athenaeum* fragments frequently questioned whether a whole exists at all. Preeminent fragment poets in the Ger. trad. are Friedrich Hölderlin and—much later—R. M. Rilke. Hölderlin, whose first fragments were posthumously published in *Berliner Ausgabe* (1913), often left unfinished lines and gaps in his pieces. Rilke, in his "Archaïscher Torso Apollos" ("Torso of an Archaic Apollo," 1908), explores the fragment theme in his *ekphrasis of a ruined sculpture. The Rus. poet Alexander Pushkin also drew inspiration from the circle, producing dozens of fragments and publishing a chapter of his novel in verse *Evgenij Onegin* (1825–32) in fragments.

In the 20th c., the fragment form was used to reflect the disjointedness of the psychological experience and convey a sense of general disorder. Guillaume Apollinaire juxtaposed fragment poems on a white page, unifying the disjunctive content of his text with white space (as in *Calligrammes*, 1918). Often lacking punctuation and connective verbs, his enigmatic poems call on the

reader to imagine transitions. The imagists frequently borrowed from Sappho's lexicon. H.D. saw in her muse a "fractured sense of eternally being on intellectual borders," while Ezra Pound channeled Sappho in "Papyrus" (1916), employing the *concision and directness that would define the imagism. Pound also drew on the Japanese *haiku trad. (see RENGA), which often employed fragmentary syntax, to juxtapose images in floating, incomplete lang. (as in "In a Station of the Metro," 1913).

T. S. Eliot, who wrote in *The Waste Land* (1922) "these fragments I have shored against my ruins," employed abrupt shifts in speaker, lang., and time to impart a sense of psychological fragmentation and to reflect a war-torn political landscape. In this spirit, poets began to experiment with internal fracturing, employing sentence fragments and broken grammar within their works. Later, the Language poets of the 1970s (incl. Bruce Andrews, Michael Palmer, Ron Silliman, and Charles Bernstein) fragmented lang. until it no longer held conventional measures of meaning; through disjunctive lists of words and phrases, these poets shifted focus to the materiality of words (see LANGUAGE POETRY). More recently, hypertext poems enable readers to reorganize the content of a fractured text; in such cases, a poem is shattered by the medium itself and then pieced together by the reader (see ELECTRONIC POETRY).

As contemp. poets continue to publish pieces entitled simply "Fragment," one such poem by Seamus Heaney poses a question that may allude to the persistence of the fragment genre: "Since when," he asked, / "are the first line and the last line of any poem / where the poem begins and ends?"

*See* IMAGINATION, QIṬA, ROMANTICISM.

■ T. McFarland, *Romanticism and the Forms of Ruin* (1981); M. Levinson, *The Romantic Fragment Poem* (1986); E. W. Harries, *The Unfinished Manner: Essays on the Fragment in the Later Eighteenth Century* (1994); M. Greenleaf, *Pushkin and Romantic Fashion* (1997); N. Saul, "Aesthetic Humanism," *The Cambridge History of German Literature*, ed. H. Watanabe-O'Kelly (1997); D. Collecot, *H.D. and Sapphic Modernism* (1999); *Del Frammento*, ed. R. M. Losito (2000); C. Elias, *The Fragment* (2004); T. Hoagland, "Fragment, Juxtaposition, and Completeness," *Cortland Review* 33 (2006); Sappho, *If Not, Winter: Fragments of Sappho*, trans. A. Carson (2009); S. Jung, *The Fragmentary Poetic* (2009).
A. SLESSAREV

## FRANCE, POETRY OF

I. Medieval to Early Modern
II. Early Modern to 20th Century

**I. Medieval to Early Modern**. To assume that *poetry* is a self-evident term, that it denotes, in Charles Baudelaire's expression, "rhythm and rhyme," or that it has inhabited since antiquity three well-defined categories—epic, dramatic, lyric—is to overestimate the transparency of these terms. Such categories are useful (e.g., scholars routinely speak about "lyric" and "epic" poetry in the Middle Ages) but even when they are applicable, these terms are unstable in meaning. The word *poète* (poet), e.g., comes into use in the 13th-c. *Roman de la Rose*, where it means "Latin poet" or "poet whom one glosses." In the 14th c., it comes to be used of vernacular poets, often with the primary sense of "allegorist." The words *poésie* or occasionally, as in the early 15th-c. poetic theorist Jacques Legrand, *poetrie* (in the etymological sense of "making" and even "feigning") also appear in the 14th c., although vernacular treatises of versification will not become *arts poétiques* until the middle of the 16th c. Indeed, *poésie* is not an esp. common term for vernacular verse in Fr. until the early mod. period.

While the earliest texts in Fr. date from the 9th c., there is almost nothing written in prose before the early 13th c. that would commonly be called "literary." In the Middle Ages, writing in verse is assimilated both to rhet. (part of the trivium of arts) and to music (part of the quadrivium of mathematical disciplines). Eustache Deschamps (ca. 1346–1407) commemorated ca. 1377 the great 14th-c. poet and composer Guillaume de Machaut in these terms: "the death of Machaut, the noble Rhetorician." In a treatise on versification, *L'Art de dictier* (1392), Deschamps defined verse as a kind of "natural music." The distinction between *verse* and *prose* was operative in the med. period. The It. scholar Brunetto Latini distinguished between these two "manners of speaking" in his 13th-c. *Li Livres dou Tresor* (ca. 1264), and the distinction had already given rise to much debate in the early 13th c.: verse had come to be seen as inherently mendacious, and many verse narrative works were translated into prose. The term *seconde rhétorique* (second rhetoric) to distinguish verse from prose, common in the 15th c., appears first in Occitan, in the *Leys d'amors* (1356) often attributed to Guilhem Molinier, probably under the influence of the verse-prose distinction found in Brunetto. Yet "rhythm and rhyme" do not always make "poetry" in the early periods. E.g., after Aristotle's *Poetics* had been rediscovered and disseminated in the Lat. West in the 16th c., much effort was expended to determine which kinds of verse qualified for the title of *poetry* by virtue of being mimetic, i.e., of following Aristotle's idea that poetry required the imitation of reality (see MIMESIS).

The tripartite division of poetic genres that mod. readers often assume to be of cl. origin—epic, dramatic, lyric—owes more to the 19th c. (esp. G.W.F. Hegel's *Aesthetics*) than to antiquity. The triad does not appear in this form in Aristotle or Horace, in the Middle Ages or the early mod. period (though Antonio Minturno [ca. 1500–74] makes what seems a similar distinction in his *De poeta* of 1559). The word *lyrique* (lyric), often applied to a large part of the med. poetic corpus, does not appear in Fr. until the early 15th c. (as a calque for the Lat. *lyrica*, in a discussion of Horace). It denotes "lyric" poetry in the vernacular only from the 1490s and remains rare enough in the mid-16th c. for the young Joachim du Bellay to be mocked in print for using it as late as 1550. The mod. sense of lyric as personal verse becomes cur-

rent in the 18th c. Similarly, *épopée* (epic) and *roman* (romance)—the latter being the more common term until the late Ren.—are not clearly distinguished either in the Middle Ages or the 16th c. (the prominent humanist poet Pierre de Ronsard called Homer's *Iliad* a "roman"). Although verse theater in Fr. certainly existed from very early times, the term *dramatic* seems to have appeared in the late 14th c. to denote verse compositions in which the several persons represented were clearly distinguished from an authorial persona. Thus, the problem of classification is a stubborn one. Familiar terminology may be useful but cannot be taken for granted.

**A. *The Middle Ages.*** A salient distinction in med. and Ren. poetics is between poetry written in rhyming couplets (*rime plate*) and that written in other schemes. The former tends to appear in longer narrative (e.g., romance) or narrative-didactic poetry (e.g., the *Roman de la Rose*) and in theater, while the latter in poetry on other topics, e.g., in amatory poetry. This distinction is not airtight: many stanzaic forms are lengthy and contain narrative and indeed "dramatic" elements (e.g., the dialogue poems, or *joc-partits*, of which there are a number of examples in Occitan and in early Fr. poetry). Moreover, *chansons de geste* are not generally written in rime plate but instead in assonant or monorhyme stanzas. Short, fixed forms are also interspersed into longer narrative works in rime plate and even with prose, notably from the 14th-c. Guillaume de Machaut (ca. 1300–77) but also in the anonymous, probably 13th-c. *prosimetrum Aucassin et Nicolette*.

The verse produced between ca. 1100 and 1470 in what is now France was written in two dialect groups, broadly speaking: OF, spoken in northern France (the *langue d'oïl*), and Occitan (what used to be called Provençal, the *langue d'oc*). A greater proportion of the narrative poetry we possess is in northern Fr. dialects, although there is a considerable corpus in both langs.

We have several hagiographic narrative poems in OF from before the turn of the millennium: the "Séquence de Sainte Eulalie," probably written at the end of the 9th c., about 50 years after the Strasburg Oaths of 842 (the first recorded text in OF and OHG), and the 10th-c. *Vie de Saint Léger*, in octosyllables. Another early saint's life is the 11th-c. *Vie de Saint Alexis*, in assonant decasyllables. Later important saints' lives include an account of St. Mary the Egyptian by the late 13th-c. poet Rutebeuf, in octosyllabic couplets.

The chansons de geste or "songs of great deeds" are patriotic accounts of aristocratic and royal valor, incl. in later cases stories of the crusades. The *Chanson de Roland* (early 12th c.), preserved in a ms. in the Bodleian Library in Oxford, recounts an episode in Charlemagne's war against the Moors in Spain. This is the earliest remaining long narrative poem in Fr. The form of the *Chanson de Roland* is a series of assonant stanzas or *laisses* of unequal length, imbricating the material from one to the next. While this version, apparently not widely disseminated, survives only in the Oxford ms., the story was adapted in the 12th c. in rhyming verse. Other chansons de geste include the royal cycle, the cycles of Guillaume d'Orange and Doon de Mayence, and two cycles narrating the exploits of the crusades.

At most, two extant chansons de geste (the Oxford *Roland* and the *Chanson de Guillaume*) predate the earliest romances we possess. Most of the production of chansons de geste is contemporaneous with that of verse romance, although it continues for longer, verse romance giving way to prose romance before chansons de geste becomes unrhymed. Romance differs from chanson de geste in subject matter: chanson de geste is generally concerned with the matter of France, romance with the matter of Britain—in particular the stories of the Arthurian court, the Round Table, and the Grail—and the matter of Rome, consisting of adaptations of Lat. lit. such as Virgil's *Aeneid*. The trad. of verse historiography, e.g., the 12th-c. Wace, a court poet to the Eng. Henry II, or Gaimar's account of the battle of Hastings, which is the earliest surviving text in octosyllabic rhyming couplets, is important to the devel. of verse romance, where octosyllabic rime plate comes to predominate, although other verse forms occasionally appear, such as the 12-syllable line of the *Roman d'Alexandre*, from which the *alexandrine gets its name. Chrétien de Troyes' five verse romances of the later 12th c., incl. *Lancelot, Erec et Enide*, and the unfinished but much continued *Li Contes del Graal*, are sophisticated examples of the "romance" genre, voluminously imitated in other Eur. langs., notably Ger., in both verse and prose. The form of the romance gave birth to perhaps the most influential long narrative poem in med. Fr.: the *Roman de la Rose*, the work of Guillaume de Lorris (ca. 1205–40) and Jean de Meun (ca. 1240–1305). Guillaume's 4,056-line version, written ca. 1230, inspired a continuation more than four times longer. Guillaume's poem is an *allegory in which a young man of 20 enters a mysterious walled garden and falls in love with a rose he espies while looking into the fountain of Narcissus. Jean de Meun's continuation (ca. 1270–80) marshals a number of personified philosophical and ethical concepts (e.g., Dangier, Faulx Semblant) in a poem of initiation and encyclopedic knowledge liberally spiced with misogyny. The *Rose* was enormously popular; Chaucer translated part of it into Eng. The *Rose* informs much of the allegorical practice of the 14th and 15th cs., and the poem was widely read as late as the 16th c. (an adaptation, often attributed to the Ren. poet Clément Marot, was published in 1526). The long *dits amoureux* of Guillaume de Machaut, often interspersed with short lyric pieces set to music of his own composition—e.g., his *Remède de Fortune* and *Voir dit*—breathe the same Ovidian atmosphere as the *Rose*, a poem that they imitate, transform, and critique (see DIT).

Smaller-scale narrative forms include, in addition to saints' lives, e.g., the shorter narrative lays attributed to a 12th-c. Anglo-Norman poet who identifies herself as "Marie" from "France" (and whom the trad. has styled Marie de France [ca. 1135–1200]) as well as numerous *fabliaux (short, often bawdy stories of the sort that in-

spired Boccaccio's *Decameron* and Chaucer's *Canterbury Tales*). The humor and irony of the fabliau blossoms in *Le Roman de Renart*, a long satirical animal epic written in several parts or "branches," probably by several poets of the 12th and 13th cs.

Short poems, often in stanzaic, sometimes *heterometric fixed forms, not usually written in rhyming couplets, are conventionally considered "lyric" forms. Many of these were sung, or at least written in forms with musical conventions such as the later med. *rondeau and *ballade. The Occitan trad. is the earlier one, its influence waning after the Albigensian crusades of the early 13th c. *Occitan poetry, long somewhat neglected by Fr. scholars constructing a homogeneous national trad., despite its centrality to the devel. of OF "lyric," has been claimed by It. and Catalan scholars for their own literary hists. (see Burgwinkle et al.). Dante and Petrarch admired and imitated the poetry of, e.g., the 12th-c. *troubadour Arnaut Daniel.

No doubt the corpus of Occitan poetry is one of the most sophisticated, influential, and intellectually ambitious poetic trads. in Eur. lit. hist. Occitan poets are troubadours or "finders" of both words and music: the production of troubadour poetry seems to have spanned the social classes from the most elevated aristocrats to indigent traveling musicians. Many of the aspects of lyric poetry that contemp. readers might take, mistakenly, as mod.—self-reference and metatextual play, the blurring of the borders between the fiction of love and the artifice of poetry, the trenchant analysis of the circulation of desire—are already present in the earliest troubadour lyrics. The works of Guilhem IX, Duke of Aquitaine, such as his "Farai un vers de dreyt nien" (I will make a poem from entirely nothing; ca. 1100), have appealed to postromantic readers, who see there a reflection of their own concerns or a premonition of Stéphane Mallarmé's poetics of negation and ling. self-containment. The terrifying, cruel distance of the object of desire, the *domna*, reduced to a ling. sign or *senhal, has inspired the psychoanalyst Jacques Lacan and, through him, readers with psychological and philosophical interests. The knotty verse of Marcabru (associated with what is called the *trobar clus* or closed style), has particularly spoken to recent readers (see the ed. [2000] by Simon Gaunt, Ruth Harvey, and Linda Paterson), although the more accessible *trobar leu*, e.g., the poetry of Bernart de Ventadorn, is also much read. Jaufré Rudel, who sang of the *amor de lonh*, or "love from afar," is perhaps the best known of the troubadours today. There is also a considerable body of troubadour lyric written by (or attributed to) women, known as *trobairitz, of whom the 12th-c. Comtessa de Dia is now perhaps most read. Unfortunately, a great number of the names of the *trobairitz* have disappeared. Still, ms. culture stressed the production of a poetic persona whose life was supposedly reflected in the poetry and tended to situate troubadours and trobairitz in a brief biographical fiction called a *vida.

Many of the early lyric songs in the langue d'oïl, OF, are anonymous *chansons de toile, *reverdies, chansons d'aube (see ALBA), or *pastourelles, dating from the 12th and 13th cs. The *trouvères, counterparts in northern France to the troubadours, took up many of the techniques and themes of troubadour poetry; these include the 13th-c. King of Navarre, Thibaut de Champagne (1201–53), a direct descendant of Guilhem IX and the great-grandson of Eleanor of Aquitaine, who wrote in Fr. (and was quoted by Dante). As was the case for the troubadours, many of the trouvères were aristocratic, although 13th-c. poets such as Rutebeuf, Gilbert de Berneville, and Adam de la Halle were commoners; the last two are associated with the flowering of Fr. poetry in the northern city of Arras, whereas Rutebeuf was Parisian.

It was esp. in the north of France that the musical trad. of med. poetry would develop in notable ways. With the refinements in mensural notation and consequently in polyphony in the 13th and 14th cs., such forms as the polytextual motet—a type of layered song counterposing several poetic texts—flourished. Adam de la Halle (ca. 1250–1306) cultivated the genre of the motet, which came to a very high level of sophistication in the works of the 14th-c. Guillaume de Machaut. Such songs, fusing Christian and cl. topoi, demand a complex process of reception. Since the texts, sung simultaneously, are not easily intelligible, interpretation depends as much on written texts (Machaut took great care in the presentation of his mss.) as on performance and requires, in particular, accounting for the text of the fragment of plainchant on which they were constructed. E.g., one of Machaut's motets, built on a fragment of *chant, the "tenor," recounting David's grief on the death of Absalom (the text is *ego moriar pro te*, "I will/would die for you"), collates two Fr. texts derived from the Ovidian myth of Narcissus and Echo. Fourteenth-c. poets also worked in the fixed forms that would be developed by late med. writers, the *virelai* and particularly the rondeau and the ballade; these were cultivated by Machaut and his contemporaries and particularly by the poets of following generations who, unlike Machaut, were not generally composers, e.g., Deschamps, Christine de Pizan (1363–1430), Alain Chartier (ca. 1385–1433), and in particular Charles d'Orléans (1394–1465), who wrote hundreds of rondeaux and ballades, both in Fr. and, during a 25-year period of captivity in England, in Eng.

For mod. readers, perhaps the best known of all late med. poets is François Villon (1431–after 1463), a young Parisian with a colorful, much romanticized life. Villon, of whose biography we know little for certain, is the author of several extended works in autobiographical guise, incl. a *Testament*, detailing the mock legacy of a poor poet and interspersing refined examples of the ballade and the rondeau. Villon, who was once condemned to death and composed a *quatrain for the occasion of his hanging later adapted by François Rabelais (fl. early 16th c.), disappears without a trace after 1463. Collections of his poems are among the first printed poetry collections of late 15th-c. France; Clément Marot published an ed. of his poetry in 1533. Villon's *Lais* (*Legacy*, composed 1456) and *Grand testament* (composed 1461) are important laboratories for the devel. of a highly stylized first-person voice, the precursor for many later writers and for the roman-

tic *poète maudit* (cursed poet). It would be a mistake to assume that the type of mock-testament that Villon composes is an entirely new devel.; the genre has important 13th-c. antecedents in Jean Bodel, Baude Fastoul, and Rutebeuf.

The 15th c. saw important devels. in verse drama, both religious (e.g., the lengthy *Mystère de la Passion*, ca. 1425, or an even longer mid-century passion play attributed to Arnoul Greban) and secular, most notably the anonymous *Farce de Maître Pierre Pathelin* (1465), which Rabelais knew and which is still performed. Devels. in theater built on a lively native Fr. trad. of mystery plays and other varieties of med. drama, the latter exemplified already in the 13th c. by Adam de la Halle's plays *Jeu de Robin et Marion*, written in Italy for Charles I of Naples, and his *Jeu de la Feuillée*.

**B. Sixteenth and Seventeenth Centuries.** Although the 16th c. is one of the richest periods in the hist. of Fr. poetry, the 17th c. is often considered an era of relative decline, at least in nondramatic poetry. There is some truth to this received notion, even if it is also informed by ideologies of literary taste inherited from that century.

The historiography of Fr. lyric poetry in the 16th-c. has long cited Joachim du Bellay's *La deffence et illustration de la langue françoyse* (1549), an aggressive plea for the foundation of a new national poetry worthy of the cl. past, as a reference point. du Bellay's treatise, along with Pierre de Ronsard's *Odes* (1550), has rather too neatly divided the century into two halves. Many earlier commentators took du Bellay's dismissal of most of the poetic production in Fr. before his time at face value, when du Bellay's treatise, a polemical response to Thomas Sébillet's erudite *Art poétique françoys* of 1548, clearly aims to establish his poetry and that of his contemporaries as the foundation of a new Fr. trad. Although the period of poetic production falling roughly between 1549 and 1585 is one of the most impressive in the entire hist. of Fr. poetry, critical work on 16th-c. Fr. poetry in the last century has demonstrated the richness of the reign of François I (1515–47), and indeed the extent to which the poets of the *Pléiade build on humanist ideas already firmly in place early in the 16th c., and in some cases in the 15th c. as well. Both the pre-Pléiade poets and their poetic descendants imported It. forms (such as the *sonnet, brought into Fr. by Marot and Mellin de Saint-Gelais in the 1530s and made Fr. by the Pléiade in the 1550s), and philosophical currents such as Ficianian Neoplatonism that had already attracted the attention of Fr. readers by the end of the 15th c.

The *Grands *Rhétoriqueurs* stand at an awkward juncture in Fr. poetic hist., on the (arbitrary) border between "late medieval" and "Renaissance" poetics. The poets of the *Grande Rhétorique*, attached to the courts of Burgundy and France, develop a particularly complex poetics, playing on the possibilities of late med. allegory in intricate ways and developing verse forms and rhyme schemes of unparalleled complexity in the Fr. trad. A volume of "arts of second rhetoric" compiled by E. Langlois in 1902 is a useful primary source for the study of 15th-c. verse. The Grands Rhé-toriqueurs, manipulating traditional fixed forms such as the rondeau and ballade, reworked these in ways that distanced them from their musical conventions. The rondeau, e.g., was reimagined in ways that made it difficult, even impossible, for the text to be set to music in the conventional way (Villon's "Mort, j'appelle de ta rigueur," from the *Testament*, is a good early example). In this, poetic practice reflects compositional practice among late 15th- and early 16th-c. composers such as Josquin des Prez (ca. 1450–1521).

The innovations of Grands Rhétoriqueurs such as Jean Meschinot, Jean Molinet, Guillaume Cretin, Jean Marot, and Jean Lemaire de Belges, poets long disparaged in the critical trad., certainly underlie many of the devels. in verse in the era of François I, most notably the work of Clément Marot (ca. 1496–1544), whose father, Jean, was also a court poet. Early poems by the young Marot show his mastery of the word games of the Grande Rhétorique, evincing as well his ability to play on the exigencies of poets obliged to curry favor with aristocratic patrons. Marot's collection *L'Adolescence clémentine* (1532) and its 1534 continuation are collectively a summa of late med. poetic forms. Marot later abandoned the fixed forms of the Middle Ages for more classically inspired ones, in particular the *epigram. He is also responsible for some of the early trans. of Petrarch's poetry into Fr. (see PETRARCHISM). A strong supporter of religious reform who spent a number of years in exile for his beliefs, Marot is the author of still-popular trans. of the Heb. Psalms, a crowning achievement of his career. Nonetheless, it would be too simple to reduce Marot's poetics entirely to his religious faith. He translated, e.g., bawdy epigrams by Martial around the same time as the Psalms, and such an alternation of the worldly and the sacred represents the period. Marot's poetry is an important influence on the philosophically minded Maurice Scève (ca. 1511–64), the author of the first Petrarchan love sequence in France and the winner of a contest for the composition of *blasons of the human body organized by Marot in 1536. The works of Scève's Lyonnese contemporaries Pernette du Guillet and Louise Labé are infused with Petrarchan lang. as well as topoi derived from Ficinian Neoplatonism. Neoplatonic ideas about music and poetry underlie much of lyric production after 1549, as in the works of the mathematician and poet Jacques Peletier du Mans (1517–82). The treatises of Scève's friend and disciple Pontus de Tyard (1521–1605) influenced the founding by Jean-Antoine de Baïf and Thibault de Courville in 1570 of a royal Academy of Poetry and Music, which was intended to resurrect the "effects of music" described in mythological stories like those of Orpheus and Amphion in the interest of promoting harmony within the kingdom.

Ronsard (1524–85) and du Bellay (ca. 1522–60) were the preeminent Fr. poets of their generation, and indeed, much of the poetry not only of the 16th but of the 17th c. should be read in relationship to Pléiade aesthetics and its rejection by 17th-c. theo-rists. Certainly, the body of Fr. poetry produced in the period of Ronsard's dominance is now among the most highly prized in the entire Fr. trad. More than any other poet, Ronsard naturalized the sonnet in Fr. in a number of important collections beginning with his *Amours* (1552), pub. with a musical supplement in 1552 and reissued in 1553 with an innovative, erudite commentary by Marc-Antoine Muret. Ronsard's contemp. du Bellay also published a number of significant sonnet collections, incl. *L'Olive* (1549), *Les Regrets* (1558), and *Les Antiquitez de Rome* (1558). Ronsard experimented with other, more metaphysically ambitious lyric works, incl. the *Odes* (1550) and *Hymnes* (1556), whereas du Bellay cultivated an intimate, "low" style and a melancholic meditation on the impermanence of things and the venal political ambitions of his contemporaries, one much inflected by Ovidian topoi. The poets of Ronsard's generation were much influenced by the distinguished humanist Jean Dorat, teacher of Ronsard and Baïf, who wrote principally in Lat. Other important members of the group initially called the *Brigade* and later the Pléiade included Pontus, Peletier, Étienne Jodelle, and Remy Belleau.

Of the generation following Ronsard, Philippe Desportes (1546–1606) and Agrippa d'Aubigné (1552–1630) are probably the most noted writers of lyric verse. The former inspired François de Malherbe's (1555–1628) call for the reform of Fr. versification often cited as the birth of neoclassicism in poetry. (In one of his most famous lines, Nicolas Boileau later praised Malherbe for bringing order to the alleged disorder of Pléiade poetics: "enfin Malherbe vint" [Finally Malherbe arrived].) Trad. has tended to situate 17th-c. poetic production between Malherbe's castigation of Pléiade and post-Pléiade verse and Boileau's orderly ideal of a balanced poetry whose regular cadences please and instruct the reader. Indeed, Boileau suggested, in his 1674 *Art poétique*, that little of note had happened in Fr. verse between Malherbe's reform in the opening years of the 17th c. and his own time. Of course, this is far from true: a number of worthy poets fit awkwardly into what has often been seen as the period's predominantly classicizing aesthetics: Théophile de Viau, Marc-Antoine Girard de Saint-Amant, Tristan l'Hermite, and Vincent Voiture are "lyric" poets whose posthumous reputations, although respectable, have suffered from ideological accounts of the Grand Siècle and its cl. rigor. In the 1630s and 1640s, Vincent Voiture resurrected late med. forms such as the rondeau in an effort to bring back the "elegant banter" (Boileau's expression) of Clément Marot's court poetry, while Viau had earlier been tried for "libertine" tendencies, in relation to the affair of the *Parnasse des poètes satyriques* (1622).

Both the 16th and 17th cs. saw the continued flourishing of *devotional poetry, a genre that often overlaps with the other lyric forms already discussed. The religious poems of Queen Marguerite de Navarre, e.g., the *Miroir de l'âme pecheresse* (1531), condemned initially by the Sorbonne and later translated into Eng. by Elizabeth I, are early 16th-c. examples. Jean de Sponde

(1557–95) is no doubt the preeminent late 16th-c. religious poet. There are also a number of collections of Christianized love poetry by poets like Ronsard, intended to be sung by the devout, often to popular tunes (see CONTRAFACTUM). The 17th c. continues the trad. of devotional verse, notably in Jean de La Ceppède's *Théorèmes* (1613, 1621) or Claude Hopil's *Les douces extases de l'âme spirituelle* (1627). Contemplative religious poetry appears throughout the 17th c.; a significant late 17th-c. example of the genre is Racine's *Cantiques spirituels* (1694).

New forms of narrative poetry also appeared during these centuries. Du Bellay had called for the writing of "long poems," new Fr. "Iliads" based on the native mythical-historiographical trads. On a royal commission, Ronsard composed four books of an unfinished epic, *La Franciade* (1572), based on the story of Francus, a traditional account, attested as early as the 7th c., of the Trojan origins of the Fr. monarchy. But it is perhaps in the trad. of all-encompassing "scientific" poetry, a form with precedents in the encyclopedic tenor of such med. long poems as the *Roman de la Rose*, that we see the most original devels. Such poems as Scève's *Microcosme* (1562), a 3,003-line account of human knowledge and the fall of humankind, and Guillaume de Salluste Du Bartas's (1544–90) much longer and more influential *La Sepmaine: ou, Creation du monde* (1578) and *Seconde Sepmaine* (1584) are important in this vein, as is the somewhat more peculiar *La Galliade, ou de la révolution des arts et sciences* (1578, expanded 1582) by Guy Le Fevre de la Boderie, which claims that France is the wellspring of worldly knowledge. D'Aubigné's seven-book *Les Tragiques*, an immensely powerful account of the religious wars from a Protestant standpoint, begun by d'Aubigné in the 1570s but published anonymously only in 1616, is probably the most significant of the early mod. narrative long poems. Later in the 17th c., there are a number of epics on national themes, e.g., in the context of the conflict with Spain (such as works by Antoine Godeau and Georges de Scudéry), none of which seems to have gained much favor among readers then or now. *Mock epic has several instances at mid-century, in particular Paul Scarron's parody of the *Aeneid* entitled *Virgile travesti* (1648–52). For all this, the great master of 17th-c. narrative poetry, working on a much smaller scale, is probably Jean de La Fontaine (1621–95), whose *Fables* show a prodigious variety of verse styles. La Fontaine became, with the prose writers François de La Rochefoucauld and Jean de La Bruyère, a preeminent commentator on the social mores of Louis XIV's France. The rise of the cl. trad. of Fr. theater, culminating in the triumvirate of Corneille, Racine, and Jean-Baptiste Poquelin (i.e., Molière), is a central aspect of the devel. of Fr. verse in the 17th c., with important predecessors in such 16th-c. dramatists as Théodore de Beza, whose *Abraham sacrifiant* of 1550 is often called the first tragedy in Fr., and Robert Garnier, whose best known play is no doubt *Les Juives* (1583). Sixteenth-c. theater often intercalates lyric forms in imitation of the ancient choral odes separating the scenes

of Gr. dramas. The regulation of verse conventions, in particular after the foundation of the Fr. Academy in 1635, means that the hist. of Fr. versification is inseparable from debates concerning the *decorum of drama.

## II. Early Modern to Twentieth Century.

A. *Eighteenth Century.* Considered by many of his contemporaries the greatest poet of the c., François-Marie Arouet, known as Voltaire (1694–1778), is best known in poetry for his verse tragedy *Zaïre* (1732), but he tried his hand at many genres and forms. His epic *La Henriade* praises the ascension of Henri IV, who brought an end to the religious wars in France. He also wrote philosophical poems, which suited his antilyrical nature, in addition to satires and occasional verses celebrating such luminaries as Isaac Newton's Fr. translator, Mme. de Châtelet. Although verse was overshadowed during the Enlightenment by prose works (e.g., Voltaire's volumes on hist., his philosophical tale *Candide*, or Denis Diderot's monumental *Encyclopedia*), a few writers became famous for their poetic meditations on nature and landscapes. Jean-François de Saint-Lambert's *Les Saisons* (1769) explores both the sensorial richness of the months' cycle and the underlying harmony of the universe. Jacques Delille tested his verse in well-known trans. of Virgil's *Georgics* and John Milton's *Paradise Lost* and then proposed his own vision of natural beauty in *Les Jardins ou L'Art d'embellir les paysages* (1782). Other poets, such as Jean-Baptiste Rousseau or Jean-Baptiste Gresset, had already made names for themselves by openly opposing the Encyclopedists or by imitating classicist writers such as Boileau.

Once the century had ended and the Fr. Revolution had overturned both political and cultural orthodoxies, one victim of the Reign of Terror gained posthumous fame both as a martyr to tyranny and as the epitome of a poet's resistance to cold rationalism. André Chénier (1762–94) was condemned to the guillotine because, in newspaper articles, he had criticized the execution of Louis XVI. Although few of his poems had been published before his death, a footnote in François-René de Chateaubriand's *Génie du christianisme* (1802) helped turn Chénier into a legend. The note recounts that, on standing next to the guillotine, the poet had moved his hand to his forehead and said, "To die! I had something there in my mind!" Not only did this help turn the poet into a hero for counterrevolutionary Royalists in the 1820s, but it led a generation of romantic poets such as Alfred de Vigny (1797–1863) to align themselves with the legend of a misunderstood poetic genius and conflate the pathos of tragedy with a putative inner voice of poetry. *Les Iambes*, which Chénier wrote while he was imprisoned, is a skillfully crafted work of satire that uses Gr. and Lat. models that the author had read in the original. His *Hymnes* and *Odes* follow the model of occasional verse from the 18th c. but are often infused with passionate appeals for justice—as in his defense of Charlotte Corday, who had assassinated Marat, or in his most famous ode "La Jeune captive," which was inspired by a young woman Chénier met in prison. The woman's appeal to have her life spared, and the poet's reflection in the last two stanzas on his verse rendition of her appeal, became a model for the heart-cries that the romantics would emulate and develop.

**B. *Romanticism*.** Jean-Jacques Rousseau's final book, *Les Rêveries du promeneur solitaire* (*Reveries of a Solitary Walker*, 1782), set the tone for Fr. poetry in the first half of the 19th c. According to this prose account of walks taken by the author in the countryside around Paris and of others taken earlier when he lived near Geneva, Rousseau (1712–78) found refuge from his critics by making forays into nature. Such occasions restored the natural calm that he craved and led him to balance the movements of nature with his own search for happiness. Following his lead, the romantic poets Alphonse de Lamartine (1790–1869) and Victor Hugo (1802–85) would turn into verse the sort of meditations on loss, self-isolation, and nature's restorative power that Rousseau developed in his last book. A second group of writers, most notably Aloysius Bertrand (1807–41) and Charles Baudelaire (1821–67), refined the formal links forged by Rousseau between the rhythms of poetic prose and the cadence of walking by developing the new medium of prose poetry (see PROSE POEM).

Despite its brevity, Lamartine's *Méditations poétiques et religieuses* (1820) immediately earned its author praise for the simplicity of its evocations of past happiness and the smooth-flowing reveries that his verse sustained. In "Le Lac," the poet laments the inevitable passage of time, echoed in a lake's lapping waves, and asks the rocks and vegetation on the shore to attest to the moment of passion that he shared there, months earlier, while rowing his beloved who has since died. "L'Isolement" and "Le Vallon" imply in their descriptions of meadows and valleys an ascent toward the Christian paradise, with death proclaimed as a joyous release. Less religious but just as poignant in their depictions of the instability of human attachments are Marceline Desbordes-Valmore's *Poésies* (1830) and *Les Pleurs* (1833). The direct evocations of hardship (e.g., the illness and death of a child, abandonment by a lover) and subtle reversals of anticipated meanings near the ends of her poems are prime illustrations of poetry's power to surprise.

Hugo placed surprise at the heart of his romantic aesthetic, writing in *Les Contemplations* (1856) that, when reading lyric verse, "Il faut que, par instants, on frissonne, et qu'on voie / Tout à coup, sombre, grave et terrible au passant, / Un vers fauve sortir de l'ombre en rugissant!" (We must, at some moments, shudder when we see / All of a sudden, the dark, somber and terrifying movement / Of a wild verse emerge from the darkness roaring!). Having published in 1822 a first volume of verse that reworked legends of folklore (*Les Odes et poésies diverses*), Hugo set a new course with his second book, *Les Orientales* (1829). In it, he depicted distant lands while working out a broad variety of verse forms that detached lyric from the dominant alexandrine line that Chénier and Lamartine had used. Embracing ex-

oticism was not a novelty, since Montesquieu had made the subject popular almost a century earlier with his *Lettres persanes* and exiled writers such as Chateaubriand had placed their prose dramas in distant countries (the latter's *René* and *Atala* are set in Amerindian territories around the Mississippi). Hugo too would undergo the rigors of exile in 1851 when he fled France to protest Napoleon III's reign, spending 19 years on the island of Guernsey. Yet by tying Hugo's poetry to a setting in Muslim North Africa and Spain, *Les Orientales* set in motion an appropriation of other cultures, epochs, and langs. that would become a hallmark of *romanticism and make its poetry a fundamentally composite genre.

In the shorter preface to *Les Orientales*, Hugo compared the new literary movement to a med. town whose irregular streets, winding between buildings of all types, and teeming citizenry, living amid disorder and change, represented the ferment of life. Instead of imitating Gr. and Roman subjects (as Chénier and earlier poets had done), Hugo challenged his contemporaries to engage readers with outbursts of energy and passion drawn not only from remote places (Egypt, Constantinople, or the Danube basin) but from different epochs (biblical times, the Middle Ages, or contemp. events). Alfred de Vigny rose to the challenge, evoking in such poems as "La Maison du berger" and "L'Esprit pur" the joy of being transported beyond the mod. world of railways and riches to seats of lasting power—nature's gradual changes or the realm of spiritual serenity. Another poet who defined poetry as a spiritual quest was Gérard de Nerval (1808–55). His two-volume *Voyage en Orient* chronicles his travels to North Africa, while his trans. of J. W. Goethe's *Faust* led him to discover Ger. mythology. In his collection of sonnets *Les Chimères* (1854), he excelled in transposing personal grief into psychological studies of heroes from ancient, Christian, or Eng. myths. Théophile Gautier (1811–72) lived for a period in Spain, and while there composed *España* (1845), which began the transpositions of paintings and sculptures that would exemplify his cult of beauty in *Emaux et camées* (1852).

Romanticism's complex appropriation of other worlds and the creation of composite verses that collated the diversity of France's colonial empire in Africa, the Caribbean, and the Pacific gained impetus from several writers who had first-hand knowledge of lands beyond Europe. Charles-Marie Leconte de Lisle's *Poèmes barbares* (1872) draws on Hindu myths, tropical vegetation, and animals common to the Asian and Af. continents, as well as elements gleaned from the first 18 years of his life on a sugar plantation in Reunion, an island in the Indian Ocean. Like J.-M. de Heredia, who left his native Cuba in 1850 at age eight, Leconte de Lisle (1818–94) wrote finely crafted poems based on myths of different civilizations, and both poets began by publishing discrete poems in an anthol. entitled *Le Parnasse contemporain* in 1866. Along with François Coppée and other poets published in the collection, both authors adopted the name *Parnassiens* (see PARNASSIANISM) and developed the doctrine of art for art's sake first proposed by Gautier in 1836. According to Gautier, poetry could attain greatness only by abandoning any claim to moral pronouncements or the analysis of sentiment and by instead transposing into words the richness of color and composition exemplified in the plastic arts (see AESTHETICISM). Another poet of foreign birth, the Uruguay-born Isidore Ducasse (1846–70), published under the pseud. Comte de Lautréamont a long prose poem in six cantos, *Les Chants de Maldoror* (1869). It recounts in graphic detail the struggle between God and a romantic hero (whose name in the book's title illustrates romanticism's privileging of liminal moments between night and day: *mal d'aurore*). The publisher decided that, given the work's seeming immorality, it was better to distribute it outside France, which meant that it was little read until Remy de Gourmont praised its formal beauty in 1891. The composite genre of poetry in prose had been tried earlier by Aloysius Bertrand in his posthumous *Gaspard de la nuit* (1842). Most of its short texts are either portraits of artisans or detailed descriptions of landscapes, so that the work in its entirety is reminiscent of paintings by Johannes Vermeer and other Dutch artists. While acknowledging Bertrand, in the preface to *Le Spleen de Paris* (1869), Baudelaire pushed the hybrid genre in a new direction and linked the fluid rhythms of poetic prose to surprises and ecstatic moments found by a man walking through Paris. Giving his book the subtitle *Petits poèmes en prose*, Baudelaire also coined the term *prose poems*.

Widely considered the most important poet of the 19th c. and the writer responsible for placing poetry at the vanguard of artistic experimentation and ethical questioning, at least up until the surrealists of the 1930s, Baudelaire led a life marked by debt, illness, and a difficult stepfather. His early publications were reviews of the annual Parisian Salons, in which painters such as Eugène Delacroix exhibited their work. The first Fr. translator of E. A. Poe and an admirer of Gautier, he reoriented romanticism with his masterpiece *Les Fleurs du mal*, which was censored two months after its publication in 1857 for causing an outrage to morality. Baudelaire maintained that the judgment betrayed a misreading of his book since the poems' depictions of sadism, prostitution, and other addictions do not glorify evil but unmask the hypocrisy of his day. The first and longest section in the book, "Spleen et Idéal," also demonstrates what prevents human beings from achieving a romantic fusion with Beauty or Nature. First there is resignation to despair and then comes the numbing effect occasioned by merely satisfying our appetites, instead of embracing life's unpredictability and its fragile richness. The two poles of human experience—ecstasy or the enslavement to false value— are evoked in the transporting rhythms and promised happiness of "L'Invitation au voyage" and in the claustrophobic melancholy of the fourth "Spleen" poem that begins "Quand le ciel bas et lourd pèse comme un couvercle . . ." (When the low and heavy sky weighs like a lid). Although famous for his poetry, Baudelaire had to write prose articles and reports to pay his creditors. His death at age 46 came two years before the appearance of his complete volume of prose poems.

Hugo outlived almost all the preceding writers, and he kept in touch with devels. in the romantic movement, from Lamartine's introspective questionings to Baudelaire's experimental fusions of verse and ethics, prose and poetry. Hugo's own verse, however, followed its own trajectory. During his exile in Guernsey, he completed not only his novels *Les Misérables* and *L'Homme qui rit* but also satirical verses against Napoleon III, *Les Châtiments*, and some of his best-known poems. These appeared in the elegiac *Contemplations* (1856) and his epic recounting of humankind's rise to spirituality, *La Légende des siècles*, the three volumes of which were published in 1859, 1877, and 1883. The pantheistic beliefs that Hugo came to espouse during his exile were further developed in poems that appeared posthumously in *Dieu* and *La Fin de Satan*. When he died in 1885, Hugo was celebrated as a national hero, for his return to France in 1870 had coincided with the abdication of Napoleon III and a humiliating defeat of the Fr. army by Prussia. His body lay in state at the Arc de Triomphe but he had insisted before his death that his corpse be laid in a pauper's coffin. The procession taking the coffin on its workhouse hearse took six hours to move through the crowd and reach the Pantheon, where Hugo was then buried alongside France's greatest.

**C. Symbolism.** Stéphane Mallarmé (1842–98) wrote in his essay "Crise de vers" (1886, 1896) that Hugo's death was the turning point for Fr. poetry, since the fixed verse patterns that Hugo and the romantics had perfected had died with him. Mallarmé's disciple Paul Valéry (1871–1945) would later characterize the contrast between Hugo and Mallarmé by an elliptical formula: "Hugo: how to say everything in verse. Mallarmé: how to say nothing except what is verse." Not only does this motto point to a radical change, underscored by Mallarmé, in the sorts of things that poems should say—not *information, facts, or what the latter termed "l'universel reportage"—but it indicates a break in the way that a poem actually says anything. Versification was altered but so too was what it served. Both of these changes reverberated throughout the loosely associated group of poets known as the symbolists.

To start with versification, the freeing of verse had begun 20 years earlier. After Paul Verlaine's *Poèmes saturniens* appeared in 1866, more poems eschewed the standard alexandrine line and used lines of ten, eight, four, seven or five syllables. The last two cases were important since an uneven number of syllables meant that verses were no longer divisible into symmetrical halves, which allowed poems where the rhythms often ran from one uneven verse line into another. Verlaine (1844–96) developed this technique in his books *Fêtes galantes* (1869) and *Romances sans paroles* (1874), and the use of uneven syllabic lines became a credo in his poem "Art poétique," which called for allying poetry with music, while loosening semantic exactitude through combinations of sounds. Arthur Rimbaud (1854–91), who accompanied Verlaine during extended stays in Belgium and England, freed the alexandrine further from its stock rhythms by using run-on lines and surprising pauses at the beginnings or ends of the lines. His poem "A la musique" (written in 1870) goes beyond Verlaine since, in all his verses, Rimbaud blended innovative rhythms with ironic twists of meaning. So, when readers reach the end of "Le Bateau ivre" or "Les Effarés," they are shocked to find that what they assumed to be either the subject or the tone of the poem is upturned. Rimbaud's extremely short poetic career, from age 16 to 18, encompassed intense spells of creativity in which he not only produced experimental verses but pushed the prose poem to new heights—in *Une saison en enfer* (*A Season in Hell*, 1873) and *Illuminations*, which was published after his death.

Common to Verlaine's moody evocations of landscapes and solitude and to Rimbaud's complex staging of sentiments is the belief that a poem's force lies not in its mode of representation (or its ability to describe everyday scenes and emotions) but in the innovative effects that the poem produces for its readers. This lies at the heart of not only the symbolists' fascination with music but their emphasis on suggesting multiple meanings in the same poem, so that the text's patternings outdo in richness the events or thoughts that led to its composition. Jule Laforgue's parodies of romantic melancholy in *Les Complaintes* (1885) give a comic tone to this self-reflexivity, while Jean Moréas (1856–1910), who wrote a symbolist *manifesto in 1886, evokes the power of fleeting illusions in his collection *Les Syrtes* (1884). It was, however, Mallarmé's poetry that exemplified a poem's ability to stand as a self-sufficient object whose sounds and senses echo each other indefinitely. Although he published relatively few verses, some prose poems, and influential essays, his reunions every Tuesday with fellow poets helped establish him as the unofficial leader of *symbolism. His one collection of poems, *Poésies*, appeared in 1899, a year after his death, and contained "L'Après-midi d'un faune" (initially written for a staged performance to be accompanied with a score by Claude Debussy) along with sonnets that illustrated his goal of "painting not the thing but the effect that it creates."

Paul Valéry gave theoretical support to the symbolists' belief that a poem could create new experiences. Setting aside poetry in 1892, he devoted the next 20 years to writing down his reflections on mathematics, philosophy, and lang. in essays such as "Une soirée avec Monsieur Teste" and in notebooks that he would work on each morning after rising at 5:00. Covering a wide range of topics, the notebooks scrutinize the symbolic transformations, or what Valéry called a calculus, that give words their power. Rather than reflect preexistent ideas or thoughts, words for Valéry are integers in pragmatic calculations whose utterances are meant to change the world, thus anticipating by 40 years Ludwig Wittgenstein's writings on lang.-games and J. L. Austin's notion of performatives (see SPEECH ACT THEORY). Valéry also recognized that poetry has more potential for transforming the meanings of utterances than any other use of written symbols. If we consider his poem of 1891 "Narcisse parle" (which the poet would revise later in his career, in order to perfect its sonic transformations), we find the Gr. mythological hero voicing his last thoughts before suicide:

Farewell, lost reflection on the sealed up waters,
Narcissus . . . this very name is a tender fragrance
To the delicate heart. Sprinkle for the shades of the
    departed
This empty grave with petals from the funereal rose.

Not only do these lines take up aspects of the tragic search for self that Mallarmé had explored in his poem "Hérodiade" (1887), but they fuse a "name," a "fragrance," and a "heart" into one symbolic evocation by which the name *becomes* the fragrance, which in turn exchanges its "delicate" nature for the "tender" one associated with the heart. The fusion is helped by the phonetic properties of the name "Narcisse" that lends its sounds *n* (*nom*, name), *ar* (*parfum*, fragrance), and *ss* (*suave*, delicate) to the words following it. It is also helped semantically by the devel. of the flower code ("fragrance," "petals," "rose"), which is both a *metaphor for transient beauty and the context for the literal meaning of the common name "Narcissus." The aural properties of this particular word, in conjunction with its verbal associations, consequently turn it into the very name for the sadness-in-perfection that the poem unfolds. Valéry later took up writing verse long enough to publish his most famous collection, *Charmes*, in 1922. "Le Cimetière marin," one of its longer poems, is considered by many to be an illustration of Valéry's definition of poetic "charms"— "a prolonged hesitation [perceived by the reader] between [a verse's] sound and sense."

Another symbolist who pushed the boundaries of thought by creating a new poetic form was Victor Segalen (1878–1919). His collection *Stèles* (1914), written while the poet worked as a doctor in China, was based in part on two long journeys he made on foot and on horseback to the center of the country. Each stele offers lapidary pronouncements about different paths to joy. Paul Claudel (1868–1955) in his finely crafted prose poems *Connaissance de l'Est* (1914) drew inspiration from walking around Chinese cities. His later verse and dramatic works would use symbolist evocations of feeling as a path to Christian spirituality. Satirical poets had already put the performative power of poetry to new uses during the final decades of the 19th c. Meeting at the Chat Noir cabaret in Paris (1885–96), such *fumiste* writers as Alphonse Allais would perform spectacles overturning romantic or cl. works. Their biting humor and riffs on advertising and popular songs prepared the way for Dadaist performances a quarter-century later.

**D.** *Avant-Gardes of the Twentieth Century.* By 1912, Paris had become the cultural capital of Europe, attracting innovators in all branches of the arts. Important collaborations ensued between artists working in different media. Painters from abroad, such as Pablo Picasso, would join experimenters such as Sergei Diaghilev and his Rus. ballet troupe to produce works that set new aesthetic standards. The poet Guillaume Apollinaire (1880–1918) wrote program notes for Diaghilev's ballet *Parade* as well as the first essays explaining cubist painting to the general public (see CUBISM).

Poetry played a key role in the devel. of these avant-garde aesthetics (see AVANT-GARDE POETICS). In 1908, the young writer Jules Romains (1885–1972) published a book-length poem in two parts called *La Vie unanime* that called for a new form of lit., unanimism. Written in verses of varying syllabic counts grouped into regular stanzas, the book demonstrates how individual consciousness can be absorbed by the various rhythms of life around it—animal, chemical, electrical, machine or human. The massed comings and goings of city crowds inspired many of Romains's pages. F. T. Marinetti's "Futurist Manifesto," pub. in Paris a year later, cut poetry free from old myths such as idealizing statuesque beauty. It proposed instead that a new cult be formed around speed and the dynamism of machines. Blaise Cendrars's 1913 poem "Prose du Transsibérien et de la petite Jehanne de France" is an account written in *free verse of a train journey across Russia, and it evokes the giddiness of hurtling through time and space that futurists valued. Nevertheless, there is a tension in the poem between nostalgia for the past and the dynamism of fast travel (see FUTURISM).

The writer who best captured the exhilaration of the new horizons made possible by mass communication, the telegraph, and travel was Apollinaire. His book *Alcools* (1913) opens with the declaration "A la fin tu es las de ce monde ancien" and goes on to praise the poetry of advertisements, catalogs, and posters. After enlisting in the Fr. army in World War I, Apollinaire would write part of his most innovative volume, *Calligrammes* (1918), while serving at the front. Printed on army paper, the third part of the book was distributed to fellow soldiers, and it contains some poems lamenting lost comrades and turning the soldiers' routine and squalid conditions into beautiful testimonials. The visual form of some *calligrammes, scattering words and letters across the page, allowed Apollinaire to embed his verses within line drawings of a heart, a fountain, or a rifle. Mallarmé's philosophical poem *Un coup de dés* (*A Throw of the Dice*, 1897) had been the first work to exploit the entire space of a page, allowing readers to scan words in multiple directions, but Apollinaire's war poems and Pierre Reverdy's book *Les Ardoises du toit* (*Roof Slates*, 1918) used new typographical arrangements to evoke simple situations that resonate through a web of strong emotions (see TYPOGRAPHY).

As the reality of the Great War's slaughter and futility became known, some artists used poetry's performative force to attack the basis of everyday lang. that for them had been contaminated by politicians' speeches and jingoistic nationalism. In April 1916, a group of performers began an entertainment review, the Cabaret Voltaire, in a Zurich café. Their rallying cry was "Dada," which they defined not as an aesthetic movement but as a systematic destruction of meaning. The *Dada manifestos were not published but proclaimed in public alongside *performance poems—sound events juxtaposing phonemes from different langs. and recited by different performers. Paris became a center of Dada creativity once Tristan Tzara came there in 1920 to join writers of an experimental review called *Littérature*. Two of the writers, André Breton (1896–1966) and Philippe Soupault (1897–1990), had developed a technique of collaboratively transcribing dreams, which they called automatic writing. Others such as Robert Desnos (1900–45), Paul Éluard (1895–1952), and Louis Aragon (1897–1982) published poems in which sounds or typographical shapes were reinvented. These innovations precipitated calls for a new lyricism that would directly express the unconscious while being a collaborative endeavor, since artistic *"genius," according to these writers, was illusory. Their rallying call appeared in 1924 under the title *Surrealist Manifesto*, which borrowed its name from a term that Apollinaire had used earlier to describe artists' refusal to slavishly copy traditional forms.

Combining the iconoclastic force of Dada (esp. in their public denunciations of idealist art) with a new cult of feminine beauty, the surrealists wrote novels, essays, and poems that gave voice to nascent desire. Love lyrics such as Éluard's "L'Amoureuse" in *Capitale de la douleur* (1926) show that refusals of conventional logic (the poem begins "She is standing on my eyelids") can allow rhetorical figures to represent the all-encompassing power of passion. Fraught by internal struggles, *surrealism lost many of its members by the mid-1930s, after expelling Aragon for putting Communism before art or attacking rival groups such as the review *Le Grand Jeu*. The latter's cofounder, René Daumal, had set the foundations for a poetry of change and a rejection of self-identity in his *Contre-ciel* (1936). Although some surrealist poems such as Éluard's "Liberté" became famous statements of resistance during the Nazi occupation of France, by 1945 the movement had ceased being a mirror for important innovations in poetry.

**E. Strands of Post–World War II Poetry.** No one movement or set of aesthetic principles characterizes the broad diversity of poems published since 1950. Yet common strands in these works emerge once we examine three types of action that mod. poetry accomplishes in its efforts to change the world—political action, transformation of a person's interactions with the material world, and the forging of new connections with other forms of expression.

Poetry's power to disrupt not only political *doxa* but facile uses of lang. is brilliantly illustrated by René Char's wartime fragments collected in *Feuillets d'Hypnos* (1946) and by his finely crafted books *La Parole en archipel* (1962) and *Aromates chasseurs* (1975). However, it was outside France that one poem gained fame as a rallying cry for justice, not only in the Caribbean of which it speaks, but across the francophone world. Aimé Césaire's *Cahier d'un retour au pays natal* (*Notebook of a Return to the Native Land*, 1939) is part narrative and part invective against the inequalities imposed by Caribbean plantation economies and colonialism. Its 174 stanzas in free verse are tightly organized around recurring phrases that rise in a concluding crescendo that calls on the black population of Martinique (and other islands) to shake off its collective shame and fight for self-determination. The first text to make use of the term \*négritude, Césaire's poem inspired many writers in and beyond France to blend poetry and political commitment. The Guadeloupean writer Édouard Glissant (1928–2011) connected the hist. of Caribbean slavery to early epochs in the trade and uses of salt throughout his \*long poem *Le Sel noir* (1960). Modeled on the renewed epic form of Saint-John Perse's *Amers* (1957), with its long stanzas of free verse and complex forms of address, Glissant scans lost civilizations of Carthage, Rome, and Celtic Brittany as well as Africa. He also turns Perse's chronicles of individual quests (most notably in *Anabase*, 1924) into a song of peoples on the move. Léopold Sédar Senghor developed Césaire's concept of négritude in his fusion of West African trads. and politically inspiring lyrics (*Ethiopiques*, 1956), while Raymond LeBlanc's *Cri de terre* (1972) unearths the violent suppression of Acadian culture in the coastal landscape of New Brunswick, Canada. Michèle Lalonde's poster-poem "Speak White" (1970) allies the call for Quebecois' self-respect to that of black pride. More recently, Herménégilde Chiasson and Robert Dickson have crafted poetic monuments to the anxieties of Fr.-speaking cultures in the anglophone Canadian Maritimes and Ontario.

A second strand of political poetry developed in the wake of Francis Ponge's (1899–1988) method of implying a materialist theory of happiness through meditations on objects and nature. The intricate prose poems of his *Le parti pris des choses* (1942) underscore modes of living that are in harmony with the rhythms of nonhuman organisms. "Notes pour un coquillage" argues that lang. should be used not as a mirror for ideas but as a tool for improving our lives with others, and this lesson was not lost on writers who turned to poetry in order to reinvigorate lang. and reconnect speakers with the material world. Eugène Guillevic (1907–97) developed his own minimalist forms of lyric that celebrate natural forces and the lessons they embody. Yves Bonnefoy (b. 1923), France's most famous poet of the second half of the 20th c., has written essays and poems in which a search for presence is the overarching goal; poets such as Philippe Jaccottet (b. 1925) have continued in this vein. André du Bouchet (1924–2001) wrote experimental poems in which the careful placement of a few words in unique typographical arrangements across entire pages is part of a conjoined exploration of lang.'s potential and of life rhythms connecting a walker to the hills he traverses. The poems of Jacques Dupin, André Frénaud, or Jacques Réda are less experimental than du Bouchet's, yet they continue to fathom the human body's relation to space, as does the work of Jacqueline Risset and James Sacré. Bernard Noël has developed a highly original form of philosophical poetry that proposes the singularity of bodily sensation as a counterweight to idealist illusions. In Noël's book *La Chute des temps* (1983), perceptions are transposed as events that allow us to escape the hold of clock time, grounding poetry in an awareness of living that is close to the self-sufficient joys described by Baudelaire.

A final group of writers has reinvented poetry's ties to other art forms. Beginning with Henri Michaux (1899–1984), the shared mechanics of writing and drawing have become central to poems that exploit typographical invention. Concrete poets Pierre Garnier (b. 1928) and Jean-Pierre Faye (b. 1925) moved beyond Apollinaire's shoehorning of spoken verses into calligrams and proposed new types of visual syntax (see CONCRETE POETRY). Pierre-Albert Jourdain (1924–91) and Michel Deguy (b. 1930) managed, in different ways, to draw innovative effects from varying their poems' visual shape. Emmanuel Hocquard (b. 1940) has experimented with poems written in a tabular form (in *Théorie des tables*) or with poetry and photography. Members of the \*Oulipo group refuse the assumption that lyric verse expresses an individual's emotions and invented numerical patterns for syllabic and linear arrangement that place mathematical properties, rather than sentiment, at the heart of a poem. For instance, Jacques Roubaud's collection of verses *Є* (1967) is structured around moves in the Japanese game Go. Michelle Grangaud's *Geste: narrations* (1991) is composed of three-line stanzas (with lines of five, five, and eleven syllables), each of which recounts a circumstance that may be combined with other stanzas to produce an indeterminate number of narratives. By bringing into question the opposition between narrative and lyric, Oulipo writers and others such as Pierre Alféri and Dominique Fourcade might be said to have brought Fr. poetry full circle, since their work recalls the formal experiments of Occitan and early Fr. writers who blended elements of the two forms.

*See* CANADA, POETRY OF; CARIBBEAN, POETRY OF THE; MEDIEVAL POETRY; NEOCLASSICAL POETICS; RENAISSANCE POETRY; ROMANTIC AND POSTROMANTIC POETRY AND POETICS.

■ **Anthologies, Manifestos, and Translations**: *Anthologie de la nouvelle poésie négre et malgache*, ed. L. S. Senghor (1942); *Modern French Verse*, ed. P. Mansell Jones (1957); *Anthologie de la poésie française du XVIème siècle*, ed. F. Gray (1962); *Anthology of Modern French Poetry*, ed. C. A. Hackett (1967); A. Breton, *Manifestoes of Surrealism*, trans. R. Seaver and H. R. Lane (1969); *La Poésie française des origines à nos jours: Anthologie*, ed. C. Bonnefoy (1975); *Modern French Poetry: A Bilingual Anthology*, ed. P. Terry and S. Gavronsky (1975); *Anthologie des grands rhétoriqueurs*, ed. P. Zumthor (1978); T. Tzara, *Sept manifestes Dada, Lampisteries* (1978); *L'Anthologie arbitraire d'une nouvelle poésie, 1960–82: Trente poètes*, ed. H. Deluy (1983); *The Random House Book of Twentieth-Century French Poetry*, ed. P. Auster (1984); *The Defiant Muse: French Feminist Poets from the Middle Ages to the Present*, ed. D. C. Stanton (1986); *Anthologie de la poésie du XVIIe siècle*, ed. J.-P. Chauveau (1987); *Anthologie de la poésie lyrique française des XIIe et XIIIe siècles*, ed. J. Dufournet (1989); *La Poésie acadienne, 1948–1988*, ed. G. Leblanc and C. Beausoleil (1992); *Poèmes de femmes des origines à nos jours*, ed. R. Deforges (1993); "La Poésie contemporaine en France," *Littéréalité*, ed. S. Villani (1994); *Anthology of First World War French*

Poetry, ed. I. Higgins (1996); *Les Poètes du Chat Noir*, ed. A. Velter (1996); *Anthologie de la poésie française*, ed. J.-P. Chauveau, G. Gros, D. Ménager (vol. 1), M. Bercot, M. Collot, C. Seth (vol. 2) (2000); *Anthologie de la poésie française du XX siècle*, ed. M. Décaudin (2000); *Anthologie de la poésie française du XVIe siècle*, ed. J. Céard and L.-G. Tin (2005); *Futurist Manifestos*, ed. U. Apollonio (2009).

■ **Criticism and History**: T. de Banville, *Petit traité de poésie française* (1935); J. Paulhan, *Clef de la poésie* (1944); S. Bernard, *Le Poème en prose de Baudelaire jusqu'à nos jours* (1959); R. Lalou, *Histoire de la poésie française* (1963); M. Sanouillet, *Dada à Paris* (1965); G. E. Clancier, *De Chénier à Baudelaire* (1970); *Essais de sémiotique poétique*, ed. J. A. Greimas (1972); G. Brereton, *An Introduction to the French Poets* (1973); *The Appreciation of Modern French Poetry: 1850–1950*, ed. P. Broome and G. Chesters (1976); M. Riffaterre, *Semiotics of Poetry* (1978); J.-M. Gleize, *Poésie et figuration* (1983); *The Prose Poem in France: Theory and Practice*, ed. M. A. Caws and H. Riffaterre (1983); M. Riffaterre, *Text Production*, trans. T. Lyons (1983); M. Bishop, *Contemporary French Women Poets* (1984–85); W. Calin, *In Defense of French Poetry: An Essay in Revaluation* (1987); R. Chambers, *Meaning and Meaningfulness* (1987); R. R. Hubert, *Surrealism and the Book* (1988); M. Collot, *La Poésie moderne et la structure d'horizon* (1989); J. Chénieux-Gendron, *Surrealism* (1990); C. Prendergast, *Nineteenth-Century French Poetry: Introductions to Close Readings* (1990); *The Ladder of High Design: Structure and Interpretation of the French Lyric Sequence*, ed. D. Fenoaltea and D. L. Rubin (1991); *Poetry in France: Metamorphoses of a Muse*, ed. K. Aspley and P. France (1992); "Mallarmè, Theorist of Our Times," ed. S. Winspur, *Dalhousie French Studies* 25 (1993)—spec. iss.; *Understanding French Poetry: Essays for a New Millennium*, ed. S. Metzidakis (1994); P. D. Cate and M. Shaw, *The Spirit of Montmartre: Cabarets, Humor, and the Avant-Garde, 1875–1905* (1995); A. Gendre, *Evolution du sonnet français* (1996); *La Poésie française du Moyen Age jusqu'à nos jours*, ed. M. Jarrety (1997); C. Scott, *The Poetics of French Verse* (1998); E. S. Burt, *Poetry's Appeal: Nineteenth-Century French Lyric and the Political Space* (1999); S. Gaunt and S. Kay, *The Troubadours: An Introduction* (1999); J.-J. Thomas and S. Winspur, *Poeticized Language: The Foundations of Contemporary French Poetry* (1999); *Poétiques de la Renaissance: Le modèle italien, le monde franco-bourguignon et leur héritage en France au XVIème siècle*, ed. P. Galand-Hallyn and F. Hallyn (2001); F. Rigolot, *Poésie et Renaissance* (2002); M. Shaw, *The Cambridge Introduction to French Poetry* (2003); *A Short History of French Literature*, ed. S. Kay, T. Cave and M. Bowie (2003); G. W. Fetzer, *Palimpsests of the Real in Recent French Poetry* (2004); J. Acquisito, *French Symbolist Poetry and the Idea of Music* (2006); C. Chi-ah Lyu, *A Sun within a Sun: The Power and Elegance of Poetry* (2006); *Sens et présence du sujet poétique: La poésie de la*

*France et du monde francophone depuis 1980*, ed. M. Brophy and M. Gallagher (2006); J. Petterson, *Poetry Proscribed: Twentieth-Century (Re)Visions of the Trials of Poetry in France* (2008); "Uncanny Poetry/Méconnaissance de la poésie," ed. C. Wall-Romana, *L'Esprit Créateur* 49.2 (2009)—spec. iss.; *Cambridge History of French Literature*, ed. W. Burgwinkle, N. Hammond, and E. Wilson (2011); A. Armstrong and S. Kay, *Knowing Poetry: Verse in Medieval France from the "Rose" to the "Rhétoriqueurs"* (2011).

> J. S. HELGESON (MED. TO EARLY MOD.);
> S. WINSPUR (EARLY MOD. TO 20TH C.)

**FRANCOPHONE POETS OF THE U.S.** While poems written in Fr. can be found in the archives of some New England newspapers or as a curiosity among the minor work of writers such as Jack Kerouac and T. S. Eliot, they form a major component of the lit. hist. of Louisiana. Until recently, this body of poetry was virtually erased from the lit. hist. of the U.S.

Louisiana was established as a Fr. colony in 1699. Two Fr.-born writers of this era produced neoclassical poems distinguished more for their New World subject matter than their literary quality. Jean François Dumont de Montigny composed a long poem in *alexandrines about the 1729 Natchez Indian massacre of Fr. settlers. In the late 1770s, Julien Poydras de Lalande, who later served in the U.S. Congress, published two anonymous verse pamphlets and a signed poem praising Sp. governor Bernardo de Gálvez.

Following the Louisiana Purchase of 1803, Fr. became a means by which "Creole" descendants of colonial settlers, whether black or white, could differentiate themselves from the Eng.-speaking "Americans" whom they perceived to be crude and lacking in culture. Francophone newspapers flourished, and from the 1830s on, they published thousands of poems and stories by local writers. "Standard" or Parisian Fr. was the norm for literary writing, regardless of the regional dialect spoken at home.

Fr. romantic poets Victor Hugo, Alphonse de Lamartine, Alfred de Musset, and Pierre-Jean de Béranger influenced Louisiana poets of the first half of the 19th c. Tullius St.-Céran, Constant Lépouzé, Urbain David, and Auguste Lussan wrote historical odes on heroic subjects like the Battle of New Orleans or the July 1830 revolution. Louisiana "Creole of color" Victor Séjour, educated in France like many young men of his social class, wrote a poem that won him political favor about the return of Napoleon's ashes to Paris; he went on to become a famous Parisian playwright.

Brothers Dominique and Adrien Rouquette, educated in France, wrote long narrative poems reflecting their fascination with Native Am. culture and the Am. wilderness: Adrien became a hermit-priest ministering to a Choctaw Indian tribe. Alexandre Latil, diagnosed with leprosy while still in his teens, moved to a remote cabin and wrote moving poems about love, time, and loss. He published *Les Éphémères* (1841), a well-received poetry collection, prior to his death at 35.

*Les Cenelles* (1845), ed. Armand Lanusse, was the

first literary anthol. by poets of color published in the U.S. Its title translates as "The Mayhaws," indigenous fruits from a prickly hawthorn shrub. The 85 poems by 17 free men of color take up typical romantic themes of love, death, and nature rather than race; but some poems present an ideal of feminine beauty that is darker than the blue-eyed blonde of continental Fr. romanticism, and others protest the hated social custom of *plaçage* between free women of color and white Frenchmen. The strongest poet in the anthol., Camille Thierry, later published the collection *Les Vagabondes* (1874) in France. Joanni Questy and Mirtil-Ferdinand Liotau contributed memorable lyrics, and Séjour's Napoleonic *ode was included.

In the second half of the century, Marxist themes appear in the works of Joseph Déjacques, Charles Testut, and Pierre-Aristide Desdunes—the latter a Creole of color. The Civil War inspired some odes to the Confederacy; those by F. Colin and Charles Délery are of better quality than most. Answering them were Joseph Chaumette's abolitionist verse pamphlet and numerous poems praising the bravery of black Civil War soldiers. During the Reconstruction, the topic of racial injustice erupted in impassioned poems by Pierre L'Hermite (a pseud.), Camille Naudin, Victor-Ernest Rillieux, and Desdunes, among others. Léona Queyrouze wrote a *sonnet sequence lamenting the 1891 massacre of 11 It. prisoners by a vigilante mob in New Orleans, while Jules Choppin published verse fables in Creole dialect.

Between 1916 and 1923, Louisiana banned the use of Fr. in schools and state facilities. Speaking Fr. became a mark of shame, the last Fr.-lang. newspaper closed down, and the francophone literary trad. all but died out. But the formation of the Council for Development of French in Louisiana (CODOFIL) in 1968 to preserve the state's Fr. heritage has reversed those trends and sparked a literary renaissance.

Unlike their predecessors, contemp. francophone poets have written most often in Cajun or Creole dialect rather than in standard Fr. The Cajun poets, descendants of the Fr. Acadians expelled from Nova Scotia by the Brit. in 1755, include the well-known musician Zachary Richard, winner of Canada's Prix Champlain for Literature; "Jean Arceneaux," the pseud. of Cajun folklorist Barry Ancelet; Beverly Matherne; Carol Doucet; Kirby Jambon; and David Cheramie. The hybrid Fr.-Af. "Creole" lang., denigrated as "dirty French" in previous century, has been the choice of poets Debbie Clifton and Sybil Kein.

■ A. Lanusse, ed., *Les Cenelles* (1848); A. Fortier, "French Literature in Louisiana," *PMLA* 2 (1886); R. L. Desdunes, *Nos Hommes et Notre Histoire* (1911); R. Caulfeild, *The French Literature of Louisiana* (1929); E. L. Tinker, *Les Écrits de langue française en Louisiane au xixe siècle* (1932); *Creole Voices*, ed. E. M. Coleman (1932); *Cris sur le bayou*, ed. B. J. Ancelet (1980); M. Fabre, "The New Orleans Press and French-Language Literature by Creoles of Color," *Multilingual America*, ed. W. Sollors (1998); *Creole*, ed. S. Kein (2000); M. Allain, ed., *Louisiana Literature and Literary Figures* (2004); N. Shapiro, ed., *Creole Echoes* (2004); C. Brasseux, *French, Cajun, Creole, Houma* (2005); D. Kress, "Pierre-Aristide Desdunes, *Les Cenelles,* and the Challenge of Nineteenth-Century Creole Literature," *Southern Quarterly* 44 (2007).

J. KANE

**FRANKFURT SCHOOL.** The unofficial, popular name for the *Institut für Sozialforschung* (Institute for Social Research), founded in 1923 and affiliated, except for its exile during the National Socialist regime and immediately thereafter, with the University of Frankfurt in Germany. The institute launched its work with the goals of innovating the methodologies and analytical possibilities for empirical social research; its work has focused on those (esp. the working class) who under duress confront the complexities of mod., industrial-capitalist society. Moreover, the Frankfurters sought to develop alternatives to what they considered the determinist rigidity of the orthodox Left and specifically Marxian theory, whether Social Democratic or Leninist. That rigidity, the Frankfurters argued, had contributed to the absence of a more robust critical consciousness and a sensing of agency among classes, groups, and individuals open to grasping and acting on the need for profound social transformation. Contesting such determinism, and esp. *conceptual* determinism, the Frankfurters began to rearticulate the importance of lit. and the other arts by noting, among other things, that Karl Marx and Friedrich Engels had themselves emphasized the links—apparently necessary, inextricable links—between imaginative/literary/aesthetic experience and the inculcation of both relentless critical thinking (the young Marx's famous call for "the ruthless critique of everything in existence") and sustained transformative action. Bringing Marx, Engels, and related precursors together with their own sense of how lit. and the other arts had sparked critical agency throughout hist. (and had done so with special urgency in the mod. period stretching from *romanticism through *modernism and *avant-garde experimentalism), the Frankfurters demonstrated their conviction that art could act decisively on structural, socioeconomic dynamics and might indeed be the means through which certain aspects of sociohistorical devel. could become apprehensible in the first place.

Institute figures contributing to Frankfurt lit. crit. and *interpretation include Max Horkheimer, Erich Fromm, Leo Löwenthal, and Herbert Marcuse. But by far the most important Frankfurt critics and interpreters of literary, aesthetic, and cultural works are Theodor W. Adorno, who was recruited by Horkheimer to join the institute, and Walter Benjamin, the institute's most significant collaborator. Benjamin's and Adorno's writings on poetry are concerned with Homer, the Occitan *troubadours, Dante, Shakespeare, J. W. Goethe, Friedrich Schiller, Friedrich Hölderlin, Heinrich Heine, P. B. Shelley, John Keats, Charles Baudelaire, Arthur Rimbaud, Stéphane Mallarmé, Eduard Mörike, Rudolf Borchardt, Georg Trakl, Stefan George, Guillaume Apollinaire, André Breton, Paul Éluard, Gottfried Benn, Ezra Pound,

Bertolt Brecht, Federico García Lorca, W. C. Williams, Wallace Stevens, Paul Celan, and others. Benjamin and Adorno esp. underscore that not only lit. but precisely lit.'s ostensibly most subjective, individualist, ephemeral, fragile literary phenomenon—mod. *lyric poetry—illuminates human beings' historical and existential experience of (and capacity to judge and thus challenge) capitalist society.

In autumn 1938, Benjamin presented to Adorno—for publication in the institute's jour., the *Zeitschrift für Sozialforschung*—"The Paris of the Second Empire in Baudelaire," Benjamin's "first" Baudelaire essay. The essay in many ways attempts to continue—or relocate on the terrain of artistic construction and lyric-aesthetic experience—Marx's historiographic masterpiece, *The Eighteenth Brumaire of Louis Bonaparte* (1852). Taking as his point of departure the *Brumaire*'s fond though unsparing critique of the *bohème*'s "conspiratorial" rebelliousness, Benjamin builds elaborate parallels and discovers the intersecting levels where Baudelaire's poetry itself becomes the intriguingly antisocial conspirator whose socioconceptual-imaginative limits are those of present society. Baudelaire's fantastic creativity, intelligence, intuition, and bitter subversiveness, gathered into and animating his unique artistic talent, yield a lyric poetry unprecedentedly mod. in its aim homeopathically to inhabit—and thereby make imagistically available—the very frame and machinations of the mod. socioeconomic limit-phenomenon at issue, *exchange value*. Baudelaire burrows into, captures, and presents exchange value's manifestation-identity in and as mechanical reproduction, in and as *commodity form*. Baudelaire does this by apparently making the poem itself into, or by greatly intensifying its already achieved status as, a commodity. Benjamin underscores Baudelaire's genius in reconjuring previous sociohistorical, sociolinguistic, and specifically *poetic* senses of what commodities (Fr. *biens, marchandises, denrées, produits*; Ger. *Waren*) have previously been (goods, services, things deemed commodious, convenient, useful, fine, desirable).

Benjamin contends that Baudelaire's poetry not only speaks of this overarching commodity hist. but devastatingly reenacts it into and as poetry's own historical trajectory. Through a time-lapse crosscutting whose unfolding logic stretches from cl. and neoclassical poetic langs. of form and style to journalistic and street argots of his own early–late 19th c. lifetime, Baudelaire re-sounds while cannily channeling, often with intended hyperostentation, those diverse poetic trads. (incl. centuries of experiment with poetry's heightening of rich and sensuous particularity, centuries of treating lyric as particularity made into poetic principle and practice) into contemp. imaginings of fashionable, materialistic-consumerist luxury. Imaginings that perversely wind up ratifying rather than contesting the very social and existential mod. abstraction, the very fact of rule by a predetermined concept (here, the mod. concept *exchange value*), that lyric's commitment to sensuous particularity presumably aims to oppose.

Consequently, the artistic-aesthetic "aura" that Benjamin famously connects to preindustrial hists. in which particularity was able (with imagination's capacity for spontaneous—neither random nor as yet conceptually predetermined—experience and judgment) to voice itself as something potentially universally communicable (although the given particular's seemingly governing or determining concept did not as yet exist): this *aura, semblance-form* or *recognized critical aesthetic illusion* that could make something seemingly glimpsed or dimly felt against the context of its empirical absence, this entire constelled dynamic of aura, critical aesthetic autonomy, and experience, Benjamin claims, "withers" in the era of mechanical reproduction, the era of exchange-commodity valuation. And so too must lyric poetry's previous life—as alpha and omega *of* aura—wither. Though shot through with a bitter irony whose strains of pathos can still register some trace of the once formidable, haunting note of protest that inhered in lyric song's traditional refusal to be bound by mere saying (by the mere denotative stating of an already determined status quo), lyric poetry—understood historically, and esp. since recent romanticism, as the artistic-aesthetic apotheosis of an emancipatory human ability to exceed or transcend given, already determined, conceptual limits, to insist on experiencing and judging past them—now confesses itself in Baudelaire to have become nothing *but* the mod. commodity or, more precisely, the final triumph of mod., mechanical, exchange-commodity valuation, as lyric's very song finds itself and its whole prior hist. unable to do more than musically describe, rather than exceed, the conceptual limits, the imprisoning walls, within which it along with everyone and everything else is now held or determined: exchange-commodity value. (Later poets' experiments in making the poem seem like, or even become fully subsumed into mod. commodity status are generally thought to trace their paths back to this Baudelairean moment, and—esp. in *postmodernism—from Benjamin's influential interpretations of it.)

But Adorno thinks that Baudelaire's poetry goes significantly further than the brilliantly symptomizing, bitter homeopathy of exchange value and commodity form that Benjamin identifies; Adorno believes that Baudelaire's lyric poetry finally stretches past exchange-commodity value limits and that some of Benjamin's earlier writings had already begun to articulate this extra, supercharged, critical distance in Baudelaire and later Baudelairean poets. Adorno therefore argues that in "The Paris of the Second Empire in Baudelaire," Benjamin now, in line with "The Work of Art in the Age of Mechanical Reproduction" (1935) and kindred essays, has unfortunately limited not only Baudelaire but himself too—has constrained his understanding of Baudelaire's, of advanced lyric's, and of mod. art's critical value—by adopting an essentially orthodox Marxist-Leninist, resolutely determinist approach to exchange-commodity value by no longer holding that the human agency potentialized in lyric/aesthetic experience, and the critical reflection thereby generated, have the capacity to project judgments and valuations that exceed the conceptual limits of exchange-commodity value. Observing that at key moments "The Paris of the Second Empire" redirects its treatment of Baudelaire's poetry back to the commodity and that Benjamin consistently claims—citing Marx—that the commodity is defined entirely by labor, Adorno insists otherwise, noting that Marx had emphatically refused to halt at such a definition.

Adorno here evokes the final movement in *Das Kapital*'s historical critique of exchange value/commodity form. Marx shows that the commodity's value derives not only from the conceptual abstraction of labor time but, crucially, from an ongoing, socially taken yet unspoken (and only recently apprehensible and, still more recently, Marx urges, *contestable*) *judgment* that this very abstraction of labor time *must or should be* the final basis for valuation/judgment.

Marx avers that this ability to transcend the conceptual abstraction of labor time as the ultimate determinant of socioeconomic value would break open—initially, via aesthetic judgment—exactly what aesthetic judgment by definition (since Kant at least) offers the *form* or *semblance* but not yet the *substance* of: an already extant, determined and determining *concept*. In such Kantian-aesthetic breaking open of extant, substantive-objective conceptual determination, the recognized and engaged *semblance-form, illusion-form*, or *aesthetic illusion* underwriting aesthetic quasi-conceptuality lets subjects feel or experience their semblance-play with conceptual *form* as if this play already *were* substantive-determinative-objective conceptuality, though a conceptuality somehow freely chosen rather than deterministically, "coercively" compelled (as almost all substantive—already determined—concepts perforce are; e.g., one is not "free" but is rather "coerced" by objective reality and the concepts that represent it to "agree" with basic concepts of mathematics that make two plus two equal four). Aesthetic judgment thus begins to enact, in *semblance-form* or the *subject's* reflective "subjective" engagement (rather than *substantive-objective*, already determined *content*), the experience and process, crucial to the sensing of critical agency, of the subject's being enabled to form, make, or construct something *not* conceptually predetermined that might yet noncoercively establish a new objectivated (genuinely universalizable) concept and/or value. Marx reiterates the need to break open this question of value when he demands that socioeconomic value be subject to a judgment process that aims for potentially universal concepts and objective realizations of them that are not required to have started from the ruling concept *exchange-commodity value based only in labor-time*. Economic modernity until his moment, Marx further argues, has been a hist. leading to capitalism's self-interested emancipation of labor-time made into exchange value; that emancipation has not only made the specific concept of exchange value decisive for capitalist socioeconomic valuation but has signified the socioeconomic triumph of determinate conceptualization itself. This enshrining *of a concept*

*or of conceptuality itself* as the source and regulative principle of socioeconomic value (as opposed to previous, precapitalist regimes' tendency to charge a person or group with representing, as sovereign, a body of beliefs or doctrines that need subjective inflection because they are not, as exchange value will be, conceptually-logically formulated and fixed) holds enormously generative possibilities for mod. socioeconomic productive capacity. But aside—or flowing—from this new "conceptualist" (and, thus, already objectively determined) mode of production's tendency to expand its social character and the quantity of goods produced while simultaneously intensifying the disparities of wealth and resource distribution comes an increasing *disappearance of particularity* (related to if not wholly caused by the *disappearance of use* as a determinant of value when value becomes subject to universal predetermination by a perforce abstract concept). This theme, already developed by Marx and Engels, famously becomes in Benjamin and then Adorno's writings "the crisis and withering of experience and aura."

Furthermore, given this historical relation between conceptual abstraction per se and exchange-value abstraction and *then* given that *lang.* is deemed by Marx, Engels, and the Frankfurters the favored *medium* for significantly communicable *conceptuality*, there is already in Marx and Engels the noteworthy intensification of a high romantic theme (rooted deeper still in cl. poetics and aesthetics): *lyric poetry bears a special, radical relationship to conceptuality as such and, hence, in modernity, to conceptuality's concretely practically realized socioeconomic identity as exchange-commodity value*. Because of its distilled relationship to the ling. medium (often seeming to be nothing but lang. itself being voiced past its object-objective status toward musical songfulness), lyric understandably figures as the artistic form closest to the medium of thought. Lyric semblance hence stands as the artistic-aesthetic experience *closest to the very act of thinking or conceiving* (albeit *thinking or conceiving* experienced *as if* not yet conceptually predetermined).

To paraphrase alternative formulations that Marx and Engels suggest and that the Frankfurters enunciate in a fuller, more sustained manner: each art has its own unique character; that of lyric is to take lang, (the presumably bottom-line medium of objectivity and conceptuality) and, first, to subjectivize it, making something that seems formally like a concept but does something that objective concepts generally do not do with their ling. medium: sing. Each of the arts has its mode or modes of semblance. In lyric, semblance primarily involves making speech acts appear, feel, as if their very logic has compelled them somehow to burst—naturally, justifiably, as it were—toward or into something within the full range of what can seem musical or songful, which, when enacted in the poem, seems necessary but not predetermined and which, in its bursting (in a manner inseparable from pleasure) the formal contours of extant conceptuality, allows subjects a renewed sense of capacity or agency vis-à-vis *materials* that can eventually, postaesthetically, be grasped as re-conceived or newly conceived sociopolitical, historical, and/or ethical *content*.

In sum, lyric's dynamic and medium uniquely capture the conceptual basis of mod. socioeconomic valuation *and*, at the same time, in extending past ling. objectivity, critically stretch experience and judgment beyond extant conceptual boundaries or determinants (incl. the socioeconomically dominant concept of exchange-commodity value).

Rearticulating and elaborating in Frankfurt vocabulary the relevant notions from Marx and Engels, Adorno highlights how Benjamin intuitively grasps that Baudelaire takes as subject matter modernity's problematic socioeconomic apotheosis of determinate conceptuality—and, vice versa, that Baudelaire's tortured explorations of infernal, experience-denying mod. determinism register an abiding reality: the nonexperience of human beings for whom judgment has by definition been made external or irrelevant to the capacity for critical agency. Adorno therefore urges Benjamin to extend the analysis to consider whether Baudelaire's wager—about making a profoundly mod. lyric poetry just when the experiential conditions for significant lyric appear to have gone missing—might *have* to inculcate critique of the concept-practice *exchange value*. Benjamin goes on to write a second essay, "On Some Motifs in Baudelaire" (1939–40), that Adorno immediately feels (as he indicates in his writings) has taken poetics, aesthetics, and critical theory to a level that Benjamin alone could have reached. The reception hist. tends to confirm Adorno's assessment; "On Some Motifs in Baudelaire" is widely regarded as one of the great 20th-c. essays on mod. poetry, social analysis, and critical theory. While not giving up on philological method and immanent engagement with materials, Benjamin alters his view of Baudelaire's enterprise. Benjamin does not move Baudelaire thematically from seductive, intriguing but commodified brasserie backrooms to more revolutionary contributions at the barricade frontlines. Instead, he shows the poetry to be struggling formally with, rather than simply reproducing, exchange value and mechanical reproduction. Confronting mechanical reproduction's and exchange value's tendency to cause the withering of charged auratic distance and reflective experience/judgment, and the withering of uncompromising, searching lyric musicality, Baudelaire's poetry discovers critical (not consolatory or redemptive but probing) formal means to wrest a sense of aura from aura's absence; it discovers how to invest the seeming unavailability of reflective experience with the charge and force *of* reflective experience (so that one can become enabled to reflect, for starters, on what it means to appear to have lost reflective capacity itself). Baudelaire's poetry—in, as, *lyric*—discovers anew how to sing song's apparent impossibility and thereby to allow subjects to begin to apprehend both extant social determinations and human beings' critical capacity to feel and think past them.

These exchanges with Adorno lead Benjamin toward the drafting of *Theses on the Philosophy of History*

(1940). Hence Benjamin's much-discussed angel of hist., hidden hunchback, and the notion of weak messianic power—and much more in the poetics of what remains to this day the Left's perhaps most celebrated self-critique of mechanistic determinism—appears to arise from intense engagement with mod. lyric's difficult explorations of aura, semblance character, and experience in confrontation with the concept-practice of exchange-commodity value. For his part, Adorno repeatedly indicates that Benjamin's acute enunciation of Baudelairean lyric's ability simultaneously to capture and exceed exchange-commodity value deeply colors everything Adorno proceeds to write not only about lyric but about the hist. and critical potential of the other arts as well. The influence evidences itself immediately in Adorno and Horkheimer's 1944 *Dialectic of Enlightenment*, in the critique of an instrumental rationality that causes conceptuality to lose contact with aesthetic-imaginative exploration of the difference and otherness residing beyond known predetermined conceptual borders, and in the text's various excursions, not least, the virtuosic treatment of the *Odyssey*'s telling of Odysseus's self-torturing experience of the Sirens' song, a foreshadowing of lyric modernity's much later retrospective explorations of its own prehists. in the division of labor, and in the self-sacrifice Western culture seems ab ovo to have needed to pit against the intrigue or pleasure involved in processes of encountering realms of experience that beckon with new knowledge.

Furthermore, Benjamin's writings on Baudelaire prove generative for some of the greatest lyric talents of the middle to late 20th c. who read them, incl. Brecht and Celan, in a process of engagement that continues in today's poetry and poetics. Picking up various suggestions from Benjamin and from Brecht's critique of an uncritical and merely "culinary" poetics and aesthetics (a term both Benjamin and Adorno adopt), Adorno goes on to hint at ways of extending a distinction in early Benjamin between genuine and false aura. Thus a real, critical attempt to engage aura is often seen to involve poems or other art works effectively evoking it by appearing provisionally to abandon it—or by appearing to abandon "culinary," formulaic, grown-sterile versions of what aura has heretofore been.

Finally and perhaps most significantly for post-1945 culture, Benjamin's unfolding of the dynamics of aura and experience in Baudelairean lyric suffuses Adorno's notorious, terribly misunderstood meditations about the "barbarism" of "poetry after Auschwitz." Adorno—notably echoed in his "after Auschwitz" ruminations by, among others, his colleague Marcuse—resists any notion that fascism and the Nazi genocide can be assimilated even to some final nightmarish stage of exchange-commodity value and capitalism. But in considering fascism's eventual rise to power and its genocidal undertakings, he and other Frankfurters emphasize the importance of decades of a prefascist "experience of non-experience," of people's increasing sense of the irrelevance to dominant socioeconomic value of their individual and collective subjectivity and critical agency, and the sense of passivity—and far worse—that emerges as a consequence. Despite fraught relations with him, Adorno understands Celan's incomparable lyric poetry as the extraordinary, and extraordinarily grim, limit-case in the Baudelairean line, whereby poetry's very humanness in some sense requires it to become unprecedentedly brutal, "barbaric," and difficult in dedicating its life-giving semblance-experience experimentalism, its agency-and-critical-subjectivity-sparking awareness, precisely to the effort of conveying a glimpse of the meaning of the inconceivable *elimination of particular life* and, of course, *particular experience and subjectivity*—the poem's *particularized* sensing of the *industrial* elimination of millions of human *subjects* (grasped, as it is so hard to grasp, as individual murder on individual murder on individual murder on individual murder . . .)—that the genocide was. If ever a mod. lyric poetry has existed whose hazarded point of departure has had to involve radically exceeding all known versions of aura, to such a degree that readers may at first believe aura simply to have been abandoned, Celan's poetry, Adorno suggests, is it. This ultimate lauding of Celan constitutes, in what turns out to be a very late moment in Adorno's career—and in lines explicitly invoking Benjamin—a rediscovery of lyric's unique role in engaging the most difficult, significant hists. that confront us.

*See* ARTIFACT, POETRY AS; FICTION, POETRY AS; INFORMATION, POETRY AS; POLITICS AND POETRY.

■ T. W. Adorno, *Prisms*, trans. S. Weber and S. Weber (1967); W. Benjamin, *Illuminations*, ed. H. Arendt (1968); K. Marx, *Critique of the Gotha Program*, ed. C. P. Dutt (1970); D. Ricardo, *On the Principles of Political Economy and Taxation*, ed. R. M. Hartwell (1971); T. W. Adorno and Max Horkheimer, *Dialectic of Enlightenment*, trans. J. Cumming (1972); T. W. Adorno, *Negative Dialectics*, trans. E. B. Ashton (1973); W. Benjamin, *Charles Baudelaire*, trans. H. Zorn (1973); T. W. Adorno, *Minima Moralia: Reflections from Damaged Life*, trans. E. Jephcott (1974); S. Buck-Morss, *The Origins of Negative Dialectics: Theodor W. Adorno, Walter Benjamin, and the Frankfurt Institute* (1977); K. Marx, *Capital: A Critique of Political Economy*, trans. B. Fowkes (1977); W. Benjamin, *Reflections*, ed. P. Demetz, trans. E. Jephcott (1978); M. Jay, *Marxism and Totality: The Adventures of a Concept from Lukács to Habermas* (1984); F. Jameson, *Late Marxism: Adorno, or The Persistence of the Dialectic* (1990); T. W. Adorno, *Notes to Literature*, trans. S. W. Nicholsen, 2 v. (1991–92); M. Jay, *The Dialectical Imagination: A History of the Frankfurt School and the Institute of Social Research*, rev. ed. (1996); T. W. Adorno, *Aesthetic Theory*, ed. G. Adorno and R. Tiedemann, trans. R. Hullot-Kentor (1997); T. W. Adorno and W. Benjamin, *The Complete Correspondence: 1928–1940* (1994), ed. H. Lonitz, trans. N. Walker (1999); W. Benjamin, *The Arcades Project* (1982), ed. R. Tiedemann, trans. H. Eiland and K. McLaughlin (1999); R. Kaufman, "Lyric Commodity Critique, Benjamin Adorno Marx, Baudelaire Baudelaire Baudelaire," *PMLA* 123 (2008); and "Poetry after 'Poetry After Auschwitz,'" *Art and Aesthetics after Adorno*, ed. J. M. Bernstein et al. (2010).

R. KAUFMAN

# FREE VERSE

I. History
II. Form

Free verse is poetry without a combination of a regular metrical pattern and a consistent line length. The exact denotation of the term has long been disputed, and usage varies in whether other organizing principles such as rhyme scheme, syllable count, or count of strong stresses are excluded. Because most definitions are negative and/or metaphorical, the positive features characteristic of free verse are somewhat undefined. Free verse is normally divided into poet-determined lines (not dependent on page width, like prose or *prose poems); beyond that aspect, certain formal structures such as syntactic *parallelism, heavy *enjambment, conspicuous use of white space, or stress clash are frequently seen, but none is definitive. Some writers have argued that free verse is not, properly speaking, a verse form at all; yet, whether one calls it a verse form, a set of verse forms, or one end of a formal continuum, it has been common in Eng. and many other langs. since the 20th c.

**I. History.** The origins of free verse predate the 20th c. Scholars have pointed to possible predecessors such as ancient Heb. lit. and its mod. trans., esp. the King James Bible; the *Epic of Gilgamesh*; very early Gr. poetry; relatively loose *blank verse from the Ren.; the choruses of John Milton's *Samson Agonistes;* Fr. *vers libres classiques* or *vers libéré* of the 17th and 18th cs.; late 18th- and early 19th-cs. innovations such as Christopher Smart's *catalogs in *Jubilate Agno*, William Blake's prophetic books, James Macpherson's Ossianic poems, and S. T. Coleridge's "Christabel"; J. W. Goethe's and Friedrich Hölderlin's poetry in Ger., Alexander Pushkin's in Rus., other romantic-era poets, and rhythmical prose from various periods. Some of these antecedents influenced mod. free verse, while others may have merely anticipated it, just as some include arguably nonmetrical verse while others are simply innovations within constrained metrical trads. The more immediate ancestors of mod. free verse in Eng. come from the mid-to-late 19th c.: Walt Whitman most important among them, but also other innovators in Eng. and other langs., esp. the Fr. symbolists. From a formal point of view, 20th-c. poetry merely extends trends that were already in process.

But self-proclaimed "free verse" in Eng. has implied not only a set of formal practices or procedures but, at various times, a movement, a group-identity marker, and a political statement. Most important, it has marked a poet as "modern." Influenced by the *vers libre* movement in Fr., which began in the 1880s, the free verse movement in Eng. began in the first two decades of the 1900s with T. E. Hulme, Ezra Pound, T. S. Eliot, W. C. Williams, H. D., D. H. Lawrence, Amy Lowell, and others. From the earliest days of the movement, poets and groups periodically published polemics arguing in favor of a line that "follows the contours of [the poet's] thought and is free rather than regular" (Hulme), "compos[ing] in the sequence of the musical phrase, not in the sequence of the metronome"

(Pound), "composition by field, as opposed to the old line, stanza . . ." (Charles Olson), "undisturbed flow from the mind of personal secret idea-words, *blowing* (as per jazz musician) on subject of image" (Jack Kerouac), etc. Prescriptions are often justified in terms of a desire for more direct expression of thought or for lang. that naturally or organically matches the form of its referent. Although the adoption of free verse has often been seen as part of a rebellion against some decadent prior order, the specific political engagement of that rebellion could range from Fascist sympathies to conservative Anglicanism to mild populism to open hedonism to mystical spiritualism to New Left activism to anarchism. All of these attitudes could also be found in metrically regular poetry of the same periods, though free verse may lend itself esp. easily to direct political statement. And free verse has always been marked by sharp differences among its practitioners over matters of both form and content. Free verse has continued to evolve, and new schools and movements (e.g., the *Beat poets, the *Black Mountain school, the *New York school, *Language poetry) have arisen periodically.

**II. Form.** Free verse allows immense formal diversity. Lines may be as short as a syllable (or even a typographical letter) or too long to fit within the margins of a printed page. Stress patterns may be as random as the lang. allows, or they may show notable parallelism. Line breaks range from emphatically *end-stopped to heavily enjambed. The visual arrangement of lines on the page may be exploited in various ways, from extra white spaces (to show pauses, create emphasis, or show different voices), to arrangement in concrete shapes, to serious derangement of syntactic structure such that the reader must piece the parts together like shards of a clay tablet (see TYPOGRAPHY, VISUAL POETRY). The syntax may be similar to that of everyday speech or that of formal prose, or it may be a specialized poetic grammar that would be considered telegraphic, ill-formed, or even incoherent in other contexts. The register may be learned and literary, colloquial and vulgar, or (often) conspicuously mixed (see DICTION). The poem may avoid traditional sound patterns such as *rhyme and *alliteration, or it may make extensive use of them. Poems may be densely rhythmic, casually conversational, or prosaically expository.

Various writers have proposed to divide free verse into categories. Many list types or schools based on a confluence of key formal features, usually identified with a particularly influential poet. Chris Beyers's *A History of Free Verse* is fairly typical in listing four such types: (1) the long line (e.g., in Whitman), (2) the short line (e.g., in Williams and H. D.), (3) verse "haunted by meter" (e.g., in Eliot), and (4) verse that "avoids tradition" (e.g., in Lawrence). Individual poets are undoubtedly influential on the practice of other poets. Furthermore, "schools" of poetry may cohere as much by ideologies, guiding metaphors about form, or social networks as by their actual poetic practice, so these relationships are important from a literary-historical point of view; however, basing a theory of formal types on

particular poets is problematic: there is no one-to-one match between poets and forms.

An alternative approach to listing a finite number of types or schools is to explore the formal features exploited to varying degrees and in various combinations by most free-verse poets. Eleanor Berry's "The Free Verse Spectrum," e.g., proposes a five-dimensional descriptive matrix based on continuous axes rather than binary divisions. Implicit in this exploration of features is often the question of what, in the absence of regular meter or rhyme, makes this lang. poetic. An exhaustive list is not possible, but some prominent features follow:

**A. *Lineation.*** Division into lines is the one feature shared by all free verse (excluding prose poetry). Different poets and theorists handle line structure quite differently, but some important aspects include *rhythm, both in terms of timing and of salience; phrasing or grouping; segmentation of *attention; and visual effects.

The line is generally considered a unit of rhythm. Some writers have claimed that all the lines in a poem take approximately equal amounts of time to say or read, but this position can be defended empirically only for a limited number of free-verse poems. Similarly, the claim that each line is one breath is plausible for some poems but not for most. Poets do not even agree, in theory or in actual oral *performance, as to whether there is or should be a *pause at the end of each line. Instead, the lines may signal a more abstract kind of equivalence, segmenting the text into comparable units of attention, emphasis, or weight. A word, image, or phrase occupying a line by itself, or ending a line, tends to receive more focus than the same item buried in a long line.

Still, we probably do tend to read or speak longer lines faster than shorter lines and to slow down, at least slightly, at line breaks, bringing unequal lines closer to temporal equivalence. This tendency helps explain why some poets and critics say shorter lines speed a poem up, while others say they slow it down: word by word, they slow it down, but line by line, they speed it up.

Line length is the most commonly cited feature distinguishing one type of free verse from another. The distinction between the long, mostly end-stopped, often parallel, oratorical long lines of Whitman and the short, often enjambed, colloquial, imagistic lines of Williams is seen as basic. Again, free-verse lines can be virtually any length, and even Williams and Whitman vary their own lines, but this long/short distinction can be a useful starting point.

In most free verse, lines tend to correspond to phrases or clauses: as a default, line breaks will coincide with the more important phrase boundaries. Where line and phrase boundaries do not correspond, the lines are enjambed, and "tension" may result. Most free verse has some enjambment, and in some poems, it is the norm rather than the exception. Critics disagree on their evaluation of this as on so many issues; some denigrate line divisions that do not reflect the "natural" units of lang.; others criticize poems for a lack of tension between line and phrase, which they find flat or boring. In either case, the decision of where to break lines is a key element of free-verse *versification.

**B. *Stanzas.*** Another grouping effect happens not within the line but between lines: some free verse is basically stichic, with no obvious grouping of lines or grouping only into long verse paragraphs (see STICHOS). Other free verse is stanzaic or strophic, with lines grouped into units of similar numbers of lines (see STROPHE). Sometimes the grouping of lines is largely a visual device, in which the stanzas do not correspond to whole units of syntax, phonology, argument, or image; in other poems, the groupings are tightly linked and structural despite not being joined by predictable patterns of meter or rhyme. In other words, just as lines may be end-stopped or enjambed, stanzas may reinforce or undercut syntactic, phonological, and semantic units.

**C. *Parallelism.*** A common feature of verbal art worldwide is parallelism: the recurrence of similar units. This is true of metrically regular verse as well as free verse, but because free verse avoids the pervasive parallel structures of meter and rhyme, other kinds, esp. syntactic parallelism, tend to become more important. Syntactic parallelism frequently occurs in combination with rhetorical figures involving repetition of words or phrases. The best known of these devices is *anaphora, the repetition of words at the beginnings of lines, sentences, clauses, or phrases. (N.B.: *anaphora* is used differently in ling.). A well-known example is Allen Ginsberg's *Howl*: in pt. 1, over 60 lines are parallel relative clauses beginning with "who." Syntactic parallelism is easiest to recognize in combination with anaphora or similar devices, but quite possible without them. An example of parallelism with only minimal repetition of words is James Wright's "Spring Images," in which each stanza is a sentence of almost identical syntax:

Two athletes
Are dancing in the cathedral
Of the wind.

A butterfly lights on the branch
Of your green voice.

Small antelopes
Fall asleep in the ashes
Of the moon.

(1971, 129)

**D. *Rhyme and Meter.*** Free verse generally avoids strict rhyme schemes, as in *sonnets or *ballads, and strict alliteration patterns, as in OE verse; however, free verse may include extensive sound patterning on an unpredictable basis. Virtually every possible type of sound repetition may occur: not only alliteration, *assonance, and rhyme but also more complex combinations of sounds. In some free-verse poems such effects are woven densely throughout, while in other poems, they are occasional ornaments. (See SOUND.)

Similarly, since free verse, by definition, avoids regular meter, there is no predictable pattern of recurrent feet (or of strong and weak positions) combined with a consistent line length; however, this statement does not mean that meter, in the sense of recurring patterns of stressed and unstressed syllables, or of rhythmic beats and offbeats, is irrelevant. First, some verse is explicitly composed in lines of a given number of strong stresses, with the total number of syllables unspecified. This patterning might qualify as an *"accentual" meter, but poems patterned this way are often called free verse. Second, recognizable metrical lines or line fragments occur prominently in some free verse; it remains free verse because these sequences are not consistent or predictable. Some critics link these flashes of metrical regularity to moments of heightened intensity in the poem or to iconic emotional values of different meters. Although the most-discussed sequences match well-known verse forms such as *iambic pentameter or *tetrameter, one also finds ad hoc metrical patterns that are repeated enough within a poem to be noticeable, but do not fit traditional metrical terminology.

On a more general, statistical level, there seem to be prosodic differences between the free verse and prose of a given poet even where no "ghosts of meter" are obvious. Some recent research suggests that free verse on average has more stress density, more stress clashes, more binary alternation of stressed and unstressed syllables, and more rhythmic units of a given number of syllables (e.g., four or six) than general prose. Certain grammatical and lexical differences correspond to these prosodic ones.

**E. *Intonation.*** Recent research has increasingly focused on intonation (pitch patterns) in free verse (see PITCH). Intonation is a factor in all speech, incl. poetry, but because it is not shown in writing, it has been underappreciated. Renewed interest has been buoyed by improved sound technology, by more sophisticated theories of intonation, and by the increased popularity of oral poetry performance—from traditional poetry readings to *poetry slams and other formats. Intonation is esp. important in free verse because, in the absence of meter and rhyme, intonation plays a primary role in signaling line ends, grouping of lines, parallelism, and other structural relationships. It also forms coherent rhythmic structures in itself, e.g., in sequences of alternating rising and falling tones, or in repeated complex contours.

**F. *Content.*** Subject matter is not necessarily different in free verse from metrically regular verse. Free verse appears to facilitate more "transparent" lang. in some poems, in which the form is hardly noticed, and this facility may have implications for the emotional effects that can be achieved. Also, the relation of form to content can be different for different types of free verse, although one can find exceptions to virtually any form–content pairing. Where lines are short, the reader's attention is drawn to individual words or short phrases, and this tendency lends itself to a focus on images or on words as words. Where lines are long, the attention is drawn more to the sweep of ideas and to larger rhythmic structures; this attraction may lend itself to a grander scale of arguments and comparisons, among other differences.

See FUTURISM, IMAGISM, LINE, METER, MODERN-ISM, OPEN FORM, PROJECTIVE VERSE, RHYME, SPRUNG RHYTHM, STANZA, SYLLABIC VERSE, VARIABLE FOOT, VORTICISM.

■ T. S. Eliot, "Reflections on *Vers Libre*," *New States-man* 8 (1917); E. Pound, "A Retrospect," *Pavannes and Divisions* (1918); H. Monroe, "The Free Verse Move-ment in America," *English Journal* 3 (1924); T. E. Hulme, "A Lecture on Modern Poetry," *Further Specu-lations* (1936); Olson; D. Levertov, "Notes on Organic Form," *Poetry* 106 (1965); P. Ramsey, "Free Verse: Some Steps toward Definition," *SP* 65 (1968); J. Wright, *Col-lected Poems* (1971); C. Hartman, *Free Verse: An Essay on Prosody* (1980); R. Hass, *Twentieth-Century Pleasures* (1984); T. Steele, *Missing Measures: Modern Poetry and the Revolt against Meter* (1990); Cureton; J. Kerouac, "Essentials of Spontaneous Prose," *The Portable Beat Reader*, ed. A. Charters (1992); S. Cushman, *Fictions of Form in American Poetry* (1993); A. Finch, *The Ghost of Meter* (1993); H. Gross and R. McDowell, *Sound and Form in Modern Poetry*, 2d ed. (1996); H. T. Kirby-Smith, *The Origins of Free Verse* (1996); D. Wesling, *The Scissors of Meter* (1996); E. Berry, "The Free Verse Spec-trum," *CE* 59 (1997); G. B. Cooper, *Mysterious Music: Rhythm and Free Verse* (1998); C. Beyers, *A History of Free Verse* (2001).

G. B. COOPER

**FREIE RHYTHMEN.** In Ger., this term refers to un-rhymed, metrically irregular, nonstrophic verse lines of varying length. These lines can usually be distinguished from rhythmical prose not only by their visual arrange-ment on the page but by a tendency toward nearly equal intervals between stressed syllables, as well as phonological and rhythmic correspondences between lines. *Freie Rhythmen* represent the only major formal innovation that Ger. lit. provided to world lit. in the 18th c. Introduced by F. G. Klopstock in the 1750s (e.g., "Dem Allgegenwärtigen," 1758; "Frühlingsfeier," 1759) as a conscious revolt against the restraints im-posed on Ger. poetry by Martin Opitz in the 17th c., freie Rhythmen are particularly appropriate as a me-dium for the free, unrestrained expression of feelings typical of the age of *sentimentality (Empfindsamkeit)*:

> Nicht in den Ozean der Welten alle
> Will ich mich stürzen! schweben nicht,
> Wo die ersten Erschaffenen, die Jubelchöre der
>     Söhne des Lichts
> Anbeten, tief anbeten und in
>     Entzückung vergehn!
>
> (Klopstock, "Frühlingsfeier")

They were used in the 1770s by J. W. Goethe in his "Great Hymns" ("Wanderers Sturmlied," "Ganymed," "Prometheus," "Mahomets Gesang," etc.) and later by Friedrich Hölderlin ("Hyperions Schicksalslied") and Novalis ("Hymnen an die Nacht"). Heinrich Heine contributed to the devel. of the form with the 22 poems

that make up the two cycles of *Die Nordsee* (*The North Sea*) in 1825–26. Such romantic uses of freie Rhyth-men influenced later Ger.-lang. poets such as Friedrich Nietzsche, Arno Holz, R. M. Rilke, Georg Trakl, and Gottfried Benn. Ger. terminology draws a clear distinc-tion between freie Rhythmen and *freie Verse*.

■ A. Goldbeck-Loewe, *Zur Geschichte der freien Ver-sen in der Deutschen Dichtung* (1891); L. Bennoist-Hanappier, *Die freien Rhythmen in der deutschen Lyrik* (1905); E. Lachmann, *Hölderlins Hymnen in freien Strophen* (1937); A. Closs, *Die freie Rhythmen in der deutschen Lyrik* (1947); F. G. Jünger, *Rhythmus und Sprache im deutschen Gedicht* (1952); W. Mohr and A. Closs, "Freie Rhythmen," *Reallexikon II*; H. Enders, *Stil und Rhythmus* (1962); L. L. Albertsen, *Die freie Rhythmen* (1971), and *Neuere deutsche Metrik* (1984); B. Nagel, *Der freie Vers in der modernen Dichtung* (1989); C. Kohl, *Rhetoric, the Bible, and the Origins of Free Verse* (1990); C. Wagenknecht, *Deutsche Metrik* (1993); D. Frey, *Einführung in die deutsche Metrik mit Gedichtmodellen* (1996); S. Elit, *Lyrik* (2008); W. Blache, *Heinrich Heine* (2009).

D. H. CHISHOLM; K. BOWERS

**FREIE VERSE** (Fr. *vers libre*). (1) Rhymed lines in either iambic or trochaic meter throughout, but with a varying number of stressed syllables and, therefore, varying in line length. They were first used in It. *mad-rigals, then in Fr. *fables and comedies, and in Ger. in the 18th c. by Barthold Brockes, Albrecht Haller, Christian Gellert, Friedrich von Hagedorn, G. E. Less-ing, and Christoph Wieland. (2) Later, the term was used more loosely to refer to lines of varying length without any metrical constraints, distinguished from *freie Rhythmen* and rhythmical prose only by rhyme and occasionally by *assonance.

See FREE VERSE, VERS LIBRES.

■ L. Ern, *Freivers und Metrik* (1970); K. Birkenhauer, *Die eigenrhythmische Lyrik Bertolt Brechts* (1971); R. Kloepfer, "Vers libre—Freie Dichtung," *Zeitschrift für Literaturwissenschaft und Linguistik* 3 (1971); H.-J. Frey and O. Lorenz, *Kritik des freien Verses* (1980); W. Deinert, "'Ist das noch ein Vers?' Tractatus metrico-poeticus: Ueber den freien Vers und seine Abkömm-linge," *Literaturwissenschaftliches Jahrbuch* 24 (1983); H. Fricke, "Moderne Lyrik als Normabweichung," *Lyrik—Erlebnis und Kritik*, ed. L. Jordan et al. (1988); D. Lamping, "Zu den Anfängen von Brechts Lyrik in freien Versen," *Wirkendes Wort* 40 (1990); *Moderne Lyrik* (1991); and *Das lyrische Gedicht* (1993); C. Wa-genknecht, *Deutsche Metrik* (1993); D. Frey, *Einfüh-rung in die deutsche Metrik mit Gedichtmodellen* (1996); S. Elit, *Lyrik* (2008).

D. H. CHISHOLM; K. BOWERS

**FRENCH POETRY.** See FRANCE, POETRY OF.

**FRENCH PROSODY.** Metrically, Fr. poetry is syl-labic, based on a fixed number of syllables in each line that need not have the same duration or pitch contour. *Rhythm is based on word order, sound devices (*alliteration, *assonance, sound symbolism, etc.), modulations of vowel pitch (such as oratorical, affective, emotional, emphatic, logical, distinctive, contrastive, social, and local accents), and the *quantity or *duration of the syllables, all these in relation to the metrical foundation of the verse line. In most Fr. poems, rhythmic factors are not periodic (i.e., a pattern does not occur at least twice in the same order); the syllable count and the *stanza are metrically determinant. This means, as Louis Du Gardin argued in *Les Premières Addresses du Chemin du Parnasse* (1620), that a Fr. verse line cannot be metrical by itself but only in relation to another line. The perception of the poem as such depends on context ("equivalences contextuelles"; Cornulier 1982, 1995). Therefore, sentences in prose texts such as "Parce que c'estoit luy, parce que c'estoit moy" (Because it was he, because it was I; Michel de Montaigne, *Essais*) or "Et qui vit sans tabac, n'est pas digne de vivre" (Whoever lives without tobacco does not deserve to live; Molière, *Dom Juan*), despite their perceptible 6 + 6 rhythm, should not be considered as verse lines (*vers blanc*; see BLANK VERSE).

From the 16th to the 19th c., certain poets (e.g., Jean-Antoine de Baïf) and theorists (e.g., Marin Mersenne) tried to promote a form of Fr. poetry (i.e., the *vers mesurés à l'antique*) based on differences in syllabic duration. They failed because this system was too complicated and too unlike the established one. The syllabic foundation of the Fr. verse line strongly prevailed over Latinate prosody: syllabation characterized the *prosody of "classical poetry" until the mid-19th c., even though, to the 18th c. at least, Fr. speakers probably differentiated heavy or long from light or short vowels.

This syllabic system is derived from med. Roman poetries. Poets of the Middle Ages produced different types of metrical combinations for which they drew on cl. Lat. prosody, Lat. prose, and a type of Lat. prosody that disregarded the position of accents or included the same number of words on each verse line (Norberg). The *Cantilène de Sainte Eulalie* (ca. 878), for instance, is a mixture of varying *couplets (lines of 10 to 13 syllables; some couplets have one *meter, others two) and of two langs. (Lat. and *langue d'oïl*), and the *Vie de Saint Léger* (1040) is made up of iambic couplets whose final assonances make them sound like a combination of two distinct metrical systems. It is likely that the syllabic system prevailed in Fr. on account of its convenience for composition and reception.

Although the notion of *accent in the Fr. lang. is strongly controversial and covers different meanings of the word, some scholars since Scoppa have argued that the syllabic foundation of the verse lines, and of the 6 + 6 *alexandrine in particular, should be complemented by a fixed or varying number of accents. Since *meters reflect speech to some degree, the *hemistichs that constitute the verse line must contain emphasized or tonic syllables. In fact, these emphasized syllables owe their existence not to metrics but to the rhythms of speech: because the last vowel pronounced in a word group is usually emphasized in Fr., the last masculine

vowel of any metrical pattern is necessarily emphasized. There is, in a word, no metrical stress. The strict cl. superimposition of syntax and meaning on the metrical pattern is not mandatory; it simply helps the reader or listener feel the rhythm:

> Mais elle était du monde où les plus belles choses
> Ont le pire destin,
> Et rose elle a vécu ce que vivent les roses,
> L'espace d'un matin.
>
> (François de Malherbe, "Consolation à M. du Périer")
>
> (But she was of the world where the most beautiful things
> Have the worst fate;
> And being a rose, she lived what roses live,
> The space of a single morning.)

From the mid-16th c. to about 1830, poets tended to place words that could potentially receive stress at the end of a given metrical pattern. This allowed them consistently to avoid filling the last position of the pattern with a determiner, a pronoun that comes before its noun, a one-syllable preposition, a countable *e*, a word crossing over between the hemistichs, etc. (Cornulier 1982, 1995; Gouvard).

As illustrated in the above example from Malherbe, Fr. poetry has two types of verse lines. The shorter *vers simples* (lines 2 and 4) have from one to eight syllables. The longer *vers complexes* (lines 1 and 3) contain nine (5 + 4, 4 + 5), ten (4 + 6, 6 + 4, 5 + 5), eleven (5 + 6, 6 + 5), or twelve syllables (6 + 6) and are divided into two hemistichs. In cl. poetry, the *caesura clearly marks the frontier between the hemistichs; this metrical mark weakens under the attacks of poets from 1850 onward. Cornulier (1982) formulated a nonmetrical principle applied to Fr. prosody, known as *la loi des huit syllabes,* or the eight-syllable law: we are unable to sense the periodicity of acoustic signals of more than eight phonetic events. In Fr., identification of the exact number of syllables in a line is limited to eight. This cognitive limit explains why lines longer than eight syllables have to be divided. Nevertheless, there are some eight-syllable lines that contain a caesura (in the Middle Ages) as well as nine-syllable lines that do not (in Pierre de Ronsard).

The unstable *e* is one the most noticeable properties of Fr. poetry (Réda).It tends to differentiate poetry and spoken lang. Some parts of southern France aside, it has not been pronounced since the mid-16th c. (as in the word *samedi*, which yields "sam'di" [samdi] in spoken lang., instead of "samedi" [samEdi] in poetic diction), but it is articulated in Fr. poetry not followed by a vowel, an aspirated consonant *'h*, or a line break:

> L'alcyon, quand l'océan gronde,
> 1 23    4    5 67    8
> Craint que les vents ne troublent l'onde
> 1    2 3 4    5    6 7    8

Où se berce son doux sommeil.
  1  2  3  4  5     6   7    8

    (Victor Hugo, "Le poète dans les révolutions")

(The Halcyon, when the ocean roars,
Fears the winds ruffle the waters
Where his sweet sleep rocks.)

By contrast, the *e* is elided before a vowel and before the nonaspirated consonant *h*:

Jeun(e) homm(e), ainsi le sort nous presse.
(Young man, thus is destiny pressing us)

At the end of the feminine verse line, the nonaspirated consonant *h* is not counted, as in the following examples from Charles Baudelaire:

*Rien n'égale en longueur les boiteuses journées.*
  1   2  3  4   5   6   7 8 9 10 11  12

                           ("Spleen")

(Nothing is as long as the limping days)

and:

*C'est le Diable qui tient les fils qui nous remuent!*
  1  2   3   4   5   6  7   8  9   10  11 12
                          ("Au lecteur")

(The Devil pulls the strings that move us!)

There is some dispute about the function of *rhyme in Fr. poetry. Some scholars, like Aquien, think it is a prosodic unit the function of which is to indicate the end of the verse line. Cornulier (1981, 2005) objects to these suggestions: if the second occurrence (the echo) may signal the end of a verse line, the first (the call) cannot. Furthermore, since this poetry is based on the repetition of a fixed number of syllables from one line to the next, the second occurrence of a stanza enables the perception of meter(s). Finally, if the last syllable of a group of words is necessarily emphasized, its repetition through rhyme has no metrical function (this is why Ronsard, Joachim du Bellay, and others could write nonrhymed poems). Rhyme, or the identity of the last counted vowel of two or more verse lines, should thus be seen as a rhetorical *ornament. Nevertheless, the *rhyme scheme has a metrical function since it guarantees the periodicity of stanzas:

| | | |
|---|---|---|
| Mignonne, allons voir si la rose | a | fem. |
| Qui ce matin avoit desclose | a | fem. |
| Sa robe de pourpre au Soleil, | b | masc. |
| A point perdu ceste vesprée | c | fem. |
| Les plis de sa robe pourprée, | c | fem. |
| Et son teint au vostre pareil. | b | masc. |

| | | |
|---|---|---|
| Las! voyez comme en peu d'espace, | a | fem. |
| Mignonne, elle a dessus la place | a | fem. |
| Las! las ses beautez laissé cheoir! | b | masc. |
| Ô vrayment marastre Nature, | c | fem. |
| Puis qu'une telle fleur ne dure | c | fem. |
| Que du matin jusques au soir! | b | masc. |

| | | |
|---|---|---|
| Donc, si vous me croyez, mignonne, | a | fem. |
| Tandis que vostre âge fleuronne | a | fem. |
| En sa plus verte nouveauté, | b | masc. |
| Cueillez, cueillez vostre jeunesse: | c | fem. |
| Comme à ceste fleur la vieillesse | c | fem. |
| Fera ternir vostre beauté. | b | masc. |

                            Ronsard, *Odes*

(Darling, let's see if the rose
that unfolded this morning
its purple robe in the sun,
has not lost tonight
the folds of its purple dress,
And its complexion, that is like yours.

Alas! see as in such a little space,
darling, on the ground,
Alas! Alas! It dropped its beauty.
Oh, really cruel mother Nature,
since such a flower lasts
from the morning through the night.

Then, if you believe me, darling:
while your age blossoms,
in its most green novelty,
pick, pick your youth.
As for this flower, old age
Will tarnish your beauty.)

The rhyme scheme (*aabccb*) and the order of feminine and masculine rhymes of the first stanza are reiterated in the following stanzas, but the graphemes included in the rhymes change from one stanza to the other. To the degree that it becomes a periodic pattern, rhyme is metrically determinant. The description of cl. stanzas by Cornulier (1995) and Aroui (2000) is probably the most relevant. Cornulier shows that there are pure simple stanzas (*aa*) (*abab*) and (*aabccb*), mixed cl. stanzas (combination of pure simple stanzas), and inverted cl. stanzas (*abba*) and (*aabcbc*).

Since the end of the 18th c. and esp. since Hugo's preface to *Cromwell* (1827), many poets have tried to regenerate Fr. prosody, arguing that the cl. metrical foundation is not musical enough and hinders the successful implementation of rhythmic poetry. They have proposed to dissociate syntax from metrics, shifted the alexandrine caesura (e.g., from 6+6 to 8+4 or 4+8), and eventually broken the metrical foundation of the verse line (Gouvard), as in Arthur Rimbaud's "Qu'est-ce pour nous mon cœur . . ." (What does it matter to us, my heart . . .):

Tout à la guerre, à la + vengeance, à la terreur,
Mon esprit! Tournons dans + la morsure : Ah!
passez,
Républiques de ce + monde! Des empereurs,
Des régiments, des co + lons, des peuples, assez!

(All to war, to vengeance, to terror,
my Soul! Let us turn in the wound: Ah! disappear,
republics of this world! Of emperors,
Regiments, colonists, peoples, enough!)

There is no easy or permanent *scansion for these lines. Rimbaud wished to destroy the alexandrine and cl. prosody with it. There is no perceptible periodicity. These lines are the culmination of what Murphy (1985) calls "déversification": between 1850 and 1870, poets gradually renewed syllabism. This led to the emergence of *vers libre* (free verse), which, as Roubaud has shown, has always been conceived in reference to the alexandrine. So deeply rooted in Fr. culture is syllabic poetry that its prosody remains the fundamental rhythmical basis even for contemp. poets.

The eight-syllable law and its consequences, or the binary foundation of cl. stanzas, suggest that a cognitive approach would be fruitful for future study of the origins and history of Fr. versification.

*See* VERS LIBÉRÉ.

■ A. Scoppa, *Vrais Principes de la versification, développés par un examen comparatif entre la langue italienne et la langue française* (1811–14); W. F. Patterson, *Three Centuries of Poetic Theory* (1935); Lote; Norberg; J. Roubaud, *La Vieillesse d'Alexandre: Essai sur quelques états récents du vers français* (1978); C. Scott, *French Verse-Art* (1980); B. de Cornulier, "La rime n'est pas une marque de fin vers," *Poétique* 46 (1981); and *Théorie du vers: Rimbaud, Verlaine, Mallarmé* (1982); H. Meschonnic, *Critique du rythme: Anthropologie historique du langage* (1982); C. Scott, *Vers Libre: The Emergence of Free Verse in France 1886–1914* (1990); J. Bourassa, *Rythme et sens: Des processus rythmiques en poésie contemporaine* (1993); B. de Cornulier, *Art poëtique* (1995); C. Gérard, "The Structure and Development of French Prosodic Representations," *L&S* 41 (1998); R. Pensom, *Accent and Metre in French* (1998); J.-L. Aroui, "Nouvelles considérations sur les strophes," *Degrés* 104 (2000); J.-M. Gouvard, *Critique du vers* (2000); *Le Vers français*, ed. M. Murat (2000); *Le Sens et la mesure: De la pragmatique à la métrique*, ed. J.-L. Aroui (2003); R. Pensom, "La poésie moderne française a-t-elle une métrique?," *Poésie* 103 (2003); S. Murphy, *Stratégies de Rimbaud* (2004); J. Réda, *L'Adoption du système métrique: Poèmes (1999–2003)* (2004); M. Aquien, *Le Renouvellement des formes poétiques au XIX<sup>e</sup> siècle* (2005); B. de Cornulier, "Rime et contrerime en traditions orale et littéraire," *Poétique de la rime*, ed. J. Dangel and M. Murat (2005); C. Scott, "*État présent*: French Verse Analysis," *FS* 60 (2006); G. Peureux, *La Fabrique du vers* (2009); T. M. Rainsford, "Dividing Lines: The Changing Syntax and Prosody of the Mid-Line Break in Medieval French Octosyllabic Verse," *Transactions of the Philological Society* 109 (2011).

G. PEUREUX

**FRISIAN POETRY.** Frisian, the nearest continental relative of Eng., was once the speech of an independent and extensive maritime nation along the North Sea coast but is today the lang. of a minority people living partly in the Netherlands and partly in Germany. It exists in three forms: East and North Frisian, spoken in Germany; and West Frisian, spoken in the Netherlands. Only West Frisian, which now has legal status both in the schools and in the public life of Netherlands Friesland (or Fryslân, its official name, in the Frisian lang.), has developed into a full-fledged literary lang. and *Kultursprache*.

As is the case with other Germanic peoples, lit. among the Frisians began with the songs of *bards celebrating the great deeds of kings and heroes, though none of those early epics has survived. What has survived is a valuable body of Frisian law, the earliest dating from the 11th c., in a distinctive form marked by such literary devices as *alliteration and *parallelism and often genuinely poetic in thought and feeling.

When, about the year 1500, Friesland came under foreign control, Frisian lost its position as the lang. of law and public life, and Frisian lit. sank to a low level. No great poetic figure appeared on the scene until Gysbert Japicx (1603–66), an eminent Ren. poet who with his *Rymlerije* (Poetry), pub. posthumously in 1668, re-established Frisian as a literary and cultural lang. The 18th c. saw the rise of many followers and imitators of Japicx; however, no outstanding poetic figure came to the fore. In the 19th c., Eeltsje Halbertsma (1797–1858) dominated the scene; much of his work is folk poetry inspired by Ger. *romanticism. Another outstanding figure is Harmen Sytstra (1817–62), a romantic inspired by his country's heroic past, whose work reveals a desire to restore the old Germanic verse forms. The latter half of the 19th c. produced many folk poets, the most popular of whom were Waling Dykstra (1821–1914) and Tsjibbe Gearts van der Meulen (1824–1906). Piter Jelles Troelstra (1860–1930), with themes centering on love, nature, and the fatherland, ushered in a second romantic period.

The 20th c. ushered in a new spirit to Frisian poetry, perhaps most evident in the work of Simke Kloosterman (1876–1938), whose poetic art is both individualistic and aristocratic. In her poems, she gives intense utterance to the longings and disillusionments of love. Rixt (pseud. of Hendrika A. van Dorssen, 1887–1979) also wrote verse characterized by emotional intensity. A first-rate poet at the beginning of the century was Obe Postma (1868–1963), whose verse has vigor, penetration, and philosophical insight. Much of it is poetry of reminiscence; still more is a paean to life and the good earth. Postma was the first to use *free verse in Frisian and to use it well.

The new spirit came to full expression and brought about a literary renaissance in the Young Frisian movement, launched in 1915 and led by the daring young nationalist Douwe Kalma (1896–1953). A talented poet and critic, Kalma sharply denounced the mediocrity and provincialism of 19th-c. Frisian letters. With him and his movement, Friesland began to have an independent voice in Eur. culture. Kalma's genius appears at its freshest in his classic *Kening Aldgillis* (King Aldgillis, 1920), a historical play in *blank verse. Kalma's lyric poetry is technically skillful but often nebulous in content. His work—like that of his school—suffers from *aestheticism and a poetic jargon laden with neologisms and archaisms.

Among the poets of merit who had their start in the Young Frisian school are R. P. Sybesma (1894–1975), an excellent sonneteer, and D. H. Kiestra (1899–1970), a poet of the soil with a vigorous talent. For decades, the most popular poet was Fedde Schurer (1898–1968), a versatile artist who preferred national and religious themes. His early poems show the influence of Young

Frisian aestheticism; those written after 1946 are more direct, unadorned, and mod. In 1946, he helped launch *De Tsjerne* (The Churn), the literary periodical with which most of the important names in Frisian letters were associated until 1968.

Around 1935, some of the younger poets, such as J. D. de Jong (1912–96), Ype Poortinga (1910–85), and G. N. Visser (1910–2001), showed signs of breaking away from the Young Frisian movement, both in spirit and in poetic diction. Douwe A. Tamminga (1909–2002) created his own poetic idiom, based largely on the lang. of the people that he transfigured and sublimated into pure art.

Since World War II, more than 600 books of poetry have been published in Friesland, half of which appeared since the 1990s because of easier ways of getting poetry into print. Postwar disillusionment and existential despair informed much of the poetry of the late 1940s and 1950s, when biting satire and experimental forms openly declared all trads. meaningless. Among the mod. voices were Anne Wadman (1919–97) and Jan Wybenga (1917–94), who led the way in experimental poetry. An experimentalist group led by Hessel Miedema (b. 1929), Steven de Jong (b. 1935), and Jelle de Jong (b. 1933) started its own jour., *Quatrebras* (1954–68). Miedema's *De greate wrakseling* (The Great Wrestle, 1963) in particular clearly demonstrated a refusal to be restricted by conventional thought or form. Sjoerd Spanninga (pseud. of Jan Dykstra, 1906–85) introduced exotic imagery from foreign cultures, esp. Asian, through a wide variety of forms. The verse of Marten Sikkema (pseud. of G. A. Gezelle Meerburg, 1918–2005), Freark Dam (1924–2002), and Klaes Dykstra (1924–97) was more traditional. Other older poets continued to write: Tamminga's *In Memoriam* (1968), written after his son's untimely death, is a masterpiece of profound thought and feeling cast in disciplined but fluid form. Tiny Mulder (1921–2010) is another distinguished poet who frequently effects a remarkable fusion of significant form and content and evinces a penetrating vision that affirms life without evading its horrors and sorrows. A similar life-affirming attitude can also be discerned in the poems by Tsjits Peanstra (pseud. of Tsjits Jonkman-Nauta, b. 1924), Berber van der Geest (b. 1938), Baukje Wytsma (b. 1946), Eppie Dam (b. 1953), and Margryt Poortstra (b. 1953). Deeply personal, erotic poetry was written by Ella Wassenaer (pseud. of Lipkje Post-Beuckens, 1908–83). A reactionary response toward earlier generations and movements can be found in the work of Tjitte Piebenga (1935–2007) and Trinus Riemersma (1938–2011), whereas a mock-serious tackling of Frisian reality pervades poems by Jan J. Bylsma (b. 1931) and R. R. vander Leest (b. 1933).

In 1967, in order to present poetry to the public at large, the idea of Dial-a-Poem was launched by F. S. Sixma van Heemstra (1916–99). This Frisian initiative, known as *Operaesje Fers*, was soon picked up all over the world. The group of poets who developed this idea included Josse de Haan (b. 1941), whose poems show affinities with *surrealism; Meindert Bylsma

(b. 1941), whose work reflects a certain playfulness; and Daniel Daen (pseud. of Willem Abma, b. 1942), who has been not only prolific but consistently impressive in his ability to fuse the concrete and abstract.

From the 1970s until the 1990s, two journals dominated the Frisian literary scene: *Trotwaer* (Sidewalk, 1969–2002) and *Hjir* (Here, 1972–2008). Whereas the first initially contained many contributions by a group of young intellectuals–de Haan and Riemersma among them—who had joined hands to start a nonprofit publishing house, the second depended mainly on work written by young teachers, such as Sybe Krol (1946–1990), Piter Boersma (b. 1947), Jelle Kaspersma (b. 1948), and Jacobus Quiryn Smink (b. 1954). One of this group, Tsjêbbe Hettinga (b. 1949), gained international renown. His compact poetic idiom throbs with the longing to travel to mythical shores. Hettinga knows how to perform; his sonorous recitations attract large crowds. Hettinga's brother Eeltsje Hettinga (b. 1955) also wrote enticing poems and initiated poetic productions, e.g. *Gjin grinzen, de reis* (No Borders, the Voyage, 2004). Following the example of Tsjêbbe Hettinga, the most recent generation of poets—such as Anne Feddema (b. 1961), Elmar Kuiper (b. 1969), Nyk de Vries (b. 1971), Tsead Bruinja (b. 1974), and Arjan Hut (b. 1976)—is in the recitation of their poems as much performers as they are poets. With poets such as Harmen Wind (1945–2010), Wilco Berga (b. 1947), Jabik Veenbaas (b. 1959), and Albertina Soepboer (b. 1969), they write both in Dutch and in Frisian, unlike the older generations who were solely committed to the Frisian lang. However, Frisian identity continues to be a recurring topic, as in the work of Bartle Laverman (b. 1948), Cornelis van der Wal (b. 1956), and Abe de Vries (b. 1965). The 21st-c. successor to *Trotwaer* is the bilingual (Frisian and Dutch) periodical *De Moanne* (The Month/The Moon), while the monolingual *Ensafh* (Etcetera) has succeeded *Hjir*.

■ **Anthologies:** *It sjongende Fryslân*, ed. D. Kalma (1917); *De nije moarn*, ed. D. Kalma (1922); *Fiiftweintich Fryske dichters*, ed. F. Schurer (1942); *Frieslands dichters*, ed. A. Wadman (1949)—poetry since 1880, Dutch trans.; *Friesische Gedichte aus West-, Ost- und Nordfriesland*, ed. Y. Poortinga et al. (1973)—Ger. trans.; *Country Fair: Poems from Friesland since 1945*, trans. R. Jellema (1985); *The Sound That Remains: A Historical Collection of Frisian Poetry*, trans. R. Jellema (1990); *Frisian Literature Today*, ed. B. Oldenhof (1993); *Hinter Damm und Deich: Die friesische Landschaft wie sie die Dichter sehen*, ed. M. Brückmann et al. (1997)—poems in East, North, and West Frisian, Ger. trans.; T. Hettinga, *Strange Shores/Frjemde kusten*, trans. J. Brockway (1999); *Gysbert Japix: Een keuze uit zijn werk*, ed. P. Breuker (2003)—Dutch trans.; *Droom in blauwe regenjas: Een keuze uit de nieuwe Friese poëzie sinds 1990*, ed. T. Bruinja and H. J. Hilarides (2004)—Dutch trans.; *Gjin grinzen, de reis/Geen grenzen, de reis/No Borders, the Voyage*, ed. E. Hettinga (2004)—Dutch and Eng. trans.; O. Postma, *What the Poet Must Know*, trans. A. Paul (2004); *Het goud op de weg: De Friese poëzie sinds 1880*, ed. A. de Vries (2008)—Dutch trans.; *Spiegel van de Friese Poëzie van de zeven-*

*tiende eeuw tot heden*, ed. P. Boorsma et al., 3d rev. ed. (2008)—Dutch trans.

■ **Criticism and History**: E. H. Harris, *Literature in Friesland* (1956); J. Piebenga, *Koarte skiednis fen de Fryske skriftekennisse*, 2d ed. (1957)—hist., http://www.sirkwy.nl/xmlboeken.html&bid=9&part=2; J. Smit, *De Fryske literatuer 1945–1967* (1968); K. Dykstra, *Lyts hânboek fan de Fryske literature*, 2d ed. (1997)—survey of Frisian lit. from beginnings to 1990s, http://www.sirkwy.nl/xmlboeken.html&bid=76; T. J. Steenmeijer-Wielenga, *A Garden Full of Song: Frisian Literature in Text and Image*, trans. S. Warmerdam (1999); *Handbuch des Friesischen/Handbook of Frisian Studies*, ed. H. H. Munske et al. (2001); *Zolang de wind van de wolken waait: Geschiedenis van de Friese literatuur*, ed. T. Oppewal et al. (2006); *Asega is het dingtijd? De hoogtepunten van de Oudfriese tekstoverlevering*, ed. O. Vries (2007).

■ **Web Sites**: Tresoar: Fries Historich en Letterkundig Centrum, http://www.tresoar.nl; Sirkwy: Fryske literatuerside, http://www.sirkwy.nl.

B. J. Fridsma; H. J. Baron; J. Krol

**FROTTOLA AND BARZELLETTA** (It. "nonsense" [poem], corresponding to German *Spass*). In the late 14th c., the *frottola* was a type of It. popular verse, satiric, rambling, and written in very irregular meters and stanzas, with analogues in other Eur. poetries. Early examples are found in the poetry of Francesco di Vannozzo (ca. 1340–after 1389) and Franco Sacchetti (ca. 1332–1400). In the 15th and 16th cs., it evolved into a kind of *ballata*, composed in octosyllables (*ottonari*), and thus came to be referred to increasingly as *frottola-barzelletta*, i.e., a joke with didactic content. In the course of the century, this became an important medium for serious moral instruction. The barzelletta is a subspecies of the It. 15th-c. carnival song (*canto carnascialesco*), written for musical setting in octosyllables and often following the structure of the *ballata grande* in which the *ritornello* or refrain often has the rhyme scheme *abba*. The barzelletta became very popular in the 15th and 16th cs. in the hands of practitioners such as Politian and Lorenzo de' Medici: one well-known example is Lorenzo's carnival poem, the "Trionfo di Bacco e Arianna."

See ADYNATON, COQ-À-L'ÂNE, DIDACTIC POETRY, FATRAS, ITALIAN PROSODY, NONSENSE VERSE.

■ V. Pernicone, "Storia e svolgimento della metrica," *Problemi ed orientamenti critici di lingua e di letteratura italiana*, ed. A. Momigliano, v. 2 (1948); M. Pazzaglia, *Teoria e analisi metrica* (1974); Spongano; Wilkins; F. P. Memmo, *Dizionario di metrica italiana* (1983); Elwert, *Italienische*; S. Verhulst, *La frottola (XIV–XV sec.)* (1990); A. Menichetti, *Metrica italiana* (1993); S. Orlando, *Manuale di metrica italiana* (1994).

T. Wlassics; C. Kleinhenz

**FU.** This Chinese literary form first obtained prominence in the Han dynasty (206 BCE–220 CE) and continued to be a major genre in the Chinese literary trad. Because the *fu* has no exact Western counterpart,

a commonly accepted Eng. name for the genre does not exist. Although the trans. "rhapsody" is appropriate for the Han fu, in which declamation and recitation were important, other Eng. names such as *rhyme-prose, *prose poem, verse essay, exposition, or poetical description are acceptable. The mature form of the fu did not emerge until the Former Han dynasty, when poets such as Sima Xiangru (179–117 BCE) and Yang Xiong (53 BCE–18 CE) wrote the long, difficult poems that became the standard against which all fu ultimately are measured. This type of fu, which later anthologists classified as *gu fu*, or "ancient-style fu," has the following features: an ornate style, lines of unequal length, mixture of rhymed and unrhymed passages, elaborate description, *hyperbole, repetition of synonyms, extensive cataloging, difficult lang., a tendency toward a complete portrayal of a subject, and often a moral conclusion. The formation of this genre is the product of multiple influences, incl. a set of rhymed riddles by the philosopher Xun Kuang (ca. 312–235 BCE), the rhetorical prose of traveling persuaders of the Warring States period, and the Qu Yuan poems in the *Chuci* (Lyrics of Chu). The earliest datable fu is the "Fu on the Owl" by Jia Yi (ca. 200–168 BCE). However, the gu fu did not reach its full devel. until the mid-2d c. BCE when writers such as Sima Xiangru composed elaborate *epideictic compositions for the court. At the end of the Western Han (206 BCE–8 CE) Yang Xiong attempted to combine effusive praise of the Han imperium with crit. of imperial extravagance. However, he soon rejected the genre for its failure to convey a moral message. It should also be noted that not all Han fu are epideictic pieces. Yang Xiong composed a personal piece on his poverty, the imperial concubine Favorite Beauty Ban (d. ca. 6 BCE) wrote about her loss of imperial favor, and Cai Yong (132–92 CE) and others composed pieces about their travels. At the end of the Han, writers began to compose much shorter pieces that are usually called *xiao fu* (small expositions). The most famous examples are "Fu on Climbing a Tower" by Wang Can (177–217) and "Fu on the Luo River Goddess" by Cao Zhi (192–232).

During the early med. period (3d to 7th c.), some writers continued to write Han-style gu fu. Examples are "Fu on the Three Capitals" by Zuo Si (ca. 250–305) and "Fu on the Yangtze River" by Guo Pu (276–324). However, most of the best-known fu are on personal subjects. These include "Fu on Living in Idleness" and "Fu on Recalling Old Friends and Kin" by Pan Yue (247–300), "Fu on Lamenting the Departed" by Lu Ji (261–303), "Fu on Stilling the Passions" by Tao Qian (ca. 365–427), and the "Lament for the South" by Yu Xin (513–81). The early med. period is also known for the emergence of the *pian fu* or "parallel-style fu." These pieces are noted for their carefully wrought parallel couplets, heavy use of *allusion, and attention to delicate phrasing. Perhaps the best writer of such pieces was Jiang Yan (444–505), whose "Fu on Separation" and "Fu on Resentment" are regarded as masterpieces of this form. Another fu type that reached maturity during the early med. period is the *yongwu fu* (fu on things). These include fu that describe natural phenomena, scenery, birds, animals, plants, insects, musical instruments, and similar objects. Although there are famous Han dynasty examples such as the "Fu on the Parrot" by Mi Heng (ca. 173–98), early med. writers composed numerous such pieces. E.g., Fu Xuan (217–78) and his son Fu Xian (249–94) between them composed almost 100 yongwu fu.

Although the conventional view is that the fu declined beginning in the Tang dynasty (618–907), recent scholars have shown that the form continued to flourish through the Qing period (1644–1911). During the Tang period, the fu was one of the two literary forms that were required for the civil service exam. This form is usually called *lü fu* (regulated fu). Candidates wrote on a prescribed topic (usually a phrase from a cl. text) and had to follow a specified rhyme. Also during the Tang, a new type of fu, the *wen fu* or "prose-style fu" was introduced. This form was influenced by the new type of prose known as *guwen* or "ancient-style prose." The best-known examples of Tang wen fu are by Han Yu (768–824) and Du Mu (803–53), whose "Fu on the Epang Palace" is a common anthol. piece. The wen fu reached full maturity during the Song dynasty. The most famous pieces of the form are the "Fu on Autumn Sounds" by Ouyang Xiu (1007–72) and the "Fu on the Red Cliff" by Su Shi (1037–1101).

■ J. Hightower, "The *Fu* of T'ao Ch'ien," *HJAS* 17 (1954); H. Wilhelm, "The Scholar's Frustration: Notes on a Type of 'Fu,'" *Chinese Thought and Institutions*, ed. J. K. Fairbank (1957); Y. Hervouet, *Un Poète de cour sous les Han* (1964); B. Watson, *Chinese Rhyme-Prose* (1971); D. Knechtges, *The Han Rhapsody* (1976); W. Graham, *"The Lament for the South"* (1980); *Wen xuan*, trans. D. Knechtges, 3 v. (1982–96); D. Knechtges, "The Old Style *Fu* of Han Yu," *T'ang Studies* 13 (1995); P. Kroll, "The Significance of the *Fu* in the History of T'ang Poetry," *T'ang Studies* 13 (1995); K. Gong, *Studies on the Han Fu*, trans. and ed. D. Knechtges (1997); P. Kroll, "Seven Rhapsodies of Ts'ao Chih," *JAOS* 120.1 (2000).

D. KNECHTGES

**FUGITIVES.** The Fugitives were a group of literary intellectuals, most associated with Vanderbilt University, who produced the short-lived but influential little magazine *The Fugitive* (1922–25). The circle's most famous members were the poets Robert Penn Warren (1905–89), Allen Tate (1899–1979), Laura Riding (1901–91), John Crowe Ransom (1888–1974), Donald Davidson (1893–1968), and Merrill Moore (1903–57). *The Fugitive* was an early publisher and champion of the poetry of Hart Crane, and the turbulent later friendship of Crane and Tate began with Tate's work on the magazine. The Fugitives influenced subsequent generations of writers and critics in the South and elsewhere, incl. Cleanth Brooks, Jesse Stuart, Randall Jarrell, Peter Taylor, and Robert Lowell.

Finding southern lit. mired in "lost-cause" sentimentality and stifling gentility, the Fugitives tried to bring to it modernity and cosmopolitanism. "*The Fugitive* flees from nothing faster than from the high-caste Brahmins of the Old South," they announced in their opening number. They rejected the lush late Victorianism of Ernest Dowson and A. C. Swinburne (although many poems influenced by those poets appeared in *The Fugitive*), with the older members turning to Thomas Hardy, W. B. Yeats, and E. A. Robinson and the younger members championing T. S. Eliot and Ezra Pound; but all of them strove, like similar circles in other cities, to flesh out the meaning of Pound's imperative to "make it new."

Although Ransom, Warren, and Brooks went on to become leading spirits of the *New Criticism, little crit. beyond reviewing went on in *The Fugitive*. Ransom did develop his idea of a tension between an abstract conception and the messy particulars of experience in his discussions with the Fugitives, ideas that bore fruit in his later thought about *concrete universals. Perhaps the movement's most important contribution to the devel. of New Criticism arose from the careful technical analysis they gave to each other's work as poets: their line-by-line attention to turns of phrase, their interest in problems of diction, their worrying of the relationship between the overall shape of a poem and of the poetic particulars that pull in other directions. It was perhaps as a writing workshop more than as a literary-critical movement proper that the Fugitives did most to shape the intellectual habits of New Criticism.

Although many of the Fugitives were later members of the *Agrarians, the Fugitives did not have the political or economic agenda of the later group. But their disciplined examination of poetry and their freedom of thought about it both began the literary renaissance of the 20th-c. South and gave the Fugitives a place in the broader literary world.

■ J. L. Stewart, *The Burden of Time: The Fugitives and Agrarians* (1965); C. Beck, *The Fugitive Legacy* (2001); M. Farrell, *Collaborative Circles* (2001).

J. BURT

**FUROR POETICUS** (Lat., "divine fury," "poetic madness," "poetic fury"; Gr. *enthousiasmos*). From Greco-Roman to early mod. times, the concept of a poet's possession by the *muses or a god such as Apollo, or later, the Christian deity. The term *furor poeticus* is not itself cl.; the exact locution appears first in humanist Neo-Lat. The most celebrated and influential treatment of this concept is found in several works by Plato. In the *Phaedrus* (244a–245a, 265a–b), furor poeticus is third of four forms of madness (*maniké*), and Plato describes the frenzied poet as insane. In the posthumous *Laws* (719c), he points out that when the poet sits on the muse's tripod, he is not in his right mind and that, unlike the legislator who must not give two rules about the same thing, the poet as imitator is often compelled to contradict himself. In the *Ion* (533d, 534b), which is perhaps the most damaging to the idea of human agency, Plato says both lyric and epic poets compose not by art but through divine possession; he compares poets to Corybantic revelers, insisting that "God" takes away the minds of poets and speaks through them while they, like divine prophets, remain in a state of unconsciousness. Poets, he adds, are holy, "winged," and unable to compose unless inspired and out of their senses. Akin to "mania" and at times "ecstasy," furor poeticus is described as a form of possession by the divine powers in which the poet is a passive vessel; the concept categorically removes human skill (and responsibility) from poetic production. Yet to understand furor poeticus only in these terms would be misleading, despite ubiquitous references to Plato throughout lit. hist. In actuality, early sources of this concept reveal no evidence of the complete surrender of human agency to the divine "breath," nor of human absence from the creative process (Tigerstedt). Homer clearly makes Demodokos a self-possessed and conscious "maker," inspired as he may be by the muse. Hesiod, though often thought to be the prime example of the possessed poet, does not demonstrate even in the *Theogony* a surrender of his poetic skills to manic, mantic, or ecstatic composition. Cicero (*De divinatione* 1:31.66) connects frenzy to the prophetic inspiration of Cassandra, noting that a god spoke through her. In a later passage (1:37.88), he links poetic inspiration to this frenzy, quoting Democritus and Plato. But he also significantly qualifies Plato's idea of frenzy by pointing out that lawyers too must have a similar passion to argue lawsuits. Placing furor poeticus in the forum or the law courts adds a grace note of balance to the sense of *furor* as divine mania. Horace quotes with some disdain Democritus's statement barring sane poets from Helicon and promises to teach Roman poets the importance of wisdom to their craft (*Ars poetica* 295–309). The elder Seneca rejects furor poeticus (*Prologue* 1ff.; *Suasoriae*, 3.7), although the younger Seneca defends it (*Epistulae Morales* 84.1–7; Burwick). The doctrine remained controversial. The myths of the *prisci poetae*, e.g., which are found in numerous ancient and Ren. sources, tend to defy the notion of madness. These inspired "first poets" such as Linus and Musaeus, however divine their auspices, clearly reflected the agency of self-conscious founders of civilization.

From Roman times onward, furor poeticus found resonance in the idea of a *vates, or prophet-poet, although the definitions were not coterminous. Statius (*Silvae* 2.7.3) contends that Lucan was the most inspired Roman poet, who like a *sacerdos* was "struck in his heart by learned frenzy" ("docto pectora concitatus oestro") and that Ennius, Varro, Ovid, and even Lucretius should yield to his madness. But Lucan himself, in a notorious address in the *Bellum Civile* (1.63-6), resisted the notion of poetic madness and claimed that Nero's divinity was all the inspiration needed to give strength to Roman poems (Hershkowitz). Nevertheless, the trad. of the vates was kept alive throughout late antiquity, as the legends attesting to Virgil's otherworldly auspices reflect. In his *Etymologiae* (book 7), Isidore of Seville (7th c.) defines the term *vates*, following Varro, as the "power of the mind" that accompanies poetic inspiration. Although he does not mention the divine or supernatural in connection with this power, he suggests the relation of the term to otherworldly intervention by placing the section on poets just before "De Sybillis" and "De magis." In the early 15th c., Coluc-

cio Salutati (*De Laboribus Herculis* 1.3) seems to merge Isidore and Cicero (from the *Pro Archia*), asserting that divine inspiration gives poets the mental power of prophecy (Scott). Also in the 15th c., Leonardo Bruni observed that the "power" of the vates was divine in nature, deriving either from Venus or (when associated with *vaticinium*) from the muses (Greenfield). Later in the century, the influential Neoplatonist Marsilio Ficino subtitled his trans. of Plato's *Ion* "*De furore poetico*" and also wrote a famous letter in 1457 (not pub. until 1495) called "De divino furore." Congratulating his young correspondent on his verse and prose, Ficino asserts that he could not achieve so much at such an early age without the addition of divine frenzy to study and technique. Following Plato, he claims that the divine frenzy brings humans back to the knowledge they possessed before being imprisoned in the body. Ficino's friend Cristoforo Landino echoes this sentiment in his celebrated edition of Dante. The source of divine inspiration would seem a foregone conclusion in Dante's case—e.g., Boccaccio saw Dante as a *poeta theologus*, a divine interpreter (*interpres divinus*). Yet the line is blurred in Landino (as with much Neoplatonic writing) between the Christian god's divine inspiration and that of rehabilitated Greco-Roman gods and muses. Landino and Bruni thought normal people could suddenly be seized by furor poeticus, which would then allow a divine force to speak through them; Angelo Poliziano believed instead that the vatic quality was inherent in particular people from birth (Greenfield). But, despite these slight differences among these humanists, they were united in their aim. The defense of the divine spirit in the poet had a practical advantage at the end of the 15th c. In establishing the curricular innovations of the *studia humanitatis*, chief among which was the addition of poetry and hist. to the med. *trivium* of grammar, rhetoric, and dialectic, humanists such as Landino and Poliziano marshaled the poet's supposed divinity as justification for raising the poetic art to a central place in Ren. epistemology.

Although divine inspiration sometimes seems a doctrine, there was probably never full commitment to furor poeticus as the sole means of composing poetry (e.g., even Ficino sets divine frenzy beside study and technique). Human agency always played a part. In *Astrophil and Stella* 74, Philip Sidney half-jokingly rejects "poet's fury"; but in his *Defence of Poesy*, he discusses the Roman vates with approval, lending credence to the humanist argument for the centrality of the poet to education and social devel. Sidney extends the earlier humanist argument, claiming that poetry alone among the human disciplines is superior to nature; he presents the poet as a self-conscious manipulator of the "zodiac of his own wit." Sidney's contemporary George Chapman went to great pains to separate inspiration and Democritan insanity; Edmund Spenser, in contrast, invokes poetic "rage" as a form of human alienation, a "divine instinct" (E. K., *The Shepheardes Calender*), although he elsewhere expresses skepticism in regard to "courtly" Platonism (Huntington). Despite continuing ambivalence, however, poets (esp. epic poets) might still claim to be mere conduits through which the divine voice issued. In *Paradise Lost* (bk. 9:21–24), John Milton insists that his muse (Urania) "deigns / Her nightly visitation unimplor'd," dictates to him "slumb'ring," and inspires his "unpremeditated verse." But such an utter deprivation of agency, even if only fanciful, is rare. The reality of poetic production tended to preclude doctrinaire belief in furor poeticus.

In the 18th c., the doctrine of furor poeticus eroded considerably, being replaced by less Neoplatonic (and more pragmatic) ideas of poetic inspiration, poetic madness, and poetic production. Joshua Reynolds (*Discourses on Art* 6), discussing *"imitation," rejected the notion of inspiration as a mysterious "gift" because it diminished the importance of labor and application. In the romantic period, however, furor poeticus was seen as a means of liberating the *imagination from conformity (Burwick), although, as interest in clinical madness grew, it tended to be linked to insanity rather than divinity or cl. *enthousiasmos*. The idea of the "vatic" also became secularized, although it was not associated a fortiori with madness; as a poetic posture, it continued to appeal to poets as late as Walt Whitman, Robinson Jeffers, Allen Ginsberg, and Bob Dylan. In the contemp. idiom, poetry and madness remain linked, as, in certain contexts, do poetic inspiration and divine auspices.

*See* GENIUS, INSPIRATION.

■ Curtius; M. Foucault, *Folie et déraison* (1961); E. N. Tigerstedt, "Furor Poeticus: Poetic Inspiration in Greek Literature before Democritus and Plato, *Journal of the History of Ideas* 31 (1970); W. Scott, "Perotti, Ficino, and Furor Poeticus," *Res publica litterarum* 4 (1981); C. C. Greenfield, *Humanist and Scholastic Poetics, 1250–1500* (1981); C. Kallendorf, "The *Poeta Theologus* in Italian Renaissance Commentary," *Journal of the History of Ideas* 56 (1995); F. Burwick, *Poetic Madness and the Romantic Imagination* (1996); J. Huntington, "Furious Insolence: The Social Meaning of Poetic Inspiration in the 1590s," *MP* 94 (1997); D. Hershkowitz, *The Madness of Epic* (1998); C. J. Steppich, '*Numine afflatur*': *Die Inspiration des Dichters im Denken der Renaissance* (2002).

R. FALCO

## FUTURISM

I. Italian
II. Russian
III. Other Futurisms

Futurism was the prototypical 20th-c. avant-garde movement in lit. and the arts, militant in its promotion of extreme artistic innovation and experimentation. Its stance was to declare a radical rejection of the past and to focus on the maximally new in art, technology, and politics, often combined with stylistic *primitivism. It rejected psychological sensitivity and the effete lyricism of *symbolism. Dynamism was glorified, as were all forms of rapid or violent movement such as war, airplanes, cars, radios, and electricity. Futurism sought out conservative social elements and confronted them

in order to provoke a violent negative response. In contrast to symbolism, which was musically oriented, futurism showed a preference for the visual arts. Many of the futurist poets were also painters.

**I. Italian.** It. futurism began with the "Fondazione e Manifesto del Futurismo" (The Founding and Manifesto of Futurism), first pub. in Fr. in *Le Figaro* in Paris, February 20, 1909; here F. T. Marinetti (1876–1944) declared that a roaring car was more beautiful than the *Victory of Samothrace*, that no work without an aggressive character could be a masterpiece, that war was hygienic, and that museums were graveyards (which should be destroyed or visited rarely). In succeeding *manifestos, Marinetti enunciated the principles of futurism in relation to poetry. *Parole in libertà* (words in freedom) denoted lang. free of syntax and logical ordering and, thus, better able to convey intense *emotion rapidly. *Immaginazione senza fili* (wireless imagination) and *analogia disegnata* (pictorialized analogy) involved maximum freedom of *imagery and *metaphor. This led to the expressive use of *typography, with fonts of various sizes and styles being used in the same line or word and free disposition of words on the printed page, sometimes resembling a typographic *collage (e.g., Marinetti's "Joffre après la Marne" or "SCRABrrRrraaNNG," both 1919). Expressive typography and syntactic and metaphoric freedom were intended to give the effect of simultaneous sense impressions and superimposed time frames (*simultaneità*), e.g., Marinetti's famous poem "Bombardamento," which recreates by onomatopoetic and typographic means the 1912 siege of Adrianopoli. This and the other poems of Marinetti's most important book, *Zang Tumb Tuuum* (1914), provide successful illustrations of futurist poetics in practice, which also includes visual poems such as "Pallone Frenato Turco" (Turkish Hot-Air Balloon). There was an active cross-fertilization among the futurists, the cubist painters (see CUBISM), and Guillaume Apollinaire with his *calligrammes.

Marinetti was a brilliant public performer who could make reading a manifesto the high point of a literary evening or evoke the sounds of a whole battlefield single-handedly. "Futurist Evenings," the first of which occurred on January 12, 1910, were designed to create a scandal and often ended in riots, official protests, and arrests of the participants. Marinetti's skill in creating and exploiting this notoriety made futurism a major cultural force in a short period of time. At the same time, his financial independence allowed him to publish his own works and those of his associates in numerous eds. through his Milan publishing house, Edizioni Futuriste di "Poesia," which also put out a poetry jour. Futurism had centers in a number of other It. cities, notably Florence, where the futurist newspaper *Lacerba* was published January 1913–May 1915; with Marinetti's transforming participation from February 1913, *Lacerba* became a leading example of innovative typography. The two major collections of futurist poetry assembled by Marinetti are *I poeti futuristi* (1912) and *I nuovi poeti futuristi* (1925).

Most futurist poetry, incl. Marinetti's own early poetry, while futurist in theme, was closer in form to *vers libre* than to parole in libertà, e.g., the works of Ernesto Cavacchioli (1885–1954), Luciano Folgore (1888–1966), and Aldo Palazzeschi (1885–1974), the last a poet of the first magnitude, esp. in his later work. Others, however, some of whom were primarily painters, produced significant works in the parolibrist manner, e.g., Carlo Carrà (1881–1966), Giacomo Balla (1871–1958), Franceso Cangiullo (1884–1977), Corrado Govoni (1884–1965), Ardengo Soffici (1879–1964), and Gino Severini (1883–1966). It is sometimes difficult to separate futurist works into poems and pictures since the two art forms were so closely intertwined. It. futurists also made innovative contributions to sculpture, architecture, theater, film, photography, and music. One other important element of It. futurism was a militaristic nationalism, which caused it to become aligned with Mussolini and Fascism for a time, this, in turn, producing an international revulsion against the movement that has only recently dissipated.

**II. Russian.** Marinetti claimed that Rus. futurism was a direct outgrowth of his It. movement. However, the chief Rus. representatives insisted that they had developed their ideas independently and differed significantly from the Italians. But little that is distinctively futurist except early poems by Velimir Khlebnikov (1885–1922) can be found in Russia before 1910. Information on It. futurism began to appear in Rus. periodicals by March 1909; thus, the influence of It. futurism on the early stages of Rus. futurism is probable. Both can be seen as emerging from symbolist antecedents in similarly traditional, preindustrial societies. Yet in quality and breadth of poetic practice, and to some extent in poetic theory, Rus. futurism clearly overshadows It. futurism. Without financial resources comparable to Marinetti's, Rus. publications had to be more modest in cost and number, but this was made a virtue by emphasis on a primitive, deliberately antielegant look. The Rus. movement has two branches, cubo-futurism and ego-futurism.

**A.** *Cubo-Futurism,* originally named Hylaea, had its first important publication in the manifesto and collection *Poščečina obščestvennomu vkusu* (A Slap at Public Taste, 1913). This manifesto, drafted in December 1912, was co-written and signed by David Burliuk (1882–1967), Aleksei Kruchenykh (1886–1968), Vladimir Mayakovsky (1893–1930), and Khlebnikov. Clearly based in style and content on the earlier It. manifestos, it advocated throwing Alexander Pushkin, Fyodor Dostoevsky, Leo Tolstoy, et al. from the "Steamship of Modernity" and attacked the leading members of the current literary establishment. It then called for increasing the vocabulary with arbitrary and derived words, declared a hatred for previously existing lang., and proclaimed the "samovitoe" (self-sufficient) word. The collection featured major poems by Khlebnikov, incl. "Bobèobi pelis' guby" (Bobeobi Sang the Lips, 1908–9), an example of cubism in verse in which

a portrait is constructed of facial features expressed in abstract sounds. Khlebnikov was recognized as the most brilliant and inventive of the group. His experiments ranged from arcane neologisms to exotic verse forms, e.g., *Razin* (1920), written in *palindromes. Imagery in his poems reflects pagan and folk sources rather than urbanism. His poems were usually too complex to be popular, but his innovations still serve as an inspiration to present-day poets.

David Burliuk, the self-styled father of Rus. futurism, had first recognized Mayakovsky's poetic genius and had suggested the idea of *sound poetry to Kruchenykh. He was also responsible for the publication of a number of important futurist miscellanies. Though primarily a painter, Burliuk was also a prolific poet, with an antiaesthetic Rimbaudian bent.

Mayakovsky was a true urbanist who read his consonant-rich poetry from the stage in a powerful bass voice. A mixture of hyperbolic, egocentric imagery and painful sensitivity, his poems have a direct emotional impact. After the revolution, Mayakovsky willingly turned his poetic talent into a tool for political propaganda, and he was posthumously canonized by Stalin as the "Great Poet of the Revolution." His poems were published in massive eds., were memorized by generations of school children, and were given extensive, though restricted, critical attention by Soviet scholars. His *lesenka* (stepladder line), introduced in 1923, was adopted by many other poets of his time and remains a common device in Rus. poetry even today.

The idea of the "self-sufficient" word developed in the hands of Kruchenykh and Khlebnikov into *zaum' (transrational lang.), which in its most radical form was pure sound poetry. Although earlier experiments by Khlebnikov have certain features of zaum', the first true example is Kruchenykh's sound poem "Dyr bul ščyl" (*Pomada*, 1913), which is prefaced by the statement that the words do not have any definite meaning. Other poems by Kruchenykh consist entirely of vowels. In the 1920s, he produced a series of useful theoretical works on futurism.

The years 1913–14 were the high point of cubo-futurism, with publication of many books and performances of the dramas *Pobeda nad solncem* (Victory over the Sun) by Khlebnikov and Kruchenykh and Mayakovsky's *Vladimir Majakovskij, Tragedija.* The end of 1913 and beginning of 1914 saw a tour of 17 provincial cities by Burliuk, Mayakovsky, and Vasily Kamensky (1884–1961), the poet-aviator who wrote typographically elaborate "ferroconcrete" poems.

Other important poets briefly associated with this movement were the theoretician Benedikt Livšic (1886–1937), the dramatist Il'ja Zdanevič (1894–1975), the impressionist Elena Guro (1877–1913), and the early Boris Pasternak (1890–1960). The devel. of Rus. formalist literary theory (see RUSSIAN FORMALISM) is closely related to cubo-futurist practice, Roman Jakobson and Viktor Skhlovsky being associates of the futurists. Jakobson's move to Prague in 1921 stimulated the rise of a similar trend there. A number of later Rus. movements are to some extent based on futurism, e.g., *constructivism, LEF, OBERIU, and the *Ničevoki* (Nothingists). The works of Igor Terent'ev (1892–1937) and Aleksandr Tufanov (1877–1941) continued zaum' practice and theory.

**B.** *Ego-Futurism.* Based in Petersburg and claiming as its founder the popular poet-aesthete Igor' Severjanin (1887–1941), who was the first to use the term *Futurizm* in the Rus. context (1911), ego-futurism emphasized extravagant urban imagery, foreign words, neologisms, egocentricity, and experimentation in rhyme. Its moving force was Ivan Ignat'ev (1882–1914), who wrote a number of manifestos and ran a publishing venture, *Peterburgskij glašataj* (Petersburg Herald), which produced several miscellanies and books by group members. The most inventive of these was Vasilisk Gnedov (1890–1978), with his famous "Poema konca" (Poem of the End, 1913) consisting of a blank page performed with a silent gesture of resignation. Gnedov also wrote poems of one letter, word, or line, sometimes bordering on zaum'. A Moscow offshoot of ego-futurism, the *Mezonin poezii* (Mezzanine of Poetry, 1913), was led by Vadim Šeršenevič (1893–1942), a prolific poet and publisher who later led the movement *Imažinizm* (Imaginism).

**III. Other Futurisms.** Futurism took root in a number of other Slavic national lits. In the Ukraine, Myxajl Semenko (1892–1937) proclaimed *Kverofuturism* (Querofuturism) in 1914, later named Panfuturism, and put out a series of books and a jour., *Nova Generacija* (New Generation, 1927–31). In Poland, futurist-style manifestos and poems were written by Jerzy Jankowski (1887–1941) as early as 1912. The Kráków poets Tytus Czyżewski (1880–1945), Bruno Jasieński (1901–38), and Stanisław Młodożeniec (1895–1959) formed a futurist group in 1919, as did the Warsaw poets Anatol Stern (1899–1968) and Aleksander Wat (1900–67), the two groups coming together in 1921–22 to produce two important collections, *Jednodniówka futurystów* (One-time Issue of the Futurists) and *Nuž w bžuhu* (Knife in the Stomach). Czech futurism, called *Poetismus* (Poetism), included among its founding members the poets Vitěslav Nezval (1900–58), Jaroslav Seifert (1901–86), Konstantin Biebl (1898–1951), and the artist and theoretician Karel Teige (1900–51). The Slovenes had Anton Podbevšek (1898–1981). Futurist movements flourished for a time (1917–23) in Georgia and Armenia as well.

In Spain, the influence of It. futurism was important to the Catalan poets Josep-María Junoy (1887–1955) and Joan Salvat-Papasseit (1894–1924) and others who wrote parolibristic poems with a strong visual dimension, as did members of the ultraist movement (1919–23), most notably Guillermo de Torre (1900–1971; see ULTRAISM). Port. futurism was short-lived, centering on the activities of José de Almada-Negreiros (1893–1970) in 1916–17. The Brazilian poet Mário de Andrade (1893–1945) and a few others also showed the influence of Marinetti. In England, *vorticism was futurist in style. Marinetti considered it a branch of his

movement, but its leaders, Ezra Pound (1885–1972) and Wyndham Lewis (1882–1957), the publisher of *Blast* (1914–15), saw themselves as independents. By the early 1920s, other Eur. movements had taken the lead away from futurism and had begun to emphasize other qualities: *Dada (nihilism, the absurd), *surrealism (the subconscious), constructivism (functionalism). Some later movements still retained noticeable elements of futurism, e.g., *concrete poetry, *lettrisme, and sound poetry.

*See* AVANT-GARDE POETICS, MODERNISM.

■ **General**: E. Falqui, *Bibliografia e iconografia del Futurismo* (1959); R. Poggioli, *The Theory of the Avant-Garde*, trans. G. Fitzgerald (1968); Z. Folejewski, *Futurism and Its Place in the Development of Modern Poetry* (1980); W. Bohn, *The Aesthetics of Visual Poetry, 1914–1928* (1986); M. Perloff, *The Futurist Moment* (1986); J. J. White, *Literary Futurism* (1990); R. Humphreys, *Futurism* (1999); *International Futurism in Arts and Literature*, ed. G. Berghaus (2000); *Futurist Performance* (2001), ed. M. Kirby; M. Puchner, *Poetry of the Revolution: Marx, Manifestos, and the Avant-Gardes* (2006); *Futurism and the Technological Imagination*, ed. G. Berghaus (2009); D. Ohana, *The Futurist Syndrome* (2010); *100 Artists' Manifestos*, ed. Alex Danchev (2011).

■ **Italian**: R. Clough, *Futurism* (1961); P. Bergman, *"Modernolatria" et "simultaneità"* (1962); *Futurist Manifestos*, ed. U. Apollonio (1970); F. Marinetti, *Selected Writings*, ed. R. Flint (1972); *Per conoscere Marinetti e il Futurismo*, ed. L. de Maria (1973); C. Tisdall and A. Bozzolla, *Futurism* (1977); *Contributo a una bibliografia del futurismo italiano*, ed. A. Baldazzi et al. (1977); N. Zurbrugg, "Marinetti, Boccioni and Electroacoustic Poetry," *Comparative Criticism* 4 (1982); G. Berghaus. *The Genesis of Futurism: Marinetti's Early Career and Writings, 1899–1909* (1995), and *Futurism and Politics* (1996); M. Bentivoglio and F. Zoccoli, *Women Artists of Italian Futurism* (1998); *Futurist Manifestos*, ed. U. Apollonio and R. Humphreys (2001); *Italian Futurist Poetry*, ed. W. Bohn (2005); *Critical Writings / F. T. Marinetti*, ed. G. Berghaus (2006); *Futurism: An Anthology*, ed. L. Rainey, C. Poggi, L. Wittman (2009); C. Poggi, *Inventing Futurism: The Art and Politics of Artificial Optimism* (2009).

■ **Russian**: *Manifesty i programmy russkogo futurizma*, ed. V. Markov (1967); V. Markov, *Russian Futurism* (1968); V. Shklovsky, *Mayakovsky and His Circle*, trans. L. Feiler (1972); E. Brown, *Mayakovsky, A Poet in the Revolution* (1973); V. Barooshian, *Russian Cubo-Futurism, 1910–1930* (1977); B. Jangfeldt, *Majakovsky and Futurism, 1917–1921* (1976); B. Livshits, *The One and a Half-Eyed Archer*, trans. J. E. Bowlt (1977); S. Compton, *The World Backwards* (1978); *Ardis Anthology of Russian Futurism*, ed. E. Proffer and C. Proffer (1980); V. Erlich, *Russian Formalism: History–Doctrine*, 3d ed. (1981); A. Lawton, *Vadim Shershenevich* (1981); G. J. Janecek, *The Look of Russian Literature* (1984); V. Khlebnikov, *The King of Time*, trans. P. Schmidt (1985); Terras, "Centrifuge," "Futurism," "Zaum'"; J. R. Stapanian, *Mayakovsky's Cubo-Futurist*

*Vision* (1986); *Russian Futurism through Its Manifestoes, 1912–1928*, ed. A. Lawton and H. Eagle (1988); L. Magarotto, D. Rizzi, M. Marzaduri, *Zaumnyi futurizm i dadaizm v russkoi kul'ture* (1991); R. Jakobson, *My Futurist Years*, ed. B. Jangfeldt and S. Rudy, trans. S. Rudy (1997); M. Shkandrii, M. Mudrak, I. Holuizky, *David Burliuk, 1882–1967* (2001); *Russkii futurizm*, ed. V. N. Terekhina and A. P. Zimenkov (2009); T. Harte, *Fast Forward: The Aesthetics and Ideology of Speed in Russian Avant-Garde Culture, 1910–1930.* (2009); B. Jangfeldt, *Stavka-zhizn': Vladimir Maiakovskii i ego krug* (2009); N. Gourianova, *Aesthetics of Anarchy* (2012).

■ **Other Futurisms:** *Polska avangarda poetycka*, ed. A. Lam, 2 v. (1969); W. Wees, *Vorticism and the English Avant-Garde* (1972); *L'avanguardia a Tiflis*, ed. L. Magarotto et al. (1982); M. Mudrak, *The New Generation and Artistic Modernism in the Ukraine* (1986).

G. J. Janecek

**FYRTIOTALISTERNA** (Swedish, "The Poets of the 1940s"). A group of modernist poets who contributed to the definitive breakthrough of lyrical *modernism in Sweden in the 1940s. The name of the group came from the jour. *40-tal* (The 40s), which was published from 1944 to 1947 and edited by some of Sweden's leading poets and critics. Several young poets of the 1940s published their first poems in *40-tal*, and the jour. played a crucial role introducing foreign modernists—such as T. S. Eliot, Federico García Lorca, Ezra Pound, Albert Camus, William Faulkner, and Franz Kafka—in Sweden by publishing trans. and critical essays. *Fyrtiotalisterna* embraced modernist styles and preferred *free verse over traditional lyrical forms. They were affected by World War II, and their poetry can be seen as a direct response to the war. Anxiety and disillusion are frequent themes, but the poems also strive to find a way out of those feelings. Fyrtiotalisterna were critical of ideologies, intellectual, analytical, and conscious of the world and its shortcomings, and their work emphasized the universal and objective over the subjective and personal. The poetry of Fyrtiotalisterna is sometimes said to be pessimistic, but it is a critical, short-term pessimism, aiming at analyzing the contemp. situation in order to move on into a better future—almost an optimistic pessimism, with hope of renewal at its core. Hope is often associated with love, which is another recurring theme in the poetry of the 1940s.

The leaders of the movement, Erik Lindegren (1910–68) and Karl Vennberg (1910–95), were critics as well as poets. Lindegren's *mannen utan väg* (The Man without a Way, 1942) became a bible for the new generation. The collection contained "shattered sonnets" in which the traditional *sonnet form was broken down into two-line stanzas without rhymes and with a compressed and violent imagery. Lindegren's next collection, *Sviter* (Suites, 1947), was less obtrusive, with a prominent love theme. Vennberg was the master of contrasts and opposites. In his poetry collections, poems that criticize contemp. society with biting irony intermingle with esoteric poems colored by mysticism. Rut Hillarp (1914–2003) wrote love poems in an analytical and problematizing spirit typical of the Swedish 1940s, using erotic imagery to explore gender and power hierarchies. The movement was broad and included numerous poets, such as Sven Alfons (1918–96), Werner Aspenström (1918–97), Ann Margret Dahlquist-Ljungberg (1915–2002), Elsa Grave (1918–2003), Ella Hillbäck (1915–79), Ragnar Thoursie (1919–2010), and Maria Wine (1912–2003). Fyrtiotalisterna have been associated mostly with poetry, but some writers connected to the group wrote prose fiction (e.g., Lars Ahlin, Stig Dagerman, Eva Neander, and Gösta Oswald).

■ L. Bäckström, *Erik Lindegren* (1962); K. E. Lagerlöf, *Den unge Karl Vennberg* (1967); I. Algulin, *Den orfiska reträtten* (1977)—on *Fyrtiotalisterna*; A. Cullhed, *"Tiden söker sin röst"* (1982)—on Lindegren's *mannen utan väg*; R. Lysell, *Erik Lindegrens imaginära universum* (1983); L. Elleström, *Vårt hjärtas vilt lysande skrift* (1992); *On Karl Vennbergs lyrik* (1992); A. Bränström Öhman, *Kärlekens ödeland* (1998)—on Hillarp; A. Johansson, *Poesins negativitetk* (2000)—on Vennberg; J. Björklund, *Hoppets lyrik* (2004)—on Hillbäck, Hillarp, Dahlquist-Ljungberg.

J. Björklund

**GAELIC POETRY.** *See* IRELAND, POETRY OF; SCOTLAND, POETRY OF.

**GAI SABER** (Occitan, Sp., "gay knowledge," also called *gaia* or *gaya sciencia*). The art of poetic composition and, thus, the skill of a lover or the knowledge of *courtly love. In the prologue to *Las razos de trobar*, an early 13th-c. grammatical manual that is the oldest in or about a Romance lang., Raimon Vidal proposes to teach lettered men the "saber de trobar" or art of poetic composition. As an address to an aristocratic Catalonian readership interested in establishing rules for the public performance and judgment of *Occitan poetry, Vidal's description is foundational for later grammatical treatises such as the Occitan *ars poetria*, the *Leys d'Amors* (Laws of Love, ca. 1330, revision 1355), attributed to Guilhem Molinier, and Enrique de Villena's *Arte de trovar* (ca. 1427–33). Referring to Vidal, these treatises develop the concept of *gai saber* as the knowledge of proper poetic composition codified through competitions (see POETIC CONTESTS), and the publication of grammatical treatises and works that cultivate its precepts. Consistent with med. principles of knowledge, this establishment and preservation of immutable rules make a science of poetry (Weiss).

The founders of the Consistori de la Sobregaia Companhia del Gay Saber (Consistory of the Merry Band of the Gay Knowledge), an academy established at Toulouse in 1323 to preserve the Occitan *troubadour lyric trad., produced the *Leys* as a poetic code that designates rules for composing Occitan poetry in annual competitions. The treatise gives descriptive definitions with examples of major poetic genres such as the *vers, *canso, *sirventes, *dansa, *descort, *tenso, *partimen, and *planh, as well as other technical terms. Although the consistory's members were composed of laymen who met unofficially to compose and perform Occitan poetry, their social profile as a confraternity and their celebration of Marian and *devotional poetry resemble the activities of the northern Fr. *Puys* founded by religious confraternities. The Toulouse Consistory aspired to give the Occitan lyric trad. a Latinate authority by emulating the ceremonies of the city's university: the competitions were treated as public examinations followed by bachelors' and masters' degrees in *gaia sciencia*. Villena refers to Raimon's *Razos* and the *Leys d'amors*, and describes the establishment of the Consistory in Toulouse and its continuation in Barcelona that includes a poetic competition, the publication of *libros del arte* (vernacular treatises), and royal sponsorship. He emphasizes the importance of complete rather than amateur poetic knowledge, giving a full account of all the rules necessary for understanding the art of poetry and of how these constitute the criteria by which poetry is judged. Poetry is regen-

erated as a branch of knowledge through not only a constant public verification of transmissible rules but the establishment of institutions and the revision of these rules in poetic treatises.

In addition to its place in med. considerations of poetic knowledge, 20th-c. thinkers turned to gay science and the consistory as a kind of "counterlaw" to the authority of the Church and Roman legal trad., one that emphasizes a wisdom found through the physical and spiritual experience of lovers (Goodrich, Dragonetti). Fascinated with the subversive spirit of gay science as erotic knowledge, Friedrich Nietzsche maintains in his *Gay Science* (1910) that any science must have a certain amount of erotic playfulness, which he associates with the art of the troubadours.

■ *Monumens de la littérature romane, I–II: Las flors del gay saber, estier dichas Las leys d'Amor, I–III: Las flors del gay saber, estier dichas Las leys d'Amors*, ed. A. Gatien-Arnoult (1841–49); *Las Leys d'Amors: Manuscrit de l'Académie des jeux floraux*, ed. J. Anglade (1919–20); *The "Razos de trobar" of Raimon Vidal and Associated Texts*, ed. J. H. Marshall (1972); R. Dragonetti, *Le gai savoir dans la rhétorique courtoise: Flamenca et Joufroi de Poitiers* (1982); *Obras completas de Enrique de Villena*, ed. P. M. Cátedra (1994); J. Weiss, *The Poet's Art: Literary Theory in Castile c. 1400–60* (1990); P. Goodrich, "Gay Science and Law," *Rhetoric and Law in Early Modern Europe*, ed. V. Kahn and L. Hutson (2001); C. Léglu, "Language in Conflict in Toulouse: *Las Leys d'Amors*," *MLR* 103 (2008).

M. GALVEZ

**GAITA GALLEGA.** A two-hemistich verse having marked ternary movement and a variable number of syllables, usually averaging about ten or eleven. It is primarily a Galician-Port. meter used in Sp. popular (rarely learned) verse. It is thought to be related to the *muiñeira*, a song to be accompanied by the bagpipe. Henríquez Ureña writes, "It seems hardly necessary to note that this meter, in spite of its relationship with the 15th-c. *arte mayor*, cannot be confused with it, because, even in the most regular forms, it employs the anapestic decasyllable; moreover, the latter becomes characteristic of the new regular form."

■ P. Henríquez Ureña, *Versificación irregular en la poesía castellana*, 2d ed. (1933).

D. C. CLARKE

**GALICIA, POETRY OF.** Spreading from the pilgrimage center of Santiago de Compostela throughout Galicia and northern Portugal, Galician-Port. *cantigas* were among the earliest lyric forms in the Iberian peninsula. Most of the secular *cantigas* are preserved in the *Cancioneiro* (Songbook) *da Ajuda* (mid-14th c.), *Cancioneiro da Vaticana* (end of 15th c.), and the

*Cancioneiro Colocci-Brancuti* (now *Cancioneiro da Biblioteca Nacional de Lisboa*, 16th c.). King Alfonso X *el Sábio* (The Wise) was responsible for the religious *Cantigas de Santa María* (13th c.). Galician poets from 1200–1350, the period of greatest achievement, include Martín Codax, Afonso Eanes de Cotón, Bernal de Bonaval, Joan (García) de Guilhade, Joan Airas, Pai Gomes Chariño, Airas Nunes, Pero García, and Pedro Amigo de Sevilla. The Galician-Port. school, although following Occitan models (see OCCITAN POETRY), is best exemplified by the apparently native *cantiga de amigo*, a song of melancholy nostalgia by a maiden for her absent lover.

After the death of Portugal's King Diniz (1325), the old lyric declined; from 1400, Castilian began to replace Galician as the lang. of poetry in the peninsula. The bilingual *Cancioneiro de Baena* (1445) still has a few Galician poems by Macias "o namorado" (fl. 1360–90), the Arcediano de Toro (fl. 1379–90), and Alfonso Álvarez de Villasandino (1340?–ca. 1428). Until the 18th c., little written Galician poetry had been preserved. Diego A. Cernadas de Castro (1698–1777), "el cura de Fruime," wrote bilingual occasional verse and with Manuel Freire Castrillón (1751–1820) marks the gradual rebirth of Galician lit.

*Romanticism brought more interest in Galicia's past and its ancient lit., folklore, and other indigenous features. Among others, Antolín Faraldo (1823–53) defended Galician autonomy and, with Aurelio Aguirre (1833–58), the Galician Espronceda, promoted literary regionalism. Francisco Añón y Paz (1812–78), "el Patriarca," is remembered for his patriotic *odes and humorous compositions. Alberto Camino (1821–61), author of sentimental and elegiac verse, is a forerunner of the *Rexurdimento* (Renaissance) led by Rosalía de Castro (1837–85). The rebirth was signaled by the Floral Games of La Coruña in 1861, the winning poems of which were published in the *Album de caridad* (1862). In 1863, Castro published *Cantares gallegos* (Galician Songs), the first book written in Galician in the mod. period. In 1880, Castro's *Follas novas* (New Leaves) appeared. Castro also wrote in Castilian, but her social concerns are most obvious in Galician. Moreover, her themes include some of the earliest feminist statements in Galicia, if not on the peninsula. Two of her important contemporaries were Eduardo Pondal y Abente (1835–1917), who wrote *Queixumes dos pinos* (Complaints of the Pines), and Manuel Curros Enríquez (1851–1908), forced to emigrate to Cuba after writing anticlerical verse. There he wrote the nostalgic *Aires da miña terra* (Airs of My Land, 1880). Valentín Lamas Carvajal (1849–1906) sang elegiacally of the peasant life in works such as *Espiñas, follas e frores* (Thorns, Leaves and Flowers, 1875). Other poets of the later 19th c. are José Pérez Ballesteros (1883–1918), known for the three-volume *Cancionero popular gallego* (1885–1912); Manuel Leiras Pulpeiro (1854–1912); and Manuel Lugrís Freire (1863–1940).

Among contemp. poets, the lang. has become more sophisticated. *Troubadour trads., *saudade*,

and Galician nationalism are still present, while numerous foreign poetic movements have also been influential. The foremost poets of the early 20th c. are Antonio Noriega Varela (1869–1947), Ramón Cabanillas (1876–1959), Victoriano Taibo (1885–1966), and Gonzalo López Abente (1878–1963). Noriega's ruralism is close to that of the previous generation, but Cabanillas and López Abente reflect Sp.-Am. *modernismo*. Taibo's peasant themes express his social commitment. The best poet of the avant-garde in Galician was the sailor Manoel Antonio (1900–30), who collaborated with the artist Álvaro Cebreiro in the iconoclastic manifesto *Mais Aĺ* (Beyond, 1922). During his lifetime, he published *De catro a catro* (Four to Four, 1928); posthumously, the nearly complete works have appeared, showing him to be a true disciple of *creationism in the manner of Vicente Huidobro and Gerardo Diego. Luis Amado Carballo (1901–27) wrote a more pantheistic, vanguard poetry. Ricardo Carballo Calero (1910–90), Florentino Delgado Gurriará (1903–86), Xulio Sigüenza (1900–65), and Eugenio Montes (1900–82) also wrote avant-garde verse before the Sp. Civil War. In the same period, there was Aquilino Iglesia Alvariño (1909–61), and above all, Luis Pimentel (1895–1958). Fermín Bouza Brey (1901–73), one of the best-known Galician writers of the postwar period, also employed elements of med. poetry in the so-called New Troubadorism; in the same vein was Álvaro Cunqueiro (1911–81). In the 1940s and 1950s, Luz Pozo Garza (b. 1922), María do Carme Kruckenberg (b. 1926), and Pura Vázquez (1918–2006) were, among others, the best-known poets, with a wide range of lyrical motives. The Galician landscape is present in the extensive works of Uxío Novoneyra (1930–99). His native mountains of Caurel were presented in a cosmogonic vision of himself. He is present in María Mariño's (1918–67) and Bernardino Graña's (b. 1932) poetry.

Since 1976, Galician poetry has undergone rapid change. The proliferation of texts and critical studies led to the identification of a Golden Age of poetry. Some, such as X. L. Méndez Ferrín (b. 1938), have followed Celso Emilio Ferreiro (1914–79) and Lorenzo Varela's (1917–78) social poetry, while others have maintained Antonio's avant-garde orientation, adding a tendency toward intimism (Claudio Rodríguez Fer, b. 1956), and biographical content (Antonio Tovar, 1911–84).

The last decades of the 20th c. saw the emergence of three poetic groups, each associated with a major metropolitan area—Vigo; A Coruña; and the spiritual and cultural center of Galicia, Santiago de Compostela—and each characterized by generational and poetic conditions. Already well established by the 1980s, the Vigo group of Víctor Vaqueiro (b. 1948) and Alfonso Pexegueiro (b. 1948) witnessed the emergence of Xavier Rodríguez Baixeiras (b. 1945) and, later, incorporated poets such as X. M. Álvarez Cáccamo (b. 1954) and Manuel Vilanova (b. 1944), who had previously written in Castilian. Also linked to the Vigo group are the younger poets of the Rompente group.

The A Coruña group, Nebulosa Poética (Nebulous Poetics), brings together a diverse stock of poets, some more representative of the group's philosophy than others. The cultural magazine *Dorna*, supported by a student group from the Universidad de Santiago de Compostela, provided a forum for mature and young voices alike: Luisa Castro (b. 1966), Ramiro Fonte (b. 1957), Luis Gónzalez Tosar (b. 1952), and Ana Romaní (b. 1962). Linked to the Cravo Fondo group are Xesús Rábade (b. 1949), Helena Villar (b. 1940), and Xulio and Xesús Valcárcel (b. 1953 and 1955, respectively). Darío Xohán Cabana's (b. 1952) excellent trans. of Dante and Petrarch were already regarded highly by the 1970s and 1980s. Cabana explores in sonnet form personal experience and the call of his homeland. And despite his meager output in Galician, José Ángel Valente (1929–2000) left a notable mark on its lyric with *Cantigas de Alén*.

Later poetic currents followed a more culturalist approach, incorporating elements of the Port., Eng., and Am. trads., as well as those associated with mod. and postmod. aesthetics. Characteristic of such a poetics are varied musical, visual, and philosophical references and the desire to establish a new, cultured discourse capable of voicing idiomatic and formal experimentation. New conceptualizations of space, metrical form, *rhythm, and *imagery accompany the assimilation and transcendence of a cl. past. Arcadio López Casanova (b. 1942) is an innovative and foundational figure in this vein. In *Mesteres*, physical and spiritual exile is embodied in a solemn soliloquy that recalls the tragic, polyphonic chorus of antiquity, as it evokes the land and men of Galicia. Also worthy of mention is the vast oeuvre of Méndez Ferrín and, no less so, the innovative work of Vilanova, whose collection *E direivos eu do mister das cobras* could be considered a Galician "happening."

The 1990s ushered in a new wave of perspectives (feminist, ecological, antimilitarist), questioned earlier modes of expression, and reread myth and trad. from a parodic, often subversive, standpoint. The written word's capacity to represent alienation and otherness is explored by María Xosé Queizán (b. 1939). Romaní projects the self onto a vast seascape through the Homeric characters Odysseus and Penelope. Chus Pato (b. 1955) prefers to transgress conventional *syntax; Marta Dacosta (b. 1966) fuses landscape and biography; and Helena de Carlos (b. 1964) is firmly anchored in a rigorous, cl. style. The poetry of Isolda Santiago (b. 1960), Yolanda Castaño (b. 1977), and Olga Novo (b. 1975) ranges from sensorial experience and preciosity to primeval, telluric, tribal eroticism. Antón R. Reixa (b. 1957) weaves colloquial, popular discourse with advertising; Xavier Santiago is drawn to the audiovisual experience of urban environments. Rafa Vilar (b. 1968) is known for his minimalist style; Martín Vega (b. 1975) for his meticulously refined, cosmopolitan style; and Xosé M. Millán Otero (b. 1964) for his seminal conception of the word. Rodríguez and Seara's anthol. (1997) draws together many of these poets who accompany a selection of their work with insightful, critical self-analysis. Still relevant is the creative voice of López Casanova, who, in *Liturgia do corpo* (Liturgy of the Body, 1983), presents a lyrical anthem of self-immersion in response to the inevitability of death. In the epic work of Manuel María (1929–2004), the voice revels before a humanized nature; and the vigor of Méndez Ferrín, in *Estirpe* (Origin, 1994), restructures origins, ethnicity, hist., and land.

Among the most critically acclaimed voices is that of Rodríguez Baxeiras, who received the leading prize for Galician poetry for *Beira norte* (North Border, 1997), a symbolic journey homeward, toward the interiority of the lyrical voice. The books of Fonte, cofounder of the poetic collective Cravo Fondo and an active participant in *Dorna*, fuse personal, intimate experience with plurality and acceptance. Miguel Anxo Fernán Vello's (b. 1958) celebratory, erotic discourse, and Pilar Pallarés's (b. 1957) life-affirming poetics have been equally successful among critics. Manuel Forcadela's (b. 1958) works pay homage and parody the early works of Román Raña (b. 1960), Paulino Vázquez (b. 1962), and Anxo Quintela (b. 1960). Rodríguez Fer combines critical essay writing with poetic, phonic, graphic, and above all, erotic experimentation. Among the poets exiled in Argentina who contributed significantly to Galician lyric are Varela, Eduardo Blanco Amor (1897–1979), and Luis Seoane (1910–79).

Several collectives have given impetus to poetic production: Brais Pinto (1950s), Rompente, Alén, and De amor e desamor. Galician jours.—*Nordés, Cen Augas, Dorna, Escrita, A nosa terra, Nó*—have provided space for both the established writers and the new. Luciano Rodríguez's anthol. *Desde a palabra, doce voces* (From the Word, Twelve Voices, 1985) gathers the most representative poetry of the early 1980s. Losada's (1990) and López-Barxas and Molina's (1991) anthols. assemble, with a few notable exceptions, a similar selection.

*See* BASQUE COUNTRY, POETRY OF THE; CATALONIA, POETRY OF; PORTUGAL, POETRY OF; SPAIN, POETRY OF.

■ **Anthologies**: *Cancionero popular gallego* (1886), ed. J. Pérez Ballesteros, 2 v. (1942); Alfonso X, el Sábio, *Cantigas de amor, de escarño e de louvor*, ed. R. Carballo Calero and C. García Rodríguez (1983); *Antología de la poesía gallega contemporánea*, ed. C. A. Molina (1984); *Desde a palabra, doce voces*, ed. L. Rodríguez Gómez (1986); *Festa da palabra*, ed. K. N. March (1989)—contemp. Galician women poets; *Poesía gallega de hoy. Antología*, ed. B. Losada (1990); R. de Castro, *Poems*, ed. and trans. A. M. Aldaz et al. (1991); *Fin de un milenio. Antología de la poesía gallega íntima*, ed. F. López-Barxas and C. A. Molina (1991); *Para sair do século. Nova proposta poética*, ed. L. Rodríguez Góez and T. Seara (1997).

■ **Criticism and History**: A. Cruceiro Freijomil, *Diccionario bio-bibliográfico de escritores*, 3 v. (1951–54); J. L. Varela, *Poesía y restauración cultural de Galicia en el siglo XIX* (1958); R. Carballo Calero, *Historia da literatura galega contemporánea* (1981); L. Méndez Ferrín, *De Pondal a Novoneyra* (1984); C. Davis, *Rosalía de Castro e o seu tempo* (1987); C. Rodríguez Fer, *A literatura galega durante a guerra civil (1936–39)* (1994); A. Tarrío, *Literatura galega* (1994); R. Raña, *A noite nas* *palabras* (1996); D. Vilavedra, *Historia da literatura galega* (1999).

A. Carreño

**GALLIAMB(US).** In *classical prosody, a catalectic *ionic *tetrameter, named after the Galli, the eunuch priests of the Gr. goddess Cybele. There is an anonymous Gr. fragment, sometimes attributed to Callimachus (from *incerti auctoris* 761 [Pfeiffer]) cited by the ancient metrist Hephaestion as an example of this meter, which, if true, would suggest it was developed by the Alexandrian poets; but the most famous example is Lat., Catullus 63. This takes the form of an anaclastic ionic *dimeter ( ◡ ◡ – ◡ – ◡ – – ) + a catalectic ionic dimeter ( ◡ ◡ – – ◡ ◡ – ) with or without *anaclasis, and with numerous resolutions. In the second dimeter, the second long syllable (longum) is almost always resolved. The first verse of the poem is typical: *super alta vectus Attis / celeri rate maria* ( ◡ ◡ – ◡ – ◡ – – | ◡ ◡ – ◡ ◡ ◡ – ). In the 19th c., both Tennyson ("Boadicea") and George Meredith ("Phaethon") experimented with accentual imitations of galliambus.

■ G. Allen, "On the Galliambic Metre," *The Attis of Caius Valerius Catullus Translated into Eng. Verse* (1892); Wilamowitz; R. Pfeiffer, *Callimachus* (1985); Halporn et al.; West.

J. W. Halporn

**GAUCHO POETRY.** Taken literally, *gaucho poetry* is the name for poetic compositions, anonymous or otherwise, that deal with the life and adventures of the Argentinean cowboy.

Popular poetry, which had its origin in the Sp. *romancero*, flourished at the end of the 18th c. and reached its peak by the middle of the 19th c. In Uruguay and Argentina, learned writers invaded the field of folk poetry and produced a number of literary imitations of the style of early *payadores* or singers of popular poetry. The first of these poets was the Uruguayan Bartolomé Hidalgo (1788–1822), whose famous dialogues expressed the sentiments of the gaucho in regard to the war of independence against Spain. He was followed by the Argentine Hilario Ascasubi (1807–75), who played an active role in the struggle against the dictatorship of Juan Manuel de Rosas and who published a number of gaucho ballads dealing with the siege of Montevideo (*Paulino Lucero o los gauchos del Rio de la Plata*, 1839–51). *Santos Vega, o los mellizos de la Flor* (1851, 1872), his greatest achievement in this type of poetry, tells the story of two brothers, one of whom becomes an outlaw. The main value of the poem resides in its colorful and accurate description of country and city life in mid-19th-c. Argentina. Estanislao del Campo (1834–80) followed the example of these writers and employed pure gaucho dialect in his *Fausto* (1866), a parody of Charles Gounod's opera.

The greatest of the gaucho poems is *Martín Fierro* (1872, 1879) by the Argentine José Hernández (1834–86). A well-educated man and a writer deeply conscious of his social mission, Hernández set out to prove the moral fortitude of the gaucho and his right to gain a respectable position in the life of his country. Dealing with the problem of civilization and barbarism in the Am. continent, he criticized the defenders of "civilization" for their irresponsibility in ruthlessly destroying the trads. of native populations, esp. the nomad gauchos. Encouraged by the success of his poem, Hernández wrote a second part (1879) in which he told of Martín Fierro's return from the Indian country where he had sought refuge from persecution by the city authorities. The tone of this continuation is no longer rebellious but moderately didactic. Hernández's poem owes its immense popularity in Sp. America to its virile exaltation of freedom and courage, to its forceful display of nationalism, popular wisdom, and pride in the virtues of a people who hold fast to the trad. of their homeland. Most critics consider *Martín Fierro* the highest achievement of popular poetry in Sp. America.

See COWBOY POETRY; SPANISH AMERICA, POETRY OF.

■ *The Gaucho Martín Fierro*, trans. W. Owen (1935); M. W. Nichols, *The Gaucho: Cattle Hunter, Cavalryman, Ideal of Romance* (1942); *Poesía gauchesca*, ed. J. L. Borges and A. Bioy Casares, 2 v. (1955); *Antología de la poesía gauchesca*, ed. H. J. Becco (1972); F. E. Tiscornia, *Poetas gauchescos* (1974); H. J. Becco, *Trayectoria de la poesía gauchesca* (1977); J. B. Rivera, *Poesía gauchesca* (1977); R. A. Borello, "El *Martín Fierro* y la poesía gauchesca," *Boletín de la Academia Argentina de Letras* 54 (1989); J. Ludmer, "The Gaucho Genre," *Cambridge History of Latin American Literature*, ed. R. González Echevarría and E. Pupo-Walker, v. 1 (1996); R. A. Borello, *La poesía gauchesca: Una perspectiva diferente* (2000); W. Katra, "The Poetic Tradition of the Gaucho," *Cowboy Poets and Cowboy Poetry*, ed. D. Stanley and E. Thatcher (2000); G. Kirkpatrick, "Romantic Poetry in Latin America," *Romantic Poetry*, ed. A. Esterhammer (2002).

F. Alegría

**GAY POETRY.** Generically, the term *gay poetry* designates poems with homosexual themes written by gay male poets or male poets who had or have sex with other men. Defining the term, however, also necessitates addressing the practice of such designation, rather than focusing exclusively on the designated topics or content. As Woods (1998) notes, a male homosexual literary trad. is actually fabricated by the construction of politically and socially validating lists of forebears and relevant texts. In this sense, readers often "claim" gay poets, regardless of the writers' own identifications, the matter of particular poems, or even their oeuvre as a whole. Characteristics marking a poet or poem as within a gay poetry trad. may include an often (but not always) positive and explicit representation of same-sex encounters, affairs, or relationships; narrators' or other figures' identification as *gay* or *homosexual* (or historical and cultural variants of same-sex sexual and emotional relations, incl. *uranian, invert, sodomite, catamite, pederast*); implicit or heavily codified representations of gays and homosexuals or same-sex attraction, practices, or relationships; or public claims, common knowledge, or newly discovered evidence of the author's homosexual self-identification or same-sex sexual practices.

Claiming an author or text to construct a trad. of gay poetry does not occur without ideological motivations. As the Am. poet Robert Duncan wrote in his pioneering essay "The Homosexual in Society" (1944), when such designations were made through World War II, it was either to "contend" apologetically that "such an undeniable homosexual as Hart Crane . . . was great despite his 'perversion'" or to promote "the growth of a cult of homosexual superiority to heterosexual values." Dissatisfied with both rationales for designating a text or author as gay, Duncan discusses his alternate vision for gay poetry as a "battlefront toward human freedom." In the wake of devels. in Western gay and lesbian politics since the early 1970s, the apologetic reference to gay poetry has largely fallen by the wayside. Instead, usage of the term negotiates a cultural humanism similar to what Duncan favored, as well as the politically driven promotion of lit. that represents a sexual minority's identity-based experiences or interests. Drawn from various historical periods and geopolitical locations, examples of gay poetry are often thought by their readers and critics to encourage individuals' and a minority group's consciousness raising by promoting the recognition of the social and cultural validity of their sexual identities and same-sex physical and emotional relationships. While such a politically charged process of culture and trad. building still continues, since the late 1980s economic motives have tended to inflect or overrun both the cultural humanism and political motivation underlying the category of gay poetry, as the publishing industry increasingly uses the term to designate a marketing category.

If readers claim as a gay poet a writer who is identifiable through some other social or cultural rubric (such as nationality, religious culture, race, or ethnicity), his work may be read as intersectional (e.g., as representative of gay Af. Am. poetry, gay Chinese poetry, gay Eastern Eur. Jewish poetry, gay Turkish Muslim poetry, gay Cuban Catholic poetry). Yet second- or third-identity categories often modify sexual identity as a primary term of identification. Thus, the rubric *gay* risks being grossly misapplied to various cultures and periods that may have recognized same-sex sexual experience as defining only a physical act, rather than a social or even ontological category of person. Often such poetry is read through a Western lens, more specifically through the lens of a white, middle-class, Am. sexual minority politics that has tended to ignore differences between local articulations of "gay" identities and same-sex practices. Critics and anthologizers have often overlooked variances—such as pederasty or a cultural understanding of "homosexuality" as sexual passivity—so as to construct a literary heritage bearing positive representations of male-male same-sex love in all its articulations. Diverse global authors, texts, and poetic figures have been misappropriated in this fashion—incl. the ancient Mesopotamian *Epic of Gilgamesh*, Ovid's representation of Orpheus in the *Meta-*

*morphoses*, the 1st-c. BCE Roman poet Catullus, the 8th-c. Persian poet Abū Nuwās, 10th-through 13th-c. Japanese samurai poetry, 13th-c. Turkish *divan poetry by Jalāl al-Dīn Rūmī and others, sonnets by Ren. luminaries Michelangelo Buonarroti and Shakespeare, and the 17th-c. devotional lyrics of Thomas Traherne and John Donne.

Building a gay trad. runs less risk of anachronism if claimants begin with the 19th c., when, according to philosopher Michel Foucault, homosexuality was "born" as an identifiable social category in the West. The juridical and medical emphasis of that categorization tended to read homosexuality as an antisocial "perversion." Some instances of 19th-c. gay poetry reinforce that understanding, such as the stormy four-year affair in the early 1870s between Fr. symbolist poets Arthur Rimbaud and Paul Verlaine. Begun with Rimbaud's self-introduction to Verlaine through a letter enclosing the renowned "Le Bateau ivre" (The Drunken Boat), their relationship, upon its ending, spawned Rimbaud's bitter prose-poem *Une saison en enfer* (*A Season in Hell*): "For I can say victory is won: the gnashing of teeth, the hissings of fire, the pestilential sighs are abating. All the noisome memories are abating." Yet not all 19th-c. gay poetry was the product of tempestuous personal passions. Indeed, later readers have claimed some of the period's gay poetry as models for nationalist and humanist political visions. The Am. Walt Whitman's long-term project *Leaves of Grass* (1855–92) joins a vision for building a national lit. and for universal betterment with a celebration of the "manly attachment" of "camerados." As he exclaims in "Scented Herbage of My Breast," "I will sound myself and comrades only, I will never again utter a call only their call, / I will raise with it immortal reverberations through the States, / I will give an example to lovers to take permanent shape and will through the States." A similarly political valence can be found in the Ir. writer Oscar Wilde's "Ballad of Reading Gaol," produced during his imprisonment in 1895 for "gross indecency." Though the poem does not comment on the homosexual nature of his offense, it is a benchmark of social protest poetry that exemplifies gay poetry's current of cultural humanism in its inveighing against the Brit. justice system: "every prison that men build / Is built with bricks of shame."

Most 20th- and 21st-c. poets claimed for a gay male poetic trad. are from the U.S. or Western Europe, although many Asians and Latin Americans are claimed as well. However, a number of early 20th-c. writers included in the gay poetic trad. wrote about erotic matters in ambiguous ways so as not to reveal them as same-sex affairs or were reticent about their own homosexuality or bisexuality until later in their careers, if at all. In the cases of writers like Jorge Luis Borges (Argentina), Stefan Georg (Germany), Marsden Hartley (U.S.), and Stephen Spender (U.K.), it is not clear why these figures may have been reticent about homosexuality in their work. Many readers and critics tend to personalize the decision of such writers to keep themselves or their poetry "in the closet" yet claim them as gay poets anyway. Based on evidence of similarly reticent gay poets, it can be noted that cultural pressures often are responsible for a reluctance to identify oneself as homosexual or to draw attention to ambiguated or even explicit same-sex content in one's work. Certainly, this is true of writers who recognized their poetry as outgrowths of religious (often Roman Catholic) cultures, such as Vicente Aleixandre (Spain), W.H. Auden (U.K.-U.S.), Gastón Baquero (Cuba-Spain), Eugénio de Andrade (Portugal), and José Lezama Lima (Cuba). Political pressures also led to gay closeting or reticence. Sometimes those pressures originated in the state, as in the threat of blacklisting that faced Am. writers such as James Merrill (U.S.) during the postwar McCarthy era. Even in leftist states, however, governments persecuted homosexuals and viewed same-sex love as incompatible with radicalism. Thus, many gay poets—such as Xavier Villaurrutia (Mexico) and Nicolás Guillén (Cuba)—remained relatively silent about homosexuality in and out of their work. At other times, political pressures combined with cultural ones, as in the desire to avoid charges of effeminacy so as to promote culturally, racially, or nationally revitalizing projects. Such a combination is witnessed in Latin Am. avant-gardists such as Mário de Andrade (Brazil) or *Harlem Renaissance poets such as Countee Cullen (U.S.), Claude McKay (Jamaica-U.S.), and Langston Hughes (U.S.). Sometimes poets' contemp. audiences simply were unable to recognize attempts at homosexual expression. The Af. Am. poet Richard Bruce Nugent, e.g., notes that his "Shadows" (1925) was well received as a race poem, but in fact he had set out to express "the lonesomeness" of being "otherwise stigmatized" as a homosexual black man.

Of course, from World War I into the early 1950s, some writers—incl. Mikhail Kuzmin (Russia), C. P. Cavafy (Greece), Fernando Pessoa (Portugal), Luis Cernuda (Spain), Paul Goodman (U.S.), Robert Duncan (U.S.), Salvador Novo (Mexico), and Robin Blaser (U.S.-Canada)—explicitly and positively represented same-sex eroticism or wrote about social struggles attending their homosexuality. Others, such as Charles Henri Ford (U.S.) and Parker Tyler (U.S.), exhibited a camp sensibility, parodying gender and sexual norms for self-identified homosexual audiences. Several U.S. homosexual poets, most notably Hart Crane, continued a visionary Whitmanic trad. during the interwar period. Whitman has greatly influenced homosexual poetry internationally as well. He is the subject of the Andalusian poet Federico García Lorca's "Oda a Walt Whitman" (1930), a critique of Americanization and commercialization and its negative effects on homosexual identity. Indeed, the poem proved a major influence for Duncan's aforementioned essay "The Homosexual in Society," since, in the ode, García Lorca attacks self-important, campy attitudes as the product of capitalist corruption and an undermining of gay poetry's potential for a humanist vision. García Lorca's engagement with Whitman was translated by Duncan's friend Jack Spicer in his pivotal book *After Lorca* (1955) and is invoked in several of his friend Stephen Jonas's odes and

*Orgasms* series. The obscenity trial concerning Allen Ginsberg's Whitmanic epic *Howl* (1956) revolutionized gay poetry, supplying a benchmark whereby the poetic expression of male same-sex desire was legally recognized as freedom of speech and thus subject to protection by the First Amendment in the U.S. Not all postwar gay poetry was visionary or Whitmanic. Some of the period's most impressive gay poetry insists on a colloquial voice and a direct poetic realism. *New York school poet Frank O'Hara's concentration on the quotidian and the poetic detailing of his everyday experience led to the incorporation of much homosexuality in his work, and he even uses slang for a homosexual threesome ("Lucky Pierre style") to describe his poetics in his tongue-in-cheek "Personism: A Manifesto" (1959, pub. 1969). John Wieners adopted a similarly frank attitude, openly writing of his own homosexuality in his autobiographical lyrics, incl. "Two Years Later" (ca. 1964), "How to Cope with This?" (1968), and "Queer" (1968).

Much gay poetry became overtly politicized in the wake of the 1969 Stonewall riots in New York City and the subsequent establishment of the Gay Liberation Front (GLF), the first radical, rather than assimilationist, gay and lesbian political organization. In the U.S. during this period, gay poetry was characterized by both sexual playfulness and political consciousness. It gave license to straight poets such as Gerard Malanga (also remembered as Andy Warhol's assistant) to explore bisexual experiences and themes in their writing. For the more politically minded, the publishing of poetry was esp. important, as is seen the gay poetry journal *Mouth of the Dragon*, as well as in the lists of poet Paul Mariah's ManRoot Press and Winston Leyland's Gay Sunshine Press. Gay Liberation media also often featured short lyrics; even if the literary quality was poor, the poetry still valuably rendered same-sex desire visible and expressed that desire as the core of a coalitional antisexist, antiracist, anticapitalist, and antiwar politics. For instance, the first issue of the GLF's newspaper *Come Out!* (Nov. 1969) includes a poem by Michael F. Boyle lamenting his struggle with the closet ("I am trapped in Society's Web of Rules / And obey them all, in abject fear"). From the same issue, Ron Ballard's short quatrain "Voice from the Closet" metaphorically comments on how, until gay liberation, anonymous public sex in "tearooms" (public restrooms or water closets) had been a kind of "closet" that let homosexuals keep their sexuality secret and thus reinforced racist and imperialist hierarchies by not challenging the core issue of sexism (homophobic and patriarchal ideologies). Incorporating poetry into New Left and Gay Liberation politics happens in a more literary manner in Ginsberg's "Graffiti 12th Cubicle Men's Room Syracuse Airport" (1969), a found poem that pointedly links repressive sexual attitudes to wartime culture by mixing messages about same-sex desire ("I want a blow job Who do I call") with commentary about Vietnam ("All power to the Viet Cong!"). Many gay literary poets writing at this time, such as James Broughton, were newly out as homosexuals. Others already had been publicly homosexual and writing explicitly gay content but discovered new liberties in a political climate emphasizing gay visibility and pride. Sometimes this resulted in a poetry that could seem to be a frivolous celebration of sex, yet its political significance rested precisely in rendering gay sex visible. For a limited press run, the *Black Mountain poet and founder of Jargon Society press Jonathan Williams wrote his *gAy BCs* (1976). In this provocative poetic primer, each letter attributes gay sexual practices to men bearing common Eng. names ("ARTHURS are a-thirst!" and "CHUCKS, of course, suck"); the poem is followed by the New York school artist and writer Joe Brainard's sexually explicit illustrations of those acts. International poets exhibiting a similar gay sensibility have been appropriated for a gay poetry trad. through trans. Such figures include the Japanese poet Mutsuo Takahashi's *The Penisist* (1975). The former *Beat poet Harold Norse celebrates gay male cruising and anonymous sex ("Let Me Love All at Stillman's Gym," 1969) yet also inveighs against homophobic violence, police entrapment, and legal prejudice ("The Queer-Killers," 1970). After illness with testicular cancer, the gay Buddhist monk and performance poet John Giorno's *Cancer in My Left Ball* (1973) matched a celebration of homosexuality with politicized meditations on the frailty of all bodies. Antler's long poem "Factory" (1970) connects his gay sexuality and continuance of Whitman and García Lorca's visionary poetics to working-class consciousness and anticapitalist protest.

As liberal gay politics have become increasingly "mainstreamed" (i.e., intertwined with capitalism and popular cultural representations), the term *gay poetry* now functions as a market category used in publishing and distribution, as well as in determining major international and national literary awards. This trend began in the 1980s, growing during the 1990s and into the 21st c. Understandably, then, the category *gay poetry* increasingly has more significance for readers, publishers, and consumers than it does for many writers. Some prominent Am. writers that lived through the heyday of gay liberation, incl. John Ashbery and Robert Duncan, were reluctant to identify themselves as "gay poets," even though they were openly homosexual. In order to advance the broader concerns of their work, rather than misreadings driven by identity politics, some have erased historical references to gay liberation, as in Ronald Johnson's revision and exclusion of poems from his *Ark: The Foundations* (1980). Still, many contemp. poets have identified or continue to identify their work as "gay" or "queer" or, in the least, do not resist such labels (Francisco X. Alarcón, Kazim Ali, Jeffrey Beam, Frank Bidart, Justin Chin, Henri Cole, CA Conrad, Dennis Cooper, Alfred Corn, Edward Field, Richard Howard, Kevin Killian, Wayne Koestenbaum, Timothy Liu, Jaime Manrique, D. A. Powell, Rodrigo Reyes, Reginald Shepherd, Aaron Shurin, and Emanuel Xavier). Many have consciously used poetry to address the impact of HIV/AIDs on gay populations (Rafael Campo, Mark Doty, Thom

Gunn, Essex Hemphill, Assoto Saint). Worldwide, other recent poets have used gay themes to intervene in homophobic perception and institutional oppression of male sexual minorities, incl. Reinaldo Arenas (Cuba), Edwin Morgan (Scotland), Danton Remoto (Philippines), Severo Sarduy (Cuba-France), and Cyril Wong (Singapore). Others, such as Agha Shahid Ali (India), are more cautious about poetically disclosing their orientation.

■ **Anthologies**: *The Male Muse*, ed. I. Young (1973); *Angels of the Lyre*, ed. W. Leyland (1975); *Orgasms of Light*, ed. W. Leyland (1977); *The Penguin Book of Homosexual Verse*, ed. S. Coote (1983); *The Son of the Male Muse*, ed. I. Young (1983); *Gay & Lesbian Poetry in Our Time*, ed. C. Morse and J. Larkin (1988); *The Road before Us*, ed. A. Saint (1991)—black poets; *Gay and Lesbian Poetry*, ed. J. J. Wilhelm (1995); *The Columbia Anthology of Gay Literature*, ed. B.R.S. Fone (1998); *A Day for a Lay*, ed. G. G. Dillard (1999); *Word of Mouth*, ed. T. Liu (2000); *The World in Us*, ed. M. Lassell and E. Georgiou (2000); *Masquerade*, ed. J. Elledge (2004); *Seminal*, ed. J. Barton and B. Nickerson (2007)—Canadian poets; *Mariposas*, ed. E. Xavier (2008)—Latino poets; *Our Caribbean*, ed. T. Glave (2008).

■ **Criticism and History**: R. Duncan, "The Homosexual in Society" (1944), *A Selected Prose*, ed. R. J. Bertholf (1985); G. Woods, *Articulate Flesh* (1987); M. Foucault, *The History of Sexuality, Vol. 1: An Introduction*, trans. R. Hurley (1990); T. Yingling, *Hart Crane and the Homosexual Text* (1990); M. Maslan, *Whitman Possessed* (1991); J. Goldberg, *Sodometries: Renaissance Texts, Modern Sexualities* (1992); M. Moon, *Disseminating Whitman* (1993); S. Jones, *Gay and Lesbian Literature since World War II* (1998); R. K. Martin, *The Homosexual Tradition in American Poetry*, rev. ed. (1998); R. Rambuss, *Closet Devotions* (1998); G. Woods, *A History of Gay Literature* (1998); S. Bruhm, *Reflecting Narcissus* (2000); E. Bejel, *Gay Cuban Nation* (2001); J. E. Vincent, *Queer Lyrics* (2002); M. Cole, *The Other Orpheus* (2003); D. R. Jarraway, *Going the Distance: Dissident Subjectivity in Modernist American Literature* (2003); A.B.C. Schwartz, *Gay Voices of the Harlem Renaissance* (2003); B. Saunders, *Desiring Donne* (2007); M. Menon, *Unhistorical Shakespeare* (2008); M. D. Snidecker, *Queer Optimism* (2008); E. Keenaghan, *Queering Cold War Poetry* (2009)—Cuba and the U.S.

E. KEENAGHAN

**GENDER AND POETRY.** Gender norms and expectations are inevitably registered in poetic texts, whether or not the poet is consciously addressing them. Because gender is a salient feature of human experience, perceptions of gender necessarily affect representations of speech, social interaction, and human reflection. A poet's gender helps shape his or her perspective, just as a reader's gender conditions her or his responses to a poem. Poetry's links to gender become particularly apparent when poetic subgenres acquire gendered associations or when gender conventions become a self-conscious concern of poets and critics. Like gender norms themselves, the particular issues involving gender that are explored in poetic works vary across time and from culture to culture.

Because the writing of poetry was limited predominantly to educated men for many centuries, early poetry reflects largely masculine pursuits and perspectives. This is evident, for instance, in religious writing such as the Upanishads and much of the Heb. Bible; in OE, Gr., or Roman *epics; in the *pastoral poetry of Theocritus or Virgil, the *odes of Pindar and Horace, and the love poems of Ovid. Nonetheless, some early poetry celebrates women's strengths. Nordic saga often presents women as economically and emotionally independent, and in some Muslim epic trads., female characters are strong-minded, intelligent, and politically independent, as manifested in the woman-warrior motif in the Turkic *Dede Korkut*, the Persian *Shahnāmeh*, and the Ar. *Sîrat al-amîra Dhât al-Himma*. In the Western written canon, Sappho's widely celebrated *lyric poems provide an exception to the norm of male authorship, giving rise to an association of the lyric genre with the feminine. Many Japanese women also wrote poetry between the 7th and 10th cs., and there are female oral trads. in many cultures. Much of this earlier lit. reinforces established cultural norms for masculine and feminine behavior.

Gender becomes a more self-conscious focus of poetry as major cultural shifts call established gender norms into question. Such changes tend to occur as cultures develop attitudes and structures supporting women's education and participation in the public sphere, which in turn lead to greater numbers of women writing and reading poetry. Cultural and philosophical paradigm shifts also directly affect gender ideologies, which in turn affect who writes poetry, who reads it, the assumptions underlying its reception, and its content. Such shifts take place during the Ren., with the turn to the use of vernacular langs.; in the early romantic period, with the devel. of a gendered aesthetics; and in the modernist era, as revolutions in technology and in legal, educational, and economic systems lead to greater equality between women and men.

Early epic and religious verse depend in fundamental ways on gender hierarchy. Epic poetry was unabashedly masculine in its narrative, typically interweaving concerns with war, kingship, national politics, men's dangerous journeys through unknown realms, and male sexual prowess—as in Homer's *Iliad* and *Odyssey*, Virgil's *Aeneid*, the *Nibelungenlied*, and the *Chanson de Roland*. Women appear in such verse primarily as love objects or as obstacles to be conquered—e.g., as seductresses who stand in the way of masculine ideals of heroism and loyalty. Sacred writing assigns gender to figures of the divine in the verse of Hindu, Judeo-Christian, Buddhist, and other trads. In these major world religions, the central deity is male, although other powerful divine figures may be female. Aside from sacred texts, religious verse in the Christian trad. glorifies a masculine "God the Father" and often invokes a warrior-Christ, as in the mystic "Dream of the Rood." Dante's *Divine Comedy* is representative in

imagining the individual's journey to God as a simultaneous journey to love, embodied for Dante in the inspirational and pure Beatrice. This narrative implicitly identifies the Christian as heterosexual male and the woman as his route to spiritual advancement. The med. *courtly love trad. secularizes this vision of ennobling love as manifest between a knight and a nobleman's wife. An alternative pattern of Christian verse represents the poetic speaker as a subservient "bride" or lover of Christ or as the ministrant of the Church, which is itself the "bride." Such gendering implies radically different stances when articulated by a man such as George Herbert in England or a woman such as Sor Juana Inés de la Cruz in Mexico, both writing in the 17th c.

John Milton's epic *Paradise Lost* combines gendered elements of the national and martial epic trad. with those of religious narrative in writing of an authoritative masculine God, battling armies of angels, and a hierarchically gendered Adam and Eve. Milton's powerful representation of this already well-established gendered narrative influenced generations of religious and secular poets. Female resistance to this view was already apparent 60 years earlier, when Aemilia Lanyer wrote "Eve's Apologie in Defense of Women" as part of her *Salve Deus Rex Judaeorum*, a poem addressed specifically to women; while accepting the traditional view of Eve's responsibility for the Fall, Lanyer argued that women should not consequently be vilified. Later poets offer bolder revisions. Two hundred years later in the U.S., a young Emily Dickinson calls herself Eve and writes several poems redefining paradise or "Eden"; more radically, at the turn of the 20th c. Jewish Ger. Else Lasker-Schüler makes Eve a model of self-creation and the original producer of lang. Notions of Eve's responsibility for the fall into sin, caused by women's purported susceptibility to evil and powers of seduction, have nonetheless continued to influence poetic representations of women up to the present, as notions of Adam as the first created human favored by God with the gift of naming have influenced representations of men.

While epic verse remained the almost exclusive domain of male poets until the 20th c., in the med. period women participated in lyric trads. in Europe, Asia, and in the Arab world, though the number of women with the education and economic privilege that would allow them to write poetry was small. In Europe, convents were the primary site of education for women, and many female poets—like Hrotsvit, a 10th-c. Ger. poet and playwright; and Hildegard of Bingen, a 12th-c. Ger. philosopher, composer, and poet—belonged to abbeys. In contrast, Chinese Li Qingzhao grew up in a family of officials and scholars, and her poetry was already well known before her marriage in 1101, although only around 100 of her poems have survived. In Arab lands, from the 6th c. CE female poets gathered in literary salons hosted by women to perform their poetry, and poetry by women about love, liberation, and spiritual matters flourished in Muslim Spain and Portugal from the 10th through the 12th cs.

Gender difference became a distinct focus of poetry

in the late med. *querelle des femmes*, a Eur. debate conducted largely among men about which sex is superior. This debate influenced numerous early mod. writers who praise women's intelligence and accomplishments and protest the social, legal, and economic restrictions imposed on them. Following this debate, Christine de Pizan's arguments against the degradation of women at the beginning of the 15th c. responded to misogynist doctrines in Jean de Meun's popular poem *Roman de la Rose*. Arguments about the capacities and nature of women also play out in such Ren. works as Ludovico Ariosto's epic *Orlando furioso*, retelling the Charlemagne legends in ways that suggest the physical, moral, and intellectual equality of women; or in Edmund Spenser's late 16th-c. epic *The Faerie Queene*, an allegorical celebration of Queen Elizabeth's monarchy. Shakespeare frequently undercuts gender conventions, as he does playfully in his verse dramas *As You Like It* and *Twelfth Night*, where male actors play women successfully impersonating men, thereby highlighting the artificiality of gender performance for both sexes.

While debates about gender are more readily inscribed in narrative, philosophical, and dramatic verse, a single perspective on gender is characteristic of the lyric because of its brevity and personal voice. The Ren. *sonnet sequence typifies the masculine perspective dominant in Western lyric trads. until at least the late 19th c. In this trad., the woman is sometimes demonized, as in Shakespeare's "Dark Lady" sonnets, but more often idealized in an objectifying way. The beloved is the usually distant object of male desire; seen through the male gaze, her beauty is celebrated—often through the *blason* or listing of the woman's body parts, at the expense of her character and agency. Some of Shakespeare's early sonnets are addressed to a male beloved, providing precedent for explicitly homosexual love sonnets by such 20th-c. poets as James Merrill. Women have written sonnets almost since the form was invented: It. courtesan Veronica Franco wrote two sonnets, and her *terza rima poems challenged idealizing clichés of the Petrarchan sonnet trad. in the mid-16th c.; the first amatory sonnet sequence by an Eng. woman was Mary Wroth's *Pamphilia to Amphilanthus* in 1621. Perhaps similarly inspired by Shakespeare, women have also written love sonnets to those of their own sex—e.g., Gabriela Mistral in her 1914 *Sonetos de la Muerte*—and by the late 20th c. poets are writing explicitly lesbian love sonnet sequences, such as Marilyn Hacker in *Love, Death, and the Changing of the Seasons* and Adrienne Rich in her modified sonnet sequence "Twenty-One Love Poems."

Lit. of the med. and early mod. period articulated gender and sexual expectations largely through the depiction of character and relationships; at the beginning of the romantic era, Ger. philosophers and poets constructed a powerfully influential aesthetic distinguishing the beautiful and the *sublime in gendered terms: the beautiful was associated with the small, contained, delicate, and "feminine"; the sublime with grandeur, natural chaos, and unboundedness—the "masculine"

(although, contrarily, women were also identified with nature, including both its nurturing and terrifying aspects). For Immanuel Kant, women were incapable of appreciating the sublime because of their limited moral capacity and weaker constitutions, while they were conceived as the embodiment of the beautiful. J. W. Goethe concludes *Faust* with reference to "das ewig Weibliche," the "eternal feminine," as drawing the striving male intellectual and artist upward to heaven, a formulation extending earlier representations of woman as the vehicle for man's access to the divine and the depths of his own soul. In Ireland Edmund Burke, in Scotland David Hume, and in the U.S., E. A. Poe articulate varieties of this assoc.—Poe famously remarking that the proper object of a poem is beauty and that the death of a beautiful woman is "unquestionably the most poetical topic in the world."

Romantic philosophical debate helped shape the gender dynamics within continental Eur., Brit., and Am. poetry of the 19th c. In the poems of William Wordsworth, P. B. Shelley, William Blake, and other Brit. romantics, nature is often a feminized other, what the (male) poet is not, typically figured as a healing force and sometimes as a terrifying one. The assoc. of women or the feminine with nature, which lacked the powers of speech, was among the cultural factors that silenced aspiring female poets in Britain or pushed potential poets toward nonpoetic genres. Am. transcendentalism also displaced women from poetic agency, in this case by conceiving poetic creativity as largely independent of all feminine presence, even as inspiration. On both sides of the Atlantic, the discourse on creativity was complex; even individual poets altered their constructions of nature and representations of the feminine, and of women, during their lifetimes. Typically, however, during this era, the poet was figured as male. Walt Whitman, who perhaps more than any other male poet attempted to acknowledge female equality and agency ("I am the poet of the woman the same as the man"), sexualizes this masculinist aesthetic in celebrating every aspect of his explicitly male body not only as part of nature but as key to his concept of the Am. "self."

Within a few decades of the earliest romantic poetry, female poets on both sides of the Atlantic were protesting aesthetic theory's implied abrogation of women's creative power. Felicia Hemans, Lydia Sigourney, Frances Harper, and others resisted romantic associations of women with passive nature in their assertion of women's subjectivity and agency, often with direct implications for public policy—as in Sigourney's poetry on Native Ams. and Harper's on slave women. E. B. Browning's long narrative poem *Aurora Leigh* constructs an ambitious female poet as its protagonist, thereby also revising the epic trad. as appropriately focused on the life of a woman. Emily Dickinson places the power and nuance of a philosophized and felt subjectivity at the heart of her experimental poetry. In the 1880s, Anglo-Jewish Amy Levy revises the dramatic monologue developed by Robert Browning so that it is spoken by a woman—e.g., "Xantippe," in the voice of Socrates' wife. As movements for greater rights for women gathered strength internationally, an increasing number of poets constructed unconventional female subjects to embody the century's social changes. Henry Wharton's 1885 trans. of Sappho also gave increased impetus to women's claims to the lyric "I" and encouraged the exploration of same-sex eroticism. At the turn of the 20th c., Nicaraguan poet Rubén Darío celebrated an almost hermaphroditic interchange of masculine and feminine principles (see MODERNISMO).

While 19th-c. thinkers typically gendered genius, the sublime, and hence the poet-as-creator as masculine, poetry itself came to be associated increasingly with the feminine and feminized *sentimentality, as did the arts of painting, dance, music, and theater. This identification occurred in part because of the growing popular and economic success of female writers, but it was also linked to larger patterns of gender anxiety, as industrialization and urbanization removed increasing numbers of men from professions requiring physical strength or associated with stereotypical masculinity. By the turn of the 20th c., cultural movements throughout the industrialized world manifested anxiety about changing gender norms through a discourse of aggressive masculinity—in religious, political, and professional as well as artistic spheres. The most authoritative discourse in the West had become that of technology and science, and as part of the devel. of modernism, male poets increasingly theorized the principles of their verse in the lang. of mathematics, science, impersonality, and abstraction in opposition to the increasingly feminized concept of sentiment. The early 20th-c. devel. of a scientific discourse of sexuality—particularly of a "third sex" or homosexuality—by writers such as Otto Weininger, Sigmund Freud, and Havelock Ellis encouraged some poets to explore sexual desire and pleasure with increasing frankness, while others perceived only greater anxiety and confusion about shifting gender norms and conceptions of the sexual. Representative of the period's (often queer) avowals of desire is Amy Lowell's 1919 "A Decade," with its representation of intercourse with her female partner of ten years: "the taste of you burnt my mouth with its sweetness." In contrast, Tristan Tzara's "Dada Manifesto" (1918) makes explicit the contrast between feminizing conceptions of the poet and an insistently masculinist *modernism, representing male sexual energy through images of speed, noise, and technological force: "We aren't sentimental," he states; we will "replace tears by sirens." Swiss and Ger. *Dada, It. *futurism, Rus. constructivism (with its commitment to abstraction), Anglo-Am. modernism, and later Fr. *surrealism all engaged in a discourse of masculinity, technology, or impersonality. Representative of this dominant masculine discourse is Ezra Pound's 1918 call for a new poetry that is "free from emotional slither." This aesthetic that devalued feeling, the popular, and the naïve and that elevated abstraction, the technical, and the complex became the cornerstone of the *New Criticism in the 1930s, leading to the mid-century canonization of poets who fit modernist criteria for greatness and to the devaluation of all poets—male and female—who participated in the 19th-c.'s popular sentimental trads. New Critical modes of reading also fostered neglect of the striking aspects of gender and sexual anxiety and of feminism manifest in some of modernism's most significant poems.

With the political movements for women's liberation and gay rights in the U.S. and Western Europe during the 1960s and 1970s, gender roles, the relation between sex and gender, and oppression based on gender or on sexual preference again became explicit concerns of much poetry. Reflecting greater social equality, women poets attempted longer, more ambitious forms, and greater numbers of women gained widespread recognition and publishing opportunities. In the closing decades of the 20th c., various forms of feminist theory, queer theory, and masculinity studies emerged. These theories and others, e.g., Donna Haraway's theory of the cyborg, have provided fresh models of psychosexual devel. and social analysis that encourage new thinking about gender in interpretations of poetic texts. Such theories have also provided new ground for poetic performance and representation of gender.

*See* FEMINIST APPROACHES TO POETRY, GAY POETRY, LESBIAN POETRY, POETESS, QUEER POETRY.

■ S. Gilbert and S. Gubar, *The Madwoman in the Attic* (1979); P. G. Allen, *The Sacred Hoop* (1986)— Am. Indian trads.; A. Ostriker, *Stealing the Language* (1986); *Rewriting the Renaissance*, ed. M. W. Ferguson, M. Quilligan, and N. J. Vickers (1986); G. Hull, *Color, Sex and Poetry* (1987)—Harlem Ren.; J. DeJean, *Fictions of Sappho, 1546–1937* (1989); M. Ross, *The Contours of Masculine Desire* (1989)—romanticism; S. Clark, *Sentimental Modernism* (1991); A. Mellor, *Romanticism and Gender* (1992); J. C. Frakes, *Brides and Doom* (1994)—med. Ger. epic; S. Gaunt, *Gender and Genre in Medieval French Literature* (1995); H. Sussman, *Victorian Masculinities* (1995); E. Stehle, *Performance and Gender in Ancient Greece* (1996); L. Keller, *Forms of Expansion* (1997)—contemp. long poems; Y. Prins, *Victorian Sappho* (1999); G. Schultz, *The Gendered Lyric* (1999)—19th-c. Fr. poetry; *Reading and Writing the Ambiente*, ed. S. Chávez-Silverman and L. Hernández (2000); M. Simpson, *Poetic Epistemologies* (2000); *Early Modern Women Poets (1520–1700)*, ed. J. Stevenson and P. Davidson (2001); *The Poetry of Arab Women*, ed. N. Handal (2001); *Writing Gender and Genre in Medieval Literature*, ed. E. Treharne (2002); P. B. Bennett, *Poets in the Public Sphere* (2003)—19th c. Am.; P. McCracken, *The Curse of Eve, The Wound of the Hero* (2003)—med. lit.; M. Davidson, *Guys Like Us* (2004); S. Wolosky, "Poetry and Public Discourse," *Cambridge History of American Literature*, ed. S. Bercovitch, v. 4 (2004); C. Miller, *Cultures of Modernism: Marianne Moore, Mina Loy, Else Lasker Schüler* (2005); J. Dowson and A. Entwistle, *A History of Twentieth-Century British Women's Poetry* (2005); C. G. Martin, *Milton and Gender* (2005); *Medieval Constructions in Gender and Identity*, ed. T. Barolini

(2005); R. B. DuPlessis, *Blue Studios: Poetry and Its Cultural Work* (2006); *Shadowed Dreams*, ed. M. Honey, 2d ed. (2006)—Harlem Ren.; C. Bates, *Masculinity, Gender, and Identity in the English Renaissance Lyric* (2007); *Deutsche Dichterinnen vom 16. Jahrhundert bis zur Gegenwart*, ed. G. Brinker-Gabler, rev. ed. (2007)—Ger. women poets from the 16th c. to present; *Japanese Women Poets*, ed. S. Hiroaki (2007); *Women and Medieval Epic*, ed. S. S. Poor and J. K. Schulman (2007); *Gender and Modernism*, ed. B. K. Scott, 4 v. (2008).

L. KELLER AND C. MILLER

**GENERATIVE METRICS.** A branch of ling. concerned with the metrical structure of poetry. Following basic tenets of generative ling., generative metrics understands poetic form as resulting from rule-governed behavior. Explicit statement of metrical competence, i.e., the native practitioners' knowledge of the system that underlies that behavior, is at the core of the research program of generative metrics. Describing and explaining variation in metrical systems within a single author, a single trad., or across trads. (typological variation) form an important part of this project because variation reveals the boundary between individual choices and the general principles grounded in the human-lang. faculty. Following early work by Roman Jakobson, generative metrics maintains that categories and properties available to natural metrical rules are those that are also independently needed in grammatical (phonological) rules of langs. This hypothesis informs the typological aspect of generative metrics and leads to a sharp distinction between natural and artificial aspects of poetic form: the former are grounded in the lang. faculty and are acquired and processed in the same unconscious way as the grammatical system, whereas the latter make part of what might be called "communicated" form (Nigel Fabb) and are subject to more explicit manipulation by the poet.

Two competing views of the nature of *meter have developed in generative metrics, namely, templatic and rhythmic theories. Originating in the early work of Morris Halle and S. J. Keyser and later advocated by Fabb, templatic (also called "serial" by Alan Prince) theories view the metrical pattern as an abstract series of positions (a template). Halle and Keyser define Eng. *iambic pentameter as a series of ten W(eak) and S(trong) slots; mapping between linguistic structure and meter is mediated by correspondence rules. Three such rules are adduced in order of increasing constraint: either stressed *syllables occur in only and in all S positions (violated by weak syllables in S positions) or in only but not in all S positions (violated by stresses in W positions); or stress maxima (fully stressed syllables falling between two unstressed syllables in the same syntactic constituent) occur in only but not in all S positions. Violations of the first two rules merely indicate metrical complexity (tension), but violations of the third render a line unmetrical.

Rhythmic theories, advocated by Paul Kiparsky, Bruce Hayes, and Prince, assume the metrical and the linguistic representations to be built out of the same basic components. In such theories, poetic meter, just like linguistic stress, is based on *rhythm (i.e., a recurring pattern). The S and W in metrical structure have the same meaning as the strong and weak syllables in the representation of stress. This devel. in metrics paralleled the new understanding of stress that was taking shape in linguistic theory in the 1970s. In contrast to earlier understanding of stress as an abstract feature, in the theory proposed by Liberman and Prince, stress was a matter of rhythm and of grouping.

Rhythm is usually (though not necessarily) understood as based on grouping of material into prosodic constituents (feet, dipodes, cola), following the traditional notion of metrical foot that had been abandoned by Halle and Keyser. (Unfortunate terminological confusion results from the fact that ling. borrowed many terms from traditional metrics, e.g., *foot, iamb, trochee*. This overlap in terminology underscores the synergy between metrics and ling.: the idea that rhythm is due to grouping originated in poetics; was adapted for its own needs by linguistic theory; and then, outfitted with new theoretical trimming, made its way back into metrics).

Tension can be expressed by the degree of agreement between the metrical and linguistic structures. In the majority of lines, there will be a mismatch between the lang. and the meter. Ling. Ss in metrical Ws cause labeling mismatches; when such Ss occur in a polysyllabic word, the line is unmetrical. Bracketing mismatches occur when the two patterns of W and S agree but the constituent structure is misaligned. Kiparsky argues that John Milton allows some labeling mismatches absent in Shakespeare, but such mismatches never occur simultaneously with bracketing mismatches. This fact would elude a theory of meter without constituent structure except by brute-force stipulation. Characteristically for generative metrics, constituent structure was reintroduced by Kiparsky not for any historical, intuitive, or ideological reason but because it allowed the theory to handle data that remained out of reach for the earlier theory.

An additional argument in favor of the rhythmic view is one of parsimony. Because rhythm is based on a recurring pattern of constituents, the range of potential meters that can be described with a rhythmic theory is smaller than what can be described using arbitrary templates. The more restrictive theory is more desirable, in absence of evidence to the contrary. But there remain some recalcitrant data. Aperiodic meters, such as the meters of Sanskrit and Gr. *lyric, appear to be based on templates consisting of a random sequence of weak and strong positions, without any pattern. Work by Ashwini Deo has shown that even such apparently "irregular" meters have an underlying rhythmic structure and, thus, are compatible with rhythmic theories.

In an important devel., Kristin Hanson and Kiparsky advanced a parametric theory of meter, using the tool developed in generative grammar to account for cross-linguistic diversity and limitations on it. A metrical system can be thought of as a set of choices in several general parameters that describe the structure of the meter and its realization. Hanson and Kiparsky argued that langs. make the choice among the available parameters in such a way as to maximize the use of the vocabulary in the meter ("metrical fit").

Later devels. in generative metrics parallel the progress in ling. Optimality theory (OT; first suggested by Prince and Smolensky in 1993), a theory of resolution of conflicting preferences, was applied to meter by Golson and Riad. Abandoning the assumption that meter is based on an underlying abstract template, these authors derive the patterns entirely from the interaction of conflicting constraints. The focus on the threshold of absolute metricality in early work in generative metrics reflected a similar trend in generative grammar; both domains have later addressed gradient acceptability. Sophisticated theories of linguistic gradience and variation have been applied to metrics. On the one hand, work by Hayes and MacEachern and by Kiparsky on folk verse has used OT to describe the way complex structural variation in quatrain types arises from a small set of conflicting general preferences. On the other hand, Fabb has argued that aspects of the metrical form that are gradient must be handled by a pragmatic component, separate from the grammatical component responsible for defining the limits of metricality.

At the core of the approach of generative metrics is the assumption of modularity, i.e., the understanding that not all aspects of a poetic work are to be explained at the same time and that poetry owes part of its complexity to the multiplicity of modules required for its processing. Because the scope of the approach is limited to structural aspects of verbal art, generative metrics represents a conspicuous example of the advantages and limitations of purely formal methods applied to problems in poetics.

*See* FOOT, FORMALISM, LINGUISTICS AND POETICS.

■ R. Jakobson, "On Czech Verse" (1923); M. Halle and S. J. Keyser, "Chaucer and the Study of Prosody," *CE* 28 (1966); "Illustration and Defense," *CE* 33 (1971); and *English Stress* (1971); K. Magnuson and F. G. Ryder, "Second Thoughts," *CE* 33 (1971); A. M. Devine and L. D. Stephens, "The Abstractness of Metrical Patterns," *Poetics* 4 (1975); P. Kiparsky, "Stress, Syntax, and Meter," *Lang* 51 (1975); R. P. Newton, "Trochaic and Iambic," *Lang&S* 8 (1975); and "The Rhythmic Structure of English Verse" *LingI* 8 (1977); M. Liberman and A. Prince, "On Stress and Linguistic Rhythm," *LingI* 8 (1977); B. Hayes, "A Grid-Based Theory of English Meter," *LingI* 14 (1983); *Rhythm and Meter*, ed. P. Kiparsky and G. Youmans (1989)—see esp. B. Hayes, "The Prosodic Hierarchy in Meter" and A. Prince, "Metrical Forms"; K. Hanson and P. Kiparsky, "A Parametric Theory of Poetic Meter," *Lang* 72 (1996); C. Rice, "Generative Metrics," *GLOT International* 2.7 (1997)—a general overview; C. Golston, "Constraint-based Metrics," *Natural Language and Linguistic Theory* 16 (1998); B. Hayes and M. MacEachern, "Quatrain Form in English Folk Verse," *Lang* 74 (1998); C. Golston and T. Riad, "The Phonology of Classical Greek Meter,"

*Linguistics* 38 (2000); N. Fabb, *Language and Literary Structure* (2002); A. Deo, "The Metrical Organization of Classical Sanskrit Verse," *JL* 43 (2006); P. Kiparsky, "A Modular Metrics for Folk Verse," *Formal Approaches to Poetry*, ed. E. Dresher and N. Friedberg (2006).

T.V.F. BROGAN; L. BLUMENFELD

**GENERIC RHYME.** A species of *near rhyme in which the rhyming syllables contain identical vowels followed by consonants that are not identical but belong generically to the same phonetic class. It is a characteristic prosodic feature of Ir. and Scottish Gaelic poetry, where, by the 8th c. CE, Ir. grammarians had differentiated six permissible rhyming groups: (1) p-t-c, (2) f/ph-th-ch, (3) b-d-g, (4) bh-dh-gh-mh-l-n-r, (5) m-ll-nn-rr-ng, and (6) s. Examples of generic rhyme also appear in passages of *Welsh poetry that may date from the 6th c. CE and involve consonant classes such as (1) d-g, (2) f-gh-w, (3) dd-l-r, (4) nt-nc, and (5) all nasal consonants and clusters of r + nasal. Among later Welsh poets, generic rhyming never became requisite, and Welsh grammarians came to refer to the device as "Irish." Occasional generic rhymes may be found in Eng. *nursery rhymes, particularly between the voiceless stops *c*, *t*, and *p* (". . . on the tree *top* /; . . . the cradle will *rock*") and between the nasal continuants *m* and *n* (". . . for my d*ame* /; . . . lives in the *lane*").

*See* CELTIC PROSODY; RHYME; SCOTLAND, POETRY OF.
■ *Canu Aneirin*, ed. I. Williams (1938); G. Murphy, *Early Irish Metrics* (1961); *Irish Syllabic Poetry*, ed. E. Knott (1981); *Early Welsh Saga Poetry*, ed. J. Rowland (1990).

C. W. DUNN; B. BRUCH

**GENEVA SCHOOL.** The Geneva school of literary crit. brought together a group of phenomenological critics with varying ties to Geneva. Marcel Raymond and Albert Béguin, the earliest Geneva school figures, and Raymond's students Jean Starobinski and Jean Rousset were all directly associated with the University of Geneva. Georges Poulet, born a Belgian, taught in Switzerland for many years and was directly influenced by Raymond; Jean-Pierre Richard, a Frenchman, and J. Hillis Miller, an Am., have recognized Poulet's influence on their work. Not a "school" in the sense of having a common doctrine or manifesto, they are linked by a vision of lit. as a network of phenomenological perceptions and expressive lang. that delineates, throughout an author's work, an individual consciousness or *cogito*. Formal concepts such as poetry and prose are not important: the Geneva reader seeks individual patterns of awareness rather than aesthetic structures. Later Geneva critics have broadened their focus beyond individual authors to examine patterns of consciousness in art, music, cultural hist. and lang. itself. (This Geneva school should not be confused with an earlier Geneva school of ling. theory associated with Ferdinand de Saussure, Charles Bally, and Albert Sechehaye.)

The literary Geneva school has its roots in existential and phenomenological theory (Edmund Husserl and Gaston Bachelard), in romantic tradition, in the thematic hist. of ideas (A. O. Lovejoy), and in Henri Bergson's analyses of the perception of time. Rejecting "objective" views of a work (whether continental *historicism or Am. *New Criticism), the Geneva critics propose alternative techniques for analyzing the written text. Two influential studies, Raymond's *From Baudelaire to Surrealism* (1933) and Béguin's *L'Âme romantique et le rêve* (The Romantic Soul and Dream, 1939), examine passages by Fr. symbolists, Ger. romantics, and mod. Fr. poets as exploratory moments in a visionary search for reality. Lit., at this level, records the evolution of a preconscious awareness to a consciousness fully situated in time and space. Poulet's *Studies in Human Time* (1949–68) outlines a systematic methodology for this approach, first documenting ways that time and space are represented throughout an author's work and then plotting the personal coordinates of a developing creative consciousness. Thus, Victor Hugo experiences space first as formless movement in a void, a vague emptiness to be populated and conquered: filling both poetry and novels with a mass of concrete details, he discovers that such details are merely deceptive images hiding a discontinuous and empty reality. Geneva crit. has no formula for stating critical results: the same perceptions and experiences may be seen from a more subjective point of view (Poulet) or in an object-centered vision that recaptures the sensual logic of the mental landscape (Richard). Separate analyses may also be grouped in a larger period hist. Since the Geneva critics believe that lit. portrays the growth of a spiritual identity, they often situate individual patterns of consciousness within metaphysical contexts: within an awareness of true presence (Poulet), of divinity (Béguin) or immanent reality (Miller's early works), and within the precarious viability of expressive forms themselves (Starobinski, Miller, Rousset). A basic metaphor is that of an inner mental space, an initial unformulated awareness from which consciousness emerges to write its own narrative.

Geneva readers undertake an act of sympathetic identification with the literary cogito. They employ an essentially hermeneutic process of suspending presuppositions and waiting for the work to "signal" a route into its mental universe (a universe that is incidentally not limited to any one text but embraces everything the author has written). Richard cites poetry, essays, reviews, correspondence, notes, and even a fashion column in his detailed thematic study, *L'Univers imaginaire de Mallarmé* (Mallarmé's Imaginary Universe, 1961). Geneva critics have been criticized for going beyond acceptable boundaries of ling. interpretation in an attempt to espouse patterns of consciousness and for not valuing the separate identities of different works. Their "criticism of identification" necessarily precludes any judgment or evaluation according to exterior criteria, whether aesthetic, sociological, or political. Those who see lit. as an objective pattern of greater or lesser beauty or as an example of cultural production will not be content.

Geneva crit. typically emphasizes individual patterns of consciousness and an opposition to objective or "exterior" readings. It is a totalizing model whose unifying and humanistic tendencies are rejected by the impersonal ling. strategies of deconstruction. Geneva critics vary in their methods, however, and several have shown interest in the impersonal or at least transindividual structures of lang. over the last decade. Starobinski's *Action and Reaction* (1999) constructs a multidisciplinary semantic hist. to illuminate the textuality of human decisions. Miller, who rejected Geneva individualism in 1970 for the impersonal textuality of deconstruction, adopted a "rhetorical" approach that emphasized lang. and defined the act of reading as a performative speech act repeated and renewed in different situations. In *The Medium Is the Maker*, he effectively inverts the Geneva concept of unifying cogito by presenting identity as a decentered, variable nexus within the larger system of ling. exchange. The Geneva focus on patterns of consciousness in lit. and on the challenges of reading remains part of the critical landscape.

■ A. Béguin, *L'Âme romantique et le rêve* (1937); M. Raymond, *From Baudelaire to Surrealism*, trans. G. M. (1950); J. Rousset, *La Littérature de l'âge baroque en France* (1953); J.-P. Richard, *Poésie et profondeur* (1955); G. Poulet, *Studies in Human Time I–IV*, trans. E. Coleman and C. Dawson (1956–77); A. Béguin, *Poésie de la présence* (1957); J.-P. Richard, *L'Univers imaginaire de Mallarmé* (1961), and *Onze Etudes sur la poésie moderne* (1964); J. H. Miller, *Poets of Reality* (1965); S. N. Lawall, *Critics of Consciousness* (1968); J. Rousset, *L'Intérieur et l'extérieur* (1968); G. Poulet, *La Conscience critique* (1971), and *Exploding Poetry*, trans. F. Meltzer (1980); J. H. Miller, *The Ethics of Reading* (1987); J. Starobinski, *Jean-Jacques Rousseau, Transparency and Obstruction* (1988), *The Living Eye* (1989), and *Blessings in Disguise* (1993), all trans. A. Goldhammer; J. H. Miller, *Theory Now and Then* (1991), *Others* (2001), and *The Medium Is the Maker* (2009); J. Starobinski, *Action and Reaction*, trans. S. Hawkes and J. Fort (2003).

S. N. LAWALL

**GENIUS.** As now understood, the term *genius* derives from two Lat. roots, *genius* and *ingenium*. The first comes from *gens*, or family, whose tutelary spirits (e.g., Penates, as found in the *Aeneid* and alluded to in Ben Jonson's "To Penshurst") are identified with and embodied in men and worshipped on each birthday. In this sense, the Roman *genius* is comparable to the Gr. *daimon* (demon), a spirit that directs one's actions. Socrates regarded himself as directed by his daimon. Genius was also identified with the character of a place, as in *genius loci*. When Christianity became the official religion of the Roman Empire, daimon came to be thought of primarily as diabolical through the influence of Augustine and other church fathers (we still have in common parlance the phrase "evil genius").

The other root of *genius*, Lat. *ingenium*, referred more clearly to "natural talent or aptitude, proficiency." While the maxim *poeta nascitur non fit* steadily increased in popularity from antiquity to the 18th c., it was sometimes countered throughout this long period by ideals of acquired skill. E.g., the classically trained Jonson in the early 17th c. insisted *poeta fit non nascitur*.

Further, although it is tempting to see *genius* as referring only to the inner world of the poet and becoming synonymous with talent, in fact the notion of an accompanying spirit is never absent. The It. word *ingegno* captures the ambiguity of *genius* in the Ren., referring at once to natural talent and to the spirit that provides that talent. This ambiguity in which genius seems to exist both inside and outside is prevalent. The 17th-c. Eng. author John Marston insists that his "*Genius*" despises "*Critickes* rage" (Wharton); in this typical case, "genius" represents a separate entity capable of individual thought. In "Lycidas," John Milton describes the resurrected spirit of the dead Edward King as the "Genius of the shore," a Christianized reference to the Roman concept of *genius loci*—in this case, a tutelary figure.

It may be that for some authors talent was beyond craft, beyond reason, even beyond the rules of art, as in Alexander Pope's "Grace beyond the Reach of Art." But it would be overstating the case to say that all authors believed in the subordination of craft to genius, even after the advent of *romanticism. It is true that the long-lasting cult of J. W. Goethe's genius reflected a belief in the author's otherworldliness, but near the same time Joshua Reynolds (*Discourses on Art*) showed contempt for those who thought great art sprang from inspiration alone. Even "romanticized," the term *genius* always contained a modicum of craft—*poeta fit*. Lost, however, was the sense of a separate, accompanying spirit.

The concept of genius is developed most fully in *neoclassical poetics and in *preromanticism. Now "genius" became more than mere "talent"—although even here, one must be wary of generalizations. For instance, in Milton's famous ambiguity of the one "talent" that is "death to hide" (sonnet 19), the poet alludes to the biblical parable while referring to his own languishing talent. It is unlikely that Milton considered his "talent" anything less than "genius." By 1775, *genius* was unequivocally associated with inventiveness, creativity, and fecundity of *imagination. Genius surpasses talent just as the *sublime exceeds the beautiful. The semantic shift is essentially from genius as denoting those at the top of the class of mortal intellects to those above the mortal class altogether.

Immanuel Kant characterized genius as "the talent [natural endowment] that gives the rule to art," adding that, because talent itself belongs to nature, "*Genius* is the innate mental predisposition [*ingenium*] *through which* nature gives the rule to art" (*Critique of Judgment*). He claimed that genius was a talent for art, not for science; distinguished from taste, by which one judged a beautiful object, genius was required to *make* a beautiful object, the chief quality of genius being "originality." Kant rejects imitation and "teachability" in genius; only natural endowment and inspiration constitute it—not even Isaac Newton qualifies in Kant's judgment because Newton could show the steps he took to reach his discoveries, whereas "no *Homer* or *Wieland*" can show how his ideas originate. J. R. Lowell's later dictum, "talent is that which is in a man's power; genius is that in whose power a man is," echoes Kant's notion of genius with slightly different emphases and clearly signals the curtailment of poetic agency. The doctrines of *spontaneity and *originality, those quintessential hieroglyphs of romanticism, degraded the idea of talent as skilled performance, highlighting a notion of creativity akin to *furor poeticus* without the balance of *imitatio*. In the Ren., and even up to the time of Reynolds, true imitation is a creative and inventive activity; after Kant, imitation loses this value. Important forces driving the shift are the 18th-c. tastes for the gothic, the *sublime, *primitivism, and other manifestations of the sub- and suprarational; and the adulation of Shakespeare as a natural genius.

Still, it can be misleading to suggest an overly schematic history or to see a petrified and polarized relationship between natural endowment and skill. Romanticism notwithstanding, the notion of skill in artistic production was reaffirmed often in the 19th and 20th cs., e.g., by W. D. Howells ("there is no 'genius'; there is only the mastery that comes to natural aptitude from the hardest study of any art or science" [Howells; Stokes]) and by Irving Babbitt in his essays on originality (1908) and on romantic genius (1919), a sweeping indictment of the romantic mythology of originality and genius.

Important documents in the hist. of the concept include Longinus, chs. 33–36 (first trans. into Eng. in 1554 and refracted for the 17th c. through Nicolas Boileau), Abbé Du Bos, *Réflexions critiques sur la poésie et la peinture* (1719), and Joseph Addison's *Spectator* essay no. 160 (Sept. 3, 1711). Between 1751 and 1774, 12 publications treat the concept of genius, incl. William Sharpe's *Dissertation upon Genius* (1755), William Duff's *Essay on Original Genius* (1767), and Alexander Gerard's *Essay on Genius* (written 1758, pub. 1774; ed. B. Fabian, 1966, with valuable intro.), the most important being Edward Young's *Conjectures on Original Composition* (1759), which is essentially a romantic manifesto. Young was a primary influence on Ger. *Sturm und Drang*, where genius becomes a key concept, reformulated in the distinction between *fancy and imagination, whence S. T. Coleridge (*Biographia Literaria*, chs. 2, 15). Kant's *Critique of Judgment* (1790) is central. An important romantic episode occurs in William Hazlitt's two essays, on "Genius and Common Sense" (*Table Talk*) and on "Whether Genius Is Conscious of Its Power?" (*The Plain Speaker*). Charles Lamb's "The Sanity of True Genius" (1826) reasserts psychic balance.

■ W. D. Howells, "Editor's Study," *Harper's Monthly* 72 (1886); O. Schlapp, *Kants Lehre vom Genie* (1901); I. Babbitt, "On Being Original," *Literature and the American College* (1908); E. C. Stedman, *Genius and Other Essays*, ed. L. Stedman and G. M. Gould (1911); I. Babbitt, "Romantic Genius," *Rousseau and Romanticism* (1919); L. P. Smith, *Four Words* (1924); E. Zilsel, *Die Entstehung des Geniebegriffs* (1926);

H. Thüme, *Beiträge zur Geschichte des Geniebegriffs in England* (1927); B. Rosenthal, *Der Geniebegriff des Aufklärungszeitalters* (1933); H. Sudhiemer, *Der Geniebegriff des jungen Goethe* (1935); P. Grappin, *La Théorie du génie dans le préclassicisme allemand* (1952); Abrams; Wellek, v. 2; G. Tonelli, "Genius, Renaissance to 1770," and R. Wittkower, "Genius, Individualism," pt. 4, *DHI*, v. 2—with biblios.; Saisselin; J. Chance, *The Genius Figure in Antiquity and the Middle Ages* (1975); K. Frieden, *Genius and Monologue* (1985); J. Schmidt, *Geschichte des Genie-Gedankens in der deutschen Literatur, Philosophie und Politik,* 2 v. (1985); C. Battersby, *Gender and Genius* (1989); *Genius,* ed. P. Murray (1989); T. F. Wharton, "'Furor Poeticus'—Marston and his Contemporaries," *Explorations in Renaissance Culture* 19 (1993); M.J.A. Howe, *Genius Explained* (1999); O.N.C. Wang, "Kant's Strange Light: Romanticism, Periodicity, and the Catachresis of Genius," *diacritics* 30 (2000); D. Dutton, "What is Genius?" *Philosophy and Literature* 25 (2001); C. Haynes, "Reassessing 'Genius' in Studies of Authorship: The State of the Discipline," *Book History* 8 (2005); C. Stokes, "In Defense of Genius: Howells and the Limits of Literary History," *American Literary Realism* 40 (2008).

T.V.F. Brogan; R. Falco

**GENRE.** Most broadly, the term *genre* designates the long and controversial hist. of literary classification from antiquity to the present. The practice of grouping individual texts into distinct categories, called *genres,* is common to writers and readers of all periods. But these genres are themselves contingent, historical. Writers' tendencies and readers' expectations regarding the identifying features of a particular genre—theme, *style, *form, vocabulary, *syntax, *address, *allusion, morphology, medium, and so forth—are highly variable, both synchronically and diachronically. While debate over the nature and attributes of particular genres sometimes devolves into a chicken-or-egg squabble (which comes first, the generic category or the individual work?), it is also one of the chief engines of lit. hist. Thinking about lit. in terms of genre both piques and gratifies the human appetite for classification—the urge to identify unidentical things. But the dynamism of generic change also drives powerful narratives of difference and autonomy. We may think of a text as an expressive (authorial) or communicative (textual) intention endowed with a form that makes its meaning intelligible to others, even across great distances of time and space. At the same time, we recognize it to be a set of discursive effects not fully reducible to recognizable intentions or formal rules. Genres insist on horizons of meaning and expectation (Jauss), but they also give rise, through each act of reading, to dialectics and questions (Conte 1986).

*Genre* means "kind" or "sort" and is etymologically related to words such as *gender, genus,* and *beget.* Not surprisingly, texts in generic groupings are often understood to possess a kin-like relation to one another. Texts in the grouping known as "epic," e.g., are commonly said to "belong" to that genre, very much as if it were a family or clan. There has been a wide variety of genealogical and biological models of generic change, from J. W. Goethe's organicism, to Ferdinand Brunetière's speciation, to Franco Moretti's stemmatism. Some—Brunetière is the chief example—have rightly been faulted for thinking too strictly in terms of naturalistic categories. But the work of recent critics as different from one another in kind as Fowler, Kristeva, and McKeon attests to the continuing viability of biological analogies for a wide variety of rhetorical, discursive, historicist, and materialist theorizations of genre that are all diachronic and antiessentialist. Even a genre theorist as profoundly skeptical of communicative intention as Jacques Derrida nevertheless speaks of genres in terms of a more generalized sociality. Like him, many readers prefer to think of a text as "participating in" rather than "belonging to" a particular genre.

Belonging, participation, and other anthropomorphisms of genre, such as miscegenation, locomotion, sterility, and even death, find a precursor in Aristotle, who, in his *Poetics* (4th c. BCE), credits the differentiation of poetic genres to differences not only in poetic objects but in poets' own characters: the kind of person you are (e.g., superior, serious, noble vs. inferior, base, vulgar) dictates, Aristotle (following Plato) reasoned, the kind of poem you will write. This characterological determinism did not uniformly dictate cl. poetic practice, which reflects more freely and self-consciously made decisions about what and how to write. But such associations between genre and human nature, behavior, and relationship nevertheless abounded in antiquity and persist in much later expressivist thinking about genre and its implications for literary studies. The mod. aestheticization of the sapphic fragment as *"lyric," for instance, has its origins in the ancient reification of the emotional timbre of the poet Sappho's voice.

What postromantics habitually call Sappho's "lyrics," however, do not find their original theorization in either Plato or Aristotle, to whom centuries of trad., as we will see, have confusingly attributed the critical establishment of a trio of "major" or "basic" genres: *epic, *dramatic, and lyric (cf. Hegel). The lyric—when characterized as poetry that is neither chiefly narrative (epic) nor chiefly imitative (dramatic), but rather directly expressive of the poet's own thoughts and feelings—is, in fact, precisely that which is absent or excluded from Aristotle's system. The genre system proper to Aristotle comprises the object (either the actions of superior characters or the actions of inferior characters) and mode (either narrative or dramatic) of poetic address. The four possible combinations are tragedy (superior-dramatic), epic (superior-narrative), comedy (inferior-dramatic), and parody (inferior-narrative). The two genres that matter most to Aristotle are epic and, above all, *tragedy. He gives *comedy and *parody short shrift, and what later theorists call "lyric" is nowhere to be found in the *Poetics.* The lit. of antiquity is full of types of poems—incl. *elegies, *odes, *epigrams, *epithalamia, and *epinikia—that, since the 16th c., have generally been classified as lyric genres. But this is a mod. classification, not an Aristotelian or aboriginal or "natural" one.

Many mod. inheritors of the *Poetics*, incl. major poets and theorists of the Ren. who got their Aristotle channeled largely through Horace's *Ars poetica* (1st c. BCE), were intensely devoted to further, more accurately construed fundamentals of Aristotelian genre theory, which included an emphasis on structural *unity and *mimesis, as well as a sense of literary kinds as both fixed in their rules and finite in their number. This devotion persisted through, and even beyond, the neoclassical era. Yet from Dante and Ludovico Ariosto to Ben Jonson (himself one of Horace's many Ren. trans.), John Dryden, Alexander Pope, and, much later, Matthew Arnold, some of the strongest advocates of cl. *decorum nevertheless insisted on maintaining a critical relation to it—reevaluating received rules and deviating from them in keeping with specific aesthetic or social goals, with the perception of a generally advancing understanding of the world, the object of poetic mimesis. As Pope puts it in his *Essay on Criticism* (1711),

> Learn hence for Ancient *Rules* a just Esteem;
> To copy *Nature* is to copy *Them*.
> Some Beauties yet, no Precepts can declare,
> For there's a *Happiness* as well as *Care*.
> *Musick* resembles *Poetry*, in each
> Are *nameless Graces* which no Methods teach,
> And which a *Master-Hand* alone can reach.
> If, where the *Rules* not far enough extend,
> (Since Rules were made but to promote their End)
> Some Lucky LICENCE answers to the full
> Th' Intent propos'd, *that License* is a Rule.

Pope's "lucky license" seems to anticipate later flowerings of arguments against inflexible and prescriptive concepts of genre—e.g., the individualistic arguments closely associated with the rise of continental and Brit. *romanticism. The late 18th and early 19th cs. saw an expansion and liberalization of genre theory and crit., an influential positing of open rather than closed generic systems. Many romantic writers felt that any historically determined set of fixed categories imposed on fresh poetic production was inadequate to new, dynamic theories of consciousness and growing confidence in the autonomy of aesthetic judgment. As human consciousness changed, they reasoned, new genres would continue to emerge. Other poets and theorists went even further, strongly resisting generic systematization of any kind (cf. Curran, Rajan). Although the idea that there exist only certain fixed, transhistorical genres has *never* been accepted without controversy, these romantic, post-Kantian devels. would be esp. consequential in the ongoing, contentious shifts in genre theory—shifts esp. visible beginning in the late 18th c.—away from taxonomics and toward *hermeneutics. Static taxonomics was largely rejected in favor of various competing historical models of generic devel. and transformation. And the principles of generic decorum that Aristotle and esp.

Horace insisted on as normative standards linking the qualitative evaluation of poetry to the realm of human conduct would never regain their former influence.

This historical change is more comprehensively reflected, in part, in the transition from prescriptive models of genre (how poetry *ought* to be written) to descriptive-prospective models (how poetry *has been* and *may yet be* written). But this transition is not simply diachronic, no straightforward triumph of the mod. over the ancient. For, although it was Horace, and not Derrida, who coined the term "the law of genre" and although he insisted in his *Ars poetica* that mixed genres were monstrous violations of generic purity, yet Horace's own poetic practice, as Farrell demonstrates, is a thick forest of generic hybridization. Cl. poetry itself, as the example of Horace makes plain, frequently destabilizes cl. norms of genre. Indeed, the lack of congruence between theory and practice is the energizing, often conflicted condition of emergence for authors' individual works and for the historical appearance and transformation, in every period, of generic norms and expectations.

Still, for the sprawling Lat. and vernacular lits. of the Middle Ages, there were little anxious reflection and debate on the priorities of cl. poetics, such as would ensue from the rediscovery of Aristotle's *Poetics* in the early 16th c. Cl. terms persisted, but without much normative force; and they were supplemented by new terms, such as *vision, legend,* and *romance*. Yet there was no free-for-all. Many aspects of ancient rhet. and poetics were transmitted and adapted as schemata. And by the 13th c., the med. obsession with classification had focused its concentrated attention on Aristotle's recently translated works on logic, politics, ethics, and zoology. Moreover, both Christian dogma and Christian discourse entailed complex thematic and structural links across late Lat. Christian antiquity and the Middle Ages. Fowler, e.g., points to the extensive modulation of *allegory at the crossings of Christian and non-Christian canons. And Jauss provides a general warning against the retrospective imposition of a distinction between "spiritual" and "worldly" genres, pointing to the extraordinary range of models for med. literary genres found in the Bible, incl. *hymns, *laments, *sagas, legends, genealogy, letters, contracts, biographies, *proverbs, *riddles, parables, epistles, and sermons. Jauss also finds in med. genres, such as the courtly lyric, signs of the coming great shifts in the perceived purposiveness and autonomy of literary genres.

Indeed, with the later rediscovery of Aristotle's *Poetics* came not only a rededication to perceived cl. norms and a consequent sense of the impropriety and even alterity of med. "mixed" genres but a radical reinterpretation—really, as we have seen, a misreading—of the *Poetics* itself. The nonrepresentational genres—Genette calls them "a cloud of small forms"—that were effectively ignored by Aristotle as neither narrative nor dramatic became an increasingly important aggregate in Ren. genre theory and beyond. They were, as Genette observes, assimilated or promoted in two ways: first, by reclassifying nonimitative genres (those that imitate no action but merely express the poet's thoughts and feelings) as being in their own way imitative of the activities of thinking and feeling; second, and more radically, by rejecting the devaluation of the nonimitative genres and by elevating the status of their aggregative identity as "lyric" to the level of "epic" and "dramatic."

The hist. of the revaluation of genres, such as that of the ascendancy of lyric, is also a hist. of the recategorization of individual works and the reconfiguration of generic categories themselves. Lucretius's *De rerum natura* (1st c. BCE), e.g., has been variously classified as didactic epic, scientific poem, and verse sermon. Lucretius himself takes pains to justify his setting forth of Epicurean doctrine in "Pierian song," and Ren. theorists debated whether *De rerum natura* counted as "poesy" at all. Yet John Milton, like Virgil before him, found it to be an essential model for his own transformation of cosmological epic. In the late 18th c., it inspired the "poeticized science" of Erasmus Darwin. In the 19th c., Karl Marx simply classed *De rerum natura* with other philosophical treatises in his Jena dissertation, while Alfred, Lord Tennyson made Lucretius the subject of a dramatic *monologue discrediting his materialism. And Lionel Johnson's *lyric sequence, "Lucretius" (1895), opens with what one could call a Lucretian *sonnet, written, like *De rerum natura*, in hexameters.

As Johnson's sonnet helps to illustrate, the conventions of a genre may include formal, thematic, stylistic, and mimetic features: like many sonnets, it has 14 lines, it is about death, its language is elevated and meditative, and it seems to avoid direct address. Most commonly, a genre is constituted and recognized through shifting combinations, or ensembles, of such features. Deviations from the conventions of a given genre are often, as in Johnson's "Lucretius," small enough or self-conscious enough to highlight, rather than obscure, a particular text's generic resemblance to other texts. And while, generally speaking, the greater the deviation, the more attenuated the resemblance, sometimes it is, in fact, the more radical deviations—such as G. M. Hopkins's *curtal sonnets and Alexander Pushkin's *Onegin stanzas (also known as "Pushkin sonnets")—that are most effective at drawing fresh attention to the durability of received conventions.

Identifying such variations, though it may sometimes seem like a very specialized, even trivial, technical matter, has significant consequences for literary hist., crit., and theory. Shakespeare's sonnet 126, e.g., quite self-consciously stops two lines short of the conventional 14, signaling, among other things, the action of the "sickle hour" of death, referred to in line two, which cuts all love—and lovers—short. In the 1609 quarto, two pairs of italic brackets stand in for the missing (if this is a sonnet, we expect them to be there) 13th and 14th lines. But many later printings do not reproduce them. Is this sonnet unfinished? Does the typographically marked absence of the final two lines finish it? Does the absence of the brackets undo it? Either way, the perception of a gap between text and generic convention is a condition of interpretation,

not only of the poem but of the published sequence of Shakespeare's *Sonnets*, to which it belongs. There are methodological consequences as well. Ignoring the typographic element means rejecting the interpretive significance of the 1609 text's nonverbal graphic elements—something to which materialist scholars would object. Accepting as a sonnet a 12-line poem embedded within a sequence of 14-line poems may call into question the integrity of the sequence. Refusing to accept a 12-line poem as a sonnet may call into question the sequence's stability and completeness.

By 1609, the sonnet was ubiquitous, and the popular *sonnet sequence was already well established as much more than a mere collection of individual poems. From their Dantean and Petrarchan models, both Philip Sidney and Shakespeare had learned a self-conscious style that begged—and sometimes beggared—the question of the relation between text-sequence and event-sequence. Structural ambiguity also helped blur the distinction between factual and fictional accounts, between author and persona. Later sonnet sequences, from John Donne's to Marilyn Hacker's, have continued to be written and read as implicit or explicit meditations, not only on autobiography but on narrative as such, and on the possible relation of nonnarrative or counternarrative poetry to themes of religious devotion, erotic love, and psychological interiority. Vikram Seth's *The Golden Gate* (1986), a book composed entirely of Pushkin sonnets, was very successfully marketed as a novel, prompting some to lament the further narrativization of all lit., while others celebrated the way novelistic discourse disseminated this traditional poetic form among new communities of readers.

Narratives may come in all sorts of genres, from the cl. epic and the Ren. sonnet sequence to the existential drama and the psychoanalytic case study. However, most theories of narrative and narrativity focus chiefly on literary fiction, esp. the novel. From the perspective of the present, the novel has become for many a *synecdoche for genre as such (cf. McKeon). When students in contemp. lit. classrooms refer to *Hamlet* or *The Waste Land* as a "novel," they are not necessarily making a simple category error but rather reflecting a broad cultural and critical shift toward treating the novel as paradigmatic of all that is interesting and dynamic in what Bourdieu calls the "literary field." Bakhtin's theory of the novel's exceptionality among other genres prompts his claim that lit. in the mod. era has undergone a process of "novelization." Not that other genres have grown to resemble novels in their features but that the nature of the novel—its status as the only "uncompleted" genre, its distinctive structural relation to the present, its fundamental plasticity, and its devotion to public autocritique—"sparks the renovation of all other genres . . . infects them with its spirit of process and inconclusiveness . . . implies their liberation from all that serves as a brake on their unique development" (Bakhtin 1981).

This remedial prescription for further generic devel. finds its counterpart in the wish to dispense altogether with the genre concept in literary analysis—a wish that had been gaining critical force since the 18th c. (cf. Schlegel) but that reached its furthest extreme in Croce's insistence that genre is a useless and even dangerous abstraction that draws attention away from each individual text's notable singularity, on which its aesthetic value, in Croce's view, depends. But Jauss and many others have given the lie to Croce's impossibly absolutist view of expressive singularity. For to be even minimally intelligible, any text, any expressive act, must refer to some set of conventions or norms against which its singularity can be noted and its novelty measured.

Post-Crocean reassertions and refutations of the meaningfulness and utility of the concept of genre are extremely diverse, ranging from Crane's neo-Aristotelianism, to Jakobson's emphasis on ling. structures and Bakhtin's on "speech genres," to Burke's posing of genres as frames of symbolic adjustment, to the competing anthropological structuralisms of Frye and Todorov, to Jauss's historical-systems model, to Miller's situational pragmatics, to Jameson's historical materialism, to Kristeva's *intertextuality, to Nelson's psychoanalytic reflections on genre as repetition compulsion, to Altman's work on film genres and Holt's on genre and popular music, to the reflexive questioning of critical genres in Stewart, Jackson, and Poovey. The diversity, sophistication, and ongoingness of such work testify to the stickiness of genre, not just as a concept that will not be shaken off but as that which provides the necessary traction for the mediation of literary and social discourse.

See CONVENTION, CRITICISM, KIND, VERSE AND PROSE.

■ K.W.F. Schlegel, *Gespräch über die Poesie* (1800); J. W. Goethe, "Naturformen der Dichtung," *Noten und Abhandlungen zu besserem Verständnis des west-östlichen Divans* (1819); F. Brunetière, *L'évolution des genres dans l'histoire de la littérature* (1890); B. Croce, *Estetica come scienza dell'espressione e linguistica generale* (1902); K. Viëtor, "Probleme der literarischen Gattungsgeschichte," *Deutsche Vierteljahrschrift für literaturwissenschaft und Geistesgeschichte* 9 (1931); *Critics and Criticism*, ed. R. S. Crane (1952); Frye; K. Burke, *Attitudes Toward History* (1959); R. Jakobson, "Linguistics and Poetics," Jakobson, v. 3; E. D. Hirsch, *Validity in Interpretation* (1967); C. Guillén, *Literature as System* (1971); P. Hernadi, *Beyond Genre* (1972); R. L. Colie, *The Resources of Kind: Genre-Theory in the Renaissance* (1973); Culler; G.W.F. Hegel, *Aesthetics*, trans. T. M. Knox, 2 v. (1975); T. Todorov, *The Fantastic*, trans. R. Howard (1975); J. Derrida, "La loi du genre / The Law of Genre," *Glyph* 7 (1980); M. M. Bakhtin, *The Dialogic Imagination*, ed. M. Holquist, trans. C. Emerson and M. Holquist (1981); F. Jameson, *The Political Unconscious* (1981); "Genre," spec. iss., *Poetics* 10.2–3, ed. M.-L. Ryan (1981); H. Dubrow, *Genre* (1982); H. R. Jauss, *Toward an Aesthetic of Reception*, trans. T. Bahti (1982); Fowler; J. Kristeva, *Revolution in Poetic Language*, trans. M. Waller (1984); C. R. Miller, "Genre as Social Action," *QJS* 70 (1984); A. Rosmarin, *The Power of Genre* (1985); M. M. Bakhtin, *Speech Genres and Other Late Essays*, trans. V. W. McGee (1986); R. Cohen, "History and Genre," *NLH* 17 (1986); G. B. Conte, *The Rhetoric of Imitation*, trans.

C. Segal (1986); S. Curran, *Poetic Form and British Romanticism* (1986); *Renaissance Genres*, ed. B. K. Lewalski (1986); T. Todorov, *Genres in Discourse*, trans. C. Porter (1990); S. Stewart, *Crimes of Writing* (1991); G. Genette, *The Architext*, trans. J. E. Lewin (1992); T. O. Beebee, *The Ideology of Genre* (1994); C. B. Conte, *Genres and Readers*, trans. G. W. Most (1994); P. Bourdieu, *The Rules of Art*, trans. S. Emanuel (1996); R. Altman, *Film/Genre* (1999); *Modern Genre Theory*, ed. D. Duff (2000); *Theory of the Novel*, ed. M. McKeon (2000); T. Rajan, "Theories of Genre," *CHLC*, v. 5, ed. M. Brown (2000); V. Nelson, *The Secret Life of Puppets* (2001); "Theorizing Genres," spec. iss., *NLH* 34.2–3, ed. R. Cohen (2003); J. Farrell, "Classical Genre in Theory and Practice," *NLH* 34 (2003); V. Jackson, *Dickinson's Misery* (2005); F. Moretti, *Graphs, Maps, Trees* (2005); J. Frow, *Genre* (2006); "Remapping Genre," spec. iss., *PMLA* 122.5, ed. W. C. Dimock and B. Robbins (2007); F. Holt, *Genre in Popular Music* (2007); M. Poovey, *Genres of the Credit Economy* (2008).

M. CAVITCH

**GEORGIA, POETRY OF.** A written Georgian lit. starts with the beginning of the Christian era (4th c.). The earliest poetic forms are *psalms and *hymns, initially trans. from Gr. Over the next four or five centuries, Georgian monks, priests, and biblical scholars created an impressive body of ecclesiastical poetry. Ioane-Zosime (10th c.) was a tireless liturgical scholar, writer, translator, and poet, and the likely author of the hymn "Kebai da dibeai kartulisa enisai" (Praise and Glory to the Georgian Language), which suggests that Christ, in his Second Coming, will address the faithful in Georgian. Gradually, spiritual songs acquired more secular coloring, evolving into *lyric poems. From the early med. period to the beginning of the 20th c., poetry persists as the predominant mode of literary expression.

In the 11th and 12th cs., narrative poems emerged as the major genre of Georgian poetry. It reached its peak in the 12th c., under Queen Tamar (1184–1213). Among the distinguished poets of her court were Chkhrukhadze, Ioane Shavteli, and Shota Rustaveli; the last is acknowledged as the greatest master of Georgian poetic art. His epic poem *Vepkhis tqaosani* (*The Man in the Panther's Skin*) recounts the adventures of a young prince who aids his friend in search of his beloved, captured by devils. The poem's exceptional richness of vocabulary, powerful images, exquisite *alliterations, and complex rhyming are unsurpassed in Georgian poetry.

Rustaveli's poem became a paradigm for poets of the following four centuries, which mark a low point in the devel. of Georgian poetry. The themes and plots of *The Man in the Panther's Skin* are imitated in lyric and narrative poems alike. In the 16th and 17th cs., several Georgian kings distinguished themselves as poets. King Teimuraz I (1588–1662) translated Persian love poems, giving them a distinctly Georgian flavor. He also wrote an epic poem *Tsameba ketevan dedoplisa* (The Martyrdom of Queen Ketevan) dedicated to his mother,

Queen Ketevan, who had been held hostage in Persia and was later tortured to death for refusing to renounce her Christian faith. King Archil II (1647–1713) wrote several didactic poems that contemplated the destiny of his country, religion, morals, and the art of poetry. Another writer of royal birth was Vakhtang VI (1675–1737), a poet, translator, and literary commentator. His refined allegorical love poems are tinged with mystical longing.

A far more radical innovator was David Guramishvili (1705–92), a Georgian nobleman who became an officer in the Rus. army. Although his major work, *Davitiani* (The Story of David), is written in traditional metrics, in his shorter lyrics he introduces a great variety of metrical forms and rhyming patterns inspired by folk poetry. *Davitiani* consists of several short narrative poems in which the author both expresses his religious and political thoughts and recounts his tumultuous and eventful life.

Bessarion Gabashvili (1740–91), better known as Besiki, was the next notable figure, a court poet of King Heraclius II. Love is the major theme of his remarkably elegant and sonorous lyrics. He also composed satirical poems aimed at his adversaries at the court.

In the early 19th c., Georgia was annexed by Russia, and Georgian nobility and intellectuals became acquainted with the literary trads. of Russia and Western Europe. Georgian poetry of the following decades displays romantic influences (see ROMANTICISM). The movement is best represented by Alexandre Chavchavadze (1786–1846), Grigol Orbeliani (1804–83), and Nikoloz Baratashvili (1817–45). Chavchavadze and Orbeliani express their pride in the Georgian heroic past or meditate on the country's lost glory. Other poems, marked with vibrant sensuality, praise the earthly joys of love, friendship, and feasting. However, Baratashvili is the epitome of Georgian *romanticism. In his best-known poem, "Merani" (The Steed), Baratashvili's poetic *persona is a passionate rebel challenging his destiny. In his only narrative poem, *Bedi kartlisa* (The Fate of Georgia), he contemplates the consequences of the last devastating battle of King Heraclius II against the Persian invaders. Baratashvili significantly reformed Georgian versification, introducing new metrical forms and integrating contemp. spoken lang.

The second half of the 19th c. is marked by increased dissatisfaction with oppressive Rus. policies. The most prominent figure of this generation was Ilia Chavchavadze (1837–1907). An outspoken critic of the policy of Russification and an advocate of an independent Georgian state, he wrote lyrical as well as narrative poems of patriotic appeal. His friend and contemporary Akaki Tsereteli (1840–1915) enjoyed far greater popularity among the general public, because of the clarity of his images, simplicity, and sonority of his lang. Many of his love poems have become popular songs. Vazha Pshavela (pseud. of Luka Razikashvili, 1861–1915) wrote poems in the vernacular of his native Pshavi, a mountainous region in Georgia. The tragic clash between the society's moral code and ethical concerns of an individual is the major theme of his narrative poems.

The first decade of the 20th c. witnessed a new surge of Western influence in a proliferation of poetic schools that assimilated simultaneously symbolist, futurist, and decadent forms and ideas. In 1916, a group of poets including Titsian Tabidze (1895–1937), Paolo Iashvili (1894–1937), and Giorgy Leonidze (1899–1966) raised the banner of the symbolist movement in Georgian poetry (see SYMBOLISM). These poets experimented boldly with vocabulary and versification and adjusted Western genres to the traditional forms of Georgian poetry. Georgian futurist poets—Nikoloz Shengelaia (1903–43), Simon Chikovani (1903–66), Shalva Alkhasishvili (1899–1980), and others—strained the potentialities of lang. to the breaking point, reflecting the same preoccupations as their Eur. and Rus. counterparts (see FUTURISM). Galaktion Tabidze (1891–1959), who did not belong to any literary group, is considered the most brilliant poet of the century. An acute sense of loneliness, mourning for loss, and at times a Baudelairean ennui and nostalgia find poignant expression in his fluid and sonorous verses.

After the socialist revolution of 1917, Georgia enjoyed a brief period of independence (1918–21), but in February 1921, the Red Army installed a Bolshevik government. A variety of poetic groups flourished through the 1920s. But the censorship's ever-tightening control resulted in the creative barrenness of the following two decades, as Georgian poets were required to extol the political and ideological superiority and economic achievements of the Soviet state. Several outstanding poets, incl. Tabidze and Iashvili, fell victim to the political purges of the late 1930s.

By the late 1950s, a new generation of poets emerged: Ana Kaladadze (1924–2008), Mukhran Machavariani (1929–2010), Otar Chiladze (1933–2009), Shota Nishnianidze (1929–99), and others. Taking advantage of the relatively liberal political atmosphere, they expressed their sentiments with remarkable vigor, imagination, and technical artistry. From the late 1960s, Lia Sturua (b. 1939), Besik Kharanauli (b. 1939), and many others embraced *vers libre. In subsequent decades, Manana Chitishvili (b. 1954), Tsira Barbakadze (b. 1965), Giorgi Lobzhanidze (b. 1974), Rati Amaglobeli (b. 1977), and others introduced new rhythms and styles. Kote Qubaneishvili (b. 1953) became the standard-bearer of the postmodernist generation whose flamboyant poetic vocabulary broke many literary taboos.

■ S. Rustaveli, *The Man in the Panther's Skin*, trans. M. S. Wardrop (1912); C. Beridze, "Georgian Poetry," *Asiatic Review* 17 (1930–31); R. P. Blake, "Georgian Secular Literature: Epic, Romance and Lyric (1110–1800)," *Harvard Studies and Notes on Philosophy and Literature* 15 (1933); J. Karst, *Littérature géorgienne chrétienne* (1934); *History of Georgian Literature*, ed. A. Baramidze, 6 v. (1962–78)—in Georgian; *Georgishe poesie aus acht Jahrhunderten*, ed. A. Endler (1971); *L'avangardia a Tiflis*, ed. L. Magarotto (1982); *The Literature and Art of Soviet Georgia*, ed. S. Dangulov

(1987); D. Rayfield, *The Literature of Georgia: A History* (1994); *An Anthology of Georgian Folk Poetry*, ed. K. J. Tuite (1994); H. I. Aronson and D. Kiziria, *Georgian Language and Culture* (1999).

D. KIZIRIA

**GEORGIANISM.** A naturalistic style associated with the five anthols. of *Georgian Poetry* (1912–22), ed. by the civil servant Sir Edward Marsh and containing poems by Rupert Brooke, Walter de la Mare, W. H. Davies, Wilfrid Gibson, D. H. Lawrence, Robert Graves, and Isaac Rosenberg, among others. Brooke, Gibson, de la Mare, and Lascelles Abercrombie were its original core, joined in 1916–17 by Graves and Siegfried Sassoon. To their discomfort, the final, weakest volume linked the Georgian brand name with J. C. Squire's *London Mercury* coterie. Lawrence welcomed the first volume as a "great liberation" from fin de siècle angst, but to its modernist enemies, *Georgianism* came to mean vague, sentimental rural lyrics in traditional forms, representing a retreat from modernity. Later defenders, however, saw it as an "English tradition" of natural speech-based verse that anticipated the *Movement's desire to return poetry to the ordinary reader. Although they were not published in *Georgian Poetry*, Edward Thomas and Robert Frost were associates of Gibson and de la Mare, and a looser sense of *Georgian* includes their style of carefully unemphatic, conversational poetry, distinct from the modernists' syntactic disorder and fragmented forms (see MODERNISM).

Modernist disagreement with Georgian poetry has tended to obscure their similarities, however. Like the imagists (see IMAGISM), the earlier Georgian volumes sought poems of intense emotion and direct impact, and in common publications like Harold Monro's quarterly jour. *Poetry and Drama*, both share a critical vocabulary of immediacy and sincerity. Ezra Pound, in fact, turned down an offer to be in the first Georgian anthol. for copyright reasons, though its success led him to adopt the anthol. format for *Des Imagistes* a year later. Whether in the amoral naiveté of the tramp-poet Davies, the mingled ecstasy and disgust of Abercrombie's verse dramas, or the abrupt *free verse of Lawrence, the Georgians' sometimes inept attempts to find poetry in the raw and unfiltered would nonetheless anticipate much later 20th-c. verse. The *war poetry of the third and fourth Georgian volumes is a natural extension of their ethos, while the recurrent Georgian interest in the uncensored imaginations of children and other nature figures would resurface a decade later among the Eng. surrealists (a connection anticipated by T. S. Eliot's 1924 Clark lectures, which compare Davies to Jean Cocteau).

Eliot's criticisms of Georgianism in the *Egoist* series "Reflections on Contemporary Poetry" (1917–19), on the other hand, detect in their tonal infelicities an emotional self-deception inherent in any mod. poet's trying to be simple in a complex society, incl. the imagists of Chicago's *Poetry* magazine. Edward Thomas

shared Eliot's distaste for John Masefield's and Gibson's theatrical sincerity, and his own uninflected, meditative style has become one influential response. But Eliot saw their emotional and stylistic defects as a symptom of the insular, rootless self-satisfaction of Georgianism's Eng. middle-class readership, implying Georgianism was a cultural problem as much as a poetic movement. Criticizing Georgianism as "a style quite remote from life" ("Prose and Verse," *Chapbook* 22 [April 1921]), Eliot and Pound's formal shock tactics still sought the same vital and unimpeded relation between art and audience as *Georgian Poetry* originally wanted. And the fact that Eliot would publish many Georgians in Faber's "Ariel Poems" series of 1927–28 suggests that they were less enemies to be eradicated than individual poets of varying talents belonging to a rival "-ism," whose cultural difficulties with being both authentic and accessible modernism would itself take over.

■ R. H. Ross, *The Georgian Revolt* (1962); D. Hibberd, *Harold Monro* (2001); A. Jaffe, *Modernism and the Culture of Celebrity* (2005); P. Howarth, *British Poetry in the Age of Modernism* (2006).

P. HOWARTH

**GEORGIC.** A type of poetry that takes its name from Virgil's *Georgics* (29 BCE), the middle work in Virgil's career between his *pastorals (*Eclogues*, 39 BCE) and his *epic (*Aeneid*, 29–19 BCE). Sometimes earlier didactic verse, such as Hesiod's *Works and Days* or Lucretius's *De rerum natura*, which influenced Virgil's poem, are named as prototypes. The four books of Virgil's *Georgics* present themselves as a set of instructions or precepts (*praecepta*) for the tending (*cultus)* of crops, vines, cattle, and bees. They mix their precepts with myth, meteorological lore, philosophy, and narrative digression in order to represent the dignity—but also the difficulty and daily care—of rural labor. However, while Virgil's poem drew carefully from Greek and Roman agricultural and scientific treatises (Aratus, Varro, and others), it would not have served the practical needs of a real farmer; its audience was learned and urban, located largely in the circle of Augustus in Rome. As Virgil's central pun on *vertere* (to turn) and *versus* (the furrow in the field and a line of written verse) emphasizes, the *Georgics* are just as much about the poet's careful labor of representation within a larger field of cultivating activities. Highlighting and reflecting on its own medium, in other words, the poem offers a complex meditation on the affinities and differences between the tending of words and the culture of the ground. It is no accident, therefore, that the *Georgics* are the most carefully wrought and densely allusive of Virgil's works or that John Dryden's 1697 Eng. rendition promoted them as the "best poem by the best poet."

Instances of georgic before Dryden include Poliziano's *Rusticus* (1489), Luigi Alamanni's *La Colitivazione* (1546), and Thomas Tusser's *Five Hundred Points of Husbandry* (1573). In 17th-c. England, however, georgic is present more often as a mode or set of themes than as strict formal imitation. In *The Advancement of Learning*, Francis Bacon promoted his new science as a "georgics of the mind, concerning the husbandry and tillage thereof," and the georgic appealed widely to Bacon's followers later in the century (Abraham Cowley, Samuel Hartlib, John Evelyn, and others), who were interested in experiment, education, and estate management. It took Dryden's version, prefaced by an influential essay on the poem by Joseph Addison, to touch off a series of marked imitations, serious and mock, and to establish the georgic as a distinctive genre during the 18th c. Examples included John Philips's *Cyder* (1708), John Gay's *Rural Sports* (1713), William Somervile's *The Chace* (1735), Christopher Smart's *The Hop Garden* (1753), John Dyer's *The Fleece* (1757), and James Grainger's *The Sugar Cane* (1764). Among the several reasons for this proliferation was the appeal of Virgil's ambivalent and plangent celebration of empire to Britons whose awareness of their own nation's territorial ambitions and liabilities was similarly vexed, esp. after the Act of Union joining Scotland to England and Wales in 1707. Less imitative but far more influential, James Thomson's *The Seasons* (1730) and William Cowper's *The Task* (1785) merged georgic elements with other descriptive genres to produce long topographical poems that were the most popular verse of the century. These shaped the meditative, descriptive verse of the first generation of romantic poets, including Charlotte Smith, S. T. Coleridge, and William Wordsworth (see esp. Wordsworth's long philosophical poem *The Excursion* [1815]). After Wordsworth, in part because of the growing prominence of the novel and other prose genres dedicated to the tasks of daily life, georgic once again appears more often as a mode; its attitudes and concerns persisted, but informing a range of poetic and prose genres. Georgic verse maintained a foothold in 19th- and early 20th-c. America, where agrarian improvement and national expansion came later than in Britain. Its presence is more or less marked in the work of Joel Barlow, Walt Whitman, Robert Frost, Lorine Niedecker, Muriel Rukeyser, and others. In mid-20th-c. Brazil, one of the definitive poems of the *Noigandres school, Décio Pignatari's "terra" (1956, pub. 1962) was called by Haroldo de Campos a "concrete 'georgic'" for the way it retrieves the notion of the line of verse as a furrow.

Addison's "Essay on the Georgics" distinguished its subject sharply from pastoral, but as the aristocratic figure of the Ren. courtier receded behind the models of the working landowner and small independent proprietor, in practice these adjacent genres overlapped. For verse written from the mid-17th c. on, pastoral and georgic mark the ends of a spectrum of possibilities for writing about the countryside, as well as for representing the vocation of the poet. If pastoral's emphasis inclines toward the sympathy of nature, the spontaneity of production, and the leisure of the singer, the attention of georgic falls on the necessity of skill and effort to counteract the wayward tendencies of nature and civilization alike.

See CALENDRICAL POETRY, DESCRIPTIVE POETRY, DIDACTIC POETRY, ECLOGUE, GENRE.

■ D. Durling, *The Georgic Tradition in English Poetry* (1934); *An Anthology of Concrete Poetry*, ed. E. Williams (1967); J. Chalker, *The English Georgic* (1969); R. Cohen, "Innovation and Variation," *Literature and History*, ed. R. Cohen and M. Krieger (1974); R. Feingold, *Nature and Society* (1978); J. Barrell, *English Literature in History* (1984); A. Low, *The Georgic Revolution* (1985); A. Fowler, "The Beginnings of English Georgic," *Renaissance Genres*, ed. B. K. Lewalski (1986); K. Heinzelman, "Roman Georgic in a Georgian Age, *TSLL* 33 (1991); F. de Bruyn, "From Virgilian Georgic to Agricultural Science," *Augustan Subjects*, ed. A. Rivero (1997); K. O'Brien, "Imperial Georgic," *The Country and the City Revisited*, ed. G. Maclean, D. Landry, and J. P. Ward (1999); R. F. Thomas, *Reading Virgil and His Texts* (1999); T. Sweet, *American Georgics* (2001); R. Thomas, *Virgil and the Augustan Reception* (2001); K. Goodman, *Georgic Modernity and British Romanticism* (2004).

K. GOODMAN

**GERMANIC PROSODY.** The earliest poetry recorded in Germanic langs. takes the form of alliterative verse (AV), in which stress, syllable weight, and the matching of syllable onsets (i.e., *alliteration) all play structural roles. Although all the Germanic langs. eventually abandoned AV during the Middle Ages and adopted poetic forms characterized by *rhyme and alternating stress at equal intervals on the basis of Lat., Occitan, and OF models, the alliterative form appears to have been the only variety in use before Christian missionaries introduced writing on parchment and Lat. poetic types. The Roman historian Tacitus (*Germania*, ca. 98 CE) describes *oral poetry (or *songs, *carmina*) as the only form of historical lore among the early Germanic peoples, and presumably the form was AV, though this cannot be proved. Neither can AV be proved in connection with any of the references to songs performed by early Germanic people (often to the accompaniment of a lyre or harp) to be found in Gr. and Lat. sources of the 2d to the 6th c., incl. works of Procopius, Jordanes, and Venantius Fortunatus.

The form is usually assumed to have originated relatively late in Germanic prehist., since varieties of it are found in several early Germanic langs., which also offer evidence of a shared poetic trad. in the form of many items of chiefly or exclusively poetic vocabulary, e.g., OHG *balo*, Old Saxon *balu*, OE *bealu*, and Old Icelandic *bǫl*, all meaning "misfortune." The AV form cannot antedate the Common Germanic shift of accent to most nonprefixal initial syllables, since both alliteration and the metrical form depend on stress placement. This accent shift appears to have been a relatively late prehistoric devel. The earliest AV attested takes the form of brief runic inscriptions, beginning with the Norwegian Tune Stone of about 400 CE. The earliest datable examples in ms. are also mostly brief, coming from England. These include the nine-line "Hymn" of Cædmon (ca. 670, first found in mss. of the 8th c.), the five-line "Death Song" of Bede (735, found in 9th-c. mss.), and the two-line "Proverb from Winfrid's Time" (757–86). In addition, the 818-line "Guthlac A," in a ms. of the 10th c., purports (plausibly) to have been composed within a life span of the saint's death in 714. Several other Anglo-Saxon poems show archaic ling. and formal features resembling those encountered in "Guthlac A," but there is no reliable basis for dating them very precisely.

Quite small is the surviving corpus of AV in OHG, fewer than 250 lines all told, amounting to two poetic *fragments of the 9th c., *Hildebrandslied* (a heroic lay) and *Muspilli* (a sermon on the Last Judgment), plus a number of shorter poems (see GERMAN POETRY). In Old Saxon are preserved the 9th-c. *Heliand* (a life of Christ) in nearly 6,000 lines and the 337-line *Genesis*; another 600 or so lines of the latter are preserved in an OE trans. A comparatively large corpus of early Germanic AV comes from England (see ENGLAND, POETRY OF). Among the more than 30,000 lines of verse in OE, all the longer poems but *Beowulf* are based on Lat. sources, while the shorter lyrics (such as "The Wanderer" and "The Wife's Lament"), heroic compositions (such as "Waldere" and "The Fight at Finnsburg"), and wisdom poetry (such as "Precepts" and "Maxims I") tend to be more original compositions. The estimable corpus of surviving AV in ME is more diverse, incl. romances (such as *Sir Gawain and the Green Knight* and *The Alliterative Morte Arthure*), historical works (such as the *Destruction of Troy* and *The Wars of Alexander*) and works of religious and/or social commentary (such as *Wynnere and Wastoure* and *Piers Plowman*). Also sizable is the body of extant Old Icelandic AV (see NORSE POETRY), which differs from West Germanic AV in that its form is stanzaic. Of the various eddic meters (see EDDA), which are preserved in about 7,100 long lines, the commonest is *fornyrðislag*, which is also the meter that most closely resembles West Germanic AV. The *dróttkvætt* meter of most skaldic verse (a corpus of nearly 6,000 *strophes, mostly of eight lines each) resembles *fornyrðislag* with the addition of a trochaic cadence, with certain alliterative and syntactic adjustments.

In the earliest poetry in ms., the alliterative long line comprises two verses, an *on-verse* and an *off-verse*, linked by alliteration. An example from the OHG *Hildebrandslied* will illustrate:

x  P x   x   P      p x x  P x
Mit gēru  scal man    geba infāhan.
(With a spear should one receive gifts.)

The alliterating words *gēru* and *geba* receive the greatest degree of stress, both being nouns. Syllables bearing a lesser degree of stress (*man* and *-fā-*, a pronoun and a verb root, respectively) are not required to alliterate; in fact, no stressed syllable after the first may alliterate in the off-verse. The remaining syllables are unstressed and alliterate only by coincidence. A vowel may alliterate with any other vowel, but each of the clusters *sp*, *st*, and *sk* (*sc*) alliterates only with itself.

Under the most widely accepted analysis of the form, that of Eduard Sievers, a typical verse comprises four metrical positions. Each position may be filled by one of three metrical entities: (1) a lift, which is usually a heavy, stressed syllable (represented by *P* in the scansion above), (2) a half-lift, which is a syllable of lesser stress, either heavy or light, or (3) a drop, which is paradigmatically one or more unstressed syllables (represented by *x* or *xx*, etc.). A stressed light syllable (represented by *p* above) may combine with another syllable to serve as a lift, a substitution known as *resolution; *geba* in the off-verse above, with a light initial syllable, is an example. In combination with the principle of four positions to the verse, restrictions on the placement of half-lifts ensure that the metrical pattern will conform to one of five types (see ENGLISH PROSODY). In addition, there are restrictions on the number of syllables that may appear in a drop, the count being more circumscribed in the coda of the verse, which, as in other IE verse forms, is more rigidly structured than the verse onset.

Alternative analyses have been proposed. Heusler (1925–29, 1941) argued that a verse comprises two isochronous measures (see ISOCHRONISM) that may be scanned using musical notation. In 4/4 time, a lift corresponds to a half note and a drop to a quarter or eighth note. Pope refined this analysis, filling the rests allowed by Heusler with notes on a lyre (though this explanation for rests will not serve for Scandinavian verse, which appears not to have been performed to the accompaniment of a musical instrument). Although isochronous theories are still discussed in some Ger.-lang. scholarship, they no longer play any prominent role in anglophone lit., in part because they are not easily reconcilable with the prevailing analysis of Sievers (despite the efforts of Pope). In particular, they ignore the requirement of four metrical positions to the verse that is fundamental to Sievers's analysis. More compatible with Sieversian approaches is the word-foot theory of Russom, according to which verses comprise feet whose contours correspond to the prosodic patterns encountered in the words of the lang. Allowable verse types are then determined by restrictions on the ways feet may be combined. Alternative analyses continue to be proposed because of the relative abstractness and complexity of Sieversian metrics, particularly because of the typological peculiarity of this approach, since quantity and stress (lexical and clausal) both play indispensable roles in the scansion. By contrast, the prosodies of related langs. are based either on syllable quantity alone (as in Gr. and Sanskrit, where the pitch accent is of no account in verse construction, and in Lat., where the stress accent plays no role) or on accent and/or syllable count alone (as in most mod. Eur. langs., in disregard of syllable *quantity). Despite its unusual nature, however, and the questions it raises about *performance and how the audience could have perceived the metrical template, the analysis of Sievers is verifiable as accurate in ways that the alternative analyses are not.

The prosodic contours allowed by the Sieversian framework dictate that the syntax of AV should differ from that of prose. Words of intermediate stress (or *particles*), such as finite verbs, pronouns, and demonstrative adverbs, are treated as stressed or unstressed in accordance with their position within the clause, as observed by Kuhn. They tend to be grouped before or immediately after the first lift, where they are unstressed; if they appear later in the clause, they bear *ictus. Two successive verses in *Muspilli* illustrate the principle: *der inan uarsenkan scal: / pidiu scal er in deru uuicsteti* (who shall let him fall: / therefore he shall on the battlefield). Here "scal" (shall) is stressed at the end of the clause in the first verse and unstressed in the first drop of the second verse. The regularity is observed with much greater fidelity in OE and in native Old Icelandic compositions in fornyrðislag than in Old Saxon and OHG; indeed, it is violated in the verses from *Hildebrandslied* cited above. It is probably no accident that in OE and Old Icelandic poetry, the use of particles is minimized: in these trads., unlike in Old Saxon and OHG, elimination of unstressed function words, esp. pronouns and articles, was plainly regarded as a stylistic virtue, with the result that Sievers's four-position principle is more plainly discernible in the verse structure.

Although a variety of AV forms arose in Scandinavia, primarily because of the thoroughgoing reduction of unstressed syllables in North Germanic, the older forms persisted nearly unchanged, at least in Iceland, until their demise (or fundamental modification) in the 14th c. The Sieversian patterns are as plain in poetry of the 10th c. as of the 14th. By contrast, even before the Norman Conquest, the form of OE AV was evolving: in some poetry of the late 10th c. and later, the four-position principle at the heart of Sievers's analysis is partly obscured, because of the increased use of particles, and most metrists agree that ME AV does not conform to this pattern at all. In form, some ME AV is less reminiscent of OE poetry than of the alliterative prose style adopted by the homilist Ælfric, ca. 1000 CE, though a genetic connection is dubitable because of the rarity of poetic vocabulary in Ælfric's works. In some other ME works descended from the OE alliterative trad., esp. Lawman's (Layamon) *Brut* (ca. 1200), even alliteration is not essential, as it may be replaced by rhyme. On the continent, where the structure of AV was looser, the appeal of Lat. forms was felt earlier: already ca. 868 (i.e., not long after the composition of the *Heliand*) the monk Otfrid in Alsace composed his *Evengelienbuch*, a gospel harmony in rhymed *couplets. By the MHG period, even alliteration had been discarded, and all that remained of the original alliterative form was the mid-line *caesura.

*See* GNOMIC POETRY, MEDIEVAL POETRY.

■ Sievers; A. Heusler, *Deutsche Versgeschichte*, 3 v. (1925–29); H. Kuhn, "Zur Wortstellung und -betonung im Altgermanischen," *BGDSL (H)* 57 (1933); A. Heusler, *Die altgermanische Dichtung*, 2d ed. (1941); J. C. Pope, *The Rhythm of "Beowulf,"* rev. ed. (1966); W. Hoffmann, *Altdeutsche Metrik* (1967); J. Kuryłowicz, *Die sprachlichen Grundlagen der altgermanischen Metrik* (1970); J. K. Bostock, "Appendix on OS and OHG Metre," *Handbook of Old High German Literature*, 2d ed. (1976); D. Hofmann, *Die Versstrukturen der*

*altsächsischen Stabreimgedichte Heliand und Genesis*, 2 v. (1991); G. Russom, *"Beowulf" and Old Germanic Metre* (1998); K. E. Gade, "History of Old Norse Metrics," *The Nordic Languages*, ed. O. Bandle et al., v. 1 (2002); S. Suzuki, *The Metre of Old Saxon Poetry* (2004); J. Terasawa, *Old English Metre* (2011).

R. D. FULK

## GERMAN POETRY

I. Medieval
II. Early Modern
III. Seventeenth Century
IV. Eighteenth and Early Nineteenth Centuries
V. Nineteenth Century
VI. Twentieth Century

**I. Medieval.** The written record of Ger. poetry begins in the early 9th c. Charlemagne's biographer Einhard attests to the emperor's interest in preserving pre-Christian poetry (*barbara et antiquissima carmina*), but no collection of vernacular poetry predating the conversion of the Germanic tribes to Christianity has survived. The written remnants of this oral culture are few. Singular in its prominence is the *Hildebrandslied* (*The Lay of Hildebrand*), a 68-line *fragment in OHG in irregular alliterative long-line verse (*Germanic prosody) recorded around 830. Also rooted in pagan oral trad. are the two *Merseburger Zaubersprüche* (Merseburg magical charms).

With the consolidation of political power under the Carolingian dynasty (752–911), monasteries became the principal site of literary activity. Almost all extant vernacular texts served religious ends, incl. the *Wessobrunner Gebet* (Wessobrunn Prayer, ca. 814); *Muspilli*, a late-9th-c. fragment employing eschatological visions to promote a godly life; and the Old Saxon (Low Ger.) *Heliand* (The Savior, ca. 830), a gospel harmony in traditional alliterative verse. Theologically learned and a key document within OHG poetics, Otfrid of Weissenburg's *Evangelienbuch* (Gospel Book, ca. 863–71) demonstrated that end rhyme, an innovation derived from Lat. *hymns, could effectively replace *alliteration as the binding structure in a modified heroic long line. Rhyme is also used in the *Ludwigslied* (Song of Ludwig, ca. 882), a poem celebrating King Louis III of France as a Christian warrior-king, and in the short *Petruslied* (Song of Peter, ca. 900), the oldest known Ger. hymn, a strophic text with neumes, or musical notation, which probably served as a processional song.

While some vernacular poetry certainly persisted during Carolingian rule and later under the Ottonian and Salian emperors, textual evidence is scarce. Lat. prevailed, memorably in the dramas and verse of the abbess Hrotsvit of Gandersheim (ca. 935–973). A substantial 11th-c. collection of Lat. lyric poetry, *Cambridge Song* includes among its many poems of Ger. origin two *macaronic poems in OHG and Lat. Several Lat. verse narratives suggest vernacular ties, incl. a heroic epic loosely based on Germanic tribal hist. (*Waltharius*, 9th–10th c.), the first med. *beast epic *Ecbasis captivi* (Flight of the Prisoner, ca. 1045), and the romance epic (*Ruodlieb*, mid-11th c.). Only in the mid-11th c. did written Ger. texts begin to reappear, initially with a religious purpose. Prominent examples include the *Ezzolied* (*Ezzo's Song*, ca. 1064), a salvation hist.; the *Annolied* (*The Song of Anno*, ca. 1080), a hagiographic poem in praise of Archbishop Anno of Cologne that is also a world chronicle; and poems and a life of Jesus by the Lower Austrian recluse Ava (ca. 1060–1127), the earliest preserved works of a Ger.-speaking woman writing in the vernacular. Mystics such as Hildegard of Bingen (1098–1179) continued to have their visions and songs recorded in Lat.

In the 11th c., powerful ducal and episcopal courts increasingly supplemented monasteries as sites of active literary interest. The Ger. lang. was changing as well. The transition from the dialects of OHG to MHG is generally dated from 1050. Verse narratives drawing on Fr. sources like Lamprecht's *Alexanderlied* (Song of Alexander, ca. 1150) and Konrad's *Rolandslied* (Song of Roland, ca. 1170) and adventure tales such as *König Rother* (*King Rother*, ca. 1150) and *Herzog Ernst* (*The Legend of Duke Ernst*, ca. 1180) registered new ling. and cultural confidence. Pointing to the future, in his *Eneit* (Aeneid, 1174–89) Heinrich von Veldeke (ca. 1150–1210) adapted the OF *Roman d'Eneas* in a polished MHG greatly admired by his contemporaries.

The courtly *epic was one of two poetic genres that flourished in the decades that followed, a 50-year period, 1170–1220, that defines the high point of MHG lit. The writers were typically aristocrats bound in service to a greater noble and writing under his patronage. Texts were performed orally, providing entertainment and instruction through an idealized fusion of Christian and chivalric principles. Poets found particular inspiration in Fr. texts (notably Chrétien de Troyes) and the Arthurian romances and Anglo-Celtic materials transmitted through them. Three poets stand out. The first, Hartmann von Aue (ca. 1160–65–after 1210), wrote two Arthurian epics (*Erec*, ca. 1180; *Iwein*, ca. 1200), a verse tract about *minne* or *courtly love (known as *Die Klage* [The Dispute] or *Das Büchlein* [The Little Book], ca. 1180–85), an atonement legend (*Gregorius*, ca. 1188), and an exemplary tale of self-restraint and compassion (*Der arme Heinrich* [*Poor Heinrich*], ca. 1195). Wolfram von Eschenbach (ca. 1170–1220), arguably the greatest of the three, is remembered principally for his *Parzival* (ca. 1210), a monumental work of some 25,000 lines in which the eponymous hero on an idiosyncratic quest finds the inner nobility and mature religious understanding essential to true knighthood. The third is Gottfried von Strassburg (d. ca. 1210), whose incomplete *Tristan* (ca. 1210) celebrates the endurance of love beyond all trial and suffering.

For one additional work of distinction, however, there is no known author. The violently tragic narrative of the *Nibelungenlied* (ca. 1200) reaches back to events and characters associated with the Germanic migrations of the 5th and 6th cs. and preserved in oral trad. Although set in the contemp. world of courtly culture, a heroic ethos motivates the action and leads to the final bloodbath. Unlike the courtly epics in rhymed tetrameter *couplets, the *Nibelungenlied* features some 2,300 four-line stanzas in the distinctive *Nibelungenstrophe.

Like the writers of courtly epics, the writers of courtly love poetry, the second major MHG genre, were primarily of knightly origin, composing and performing their works with musical accompaniment within aristocratic circles. A significant selection of their poetry, known collectively as *Minnesang, remains, although little of their music has been preserved. Early examples are localized in Upper Austria/Bavaria, 1140–70, where relatively simple poems employed the Nibelungenstrophe and featured indirect exchanges between male and female voices and other native forms. After 1170, *Occitan poetry mediated by *troubadours and *trouvères prompted more complex content based on courtly love conventions and formally sophisticated stanza structures. The Minnesang poet typically placed himself in service to a high-born lady of exceptional beauty and virtue, unattainable despite his musical wooing and display of virtuosity. Major poets among the some 150 whose works have been preserved include Friedrich von Hausen (d. 1190), Heinrich von Morungen (d. 1222), Reinmar the Elder (d. ca. 1205), and three poets also known for their courtly epics: Wolfram, master of the subgenre known as *tagelied (dawn song, *alba) in which lovers must part at daybreak; Heinrich von Veldeke; and Hartmann von Aue. The greatest is Walther von der Vogelweide (ca. 1170–1230), a professional poet who reinterpreted courtly trads. and expanded Minnesang to praiseworthy women of lower social standing. Walther also provided his patrons with encomiastic tributes and offered social-critical judgments in shrewd single- and multistanza poems (*Spruchdichtung), a flexible didactic genre of growing importance in the 13th c. He is the first important political poet in Ger.

Courtly love poetry had a long life. Poets sustained and modified its conventions for several centuries. Esp. in later decades, but already in the poems attributed to Neidhart (ca. 1185–1240), more patently sexualized encounters with villagers led to greater realism and also to parody and a trad. of bawdy satire. The images of courtly love were adapted to religious use by the visionary mystic Mechthild of Magdeburg (ca. 1207–1282). Minnesang is the first Ger.-lang. poetry to be preserved in elaborate ms. collections; the most important is the *Grosse Heidelberger Liederhandschrift* (Great Heidelberg Songbook, ca. 1300), also known as the Codex Manesse. Somewhat earlier, some 52 MHG stanzas were recorded in the Codex Buranus (ca. 1230), a compilation largely of Lat. *Goliardic verse best known as the textual source for Carl Orff's 1937 cantata *Carmina Burana*.

The 13th c. saw an expansion of didactic poetry. Spruchdichtung was used for tributes; *laments; and religious, moral, and political commentary. The most prominent practitioner was the widely admired Heinrich von Meissen, known as Frauenlob (Praise of Our

Lady, ca. 1250–1318). The prolific and witty poet known as Der Stricker (The Weaver, ca. 1190–1250) spanned many genres, incl. *fables, romances, and short poems. Like a growing number of poets, he was not of knightly origin. Indeed, the world of chivalric valor was becoming increasingly anachronistic. In his satirical narrative *Meier Helmbrecht* (Farmer Helmbrecht, ca. 1268), Wernher der Gartenaere (mid- to late 13th c.) addressed the general social decay. Others settled for adventure and entertainment, writing romances, farcical tales, and continuations of popular epic material. Influential didactic works of the 13th and 14th cs. include Freidank's gnomic *Bescheidenheit* (Sagacity, ca. 1215–30), Hugo von Trimberg's (b. ca. 1230) moral sermon *Der Renner* (The Runner, 1300), and Heinrich der Teichner's (ca. 1310–1378) scolding *Reimreden* (Rhymed Speeches, 1350). The multistrophic *leich* also flourished in the 13th and 14th cs., a virtuoso form employed in musical performance for large-scale themes, both religious and secular.

A growing body of vernacular religious poetry, largely trans. from Lat., served as popular paraliturgical aids: processional songs, pilgrimage hymns, Marian hymns and prayers, confessional poems and sequences. Several well-known hymns of anonymous provenance, incl. the 12th-c. "Christ, der ist erstanden" (Christ, he is risen; later expanded) and the 14th-c. Lat.-Ger. Christmas hymn "In dulci jubilo," remain in active use.

A belated and final example of the great med. poets of aristocratic origin, the Tyrolean Oswald von Wolkenstein (1377–1445), successfully recapitulated the major genres of MHG poetry. He also experimented with polyphonic structures, esp. in two-voiced love songs. But like so much written before 1450, Oswald's work was soon forgotten. A sustained recovery of MHG poetry would begin in the 18th c.

**II. Early Modern.** In the transition from late med. to early mod. society, the new urban centers and their interests came to dominate literary activity. Didactic poetry was retooled for the urban setting. Writing for a clerical and courtly audience, Heinrich Wittenwiler (ca. 1395–1426) had used a peasant wedding and ensuing conflict to depict a world of grotesque madness in his verse satire *Der Ring* (ca. 1410). In contrast, the Basel humanist Sebastian Brant (1457–1521) populated his *Narrenschiff* (*The Ship of Fools*, 1494) with fools from all social strata. The work achieved unprecedented renown, its verse couplets and woodcuts illustrating human folly (many by the young Albrecht Dürer) reprinted and trans., incl. a Lat. version that made it a Eur.-wide success. Amid a general proliferation of narrative verse in rhymed couplets, the Low Ger. animal fable *Reinke de Vos* (*Reynard the Fox*, 1498) proved esp. popular.

Secular and religious songs also flourished, many compiled in hand-copied mss. and after 1520 in print. Forms ranged from simple strophic songs (later idealized as folk songs, although largely of urban middle-class origin) to the complex stanza structures codified by the *Meistersingers, artisan poets who organized instructional schools to pass on their poetic and musical craft. The most famous was the Nürnberg shoemaker Hans Sachs (1494–1576). In *Meistersang*, religious topics dominated. In popular song, sociability was at the fore, even in the laments about the vicissitudes of love, in ballads narrating remarkable events, and in evocations of the solitary life of the journeyman.

A final major devel. in the transition to the new urban culture was the growth after 1400 of humanistic studies. In prosperous cities in the southwest of Germany, an educated elite promoted renewed attention to the ancients and to the poetics of a polished Lat. The new learning imported from Italy also found advocates in progressive courts and bishoprics and, less quickly, selected universities (Heidelberg, Erfurt, Tübingen, Wittenberg, Ingolstadt). The humanist vision would link learned culture across Europe and decisively affect the devel. of Ger. poetry in the 17th c. In the 16th c., however, urbane Neo-Lat. poetry, with its metrical and ling. virtuosity, remained a separate sphere from vernacular verse. The leading Ger. humanist Conrad Celtis (1459–1508), known for his erotic *Amores* (Loves, 1502), recovered forgotten Lat. texts from the Ger. past (incl. the dramas of Hrotsvit of Gandersheim). Celtis was crowned *poeta laureatus* (*poet laureate) by Emperor Friedrich III in 1487, the first Ger. to receive the honor.

The finest and most influential poet of the 16th c. was Martin Luther (1483–1546). In his Bible trans. (1522, 1534), Luther affirmed the vernacular and contributed to the gradual standardization of New High Ger. in his attempt to reach a transregional audience. His vividly powerful hymns, many using familiar melodies from religious and secular sources, include "Ein feste burg ist unser Gott" ("A Mighty Fortress Is Our God," 1528) and the Christmas hymn "Vom Himmel hoch da komm ich her" ("From Heaven Above," 1533). His activity led to a radical increase in literacy and set off a wave of song production.

Among the poets who responded with enthusiasm to the reform movement unfolding around Luther, the scrappy humanist Ulrich von Hutten (1488–1523) trumpeted his allegiance in his Ger. poem "Ain new Lied" (A New Song, 1521). A staunch defender, Hans Sachs greeted Luther as "Die Wittembergisch Nachtigall" ("The Wittenberg Nightingale," 1523) in an *allegory first written as a Meistersang but then refigured for popular distribution in *Knittelvers*, a simple rhymed form that served as the common verse throughout the 16th c., later becoming directly associated with Sachs and his tone of homespun good humor.

The Reformation and the conflicts that it unleashed provided subject matter for Ger. poetry for the next 100 years. *Invectives flew off the presses. Internal strife among the reformers and counterattacks from Catholic intellectuals accompanied the violence and confusion of the late 16th c. Economic and social crises led to an increase in penitential poetry and expressions of a more individualized piety among Lutheran hymn writers, incl. women who also wrote hymns and *devotional poetry. Verse narratives continued to enjoy wide popularity, esp. those with a satirical purpose.

**III. Seventeenth Century.** What decidedly altered Ger. poetry in the 17th c. was the question of how the cultural practices of the learned elite who were writing a polished and erudite Lat. might be realized also in Ger. On the example of Ital., Fr., and Dutch poets who demonstrated that a learned vernacular literature was possible, the new standard was set by Martin Opitz (1597–1639) in his handbook *Buch von der Deutschen Poeterey* (Book of German Poetics, 1624). The reforms that Opitz introduced privileged alternating meters, pure rhymes, mastery of grammar and rhet., and a general literacy in the cl. and Neo-Lat. trads. He insisted on the coincidence of word accent and metric stress. If he was subsequently faulted for his overly prescriptive pronouncements, Opitz's larger vision of how the Ger. lang. might become an apt vehicle for learned culture unquestionably prevailed.

In the new Ger. poetry, eloquence and polish were highly prized but also *wit and conceptual *invention. Two of the most common genres emphasized the order and constraint of lang.: the *epigram and the *sonnet. But *Renaissance poetics and It. example legitimated a range of options, some defined by formal features and others by content. *Occasional verse and poetry with a didactic purpose flourished in all genres. *Emblem books, starting with Andrea Alciato's Lat. collection published in 1531 in Augsburg, made ideas and visual materials from the Ren. and classics widely available. After 1617, societies dedicated to the cultivation of the Ger. lang. (*Sprachgesellschaften*) served as intellectual and social networks in selected principalities and urban centers.

Yet Germany itself was split by confessional allegiances and divided into some 300 territories and principalities. In the absence of a single cultural center, regionalism prevailed. The Thirty Years' War (1618–48) devastated both the countryside and the cities, introducing financial chaos, famine, and widespread suffering. Unsurprisingly, poetry also displayed regional and confessional differences. While the widely used term *baroque* usefully signals Ger. poetry's common cause with numerous Eur. vernacular lits., it should not obscure the diversity of texts written between 1600 and 1700.

Major poets after Opitz include Paul Fleming (1609–40), initially a Neo-Lat. love poet, who wrote elegant Ger. verse on Ren. models. The greatest poet of the 17th c., the Silesian Andreas Gryphius (1616–64), wrote rhetorically powerful sonnets, largely on somber themes capturing the traumas of the age and the transitory nature of human experience. The Silesian courtier Friedrich Logau (1604–55) mastered the epigram. Attentive to *pastoral themes as well as acoustic effects, the Nürnberg poets, incl. Georg Philipp Harsdörffer (1607–58) and Johann Klaj (1616–56), promoted dactylic verse, as did Philipp von Zesen (1619–89), and they developed a more mannerist style (see MANNERISM). The Breslau patrician Christian Hofmann von

Hofmannswaldau (1617–79) proved a virtuoso master, intellectual, highly sensual, and ironic. His gallant verse, together with the works of his fellow Silesian Daniel Caspar von Lohenstein (1635–83), embodied the excesses of baroque poetry in the eyes of 18th-c. neoclassicists. A simpler, more personal tone was created by Johann Christian Günther (1695–1723), esp. in his love poetry.

Almost all 17th-c. poets wrote religious as well as secular poetry. The Jesuit Friedrich Spee (1591–1635) wrote mystical poetry blending pastoral and Petrarchan elements in his *Trutz-Nachtigall* (Defiant Nightingale, 1649). Johannes Scheffler (1624–77), who took the name of Angelus Silesius when he converted to Catholicism, collected his intellectually paradoxical epigrams and sonnets in his *Cherubinischer Wandersmann* (*The Cherubinic Wanderer*, 1675). The learned Lutheran mystic Catharina Regina von Greiffenberg (1633–94) wrote sonnets and songs marked by metaphorical inventiveness and evident delight in the natural world. The Lutheran pastor Paul Gerhardt (1607–76), the most significant hymnist since Luther, achieved a tone of simple devotion and clarity. Many of his hymns are still sung today, incl. his free trans. of "Salve caput cruentatum" as "O Haupt voll Blut und Wunden" ("O Sacred Head now wounded"), the anchoring chorale in J. S. Bach's *St. Matthew Passion*.

Participation in the literary culture of 17th-c. Germany required education. Its formal institutions were closed to women, and only a few women were afforded the luxury of private tutoring enjoyed by Greiffenberg or Sibylle Schwarz (1621–38), daughter of a Greifswald patrician. Religious experience, however, increasingly legitimated the individual voice, and both men and women responded. The devotional hymns and poems by the Schleswig-Holstein dissenter Anna Ovena Hoyers (1584–1655) lacked metrical regularity and other signs of Opitz's reforms, but she was capable of an assertive verse in defense of her sectarian commitments. At the end of the 17th c., the introspection and emotionality of Pietist worship impelled Gottfried Arnold (1666–1714), Gerhard Tersteegen (1697–1769), Count Nikolaus Ludwig von Zinzendorf (1700–60), and some 100 new poets to song.

**IV. Eighteenth and Early Nineteenth Centuries.** The 18th c. witnessed broad social and intellectual changes incl. the postwar economic recovery of urban centers, the growing cultural influence of middle-class professionals, and the expansion of the book trade. Scientific wonder combined with a vital interest in perception to modify the lang. of theology and bring new visual energy to poetry. The Swiss scientist Albrecht von Haller (1708–77) probed central issues of moral philosophy in his verse treatises and celebrated the sublimity of *Die Alpen* (*The Alps*, 1729). The Hamburg patrician Barthold Heinrich Brockes (1680–1747) published nine volumes of his *Irdisches Vergnügen in Gott* (Earthly Delight in God, 1721–48) in which his physicotheological poetry proclaimed evidence of divine providence in every aspect of the natural order. The call of the Frenchman Nicolas Boileau and others for a renewed commitment to the classics was answered as poets polished the vernacular in trans. and adaptations from Lat. and Fr. In his *Versuch einer critischen Dichtkunst* (Attempt at a Critical Poetics, 1730), the Leipzig professor Johann Christoph Gottsched (1700–66) defined *neoclassical norms in a Ger. context and struggled to give order to the abundance of poetic forms. The poetic values of gallant verse found middle-class adaptation in the polished social songs of Friedrich von Hagedorn (1708–54) and in the playfully erotic *anacreontic poetry of Johann Wilhelm Ludwig Gleim (1719–1803) and many others. Christian Fürchtegott Gellert (1715–69) gave didacticism new poetic grace in his *Fabeln und Erzählungen* (Fables and Tales, 1746), the best seller of the century. In his verse narratives, Christoph Martin Wieland (1733–1813) combined a cultivated, elegant wit with urbane sensuality and accelerated the devel. of a transregional readership for Ger. poetry in his jour. *Der Teutsche Merkur* (The German Mercury, 1773).

Women were increasingly among the readers of poetry and, if more slowly, among its writers. Anna Luise Karsch (1722–91), a self-taught poet of humble origins and a voracious reader, was the most famous woman poet of the era, celebrated for her "native genius." After 1740, Eng. poetry joined Fr. and It. as models for emulation. John Milton's *Paradise Lost* became the focus of heated debates on the limits of the creative imagination. The new and the marvelous gained footing within a poetological discourse previously constrained by rationalist principles.

At midcentury, F. G. Klopstock (1724–1803) revealed the eruptive power of poetic lang. in the opening cantos of *Der Messias* (The Messiah, 1748–73), his epic of Christ's passion and triumph. In his bid to create the great Ger. epic, Klopstock introduced the *hexameter line and intensified syntax and diction. His imaginative breadth and affective rhet. offended those committed to neoclassical reforms but attracted readers putting the text to devotional use and writers eager to enhance Ger.'s expressive capacity. His *Oden* (Odes, 1771) became the basis for enthusiastic and even brash critical pronouncements, the most important by J. G. Herder (1744–1803), and accelerated discussion about original *genius and the *sublime. Klopstock eschewed rhyme and the simple alternating rhythms that dominated 18th-c. poetry and instead wrote *odes and *elegies in adapted cl. meters, in original meters of his own definition, and in free rhythms legitimated by the example of Pindar and the Psalms (see FREIE RHYTHMEN). He demonstrated how Ger. might serve as a vehicle for the depths of sentiment as well as hymnic sublimity, stimulating a vast poetry of sensibility (*Empfindsamkeit*) with its trope of heartfelt emotion.

On Klopstock's example, Herder proclaimed the ode and, with it, all lyric poetry, the highest of the literary genres. For Herder, true poetry resided in the premod. era, with Homer, the Hebrew Psalms, the songs of Germanic bards, Ossian, and similar works valued as songs of the people (*Volkslieder*). In his estimation, Klopstock came the closest of any mod. writer to recovering their lost immediacy and enthusiasm. Klopstock became the idol of many younger poets, incl. those in

Göttingen who formed a fellowship around his example (the *Hainbund*), and who featured his poetry in a new transregional *Musenalmanach*. Such poetry almanacs became the principal vehicle for the distribution of poetry in the next decades. Ludwig Christoph Heinrich Hölty (1748–76), the strongest lyric talent in the group, followed Klopstock's example by employing cl. meters in his odes. Johann Heinrich Voss (1751–1826) later distinguished himself for his *idylls and his hexameter trans. of Homer. Friedrich Stolberg (1753–1835) and his brother Christian (1748–1821) enthusiastically echoed Klopstock's patriotic poetry. On the fringes of the Göttingen circle, Gottfried August Bürger (1747–94) made his name on the basis of his ballads and love poems.

J. W. Goethe (1749–1832) is not only the single most important heir to these midcentury transformations of Ger. poetry but a major participant in them. His specific attentiveness to Klopstock is evident in the remarkable free-rhythm poems written between 1772 and 1774, in which he probed the construction of poetic enthusiasm and emotional immediacy, incl. "Wandrers Sturmlied" ("The Wanderer's Storm Song"), "Ganymed," and "An Schwager Kronos" ("To the Postilion Chronos"). But unlike his peers, Goethe moved with decisive energy to create a poetry apart from and, indeed, well beyond the 18th-c. example. A dramatist, novelist, scientist, and court administrator in Weimar, as well as a poet, Goethe constantly experimented in terms of *genre, *voice, and *form, absorbing and reworking all that he appreciated from the most colloquial style to the highest hymnic verse and making most of what he wrote seem utterly effortless. What he created frequently became the genre's new paradigm, as, e.g., his recreation of the Lat. love elegy in mod. setting in the *elegiac distichs of the *Römische Elegien* (Roman Elegies, 1795) or the classic epic in the hexameters of *Hermann und Dorothea* (1797) with its response to the dislocations of the Fr. Revolution. Unlike Klopstock, Goethe remained appreciative of rhyme, although not wedded to its use. The relationships of love, desire, and creativity and the continuity and coherence of the natural world, with its analogues in human experience, became his greatest themes, to which he returned again and again. In *Faust* (1808, 1832) Goethe programmatically recapitulated much of the Eur. poetic trad. from Gr. trimeter, through folk song, Minnesang, Knittelvers, to Sp. trochees, Fr. *alexandrines, Eng. *blank verse, and It. *ottava rima* and *terza rima*. In his middle years, he turned to Persia and the Near East, engaging the poetry of Hāfiz (d. 1389) in a substantial lyric cycle, the *West-östlicher Divan* (West-Eastern Divan, 1819). He later wrote a smaller cycle evoking Chinese poetry, *Chinesisch-Deutsche Jahres- und Tageszeiten* (Chinese-German Seasons of the Year and Day, 1827), and he actively promoted his notion of world lit., envisioning dynamic exchange among literary cultures large and small with salutary political influence. With Goethe, Ger. poetry decisively achieved full Eur. stature.

No single poet has had as major an impact on Ger. poetry as Goethe. Consequently, it can be easily forgotten that, in the 1780s, Bürger, Hölty, Voss, even the early Friedrich Schiller (1759–1805) were better known as poets. Goethe was celebrated primarily as a novelist and dramatist in his first decades of writing. In the 19th c., he came to dominate Ger. letters and, in particular, Ger. poetry.

Schiller, primarily a dramatist and theorist, published poetry in the 1780s that seemed unlikely to compel broad interest; much was rhetorically cumbersome, sober, and overtly philosophical. But his lament at the loss of Gr. antiquity with its divinity-filled world in "Die Götter Griechenlands" ("The Gods of Greece," 1788) proved electrifying in its indictment of contemp. society for its mechanistic notions of nature and impoverished abstractions; and his hymnic "An die Freude" ("An Ode to Joy," 1785) sparked utopian dreams. (Ludwig van Beethoven's setting in his Ninth Symphony serves as the new Eur. anthem.) In partnership with Goethe after 1794, Schiller used his poems and essays to articulate an agenda for the renewal of Ger. culture that has become known as Weimar Classicism. "Das Ideal und das Leben" ("The Ideal and the Actual Life," 1795) can stand for multiple poems proclaiming the mediating function of aesthetic experience between the material and the ideal. In "Der Spaziergang" ("The Walk," 1795), an elegy in cl. distichs in which landscape poetry is recast for philosophical purposes, Schiller provides a cultural-historical meditation on human devel. from the blissful constraints of primitive experience through mod. alienation to the recovery of harmony at the heights of poetic consciousness. Both were published in *Die Horen* (The Hours), his high-minded but short-lived periodical, where he also published his theory of *naïve and sentimental poetry and other aesthetic treatises.

Schiller and Goethe collaborated on a collection of ballads that appeared in Schiller's *Musenalmanach* in 1797. The mod. *ballad rightly claims its generic roots in med. and early mod. oral trad. In its 18th-c. revival, Bürger's "Lenore" (1773) and Goethe's "Der König in Thule" ("The King of Thule," 1774) and "Erlkönig" ("The Elf King," 1782) consciously evoked earlier stylistic gestures and supernatural strains. The ballads of 1797, incl. Goethe's "Die Braut von Korinth" ("The Bride of Corinth") and "Der Zauberlehrling" ("The Sorcerer's Apprentice") and Schiller's "Die Kraniche des Ibykus" ("The Cranes of Ibykus"), are more intellectually self-conscious. The ballad, and its variant the "Romanze" with generic links to Sp. and other Romance models, would prove to be a favored vehicle of the romantic poets, who emphasized its affinities with the folk song.

In his laments about the mod. age, its alienation and fragmentation, its deadening materialism and rationalism, Schiller inspired an entire generation of romantic poets. Their core narrative of a primal unity once experienced in nature, in childhood, in ancient Greece, the Middle Ages, and other cultural-historical moments given Edenic status, but now lost in the present, found endless variation in the expression of crisis and the quest for renewal and restoration. Aesthetic experience, the *imagination, and, above all, poetry itself became potential agents of redemption.

The single most compelling representation of the poet's plight in the present moment, intensified by acute knowledge of the richness of what has been lost appears in the works of Friedrich Hölderlin (1770–1843). The lost ideal is figured in images of plentitude, in a personalized and benevolent natural world vibrant with divinity, in the cultural-historical ideal of cl. Greece, and in idyllic images of childhood, home, and loving embrace. Hölderlin assigned heroic stature to the *poet, who most urgently and painfully bears the knowledge of the mod. day's impoverishment. The poet is also the purveyor of hope as he creates a remnant in poetic speech of what once was and anticipates what might yet be. Like that of many romantics, Hölderlin's vision of hist. was deeply rooted in Christian eschatological structures, an appropriation evident in his great elegy "Brod und Wein" ("Bread and Wine," 1800–01) and the late hymns such as "Patmos" (1802–03). The verbal power of his poetry is based on a richly inflected lang. indebted to Klopstock's example and his own intensive study of Gr. poetry, esp. Pindar and Sophocles; on intentional musicality; on the use of cl. forms; and on tautly structured lines with resonant symbolic *metaphors. Although 70 of Hölderlin's poems were published before his confinement in 1806 due to recurring mental illness, which lasted until his death, they were scattered and largely unknown. Appreciation for his great elegies and hymns and later fragments was made possible by the rediscovery of his works in the early 20th c.

Like Hölderlin, Friedrich von Hardenberg (1772–1801), who published as Novalis, transformed existing religious discourse to shape a syncretistic vision with a Christian core. Reversing the spatial trajectory of key Enlightenment terms, the quest in Novalis's single most important piece, "Hymnen an die Nacht" ("Hymns to the Night," 1800), a six-part *prose poem with lyric inserts, leads downward into the darkness of earthly despair and eroticized longing. Out of individualized anguish arises the emotionalized certainty that death marks the recovery of wholeness in the final mystical union with Christ as beloved. The poem was published in the *Athenaeum*, the principal organ of the romantic writers in Jena who sought to revolutionize philosophy and lit. by freeing them from rationalist and classicist constraints, and more boldly, to transform the human spirit.

Within the Jena circle, August Wilhelm Schlegel (1767–1845), in particular, worked to expand Ger. poetic forms by promoting Romance models. The Petrarchan sonnet became the signature genre of the romantic movement, produced in staggering quantity, and a lightning rod for attacks on its new poetic directions.

In Heidelberg, the second principal site of romantic activity, an enthusiasm for recovery of the Ger. past also had immediate impact on poetry. Achim von Arnim (1781–1831) and Clemens Brentano (1778–1842) gathered more than 700 poems from printed and oral sources and edited these "songs of the people" to make them compelling for mod. readers, to publish the landmark anthol. *Des Knaben Wunderhorn*

(The Youth's Magic Horn, 3 v., 1805–08). Herder had provided a precedent in 1778–79 with his successful two-volume collection of folk poetry drawn from international sources. But it is the Ger.-speaking world that is monumentalized in these "old German songs," the collection's subtitle. The simple strophic song, with its accessible diction, generally naïve tone, suggestion of orality, abundant rhyme, and thematic preoccupation with ordinary people and nature, became in the next decades a vehicle by which multiple poets sought to create a new Ger. poetry.

There was a precedent. In a large body of poetry that is mostly forgotten today, Ludwig Tieck (1773–1853) had scripted new formulas and metaphors for romantic verse devoid of cl. forms and mythology and inserted examples into his early narrative works. Brentano readily absorbed the new lang., but he also strained the simplicity of the folk-poetry model in his musically evocative verse, where his virtuosity was enhanced by the legacy of baroque and med. poetry. In repeating laments of estrangement and loss, he attested to the inadequacy of romantic aesthetic solutions to human existential need. After returning to his Roman Catholic faith in 1817, Brentano readdressed much of his creative effort to religious purposes. Joseph von Eichendorff (1788–1857) also adapted the forms and ambience of folk song in his ostensibly artless but carefully crafted poetry. His poems convey a pervasive longing for something beyond reach and definition and feature beautiful, ominous enticements from the imaginative depths, often explicitly erotic, that promise consolation and release. The answer Eichendorff endorsed in his poetry lay elsewhere, heavenward and in the future, located for him by his firm Catholic faith. But he never ceased evoking the attraction of the earthly enchantments whose power he repeatedly sought both to awaken and to constrain in his highly musical poetry.

Tieck, Arnim, Brentano, and Eichendorff all embedded their poems and songs in their novels (as did Goethe in *Wilhelm Meisters Lehrjahre* [*Wilhelm Meister's Apprenticeship*, 1795]). Single collected volumes of poetry were still relatively rare. The most enduring legacy for this large body of romantic poetry is musical; Beethoven, Franz Schubert, Robert Schumann, Johannes Brahms, Hugo Wolf, Gustav Mahler, Richard Strauss, and many lesser composers have guaranteed its international fame as the Ger. *lied*. Some poets, such as the epigonal romantic Wilhelm Müller (1794–1827), author of the cycles *Die schöne Müllerin* (*The Beautiful Maid of the Mill*, 1821) and *Die Winterreise* (*Winter Journey*, 1824), are known primarily through the musical settings of their works.

**V. Nineteenth Century.** In response to the events of the Fr. Revolution, Klopstock wrote a substantial number of poems celebrating its promise and later condemning its excesses. The Napoleonic invasion and the Wars of Liberation (1805–15) again led to excited poetic responses. Ernst Moritz Arndt (1769–1860), Friedrich de la Motte-Fouqué (1777–1843), and Theodor Körner (1791–1813) joined in the poetic call to arms. Unlikely forms such as Friedrich Rückert's (1788–

1866) *Geharnischte Sonette* (Armored Sonnets, 1814) were also fielded in the fight for "folk and fatherland." The ballads and earnest folk songs of Ludwig Uhland (1787–1862) served political ends in gentler more conservative ways. Rückert later turned his attention as a scholar to irenic purposes, finding refuge in the rich poetic world of Persia and the Near East. Near Eastern forms, prominently the *ghazal*, were popularized by him and August von Platen (1796–1835).

After 1815, most poets were keenly aware that not only a political era had passed but a poetic one; they were uncertain about the future and the status of poetic lang. An heir to the legacy of romantic tropes and forms and a master in his demonstration of the artifice as well as the seductive attraction of the world constructed from them, Heinrich Heine (1797–1856) used irony and self-deprecating humor to define dissonance and disillusionment as the 19th-c. poet's plight. His early collection *Das Buch der Lieder* (*The Book of Songs*, 1827) provides multiple variants on the theme of unrequited love, incl. the well-known "Loreley" and the rhythmically agile two-part cycle *Die Nordsee* (*The North Sea*, 1825–26). His verse satires *Atta Troll* (1843, rev. 1847) and *Deutschland. Ein Wintermärchen* (*Germany: A Winter's Tale*, 1844) written after emigration to Paris in 1831, where he lived out his life as a journalist and writer in political exile, mark his critical hostility to the political verse of his contemporaries as well as to the philistine culture of bourgeois Ger. society. In the freshest components of his *Neue Gedichte* (*New Poems*, 1844), *Romanzero* (1851), and later poems, Heine delivered sharp political and social commentary, grappled with his Jewish identity, and registered the suffering of debilitating illness that confined him to bed in his final eight years.

August Heinrich Hoffmann von Fallersleben (1798–1874), Ferdinand Freiligrath (1810–76), Georg Herwegh (1817–75), and others writing in the 1840s, the so-called *Vormärz* of optimism that preceded the failed revolution of 1848, produced rousing, occasionally bombastic songs to promote the liberal vision of Germany unity and radical reform. Many were set to familiar tunes, such as Hoffmann von Fallersleben's "Deutschland, Deutschland über alles" (1841), which became the national *anthem, 1922–45 (the third stanza serves as the current national anthem of the Federal Republic of Germany). After 1849, bitterness and silence largely replaced their boisterous verse.

Most poetry of the mid-19th c. registered Germany as a political and cultural backwater. In this period of resignation and restraint, the so-called *Biedermeier* era, poets turned inward, socially and psychologically. The carefully ordered life and the cultivation of the home-grown idyll were accompanied by pronounced strains of melancholy, psychological frailty, and unsettling premonitions of unseen menace. Poets typically had a narrow range and used their art in varying ways to flee lives they experienced as deficient and distasteful. Platen polished his sonnets, odes, and imported verse forms, seeking an aesthetic refuge from life's muddle and guilt. Nikolaus Lenau (pseud. of Franz Nikolaus Niembsch, 1802–50), first built a reputation on evocations of the Hungarian landscape of his childhood and then made melancholy and despair the thematic core of his culturally pessimistic work. The best poets, such as Eduard Mörike (1804–75), demonstrated new ways to express elusive sensations, fleeting perceptions, and fragile moments of aesthetic pleasure. Mörike stands out for his exceptional facility in a range of inherited genres and verse forms, from cl. meters and sonnets to folk song, and for the evocative lyricism of his verse. Whether probing the unconscious or evoking the biological world of her beloved Westphalia in precise realist diction or grappling with received religious lang. to express faltering conviction, the lyric poetry and ballads of Annette von Droste-Hülshoff (1797–1848) reveal an interest in interiority, the instability of human identity, and the ambivalence of perception. Anchored and constrained by class and gender, the aristocratic Droste-Hülshoff repeatedly staged a surrendering to imaginative depths with varying consequences: fright, guilt, unresolved longing, and resignation or relief on return to the familiar but rarely any alteration in the external world of her poetic protagonists.

Even though the second half of the 19th c. has been widely considered hostile to poetry, epigonal poets such as the immensely popular and now forgotten Emanuel Geibel (1815–84) prospered. Poets remained largely unresponsive to industrialization, urbanization, secularization, and other large-scale social changes. Lyric poetry was confirmed as a refuge, domestic and psychological, from all that was shifting in the public sphere. Exceptions such as the Swiss realist Gottfried Keller (1819–90) struggled to find appropriate poetic voice. The period 1840–1914 witnessed an enormous growth in poetic anthols., which were deemed supremely fit for moral improvement, educational purposes, and social entertainment.

**VI. Twentieth Century.** The notion that poetry, and more broadly art and beauty itself, must proclaim a timeless realm apart from public and political life was embraced not only by middle-class readers but also by fin de siècle artists who otherwise rejected bourgeois notions of artistic consumption. They radicalized the claim: only apart from all things external and contingent can true art flourish. Mörike's "Auf eine Lampe" ("To a Lamp," 1846) and the Swiss Conrad Ferdinand Meyer's (1825–98) "Der römische Brunnen" ("The Roman Fountain," 1882) had prefigured the interest in self-sufficient artifacts and symbolic lang. transcending ephemeral experience. Stefan George (1868–1933) embodied aesthetic *modernism in its most elitist expression. From 1890 onward, he carefully printed his poems in stylized orthography in limited editions on fine paper as repositories of a poetic beauty otherwise lost to what he saw as a debased and vulgar civilization. Poetry served a sacred function in a sectarian cult with strong homoerotic attachment and messianic zeal. His collections include *Das Jahr der Seele* (The Year of the Soul, 1897) with its refined symbolic landscapes, and *Der siebente Ring* (The Seventh Ring, 1907) with its dreams of civilization renewed. Among the younger

writers attracted to the aestheticist vision was the Viennese prodigy Hugo von Hofmannsthal (1874–1929), who wrote exquisite and surprisingly mature poetry while still of school age. In the ten years of his poetic production after 1890, Hofmannsthal evoked a world of impression in which the formal perfection of the poem served as the sole site of stability in a transient phenomenal world. Later, Hofmannsthal rejected this aestheticist vision—and with it, lyric poetry—on ethical grounds, turning to drama, opera, and other forms.

Rainer Maria Rilke (1875–1926), who began in Prague as a prolific but unexceptional poet, ended his career acclaimed as the major lyric voice of the early 20th c. A search for meaning distinguished each phase of Rilke's devel. and repeatedly altered his stylistic choices. His poems trace a general path from subjectivity and emotionalism in *Das Stunden-Buch* (*The Book of Hours*, 1905) via *Das Buch der Bilder* (*The Book of Images*, 1902, 1906) to a focus on external objects, particularly works of aesthetic value, in *Neue Gedichte* (*New Poems*, 2 v., pub. 1907–08). His *Dinggedichte* implicitly underscore how alienated he believed mod. humans to be from the integrity and intensity of the phenomenal world. In the *Duineser Elegien* (*Duino Elegies*, 1923), a ten-poem cycle in free-rhythm verse, and the two-part cycle *Sonette an Orpheus* (*Sonnets to Orpheus*, 1923), works that are generally considered Rilke's greatest achievement, solutions for the human plight are proclaimed in the creative and transforming word, an aesthetic redemption that turns the visible world into an inner invisible one, bestowing purpose in the face of transience.

The creative energy that surged through the Ger.-speaking world after 1890 did not run its poetic course with George, Hofmannsthal, and Rilke. There was scarcely a poet of note who did not share a fundamental antipathy toward the perceived self-satisfactions of bourgeois society, with its sentimental heroic trappings, growing bureaucracy, philistine if prosperous tastes, and enforced propriety. Some marked their distance through fanciful ling. play, like Christian Morgenstern (1871–1914), best known for his humorous *Galgenlieder* (*Gallows Songs*, 1905). Others fashioned their lives as well as their poetry around imaginary identities and exotic alternatives to Wilhelmine society, such as the unconventional feminist Else Lasker-Schüler (1869–1945), whose protective disguises and ling. creativity could not, in the end, ward off forced exile as a Jew.

After 1910, a poetic explosion signaled the arrival of new, determinedly disruptive voices. *Expressionism was edgy and assertive; it broke decisively with the cadences of *aestheticism and the cult of the beautiful. Jakob van Hoddis's (1884–1942) disjunctive images ordered in simple rhymed stanzas in "Weltende" ("End of the World," 1911) became a model for multiple poetic collages, half-real, half-surreal. Apocalyptic anticipation marked the work of Georg Heym (1887–1912), and ling. experiments honed lang. to maximize intensity in the futurist poetry of August Stramm (1864–1915). Ernst Stadler (1881–1914) filled long irregular lines with vitalistic assertions. Expressionist poetry burned brightly and quickly. By the end of World War I, it yielded center stage to drama, where calls for a new man and a new community continued to be sounded. *Menschheitsdämmerung* (*Dawn of Humanity*, 1920), its signature anthol., was assembled retrospectively by Kurt Pinthus (1886–1975).

The Salzburg medical orderly Georg Trakl (1887–1914), who died from a drug overdose after the battle of Grodek, wrote purposefully hermetic poetry. Trakl employed resonant lang. with self-consciously repetitive and derivative images (often from the poetic repertoire of Hölderlin and the romantics), reassembled like fragments in associative structures. He obsessively filled his symbolic landscapes with signs of decline, disintegration, and guilt only partially clarified.

In terms of cynicism, Gottfried Benn (1886–1956), a physician, surpassed the provocations of his contemporaries in his early collections beginning with *Morgue* (1912). Benn later insisted on a stern and individualized cerebralism, denying the mod. human any consolation in nature or sentiment, religious community or social program of salvation (his public, if short-lived, affiliation with National Socialism notwithstanding). In his *Statische Gedichte* (Static Poems, 1948) largely written between 1935 and 1945, the poetic word in abstracted form is considered the sole authentic bulwark against nihilism and pure of the deceits of cultural hist. His late poems and his theory of absolute poetry in *Probleme der Lyrik* (Problems of Lyric, 1951) proved esp. attractive to young writers in postwar Germany, where he replaced Rilke as a poetic example.

But in the era of the Weimar Republic, other alternatives to Benn's stern modernism existed. The most radical was the short-lived culture of *Dada, created in 1916 by avant-garde artists in Zurich, the center of political and intellectual exile. Under Hugo Ball, the Cabaret Voltaire offered soirées pillorying established culture. Poetry performances included *sound experiments (from phonetic patterning to pure noise), repudiation of ling. sequencing (play with simultaneity and with stasis), and montage. Dada with a more political edge followed in Berlin in 1918 and other Eur. cities.

In other ways, poetry became more public. Cabarets and revues brought poetry onto the stage in the form of chansons and songs. Joachim Ringelnatz (pseud. of Hans Bötticher, 1883–1934), poet and cabaret performing artist, added humor to the scene, as did Erich Kästner (1899–1974). Kurt Tucholsky (1890–1935) wrote satirical poems with pointed political purpose.

The most important poet to arise out of this milieu was Bertolt Brecht (1898–1956). In his early collection *Hauspostille* (*Devotions for the Home*, 1927), Brecht deftly subverted a range of bourgeois pieties, incl. religious sentiment and idealizations of landscape and love. Under the banner of *Gebrauchslyrik* (useful lyric), he developed a verse free of psychological excess, public in its reporting, and often polemical in its instructional intent. Brecht typically set his understated speech in simple rhymed stanzas, largely devoid of metaphor but enriched by colloquial phrases, biblical lang. and hymns, and citations of well-known poems. Many of his social-critical songs and ballads were in-

serted into his plays. Substantial collections include the *Svendborger Gedichte* (*Svendborg Poems*, 1939), written in Danish exile after he fled Nazi Germany in 1933, and the laconic *Buckower Elegien* (*Buckow Elegies*, 1953) written after his 1948 return to East Berlin. Brecht's impact on poets both East and West in the second half of the 20th c. was singular.

With the founding of the German Democratic Republic (GDR) and the Federal Republic of Germany (FRG) in 1949, two separate political cultures laid claim to the poetic past. The GDR proclaimed itself heir to all things progressive within Ger. lit., celebrating in particular the legacy of Weimar Classicism, Heine and the Young Germans, and the realistic-critical lit. of the Weimar Republic. Johannes R. Becher (1891–1958), who began as an expressionist poet, emerged as the embodiment of orthodox GDR verbal culture, embracing the forms and diction of traditional poetry to promote a new socialist society. He wrote the national anthem and became the minister of culture in 1954. Less orthodox but astute and inventive to the end, Brecht was the undisputed literary star and a major example for the next generation of GDR poets, incl. the laconic skeptic Günter Kunert (b. 1929) and the antiestablishment songwriter and performer Wolf Biermann (b. 1936). Modernism was suspect. Nature poets Peter Huchel (1903–81) and Johannes Bobrowski (1917–65) reinvigorated their genre as well as the landscapes they evoked with a sharpened focus on human activity and hist. In the 1960s, a younger, energetic generation of poets born in the 1930s altered the ongoing debate about poetry's function within socialist society by pressing the question of subjectivity and the expression of individual experience. The new poets wrote poetry that proved more critical, experimental, and personal than the conservative GDR cultural authorities desired. Within a decade, political realities led to censorship, harassment, and mounting disillusionment with the East German state and, after 1970, multiple relocations to the West. The forced expatriation of Biermann in 1976 proved a watershed. In the end Huchel, Kunert, and, from the 1930s generation, Reiner Kunze (b. 1933), Bernd Jentzsch (b. 1940), Sarah Kirsch (b. 1935), and Kurt Bartsch (1937–2010) left. Volker Braun (b. 1939), Heinz Czechowski (1935–2009), Rainer Kirsch (b. 1934), and Karl Mickel (1935–2000) remained. The 1980s saw growing disengagement. Younger poetic voices, uneasy within inherited ling. and political boundaries, placed a renewed emphasis on formal experimentation that would continue after the collapse of the GDR in 1989.

After the formation of the FRG in 1949, it was Benn who first dominated poetic discussion. His emphasis on form above content, on hist.'s emptiness, and on words stripped of ideology attracted younger writers seeking refuge from the trauma of the war years. Similarly, nature poetry seemed to offer a refuge, evoking a world of tangible plants and animals. Here also was continuity with the past. Among the authors associated with the example of Oskar Loerke (1884–1941) and the prewar jour. *Kolonne* (Convoy, 1929–32), the mythopoetic Wilhelm Lehmann (1882–1968) and Catholic Elisabeth Langgässer (1899–1950) evoked a natural world largely apart from human activity. Günter Eich (1907–72) proved more overtly political; Eich developed a terse, minimalist style that secured his postwar reputation. Writing in a lang. uncontaminated by National Socialism became a priority. *Gruppe 47* (Group 47), a gathering of authors committed to renewing democratic lit. first convened by Hans Werner Richter (1908–93) in 1947, established a general modernism and encouraged critical opposition to the political restoration.

The most important new poetic voices came from outside the FRG. Austrian-born Ingeborg Bachmann (1926–73) asserted the need to reclaim poetic lang. in the present setting of disillusionment with bold metaphors and a desire for utopian dreaming coupled with fundamental unease about the present. Nobel laureate of 1966 Nelly Sachs (1891–1970) wrote more directly from her Swedish exile, where she survived the war, straining to say the unspeakable not only about the Shoah but about personal suffering. Romanian-born Paul Antschel, who changed his name to Celan (1920–70), witnessed to the past in a lang. that he experienced as both essential and suspect. The son of Ger.-speaking Jews who died in the Holocaust, Celan moved after the war to Paris and became a Fr. citizen. His early and best-known poem "Todesfuge" ("Death Fugue") in *Mohn und Gedächtnis* (Poppy and Memory, 1952) evoked the death camps in a musical counterpoint atypical in its fluidity and accessibility. Later works, such as the collections *Sprachgitter* (*Speech-Grille*, 1959), *Atemwende* (*Breathturn*, 1967), and *Fadensonnen* (*Threadsuns*, 1968), testified to growing despair and silence communicated in a lang. that had become fragmented, compounded, and parched. An accomplished translator of the Fr. symbolists as well as contemp. poets, the polyglot Celan estranged lang. to the limits of comprehension while underscoring the urgency of dialogue.

Lang. was also the immediate concern of poets reviving the international avant-garde trads. of ling. experimentation. They privileged phonetic, graphic, and morphological elements in order to liberate lang. from grammatical convention. Eugen Gomringer's (b. 1925) *concrete poetry isolated verbal materials in visual settings. Helmut Heissenbüttel (1921–96) inventoried words, writing "texts" rather than poems; Jürgen Becker's (b. 1932) "texts" also ignored traditional genre boundaries. In Austria, the *Wiener Gruppe* (Vienna Group) initiated bohemian events. H. C. Artmann (1921–2000) exploited dialect, and Friederike Mayröcker (b. 1924) experimented widely, incl. with montage. Ernst Jandl (1925–2000) evidenced humor as well as self-irony in performance and in his collections of sound poetry.

By the mid-1960s, ever more politically potent poetry was appearing. Already in the mid-1950s Hans Magnus Enzensberger (b. 1929) had faced the emerging social and political reality of postwar Germany more resolutely than most of his contemporaries. Versatile and ironic, he provoked and prodded in his richly allusive verse. Brecht's influence was increasingly evident. Günter Grass (b. 1927), Peter Rühmkorf (1929–2008), and Biermann, performing and publishing in the West, mobilized political sentiment in print and in concert. Erich Fried (1921–88), living in Great Britain, wrote outspoken political poetry, incl. *Warngedichte* (Poems of Warning, 1964) and *und Vietnam und* (and Vietnam and, 1966).

In counterpoint, the new subjectivity of the 1970s focused on everyday needs and personal experience. Rolf Dieter Brinkmann (1940–75), emerging from the counterculture, used seemingly banal moments to capture "snapshots" of everyday reality. Sarah Kirsch had long reflected on nature and love; her collection *Katzenleben* (*Catlives*, 1984), pub. after her 1977 departure from the GDR, marked a personal coming to terms with the writers' life within political and social constraints. The women's movement and the question of female subjectivity led both writers and critics to new appreciation of forgotten poets such as Karoline von Gunderrode (1780–1806) and to recognition of common themes of identity, exile, and loss in the poetry of Jewish women writers such as Lasker-Schüler, Sachs, Gertrud Kolmar (1894–1943), Rose Ausländer (1901–88), Mascha Kaléko (1907–75), Hilde Domin (1912–2006), and Ilse Aichinger (b. 1921).

Others shifted gears. Karl Krolow (1915–1999), known for modernist poems such as *Fremde Körper* (*Foreign Bodies*, 1959), grew more laconic and elegiac. In the 1980s, a general disillusionment characterized the work of many older and still-productive poets, who approached the future with apocalyptic visions and dire warnings. In contrast, younger poets writing in the 1980s and 1990s evidenced wider stylistic modes, a revival of hermetic poetic gestures, more explicit citations of the larger poetic trad., and a return to overt demonstrations of formal virtuosity. Technology often replaced nature as an imagery source. Thomas Kling (1957–2005) experimented with *typography and orthography, fractured syntax, and intertextual citations. Former East German Uwe Kolbe (b. 1957) combined radical subjectivity with ling. play.

In the 21st c., Ger. poetry continues to prosper, despite repeated assertions about its decline. Durs Grünbein (b. 1962) can be seen as representative of a great many poets working with questions of postunification culture who seek to keep alive the recent past and yet reclaim the larger Ger. poetic trad. The number of new poets continues to increase in a highly educated society, where their work is supported by a well-established system of jours., publishing houses, prizes, academies, civic grants, and media.

*See* AUSTRIA, POETRY OF; GERMANIC PROSODY; GESELL-SCHAFTSLIED; ROMANTIC AND POSTROMANTIC POETRY AND POETICS; SWITZERLAND, POETRY OF.

■ **Anthologies.** *German*: *Epochen der deutschen Lyrik*, ed. W. Killy, 10 v. (1969–77); *Seventeen Modern German Poets*, ed. S. Prawer (1971); *Lyrik des Barock*, ed. M. Szyrocki, 2 v. (1971); *Spätmittelalter, Humanismus,*

*Reformation*, ed. H. Heger, 2 v. (1975–78); *Deutsche Dichterinnen vom 16. Jahrhundert bis zur Gegenwart*, ed. G. Brinker-Gabler (1978); *Lyrik-Katalog Bundesrepublik*, ed. J. Hans, U. Herms, R. Thenior (1978); *Lyrik für Leser: Deutsche Gedichte der siebziger Jahre*, ed. V. Hage (1980); *Modern deutsche Naturlyrik*, ed. E. Marsch (1980); *German Poetry*, ed. M. Swales (1987); *Deutsche Gedichte von 1900 bis zur Gegenwart*, ed. F. Pratz, 2d ed. (1987); *Frühe deutsche Literatur und lateinische Literatur in Deutschland 800–1150*, ed. W. Haug and B. K. Vollmann (1991); *Deutsche Lyrik des frühen und hohen Mittelalters*, ed. I. Kasten (1995); *Humanistische Lyrik des 16. Jahrhunderts*, ed. W. Kühlmann, R. Seidel, and H. Wiegand (1997); *Deutsche Lyrik des späten Mittelalters*, ed. B. Wachinger (2006); *Reclams grosses Buch der deutschen Gedichte*, ed. H. Detering (2007); *In welcher Sprache träumen Sie? Österreichische Lyrik des Exils und des Widerstands*, ed. M. Herz-Kestranek and K. Kaiser, D. Strigl (2007). **English**: *The Penguin Book of German Verse*, ed. L. Forster, rev. ed. (1959); *Anthology of German Poetry from Hölderlin to Rilke*, ed. A. Flores (1960); *The German Lyric of the Baroque in English Translation*, ed. and trans. G. Schoolfield (1961); *Modern German Poetry 1910–1960*, ed. M. Hamburger and C. Middleton (1962); *Twentieth-Century German Verse*, ed. P. Bridgwater (1963); *Anthology of German Poetry through the 19th Century*, ed. A. Gode and F. Ungar (1964); *The Penguin Book of Lieder*, ed. and trans. S. Prawer (1964); *An Anthology of Concrete Poetry*, ed. E. Williams (1967); *Medieval German Lyric Verse in English Translation*, ed. and trans. J. Thomas (1968); *German and Italian Lyrics of the Middle Ages*, ed. and trans. F. Goldin (1973); *East German Poetry*, ed. M. Hamburger (1973); *Twenty-five German Poets*, ed. and trans. W. Kaufmann (1975); *German Poetry, 1910–1975*, trans. M. Hamburger (1977); *German Poetry from 1750 to 1900*, ed. R. Browning (1984); *Austrian Poetry Today*, ed. and trans. M. Holton and H. Kuhner (1985); *Contemporary Austrian Poetry*, ed. and trans. B. Bjorklund (1986); *The Defiant Muse: German Feminist Poems from the Middle Ages to the Present*, ed. S. Cocalis (1986); *Evidence of Fire: An Anthology of Twentieth-Century German Poetry*, ed. R. Ives (1988); *German Lieder*, ed. P. Miller (1990); *Menschheitsdämmerung/Dawn of Humanity*, ed. K. Pinthus, trans. J. M. Ratych, R. Ley, R. C. Conard (1994); *The Cambridge Songs*, ed. and trans. J. Ziolkowski (1994); *German Epic Poetry*, ed. F. Gentry and J. Walter, trans. F. Ryder and J. Walter (1995); *German Poetry in Transition, 1945–1990*, ed. and trans. C. Melin (1999); *Sovereignty and Salvation in the Vernacular, 1050–1150*, ed. and trans. J. Schultz (2000); *After Every War: Twentieth-Century Women Poets*, ed. and trans. E. Boland (2004); *The Faber Book of Twentieth-Century German Poems*, ed. M. Hofmann (2005).

■ **Criticism and History. German**: *Geschichte der politischen Lyrik in Deutschland*, ed. W. Hinderer (1978); *Die deutsche Lyrik, 1945–75*, ed. K. Weissenberger (1981); *Gedichte und Interpretationen*, ed. V. Meid et al., 7 v. (v. 1–6, 1982; v. 7, 1997); *Geschichte der deutschen Lyrik vom Mittelalter bis zur Gegenwart*, ed. W. Hinderer (1983); G. Schulz, *Die deutsche Literatur zwischen Französischer Revolution und Restauration*, 2 v. (1983, 1989); B. Sorg, *Das lyrische Ich* (1984); H.-G. Kemper, *Deutsche Lyrik der frühen Neuzeit*, 6 v. (1987–2002); G. Kaiser, *Augenblicke deutscher Lyrik* (1987); *Deutsche Lyrik nach 1945*, ed. D. Breuer (1988); *Gedichte und Interpretationen: Deutsche Balladen*, ed. G. Grimm (1988); W. Haubrichs, *Die Anfänge: Versuche volkssprachiger Schriftlichkeit im frühen Mittelalter* (1988); G. Kaiser, *Geschichte der deutschen Lyrik von Goethe bis Heine*, 3 v. (1988); *Frauen dichten anders*, ed. M. Reich-Ranicki (1998); *1400 Deutsche Gedichte und ihre Interpretationen*, ed. M. Reich-Ranicki, 12 v. (2002); F.-J. Holznagel et al., *Geschichte der deutschen Lyrik* (2004); H. Korte, *Deutschsprachige Lyrik seit 1945*, 2d rev. ed. (2004); H. Hiebel, *Das Spektrum der modernen Poesie*, 2 v. (2005); B. Böschenstein, *Von Morgen nach Abend* (2006); R. Klüger, *Gemalte Fensterscheiben* (2007). **English**: P. Demetz, *Postwar German Literature* (1970); R. M. Browning, *German Baroque Poetry, 1618–1723* (1971); G. Gillespie, *German Baroque Poetry* (1971); A. De Capua, *German Baroque Poetry* (1973); E. Blackall, *The Emergence of German as a Literary Language*, 2d ed. (1978); R. Browning, *German Poetry in the Age of the Enlightenment* (1978); Sayce, *German Baroque Literature*, ed. G. Hoffmeister (1983); S. Jaeger, *The Origins of Courtliness* (1985); P. Demetz, *After the Fires: Recent Writing in the Germanies, Austria and Switzerland* (1986); M. Hamburger, *After the Second Flood* (1986); *German Poetry through 1915*, ed. H. Bloom (1987); B. Peucker, *Lyric Descent in the German Romantic Tradition* (1987); J. Rolleston, *Narratives of Ecstasy* (1987); *Modern German Poetry*, ed. H. Bloom (1989); K. Leeder, *Breaking Boundaries: A New Generation of Poets in the GDR* (1996); D. Wellbery, *The Specular Moment* (1996); M. Gibbs and S. Johnson, *Medieval German Literature* (1997); W. Haug, *Vernacular Literary Theory in the Middle Ages* (1997); M. Lee, *Displacing Authority* (1999); *Landmarks in German Poetry*, ed. P. Hutchinson (2000); R. Owen, *The Poet's Role: Lyric Responses to German Unification by Poets from the G.D.R.* (2001); I. Stoehr, *German Literature of the Twentieth Century* (2001); C. Edwards, *The Beginnings of German Literature* (2002); *Literature of the Sturm und Drang*, ed. D. Hill (2003); A. Classen, *Late-Medieval German Women's Poetry* (2004); *Early Germanic Literature and Culture*, ed. B. Murdoch and M. Read (2004); *German Literature of the Early Middle Ages*, ed. B. Murdoch (2004); *The Literature of German Romanticism*, ed. D. Mahoney (2004); *A New History of German Literature*, ed. D. Wellbery (2004); *German Literature of the Eighteenth Century*, ed. B. Becker-Cantarino (2005); *German Literature of the Nineteenth Century, 1832–1899*, ed. C. Koelb and E. Downing (2005); *The Literature of Weimar Classicism*, ed. S. Richter (2005); *German Literature of the High Middle Ages*, ed. W. Hasty (2006); *Early Modern German Literature 1350–1700*, ed. M. Reinhart (2007); B. Bennett, "Histrionic Nationality: Implications of the Verse in *Faust*," *Goethe Yearbook* 17 (2010).

M. Lee

**GESELLSCHAFTSLIED.** A term narrowly applied to a four-part, polyphonic song, composed and performed by and for educated society during the *rococo and *baroque periods in Germany. Musical forerunners include It. part songs: the courtly, non-strophic *madrigal, the strophic Neapolitan *villanella* (street song), and the *canzone. Gesellschaftslieder* are usually composed to an existing melody sung by the tenor or the discantus but occasionally in one of the middle voices. Sixteenth-c. Gesellschaftslieder, commonly composed in bar form, are characterized by the melodic quality of all voices in the imitative style of the Fr. *chanson*. Although distinct from the *Hofweise* (court song) and the *Volkslied* (folk song), Gesellschaftslieder share thematic concerns of both genres, most prominently the pain and pleasure of love, as well as drinking songs. As in the 19th c., there was a close connection between the Gesellschaftslied and the flowering of Ger. lyrical poetry from 1620 to 1680 (e.g., Simon Dach, Martin Opitz, G. R. Weckherlin). Among important composers of the genre, Ludwig Senfl was the most prolific.

The term is more popularly used as a synonym for the 19th-c. *geselliges Lied* (sociable song)—a term also loosely employed for the *Tafellieder* of the late 18th and early 19th cs.—but usually refers to solo song with piano (or guitar or harp) accompaniment, performed in Ger. drawing rooms. The sociohistorical context into which the Gesellschaftslied was born witnessed J. W. Goethe's contribution to Ger. lyric poetry, the Enlightenment emphasis on *Bildung und Kultur* (education and culture), the rise of music printing, the devel. of the pianoforte, and the accompanying expectation of a modest musical ability in polite young men and women. Such a confluence of factors inspired the Goethe settings of J. F. Reichardt and C. F. Zelter, strophic songs that reflected textual nuances and were written for the amateur performer. Amateur performance has always had two levels—the safe and the accomplished, which reaches professional standards. Whereas the first is purely a source of entertainment, the second, while sharing this function, has a very strong educative value that improves the quality of music making in society in general. This interlocking dynamic existed in 19th-c. Germany, and an enormous difference in standards of performance and composition fall under the one rubric of *Gesellschaftslied*.

■ A. Reissmann, *Das deutsche Lied in seiner historischen Entwicklung* (1861); F. W. von Ditfurth, *Deutsche Volks–und Gesellschaftslieder des 17. und 18. Jahrhunderts* (1872); M. Friedlaender, *Das dt. Lied im 18. Jh.*, 2d ed., 2 v. (1908); R. Velten, *Das Ältere dt. Gesellschaftslieder unter dem Einfluss der italienischen Musik* (1914); M. Platel, *Vom Volkslied zum Gesellschaftslied* (1939); W. Flemming, "Gesellschaftslied," *Reallexikon II*; W. Kayser, *Gesch. des deutschen Verses* (1960); *Die Lautenhandschrift des Prämonstratenserstiftes Strachov (Prag)*, ed. J. Klima (1976); M. M. Stoljar, "*Speculum ludi*: The Aesthetics of Performance in Song," *Music and German Literature*, ed. J. M. McGlathery (1992); L. Finscher, "Lied und Madrigal, 1580–1600,"

*Music in the German Renaissance*, ed. J. Kmetz (1994); J. Steinheuer: "Zum Wandel des italienisches Einflusses auf das deutsche Gesellschaftslied und vor allem das Quodlibet in der ersten Hälfte des 17. Jahrhunderts," *Relazioni musicali tra Italia e Germania nell'età barocca: Loveno di Menaggio*, ed. A. Colzani (1997).

L. BYRNE BODLEY

**GHAZAL.** A *monorhyme (*aa ba ca*, etc.) *lyric poem originating in Arabia as a thematic genre on love and later developed into a fixed form in Persian, Turkish, Urdu, and most other Islamicate lits. The Ar. root *gh-z-l* semantically encompasses the gazelle, the act of spinning/weaving, and, eventually, amorous talk with a woman; as a poetic genre, *ghazal* ranges in mood from elegiac to *anacreontic, from defeatist to mystically ecstatic. The ghazal motifs and imagery already appear in the *nasīb* of the pre-Islamic Ar. *qaṣīda, evoked both as the poet's pain at separation from his beloved and as nostalgic reverie of their youthful amorous exploits. In the Umayyad period (660–750), the ghazal developed into a stand-alone love poem, prosodically similar to the qaṣīda but shorter and preferably in meters suitable for singing. The early Ar. ghazal reflects two major schools or ideals of love, Hijazi and 'Udhrī. In the Hijazi ghazal, at Mecca and Medina, an urbane and lighthearted mood prevailed, with poets like 'Umar ibn Abī Rabī'a (d. 712 or 721) often admiring and wooing the female pilgrims. Aristocratic beloveds were usually mentioned by name in the early ghazal, perhaps contributing to social and political problems for poets like al-'Arjī (d. 737) and al-Aḥwaṣ al-Anṣārī (d. 729), who both wound up in prison. The Hijazi lover is deferential to his lady in the ghazal but hopes for and can achieve consummation of his love, while generally avoiding bawdry (obscene matter is the purview of the *mujūn* genre), though in the ghazals of Bashshār ibn Burd (d. 784) or in certain bacchic ghazals, this boundary is blurred. By contrast, the 'Udhrī poets love chastely (famous among Eur. romantics through Stendhal's *De l'amour* and Heinrich Heine's *Der Asra*, "Welche sterben, wenn sie lieben"), separated by circumstance from their ladies and dying as ennobled martyrs to unfulfilled love—at least as portrayed in the vitas that later attached to ghazal poets like Jamīl (d. 701), or the legendary Majnūn, driven mad by his love for Laylā and proverbially known in Islamicate trads. for unwavering devotion. In the early Abbasid period (750–1258), the courtly ideal of unattainable love is exemplified in al-'Abbās b. al-Aḥnaf (d. ca. 808), whereas with Abū Nuwās (d. ca. 814), the ghazal turns away from naming an aristocratic lady toward an anonymous beloved who may be a slave or a server in the wine tavern and not infrequently male. The homoerotic environment and the anonymous beloved characterize the later ghazal trad., esp. in Persian, Turkish, and Urdu. Meanwhile, the elaboration of literary, legal, and medical theories of the stages and kinds of love, esp. eros, enabled Neoplatonic and mystical symbolism to attach to the ghazal during the 10th and 11th cs., particularly in Sufi circles. The ghazal ethos was acutely expressed in Andalusia by Ibn Zaydūn (d. 1071) and others, where the thematics also found expression in new fixed forms (e.g., *muwashshaḥ*, *zajal*; see ZÉJEL).

Persian *love poetry has roots in the Sasanian minstrel trad., incl. musical performance; but the images, motifs, and prosodic structures of Ar. were fundamental to the devel. of the Persian ghazal. From Persian poetry's earliest emergence in the 10th c., *ghazal* is an integral concept and technical term distinguishing the mode of love poetry from modes of *panegyric, *elegy, or *satire across a variety of verse forms (qaṣīda, *rubāʿī, *qiṭa). Persian poetry of the 9th–10th cs. produced many shorter poems focused on amorous themes, often for a wine symposium or royal banquet. Without abandoning its earthly and epicurean associations, love was, however, increasingly understood, esp. in the expanding Sufi contexts, as susceptible of pointing symbolically to the transcendental. Furthermore, by the 12th c., esp. in the work of Sanāʾī (d. ca. 1131), the Persian ghazal assumed the contours of a fixed form, later defined as a monorhyme poem (*aa ba ca*, etc.) of 5 to 14 lines, incl. a line, usually the last or penultimate, mentioning the poet's pen name (*takhalluṣ*). This last feature developed perhaps as a seal of authorship for ghazals sold to musicians as lyric texts, to be performed in the poet's absence. This "clasp line" also served as a device of *closure, for the poet to exit the mood of reverie, comment on the theme, or possibly dedicate the poem to a patron. Almost all subsequent Persian poets practiced this fixed-form ghazal, incl. Saʿdī (d. 1292), known for his inimitable simplicity and cultivation of both earthly and ethereal beloveds; Jalāl al-Dīn Rūmī (d. 1273), who mastered the ecstatic mystical expression of the religion of love in the ghazal; Ḥāfiz (d. 1389), who turned the ghazal into a deep, complex meditation, at once carnal, sociopolitical, and mystical; and Ṣāʾib (d. ca. 1676), a prolific and careful craftsman of lang. who plumbed conventional motifs and images for new meanings.

This fixed-form ghazal spread to many kindred lits. in central and south Asia, incl. Anatolian (13th c.) and Chaghatay (15th c.) Turkish, as well as to Urdu (15th c.), where the influence of the Persian poets of the "Indian style" provided the model for Walī Dakanī (d. before 1725) but took on increasingly modernist casts in the ghazals of Mīrzā Ghālib (d. 1869) and Muḥammad Iqbāl (d. 1938). Though some contemp. Persian poets have excelled at the ghazal form (e.g., Sayyid Muḥammad Ḥusayn Shahryār [d. 1988] and Sīmīn Bihbahānī [b. 1927]), it remains most vital in the Urdu tradition. Ger. trans. of the Persian ghazal deeply influenced J. W. Goethe, August von Platen, Friedrich Rückert, and the musical *lieder*; since about 2000, Am. poetry has witnessed a vibrant ghazal scene, largely informed by a 1969 experiment in New York involving Adrienne Rich, W. S. Merwin, William Stafford, and Mark Strand and their adaptations of Ghālib's poetry from literal trans. (pub. as *Ghazals of Ghālib*).

Once established as a fixed form, the cl. ghazal was no longer bound thematically to love, and a range of themes, esp. mysticism and speculative philosophy, panegyric, and politics, could be expressed. Typical locales of the cl. ghazal include the garden, the royal banquet or symposium, and the wine tavern, often in the spring at dawn after a sleepless night. The main characters include the lover, typically identified with the voice of the poet, at least until the takhalluṣ creates some distance from the speaking *persona of the poem. Usually enthusiastic and determined, he is, however, not often successful because of several factors: the beloved's hauteur, indifference, and downright cruelty; the watchful eye of the beloved's kinsmen or the presence of rivals; and the night watchman or morals police. The lover/drunkard is castigated by various blamers—kinsmen attempting to rescue the lover from irresolute self-destruction or religious and political figures of authority. Esp. in mystical poems, this is manifested as an antinomian revelry, with the poetic persona, often a *qalandar* dervish, exalting in his irreligion, loving an idol, abandoning the mosque for the tavern, and learning the secrets of life from a social outcast (*rind*), a tavern owner, or a Zoroastrian magus, in the role of saint and mystagogue.

See ARABIC POETICS, ARABIC POETRY, PERSIAN POETRY, TURKISH POETRY, URDU POETRY.

■ A. J. Arberry, "Orient Pearls at Random Strung," *Bulletin of the School of Oriental and African Studies* 11 (1943); A. Pagliaro and A. Bausani, *Storia della letteratura persiana* (1960); E. Yarshater, "The Theme of Wine-Drinking and the Concept of the Beloved in Early Persian Poetry," *Studia Islamica* 13 (1960); *History of Iranian Literature*, ed. J. Rypka (1968); *Ghazals of Ghālib*, ed. A. Ahmad (1971); A. Hamori, *On the Art of Medieval Arabic Literature* (1974); M. Hillmann, *Unity in the Ghazals of Ḥāfiz* (1976); A. Schimmel, "The Emergence of the German Ghazal," *Studies in the Urdu Ghazal and Prose Fiction*, ed. M. Memon (1979); A. E. Khayrallah, *Love, Madness and Poetry: An Interpretation of the Magnūn Legend* (1980); G. J. van Gelder, *Beyond the Line: Classical Arabic Literary Critics on the Coherence and Unity of the Poem* (1982); R. Dankoff, "The Lyric in the Romance: The Use of Ghazals in Persian and Turkish Masnavīs," *Journal of Near Eastern Studies* 43 (1984); W. Skalmowski, "The Meaning of the Persian Ghazal," *Orientalia Lovanensia Periodica* 18 (1987); H. Moayyad, "Lyric Poetry," *Persian Literature*, ed. E. Yarshater (1988); W. Andrews, *Poetry's Voice, Society's Song* (1985); W. Feldman, "A Musical Model for the Structure of the Ottoman Gazel," *Edebiyât* 1 (1987); *Intoxication: Earthly and Heavenly: Seven Studies on the Poet Hafiz of Shiraz*, ed. M. Glünz and J.C. Bürgel (1991); *The Legacy of Mediæval Persian Sufism*, ed. L. Lewisohn (1992); C. Petievich, *Assembly of Rivals: Delhi, Lucknow and the Urdu Ghazal* (1992); R. Russell, *The Pursuit of Urdu Literature* (1992); R. Jacobi, "Theme and Variations in Umayyad G. Poetry," *Journal of Arabic Literature* 23 (1993); J. Stetkevych, *The Zephyrs of Najd: The Poetics of Nostalgia in the Classical Arabic Nasīb* (1993); R. Zipoli, *Technique of the Ǧawāb: Replies of Nawāī to H̱āfiz̤ and Ǧāmī* (1993); F. Pritchett, *Nets of Awareness: Urdu Poetry and Its*

*Critics* (1994); S. Enderwitz, *Liebe als Beruf: ʿAbbās ibn al-Aḥnaf und das Ġazal* (1995); J.T.P. de Brujin, *Persian Sufi Poetry* (1997); T. Bauer, *Liebe und Liebesdichtung in der arabischen Welt des 9. und 10. Jahrhunderts* (1998); P. Losensky, *Welcoming Fighānī: Imitation and Poetic Individuality in the Safavid-Mughal Ghazal* (1998); *Encyclopedia of Arabic Literature*, ed. J. S. Meisami and P. Starkey (1998); H. Mukhia, "Failure as Dissent in Urdu Ghazal," *Modern Asian Studies* 33 (1999); *Ravishing Disunities: Real Ghazals in English*, ed. S. A. Agha (2000); S. Shamīsā, *Sayr-i ghazal dar shiʿr-i fārsī* (2001); J. S. Meisami, *Structure and Meaning in Medieval Arabic and Persian Poetry* (2003); S. R. Faruqi, "A Stranger in the City: The Poetics of Sabki Hindi," *Annual of Urdu Studies* 19 (2004); C. M. Naim, *Urdu Texts and Contexts: The Selected Essays of C. M. Naim* (2004); *Ghazal as World Literature 1: Transformations of a Literary Genre*, ed. T. Bauer and A. Neuwirth (2005); W. Andrews and M. Kalpakli, *The Age of Beloveds* (2005); F. Lewis, "The Transformation of the Persian Ghazal: From Amatory Mood to Fixed Form," *Ghazal as World Literature II: From a Literary Genre to a Great Tradition*, ed. A. Neuwirth et al. (2006); *Hafiz and the Religion of Love in Classical Persian Poetry*, ed. L. Lewisohn (2010); J.T.P. de Brujin and E. Yarshater, "Ghazals i and ii," *Encyclopaedia Iranica*, ed. E. Yarshater, http://www.iranicaonline.org/articles/gazal-1-history and http://www.iranicaonline.org/articles/gazal-2; R. Blachère, A. Bausani, F. Īz, "Ghazal," *Encyclopaedia of Islam*, 2d ed., ed. P. Bearman et al., Brill Online (2002– ).

F. D. Lewis

**GLOSA.** A Sp. metrical form, also called *mote* or *retruécano*, closely related to the *cantiga, introduced in the late 14th or early 15th c. by the court poets. In its strict form, it is a poem consisting of a line or a short stanza, called *cabeza* (also *mote*, *letra*, or *texto*), stating the theme of the poem, and followed by one stanza for each line of the cabeza, explaining or glossing that line and incorporating it into the explanatory stanza, often at the end as a refrain. *Strophes may be of any length and rhyme scheme. Loosely, the *glosa* is any poem expanding on the theme presented in the opening stanza and usually repeating one or more lines of that stanza. A famous late 16th-c. glosa is one by Vicente Espinel beginning "Mil veces voy a hablar / a mi zagala."

■ H. Janner, "La glosa española. Estudio histórico de su métrica y de sus temas," *Revista de Filología Española* 27 (1943); Le Gentil; Navarro.

D. C. Clarke

**GLOSSOLALIA** (Gr. *glossa*, "tongue," and *lalein*, "to speak"). *Glossolalia* or *glossolaly* denotes "speaking in tongues" or "the gift of tongues." These two etyma occur together in 1 Corinthians 14:2 ("one who speaks in a tongue [*lalein glosse*] speaks not to men but to God; for no one understands him, but he utters mysteries in the Spirit"), though the term *glossolalia* gained quasi-technical connotations only when the Christian universalist William Fredric Farrar defined it as "soliloquies of ecstatic spiritual emotion" in his *Life and Work of St. Paul* (1879). In addition to its role in Christian thought and practice from Paul down to the mod. Pentecostal and charismatic movements, glossolalia has also been observed historically in Egyptian, Gr., Judaic, Islamic, and Nordic ceremonial trads. and in 19th-c. spiritualism, as well as ethnographically across the globe. Since the late 19th c., mod. poetic practice has made use of glossolalic speech codes for a range of deliberate purposes.

Interpretations of glossolalia can be grouped into three main arenas: theology, psychology, and ling. Theology understands glossolalia as credulous, inspired conversation with God occurring outside the domain of natural, intelligible lang. (although religious communities often believe such utterances can be "understood"). While psychology and anthropology both define glossolalia as vocalization born of a "disassociated" mental state, psychology has tended to pathologize glossolalia and anthropology to regard it more neutrally as ritual practice (e.g., "trance"). To linguistically inclined theorists from Roman Jakobson to W. J. Samarin to Michel de Certeau, glossolalia belongs to a family of practices that fabricate the semblance or "facade" of a lang. bereft of structural rules or referential functions, thus, one not causally linked to enthusiasm, belief, or disassociation. The extent to which such theorists distinguish glossolalia proper from other vocal manifestations (e.g., *xenoglossia, *nonsense, ventriloquism, skat, aphonic noise, invented langs., archaic sacerdotalism), as well as from other disassociative states (e.g., spiritual possession, vision, catatonia, hysteria), can differ. Certeau persuasively theorizes glossolalia as a ritual practice resulting from both a "need" or "imperative" to speak ("speaking in tongues" transgresses the order through which an individual is capable of "holding one's tongue") and a "belief" in speech (compensating for the meaninglessness of that which is spoken). He thus regards glossolalia as "vocal utopia"—a "non-language" within the realm of oral communication analogous to the "non-place" of utopia within society writ large. It is chiefly with this third, ling. inflection that glossolalic speech codes have been employed by mod. poets.

Perhaps owing to shifts in the fin de siècle economy of authority among the disciplines of ling., psychology, theology, poetry, and spiritualism, the late 19th and early 20th cs. may be regarded as a heyday for both the social-scientific theory and poetic practice of glossolalia. In the spiritistic milieus of Western Europe (esp. France and Germany), popular cases of glossolalic mediums were widely reported, most famously Flournoy's "Mlle. Helene Smith," whose "Martian" lang. Flournoy described as a "typical case of 'glosso-poesy,' of complete fabrication of all the parts of a new language by a subconscious activity." Oskar Pfister, an associate of Sigmund Freud, devoted considerable energy to the psychoanalytic interpretation of glossolalia, misguidedly attempting strategies of decipherment.

Instances of glossolalia abound in the poetry of the historical avant-garde (see AVANT-GARDE POETICS), as well as in the work of its predecessors and successors (from Christian Morgenstern [Germany] to Claude Gauvreau [Quebec]), and its hist. overlaps significantly with that of the global devel. of *sound poetry. Most of these poems contain an ambition to sacralize (or resacralize) instrumentalized lang. by conceptualizing poetry as ritualistic social communion predicated on words transcending their constitutive mundanity (e.g., Velimir Khlebnikov's *zaum*, which engages forms of glossolalic Rus. occultism—see RUSSIA, POETRY OF). "Gadji beri bimba," the characteristic glossolalic poems of Ger. Dada (see DADA), emerged from Hugo Ball's work on a burlesque manger play (some of its onomatopes, like "tumba ba-umf," are those of a trumpeting pachyderm in the caravan of the magi) and were vocalized in a liturgical register by Ball, who was dressed as a "magic bishop." These poems might even be characterized as *metaglossolalia*, acting out glossolalia itself by means of phonosymbolic motifs such as *galassassa*, *glassala*, and *sassala*.

The most systematic, self-conscious marriage of poetic art with glossolalic speech belongs to the Rus. symbolist Andrei Bely. His *Glossalolija: Poema o zvuke* (*Glossalalia: A Poem about Sound*), written in 1917 under the sway of anthroposophy and pub. in 1922, is an extensive exercise in glossolalic vocalization in the service of a ling. creation myth, in which the "eurhythmic" tongue is cast as protagonist: "before there were distinct sounds the tongue would leap, like a dancer, in its own enclosed sphere." Bely describes the poet-glossolalist as a gestural, historical linguist, who is "free to meditate for hours on the alternations of roots—across languages, throughout the centuries." But he ultimately privileges poet over linguist, owing to the poet's ability to "hear in the shudderings of the air the imprint of ancient meaning; and, by wrapping oneself in the image of muttering bygones, to resurrect that which has gone by." Bely implicitly argues what Jakobson expounds explicitly: that auditory *iconicity (i.e., phonosymbolism) is a dynamic generator of meaning in all lang. systems. This distinguishes Bely from his Fr. symbolist coevals, for whom poetic sound patterning is an impressionist gesture rather than a systemic object of fascination (see SYMBOLISM).

The introduction of recording technology to field ethnography by anthropologists (e.g., Felicitas Goodman's and W. J. Samarin's recordings or Peter Adair's classic cinema verité depiction of Appalachian snake-handler glossolalists) provided the necessary material conditions for later 20th-c. insights regarding the status of glossolalia as a ling. performance of pancultural proportions. Following Goodman's cross-cultural account, Paz argued that glossolalia is always attended (i.e., cross-culturally) by the story of "the reconciliation of languages" that traditionally opposes Babel: "the Gospel counters the diabolical cosmopolitanism of Babel with the spiritual cosmopolitanism of Jerusalem, and the confusion of tongues with the wondrous gift of speaking

other tongues." However, in furnishing glossolalia with a genetic myth of cosmopolitanism (*other* tongues), Paz risks conflating glossolalia with xenoglossia.

Even as large communities of believers continue to speak in tongues, recurrent interest in glossolalia within ling., *poststructuralism, and postmod. poetics suggests the persistence of glossolalic longings in secular modernity (see POSTMODERNISM). Barth's postmodernist account ("The senselessest babble, could we ken it, might disclose a dark message, or prayer") stages lit. as the site of an attempted rapprochement between these seemingly antithetical domains. So too do some elements of a so-called postmod. poetics, from Allen Ginsberg's shamanic rituals (see Hungerford) to the ethnopoetic recordings of poets such as Maria Sabina.

*See* ONOMATOPOEIA, SOUND, TIMBRE.

■ T. Flournoy, *From India to the Planet Mars: A Study of a Case of Somnambulism with Glossolalia*, trans. D. Vermilye (1900); O. Pfister, *Die psychologische Entratselung der religidsen Glossolalie und der automatischen Kryptographie* (1912); Jakobson, v. 4, "Retrospect"; P. Adair, *Holy Ghost People* (1967); J. Barth, *Lost in the Funhouse: Fictions for Print, Tape, Live Voice* (1968); F. D. Goodman, *Speaking in Tongues: A Cross-Cultural Study of Glossolalia* (1972); W. J. Samarin, *Tongues of Men and Angels* (1972); and "*Glossolalia* as Regressive Speech," *Language and Speech* 16 (1973); R. Jakobson and L. R. Waugh, *The Sound Shape of Language* (1979); G. Rouget, *Music and Trance*, trans. B. Biebuyck (1985); O. Paz, *Convergences*, trans. H. Lane (1992); T. R. Beyer Jr., "Andrej Belyj's Glossalolija: A Berlin Glossolalia," *Europa Orientalis* 14 (1995); M. de Certeau, "Vocal Utopias: Glossolalias," *Representations*, trans. D. Rosenberg (1996); E. W. White, *The Magic Bishop: Hugo Ball, Dada Poet* (1998); A. Bely, *Glossolalie*, trans. T. Breyer (2004); A. Hungerford, *Postmodern Belief* (2010).

H. FEINSOD

**GLYCONIC.** Named after Glycon, a Gr. poet whose date and place are unknown, this metrical colon (x x – ◡ ◡ – ◡ –) was basic to *aeolic meters and so became common in Gr. and Lat. lyric poetry. It was used by the Gr. melic poets Alcaeus and Sappho and by later Gr. and Roman poets both for *monody and choral lyric (see MELIC POETRY). In lyric, the number of syllables is fixed; in choral lyric and drama, *resolution is permitted. Horace began his glyconics with two long syllables.

The catalectic form of the glyconic, x x – ◡ ◡ – –, is called the Pherecratean, after the Gr. comic poet Pherecrates (fl. late 5th c. BCE). Apart from *anceps in the final syllable, the Pherecratean permits resolution only in the quantities of the base (the first two syllables) and occurs, usually with one or more glyconics, chiefly in Anacreon, in the choruses of Gr. tragedy, and in Horace (in whom the base is regularly spondaic). An example is Horace's *Odes* 1.5.3. The hypercatalectic form of the glyconic (x x – ◡ ◡ – ◡ – –) is called the hipponactean.

■ Wilamowitz, pt. 2, ch. 4; Maas; Koster; Dale; Halporn et al.; Snell; West; K. Itsumi, "The Glyconic in Greek Tragedy," *CQ* 78 (1984); Gasparov, *History*; A. P. David, *The Dance of the Muses* (2006).

R. J. Getty; P. S. Costas; J. W. Halporn

**GNOMIC POETRY.** A gnome is a "short pithy statement of a general truth; a proverb, maxim, aphorism, or apophthegm" (*OED*). The name *gnomic* was first applied to a group of Gr. poets who flourished in the seventh and sixth cs. bce, incl. Theognis, Solon, Phocylides, and Simonides of Amorgos. But gnomes were popular in ancient Egyptian, Chinese, Sanskrit, and Heb. lits. In the West, the poet Horace frequently employed gnomes, as did such Lat. authors as Cicero and Tacitus. A number of poetic collections of gnomes are preserved in early Germanic and Celtic lits., incl. the Old Ir. *Instructions of King Cormac Mac Airt*, several Middle Welsh gnomic poems, the ON *Hávamál*, and two OE poems known as *Maxims I* and *Maxims II*; gnomes occur frequently in OE narrative poems, incl. *Beowulf*. In the ME period, many gnomic utterances attributed to King Alfred the Great and others were gathered in poetic collections. Gnomic poetry was later cultivated in England by Francis Quarles (*Emblems*, 1633) and in France by Gui de Pibras, whose *Quatrains* (1574) imitated the gnomic poets.

*See* EPIGRAM, PROVERB, RIDDLE.

■ B. C. Williams, *Gnomic Poetry in Anglo-Saxon* (1914); K. Jackson, *Early Welsh Gnomic Poems* (1935); C. Larrington, *A Store of Common Sense: Gnomic Theme and Style in Old Icelandic and Old English Wisdom Poetry* (1993); S. Deskis, *Beowulf and the Medieval Proverb Tradition* (1996).

R. P. ApRoberts; P. S. Baker

**GOLIARDIC VERSE.** *Goliardus* (from which derive the Eng. *Goliardic* and *Goliard*) may be owed to the Lat. *gula* (gluttony), or *Golias*, the Lat. for Goliath, the OT figure famously slain by David (1 Sam. 17). The term may also have affiliations with the Ger. *goljan* (to sing), or the Fr. *gailliard* (happy man). Some have attributed the popularity of the term in the 12th c. and its application to a kind of writing to a letter in which Bernard of Clairvaux famously condemned Peter Abelard as a "Goliath" figure.

Whatever the origin of the term, the poetry designated by it has long been associated with the *Ordo Vagorum*, a counterfeit religious "order" of students joined by a love of poetic composition and anticlerical views, who, so the trad. holds, moved in the 12th and 13th cs. from one intellectual center to the next in search of like-minded companions and poetic inspiration. Closer to the truth is the idea that, in these centuries, students and their teachers, inhabiting the great centers of learning in France, Germany, and England and inspired by the new secularism, produced a form of poetic satire that loosely took as an organizing emblem the figure of Goliath.

That Goliath should become a central figure in a new poetic movement is perhaps owed less to Bernard of Clairvaux's influence and more to a med. trad. of viewing Goliath as a symbol of evil (and of seeing David as a prefiguration of Christ). And yet in the 12th c., this rather narrow identification was expanded and somewhat softened: Goliath became a figure in, or the "author" of, a new strain of satiric verse, while his persona, remaining fundamentally negative, came to include the learning associated with the schools attended by those of his "order." As Christian *exegesis transmogrified into a literary procedure, his personality thus became more complex.

Complex, too, are the themes of the poems organized under the Goliardic rubric. Some celebrate the pleasures of love and of drinking; some take to task the worst foibles of monastic and ecclesiastical corruption; others notice the beauties of nature. Of the more famous Goliardic poets, Walter of Châtillon, Hugh Primas of Orléans, and the Archpoet stand out as exemplars of a kind of poetic composition that negotiates the space between crit. of authority and the articulation of a discrete and even likeable subjectivity.

Part of that subjectivity is resident in and expressed by the so-called Goliardic meter. Lacking any direct connection with the cl. quantities of Greco-Roman versification (see QUANTITY), this meter is based instead on word accent (see ACCENTUAL VERSE), and its typical configuration consists of a stanza of four lines of 13 syllables each, with a *caesura after the seventh syllable and end rhyme consistent within each *strophe. Sometimes the fourth line of the stanza is a hexameter (called an *auctoritas*).

Goliardic verse is found in many places but most famously in the so-called *Carmina Burana* collection, an anthol. of 228 poems, many (though not all) of which are either properly Goliardic by dint of meter or in terms of theme or both, esp. poems 187–228. In fact, poem 219 of the collection famously announces the "formation" of the Ordo Vagorum by parodying Mark 16.15 while demolishing in its many lines the pretenses of ecclesiastical superiority, esp. against the backdrop of monastic reform, of which the *Ordo Vagorum* is but the latest instance.

*See* SATIRE.

■ H. Waddell, *The Wandering Scholars* (1927); G. F. Whicher, *The Goliard Poets* (1949); *Carmina Burana*, ed. A. Hilka, O. Schumann, and B. Bischoff, Band 1, v. 1–3 (1930–70), with commentary in Band 2, v. 1 (incomplete, 1961); Raby, *Secular*; P. G. Walsh, "Golias and Goliardic Poetry," *Medium Aevum* 52 (1983); P. G. Walsh, *Love Lyrics from the Carmina Burana* (1993); *Hugh Primas and the Archpoet*, trans. F. Adcock (1994).

J. Pucci

**GRAMMATICAL RHYME** (Fr. *rime grammatical*; Ger. *grammatischer Reim*, It. *replicatio*), sometimes *etymological rhyme*. Rhymes that employ related forms derived from a common root syllable or etymon, such as a verb and a noun, or otherwise play on the varying lexical forms of a stem, esp. by repeating the same rhyme word in a run of lines but in a different case each time, so with different inflectional endings: the effect is close to that of *monorhyme. This kind of rhyming would be regarded by most mod. poets as scarcely rhyme at all, for being too easy, but it was practiced in Occitan by the *troubadours, in OF (Chrétien de Troyes), and by the *rhétoriqueurs*, e.g., Rutebeuf and Mousket; it can be effective still in short runs. Austin has also noted grammatical rhyme in the collection of Gr. oracular writings know as the Sibylline books and Virgil's *Eclogues*. Mod. and contemp. examples appear often in Rus. poetry, notably, according to Worth, in Alexander Pushkin's *Evgenij Onegin* and in a more limited way, according to Wachtel, in Joseph Brodsky, whose grammatical rhymes in *A Part of Speech* are based less on morphology than on approximate grammar and etymology. Grammatical rhyme is not to be confused with *homoeoteleuton*, "case rhyme," which is the Gr. term for agreement of inflectional endings on words, without any intent at rhyme strictly speaking: grammatical rhyme uses the identity of roots (whether obvious or not) counterpointed with the difference of endings precisely in a rhyme-like fashion, though on the grammatical-category level and expressly for a rhyme-like effect: it is, therefore, a lexical analogue of (phonic) rhyme, while homoeoteleuton is not. *Equivocal rhyme* (Fr. *rime équivoque*), closely related and very popular among the *Grands *Rhétoriqueurs* is discussed elsewhere (see MOSAIC RHYME). The structure treated as grammatical rhyme in *prosody is treated as *polyptoton in rhet.

■ A. Tobler, *Le Vers français* (1885)—177–78; R. Austin, "Virgil and the Sibyl," *CQ* 21 (1927); Patterson; D. Worth "Grammatical Rhyme Types in *Evgenij Onegin*," *Alexander Pushkin: Symposium II*, ed. A. Kodjak, K. Pomorska, and K. Taranovsky (1980); M. Wachtel, *The Cambridge Introduction to Russian Poetry* (2004).

T.V.F. BROGAN; J. CHANG

**GRAVEYARD POETRY.** A type of meditative poetry, graveyard poetry takes as its major themes a melancholy sense of mutability, the inevitability of death, and the hope of a future life, arriving at such moral generalizations as Thomas Gray's "The paths of glory lead but to the grave" and "Even from the tomb the voice of nature cries." Although there are some earlier examples (e.g., Andreas Gryphius's *Kirchhofs Gedanken* in the mid-17th c. in Germany), Thomas Parnell's "Night-Piece on Death" (1721) first develops the type that became fully established with Edward Young's *Night-Thoughts* (1742), Robert Blair's "The Grave" (1743), and Gray's "Elegy Written in a Country Churchyard" (1750). In the latter half of the 18th c., graveyard poetry became widespread in Germany, the Netherlands, Sweden, France, and Italy, the best-known examples being Friedrich Karl Kasimir von Creutz's "Die Gräber" (1760) and Ugo Foscolo's "Dei Sepolcri" (1807).

■ P. von Tieghem, *Le Préromantisme*, 3 v. (1924–47) J. W. Draper, *The Funeral Elegy and the Rise of English Romanticism* (1929); E. Sickels, *The Gloomy Egoist* (1932); C.A.D. Fehrman, *Kyrkogårdsromantik* (1954); H. Weinbrot, "Gray's *Elegy*: A Poem of Moral Choice

and Resolution," *SEL* 18 (1978); *Studies in the Literary Imagination* 39.1 (2006)—spec. issue on lit. and graveyards.

F. J. WARNKE; A. PREMINGER; L. METZGER

**GREEK ANTHOLOGY.** The *Greek Anthology* is a collection of more than 4,000 Gr. short poems (or *epigrams*, a term that had a wide and disputed application), mainly composed in elegiac couplets and written between the 7th c. BCE and the 10th c. CE. It exists in two versions: the *Palatine Anthology*, which was an expansion, made around 940 CE, of a prior compilation made by Constantine Cephalas around 900 CE; and the *Planudean Anthology*, made in 1301 by Maximus Planudes and based on an abridged version of Cephalas's collection. Cephalas himself drew on a wide variety of sources, incl. anthols. of epigrams made by Meleager around the beginning of the 1st c. BCE, Philip of Thessalonica under Nero, Strato probably at the time of Hadrian, Agathias in the mid-6th c. CE, and others.

Mod. eds. of the *Greek Anthology* print the 15 books of the *Palatine Anthology* (it is named after the ms., which was found in the Palatinate Library of Heidelberg), and they add in an appendix (or book 16) several hundred poems in the *Planudean Anthology* that do not appear in the *Palatine*. The 15 books are arranged by subject, from the Christian epigrams of the first book to the *riddles of the 14th and the miscellany of the 15th (which includes shaped poems; see TECHNOPAEGNION). Among the most influential are book 5, *erotic poetry; book 6, dedicatory and votive epigrams; book 7, *epitaphs and other poems on death; book 9, "epideictic" pieces (descriptions of natural objects and works on art, stories, imagined speeches, inscriptions, and others); book 10, "protreptic" poems, which exhort or instruct readers; book 11, sympotic and satirical epigrams; and book 12, pederastic poetry.

The *Planudean Anthology* was arranged in a different order (in seven books), and it omitted or bowdlerized much material. This version was the source for almost all readers until the 19th c., so it was mainly in this form that the *Greek Anthology* exercised its enormous influence on Eur. poetry. After the first printing in 1494, poetry from the *Greek Anthology* was widely translated and adapted into Neo-Lat. and the Eur. vernaculars, and it spurred devels. in many kinds of short poems, incl. the *sonnet, *emblem, and *madrigal. It had its largest impact on the epigram, often being taken to represent a sweet, naïve, or charming alternative to the pointedness of Roman epigrams (esp. Martial's).

See ANTHOLOGY, BYZANTINE POETRY, ELEGIAC DISTICH, EPIDEICTIC POETRY, GREEK POETRY.

■ **Complete Editions**: *Greek Anthology*, ed. W. R. Paton, 5 v. (1916–18); *Anthologie grecque*, ed. P. Walz et al., 2d ed., 12 v. (1960–); *Anthologia graeca*, ed. H. Beckby, 2d ed., 4 v. (1965).

■ **Selected Editions**: *Select Epigrams from the Greek Anthology*, ed. J. W. Mackail, 3d ed. (1911); *The Greek Anthology: Hellenistic Epigrams*, ed. A.S.F. Gow and D. L. Page, 2 v. (1965); *The Greek Anthology: The Gar-*

*land of Philip*, ed. A.S.F. Gow and D. L. Page, 2 v. (1968); *Further Greek Epigrams*, ed. D. L. Page (1981).
■ **Criticism and History**: J. Hutton, *The Greek Anthology in Italy to the Year 1800* (1935); and *The Greek Anthology in France and in the Latin Writers of the Netherlands to the Year 1800* (1946); A. Cameron, *The Greek Anthology from Meleager to Planudes* (1993); *Brill's Companion to Hellenistic Epigram*, ed. P. Bing and J. Bruss (2007).

K. HAYNES

**GREEK POETICS.** *See* ALEXANDRIANISM; BYZANTINE POETRY; CLASSICAL POETICS.

## GREEK POETRY

I. Classical
II. Medieval. *See* BYZANTINE POETRY.
III. Modern

### I. Classical

**A.** *The Preliterate Period (ca. 2000–750 BCE).* The earliest Gr. verses preserved in writing date from the 8th c. BCE, and poetry has continued to be composed in Gr. from that time until the present day. But mod. research (see ORAL-FORMULAIC THEORY) indicates that the Gr. poetic trad. is, in fact, far older than the introduction of writing. The nature of the word groups of which the Homeric *epics are largely composed (see FORMULA), as well as the content of those epics, imply a preexisting oral trad. of dactylic heroic poetry extending back into the Bronze Age civilization of the Mycenaeans, which came to an end about 1100 BCE (see ORAL POETRY). The *aeolic meters that are widely used in extant Gr. poetry, notably by Sappho and Alcaeus, presuppose an even more ancient oral trad. of *song, for they show clear affinities with the meters of the Indian Vedas; their ultimate origins may, therefore, date back as far as about 2000 BCE. It is also now generally recognized that Gr. poetry emerged from and participated in an ancient Near Eastern and Eastern Mediterranean cultural koiné. These links with the music, poetry, and culture of the ancient Near East are strongest perhaps in the preliterate and earlier archaic periods, but various kinds of cultural interaction almost certainly continued to influence Gr. verse throughout its hist.

The introduction of an alphabet specifically adapted to the recording of Gr., which took place not later than the mid-8th c. BCE, was no doubt the most important single event in the hist. of Gr. poetry. Gr. (and Eur.) lit. begins here, at the point where the songs could be fixed in permanent form and transmitted to posterity. Yet for many centuries after, Gr. poetry continued to bear the deep imprint of ancient oral trad., incl. two of its most distinctive characteristics: (1) its mythological and heroic content and (2) its long dependence on oral *performance as the means of reaching its public.

Ancient Gr. poetry in nearly all genres worked within a frame of reference provided by the traditional gods and the heroes of the Bronze Age. That mythic-

legendary world afforded the poets both their basic story patterns and their paradigms of conduct. Heroic epic, many forms of choral *lyric, and *tragedy directly represented characters and incidents drawn from that world; epinikion and monodic lyric (see EPINIKION, MONODY) constantly evoked it as a standard against which the human condition might be measured.

For more than three centuries after the introduction of writing, Gr. poetry continued as before to be enacted orally, often with the accompaniment of music or dancing or both, before audiences as small as dinner parties and as large as the vast crowds at religious festivals—Plato (*Ion* 535d) mentions audiences of 20,000 for performances of epic at such festivals. Thus, Gr. poetry of the archaic and high cl. eras combined features that may at first sight seem contradictory. It had the elaboration, finish, and durability that belong to book poetry as opposed to oral poetry, yet insofar as its intended public was concerned, it remained an oral and often even visual and quasi-dramatic entertainment.

To this inheritance from the preliterate trad. may also be attributed certain other characteristics of archaic and high cl. Gr. poetry: its richness in aural effects (the immense variety and musicality of its quantitative meters, for instance, are unmatched in any Eur. poetry—see METER, QUANTITY); the prominent part it played in the cultural life of the society as a whole; and the wide range of its human appeal, particularly in its most popular genres, epic and drama.

In dealing with ancient Gr. poetry, it must always be borne in mind that we have less than 5 percent of all that was originally produced—the tiny proportion that has made it through the processes of selection, reperformance, and preservation spanning the more than 2,500 years since the invention of the Gr. alphabet. This means that our story necessarily tracks and depends on the Greeks' own processes of *canon formation, which probably had their start already in the education system of 5th-c. Athens, continued in the work of the Hellenistic scholars in the 3d and 2d cs. BCE, and finally depended on whether Gr. texts made the crucial transition from papyrus (the writing material of the ancient world) to longer-lasting vellum in the 4th c. CE. Over the last 150 years, however, substantial ancient papyrus finds preserved in Egypt have significantly enhanced and diversified our knowledge of Gr. poetry, both supplementing our corpora of canonical poets and offering us vivid glimpses of the kaleidoscopic range and variety of Gr. verse beyond the cl. canon.

**B.** *The Earlier Archaic Period (ca. 750–600 BCE).* Thanks (it seems) to the introduction of writing, a great number of poems dating from this period were known to the later Greeks. With the exception of the major poems attributed to Homer and Hesiod, however, most of this work survives only in quotations, summaries, and allusions (and now, to some extent, in fragmentary papyrus finds), but these are enough to permit a sketch map, at least, of a complex literary landscape. All the major nondramatic genres of subsequent cl. poetry are already in existence, but they tend to be associated with particular regions. Of these, four stand out: Ionia, Lesbos, Sparta, and Boeotia.

The Ionic-speaking region embraced the central part of the west coast of Asia Minor and the islands that stretch from there toward Greece proper. Here, the most important and longest-lasting of all Gr. and Lat. verse forms—the dactylic *hexameter ($- \smile\smile \, | - \smile\smile \, | - \smile\smile | - \smile\smile | - \smile\smile | - -$)—seems to have achieved its definitive form. The "formulas" of which the hexameters of Homer are largely composed show elements of several Gr. dialects, but the predominant and apparently latest stratum is Ionic. It is generally inferred that the trad. of hexameter composition, after passing through the bards of one or two other dialectal regions, culminated in Ionia; and, in fact, the oldest Gr. trads. concerning Homer place him in Chios or Smyrna, cities that belong to this region. Ionia, then, was the probable birthplace of the two great epics that later Greece, and later Europe, perceived as the fountainhead of their lit., the *Iliad* and the *Odyssey*. Since the 18th c., a debate has raged over the genesis, authorship, unity, and dates of completion of these poems (see the fourth section of the bibl., esp. the intro. to Parry). But one certainty at least remains: from the earliest period, they stood as models of the poetic art, above all for the satisfying *unity of their *plots and for their brilliant technique of characterization through speeches.

Also from Ionia during this period come the first examples of *iambic and elegiac poetry (see ELEGY). In both these genres, the poems were relatively short *monologues, predominantly concerned with war, political and personal *invective, and love; but the elegiac tended more than iambic to include a gnomic element, i.e., meditation and advice on various aspects of the human condition. Metrically speaking, *iambic* by the ancient Gr. definition embraced poems composed in the iambic trimeter (a three-metron or, in mod. parlance, six-foot iambic line: $\smile - \smile - | \smile - \smile - | \smile - \smile -$) and in the trochaic tetrameter catalectic ($- \smile - \smile \, | - \smile - \smile \, | - \smile - \smile \, | - \smile -$). The first of these was to have a rich afterlife in cl. (and to some extent later Eur.) lit. as the standard verse form for dialogue in drama. Elegiac poetry was composed in *elegiac distiches—a dactylic hexameter followed by a dactylic *pentameter, so-called ($- \smile\smile - \smile\smile - | - \smile\smile - \smile\smile -$); this meter also was to become an enormously important medium, not least in the *epigrams of the *Greek Anthology*.

The most famous and, so far as the Greeks were in a position to know, the first composer in both genres was Archilochus, of the Ionic island Paros (fl. 648 BCE). Some Gr. authors actually put his poetry on a level with that of Homer, in its very different way; the intensity and metrical perfection of his surviving *fragments seem to confirm that judgment. Archilochus was also the earliest known composer of a third variety of "iambic" poetry as anciently defined, the *epode, which consisted of alternating long and short lines predominantly in iambic or dactylic meters; this was a superb instrument for invective from Archilochus to

the Roman Horace. Several other iambic and elegiac poets flourished in 7th-c. Ionia, esp. Semonides, Callinus, and Mimnermus. The only distinguished elegiac poet working on the Gr. mainland during this period was Tyrtaeus (fl. ca. 640 BCE), whose martial and political poems, composed in Sparta, survive in several extensive fragments.

The poetry of the Ionian region in all its genres is remarkable for the clarity of its expression and metrical form (the repeated line and the repeated *couplet are the only options available) and for a rather sophisticated realism. For lyricism during this period, one must turn elsewhere. Gr. lyric (or *melic) poetry by the ancient definition was poetry sung to instrumental accompaniment. In practice, it fell into two broad categories: choral lyric, which was normally a dance as well as a song and might be composed in an almost infinite variety of meters and stanza forms, and solo lyric (sometimes misleadingly called *personal lyric*), composed for accompanied singing only, in a more limited though still extensive range of meters, and falling into short stanzas, most often quatrains. Both kinds of lyric emerge from the mists of preliteracy during this period, primarily in two centers, Aeolic-speaking Lesbos and Doric-speaking Sparta.

From the late 8th into the early 6th c., a series of choral and solo lyric poets is recorded on the isle of Lesbos. Most of them, such as Terpander and Arion, are now scarcely more than sonorous names, but Sappho and Alcaeus, who both flourished ca. 600 BCE, have left many fragments of solo lyric poetry. Both composed in approximately the same range of aeolic lyric meters (two of the most famous aeolic stanza forms, the *sapphic and the *alcaic, are named after them), and in the same soft and musical Aeolic brogue, but, in content and tone, they are vastly unlike each other. For the power and beauty of her songs of love and loss, Sappho has no peer in Gr. lit. Alcaeus's songs on the turbulent politics of the island, his hymns to the gods, and, above all, his drinking songs, crisply and forcefully composed, were to prove of great influence on later Eur. lyric.

Seventh-c. Sparta was famed for the competitions in choral lyric at its great religious festivals (see POETIC CONTESTS), but the only one of its poets about whom anything significant is known is Alcman (second half of the 7th c.). From his numerous and in some cases quite substantial fragments, it can be deduced that his choral lyrics already embodied the most striking characteristics of the choral lyric genre as it was later known. The long polymetric stanzas of his First Partheneion, e.g., its extensively narrated examples from *myth or saga, its *gnomic passages in which the singers reflect on the universal meaning of their tale, can still find parallels in Pindar and Bacchylides a couple of centuries later.

In central Greece, Boeotia in this period saw the composition of a great number of poems; only three survive complete—the *Theogony*, the *Works and Days*, and the *Shield of Herakles*—but a fourth, the *Ehoiai* or *Catalogue of Women*, can now be restored to a considerable extent from papyrus fragments. Both the lost and the surviving poems of the Boeotian corpus were generally ascribed in ancient times to the great Hesiod, who seems to have flourished ca. 700 BCE, but most mod. critics deny the authenticity of the *Shield* and several that of the *Ehoiai*. In any case, all are composed in a medium that is virtually indistinguishable from that of the Homeric epics: the meter is the same, almost the same formulary is employed, and the same mixture of dialects is evident. But there the resemblance ends. The Hesiodic works show nothing of the architectonic skill of Homer or of his genius for realizing character through speech. They are essentially episodic codifications of ancient lore. The *Theogony* presents the origin and hist. of the Greek gods, organizing the material by generations; the *Ehoiai* followed the hist. of the heroic families by clans and, within clans, by generations; the *Works and Days* is a manual of the art of living, proceeding from ethical and political considerations to practical instruction in farming, navigation, and the rules of daily conduct. But this essentially catalogic principle of composition does not mean that Hesiod lacks art. Largely through the characteristically archaic techniques of *ring composition and significant *repetition, he succeeds in making his topics and episodes cohere within themselves and between each other. In addition, it is sometimes claimed that Hesiod represents the first self-conscious authorial "I" in Eur. lit.: thus, in the *proem to the *Theogony* and in a couple of metapoetic passages in the *Works and Days*, he builds up an impressive *persona of "Hesiod." But this claim to innovation over Homer is largely a mirage of historical preservation. It seems likely that ancient *bards in performance particularized themselves and their songs in *prooimia* or proems adapted to a local audience. While we have lost these prooimia for Homeric epic, we have them preserved for Hesiod; hence, the apparent difference of the lofty, seemingly anonymous third-person narration of Homeric epic vs. the self-revelatory intimacy and immediacy of the Hesiodic persona. Though debate still rages on this point within mod. scholarship, it seems likely that "Hesiod" and his foolish brother "Perses" (the addressee of the *Works and Days*) are fictive personae adapted to the needs of the didactic genre.

Much other hexameter poetry was composed in various regions of Greece during this period; the hexameter, in fact, seems early on to have become a kind of poetic koiné. Particularly important in its time was the Epic Cycle, a catena of medium-length epics by various hands that covered the entire Troy saga. Other epics since lost are known to have told of the legendary hist. of Corinth, the story of the Argonauts, and the house of Oedipus. Other extant examples of early hexameter poetry are certain poems in the heterogeneous collection that has come down to us under the title of the *Homeric Hymns*: at least Hymns II (to Demeter), III (to Apollo), and V (to Aphrodite) probably belong to this period. It is a remarkable fact that by about 600 BCE all the major nondramatic genres of Gr. poetry were already in existence: heroic epic, iambic, elegiac, solo and choral lyric, and, at least in some sense, *didactic (for Hesiodic poetry, though far wider in scope than the didactic poetry of later antiquity, was certainly its inspiration).

**C. *The Later Archaic Period (ca. 600–480 BCE).*** The diversity of later archaic Gr. poetry was great, but three general trends may be distinguished: the major poetic genres become less tied to specific regions of Greece (or more "Panhellenic"), and lyric poetry in particular shows a growing sophistication, metrically as well as intellectually. Also in this period, real, historically verifiable authors and poets first emerge into the full light of hist., since, in many cases, the earlier authors' names seem to be fictions standing for the poetic trads. and genres they are said to have invented or in which they were thought to excel. Composition in epic hexameters continued in many parts of Greece; some poems of the Epic Cycle and of the Hesiodic corpus, as well as several of the Homeric hymns, probably belong to the earlier part of this period. The most significant discernible devel. is the gradual disintegration of the system of formulas characteristic of the older epics. By the late 6th c., the first tentative signs of a "literary" or "secondary" epic may perhaps be made out in the work of Panyassis of Halicarnassus, an uncle or cousin of the historian Herodotus.

An outstanding exponent of both elegiac and iambic poetry was the statesman Solon (fl. 594 BCE), the earliest recorded Athenian poet. The quite substantial fragments of his work are partly gnomic or personal in content—in this, conforming to Ionian precedent—but the majority addresses political principles and issues connected with Solon's famous reforms of the Athenian economy and constitution. Across the Aegean, Hipponax of Ephesus (fl. 540 BCE) culminated the Ionian trad. of iambic invective and lampoon. His favorite meter was one that now appears for the first time, the *scazon* or limping iambic trimeter ($\smile - \smile - \mid \smile - \smile - \mid \smile - - -$; see CHOLIAMBUS). The last of the major archaic elegists, Theognis of Megara (second half of the 6th c.?), is represented by a large number of poems, predominantly gnomic in character, in the 1,300-line anthol. of elegiacs that somehow survived the Middle Ages and now goes under the title of the *Theognidea*, the only corpus of archaic elegiac poetry to be preserved through continuous ms. transmission. Finally, the elegiac, iambic, and hexameter fragments of Xenophanes of Colophon (ca. 570–478 BCE) open a new dimension in poetry, the philosophic and scientific; his penetrating physical and ethnographic observations and his crit. of Gr. anthropomorphic religion are expressed in lively and elegant verse. The two other poet-philosophers who followed him, Parmenides and Empedocles, belong rather to the hist. of philosophy than to that of poetry.

In lyric poetry, there were spectacular devels. Papyrus discoveries of the 1970s and 1980s have greatly enriched our knowledge of Stesichorus of Himera in Sicily, who seems to have flourished in the first half of the 6th c. They fully confirm the ancient trads. that he composed songs very much in the epic manner, and even approaching the epic scale, and also that he adopted or perhaps invented the practice of composing choral lyric by triads (*strophe, metrically responding *antistrophe, nonresponding epode), which is the most striking formal characteristic of subsequent Gr. choral lyric. Ibycus of Rhegium in southern Italy (fl. ca. 535 BCE) and Simonides of the Aegean isle of Ceos (556–468) each left superb fragments of lyric. Simonides, in particular, seems to have been a great innovative master, turning his hand to many different varieties of choral lyric, incl. the epinikion (which he may have originated) and the short epigram in elegiac distiches, a form that had an immense literary future before it.

Anacreon of Teos in Ionia (ca. 575–490) brought solo lyric poetry to heights of wit and technical polish that were matched in cl. times perhaps only by the Roman poets Catullus and Horace. His many brilliant fragments sing mostly of love and wine but also occasionally flare with trenchant abuse or touch on more somber themes of old age and death. Metrically, he was not a great innovator, but he seems to have been the first poet to make extensive use of the catchy rhythm ◡◡−◡−◡−−, later called the *anacreontic after him. (This meter plays a great part in the extant collection of *light verse that seems to have been continuously composed in imitation of Anacreon through the Roman and Byzantine periods; this collection, which goes under the title *Anacreontea*, had great popularity and influence in 16th- to 18th-c. Europe.)

The most momentous poetic devel. in this period was the introduction of poetic drama. Officially sponsored performances of tragedy at the Great Dionysia festival in Athens are first attested in ca. 534 BCE and of *comedy in 486 BCE. The ultimate origins of both genres and their hists. down to the time of the great Persian invasion of Greece in 480–79 BCE are still problematic for want of adequate evidence; the archaeological evidence and (often contradictory) ancient accounts of the origins of drama are collected in Csapo and Slater. Our extant examples of tragedy and comedy date only from the ensuing period. In antiquity, Athens proudly claimed the invention of both tragedy and comedy, but this claim was not uncontested. In fact, abundant ancient evidence suggests that many different Gr. cities may have been developing different forms of choral drama more or less simultaneously in the 6th c. BCE. Thus, Herodotus (5.67) mentions "tragic choruses" performed in honor of a cult hero in 6th-c. Sicyon in the Peloponnese, while we have reports of early comic performances in Megara, in the Gr. city of Syracuse on Sicily, and of early satyr plays in Phleius (also in the Peloponnese). It is, moreover, noteworthy that, even in Athens, almost a third of the poets whose names are preserved as practicing tragic playwrights in the 5th c. are non-Athenian. The fact that we have extant dramas from Athens alone—that Athens essentially wins this ancient contest—may have more to do with political, economic, and military factors discussed below than with issues of literary or aesthetic quality. But once

developed, the arts of tragedy, comedy, and satyr play were elaborated by the Athenians with great energy and success, so that drama (along with painted pottery) became one of Athens's great export commodities. Ancient evidence suggests that, already by the last two decades of the 5th c., Attic tragedy was being performed in southern Italy (and probably many other places in the Gr. world), while the 4th c. witnessed an explosion in the building of monumental stone theaters throughout the Gr. cities of the Mediterranean that scholars have connected with the expanding performance horizons of Attic drama.

**D. *The High Classical Period (ca. 480–400 BCE).*** After the Persian Wars, Athenian power and dominance reached their peak. The years between 479 and Athens's defeat by Sparta in 404 saw the creation of a naval empire in the eastern Mediterranean, the exaction of "tribute" from the allied Gr. cities of the empire, the Periclean democracy, the erection of the great buildings and sculptures on the Acropolis—and the composition of all the surviving masterpieces of Attic tragedy. Elsewhere in Greece, choral lyric continued to be practiced with great success. Our firsthand knowledge of the tragic art depends almost exclusively on the extant plays of the three most famous Attic tragedians, Aeschylus (525–456), Sophocles (496–406), and Euripides (ca. 480–406); the earliest surviving example, Aeschylus's *Persians*, was produced in 472. On the strictly *dramatic* aspects of the art, much is to be found elsewhere (see Lesky, Goldhill). Viewed in the context of Gr. poetry, tragedy is remarkable for the manner in which it appropriated and combined so many existing poetic genres. In tragic tone, in characterization through speech, and to some extent even in plot construction, the tragedians picked up and developed precedents in Homeric epic (as Aristotle implies throughout the *Poetics*, e.g., 1449b17: "anybody who can tell a good tragedy from a bad one can do the same with epics"). In metrics, they owed less to the epic than to iambic, solo lyric, and choral lyric. They added little to the existing repertoire of Gr. meters but combining freely metrical elements that had previously been confined to separate genres. The result, esp. in the choral odes and the arias of tragedy, is a poetry of unprecedented richness and variety in tone, tempo, and rhythm. Fifth-c. Attic tragedy is, thus, both a synthesis of all the earlier modes of Gr. poetry and the starting point of Eur. drama.

Probably an art of such power and wide popular appeal was bound, in time, to overshadow the traditional genres of Gr. poetry, and by the end of the 5th c., this process had taken place. Elegiac and solo lyric continued to be practiced until the last few decades but only falteringly. Choral lyric alone was still able to reach great heights, but even that genre faded out of hist. with the death of Pindar of Thebes (ca. 522–443). The most famous of all the choral lyricists, Pindar was master of a great range of song types for a variety of occasions. When the Hellenistic scholars came to edit his complete poems, they grouped them under the headings of *hymns, *paeans, *dithyrambs, partheneia (songs for girl choruses), *hyporchemes (dance poems), *encomia, threnoi (death laments), and epinikia (victory *odes); the titles may not in every case have reflected Pindar's intent, but they give a vivid notion of the diapason of Gr. choral lyric. Of all these, only the Epinikia, praising the victors at the four great athletic festivals, have survived intact through direct ms. transmission. Varying in length from one to thirteen triads, these odes concentrate not so much on the transient details of the athletic success as on its significance in the divine and human cosmos: the human victory is measured against mythological precedents the evocation of which—sometimes continuously, sometimes only in brief glimpses of dazzling vividness—may occupy much of the ode.

Pindaric poetry is not easy reading. It may well have been more readily comprehensible in its original performance, when it was *heard* and its message was reinforced by music and choral dancing; its allusiveness, the intricacy of its word placing and metrics, and the never-failing originality and precision of its diction keep a reader in constant tension. But it is poetry of unsurpassed metaphorical richness, intensity, and visionary power. Far more accessible is the choral lyric of Bacchylides of Ceos, many of whose songs—mostly epinikion odes and dithyrambs—have been discovered on papyri in mod. times. Bacchylides was a younger contemporary of Pindar, all of whose datable poems fall within the period 485–452. Clarity and grace mark his poetry; his meters are simple and tuneful, his mythical narratives interestingly chosen, visually evocative, and delicately ambiguous.

The first extant Gr. comedy is Aristophanes' *Acharnians*, produced in Athens in 425. Since antiquity, it has been customary to divide the hist. of the Attic comic art into three phases: Old, Middle, and New. Old Comedy extended from the institution of the comic contests at the Great Dionysia in 486 until the opening decades of the 4th c., but most of our knowledge of it depends on Aristophanes' 11 surviving plays. Of all the poetry created by the Greeks, Old Comedy has the widest metrical and stylistic range and allows by far the freest play of fantasy. Its basic dialect is the local vernacular—colloquial Attic speech in all its vigor and explicitness, sexual and scatological. Further, the extant Aristophanic comedies display an extraordinary aptitude for the *parody of every other poetic genre, not least of tragedy. But Old Comedy's single most extraordinary feature was its total freedom to create characters and situations. In most Gr. poetry up to that time, the basic narratives and characters were drawn from the ancient myths and sagas. The majority of Old Comic plots, however, seem to have been free fictions, some of them blossoming into poetic fantasies that might embrace Hades (as in Aristophanes' *Frogs*) or the entire universe (as in his *Birds*).

The last two or three decades of this period saw a revolutionary movement in Gr. music and poetry that is known to us primarily from allusions in Old Comedy, from a partially preserved lyric text, *The Persians*, by Timotheus of Miletus (fl. ca. 450–360), and from some of the songs in Euripides' late plays (as well as references to it by Plato, Aristotle, and later writers on music). This seems to have been mainly a musical revolution, provoked by the increasing professionalization of musicians—esp. pipe or aulos players—that resulted from the enormous, expanding popularity of tragedy and choral dithyramb throughout the Gr. world. Professional musicians were interested in developing a freer, more virtuoso style to showcase their skills. The references to this New Music outside of Timotheus and Euripides tend to be disapproving but are clearly tendentious and ideologically driven, an elite reaction to the rise to prominence of lower-class professional musicians. In relation to poetry, the most remarkable technical features of the New Music were its abandonment of the triadic arrangement of responding stanzas that had characterized all earlier lyric verse and the opening of a split between the words and the melody of a lyric (see MUSIC AND POETRY). For the first time, the evidence suggests, one syllable, instead of being set to one note, might be extended over several notes, as in the melisma of mod. song. These and other innovations in the instrumentation and performance of poetry effectively created a permanent break with the trad. of archaic and high cl. lyric poetry that had flourished since at least the early 7th c. In terms of preservation and posterity, these New Musical experiments were ultimately undone by a hostile conservative trad. Thus, although there is evidence that the songs of Timotheus continued to be learned and performed throughout the Gr. world for six centuries (until the 3d c. CE), they failed to make the crucial transition to vellum in the late antique period and so are almost entirely lost to us. For the Greeks (and so necessarily for us), the "lyric age" ended in 450 BCE, with Pindar and Bacchylides, the last of the canonical "lyric nine."

**E. *The Fourth Century* BCE.** From the perspective of what the Greeks canonized and preserved, the outstanding event in Gr. lit. of this period is the triumph of prose. Prose as a literary medium had developed rather slowly in the outer regions of the Gr. world from the mid-6th c. BCE onward. In Athens, it did not establish itself until the second half of the 5th c.; only in the 4th c.—and above all in the works of Isocrates, Plato, Xenophon, and Aristotle—did it acquire an unchallengeable position as the medium for the exploration of the deepest human concerns, philosophical, psychological, and political. Accordingly, the poet was gradually forced from his supreme role as universal teacher into the role of, at most, entertainer. The most flourishing variety of Gr. poetry in the 4th c. was comedy. Aristophanes' last surviving play, the *Ploutos* or *Wealth* (388), is often taken to mark the transition from Old to Middle Comedy. Certainly, the relative tameness of its central comic fantasy, its drastic reduction of the chorus's role, and its almost total elimination of any lyric element all seem to have been characteristics of Middle Comedy, which is conventionally dated ca.

380–320. New Comedy (ca. 320–250) is much more accessible to us, thanks to extensive papyrus discoveries. Most of these are plays by the most famous of the New Comic poets, Menander (ca. 342–291). The New Comic plots continue the trad. of Old Comedy in that they are fictional and set in contemp. Greece, but the fictions are now much more realistic, closer to mod. romantic comedy or situation comedy. Within this frame, Menander crafts exquisite plots and creates a long series of delicately shaded character studies. The predominant meter of his comedies is the iambic trimeter. Lyric now has no place in the fabric of the comedies, although they are divided into acts (regularly, it seems, five) by pauses in the scripts marked *Khorou*— "[song] of a chorus"—apparently songs unrelated to the dramatic action and probably not composed by the playwright. This last traceable phase of Gr. poetic drama, through the Lat. adaptations by Plautus and Terence, was to provide the formal model for both the tragedy and comedy of Ren. Europe: the five-act play in iambic verse.

Noncomic poetry apparently continued robustly throughout the 4th c., but the preserved remnants are pitifully meager. Tragedies continued to be produced in large numbers at the Great Dionysia in Athens, though, perhaps significantly, canonization of the three great 5th-c. tragedians was already taking place through reperformance of their plays alongside new compositions. The New Music movement in lyric poetry (see above) had apparently run its course by the middle of the century. The epic and elegiac poems by Antimachus of Colophon (fl. ca. 400) had their admirers in later antiquity. But at least to the Greeks' own perception (what they considered worth canonizing and preserving), the great era of Gr. poetry (dramatic and nondramatic) that had sustained itself continuously from the preliterate period had come to an end. The stage was clear for a new kind of poetry.

F. *The Hellenistic Age (ca. 300–21 BCE).* In Athens, New Comedy—the last survivor of any of the publicly performed cl. genres—continued in full vigor during the earlier part of this period. Elsewhere, the circumstances and character of Gr. poetry changed radically. The conquests of Alexander the Great (d. 323) had extended the power, and with it the lang., of the Greeks into the Near and Middle East, a shift soon followed by a shift in the focuses of literary activity. The newly founded Gr. metropolises, above all Egyptian Alexandria, attracted talent of every kind from wherever Gr. was spoken. But the new poetic culture that arose in those vast cities, with their diverse mixture of Gr.-speaking immigrants and native populations, was necessarily a culture of the book; its audience was no longer the citizen in the marketplace. The result was a learned poetry of exquisite technical finish and literary allusiveness—a poetry, for the first time in this story, analogous to that of Virgil, John Milton, or T. S. Eliot. At the same time, however, the Hellenistic poets were very conscious of the need to validate the new kind of poetry by ensuring the *appearance* of continuity with the older Gr. poetic trad. Many of the archaic genres were now revived in form, if transfigured in scope and tone. The most versatile of the Hellenistic poets, Callimachus (active in Alexandria ca. 280–245), offers a good example of the process. His *Hymns* deliberately recall the Homeric hymns of archaic Greece. Yet these Callimachean counterparts are not so much acts of piety as masterpieces of delicate wit and fantasy; and more than one of them incorporates a literary evocation of the festival at which it was to be *imagined* as delivered. Similar imitations and transpositions are to be found in Callimachus's *Iambi*, where Hipponax is an acknowledged model, and in his *Aetia*, where he invokes the precedents of Mimnermus and Hesiod.

In this general revival of the archaic genres, it was impossible that Homer should be neglected, but he now elicited very diverse literary responses. To Callimachus and many other Hellenistic poets, notably Theocritus, the vast scale and heroic temper of Homeric epic were no longer achievable or even desirable, for these men aimed above all at brevity, polish, and realism. They devised their own brand of narrative poetry, the brief epic, adopting (with refinements) the Homeric medium, the hexameter, but limiting the scale to a few hundred lines (see EPYLLION). Within this space, there could be no question of retelling a heroic saga; rather, the poet would illuminate a single heroic episode, bringing out its full color and detail. Examples of this form are Callimachus's fragmentary *Hekale*, Theocritus's *Idyll* 13 on Herakles and Hylas, and, at a later date, Moschus's *Europa*. A number of Hellenistic poets, however, did compose large-scale epics, though the only one that survives is the *Argonautica* of Apollonius Rhodius, a younger contemporary of Callimachus. In its versification, its lang., and its similes, this poem abundantly testifies to Apollonius's long study of Homer, yet in content and tone it is utterly un-Homeric. Apollonius's passive and hesitant hero, Jason, belongs rather to our world than to the world of Achilles and Odysseus, and the depiction in book 3 of Medea's love for him is a breakthrough in the psychological depiction of passion, at least in the epic context.

Hesiod was the alleged model for the many didactic poems composed in the Hellenistic period, though the wide human scope of Hesiodic poetry tended to be reduced simply to the versification of this technology or that. The most notable surviving example is Aratus's *Phainomena*, on astronomy and meteorology. The only altogether new genre created by the Hellenistic poets (or, if not created, adapted from subliterary songs and mummings of an earlier period) was *pastoral poetry. The earliest known examples are the work of Theocritus, who was approximately a contemporary of Callimachus and Apollonius. The collection of his poems that has reached us under the title of *Idylls* consists of relatively short pieces, mostly in hexameters, but only a minority of them are pastorals, and one of Theocritus's most brilliant dialogue poems, *Idyll* 15, is set in the multicultural hubbub of Alexandria itself. Both the nonpastoral and the pastoral poems display the Callimachean preference for brevity and precise detail, but, in his control of verbal music, Theocritus may be thought to surpass even Callimachus.

The great creative impetus of Hellenistic poetry was limited to the first half of the 3d c. BCE. Thereafter, very little new ground was broken. The various genres that were then reestablished or created continued to be practiced, but the surviving examples are of little poetic significance (see ALEXANDRIANISM).

**G. *The Roman Imperial Period.*** With the battle of Actium in 31 BCE, Rome's empire over the Mediterranean and Near East was decisively established. Paradoxically, it was the *Roman* poets who henceforth most successfully exploited the legacy of Hellenistic Gr. poetry; the three great poems of Virgil himself, for instance, would be inconceivable but for the precedents of Hellenistic pastoral, didactic, and epic. Though a great many poems were composed in Gr. under the empire, none matches the work of the major Roman poets in intrinsic interest or influence on subsequent Eur. poetry. Thus, the trad. of ancient Gr. poetry, while competently perpetuated during this period, was gradually losing its momentum. Two slow but steady devels., one ling. and the other social, were finally to bring that trad. to an end: a change in the pronunciation of Gr., whereby quantity is replaced by stress (see ACCENT), and the triumph of the Christian imagination over the pagan. From about the beginning of the Christian era, the distinction in colloquial Gr. speech between long and short vowel quantities began to disappear, and the musical pitch accent that had prevailed since archaic times began to be replaced by a tonic stress accent similar to that of mod. Gr. or Eng. Literary Gr. poetry responded only very slowly to these changes, but by the 6th c. CE, the characteristic Byzantine versification was well established, its guiding principle no longer syllable quantity but recurrent stress accent. In this fashion, Gr. poetry gradually lost the superb metrical system that, in the hands of Pindar, the Attic tragedians, and Theocritus, had generated such an incomparable wealth and variety of verbal music. Simultaneously, Gr. poetry was also being gradually distanced from pagan mythology—from the rich intellectual and imaginative resource that had provided it with its themes since the preliterate era. As a consequence of these two devels., Gr. poetry was no more the same art. No absolute date can be set to that final transformation, and exceptions to the general trend can always be found: for instance, scholars continued to compose verses in quantitative Gr. meters down through the Middle Ages and Ren. (see CLASSICAL METERS IN MODERN LANGUAGES). But, effectively, the change had taken place by the end of the 6th c. CE.

Most of the Gr. poetry that survives from the Roman imperial period falls under one of three genres: didactic, epic, and epigram. Tragedy and comedy were no longer composed, and the few known examples of lyric poetry are not very striking either in substance or metric. The didactic poets followed closely in the steps of their Hellenistic predecessors, composing versified textbooks of varying interest and merit on such sub-

jects as geography and fishing. Epic both mythological and *panegyric (i.e., celebrating the exploits of some political figure) was very widely composed. Much the most interesting example is the *Dionysiaca* composed by Nonnus of Panopolis in Egypt in the early 5th c. This story of the triumphant career of Dionysus, in 48 books (matching the total number of books in the *Iliad* and the *Odyssey*), is the last major Gr. poem in hexameters.

Alone among the Gr. genres, the epigram never fell out of fashion. This kind of brief, finely worked, and pointed poem, somewhat comparable in finish and compactness to the *haiku (see RENGA) or the *heroic couplet, most often took the form of one to four elegiac distichs. The earliest examples are inscriptions (*epigrammata*) on gravestones or votive objects of the archaic period. During the 5th c. BCE, the form was increasingly adapted to literary purposes, and the range of its content was extended beyond the funereal and dedicatory to many other human concerns—above all, love, humor, and wine. The great surviving corpus of epigrams, the *Greek Anthology*, put together for the most part by the 10th c. CE, is one of the most moving and impressive of all the monuments of ancient Gr. poetry. Within it are found epigrams by most of the famous poets, and philosophers too, composed over a span of approximately 14 centuries.

**II. Medieval.** *See* BYZANTINE POETRY.

**III. Modern.** As Greece's modernity is dated along with national independence (1828), any discussion about lit. in the expansive terrain of the post-Byzantine period necessarily concerns poetic instances of vernacular expression and is specifically tied to the multifarious uses of the Gr. lang. The institution of mod. Gr. lit. cannot be separated from the problem of the "proper" Gr. literary lang., and it can just as easily be said that the very hist. of mod. Gr. lit. (esp. poetry) ultimately decides the thorny issue identified as "the language question." This polemic involves advocates of the formal idiom (*katharevousa*—a constructed form with archaic resonance that literally means "pure") against advocates of the quotidian spoken idiom (*dēmotikē*—demotic), a fierce battle that began in mid-19th c. and ended, in favor of the second, with 1930s *modernism, even though katharevousa remained the official state lang. until 1976. But the overarching problematic of mod. Gr. poetry also involves an array of other lang. uses, from local dialects to diasporic idioms, which enable the coincidence of numerous ling. registers, much to the benefit of poetic creativity. This gives Gr. poets an extraordinary expressive range, often impossible to render in trans.

Between the fall of Constantinople to the Ottomans (1453) and the Greek War of Independence (1821–28), literate poetry flourished mainly in Gr. lands under Venetian influence, esp. Crete. What was later named the Cretan Renaissance is standard reference to the production of poetic romances that draw a great deal on It. models but have a distinctive character. The exemplary poet of the Cretan Ren. is Vitsentzos Kornaros (1553–1613), whose genre-defining epic romance *Erot-*

*okritos*—a poem of 10,000 rhyming 15-syllable iambic verses in the Cretan dialect—narrates the chivalrous love of Erotokritos for the princess Aretousa and their union after long and arduous adventures of deception and intrigue. The most recognized antecedent is the Frankish romance *Paris et Vienne* (1487), with additional influences traceable to Ludovico Ariosto and the Cretan folk-song trad., but Kornaros forges a poetic idiom, whose innovation, within the parameters of the Gr. lang., is broadly recognized, thanks to Gr. modernist interpretations.

In the rest of the Gr. world under Ottoman rule, poetry flourishes in the folk-song form. From the painstaking collection of folk songs by folklorist Nikolaos Politis (1852–1921), we now recognize the heyday of this anonymous popular poetic form to be the 18th c., when a vast range of improvised love songs, songs of travel, *lullabies, and *dirges comprise poetic material of profound beauty and innovation, arguably superior to any poetry in Gr. since the close of the 9th c. In terms of both form and poetic lang., the Gr. folk song proved remarkably influential, even in the most experimental of romantic and modernist expressions.

The inaugural modernity of Gr. poetry belongs to Dionysios Solomos (1798–1857). Although Solomos was established as national *poet laureate because the first two stanzas of his "Hymn to Liberty" (1823—one of few poems completed and pub. in his lifetime) became the Gr. national *anthem, he is nonetheless characterized by inimitable experimentalism in both lang. and form, having introduced into Gr. a number of Western metrical forms (*sestina, *ottava rima, *terza rima) that freed Gr. poetry from the compulsion toward the 15-syllable verse. As a member of the Ionian aristocracy (the Ionian islands were never under Ottoman rule), Solomos was bilingual and certainly more adept in It. than Gr. Because of his struggle with the Gr. lang., he wrote in dēmotikē, itself a groundbreaking gesture in the devel. of mod. Gr. poetry. He was influenced philosophically by G.W.F. Hegel and Ger. *romanticism and, in literary terms, by cl. It. and his sparse knowledge of the Gr. folk-song trad. His Gr. poetic oeuvre is comprised of an extraordinary series of fragments and voluminous marginal notes in It., the ensemble constituting an as yet unmatched experiment in poetic modernity. Solomos's idiosyncratically inventive way of creating composite words in several ling. registers makes trans. exceedingly difficult. The pinnacle of Solomos's achievements is *The Free Besieged*, a long unfinished poem drafted between 1833 and 1847 in several versions that include rhymed 15-syllable and *free verse, single-verse fragments, interspersed prose, and a theoretical preamble—all experimenting with lyric, epic, and dramatic styles in order to capture the atmosphere of the heroic resistance and exodus of Messolonghi (1826) during the Greek War of Independence. Messolonghi, as the site of Lord Byron's demise, also inspired Solomos to a series of odes and fragments in Byronic style.

The other groundbreaking poet of this era, Andreas Kalvos (1792–1869), was also Ionian, and he, too, wrote his first texts (tragedies and dramatic monologues) in It. Later in life, he also wrote prose texts in Eng., having spent a good part of his life in England as a country squire. His only poetic output in Gr. is a book of *Odes and Lyrics* (1826), which was rejected by the Gr. intelligentsia of his day but granted him instant recognition in Fr. trans. Kalvos, too, is characterized by an idiosyncratic poetics that combines archaic and demotic metrics and ling. registers to produce an unusual manner, simultaneously stern and sentimental, intellectual and lyric, pagan and traditionally romantic. Kalvos's influence is traced explicitly in various modernist and contemp. experiments (notably the prosody movement of the 1990s), but his poetic legacy continues to produce vehement disputes. Both Solomos and Kalvos (like C. P. Cavafy later) wrote outside the national territory and in idiomatic Gr., prompting George Seferis to claim in 1936 that the inauguration of contemp. Gr. poetics belonged to "our three great deceased poets who did not know Greek."

In the aftermath of national independence, canonical Gr. romanticism flourishes in Athens, at the heart of national-cultural and intellectual life. The founder of the romantic school of Athens was Alexandros Soutsos (1803–63), a fervent admirer of Victor Hugo and Byron, whose exuberant romantic and patriotic writings, however, do not capture the spirit of their models. Though he was terse and vigorous as a satirist, Soutsos exercised a stultifying influence on Gr. poetry. Most representatives of this school were bound to an exaggerated romanticism, using a stilted formal idiom (katharevousa) for painstakingly patriotic poetry. Achilleas Paraschos (1838–95) is the leading figure in the last period of the school. His contemporaries were all overshadowed by his reputation, in spite of the greater sincerity and more delicate technique of many of their works. Some of them have come to be appreciated in recent years—Demetrios Paparrhegopoulos (1843–73) as a refined lyricist, Alexandros Vyzantios (1841–98) as sharp-witted satirist, and Georgios Vizyenos (1849–96) as the most important 19th-c. innovator of the short-story form.

About 1880, a young group of poets, influenced by the virulent crit. of Emmanuel Roidis (1836–1904), a brilliant novelist and public intellectual, formed the New School of Athens. They aspired to become the Gr. Parnassians (see PARNASSIANISM), masters of a restrained and objective art. The central figure was Kostis Palamas (1859–1943), a man of wide learning whose works blended not only the ancient and mod. Gr. trads. but the social and spiritual convulsions of the late 19th and early 20th cs. *The Dodecalogue of the Gypsy* (1907) is perhaps his crowning achievement. Its hero, the Gypsy musician, a symbol of freedom and art, gradually deepens into the patriot, the Greek, and finally the Hellene—citizen and teacher of the world. This powerful epic-lyric, together with *The King's Flute* (1910), a historical epic, and *Life Immovable* (1904), the most important of his lyric collections, solidified an enormous influence both on contemporaries of the school and their immediate successors. The poets of this generation should be credited for introducing *symbolism and free verse into Gr. poetry, much to the benefit of their 20th-c. counterparts.

Yet arguably the greatest poet of the mod. Gr. trad. remained untouched by Palamas's influence. C. P. Cavafy (1863–1933) was an Alexandrian by both birth and sensibility. His inimitable achievement was the creation of a mythical world of diasporic Hellenism characterized by *irony, eroticism, and a tragic vision that celebrates those who gracefully deviate from the norm or singularly embody what is fleeting and irreproducible or face disaster with honest self-awareness. Cavafy's mythographic universe parallels those fashioned by eminent contemporaries (W. B. Yeats, Ezra Pound, T. S. Eliot) and has thus gained him a place in the pantheon of modernist poetry worldwide. Cavafy wrote both historical and lyric poetry with equally erotic sensibility and, more than any other Gr. poet, he can be said to embody a pagan spirit, unperturbed by the social and cultural institutions of his day. He remained uninterested in publishing and preferred to distribute his poetry in folios he variously assembled on his own, following no chronological order. He is, thus, quintessentially modernist in disregarding both the commercial sphere and the establishment of a legacy.

Cavafy exercised no influence on his contemporaries, although his influence on subsequent generations to this day is unsurpassed. The most significant of early 20th-c. poets succeeded in distinguishing themselves from the dominance of Palamas's poetics. Kostas Varnalis (1884–1974) rivals Palamas as a socially conscious poet, the first to bear a strong political voice and the inaugural figure in the long trad. of 20th-c. leftist poetics. Less directly influential but more poetically significant is Kostas Karyotakis (1896–1928). A complex man of great talent and fragile sensibility, Karyotakis wrote lyric and satirical poems with equal skill: witness *Elegies and Satires* (1927). His unfortunate liaison with the lyric poet Maria Polydouri (1902–30), his rejection of bourgeois patriotic propriety, and his subsequent suicide were later recognized to reflect a poetic sensibility of unusual daring, reversing belief that he epitomized the Gr. malaise of post-Asia Minor Catastrophe (1922). Counterposed to Karyotakis's sensibility is Angelos Sikelianos (1884–1952). Powerfully elegiac, Sikelianos construes Gr. nature and hist. in both Apollonian light and Dionysian mystery. With a rich diction and avowedly Delphic spirit, the natural landscape, the human form, and abstract thought are all brought into clear-cut relief in exceedingly singular lyrical form. Additionally, Nikos Kazantzakis (1885–1957), renowned as a novelist, deserves mention for the most conceptually daring work of his time: a formidable 33,333-line mod. sequel to the *Odyssey* (1938), written in Cretan dialect and radical (bordering on artificial) dēmotikē, in which the Odyssean hero, haunted by Nietzschean nihilism, searches for existential salvation in an incessant journey through various modes of thought.

The modernist movement, known as the Generation of the 1930s, having reconfigured the terms of the entire mod. Gr. poetic trad., still exercises a catalytic influence. Accordingly, it produced two Nobel Prize winners, George Seferis (1963) and Odysseus Elytis (1979), and the Lenin Prize recipient Yiannis Ritsos (1977); all three poets saw their work set to music by the composer Mikis Theodorakis in a gesture that brought the sensibility of Gr. modernism to a broad public. Seferis (1900–71) ushers a style, method, and vision in conversation with Eliot and Paul Valéry, by casting the mod. predicament in a Gr. literary landscape that encompasses ancient epic and tragic poetics, the Cretan Ren., and the entire demotic trad. in order to produce a new mythical lang. in dramatic free verse, rich in nuance while spare in decoration, which poeticizes a Gr. psyche in the midst of a ruined past to be overcome. This poetic project enhanced with carefully timed publications of literary essays, over a 30-year period, which sealed Seferis's unparalleled hegemonic influence on Gr. letters. Similarly committed to the project of Gr. modernism but in an entirely different style, Elytis (1911–96) wielded his influence more by virtue of a lyrical technique that crafts a personal mythology in celebration of the natural-material features of the Gr. imagination. Initially following a surrealist juxtaposition of disparate images in flamboyant lyricism, Elytis's gravity is measured by the intricate poetics of *Axion Esti* (1960), an extended secular hymn that draws on Gr. Orthodox liturgy, 19th-c. demotic trad., dramatic prose, and historical material from World War II to sculpt and praise the spiritual dimension of the Gr. psyche in the world of the senses.

Gr. *surrealism in this generation (in direct association with its Fr. strains) is exemplified by Andreas Embeirikos (1901–75), who was also the first Gr. psychoanalyst and who wrote in exceedingly ornate lang., occasionally adopting *archaisms with unabashed relish; and Nikos Engonopoulos (1910–85), who was also the most radical and yet most representative painter of his generation. Initially of this group, Nikos Gatsos (1911–92), who published only one poetry book in his lifetime, the sumptuous *Amorgos* (1943), is nonetheless considered one of the most influential figures of this generation because of his production of several hundred song lyrics, written with remarkable skill, imagination, and grace (and set to music by many Gr. composers, notably Manos Hatzidakis) that singlehandedly raised the genre to a high art form. Certainly worth mentioning here is Giorgos Sarantaris (1908–41), whose hapless death brought to an unjust end the work of the most important philosopher-poet in 20th-c. Greece.

The magnitude of this generation is sealed by Ritsos (1909–90), who, along with Cavafy and Seferis, is the most influential Gr. poet worldwide. An inordinately prolific poet, Ritsos excelled in several forms: traditional folk metrics (*Epitaphios*, 1936), long-form dramatic verse (*Moonlight Sonata*, 1956), and short, sparse object-oriented poems (*Gestures*, 1972), as well as a variety of theatrical and prose pieces. What unites these concerns is an overt political voice, for which Ritsos was exiled and interned in concentration camps for most of his life as an avowed communist. Ritsos favors tragic landscapes, where the old gods no longer survive, while dispossessed humans, wounded and still threatened by the civilization they inhabit in ruined cities and arid plains, envision alternate universes in material household details, dreamlike encounters, and new myths.

Ritsos's figure permeates the post-Civil War generation of leftist poets, who wrote in conditions of persecution what was named the *poetry of defeat*: poetry of profound irony and self-critique against the backdrop of the bleakest landscape, where glimpses of real friendship provide the only possible resistance. This reticent poetry of extreme talent, sensitivity, and responsibility is exemplified by Manolis Anagnostakis (1925–2005), Aris Alexandrou (1928–78), Tasos Leivaditis (1922–88), and Titos Patrikios (b. 1928). Also writing in this period, Miltos Sahtouris (1919–2005), Nikos Karouzos (1926–90), and Eleni Vakalo (1921–2001) are three major poets who work in a postsurrealist mode but cannot be categorized. Sahtouris paints nightmare dreamscapes of a world that appears to have survived the destruction of humanity, often with characteristic humor. Karouzos favors a highly personal idiom, sometimes cryptically invoking a pre-Socratic sense of the universe. Vakalo, also the premier art critic of her time, engages in a self-conscious poetry of the object, which implicates a beautifully open-ended, if stark, poetic persona.

The generation following, known as the Generation of the 1970s, wrote out of the experience of the Gr. Junta years (1967–74) and in the atmosphere of global youth culture, in the aftermath of an internationalist antiestablishment poetics that spans the range from *Beat poetry to rock-music aesthetics. This uncategorizable poetry incorporated a generally irreverent attitude toward bourgeois consumerist complacency by exploiting the full riches of colloquial speech, incl. imported terms and commercial monikers, and calling into question all orthodox beliefs and established positions, incl. gender roles and dogmatic political commitments. The tendency was to elucidate a bereft and absurd world in a lang. as contemporary as the drifting scene it depicted. Of the great number of poets in this generation, who emerged (often to submerge again in silence or long absence), it is worth noting, not as representative but by virtue of singular achievement and uniqueness, Dimitris Kalokyris (b. 1948), whose additional inordinate talents as storyteller, artist, art designer, pioneering publisher, and translator of Jorge Luis Borges are encapsulated in a poetry of magical effect; Maria Laina (b. 1947), who perfected a subtle, laconic, yet pulsating lyricism; and Dionysis Kapsalis (b. 1952), whose theoretical learning, studious contemplation of even minor traditional elements, and unequaled skill in the rhythmic use of the Gr. lang. (evident in his trans. of Emily Dickinson and Shakespeare's sonnets) pioneered a contemp. return to metrics.

The proliferation of poetic writing worldwide, aided by electronic media even if in the context of poetry's increasing irrelevance to popular art, renders all assessment of contemp. poetic production in Greece difficult. Yet there is no doubt that, of all literary forms, poetry has wielded the most decisive force in mod. Gr. culture. This gravity cannot be outmaneuvered. In the end, the future of Gr. literary expression will be waged on the permutations of continuing to fashion Gr. poetic lang., in whatever form this is to be actualized.

*See* CHORUS, CLASSICAL POETICS, CLASSICAL PROSODY, CLASSICISM, DRAMATIC POETRY, LATIN POETRY, NARRATIVE POETRY, TRAGICOMEDY.

■ **Classical**. *Anthologies*: *Greek Lyric Poetry*, ed. D. Campbell (1982)—Gr. text and commentary; *Penguin Book of Greek Verse*, ed. C. A. Trypanis, 3d ed. (1988); *Hellenistic Poetry* (1990) and *Archaic Greek Poetry* (1992), both ed. and trans. B. Fowler; *Greek Lyric Poetry*, ed. G. Hutchinson (2001)—Gr. text and commentary. *Bibliographies*: *L'Année Philologique: Bibliographie critique et analytique de l'antiquité gréco-latine* 1–(1927–), http://www.annee-philologique.com/aph/. *Criticism and History*: D. L. Page, *Sappho and Alcaeus* (1955); A. E. Harvey, "The Classification of Greek Lyric Poetry," *CQ* n.s. 5 (1955); W. B. Stanford, *The Sound of Greek* (1967); Parry; F. Cairns, *Generic Composition in Greek and Roman Poetry* (1972); K. J. Dover, *Aristophanic Comedy* (1972); M. L. West, "Greek Poetry 2000–700 BCE," *CQ* 23 (1973); and *Studies in Greek Elegy and Iambus* (1974); H. F. Fränkel, *Early Greek Poetry and Philosophy*, trans. M. Hadas and J. Willis (1975); W. G. Arnott, "Introduction," *Menander*, v. 1 (1979)—comedy; R. Janko, *Homer, Hesiod, and the Hymns* (1982); T. G. Rosenmeyer, *The Art of Aeschylus* (1982); A. P. Burnett, *Three Archaic Poets* (1983); M. Griffith, "Personality in Hesiod," *Classical Antiquity* 2 (1983); A. Lesky, *Greek Tragic Poetry*, trans. M. Dillon (1983); A. P. Burnett, *The Art of Bacchylides* (1985); T. Figueira and G. Nagy, *Theognis of Megara* (1985); J. Herington, *Poetry into Drama* (1985); E. L. Bowie, "Early Greek Elegy, Symposium and Public Festival," *JHS* 106 (1986); E. Bundy, *Studia Pindarica*, 2d ed. (1986); S. Goldhill, *Reading Greek Tragedy* (1986); G. F. Else, *Plato and Aristotle on Poetry* (1987); M. W. Edwards, *Homer* (1987); H. White, *Studies in Late Greek Epic Poetry* (1987); B. Gentili, *Poetry and Its Public in Ancient Greece*, trans. A. T. Cole (1988); G. O. Hutchinson, *Hellenistic Poetry* (1988); R. Lamberton, *Hesiod* (1988); R. Hamilton, *The Architecture of Hesiodic Poetry* (1989); R. P. Martin, *The Language of Heroes* (1989)—*Iliad*; A. W. Pickard-Cambridge, *The Dramatic Festivals of Athens*, 2d ed. (1989); G. Nagy, "Hesiod and the Poetics of Pan-Hellenism," *Greek Mythology and Poetics* (1990); S. Goldhill, *The Poet's Voice* (1991); L. Kurke, *The Traffic in Praise* (1991)—Pindar and choral lyric; J. Redfield, *Nature and Culture in the "Iliad,"* 2d ed. (1994); A. Cameron, *Callimachus and His Critics* (1995); E. Csapo and W. J. Slater, *The Context of Ancient Drama* (1995); P. DuBois, *Sappho Is Burning* (1995); D. Konstan, *Greek Comedy and Ideology* (1995); M. Detienne, *The Masters of Truth in Archaic Greece*, trans. J. Lloyd (1996); R. Hunter, *Theocritus and the Archaeology of Greek Poetry* (1996); G. Nagy, *Poetry as Performance* (1996); F. I. Zeitlin, *Playing the Other* (1996); E. Bakker, *Poetry in Speech* (1997)—Homer; E. Stehle, *Performance and Gender in Ancient Greece* (1997); M. L. West, *The East Face of Helicon* (1997); A. Carson, *Eros the Bittersweet*, 2d ed. (1998); K. Gutzwiller, *Poetic Garlands* (1998)—

Hellenistic epigrams; D. Selden, "Alibis," *Classical Antiquity* 17 (1998); A. Carson, *Economy of the Unlost* (1999); G. Nagy, *Best of the Achaeans*, 2d ed. (1999); S. Stephens, *Seeing Double* (2003)—Hellenistic poetry in Egyptian context; E. Csapo, "The Politics of the New Music," *Music and the Muses*, ed. P. Murray and P. Wilson (2004); C. A. Faraone, *The Stanzaic Architecture of Early Greek Elegy* (2008); D. J. Mastronarde, *The Art of Euripides* (2010). *General Histories*: *CHCL*, v. 1; A. Lesky, *History of Greek Literature*, 2d ed. (1996). *Primary Texts*: Bibliotheca Teubneriana series (1888–)—crit. texts without trans.; Loeb Classical Library series (1912–)—texts, with facing trans., of all the major poets, incl. D. A. Campbell, *Greek Lyric* 5 v. (1982–93); D. E. Gerber, *Greek Elegiac Poetry*; and *Greek Iambic Poetry* (both 1999); *Callimachus*, ed. R. Pfeiffer, 2 v. (1949); *Theocritus*, ed. A.S.F. Gow, 2 v. (1950); D. L. Page, *Poetae Melici Graeci* (1962); M. L. West, *Iambi et Elegi Graeci ante Alexandrum cantati*, 2d ed. (1989–92); Oxford Classical Texts series (1980–)—good critical texts without trans. *Prosody*: Wilamowitz; Dale; Halporn et al; Snell; West.

■ **Modern**. *Anthologies*: *Anthologia 1708–1933*, ed. E. N. Apostolidis (n.d.); *Modern Greek Poems*, trans. T. Stephanidis and G. Katsimbalis (1926); *Eklogai apo ta tragoudia tou Hellenikou Laou*, ed. N. Politis, 3d ed. (1932); *Modern Greek Poetry*, trans. K. Friar (1973); *Voices of Modern Greece*, trans. E. Keeley and P. Sherrard (1981); *Greek Poetry: New Voices*, ed. D. Connolly (1999); *A Century of Greek Poetry 1900–2000*, ed. P. Bien et al. (2004); *The Greek Poets: Homer to the Present*, ed. P. Constantine et al. (2009). *Criticism and History*: P. Sherrard, *The Marble Threshing Floor* (1956); G. Seferis, *On the Greek Style: Selected Essays in Poetry and Hellenism*, trans. R. Warner and T. D. Frangopoulos (1966); M. Vitti, *Storia della letteratura Neogreca* (1971); C. T. Dimaras, *A History of Modern Greek Literature*, trans. M. Gianos (1972); L. Politis, *A History of Modern Greek Literature*, trans. R. Liddell, 2d ed. (1975); A. Karantones, *Eisagoge ste neoteri poiese*, 4th ed. (1976); R. Beaton, *Folk Poetry of Modern Greece* (1980); Z. Lorenzatos, *The Lost Center* (1980); E. Keeley, *Modern Greek Poetry: Voice and Myth* (1983); D. Tziovas, *The Nationism of the Demoticists* (1986); G. Jusdanis, *The Poetics of Cavafy* (1987); V. Lambropoulos, *Literature as National Institution* (1988); D. Ricks, *The Shade of Homer* (1989); S. Gourgouris, *Dream Nation* (1996); D. Dimiroulis, *O poiētēs ōs ethnos* (1997); K. Van Dyck, *Kassandra and the Censors* (1998); D. Holton, *Literature and Society in Renaissance Crete* (2006).

C. J. HERINGTON, L. KURKE (CL.); E. KEELEY,
S. GOURGOURIS (MOD.)

**GREGUERÍA.** This Sp. word, which originally meant "confused outcry or vociferation," was used by the Sp. avant-garde writer Ramón Gómez de la Serna to designate short, witty prose texts he began producing around 1910. After Gómez de la Serna, many other writers cultivated this genre, incl. members of the Sp. poetic Generation of 1927. Gómez de la Serna first published stand-alone *greguerías* in periodicals and later as book-length collections. They are also the basic structure of many of his essays, short stories, biographies, novellas, and novels. Greguerías display a wide variety of forms and techniques and address many subjects, which makes the task of classification risky and endless. Some approaches have treated the greguería as an entirely new genre; others see it as related to aphorisms, proverbs, and maxims; still others have emphasized its humorous and imagistic or metaphoric qualities. The polymorphous nature of the greguería seems to defy all monolithic approaches. Some greguerías are related to the Spanish *baroque, specifically to *conceptismo and Baltasar Gracián's *agudeza, roughly equivalent to the Eng. notions of *conceit or *wit. They are also analogous to the romantic notion of the *fragment and to 20th-c. *imagism. Many of Gómez de la Serna's greguerías create witty *metaphors whose terms are dissimilar objects in the world, employing the form of the apposition (*A:B*): "Poplar: tree with green butterflies"; "Owl: feathered cat"; "Microphone: everyone's ear." Others exploit uncomplicated and humorous visual assocs. of letters and numbers: "8 is the hourglass of the digits"; "B is the wet nurse of the alphabet"; "The swan is the capital S of the lake's poem"; "q is p coming back from a stroll." Some constitute complex puns and alliterative word games: "*Idem* is a thrifty word"; "Wednesday: a long day by definition"; "Reminiscence: ruminating recollections." A vast number consists simply of striking concrete *images, mostly visual or synaesthetic, that combine sound, smell, and tactile sensations: "A tapping on the strainer: orange juice"; "Velvet of silence"; "Violets give off blue perfume" (see SYNAESTHESIA).

*See* AVANT-GARDE POETICS; SPAIN, POETRY OF.

■ R. L. Jackson, "Toward a Classification of the 'Greguería,'" *Hispania* 48 (1964); R. Gómez de la Serna, *Greguerías: Selección 1910–1960*, ed. S. Prieto Delgado (1977); M. Durán, "Origen y función de la greguería," *Studies on Ramón Gómez de la Serna*, ed. N. Dennis (1988); *Aphorisms: Ramón Gómez de La Serna*, trans. M. González-Gerth (1989); W. Redfern, "Greguerías: Squeals/Pipsqueaks? The Work of Ramón Gómez de la Serna," *Verbatim* 28 (2003); "Greguerías by Ramón Gómez de la Serna," *Translation: A Translation Studies Journal* 1, trans. O. Cisneros (2005).

O. CISNEROS

**GUARANÍ POETRY.** Though spoken in neighboring countries, Guaraní is present primarily in Paraguay, where, unique among Amerindian langs., it is the majority tongue of a nonindigenous and mestizo population of several million.

Of the considerable lit. in Guaraní, poetry is the dominant genre and the one that most exhibits Paraguay's historical spectrum from indigenous to nonindigenous. As sacred indigenous song of *ñe'ẽ* (word/soul), poetry has been present from the beginning, explaining and celebrating a vast cosmology that flows from the moment when Ñamandu Ru Ete (True Father Ñamandu) set life in motion by forming in himself the foundation of the word. Paralleling this trad., a corpus of *campesino* oral verse also developed in the colonial period, expressed often in the Guaraní-Sp. blend known as *jopara*, with a frequent focus on Christian religious themes.

Unfortunately, much remains unknown about this orature, and it was not accompanied by a significant written counterpart until after the catastrophic War of the Triple Alliance (1864–70), when Guaraní assumed greater importance as an emblem of nationalism. The decades between 1870 and the Chaco War against Bolivia (1932–35) saw themes of nature, love, war, and poverty woven into verse by Narciso R. Colmán, Manuel Ortiz Guerrero, Emiliano Fernández, and others. Following Paraguay's victory in the Chaco War, Guaraní's role in lit. expanded. Poets of the mid-20th c., among them Darío Gómez Serrato, Pedro Encina Ramos, Epifanio Méndez Fleitas, and Teodoro Mongelós, elaborated their predecessors' themes while adding distinctive experiments with rhyme, phrasing, and lineation.

The hardships of the Alfredo Stroessner dictatorship (1954–89) and the post-Stroessner period have seen considerable efforts to define a Guaraní poetics rooted in campesino life and Paraguay's diverse heritage. Protagonists in this effort have included Gumersindo Ayala Aquino, Félix de Guarania, Juan Maidana, Carlos Martínez Gamba, Lino Trinidad Sanabria, and Rudi Torga, all of whom use the Guaraní lang. as a conduit to express Paraguay's authentic *teko* (character).

What role Paraguay's indigenous heritage plays in this *teko* continues to be debated. The anthropological writings of Kurt Unkel Nimuendaju and León Cadogan concerning, respectively, the concepts of *Yvy Marae'y* (the Land without Evil) and *ayvu rapyta* (the basis of language) have encouraged much discussion. Whereas writers such as Encina Ramos used Eur.-inspired prosody to romanticize Guaraní mythology, recent poets like Susy Delgado, Ramón Silva, and Zenón Bogado Rolón have sought a deeper synthesis. They and others, incl. Miguelángel Meza, Feliciano Acosta, and Mario Rubén Álvarez, continue to explore the singular capacity of Guaraní to express Paraguay's particular confluence of cultures.

*See* COLONIAL POETICS; INDIGENOUS AMERICAS, POETRY OF THE.

■ T. Méndez-Faith, *Breve diccionario de la literatura paraguaya* (1996); *Poesía paraguaya de ayer y de hoy: tomo II, guaraní-español*, ed. T. Méndez-Faith (1997); *Antología de las mejores poesías en guaraní*, ed. R. Torga (1998); F. Acosta, *Ñe'ẽporãhaipyre guaraní, literatura guaraní* (2000); *Forjadores del Paraguay: Diccionario biográfico* (2000); *Antología de la poesía culta y popular en guaraní*, ed. R. Bareiro Saguier and C. Villagra Marsal (2007); *Literatura oral y popular del Paraguay*, ed. S. Delgado and F. Acosta (2008); Portal Guaraní, http://www.portalguarani.com/autores.

T. K. LEWIS

# GUATEMALA, POETRY OF

I. The Precolonial Period to the Nineteenth Century
II. The Mainstream Tradition (1920s–2010)
III. New Women's and Indigenous Poetry in Guatemala

**I. The Precolonial Period to the Nineteenth Century.** Poetry in Guatemala has served as a vehicle of emergent national expression, with the marked limitation that a great part of Guatemala's population has been made up of non-Sp.-speaking Indian peoples whose writings have disappeared. Even the *Popol Vuh*, the most important work in the Quiché lang. and a veritable storehouse of images that constantly reemerged in the poetry of the 20th c., was written after the arrival of the conquistador Pedro de Alvarado. The *Rabinal Achí*, a dramatic work involving dance and poetry, is thought to date from the 15th c. The administrative seat of Spain's Central Am. colonial rule, Guatemala dominated regional discourse for over 400 years, generating a canon of lit. based on Eur. models and centered on prose. From the 16th to the 19th c., poetic production took forms such as the *villancico*, the *sainete*, the *jácara*, the *tonada*, and the *cantata*, with poets such as Rafael Antonio Castellanos (ca. 1725–91) and Manuel José de Quirós (ca. 1765–90) writing music as well as verse.

In the 18th c., Rafael Landívar (1731–93) wrote his *Rusticatio mexicana* (1782) in Lat.; and in the early 19th, the Sp.-born Pepita Garcia Granados (1781–1845) broke religious and sexual taboos with her scandalous, salacious verse, while José Batres Montúfar (1809–44), influenced by Eur. *romanticism, wrote verse of satire, irony, wit, and political commentary. However, while the Nicaraguan modernist Rubén Darío drew on Fr. *symbolism as opposed to the Sp. trad., to provoke a virtual revolution involving an aesthetically driven poetry, called *modernismo, in much of Latin America and extending back to Spain, Guatemala's most important *modernistas*, Enrique Gómez Carrillo (1873–1927) and Rafael Arévalo Martínez (1884–1975), as well as most later Guatemalan writers, were better known for their prose than for their poetry.

**II. The Mainstream Tradition (1920s–2010).** The *vanguardismo* movement, Latin America's response to Eur. and U.S. avant-garde trends, saw the emergence of the first two Guatemalan poets of international stature, Miguel Ángel Asturias (1899–1974) and Luis Cardoza y Aragón (1901–92), both of whom began their careers as students living in Paris, studying pre-Columbian culture and absorbing the fashionable literary trends in the city's émigré community during the post-World War I period. The two writers shared an interest in *primitivism, *surrealism, and other avant-garde movements, as well as in Indian themes (*indigenismo*) that they related to such political themes as Central Am. unionism and democratic reforms. While Cardoza was perhaps Guatemala's greatest poet, bringing surrealism to bear on Latin Am. themes, he is better known for his memoirs and his essays on Guatemalan hist. and culture, as well as on the Mexican mural movement, esp. during his long period of exile in Mexico after the 1954 military coup in his native country. Asturias, a Nobel Prize laureate mainly known for his novels, became the most famous of the *vanguardistas*. While most of his poetry is forgotten, his work often figures in discussions of the representation of Mayan life and culture in contemp. Guatemalan lit.

The 1930s saw a growing emphasis on indigenismo in the work of *Grupo Tepeus* and other writers. The key figure was novelist Mario Monteforte Toledo (1911–2003), but the leading poets were Alfredo Balsells Rivera (1904–40) and Oscar Mirón Álvarez (1910–38), who frequently wrote on life in Guatemala City under the dictatorship of Jorge Ubico (1931–44).

The October Revolution of 1944 led to Juan José Arévalo's reform government (1945–51) and a new poetry alive to the moment. Inspired by Pablo Neruda's most militant poetry, Enrique Juárez Toledo (1910–99), Raúl Leiva (1916–74), and Otto Raúl González (1921–2007) formed *Grupo Acento* (Focus Group). Some years later, several group members joined *Saker-ti*, a literary-cultural group comprised mainly of young students and cultural workers, which sought to create a "democratic, nationalist and realist art" just as Jacobo Árbenz came to power (1951). Saker-ti included the poets Miguel Ángel Vazquez (b. 1922), Julio Fausto Aguilera (b. 1929), Melvin René Barahona (1931–65), Augusto Monterroso (1921–2003), and Carlos Illescas (1918–98), while the group's leading ideologue was the left-wing activist and polemicist Huberto Alvarado (1927–74). But the U.S.-supported coup of 1954 led to the silence or exile of many of the writers, some of whom pursued their work in Mexico and elsewhere.

With the 1954 coup, *La Generación Comprometida* (the Committed Generation) emerged in the 1960s as a new group of writers who questioned both U.S. imperialism and the political consensus represented by the October Revolution. Repudiating Asturias for accepting an ambassadorship in France, the group adopted his motto "the poet is a form of moral behavior" in their argument for poetry in the name of armed struggle. Otto René Castillo (1934–67) became the leader of the group, and his poem "Intelectuales apolíticos" (Apolitical Intellectuals) served as their poetic manifesto. Castillo's poetry, framed by simple metrical forms and emotionally direct lang., is more lyrical and metaphorical than epic and historical. In this, he typified his generation's reaction against the grand Nerudian model of political poetry, and the group's turn to a conversational tone popular in the early years of the Cuban Revolution. Castillo's book *Vámonos patria a caminar* (*Let's Go!*, 1965) contains themes of love and commitment, injustice and tragedy, revolutionary hope and death—incl. the premonition of his own end (he was executed by the military in 1967)—as part of the process leading to social transformation.

Meanwhile, poets such as Edwin Cifuentes (b. 1926), Arturo Palencia (1931–81), and Marco Antonio Flores (b. 1937) explored themes of alienation, conquest, subjugation, and rebellion. Gradually disillusioned with the Left in the late 1960s, Flores turned from poetry to the acidic, disenchanted prose fiction represented by his novel *Los compañeros* (*Comrades*, 1976). However, three poets of La Generación Comprometida—Luis Alfredo Arango (b. 1936), Francisco Morales Santos (b. 1940), and Roberto Obregón (b. 1946)—joined three

older writers—Antonio Brañas (1920–98), Fausto Aguilera (b. 1928), and José Luis Villatoro (1932–98)—and one younger woman writer, Delia Quiñónez (b. 1946), to form the group *El Nuevo Signo* (The New Sign) in 1968.

The Nuevo Signo poets explored the crisis of conscience in the face of militarized society, lending their poetry a testimonial and denunciatory function. They sought to identify alternatives to continued military rule and explored the lang. and themes of the rural Guatemalan experience. Several members of the group came from poor, rural backgrounds and tended to focus on peasant themes. But Nuevo Signo's poetry was also a response to previous indigenist discourse in Guatemala. In place of Asturias's "lyric exaltation" of Indian and pre-Columbian myth and Castillo's celebration of Mayan roots, the Nuevo Signo writers strove for a more sober treatment of Indian realities.

Obregón began to publish in his teens, when he went to study in Moscow. In 1970, working with the guerrillas, he was "disappeared" by a Salvadoran army patrol. His surviving poetry exhibits a flair for dramatic and extreme metaphors centered on blood and fire, death and rebirth. Most of the Nuevo Signo writers tried to avoid partisan poetry, however, electing instead to explore the broader forces operating in Guatemalan society, with Arango emerging as the crucial master poet of his generation and Morales as the group's leading spokesperson. Nuevo Signo poets also sought to explore complex states of subjectivity while observing the 1960s idea that the personal is political.

Headed by Manuel José Arce (1935–85) and Carlos Zipfel (b. 1937) and joined by Margarita Carrera (b. 1929), Luz Méndez de la Vega (b. 1919), and others, *Grupo Moira* represented cosmopolitan, modernizing concerns defined by their interest in existentialist, psychological, and aesthetic themes. Arce and Zipfel were major lyric poets in the intimist mode. Before his death in 1985, Arce produced a remarkable body of political poetry. Meanwhile, Carrera and Méndez cultivated Freudian and feminist perspectives that opened the way to a serious body of women's poetry.

Two literary groups—*La Galera* (The Galley) and *Grupo Literario Editorial RIN-78*—emerged in the wake of the 1976 earthquake and continued military rule. Incl. writers such as Luis Eduardo Rivera (b. 1949), Roberto Monzón (1948–92), Otoniel Martínez (b. 1953), and Aida Toledo (b. 1952) and heralded by Enrique Noriega Jr.'s (b. 1949) *¡Oh banalidad!* (1975), La Galera rejected the lit. of political denunciation and national transformation, expressing disillusionment with life in the nation and the lit. expressing it and valorizing poetry, aesthetics, and bohemianism.

Under Efraín Ríos Montt's dictatorship, several writers of varying political tendencies joined together in a kind of literary popular front to maintain a culture of writing and publishing activities in a period of retrenchment. Taking on the name of Grupo Literario Editorial RIN-78, the project included poets associated with Nuevo Signo and the new feminist poetry, as well as younger writers. The term RIN came from a

Japanese *ideogram standing for unity, toleration, and diversity. Thus, the group did not attempt to articulate any particular political ideology but rather outlined goals that were "cultural and promotional." In a short period, they produced 36 books, incl. 15 of poetry.

After the failed military coup against the reformist government of Marco Vinicio Cerezo in 1987, a new group emerged playfully calling itself *La Rial Academia* (i.e., not the Royal [Real] but the Laughable Academy) and dedicating itself to attacking RIN-78's neutrality. While several of its members wrote about poetry, René Leiva (b. 1947) was one of the few to publish volumes of verse.

### III. New Women's and Indigenous Poetry in Guatemala.

There are some antecedents for women's poetry in 20th-c. Guatemalan lit. hist. Luz Valle (1896–1971), Magdelena Spinola (1886–1975), Romelia Alarcón de Folgar (1900–70), and Alaide Foppa (1914–80) were prominent women writers who sought to rise above the quietistic "feminine as opposed to feminist" mode of the upper-class *poetisa* model prevalent in Central America. Antimilitary resistance emerging among Guatemalan women poets of the 1970s would change that identification dramatically. A well-known feminist, Foppa became a political force in life and poetry after her children *were disappeared* and until she herself *was disappeared* in 1980. The youngest member of Nuevo Signo and the only woman among its founders, Quiñónez went to the forefront of an emerging movement of Guatemalan women's poetry. Ana Maria Rodas's (b. 1937) militant *Poemas de la izquierda erótica* (Poems of the Erotic Left, 1973) rebuked the *machismo* of the male revolutionary Left. More recently, several women poets—incl. Carmen Matute (b. 1944), Isabel de los Ángeles Ruano (b. 1945), and Aida Toledo (b. 1952)—showed their ability to write a richly layered, imagistic, and subjectivist poetry, often expressing eroticism, deep psychic disturbance, and metaphysical explorations while registering a political, specifically feminist agenda.

The most significant new devel. of the 1980s was, however, the appearance of a Mayan testimonial poetry practiced by men and women alike, incl. Nobel Peace Prize-winner Rigoberta Menchú (b. 1959). The first mod. indigenous voice was the Nuevo Signo member Luis de Lión (1940–84), an only partially ladinized Indian, who was disappeared by the military. After him came one of the initial members of RIN-78, Enrique Luis Sam Colop (b. 1955).

These three writers drafted their poems in Sp., offered as "translations" from the Quiché, in an invented indigenous tonality expressing the pain and resistance of their people. Similarly, Humberto Ak'abal (b. 1952) emerged in the 1990s as the first fully celebrated indigenous poet. In his work, the indigenous question is one not of radical separatism but of the creation of conditions for mutual recognition and respect. His poems draw upon Quiché trads. to reshape ling. and poetic norms in relation to dimensions of indigenous culture, emphasizing city versus country, the struggle against communal destruction, and the capacity of modernity and globalization to deepen rather than dilute indigenous cultural devel. Ak'abal includes elements of shamanism and magic in his texts, but he also employs ladino poetic trads. and tropes, enmeshing them with indigenous images.

In these indigenous writers and the new women poets, incl. many appearing in the 21st c., we see fresh beginnings for poetry in Guatemala's future. In the midst of globalization and local power struggles, poets shift their focus from national identity to more panindigenous and universal themes, linking Guatemala to the larger world, but never losing sight of their own local issues.

*See* AVANT-GARDE POETICS; COLONIAL POETICS; INDIGENOUS AMERICAS, POETRY OF THE; SPANISH AMERICA, POETRY OF.

■ *Poesía revolucionaria guatemalteca*, ed. M. L. Rodríguez Mojón (1971); F. Albizúrez Palma and C. Barrios y Barrios, *Historia de la literatura guatemalteca*, 3 v. (1981–87); R. Armijo, "Introducción," *Poesía contemporánea de Centro América*, ed. R. Armijo and R. Paredes (1983); A. Chase, "Prólogo," *Las armas de la luz: Antología de la poesía contemporánea de la América Central*, ed. A. Chase (1985); D. Vela, *Literatura guatemalteca* (1985); *Ixok amar·go: poesía de mujeres centroamericanas por la paz. Central American Women's Poetry for Peace*, ed. Z. Anglesey (1987); *Exodus: An Anthology of Guatemalan Poets*, ed. A. Saavedra (1988); D. Liano, "Studio introduttivo," *Poeti di Guatemala: 1954–86*, ed. D. Liano, trans. A. D'Agostino (1988); J. Beverley and M. Zimmerman, *Literature and Politics in the Central American Revolutions* (1990); *Nueva poesía guatemalteca*, ed. F. Morales Santos (1990); M. Zimmerman, *Literature and Resistance in Guatemala: Textual Modes and Cultural Politics from El Señor Presidente to Rigoberta Menchú* (1995); *Voices from the Silence: Guatemalan Literature of Resistance*, ed. M. Zimmerman (1998).

■ **Web Sites**: B. Mateos, *Palabra virtual: voz y video en la poesía iberoamericana*, http://www.palabravirtual. com—sections on Guatemala; *Poesía guatemalteca*, http://www.poesiaguatemalteca.com/.

M. ZIMMERMAN

**GUJARATI POETRY.** For many years, Narsinh Mehta (15th c.) was the first known poet in the hist. of Gujarati lit., but after dozens of mss. of old Gujarati lit. were recovered from the protected Jain scriptoria at Jesalmer, the record of Gujarati poetic hist. was extended to the 11th c. CE. This new literary era was called the pre-Narsinh or Rāsā period and included many Jain and a few non-Jain texts. Among them, Jain texts such as Jinpadmasūri's *Sirithulibhadda Fāgu* (ca. 1334) and Rahshekhar's *Nemināth Fāgu* (ca. 1344) and non-Jain texts such as the anonymous *Vasant Vilās* (1452) stand out for their creative fervor. The med. Gujarati lit. that followed is divided into the Bhakti, Akhyān, and Vairagya periods. The sweet feminine melancholy of Mīrābāī, the master narratives of Premanand Bhatt (1649–1714), the exotic storytelling of Sāmal Bhatt

(1718–65), the philosophical sarcasm of Akho, and the devotional eroticism of Dayārām enriched the med. canvas. The transcendental vision of med. Gujarati poetry was conveyed with native lyricism in varied oral and singable verse forms.

Under Brit. rule, new technological advances and educational policies and, in particular, the imported model of Eng. romantic poetry (see ROMANTICISM) brought the med. Gujarati era to an end. The literary period that followed continued until shortly after the departure of Brit. rule in 1947. This era is divided into three parts: the Reformist (1850–85), Pandit (1885–1915), and Gandhi (1915–45) periods.

Dalpatrām (1820–98) and Narmad (1833–86) emerged as the most significant poets of the Reformist period; the former was a conservative, and the latter was a radical reformer. Uneducated in Eng., Dalpatrām was influenced by Vraj poetics and was a master of prosody. His poetry was distinguished by wit and satire. Narmad, the first pioneer of the mod. era, adopted the Eng. romantic model and dealt with personal topics such as love and nature. In spite of his enthusiasm and quest for beauty, his verse is often considered inexpert.

The Pandit period was characterized by a discriminatory attitude toward Eng. values. Poets of this period chose instead to assimilate the Sanskrit and Persian trads. Narsinhrao Divetiā (1859–1937) continued in the romantic model, but other poets soon complicated this conservatism. The sculpturelike structure of Kavi Kānt's (1867–1923) *Khandkavya*, the verseless outburst of Nānālal's (1877–1946) platonic idealism, the pensive juvenile world of love and separation built by Kalāpi (1874–1900), and the robust poetic lang. of run-on verses inscribed by B. K. Thākore (1869–1952) were remarkable landmarks of the Pandit period of Gujarati poetry.

As Mohandas K. Gandhi entered the Indian political scene, the new themes of truth and nonviolence pervaded all spheres of life. While combating Brit. rule, Gandhi confronted the cardinal issues of untouchability, village reforms, and the unequal distribution of wealth. He aimed at simplicity and compassion and ultimately aspired to forge a universal brotherhood. The Gujarati poetry in this period appropriated the Gandhian vision. Two major poets, Sundaram (1908–91) and Umāshankar Joshi (1911–88), made experimental and often eclectic poetry in this vein. Their poetry railed against political and social inequality, calling for a humane and compassionate approach toward the downtrodden and the exploited. Meanwhile, the Bengali poet Rabindranath Tagore's (1861–1941) aesthetic theories were at work during this period.

Umāshankar Joshi, recipient of the prestigious Jnānpith Award, lived in three successive literary periods (the premodernist, modernist, and postmodernist periods). His poem "Chhinnabhinna Chhun," one of the seven components of his influential long poem *Saptapadi*, became the harbinger of the modernist period. Suresh Joshi (1921–86), who discarded much of the idealism of the Gandhian period; Rājendra Shāh (1913–2010), another Jnānpith Award-winner; and

Niranjan Bhagat (b. 1926), a premodernist poet of urban inclination, provided the springboard for a new period of international poetry. Poetry of this era was concerned with pathos and the meaninglessness of contemp. life, private idiosyncrasy, repressed psyche, the subconscious, the inwardness of individual experience, the dislocation of logic, and the use of associative lang. Lābhshankar Thākar (b. 1935), with his *dissociation of sensibility, and Sitanshu Yashaschandra (b. 1941), with his surreal verve and apolitical tone, confidently carry on this trad.

In the latest phase of postmodernity, Gujarati poets explore new themes, such as Dalitism and feminism, in traditional forms such as *ghazals and songs. Meanwhile, Gujarati poetry continues to look toward new gravity and grandeur.

*See* BENGALI POETRY; INDIA, POETRY OF; SANSKRIT POETICS; SANSKRIT POETRY.

■ N. Bhagat, "Experiments in Modern Gujarati Poetry," *Indian Literature* 21 (1978); R. Joshi, "Recent Trends in Gujarati Literature," *Indian Literature* 27 (1984); *Modern Gujarati Poetry*, trans. S. Ramanathan and R. Kothari (1998).

C. TOPIWALA

**GUSLAR.** An oral epic poet from the area known for much of the 20th c. as Yugoslavia; the trad. flourished in various regions from at least the 15th through the early 20th c., before becoming moribund. The term derives from the accompanying *gusle*, a (usually) one-stringed, lute-shaped instrument bowed by the singer, although some epic poets performed without the gusle, according to Murko. In the Ottoman Empire, Muslim guslars were attached to Turkish courts but later plied their trade chiefly in coffeehouses, esp. during Ramadan. In the Christian areas, performances took place at social gatherings and were attended by a cross-section of the village population. The singer's craft, most often a masculine avocation, was passed from father to son or from one guslar to another; learning the singing trad. was an informal process, with certain stages of private and public performance (Lord).

It was the guslars with whom Parry and Lord worked in evolving the *oral-formulaic theory, assisted by Nikola Vujnović, their native translator, interviewer, and transcriber, who was also a guslar himself. The Parry-Lord guslars from Novi Pazar, Bijelo Polje, and elsewhere are selectively represented in the series *Serbo-Croatian Heroic Songs*; a full ed. of the guslar Halil Bajgorić's *The Wedding of Mustajbey's Son Bećirbey* is available in book form (Foley 2004) and online as a hypertext edition with audio. The classic collection of epic performances from the Christian areas is Karadžić's *Srpske narodne pjesme* (selective trans. in Holton and Mihailovich). The most important mod. guslar was the Bosnian Avdo Medjedović, an illiterate singer who composed epics as lengthy as 18,000 lines. On the role of the guslar in the comparative study of oral trads., see studies below by Lord, Koljević, and Foley.

■ V. Karadžić, *Srpske narodne pjesme* (1841–62); *Serbo-Croatian Heroic Songs* (*Srpskohrvatske junačke pjesme*), ed. and trans. M. Parry, A. Lord, and D. Bynum

(1953–); Lord; S. Koljević, *The Epic in the Making* (1980); J. M. Foley, *The Theory of Oral Composition* (1988); M. Murko, "The Singers and Their Epic Songs," trans. J. M. Foley, *Oral Tradition* 5 (1990); J. Foley, *Traditional Oral Epic* (1990), *Immanent Art* (1991), and *The Singer of Tales in Performance* (1995); *Songs of the Serbian People*, trans. M. Holton and V. Mihailovich (1997); J. M. Foley, *Homer's Traditional Art* (1999) and *How to Read an Oral Poem* (2002); *The Wedding of Mustajbey's Son Bećirbey as Performed by Halil Bajgorić*, ed. and trans. J. M. Foley (2004), http://oraltradition.org/zbm.

J. M. FOLEY

**GYPSY POETRY.** *See* ROMANI POETRY.

# H

**HAIBUN.** A literary form developed in Japan that employs a combination of prose and haiku. A haibun may be as brief as a single terse paragraph followed by a single haiku or an extended work involving an alternation of prose and verse. Accordingly, the haikus may occur singly, in groups, or in linked series, between prose passages. The best known examples are the travel jour. *Narrow Road to the Interior* by Bashō (1694) and the autobiographical *The Year of My Life* by Issa (1819). The prose and verse sections of a haibun are intended to function discretely as self-contained texts; however, in combination, they enact a kind of dialogue between them, a compounding of points of view on the same situation or topic. While the form was developed by Bashō out of the haikai trad. of linked verses employing commonplace diction and a light-hearted tone, it has been used for a range of tones and themes; however, personal themes predominate. As with haiku, haibun has been adapted into many langs. and cultures. Its practice is cultivated by haiku societies, jours., and web sites; it is also practiced by poets such as James Merrill, Robert Hass, and Rachel Blau DuPlessis. The form has undergone variations as well: in Merrill's "Prose of Departure," the haiku and prose are connected syntactically, rather than being discrete elements; also, the first and third lines of each haiku rhyme. Others vary the form by not keeping to the strict syllable count of haiku or more flexibly employing *free verse.

*See* HAIKAI, RENGA.

■ K. Issa, *The Year of My Life*, trans. N. Yuasa (1972); E. Miner, *Japanese Linked Poetry* (1979); B. Ross, "North American Versions of Haibun and Postmodern American Culture," *Postmodernity and Cross-Culturalism*, ed. Y. Hakutani (2002); M. Bashō and D. L. Barnhill, *Bashō's Journey: The Literary Prose of Matsuo Bashō* (2005).

W. WENTHE

# HAIKAI

   I. Introduction
   II. Formal Characteristics
   III. History

**I. Introduction.** *Haikai* (literally, "comic"), more properly called *haikai no renga* (comic linked verse), refers to a number of poetic forms that emerged in the early mod. period in Japan (1615–1868). The term is used in *Kokin waka shū* (Ancient and Modern *Waka* Anthology, ca. 905; see KOKINSHŪ) to refer to unconventional or humorous *waka. With the devel. of *renga* (linked verse) in the med. period (1185–1600), the term *haikai no renga* denoted a variety of humorous linked verse that was written between sessions of orthodox renga composition. As a courtly form, orthodox renga forbade the use of nonelegant words (such as Buddhist

terms and Chinese compounds); haikai no renga, however, permitted it.

In the early mod. period, haikai no renga evolved into a form independent of both waka and renga. It held a special appeal for commoners, though members of all social status groups composed it. Haikai was most popular from the middle of the 17th to the end of the 18th c.; by the end of the 19th c., literary reformers abandoned it in favor of its modernized form, haiku (see JAPAN, MODERN POETRY OF).

**II. Formal Characteristics.** The main categories of haikai are linked verse (haikai no renga, *renku*) and *hokku* ("starting verse").

**A. *Linked Verse.*** Linked verse derives most closely from its med. ancestor, orthodox renga, and shares many of its conventions, such as the necessity of including a *kigo* (seasonal word or phrase) and the basic pattern of alternating verse links (*ku*), each 5-7-5 and 7-7 moras long. These links were usually composed by two or more poets working collaboratively in a single session. While, following renga conventions, it was possible to construct sequences of 50, 100, or even 10,000 links in length (or, at the other extreme, as few as two or three), the most common linked verse form was the *kasen*, the 36-link sequence that was the favorite of the Bashō school.

As in renga, haikai verse links were composed on the spot in a group setting; also, like renga poets, haikai poets commonly composed verses that were ambiguous enough to allow for multiple interpretations, thus maximizing the possibilities for linking. However, haikai differed from renga in two important ways: haikai-linked verse used *haigon* (haikai lang.); put another way, it could refer to "vulgar" (*zoku*) topics and situations that were not allowed in courtly verse. This included not only references to the everyday lives of commoners, incl. sexuality, but words of Chinese origin and Buddhist expressions. Furthermore, unlike orthodox renga, haikai-linked verse was expected to be humorous: this ranged from subtle, intellectual allusiveness to outrageous puns and coarse ribaldry.

The following are the two verses that begin a 36-link Bashō-school sequence. The sequence is included in *Sumidawara* (Charcoal Sack, 1694):

| | |
|---|---|
| ume ga ka ni | amid the scent of plum blossoms |
| notto hi no deru | the sun rises, pop! |
| yamaji kana | mountain path |
| | Matsuo Bashō |
| | |
| tokoro dokoro ni | here and there |
| kiji no nakitatsu | pheasants cry out, flying |
| | Shida Yaba |

Bashō's verse is typical of haikai in the sense that it employs a haigon, the colloquial expression *notto* (to rise effortlessly), creating a sense of immediacy and freshness as well as gentle humor. Such a word would have been prohibited in waka and renga. Yaba's verse links to it by adding another detail to the scene: birds that one would be likely to encounter on a mountain path. The pheasants' piercing cry resonates with the sharp surprise of the sun's sudden appearance.

**B. *Hokku.*** While Bashō and his disciples are regarded as the greatest proponents of linked verse, his school is also credited with the establishment of the hokku as an independent verse form. Hokku refers to the 17-mora-long verse (i.e., 5-7-5) that starts a sequence; it is the only verse of the sequence that can be composed outside of a haikai session by a poet working alone. For this reason, it originally became important as a means for teachers to instruct their disciples and for established poets to hone their skills. By the late 17th c., haikai enthusiasts had taken to experimenting with forms besides the long linked-verse sequences, and the autonomous hokku emerged as a favorite of poets like Bashō, who aimed to bring the standards of haikai more in line with those of the courtly forms waka and renga.

Like verses used in longer sequences, hokku are expected to include seasonal words and haikai lang. Hokku are also distinguished by the use of *kireji* (literally, cutting characters) that allow this short verse form to create a two-part structure that juxtaposes contrasting images:

| hana ibara | brambles in bloom |
|---|---|
| kokyō no michi ni | as I climb the hill |
| nitaru kana | to my hometown |
| | Yosa Buson |

Here the seasonal word is "ibara," brambles. The kireji, "kana," comes at the end, setting the seasonal word apart from "kokyō no michi ni nitaru" (just like the ones on the road to my hometown) and inviting the reader to consider the connection between them.

As these examples show, the humor of haikai is often subtle, particularly in the verse of the poets that are most admired by mod. scholars and critics. Indeed, in most cases, it would be better to associate the most sophisticated haikai with the expression of a moment of insight or perception, esp. resulting from the juxtaposition of two incongruous images.

**III. History.** The earliest proponents of haikai no renga as a verse form independent of renga were Yamazaki Sōkan (1465–1553) and Arakida Moritake (1473–1549), both of whom are credited with beginning the process of extracting from haikai no renga the coarseness that often characterized it when it was composed as part of an orthodox renga session, yet retaining its appealing wittiness. Sōkan's *Inu Tsukuba shû* (Dog Renga Anthology, ca. 1540) is often called the first collection of verse in the new genre. Nearly a century later, Matsunaga Teitoku (1571–1653), an immensely learned scholar who excelled at nearly all forms of cl. Japanese verse, lent more prestige to the form with the publication

of his haikai collection *Enoko shū* (Puppy Anthology, 1633). He also established a set of rules (*shikimoku*) for haikai composition such as had long existed for waka and renga. Teitoku sought to retain the elegant aspects of renga while allowing the use of haigon—making the existence of the haigon, rather than the presence of humor, the distinguishing feature of haikai. In doing so, Teitoku expanded the appeal of the genre beyond commoners; his own reputation for literary excellence was such that his school attracted socially elite samurai, scholars, and aristocrats.

Teitoku's success in attracting practitioners to the form was followed by that of Nishiyama Sôin (1605–82). Sôin's followers, called the Danrin school, regarded the Teitoku style as somewhat staid and dour; they instead emphasized haikai's comic possibilities, exulting in its potential for word play, wit, and bawdiness. The Danrin style was in keeping with the exuberance and flash of early mod. urban culture. Indeed, one of the Danrin school's most famous adherents, the popular fiction writer Ihara Saikaku (1642–93), was said to have been so skilled at *yakazu* (rapid-fire) haikai composition that he composed 23,500 verses at a public event that lasted a single day and night. Nevertheless, the Danrin school's lack of restraint was not to everyone's tastes, and there was considerable rivalry within the haikai community. By the late 17th c., while many haikai practitioners were drawn to the Danrin school's tendency to frivolity and others held fast to the Teitoku school's more conservative tastes, some poets, like Uejima Onitsura (1661–1738) took another route, aiming to infuse their verse with the authenticity (*makoto*) of expression that was the hallmark of courtly verse.

However, most of the credit for transforming this still somewhat disreputable offshoot of cl. renga into a serious literary form goes to Matsuo Bashō (1644–94). Bashō's reputation as the "saint" of haikai is in part due to the brilliance of his verse and in part due to the extreme devotion that he was able to inspire in his many followers. Bashō, esp. famous for his hokku, linked verse, and haibun (haikai prose, incl. the famous travel journal *Oku no hosomichi* [*Narrow Road to the Interior*]), distinguished himself not just as a writer but as the originator of an image of haikai poets as free-spirited vagabonds in the mode of med. pilgrim poets like Saigyō. He claimed that a similar aesthetic quality was present in "the *waka* of Saigyō, the *renga* of Sōgi, the paintings of Sesshū, and the tea ceremony of Rikyū" (in *Oi no kobumi* [Rucksack Notebook, 1687]) and argued that haikai also shared this quality. Bashō's habit of traveling earned him students throughout Japan. The most prominent among them (called Bashō's Ten Disciples, alluding to the famous students of Confucius) became instrumental in spreading his reputation; they were Takarai Kikaku, Mukai Kyorai, Naitō Jōsō, Sugiyama Sanpū, Hattori Ransetsu, Morikawa Kyoriku, Kagami Shikō, Shida Yaba, Nozawa Bonchō, and Tachibana Hokushi.

After Bashō's death, the humorous, gamelike aspect of haikai attracted large numbers of followers, and they treated it as a parlor game and occasionally even as a form of gambling. However, a countertrend emerged in the middle of the 18th c., centered around Yosa Buson (1716–83). Buson, more famous during his lifetime as a painter than a poet, was the most outstanding member of a group of latter-day Bashō admirers who sought to reclaim for haikai the gravity and seriousness to which Bashō-school poets aspired. Collectively known as the Bashō Revival movement, these poets—among them Ōshima Ryōta (1718–87), Tan Taigi (1709–71), and Katō Kyōtai (1732–92)—wrote verse that did not stylistically resemble that of the Bashō school but rather shared the view that haikai was an appropriate medium for the expression of sensitive emotions and profound insights.

By the beginning of the 19th c., the practice of linked-verse composition had almost completely disappeared. While there were still some impressive adherents of the genre, most notably Iwama Otsuni (1756–1823) and Kobayashi Issa (1763–1827)—the latter particularly famous for his verse focusing on simplicity and poverty—haikai lost a good deal of its momentum. A related form, senryū—humorous hokku without seasonal words—began to compete with haikai for followers. Haikai retained considerable popularity, but its practice was so centered on tsukinami (monthly) group meetings in which aspiring poets followed their teachers' directions dutifully and unimaginatively that in later decades the term tsukinami itself became derogatory. Late 19th-c. reformers, like Masaoka Shiki (1867–1902) and Naitō Meisetsu (1847–1926) revitalized haikai into a modernized genre, which they renamed "haiku."

*See* HAIKU, WESTERN; JAPAN, POETRY OF; JAPANESE POETICS.

■ R. H. Blyth, *Haiku* (1949–52); K. Yasuda, *The Japanese Haiku* (1957); H. Henderson, *An Introduction to Haiku* (1958); E. Miner, *Japanese Linked Poetry* (1979); *From the Country of Eight Islands*, ed. and trans. H. Sato and B. Watson (1981); *The Monkey's Straw Raincoat*, ed. and trans. E. Miner and H. Odagiri (1981); W. Higginson, *The Haiku Handbook* (1985); H. Shirane, "Matsuo Bashō and the Poetics of Scent," *HJAS* 42 (1992); *Bashō and His Interpreters*, trans. M. Ueda (1992); W. Higginson, *The Haiku Seasons* (1996); H. Shirane, *Traces of Dreams* (1998); *The Path of Flowering Thorn*, trans. M. Ueda (1998)—on Buson; *Early Modern Japanese Literature*, ed. H. Shirane and B. James (2002); D. L. Barnhill, *Bashō's Haiku* (2004); M. Ueda, *Dew on the Grass* (2004)—on Issa; C. A. Crowley, *Haikai Poet Yosa Buson and the Bashō Revival* (2007).

C. A. CROWLEY

## HAIKU, WESTERN

I. Before 1910
II. Through the Two World Wars
III. Resurgence in the 1950s

From the time of *Japonisme* in painting (1850–1910), Japanese arts began to exert an unprecedented influence on Western art and artists. In the exchange between Japan and the West, the verse practice known as *haiku*—the term was coined by Masoka Shiki about 1900—would come to exert great influence over the entirety of the 20th c. and after. In Western langs., haiku is commonly arranged into three lines, a rendition of the Japanese syllabic pattern of five, seven, and five *moras, although, in Japanese, these often appear in a single line. An alternate designation is *hokku* (first verse), which implies a longer string of linked verses known as *renga. Haiku practice in the West typically presents verses rich in *imagery, often juxtaposed in startling combinations. Furthermore, "stepping stones" of images running through longer verses (as Allen Ginsberg called Ezra Pound's practice) bring Western haiku into resemblance to traditional Japanese renga, the collaborative linked verse form of which *haikai was a subgenre—albeit the Western adaptations are typically the product of a single poet rather than a group. The following article outlines some prominent adaptations of haiku into Fr., Am., Sp., and Lat. Am. poetry.

**I. Before 1910.** The Western adoption of haiku poetry began in 1905 when Paul-Louis Couchoud (1879–1959), who was also among the first translators of haiku, composed poems in Fr. in the fashion of haiku (pub. in 1905 in a booklet titled *Au fil de l'eau*). Other minor poets in France followed Couchoud's lead, copying and modifying his Fr.-lang. haiku poems and trans. A 1902 ms. of José Juan Tablada (1871–1945) of Mexico, *Nao de China,* reportedly included Sp.-lang. haiku, which would make him the first to adapt haiku to another lang. It is referred to as if it had been published, although it seems never to have been. Nonetheless, Tablada translated and published original haiku in the second decade of the 1900s, and, by the following decade, he had developed into an energetic promoter of the practice. Antonio Machado (1875–1939) of Spain was another early participant in haiku. His 1907 *Soledades, Galerías, Otros poemas* contains poems that were most likely haiku-inspired, although there is speculation that they derive from Sp. folk genres. The early imagists in London, encouraged by T. E. Hulme (1883–1917), adapted the extremely brief Japanese poetic forms of *tanka* and haiku to their experimental poetry (see IMAGISM).

**II. Through the Two World Wars.** From 1910 to 1919, many imagist poets produced poems with haiku-like juxtapositions. Imagist experimentation included Amy Lowell's (1874–1925) visual Japonisme in *Pictures of the Floating World* and Ezra Pound's (1885–1972) "hokku-like" "In a Station of the Metro." The depth of imagist engagement with haiku was indicated by Fletcher (1946): "I should say that the influence of haiku on the Imagists was more considerable than almost anyone has suspected." After imagist experiments, two Fr. poets, Julien Vocance (1878–1954) and Paul Éluard (1895–1952), became prominent. Both contributed haiku to the 1920 issue of *Nouvelle Revue Française* that declared 1920 "the year of haikai in France." Éluard's hybrids have elements of *Dada and nascent *surrealism. Publications in Spain and Mexico carried Tablada's haiku starting in 1919. Also in Spain, haiku found its way into the brevity of line and image formation of many of the Generation of 1927, incl. Federico García Lorca (1898–1936), and the poet at the forefront of avant-gardism in Spain, Guillermo de Torre (1900–71; see ULTRAISM). De Torre's haiku was hybrid with *visual poetry, bringing his accomplishments beyond what others had achieved. While the years of World War I and between the wars were very fertile times for the spread of haiku, from the mid-1930s and the Sp. Civil War, and to the end of World War II, the atmosphere that had fostered such international activities turned inhospitable; the activities of vanguard artists were viewed with distrust; and rather than risk the same fate as Lorca, many artists abandoned their avant-garde activities.

**III. Resurgence in the 1950s.** The 1950s saw a resurgence of avant-garde activity that generally included the writing of haiku. There was renewed interest in Japanese culture, Zen Buddhism, trans. of Japanese lit., and scholarly tracts on Japan. Among those in the *Beat movement, Jack Kerouac (1922–69), Allen Ginsberg (1926–97), and Gary Snyder (b. 1930), who resided in Kyoto for years, demonstrated great interest in Asia and Buddhism. Kerouac put haiku to jazz accompaniment in the late 1950s, but his haiku were collected and published only in 2003. Ginsberg discussed his connection to haiku as a connection between what he called "ellipsis" and condensed images. Snyder had been a student of East Asian langs.; his engagement with East Asian poetry is perhaps the greatest among all Western poets. However, it was not only North Americans who were haiku transformers in the 1950s. The concrete poets of Brazil, in particular Haroldo de Campos (1929–2003) and Pedro Xisto (1901–87), wrote haiku and engaged Asian poetics in their practice and theoretical writings (see CONCRETE POETRY). Furthermore, literary giants such as Jorge Luis Borges (1899–1986) wrote haiku in both the 1920s and the 1950s. In Mexico, Octavio Paz (1914–98) picked up the thread of avant-gardism as well as the haiku torch from his countryman Tablada. Paz's "Bashō An" contains the lines "vowels, consonants: / the house of the world" that, like the entire poem, self-consciously oscillate among ling. construct (haiku), its architectural, physical counterpart (Bashō's hut), and the phenomenological world. In so doing, they raise the Buddhist question of the relationship among conjurer-poet, poetic product, and constructing the greater world, a question that has long been at the heart of East Asian poetry. "Bashō An" simultaneously constitutes a tribute to and an enactment of haiku poetics and stands as a bridge between East and West of haiku image-pillars supporting poetics suspended across space-time.

*See* JAPANESE POETICS.

■ A. Neuville, *Haïkaï et Tankas: Epigrammes à la japonaise* (1908); *Anthologie de la littérature japonaise des origines au XXe siècle*, ed. M. Revon (1910); E. Pound, "Vorticism," *Fortnightly Review* 571 (1914); J. Vocance, "Cent Visions de Guerre," *Grande Revue* 5 (1916); and "Haï-kaïs," *Nouvelle Revue Française* 15 (1920); W. L. Schwartz, *The Imaginative Interpretation of the Far East in Modern French Literature, 1800–1925* (1927); J. G. Fletcher, "The Orient and Contemporary Poetry," *Asian Legacy in American Life*, ed. A. Christy (1945); K. Yasuda, *A Pepper Pod: Classic Japanese Poems Together with Original Haiku*, trans. A. Neuville (1946)—foreword by J. G. Fletcher; R. H. Blyth, *Haiku* (1949); *Breve Antologia Brasileira de Haikai*, ed. E. Martins (1954); E. Miner, "Pound, Haiku, and the Image," *HudR* 9 (1956–57); G. Brower, *Haiku in Western Languages* (1972); J. R. Jiménez, "La difusión del *haiku*: Díez Canedo y la revista *España*," *Cuadernos de Investigación Filológica* 12–13 (1987); J. Johnson, *Haiku Poetics in Twentieth-Century Avant-Garde Poetry* (2011).

J. JOHNSON

**HAITI, POETRY OF.** *See* CARIBBEAN, POETRY OF THE.

**HARLEM RENAISSANCE.** *Harlem Renaissance* must be taken as a synecdochal term in which Harlem, a neighborhood in New York City, stands for the variety of outposts of Af. Am. cultural production in the United States and abroad from the turn of the 20th c. into the late 1930s. The devels. that swelled the ranks of Af. Ams. in Harlem from 1915 to 1930—incl. the Great Migration; Harlem's international pan-Af. presence; middle-class social, political, and educational uplift organizations; strong newspaper outlets; and coteries of artists served well by a variety of theatrical and cultural institutions, as well as wealthy white patrons—were mirrored to lesser degrees in other locations such as Lynchburg, Virginia; Philadelphia; Washington, D.C.; and Chicago. Both Claude McKay and Langston Hughes spent substantial amounts of time in Europe. Thus, the term *New Negro*, given currency previously by John M. Henderson, Booker T. Washington, Sutton E. Griggs, and Hubert Harrison before becoming the title of renaissance-movement aesthetician Alain Locke's groundbreaking collection of art and essays, is more technically appropriate. It was a loosely cohesive movement, drawing variously on a variety of elements. Af. Am. *blues, *ballads, hollers, work songs, and game songs collected by folklorists or recorded commercially exerted their influence on writers such as Hughes, Sterling Brown, and Zora Neale Hurston. The local color and realist challenges to the plantation trad. by Frances Ellen Watkins Harper, Paul Laurence Dunbar, and Charles Chesnutt and the uplift and protest activities of Griggs, Ida B. Wells, Marcus Garvey, and W.E.B. Du Bois helped usher in elements of direct protest as well as a realistic focus on the dilemmas of rural citizens and the newly transplanted urban Af. Am. The New Poetry of writers like E. A. Robinson, Carl Sandburg, Vachel Lindsay, and Edgar Lee Masters—along with a strong strain of traditional Brit. romantic and Victorian poetry, all championed by anthologist William Stanley Braithwaite—helped create a strong variety of poetic expression. Run through the alembic of Af. Am. diversity and originality, these influences helped to give voice, much in the manner of the Ir. literary renaissance, as James Weldon Johnson pointed out, to proud nationalistic feelings among Af.

Ams. who sought appropriate group spirit and expression in their work.

Championing black artistic productions as a way of attaining full rights and participation in Am. society, the leading lights of the movement helped produce works that were varied in their consideration of "The Negro in Art: How Shall He Be Portrayed"—the title of a feature in one of the major jours. of the renaissance, *The Crisis,* ed. by Du Bois and Jessie Fauset for the NAACP (*Opportunity, The Survey Graphic, Fire!!, Negro World,* and *The Messenger* were the other major jours.). Du Bois insisted that "all art is and must be propaganda," while Locke argued for aesthetic expression and freedom, but both clearly valued art for its aesthetic and political value in varying degrees. In poetry and prose, Johnson provided important early examples for younger artists to follow. Younger writers learned to explore character devel. and more subtly to employ the artistic nature of Af. Am. folk materials as a result of the variety of Johnson's achievements. He created more nuanced minstrel songs for the stage and cowrote the Negro national *anthem, "Lift Ev'ry Voice and Sing" (1899). His psychological devels. of the "tragic mulatto" character and use of ragtime elements in *Autobiography of an Ex-Colored Man* (1912) showed how such materials could be referenced and developed. He published an influential selection and intro. to *The Book of American Negro Poetry* (1922, 1931), promoted oral sermons in *The Book of American Negro Spirituals* (1925) and *The Second Book of American Negro Spirituals* (1926), and created his own poetic versions of the sermons in his masterful *God's Trombones* (1927).

The radical experimentation in the poetry of Jean Toomer stemmed from his connection with Af. Am. folk roots in Georgia work songs, field hollers, and spirituals ("Cotton Song"), as well as his immersion in orientalism, *imagism, and symbolist techniques culled from his involvement in avant-garde literary movements and associations with Waldo Frank and Sherwood Anderson ("Sound Poem"). Though poets such as Hughes and Brown are frequently identified with the heavy use of blues, jazz, and spiritual materials in their work—often as these genres interact and overlap with each other—both also composed poetry in traditional Eur. forms, as Hughes insisted he be able to do in his seminal essay "The Negro Artist and the Racial Mountain" (1926). Brown himself made brilliant use of a black folk hero in his sequence of "Slim" poems, while mixing iambic pentameter, standard Eng., and folk elements in "Virginia Portrait" and "Strange Legacies." Hughes mixed poems with 12-bar blues structures as in "Morning After"; with blues dialogues as in "Early Evening Quarrel"; and with standard-Eng. poems as in "Negro," with its Chinese-box structure. Claude McKay, often typed as a traditionalist for his extensive use of the *sonnet form, was actually an experimental practitioner of the form, bringing new passions and hues into its domain ("If We Must Die"). Regarded through the lens of his early dialect poetry, the colonial background and training grafted onto his Am. and international experiences with socialism, and his clear appreciation for simple folk creation ("Negro

Spiritual"), McKay's work reveals a sometimes radical use of traditional forms. Countee Cullen, the darling of the middle-class Af. Am. seeking educational credentials (Phi Beta Kappa) and traditional Eng. aesthetics in poetry (idolizing John Keats), introduced stark Af. Am. experiences into Eur. forms in poems like "Incident" and "Heritage," while not ignoring the experiences of folk-cultural figures such as the "Colored Blues Singer." Women poets of the era, published in the jours. and anthols. nearly as frequently as the men yet marginalized as overly genteel in subsequent crit., combined traditional themes (nature, love, heritage) and forms (sonnet, couplet, quatrain) with an Af. Am. focus in such poems as Angelina Weld Grimké's "Tenebris" and Gwendolyn Bennett's "Fantasy," while adding starker protest (Anne Spencer's "White Things"), introducing feminist issues and open forms (Spencer's "Before the Feast at Shushan"), and using colloquial diction (Bennett's "Song") in their work as well.

Although sometimes thought to have ended with the stock market crash in 1929, the renaissance continued to produce into the 1930s—Brown's *Southern Road* (1932), Hughes's *The Dream Keeper and Other Poems* (1932), and Mae Cowdery's *We Lift Our Voices and Other Poems* (1936), along with important prose volumes. Even beyond the 1930s, however, Harlem Renaissance writers continued to resonate with audiences and succeeding generations of artists such as Richard Wright and Gwendolyn Brooks in the Black Chicago Renaissance and Amiri Baraka and Sonia Sanchez in the *Black Arts movement; they had a profound influence on the hispanophone Caribbean *Negrismo* movement and the francophone *Negritude movement as well.

*See* AFRICAN AMERICAN POETRY, AVANT-GARDE POETICS, DIALECT POETRY, JAZZ POETRY, ORAL POETRY.

■ *The Harlem Renaissance Remembered*, ed. A. Bontemps (1972); A. Rampersad, *The Life of Langston Hughes* (1986); G. T. Hull, *Color, Sex, and Poetry* (1987); S. C. Tracy, *Langston Hughes and the Blues* (1988); *Women's Poetry of the Harlem Renaissance*, ed. M. Honey (1989); G. Hutchinson, *The Harlem Renaissance in Black and White* (1995); *The Best of the Brownies' Book*, ed. D. Johnson-Feelings (1996); *The Harlem Renaissance, 1920–1940*, ed. C. D. Wintz, 7 v. (1992–96); *Rhapsodies in Black: Music and Words from the Harlem Renaissance*, comp. and prod. S. Amos (2000)—4-CD set; A.B.C. Schwarz, *Gay Voices of the Harlem Renaissance* (2003); *Encyclopedia of the Harlem Renaissance,* ed. C. D. Wintz and P. Finkelman, 2 v. (2004); *Harlem Speaks*, ed. C. D. Wintz (2007); *After Winter: The Art and Life of Sterling A. Brown*, ed. J. E. Tidwell and S. C. Tracy (2009).

S. C. TRACY

**HAUSA POETRY.** In the Hausa lang. as spoken in Nigeria, Niger, and parts of Ghana, the single term *waka* is applied to two closely related trads., song and written poetry (verse). Popular song and courtly praise singing are oral, professional, and instrumentally accompanied, typically with interaction between lead singer(s) and chorus. Poetry, on the other hand, is chanted without accompaniment, and reward for performance is not usually sought. Poems are composed in roman or in *ajami* (Ar.) script and often circulate in ms. or in printed form. Both song and poetry can be scanned according to patterns of heavy and light syllables. Song follows traditional patterns (Greenberg) or parallels instrumental accompaniment. Poetry usually has scansions corresponding to those of cl. Ar. meters. In song, the words of the lead singer are interrupted by the *refrains or repetition of the *amshi* (chorus); this may occasion variation in the length of "verses" between choruses. Commonly, poetry is in *couplets displaying syllable end rhyme or in five-line stanzas with end rhyme in the final line, supplemented by *internal rhyme in the first four lines. It has been claimed that, in some cases, tonal rhyme can accompany syllable rhyme.

Of the 16 cl. Ar. meters, nine are found in Hausa poetry (in descending order of frequency), *kaamil, mutadaarik, mutaqaarib, rajaz, basiiṭ, waafir, khafiif, ramal*, and *ṭawiil*. Claims for other meters require liberal interpretation of the cl. Ar. form. There is some controversy over whether the traditional Ar. method of analysis is appropriate to Hausa, even for meters of Ar. provenance (Galadanci, Schuh). Since at least the latter part of the 20th c., there has been cross-fertilization between song and poetry, with poets adopting meters that originated in song (Muhammad 1979).

Mod. poetry in roman script (starting in 1903) developed from the trad. of Islamic religious verse in ajami of the 19th c. Since at least the time of the Islamic *jihaad* (holy war) of Shehu Usman dan Fodio (1804), the propagation of the faith has involved the writing of Hausa poetry that circulated both in ms. form and through the performances of religious mendicants, often blind. Such poetry fell broadly into the categories of theology, praise of the Prophet, biography of the Prophet and his companions, admonition and exhortation, religious obligations, law, and astrology. While strictly religious poetry continues to be written, the 20th c. saw a great broadening in themes, which now cover such diverse subjects as Western education, hygiene, the evils of drink, filial piety, and many topical subjects such as the population census and the introduction of new currency. Poetry writing along with song has been an important part of the political process with the approach of Nigerian independence (1960); the Civil War (1967–70); the rise of political parties in northern Nigeria during the civilian political eras of the 1960s, 1980s, and 2000s; and the creation of new states in the 1980s and 1990s. To a considerable extent, Hausa poetry retains, as its most prominent characteristics, didacticism and a concern for social issues inherited from Islamic trad. Personal lyrical expression has traditionally been restricted to the category of *madahu* (praise of the Prophet), where the lang. of deep personal devotion, longing, and desire was both legitimate and appropriate. More recently, however, love poetry, which had in the past been private, entered the public arena through the publication of the anthol. *Dausayin Soyayya*.

Mod. Hausa poetry has been published regularly in the newspaper *Gaskiya Ta Fi Kwabo* (founded 1939), and prominent poets such as Akilu Aliyu, Mudi

Sipikin, Na'ibi Wali, Salihu Kwantagora, and others have reached a wider audience in broadcasts over radio stations in northern Nigeria. Poetry-writing circles have been formed and have access to radio. While the majority of poets have been men, women such as Hauwa Gwaram and Alhajiya 'Yar Shehu have written on contemp. social and religious issues, following in the footsteps of the poet and translator Nana Asma'u, daughter of Shehu Usman dan Fodio, leader of the jihaad of 1804, and scholar in her own right (Boyd and Mack).

Song has been available on recordings since the 1950s and is a mainstay of radio programming and, more recently, television. The popular music of northern Nigeria is that of singers in traditional soloist and chorus ensembles, such as Mamman Shata and Musa Dan Kwairo (succeeded by his sons), and soloists accompanying themselves on stringed instruments, such as Dan Maraya Jos and Haruna Oji. A more recent devel., thanks to the burgeoning film and video industry, is film music, often in imitation of Indian film music but with Hausa metrical forms.

■ **Anthologies**: *Wakokin Mu'azu Hadejia* (Poems of Mu'azu Hadejia, 1955); N. Sulaimanu, et al., *Wakokin Hausa* (Poems in Hausa, 1957); *Wakokin Sa'adu Zungur* (Poems of Sa'adu Zungur, 1966); *Tsofaffin Wakoki da Sababbin Wakoki* (Old and New Poems of Mudi Sipikin, 1971); *Wakokin Hikima* (Poems of Wisdom, 1975); A. Aliyu, *Fasaha Akiliya* (The Skill of Akilu, 1976); *Zababbun Wakokin Da da na Yanzu* (Selected Poems of Yesterday and Today), ed. D. Abdulkadir (1979); B. Sa'id, *Dausayin Soyayya* (The Mellowness of Mutual Love, 1982); *The Collected Works of Nana Asma'u*, ed. J. Boyd and B. B. Mack (1997).

■ **Criticism and History**: J. H. Greenberg, "Hausa Verse Prosody," *JAOS* 69 (1949); D. W. Arnott, "The Song of the Rains," *African Language Studies* 9 (1969); M.K.M. Galadanci, "The Poetic Marriage between Arabic and Hausa," *Harsunan Nijeriya* 5 (1975); M. Hiskett, *A History of Hausa Islamic Verse* (1975); D. Muhammad, "Interaction Between the Oral and the Literate Traditions of Hausa Poetry," *Harsunan Nijeriya* 9 (1979) and "Tonal Rhyme: A Preliminary Study," *African Language Studies* 17 (1980); G. L. Furniss, *Poetry, Prose and Popular Culture in Hausa* (1996); R. G. Schuh, "Metrics of Hausa and Arabic poetry," *New Dimensions in African Linguistics and Languages*, ed. P.F.A. Kotey (1999).

G. Furniss; R. G. Schuh

# HEBRAISM

I. Hebraism as a Form of Language
II. Hebraism and Hellenism
III. Hebraism as a Critical Term
IV. Christian Hebraism
V. Midrash and Kabbalah

**I. Hebraism as a Form of Language.** A *Hebraism* is a speech form in common use that has its origin in the Bible, particularly in the OT. Such Hebraisms are pervasive in all Eur. langs., particularly Ger. and Eng. In Ger., this is to be accounted for by the powerful and continuing influence of Martin Luther's Bible trans. (1522, 1534); in Eng., the trans. and paraphrasing of books of the Bible go back to the very beginnings of the lang. in OE and continue to the King James version of 1611 and beyond. The result is that Heb. speech forms, ranging from brief phrases to *proverbs, have become naturalized and are produced for the most part without users being aware of their Heb. origin. Examples are to escape "by the skin of one's teeth," "to go from strength to strength," "the ends of the earth," "out of the mouths of babes," to "wash one's hands of," "to be clothed in scarlet," "no rest for the wicked," "the way of a man with a maid."

In literary lang., Hebraisms are a constant presence for writers of all periods, but particularly concentrated use in Eng. may be noted in Francis Bacon, John Bunyan, William Blake, William Wordsworth, and D. H. Lawrence. William Tyndale claimed that "the properties of the Hebrew tongue agreeth a thousand times more with the English than with the Latin" (*The Obedience of a Christian Man*, 1528). Even Joseph Addison, a writer of more cl. taste, remarked that "it happens very luckily that the Hebrew idiom turns into the English tongue with a particular grace and beauty" (*Spectator*, no. 405).

## II. Hebraism and Hellenism.

As an abstract noun, *Hebraism* denotes the Heb. or biblical component in Western culture. Hebraism is often perceived as the opposite of Hellenism. Matthew Arnold popularized and sharpened this distinction in *Culture and Anarchy* (1869). The Hellenic legacy, he claimed, is aesthetic; the Hebraic legacy, moral: "The governing idea of Hellenism is spontaneity of consciousness; that of Hebraism, strictness of conscience." While the future of the human race is inconceivable without the passion for righteousness of the Heb. prophets, the exclusive emphasis on this aspect leads to the impoverishment of science, art, and lit. Arnold derived his ideal of Hellenism largely from the Ger. Hellenists, J. J. Winckelmann and J. W. Goethe, and his own contemporaries, Heinrich Heine and Wilhelm von Humboldt. But Arnold drew short of Winckelmann's radically antiChristian sentiments and was not entirely comfortable with Humboldt's aim of ridding Christianity of its "Semitic" element in order to bring it closer to the Hellenistic ideal of human perfection to which he felt the IE peoples were naturally attuned.

Arnold's real target was evidently the Puritanism of the Victorian middle class, whom he spoke of as "Philistines"—borrowing the term from Heine. Their type of piety, he said, called for self-conquest—the Old Adam laboring under the burden of sin had to be "delivered from the body of this death." But it is questionable whether such evangelical piety—exemplified, as Arnold notes, by the letters of the apostle Paul and the writings of St. Augustine—really characterizes the cultural and religious message of the Heb. scriptures. Powys had a truer sense of the essentials of Hebraism when he spoke of "the human wisdom, the human sensuality, the human anger, the human justice . . . of this old shameless literature of the Old Testament." In this light, Hebraism has at least as much reference to the Old Adam as to the regenerate human being of Pauline Christianity.

Arnold modified his view of Hebraism in *Literature and Dogma* (1873), where he speaks of the prophets as using literary lang.; we must understand their words as human poetry rather than dogma. In fact, we need to bring to such texts an aesthetic taste no less refined than that required for the appreciation of the great texts of the Hellenic trad.

## III. Hebraism as a Critical Term.

The use of *Hebraism* in the general senses discussed above has often led to distortion. Critics have, however, also pointed to specific literary forms and modes of discourse associated with Hebraism or derived from Heb. sources, an attention that, increasing in recent years, has yielded a more discriminating and finely gauged understanding of the nature of Hebraism and its place in Western lit.

In the 3rd c., Longinus in a famous passage of his *Peri hypsous* (*On the Sublime*) had associated the *sublime with Hebraism, pointing to the first verses of Genesis as an example of grandeur of vision and lang. With the awakening of interest in Longinus starting with Nicolas Boileau (1674), increasing attention was given to Heb. examples of sublimity. Robert Lowth in his *Lectures on the Sacred Poetry of the Hebrews* (1753) proposed biblical prophecy with its vehemence and passion as the perfect model of sublime poetry. Edmund Burke in defining the sublime (1757) cited passages from Job marked by power, darkness, and terror. Following Lowth's lead, the Ger. romantic philosopher J. G. Herder wrote a treatise (*Vom Geiste der hebräischen Poesie*, 1782) ardently praising the poetic *genius of the Hebrews; he viewed the Bible as a body of *national poetry that his own compatriots might emulate. Earlier he had written of the Song of Songs as an impassioned, oriental love poem. Hebraism, in short, provided a heady mixture of sublimity, *primitivism, and orientalism to offset the neoclassical tenets of the 18th c. Blake went even further: revising Longinus, he dismissed Homer, Ovid, Plato, and Cicero and declared "the Sublime of the Bible" to be the only true standard (Preface to *Milton*). He had in mind the "terrific" parts of his own longer poems, which consistently echo the lang. of the Heb. prophets and escape "the modern bondage" of rhyme and *blank verse (Preface to *Jerusalem*) to reproduce the effect of Heb. *parallelism. S. T. Coleridge in his *Table-Talk* likewise took it for granted that "Sublimity is Hebrew by birth." Hebraism thus helped to bring about a loosening of cl. restraints, an increasing preference for emotional intensity, and a freer prosody in the romantic period.

While this appreciation gave Heb. poetry an important role in the hist. of Eur. lit., the emphasis on sublimity suggests a somewhat limited understanding of Hebraism. Throughout his treatise, Longinus stressed "height of style," i.e., grandiloquence, finding his chief examples in Homer. The passage he chose from Genesis is from this point of view clearly untypical. "God said let there be light and there was light" is marked by extreme simplicity rather than grandiloquence. In the end, the rules and figures of rhet. listed by Longinus do not match such examples. And even when applied by Lowth and others to the more heightened examples of biblical poetry, something essential seems to be lost in the process of systematizing.

A different literary evaluation is that of Augustine, who in his *Confessions* (ca. 397) describes how disagreeably low and simple he found scripture on first encounter: "I could not bend down my neck to its humble pace." High though the meaning seemed to be, the lack of grandiloquence in the Psalms and Gospels offended his sense of *decorum. Later, as Auerbach has shown (1965), Augustine came to appreciate the power of this "humility," which challenged the cl. division of style into three types (high, middle, and low), as well as the artificial social structure that supported that division. The biblical style, combining as it did the sublime and the everyday, was thus an essentially subversive model, leading in the direction of a radical simplicity and realism both in prose and poetry. This model influenced the literary lang. of Europe in the Middle Ages and remained a latent force in the Ren. in spite of the moderating influence of other models and styles.

The Psalms in their simplicity and directness were perceived as a special example of this mode of Hebraism. Beginning with Petrarch (*Salmi penitenziali*, in Lat., 1347), many leading poets turned to them as a primary lyric model (see PSALM). In the 16th c., Clément Marot in France, and Thomas Wyatt, the Earl of Surrey (Henry Howard), and Philip Sidney in England found their poetic voices in their psalm paraphrases and trans. (see PSALMS, METRICAL). But the supreme achievement was that of the 17th-c. Eng. poets George Herbert, Francis Quarles, and George Wither. Herbert's collection *The Temple* (1633) shows the subtlest and most pervasive use of the psalter in this period. Responding to the dialogic character of the Psalms, Herbert achieved a dramatic tension lacking in other strains of lyricism in Eng.

> Look on my sorrows round!
> Mark well my furnace! O what flames,
> What heats abound!
> What griefs, what shames!
> Consider, Lord; Lord, bow thine eare,
> And heare!

("Longing")

In addition to other echoes, the last two lines of this example paraphrase the opening of Psalm 86, yet what we hear is Herbert's personal, authentic voice.

**IV. Christian Hebraism.** The 17th c. constitutes the apotheosis of Hebraism in Brit. lit. and in its political thought. In the Latin version of John 5:39, Jesus tells his disciples, "Scriptamini scripturas" (You search the scriptures), and the misinterpretation of this present indicative as an imperative led John Selden to lament, "These two words have undone the world. Because Christ spake it to his disciples, therefore we must all, men, women, and children, read and interpret the Scriptures" (*Table Talk*). But the theological

aristocrats of the Reformation searched and found, in the Heb. Bible and in postbiblical rabbinic sources, the Jewish roots of Christianity. And where the political science of the earlier Ren. humanists, influenced by Greece and Rome, was secular in character, the later political works of Hugo Grotius, Selden, John Milton, and John Locke, crowded with references to the Heb. Bible, reflect the belief that it contains a political constitution, designed by God for the children of Israel (Nelson). And although its detractors may complain that the King James Bible of 1611 turns Heb., Aramaic, and koiné Gr. into a single ling. code rapidly adopted as "Church English," the lit. inspired by the King James Bible attests to its magnificence.

That inclusive lit. includes productions by Christian Hebraists such as Bishop Lancelot Andrewes, who contributed to the King James Bible trans., although his sermons, even after 1611, continue to refer to the Geneva Bible; and John Donne, whose sermons on the *penitential psalms reveal familiarity with rabbinic sources. At the other end of the religious and political spectrum is John Bunyan, "this soldier of Cromwell's New Model Army and nonconformist preacher," whose lang. and thought are nevertheless informed by the Bible trans. most closely associated with the monarchy and the established Church of England (Hamlin).

Milton is the most learned and most biblicocentric of the great Brit. poets. He composed his earliest surviving poems, paraphrases of Psalms 114 and 136, at age 15. His headnote to his 1648 metrical trans. of Psalms 80–88 calls attention to his "translat[ion] from the original," as do his marginal notations, incl. 18 separate transliterations of Heb. words and phrases and eight literal Eng. trans. that he explicitly states come directly from the Heb. Milton strives heroically to achieve Judaic self-understanding in *Samson Agonistes*. He changes details in his source, Judg. 13–16, but he determinedly retains as much of the original as is compatible with his vision. Milton's virtual obsession with the Bible—he refers or alludes to it 9,000 times in his *De doctrina christiana* alone—suggests that Samson, the primitive ruffian who so appalls some present-day readers, might not have appalled Milton. A Hebraic rather than an ironic reading would acknowledge the humanity of the chorus despite its flawed understanding, its capacity for fellow feeling, and its considerable spiritual and intellectual devel.; and while recognizing Manoa's shortcomings, it would also understand the love expressed by laying out money for one's child instead of laying it up for oneself and by preparing to devote the rest of one's life to nursing that child (1485–89). And since devaluing the chorus and Manoa devalues their ethnicity, a corrective reading compatible with a charitable rather than triumphalist Christianity would recognize Milton's use of a positive typology (congruity rather than disparity) and his transfer of terms from the Heb. Bible to the NT in order to emphasize God's ways with his faithful.

The great natural law theorists of the 17th c., such as Grotius and Selden, attempt to discover shared moral rules in the natural, precivil state of humankind that would provide a basis for relationships among human beings anywhere in the world. This is in part what makes their work a pioneering contribution to international relations. Instead of a Pauline dualism that pits the carnal children of loins against the spiritual children of faith, Grotius and Selden look for continuities among the cultures and religions of pagans, Jews, Muslims, and Christians. Their positive influence on Milton's poetry and prose is evident in his best work that, instead of eliding the Hebraic factor in a nature-grace dichotomy, emphasizes the compatibility of pagan natural law, Hebraic Mosaic law, and Gospel. The right order of ascending value in Milton's monistic prose treatises (*Doctrine and Discipline of Divorce, Tetrachordon, Areopagitica, Tenure of Kings and Magistrates*) includes the lower in the higher without a turning away or rejection. This tripartite crescendo arrangement also informs some of Milton's most successful poetry: the devel. of the idea of *katharos* (pure) in the successive quatrains of his last sonnet, which begins with Euripides' *Alcestis*, extends to the levitical rites of purification after childbirth under "the old Law," and concludes with a vision of absolute purity in a Christian heaven; and the continuous but developing sense of the pastoral in "Lycidas," narrated by a shepherd whose consolation is measured, at least in part, by the progression in meaning of the very words *shepherd* and *pastoral*, from cl. aesthetics (64–84) through Hebraic-prophetic ethics (113–31) to the limitless reward of a Christian heaven purged of evil (165–85).

The first four books of *Paradise Lost* derive primarily from pagan authors, who are governed by natural law. The middle books draw most heavily on Hebraic revelation beyond nature's law, provided by the "Divine Interpreter," Raphael. The last books attempt systematically to debase the others by submitting both natural law and the Mosaic law to the judgment of Christian experience. *Paradise Lost* is a radically nostalgic work that insists relentlessly on the discontinuity between Christianity and earlier dispensations and thus between Christian postlapsarian life and a Hebraic paradise before the Fall. But the doctrinal use of negative typology contrasts with a synthesizing poetic imagination. Milton's most beautiful poetry can mingle the voices of Homer (the descent of Hermes) and Genesis (the visit of the three angels to Abraham) with his own (Raphael's descent to Paradise in book 5); or, with equal brilliance, Wisdom in Prov. 8:30–31 ("Then I was by him as a nurseling, and I was daily his delight, playing always before him"), the *muse Urania in book 7 of *Paradise Lost*, and Milton's Samson ("I was his nursling once and choice delight, / His destined from the womb" [633–34]).

**V. Midrash and Kabbalah.** A uniquely Heb. mode of discourse that has attracted critical attention in recent years is midrash. This term refers originally to the scriptural exegesis practiced by the Talmudic rabbis, involving homilies, parables, and the imaginative interweaving of different texts. It was further developed

in later centuries by the Hasidic masters. Midrash is something between interpretive and creative writing. Kermode (1979) applies the term to the different versions of the Passion narrative. Thus, Matthew offers us a "midrash" on Mark: we have to do with retold tales, reinvented for new audiences. Such interpretive fiction is found in many literary genres. *Samson Agonistes* is a kind of midrash on Judg. 13–16, and *Paradise Lost* is a midrash on Gen. 1–3. The midrashic mode is of great importance for such mod. writers as S. Y. Agnon (Israel) and Jorge Luis Borges (Argentina) and is manifestly the basis of the work of the Fr. writer Edmond Jabès. Frye speaks of Franz Kafka's *The Trial* as a kind of "midrash" on Job. This model of interpretive or *hermeneutic discourse is congenial to some mod. theorists who welcome the merging of the critical and creative functions. It also sits well with the contemp. emphasis on *intertextuality. Meaning is thought to inhere not in texts but in the interrelations between them—as Bloom (1973) has it, "the meaning of a poem can only be another poem."

The last type of Hebraism to be noted is Kabbalah. In its origin, Kabbalah is simply an esoteric form of midrash. Its classic text, the *Zohar* (*Book of Splendor*), is a commentary on the Pentateuch aimed at uncovering its occult meaning, which has to do with the dynamic structure of the divine world itself and with primordial beginnings, rather than with hist. It has links with Gnosticism. Kabbalah aroused a great deal of interest among the humanists of the Ren., esp. Johann Reuchlin in Germany and Giovanni Pico della Mirandola and Francesco Giorgi in Italy. Its ideas gained currency (though often in distorted form) in the 16th and 17th cs. in combination with elements of alchemy and Neoplatonism.

The first major poet to give powerful expression to kabbalistic ideas and symbols was Blake. His notion of the giant Albion is derived from the kabbalistic Adam Kadmon, who "anciently contain'd in his mighty limbs all things in Heaven and Earth," while the mythological drama involving Blake's "Zoas" and their female "Emanations" bears a striking resemblance to the sexual inner life of the kabbalistic Sefirot. Similarly kabbalistic is Blake's notion of a primordial Fall from which all evil flows in the divine and human realms. These ideas (drawn intermediately from Emanuel Swedenborg and others) had a central influence on shaping Blake's poetry as a whole. Kabbalistic notions and images also emerged in the work of Victor Hugo, esp. his later, apocalyptic poems, and in the occult system developed by W. B. Yeats. In literary theory, Kabbalah has been claimed by Bloom (1975) as a crucial example of creative "misreading" and consequently as a model for "strong" poetry. Kabbalistic "misreadings" involving the radical subversion of normal lang. have also been seen as an anticipation of mod. trends. Idel speaks of Abraham Abulafia as "deconstructing language as a communicative instrument into meaningless combinations of letters." New meanings are then discovered from the resulting verbal fragments by a kind of free association.

In his final major work, Fisch (1999) engaged passionately with the erotics of Blake and P. B. Shelley. One of his central ideas is that Blake hated the law of the Heb. Bible both in itself and as it affected Milton but was in thrall to the Bible's Heb. poetry and to Milton's biblical poetry, which he identified with the sublime. And where Fisch himself points out the harm of Blake's thought, which ecstatically fuses self-knowledge, eros, and death, he also responds passionately to the beauty of Blake's poetry.

See CLASSICAL POETICS, CLASSICISM, HEBREW POETRY, HEBREW PROSODY AND POETICS.

■ **Background Studies:** *The Legacy of Israel*, ed. E. R. Bevan and C. Singer (1928); D. Daiches, "The Influence of the Bible on English Literature," and F. Lehner, "The Influence of the Bible on European Literature," *The Jews*, ed. L. Finkelstein, 3d ed. (1960); S. W. Baron, *A Social and Religious History of the Jews*, 2d ed., v. 13 (1969), 160–201; and v. 15 (1973), 141–55; *Literary Guide to the Bible*, ed. R. Alter and F. Kermode (1987)—esp. the appendix, "General Essays."

■ **Specialized Studies:** J. C. Powys, *The Enjoyment of Literature* (1938); Leo Spitzer, "Understanding Milton," *Essays on English and American Literature*, ed. A. Hatcher (1962); Auerbach; D. Hirst, *Hidden Riches* (1964)—on occultism in Blake; H. Fisch, *Jerusalem and Albion* (1964)—on 17th-c. Heb.; F. Secret, *Les Kabbalistes chrétiens de la Renaissance* (1964); M. Roston, *Prophet and Poet* (1965)—on Lowth and the beginnings of romanticism; E. Auerbach, *Literary Language and Its Public in Late Latin Antiquity and in the Middle Ages,* trans. R. Manheim (1965)—ch. 1; D. J. DeLaura, *Hebrew and Hellene in Victorian England* (1969); A. A. Ansari, "Blake and the Kabbalah," *William Blake*, ed. A. H. Rosenfeld (1969); H. Bloom, *The Anxiety of Influence* (1973), and *Kabbalah and Criticism* (1975); F. S. Heuman, *The Uses of Hebraisms in Recent Bible Translations* (1977); F. Kermode, *The Genesis of Secrecy* (1979); J. L. Kugel, *The Idea of Biblical Poetry* (1981), and "On the Bible and Literary Criticism," *Prooftexts* 1 (1981); N. Frye, *The Great Code* (1982); S. A. Handelman, *The Slayers of Moses* (1982); G. H. Hartman, "On the Jewish Imagination," *Prooftexts* 5 (1985); C. Bloch, *Spelling the Word* (1985)–on Herbert and the Psalms; *Midrash and Literature*, ed. G. H. Hartman and S. Budick (1986)—valuable bibl.; H. Fisch, *Poetry with a Purpose* (1988); *Critics of the Bible 1724–1873*, ed. J. Drury (1989); M. Idel, *Language, Torah, and Hermeneutics in Abraham Abulafia* (1989); E. Aizenberg, "Hebraism and Poetic Influence," *Borges and His Successors*, ed. E. Aizenberg (1990); D. Boyarin, *Intertextuality and the Reading of Midrash* (1990); J. P. Rosenblatt, *Torah and Law in "Paradise Lost"* (1994); H. Fisch, *The Biblical Presence in Shakespeare, Milton, and Blake* (1999); J. Kugel, *The Bible as It Was* (1999), J. Rosenblatt, *England's Chief Rabbi: John Selden* (2006); G. Toomer, *John Selden: A Life in Scholarship,* 2 v. (2009); C. Goodblatt, *The Christian Hebraism of John Donne* (2010); E. Nelson, *The Hebrew Republic: Jewish Sources and the Transformation of European Political Thought* (2010); H. Hamlin, "*The Pilgrim's Progress* and the King James Bible," *The King James Bible after Four Hundred Years*, ed. H. Hamlin and N. W. Jones (2011).

H. FISCH; J. ROSENBLATT

## HEBREW POETRY

I. Introduction
II. Biblical and Medieval
III. Modern

**I. Introduction.** Heb. lit. spans three millennia and ranks among the world's oldest. Heb. poetry began to appear at least by the 11th c. BCE and flourishes in contemp. Israel. Whatever gaps disrupted this virtually continuous literary flow should be attributed more to the loss of linking texts than to a diminution of creativity. Heb. poets may not always have been aware of their entire literary heritage, but most often they did have both a diachronic and synchronic knowledge of much of it.

In every age, the Heb. Bible has constituted the foundation and principal component of that heritage, a major source for literary forms, *symbols, rhetorical *tropes, syntactic structures, and vocabulary. There has been, however, no uniformity in metrical systems: these have varied from age to age and, following the biblical period, were usually adapted from those employed in the area where the Heb. poet happened to reside. In the Persian period (5th–4th cs. BCE), Aramaic began to replace Heb. as the vernacular in Palestine, continuing as the spoken lang. long into the Byzantine period (4th–7th cs. CE), while Gr. prevailed in the Mediterranean diaspora. With the rise of Islam in the 7th c., Ar. became the lingua franca for Jews of the Middle East, North Africa, and Spain. In Christian Europe, the various IE langs. were adopted. From the Middle Ages until the early 20th c., Yiddish was the vernacular used by the majority of Eur. Jewry as the centers of Jewish population shifted to Central and Eastern Europe. The interplay of these non-Hebraic langs. and lits. with Heb., the literary lang. of the Jews, broadened and altered Heb. poetry, affecting its syntax, vocabulary, themes, and genres.

The scope and variety of these phenomena make it as difficult to formulate a single comprehensive definition of Heb. poetry as it is to formulate one for world poetry. Still, the definition of poetry proposed by Barbara Herrnstein Smith is sufficient to accommodate the entire gamut of Heb. poetry: "As soon as we perceive that a verbal sequence has a sustained rhythm, that it is formally structured according to a continuously operating principle of organization . . . we are in the presence of poetry and we respond to it accordingly, expecting certain effects from it and not others" (*Poetic Closure*, 1968).

## II. Biblical and Medieval

**A. Biblical Poetry (1100 BCE–150 BCE).** The Heb. Bible (or OT) is an assemblage of sacred texts composed over a span of about a thousand years. The earliest mss.—

primarily the Dead Sea Scrolls—date only from the 2d–1st c. BCE, but ling. and historical considerations provide a basis for ascribing the composition of most of the included texts to earlier centuries. The relative date and general period of most texts can be determined with some assurance, but the date of many poems and even of books remains controversial. Close to a third of the Heb. Bible is poetry. Many scholars believe the most salient feature of biblical poetry, like the Semitic, and esp. Ugaritic (13th-c. North Canaanite), poetry that preceded it, is *parallelismus membrorum* (Lowth) or *parallelism. There also appears to be a quasi-metrical feature in this poetry, in that the lines forming most *couplets and the occasional triplet are of similar length (Herder). Efforts to define the prosodic component more precisely are, however, unconvincing, usually involving manipulations of the received text to suit a particular theory. And no early Heb. poem maintains a consistent line length throughout.

No poetics of Heb. poetry was transmitted in ancient times. The earliest attempts to describe biblical *prosody were performed by some of the church fathers, who tended to compare contemp. Gr. and Lat. forms, and more extensive treatments by Jewish scholars began only in the Middle Ages (Cooper, Kugel 1979, Berlin 1991, Harris). Recent decades have seen several substantial efforts to describe biblical poetry (e.g., O'Connor, Alter, Berlin 1985, Watson, Pardee, Alonso Schökel).

Defining the basic components of biblical Heb. poetry depends on how one views the matter of *meter. Phonological meter in the strict sense, although proposed in one way or another since Sievers (1901; see, e.g., Stuart), cannot be established. Counting major words or word accents as one beat each, or counting syllables with or without attention to phonemic *accent, does not yield convincing results (Pardee, Vance). O'Connor has suggested instead a meter founded on syntactic constraints—only so many words, so many constituents, so many clauses within a line. The wide flexibility of the poetic line in the Bible leads Hrushovski to conceive of free rhythms ("rhythm[s] based on a cluster of changing principles") for biblical verse (cf. Dobbs-Allsopp 2009). Nevertheless, taken by itself, no prosodic or purely syntactic meter can be used to characterize a single line of biblical text as poetic. For that reason, most students of biblical poetry define the basic unit of verse as a two-part line (comprised of cola, *hemistichs, or *versets) or simply a couplet (of two lines). The poetic line is usually composed of two cola—sometimes three or four—that are parallel to each other.

While most descriptions of biblical parallelism up through the mid-20th c. focus on a reiteration of semantic sense and/or sentence structure, more recent accounts, influenced by Roman Jakobson's seminal work, highlight repetitions of ling. features in all areas of lang. Hrushovski summarizes the possibilities: "It may be a parallelism of semantic, syntactic, prosodic, morphological, or sound elements, or of a combination of such elements." Observing that there is more often repetition of sound within the line than between lines, Greenstein (1986–87) downplays the phonological element. He also separates out semantic content, which is context-dependent and unquantifiable, from the other, properly formal components and points to three primary features of biblical parallelism: first and foremost, relative balance of line length; second, a repetition of syntactic structure, on either the surface or underlying (deep) level, from line to line; and third, a distribution of conventionally associated words or phrases between the lines of the couplet. These can be a paradigmatically related set of words paired in the poetic trad. For example, *rosh-qodqod* (head, pate); *yayin-dam ʿanavim* (wine, blood of grapes); *shamaʿ -bin* (hear, discern) or a syntagmatically related set of words, known in biblical studies (Melamed) as the breakup of a stereotyped phrase (e.g., "Balaam son of Beor" split into "Balaam"—"son of Beor"). All parallel lines have at least one, and ordinarily more than one, of these three features.

Some of the repetitive patterns that constitute parallelism occur in biblical prose, esp. in legal formulations. However, this does not mean that the boundary between prose and poetry in the Bible is indistinct. For one thing, although an umistakably poetic couplet may be embedded within a distinctly prose context (e.g., Gen. 7:11b), in a full poem, the parallelisms occur in an uninterrupted series of couplets, triplets, and an occasional single line. For another, in addition to the properties of parallelism, biblical poetry is typically characterized by a number of optional tropes, incl. but not limited to syntactic deletion in the second line with lengthening of a nondeleted constituent as "compensation" to maintain the balance of line length (Geller); variations in word order (e.g., *chiasmus); *alliteration, *assonance, and *rhyme; *figuration; distinctively poetic *diction (e.g., *tehom* [sea, subterranean ocean]; *maḥats* [smite]); *ambiguity or double entendre; *paronomasia; terseness or *concision of expression—and more specifically, parataxis (see HYPOTAXIS AND PARATAXIS) and nonuse of the relative pronoun (*asher*), the direct-object marker (*ʾet*), and the definite article (*ha-*)—and other archaic ling. features (Robertson).

Moreover, in early biblical poetry, and in many later poems as well, there is a different, more archaic verbal system. In the earlier system, the present and future, or foreground, are expressed by the prefixed form *yiqtol* (old West Semitic *yaqtulu*), while the past, or background, is expressed by the suffixed form *qatal* (old West Semitic *qatala*). This system contrasts with that of biblical prose, in which the past is conveyed by *way-yiqtol* in clause-initial position and *qatal* in noninitial position, and the future by *we-qatal* clause-initially or *yiqtol* noninitially (Niccacci). Last but not least, biblical poetry is composed largely of verbal clauses with little embedding, while biblical prose tends to have nominal chains and embedded clauses. As Polak has shown, there is a direct correlation between the syntactic simplicity of poetic lines in the Bible and the oral character of Heb. verse. Be that as it may, if we bear all these criteria in mind, it is difficult not to recognize a biblical Heb. poem, or even a couplet, when we see one.

Consider this short song, which is quoted with an introduction in a prose narrative context (Num. 21:17–18):

*'alí be'ér / 'enú-láh*
*be'ér haparúha sarím*
*karúha nedibé ha'ám*
*bimhoqéq / bemish'anotám*

(Arise, O well! / Sing to it!
The well the princes have dug,
[The well] the people's leaders have excavated,
With their staffs, / with their walking-sticks.)

The poem is constructed of four couplets in parallelism. The first and last are either brief couplets or lines featuring internal parallelism. The middle two lines, longer than the first two but balanced between themselves, are a couplet, two roughly synonymous relative clauses with "well" as their head, each formed of the same syntactic pattern, except that the head ("well") is deleted in the second line. Note that the subject noun-phrase in the second line is longer than that in the first line, compensating for the quasi-metrical weight that is lost as a result of the deletion. The last line (or couplet) comprises two fairly synonymous adverbial complements, which are structurally as well as lexically (the anaphoric preposition *bi*) repetitive. There is sound repetition in the first couplet between the first and last syllables. There is word repetition (*be'ér*) from the first couplet to the second. In the second couplet, the first line displays assonance between the first two words (*b-r* followed by *p-r*), while the verb in the second line echoes and rhymes with the verb in the first line. Archaic features include the omission of the definite article (*ha-*) in all but the third line (*ha'am*) and of the relative pronoun in both lines of the middle couplet. Each couplet is syntactically dependent on the preceding one, but from a purely semantic perspective, the second line of each couplet adds little to the sense. The entire song boils down to a single sentence—*Arise, O well that the princes have dug with their walking sticks!* It is typical of biblical poetry, however, to advance the message in steps, adding a point or a nuance here, burnishing or refining an image there. In this poem, parataxis governs the whole; there are no connectives. In later biblical poetry, parataxis decreases and variety and flexibility increase, but the essential features remain the same.

In ancient Semitic poetry preceding the Heb. Bible, such as the strongly cognate verse from Ugarit (see above), poetry serves as a narrative mode, as in an *epic as well as a *lyric mode, as in *hymns and prayers. Biblical poetry is characteristically nonnarrative. In biblical poetry, events are not recounted but dramatized (Lichtenstein). Moreover, poetry of any length in the Bible is always discourse—it is spoken by a named or implied speaker (Greenstein 2000). When the speaker expresses thoughts and feelings, it may be lyric (Dobbs-Allsopp 2006, Linafelt). When the speaker gives instructions or advice, it may be *gnomic. The poetic discourse may take the form of hymns or *songs embedded in narratives (e.g., the Song at the Sea in Exod. 15, the Song of Deborah in Judg. 5, the prayer of Jonah in Jon. 2) or collected in the book of *Psalms; or of prophetic oracles, mostly assembled in the books of the prophets; or of *epigrams, as in the book of Proverbs. The *elegies of the book of Lamentations and the rhapsodies of the Song of Songs are in poetry. The contrasting functions of prose for narrative and poetry for discourse are well exemplified by the book of Job, whose narrative framework is prose and whose lengthy speeches are in poetry. There is a tendency toward parallelism, the hallmark of biblical poetry, in discourse within prose narrative as well.

*Imagery and *metaphor, though not invariably present in biblical poetry, are prominent in many genres and poems. Some metaphors, such as the wicked as a predator and the needy as vulnerable sheep, are the biblical poet's stock in trade. Most often, a particular figuration will not be employed for more than one instance at a time. Even in Psalm 23, the image of God as shepherd gives way to that of host, spreading out a table for the speaker in view of his adversaries. In the poetry of some of the prophets, Job, and other texts, however, an image or metaphor may pervade a large stretch of verse (e.g., Isa. 5:1–4) or even several chapters (for Jeremiah, see Jindo).

**B. *Extracanonical Works*** (i.e., works not included in the Heb. biblical canon). The book of Sirach (the sole apocryphal work, a substantial part of which is preserved in the Heb. original) and the Dead Sea Scrolls discovered in 1947–48 indicate that poetic activity did not cease after the canonization of the Heb. Bible in the 2d c. BCE Most scholars ascribe the apocryphal works to the 2d or 1st c. BCE, and their poetry is akin to that found in the wisdom lit. The author of Sirach at times displays a remarkable fluency and originality, as when he describes the High Priest's entry into the Holy of Holies on Yom Kippur:

> How glorious (he was) when he emerged from the Sanctuary
> And stepped out from inside the curtain;
> Like a star shining through thick clouds,
> Like a full moon on feast days,
> Like the sun combing the King's palace,
> Like a rainbow seen in the cloud,
> Like a lily by a flowing stream,
> Like a flower of Lebanon on a summer's day
> Like the fire of frankincense upon the offering.
>
> (50:5–9)

**C. *The Mishnaic and Talmudic Period (ca. 100 BCE–500 CE).*** The lit. that has survived from the Mishnaic-Talmudic era is primarily legal or homiletic, but it contains several *occasional poems celebrating important events in life: births, circumcisions, marriages, and epitaphs. These were preserved not for their aesthetic quality but because they honored important scholars. Stylistically, they mark a break with the biblical trad. Instead of parallelism, many use a four-colon line. The poems are not laced with biblical quotations, their vocabulary is a mixture of biblical and postbiblical words, and their syntax is late Heb.

**D. *The Byzantine Period (500–800).*** *Piyyut* (derived from Gr. *poiētēs*) or synagogue hymnography is distinctive in both its volume and its focus from biblical psalmody and poetry. This type of poetry was produced since the late Roman period in Jewish communities and congregations where poetry was allowed to embellish Jewish liturgy. Such compositions were preferably written for the Sabbath and festivals when statutory prayers were supposed to have a link with the theme of the day. The majority of Jewish liturgical poems (*piyyutim*) for the Sabbath relates to biblical topics or addresses ways of *exegesis with regard to biblical themes, whereas festival compositions extensively deal with the aspects of the holiday involved. Since the early 20th c., tens of thousands of piyyutim have been re-collected from the Genizah mss., deciphered, reconstructed, and edited in critical eds., with important results in particular for our knowledge of Byzantine-Jewish and Babylonian-Jewish liturgy and hymnology. By virtue of these textual studies, names and works of long-forgotten synagogue poets (*paytanim*) in different temporal and regional settings have been added to the corpus, leading to great progress in the knowledge about distinct piyyutic genres and forms. We would not have known otherwise about the significance and growth of the early *qinot* (threnodies), *selihot* (penitential hymns), *'avodot* (compositions for the Day of Atonement), *qedushta'ot* or *yozrot* (multipart hymns for the Sabbath and festival morning services); nor would we have been acquainted with the names of great hymnists who were crucial for the trad. of Piyyut.

Piyyut as a phenomenon in Jewish culture and lit. deserves further investigation concerning its interactivity with surrounding cultures and religions. Themes and motifs are not exclusively versified recounts of rabbinic-midrashic materials but also draw on other noncanonical and nonrabbinic sources or can be considered as intrinsically paytanic. Piyyut lang. is a fascinating combination of biblical, rabbinic, and "jargonic-piyyutic" grammar and vocabulary, at times mixed with elements from Aramaic and Gr.

Yose ben Yose (4th c.) is the first *paytan* whose name is known. He heads a line of major composers who wrote in Palestine between the 6th c. until after the Muslim conquest of Jerusalem in 636 CE, the most famous among them being Yannai (6th c.), Simeon bar Megas (6th c.), Yehudah (6th c.), Eleazar birabbi Qillir (7th c.), Yohanan ha-Kohen (7th c.), and Joseph ben Nisan (7th c.). During the 5th and 6th cs., the various piyyut forms became standardized and were usually inserted into key sections of the synagogue liturgy. These hymnists introduced consistent strophic and rhyme schemes; they also favored other intricate poetic structures and employed a rich variety of prosodic

devices and lexical patterns. There can be little question that the cantor-poets were widely regarded as the mouthpiece of their communities. The med. *Chronicle of Ahima'ats* (1017–60) proves to be particularly informative in this regard, since it preserves an account of the Palestinian *hazzan* Ahima'ats who, during his visit to southern Italy, was invited to recite in synagogue the poems of other hymnists, incl. the poem of a locally rejected paytan called Silano. By adapting some of Silano's verses accusing the Karaites of heresy and favoring the Rabbanites, Ahima'ats succeeded in regaining the confidence of the Jerusalem rabbis, and he eventually rehabilitated Silano's piyyutim in his hometown. The story affords us some idea of the socioreligious context in which the cantor-poets functioned.

**E. *Muslim Spain (900–1100).*** The ling. studies of Heb. in the Islamic East in the hands of Saadia Gaon (882–942), Dunash Ibn Labrat (920–90), and others—some of them migrated from Iraq to Spain—stimulated the Jews of Muslim Spain to engage in a renaissance of Heb. lang. and lit. Andalusian-Jewish poets combined the role of poet and philologist and earned a living by their work by the patronage of Jewish aristocratic courtiers, who employed them for the sake of their status and position. The most famous example is Hasday Ibn Shaprut (ca. 915–975), the Jewish counselor of Caliph Abdarahman III of Córdoba, who maintained a coterie of Jewish poets at his court. These composers were aware of contemp. tastes as well as of the Jewish poetic trad., inducing them to emphasize a greater purity of Heb. in the biblical sense. Grammatical correctness was appreciated and a biblicist style was applied. However, they were also eager to invent new ways of composing in Heb. in close familiarity with the themes and techniques of Ar. poetry and poetics. Ar. influence is particularly felt in the description of themes such as love, wine, and nature in secular verse and in the use of metrical schemes that became standardized in both secular and liturgical poetry. But it was not only the new metrical forms that were borrowed from the Arabs: Heb. poets adopted the rules of composition fixed by the Arab rhetoricians, their rhyme patterns, and various other themes. They also favored the local Sp. version of the popular "girdle" poems or *muwashshahat*. The last couplets of these compositions were often written in either Ar. or Sp., mostly derived from popular lyrics. These parting lines (see KHARJA) are very instructive for the comprehension of some of the surviving Ar. or Romance vernacular. Only when they wrote piyyutim or synagogue hymns did they sometimes adhere to traditional models. More often than not, they employed the Arab structures and techniques even in the religious domain. In terms of their Heb. diction, they eschewed the cavalier way by which the paytanim constructed words and phrases, considering these to be barbarisms. If the Arab rhetoricians had insisted that the lang. of the Qur'an was the epitome of good writing, their Heb. counterparts adhered to the biblical models, though on rare occasions they allowed themselves to draw their vocabulary from Talmudic sources. Because Heb. and Ar. are both Semitic langs., they infused Heb. words at times with Ar. connotations.

One of the most common genres was the Ar. *ode or *qaṣīda, which soon became the vehicle for *occasional verse written to celebrate an important event or to praise a patron (see EPIDEICTIC POETRY). The Heb. imitations of such poems would begin in a purely lyrical vein, describing the beauties of nature, a drinking party, or a meeting of friends or would develop a philosophical meditation; the poet would then shift into a laudatory mode praising a patron or colleague. A prolific poet was Samuel the Prince, Samuel Ibn Nagrela ha-Nagid (993–1056), who attained the powerful position of chief vizier of Granada and head of the Muslim army of the Berber king Habbus. Because of his military career, he wrote a great deal of secular poetry on the battlefield, a phenomenon never repeated by any other med. Heb. poet. He was followed by Solomon Ibn Gabirol (ca. 1021–55) from Malaga, a philosopher and poetic genius. His secular poetry includes amatory poems of much beauty, while his religious works give expression to his Neoplatonic ideas. In his lyric-cosmological composition *Keter Malkhut* (Kingly Crown, ca. 1041), he contrasts the glory of God the Creator with the tragic shortcomings of the human. Moses Ibn Ezra (1055–1135) was noted for his deep familiarity with Ar. poetry. Ibn Ezra is the leading theoretician of the Andalusian-Heb. school of poetry. His *Sefer ha-ʿIyyunim we-ha-Diyyunim* (Book of Discussion and Commemoration, ca. 1135) is a valuable source for the study of aesthetic principles of Heb. secular poetry based on Ar. poetics. The standards of purity listed by Ibn Ezra were, in fact, valid for both liturgical and secular verse. A protégé of Ibn Ezra and the most renowned of all Andalusian-Heb. poets was Jehudah Halevi (ca. 1074–1141), born in the Christian north of Spain and also acclaimed as the author of a widely read philosophical treatise entitled the *Kuzari* (ca. 1140). His poem "Tsiyyon ha-lo tish'ali" (Zion, will you not ask; 1120–40), a song of love and longing for the land of Israel, was widely known and inspired many imitators. At the end of his life, Halevi indeed traveled to the crusader's kingdom of Palestine, reached Jerusalem, and died under unknown circumstances. The Andalusian school of Heb. poetry, of which Halevi undoubtedly is the most illustrious example, had a continuing influence on the trends emerging in Heb. secular poetry of Christian Spain.

**F. Italian.** The It. Jewish community was established in Roman times. Although it was small in numbers, it was highly cultured and, until the 19th c., made important contributions to the corpus of Heb. poetry. The first It. poet known to us is Silano of Venosa (9th c.), who wrote piyyutim in the style of the Palestinian school that had dominated It. Heb. poetry until the 12th c. Among Italy's leading paytanim were Shephatiah ben Amittai (d. 886) and Amittai ben Shephatiah (9th c.) of the Ahima'ats family and Meshullam ben Qalonymos (10th c.).

Between the 12th and 15th cs. the influence of Sp.-Heb. poetry—its syllabic meters, subject matter, and structures—prevailed, but vernacular It. forms were gradually introduced, esp. the *sonnet in the 14th c. and *terza rima in the 15th. The leading poets of this period were Benjamin ben Abraham degli Mansi (13th c.) and the renowned Immanuel of Rome (see below).

The final period begins at the close of the 15th c. and ends at the opening of the 20th. At first, we feel the impact of the Sp. Jewish exiles who reached Italy after 1492. Religious poetry is now dominated by the Kabbalah or Jewish theosophy. Secular poetry, on the other hand, reflected the increasing contact with It. culture. More It. poetic forms are introduced: the *ottava*, the *canzone, the *canzonetta*, the *madrigal, and *blank verse (*versi sciolti*). Heb. poetic drama appears in the 17th c., to be followed by many such works in the 18th and 19th cs. Ar. quantitative meter is soon modified by the elimination of the distinction between short and long syllables so that the lines began to resemble the It. *endecasillabo* (see HENDECASYLLABLE; Pagis 1976). The 17th-c. poet Nathan Jedidiah of Orvieto even made an attempt to write poems in accentual meter (see ACCENTUAL VERSE), but the hendecasyllabic line prevailed.

Four poets stand out: Immanuel of Rome (1261–1332), Jacob and Immanuel Francis (16th c.), and Moses Hayyim Luzzatto (1707–46). Immanuel of Rome was undoubtedly the greatest of the Italians. His *Mahberot Immanuel* (Immanuel's Compositions) is a collection of *maqamot* containing 28 sections, the last of which, *ha-tophet we-ha-Eden* (Hell and Paradise), was inspired by Dante's *Divina commedia*. Immanuel first introduced the sonnet into Heb. poetry. His supple verse reflects the culture of the Ren.; his bawdy verses are a rarity in Heb. letters. Immanuel composed a rhetorical work in which he described the new forms in It. verse and insisted that the *acutezza* (*agudeza or *wit) of the poem's *diction and subject matter must be primary. By this term, he meant the use of surprise, either formally (*oxymoron) or conceptually (*paradox), by strange and complex metaphors or uncommon *conceits. In this, he was faithful to the *baroque school then current in Italy and Spain. Jacob and Immanuel Frances of Mantua wrote polemic satires against the supporters of Shabtai Zevi (17th c.), the mystical Messiah.

Luzzatto composed poems and allegorical *closet dramas similar to the It. works of his day. His first play, *Migdal ʿOz* (Tower of Strength, 1737), was modeled after Giovanni Battista Guarini's *Il pastor fido*. Luzzatto combined an awareness of 18th-c. science with a deep Kabbalistic faith. His achievement lies on the border between a late Ren. and a mod. worldview.

The Heb. poetry produced by premod. Ashkenazi Jewry was almost entirely religious, influenced by the Palestinian and It. schools. It consisted of liturgical hymns and dirges commemorating the massacres during the Crusades. A particular genre of martyrological poetry was the ʿaqedah, which celebrated the sacrifice of Isaac as a symbol of the martyrdom of Jews.

Ephraim of Bonn (12th c.) has a fine example of this genre (discussed by Shalom Spiegel, *The Last Trial*), and *U-netaneh toqef* (10th c.), a prayer attributed to the martyr Amnon of Mayence, which still holds a prominent place in the Yom Kippur liturgy.

By the 16th c., the center of Ashkenazi Jewry had moved from Germany to Eastern Europe. The Jews in the Polish-Lithuanian kingdom expressed their piety by the meticulous observation of the *halakhah* (Jewish Law) and by the study of religious texts. They inhabited a cultural milieu that infrequently resorted to the arts—not even to the composition of religious hymns.

## III. Modern

**A. *The European Period (1782–1918)*.** At the end of the 18th c., a new kind of Heb. poetry emerged in Central Europe. This poetry was part of the Jewish Enlightenment, or *Haskalah*, a term derived from the Heb. word for intellect. From the Middle Ages until the 1780s, Heb. had been used primarily for religious texts, with the exception of works by the aforementioned It.-Jewish poets. The Jewish Enlightenment, in contrast, promoted the use of Heb. for educational, scientific, philosophical, and aesthetic works. The poems of the Haskalah, thus, came to be viewed as an alternative to the religious Heb. canon.

The Haskalah movement began in Germany with influential figures such as the philosopher Moses Mendelssohn (1729–86) and the Ger. Jewish Hebraist, educator, and poet Naphtali Hirz Wessely (1725–1805). Wessely published the *manifesto of the movement, *Divre Shalom ve-Emet* (Words of Peace and Truth, 1782). Other important figures of the early movement were Isaac Eichel (1756–1804), a student of Immanuel Kant, and Baruch Lindau (1759–1849). Together they founded the first club of Enlightenment poets and thinkers, known as the *Maskilim* (Enlighteners or Proponents of Enlightenment); the club published the first Heb. periodical, *Ha'me'asef* (The Gatherer), a collection of mostly didactic Heb. poetry by contemp. writers.

The Haskalah soon spread to Jewish communities in Vienna and Prague and expanded eastward from there to the region of Galicia in Eastern Europe. By the middle of the 1820s, the movement had reached Russia. In all these places, the Maskilim advocated a rationalist intellectual Heb. discourse espousing universal and humanistic values, a strong commitment to Jewish society, and a wish to reform its traditional structures. They promoted openness to the ideas of the local Western culture; however, when it came to poetic form, they strictly followed the syllabic meters of the It. Heb. poets of the previous century. The Maskilim poets developed a new style of writing, a *collage of biblical Heb. phrases called *melitsah*. This style was described by the poet and thinker Shlomo Levisohn (1789–1821) in his 1816 book *Melitsat Yeshurun* (The Eloquence of Yeshurun).

While literary historians generally agree about the role of the Haskalah in the devel. of the new poetry, some date the emergence of mod. Heb. poetry only to the middle of the 19th c., while others place it as late as the end of the century. However, there is no doubt that the 1850s and 1860s saw rapid growth in the community of readers and in the publication of Jewish poems, poetry books, and periodicals such as *Ha'magid* (The Preacher), *Ha'carmel* (The Carmel), and *Ha'melitz* (The Advisor). A new Heb. lit. crit. also arose. In terms of style, the didactic epos of the Haskalah was replaced in prose with the new Heb. novel and in poetry with the modern *long poem.

In the mid-19th c., Heb. poetry grew to include a wider scope of themes and genres. Talented new poets soon established themselves as major Heb. writers, among them Micha Joseph Levenson (also known as Michal, 1828–52) and the most renowned poet of the Haskalah, Judah Leib Gordon (1830–92). Gordon's long poems were mostly on biblical themes. Some of his writings, however, included strong social and political messages, referring, e.g., to the condition of women in religious Judaism in *Kutzo Shel Yod* (The Point on Top of the Yod, 1878); criticizing religious dogmatism; or calling on the Jewish people to emancipate themselves (while also questioning their ability to do so), as in his poem "Hakitza Ami" (Awake My People, 1863).

Another strand of mod. Heb. poetry emerged with the pre-Zionist national movement, *Hibbat Zion*, in Eastern Europe, which brought about a wave of sentimental Heb. poems addressing or describing the national homeland. Poets writing about and to Zion included Mordecai Zevi Manne (1859–86), Naphtali Herz Imber (1856–1909), and Menahem Mendel Dolitzki (1856–1931).

In Italy, meanwhile, a few poets continued to write in Heb. Rachel Luzzatto Morpurgo (1790–1860), for instance, wrote mostly sonnets on religious, mystical, and secular themes. The work of the It. poet, philosopher, and biblical commentator Samuel David Luzzatto (also known as Shadal, 1800–65) reached Jewish communities beyond Italy and influenced the devel. of Jewish nationalism in lit. Mod. Heb. poets such as Hayyim Nachman Bialik were influenced also by the earlier work of Moses Hayyim Luzzatto (also known as Ramchal), a major It. Jewish writer who was considered by some to be the first mod. Heb. poet, predating even the works of the Haskalah poets. However, by the second half of the 19th c., Heb. poetry in Italy had declined, and Eastern Europe became its main center. Additionally, in the 19th c., a number of non-Eur. Jews composed Heb. verse. The Baghdadi-born Palestinian poet Avraham Barukh Mani (1854–82), e.g., wrote poetry in the It. Heb. style.

A major shift in Heb. poetry and in Jewish hist. took place around 1881–82, following the pogroms in Russia. These years mark the beginning of what Harshav has called the Modern Jewish Revolution, when ideas that had developed in relatively small circles for many years were rapidly adopted by millions of Jews. It was in this period that Hayyim Nachman Bialik (1873–1934) published his first poems. Bialik's poetry combined *accentual-syllabic meters from Rus. poetry with the rich sounds of the Ashkenazi pronunciation of Heb. In his poems, Heb. was not restricted to the vocabulary and syntax of the Bible but drew on the entire spectrum of Heb. lit. Bialik wrote about longing for Zion and life in the diaspora, about love, the struggle with faith, the pogroms, and much more.

Bialik's contribution to Heb. lit. included not only poetry, but major essays on lang. and lit. He was an influential ed. and publisher in Russia, Berlin, and, later, Tel Aviv. Though his production was relatively small, the quality and importance of his work, along with the prophetic tone of some of his poems, earned him the title of the Heb. *poet laureate. Many historiographies of Heb. poetry consider him the father of mod. Heb. poetry.

Bialik's contemp. Saul Tchernikhovsky (1875–1943) also furthered the devel. of an accentual-syllabic Heb. poetry and greatly enriched Heb. lit. with sonnets, *idylls, and other poetic forms. His trans. from ancient Gr., Akkadian, and Finnish, and his original poetic work in Heb., introduced his readers to Eur. myths, ideas, and verse forms. Bialik and Tchernikhovsky as well as other poets of the Heb. revival juxtaposed historical and national themes with a growing focus on the individual. Some of these poets were influenced by Eur. romanticisms and introduced to Heb. lit. elaborate descriptions of nature, thus expanding the vocabulary of the lang. to include names of flora and fauna. In this way, the Heb. poetry of this period contributed significantly to the revival of Heb. as a spoken lang.

Tchernikhovsky and Bialik were followed by major writers such as Jacob Fichman (1881–1958), Yehuda Karni (1884–1949), Zalman Shneor (1887–1959), and Jacob Steinberg (1887–1947).

**B. _Europe, 1918–48._** The school of Bialik dominated Heb. poetry until the 1930s. By then, younger Heb. poets, many of whom had arrived in Israel following World War I and the Rus. Revolution, had begun to rebel against the older poets' linear and symmetrical forms, as well as their traditional sources and themes. Once used almost exclusively for rabbinical writings, Heb. had now become a full-fledged spoken lang., and the new poetry was tempered by the vernacular. It also reflected the Socialist-Zionist ideology of the pioneer culture, which was far less traditionally "Jewish" in theme and was permeated by the new Mediterranean landscape.

The most prominent "pioneer" poets were Nathan Alterman (1910–70) and Abraham Shlonsky (1900–73). Both were influenced by the Rus. revolutionary poets Alexander Blok, Vladimir Mayakovsky, and Sergei Esenin and by *expressionism. In their work, the ennui of the disintegrating urban Eur. culture, the destruction wrought by war, and the impending Holocaust vied with enthusiasm for the daring novelty of the reborn homeland, its bright but uncompromising colors, its sand dunes, and its sea. Another pioneer poet, Rachel Bluwstein Sela (1890–1931), wrote lyrical short poems in a clean and precise lang. that was influenced by the Rus. poet Anna Akhmatova and Rus. *acmeism. Rus. influence also made its way into Heb. poetry in Palestine through the works of the communist poet Alexander Penn (1906–72), who translated poems by

Mayakovsky to Heb., and by Leah Goldberg (1911–70), a scholar, writer, and trans. (see RUSSIA, POETRY OF).

The uprooted poets of this generation wandered through the capitals of Europe, absorbing the cultures of their temporary homes. They were exposed not only to Rus. poetics but to Ger. expressionism, Fr. *symbolism, the existentialism of R. M. Rilke, Freudian and Jungian views of the arts, and much more. Many of these poets translated poems and plays from It., Fr., Rus., and Eng. into Heb. Shlonsky and Goldberg wrote poems and plays for both adults and children; Alterman published a highly influential political and satirical newspaper column in verse called _Hatur Hashvi_ (The Seventh Column). Thus, in a relatively short period, these poets created a large canon of native Heb. _Eretz Israeli_ poetry.

Another major figure in the devel. of Heb. poetry in Eretz Israel was the poet and activist Uri Zvi Greenberg (1894–1981). Greenberg broke away from Socialist-Zionist ideology to create a new poetic style with a messianic tone. For him, the "return" to the land was a return to God's historic covenant, a rejection of what he perceived as the "false" morality of the gentiles, and a dedication to the miracle of divine providence. Greenberg's style is often extravagantly Whitmanian. He eschews foreign verse forms, preferring the cadences of the biblical peroration and Jewish liturgical verse (piyyutim). His vocabulary is sometimes drawn from Kabbalistic texts.

Jonathan Ratosh (1908–81) and the Canaanite movement represented still another ideological direction in Heb. poetry. This movement tried to create a strong connection among land, lang., and poetry by reviving Canaanite sounds and the Canaanite pantheon. A very different connection between the land and poetic style can be found in the work of Esther Raab (1894–1981), Israel's first native-born woman poet, who was also the first to describe the landscape of Israel without the ambivalence of the immigrant poets.

While Heb. poetry of the early 1920s is characterized by modernist and experimental styles (see MODERNISM) and by its break from the rhythms and meters of the Ashkenazi pronunciation of Heb., much of the poetry written in the late 1920s, 1930s and even 1940s—esp. by poets from the Shlonsky-Alterman-Goldberg school—represented a return to constrained poetic expressions, to postsymbolism, and to the prosodic forms of the now established Eretz Israeli pronunciation.

While some poets from the 1920s onward wrote in *free verse, most were considered minor voices at the time. E.g., in 1923 in Vienna, David Vogel (1891–1944) published a collection of modernist lyric poems in free meter titled _Lifnei Sha'ar ha-Afel_ (In Front of the Dark Gate). In Palestine, Avraham Ben-Yitzhak (1883–1950) experimented with a mod. form of biblical parallelism in "Bod'dim Omrim" (Loners Say, 1918) and in "Ashrei Hazor'im v'lo Yiktzoru" (Happy Are They Who Sow, 1930). Avot Yeshurun (1904–92) challenged readers with enigmatic, idiosyncratic, and complex poems and forms. Contrary to the ruling conventions of his time, he wrote in a lang. that openly reflected the multilingualism of both the immigrant writer and the land by including Yiddish and Ar. sounds and words. These poets were at the margins of the canon when their works were published; but the poets and critics of the next generation moved them to the center, as part of their revolt against Alterman, Shlonsky, and Goldberg.

**C. Israeli Poets (1948–2010).** With Israel's War of Independence in 1948, a new generation of Heb. poets arose. These were either native Israeli poets or products of the Heb. school system that the Zionists had established in Eastern Europe, who arrived in Palestine as young pioneers before the outbreak of World War II. For them, Heb. was a vibrant spoken lang., and Israel's landscape was the landscape of their youth, if not their infancy. While most no longer drew from the traditional religious world of Eastern Europe, the Bible and the Prayer Book (*Sidur*) continued to serve them as major sources, and biblical phrases, allusions, forms, and myths continued to occupy much of their poetry.

The older writers of the Israeli generation who began as junior members of the Shlonsky-Alterman school, such as Haim Guri (b. 1923), remained committed to the Socialist-Zionist ideology. Following the War of Independence and the mass immigration to Israel, however, many discovered that there were no simple solutions to the problems of their new society. Once independence was attained, individualism, which had been suppressed during the struggle, broke loose, and subjectivism became the rule.

In this era, poets such as Yehuda Amichai (1924–2000), Amir Gilboa (1917–84), and Abba Kovner (1918–87) abandoned the strict metrical and stanzaic patterns to which the Shlonsky-Alterman generation had adhered. Amichai chose his metaphors from quotidian experience—a newspaper headline, the terms of a contract, a cliché—as well as from traditional Jewish texts, to which he often gave an ironic twist. His poetry evoked a tension between the sacred and profane experiences of the mod. poet as a Jew, an Israeli, a Jerusalemite, and a human being.

By the 1950s, literary influences on Heb. poetry had become less Ger. or Rus., and more Anglo-Am. The poets known as the Statehood Generation, such as Amichai, Nathan Zach (b. 1930), Moshe Dor (b. 1932), David Avidan (1934–95), and Dahlia Rabikovitch (1936–2005), rebelled against the poetic style of Shlonsky and Alterman. Zach attacked what he termed the monotonous rhythms of Alterman and called for a new poetry in which line and stanza were freed from traditional rules. He also called for a new poetic diction characterized by semantic significance rather than mechanical regularity. He believed that poems should be not neatly rounded to a close but fluid and open-ended. Figurative lang. should be used sparingly: i.e., the poet should avoid manifestly poetic diction and syntax and draw upon everyday speech, incl. slang. Zach also attacked "objective" or "ideological" poetry: the artist, he believed, should concentrate on the subjective, existential experience of a complex mod. world. While not all the poets of the Statehood Generation followed Zach's views, most of them saw their work as an attempt to focus on the concrete, on the "here and now." In some of the poems of Avidan, e.g., the focus on the "now" meant constant questioning of the boundaries of the poetic lang. and form and bringing into poetry some of the sounds and patterns of the media and technology of a rapidly changing world. Toward the end of the 1960s, Avidan's poetry became even more concrete in an objectivistic and even pseudo-Talmudic manner.

Rabikovitch, a feminist poet whose sophisticated naïf poems have been widely acclaimed, focused on concrete and subjective experiences but in a rich lang. that drew from the many historical layers of Heb. Her collection *Ahavat Tapu'ach Hazahav* (The Love of the Orange, 1959) is lush with musical patterns. It is one of the most influential poetry collections of the later 1950s and the beginning of the 1960s, together with Zach's *Shirim Shonim* (Different Poems, 1960), Amichai's *Shirim 1948–1962* (Poems), and Avidan's *Masheu Bishvil Misheu* (Something for Somebody, 1964).

In the 1960s, the poets Meir Wieseltier (b. 1941), Yair Horvitz (1941–88), and Yona Wallach (1944–85) created the Tel Aviv Circle and published some of the major works in mod. Heb. poetry. Wallach shocked Israeli readers with her daring expressions of sexuality and the decidedly Jungian bent of her poetry.

With the Lebanese War of the 1980s, Heb. poets reverted to more directly political poetry. In the wake of the war, several volumes of protest poetry appeared in which Zach and Rabikovitch, once the apostles of subjectivism, and younger poets such as Yitzhak Laor (b. 1948) participated. For Rabikovitch, this meant protesting oppression and suffering through intimate situations and the experiences of women and children. Political poetry, from both the Right and the Left, held sway until the 21st c. (see e.g., the work of Aharon Shabtai [b. 1939]).

Heb. poetry of the later 20th and early 21st cs. has been enriched by the interplay among multicultural Israeli voices. The works reflect the varied origins of both immigrants and their children and of different social and ethnic groups: the religious world of Zelda Mishkovsky (1914–84); the middle Eur. roots of Zach, Amichai, and Dan Pagis (1929–86); the Rus. Polish milieu from which sprang Kovner and Gilboa; the Anglo-Am. influences on T. Carmi (1925–94), Gabriel Preil (1911–93), who lived in New York, and Simon Halkin (1898–1987); the Mediterranean world of Mordecai Geldman (b. 1946); the Maghrebian world of Erez Biton (b. 1942); and the Arab-Jewish roots of Ronny Someck (b. 1951), Amira Hess (b. 1956), Haviva Pedaya (b. 1956), and Almog Behar (b. 1978).

Periodicals and jours. had been major venues for mod. Heb. poetry from its beginning, but the end of the 20th and beginning of the 21st cs. demonstrated a sudden growth in new jours. and a slight change in their role and format. It is difficult to predict which of the current directions in Heb. poetry will have a lasting influence, but the jour. appears to reflect a need for literary spaces that accommodate a diverse range of social, ethnic, and political affiliations, as well as the search for new poetic styles. Some of the jours. embodying these sentiments include *Ha'Kivun Mizrach* (To the East), a jour. focusing on Mizrahi and Arab-Jewish issues and questions of identity; *Mashiv Haru'ach* (Make the Wind Blow), a jour. devoted primarily to religious Heb. poetry; *Mita'am: A Review of Literature and Radical Thought*, ed. by Laor; *Emda* (Position), ed. by Ran Yagil, which calls for a return to modernist poetic values and to a new kind of poetic (but not social) elitism; *Maayan* (Spring), a forum for poetry in Israel and beyond; and the renewed format of *Achshav* (Now), a jour. that was instrumental in the devel. of Israeli poetry for many years and now appears in a new format. In 2005, a small group of poets and writers became associated with a new literary jour. titled *Ho!* Poets in *Ho!* strive to restore formal rhythms and rhymes to Heb. poetry and to create a poetry that is not specifically Israeli but more "cosmopolitan."

See AL-ANDALUS, POETRY OF; HEBREW PROSODY AND POETICS; JUDEO-SPANISH POETRY; YIDDISH POETRY.

■ **I. Biblical**: R. Lowth, *Lectures on the Sacred Poetry of the Hebrews*, trans. G. Gregory (1787); J. G. Herder, *The Spirit of Hebrew Poetry* [1783], trans. J. Marsh (1833); E. Sievers, *Metrische Studien I–II* (1901–7); G. B. Gray, *The Forms of Hebrew Poetry* (1915); T. H. Robinson, *The Poetry of the Old Testament* (1947); E. Z. Melamed, "Break-up of Stereotyped Phrases as an Artistic Device in Biblical Poetry," *Studies in the Bible*, ed. C. Rabin (1961); S. Gevirtz, *Patterns in the Early Poetry of Israel* (1963); R. Jakobson, "Grammatical Parallelism and Its Russian Facet," *Language* 42 (1966); B. Hrushovski, "Prosody, Hebrew," *Encyclopedia Judaica* (1971); D. A. Robertson, *Linguistic Evidence in Dating Early Hebrew Poetry* (1972); A. M. Cooper, *Biblical Poetics* (1976); D. K. Stuart, *Studies in Early Hebrew Meter* (1976); S. A. Geller, *Parallelism in Early Biblical Poetry* (1979); J. L. Kugel, "Some Medieval and Renaissance Hebrew Writings on the Poetry of the Bible," *Studies in Medieval Jewish History and Literature*, ed. I. Twersky (1979); and *The Idea of Biblical Poetry* (1981); E. L. Greenstein, "How Does Parallelism Mean?" *A Sense of Text* (1983); M. H. Lichtenstein, "Biblical Poetry," *Back to the Sources*, ed. B. W. Holtz (1984); R. Alter, *The Art of Biblical Poetry* (1985); A. Berlin, *The Dynamics of Biblical Parallelism* (1985); W.G.E. Watson, *Classical Hebrew Poetry* (1986); E. L. Greenstein, "Aspects of Biblical Poetry," *Jewish Book Annual* 44 (1986–87); L. Alonso Schökel, *A Manual of Hebrew Poetics*, trans. L. Alonso Schökel and A. Graffy (1988); D. Pardee, *Ugaritic and Hebrew Poetic Parallelism* (1988); A. Niccacci, *The Syntax of the Verb in Classical Hebrew*, trans. W.G.E. Watson (1990); A. Berlin, *Biblical Poetry through Medieval Jewish Eyes* (1991); S. E. Gillingham, *The Poems and Psalms of the Hebrew Bible* (1994); M. O'Connor, *Hebrew Verse Structure*, 2d ed.

(1997); F. H. Polak, "The Oral and the Written: Syntax, Stylistics, and the Development of Biblical Prose Narrative," *Journal of the Ancient Near Eastern Society* 26 (1998); E. L. Greenstein, "Direct Discourse and Parallelism," *Studies in Bible and Exegesis* 5 (2000—in Heb.); D. R. Vance, *The Question of Meter in Biblical Hebrew Poetry* (2001); R. A. Harris, *Discerning Parallelism* (2004); F. W. Dobbs-Allsopp, "The Psalms and Lyric Verse," *The Evolution of Rationality*, ed. F. L. Shults (2006); T. Linafelt, "Lyrical Theology: The Song of Songs and the Advantage of Poetry," *Toward a Theology of Eros*, ed. V. Burrus (2006); F. W. Dobbs-Allsopp, "Poetry, Hebrew," *New Interpreter's Dictionary of the Bible*, v. 4 (2009); J. Y. Jindo, *Biblical Metaphor Reconsidered* (2010).

■ **II. Medieval**. *Anthologies and Editions, in English*: *A Treasury of Jewish Poetry*, ed. N. and M. Ausubel (1957); *An Anthology of Modern Hebrew Poetry*, ed. S. Y. Pnueli and A. Ukhmani (1966); *The Penguin Book of Hebrew Verse*, and trans. T. Carmi (1981); *Wine, Women, and Death,* ed. R. P. Scheindlin (1986); R. Loewe, *Ibn Gabirol* (1989); *The Gazelle*, ed. R. P. Scheindlin (1991); A. Schippers, *Spanish Hebrew Poetry and the Arabic Literary Tradition* (1994); *The Modern Hebrew Poem Itself*, ed. S. Burnshaw, T. Carmi, E. Spicehandler (2003); D. Bregman, *The Golden Way*, trans. A. Brener (2006); *The Dream of the Poem*, ed. and trans. P. Cole (2007). *In Hebrew*: *Diwan of Yehudah ha-Levi*, ed. H. Brody, 2 v. (1894–1930); J. Schirmann, *Hebrew Poetry in Spain and Provence*, 4 v. (1954–56); *New Hebrew Poems from the Genizah*, ed. J. Schirmann (1965); *Israel Levin Jubilee Volume*, ed. R. Tsur and T. Rosen (1994); *Eretz Israel and Its Poetry, Studies in Piyyutim from the Cairo Geniza*, ed. M. Zulay (1995); *Jewish Palestinian Aramaic Poetry from Late Antiquity*, ed. J. Yahalom and M. Sokoloff (1999); *Tahkemoni or Tales of Heman the Ezrahite*, ed. J. Yahalom and N. Katsumata (2010). *Criticism and History, in English*: S. M. Stern, *Hispano-Arabic Strophic Poetry* (1974); R. Brann, *The Compunctious Poet* (1990); Á. Sáenz-Badillos, *A History of the Hebrew Language* (1993); R. Drori, *Models and Contacts* (2000); *The Literature of Al-Andalus*, ed. M. R. Menocal, R. P. Scheindlin, M. Sells (2000); J. Tobi, *Proximity and Distance: Medieval Hebrew and Arabic Poetry* (2004). *In Hebrew*: E. Fleischer, *Hebrew Liturgical Poetry in the Middle Ages* (1975); D. Pagis, *Change and Tradition in the Secular Poetry* (1976); J. Schirmann, *Studies in the History of Hebrew Poetry and Drama* (1979); T. Rosen-Moked, *The Hebrew Girdle Poem (Muwashshah) in the Middle Ages* (1985); J. Yahalom, *Poetic Language in the Early Piyyut* (1985); D. Pagis, *Hebrew Poetry of the Middle Ages and the Renaissance* (1991), and *Poetry Aptly Explained* (1993); J. Schirmann and E. Fleischer, *The History of Hebrew Poetry in Muslim Spain* (1996); J. Schirmann and E. Fleischer, *The History of Hebrew Poetry in Christian Spain and Southern France* (1997); J. Yahalom, *Poetry and Society in Jewish Galilee of Late Antiquity* (1999); J. Yahalom, "Poet-Performer in the Synagogue of the Byzantine Period,"

*Continuity and Renewal*, ed. L. I. Levine (2004); M. Rand, *Introduction to the Grammar of Hebrew Poetry in Byzantine Palestine* (2006). **Byzantine Period and Muslim Spain**: I. Davidson, *Thesaurus of Mediaeval Hebrew Poetry* (1924); J. Schirmann, "The Research on Spanish-Hebrew Poetry 1919–1939," *Sedarim* (1942); *J. Schirmann's Bibliography of Studies of Mediaeval Hebrew Poetry 1948–1978: Accumulative Index*, ed. E. Adler et al. (1989); *Ma'agarim Online Historical Dictionary*, http://hebrew-treasures.huji.ac.il (in Heb.); Piyyut Project of the Institute for the Research of Hebrew Poetry.

■ **III. Modern**. *Anthologies, in English*: *Modern Hebrew Poetry*, ed. and trans. R. F. Mintz (1966); "Israel," *Modern Poetry in Translation*, ed. R. Friend (1974); *Modern Hebrew Literature*, ed. R. Alter (1975); *Fourteen Israeli Poets*, ed. D. Silk (1976); *Contemporary Israeli Literature*, ed. E. Anderson (1977); *Modern Hebrew Poetry*, ed. and trans. B. Frank (1980); *Modern Hebrew Poetry*, ed., A. Mintz (1982); *Israeli Poetry*, ed. W. Bargad and S. F. Chyet (1986); *Modern Hebrew Literature in English Translation*, ed. L. I. Yudkin (1987); *No Rattling of Sabers*, ed. E. Raizen (1996); *Found in Translation*, ed. E. Friend (2007); *Poets on the Edge*, ed. T. Keller (2008). **In Hebrew**: *Sifruthenu ha-Yafah*, ed. J. Lichtenbaum, 2 v. (1962)—mod. *Shirah Tse'irah*, ed. B. Yaoz and Y. Kest (1980). **Bibliographies, in English**: Y. Goell, *Bibliography of Modern Hebrew Literature in English Translation* (1968)—7,500 items from 1880–1965; *Bibliography of Modern Hebrew Literature in Translation* (1975)—700 items since 1917; I. Goldberg and A. Zipin, *Bibliography of Modern Hebrew Literature in Translation* (1979–)—series providing current bibl. and extensive retroactive coverage. **In Hebrew**: *Shishim ve-shisha Meshorerim*, ed. Z. Stavi (1996); *Shira Chadasha*, ed. M. Izakson and A. Kosman (1997); *Shirat Ha'tchiya Ha'ivrit*, ed. B. Harshav (2000); *Lanetsach Anagnech*, ed. M. Shaket (2003); *Ve-karati Lecach Ahava*, ed. M. Dor (2008). **Criticism and History, in English**: D. Goldstein and B. Hrushovski, "On Free Rhythms in Modern Poetry," Sebeok; S. Halkin, *Modern Hebrew Literature*, 2d ed. (1970); E. Spicehandler, "Hebrew Literature, Modern," *Encyclopaedia Judaica* (1971–92); I. Zinberg, *A History of Jewish Literature*, ed. and trans. B. Martin, 12 v. (1972–78); E. Silberschlag, *From Renaissance to Renaissance*, 2 v. (1973–77); C. Kronfeld, *On the Margins of Modernism* (1996); D. Jacobson, *Does David Still Play before You?* (1997); R. Kartun-Blum, *Profane Scriptures* (1999); M. Gluzman, *The Politics of Canonicity* (2002); D. Miron, *The Prophetic Mode in Modern Hebrew Poetry* (2009). **In Hebrew**: J. Klausner, *Historiyah Shel-ha-Sifrut ha-Ivrit ha-Hadashah*, 6 v. (1930–50)— F. Lachover, *Toldot ha-sifrut ha-Ivrit ha-Hadashah*, 4 v. (1936–48)—mod.; A. Ben-Or, *Toldot ha-Sifrut ha-Ivrit be-Dorenu*, 2 v. (1954–55)—D. Miron, *Arba' Panim ba-Sifrut ha-Ivrit Bat Yamenu* (1962)—contemp.; A. M. Habermann, *Toledoth Hapiyyut Vehashir* (1970).

E. Spicehandler (intro., extracanonical, It., mod.); E. L. Greenstein (bib.); W. van Bekkum (med.); V. K. Shemtov (mod.)

# HEBREW PROSODY AND POETICS

I. Biblical
II. Medieval
III. Modern

## I. Biblical

**A. *Prosody*.** Approximately one-third of the Heb. Bible (to which discussion is here confined) in many eds. is presented in a format that suggests that the content is to be viewed as verse. In fact, all talk of "verse" or "poetry" in the Bible is the result of mod. scholarly hypothesis, so that no discussion of biblical prosody can be entirely descriptive. No trad. about the nature of biblical prosody has survived for the received Masoretic text. To be sure, a number of passages termed "song" (*shirah*)— like the "Songs" of Miriam (Exod. 15), of Moses (Deut. 32), of Deborah (Judg. 5), and of David (2 Sam. 22), as well as a few Dead Sea texts—are so arranged as to suggest an effort at indicating verse. The special system of punctuation in the so-called "poetic books" (Psalms, Proverbs, and Job) as well as the format of their text in some biblical mss., incl. the Aleppo Codex (the earliest nearly complete form of the Masoretic text), may point in a similar direction; but we have no explicit statement of underlying prosodic principles. Early references by authors such as Josephus and the church fathers to cl. meters like *hexameters and *pentameters in the Bible are simply apologetic in nature, designed to appropriate for the Bible the heritage of the cl. Gr. trad., comprehensible to the Hellenistic audience and intended to elicit its respect.

Biblical study in the 18th and 19th cs. also attempted to force passages considered "poetic" into approximations of cl. meters. But by the late 19th c. and despite the efforts of no less a metrist than Eduard Sievers, it was generally recognized that prospects for exact scansions were chimerical, not least because of uncertainties in regard to key aspects of ancient Heb. pronunciation. A loose working hypothesis was reached that, without claiming to be an adequate statement of biblical prosody, still allowed prosodic considerations to play a role in practical exegesis.

An essential empirical fact is the general symmetry in clause length displayed in most passages that, on other grounds, might reasonably be termed "poetic." In books like Job or Psalms, most clauses consist of from two to six words, the majority having from three to five. (By contrast, in books like Genesis or Judges, mainly narrative in content, clause length seems to be random.) It is reasonable to suppose that passages with such symmetry form an expectation in the reader's mind that, after a certain number of words, a *caesura or line break will occur. The specific phonetic, and therefore prosodic, aspect is the silence, real or potential, awaited at the limit of expectation, which usually corresponds to clause closure. The unit so delimited is the line (in other common terminologies, *colon, *stichos, *hemistich, *verset). So firm is the perceptual base that long clauses tend to be analyzed as two enjambed lines: "wa'ani nasakti malki / ál ṣiyyon har qodši"

(For I have anointed my king / On Zion, my holy mountain [Ps. 2:6]).

Within lines, a meter might potentially be either iso-syllabic or accentual. Syllabic analysis has been attempted several times, esp. for some early verse (Freedman, Stuart). But even recourse to a reconstructed ancient pronunciation cannot remove the many examples of syllabic asymmetry between lines. For this reason and many others, it is better to speak of rhythm rather than meter in discussing biblical prosody. The consensus has long been that the rhythmical basis for biblical prosody lies in the stresses of speech (the Ley-Sievers system). Heb. is a lang. with a strong stress accent that is phonemic (e.g., *qáma*, "she arose," vs. *qamá*, "rising" [participle]). The system may be summarized as follows: lines contain from two to six stresses, the great majority having three to five. Each metrical unit, or foot, receives a single stress, although long terms, usually of five or more syllables, may have two stresses. By "metrical unit" is meant in most cases what is commonly presented as a "word" in the Masoretic graphemic system.

The overall system has rightly been termed "semantic-syntactic-accentual" (Hrushovski). The essential device for linking verses or sense units together within the system is *parallelism of the *couplet (in other terminologies, bicolon, *distich, stichos). The great majority of couplets can be represented as 3:3, 2:2 (often doubled to 2:2::2:2, sometimes best analyzed as 4:4), and 3:2 (often analyzable as 5), where the numbers refer to words or stresses. Also present are slightly asymmetrical couplets like 2:3 or 4:3, etc. Extreme asymmetries like 4:2 or 2:4 are likely to be "regularized" by emendation *metri causa*, but the asymmetry may have been obscured in sung or chanted performance. A unit of three lines, the *triplet (tricolon, tristich) is also common, as well as the *quatrain. Larger units like *strophes are frequently discernible in context. Biblical verse rarely employs a single meter throughout a poem, although 3:3 is so common as to appear dominant. Alternations of 3:3 and 2:2 seem to occur esp. in early poems. Scansion of a given passage, therefore, often depends on one's assessment of the soundness of the text, interpretation of the meaning, and willingness to view certain elements as "extra-metrical." E.g., Isa. 1:1–2:

> Hear O-heavens/And give-ear, O-earth,
> For-YHWH has-spoken:
> Sons I-have-reared and-raised,
> But-they have-rebelled against-me!

may be scanned in several ways: as 2:2:2 + 3:3; or, if "For-YHWH has-spoken" is viewed as extrametrical, as 2:2 + 3:3; or, if one joins the monosyllabic preposition in the final line to its verb ("have-rebelled-against-me"), as 2:2 + 3:2. Such a loose system will never satisfy purists, who can point to passages in supposed "prose" that also scan quite regularly. Some have despaired of uncovering *any* biblical rhythm, and some have denied the very possibility of its existence. But since there are rhythmic symmetries accompanied usually by parallelism and a host of devices often associated with verse in other prosodies—*alliteration, *assonance, rhyme (all common if random in biblical verse), *archaisms, and *tropes—it has seemed to most scholars satisfactory as a general or working hypothesis to speak of biblical rhythm, if not meter, and prosody.

Parallelism is commonly included in discussions of biblical prosody because of the constitutive role it clearly plays in the rhythm of biblical verse. Most scholars include both grammatical and semantic aspects in parallelism. Aside from sporadic examples of earlier awareness, the concept and term of parallelism were introduced by Bishop Robert Lowth in the mid.-18th c. Lowth recognized two aspects of *parallelismus membrorum*: "constructive" (i.e., grammatical) or parallelism of form; and semantic or parallelism of meaning. He isolated three categories: "synonymous," "antithetic," and (a catchall) "synthetic." Despite the fact that the last category in particular was unclear, Lowth's classification remained basically unchanged until refined by G. B. Gray in the early 20th c. It is now generally recognized that the term "synthetic parallelism" has no real meaning.

The basic unit of parallelistic verse is the couplet, with its A and B lines (a triplet adds a C line, a quatrain a D line). Parallelism between individual members of the lines may be complete—a situation commonly represented by the schema *abc/a'b'c'* (each letter stands for a stressed metrical unit, those in the B line being marked with a prime)—but it is frequently partial or incomplete. The most common type involves *ellipsis, or "gapping," of an A-line term in the B line, in the deep structure of which it is, however, still present or "understood" (O'Connor). Apparently from a desire to maintain general syllabic symmetry, the approximate number of syllables in the gapped term may be "compensated" for by an expanded or longer B line parallel ("ballast variant"). A typical schema is *abc/b'c'2*.

Semantic correspondence between parallel terms extends from actual identity via repetition to varying degrees of synonymity and antonymity, to relationships that may be labeled complementary (*eat/drink*), merism (*heaven/earth*), whole-part or part-whole (*Pharaoh and his hosts/his chief officers*), metaphorical (*the wicked/chaff*), and epithetic (*God/the Holy One of Israel*), among others. Some parallel pairs, e.g., silver/gold or heaven/earth, are so common as to become virtual formulas. Such A- and B-line "word pairs" may stem from oral composition, but in most biblical verse represent merely a form of poetic diction. It is now known that word pairs and many other features of parallelism go back at least as far as the Ugaritic texts of the 13th c. BCE and form part of the extensive Canaanite heritage of biblical verse. Among the most striking parallel patterns is "climactic parallelism," which may be represented by the schema *abc/abd*, in which the first two words of the A line are repeated, but the last term is gapped and replaced at the end of the B line by another term. E.g., Ps. 92:10: "For-behold your-enemies, O Lord, // For-behold your-enemies shall-perish!"

Little work has been done on the hist. of biblical parallelism, although it is possible to discern a difference between an earlier, stricter form in which parallelism is mainly between individual constituents of the couplet and a later, looser form in which whole lines, or even couplets, are merely general semantic equivalents of other lines and couplets, as in Ps. 23:3–6. In general, parallelism allows almost endless variation without obscuring its basic contours. Roman Jakobson, who viewed parallelism as the basic device of all poetry, said that it activates all levels of lang.

**B. Poetics.** The Bible contains no explicit statements about poetics in regard to the nature of either poetry or poetic composition. However, an implicit poetics may be inferred from the complaint of the prophet Ezekiel that people consider him a mere "maker of parables" (Ezek. 21:5), a singer of "love songs, sweetly sung and skillfully played" (Ezek. 33:32). "Parables" (Heb. *mashal*, the meaning of which extends from "proverb" to larger literary compositions of several types) and secular song were the province of Wisdom in Israel, as was elsewhere in the ancient Near East the trad. of science, intellect, and conscious literary art. Although the "wise" probably claimed some type of inspiration for their productions, their art was viewed predominantly as an expression of human skill. Prophets, on the other hand, although employing the forms of poetic expression cultivated by the "wise," were believed to be mere "mouths," passive transmitters of divine messages. To view their oracles as "art" violated their prophetic function, even though, as Fisch has observed, their message achieved its effect partly via the literary artifice employed. Implicit in the conflict between prophecy and poetry is a poetics of tension between aesthetics and religion that has had a profound influence on Western culture. Meir Sternberg has explored similar tensions in the poetics of biblical narrative. Related to this is the Bible's remarkably free use of genre. Although form critics long ago isolated most of the genres used by biblical authors and related them to their analogues in the ancient Near East, analysis often shows that the traditional forms have been "sprung" or "undermined" (Fisch) by introducing an element of tension, esp. in hymns, where myth is combined with hist. in a manner unattested elsewhere in the ancient world. F. M. Cross has explored the historicizing of myth in Heb. texts. E.g., a key myth found in many places in the Heb. Bible centered on a cosmic battle between the deity and a sea monster (representing Chaos), followed by creation and, as a capstone, the erection of the divine palace, the shrine. These traditional elements are applied in a cl. biblical hymn, the "Song of the Sea" (Exod. 15), to the formative events of the "creation" of Israel—the exodus from Egypt and conquest of Canaan. However, the old mythical motifs of the theme are radically redefined, so that the cosmic foe, the sea, becomes the natural agent of the destruction of Pharaoh and his army, while the conquest is described in quasi-mythic terms as the establishment of a shrine on the hills of Canaan. The ambiguity that arises from the indeterminacy of hist. and myth results in that tension that gives the poem, as so much of biblical poetry, its transcendent dimension.

**II. Medieval.** Med. Heb. poetry comprises two distinct branches of verse, each governed by its own characteristic poetics and systems of versification. Generically speaking, these branches are *piyyut* (Gr. *poesis*, liturgical poetry) and nonliturgical or secular poetry. The poetic styles and verse forms developed by each branch varied widely according to epoch, historical school, and geographic center.

**A. Prosody.** Until the High Middle Ages, liturgical poetry predominated in Heb. writing to the complete exclusion of the secular. Piyyut emerged in Palestine (probably in the 4th c.) as a popular supplement to the increasingly standardized and fixed (prose) prayer. Additionally, complex poetic cycles (*yotser* and *qedushta*) whose themes were related to the weekly recitation of scripture were incorporated into the synagogue service. The genres of piyyut were thus determined by specific liturgical contexts, and piyyut texts were always intended for public recitation. The rules pertaining to form (most *piyyutim* were strophic), structure, and rhyme were also closely tied to the liturgical function of the poem. Idiosyncratic and complex rhymes (initial, internal, and terminal) are characteristic of early piyyut, but end rhyme eventually became the prevalent form. *Acrostics based on the 22-letter Heb. alphabet or the poet's name constituted an important formal feature of nearly all piyyut.

Over the course of its long evolution, piyyut came to employ four distinct systems of versification. In its earlier phases, it was composed in two verse forms similar to those found in the Heb. Bible, one based on an equivalent number of words in parallel versets, the other an accentual system based on three to five word stresses per line. Later, in a postclassical devel. (Spain, 10th c.), syllabic meters, which make no distinction in vowel length but fix the number of syllables per line (six to eight syllables per verset or line is common), were used extensively (see SYLLABIC VERSE). Finally, the quantitative meters associated with secular poetry (see below) were employed sporadically in strophic liturgical verse after the 10th c. (see QUANTITY).

Secular Heb. poetry emerged in Muslim Spain in the 10th c. as a subcultural adaptation of *Ar. poetry. Two main verse forms were cultivated. The predominant type, written in the cl. mold of Ar. courtly poetry, forms one continuous sequence of lines, ranging from an epigrammatic couplet to a formal ode (*qaṣīda) of more than 50 lines. Regardless of length, this type of composition is governed by a single meter and end rhyme that are carried through every line of verse without variation. Rhyme words ending in a vowel include the consonant preceding the vowel (CV); for words ending in consonants, the rhyme must encompass the preceding vowel and antepenultimate consonant (CVC). (See AL-ANDALUS, POETRY OF.)

The second type of secular composition was strophic in form and closely connected to musical performance. The *muwashshah*, as it was known in Ar. (Heb. *shir ezor*, "girdle poem"), was usually devoted to the genre of *love poetry or, in a secondary devel., to *panegyric. Conservative Ar. literati tended to regard the muwashshaḥ with disdain because it did not meet the strict prosodic requirements of cl. Ar. poetry. Jewish courtly circles, however, enthusiastically accepted it (11th c.), possibly on account of the prevalence of similar strophic forms in the pre-Andalusian piyyut. The muwashshaḥ employed the quantitative meters used in the cl. monorhyming poem but did so in a highly irregular fashion: i.e., the meter of the first part of a strophe often differed from that of the second part of the strophe. Additionally, the muwashshaḥ used quantitative meters in nonstandard patterns. Tonic elements may also have come into play, though this is a matter of dispute. Muwashshaḥāt also differed from poems of the cl. type in allowing great flexibility in the use of rhyme. One rhyme of the muwashshaḥ (that of the first part of the strophe) varies from strophe to strophe; a second rhyme (that of the last part of each strophe) remains fixed throughout the poem (e.g., *aaabb, cccbb, dddbb*). In addition to its appealing rhyme schemes and often complex metrical patterns, a striking feature of the muwashshaḥ is its *\*kharja* (exit) or envoi. Heb. muwashshaḥāt frequently conclude with romance or colloquial Ar. kharjas (in Heb. script), usually in the form of a quotation from a popular Old Sp. or Hispano-Ar. love song.

The quantitative meters employed in both types of secular composition, as well as in some liturgical poetry, were created by means of an artificial system that transposed the distinctive prosodic patterns of Ar. into Heb. In Ar., as in cl. Gr., quantitative meters are based upon the distinction between long and short syllables. It is the pattern of long and short syllables that creates the different meters. A line of verse (Ar. *bayt*; Heb. *bayit*, "house") was typically composed of metrically equivalent versets made up of from two to four metrical feet (*čamudim*). Since cl. Ar. preserved the phonological values of long and short vowels to a greater degree than biblical Heb., the system required that certain liberties be taken with Heb. grammar and phonology. Twelve of the 16 basic cl. Ar. meters were reproduced in simplified form; with variants (lengthened or shortened metrical feet), the number of Heb. quantitative meters amounted to approximately 60. This Ar.-style quantitative prosody subsequently attained a normative status in various Near Eastern, Eur., and Mediterranean communities. It was still popular in Italy in the Ren., when Heb. poetry came under the influence of It. There, It. verse forms and poetic styles were assimilated into Heb.; eventually, quantitative metrics was exchanged for purely syllabic schemes akin to those employed in It.

**B. Poetics.** Secular poetry, which represented a fusion of Ar. form and style with biblical Heb. diction and imagery, was conventional in content and stylized in form. Its modes of expression and choice of themes were generally lyrical and descriptive (love and wine poetry as well as panegyric are well represented genres), and its purpose was to entertain and persuade. Manneristic virtuosity and rhetorical ornamentation were highly prized in secular verse, but, at least among the better poets, the importance attached to conventionality, rhetorical technique, and florid style did not preclude the expression of intense feeling, particularly in poems of a personal and occasional nature.

Piyyut, by contrast, was conceived as an ennobling poetry given over to the communal passion to draw closer to God. Until the 9th c., piyyut tended to be esoteric and elusive; it was suffused with arcane references to Talmudic texts and rabbinic interpretation of scripture and consciously lacking in metaphor and simile. After the 10th c., when liturgical poets of the Mediterranean lands were frequently engaged in the production of the prestigious secular verse, the prosody and style of secular poetry cross-fertilized piyyut. The old type of piyyut continued to be composed alongside newer, more intelligible piyyutim. The poets of Muslim Spain led the way, using many of the forms and genres of the postcl. Iraqi piyyut and creating some new ones of their own (notably the *rĕshut*, a short poetic meditation on the theme of the prose prayer), but they abandoned the eclectic and inventive lang. of early and cl. piyyut for the biblical purism they propagated in secular verse. Similarly, they revamped the austere poetics of the earlier piyyut trad., replacing it with the ornamental and decorative approach of their secular poetry. For most of the High and later Middle Ages, then, piyyut and secular poetry coexisted in "creative dissonance."

### III. Modern

**A. Prosody.** Heb. prosody has not stagnated over the past 200 years. On the contrary, it has passed through stages of quick devel. and has changed to some extent at each of the major centers of Heb. poetry. From the beginning of the Ren., Heb. poetry—centered in Italy after the Jews were expelled from Spain—began to assimilate Eur. poetic styles and conventions. Immanuel of Rome (ca. 1261–1332), a contemporary of Dante, used the It. *sonnet form for lines written in Gr. meters. However, the natural accents of the Heb. lang. made it difficult to assimilate quantitative meter. Apparently, the pronunciation of long and short vowels in Heb. had been forgotten during the Middle Ages. The accepted substitution for the difference in length between parts of the foot, the *t'nua* (vowel) and the *yated* (one long and one short syllable), served Heb. poetry in Italy until the beginning of the 20th c. Hence, for 600 years (until 1900), the accepted meter of the Heb. sonnet was a hendecasyllabic line with a stress on the penultimate syllable (Landau).

The harbinger of mod. Heb. prosody was N. H. Weizel (1725–1805) in his *Shirey Tiferet* (1785–1805 [Songs of Glory]). Weizel sensed the strangeness of the meter used for Heb. poetry in Spain and also the difficulty of assimilating Gr. meter. In his desire to write a Heb. epic in a form similar to the Gr. hexameter, he devised a line of 13 syllables with a strong caesura and penultimate stress. He used couplets separated by unrhymed lines and at times the *envelope rhyme scheme, *abba*.

This system remained in effect until the Hibat Zion period (1881–97), though with variations.

During the Hibat Zion period, meter began losing its independence, and poetics increased its influence on prosody. In addition to the lyrical-didactic fusion that appeared during the Enlightenment, rhythm was introduced in questions and answers as composed by Abraham Ber Gotlover: "Why are you weeping, my People, and why are you crying out?" ("Nes Ziona," in Karton-Blum). This is even more apparent in Judah Leib Gordon: "What are we, you may ask; what is our life? / A People are we, like the Peoples around us?" (*Eder Adonai* [The Flock of God] in Karton-Blum). The dialogue, the quotations, the succession of ideas or feelings came to occupy a strong position and determined the nature of the meter and rhythm. Prosody was set aside and played a decreasing role in poetry, while the rhythm of the contents took its place. The stress on the contents intensified the persona of the artist and highlighted the new positive approach to what is holy to Israel and to the Zionist feelings expressed in the poetry (Karton-Blum).

After Weizel, all the common stanza forms of Eur. lit. appeared in Heb. poetry (Shpan). But today Weizel's meter seems something artificial, for it does not distinguish between naturally accented syllables and those whose accent is weak. The blurring of the tonic differences renders this meter as monotonous as the Heb.-Ar. meter of the Middle Ages. Only during the period of Hayyim Nachman Bialik (1873–1934) was a way found to absorb Gr. meter into Heb. poetry: accented syllables were treated as long, while unaccented syllables (or ones with a secondary accent) were treated as short.

During Bialik's generation, the dominant Ashkenazi vocalization of Heb. affected the poetry. This system stresses the penultimate vowel and pronounces certain vowels and consonants differently from the Sephardic pronunciation. For example, the vowel *o* is pronounced *oy*, and the consonant *th* is pronounced *s*. The tonic meter merged well with Ashkenazi pronunciation. One esp. notes the flexibility of the *amphibrach, well loved by Bialik (Benshalom). Use of the Sephardic pronunciation accepted in Israel today did not become widespread until the following generation (Shavit).

Saul Tchernikhovsky (1875–1943) trans. Gr. epic poetry into Heb. and thereby created the Heb. dactylic hexameter, in which *trochees take the place of *spondees (Shpan). The following generation (Jacob Kahan [1881–1967] and Jacob Fichman [1881–1958]) preserved the traditional rhythms; only Uri Zvi Greenberg (1895–1981) and Abraham Shlonsky (1900–73) completely broke with the earlier framework. Greenberg abandoned regular meter and rhyme to create an extended rhythm, which was the only means, he felt, to create a poem with the pathos necessary to express this generation's pain (Hrushovski). Shlonsky, on the other hand, disregarded meter altogether. After an extended struggle, Greenberg and Shlonsky succeeded in exchanging the Ashkenazi vocalization with the Sephardic pronunciation and began a new era in Heb.

poetics and prosody. Jonathan Ratosh's (1908–61) poems are distinguished by a virtuoso rhythm built on repetition of sounds, words, and sentences that flow at a dizzying, intoxicating tempo. It is interesting that Nathan Alterman (1910–70), who is an extreme modernist with regard to lang., reverted to regular meter, esp. the *anapest, and to regular rhyme (though a certain estrangement is expressed in his use of assonance), but he found few disciples.

In contrast to Alterman, Nathan Zach (b. 1930) gave up all the forms of harmony, even the standard harmony of the stanza (the length of the lines, rhyming, assonance, etc.). Zach even criticized Bialik's rhythms as schematic and boring. Though he dealt at great length with the problems of prosody, it seems that poems whose contents had a dramatic flair affected his changes in prosody. In consequence of this trend, traditional prosody lost most of its effect on Heb. poetry. In contrast, Martin Buber, in his essay "On Culture" (*Pnei Adam*, [The Face of Man]) established the rule of rotation in culture. He maintains that when a culture declines to its low point or becomes most distant from its original sources, a striving toward rising higher develops and a desire to return to its sources. Something like this occurred also to the prosody and poetics of Heb. Apparently in line with this conception, at the height of Shlonsky's rebellion in prosody, there were already in Heb. lit. restrained artists such as Shin Shalom (1905–90) and Leah Goldberg (1911–70) who refrained from utilizing strangeness in their lang.; indeed, they returned to rhyming and meters within their poetic stanzas and even composed sonnets. Sonnets can be found even by the ironic and bitter Yehuda Amichai (1924–2000). Since the 1980s, restrained *modernism has played a dominant role in the prosody of Heb. poetry (rendering it meterless, rhymeless, and structureless).

In an insightful study, Aharon Mirsky revealed that the structure of the Heb. lang. creates a rhythm that can serve as an alternative to punctuation. This characteristic of the Heb. lang. has been exploited by end-of-the-century poets in order to create a mod. rhythm that is both moderate and pleasant to the ear and that relies on daily speech rhythms. This is how Zelda constructed her poems, basing them on the rhythm of speech and on functional rhythm (Bar-Yosef).

**B. Poetics.** The poetics of mod. Heb. has also been dynamic, changing from period to period in accord with its prosody. Moses Hayyim Luzzatto (1707–46) viewed lit. as "the creation of something good and pleasant," thus equating the artist with the aesthete. His conceptions of figurative lang. were derived from cl. rhet. His explanations were based on the Bible, and they concur with the approach that views the arts as decorative. Shlomo Levisohn (1789–1821) regarded the Bible as an example of the poetics of the sublime. The trans. of the Bible into Ger. and the preparation of the "Commentary" during Moses Mendelssohn's period (1729–86) created a poetics that also served the new poetry. Such poetry attempted to educate the Jewish nation and, therefore, had to be expressed in Heb., for it alone was understood by all Jewish people. At first, the poetry was composed in the lang. of the Bible, but this archaic diction reminded one more of ancient landscapes than of the current world. Words integrally linked in a poem proved to mean something else when taken out of context and thus distanced the poem from real life; the rhet. (*melitsa*) remained meaningless to most of its readers.

It was Bialik who created the synthesis of the lang. of the Bible, the sages, and the Middle Ages; he even created new words. His symbols are rich and romantic. His lang. is not built on completely figurative elements taken from ancient sources: his sources are familiar to us, yet they do not stand out in his poetry. Greenberg created symbols, such as "Sinai," "Jerusalem," "Massada," "light," "yearning," and "sublime," which refer to national myths (Kurzweil). Shlonsky rebelled against the poetic conventions of Bialik's period. He opposed usage of biblical similes; he drew his imagery from his current surroundings. He created metaphors and similes open to variable interpretation, such as "breasts of the night" and "night like the altar stone." Yet despite his estrangement from Bialik's style, there are those who speak of "Shlonsky in Bialik's bonds" (Hagorni).

The world wars, the Holocaust, and existentialism stimulated—though relatively late—the appearance of an expressionist poetics in mod. Heb. poetry (see EXPRESSIONISM). In this mode, the sentence, the word, and even sense are broken, incomplete. Following Shlonsky and Greenberg, Amir Gilboa (1917–84) and others use ambiguity for effect: at times a word is linked to what precedes it as well as what follows, as, e.g., "Also in the city on sidewalks you will run from them." The expression "you will run" (a single word in Heb.) is linked to "sidewalks" as well as "from them" (Barzel). For the same reasons noted above, *bathos is dominant in recent Heb. poetry, as in the poetry of Yehuda Amichai who writes, "The memory of my father is wrapped in white paper / Like slices of bread for the working day."

The poetry of the Holocaust, its symbols and metaphors, returned to Heb. poetry its exaltedness and pathos, esp. with regard to death, and thus Itamar Yaoz-Kest wrote in his Bergen-Belsen poems: "It seems that we were thrown into a fiery flame / Yet meanwhile we reflected on life and death" (in Österreich). Avner Treinin used allusions even to the stories of Joseph in his poem "The Striped Coat of the Man in the Camp": "And his brothers did not envy him / his striped coat / in which they, too, were dressed / when lowered from the [railroad] lines." The atmosphere in this poem is melancholy and elegiac, with no sarcastic attitude toward the terrors of the Holocaust.

Toward the close of the 20th c., the canon of Heb. poetry accepted even poems with a religious undertone such as those by Yosef Zvi Rimon, Aharon Mirsky, Zelda, Yaoz-Kest, and others. It seems that Heb. poetry continues to stream in two channels. On the one hand, we find leftist poetry with what remains of mod. rebellious poetics and prosody accompanied by a distancing from the lang. and culture of national sources. On the other hand, we find the minor conservative channel of poetics with restrained modernism that preserves the traditional character. The poets Yaoz-Kest, Mirsky, Zelda, Tuvia Ribner, Dan Pagis, Shlomo Zamir, Shalom Ratzabi, and others stand out in this trend.

*See* CLASSICAL POETICS, HEBRAISM, HEBREW POETRY, YIDDISH POETRY.

■ **Biblical:** R. Lowth, Lecture 19, *De sacra poesi Hebraeorum*, trans. G. Gregory (1753), "Preliminary Diss.," *Isaiah* (1778); E. Sievers, *Metrische Studien* (1901–7); G. B. Gray, *The Forms of Hebrew Poetry* (1915, rpt. 1972 with essential "Prolegomenon" [with bibl.] by D. N. Freedman); T. H. Robinson, "Basic Principles of Hebrew Poetic Form," *Festschrift Alfred Bertholet*, ed. W. Baumgartner et al. (1950); P. B. Yoder, "Biblical Hebrew [Versification]," in Wimsatt; B. Hrushovski (in bibl. to sect. II below); F. M. Cross, *Canaanite Myth and Hebrew Epic* (1973); F. M. Cross and D. N. Freedman, *Studies in Ancient Yahwistic Poetry* (1975); D. Stuart, *Studies in Early Hebrew Meter* (1976); S. Geller, *Parallelism in Early Biblical Poetry* (1979), pt. 1 and app. B; D. N. Freedman, *Pottery, Poetry, and Prophecy* (1980); M. O'Connor, *Hebrew Verse Structure* (1980); J. Kugel, *The Idea of Biblical Poetry* (1981), incl. survey of theories in sect. 7.2; W. Watson, *Cl. Heb. Poetry* (1984); R. Alter, *The Art of Biblical Poetry* (1985); A. Berlin, *The Dynamics of Biblical Parallelism* (1985); *The Hebrew Bible in Literary Criticism*, ed. A. Preminger and E. Greenstein (1986); M. Sternberg, *The Poetry of Biblical Narrative* (1985); H. Fisch, *Poetry with a Purpose* (1988); L. Schoekel, *A Manual of Hebrew Poetics* (1988); W. Watson, *Traditional Techniques in Classical Hebrew Verse* (1994); J. P. Fokkelman, *Major Poems of the Hebrew Bible*, 3 vols. (1998–2003); *Poetry of the Hebrew Bible*, ed. D. Orton (2000); D. Vance, *The Question of Meter in Biblical Hebrew Poetry* (2001).

■ **Medieval:** B. Hrushovski, "Ha-shitot ha-ra'shiyot shel heharuz ha-'ivri min ha-piyyut' ad yameinu," *Hasifrut* 2 (1970–71); and "Prosody, Heb.," *Encyclopaedia Judaica* 13 (1971–72), 1203–24; E. Fleischer, *Shirat ha-qodesh ha-'ivrit bi-ymei ha-beinayim* (Hebrew. Liturgical Poetry in the Middle Ages), (1975); D. Pagis, *Ḥiddush u-masoret be-shirat ha-ḥol ha-'ivrit bi-ymei ha-beinayim* (Change and Tradition in Secular Poetry: Spain and Italy), (1976); R. Brann, *The Compunctious Poet* (1990); Joseph Tobi, *Proximity and Distance* (2004).

■ **Modern:** B. Z. Benshalom, *Mishkalav shel Bialik* (Bialik's meters, 1942); B. Kurzweil, *Sifrutenu Hahadasha Hemshekh o Mahapekha* (Our new literature—Continuation or revolution, 1959); S. Shpan, *Masot Umehkarim* (Essays and Studies, 1964); M. M. Buber, *Pnei Adam* (The Face of Man, 1965); N. Zakh, *Zeman Veritmus Etzel Bergson Uvashira Hamodernit* (Time and Rhythm in Modern Poetry, 1966); R. Karton-Blum, *Ha- Shirah ha-'ivrit bi-tekufat Hibat Tsiyon* (Hebrew Poetry during the Hibat Zion period, 1969); D. Landau, *Hayesodot Haritmiyim shel Hashira* (The Rhythmic

Elements of Poetry, 1970); and "Hitpathut Hason-neta Basifrut Haivrit" (Development of the Sonnet in Hebrew Literature), diss., Univ. Bar-Ilan, Israel (1972); B. Hrushovski, *Ritmus Harakhavut* (The Rhythm of Extensity, 1978); U. Shavit, *Hamahapekha Haritmit* (The Rhythmic Revolution, 1983); H. Barzel, *Amir Gilbo'a* (1984); A. Hagorni, *Shlonski Be'avotot Byalik* (Shlonsky in Bialik's bonds, 1985); R. Tsur, *On Met-aphoring* (1987); Ch. Bar-Yosef, *Al Shirat Zelda* (On the poetry of Zelda, 1988); D. Landau, *Iduna shel Sheaga* (The Refinements of Roars, 1990)—on lyric poetry; R. Tsur, *Toward a Theory of Cognitive Poetics* (1992), and *Rhythm, Structure and Performance* (1998); A. Mir-sky, *Signon Ivri* (Heb. style, 1999).

S. A. GELLER (BIBLICAL); R. BRANN (MEDIEVAL); D. LANDAU (MODERN)

**HELLENISM.** *See* CLASSICISM; GREEK POETRY; HEBRAISM.

**HELLENISTIC POETICS.** *See* ALEXANDRIANISM; CLASSICAL POETICS.

**HELLENISTIC POETRY.** *See* ALEXANDRIANISM; GREEK POETRY.

**HEMIEPES** (Gr., "half-hexameter"). In cl. Gr. poetry, the metrical sequence $- \cup \cup - \cup \cup -$, which corresponds to the first half of a dactylic *hexameter, before the penthemimeral *caesura. This sequence took on a life of its own; it occurs alone and in various combinations with other cola in Gr. lyric verse. West suggests that, al-though it is conventional to think of the hexameter as six dactylic feet, in fact, it might better be thought of as two cola, hemiepes plus a *paroemiac, spliced together at the caesura with one long or two short syllables.
■ Wilamowitz; West; J. L. López Cruces, "Sobre la co-lometría de PMG 836 a (Philoxenus Leucadius) y SH 737 (Stratonicus Atheniensis)," *Florentia Iliberritana* 2 (1991); C. O. Pavese, "A tavoletta KN V(1) 114 + 158 + 7719 e l'origine dell'esametro dattilico," *Atti e memorie del secondo congresso internazionale di micenologia*, ed. E. De Miro et al. (1996).

R. J. GETTY; T.V.F. BROGAN

**HEMISTICH** (Gr., "half line"). A half line of verse; the two hemistichs are divided by the *caesura. In Gr., it usually forms an independent *colon. The device is used in Gr. and subsequent drama whenever characters exchange half lines of dialogue rapidly, giving the ef-fect of sharp argument; in Gr., such a series is called *hemistichomythia* (see STICHOMYTHIA, SPLIT LINES). In other types of poetry, an isolated hemistich may give the effect of great emotional or physical disturbance, e.g., Virgil's isolated half lines in the *Aeneid* (1.534, 2.233), whence Shakespeare may have learned the de-vice, but John Dryden eschews isolated hemistichs as "the imperfect products of a hasty Muse" (dedication to the *Aeneid*).

In Old Germanic poetry—i.e., in OE, OHG, and ON—the hemistich is the primary structural unit of the meter (see ENGLISH PROSODY, GERMANIC PROSODY, NORSE POETRY). The first hemistich is technically called the a-verse (or on-verse), the second hemistich the b-verse (or off-verse). In the definitive typology of OE meter, Sievers showed that all the hemistichs in *Beowulf* could be reduced to orderly variations of only five types (A-E). Further, although each half line in *Beowulf* generally contains metrical patterns that could occur in the other half (disregarding *alliteration), hemistichs are by no means metrically interchange-able. A few hemistichs are exclusively first half-line types (e.g., type A with a light first lift and the ex-panded type D), and studies have shown that certain combinations of first and second half lines, while not prohibited, are avoided (e.g., two type As or two type Bs); consequently, the structure of the long line is far from being a random mixture of self-contained hemis-tichs. All this seems to imply that the poet put together hemistichs according to some definite principles as yet undiscovered. Recent studies have also shown the ME alliterative line to have a clearer hemistichic struc-ture than was assumed by most 19th- and 20th-c. scholars.
■ Sievers; J. L. Hancock, *Studies in Stichomythia* (1917); A. J. Bliss, *The Metre of "Beowulf,"* 2d ed. (1967); T. Cable, "Middle English Meter and Its Theoretical Implications," *YLS* 2 (1988).

T.V.F. BROGAN; R. A. HORNSBY; T. CABLE

**HENDECASYLLABLE.** A line of 11 syllables, the hen-decasyllable is significant in both the quantitative verse of Gr. and Lat. and in the accentual and syllabic proso-dies of the mod. Romance langs., though as different meters. In *classical prosody, the hendecasyllable is the *phalaecean, which has the pattern $\cup \cup$ (or $\cup -$; $- \cup$; $- -$) $- \cup \cup - \cup - \cup - \cup$ and is chiefly associated with Catullus. But in the Middle Ages, as the quantitative or "metrical" Lat. verse was transformed into the accentu-ally based "rhythmic" verse of the vernaculars, the It. *endecasillabo* seems to have evolved from the cl. *sap-phic or iambic *trimeter; its relation to the Fr. *déca-syllabe* in the earliest stages is disputed. In *De vulgari eloquentia* (*On Vernacular Eloquence*, 2.5, 2.12; ca. 1304), Dante defined the hendecasyllable as the most noble line of *Italian prosody, the one most suitable for the highest forms of poetic expression in the vernacular and, as such, the preferred line for the *canzone, the most illustrious of *lyric forms; the hendecasyllable has been the staple line of It. poetry since the 13th c. The names of the line forms in It. prosody are established by the place of the principal accent; thus, the normal hendecasyllable has 11 syllables, with a fixed stress fall-ing on the tenth (the *endecasillabo piano*); normally in this form of the meter, the final word in the line is paroxytonic. Occasionally, lines of ten syllables occur; these are the analogues of the Romance *decasyllables and, in their unrhymed form and more distantly, the Eng. *iambic pentameter. Lines of 12 syllables also occur, the final word then being proparoxytonic. In ad-dition to the major stress on the tenth syllable, the It. hendecasyllable is divided by a variable *caesura into two *hemistiches of unequal length, one a *settenario* and the other a *quinario*—with a corresponding secondary stress on either the sixth syllable (*endecasillabo a maiore*: "nel mezzo del cammín / di nostra vita") or the fourth (*endecasillabo a minore*: "mi ritrovái /; per una selva oscùra"). In the former, the settenario comprises the first hemistich, followed by the quinario, and vice versa in the latter. Given the large number of dispositions of the secondary stresses in the line, the hendecasyllable is the most versatile meter in It. prosody, being used in virtually every genre (canzone, *ballata*, *sonnet*, *terza rima*, *ottava rima*, *madrigal*, and others) and for all subjects by most It. poets. A distinctive feature of many It. stanza forms is "the harmony of eleven and seven" (Ker), a mixing of hendecasyllables and *heptasyllables* that carried over into Sp. prosody as well.

The Marqués de Santillana adapted the hendecasyllable to the Sp. sonnet form in 1444, and in general, the devel. of the hendecasyllable in Spain followed the same pattern as that in Italy. Heinrich Heine and J. W. Goethe imitated the It. hendecasyllable in Germany. In England, the iambic pentameter was influenced in its early stages (i.e., in both Chaucer and Thomas Wyatt) by the It. endecasillabo, but 11-syllable lines in Eng. are usually simply pentameters with an (extrametrical) feminine ending (see MASCULINE AND FEMININE): true hendecasyllables in Eng. after the Ren. are usually trans. or imitations of Catullus.

See CLASSICAL METERS IN MODERN LANGUAGES, VERSI SCIOLTI, VERSO PIANO, VERSO SDRUCCIOLO, VERSO TRONCO.

■ W. Thomas, *Le Décasyllabe roman et sa fortune en Europe* (1904); F. D'Ovidio, *Versificazione italiana e arte poetica medievale* (1910); W. P. Ker, "De superbia carminum," *Form and Style in Poetry* (1928); M. Serretta, *Endecasillabi crescenti* (1938); A. Monteverdi, "I primi endecasillabi italiani," *Studi romanzi* 28 (1939); V. Pernicone, "Storia e svolgimento della metrica," *Tecnica e teoria letteraria*, ed. M. Fubini, 2d ed. (1951); M. Burger, *Recherches sur la structure et l'origine des vers romans* (1957); D. S. Avalle, *Preistoria dell'endecasillabo* (1963); G. E. Sansone, "Per un'analisi strutturale dell'endecasillabo," *Lingua e Stile* 2 (1967); A. D. Scaglione, "Periodic Syntax and Flexible Meter in the *Divina Commedia*," *RPh* 21 (1967); I. Baldelli, "Endecasillabo," *Enciclopedia Dantesca*, ed. U. Bosco, v. 2 (1970); P. Boyde, "The Hendecasyllable," *Dante's Style in his Lyric Poetry* (1971); A. B. Giamatti, "Italian," in Wimsatt; F. Caliri, *Tecnica e poesia* (1974); Spongano; Wilkins; P. G. Beltrami, *Metrica, poetica, metrica dantesca* (1981); Elwert, *Italienische*; A. Menichetti, *Metrica italiana* (1993); S. Orlando, *Manuale di metrica italiana* (1994).

T.V.F. BROGAN; R. A. SWANSON; C. KLEINHENZ

**HENDIADYS** (Gr., "one through two"). The use of two substantives (occasionally two adjectives or two verbs), joined by a conjunction, to express a single but complex idea: one of the elements is logically subordinate to the other, as in "sound and fury" (*Macbeth* 5.5.27) for "furious sound." The figure appears in the Bible and in Gr. verse and prose but is not referred

to before Servius (4th c. CE), who notes it in Virgil (e.g., *pateris libamus et auro*: we pour our libations from cups and gold = from golden cups—*Georgics* 2.192). In Gr., according to Sansone, hendiadys typically shows a "reciprocal" (21) relation between its two elements, "*either of which* could be logically and grammatically subordinated to the other" (19): thus *pros haima kai stalagmon* (A. *Eumenides* 247) may mean both "the dripping of the blood" and "the dripping blood" (20).

Virgil's hendiadys sometimes involves two distinct ideas (Hahn)—from cups and from gold—as well as a third that fuses them. The sum is elusive and complex. Shakespeare, mining the figure's mysterious and antilogical overtones, uses hendiadys far more than any other Eng. writer, often in conjunction with other kinds of doublets, to cast doubt on the authenticity of linguistic and social unions (couplings, contracts, marriages) and to provide a linguistic mirror for the internal agitation and ambivalence of troubled characters and plays. See esp. *Hamlet* (Wright, Kermode). Vickers, citing Kerl and Empson, disputes this view. Housman parodies Gr. hendiadys in "I go into the house with *heels and speed*"(emphasis added).

■ A. E. Housman, "Fragment of a Greek Tragedy," *Bromsgrovian* (1893), rpt. in *Parodies*, ed. D. Macdonald (1960); H. Poutsma, "Hendiadys in English . . . ," *Neophilologus* 2, no. 1 (1917); E. A. Hahn, "Hendiadys: Is There Such a Thing?" *CW* 15 (1921–22); E. Kerl, "Das Hendiadyoin bei Shakespeare," diss., U. of Marburg (1922); Empson; G. T. Wright, "Hendiadys and *Hamlet*," *PMLA* 96 (1981); K. T. Loesch and G. T. Wright, "Forum: Hendiadys," *PMLA* 97 (1982); D. Sansone, "On Hendiadys in Greek," *Glotta* 62 (1984); F. Kermode, "Cornelius and Voltimand," *Forms of Attention* (1985), and *Shakespeare's Language* (2000); B. Vickers, *"Counterfeiting" Shakespeare* (2002).

G. T. WRIGHT

**HEPTAMETER.** This term means a line of seven feet, but metrists have at times termed *heptameters* meters that have little resemblance to each other beyond syllable count, so the term is perhaps better avoided. It is occasionally used to refer to cl. meters such as the Lat. *septenarius*, which is a brachycatalectic line of seven *trochaic* feet, and it has been used by some prosodists for mod. meters such as the Ren. *fourteener*, as in George Chapman's trans. of Homer, but this is not the same type of meter, has a different rhythm, and is used in radically different contexts. Still less is it an appropriate term for Eng. *ballad meter, which in its most common form is set in *quatrains of lines of 4-3-4-3 *accentual verse. Schipper uses this term more or less synonymously with *septenary* for ME poems in 14–15 syllables such as the *Poema morale* and *Ormulum*, but here too terminology implies a derivation and structure that now seem problematic. In mod. Eng. verse, the term is applicable mainly to the long line of William Blake's later prophetic books, a line that Blake said "avoided a monotonous cadence like that of Milton and Shakespeare" by achieving "a variety in every line, both in cadence and number of syllables." Syllable count actually ranges as high as 21. Blake's sources would seem to be the Bible (see VERSET), James Macpherson, and late 18th-c. Ger. experiments in long-lined verse such as those in Friedrich Hölderlin's *Hyperion*, but Blake himself claimed that the form was given him in automatic writing. Other 19th-c. instances are William Wordsworth's "The Norman Boy" and "The Poet's Dream" (coupleted quatrains); Lord Byron's "Stanzas for Music"; Walter Scott's "The Noble Moringer"; Elizabeth Barrett Browning's "Cowper's Grave"; and J. G. Whittier's "Massachusetts to Virginia."

■ Schipper; A. Ostriker, *Vision and Verse in William Blake* (1965); K. Raine, "A Note on Blake's 'Unfettered Verse,'" *William Blake: Essays for S. Foster Damon*, ed. A. H. Rosenfeld (1969).

T.V.F. BROGAN

**HEPTASYLLABLE.** In most metrical systems, lines of seven syllables are almost always variants of *octosyllables, not an autonomous meter. In Eng., such lines appear most prominently in the verse form known as "8s and 7s," as in John Milton's "L'Allegro" and "Il Penseroso." In Fr., they are one form of *vers impair*, though the heptasyllables in Pierre de Ronsard's *odes are a deliberate imitation of Pindar, whose odes were printed in short lines in the 16th c. Only in *Italian prosody is the heptasyllable or *settenari* a major line form, being used in alternation with the *hendecasyllable, the *endecasillabo*. This mixing of lines of 7 and 11 syllables in stanzas is distinctive to It. prosody and very much exploited by poets. In the Welsh *englynion*, they were perhaps the original line length, later to be combined with 10s and 6s (see ENGLYN). Seven syllable lines are also prominent in Vietnamese poetry. Some 20th-c. Eng. poets such as Thom Gunn developed a basically syllabic heptasyllable line as kind of transitional form between meter and *free verse.

■ M. F. Moloney, "The Prosody of Milton's 'Epitaph,' 'L'Allegro,' and 'Il Penseroso'," *MLN* 72 (1957); R. Nelli, "Remarques sur le vers heptasyllabique français et occitan," *Mélanges offerts à; Rita Lejeune*, vol. 1 (1968); B. Vine, "On the Heptasyllabic Verses of the *Rig-Veda*," *ZVS* 91 (1977); Elwert, *Italienische*.

T.V.F. BROGAN; P. WHITE

## HERMENEUTICS

 I. Definition and Etymology
 II. Ancient and Medieval
 III. Modern
 IV. Contemporary
 V. Future Tasks

**I. Definition and Etymology.** Hermeneutics is sometimes understood as an art practiced by every human being engaging in social interactions, sometimes as a discipline of the humanities that builds on that art and elaborates explicit rules, sometimes as that discipline's philosophical justification. Hermeneutics deals not with unformed natural objects but with products

of rational agents to which a meaning can be ascribed (*interpretanda*). Its basic operation is not explanation, as in the natural sciences, but understanding. A causal explanation of the genesis of the interpretandum is thereby not excluded, but it differs from the explanation of natural events (see Wright, Apel 1984). The products to be understood are not limited to texts: Hermann Kretzschmer published on musical and Carl Robert on archaeological hermeneutics. Also mute actions, perhaps even dreams and lapses, can be understood insofar as they express, according to Sigmund Freud, unconscious intentions. But since hermeneutics in its higher forms is itself a ling. activity, the understanding of products in the form of spoken or written lang. is its most congenial task. *Interpretation is itself a product of rational agents; thus, it can itself become the object of an interpretation. Since interpretation occurs in a lang., it presupposes antecedent, often unconscious hermeneutic acts that led to the interpreter's mastery of his own lang. On the other hand, the failure of our normal hermeneutic acts facing a novel interpretandum leads to the genesis of hermeneutics as theory. Thus, hermeneutics deals mainly with difficult interpretanda, either in a different or outdated lang. or in the same lang., but with various layers of meaning, such as in poetry. Poetry has, therefore, always been a privileged object of hermeneutics. Traditionally, hermeneutics has often focused on texts with authoritative claims, either religious or legal, whose interpretation was crucial for a culture. The desire to adjust the authoritative texts to the needs of the present often led to transcending what was intended by the text. The understanding of an interpretandum, however, has to be distinguished both from the constitution of its physical basis and the evaluation of its meaning, e.g., according to its truth or its aesthetic value. In the case of texts, the first task is fulfilled by *textual criticism. Even if the three tasks are conceptually different (understanding a text presupposes its establishment, and its evaluation presupposes its appropriate interpretation), in real life they are connected: textual crit. is not simply a mechanical work but has to look at the meaning of the words in order to constitute the most likely text; and often only the recognition of the truth of an assertion can convince us that we have really understood its meaning.

Etymologically, the term *hermeneutics* goes back to the Gr. *hermēneutikē téchnē*. There is a family of related terms, such as the verb *hermēneúein* (translate, interpret, explain, express, describe) and the nouns *hermēneuma*, *hermēneía*, and *hermēneús*. The last one is the oldest word (but not found earlier than in the 5th c. BCE) and has the original meaning "interpreter" (later also "agent," "broker"), coined with reference to the god Hermes, a mediator between gods and humans. In Plato's *Statesman*, a hermeneutic art is mentioned in connection with the mantic art (260d, cf. 290c); it is probably the art of interpreting divine signs, for, within a religious view, what are for us purely natural events can be interpreted since they appear as manifestations of the gods. In the (probably spurious) *Epinomis*, the hermeneutic and the mantic arts are criticized for knowing only what has been said but being unable to determine whether it is true (975c). In Gr., *hermēneía* signifies also the capacity for communication (Xenophon, *Memorabilia* 4.3.12), stylistic expression or gift of style (so in the title of the rhetorical work ascribed to Demetrius or in Dionysius of Halicarnassus's *Pros Gnaion Pompēion epistolē* [Letter to Pompey, 1.2]), or enunciation: so in the (probably later) title of Aristotle's work, translated as *De interpretatione* (On Interpretation) by Boethius, although it is hardly a hermeneutic work in the sense defined above. For poetics, Demetrius's work is the most important treatise of antiquity using the term *hermēneía*.

**II. Ancient and Medieval.** Even if the ancients do not have a discipline called *hermeneutics* corresponding to the mod. one, we find scattered hermeneutic reflections in their philosophical, poetological, rhetorical, mythographic, theological, juridical, and mantic lit. (Of the latter, oneiromantic works, dealing with dreams, may overlap with mod. hermeneutic interests.) Plato criticizes poets and rhapsodes for not really understanding what they say, since they are inspired by the gods (*Apology* 22a ff., *Ion* 533d ff.). In the *Ion*, terms related to *hermēneús* are used five times (534e f.); the rhapsodes are called interpreters of the interpreters, since the poets are interpreters of the gods (see also 530c). At the same time, Plato's Socrates hardly believes that his grammatically impossible interpretation of *hekōn* in Simonides' poem in accordance with Socrates' own ethical theory (*Protagoras* 345d ff.) captures the poet's *intention. He wants to show that the philosophical quest is independent of the interpretation of traditional authoritative texts: philosophy should be the standard of interpretation, rather than the other way around. In fact, Plato's Socrates mocks persons who hide behind the interpretations of poets and exhorts them to expose their own ideas, since it is not possible to find out what absent people believe (*Hippias minor* 365c f., *Protagoras* 347e). This is linked to Plato's privileging oral conversation ahead of all forms of written communication (*Phaedrus* 274b ff.), for only in conversation can the author react to crits. and expose what he really intends. Although this renders it likely that, as the Tübingen school, which focused on Plato's esoteric doctrines, teaches, Plato did not entrust all his philosophical beliefs to writing, the choice of the literary dialogue must have been motivated by the desire to imitate that form of intellectual exchange where the most thorough interpretation of the interlocutor's ideas is possible. At the same time, the anonymity of Plato's dialogues (not shared by Aristotle's and many of Cicero's dialogues, where the author is one of the interlocutors) makes it difficult to discern which position Plato himself supports. The differentiation between dialogical works and works in the first person (*autoprósōpa*) is ancient (Ammonius, *Eis tas tou Aristotelous Katēgorias hypomnēma* [Commentary on Aristotle's Categories]); no less is the distinction between the author's position and that of the interlocutors in his dialogues (Aristides Quintilianus, *Peri mousikēs* [On

music]), even if an assertion by an interlocutor may also be on a different level a statement by the author himself (Cicero, *Orator* 13.42). Plato's crit. of poetry is not incompatible with his dialogues being themselves some of the artistically most complex works of antiquity. Plato does not want to eliminate poetry; he aims at a synthesis of *philosophy and poetry. Some of his remarks about poetry apply to his own work and are hints on how to interpret him (e.g., *Symposium* 223d, *Republic* 393c).

Not surprisingly, Plato's dialogues became themselves one of the favorite interpretanda of ancient hermeneutics (also two of the most influential theorists of hermeneutics in the 19th and 20th cs., Friedrich Schleiermacher and Hans-Georg Gadamer, were renowned Plato scholars). Albinus's *Prologos*, the anonymous *Prolegomena tēs Platōnos philosophias* (Prolegomena to Plato's Philosophy, earlier ascribed to Olympiodorus), and many individual commentaries of Platonic dialogues by Neoplatonists deal with the varieties of the dialogue form as well as with the concrete meaning of intricate passages. Sometimes later doctrines are read into them, but Proclus rightly insists on the hermeneutic maxim that the preludes of the Platonic dialogues must be connected with their main topics and deduces this from Plato's own statement in the *Phaedrus* (264c) that speeches are like organisms (*Eis ton Platōnos Parmenidēn* [Commentary on Plato's Parmenides]). Hereby he seems to imply the canon that an author's interpretation has to take into account his own remarks about interpretation.

The other great interpretanda of the ancients were religious texts. The allegorical interpretation of pagan myths began probably with Theagenes of Rhegium in the 6th c. BCE; it was fully elaborated by the Stoics. Lucius Annaeus Cornutus's work is preserved; it offers, based on mostly invalid etymologies, an interpretation of the divinities as natural elements. The Neoplatonic interpretation of the gods connects them to metaphysical strata of reality. Since only the Jewish and Christian religions are based on sacred books, the hermeneutics of the OT and NT are far more complex than the approach to pagan myths. Already the Hellenized Jew Philo of Alexandria offers, influenced by Plato and the Stoics, a philosophical interpretation of the OT, which recognizes a higher spiritual beyond the literal or sensual meaning (see, e.g., *Peri Abraam* [On Abraham] §200) and, thus, frees the Bible from statements either contradictory or morally unworthy of God; particularly extensive is Philo's *Nomōn hierōn allegoria* (Allegorical Interpretation of the Laws). Philo's philosophical approach had little impact on the rabbinic interpretation collected in the Mishnah and the Gemara, although the Talmudical hermeneutics also develops, from Hillel to Eliezer ben Jose, explicit rules to deal, e.g., with contradictions between biblical passages. Philo exerts a strong influence on Clement of Alexandria and Origen, the first systematic Christian theologian, who in *Peri archōn* (*On First Principles*) 4:1–3 articulates an analogous biblical hermeneutics, subordinating the literal to the allegorical sense (the first not always being present; see ALLEGORY), and adding a third, psychic sense between the somatic and the pneumatic. Origen teaches that the literal interpretation may lead to Gnosticism (4:2,1,4) and insists that scripture offers rules for its own interpretation. In opposition to the school of Alexandria, the school of Antioch (Theodore of Mopsuestia) limits the allegorical interpretation. It was Ambrose's defense of an allegorical meaning in the Bible that facilitated Augustine's conversion, since he had been alienated by a literal interpretation of several of its passages (*Confessions* 5.14). The later Augustine not only dedicated several works to biblical *exegesis, but developed a biblical hermeneutics, particularly in the 12th book of the *Confessiones* (*Confessions*) and in *De doctrina christiana* (*On Christian Doctrine*). Its first book deals with the objects of Christian doctrine, its second and third with its signs, mainly with obscurities arising from unknown or ambiguous signs, respectively. At the end of the third book, which warns against interpreting literal expressions figuratively and vice versa, Augustine recommends the seven rules of Tichonius. From Johannes Cassianus onward, Christian biblical hermeneutics has known four senses: the literal, allegorical, tropological (moral), and anagogical (relating to the eschatology). (Also the rabbinical exegesis developed a fourfold approach to the Bible in the Pardes typology.) The second sense is linked to the interpretation of events of the OT as prefiguration of events in the NT, a doctrine present both in the Gospels and in the letters of Paul (Rom. 5:14, 1 Cor. 10:6; cf. Gal. 4:24 on allegorical interpretation). The theory of the fourfold sense determines the whole Middle Ages. Thomas Aquinas insists that the literal meaning, under which he subsumes the parabolic sense, must be the basis of all other senses (*Summa Theologica* 1q.1a.10). But there is also an allegorical sense since things, insofar as they are created by God, may be themselves signs of other things. Aquinas explains the use of metaphors in the Bible partly with human nature, partly with the necessity to address ignorant people (1q.1a.9, q.61a.1ad1, q.67a.4, 1/2q.98a.3ad2). In *De Genesi* (On the Genesis), Nicholas of Cusa extends the latter idea so far as to take seriously the possibility that the chronology of the OT may be completely wrong. But not only the Bible triggered complex hermeneutic efforts; no less impressive was the disagreement of ecclesiastical authorities. The prologue of Peter Abelard's *Sic et non* (Yes and No) discusses various strategies to overcome apparent contradictions: the text may be unreliable; the words may have a different meaning from other authors; the authority may have only quoted someone else without agreeing with him; he may have later revoked his earlier position; what comes across as a general statement may have been intended only with restrictions.

The importance of allegory was not limited to theology. The most original work of med. poetics, Dante's uncompleted *Convivio* (*The Banquet*), offers allegorical interpretations of three of his poems. In the "Letter to Can Grande" (if authentic), Dante defends the polysemous nature of the *Divine Comedy*, connecting its allegorical interpretation with the doctrine of the fourfold sense in scripture. Already in *Vita nuova* (*New Life*), Dante offered, for the first time in Western hist., interpretations of his own lyric in an autobiographical context. A complex doctrine of poetry is not limited to the Eur. Middle Ages but was also developed in the Kashmir school of lit. crit. by Ānandavardhana in the *Dhvanyāloka* (Light on Suggestion, 9th c.) and by his commentator Abhinavagupta in the *Locana* (The Eye, 10th to 11th c.), focusing on the concept of *dhvani* or suggestion: the poetic value consists not in what is explicitly said but in what is only evoked.

**III. Modern.** While med. and large parts of ancient hermeneutics search mainly for the truth in paradigmatic texts, mod. hermeneutics develops methods for approaching the meaning of a text, while abstracting from its truth-claim. The humanities owe to this turn a new rigor; at the same time, the social cost was enormous, since now it was no longer possible to transform the trad. with the sincere belief that one still continued it: fundamentalism and revolutionary break became the alternatives. This turn had various causes, one being the Reformation's interest in the "real meaning" of the Bible against the constructions of the Catholic Church and Scholasticism (Matthias Flacius). Needless to say, Protestant hermeneutics was still oriented toward theological truth, but it had to develop philologically more reliable methods in order to grant its new claims plausibility. But also outside theology, progress in textual crit., new discussions of logic, the reception of Roman law, as well as the study of Aristotle and his commentators, led to the turn. J. C. Dannhauer's *Idea boni interpretis* (Idea of the Good Interpreter) of 1630, one of the first universal hermeneutics, and his *Hermeneutica Sacra* (Sacred Hermeneutics) of 1654 manifest this turn within the Lutheran church. Also important is the Cartesian Johannes Clauberg, who in his *Logica vetus et nova* (Old and New Logic) of 1654 wants to go beyond René Descartes, who had focused on the lonely subject. In Baruch Spinoza's *Tractatus theologico-politicus* (*Theological-political Treatise*), the new hermeneutics is directed against Maimonides who had read into the Bible his own philosophical convictions—now, however, to justify not a new form of religious orthodoxy but a detachment from the trad. According to Baruch Spinoza, nothing guarantees that the biblical texts contain truth, while at the same time it cannot be denied that, e.g., Joshua and probably the author of the text believed that the sun moved around the earth. This sharp distinction of the meaning of a text from its truth leads to the demand for a historical analysis of the single books of the Bible and to the denial of Moses's authorship of the Pentateuch. Giambattista Vico's *Scienza nuova* (*New Science*), which anticipates central tenets of J. G. Herder's philosophy, contains the seminal idea that the worldview of the archaic human (which returned in the Middle Ages) markedly differs from that of the mod. human. To understand the former, we need to translate the poetical statements in which he grasped the world into the rational lang. of modernity.

Thus, Vico finds historical events expressed by *myths. Eighteenth-c. rationalism fostered hermeneutic reflections, which can be found in scattered form in Christian Thomasius and Christian Wolff, in elaborated form in J. M. Chladenius's *Einleitung zur richtigen Auslegung vernünftiger Reden und Schriften* (Introduction to a Correct Interpretation of Rational Speeches and Writings) of 1742 and in G. F. Meier's *Versuch einer allgemeinen Auslegungskunst* (Essay of a General Art of Interpretation) of 1757. (Meier was a pupil of A. G. Baumgarten, who gave a new meaning to the word *aesthetics*, first in his *Meditationes philosophicae de nonnullis ad poema pertinentibus* [Philosophical Meditations on Some Aspects Belonging to Poetry] of 1735.) Both Chladenius and Meier are inspired by G. W. Leibniz, Chladenius particularly by Leibniz's *Monadology* when he speaks of the point of view (*Sehepunckt*) of the interpreter. In *Der Streit der Fakultäten* (*The Conflict of the Faculties*), Immanuel Kant developed hermeneutic rules to deal with the Bible, but neither he nor the Ger. idealists published separate books on hermeneutics. Still, J. G. Fichte, F.W.J. Schelling, and G.W.F. Hegel engage in interpretative activities of great complexity, among which Schelling's attempt to make sense of myths in his *Philosophie der Mythologie* (*Philosophy of Mythology*), posthumously pub. in 1856–57, deserves special mention because it addresses again the theoretical problem of understanding what seems alien to reason, myth. Both Schelling and Hegel have a profound interest in all the arts, particularly in lit., to which early *romanticism opened a new access. Inspired by the general philosophical revolution as well as the enormous growth in historiographic knowledge in the 18th c., around 1800 an explicit interest in hermeneutics arose, mainly among philologists, such as F. A. Wolf (*Darstellung der Altertumswissenschaft* [Exposition of the Science of Antiquity], 1807) and Schelling's pupil Friedrich Ast (*Grundlinien der Grammatik, Hermeneutik und Kritik* [Outlines of Grammar, Hermeneutics, and Criticism], 1808), who discusses the hermeneutic circle. Schleiermacher's *Hermeneutik und Kritik mit besonderer Beziehung auf das Neue Testament* (Hermeneutics and Criticism with Special Reference to the New Testament), pub. posthumously in 1838 but going back to studies begun in 1805, wrongly claims to be the first general hermeneutics. But it is a highly innovative work, partly thanks to the method of concept formation inspired by Ger. idealism. It stands on the ground of the mod. separation of meaning and truth: in theology, the philological and the dogmatic procedure are utterly different, and the interpreter must know which one he or she is following. Thus, Schleiermacher rejects the old doctrine of the fourfold sense and warns against projecting later religious ideas back into the NT. His book subdivides interpretation into grammatical and psychological, dealing with the general lang. and the individual peculiarities of the author, respectively. The psychological interpretation is further subdivided into psychological in the narrower sense and technical interpretation; while the first focuses on the stream of consciousness of the author, the second addresses his

deliberate strategies of structuring his thoughts. Schleiermacher sometimes seems to suggest that the *mens auctoris*, the mental state of the author, is the last criterion for the correctness of an interpretation. At the same time, he speaks of unconscious acts of an author that the interpreter may reconstruct and recognizes the truth of the old saying that an interpreter can understand an author better than the author did himself, namely, by rendering things conscious in us that were unconscious in the author. On a methodological level, Schleiermacher favors both comparison and divination, the former being regarded as the male, the second as the female form of cognition. The 19th c. brings forth further attempts to found the historical and philological sciences, J. G. Droysen's *Grundriss der Historik* (*Outline of the Principles of History*) of 1868 and P. A. Boeckh's *Encyklopädie und Methodologie der philologischen Wissenschaften* (Encyclopedia and Methodology of the Philological Sciences) being the most prominent ones. Confronted with the quick ascent of the natural sciences, both neo-Kantianism (Wilhelm Windelband and later Heinrick Rickert) and Wilhelm Dilthey defend the autonomy of the *Geisteswissenschaften* (called "moral sciences" in contemp. Eng. discourse) in opposition to the natural sciences. Dilthey, himself an expert in the hist. of hermeneutics, tries to found the humanities in a philosophy of life that links understanding to an analysis of experience and expression. His *Einleitung in die Geisteswissenschaften* (*Introduction to the Human Sciences*) of 1883, however, never went beyond the first volume, even if the late Dilthey still published in 1910 the long essay *Der Aufbau der geschichtlichen Welt in den Geisteswissenschaften* (*The Formation of the Historical World in the Human Sciences*). The difficulties of the project have partly to do with Dilthey's growing insight into the paradoxes of *historicism: if everything is historically conditioned and relative, how can the idea of a valid foundation for historical work make any sense?

**IV. Contemporary.** The great trad. of rationalist hermeneutics from the 17th to the 19th c. came to a halt in the 20th c., and the disarray in which the humanities find themselves in the 21st c. is partly a consequence of the lack of a generally shared hermeneutic theory. Probably, the most important single figure responsible for its crisis is Martin Heidegger. Influenced by Dilthey's philosophy of life, Heidegger, in his 1927 work *Sein und Zeit* (*Being and Time*), embeds *Verstehen* (understanding) in *Dasein* (being-there, existence). Existence itself is a process trying to understand itself; thus, understanding is no longer an intellectual operation subject to a cognitive standard. Heidegger rejects the idea that the hermeneutic circle could be avoided; on the contrary, we should enter into it in the right way. The late Heidegger radicalizes the historicism that had come to dominate Ger. culture and offers a vision of intellectual hist. as discontinuous but at the same time leading away from an original contact with Being. His interpretations of pre-Socratic philosophy as well as mod. poets, such as Friedrich Hölderlin and R. M. Rilke, try to capture the hist. of this loss. His discussions of cl. philosophy seek to overcome the trad. of metaphysics by pointing to inner tensions and contradictions in the interpretanda (*Verwindung*)—a method perfected later by Jacques Derrida's deconstruction, which Derrida presented in texts themselves innovative from a literary point of view. Another attack on traditional hermeneutics came from political philosopher Leo Strauss, who pointed to the fact that the fear of persecution can lead authors to disguise their thought in their texts. It was, however, Heidegger's pupil H. G. Gadamer who in 1960 applied in *Wahrheit und Methode* (*Truth and Method*) Heidegger's basic starting point to a theory of the humanities. Gadamer starts his enterprise with an ontology of the artwork, which explains the importance of his book for aesthetics, but gives a bias to his later approach to the humanities in general. For while the illegitimacy of the *intentional fallacy is manifest in dealing with artworks, where the intention of the author cannot be the ultimate standard of interpretation, there may well be other forms of understanding in which this standard is appropriate. Gadamer's narrative of the hist. of hermeneutics is supposed to prove the mere historicity of the mod. objectifying method; he himself wants to return to a hermeneutics that sees the interpretanda primarily as places of possible manifestation of truth, to be discovered in a dialogical process in which the interpretanda are applied to contemp. concerns. His idea of the foreconception of completeness (*Vorgriff der Vollkommenheit*) is somehow analogous to the analytical philosopher Donald Davidson's principle of charity, according to which we have inevitably to presume that the bulk of the statements of an unknown lang. is true if we are to have a chance to learn to understand it. With this idea, both Gadamer and Davidson challenge the starting point of mod. hermeneutics and somehow return, even if on a higher level, to the earlier form that connected understanding to the grasping of truth. But whereas Davidson's argument is a transcendental one, Gadamer rejects any search for the justification of a concrete interpretation: understanding is, as in Heidegger, an event, not in need of criteria or methods. Instead, Gadamer relies on effective hist. (*Wirkungsgeschichte*), even if this means that he deprives himself of the possibility of distinguishing between correct interpretation and historically influential misunderstanding. Gadamer's approach was criticized early on by the It. legal historian Emilio Betti and the Am. E. D. Hirsch and most recently by Hans Krämer. Of particular importance in Germany was the crit. by Apel and Habermas. The latter reproached Gadamer for uncritically supporting trads. and introduced psychoanalysis and critique of ideology as intermediate forms between the natural sciences and the humanities. But the strongest defense of the hermeneutic relevance of psychoanalysis came from the Fr. philosopher Paul Ricoeur in *De l'interprétation. Essai sur Freud* (*Freud and Philosophy: An Essay on Interpretation*) of 1965 with the famous classification of Karl Marx's, Friedrich Nietzsche's, and Sigmund Freud's hermeneutics as one of suspicion. In the later *Le conflit des interprétations* (*The Conflict of Interpretations*), Ricoeur shows an extraordinary capacity of moving between hermeneutics, on the one hand, and *structuralism, psychoanalysis, phenomenology, and religion, on the other hand.

Analytical philosophy has for a long time shunned hermeneutics. When Richard Rorty took his leave from analytical philosophy, which he regarded as hopelessly committed to representationalism, he proposed hermeneutics as an alternative: not, however, as an alternative foundational enterprise but as a form of conversation and edification. But it is important to understand that hermeneutics as such is not committed to antifoundationalism, as we find it, e.g., in Stanley Fish's work: only its post-Heideggerian turn is. After Donald Davidson and Paul Grice, Robert Brandom's complex form of inferentialism, in which the undertaking and attributing of commitments play a decisive role, is an example of how contemp. analytical philosophy has developed a new interest in hermeneutics, while not being willing to relinquish the normative stance.

**V. Future Tasks.** Probably the most important task of a hermeneutics of the future that tries to mediate between the mod. and the contemp. approach is a systematic differentiation between the various functions of understanding. While some forms of understanding are inevitably oriented toward the mens auctoris, other forms are oriented toward the content with which the mens auctoris is struggling; therefore, they can transcend what the author has in mind and point to the unintended consequences of his speech acts. In both cases, however, an interpretation can succeed or fail, and it is hard to see how such a statement is legitimate without a commitment to some form of realism and to some methods that allow us to evaluate whether an approximation to reality has occurred. Since a correct interpretation presupposes familiarity with the topic of the interpretandum and since sometimes such knowledge may be fostered by a misunderstanding of the author's intention, there can occur fruitful misunderstandings that allow a new understanding on a deeper level. Furthermore, every hermeneutic effort has to recognize that expression may be distorted by fear but also by techniques of detachment, such as *irony and the deliberate use of fictionality, by which some truth is hinted at in an indirect way. In this sense, the hermeneutics of the artwork is the discipline's most complex and elusive task.

■ F.W. Farrar, *History of Interpretation* (1886); H. Kretzschmar, "Anregungen zur Förderung musikalischer Hermeneutik," *Jahrbuch der Musikbibliothek Peters* 9 (1902); C. Robert, *Archaeologische Hermeneutik* (1919); J. Wach, *Das Verstehen*, 3 v. (1926–33); B. Smalley, *The Study of the Bible in the Middle Ages* (1941); L. Strauss, *Persecution and the Art of Writing* (1952); M. Heidegger, *Being and Time*, trans. J. Macquarrie and E. Robinson (1962); E. Betti, *Allgemeine Auslegungslehre als Methodik der Geisteswissenschaften* (1967); E. D. Hirsch, *Validity in Interpretation* (1967); P. Ricoeur, *Freud and Philosophy*, trans. D. Savage (1970); K.-O. Apel et al., *Hermeneutik und Ideologiekritik* (1971); J. Habermas, *Knowledge and Human*

*Interests*, trans. J. J. Shapiro (1971); D. Ihde, *Hermeneutic Phenomenology* (1971); G. H. von Wright, *Explanation and Understanding* (1971); H.-E. H. Jaeger "Studien zur Frühgeschichte der Hermeneutik," *Archiv für Begriffsgeschichte* 18 (1974); P. Ricoeur, *The Conflict of Interpretations*, ed. D. Ihde (1974); H.-G. Gadamer, *Truth and Method*, trans. G. Barden and J. Cumming (1975); P. Szondi, *Einführung in die literarische Hermeneutik* (1975); D. C. Hoy, *The Critical Circle* (1978); R. Rorty, *Philosophy and the Mirror of Nature* (1979); H. Brinkmann, *Mittelalterliche Hermeneutik* (1980); J. Derrida, *Margins of Philosophy*, trans. R. Bass (1982); R. J. Bernstein, *Beyond Objectivism and Relativism* (1983); K.-O. Apel, *Understanding and Explanation*, trans. G. Warnke (1984); D. Davidson, *Inquiries into Truth and Interpretation* (1984); J. Caputo, *Radical Hermeneutics* (1987); S. Fish, *Doing What Comes Naturally* (1989); P. Grice, *Studies in the Ways of Words* (1989); G. Bruns, *Hermeneutics, Ancient and Modern* (1992); *Legal Hermeneutics*, ed. G. Leyh (1992); J. E. Malpas, *Donald Davidson and the Mirror of Meaning* (1992); W. Alexander, *Hermeneutica generalis* (1993); J. Weinsheimer, *Eighteenth-century Hermeneutics* (1993); R. Brandom, *Making It Explicit* (1994); J. Grondin, *Introduction to Philosophical Hermeneutics* (1994); G. Scholz, *Ethik und Hermeneutik* (1995); W. Dilthey, *Hermeneutics and the Study of History*, ed. R. A. Makkreel and F. Rodi (1996); P. Redding, *Hegel's Hermeneutics* (1996); V. Hösle, "Philosophy and the Interpretation of the Bible," *Internationale Zeitschrift für Philosophie* 2 (1999); O. R. Scholz, *Verstehen und Rationalität* (1999); *Biblical Hermeneutics*, ed. B. Corley, S. Lemke, G. Lovejoy (2002); *The Cambridge Companion to Gadamer*, ed. R. L. Dostal (2002); *Is There a Single Right Interpretation?* ed. M. Krausz (2002); G. Abel, *Zeichen der Wirklichkeit* (2004); T. M. Seebohm, *Hermeneutics* (2004); V. Hösle, *Der philosophische Dialog* (2006); H. Krämer, *Kritik der Hermeneutik* (2007); A. Spahn, *Hermeneutik zwischen Rationalismus und Traditionalismus* (2009).

V. Hösle

**HERMETICISM.** This trans. of the It. term *ermetismo* (derived from the name of the Egyptian god Thoth, Gr. Hermes Trismegistus, the mythical author of occult texts) is used to refer to the most widely known autochthonous trend in 20th-c. It. poetry and extended by analogy to describe the general tendency of contemp. poetry toward inaccessibility of lang. and multivalence of meaning. The term gained wide critical currency after the publication of Flora's study *La poesia ermetica*, but the "school" had identified its origins in a group of poets gathered around the Florentine literary review *La voce* (1908–13), as well as in the Orphism (*orfismo*) professed by Arturo Onofri and Dino Campana. The *Canti orfici* (1914) of the latter is now regarded as the first full manifestation of the new trend. The main exponents of the school between the two wars were Giuseppe Ungaretti and Eugenio Montale. Its third-wave representatives include Mario Luzi, Sandro Penna, Alfonso Gatto, and Piero Bigongiari.

Salient features of the *ars poetica* of the *ermetici* are a

blind faith in the miraculous virtues of the Word, often considered more as sound than as sense (poignant instances are some of Ungaretti's programmatic poems in *L'Allegria*: "Il porto sepolto" or "Commiato"); a renewed awareness of the polysemous nature of all utterance (see POLYSEMY); a reliance on the subconscious and irrational drives of the psyche; a partiality for mental processes based on intuition rather than logic and, hence, a favoring of oneiric techniques of description (good instances are the first two poems in Salvatore Quasimodo's *Acque e Terre*). The great tool of the hermeticist poetic discourse is the analogue, the art of the *simile, in the Aristotelian sense of the sudden grasp of "similarity in things dissimilar." Arthur Rimbaud and Georg Trakl are figures often mentioned, esp. in relation to Campana's poetic chimaeras; the roots of the hermetic movement have also been traced to E. A. Poe and Novalis. The parallels with Fr. *symbolism, esp. Stéphane Mallarmé and Paul Valéry, are evident.

In contemp. It. literary historiography, a sociological-political interpretation of hermeticism has taken hold. The only "form of rebellion" (Tedesco) available to the poet in totalitarian times is an "evasion into the self," a solipsistic *clausura*, "an island of salvation" (Bo). The historicist interpretation has even been extended to the positing of a secret code, allegedly worked into hermetic texts by secretly antifascist authors. Similar trends exist in countries with widely differing sociopolitical situations (e.g., Ezra Pound, T. S. Eliot, H.D. and Wallace Stevens in Eng.; Federico García Lorca and Juan Ramón Jiménez in Sp.; Paul Éluard in Fr.; Osip Mandelstam in Rus.). Hermeticism was part of a cyclical recurrence of *trobar clus*, a concept of poetry as magic and hypnosis, keyless mystery, Orphic descent into the dark nether regions of the soul.

*See* OBSCURITY.

■ A. Onofri, *Il nuovo Rinascimento e l'arte dell'Io* (1925); F. Flora, *La poesia ermetica* (1936); M. Apollonio, *Ermetismo* (1945); F. Giannessi, *Gli ermetici* (1951); M. Petrucciani, *La poetica dell'ermetismo italiano* (1955); O. Ragusa, "French Symbolism in Italy," *RR* 46 (1955); V. Orsini, *Ermetismo* (1956); S. Ramat, *L'ermetismo* (1969); C. Bo, "Due testimonianze di letteratura contemporanea," *Letteratura Italiana* 24 (1970); N. Tedesco, *La condizione crepuscolare* (1970); L. Anceschi, *Le poetiche del Novecento in Italia* (1973); M. P. Predmore, *La poesía hermética de Juan Ramón Jiménez* (1973); M. Strazzeri, *Profilo ideologico dell'ermetismo italiano* (1977); D. Valli, *Storia degli ermetici* (1978); *La critica e gli ermetici*, ed. M. Fioravanti (1978); F. Di Carlo, *Letteratura e ideologia dell'ermetismo* (1981); L. Woodman, *Stanza My Stone: Wallace Stevens and the Hermetic Tradition* (1983); J. Cary, *Three Modern Italian Poets: Saba, Ungaretti, Montale*, 2d ed. (1993); A. Dolfi, *Terza generazione* (1997).

T. WLASSICS; E. LIVORNI

**HEROIC COUPLET.** A rhyming pair of Eng. heroic (that is, *iambic *pentameter) lines, most often used for *epigrams, verse essays, *satires, and narrative verse and the dominant form for Eng. poetry from ca. 1640 to ca. 1790. The Eng. created the heroic couplet in the

16th c. by imposing a regular iambic stress pattern and a regular *caesura (falling normally after the fourth, fifth, or sixth syllable) on the old Chaucerian decasyllabic line (see DECASYLLABLE) and by imposing on the Chaucerian couplet (called "riding rhyme" by George Puttenham and George Gascoigne) a regular hierarchy of pauses—respectively, caesural, first-line, and end-of-couplet—adapted from the Lat. *elegiac distich. This form, in which the end of the couplet regularly coincides with the end of a sentence, would later be called "closed," as opposed to the "open" type, in which there is no such coincidence of line and syntax.

The transformation of the Chaucerian line into what Puttenham and John Dryden called the "heroic" line was evolutionary, spanning the 16th c. from ca. 1520 to 1600 (Thompson). But the imposition of the hierarchy of pauses on the loose couplet inherited from Chaucer was more dramatic, taking place almost explosively between 1590 and 1600, when numbers of Eng. poets translated and adapted Lat. poems in elegiac distichs—chiefly the *Amores* and *Heroides* of Ovid and the *Epigrammaton* of Martial—achieving or approximating a correspondence of couplet to distich. Christopher Marlowe's trans. of the *Amores* accomplishes a virtually unexceptionable equivalence:

> sive es docta, places raras dotata per artes;
> sive rudis, placita es simplicitate tua.
> est, quae Callimachi prae nostris rustica dicat
> carmina—cui placeo, protinus ipsa placet.
> est etiam, quae me vatem et mea carmina culpet—
> culpantis cupiam sustinuisse femur.
> molliter incedit—motu capit; altera dur est—
> at poterit tacto mollior esse viro.
>
> (If she be learn'd, then for her skill I crave her,
> If not, because shees simple I would have her.
> Before *Callimachus* one preferres me farre,
> Seeing she likes my bookes why should we jarre?
> An other railes at me and that I write
> Yet would I lie with her if that I might.
> Trips she, it likes me well, plods she, what then?
> Shee would be nimbler, lying with a man.)

Other poets significant for the devel. of the form were Nicholas Grimald (who preceded the wave), John Harington, John Marston, Thomas Heywood, Joseph Hall, Michael Drayton, Ben Jonson, and John Donne.

The immediate result of this structural imitation was the affixing onto Eng. couplets of the Lat. distich's hierarchy of pauses and of a correspondingly balanced rhet. Note the balances above between the sharply demarcated lines of single couplets—"If . . . / If not . . ."—and the sharply divided halves of single lines—"If . . . then"; "Trips . . . plods." Eng. rhyme, which had the same closural power as the recurrent half-line pattern in the *pentameter of the Lat. distich, allowed the Eng. measure, once it outgrew its dependence on the Lat. model, to become much more flexible and thus absorb the modifications by which successive Eng. poets from Donne to George Crabbe transformed it into a medium of great expressive power.

At the same time, the heroic couplet also underwent a second major devel., beginning with Marlowe's *Hero and Leander* (1593) and extending until about 1660, in which the formal elements, the rhyme, and all the pauses were subsumed and all but concealed. This process, which Marlowe himself practiced cautiously, was carried further by George Chapman in his trans. of the *Odyssey* (1614) and in William Chamberlayne's long romance *Pharonnida* (1659). This "romance" or "open" couplet pointedly rejected the emphasis and definition established by the closed couplet; here, rhyme and syntax do not parallel and reinforce each other, and the formal elements work against sense, creating mystery and remoteness instead of clarity and precision. But the romance couplet vanished from Eng. poetry before the Restoration, to be revived—briefly, and appropriately—by such romantic poets as John Keats (*Endymion*), Leigh Hunt (*The Story of Rimini*), and Thomas Moore (*Lalla Rookh*).

Meanwhile, the closed couplet was refined and extended in the 17th c. by such poets as Francis Beaumont and George Sandys, then Edmund Waller, John Denham, and Abraham Cowley, and thus handed on to Dryden (practicing 1660–1700) and Alexander Pope (practicing ca. 1700–45). The heroic couplet as all these poets understood it is both described and exemplified in the famous lines from "Cooper's Hill" (1642) that Denham addressed to the Thames:

> O could I flow like thee, and make thy stream
> My great example, as it is my theme!
> Though deep, yet clear, though gentle, yet not
>     dull,
> Strong without rage, without ore-flowing full.

As this widely known and widely imitated little passage illustrates, the closed couplet provides continuous support in its half line, line, and couplet spans for certain rhetorical devices and corresponding intellectual procedures, particularly *parallelism ("deep . . . gentle . . . / Strong . . . full"), with which poets enforced systems of induction, and *antithesis ("gentle . . . not dull"), with which they determined comparisons and refined analyses. They often intensified such patterns with the elliptical figures *zeugma and *syllepsis ("O could I flow like thee, and [could I] make thy stream") and with inversion ("Strong without rage, without ore-flowing full"). The argumentative and persuasive implications of such practices were esp. pertinent to an age empirical in intellectual tendency and social in cultural orientation.

Dryden chiefly developed the oratorical possibilities of the heroic couplet, addressing large, potentially turbulent groups: in theatrical prologues, men and women, or fops and gentlemen; in satires, Whigs and Tories, or Puritans and Anglicans. He projected himself not as an individual but as a spokesman, a representative of one faction or, if possible (as in the opening of *Astraea Redux*), of sensible Englishmen in general. In *Religio Laici*, he concludes his exposition of how Catholics and Protestants both in their own way abuse the Bible:

So all we make of Heavens discover'd Will
Is not to have it, or to use it ill.
The Danger's much the same; on several Shelves
If *others* wreck *us*, or *we* wreck our *selves*.

Notice, first, Dryden's use of the formal aspects of the closed couplet—the definitive use of caesura in the second and fourth lines and the emphasis of the rhymes—and, second, the way he unifies the two sides, partially by using plural pronouns, himself taking the position of spokesman for both.

Pope developed the heroic couplet into a primarily social—as opposed to Dryden's political—instrument. He presented himself as a sensible gentleman addressing either an intimate friend—as in the opening lines of the *Essay on Man*—or an attentive society—as in the *Essay on Criticism*—or, as in his mature essays and epistles, both at once. In this conversational exchange with his friend Dr. John Arbuthnot, the sensible (if sensibly exasperated) gentleman asks who has been hurt by his social satire:

Does not one Table *Bavius* still admit?
Still to one Bishop *Philips* seems a Wit?
Still *Sappho*—'Hold! for God-sake—you'll offend:
No Names—be calm—learn Prudence of a Friend:
I too could write, and I am twice as tall,
But Foes like these!—One Flatt'rer's worse than all;
Of all mad Creatures, if the Learn'd are right,
It is the Slaver kills, and not the Bite.

Notice, first, the caesura-defined parallel in line 5, and the formally illuminated antithesis, dividing both "Foes . . . [and] Flatt'rer" and the two conversationalists, in line 6; and, second, Pope's and his friend's awareness, although they are in intimate talk, that the walls have ears. Dryden in his most characteristic achievements aimed at political harmony or what he called "common quiet." Pope aimed, rather, at generally shared understanding or what he called "common sense."

The heroic couplet, modified in various ways, supported the generation of great poets who followed Pope, esp. Samuel Johnson, Charles Churchill, Oliver Goldsmith, and Crabbe. And even when Eng. culture shifted its focus from general understanding to individual expression—and quite properly revived the open couplet—several poets, chief among them Lord Byron, still found the closed couplet useful for public satire. Robert Browning ("My Last Duchess") and Matthew Arnold used the heroic couplet in the Victorian period; T. S. Eliot composed a heroic couplet section for *The Waste Land*, which he wisely excised when Ezra Pound made him see that he could not compete with Pope; and Robert Frost produced several exemplary heroic couplet poems (e.g., "The Tuft of Flowers"). Among more recent examples (see Steele, Caplan), A. D. Hope's extended use of the heroic couplet in *Dunciad Minor* stands out.

*See* BLANK VERSE, HEROIC VERSE.

■ Schipper; F. E. Schelling, "Ben Jonson and the Classical School," *PMLA* 13 (1898); G. P. Shannon, "Nicholas Grimald's Heroic Couplet and the Latin Elegiac Distich," *PMLA* 45 (1930); R. C. Wallerstein, "The Development of the Rhetoric and Metre of the Heroic Couplet," *PMLA* 50 (1935); G. Williamson, "The Rhetorical Pattern of Neo-classical Wit," *MP* 33 (1935–36); E. R. Wasserman, "The Return of the Enjambed Couplet," *ELH* 7 (1940); Y. Winters, "The Heroic Couplet and Its Recent Revivals," *In Defense of Reason* (1943); W. C. Brown, *The Triumph of Form* (1948); W. K. Wimsatt, "One Relation of Rhyme to Reason," *The Verbal Icon* (1954); J. H. Adler, *The Reach of Art* (1964); J. A. Jones, *Pope's Couplet Art* (1969); W. B. Piper, *The Heroic Couplet* (1969); G. T. Amis, "The Structure of the Augustan Couplet," *Genre* 9 (1976); H. Carruth, "Three Notes on the Versewriting of Alexander Pope," *Michigan Quarterly Review* 15 (1976); *An Heroic Couplet Anthology*, ed. W. B. Piper (1977); Thompson; Brogan, 389 ff.; P. Deane, *At Home in Time: Forms of Neo-Augustanism in Modern English Verse* (1994); T. Steele, " 'The Bravest Sort of Verses': The Heroic Couplet," Finch and Varnes; D. Caplan, *Questions of Possibility* (2005), ch. 4.

W. B. PIPER; S. CUSHMAN

**HEROIC VERSE,** heroic meter, heroic poetry. The term came to be used for *epic in the Middle Ages and after. Isidore of Seville in his *Etymologiae* (7th c. CE) defines *heroic poetry* (*carmen heroicum*) as being so named "because in it the affairs and deeds of brave men are narrated (for heroes are spoken of as men practically supernatural and worthy of Heaven on account of their wisdom and bravery); and this meter precedes others in status." In the Ren., Marco Girolamo Vida proclaims the subject of his *De arte poetica* (On Poetic Art, 1527) to be heroic poetry, though, in fact, it consists mainly of practical advice for poets derived from Horace and Quintilian. Torquato Tasso in his *Discorsi del poema eroico* (Discourses on the Heroic Poem, 1594) advocated a more romantic conception of epic but also insisted on accurate depiction of historical reality; he also wrote "heroic sonnets" celebrating great men and events of the past. John Dryden opens the Preface to his trans. of Virgil (1697) with the statement that "a heroick Poem, truly such, is undoubtedly the greatest Work which the Soul of Man is capable to perform."

Heroic meter is the *meter characteristic of heroic poetry: in cl. Gr. and Lat., this was, of course, the (dactylic) *hexameter. With the emergence of the Romance vernaculars from low Lat., however, poets in each lang. sought a line form that would represent the equivalent or analogue of the noblest meter of antiquity, the hexameter, the canonical meter of the epic trad. These were the *hendecasyllable (*versi sciolti*) in It.; first the *alexandrine, then the *décasyllabe* in Fr.; and first the *fourteener, then *blank verse in Eng. Thomas Sébillet and Joachim du Bellay brought into Fr. use the term *vers héroique* for the décasyllabe, but Pierre de Ronsard, opposing the *decasyllable, used it rather for the alexandrine.

*Heroic verse* is still today the most neutral term for the ten-syllable, five-stress line in Eng. otherwise called *iambic pentameter* or *decasyllable*. Each of the latter two terms, while acceptable for general usage, carries with it connotations that are not historically accurate in every age and, hence, should be used with care. The former implies associations with *classical prosody that many now feel inappropriate ("feet"), while the latter implies ones with Romance prosody that are equally inappropriate (syllabism as the chief criterion). It is certainly true that, in the first half of the 16th c., when Eng. poets were rediscovering or simply constructing the line that was to become the great staple of Eng. poetry, most of them had been given training at school in Lat. metrics. Others, however, were very familiar with continental verse models, chiefly It. and Fr., that offered a line of 10 to 12 syllables with variable stressing equally available for adaptation into Eng. The point is that all the Romance models were isomorphs of the cl. line that adapted itself to the varying ling. constraints of each new lang. into which it was imported.

■ R. C. Williams, *The Theory of the Heroic Epic in Italian Criticism of the 16th Century* (1921); Curtius, ch. 9; Weinberg; *Concepts of the Hero in the Middle Ages and Renaissance*, ed. N. T. Burns and C. J. Reagan (1975); J. M. Steadman, *Milton and the Paradoxes of Renaissance Heroism* (1987); *Heroic Epic and Saga*, ed. F. J. Oinas (1978)—surveys 15 national lits.; G. T. Wright, *Shakespeare's Metrical Art* (1988); O. B. Hardison Jr., *Prosody and Purpose in the English Renaissance* (1989); W. J. Kennedy, "Heroic Poem before Spenser," and M. A. Radzinowicz, "Heroic Poem since Spenser," *The Spenser Encyclopedia*, ed. A. C. Hamilton et al. (1990); B. Murdoch, "Heroic Verse," *Camden House History of German Literature, Vol. 2: German Literature of the Early Middle Ages*, ed. B. Murdoch (2004).

T.V.F. BROGAN

**HETEROGRAM** (Gr. *éteros*, "another"; *gram*, "writing"). A text in which no letter of the alphabet appears more than once. One of many forms of *constraint that were adopted by the *Oulipo group in France, the heterogram became the basis for heterogrammatic verse (also known as *threnodials*), an extremely demanding poetic form invented by Georges Perec (1936–82) and illustrated in four works, *Ulcérations* (Bleedings, 1974), *Alphabets* (1976), *La clôture* (In Closure, 1980) and *Métaux* (Metals, 1985). In its most basic form, Perec's heterogram is a cube consisting of 11 poems of 11 lines; each line is written from an isogram or a series of the 11 most common letters in a given lang. Each line of the poem is an *anagram of the isogram. In Fr., the most commonly used letters are all present in the title *Ulcérations*, Perec's first heterogrammatic cycle. In Eng., the most felicitous name for the practice, a single word made up of the 11 most commonly used letters, is *threnodials*, which derives from *threnody*, meaning a *lament or a *dirge. Though heterogrammatic verse is composed on a grid that displays the anagrammatic matrix, the poem also enjoys a second, free-verse lineation in print, one that is capitalized, punctuated, and more legible to the eye. In some cases, heterogrammatic verse is printed separately from its block-shaped blueprint.

After having established the basic rules of the form,

Perec further experimented with its potentiality: in *Alphabets*, he reduces to ten the letters in the basic isogram and proceeds to write 16 chapters of eleven 11-line stanzas, each of which includes one of the 16 letters not included in the base isogram; in the 17-poem cycle *La clôture*, he returns to the original 11-letter isogram, but he introduces the principle of a joker, adding one additional letter to the series (printed as §) and extends the matrix by one line; finally, in *Métaux*, Perec uses a 12-letter isogram (an allusion to the *alexandrine verse form), and two jokers per line, in order to craft seven heterogrammatic *sonnets consisting of 14 matrix lines of 14 letters each. The novelty and highly restrictive difficulty of heterogrammatic verse may explain why few others have practiced the form. Among the few exceptions are Oskar Pastior's (1927–2006) Ger. adaptations of Perec's form in *Okular ist eng oder Fortunas Kiel* (The Narrow Eyepiece or Fortune's Keel, 1992) and Ian Monk's (b. 1960) "A Threnodialist's Dozen" (1998), the first poem of which is printed below as illustration of the heterogram:

```
S L I T H E R O N D A
S H I N D A R E T O L
E A D T H I S L O R N
A R T S L I N E D O H
T O S I L A N D H E R
N O T E S H A R D L I
L T O N E S H A R D I
N H A L E D I T S O R
D E R S L A I N T O H
A N D S O R E L T H I
S T H R E N O D I A L
```

Slither on, dash in,
Dare to lead this lorn art's
line
              doh to si
land her notes' hard lilt.

One shard inhaled,
              its order's lain,
to hand Sorel
this threnodial.

*See* ALEATORY POETICS, AVANT-GARDE POETICS, CONCEPTUAL POETRY, FORMALISM, LIPOGRAM, MODERNISM, MORALE ÉLÉMENTAIRE.

■ W. F. Motte, "Georges Perec on the Grid," *French Review* 57 (1984), and *The Poetics of Experiment: A Study of the Work of Georges Perec* (1986); B. Magné, "Quelques considérations sur les poèmes hétérogrammatiques de George Perec," and M. Ribière, "*Alphabets* déchiffré," *Cahiers Georges Perec* 5 (1992); J.-J. Poucel, "The Arc of Reading in Georges Perec's *La Clôture*," *YFS* 105 (2004).

J.-J. POUCEL

**HETEROMETRIC,** heterometrical, polymetric; technically, "anisometrical" (as in Schipper). (1) Of stanzas taken singly or nonstanzaic poems: composed of lines of differing lengths and metrical structures. The *sapphic, the Lat. *elegiac distich, and *tail rhyme are examples of stanzaic forms that mix longer and shorter lines. Variation of line length has been a significant factor in a number of lyric genres that have metrical form, certainly in cl. and in med. Lat. poetry, but particularly so after the flowering of *Occitan poetry in the 12th–14th cs. (Elwert). The interplay between long lining and short may take three forms: alternation, as in the elegiac distich and one important type of *ballad meter; longer lines punctuated by short ones—the general phenomenon of "tailing"; and short lines closed by longer ones, as in the *Spenserian stanza. Fr. *vers mêlés* are heterometric (see VERS LIBRES CLASSIQUES). Sense (1) is what is usually meant by the term *heterometric*. (2) Of stanzaic poems: heterostrophic—i.e., subsequent stanzas not in correspondence or *responsion to the first. In strophic compositions that consist of more than one stanza, it is the norm that whatever metrical pattern is established in the first stanza will be duplicated in subsequent ones (they are said to *respond*). Most often the first stanza is *isometric, but even if it is heterometric, all following stanzas in an isometric (isostrophic) poem are identical, i.e., heterometric in precisely the same way: in Eng. poetry, the great masters of the isometric poem in heterometric stanza are John Donne, Thomas Hardy, and W. H. Auden. Note that, in the regular ode, the *antistrophe responds metrically to the opening *strophe, and even in some *free verse, which is not metrical and is built on a base not primarily aural but visual, the poet will establish a visual shape—the equivalent of a stanza—and then reiterate that shape exactly, giving a visually isometric effect. In some radical genres such as the *descort*, however, each stanza is different metrically from every other—i.e., the poem as a whole is truly heterometric. Such forms are rare, but one conspicuous example is the irregular or *Pindaric ode. In cl. prosody, older terms for isometric and heterometric are *homoeomeral* and *polyrhythmic*.

*See* RHYME COUNTERPOINT, STANZA.

■ Schipper; Elwert; K. D. Vishnevsky, "The Law of Rhythmical Correspondence in Heterogeneous Stanzas," *Metre, Rhythm, Stanza, Rhyme*, ed. G. S. Smith (1980).

T.V.F. BROGAN

**HETERONYM.** This concept enters poetry primarily through the work of the Port. modernist Fernando Pessoa. Pessoa composed verse under his own name (*orthonym*) as well as heteronyms or discrete personalities, each with his own *biography, poetic *voice, and engagement with the traditional genres of the Western literary trad. The main heteronyms are Alberto Caeiro, Ricardo Reis, and Álvaro de Campos. Pessoa's fictitious but independent poets emerge from the depersonalization of mod. consciousness, self-estrangement, and the dismantling of *romanticism's "I." In effect different lyric subjects, the heteronyms are autonomous of Pessoa's own poetic identity. As one among many poets, Pessoa himself may be yet another heteronym. The multifaceted, centerless poetic project reveals a crisis or emptiness of being, a negation of a coherent literary selfhood. Pessoa encapsulates the essence of heteronymy with his injunction "Be plural like the universe."

*See* PERSONA; PORTUGAL, POETRY OF.

■ K. D. Jackson, *Adverse Genres in Fernando Pessoa* (2010).

J. BLACKMORE

**HEXAMETER.** Strictly speaking, any line of verse composed of six metrical feet. The only such line with a major role in lit. hist. is dactylic hexameter, for which *hexameter* is usually shorthand. It was the meter of the earliest and most prestigious poetry of cl. antiquity and became the dominant meter for nondramatic verse in cl. Gr. and Lat. lit. The basic template is a 17-syllable line of five *dactyls (– ⌣ ⌣) and a concluding *spondee (– –); individual lines occasionally show that pattern: "quadrupedante putrem sonitu quatit ungula campum" (*Aeneid* 8.596). For individual dactyls, spondees can be substituted, though never for all five and seldom in the fifth foot; a line can, in fact, be as short as 13 syllables: "monstrum horrendum, informe, ingens, cui lumen ademptum" (*Aeneid* 3.658, with vowels elided in the first three feet). Most lines are from 14 to 16 syllables, and variation of dactyls and spondees is part of the craft: "aurea subnectens exsertae cingula mammae" (*Aeneid* 1.492: – ⌣ ⌣ | – – | – – | – – | – ⌣ ⌣ | – –). In most cases the conclusion of the line is marked by the regular cadence – ⌣ ⌣ | – x (the so-called adonean *colon), though a spondee in the penultimate foot is occasionally used for special effect. Rhythmic pacing is also managed by shifting the location of a *caesura. It usually occurs within the third, less often within the fourth foot; a caesura between the third and fourth feet, which would divide the line in two, is avoided. A caesura bisecting the third foot is called penthemimeral, one bisecting the fourth is called hephthimeral. The portion of a line preceding a penthemimeral caesura (the pattern – ⌣ ⌣ – ⌣ ⌣ –) is known as a *hemiepes (half-epic) and is used as a building block in other cl. meters. A word break between the fourth and fifth feet, rare in Homeric epic, is associated with *pastoral poetry and is known as the bucolic diaeresis.

At some times and places, stricter rules are also observed; a particularly stringent set is employed for one of the last great effusions of cl. Gr. poetry, the 48-book *Dionysiaca* of Nonnus from the 5th c. CE. The meter in its basic form, however, appears fully developed no later than 700 BCE as the meter of the Homeric epics; Hesiod also uses it exclusively. By the 6th c. BCE, it has been adapted to a couplet form, the so-called *elegiac distich, which consists of a dactylic hexameter and a truncated version of itself that is called a *pentameter (in effect, a double hemiepes); this meter has its own hist. as the meter of epigram and love poetry. Both meters are used in Lat. by Ennius in the early 2nd c. BCE. Throughout cl. antiquity, dactylic hexameter proper remains the almost exclusive meter of narrative verse, as well as pastoral and didactic poetry and, in Lat., *satire. As Lat. shifts over to qualitative rhymed verse in the Middle Ages, a hybrid form known as *leonine verse becomes popular, though its regular use of internal rhyme has the significant effect of breaking the august long line into smaller units: "Orpheus Eurydice sociatur, amicus amice, / matre canente dea, dum rite colunt hymenea" (Hugh Primas). Unrhymed quantitative hexameter poems such as Virgil's *Aeneid* and Ovid's *Metamorphoses* nevertheless continue to be read as major embodiments of the prestige of cl. civilization, and new poems in the meter continue to be written. It is still the main vehicle for Lat. verse composition (some productions by the young Arthur Rimbaud were his first pub. works).

With the Ren. come both a revived use of the hexameter in Neo-Lat. poetry and attempts to transfer it in some form into the vernaculars: as a vehicle for translating cl. poetry and potentially as an authoritative verse form for the developing national lits. *Esametri italiani* are debuted in the *Certame Coronario*, a public literary contest staged by Leon Battista Alberti and Leonardo Dati in 1441 to promote poetry in the vernacular; there is some follow-up by other It. poets into the next century. An ambitious attempt is mounted by the *\*Pléiade* poet Jean-Antoine de Baïf, who founds an Académie de Poésie et de Musique (1567–73) expressly to develop and promulgate rules for truly quantitative Fr. verse on the cl. model (*\*vers mesurés à l'antique*); the results are modest but still command respect. In England, the linguistic change from ME to mod. Eng. seems to open the possibility of a comparable shift in *\*Eng. prosody. The hexameter, as it happens, falls exactly between the two indigenous claimants to Eng. poetry's dominant meter: the *\*iambic pentameter that is Chaucer's principal medium and a seven-beat iambic line—the *\*fourteener—that is a typographical rearrangement from the traditional 4-3 *\*ballad stanza. Both were used for trans. of the *Aeneid* published in the course of the century—the former by Gavin Douglas (1553) and (without rhyme) Henry Howard, the Earl of Surrey (1554–57), the latter by Thomas Phaer (1562) and Thomas Twynne (1573)—but in humanist circles, there was influential opinion that an appropriately anglicized dactylic hexameter was needed. Roger Ascham quotes in his *Scholemaster* (1570) from an Eng. *Odyssey* in purportedly quantitative hexameters; in 1582, Richard Stanyhurst publishes four books of the *Aeneid* in his version of the original meter, together with his own detailed rules for determining Eng. *\*quantity. The eccentricity of those rules and the bizarreness of Stanyhurst's diction ("Lyke bandog grinning, with gnash tusk greedelye snarring") attract a good deal of mockery, but better poets—Philip Sidney and Thomas Campion most notably—are also drawn to the possibility of Eng. quantitative verse and experiment with it in various meters, with varying degrees of success. Two of the embedded poems in the first version of Sidney's prose romance *Arcadia* (1590, 1593) are in hexameters written to his own quantitative rules, though quantity has a way of coinciding with stress: "When that noble toppe doth nodd, I beleeve she salutes me; / When by the winde it maketh a noyse, I do thinke she doth answer." By the 17th c., however, the

effort has run its course, and the accentual-syllabic iambic pentameter is firmly established as the touchstone meter for Eng. poetry.

More straightforwardly qualitative but unrhymed dactylic hexameters (with an accentual trochee generally acceptable as the equivalent of a spondee) make a place for themselves in later periods. The publication of the first three cantos of F. G. Klopstock's *Der Messias* in 1748 establishes the meter as a viable one in mod. Ger. J. W. Goethe uses it successfully for his epic *Hermann und Dorothea* (1797), where part of the effect is the way in which the classicizing form plays off against the contemp. setting of the French Revolution. The unrhymed elegiac distich also takes root in Ger. Goethe employs it for some of his most personal poems; at one point in his *Römische Elegien*, he represents the composition of dactylic hexameters as love play: "Oftmals hab ich auch schon in ihren Armen gedichtet / Und des Hexameters Mass leise mit fingernder Hand / Ihr auf den Rücken gezählt" (even in her arms I have often composed poetry and, tapping with my hand, softly counted out the beat of the hexameter on her back; 5.15–17). A trans. of the *Iliad* into hexameters by Nikolai Gnedich, completed after 20 years of work in 1829, made a big impression in Rus. literary circles. Alexander Pushkin praised it extravagantly and was moved to experiments of his own in unrhymed hexameters and elegiacs. Both meters are used in Rus. poetry into the 20th c., esp. for trans.; Valery Bryusov, a leader of the symbolist movement, produced an esp. striking hexameter trans. of the *Aeneid* (pub. posthumously in 1933). Robert Southey's *Vision of Judgment* (1821; famously parodied by Lord Byron the next year in a poem of the same name) is the first of a line of 19th-c. Eng. poems in unrhymed hexameters. The best known is H. W. Longfellow's *Evangeline* (1847), a love story set in mod. hist., somewhat on the model of *Hermann und Dorothea*. The effect of the meter there is largely one of solemnity: "This is the forest primeval. The murmuring pines and the hemlocks, / Bearded with moss, and in garments green, indistinct in the twilight, / Stand like Druids of eld, with voices sad and prophetic." Alfred, Lord Tennyson, on the other hand, decided that hexameters in Eng. are "only fit for comic subjects"; his mockery of some attempts to have it otherwise became famous: "These lame hexameters the strong wing'd music of Homer! / No—but a most burlesque barbarous experiment" ("On Translations of Homer"). Tennyson's distaste is related to the seriousness with which he regarded quantity. The late 19th and early 20th cs. saw renewed attempts, by Robert Bridges and others, to reestablish Eng. verse, and with it the Eng. hexameter, on a quantitative basis, but they proved infertile. Cecil Day-Lewis was more influential in using a loosely defined six-stress line, suggesting the cl. meter but not attempting any strict observance of its rules, for his trans. of Virgil (1952): "I tell about war and the hero who first from Troy's frontier, / Displaced by destiny, came to the Lavinian shores." Such a form has proved very popular for trans. from cl. epic and continues to be used. The unacknowledged contours of the ancient meter can at times be sensed beneath the verse and prose of mod. writers, esp. those with cl. training. James Joyce's *Ulysses* (1922) opens with 14 syllables cadenced as a dactylic hexameter, spondaic in the fifth foot.

See CLASSICAL METERS IN MODERN LANGUAGES.

■ Omond; R. Burgi, *A History of the Russian Hexameter* (1954); Maas; W. Bennett, *German Verse in Classical Metres* (1963); J. Thompson, *The Founding of English Metre* (1961); D. Attridge, *Well-weighed Syllables* (1974); West; Gasparov, *History.*

G. BRADEN

**HIATUS.** The grammatical and metrical term for the gap that is created by pronunciation of contiguous vowels, either within a word or (more commonly) word-terminal and following word-initial. The effect of the juncture is a slight catch or pause in delivery. The alternative is to remove one vowel via *elision. In Eng. like other langs., the indefinite article (*a*) has an alternate form (*an*) that exists specifically to prevent hiatus. In both prose and poetry, hiatus has been deemed a fault since at least the time of Gorgias and Isocrates; Cicero and Quintilian (*Institutio oratoria* 9.4.34 ff.) discuss it at length. In the cl. langs. (see CLASSICAL PROSODY), hiatus was common in Gr. epic poetry, with and without shortening of the first vowel, but rarer in Lat. Occitan had no strict rules about elision and hiatus; in OF, hiatus was generally tolerated until the 14th c.: there is no elision to prevent hiatus in the *Saint Alexis* (about 1040), but in Jean Froissart, there are 132 cases of elision against five of hiatus (Lote). In *French prosody since François de Malherbe (17th c.), the use of hiatus was proscribed. In It., hiatus is generally avoided, as it is in Sp., though in Sp. it was the rule into the late 14th c., after which time its frequency waned. Richter summarizes the cl., Ren., and Fr. views; distinguishes nine types of hiatus; and gives statistics and examples for each type. Pope's mimetic example, "Though oft the ear the open vowels tire" (*Essay on Criticism* 2.345), is more famous than it is offensive, and indeed the strict censuring of hiatus in Fr. and Eng. neoclassical crit. seems mainly genuflection to the ancients, for elision is common in speech.

Debra San classifies two other types of hiatus: narrative and grammatical. Narrative hiatus is the logical or chronological interruption of story line by flashbacks, tangents, and authorial commentary. Grammatical hiatus varies from the insertion of an adjective between an article and the following noun to the more noticeable *tmesis. Subject-verb hiatus, a form of grammatical hiatus, is the syntactical interruption between the subject and verb in a sentence over a number of poetic lines by subordinate clauses, parenthetical insertions, and other phrases.

■ A. Braam, *Malherbes Hiatus Verbot* (1884); A. Pleines, *Hiat und Elision im Provenzalischen* (1886); J. Franck, "Aus der Gesch. des Hiat im Verse," *ZDA* 48 (1906); Thieme, 370—cites 12 Fr. studies; Bridges; J. Pelz, *Der prosodische Hiat* (1930); W.J.H. Richter, *Der Hiat im englischen Klassizismus (Milton, Dryden, Pope)* (1934); Lote 3.87; A. Stene, *Hiatus in English* (1954); P. Habermann and W. Mohr, "Hiat," *Reallexikon II*; Maas, sect. 141; Elwert, 62–67; Morier; D. San, "Hiatus of Subject and Verb in Poetic Language" *Style* 39 (2005).

T.V.F. BROGAN; D. VERALDI

**HIEROGLYPH** (Gr., "sacred carving"; Fr. *hiéroglyphique,* for the style of writing used by ancient Egyptians among other cultures to represent abstract ideas, sounds, or objects through graphic figures). A ling. or anthropological account of hieroglyphs might begin with the recovery of the Rosetta Stone in 1799, which led Jean-François Champollion to recognize the previously undetected phonetic function of the script. An account of how hieroglyphs influenced poetic and philosophical currents from Plato through postmodernism, however, must concentrate on how their assumed symbolic function inspired a range of metaphorical, often mystical interpretations.

Although Plato remained skeptical of the illusory truths bodied forth in writing, his method of allegorical interpretation (see ALLEGORY, CLASSICAL POETICS) and his conception of Egypt as a land of ancient learning remained foundational for Neoplatonic and hermetic philosophers through late antiquity who saw the hieroglyph as a lost, ideal lang.—a sacred carving, as its etymology suggests, that required decoding. After fading from view during the Middle Ages, hieroglyphs and the philosophies that engaged them emerged again in the early Ren. with the recovery of Horapollo's *Hieroglyphica* in 1419. Horapollo's inventive, though often spurious, interpretations inspired widespread fascination with hieroglyphs among humanist philosophers, artists, and writers. This fascination revitalized interest in med. nature symbolism, increased the repertoire of symbols for painters and writers, and lent the act of inventing and interpreting such symbols an air of ancient authority rooted in the origins of lang. and learning.

As the Ren. spread across Europe, attention to hieroglyphs themselves was gradually displaced by a more diffuse brand of hieroglyph-inspired thinking. Thus, hieroglyphs came to influence all kinds of cultural productions, from *visual poetry and the finely wrought *conceits of *metaphysical poetry to painting and the popular *emblem trad., and from commemorative medals and cryptic *imprese* to academic debates about the possibility of a universal system of symbols.

As the Ren. gave way to Enlightenment reason, the influence of hieroglyphs receded. In reaction to the cultural prominence of strict rationality, however, renewed forms of hieroglyphic thinking emerged in Ger. *romanticism, Am. transcendentalism, Fr. *symbolism, and related movements where the hieroglyph again became the specimen of an idealized, more immediate relationship between word and world, human beings and nature, sign and signified (see SIGN, SIGNIFIED, SIGNIFIER).

In the 20th c., hieroglyphs continued to inform a range of work. Guillaume Apollinaire's *Calligrammes* (1918), e.g., consciously engages the hieroglyphic trad.

(see CALLIGRAMME), and Ezra Pound turned to Chinese characters as earlier writers turned to the hieroglyphs, exaggerating their pictorial quality to divine an ideal model for poetic expression. Focusing on the Americas, Charles Olson developed a poetics inspired by Mayan hieroglyphs. In Brazilian *concrete poetry and other visual poetries of the later 20th c., hieroglyphic thinking persists in the desire to get beyond words to something more originary and authentic.

■ E. Iversen, *The Myth of Egypt and Its Hieroglyphs* (1961); L. Dieckmann, *Hieroglyphics* (1970); *Speaking Pictures*, ed. M. Klonsky (1975); J. T. Irwin, *American Hieroglyphics* (1980); T. C. Singer, "Hieroglyphs, Real Characters, and the Idea of Natural Language in English Seventeenth-Century Thought," *Journal of the History of Ideas* 50 (1989).

A. VANDER ZEE

**HINDI POETRY.** The heritage of Hindi lit. is a palimpsest inscribed with a range of dialects and with multiple sensibilities. Though the contemp. poetry mostly reflects a standardized mod. lang. and articulates ideas parallel to those of many mod. lits., it also contains deep resonances of its premod. legacy. An outline of Hindi poetry must, therefore, survey a period of several centuries, from the time that Hindi and other northern Indian langs. first emerged as distinct forms of regional speech from earlier Sanskrit-derived langs. such as Prakrit and Apabhraṃsha.

One of the greatest strengths of premod. culture—its often oral medium—is also one of the greatest impediments to our knowledge of its early circumstances. The ebullient genres of *ballads of the seasons, marriage songs (see EPITHALAMIUM), versified saws and aphorisms, bardic *panegyrics, devotional *hymns and prayers, and many other such phenomena typical of Indian culture certainly predate any written record of their existence. Only in recent times has this oral trad. begun to fade, eclipsed by the easy seductions of the mod. media (see ORAL POETRY).

Following these dimly perceived early genres of Hindi verse that left little written record of their existence, the most powerful catalyst to the trad. was a flowering of devotional religion, or *Bhakti*, in northern India in the 15th and 16th cs. (see DEVOTIONAL POETRY). This period saw the emergence of a newly "emotional" style of devotionalism in which human relationships served as paradigms for the love of God; though primarily Hindu in orientation, it shared many general characteristics with parallel trads. of ecstatic Sufism. The image of Viṣṇu (Vishnu) as a compassionate deity, esp. in his incarnations as Kṛṣṇa (Krishna) and as Rāma, was a compelling focus, and the loci of the earthly lives of these deities, earlier recorded in the sacred geographies of Sanskrit lit., were transformed from textual abstractions into palpable centers of devotional worship and pilgrimage.

Descriptions of the sports of the heroic and sublimely beautiful Kṛṣṇa in the bucolic setting of Braj, Kṛṣṇa's "earthly paradise" on the banks of the river Ya-muna to the south of mod. Delhi, had long featured in such Sanskrit texts as the *Purāṇa*s (esp. 4th–9th cs. CE). In the 12th c., Jayadeva's sensuous Sanskrit poem *Gītagovinda* added Kṛṣṇa's consort Rādhā to the picture. The love of Rādhā and Kṛṣṇa became a favorite theme for generations of "poet-saints" in successive centuries, with figures such as Sūrdās (early to mid-16th c.) achieving fame for the beauty of their compositions and the incisiveness of their devotional vision. Their poems were mostly written in Braj Bhasha, the dialect of Hindi that was and is spoken in the Braj region, sometimes assumed (ahistorically) to be Kṛṣṇa's own lang. With the exception of some exegetical commentaries, most composition was in rhymed verse, and many genres were intended for singing. The poetry was typically eulogistic, sweetly celebratory, and ecstatic in tone: and though the Braj poets inherited aesthetic codes and literary tropes from the Sanskrit trad., they showed enormous creativity in their evocations of Kṛṣṇa as the divine lover who was simultaneously the supreme deity—God himself. Certain themes became firm favorites: the pranks of Kṛṣṇa the child-god; the sensuality of his persona as a voluptuous youth; the appeal of his seductive flute; his moonlit "round-dance" with the *gopīs*; his secluded assignations with Rādhā; and in thematic counterpoint, his status as a savior who bestows grace on his devotees.

The most popular genre consisted of individual songs, *bhajan*s, which were disseminated by performance, eventually to be written down and compiled in anthols. The sacred content of the songs made ms. copying an act of piety that brought its own rewards; written and oral recensions would often develop side by side. For all the prestige of the great poets, matters of authorship counted for little, and many a poet's corpus grew steadily over the centuries. Textual ascription can sometimes be validated on the basis of whatever mss. have survived the rigors of climate, the appetites of insects, and the indifference of custodians. For most devotees of such poetry, however, authenticity depends on spiritual potency rather than dry historiography.

The asocial mores of Kṛṣṇa-as-lover were complemented by the impeccable moral rectitude of Rāma, hero of the epic *Rāmāyaṇa*. Told in many langs. over at least two millennia, this narrative found its vernacular exemplar in the *Rāmcaritmānas*, a magisterial poem by the brahmin Tulsīdās (1532–1623) begun in 1574. Tulsī's epic was written in Awadhi, the dialect spoken around Rāma's capital of Ayodhya toward the eastern end of the Hindi area; but in his choice of both lang. and poetic form, Tulsī was also following the precedent of such Sufi poets as Manjhan (fl. mid-16th c.) and Jāyasī (b. ca. 1494) whose allegorical Awadhi romances *Madhumālatī* and *Padmāvat* (respectively) had pioneered this epic format some decades earlier. This formal connection between genres whose communities have become differentiated—if not mutually alienated—in more recent times reminds us that a rich symbiosis existed between various different religious paths in premod. India. Today's misplaced association of Tulsīdās with an intolerant Hindu chauvinism is be-lied by the wit, subtlety, and sublime perceptiveness of his poetic voice.

Another strand in the fabric of premod. poetry is of similarly devotional character but has a different coloration. Throughout the late med. period, a loose grouping of poets known as the *sants*, typically from the lower strata of society (as opposed to the mostly high-born Kṛṣṇa and Rāma poets), chose a more un-comfortable, abstract, and hard-hitting rhet. for their religious songs and verse. The best-known figure in this trad. is the weaver Kabīr, born in the mid-15th c. Kabīr's poetic vision perceives God as transcending all form, whether anthropomorphic or otherwise; the poet roundly excoriates priesthood, ritual, scriptures, and all the trappings of organized religion advocating a personal search for the divine within the human soul. Kabīr's *bānī* or sacred utterances are recorded in three main recensions with little material held in common between them. One of the three is the *Gurū Granth Sāhib* of the Sikh faith that was founded by another *sant* poet, Kabīr's contemp. Gurū Nānak (1469–1539), who wrote in Punjabi (see PUNJABI POETRY).

Religion was not the only theme in premod. poetry. With the enrichment of courtly culture during the Mughal period, poets enjoying the *patronage of local kingdoms began to compose highly sophisticated verse with a more worldly flavor and a more self-consciously literary orientation. The subject of their brilliantly or-nate verse was often poetry itself, and in their elabo-ration of tropes, they drew on two complementary aspects of Indian literary trad. First, their rhetorical typologies embroidered the age-old poetics of Sanskrit lit.; and second, the well-established figures of Kṛṣṇa and Rādhā became the perfect hero and heroine to model these elegant tropes. Braj Bhasha continued to serve as the dialect of choice for poetic composition, regardless of the native tongue of the individual poet. This new mode of poetry, written for (and sometimes by) the regional kings of northern India, came to be called *rīti*—a "stylist" mode, an embodiment of literary style; but the borders between this and devotional verse were always porous, with traffic flowing continuously between the complementary genres.

The 19th c. saw deep-seated changes in Indian so-ciety as Eng.-lang. culture made its presence felt with increasing strength. Interregional communications improved, the printing press arrived, a middle-class disposition developed, the small minority of Indians literate in Eng. grew steadily; and as the century pro-gressed, a Victorian ethos penetrated deep into the consciousness of many writers. Lit. came to be seen as a medium through which social change might be ef-fected; and as though to distance this new conscious-ness from the old tropes of *rīti* and devotional poetry, writers began to switch dialects, forsaking the sweetly lyrical associations of Braj Bhasha for a more utilitar-ian idiom in Khari Boli, the dialect from the Delhi re-gion that already served as a lingua franca across the Hindi-speaking north. Poetry found a new rival in

the rapid devel. of prose genres, often inspired by new models in Western fiction and polemics and expressed in the nascent media of Hindi newspapers and jours. The spirit of the age was represented in the person of the polymath Bharatendu Harishchandra of Banaras (1850–85), who maintained the old Braj idiom in his verse while leading a generation of writers in the new style of Khari Boli prose.

Unsurprisingly, new poetic conventions in Khari Boli took some time to find their feet, and the early accomplishments were to have little enduring appeal for Hindi readers; few poets from the opening years of the 20th c. are enjoyed today. But a confident new style was not long in coming, with poets such as Suryakant Tripathi "Nirala" (1896–1961) and Mahadevi Verma (1907–87) writing Khari Boli verse of great power and personality. The headstrong, eccentric Nirala strode the literary stage in moods of anger, sadness, and deeply humanist compassion, while the lyrical laments of Ma-hadevi reminded readers of the passionate outpourings of a 16th-c. forebear, the Rajasthani princess Mīrābāī, whose Kṛṣṇa songs are among the most enduring voices from any period of Hindi poetry. The roman-ticist idiom of Mahadevi and other like-minded poets writing in the 1920s was dubbed *Chāyāvād* (Shadow-ism); but like many a derogatory sobriquet, the name stuck, becoming a neutral title for this loosely affiliated group of poets. A more populist style was that of Har-ivansh Rai Bachchan (1907–2003), a teacher of Eng. lit. at Allahabad University; his romantic, Khayyām-and-Fitzgerald-inspired *Madhuśālā* (The House of Wine), won him a huge following at *kavi sammelan*s or poetic symposia, which have always been successful in pro-jecting Hindi poetry well beyond the small cliques of intellectual literati.

Following Chāyāvād, several schools of poetry rose and set. *Pragativād* enshrined a progressivist agenda, and the subsequent *Prayogvād* was experimentalist in character: such labels and themes show the Hindi poets' engagement with Western literary trends. But rather than pursuing the ephemeral fashions of modernist idiom, we may rather mention a single voice, one that defines the mid-20th c. more than any other. S. H. Vat-syayan (1911–87) was a champion of the so-called *Nayī Kavitā* or New Poetry, and perhaps its finest exponent also. His pseud. Agyeya (also transliterated Ajneya, and meaning "the unknowable"), alludes to the secret smuggling of his early nationalistic writing from a Brit-ish jail cell during the independence struggle. Agyeya was both a novelist and a poet. Like many of the other poets featured in the volumes of verse compiled under his editorship, he wrote in a style that combines the so-norous grandeur of the cl. Sanskritic heritage with the variously gritty, sweet, and forceful vernacular idiom of contemp. Hindi speech. This combination is seen in its fullest glory in his long poem *Asādhya Vīṇā* (The Unmastered Veena, alluding to the most cl. of India's lutes), a long and deeply emotive poem written in 1961. Rich with description and allusion, this poem func-tions as a summation of the Hindi poetic trad. thus far, ranging from the humanist concerns of today, through the romanticism of earlier decades, back to the diction and musical phrasing of the premod. poets; echoing through all these modalities is an apprehension of the broader Indian trad., rooted in its cl. past and flowering in the creative energy of a forward-looking present.

Contemp. Hindi poetry has many moods, registers, and styles—from the popular lyrics of cinema (themselves rooted in traditional genres of music and poetry) to the intellectually rigorous verse of such poets as Muktibodh (pseud. of Gajanan Madhav, 1917–64), Raghuvir Sahay (1929–90), and Kunwar Narain (b. 1927). The parallel trad. of Urdu verse is also accessible to speakers of Hindi, esp. when performed at recitals where distinctions of script (Devanagari for Hindi, Persian for Urdu) melt away. The old devotional poetry of Braj and Awadhi may no longer be popular with mainstream writers, but its echoes still resound, and it has never been relinquished by the Hindi-speaking public. Thus, inscriptions from every layer of Hindi's poetic palimpsest remain visible to the readers of today, inspiring many to wield pens of their own.

*See* INDIA, POETRY OF; RĀMĀYAṆA POETRY; SANSKRIT POETICS; SANSKRIT POETRY; URDU POETRY.

■ Ajneya, *Nīlāmbarī* (1981)—Eng. trans.; K. Schomer, *Mahadevi Varma and the Chayavad Age of Modern Hindi Poetry* (1983); R. S. McGregor, *Hindi Literature from Its Beginnings to the Nineteenth Century* (1984); *Songs of the Saints of India*, trans. J. S. Hawley and M. Juergensmeyer (1988); D. Rubin, *The Return of Sarasvati: Translations of the Poems of Prasad, Nirala, Pant and Mahadevi* (1993); Manjhan, *Madhumālatī: An Indian Sufi Romance*, trans. A. Behl and S. Weightman (2000); *New Poetry in Hindi: Nayi Kavita, an Anthology*, ed. and trans. L. Rosenstein (2003); K. Narain, *No Other World: Selected Poems,* trans. A. Narain (2008).

R. SNELL

**HIP-HOP POETICS.** The terms *hip-hop* and *rap* are sometimes used as synonyms. Adding to the confusion, the definitions of both forms remain in flux, since the music continues to develop with impressive speed. In a widely held formulation, though, *rap* refers to syncopated verbal performance, while *hip-hop* refers to a broader movement of music, fashion, and culture, incl. MC and DJ performances, graffiti, and breakdancing. According to this definition, rap constitutes an aspect of hip-hop. Hip-hop also includes many subgenres, whether based in regions (such as East Coast, West Coast, and Dirty South), styles and themes (such as crunk, gangsta, political, neosoul, club bangers, and reggaetón) or period (such as old school and new school).

One way to understand hip-hop is to trace its historical devel. In the 1970s, the music arose from postindustrial urban environments, most notably, the South Bronx (Rose 1994). Credited to the Sugarhill Gang, a band assembled for a 1978 studio session, the song "Rapper's Delight" is often cited as introducing hip-hop, largely an underground, local art form, to a broader audience. (Conflating the terms, the title mentions "rapper" and the opening words name "hip-hop.") Set to the beat of Chic's song "Good Times," "Rapper's Delight" offered party music designed for the dance floor. Recorded in a studio, the song signaled a change. Suggesting hip-hop's commercial potential, it inspired a host of new recordings, several of which produced more distinguished songs. (Chuck D of Public Enemy, for instance, called the song "a miracle" [quoted in Chang, 2005]). As a consequence, songs recorded in studios gained popularity, and hip-hop recording artists claimed the top status previously afforded to DJs performing in local venues.

From its beginning, hip-hop has exploited emerging technologies, most notably turntable and sampling techniques. The sources for sampling ranged from the political to the funky. Public Enemy, for instance, sampled speeches by Louis Farrakhan and songs by James Brown, whose drumbeats and shouts became an industry staple. Technology introduced new means of distribution and promotion, as well as new recording techniques. Hip-hop developed into an art both "transnational" and "multiregional" (Perry 2004, 10). Thriving hip-hop scenes exist in countries as culturally different as France, Germany, and Japan, as well as in many Ar.-speaking nations.

Many of the early songs featured loose, four-stress, *end-stopped lines. For instance, in "Proud to Be Black," Run-DMC addressed the audience, "Listen party people here's a serious song / It's right not wrong, I should say right on." As hip-hop developed, the artists favored more extravagant rhyming, piling *internal rhyme upon external and rhyming several consecutive lines. Multiple unstressed syllables allow the artist to accelerate his or her delivery, speeding over the words in a tour de force. Accordingly, the speed of the performances increased, presenting a dense field of *rhyme, not a numerically patterned scheme. Many performers employ rhyme in several distinctive ways. Occasionally, they wrench the rhymes, adding stress to a syllable or changing pronunciation (see WRENCHED ACCENT). Other performers rhyme with a pointedly regional accent. At such moments, they express an identity rooted in a particular place, often defined against other hip-hop scenes. Finally, some artists pause within end words in order to achieve a punning effect, producing an effect akin to a heavy *enjambment. In a famous example, Jay-Z boasts in Kanye West's "Diamonds from Sierra Leone (Remix)," "I'm not a businessman, / I'm a business, man!"

Hip-hop has generated much controversy over its expressions of misogyny, homophobia, and incitements to violence. (One of the music's fiercest critics, Stanley Crouch, decries "the aggressive, hedonistic vision of rap" and "the conventional amorality of gangster rap" [Crouch 2004]). In the more limited sphere of poetics, it faces the question of whether it should be classified as poetry. Such debates often reveal more about the participants' aesthetic commitments than about the work under discussion. In several notable ways, the procedures of hip-hop artists differ from those of print-based poets. In the most manifest difference, contemp. poets generally write for the page, while hip-hop artists perform their words (see PERFORMANCE). Yet this distinction hardly remains absolute. Numerous Web sites feature countless hip-hop lyrics for listeners to study apart from the music. In this respect, the listeners respond to the performers' ambition: many hip-hop artists eagerly claim the status of the poet. Indeed, the Am. context witnesses a historical reversal, as hip-hop artists often remain more committed to verse's most visible markers than many poets do. Hip-hop artists employ rhyme much more frequently, blending comic and serious verse techniques. Rare in contemp. poetry, *doggerel remains a prominent mode in hip-hop. In short, hip-hop artists delight in verse techniques and attitudes often decried as either old fashioned or déclassé; in the process, they show how vital they remain and how contemp. they sound.

See CLOSE RHYME.

■ T. Rose, *Black Noise* (1994); S. Crouch, *The Artificial White Man* (2004); I. Perry, *Prophets of the Hood* (2004); J. Chang, *Can't Stop Won't Stop* (2005).

D. CAPLAN

**HISPANO-ARABIC POETRY.** *See* AL-ANDALUS, POETRY OF.

**HISTORICISM.** A critical mode that argues that the ultimate meaning of a poem is located in hist. Historicism places poetry within specific social and cultural configurations of the past, as well as within the narratives conceived to describe that past. It tends to be defined against a formalist trad. that stresses the most valuable thing about poetry is that it is not historical, that it is not tied to time, that it gestures or even stands beyond the mutability of hist. to articulate eternal truths about God, nature, or human beings. Historicism and *formalism, nevertheless, are not distinct; they regularly interpenetrate one another in a variety of ways. One way of defining the hist. of historicism, then, is to chart the shifting interdependence of *form and hist.

This interpenetration begins with the theories of mimesis put forth by Plato and Aristotle. In the *Republic*, Plato's Socrates bans from the community all poets (except those writing hymns to the gods or eulogies of virtuous men) because poets try to pass off representations as true things. Using poetry's mimesis as a guide for living seems to make the historical conditions of pleasure and pain, rather than ahistorical reason, the guides to life. Plato's denunciation of poetry, nevertheless, tends to be poetic: poets are ironically denounced in Plato's artfully constructed dialogue (Derrida 1981; Else). In the *Poetics*, Aristotle instead stresses that human beings are naturally given to representation, and he distinguishes poetry as a more philosophical form of mimesis than hist. because it speaks of universals. Hist. relates things that have happened, while poetry speaks of things that may happen or should hap-

pen. Poetry overcomes hist. and gestures at the ideal through unified form: the integrity of art, its status as discrete object (e.g., the logic of a plot having a beginning, a middle, and an end) is a means of overcoming historical particularity toward universal truths (Else).

The arguments of Plato and Aristotle are influential in the debates concerning scriptural interp. of later antiquity and the Middle Ages, particularly as articulated by Augustine, Anselm, and Aquinas; the line between sacred and secular-historical is complexly rethought as the line between *sign and signification (Colish). With the flourishing of vernacular lits. in the later Middle Ages and Ren., the arguments surrounding scriptural interp. were applied increasingly to poetry. The most influential example is Dante's argument in *Convivio* that poetry, like scripture, is allegorical and points beyond itself to sacred truths (Colish; Auerbach 1961). Nevertheless, Ren. writers, esp. Petrarch, often stressed that poetry could be a worthwhile activity in itself that pointed only to its own negotiated meanings (Freccero). Philip Sidney's *Defence of Poesy* summarizes many Ren. commonplaces when he insists that poetry is superior because it has nothing to do with hist.: loosely following Aristotle, he argues that while historians are tied to nature, to a narration of things as they happened, poets are tied only to "the zodiac of [their] own wit" and are able to imagine things better than they ever were. This argument becomes specifically historical, though, when Sidney insists that poetry has a didactic function: to teach by delighting. While he initially argues that poetry is not mimetic—it does not follow nature—he concludes, contradictorily, by suggesting that the unusual mimesis of poetry has a historical function (Miller).

These ancient, med., and Ren. arguments continue to form the basis of understandings of the interrelation of hist. and poetry. But the emergence of science in the 17th and 18th cs. promised something else: an account of poetry that was true according to scientific method. This scientific account emerged in tandem with a reconceptualization of "history" itself, which became increasingly theorized according to Giambattista Vico's *verum et factum* principle: "the true and the made are interchangeable" (Jay). Hist. (what Vico called the world of nations) was comprehensible to humankind because the human mind was itself a product of the hist. it sought to understand. Nevertheless, this reconceptualization of hist. and the scientific method that accompanies it have had a complex relationship. As Auerbach noted, "strict scientific methods are not applicable to historical phenomena or to any other phenomena [such as poetry] that cannot be subjected to the special conditions required by scientific experimentation." Though historical research is exacting and attempts to set in motion scientific criteria, it is also always "an art that works with scholarly material" (Auerbach 1965). The status of hist. and lit. as both social entities and scholarly disciplines, as well as the general mod. project of historicism itself, is predicated upon the uneasy triumph of scientific empiricism and the division of knowledge that accompanies it. The burden of literary historicism since the Enlightenment has been an effort to coordinate the goal of empiricism in historiography with the reconceptualization of lit. as an ahistorical entity (McKeon).

This combination of cl. theories of mimesis coupled with mod. conceptions of objectivity has resulted in a number of paradoxical reconfigurations of the long-standing tension between poetry and hist. There emerges an often uneasy alliance between, on the one hand, conceptions of poetic inspiration, individual genius, cults of beauty, and emphases on poetic form and autonomy; and on the other hand, a stress on art's imitation of life and nature, on the importance of realism, on art's social function, and of a spirit of an age (zeitgeist) that fundamentally determines the meaning of art. The first of these alliances finds an origin in Immanuel Kant's *Critique of Judgment*, which emphasizes the autonomy and sublimity of aesthetic experience. Kant outlines the operation of the mind of a subject to argue that taste is disinterested and objective. This theory becomes forcefully expressed first in the *Sturm und Drang* movement and later in romanticism generally. The source of a poem is neither the representation of the historical world nor the representation of a higher ideal (God or a Platonic form). Rather, poetry originates in the inner feelings and mental operations of the poet. Poetry, and aesthetic expression generally, is thus seen as radically separate from the historical world. Indeed, for Victorian writers such as John Ruskin and Oscar Wilde, beauty in art becomes an end in itself. Echoing Sidney, Wilde asserts in the preface to *The Picture of Dorian Gray* that "the artist is the creator of beautiful things" and "no artist desires to prove anything" (see AESTHETICISM). This stress on form apart from hist. likewise is a principle of the *New Criticism of the 20th c., as well as, to a lesser extent, *Russian formalism (Jameson 1972). Despite their assault on romantic conceptions of poetic inspiration, the New Critics held on to the sense of art as radically distinct from hist. by shunning all extrinsic features and focusing only on the so-called intrinsic features of a poem (Brooks, Wimsatt).

Against this loose alliance of formalism has played out an equally loose alliance of historical crit. that has sought as its ideal an objective account of a work of art as a function of historical process. Eighteenth-c. critics' stress on "taste" is also a stress upon following what they imagined to be natural. Art itself should be "Nature to advantage dressed, / What oft was thought, but ne'er so well expressed," as Alexander Pope insisted in *An Essay on Criticism*. Samuel Johnson insisted that lit. should be "a just representation of things really existing and actions really performed" (Wellek), which led him to decry John Milton's "Lycidas" as artificial and insincere. Likewise, in the realism of the 19th-c. historical novel (Lukács 1962) and in Matthew Arnold's insistence that lit. can guarantee social stability by inculcating the best that is thought and said, the governing assumptions are that lit. is a historical force. In the 20th c., the treatment of lit. as an expression of a period stands behind the History of Ideas school (Love-

joy) and Tillyard's *Elizabethan World Picture*. Despite its vilification of the hist. of ideas, Marxist ideological critique shares the assumption that a work of art can be demystified to reveal the historical operations that set it in motion. Recalling Plato, some Marxists see works of art as misleading expressions of a dominant ideology that turn people (or actively dupe them) from a historical truth—the operation of class struggle (Eagleton).

Yet if these two strands of formalism and historicism are distinct, they have never been separable. As in Sidney's *Defence of Poesy*, the assertion of poetic autonomy tends to reveal its own historicity. William Wordsworth insisted in the Preface to the *Lyrical Ballads* not only that poetry originates in "the spontaneous overflow of powerful feelings" but that this "emotion" must be "recollected in tranquility." This insistence imagines less an isolated genius than a particular historical imagination (Liu), and it recalls Vico's conception of hist. as made by humans. The aestheticism of Ruskin and Wilde is likewise inseparable from their outspoken socialism. And the New Critical stress on poetic autonomy and objective analysis is regularly invoked less as an end in itself than as a means of overcoming the shattered, fragmented consciousness of modernity (Adorno 1981, Lukács 1964).

The historical view likewise has been shown to have a formalist or idealist logic of its own. The great Ger. historian Leopold von Ranke insisted that historical writing ought to show "wie es eigentlich gewesen." Am. historians in particular took that phrase as a call for empiricist objectivity—to describe an event "as it really was." But "eigentlich" also meant "essentially" in a Hegelian sense. In Ranke's reception and in putatively empirical historicism generally, idealism and objectivity keep moving in and out of each other (Novick). Similarly, White stresses that historical writing tends to depend on particular literary genres (tragedy, comedy) as much as on a clear account of events "wie es eigentlich gewesen," really or essentially.

If poetry and hist., then, have always been complexly intertwined concepts and practices, the most compelling historical crit. has tended to begin with this recognition and attempted to clarify a particular manifestation of this old problem. Certainly, the most influential account of art's relation to hist. has been by G.W.F. Hegel, whose conception of art is based in large part upon Kant's *Critique of Judgment*. Hegel's use of Kant may initially seem surprising because the third critique has also become the basis of a formalist trad. indifferent, or actively hostile, to historicized understandings of art. In *Critique of Judgment*, Kant famously describes aesthetic objects as "purposiveness without purpose" ("Zweckmäßigkeit ohne Zweck"). Artworks cannot be subsumed under another concept but should be enjoyed in themselves. Nevertheless, Hegel incorporates this Kantian argument into his philosophy of hist., where "history" names the gradual unfolding of Spirit. Hegel too insists that art is purposeless, in the sense that it cannot be said to have utility. But it does exhibit an "internal teleology," a logic that is the operation of Spirit. Art is, thus, a contemplative consciousness that comes to know Spirit and does this through its form.

Whereas Aristotle sees such objectification as a question of mimesis, Hegel sees art, and the internal logic of a particular work, as an ontological concern. As a result, it is not accurate to say that a work "represents" Spirit. Rather, a work *is* a particular mode of consciousness. Art for Hegel is, thus, not *Vorstellung* (representation) but *Darstellung* (presentation) or *Scheinen* (manifesting). Art manifests or embodies, rather than represents, and what it ultimately manifests, for Hegel, is Spirit. And since hist. is the unfolding of Spirit, art likewise manifests a particular historical stage of consciousness (Taylor).

Hegel's rewriting of the formal integrity of an art object as an expression of a historical consciousness has been the basis of many 20th-c. aesthetic theories. What changes is what exactly is expressed in the form of a work of art, and here Karl Marx's critique of Hegel has been deeply influential. For Marx, Hegel has everything upside down: rather than imagining the material world as an expression of an abstract spirit, the abstract spirit expresses a historical, material world. What is expressed in a commodity, or in a work of art, is not Spirit but a mode of production: a system of making, reproducing, and distributing the things that are necessary for people to live. Certainly the theorist who propounded and advanced this conviction more than any other was Theodor Adorno, who insisted that any historical analysis must be formalist. The logic of the work is the social logic of the world that produced it, a logic that is otherwise not available for analysis (Adorno 1997, Jameson 1990).

Recent returns to historicism in the last 40 years ought to be seen in this broader perspective. What has changed significantly is the concept of hist. and the Enlightenment criteria of objectivity. As Montrose argued, poststructuralism, and New Historicism esp., focused on both the "historicity of texts" as well as the "textuality of history" (see also Attridge, Bennington, and Young). Hist. became imagined as a text that is, consequently, subject to the hermeneutic and epistemological difficulties of any text (Derrida, Dilthey, Fish), rather than as a spiritual manifestation, a mode of production, or a series of objective facts. Most critical schools of the last 40 years have emerged in part to amplify or address this shift (reader response, New Historicism, systems theory; see Fish; Gallagher and Greenblatt; and Luhmann). Particularly influential have been Althusser's reimagination of hist. through a Lacanian conception of lang., so that, as Jameson (1981) argues, lit. expresses the "political unconscious," the otherwise unrepresentable manifestation of hist. itself; and Foucault's devel. of an "archeology of knowledge" that examines the intersection of power and knowledge. The textualization of hist. has meant that questions of mimesis have acquired renewed force. The Platonic and Aristotelian conceptions of mimesis remain crucial but have been rethought through Foucault's concept of "discourse" (see also Gallagher and Greenblatt). Thus, poetry is imagined in relation to an *epistemē* or system of knowing. And yet this imagining of epistemēs has set the uneasy relation of formalism and historicism in motion once again. On the one hand, an epistemē ends up closely resembling the integrity of a work of art: it has an immanent logic that controls operations within it. The textualization of hist. threatens to end historical thinking itself by collapsing temporal difference into textual difference: a triumph of a new, ahistorical formalism (Jameson 1991). Conversely, the question of how to demarcate an epistemē or field reintroduces the difficulties of objective historical analysis as such and reanimates the effort to create a historicism that is a science and an analysis of aesthetic judgment that is objective (Bourdieu).

*See* HISTORY AND POETRY, MARXISM AND POETRY, NEW HISTORICISM.

■ M. Arnold, *Culture and Anarchy* (1869); E.M.W. Tillyard, *The Elizabethan World Picture* (1943); A. O. Lovejoy, *The Great Chain of Being* (1950); C. Brooks, "The Formalist Critic," *KR* 13 (1951); W. K. Wimsatt, *The Verbal Icon* (1954); Wellek, v. 1; E. Auerbach, *Dante, Poet of the Secular World*, trans. R. Manheim (1961); G. Lukács, *The Historical Novel*, trans. H. and S. Mitchell (1962), and *Realism in Our Time,* trans. J. and N. Mander (1964); E. Auerbach, *Literary Language and Its Public in Late Latin Antiquity and in the Middle Ages*, trans. R. Manheim (1965); M. L. Colish, *Mirror of Language* (1968); L. Althusser, *Lenin and Philosophy and Other Essays*, trans. B. Brewster (1971); M. Foucault, *The Archeology of Knowledge and the Discourse on Language*, trans. A. M. Sheridan Smith (1972); F. Jameson, *The Prison-House of Language* (1972); H. White, *Metahistory* (1973); J. Freccero, "The Fig Tree and the Laurel: Petrarch's Poetics," *Diacritics* 5 (1975); C. Taylor, *Hegel* (1975); T. Eagleton, *Marxism and Literary Criticism* (1976); J. Derrida, *Writing and Difference*, trans. A. Bass (1978); Fish; T. W. Adorno, "Cultural Criticism and Society," *Prisms*, trans. S. and S. Weber (1981); J. Derrida, *Dissemination*, trans. B. Johnson (1981); F. Jameson, *The Political Unconscious* (1981); P. Bourdieu, *Distinction*, trans. R. Nice (1984); M. Jay, *Marxism and Totality* (1984); G. F. Else, *Plato and Aristotle on Poetry* (1986); J. T. Miller, *Poetic License* (1986); L. Montrose, "The Elizabethan Subject and the Spenserian Text," *Literary Theory / Renaissance Texts*, ed. P. Parker and D. Quint (1986); *Post-Structuralism and the Question of History*, ed. D. Attridge, G. Bennington, and R. Young (1987); P. Novick, *That Noble Dream* (1988); W. Dilthey, *Introduction to the Human Sciences [1883], Selected Works*, ed. R. A. Makkreel and F. Rodi, v. 1 (1989); A. Liu, *Wordsworth and the Sense of History* (1989); F. Jameson, *Late Marxism* (1990), and *Postmodernism, or, The Cultural Logic of Late Capitalism* (1991); M. McKeon, "The Origins of Interdisciplinary Studies," *Eighteenth-Century Studies* 28.1 (1994); T. W. Adorno, *Aesthetic Theory*, trans. R. Hullot-Kentor (1997); Derrida; C. Gallagher and S. Greenblatt, *Practicing New Historicism* (2000); N. Luhmann, *Art as a Social System*, trans. E. M. Knodt (2000).

C. WARLEY

**HISTORY AND POETRY.** The distinction between hist. and poetry is a traditional subject of debate, and it continues to matter because it has been so difficult to establish. Historians often defend the veracity of their discipline by distinguishing it from poetry, but this would not be necessary if their work were not also literary in some essential way. Poets often call on the time-honored opinion of Aristotle, who placed poetry above hist., though these appeals to authority only show how hard it is to define the special claims of poetic lang. Thus, hist. and poetry serve as foils for one another, pushed together or pulled apart by the intellectual and polemical needs of the time.

In the beginning, there was no difference between hist. and poetry. Though most organized societies established some sort of rote record keeping at a very early stage, the first narrative hists. were poetic. In Europe, Homer established a record of the heroic past that became the accepted starting point for centuries of later hists. In India, the same role was played by the *Mahābhārata* and the *Rāmāyaṇa*. Even in China, where precise court records were essential to the legitimacy of a reign, the scribes who kept these records also sang and transcribed historical poems. Confucius is said to have arranged and edited the two great anthols. of their work, one historical, the *Classic of Documents*, and the other poetic, the *Classic of Odes* (Ng and Wang). The authority of such foundational works affected historical accounts in many cultures for centuries: even John Milton's *History of Britain* includes an account of the mythical Brutus, who was supposed to have linked the founding of Britain back to the *Aeneid*.

In ancient Greece, the earliest historians cast themselves as rivals to and substitutes for Homer. The opening lines of Herodotus's *Histories* echo the beginning of the *Iliad* and also state the specific claims of *historiê*, a term that originally meant "inquiry." Though Herodotus accepts the basic historicity of the Homeric accounts, he also corrects them where necessary. In doing so, he establishes a basic distinction between the authority of the poet and that of the historian. The poet of the *Iliad* invokes the muses and bases his account on the inspiration they provide. Thus, his knowledge exceeds that of an ordinary human, and his vantage point on events is essentially unlimited. Herodotus, on the other hand, relies on autopsy, testimony, and common sense; thus, he is limited to what human beings might themselves have witnessed. The limitations of this sort of account, however, are supposed to be outweighed by its veracity. Thucydides, therefore, disdains the accounts of poets because their claims cannot be verified (*Peloponnesian Wars* 1.21).

The most famous and influential distinction between hist. and poetry, that of Aristotle in the *Poetics*, codifies this difference in authority. Hist., in this account, relates what has happened, whereas poetry can also relate what may happen or what should happen (1451b). Poetry, therefore, is the higher art; untethered to the actual, it can ascend from the particular to the universal. Actually, despite its great authority, Aristotle's definition is itself quite particular. Enclosed as it is within a larger discussion of unity of action, one that takes tragedy as its normative example, Aristotle's discussion is swayed by the threat of aesthetic disunity. "Of all plots and actions," he says, "the episodic are

the worst" (1452a). A literary form such as hist., in which events are transcribed for no other reason than that they happened and in no other order than the one in which they occurred, violates Aristotle's notions of the shapeliness of art.

Thus, a great deal of the territory between hist. and poetry is left untouched by Aristotle's famous distinction. Since the point at issue is the shape of narrative, lyric poetry is ignored. Though the shift from verse to prose seems momentous, and not unrelated to other distinctions between inspired accounts and verifiable ones, Aristotle dismisses it. On the other side as well, Aristotle leaves out a good deal of what is now implied by the term *history*. He approaches it simply as a kind of writing, one that had still to establish itself. There is, in fact, no notion in Eur. antiquity generally of hist. as a pattern of events quite separate from particular historical accounts, no sense of hist. as a mode of explanation or a kind of knowledge (Press, Unger). For this reason, Aristotle's distinction did not matter much until it had been pulled from its own time and context and reapplied in the Ren.

As long as hist. is nothing more than a kind of writing, as it was for Eur. antiquity, then it will naturally share a great deal with poetry. Thus, Lucian's *How to Write History* (ca. 165 CE) suggests that the historian should "have a touch and share of poetry," though it also cautions against "poetry's wild enthusiasm." Quintilian also considered hist. "a kind of prose poem" (10.1.31). Hist. and poetry differ in degree but not in kind; even so fundamental a distinction as that between fact and fancy is of little use in distinguishing them. Ancient historical accounts showed a marked tolerance for mythic material, as long as it was generally received as if true, and the crucial distinction in judging competing accounts was objectivity rather than factuality (Marincola, Unger). Since hist. and poetry were thought of as rhetorical arts, both were expected to use figurative lang. for persuasive and decorative purposes, though perhaps in varying concentrations.

Only in Christian historiography does the figurative achieve an importance sufficient to affect the relation of hist. to poetry, perhaps even to determine the difference between them. Typological interpretations of the Bible, meant to link the OT to the NT as prophecy to fulfillment, also ascribed a particular shape to the passage of time, one not apparent on the face of events. Within the apparent welter, leading nowhere, there was a pattern and a direction. For Augustine, it was this pattern, read figuratively, that distinguished the hist. of the City of God from the literal passage of time (Press). Thus, Christian historiography proposed a kind of hist. quite different from the mere aggregate of temporal accounts and a meaning of the term *history* distinct from literary composition altogether. "History," as a meaningful movement in time, now became the object of study for hist., a scholarly discipline. And though this lifted hist. out of the ruck of literary rhet., the distinction between mere events and "History" was itself inherently figurative and thus implicitly poetic.

Since historical research and interest were preconditions of the rebirth of ancient scholarship in the Ren., the discipline of hist. enjoyed a singular authority among Ren. humanists. In this context, the dignity of hist. depended on its truthfulness, in contradistinction to the fables and romances of the Dark Ages. For the first time in the writing of Eur. hist., the discovery and evaluation of documentary evidence and the weighing of different sources—and not eyewitness testimony—formed the basis of the historian's authority. For the It. humanists in the *ars historica* trad., figurative lang. was disdained as useless ornament, and hist. was placed above poetry because truth was more effective at teaching and motivation (Cochrane). However, some humanist scholars defended the use of retrospectively composed speeches in works of hist. on the grounds that these offered the same sort of general truth as poetry (Grafton). A contemporaneous but unrelated movement in China resulted in the removal of poetry, as frivolity, from the civil examinations, in favor of cl. and historical knowledge as applied to current events (Ng and Wang).

In both Europe and China in the early mod. period, the systematization of knowledge resulted in various schemes of codification, in which poetry and hist. were usually assigned to different columns. Francis Bacon's *The Advancement of Learning* (1605), e.g., divides human knowledge into the categories of philosophy, poesy, and hist. Bacon defines poetry as "feigned history," higher in one way than real hist. because it can offer a moralized presentation of events, lower in another since it is not true (2.4.1). For other Ren. writers, the use of "fained materials" was to be reprehended, along with "Oratorial or Poetical Notions" (Lowenstein). When Ren. poets called on Aristotle, then, it was because the art of *"feigning" seemed in need of defense. Edmund Spenser, George Puttenham, and Philip Sidney all relied on Aristotle in claiming an aesthetic advantage for poetry, as more able to rearrange events into pleasing patterns, and a moral advantage, as capable of showing what ought to be or can be as well as what is (Levine).

In his *Defence of Poesy* (1595), Sidney also claimed that the best historians of the cl. past had written poetically and not just factually. This was literally true in his own time, when many of the most prominent historians were also poets and vice versa. Walter Ralegh, Samuel Daniel, and Milton all composed national or universal hists., while later John Dryden was poet laureate and historiographer royal. This is the situation that obtained commonly in China as well, where many court historians were also distinguished poets (Ng and Wang). In fact, despite the energy used in early mod. Europe attacking and defending the art of feigning, it proved quite difficult to draw a definitive line between hist. and poetry. Since even Bacon accepted certain fables and marvels as fact, and even the most rigorous hist. depended inevitably on rhetorical devices of some kind, hist. and poetry seemed to differ in degree and not in kind. Even Lodovico Castelvetro, one of the most adamant of humanists where hist. was concerned, could only claim meekly that "the subject matter of po-

etry ought to be similar to that of history, and resemble it, but it should not be identical" (MacLean).

The *philosophes* of the Enlightenment were even more adamant in their preference for fact and somewhat more specific in their dislike of figurative lang. In the entry on the topic in his *Philosophical Dictionary* (1764), Voltaire refused to admit figurative lang. into hist., "for too many metaphors are hurtful, not only to perspicuity, but also to truth, by saying more or less than the thing itself." Poetic accounts, like fabulous ones, were relegated to a past that had not enjoyed the benefits of Newtonian science. Even in the case of epic poetry, Voltaire preferred work that was based on fact. But he was willing to admit as "fact" unprovable accounts that had long been accepted, and he was also concerned to distinguish his own historical work, which had been shaped so as to rival the drama and dignity of tragedy, from mere chronicle (White 1978). Historical writing, in other words, was still considered a branch of lit. and was taught as such, and it was just as difficult for Voltaire as it had been for Castelvetro to differentiate the literary techniques of the historian from those of other writers.

The increasing rationalization and specialization visible since the Ren. did inevitably have the effect of forcing each kind of learning to define its own domain. For the romantics, then, the tension between hist. and poetry was part of a larger conflict between reason and emotion, fact and fancy, science and lit. Writing the entry on "Hist." for the *Encyclopedie moderne* (1828), Prosper de Barante dated this split to the moment at which Herodotus took his departure from heroic poetry. Thus, "the real was separated from the ideal, poetry from prose, the pleasures men allow themselves in the domain of the spirit from the positive aspects of life" (Gossman). When William Wordsworth refers to Aristotle's distinction in the Preface to the 2d ed. of *Lyrical Ballads* (1800), he augments the traditional reasons for the superiority of poetry over hist. by claiming that, in the former, the past is "carried alive into the heart by passion." Poetry, he claims, effects an immediate and affective tie, unencumbered by all the obstacles placed in the way by the historian's lumber. To T. L. Peacock's charge that poetry is nothing more than defective hist., P. B. Shelley's *Defence of Poetry* (1821) responds by claiming that it effects an emotional identification across time that is stronger and more profound than factual hist. can ever be: "it arrests the vanishing apparitions which haunt the interlunations of life, and veiling them, or in language or in form, sends them forth among mankind."

Shelley claims that "all the great historians, Herodotus, Plutarch, Livy, were poets," creators of "living images," though held back by the limitations of historical form, and many of his contemporaries who wrote hist. aspired to escape those limitations and achieve the immediacy of the poetic image. Thomas Carlyle, e.g., declared in an 1834 letter to his brother that his *French Revolution* was to be "an epic poem." In his 1830 essay "On History," he saw the past as "a real Prophetic Manuscript," a kind of poem in itself, available in full to no one but obscure in particular to anyone who approached it as mere fact. Thus, the gap between hist. and poetry was closed from the far side, as it were, and the romantic historian took a role "similar to that of the Romantic poet" (Gossman). In this context, to reconnect past with present was to restore a more general unity, lost as human faculties grew farther apart over time. For Jules Michelet, e.g., the work of a genuine historian was to effect a spiritual resurrection, not only to recount some facts about the past (White 1978).

At the same time, a very different kind of hist. writing arose, partly in response to romantic fiction. Drawn to the novels of Walter Scott, Leopold von Ranke was shocked to discover that the Middle Ages as represented in contemp. documents bore little resemblance to their fictionalized counterpart. His determination to see the past "wie es eigentlich gewesen," lifted free of its original context and freely trans. as it was, became the motto for academic hist. in Europe (Bentley). Though Ranke's immediate influence was limited to Europe, the trend toward an academic, purely factual hist. was worldwide, and the remains of traditional poetic forms were removed from Arab and Bengali hist. as well (Iggers and Wang). And yet Ranke himself was not at all antipathetic to poetry, nor did he believe that hist. should be told without recourse to larger patterns of meaning, figurative or symbolic (Braw, Breisach). Even for Ranke, the distinction between mere recording and actual hist. lay in the ability of the latter to "recreate" and to do so in a way "related to poetry" ("On the Character of Historical Science").

Nonetheless, the 20th c. began with positivist hist. posed starkly against a poetic trad. for which the *lyric was the paradigmatic form. J. B. Bury's 1903 address, "The Science of History," forthrightly declared the claims of historical science, free of speculative metaphysics and of poetic ornament (Breisach), while Ezra Pound's disdain for the " 'germanic' system of graduate study" can represent the poet's response. And yet many historians, led chronologically if not intellectually by Benedetto Croce, attacked the positivist definition of hist. as a science, while many mod. poets, Pound foremost among them, were inspired methodologically by historical research into the past. Pound particularly revered Lorenzo Valla, who gave humanist hist. its illustrious beginning by exposing the donation of Constantine as a forgery. Though *modernism may seem to be antihistorical by definition, Pound was hardly the only modernist who aspired to write "a poem including history." Mod. poets such as Pound, W. B. Yeats, and T. S. Eliot shared with their Victorian predecessors a desire to make the past speak, one so strong it strained against the constraints of lyric form and brought forth time-traveling works like *The Cantos* and *The Waste Land*.

In recent times, the notion that the writing of hist. is inevitably a rhetorical task has been presented by Hayden White as if it also meant that the writing of hist. is essentially rhetorical. This position has attracted much opposition from historians for whom an admission of the rhetorical, the figurative, and the poetic into their work seems to mean the abandonment of truth. Still, historians continue to call upon some form of literary distinction to differentiate their work from mere chronicle. And it remains difficult to distinguish hist., as a pattern of events and a form of knowledge, from the group of writings called hists. without some recourse to figurative understanding of a kind difficult to distinguish from that of the poets.

■ R. Unger, "The Problem of Historical Objectivity," *History and Theory* 11 (1971); H. White, *Metahistory* (1973); G. Press, "History and the Development of the Idea of History in Antiquity," *History and Theory* 16 (1977); H. White, *Tropics of Discourse* (1978); E. Cochrane, *Historians and Historiography in the Italian Renaissance* (1981); J. Kenyon, *The History Men* (1983); L. Gossman, *Between History and Literature* (1990); H. Lindenberger, *The History in Literature* (1990); D. Lowenstein, *Milton and the Drama of History* (1990); G. MacLean, *Time's Witness* (1990)—Eng. poetry, 1603–60; S. Lu, *From Historicity to Fictionality* (1994)—on China; J. Marincola, *Authority and Tradition in Ancient Historiography* (1997); J. Levine, *The Autonomy of History* (1999); F. Ankersmit, *Historical Representation* (2001); *Turning Points in Historiography*, ed. Q. Wang and G. Iggers (2002); M. Bentley, *Modernizing England's Past* (2005)—Eng. historiography, 1870–1970; O. Ng and E. Wang, *Mirroring the Past* (2005)—imperial China; J. D. Braw, "Vision as Revision: Ranke and the Beginning of Modern History," *History and Theory* 46 (Dec. 2007); E. Breisach, *Historiography*, 3rd. ed. (2007); A. Grafton, *What Was History?* (2007); *A Global History of Modern Historiography*, ed. G. Iggers and Q. Wang (2008).

M. North

**HITTITE POETRY.** The great bulk of the lit. recovered from Hattusa (Boğazköy/Boğazkale, located about 62 miles northeast of Ankara), capital of the Hittites from the 17th to the early 12th c. BCE, was written in prose. A metrical analysis of those texts definitely composed in bound lang., such as the mythological compositions known as "Songs," is difficult because of a number of technical characteristics of the script in which they are written: as a syllabary, cuneiform is unable to render precisely the phonology of an IE lang. such as Hittite, since it cannot express consonant clusters adequately, esp. at the beginning or end of words. Furthermore, the Hittite scribes often used *ideograms for many common lexemes, thus concealing their phonological shape from the uninitiated reader. Finally, breaks between lines of poetry are quite often not indicated either by line breaks or by punctuation, which was not a feature of cuneiform texts in any event.

The earliest scrap of Hittite poetry we possess, a soldier's *lament, is included in an historical text composed in the 16th c. BCE:

Nesas waspus[1] Nesas waspus[2] // tiya-mu[3] tiya[4]
nu-mu annasmas[1] katta arnut[2] // tiya-mu[3] tiya[4]
nu-mu uwasmas[1] katta arnut[2] // tiya-mu[3] tiya[4]

(Clothes of Nesa, clothes of Nesa—approach me,
    approach!
Bring me to my mother—approach me, approach!
Bring me to my *uwa*—approach me, approach!)

The basic principle underlying this Hittite versification is phrasal stress, namely, regular lines of four stresses each, falling into two cola (see COLON). The rules governing the presence or absence of stress (on, e.g., enclitics, noun phrases, and adverbs)—whose details still remain somewhat obscure to mod. scholars—have been shown to be applicable in Hittite prose as well. Therefore, this type of poetry is a native Anatolian ling. phenomenon and not, as had been suggested previously, the result of trans. into Hittite of poems originally composed in the Hurrian or Akkadian langs. It seems that *assonance, *alliteration, *rhyme, and synonymous *parallelism also played some role in Hittite poetry, but none of these techniques was structural to its practice.

Many of the *incantations and short hymns featured in Hittite ritual and cult employ at least some elements of poetic lang., but it is the "Songs" adapted from Hurrian-lang. forerunners that best illustrate Hittite poetry. These include the constituents of the Kumarbi Cycle: the "Song of Emergence" (often referred to today as "Kingship in Heaven"), the "Song of Hedammu," the "Song of Ullikummi," the "Song of Silver," the "Song of the Protective Deity," as well as the "Song of the Sea" and the Hurro-Hittite bilingual "Song of Release."

Despite the seeming aberrance of the final line, this quatrain from the "Song of Ullikummi" provides a good impression of the style of Hittite *epic poetry:

Kumarbis[1]-za hattatar[2] // istanzani[3] piran daskizzi[4]
nu idalun[1] siwattan[2] // huwappan[3] sallanuskizzi[4]
nu-za Tarhuni[1] menahhanda[2] // idalawatar[3]
    sanhiskizzi[4]
nu Tarhuni[1] // tarpanallin[2] sallanuskizzi[3]

([The god] Kumarbi takes wisdom into his mind.
He rears a bad day as Evil.
He seeks evil for the Storm-god.
He rears a rival for the Storm-god.)

*See* SUMERIAN POETRY.

■ H. Th. Bossert, "Gedicht und Reim im vorgriechischen Mittelmeergebiet," *Geistige Arbeit* 5 (1938); H. G. Güterbock, "The Song of Ullikummi," *Journal of Cuneiform Studies* 5 (1951); I. McNeill, "The Metre of the Hittite Epic," *Anatolian Studies* 13 (1963); S.P.B. Durnford, "Some Evidence for Syntactic Stress in Hittite," *Anatolian Studies* 21 (1971); H. Eichner, "Probleme von Vers und Metrum in epichorischer Dichtung Altkleinasiens," *Hundert Jahre Kleinasiatische Kommission*, ed. G. Dobesch and G. Rehrenböck (1993); O. Carruba, "Poesia e metrica in Anatolia prima dei Greci," *Studia classica Iohanni Tarditi oblata*, ed. L. Belloni et al. (1995); O. Carruba, "Hethitische und anatolische Dichtung," *Intellectual Life of the Ancient Near East*, ed. J. Prosecky

(1998); H. A. Hoffner, *Hittite Myths*, 2d ed. (1998); H. C. Melchert, "Poetic Meter and Phrasal Stress in Hittite," *Mír Curad*, ed. J. Jasanoff et al. (1998); R. Francia, "'Montagne grandi (e) piccole, (sapete) perchè sono venuto?' (in margine a due recitativi di Iriya, CTH 400–401)," *Orientalia* 73 (2004); G. Beckman, "Hittite and Hurrian Epic," *A Companion to Ancient Epic*, ed. J. M. Foley (2005); G. Beckman, "Hittite Literature," *From an Antique Land*, ed. C. S. Ehrlich (2008).

G. BECKMAN

**HOMODYNE AND HETERODYNE.** Terms taken from the science of radio waves by Knight in 1939 to describe the coincidence (homodyne) and conflict (heterodyne) between word accent and (quantitative) verse *ictus in the Lat. *hexameter of Virgil, and from this usage expanded to refer to other patterns of alignment between accent and ictus in Gr. and Lat. poetry. Knight and others have argued these concords and discords were used by Virgil and other poets for expressive purposes, as instanced, e.g., in the distinctive discord in the fourth foot of the Virgilian hexameter. Other scholars have questioned such a view, finding the coincidences and conflicts fortuitous.

■ W.F.J. Knight, *Accentual Symmetry in Vergil*, 2d ed. (1950; rpt. with corrections, 1979); L. P. Wilkinson, *Golden Latin Artistry* (1963), 89–134; Allen.

J. W. HALPORN

**HOMOEOTELEUTON** (or *homoioteleuton*, Gr.; "similar endings"; cf. *homoioptoton*). This term first occurs in Aristotle (*Rhetoric* 5.9.9; 1410b2) but (though the phenomenon may be found in Gorgias) is normally applied to cl. Lat. (see Quintilian 9.3.77–80). It describes identical or similar inflectional case endings on words in proximity, whether in prose or verse, as in Cicero's famous "Abiit, abscessit, evasit, erupit"; most often the words are at the ends of cola (in prose) or lines (in verse). Aristotle distinguishes three types of sound similarity in endings. When homoeoteleuton occurs at the end of two or more lines in succession, it becomes "case rhyme"—as when Cicero ends three consecutive *hexameters with *monebant, ferebant,* and *iubebant.* But it should be understood that homoeoteleuton is not an instance of *rhyme, strictly speaking, for, in inflectional langs., similarity of word ending is the rule rather than the exception, so often can scarcely be avoided. In noninflected, positional langs., such as Eng., by contrast, the poet must labor for the phonic echo. Word endings in homoeoteleuton bear grammatical information, but that is all. In a system where these do not exist, rhyme poses phonic similarity precisely to point up the semantic difference of the roots. Homoeoteleuton is chosen by the lang.; rhyme is chosen by the poet. True rhyme first appears in the Christian Lat. hymns of the 3rd to 4th cs. CE. Still, it is clear that homoeoteleuton was a distinct and intentional stylistic device and was capable of some range of effect. It is more common by far in Lat. than in Gr. By a curious turn, something of the same effect was later achieved in *rime grammaticale* as practiced in 15th- and 16th.-cs. Fr. poetry by the *\*rhétoriqueurs*. The general association of homoeoteleuton with grammatical necessity (i.e., similarity) and rhyme with intentional artfulness (i.e., semantic difference) is evident in the problematic proposition by W. K. Wimsatt, a proponent of \*New Criticism, of the difference between homoeoteleuton and rhyme as a figure for the difference between prose and poetry.

*See* GRAMMATICAL RHYME.

■ P. Rasi, *Dell'omoeoteleuto latino* (1891); W. K. Wimsatt, "One Relation of Rhyme to Reason," *MLQ* 5, no. 3 (1944); N. I. Herescu, *La Poésie latine* (1960); E. H. Guggenheimer, *Rhyme Effects and Rhyming Figures* (1972); Lausberg, 360–63; L. Håkanson, "Homoeoteleuton in Latin Dactylic Verse," *Harvard Studies in Classical Philology* 86 (1982); Lanham; Norden; D. R. Shackleton Bailey, *Homoeoteleuton in Latin Dactylic Verse* (1994); S. Friedberg, "Prose and Poetry," *PoT* 26 (2005).

T.V.F. BROGAN; N. GERBER

**HOVERING ACCENT** (Ger., *schwebende Betonung*). A term taken up by Jakob Schipper from F. B. Gummere and embraced by his students and a number of 19th- and 20th-cs. metrists (e.g., E. W. Sievers, B. ten Brink, M. Kaluza, R. M. Alden, J. Malof, D. Attridge) for cases in \*scansion where stress seems to be equally disposed on two adjacent syllables. Originally, the concept was offered to solve the problem of a word stress not in alignment with metrical \*ictus. Ten Brink confined "level stress" to equal manifestation of both stress and ictus "in delivery," but to later metrists, it meant that "the stress seems to hover over two syllables, uncertain upon which it should alight" (G. R. Stewart), i.e., in scansion. Seymour Chatman has attacked it as a purely paper ambiguity. G. M. Hopkins employs contiguous strong stressing in that his whole aim is to "spring" loose the alternating stresses of Eng. metrical verse.

*See* ACCENT.

■ Schipper 1.91; Schipper, *History* 138; A. Eichler, "Taktumstellung und schwebende Betonung," *Archiv* 165 (1934): G. B. Erné, "Die schwebende Betonung als Kunstmittel in der Lyrik," Diss., Berlin (1944); Chatman; G. R. Stewart, *The Technique of English Verse* (1966); Wimsatt and Beardsley.

T.V.F. BROGAN

**HUDIBRASTIC VERSE.** A specific form of octosyllabic verse with distinctive polysyllabic and mosaic rhymes, a satirical tone, and frequently impious imagery—widely imitated but never equaled—employed by Samuel Butler (1612–80) in his popular *Hudibras* (1663–78). The meter would appear joggingly monotonous were the reader not kept constantly engrossed in the conversational, sparkling wit and constantly alert for the unexpected rhymes, many of them feminine (see MASCULINE AND FEMININE), which, as an anonymous writer has remarked, "seem to chuckle

and sneer of themselves." Butler speaks, e.g., of Dame Religion,

> Whose honesty they all durst swear for,
> Tho' not a man of them knew wherefore;

and of a time when

> The oyster women picked their fish up
> And trudged away to cry, No Bishop.

*See* MOCK EPIC.

■ E. A. Richards, *Hudibras in the Burlesque Tradition* (1937); I. Jack, "Low Satire: *Hudibras*," *Augustan Satire, 1660–1750* (1952); C. L. Kulisheck, "Swift's Octosyllabics and the *Hudibras* Tradition," *JEGP* 53 (1954); Saintsbury, *Prosody*; L. S. Catlett, "An Odde Promiscuous Tone: A Study of the Prosody of *Hudibras*," *DAI* 32 (1971).

L. J. ZILLMAN

**HUITAIN.** In Fr. poetry, an eight-line \*strophe (see OCTAVE) in eight- or ten-syllable lines, written on three rhymes, with one of these appearing four times and with the same rhyme for the fourth and fifth lines. The order is commonly *ababbcbc*, sometimes *abbaacac*. The *huitain* may be a complete poem in eight lines, or it may be employed as the structural unit for longer poems. In the 15th c., François Villon wrote his *Lais* and the body of *Le grand testament* and most of its \*ballades in huitains. The form was popular in France in the first half of the 16th c. (e.g., Clément Marot), and it was sometimes employed in 18th-c. \*epigrams. In his *Petit traité de poésie française* (1872), Théodore de Banville regrets the abandonment of the huitain by mod. Fr. poets and calls it (with the \*dizain) "perhaps the most perfect thing our lyric art has produced."

■ Kastner; Patterson.

A. G. ENGSTROM

**HUMORS.** The idea that a person's traits of character and behavior depend on a balance of four bodily fluids or "humors"—blood, phlegm, and black and yellow bile—can be traced to Hippocrates (5th c. BCE), though it finds its main exponent in Galen (2d c. CE), the Gr. physician who systematized medical knowledge. In *The Anatomy of Melancholy* (1621), Robert Burton explored the effects of melancholy, which was caused by an excess of black bile. Phlegm created a phlegmatic character; yellow bile, a choleric character; blood, a sanguine character. Burton and other such Ren. writers as Thomas Linacre, Thomas Elyot, and Thomas Wright adapted and explored these theories and emphasized the connection between physical and psychological balance that led to a well-balanced personality and to \*decorum.

In 1597, George Chapman dramatized the theory in *A Humourous Day's Mirth*. Following Chapman's lead, Ben Jonson wrote a number of comedies of humor: *Every Man in His Humour* (1598) and *Every Man out of His Humour* (1599) are the clearest examples; but in his introduction to *The Magnetic Lady* (1641), Jonson suggests that all his comedies have been studies of humors.

In the "Induction" to *Every Man out of His Humour*, Jonson says that a person suffers from a humor

> when some one peculiar quality
> Doth so possess a man, that it doth draw
> All his affects, his spirits, and his powers,
> In their conflutions, all to run one way,
> This may be truly said to be a humor.

He also derides those who have overused the term *humor* until it has become commonplace and those who affectedly claim a humor when they have a small idiosyncrasy. To Jonson's mind, a true humor is a dangerous and corrupting sickness; the *comedy takes root in the process of its correction.

Restoration comedy revived and altered humors comedy, with Thomas Shadwell's claim to be Jonson's heir nearly devastated by John Dryden in "MacFlecknoe" (1682). In the comedies of both and of their successors, humoral characters shade into the Witwouds, Horners, Lovewells, and Lady Cockwoods of comedy of manners. From that devel., eccentric characters or characters dominated by single pronounced traits populate novels from Henry Fielding to Charles Dickens.

■ P. V. Kreider, *Elizabethan Comic Character Conventions* (1935); J. J. Enck, *Jonson and the Comic Truth* (1957); J. D. Redwine Jr., "Beyond Psychology," *ELH* 28 (1961); N. G. Siraisi, *Medieval and Early Renaissance Medicine* (1990); G. K. Paster, *The Body Embarrassed: Drama and the Disciplines of Shame in Early Modern England* (1993); M. C. Schoenfeldt, *Bodies and Selves in Early Modern England* (1999); L. García-Ballester, *Galen and Galenism*, ed. J. Arrizabalaga et al. (2002); M. Floyd-Wilson, *English Ethnicity and Race in Early Modern Drama* (2003); G. K. Paster, *Humoring the Body: Emotions and the Shakespearean Stage* (2004).

F. TEAGUE

**HUNGARY, POETRY OF.** The origins of Hungarian poetry can be traced back to the oral trad. of tribes that settled in the Carpathian basin around the 9th c., although there is no record of these primarily shamanistic songs and their afterlife is part of Hungarian folklore, not lit. The trad. of pagan *bards was, after the establishment of a Christian Hungarian state at the end of the 10th c., slowly absorbed by entertainers of the Middle Ages (see JONGLEUR). The first literary record can be dated from the end of the 12th c. (a funeral sermon) and the first instance of lyric poetry, *The Lament of Mary*, from the second half of the 13th c. This *lament, like most early Hungarian poetry, is based on Lat. models; however, it is not a trans. in the mod. sense of the word but a re-creation, a poetically powerful rendering of Mary's loss, using both rhyme and *alliteration. Chronicles from the 11th to the 14th c. frequently recorded ancient legends ("The Legend of the Miracle Stag," "The Legend of Álmos") that became part of the poetical trad. and formed the basis for later retellings, most notably by the 19th-c. poets Mihály Vörösmarty (1800–55) and János Arany (1817–82).

The early poetry of Hungary was predominantly Lat., and the first significant Hungarian poet, Janus Pannonius (pseud. of János Cseszmiczei, 1434–72) wrote exclusively in Lat. His poetry is steeped in Ren. humanism; after completing his education in the cultural centers of Italy, he became bishop in the southern city of Pécs. The poetry of Pannonius follows cl. antiquity in its form (*epigrams and *elegies were favored) and the humanist rhet. of 15th-c. Lat. in its lang. but stays connected to Hungarian topography and experiences. His accomplishment was to bring Ren. humanism to Hungary and to leave the first body of work to bear the mark of an independent poetic voice.

The Reformation saw the first partial, and later complete, trans. of the Bible (the work of Gáspár Károli [1529?–91], pub. 1590), which instantly enriched the poetic trad. of Hungary. A notable example of this influence can be seen in the Psalm trans. of Albert Szenci Molnár (1574–1639). Other important figures of this period include the writer and publisher Gáspár Heltai (ca. 1490–1574), the Bible translator János Sylvester (ca. 1504–1551), and Péter Bornemissza (1535–84). An important evolving poetic genre of the period is the *song, often accompanied by music, with Sebestyén Tinódi Lantos (1510?–56) as its most important contributor. The main theme of his collected songs (*Cronica*, 1554) is the struggle against Turkish rule, thus establishing an important strand in Hungarian lit. concerned with the country's independence and the fate of its inhabitants. Another important new genre emerging at the end of the 16th c. is that of versified narratives, best exemplified by Péter Ilosvay-Selymes's *The Story of the Remarkable Miklós Tholdi's Extraordinary and Brave Deeds*, and with the work of Albert Gergei, whose *The Story of Prince Argirus and a Fairy Virgin* is based on the It. *bella istoria*. This secular narrative poetry is devoid of didactic elements and, through its concise style and colorful descriptions, marks an important moment in the devel. of Hungarian lit.

Although not the first to write lyric poetry in Hungarian, Bálint Balassi (1554–94) is the first outstanding lyricist of the Hungarian lang. His oeuvre consists of martial poetry (he was active in politics and warfare against the Turks; "In Praise of the Outposts"), love songs ("When He Met Julia, He Greeted Her Thus"), and religious poetry ("He Prays to God"); and his innovations include a new verse form (the Balassi stanza) and the conscious composition of complete sets of poems, with cycles arranged into tightly structured eds. With Balassi, Hungarian poetry reaches maturity in both lang. and form, and his poetry can be compared to accomplishments in other Eur. langs. in the 16th c. He inspired a group of followers, notably János Rimay (1569–1631), a mannerist poet who exemplifies the transition from the late Ren. to the *baroque.

The major poet of the baroque era is Count Miklós Zrínyi (1620–64); his 15-canto *epic *The Siege of Szigetvár* follows the epic ideals exemplified by Virgil and the It. Torquato Tasso but adapts them into a uniquely Hungarian version, with the heroic battle of his great-grandfather against the army of the Ottoman Empire as its subject. Zrínyi himself became an accomplished general in the fight against the Turks and a leading political figure of his time; although poetry was not his primary concern, he was conscious of the importance of a literary legacy and published his epic, along with his love poems, in 1651. *The Siege of Sziget-vár* is built around cl. norms but also uses the rhyming and compositional patterns of earlier Hungarian narrative poetry. The epic form remains an important element in 17th-c. Hungarian poetry; besides Zrínyi, the most important contributor is István Gyöngyösi (1629–1704), whose pseudoepics focus on current events and are characterized by both rich baroque lang. and a political purpose.

Popular poetry of the 17th c. is mostly political in its nature, as Hungary's quest for independence remained a major concern. Anti-Turkish and anti-Hapsburg sentiments are at the core of the so-called *kuruc* poems, a collection of popular songs from the decades between 1670 and 1710, the time of the freedom fights that ended with the armed struggle led by Count Ferenc Rákóczy II (1676–1735). As often happens in Hungarian hist., the efforts for independence ended in heroic defeat; this further strengthened the important thematic trad. of defeat and loss in the poetry of Hungary. Mod. philology has proved many of the *kuruc* songs to be the fabrications of Kálmán Thaly (1839–1909), not unlike James Macpherson's *Ossian*; but, as a cultural idiom, it is part of Hungarian lit.

The intellectual hist. of 18th-c. Hungary followed major Eur. trends. By the century's end, Enlightenment ideals were increasingly accepted, culminating in the movement of the Hungarian Jacobins, heavily influenced by the Fr. Revolution. As the official langs. of the country were still Ger. and Lat., the establishment of the Hungarian vernacular became a goal of the progressive intelligentsia, effectively uniting political and literary goals. The most important representatives of this movement were Ferenc Kazinczy (1759–1831) and János Batsányi (1763–1805), both of whom made invaluable contributions toward establishing an independent Hungarian literary community, with proper institutional support.

The most important lyric poet after Balassi is Mihály Csokonai Vitéz (1773–1805); despite many hardships and a brief life, he was able to produce remarkable poetry that is characterized by strong musical qualities, a *rococo playfulness, and great symbolic power ("To the Echo of Tihany," "To Hope"). His love poetry (addressed to Julianna Vajda, whom he called *Lilla*) is among the best ever written in Hungarian. Csokonai was a great innovator, who used his knowledge of Eur. artistic and philosophical trends of his time to enrich the poetic trad. of his native tongue. An admirer of Jean-Jacques Rousseau, Csokonai appears at the end of the Hungarian Enlightenment. The other important poet at the turn of the 18th and 19th cs. is Dániel Berzsenyi (1776–1836), a reclusive nobleman who became the greatest master of cl. verse forms in Hungarian, successfully transplanting the most difficult Gr. and Lat. metrics into a Hungarian poetic idiom ("The Approaching Winter"). Berzsenyi is not a pure classicist, however; his poetry demonstrates preromantic tendencies, and his influence can be felt well into the 20th c.

The Reform Age, as the first half of the 19th c. is commonly called in Hungarian intellectual hist., was focused on the political progress championed by the liberal nobility. The literary achievements are grouped under the label of *romanticism, and this period is arguably the golden age of Hungarian poetry, with a wealth of canonized masterpieces. Ferenc Kölcsey (1790–1838), a critic, poet, and leading literary figure, became the author of the national *anthem; his poetry is marked by both *classicism and romanticism ("Vanitatum Vanitas," "Huszt"). The poetic oeuvre of Vörösmarty is probably closest in its qualities to Eur. romanticism, both in voice and scope. He began with epic poetry; his *The Flight of Zalán* (1825), a heroic epic written in *hexameter, made his reputation in literary circles, although it is less often read than his later lyric and philosophical poetry ("Appeal," "Thoughts in the Library," "On Mankind"). His late masterpiece "The Ancient Gypsy" is one of the greatest expressions of the desperation following the failure of the 1848–49 War of Independence. The poet forever associated with this war and the preceding revolution of 1848 and one of the best-known poets both in and outside Hungary is Sándor Petőfi (1823–49). Petőfi was the first true Hungarian literary celebrity and the first national poet who tried to earn his living as a writer. His life and death at the battle of Segesvár are part of the nation's cultural memory. Petőfi's poetry is influenced by folk poetry; he transformed the short song into an expression of his poetic *persona, while also creating longer, narrative poetry, incl. the remarkable "John the Valiant" and "The Hammer of the Village." His love poems are classics of the genre ("At the End of September"), and the most important political poem in the Hungarian trad. is his "National Song," written and performed on the outbreak of the 1848 revolution. A counterpoint to Petőfi's short life and popular oeuvre is that of his friend Arany, who created the greatest examples of the *ballad in Hungarian ("Bards of Wales," "The Two Pages of Szondi"), and wrote superb epic poetry (*Toldi Trilogy*). His late poetry ("Autumn Bouquet") shows great emotional and lyrical maturity and successfully redefines the cliché of the young romantic poet. Arany is known for his intellectual integrity, and his impact on the devel. of the Hungarian poetic lang. cannot be overestimated.

The second half of the 19th c. sees the disillusionment after the failed War of Independence slowly diminish, as economic progress transforms the Austro-Hungarian Empire into a mod., developing state. János Vajda (1827–97), a major, if uneven, poet, is known for his philosophical pessimism; while József Kiss (1843–1921) became the first Hungarian poet with a Jewish background and an interest in representing the urban experience. The century's turn saw an unprecedented rise in the numbers of literary publications and marks the start of the golden age of mod. Hungarian lit., which centers around the writers associated with the literary review *Nyugat* (The West), published between 1908 and 1941. The goal of *Nyugat* was to introduce the achievements of Eur. lit. through trans. and to create a platform for the progressive elite of Hungarian lit. Like many in his generation,

Endre Ady (1877–1919) was heavily influenced by Fr. *symbolism; his poetry is considered the starting point for the mod. age in Hungarian lit. His unique style is easily recognizable; his main themes are the backwardness of his country ("At the Gare de l'est," "Upward Thrown Stone"), and his love for Léda ("Beautiful Farewell Message"), along with religious poetry. Ady provokes both controversy and admiration, and his legacy has undergone several changes, but his influence on his contemporaries is undeniable. Árpád Tóth (1886–1928) is best described as a melancholy symbolist, whose basic mood is one of sad longing; part of his poetic oeuvre, as is typical for the *Nyugat* generation, is trans. from Eng., Fr. and Ger. Gyula Juhász's (1883–1937) lifelong battle with depression left a mark on his musical, art nouveau-influenced poetry; besides the Anna cycle (chronicling his unfulfilled love), he is known for his landscape poetry depicting the river Tisza around the southern town of Szeged. The two greatest poets belonging to the first generation of *Nyugat* are Mihály Babits (1883–1941) and Dezső Kosztolányi (1885–1936). Babits, who translated Dante's *Divine Comedy*, was a true *poeta doctus* whose erudition influenced the themes and style of his poetry. He spoke out against World War I in "Before Easter," and his late masterpieces "The Book of Jonah" and "Jonah's Prayer" foreshadow the looming catastrophe of Europe in a beautiful biblical voice. Kosztolányi has a different poetic persona; his early "Laments of a Poor Little Child" show the influences of modernist trends such as *impressionism and *expressionism, while his late poetry is focused on death and the great questions of life, in part following stoic sentiments. Kosztolányi's writing is always crafted with great attention to the poetic medium, his beloved Hungarian lang.

The most important poetic genius of the interwar period is Attila József (1905–37), a tormented man with a difficult upbringing who suffered from psychosis: his genuine, sincere poetry is a towering achievement. He wrote in many forms, with a keen sense of composition, while experimenting with varied poetic sensibilities. Some of his poetry is politically charged, as he sought to give voice to the working poor; more important, though, his poetry can be characterized as an honest exploration of the depths of torment, sometimes presented in a seemingly simple and straightforward manner ("With a Pure Heart," "Ode," "For My Birthday," "By the Danube"). He took his own life at the age of 32, leaving a poetic heritage that has never been surpassed.

The international avant-garde (*futurism and expressionism) is the main influence on the poetry of Lajos Kassák (1887–1967), who chiefly employed *free verse. His style changed during his lifetime, but his political activism was always tied to a search for progressive forms of literary expression ("The Horse Dies, the Birds Fly Away"). Kassák was also a painter, typographer, and graphic artist, with an interest in the visual qualities of poetry, and promoted early avant-garde art forms through the jours. he edited.

A member of the second generation of the *Nyugat*, the poet Lőrinc Szabó (1900–57) chronicled the evolution of his own self and the hist. of his relationships. Szabó became a master of the *sonnet, which he arranged into book-length cycles, besides being a prolific translator. The fate of Miklós Radnóti (1909–44) was marked by his heritage: as a baptized Jew, he fell prey to the discriminatory Jewish laws introduced in the 1930s and died in a forced-labor camp, leaving behind the most significant Hungarian Holocaust poetry ("Forced March," "Razglednica"). He was a classically oriented poet, who used cl. forms as a refuge against the ever-growing horrors of Nazi Europe. Another representative of this generation, Gyula Illyés (1902–83), wrote mostly in free verse, under the influence of Fr. surrealism and expressionism, and later became part of the populist writers' movement. He was well regarded by the socialist government of the postwar period, though he struggled to maintain his independence. Sándor Weöres (1913–89), the creator of *nursery rhymes that are known to almost all Hungarians, is a poet of immense erudition and great talent, who has an unparalleled ability to evoke musical qualities in his complex, universal poetry influenced by both Eastern philosophies and Western mysticism. A very different kind of poet, János Pilinszky (1921–81), used a reduced, bare lang. to comunicate the anxieties of a moral being in the 20th c., always struggling with questions of faith. He belonged to a group of poets gathered around *Újhold* (New Moon), the short-lived but significant postwar literary magazine; it also included the poet Ágnes Nemes Nagy (1922–91).

The great survivor of 20th-c. Hungarian poetry is György Faludy (1910–2006), who was acquainted with József yet lived into the 21st c. His poetic persona can be described as a vagabond, traveling and experiencing life to the fullest. He spent a considerable part of his live in exile (after being imprisoned by the communist regime) but returned in 1988, before the political changes. Among his best known work is his trans. of François Villon, first pub. in 1934.

An important part of Hungarian culture comes from Transylvania, now part of Romania, where the greatest number of Hungarians live outside Hungary. Domokos Szilágyi (1938–76) should be mentioned as a poet from this region whose ling. and formal invention is noteworthy, while András Ferenc Kovács (b. 1959) is a living Transylvanian poet who reinterprets (through palimpsest and *pastiche) the greater heritage of Eur. poetry with considerable poetic force.

A humorous tone, political engagement, and confessional themes dominate the poetry of György Petri (1943–2000), who was part of the antiestablishment of the 1970s and 1980s. The leading female poet of the contemp. era is Zsuzsa Rakovszky (b. 1950), a careful examiner of the fragility and insecurity of human experience. A prolific, though uneven, contemp. poet well known for his philosophical yet playful poetry, Dezső Tandori (b. 1938) is associated with the renewal of the poetic idiom in the 1970s. Two notable contemp. poets are János Térey (b. 1970), who experiments with longer verse narratives, and Dániel Varró (b. 1976), whose sense of rhyme and poetic tone is displayed in his playful and often intertextual poetry.

Since 1989, Hungary has undergone many transformations, and Hungarian poets are trying to find their role and tone in a world marked by new and powerful modes of communication, a new evolving social structure, and changes in the consumption of lit. Because of its relative ling. isolation, Hungarian poetry is still not widely known in the outside world, although new anthols. have been published and recent trans. may bring new audiences to its hidden gems.

■ **Anthologies:** *Magyar Poetry* (1908), *Modern Magyar Lyrics* (1926)—both trans. and ed. W. N. Loew; *The Magyar Muse*, ed. and trans. W. Kirkconnell (1933); *Magyar versek könyve*, ed. J. Horváth (1942); *A Little Treasury of Hungarian Verse*, ed. and trans. W. Kirkconnell (1947); *Hungarian Poetry*, ed. E. Kunz (1955); *Hét évszázad magyar versei*, ed. I. Király et al., 4 v. (1978–79); *Old Hungarian Literary Reader*, ed. T. Klaniczay (1985); *The Face of Creation: Contemporary Hungarian Poetry*, ed. and trans. J. Kessler (1988); *In Quest of the "Miracle Stag,"* ed. A. Makkai (1996); *The Colonnade of Teeth: Modern Hungarian Poetry*, ed. G. Gomori and G. Szirtes (1997); *Magyar nőköltők a XVI. századtól a XIX. századig*, ed. M.S.Sárdi (1999).

■ **Bibliographies:** *Bibliography of Hungarian Literature*, ed. S. Kozocsa (1959); A. Tezla, *An Introductory Bibliography to the Study of Hungarian Literature* (1964)—annotated; and *Hungarian Authors: A Bibliographical Handbook* (1970).

■ **Criticism and History:** F. Toldy, *A magyar költészet története* (1867); G. Király, *Magyar ősköltészet* (1921); J. Horváth, *A magyar irodalmi népiesség Faluditól Petőfiig* (1927), and *A magyar irodalmi műveltség kezdetei* (1931); A. Schöpflin, *A magyar irodalom története a XX. században* (1937); T. Kardos, *Középkori kultúra, középkori költészet* (1941); J. Horváth, *A magyar vers* (1948); J. Waldapfel, *A magyar irodalom a felvilágosodás korában* (1954); T. Kardos, *A magyarországi humanizmus kora* (1955); A. Szerb, *Magyar irodalomtörténet* (1958); *A magyar irodalom története*, ed. M. Szabolcsi, 4 v. (1966); P. Rákos, *Rhythm and Metre in Hungarian Verse* (1966); J. Horváth, *Rendszeres magyar verstan* (1969)—systematic Hungarian poetics; A. Karátson, *Le symbolisme en Hongrie* (1969); A. Kerek, *Hungarian Metrics* (1971); *L'Irréconciliable: Petőfi, poète et révolutionnaire*, ed. S. Lukácsy (1973); M. Szegedy-Maszák, *Világkép és stílus* (1980); *Pages choisies de la litterature hongroise des origines au millieu du XVIIIe siècle*, ed. T. Klaniczay (1981); *Vándorének*, ed. M. Béládi (1981)—Hungarian poets in Western Europe and overseas; *A History of Hungarian Literature*, ed. T. Klaniczay (1982); B. Pomogáts, *A nyugati magyar irodalom története* (1982); L. Czigány, *The Oxford History of Hungarian Literature* (1984); *A nyugati magyar irodalom 1945 után*, ed. M. Béládi et al. (1986). E. Kulcsár Szabó, *A magyar irodalom története 1945–1991* (1993); M. Szegedy-Maszák, *Literary Canons: National and International* (2001); G. Szirtes, *An Island of Sound: Hungarian Poetry and Fiction before and beyond the Iron Curtain* (2004); *A magyar irodalom történetei*, ed. M. Szegedy-Maszák et al. (2007); L. C. Szabó, *A magyar költészet századai* (2008).

V. VARGA

**HYBRID POETRY.** The term *hybrid poetry* came to be used informally in the 1990s to describe a growing stylistic eclecticism in late 20th-c. poetry of the U.S. It refers to the fusion of styles that had been experienced by some as separate polarities before the 1980s. With the publication of the anthology *American Hybrid*, the term began to receive wider attention. In her intro., Cole Swensen notes that "while extremes remain, and everywhere we find complex aesthetic and ideological differences, the contemporary moment is dominated by rich, uncategorizable writings, often hybrids that mingle attributes from previous 'camps' in diverse and unprecedented ways." Although in a practical sense all poetry is *hybrid*, the term hybrid proposes a botanical conceit to explain how apparently competing strains might have influenced each other in the evolving course of the art.

What is hybridized in hybrid poetry? A form that passed into Am. poetry in the 1980s might be described something like this: on the one hand is poetry that emphasizes personal or emotional expressiveness, often with a first-person, apparently autobiographical speaker. It ranges in style from the restrained writings of Elizabeth Bishop to the intimate poems of James Schuyler and Frank O'Hara to the explosive poetry of Robert Lowell, Allen Ginsberg, and their heirs. Though it sometimes uses *surrealism, it mostly employs tropes of *realism. Poetry from the other strain foregrounds, rather than emotional expression, the materiality of lang. It is attracted to procedures that call into question the authority of a subjective speaker and representation itself; it points to its own processes of composition, employing disjunctive or fragmentary syntax as an alternative to conventional grammar.

How these different strains arose will be a source of historical inquiry as the poetic canon is continually reconstituted. As Swensen notes, mid-19th-c. poetry provides one point of entry: the turbulent, often revolutionary values of romantic poets were taken up, addressed, and often opposed by other writers, particularly by symbolists after Charles Baudelaire—including Arthur Rimbaud and Stéphane Mallarmé—who tried to establish distance from the personal expressiveness of *romanticism; the sense of poetry as oppositional was brought forward into the modernist enterprise. Yet if the Fr. symbolist avant-garde questioned the values of romantic poetry—the idea of nature as an ally, an emphasis on subjective experience, and the primacy of the feeling function—they also embodied many romantic values in their own practices, desiring freedom to choose subject matter and style, promoting the belief in the power of art and imagination to be forces of change. Romantic and postsymbolist poetry were hybridized, even as some of their features—esp. attitudes toward nature and urbanity—were not.

In the Anglo-Am. *modernism of the 1920s and 30s, braiding poetic practices from the previous century was also common. Robert Frost and E. A. Robinson created the clear traditions of naturalism in narrative poetry. T. S. Eliot's poetry, using images from Fr. *symbolism to render mod. urban atmospheres, attracted disciples from the *Fugitives to Robert Lowell and beyond. Ezra Pound collaged fragments of pastoral, medieval voices and urban song for his *Cantos*, and the self-proclaimed Objectivists identified Pound and W. C. Williams as twin progenitors. Gertrude Stein's abstract, cubist experiments resurfaced in the feminist lyric innovation of the 1980s as well as in *Language poetry. Indeed, techniques such as *collage and *cubism accelerated processes of poetic hybridization.

The 1950s and 60s saw a number of attempts to discern (and sometimes to reconcile) the two strains—perhaps most notably, Robert Lowell's acceptance speech for the National Book Award of 1960, in which he situated his work between what he called "the raw and the cooked" in contemporaneous poetry. In *American Hybrid*, Swensen notes the significance of the publication of Donald Allen's 1960 anthology *The New American Poetry 1945–1960*, which "brought all marginal poetries together, naming them and throwing them into sharp focus, [marking] the beginning of their demarginalization." In 1965 Robert Kelly and Paris Leary's anthology *A Controversy of Poets* arguably tried to hybridize the prevailing divisions. Beginning with the early 1980s, continual shifts not only in aesthetic values but in the polarization of camps give rise to complexly hybridized poetic practices. Much new poetry of the 21st c.— particularly that of lyric innovation—reflects oppositional features of avant-gardes, including an interest in the materiality and structure of language, without sacrificing emotional content or topical subject matter.

*See* AVANT-GARDE POETICS, BLACK MOUNTAIN SCHOOL, OBJECTIVISM.

■ *The New American Poetry 1945–1960*, ed. D. Allen (1960); *A Controversy of Poets*, ed. P. Leary and R. Kelly (1965); *An Exaltation of Forms*, ed. A. Finch and K. Varnes (2002); *American Women Poets in the 21st Century*, ed. C. Rankine and J. Spahr (2002); C. Rankine and L. Sewell, *American Poets in the 21st Century: The New Poetics* (2007); *American Hybrid*, ed. D. St. John and C. Swensen (2008); R. Shepherd, *Lyric Postmodernisms* (2008).

B. HILLMAN

**HYMN.** An ancient Gr. liturgical and literary genre that assimilates Near-Eastern and specifically Heb. trad. in the Septuagint trans. (LXX) of the OT, the hymn was introduced into Christian trad. in the Gr. NT and the Lat. Vulgate Bible and by the Gr. and Lat. fathers, and has continued to flourish in Western culture in both liturgical and literary trads. down to the 21st c. Other trads. represented in Asian and in early Am. cultures, as well as in those of ancient Akkad, Sumer, and Egypt that influenced Heb. trad., are important but lie beyond the scope of this entry.

The Gr. noun *hymnos* refers to a song, poem, or speech that praises gods and sometimes heroes and abstractions. Hymns are in lyric measures, *hexameters, elegiac couplets, and even prose in late antiquity; the longest critical discussion of the hymn by the rhetorician Menander, *Peri Epideiktikon* (3d c. CE), makes no distinction between prose and verse. Most of the Gr. lyric hymns (mainly fragments by Alcaeus, Simonides, Bacchylides, Timotheus, and Pindar) were probably sung in religious worship. Similarly, the hexameter *Orphic Hymns* with their markedly theurgic emphasis may have been designed for religious purposes, although such abstractions as Justice, Equity, Law, and Fortune, as well as the Stars, Death, and Sleep, are subjects of praise. Thucydides refers to one of the hexameter *Homeric Hymns* as a prelude or preface; these presumably were literary introductions to epic recitations. The famous philosophic hymn by the Stoic Cleanthes (4th–3d c. BCE) is probably literary rather than liturgical in intention, as are the *Hymns* by the Neoplatonic philosopher Proclus (5th c. CE), although there is a significant theurgic element in the latter. The six extant *Hymns* of the Gr. poet Callimachus, in hexameters and elegiac couplets, are certainly literary emulations of the *Homeric Hymns*, and the long prose hymns of the apostate Emperor Julian (4th c. CE) could not have been used in worship.

When the LXX translators came to the Heb. OT, they used the nouns *hymnos*, *psalmos* (song or tune played to a stringed instrument), *ode* (song), and *ainesis* (praise), and the related verbs (*hymneo*, etc.) to translate a variety of Heb. words for praise, song, music, thanksgiving, speech, beauty, and joy. Several psalms are identified in their titles as hymns (e.g., 53, 60), incl. sometimes the explicit use of both words, *psalmos* and *hymnos* (6, 75; see PSALM). The psalms are also identified with odes or songs in several titles (e.g., 51), sometimes in the expression "a song of a psalm" (*ode psalmou*, 65), at others as "a psalm of a song" (*psalmos odes*, 67 and 74). Psalm 136.3 connects *ode* and *hymnos*; and, in two similar NT passages, all three terms are mentioned together with the implication of rough equivalence (Eph. 5:19, Col. 3:16).

While literary hymns were not a popular or important genre in pagan Roman adaptations of Gr. literary forms, Lat. Christians of the 4th c., influenced by the hymn singing of the Eastern Church, revived and introduced both literary and liturgical hymns into the Lat. West. This revival is also reflected in Jerome's Vulgate trans. of the Bible, where the transliterations *hymnus* and *psalmus* are regularly employed (along with a more accurate and consistent trans. of the OT Heb.). In his *Confessions* (9.7), Augustine remarks on the introduction of the singing of hymns and psalms in Milan by Ambrose. Isidore's influential *Etymologiae* (7th c.) identifies the Psalms of David as hymns (1.39.17) and asserts that, properly speaking, they must praise God and be sung, although in another work he notes that Hilary of Poitiers (also 4th c.) first composed hymns in celebrations of saints and martyrs (*De ecclesiacis officiis* 1.7).

Ambrose's short hymns (eight quatrains of iambic dimeter) are explicitly trinitarian and were intended to counteract Arian doctrine, which had itself apparently been fostered by hymns of an Arian bent. Considerable suspicion remained in the 6th and 7th cs. over the liturgical use of hymns composed by men as opposed to the divinely inspired Psalms of the Bible. But the unquestioned orthodoxy of Ambrose himself probably helped the hymn become accepted as a regular part of the liturgy along with the psalmody. As the Middle Ages progressed, many brilliant new hymns were added to the Lat. hymnody, from the great passion hymn "Vexilla regis prodeunt" by Fortunatus (7th c.) and the "Veni, Creator Spiritus" (trans. by John Dryden) to Thomas Aquinas's hymns for Corpus Christi day and the Franciscan "Stabat mater." Closely related to the hymn is the med. "prose" or sequence. Noteworthy are the works of Notker Balbulus (9th–10th cs.) and of Adam of St. Victor (12th c.), and the magnificent Franciscan "Dies irae."

The Reformation renewed the suspicion of hymns among many Protestants. Although Martin Luther composed hymns from paraphrases of the Psalms and other portions of the Bible, he also translated hymns from the Roman breviary and wrote original ones. John Calvin, on the other hand, who opposed the use of man-made hymns in congregational worship, retained the poet Clément Marot to create a metrical psalmody or psalter in Fr., and the Calvinistic position strongly influenced the Anglican and Presbyterian churches in Great Britain in the 16th and 17th cs. The renderings of the Anglican psalmody by Thomas Sternhold and John Hopkins (2d ed., 1549), generally infelicitous but set in *ballad meter, may have prompted many Eng. poets of the Elizabethan and Jacobean periods to experiment with trans. of the Psalms (Philip and Mary Sidney produced an entire psalter, while John Milton translated 17 psalms in a variety of verse forms); but in popular terms, the Sternhold-Hopkins psalter was enormously successful.

The Roman Catholic Church experienced a different problem. The great influence of Ren. humanism led to a succession of more or less unfortunate revisions of the hymnody beginning with that by Leo X in 1525 and ending with Urban VIII's in the early 17th c. The motive was to turn the late cl. and med. Lat. of the hymns and sequences into good cl. Lat.

It remained for the Eng. nonconformist minister Isaac Watts to revive the writing of original hymns in the 18th c. and turn the primary focus of hymns away from literary artistry back to the rugged emotional expression of strong religious beliefs (*Hymns and Spiritual Songs*, 1707–9). As the 18th c. progressed, there occurred an enormous outpouring of hymns, along with new metrical versions of psalms, in the works of John and Charles Wesley, John Newton, Augustus Montague Toplady, Edward Perronet, the poet William Cowper, and many others, some of which (e.g., those by Charles Wesley) have great lyric power.

This outpouring continued in the 19th c. The works of Fanny Crosby and Katherine Hankey and the musical arrangements of W. H. Doane are preeminent among those of literally hundreds of writers and composers. New hymns were composed to the end of the 20th c. (e.g., by Doris Akers and Stuart Hamblen) and continue to this day (e.g., by Andraé Crouch and Ralph Carmichael). New and revised hymnals are still being arranged.

At about the same time that Ambrose introduced congregational hymn singing to the Christian church

in Milan, the Christian poet Prudentius (ca. 348–405) wrote Christian literary hymns in the manner of the pagan poets of antiquity. Although some of Prudentius's creations are brief enough to be sung congregationally, many of his hymns are much too long for worship, and all have obvious literary and poetic pretensions. The fine lyric measures in two of his collections (*Peristephanon* and *Cathemerinon*) celebrate mainly saints and martyrs.

The cl. literary hymn was revived during the Ren. in both its Prudentian and secular forms. Pope Paul II's 140-line *sapphic "Hymnus de passione" (15th c.) could have been written by Prudentius, but Giovanni Pontano's (1426–1503) sapphic "Hymnus in noctem" (from his *Parthenopei*) imitates Catullus's lyric celebration of Diana. Pontano also wrote Christian literary hymns in Lat. elegiacs. Another Neo-Lat. poet, Marcantonio Flaminio (1498–1550), who wrote probably the best liturgical hymns of the Ren. (in Ambrosian dimeters), also composed a celebrated literary lyric, "Hymnus in Auroram."

Michele Marullo's 15th c. *Hymni naturales* were found by many in the Ren. to be too thoroughly pagan in subject and tone as well as form. There were other celebrated Christian literary hymns in the Ren., esp. those by Marco Girolamo Vida in the early 16th c. (*Hymni*, 1536). The later vernacular poets follow the lead of the Neo-Latinists. Pierre de Ronsard, along with Marullo the most prolific writer of literary hymns, composes both explicitly Christian and secular, philosophical hymns along with mythological celebrations. The first two of Edmund Spenser's *Four Hymns* celebrate love and beauty in a cl. philosophical (and Petrarchan) way, while the latter two celebrate heavenly (i.e., Christian) love and beauty.

These two trads. continue in Neo-Lat. and the vernacular lits., most notably in George Chapman's two long hymns in *The Shadow of Night* (1594), in Raphael Thorius's celebrated *Hymnus tabaci* (1625), in several of Richard Crashaw's long Christian literary hymns, James Thomson's "A Hymn on the Seasons," John Keats's "Hymn to Apollo," and P. B. Shelley's "Hymn to Intellectual Beauty," "Hymn of Apollo," and "Hymn of Pan."

While liturgical hymns tend simply to start and stop, the literary hymn frequently has an Aristotelian coherence—a beginning, middle, and end. Typically, it begins with an invocation and *apostrophe. The main body will narrate an important story or describe some moral, philosophic, or scientific attribute. A prayer and farewell provide the conclusion. The hist. of literary hymns is marked by great stylistic variation and rhetorical elaboration, depending on the writer's object of praise and his conception of the relation of style to content. The definitive survey of this trad. remains to be written.

See ASSYRIA AND BABYLONIA, POETRY OF; EGYPT, POETRY OF; GREEK POETRY; HEBREW POETRY; INDIA, POETRY OF; INDIGENOUS AMERICAS, POETRY OF THE; LATIN POETRY; LAUDA; SUMERIAN POETRY.

■ **Anthologies and Primary Texts**: *Analecta hymnica medii aevi* (1886–1922); *Early Latin Hymns*, ed. A. Walpole (1922); *Mystical Hymns of Orpheus*, trans. T. Taylor

(1896); *Lyra Graeca*, ed. and trans. J. Edmonds, 3 v. (1922); *Proclus's Biography, Hymns, and Works*, trans. K. Guthrie (1925); *Poeti Latini del Quattrocento*, ed. F. Arnaldi et al. (1964); *Hymni latini antiquissimi XXV*, ed. W. Bulst (1975); *Hymns for the Family of God*, ed. F. Bock (1976); *New Oxford Book of Christian Verse*, ed. D. Davie (1981); *English Hymns of the Nineteenth Century*, ed. R. Arnold (2004).

■ **Criticism and History**: G. M. Dreves, *Aurelius Ambrosius* (1893); R. Wünsch, "Hymnos," Pauly-Wissowa, esp. 2.119, 3.145 ff.; Manitius; "Psalters," *Dictionary of Hymnology*, ed. J. Julian, 2d ed., 2 v. (1907); L. Benson, *Hymnody of the Christian Church* (1927); P. Von Rohr-Sauer, *English Metrical Psalms from 1600 to 1660* (1938); O. A. Beckerlegge, "An Attempt at a Classification of Charles Wesley's Metres," *London Quarterly Review* 169 (1944); H. Smith, "English Metrical Psalms in the Sixteenth Century and Their Literary Significance," *Huntington Library Quarterly* 9 (1946); R. E. Messenger, *The Medieval Latin Hymn* (1953); Raby, *Christian*; *Reallexikon II* 1.736–41; Bowra; L. Benson, *The English Hymn* (1962); J. Szövérffy, *Die Annalen der lateinischen Hymnendichtung*, 2 v. (1964–65); C. Maddison, *Marcantonio Flaminio* (1966); H. Gneuss, *Hymnar und Hymnen im englischen Mittelalter* (1968); P. Rollinson, "Renaissance of the Literary Hymn," *Renaissance Papers* (1968); C. Freer, *Music for a King* (1971); J. Szövérffy, *Iberian Hymnody: Survey and Problems* (1971); J. Ijsewijn, *Companion to Neo-Latin Studies* (1977); J. Szövérffy, *Guide to Byzantine Hymnography* (1978); *Menander Rhetor*, ed. and trans. D. Russell and N. Wilson (1981); J. Szövérffy, *Religious Lyrics of the Middle Ages: Hymnological Studies and Collected Essays* (1983); P. S. Diehl, *The Medieval European Religious Lyric* (1985); J. Szövérffy, *Concise History of Medieval Latin Hymnody* (1985); and *Latin Hymns* (1989); W. D. Furley, "Praise and Persuasion in Greek Hymns," *JHS* 115 (1995); D. Sheerin, "Hymns," *Medieval Latin*, ed. F.A.C. Mantello and A. G. Rigg (1996); M. Depew, "Enacted and Represented Dedications: Genre and Greek Hymn," *Matrices of Genre*, ed. M. Depew and D. D. Obbink (2000); C. Léglu, *Between Sequence and Sirventes* (2000); J. R. Watson, "Hymn," *A Companion to Victorian Poetry*, ed. R. Cronin, A. Chapman, A. H. Harrison (2002); *Sapientia et Eloquentia*, ed. G. Iversen and N. Bell (2009).

P. ROLLINSON

**HYPALLAGE** (Gr., "exchange"). A device of syntactic displacement that changes the reference of words in syntagms or sentences: a word, instead of referring to the word it logically qualifies, is made to refer to some other. As such, hypallage is one species of *hyperbaton. Henry Peacham, the Tudor rhetorician, writes, "Open the day and see if it be the window." Shakespeare found many uses for the device; many of them exhibit, in the misplacing of the words, mental disturbance or confusion or (witty) dimness of wit. Bottom, appropriately, has several, incl. "I see a voice. Now will I to the chink, / To spy and I can hear my Thisby's face" (*A Midsummer Night's Dream* 5.1.189–90). Hypallage indicates the speaker's mental confusion in Slender's remark, "All his

successors (gone before him) hath done't; and all his ancestors (that come after him) may" (*Merry Wives of Windsor* 1.1.13). The most common example of hypallage is the transferred epithet, a figure characteristic of Virgil, Edmund Spenser, Shakespeare, and John Milton, which has some effects of *personification. Lausberg, discussing "die metonymischen Epitheta," distinguishes syntactical and other varieties, e.g., Caesar's "This was the most unkindest cut of all" (*Julius Caesar* 3.3.188) and Othello's "Alas what ignorant sin have I committed?" (4.2.70). T. S. Eliot has "Winter kept us warm, covering/Earth in forgetful snow" (*The Waste Land*). We would today be tempted to call many examples spoonerisms.

■ M. Joseph, *Shakespeare's Use of the Arts of Language* (1947); Lanham; Lausberg; Morier; A. Quinn, *Figures of Speech* (1982).

R. O. EVANS; T.V.F. BROGAN; A. W. HALSALL

**HYPERBATON.** A technical term from the cl. art of rhet., hyperbaton is a generic name for a variety of figures of speech that transpose words within a sentence. Figures contained under the umbrella of hyperbaton include anastrophe (transposition of two words in a sentence); *hysteron proteron (syntax or sense placed out of logical or temporal order); *hypallage (transposition of the natural relationship between two elements in a proposition); *tmesis (separation of a compound word by the insertion of another word); and *parenthesis (insertion of a word, phrase, or sentence into an already complete sentence), among others. These figures deviate from ordinary word order by means of reversal, transposition, and interruption; together they constitute some of the most widely used rhetorical devices in poetry. Although hyperbaton is more common in Gr. and Lat. writing than in noninflected langs. that depend on word order for sense, poets writing in the Eur. vernaculars have nevertheless made frequent use of its constructions. Through syntactical displacements, hyperbaton may emphasize a particular word or idea, convey an emotional state, or fulfill the demands of poetic meter. The result may be humorous—as in Shakespeare's *A Midsummer Night's Dream*, when Bottom cries, "I see a voice. Now will I to the chink, / To spy and I can hear my Thisby's face"—as well as lyrical—as in Emily Dickinson's poem, "From cocoon forth a butterfly / As lady from her door / Emerged—."

Longinus offers the most extensive ancient discussion of hyperbaton, calling the figure "the truest mark of vehement emotion." According to this view, the figure imitates the speech of a person who has been carried away by a violent feeling: "while under the stress of their excitement, like a ship before a veering wind, they lay their words and thoughts first on one tack then another, and keep altering the natural order of sequence into innumerable variations" (*Peri hypsous* [*On the Sublime*]). Such a conception of hyperbaton indicates how the figure could be included in the list of syntactical displacements through which psychoanalytic crit. reads the unconscious intentions of the subject (Lacan). However, although hyperbaton may imitate the natural speech of a person afflicted with great emotion, cl. theory understands it to be the product of rhetorical technique. Quintilian claims that, without figures such as hyperbaton, lang. would be "rough, harsh, limp, or disjointed," with words "constrained as their natural order demands" (*Institutio oratoria*).

Like other rhetorical figures, definitions of hyperbaton rely upon an idea of ordinary, natural, or normal lang. against which its lexical transpositions can become legible. The Gr. word literally means "to overstep," and Lat. and Eng. trans. of hyperbaton—such as *transgressio* and "the trespasser"—convey its association with acts of transgression (Quintilian, *Institutio oratoria*; George Puttenham, *Arte of English Poesie*). This thematic of transgression can become a part of the figure's meaning in a poetic context, as when Edmund Spenser uses hyperbaton to describe the actions of a deceitful man in bk. 6 of *The Faerie Queene*:

> For to maligne, t'envie, t'use shifting slight,
> Be arguments of a vile donghill mind,
> Which what it dare not doe by open might,
> To worke by wicked treason wayes doth find,
> By such discourteous deeds discovering his base kind.

The grammatical disorders of hyperbaton may also imply a corresponding social disorder, as suggested in Winston Churchill's reputed comment to an officious newspaper editor: "This is the kind of impertinence up with which I will not put." Hyperbaton is rarely used today as a term of literary analysis, as deviations in word order now seem coincident with poetic lang. itself, rather than a particular form of figuration.

*See* ORNAMENT, RHETORIC AND POETRY, SCHEME.

■ J. Lacan, "The Insistence of the Letter in the Unconscious," *YFS* 36–37 (1966); H. Weil, *The Order of Words in the Ancient Languages Compared With That of the Modern Languages* (1978); B. Vickers, *In Defense of Rhetoric* (1988); B. Dupriez, *A Dictionary of Literary Devices* (1991); Lanham; G. Burton, "Silva Rhetoricae" (rhetoric.byu.edu).

J. C. MANN

**HYPERBOLE** (Gr., "throwing beyond"). Hyperbole is a figure of speech marked by flagrant exaggeration. From Deut. 1:28 where "cities are fortified to heaven" to Virgil's "Twin rocks that threaten heaven" (*Aeneid* 1.162) to Shakespeare's "it smells to heaven" (*Hamlet* 3.3), hyperbole is common across all lits. Isocrates invokes the trope by name, calling his subject "a god among men" (*Evagoras* 72). Aristotle recognized it as a type of metaphor and suggested it demonstrates a vehemence associated with youth or anger (*Rhetoric* 1413a). Quintilian identifies it with comic wit as "an elegant straining of the truth" (*Institutio oratoria* 8.6.67).

Because hyperbole pushes comparison past simple credibility, the Ren. critic George Puttenham designated it as a figure of "immoderate excesse" and dubbed it the "over reacher" (*The Arte of English Poesie* 3.7). Though the suitability of diction to subject matter has

been a primary topic among critics from antiquity to today, the distortion of truth in hyperbole is instantly recognizable. Hyperbole succeeds by making propositions that are either impossible—"What is he ... whose phrase of sorrow / Conjures the wandering stars, and makes them stand / Like wonder-wounded hearers?" (*Ham.* 5.1)—or that are linked to a "comparative absolute": "Zenocrate, the loveliest maid alive, / Fairer than rocks of pearl and precious stone" (Christopher Marlowe's *Tamburlaine*, 1.1.3). The use of hyperbole in drama produces different effects from those it produces in poetry; overextension may be less tolerable in a poetic speaker than a tragic protagonist, for whom the added dimension of action may be measured against expression in ways unavailable to the poet.

Hyperbole achieves its end by a seeming contradiction, as a truth is nonetheless understood somewhere short of the false mark. Beyond speech, it is considered a "figure of thought" and is related to the forms of understatement *litotes and *meiosis.

■ G. Genette, "Hyperboles," *Figures I* (1966); G. V. Stanivukovic, "'Mounting above the Truthe': On Hyperbole in English Renaissance Literature," *Forum for Modern Language Studies* 43 (2007).

K. McFADDEN

**HYPERMETRIC** (Gr., "beyond the measure"). A line that has at least one extra syllable that is not part of the regular metrical pattern. The term is used in two distinct ways in cl. poetry. In lyric meters, particularly *ionics, hypermetric refers to a line that has one or more extra syllables at its beginning (see ANACRUSIS). The second application of the term is to an extra syllable at the end of the line. This extra syllable, however, elides with the initial syllable of the next line so that, prosodically, the extra final syllable is not counted. A line that does have an extra felt syllable at the end is properly called hypercatalectic. An elided final syllable is relatively common in lyric but very rare in epic. Because it does not occur in Gr. hexameter, its appearance in some 20 lines of Virgil's poetry has attracted considerable attention.

In OE poetry, the term denotes a half line expanded by means of an additional stress (see ENGLISH PROSODY, GERMANIC PROSODY). In OE poetry, particularly in *Beowulf*, hypermetric lines have occasioned considerable prosodic dispute. Attempts have been made to find a theoretical origin for the practice of hypermetrics, as well as to construct a taxonomy for hypermetric lines, studying, among other things, the relationship between extra stresses and patterns of *alliteration.

■ Sievers; A. J. Bliss, *The Metre of "Beowulf,"* 2d ed. (1962); J. C. Pope, *The Rhythm of "Beowulf,"* 2d ed. (1966); Brogan; West; G. Russom, *Old English Meter and Metric Theory* (1987); G. P. Goold, "Hypermeter and Elision in Virgil," *Vertis in usum*, ed. J. F. Miller, C. Damon, and K. S. Myers (2002); T. A. Bredhoft, "The Three Varieties of Old English Hypermeter Versification," *N & Q* 50 (2003).

R. A. HORNSBY; T.V.F. BROGAN; D. KUTZKO

**HYPOGRAM** (Gr., "subscription" or "something written below"; de Man trans., "sub-text or, better, infra-text"). *Hypogram* came into use among 20th-c. semioticians to describe the "theme-word" (*mot-thème*) or absent text, seme, or presupposition that furnishes a nucleus from which a poem's "given" structure (see MATRIX) takes its form. According to the hypothesis guiding Ferdinand de Saussure's study of Lat. verse between 1906 and 1909, words, names, or *clichés hide below the surface of a text, identifiable only by distributions of ungrammatical phonemic features in the surface text. Saussure variously employed the terms *anagram, paragram*, and *hypogram* to describe this encoded dissemination of a key term, reserving the latter esp. for the instance of a proper name or master word (as when the name *Pindarus* is dispersed through the opening verses of the *Aeneid*). Saussure may first have theorized the hypogram in work on Vedic hymns and subsequently discovered them in a transhistorical range of Gr. and Lat. poetry from *Saturnian verse to Angelo Poliziano. He searched for but found no cl. doctrine governing the use of hypograms; rebuffed by the few contemporaries he queried about their existence (incl. It. poet Giovanni Pascoli, perhaps the last celebrated Lat. versifier), Saussure abandoned his search. Saussure's notions, which contradicted his contemporaneous theory of the arbitrariness of the ling. sign (*l'arbitraire du signe*), were both ridiculed and mythologized by commentators after the rediscovery of his notebooks in the 1960s and subjected to the critique that the limited phonetic distribution of a particular lang. made it possible to find unlimited patterns absent of authorial intention. For such critics, Saussurean hypograms are the result of subjective modes of reading, rather than intrinsic aspects of a text discoverable by an empirical method.

Nevertheless, semioticians in the 1970s, esp. Riffaterre, shifted and extended the definition of *hypogram* to describe the way in which any poem is produced around an absent semantic nucleus. Whereas Saussure stressed a particular keyword distributed phonemically throughout the text, Riffaterre described the hypogram as a "unit of readable meaning susceptible of grammatical predication." When *hunger*, e.g., is granted as the hypogrammatic nucleus of Arthur Rimbaud's poem "Fêtes de la faim" or *nothing* in Stéphane Mallarmé's "*-yx*" sonnet, the poem's many ungrammatical features become intelligible. The purpose of the poem is not to reveal the hypogram but to hide it. Reading practices defined by a search for a hypogram substitute figurative elaboration for referential reading. De Man considered Riffaterre's to be "the most reliable didactic model" in its day, but Culler observes that Riffaterre's reduction of poetic structure to a game or experiment ("a calisthenics of words") can diminish *interpretation into the puzzling out of a proper "solution." Hypogrammatic interpretation has also been called "cipher-type montage" and has a legacy in the compositions of the contemp. Fr. poet Jacques Roubaud.

*See* SEMIOTICS AND POETRY.

■ T. Blount, *Glossographia* (1656); F. de Saussure, *Cours de linguistique générale*, ed. C. Bally and A. Seche-haye [1916], trans. W. Baskin (1974); J. Starobinski, *Les Mots sous les mots: Les anagrammes de Ferdinand de Saussure*, trans. O. Emmet (1979); M. Riffaterre, *Semiotics of Poetry* (1978); J. Culler, *The Pursuit of Signs* (1981); D. Shepheard, "Saussure's Vedic Anagrams," *MLR* 77 (1982); P. de Man, "Hypogram and Inscription," *The Resistance to Theory* (1986); W. Gordon and H. Schogt, "Ferdinand de Saussure: The Anagrams and the *Cours*," *The Emergence of the Modern Language Sciences*, ed. S. Embleton et al. (1999); J.-J. Thomas and S. Winspur, *Poeticized Language: The Foundations of Contemporary French Poetry* (1999); S. Metzidakis, "Replacing Literary History: With Hypograms or Paragrams?" *L'Esprit Créateur* 49 (2009).

H. FEINSOD

**HYPOMETRIC** (Gr.; "less than a measure"). Poetic forms lacking in prosodic fullness in relation to the norm; contrast *hypermetric. The nature of the lack varies from *prosody to prosody. Quantitative: in *Amores* 1, Ovid wittily announces he set out to write of heroic matters in *hexameters, but Love stole a foot from every other line—so yielding the *elegiac distich he had in mind all along. Accentual: Shakespeare's sonnet 145 is in *iambic *tetrameter rather than in the conventional *pentameter—the only hypometric sonnet in the sequence. Syllabic: early Japanese poetry often used lines shorter or longer than the normal fives and sevens; from about the 9th c., however, the hypermetric (*ji amari*) was allowed, whereas the hypometric (*ji tarazu*) was proscribed, a rule followed rigorously until recent times. *Catalexis, by contrast, refers to a specific line or colon short on its end in an otherwise regular poem.

*See* ACEPHALOUS.

E. MINER

**HYPORCHEMA** (Gr., pl. *hyporchemata*). Gr. choral song accompanied by dancing. Hyporchema was supposed to have been invented by Thaletas of Gortyn in Crete (7th c. BCE), but Athenaeus found its origins in Homer (cf. *Odyssey* 8.261 ff.). It was characterized by its use of *cretic measures. As a hymn, the hyporchema was akin to the *paean in honor of Apollo, as it was later to the *dithyramb in praise of Dionysus. Pindar, e.g., wrote both hyporchemata and paeans. In *tragedy, the term was applied by Eucleides, an authority cited by Tzetzes, to lyric passages where the chorus was evidently dancing. Consequently, some mod. scholars have unnecessarily imagined it as a kind of lively *stasimon, e.g., in several passages of Sophocles, where jubilation of the chorus at the arrival of glad tidings is followed by the catastrophe of the play.

■ E. Diehl, "Hyporchema," Pauly-Wissowa; Schmid and Stáhlin; A. M. Dale, *Collected Papers* (1969)—esp. ch. 3; R. Seaford, "The Hyporchema of Pratinas," *Maia* 29 (1977–78); Michaelides; A. W. Pickard-Cambridge, *The Dramatic Festivals of Athens*, 2d ed. (1989).

R. J. GETTY; T.V.F. BROGAN

**HYPOTAXIS AND PARATAXIS.** Contrasting ways of connecting clauses or phrases, whether in prose or in verse. In a hypotactic style, one specifies the logical relationships among elements, rendering the entailments and dependencies among them explicit by placing them in a hierarchy of levels of grammatical subordination. The main clause is connected to the dependent elements by subordinating conjunctions (*while*, *because*, *if*, etc.) or by relative pronouns (*who*, *which*, *that*, etc.). Hypotaxis also may extend beyond the sentence boundary, in which case the term refers to a style in which the logical relationships among sentences are explicitly rendered.

In a paratactic style, the logical relationships among elements are not specified but are left to be inferred by the reader. Within the sentence, a paratactic style may connect clauses or phrases at the same grammatical level with coordinating conjunctions (employing *polysyndeton) or without coordinating conjunctions (employing *asyndeton). The relationships among sentences can be paratactic as well, as in Caesar's famous claim, *"veni, vidi, vici."*

Hypotaxis and parataxis are each capable of varied poetic uses. Because hypotactic styles specify the logical connections among their elements, they lend themselves to establishing the sense that the main poetic idea has been meditated upon and seen from all its angles. Hypotaxis can also suggest that the speaker is somewhat detached from the immediacy of the action, perhaps to enable a deeper purchase upon its nature or a more reflective account of its meaning. Finally, a hypotactic style lends itself to registering qualifications, hesitations, and mixed feelings since it provides the grammatical means of weighing conflicting moments against each other.

Parataxis, by contrast, is esp. suited to rendering thoughts and actions from the urgent perspective of a participant caught in the immediate flow of events. As a hypotactic style lends itself naturally to an analytical point of view, so a paratactic style lends itself naturally to the rush and chaos of life as it is lived in the immediate first-person. A hypotactic style sometimes indicates the desire to evaluate the subject of the poem with a this-worldly intellect; a paratactic style sometimes indicates the desire to gain poetic access to the otherworldly power readers associated with archaic or primitive texts.

Because it leaves the logical relationship among terms unspecified, a paratactic style is useful in circumstances where the meaning of an event or the nature of its connections should be suggested by the author or inferred by the reader, as in the "subverted metaphors" frequently employed in *haiku (see JAPAN, MODERN POETRY OF) or in *pantun, where the relationship between two observations (in the first form) or between two couplets (in the second) is implied but unstated. The tendency to leave the connections implicit also makes possible a slightly different relationship between author and reader since the author does not so much explain a thought as require the reader to achieve that thought by a leap of imagination. Thus, parataxis is particularly useful when a meaning is designed to be shown rather than said, as in the famous example of Ezra Pound's "In a Station of the Metro." That the connections must be suggested rather than defined makes a paratactic style also capable of implying that the poem registers a power beyond its ability to articulate, that it sees its elements as brightly lit particulars that direct the attention into a fraught and unspeakable background where the power of the narration is, as in the Abraham episode in Genesis (in Auerbach's famous reading of that episode in *Mimesis*), a function of the disparity between the terseness of the narration and the immensity and obscurity of the ultimate subject of that narration. Auerbach says of this kind of parataxis that "it is precisely the absence of causal connective, the naked statement of what happens—the statement which replaces deduction and comprehension by an amazed beholding that does not even seek to comprehend—which gives this sentence its grandeur."

Many interesting effects can be achieved by playing the tone against the grain of the syntax. In a letter to Sidney Cox in 1915, Robert Frost jeered at "Solway Ford" by Wilfred Gibson, noting that if one were to "look at the way the sentences run on," one would discover that "they are not sentences at all in my sense of the word." Clearly, Frost did not mean that the sentences were ungrammatical but that they did not have what he calls the "sentence sound," the unmistakable syntactic tang of living utterance. Part of the problem seems to be the unintentionally comic disparity between the syntax of the passage and its intended tone. The poem turns on a moment of violence in which the protagonist's horse rears and breaks free, overturning his wagon upon him and leaving him pinned beneath it, to await the incoming tide by which he will be drowned. Gibson is horrified by the scene and wishes us to feel that horror. But the sentence in which this violent action is rendered is a stately, complexly hypotactic word temple. The effect of adopting a hypotactic rather than a paratactic syntax is to distance the observer and the poet from the action. One might imagine wishing to do so for purposes of irony, but it is hard to see irony in the long sentence that Gibson actually wrote, which begins, "The empty wain made slowly over the sand." Compare, for instance, the syntax in the moment of violent action in Wilfred Owen's "Dulce et Decorum Est," in which a column of retreating British soldiers during World War I is suddenly caught up in a barrage of gas shells. In the passage beginning "Gas! GAS! Quick, boys!" the sentences are long, but the syntax is intensely paratactic. Later in the poem, Owen adopts a pointedly hypotactic syntax, meant to reflect bitterly not only upon the distance between the civilian's point of view and the soldier's but also upon the meaning of the heritage of cl. eloquence summed up in Horace's motto that it is sweet and fitting to die for one's country. Frost himself renders the chainsaw accident in "Out, Out—" in surprisingly hypotactic lang.; but in that poem, the tension between the syntax and the meaning is meant to capture the speaker's inability to come to terms with the violence of the scene. Unlike Gibson, Frost is well aware of the strangeness of the syntax he uses, and he exploits it to give a nightmarish unreality to the moment of the accident. Although the sentences are quite short, they all seem to be fragments of a longer hypotactic sentence the speaker cannot get straight.

Paratactic styles are often underlined by anaphora (repeated words or phrases at the beginning of sentences or verses). Anaphora is particularly characteristic of folk or archaic styles of narration—the Bible, say, or the Child ballads. Anaphora often places events in a flow of rhapsody where the coherence of the passage is provided not by articulating the logical connections among the events but by tapping into the sense that this story has been retold so often that its inevitabilities go without saying. Anaphora initiates a flow of eloquence that presumably can just keep on going—it may not articulate the relationships among the successive objects, but it places them in a context of unending rhetorical abundance. Walt Whitman's anaphoric catalogs are a good example of the alliance between parataxis and anaphora.

*See* ANAPHORA, CATALOG.

■ Auerbach; T. W. Adorno, "Parataxis: Zur späten Lyrik Hölderlins," *Gesammelte Schriften*, ed. R. Tiedemann and H. Schweppenhäuser, v. 11 (1974); R. Alter, *The Art of Biblical Narrative* (1981); J. L. Jugel, *The Idea of Biblical Poetry* (1981); A. Easthope, *Poetry as Discourse* (1983); R. Silliman, *The New Sentence* (1987); F. Jameson, *Postmodernism, or, The Cultural Logic of Late Capitalism* (1991); B. Perelman, *The Marginalization of Poetry* (1996); L. Hejinian, *The Language of Inquiry* (2000); Lord.

J. BURT

**HYSTERON PROTERON** (Gr., "the latter [as] the earlier"). A specific type of *hyperbaton or syntactic dislocation: the figure in which the natural order of time in which events occur is reversed, usually because the later event is considered more important than the former, e.g., Xenophon, "trophe kai genesis" (*Memorabilia* 3.5.10)—in William Shakespeare's phrase, "for I was bred and born"; and Virgil, "Moriamur et in media arma ruamus" (*Aeneid* 2.353)—"Let us die and rush into battle." George Puttenham, recalling the Eng. proverb "the cart before the horse," calls it "the preposterous" (*Arte of English Poesie*, 1589) but distinguishes between effective and ludicrous examples. Hysteron proteron may also represent inversion of the social or natural order: "How wild a Hysteron Proteron's this, which Nature crosses, / And far above the top the bottom tosses" (Joseph Beaumont, *Psyche* 1.85). But in poetry, the device may be highly effective without seeming preposterous, as in P. B. Shelley's "I die! I faint! I fail!" ("The Indian Serenade"). Compare the logical fallacy of *petitio principii*.

■ S. E. Bassett, "H. P. Homerikos," *HSCP* 31 (1920); Lausberg; P. Parker, *Shakespeare from the Margins* (1996), chap. 1.

R. O. EVANS; A. WATSON

**IAMBE.** A Fr. satiric poem of variable length in *rimes croisées* (*abab cdcd*, etc.), in which *alexandrines alternate throughout with *octosyllables. The iambe, whose name is rooted in the satirical trad. going back to the bitter iambics of the Gr. poet Archilochus (fl. 648 BCE), came into Fr. as a generic term with the posthumous publication of the *Iambes* of André Chénier (1762–94) and *Les Iambes* (1830–31) of Auguste Barbier. Isolated examples of the form are also to be found in Victor Hugo ("La Reculade," *Les Châtiments*) and Théophile Gautier ("Débauche," *Premières poésies*). Violent contrasts in rhythm from line to line make the Fr. iambe a remarkably appropriate vehicle for satire; the brevity of the octosyllable interrupts the amplitude of the alexandrine with a sense of urgency and exasperation; the broad, oratorical movement of the longer line gives way to the looser rhythms and private voice tones of the shorter one:

> Nul ne resterait donc . . .
> Pour cracher sur leurs noms, pour chanter leur
>     supplice?
> Allons, étouffe tes clameurs;
> Souffre, ô coeur gros de haine, affamé de justice.
> Toi, Vertu, pleure si je meurs.

(A. Chénier, Iambes XI)

■ T. de Banville, *Petit traité de poésie française* (1872); Kastner; A. Chénier, *Oeuvres complètes* (1958); M. Grammont, *Le Vers français*, rev. ed. (1961), and *Petit traité de versification française*, 10th ed. (1982).

A. G. ENGSTROM; C. SCOTT; D. EVANS

**IAMBIC** (Gr. *iambos*; Ger. *Jambus*). The chief meter in most cl. and mod. prosody. Iambic meter is based on the iamb, a metrical *foot consisting of a short or unstressed syllable followed by a long or stressed syllable. In Lat. poetry, the iamb was comprised of this short and long syllable pair; in Gr. it was a *metron consisting of this plus a preceding *anceps and long syllable: x – ◡ –. The word *iambos* (pl. *iamboi*) first appears in Archilochus and is used for a distinct genre of poetry, namely, *invective; this generic association was carried into Roman times. The name for the meter thus derived from the genre with which it was originally associated, not vice versa. Originally, the word *iambic* may have arisen from occasions on which ritual songs (some of them lampoons) were sung and danced. Archilochus uses iambic metra in *trimeters, *tetrameters, and *epodes; and the Ionian poets who preferred it have come to be known as "iambographers."

Iambic was thought in antiquity to be the rhythm nearest to common speech. Throughout Gr. and Lat. poetry, iambic in trimeter and tetrameter is the standard meter for recitation forms, esp. dramatic *dialogue. The Lat. iambic dimeter became, with Augustine, Ambrose, and Hilary of Poitiers, the standard line for the early Christian *hymn, making it perhaps the chief meter of the Middle Ages and the ancestor of the mod. tetrameter, very important in Rus., and second only to the pentameter in Eng. and Ger. The same claim has been made in mod. times about Eng. as was made by the ancients about Gr. (Aristotle, *Rhetoric*, bk. 3)—namely, that iambic is the rhythm of common speech.

This view—that much poetry is iambic because lang. is iambic—may be bolstered by the recognition that iambic rhythm is, more simply, an alternating pattern and that, given any system of two values (on-off, long-short, stressed-unstressed), alternation is the simplest pattern capable of being generated. On the other hand, alternation clearly describes *trochaic meters just as well as it does iambic. Several important psychological experiments in the 20th c. showed that when auditors are presented with an alternating series of weak and strong tones that are perfectly isochronous (equidistant), they invariably *hear* them as grouped into binary units—i.e., iambic or trochaic, most often trochaic. When the intensity of the stress is increased, the units are perceived as trochaic. When the stress, or the interval after the stress, is lengthened, the units are perceived as iambic. In general, when intervals are irregular, the series will be heard as trochaic. More recently, Hayes has claimed that the apparent asymmetry between iambs and trochees is based on an extralinguistic principle of rhythmic grouping called the iambic/trochaic law. According to this model, the basic properties of rhythmic structure may determine ling. stress.

All these experiments report on only primary (simple) rhythmic series and not on lang. In contrast, it has also been argued that lang. itself is in fact a secondary rhythmic series where multiple rhythms are enacted, and interact, across the same space simultaneously. When the events are words, lang. imposes a secondary or counterrhythm on top of the phonological rhythm of stresses and unstresses that is morphological and syntactic (see RISING AND FALLING RHYTHM); here, word types and word boundaries matter. Morphological factors have been shown to be real and important forces in cl. meters (see BRIDGE). We must realize that readers' and auditors' perceptions of lines as "iambic" or "trochaic" depend on both phonotactics and morphotactics within the metrical frame. Trochaic rhythms are sensitive to (1) the word shapes used to fill the pattern (trochaic words are needed frequently) and (2) alteration of the beginnings or ends of the sequences (*catalexis is important), whereas iambic rhythms seem not to be sensitive to either. *Anacrusis is common in iambic verse but virtually impossible in trochaic, catalexis is unusual, and word shapes are largely immaterial—iambic verse accepts virtually any. Halpern argues persuasively that iambic meter is a more complex and subtle meter because it is capable of effects of modulation not possible in any other meter, whether trochaic, ternary, or purely accentual. Iambic meter, i.e., is not the reverse of trochaic but rather in its own class altogether.

Disruption of an iambic meter might seem attainable in several ways: extra stresses in the line, missing stresses in the line, or extra unstressed syllables without loss of stresses (extra syllables). But iambic generally tolerates occasional extra syllables and dislocations of stress placement very well, esp. at major syntactic boundaries such as the beginning of the line and the *caesura. In general, contiguous stresses are the most serious problem for iambic meters. The general principles of rhythm apply: as long as the reader's perceptual frame, the "metrical set," is not broken, considerable variation is possible. Further, the lang. has an efficient mechanism for demoting heavy contiguous stresses and for promoting weak stresses in runs of unstressed syllables so as to even out the rhythm. Older prosodists who advocated the notion of trochaic "substitutions" in iambic verse perhaps failed to grasp that such feet are not trochaic; so long as the iambic metrical set is preserved, they are perceived as complications, not violations. This suggests that the terms *iambic* and *trochaic* should be applied only to meters, not units of meters.

Several important poets have felt that iambic rhythm is tyrannous: Ezra Pound observed that "the god damn iamb magnetizes certain verbal sequences" (*Letters* 1950); for the *vers-librists* and imagists, then, "to break the pentameter, that was the first heave" (Canto 81), and the means were "to compose in the sequence of the musical phrase, not in sequence of a metronome" ("A Few Dont's by an Imagiste" [1913]), means Pound claimed to have found in *Occitan poetry and Chinese. Breaking the iambic rhythm is precisely the effect G. M. Hopkins sought to achieve with *"sprung rhythm."

Various iambic meters have now been identified both in poetry and in common speech patterns (by literary scholars and linguists, respectively) across a diverse range of lang. contexts, incl. Korean, Somali, Paumari, and Hungarian.

*See* BINARY AND TERNARY; DIPODISM, DIPODIC VERSE; PYRRHIC; SPONDEE.

■ J. M. Edmonds, *Elegy and Iambus* (1931); A. D. Knox, "The Early Iambus," *Philologus* 87 (1932); E. Pound, "Treatise on Metre," *ABC of Reading* (1934); H. Woodrow, "Time Perception," *Handbook of Experimental Psychology*, ed. S. Stevens (1951); J. Thompson, "Sir Philip and the Forsaken Iamb," *KR* 20 (1958); Maas; M. Halpern, "On the Two Chief Metrical Modes in English," *PMLA* 77 (1962); D. W. Cummings and J. Herum, "Metrical Boundaries and Rhythm-Phrases," *MLQ* 28 (1967); Dale; M. L. West, *Studies in Greek Elegy and Iambus* (1974); P. Fraisse, *Psychologie du rythme* (1974); G. Nagy, "Iambos: Typologies of Invective and Praise," *Arethusa* 9 (1976); Halporn et al.; Brogan; M. L. West,

*Introduction to Greek Metre* (1987); J. Thompson, *The Founding of English Metre*, 2d ed. (1989); B. Hayes, *Metrical Stress Theory* (1995); G. Powell, "The Two Paradigms for Iambic Pentameter and Twentieth-Century Metrical Experimentation," *MLR* 91 (1996); M. J. Duffell, "'The Craft So Long to Lerne': Chaucer's Invention of the Iambic Pentameter," *Chaucer Review* 34 (2000); *Iambic Ideas*, ed. A. Cavarzere, A. Aloni, and A. Barchiesi (2001); *Formal Approaches to Poetry*, ed. B. E. Dresher and N. Friedberg (2006); Duffell.

T.V.F. BROGAN; S. S. BILL

**IAMBIC SHORTENING** or *brevis brevians* (Lat., "a short syllable shortening"). A linguistic phenomenon whose consequences are of special importance for the metrics of early Lat. poetry. In the syllabic series ∪ − or ∪ − x, the syllable immediately preceding or following the natural word accent may be counted short; thus ∪̆ − may become ∪̆ ∪, as in Terence, *Eunuchus* 8: *ex Graecis bŏnĭs*, where the final syllable of *bonis* (naturally long) counts as short because the word accent falls on *bo*-; or ∪ − x̌; may become ∪ ∪ x̌, as in Terence, *Eunuchus* 22: *stratus măgĭstrátus*, where the second syllable of *magistratus* though long counts as short because the natural word accent falls on the following *a*. A short monosyllable, or a disyllable with the first syllable short and the second elided, can alter a following long to a short, e.g., Plautus, *Aulularia* 483: *ĕt illae*. It is then a phenomenon of juncture (*sandhi*) and involves more than a preceding short.

■ W. M. Lindsay, *Early Latin Verse* (1922); E. Fraenkel, *Iktus und Akzent im lat. Sprechvers* (1928); H. Drexler, *Plautinische Akzent Forschungen*, I, II (1932), index (1933); O. Skutsch, *Prosodische und metrische Gesetze der lambenkürzung* (1934); C. Questa, *Introduzione alla metrica di Plauto* (1967), 31–70; W. Mańczak, "Iambenkurzung im Latin," *Glotta* 46 (1968); Allen; A. M. Devine and L. D. Stephens, "Latin Prosody and Metre: Brevis Brevians," *CP* 75 (1980).

J. W. HALPORN

**ICELAND, POETRY OF.** (For information on Icelandic poetry before 1550, see NORSE POETRY.) Considering the difficult living and cultural conditions in Iceland after its literary peak in the 12th to 14th cs., and esp. the period from 1600 to 1800, with its severe cold, epidemics, famines, volcanic eruptions, and oppressive political conditions under Danish rule, it is remarkable that there was any Icelandic poetry at all at this time. Poetry's success was facilitated by a fairly high rate of literacy as well as an almost universal custom of composing, memorizing, and reciting verse.

Whether oral or literary, secular or religious, popular or learned, poetry was to remain the principal genre of Icelandic lit. for centuries after the Reformation in 1550, only giving way to works of prose in the late 19th and early 20th cs. One notable feature is Icelandic poets' use of *alliteration, a poetical device common to many Germanic literary trads. in the Middle Ages but surviving into the mod. period only in Iceland. Traditional alliteration was not seriously challenged until

Icelandic modernists started advocating and practicing *free verse around the middle of the 20th c., and it is still used sporadically in mod. Icelandic poetry and lyrics.

The introduction of paper in the 16th c. had a greater impact on Icelandic poetry than two other phenomena from the same period, the introduction of Danish Lutheranism and printing (which was monopolized by the Church until 1772). Paper made it economically feasible for farmers and priests all over the country to copy mss., and through these copies, as well as extensive memorization, secular lit. was disseminated. The *kenning-based, alliterative and rhymed narrative poetry known as *rímur held sway over other kinds of secular poetry from the 14th to the 19th cs., whereas Lutheran *psalms came to prominence in religious poetry during the Reformation; their impact proved enduring.

Bishop Guðbrandur Þorláksson (ca. 1541–1627) laid the foundations for the reformed lit. of the country by publishing and commissioning psalms and other religious poetry. His *Vísnabók* (Book of Poems) of 1612 bears witness to the strength of the poetic trad. in Iceland. Whereas in countries such as Denmark and Germany clerical writings shaped the lang., in Iceland the Church had to rise to the level of the vernacular. Earlier trans. of Lutheran hymns into Icelandic had failed miserably in this respect. Bishop Guðbrandur thus enlisted the service of the best poets he knew for this volume, such as the Reverend Einar Sigurðsson (1538–1626), among whose poems is a tender *lullaby on the birth of Jesus, "Kvæði af stallinum Kristí" (Poem on Christ's Cradle) in the popular dance meter *vikivaki*. His son, the Reverend Ólafur Einarsson (1573–1659), also a notable poet, contributed a gloomy complaint on the times to *Vísnabók*. In a rare instance of poetic genius passing from parents to children through three generations, Ólafur's son, the Reverend Stefán Ólafsson (ca. 1619–88), became one of the leading poets of the 17th c. He wrote, as did his father, complaints on laborers and Icelandic sloth, as well as love lyrics and poems about the pleasures of tobacco, drink, and horses.

A poet who wrote little in this light, worldly vein was the Reverend Hallgrímur Pétursson (1614–74), indubitably the major poet of the 17th c. in Iceland. He did not, like Stefán Ólafsson, mock the common people, but he was not shy about attacking the ruling classes. After commenting on Pilate's error in consenting to Jesus' death in his 50-poem cycle *Passíusálmar* (*Hymns of the Passion*, 1666), Hallgrímur adds, "God grant that those in power over us avoid such monstrous offenses" (hymn 28). As a religious work, the *Passíusálmar* is unsurpassed in Icelandic lit. and a *baroque tour de force, full of striking imagery. An excellent shorter hymn, "Um dauðans óvissan tíma" (On the Uncertain Hour of Death), is still sung at funerals, a good example of the role that poetry of a high order has played in Icelandic life. Hallgrímur also wrote three rímur cycles and other secular poems, such as "Aldarháttur" (Way of the World), contrasting the degenerate present with the glorious period of the past Icelandic Commonwealth.

Two figures stand out in 18th c. Icelandic poetry. Jón Þorláksson (1744–1819) wrote several popular short poems, incl. one on a dead mouse in church ("Um dauða mús í kirkju"), and long trans. of Alexander Pope's *Essay on Man*, John Milton's *Paradise Lost*, and F. G. Klopstock's *Messias*, the latter two in *fornyrðislag*. Eggert Ólafsson (1726–68) was a child of the Enlightenment who, having studied natural hist. in Copenhagen and made a survey of Iceland, preached the beauty and usefulness of Icelandic nature in poems such as "Íslandssæla" (Iceland's Riches) and the long *georgic "Búnaðarbálkur" (Farming Poem).

This positive attitude toward Icelandic nature, along with a yearning for independence, became an important feature of Icelandic *romanticism, whose major poet is Jónas Hallgrímsson (1807–45). Apart from his lyrical descriptions of nature, which tend toward the *pastoral but also include sublime elements, as in "Ísland"—which begins "Iceland, frost-silvered isle! Our beautiful, bountiful mother!"—he is remembered for his poems on the pain of lost love and for his mastery of many poetic forms, incl. (for the first time in Iceland) the *sonnet and *terza rima. The other great romantic poet is Bjarni Thorarensen (1786–1841), who portrayed nature in *similes and *personifications and tended to glorify winter rather than summer, esp. in his poem "Veturinn" (Winter). He also raised a traditional Icelandic genre, the memorial poem, to a new height. Quite different from these Copenhagen-educated men is the poor folk poet and wood-carver Hjálmar Jónsson (1796–1875), known as Bólu-Hjálmar. His large body of verse includes personal invective, rímur, bitter complaints about poverty, and poems about death.

One of the greatest poets of the later 19th c. is Matthías Jochumsson (1835–1920), a free-thinking parson and newspaper ed. who wrote inspired lyrics, hymns, and memorial poems and also made masterful trans. of four of Shakespeare's tragedies. Around the turn of the century, Einar Benediktsson (1864–1940) was a powerful figure who, as a kind of latter-day Eggert Ólafsson, sought to improve Iceland by forming international corporations to mine gold and harness water power. He used lang. as he used wealth, to gain power, and his nature poems, like "Útsær" (Ocean), are rich with the imagery of opposing elements in nature and his view of the pantheistic force uniting all things.

As the 20th c. wore on, Icelandic poetry was pulled in two opposite directions, toward social engagement or a kind of realism on the one hand and introspective lyricism or *modernism on the other. A number of poets took sides in this respect, but some swung between the opposing poles throughout their careers. Steinn Steinarr (1908–58) came to the rapidly modernizing town of Reykjavík as a poor youth in the late 1920s, and in his first collection (1934), he produced poems of social protest, sympathizing with hungry workers who "don't understand / their own relationship / to their enemies." This same poem, "Veruleiki" (Reality), in free verse, goes beyond skepticism of the social order, however, to speak of the illusory nature of existence itself. This note of doubt, alienation, and nihilism later became predominant in Steinn's finely pruned, paradoxical poems, the longest and most highly regarded of which is the poetic cycle *Tíminn og vatnið* (Time and the Water, 1948), an enigmatic and symbolic meditation probably meant to be sensed rather than comprehended.

Many poets followed the example of the modernists of the 1950s—the so-called *Atómskáld* (Atom Poets) such as Sigfús Daðason (1928–96)—and tried to break with trad., experimenting with various poetic practices of modernism. Others tried to merge the mod. with the traditional in order to benefit from both. Hannes Pétursson (b. 1931) has produced sensitive and meticulously crafted lyrics on a variety of subjects incl. Icelandic folklore, historically charged Eur. locations (the prison camp at Dachau, the Strasburg cathedral), and cl. figures like Odysseus. He writes on such themes as the emptiness of lang. and humankind's separation from nature. His poetical cycle *Heimkynni við sjó* (Living by the Sea, 1980) marks a return to nature and a new awareness of surroundings and oneself, rendered through arresting images and metaphors. More often, however, the city shows itself to be the natural habitat of the mod. poet, as witnessed by the urbane and imaginative poetry of Kristján Karlsson (b. 1922) and Sigurður Pálsson (b. 1948). But Gyrðir Elíasson (b. 1961) has also proved that a fresh look at nature is still possible in postmod. times, tinged though it may be with romantic sympathies and otherworldly broodings.

Women were instrumental in transmitting and developing folk poetry through the centuries, but few became prominent as poets in their own right until the 20th c. Unnur Benediktsdóttir Bjarklind (1881–1946), who published under the pseud. Hulda, revived and developed such rhapsodic folk-poetry genres as *þulur* (sing. *þula*) and also became one of the main proponents of *symbolism (or neoromanticism) in Iceland. Another breakthrough in women's poetry came with the first volumes of the poems of Vilborg Dagbjartsdóttir (b. 1930), published in the 1960s. Since then, many Icelandic women have made their name as poets, with work ranging from the sensual lyricism of Nína Björk Árnadóttir (1941–2000) to the clear-eyed and socially engaged poetry of Ingibjörg Haraldsdóttir (b. 1942) to the poetical playfulness of Steinunn Sigurðardóttir (b. 1950).

■ **Bibliographies:** P. Mitchell and K. Ober, *Bibliography of Modern Icelandic Literature in Translation*, 3 v. (1975–97)—trans. of works since the Reformation to the late 20th c.
■ **Criticism and History:** *A History of Icelandic Literature*, ed. D. Neijmann (2006); *Íslensk bókmenntasaga*, ed. V. Ólason, H. Guðmundsson, and G. A. Thorsson, 5 v. (1993–2006); M. Eggertsdóttir, *Barokkmeistarinn* (2005)—Hallgrímur Pétursson and baroque poetry; S. Y. Egilsson, *Arfur og umbylting* (1999)—Jónas Hallgrímsson and Icelandic romanticism; E. Þorvaldsson, *Atómskáldin* (1980)—modernism in Iceland; Þ. Þorsteinsson, *Ljóðhús* (2007)—on Sigfús Daðason.
■ **Primary Texts:** *Bishop Guðbrand's "Vísnabók" 1612*, ed. S. Nordal (1937)—facsimile with Eng. intro.; *Hymns of the Passion by Hallgrímur Pétursson*, trans.

A. C. Gook (1966); *Íslenzkt ljóðasafn*, ed. K. Karlsson, 6 v. (1974–78)—comprehensive anthol. of Icelandic poetry; *Bard of Iceland: Jónas Hallgrímsson, Poet and Scientist*, ed. and trans. D. Ringler (2002); *Stúlka: Ljóð eftir íslenskar konur*, ed. H. Kress, 2d ed. (2001)—an anthol. of poetry by Icelandic women; *The Postwar Poetry of Iceland*, trans. S. A. Magnússon (1982); *Brushstrokes of Blue: The Young Poets of Iceland*, ed. P. Valsson, trans. D. McDuff (1994).

R. Cook; S. Y. Egilsson

**ICONICITY.** A natural resemblance or analogy of form between a word (the signifier) and the object it refers to (the signified; see SIGN, SIGNIFIED, SIGNIFIER). In the semiotics of C. S. Peirce, every sign mediates between its referent and a meaning; the relation among signifier, signified, and meaning is, in effect, triangular. Three types or modes of representation are recognized; hence, three possible relationships may obtain between the sign and its object. If the relation is cognitive (thought) but arbitrary, the sign is a *symbol*. Thought is carried on in terms of signs; hence, meaning itself is a sign relation. If the sign is in physical proximity to its object, then the sign is an *index*: smoke is an index of fire. If there is resemblance between sign and object, the sign is an *icon*: mimicry by a professional mime is iconic. Icons, like indexes, are not genuine or full-bodied signs for Peirce but are inferior, though they may be common or even prolific; icons "can represent nothing but Forms and Feelings."

Peirce's concept of iconicity is important because it refutes the traditional critical denigration of mimetic sound effects in poetry such as *onomatopoeia by showing that the mimetic function is a key component of the representational system itself. Mimetic effects in poetry may now be seen not as quaint aberrations or mere "poetical" devices but, rather, natural extensions of a process always at work in lang. Considerable ling. research in the 20th c. confirmed that iconicity operates at every level of lang. structure (phonology, morphology, syntax) and in virtually every known lang. worldwide. Beyond speech itself, iconicity also functions in visual representations of lang., e.g., sign lang. (particularly evident), and in several writing systems and writing-based picture-signs (*hieroglyph, *ideogram, phonogram, rebus). And verbal iconicity can be correlated with visual forms of iconicity in painting and poetic imagery.

In poetry, prosodic iconicity can be found operating at every level of the text, from a wide range of mimetic sound effects to expressive rhythms and "representative meter," to iconic syntax; and in the visual mode of the poem, from mimetic subgenres such as *concrete poetry to mimetic strategies of deployment in *free verse (see VISUAL POETRY).

*See* COGNITIVE POETICS; ICONOLOGY; MIMESIS; SEMIOTICS AND POETRY.
■ C. S. Peirce, *Collected Papers*, ed. C. Hartshorne and P. Weiss, 8 v. (1931–58); D. L. Bolinger, *Forms of English* (1965); R. W. Wescott, "Linguistic Iconism," *Lang* 47 (1971); S. Ullmann, "Natural and Conventional Signs," and T. Todorov, "Literature and Semiotics," *The Tell-Tale Sign*, ed. T. A. Sebeok (1975); T. A. Sebeok, "Ico-

nicity," *MLN* 91 (1976); W. K. Wimsatt, "In Search of Verbal Mimesis," *Day of the Leopards* (1976); Y. Malkiel, "From Phonosymbolism to Morphosymbolism," *Fourth LACUS Forum* (1978), supp. by D. B. Justice, "Iconicity and Association," *RPh* 33 (1980); R. Cureton, "e e cummings: A Case Study of Iconic Syntax," *Lang&S* 14 (1981); J. N. Deely, "Antecedents to Peirce's Notion of Iconic Signs," *Semiotics 1980*, ed. M. Herzfeld and M. D. Lenhart (1982); J. Haiman, *Natural Syntax: Iconicity and Erosion* (1985); *Iconicity in Syntax*, ed. J. Haiman (1985); M. Nänny, "Iconic Dimensions in Poetry," *On Poetry and Poetics*, ed. R. Waswo (1985); W. Bernhart, "The Iconic Quality of Poetic Rhythm," *Word and Image* 2 (1986); W. Nöth, *Handbook of Semiotics* (1990); *European Journal of English Studies* 5.1 (2001)—spec. issue on iconicity; *From Sign to Signing*, ed. G. W. Müller et al. (2002); *Outside-In-Inside-Out*, ed. C. Maeder et al. (2005); M.-Y. Tseng, "Common Foundations of Metaphor and Iconicity," *Cognitive Poetics*. ed. G. Brône and J. Vandaele (2009); *Signergy*, ed. J. Conradie et al. (2010).

T.V.F. BROGAN

**ICONOLOGY.** The study of icons (images, pictures, or likenesses). It is thus, as Gombrich argues in *Art and Illusion*, a "science" of images, which not only "investigates the function of images in allegory and symbolism" (see ALLEGORY, SYMBOL) but explores what we might call "the linguistics of the visual image," the fundamental codes and conventions that make iconic representation and communication possible. Iconology, thus, has links with philosophy, esp. the field of *semiotics or the general science of signs, as well as with psychology, particularly the analysis of visual perception (Arnheim) and the imaginary (see IMAGE, IMAGERY, IMAGINATION). More modestly, *iconology* may be described as a "rhetoric of images" in a double sense: first, as a study of "what to say about images"—e.g., the trad. of "art writing" that goes back to Philostratus's *Imagines* (ca. 220 CE) and is centrally concerned with the description and interpretation of a work of visual art; second, as a study of "what images say"—i.e., the ways in which images speak for themselves by persuading, telling stories, or describing states of affairs. Iconology also denotes a long trad. of theoretical and historical reflection on the concept of imagery, a trad. that, in its narrow sense, probably begins with such Ren. handbooks of symbolic imagery as Cesare Ripa's *Iconologia* (1592) and culminates in Panofsky's influential *Studies in Iconology*. In a broader sense, the critical study of the icon extends to theological and philosophical concepts such as the biblical concept of the *imago dei*, the notion that human beings are created "in the image and likeness" of God. The Platonic concept of the *eikon* crops up in the notion of *eikasia* (cf. Eng. "icastic"), the perception of images, appearances, and reflections (*Republic* 509e); in the theory of art, where it is linked with *mimesis (*Republic* 598e–99a; see IMITATION); and in basic models of being and knowing. Peters notes that, for Plato, "the visible universe is the *eikon* of the intelligible one."

The concept of the icon may best be understood as oscillating between a very general sense (the notion of "likeness" or "similitude") and a fairly specific reference to visual representations *by means of* likeness (e.g., paintings, statues, photographs). Peirce's semiotic theories and mod. ling. research provide the foundation for the mod. understanding of iconicity: in Peirce's theory, iconic signs include such things as algebraic equations, diagrams, phonetic mimicry, and sugar substitutes. The notion of the icon enters poetics in both its general and specific senses. Theories of *metaphor, figurative lang., and allegory, all of which involve the analysis of verbal analogies, similitudes, and comparisons, invoke the general sense of the icon as a relationship of likeness. The New Critical idea of the poem as a "verbal icon" (Wimsatt) whose formal structure incarnates its propositional content is the formalist version of poetic iconicity (see NEW CRITICISM). The more specific sense of the poetic icon conceives it as a poetic "image," not in the sense of similitude but as a verbal representation of a concrete (usually visual) object. Vivid descriptions of places, objects, works of art (see EKPHRASIS), and persons, while not themselves "iconic" in the general sense, are seen as eliciting mental images in the reader, evoking a kind of secondary visual representation. Sometimes the notion of an "iconic" poetic image may be reserved for highly charged symbolic objects (John Keats's urn, S. T. Coleridge's albatross), but it may equally well be applied to more common materials. Experimental genres such as *concrete poetry, pattern poetry, and *visual poetry that array the text into the visual shape of an object are of central interest for the ways they combine the general notion of iconic likeness with the specific strategies of visual representation.

Poetics often moves between these two senses without much critical self-awareness. Aristotle's *Rhetoric* (3.4) uses *eikon* in the general sense to denote comparison or *simile; Quintilian calls it a kind of comparison "which the Greeks call *eikon* and which expresses the appearance of things and persons" (*Institutio oratoria* 5.11.24); Henry Peacham defines *icon* as a "forme of speech which painteth out the image of a person or thing by comparing forme with forme, quality with quality, one likeness with another" (*Garden of Eloquence*, 1577). As the Ren. interest in the naming and classifying of stylistic and rhetorical devices waned, the term *icon* almost disappeared from poetics. The all-purpose term *image* took its place in poetic theory until the mod. revival of semiotics reopened the question of iconicity as a general problem.

Most early mod. studies of literary or poetic iconology, e.g., Tuve, are compilations of specific symbolic motifs (see also Aptekar, Frye, Landow, Ziolkowski). These studies, which generally attempt to reconstruct the meanings associated with particular visual images, might better be called "iconographies," reserving the term *iconology* for studies that raise more general questions about the conditions under which poetic images acquire meaning and of the nature of literary similitude, resemblance, and iconicity (see Panofsky, Bialostocki, and Mitchell for discussion of the distinction between *iconography* and *iconology*). Panofsky, most famously, treats *iconography* as a kind of dictionary of visual motifs that can be translated into words, reserving *iconology* for the larger sphere of the grammar, syntax, and even the ontology of images in their broad historical and cultural context. Most comparative studies of the "sister arts" of poetry and painting, regulated by the Horatian maxim *ut pictura poesis*, are poetic "iconographies" that try to clarify the meaning of poems by reference to the pictorial scenes or works of art they describe. *Iconology* in its more general sense would raise questions about the status of iconic representation in the specific text, its genre, and its cultural context, as in Gilman's exemplary study, which not only provides a great deal of information about the iconographic resources of Eng. poetry in the 17th c. but situates these data in the context of the religious and political struggles over the relative value of visual and verbal representation.

Iconology, then, is not just the interdisciplinary study of imagery in a variety of media but a historical and theoretical inquiry into the nature of imagery, with special emphasis on the difference (as well as the similarity) between iconic and verbal representation. Images and words, despite their easy conflation in phrases like "poetic imagery" or "verbal icon," carry with them a hist. of radical differentiation, articulated in oppositions such as *nature and *convention, space and time, the eye and the ear—what Rancière has called "the distribution of the sensible." These oppositions are frequently associated with distinctions of class, race, gender, and political or professional identity (Mitchell 1986). What Leonardo da Vinci (or his 19th-c. eds.) called the *paragone* or contest of poet and painter, verbal and visual artist, often becomes a figure for competing if not antithetical modes of being and knowing, most fundamentally the gap between the speaking self and the seen or imagined other. Ultimately, the word-image difference inscribed in the concept of iconology finds itself mapped on to *species* difference, and the ling. barrier between human beings and animals is overcome by their shared participation in the world of images and visual perception.

Iconology, thus, comes to lit. and poetry with a sense of its own impropriety, as a discipline focused on nonverbal forms of representation. It is the intrusion of the visual and pictorial into the realm of voice, hearing, and lang., the entrance of similitude into the (ling.) territory of "difference," the colonization of writing by painting (or vice versa). The subject matter of iconology is both the desire for and resistance to the merging of lang. and imagery. The political psychology and anthropology of iconic representation—the analysis of such phenomena as idolatry, iconoclasm, iconophobia, fetishism, scopophilia, voyeurism, and iconophilia—are as important to the discipline of iconology as the meaning of any particular image.

*See* EMBLEM, FIGURATION, PAINTING AND POETRY, SOUND.

■ C. S. Peirce, "The Icon, Index, and Symbol," *Collected Papers*, ed. C. Hartshorne and P. Weiss, 8 v. (1931–58), v. 2; C. Morris, "Aesthetics and the Theory of Signs," *Journal of Unified Science* 8 (1939); E. Panofsky, *Studies in Iconology* (1939); E. H. Gombrich, "Icones Symbolicae: The Visual Image in Neo-Platonic Thought," *Journal of the Warburg and Courtauld Institutes* 11 (1948); R. Arnheim, *Art and Visual Perception* (1954); W. K. Wimsatt, *The Verbal Icon* (1954); E. Panofsky, "Iconography and Iconology," *Meaning in the Visual Arts* (1955); Frye; J. Hagstrum, *The Sister Arts* (1958); E. H. Gombrich, *Art and Illusion*, 2d ed. (1961); J. Bialostocki, "Iconography and Iconology," *Encyclopedia of World Art*, ed. B. S. Myers (1963); H. Weisinger, "Icon and Image: What the Literary Historian Can Learn from the Warburg School," *Bulletin of the New York Public Library* 67 (1963); J. Hagstrum, *William Blake* (1964); R. Tuve, *Allegorical Imagery* (1966); F. E. Peters, *Greek Philosophical Terms* (1967); J. Aptekar, *Icons of Justice* (1969); J. V. Fleming, *The "Roman de la Rose": A Study in Allegory and Iconography* (1969); G. Hermeren, *Representation and Meaning in the Visual Arts* (1969); U. Eco, *A Theory of Semiotics* (1976); W.J.T. Mitchell, *Blake's Composite Art* (1978); T. Ziolkowski, *Disenchanted Images* (1977); W.J.T. Mitchell, *Iconology* (1986); *Ikonographie und Ikonologie*, ed. E. Kaemmerling (1979); B. Bucher, *Icon and Conquest* (1981); *Image and Code*, ed. W. Steiner (1981); G. C. Argan, "Ideology and Iconology," *The Language of Images*, ed. W.J.T. Mitchell (1982); G. Landow, *Images of Crisis: Literary Iconology, 1750 to the Present* (1982); Ransom, esp. "Wanted: An Ontological Critic"; E. Gilman, *Iconoclasm and Poetry in the English Reformation* (1986); K. Moxey, "Panofsky's Concept of 'Iconology,'" *NLH* 17 (1986); W.J.T. Mitchell, "Iconology and Ideology," *Works and Days* 11–12 (1988); J. Rancière, *The Politics of Aesthetics*, trans. G. Rockhill (2004).

W.J.T. MITCHELL

**ICTUS** (Lat., "beat"). Long disputed as a term, the concept of *ictus* goes by a variety of other less satisfactory names, esp. *metrical accent*, *prosodic accent*, and *metrical stress*. As it is currently conceived, *meter is a pattern of prominent and nonprominent, or marked and unmarked, positions that together form a distinct pattern, the *line. *Ictus* is the most neutral term for each marked or prominent position. As an element of the abstract pattern that is meter, ictus is marked in each verse system by the phonological feature that is phonemic for its lang.—*accent in stress-based langs., *pitch in tone langs., length or *duration in quantitative langs. In the Eng. iambic pentameter, e.g., the five even syllables are ictic, meaning that, in the most neutral or normative realization of this meter, these syllables will be stressed. According to the traditional account, some variations from this pattern were allowed for, esp. reversing the stressing on the first and second syllables. It was disputed whether this should be accounted for at the level of realization, i.e., in the actual line (in which case a stress falls under nonictus and a slack under ictus) or at the level of meter, by positing the permissibility of *substitution (a *trochaic foot could be substituted for an *iambic one, with stress now agreeably falling under ictus). The former option seems very undesirable, but the difficulty with the latter option lies in explaining why only some substitutions seem to be allowed and why their frequencies in the five feet of the line are very differential.

Neither option, however, infringes on the fundamental distinction between meter, as an abstract pattern applicable to all lines, and rhythm, the actualization in each specific line. In the cl. Gr. *hexameter, the first five of the six feet may be *dactyls or *spondees; the sixth must be a spondee. The number of syllables is thus variable, but the first position in each foot is ictic. On this analysis, it would seem that ictus corresponds to the concept of *arsis* (in mod. usage) and *thesis* in ancient usage, namely, a subdivision of the *foot into two elements (regardless of how many syllables occupy each element) of which only one is prominent (see ARSIS AND THESIS). In antiquity, the terms *arsis* and *thesis* were used to describe the movement of the foot or the hand in keeping time with the rhythm of a verse; Roman writers like Horace and Quintilian, however, used them in the sense of a raising or lowering of the *voice* and so reversed their senses from Gr. usage, a confusion brought into the mod. world by Richard Bentley and others in the 18th c. Nevertheless, *ictus* denotes the marked or prominent position in the foot.

It is important to remember that, at the level of meter, all ictuses are equal, whereas, in the rhythm of the actual line, stresses often vary considerably in their weights, some primary, some secondary, some even weaker. It was the signal accomplishment of mod. metrics to articulate the relation between the latter and the former as the *relative stress principle: it does not matter how strong, in absolute terms, a stress under ictus is so long as it is stronger—even if by a hair—than the syllable under nonictus. In the account given by structural metrists, stresses under nonictus can undergo *demotion and weak stresses under ictus *promotion; effectually, this means that ling. stresses are altered or adjusted in weight under the influence of the metrical grid.

In *classical prosody, the term was used in the 20th c. by scholars who held that the quantitative meter of Lat. poetry was, in fact, made audible not by length but by a stress accent. Beare, however, thinks that such an assumption "may be due merely to our craving to impose on quantitative verse a rhythm which we can recognize." Discussion of the controversy may be found in Allen.

*See* HOMODYNE AND HETERODYNE.

■ C. E. Bennett, "What Was Ictus in Latin Prosody?" *AJP* 19 (1898), with crit. by G. L. Hendrickson in 20 (1899); E. H. Sturtevant, "The Ictus of Classical Verse," *AJP* 44 (1923); E. Kapp, "Bentley and the Modern Doctrine of Ictus in Classical Verse," *Mnemosyne* 9 (1941); Beare, esp. chs. 5, 14; P. W. Harsh, "Ictus and Accent," *Lustrum* 3 (1958); P. Habermann and W. Mohr, "Hebung und Senkung," *Reallexikon II* 1.623–28; A. Labhardt, "Le Problème de l'Ictus," *Euphrosyne* 2 (1959); O. Seel and E. Pöhlmann, "Quantität und Wortakzent im horazischen Sapphiker," *Philologus* 103 (1959); H. Drexler, "Quantität und Wortakzent," *Maia* 12 (1960); L. P. Wilkinson, *Golden Latin Artistry* (1963); Allen, esp. 276 ff.; E. Pulgram, *Latin-Romance Phonology: Prosodics and Metrics* (1975); Morier; Brogan; J. Luque Moreno, *Arsis, Thesis, Ictus* (1994); R. P. Sonkowsky and F. Halberg, "Latin Verse-Ictus and Multimodal Entrainment," *Electronic Antiquity* 2 (2005).

T.V.F. BROGAN

**IDENTICAL RHYME.** Prototypical "exact" rhymes, e.g., *cat / bat*, require sonic likeness (*at/at*) paired with sonic difference (*c/b*). In *rich rhyme, sonic difference may disappear, but clear semantic difference remains, e.g. *may / May*. Identical rhyme (sometimes *tautological rhyme*) extends the likeness of rich rhyme further, indicating a repetition not just of the sound and spelling of a word but of its meaning. The very existence of identical rhyme has been a source of significant critical disagreement, as has the question of its desirability.

In his influential essay on rhyme, W. K. Wimsatt asserted that "[e]ven identical words may rhyme." Many critics, however, argue that a repeated word cannot be identical to the word that precedes it: if a word is repeated, it is necessarily in a new context with a new meaning. If nothing else, the repeated word registers as a repetition. Lotman argues that "[i]dentical (repeating) elements are functionally not identical if they occupy different structural positions."

If the status of identity in identical rhyme is one issue, its status as rhyming is another: many critics have argued over whether identical rhyme ought to be called rhyme at all. Abernathy points to the presence of ostensibly identical rhymes in otherwise unrhymed poems, such as the blank verse of Robert Browning's *The Ring and the Book* and even John Milton. Since these repetitions occur in verse contexts in which rhyming is forbidden, it becomes clear that they do not count as rhyme. If the formal characteristics of Abernathy's blank-verse examples suggest that identical rhyme is not rhyme, however, others point to the example of fixed forms such as the *sestina and the *ghazal to suggest that identical rhymes exemplify the best qualities of rhyme. In the sestina, W. K. Wimsatt argues, "[T]he same set of rhyme words is repeated in six different stanzas. But here the order changes, and so does the relation of each rhyme word to the context. That is the point of the sestina." For Lotman, the repetition of words in the ghazal "reveals the diverse aspects of one concept." J. I. Wimsatt, however, cautions against using the refrain words of fixed forms as exemplars of identical rhyme. Refrain words are "systematic, part of the form," but identical rhyme "is unsystematic, and as a result confusing and fatiguing." From this perspective, much of what has been explored as identical rhyme might more productively be called *refrain.

Other possibilities for classifying identical rhyme as something other than rhyme have also been suggested. Rhetorical *antistrophe is one possibility. Scott uses the term "terminal repetition," which raises the question of how identical rhyme is to be distinguished from simple *repetition. Scherr distinguishes rich from identical rhyme in Rus. poetry as "homonymic" versus "repetend" rhyme.

Whether one believes that identical rhyme exists, it seems clear that some spectrum runs from rich rhymes, in which words are used in two unquestionably different senses, to cases that approach identical rhyme. If one assumes the existence of such a spectrum, something like identical rhyme appears to be more frequent in Eng., esp. in Chaucer and John Gower, than might be supposed. Both rich rhyme and identical rhyme have been more freely accepted in several other trads., incl. OF and MHG. And if, as has been suggested, the refrain words of fixed forms are if nothing else theoretically similar to identical rhyme, the phenomenon has a global scope: the ghazal, e.g., is prevalent in several Middle Eastern trads.

■ E. Freymond, "Über den reichen Reim bei altfranzösichen Dichtern bis zum Anfang des XIV Jahrh," *ZRP* 6 (1882); A. Tobler, *Le Vers français* (1885); J. Möllmann, *Der homonyme Reim im Französischen* (1896); C. von Kraus, "Der rührende Reim im Mittelhochdeutschen," *ZDA* 56 (1918); J. Fucilla, "*Parole identiche* in the Sonnet and Other Verse Forms," *PMLA* 50 (1935); W. K. Wimsatt, "One Relation of Rhyme to Reason," *MLQ* 5 (1944); A. Oras, "Intensified Rhyme Links in the *Faerie Queene*," *JEGP* 54 (1955); P. Rickard, "Semantic Implications of Old French Identical Rhyme," *NM* 6 (1965); R. Abernathy, "Rhymes, Non-Rhymes, and Antirhyme," *To Honor Roman Jakobson*, v. 1 (1967); J. M. Lotman, *The Structure of the Artistic Text*, trans. G. Lenhoff and R. Vroon (1977); Scott; Scherr; A. H. Olsen, *Between Earnest and Game* (1990)—homonymic rhymes in Gower; J. I. Wimsatt, "Rhyme/Reason, Chaucer/Pope, Icon/Symbol," *MLQ* 55 (1994).

T.V.F. BROGAN; E. J. RETTBERG

**IDEOGRAM.** Thought to be ancient and exotic, the ideogram is best seen as a productive mod. Eur. fiction. Invented by Jean-François Champollion in the course of deciphering the Egyptian hieroglyphics, which were used sometimes to represent sounds and sometimes to represent ideas, the term *ideogram* is now commonly associated with the Chinese writing system and its derivatives. Its use in poetry and poetics derives from Ezra Pound's efforts to found a modernist poetic on the *"image," defined as "that which presents an intellectual and emotional complex in an instant of time." Visual *imagery had long been a distinguishing mark of poetry in Western theory; Pound's extension of the concept was suggested by Ernest Fenollosa's essay *The Chinese Written Character as a Medium for Poetry* (1903, pub. 1919). Fenollosa saw in "Chinese writing . . . something much more than arbitrary symbols. It is based upon a vivid shorthand picture of the operations of nature. . . . It speaks at once with the vividness of painting and with the mobility of sounds."

Although Chinese philology includes in its classification of written characters the categories "pictogram" (*xiangxing*), "index" (*zhishi*), and "semantic compound" (*huiyi*), the ideogram results from the contact of langs. and writing systems. It compensates for a perceived weakness in alphabetic writing. Fenollosa, followed by Pound, conceives the ideogram to transcend the condition of representation altogether:

"In reading Chinese we do not seem to be juggling mental counters, but to be watching *things* work out their own fate." For his *Cantos*, Pound developed an "ideogrammic method" of juxtaposition of "luminous details," eschewing syntactic subordination and building structures of association through conceptual rhyme. This composition method has been adopted for many subsequent long poems, e.g., Charles Olson's *Maximus* sequence.

Fenollosa's account of Chinese writing combined painting, motion, and sound, alluding to the infant cinema. Sergei Eisenstein, apparently independently, drew on the "ideogram" (in his usage chiefly the compound or *huiyi* character, joining two meanings to make a third) in his theory of cinematic montage. Inherently a multimedia object as well as an interlinguistic one, the ideogram concentrates the energies of *modernism, covering all the arts and the 20th-c. political spectrum from communism to fascism. Having outlasted its original purpose of dislodging Edwardian standards of verse decorum, it contributes to the syntax of every subsequent movement.

*See* CHINESE POETRY IN ENGLISH TRANSLATION.

■ S. Eisenstein, *Film Form*, trans. J. Leyda; (1949); E. Pound, *Selected Prose 1909–1965*, ed. W. Cookson (1975); Welsh; L. Géfin, *Ideogram* (1982); E. Fenollosa and E. Pound, *The Chinese Character as a Medium for Poetry*, ed. H. Saussy et al. (2008); C. Bush, *Ideographic Modernism* (2010).

H. SAUSSY

**IDYLL,** idyl (Gr. *eidyllion* [diminutive of *eidos*, "form"], "short separate poem"; in Gr., a pastoral poem or idyll is *eidyllion Boukolikon*). One of the several synonyms used by the Gr. grammarians for the poems of Theocritus, Bion, and Moschus, which at other times are called *bucolic, *eclogue, and *pastoral. Theocritus's ten pastoral poems, no doubt because of their superiority, became the prototype of the idyll. In the 16th and 17th cs., esp. in France, there was frequent insistence that pastorals in dialogue be called *eclogues*, those in narrative, *idylls*. In Ger., *Idylle* is the ordinary term for pastoral. Two biblical books—Ruth and Song of Songs—are sometimes called *idylls*, which may be taken to illustrate the latitude of the term. Note that Alfred, Lord Tennyson's *Idylls of the King* (1859) is hardly pastoral. Perhaps Tennyson thought that the use of the term was appropriate: each idyll contains an incident in the matter of Arthur and his knights that is separate (or framed) but at the same time connected with the central theme; the contents treat the Christian virtues in an ideal manner and in a remote setting. But there is very little in Robert Browning's *Dramatic Idylls* (1879–80), which mainly explore psychological crises, to place them in the pastoral trad. The adjectival form, *idyllic*, is more regularly and conventionally applied to works or scenes that present picturesque rural scenery and a life of innocence and tranquillity, but this has little specific relation to any poetic genre.

*See* GEORGIC.

■ M. H. Shackford, "A Definition of the Pastoral Idyll," *PMLA* 19 (1904); P. van Tieghem, "Les Idylls de Gessner et le rève pastoral," *Le Préromantisme*, v. 2 (1930); P. Merker, *Deutsche Idyllendichtung* (1934); E. Merker, "Idylle," *Reallexikon II* 1.742–49; J. Tismar, *Gestörte Idyllen* (1973); T. Lange, *Idyll und exotische Sehnsucht* (1976); K. Bernhard, *Idylle* (1977); R. Böschenstein-Schäfer, *Idylle*, 2d ed. (1977); V. Nemoianu, *Micro-Harmony: Growth and Uses of the Idyllic Model in Literature* (1977); J. B. Pearce, "Theocritus and Oral Tradition," *Oral Tradition* 8 (1993); S. Halse, "The Literary Idyll in Germany, England, and Scandinavia, 1770–1848," *Romantic Prose Fiction*, ed. G. Gillespie (2008).

T.V.F. BROGAN; J. E. CONGLETON

**IMAGE.** *Image* and *imagery* are among the most widely used and poorly understood terms in poetic theory, occurring in so many different contexts that it may well be impossible to provide any rational, systematic account of their usage. A poetic image is, variously, a *metaphor, *simile, or figure of speech; a concrete verbal reference; a recurrent *motif; a psychological event in the reader's mind; the vehicle or second term of a metaphor; a *symbol or symbolic pattern; the global impression of a poem as a unified structure.

The term's meaning and use have also varied radically depending on time and place. While the concept has been at the center of *Chinese poetics for centuries, for instance, its prominence in Western criticism is a relatively mod. phenomenon. Frazer argues that the term first becomes important to Eng. crit. in the 17th c., perhaps under the influence of empiricist models of the mind. Thomas Hobbes and John Locke use the term as a key element in their accounts of sensation, perception, memory, imagination, and lang., developing a "picture-theory" of consciousness as a system of receiving, storing, and retrieving mental images. The term continues to play an important role in *neoclassical poetics, usually in accounts of description. Joseph Addison, in the *Spectator* papers on the "Pleasures of the Imagination" (nos. 411–21, 1712), argues that images are what allow the poet to "get the better of nature": "the reader finds a scene drawn in stronger colors and painted more to the life in his imagination by the help of words than by an actual survey of the scene which they describe."

In *romantic and postromantic poetry and poetics, the image persists in a sublimated and refined form and is often defined in opposition to "mental pictures" (Edmund Burke) or to the "merely descriptive" or "painted," ornamental images of 18th-c. poetry. S. T. Coleridge's distinctions between symbol and *allegory ("living educts" versus a mere "picture language") and *imagination and *fancy (creative versus remembered images) consistently appeal to a difference between a "higher," inward, intellectual image and a lower, outward, sensuous one. The notion of the poetic symbol, along with the poetic process as an expressive rather than mimetic endeavor, helps to articulate the notion of the romantic image as something more refined, subtle, and active than its neoclassical predecessor. Modernist poetics often combines (while claiming to transcend) the neoclassical and romantic concepts of the image, urging poets to make their lang. concrete and sensuous

while articulating a theory of poetic structure that regards the entire poem as a kind of matrix or crystallized form of energy, as if the poem were an abstract image (see MODERNISM). Thus, Ezra Pound stresses the importance of both the psychological and structural features of the image when he famously defines it as "that which presents an intellectual and emotional complex in an instant of time." In part because of the powerful influence of *imagism as propounded by Pound and others, *image*, however ambiguously defined, is treated in much 20th-c. crit. as though it were synonymous with poetry itself. Lewis offers a declaration that could stand in for any number of mod. and contemp. poets: "the image is the constant in all poetry, and every poem is an image."

Understandings of *image* shifted through the 20th c. and into the 21st as critics grappled with the increasing prominence of visual media. Whereas at the beginning of the century, modernists turned to the visual image as a source of immediacy and presence, an increased sensitivity to forms of mechanical and later digital reproduction made it seem inevitable that the image would offer a different lesson: that images do not offer direct access to reality but point always instead to other images. Like words, they are governed by their own grammars and rhets. and must be interpreted according to specific conventions. Rather than strive for the iconicity of the image, then, postmodern critics stress the etymological relation between *image* and *imitation*. Words and images share the common condition of all representation, woven together into a mediated web of signs and simulations.

A critique of the concept of the poetic image would probably begin by noting that it tends to blur a distinction that underlies a large tract of poetics, namely, the difference between literal and figurative lang. An image is, on the one hand, "the only available word to cover every kind of simile [and] metaphor" (Spurgeon); on the other hand, it is simply "what the words actually name" (Kenner), the literal referents of lang., concrete objects. Pound's treatment of the concept is again illustrative. One of his instructions for would-be imagists is that a poem should offer a "direct treatment of the 'thing' whether subjective or objective." Emphasizing at once its immediacy and, by putting "thing" in quotation marks, calling that directness into question, Pound suggests that the image can reconcile the subjective and objective character of *representation. The image, in other words, designates both metaphor and description, both a purely ling. relation between words and a referential relation to a nonlinguistic reality, both a rhetorical device and a psychological event. This confusion is most evident in theories of metaphor that follow Richards's influential distinction between *tenor* and *vehicle*. Is Shakespeare's metaphor "Juliet is the sun" to be understood as an image because "sun" is a concrete noun that evokes a sensuous picture in the reader's mind? Or is the whole expression an image because it insists on a "likeness" between two unlike things? Is an image, in short, a bearer of sensuous immediacy and presence or a relationship formed by the conjunction of two different words and their associated vocabularies? Is it a mode of apprehension or a rhetorical device? Whatever we may understand as the meaning of the term *image* in any particular context, it seems clear that the general function of the term has been to make this distinction difficult, if not impossible.

What could be at stake in perpetuating confusion between metaphor and description or between figurative and literal lang.? One possibility is that the figurative-versus-literal-lang. distinction is itself untenable, and the ambiguous use of the term *image* is simply a symptom of this fact. *Image*, understood in its narrow and literal sense as a picture or statue, is a metaphor for metaphor itself (a sign by similitude or resemblance) and for mimetic representation or *iconicity. Since literary representation does not represent by likeness the way pictorial images do, literary representation is itself only and always metaphorical, whether or not it employs particular figures. (Goodman argues, for instance, that representation, properly speaking, only occurs in dense, analogical systems like pictures and that a verbal description, no matter how detailed, never amounts to a depiction). The literal-figurative distinction itself appeals to an implicit distinction between "letters" (writing) and "figures" (images, pictures, designs, or bodies in space). The concept of "poetic imagery" is, thus, a kind of *oxymoron, installing an alien medium (painting, sculpture, visual art) at the heart of verbal expression. The motives for this incorporation of the visual arts are usually clear enough: the whole panoply of values that go with painting—presence, immediacy, vividness—are appropriated for poetry. But there are equally powerful motives for keeping the incorporation of the visual under control, for seeing the visual arts as a dangerous rival as well as a helpful ally. G. E. Lessing, in *Laokoön* (1766), thought that the emulation of the visual arts by lit. would lead to static, lifeless description, while Burke (*A Philosophical Enquiry into the Origin of Our Ideas of the Sublime and the Beautiful*, 1757) argued that visual imaging was a vastly overrated aspect of literary response, incompatible with the opacity he associated with true literary sublimity. Within this trad., the rivalry between word and image is frequently animated by anxieties about other forms of difference, chiefly those related to race, gender, and sexuality. Thus, as both Mitchell and Heffernan demonstrate, *ekphrasis* is often understood as a struggle between masculine poet and feminized image. The recurrent figure of the blind poet, whose blindness is a crucial condition of his insight and freedom from merely "external" visual images, reminds us that the boundaries between images and texts, figures and letters, the visual and the verbal are not so easily breached in Western poetics.

Another place where the contradictory tendencies of poetic imagery may be glimpsed is in the area of reader response. Here the image plays the role of a supplement to the poetic text (Derrida). It opens an empty space to be filled by the activity of the reader's imagination. Ideally, it completes the text in the reader's mind, in the world it projects, in the "spaces" between its words, bringing the "vision" of the poem sensuously, perceptually alive; but it may equally well open a threatening space of indeterminacy. Thus, the voice and sound—aural "images" such as *rhyme, *rhythm, *onomatopoeia, and *tone—are the first place to look for perfect iconicity in poetry. But what of the imperfect, secondary icons—the "mental pictures" that voice and sound produce, the imaginary spaces—theater, dream vision, movie, map, or diagram—that arise out of the reading experience? Poetics discloses a certain ambivalence toward these phenomena. While visualization, for instance, is universally acknowledged as an aspect of reader response, there is still considerable resistance to treating it as a legitimate object of literary study. The supposed "privacy" and "inaccessibility" of mental images seem to preclude empirical investigation, and the supposed randomness of visual associations with verbal cues seems to rule out any systematic account. But mental imagery has taken on a whole new life in the work of postbehavioral cognitive psychology. Literary critics who want to talk about poetic imagery in the sense of readers' visual response would do well to consult the work of philosophers and psychologists such as Jerry Fodor, Nelson Goodman, Ned Block, and Stephen Kosslyn, who have conducted experimental studies of visualization and mental imaging. Ludwig Wittgenstein's critique of the "picture theory" of meaning (*Philosophical Investigations*, 1957) also ought to be required reading for those who think of images as private. If mental images are an essential part of the reading experience, why should it be any more difficult to describe or interpret them than the images offered in Sigmund Freud's *The Interpretation of Dreams*?

At the same time, psychologists experimenting in the field of mental imaging might attend to poets and critics who have dealt with this question. It seems obvious, for instance, that mental imaging cannot be a subject of laboratory investigation alone but must be understood in the context of cultural hist. Some cultures and ages have encouraged reader visualization far more extensively than others: "quick poetic eyes" and the "test of the pencil," e.g., were the slogans of 18th-c. poetics, which urged the reader to match his or her experience with conventional, public models from painting and sculpture. We might ask why Shakespeare seems to have been singled out as the principal object of traditional image studies in Eng. crit. One answer may be that the study of imagery is part of the transformation of each Shakespearean play from a promptbook for the theater into a printed text for private reading. The first such study, Walter Whiter's *A Specimen of a Commentary on Shakespeare* (1794), was published in the same era that saw Shakespeare move from the playhouse to the study and heard Charles Lamb's famous argument that "the plays of Shakespeare are less calculated for performance on a stage, than those of almost any other dramatist whatever" ("On the Tragedies of Shakespeare," 1811; see CLOSET DRAMA). For Lamb, the inadequate visual and aural presence of mere actors on stage was to be replaced with "the sublime images, the poetry alone . . . which is present to our minds in the reading." Whatever its merits, Lamb's argument makes it clear that the issue of mental imaging is not solely a matter for experimental investigation but entails deeply disputed cultural values—the rivalry of visual and aural media (incl. the "breach" or "hinge" between written and spoken lang. explored by Derrida); the contest between art understood as a public, performative mode and its role as a private, subjective refuge; the notion of authorial *intention as a mental representation ("vision" or "design") that stands before or behind the poem.

The very idea of the mental image seems inextricably connected with the notion of reading as the entry into a private space (the Lockean metaphor of the mind as a *camera obscura* or "dark room" into which ideas are admitted through sensory apertures reinforces, with a kind of metaimage, this picture of mental solitude in an interior space filled with representations). It is not surprising, then, that the concept of the poetic image in all its ambivalence holds part of the central ground of poetics, serving as both the mechanism of reference to and deferral of an external, imitated or projected reality; as the projection of authorial intention (but also of unauthorized "unconscious" meaning); as the ling. ligature that composes figures of speech and thought and decomposes them into a general condition of lang. and consciousness; as the realm of freedom and dangerous uncertainty in reader response. Future crit. of the poetic image must, at minimum, take account of the historical variability of the concept and resist the temptation to dissolve poetic expression into the universal solvent of "the image."

See DESCRIPTIVE POETRY, ENARGEIA, FIGURATION, IMITATION, MIMESIS, PAINTING AND POETRY, UT PICTURA POESIS.

■ E. Pound, *Pavannes and Divisions* (1918); H. W. Wells, *Poetic Imagery* (1924); S. J. Brown, *The World of Imagery* (1927); O. Barfield, *Poetic Diction* (1928); J. Dewey, "The Common Substance of All the Arts," *Art as Experience* (1934); C. Spurgeon, *Shakespeare's Imagery and What It Tells Us* (1935); I. A. Richards, *The Philosophy of Rhetoric* (1936); C. Brooks, "Metaphor and the Tradition," *Modern Poetry and the Tradition* (1939); L. H. Hornstein, "Analysis of Imagery: A Critique of Literary Method," *PMLA* 57 (1942); C. D. Lewis, *The Poetic Image* (1947); R. B. Heilman, *This Great Stage: Image and Structure in "King Lear"* (1948); R. H. Fogle, *The Imagery of Keats and Shelley* (1949); W. Clemen, *The Development of Shakespeare's Image* (1951); Abrams; Wellek and Warren, ch. 15; Frye; F. Kermode, *The Romantic Image* (1957); H. Kenner, *The Art of Poetry* (1959); R. Frazer, "The Origin of the Term *Image*," *ELH* 27 (1960); M. Hardt, *Das Bild in der Dichtung* (1966); P. N. Furbank, *Reflections on the Word "Image"* (1970); J. Derrida, *Of Grammatology*, trans. G. C. Spivak (1974); N. Goodman, *Languages of Art* (1976); S. Kosslyn, *Image and Mind* (1980); T. Ziolkowski, *Disenchanted Images* (1977); *The Language of Images*, spec. iss. of *CritI* 6.3 (1980); N. Block, *Imagery* (1981); M. A. Caws, *The Eye in the Text* (1981); *Image and Code*, ed. W. Steiner (1981); W. Steiner, *The Colors of Rhetoric* (1982); *Articulate Images*, ed. R. Wendorf (1983); P. de Man, "Intentional Structure of the Romantic Image," *The Rhetoric of Romanticism* (1984); *Image/Imago/Imagination*, spec. iss. of *NLH* 15.3 (1984); W.J.T. Mitchell, *Iconology* (1987); P. Yu, *The Reading of Imagery in the Chinese Poetic Tradition* (1987); J. Heffernan, *Museum of Words* (1993); H. Belting, *Likeness and Presence*, trans. E. Jephcott (1994); W.J.T. Mitchell, *Picture Theory* (1994); S. Durham, *Phantom Communities* (1997); K. Jacobs, *The Eye's Mind* (2001); J. Rancière, *The Future of the Image*, trans. G. Elliott (2007); E. B. Loizeaux, *Twentieth-Century Poetry and the Visual Arts* (2008).

W.J.T. MITCHELL; B. GLAVEY

## IMAGERY

I. Culture and Criticism
II. Sense, Mind, and Language
III. Imagery and Discourse

**I. Culture and Criticism.** *Imagery*, like the related word *imitate*, invokes the power of imagination, the cultural uses and dangers of likeness, and the baffling confluence of concrete and abstract, literal and figurative, body and mind, matter and spirit. One index of the cultural volatility of imagery is its place in religions. Religious trads. such as Judaism oppose the worship of images as false; Islam avoids the representation of all divinely created forms, although Islamic exegesis addresses the uses and limits of inner and outer meaning; Hinduism and Buddhism embrace imagery; and many shamanistic religions employ totemic images. Rich Christian trads. of sacramental imagery are accompanied by strong countercurrents of iconoclasm, as in the Iconoclastic Controversy of the 8th and 9th cs. in the Eastern Church and the Protestant Reformation. Problems of imagery are implicit in Midrash and in patristic and med. biblical exegesis, esp. in the devel. of the four senses of scripture.

Images occupy a critical place in the Gr. philosophical mediation of the material and the ideal. Plato distinguishes true ideas from false likenesses, images being at a double remove from reality, and he credits neither painting nor poetry as knowledge. Aristotle recognized the central role of imagery in the formation of thought, and by identifying structures of representation, he legitimized the arts as forms of truth. Roman commentators such as Horace, Longinus, and Quintilian spoke of imagery and its uses in poetry and *rhetoric. Horace coined the formula **ut pictura poesis* (as is painting, so is poetry), drawing upon an aphorism attributed to Simonides of Ceos by Plutarch, who praised the historians whose lively prose made readers see actions described in words. The rhetorical figure *ekphrasis* was widely used by Gr. and Roman writers for imagery that makes something appear in poetry as if present, "laying it out before the eyes," in the words of Cicero's *De oratore*.

The genre of the *dream vision and med. descriptive formulas like the *blason or *laisses similaires* are rich sources for imagery in theory and practice. In the widely disseminated Ren. convention of *Petrarchism, description of the *imago vera* of the beloved object erects a symbolic infrastructure embodying subject and object, and the theoretical structure of Petrarchan imagery is a major source of *Renaissance poetics. But the consideration of imagery as a category in literary theory and practice begins with early mod. lit. crit., Frazer argues, in the 16th and 17th cs. (also Furbank, Legouis [in Miner], and Mitchell [1986]).

The functions of the term during the Ren. were still largely fulfilled by the figures of rhetorical *copia*, a persuasive writing style marked by abundant *schemes and *tropes. Figurative lang. was viewed as both an *ornament and a means of embodiment. Erasmus and other Ren. practitioners promoted *enargeia*, vivid, pictorial imagery that achieves copia through its sheer quantity and detail.

Philip Sidney's *Defence of Poesy* (1595) makes a paradoxical claim for the excellence of poetry among the rival arts: he contends that the poet "nothing affirms, and therefore never lieth," for poets work through the senses to move a will infected by the passions away from vice through images of virtue. For Sidney, the delightful instruction of imagery fuses the abstraction of philosophy and the concrete example of hist. Nicolas Boileau similarly calls on the animation and warmth of imagery as a source of poetic power.

**II. Sense, Mind, and Language.** With the growth of skepticism and empiricism in the late 17th and early 18th cs., interest turned to the cognitive function of imagery. The epistemology of Thomas Hobbes and the associationist psychology of John Locke led to a way of looking at poetry in which the image was the connecting link between experience (object) and knowledge (subject). An image was reproduced in the mind as an initial sensation was produced in bodily perception. Thus, when the eye perceives a certain color, a person will register an image of that color in the mind—"image" because the subjective sensation experienced will be a copy of the objective phenomenon of color.

Of course, the mind may also produce images when remembering something once perceived but no longer present or reflecting on remembered experience or combining perceptions and the products of imagination or hallucinating out of dreams and fever. In literary usage, *imagery* thus comes to refer to images produced in the mind by words that refer to sense perceptions and to the many artistic permutations of sense impression, memory, and fabrication.

G. E. Lessing's *Laokoön* (1766), an influential critique of the arts as systems of signs, argues against the equation of imagery in the visual and verbal arts, distinguishing time and space as the proper places of poetry and painting. The descriptive poetry of the 18th c. often dwelt on imagery of landscape in the memory and words of the observing subject. Creative power was assumed to reside in the *"imagination," a volume of images entering and circulating in the mind. With romantic transcendentalism, the world appeared as the garment of God, the abstract and general resid-

ing in the concrete and particular, and Spirit was felt to be immanent in Matter. *Nature was itself divine, and nature poetry, a way to body forth the sacred. Imagery, therefore, was elevated to the level of *symbol, to become an embodiment of truth and a central issue of poetry and crit. In "Tintern Abbey," William Wordsworth claims to find in the contemplation of sensual experience a source of conscious life: "While with an eye made quiet by the power / Of harmony, and the deep power of joy, / We see into the life of things."

Science and lit. shared an interest in the powers of imagery during the latter 19th c. The philologist Max Müller accounted for metaphorical imagery as an organic part of the growth of lang., rather than as an *ornament. To conceive of immaterial things, human beings must express them as images of material things because human lang. lags behind conceptual needs. So lang. grows through *metaphor, from image to idea. The word *spirit*, e.g., has as its root meaning "breath"; as the need to express an immaterial conception of soul or deity emerged, an existent concrete word stood for the new abstract meaning.

Francis Galton's experiments in the psychology of perception (1880) suggested that people differ in their image making. While one person may reveal a predominant tendency to visualize his or her reading, memories, and ruminations, another may favor the mind's "ear," another the mind's "nose," and yet another may have little imagery at all. Other psychologists, such as the Am. Joseph Jastrow, became interested in ambiguous images, suggesting that perception was not just the result of external sense data but also a product of the mind.

Symbolist poets frequently turned to *synaesthesia* to confound the separate senses of experience and to expose the richness of the poet's soul (see SYMBOLISM), as in Charles Baudelaire's poem "Correspondances," which evokes forests of symbols that have powers of infinite expansion; exotic and unfathomable things, like amber, musk, and incense, enrapture the soul and senses. Arthur Rimbaud's "Voyelles" ("Vowels") seeks an arbitrary dislocation of perceptions and understanding: "A black, E white, I red, U green, O blue."

Psychology often categorizes images through the senses: visual (sight, brightness, clarity, color, and motion), auditory (hearing), olfactory (smell), gustatory (taste), tactile (touch, temperature, texture), organic (awareness of heartbeat, pulse, breathing, digestion), and kinesthetic (awareness of muscle tension and movement). The role of different senses emerged as one way of categorizing poetic imagery early in the last century of crit. A line of John Keats's poetry might be tactile and organic—e.g., "For ever warm and still to be enjoy'd, / For ever panting, and for ever young" ("Ode on a Grecian Urn"). Themes such as behavior, location, and time may also classify imagery in relation to such matters as warfare, eating, hair, the domestic, the urban, birds, mountains, morning, or summer.

Critics in the early 20th c. cataloged images and identified dominant sets or clusters of images within a poem or a poet's oeuvre, a *genre, or a literary period or style, drawing analogies to themes, authorship, historical or biographical origins, organic form, or the symbolic organization of cultural forms like *myth or *archetype. When the meaning and function of imagery were adapted as markers of the literary in theories about poetic lang. and creation, imagery became one of the key terms of the *New Criticism. Knight (1930) found in imagery a pattern below the level of plot and character that is an index of the intellectual content of Shakespeare's plays. Warren (1946) saw in the *Rime of the Ancient Mariner* a symbol of the artist-archetype, embodied in the figure of the Mariner, torn between the conflicting and ambiguous claims of reason (symbolized by the sun) and the imagination (symbolized by the moon). Burke (1941) compared S. T. Coleridge's letters with image-clusters in the *Ancient Mariner* and concluded that the albatross symbolizes the poet's guilt over his addiction to opium, thus illuminating the motivational structure of the poem. But I. A. Richards in *Principles of Literary Criticism*, like Galton, found that the sensual perception of images in poetry differed radically from one reader to another and excluded visual imagery from crit., focusing instead largely on the semantic operations at work in imagery.

Sensory imagery, however concrete or referential, comes to be seen in many forms of 20th-c. crit. as exercising complex figurative functions. Freudian and Jungian theories of mind look toward the complex function of images in personality and culture. Structuralist ling. theory defines lang. as an arbitrary system of signs through which reference is always mediated, and the understanding of imagery as a system of signs is similarly transformed. Verbal and visual imagery in ling. and philosophical theory offered famous illustrations of the function of the sign. Ferdinand de Saussure, e.g., produces a diagram of the tree, and Ludwig Wittgenstein borrows from Jastrow the image of the duck-rabbit to explore the roles of mind, lang., and sense.

Richards introduced terms such as *tenor and vehicle* that often came to be used to explain the structure of imagery not as purely sensual but as figurative lang., and similar terms may be found in structuralist poetics. In Robert Burns's *simile "my love is like a red, red rose," images like the color, texture, or odor of a rose are figures for a lady's blush, her delicate skin, her fragrance. Burns's speaker is saying that his lady is to him as June is to the world, bringing rebirth and joy. The lady makes him feel as spring makes him feel: the ground of comparison is a set of feelings and associations. The imagery of the vehicle (the rose) and of the tenor (my love) are discrete objects related by thinking and feeling and writing and reading human subjects. Those associations are the ground of the simile that connects vehicle and tenor. The poem presents imagery of rose and of lady, and the qualities attributed to these objects intersect. But the rose and the lady are not images of one another. As Gertrude Stein observed, a rose is a rose is a rose.

Yet powerful imagery invites us to forget that distinction. An image involving *synecdoche, e.g., blurs the distinction of part and whole or container and thing contained—as in a ruby-red glass of wine. Just which object is ruby red, the glass or the wine? Where is the ruby if one cannot drink or taste it and it will not hold liquid? Or would a red object that has a taste, like a cherry, create likewise illogical imagery?

The mixing of images can be comical when it produces a material absurdity, as in the line "I smell a rat, Mr. Speaker; I see him floating in the air, but I will yet nip him in the bud." But Quintilian (see CATACHRESIS) argued that such imagery may be effective when it borrows an available term for one that does not exist, and such fused images easily enter the canon of poetry, as in Hamlet's "to take arms against a sea of troubles." Here if we do not imagine from the lang. of the character a demented warrior slashing at the sea with his sword, we may imagine two separate sets of images related in metaphor—feeling overwhelmed by troubles as by the inundation of the sea and doing something about them as when a warrior arms himself and marches out to meet the enemy.

Such understanding of imagery reflects a social and historical understanding of lang. Even decorous poetic imagery may violate the norms of sense perception, as when poetry flattens images into the merely picturesque, a danger Wordsworth contemplates in the lines "hedgerows hardly hedge-rows, little lines / Of sportive wood run wild: these pastoral farms, / Green to the very door" ("Tintern Abbey"). Precious imagery eclipses the role of the senses in description, as in Belinda's awakening in Alexander Pope's *Rape of the Lock*: "Sol thro' white curtains shot a tim'rous ray." In satiric or grotesque poetry (see SATIRE), imagery often conjoins visual objects incongruously, piling them up, or exposing shame or weakness for comic or absurd effect and challenging norms of *decorum and belief, as in the gutters of Jonathan Swift's "Description of a City Shower," where "dead cats and turnip-tops come tumbling down the flood."

In some imagery like the metaphysical *conceit, a trope that marks one of the major interests of early 20th-c. crit. (Wells, Rugoff, Tuve, Miller; see METAPHYSICAL POETRY), poets are licensed to challenge the reader with an image that reveals a significance that first appearances would make seem unlikely.

Similar interest in overlapping imagery may be seen in the imagist movement of the early 20th c., where one image may be defined through another distinctly apart from it as an "intellectual and emotional complex" perceived through lang. "in an instant of time" (see IMAGISM). In Ezra Pound's "In a Station of the Metro," for instance, faces in a crowd are seen as petals on a bough. According to Pound, a poem of this sort tries to record the precise instant in which a thing outward and objective transforms itself or darts into a thing inward and subjective.

Critics such as Roman Jakobson working in the school of *Russian formalism approached lit. as organized violence committed on ordinary speech. Lit. deviates from and thus empowers speech through devices such as *meter or imagery—these deviations make it lit.

**III. Imagery and Discourse.** Mid-20th-c. devels. in speculative and experimental psychology, involving phenomenology, epistemology, and cognitive psychology, questioned what mental imagery is. Block, e.g., argued against the objection that internal pictures are nonexistent because we do not have pictures in the brain and an inner eye with which to see them. Images are verbal and conceptual to Block, who proposed that there are two kinds of imagery, one that represents perception in roughly the same way pictures do, the other that represents as lang. does, i.e., conceptually. Block also contended that some images combine pictorial and verbal elements and that the real question is what types of representation are possible. Furbank, on the other hand, after giving a very useful hist. of the term *image* to the imagists, reveals the ambiguities and confusions involved in using the terms *image* and *concrete* to describe qualities of the verbal medium. We should not confuse *abstract* with *general* or *concrete* with *specific*. *Concrete*, e.g., does not necessarily mean "sensuous," and that which is *specific* may very well also be *abstract*. The only actual physical element of poetry is found in the subvocal or silent actions of tongue and larynx as a poem is recited or read. Furbank has suggested that we drop the term *imagery* altogether. Cognitive psychologists and neuroscientists over the second half of the 20th c. revived interest in imagery and gathered empirical evidence about the status of sense imagery and mental imagery, looking at the interference of motor and visual perception, e.g., or at examples of mental rotation or analogue images.

Mitchell (1986) places the entire issue of imagery within the broad historical context of knowledge as a cultural product (see ICONOLOGY, IMAGE). He has provided a chart of the "family of images" to indicate the different meanings of *imagery*: graphic images (pictures, statues, designs) are found in art hist.; optical images (mirrors, projections) in physics; perceptual images (sense data, "species," appearances) in philosophy and theology; mental images (dreams, memories, ideas, phantasmata) in psychology and epistemology; and verbal images (metaphors, descriptions, writing) in lit. crit.

Imagery frequently enters into deconstructive philosophy and crit. as an occurrence of false origins or priority. Images may be the necessary supplements of originals (like the Platonic "Form of the Good") that cannot be otherwise known. Images involving binaries (such as black and white) include their opposites as a black or white object does not. In work such as "Plato's Pharmacy," Jacques Derrida offers a critique of the logic of Plato's imagery; Derrida's own work often relies on playful images to unsettle received ideas, as in the image of Plato dictating to a writing Socrates in *The Post Card*. P. de Man's work deconstructs the unity of the figural icon or the notion of dominant figures and looks to ways in which critical insight depends on blindness to assertion and yielding to the knots of lang.

One feature of postmod. *Language poetry of recent decades is an emphasis on the materiality of the signifier rather than its reference to a prior material object or experience; here, imagery is not the product of a material sense perception but a material function of lang., as in Lyn Hejinian's claim in "Happily" (2000) to write with inexact straightness in a place between phrases of the imagination.

Mitchell (1986) has promoted the study of iconology across the media and of the relations of visual and verbal representations in the context of social and political issues. His argument concerning the nature and function of imagery averts a mere binary between the empiricist positivism and deconstruction. Both our signs and the world they signify are a product of human action and understanding, and although our modes of knowledge and representation may be arbitrary and conventional, they are the constituents of the forms of life—the practices and trads. within which we make epistemological, ethical, and political choices. The question is, therefore, not simply "what is an image?" but more "how do we transfer images into powers worthy of trust and respect?" Discourse, Mitchell concludes, projects worlds and states of affairs that can be pictured concretely and tested against other representations.

Approaching the problem from a sociopolitical-historical perspective, Weimann would remind us that, while for mod. critics the meaning of a poem is secondary to its figures, for Ren. and metaphysical poets the meaning was primary. Here he agrees with Tuve that mod. interpretations fail to do justice to the intentions and structures of earlier works. Metaphor, he says, is neither autonomous nor decorative; rather, it relates human and universe, and the link or interaction between tenor and vehicle is the core. Hist. is part of the meaning of a metaphor. Shakespeare's freedom of ling. transference reflects the social mobility of his era, an age of transitions and contradictions. That neoclassical critics did not value Shakespeare's rich imagery but preferred plot over diction reflects their own view of the person in society. This valuation was reversed during the romantic age, but even the romantics did not place form over meaning. Modernist poets and critics, Weimann argues, emphasizing the autonomy of a literary work and its spatial patterns, have removed lit. from both hist. and its audience (see AUTONOMY; MODERNISM). In seeking liberation from time and space and from hist. into myth, this trad. has rejected the mimetic function of lit. in cl. crit. (see MIMESIS), as well as the expressive principle of *romanticism. Metaphor is now seen as an escape from reality and has become severed from its social meaning. In reply, Weimann calls for an integration of the study of imagery within a more comprehensive vision of lit. hist.

Yu's analysis of Chinese imagery suggests ways in which the study of poetic imagery can be enriched further by means of comparative studies. She sees a fundamental difference between "attitudes toward poetic imagery in classical China" and "those commonly taken for granted in the West." Western conceptions are based on the dualism of matter and spirit and on the twin assumptions of mimesis and fictionality: poetry embodies concretely a transcendent reality, and the *poet is a creator of hitherto unapprehended relations between these two disparate realms. The Chinese assumption, by contrast, is nondualistic: there are indeed different categories of existence—personal, familial, social, political, natural—but they all belong to the same earthly realm, and the poet represents reality both in a literal sense and by joining various images that have already been molded for him by his culture. Thus, the Chinese poetic and critical trads. reveal the conventional correspondences used by the poets in their efforts to juxtapose images so as to suggest rather than explain meaning.

■ **Criticism and History**: W. Whiter, *A Specimen of a Commentary on Shakespeare* (1794); W. Spaulding, *A Letter on Shakespeare's Authorship of "The Two Noble Kinsmen"* (1876); Richards; S. J. Brown, *The World of Imagery* (1927); F. C. Kolbe, *Shakespeare's Way* (1930); C. Spurgeon, *Shakespeare's Imagery and What It Tells Us* (1935); U. Ellis-Fermor, *Some Recent Research in Shakespeare's Imagery* (1937); K. Burke, *Attitudes toward History* (1937); G. W. Knight, *The Burning Oracle* (1939); M. B. Smith, *Marlowe's Imagery and the Marlowe Canon* (1940); K. Burke, *The Philosophy of Literary Form* (1941); L. H. Hornstein, "Analysis of Imagery," *PMLA* 57 (1942); G. W. Knight, *The Chariot of Wrath* (1942); E. A. Armstrong, *Shakespeare's Imagination* (1946); Brooks; R. B. Heilman, *This Great Stage* (1948); D. A. Stauffer, *Shakespeare's World of Images* (1949); T. H. Banks, *Milton's Imagery* (1950); W. H. Clemen, *The Development of Shakespeare's Imagery* (1951); F. Marsh, *Wordsworth's Imagery* (1952); J. E. Hankins, *Shakespeare's Derived Imagery* (1953); Frye; J. W. Beach, *Obsessive Images* (1960); R. Frazer, "The Origin of the Term 'Image'," *ELH* 27 (1960); G. W. Knight, *The Crown of Life* (1961); G. W. Williams, *Image and Symbol in the Sacred Poetry of Richard Crashaw* (1963); D. A. West, *The Imagery and Poetry of Lucretius* (1969); P. N. Furbank, *Reflections on the Word "Image"* (1970); S. A. Barlow, *The Imagery of Euripides* (1971); *Seventeenth-Century Imagery*, ed. E. Miner (1971); W. E. Rogers, *Image and Abstraction* (1972); J. Doebler, *Shakespeare's Speaking Pictures* (1974); R. Weimann, *Structure and Society in Literary History* (1976); J. H. Matthews, *The Imagery of Surrealism* (1977); V. N. Sinha, *The Imagery and Language of Keats's Odes* (1978); R. Berry, *Shakespearean Metaphor* (1978); T. Cave, *The Cornucopian Text* (1979); de Man; V. S. Kolve, *Chaucer and the Imagery of Narrative* (1984); J. Steadman, *Milton's Biblical and Classical Imagery* (1984); J. Dundas, *The Spider and the Bee* (1985); W.J.T. Mitchell, *Iconology* (1986), *Art and the Public Sphere* (1993), and *Picture Theory* (1994); V. A. Kolve, *Telling Images* (2009).

■ **Figurative Language**: M. Müller, *Lectures on the Science of Language*, 2d ser. (1894); F. I. Carpenter, *Metaphor and Simile in Minor Elizabethan Drama* (1895); G. Buck, *The Metaphor* (1899); J. G. Jennings, *An Essay on Metaphor in Poetry* (1915); H. W. Wells, *Poetic Imagery* (1924); O. Barfield, *Poetic Diction* (1928); E. Holmes, *Aspects of Elizabethan Imagery* (1929); I. A. Richards, *The Philosophy of Rhetoric* (1936), and *Interpretation in Teaching* (1938); M. A. Rugoff, *Donne's Imagery* (1939); C. Brooks, *Modern Poetry and the Tradition* (1939); R. Tuve, *Elizabethan and Metaphysical Imagery* (1947); C. D. Lewis, *The Poetic Image* (1947); H. Coombs, *Lit-*

*erature and Criticism* (1953); W. K. Wimsatt, *The Verbal Icon* (1954); F. Kermode, *The Romantic Image* (1957); C. Brooke-Rose, *A Grammar of Metaphor* (1958); O. Barfield, "The Meaning of the Word 'Literal'," *Metaphor and Symbol*, ed. L. C. Knights and B. Cottle (1960); M. Peckham, "Metaphor," *The Triumph of Romanticism* (1970); E. E. Ericson, "A Structural Approach to Imagery," *Style* 3 (1969); G. Lakoff and M. Johnson, *Metaphors We Live By* (1980); R. J. Fogelin, *Figuratively Speaking* (1988); J. Witherow, "Anger and Heat: A Study of Figurative Language," *Journal of Literary Semantics* 33 (2004).

■ **Journals**: *Journal of Mental Imagery; The Literary Image; Word & Image*.

■ **Mental Imagery**: F. Galton, "Statistics of Mental Imagery," *Mind* 5 (1880); G. H. Betts, *The Distributions and Functions of Mental Imagery* (1909); J. K. Bonnell, "Touch Images in the Poetry of Robert Browning," *PMLA* 37 (1922); E. Rickert, *New Methods for the Study of Literature* (1927); J. E. Downey, *Creative Imagination* (1929); R. H. Fogle, *The Imagery of Keats and Shelley* (1949); R. A. Brower, *The Fields of Light* (1951); Wellek and Warren, ch. 15; *The Language of Images*, ed. W. T. J. Mitchell (1980); *Imagery*, ed. N. Block (1981); P. Yu, *The Reading of Imagery in the Chinese Poetic Tradition* (1987); W.J.T. Mitchell, "The Pictorial Turn," *Artforum* 30.7 (1992); M. Tye, *The Imagery Debate* (1992); W.J.T. Mitchell, "What Do Pictures Want?" *October* 77 (1996); N.J.T. Thomas, "Mental Imagery," *Stanford Encyclopedia of Philosophy*, ed. E. N. Zalta, http://plato.stanford.edu/archives/fall2010/entries/mental-imagery.

■ **Symbol and Myth**: O. Rank, *Art and Artist*, trans. C. F. Atkinson (1932); R. P. Warren, "A Poem of Pure Imagination," *The Rime of the Ancient Mariner by Samuel Taylor Coleridge* (1946); Crane; P. Wheelwright, *The Burning Fountain* (1954); H. Musurillo, *Symbol and Myth in Ancient Poetry* (1961); P. Wheelwright, *Metaphor and Reality* (1962); K. Burke, *Language as Symbolic Action* (1966); A. Cook, *Figural Choice in Poetry and Art* (1985).

S. FOLEY

# IMAGINATION

I. Distinctions from Fancy; General Scope
II. Ancient, Classical, and Medieval
III. Renaissance and 17th Century
IV. 18th Century and Romanticism
V. Later 19th and 20th Centuries

**I. Distinctions from Fancy; General Scope.** Imagination derives from Lat. *imaginatio*, itself a substitute for Gr. *phantasia*. During the Ren., the term *\*fancy*—connoting free play, mental creativity, and license—often eclipsed imagination, considered more as reproducing sense impressions, primarily visual images. By ca. 1700, empirical philosophy cast suspicion on fancy; imagination seemed preferably rooted in the evidence of sense data. Thomas Hobbes, nevertheless, retains "fancy" and is perhaps the last Eng. writer to use it to signify the mind's greatest inventive range. John Dryden describes imagination as a capacious power encompassing traditional stages of composition: *invention, fancy (distribution or design), and elocution (style). G.W. Leibniz contrasts *les idées réelles* with *les idées phantastiques ou chimériques* (*Nouveaux essais*). Many, incl. Joseph Addison, use fancy and imagination synonymously, but Addison calls his important *Spectator* series (nos. 409, 411–21) "Pleasures of the Imagination." More susceptible to prosodic manipulation in verse, the term retains a higher place in poetic diction than in crit. (e.g., William Collins's "Young Fancy thus, to me divinest name"). But in England and particularly in Germany, writers increasingly distinguish the terms before S. T. Coleridge's definitions in *Biographia Literaria* (1817). By 1780, Christian Wolff, J. G. Sulzer, J. N. Tetens, and Ernst Platner make explicit distinctions. Coleridge recognizes this by claiming himself the first "of my countrymen" to distinguish fancy from imagination. But several Eng. writers record distinctions between 1760 and 1800.

Since 1800, and to some degree before as well, poets and critics have considered imagination the chief creative faculty, a "synthetic and magical power" responsible for invention and originality (Coleridge). Writers have associated or identified imagination with *genius, *inspiration, *taste, visionary power, and prophecy (see also EXPRESSION, IMITATION, ORIGINALITY). During the past three centuries, no other idea has proved more fruitful for poetics and critical theory or for their intersection with psychology and philosophy. Before the watershed in the hist. of the idea during the late 17th–19th cs., commentaries and poetics generally accord imagination an important but ambivalent role: judgment or understanding must trim its vagaries and correct its wayward force. Ancient poets, philosophers, and psychologists consider imagination a strong and diverse power; but, unregulated, it produces illusion, mental instability (often melancholy), bad art, or madness. Yet imagination becomes the chief criterion of Eur. and Am. *romanticism. Even if we speak of romanticisms in the plural, imagination is important to each one. Not only philosophers and psychologists, but critics and poets elevate it as a prime subject of their vital work. William Wordsworth's *The Prelude* proclaims imagination as its main theme; John Keats's "Lamia" and great odes debate in symbolic terms the function and worth of imaginative art. To a surprising extent, the transcendental or "critical" philosophy in Germany and America explores and elaborates the idea, spawning theories that champion the process and function of art as the final act and highest symbolic expression of philosophizing.

**II. Ancient, Classical, and Medieval.** In the book of Genesis, two forms of imagination emerge, *bara*, which signifies *creatio ex nihilo* (Gen. 1:27), and *yatsar*, the creation of the human from the dust of the earth (*human* shares a root with *earth*, *dust*, or *soil*). The Western trad. usually reserves *creatio ex nihilo* for God alone, with human imagination as an echo or lesser ex-

ercise of it. However, the myths of Prometheus, Faust, and Frankenstein challenge this. Some critics detect a challenge, too, in writers such as J. W. Goethe and even John Milton. Ancient stories and myths of a demiurge or figure, often in female form, necessary to inspire and actually to carry out divine creation, find expression in later writers (e.g., P. B. Shelley, W. B. Yeats). Similarly, the Gr. *muses are all female.

Ancient religious texts can criticize imagination: "the imagination of man's heart is evil from his youth" (Gen. 8:21). Yet the same texts are interpreted to provide for a positive imagination that facilitates a dialogue between the human and divine. Coleridge identifies *Logos* as the communicative intellect in God and man and suggests that it is the ultimate power of making, "the Creator! and the Evolver!"

What may be called a mystical sense of imaginative unity joining the divine or universally creative with the human emerges in poets such as Rūmī and William Blake, for each uniquely so. Sufi teaching approximates imagination with the idea of *barzakh*, a realm partaking of spirit and matter. The Vedic trad. presents imagination, too, as the higher power of the gods creating and sustaining all reality, as well as a human power realizing and partaking of this larger harmony.

Aristotle advances in *De anima* the cl. definition of imagination: mental reproduction of sensory experience. In this elegant simplicity, imagination registers sensory impressions immediately present in the act of perception. With sense data absent, imagination becomes a form of memory, mother of the Muses. Aristotle discusses the role of imagination in what John Locke will call "the association of ideas," central to empirical psychology. David Hume, Joseph Priestley, the associationists in general, William Hazlitt, and to some degree Wordsworth will later view imagination in terms of heightened associations of ideas (either unconscious or determined by conscious choice) coexisting with feelings and passions, thus giving all associative operations a subjective and affective element. Imagination thus forms the basis of taste, by definition grounded in the perceiving subject, an argument Edmund Burke broaches in his *Enquiry into the Sublime and Beautiful* (1757) and later at the core of Immanuel Kant's *Kritik der Urteilskraft* (*Critique of Judgment*, 1790).

But in the *Poetics*, where Aristotle pursues a structural or generic approach based on dramatic texts, he skirts the function of imagination. The audience's imaginative response projecting sympathy and identification (pity and fear) may be inferred, but Aristotle does not analyze imagination as crucial to either reception or production.

Plato distrusts the artist's imagination and assigns it an essentially reproductive duty (copying a copy). In psychological terms, the soul passively receives an image, which reflects an idea. However, the Platonic *nous* (reason) carries a force similar to later conceptions of creative imagination. Philip Sidney and F.W.J. Schelling, among others, will later interpret Plato's thought and image-laden writing to counter Plato's own condemnation of poetry and poets. For Plotinus, the imagination (phantasy) is a plastic, constructive faculty that can change and alter experience, permit or realize a form of intellectual intuition or insight. Phantasy comes in two forms. The lower—linked to sense and the soul's irrational power—may harmonize with the higher, which reflects ideas and the rational. Plotinus and Proclus are among several who provide antecedents for Coleridge's "primary" and "secondary" imagination. As Plotinus considers nature an emanation of soul and soul an emanation of mind, his thought adumbrates a large system of nature and sense, idea and soul, cosmos and mind, creator and creativity, all interconnected through imaginative power. Elements of this thought recur in the hermetic philosophers, Jakob Boehme, Blake, Schelling, and Coleridge. Plotinus provides implications for mimetic theory and for a poetics that spills into theodicy, where the external world is "the book of nature" or, as Goethe and others later express it (before the Rosetta Stone is deciphered), a divine "hieroglyphic." Using this general idea, R. W. Emerson and H. D. Thoreau develop their own angles of vision, as do the *Naturphilosophen* in their search for connections between the forces and laws discovered by natural science and poetry conceived as an inventive power creating its own related—but original—nature.

From the beginning, imagination thus possesses roots both in empiricism based on sense experience and in transcendentalism. Its function may be seen in terms of natural and psychological phenomena, perception, acquisition of knowledge, creative production of art, and even, as Baruch Spinoza says, the prophets who receive "revelations of God by the aid of imagination" (*Tractatus theologico-politicus*, 1670). These manifestations are not mutually exclusive but interact, as in the thought of Giordano Bruno, who conceives of sense, memory, emotion, cognition, and the divine mind all linked through imagination. Many writers divide the power into levels or degrees, with adjectives denoting particular functions (e.g., re/productive, *erste/zweite/ dritte potenz*, primary or secondary, creative, sympathetic, perceptive). *The Prelude* traces a maturation of the power through different stages. The explosion of Ger. analytical terms for imagination in the 18th c. is staggering (*Einbildungskraft, Phantasie, Imagination, Fassungskraft, Perceptionsvermögen, Dichtungsvermögen,* or *Dichtkraft*—with variants, and more). Since antiquity, then, images produced by this power have been variously considered as materially real or as appearances and pure illusion or even as idealized forms. Poetry, dreams, divine inspiration (madness and prophecy), delusion, and emotional disturbances—all involve one or more activities of imagination. It therefore harbors the greatest potential not only for insight and intuition but for deception and illusion.

Horace, long influential in Western poetics, barely mentions imagination in his *Ars poetica*. This absence, coupled with Platonic distrust of imagination and later neoclassical emphasis on verisimilitude and *decorum in imitation (what much 18th-c. and romantic theory scorns as mere "copy"), diminishes the place of imagination in poetic theory for centuries after Horace. Although Philostratus declares imitation inferior to

phantasy and Quintilian connects imagination (*visiones*) with raising absent things to create emotion in the hearer, not until the rediscovery in the 16th c. of the *Peri hypsous* (*On the Sublime*) attributed to Longinus do Eur. critics turn more to the power he describes: "moved by enthusiasm and passion you seem to see the things whereof you speak and place them before the eyes of your hearers." Nicolas Boileau translates Longinus; in England, John Dennis and Alexander Pope spread his views. The useful, if rough, distinction between "Aristotelian" and "Longinian" crit. stems largely from divergent emphases on imagination and its corollaries for mimetic theory.

Med. views of imagination vary, with Aristotelian rather than Platonic influence dominating. Yet, both emerge in Thomas Aquinas and Moses ben Maimon (Maimonides). Ibn Sīnā (Avicenna) and Rūmī place imagination above intellectual reason in pursuing knowledge and enlightenment. In Scholastic thinkers, imagination continues its role of connecting and representing a link between the material and the spiritual. Although they theorize little, writers such as Dante, Chaucer, and the poet of *Piers Plowman* create a visionary or comprehensively imaginative rendering of experience.

**III. Renaissance and 17th Century.** Giovanni Pico della Mirandola's *De imaginatione sive phantasia* (ed. and trans. H. Caplan, 1971) collects from the cl. and med. trads. but stresses vision as the primary or archetypal sense, circumscribing the possibility of a larger poetics founded on imagination. George Puttenham summarizes Ren. notions of imagination in the production of poetry and emphasizes the link between poet as creator and a divine creator (see RENAISSANCE POETICS). Sidney and J. C. Scaliger call the poet a "creator" (Ben Jonson calls him a "maker"), implying that such creation imitates or follows nature rather than copies it. Hence, a dichotomy should not be established between imitation and creative imagination; it is possible to ally them, as Coleridge does in *On Poesy or Art*. As Coleridge frequently says, to distinguish is not necessarily to divide. Even with Sidney (and later Leibniz, Joshua Reynolds, Shelley, and Thomas Carlyle), imitation not so much duplicates nature as it echoes divine creative power. The 19th-c. Platonist Joseph Joubert will claim that the poet "purifies and empties the forms of matter and shows us the universe as it is in the mind of God. . . . His portrayal is not a copy of a copy, but an impression of the archetype." Thomas Macaulay will call this the "imperial power" of poetry to imitate the "whole external and the whole internal universe." For Anthony Ashley Cooper, the third Earl of Shaftesbury, the poet is a "just Prometheus under Jove," and the variation on the Ovidian phrase—a god or daemon in us—becomes common in discussions of imagination. During the *Sturm und Drang* and romantic eras, the theme of Prometheus further modifies the connection between divine creative energy and human poetry. In Blake's Christian vision, these powers merge as the "divine-human imagination"; Schelling calls genius "a portion of the Absolute nature of God." Poetry for Shelley elicits "the divinity in man." Coleridge considers the secret of genius in the fine arts to make the internal external and the external internal; in religious terms, Jesus is the living, communicative intellect in God and man—suggestively phrased in Emerson's "living, leaping Logos."

Ren. psychologists, among them Philipp Melancthon, Veit Amerbach, and esp. Juan Luis Vives, advance increasingly sophisticated views of the mind wherein imagination and the association of ideas play important roles. Sidney and Edmund Spenser consider imaginative power central to both theory and practice. Shakespeare uses imagination (or fancy as its equivalent) suggestively, as in the Chorus of *Henry V*. In Eng. critical discussion of imagination, Theseus's lines in *A Midsummer Night's Dream* (5.1) become the most-quoted verses (Milton's *Paradise Lost* also figures prominently). Although close reading reveals Theseus's distrust of "strong" imagination and its "tricks," identifying imagination with madmen, lovers, and poets—whose tales may never be believed—Hippolyta reinterprets all the players and the night's action as a totalized myth which "More witnesseth than fancy's images, / And grows to something of great constancy."

Francis Bacon's view of rhet. and poetry must be spliced together from many writings. Two trends emerge. He splits rational or scientific knowledge from poetic knowledge, which is "not tied to the laws of matter." But this bestows greater freedom on imagination to join and divide the elements of nature, to appeal to psychological satisfaction rather than verisimilitude, and to permit the imitation of nature to differ from nature itself not only in the medium of presentation but in its appeal to moral value—and to what would later be called aesthetics and the sublime. Later these premises resurface often, incl. Addison's "Pleasures of the Imagination," Hume's "Of the Standard of Taste," and Reynold's *Discourses* (esp. 6, 7, and 13), where imagination rather than the matter-of-fact becomes "the residence of truth." In *The Advancement of Learning*, Bacon mentions an "imaginative or insinuative reason," a concept Matthew Arnold repeats. But Bacon concludes, "I find not any science that doth properly or fitly pertain to the imagination."

Hobbes fails to see the capacious possibilities of Bacon's scheme for crit. or the arts, but his contributions to empirical psychology open other avenues and begin to supply the science Bacon found wanting. For Hobbes, the "compounded imagination" forms "trains of ideas" or "mental discourse" that evolves into judgment or *sagacitas*. In "compounding" images and directing these associations to larger designs, the "contexture" of imagination offers a picture of reality. This suggests what thinkers in the next century commonly express: imagination subsumes judgment. In 1774, Alexander Gerard's *Essay on Genius* explicitly declares this.

Locke coins the phrase "association of ideas" in the *Essay Concerning Human Understanding* (4th ed., 1700). Originally, he means idiosyncratic links between mental representations peculiar to an individual, a process Laurence Sterne explores in *Tristram Shandy*. But the phrase, like William James's "stream of consciousness," changes signification and soon stands for a pervasive habit of mind, both conscious and unconscious, akin to Hobbes's mental discourse and trains of compounded ideas. Locke receives little credit for recognizing imagination as a strong faculty because he criticizes poetry and shows scant sympathy for art and he distrusts figuration in lang. But the "tabula rasa" tag oversimplifies his epistemology and psychology. He states that "the mind has a power," an innate power (distinguished from innate ideas, which it never possesses) "to consider several" simple ideas "united together as one idea; and that not only as they are united in external objects, but as itself has joined them." As in Bacon, the active formation of complex ideas in "almost infinite variety" need not correspond to nature.

Replying to Locke's difficult arguments about innate ideas, Leibniz in his *Nouveaux essais* quotes Aristotle's *De anima*: "There is nothing in the mind not previously in the senses—except the mind itself." Here, as George Santayana later notes, Leibniz uncovers the germ of Kant's critical philosophy. In Leibniz—and in Hobbes's and Locke's ascription of an active power forming complex ideas or trains of them—imagination acquires a central position in a new, flexible faculty-psychology with its accompanying facultative logic.

**IV. 18th Century and Romanticism.** Addison brings these concepts within the ken of critical theory and poetics. "The Pleasures of the Imagination" arise from comparing our imaginative perception of nature with our perception of art, where art is itself an imitation of nature achieved through the artist's imaginative production that "has something in it like creation; it bestows a kind of existence. . . . It makes additions to nature." The interest rapidly becomes psychological and involves a projective faculty, active and passive, productive and reproductive. Like Pico, Addison emphasizes vision but remarks that the pleasures of imagination

> are not wholly confined to such particular authors as are conversant in material objects, but are often to be met with among the polite masters of morality, criticism, and other speculations abstracted from matter, who, though they do not directly treat of the visible parts of nature, often draw from them their similitudes, metaphors, and allegories. . . . A truth in the understanding is . . . reflected by the imagination; we are able to see something like colour and shape in a notion, and to discover a scheme of thoughts traced out upon matter. And here the mind . . . has two of its faculties gratified at the same time, while the fancy is busy in copying after the understanding, and transcribing ideas out of the intellectual world into the material.

The material and the intellectual or passionately moral worlds fuse through imagination; matter and spirit find a common faculty and may be represented by a single image.

In part derived from Addison's crit., Mark Akenside's popular poem *The Pleasures of the Imagination* combines empirical and Platonic elements. Imagination "blends" and "divides" images; its power can "mingle," "join," and "converge" them—phrases that anticipate Coleridge's "secondary" imagination. Collins and Joseph Warton downgrade satiric and didactic verse; Warton proclaims that "invention and imagination" are "the chief faculties of a poet." Edward Young links originality and genius with imagination; Gerard, whom Kant later praises as "the sharpest observer of the nature of genius," says, "it is imagination that produces genius." Gerard, Priestley, and William Duff extend associationist and empirical psychology to give a fluid model of the mind, not rigid or compartmentalized. Hazlitt concludes, "the imagination is an *associating* principle" assuring "continuity and comprehension of mind," a definition allied with his remark that poetry portrays the flowing, not the fixed. Emerson gives a twist to this organic process by hinting at a Neoplatonic foundation in "The Poet": "the endless passing of one element into new forms, the incessant metamorphosis, explains the rank which the imagination holds in our catalog of mental powers. The imagination is the reader of these forms."

In Italy, L. A. Muratori advances a mutually beneficial combination of intellect and imagination to produce "artificial" or "fantastic" images applied metaphorically and charged with emotion. Vico's *Scienza nuova* (1725, 1744) mentions a recollective *fantasia* but, more important, examines how poetic imagination creates the basis for culture through the production of myths and universal patterns that shape understanding of both nature and human nature. Largely ignored during his lifetime, Vico produced ideas that continue to influence historiography, anthropology, education, and imaginative writers such as James Joyce.

While Samuel Johnson and Hume generally distrust the imagination, they stress its pervasive ability to supplant reason. Imagination for Hume becomes the central faculty and for Johnson, in his morality and psychology, the main concern. Both appreciate the role of the passions in strengthening imaginative activity and the association of ideas. They yoke the cl. theory of passions, further developed in the Ren., to empirical psychology. Hume sees imagination as a completing power acting on suggestiveness; he claims that the elements a writer creates "must be connected together by some bond or tie: They must be related to each other in the imagination, and form a kind of *unity* which may bring them under one plan or view." As Coleridge defines "the secondary" imagination, it "dissolves, diffuses, dissipates, in order to re-create; or where this process is rendered impossible, yet still at all events it struggles to idealize and to unify."

The associationists—among them Lord Kames (Henry Home), Archibald Alison, Hugh Blair, Gerard, Hazlitt (to some extent), and others—stress imaginative association as pervasive; it determines taste. Images and sense data receive modifying "colors" of feeling and passion, a notion Wordsworth uses. The emphasis on feeling fused with perception or cognition may be compared with Richards's (1929) later discussion of "emotive" versus "intellectual" belief or T. S. Eliot's *"dissociation of sensibility."

In Burke's *Enquiry*, the imaginative arts become the "affecting arts." Because they trigger the completing imagination of reader or audience, "suggestion" and *"obscurity" attain positive value in poetry and visual art. This helps explain the growing interest in literary forms and genres not rigidly fixed but fluid, also the fascination in Blake, Novalis, and others for aphorism and the importance of the literary *fragment in the early 19th c. The imagination of the reader becomes regarded as an important critical concept, too, ranging from Dryden's and Locke's "assent" to Coleridge's "willing suspension of disbelief." Sulzer, in his *Allgemeine Theorie der Schönen Künste*, notes, "the imagination of those who hear or see the artist's work comes to his aid. If through any of the latent qualities in the work this imagination takes on a vivid effect, it will thereupon complete what remains by itself."

Sensing expansion of the idea, Burke claims in his *Enquiry* (6th ed., 1770) that to imagination "belongs whatever is called wit, fancy, invention, and the like." Hazlitt later remarks, "this power is indifferently called genius, imagination, feeling, taste; but the manner in which it acts upon the mind can neither be defined by abstract rules, as is the case in science, nor verified by continual unvarying experiments, as is the case in mechanical performances." Critics analyze passages of poetry as reflecting the pervasive operation of imagination, one aspect of what Coleridge first calls "practical criticism," a forerunner of the *New Criticism.

Adam Smith bases his *Theory of Moral Sentiments* (1759) on the sympathetic identification that imagination allows us to extend to others. As James Beattie says, "the philosophy of Sympathy ought always to form a part of the science of Criticism." Hazlitt later states that "passion, in short, is the essence, the chief ingredient in moral truth; and the warmth of passion is sure to kindle the light of imagination on the objects around it." The application in crit. is found in Wordsworth, Coleridge, and Keats, culminating rhetorically (along with much else) in Shelley's *Defence of Poetry*: "the great secret of morals is love; or a going out of our own nature, and an identification with the beautiful . . . not our own. A man . . . must imagine intensely and comprehensively; he must put himself in the place of another and of many others. . . . The great instrument of moral good is the imagination; and poetry administers to the effect by acting upon the cause. Poetry enlarges the circumference of the imagination." Applications of what Coleridge calls "sympathetic imagination" are crucial to changes in dramatic crit. Before 1800, William Richardson, Thomas Whatley, and Maurice Morgann approach Shakespeare in this fashion, and Coleridge becomes the most brilliant exponent of such psychologically based crit., a forerunner of the psychological criticism of the 20th c.

The idea of imaginative sympathy also affects theories of poetic lang.: it should be "natural" and "spontaneous." *Metaphor, *personification, and figurative writing in general are now viewed less as *ornament and more as essential to impassioned "natural lang." Theories of the primitive origin of lang. (Jean-Jacques

Rousseau, J. G. Herder, Duff, Lord Monboddo [James Burnett], and many recapitulations, incl. Shelley's and G.W.F. Hegel's) strengthen connections between imagination, poetry, early develop. of societies and their langs., and figurative speech in general (see ROMANTIC AND POSTROMANTIC POETRY AND POETICS). As Hazlitt says, exemplifying the connection between imagination and the fascination with figurative lang., a metaphor or figure of speech requires no proof: "it gives *carte blanche* to the imagination." In the best poetry, images are "the building, and not the scaffolding to thought." What is true not only may but must be expressed figuratively and is a specially valid form of knowledge. Hazlitt, neither a religious enthusiast nor a transcendentalist, even says imagination holds communion with the soul of nature and allows poets "to foreknow and to record the feelings of all men at all times and places."

Blake's emphasis falls heavily on imagination as a power ultimately communicating and sharing with the holy power of creation, a vision that culminates in an Edenic state. "All things Exist in the Human Imagination," "Man is All Imagination," so also "God is Man & exists in us & we in him." "The Eternal Body of Man . . . The Imagination, that is, God himself," is symbolically "the Divine Body of the Lord Jesus." We are "Creating Space, Creating Time according to the wonders Divine of Human Imagination."

Wordsworth's ideas of imagination evolve from the Preface to the 2d ed. of *Lyrical Ballads* (1800), through its 1802 version, to a new preface and "Essay Supplementary" in 1815. In *The Prelude*, he describes the infant:

> . . . his mind
> Even as an agent of the one great mind,
> Creates, creator and receiver both,
> Working but in alliance with the works
> Which it beholds.—Such, verily is the first
> Poetic spirit of our human life.

Cf. Coleridge's definition of "primary" imagination: "the living Power and prime Agent of all human Perception, and . . . a repetition in the finite mind of the eternal act of creation in the infinite I AM." Coleridge began the *Biographia* as a preface to his own volume of verse, in part answering and modifying Wordsworth, but expanded it to a critical exposition and autobiography of his *literary* life that pivots on a reply to Wordsworth's published ideas concerning fancy and imagination. Coleridge considers that Wordsworth too closely links fancy and imagination and explains imagination too exclusively via associationism.

In the 1815 Preface, Wordsworth tries to explain how imagination creates as well as associates. The power becomes for him so vast it challenges all conception, as with the apostrophe in *The Prelude* after crossing the Alps, or later: "Imagination, which, in truth, / Is but another name for absolute power / And clearest insight, amplitude of mind, / And Reason in her most exalted mood." Wordsworth also claims: "Imagination having been our theme, / So also hath that intellectual Love, / For they are each in each, and cannot stand / Dividu-

ally." He uses his idea of imagination to establish new grounding in poetic lang. and vindicates it in his practice (though not always in perfect conformity with his theoretical statements). He chooses not to exert a systematic philosophical concern for the idea as Coleridge does. He even considers that the word *imagination* "has been overstrained . . . to meet the demands of the faculty which is perhaps the noblest of our nature."

Keats explores the idea of sympathetic imagination and *"negative capability," a search for truth or reality without any compulsive reaching after fact. Many of his letters and poems are undogmatic speculations on the value, "truth," and nature of the imaginative inner life. Shelley, regarding reason more in its deductive and experimental mode, contrasts it sharply with imagination and, on this distinction, builds his *Defence of Poetry*. The essay recapitulates many earlier devels. He constructs his argument through powerful images and analogies rather than by Keats's "consequitive reasoning." Shelley's impassioned and figurative prose actualizes its own subject. He emphasizes the unconscious power of imagination over the conscious will in poetic composition.

Coleridge, familiar with philosophical devels. of the idea since Plato and Aristotle, fuses and transforms them into the most suggestive and fruitful critical observations of Eng. romanticism. Though he never completes a systematic work that includes extended discussion of imagination, his theoretical pronouncements and practical insights provide rich ground. He combines Brit. empirical psychology, Platonism and Neoplatonism Scholastic and hermetic philosophies, and Ger. transcendentalism. The result is more than an admixture: he crystallizes and connects issues of perception and constitutive or regulative ideas, of associationism, of theories of lang. and poetic diction, and of the function of imagination into a mimesis that "humanizes" nature not only by reproducing natural objects and forms (the "fixities and definites" manipulated by fancy) but also by imitating the living process through which they exist and through which we feel and realize them. Unlike many contemp. Ger. writers (e.g., J. G. Fichte or Schelling), he applies the theory of imagination at the level of individual phrase and *image in the crit. of poetry.

Symbols for Coleridge are "living educts of the imagination, of that reconciling and mediatory power which, incorporating the reason in images of the sense, and organizing (as it were) the flux of the senses by the permanence and self-encircling energies of the reason, gives birth to a system of symbols, harmonious in themselves and consubstantial with the truths of which they are the conductors" (*The Statesman's Manual*). This definition is virtually identical to Bishop Robert Lowth's discussion of "mystical allegory" in *De sacra poesi Hebraeorum* (1753). Thus, even in the symbol as defined by Coleridge, we see elements of prophecy and its earlier critical devel. Various romantic definitions of symbol, allegory, myth, and schema, whether from Kant, Schelling, K.W.F. Solger, Hegel, or others, rely on imagination. Coleridge enlarges, reformulates, and applies the idea of imagination in ways seminal for poetics. He may be regarded as the most important progenitor of the New Critical valuation of *organicism and of *unity.

The Brit. devel. of the idea thus draws from both Platonic and Neoplatonic strains as well as from the line of 18th-c. empiricism initiated by Hobbes and Locke. With Coleridge, and to some extent Shelley and Carlyle, Ger. transcendental philosophy further enriches the anglophone trad., just as Brit. writing on the subject vitalized Ger. thought in the 18th c. The Ger. background draws heavily on Spinoza, Locke, Leibniz, Wolff, Addison, Shaftesbury, the "Swiss Critics" J. J. Bodmer and J. J. Breitinger, A. G. Baumgarten, Hume, and the associationists (histories of associationism are written in 1777 by Michael Hissmann and in 1792 by J.G.E. Maass). In the later 18th c., Ernst Platner, Herder, and Sulzer extend discussion into psychology, lit., culture, and myth. Sulzer declares that "mythological poems must be considered as a lang. of imagination. . . . They make a world for themselves." Tetens, the most eminent psychologist of the era, breaks the power of imagination into different levels responsible for perception, larger associations and cognition, and ultimate poetic power. He profoundly influenced Kant, and Coleridge read him carefully.

The issue in Kant is central and vexing; his presentations of imagination are multiple. Taking a less than clear-cut but prominent place in the *Critique of Pure Reason*, imagination is "an active faculty of synthesis" operating on sense experience, "a necessary ingredient of perception itself" that mediates between senses and understanding. But "a transcendental synthesis of imagination" also exists, so that, again, imagination is both an empirical and a transcendental faculty or power. In the *Critique of Judgment*, imagination is vital to the analytic of both beauty and the sublime. It is not simply reproductive and operating under "the laws of association" but also "productive and exerting an activity of its own." Kant tries to reconcile empirical views of the "reproductive" imagination with those derived from imagination in its "pure" or "productive" mode; this leads to a "tertium medium" joining the two, an idea Coleridge also suggests in the *Biographia*. In our perceptions, Kant claims, we "introduce into appearances that order and regularity which we name nature." In aesthetic theory, he stresses the "free play" of imagination and how, combined with taste, it draws an analogy between beauty and morality through the medium of the symbol.

Fichte proclaims "all reality is presented through the imagination." On the faculty of "*the creative imagination . . .* depends whether we philosophize with or without spirit . . . because the fundamental ideas . . . must be presented by the creative imagination itself. . . . The whole operation of the human spirit proceeds from the imagination, but an imagination that can be grasped no other way than through imagination." He elevates imagination as the most important epistemological faculty and bases philosophy on it. In part to resolve potential contradictions or dualities in Kant and to escape Fichte's more abstract epistemology, Friedrich Schiller writes his *Ästhetische Erziehung des Menschen* (1795), where free play of imagination becomes *Spieltrieb* (the "play drive"). With antecedents of imagination as "play" or "free play" in Bacon, Kant, C. M. Wieland, and G. E. Lessing, Schiller explores imagination as an aesthetic state of being that oscillates (recalling Fichte's "schweben der Einbildungskraft") between "form" and "sense" drives. This aesthetic imagination renovates the soul and permits it to be "fully human," opening a line of utopian thought. An extensive transcendental poetics develops with Schiller, the Schlegels (A. W. and Friedrich), and Novalis. They all hold imagination to be of supreme importance in the psychological and epistemological grounding of art.

Schelling constructs his *System des transzendentalen Idealismus* (1800) on the idea of imagination, which in that and other works he carries further than perhaps any other thinker. It is central to his philosophy of nature and of mind as one larger system ensured by the unifying revelation of the work of art. The *Kunstprodukt* combines the force of nature with that of mind into something that had not previously existed in either. Imagination creates the myths that secure all cultural and spiritual significance. Finally, the artist's imagination generates the most comprehensive symbols; in them, knowledge realizes its highest manifestation. Art becomes necessary to complete philosophy; philosophy's highest goal is the philosophy of art, ultimately based on imagination in divinity, artist, philosopher, and audience.

Hegel's *Aesthetik* (1835) utilizes imagination or "Geist" (spirit) as a key element for his historical and critical views but does not much enlarge the theory of imagination. Goethe emphasizes imagination, though in unsystematic fashion. The hermeneutic trad. from Friedrich Schleiermacher through Wilhelm Dilthey and down to Hans-Georg Gadamer relies on imagination as an instrument of knowledge and interpretation, with Gadamer roughly retaining the older distinction between imagination and discursive reason as that between *Wahrheit* (truth) and *Methode* (method). (See HERMENEUTICS.)

Romantic writers provide the idea with its most comprehensive formulation and make the highest claims for imagination. It stands directly related to—and necessary for—perception, memory, sympathy, images, ideas, knowledge, morality, worldviews, poetry, prophecy, and religion. Santayana proclaims Emerson the first mod. philosopher to base a system on imagination rather than reason. Schelling or Coleridge may have a stronger claim, though Coleridge's later thought increasingly grasps a fuller reason, both discursive and intuitive, as subsuming imaginative power. Even a brief review of romantic manifestations of imagination threatens to expand infinitely.

Perhaps the greatest "romantic" claim is that imagination resolves contradictions and unifies the soul and being of creator and receiver, writer and reader, subject and object, and human nature and *Naturgeist* alike. Imagination, says Coleridge, "reveals itself in the balance or reconciliation of opposite or discordant qualities: of sameness, with difference; of general, with the concrete; the idea, with the image; the individual, with the representative." Coleridge, Schelling, Schiller, and Shelley all say that imagination or poetry calls upon the "whole" soul or individual. To characterize this activity Coleridge coins two words: in an 1802 letter, "co-adunating" (from the Lat. "to join" or "to shape into one"); and in the *Biographia*, the famous "esemplastic" (with its analogous Gr. basis). Schelling notes an actual etymology reminiscent of Herder: "In-Eins-Bildung" (making into one) for "Einbildungskraft." The traditional way of expressing this unifying action, recognized in Neoplatonic and hermetic circles, was to say, as Wordsworth does, that imagination "modifies" or throws "one coloring" over all its productions. As the resolution of contradictions or antinomies, imagination could be seen as a metaphysical, psychological, and artistic principle—as Kant said, a "blind power hidden in the depths of the soul"—that unifies noumenal and phenomenal, sensory and transcendental, mind and spirit, self and nature (e.g., Fichte's *Ich* and *Nicht-Ich*), even freedom and necessity. The power thus resolves Cartesian dualism and all subject/object, ego/world, Aristotelian/Platonic or Neoplatonic divisions. It drives all dialectical process and provides genuine knowledge. However, this view is tempered; Coleridge often stresses the reconciliation of opposites as much as their unity.

**V. Later 19th and 20th Centuries.** Such full-dress syntheses left scant room for further analysis or higher claims. Arguably, imagination had come to stand for many ideas, not one. The associated terms and adjectives grew confusing, and G. H. Lewes remarked that "there are few words more abused."

John Ruskin posits three modes of imagination and an elaborate, schematic division of fancy and imagination. He stresses the intuitive grasp of art rather than its reasoning or analysis. Walter Pater echoes Coleridge to some degree, as Wallace Stevens will, but neither adds a new dimension to the theory of imagination. In Germany, Theodore Lipps's studies of *Einfühlung* or *empathy are related to an imaginative grasp of living truth; in this connection, G. M. Hopkins's *"inscape" also suggests an intuition of object and the feelings it arouses. Oscar Wilde's simultaneous attacks on realism and on unrealistic romances in "The Decay of Lying" are playful defenses of what earlier had been called "feigning," now phrased in more provocative and paradoxical lang. than Sidney's or Shelley's.

Babbitt, while unsympathetic to romanticism, nevertheless develops a theory of ethical imagination similar to 18th-c. discussions. Benedetto Croce's aesthetics and poetics lean heavily on a productive imagination ( *fantasia*) that acts under the influence of intuition and feeling to produce a unifying image. Though without extensive elaboration on the theory of imagination as such, anthropological, psychological, and psychoanalytical studies by J. G. Frazer, Claude Lévi-Strauss, Sigmund Freud, Carl Jung, Mircea Eliade, and others

have significantly deepened concerns voiced by Vico and Thomas Blackwell. The interest here, as to some extent with Ernst Cassirer's theory of the symbol, is more with the formation and importance of the individual image or myth than with all the powers once attributed to imagination. The study of dreams and artistic creativity draws more attention to imagination. Richards, through his scholarship and crit. of late 18th-c. figures and esp. through *Coleridge on Imagination*, combines elements of a romantic aesthetic with mod. psychology and helps create the New Criticism.

Collingwood, positing imagination as a mediating faculty between sense and intellect, refashions romantic theory and attempts to give it consistent shape. Imagination provides knowledge guaranteed by the work of art, which raises perception, feelings, creation, and expression to consciousness through a concrete act. He jettisons higher claims and focuses on a comprehensive aesthetic, but the currency and effect of his views—fundamentally out of step with *postmodernism—diminish in the second half of the 20th c. More recently, neurophysiologists have attempted to analyze areas of the brain, while developmental psychologists have empirically studied artists', scientists', and children's creative activities to determine the functions played by brain hemispheres, biochemistry, the environment, habit, and association in the imaginative process, incl. poetry. Results have been mixed, with no single theory or explanation emerging.

But the notion of imagination as a reconciling or unifying power is generally opposed to the spirit of literary *modernism and postmodernism. Nor is it central to phenomenological approaches. More stress falls on the power of the individual image, or images juxtaposed, e.g., in *imagism or the metaphysical revival. Claims for art to save and enlighten, or to provide special knowledge, are reduced. Detractors of the New Criticism simplify and attack the concept of organic unity. However, though less massively than in romantic poetics, the idea of imagination continues to play a role in postmodernism. *Structuralism offers affinities with romantic organicism and an imaginative, intellectual reconstruction of reality, the creation of this "simulacrum," itself an imitation and not a copy. In mod. crit., studies of imagination in individual writers continue to proliferate. Paul Ricoeur, Emmanuel Levinas, and Jacques Derrida engage the idea. Deconstruction shuns any unifying power to resolve contradictions and builds itself—or rather deploys its various moves and strategies—in part by exploiting those contradictions or divisions. But while deconstruction seems a polar opposite of imaginative unity and organic synthesis, the romantic theory of imagination itself thrives on such contradictions and polarities. In one sense, imagination and deconstruction are allied: in crit. or philosophy, they distrust any formal system for either analysis or creativity; they rejoin poetry and philosophy through the medium of words and through a consideration of the nature and the hist. of writing in general, and figurative lang. in particular. Artists consistently retain faith in imagination, as does Doris Lessing in her

2007 Nobel lecture: "But the storyteller will be there, for it is our imaginations which shape us, keep us, create us—for good and for ill. It is our stories that will recreate us, when we are torn, hurt, even destroyed. It is the storyteller, the dream-maker, the myth-maker, that is our phoenix, that represents us at our best, and at our most creative."

■ I. Babbitt, *Rousseau and Romanticism* (1919); G. Santayana, *Character and Opinion* (1921); H. C. Warren, *History of Association Psychology* (1921); B. Croce, *Aesthetic*, trans. D. Ainslie (1922); Richards, esp. ch. 32; L. P. Smith, "Four Romantic Words," *Words and Idioms* (1925); M. W. Bundy, *The Theory of Imagination in Classical and Modern Thought* (1927); I. A. Richards, *Practical Criticism* (1929); M. W. Bundy, "'Invention' and 'Imagination' in the Renaissance," *JEGP* 29 (1930), and "Bacon's True Opinion of Poetry," *SP* 27 (1930); R. Wellek, *Kant in England* (1931); A.S.P. Woodhouse, "Collins and the Creative Imagination," *Studies in English*, ed. M. Wallace (1931); I. A. Richards, *Coleridge on Imagination* (1934); D. Bond, "'Distrust of Imagination' in English Neoclassicism," *PQ* 14 (1935), and "Neoclassical Psychology of the Imagination," *ELH* 4 (1937); R. G. Collingwood, *Principles of Art* (1938); C. D. Thorpe, *The Aesthetic of Hobbes* (1940); K. R. Wallace, *Bacon on Communication and Rhetoric* (1943); W. J. Bate, "Sympathetic Imagination in 18th-Century English Criticism," *ELH* 12 (1945); W. J. Bate and J. Bullitt, "Distinctions between Fancy and Imagination," *MLN* 60 (1945); W. J. Bate, *From Classic to Romantic* (1946); W. Stevens, *The Necessary Angel* (1951); A.S.P. Woodhouse, "Romanticism and the History of Ideas," *English Studies Today*, ed. C. Wrenn and G. Bullough (1951); Crane; Abrams; E. L. Fackenheim, "Schelling's Philosophy of the Literary Arts," *PQ* 4 (1954); Wellek, v. 1; M. H. Nicolson, *Science and Imagination* (1956); R. Cohen, "Association of Ideas and Poetic Unity," *PQ* 36 (1957); Wimsatt and Brooks; E. D. Hirsch Jr., *Wordsworth and Schelling* (1960); E. Tuveson, *The Imagination as a Means of Grace* (1960); W. P. Albrecht, *Hazlitt and the Creative Imagination* (1961), chs. 1, 3, 5; F. Yates, *The Art of Memory* (1966); T. McFarland, *Coleridge and the Pantheist Tradition* (1969); H. Mürchen, *Die Einbildungskraft bei Kant* (1970); R. Barthes, "The Structuralist Activity," *Critical Essays*, trans. R. Howard ([1963] 1972); W. Wetherbee, *Platonism and Poetry in the Twelfth Century* (1972)—for imagination and *ingenium*; R. Scholes, *Structuralism in Literature* (1974), ch. 6; E. S. Casey, *Imagining* (1976); M. Warnock, *Imagination* (1976); J. Derrida, *Writing and Difference*, trans. A. Bass (1978); J. Engell, *The Creative Imagination* (1981); D. Tracy, *The Analogical Imagination* (1981); D. P. Verene, *Vico's Science of Imagination* (1981); T. Todorov, *Theories of the Symbol*, trans. C. Porter ([1977] 1982); P. de Man, *The Rhetoric of Romanticism* (1984); E. Dod, *Die Vernünftigkeit der Imagination* (1985)—on Schiller and Shelley; T. McFarland, *Originality and Imagination* (1985); M. Kipperman, *Beyond Enchantment* (1986)—Eng. poetry and Ger. idealism; C. G. Ryn, *Will, Imagination and Reason* (1986)—on Babbitt; W. C. Chittick, *The Sufi Path of Knowledge* (1989); *Coleridge, Keats, and the Imagination*, ed. J. R. Barth and J. L. Mahoney (1989); *Coleridge's Theory of Imagination Today*, ed. C. Gallant (1989); B. Croce, *Essays on Literature and Literary Criticism*, ed. and trans. M. E. Moss (1990); R. Kearney, *The Wake of Imagination* (1994); F. Burwick, *Poetic Madness and the Romantic Imagination* (1996); W. K. Mahony, *The Artful Universe* (1998)—Vedic imagination; J. R. Barth, "Imagination," *New Dictionary of the History of Ideas*, ed. M. C. Horowitz (2004).

J. ENGELL

**IMAGISM.** A school of *free verse that developed between 1912 and 1917; it originated in London but developed largely in the U.S., where it had a stronger impact. Imagism opposed the excesses of Victorian poetry by insisting upon an ascetic, disciplined poetic technique; Kenner famously called its stress upon compression and direct presentation a form of "technical hygiene." Equally important, however, was the example imagism set for the promotion and circulation of modernist verse. As early as 1917, Harold Monro could write that the imagists "took every possible opportunity of preparing themselves a public." Instrumental in both respects were the numerous critical and polemical writings issued on imagism's behalf by Ezra Pound and others, documents that have been as influential as the poems themselves.

Imagism was initially disseminated through the cultivation of relationships (and controversies) through a few key modernist "little magazines": *Poetry: A Magazine of Verse, The Glebe,* and *The Little Review* in the U. S.; and *The New Age* and *The New Freewoman* (later *The Egoist*) in Britain. The January 1913 issue of *Poetry* featured three poems by Hilda Doolittle, signed "H.D., 'imagiste,'" and a report on the London scene by Pound mentioned "[t]he youngest school . . . that has the nerve to call itself a school." The March 1913 *Poetry* included F. S. Flint's essay "Imagisme" and Pound's "A Few Don'ts by an Imagiste." Flint reported that, rather than producing a *manifesto, the school had come up with only a few rules: "1. Direct treatment of the 'thing,' whether subjective or objective. 2. To use absolutely no word that did not contribute to the presentation. 3. As regarding rhythm: to compose in sequence of the musical phrase, not in sequence of a metronome." He also mentioned a fourth principle, "a certain 'Doctrine of the Image,'" which they had not committed to writing [and which] did not concern the public." This hermetic quality, like H.D.'s identity, was a calculated effect of imagist self-promotion, but it also pointed to a visionary aspect of imagism that was evident in "A Few Don'ts." Here, Pound defined the image as "that which presents an intellectual and emotional complex in an instant of time" before providing a new list of technical proscriptions.

Whereas imagism has been called the first Eng.-lang. avant-garde, it can also be understood as a reaction against Eur. avant-garde movements (see AVANT-GARDE POETICS). Rainey, for instance, has shown how Poundian imagism developed in direct response to the sensational London reception of F. T. Marinetti's *futurism. Whereas futurism called for the destruction of the past, Flint's essay posited that the imagists "were not a revolutionary school; their only endeavor was to write in accordance with the best tradition." Yet if imagism was intended to be, in Rainey's phrase, "the first anti-avant-garde," it nevertheless circulated with the currency of an avant-garde movement.

The first phase of imagism culminated in the anthol. *Des Imagistes* (1914), which included poems by Flint, Amy Lowell, W. C. Williams, Allen Upward, Ford Madox Hueffer, and James Joyce, in addition to those of Pound, H.D., and Richard Aldington. The *anthol. form testified to imagism's ambiguous attitudes toward modernity and trad. On one hand, the anthol. was a patently commercial form that had been exploited for the avant-garde by Marinetti and whose economic potential had been realized by Edward Marsh's much more conservative *Georgian Poetry* collection (see GEORGIANISM). On the other hand, the anthol. had been the form that preserved the ancient trads. upon which the core imagists had drawn and this authenticated their deepest aspirations in a way that would not have been true for Marsh or Marinetti. Aldington and H.D. had strongly relied on the *Greek Anthology* (H.D.'s first poems appeared under the title "Verses, Translations, and Reflections from 'The Anthology'"), and Pound and Upward's Chinese sources had been, as they knew, preserved in two ancient anthols., one compiled by Confucius, the other by Qu Yuan. This particular admixture of ancient Gr. and Asian sources pointed to the movement's origins at the heart of the Brit. Empire.

Such dynamics were less characteristic of imagism's second phase. Pound abandoned the movement following a bitter dispute with Amy Lowell concerning the group's leadership. A special issue of *The Egoist* ed. by Aldington in 1915 attempted to consolidate the movement while charting new directions, notably engagement with World War I. Instituting a more democratic representation of the poetry, Lowell made imagism the financial success *Des Imagistes* had not been with three annual anthols. titled *Some Imagist Poets* in 1915, 1916, and 1917. These included the imagists' own programmatic prefaces, but their earlier strictures were relaxed to enable them to claim a place within a continuum of "all great poetry." Lowell's promotional genius inspired a wide readership but also a host of recruits (and parodists); although Lowell had archly told Pound that he could not copyright the word *imagism*, she eventually would look into the possibility of copyrighting the name herself.

The Lowell-Aldington regime attenuated imagism's earlier visionary, psychological claims. Pound's first citation of the "School of Images" had situated "*Les Imagistes*" as "the descendants of the forgotten school of 1909," the Poets' Club led by the philosopher T. E. Hulme. Inspired by Henri Bergson, Hulme had stressed the centrality of an "intuitive language" comprised of "visual concrete" poetic images. Whereas an older trad. of crit. focused on the deeply materialist and antiromantic quality of the image (qualities that

highlighted its differentiation from Fr. *symbolism), a more recent phase, led by Tiffany's study of Pound, has given renewed attention to the image's simultaneously material and metaphysical character and has drawn it into conversation with Marxian and Freudian theory. Pound's famous juxtaposition of natural and metropolitan images in the haiku-inspired "In a Station of the Metro" can thus be understood as the means of summoning an archaic vision of the dead. An appreciation of the simultaneously objective and visionary character of the image is equally essential for reading H.D., whose work remains the preeminent embodiment of imagist doctrine. In the early "Epigram (After the Greek)," H.D.'s condensation of an ancient, anonymous epitaph endows the original with a new emphasis upon the union of love with absence and death:

> The golden one is gone from the banquets
> She, beloved of Atimetus,
> The swallow, the bright Homonoea:
> Gone the dear chatterer;
> Death succeeds Atimetus.

H.D.'s poem makes explicit the fascination with dead cultures implicit in Pound's poem, doing so in a series of rhythmic cadences, with the single metaphor of a bird that has taken flight.

*See* CHINESE POETICS.

■ E. Pound, *Ripostes* (1912); F. S. Flint, "Imagisme," *Poetry* 1 (1913); *The Egoist*, Special Imagist Number (May 1, 1915); T. E. Hulme, *Speculations*, ed. H. Read (1924); E. Pound, *Letters*, ed. D. D. Paige (1950); S. K. Coffman, *Imagism* (1951); E. Pound, *Literary Essays* (1954); F. Kermode, *The Romantic Image* (1957); H. Kenner, *The Pound Era* (1971); D. Perkins, *A History of Modern Poetry*, v. 1 (1976), ch. 15; H.D., *End to Torment* (1979); M. Levenson, *A Genealogy of Modernism* (1984); S. S. Friedman and R. B. DuPlessis, *Signets* (1990); R. G. Babcock, "Verses, Translations, and Reflections from 'The Anthology,'" *Sagetrieb* 14 (1995); Z. Qian, *Orientalism and Modernism* (1995); D. Tiffany, *Radio Corpse* (1995); L. Rainey, *Institutions of Modernism* (1998); *Amy Lowell*, ed. A. Munich and M. Bradshaw (2004); A. Thacker, "'Mad after Foreign Notions,'" *Geographies of Modernism*, ed. P. Brooker and A. Thacker (2005).

J. BRADDOCK

**IMITATION.** Refers to three broad facets of poetics—theories of *representation, practices of instruction, and strategies for writing in response to authorial and textual models. These senses can be distinguished analytically, but historically and conceptually they share a large measure of overlap. Though much critical reflection focuses on the status of representation, imitation has a significant performative dimension as a means to constitute and shape modes of identity, expression, and imagination. From cl. antiquity through the Enlightenment, imitation is a central feature in discussions of lit. and the arts (particularly the visual arts and music) as well as education, social and political institutions, and scientific understanding. From the romantic era onward, it is generally eclipsed by *originality or *imagination as a heuristic category for describing, analyzing, and evaluating artistic production. Imitation remains, however, a key for engaging trad. in mod. lit. and for positioning works and performance in *postmodern, *postcolonial, and globalized culture.

In theories of representation, imitation conventionally translates Gr. *mimesis. Mimesis probably referred originally to ritual impersonation involving masks, gestures, music, song, and dance. Plato expands this range of meaning and reveals some of the abiding contradictions and tensions within imitation. In books 2 and 3 of the *Republic*, he voices concern over the power exercised by *myths as cultural narratives and by the speeches in *tragedy as they shape the character of future guardians of the city. The prime issue is the content of verbal imitation: violent and disgraceful episodes in Homer, Hesiod, and the tragic poets can potentially corrupt the young by offering examples that compromise a heroic ethos. In book 10, Plato tries through dialectic to establish the truth-value of imitation, hence the credibility and utility of artistic representation. He locates mimesis at a third remove from reality (after the ideal Form and its concrete embodiment in the object represented through art). His exemplary agent in this discussion is the painter who, like the poet, deals with appearance instead of being and appeals to passions rather than the higher principle of reason. In late dialogues (notably the *Sophist* and the *Timaeus*), Plato seems to hold open some possibilities for imitation as a means of grasping reality. It applies, for instance, to explaining institutions and first principles. But he never fully resolves the questions raised in the *Republic*. In later thinkers, Plato's critique of imitation as a copy or counterfeit of reality sustains a long trad. of skepticism about art as well as a troubled recognition of its capacity to influence belief and action.

Aristotle approaches imitation in the *Poetics* by distinguishing its medium, objects, and mode, and he implicitly addresses the concerns raised by Plato. Defining the objects of imitation as the actions of greater and lesser men, he finds a place for the passions in the theory of *catharsis and asserts the power of verbal imitation to portray (at least in tragedy) what we would not want otherwise to see or endure—precisely the content that generates anxiety in the *Republic*. At the same time, he shifts the philosophical basis of imitation by associating poetry with universals and hist. with particulars as objects of knowledge. Imitation, he argues, is not a condition of misapprehension but the product of two human instincts, a pleasure in learning and an innate attraction to harmony and *rhythm. It does not copy nature or reproduce a chronology of events but presents instead a transposed, artificial rendering of action with its own internal, structural coherence.

A double trad. follows from Plato and Aristotle. By one account, imitation is an imperfect and derivative copy of reality that can produce only illusion. By the other, imitation is a craft of making verbal structures and artifacts that exhibit organization and *unity and correspond meaningfully to human action and expe-

rience. These positions share important ground with other trads. that emerge in antiquity and the Middle Ages. Neoplatonic imitation reflects the hierarchy of Plato's Forms. In Boethius's 6th-c. *De musica*, the mathematical proportion of sounds mirrors relations such as those of body to soul or the rational order of the created universe. Christian writers approach ludic imitation in starkly diverging ways. Paul sees the Apostles as men doomed to die in a spectacle of martyrdom for the world, angels, and humankind (1 Corinthians 4:9). Bernard of Clairvaux (*Epistula* 87) amplifies Paul's metaphor of ludic imitation into an ironic form of humility in which suffering provokes ridicule in the secular world but joy when seen from a divine perspective. Tertullian (*De spectaculis*) rejects ritual and theatrical imitation as idolatry.

Augustine offers a notable example of the profound ambivalence attached to imitation. In his *Confessions*, he records his pleasure and moral confusion at seeing the death of Dido enacted on the stage and following the wanderings of Aeneas, ignorant all the while, he says, of his own spiritual death and moral vagrancy. He finds the danger repeated in the effects of imitation on his friends at public games and the theater. In his *De musica*, poetry is said to produce not only deceptive images but images of images (*phantasmata*) that lie at the very entrance of error. The med. encyclopedists Isidore of Seville and Hrabanus Maurus carried forward Augustine's critique of imitation in their descriptions of theater. By contrast, in the widely cited definition of *comedy ascribed to Cicero by the grammarian Donatus, imitation operates as a reliable guide to knowledge of the social world: comedy is "an imitation of life, a mirror of custom, and image of truth." The key terms of this formulation—"imitation," "mirror," and "image"—apply equally, of course, to the critique and defense of imitation, depending on the value ascribed to *figuration. In the *De vulgari eloquentia*, the first vernacular poetics, Dante gives a "true definition of poetry" as "a fiction expressed in verse according to rhetoric and music." His definition follows in the general line of Aristotle's view and assumes that imitation produces a "construction" (in this case the form of the It. *canzone) that derives from the objectified, externalized art of making things.

Horace's *Ars poetica* effects a decisive trans. of theories of imitation from cl. antiquity to later literary periods. Among the precepts he offers, Horace directs "the schooled imitator [*doctum imitatorem*] to look toward the model of life and manners and create lively expression there" (317–18). Amplifying his dictum that poets wish either to benefit or please their audiences, he urges, "Let whatever is made with the aim of pleasing be close to true things [*proxima ueris*]" (338). Horace follows the doctrine of literary *decorum to regulate imagination and expression and to communicate with an audience by recognizing its expectations. At the same time, he gestures toward a criterion of verisimilitude, in which art reflects nature and social behavior and can be judged by its correspondence to commonly perceived reality. A crucial displacement occurs, however, from Aristotle's definitional approach to imitation. Horace presents a rhetorical understanding of the persuasive, socially constituted congruence thought to hold between representation and reality.

Horace's view established a framework in which Aristotelian imitation was received in the Middle Ages and the Ren. Although William of Moerbeke produced an accurate Lat. trans. of the *Poetics* (1278), the version that exercised some limited influence was Herman Alemannus's trans. of Averroës's Ar. *Middle Commentary on the "Poetics"* (1256). In Herman's trans., imitation is *assimilatio* (likening), and it draws on common experience and appeals to the faculty of imagination in the service of reaching moral judgments and apportioning praise and blame. The synthesis of Aristotle and Horace continues in the early mod. period in Antonio Minturno's assertion that imitation involves recognition chiefly based on manners and morals (*De poeta*, 1559). Lodovico Castelvetro's trans. of and commentary on the *Poetics* (1570, rev. 1576) renders imitation as *rassomiglianza* (likeness) and bases the concept on verisimilitude, though it distinguishes literal copying from the craft required of the poet. J. C. Scaliger's *Poetices libri septem* (1561), while asserting the primacy of art over nature, equates imitation with verisimilitude and argues for the didactic ends of representation.

In Ren. England, Roger Ascham's *The Scholemaster* (posthumously pub. in 1570) touches briefly on the theoretical dimensions of imitation in comedy and tragedy, citing Plato's discussion and evoking the analogy between poetry and painting. The analogy recurs in Philip Sidney's definition of *poetry* in his *Defence of Poesy* (1595), where it joins Aristotelian mimesis to serve the Horatian ends of instruction and pleasure: "Poetry therefore is an art of imitation, for so Aristotle terms it in the word mimesis—that is to say a representing, counterfeiting, or figuring forth to speak metaphorically, a speaking picture with this end, to teach and delight." Sidney goes beyond the idea of imitation as a reproduction, however, as he places the work of art created by poetic imagination (the "golden" world) above nature (the "brazen" world). George Puttenham (*The Arte of English Poesie*, 1589) judges poetry "an art not only of making, but also of imitation" but establishes a hierarchy that locates divine and natural instincts as the highest causes of aesthetic creation, followed by experience, and ending in imitation.

Imitation as an instructional practice is already implicit in Plato's moral concerns with the effects of representation. It becomes especially prominent in the rhetorical pedagogy of antiquity and the Middle Ages, in which it supplements talent (*ingenium*), curricular instruction (*ars*), and practice (*exercitatio*). Within pedagogy, imitation divided into two complementary spheres: it taught morals by copying the example of virtuous men and shaped rhetorical and literary style by following models from a *canon of orators and authors. The connection between morals and acquired verbal facility begins at least with Isocrates and remains a constant feature of the trad. In Cicero's *De oratore* (2.22–23), the first step toward the formation of an orator is

the choice of someone to imitate, the second is practice, and the third is written composition. Imitation, building on the instructional techniques of grammar, involves a close analysis of texts. Writing extends to paraphrase and trans., in verse and prose, as well as to set exercises and invented speeches. Seneca's *Epistula* 84 (to Lucilius) offers three metaphors for imitation widely cited in the Ren., the Enlightenment, and beyond: writers should copy bees who gather their materials from many sources and blend them into one compound; like food in the body, materials must be digested and made into one substance; and the mind should hide what it has used and bring forth what it has made, in a relation like that of child to father.

In its dual sense of imitation, the rhetorical trad. significantly broadens the scope of imitation beyond copying or representation. Models of conduct and style are embodied and performative. One decides whom to imitate and, thus, absorbs and produces an ethical *persona and a style of expression—or, better, a repertoire of expressive styles. Henry Peacham's *The Garden of Eloquence* (1577, 1593) follows cl. doctrine in saying that an orator reproduces not only what was said previously by his model but his utterance, *pronunciation, and gesture. (Ovid ascribes these skills to Morpheus, the son of Somnus, in *Metamorphoses* 11.) Models of rhetorical imitation also have an acknowledged hist. In the *Brutus*, Cicero gives an account of orators and public figures, which includes exemplary practitioners, monitory cases, and even examples of the risible and ridiculous. The creation of a moral agent, speaker, or poetic stylist is thus a dynamic interchange between examples and living beings who absorb and transform influences. While Quintilian acknowledges that a significant portion of art depends on imitation, he holds that imitation by itself is not adequate (*Institutio oratoria* 10.2.4), any more than authoritative models are themselves without blemishes. His discussion turns fundamentally on the reciprocity of imitation and *invention and on the exercise of judgment (10.2.14). *Emulation* serves as a middle term between imitation and invention; it reflects, moreover, the shifting ratios of deference and assertive rivalry by which one establishes authority and becomes in turn a model for imitation. This process depends not merely on the ability to internalize models but on the critical capacity to analyze their grammatical and rhetorical structures and to locate them within social and political hist.

The Ren. debate on *Ciceronianism reframes the issues that emerged in antiquity. Unlike Cicero and Quintilian, who confronted the authority of Gr., humanists faced a practice of Lat. writing already securely in place within nearly every facet of official culture, as well as vernaculars with growing claims to documentary functions and literary prestige. Cicero's Lat. offered a standard for prose, as did Virgil's for poetry. Ciceronians argued for an absolute standard of correctness, while their opponents, perhaps most notably Erasmus in his satirical dialogue *Ciceronianus* (1528), emphasized the radical contradiction of restricting imitation to one source while expecting writers to exercise critical judgment, emulate the ancients, and generate an authentic but independent equivalent to the original. The pragmatic resolution for most theorists was to admit a multiplicity of models for imitation. If this step led away from an impossible standard, it did not fully resolve other problems, such as locating selfhood within a derivate writing and speaking subject, assimilating the Bible and Christian authors into a canon, dealing with historical changes in lang., or decontextualizing vocabulary and phrasing in order for them to remain useful as sources for expression.

Imitation serves a variety of performative aims besides rhetorical training. In med. Lat., the verb *imitari* is used in the ceremony of ordination in the sense of realizing an ideal that has grown out of faith and teaching. The 12th-c. Tegernsee *Accessus ad auctores*, an introduction to canonical authors for schoolboys, credits Ovid with writing in imitation of women's voices in the *Heroides* for the purpose of demonstrating which ones should and should not be imitated. A 13th-c. commentary on Geoffrey of Vinsauf's *Poetria nova*, the most influential of the med. prescriptive "arts of poetry," praises Geoffrey as both a rhetor and an orator and observes of the latter, "to speak artfully is to imitate the precepts of art [*artis precepta*]." Dante sets out the principle that vernacular poets should imitate the ancients, who drew on grammar and rules, while he in his role as commentator is bound to imitate learned works on poetic doctrine (*De vulgari eloquentia* 2.4.3). In the *Canterbury Tales*, the frame tale for Chaucer's narrative is premised on imitating fictional characters performing speech acts: "Whoso shal telle a tale after a man, / He moot reherce as ny as evere he kan / Everich a word, if it be in his charge" ("General Prologue," 1731–33). In preaching and devotion, Catholics and later Protestants find models for spiritual imitation in Christ, the saints, and the martyrs.

Several challenges to the pedagogy of imitation arise within the rhetorical trad. In his treatise *Peri hypsous* (*On the Sublime*; discovered by Francesco Robortello in 1554 and widely promulgated by Nicolas Boileau's trans. of 1674), Longinus treats the violent feelings created by great writing and lang., which aim at emotional transport and ecstasy rather than persuasion. Imitation and emulation are means by which the soul can shape itself imaginatively from the models of great writers in order to produce this effect and communicate it to an audience. Longinus's comparison for the *sublime is the inspiration of the Pythian priestess who delivers her oracles, as if divinely impregnated by the vapors of Apollo's sacred cave. His method is to imagine what Homer, Plato, Demosthenes, or Thucydides would have said when elaborating and expressing an elevated idea. In the 16th c., Michel de Montaigne, by contrast, exploits the potential of imitation and the emulation of style to a radically different end from transport and ecstasy. Ostensibly subordinated to the authors yet able to conceal his borrowings from them, he argues in his essay "On Books"

(*Essais* 2.10) that his object is to know his natural rather than acquired faculties. He resituates the Horatian formula so that he reads intermittently and selectively for pleasure and for the usefulness of self-knowledge and the conduct of life. The "maistres du mestier" (for him Lat. writers) serve not as models to absorb but as known points against which to measure a self at once deferential and resistant to the influences that have helped shape it. Besides the challenges represented by Longinus and Montaigne, imitation comes under the pressure of historical shifts both within and against the project of Ren. humanism. The *querelle des anciens et des modernes* (quarrel of ancients and moderns), begun in late 17th-c. France and continued in England, had as its immediate question whether to follow the models of cl. writers or the new learning derived from method and science. Behind that question lay foundational disputes over imitation. Were the models of the ancients common to human nature and, therefore, immediately applicable, even familiar (as they were to Petrarch and others), or were they historically specific and in some measure remote? What kind of learning might imitation of the ancients convey to an age that had begun to distinguish science and the arts as increasingly distinct realms of knowledge?

Imitation as a strategy of writing emerges from the instructional practice of grammar and rhet. The aim is to produce a work that stands in some significant relation to canonical masterpieces, whether as a text that appropriates the prestige of its literary predecessors or as one that seeks to rival them. In this respect, imitation becomes a form of invention, the discovery of the materials and informing plan of a work. Horace's advice on depicting character—either follow convention or devise something self-consistent (*Ars poetica* 119)—expanded to include the entire project of composition. It underwrites the distinction that appears in med. prescriptive poetics between *materia executa* or *pertractata* (subject matter already treated) and *materia illibata* (subject matter not yet treated in poetry or prose). Both kinds require imitation, though their strategies of composition differ.

For materials treated by earlier writers, Geoffrey of Vinsauf urges his students not to follow the *vestigia verborum* (the footsteps of the words) but to be silent where the source text speaks and to speak where it is silent. Geoffrey's term *vestigia* is itself a gesture toward literary imitation, for it evokes the ending of the *Thebaid* where Statius directs his poem to follow Virgil's *Aeneid* at a distance and always honor (or speak to) its footprints: "longe sequere et uestigia semper adora" (*Thebaid* 12.817). Following a text, in this sense, implies a critical reading of the source and a recognition of what the source leaves unexamined or unexpressed. For materials not yet treated, the process of composition depends on a form of imitation that likewise generates a parallel work, often in style or genre. The *rota virgiliana* described in John of Garland's *Parisiana poetria* sets out three corresponding lists of topics for *pastoral, *georgic, and *epic poetry according to rank, place, occupation, and accoutrements; in so doing, it charts a course for a poetic career (the *cursus honorum* by which a writer advances from lower to higher genres), and it offers an image of the social order. Such "material" invention originates in the Virgil commentaries of Donatus and Servius, and the authorial paradigm remained vital for Jacopo Sannazaro, Pierre de Ronsard, Torquato Tasso, Edmund Spenser, Miguel de Cervantes, and John Milton among others. The writer of new materials composes his work within discursive conventions that immediately link it to generic intertexts.

Imitation depends on a relocation of authorial and textual models, and it seeks to create not replicas but counterparts responsive to changed historical contexts. Virgil appropriates Homer's *Odyssey* and *Iliad*, respectively, in the two halves of the *Aeneid*. Dante redirects Virgil's unfinished imperial epic to a Christian cosmos in the *Divina commedia*, while Mapheus Vegius offers a form of narrative closure by adding a 13th book to Virgil's poem. The poet Prudentius (ca. 348–405) composes a body of work informed by the idea of creating Christian equivalents to cl. genres, notably but not exclusively in rewriting Virgil's battle scenes as contests between virtues and vices in the *Psychomachia*. Ovid's *Ars amatoria* provides a model for med. Lat. homoerotic verse and material for generic imitations such as the elegiac *comoediae*. The stories of Thebes, Troy, and Rome, which served as the mythical-historical foundation of Eur. political narratives, found vernacular expression and chivalric contexts in the 12th-c. Fr. *romans d'antiquité*. Chaucer's self-appointed disciple John Lydgate calls his master "Dant in Englyssh," by which he means to recognize Chaucer's overt gestures toward Dante and perhaps to identify the *dream vision of the incomplete *House of Fame* as a functional analogue to the *Commedia*, different in scale but comparable in theme. Boccaccio, Ariosto, Tasso, Spenser, and Cervantes negotiate a different ratio of genre and literary prestige by adapting the popular and chivalric romance to epic and the novel.

Ren. writers show a particularly keen understanding of what imitation involves as a principle of composition, particularly as it grows out of pedagogy and a curriculum of reading. Ascham emphasizes the faculty of judgment required to follow a literary model, and he describes two approaches to imitation, one a dissimilar treatment of the same material and the other a similar treatment of different material. Ben Jonson follows the same principles in asserting that a poet or maker must "bee able to convert the substance, or Riches of an other *Poet* to his owne use" (*Timber*). Focusing on Petrarch's ambitious body of writing, Greene (1982) proposes that four kinds of imitation can be distinguished within the humanist trad.: reproductive (following a cl. subtext with reverential fidelity), eclectic (mixing a variety of allusions and sources), heuristic (revealing yet distancing subtexts), and dialectical (staging the resistance or ambivalence of a work to its subtext).

In later periods, imitation has a diminished though continuing presence in poetic theory and literary production. John Dryden sees imitation as a form of trans. in which a writer can diverge from the words and sense of the source and take "only some general hints from the Original" ("Preface Concerning Ovid's Epistles," 1680). The imitation of nature is a commonplace of aesthetic theory through the neoclassical period. In the early 19th c., William Hazlitt's "On Imitation" (1817) contends that imitation excites curiosity and comparison, and so "it opens a new field of inquiry, and leads the attention to a variety of details and distinctions not perceived before." Romantic, postromantic, and mod. writers employ imitation to evoke rather than recreate earlier works and to delineate their own modernity (see MODERNISM, ROMANTIC AND POSTROMANTIC POETRY AND POETICS). Imitation designates the unclosed gaps with the original texts in Ezra Pound's trans. of the OE "Seafarer" (1911) and James Joyce's *Ulysses* (1922), in surrealist retellings of cl. tragedy and myth (see SURREALISM), and in Robert Lowell's *Imitations* (1961). In postmod. writing and performance, imitation stands behind the principle that cultural expression depends on reproducing earlier cultural forms. In Af. Am. lit. and culture, *signifying operates as a practice of simultaneous imitation and troping. Postcolonial writing takes the dominant forms and myths of Eur. lit. as one point of departure for recontextualizing and challenging the legacy of imperialism.

The mod. critics most committed to revisiting imitation are the mid-20th-c. *Chicago school, notably R. S. Crane, Richard McKeon, and Elder Olson, who proposed a neo-Aristotelian emphasis on imitation of human actions as the basis of literary art (contra the then-dominant attention of the *New Criticism to *form, rhet., and figuration); and the Fr. critic René Girard, who developed an ambitious theory according to which the literary imitation of reality reveals the more profound processes of imitation—of desire for an object, and finally of violence against an enemy—at the root of culture itself. The Canadian critic Northrop Frye placed imitation near the center of a systematic account of the distinctiveness of lit., which as an imitation of typical (rather than particular) action is more philosophical than hist. and as an imitation of general (rather than specific) thought is more historical than philosophy; but Frye was more interested in the genres, forms, and modes that result from imitation than the process itself. The Ger. philologist Erich Auerbach was less thoroughgoing than these contemporaries, but his *Mimesis* (1946, trans. into Eng. 1953), which concerns the interpretive rather than theoretical issues occasioned by imitation, is probably the most influential treatment of the concept in the 20th c. The concept of *intertextuality devised by Julia Kristeva and adapted by Roland Barthes, Gérard Genette, and other poststructuralist theorists provides a means for situating the literary *work within a network of previous *texts, *conventions, and codes (see POSTSTRUCTURALISM). The anxiety of *influence plotted by Harold Bloom as a struggle of assertion and belatedness operates within the dialectical structure of imitation. In recent theorizing about authorship, imitation emerges not only as a means of self-definition but as a gesture toward hist., culture, and politics.

See FEIGNING, REPRESENTATION.

■ H. Gmelin, "Das Prinzip der Imitatio in den romanischen Literaturen der Renaissance," *Romanische Forschungen* 46 (1932); R. McKeon, "Literary Criticism and the Concept of Imitation in Antiquity," *MP* 34 (1936); J. De Ghellinck, "Imitari, Imitatio," *Bulletin du Cange* 15 (1941); R. S. Crane, *The Languages of Criticism and the Structure of Poetry* (1953); Curtius; Weinberg; R. Girard, *Deceit, Desire, and the Novel*, trans. Y. Freccero (1961), and *To Double Business Bound* (1978); D. A. Russell, "De imitation," *Creative Imitation and Latin Literature*, ed. D. West and T. Woodman (1979); G. W. Pigman III, "Versions of Imitation in the Renaissance," *RQ* 23 (1980); T. M. Greene, *The Light in Troy: Imitation and Discovery in Renaissance Poetry* (1982); J.-C. Carron, "Imitation and Intertextuality in the Renaissance," *NLH* 19 (1988); *CHLC*; G. Gebauer and C. Wulf, *Mimesis: Culture—Art—Society*, trans. D. Reneau (1995); J. M. Ziolkowski, "The Highest Form of Compliment: *Imitatio* in Medieval Latin Culture," *Poetry and Philosophy in the Middle Ages*, ed. J. Marenbon (2001); *European Literary Careers: The Author from Antiquity to the Renaissance*, ed. P. G. Cheney and F. A. de Armas (2002).

R. R. EDWARDS

**IMPRESSIONISM.** *Impressionism* as a term related to poetry owes its existence to a poetic ambition, prevalent roughly between 1890 and 1910, inspired by the visual arts and focused on achieving ever neater verbal subtlety and nuances in poems, novellas, and lyrical, mainly one-act, plays. It exemplified the Horatian conception of *ut pictura poesis*, although with a specific emphasis on subjectivity in expression. But impressionism also suggested the possibility of blending inwardness with expressiveness. Claude Monet's painting *Impression: Soleil Levant* (1874) exposed this new style for the first time to viewers who were mainly used to mimetic renderings of nature and social life in the visual and literary arts.

Etymologically speaking, phrases like "making an impression," "being impressionistic," or creating something in an "impressionist style" offer three different categories related to the concept and conception of impressionism. The Latin word *impressio*, from which *impressionism* derives, contains a range of meanings itself. It refers to the art of rhetorical articulation, to traces of particular phenomena and their imprint on the soul, and to a military attack. Even the latter is of interest here in view of the way that impressions are intended to strike, if not overwhelm, the spectator.

"Being impressionistic" is a postimpressionist quality judgment of some ambiguity, for it suggests texts or arguments that are highly illustrative or colorful but also lack coherence and discursive stringency. "Making an impression" is normally associated with a person's making his or her mark. In aesthetic terms, however, it is the artistic object and, through it, the work of art that impresses the viewer or, in more general terms, the recipient.

Impressionism is the theory of visual impact in the arts connected with a sense of the incomplete; after all, the impressionist only wishes to give a particular impression of the artistic object. That is to say, impressionism is a fundamental expression of a subjective point of view. The evocative yet subtle use of color, light, shade, and often blurred contours in paintings by Claude Monet, James Whistler, or Max Liebermann emphasizes the representation of mere segments of a broader picture.

The poetics of impressionism considers mainly atmosphere and objects as well as the effective emancipation from their "real-world" surroundings. Impressionism is, therefore, antimimetic but also antihistorical. It was as much a reaction against *realism in art and lit. as a rejection of *historicism. Instead, it favored challenging the receptive capacity of the senses as well as the sheer feeling for things and situations. Therefore, the Goncourt brothers, e.g., as historians of the present, were in their personal journals as impressionist as Marcel Proust, Peter Altenberg, or even Franz Hessel, whose book *Spazieren in Berlin* (1929), recognized by Walter Benjamin as a literary masterpiece, represents perhaps the last example of a distinctly impressionist approach to modernist writing. Benjamin himself, like K.W.F. Schlegel and Friedrich Nietzsche before him, exemplified and practiced impressionism in philosophy, or rather he treated thought as if it were an intellectual impression. In turn, this approach illustrated the tension between the "ideal" of ideological stringency—in Benjamin's case, Marxism—and the attraction of plurality offered by impressionism. In intellectual terms, then, impressionism was, in the age of *isms*, essentially an anti-ideological ideology.

In poetry and poetic prose, though, impressionism lived off the suggestiveness of sound and rhythm supported by tantalizing verbal images (e.g., in Stéphane Mallarmé's "L'Après-midi d'un faune," 1876). By 1900, literary impressionism had become a genuinely Eur. literary phenomenon, with Gabriele D'Annunzio in Italy; Paul Verlaine, Paul Bourget, early André Gide, and Marcel Proust in France; Maurice Maeterlinck in Belgium; J. P. Jacobsen and Herman Bang in Denmark; and Knut Hamsun in Norway. But the hub of literary impressionism lay in Ger.-lang. cultures with, to mention but a few names, Detlev von Liliencron, early Hugo von Hofmannsthal and R. M. Rilke, Richard Dehmel, Max Dauthendey, Eduard Keyserling, early Robert Walser, Leopold von Andrian, and early Stefan Zweig. The crossovers among impressionism, *symbolism, and *Jugendstil* are of particular interest, as is the way in which impressionism transformed into *expressionism. In England, the most elaborate *manifesto on impressionism can be found in Ford Madox Ford's essay pub. under the same title in 1914. Together with Verlaine's "Art poétique" (1884), it provides the poetological framework for a conception of artistic expression that never really obtained the status of a movement. Ford traces impressionism back to William Hogarth and his *Analysis of Beauty* (1753) but argues "that one is an Impressionist because one tries to produce an illusion of reality—or rather the business of Impressionism is to produce that illusion." Arguably, the greatest illusion of the impressionists was to think that this position could be maintained.

■ R. Hamann, *Der Impressionismus in Leben und Kunst* (1907); A. Soergel, *Dichtung und Dichter im Impressionismus* (1911); M. Picard, *Das Ende des Impressionismus* (1920); H. Breysig, *Eindruckskunst und Ausdruckskunst* (1927); K. Brösel, *Veranschaulichung im Realismus, Impressionismus und Frühexpressionismus* (1928); L. Thon, *Die Sprache des deutschen Impressionismus* (1928); O. Walzel, *Wesenszüge des deutschen Impressionismus* (1930); R. Moser, *L'Impressionisme français* (1951); J. Gibbs, "Impressionism as a Literary Movement," *Modern Language Journal* 36 (1952); J. Lethève, *Impressionistes et symbolistes devant la presse* (1959); K. Brinkmann, *Impressionismus und Expressionismus in deutscher Literatur* (1960); H. Sommerhalter, *Zum Begriff des literarischen Impressionismus* (1961); R. Hamann and J. Hermand, *Impressionismus* (1972); U. Karthaus, *Impressionismus, Symbolismus und Jugendstil* (1977); H. Marhold, *Impressionismus in der deutschen Dichtung* (1985); *Geschichte der deutschen Literatur, vom 18. Jahrhundert bis zur Gegenwart, band II/2*, ed. V. Žmegac (1995).

R. GÖRNER

**INCANTATION** (Lat. *incantare*, "to chant, bewitch, cast a spell"). Use of a ritualistic formula spoken or chanted to produce a magical effect or *charm; more generally, a *chant used in magical ceremonies or sorcery: "With nigromaunce he wolde assaile / To make his incantacion" (John Gower, *Confessio amantis* 3.45). Also the magical spell itself: "Double, double, toil and trouble" (Shakespeare, *Macbeth* 4.1.10, 20, 35). Frazer discusses incantation under homeopathic magic, though several of his examples are not magic but simply petitions to gods or spirits to undertake a desired action. Similar are other ancient examples such as the Babylonian incantations, which are ritualistic formulas associated with the act of burning images of one's enemies (the great Mesopotamian series of incantations are known as the *Surpu* and *Maqlû*, both words meaning "burning"); the verbs are usually in the optative rather than the indicative mood ("may it happen" rather than "it will happen"), suggesting prayer rather than magic. In Hittite, at the dedication of a building, a piece of copper is deposited in the foundation with the incantation, "as this copper is firm and sound, so may the house be firm and sound." Related are such voodoo practices as thrusting pins into a doll to cause pain or death, usually accompanied by an incantation.

*See* SOUND.

■ J. G. Frazer, *The Golden Bough*, 3d ed., 12 v. (1905–15); B. Meissner, *Babylonien und Assyrien* (1920–25); G. Meier, *Die assyrische Beschwörungssammlung Maqlû* (1937); R. Lesses, "Exe(o)rcising Power: Women as Sorceresses, Exorcists, and Demonesses in Babylonian Jewish Society," *Journal of the American Academy of Religion* 69 (2001); A.-L. Siikala, *Mythic Images and Shamanism: A Perspective on Kalevala Poetry* (2002).

R. O. EVANS

**INCA POETRY.** *See* INDIGENOUS AMERICAS, POETRY OF THE.

**INCREMENTAL REPETITION.** F. B. Gummere's phrase for a rhetorical device he believed to be a distinguishing feature of the Eng. and Scottish popular *ballads. In incremental repetition, a line or stanza is repeated successively with some small but material substitution at the same crucial spot. A sequence of such repetitions accounts for the entire structure of some few ballads, incl. "Edward" and "Lord Randall." The latter uses incremental repetition in the form of question and answer; "The Maid Freed from the Gallows" combines this with the "climax of relatives," another typical form. More commonly, though, incremental repetition spans a passage of only three or four stanzas, and it is frequently confined to the lines of a single quatrain, as in the following stanza from "Sir Hugh; or, The Jew's Daughter":

> Then out and came the thick, thick blood,
> Then out and came the thin;
> Then out and came the bonny heart's blood,
> Where all the life lay in.

This kind of repetition is different from the kind of additive repetition found in "This is the House that Jack Built" or "The Twelve Days of Christmas." Gummere thought incremental repetition a test of a true oral ballad, but later scholars have demurred (Gerould); Bertrand H. Bronson shows the influence of the music.

Though incremental repetition is common in the Eng. and Scottish ballads, it is also found in much *oral poetry or oral-derived poetry, from the ancient Sumerian *Epic of Gilgamesh* to Old Welsh poetry to Port. folk song to Zulu song to songs of the Teleut in Siberia, not to mention other Anglo-Am. folksongs that are not ballads. It is also occasionally used as a prose device, e.g., by James Joyce. Incremental repetition is but one of a number of devices characteristic of oral poetry and *song that facilitate composition and memorization; in audition, it sometimes produces an effect of suspense or emotional intensification. In songs and ballads, it can enhance the music by reducing the density of the verbal component and by reinforcing parallels established by the repeated melody.

■ F. B. Gummere, *The Popular Ballad* (1907), esp. 117–24; L. Pound, *Poetic Origins and the Ballad* (1921)—sharply critical; G. H. Gerould, *The Ballad of Tradition* (1932), 105ff.; K. Jackson, "Incremental Repetition in the Early Welsh Englyn," *Speculum* 16 (1942); B. H. Bronson, *Traditional Tunes of the Child Ballads* (1959); D. K. Wilgus, *Anglo-American Folklore Scholarship since 1898* (1959); R. D. Abrahams and G. Foss, *Anglo-American Folksong Style* (1968); B. H. Bronson, *Ballad as Song* (1969); W. F. H. Nicolaisen, "How Incremental Is Incremental Repetition?" *Ballads and Ballad Research*, ed. P. Conroy (1978); R. B. Kershner, "The Artist as Text: Dialogism and Incremental Repetition in Joyce's *Portrait*," *ELH* 53 (1986).

A. B. Friedman; E. Doughtie;
T.V.F. Brogan; A. Watson

**INDETERMINACY.** Denotes a lingering state of indecision with regard to the meaning of a given sign, statement, or text, marking the lack of a stable context for *interpretation. Indeterminacy tends to be an exclusive category that implies an irresolvable conflict between discrete meanings and interpretations (i.e., the four irreconcilable meanings that Miller finds in William Wordsworth's "Resolution and Independence"), as opposed to *polysemy, which is often an inclusive category that implies a plurality of meanings and contexts for interpretation where their sheer proliferation, not their irresolvability, is the central issue. Indeterminate texts are composed of terms that do not cohere in a consistent interpretation and, therefore, remain obscure and enigmatic, leading to a suspension of meaning. As a critical term, *indeterminacy* gained currency in poststructuralist lit. crit. (see POSTSTRUCTURALISM), which emphasized what Hartman called "a hermeneutics of indeterminacy" or "a type of analysis that has renounced the ambition to master or demystify its subject (text, psyche) by technocratic, predictive, or authoritarian formulas."

Indeterminacy is brought about when no single meaning or interpretation may be adequately fixed around a given text, because of a radical separation of signifiers from their signifieds. Indeterminate texts are, thus, characterized not by the "depth" of complex intertextual relations and different associative and metaphoric connections but by disjunctive metonymic relations that give rise to a peculiar "surface tension." In indeterminate texts, the symbolic evocations generated by words on the page are no longer grounded in a coherent discourse, so that it becomes impossible to decide which of these associations are relevant and which are not. This displacement of meaning corresponds to the basic situation of Saussurean ling. in which "there are only differences without positive terms." The ling. sign is reduced to an ultimate differential unit, which is then combined with other differential units in a signifying chain according to the laws of a closed system. Lacan has termed this phenomenon "the sliding of the signified under the signifier" and claimed that it is the outcome of the nature of the signifier, which "always anticipates meaning by deploying its dimension in some sense before it." Thus, e.g., at the level of the sentence, one might consider a chain of signifiers that is interrupted before the significant term is introduced (in such combinations as "The fact remains . . .," "For example . . .," "Still perhaps . . .," etc.). According to Lacan, these chains of signifiers, supposedly meaningless, make sense, despite lacking an explicit reference, and that sense becomes all the more oppressive for having been denied. Similarly, in indeterminate texts, signifiers cease to be "signifiers of something" and become "signifiers to someone"; while they may have no clear referential function, they retain emotive and conative functions (see POETIC FUNCTION). The definitive discussion of indeterminacy in mod. poetry is that of Perloff.

*See* APORIA; DIFFICULTY; SIGN, SIGNIFIED, SIGNIFIER.

■ M. Perloff, *The Poetics of Indeterminacy* (1981); F. de Saussure, *Course in General Linguistics*, ed. C. Bally and A. Sechehaye, trans. R. Harris (1983); J. H. Miller, *The Linguistic Moment* (1985); B. J. Martine, *Indeterminacy and Intelligibility* (1992); G. Graff, "Determinacy/Indeterminacy," *Critical Terms for Literary Study*, ed. F. Lentricchia and T. McLaughlin, 2d ed. (1995); *Artifice and Indeterminacy: An Anthology of New Poetics*, ed. C. Beach (1998); J. Ashton, "'Rose Is a Rose': Gertrude Stein and the Critique of Indeterminacy," *Modernism/Modernity* 9 (2002); U. Wirth, "Derrida and Peirce on Indeterminacy, Iteration, and Replication," *Semiotica* 143 (2003); J. Lacan, "The Instance of the Letter in the Unconscious," *Écrits: A Selection*, trans. B. Fink (2004); J. Medina, "Anthropologism, Naturalism, and the Pragmatic Study of Language," *Journal of Pragmatics* 36 (2004); G. Hartman, *Criticism in the Wilderness*, 2d ed. (2007); J. Lezra, "The Indecisive Muse: Ethics in Translation and the Idea of History," *CL* 60 (2008).

N. Pines

**INDIA, ENGLISH POETRY OF.** Two figures dominate 19th-c. Indian poetry in Eng.: Henry Louis Vivian Derozio (1809–31), a Eurasian of Port. descent, and Toru Dutt (1856–77). There could have been a third, Michael Madhusudan Dutt (1824–73, no relation to Toru); but after publishing one book, he more or less gave up writing in Eng. in favor of his native Bengali, becoming the first great mod. poet in that lang.

"Born, and educated in India, and at the age of eighteen he ventures to present himself as a candidate for poetic fame," Derozio wrote in the preface to *Poems* (1827), his first book. It bore the impress of its times: the Scottish Enlightenment, the poetry of Lord Byron and P. B. Shelley, and the Gr. war of independence all found their way into it. The new lit. that marks its beginning with Derozio has since had many unsatisfactory names: Indo-Eng., India-Eng., Indian Eng., Indo-Anglian, and even Anglo-Indian. In "The Harp of India," the famous opening *sonnet of *Poems*, the poet sang of India before there was an India to sing of or sing to: "Thy music once was sweet—who hears it now?" Later, often decades later, others in the Indian langs. picked up the nationalist theme. An irony of Brit. colonialism was that, as it expanded, it also, through education, spread the Eng. lang. among Indians, which, in the argumentative Indian mind, planted the seed of freedom not only from colonial rule but from religious and social orthodoxies. Derozio taught at the Hindu College in Calcutta, where his radical ideas greatly influenced his students, some of whom were among the earliest Indian poets and prose writers in Eng.

Derozio died at 22, of cholera. Toru Dutt was 21 when she died of tuberculosis; her only book to be published during her lifetime was a volume of trans.

of Fr. poetry. The poets in Dutt's *A Sheaf Gleaned in French Fields* (1876) include Victor Hugo, Alphonse de Lamartine, Gérard de Nerval, Charles Baudelaire, and Charles-Marie Leconte de Lisle. Dutt clearly was a poet of wide literary tastes and, as a translator, handled a variety of verse forms with ease, unafraid to use the spoken idiom when required. All this is evident in her own poems as well. "Sita," "Baugmaree," and "Our Casuarina Tree," which appeared in the posthumous volume *Ancient Ballads and Legends of Hindustan* (1882), are among the finest lyrics in Indian poetry. As A. Chaudhuri pointed out, in "Baugmaree," which is the name of the Calcutta suburb where the Dutt family had its country house, the poet adapts the sonnet in ways that It., Eng., and the other Western Eur. poetries had not seen.

During the last decades of the 19th c. and in the first half of the 20th, much poetry was written that is now forgotten but not entirely forgettable. Fredoon Kabraji's (1897–1986) self-deprecating title *A Minor Georgian's Swan Song* (1938) is representative—but he is a better poet than the title suggests. The postindependence poets—Nissim Ezekiel (1924–2004), Jayanta Mahapatra (b. 1928), A. K. Ramanujan (1929–93), Arun Kolatkar (1931–2004), Kamala Das (1934–2009), Keki N. Daruwalla (b. 1937), Dom Moraes (1938–2004), Dilip Chitre (1938–2009), Eunice de Souza (b. 1940), Adil Jussawalla (b. 1940), Arvind Krishna Mehrotra (b. 1947), Agha Shahid Ali (1949–2001), Manohar Shetty (b. 1953), Imtiaz Dharker (b. 1954)—had little to do with the 150-year-old trad. of Indian poetry in Eng. In the absence of critical eds. or even anthols., most of this poetry was unavailable to them anyway. Like the 19th-c. poets, they had to start afresh, assembling their trad. however they could. They fashioned it from what they found at hand (the *Bhakti* poets) and farther afield (G. G. Belli, Robert Browning, W. B. Yeats, André Breton, T. S. Eliot, Ezra Pound, W. C. Williams, Robert Lowell).

"My backward place is where I am," Ezekiel, the preeminent Indian poet in Eng. after independence, wrote in "Background, Casually" (1976), both describing his location and stating its centrality to his poetics. His low-key, plain style marked a clear shift away from poets like Sarojini Naidu (1879–1949), whom Mahatma Gandhi called the nightingale of India, and Sri Aurobindo (1872–1950), who had preceded Ezekiel. Ezekiel called his first book *A Time to Change* (1952). Staying clear of Indian myths and legends, he is also the first poet to write about the Indian city, in his case Bombay, a "Barbaric city, sick with slums, / Deprived of seasons, blessed with rains," as he called it in "A Morning Walk" (1959).

Kolatkar, Chitre, Mahapatra, and Ramanujan, like M. M. Dutt, wrote in Eng. as well as in their native tongues (Kolatkar and Chitre in Marathi, Mahapatra in Oriya, Ramanujan in Kannada). Das, under the pseud. Madhavikutty, was a renowned writer of short fiction in Malayalam, a fact largely unknown to her Eng. readers. Ramanujan, Kolatkar, Chitre, and Mehrotra also translated from the Indian langs. (Tamil Sangam poetry, Prakrit love poetry, the Bhakti poets Nammal-

var, Tukaram, and Kabīr). Their trans. mirrored their Eng. poems, just as their Eng. poems mirrored their trans. Poets also ran publishing cooperatives (Clearing House, Newground, Praxis) and edited magazines (*Poetry India, Chandrabhāgā*) and anthols. The canon of Indian poetry in Eng. has been shaped not by Indian scholars but by the poets.

Ramanujan wrote a poetry of self-revealing masks. Even his inventive stanza shapes were another mask in his poetic wardrobe, behind which the falling, plunging self was terrifyingly visible. Ramanujan's reputation as a poet, at least in the United States, where he taught at the University of Chicago, has been eclipsed by his reputation as a folklorist, essayist, and trans., as the inventor of Tamil poetry for contemp. times.

The most remarkable Indian poet of the 20th c. was Kolatkar, who created two independent, major bodies of work in two langs., Eng. and Marathi. *Jejuri* (1976), a sequence of 31 poems about a visit to a temple town of the same name in Maharashtra, established his international reputation. He published three more volumes, two of which appeared in the year he died and the third posthumously. He was an elusive figure who had a horror of mainstream publishers. At the heart of his work lies a moral vision, the basis of which is the things of this world, precisely, rapturously observed: "A sawed off sunbeam comes to rest / gently against the driver's right temple" ("The Bus," 1976).

The postindependence poets and their 19th-c. predecessors may seem to have little in common, but the parallels of cosmopolitanism, bilingualism, and trans. are too striking to be missed.

*See* ASSAMESE POETRY; BENGALI POETRY; GUJARATI POETRY; HINDI POETRY; INDIA, POETRY OF; KANNADA POETRY; KASHMIRI POETRY; MALAYALAM POETRY; MARATHI POETRY; NEPALI AND PAHARI POETRY; NEWAR POETRY; ORIYA POETRY; PUNJABI POETRY; RĀMĀYAṆA POETRY; SANSKRIT POETICS; SANSKRIT POETRY; TAMIL POETRY AND POETICS; TELUGU POETRY; URDU POETRY.

■ *Ten Twentieth-Century Indian Poets*, ed. R. Parthasarathy (1976); N. Ezekiel, *Collected Poems* (1989); *The Oxford India Anthology of Twelve Modern Indian Poets*, ed. A. K. Mehrotra (1992); B. King, *Modern Indian Poetry in English*, rev. ed. (2001); J. Ramazani, "Metaphor and Postcoloniality: A. K. Ramanujan's Poetry," *The Hybrid Muse* (2001); A. Chaudhuri, "A State of Commerce," *The Telegraph* (April 7, 2002); *A History of Indian Literature in English*, ed. A. K. Mehrotra (2003); *Early Indian Poetry in English*, ed. E. de Souza (2005); B. King, *Three Indian Poets*, rev. ed. (2005); *The Bloodaxe Book of Contemporary Indian Poets,* ed. J. Thayil (2008); A. K. Mehrotra, "The Emperor Has No Clothes," *Partial Recall* (2011).

A. K. MEHROTRA

## INDIA, POETRY OF

I. Ancient Period (ca. 1200 BCE–1200 CE)
II. Middle Period (ca. 1200–1800 CE)
III. Modern Period (since ca. 1800)

The term *Indian poetry* commonly refers to an immense and diverse body of poetry produced on the Indian subcontinent and by authors of subcontinental origin, since about 1200 BCE. Also known as South Asia, this region is now divided into seven nations (incl. India, Pakistan, Bangladesh, Nepal, and Sri Lanka) and is as large and varied as western Europe. Indian poetry does not belong to a unified, monolingual trad. but rather is a constellation of interacting trads. in about 25 major lit. langs., many of which are used widely for everyday communication in South Asia in mod. times.

The subcontinental langs. have preserved their poetic trads. in oral as well as written forms, using a dozen different script systems of indigenous and foreign origin. The langs. belong to four families: Indo-Aryan, Dravidian, Austro-Asiatic, and Sino-Tibetan. Of these, the Indo-Aryan and Dravidian langs. have been predominant as literary media and, since about 1000 CE, they have been strongly associated with specific geographical regions within the subcontinent. At the same time, langs. from abroad, such as Persian (between the 13th and 19th cs.) and Eng. (since the late 18th c.), have periodically come into widespread use, greatly complicating Indian ling., regional, national, and cultural identities, as well as conceptions of poetry, genre, and aesthetics.

This article surveys the general patterns and transformations in poetry of the subcontinent as a well-defined multilingual area over time. It focuses on the most important poetic practices and innovations of each historical period and on changes in poetics and in historical and cultural circumstances. The broad historical divisions here are the ancient period (ca. 1200 BCE–1200 CE), which includes the early *epic period (ca. 600 BCE–400 CE) and the cl. Sanskrit period (ca. 400–1200 CE); the middle period common to many langs. (ca. 1200–1800); and the mod. period (ca. 1800 to the present). For details of particular Indian poetic trads., consult the entries by lang.

## I. Ancient Period (ca. 1200 BCE–1200 CE)

**A. Conceptions of Poetry.** For about 2,500 years, Indian theorists and literati have frequently used the word *kāvya* for poetry to distinguish it from other kinds of verbal composition. In its earliest and narrowest meaning (ca. 600 BCE), kāvya characterizes the poetry of the *Rāmāyaṇa*, which is epic in scope, narrative in structure, and lyrical in effect, with relatively straightforward *syntax and *diction. In a second, wider meaning (ca. 200 CE onward), kāvya signifies composition in verse or prose, designed to give its audience an experience of *rasa*, the aesthetically fashioned representation of emotions.

In its widest sense (popular ca. 700–1200 CE), kāvya designates the full range of imaginative composition, in verse (*padya*), prose (*gadya*), and mixtures of the two (*miśra'*, *campu*). It includes drama and performance texts, which often are multilingual in the cl. period, with different characters speaking in different langs. or social and regional dialects for verisimilitude. Kāvya in this sense further includes prose narrative, both "fictional" (*kathā*) and "nonfictional" (*ākhyāyikā*), covering what we now call *myth, legend, short story, novella, novel, moral tale, fable, biography, and history. Kāvya

in the latter part of the ancient period thus coincides with the meaning of lit. itself (*sāhitya*), although the term still does not cover the "total order of words" (*vānmaya*) in a given lang. Within this framework, Indian theorists distinguish between *dṛśya kāvya*, poetry that has to be "seen" to be properly understood (*dramatic poetry and *performance), and *śravya kāvya*, poetry that needs only to be "heard" to be grasped fully (epic, *lyric, prose).

**B. Early Epic.** The period during which the major epics, the *Rāmāyaṇa* and the *Mahābhārata*, were probably composed (ca. 600 BCE–400 CE) constitutes an essential backdrop for later Indian poetry. Society at this time is almost entirely Hindu, with the institutions of caste, endogamy, and Vedic ritual already in place, along with the proscriptions against pollution. The two epics represent a world in which Hinduism as a polytheistic way of life was divided mainly between followers of the major gods Viṣṇu and Śiva and in which the subcontinent is organized politically into small and large republics ruled by dynasties of kings. Works belonging to this period are composed, preserved, and transmitted orally, using elaborate techniques of memorization and verification; indigenous script systems and writing (with a stylus, on prepared bark or palm leaf) become available only around the 2d c. BCE. In this setting, the *Rāmāyaṇa* and the *Mahābhārata* appear as heroic *sagas in verse that draw on bardic materials and conventions, folklore, romance, and hist., with many themes resonating strongly with the Troy cycle of stories and Gr. and Roman myths, and hence pointing to shared IE sources.

Vālmīki, the original author of the *Mahābhārata*, is recognized as the "first *kavi"* or ur-poet, and the poem itself is the "original kāvya," standing at the head of the subcontinent's lit. trads. Vālmīki defines the *śloka* as the ideal vehicle for poetic emotion as well as verse narrative, and his virtuoso handling of this unrhymed metrical verse form (resembling a closed *couplet, divided by *caesuras into quarters) becomes an enduring model for subsequent craftsmanship in narrative, dramatic, and lyric verse. The *Rāmāyaṇa* and the *Mahābhārata* together define some of the overarching subjects of Indian poetry: *dharma* (law, duty, obligation), justice, war, love, and the irrevocability of vows, curses, and promises. Most important, they become reservoirs of stories from which poets of all subsequent generations draw. At the level of technique, they invent framed narratives, in which smaller stories are nested inside larger tales, and the outermost frame gathers them all into a cohesive poetic structure. Emboxed narratives find their way from the epics into the Buddhist *Jataka* tales (4th c. BCE) and the Hindu *Panchatantra* fables (2d c. CE), and ultimately into Somadeva's *Kathasaritsagara* (11th c. CE); from these widely circulated texts, the device then migrates to Persian, Ar., the Romance langs., and Eng., influencing the poets of the *1001 Nights* as well as Giovanni Boccaccio and Chaucer.

**C. Classical Sanskrit.** By the cl. period (ca. 400–1200 CE), Indian society had become more varied; besides numerous caste divisions (*jatis*), it included many new ethnic communities with distinctive ways of life. The primeval forests had been cleared; the Indo-Gangetic plains and the Deccan Plateau were well populated; networks of roads connected market towns, pilgrimage centers, ports, and royal capitals, signifying a shift toward urban culture, travel, and prosperity. Politically, republics had given way to imperial formations covering large portions of the subcontinent. Hinduism was still the predominant religion, but it now emphasized large public temples, pilgrimage sites, and domestic rituals and flourished alongside Buddhism and Jainism as alternative worldviews.

In verse, cl. Sanskrit poetry centered around three primary classes of texts. (1) The category of *mahākāvya* and *dirgha-kāvya*, poems in "major forms" divided into *sargas* (cantos, chapters, sections), which devised large-scale structures for the saga of a royal clan, the heroic battle poem, and the courtly epic (written to order for a patron), among other subgenres. (2) The category of *laghukāvya* and *khanda-kāvya*, which consisted of short and medium-length poems, poetic segments, and fragments and extracts from longer works. It included the *subhāṣita*, a beautifully crafted verse that could stand on its own, as well as the poetic sequence, a thematic arrangement of separate verses or passages. (3) The category of *kośa* or edited *anthology brought together short poems, either by a single author or by many hands, often arranged by form and theme. In later centuries, the cl. mahākāvya and dirgha-kāvya (rather than the *Rāmāyaṇa* and the *Mahābhārata*) became the practical models for epics and long poems in the mod. Indian mother tongues; the subhāṣita served as the norm for brevity, elegance, and lyricism; and the kośa, secular and inclusive, defined the ideal anthol. of poetry.

In addition, cl. Sanskrit expanded the concept of kāvya to include prose works as well as drama. The *ākhyāyikā* (the short or extended "true story") provided new frameworks for biographical and historical writing, whereas the *kathā*, a short tale that retells a received narrative or narrates an invented fiction, showcased fantastic events as well as verisimilar representations of human characters (both individuated figures and stock types), together with social and psychological realism. The *nataka* or poetic play in several acts (a variety of dṛśya kāvya) created the model of multilingual drama in a mixture of prose and verse, with the former utilized for dialogue and the latter for emotional intensity, foregrounding, and *allusion. While ancient Gr. drama is distinguished by its invention of *tragedy and Aristophanic *comedy, the distinction of cl. Sanskrit drama lies in its invention on stage of the heroic romance, the farce, and esp. the romantic comedy (as in Kālidāsa's [4th c. CE] *Śakuntalam*).

As a distinctive style, kāvya in its cl. phase sought to create a verbal texture pleasing to both the ear and the mind and became an aesthetic model for the later Indo-Aryan and Dravidian langs. It involved not only rasa but extensive figuration and embellishment (*alaṃkāra*), the use of indirect suggestion (*dhvani*) over and above *connotation and denotation to convey meaning, a display of learning in the arts and sciences, an intricate syntax and an enormous

vocabulary, and a wide variety of complicated *meters and verse forms. Thematically and formally, esp. in the category of short or fragmentary poems, cl. kāvya opened up a fresh range of generic possibilities for subsequent Indian poetry, from descriptions of the seasons, *confessional poetry, *epigrams, and *erotic poetry to *hymns and prayers, philosophical reflections, *didactic poetry, and even short dramatic *monologues. The richness of cl. kāvya style revolved around concrete *imagery, precise representation, nuanced *emotion, refinement of sensibility, and memorability.

Passing through a number of well-defined phases (in Sanskrit, from Vedic to epic to cl.; in cl. Tamil, from *caṅkam* to epic to devotional), Indian poetry of the ancient period came to constitute a massive, multiform body of verbal composition. In the middle and mod. periods, this body became a repository of *commonplaces for poets and audiences to tap and a *canon to which they could respond, as they created fresh configurations of lang., theme, aesthetics, religious belief, social thought, and politics.

## II. Middle Period (ca. 1200–1800 CE)

A. *Historical and Cultural Changes.* The middle period begins and ends at different times for langs. and regions of the subcontinent; but most poetic trads. undergo vital transitions in the late 12th and late 18th cs., so its common historical span may be specified as 1200–1800. In the largest internal change marking the end of the cl. and the beginning of the middle period, Sanskrit ceases to be the primary medium of literary composition, giving way to writing in about 15 mother tongues. Similar to the transition from Lat. to the vernaculars in Europe around the same time, this ling. and literary shift is accompanied by a selective but concerted devaluation of the ancient Indian past and particularly by the rise of new chauvinisms centered around the geographical domains of the various mother tongues.

This cultural transformation coincides with several other historical changes. By about 1200, gradual Muslim conquest, migration, and settlement on the subcontinent had led to Muslim imperial rule, which lasted for six centuries. Indian society was more mixed and fragmented, being characterized by a foreign ruling elite, new immigrant and settler communities from central and western Asia, and segregation among different races, religions, and langs. By the 13th c., Islam was the religion of power, Buddhism had migrated out of the Indian mainland, and Hinduism had been altered by the emergence of *Bhakti*. Islam brought its own divisions: the Sunni, Shi'a, and Sufi religious communities, as well as the Ar., Persian, and Turkish ling. communities (each with its own literary trads.). Moreover, by the 13th c., the technology of writing with reed pen and ink on paper had arrived on the subcontinent, drastically altering the material existence and possibilities of lit. Under such circumstances, the change of verbal medium, from half a dozen ancient literary langs. dominated by Sanskrit to about 15 regional mother tongues and two or three foreign langs., engendered far-reaching changes in the very conception of poetry and its functions.

**B.** *Bhakti Poetry.* The most prominent literary, religious, and social movement of the middle period is Bhakti ("devotion" to a god, often classified as theism), which began in the far south (the Tamil region) after the 6th c. and spread with surprising success over the subcontinent by the 16th c. Despite ling. diversity and local and regional variations, Bhakti poetry has common features across a dozen major langs. The movement involves several thousand poets, called *bhaktas* and *sants,* as well as many disparate "communities" or "paths" (*sampradayas, panthas*) focused variously on Viṣṇu and his avatars, Śiva, Devi (the universal goddess), or an undifferentiated godhead.

In Bhakti poetry, which strongly parallels Christian mystical poetry in late med. and early mod. Europe, a poet expresses his or her intensely personal devotion to a particular god, goddess, or godhead. True poetry in this trad. must be spontaneous, urgent, personal, and "divinely inspired" and should be composed in the more natural mother tongue than in an artificial lang. like Sanskrit. Bhakti poets and poems, therefore, tend to be more immediate, colloquial, autobiographical, confessional, and dramatic than many of their cl. counterparts, swerving away from impersonal kāvya on a significant scale. Most Bhakti poetry is composed in short or minor forms of local or regional origin (not borrowed from Sanskrit), and it is usually metrical and uses verse forms with end rhyme (rare in the cl. langs.). Many poems in the trad. are addressed to fellow worshippers; others are addressed to a god or to the poet's audience and, hence, are unlike Western lyrics. Short Bhakti poems are set to music and sung, often in a congregation; and they are also used frequently in such performance arts as dance, dance-drama, and folk theater (see DEVOTIONAL POETRY).

Bhakti alters the historical evolution of poetry on the subcontinent on several fronts. It is the first comprehensive movement in the new regional lits. emerging at the end of the cl. period, and it shapes their characteristic *topoi* and themes, forms and genres. Socially and politically, many bhaktas and sants are radicals who substantially modify or even reject the Hinduism and priestly culture of the ancient period; some belong to very low or "untouchable" castes, and they participate fully in the movement's outspoken "counterculture." In religious, theological, and philosophical terms, Bhakti defines a major alternative to ritualized "salvation" in ancient Hinduism, and it provides the central impetus for Sikhism, a new religion that arose in the 16th c. Notable formal innovations in short Bhakti poems include an opening *refrain, which becomes prominent in musical performance; and a concluding signature line that explicitly identifies its author, in marked contrast to the impersonality of the subhāṣita and of laghukāvya in cl. Sanskrit.

### III. Modern Period (since ca. 1800)

**A.** *Colonization and Modernity.* For large parts of the subcontinent, the mod. period of hist. begins with Brit. rule in the mid-18th c., whereas literary modernity appears only in the 19th. Many material, ideological, and practical factors contribute directly and indirectly to this large-scale transition from a "traditional" to a "modern" society: the military success of a foreign power on the subcontinent; the establishment of a rationalized system of administration (in contrast to the disarray of late Mughal administration in the 18th c.); the introduction of journalism, newspapers, and periodicals, as well as of a comprehensive postal system; the formation of a full-fledged, multilingual print culture; the emergence of a public sphere that allowed rational debate on issues of common concern (in spite of colonial censorship); the popularity of civic associations and literary societies, modeled on Eur. institutions; Brit. and Eur. critiques of traditional Indian culture; and esp. the availability of Western-style education in schools, colleges, and universities.

In the later 19th c., Indian poets began encountering Anglo-Am. literary works and reading Eng. trans. of Gr., Roman, and mod. Eur. lits. Many of them subsequently began to imitate their Western predecessors and contemporaries, significantly changing the formal, thematic, and generic complexion of the lits. in indigenous langs. The Westernization of India under Brit. rule also went one step further: it created the poet who wanted to write poetry of the Anglo-Am. kind directly in the Eng. lang. But the modernity of Indian writing after about 1800 does not consist solely in its Westernization, and Indian writers did not become mod. merely by imitating Euro-Am. writers. In most Indian mother tongues, the 18th and 19th cs. were largely periods of very complex, creative interaction among local, regional, subcontinental, and international trads., leading as much to reactionary traditionalism and reactive nationalism as to stimulating cultural syncretism.

The overall effect of colonization on Indian poetry was thus multifaceted and far-reaching: the encounter with Eur. cultures drove Indian writers to experiment with poetry markedly different from anything the Indian trads. themselves had invented; it went hand in hand with a renewed interest in their own trads. of the ancient and middle periods; and it introduced yet another foreign literary lang., Eng., into the Indian babel. These effects have continued from the early 19th c. to the present, and the grafting of Western "influences" onto "indigenous" sensibilities has resulted in a hybrid lit. that has broken away sharply from many of the patterns in Indian poetry of the preceding three millennia. *Ādhunik kāvita* (mod. poetry) swerves away in complicated ways from *prācīn kāvya* (ancient or old poetry), whether that of cl. Sanskrit or of the Bhakti movement, and pushes kāvya and kavitā across new frontiers.

**B.** *Modern Poetic Genres.* The shift away from the poetry and poetics of the middle period was signaled by a concerted change in poetic forms, themes, conventions, images, metrical frames, and structural principles, as well as by radical changes in the conception of who the poet (*kavi*) is, what his or her functions are, and how his or her audience is constituted. Moreover, the transformed situation of Indian poets in the 19th and early 20th cs. generated new attitudes, concerns, tones, and voices: they explored enjambed lines (see ENJAMBMENT), Elizabethan *blank verse, Eng. epic conventions, Miltonic *similes, and romantic lyrics; experimented with specific Eur. and non-Indian verse forms grafted onto Sanskrit-based prosody; and elaborated themes related to nation, identity, and social, religious, and political change. This multifarious transition led to writing that, when placed beside earlier Indian poetry, strikes a remarkably cosmopolitan, mod. note; but its novelty, whether in the indigenous langs. or in Eng., does not result simply from a rejection of the Indian past.

The varieties of creative synthesis in mod. Indian poetry are evident in the new genres that appeared in the 19th and 20th cs. Among them are the long philosophical or speculative poem, epic in size and scope and envisioning a new worldview (e.g., Aurobindo Ghose's [1872–1950] *Savitri* in Eng., G. M. Muktibodh's [1917–64] *Andhere men* in Hindi); the nationalist epic, retelling an ancient Hindu myth or story, esp. from the *Rāmāyaṇa* or the *Mahābhārata* (e.g., Michael Madhusudan Dutt's [1824–73] *Meghanādvadha* in Bengali, Jaishankar Prasad's [1889–1937] *Kāmāyanī* in Hindi); the long sequence of short poems, whether religious, philosophical, satiric, or personal in theme, modeled on the Western poetic sequence as well as on premod. Indian sequences (e.g., Rabindranath Tagore's [1861–1941] *Gitanjali* in Bengali; Subramania Bharati's [1882–1921] "prose poems" in Tamil; Rajagopal Parthasarathy's [b. 1934] *Rough Passage* in Eng.); the short metrical lyric in a mod. rhymed stanza form, sometimes set to music, as well as the modernized lyric based on premod. Indian and foreign verse forms (e.g., Faiz Ahmed Faiz's [1911–84] *ghazals, nazms,* and *gits* in Urdu; B. S. Mardhekar's [1909–56] and Vinda Karandikar's [1918–2010] *abhangas* in Marathi; Buddhadev Bose's [1908–74] *sonnets in Bengali); and the "free-verse" poem, varying in length from a few lines to several hundred and ranging in theme from autobiographical and confessional to mythological, political, and historical (e.g., the love poems of P. S. Rege [1910–78] in Marathi; the political poems of Dhoomil [1936–75], Shrikant Verma [1931–86], and Raghuvir Sahay [1929–90] in Hindi; the bilingual poetry of A. K. Ramanujan [1929–93] in Eng. and Kannada and of Arun Kolatkar [1932–2004] in Eng. and Marathi; and *protest poetry, Dalit poetry, and contemp. feminist and women's poetry in most langs.).

In the course of these devels., the tensions between modernity and trad., Indianness and Westernization, have played a shaping role. Like many of their 19th-c. predecessors, 20th- and 21st-c. Indian poets reject certain aspects of their past but at the same time make use of it, achieving a modernity in which Westernization and Indianness stand in a constant and constantly productive conflict. As a result, mod. Indian writers, critics, and common readers now refer to all varieties of

poetry as *kāvya*; in its broadest usage around the millennial moment, kāvya, thus, embraces a vast quantity of diverse poetry in about 25 major langs. produced over some 3,000 years.

*See* ASSAMESE POETRY; BENGALI POETRY; GUJARATI POETRY; HINDI POETRY; INDIA, ENGLISH POETRY OF; KANNADA POETRY; KASHMIRI POETRY; MALAYALAM POETRY; MARATHI POETRY; NEPALI AND PAHARI POETRY; NEWAR POETRY; ORIYA POETRY; PUNJABI POETRY; RĀMĀYAṆA POETRY; SANSKRIT POETICS; SANSKRIT POETRY; TAMIL POETRY AND POETICS; TELUGU POETRY; URDU POETRY.

■ A. B. Keith, *A History of Sanskrit Literature* (1928); *An Anthology of Sanskrit Court Poetry*, trans. D.H.H. Ingalls (1965); *The Mahābhārata*, trans. C. V. Narasimhan (1965)—handy abridgement; A. K. Ramanujan, *Speaking of Śiva* (1973); *The Mahābhārata*, trans. J.A.B. van Buitenen, 3 v. (1973–80); E. C. Dimock et al., *The Literatures of India* (1974)—compact intro.; E. Zelliot, "The Medieval *Bhakti* Movement in History," *Hinduism*, ed. B. L. Smith (1976)—a balanced subject guide; D. Kopf, *The Brahmo Samaj and the Shaping of the Modern Indian Mind* (1979)—historical and cultural contexts; *Hymns for the Drowning*, trans. A. K. Ramanujan (1981); S. Lienhard, *A History of Classical Poetry* (1984); *The Rāmāyaṇa of Vālmiki*, trans. R. Goldman et al., 5 v. (1984–2005); *The Bhagavad-Gītā*, trans. B. S. Miller (1986); *Poems of Love and War*, trans. A. K. Ramanujan (1986)—from cl. Tamil; *Songs of the Saints of India*, ed. and trans. J. S. Hawley and M. Juergensmeyer (1988); S. K. Das, *A History of Indian Literature*, 3 v. (1991–2005)—incomplete but informative; *The Oxford Anthology of Modern Indian Poetry*, ed. V. Dharwadker and A. K. Ramanujan (1994)—selections from 15 langs.; A. K. Ramanujan, *Collected Essays* (1999); *Kabir: The Weaver's Songs*, trans. V. Dharwadker (2003); *Literary Cultures in History: Reconstructions from South Asia*, ed. S. Pollock (2003)—best crit. overview of major Indian lits.; S. Pollock, *The Language of the Gods in the World of Men* (2006)—excellent, comprehensive.

V. DHARWADKER

# INDIAN PROSODY

  I. Classical Languages: Sanskrit, Prakrit, and Tamil
  II. The Modern Vernaculars

**I. Classical Languages: Sanskrit, Prakrit, and Tamil.** Indian metrics is one of the world's most complex prosodic trads. Though perhaps best treated historically, it must in an article such as this be surveyed formally. Indian meters fall into three main types: (a) those that fix the *quantity of each syllable (varṇavṛtta), (b) those that fix the total quantity of each line (mātrāvṛtta), and (c) those that appear to mix the two types (śloka). Like the metrics of Gr. and Lat., Indian versification is based on a prosodic distinction between *heavy* and *light* syllables. A heavy syllable contains a long vowel or a short vowel followed by two or more consonants. A light syllable contains a short vowel followed by at most one consonant. The distinction of vowel quantity is inherent in the phonology of Sanskrit and the other Indian langs.

**A. Fixed-syllable Meters.** The elegant meters of cl. Sanskrit poetry are of this type. The general formula calls for four usually identical feet (*pāda*), which in practice may vary from eight to 21 or more syllables each. *Mandākrāntā* (the meter of Kālidāsa's *Meghadhūta*) may be taken as an example. Each of its four 17-syllable feet realizes the following pattern: G G G G L L L L L G / G L G G L G x (G = *guru*, or heavy syllable; L = *laghu*, or light syllable; x = a syllable of variable quantity; "/" marks the *yati*, or *caesura). Less common meters may vary identical first and third feet with identical second and fourth feet or may have four different feet, but the principle remains the same: the quantity of each syllable is predictable and the sequence or pattern is fixed. In *recitation, a chanting intonation is usually employed, modeled on the quantitative sequence of the line. Though some common recitative patterns are noticeable, each reciter may also cultivate a personal style. The names of the meters generally scan in the meter and often suggest appropriate associations: *mandākrāntā*, ([a lady] slowly approaching).

**B. Fixed-Line or Moric Meters.** Here the quantity of the total line is fixed by considering a laghu worth one "measure" (*mātrā*; cf. Lat. *mora) and a guru two. Free variation of syllables within the line is, however, restricted by several conventions, which demonstrate the influence of a regular *beat—indicating that these meters were probably sung. It is forbidden, for instance, that the beat fall on the second half of a guru syllable. If we assume one beat every four mātrās (three, five, and six are also possible), this convention will, in effect, articulate the line into groups (*gaṇa*) of four mātrās each, which have only the shapes G G, G L L, L G L, L L G, or L L L L, each signaled by an initial beat. The *āryā*, which probably originated in popular, non-Sanskritic milieux and remained the meter of choice for cl. Prakrit poetry, may serve as a typical example: it is composed of two lines, the first of which must contain 30 mātrā, the second 27. The simple tetramoric pattern (above) is, however, complicated (and syncopated) by adding to seven of these gaṇa an eighth (or two mātrās (for a total, in the first line, of 30) and, further, in the second line, by reducing the sixth gaṇa to a single laghu (i.e., 27). Convention also restricts the kinds of gaṇa that do, in fact, occur in given loci in the verse; e.g., in the āryā, L G L is possible only for the second and fourth gaṇa. The meters of the songs of the *Gītagovinda* (13th c.) and those employed in middle Indic *devotional poetry and in the mod. north Indian langs. are generally of the moric type, which is subject to extreme variation. Beginning with the *Gītagovinda*, end rhyme is frequently associated with moric meter, and later vernacular poetry is regularly rhymed. *Alliteration, though not unknown in earlier poetry, also becomes an increasingly prominent feature of moric verse. As may be surmised, the correlation of moric meter with song is in the mod. period even more marked.

The meters of the Dravidian langs. of the south (Tamil, Telugu, Kannada, Malayalam) are based on a somewhat more complicated *scansion (in certain circumstances, treating as light even a syllable containing a long vowel); but during the long course of coexistence and mutual contact, there has been a give and take of both theory and practice with the Sanskritic north. The oldest Dravidian (viz., Tamil) meters greatly resemble the moric meters of the Prakrits, employ alliteration with great effect, and are definitely rhythmical (cf. again the *Gītagovinda*). On the other hand, they often feature initial rhyme, based on the first interior consonant of the line—virtually unknown in the north. Lines most commonly consist of four feet (*cīr*) comprising two or three syllables (*acai*). The earliest treatise on prosody in the Dravidian langs. is the *Ceyyuḷiyal* chapter of the Tamil *Tolkāppiyam* (3d to 5th cs. BCE). The cl. meters prevailed until the end of the first millennium CE, when folk meters were popularized by devotional poets.

**C. Śloka.** The most common Sanskrit meter is partly fixed, partly free. Śloka (praise) is both a type and a species, deriving in its special *epic and later form (after 500 BCE) from the meters found in the oldest extant Indic text, the *Rig Veda* (ca. 1500–1000 BCE). The cl. śloka is like type (a) in that it is composed of four feet, each of which must have eight syllables; but it is like (b) in that its line appears to fall into two four-syllable halves, the first of which is quantitatively quite free (though x L L x does not normally occur), the second of which is obligatorily L G G x in odd feet and in even feet L G L x. A "trochaic" cadence, thus, alternates with an "iambic." Many variations on this pattern are, however, found. The older Vedic meters (*chandas*) are composed generally of feet with 8, 11, or 12 syllables. Of the eight-syllable meters, some have three feet (*gāyatrī*), some four (*anuṣṭubh*). This latter is evidently the ancestor of the cl. śloka, but it lacks, along with the other Vedic meters, the contrast between even and odd feet. Its usual shape is x G x G /L G L x. The 11-syllable meters (*triṣṭubh*) generally have the same attack and the same cadence but add a middle sequence of L L G (/). The *jagatī* adds a syllable to the triṣṭubh but is otherwise like it. Like the anuṣṭubh, the triṣṭubh and jagatī have descendants in the cl. metrics—the family of 11-syllable meters called *upajāti*, and 12-syllable meters such as the popular *vaṃśastha* and *drutavilambita*. The style of śloka recitation is more or less uniform over all of India, testifying to its antiquity. The Vedic meters have been deformed by the superimposition of later prosodic features, such as the obligatory *sandhi* (ling. junctures) of the cl. lang. and are only dimly perceptible in the (otherwise) beautiful ritual chanting of the Vedic priest, itself the likely precursor of cl. Indian music.

The śloka is not "poetic" in the usual Western

sense, however. Though it is metrical, it is functionally the equivalent of Western prose in that it is the mode of choice for an entire range of literate composition, from epic (*Mahābhārata, Rāmāyaṇa*) and *fable (*Kathāsaritsāgara*) to grammar (*Vākyapadīya*) and astronomy (*Sūryasiddhānta*)—doubtless reflecting the importance of memorization in Indian religious and cultural trad.

The study of prosody is very old in India, being counted as one of the six "ancillaries of the Veda" (*vedāṅga*). A *sūtra* attributed to Piṅgala, portions of which may be as old as 600 BCE (the rest as late as 500 CE), describes about 160 meters, but surprisingly not the śloka that we know. In the late cl. period (after 900 CE), an elaborate technical lit. (*chandaḥśāstra*) grew up, based on Piṅgala, wherein were defined the various meters in actual use and, with mathematical completeness, many meters merely possible. Associations with moods, time of day, and colors were sometimes also made, testifying to an effort to integrate metrics into the larger domain of aesthetics.

## II. The Modern Vernaculars.

Throughout the med. and early mod. periods, the end-stopped rhyming couplet was the preferred medium of expression for poets in the New Indo-Aryan langs. (Hindi, Punjabi, Gujarati, Marathi, Bengali, Assamese, and Oriya). As in cl. Sanskrit, lines are usually divided by caesurae into two, three, or four feet (*pāda* or *caraṇ*). The most popular verse form for the vast number of devotional lyrics produced in this period is the *pad*, a stanza of from four to eight lines (but often extended to several more), all having the same metrical structure and frequently the same rhyme. Often the lyric begins with a shorter line that in *performance serves as a *refrain. Alliteration is prevalent throughout the med. period; among the poets of Rajasthan, it becomes obligatory.

On the whole, Hindi poets favored moric meters, esp. those with a tetramoric pattern. It appears that the poets normally had a specific rhythmic cycle (*tāla*) in mind when they chose the meter. Often this was a cycle of 16 beats divided into four equal sections, the common time of Indian music. The majority of lyrics have 16 morae in the first foot of each line and from 10 to 16 in the second.

The *dohā* is a rhyming couplet commonly used for aphorisms, as well as for longer narrative and *didactic poetry. The first foot of each line has 13 morae and the second 11. In the case of Kabīr and other *sant* poets, it is called *sākhī*, and in the *ādigranth* of the Sikhs, it is termed *salok* (from Sanskrit *śloka*, of which it was the vernacular equivalent). The basic unit of the narrative poems composed in the Avadhī dialect of Hindi (notably the Sufi romances and the *Rāmcaritmānas* of Tulsīdās) was a stanza of from five to eight distichs in the 16-moric *caupāī* meter followed by a dohā.

Hindi poets also used syllabic meters, the most common being two types of quatrains called *savaiyā* and *ghanākṣarī*. The former has lines of 22–26 syllables with a trisyllabic rhythm and a medial caesura; the ghanākṣarī line has three feet of eight syllables and a fourth of seven or eight. The tetrasyllabic rhythm of the latter prevailed in other vernaculars, which used mainly syllabic meters. The most common meter in Eastern India (Bengali, Assamese, and Oriya) was the *payār*, a rhyming couplet used for both lyric and narrative poetry. Here, each line has 14 syllables divided 8 + 6 but subdivisible into a 4 + 4 + 4 + 2 structure. Another popular couplet form was the *tripadī*, of which each line has two feet of equal length, often with end rhyme, followed by a third that is slightly longer, e.g., 6 + 6 + 8 or 8 + 8 + 10.

Similar to the payār are the *abhaṅga* and the *ovī*, the most popular forms used by Marathi poets. The shorter type of abhaṅga is composed of rhyming octosyllabic sections; the longer abhaṅga has lines of four feet (6 + 6 + 6 + 4 syllables) with the second and third rhyming. The ovī is considered a folk meter from which the abhaṅga derived. Its first three feet are of equal length and have end rhyme, while the fourth is slightly shorter and rhymeless.

These are the most common types of meter. The theorists describe many more, of which several are adaptations of Sanskrit meters or permutations of the basic vernacular ones, but the more recondite meters are usually confined to the work of scholastic court poets. Poetry in Urdu stayed within the Perso-Ar. trad., using principally the *ghazal and *masnavī forms.

Med. and mod. Tamil poets retained their purely indigenous meters, those who composed in the other Dravidian langs. (Kannada, Telugu, Malayalam) more readily assimilated the meters and vocabulary of Sanskrit. Kannada and Telugu poetry, of which the earliest examples emerged about a thousand years ago, used meters derived from Sanskrit as well as Dravidian meters that are found earlier in Tamil, adapting some of them to the Sanskrit method of *scansion. Though Telugu poets were stricter in observing metrical rules, they modified the Sanskrit meters more than their Kannada counterparts and also accepted *enjambment. Many of the meters used in Malayalam bear Sanskrit names but are freer than Sanskrit in their syllabic structure.

A form of *prose poem in Kannada is found in the short *vacana* (utterances) of Basavaṇṇa (12th c.) and subsequent Vīraśaiva poets of Karnataka. Comparable, though more regular, are the *vākh* of the Kashmiri female saint Lalla (or Lal Ded; early 14th c.): these are quatrains of approximately seven syllables and four stresses in each line with occasional rhyme. In the 19th c., familiarity with Eng. poetry encouraged Bengali poets, and later those writing in other langs., to experiment with *blank verse and enjambment. Rabindranath Tagore, besides writing blank and *free verse, maintained the moric trad. but simplified the rules for measuring quantity by giving all open syllables the value of one mora and all closed syllables two.

*See* ASSAMESE POETRY; BENGALI POETRY; CLASSICAL PROSODY; GREEK POETRY; GUJARATI POETRY; HINDI POETRY; INDIA, POETRY OF; KANNADA POETRY; MALAYALAM

POETRY; MARATHI POETRY; ORIYA POETRY; PUNJABI PO-
ETRY; TAMIL POETRY AND POETICS; TELUGU POETRY.

■ E. W. Hopkins, *The Great Epic of India* (1901), esp.
ch. 4; E. V. Arnold, *Vedic Metre* (1905)—the standard
authority; A. B. Keith, *A History of Sanskrit Literature*
(1920), esp. ch. 20, secs. 3–4; H. Weller, "Beiträge zur
Metrik der Veda," *Zeitschrift für Indologie und Iranis-
tik* 12 (1922); J. Hermann, "Über die älteste indischer
Metriker und ihr Werk," *Indian Linguistics* 3 (1933);
H. D. Velankar, "Apabhraṁśa Metres," *Journal of the
University of Bombay (Arts)* 131 (1933), 137 (1936); and
"Chandaḥ kośa," *Journal of the University of Bombay
(Arts)* 131 (1933)—rpt. as App. 2 to his *Kavidarpaṇa*
(1960); A. C. Chettair, *Advanced Studies in Tamil Poetry*
(1943); H. N. Randle, "Sanskrit and Greek Metres,"
*Journal of Oriental Research* 17 (1947); H. D. Velankar,
"Prosodical Practices of Sanskrit Poets," *Journal of the
Bombay Branch of the Royal Asiatic Society* n.s. 24–25
(1948–49); H. Weller, "Metrica," *Beiträge zur indischen
Philologie und Altertumskunde* (1951); V. Raghavan,
"Sanskrit and Prakrit Metres," *Journal of the Madras
University* 23 (1952–53); L. Renou, *L'Inde Classique*,
v. 2 (1953), App. 2, and "Sur la Structure du Kavya,"
*Journal Asiatique* 247 (1959); M. Sinha, *The Histori-
cal Development of Medieval Hindi Prosody* (1964);
A. K. Warder, *Pali Metre* (1967); A. D. Mukherji,
"Lyric Metres in Jayadeva's Gitagovinda," *Journal of the
Asiatic Society of Bengal* (1967, pub. 1969); H. Jacobi,
*Kleine Schriften* (1970); P. Kiparsky, "Metrics and Mor-
phophonemics in the *Rigveda*," *Contributions to Gener-
ative Phonology*, ed. M. K. Brame (1972); D. Matthews
and C. Shackle, "Note on Prosody and Metre," *An An-
thology of Classical Urdu Love Lyrics*, ed. D. Matthews
and C. Shackle (1972); *Indian Literature*, ed. A. Pod-
dar (1972); N. Sen, *Early Eastern New Indo-Aryan Ver-
sification* (1973); Allen; G. Nagy, *Comparative Studies
in Greek and Indic Metre* (1974); S. Pollock, *Aspects of
Versification in Sanskrit Lyric Poetry* (1977); S. Subrah-
manyan, *The Commonness in the Metre of the Dravidian
Langs.* (1977); J. F. Vigorita, "The Trochaic Gayatri,"
*ZVS* 93 (1979); C. E. Fairbanks, "The Development
of Hindi Oral Narrative Meter," *DAI* 42 (1982);
S. Lienhard, *A History of Classical Poetry: Sanskrit–Pali–
Prakrit*, ed. J. Gonda (1984); E. Gerow, "Jayadeva's Po-
etics and the Classical Style," *JAOS* 109.4 (1989)—spec.
iss.; J. S. Klein, *On Verbal Accentuation in the Rigveda*
(1992); W.P. Lehmann, "Poetic Principles in the South
Asian Literary Tradition: Interrelatedness of Grammar,
Prosody, and Other Elements of Language," *College Lit-
erature* 23.1 (1996); M. Witzel, "Sarama and the Panis:
Origins of Prosimetric Exchange in Archaic India,"
*Prosimetrum: Crosscultural Perspectives on Narrative
in Prose and Verse*, ed. J. Harris and K. Reichl (1997);
U. Niklas, "A Short Introduction to Tamil Prosody,
Part I," *Kolam* 3 (1999); A. Sharma, "Of Śūdras, Sūtas,
and Ślokas: Why is the Mahābhārata Preeminently in
the Anuṣṭubh Metre?" *Indo-Iranian Journal* 43 (2000);
A. S. Deo, "The Metrical Organization of Classi-
cal Sanskrit Verse," *JL* 43 (2007); A. Mahoney, "The
Feet of Greek and Sanskrit Verse," *Greek and Latin

*from an Indo-European Perspective*, ed. C. George et al.
(2007).

E. GEROW (CL. LANGS.);
A. W. ENTWISTLE (MOD. VERNACULARS)

## INDIGENOUS AMERICAS, POETRY OF THE

I. Amazonia
II. Tahuantinsuyu
III. Anahuac
IV. Turtle Island

Knowing what may or may not constitute the roots
of poetry and poetics indigenous to America involves
factors specific to the continent. The first issues from its
sheer size and shape, esp. in the midriff tropical zone.
Extending northwest from Brazil, the Am. tropics
cover one fifth of the globe, an ancient, unbroken, and
culturally rich landmass found on no other continent.
Then, from Alaska to Tierra del Fuego, confidently
identified langs. and even lang. families are myriad,
some written long before Rome could impose its alpha-
bet. In Mesoamerica (roughly the tropics north of the
isthmus and self-defining as *Anahuac*), stone inscrip-
tions written in the visible lang. known as *tlacuilolli*
in Nahuatl—a script that may represent sound while
depending on the phonetics of no particular speech—
date back more than two millennia and find elaborate
expression in scrolls, maps, and screen-fold books of
native paper and deerskin (known as the *codices*). Be-
fore and after the Classic Period (3d to 10th c. CE), the
related story of lowland Maya *hieroglyphs is similar.
Their speech-specific phonetics were transcribed into
the Roman alphabet after the invasion, in the *Chilam
Balam* books of Chumayel and other Yucatecan towns,
notable for their poetic wordplay with philosophical
paradoxes and puns emanating from understandings of
time both long resident and Eur.

Once arrived, the Eur. invaders are notorious for
having burned whole libraries of books in Mesoamer-
ica. On the Pacific Rim, the same fate was accorded
in the Andes to libraries of Inca texts written in the
knotted cord script known in Quechua as the *quipu*.
It is now slowly becoming apparent (Julien, Brokaw)
that the quipu recorded in Quechua—besides statisti-
cal information pertinent to the pastoral economy and
subjects of the Inca Tahuantinsuyu and their calendar—
kingship drama, chronicles, and liturgy, notably the
*hymns in praise of the supreme Inca, sun king and
shepherd/llama herder. In 18th-c. Europe, these served
as a source for the *Encyclopédie* (notably in its entry on
script) and inspired the royal performances at Versailles
known as *Indes galantes* that were enhanced by Jean-
Philippe Rameau's music and Jean-François Marmon-
tel's prose.

Besides cultural geography, ling. diversity, and writ-
ten precedent, most telling of all these given factors in
America are the recent revisions of the archaeological
underpinnings on which lit. hist. and geography ulti-
mately rely. Most salient is the case of Amazonia now
recognized as the site of the continent's oldest ceram-

ics (Neves), while the clarification of texts inscribed at Chavin de Huantar, the metropolis on the uppermost Amazon that served as portal to the Pacific Ocean, confirmed them as an enduring ideological premise (Burger, Salomon 2004). In the isthmus that joins South America to Anahuac east to west, pointers to ancient travel routes in fresh eds. of classic texts such as the Toltec lament (*Popol Vuh*, 6065–67; *Cantares mexicanos*, folio 26v) are corroborated in the 1570 *Relaciones geográficas* of Cholula and Tepeaca and by archaeology at San Agustín (Colombia), Subtiaba (Nicaragua), and Yojoa (Honduras). Similar attention has been paid to the northwest continuations of Mesoamerica (Neurath), long distorted by U.S. discourse on its Southwest, esp. when it touches the open wound of Turtle Island's Ghost Dance. Chosen in 1825 by the Iroquois historian David Cusick to refer to America north of Mexico, *Turtle Island* has long been the term used by the Algonkian peoples to refer to the widespread territory of their langs.

In this predicament, a useful way to proceed is to rely wherever possible on native authority and start by acknowledging a category of classic texts that weld political hists. onto the world ages of Am. genesis, whose conception and scope make them poetry in the fullest sense. At the same time, we need not relinquish that wondered sense of a New World that animated thinkers in the late 16th c., before the fetters of Eur. ideology and social control (let alone mapping) had tightened. Of these, Michel de Montaigne merits close attention, for the pair of Am. *Essais* that effectively chart the continent, profoundly unsettling the authority of the Bible and the Greco-Roman classics. "Des cannibales" (1580) acknowledges the lowland rainforest of America as a prime source of poetry. "Des coches" (1588) does the same for the Inca and the Aztec empires along the continent's Pacific Rim, Montaigne having read in the meantime Francisco López de Gómara's *Historia general de las Indias* (1552).

With Montaigne and native validation in mind, we proceed, then, by discussing in turn four first sources of New World poetry: Amazonia, Tahuantinsuyu, Anahuac, and Turtle Island, each in its way an indispensable precedent for poetry composed in indigenous speech and in imported Port., Sp., and Eng. A corresponding range of poems trans. and in the original is available in Alcina Franch, Péret 1969, Rothenberg 1972, and Dorn and Brotherston, while Tomlinson provides wide overall contextualization. For drama in verse, see Meneses.

**I. Amazonia.** As the allies of the Fr. who ensured them victory over the Tupiniquin and the Port., the Tupinamba of Brazil (or France Antarctique) were invited to Henry II's court at Rouen in 1550, where they reenacted their triumph in a rainforest setting, singing songs of victory in their lang. A precedent for Montaigne, the event effectively belonged to the Americanist royal court trad. furthered at Versailles in the Indes galantes performances, which lauded Louis the Sun King in terms borrowed from Inca liturgy. Direct contact with the Tupinamba at Rouen under Charles IX and acquaintance with someone who had lived in their territory provided Montaigne with the two examples of native poetry that he included in "Des cannibales."

In the genre of the taunt (*carbet*), Montaigne's first cannibal poem fuses standard Eur. fear of naked savages who terrify enemy captives by threatening to eat them with the core drama of the Christian Eucharist and actual instances of anthropophagy among the Europeans of Montaigne's day. For their part, as members of the Tupi-Guaraní lang. family and culture, the Tupinamba authors of the taunt explicitly draw on notions of transubstantiation and eschatology widespread in extensive poetic texts composed in Tupi terms and in the Tupi tongue. In them, a principal reference is the *yvy tenonde* (Land without Ill), an obtainable earthly paradise that has for centuries inspired pilgrimage along the length of the Amazon. Fleeing Eur. invaders in 1549, a group of coastal Tupi are reported to have traveled up to Chachapoyas, the ancient Andean city of circular ruins. After missionary beginnings, these texts have come to constitute an enduring focus for anthropology in Brazil, in the work of Egon Schaden, Curt Nimuendajú, and more recently Eduardo Viveiros (Sá). They are usefully complemented in Eng. by Whitehead's ed. of the autobiographical *Warhaftige Historia* (1557) by Hans Staden, who, when captive, heard Tupi taunts firsthand, in the flesh as it were.

In his essay, besides the taunt, Montaigne dwells on a Tupi poem he called *anacreontic, which asks a snake to allow the speaker to copy the exquisite designs on its skin, in a girdle he would give to his lover. Reviled in biblical teaching, the snake here is honored in an interspecies dialogue characteristic of Amazonian poetics. It plays on the idea of the snake's pride in its speckled hue, paying keen attention to visual design in the serpentine labyrinths likewise found on the continent's oldest known ceramics. In Marajó, the island at the river's mouth, these reached extremes of sophistication.

The Tupi trad., which includes Guaraní, the first lang. of Paraguay, for centuries served as the lingua franca or *Lingua Geral* of lowland South America. In the 20th c., it was enriched by no less than two trans. (by Eduardo Saguier in 1951 and Dacunda Díaz in 1996) of José Hernández's *Martín Fierro*, the great gaucho epic of the Argentinean pampa (see GAUCHO POETRY), being ethnically the despised mother tongue of the eponymous hero; more recently, it has come to play a role in the cultural politics of MercoSur. The poetics of this trad. delights in exploring how word concepts are born in the first place and inhere in trains of thought. These are superbly exemplified in the classic work *Ayvu rapyta* of the Mbya Guaraní, a title that means something like the source of human lang.; through intense cogitation, it establishes the rain forest itself as the mid-earth from whose trees lang. flows.

The concentration on dream and the flow of thought, the dreaming of the world into existence seen as a precondition for deed and creation, may be held to typify Amazonian genesis and characterize work of Umasin Panlon and other authors of FOIRN (Federação das Organizações Indígenas do Rio Negro). Musings on these beginnings by the Witoto gathered by Preuss begin thus:

> a phantasma, naino, nothing else
> the father touched the image of the phantasm
> touch a secret, nothing else
> the father Nainu-ema, who-has-the-phantasm,
>     held it by a dream
> to himself
> thought hard about it

Rothenberg translated Preuss's text to great effect in *Technicians of the Sacred*, a foundational work of *ethnopoetics.

Studies and anthols. of Tupi-Guaraní poetry and poetics (Cadogan 1959, Bareiro Saguier) have abounded since Montaigne's pioneer commentary, and the trad. has been indispensable to the growth of Brazilian lit. Poems and songs in Lingua Geral were collected in the late 19th c. by João Barbosa Rodrigues, when they could still be heard in the markets and festivals in the lower Amazon. He gave the result of his labors under the hybrid title *Poranduba amazonense*, an abundant anthol. of texts that reserves a special place for the Amazonian midwife. We learn of the greenstone *muiraquitã*, the charm typically carved in the form of early vertebrates like the frog or the fish and bestowed on the father of the female rather than the male child; the lean new moon and the full moon mirrored in the lake that yields the *muiraquitã*; moons as measures of time, sidereal (27.32 nights) when blackfaced incestuous male and synodic (29.54 nights) when female lying in her hammock; and the armadillo (*tatu*), whose dance leads to safety deep in the forest.

In their ed. of Joaquim de Sousândrade's substantial epic *O Guesa* (1888), Augusto and Haroldo de Campos have drawn out the significance of these precedents for the remarkable sequence of cantos known as Tatuturema, the armadillo dance-song that celebrates local understandings of genesis. In the complex societies characteristic of Manaus and the confluence of the Amazon with the Rio Negro, Lingua Geral also preserved the legends and the night music generated by the "devil" Jurupari (Medeiros).

Jurupari, himself a recalcitrant product of the midwife cult and the focus of a major epic, affirms his gender and his origins by tracing them to the Milky Way and a gestation period said to last ten (sidereal) moons rather than the usual nine (synodic). He does this when literally orchestrating his federation. He bestows on each of its 11+3 wind instruments, seen and played exclusively by males, word-poem definitions, each belonging to a distinct lang. or dialect of multilingual Manaus, overall Arawak to the east and Tucano to the west. Jurupari appears as the lure in the *Travels on the Amazon and Rio Negro* of Charles Darwin's contemp. A. F. Wallace (ch. 17) and, after him, in Oscar Wilde's *The Picture of Dorian Gray* (ch. 11).

The Mbya Guaraní *Ayvu rapyta* epitomizes lowland South America as a poetics of dreaming the world into being that is simultaneously cosmogony, a genesis poetic in dealing with primordial origins (Cadogan 1959). In the Carib trad., it is matched as such by *Watunna* of the Soto and by the Makunaima corpus of their Pemon neighbors. Recalled in poetically dense Adeni (a kind of script within speech) and ritually recited at the annual harvest festival of its name, *Watunna* (Civrieux) recounts the felling of the great tree whose branches and roots conjoined sky and earth and whose petrified stump is the Marahuaca massif, the Soto homeland in Venezuela. The felling precipitates a great flood and reveals Marahuaca to be a watershed common via the (hydrographically improbable) Casiquiare canal to both the Amazon and the Orinoco.

The felled tree also initiates the saga of agriculture, the first seedlings being brought from Roraima, a petrified tree stump to the northeast and a botanical El Dorado fondly recalled in Pemon dream songs. While people work in the fields learning to plant from the birds, the known loners tapir and jaguar engage in a wry dialogue that opposes the former's slow wits with the keen senses of the latter in the wild forests of the night (William Blake's bright-burning tiger began life as a jaguar from Surinam). The climax of the whole planting saga comes when Huioo, the great water snake, seeing all the birds flying resplendent above, leaps up in the air to join them, crying "I want my feather crown." There could hardly be a clearer pointer to the multiple meanings embodied in the hybrid bird-reptile figure revered throughout the continent and seminal in Mesoamerican genesis as the plumed serpent Quetzalcoatl.

Gathered by Theodor Koch-Grünberg, the Pemon texts deal with these and cognate motifs, like love for an evanescent fish bride, a fearsome father-in-law figure, and the trickster evident elsewhere in Carib lit. that came to inspire Mário de Andrade's epochal novel *Macunaíma* (1928).

In Surinam, the story of the Trio culture hero Pereperewa lends Carib creation a particular resonance at the moment when he is taken by his fish bride to meet her alligator father, who proves to be a creature of many simultaneous identities (Rivière). Reflected in the dark waters of the river, his red cayman eyes produce terror, as does his size as he rises to reveal the load he carries on his back like a canoe, a word synonymous with *alligator*. Surviving the encounter, Pereperewa learns the advantages of cultivation, in food he is able to take back to his people: peanuts, chili peppers, squash, and the Amazonian staple manioc.

Archaeology is now corroborating the deeper reverberations of the Pereperewa story, fine example of Carib poetry that it is, in a cultural coherence that runs for millennia along the entire length of the Amazon. Toward the headwaters in the west, in the ancient city of Chavin, an obelisk carved about three millennia ago to represent two caimans and named after the Peruvian who excavated the city in the 1920s, Julio Tello, identifies the achievements of Amazonian agriculture as the "gifts of the caiman," specifying exactly the same examples as the Trio do today, far away toward the mouth of the Amazon.

If Tupi-Guaraní and Carib texts indicate the ancient and rich relationship between lowland South America and the Andes, so too do those of a third major Amazonian group, the Bororo-Gé, with whom Claude Lévi-Strauss in the 1930s began the work that culminated in the four volumes of *Mythologiques* (1964–71), the Bororo being the author of his primary myth. In their own *Enciclopédia* (1962–76), the Bororo highlight the dual role of the jaguar, founding father both terrestrial as the occupant of the last of the 7 caves and celestial as the first of the 11 constellations to rise over the eastern horizon. Implicit throughout their culture and songs and quite explicit in their painted jaguar skins (*adugo biri*), the significance of the Bororo pair of prime numbers 7 and 11 can, in its turn, be traced back to stonework at Chavin. There, to either hand in the great circular court, pairs of jaguars with such night-sky identification process toward the exit.

In the Muisca kingdoms that are now Colombia (Krickeberg), lowland precedent is celebrated in the corpus of greenstones directly reminiscent of the muiraquitá. One such from Sopó, adorned with the customary midwife motifs of frog and fish, is illustrated in Alexander von Humboldt's great work *Vues des cordillères et monuments des peuples indigènes de l'Amérique* (1810, plate 44), where it merits a commentary as substantial as that he accords to the Mexica Sunstone (plate 23). This logs the Guesa's indiction at 15 years (when the annual difference between sun and moon amounts to 15 nights and the difference between synodic and sidereal cycles of the moon amounts to 15 moons). Drawing on accounts of Muisca belief recorded by Pedro Simón and others, Humboldt's commentary on this greenstone directly inspired the first attempts in independent Latin America at the cl. Eur. epic genre, not only *O Guesa* but Andrés Bello's *Silvas americanas* (1823).

Within the larger Chibcha category, in lang. the Muisca are kindred of the Kogi of northern Colombia, the Cuna of Panama, and the Talamanca of Costa Rica. Kogi songs and legends are notable for naming the 11 constellations that match those of the Bororo and Desana in Amazonia and for monitoring the now ever-higher snow line in their mountains. A prime focus for the Cuna is the declaration by Nele de Kantule of the isthmian republic in 1925 within but independent of Panama.

Extensive and often recorded as verse or incantation in its own local script, Cuna lit. hinges on the *ikala* or "way," a mode proper to curing, initiation, the rhythms of the moon (*Ni*), childbirth (*Mu*), supporting the dead on the journey into the afterlife (*Serkan*), therapy, cosmogony (*Pap*), and political hist. that, in being inseparable from *myth*, is necessarily poetic. Performed over the course of a night once every moon, women sitting in a middle circle with men on three sides of the room, the most comprehensive is the *Tatkan ikala*, which stretches from beginnings of the world to the present. It falls into four parts: cosmic comings into being; epic deeds of culture heroes (*Neles*); migrations

and foundings of villages; and the invasion from Europe and its current consequences (Kramer).

Echoes of Amazonia are constant: the first forefather's two wives, one brown/black, the other white; the felling of the great tree of life, *Palu uala*, and the consequent flood; lunar incest instigated by the brother who advances on his sister's hammock in the dead of night, she being able to stain his face black, the whole being explicitly referred to the female synodic moon and the quicker male sidereal moon; and successive catastrophes inflicted on the world (flood, darkness, storm, warfare) that elaborate the world-age genesis story.

Diagnostic of the Chibcha territory common to the Muisca and the Cuna are creatures and objects formed of gold, the man named El Dorado celebrated in Muisca myth and goldwork and known as Organ in the ikala, and the specifically Cuna *Olopatte*, the golden platter on which early heroes arrive on earth. Also, explicit in the *Pap ikala*, though rare in world-age genesis in South America, is the epic that follows the course of the inner planets (Mercury and Venus), which appear to pass through the underworld in moving from the western sunset to the eastern dawn.

**II. Tahuantinsuyu.** In Quechua, the lang. of the Inca empire, *Tahuantinsuyu* means four districts. Montaigne finds poetry in its road system and sheer social organization: the causeway that ran "straight, even and fine" from Quito to Cuzco and the well-stocked palatial inns (*tambos*) along the way. Returning in conclusion to his title and theme ("Des coches"), he admires the blind courage of those who tried unsuccessfully to save Atahuallpa, in his litter, from Francisco Pizarro, in a tragedy that, unknown to Montaigne, entered the cycle of Quechua kingship drama (Lara 1957, 1969).

The early 17th-c. Quechua text known as the *Huarochirí Manuscript* (1991) makes clear the antiquity of the Tahuantinsuyu concept, tracing its beginnings to the deeds of Huarochirí's own culture hero Pariacaca. Commemorated by a stairway that joins Apurimac and the headwaters of the Amazon to Rimac (Lima) on the Pacific coast, Pariacaca starts life as a glorious snow-covered mountain on Huarochirí's horizon. With cosmic force, Pariacaca tames both the rainforest Antisuyu and the coastal Condesuyu, the latter supplying his demand for spondylus or thorny redshell oyster. Brought fresh to the highlands from the equatorial seas of Ecuador, spondylus had value as shell adornment and as shellfish delectable to eat. The bivalve spondylus (*mullo*) stands most tellingly as the initial glyph on the Tello obelisk at Chavin, and its mouth-womb is a motif in coastal ceramics, notably among the Moche, 1–500 CE.

Through his son, Pariacaca sets up the first Tahuantinsuyu dynasty, which passing through Ayacucho and other centers, eventually becomes Inca in Cuzco. Archaeologically, the fourfold Tahuantinsuyu emblem—the open Andean cross—is to be seen on the Tello obelisk, opposing Antisuyu caiman to Condesuyu spondylus, with Chinchasuyu extending to the north and Collasuyu to the south. Unambiguous and unmistakable, this open-cross emblem is also found in the isthmus, suggesting widespread recognition north and west of Chinchasuyu, to the very threshold of Anahuac.

As evidence of idolatry gathered by the mestizo priest Francisco de Ávila (who provided a brief Sp. trans. of the earlier chapters), the *Huarochirí* text leaves little doubt about the power of pagan belief in world-age genesis expressed through worship of *huacas* (phenomena, natural and constructed, of imposing size and significance), in cults centered typically on mountains like Pariacaca, the stairway over its shoulder that links Amazonian Apurimac with Rimac and canals on the continental watershed engineered to reverse the water flow in favor of Antisuyu and Amazonia. The narrative begins with the initial pair of destructions of the world through flood and solar eclipse; before each, a llama, through its finer senses, warns its duller human masters of approaching catastrophe, and each is tied to a period of five days. Though the biblical parallel is acknowledged in the flood, in the Andes, people are saved not by Noah but a mountain they flee toward. The eclipse provokes the uprising of pastoral creatures like the llama who foresaw it, a rebellion that results from the breaking of the interspecies contract that enables pastoralism in the first place. Christian ideology was seen to have broken this contract by privileging human over other life.

Thereafter, attention focuses on Pariacaca himself as main actor in the world-age genesis. Raining down volcanic fire, he destroys the primeval cannibal Caruincho, along with Caruincho's consort, and sets up Huaca guardians toward both Amazonia (Antisuyu) and the ocean (Condesuyu), thereby explicitly establishing the beginnings of Tahuantinsuyu. He then punishes the neighboring Colli for failing to respect fundamental laws of hospitality, sending them winds of hurricane force, evidence being found in eroded rocks of human shape. Like the first pair of catastrophes of flood and eclipse, this pair of events—rain of fire and hurricane—too is tied to periods of five days each, a score in all.

A first concern in the *Huarochirí* text is Pariacaca's precedence over the main god in the Inca system, Viracocha. In Quechua, Viracocha is the focus of extensive liturgy, most concisely the hymns or prayers of the Zithuwa ritual (Rowe 1953) that accords him the *epithets earth-maker, lightning, guardian of crops,* and *herder of humans and llamas alike.*

A work contemp. with the *Huarochirí* narrative, Guáman Poma's (ca. 1535–1616) *El primer nueva corónica y buen gobierno* (ca. 1615; see Murra and Adorno), registers the very geography of the Inca Tahuantinsuyu in terms of the music, dance, and song characteristic of each quarter and the metropolitan center, Cuzco. Intercalated with page-framed images, this alphabetic text in Quechua and Sp. notes its immediate source as quipu records. In its own version of world-age genesis, people of each successive world age are distinguished by such features as clothing, houses, and style of prayer. Poma's work reveres the pastoral llama, who at the *raymi* solstice festival literally gives the keynote for the Inca emperor to begin the songs and music proper to Cuzco at the center of the four *suyu.*

El Inca Garcilaso de le Vega (1539–1616) gives a privileged version of this heritage in his *Comentarios reales* (1609), also contemp. with the *Huarochirí* narrative and Poma's *Corónica.* Garcilaso confirms the literary functions of the quipu in recording poetry and chronicle, as well as counts of llama herds and people. He includes a hymn collected by Blas Valera (1545–97) in a trilingual version—Quechua, Sp., and Eng.—as well as a love poem, measures of his taste as courtly scion of the imperial Inca. The two Quechua poems quoted by Garcilaso had the egregious distinction of being chosen by J. G. Herder as "voices of the people in song" (*Stimmen der Völker in Liedern*), songs of wild Am. people at that ("die Wilden"). Persuasive as Herder's sense of *Stimmen* may be, his venture into Inca hymnology exemplarily signals a mismatch between beginnings of Eur. romantic need and this branch of Am. poetics with its courtly pastoral underpinnings:

> Viracocha, you say
> may the sun be, may the night be
> in peace, in safety
> sun, shine on and illume
> the Incas, the people, the servants
> whom you have shepherded

The kingship verse drama *Apu Ollanta* (1735) exerted such strong appeal in colonial times that Spain outlawed performances of it after Tupac Amaru II's uprising of 1780, which foreshadowed independence. Deriving from the Quechua *haraui* (elegiac song; cf. *haravek,* the term for poet) and integrated early into *Spanish prosody, the verse form known as the *yaraví* enjoyed great appeal during this period, thanks initially to the martyr poet Mariano Melgar (1790–1815), while Wallparamachi and his guerrilla fighters sang in Quechua to further their struggle. Extremely sensitive accounts of similar forms in context, like the *huayno* and the *jailli,* are found in the novels and essays of José María Arguedas (1911–69), the anthropologist-poet who compiled the landmark collection *Canto Kechwa* (1938). The resilient huayno conjoins native and mestizo and respects distinctive styles in Huamanga, Apurimac, and elsewhere (Rowe 1996). Some idea of the powerful political charge these trads. acquired during the Sendero Luminoso (Shining Path) era can be had from the well-titled volume *Sangre de los cerros* (1987) by the Montoya brothers. Their broader aesthetic potential is patent in the work of Odi González (b. 1962) and the trilingual (Quechua, Sp., Eng.), New York-based Fredy Amilcar Roncalla (b. 1953), among others. At the turn of the century (1905), Alencastre, a landowner from Cuzco (see Warak'a 1999), had been preceded at the other end of the social scale by *Tarmap pacha huaray,* an anthol. of Quechua poems from Tarma got together by self-professed pariahs ("unos parias").

Expatriate for much of his life in Paris, the poet César Vallejo (1892–1938) repeatedly acknowledged a debt to his Andean birthplace, from the exquisitely figured gold panels of the Cuzco Coricancha (*Nostalgias imperiales,* 1918) and the wave-and-step motifs of the coastal architecture (*Escalas melografiadas,* 1923) to the drama of Inca power (*La piedra cansada*, 1938), based on a legend told in Poma's chronicle.

Poetry in Ecuador is known in Quichua, a version of the Inca Quechua that, dating back to Atahuallpa's Quito, has its own Amazon approaches (Harrison). As for Bolivia, the superbly documented study of indigenous lits. in the Andes by Arnold and Dios Yapita has made it possible for the first time in Eng. to appreciate the immense wealth and complexity of the entire region's poetry and poetics. This is strikingly so with regard to the Aymara and Collasuyu precedent for Inca and Quechua practice, within the pastoral economy and ideology characteristic of the Andes, starting with Cuzco's appropriation of Tiahuanaco herds. The authors are able to show how much is owed in Andean song and drama to the Aymara, from the quipu numeracy of tethering and the weft and warp of the textile text to principles of origin and rulership.

Diagonally opposite Chinchasuyu and its extension into Colombia and the isthmus, Collasuyu has its heart in Lake Titicaca and the pastoral wealth of the Aymara in Bolivia (Lara 1947) and finds its southern frontier in what is now Chile. On the other side of this Tahuantinsuyu frontier stand the fiercely resistant Mapuche, who, having held off the Inca, did the same when the Spaniards arrived, to be commemorated in Alonso de Ercilla's epic *La Araucana* (1569–89).

Known as *Ftah Mapu* in their lang. (Mapudungun), Mapuche territory concentrates in the landscape of the southern cordillera (Pire Mahuida) around Lacar and the lakeland passage between Chile and Argentina, which functions likewise as the setting for world-age genesis far more ancient than those nation states. In this case, refuge from the flood is sought in Mount Threng Threng and the fossil-rich strata of Trompul, bones of the fish to which protohumans reverted. *Foro-lil* (bone-stone), these fossils kilometers above sea level correspond to nocturnal shades who emerge to haunt as snake, bird, and vampire, with fin-wings and beady eyes that stare back through time (it was here that such fossils were shown to Darwin during his voyage on the *Beagle*). The floodwater threshed up by the snake Kai-Kai in the mountain lakes finds parallels along the ocean coast in terrifying tidal waves and tsunami known as *tripalafken*. After the catastrophes of the world ages, the Mapuche community clusters around the emblematic tree of the Pacific coastal forests as the face carved in the east-facing Rehue and defers to the insight and curing power of the Machi shaman (most often a woman).

Reflecting the cultural resilience and political wisdom that has enabled them still to defend at least some small part of their territory, the poetry of the Mapuche, reborn in 1966 in the work of Sebastián Queupul (b. 1944), stands out on the continental map. *Ül* (Song) is the title of a 1998 collection of four poets: Leonel Lienlaf (b. 1969), Elicura Chihuailaf (b. 1952), Jaime Luis Huenún (b. 1967), and Graciela Huinao (b. 1956), whose work privileges their native tongue (Vicuña).

Previously recognized and translated into Sp. by the Chilean poet Raúl Zurita (1989), Lienlaf contrives to recover the sensibility that brings together for the Mapuche, in their lang., world-age genesis, military struggle initially against the sword and the Christian cross, and then "pacification" by machine gun on both sides of the Andes. Enduring over "a hundred generations" and threaded into the Rehue and the Machi chant, time is marked in tree growth by *rupamum* (footsteps). This is the time of ancient trans-Andean memories, recorded just after World War I by Kössler-Ilg, that extend from world-age genesis to the late 19th-c. resistance led by Calfucurá.

Chihuailaf is notable for choosing to translate into Mapudungun the fellow Chilean poet Pablo Neruda (1904–73) in *Ti kom vl* (1995). The poems and volumes of Neruda's that Chihuailaf selects, and the way he plays Mapudungun against Sp., brilliantly begin to recover for Chile exactly the imaginative possibilities that Neruda came to dream of during and after his Am. epic *Canto general* (1950). Translated as "Todos los cantos," the title poem breathes local life and hist. into the elegiac image of the trees and stones of Arauco that closes the first canto of Neruda's epic, peopling and enlivening them in ways unsuspected half a century ago.

**III. Anahuac.** Known as *Anahuac* between the seas, Atlantic to the north and Pacific to the south, and as *Amoxtlan* (the "land of books" in Nahuatl), Mesoamerica has long held a special position in the geography of the continent. Montaigne's encounter with it is striking, since, as proof of its high civilization, in his second Am. essay he actually cites the cosmic poem of world-age genesis: "They believed the state of the world to be divided into five ages, as in the life of five succeeding Suns, whereof four had already ended their course or time." Montaigne had translated his text from Gómara's Sp., who, in turn, had drawn on Motolinía (pseud. of Fray Toribio de Benavente, 1482–1568), an early extirpator of idolatry in Cholula, deeply familiar with the Nahuatl lang. inherited by the Mexica or Aztecs.

The extant version of this cosmic poem closest to the Nahuatl trad. of the Aztecs and their predecessors is found in the *Cuauhtitlan Annals* (ca. 1570; Bierhorst 1992) and begins:

Y ynin ce tonatiuh onmanca yn itzinecan
4 atl yn itonal
. mitoa atonatiuh
yc ipan in ye yquac
yn mochih yn atocoac.
Yn anenenztihuac
yn tlaca michtihuac

Y ynic ome tonatiuh onmanca
4 ocelotl yn tonal catca
motenehua ocelotonatiuh
ypan mochiuh
tlapachiuh yn ylhuicatl

(The first sun to be founded
has the Sign Four Water,
it is called Water Sun.
Then it happened
that water carried everything away

everything vanished
people changed into fish.

The second sun to be founded
has the Sign Four Jaguar
it is called Jaguar Sun.
Then it happened
that the sky broke down)

The Nahuatl text goes on to tell how, since the sun no longer followed its course, night came and, in the dark, people were torn to pieces by jaguars plunging from the sky; this was the time of the giants. In the third sun, called 4 Rain, fire and volcanic ash (*tezontli*) rained down, and rocks boiled and twisted up; in the fourth, 4 Wind, wind carried everything away, and people changed into monkeys. Having of its own accord started to move (a pun on *ollin*, which also denotes both rubber and earthquake), the current fifth sun, 4 Ollin, will end in earthquake and hunger.

Anticipating Western geology and evolutionary theory by several centuries, the cataclysms and metamorphoses of Anahuac genesis take us back to tlacuilolli, the visual lang. of Mesoamerica from which the Nahuatl had been transcribed. Of the several examples of this world-age story that exist on paper and in stone in tlacuilolli, easily the most monumental is the Aztec or Mexica Sunstone or *Piedra de los soles*, the inscribed basalt disk that before the invasion proclaimed the world-age story in Tenochtitlan's Templo Mayor. In chronological terms, the sunstone locates the 5,200 or so years of our current fifth world age, named Nauh (4) Ollin, as a fifth (in the thumb-fingers proportion 1:4) of the precessional year that, in turn, forms a core unit of the many millions of years of genesis inscribed in Maya hieroglyphs and reflected in tlacuilolli.

The recovery of the sunstone in 1790 from under a corner of Mexico City's nearby cathedral enabled Humboldt to publish an image of it with an extensive commentary in his *Vues des cordillères*. Ideologically, the event fomented the independence cause. In poetics, susceptible to decipherment in many pages of alphabetic prose yet succinct and synchronic in its circular form, a map of simultaneity, the sunstone has come to be acknowledged as a superb poem in the visual lang. tlacuilolli. In early 20th-c. Europe, it became the prompt for the first of Guillaume Apollinaire's "concrete" *Calligrammes*, "Lettre-Océan" (see CALLIGRAMME, CONCRETE POETRY, VISUAL POETRY).

In Anahuac, the fullest alphabetic account of this cosmic saga can be found in the *Popol Vuh*, the "Bible of America" written in the mid-16th c., in their lang., by the Maya Quiché of Guatemala. A narrative in paired verses, this text starts from the very beginnings of time and falls into two parts. These hinge on the creation of humankind from maize, a motif developed, e.g., in Classic Period hieroglyphic texts at Palenque that correlate the event with the start of the Olmec and Maya Era just less than 5,200 years ago. In the ingenious way that the text itself offers clues about how they connect and interweave, the main phases of part I

can be seen to correspond to the sunstone, notably the metamorphoses into fish in the flood of the first age and into monkeys (elder brothers of the Hero Twins) in the hurricane of the fourth; these events are recounted in Nahuatl in the *Cuauhtitlan Annals* and *Leyenda de los soles*. Esp. vivid and also reflected in Maya art are the domestic revolt in the eclipse in the second age, the Twins' childhood taming of bird-reptile monsters in the volcanic landscape of the third age, and their epic descent to the underworld Xibalba that prepares for the maize creation.

The line of tlacuilolli texts to which the sunstone account belongs begins in the east with the world-age *Map of Coixtlahuaca*, the town that controlled the east-west tribute road taken by the Mexica in the reign of Moctezuma I (1440–69).

At the first level, the *Coixtlahuaca* text is overtly a map of four places subject to that city, which, again in the simultaneity characteristic of tlacuilolli, may be read both as town toponyms and as emblems of the world ages. Mictlan (southeast) and Teotlillan (northeast) recall flood and eclipse, while Nexapa (southwest) and Tepexic (northwest) recall rain of fire and hurricane. While this is the pattern inherited in the sunstone, the Mexica make one critical change. For Coixtlahuaca, the fish-tail caiman seen rising from volcanic ash in Nexapa (curiously reminiscent of the life form inscribed on Chavin's obelisk) reappears above in Tepexic, endowed with Quetzalcoatl feathers, atop a twin peak baring tooth and claw. For Tenochtitlan, the two caimans encircle the disk with imperial might, fish tails above, arms and heads (crowned by the septentrion) below. Moreover, their form invokes the metamorphic Xiuhcoanahual, the ophidian familiar that, for the Mexica, configures world-age genesis and the gyres of time counted out on the literal scales of the sunstone caiman.

The sunstone likewise reworks the central chapter of *Codex Borgia* of Cholula, whose chronicles tell of the road east toward the isthmus and beyond, to Popayan and South America. Like the affine screen-folds *Cospi* and *Vaticanus B*, *Codex Borgia* opens with an eight-page chapter based on human gestation, the 9x29 nights of the *tonalpoualli*, which simultaneously may be read as the succession of suns and in space as a map of Anahuac between north and south seas, dazzling tlacuilolli prospects of tropical America seen from south (east to right) and north (east to left). Read from top to bottom, the 10 + 8 pages of *Borgia*'s central chapter focus rather on Mesoamerica's other main time cycle, the year of 18 Feasts each of 20 days, beginning with the summer solstice, and involve a turn at midwinter from the end of one side of the screen-fold text to the start of the other. In the switch from recto to verso, the text even contrives visually to register the winter solstice as the passage through the underworld followed by the inner planets and the hero twins of the *Popol Vuh*. The codex pages configure a supremely elegant time map of tropical America.

The highland Maya *Popol Vuh* of the Quiché coincides with and interestingly differs on doctrinal points of diet from the genesis account of the neighboring Cakchiquels, on the shores of Lake Atitlan. This focus is also that of the Quiché dance drama *Rabinal Achí*. Like *Ollanta* and other Inca kingship propaganda and like an abundance of missionary plays in Quechua, Tupi, Nahuatl, and other langs. whose roots are deeply pre-Cortesian, this highland Maya work explores the boundaries between verse and theater, as Tedlock expertly shows in his ed. (2003).

The lowland Maya version of world-age genesis, transcribed in part into the alphabet from hieroglyphic stanzas (Alvarez), is found in the *Chilam Balam* books of the towns of Yucatan (Barrera Vásquez and Rendón). The *Book of Chumayel* excels in its witty play with biblical notions of time, the successive invasions of the peninsula in which the Christians come third, and the riddles of Zuyua that are invitations to brilliant conceptual insight formally derived from political tests of candidates for official position in the Katun calendar system.

In the dense polyphonic epic that issues into the current world age and Era, the hieroglyphic antecedent (Dresden Codex) has recently been shown to resolve the long-standing debate about correlating its inaugural date (4 Ahau 8 Cumku) with the Roman calendar (Julian day 584.283 in the year 3114 BCE).

Reflecting on the consequences of Eur. arrival, the *Book of Chumayel* draws on the hieroglyph-based prophecy chronicles of the Katun and Tun calendar cycles. (As *Cuceb*, the latter are meticulously edited in Bierhorst's *Four Masterworks*). One such prophecy chronicle begins thus:

> [T]he true God, the true Dios, came, but this was the origin too of affliction for us. The origin of tax, of our giving *them* alms, of trial through the grabbing of petty cacao money, of trial by blowgun, stomping the people, violent removal, forced debt created by false testimony, petty litigation, harassment, violent removal . . .

Such incredulous pain echoes that expressed in Nahuatl in the *Tlatelolco Annals* (1528) and indeed exemplifies a whole mode of postinvasion composition (León-Portilla 1964a).

Because of its scale and ambition in presenting world-age genesis in sharply poetic terms, the *Huarochirí Manuscript* has been referred to as the *Popol Vuh* of the Andes. Apt, the comparison requires that we acknowledge the level of theoretical understanding that, during the second world-age eclipse, may equate the pastoral llamas who rebelled in the Andes with their nearest domesticated equivalents in Mesoamerica, dogs and turkeys.

As the provenance of screen-fold books, notably *Codex Borgia*, Cholula was known as the Rome of New Spain. Guardian of cults stemming from the Olmec, this pyramid city was a major precedent for the Mexica, as they make clear in postinvasion codices like *Telleriano Remensis* and in the Nahuatl of their "Twenty Sacred Hymns."

Looking for evidence of idolatry, the Franciscan missionary Bernardino de Sahagún (ca. 1499–1590), whose 12-book *Florentine Codex* (completed 1577) grew from the four, dense tlacuilolli chapters of the *Tepepulco Manuscript*, found these hymns so devilish and difficult that he refrained from trying to translate them from Nahuatl. He left the originals to an appendix to book 2, while book 6 deals with the challenges posed by Nahuatl poetics. Their huge poetic power was acknowledged by D. G. Brinton in the title he gave to his Eng. trans. *Rig Veda Americanus*, a key volume in his Philadelphia Library of Aboriginal American Literature series (1882–90). An important way of facing the difficulty posed by the hymns has proved to be recognizing their dependence on the rich poetic capacity of tlacuilolli. The hymn to the rain god Tlaloc, e.g., relies on a multiple pun involving the semantics of the XX Signs, their respective numbers in the series as Snake lightning (V), Jaguar thunder (XIV), and Rain (XIX), and the sheer phenomenon of storm. The arithmetic (V + XIV = XIX) is clearly legible in the hypnotic image of Tlaloc seen on the penultimate page of a book from Teotlillan (*Codex Laud* 45), where this rainmaker is revered as *ocelocoatl*, the Jaguar-Snake of the Nahuatl hymn, and can be seen roaring thunder from under his elaborate Jaguar headdress, while holding the Snake scepter of lightning.

A similar case is the celebration of Itzpapalotl, the Obsidian Butterfly (hymn 4), whose name in tlacuilolli when read as a calendrical date comprises numbers belonging to the set of 9 Night Powers (*Yoalitecutin*) and the 13 Fliers (*Quecholli*). Central to these 13 as number 7, the butterfly's metamorphic body conjoins the vitreous edge that, like obsidian, is sharp but brittle with the beauty of the wing that, lacking the vertebrate strength of the other 6+6 fliers, is easily damaged. Relying on the fact that Hermes (Mercury) goes around the sun 22 times every seven years, Itzpapalotl's hermetic teachings underlie the considerable corpus of Chichimec lit. in which, abused and seeking vengeance, she leads the Chichimec archers south into the tropics from Chicomoztoc, their desert fastness that translates as "Seven Caves." As the eponymous *Mariposa de obsidiana* (in Garibay's trans., 1958), Itzpapalotl also prompted one of the most powerful poems in Octavio Paz's (1914–98) *Águila o sol* (1950).

In order to function practically, the Mexica tribute system relied on a multilevel arithmogram that correlates the districts in the quarters west, south, east, and north of Tenochtitlan with the tonalpoualli nights of human gestation, synodic and sidereal moons, and the days of the year. The tribute due from each district is listed in the tlacuilolli *Matrícula de tributos*, to which *Codex Mendoza* adds a map (a quincunx oriented to west). The analogies to Cuzco's Tahuantinsuyu are strong, and, in each case, songs served as tribute items of value that characterized cultural geography. Demanding the performance of a song in the lang. and style of a region was a right of conquest in Cuzco and Tenochtitlan alike, which links further back again to the Tupi carbet.

In the imperial court of Tenochtitlan, this practice

helped form the collection of poems known as *Cantares mexicanos*. Copious, this Nahuatl work encompasses poems both ancient, like a Toltec lament that also appears in the *Popol Vuh*, and mod., like those that parody Christian liturgy. Revealing overall the immense richness inherent in the Nahuatl term for poetry itself (*xochi-cuicatl*, "flower-song"), it draws on well-recognized modes proper to mourning ("orphan"), planting ("green"), and war ("enemy").

After the invasion, analogous encodings of precious knowledge in concept and number continue to inform the shamanic rhetoric of ritual cure, as in the Maya *Ritual of the Bacabs* (Arzápalo) and the Nahuatl *Tratado* of 1629.

The range and power of native poetry in contemp. Mexico are evidenced in the first volume of Carlos Montemayor's *Escritores indígenas actuales* (1992). A strength of this volume is to show the survival of poetic speech in the three main lang. families of Mexico, Otomanguan, Maya, and Nahuatl. In Otomi, Thaayrohyadi Bermúdez appeals to that people (and their Purépecha neighbors) who have lived longest along its banks for the life and health of the river Lerma, threatened as it increasingly is by attitudes and policies rooted in the exploitative ideology of the invasion begun by Christopher Columbus. Its concentration on the idea of water, primal and unpolluted, curiously echoes what is known of the celebrated poet-king of Texcoco, Nezahualcoyotl (1402–72), named in the *Cantares mexicanos*, whose first compositions are recorded in Otomi.

We have seen the bridging role of the isthmus between Meso- and South America corroborated from the east in the Andean cross emblem *chakana* found in the ceramic codex of Yojoa in the ambit of the Maya metropolis Copan (Honduras), while from the west, Nahuatl lies at the root of the names *Guatemala*, *Cuzcatlan* (El Salvador), and *Nicaragua*. A theater piece focused on the tall tales of the widely traveled *pochteca* (trader and tax collector) published in Brinton's library as *The Gueguënce: A Comedy-Ballet in the Nahuatl-Spanish Dialect of Nicaragua* (1883) reveals wit sustained by the intense cultural traffic to and fro along the isthmus. For its part, the ceramic codex of Yojoa in the Ulua homeland of the Lenca juxtaposes motifs that include the Olmec caiman whose maw is a cave, the dancing armadillo of the Amazonian midwives, the literal runner bean of coastal Peruvian ceramics, the jaguar defending the night with tooth bared and claw unsheathed, the monkey *pochteca*, the rebellious turkey of the eclipse, the craftsman whose deep inspiration flows vertebrally from a fishy forebear, and well-dressed Maya dignitaries of the nearby metropolis Copan, also in Honduras.

In mod. times, the isthmus spirit can be seen to suffuse the remarkable line of Nicaraguan poets Rubén Darío (1867–1916), Pablo Antonio Cuadra (1912–2002), and Ernesto Cardenal (b. 1925), who have all recognized native America as a chief source. The poems in Cardenal's *Homenaje a los indios americanos* (1970) work directly from native texts from the entire continent. Before him, Cuadra had found a manifold reference for his poetry in the *doble yo* (double I) concept, a human head that is shielded by and beneath a back and head that belong to a powerful beast. This motif is seen alike in Amazonian stone sculpture, in San Agustín at the headwaters of the Magdalena in Colombia, in the isthmus and, most magnificently, in the statues of Maya potentates. As for Darío, the *modernista* founder of Sp. Am. poetry (see MODERNISMO), he spoke for his work and the movement as a whole when, in the "Palabras liminares" to *Prosas profanas* (1896), he wrote that, if poetry was to be found in "nuestra América," then it would be in the old things, in the legendary Indian, the refined and sensual Inca, the lowland and highland Maya cities of Palenque and Utatlan, and the great Moctezuma's golden throne. The Otomanguan family is also represented by Zapotec, in Victor de la Cruz's (b. 1948) *Guchachi' Reza*, supported by artist Francisco Toledo, which has included trans. of Bertolt Brecht's poetry. For its part, like that of Rigoberta Menchú (b. 1959), the work of the contemp. Maya Quiché poet Humberto Ak'abal (b. 1952) defends the Maya world in his native lang. and in Sp. as living perception.

**IV. Turtle Island.** A century and a half after Montaigne, Anahuac's northern continuity with parts of America now occupied by the U.S. and Canada inspired Lorenzo Boturini (1702–1753), a student of Giambattista Vico, to write *Idea de una nueva historia de la América septentrional* (1746). The base of mod. codices scholarship, this "new idea" relies heavily on the royal library built up by Nezahualcoyotl (Lee) in Texcoco, on the east bank of the highland lake, which Boturini cataloged and tried to reassemble. Texcoco is the focus of the *Romances de los Señores de la Nueva España*, an extensive anthol. of Nahuatl poetry that complements the *Cantares mexicanos* of Tenochtitlan on the west bank, being similarly based on both ancient memory and current tribute practice (Garibay 1964–68).

In documenting their origins in Texcoco, Nezahualcoyotl and his ancestors celebrated the Chichimec saga that had first brought them south across the tropical line from the 7th c. on, led by the obsidian butterfly Itzpapalotl from their homeland Chicomoztoc (Seven Caves). Visually, the most brilliant version of this saga is to be found in *Codex Borgia*, where the butterfly is seen about to emerge from her cocoon under seven caves marked by the stars of the septentrion, on a path that leads east, north, and west before plunging south. For its part, at Tepexic the Coixtlahuaca map establishes the hermetic nature of her teachings, literally, by correlating in Seven Caves the cycles of the moon and the planet Mercury (Hermes), in the synodic formula that approximates the nights of four moons with the 116 of the planet, and the sidereal formula that does the same for three moons and 88 nights of the planet.

Exactly this hermetic logic pervades corresponding sagas of crossing the tropical line told by those who live north of it, northwest of Mesoamerica. The exemplary case is that of the Zuni, who as neighbors have the Keres-speaking Pueblo to the east and the Hopi (in speech, kin to the Nahua) to the west. Culturally, the coherence of this landscape has long been embodied in the quincunx of mountains seen in Pueblo murals, which later gave shape to the sand or dry paintings of the Navajo, and their corresponding chants or ways (Wyman). The novel *Ceremony* (1976) by the Laguna Pueblo Leslie Marmon Silko (b. 1948) focuses on Tsepina, the turquoise mountain closest to home, later called Tsodzil by the Navajo, where it generates power both poetic and therapeutic. The same power imbues the verse in her *Storyteller* (1981).

In their genesis, the Zuni emerge through rooms that are world ages, upward, as in the architecture of multistory Pueblo houses. They then migrate to find their location on the Continental Divide, between the headwaters of the Rio Grande (southeast) and those of the Colorado River (southwest). Recalled in ceremonies over the year and in corresponding iconography in underground *kiva* temples, the story falls into episodes and culminates in the arrival of Sp. invaders from Mexico, who were successfully resisted, and then of the U.S. in the last years of the 19th c. When the U.S. was still invading, a particularly sensitive account of this trad. was given by Frank Cushing, who learned the Zuni lang. and went to live among them. A century later, Tedlock published versions performed in his presence in *Finding the Center*, a magnificent work that adjusts typography to the needs of ethnopoetics.

Identified at dawn by the macaw feather he wears in his hair as he rises before the sun heliacally, the Zuni hero Nepayatamu by night is honored at the kiva shrine of the Milky Way Newekwe. From the four sides of Newekwe and after four moons, he hails his planet's return, sheltering the metamorphic butterfly in his flute. He shares these hermetic characteristics with counterparts among the Pueblo to the east like the "Sun youth" in Boas's *Keresan Texts* and among the much-visited Hopi, where the butterfly is enshrined at Awatobi and where, journeying back and forth across the tropical line, it is inseparable from genesis and the birth of maize. Throughout this territory, in the hermetic butterfly complex, there are specific and striking echoes of the poetry and visual art of Anahuac, particularly the major cities of Teotihuacan and Cholula.

In the story they tell of themselves as invaders of the Pueblo in *Diné Bahane'* (Zolbrod), the Navajo make many of these connections plain. The case of the Apache is comparable, and as Athapaskan relatives, they defended together a last frontier that stretched from Mexico and Apacheria to the Black Hills of Dakota.

The debt to the Anahuac codices, esp. their quatrefoil and quincunx maps, is patent in the sand or dry paintings laid out on the hogan floor to complement the therapeutic chants of the Navajo ways over as many as nine nights. Mutually enriching each other as they do in tlacuilolli fashion as visual and verbal lang., the dry paintings and the chants may fairly be regarded as literary bedrock among the Navajo, a celebrated example being the *Kledzhe Hatal* (*Night Chant*, last of Bierhorst's four masterworks). Moreover, this is a living trad., from which poets who write in Navajo, like Luci Tapahonso (b. 1953), may draw strength.

In defining territory, the Navajo paintings serve as an excellent guide to cultural hist. Toward the Great Plains that stretch northeast beyond the mountains, we see and hear the buffalo. Shot steadily after 1864 from transcontinental trains so as to starve still-resistant Indians to death, the buffalo embodies time and life itself on the plains. According to the Sioux Winter Counts by High Hawk and Brown Hat (Mallery), it is Buffalo Woman who brings the first gifts to the peoples of the plains, the tobacco peace pipe, maize of four colors and in all its preparations, the tipi circle, and their respective songs, which become a main ingredient in the dazzling visions of Black Elk.

Belief in the return of the buffalo to the plains was fundamental to the Ghost Dance of 1890, coincident with the Wounded Knee massacre. To remain undaunted in the face of ever more violent white assault, tribes from Mexico to Canada and from California to Oklahoma gave each other their songs, ascribing to them the value they had had as tribute items among the Aztecs and the Inca. The trance sought in the songs brought back, too, the ghosts of many thousands of the fallen. On those grounds, Bierhorst (1985) has argued strongly for detecting a similar dimension in the *Cantares mexicanos*.

"We shall live again," a main refrain in the songs heard by such poets as Gary Snyder (b. 1930) and echoed repeatedly in subsequent U.S. mass movements, implies concern with beginnings, notably among the Arapaho and Cheyenne, a principal contingent in the dance (Mooney 1896). The tongue of both is Algonkian, called the "language of America" by Roger Williams in 1643, which stretches east across the continent to include those who first encountered the Eng. in Massachusetts, in Manhattan, and with Powhatan. Algonkian genesis is typified in the song to the turtle (Bruchac), which, floating in the cosmic ocean, has borne the weight of the earth itself since "the beginning of human existence."

Adherence to this "floating island" version of Am. genesis became paramount among the Algonkian-speaking Ojibwa, midway between west and east around the frontier lakes that feed the uppermost Mississippi (a focus mapped in Lévi-Strauss's *Mythologiques*). Before Europeans arrived, these beliefs sustained the Midewiwin, a shamanic society where initiation demanded knowledge of sacred songs whose syllables and stanzas correspond to designs inscribed on birch-bark scrolls (Dewdney). This Mide writing seemed dangerous enough to Anglican missionaries to warrant suppression and Christian replacements, likewise on birch bark but printed alphabetically. Through his Ojibwa wife, Schoolcraft gained privileged insight into this trad. (see also Carr).

Among much else, texts in Mide script graphically chart the chants of genesis, the trance journey through zenith and nadir (in which in shamanic time nights are years, as they can be in the Winter Counts, as indeed they actually are near the pole), and the power of Manito. Widely shared Algonkian belief in the trance journey much strengthened the uprisings led by the

Ottawa Pontiac in 1761 and by his Shawnee successor Tecumseh. Depicted in the scrolls, one of the five most powerful Manitos is the turtle who sustains the earth. Represented ubiquitously in the artwork of Turtle Island, this creature inaugurates the epic of the Lenape (Delaware), of which Constantine Samuel Rafinesque provided a version in Mide script entitled *Walum Olum* (1836; later included in Brinton's Philadelphia library). The importance of these precedents today are made clear in the example of Gerald Vizenor (b. 1934), the Ojibwa novelist who began his career by compiling an anthol. of poetry in his lang.

In northern Appalachia, these beliefs were incorporated into the Iroquoian genesis, which is why, in his *Sketches of Ancient History of the Six Nations* (1825), the Iroquois historian Cusick referred to the whole of America north of Mexico as Turtle Island, distinguishing it from lands farther south with their early knowledge of maize and of humankind's simian forebears (this before Darwin). Belief among the Canadian Iroquois in the turtle that created the island which became the first earth was noted by the Jesuit Joseph-François Lafitau (1681–1746) in 1724. The turtle that can burrow to the very heart of the earth is invoked in the curing chants written by the Cherokee (Iroquoian neighbors in Appalachia) in their Sequoya syllabary (Mooney 1992). The syllabary texts draw likewise on shared Iroquoian reverence for maize as one of the three sisters who are the "three graces" in their common agricultural hist., maize, beans, and squash. Graphic antecedents may be found in the mound culture ceramics at Cahokia.

The syllabary texts also respect the power of moundbuilder forebears in southern Appalachia who, according to the chants, still live inside the Cherokee mounds, as a hidden resource in defense. Thereby they establish effective links, often in precise detail, with cultural norms current over a thousand years ago, detected today also among the Yuchi and the Musgokee and their neighbors.

Apart from impinging on the initial framing of the U.S. constitution, the Five (later Six) Nations of the Iroquois left a magnificent record of themselves in their *Ritual of Condolence*, another of Bierhorst's four masterworks. The rhet. relied on what Lafitau called the council style of the Iroquois; its chronology was extensive, and, in it, nights could count for years.

Farther west, connections can be made with Iroquoian speakers beyond the Mississippi, such as the Caddo and the Pawnee, whose Hako ceremony entered western poetics in 1900, having been recorded on the ethnologist Alice Fletcher's (1838–1923) phonograph.

At the turn on the 20th c., H. W. Longfellow's "Song of Hiawatha" (1855) was massively propagated throughout the U.S. school system and was the most read and performed poem of its day. Founder of the Iroquois League of Nations, its eponymous hero lives a life heavily reliant on Algonkian legend, as critics never tire of noting. What tends to be less noticed is the imaginative precision of Mide song symbols in the Eng.-lang. poem and Turtle Island perspectives that had been shared in any case by both Algonkian and Iroquois. Perhaps yet more consequentially, *Hiawatha* proved to be a major factor in Carl Jung's hypothesis of the collective unconscious and his break with Sigmund Freud.

*See* GUARANÍ POETRY, INUIT POETRY, MAPUCHE POETRY, NAVAJO POETRY.

■ H. R. Schoolcraft, *Historical and Statistical Information Respecting the History, Condition and Prospects of the Indian Tribes of the United States* (1851–57); H. Hale, *The Iroquois Book of Rites* (1883); *The Lenape and Their Legends* (1884); *Ancient Nahuatl Poetry* (1887); and *Rig Veda Americanus: Sacred Songs of the Ancient Mexicans* (1890), all ed. and trans. D. G. Brinton; G. Mallery, *Picture-Writing of the American Indians* (1893); J. Mooney, *The Ghost-Dance Religion and the Sioux Outbreak of 1890* (1896); A. C. Fletcher, *Indian Story and Song from North America* (1900); K. T. Preuss, *Die Religion und Mythologie der Uitoto* (1921); M. Austin, *The American Rhythm* (1923); R. Harcourt and M. d'Harcourt, *La musique des Incas et ses survivances* (1925); F. Boas, *Keresan Texts* (1928); W. Krickeberg, *Märchen der Azteken und Inkaperuaner, Maya und Musica* (1928); J. M. Arguedas, *Canto Keshwa* (1938); A. M. Garibay, *Poesía indígena de la Altiplanicie* (1940); J. Lara, *Poesía popular quechua* (1947); A. G. Day, *The Sky Clears: Poetry of the American Indians* (1951); N. M. Holmer, *The Complete Mu-Igala in Picture-Writing: A Native Record of a Cuna Indian Medicine Song* (1953); J. H. Rowe, "Eleven Inca Prayers from the Zithuwa Ritual," *Kroeber Anthropological Society Papers* 8–9 (1953); B. Kössler-llg, *Indianermärchen aus den Kordilleren* (1956); *El libro de los cantares de Dzitbalche*, ed. A. Barrera Vásquez (1956); J. M. Arguedas, *The Singing Mountaineers: Song and Tales of the Quechua* (1957); and *Floresta literaria de la América indígena* (1957); J. Alcina Franch, *Floresta literaria de la América indígena* (1957); J. Lara, *Tragedia del fin de Atawallpa* (1957); A. M. Garibay, *Veinte himnos sacros de los nahuas* (1958); *Ayvu rapyta*, ed. L. Cadogan (1959); *Anthologie des mythes, legends et contes populaires d'Amérique*, ed. B. Péret (1960); M. A. Asturias, *Poesía precolombina* (1960); K. A. Nowotny, *Tlacuilolli: Die mexikanischen Bilderhandschriften, Stil und Inhalt* (1961); A. Barrera Vásquez and S. Rendón, *El libro de los Libros de Chilam Balam* (1963); N. M. Holmer, *Dos cantos shamanísticos de los indios cunas* (1963); A. M. Garibay, *Poesía náhuatl* (1964–68); M. León-Portilla, *Las literaturas precolombinas de México* (1964a); and *El reverso de la conquista: Relaciones aztecas, mayas e incas* (1964b); *La literatura de los Guaraníes*, ed. L. Cadogan (1965); J. Lara, *La literatura de los quechuas* (1969); P. Rivière, *Marriage among the Trio* (1969); M. de Civrieux, *Watunna: An Orinoco Creation Cycle*, trans. D. Guss (1970); F. W. Kramer, *Literature among the Cuna Indians* (1970); M. Edmonson, *The Book of Counsel: The Popol Vuh of the Quiché Maya of Guatemala* (1971); G. Reichel-Dolmatoff, *Amazonian Cosmos: The Sexual and Religious Symbolism of the Tukano Indians* (1971); J. Rothenberg, *Shaking the Pumpkin: Traditional Poetry of the Indian North Americas* (1972); D. Tedlock, *Finding the Center: Narrative Poetry of the Zuni Indians* (1972); E. Cardenal, *Homage to the American Indians*, trans. M.

Altschul and C. Altschul (1973); M. C. Alvarez, *Textos coloniales del Libro de Chilam Balam de Chumayel y textos glíficos del Códice de Dresde* (1974); J. Bierhorst, *Four Masterworks of American Indian Literature: Quetzalcoatl, The Ritual of Condolence, Cuceb, The Night Chant* (1974); S. Dewdney, *The Sacred Scrolls of the Southern Ojibway* (1975); G. Brotherston, *Image of the New World: The American Continent Portrayed in Native Texts* (1979); R. Bareiro Saguier, *Literatura guaraní del Paraguay* (1980); G. Poma, *El primer nueva corónica y buen gobierno*, ed. J. V. Murra and R. Adorno (1980); *"In Vain I Tried to Tell": Essays in Native American Ethnopoetics*, ed. D. H. Hymes (1981); G. Vizenor, *Summer in the Spring: Ojibwa Lyric Poems and Tribal Stories* (1981); P. G. Roe, *The Cosmic Zygote: Cosmology in the Amazon Basin* (1982); T. Meneses, *Teatro quechua colonial* (1983); *Songs from This Earth on Turtle's Back*, ed. J. Bruchac (1983); L. C. Wyman, *Southwest Indian Dry Painting* (1983); *Treatise of Ruiz de Alarcón* [1629], ed. J. R. Andrews and R. Hassig (1984); *Diné Bahané: The Navajo Creation Story* (1984), trans. P. Zolbrod; J. Bierhorst, *Cantares mexicanos: Songs of the Aztecs* (1985); *Technicians of the Sacred*, ed. J. Rothenberg, 2d ed. (1985); M. León-Portilla, *Coloquios y doctrina Cristiana: Los diálogos de 1524* (1986); R. Arzápalo Marín, *El ritual de los bacabes* (1987); R. E. Montoya and L. Montoya, *La sangre de los cerros* (1987); J. Sherzer and A. C. Woodbury, *Native American Discourse: Poetics and Rhetoric* (1987); R. Harrison, *Signs, Songs and Memory in the Andes: Translating the Quechua Language and Culture* (1989); F. Salomon, *The Huarochirí Narrative: A Testament of Ancient and Colonial Andean Religion*, trans. F. Salomon and G. L. Urioste (1991); J. Bierhorst, *History and Mythology of the Aztecs: The Codex Chimalpopoca* (1992); G. Brotherston, *The Book of the Fourth World: Reading the Native Americas through Their Literature* (1992); R. L. Burger, *Chavin and the Origins of Andean Civilization* (1992); J. Mooney, *History, Myths and Sacred Formulas of the Cherokee* (1992); H. Carr, *Inventing the American Primitive: Politics, Gender and the Representation of Native American Literary Tradition* (1996); W. Rowe, *Ensayos arguedianos* (1996); D. Bahr, L. Paul, V. Joseph, *Ants and Orioles: Showing the Art of Pima Poetry* (1997); G. Brotherston, *Painted Books from Mexico* (1997); E. Chiauilaf, *Ti kom ül: Todos los cantos* (1998); C. Vicuña, *Ül: Four Mapuche Poets* (1998); *The Sun Unwound: Original Texts from Occupied America*, trans. E. Dorn and G. Brotherston (1999); K. Warak'a, *Taki Parwa/22 Poemas*, trans. O. Gonzáles (1999); C. Julien, *Reading Inca History* (2000); J. de Sousândrade, *O Guesa* [1888], ed. A de Campos and H. de Campos (2002); S. Medeiros, *Makunaíma e Jurupari: Cosmogonias ameríndias* (2002); M. León Portilla, *Códices: Los antiguos libros del Nuevo Mundo* (2003); *Rabinal Achi: A Mayan Drama of War and Sacrifice*, ed. and trans. D. Tedlock (2003); D. Arnold and J. de Dios Yapita, "The Nature of Indigenous Literatures in the Andes," *Literary Cultures of Latin America*, ed. M. J. Valdés and D. Kadir (2004); L. Sá, *Rain Forest Literatures: Amazonian Texts and Latin American Culture* (2004); F. Salomon, *The Cord Keepers* (2004); G. Brotherston, *Feather Crown* (2006); E. G. Neves, *Arqueologia da Amazônia* (2006); G. Tomlinson, *The Singing of the New World: Indigenous Voice in the Era of European Contact* (2007); J. Lee, *The Allure of Nezahualcoyotl: Pre-Hispanic History, Religion, and Nahua Poetics* (2008); J. Neurath, *Por los caminos del maíz: Mito y ritual en la periféria septentrional de Mesoamérica* (2008); H. Staden, *Warhaftige Historia* [1557], ed. N. Whitehead (2008); G. Brokaw, *A History of the Khipu* (2010).

G. BROTHERSTON

**INDONESIAN POETRY** is written in Bahasa Indonesia, the national lang. of the Republic of Indonesia and a distinct dialect of Malay. There are approximately 740 different langs. spoken across the archipelago; although most of these have had extensive oral poetic trads., only eight have longstanding written lits.—Javanese, Balinese, Sundanese, Malay, Minangkabau, Batak, Macassarese and Buginese (McGlynn). A "mod. Indonesian poetry" is the product of sociopolitical and educational changes that gathered momentum from the beginning of the 20th c. Indonesia became a unitary state in 1945; the Indonesian lang. was defined as separate from Malay in 1928 during the emerging nationalist movement and has developed its own lit., most commonly written by young, well-educated, urbanized men and relying on the market distribution of printed books and literary magazines.

Mod. Indonesian poetry is conventionally considered to have begun in 1922 with the publication of *Andalas Nusa Harapan* (Sumatra, Island of Hope) by the Sumatran-born poet Muhammad Yamin (1903–62). The poems collected in this brief anthol. combine the traditional four-line couplets of the indigenous *\*pantun* with the longer sonnet form characteristic of the Dutch Neo-romantic movement of 1880 that the emerging Indonesian poets had studied in school. Driven by powerful emotions (real or imagined), this first generation of Indonesian poets contemplated the beauty of nature from a careful distance and were commonly left in a condition of profound melancholy connected to a nostalgia for previous states of emotional comfort. Such longing (*rindu*) found its origins variously in memories of one's parents, childhood, home village, local scenery, cl. monuments, and religious certainty. Yamin's "Sedih" (Sorrow, 1934) is typical of this poetry. The sonnet opens with an evocation of the Barisan Mountain ranges of Central Sumatra and of a distant village that seems to be calling the wanderer home. Alone and uncared for, he sadly remembers his father, now deceased, lying in a grave covered with a basil plant and a single frangipani. The form and lang. are reasonably mod.; the concluding images are common pantun images: the frangipani is found in cemeteries, and the word for "basil" (*selasih*) rhymes with "love" (*kasih*).

The outstanding poet of the 1920s to 1930s was Amir Hamzah (1911–46). A prince deeply steeped in traditional Malay lit., Hamzah imbued these romantic conventions with deeply felt grief arising from his own failed relationships. In his youthful poetry, *Buah Rindu* (Fruits of Melancholy, not pub. until 1941), the relationships were with his mother, his home in East Sumatra, and the woman with whom he had fallen in love only to lose her in her unwilling marriage to another. In his mature verse, *Nyanyi Sunyi* (Songs of Loneliness, pub. earlier, 1937), Hamzah channeled his frustration into an angry, empty search for an absent God. While other poets of this period—Rustam Effendi (1903–79), Sanusi Pane (1905–68), and Sutan Takdir Alisjahbana (1908–94)—were struggling to find more contemp., though still elegant, forms of Indonesian, Hamzah is sometimes considered "the last Malay poet" because of his use of a vast cl. vocabulary, trad. quatrains, and familiar patterns of imagery.

Indonesia was occupied by Japanese military forces from 1942 to 1945 and fought for its independence from the Dutch from 1945 to 1949. Such circumstances obviously made beauty and melancholy into more difficult topics. A complete change in form, subject matter, and emotional content was brought about in a short period by the bohemian poet Chairil Anwar (1922–49). Writing under the influence of Eur., particularly Dutch, poetry of the 1930s, Anwar used *free verse to describe feelings of alienation and desolation (*sepi*) experienced in dark, tightly confined, urban settings. Anwar's influence was powerful and can be discerned in the work of his close peers Asrul Sani (1926–2004) and Rivai Apin (1927–95). The name of Sitor Situmorang (b. 1924) is particularly worthy of note: Sitor has intensively explored themes of place and love over five decades.

A middle position was achieved with the emergence of a New Generation of poets in the 1950s. Relatively free of Eur. models and confident in their use of Indonesian, they turned to regional themes. Ajip Rosidi (b. 1938) dealt in depth with the society, as well as the folk and Islamic spirituality, of West Java; he was also a strong proponent of writing in Sundanese. W. S. Rendra (1935–2009) was both a major poet and dramatist; his work focused on the lives of "the ordinary people" of Central Java. He also wrote personal love poems and more widely based works drawing on a Catholicism colored by pantheism. In the poem "Litani Domba Kudus" (Litany for the Holy Lamb, 1955), Christ is a white flower, an ivory dove, a king dwelling among paupers, and a golden deer. "Sebuah Dunia Yang Marah" (An Angry World, 1960) concludes:

God always weeps and understands.
Is always stabbed. Always betrayed.

In these poems, God is most to be found in "the enemies of the police": soldiers, prostitutes, the unemployed and beggars ("Masmur Mawar" [Rose Psalm], 1959).

Free literary expression was increasingly suppressed under the later regime of Sukarno (president from 1945 to 1967). As the nation moved increasingly to the Left, major themes became "heroism," "social destiny," "great principles," and "praise of the fatherland and the masses, and historical optimism" (Mohamad). These same themes continued to be prominent in the early work of the Generation of 1966, under the second Indonesian president Suharto (president from 1967 to 1998), only to be almost completely dropped in a second wave of personal poetry that developed after 1968. The one outstanding exception was Taufiq Ismail (b. 1937), who was able to carry his political concerns into a humorous and wide-ranging social analysis of the problems of the Suharto era.

Three major directions can be discerned in this newer work. The first was the gentle lyricism of Sapardi Djoko Damono (b. 1940), esp. as found in his anthol. *dukaMu abadi* (the Eternal Sorrow of God, 1969). Sapardi developed a carefully contrastive pattern of imagery, describing the human pilgrimage between life and death in terms of the natural progression of day to night.

A second direction was the emergence of a strong female voice for the first time. Particularly important was the work of Toeti Heraty (b. 1933). Sapardi searched for a God whom he doubts exists; in *Sajak-sajak 33* (33 Poems, 1971), Toeti sought an equally impossible object—a love in which she could participate as an equal and not as an object. The rituals of status, role-playing, and emotional control are analyzed in her poetry as the tools by which open and honest relationships are avoided.

The third direction was the move toward "concrete absurdist" poetry, esp. at the hands of Sutardji Calzoum Bachri (b. 1942). Sutardji's poetry emphasized sound at the expense of meaning and claimed to be returning poetry to the realm of the preliterate spell. His major topics were the violence of sexual relations, the pain of everyday existence, and the awesome arbitrariness of the divine. Perhaps his most intriguing poem is "Q," composed of the Ar. letters "alif," "lam," "mim" (known in the Qur'an as "the mysterious letters"), and a series of exclamation marks. The letters may stand for "Allah" and "Muhammad."

The mid-1980s mark a further turning point in the devel. of mod. Indonesian poetry. The poets who emerged during this decade had been born after independence, wrote naturally in Indonesian, and had been formed by Indonesian lit. Their work moved in two different directions. Some were caught up in the worldwide Islamic Revival, bringing an affirmative Muslim orthodoxy to the center of Indonesian poetry, contrary to the "mod." secularism or doubt that had prevailed throughout the rest of the century. Among the New Sufis were Emha Ainun Nadjib (b. 1953), Ahmadun Yosi Herfanda (b. 1956), and Acep Zamzam Noor (b. 1960). Others, such as Sitok Srengenge (b. 1965) and Dorothea Rosa Herliany (b. 1963), remained defiantly concerned with the complexities of their own emotions and the repressive environment of the late Suharto era. Herliany rejected the uncertainty about relationships that characterized Toeti Heraty's poetry and in *Kill the Radio* demanded dominance rather than equality.

The decade after the Reformation movement of 1998 has seen all these writers continue to grow in depth and subtlety. New writers have, of course, continued to appear, including a significant number of women writers, esp. Rieke Diah Pitaloka (b. 1974), Shinta Febriany (b. 1979), and Putu Vivi Lestari (b. 1981). Indonesian lit. has also begun to move into cyberspace. Together, the writers of the 1980s and their new peers are described as the Generation of 2000, a reference not to their set place in Indonesian writing but to their future promise.

■ **Anthologies and Translations**: *Pujangga Baru* (1962); *Gema Tanah Air* (1948); *Angkatan 66* (1968), all ed. H. B. Jassin; *Anthology of Modern Indonesian Poetry,* ed. B. Raffel (1970); *Complete Poetry and Prose of Chairil Anwar,* ed. and trans. B. Raffel (1970); *Ballads and Blues: Selected Poems of W. S. Rendra,* ed. and trans. B. Raffel and H. Aveling; *Contemporary Indonesian Poetry* (1975), *Arjuna in Meditation* (1976), *Secrets Need Words* (2001), all ed. and trans. H. Aveling; *Angkatan 2000 dalam Sastra Indonesia,* ed. K. L. Rampan (2000); D. R. Herliany, *Kill the Radio* (2001), *Saint Rosa* (2006), both trans. H. Aveling.

■ **Criticism and History**: H. B. Jassin, *Chairil Anwar* (1954), and *Amir Hamzah* (1962); A. Teeuw, *Modern Indonesian Literature,* 2 v. (1967, 1979); B. Raffel, *The Development of Modern Indonesian Poetry* (1967); G. Mohamad, "Njanji Sunji Kedua," *Horison,* April (1969); H. Aveling, *A Thematic History of Indonesian Poetry: 1920 to 1974* (1974); M. H. Salleh, *Tradition and Change in Contemporary Malay-Indonesian Poetry* (1977); *Indonesian Heritage,* ed. J. McGlynn (1998); *Cyber Graffiti,* ed. S. Situmorang (2004).

H. Aveling

**INFLUENCE.** A term in mod. critical theory that offers a specific account of both the origin and nature of literary works, incl. poetry. In particular, the term accounts for a *poet's making of a *poem out of an antecedent work. E.g., when John Milton produced a milestone in Eng. poetry, his *pastoral *elegy "Lycidas" (1637), we often say that he was influenced by the major pastoral elegy of the previous century in Eng., the "November" *eclogue of Edmund Spenser's *Shepheardes Calender* (1579). The nature of that relation—encompassing *imitation, *invention, citation, and many other modes of appropriation and creation—is what the term *influence* entails.

According to the *OED,* the word *influence* means "flow in" and thus has a hydrologic etymology, splitting along two courses, designated 1 and 2a: "The action or fact of flowing in; inflowing, inflow, influx: said of the action of water and other fluids" and "in *Astrol.* the supposed flowing or streaming from the stars or heavens of an etherial fluid acting upon the character and destiny of men." In both cases, *influence* functions as a figure for the idea of a clear trajectory, route, or path connecting one point with another; the points form "dyads of transmission, from one unity (author, work, tradition) to another" (Clayton and Rothstein). In poetic theory, the concept shows how one poet influences another or, to reverse the trajectory, how one poet is influenced by another: critics speak of Spenser's influencing Milton and of Milton's being influenced

by Spenser. Hence, *influence* becomes a key term for discovering the presence of a previous poet or poem in a later author or work; it constitutes one of the most potent principles of literary analysis from the 14th c. into the 21st: that works of lit. originate in previous works of lit. As such, influence suggests a clear practice for *interpretation: we are to read a poem in terms of the major influences on it.

According to the *OED,* the meaning of *influence* as "the flow of water" dates to the 16th c., when, e.g., William Harrison writes in *Holinshed's Chronicles* (1577–87), "The Towie [River] . . . taketh in the influences of diverse waters in one chanell"; the astrological meaning traces to the 14th c., when Chaucer writes in *Troilus and Criseyde* (ca. 1374), "O Influences of thise hevenes hye! / Soth is, that vnder God ye ben oure hierdes" (3.618–19). Starting in the 15th and 16th cs., poets use the term in its more literary sense. For instance, John Lydgate in his *Lyfe of St. Albon* (1439) writes, "I stande in hope his influence shall shyne / My tremblyng penne by grace to enlumyne" (Aij, cited *OED*). In the 17th c., writers often use the astrological meaning to represent literary influence, as Nathaniel Baxter does in *Sir Philip Sidney's Ourania* (1606) when speaking of "Spencers influence."

As a term of mod. critical theory, however, *influence* traces to the 18th c. and fundamentally to the 19th. Neither John Dryden nor Alexander Pope uses the word, although S. T. Coleridge uses it much as we do today (Bloom 1973). All these writers are intensely interested in a single historical problem: how to create a great work of lit. in the aftermath of the Ren., when writers such as Spenser in *The Faerie Queene* (1590, 1596), Shakespeare in *Hamlet* (1601), and Milton in *Paradise Lost* (1667, 1674) cast such a luminous shadow across the literary landscape. The Ger. poet J. W. Goethe felt himself lucky precisely because he was not Eng. Writers during the Augustan and romantic eras begin to suffer considerable "anxiety" about the influence that past Eng. poets such as Milton were exerting on them, and the problem continues into the Victorian era and on into the 20th c. As John Keats summarizes the issue, when confiding to Richard Woodhouse in 1818, "there was nothing original to be written in poetry; . . . its riches were already exhausted—and all its beauties forestalled."

Not until the 20th c., however, does the concept of poetic influence get fully theorized. Reacting to the Ger. trad. of *Quellenforschung* (source study), three major coordinates are the lit. crit. of Eliot, Bate, and Bloom. In "Tradition and the Individual Talent," Eliot famously confronts the problem that "tradition" poses to the poet's "individual talent." For Eliot, individual talent is the problem that poets inherit in the romantic notion of an autonomous poetic *genius, according to which the poet creates a poem out of the crucible of his own imaginative *inspiration, detached from what Eliot calls "predecessors." A solution lies in the poet's conscious decision to work from the literary trad.: "we shall often find that . . . the most individual parts of his work may be those in which the dead poets, his ancestors, assert their immortality most vigorously." Hence, "No poet . . . has his complete meaning alone. His significance . . . is the appreciation of his relation to the dead poets." In this way, "The progress of an artist is a . . . continual extinction of personality."

In *The Burden of the Past and the English Poet* (1970), W. J. Bate calls that burden "the greatest single problem that modern art . . . had to face." Locating the problem in "the remorseless deepening of self-consciousness" in the 18th c., Bate explores "the writer's loss of self-confidence as he compares what he feels able to do with the rich heritage of past art and literature." The 18th c. forms "the essential crossroad between . . . the . . . 'Renaissance' and . . . the 'modern,'" becoming "the first period in modern history to face the problem of what it means to come *immediately* after a great creative achievement." According to Bate, the solution to the problem lies in "something ancestral rather than parental": the poet relies on "the 'leapfrog' use of the past for authority or psychological comfort: the leap over the parental—the principal immediate predecessors—to what Northrop Frye calls the 'parental grandfather.'" Bate's emphasis on "anxiety" responds to previously idealizing models of literary transmission, such as E. R. Curtius's *European Literature and the Latin Middle Ages* (trans. 1953), which presents the literary trad. as "the medium by which the European mind preserves its identity through the millenniums." Bate's deidealizing approach lays the foundation for the most important theorist of influence in the 20th and 21st cs.

Bloom has written several books on "the anxiety of influence"—the title of his most famous book, which is subtitled "a theory of poetry." Bloom's equation of "influence" with "theory" is bold and decisive: "this short book offers a theory of poetry by way of a description of poetic influence, or the story of intra-poetic relationships." "Poetic history, in this book's argument," he continues, "is held to be indistinguishable from poetic influence, since strong poets make that history by misreading one another, so as to clear imaginative space for themselves." The act of misreading, which Bloom terms "misprision," allows the poet to contend with his anxiety in confronting a strong predecessor. In fact, Bloom moves Bate's project ahead to the romantic poets, and he develops his model of misprision into "six revisionary ratios," which he terms "clinamen," "tessera," "kenosis," "daemonization," "askesis," and "aprophrades"—terms designed to trace a complex process by which the *ephebe* or young poet revises the precursor or strong poet: (1) the poet begins by "swerving" from his precursor; (2) he "completes" the precursor by fulfilling something not in the original; (3) he creates "discontinuity" with the precursor; (4) he counters the precursor's "sublimity"—his highest artistic achievement; (5) he puts himself in a position to create "solitude" from the precursor; and (6) finally, he has the confidence to reopen his work consciously to the precursor as an act of will.

Bloom derives his theory of influence in response to three major strands of poetic theory: the romantic notion of autonomous genius; "the impasse of Formalist criticism"; and the universalizing of "Archetypal criticism" (see ARCHETYPE, FORMALISM). As the concept of "struggle" at the heart of the process indicates, Bloom relies on the psychoanalytic theory of Sigmund Freud, in particular the Oedipus complex: just as a son struggles with his father, so the strong poet struggles with his predecessor. But whereas Freud turns the struggle into a comedy or romance, by which the process of "sublimation" is "the highest human achievement," involving "the yielding-up of more primordial for more refined models of pleasure," Bloom refuses to abandon the dark melancholy of the poet's struggle.

As this short hist. indicates, a theory of poetic influence tends to focus on the figure of the poet, in particular on his mind, and to emphasize psychic and compositional agency. As such, influence is an "author-centered" and "evaluative concept" (Clayton and Rothstein). Following from Freud, Bloom's model centers on the poet's consciousness as an agent of creation—what goes on inside the psyche of the strong poet as he tries to invent a poem out of his titanic wrestling match with a father-poet. At the heart of influence, then, is the poet's creative psychology, the crucible out of which a poem is born.

Moreover, Bloom's model of influence can be "a theory of poetry" because he insists that the only point of reference for a poem can be another poem (the cardinal principle of *structuralism), not culture, hist., or politics. When Bloom was theorizing influence, a countertheory was emerging, known as *New Historicism, which reads poems by eschewing "intra-poetic relationships" to foreground the effects of social, political, and economic institutions. The overwhelming influence of New Historicism has likely inhibited further theorizing of influence.

Bloom's model rejects the ethical program assigned to poetry by Aristotle and Horace and later by a number of early mod. theorists who argue that the pleasure of poetry has utility in society, that it promotes virtue or civic duty. "The poet," summarizes the romantic poet P. B. Shelley, "is the unacknowledged legislator of the world." In contrast, Bloom's theory derives from a much less studied theorist of poetry, Longinus, who seeks to account for the greatness of literary works through the poet's imitation of another poet's work, a phenomenon Longinus calls the *sublime, a heightened mode of discourse that aims for spiritual transport, not ethical conduct.

As the terms of this discussion intimate, influence has historically been gendered. For Bloom, the strong poet and the precursor poet are both male. However, feminist critics from the 1970s on have made a major contribution to influence studies. Working from Virginia Woolf's *A Room of One's Own* (1929), which emphasizes the absence of strong female writers as a model for contemp. women, feminists question Bloom's male-centered approach, as Kolodny does; and they conceive how women poets influence one other, as Showalter (1977) does. Such an appropriation quickly extended to theories of minority writing—for instance, in Smith's manifesto for a black feminist criticism.

The theory of influence plays a significant role in current critical practice, if less so in theory. For, except for Bloom and his immediate heirs, no significant theory of influence has emerged in the 21st c. (The New Critical Idiom series does not include a volume on "Influence," instead subsuming the topic under *"Intertextuality.") Nonetheless, scholars and literary critics continue to cite Bloom; to work on relations among poets (and poems) in terms of influence, incl. preromantic authors; and to apply its specific principles: imitation, *allusion, echo. One extension of the Bloomian theory of influence comes with what classicists term "double allusion," by which one poet uses a single point of reference to allude to or show his or her influence by more than a single precursor (McKeown) and sometimes to allude to one precursor in order to target another (Cheney 1997).

Since influence posits the poet's mind in relation with a precursor, it continues to have a vital connection to the concept it most often is understood to oppose, intertextuality. Strange bedfellows, influence and intertextuality form a concerted project to disrupt the unitary notion of autonomous authorial genius; together, they buttress one of the seminal undertakings of literary theory in the late 20th c.: the "death of the author," announced by the Fr. theorist Roland Barthes.

Curiously, most theorizing about influence neglects writers' own fictions of influence, together with their supporting metaphors. While *influence* is itself a *metaphor, poets have been representing the concept for centuries. To take a single example, in *The Faerie Queene* (4.2.34), Spenser pauses to record the influence of Chaucer, because England's new national poet wishes to continue a story that Chaucer left unfinished in "The Squire's Tale":

> Then pardon, O most sacred happie spirit,
>   That I thy labours lost may thus revive,
>   And steale from thee the meede of thy due merit,
>   That noen durst ever whilest thou wast alive,
>   And being dead in vaine yet many strive:
>   Ne dare I like, but through infusion sweete
>   Of thine owne spirit, which doth in me survive,
>   I follow here the footing of thy feete,
>   That with thy meaning I may the rather meete.

Here, Spenser uses a principle of "infusion sweete" to show how the poetic "spirit" of Chaucer "survive[s]" in him. The word *infusion* has a hydrologic etymology and means "the action of pouring in (a liquid)" (*OED*, def. 1), although it also has a theological significance, namely, "the action of infusing some principle, quality, or idea, into the mind, soul, or heart; esp. the imparting of *a priori* ideas or of divine grace" (def. 2). Hence, Spenser imagines the pouring of Chaucer's spirit into his own as a providentially ordained process of influence, an act of grace that leads to the creation of great nationalist verse. In accord with this etymology, Spenser speaks of "Dan Chaucer, well of English undefyled" (4.2.32.8), thereby identifying his precursor as an Eng. fountain of purified influence. For poets interested in tracing their artistic genealogy, as well as for critics interested in lit. hist., literary relations, authorial agency, and *close reading of poetic texts, influence continues to be a major tool of invention and crit.

*See* EVALUATION, HERMENEUTICS, HISTORICISM, MUSE, ORIGINALITY, PARODY, PASTICHE, ROMANTICISM.

■ T. S. Eliot, "Tradition and the Individual Talent," *The Egoist* 6 (1919); Frye; C. Guillén, "The Aesthetics of Literary Influence," *Literature as System* (1971); H. Bloom, *The Anxiety of Influence* (1973), *A Map of Misreading* and *Kabbalah and Criticism* (both 1975), *Poetry and Repression* and *Figures of Capable Imagination* (both 1976), and *Wallace Stevens* (1977); E. Showalter, *A Literature of Their Own* (1977); S. M. Gilbert and S. Gubar, *The Madwoman in the Attic* (1979); J. Hollander, *The Figure of Echo* (1981); H. Bloom, *Agon* and *The Breaking of the Vessels* (both 1982); T. M. Greene, *The Light in Troy: Imitation and Discovery in Renaissance Poetry* (1982); J. Guillory, *Poetic Authority* (1983); R. Helgerson, *Self-Crowned Laureates* (1983); J. Loewenstein, *Responsive Readings* (1984); *The New Feminist Criticism*, ed. E. Showalter (1985)—esp. A. Kolodny, "A Map of Reading: Gender and Interpretation of Literary Texts," and B. Smith, "Toward a Black Feminist Criticism"; N. Lukacher, *Primal Scenes* (1986); *Ovid: "Amores,"* ed. J. C. McKeown, 4 v. (1987–); H. Bloom, *Poetics of Influence* (1988) and *Ruin the Sacred Truths* (1989); R. R. Edwards, *The Dream of Chaucer* (1989); *Intertextuality, Allusion, and Quotation*, ed. U. J. Hebel (1989); *Influence and Intertextuality in Literary History*, ed. J. Clayton and E. Rothstein (1991); R. Greene, *Post-Petrarchism* (1991); J. Shapiro, *Rival Playwrights* (1991); P. Hardie, *The Epic Successors of Virgil* (1993); C. Martindale, *Redeeming the Text* (1993); G. Allen, *Harold Bloom* (1994); W. J. Kennedy, *Authorizing Petrarch* (1994); H. Bloom, *The Western Canon* (1995); L. A. Renza, "Influence," *Critical Terms for Literary Study*, ed. F. Lentricchia and T. McLaughlin, 2d ed. (1995); P. Cheney, *Marlowe's Counterfeit Profession* (1997); S. Hinds, *Allusion and Intertext* (1998); H. Bloom, *Genius* (2002); R. R. Edwards, *Chaucer and Boccaccio* (2002); P. Hardie, *Ovid's Poetics of Illusion* (2002); C. Ricks, *Allusion to the Poets* (2002); W. J. Kennedy, *The Site of Petrarchism* (2003); M. Orr, *Intertextuality* (2003); C. Martindale, *Latin Poetry and the Judgement of Taste* (2005); P. Cheney, *Shakespeare's Literary Authorship* (2008); H. Dubrow, *The Challenges of Orpheus* (2008); H. Bloom, *The Anatomy of Influence* (2011).

P. CHENEY

**INFORMATION, POETRY AS.** John Guillory defines *information* as "any given (datum) of our cognitive experience that can be materially encoded for the purpose of transmission or storage"—distinct from *fact* on the one hand and *knowledge* on the other. The study of poetry of information accommodates two senses of *information*: one is quantitative and is derived from information theory, the influential branch of applied mathematics founded by C. E. Shannon after World War II, while the other is qualitative, concerned with the nature and application of information in poetry. From the standpoint of information theory, information, like matter or energy, is an object of quantitative analysis; for instance, it is a constitutive factor in feedback and equilibrium, the concepts developed by cybernetics that enable study of control and communication systems in animals, human beings, and machines. The Rus. linguist Roman Jakobson, whose intellectual formation was in structuralist ling. and *semiotics, was influenced by information theory from about 1950, and its assumptions (compounded by his interpolations) color some of his important work of that era, such as his description of the binary character of phonology in *Fundamentals of Language* (1956). After Jakobson, the earliest adaptations of information theory to poetics were the Ger. philosopher Max Bense's theory of "aesthetic information" and the Brazilian poet Haroldo de Campos's extension of that concept to the severely minimal poems of Stéphane Mallarmé, Gertrude Stein, and his *Noigandres group—all instances of what Campos calls, following Bense and the mathematician Benoît Mandelbrot, a "low informational temperature."

By contrast, the qualitative approach to the poetics of information often recognizes a more inclusive definition of the term (with less distinct boundaries against fact and knowledge) and theorizes a practice by which the poem includes, sometimes by parataxis (see HYPOTAXIS AND PARATAXIS) or juxtaposition, reportage, statistics, or other kinds of information that are usually considered nonpoetic or even antipoetic. This approach considers *information* a discourse or idiolect among others available to the poem (e.g. *confessional, *descriptive, or *prophetic); it is a rejoinder to Ludwig Wittgenstein's famous declaration that "a poem, even though it is composed in the language of information, is not used in the language-game of giving information" (*Zettel*, 1967). A poem of information in this sense may be long or short, lyrical or discursive, subjective or impersonal. But it tends to test the boundaries of poetic or *lyric convention, esp. the distinction between what Jakobson called the *poetic function and the corresponding "referential" function, in which content is communicated for its factual value. A poem of information, we might say, brings the referential function into poetic lang. in a vivid, sometimes an aesthetically or socially radical way. (While this poetics of information partly coincides with *documentary poetics, the latter tends to be based more often in actual documentary sources such as government records and archival material.)

The poetry of information has a long hist. in versified genealogies, almanacs, and other poems for use; but it is esp. visible in mod. and postmod. poetry in the U.S. and elsewhere, where it occupies several modes. Walt Whitman initiates the modernist poetry of information in "Song of Myself" (1855). From a certain angle, public poetry has always been a poetry of information. However, Whitman stretches *mimesis so that the social space of the poem indicates the possibility of—and the need for—lyric structures that embody new ranges of information. Whitman's *catalogs assemble a great deal of factual observation:

> The crew of the fish-smack pack repeated layers of
> halibut in the hold,
> The Missourian crosses the plains toting his wares
> and his cattle,
> The fare-collector goes through the train—he gives
> notice by the jingling of loose change,
> The floormen are laying the floor—the tinners are
> tinning the roof—the masons are calling for
> mortar,
> In single file each shouldering his hod pass onward
> the laborers; . . .
>
> (307–11)

What is important here is not the information itself but a new paradigm of social lyric, in which information comes between the "I" and the "you" as an object of exchange, an idiolect within the general lang. of the poem, and finally a medium of disjunction and connection. Whitman's representative "I" makes a social contract with a representative "you"—a subject position many readers, many citizens, may enter. Where information appears, this contract is often enacted through parataxis, one observation following another in parallel constructions that can seem direct and unmediated. And yet the paratactic logic of observation and enumeration does more than assemble facts; its juxtaposition of information about sexes, classes, occupations, and regions opens a virtual social space in the poem, making the poem a figure of society. E.g., Whitman writes,

> The blab of the pave . . . tires of carts and sluff of
> boot-soles and talk of the promenaders,
> The heavy omnibus, the driver with his interrogating thumb, the clank of the shod horses on the
> granite floor,
> The carnival of sleighs, the clinking and shouted
> jokes and pelts of snowballs,
> The hurrahs for popular favorites . . . the fury of
> roused mobs,
> The flap of the curtained litter—the sick man inside, borne to the hospital . . .
>
> (146–50)

Such information had not been previously considered fit for lyric poetry, esp. in such a paratactic, telegraphic presentation. Whitman's poetics of information has antecedents in *narrative poetry, for instance in the catalogs, lists, and descriptions of *epic; but in the context of his interest in representativeness as both an aesthetic and a political dimension of the poem, Whitman's paratactic juxtapositions inspired a modernist exploration of poetry as including society and hist. in new ways. In the spirit of Whitman's poetics of information, Ezra Pound articulated the possibility of long poems "including history" (*ABC of Reading*, 1934). Many of Pound's poems accommodate a more radical notion of inclusion than the conventional model of *occasional verse allows; while Alfred, Lord Tennyson's "The Charge of the Light Brigade" (1854) or Thomas Hardy's "The Convergence of the Twain" (1915) can be said to refer to hist., Pound's *Cantos* (1925–72) attempt to make historical consciousness actual in a construct of words, instructing and engaging a more active reader. Many U.S. poets continued to develop the capacity for fact and observation—and with it, the fullness of *representation—opened by Whitman and Pound. An anecdotal approach to the poetry of information can be found in the work of Charles Reznikoff (see OBJECTIVISM), esp. in *Testimony* (1934) and *Holocaust* (1975).

In the early 21st-c. U.S., the poetics of information can connect with approaches to poetries as different as neo-Marxism and Buddhism: as they do in their own ways, it analyzes and critiques the politics of subjectivity, discourse, and visibility. The poetics of information may also engage with ecopoetics, as poets inform their readers about climate change or the age of the earth in the social space of the poem (see ENVIRONMENT AND POETRY). In an "information society" in which information is monetized, politicized, and weaponized, recent U.S. poetry has increasingly embraced its role as a channel for conveying and a ground for critical reflection on the politics and economics around data of all sorts. Among the many mod. and contemp. U.S. poets in this mode are Lorine Niedecker, Muriel Rukeyser, Robert Hayden, Amiri Baraka, Michael S. Harper, Laura Mullen, Joseph Lease, Eleni Sikelianos, Julie Carr, Brenda Coultas, Camille Dungy, and Juliana Spahr.

Outside the U.S. and the trad. begun by Whitman, the poetics of information tends to emerge irregularly, in response to social circumstances and aesthetic impulses. Two examples follow. The Fr. poet Francis Ponge developed a definitional poetry, notably in *Le parti pris des choses* (*Siding with Things*, 1942), where poems describing oysters, snails, or bread are both objective, following the bodies and uses of these objects with minute attention in the tone of a lecture, and stubbornly subjective. "Neuer Zweck der Armee Hadrians" (The New Purpose of Hadrian's Army, 1979), by the Ger. poet Volker Braun, is based on an extended anecdote from Roman antiquity that would not be out of place in a work of hist. except for the speaker's avowal that he reads the anecdote "between the lines," thus acknowledging that historical information has been adapted not only materially to verse but to the inferential perspective of poetry.

*See* ARTIFACT, POETRY AS; FICTION, POETRY AS; KNOWLEDGE, POETRY AS; PHILOSOPHY AND POETRY; POIĒSIS.

■ L. Spitzer, *La enumeración caótica en la poesía moderna* (1945); C. E. Shannon, "A Mathematical Theory of Communication," *Bell System Technical Journal* 27 (1948); N. Wiener, *Cybernetics* (1948); Jakobson and Halle; M. Bense, "Klassifikation in der Literaturtheorie," *Augenblick* 2 (1958); J. L. Foster, "Pound's Revision of Cantos I–III," *MP* 63 (1966); R. Jakobson, G. Fant, and M. Halle, *Preliminaries to Speech Analysis*, 9th ed. (1969); R. P. Creed, "*Beowulf* on the Brink: Information Theory as Key to the Origins of the Poem," *Comparative Research on Oral Traditions*, ed. J. M. Foley (1987); W. R. Paulson, *The Noise of Culture: Literary Texts in a World of Information* (1988); N. Wiener, *The Human Use of Human Beings: Cybernetics and Society* (1989); *Chaos and Order*, ed. N. K. Hayles (1991); E. Grimm, "Mediamania? Contemporary German Poetry in the Age of New Information Technologies: Thomas Kling and Durs Grünbein," *Studies in Twentieth-Century Literature* 21 (1997); N. K. Hayles, *How We Became Posthuman: Virtual Bodies in Cybernetics, Literature, and Informatics* (1999); J. Guillory, "The Memo and Modernity," *CritI* 31 (2004)—the poetics of the memo; P. Laszlo and R. Lapidus, "Nothing Added, Nothing Subtracted," *SubStance* 33 (2004)—spec. iss. on "overload"; T. Terranova, "Communication beyond Meaning: On the Cultural Politics of Information," *Social Text* 22 (2004); H. de Campos, "The Informational Temperature of the Text," trans. J. Tolman, *Novas*, ed. A. S. Bessa and O. Cisneros (2007); S. McCaffery, "From Muse to Mousepad: Informatics and the Avant-Garde," *Phrasis* 49 (2008); J. Van de Walle, "Roman Jakobson, Cybernetics and Information Theory: A Critical Assessment," *Folia Linguistica Historica* 29 (2008); A. Galey, "Networks of Deep Impression: Shakespeare and the History of Information," *ShQ* 61 (2010); L. H. Liu, "The Cybernetic Unconscious: Rethinking Lacan, Poe, and French Theory," *CritI* 36 (2010).

J. LEASE

**IN MEDIAS RES** (Lat., "into the middle of things"). The device of beginning an *epic poem, drama, or work of fiction at some crucial point in the middle of a series of events that both initiates a subsequent chain of incidents and at the same time follows as the result of preceding ones. Thus, the author may work forward and backward in time to narrate the story or action. The effect is to arouse the reader's suspense and interest quickly. The phrase is taken from Horace's *Ars poetica* (147–48): "Always [the poet] hastens to the outcome and plunges his hearer into the midst of events as though they were familiar, and what he despairs of treating effectively he abandons." The suggestion that a poet should not begin "at the beginning" derives from Aristotle's argument in the *Poetics* that a plot is a specific arrangement of incidents unified by probability and necessity, not by sequence. Aristotle is recalling Homer: the *Odyssey* begins with the shipwreck of Odysseus after some ten years of wandering the Mediterranean, and the *Iliad* is not about the entire siege of Troy but a single episode in the last year of the war.

Horace's formulation became a standard convention and was discussed as such throughout the Middle Ages. During the Ren. *in medias res* was revived, critics distinguishing between "natural" (i.e., chronological) and "artificial" order. The effect of "artificial" order is to fold the temporal sequence of the narrative so that the poem opens at an esp. dramatic moment and then, at a later moment, includes a retrospective episode that recounts the origin of the events. The events depicted in John Milton's *Paradise Lost*, e.g., begin chronologically with the rebellion of Satan, the war in heaven, and the expulsion of the fallen angels; but the poem itself opens with the activities of the fallen angels in hell (books 1–2) after the expulsion. The plot moves forward from this point until books 5 and 6, when Raphael tells Adam of the dire consequences of disobeying God's laws. In other words, the convention has made it more complex, more polyvalent.

By contrast, a simpler version of in medias res is invoked by Edmund Spenser in the "Letter to Ralegh" purporting to explain *The Faerie Queene*. Spenser explains that the final meaning of all the adventures will be withheld until the last (12th) book of the poem—which, however, he never completed. The model of in medias res adopted by Ludovico Ariosto in *Orlando furioso* is a more complex variation on the convention: "artificial" order justifies multiple plotting, frequent digressions, and a mosaiclike arrangement of flashbacks and continuing narratives.

After the neoclassical period, the formal requirement of in medias res was ignored, but the precedent it established for complex enfoldings of narrative time is preserved in the device of flashback and the narrative reminiscence, as, e.g., in William Faulkner's novel *The Sound and the Fury*.

■ J. W. Draper, "The Narrative Technique of the *Faerie Queene*," *PMLA* 39 (1924); C. O. Brink, *Horace on Poetry*, 2 v. (1963–71); F. Quadlbauer, "Zur Theorie der Komposition in der mittelalterlichen Rhetorik und Poetik," *Rhetoric Revisited*, ed. B. Stock (1982); O. B. Hardison Jr., "*In medias res* in *Paradise Lost*," *Milton Studies* 17 (1983).

O. B. Hardison; R. A. Hornsby

**IN MEMORIAM STANZA.** A four-line stanza in iambic tetrameter, rhyming *abba*; so called from its use in Alfred, Lord Tennyson's *In Memoriam* (1850):

> I hold it true, whate'er befall;
> I feel it, when I sorrow most;
> 'Tis better to have loved and lost
> Than never to have loved at all.

Although Tennyson believed himself the originator of the stanza, it may be found in 17th-c. poetry, notably Ben Jonson ("An Elegy": "Though beauty be the mark of praise") and Lord Herbert of Cherbury ("An Ode upon a Question moved, whether Love should continue for ever?"). Before *In Memoriam*, Tennyson used the stanza in a few political poems. Early fragments of *In Memoriam* employ an *abab* stanza.

The *abba* form evokes traditional love poetry by recalling the octave of the Petrarchan *sonnet. The "measured" lang. of the tetrameter line, in contrast to the pentameter line of sonnets, produces a sense of something lost; the line's curtness suggests the poet's skepticism about the efficacy of lang. to express feeling and meaning, and implies an effort toward self-control.

Later uses of the stanza are rare; they include Oscar Wilde's "Symphony in Yellow" and Philip Larkin's "The Trees."

■ Schipper, *History*; E. P. Morton, "The Stanza of *In Memoriam*," *MLN* 21 (1906), and "Poems in the Stanza of *In Memoriam*," *MLN* 24 (1909); Saintsbury, *Prosody*; S. Gates, "Poetics, Metaphysics, Genre: The Stanza Form of *In Memoriam*," *VP* 37 (1999).

A. Preminger, E. T. Johnston

**INSCAPE AND INSTRESS.** In his essay "Poetry and Verse," G. M. Hopkins defines poetry as "speech only employed to carry the inscape of speech for the inscape's sake." *Inscape* is the central term in Hopkins's personal metaphysics. He coined the word by analogy with *landscape* to signify the cosmic patterns that structure the world. Just as he can speak of an Alpine glacier that is "swerved and *inscaped* to the motion of the mass," so too his theory holds that poetry (as speech) can discover deep affective meaning in patterns of human lang. sound. "Some matter and meaning is necessary," but such meaning has only an ancillary function as "an element necessary to support the shape which is contemplated for its own sake."

Hopkins's coinage of inscape antedates his discovery of the works of the Scholastic philosopher Duns Scotus, which he felt was "a mercy from God." After that, he reports, "When I took in any inscape of the sky or sea I thought of Scotus" (*Journal*, August 3, 1872). Scotus's realism enriched and valorized his concept. Louis Mackey comments that the "inscape" Scotus enabled Hopkins to see was "the network of forms [Scotistic "formalities"] that you see when you look at a thing through its haecceity [thisness]. . . . For Scotus insists on the full reality and intelligibility of the individual, the reality of the formalities discerned in things by the mind and the unity of the individual."

Hopkins often uses the term *instress* together with *inscape*. Instress is the force that vitalizes inscape for the perceiver. In his writings, Hopkins uses both terms for the first time in a note on the realism of the 5th c. BCE philosopher Parmenides, written around 1868: "I have often felt when I have felt the depth of an instress or how fast the inscape holds a thing that nothing is so pregnant and straightforward to the truth as simple *yes* and *is*." Of the numerous times the poet employs the terms in his writings, a jour. entry of Dec. 12, 1872, is one of the more suggestive. He reports closely observing the grass of the fells while walking with a Mr. Lucas: "I saw the inscape . . . freshly, as if my eye were still growing, though with a companion the eye and the ear are for the most part shut and instress cannot come."

■ *The Correspondence of Gerard Manley Hopkins and Richard Watson Dixon*, ed. C. C. Abbott (1935); *The Letters of Gerard Manley Hopkins to Robert Bridges,* ed. C. C. Abbott (1935); C. Devlin, "The Image and the Word," *Month* 3 (1950); G. Hartman, *The Unmediated Vision* (1954); *The Journal and Papers of Gerard Manley Hopkins,* ed. H. House (1959); M. Lichtmann, *The*

*Contemplative Poetry of Gerard Manley Hopkins* (1989); D. Brown, *Hopkins's Idealism* (1997); L. Mackey, *Peregrinations of the Word* (1997); J. Wimsatt, *Hopkins's Poetics of Speech Sound* (2006).

J. I. Wimsatt

**INSPIRATION** (Lat., "breathing in"). A concept that explains how a poet harnesses psychic and corporeal energies to make a poem. It often refers to a heightened state of being, through which the poet gains expressiveness and fluency. The typical scene of inspiration involves a subject who composes by encountering something outside common human experience, a force of alterity that can be integrated into a poetic process.

The Western concept of inspired poetics has roots in the Homeric epics, the *Iliad* and the *Odyssey* (ca. 800 BCE). Both begin with invocations to the supernatural Muses, a central trope of inspiration (see MUSE). Hesiod's *Theogony* (ca. 700 BCE) opens with a description of the Muses' breathing (*empneō*) a divine voice into the poet. In these works, the inspired state enhances memory, accuracy of description, and fluidity of speech.

Plato's dialogue *Ion* (4th-c. BCE), in which Socrates engages with a *rhapsode, established and perpetuated the concept of inspiration as *enthousiasmos*. Enthousiasmos, literally being filled with a divinity, connects poetic inspiration with possession, pure passivity, and ecstatic recitation. This version—known later as *furor poeticus* or poetic frenzy—became a dominant model for inspiration, although it is not exactly the same version reflected in Homer or Hesiod's inspired poetics. After Plato's influential dialogues, incl. the *Symposium* and *Phaedrus*, inspiration is equated with ecstasy.

The association of inspiration with divination manifests itself in the concept of the Roman *vates or poet as divine seer. Virgil, e.g., opens the *Aeneid* (29–19 BCE) with an invocation to the Muse and later in the poem claims the visionary power of the vates (7.41). Ovid, like Hesiod, asks the gods to "breathe into" his poetic work in the first lines of the *Metamorphoses* (1.3). Cicero uses the term *afflatus* (a blowing or breathing upon) for *inspiration* in his influential treatise on rhetoric *De oratore* (2.194).

A divine spirit that fills and overwhelms a composing subject also appears in early Heb. poetics and has a relationship to the originary animating breath of God described in Genesis. Figures like the poet-prophet David embody a dynamic between active and passive composition that resonates with poetic frenzy, even though the word *inspiration* itself is not used in the Hebraic trad. When God inspires prophets, the result is often a physiological experience that intensely affects the body (Is. 21:3, Jer.).

Inspiration persists and evolves after antiquity. The Ar. poet-critic Ibn Shuhayd, writing in med. Cordoba, discusses poetic inspiration at length in his *Treatise of Familiar Spirits and Demons* (ca. 1025). He advocates for poetry that is inspired, rather than simply a display of technical skill. This text fuses a pre-Islamic belief that each Ar. poet has an individual, inspiring genie

with an Islamic brand of Neoplatonism. Med. Christian poets also labored to reconcile their religious belief with figures like the Muses. Dante negotiates sacred and secular inspiration (as well as the inspiring influence of Christian and non-Christian poets) throughout the *Divine Comedy* (written 1307–21).

The attempt to rework cl. concepts of inspiration continued in the Ren. Marsilio Ficino made a major contribution to this project when he translated Plato's dialogues, incl. *Ion* (1484), into Lat. Later works by Pontus de Tyard (*Le solitaire premier*, 1552) and Francesco Patrizi (*Discorso della diversità de' furori poetici,* 1553) further adapted and promoted inspiration as Neoplatonic poetic frenzy. Guillaume de Salluste du Bartas's influential *La Muse Chrestiene* (1574) christianizes the Muse in the figure of Urania. This kind of syncretism also appears in Philip Sidney's *Defence of Poesy* (1595), in which he aligns the biblical poet-prophet David with the Roman vates. These treatises on inspiration reflect the changing and contested status of poets in the early mod. cultural moment, as well as larger debates on the social use of poetry.

The Sp. humanist and physician Juan Huarte moved toward a new model of inspiration in his work *Examen de ingenios* (1575), by developing a physiological account of poetic fury aligned with Galenic humoral theory. Writing in the same moment that the Port. poet Luís de Camões invokes the Muses for his epic *The Lusiads* (1572), Huarte's analysis of most poets' "overheated" temperaments emphasizes their inborn talent and anticipates significant shifts in the concept of inspiration that would fully develop in the 18th c. When John Milton invoked a Protestant Muse for his Christian theodicy *Paradise Lost* (1667, 1674) and claimed that his epic was "unpremeditated verse" (9.24), he made one of the last clear expressions of a Ren. trad. of inspired poetics. Late 17th-c. interest in Longinus's 1st-c. treatise *Peri hypsous* (*On the Sublime*) demystified inspiration, recasting it as an aesthetic and rhetorical effect of the *sublime. This secular brand of inspiration sprung from the poet's own mind, rather than arriving from the outside, through external forces (i.e., the Muses, God). Inspiration became the product of native *genius and *imagination, the mark of expansive human creative potential.

*Romanticism embraced inspiration as a dominant poetic mode, often involving an encounter with nature. P. B. Shelley reworks the model of Neoplatonic unbidden authorship and makes a forceful claim for the inspired poet's cultural authority in his treatise *A Defence of Poetry* (1821). He describes inspiration as arising within the poet, ignited by an external force, in a figure similar to the commonplace of the Aeolian harp. S. T. Coleridge's "Kubla Khan" (written 1797–98, pub. 1816) refigures ecstatic composition as a kind of dream work, exploring poetic imagination's potential. Working within a strain of Ger. romanticism, Friedrich Hölderlin aligns inspiration with a philosophical practice that collapses the opposition between the unbridled genius and the poetic technician.

Literary *modernism resisted the elevated status of inspiration that romanticism had produced, by further anchoring it in the psyche's operations. Sigmund Freud's theory of the unconscious resonated with postromantic theories of inspiration, and T. S. Eliot argued against a mystified sense of inspiration, characterizing it in psychological terms as "the sudden lifting of the burden of anxiety and fear"—in short, a lifting of repression. Laura Riding Jackson, writing in the 1920s, encapsulates this line of modernist thought in one sentence: "mystery was replaced by science; inspiration by psychology." Paul Valéry characterized inspiration as a naïve theory of creativity, yet the term eventually reemerged in his work as viable, but only when displaced from the poet onto the reader; Valéry likened the poet to a technician and the poem to "a kind of machine" designed to give the reader an inspired feeling. André Breton and the surrealist movement further stripped inspiration of its spiritual connotations and reframed it as an experimental dispossession and loss of authorial control, through techniques such as automatic writing (see SURREALISM).

In a different mode, the Beat poet Allen Ginsberg embraced a sacred poetic register and adopted a prophetic tone; the title of his collection *Mind Breaths* (1978) also reestablished the etymological connection between inspiration and breath. Such figures of inspiration continued to develop in tandem with changing social roles for the poet, from political commentator to 20th-c. mystic. The poet-prophet, however, became an exception in a period of emergent *poststructuralism that emphasized textuality over authorship or voice.

Postmod. poets, like modernists before them, resisted traditional figures of inspiration. And yet, poetics after the 1950s returned to breath itself as a principle of composition—as exemplified by Charles Olson's influential essay "Projective Verse" (1950)—suggesting the literal sense of inspiration. The movement of experimental Am. *oral poetry, represented by the postmod. poet David Antin's improvised "talk-poems," evokes ancient connections between inspiration and breath in "live" performances that recall the oral composition of Gr. epic. Juliana Spahr's work *This Connection of Everyone with Lungs* (2005), though following a trad. of poststructuralist inflected *Language poetry, explores breath as an organizing principle for poetry and politics. For Spahr—who writes against a notion of self-contained *originality that has a long hist. as the antithesis of inspiration—the act of drawing in a breath situates the poet in an environment of interconnected human and nonhuman beings.

Literary theorist Maurice Blanchot anticipated such repurposing of inspiration when he returned to the foundational myth of Orpheus in his critical work *The Space of Literature*. For Blanchot, the arrival of inspiration is a "désoeuvrement": a moment of "unworking" or a "non-event" that affirms the work of poetry in an undoing of the poet's subjectivity. Blanchot shifts away from the bounded agency of the "productive" poet and refocuses instead on the nonteleological and even "posthuman" potential revealed in the moment of inspired composition. Blanchot's intervention, like the work of some postmod. poets, reaffirms inspiration as a concept that continues to inform poetic discourse in the 21st c.

*See* INFLUENCE, INVENTION, PSYCHOLOGY AND POETRY, WIT.

■ A. Avni, "Inspiration in Plato and the Hebrew Prophets," *CL* 20 (1968); M. Blanchot, *The Space of Literature*, trans. A. Smock (1982); J. Guillory, *Poetic Authority: Spenser, Milton, and Literary History* (1983); P. Valéry, "Poetry and Abstract Thought," *The Collected Works of Paul Valéry*, ed. J. Mathews (1985); J. M. Ziolkowski, "Classical Influences on Medieval Latin Views of Poetic Inspiration," *Latin Poetry and the Classical Tradition: Essays in Medieval and Renaissance Literature*, ed. P. Godman and O. Murray (1990); R. Macksey, "Longinus Reconsidered," *MLN* 108 (1993); F. Burwick, *Poetic Madness and the Romantic Imagination* (1996); T. Clark, *The Theory of Inspiration* (1997); J. Huntington, "Furious Insolence: The Social Meaning of Poetic Inspiration in the 1590s," *MP* 94 (1997); P. Murray, "Poetic Inspiration in Early Greece," *Oxford Readings in Ancient Literary Criticism*, ed. A. Laird (2006); G. Regn, "Double Authorship: Prophetic and Poetic Inspiration in Dante's Paradise," *MLN* 122 (2007); J. Rasula, *Modernism and Poetic Inspiration* (2009).

M. URSELL

**INTENSITY.** Intensity, although chiefly a romantic standard of poetic excellence, has a long hist. Its most famous cl. statement is in Longinus's *Peri hypsous* (*On the Sublime*, 1st c. CE) with its emphasis on the superiority of original *genius to trad., of strong emotion to restraint. Philip Sidney's *Defence of Poesy* (1595) similarly underlines the superiority of the poet to the philosopher partly on grounds of intensity that can "strike, pierce, [or] possess the sight of the soul." John Dryden's recognition in his *Essay of Dramatic Poesy* (1668) of the intensity of Shakespeare's imagery can be seen in Neander's observation that "when he describes anything, you more than see it, you feel it too." Thomas Hobbes and John Locke among other Brit. empirical philosophers did much to challenge 18th-c. rationalism and to emphasize the power of sensation. Nicolas Boileau's trans. of Longinus in 1674 stirred wide interest in literary circles; but Edmund Burke's treatise *On the Sublime and the Beautiful* (1757) was even more influential, with its characterization of the sublime as "productive of the strongest emotion which the mind is capable of feeling" or as producing "astonishment."

It is among the romantics that intensity receives its fullest expression. William Wordsworth speaks of poetry as "the spontaneous overflow of powerful feelings" (Preface to *Lyrical Ballads*, 1800). P. B. Shelley contends that it is impossible to read the most celebrated writers of his day "without being startled with the electric life which burns within their words" (*A Defence of Poetry*, 1821). William Hazlitt's "gusto" embodies one of the most powerful descriptions of intensity in art—"power or passion defining any object" ("On Gusto," 1816).

His emphasis on poetry's need for a firm grasp of reality is reflected in John Keats's idea of *negative capability— "the excellence of every art is its intensity capable of making all disagreeables evaporate from their being in close relationship with Beauty and Truth" (letter of 1817).

E. A. Poe's attraction to intensity is evidenced in his requirement that poems be short, that stories be such that they can be read in one sitting ("The Poetic Principle," 1848). Subsequent 19th-c. advocates of art for art's sake continued this trad., with Walter Pater searching for "the focus where the greatest number of vital forces unite in their purist energy," arguing that "to burn always with this hard, gemlike flame, to maintain this ecstasy is success in life" (Preface, *The Renaissance*, 1873).

But, in general, the late 19th c. saw a marked shift away from the emphasis on intensity in art. Major examples include Matthew Arnold's praise for great human actions and his unhappiness with situations where "suffering finds no vent in action" (Preface, *Poems*, 1853); the more scientific methodology of C. A. Sainte-Beuve and Hippolyte Taine in studying connections between work and author, work and the spirit of the age; and Leo Tolstoy's stress on the social responsibility of art. More notable still is the critical writing of T. S. Eliot, with its focus on trad., on objectivity, on intelligence in the poet, and on the idea of the *objective correlative. The increasingly scientific and textually oriented approaches of the Am. *New Criticism downplayed intensity in favor of *irony and structure, while *poststructuralism and esp. deconstruction questioned fundamental presumptions of authorial presence and textual meaning, offering, instead of perceived intensity, delight in the play of lang.

■ T. R. Henn, *Longinus and English Criticism* (1934); S. Monk, *The Sublime* (1935); W. J. Bate, *From Classic to Romantic* (1946); Abrams; W. Jackson, *Immediacy* (1973); J. Engell, *The Creative Imagination* (1981); J. L. Mahoney, *The Whole Internal Universe* (1985); P. Veyne, Epilogue, *Roman Erotic Elegy*, trans. D. Pellauer (1988); T. McFarland, *William Wordsworth* (1992); F. Ferguson, *Solitude and the Sublime* (1992).

J. L. Mahoney

**INTENTION.** The question of the relevance and value of intention has been at the center of debate in literary theory for well over half a century, and the controversy is far from reaching a satisfactory resolution. In Anglo-Am. literary theory, the debate found its central terms in W. K. Wimsatt and M. C. Beardsley's well-known essay, "The Intentional Fallacy." Here Wimsatt and Beardsley characterize all crit. that takes account of authorial intention in the production of a literary work as committing a serious "fallacy" and resolve the question in favor of New Critical formalism (see NEW CRITICISM).

Wimsatt and Beardsley deny not the presence of intention in the structure of a poem, but the usefulness of any genetic analysis of intention. A genetic analysis attempts to give a causal explanation of how literary works are created. Many genetic theorists claim that their accounts provide criteria for deciding whether the poet succeeds in producing the poem he or she intends to produce and that such criteria also provide a more valid (because more objective) methodology for the appreciation and judgment of the poem. Wimsatt and Beardsley reject this claim.

The anti-intentionalist position denies that knowledge of a poet's intention is necessary to the proper critical appreciation and judgment of a poem. It extends this denial to the romantic claim for the relationship of the poet's personality to his poems. Wimsatt and Beardsley further argue that poems are verbal structures made out of public lang., which is governed by the conventions of a lang. community; any ambiguity or obscurity in a poem occurs not because a private lang. has crept into the poem but because the conventions of a lang. community permit it, since it adds to the poem's aesthetic richness. Anti-intentionalists such as Wimsatt and Beardsley argue that a great deal of crit. confuses inquiries beginning with "why" (our reasons for finding a poem interesting and successful) with inquiries beginning with "how" (the way the poem came about).

The rejection of intentionalist crit. was part of a more comprehensive attack on *romanticism launched earlier in the 20th c. by T. E. Hulme and T. S. Eliot. For the modernists, romantic critics such as Walter Pater, C. A. Sainte-Beuve, and Hippolyte Taine are the antagonists whose method of appreciation and judgment of poetry is genetic. The romantic writers and critics place great emphasis on individual experience and inner vision, which constitute for them central aspects of the work an artist produces. Consequently, artists no longer have a common set of problems that critics can understand and appraise. Given the emphasis on the peculiar qualities of a poet's vision, *sincerity, *originality, *spontaneity, and adequacy become the romantic criteria of crit. Wimsatt and Beardsley and other modernist critics reject these criteria as irrelevant to the interpretation of literary works.

Anti-intentionalists argue that, in the process of writing, poets often abandon their original intention or include elements not central to that intention. If a poet changes intention in the course of writing a poem, we can no longer consider the original intention as the standard for judging. On this view, authorial intentions are at best a posteriori ratiocinations important to take into account but also subject to scrutiny in the light of the finished work of art. Moreover, in the cases of anonymous poetry, of Homer and Shakespeare, and of most other poetry of the past, there is no way of determining the poet's intention. Finally, there is the Socratic argument about the inherent unreliability of the poet's capacity to explain his or her intention.

The controversy over the role of intention is part of a larger dispute on more fundamental questions about what a work of art is and what is proper to crit. The anti-intentionalist position conceives the theoretical problems of creativity and crit. as definitional and conceptual ones to be settled by rigorous logical scrutiny;

Wimsatt and Beardsley, therefore, assert that "it is not so much a historical statement as a definition to say that the intentional fallacy is a romantic one."

Romanticism, however, is a historical phenomenon that gave rise to a host of conceptual and definitional problems not resolvable by some unitary and objective logical procedure. Moreover, intentionalists such as E. D. Hirsch Jr. question Wimsatt and Beardsley's distinction between poetic lang. and ordinary lang. Hirsch insists that all uses of lang. "are ethically governed by the intention of the author." On this view, the author is the determiner of the meaning of his or her work because, without that, we have no compelling normative principle for validating one interpretation and rejecting others. Without some knowledge of what an author set out to do, we cannot reasonably judge how well she did it; otherwise, a critic is liable to condemn the work for not being the kind of work the critic happens to approve of—i.e., the kind of work the author never set out to create in the first place.

In much broader studies of lang. and discourse, philosophers and theorists such as Michel Foucault and Jacques Derrida have proposed radically anti-intentionalist views that contest any notion of author, origin, intention, the literary, or oeuvre. Poststructuralist forms of crit. characterize the author as a product of the work rather than the other way around (see POST-STRUCTURALISM). Thus emerged a powerful view that there can be a thought without a thinker, an action without an agent, a poem without a poet. On this view, literary works are necessarily a part of lang. as autonomous discourse that cannot be constrained by presumably unassailable objective criteria of crit. Once critics reject the poet's own intention for interpretation of her literary work, there is no way to curtail the freedom critics acquire in interpreting the work. In contrast to this structuralist and poststructuralist anti-intentionalist position, the anti-intentionalist formalist position supports and consolidates modernist aesthetics, in an attempt to elaborate objective criteria for interpretation and evaluation of texts. For modernist literary theorists and critics, the poststructuralist conception of lang. operates at a level where it essentially undermines the very conception of crit. as a discipline.

In this context, P. de Man, although a strong deconstructive critic, is a thoroughgoing anti-intentionalist throughout his work in a rather formalist sense. From his *Blindness and Insight* to his radically deconstructive phase, he distinguishes between ordinary and literary lang. For de Man, the everyday use of lang. is marked "by the duplicity, the confusion, the untruth" (1971), whereas literary lang. is characterized by "its separation from empirical reality" (1971). This view is affirmed in his *Allegories of Reading* where de Man stresses the absolute centrality of the nonempirical mechanisms of literary lang. Holding a strict notion of authorial impersonality, de Man argues that the relation of the author's intention to her work is always a contingent one. In effect, although radically opposed to New Critical formalism in terms of his overall deconstructive perspective, de Man remains closely allied to the New Critical anti-intentionalist stance and, thus, to the importance of the uniquely self-contained nature of the literary work. Consequently, the real opposition in the context of intention is not between de Man and the New Critics but between New Criticism and those influenced by such poststructuralist thinkers as Foucault and Derrida.

However, not all forms of contemp. crit. reject the concept of intention. In fact, whenever feminist scholars, pursuing a form of *New Historicism, underline the importance of women's agency and, therefore, of intention, causality, and change, they refuse to take a Foucauldian New Historicist stance that conceptualizes power as faceless, anonymous, and irresistible. There is, of course, no consensus among scholars within feminist studies, postcolonial studies, Af. Am. studies, Latin Am. studies, and Af. studies, among others, on the question of intention, and they do not all take a strictly Derridean or Foucauldian stance. Indeed, since critics within these and other related fields seek to explore the relationship of literary texts to extraliterary and extradiscursive forces and pressures and to the material world, they cannot altogether avoid—and they often embrace—concepts of agency, identity, intention, experience, and event.

Whenever we talk about a literary work's ability not just to adapt and vary received or currently dominant discourses and practices but actually to create new ones, we are talking about its writer's ability to intervene into discourse and thus into literary history and politics. Such an intervention cannot always avoid intentional considerations. One of the crucial premises of at least some inquiries in feminism, postcolonial studies, and Af. Am. studies is that literary writers within their fields are able to give voice and form to aspects of experience rarely articulated in lang. and lit. Moreover, when we talk about the historicity of every text's production and reception, the needs and interests of its author and readers can play a role in the construction and interpretation of that text, even when these interests and needs are produced by a multiplicity of social and historical forces.

In sum, modernist anti-intentionalists give considerable logical power and coherence to their position and its formalist and organicist criteria, and they succeed in showing the limitations of romantic criteria. Structuralists and poststructuralists, from their different philosophical perspectives, also propose views of lang. and discourse that radically question the category of intention but in ways that would also reject New Critical formalism. Yet none of these forms of crit. can succeed in showing that intentionalists are entirely wrong, for there are always numerous ways by which other critics can show how art, personality, and consciousness are indissolubly linked together, making it important and sometimes indispensable for the critic to take into account historical, cultural, material, and biographical contexts for the proper interpretation and judgment of literary works. The category of intentionality itself cannot be eliminated completely from literary crit. because, at some level, we are always aware of the distinction between nonhuman and human products. The conflict between intentionalists and anti-intentionalists arises because they hold different theories about the nature of works of art and about lang.; given their conflicting perspectives, neither position can be reduced to a version of the other or eliminated. The dispute about the relevance of intention is a peculiar one, for the conflict about the nature of literary works is not empirical, resolvable by standard modes of observation and confirmation, but fundamental and conceptual.

*See* BIOGRAPHY AND POETRY; INTERPRETATION.

■ T. S. Eliot, *The Use of Poetry and the Use of Criticism* (1933); *The Critic's Notebook*, ed. R. W. Stallman (1950), ch. 8; Abrams; W. K. Wimsatt and M. C. Beardsley, "The Intentional Fallacy," *The Verbal Icon* (1954); I. Hungerland, "The Concept of Intention in Art Criticism," *Journal of Philosophy* 52 (1955); M. C. Beardsley, *Aesthetics* (1958); E. D. Hirsch Jr., *Validity in Interpretation* (1967); R. Maier, " 'The Intentional Fallacy' and the Logic of Literary Criticism," *CE* 32 (1970); P. de Man, *Blindness and Insight* (1971); J. Derrida, *Speech and Phenomena*, trans. D. B. Allison (1973)—critique of authorial intention in the phenomenology of Husserl; G. Hermeren, "Intention and Interpretation in Literary Criticism," *NLH* 7 (1975); E. D. Hirsch Jr., *The Aims of Interpretation* (1976); *On Literary Intention*, ed. D. Newton-de Molina (1976); W. K. Wimsatt, "Genesis: An Argument Resumed," *Day of the Leopards* (1976); J. W. Meiland, "Interpretation as a Cognitive Discipline," *Philosophy and Literature* 2 (1977); P. de Man, *Allegories of Reading* (1979); K. K. Ruthven, *Critical Assumptions* (1979), ch. 9; P. D. Juhl, *Interpretation* (1980); S. Raval, "Intention and Contemporary Literary Theory," *JAAC* 38 (1980); J. M. Ellis, "Wittgensteinian Thinking in Theory of Criticism," *NLH* 12 (1981); M. C. Beardsley, *The Aesthetic Point of View* (1982), ch. 11; J. Searle, *Intentionality* (1983); H. P. Grice, *Studies in the Way of Words* (1989); A. Patterson, "Intention," *Critical Terms for Literary Study*, ed. F. Lentricchia and T. McLaughlin, 2d ed. (1995); J. T. Shawcross, *Intentionality and the New Traditionalism* (1992); J. Farrell, "Intention and Intertext," *Phoenix* 59 (2005).

S. RAVAL

**INTENTIONAL FALLACY.** "The Intentional Fallacy" is the title of a 1946 article by William K. Wimsatt, Jr. and Monroe C. Beardsley. The essay argues against the notion that literary texts should be interpreted in light of authorial intention, understood as an independent design or plan in the author's mind. Authorial intention, they argue, is inaccessible to the reader outside of the evidence present in the poem itself. When critics appeal to intention, they are, therefore, asking readers to turn away from the poem toward supplementary texts such as jours., notebooks, and letters. In contrast, Wimsatt and Beardsley argue that poems are public productions, separable from their moments of creation.

The essay established many of the key tenets of the *New Criticism. In particular, it solidified the idea that poems are autonomous organic structures, to be evaluated based upon the critic's assessment of their internal patterns of sound and meaning. The essay also reaffirmed the New Critics's distrust of biographical and historical crit., as well as their attraction to the antiro-

mantic, impersonal aesthetic developed by writers like T. E. Hulme and T. S. Eliot.

Since its publication, "The Intentional Fallacy" has set the terms for much subsequent debate about the nature of *interpretation. In particular, its critique of the romantic myth of authorship prefigures the "death of the author" thesis popularized by Roland Barthes. Other critics, esp. those associated with neopragmatism, challenged Wimsatt and Beardsley's work. In particular, Steven Knapp and Walter Benn Michaels argue that the intentional fallacy depends upon an incoherent distinction between textual meaning and authorial intention. This distinction leads critics to believe that they must access an author's innermost thoughts before accurately interpreting the words on the page. For Knapp and Michaels, in contrast, there is no such thing as intentionless meaning; all literary interpretation is oriented toward determining authorial intention.

*See* INTENTION.

■ W. K. Wimsatt and M. C. Beardsley, "The Intentional Fallacy" and "The Affective Fallacy," *The Verbal Icon* (1954); R. Barthes, "The Death of the Author," *Image-Music-Text*, trans. S. Heath (1977); S. Knapp and W. B. Michaels, "Against Theory," *Against Theory*, ed. W.J.T. Mitchell (1985).

S. SCHRYER

**INTERNAL RHYME** (Ger. *Inreim, Binnenreim*; It. *rimalmezzo*). Refers to the Eng. cover term for a variety of rhymes that occur not at the end of the line but within the line. Internal rhyme, therefore, shifts emphasis away from line endings and often away from the interplay between lines to the interplay between words. While the terminology is not standardized across prosodies, the typology of forms includes (1) rhyming (a) a word at line end with a word or words in the same line or (b) in another; or (2) rhyming (a) words within a line with each other but not with a word at line end or (b) a word or words within one line with a word or words in another but not with a word at line end. E.g., G. M. Hopkins uses types (1a) and (2a) in "Carrion Comfort": "That my chaff might fly; my grain lie, sheer and clear. / Nay in all that toil, that coil." Charlotte Smith employs internal rhyme more subtly with type (2b) in "Ode to Death":

> Friend of the wretched! wherefore should the eye
> Of blank Despair, whence tears have ceased to
>     flow,
> Be turned from thee?—Ah! wherefore fears to die
> He, who compelled each poignant grief to know,
> Drains to its lowest dregs the cup of woe?

Types (1a) and (2a) occur within a single line, types (1b) and (2b) usually in two consecutive lines. Type (1a), Ger. *Inreim* or *Mittelreim*, Fr. *rime léonine* or *renforcée*, most often rhymes the word at line end with the word at the *caesura: this form developed in the Middle Ages and is known as *leonine rhyme and the form that in English prosody is usually meant by the phrase *internal rhyme*. Type (2a), Ger. *Binnenreim*, most often rhymes two words inside the same line and is sometimes in Eng. called *sectional rhyme*; if the rhyming in a long-line couplet is ——*a* ——*a* —— *b* / ——*a* ——*a* ——*b*, splitting into short-line verse will give *tail rhyme. Type (1b), Ger. *Kettenreim* or *Mittenreim*, Fr. *rime batelée*, most often rhymes the line-end word of one line with the caesural word of the next or vice versa; Eng. prosodists sometimes call this *caesura rhyme*. In the Fr. *rime brisée*, caesura rhymes with caesura and end with end; this was already developed in leonine verse and is treated here as *cross rhyme. Both Fr. and Ger. forms developed from med. Lat.; Meyer gives a full taxonomy of types. The Fr. terms for these elaborately interlaced sound patterns were developed mainly by the *Grands* *Rhétoriqueurs* of the late 15th and early 16th cs. Internal rhyme has also been an important structuring agent in non-Western oral poetries. Lao and Thai poetries, e.g., feature yoked-word rhyme, which strings together rhyme after rhyme to heighten musical-performative aspects of lang. and which has been difficult to replicate in Eng. trans. Internal rhyme is also a chief characteristic of *hip-hop poetics.

■ K. Bartsch, "Der innere Reim in der höfischen Lyrik," *Germania* 12 (1867); Meyer; Patterson; W. Vogt, "Binnenreime in der Edda," *Acta Philologica Scandinavica* 12 (1938); H. Forster, "Der Binnenreim (Reimformel)," *Sprachspiegel* 37 (1981); Brogan; C. Compton, "Lao Poetics: Internal Rhyme in the Text of a *Lam Sithandone* Performance," *Papers on Tai Languages, Linguistics, and Literatures*, ed. C. J. Compton and J. F. Hartmann (1992); A. Bradley, *Book of Rhymes: The Poetics of Hip Hop* (2009).

T.V.F. BROGAN; J. CHANG

**INTERPRETATION.** Arguably the first, or earliest, principle of interpretation is that one understands a text—an oracle, a commandment, a scriptural parable— when one recognizes how it applies to oneself. For St. Augustine and Martin Luther, among many others, to interpret is (for better or worse) to see one's life in light of the text. Such a principle is foundational for legal hermeneutics, where interpretation always involves the application of texts to situations at hand. Mod. hermeneutics is often said to begin with the recognition that texts are, nevertheless, historical documents whose intelligibility belongs to the time and place of their composition. Friedrich Schleiermacher (1786–1834) attempted to square ancients and moderns by distinguishing between historical and psychological dimensions of interpretation. E.g., he formulates the basic principle of cl. philology as follows: "To understand the text at first as well as and then even better than its author" ("Compendium of 1819"). As in Petrarch's reading of Cicero, this means learning to inhabit the world of another person—bridging time, not piercing a veil. But Schleiermacher gives this idea a strong subjective turn when he proposes that, in addition to historical research, there is "a divinatory method [that] enables us to reconstruct the creative act that begins with the generation of thoughts which captivate the author and to understand how the requirement of the moment could draw upon the living treasure of

words in the author's mind in order to produce just this way of putting it and no other" ("The Academy Addresses of 1829"). In the words of Wilhelm Dilthey (1833–1911), "we strain to get inside a speaker" (1996). Interpretation is more than the *exegesis of meanings because meaning is not just a logical entity but is a life expression (*Lebenäusserung*), i.e., an expression of the lived experience (*Erlebnis*) of someone from the past. Experience is something that can be understood not from the outside or at a distance but only by living through it; and insofar as hist. is composed of experiences, it can only be understood internally, i.e., by reliving it, or what Dilthey calls *Nacherleben*, the key word of Dilthey's hermeneutics. *Nacherleben* means projecting oneself into the expressions that come down to us from the past, breathing one's life into them, and making them live again as they did when they were first composed.

Twentieth-c. thinking, by contrast, has stressed the historical limitations of such a task. As G.W.F. Hegel (1770–1831) had already insisted, "No one can escape the substance of his time any more than he can jump out of his own skin" (1985). Thus, for Martin Heidegger (1889–1976), interpretation can proceed only according to suppositions that our own cultural horizon makes available to us: "If, when one is engaged in a particular concrete kind of interpretation, one likes to appeal [*beruft*] to what 'stands there,' [but] then one finds that what 'stands there' in the first instance is nothing other than the obvious undiscussed assumption [*Vormeinung*] of the person who does the interpreting" (1962). This poses, however, a fundamental difficulty, familiar to anthropologists: how can we understand things that are not of our world? Heidegger's idea is analogous to the ancient practice of *allegory: understanding means the appropriation and integration of what is alien into our scheme of things. All interpretation is a form of trans.—hence, Hans-Georg Gadamer's (1900–2002) famous line, "We understand in a different way if we understand at all" (1989).

What interests Gadamer, however, is the question of what happens when texts refuse to be appropriated in this way. Gadamer identifies the "classical text," e.g., as one that causes us to reflect critically on the concepts and categories by which we usually make sense of things. Paradoxically, a "hermeneutical experience" is not an experience of intelligibility; it is rather "the experience of being brought up short by the text" (1989), something that is closer to the Socratic experience of being called into question than to Dilthey's notion of Erlebnis. Indeed, Gadamer refers explicitly to Hegel's concept of experience as *Erfahrung*, which entails the sense of undergoing a journey, trial, or crisis in which we leave behind some prior certainty or ground, some settled belief or self-understanding. Gadamer's point is that the cl. text makes a normative claim on us that requires a reinterpretation of ourselves, which means an alteration not just of our subjective disposition or perspective but of the world we inhabit. Paul Ricoeur (1913–2005) makes a similar point when he figures the text not as an author's originating intention but as the projection of a possible world that invites a critical comparison with our own. The aim of interpretation, Ricoeur says, "is no longer an intention hidden behind the text, but a world unfolded in front of it. The power of the text to open a dimension of reality implies in principle a recourse against any given reality and thereby the possibility of a critique of the real," to which he adds this interesting point: "It is in poetic discourse that this subversive power is most alive" (1981). By "poetic discourse," Ricoeur means principally narrative texts, whose mimetic power is oriented toward the future insofar as it projects a possibility that we might take up and put into play in order to change the world we inhabit. Fredric Jameson (b. 1934) proposes a comparable idea when he speaks of the potentially utopian character not just of narratives but of cultural artifacts in general. Imagine interpretation as the devel. of alternative forms of life.

For Gadamer, it is not only the text that comes down to us from the past (or from any time or place other than our own) that requires us to alter our way of thinking in order to comprehend it. In "The Relevance of the Beautiful," he argues that the same is true of the modernist work of art—the "hermetic" poetry of Stéphane Mallarmé, the cubist *collage, Marcel Duchamp's Readymades, and atonal music are among his examples. Here it appears that what understanding is called on to understand are its limits, its finitude, perhaps even its own impossibility. As Theodor Adorno (1903–69) says in his *Aesthetic Theory*, "Aesthetics cannot hope to grasp works of art if it treats them as hermeneutical objects. What at present needs to be grasped is their unintelligibility." There is nothing self-evident about artworks, particularly in our time when, as Adorno says, the task of the artist is "to make things of which we do not know what they are." Gadamer's response to this interpretive antinomy is to say that we can no longer regard the artwork from a distance as if it were a contemplative object, much less a bearer of meanings. On the contrary, in order to experience the work at all, we need to situate ourselves as participants in the temporality of its formal construction. To elucidate this idea, Gadamer invokes the model of the festival that invites us to enter into the play of its events, where play is not a rule-governed activity but is rather a form of Aristotle's *phronesis* or practical wisdom, knowing (or, more often, learning) how to make one's way in an unprecedented situation where familiar concepts and categories no longer apply. Openness to what is singular and irreproducible, unpredictable and offering no return on investment, is what makes the experience of *modernism, and perhaps of all art, possible. But this openness leads to a two-way street: "Every work," Gadamer says, "leaves the person who responds to it a certain leeway, a space to be filled in by himself" (1986). The work is more event than entity; its form is always open to the future, and so is our relation with it: "It is important to note that all interpretation points in a direction rather than to some final endpoint, in the sense that it points toward an open realm that can be filled in a variety of ways" (1976). In this re-

spect, the interpretation of the work, and indeed the work itself, is always an ongoing project—an idea that has considerable prominence in contemp. North Am. poetics, with its notion of *"open form." E.g., in "The Rejection of Closure," the poet Lyn Hejinian (b. 1941) writes, "The 'open text,' by definition, is open to the world and particularly to the reader. . . . [It] often emphasizes or foregrounds process, either the process of the original composition or of subsequent compositions by readers, and thus resists the cultural tendencies that seek to identify and fix material and turn it into a product; that is, it resists reduction and commodification."

Just so, for Gadamer the model of the festival implies that the experience of the work is not a private, subjective experience; rather, "it consists in the experience of community" (1985). In this sense, understanding is, as he says elsewhere, more "a mode of being [than] a consciousness of something" ("The Philosophical Foundations of Twentieth-Century Philosophy"). Recall Ludwig Wittgenstein's (1889–1951) famous remark from his *Philosophical Investigations*: "To imagine a language is to imagine a form of life." The same principle applies to the work of art, as Stanley Cavell (b. 1926) argues in an essay on atonal music: "The language of tonality is part of a particular form of life, one containing the music we are most familiar with. . . . No wonder we want to preserve the idea of tonality: to give all *that* up seems like giving up the idea of music altogether." However, the problem in this event is not with atonality but with ourselves insofar as we are just fixed in place, schooled in received ways of experiencing music. Cavell thinks of this as an anthropological problem in which understanding atonality, being able to experience it as music, means "naturalizing ourselves to a new form of life, a new world." To make sense of anything new, we must change.

Art historians often take a more conceptual approach to the question of what counts as art. In "The Artworld," Arthur Danto (b. 1924), referring to Andy Warhol's pop art, puts it this way: "What in the end makes the difference between a Brillo box and a work of art consisting of a Brillo box is a certain theory of art. It is the theory that takes it up into the world of art, and keeps it from collapsing into the real object which it is. . . . Of course, without the theory, one is unlikely to see it as art, and in order to see it as part of the artworld, one must have mastered a good deal of artistic theory." In other words, one cannot tell that a thing is an artwork just by looking at it. One has to see the work as the instantiation of an art concept. Indeed, conceptual artists like Sol Lewitt go even further: "Ideas alone can be works of art: they are in a chain of development that may find some form. All ideas need not be made physical."

Danto's idea of the priority of the "artworld" is sometimes called an "institutional" theory of art, where the question of what counts as art is answered by galleries, museums, auctions, and art historians. This is not entirely wrong, but it would be more fruitful to recall the historical interdependence of poetry and poetics, where *poetics* refers to what poets themselves, in contrast to literary critics and historians, have written about poetry—Horace, Dante, Edmund Spenser, William Wordsworth, Mallarmé. The poem is, whatever else it is, the instantiation of its poetics, and this fact calls for study. From the *zaum'* poems of the Rus. futurists to the recent ling. experiments of the North Am. Language group (see LANGUAGE POETRY), we find multiple and heterogeneous variations on Mallarmé's idea that poetry is made of words but not of what we use words to produce—meanings, descriptions, self-expressions ("Crisis in Poetry"). Not that the poem excludes these things, but one misses the point if one construes the poem simply as a form of mediation (the argument, interestingly of a famous essay by Susan Sontag [1933–2004], "Against Interpretation"). The point is to find new ways of experiencing what the Rus. futurists called the "word as such."

One could go from here to investigate such innovations as *visual poetry or *concrete poetry, *sound poetry, and recent experiments in holography in which one alters a poem as one proceeds through its virtual space. In each of these cases, but particularly in "holopoetry," our relation to the work becomes a matter of increasing complexity. As the Brazilian poet and media artist Eduardo Kac (b. 1962) explains, "I try to create texts which can only signify upon the active perceptual and cognitive engagement on the part of the reader or viewer. This ultimately means that each reader 'writes' his or her own texts as he or she looks at the piece." Here surely is a telling example of Gadamer's idea that understanding the modernist work means entering into the temporality or play of its formation. Indeed, one could say that "holopoetry" embodies the regulating idea of the entire hist. of interpretation, which is that there is no making sense of anything from a distance. One always has to enter a new world, a new form of life, and make the thing one's own.

*See* CRITICISM, HERMENEUTICS.

■ L. Wittgenstein, *Philosophical Investigations*, trans. G.E.M. Anscombe (1953); S. Mallarmé, "Crisis in Poetry" [1896], *Selected Prose Poems, Essays, and Letters*, trans. A. Cook (1956); M. Heidegger, *Being and Time* [1929], trans. J. Macquarrie and E. Robinson (1962); A. Danto, "The Artworld," *Journal of Philosophy* 61.19 (1964); F. Petrarca, *Letters from Petrarch*, trans. M. Bishop (1966); S. Sontag, "Against Interpretation" [1964], *Against Interpretation and Other Essays* (1966); W. Dilthey, "The Construction of the Human World in the Human Sciences" [1916], *Dilthey: Selected Writings*, ed. and trans. H. P. Rickman (1976); H.-G. Gadamer, "Composition and Interpretation" [1961], *Philosophical Hermeneutics*, trans. D. E. Linge (1976); F. Schleiermacher, "Compendium of 1819" and "Academy Addresses of 1829," *Hermeneutics: The Handwritten Manuscripts*, ed. H. Kimmerle, trans. J. Duke and J. Forstman (1977); F. Jameson, *The Political Unconscious* (1981); P. Ricoeur, *Hermeneutics and the Human Sciences*, ed. and trans. J.B. Thompson (1981); *The L=A=N=G=U=A=G=E Book*, ed. B. Andrews and C. Bernstein (1984); H.-G.

Gadamer and F. Hegel, *Introduction to the Lectures on the History of Philosophy* [1839], trans. T. M. Knox and A. V. Miller (1985); H.-G. Gadamer, "The Relevance of the Beautiful" (1974), *The Relevance of the Beautiful and Other Essays*, ed. R. Bernasconi, trans. F. G. Lawrence (1986); M. Perloff, *The Futurist Moment* (1986); T. W. Adorno, *Aesthetic Theory* (1970), ed. G. Adorno and R. Tiedemann, trans. R. Hullot-Kentor (1987); H.-G. Gadamer, *Truth and Method* (1960), 2d ed., trans. J. Weinsheimer and D. G. Marshall (1989); G. L. Bruns, *Hermeneutics: Ancient and Modern* (1992); E. Kac, "Holopoetry, Hypertext, Hyperpoetry," *Holographic Imagining and Materials*, ed. T. H. Jeong (1993); J. Drucker, *The Visible Word: Experimental Typography and Modern Art, 1909–1923* (1994); W. Dilthey, "The Development of Hermeneutics" (1900), *Hermeneutics and the Study of History*, ed. R. Makkreel and F. Rodi (1996); S. Lewitt, "Sentences on Conceptual Art" (1969), *Conceptual Art: A Critical Anthology*, ed. A. Alberro and B. Stimson (1999); L. Hejinian, "The Rejection of Closure" (1983), *The Language of Inquiry* (2000); S. Cavell, "Aesthetic Problems of Modern Philosophy," *Must We Mean What We Say?*, rev. ed. (2002); R. D. Hume, "The Pitfalls of 'Historical Interpretation,'" *PQ* 89 (2010).

G. L. BRUNS

**INTERTEXTUALITY.** A term in mod. critical theory that defines a *text (incl. a poem) in terms of its relation to other texts. In particular, the term characterizes the nature of a work as constituted by other texts, rather than originating in a precursor text or being made up of words that refer to something outside textuality.

In the late 1960s, the Bulgarian-Fr. cultural critic Julia Kristeva coined the term *intertexuality* in response to "traditional" models of *interpretation. Such models grant agency to the author, who controls the work through conscious design, relying on "intentional" *allusions to verifiable authors and works. Kristeva uses intertexuality to challenge this unitary notion of the autonomous author in command of an individuating authority. For her, all texts are necessarily "dialogic": "any text is constructed as a mosaic of quotations; any text is the absorption and transformation of another . . . , and poetic language is read as at least *double*." Specifically, she imagines the poetic field in terms of "three dimensions of textual space": "writing subject, addressee and exterior texts." This field operates along two axes. A horizontal axis connects the writing subject and the addressee via the word, while a vertical axis connects the word with exterior texts (Kristeva 1986). By placing the word at the crossroad of the poetic field, Kristeva replaces the traditional notion of *poetic origin* with an "impersonal field of crossing texts" (Clayton and Rothstein), at once downplaying the role of the author and reader and compelling the text itself to come into view: "The notion of *intertextuality* replaces that of intersubjectivity" (Kristeva 1986).

In Kristeva's original formulation (1967), the Fr. word *intertextualité* combines the preposition *inter* (between, among) with the noun *textualité* (textuality). But, as Miller observes, the word originates in the Lat. *intertextos*, "intertwined," and derives from Ovid's *Metamorphoses*. Ovid tells how the female weaver Arachne challenges the goddess Athena to a weaving contest by producing a tapestry woven with stories of gods and mortals: "The edge of the web with its narrow border is filled with flowers and clinging ivy intertwined [*intertextos*]" (6.126–27). For Miller, Kristeva, and others, *intertextuality* becomes a term for speaking about the *wovenness* of texts, their *interconnectedness*, their participation in a *web* of discourse—replacing the conventional metaphor of path, road, or route. A text is always an intertext, a part of a network of other texts. Consequently, a commentator should abandon "source-hunting" (*Quellenforschung*), allusion-identification, and *imitation as a viable hermeneutic.

Kristeva develops intertextuality by combining the ideas of Fr. structuralist linguist Ferdinand de Saussure with those of the Rus. formalist critic Mikhail Bakhtin. Saussure emphasizes the *relational* nature of meaning and of texts, which he understands to be largely free of social situations. For Saussure, the arbitrary relation between the "signifier" (the pure sound) and the "signified" (a category of things: a horse standing for all horses) constitutes the ling. sign, and the sign designates real-world referents. In contrast, Bakhtin emphasizes the *situational* nature of meaning and texts, arguing that lang. is always embedded in its social environment. This means that the relation between signifier and signified, word and object, is not clear-cut, but is, rather, characterized by "ambivalence." By combining the views of Bakhtin and Saussure, Kristeva develops an "intertextual" theory of lang. and texts, at once relational and situational.

In a hist. of intertextuality, Kristeva's Fr. colleague Roland Barthes is instrumental in developing the theory: "any text is an intertext . . . a new tissue of past citations. Bits of codes, formulas, rhythmic models, fragments of social languages, etc., pass into the text and are redistributed within it" (1981). The tissues are always both countless and anonymous. Since texts are "intertextual," they can have no single origin in the *genius of an autonomous author; therefore, they cannot be stabilized for the reader. Yet Barthes goes beyond Kristeva by relocating agency in the receiver rather than in either the text or the creator of texts. This shift leads Barthes to speak famously of "the death of the author"—one of the most potent phrases in mod. critical theory. Readers, rather than authors, are responsible for the pleasure derived from a text (as opposed to its "meaning"), and the reader's task begins by abandoning faith in any pathway connecting the author with earlier authors, the text with previous texts, or the text with the world.

Yet not all theorists of intertextuality have been willing to give up either the author or the notion of stabilized meaning. Decisively, both Genette and Riffaterre return the concept of intertextuality to Saussurean stability: texts are intertextual, but the intertext has a definite meaning; thus, the reader can track its significance. In this way, Genette and Riffaterre overcome one of the gravest liabilities of Kristeva and Barthes: the impracticality of any definition of *intertextuality* that sees the text as made up of countless, anonymous bits.

The work of Genette and Riffaterre rubs shoulders with that of Bloom on *"influence," the traditional term that Kristeva and her colleagues combat. Bloom argues for what Barthes (1981) calls a "myth of filiation" as the crucible of poetic creation: a "strong poet" invents a work in a conscious "misreading" of his "precursor" (Bloom 1973)—a literary relationship between one poet and another modeled on Sigmund Freud's Oedipus complex. While Bloom shares with Genette and Riffaterre the fundamental *knowability* of texts, rather than the famed "undecidability" posited by the Fr. critic Jacques Derrida, he joins Kristeva and Barthes in dismantling the romantic notion of the solitary poet's genius.

Recent writers also use Kristevan intertextuality to retheorize modernity as *"postmodernism," breaking down the usual binaries between the two (e.g., between "works" that serve a "purpose" and "texts" that are endlessly in "play"), instead emphasizing interconnectedness. Since postmodernism "works within the very system it attempts to subvert," writes Hutcheon (1985), it is double-coded. Hutcheon's theory of "parody" has been esp. compatible with the intertextuality at the heart of postmodernism. She recalls that "*para* in Greek can also mean 'beside,' and therefore there is a suggestion of an accord or intimacy instead of a contrast. . . . Parody, then, . . . is repetition with difference" (Hutcheon 1985). As such, parody "is the perfect postmodern form": "it paradoxically both incorporates and challenges that which it parodies. It also forces a reconsideration of the idea of origin or originality that is compatible with other postmodern interrogations of liberal humanist assumptions" (Hutcheon 1988).

Kristeva's revolutionizing of lang. and meaning has had two other important extensions. First, feminism also returns agency to intertextuality. In "Arachnologies," Miller uses Ovid's Arachne myth to contest postmodernism's suspicion about "the subject," thereby creating space for female autonomy in a patriarchal world. Second, postcolonialism rejects the emancipatory celebration claimed by Barthes and his heirs when decentering the authorial subject. For Bhabha, as for Gates and others, such decentering furthers the Western project oppressing minorities—a project charted by Michel Foucault, who emphasizes the restrictions placed on the subject by institutions that "discipline and punish." Specifically, Gates argues that Af. Am. writing has a double *voice and, thus, is deeply intertextual, self-conscious in its discourse of both a black vernacular and standard Eng.

If theories of influence locate "struggle" in the mind of the author, theories of intertextuality feature an ideological struggle: "All texts, therefore, contain within them the ideological structures and struggles expressed in society through discourse" (Allen 2000). Such struggles have both a political and a gender dynamic: a "gender politics." Sexuality is a recurrent topic in such theorizing, as Miller and Bloom intimate. Yet it is Freud's Fr. psychoanalytic heir Jacques Lacan who influentially theorizes textuality in terms of the subject's *desire* for a "lack" it cannot fulfill. Like Derrida, Barthes, Kristeva, and Foucault, Lacan mounts a major critique of the master-myth of Western culture, *patriarchal logocentrism* (the authority of the father's word), emphasizing instead a *feminizing intertexual "otherness."*

The revolution mounted in France toward the end of the 20th c. should not elide what Miller uncovers in Ovid: that intertextuality traces to cl. culture, in particular to the Socratic dialogue and Menippean satire. Scholars find versions in the other main cl. literary critics, Aristotle, Horace, and Longinus, as well as in the Roman rhetoricians Cicero and Quintilian, and in such early mod. Eur. writers as Dante and Michel de Montaigne. Arguably, the greatest "theorist" for intertextuality is the author who has proved most impermeable to both textual origins and stability: Shakespeare (Garber).

Intertextuality has underwritten a vast change in how culture sees the world, from the new gold standard, global interdisciplinarity, to the World Wide Web, acmes of ideological and electronic intertexts, respectively. Intertextuality proves invaluable for the study of poetry and poetics because it challenges the simplistic notion of a text's having a stable origin, instead recognizing poetry's dialogism. In intertextuality, texts are interconnected, interdependent, polyvocal, part of a network of authors, works, and readers. Most usefully, however, intertextuality can become a critical helpmeet to influence, allowing the reader to recognize in a given text both a clear myth of filiation and an intricate network of connection. In practice, critics now attend to both "allusion and intertext" (Hinds). For instance, John Milton is well known in *Paradise Lost* to appropriate an *inward hell* from Christopher Marlowe's *Doctor Faustus*, but this does not mean that Milton's tormented Satan originates solely in Marlowe's devil Mephistopheles. For Marlowe did not invent an inward hell, although we no longer know what he read when he put the idea onto the Elizabethan stage. Instead, the best we can do is locate origins in such figures as John Calvin, Thomas Aquinas, and Bonaventure, and trace its afterlife to Milton. In this way, our reading of Satan's *agon* can depend on both theories of influence and theories of intertextuality. Both theories seem required to read the poem with care.

*See* FORMALISM, HERMENEUTICS, POSTSTRUCTURALISM, STRUCTURALISM.

■ J. Lacan, *Écrits* (1966); J. Kristeva, "Bakhtin, le mot, le dialogue et le roman," *Critique* 239 (1967), and *Semeiotikè* (1969); H. Bloom, *The Anxiety of Influence* (1973); F. de Saussure, *Course in General Linguistics*, ed. C. Bally and A. Sechehaye, trans. W. Baskin (1974); J. Culler, "Presupposition and Intertextuality," *MLN* (1976); J. Derrida, *Of Grammatology*, trans. G. C. Spivak (1976); M. Foucault, *Discipline and Punish*, trans. A. Sheridan (1977); M. Riffaterre, *Semiotics of Poetry* (1978); M. M. Bakhtin, *The Dialogic Imagination*, ed. M. Holquist, trans. C. Emer-

son and M. Holquist (1981); R. Barthes, "Theory of the Text," *Untying the Text*, ed. R. Young (1981); M. Foucault, "What Is an Author?" *The Foucault Reader*, ed. P. Rabinow (1984); J. Kristeva, "Word, Dialogue, and Novel," *The Kristeva Reader*, ed. T. Moi (1986); N. K. Miller, "Arachnologies," *Subject to Change* (1986); M. Garber, *Shakespeare's Ghost Writers* (1987); H. L. Gates Jr., *The Signifying Monkey* (1988); L. Hutcheon, *A Poetics of Postmodernism* (1988); *Intertextuality, Allusion, and Quotation*, ed. U. J. Hebel (1989); *Intertextuality*, ed. M. Worton and J. Still (1990); *Influence and Intertextuality in Literary History*, ed. J. Clayton and E. Rothstein (1991)—esp. "Figures in the Corpus: Theories of Influence and Intertextuality"; C. Martindale, *Redeeming the Text* (1993); G. Allen, *Harold Bloom* (1994); G. Genette, *Palimpsests*, trans. C. Newman and C. Doubinsky (1997); S. Hinds, *Allusion and Intertext* (1998); G. Allen, *Intertextualty* (2000); L. Hutcheon, *A Theory of Parody*, 2d ed. (2000); R. Barthes, "The Death of the Author," *Norton Anthology of Theory and Criticism*, ed. V. B. Leitch et al. (2001); M. Orr, *Intertextuality* (2003); H. K. Bhabha, *The Location of Culture*, rev. ed. (2004); P. Cheney, "Milton, Marlowe, and Lucan: The English Authorship of Republican Liberty," *Milton Studies* 49 (2008); M. Juvan, *History and Poetics of Intertexuality*, trans. T. Pogacar (2008).

P. CHENEY

## INTUITION

I. In Aesthetics and Poetics
II. In Poetry

**I. In Aesthetics and Poetics.** The term *intuition* owes its importance in mod. poetics to Benedetto Croce's use of it in his *Estetica come scienza dell'espressione e linguistica generale* (*The Aesthetic as the Science of Expression and of the Linguistic in General*, 1902), where he identifies it with *expression. Rejecting as naïve the popular view of intuition as a completely subjective phase of the cognitive process, Croce lays down this warning: "it is impossible to distinguish intuition from expression in this cognitive process. The one appears with the other at the same instant, because they are not two, but one." Also, "to intuit is to express; and nothing else (nothing more but nothing less) than to express." In 1915, Croce acknowledged that his own dissatisfaction with his 1902 account of intuition had led to its "conversion" into the "further concept of pure or lyrical intuition." Under the influence of Giovanni Gentile (*La filosofia dell'arte* [*Philosophy of Art*], 1931) as well as Giambattista Vico and G.W.F. Hegel, Croce had delivered his Heidelberg lecture in 1908 on "Pure Intuition and the Lyrical Character of Art," where the term's meaning deepens to include the "successful union of a poetic image with an emotion."

By the time he is done, Croce has given an aesthetic theory of intuition that is a theory of expression and of *imagination as well. By identifying it with expression and imagination, Croce was able to give his use of intuition a measure of variety and novelty it probably could not have sustained on its own. Croce nearly makes us forget that, before Immanuel Kant took it up with fresh insight, the concept had already had a long hist. in med. Lat. as *intuitus*, and an even longer hist. in its original Gr. form, *nous*.

It was C. S. Peirce who pointed out that the Lat. term *intuitus*—which Kant puts in parentheses after the Ger. equivalent, *Anschauung*—first occurs as a technical term in Anselm's *Monologium* (11th c.). Anselm, Peirce explains, had tried to draw a clear distinction between seeing things through a glass darkly (*per speculum*) and knowing them "face to face," calling the former *speculation* and the latter *intuition*. In a famous passage of the *Monologium*, Anselm writes, "[T]o the supreme Spirit, expressing [*dicere*] and beholding through conception [*cogitando intueri*], as it were, are the same, just as the expression of our human mind is nothing but the Intuition of the thinker." Some students of Ezra Pound's *Cantos*, commenting on the so-called Anselm canto (105), have suggested that the entire *Monologium* may be read as an adumbration of what T. S. Eliot called the *objective correlative.

In the *Proslogium*, Anselm would later attempt to show that, in the concept of God intuited through Christian faith, enough is contained to "prove" discursively that anything so conceived must not only be thinkable but exist. Pressing his argument (against the fool who has said in his heart "there is no God"), Anselm compares the human intuition of God with a painter's intuition of a painting he has actually painted, as contrasted with his intuition of the same before he has painted it. This so-called ontological "proof" of God's existence, later advanced by René Descartes, G. W. Leibniz, and Baruch Spinoza, prompted many later critics to attack Anselm. And foremost among them was Kant.

Intuition lies at the heart of Kant's entire intellectual paradigm. In his first critique, the *Critique of Pure Reason* (1781), Kant is at pains to distinguish two kinds of intuition: first, a *receptive* kind, which enables the understanding (*Verstand*) to take in phenomenal sensations in the a priori forms of space and time and as related to one another causally; and second, a *nonreceptive* kind, which Kant does not hesitate to characterize as a "productive imagination." It provides the understanding with a store of supersensory things-inthemselves, not knowable through sensory experience. A proper name for it, says Kant, is "intellectual intuition." The chief supersensory ideas it provides are soul, world, and God. However grand their suggestiveness, those ideas have no empirical validity: they belong entirely to intellectual intuition. The understanding cannot "prove" to itself whether they exist.

In Kant's second critique, the *Critique of Practical Reason* (1788), the entire context of his argument derives from one of the three supersensory ideas provided by intellectual intuition, namely, the soul or human psyche. As the subjectivity of reason, the soul is made "aware" of itself not in the process of trying to know itself but in that of being or willing itself. Kant's critique shows that, for the practical reason, the will can in no

sense be a phenomenon related by laws of necessity to other phenomena; on the contrary, it is a *noumenon* or thing-in-itself, unaffected by anything external to it and, therefore, completely free, answering only to itself for how it responds to the a priori "categorical imperative" by which its ends are determined intuitively.

But intuition rises to a still higher level in Kant's third essay, the *Critique of Judgment* (1790). At the outset, Kant speaks of a "great gulf" yawning between the two previous critiques, "between the realm of the natural concept, as the sensible, and the realm of the concept of freedom, as the supersensible." What is needed, he says, is "a third mediating principle," an a priori intuitive synthesis of the opposed perspectives of nature (which mind comprehends only through its phenomenal impressions on the understanding) and freedom (where mind is at home with itself in its inner, noumenal reality). A table at the beginning of the third critique shows it is "art and beauty in general" that must "bridge the gap" between the two.

Only art or aesthetic experience, Kant explains, can provide the needed a priori intuitive synthesis, precisely because it is neither natural nor free in itself and yet participates, at least apparently, in both. In nature, the mind seeks knowledge; in freedom, it wills or desires; in art, it neither seeks knowledge nor wills, but rather finds itself viewing things intuitively—William Wordsworth in his *Excursion* (4.1295) will call it a "passionate intuition"—so as to link the realms of nature and freedom together in what amounts to a great *metaphor or intuitive synthesis. Despite his Humean skepticism, Kant allows himself to speak of the "divine mind" as author of that "highest synthesis of the critical philosophy." Having identified it as "that reason which creates the content at the same time with its forms," Kant adds that it here appears at last as "intellectual perception or intuitive understanding."

Hegel remarked that, in rising through his three critiques to the concept of intellectual intuition or intuitive understanding as the governing principle of the experience of purposiveness and beauty in nature and art, Kant merits the kind of praise Aristotle accorded Anaxagoras in Gr. antiquity. When Anaxagoras first said that nous (understanding in general or reason) rules the world, "he appeared," says Aristotle, "like a sober man among drunkards." Awed, like Kant, by the spectacle of the night sky with its "undisturbed circling of countless worlds," Anaxagoras had concluded that it could only be the result of a mind or nous, a divine intuitive reason that sorts out the original constituents of things in order to join like to like in a well-ordered whole (*kosmos*). Still, as Aristotle notes, Anaxagoras wavers between assigning his nous completely to the human being's thinking soul (like Kant in his first critique) and proclaiming its total objectivity as the "soulstuff" of the sensory world of nature.

In Plato and, even more, in Aristotle and the Neoplatonists, the nous of Anaxagoras retains its original significance as the divine mind that gives order to all things. It comes finally to be conceived as a pure act of "thinking thinking about thinking" (*nóesis noéseos nóe-*

*sis*). The human soul or psyche, like everything else that is, "imitates" or "participates" in that pure act in the measure of its natural potencies. The psyche receives intuitively—quite as Kant will later explain it—the principles of its theoretical, practical, and productive kinds of rational activity. Through rational making, men and women build the cities or states in which they are able, individually and collectively, to behave rationally. And it is only when their making and behaving have acquired habitual excellence that human beings can have the experience of sharing, however briefly, in the divine existence of thinking, thinking about thinking, which is the height of *sophia* or wisdom. The good habit or virtue of making well is *technē* or art; of behaving well, it is *phronesis* or prudence; of explaining well, it is *epistemē*, or excellence in discursive reasoning. Nous or intuitive reason is what ultimately activates all three; but when the three become one at the pole, like the meridians on the globe, it is sophia, the highest intuitive reason joined with the highest discursive reason, that absorbs the other two (the highest good and the highest beauty) in its highest truth.

Through Jerome, Augustine, and Thomas Aquinas, the form of rational intuition that activates practical reason will get a special name: *synderesis*. But it will be left to Dante to do the same for the productive reason, or fine art. Dante will dare to say that his whole *Divina commedia*, in which he sought to "write like God," was for him a metaphoric, intuitive vision, completed to perfection in his "creative imagination" (*alta fantasia*), before he applied himself to the task of writing it down. Love, he says, helped him to turn his vision into poetry by dictating words in his heart (see INSPIRATION). Fortunately, he had native talent—*ingenium* or *genius—and had acquired the traditional poetic skills (*ars*) through long practice (*usus*), to be able to do some justice to love's divine dictation; otherwise, as he says, his trying to write like God might have looked rather like the efforts of a goose to fly like an eagle.

For a rounded view of the importance of intuition as an aesthetic concept that does full justice to its long hist., one must turn to Hegel's *Aesthetics*. Hegel makes use of intuition to distinguish the three great kinds of art that have characterized the civilizations of ancient Greece, the Near and Far East, and Eur. Christendom. The three are the cl., with its ideal reciprocal adequacy of content and form; the symbolic, which falls short of that ideal, presenting a reciprocal inadequacy of constituents, the results of which are sometimes ugly but sometimes tremulously *sublime in Kant's sense of the term; and the romantic, which transcends the cl. reciprocal adequacy—as Shakespeare does in his characterizations of Falstaff and Hamlet and Dante does at the close of his *Paradiso*, where, after telling us that his creative imagination finally experienced a vast intuitive power shortage (*all'alta fantasia qui mancò possa*), he permits us to share with him, intuitively, the dizzying heights of art in the process of transcending itself as art.

The same insight permits Hegel to treat comprehensively the great *epic, *lyric, and dramatic genres or voices of poetry and to predict that poets of the future

in the Western world are apt to find the lyric *voice more vital than the other two voices of poetry. As a living experience, epic poetry belongs to the beginnings of a people's national hist., just as *dramatic poetry does to the decades of its full maturity. Lyric poetry has no special time in a people's hist.; therefore, its voice is never silent. From that Hegelian vantage point, it is possible to explain why theorists of art since Kant who have counted on intuition to tell them what is actually living for them in aesthetic experience have tended to emphasize the ideal of the lyric in poetry and of musical subjectivity among all the arts. That has been so from Arthur Schopenhauer and Friedrich Nietzsche down through Henri Bergson (*The Creative Mind*) and Jacques Maritain (*Creative Intuition in Art and Poetry*, 1953). René Wellek saw in it a tendency to abolish the "whole concept of art as one of the distinct activities of man" by collapsing the rich legacy of traditional artistic distinctions into a crude "unity of experience" that makes all things subjectively and intuitively one. Still, Hegel's best insights permit us to say on Croce's behalf that, when he faithfully scrutinized his personal aesthetic experience, he found indeed that its depths resounded, for him at least, with a voice of singularly lyrical intuitive inspiration.

**II. In Poetry.** Poetic intuition differs from sensation because it is neither passive nor psychological; it is a oneness of person and world expressed in lang. In the other arts, its lang. may be song or shape or gesture. It is knowledge, but of an immediate kind and, thus, is prior to conceptual, judgmental, discursive knowledge. There is no claim in poetic intuition that its world is either real or unreal or that that world and the experiencing person are distinct; because it is not a self-conscious experience, it does not even contain the claim that it is itself poetic intuition. Although it is possible to extract concepts and abstract ideas from a poem, in the poem experienced as a poem, these ideas are fused within the intuition.

Vico, who may be credited as the originator of this conception of poetry, argued that Homer conceived of Achilles not as a courageous individual or as an example of courage or as courage itself but as an utter fusion of all of these. In poetic intuition, in other words, individuality and universality are identical (see CONCRETE UNIVERSAL). Poetic intuition, moreover, is radically distinct from perception, which is the basis of empirical knowledge. If one perceives "the blue spot here and now," one observes it as part of a spatial and temporal and chromatic framework, a structure already composed by conceptual thought. It is, of course, possible to perceive rather than intuit poems, to consider their space and time as part of some large, conventional structure within which we live our days. But to do so is to miss the poems as poems. Space and time are abstractions by means of which we think and perceive the world. But poetic intuition creates the world and, with it, our living sense of space and time. The crudeness or fineness of our very ideas of space and time is, thus, derivable from the quality of our poetic, intuitive experience. Finally, in its purest form, the concept of poetry as intuition is at odds with the idea of poetry as self-expression. In a poetic intuition, self and world, subject and object, are immediately identical. This is the way the world begins. This is the way the self begins. On its basis alone, we construct our distinctions, self and world, space and time, real and unreal, truth and error, even beauty and ugliness.

After Croce, theories of intuition in the 20th c. were pursued from directions he might never have anticipated but with results that, in some cases at least, he would have found congenial. Expressionist theories of poetry, which are the last inheritors of *romanticism and of which poetic intuition is one, had surprising strength through much of the 20th c. In Italy, the publication of Gentile's *Philosophy of Art* in 1932 effectively put an end to the currency of Crocean expressionism; but in Switzerland and France, the rise of the *Geneva school of critics during the same decade produced a strong form of intuitivist crit. This, however, is based now on Bergson, existentialism, and (esp.) phenomenology. Here too the operating assumption is that a reader will, through inseeing or intuition, come into a rapport with the imaginative space of the text and, through it, that of the poet, the authenticity of which is taken as guaranteed. On the basis of this guarantee, one can then say that the ordinary category boundaries between subjective and objective are indeed dissolved, and along with them the usual concerns of critics with the gaps or spaces between the world and the world as embodied in words. In such intuition, one is literally seeing through words into the very life of things. Eng. trans. of *Geneva school phenomenological crit. brought its methods into currency in America in the 1960s. The subsequent assaults on referentiality and determinate meaning that were associated with deconstruction (see POSTSTRUCTURALISM), however, sought to dissolve all possibility of intuitive readerly rapport with the text, much less with the poet, as convenient but vain delusions built on a one-sided metaphysics. Perhaps more productive were devels. in reader-response crit., which sought to reestablish links between particular readers and works, at least, and perhaps even to restore links among readers themselves, and so guarantee intuitive authenticity, via the concept of readerly and social *convention. Nevertheless, intuitivist theories of poetry, like phenomenological philosophy, provide the most radical alternative to traditional Western dualist metaphysics. Most of the great Western poets have indicated implicitly or explicitly their belief in the power of intuition to bypass the circuits of feeble human rationality and fickle human perception, going straight to the source. "If a sparrow come before my window," said John Keats, "I take part in its existence and pick about the gravel." Whether such entering-in upon the conscious lives of other selves, other beings not human, and even events beyond all selfhood be dream or truth is a question that seems, finally, less important than the evident fact that it proceeds from a human capacity certain beyond cavil and one that poetry above all arts, for some reason, makes central.

*See* INVENTION.

■ G.N.G. Orsini, *Benedetto Croce* (1961); M. E. Brown, *Neo-Idealistic Aesthetics: Croce, Gentile, Collingwood* (1966); M. R. Westcott, *Psychology of Intuition* (1968); B. M. Reed, "Carry on, England: Tom Raworth's 'West Wind,' Intuition, and Neo-Avant-Garde Poetics," *Contemporary Literature* 47 (2006); A. Piper, "Intuition and Concrete Particularity in Kant's Transcendental Aesthetic," *Rediscovering Aesthetics*, ed. F. Halsall, J. Jansen, and T. O'Connor (2009).

A. PAOLUCCI; H. PAOLUCCI (AESTHETICS AND POETICS); M. E. BROWN; T.V.F. BROGAN (POETRY)

# INUIT POETRY

I. Traditional Song and Poetry
II. Contemporary Song and Poetry

The Inuit (pl. form; sing. Inuk), formerly called *Eskimos*—a term considered offensive by many Inuit—live along some 5,000 miles of Arctic coastline, so comments about any one aspect of their culture are generalizations. As noted by both anthropologists and Inuit political organizations, however, the Inuit have a strong ling. and cultural connection across the circumpolar world. The Inuit lang. belongs to the Eskimo side of the Eskimo-Aleut family, and it has two branches: Inuit—known as *Kalaallisut* in Greenland; *Inuktitut*, *Inuinnaqtun*, or *Inuvialuktun* in Canada; and *Iñupiaq* in Alaska—and *Yup'ik*, spoken in several varieties in Alaska and Siberia. Traditional Inuit poetry is generally performed, rather than written and read, and it is often accompanied by drum, choral background, or dance. While the contemp. corpus includes verse written in the Western trad., Inuit poetry continues to be a highly musical production, with an emphasis on *performance and the sung and spoken word.

**I. Traditional Song and Poetry.** Traditional Inuit poetry takes a variety of forms and was often composed to be performed in the *qaggiq* (communal celebration house). As Lowenstein points out, many of the songs reflect on the process of song-making, often via comparison to a task such as hunting or to material objects or crafts. This practice of *metaphor illustrates both the skill required to create songs that would be subject to public evaluation and the extent of their value or usefulness to the community. Inuit poetry was ceremonial, possessing powers to make changes in the physical world, but it was also commonplace, a part of everyday life.

The Inuit songs known best to outsiders were recorded in the early 20th c. by the anthropologist Diamond Jenness and by the Greenlandic poet and scholar Knud Rasmussen. Rasmussen's trans., in particular, have been widely disseminated and republished, though they have often been stripped of important contextual information in the process. Rasmussen attempted to organize Inuit poetry into the following four categories: *charms, hunting songs, songs of mood, and songs of derision. More recently, Emile Imaruittuq, an elder from Igloolik, described the following three categories of songs:

**A.** *Pisiit* (pl. form; sing. *pisiq*), or personal songs. Although the term *pisiit* is now often used to refer to *hymns, the more traditional pisiit tell stories and express the singer's feelings and often make use of the *ajaajaa* (*refrain). This category would encompass Rasmussen's songs of mood and hunting songs. According to Imaruittuq, pisiit can also be called *qilaujjarusiit*, which indicates that they are performed with a drum dance. In terms of content, the lyrics are often highly metaphorical, and they may contain a lesson for the listeners. Imaruittuq notes that while pisiit could be performed by someone other than the owner or composer, credit was always given before the singing. A song whose lyrics have been altered by successive singers is called an *ikiaqtagaq* (split song). In the western (Copper Inuit) region, Jenness noted a variety of drum song called *aton* but was unable to distinguish it from the pisiq.

**B.** *Iviutiit* (pl. form; sing. *iviutiq*), or songs used to ridicule or embarrass people, often as part of a duel. Called "songs of derision" by Rasmussen, these song duels have a judicial function in that each singer is allowed to voice complaints against the other in public, and each is given an opportunity to respond. They may provide a cheerful, loving correction or a vicious assault on a reputation. The song duel varies greatly from one area to another, occasionally involving boxing, and is usually also considered entertainment. Iviutiit make use of comical euphemisms, often explicit in content (see POETIC CONTESTS).

**C.** *Sakausiit* (pl. form; sing. *sakausiq*), or songs used by *angakkuit* (shamans). Rasmussen called these charms or magic songs and recorded several examples. The Igloolik shaman Avva, for instance, knew songs that could be used to stop bleeding, to make heavy things light, to call spirit helpers, or to attract game. These powerful tools were guarded by their owners (though Rasmussen succeeded in trading for some of them). The use of obscure or archaic *diction—the highly metaphoric lang. of the angakkuit—frequently makes the sakausiit incomprehensible even to native speakers.

**II. Contemporary Song and Poetry.** As soon as Christian missionary projects and whalers brought written texts to the Arctic, Inuit began using syllabic and alphabetic orthographies to write their langs. The technology of writing, however, was more often employed pragmatically and rhetorically in the composition of letters, diaries, and political documents, rather than in the creation of books of poetry. As the Church became a dominant force in the Arctic, the performance of pisiit, iviutiit, and sakausiit fell out of favor, even as many elders continued to compose and sing songs. The older song texts, meanwhile, have been extensively collected, translated, and republished by eds. such as Jerome Rothenberg, James Houston, Guy-Marie Rousselière, Charles Hoffman, Edward Field, John Robert Colombo, Edmund Carpenter, and Tom Lowenstein. McCall and others have pointed out, however, that the publishing process, while well intentioned, has tended to strip songs of the context that gives them meaning—esp. in cases where the identity of the composers has been omitted. In this form, they appear more like *lyric poems than an accurate representation of Inuit poetry.

As McGrath observes, there is not a large body of Inuit poetry well known outside the Inuit homeland, but within Inuit communities, the trad. is flourishing. Inuit poetry is rarely published in chapbooks or in collections, but some writers, such as Greenland's Aqqaluk Lynge or Labrador's Philip Igloliorti, have published books of verse. More commonly, Inuit poetry can be found in smaller, community-based publications or online. McGrath has argued that the four genres identified by Rasmussen can also be applied to the contemp. corpus. The mood poems, she observes, are now written about mod. life in the communities and are often worked into photographs, drawings, or prints so that illustration and text are indivisible. Magic chants and incantations are no longer evident, but Christian hymns, trans. or adapted from Eng. and Danish or composed originally in Inuit lang., are widely promulgated. The hymns of Rasmus Berthelsen are known throughout Greenland, while in Canada, Armand Tagoona was a well-known composer of Christian songs. Hunting continues to be a major theme in Inuit poetry, but rather than being memorial or personal, hunting poems now tend to express a longing by young, urban writers for the old way of life. Many of these works also carry an environmentalist message, reflecting larger concerns in the North about the impacts of resource devel. and climate change (see ENVIRONMENT AND POETRY). In mod. Inuit poetry, the song duels and derisive poems generally do not exist in their traditional form, having been banned by Christian missionaries, but certain elements have survived. The question-answer sequence and the repeated use of the interrogative are features of contemp. Inuit political poetry, though the respondent is as likely to be a garbage can or an alien from Mars as a snowy owl or an offended husband.

The devel. of the *epic is a major innovation in mod. Inuit poetry; Frederik Nielsen's trilogy on Qitdlaussuaq traces the 18th-c. Inuit migration from Canada to Greenland; Alootook Ipellie's long poem "The Strangers" describes the Inuit occupation of the Arctic from ancient times and examines the consequences of Eur. contact; Villads Villadsen's Christian epic *Nalusuunerup Taarnerani* (In Heathen Darkness) describes the death of the last Norseman in Greenland and the eventual conversion and baptism of Aattaaritaa the exorcist. The politically inspired poems are sometimes purely *didactic but are more frequently satiric and ironic.

Even in the 21st c., written Inuit poetry does not entirely represent the contemp. Inuit poetic corpus. Indeed, the most vibrant Inuit poetry continues to be sung and performed rather than confined to the page. Despite the interventions of the Church and of the schools, the somewhat isolating activities of reading and writing are not esp. popular in many Inuit communities; instead, the works of musical performers such as Charlie Adams, Charlie Ningiuk, Henoch Townley,

Tumassi Quitsaq, Laina Tullaugak, Leena Evic, Susan Aglukark, Elisapi Isaac, Lucie Idlout, Tumivut, and Beatrice Deer are recognized throughout the Arctic; and the lyrics of their songs constitute a poetic trad. that is constantly being revised, referenced, and reperformed by other Inuit artists—rather like the traditional *ikiaqtagaq* or adapted song. This is not to say that Inuit poets are traditional; rather, they braid their song trads. with other musical and poetic influences. As documented by Inuit circumpolar music blogger Stéphane Cloutier, the extensive music scene in Kalaallit Nunaat (Greenland) features many *hip-hop artists. Increasingly, even Inuit writers do not seem to be relying on print publication to disseminate their work, as spoken-word artists like Mosha Folger and Taqralik Partridge are already acquiring a significant following through the use of online media sites. These younger artists expand on a range of themes related to contemp. Inuit life and identity, and, notably, many of them continue to compose in their own lang. This ling. persistence ensures that the audience of contemp. Inuit poetry is primarily Inuit, unlike the Eng.-lang. poetry of other contemp. indigenous trads., which is more readily accessible to mainstream readers.

See ANTHROPOLOGY AND POETRY; CANADA, POETRY OF; ETHNOPOETICS; FLYTING; INDIGENOUS AMERICAS, POETRY OF THE; MUSIC AND POETRY; ORAL POETRY; POETRY SLAM.

■ **Anthologies and Primary Texts**: H. Rink, *Tales and Traditions of the Eskimo*, trans. R. Brown, 2 v. (1875); W. Thalbitzer, "Old Fashioned Songs," *Phonetical Study of the Eskimo Language* (1904); H. Roberts and D. Jenness, *Songs of the Copper Eskimos* (1925); K. Rasmussen, *Report of the Fifth Thule Expedition*, 1921–24, v. 7–9 (1930–32); *Anerca*, ed. E. Carpenter (1959); *I Breathe a New Song*, ed. R. Lewis (1971); *Eskimo Poems from Canada and Greenland*, ed. T. Lowenstein (1973); *Kalaallit Taallaataat Nutaat INUIT Ny Gronlandsk Lyrik*, ed. K. Norregaard (1980); *Paper Stays Put*, ed. R. Gedalof (1980); *Poems of the Inuit*, ed. J. R. Colombo (1981); C. Berthelsen, *Gronlandsk Litteratur* (1983); "Alaska Native Writers, Storytellers and Orators," spec. iss. of *Alaska Quarterly Review* 4.3–4 (1986); *Northern Voices*, ed. P. Petrone (1988); M. Aupilaarjuk, E. Imaruittuq, et al., "Pisiit, Songs," *Perspectives on Traditional Law*, ed. J. Ooste, F. Laugrand, W. Rasing (2000); *Words of the Real People*, ed. A. Fienup-Riordan and L. Kaplan (2007).
■ **Criticism and History**: S. Frederiksen, "Henrik Lund, A National Poet of Greenland," *American Philosophical Society* 96 (1952); and "Stylistic Forms in Greenland Eskimo Literature," *Meddelser om Gronland* 136 (1954); E. Carpenter, "Eskimo Poetry: Word Magic," *Explorations* 4 (1955); H. Lynge, "The Art and Poetry of Greenland," *Greenland Past and Present*, ed. K. Hertling et al. (1971); R. Wiebe, "Songs of the Canadian Eskimo," *Canadian Literature* 52 (1972); R. McGrath, *Canadian Inuit Literature* (1984); R. Pedersen, "Greenlandic Written Literature," *Handbook of North American Indians*, ed. D. Damas, v. 5 (1984); C. Berthelsen, "Greenlandic Literature: Its Traditions, Changes, and Trends," *Arctic Anthropology* 23 (1986); R. Hulan,

*Northern Experience and the Myths of Canadian Culture* (2002); S. McCall, "I Can Only Sing This Song to Someone Who Understands It," *Essays on Canadian Writing* 83 (2004); *Uqalurait: An Oral History of Nunavut*, ed. J. Bennett and S. Rowley (2004); D. Serkoak, A. Meekitjuk-Hanson, P. Irniq, "Inuit Music," *Nunavut Handbook*, ed. M. Dewar (2004); S. Cloutier, "Inuit Circumpolar Music" (2010), http://pisiit.blogspot.com/; K. Martin, "Is an Inuit Literary History Possible?" *American Indian Culture and Research Journal* 34 (2010); L. J. Dorais, *The Language of the Inuit* (2010).

R. McGRATH; K. MARTIN

**INVECTIVE.** A personal attack or *satire, often scurrilous, formerly written mainly in verse. Invective is to be differentiated from satire on the grounds that it is personal, motivated by malice, and unjust; thus, John Dennis remarks that satire "can never exist where the censures are not just. In that case the Versifyer, instead of a Satirist, is a Lampooner, and infamous Libeller." Invective is as old as poetry and as widespread; in the West, it appears (if not in the Homeric *Margites*) at least as early as Archilochus, who wrote an invective against Lycambes; other notable Gr. examples include those by Hipponax against Bupalus, by Anacreon against Artemon, and others by Xenophanes, Timon of Phlius, Sotades (see SOTADEAN), Menippus, and (less virulently) Callimachus. Indeed, iambic meter itself (see IAMBIC) is in its earliest, Ionian form so called specifically because of its association with invective, which has the specific characteristics both of a speaker giving vent to personal hatred and of common speech for its vehicle, to which iambic meter was thought by the ancients to conform. In Lat., invective is written, though in a wider variety of meters, chiefly by Catullus (see CHOLIAMBUS), Ovid (*Ibis*), Martial, and Varro. In the Middle Ages, Petrarch's invective against doctors, *Invective contra medicum*, is notable; in the Ren., the scope of personal invective was expanded considerably by the invention of printing, which provided broadsides, bills, and *ballads particularly well suited for rapid and wide dispersal of political invective and satire. Eng. invective of this sort abounds particularly in the Restoration and 18th c.; indeed, the Eng. word *lampoon* (from the Fr. slang term *lamper*, "to guzzle, swill down") dates only from the mid-17th c. John Wilmot, the Earl of Rochester's *History of Insipids, a Lampoon* (1680) is but one of many of his and of others. John Dryden, a master of invective, nevertheless deplores it in his "Discourse concerning the Original and Progress of Satire" (1693) as both illegal and dangerous. After 1750, however, verse invective, like other verse genres such as *narrative poetry, rapidly gave ground to prose as the medium of choice, except in the (remarkably durable) trad. of the *epigram, incl. scurrilous and vindictive epigrams, which were produced in the 20th c., notably by J. V. Cunningham.

See DOZENS, FLYTING, TOAST.

■ J. Addison, *Spectator*, no. 23; *An Anthology of Invective and Abuse* (1929) and *More Invective* (1930), both ed. H. Kingsmill; J. C. Manning, *Blue Invective*

(1973); *The Book of Insults, Ancient and Modern*, ed. N. McPhee (1978); *Tygers of Wrath: Poems of Hate, Anger, and Invective*, ed. X. J. Kennedy (1981); A. Richlin, *The Garden of Priapus* (1983); *The Devil's Book of Verse*, ed. R. Conniff (1983); *The Blasted Pine: An Anthology*, ed. F. R. Scott and A. J. M. Smith (1965)—Canadian; R. M. Rosen, *Old Comedy and the Iambographic Tradition* (1988); H. Rawson, *Wicked Words* (1989); G. J. van Gelder, *The Bad and the Ugly: Attitudes towards Invective Poetry (Hijaʾ) in Classical Arabic Literature* (1989); K. Swenson, *Performing Definitions* (1991); L. Watson, *Arae: Curse Poetry in Antiquity* (1991); A. Sáenz-Badillos, "Hebrew Invective Poetry: The Debate between Todros Abulafia and Phinehas Halevi," *Prooftexts* 16 (1996); G. Nagy, *The Best of the Achaeans*, 2d ed. (1999)—chs. 12–13; P. M. Thornton, "Insinuation, Insult, and Invective: The Threshold of Power and Protest in Modern China," *Comparative Studies in Society and History* 44 (2002); I. Ruffell, "Beyond Satire: Horace, Popular Invective and the Segregation of Literature," *Journal of Roman Studies* 93 (2003); M.-H. Larochelle, "L'Invective ou le rapprochement conflictuel," *Dalhousie French Studies* 74 (2006).

T.V.F. Brogan

**INVENTION** (Lat. *invenire*, "to come upon"). The practical discovery and gathering of materials that constitute a discourse or, alternately, a faculty of the poet or rhetor to make something new of existing matter or ex nihilo. In poetic composition, *invention* variously describes the discovery or creation of subject matter, as well as the formal and structural handling of that subject matter. Examples of *invention* as poetic form and structure are Aristotle, *Poetics* 14; Boccaccio, *Genealogia deorum gentilium* 14.7 (1360); Joachim du Bellay, *La Deffence et illustration de la langue françoyse* 1.8 (1549); J. C. Scaliger, *Poetices libri septem* 1.1 (1561); and Alexander Pope, Preface to the *Iliad* (1715).

Ancient theories of rhet. named *inventio* (discovery) as the first step in the construction of an oratorical or literary work, followed by *dispositio* (arrangement), *elocutio* (expression), *pronuntiatio* (delivery or *pronunciation), and *memoria* (memory). Inventio is the most complex and significant of the steps; it refers not only to finding out a topic for composition but to devising the materials for composition through compilation, exploration, and discovery. Inventio, as Cicero explains, is "the excogitation of true or plausible things which render one's cause probable." The foundational texts on rhetorical inventio are Aristotle, *Rhetoric* 1–2; the anonymous *Rhetorica ad Herennium* 1.2.3; Cicero, *De inventione* 1.7.9 and *De oratore* 1.3.142, 2.19.79; and Quintilian, *Institutio oratoria* 3.3.1.

During the Ren., the rhetorical understanding of invention is coupled with, and to some extent supplanted by, the mod. notion of invention as innovation. In *The Advancement of Learning* (1605), Francis Bacon argues that "the invention of speech or argument is not properly an invention, for to *invent* is to discover that which we know not, and not to recover or resummon that

which we already know" (2.13.6). *Invention* continues thereafter to be used to describe poetic composition. But whereas poetic invention had once indicated the process of allowing a topic to emerge out of the materials at hand, it now begins to signify the original innovation of an author working on those materials. Ancient theories of rhetorical inventio had always acknowledged the ingenuity of the rhetor, though it was the ingenuity of discovering an already extant truth. When *invention* comes to be associated with empirical and technological ingenuity, *poetic invention*, for its part, begins to connote creation as well as discovery. Invention remains bound to matter, but differently so. In the mod. era, the term *invention*, already important to the arts of lang., becomes common to the lexicons of science and technology as well.

In the premod. era, by comparison, *invention* was a term that crossed over between rhet. and logic. Distinguished from techniques of *style and eloquence, inventio involves that part of rhet. most connected with the intellect. Despite the relative demotion of rhet. within the Scholastic trad. that flourished in Eur. universities from 1100 to 1500, theories of invention continued to be developed in that trad. precisely because invention was identified as the logical aspect of rhet. The Scholastics tended to focus on the character of invention in judicial (or forensic) oration at the expense of the other branches of rhet.: deliberative (political and legislative) and demonstrative (epideictic and poetic) oration. But when humanists like Rodolphus Agricola and Peter Ramus moved to reassign inventio and dispositio or *judicium* to the field of logic, thereby limiting rhet. to pronunciatio and elocutio alone, all three branches of oratory (juridical, legislative, and poetic) were implicated in the move. This had the paradoxical effect of restoring credit to poetic invention for having a logical and intellectual character, rather than a strictly rhetorical function. The isolation and elevation of inventio and dispositio (or judicium) also inaugurated a new interest in defining the difference between them. And that distinction between inventio and judicium would eventuate in a trad., culminating in the 18th c., that sought to define poetic invention over and against judgment (Pope, *Essay on Criticism* 1.114 [1711], Preface to the *Iliad*; Alexander Gerard, *Essay on Genius* [1774]). The peculiar legacy of invention, and esp. poetic invention, has to do with its characterization as the logical part of rhet. and the rhetorical part of logic.

Even as inventio was being brought under the aegis of logic, commentators were concerned to preserve the understanding of inventio as the discovery of matter, rather than a purely abstract or intellectual initiative. In his *Rule of Reason* (1551), Thomas Wilson, pace Agricola, reverses the order of inventio and dispositio to indicate that invention derives its matter out of the arrangement and organization of prior discourses and arguments. Invention might be reassigned to logic—in effect, rescuing rhet., or at least certain fundamental rhetorical practices, from ill repute—as long as the fundamentally material and practical character of inventio was reiterated.

An analogous set of tensions can be glimpsed in the question of whether poetic invention should concern itself with the proper imitation of *nature. Some poets and critics have made a point of differentiating *invention* from *imitation, understanding the very nature of invention to be autonomous rather than derivative in its production of subject matter (Horace, *Ars poetica* 119–20; Quintilian, *Institutio oratoria* 10.2.12; Samuel Johnson, *Rambler* no. 121 [1751]; Edward Young, *Conjectures on Original Composition* [1759]). Others have indicated that poetry can achieve its desired effects only through the proper imitation of past works or of nature (Plutarch, *Moralia* 17–18; Aquinas, *In libros posteriorum analyticorum expositio* 1, Lectio 1 [ca. 1268]; Pierre de Ronsard, *Abrégé de l'art poétique françois* [1565]; John Dryden, *Parallel betwixt Poetry and Painting* [1695]; and Johnson, "Preface to Shakespeare" [1765]). Philip Sidney conceives of poetic invention as a kind of autonomous form of imitation: "only the poet [of all human artists] . . . lifted up with the vigor of his own invention, doth grow in effect another nature, in making things either better than nature bringeth forth, or, quite anew, forms such as never were in nature" (*Defence of Poesy*, 1595). *Imitation* is a relatively flexible category in Western mimetic theories (see MIMESIS), since it can refer to the *representation of both the physical world and potential or imagined worlds. In Sidney's formulation, invention imitates "what may be or should be": the "golden world" that poetry brings into being.

If in the Ren. a principle of innovation was brought forward out of the cl. concept of invention as discovery, it was *romanticism that brought forward the sense of poetic invention as an *expression of mind, though this emphasis on poetic invention as creative or divine genius can be found in Longinus's treatise *Peri hypsous* (*On the Sublime*) and Seneca's moral epistles (see ROMANTIC AND POSTROMANTIC POETRY AND POETICS). Mind, rather than matter, became the primary touchstone for romantic theories of poetic invention; indeed, the mind itself rivals the vital *organicism of nature. The poet invents by transcending ordinary thought and by transforming ordinary matter, through *imagination as distinct from imitative *fancy or mechanistic reason (S. T. Coleridge), through spontaneous and original thought and feeling (William Wordsworth), or through an empirically derived but ultimately intuitive vision of ideal reality (P. B. Shelley). Invention is still strongly identified with intellection, but, for the romantics, poetic style and figure, rather than logic, define that identity.

The Sophists used the term *kairos* to indicate an aptness of rhetorical composition that occurs at the right moment and in the right place: a kind of serendipity. Invention, as Attridge has observed, "is an experience of coming upon a form, a phrase, a solution that seemed, in retrospect, to have been waiting in advance, or even one of being *found by* the form, phrase, or solution in a moment of illumination." And yet, "What is an invention in the eyes of its creator . . . actually becomes one only in its reception by the culture at large." *Invention*, Attridge points out, is a term that refers to both the event and its result. Whether it is the ancient rhetorical understanding of *invention* as finding out the extant matter for a discourse or the Ren. understanding of *invention* as bringing forth new meaning out of matter or the romantic understanding of *invention* as the original expression of mind, invention occurs when an act of composition rightly coincides with an act of observation or reception. And *invention* names the quality of a composition that is new but makes one think it was always there to be discovered.

*See* AGUDEZA, PRONUNCIATION, WIT.

■ D. L. Clark, *Rhetoric and Poetry in the Renaissance* (1922); C. S. Baldwin, *Ancient Rhetoric and Poetic* (1924), and *Medieval Rhetoric and Poetic* (1928); M. W. Bundy, "'Invention' and 'Imagination' in the Renaissance," *JEGP* 29 (1930); W. G. Crane, *Wit and Rhetoric in the Renaissance* (1937); F. Solmsen, "The Aristotelian Tradition in Ancient Rhetoric," *AJP* 62 (1941); M. Joseph, *Shakespeare's Use of the Arts of Language* (1947); Abrams; R. McKeon, "Imitation and Poetry," *Thought, Action, and Passion* (1953); W. S. Howell, *Logic and Rhetoric in England, 1500–1700* (1956); W. J. Ong, *Ramus, Method and the Decay of Dialogue* (1958); Weinberg; G. A. Kennedy, *The Art of Persuasion in Greece* (1963); C. Vasoli, *La dialettica e la retorica dell'Umanesimo: 'Invenzione' e 'Metodo' nella cultura del XV e XVI secolo* (1968); E. J. Ashworth, *Language and Logic in the Post-medieval Period* (1974); L. Jardine, *Francis Bacon: Discovery and the Arts of Discourse* (1974); Murphy; L. D. Martin, "Literary Invention," *CritI* 6 (1980); P. Bagni, "L'Inventio nell'ars poetica latino-medievale," *Rhetoric Revalued*, ed. B. Vickers (1982); G. Bruns, *Inventions* (1982); S. Crowley, *The Methodical Memory* (1990); Lausberg; D. Attridge, *The Singularity of Literature* (2004); J. Lauer, *Invention in Rhetoric and Composition* (2004); R. Greene, *Five Words* (2013).

R. KALAS

**IONIC.** The metrical unit ◡ ◡ – –, and meters composed in such metra (see METRON) or derived from it. In Gr. poetry, pure ionic meters found wide use in *monody (esp. Anacreon), choral lyric, and the choruses of Gr. tragedy (particularly Euripides) and comedy. For other varieties of ionic rhythms, see GALLIAMB(US), ANACREONTIC. *Aeolic and ionic meters are closely related and were often confused with one another by the ancient grammarians. Pure ionics are found in Horace, *Odes* 3.12 (probably an imitation of Alcaeus, from 108 [Lobel-Page]), but mixtures of ionics and other meters are found in Plautus. The pure ionic is sometimes called the "lesser ionic" or ionic *a minore*. The so-called "greater ionic" or ionic *a maiore* ( – – ◡ ◡ ) is a later Hellenistic devel., found particularly in the *sotadean, which also had its Lat. imitators; an example is provided by Varro, *Satirae Menippeae* 489. Accentual imitations of lesser ionics in Eng. poetry include Robert Browning's "In the midnight, in the silence of the sleep-time" and John Frederick Nims's "The Young Ionia" (*Knowledge of the Evening* [1960]). Some mod. metrists have entertained the idea that the sequence xx// in the first four syllables of the Eng. *iambic *pentameter is a kind of analogous ionic foot.

■ Hardie; Wilamowitz, pt. 2, chap. 9; Koster, chap. 9; Crusius; Dale, chap. 8; Halporn et al.; West.

J. W. Halporn; T.V.F. Brogan

**IRANIAN POETRY.** *See* persian poetry.

## IRELAND, POETRY OF

I. Poetry in Irish: Sixth to Ninth Centuries
II. Poetry in English: Eighteenth Century and the Celtic Revival
III. Irish Poetry: After Yeats (Irish and English)

**I. Poetry in Irish: Sixth to Ninth Centuries.** As the oldest vernacular lit. north of the Alps, Ir. poetry, according to the Old Ir. *Auraicept na n-Éces* (*Primer of the Poets*), consisted of "what was best then of every language . . . what was widest and finest was cut into Irish" (Ó Cathasaigh). Although the country was never colonized by Rome, the native Ir. nevertheless adapted an alphabet from some knowledge of Lat., perhaps as early as the 2d c. ce, called *ogam*, inscribed on upright stones. Oral Ir. lit. is believed to long precede the 5th c. arrival of the literate Lat. culture of such missionaries as Patrick; but in the oldest existing tablets and vellum (from the 6th and 7th cs., respectively), the vernacular tongue, often expressed in verse, already coexists with ecclesiastical texts in Lat. By the 8th c., missionaries from Ireland reversed the direction of literary exchange, carrying back to Europe instruction in cl. learning as they founded monasteries in Scotland and on the continent. With the displacement of their Druidic religion by Christianity in the 5th c., Ir. poets who composed orally (*filid*, sing.*fili*) maintained their identity as scholars and poets, even as their verse now shared the meters of church and legal texts (Ó Cathasaigh).

The earliest Ir. verse, which had originated in the same IE system as did Sanskrit and Gr. verse (see celtic prosody; also Watkins), was gradually incorporated into complex rhyming syllabic meters. Scholars once thought that this change occurred under the influence of late Lat. verse, but more recent scholarship argues, to the contrary, that the versification of early Ir. poetry influenced med. Lat. verse. In Ireland, the most famous collection of poems in this style by the Ir. Latinists is *Hisperica Famina* (Western Orations; 7th c.). This Hisperic or rhyming style was subsequently employed in the OE "Rhyming Poem." As Christianity became established in Ireland in the 6th c., the roles of the native filid coexisted with those of monastic clerics and jurists in a system of aristocratic *patronage, but it was to the scholars of the monasteries that this task largely fell. Clerics in the Ir. monasteries who copied, for preservation and dissemination, sacred texts also compiled the pre-Christian lit. of Ireland, incl. tales of destructions, cattle raids, and wooings (Ó Cathasaigh). At this time, the poems being composed by the Ir. filid, patronized to promote the

claims to property and power of his king (MacCana, Caball and Hollo), consisted typically of encomiastic genealogies and hists., but they also included more fanciful narratives, incl. the voyage saga (*echtrae*). From the 6th to the 12th c., verse is introduced into what is predominantly prose (Ni Mhaonaigh) in what is called *prosimetrum. E.g., in the voyage tales to the Otherworld (*immrama*) and in *Buile Shuibne* (Sweeney's Frenzy, the tale of an exiled king who achieves enlightenment in the wilderness), poetic passages give emphasis to already heightened emotion. Predominantly alliterative and unrhymed (*retoiric*), the poetry of this period also included rhyming syllabic forms (*nuachrotha*, "new forms"). The use of *roscad*, a form of obscure verse, was restricted to esoteric contexts.

Lyrics from med. Ir. scribes also survive, much of it in the margins of Lat. mss., escaping not just the task at hand but also the traditionalism of the filid. Early Ir. nature poetry at its best can be seen in the 9th or 10th c. Writing during a period of Viking raids on Ireland, the poet describes the reddened bracken, "its shape hidden; / The wild goose has raised his familiar cry" (MacCana, trans. G. Murphy).

Bardic or cl. Ir. poetry is usually dated from 1200–1600, a period in which the turmoil of the Norman invasion was exacerbated by the displacement of the native monasteries with continental institutions. The important role of the *poet in sustaining the social order was reinforced under a new confederation of learned families, contributing to the standardization of poetic forms in the aristocratic families of Scotland as well as Ireland. In families that came to include assimilating Anglo-Norman Catholics, poetry was the hereditary vocation of professional poets. The once separate functions of the learned filid and the nonliterate *bard now merged in the figure of the poet whose verse is both composed and performed orally, the latter accompanied by harp, even though a written record often would follow (Wong). *Dán díreach* (strict verse) is the generic name for the syllabic meters that were to be the hallmark of Ir. poetry in religious verse as well as court poetry until the 17th c. Virtuosity and artifice, learned lang. and ornateness were prized, contributing to the distinctive styles of the lore of places (*dindshenchas*, mod. spelling *dinnseanchas*) and the narrative or *laoithe* poems concerning roving warriors (*fiana*) known as *fianaigheacht*. They included *ballads, a "vibrant and earthy manifestation of popular Gaelic culture" (Caball and Hollo), and they retained their popularity in high as well as low culture (see James Joyce's *Finnegans Wake*). Less elaborate forms were employed, however, as early as the 12th c. in love poems termed *dánta grádha*, which were once believed to have been composed contemporaneously with the *amour courtois* of Fr. trad. (see courtly love), arriving in Ireland with Norman settlers. The trad. in Ir. now seems more likely to have been a "nonprofessional stream of Gaelic literary culture coterminous with the professional," what Caball and Hollo call an "amalgam of traditions" in which the earliest datable poem was composed by the Anglo-Norman Gerald fitz Maurice (1357–98). It was a "cosmopolitan combination of Gaelic, English and broader Eur. literary cultures," according to Caball and Hollo, to which aristocratic women as well as men contributed. Adapting to Ir. such forms as the *echo poem (echoing the beginning and ending of *quatrains), poems written by both sexes explore more personal subjects such as the impact of sectarian difference in relationships, and they came to include poems of male friendship (see Piaras Feiritéar [ca. 1600–53]).

After the military defeat of the Ir. chieftains at Kinsale in 1601 and the flight of the earls in 1607 to the courts and armies of Catholic Europe, for some decades Ir.-lang. writers often wrote from the courts, monasteries, and battlegrounds of Europe, preserving and expanding the filid trad., incl. the ongoing chronicling of Ir. hist. since antiquity. But with the Cromwellian settlements of 1652–54, the defeat of James II in 1690, and the ensuing Penal Laws, the economic structure that had supported the privileged status and function of the poet crumbled. Thus, much of the poetry of the 17th and 18th cs. is overtly political, a poetry of defiance, of mourning for the old order and contempt for the new. Aogán Ó Rathaille (ca. 1670–1729) and his contemporary Dáibhí Ó Bruadair (ca. 1625–98) inherited the residual role of the fili that in their own lifetime was abruptly withdrawn. Ó Bruadair, reduced to agricultural labor, in a trans. by the 20th-c. poet Michael Hartnett ruefully remembers the pen he once wielded: "From guiding the run of the clay-blade my knuckles all swollen are / And the spadeshaft hath deadened my fingers" (cited in Wong). By the 18th c., the poet Eoghan Rua Ó Súilleabháin (ca. 1748–84) makes a colorful poetic *persona of his life as a *spailpín* (itinerant laborer) in Munster. Reflecting the massive social and political upheaval of the 17th c., the form and content of postbardic poetry remains ornate, but increasingly, like the folk poetry of the period, it is colloquial in diction and tone and is composed in accentual rather than syllabic verse. It is also adapted to the purposes of *satire. If Jonathan Swift, a Dublin contemporary of Ó Rathaille's, was notorious for Eng.-lang. love poems that convert feminine allure into sexual threat, Brian Merriman (1750–1805) in a mischievous poem titled *The Midnight Court* written in Ir. in 1780 (but drawing on the Eur. trad. of the court of love) offered such an explicit and exuberant sexual empowerment of women, led by the goddess Aoibheall, that it would be censored in Eng. trans. well into the 20th c.

Already by the beginning of the 18th c., there is a different use of the pre-Christian myth of "Ireland" as the goddess Sovereignty or *Ériu,* the possession of whom legitimates Ir. kinship. Now personified as captive to a foreigner, she appeals to the poet in *dream visions to win her freedom. The vision, or *aisling,* poem, derived from Jacobite trads., would culminate in the 18th c. with such poems as "The Churchyard of Creagán" by Art Mac Cumhaigh (ca. 1738–73) and "Gile na Gile," ("Brightness Most Bright") by Ó Rathaille in which "our mild, bright, delicate, loving, fresh-lipped girl" falls prey to "that black, horned, foreign, hate-crested crew" (Kinsella 1981). There is a decline of literacy in the Ir. lang., such that, by the 19th c., Eng.

was rapidly becoming the vernacular lang. of Ireland, a process accelerated by the famine of the 1840s and the massive emigration that followed. In the poetry and in the life of the blind poet and musician Antaine Raifteararí (1779–1835) may be seen the merging of literary style with folk music and *ballad but also the invention of a new trad.: the sorrowful last survivor of a noble past. It was once presumed by scholars that Gaelic culture had sunk to that of an impoverished and oppressed peasantry. Poets were, it is true, reduced to employment as hedge-school masters, minstrels, or (as in Ó Bruadair's example) agricultural laborers, and certainly poetry moved closer to the people and the oral trad., even employing song meter (*amhrán*). But Denvir questions the widespread notion that the Ir.-lang. poet had become, as in James Macpherson's enormously popular reclamation for Scots (and Brit.) heritage of the Fenian warrior-poet Ossian, merely a moribund relic of a dying culture. "Celticism," which, in the late 18th-c. idiom of *romanticism, promoted the stereotype of the bard as a living relic, belies the lively exchanges across ling. borders in the everyday life and the lit. of Ireland at that time as well as the ongoing vitality of the filid heritage, both in the poems and ballads being written and in the oral contributions by storytellers (*seanchai*).

An example of the interfusion of the two may be witnessed in a major example of the bardic lament of the 18th c. as it was influenced by the oral keening trad. of women. Eibhlín Dubh Ní Chonaill's (c. 1743–c. 1800) celebrated *Lament for Art O'Leary* was occasioned by the murder of her husband, who resisted compliance with the Penal Laws. It survived through oral performances into the 20th c. The success of such poetry in the trad. of the filid was facilitated by devices that include the *repetition of the beginning in the ending lines and *conchlann,* the repetition of the last word of a stanza to initiate the stanza that follows (devices still employed by such 21st-c. poets as John Montague and Paul Muldoon). If in the 18th and 19th cs. the forms of high culture enter into popular usage, anonymous folk poetry written in the 17th and 18th cs. was itself sometimes composed mainly in accentual meters in forms that were technically sophisticated. "Roísín Dubh" ("Dark Rose") extends the aisling trad., but there are also homelier love poems of the time such as "Remember that Night," in which the speaker urges her beloved to "come some night soon / when my people sleep." She promises, on that night, to "put my arms round you / and tell you my story" (Kinsella 1981). Such continuity with the cultural wealth of the past was enabled in the 19th c. by a scribal culture in the Ir. lang. that was given new life by such Eng. institutions in Ireland as the Ordnance Survey, to which local poets contributed. It also, however, as Denvir notes, meant that the poetry largely sought "Gaelic and Catholic triumphalism" rather than the republicanism of the largely Eng.-speaking United Irishmen.

## II. Poetry in English: Eighteenth Century and the Celtic Revival.
The devel. in Ireland of a literate, middle-class, and urban Eng. lang. culture, Catholic as well

as Protestant, early in the 18th c. supported a growing publishing industry. Jonathan Swift (1667–1745) ambivalently acknowledged the vitality of ongoing Ir.-lang. social mores in poems such as "The Description of an *Irish-Feast*" (1720), and he translated at least one song by the blind Ir. harper Turlough Carolan (ca. 1670–1738). Swift, if less hostile than Edmund Spenser (1552–99), who wrote *The Faerie Queene* from the rebellion and plantation of Munster, enlarges a trad. where alienation was often the defining experience for the nonnative, expatriate, or Anglo-Irish poet. For Swift's contemporary Mary Barber (ca. 1685–1755), the troubles of Ireland are a metaphor for the straitened domestic circumstances of women. Indeed, political sovereignty in Ireland, in the bardic past underwritten by the sexual union of the native leader to "Sovereignty," making fecund the soil, becomes an ironic dream.

While the Gaelic Revival at the end of the 19th c. would celebrate a demotic trad. "racy of the soil," (Denis Florence MacCarthy, 1817–82), a more complicated picture is already available at the end of the 18th c. in a poem, written by an Irishman living in England, that at once celebrates and mourns a struggling rural culture: "The Deserted Village" by Oliver Goldsmith (1728–74). A half century later, the Great Famine, in which at least half a million Ir. people died and hundreds of thousands emigrated on less favorable terms than did Goldsmith, would devastate Ir. culture on all levels. While such poets as Jeremiah Joseph Callanan (1795–1829) would collect from Ir. speakers the fairy tales circulating in a still-populous countryside that would soon be deserted, by 1850 the Famine had produced a veritable subgenre of rural lit. in such notable works as the 1849 "The Year of Sorrow" by Aubrey de Vere (1814–1902); "The Famine Year" by the mother of Oscar Wilde, Jane Elgee Wilde (Speranza, ca. 1821–96); and a decade later the publication of *Laurence Bloomfield in Ireland*, one of the major long poems in Eng. of the century, by William Allingham (1824–89).

Before the Famine, Ireland produced poets whose work parallels that of the Eng. romantic period: Mary Tighe (1772–1810), whose *Psyche* influenced John Keats; and two members of the United Irishmen, William Drennan (1754–1820) and James Orr (1770–1816). The most celebrated Ir. poet of the period was Thomas Moore (1779–1852), a close friend of Lord Byron's but also of Robert Emmet's, the executed leader of the 1803 uprising. Moore in his 1807 elegy for Emmet, "Oh! Breathe Not His Name," established the tone and theme of the Ir. political *elegy, praising self-sacrifice as an act of national renewal. Moore's unabashedly sentimental lyrics set to music, *Irish Melodies*, stoked an ongoing enthusiasm for ballads, incl. nationalist ballads revived from 1798. The continuing frequency of anonymous or pseudonymous publication in 19th-c. Ireland, contrary to what we might expect, may have proved poetically enabling for poets such as James Clarence Mangan (1803–49), who, under other names and in voices shaped by different langs., forged a distinctively "non-English" voice out of estrangement from his own speech, incl. in his

revivals of the Ir. aisling in his version of the anonymous "Roísín Dubh" ("Dark Rose") and "Kathleen Ny-Houlahan." If for Mangan and Young Ireland the personal lyric of Eng. romanticism had become a mask that questioned "authenticity," such masks become ostentatious in the prose of Oscar Wilde (1854–1900). In Wilde's own Ir. ballad, however, "The Ballad of Reading Gaol," the anger is undisguised. Samuel Ferguson (1810–86), who wrote "Dialogue between the Heart and Head of an Irish Protestant," would provide W. B. Yeats (1865–1939) with another poetic counter to the stereotype of the ardent, heartfelt, and bardic Celt.

Yeats, Ireland's most celebrated poet, collected rural folk tales even as he promoted the poetry, and the nationalist politics, of Young Ireland. At the same time, in his own, early poems, he cast these Ir. themes in relation to those of the Eng. romantic poets he admired, P. B. Shelley and William Blake. Yeats sought to enlarge the scope of Celticism—in his poems but also in the Ir. nation—by promoting two other commitments to which he would devote his life. The first was to the occult, which culminated with *A Vision* (1925, rev. 1937), an ambitious recasting into the "gyres" of temporal change his lifelong investigation of historical patterns first cast in such notions as the mask, the phases of the moon, and the construction of individual identity within larger structures of fate. Its influence may be seen in "The Second Coming" with its concluding lines "And what rough beast, its hour come round at last, / Slouches towards Bethlehem to be born?" The second, more personal commitment was to the militant nationalist Maud Gonne (1866–1953), famous for her courage and her beauty, who, in refusing his repeated proposals of marriage, forced Yeats to make of "mere words" a model for the mod. love poem in Eng. As Yeats came to find aesthetically and intellectually crippling both Fenian nationalism and the Gaelic League with which he had allied his early literary interests, he developed a style that he hoped would seem "a moment's thought" ("Adam's Curse"), a poetry "as cold / And passionate as the dawn" ("The Fisherman"). Such art in its "arrogance" returned to the Protestant and Ascendancy heritage of Swift's savage indignation, even as Yeats assumed, as poet, the mask of "the wise and simple" figure of the "folk" in "The Fisherman." "All those things whereof / Man makes a superhuman, / Mirror-resembling dream" ("The Tower") Yeats claimed for the Ir. poet, even in the face of a world war larger than Ireland's "Troubles," for "All things fall and are built again / And those that build them again are gay" ("Lapis Lazuli").

**III. Irish Poetry: After Yeats (Irish and English).** The event that gave Yeats the title of perhaps the best-known elegy of the 20th c., "Easter, 1916"—with its *refrain "All changed, changed utterly: / A terrible beauty is born"—ended early the life of Patrick Pearse (1879–1916), the poet who gave to the Ir. lang. revival, as O'Leary writes, "a personal, and recognizably modern, voice." Pearse was best known for his overtly patriotic "Mise Eire." The Ir.-lang. trad. gathered new strength by the middle of the 20th c. in poems that responded to contemp. life in Ireland, and beyond, as in Máirtín Ó Direáin's (1910–88) "All This and the Hydrogen Bomb Too." Máire Mhac an tSaoi (b. 1922), celebrated for producing a poetic subject subversive of narrow attitudes toward women and sexuality in Ir. lang. culture, is followed by one female successor, Biddy Jenkinson (b. 1949), who has said that the Ir.-lang. poet should be a "trouble-maker." Nuala Ní Dhomhnaill (b. 1952), the most celebrated Ir.-lang. poet of her generation, puts the "language issue" (in a poem so titled, in Eng.) into "the lap, perhaps, / of some Pharaoh's daughter" ("Ceist na Teangan") while in "Dubh" (Black), she writes powerfully of ethnic violence in mod. Europe while echoing the figure of the Roisín Dubh (see Mangan). Ní Dhomhnaill—with Michael Davitt (1950–2005), Gabriel Rosenstock (b. 1949), and Cathal Ó Searcaigh (b. 1956)—emerged in the generation of Ir.-lang. poets influenced at University College Cork by Seán Ó Riordáin (1916–77) and Sean Ó Tuama (1926–2006). Michael Hartnett (1941–99), already a distinguished writer of poetry in Eng., at mid-career published critically acclaimed collections in Ir.

Samuel Beckett (1906–89), was—like many 20th-c. Ir. poets—influenced by the Irishman best known for his prose and his facility with langs., James Joyce (1882–1941). Perhaps following their examples in prose, and in personal mobility, more than their poetry, their successors, sharing a cosmopolitan skepticism of cultural nationalism and an awareness of how insularity may look from elsewhere, include Denis Devlin (1908–59), Pearse Hutchinson (b. 1927), and a few modernist contemporaries, such as Trevor Joyce (b. 1947), but also, and more vitally, such recent Ir. poets as Harry Clifton (b. 1952), Peter Sirr (b. 1960), Vona Groarke (b. 1964), Conor O'Callaghan (b. 1968), Justin Quinn (b. 1968), Catriona O'Reilly (b. 1973), David Wheatley (b. 1970), Sinead Morrissey (b. 1972), and Leontia Flynn (b. 1974).

Of the distinguished poets writing immediately after Yeats (one of whom was Padraic Fallon [1905–74]), it was the native Dubliner Austin Clarke (1896–1974) who brought Joyce's polyvocal playfulness and criticism of sexual hypocrisy into his poetry, even as he drew authoritatively on prosodic devices from the Ir. and, in poems such as "Aisling" and "The Straying Student," Gaelic themes. Another satirist of an Ireland isolated from Europe by neutrality in the war and culturally restricted by Catholicism at home was a poet who grew up in rural Monaghan, Patrick Kavanagh (1904–67), best known for the scathing rural realism of *The Great Hunger* but late in life a celebrant, like Clarke, of sexual love and bodily realities in "Canal Bank Walk" and "The Hospital." From the North, Louis MacNeice (1907–63), who made his reputation as a chronicler, in verse and in radio drama, of wartime and postwar London, wrote with equal deftness of the languid satisfactions of the Eng. suburbs and his own aversion and devotion to an Ireland of "dolled up Virgins / and your ignorant dead" ("Valediction"). He is particularly remembered for his ambitious and emotion-

ally nuanced *Autumn Journal*, which follows into its private, fragile places the waxing and waning of love during the months, in London, when the rumblings of war cast in new light the day to day. MacNeice wrote memorable lyrics, precise in diction, elegant but informal in voice, and almost always tonally dark—such as "Snow," "Meeting Point," "Sunday Morning," and "The Sunlight on the Garden"—that particularly influenced the poets of the North of the next generation. A Protestant contemporary who stayed in Ulster, John Hewitt (1907–1987) was another source of influence in the North.

On both sides of the Ir. border poets emerged in the postwar decades who, by the early 1970s, had received such international acclaim that a second 20th-c. revival in Ireland was proclaimed in the Am. popular press, one that has been too restrictively called the Ulster Renaissance. In the South, the writers included John Montague, born in America in 1929 and raised in the North, and the author of the major historical narrative of the Ir. Troubles, *The Rough Field*, a sequence that is modernist and even postmodernist in its juxtaposition of past and present, of historical voices and artifacts, family lore, and personal lyric. Richard Murphy (b. 1927), who has written with frankness and stark beauty about the natural world and sexuality and about relationships with men as well as women, has evoked his own haunting by the land, sea, and cultural life of the west of Ireland. The leading Ir. poet of his generation, Thomas Kinsella (b. 1928), has made the Dublin of his ancestors a topos as memorable as Joyce's, where what he calls "established personal places" may "receive our lives' heat" and, in so doing, "adapt in their mass, like stone" ("Personal Places"). At the same time, he has been, after Yeats, the poet in Ireland who has combined with a personal, and sometimes angry, voice—cadenced so naturally, often in *free verse, that its rhetorical power and even eloquence follows an innate urgency—with an effort to imagine sweeping, transhistorical patterns of recurrence, repossession, and renewal that give purpose to the most intimate and sometimes brutal acts of kinship and conquest. A translator and scholar of Ir.-lang. poetry (incl. a major trans. of *The Tain*), adopting for his own themes the early Ir. *Book of Invasions*, Kinsella has resourcefully exploited what he has called the "gapped and polyglot" trad. of Ir. poetry. The strength of poetry south of the border, and its international reach, may be witnessed in such successors as Brendan Kennelly (b. 1936), Eamon Grennan (b. 1941), Paul Durcan (b. 1944), and Dennis O'Driscoll (b. 1954).

*Site of Ambush*, a formally achieved and historically precise rendering of an ambush in the Ir. War for Independence, was published in 1975 by a young (and polyglot) scholar of the Eng. Ren., Eiléan Ní Chuilleanáin (b. 1942). She writes with equal poise and power of the quiet heroism of women's lives, sometimes in traditional roles of mourning and in preserving and renewing the past, as in "The Architectural Metaphor," which reminds us that, however "out of reach" might be the help we seek, we may see, through metaphor, where we dwell with fresh vision, "the world not dead after all." In the first Ir. revival, there were, of course, women poets, incl. Katharine Tynan (1861–1931) and Dora Sigerson Shorter (1866–1918); they were followed by mid-century by the example of Mhac an tSaoi and Blanaid Salkeld (1880–1959). The arrival of Ní Chuilleanáin and of Eavan Boland (b. 1944), the latter assuming the role of spokesperson for what she calls, in the subtitle of her 1995 *Object Lessons*, "the life of the woman and the poet in our time," ushered in a new perspective on Ir. trads. Boland's version of Pearse's "Míse Eire" is, e.g., an ironic overturning of the aisling convention. Boland in particular has inspired Paula Meehan (b. 1955), even as Meehan also has developed an inimitable idiom by drawing on trads. from Am. poetry, Buddhism, and proletarian North Dublin. Of that same generation of distinguished Ir. women poets is Moya Cannon (b. 1956) and the Ger.-born Eva Bourke (b. 1946). Medbh McGuckian (b. 1950), a Catholic poet from the North, praised for poems that seem postmod. in shifting rapidly between abstraction and intimate, sensual particularity, evokes political threat—with an increasing attunement in later volumes to republican hist. as it enters into male bodiliness—but always with a sense of the possibility that lang. may itself alter ("radicalize") the very root of the speaking tongue or metric foot or native culture, offering "a seed-fund, a pendulum / pressing out the diasporic snow" ("Dream-Language of Fergus").

Seamus Heaney (b. 1939), a Nobel laureate and the best-known Ir. poet of the current age, was part of the Belfast scene in the early 1970s that encouraged McGuckian and fellow students at Queens University, Paul Muldoon (b. 1951) and Ciaran Carson (b. 1948). Heaney, from his first poems, made palpable and universal the rituals of daily life on a Derry Catholic farmstead. Yet he also writes movingly of sorrow in such communities, whether the deaths are political or personal, as in "Clearances:" "A soul ramifying and forever / Silent, beyond silence listened for." Of Heaney's own generation, which included the *Honest Ulsterman* founder James Simmons (1933–2001), and a little later Tom Paulin (b. 1949), two other poets have enjoyed distinguished careers and international reputations. Derek Mahon (b. 1941) combined the forms of high Yeatsian rhet. with a voice that undercut its own stance, calling "poetry" a "dying art / An eddy of semantic scruple" ("Rage for Order"), driven by a postapocalyptic vision in which in "a lost hub-cap is conceived" whatever "ideal society" will "replace our own" ("After Nerval"). Michael Longley (b. 1939) is a keen observer of a quieter, more humane nature in such poems as "Madame Butterfly," yet his "Ceasefire" is perhaps the poem most often quoted on the Troubles and the hopes that followed the event that gave the 1994 poem its title.

Muldoon, while he has approached the Troubles more obliquely than these Northern predecessors, has developed dazzling, dizzying rhyme schemes (as in the 150-page *sestina "Yarrow"). His formal ingeniousness, combined with liberties taken with the *sonnet and with Yeats's *ottava rima* (and with bodies that are, like his own previous themes and even phrases, subject to disfigurement), has driven Muldoon's inimitable and arresting explorations of love and abjection in a time of violence, a hist. that he does not limit geopolitically to the North of Ireland. As much a poet of the cold war (and later the Am. wars in the Islamic world) as of the Troubles that he knew close up in rural Armagh, Muldoon's "voice" is thrice removed and yet intimate and invasive when the imprisoned hunger strikers speak (as mushrooms) in "Gathering Mushrooms": "lie down with us now and wrap / yourself in the soiled grey blanket of Irish rain." Carson, who learned Ir. in his Belfast home, has made a dual career as a prolific producer of musical and verbal arts that cross the boundaries among poetry, prose, song, trans., and even ethnography, suggesting new possibilities for imagining trads. in both langs., Ir. and Eng., as they spar with and spur one another. As he writes in "Hamlet," in passing the time at the local pub, hist. itself comes alive, proposing new endings to tragic episodes, because conversation *is* itself time, so the past, hedged by words that "blossom" in creative, oral exchange, "flits incessantly into the present."

■ **Anthologies in English and Translations from Gaelic:** *The Love Songs of Connacht* and *The Religious Songs of Connacht*, ed. and trans. D. Hyde (1893, 1906); *Bards of the Gael and Gall*, ed. and trans. G. Sigerson (1897); *Selections from Ancient Irish Poetry*, ed. and trans. K. Meyer (1911); *An Anthology of Irish Verse*, ed. P. Colum (1922); *Love's Bitter-Sweet*, ed. and trans. R. Flower (1925); K. A. Jackson, *Studies in Early Celtic Nature Poetry* (1935); *1000 Years of Irish Poetry*, ed. K. Hoagland (1947); *A Celtic Miscellany*, ed. and trans. K. A. Jackson (1951); *Irish Poets of the Nineteenth Century*, ed. G. Taylor (1951); *Early Irish Lyrics*, ed. and trans. G. Murphy (1956); *Kings, Lords and Commons*, ed. and trans. F. O'Connor (1959); *Love Poems of the Irish*, ed. and trans. S. Lucy (1967); *The Penguin Book of Irish Verse*, ed. B. Kennelly (1970); *The Book of Irish Verse*, ed. J. Montague (1974); *An Duanaire, 1600–1900: Poems of the Dispossessed*, ed. and trans. T. Kinsella and S. O'Tuama (1981); *Early Irish Verse*, ed. and tran. R. Lehmann (1982); *Poets of Munster*, ed. S. Dunne (1985); *The Bright Wave*, ed. D. Bolger (1986); *The New Oxford Book of Irish Verse*, ed. T. Kinsella (1986); *Contemporary Irish Poetry*, ed. A. Bradley (1988); *Contemporary Irish Poetry*, ed. P. Fallon and D. Mahon (1990); *Field Day Anthology of Irish Writing*, ed. S. Deane, 3 v. (1991); *Modern Irish Poetry*, ed. P. Crotty (1995); *Wake Forest Anthology of Irish Women's Poetry, 1967–2000*, ed. P. O'Brien (1999); *Writing Irish*, ed. J. Myers Jr. (1999); *Field Day Anthology of Irish Literature: Vols. IV–V: Irish Women's Writing and Traditions*, ed. A. Bourke et al. (2002); *In the Chair: Interviews with Poets from the North of Ireland*, ed. J. Brown (2002); *The New Irish Poets*, ed. S. Guinness (2004); *Irish Literature, 1750–1900*, ed. J. Wright (2008); *Anthology of Modern Irish Poetry*, ed. W. Davis (2010); *The Penguin Book of Irish Verse*, ed. P. Crotty (2010).

■ **Bibliographies:** R. I. Best, *A Bibliography of Irish*

*Philology and of Printed Irish Literature* (1913); K.G.W. Cross and R.T.A. Dunlop, *A Bibliography of Yeats Criticism, 1887–1965* (1971); R. Bromwich, *Medieval Celtic Literature: A Select Bibliography* (1974); M. Lapidge and R. Sharpe, *A Bibliography of Celtic-Latin Literature, 400–1200* (1985); K.P.S. Jochum, *W. B. Yeats: A Classified Bibliography of Criticism* (1990).
■ **Criticism and History**: E. O'Reilly, *A Chronological Account of Nearly Four Hundred Irish Writers* (1820); E. A. Boyd, *Ireland's Literary Renaissance* (1916); D. Corkery, *The Hidden Ireland* (1924); A. De Blacam, *Gaelic Literature Surveyed* (1929); R. Flower, *The Irish Tradition* (1947); M. Dillon, *Early Irish Literature* (1948); E. Knott, *Irish Syllabic Poetry, 1200–1600* (1957); C. Watkins, "Indo-European Metrics and Archaic Irish Verse," *Celtica* 6 (1963); C. Donahue, "Medieval Celtic Literature," Fisher; *Early Irish Poetry*, ed. J. Carney (1965); P. L. Henry, *The Early English and Celtic Lyric* (1966); P. Power, *A Literary History of Ireland* (1969); O. Bergin, *Irish Bardic Poetry* (1970); H. Bloom, *Yeats* (1970); J. E. Stoll, *The Great Deluge: A Yeats Bibliography* (1971); T. Brown, *Northern Voices: Poets from Ulster* (1975); *Two Decades of Irish Writing*, ed. D. Dunn (1975); R. Finneran, *Anglo-Irish Literature: A Review of Research* (1976); D. Perkins, *A History of Modern Poetry*, 2 v. (1976, 1987); S. O'Neill, "Gaelic Literature," *Dictionary of Irish Literature*, ed. R. Hogan et al. (1979); G. J. Watson, *Irish Identity and the Literary Revival* (1979); R. Welch, *Irish Poetry from Moore to Yeats* (1980); T. Kinsella and S. Ó Tuama, *An Duanaire: Poems of the Dispossessed, 1600–1900* (1981); *Ireland: A Social and Cultural History, 1922–79*, ed. T. Brown (1981); A. N. Jeffares, *Anglo-Irish Literature* (1982); *The Pleasures of Gaelic Poetry*, ed. S. MacReammoin (1982); S. Deane, *Celtic Revivals* (1985), and *A Short History of Irish Literature* (1986); R. Garratt, *Modern Irish Poetry* (1986); D. Johnston, *Irish Poetry after Joyce* (1986); E. Longley, *Poetry in the Wars* (1986); P. L. Marcus, *Yeats and the Beginning of the Irish Renaissance*, 2d ed. (1987); *Tradition and Influence in Anglo-Irish Poetry*, ed. T. Brown and N. Grene (1989); P. MacCana, "Introduction: Early and Middle Irish Literature (c. 600–1600)," *Field Day Anthology of Irish Writing*, ed. S. Deane, v. 1 (1991); *The Chosen Ground*, ed. N. Corcoran (1992); *Improprieties*, ed. C. Wills (1993); E. Boland, *Object Lessons: The Life of the Woman and the Poet in Our Time* (1995); D. Kiberd, *Inventing Ireland* (1995); T. Kinsella, *The Dual Tradition* (1995); *Modernism and Ireland*, ed. P. Coughlan and A. Davis (1995); S. Ó Tuama, *Repossessions* (1995); P. Haberstroh, *Women Creating Women* (1996); B. Howard, *The Pressed Melodeon* (1996); S. Deane, *Strange Country* (1997); S. Matthews, *Irish Poetry* (1997); P. McDonald, *Mistaken Identities* (1997); G. Schirmer, *Out of What Began* (1998); A. Fogarty, " 'The Influence of Absences': Eavan Boland and the Silenced History of Irish Women's Poetry," *Colby Quarterly* 35 (1999); E. Grennan, *Facing the Music* (1999); *Poets of Modern Ireland*, ed. N. Corcoran (1999); F. Brearton, *The Great War in Irish Poetry* (2000); J. Goodby, *Irish Poetry since 1950* (2000); D. Kiberd, *Irish Classics* (2000); D. O'Driscoll, *Troubled Thoughts, Majestic Dreams* (2001); N. Vance, *Irish Literature after 1800* (2002); *Cambridge Companion to Contemporary Irish Poetry*, ed. M. Campbell (2003); A. Gillis, *Irish Poetry of the 1930s* (2005); H. Clark, *The Ulster Renaissance* (2006); *Cambridge History of Irish Literature*, ed. M. Kelleher and P. O'Leary (2006)—esp. essays by T. Ó Cathasaigh, M. Ní Mhaonaigh, M. Caball, K. Hollo, A. Fogarty, N. Buttimer, M. Campbell, G. Denvir, D. Wong, P. O'Leary, L. de Paor, D. Johnston, G. Batten, and B. Nic Dhiarmada; *A Companion to Irish Literature*, ed. J. Wright, 2 v. (2010).

G. BATTEN

**IRONY.** According to the Roman rhetorician Quintilian (ca. 35–100 CE), *irony* is saying something other than what is understood. By the time Quintilian offered this definition, there were already two intertwined philosophical and rhetorical trads. considering the scope and definition of *irony*, and this twin hist. continues to this day. Irony is at once a general attitude and a localized figure of speech; it can be as broad as the Socratic commitment to knowing that one does not know and as specific as substituting one word for its opposite.

Irony can be considered philosophically as a mode of life or a general relation to knowledge and understanding. It is usually accepted that this philosophical trad. begins with Plato's Socrates, whose mode of questioning in Plato's dialogues is to accept the terms of his interlocutors' definitions and then to push those definitions (occasionally) to the point where the meaning of the discussed term either dissolves completely, leaving only a gap (*aporia*), or at least points to the need to create a definition that is more adequate than the common acceptance of a term's use. Socrates is described in the dialogues as deploying *eironeia*, which in the Gr. tragedies prior to Plato had designated deception or lying but which in the dialogues comes to refer to a strategy for attaining truth, a strategy that *appears* to accept the terms of common sense and received wisdom but ultimately exposes ordinary lang. to be inadequate. When Socrates asks Thrasymachus, in Plato's *Republic* (ca. 380 BCE), for a definition of "justice" and Thrasymachus replies that "justice is the advantage of the powerful" or "justice is paying back what one owes," Socrates accepts these definitions and then goes on to ask whether one would still call "just" actions undertaken by those in power who were mistaken about their own interests or whether returning an ax to a madman could still be a case of justice. Thrasymachus is baffled and *accuses* Socrates of irony, suggesting that (for Thrasymachus, at least) there is something pernicious about Socrates' undermining of everyday lang. and accepted usage. This sense that irony is undermining and linguistically and socially pernicious begins with Plato and continues into the 21st c. Aristotle (384–322 BCE), in his *Ethics* and *Rhetoric*, after Plato, suggested that the responsible citizen of good character should not remain distant and detached from everyday truth claims, norms, and conventions. Irony is socially irresponsible in its undermining of shared political conventions. Cicero (106–43 BCE) also claimed in *De oratore* that the active and engaged participant in a polity would use rhetorical strategies within his own context but would not, as Socrates seemed to do, have such a distanced attitude to the entire lang. that no engagement or meaning would ever be possible or secure. In the 19th c., both philosophers (Søren Kierkegaard, 1813–55) and literary critics (such as the Ger. romantics associated with the *Athenaeum* jour.) celebrated Socrates as the only "true" character insofar as he lived his life aware of the impossibility of coinciding completely with everyday lang. In the 21st c., both celebrations and denunciations of Socratic irony remain in force. The Am. pragmatist Richard Rorty (1931–2007) suggested that, given the necessary impossibility of establishing an absolute truth on which a society might establish its norms, all we can do is adopt our norms and political vocabularies, remaining aware that there is a certain provisional and contingent nature to all truth claims. We may be publicly sincere but privately ironic. Rorty endorses a Socratic mode of irony as a general attitude toward life and knowledge, and an acceptance that everyday definitions and conventions can never be adequate to some putative universal and final sense. Rorty's irony has been criticized as an abandonment of philosophical responsibility and as an overly postmod. failure to consider the difficult questions of truth, legitimation, and justification (just as Socrates was ultimately deemed by the court of Athens to have corrupted the youth). Yet Rorty himself criticizes one of the more complex aspects of Socrates' irony: by suggesting that everyday definitions are inadequate to define or establish a final sense for concepts such as justice, truth, beauty or the good, Socratic irony assumes that, when one uses irony to negate or distance oneself from everyday understanding, there will emerge some other, better, universal meaning.

Rorty is in keeping with post-20th-c. refusals to consider that a meaning or sense might transcend ordinary usage and conventions. There has been a widespread rejection of any such "Platonism," any idea that there might be a universal meaning for concepts, such as "justice," and that ordinary lang. ought to be corrected by an appeal to some proper and essential sense. For this reason, many of the 20th-c. and contemp. readings of the two modes of irony, either as a limited rhetorical device or as a style of living whereby one distances oneself from conventions, have been negative. That is, it is not assumed that when one "says something other than what is understood," there is some proper or universal sense that lies outside common sense. For Rorty, this attempt to " 'eff' the ineffable" is a mistake that irony ought to cure. Irony should destroy rather than encourage the demands for universal truth claims. Accordingly, Socratic irony was reinterpreted in the 20th c., with philosophers and literary critics arguing that Socrates indicates a specific way of life, an awareness that there is no ultimate truth or essence of humanity and that one must simply form oneself as a literary character.

In addition to being a general attitude or point of view whereby one might characterize entire texts as ironic—such as Jonathan Swift's *Modest Proposal* of 1729 and its "logical" argument for cannibalism as a means of solving the problem of hunger and poverty—irony is also a *trope. Socrates' use of irony was wide ranging, sometimes encompassing a critical attitude toward knowledge—accepting that one uses a lang. even if it remains inadequate to capture the higher and essential truths of concepts such as truth and beauty—but sometimes restricted to specifically rhetorical cases of irony. Here, rather than the mode of a character or way of life, there is the substitution of one term for its opposite, so that Socrates will hail a sophist as "wise" when the context of the dialogue and its devel. suggest otherwise. One way in which this contrariness of meaning—Quintilian's "saying something other than is understood"—can be explained is through a theory of tropes. If other figures, such as *metaphor, substitute like for like, irony substitutes opposites. Irony differs from other tropes or figures in its capacity to work differently according to context and differently within context, depending on who is reading or listening and how one is situated in relation to the speaker. Jane Austen's opening of *Pride and Prejudice* (1813)—"It is a truth universally acknowledged, that a single man in possession of a good fortune, must be in want of a wife"—is read as irony only if one does not accept the economic norms of the bourgeois marriage market. James Joyce's opening sentence of "The Dead" (1914)—"Lily, the caretaker's daughter, was literally run off her feet"—is marked as ironic only if one has the ling. resources to know that one cannot be *literally* run off one's feet. Irony has a hierarchical dimension, excluding some members of the audience from its "other" or implied sense.

That "other sense" remains difficult to secure and accounts for the multiple senses and levels of irony. These could be summarized as the following:

1. Simple rhetorical irony, the substitution of one sense for another. (Samuel Johnson's example from the dictionary of 1755 was "Bolingbroke was a holy man," an example that demonstrates that the implied sense would always depend on context and assumed values.)

2. Dramatic irony, where a character speaks in such a manner that the audience or reader recognizes the limited or contradictory nature of his or her speech. This occurs in Shakespeare's *Julius Caesar* when Marc Antony repeatedly declares that "Brutus is an honorable man" while detailing Brutus's duplicity. In this case, a character is *using* irony as a figure within his own context. More complex dramatic irony occurs in *Macbeth* where the audience hears the witches' predictions in one sense, Macbeth in another; and this is compounded if we anticipate the tragic course of events to follow. Dramatic irony is not confined to on-stage drama. It includes cases in which the audience or reader understands something quite different from the speaker's intended sense and can include nonfictional cases. We can perceive an irony in Martin Luther King's famous "I have a dream" speech, e.g., if we know that, for all his hope, events would run entirely contrary to his envisioned and expected future. In cases of fictional texts,

characters such as those in Robert Browning's dramatic monologues can express extreme religious propriety or love, while the events narrated by that very character reveal the opposite. In "My Last Duchess," the character declaring his love reveals himself to be violently controlling, while "In the Spanish Cloister" is spoken from the point of view of a morally zealous monk whose accusations of his fellow monastery inhabitants disclose his own envy and malevolence.

3. Tragic irony, where events follow a course despite, and often because of, characters' attempts to control their own fate. The audience sees a course of events unfolding, despite the characters' efforts to command their own destiny. It is Oedipus's attempt to avoid the predicted killing of his own father, e.g., that leads him to pursue the course of events that he has sought to avoid.

4. Cosmic irony occurs when the universe or cosmos appears to correct, or fly in the face of, our expectations. This has a literary mode, as in Thomas Hardy's novel *Tess of the D'Urbervilles* (1891), in which the peasant family's attempt to regain its honorable lineage results in the ruin of the well-meaning and noble Tess. This sense of cosmic contrariness captures one of the dominant popular uses of the word *irony*, when sports commentators, newscasters, or popular songwriters use *ironic* to signal that, despite our intentions, life plays itself out in a contrary direction.

5. Romantic irony is defined by the Ger. literary theorists of Jena in the *Athenaeum* jour. and taken up by 20th-c. theorists such as Paul de Man, Philippe Lacoue-Labarthe, and Jean-Luc Nancy, defines *irony* as the "permanent parabasis of tropes," suggesting that irony is not limited to a figure of speech within a text but opens a point of view outside the text's own frame—*parabasis—in which the reader or audience gains a sense of the text *as text*, not as a sign referring to some proper sense or meaning.

6. Postmod. irony is generally diagnosed or celebrated as the recognition of a loss of stable or shared meaning. Those like Rorty or (in different ways) de Man regard irony as a liberation from the idea that words are direct markers of some underlying meaning or natural referent. Others regard postmod. irony as nihilistic, as evidence for a loss of faith in public legitimation and shared understanding.

7. Irony as a trope or the substitution of a word for its opposite can range from sarcasm, the aim of which is usually to wound, such as John Searle's "That was a brilliant thing to do," to a negation without a secure opposed sense as in W.H. Auden's use of the word "clever" in his poem "September 1, 1939": "as the clever hopes expire / Of a low dishonest decade."

*See* NEW CRITICISM, PHILOSOPHY AND POETRY.

■ *Instituto oratoria of Quintilian*, trans. H. Butler (1921); D. Muecke, *Irony* (1970); W. C. Booth, *A Rhetoric of Irony* (1974); A. Mellor, *English Romantic Irony* (1980); D. Muecke, *Irony and the Ironic*, 2d ed. (1982); P. de Man, *The Rhetoric of Romanticism* (1984); J. Searle, *Expression and Meaning* (1985); P. Lacoue-Labarthe and J. Nancy, *The Literary Absolute*, trans. P. Barnard and C. Lester (1988); C. Lang, *Irony/Humor: Critical Paradigms* (1988); S. Kierkegaard, *The Concept of Irony, with Continual Reference to Socrates*, trans. L. M. Capel (1989); R. Rorty, *Contingency, Irony, and Solidarity* (1989); E. Behler, *Irony and the Discourse of Modernity* (1990); G. Vlastos, *Socrates, Ironist and Moral Philosopher* (1991); C. Colebrook, *Irony* (2004).

C. COLEBROOK

**ISOCHRONISM OR ISOCHRONY.** Refers to the rhythmic organization of speech into equal intervals of time. Most mod. discussions derive from Kenneth Pike's distinction between "stress-timed" and "syllable-timed" langs. Proponents of isochronism claim that, in stress-timed langs. (incl. Eng.), isochronism operates in such a way that the distance between stressed syllables is held constant in speech regardless (within limits) of the number of syllables between them; unstressed syllables between stresses are either lengthened or shortened in timing in order to keep the intervals isochronous. (Notice that isochronism is operative in music: musical bars are all equal in duration regardless of how many notes actually fill each one, and by convention, the first note in every bar bears a stress.)

A considerable amount of recent research into speech rhythm has been devoted to the phonetic reality behind the concepts of stress-timing and syllable-timing. In an analysis of large corpora from Chinese and Eng. natural speech (Benton et al., 2007), it was found that Chinese and Eng. fall into distinct rhythm categories. But a comparison of individual speaker data showed an overlapping continuum across both langs. The results thus remain ambiguous, and within certain more localized contexts, isochrony does seem to occur. And it may not be necessary that the intervals be objectively equal, so long as they are perceived to be equal. Acoustic measurements have failed to confirm perfect isochrony in speech production, but there is evidence that listeners impose rhythmic structure on sequences of interstress intervals. In the syllable-timed langs. such as Fr., by contrast, it is the syllables that are evenly spaced. Here isochrony comes closer to having both objective and subjective reality.

Some temporal prosodists, who hold that timing rather than stressing is the basis of meter, have applied the concept of isochronism to the *scansion of Eng. poetry. This approach has not worked well on *accentual-syllabic verse, but most types of *accentual verse, by contrast, probably show some degree of isochronism because they are not far removed from song. A good example is *ballad meter: since ballad texts were originally almost always set to music, the isochronism probably derives from the residue of the musical structure. However, some metrists insist that isochronism can only be a feature of *performance, never of meter.

■ C. Patmore, "English Metrical Critics," *North British Review* 27 (1857); P. Verrier, *Essai sur les principes de la métrique anglaise*, 3 vols. (1909–10)—esp. vol. 3; J. E. Duckworth, "An Inquiry into the Validity of the Isochronic Hypothesis," *DAI* 26 (1966), 5424A; J. S. Hedges, "Towards a Case for Isochronous Verse," *1975 Mid-American Linguistics Conference Papers*, ed. F. Ingemann (1976); I. Lehiste, "Isochrony Reconsidered," *JPhon* 5 (1977); C. Bouzon and D. Hirst, "Isochrony and Prosodic Structure in British English," *Speech Prosody*, Nara, Japan (2004); M. Benton, L. Dockendorf, W. Jin, et al., "The Continuum of Speech Rhythm: Computational Testing of Speech Rhythm of Large Corpora from Natural Chinese and English Speech," *ICPhS* 16 (2007), Saarbrücken: 1269–72; V. Dellwo, A. Fourcin, and E. Abberton, "Rhythmical Classification of Languages Based on Voice Parameters," *ICPhS* 16 (2007).

T.V.F. Brogan; I. Lehiste

**ISOCOLON AND PARISON.** *Parison* (Gr., "almost equal") describes syntactic members (phrases, clauses, sentences or lines of verse) showing *parallelism of structure. In short, they are identical in grammar or form. *Isocolon* (Gr., "equal length") denotes members that are identical in number of syllables or in *scansion. Two members could show parison without isocolon: the number and types of words would match identically, but the words themselves would not match in number of syllables. Conversely, two members could be isosyllabic and even identical rhythmically without having exact correspondence of members. But normally *parison* implies *isocolon* as well. Sometimes an obvious word is elided in the second member: "The ox hath known his owner, and the ass his master's crib." Isocolon is particularly of interest because Aristotle mentions it in the *Rhetoric* as the figure that produces symmetry and balance in speech and, thus, creates rhythmical prose or even measures in verse; cf. Quintilian 9.3.76. In rhythmical prose, it is important for establishing the various forms of the cursus. Vickers gives examples of parison: "As Caesar lov'd me, I weep for him; as he was fortunate, I rejoice at it; as he was valiant, I honour him; but as he was ambitious, I slew him" (*Julius Caesar* 3.1.24); and of isocolon: "Was ever woman in this humour woo'd? / Was ever woman in this humour won?" (*Richard III* 1.2.227). The parison by Nathaniel in *Love's Labour's Lost* (5.1.2) is famous.

◼ Norden; A. Quinn, *Figures of Speech* (1982)—esp. 77–79; Vickers; B. Vickers, *Classical Rhetoric in English Poetry*, 2d ed. (1989).

T.V.F. Brogan

**ISOMETRIC,** isometrical (from Gr., "equality of measure"); in cl. prosody, "homoeomeral." The OED dates the earliest uses of "isometric" and "isometrical" to the first half of the 19th c. Although cl. stichic verse is isometric, every line having the same length and meter (see STICHOS), sequences of metrical lines unbroken by stanzas would not necessarily have to be isometric. Most stanzaic poems are isometric: the metrical structure of the

first stanza is repeated identically in subsequent ones. A few—e.g. *tail rhyme and the *sapphic—are not.

*See* HETEROMETRIC, STANZA.

T.V.F. Brogan; S. Cushman

## ITALIAN PROSODY

I. Introduction
II. Meter
III. Rhyme
IV. Poetic Forms

**I. Introduction.** At its beginnings in the 13th c., It. poetry imitated many of the themes and forms of Occitan and OF poetry (see OCCITAN POETRY; FRANCE, POETRY OF). Med. Lat. rhythmical verse also exerted a strong formal influence on many of the nascent vernacular lyrical modes in Italy. In addition to his preeminence as Italy's leading poet, Dante (1265–1321) was the first among many well-known theoreticians of prosody. In the *Vita nuova* (ch. 25), Dante expresses his views on the hist. of poetic composition in the Eur. vernaculars and argues that, on the model of their Gr. and Lat. predecessors, It. poets should be allowed to use rhetorical figures. He also recognizes not only the seriousness of lit. but his own role as an inventive artist and his place in the literary trad.

Dante's literary career essentially retraces the trajectory of *lyric poetry in 13th-c. Italy, from the *Sicilian school through the *Dolce stil nuovo*; thus, his remarks on and practice of *versification are of particular importance for the It. poetic trad. In his unfinished treatise, *De vulgari eloquentia* (*On Vernacular Eloquence*, ca. 1304), Dante situates poetic praxis within a more theoretical discussion of the nature of poetic lang., esp. the search among the various It. dialects for a sufficiently noble literary lang., one that would be, in his terms, "illustrious, cardinal, courtly, and curial" (1.17.1; see DIALECT POETRY). Such a lang. would be the proper medium for refined lyric poetry in the "high" or "tragic" style on one of the three noble themes: prowess in arms, love, and moral virtue (2.2.7). From the "question of language," Dante passes to an extended discussion of metrical forms (2.3.1–3), particularly the construction of the *canzone*: the grammatical structure of the verse period, the qualities of words, varying line lengths, the *aab* structure of the canzone stanza, and the particular nature of rhyme words and rhyming devices. While intending to treat this last point in the (unwritten) fourth book of the treatise, Dante discusses the ordering of the canzone through placement of rhymes and discourages certain practices: excessive use of the same rhyme, equivocal rhymes, and rhymes with harsh sounds. Not extant—if they were ever written—are sections on the *ballata* and *sonnet, both of which belong to the "middle" style. Nevertheless, Dante's codification of It. prosody served as a touchstone for centuries of both praxis and crit.

**II. Meter.** It. metrics is based both on number of syllables and on the position of the primary accent in the line, the latter being the determining factor in meter. Syllables are counted only up to the last accent; if any follow it, they are ignored. Hence, the *hendecasyllable (*endecasillabo*), the most excellent of meters according to Dante and the one most appropriate for subjects in the high style, is not necessarily determined by the presence of 11 syllables, as its name implies, but rather by the placement of the primary accent on the tenth syllable and a secondary stress on either the fourth or sixth syllable. While a "normal" hendecasyllable (*endecasillabo piano*) adheres to the 11-syllable model, it may have as few as 10 syllables (*endecasillabo tronco*) or as many as 12 or 13 (*endecasillabo sdrucciolo* or *bisdrucciolo*). Contiguous vowels must often be elided for a verse to scan (see ELISION), via either *synaloepha or *synaeresis. At other times, such vowels must be pronounced separately, via dialoepha (across a word boundary) or *diaeresis (within a word).

After the hendecasyllable, the seven-syllable line (*settenario*) is the next most popular It. meter, with the principal stress always on the sixth syllable, as in "Il Cinque Maggio" by Alessandro Manzoni (1785–1873). Dante notes that verses with an odd number of syllables (3, 5, 7, 11) are generally to be preferred; thus, we find verses in all periods of It. lit. with five syllables (*quinario*: major stress on the fourth), as, e.g., in "La pioggia nel pineto" by Gabriele D'Annunzio (1863–1938). Although in early It. poetry the *trisillabo* (major accent on the second syllable) is generally found only as a rhyming component (internal rhyme: *rimalmezzo*) of a longer verse, it sometimes appears as a separate verse. The trisillabo, however, occurs with some frequency in mod. poets, as in D'Annunzio's "La pioggia nel pineto" (14–15), where he combines a quinario with a trisillabo. Dante holds the nine-syllable line (*novenario*: major accent on the eighth syllable) in contempt for giving "the impression of being three lines of three syllables" (*De vulgari eloquentia* 2.5.6; trans. Haller), but it has been used by Gabriello Chiabrera (1552–1638), Francesco Redi (1626–98), Giosuè Carducci (1835–1907), Giovanni Pascoli (1855–1912), and D'Annunzio.

Dante considers lines with an even number of syllables decidedly less noble (2.5.7), perhaps because the regularity of the stress pattern led to a monotonous cadence. Nevertheless, there are numerous examples of octosyllabic verse (*ottonario*, accent on the seventh syllable), esp. in poems of popular inspiration; similarly, we have examples of six-syllable verses (*senario*, accent on the fifth syllable) and four-syllable verses (*quadrisillabo*, accent on third).

Many early narrative poems were written in stanzas composed of 14-syllable lines, *alessandrini*, which imitate OF verses; these are essentially double *heptasyllables (*doppi settenari*, accents on the sixth and thirteenth syllables) with a *caesura after the first *settenario*. They were also called *versi martelliani*, after Pier Jacopo Martelli (1661–1727), who composed tragedies in this meter based on the model of Pierre Corneille and Jean Racine, and were used subsequently by Carlo Goldoni (1707–93) and Giuseppe Giacosa (1847–1906) in their comedies and by Carducci in his *Rime nuove*. Decasyl-

lables (*decasillabi*, accent on tenth syllable) also were first modeled on OF meters; these enjoyed a certain popularity in the 19th c. with Manzoni, Giovanni Berchet (1783–1851), Giuseppe Giusti (1809–50), and Pascoli.

Both in the Ren. and in the 19th c., we find examples of the imitation of cl. meters. The first conscious attempts were made by Leon Battista Alberti (1404–72) and Leonardo Dati (1360–1425), who composed It. *hexameters for the poetry contest—the *certame coronario*—of 1441. Ludovico Ariosto (1474–1533) tried his hand at reproducing the Lat. *iambic *trimeter in hendecasyllables. In the 16th and 17th cs., Claudio Tolomei (1492–1555) and Chiabrera attempted to resolve the conflict between the Lat. quantitative and the It. accentual systems. Carducci also experimented with "barbarian" poetry (*metrica barbara*)—for such it would have appeared and sounded to the ancients—based on accentual imitations of cl. meters, e.g. Virgilian hexameters and Catullian *elegiac distichs. In his *Odi barbare*, Carducci is esp. indebted to Horace.

**III. Rhyme.** Rhymes in It. are exact. Rhyme sounds are identical from the major stress to the end of the word: *amóre / dolóre*; *compí / sentí*; *cántano / piántano*. *Eye rhymes (*rime all'occhio*), which are apparently but not actually identical, are infrequent (*pálmi / sálmi / almí*; Dante, *Inferno* 31.65, 67, 69). Examples of composite rhymes (*rime composte*) may be found in early poetry (*chiome / oh me*; *Inferno* 28.121, 123) and esp. in the poetry of Guittone d'Arezzo (ca. 1225–93) and his followers. Other unusual sorts of rhyme found among the early lyrics include equivocal rhyme (*traductio*, where the word is the same but has a different meaning), derivative rhyme (*replicatio*, where the rhyme words have the same root), and *rich rhyme (*rima cara, ricca*, where an uncommon word form is used).

In the early lyrics, there is a phenomenon known as Sicilian rhyme (*rima siciliana*), which refers to words that in the dialect of the Sicilian poets would have rhymed because of the identity of the vowels *e* and *i*, and *o* and *u*. Thus, *diri* (= *dire*) and *taciri* (= *tacere*), as well as *tuttu* (= *tutto*) and *muttu* (= *motto*), rhyme in Sicilian, but not in It. When the Sicilian lyrics were copied into mss. by late 13th-c. Tuscan scribes, these forms were "Tuscanized," i.e., regularized orthographically, and thus emerged rhymes such as *ride / vede* (Sicilian *ridi / vidi*) and *ascoso / incluso* (Sicilian *ascusu / inclusu*).

Generally speaking, most med. It. poetry is rhymed, although we do find occasional examples of *assonance or *consonance, as e.g., in the *Laudes creaturarum* of St. Francis of Assisi (1182–1226), and some examples of *versi sciolti*, poems with unrhymed lines, the first example of which is the anonymous 13th-c. poem "Il mare amoroso." This It. variety of *blank verse was reintroduced in the Ren., first by Giangiorgio Trissino (1478–1550) in his *epic *L'Italia liberata dai Goti*.

**IV. Poetic Forms.** For Dante, the canzone represents the height of artistic perfection. It developed in Italy under the direct influence of the Occitan *canso*, the

OF *chanson*, and the German *Minnesang*. Canzoni generally have several *strophes composed mainly of endecasillabi and settenari, all of which follow the same structure (a one-stanza canzone is called a *cobbola*). Canzoni composed entirely of shorter meters are called by the diminutive *canzonette*; these were esp. privileged in the 17th and 18th cs. by Chiabrera, Carlo Innocenzo Frugoni (1692–1768), Pietro Metastasio (1698–1782), and Giuseppe Parini (1729–99).

The essential division of the canzone strophe is bipartite, the first part being termed the *fronte* and the second the *sirma*. The fronte usually divides into two (sometimes three) equal parts called "feet" (*piedi*); the sirma sometimes divides into two equal parts called *volte* or *giri*. The passage from fronte to sirma, which marks the change from one musical pattern to another, is generally known as the *diesis*. Some canzoni conclude with a *commiato* (*envoi*), a short stanza generally having the same pattern as the sirma (or a part of it), in which the poet sometimes addresses his composition and instructs it where it should go, with whom it should speak, what it should say, and so on.

These rules were followed rigidly until the 17th c., when the rise of the *canzone libera* signaled the abandonment of prosodic uniformity among strophes. Poets were thus presented with two possibilities: following the older, traditional forms or the newer, freer models. While some poets adhered in part to the earlier modes (Vittorio Alfieri [1749–1803], Vincenzo Monti [1754–1828], Ugo Foscolo [1778–1827], Manzoni, Carducci), most followed the newer forms, perhaps best exemplified by Giacomo Leopardi (1798–1837) in his *Canti*.

Other important forms include the ballata, which arose in the mid-13th c. as a song to accompany a dance and has essentially the same form as the canzone, except that the ballata begins with a *refrain, the *ritornello* or *ripresa*, which in performance was repeated after each stanza and the last rhyme(s) of which recurs at the end of each stanza. The ballata was very popular in the Middle Ages and Ren. and found illustrious practitioners in Dante, Petrarch (1304–74), Lorenzo de' Medici (1449–92), Angelo Poliziano ([Politian] 1454–94), and Pietro Bembo (1470–1547). It was revived briefly in the late 19th c. by Carducci, Pascoli, and D'Annunzio. The *lauda* adopted the metrical form of the secular ballata under the guidance of its first great practitioner, Jacopone da Todi (1236?–1306), but its very popular use for religious subjects did not extend past the 15th c. In imitation of the Occitan *troubadour Arnaut Daniel (fl. 1180–95), Dante introduced the *sestina; later practitioners include Petrarch, Michelangelo (1475–1564), Carducci, D'Annunzio, and Giuseppe Ungaretti. The 14th c. saw the advent of other lyrical modes, esp. the *madrigal and *caccia. In the 16th and 17th cs., the madrigal became the preferred form to be set to music, e.g., by Giovanni Palestrina (ca. 1525–94) and Claudio Monteverdi (1567–1643); the caccia disappears after the 16th c.

The sonnet, arguably the single most important

creation of It. prosody, was apparently invented in the second quarter of the 13th c. by Giacomo da Lentini (fl. first half of 13th c.), a notary at the court of Frederick II in Sicily. Although perhaps formed by the reduction of two *strambotti* (see STRAMBOTTO), it more likely developed in imitation of the strophe of the canzone. In early It. lit., the rhyme schemes of the quatrains and tercets are more flexible than later. The sonnet was also used as the vehicle for *verse epistles in the *tenzone* (see TENSO), an exchange of sonnets in which a topic or question was proposed for discussion to one or more poets. (Generally, as the tenzone developed, it became the rule that the response would have the same rhymes and metrical scheme as the initial sonnet, hence the phrase "rispondere per le rime," to reply by the rhymes.) Under the influence of Petrarch, perhaps its most important practitioner, and *Petrarchism, the *sonnet sequence spread throughout Europe. It. poets who have cultivated the sonnet include Michelangelo, Torquato Tasso (1544–95), Alfieri, Foscolo, Carducci, and D'Annunzio, although its popularity in It. has steadily diminished since the 17th c.

In narrative poetry, *ottava rima*, used first by Giovanni Boccaccio (1313–75) for his verse narratives (*Teseida, Filostrato, Ninfale fiesolano*), became the staple for both the epic and the popular *cantare*, which had for its subject matter cl. and med. myths and legends, as well as contemp. political events and humorous tales. Following Boccaccio's lead, the great epic poets of the Ren. used ottava rima for their chivalric poems (Matteo Maria Boiardo [1441–94], *Orlando innamorato*; Ariosto, *Orlando furioso*; and Tasso, *Gerusalemme liberata*), as did other poets such as Luigi Pulci (1432–84, *Morgante*), Politian (*Stanze per la giostra*), Giambattista Marino (1569–1625, *Adone*), and Alessandro Tassoni (1565–1635, *La secchia rapita*).

*Allegory, *didactic poetry, and the *dream vision generally were composed in *terza rima, following the great model of Dante's *Divina commedia*. Thus, Boccaccio used terza rima in the *Amorosa Visione*, Petrarch in the *Trionfi*, and Fazio degli Uberti (ca. 1307–70) in the *Dittamondo*. In later centuries, terza rima, often in the form of the *capitolo*, was incorporated by poets for a variety of compositions: *satires (Ariosto, Francesco Berni [?1497–1535], Alfieri, Leopardi), historical fictions (Niccolò Machiavelli [1469–1527]), *eclogues (de' Medici), amorous elegies (Ariosto, Foscolo, Carducci), and political allegories (Monti).

The rules of It. prosody were essentially fixed for subsequent poets in the first two centuries of It. lit., because of the examples of Dante, Petrarch, and Boccaccio and due to the work of early compilers of metrical treatises such as Francesco da Barberino (1264–1348; *Documenti d'Amore* [1306–13]), Antonio da Tempo (ca. 1275–1336; *Summa artis rithimici vulgaris dictaminis* [1332]), and Gidino da Sommacampagna (fl. late 14th c.; *Trattato dei ritmi volgari* [1381–84]). To be sure, metrical innovation has always taken place, particularly in the 20th c. with literary movements such as *futurism and *hermeticism. Nevertheless, while prosodic forms are no longer followed strictly, poets still imitate, albeit unconsciously, the cadences of traditional verse.

See CLASSICAL METERS IN MODERN LANGUAGES; FROTTOLA AND BARZELLETTA; GRAMMATICAL RHYME; HIATUS; ITALY, POETRY OF; MOSAIC RHYME; VERSO PIANO; VERSO SDRUCCIOLO; VERSO TRONCO.

■ G. da Sommacampagna, *Trattato dei ritmi volgari*, ed. G.B.C. Giuliari (1870); P. E. Guarnerio, *Manuale di versificazione italiana* (1893); F. Flamini, *Notizia storica dei versi e metri italiani* (1919); R. Murari, *Ritmica e metrica razionale italiana* (1927); V. Pernicone, "Storia e svolgimento della metrica," *Problemi ed orientamenti critici di lingua e di letteratura italiana*, ed. A. Momigliano, v. 2 (1948); M. Pazzaglia, *Il verso e l'arte della canzone nel "De vulgari eloquentia"* (1967); A. B. Giamatti, "Italian," in Wimsatt; *La metrica*, ed. R. Cremante and M. Pazzaglia (1972); D. S. Avalle, *Sintassi e prosodia nella lirica italiana delle origini* (1973); F. Caliri, *Ritmica e metrica* (1973); Spongano; M. Fubini, *Metrica e poesia*, 3d ed. (1975); *Literary Criticism of Dante Alighieri*, ed. and trans. R. S. Haller (1977); Antonio da Tempo, *Summa artis rithimici vulgaris dictaminis*, ed. R. Andrews (1977); L. Castelnuovo, *La metrica italiana* (1979); D. Alighieri, *Opere minori*, ed. P. V. Mengaldo (1979); M. Shapiro, *Hieroglyph of Time: The Petrarchan Sestina* (1981); Brogan—bibl. to 1981, supp. in *Verseform* (1988); F. P. Memmo, *Dizionario di metrica italiana* (1983); Elwert, *Italienische*; A. Menichetti, *Metrica italiana* (1993); S. Orlando, *Manuale di metrica italiana* (1994).

C. KLEINHENZ

## ITALY, POETRY OF

I. Duecento: The 1200s
II. Trecento: The 1300s
III. Quattrocento: The 1400s
IV. Cinquecento: The 1500s
V. Seicento: The 1600s
VI. Settecento: The 1700s
VII. Ottocento: The 1800s
VIII. Novecento: The 1900s

I. Duecento: The 1200s. The Middle Ages, from the fall of the Roman Empire to the 1300s, was long regarded as merely an epoch of barbarism. Mod. historiography, however, has rediscovered the period from Charlemagne to the birth of the Romance vernacular lits. as a time of fervent incubation, a preparation for the cultural rebirth of the 13th and 14th cs. During this period, the autonomous existence of the Neo-Lat. langs. became evident. The first documents of It. lang. and lit.—from the doubtful *Indovinello veronese* (Veronese Riddle, 9th c.) and the *Ritmo laurenziano* (Laurentian Verse, ca. 1150) to St. Francis's "Hymn," Jacopone's poems, and the Sicilian and Tuscan love lyrics—should be examined in the light of three conditioning facts: (1) the political conformation of the It. Peninsula—the constant tension between temporal and ecclesiastical power and its result, the Guelph-Ghibelline wars;

(2) the influence of Fr. and Occitan literary models—the Fr. lang. precedes It. by a century or more, the delay usually being attributed to a tenacious survival of Lat., though it also reflects the absence of a central power, hence a slower evolution of feudal structures in the peninsula; and (3) the widespread religious revival beginning around the year 1000 and its vast influence throughout the 1300s.

Directly related to the latter is the religious order founded by Francis of Assisi (1182–1226), who is also the first It. poet worthy of note. His "Cantico delle creature" (Song of the Creatures, also known as the *Laudes creaturarum*), a thanksgiving hymn by and for the creature to the Creator, reflects a spirit of humility and simple faith, as well as a newfound wonder at the beauty of the creation and an implicit refusal to see earthly life as a mere valley of tears. The primitive diction should not mislead the reader: Francis is a conscious inventor of poetry. This can be seen in the careful structure of the hymn, in the purposeful ambivalence of word choice, and in the celebrated adjectival series that define each "member" of the grace-giving choir.

The genre of the *lauda, enriched by the example of med. Lat. liturgical lit., became high poetry in the hands of Jacopone da Todi (1236?–1306), an attorney spiritually reborn after the tragic death of his wife. Jacopone vigorously opposed the power plays of Pope Boniface VIII (Dante's archenemy) and was excommunicated and imprisoned by him; a number of the approximately 100 extant laude by Jacopone are against the simony of the Church (e.g., "O Papa Bonifazio"). Jacopone's best poetry is inspired by his feeling of isolation in his mystical passion, and his masterpiece, the "Donna del Paradiso" (Lament of Mary), presents Christ's passion as seen through the eyes of his mother. Here Jacopone reaches lyric heights never before attained in It. poetry.

The first matrix of It. literary trad. is the *Sicilian school. Centered at the court of Frederick II (1194–1250), the group devolved from the Occitan *troubadour trad., superimposing the rituals of feudal bondage and court protocol onto a concept of love, its only topic, in which the perfect submission by the lover corresponds to the heavenly perfection of the lady. The school had great cultural importance, and its major exponent, the notary Giacomo da Lentini (first half of 13th c.), probably invented the *sonnet. Mentioned by Dante as the foremost poet of the Magna Curia, Giacomo was a faithful adapter of the troubadours' and *trouvères' schemata of *fin'amors* (see COURTLY LOVE). Other members of the Sicilian school were Giacomino Pugliese (fl. 1325–50), Rinaldo d'Aquino (?1227–81), and Pier delle Vigne (ca. 1190–1249?).

The emperor Frederick, himself a poet, had vainly attempted to unify his Ger. and It. domains against violent ecclesiastical opposition. During his reign arose the Ghibelline (imperial) and Guelph (papal) factions, antagonists for over a century in It. politics. After the battle of Benevento (1266), which marked the end of the Hohenstaufen dynasty, the practice of poetry survived but was transplanted to Tuscany in central Italy. Its first noteworthy heir, Guittone d'Arezzo (ca. 1225–93), a Guelph exiled from his homeland, renewed and enriched the earlier *lyric trad. by extending its topics to ethical and social concerns. As an extension of the *trobar clus, Guittone's hermetic poems sound cold and artistically stifling. His technically complex style attracted imitators, such as Chiaro Davanzati (d. 1304) and the abstruse Monte Andrea (fl. 2d half 13th c.). Guittone's poetic corpus is both a bridge and a hurdle to be overcome between the Sicilians and the first great flowering of It. lyric, the school of the Sweet New Style, the *Dolce stil nuovo.

The very existence of such a "school," posited only by a vague reference in Dante's Purgatorio, is unsure. Certain, however, is a common conception of love as "dictator" (inspirer and despot). The Bolognese judge Guido Guinizzelli (ca. 1240–76), praised by Dante as the father of the style dolce (sweet, not bitterly harsh, as in Guittone) and nuovo (original), left a celebrated summary of the new amorous ars poetica in his *canzone "Al cor gentil": true nobility comes not from lineage but from virtue; love is a positive force: through the lady, admired from afar, the lover with a "noble heart" attains spiritual perfection. Guido's corpus (about 20 extant texts) shows a youthful vitality, also present in Dante's Vita nuova. Among the numerous adepts of the Sweet New Style are Lapo Gianni (d. after 1328), Gianni Alfani (fl. late 13th–early 14th cs.), Dino Frescobaldi (1221–1316), and the prolific Cino da Pistoia (ca. 1270–1336), usually viewed as a link between Dante and Petrarch. The maturity of the school is represented by Guido Cavalcanti (ca. 1255–1300), Dante's "primo amico" (first friend), whom legend depicts as a haughty loner, an image probably inspired by his poems (52 extant), his ars poetica, and theory of love, captured in the complex canzone "Donna me prega." Cavalcanti's interest in the mechanics of feelings, esp. the anguish of love, gives him a "morbid and mournful" air, as he observes the torment of his own soul. In his concept of love, the sight of a "real" woman stimulates the lover to form an idea of beauty that pervades his soul and, in turn, prods him to strive vainly toward the "original."

Parallel to the stilnovo, a trad. of jocose (or bourgeois) poetry developed. The "Contrasto" by Cielo d'Alcamo (ca. 1200–50) is a highly artistic, lively amorous dialogue between a cynical minstrel and a clever young woman. The Sicilian court poets' recurrent topics (praise, submission) and artful ling. koiné are the ironic subtext to this still-enjoyable little masterpiece. *Parody of stilnovo themes results in shrill outbursts in Cecco Angiolieri (1260–1313?), the skilled Sienese sonneteer (over 100 extant poems), whose themes include wild quarrels with his lady (Becchina, who is no lady), tavern brawls, the sorry state of his purse, and the stinginess of his parents. Cecco is no Italian Villon, as he has been called. His texts are meant for recital in the inn or square; the punch lines are ideally completed by guffaws from the guzzlers. A gentler realism inspires the sonnets of Folgóre, poet of San Gimignano (ca. 1265–before 1332), reflecting the chivalric ceremonies of polite society. The frank pursuit of pleasure here is tempered by a code of behavior based on good taste.

**II. Trecento: The 1300s.** In retrospect, the first hundred years of It. lit. appear as preparation for Dante's poetry. This perception, philologically speaking, is quite correct. Aesthetically, however, a veritable chasm separates Duecento poetry from the Divina commedia (Divine Comedy). For valid parallels, one must turn to the fine arts and Giotto (ca. 1267–1337) or to philosophy and Thomas Aquinas (1225–74).

Little is known of Dante Alighieri's life. Born in 1265 in Florence into a Guelph-leaning family of lesser nobility, he studied rhet. with Brunetto Latini (ca. 1220–94). Lasting influences on his youth included his friendship with Cavalcanti; his discovery of his own talent for poetry; and, esp., his love for a Beatrice Portinari, wife of the banker Simone dei Bardi. Remaining devoted to Beatrice in her life and after her death, Dante recounts their lopsided love story in the Vita nuova (New Life); in his magnum opus, written to honor this young woman who died at 25, Beatrice is present from beginning to end. Dante never mentions his wife Gemma and their children (two sons, Jacopo [1289–1348] and Pietro [1300–64], wrote commentaries on their father's work). After 1295, documents attest to Dante's participation in the civic life of his city; in 1300, he became one of six priori (cabinet members) in a Florence torn between the two factions of the Guelph party: Blacks, subservient to Rome, and Whites, anti-imperial but resistant to papal hegemony. Dante sided with the latter. In 1301, he was sent by his party, then in power, as ambassador to Pope Boniface VIII, who promptly detained him, while the Blacks, with Fr. and papal help, seized power in Florence. Dante, sentenced in absentia to be burned at the stake, never again set foot in his city. In exile over 19 years, he hoped at first to deserve recall on the strength of his learning: he produced works on lings. (De vulgari eloquentia [On Vernacular Eloquence], in Lat., incomplete), philosophy (Convivio [The Banquet], unfinished), and political science (Monarchia). Scholars date the composition of the Divine Comedy from 1307 to the year of Dante's death in Ravenna, 1321.

The Vita nuova (1292–93) is a collection of poems connected by prose passages relating a tenuous love story from the meeting between Dante and Beatrice, both aged nine, to her death in 1290 and beyond. It is a story made up of abstract emotions, the most daring "real" event being Beatrice's one-time reciprocation of Dante's greeting. Neither autobiography nor total fiction, the Vita nuova is rather a typology of youthful love, pervaded by a quasi-religious, mystical solemnity and by an oneiric vagueness of detail. Dante's Rime comprise the poems excluded from the Vita nuova and those written after 1293, incl. the canzoni of his maturity and exile; closest to the inspiration of the Comedy is the poem "Tre donne" ("Three Women").

The 14,233 verses of the Comedy (for Dante, comedy and tragedy refer to both content and style) took 15 years to compose. In addition to the glorification of Beatrice and the exile's wish to show his worth, the purpose of the poem is expressed in Dante's letter to Can Grande (*Epistle* 13, of debated attribution) as the messianic mission "to lead the living out of a state of misery into a state of bliss." The poet achieved his literary purpose of fashioning with words a world that in its miraculous credibility vies with God's own creation. We must remember that the *Comedy* is a fiction, the work of a poet and master storyteller, not of the Holy Spirit. This obvious truth sets a limit to symbolic interpretation, even though the med. practice of *allegory is ever-present in the text. What distinguishes Dante's from earlier otherworldly journeys is that his predecessors are *all* allegory; we read Dante after seven centuries for what we find beyond his didactic purposes. Allegory is a premise of the *narratio*, flexible and often ambiguous: it is part of the polyvalence present in all enduring poetry. While Beatrice and Virgil may be, respectively, "theology" and "reason," we believe and love them primarily because Dante "forgot," more often than not, their roles as abstractions.

The *Comedy* is the fictive, visionary account of a redemptive journey through hell and purgatory to paradise and God, by a pilgrim, Dante Alighieri, who is guided first by Virgil, later by Beatrice, and finally by St. Bernard. Hell holds the souls of the damned, distributed into nine "circles" set up according to Aristotle's categories of sin (incontinence, violence, fraud [heresy was unknown to the Greek]). Purgatory is segmented into the seven deadly sins of Christian dogma (with Ante-Purgatory and Earthly Paradise bringing the number of divisions to nine). Paradise comprises the nine heavens of Ptolemy's geocentric universe, from the seven planetary spheres to the fixed stars, the *Primum Mobile*, and the Empyrean, abode of all the souls happy in the sight of God. The recurrence of the number three and its multiples, as well as other divisions in the edifice, such as the 100 *canti* or the strophic scheme of three lines of eleven syllables each—*terza rima*—or the *canto and episode parallelisms and contrasts at corresponding "locations" in the three *cantiche* are important for Dantean exegesis.

Of the three canticles (34 + 33 + 33 canti), *Inferno* is the most dramatic and suspenseful. Memorable characters and events dominate several canti: Francesca's story of love and death, Farinata's "war memoirs," Chancellor Pier delle Vigne's suicide, Ulysses's last voyage, the prison "cannibalism" of Count Ugolino of Pisa. *Purgatorio* is the realm of elegy, subdued sadness, and hopeful yearning: it is the most "earthly" cantica, with feelings of brotherly affection. *Paradiso* is the triumph of Beatrice, who is both symbol and real woman. Among the blessed, absolute equality is the rule: no character should emerge. The sequence of heavens is transformed into a transcendental fireworks display of growing intensity. Humanity is never absent from the rarefied mysticism signaling God's presence. And the great saints appear in person to test, prod, warn, and guide the pilgrim toward fulfillment. God, thanks to Dante's magnificent intuition, is depicted here not as the bearded elder of Judeo-Christian iconography but

as a blinding point of light immeasurably both far and near. In *Paradiso*, Dante gives evidence of his most sublime, mature genius.

Dante's robust spirituality, unshaken religious convictions, and firm belief in the continuity of social structures were rooted in the apparent stability of the "old" world, the thick Ages in the Middle. The *curriculum vitae* of Francesco Petrarca (Petrarch, 1304–74) coincides with a historical moment of accelerated change and crumbling certainties. Petrarch appears much closer to us than does Dante: closer than the generation or two that actually separate these two quasi-contemporaries. The mod. instability of Petrarch's psychic makeup is manifest in his vast correspondence, in his treatises (e.g., on "solitude," on the "remedies against Fortune"), and esp. in his Lat. *Secretum* (*Confessions*), which is a microscopic analysis of that nameless something that forever anguished his soul. Born in Arezzo of a Florentine bourgeois family in exile, Petrarch was brought up in southern France. He studied jurisprudence at Montpellier and Bologna. On April 6, 1327, his destiny was redirected when he met, in Avignon, Laura, the unidentified woman whom he loved in life and in death (she died of the plague in 1348) and whom he immortalized in his poetry. Petrarch is the forefather of humanism, the revival of Greco-Roman culture that would dominate the next century. His work in Lat. is immense, esp. his epic in hexameters, *Africa*, which procured him the title and crown of *poet laureate conferred by the Senate of Rome on April 8, 1341. The uncontested arbiter of Eur. lit., Petrarch lived the latter half of his life mainly in Italy.

Petrarch expected enduring fame from his Lat. work; immeasurably superior are his modestly titled (with affected scorn) *Rerum vulgarium fragmenta* (freely rendered, "Italian bits and pieces") or *Canzoniere*. In spite of his expressed desire to burn the collection, he kept revising and perfecting the ms. to his dying day. The 366 poems (317 sonnets, plus 29 canzoni, nine *sestinas, seven *ballate*, and four *madrigals) record the earthly (not at all merely spiritual) passion inspired by Laura, even after her "flight to heaven." Petrarch is the last great representative of the troubadour trad. (afterward there will be epigones and *Petrarchism). Some critics have doubted the very existence of Laura, assuming her to be a composite of the poetic trad. While the "love story" behind the stylized abstractions is clearly an unrequited love, the human passion of the poet, with its ebb and flow over the years, its brief joys and long despair, its cries and silences, and its phases of resignation and rebellion, recreates the anonymous Beloved, body and soul. Although Petrarch veils and stylizes his earthly model, the living warmth of his words makes the reader mentally recreate Laura. There is no direct description of her in the *Canzoniere*, yet we never lose sight of her.

There is something artful if not artificial in this process—the something that made De Sanctis remark that, while Dante was more poet than artist, Petrarch was more artist than poet. Nevertheless, readers have always privileged the poems written about Laura and the self-analytic pauses. Set aside the opening and closing pieces as well as the few nondirectly Laura poems, and what remains engraved in memory are the dreamy evocation of the fateful day (no. 2); the old pilgrim (16) on his way to Rome; a *solo e pensoso* walk across the fields (35); the tired prayer of the penitent (62); a lovely shape made of transparencies (90 and the famous 126); the *cameretta* (little room) of the poet (234); and, in the death of Laura, the inexorable march of days and years (272), the useless return of spring (310), and the sad song of a nightingale telling us that "nothing here below delights—and lasts" (311). A certain repetitiveness has been observed in the *Canzoniere*; but, in fact, the work was meant to be sampled in small doses, rather than by continued perusal. A monochrome uniformity is genuine in Petrarch's only other It. verse work, the later *Trionfi*. Heavily allegorical, unfinished and unrefined, these series of Dantesque *terzine* sing the "triumphs" of Love, Chastity, Death, Fame, Time, and Eternity.

Among the minor *Trecento* poets are the late *stilnovista* Fazio degli Uberti (ca. 1305–67) from Pisa; the courtly poet Antonio Beccari (1315–before 1374) from Ferrara; the prolific Florentine popularizer of vernacular lit., Antonio Pucci (ca. 1310–88); and the fine author of ballads Franco Sacchetti (ca. 1330–1400). The third component of the great *Trecento* triumvirate, Giovanni Boccaccio (1313–75), father of mod. storytelling, was an uninspired but evidently inspiring versifier—e.g., Chaucer's vast and undervalued debt to Boccaccio's *Filostrato* (1336?), the romance of Troilus in octaves and *Teseida* (1341?), an epic, the Palamon and Arcite story. Boccaccio's own "Vita nuova" (*Commedia delle ninfe*, 1341) and allegorical vision in *terzine* (*Amorosa visione*, 1343?) influenced in turn Petrarch's *Trionfi*. There are more than 100 lyric compositions also attributed to Boccaccio, counting the ballads from the frame of the *Decameron*.

**III. Quattrocento: The 1400s.** The sudden blossoming of vernacular lit. in the 14th c. carried in it the seeds of decadence or rather of exhausted retrenchment during the first half of the next century. Petrarch and Boccaccio (and protohumanist Dante) were indeed the fountainhead of the cultural movement called *humanism*, essentially an enthusiastic revival of Lat. lit. (as opposed and "superior" to It. lit.). The trend, initially a passion for cl. learning and a rediscovery of many major texts of Lat. and Gr. antiquity, by degrees became a belief in the panacea of cl. education, capable of "freeing" humankind. The main creative tenet of this new *classicism* was *imitatio*, theorized by Petrarch and the basis for the later Petrarchism. The new blooming of Lat. lit. highlights such well-known humanists as Giovanni Pico della Mirandola (1463–94), Lorenzo Valla (1406–57), Coluccio Salutati (1331–1406), Giovanni Pontano (1426–1503), and Marsilio Ficino (1433–99). Far from being slavish imitators, the humanists in fact ended by "dethroning the ancients from their exalted position" (Guarino, in Bondanella) by reexamining under the microscope of philology the old texts and by historicizing classicism. Humanism was nothing short of a discovery of hist. in the mod. sense of the word.

Poetry in It. continued to be produced, marginally as it were, often in its "lower" species as imitations of popular song. The Venetian patrician Leonardo Giustiniani (1338–1446) became a sort of bestseller on account of his talent for reproducing the sonorities and easy grace of the *canzonette* sung by gondoliers on the *laguna*. The same taste for the simple diction of popular genres inspired the Florentine Luigi Pulci (1432–84), but with a different result. Pulci is a "humorist" in the true sense of the word: for him, life was a "harmonious mixture of sweet and bitter and a thousand flavors." Not merely a parody of the solemnities of the Fr. *chansons de geste, Pulci's mock-heroic "epos" *Morgante* is the amusing product of a whimsical comic genius. Its rough model is enriched by characters alive on the page—in spite of their irrational capriciousness. In addition to the usual types, Pulci introduced Morgante, the giant, inspirer of Rabelais; the ribald monster Margutte who dies of immoderate laughter at a gross practical joke; and the amusing "logician" fiend Astaroth, spokesman for Pulci's religious doubts and occult leanings.

Matteo Maria Boiardo (1441–94) made reference in a serious vein to the same material. Pulci's attitude toward the Carolingian sources had reflected popular Tuscan city-bred tastes; Boiardo brought to them the conservative provincial atmosphere of northern courtly life. The incomplete *Orlando innamorato* (Roland in Love) injects Arthurian elements into the chivalric material: all-conquering love now presides over the knights' and ladies' adventures. The poem is a whirlwind of disparate episodes, unified, if at all, by overwhelming passion and vigorous action. The idiom, of strong regional flavor, hindered wide diffusion of the original; up to the 19th c. *Orlando* was read in Tuscanized versions done by Francesco Berni and others.

Florence, transformed from Dante's *comune* into a *signoria* under the Medicis, reacquired its cultural centrality during the second half of the century. Pulci's lord protector, Lorenzo de' Medici (1449–92, known as Il Magnifico), was himself a versatile poet. Critical appraisals of Lorenzo's poetry range from enthusiastic endorsement of his artful masquerades to viewing his output as the pastime of a statesman, the amusement of a dilettante. In truth, he was simply one of the many skillful literati of his court. His principal merit, other than his all-important patronage, lies in his vigorous defense of literary It.: Lorenzo contributed in a decisive way to the final prevalence of the Tuscan-Florentine trad. and the decline of literary writing in Lat.

Still, it may well be that Lorenzo's most enduring achievement was the discovery of the poetic talent of Politian (Poliziano), pseud. of Agnolo Ambrogini (1454–94) from Montepulciano (hence the name). Politian became a leading humanist, rediscovering and editing ancient texts. Apart from his poetry in Lat. and Gr., Politian wrote canzoni and other lyric poems. In his masterwork, the unfinished *Stanze* (Strophes, in *ottave*), he retells allegorically the meeting between Giuliano de' Medici, a youth devoted to pleasure and adventure, and the nymph of unearthly beauty Simonetta (Vespucci). The airy lightness of the *Stanze* is a poetic miracle, every octave a mixture of reminiscences, references, and reminders (Homer, Horace, Virgil, Dante, Petrarch, and many others), but the result appears perfectly natural. Moments of noble melancholy accent the pellucid text, mementos of the fragility and transience of all earthly things. Politian is the first poet of mod. times whose subject is poetry; a poet's poet, he saw lit. as the essence of life.

Composed during the last two decades of the century, the *Arcadia* of Jacopo Sannazaro (1458?–1530), a mixture of prose tales and *pastoral songs, has enjoyed great fortune over the years, cyclically renewed and, in a way, enduring into our own times of recurrent ecological lamentation. "Antimetropolitan" yearnings (anachronistic already at inception) for a nonexistent rural simplicity, together with the immemorial myth of a lost Golden Age, inspire this early environmental manifesto.

**IV. Cinquecento: The 1500s.** The *Rinascimento*, the It. Ren., is the age of artistic and literary splendor between the age of humanism and the advent of *baroque. Its poetic practice is pervaded by the heritage of the Trecento, esp. Petrarch (Dante was considered a "primitive" by this age of refinement), filtered through the classicism that prevailed in the 15th c. The Rinascimento is the age of Petrarchism, an age not only of servile *imitation of the themes and style of the *Canzoniere*, not only the fashionable organization of one's poetic output into an ideal love story, but an adherence to the Platonic ideal of love and to the ling. ideal of purity, harmony, and elegance of expression, which later deteriorated into mere technical virtuosity. The patron saints of the Eur. 1500s were Petrarch and Plato; however, Aristotle's *Poetics* was also rediscovered and deeply, at times obsessively, studied—and in part misconstrued. The tenet of imitatio became paramount. Literary genres were rigidly codified, just as social behavior came to be governed by a code—its great documents are Baldassare Castiglione's *Il Cortegiano* (*The Courtier*, 1528) and Niccolò Machiavelli's *Il Principe* (*The Prince*, 1532). At the threshold of this great age stands the historically important but poetically insignificant Cardinal Pietro Bembo (1470–1547), friend of Lorenzo and Politian. Bembo, as codifier of Petrarchism and Platonism, is the embodiment of the Ren. His *Rime* (Poems) are little more than textbook examples to illustrate his theories, but his treatise, *Prose della volgar lingua* (Writing in the Vernacular, 1525), became something of a bible for the literati of the century. This inclusive codification of literary taste and ling. choice had a decisive influence on the diction of authors from Ludovico Ariosto to Torquato Tasso.

The essence of the Rinascimento is best revealed in the epic romance *Orlando furioso* (The Frenzy of Roland), whose author, one of the most likeable figures in the annals of It. lit., is Ludovico Ariosto (1474–1533). Ariosto's minor work illustrates the frustrations of a harried existence. His lyric poetry was inspired by his lifelong devotion to Alessandra Benucci, whom he married secretly so as not to forfeit ecclesiastical benefits. The seven *Satire* recount his travels and reflections. The last years of life were devoted to the definitive revision of his epic poem (pub. in 1532 in 46 canti). *Orlando*, 30 years in the making, pools the experience of the minor work, the warmth and immediacy of the love poetry, the detached and smiling wisdom of the *Satire*, and the character sketching of his theatrical pieces. The external occasion for the poem was Boiardo's unfinished *Orlando innamorato*: the *Furioso* completes the story, closely following its sources in the Carolingian epic cycle and the Celtic Arthurian legends in narrative detail but renewing the material with poetic license. This master storyteller holds hundreds of threads in hand at once and unerringly weaves them into an immense coherent tapestry. The great movers of the threefold plot are Ariosto's passions: first, love conceived as an earthy emotion, frankly sensual; second, the forms of knightly behavior and of court ritual; third, an insatiable appetite for adventure. Voltaire noted that Ariosto is always "superior" to his material: he tells his story "jokingly"— taking seriously and yet mocking his inventions: hence, the frequent authorial intrusions (comments, tongue-in-cheek explanations, ironic misdirection); hence, the fable-like and dreamy atmosphere around Ariosto's knights and ladies. Painstaking realism of detail fuses with an oneiric vagueness of context. The description of Atlante's castle and the invention of the lunar travels of Astolfo are emblematic of this attitude.

The form of the *Orlando furioso* is nothing short of prodigious. The octaves of *narrative poetry—woody and lagging in Boccaccio's youthful poems, prosily stammering in Pulci's *Morgante*, loosely dressing Boiardo's laborious inventions—coincide here, for the first time in It. poetry, with the "breathing" of author and reader. Ariosto lives in his octave, in the six (the alternately rhymed verses) plus two (the clinching couplet) pattern of his *strophe, each one a microcosm, in its perfectly controlled and yet wondrously airy architecture, of the entire magnificent construction.

Ariosto's Petrarchan love lyrics are undistinguished products of the age, similar to myriads of contemp. songbooks. Little talent emerges from the crowd of the *Cinquecento petrarchisti*. Monsignor Giovanni della Casa (1503–56), remembered for his *Galateo* (Book of Manners), shows a nostalgia for robust emotions and monumental imagery. Two women poets introduce a welcome variation in a field dominated by the stylized male psychology of emotions: Vittoria Colonna (1492–1547), of aristocratic family and patroness of artists, authored a conventional songbook; Gaspara Stampa (1523–54), probably of low social standing, occasionally allows life to show through her imitative verse. Even more creatively, the feverish and disordered rhythms of a passionate existence seem to influence her songs, which are suggestive of entries in a love diary.

Intimations of the incipient baroque taste have been

detected in Luigi Tansillo (1510–68). His too-easy sonorities, abuse of color, predilection for horrid landscapes, and colloquial touch seem, indeed, to point toward Giambattista Marino. But more noteworthy than the lyric output of the age and its vast and forgotten epic feats (the best are Giangiorgio Trissino's *L'Italia liberata dai Goti* [Italy Freed from the Goths], Luigi Alamanni's *Avarchide*, and Bernardo Tasso's *Amadigi*) is its humorous or light verse. Two cultivators of this genre had vast influence throughout the following century. Francesco Berni (1498–1535), Tuscan refurbisher of Boiardo's epic, is the wellhead of the *bernesco* poem, still jokingly cultivated in Italy—a buffoonery of "sitcom" heavy on puns. Written in an irresistibly funny It. modeled on Lat. (or a Lat. bastardized by It.), the mock-heroic epic *Baldus* by Merlin Cocai (pseud. of the rebellious Benedictine monk Teofilo Folengo, 1491–1544) extends Pulci's *Morgante* by recounting the farcical adventures of Baldus, a descendant of Rinaldo.

The last great poetic voice of the Ren., Torquato Tasso (1544–95), is the spiritual forerunner of baroque poetics. Most likely inheriting a psychic disorder, he became distraught by the mental effort required to produce his masterwork, the epic *Gerusalemme liberata* (*Jerusalem Delivered*, 1581). Episodes of irrational behavior at the court of Ferrara and aimless excursions across the peninsula eventually led to Tasso's confinement for seven years in the dungeon asylum of Sant'Anna. Pirated eds. of his poem, attacks from pedantic critics, and obsessive religious doubts exacerbated his illness; he died in Rome. His minor work alone would be sufficient to give him a high rank among the Petrarchans and epic poets of his century. His nearly 2,000 lyrics (*Rime*) are a workshop in which the poet perfected techniques and experimented with sentimental situations; these are interspersed with lyrics of admirable invention and masterful execution, esp. his madrigals, a genre congenial to Tasso's evanescent moods. The Petrarchan model here appears at one remove, filtered through the Petrarchans of the early 1500s—Bembo, della Casa—as indeed Petrarch will be read through Tasso by the next generation of poets, Marino and his school. The chivalric poem *Rinaldo* (12 canti of ottave) betrays the adolescent's hand as well as features that will later govern the inspiration of his epic. Already here, the war chronicle of the sources is constantly squeezed out by courtly love. Tasso first favored the *idyll, and his pastoral play *Aminta* is rightly spoken of in the same breath with his lyric output: its theatrical pretext gives way to the emotional situations and flights of pathos in the *Rime*.

Whether *La Gerusalemme liberata* is the first full poetic manifestation of the incipient baroque age (some critics hold that the very terms *baroque* and *Marinism* are misnomers for "Tassism" and "Tassomania") or, inversely, the last bloom of the "sane" Rinascimento is an academic question; and interestingly, it parallels the great 17th-c. controversy (which engaged Galileo Galilei) on the relative worth of the two great narrative poems of the preceding age, those of Ariosto and Tasso. Tasso's epic, its pretext the last phase of the First Crusade, has a cast composed of both lifeless historical characters and fictive personae of the poet himself, each endowed with throbbing life. To Ariosto's objectivity, detachment, and *irony, Tasso opposes his subjectivity, participation, and sentimentality. All the great passionate characters of the oft-abandoned plot are facets of Tasso's psychic makeup, exhibiting the excesses and morbidity that landed their creator in Sant'Anna. The *Gerusalemme* is, in this sense, a truly autobiographical epos. Long traverses through Aristotle's poetics and the theory of the epic preceded and accompanied the feverish composition, but the rules reaffirmed were soon discarded by Tasso's more powerful sentimental inspiration. The Crusade cedes place to the multiple, strangely disturbed love stories of the variously and wrongly assorted couples. The whole is immersed in an overheated atmosphere of gratuitous heroism, white and black magic, cliffhangers cum heavenly intervention, duels to the death, and battle scenes of vast confusion. In the *Orlando furioso*, the good-natured "colloquial" voice of Ludovico the Amiable constantly tended to overdub the narrator, while in the *Gerusalemme*, Torquato's falsetto breaks through, fitfully as it were, to lend his creations a hundred diverse intonations of emotional disorder.

Tasso's *ottava*, ordered into obsessive parallelisms and chiastic contrasts, offers an ineffable musicality and a psychomimetic finesse never before heard. It is masterfully torn by the high drama of *enjambments. Indeed, Tasso addresses his poem to a new audience of a new age and sensibility, that of the Counter-Reformation, an age of earthshaking upheavals. This critical view allows us to reevaluate Tasso's reworking of *Gerusalemme conquistata* (Jerusalem Recovered), a text of vaster and more solemn architecture, characterized by a baroque heaviness of pace and expression and universally judged a complete failure until the late 20th c. The characteristics of *Gerusalemme conquistata* are in evidence in Tasso's late poem *Il mondo creato*, a ponderous account of the Creation similar in flavor to an overripe fruit.

**V. Seicento: the 1600s.** The 17th c., a Golden Age in the Spain of Luis de Góngora and Miguel de Cervantes, in the France of Jean Racine and Jean de La Fontaine, and in the England of the metaphysical poets, was long considered to have been an age of decadence in Italy. Its dominant Tassesque aesthetics certainly revealed the exhaustion of a long-mined vein, an exasperation of the drive for outward perfection yearned for by the Ren. The age frittered away its heritage in an obsessive search for originality and "marvels." Foreign (Sp.) and papal domination in the peninsula, the newborn religious dogmatism imposed by the Counter-Reformation, the general lowering of ethical standards owing perhaps to the riches from the New World, and the universal instability of ideas in this age of scientific revolution have all been indicated as causes for the alleged poetic aridity of the age. The baroque age in Italy adopted the ars poetica of the late Ren., developing Tasso's theories and example toward a concept of poetry as a nonrational activity, and it endorsed a view of literary production and appreciation based on *taste and feeling.

Giambattista Marino (1569–1625), a Neapolitan, became the high priest of the new school of writing usually called *Marinism (also *Seicentismo*, conceptism, and *manierismo*). He was the theorizer and the most prolific practitioner of the poetics of *meraviglia* (of astonishment—at all costs), a style in search of the arduous and the complex. A genre loved by Marino and the *marinisti* was poetry on art (e.g., his collection *Galleria*), a species of poetry feeding on itself (his *Lira*, [Lyrics]) and pillaging all preexistent lit.—as does Marino's masterpiece the *Adone* (Adonis), in almost every one of its 40,000 verses. The poem is truly a miracle of words growing on words and never managing to cover the void under them.

Among Marino's contemporaries, two poets sought independence from the master: Gabriello Chiabrera (1552–1638), whose *anacreontic songs are another "reading" of Tasso, and Alessandro Tassoni (1565–1635), remembered for his mock-heroic *Secchia rapita* (The Ravished Pail, 1622). The most notable recovery of late-20th-c. crit. is the poetry of the philosopher Tommaso Campanella (1568–1639), whose work closely parallels the metaphysical songs of John Donne, George Herbert, and Richard Crashaw (see METAPHYSICAL POETRY). This Calabrese monk suffered a monstrous fate, 30 years in prison (several years in the flooded underground dungeon of St. Elmo with hands and feet chained) for heresy and rebellion. Campanella's poems, owing to their forbidding complexity of concepts and diction, were judged by their rare readers almost devoid of interest. But today these canzoni, esp. the beautiful "Hymn to the Sun," composed in the depth of St. Elmo, strike us as the "missing link" in It. baroque poetry. In his translucent verses, the chained poet attains the lyrical height for which Marino always strove but rarely reached.

**VI. Settecento: The 1700s.** The latter half of the 1600s produced a general decadence in poetry. The antibaroque backlash came as a call to "return to nature," to observe the limits of good taste and common sense, and to renew imitatio and the cult of the classics. The adepts of this neoclassical revival congregated in the Academy of Arcadia (a loose association of literati, self-defined "shepherds"), founded in 1690 by Queen Christina of Sweden, then in exile in Rome. Arcadia promoted pastoral poetry, sobriety of lang., and faithfulness to trad., discarding the whole Marinist century to hark back to Sannazaro's Cinquecento. However, this school also became in turn the matrix of mediocre versifiers of derivative bucolic idylls. An intermittently genuine poetic voice is heard in the tenuous lyrics of the great libretto dramatist Metastasio (pseud. of Pietro Trapassi, 1698–1782), poet-in-residence for most of his life at the Hapsburg court in Vienna. His many melodramas (e.g., *Didone abbandonata, Olimpiade, Demoofonte,* and *Demetrio*) are deservedly famous. In his *Canzonette* (Songs), Metastasio introduced a facile sentimentalism and an evanescent lyricism that he, unlike his predecessors, couched in down-to-earth lang.

René Descartes' rationalism influenced practically all intellectual trends in 18th-c. Italy. The influence of the Fr. Encyclopedists—Voltaire, Montesquieu, and Denis Diderot—on the one hand and of the Ossian craze, with the nocturnal and sepulchral fashion it brought with it, on the other, became paramount. The first civic poet of Italy, the Lombard Giuseppe Parini (1729–99), represents the sober awakening of the age leading to the Fr. Revolution. A seriousness of ethical purpose and a sense of mission in his social crit. distinguish this Catholic priest, ed., and schoolteacher. Parini is remembered for his long and unfinished poem of bitter social comment, *Il giorno*, depicting one day in the life of a "giovin signore," a young man about town. The satire, ferociously allusive and resentful, and seldom attenuated by the smile of superior comprehension, seems at times shot through by a secret nostalgia for the world of fashion and elegance. Parini is the first in the hist. of It. poetry to have obtained from the "short" hendecasyllable effects vying with those of the flexible cl. hexameter.

The essence of pure poetry—as opposed to the practically ambitious *engagé* verse of Parini—is represented by the domineering figure of the preromantic playwright Vittorio Alfieri (1749–1803), scion of an old aristocratic family from Italy's Piedmont region. The first fruit of his illumination, the tragedy *Cleopatra*, was followed by a feverishly fertile decade of dramatic production (1776–86): 18 more tragedies, dramatic verse in dialogue form. The Alfierian hero, a pure revolutionary, acts out the abstract libertarian rebellion of the poet's soul, scornful of any pragmatic effort at real social progress. Alfieri's stay in Tuscany afforded him time to refine his Piedmontese, Frenchified ling. and cultural background. In Paris in 1789, he was at first wildly enthusiastic about, then bitterly disappointed in, the Fr. Revolution. In 1792, he escaped the Terror to spend his last years in Florence writing six comedies, his violent anti-Fr. *Il misogallo* (The Francophobe), and his celebrated *Vita* (Memoirs), with its relentlessly, almost breathlessly drawn portrait of the poet-hero.

Alfieri represents the *Sturm und Drang* of It. poetry. His collection of lyrics (*Rime*) amounts to a spiritual autobiography of a soul tormented by dreams of immensity. The idealized and idolized figure of the poet, alone, in haughty solitude, looms large. The Petrarchan subtext of these poems signifies a return to the source; it is the manifestation of a genuine "elective affinity" rather than the obligatory imitation of an earlier century. However, the greatest lyric poetry of this "lion of Asti" is to be found in his tragedies, texts of a lyrical essentiality, of an elliptic diction, a barebones structure, and an unrelenting pace. By critical consensus, Alfieri's most acclaimed tragic pieces, *Saul* (1882) and *Mirra* (Myrrha, 1887), are staged poems on the *sublime.

**VII. Ottocento: The 1800s.** The Arcadian trend had sown the seeds of a rebirth of taste for cl. ideals of beauty. In Italy, these preromantic stirrings coincide with a short period of neoclassical predominance in art (Antonio Canova) and lit. concurrent with the Napoleonic age. The two movements, Arcadism of the late 1700s and *neoclassicism of the early 1800s, shared an attention to form, an aesthetics based on the renewed concept of the sublime, a taste for the genuine and primordial, and a purism in the medium of art. Ippolito Pindemonte (1735–1828), remembered for his *Poesie campestri* (Rustic Verses), and Vincenzo Monti (1754–1828) were the most coherent adepts of the new trend.

The poetic genius of the imperial *intermezzo* was Ugo Foscolo (1778–1827). His poetry fuses the classicist's love for perfection of form with the heritage of Parini and Alfieri and with Eur. *romanticism. Born of a Gr. mother on the Ionian island of Zante, Foscolo was, so to speak, a congenital classicist in his psychic makeup. His tempestuous age provided the background for a truly romantic curriculum of wars and turbulent loves. In 1802, he published *Ultime lettere di Jacopo Ortis* (Last Letters of Jacopo Ortis), an epistolary novel of love and suicide inspired by J. W. Goethe's *Werther*. Foscolo's 12 sonnets (among them the masterpieces "Alla Musa," "A Zacinto," "Alla sera," and "In morte del fratello Giovanni") and his two major *odes (1800–03) are perfect expressions of the cl. ideal implanted in a romantic soul. His principal claim to posthumous glory should have been the three-part hymn *Le Grazie* (The Graces), a vast corpus of *fragments composed over the course of 20 years. The immaterial lightness of diction and verse can only increase our regret at the structural sketchiness of the magnificent torso. Though 20th-c. exegesis, with its bias for the fragmentary, has rediscovered this great mass of poetic wreckage, attempts at a coherent reconstruction have not been wholly convincing. The entire experience of the poet's "life in art" is the true theme of the poem.

Foscolo remains best known for his "Dei sepolcri" (On Tombs, 1806), written in 295 blank verses. The theme, occasioned by the Napoleonic decree prohibiting burial within urban limits, is left behind, replaced by a poetic meditation on life and death, on the immemorial rites of burial, on fame surviving the tomb, and on the great men of the past and their sepulchers. The evocation of the nocturnal cemetery, the "triumph" in the Petrarchan sense of posthumous glory over death, the celebration of memory as a cenotaph to greatness, the motif of tears and consolation—all are close to the central topics of romanticism. In his "Sepolcri," Foscolo emerges as the "father of Italian romanticism."

The new mode of conceiving the human condition given by romanticism, with its components of Enlightenment rationalism and Restoration *historicism, with its taste for the unsophisticated and primordial, and with its repertory of lugubrious themes came of age in Italy in the 1820s. It. romantics, who first gathered around the Florentine periodical *Conciliatore* (1818–19), distinguished themselves from their fellows in Germany and England by their concern with the social and ethical role of lit. The Risorgimento (It. national "Resurgence," a movement that would result in 1860 in the birth of a unified mod. Italy) was an important factor, mainly through the educative influence of such protagonists as the patriot Giuseppe Mazzini (1805–72), the publicist Vincenzo Gioberti (1801–52), and the literary historian Francesco De Sanctis (1817–83).

The great models—Friedrich Schiller, Lord Byron, François-René de Chateaubriand, and Walter Scott—had only limited direct influence on literary works. The most conventional It. romantic poet, Giovanni Berchet (1783–1851), left a thin collection of songs and ballads, which is a veritable index of the items dear to Eur. romanticism. Berchet's theoretical *Lettera semiseria* (Semiserious Letter) had a lasting impact on the reception of romantic ideology. A more interesting figure is Niccolò Tommaseo (1802–74), the blind lexicographer and Dante scholar and author of lyric poetry of "cosmic nostalgia" and a prophetic tone. The bitterness of a bleak existence inspired the Tuscan Giuseppe Giusti (1809–50), who wrote poetry marked by sarcasm and despair. Alessandro Manzoni (1785–1873) is best known for his great novel *I promessi sposi* (*The Betrothed*); his verses are marginal products, but his five "Hymns" (1812–22), of deep religious inspiration, his commemorative poems, and the choral passages from his plays *Carmagnola* (1820) and *Adelchi* (1822) show the great novelist's precise diction as well as the characteristic undercurrent of *I promessi sposi*: compassion for the humble, the disinherited, and the marginal.

The realistic penchant of the romantic movement in Italy, its bias for the popular and immediate, favored the flowering of *dialect poetry. The traits of dialectal speech included a down-to-earth tone, a direct documenting of life, and a built-in smile owing to the use of dialectal variation as a vehicle of low humor. The two greatest It. dialect poets show a taste for the "slice of life," for a ready plebeian wit, and for the antiliterary spirit congenial to the realistic facet of romanticism. Carlo Porta (1775–1821) derived some of his inspiration from the decidedly nonpoetic contacts through his clerk's window in the Milan tax offices. His masterworks are versified *novelle*: the "disasters" of a semiderelict (the "Giovannin Bongee" stories), the "lamentations" of a poor street fiddler (bow-legged "Marchionn"), and the tale of a streetwalker ("Ninetta del Verzee"). Porta's laughter never becomes a sneer; behind his smile, one often senses the sadness of the wise. The encounter with Porta freed Giuseppe Gioacchino Belli (1791–1863) from his failed attempts at It. verse and opened up the dialect of the Roman plebs as inspiration. A minor cleric, Belli left behind about 2,000 sonnets (pub. in the 1880s) inspired by a violent anticlericalism, irreverent and often obscene. He too is a poet of metropolitan low-class life—vagrants and beggars, monks and spies, flunkeys and whores—with an infusion of prelates.

The greatest poet of mod. Italy, Giacomo Leopardi (1798–1837) was born to an impoverished aristocratic family in Recanati. The poet's professed revulsion for his backward hometown and his disciplined upbringing (esp. the conservatism of his father) have been made much of in critical attempts to trace the roots of his cosmic pessimism. Young Giacomo spent his adolescence in obsessive studies, amassing an astonishing amount of writing: verses, plays, and learned (though all compilative) essays and treatises, almost blinding himself in the process. Though merely the products of a pedantic youth, the early works have been shown to contain the germ of Leopardi's later and most persistent *leitmotif:* the attraction to illusions and delusions, the heroic striving toward an abstract glory marking one's passage on earth (for Leopardi, humankind's only existence). These *motifs are recurrent in the immense notebook collection, the *Zibaldone* (1815–32). The clash of nature and reason, the dominant theme of the Enlightenment, was at first given by young Leopardi a Rousseauian solution (benign nature vs. the ills brought on by human reason), but the contrary prevails in his later work: hostile nature, a "stepmother" for humankind, undermines all human endeavors. The romantic elements influencing Leopardi's system underwent a characteristic transformation: the denial of the poet's social role (and the belief in *pure poetry, anticipating the "decadent" poetics to come), a materialistic worldview, a refusal of almost all nonlyric content, and a bias for the "pathetic" based on "immediacy" of feeling.

The concepts of "infinity" and "remembrance" are the cornerstones of Leopardi's best verse and are strongly present in his poetry until 1821, when the poet "escaped" from Recanati. "Rimembranze" (Recollections) and "Appressamento della morte" (Nearness of Death), written at age 18, experiment with fashionably lugubrious topics; a number of *engagé* compositions and poetic meditations show Leopardi's search for his poetic voice. He discovers it in the idyll "La Vita solitaria" (Life of Solitude) and esp. "La Sera del dì di festa" (Sunday Night). The tension is maintained through the whole (short) poem in the admirable "Alla luna" ("To the Moon"); however, "L'Infinito" ("The Infinite"), a poem of a mere 15 lines written before the poet's flight from his family, is universally recognized as his masterwork—it is, with Dante's "Tanto gentile," the most renowned It. lyric. Its contents are of a lightness and evanescence that elude paraphrase. Its last line with its sign of *cupio dissolvi* (the "sweetness of shipwreck") ties Leopardi to such key texts of mod. poetry as Arthur Rimbaud's "Le Bateau ivre" and Stéphane Mallarmé's "Brise marine."

The years 1822–28, a period of uneasy independence interrupted by desperate returns to Recanati, mark an intermission in Leopardi's poetry. He fitfully produced the *Operette morali* (Little Moral Exercises, 1824), pensive and ironic dialogues on ontological questions, in this pause, a gathering of strength before his second creative period (ca. 1828–30), an economically forced return to Recanati for 16 months of ennui. The cosmic meditation of "Canto notturno" (Nocturne of a Nomadic Shepherd in Asia) is "one of the supreme mod. songs of existential anguish" (Perella, in Bondanella). "A Silvia" (written in Pisa, "perhaps the most poignant elegy in the Italian language"), "Le Ricordanze" (Memories), and "Il Sabato del villaggio" (Saturday in the Village) are the most characteristically Leopardian texts in his collection of *Canti* (1831), with their tone of thoughtful melancholy and disconsolate contemplation of the nullity of all things under the empty heavens. The elegy "La Quiete dopo la tempesta" (The Calm after the Storm) looks for happiness in death.

Leopardi lived to see his *Canti* published in a definitive ed. in 1836. Their themes have a common denominator: the loss of dreams—of youth, of happiness, of heroic existence—a loss restated with calm despair in the cruel light of cold and godless reality. The meter is a kind of early *free verse: discarding the strophic models of the past, Leopardi relied on a loose rhythm, now expanded freely, now suddenly restrained. While the incisive "A se stesso" (To Himself) is a pitiless spiritual self-portrait, the poet facing his bleak universe and murmuring his final renunciation, the late elegies "Amore e morte" (Love and Death) and "Tramonto della luna" (Moon Setting), as well as his last poem, "La ginestra" (The Desert Flower), seem to be not only the conclusion of an experience but a hint at another incipient search for new directions.

The reaction to the excesses of romanticism, such as the lachrymose sentimentalism of the Prati-Aleardi school, took place in Italy under a double flag, *realism and classicism. On the one hand, the call for a return to the sanity of everyday life as the master theme of literary *mimesis was spread by a largely Lombard group of poets known as *Scapigliati* (the unkempt ones)—a movement parallel to the Fr. *Bohème.* The salient figures of the movement, the Boito brothers, Camillo (1836–1914) and Arrigo (1842–1918, also remembered for his librettos); Emilio Praga (1839–75); and Carlo Dossi (1849–1910) professed an ars poetica based on the "slice of life." For the most part, they produced "little proses in verse," unwittingly turning upside down Charles Baudelaire's ambition of *petites poèmes en prose.*

The classicists' reaction, on the other hand, to the romantic mania for *originality had at first a rather ineffectual leader in Giacomo Zanella (1820–88), who revived the minor neoclassical trad. of Monti and Pindemonte, a trend largely exhausted by mid-century. The heritage of classicism in Alfieri and Foscolo, and even in the young "civic" Leopardi, was pressed into the service of antiromanticism by Giosuè Carducci (1835–1907), a poet of vast authority who was the uncontested focal point of It. fin de siècle poetry. Carducci attempted to confer dignity and discipline on a field that, by his maturity, had lost or refused both. Carducci, chair of It. at Bologna, was "the last great *literatus*" Italy had. His professed ideal of a "sane, virile, strong-willed" lit. has lost most of its appeal in mod. times; his reclaiming for the poet the immemorial function of *vates has an archaic flavor. His lyric production in traditional form appeared in the collections *Levia gravia* (Light and Heavy, 1861–71), *Giambi ed epodi* (Iambs and Epodes, 1867–69), and *Rime nuove* (New Verses, 1861–87). Carducci believed in the possibility of transplanting Greco-Lat. metrics into It. versification; while probably overrated as a prosodic experiment, it makes an interesting *curiosum* out of his most discussed volume, *Odi barbare* (Barbaric Odes, 1877–89).

**VIII. Novecento: The 1900s.** Currents as diverse as positivism and *decadence, the *Voce* and the *Ronda* groups, the Twilight poets and the futurists, *hermeti-cism and neorealism not only coexist but in retrospect appear to be interdependent elements of the same whole. Two monumental figures, Gabriele D'Annunzio and Giovanni Pascoli, preface and condition contemp. poetry; neither strictly belongs to a "school," but each recapitulates and anticipates several.

Carducci today appears firmly rooted in the century of Leopardi and Manzoni, while the poetry of Giovanni Pascoli (1855–1912), his successor at Bologna, stretches far into our own. Some of his best-known pieces from *Poemetti* (1897) and *Canti di Castelvecchio* (1903) most surely have been swept away by the tears shed over them (e.g., "Cavallina storna" [The Dappled-Gray Pony], memorized by generations of schoolchildren). But his thin first collection, *Myricae* (1891), remains the cornerstone of mod. It. poetry. The title "Tama-risks" hints at the "lowly shrubs" of the fourth eclogue, but this "last descendant of Virgil" is not merely a poet of simple rustic scenes, as his themes seem to suggest. His quaint syntax and vocabulary, invasive *onomato-poeia, dialect and Lat. words, and exotic and techni-cal terms, e.g., signal the complexity underlying his deceptively simple landscapes. Pascoli's interest never fixes on the positive spectacle of human labor in the fields; his rural tableaux radiate a mysterious feeling, an almost religious stupor. A pattern in Pascoli's construc-tions may be discerned: a rural view is sketched out by broad brush strokes, then filtered and "undefined" through some optical disturbance: haze, mist, fog. A minimal sign of life appears, slowed at once almost to a standstill. The *cadence remains "the beating of his own heart" (Garofalo, in Bondanella)—though with the constant sinking feeling of skipped beats. At last, a tiny acoustic element is added to the landscape— the chirping of a bird, the rustle of leaves, a snatch of faraway singing. That is all, but the whole remains miraculously suspenseful, suggestive not of something "else" but of itself. Even the most allegorical-seeming texts of Pascoli—e.g., his best *poemetti*, "Il vischio" (Mistletoe) and "Digitale purpurea" (Foxglove)— suggest, rather than a meaning, an abstract horror, a visionary experience of evil. The tragedy of Pascoli's life, the unsolved murder of his father in 1867, fixed his poetic age at 12: there is a sense of bewildered won-der in front of an uncomprehended world, the urge to escape, the need for refuge—a need he soon identified with poetry. In the poet's psyche, the unknown assassin assumes the features of humankind, driven on by the eternal enigma of evil. In an 1897 essay, "Il fanciullino" (The Child), Pascoli shaped this very concept into an ars poetica.

If Pascoli's "life in art" had few events, D'Annunzio (1863–1938) construed his life as a work of art. A cross between Friedrich Nietzsche's "superman" and J. K. Huysman's Des Esseintes (*À rebours*, 1884), he was the last vates of It. lit. "More a rhetorician than poet" (Sapegno), a "dilettante di sensazioni" (Croce), D'Annunzio titled his mature collection *Laudi* (1903–4). Composed of three parts, *Maia, Electra*, and *Alcyone*, it is a *laus vitae*, a celebration of life, in which he seems intoxicated by his own exultation. His extraordinary

imitative skill fills his writing with disparate echoes: some from the Fr. and Eng. Parnassians (see PARNAS-SIANISM) and *Pre-Raphaelites, some deliberate imper-sonations of stilnovo and OF masters. This mimetic bent reflects D'Annunzio's principal characteristic, the musicality of his verse. The best of D'Annunzio is often his most extreme: poems in which the thematic pretext is at its baroque flimsiest and the text a polyphony, as in "La pioggia nel pineto" (Rain on the Pine Trees).

In a 1910 article ("Poets on the Wane," in De Ber-nardi) Borgese defined as *crepuscolari* a group of young poets whose cult of quotidian themes and slipshod ex-pression seemed to signal the end of a great lyric trad. The term took root without its negative connotation and denotes a tone shared by most verse published in the decade preceding World War I. Not a formal school, Waning Poetry was as much a derivation from as a reaction to Pascoli's mystic rusticism and D'Annunzio's pompous alexandrinism. *Poesie scritte col lapis* (Poems Written with a Pencil) by Marino Moretti, *Armonie in grigio et in silenzio* (Harmonies in Gray and Silence) by Corrado Govoni, *Piccolo libro inutile* (Use-less Booklet) by Sergio Corazzini—the very titles of these slim volumes announce deliberate colorlessness and monotony, everyday emotions about banal objects. The most versatile member of the group was Corrado Govoni (1884–1965), who later became a futurist. Dying at 20, a consumptive Sergio Corazzini (1886–1907) declined the title of poet for that of a "weep-ing child" who "knows nothing but how to die." Two poets of the first rank are customarily included here: Aldo Palazzeschi (1885–1974) exceeds all labeling and warrants treatment apart; Guido Gozzano (1883–1916) survived tuberculosis long enough to see the success of his *Colloqui* (1911). Gozzano's mild irony blends with his mild yearning.

Historically, "crepuscularism" and *futurism rise from the same impulse, the need to escape D'Annunzio's dominance and Pascoli's classicism. Futurism burst on the scene with the 1909 *manifesto of F. T. Marinetti (1887–1944). Marinetti trumpeted activism at all costs, adventure and aggression, speed and the triumph of the machine, destruction of the past, war as the "hy-giene" of hist., and scorn for women and sentiment. The very scope of its ludicrous claims killed the school; after its disintegration (1915), however, futurism was adopted by National Socialism, Marinetti becom-ing a sort of poet laureate of the regime. Still, Mari-netti's poetics had a vast and, on the whole, salutary influence. His main thesis—simultaneity of impression and expression (hence, fusion of object and image)— influenced Guillaume Apollinaire's *calligrammes, *Dada, *cubism, and Vladimir Mayakovsky. In Italy, futurism's best adherents soon developed in different directions, turning against its ontological claims (Gian Pietro Lucini, Ardengo Soffici [1879–1964]) or deriv-ing from its libertarian impulse a ludic concept of po-etry (Govoni, Palazzeschi).

Gian Pietro Lucini (1867–1914), between his early Parnassian sonnets and his late antifuturist stance, published his theory of free verse in Marinetti's review ("Poesia," 1908) and then his *Revolverate* (Gunshots,

1909). Resistance to time attests to the greatness of Palazzeschi, a much appreciated novelist. The production of his "poetic" decade (1905–15) differs from the humorless declamation of mainline futurists. Its wit and charm are seen in his celebrated phono-mimetic "Fontana malata" (Ailing Fountain). His "L'incendiario" (The Arsonist) records the urge to break with trad.—without the obsessive need for activism or ling. anarchy.

A flourishing literary culture in the years preceding World War I gave rise to a number of periodicals, many of them Florentine. The most influential, *La voce* (1908–13), was directed by Giuseppe Prezzolini (1882–1982), who gathered together a heterogeneous group of collaborators. *La voce* became associated with nearly all the trends in vogue during its run. It offered a first forum to the best-known autochthonous poetic movement in 20th-c. Italy, later called *hermeticism*. The forefather of this novel trobar clus, Dino Campana (1885–1932), came to notice after the "school" had gained notoriety with Giuseppe Ungaretti and Eugenio Montale. Campana is often compared to Rimbaud and Georg Trakl for his aimless wanderings over the world, interrupted only by his stays in mental asylums (he was permanently committed in 1918), and for his poetics of total faith in the magic of the word. The *Canti orfici* (1914) refer to Orpheus: here poetry is a descent into hell and a religion for initiates.

Two other influential poets who matured in the *La voce* context produced poetry in a vein related to Campana's. The existential adventure of Clemente Rébora (1885–1957), not less erratic than Campana's, took place all *within*, as a lifelong struggle with his own soul and a periodically despairing search for superior truth. Rébora's only inspiration is his need to find the all-encompassing word. His aptly titled *Frammenti lirici* (1913) and *Canti anonimi* (1922) record in their daring analogies, in Rébora's characteristic "*imagine tesa*" (taut imagery), a "sort of transcendental autobiography" of powerful originality (Contini). Camillo Sbárbaro (1888–1967) sang the "monotonous recurrence of indifferent life," withdrawing from the bustle into his private drama, in *Resine* (Amberdrops, 1911) and *Pianissimo* (1914).

The review *La ronda* (1919–23) welcomed the voices of reaction to the cult of originality in prewar poetry. Its founder, Vincenzo Cardarelli (1887–1959), advocated a return to the classics (esp. Leopardi and Manzoni), i.e., to syntax, logic, and immediate comprehension. The progress of hermetic poetry, supported by parallel trends abroad among the Fr. and also in T. S. Eliot and Ezra Pound, proved irresistible. Its principal exponents are less typical of its program than its lesser adepts (Salvatore Quasimodo [1901–68], Alphonso Gatto [1909–76], Mario Luzi [1914–2005], Leonard Sinisgalli [1908–81], Vittorio Sereni [1913–83]). All share the quasi-mystical concept of "poetry as life," as a magic formula capable of revealing, under the semblances of this phenomenal world, "universal reality" (Manacorda).

Giuseppe Ungaretti (1888–1970) will be long appreciated for his prosodic innovation, based on the lesson of Rimbaud's *Illuminations* and Mallarmé's *Un coup de dés* (*A Throw of the Dice*). Fragmenting the *vers libre* of his futurist beginnings, Ungaretti eliminated punctuation and transformed poetic diction into a series of fragments lit up by intermittent floodlights. His first book of verse, *Allegria* (1916; repub. in 1923 with a preface by Benito Mussolini) remains the overture to a new phase of It. poetry. The title of his collected poems, *Vita d'un uomo* (A Man's Life), points to his dominant theme, the sublimation of his experiences, though these, esp. in the verse of the 1930s and 1940s, at times remain untranslated into poetry.

Eugenio Montale (1896–1981) may well be perceived as the true heir to Pascoli. His poetry is Pascolian in its resignedly hopeless scrutiny of the "ontological mystery," its vague desire for an escape route from the *male di vivere* (both "pain of life" and "evil of living"), for a "broken seam / in the net that constrains us." Pascolian, too, is Montale's characteristic of transforming emotion into landscape. Pascolian is, in his epoch-making *Ossi di seppia* (*Cuttlefish Bones*, 1925), Montale's metaphysical and baroque mythmaking, soberly desolate as it is. Much has been made of the political texts by antifascist Montale (from *Occasioni*, 1939, to *Satura*, 1971), endlessly deciphered by immense and often too-hermetic exegesis.

Variously related to hermeticism are four poets: Umberto Saba (1883–1957), Cesare Pavese (1908–50), Sandro Penna (1906–77), and Pier Paolo Pasolini (1922–75). Saba was in a sense prehermetic; his *Canzoniere* (*Songbook*) "reads as a 19th-century work" (Debenedetti). His simplicity and trite diction prompted critics to see in him an authentically popular poet. It slowed recognition and led Saba to publish a chronicle (1948) effectually advertising his own songbook. A typical motif is animal life related to human behavior. Pavese offered a model of antihermetic poetry in his realistic and matter-of-fact *poesie-racconto* (story-poems) in *Lavorare stanca* (*Hard Labor*, 1936), but the project failed both in this role and as a matrix of poetry.

"Hermetic" in a special sense ("coding" for this gay poet was a must), Penna's only topic is love, *dolce pena*, "cross and delight," "strange joy" (the last two are titles of collections). This "vigorous outsider" was also an *ermetico* in his refusal of easy legacies, in his ironclad rule of conciseness, and in his stenographic imagery. His best poems, always centered on his beloved *ragazzi*, are prodigies of a balanced moment suspended in timelessness. Everything is burned off in the white heat of the poet's dogged hammering at the "right word." Pasolini, the filmmaker whose 1957 *Le ceneri di Gramsci* (Gramsci's Ashes) is widely acknowledged as one of the most important collections of poetry published in the postwar period, had a different and more tragic purity of voice. Paroxysms of paradox interrupt his song. The popular brand of Marxism he professed never overcame his bourgeois values. Pasolini took idiosyncrasy for ideology: the pangs of libido appear in some of his purposely controversial and perhaps less enduring pieces as the stirrings of hist.

Around the critic Luciano Anceschi (1911–95) and his influential periodical *Il Verri* sprang into being the self-styled Gruppo 63 (so called from its founding meeting at Palermo in 1963). Three poets associated with it are likely to mark the last decades of the 20th c. with their names: Antonio Porta (1935–89), Andrea Zanzotto (1921–2011), and Edoardo Sanguineti (1930–2010). In their verse, the ling. revolution begun by Pascoli comes full circle; his weakening of the tie between signifier and signified reaches the final stage of divorce. The movement has been compared in its sound and fury to futurism; however, the poetry initially born out of and later in some cases opposed to Gruppo 63 is distinguished by a theoretical rigor unknown to Marinetti et al. Porta was first brought to critical notice by the collective volume *I novissimi* (1961). His poems reveal a strongly individual voice and have an eerie capacity to suggest, behind a deliberately gray diction, vast threatening conspiracies by unknown objects and persons. Porta went beyond his *novissimi* origins and alliances. Some critics distinguish his poetry as the first real novelty after hermeticism.

Zanzotto "joined" the group after the fact, as it were. His early collections—*Dietro il paesaggio* (Behind the Landscape, 1951), *Elegia* (1954), *Vocativo* (1957), and *IX Ecloghe* (1962)—are characterized by traditional form (Zanzotto even wrote Petrarchan sonnets, the only 20th-c. poet to do so outside of parody). Zanzotto's arcane Arcadia suggests spectral visitations, séances of literary ghost-evoking. Lang. acts here as a trance-inducing drug. New revolutionary techniques appear with *La beltà* (Beauty, 1968) and subsequent collections of ever-increasing textual complexity.

An original member of the Palermo group, Sanguineti had anticipated in his *Laborintus* (1956) its ideological and technical characteristics. A shocked Pavese refused to consider seriously Sanguineti's early samples, and Zanzotto later called them the "record of a nervous breakdown." Sense in *Laborintus* is replaced by obsessive *paronomasia. Sanguineti's collected poems, *Segnalibro* (Bookmark, 1982), and esp. his *Novissimum Testamentum* (1986), rank him with the best of contemp. Eur. poets.

Among the poets active in the second half of the 20th c., Franco Fortini (1917–94) and Paolo Volponi (1924–94), *engagé* writers of the older generation, deserve more than a summary listing, as well as Luciano Erba (1922–2010), Maria Luisa Spaziani (b. 1924), Giovanni Raboni (1932–2004), Dario Bellezza (1944–96), and Fabio Doplicher (1938–2003). Curiously, while the dialects of the peninsula had seemed doomed by 20th-c. mass education and media diffusion, poetry in dialect shows no sign of decadence. Among its practitioners, heirs to Meli, Porta, and Belli, were the first-rate poets Virgilio Giotti (1885–1957) and Giacomo Noventa (1898–1960). A generation of younger poets is gathered in the anthol. ed. by Giancarlo Pontiggia and Enzo Di Mauro, *La parola innamorata* (The Enamored Word, 1978): Maurizio Cucchi (b. 1945), Giuseppe Conte (b. 1945), Milo De Angelis (b. 1951), Valerio Magrelli (b. 1957), and Cesare Viviani (b. 1947).

*See,* ITALIAN PROSODY, RENAISSANCE POETICS, ROMANTIC AND POSTROMANTIC POETRY AND POETICS.

■ **Criticism; History, Specialized; Primary Texts**: E. Underhill, *Jacopone da Todi, Poet and Mystic* (1919); E. Garin, *Il Rinascimento italiano* (1941); F. Flora, *La poesia ermetica* (1947); C. Calcaterra, *Il Barocco in Arcadia* (1950); A. Momigliano, *Saggio sull' "Orlando Furioso"* (1952); A. Bobbio, *Parini* (1954); A. Galletti, *Il Novecento* (1954); *Marino e marinisti: opere scelte*, ed. G. Getto, 2 v. (1954); *Lirici del Settecento*, ed. B. Maier (1960); *Poeti del Duecento*, ed. G. Contini, 2 v. (1960); A. Viscardi, *Storia della letteratura italiana dalle origini al Rinascimento* (1960); E. H. Wilkins, *The Life of Petrarch* (1961); *Leopardi's Canti*, trans. J. H. Whitfield (1962); G. Santangelo, *Il secentismo* (1962); M. Bishop, *Petrarch and His World* (1963); J. V. Mirollo, *The Poet of the Marvelous: Giambattista Marino* (1963); G. Petronio, *Il Romanticismo* (1963); A. Del Monte, *Le origini* (1964); B. Maier, *Il Neoclassicismo* (1964); G. Singh, *Leopardi and the Theory of Poetry* (1964); J. H. Whitfield, *Giacomo Leopardi* (1964); T. G. Bergin, *Dante* (1965); C. P. Brand, *Torquato Tasso . . . and His Contribution to English Literature* (1965); *Complete Poems and Selected Letters of Michelangelo*, trans. C. Gilbert (1965); G. Pozzi, *La poesia italiana del Novecento* (1965); *Dante's Lyric Poetry*, ed. K. Foster and P. Boyde (1967); M. Fubini, *Ritratto dell'Alfieri* (1967); G. Getto, *L'interpretazione del Tasso* (1967); G. Contini, *Letteratura dell'Italia unita, 1861–1968* (1968); G. Manacorda, *Storia della letteratura italiana contemporanea* (1968); P. Nardi, *La Scapigliatura* (1968); W. Binni, *Saggi alfieriani* (1969); P. Dronke, *The Medieval Lyric* (1969); T. G. Bergin, *Petrarch* (1970); *Tasso's "Jerusalem Delivered,"* trans. J. Tusiani (1970); *Enciclopedia dantesca*, ed. U. Bosco, 5 v. (1970–78); A. Vallone, *Dante* (1971); L. Anceschi, *Le poetiche del Novecento in Italia* (1973); M. Marti, *Storia dello stil nuovo* (1973); C. P. Brand, *Ludovico Ariosto: A Preface to the "Orlando Furioso"* (1974); G. Debenedetti, *Poesia italiana del Novecento* (1974); R. Griffin, *Ludovico Ariosto* (1974); *Francis Petrarch Six Centuries Later: A Symposium*, ed. A. Scaglione (1975); M. Fubini, "Arcadia e Illuminismo," *Dal Muratori al Baretti* (1975); A. Seroni, *Il decadentismo* (1975); *Ariosto's "Orlando Furioso,"* trans. B. Reynolds (1975–77); *Petrarch's Lyric Poems*, trans. R. M. Durling (1976); U. Bosco, *Petrarca* (1977); G. Getto, *Carducci e Pascoli* (1977); M. Fubini, *Ugo Foscolo* (1978); *Il Novecento*, ed. G. Grana, 10 v. (1980); *The New Italian Poetry: 1945 to the Present*, ed. and trans. L. R. Smith (1981)—bilingual anthol.; T. Barolini, *Dante's Poets* (1984); K. Foster, *Petrarch* (1984); U. Foscolo, *Poesie e carmi*, ed. F. Pagliai et al. (1985); C. Kleinhenz, *The Early Italian Sonnet* (1986); A. R. Ascoli, *Ariosto's Bitter Harmony* (1987); P. Hainsworth, *Petrarch the Poet* (1988); *New Italian Poets*, ed. D. Gioia and M. Palma (1991); *Shearsmen of Sorts: Italian Poetry 1975–1993*, ed. L. Ballerini (1992); S. Sturm-Maddox, *Petrarch's Laurels* (1992); Dante, *Vita Nuova, Rime*, ed. D. De Robertis and G. Contini (1995); Petrarch, *The Canzoniere*, trans. M. Musa (1996); *Come leggere la poesia italiana del Novecento*, ed. S. Carrai and F. Zambon (1997); L. Pulci, *Morgante*, trans. J. Tusiani (1998); *Gruppo 63:*

*l'antologia*, ed. N. Balestrini and A. Giuliani (2002); G. Pascoli, *Poesie*, ed. M. Pazzaglia (2002); M. Arcangeli, *La Scapigliatura poetica Milanese e la poesia italiana fra Otto e Novecento* (2003); *Gruppo 63: critica e teoria*, ed. R. Barilli and A. Guglielmi (2003); *La poesia italiana del Novecento*, ed. M. Bazzocchi and F. Curi (2003); N. Merola, *Poesia italiana moderna: da Parini a D'Annunzio* (2004); *Dopo la lirica: poeti italiani 1960–2000*, ed. E. Testa (2005); A. Manzoni, *Le poesie*, ed. V. Marucci (2005); *La poesia italiana del secondo Novecento*, ed. N. Merola (2006); S. Zatti, *The Quest for Epic: From Ariosto to Tasso*, trans. S. Hill (2006); *Twentieth-Century Italian Poetry*, ed. E. Ó Ceallacháin (2007); G. Leopardi, *Canti*, trans. J. G. Nichols (2008); *An Anthology of Modern Italian Poetry in English Translation*, ed. and trans. N. Condini (2009).

■ **History, General**: A. Momigliano, *Storia della letteratura italiana* (1936); F. Flora, *Storia della letteratura italiana*, 4 v. (1940–41); N. Sapegno, *Compendio di storia della letteratura italiana*, 3 v. (1954); J. H. Whitfield, *A Short History of Italian Literature* (1960); F. De Sanctis, *History of Italian Literature* (1870), trans. J. Redfern (1968); *Storia della letteratura italiana*, ed. E. Cecchi and N. Sapegno, v. 8–9 (1969); *I classici italiani nella storia della critica*, ed. W. Binni, 3 v. (1971–77); *Dizionario critico della letteratura italiana*, ed. V. Branca (1973); Wilkins; *Orientamenti culturali: La Letteratura italiana: I maggiori, I–II; I minori, I–IV; Le correnti, I–II; I contemporanei, I–VI* (1975–); *Letteratura italiana, profilo storico*, ed. I. De Bernardi et al., 3 v. (1980); M. Puppo, *Manuale critico bibliografico per lo studio della letteratura italiana* (1985); B. Croce, *Essays on Literature and Literary Criticism* (1972), ed. and trans. M. E. Moss (1990); *Storia della civiltà letteraria italiana*, ed. G. Bárberi Squarotti, F. Bruni, and U. Dotti (1990–96); *Storia della letteratura italiana*, ed. E. Malato (1995–); *Dictionary of Italian Literature*, ed. P. and J. C. Bondanella, rev. ed. (1996); *Storia generale della letteratura italiana*, ed. N. Borsellino and W. Pedullà (1999); *Medieval Italy: An Encyclopedia*, ed. C. Kleinhenz et al., 2 v. (2004); *Encyclopedia of Italian Literary Studies*, ed. G. Marrone et al., 2 v. (2007); *Seventeenth-Century Italian Poets and Dramatists*, ed. A. N. Mancini and G. P. Pierce (2008).

T. Wlassics; C. Kleinhenz; E. Livorni

**ITHYPHALLIC** (Gr., "erect phallus"). An iambotrochaic *colon of the form – ◡ – ◡ – x, which can be regarded as the remainder of a catalectic iambic *trimeter after the *caesura after the second *anceps. According to the scholia to the ancient metrist Hephaestion, the ithyphallic received its name from its use in the procession of the phallos at the festival of Dionysus (cf. Aristophanes, *Acharnians*). It is often used as a colon or a closing element (*clausula) in the iambic songs in Gr. drama (see DACTYLO-EPITRITE); in Aristophanes' *Wasps* (248–72), it is used with a colon consisting of an iambic *dimeter. It is also used in the *epodes of Archilochus and the epodic forms Horace derived from him. An ithyphallic of the form – x – x – – is often used by Plautus with *cretics ( – ◡ – ), and sometimes it is used as a clausula in a short cretic system (*Pseudolus* 921) or together with iambic quaternarii (*Curculio* 103–04).

■ W. M. Lindsay, *Early Latin Verse* (1922); Maas; C. Questa, *Introduzione alla metrica di Plauto* (1967); Dale; Halporn et al.; Snell; West.

J. W. Halporn

# J

## JAPAN, MODERN POETRY OF

I. Tanka
II. Haiku
III. Free Verse

While many mod. Japanese poets adapted traditional forms such as tanka (see WAKA) and haiku (see HAIKAI) in directions compatible with mod. concerns and interests, others cultivated mod. verse forms influenced by the West. The following traces the devel. of mod. tanka, mod. haiku, and mod. free verse.

**I. Tanka.** Mod. tanka began with an explosion of polemic stimulated by the introduction of new literary forms and ideas that accompanied the opening of Japan to the world in the mid-19th c. A tanka is simply a different name for the *waka*, a term dating back to the beginning of the genre, meaning a short poem written in a fixed pattern of 5-7-5-7-7 syllables, with various conventions relating to subject, vocabulary, and so on. In the closing years of the 19th c., both terms were used simultaneously to refer to the same verse genre, but the word *tanka* was preferred by poets who considered themselves reformers. Old-style tanka known as *kyūha-waka* had been dominated by the Outadokoro (Palace School) poets who were associated with courtier families and with the imperial family itself, which had authorized the establishment of the office of Palace Poetry in 1871. Opposed to the hidebound, moribund mode of expression favored by these poets, such young iconoclastic writers as Ochiai Naobumi (1861–1903), his pupil Yosano Tekkan (1873–1935), and Masaoka Shiki (1867–1902), better known as a haiku reformer but who also took up the banner of tanka renewal, wrote several critical essays arguing for tanka as high lit. open to the new intellectual currents from the West, rather than an exercise in trad. Tekkan's "Bōkoku no On" (Sounds Ruinous to the Country, 1895) and Shiki's "Utayomini atauru Sho" (Letters to a Tanka Poet, 1898) are typical of the attacks launched by reformers in their attempts to revivify tanka composition. A number of the reformers advocated the explicit linking of tanka to *shintaishi* (new-style verse), the new free-verse form imported from the West, esp. Tekkan who called for tanka to be renamed *tanshi* (short poems). In their efforts to dissolve the barriers hitherto existing between traditional modes of poetry like tanka and the new *free verse modeled on Western poetry, several of the reformist poets also composed free verse and prose to stake their claims for tanka as art. The first fruits of this new style of tanka came from poets associated with the *Myōjō* (Morning Star) magazine, above all from the brush of Yosano Akiko (1878–1942), the wife of Tekkan. Akiko's first tanka collection *Midaregami* (Tangled Hair, 1901) shocked the traditional tanka world with its daring, sensual poems openly celebrating female sexuality and its use of diction and imagery never seen before in tanka.

By 1910, literary naturalism had become all the rage in Japan and tanka poets moved variously to embrace a plainer, more naturalistic style of expression. By this time the leadership role in tanka composition had passed from poets associated with *Myōjō* to poets associated with the *Araragi* (Japanese Yew Tree) magazine. The most important poet of the period was Ishikawa Takuboku (1886–1912), who was originally linked to *Myōjō*. Takuboku's first tanka collection, *Ichiaku no Suna* (A Handful of Sand), was published in 1910 and focused in clear, limpid verse on the poet's sensibility: his existential loneliness and spiritual malaise. The following tanka by Takuboku, first pub. in 1909, is typical of his poetry:

| Jinjō no odoke naramu ya | Not just a common buffoon |
| Naifu mochi shinu mane | Knife in |
| o suru | hand, faking suicide |
| Sono kao sono kao | That face that face |

Takuboku popularized the fashion for writing tanka as a three-line verse (earlier it had been written in a single unbroken line), and his intensely personal angst amid the new, mighty metropolis of Tokyo captured legions of readers.

The leading poet of the Araragi coterie was Saitō Mokichi (1882–1953) who emerged as one of the greatest tanka poets of the 20th c. Trained as a psychiatrist, Saitō was originally attracted to modernist modes of writing imported from the West, although he eventually rejected modernist poetics in favor of a more traditional aesthetic (see MODERNISM). The greatest modernist poet of the prewar period was Maekawa Samio (1903–90), who originally came to attention because of his "proletarian" tanka, written in a free meter, that extolled left-wing activism. In 1930, Samio turned his back on his proletarian comrades with the publication of his first volume of tanka, *Shokubutsusai* (Botanical Revels). This collection of 574 tanka was imbued with the modernist poetics of writers like Jean Cocteau. Samio openly embraced Fr. surrealist techniques (see SURREALISM), as the following dislocatory verse from this volume demonstrates:

| Toko no ma ni | In the alcove |
| Matsurarete aru | Placed on a pedestal |
| Waga kubi o | My head. |
| Utsutsu naraneba | Because this is not real |
| Naite miteishi | In tears I stared at it. |

In 1926, the famous tanka poet Shaku Chōkū (better known as Orikuchi Shinobu, 1887–1953) had declared the tanka was well on the way to extinction. Samio's riposte in the form of modernist verse was itself criticized in Matsumura Eiichi's 1934 article titled "Tanka Sanbunka" (Prosifying Tanka), which took Samio as well as other poets like Mokichi to task for using foreign vocabulary in their verse (see XENOGLOSSIA). What actually brought tanka to the brink of extinction was World War II. The mass of xenophobic prowar tanka penned by Samio and Mokichi, and just about everybody else, led to a disastrous drop in artistic standards and provoked revulsion on the part of postwar poets against the tanka genre itself and its long association with Japanese trad. The first substantial attack on tanka appeared in May 1946. The critic Usui Yoshimi (1905–87), in an article titled "Tanka e no Ketsubetsu" (Farewell to Tanka), criticized tanka poets for their unquestioning support of the war and for the awful verse produced as a result. The philosopher Kuwabara Takeo (1904–88) followed up a like-minded attack on haiku with an article in January 1947, titled "Tanka no Unmei" (The Fate of Tanka), that argued the tanka form itself was unable to express the mod. world or the mod. spirit. Other attacks on tanka swiftly followed. This storm of crit. led to a loss of confidence among tanka poets esp. younger poets only beginning to come to notice. Established poets like Kondō Yoshimi (1913–2006) and Miya Shūji (1912–86) led the counterattack and revived tanka by composing verse simultaneously celebrating and criticizing the U.S. occupation, which lasted until the end of 1951. Poets such as these also attempted to document the war in their tanka, realistically and graphically expressing the emotions of the Japanese people.

Tsukamoto Kunio (1922–2005) was the leading avant-garde tanka poet in the immediate postwar period. Such tanka had been suppressed during wartime because of its connections to Western art and lit. Tsukamoto sought to reestablish the literary credentials of tanka in the face of attacks on the genre itself by emphasizing the literary and artistic qualities of the genre. By the 1960s and 1970s, tanka had been restored to legitimacy as a literary art but the genre did not regain the prestige and influence that it had wielded before and during the war. Poets like Terayama Shūji (1935–83), who was also active as a free-verse poet and dramatist, wrote innovative and fresh tanka that in its use of free meter and subject seemed appropriate to the new age. Women tanka poets also occupied a larger part of the poetry scene than before. Baba Akiko (b. 1928) became a powerful presence from this period onward not only for the cl. elegance of her verse that hearkened back to the waka trad. but for her tanka crit. and scholarship. Tawara Machi (b. 1962) created a sensation with her debut volume *Sarada Kinenbi* (Salad Anniversary, 1987), which sold over a million copies and became the most successful tanka collection of the mod. era. Composed in simple colloquial diction, this collection told of the love affair of the young woman narrator, breaking completely with the more ornate style of older tanka still favored occasionally by mod. poets. A flood of similar collections followed, most of which imitated Machi's style. The 100-year debate over whether to compose tanka in colloquial rather than cl.

lang. seemed by the 21st c. to have been won in favor of the former, with the success of Machi and her followers. But many amateur tanka poets prefer to cleave to older models of tanka; and as cl. waka are still widely read and also taught in schools, there seems little possibility that the cl. style will disappear altogether. In that respect, tanka still retains a sense of continuity with cl. waka poetry, linking the poetry of the present with the literary legacy of a past over a millennium in length.

**II. Haiku.** By the mid-19th c., haiku was trapped in a cultural discourse that saw the genre as something more than lit.; indeed, some schools of traditional haiku argued that haiku was not lit. at all but a unique expression of the Japanese spirit, something akin to religion. Such schools saw great haiku masters like Matsuo Bashō (1644–94) as spiritual gurus rather than excellent poets. On the other hand, haiku was composed by a host of ordinary people as a pastime or hobby expressing their personal feelings or simply documenting the events in their lives. This led to a crisis of legitimacy about whether haiku could actually be described as a serious literary art, a crisis that was exacerbated by the introduction of Western poetry and ideas that accompanied the opening of Japan to the world in the mid-19th c. (in some respects, the debate is still ongoing). By and large, serious haiku poets themselves did not share in this pessimism about the nature of the genre (arising primarily out of its extreme brevity, only 17 syllables in total), but a number of haiku poets felt the need to address the issue.

Masaoka Shiki, the most important haiku poet and reformer of the late 19th c., took up this issue in a series of essays pub. between 1889 and 1895 and argued not only that the haiku of his time was banal, nothing but *doggerel, but that Matsuo Bashō, the saint of haiku himself, wrote mostly rubbish. Shiki took the view that, for haiku to be considered as lit., it needed to be evaluated by literary criteria, not by extraliterary considerations that had elevated Bashō to sainthood and that maintained the moribund schools of traditional haiku of the day.

In the first few decades of the 20th c., Shiki's legacy was split into two schools or factions: one led by Kawahigashi Hekigotō (1873–1937), who advocated haiku written in a mod. free meter format, and the other led by Takahama Kyoshi (1874–1959), who defended the traditional diction of haiku with its fixed syllabic 5-7-5 pattern, season words, and fixed topical themes. Both poets claimed the mantle of Shiki's successor, and for most of the 20th c., the two schools continued to flourish independently. Hekigotō preferred to call his poems *tanshi* (short free verse), following some early tanka poets, rather than haiku. Among Kyoshi's followers, the names of Murakami Kijō (1865–1938) and Iida Dakotsu (1885–1962) are prominent. Both poets composed haiku along traditional, conservative lines, with a strong focus on nature and natural phenomena, incl. animals and insects. Hekigotō's free-verse school included radical poets like Ogiwara Seisensui (1884–1976), who did away with season words, for instance, and also Nakatsuka Ippekirō (1887–1946), whose poetry took haiku to a new depth of experimentation where the verse becomes almost abstract. The traditional school was centered on the magazine *Hototogisu* (Cuckoo) founded by Kyoshi. Kyoshi's preferred aesthetic was *shasei* (sketching from life) advocated by his master Shiki, but Kyoshi interpreted this in a more conservative manner, stressing how haiku should evoke past literary assocs. Although the Cuckoo school dominated prewar haiku circles, by the 1930s a number of poets had turned against its traditional aesthetic in favor of a more modernist style closer to the free-verse school. Mizuhara Shūōshi (1892–1981) and Yamaguchi Seishi (1901–94) led the charge. These two poets stressed musical rhythm and unconventional subjects, respectively. In the late 1920s and 1930s, a school of proletarian haiku emerged, based in Kyoto University, which stressed working-class topics. The poets in the Kyoto school achieved fame by being arrested in 1940 as "spies," presumably because of their left-wing sympathies.

During World War II, in common with tanka poets, haiku poets produced a prodigious quantity of prowar, xenophobic verse mostly devoid of literary merit, and this led to fierce attacks on the genre after the war's end. The Kyoto University philosopher Kuwabara Takeo's famous essay "Dainigeijutsuron—Gendai Haiku ni tsuite" (A Second-Class Art—On Contemporary Haiku), pub. in November 1946, argued that haiku was a mere craft, not lit. Kuwabara used the technique developed by the Brit. lit. critic I. A. Richards to ask a group of intellectuals to evaluate 15 haiku by various famous haiku poets and a few completely unknown amateurs. The result was that practically none of the intellectuals could tell the difference between the haiku "masterpieces" and the unknown works. Kuwabara's attack plunged the contemp. haiku world into despair and undermined many of the tenets of traditional haiku. Consequently, conventions relating to fixed topics, meter, and so forth were largely abandoned by postwar poets, who composed difficult, abstract verse close to the kind of free verse (*shi*) composed by various mod. poets. Two prominent postwar poets whose poetry can stand for this trend (at times their verse can be very demanding) and who were esp. celebrated for their literary skills are Nakamura Kusatao (1901–83) and Kaneko Tōta (b. 1919).

Contemp. haiku is notable for the large number of women poets now composing verse. Fujiki Kiyoko is an example of a poet who has become increasingly recognized as an important writer. Fujiki's first book of haiku appeared in 1934, and her wartime verse and erotic poetry have become esp. acclaimed. Her poetic trajectory parallels the practice of many contemp. female tanka poets who also write explicitly erotic verse. Kadokawa Haruki (b. 1942) is another important contemp. haiku poet. The heir to the Kadokawa publishing empire, he has also achieved success as a businessman, film director, and producer. Kadokawa has won many awards for his haiku, which treat a variety of themes in powerful, terse lang., incl. his 2004 collection about life in prison (he was jailed for possessing cocaine).

The association between haiku and autobiographical themes seems inescapable given the brevity of the form and the long association of the genre with the life journeys of many famous poets. For this reason, haiku still retains a strong attraction for millions of amateurs who use haiku to record and explore their inner lives in workmanlike lang. with no particular ambition to imitate the austere beauty achieved by haiku masters.

**III. Free Verse.** Japanese free-verse poetry (shi) originally began from trans. of a group of mostly Eng. poems, which were collected into a single volume (also containing some original poetry), entitled *Shintaishi Shō* (A Collection of Poetry in the New Style, 1882). Three scholars translated these poems into Japanese, none of whom had any reputation as poets. The trans. poetry came from a variety of authors and included extracts from various of Shakespeare's plays and poetry by H. W. Longfellow; Charles Kingsley; Alfred, Lord Tennyson; and Thomas Gray. Many of the poems were translated into a 7-5 syllabic sequence based on the traditional meter of waka. Other influences helped shape the devel. of Japanese "new-style" verse: trans. of hymns, poetry composed in Chinese by Japanese poets (called *kanshi* in Japanese—the word for free verse, *shi*, arises from this; see CHINESE POETRY IN JAPAN), trans. of Brit. military ballads, and songs for children written in simple colloquial Japanese. The chief difference between "new-style" verse and traditional genres of poetry like tanka and haiku was the length and structure of the poems: new-style verse could continue for many stanzas, unlike the exceedingly brief verse of trad. poetry, and did not necessarily follow the metrical structure of traditional genres of poetry. Shimazaki Tōson (1872–1943) was the first major poet to compose verse using the new style. He wrote four volumes of poetry between 1897 and 1904 (when his collected poetry appeared) before he abandoned poetry for fiction and subsequently achieved fame as a novelist. Tōson's musical, romantic verse used the diction of cl. Japanese to achieve a fresh yet elegant tone. He borrowed themes and imagery from cl. lit. as well as phrases from trans. of Western verse and hymns. His success spawned numerous imitators who followed their master in blending elements from cl. waka with themes taken from trans. of Western verse to produce new-style poetry that was pleasing to the ear but still managed to suggest something of the novelty of Western verse. A number of leading new-style poets like Yosano Akiko, Ishikawa Takuboku and Kitahara Hakushū (1885–1942) also wrote tanka, confirming that new-style verse was an intermediate or hybrid form bridging the gap between cl. poetry and free verse.

The first collection to be written entirely in free verse, defined here as poetry composed not in the 7-5 meter and using colloquial rather than cl. grammar, was Kawai Suimei's (1874–1965) volume *Kiri* (Mist), which was published in May 1910. However, another poet called Kawaji Ryūkō (1888–1959), who belonged to Kawai's circle, also wrote a celebrated volume of free verse, titled *Robō no Hana* (Wayside Flowers) that came out a mere three months later and is often cited as the first volume of free verse to appear in Japan. Kawai's poems are mostly *prose poems, and Kawaji's collection contains poetry first published in 1907, so this may explain the reason for Kawaji's prominence. Various manifestos arguing for free verse rather than new-style verse or traditional genres of poetry had already appeared, the earliest being Toyama Masakazu's (1848–1900) 1895 essay advocating a movement to write poetry using contemp. Japanese. Also, in 1892, the famous novelist Natsume Sōseki (1867–1916) issued a call for poetry to follow the example of Walt Whitman's free verse. The movement toward free verse had several consequences. A number of outstanding collections of free verse soon resulted, incl. Takamura Kōtarō's (1883–1956) *Dōtei* (The Journey, 1914); Hagiwara Sakutarō's (1886–1942) *Tsuki ni Hoeru* (Howling at the Moon, 1917); and Miyazawa Kenji's (1896–1933) *Haru to Shura* (Spring and Ashura, 1924). Many poets were reluctant to abandon the elegant beauty of cl. diction and continued to compose verse in a mixture of cl. and colloquial syntax or composed verse in both modes. E.g., Hagiwara's last collection *Hyōtō* (The Iceland, 1934) was written entirely in cl. Japanese, unlike the bulk of his earlier collections. Inspired by trans. of Paul Verlaine, Charles Baudelaire, and like-minded Fr. and Ger. symbolist poets, poets belonging to the Japanese symbolist school were esp. noteworthy for their mixture of cl. and colloquial. The two most prominent such poets were Susukida Kyūkin (1877–1945) and Kambara Ariake (1875–1952). Later poets inherited their mantle, most notably Murō Saisei (1889–1962) and Miyoshi Tatsuji (1900–64). Japanese modernist poetry also embraced free verse enthusiastically—avant-garde poets like the Dadaist Takahashi Shinkichi (1901–87; see DADA) and the surrealist poet Nishiwaki Junzaburō (1894–1982; see SURREALISM) produced powerful dislocatory collections. Takahashi's self-proclaimed Dadaist collection published in 1923 and Nishiwaki's 1933 collection *Ambarvalia*, which explored the landscape of Tokyo devastated by the 1922 earthquake using techniques developed during his stay in Europe, are both landmark works of poetry.

The advent of World War II inspired a vast outpouring of patriotic and xenophobic verse. After the war, many poets sought to conceal their wartime verse (generally marked by its lack of literary merit) by deleting such poetry from their later collections. In the 1950s and 1960s, the poet and critic Yoshimoto Takaaki (1924–2012) led the charge to expose the wartime writings of these poets as part of the resurgence of the Left (Yoshimoto was widely acknowledged as the leader of the Japanese New Left) in intellectual circles. Yoshimoto did have some sympathy for those poets who underwent a mea culpa and renounced their wartime writings, esp. the poet Takamura Kōtarō, whose verse he championed. The school of poets obsessed with the war and its aftermath has become known as the "postwar" school, although originally they were called the Arechi (Wasteland) group, after the name of the journal in which their poetry was published. These poets and their successors wrote only free verse, thus assuring the victory of this form over hybrid varieties of poetry incorporating cl. diction. Prominent among this group

were Tamura Ryūichi (1923–98), Ayukawa Nobuo (1920–86), Kuroda Saburō (1918–80), and, later, Yoshimoto Takaaki. Their premise was that postwar Japan was a wasteland, virtually a colony of the U.S., so in order to write poetry it was necessary to take up issues such as the war and the suffering it entailed, as well as the legacy of the U.S. occupation. Women poets like Ibaragi Noriko (1926–2006) and Ishigaki Rin (1920–2004) who achieved prominence from the 1950s onward wrote verse with similar concerns but with a stronger focus on the role of women in daily life and society at large.

Opposing the "ideology" of this school, which dominated postwar poetry for a decade or more, was an eclectic group of poets united in very little save their concern with poetic lang. and its limits. Inheriting Nishiwaki's surrealist bent, Yoshioka Minoru (1919–90) dominated poetry circles in the 1950s and 1960s; his powerful style used the ambiguity and indeterminacy of lang. in a masterful way and captured the allegiance of many contemp. poets. His 1958 collection *Sōryo* (Monks) successfully imported the older, prewar modernist trad. into the postwar era. Other poets who were obsessed with lang.—so much so that later critics have called them the "language school"—include Suzuki Shiroyasu (b. 1935) and his successor Nejime Shōichi (b. 1948) who used poetry to transgress the accepted boundaries of decorum concerning sexuality and violence. Like Nejime, Tomioka Taeko (b. 1935) has gone on to a successful career as a novelist, but her poetry of the 1960s established a powerful precedent for women poets to follow, with her long, trademark *monogatari* (tale) poems—seemingly endless dialogues defamiliarizing gender, among much else. One of her successors, Isaka Yōko (b. 1949) has extended this technique to everyday life and achieved a solid reputation from the 1970s onward. Irisawa Yasuo (b. 1931) also explored the long "tale" poem, concentrating on Japanese trad. in his celebrated 1968 collection *Waga Izumo Waga Chinkon* (My Izumo, My Requiem), which could also be read as a parodic homage to T. S. Eliot's *The Waste Land*. Yoshimasu Gōzō (b. 1939) also works in this vein, reading his saga-style poetry aloud to receptive audiences who come to hear his famous oral performances. Shiraishi Kazuko (b. 1931) writes long poetry that seems as much utterances of a seer as anything else and has also been acclaimed by her peers for her achievements.

Tanikawa Shuntarō (b. 1931) has often been mentioned as a possible candidate for the Nobel Prize in Literature, a tribute to his extraordinary gifts as a poet. From his first collection *Nijū Oku Kōnen no Kodoku* (20 Billion Light Years of Loneliness, 1952) to his famous 1968 collection *Tabi* (Journeys) and his award-winning 1993 collection *Seken Shirazu* (The Naïf), his journey as a poet has traversed the entire half-century since the war. A master of verse form, Tanikawa has often experimented with rhymes and other complex metrical devices, exploring the beauty and pathos of everyday life in lang. as fresh as it is readable.

Poets since the 1970s have generally acknowledged Tanikawa's preeminence as a poet but often dispute his emphasis on audience-oriented *performance poetry, instead emphasizing poetry as conceptual art, a kind of abstract art marked by difficulty and indeterminancy. "Language" poets of the 1970s and 1980s like Arakawa Yōji (b. 1949) and Iijima Kōichi (b. 1930) have been succeeded by like-minded poets of a younger generation, most notably Inagawa Masato (b. 1949) and Hiraide Takashi (b. 1950). Itō Hiromi (b. 1955), now resident in the U.S. and active also as a novelist, was the quintessential feminist poet of the 1980s and 1990s, with volumes like *Teritorii Ron II* (On Territory 2, 1985) establishing her mastery of disruptive, *collage-style verse questioning gender and the self itself. Since the dawning of the 21st c., Japanese poets have moved more in the direction of *performance than abstract art, but the challenge of poetry competing in the crowded space of print publication, whether printed paper or cybertext, continually stimulates poets to go beyond recognized boundaries of lang. and convention to stake a claim for poetry as significant art.

■ M. Ueda, *Modern Japanese Haiku* (1976); J. Beichmann, *Masaoka Shiki* (1982); A. Heinrich, *Fragments of Rainbows* (1983); D. Keene, *Dawn to the West: Japanese Literature in the Modern Era,* v. 2 (1984); M. Saitō, *Red Lights,* trans. S. Shinoda and S. Goldstein (1989); *An Anthology of Contemporary Japanese Poetry,* ed. and trans. L. Morton (1993); *Modern Japanese Tanka,* trans. Makoto Ueda (1996); S. Shimaoka, *Shi to wa Nanika* (What Is Poetry?, 1998); J. Beichman, *Embracing the Firebird* (2002)—on Yosano Akiko; H. Kawana, *Modan Toshi to Gendai Haiku* (The Modern City and Contemporary Haiku, 2002); L. Morton, *Modern Japanese Culture* (2003); L. Morton, *Modernism in Practice: An Introduction to Postwar Japanese Poetry* (2004); *Columbia Anthology of Modern Japanese Literature,* ed. J. Rimer and V. Gessel, 2 vols. (2005–7); T. Saigusa, *Shōwa Tanka no Seishinshi* (A Spiritual History of Shōwa Tanka, 2005); N. Ōta, *Nihon Kindai Tankashi no Kōchiku* (The Construction of Modern Tanka History in Japanese, 2006).

L. MORTON

**JAPAN, POETRY OF.** Japanese poetry has a recorded hist. of approximately 1,500 years, and the art has occupied a central position in the nation's cultural life. While the term *Japanese poetry* generally applies to verses in the vernacular, i.e., poetry *in* Japanese, it also refers in its most inclusive sense to poetry *by* Japanese, incl. that written in Chinese, which until mod. times was the lingua franca of East Asian literati. Vernacular poetry is called *waka (or *yamato uta,* Japanese poem or Japanese song) or simply *uta* (poem or song); poetry in Chinese by Japanese poets is called *kanshi* (see CHINESE POETRY IN JAPAN), though that term is also used in Japan for Chinese poetry composed by Chinese. Many Japanese poets composed in both langs. When considered in the context of the geographical boundaries of the Japanese archipelago, the term *poetry of Japan* also includes other poetic trads., incl. those of the Ryūkyū Islands and the Ainu, which are beyond the scope of the discussion below.

The evolution of premod. Japanese vernacular poetry is characterized by shifting ratios of oral versus written expression, native inspiration versus foreign assimilation, public versus personal subject matter, "high" versus "low" topics, court versus plebeian poetic practice, ritual or political versus belletristic purpose, and conventionality versus originality. And yet it maintains certain consistencies throughout, the predominant one being the lyric *voice—the ostensibly personal expression of emotion. The premod. Japanese poet generally reserved more discursive or philosophical matters for poetry in Chinese (which, to be sure, also employed the lyric approach). The emotions expressed in vernacular poetry, furthermore, were inspired most importantly by the four seasons and by love, the latter often conveyed through metaphors drawn from nature. Other important topics were lamentation, travel, and congratulation. Though early song included various other topics, such as warfare, those considered appropriate for orthodox vernacular poetry generally came to be fixed early in the written hist. of the medium, as did acceptable treatments, images, and vocabulary. Although Japanese poetic practice could encompass original inspiration, it also placed great store on the conventional, esp. in public, multipoet settings where it might be more desirable to fit in than to stand out. After standardized poetic forms and meter coalesced from irregular preliterate songs, they too remained constant, nearly always being based on alternating segments of five and seven morae (see MORA). *Hypermetric or *hypometric segments sometimes occurred. Both short and long segments have an underlying four-beat rhythm, with the last beat of a short segment being a rest. Early Japanese poetry, most of which dates from the 7th and 8th cs. CE, includes the *chōka* (long poem) of an unfixed number (usually a few dozen) of alternating five- and seven-morae segments and two final segments of seven morae; the *sedōka* (head repeating poem) of 5-7-7-5-7-7 morae segments; the *katauta* (half poem) of 5-7-7 morae segments; the *bussokusekika* (Buddha's footstone poem) of 5-7-5-7-7-7 morae segments; and most notably the *tanka* (short poem) of 5-7-5-7-7 morae segments. The last of these became so popular in the ensuing Heian period (794–1185) that the term *waka* grew to be generally synonymous with it, and that is how it will be used below. The chōka came to be employed only infrequently, and the sedōka, katauta, and bussokusekika disappeared entirely. The 31-morae waka retained its creative vitality through the med. era (1185–1600), though as that era progressed, many of the finest poetic minds increasingly turned to linked verse (*renga), in which a group of poets alternately linked 17- and 14-morae poems into hundred-verse chains. But even linked-verse poets also composed waka. After the turn of the 17th c., orthodox waka was eclipsed in popularity by other poetic forms such as comic waka (*kyōka), *haikai linked verse (*haikai [no] renga or renku), and haiku (see below), though it continued to be widely composed.

The visual layout of a Japanese poem on the page is

variable and not necessarily reflective of the 5-7 morae structure. It may be written in one or several lines or artfully arranged on a page decorated with colored underpainting. But no matter how it is recorded on paper, the oral qualities of vernacular Japanese poetry remain vital. These include *alliteration and *assonance, but generally not end rhyme, since the fact that nearly all morae in Japanese end with one of a small number of vowels makes rhyme altogether too facile.

Waka poetry also figured prominently in other literary genres, e.g., poem tales (*utamonogatari*, short narratives that hinge on a poem or poems), diaries and travel lit. (see JAPANESE POETIC DIARIES), prose fiction (*monogatari*, such as *Genji monogatari* [*The Tale of Genji*], ca. 1008 CE, which contains hundreds of waka poems), and drama (such as *nō* plays). While poetic composition in Chinese was generally the domain of certain highly literate courtiers and clerics, mostly male, the ability to compose waka was for centuries a necessary polite accomplishment of all court men and women, being central to their education, social interaction, and self-definition. Therefore, unlike other Japanese literary arts such as the nō drama or monogatari recitation, Japanese court poetry was practitioner-oriented, its makers constituting its audience. This resulted in a very sophisticated level of reception and crit., and there remains an enormous body of theoretical and commentarial work (*karon*, literally, "treatise on Japanese poetry"; see JAPANESE POETICS). As the med. period progressed, Japanese poetry became an object of study and enjoyment among warriors and commoners, who likewise began to contribute to the corpus of anthols. and commentaries.

The hist. of Japanese poetry began before the advent of a Japanese writing system, with anonymous bards composing orally on concerns commonly held by the communities they served. These early vernacular songs were simple and declarative, and some of their basic topics, such as love, death, and travel, remained central to the vernacular poetic trad. thereafter, as did the tendency to express those topics against a backdrop of nature. They also dealt frequently with relations between gods and the human world, the border between poetry and religious ritual being porous. With the gradual acquisition of the Chinese writing system, the Japanese began to read Chinese poetry and prose, and the continental example thereafter provided an ever-growing resource through which—and against which—Japanese poetry developed. The 8th c. saw the compilation of the oldest extant anthols. of poetry by Japanese in Chinese (*Kaifūsō* [Florilegium of Cherished Airs], 751 CE) and in the vernacular (*Man'yōshū*, Anthology of Ten Thousand Leaves; last dated poem, 759), both of which include verses of earlier origin. The approximately 4,500 poems in *Man'yōshū* bear witness to the transition during the 7th and 8th c. from early oral vernacular song to a rich and complex written vernacular poetic trad., in which anonymous and communal expression gave way to highly wrought works by named individuals who possessed a sense of historical poetic devel. Increasing

courtly sinophilia produced three anthols. of kanshi in the early 9th c., but thereafter the vernacular voice resurfaced publicly in the first imperially sponsored collection of Japanese verse, *Kokin wakashū* (Anthology of Ancient and Recent Japanese Poetry [abbreviated *Kokinshū*], 905), which established the basic orthodox lexicon, topics, and treatments for the subsequent 20 imperially commissioned anthols. (the last being *Shinshoku kokin wakashū* [New Continued Anthology of Ancient and Recent Japanese Poetry, 1439]), as well as the vast number of anthols. that poets privately compiled. The preface to *Kokinshū* is important for its expression of the character and desiderata of the native poetic idiom, notably the idea (itself borrowed from China) that poetry is essentially lyrical, that it "takes the human heart as seed, which burgeons forth in myriad words as leaves." This affective-expressive nexus characterizes the essence of the Japanese poetic medium. But even as it exploited certain approaches from Chinese verse of the Six Dynasties (222–589 CE), *Kokinshū* poetry rigorously excluded Sino-Japanese vocabulary and natural imagery not found in the archipelago. Orthodox waka retained this unadulterated native lexicon throughout the premod. era.

In the late Heian and med. periods, Japanese poetry became increasingly intertextual, expanding the boundaries of the 31-morae form through quotations from earlier waka. The eighth imperial poetic anthology, *Shinkokin wakashū* (or *Shinkokinshū*, New Anthology of Ancient and Recent Japanese Poetry, 1217), is emblematic of this shift. At this time as well, hereditary poetic houses developed, as did secret trads. that were handed down within those houses to buttress their authority. The tone of waka poetry became more melancholic and the Buddhist sense of evanescence more pronounced. This med. aesthetic of bittersweet beauty in perishability is also seen in the nō drama and tea culture, as well as in formal linked verse. Vast numbers of kanshi also continued to be composed, however, notably within the Zen establishment, and later among literati of the early mod. (Tokugawa or Edo) period (1600–1868).

But orthodox Japanese poetic composition was always paralleled by unconventional haikai forms that flouted the topical, thematic, and lexical strictures of formal work. During the social upheaval of the late med. period, such poetry came increasingly to be seen as its own legitimate poetic way, wherein Sino-Japanese vocabulary and aspects of daily life or bawdy humor could be celebrated, just as *kyōgen* comic plays came to coexist with the classic nō theater. Though the term *haikai* was also used in reference to unconventional waka, it was more frequently employed in the context of linked verse, and eventually the first verse of such sequences, the *hokku*, came to stand alone and later be termed *haiku*. Matsuo Bashō (1644–94), who became Japan's most famous premod. poet, participated in numerous haikai linked-verse sessions, and some *hokku* originally composed to initiate 36-verse sequences were later used alone in other contexts. But even as the short 17-morae form was coming into its own, the poet and fiction writer Ihara Saikaku (1642–93) was working in the other direction, single-handedly creating sequences of linked haikai that reached many hundreds of verses in length. Bashō also introduced poetic meter and techniques from haikai into his prose writing, creating a genre known as *haibun.

With the collapse of the Tokugawa shogunate and the restoration of ostensibly direct imperial rule under Emperor Meiji in 1868, the predominant foreign literary influences no longer entered from China but from Europe and the United States, and Japanese poets began experimenting with new forms (shintaishi) and new approaches such as *surrealism (see JAPAN, MODERN POETRY OF). While orthodox waka and composition in Chinese gradually declined in popularity, haiku remains widely practiced. Contemp. Japanese poets have also experimented with modernizing the waka through the use of new vocabulary and topics. Japanese poetry, which during the premod. period was almost entirely contained within the boundaries of the archipelago, has also begun to exert an influence outward, evidenced notably by the composition of haiku and linked verse in other langs.

■ **Criticism and History**: R. H. Brower and E. Miner, *Japanese Court Poetry* (1961); E. Miner, *An Introduction to Japanese Court Poetry* (1968); J. T. Rimer and R. E. Morrell, *Guide to Japanese Poetry* (1975); D. Keene, *World within Walls: Japanese Literature of the Pre-Modern Era, 1600–1867* (1976); J. Konishi, *A History of Japanese Literature*, v. 1, trans. A. Gatten and N. Teele (1984), *A History of Japanese Literature*, v. 2, trans. A. Gatten (1986), *A History of Japanese Literature*, v. 3, trans. A. Gatten and M. Harbison (1991); H. C. McCullough, *Brocade by Night: "Kokin Wakashu" and the Court Style in Japanese Classical Poetry* (1985); Miner et al; M. Morris, "Waka in Form, Waka in History," *HJAS* 46.2 (1986); D. Keene, *Seeds in the Heart: Japanese Literature from Earliest Times to the Late Sixteenth Century* (1993); D. Keene, *Dawn to the West: Japanese Literature of the Modern Era* (1999); *Medieval Japanese Writers*, ed. S. D. Carter, v. 203 of *Dictionary of Literary Biography* (1999); K. Kawamoto, *The Poetics of Japanese Verse*, trans. S. Collington, K. Collins, and G. Heldt (2000).

■ **Translations**: *Japanese Literature in Chinese*, trans. B. Watson, 2 v. (1975–76); *Songs of Gods, Songs of Humans: The Epic Tradition of the Ainu*, trans. D. L. Philippi (1979); *From the Country of Eight Islands: An Anthology of Japanese Poetry*, trans. H. Sato and B. Watson (1981); *Waiting for the Wind: Thirty-Six Poets of Japan's Late Medieval Age*, trans. S. D. Carter (1989); C. Drake, "A Separate Perspective: Shamanic Songs of the Ryukyu Kingdom," *HJAS* 50:1 (1990); *Classical Japanese Prose*, trans. H. C. McCullough (1990); *Classical Japanese Poetry*, trans. S. D. Carter (1991); *A Waka Anthology, Volume One*, trans. E. A. Cranston (1993); *Early Modern Japanese Literature: An Anthology, 1600–1900*, ed.

H. Shirane (2002); *Dance of the Butterflies: Chinese Poetry from the Japanese Court Tradition*, trans. J. N. Rabinovitch and T. R. Bradstock (2005); *A Waka Anthology, Volume Two*, trans. E. A. Cranston (2006); *Traditional Japanese Literature*, ed. H. Shirane (2007).

H. M. HORTON

**JAPANESE LINKED VERSE.** *See* RENGA.

**JAPANESE POETIC DIARIES.** The Eng. term *Japanese poetic diaries* translates no single term used with consistency across the hist. of "diaries" (niki, nikki; ki, kikō) in Japanese trad. The practice of keeping more or less dated or dateable records, in either cl. Japanese or Chinese, that include poetry texts of one or more genres was practiced among imperial court officials and the aristocratic elite of the Heian period (794–1185). It continued to flourish and evolve as a mode of cultural production that marries writing in prose with the collection and contextualization of poetry in many different forms serving various purposes throughout Japan's premod. hist. While the practice has never completely died out—examples can be found for Meiji (1868–1912) and later years as well—it no longer forms a main current of Japanese cultural production.

Poetic diaries that have survived from the early 10th c. point to the function of poetry—both native *tanka* or *waka (short verse in Japanese) and *kanshi* (verse in Chinese; see CHINESE POETRY IN JAPAN)—as an important form of cultural capital in the shifting rivalries between members of the Fujiwara regental house and the imperial family (reigning sovereigns as well as still-active abdicated or "retired" ones). Diaries, as well as poetic collections (kashū or ie no shū) with more or less extended headnotes, were produced by members of all three groups: the regents' households as well as the entourages of sitting and abdicated emperors. The 10th-c. practice of diary keeping by writers associated with the Fujiwara and other aristocratic families provided a patrimony of precedents for future clan heads to consult. As Heldt has argued in *The Pursuit of Harmony*, it also may have implied—because it mimicked the practice of diary keeping that had been carried on by court officials historically within the imperial palace—a symbolic equivalence between the regental and the imperial households. Heldt reads Ki no Tsurayuki's *Tosa nikki* (The Tosa Diary, 935) within this context as the attempt of a middle-ranking courtier to engage or maintain patronage ties with the high aristocracy via the display of his own talents as a desirable member of the entourage of proxy poets, scribes, and calligraphers surrounding the regent's and its rivals' households. Others have called attention to the impact of male-authored "poetic diaries" (also sometimes labeled "poetic tales" [uta monogatari]) composed by writers associated with the Fujiwara regents throughout the 10th c., culminating in the well-known *Kagerō nikki* (The Gossamer Diary, after 974), a poetic diary by a secondary wife of Regent Fujiwara Kaneie (see Mostow).

The *Kagerō nikki* fits easily within a genealogy of Fujiwara cultural production. It narrates its author's

21 years of marriage to Fujiwara Kaneie, highlighting in part the amorous and poetic talents of Kaneie. Just as important, it displays the poetic skills of the diarist herself, a valuable member of Kaneie's extended household. Yet the complexity of the *Kagerō nikki*'s prose and its apparent influence on poetic diaries by later aristocratic wives and ladies-in-waiting suggest the devel. of a differently configured set of motives, forms, and implied readers in the 11th c.

At the outset of her diary, the *Kagerō* author explicitly signals her engagement with the genre of fictional tales. She writes in opposition to the "empty words" of the old tales, she claims, "in the form of a memoir" for those who might ask about "the lives of the well-born." But in fact the rhetorical density of the *Kagerō*'s narrative portions heralds the sophisticated intertexual play between diary and tale genres that will characterize a number of subsequent poetic diaries, most notably the *Sarashina nikki* (The Sarashina Diary, after 1058), and the *Izumi Shikibu nikki* (The Diary of Izumi Shikibu, late 11th c.?; see Sarra). Deliberate blurring of generic boundaries between poetic diaries and fictional narratives (*tsukuri monogatari*) by women from middle-ranking families is visible as late as *Towazugatari* (An Unrequested Tale, after 1306), the memoir of a lady-in-waiting who drew self-consciously on episodes from *The Tale of Genji* (ca. 1008) to craft a record of her life at court and her wanderings as a Buddhist nun. Poetic diaries by mid-Heian and Kamakura period women (1185–1336) often call attention to the diarist's talent in both poetry and prose narrative, with the increased emphasis on narrative implying perhaps the importance of imperial and high-aristocratic women as the diarists' primary audience.

With the establishment of the military government at Kamakura and the increased physical mobility of the literate elite throughout the Kamakura and Muromachi periods (1336–1573), the practice of writing poetic travel diaries (kikō) proliferated. These diaries include not only the traditional courtly waka but the med. genre of *renga (linked verse), and finally in the Tokugawa period (1600–1867) *haikai (comic linked verse) and *haibun (poetic prose), which the poet Matsuo Bashō (1644–94) brought to such ripeness. Med. and early mod. poetic diaries bespeak their authors' involvement in establishing or perpetuating their reputations as heads of poetic schools. Their intended readers were other poets and aspiring practitioners of poetry.

One rhetorical feature linking med. poetic travel diaries to each other as well as to earlier and later diaries is the trad. of utamakura (poetic toponyms) that informs many of them. An itinerary of actual sites conventionally associated with specific poetic images as far back as the Heian period or earlier provides a structural framework for many poetic travel diaries. Thus, when the poet-nun Abutsu visited Yatsuhashi on her journey to Kamakura, recorded in *Izayoi nikki* (Diary of the Waning Moon, ca. 1283), the poem she composed on the place/place-name deliberately echoes earlier poets' compositions on the same site. Each poem memorializing such sites records the moment at which the diarist's composition joins a poetic dialogue about the place that had been ongoing for centuries. Such poems were also understood to function as ritualized forms of greeting to the resident spirit or deity of the place. The early 17th c. saw the rise of print culture and the spread of literacy beyond the courtly and warrior elites. Along with these profound sociohistorical shifts, a new spirit of parody and linguistic play informs the practice of poetic diaries, as it does so many other early mod. cultural practices. Bashō's poetic diaries sometimes self-ironically record the bouts of performance anxiety that encounters with utamakura inspired in him. He famously laments his failure to produce a poem at Yoshino in *Oi no kobumi* (Rucksack Notebook, 1687). Although poems by Bashō are conspicuously absent in his account of his visit to Matsushima in *Oku no hosomichi* (*Narrow Road to the Interior*, 1689), with its rich Chinese-influenced parallel constructions and allusions, his prose description of the place is a tour de force of the new form of haibun he pioneered in this, his most famous poetic diary.

Bashō's poetry and poetic diaries ultimately found readers beyond Japan, becoming central texts in the 20th-c. cross-cultural trad. of haiku poetry first promoted by the *imagistes*, a group of Anglo-Am. modernist poets publishing under the leadership of Ezra Pound immediately before World War I (see IMAGISM). The influence of poetic diaries by Heian and early med. women writers has been similarly far-reaching. Canonized by mod. scholars of "national literature" in Japan, early Japanese "women's memoir literature" became a vital source of inspiration for Japanese women writers throughout the 20th c.

*See* JAPAN, POETRY OF.

▪ *The Izumi Shikibu Diary*, trans. E. Cranston (1969); *Lady Daibu's Poetic Memoirs*, trans. P. Harries (1980); L. Miyake, "The Tosa Diary," *The Woman's Hand*, ed. P. Schalow and J. Walker (1996); H. Shirane, *Traces of Dreams* (1998); E. Sarra, *Fictions of Femininity* (1999); T. Suzuki, "Gender and Genre," *Inventing the Classics*, ed. H. Shirane and T. Suzuki (2000); M. Horton, *Song in an Age of Discord* (2002); *The Journal of Sōchō*, trans. M. Horton (2002); *At the House of Gathered Leaves*, trans. J. Mostow (2004); T. Yoda, *Gender and National Literature* (2004); J. Wallace, *Objects of Discourse* (2005); R. Kubukihara, "Aspects of Classical Japanese Travel Writing," spec. iss. of *Review of Japanese Culture and Society* 19 (2007); G. Heldt, *The Pursuit of Harmony* (2008).

E. SARRA

**JAPANESE POETICS.** Japanese poetics was shaped by the nature of poetic composition as a social practice among the Heian (794–1185) court aristocracy. The practice spread among the warriors and monks in the castle towns and temples of the med. age (1186–1600) and came to include merchants and commoners of the Edo period (1600–1868). *Waka or tanka*, the five-line poem of 5-7-5-7-7 syllables, recorded since the early 8th c., remained the cl. genre, with earlier forms like the long poem (chōka) and later genres like *renga and *haikai* (linked poetry) and *hokku* (or *haiku) being variations of it. This means that, apart from subtle historical changes, poetic lang. and themes remained largely the same, with the only revolutionary change occurring when the formerly barred Chinese loan words and daily-life vocabulary came to be included in the Edo period. The authors of poetic treatises were practicing poets themselves, and their readers were students or disciples who needed to acquire the art as a social skill, proof of their qualification as civilized persons. Many of the treatises were like textbooks devised for pedagogical purposes. They invariably included a brief hist. of the practice, usually tracing its primordial origins in the age of the gods as recorded in the first hist. books (*Kojiki*, 712; *Nihongi*, 720) or citing earliest examples from the first poetry anthol., the *Man'yōshū* (ca. 759), and from the 21 imperial anthols. commissioned by successive emperors until 1433. Other sections would consist of long passages of citation of exemplary poems, often with critical comments; equally numerous were stories or anecdotes (*utamonogatari*, *setsuwa*) about the circumstances in which a poem was composed or about particular poets and their deep devotion to the art. A significant portion was devoted to practical instruction about poetic diction and techniques, such as the use of "pillow words" (*makura kotoba*), conventional epithets associated with particular words—e.g., "Izumo, of the rising eight-fold clouds" or "Nara, of the good blue earth"; the use of *joshi* or preface, a metaphorical intro. to the main statement of the poem; the technique of punning or double meaning (*kakekotoba*); and the deploying of word pairs linked by association (*engo*). There was from early on a penchant for numerical categories and classifications such as "the nine grades of waka" (*waka kuhon*) or "the six types of poetry" (*rikugi*)—they were useful for distinguishing among the countless riches of the accumulated archives—and always, in the endeavor to define the appeal of specific poems and styles, a nurturing of the aesthetic sensibility.

There were also treatises, however, that dealt with first-order questions such as the essential nature and function of poetry. The *Kokinshū* Preface (905), written by Ki no Tsurayuki at the beginning of Japanese poetics, is a case in point:

> Japanese poetry has its seed in the human heart-mind [*kokoro*], which sprouts into a myriad leaves of words [*koto no ha*]. The person who lives in this world, faced with life's teeming events and circumstance, expresses what he feels in his heart through the medium of things visible and audible. Listen to the warbler crying among the flowers, the croaking of the frog dwelling in the waters—is there any among creatures vital and alive that does not break out in song? It is poetry that moves heaven and earth without the use of force, stirs to compassion the demons and deities invisible to the eye, harmonizes relations between men and women, and pacifies the heart of raging warriors.

As is often observed, this opening passage compre-

hends all the elements of a poetic performance: the world, the poet's inner response to it, the lang. he or she uses to communicate it, and the natural imagery that is its embodiment or figure. This is essentially a lyrical poetics: a poem is an effluence of the heart in response to being moved by experience; it comes into being as a natural process. Further, its primary method is imagistic *figuration. Finally, the Preface defines the social aspect of poetic function as persuasion without physical force, the pacific containment of violence, be it political or sexual. In sum, poetry is the quintessential art of civility, as confirmed by its social usages, whether in ritual ceremonies, banquets, or quotidian communication, or as the lang. for negotiating the complications of a private relationship.

The *Kokinshū* preface established the parameters of poetics on the twin concepts of the heart-mind and lang., or content and form, requiring a judicious balance between them. Its understanding of poetry as lyric was modified crucially by the leading *Shinkokinshū* (1201) poets in the early med. period. Shunzei, in particular, redefined the poem as an impersonal symbolic construct of the true nature of reality as apprehended in the Tendai Buddhist philosophy of the three truths, i.e., phenomena apprehended according to three orders of understanding as (1) empty in lacking an inner unchanging core; (2) provisionally real in arising and disappearing according to mutable circumstance; and (3) middle or ambiguous in being beyond the dualism of the first two orders while encompassing them. In this new poetics, the process of composition is likened to meditation (*shikan*, literally, stillness and insight), and the poem is seen as the figuration of that deep and concentrated state of mind. Shunzei writes in *Korai fūteishō* (Poetic Styles from Antiquity to the Present, 1197, rev. 1201):

> In the opening passage of the work called *Tendai shikan*, there are these words written by Shōan Daishi: "The luminous tranquility of stillness and insight was yet unheard of in ages past." The very sound of these words, evoking limitless depths, fathoming a remotely inward significance, awesome and splendid, is like the good and bad in poetry, the endeavor to know its deep mind, difficult to convey in words; and yet it is precisely this analogy that enables us to comprehend it in the same way. . . .
>
> It is true that the one are golden words of Buddhist scripture, full of a deep truth, while the other seems to be but an idle game of empty words and fine phrases. And yet it manifests a profound significance in things and can be the circumstance which leads one to the Buddhist way. Moreover, because delusion is of itself wisdom, the *Lotus Sutra* says, "Properly explained, the secular classics . . . and the actions of mundane existence are all following the True Dharma." And the *Fugenkan* teaches, "What is the thing that is designated sinful, what designated fortunate? Neither sin nor fortune possesses a subject; the mind is of itself empty." Consequently, here also in speaking of the deep way of poetry, I draw upon

its similarity to the three truths of the empty, the contingent, and the middle [*kū.ke.chū no sandai*] and write of it in the same terms.

The med. theory of a symbolic poetry produced an aesthetics of evocation manifest in the pursuit of such qualities as aura or overtones (*omokage, yojō*) and ineffable depth (*yūgen*), and the eschewing of clarity of meaning as banal.

In the treatise *Sasamegoto* (*Murmured Conversations*, 1463–64), the renga poet-monk Shinkei would found poetic process on discipline in the mind-ground (*shinji shugyō*) and describe the highest poetry as one that is "constituted solely of nuance," with no specific meaning to convey but with the power to evoke an experience of ultimate reality. Similarly, while maintaining impartiality as a general principle, he drew attention to the marvelous effects produced by *soku* (the distant link), as distinct from *shinku* (the close link), in the structure of waka and renga. *Distant* and *close* name the perceived space between the upper and lower parts of a waka or between any two contiguous verses in a linked poetry sequence. This mediate space will seem close when the poem's lines, being closely connected phonologically, syntactically, and semantically, constitute an integral unity, but distant when a *caesura divides the poem into two disparate parts and there is no overt semantic connection between them. Instead, the silent link demands to be intuited or interpreted by the audience.

The use of hidden or subtle linkages between verses in Bashō-school haikai of the Edo period, called variously *nioi*, fragrance, or *hibiki*, resonance, manifests the same preference and is similarly motivated by a desire to evoke the interpenetrability of all phenomena or the boundlessness of the mundane when seen through enlightened eyes. Haikai began as a rebellion against the extreme refinement of cl. renga and the proliferation of minute rules of composition in its late stages. Haikai reveled in the low and vulgar aspects of ordinary life, eschewed the pure Japanese of cl. poetic diction, and favored harsh-sounding Chinese compounds and nonsensical colloquial expressions. Edo poetics was divided between high and low, the refined and the vulgar (*ga* and *zoku*), and derived great amusement in the incongruous mixing of the two orders of social reality. But Bashō later tired of amusement for its own sake and succeeded, after much struggle, in elevating the mundane by giving it a sheen of numinosity learned from Taoism, Zen, and med. aesthetics, such that, to the poet, there is nothing that does not own its own unique beauty in the larger scheme of things. As he writes in *Oi no kobumi* (Rucksack Notebook, 1687):

All art is one in nature, whether in Saigyō's waka, Sōgi's renga, Sesshū's painting, or Rikyū's tea. In matters of art, one follows the dynamic creativity of nature and makes a friend of the four seasons. The man of art sees nothing that is not a flower, longs for nothing but is a moon. Those who do not see flowers are like barbarians, those who do not long for the moon are akin to the birds and beasts. One must leave the barbarians and leave the company of beasts, constantly pursuing nature, always returning to the four seasons.

■ J. Konishi, "Association and Progression," *HJAS* 21 (1958); *Fujiwara Teika's Superior Poems of Our Time*, ed. and trans. R. H. Brower and E. Miner (1967); "The *Mumyōshō* of Kamo no Chōmei and Its Significance in Japanese Literature," trans. H. Katō, *Monumenta Nipponica* 23 (1968); E. Cranston, "Water Plant Imagery in *Man'yōshū*," *HJAS* 31 (1971); "Ex-Emperor Go-Toba's Secret Teachings," ed. and trans. R. H. Brower, *HJAS* 32 (1972); E. Cranston, "The River Valley as *Locus Amoenus* in Man'yō Poetry," *Studies in Japanese Culture*, ed. Japan P.E.N. Club (1973); W. LaFleur, "Saigyō and the Buddhist Value of Nature," *History of Religions* 13 (1973–74); E. Cranston, "The Dark Path: Images of Longing in Japanese Love Poetry," *HJAS* 35 (1975); J. Konishi, "The Art of Renga," *Journal of Japanese Studies* 21 (1975); "Rules for Poetic Elegance," trans. N. Teele, *Monumenta Nipponica* 31 (1976); E. Ramirez-Christensen, "The Essential Parameters of Linked Poetry," *HJAS* 41 (1981); S. Carter, "Rules, Rules, and More Rules: Shōhaku's *Renga* Rulebook of 1501," *HJAS* 43 (1983); W. LaFleur, *The Karma of Words* (1983); J. Wixted, "The *Kokinshū* Prefaces: Another Perspective," *HJAS* 43 (1983); *On the Art of the Nō Drama: The Major Treatises of Zeami*, trans. J. Rimer and M. Yamazaki (1984); "Fujiwara Teika's *Maigetsushō*," ed. and trans. R. H. Brower, *Monumenta Nipponica* 40 (1985); "*Tamekanekyō Wakashō*," trans. R. Huey and S. Matisoff, *Monumenta Nipponica* 40 (1985); M. Morris, "Waka and Form, Waka and History," *HJAS* 46 (1986); "The Foremost Style of Poetic Composition: Fujiwara Tameie's *Eiga no Ittei*," ed. and trans. R. H. Brower, *Monumenta Nipponica* 42 (1987); T. Ikeda, "Continuity and Discontinuity in Renga," *Acta Asiatica* 56 (1989); E. Miner, "Waka: Features of Its Constitution and Development," *HJAS* 50 (1990); J. Rabinovitch, "Wasp Waists and Monkey Tails," *HJAS* 51 (1991); I. Smits, "The Poem as a Painting: Landscape Poetry in Late Heian Japan," *Transactions of the Asiatic Society of Japan*, 4th ser., 6 (1991); M. Ueda, *Literary and Art Theories in Japan* (1991); C. Drake, "The Collision of Traditions in Saikaku's Haikai," *HJAS* 52 (1992); M. Horton, "Renga Unbound," *HJAS* 53 (1993); D. Bialock, "Voice, Text, and the Question of Poetic Borrowing in Late Classical Japanese Poetry," *HJAS* 54 (1994); R. Bundy, "*Santai Waka*: Six Poems in Three Modes," *Monumenta Nipponica* 49 (1994); *Conversations with Shōtetsu*, ed. S. Carter, trans. R. Brower (1994); R. Raud, *The Role of Poetry in Classical Japanese Literature* (1994); C. Crowley, "Putting *Makoto* into Practice: Onitsura's *Hitorigoto*," *Monumenta Nipponica* 50 (1995); *The Distant Isle*, ed. T. Hare et al. (1996); E. Kamens, *Utamakura, Allusion, and Intertextuality in Traditional Japanese Poetry* (1997); K. Kawamoto, *The Poetics of Japanese Verse* (2000); S. Carter, "Chats with the Master: Selections from *Kensai zōdan*," *Monumenta Nipponica* 56 (2001); M. Meli, "'Aware' as a Critical Term in Classical Japanese Poetics," *Japan Review* 13 (2001); P. Qiu, "Aesthetic of Uncoventionality: *Fūryū* in Ikkyū's Poetry," *Japanese Language and Literature* 35 (2001); R. Huey, *The Making of the Shinkokinshū* (2002); S. Klein, *Allegories of Desire* (2002); P. Atkins, "The Demon-Quelling Style in Medieval Japanese Poetic and Dramatic Theory," *Monumenta Nipponica* 58 (2003); *Japanese Poeticity and Narrativity Revisited*, ed. E. Sekine (2003); R. Raud, "The Heian Literary System: A Tentative Model," *Reading East Asian Writing*, ed. M. Hockx and I. Smits (2003); *Hermeneutical Strategies: Methods of Interpretation in the Study of Japanese Literature*, ed. M. Marra (2004); K. Kimbrough, "Reading the Miraculous Powers of Japanese Poetry," *Japanese Journal of Religious Studies* 32 (2005); R. Bundy, "Solo Poetry Contest as Poetic Self-Portrait," *Monumenta Nipponica* 61 (2006); *Matsuo Bashō's Poetic Spaces: Exploring Haikai Intersections*, ed. E. Kerkham (2006); W. Denecke, "'Topic poetry is all ours': Poetic Composition on Chinese Lines in Early Heian Japan," *HJAS* 67 (2007); G. Heldt, *The Pursuit of Harmony* (2008); *Literature and Literary Theory*, ed. A. Ueda and R. Okada (2008); E. Ramirez-Christensen, *Emptiness and Temporality* (2008); Shinkei, *Murmured Conversations*, ed. and trans. E. Ramirez-Christensen (2008); R. Thomas, *The Way of Shikishima* (2008).

E. RAMIREZ-CHRISTENSEN

**JAVA, POETRY OF.** *See* INDONESIAN POETRY.

**JAZZ POETRY.** The diverse range of instrumental and vocal music categorized as *jazz* (and its precursor and counterpart, *\*blues*) functioned throughout much of the 20th c. as a colorful symbol, a structuring principle, and a totalizing—and tantalizing—trope for writers, filmmakers, visual artists, and even (when considering the age of art deco) architects. Jazz has greatly influenced other literary genres such as the novel (consider Ralph Ellison's treatment of Louis Armstrong in *Invisible Man* or Toni Morrison's *signifying on "The Trombone Blues" in the novel *Jazz*). Yet poetry is arguably the genre through which we can best see and hear how the divergent improvisatory stylizations of jazz aesthetics permeate America's literary and cultural landscape.

What would America be without jazz music? Less rhythmically complex and conceptually daring. What would Am. poetry be without jazz poetics? Less performatively vibrant and innovative. The invigorating, if originally contested, presence of jazz as the muse for a substantial body of Am. poetry can be traced back to the art form's emergence in the early 1920s. The revolutions of *modernism and the *Harlem Renaissance (also known as the New Negro Renaissance)—parallel and intersecting youth movements—marked shifts in *taste, culture, mood, art, and, of course, music that altered the content, form, and *performance of poetry. The devels. in jazz and the evolution of Am. poetry had related trajectories that were not lost on writers of the time. Other periods in which jazz poetry has flourished as a style and in performance were the eras of the *Beats and the *Black Arts movement, and, more recently, the New Renaissance movement in black writing from the 1990s to the present.

Jazz poems are animated esp. by the productive tension between what is written and what is spoken. They blur the boundaries between what is seen and what is heard. Yet do recitals of jazz-influenced poems remain consistent irrespective of the performance venue, or do they change over time and under different circumstances? Performance is central to jazz composition because improvisation produces innovation. The demands for improvised jazz poetic forms might require that each performed iteration of the poem be recognizably different from the previous one. In some instances, collaborative endeavors between poets and jazz musicians have produced compositions that, in live or recorded form, establish a new poetic work. Yet many poets deeply influenced by jazz tend to perform their verses without substantial changes, whether they perform with or without musical accompaniment. Moreover, requiring such continual variation would preclude an appreciation of other ways that improvisation enters jazz poetry at the moment of composition, a moment of performance on the page or the computer screen.

In the musico-cultural climate of the early 21st c., jazz music is typically associated with virtuosic performance, rigor, and sophistication. Thus, the quibble over whether verse alluding to or incorporating jazz aesthetics merits the label *jazz poem* reflects the creative prestige associated with this music. However, in part because the earliest venues for jazz (and ragtime—and blues for that matter) performances were often bordellos, after-hours juke joints, and cabarets, the music's association with sex and licentious or illicit behavior greatly influenced the less-than-enthusiastic response to poets, such as Langston Hughes, who used jazz early and often in their work. "To A Black Dancer in 'The Little Savoy,'" from Hughes's *The Weary Blues* (1926), e.g., isolates key corporeal features celebrating a dark "Wine-maiden / Of the Jazz-tuned night" whom Hughes apostrophizes: "Lips / Sweet as purple dew, / Breasts / Like the pillows of all sweet dreams . . ."

Hughes's contemporary Countee Cullen eschewed jazz poetry. In the February 1926 issue of *Opportunity*, in a review of *The Weary Blues*, Cullen questioned whether "jazz verse" could ever belong to "that dignified company, that select and austere circle of high literary expression which we call poetry" and regarded Hughes's "jazz poems as interlopers in the company of the truly beautiful poems in other sections of the book" (O'Meally). In fact, Hughes's response to Cullen and others such as the archetypal "Philadelphia club-woman" representing those who were "ashamed" that Af. Americans "created jazz" was to assert an intrinsic connection between racial "theme and treatment" and "the meanings and rhythms of jazz" in his poetry. As he observed in "The Negro Artist and the Racial Mountain" (1926), "[J]azz to me is one of the inherent expressions of Negro life in America; the eternal tom-tom beating in the Negro soul."

Hughes's essentialist link between black expressive culture and jazz emphasizes its racial dimensions. True enough, black expressive culture has placed a distinct value on oratorical, rhetorical, and musical virtuosity that has influenced the hist. of poetic performance. Jazz has expressed not only in Hughes's terms "Negro life" and "Negro soul" but the heart and soul of America. Some of the first white Am. poets to allude to jazz music or its milieu included Vachel Lindsay, Carl Sandburg, Mina Loy, and Hart Crane. This does not mean that their poems were composed in a way that fully embodied and respected the jazz ethos. Loy and Lindsay both tended to associate jazz with *primitivism and *decadence.

Until the recent advent of hip-hop's globalization (itself an outgrowth of jazz; see HIP-HOP POETICS), jazz was arguably the U.S.'s best-known indigenous art form. Yet the jazz cadence of Am. lit. and culture extends beyond geographic boundaries (O'Meally). Anderson describes how the "jazz poet draws upon the various traditional/nontraditional (African and/or European) cultural elements and forges a unique expression of individual and racial or musical identity through his or her poetry." While the poetry of Hayden Carruth, Robert Creeley, and Clark Coolidge has long been associated with jazz influence, many poets from diverse multiethnic cultures within and beyond the Americas, such as Lawson Fusao Inada, Joy Harjo, Sherman Alexie, and Matthew Shenoda, are deeply engaged in blues and jazz poetics. Jazz and its lit. transcend black/white and Af./Eur. dichotomies.

In jazz poetry, poetic structure thrives on the artful balance between discipline and freedom, silence and noise, and presence or absence of notation. The white space beyond and between lines informs pacing within the poem. Jazz music embodies a comparable balance between creative freedom and disciplined restraint that is essential to crafting verse, whether in *meter, *free verse, or more experimental prosodies. Fundamental protocols of jazz are improvisation, collaboration, and live performance. Each of these involves an explicit expressive exchange among the musicians and an implicit dynamic exchange between the performers and the audience.

The emphasis on mutually attentive listening means that the often-used term *jazz accompaniment* is not adequate to describe jazz poetry performances. Given the catalyzing effect of collaboration, *jazz interaction* or *jazz communication* more suitably denotes what, ideally, occurs between poets and musicians. The dynamic range of this communicative style can be heard in Langston Hughes's collaboration with the bassist Charles Mingus, among others, on the album *The Weary Blues*, recorded in the wake of bebop and at the height of the poetry-read-to-jazz movement closely associated with the Beat poets. Other poets whose collaborative performances and jazz verse deserve mention are Amiri Baraka (and his New Ark Orchestra), Jayne Cortez (who recorded eight jazz and poetry albums with her band the Fire Spitters), Yusef Komunyakaa, Ntozake Shange, Michael S. Harper, Sonia Sanchez, Al Young, Quincy Troupe, and Tracie Morris.

The emphasis on rendering collaborative and solo versifying audible within a legible medium is best seen in poems written about jazz figures such as John Coltrane, Billie Holiday, Charlie Parker, and Thelonious Monk. In fact, the Coltrane poem is a subgenre in the poetry about musicians. During the Black Arts era, Sanchez, Baraka, and Haki Madhubuti (Don Lee) often wrote poems about Coltrane that used excessive orthographic and phonological alteration and included marginalia as performance cues to overcome what Henderson called "the cold technology of the printed page." Lee's "Don't Cry, Scream" informed readers to "sing / loud / & / high"; his tribute in "the sixties" (when "a trane / came / out") uses *epenthesis to signal Coltrane's sound "screameeeeeeeeeeeeeee-ing." Baraka's poem "AM/TRAK" exhibits a comparable protraction of vowels and consonants in his echo of Coltrane's "scream": "blow, oh honk-scream (bahhh-hhhhhh—wheeeeeeeeee)"!!! . . . (*Black Art*). Likewise, Sanchez parenthetically instructed her readers to sing "slowly to the tune of my favorite things" in "a / coltrane / poem." Her poem aims to transcribe a particular movement in Coltrane's "My Favorite Things"—as well as the tune's triple-meter feel—through the spacing and stressing of "dum" and "da":

```
(softly      da-dum-da da da da da da da da da /
             da-dum-a
till it       da da da da da da da da da
builds up)    da-dum-da da da.
```

Baraka, Sanchez, and other poets attempting to evince oral effects in a textual medium chose jazz tunes that were well known beyond aficionados so that the effectiveness of their phonological and orthographic techniques could be better realized. However, as the popularity of jazz decreased, both a tonal and formal shift became evident in Coltrane poems from the 1980s and 1990s to the present; these poems became less "visually aggressive on the page" than those of the Black Arts era. Indeed, Elizabeth Alexander's poem "John Col" demonstrates this change, while alluding to W. B. Yeats's "Easter, 1916" and a slogan of the Black Arts and Black Power movements:

the bloody foot-
lights cup the dark
where red and black
are beautiful

a terrible beau-
ty a terrible
beauty a terrible
beauty a horn

And this brass heart-
beat this red
sob    this    this
John Coltrane Col
trane song.

In contrast to "sheets of sound"—the description of Coltrane's rapid-fire succession of notes in his style of the 1950s, first used by Ira Gitler, the jazz critic of *Down Beat* magazine, on the liner notes to Coltrane's 1958 album *Soultrane*—Alexander's poem is pared down to a minimal number of words. Other recent poets involved in versifying Coltrane's evolutions in musical style, form, and technique include Kamau Daood, Nathaniel Mackey, Cornelius Eady, A. Van Jordan, and Linda Susan Jackson.

Much of the poetry driven by jazz music has been influenced by its male-centered homosocial milieu. Yet poets have offered distinct challenges to the conventional conflation of instrumental virtuosity with masculine virility. Close attention to the poetic visualizations of the jazz instrumentarium by poets such as Cortez and Shange sheds light on the existence of a corporeality that stretches beyond the hegemonic representations of the trumpet's shape and sound and of the embodiment of jazz more generally. Cortez explores the symbolic implications of Duke Ellington's album of jazz and narrative text *The Drum Is a Woman* when she asks, "If the drum is a woman,"

> why are you pounding your drum into an insane
>     babble . . .
> why are you choking your drum
> why are you raping your drum
> why are you saying disrespectful things
> to your mother drum your sister drum
> your wife drum and your infant daughter drum

Cortez does not reject the masculinist metaphor but embraces it figuratively to protest violence against women. Considering gender and sexuality reveals other striking facets of jazz poetics—for instance, how many poets identify the curvilinear shape of musical instruments as voluptuous female lovers and muses. Shange, e.g., maps various jazz instruments onto the territory of the body in her poem "I Live in Music." She draws on the physical shape of brass and string instruments for visual effect, claiming "i got 15 trumpets where other women got hips / & an upright bass for both sides of my heart." In so doing, Shange reappropriates the woman as aesthetic object of the male instrumentalist in jazz poetics.

The so-called renaissance in black writing from the 1990s to the present reflects a continuum and expansion of jazz aesthetics developed during the New Negro and Black Arts periods. All the recent poets named are heirs to the advances in techniques for translating musical forms into poetic performance made by Hughes, Shange, Troupe, and others. Of special note is the emergent movement from improvisatory aesthetics and instrumentality in jazz poetics to stylistic looping and percussive thematics in sound-directed hip-hop poetics. The writing and performances by poets Tracie Morris, Saul Williams, and Jessica Care Moore offer examples.

Although jazz poetry has existed since the beginning of the 20th c., efforts to compile and categorize it did not flourish until near the end. In the 1990s, several anthols. appeared, incl. Sasha Feinstein and Yusef Komunyakaa's two-volume *Jazz Poetry Anthology* (1991, 1996) and Nathaniel Mackey and Art Lange's hybrid anthol. *Moment's Notice: Jazz in Poetry and Prose* (1992).

*See* AFRICAN-AMERICAN POETRY; UNITED STATES, POETRY OF THE.

■  S. Henderson, "The Forms of Things Unknown," *Understanding the New Black Poetry* (1973); *The Jazz*

*Cadence of American Culture*, ed. R. G. O'Meally (1998); T. J. Anderson, *Notes to Make the Sound Come Right: Four Innovations of Jazz Poetry* (2004); M. D. Jones, *The Muse Is Music: Jazz Poetry from the Harlem Renaissance to Spoken Word* (2011).

M. D. JONES

**JE NE SAIS QUOI** (Fr., "I know not what"). Refers to a first-person experience of a "certain something" with intense effects that is difficult to explain or even express. Since the 18th c., it has been used principally as a literary term and an aesthetic response, but it was always and remains able to articulate problems of explanation and expression in a wide range of contexts. The very elusiveness inherent in the term divides opinion: some dismiss the je ne sais quoi as a refuge of ignorance concealed in an affectation; others prize its poetic potential to trace in lang. the shape and feel of phenomena that cannot be fully known but that change everything.

Precursors—the Lat. *nescio quid* (Cicero, Augustine), It. *non so che* (Ludovico Ariosto, Ludovico Dolce, Torquato Tasso), and Sp. *no sé qué* (Teresa of Ávila, St. John of the Cross)—are applied disparately to love, religious experience, and art. Sixteenth-c. uses of the Fr. phrase (Joachim du Bellay, *Les Regrets*, 1558; François Rabelais, *Cinquiesme livre*, 1564; Michel de Montaigne, *Essais*, 1580), while similarly disparate, are lexically inventive and semantically rich: in *Essais* (1.28), e.g., Montaigne conjures with adjectival forms of the phrase ("c'est je ne sçay quelle quinte essence de tout ce meslange" [It is I know not what kind of quintessence of all this commixture]) to capture the "nescioquiddity" of perfect friendship. The je ne sais quoi first attains prominence as a substantive and a concept in 17th-c. France. As in Montaigne, it animates poetic explorations of human *affect in all its enigmatic power (Pierre Corneille, *Rodogune*, 1645; Blaise Pascal, *Pensées*, 1670); but it also features in philosophical disputes about occult qualities (René Descartes, *Principes de la philosophie*, 1647; Jacques Rohault, *Entretiens sur la philosophie*, 1671; Gabriel Daniel, *Suite du voyage du monde de Descartes*, 1696) and looms ever larger in discussions of literary and social distinction (François Ogier, *Apologie pour M. de Balzac*, 1628; Claude Favre de Vaugelas, *Remarques sur la langue française*, 1647; Chevalier de Méré, *Lettres*, 1689). The Fr. term enters Eng. as "four French words, contracted as it were into one" (Thomas Blount, *Glossographia*, 1656), an elegant neologism with sublime possibilities. It receives its most extensive treatment in a text that bears its name, the fifth conversation of Dominique Bouhours's *Entretiens d'Ariste et d'Eugène* (1671), which urbanely presents the je ne sais quoi as a concept applicable to all enigmas. Bouhours's treatment is immediately attacked for its mixture of the sacred and profane ( Jean Barbier d'Aucour, *Sentiments de Cléante*, 1671), and the je ne sais quoi soon appears overstretched and undone by its own success as a word in literary vogue, ridiculed—in an age of *préciosité when poetic posture often betrays social position—as a vacuous affectation of the polite circle (Molière, *Les Femmes savantes*, 1672; Thomas Shadwell, *The Virtuoso*, 1676; Abbé d'Ailly, *Pensées diverses*, 1678; William Congreve, *Double Dealer*, 1694). Later authors have portrayed it variously as the properly enigmatic quality at the heart of aesthetic experience or philosophical endeavor (B. J. Feijóo, "El no sé qué," 1733; Pierre de Marivaux, *Le Cabinet du philosophe*, 1734; Montesquieu, *Essai sur le goût*, 1757; Vladimir Jankélévitch, *Le Je-ne-sais-quoi et le Presque-rien*, 1980) and that a poetic style may be best equipped to put into words.

*See* NEOCLASSICAL POETICS, SUBLIME, TASTE.

■ E.B.O. Borgerhoff, *The Freedom of French Classicism* (1950); G. Natali, "Storia del 'non so che,'" *Lingua Nostra* 12 (1951); E. Köhler, "*Je ne sais quoi*," *Romanistisches Jahrbuch* 6 (1953–54); E. Haase, "Zur Bedeutung von 'je ne sais quoi' im 17. Jahrhundert," *Zeitschrift für französische Sprache und Literatur* 67 (1956); A. Porqueras Mayo, "Funcion de la formula 'no sé qué' en textos literarios españoles (siglos XVIII–XX)," *Bulletin hispanique* 67 (1965); L. Marin, *Sublime Poussin* (1995); N. Cronk, *The Classical Sublime* (2002); R. Scholar, *The "Je-Ne-Sais-Quoi" in Early Modern Europe* (2005); E. Camp, "Metaphor and That Certain 'Je Ne Sais Quoi,'" *Philosophical Studies* 129 (2006).

R. SCHOLAR

**JINDYWOROBAK.** An Adelaide-based nationalist movement in Australian poetry that flourished from the late 1930s to the 1950s. Its chief theorist was Rex Ingamells (1913–55), who, in his keynote essay "Conditional Culture" (1938), wanted "to free Australian art from whatever alien influences trammel it." The emphasis was on "environmental values," and Ingamells sought to banish Brit. poetic idioms in a deeper artistic engagement with Australia's own landscape and hist., ancient as well as mod.—hence, *Jindyworobak*, an Aboriginal word from the Wuywurrung lang., meaning "to annex, to join" (Ingamells).

Aboriginality was crucial to Ingamells's radical project, serving to define its mixed legacy. Sharing the then-common view that Aborigines were a dying race, the Jindyworobaks felt free to appropriate indigenous culture for literary purposes, notably the concept of *Alchera* or *Alcheringa*—obliquely trans. from the Arrernte lang. as the "Dreamtime"—which they celebrated in purely figurative terms as the spirit of the land.

Though the Jindyworobaks' primitivism has some affinities with *modernism, their poetry was broadly traditional in form, ranging from nationalistic stridency to intimate lyricism. Initially, some use was made of Aboriginal words, Ingamells's experimental poems in this vein being much derided. However, the verse of Roland Robinson (1912–92) continues to attract interest, incl. his respectful poetic transcriptions of Aboriginal Eng. Other major Jindyworobak poets were Ian Mudie (1911–76), William Hart-Smith (1911–90), and Flexmore Hudson (1913–88).

Many poets of varied commitment passed through the pages of the annual *Jindyworobak Anthology* (1938–53), and they contributed to the *pastoral emphasis in much postwar Australian poetry. With the rise of indigenous poets since Oodgeroo Noonuccal (Kath Walker, 1920–93) in the 1960s, fewer nonindigenous Australian poets have attempted Aboriginal themes, yet Jindyworobak elements arguably abide in the poetry of Les Murray (b. 1938) and Billy Marshall-Stoneking (b. 1947), among others.

*See* AUSTRALIA, POETRY OF; PRIMITIVISM.

■ R. Ingamells, "Conditional Culture," *The Writer in Australia*, ed. J. Barnes (1969); *The Jindyworobaks*, ed. B. Elliott (1979); H. McQueen, "Inadvertent Grandeur," *The Black Swan of Trespass* (1979); L. Murray, "The Human-Hair Thread," *Persistence in Folly* (1984); R. Sellick, "The Jindyworobaks and Aboriginality," *Southwords*, ed. P. Butterss (1995).

P. KIRKPATRICK

**JINGLE** (ME *gyngle*). Any verse that catches the listener's ear, often through bouncy rhythms and exaggerated sound repetition, esp. *rhyme and *alliteration. Some jingles verge on *nonsense, emphasizing sound qualities over meaning, e.g., the classic nursery rhymes "Eeny meeny miny mo" and "Hickory dickory dock." Jingles are easily memorized and repeated, but they tend to achieve their staying power less through *euphony than through insistence. The initial pleasantness of a jingle may quickly turn toward irritation: in "Punch, Brothers, Punch" (*Tom Sawyer Abroad*), e.g., Mark Twain recounts a comic incident in which the lines "Punch, brothers! Punch with care! / Punch in the presence of the passenjare!" invaded his mind, creating an "idiotic burden" in which he "suffered, and cried, and jingled all through the evening." Twain's unwelcome mental refrain comes from a newspaper advertisement, but the most prominent instance of mod. jingles is in television and radio advertising, where companies exploit the mnemonic qualities of jingles in the hope of selling products. The term has long had pejorative connotations. Joseph Addison (*Spectator* no. 297) criticizes John Milton for often affecting "a kind of Jingle in his Words" in *Paradise Lost*, but Milton himself had prefaced his *epic by scorning the "jingling sound of like endings" represented by end rhyme.

■ *Oxford Book of Nursery Rhymes*, ed. I. Opie and P. Opie (1951); L. M. Scott, "Understanding Jingles and Needledrop: A Rhetorical Approach to Music in Advertising," *Journal of Consumer Research* 17 (1990); R. F. Yalch, "Memory in a Jingle Jungle," *Journal of Applied Psychology* 76 (1991)—psychological study of jingle as mnemonic.

L. PERRINE; T.V.F. BROGAN; E. J. RETTBERG

**JITANJÁFORA.** A kind of *sound poetry where words invented for their acoustic qualities may alternate with or imitate real ones. The term was borrowed in 1929 by the Mexican critic Alfonso Reyes from the first stanza of "Leyenda," a poem by the Cuban Mariano Brull: "Filiflama alabe cundre / ala olalúnea alífera / alveola jitanjáfora / iris salumba salífera." In several articles that Reyes later republished in 1942 as "Las jitanjáforas," he called them "[c]reations that address not reason, but rather the senses and the imagination. Words here do not seek a useful goal. They play on their own." The emergence of the *jitanjáfora* in avant-garde Cuban poetry of the 1920s has been linked to a nationalist desire to imitate the music and dance of Afro-Cuban rituals; however, Brull admired Paul Valéry's notions of *pure poetry, and Emilio Ballagas was aware of Gertrude Stein's avant-garde writing that played with sound and nonsense. Besides Brull and Ballagas, other Cuban poets such as Ramón Guirao, José Tallet, and Nicolás Guillén cultivated the genre, but jitanjáforas can also be found in other poets, incl. canonical figures of the Hispanic trad., such as Félix Lope de Vega and Sor Juana Inés de la Cruz, as well as in Eur. *Dada poets and many other literary trads.

*See* AVANT-GARDE POETICS; DANCE AND POETRY; MUSIC AND POETRY; NONSENSE VERSE; SPANISH AMERICA, POETRY OF.

■ A. Reyes, "Las jitanjáforas," *La experiencia literaria* (1942); C. Bousoño, *El irracionalismo poético* (1977); M. J. de Navascués, "Hacia una estilística de la jitanjáfora," *Revista de literatura* 53 (1991); M. Arnedo, "'Afrocubanista' Poetry and Afro-Cuban Performance," *MLR* 96 (2001).

O. CISNEROS

**JONGLEUR** (Fr. *jongleur*, Occitan and Catalan *joglar*, Sp. *juglar*, Port. *jogral*, It. *giullare*). A med. *minstrel in France, Spain, Portugal, or Italy. Although the word dates only from the 8th c., jongleurs seem to have existed in France from the 5th c. to the 15th. The term was applied to performers of various kinds—acrobats, actors, and entertainers in general, as well as musicians and reciters of verse. Like minstrels, jongleurs were often condemned for irregular behavior but sometimes found to have a role in salvation. Chaucer used Eng. *janglere* (from the Fr.) for a tale teller like himself; *juggler* meant an entertainer, one who amuses people, until it came to mean "one who practices juggling" in the 19th c. (*OED*). See the OE *scop, the Celtic *bard, and the ON *skald (see NORSE POETRY).

The Occitan *joglar* performed lyrics composed by a *troubadour whom he served as a singing messenger, perhaps accompanying himself with an instrument or alternating song with instrumental performance. The troubadour might name the jongleur in the *tornada, with instructions to take the song to an addressee who could be expected to reward him for it. Thus, a given song was usually entrusted to one jongleur, but the troubadour might commission several jongleurs with different songs during his career, occasionally revising a given song for a second performer. During the 12th and 13th cs., the relative frequency of such mentions of jongleurs declined, suggesting that oral diffusion was being gradually replaced by written transmission.

The OF jongleur performed not only the lyrics of the *trouvères but *chansons de geste, *medieval romances, saints' lives, *fabliaux, miracle plays, and other narratives. The chansons de geste were originally performed to a simple melody and, according to the *oral-formulaic theory, were composed in performance by a technique similar to that of the 20th-c. illiterate Yugoslavian *guslar (Lord, Duggan); but some scholars maintain that the jongleurs read the chansons de geste from a book even in the earliest times. They probably

did the same with romances and saints' lives, texts that frequently depict the narrator as a jongleur.

*See* MEDIEVAL POETRY.

■ E. Faral, *Les Jongleurs en France au moyen âge* (1910); Jeanroy; R. Morgan, "Old French Jogleor and Kindred Terms," *RPh* 7 (1954); R. Menéndez Pidal, *Poesía juglaresca y orígenes de las literaturas románicas* (1957); J. Duggan, *The Song of Roland: Formulaic Style and Poetic Craft* (1973); W. D. Paden, "The Role of the Joglar," *Chrétien de Troyes and the Troubadours*, ed. P. S. Noble and L. M. Paterson (1984); W. A. Quinn, "Chaucer's Janglerye," *Viator* 18 (1987); R. E. Harvey, "Joglars and the Professional Status of the Early Troubadours," *Medium Aevum* 62 (1993); P. Dronke, *The Medieval Lyric*, 3d ed. (1996); J. W. Baldwin, "The Image of the Jongleur in Northern France around 1200," *Speculum* 72 (1997); I. Marchesin, "Les Jongleurs dans les psautiers du haut moyen âge," *Cahiers de civilisation médiévale* 41 (1998); G. Noto, *Il giullare e il trovatore nelle liriche e nelle biografie provenzali* (1998); S. Orlando, "Letteratura e performance in antichi testi romanzi (spagnoli e italiani)," *European Medieval Drama* 3 (1999); Lord; S. Menegaldo, *Le jongleur dans la littérature narrative des XIIe et XIIIe siècles* (2005); C. Symes, *A Common Stage: Theater and Public Life in Medieval Arras* (2007).

W. D. PADEN

**JUDEO-SPANISH POETRY.** Poetry sung, recited, or written in the Judeo-Sp. (Judezmo, Ladino) dialect, in the various postdiasporic communities of the Sephardic Jews—North Africa (Morocco, Algeria) and the Eastern Mediterranean (the Balkans, Greece, Turkey, Israel)—after their exile from Spain in 1492. By contrast, in Western Eur. centers such as Amsterdam, Bayonne, and Leghorn, there were Jewish authors who did not write in the Judeo-Sp. dialect but continued to form part of the Hispanic (Sp. or Port.) literary trads. Judeo-Sp. poetry may be organized into the following generic categories: *complas* (popular religious or didactic songs), *cantigas (*lyric songs), *romansas* (traditional *ballads), *endevinas* (*riddles), and *refranes (*proverbs). Complas can be considered essentially written lit.; the other genres are oral (see ORAL POETRY). Following World War II, a special subgenre of Sephardic poetry, written in Judeo-Sp. and in Fr., commemorated the tragic events of the Holocaust. In recent decades, poets and singers working both within and without the Sephardic trad. have adopted Judeo-Sp. as a poetic lang. According to Balbuena, this late wave of poetic production in Judeo-Sp. shows how the lang. is used as a tool for creating Sephardic identity in the diaspora. Traditional Sephardic romansas and cantigas have been increasingly recorded by contemp. artists whose musical reconstructions of traditional settings have been studied by Cohen and by Gutwirth.

Complas (Sp. *coplas) are strophic poems usually of paraliturgical content, by both known and anonymous authors, and are the most characteristic Sephardic genre. Typically, they are sung and often are *acrostic poems presenting the letters of the Heb. alphabet or of the author's name. Since they are essentially part of a written trad., they are generally sung by men, unlike the romansas, which are usually performed by women. Among the most traditional complas are those for the festivity of Purim, composed in the 18th and 19th cs., that relate the biblical story of Esther or evoke the joys of the holiday in *strophes of varying lengths, with short or long verses in zéjelesque rhyme (*aaab*; see ZÉJEL), often incl. a *refrain (cf. It. *ballata*; see ITALIAN PROSODY). Other complas celebrate the festivities of Hanukkah, Passover, Pentecost, the Sabbath, the Rejoicing of the Torah, and Arbor Day. There are also dirgelike complas (*Kinot*) that commemorate the destruction of the Temple (70 CE) and other tragic events in ancient Jewish hist. Other complas of a moralizing, admonitory bent (*complas de castiguerio*) preach the glories of God and warn against the illusory nature of worldly attractions. *Complas del felek* (destiny) present the life and customs of late 19th- and early 20th-c. Sephardic Jewry from a satirical or humorous perspective. In *complas de Tebariá* are celebrated the praises of the city of Tiberias, of venerable sages who lived there, and of miracles concerning its Jewish population. Attias and Peretz published another group of poems, *Complas de 'Aliyá* (Songs of Return to Zion, 1996), which give voice to the Jews' longing for redemption and return to Jerusalem in all its glory. Those complas by Abraham Toledo, devoted to the life of Joseph and first published in 1732—part of a subgenre designated as *complas hagiográficas*—constitute for Hassán (1982) perhaps the single greatest poem in Judeo-Sp. In reworking the biblical account of Joseph's life (Gen. 37: 39–45), Toledo used numerous elements from folklore, rabbinical commentaries, and traditional life, presented with lyrical verve, lexical versatility, and rhetorical strength. In comparison to such genres as ballads and proverbs, which have strong Hispanic connections, the study of complas has, until recently, been gravely neglected.

Cantigas are traditional lyric songs, frequently of Hispanic origin in form and content, but, in the Eastern trad., with significant Gr. and Turkish lexical, structural, and thematic influences. Although love in all its vicissitudes is the predominant theme, there are also lyric songs devoted to various functions in the traditional life cycle: *cantigas de boda* (wedding songs), *de parida* (birth songs), and *endechas* (*dirges). Romero (2009) has published a collection of mod. Balkan cantigas on the subject of women's liberation. Many Sephardic lyric songs, esp. in the Eastern communities, are of relatively recent origin (late 19th and early 20th c.) and often consist of *quatrains in *couplets with *assonance; some are modeled on Gr. originals, while others are imported from Spain or Sp. America. But other lyric songs attest to a venerable Sephardic trad. going back to med. Hispanic origins. The parallelistic rhymes of some Eastern poems and of many Moroccan wedding songs—similar to that of the primitive Sp. and Port. lyric—confirm the med. character of the Judeo-

Sp. cantiga trad. Some of these songs, given esoteric kabbalistic interpretations, eventually formed part of the liturgy of the Sabbatean *donmeh* sect of Islamized Jews in Turkey and have been edited and translated by Peretz.

Romansas (Sp. *romances*) are traditional ballads in assonant octosyllabic verse. In content, they are essentially similar—in some cases, genetically related—to *narrative poetry current in other Eur. communities. No other Sephardic genre is so closely linked to its med. Hispanic origins, and none has received as much scholarly attention. Judeo-Sp. ballads can be documented from as early as 1525 through verses used as tune indicators in Heb. hymnals. Several 18th-c. mss. are known, and numerous Eastern ballads were collected and printed in popular Heb.-letter chapbooks in the late 19th and early 20th cs., most recently anthologized by Weich-Shahak (1997, 2010). There are Sephardic ballads derived from med. Sp. and Fr. *epics; others concern events in Sp. and Port. hist. or tell stories from the Bible, cl. antiquity, or med. adventure romances (see MEDIEVAL ROMANCE); still others concern a variety of *topoi (prisoners and captives, the husband's return, faithful or tragic love, the unfortunate wife, the adulteress, amorous adventures, tricks and deceptions). Some ballads function as *epithalamia (wedding songs), others as dirges, still others as *lullabies. Though a majority of Sephardic ballads have med. or 16th-c. Sp. counterparts, others can be shown to derive from mod. Gr. narrative poetry; some were undoubtedly created in the exile communities by the Sephardim themselves. Bénichou's studies of oral trad. as a creative artistic process are essential to ballad crit.

Endevinas (riddles) are often rhymed and, like *proverbs, should count as a part of Sephardic traditional poetry. Of all genres, the riddle has been the most gravely neglected by scholarship. Little fieldwork has been done to collect riddles, and the known Eastern repertoire is still radically limited. Nothing is presently known of the Moroccan Sephardic riddle trad. As far as origins are concerned, a preliminary assessment indicates that Eastern Judeo-Sp. riddles are about evenly divided between texts of med. Hispanic origin and adaptations from Turkish and Gr. In many cases, however, it is impossible to point to a specific origin.

Refranes (proverbs) have been abundantly collected in Heb.-letter chapbooks since the late 19th c. by the Sephardim themselves and also by Western scholars such as Foulché-Delbosc and more recently by the Israeli scholar Tamar-Frizer. Some Sephardic proverbs agree exactly with their Sp. counterparts, while others have obviously been taken over from Gr., Turkish, or biblical Heb. sources.

*See* HEBREW POETRY; LITURGICAL POETRY; PORTUGAL, POETRY OF; SPAIN, POETRY OF.

■ M. Attias, "Shelôshah shîrê Tsîyôn," *Shevet va-'Am* 4 (1959); P. Bénichou, *Creación poética en al romancero tradicional* (1968); M. Alvar, *Endechas judeo-españolas* (1969), and *Cantos de boda judeo-españolas* (1971); S. Armistead, J. Silverman, I. Katz, *Folk Literature of the*

*Sephardic Jews* (1971–94); M. Attias, *Cancionero judeo-español* (1972); E. Romero, "Complas de Tu-Bishbat," *Poesía: Reunión de Málaga*, ed. M. Alvar (1976); L. Carracedo and E. Romero, "Poesía admonitiva," *Sefarad* 37 (1977); S. Armistead et al., *El romancero en el Archivo Menéndez Pidal* (1978); I. Hassán and E. Romero, "Quinot paralitúrgicos," *Estudios Sefardíes* 1 (1978); S. Armistead and J. Silverman, "El antiguo romancero," *Nueva revista de filología Hispánica* 30 (1981); L. Carracedo and E. Romero, "Refranes," *Sefarad* 41 (1981); P. Díaz-Mas, "Romances de endechar," and E. Romero, "Las coplas sefardíes," *Jornadas*, ed. A. Viudas Camarasa (1981); S. Armistead and J. Silverman, *En torno al romancero* (1982); I. Hassán, "Visión panorámica," *Hispania Judaica*, ed. J. M. Solà-Solé (1982); S. Armistead and J. Silverman, "Adivinanzas," *Philologica Hispaniensia in Honorem Manuel Alvar*, ed. M. Alvar (1983); *And the World Stood Silent: Sephardic Poetry of the Holocaust*, trans. I. J. Lévy (1989); M. Attias and A. Peretz, *Shire 'aliyah* (1996); S. Armistead, "Nueve adivinanzas de Estambul," *Sefarad* 58 (1998); J. Cohen, "Review of Judeo-Spanish ('Ladino') Recordings," *Journal of American Folklore* 112 (1999); M. Balbuena, *Diasporic Sephardic Identities* (2003); H. Pomeroy, *An Edition and Study of the Secular Ballads in the Sephardic Ballad Notebook of Halia Isaac Cohen* (2005); R. Foulché-Delbosc, *1313 proverbios judeo-españoles* (2006); *Las coplas de Yosef*, ed. L. Girón-Negrón and L. Minervini (2006); A. Peretz, *Mayim, esh ve-ahavah* (2006); M. Ha-'Elion, *En los kampos de lah muerte* (2008); A. Tamar-Frizer, *La palabra en su hora es oro* (2008); E. Romero, "Textos poéticos," *Sefarad* 69 (2009); S. Weich-Shahak, *Romancero sefardí de Oriente* (2010); E. Gutwirth, "Archival Poetics," *Bulletin of Spanish Studies* 88 (2011).

S. G. ARMISTEAD; J. H. SILVERMAN; D. A. WACKS

**KANNADA POETRY.** Kannada, belonging to the Dravidian family of langs., has the second oldest lit. among all the living langs. of South Asia. The earliest specimen of Kannada writing, the Halmidi inscription (ca. 450 CE), shows that Kannada must have been in use as a medium of poetry for some time already. The earliest complete extant text, the *Kavirājamārga* (9th c., the oldest work in Kannada on poetics, largely following the theories of the Sanskrit author Daṇḍin), gives the names of many older poets of whose works only the fragments that are quoted in this text remain. The meters of this earliest Kannada poetry resemble those of Old Tamil to some extent but are a clearly independent devel. of Dravidian prosody. In 2008, the government of India granted Kannada the official status of "classical language."

Jainism was the dominant religion in the Kannada-speaking part of India until the 12th c. CE, and correspondingly the oldest period of Kannada lit. hist. is dominated by Jaina authors. The oldest independent poetic works that have been preserved in their entirety are the two writings of Paṃpa (10th c.), whom still today some critics consider the greatest Kannada poet. His *Ādipurāṇa* (completed 942), containing the hagiographical account of the life of the first Tīrthaṅkara, one of the holiest persons in Jainism, and his *Vikramārjunavijayam* (959), based on the *Mahābhārata*, are considered the greatest masterpieces of Old Kannada poetry. Paṃpa and his contemps. Ranna and Ponna are commonly referred to as the *ratnatraya* or "three jewels" of Kannada lit. Other Jaina *purāṇa*s in the same *campu* style (a mixture of poetry and prose) continued to be written for several centuries.

The best known works of Kannada poetry in and out of India are the *vacana*s, which are among the most influential literary works in the lang. The vacana (saying) is a particular genre that originated in Kannada in the 11th c. and rose to immense popularity in the 12th c. because of its use as a medium of religious communication in Vīraśaivism, a Śaivite Hindu reform movement. A vacana is a *prose poem, usually a few dozen words in length; it lacks audible rhythmical structural elements but as a rule does have a rhythmic structure in its syntax, with syntactic structures being repeated as a device for underlining parallel metaphorical expressions. Thousands of vacanas from the 12th c. have been preserved. The most prominent *vacanakāra*s (vacana poets) are Basava, who was the main organizer of the Vīraśaiva movement; his spiritual teacher Allama Prabhu; his nephew, the theologian Cennabasava; and the female mystic Mahādēviyakka. The vacana lit. also marks an important turning point in Kannada ling. hist., and a Kannada speaker today can read and understand the majority of 12th-c. vacanas more or less without the help of special aids. Several excerpts from vacanas have become popular sayings far beyond the Vīraśaiva community. Vacanas are still written today.

Another high point in Kannada lit. hist. was reached in the writings of the *haridāsa*s or "servants of Hari," i.e., devotees of the god Viṣṇu. This devotional lit. is associated with the Vaiṣṇava (Viṣṇuite) Hindu reform movement initiated by the philosopher Madhva (1238–1317). The highly lyrical compositions of the haridāsas were in part inspired by earlier Vaiṣṇava devotional poetry by the Ālvārs in Tamil, esp. by the writings of the aforementioned Kannada *vacanakāra*s. Puraṃdaradāsa (1485–1565) is generally considered the foremost among the haridāsa poets, for his poetic imagery and the musicality of his writings; he is also considered the father of Carnatic [South Indian cl.] music. Comparable in fame is his contemp. Kanakadāsa (1491–1580), who wrote not only short lyrical pieces but longer narrative and allegorical poems.

The high quality of mod. poetry in Kannada has been recognized on an Indian national level: the most prestigious national literary award, the Jnanpith Award, has been awarded to seven Kannada writers, among them the three poets Kuveṃpu (pseud. of K. V. Puṭṭappa, 1904–94, known mainly for his rewriting of the *Rāmāyaṇa* epic in Kannada) in 1967; Aṃbikātanayadatta (pseud. of D. R. Bendre [Dattātreya Rāmacaṃdra Bēṃdre], 1896–1981, linguistically the most virtuosic poet in mod. Kannada) in 1973; and Vināyaka (pseud. of V. K. Gokak [V. K. Gōkāka], 1909–92, epic poet) in 1990. Other leading poets of the 20th c. were Gopalakrishna Adiga [Gōpālakṛṣṇa Aḍiga] (1918–92), who is considered the most important representative of the navya or modernist movement, and the highly popular romantic lyricist K. S. Narasimhaswamy [K. S. Narasiṃhasvāmi] (1915–2003), famous esp. for his collection *Maisūru mallige*, (1942). In most recent devels., the socially critical *dalita* movement has produced one noteworthy poet, Siddalingaiah [Siddhaliṃgayya] (b. 1954).

*See* INDIA, POETRY OF; TAMIL POETRY.

■ R. Narasimhacharya, *Karṇāṭaka kavicarite*, 2d ed. 3 v. (1972); A. K. Ramanujan, *Speaking of Śiva* (1973)—selected vacanas; R. S. Mugali, *History of Kannada Literature* (1975); *Modern Kannada Poetry*, ed. C. Kanavi and K. Raghavendra Rao (1976)—bilingual Kannada-Eng. anthol.); *60 Years of Kannada Poetry*, ed. G. S. Sivarudrappa and L. S. Seshagiri Rao (1977); K. V. Zvelebil, *The Lord of the Meeting Rivers* (1984)—selected vacanas of Basava; *A String of Pearls*, ed. H. S. Shivaprakash and K. S. Radhakrishna (1990); W. J. Jackson, *Songs of Three Great South Indian Saints* (1998)—incl. sects. on Puraṃdaradāsa and Kanakadāsa; *The Epic of Nēmi (Nēminātha-purāṇa) of Karṇapārya*, trans. S. Anacker (2002).

R. ZYDENBOS

**KASHMIRI POETRY.** *Kashmiri poetry* is a multiply referential term: geographically, signifying poetry written from the Kashmir Valley or from the wider region of Jammu and Kashmir that has been territorially disputed between India and Pakistan since 1947; linguistically, signifying poetry written in Koshur, the lang. indigenous to the valley or poetry written in the other langs. in use in Jammu and Kashmir, incl. Persian, Urdu, Hindi, and Eng. Arising from a threshold region between Central and South Asia, the term *Kashmiri poetry* in all senses testifies to a multiethnic *ecumene* defined by cultural diversity and political instability. Iconic within this rich poetic corpus are the med. Sufi philosopher-poets writing in Koshur: Lalleshwari or Lal Ded (b. ca. 1335; she is known by both her Sanskritized name Lalleshwari and its more affectionate, vernacularized version Lal Ded [grandmother Lal] in Koshur), who used the gnomic quatrain form *vakh* (see GNOMIC POETRY); Noor-ud-Din or Nund Rishi (1377–1438), composing in another quatrain form, *shrukh*; and Habba Khatoon (fl. late 16th c.), who perfected the lyrical *lol* form. On this vernacular Sufi trad. was erected a literary modernism, from the foundational Ghulam Husain Mahjoor (1885–1952) to the contemp. poet Abdul Rahman Rahi (b. 1925), creators of a poetry that laments in and exalts the Kashmiri mother tongue within a competitive multilingualism. Since the 1990s, a Hindi poetry of exile has been developed by Agni Shekhar (b. 1956), among others, testifying to a specific Kashmiri Hindu subjectivity. The Kashmiri-Am. poet Agha Shahid Ali (1949–2001) transformed these affective complexities by expressing them in a finely wrought Eng.-lang. idiom that united Eur. (e.g., \*canzone) and Urdu (e.g., \*ghazal) poetic forms, paid homage to poets of exile worldwide, from the Palestinian Maḥmūd Darwīsh (1941–2008) to the Russian Osip Mandelstam (1892–1938), and infused Islamic sacred hist. with a sharp awareness of the politics of nationalism. Ali's anthols. *The Country without a Post Office* (2000) and *Rooms Are Never Finished* (2002) constitute an exquisitely refined, poignant, and haunting lyrical record of the Kashmir conflict, its roots and its emotional consequences.

*See* HINDI POETRY; INDIA, ENGLISH POETRY OF; INDIA, POETRY OF; PERSIAN POETRY; SANSKRIT POETICS; SANSKRIT POETRY; URDU POETRY.

■ G. Grierson, *Lalla-Vakyani or The Wise Sayings of Lal-Ded—A Mystic Poetess of Ancient Kashmir* (1920); G. M. Sufi, *Kashir* (1948); N. C. Cook, *The Way of the Swan: Poems from Kashmir* (1958); T. Raina, *An Anthology of Modern Kashmiri Verse, 1930–1960* (1972); B. B. Kachru, *Kashmiri Literature* (1981); C. Zutshi, *Languages of Belonging: Islam, Regional Identity and the Making of Kashmir* (2004); A. J. Kabir, *Territory of Desire: Representing the Valley of Kashmir* (2009).

A. J. KABIR

**KENNING** (pl. *kenningar*). A multinoun substitution for a single noun, e.g. "din of spears" for battle.

Although found in many poetries, the kenning is best known from Old Germanic verse. Kennings are common in West Germanic poetry, and scholars have recognized a kenning in the expression of "corpse-sea," i.e., "blood," on the Eggjum runic inscription from western Norway, ca. 700 CE. ON eddic poetry (see EDDA) also makes use of kennings, but their greatest importance was in skaldic poetry.

In med. Icelandic rhet., the verb *kenna* (*við*), "make known (by)," was used to explain these expressions: "din" (the base word in mod. analysis) is "made known" as battle by "of spears" (the determinant). The determinant may be in the genitive case, as here, or may attach to the base word to form a compound (spear-din); the base word takes the morphological and syntactic form of the concept the kenning replaces. In skaldic poetry, the determinant could, in turn, be replaced by another determinant; if "flame of battle" means "sword," then "flame of the din of spears" makes an acceptable kenning. Snorri Sturluson, the 13th-c. poet and man of letters and the first to attempt a rhet. of kennings, called this example *tvíkennt* (twice-determined) in the commentary to *Háttatal* in his *Edda*. If another determinant were added, to make a four-part kenning, he would call it *rekit*, "driven." Snorri cautioned against "driven" kennings with more than six parts.

The relationship between the base word and determinant(s) could be essentially metonymic, as in "Baldr's father" for Odin, or metaphoric, as in the examples above. The kennings of West Germanic poetry, frequently used in connection with variation, tend toward the first category, those of skaldic poetry toward the second. Many skaldic kennings rely on Norse mythology or heroic legend for the links between the parts; thus, poetry is the "theft of Odin" because he stole it from the giants. In skaldic poetry, the number of concepts for which kennings may substitute is limited to about 100, among which warrior, woman, weapons, and battle are well represented. Since the base words tend to be fairly stereotyped (kennings for "woman" often have the name of a goddess as base word, e.g.), the system is relatively closed, but kennings make up nearly all the nouns in skaldic poetry, and the verbs are not important. Having imposed on themselves this closed system, the skalds exploited it brilliantly. In skaldic poetry, the sum of the kennings is, to be sure, greater than their parts, but the best skalds made every word count.

*See* NORSE POETRY.

■ R. Meissner, *Die Kenningar der Skalden* (1921); H. van der Merwe Scholtz, *The Kenning in Anglo-Saxon and Old Norse Poetry* (1927); H. Lie, *"Natur" og "unatur" i skaldekunsten* (1957); R. Frank, *Old Norse Court Poetry* (1978); Snorri Sturluson, *Edda,* ed. A. Faulkes (1982–98); E. Marold, *Kenningkunst* (1983); M. Clunies Ross, *Skáldskaparmál* (1986); F. Amory, "Kennings, Referentiality, and Metaphors," *Arkiv för nordisk filologi* (1988); G. Holland, "Kennings, Metaphors, and Semantic Formulae in Old Norse dröttkvætt," *Arkiv för nordisk filologi* (2005).

J. LINDOW

**KHARJA** (also *xarja*; Sp. *jarcha*). The term *kharja*, along with its less common variant, *markaz*, refers to the final segment (Ar. *qufl*) of the Andalusi poetic form known as the *muwashshah* (Sp. *moaxajá*). Developed in *Al-Andalus (i.e., Muslim Iberia) as a performative poetic genre in cl. Ar. and Heb. during the 10th c. CE, the muwashshah is characterized by its highly structured strophic form. In Ar., the noun *kharja* can mean "exit" or "departure," as well as "projection" or "conspicuous part," and both semantic domains have more or less equal importance for the kharja, given its placement at the end of the muwashshah (a kind of "exit segment") and the ling., discursive, and thematic prominence that the kharja enjoys within the poem as a whole. For scholars of med. Iberian lit., the kharja is significant because of its early devel., as well as the fact that just over 60 of them were composed (at least partially) in a Romance dialect particular to Muslim Iberia.

Perhaps the most polemical aspect of kharja research over the past several decades has been the question of its origins. The pressing question for scholars concerned with Romance lit., e.g., has been whether the Ibero-Romance kharjas emerge from a preexisting popular lyric trad. (Armistead 1982, 1985, 1987; García Gómez; Lapesa; Menéndez Pidal 1951; Monroe, 1982, 1985). For Arabists, the issue of primary interest has been to determine how Andalusi strophic poetry in general derived from Ar. poetic genres inherited from the East (Abū Haidar 2001, 2005; Hitchcock 1973, 1977, 1980, 1985; Jones). Much of the debate surrounding the kharjas, which reached its highest levels during the 1980s, has been the result of the perceived incommensurability of these two scholarly projects. Recent scholarship has sought to bring together arguments from both disciplines to form a more contextualized, performance-oriented understanding of Andalusi lang. and culture (Corriente, Rosen, Zwartjes).

Scholarly interest in the kharjas grew dramatically after the publication in 1948 of Samuel M. Stern's discovery of a relatively large number of Romance kharjas in the Heb. muwashshahāt found in the Cairo Geniza. This interest quickly prompted eds. in Spain to begin to include the Romance kharjas in literary anthols.; thus, what are essentially the final verses of cl. Ar. and Heb. strophic poems soon became a mainstay within poetic collections aimed at university and secondary-school students in Spain and beyond. In almost all cases, these kharjas were published without the muwashshahāt from which they had been extracted, and in mod. Sp. trans.

In his late 12th-c. treatise on Ar. poetry, Ibn Sanā' al-Mulk (1155–1211) argues that "the *kharja* is the spice of the *muwashshah*, its salt and sugar, its musk and amber.

It is the close of the *muwashshah*; it must, therefore, be beautiful; it is its seal; nay, it is the beginning, although it is at the end" (trans. Stern 1974). Unavoidably recontextualized and multilingual components of Andalusi strophic poems, the kharjas—whether written in Romance, Andalusi Ar., or some combination of the two (leaving aside the small subgroup of *panegyric and religious kharjas written in cl. Ar. and Heb.)—provide a potentially rich and complex textual locus for the study of Andalusi lang. use, musical composition, and communicative practice.

■ R. Menéndez Pidal, *Discurso acerca de la primitiva poesía lírica española, leído en la inauguración del curso de 1919 a 1920* (1919); S. M. Stern, "Les vers finaux en espagnol dans les *muwaššahs* hispano-hébraïques: Une contribution à l'histoire du *muwaššah* et à l'étude du vieux dialecte espagnol 'mozarabe,'" *Al-Andalus* 13 (1948); R. Menéndez Pidal, "Cantos románicos y andalusíes, continuadores de una lírica latina vulgar," *Boletín de la Real Academia Española* 31 (1951); R. Lapesa, "Sobre el texto y lenguaje de algunas jarchas mozárabes," *Boletín de la Real Academia Española* 40 (1960); R. Hitchcock, "Some Doubts about the Reconstruction of the *Kharjas*," *BHS* 50 (1973); E. García Gómez, "Métrica de la moaxaja y métrica española: Aplicación de un nuevo método de medición completa al 'Ġaiš' de Ben al-Jaṭīb," *Al-Andalus* 39 (1974); S. M. Stern, *Hispano-Arabic Strophic Poetry* (1974); R. Hitchcock, "Sobre la 'mama' en las jarchas," *Journal of Hispanic Philology* 2 (1977); A. D. Deyermond, *Las jarchas y la lírica tradicional* (1979); R. Hitchcock, *The Kharjas as Early Romance Lyrics* (1980); and "Las jarchas treinta años después," *Awraq* 3 (1980); A. Jones, "Romance Scansion and the *Muwaššahāt*: An Emperor's New Clothes?" *Journal of Arabic Literature* 11 (1980); and "Sunbeams from Cucumbers? An Arabist's Assessment of the State of *Kharja* Studies," *La Corónica* 10 (1981); S. G. Armistead, "Speed or Bacon? Further Meditations on Professor Alan Jones," and J. T. Monroe, "¿*Pedir peras al olmo*? On Medieval Arabs and Modern Arabists," *La Corónica* 10 (1982); A. Jones, "Eppur si muove," *La Corónica* 12 (1983); S. G. Armistead, "Pet Theories and Paper Tigers," *La Córonica* 14 (1985); R. Hitchcock, "The Interpretation of Romance Words in Arabic Texts: Theory and Practice," *La Corónica* 13 (1985); S. G. Armistead and J. T. Monroe, "Beached Whales and Roaring Mice: Additional Remarks in Hispano-Arabic Strophic Poetry," *La Corónica* 13 (1985); and "Poetic Quotation in the *Muwaššah* and Its Implications: Andalusian Strophic Poetry as Song," *La Corónica* 14 (1986); S. G. Armistead, "A Brief History of Kharja Studies," *Hispania* 70 (1987); F. Corriente, *Modified 'Arūḍ: An Integrated Theory for the Origin and Nature of Both Andalusi Arabic Strophic Poetry and Sephardic Hebrew Verse* (1991); J. T. Monroe, "Zajal and Muwashshaha: Hispano-Arabic Poetry and the Romance Tradition," *The Legacy of Muslim Spain*, ed. S. K. Jayyusi (1992); A. Sáenz-Badillos, "Nueva propuesta de lectura de las xarajāt con texto romance de la serie hebrea," *Revista de Filología Española* 74 (1994); O. Zwartjes, *The Andalusian Xarja-s: Poetry at the Crossroads of Two Systems?* (1995); F. Corriente, *Poesía dialectal árabe y romance de Alandalús* (1997); O. Zwartjes, *Love Songs from al-Andalus: History, Structure and Meaning of the Kharja* (1997); A. P. Espósito, "The Monkey in the *Jarcha*: Tradition and Canonicity in the Early Iberian Lyric," *Journal of Medieval and Early Modern Studies* 30 (2000); T. Rosen, *The Muwashshah* (2000); J. A. Abū Haidar, *Hispano-Arabic Literature and the Early Provençal Lyrics* (2001), and "The Muwashshahat and the Kharjas Tell Their Own Story," *Al-Qantara* 26 (2005).

V. BARLETTA

**KIND.** Essential to both the production and reception of lit. during the Ren., *kind* (sometimes *species*) was the Eng. term for *genre or the grouping of works into types according to a variety of characteristic properties. Some of the variables that informed judgment on kind include manner of representation (narrative, dramatic, "mixed," *lyric), style of *diction (high, middle, or low), the nature and scope of subject matter, prosody, plot structure, social status of characters, and length. The concept of kind encompassed prescriptive guidelines for composing poetry that would bring about certain affective outcomes (e.g., *satire is supposed to hold up vice to ridicule), as well as evaluative descriptions of the qualities deemed to be held in common. Major poetical kinds of the period, e.g., *epic, *tragedy, *comedy, *pastoral, and the *sonnet, were often placed in a hierarchy of cultural value—with epic, tragedy, and *hymn vying for supremacy. Several kinds either new (e.g., the *emblem) or revived from antiquity (e.g., the essay, the *encomium) flourished in the Ren., though some burgeoning kinds, such as the *tragicomedy, were the subject of critical controversy for their hybridity. Theorists of poetry (esp. in Italy, where such theorizing proliferated in the 16th c.), notably J. C. Scaliger (*Poetices libri septem*, 1561), Lodovico Castelvetro (*Poetica d'Aristotele vulgarizzata e sposta*, 1570, 1576), and Antonio Minturno (*De poeta*, 1559), developed their ideas about kind chiefly in dialogue with Aristotle, whose *Poetics* had established a scheme for poetic kinds. In the second half of the 20th c., literary scholars by and large claimed that kinds are properly understood to be "instrument[s] . . . of meaning" (Fowler 1982), interpretive "frames" for looking onto the world (Colie), and "shared assumptions" about how lit. was supposed to function (Orgel). *Kind* was itself a *topos* in which ideas were exchanged about the historical devel. of, and contemp. relationship among, literary forms.

■ J. C. Scaliger, *Select Translations from Scaliger's Poetics*, trans. F. M. Padelford (1905); J. E. Spingarn, *A History of Literary Criticism in the Renaissance*, 2d ed. (1924); N. H. Pearson, "Literary Forms and Types; or, A Defense of Polonius," *English Institute Annual 1940* (1941); Weinberg; R. L. Colie, *The Resources of Kind* (1973); T. Todorov, "The Origin of Genres," *NLH* 8 (1976); S. Orgel, "Shakespeare and the Kinds of Drama," *CritI* 6 (1979); H. Du-

brow, *Genre* (1982); A. Fowler, *Kinds of Literature* (1982); L. Castelvetro, *Castelvetro on the Art of Poetry*, trans. A. Bongiorno (1984); *Renaissance Genres*, ed. B. K. Lewalski (1986); *English Renaissance Literary Criticism*, ed. B. Vickers (1999); L. Danson, *Shakespeare's Dramatic Genres* (2000); A. Fowler, "The Formation of Genres in the Renaissance and After," *NLH* 34 (2003); *La notion de genre à la Renaissance*, ed. G. Demerson (2004); *The Formation of the Genera in Early Modern Culture*, ed. C. L. Guest (2009); J. Roe, "Theories of Literary Kinds," *A New Companion to English Renaissance Literature and Culture*, ed. M. Hattaway (2010).

F. L. BLUMBERG

**KNITTELVERS** (also *Knüttelvers*, *Knüppelvers*, *Klippelvers*, *Reimvers*). Originally a Ger. verse measure from the 15th to the early 17th c. that appeared in all poetry that was not sung and thus had great influence on the devel. of lyric, epic, and dramatic verse. From the Middle High Ger. *knittel*, meaning "rhyme," but also sometimes called *Knüttelvers* (from *knüttel* or *keule* meaning "club") because of its irregular rhythm.

Since the 18th c., the term *knittelvers* (originally a Ger. designation for Lat. verse in leonine hexameters) has been used to describe two types of four-stressed rhymed couplets in Ger. and Scandinavian verse: "free Knittelvers" (*freier Knittelvers*) consists of lines varying in number of syllables (usually 6–15 per line); "strict Knittelvers" (*strenger Knittelvers*), primarily a 16th-c. phenomenon sometimes called *Hans-Sachs-Vers*, consists exclusively of eight-syllable masculine and nine-syllable feminine lines in couplets. Knittelvers can be traced back to Otfrid of Weissenburg who, using Lat. verse as a model, introduced couplets into Ger. verse in the 9th c. Free Knittelvers predominates in the Shrovetide plays (*Fastnachtsspiele*) of Hans Rosenplüt and Hans Folz in the 15th c.; strict Knittelvers prevails from the late 15th to the late 16th c. (e.g., Sebastian Brant, Hans Sachs, Johann Fischart). Led by Martin Opitz, 17th-c. poets rejected both forms and used *Knittelvers* as a derogatory term to refer to the unwieldly rhythms and crude subject matter—usually humorous or satirical, often earthy and pithy, sometimes even obscene—of these 16th-c. couplets.

In the 18th c., free Knittelvers was revived by J. C. Gottsched and used later by J. W. Goethe (*Hanswursts Hochzeit*, *Jahrmarktsfest zu Plundersweilern*, and parts of *Urfaust*, *Faust*, and the *West-östlicher Divan*), Friedrich Schiller (*Wallensteins Lager*), and other poets (J. G. Herder, G. A. Bürger, J.M.R. Lenz), e.g.:

> Habe nun, ach, die Philosophie,
> Medizin und Juristerei,
> Und leider auch die Theologie
> Durchaus studiert mit heißer Müh.
> Da steh ich nun, ich armer Tor,
> Und bin so klug, als wie zuvor.
>
> (Goethe, *Urfaust*)

In general, the metrical form of 19th-c. Knittelvers (as in J. F. Eichendorff, Heinrich Heine, Eduard

Mörike, Friedrich Hebbel, Theodor Storm, Gottfried Keller, and Theodor Fontane) and turn-of-the-century Knittelvers (Detlev Liliencron, Richard Dehmel, Arno Holz, Arthur Schnitzler) is quite similar to that written in the late 18th c. In the 1780s, however, Goethe's contemporary Karl Arnold Kortum developed a new form of Knittelvers (*Die Jobsiade*, 1784, 1799) consisting of quatrains in which a masculine couplet is followed by a feminine couplet. Many lines are extremely long (15 or more syllables), with the result that syllables bearing word-stress often occur in metrically unstressed positions:

>     /        /    /    /
> So kann man nur hier das Rätsel lösen
>     /           /
> Was die *Kapitel* sechs und sieben
>      /        /
> *beschreib'ne* Krankheit gewesen
>
>                     (*Die Jobsiade*)

Kortum's variant of Knittelvers was later imitated by Wilhelm Busch, Julius Bierbaum, and most successfully by Frank Wedekind (*Santa Simplicitas*; *Politische Lieder*), but it has not been used since.

In the 20th c. Gerhart Hauptmann, Hugo von Hofmannsthal, Max Mell, Peter Weiss, and Peter Hacks have used Knittelvers in dramatic works, and poets such as Bertolt Brecht, Karl Kraus, Peter Huchel, Wolf Biermann, and Christoph Meckel wrote short poems in this verse form. Knittelvers was used by Kurt Tucholsky for a number of cabaret texts and a long political-satirical poem (*Die verkehrte Welt in Knüttelversen dargestellt von Kaspar Hauser*, 1922). Today, Knittelvers continues to be used as a medium for political and social *satire and *parody, and to depict lower-class people in burlesque, *mock-heroic, and tragicomic situations. These couplets are often used in children's verse and are spoken at carnival festivities (*Fasching*) in Mainz and elsewhere in local dialects as well as in standard Ger.

■ O. Flohr, *Gesch. des Knittelvers vom 17. Jahrhundert bis zur Jugend Goethes* (1893); E. Feise, *Der Knittelvers des jungen Goethe* (1909); A. Heusler, *Deutsche Versgesch.*, 3 v. (1925–29), esp. v. 3; W. Kayser, *Gesch. des deutschen Verses* (1960); H.-J. Schlütter, "Der Rhythmus im strengen Knittelvers des 16. Jahrhunderts," *Euphorion* 60 (1966); H. Heinen, *Die rhythmisch-metrische Gestaltung des Knittelvers bei Hans Folz* (1966); D. Chisholm, *Goethe's Knittelvers* (1975), "Der deutsche Knittelvers—alt und neu," *Akten des VII* (1985), and "Prosodic Aspects of German Hexameter Verse," *PoT* 16.3 (1995); C. Wagenknecht, "Knittelvers, Meistersang, Kirchenlied," *Deutsche Metrik* (2007).

                   D. H. CHISHOLM; K. BOWERS

**KNOWLEDGE, POETRY AS.** What does a poet want? W. H. Auden asks himself that in a brief, cryptic, question-filled poem of 1937 titled "Orpheus." "What does the song hope for?" he wonders. A simple, crea-turely joy? Or a deep, human level of understanding? Does the poet desire "To be bewildered and happy?" Or, Auden speculates, does the poet seek "most of all the *knowledge of life*?" (italics added).

In lang., the mirror opposite of the social world, pride of place comes last. Auden's "Orpheus" locates the notion that poets might most intensely crave "the knowledge of life" at the end of its array of questions. The idea concludes a stanza, and the sonorous disyllabic ripple of the word "knowledge" in a line otherwise entirely filled with staccato monosyllables gives that term a formal idiosyncrasy implying authorial endorsement. According to the hints "Orpheus" gives, poets go down into the compositional underworld of poetry not for love or happiness or melody but to win the darker, deeper prize of "knowledge."

Auden's bold poetic claim resonates interestingly with its critical moment. A long vernacular trad. extending from the *troubadours through *medieval poetics and *Renaissance poetics and best articulated in Auden's time by the *New Criticism insists that poetry bears or offers a distinctive kind of knowledge about the world. The New Critics' position, developed by John Crowe Ransom and Allen Tate, among others, was that poetry creates "a kind of knowledge which is radically or ontologically distinct" from science or other disciplines (Ransom 1941). Science, hist., and other discourses give us the world in diagram or abstract, but poetry provides what Ransom called "the world's body" and Tate, "a whole object."

This idea has survived only fitfully among the influential critical preoccupations of the past two generations. True, a certain strand of writing within both recent and contemp. poetry crit. focuses on the philosophical dimensions of poetry. The etymological roots of *philosophy* notwithstanding, however, this approach does not strictly relate to an interest in poetry encoded with any specific body of expertise or set of beliefs. Instead, with subject matter positioned as little more than the necessary enabling pretext for reflection, like the insignificant grain of grit stimulating the oyster, philosophical crit. typically focuses on a special kind of thought process that poetry is supposed to dramatize or enable, leading to a "thinking more rigorous than the conceptual," as Martin Heidegger asserted in "Letter on Humanism" (1947). Academic critics still write about poets' knowledge of their precursors or of, say, astrological or medical discourse. But since the critical focus on a poet's understanding of an intellectual trad. or a political moment almost always correlates with deference to his or her conscious *intentions in a poem, this procedure has become almost suspect in a discipline troubled by issues of ling. referentiality and wary over biographical or intentionalist reductions of literary texts (see BIOGRAPHY AND POETRY).

To compound these difficulties, granting poetry—the most archaic of the major *genres—a special, privileged epistemological status or advocating for it as the embodiment of knowledge (or any of the related concepts in the general semantic field, such as *belief, *information, or wisdom) sometimes suggests a retro-grade cultural stance. Ludwig Wittgenstein's delphic warning not to forget "that a poem, even though it is composed in the language of information, is not used in the language-game of giving information" (*Zettel*, 1967) is one that a reader encounters almost monotonously in the pages of contemp. scholarship on poetry.

Indeed, for some commentators, poetry has been defined precisely by its opposition to a certain kind of positivistic knowledge. This trad. goes back at least as far as Samuel Johnson's Imlac, who tells Rasselas that it is not the business of the poet to "number the streaks of the tulip, or describe the different shades of the verdure of the forest" (*Rasselas*, 1759). For Theodor Adorno and Max Horkheimer, writing in the immediate postgenocidal, post-Hiroshima period, knowledge was tyranny, and poetry was its antithesis: "For the Enlightenment, anything which cannot be resolved into numbers, and ultimately one, is illusion; modern positivism consigns it to poetry" (*Dialectic of Enlightenment*, 1947). From the mid-20th c. on, critics have frequently spoken of poetry, tacitly or explicitly, dismissively or honorifically, as the negation of knowledge, as a content- and proposition-empty genre, freighted with seams of *irony, *indeterminacy, and *ambiguity that seem antithetical to the pursuit of truth. Indeed, in some of the most influential crit. of the last 50 years, poetry has come to seem like a track leading away from intellectual or empirical clarities and from any specific knowledge about the world. That is the case, e.g., with Hartman's account of William Wordsworth's disengagement from the natural scene he found spread before him in the Alps and Hartman's claim that this disengagement was the precondition for Wordsworth's growth as a poet. This was so, Hartman argued, because "blindness to the external world" constituted "the tragic, pervasive and necessary condition of the mature poet."

But what many critics for many reasons have demurred from, many poets have endorsed. For them, Auden's suggestion (that poets want to achieve a "knowledge of life") remains beautiful and appealing because it remains central to the poetic calling. Whether esoteric or exoteric, intellectual or practical, universal or personal, the drive for knowledge is enduringly one of the announced ambitions of *lyric poetry. It might even seem that part of every poet whom anyone has felt it worth thinking about could be represented by Alfred, Lord Tennyson's Ulysses, whose hopeless but heroic quest is to "To follow knowledge like a sinking star, / Beyond the utmost bound of human thought."

Occasions when poets assertively link poetry to some species of knowledge are widely distributed through lit. hist., esp. in the works of self-consciously and ambitiously learned writers. John Milton, for instance, stressed the connection between knowledge and a personal knowing of God. And, at the opening of *Paradise Lost*, he prayed for metaphysical inspiration (or divine knowledge), asking "What in me is dark / Illumine, what is low raise and support, / That to the height of this great argument / I may assert eternal Providence." Across the subsequent centuries, other poets have returned repeatedly, if from very different angles, to the

strong relation between poetry and knowledge. Johnson (a poet) censured Alexander Pope's *Essay on Man* because its "penury of knowledge" vitiated its formal beauties ("Life of Pope," 1781). "Poetry is the breath and finer spirit of all knowledge," Wordsworth wrote (Preface to the 2d ed. of *Lyrical Ballads*, 1800), and P. B. Shelley claimed that poetry is "the centre and circumference of knowledge" (*A Defence of Poetry*, 1821). Their successor, Matthew Arnold, sustained the romantic affiliation of knowledge with poetry while faulting *romanticism because "with plenty of energy, plenty of creative force, [it] did not *know enough*" ("The Function of Criticism at the Present Time," 1864; italics added).

What *knowledge* meant for each of these writers varies considerably. E.g., its unspoken ground alters from biblical certainties in Milton's case through humanistic learning with Johnson and something akin to experience or observation in Wordsworth on to a revolutionary, counterempirical mysticism in Shelley and a bedrock of socially acceptable literary touchstones and periodical learning in Arnold. But the thrust of ideas about a singular correlation between poetry (itself a term with many meanings) and knowledge is persistent.

Poetic claims to knowledge have hardly diminished during the century of *modernism and its aftermath, nor has this linking of poetry and knowledge ever been a purely anglophone phenomenon. It is hard for many readers of mod. poetry to think about knowledge in poetry without remembering T. S. Eliot's "After such knowledge, what forgiveness?" and Elizabeth Bishop's "At the Fishhouses," in which the abstract word "knowledge" sounds out starkly among Bishop's welter of naturalistic detail: "It is like what we imagine knowledge to be . . . / and since / our knowledge is historical, flowing, and flown." During the same era, poets of many trads. and cultures were making similar claims and connections. Thus, in 1944, the Martinican poet Aimé Césaire insisted that "poetic knowledge [*connaissance*] is born in the great silence of scientific knowledge." And for the Mexican poet Octavio Paz (in the opening words of *The Bow and the Lyre* [1956]), "[P]oetry is knowledge [*conocimiento*], salvation, power, abandonment." Here again, what each poet means by the umbrella term "knowledge" varies considerably, but each identically insists on the presence of a special kind of significant content in poetry.

If we accept for a moment the poets' declarations that poetry *is* knowledge, then this must mean that the knowledge in question is a justified and correct belief *about* something in particular. This is because knowledge always has a subject. (We can know nothing about something, but it is impossible to know something about nothing.) The types of knowledge in which poetry has traditionally dealt can be broadly divided into five categories. First, there is poetic knowledge as mythic or historical memory or as "the tale of the tribe" (Kipling via Pound, *Guide to Kulchur*, 1938). This is the kind of knowledge that the *Epic of Gilgamesh* records for posterity in its tales about the triumphs of the eponymous king of Uruk or that the Homeric *epics codify in their accounts of the war between the Greeks and the Trojans and its consequences. (This knowledge-as-memory trad. reaches a parodic termination in Eliot's pathos-filled attempt to cram a massively fragmented and enigmatic account of several millennia's worth of Western cultural memory into *The Waste Land*.) Second, poetic knowledge can be the result of access to supernatural or divine truth, as when Dante explains to the reader at the start of the *Paradiso* that he has been "in that Heaven that knows His light most, and [has] seen things, which whoever descends from there has neither power, nor knowledge, to relate." Nevertheless, he adds, "whatever, of the sacred regions, I had power to treasure in my mind, will now be the subject of my labour." (This metaphysical trad. ramifies into the multiple branches of heterodox knowledge secreted in subsequent poetry, from the "continued Allegory, or darke conceit" supposedly ciphered into *The Faerie Queene* [Edmund Spenser, "Letter to Ralegh"] through to the intricate occult symbolism woven into the work of later writers such as Stéphane Mallarmé, W. B. Yeats, and Robert Duncan.) Third, poetry has been on occasion a means of recording a body of practical expertise or experience, a poetry *of* knowledge as it were, such as one finds in the accounts of sowing and harvesting in James Thomson's *The Seasons* or in Thomas Hardy's poetry about rural labor. (It is from this trad. that the modes of *confession and witness in poetry—so crucial to the writing of poets as diverse as Wilfred Owen, Paul Celan, and Adrienne Rich—derive.) And fourth, knowledge and poetry can commingle as knowledge *of* poetry, a discernible impression within a poem of expertise or adroitness with the genre itself. This kind of knowledge manifests internal self-awareness through allusions that demonstrate a familiarity with past poetic trads. or through overt technical virtuosity, whether of a traditional kind, using "[c]omplicated verse forms of great technical difficulty, such as Englyns, Drott-Kvaetts, Sestinas" (Auden, "Making, Knowing and Judging," 1956), or of an experimental and individualistic kind, as in the "mak[ing] it new" of Walt Whitman, Emily Dickinson, and innumerable later poets.

Finally, there is one other important kind of knowledge found in poems, a kind both pervasive and elusive, which stands at an angle to the trads. of substantive knowledge in poetry just described and which is perhaps a subtle counterpoint to those trads. That is the knowledge that simultaneously recognizes its own literal untruthfulness and its figurative veracity. Some have called it "poetic fiction," and virtually all poets, not least the erudite poets of the knowledge trad., have indulged in it seriously and to the genre's immense benefit.

Contemplating the multiplicity of assertions from poets across many centuries about how poetry and knowledge are deeply interconnected with one another, it is hard not to wonder whether some critics' distaste for the idea is not an aberration, like a brief interlude of *Alexandrianism within a larger epoch of dogmas. The necessary relations between a claim to special knowledge and a claim to special authority make the subject a politically ambiguous one. But enough practitioners have argued that poetry seeks a unique knowledge that it is difficult to dismiss such

an idea out of hand. To an extent, the assertion that poetry directly knows anything specific as a genre or that particular poems contain some unique or particular kind of knowledge is hard to analyze in the medium critics write in, prose. And yet poets keep returning to the theme of knowledge in poetry and keep insisting on its importance. Given this reality, one way of thinking about the presence of knowledge in poetry might be to search for its aura or haze rather than for its exact location. Like it or not, poetry has a species of knowledge in the way that Joseph Conrad's narrator, using a poetic *metaphor, said that Marlow had a species of understanding: "to him the meaning of an episode was not inside like a kernel but outside, enveloping the tale which brought it out only as a glow brings out a haze, in the likeness of one of these misty halos that sometimes are made visible by the spectral illumination of moonshine" (*Heart of Darkness*, 1902).

Auden implied that poets will always be intoxicatingly tempted to search for a "knowledge of life." As long as that search lasts, scholars reading poets' works will continue to be provoked, discomfited, and inspired by their diligent hunts for the life (or the afterlife) of knowledge.

*See* ARTIFACT, POETRY AS; FICTION, POETRY AS; GAI SABER; INFORMATION, POETRY AS; PHILOSOPHY AND POETRY; POET.

■ J. C. Ransom, *The World's Body* (1938), and *The New Criticism* (1941), esp. "Wanted: An Ontological Critic"; Brooks; G. Hartman, *Wordsworth's Poetry: 1787–1814* (1964); A. Tate, "Literature as Knowledge" and "Tension in Poetry," *Essays of Four Decades* (1968); O. Paz, *The Bow and the Lyre*, trans. R.L.C. Simms (1973); E. Miner, "That Literature Is a Kind of Knowledge," *CritI* 2 (1976); *Poetic Knowledge*, ed. R. Hagenbüchle and J.T. Swann (1980); *Poetry and Epistemology*, ed. R. Hagenbüchle and L. Skandera (1986); J. Simpson, "Poetry as Knowledge: Dante's *Paradiso* XIII," *Forum for Modern Language Studies* 25 (1989); A. Césaire, "Poetry and Knowledge," *Lyric and Dramatic Poetry 1946–1982*, trans. C. Eshleman and A. Smith (1990); M. Scroggins, *Louis Zukofsky and the Poetry of Knowledge* (1998); R. Geuss, "Poetry and Knowledge," and G. W. Most, "Poetry, Knowledge, and Dr. Geuss," *Arion* 11 (2003); R. von Hallberg, "Lyric Thinking," *TriQuarterly* 120 (2005); *Poetry, Knowledge and Community in Late Medieval France*, ed. R. Dixon and F. E. Sinclair (2008); T. Pfau, "'All Is Leaf': Difference, Metamorphosis, and Goethe's Phenomenology of Knowledge," *SIR* 49 (2010); R. Scharfman, "Aimé Césaire: Poetry Is/ and Knowledge," *Research in African Literatures* 41 (2010).

N. JENKINS

**KOKINSHŪ.** The *Kokinwakashū* (Collection of Old and New Japanese Poems), often known as *Kokinshū*, is an anthol. of Japanese court poetry (*waka*) compiled ca. 905. The most widely circulated version of the text consists of 1,111 poems in 20 volumes, plus prefaces in Japanese and Chinese. Compiled by a committee of poets headed by Ki no Tsurayuki (ca. 868–945), following a command from Emperor Daigo (r. 897–930), the *Kokinshū* occupies a uniquely significant position in Japanese lit. hist. as the first imperially commissioned anthol. (*chokusenshū*) of waka. The *Kokinshū* represented a reemergence of waka into public life following a period in which poetry in Chinese (*kanshi*; see CHINESE POETRY IN JAPAN) had enjoyed overwhelming popularity at court and came to be heavily canonized and vastly influential, regarded by later Japanese poets as a seminal text in the hist. of waka.

The poems of the *Kokinshū* are almost all in the standard 31-syllable form of court waka, although the collection also includes a handful of poems in other, older forms rarely seen in later chokusenshū. *Kokinshū* poetry uses refined and elegant lang., frequently has a witty or questioning tone, and is often characterized by intricate wordplay, a feature greatly facilitated by the rhetorical device most often associated with *Kokinshū* poetry, the "pivot word" (*kakekotoba*), a type of literary pun. Poems are typically preceded by a headnote identifying their author, topic, and the circumstances of their composition.

Commissioned to preserve for posterity "old poems" not included in the *Man'yōshū* and their own poems, the compilers of the *Kokinshū* selected compositions that can be broadly classified into three groups: older poems, from before the mid-9th c.; poems by court poets from the recent past (mid- to late 9th c.) and poems by contemp. poets, incl. Tsurayuki and the other *Kokinshū* eds. The *Kokinshū* includes works by 130 named poets, while approximately 450 poems are recorded as anonymous compositions. Much editorial attention was paid not only to the selection of poems but to the arrangement and sequencing of poems within the volumes of the anthol. The two main topics of poetry in the *Kokinshū* are the seasons (v. 1–6) and love (v. 11–15); other topics include felicitations (v. 7), travel (v. 9), laments (v. 16), and miscellaneous subjects (v. 17–19). Poems are assigned to each volume based on their topics and carefully ordered within each volume. For instance, the first volume of spring poetry starts with poems mentioning New Year's Day (the first day of spring under the lunar calendar), then continues with poems featuring various spring phenomena—flora, fauna, court festivals—in the order in which they were conventionally supposed to occur. A similar pattern is seen in the other books of seasonal poetry. Poems in the volumes of love poetry follow a loose narrative arc, moving from the first stirrings of desire in volume 11 to the aftermath of separation in volume 15.

The importance of *Kokinshū* in the later court-poetic trad. is due not only to its poetry but in large part to the influence of its prefaces in presenting an idealized view of waka. Drawing in part on Chinese models, including the Great Preface to the *Shijing* (*Classic of Poetry*, also known as the *Book of Songs*), Tsurayuki's Japanese preface, starting with the famous declaration that "Japanese poetry takes the human heart as its seed, becoming myriad leaves of words," came to be revered by later poets as the definitive statement on the divine origins, illustrious hist., and expressive and pragmatic nature of Japanese court poetry. In addition to its literary qualities, the *Kokinshū*, like other chokusenshū, had an important sociopolitical function by virtue of its connection to the imperial line. A chokusenshū served to demonstrate the prestige of the commissioning emperor by presenting outstanding poems as representative of his reign, while simultaneously affirming the social order engendered by his rule.

Initially legitimized as an authoritative text by its imperial commission, the *Kokinshū* was recanonized in the late 12th c. as a poetic classic of unrivalled prestige and remained at the apex of the poetic canon for centuries to come. The structure and lang. of the *Kokinshū* served as models for later chokusenshū and for acceptable waka diction in general, and within the highly intertextual poetics of cl. waka, the *Kokinshū* became a major source of allusion for later poets. A large body of commentarial texts and ritual practices known as the "transmissions on the *Kokinshū*" (*kokin denju*) developed around the *Kokinshū*, passed down through generations of waka poets. As the composition of waka came to be seen as tantamount to a religious vocation and poets came to be worshiped as deities, the *Kokinshū* came to be revered almost as a sacred text. Although the *Kokinshū* was decanonized in the late 19th c., supplanted in critical esteem by the earlier *Man'yōshū*, its authority in matters relating to the composition and crit. of Japanese court poetry for the preceding eight centuries had been without parallel.

*See* JAPANESE POETICS.

■ J. Konishi, "The Genesis of the *Kokinshū* Style," *HJAS* 38 (1978); *Kokinshū*, trans. L. Rodd and M. Henkenius (1984); H. McCullough, *Brocade by Night* (1985); *Kokin Wakashū*, trans. H. McCullough (1985); G. Heldt, *The Pursuit of Harmony* (2008).

A. E. COMMONS

**KOOTENAY SCHOOL.** The Kootenay School of Writing (KSW) is a nonprofit writer-run center in Vancouver, British Columbia, formed in 1984 that has promoted *avant-garde poetics in Canada. Uniquely organized as a collective with a small but constantly fluctuating membership, KSW has been long associated with a "politicized understanding of . . . art and literary production" (Klobucar and Barnholden). The school was formed in Vancouver in 1984, after the closure of David Thompson University College in Nelson, British Columbia, by former DTUC instructors and students, including poets Tom Wayman (b. 1945), Colin Browne (b. 1946), and Jeff Derksen (b. 1958). Important KSW poets, in its early phase, include Dorothy Trujillo Lusk (b. 1953), Colin Smith (b. 1957), Peter Culley (b. 1958), Kevin Davies (b. 1958), and Deanna Ferguson (b. 1962). In the 1990s, a number of important feminist poets became associated with the school, incl. Melissa Wolsak (b. 1947), Lisa Robertson (b. 1961), Nancy Shaw (1962–2007), Catriona Strang (b. 1966), and Susan Clark (b. 1954). Later members of the KSW collective have included Edward Byrne (b. 1947), Michael Barnholden (b. 1951), Stephen Collis (b. 1965), Andrew Klobucar (b. 1967), Reg Johanson (b. 1968), Roger Farr (b. 1970), Aaron Vidaver (b. 1970), and Donato Mancini (b. 1974). KSW has been associated with several jours., incl. *Writing Magazine* (1980–92), *Raddle Moon* (1983–2002), and *W* (1999–), as well as the small press Tsunami Editions (1986–2001), which published first books by a number of KSW poets. Often eschewing its status as a cultural institution, KSW has, nevertheless, developed a considerable international reputation.

See CANADA, POETRY OF.

■ *Writing Class: The Kootenay School of Writing Anthology*, ed. A. Klobucar and M. Barnholden (1999); J. Wiens, *The Kootenay School of Writing* (2002); P. Butling and S. Rudy, *Writing in Our Time: Canada's Radical Poetries in English, 1957–2003* (2005); C. Burnham, *The Only Poetry That Matters: Reading the Kootenay School of Writing* (2011).

S. COLLIS

# KOREA, POETRY OF

I. Classical Period
II. Modern Period

**I. Classical Period.** Cl. Korean poetry pre-20th c. is divided into two categories according to medium: one written in Korean and the other, *hansi*, written in cl. Chinese. Prior to the creation of *han'gŭl*, the Korean alphabet, in the mid-15th c., Korean-lang. poetry was transcribed in Chinese characters, sometimes with variations in the system, borrowing sounds and meaning to signify the original Korean. Even after the promulgation of the Korean alphabet, however, cl. Chinese maintained its prestige as the official written lang. of the ruling class until 1894, the year of the Kabo Reform, when Korea officially adopted han'gŭl as the national alphabet.

**A. Silla Dynasty.** Historical records witness singing and dancing as significant aspects of ancient Korean life. Koreans believed in the power of singing, music, and dance as ways to communicate with humans or the heavenly spirits. There are, however, few direct literary records from before the establishment of the Unified Silla kingdom (668–918).

The first Korean literary genre is Silla's most noteworthy, the songs called *hyangga* or "native songs." Fourteen hyangga are included in the monk Iryŏn's book *Samguk yusa* (Remnants of the Three Kingdoms, late 13th c.). The songs range in style and subject matter, from playful folk songs such as the "Sŏdongyo" (Song of Sŏdong) and "Hŏnhwaga" (Flower Offering Song), which suggest that folk songs were absorbed into the hyangga repertoire, to Buddhist devotional hymns and songs dedicated to exemplary *hwarang* (young knights). These hyangga were recorded in *hyangch'al*, a method using Chinese characters to represent sounds and meanings of the Korean lang. rather than as Chinese trans.

Folk songs ascribed to the Koguryŏ (37 BCE–

668 CE) and the Paekche kingdoms (18 BCE–663 CE), with titles only, are included in the 15th-c. *Koryŏ sa* (History of Koryŏ); the text of one Paekche song is found in the *Akhak kwebŏm* (Primer for Music Studies, 1492). *Quan Tang shi* (Complete Tang Poetry), a Chinese compilation, includes works by several Silla poets such as Ch'oe Ch'i-wŏn (b. 857) and Kim Ka-gi (d. 859), while the 8th-c. *Nihon shoki* (Chronicles of Japan) refers to a Paekche man who taught Chinese-style *gigaku*, or Buddhist ceremonial dance, in Japan.

**B. Koryŏ Dynasty.** The Koryŏ dynasty (918–1392) instituted a state civil-service examination in 958, patterned on the Chinese system, which used Chinese literary, philosophical, and historical sources and materials. One result of this official centering of Chinese materials was the importance of *hansi* (the Chinese *shi* and *fu*, poetry and rhyme prose) in Korean literary compositions. A multiplication of individual works and anthols. and the emergence of writers like Yi Kyu-bo (1168–1241), Ch'oe Ch'ung (984–1068), Kim Hwang-wŏn (1045–1117), and Chŏng Chi-sang (d. 1135), as well as the *Chungnim kohoe* (Bamboo Grove Assembly), a group of seven highly regarded poets of the late 12th c., are a few examples of Koryŏ interest in hansi genres.

The hyangga trad. continued into Koryŏ, the best-known example being the series of 11 devotional hymns composed by the Buddhist monk Kyunyŏ (923–73). The monk Chinul's (1128–1210) disciple Hyesim (1178–1234) wrote hansi poems on sŏn (Zen) subjects and collected Buddhist tales, meditation puzzles, *allegories, and poems in a 30-v. anthol. *Sŏnmun yŏmsong* (1226) or "Praise and Puzzle in Sŏn Literature." The monk Ch'ungji (1226–93) focused in his poetry on the plight of the Korean people during the late 13th-c. Mongol campaign against Japan, when they were forced to build and man an invasion fleet. References to other Buddhist monks are included in the *Haedong kosŭng chŏn* (Lives of Eminent Korean Monks, 1215).

Notable among Koryŏ writings and lit. were the mostly Chinese-lang. (with Korean-lang. refrains) *kyŏnggi*-style songs, or *kyŏnggich'e ka*, of which the "Hallim pyŏlgok" (Song of the Capital, 13th c.) is exemplary. Koryŏ-era popular songs in Korean, *sogyo*, mostly about love, collected in the *Akchang kasa* (Lyrics for Akchang, 16th c.), include "Kasiri" (Would You Go?) and "Ch'ŏngsanpyŏlgok" (Song of the Green Hills). Kim Pu-sik's (1075–1151) *Samguk sagi* (History of the Three Kingdoms) and Iryŏn's (1206–89) *Samguk yusa*, a compilation from many sources of Korean legends, myths, hists., biographies, songs, and spells, are major landmarks in Korea's political, cultural, and lit. hist.

**C. Early Chosŏn.** The first two hundred years of the Chosŏn dynasty, from its founding in 1392 until the invasions by the Japanese armies of Hideyoshi in 1598, was a period of great artistic creativity and accomplishments, both cultural and scientific. The new dynasty was only 50 years old when its fourth king, Sejong (r. 1418–50), promulgated a new phonetic alphabet, now known as han'gŭl, for the Korean lang. Composition in the Korean vernacular flourished, esp. in two verse forms, the three-line *sijo* and the longer *kasa*. Many anthols. of these works were assembled and published later, in the 18th and 19th cs.; various groups coalesced around schools of literary thought, preferences for Chinese or Korean forms of expression, and not infrequently, political-philosophical outlooks.

*Akchang* was a verse form written for performance at state ceremonies with a distinct political purpose to praise the founding of the dynasty. The two best-known examples are associated with King Sejong. The first, *Yongbi ŏch'ŏn ka* (Song of the Dragons Flying to Heaven), was composed at Sejong's order, to praise the dynasty's founders while presenting a ceremonial alternative to resentments still lingering at the overthrow of the preceding Koryŏ dynasty. It was completed in 1445 as hansi, then translated into Korean, annotated, and finally published two years later in an ed. of 550 copies, distributed at court. Sejong himself is said to have written the other notable akchang, *Wŏrin ch'ŏn'gang chi kok* (The Song of Moonlight on One Thousand Waters, 1449) a remembrance of Queen Sohŏn, who had died in 1446.

The sijo is a three-line verse form, originally composed for musical performance. There are several ways of singing, characterized by a deliberate slowness. In singing 40 to 50 syllables, the popular *sijo ch'ang* (sijo song) style takes three to four minutes, while *kagok*, the style performed by professional singers, takes as much as ten. The deliberate slowness of a sijo performance is said to bring the performer and audience into a state of tranquility and profound concentration. While syllable count is not fixed, it does play a role in patterns of syllable distribution among the four phrases that constitute the sijo lines. For the first two lines, the usual syllable count is 3-4-3 (or 4)-4. The third line, with a regular sequence of 3-5-4-3 syllables coupled with a "twist" or "turn" at the beginning of the line, brings the poem to a conclusion. Though sijo is widely believed to date back to the late Koryŏ period, its historical origins are obscured by the relatively late creation of the Korean alphabet. The *yangban* gentry class provided its main authors at least until the 19th c., while most of the sijo anthols. date from the 18th c. or later.

Even though many sijo and vernacular Korean poems are about the enjoyment of life, one characteristic feature of Korean lit. is a seriousness of literary expression, esp. in the works of the ruling class. One of the most famous examples is the exchange between the Koryŏ loyalist Chŏng Mong-ju (1337–92) and Yi Pang-wŏn (1367–1422), son of the founding Chosŏn king Yi Sŏng-gye. The story associated with Chŏng's famous sijo relates that the king's son organized a banquet and invited Chŏng, then offered a somewhat mocking, metaphorical toast couched in a sijo, urging Chŏng to stop his resistance to the changing times. Chŏng's reply has become known as the "Tansim ka" or "Song of a Loyal Heart":

> Though this body die
> and die a hundred times again,
> White bones become but dust,

> a soul exist, then not,
> Still, this heart wholly for my lord:
> How could it ever change?

> (trans. D. McCann)

In 1416, in the aftermath of Sejo's (r. 1455–68) usurpation of the throne and assassination of its occupant, his own nephew Tanjong (r. 1452–55), Sŏng Sam-mun (1418–56), one of the "Six Martyred Ministers" put to death for a plan to return Tanjong to the throne, composed on the eve of his execution a sijo that echoes Chŏng's:

> Once this body is dead and gone
> you ask, what will it be?
> On the highest peak of Pongnae Mountain
> a towering, spreading pine tree.
> When sky and earth are filled with white snow,
> alone and green, green I shall be.

> (trans. D. McCann)

Yi Hwang (1501–70), one of the great neo-Confucian philosophers of Chosŏn Korea, loved the song aspect of sijo and the positive effect that singing and listening could have on both the performer/composer and the audience. The woodblocks carved from Yi's own calligraphy for his *Tosan sibigok* (Twelve Songs of Tosan, 1565) are the oldest of all sijo source materials. Another prominent neo-Confucian scholar Yi I's (1536–84) "Kosan kugok ka" (Nine Songs from Kosan), which echoed a similar work by the Chinese philosopher Zhu Xi, also connotes the popularity of sijo among yangban elites. Chŏng Ch'ŏl (1536–93) composed dozens of sijo, in addition to four famous kasa poems. Some reflect his difficult political circumstances, others a more general philosophical outlook, and still others a directly didactic intent, as in the series written to instruct the people of the province where he had been sent as governor.

It is noteworthy that many sijo were ascribed to *kisaeng*, the female entertainer, some of whom must have been professional sijo performers. The most famous of all is Hwang Chini, the legendary author—in the absence of contemp. documentation, it is impossible to establish her authorship—of a half dozen truly remarkable sijo and a number of poems in cl. Chinese, a woman with a reputation for beauty, artistic accomplishments, as well as a singularly independent mind and will. One of her sijo reads,

> Alas! What have I done?
> Didn't I know how I would yearn?
> If only I'd said, *Just stay*,
> how could he have gone? But stubborn
> I sent him away, and know now
> I never knew what it is to yearn.

> (trans. D. McCann)

The kasa is the other major Korean vernacular verse form. It too uses a four-part line. Narrative and discursive, without stanza divisions, it was often used for travelogues, while upper-class women used the form to express their thoughts at the restraints of social norms. Some went on for hundreds of lines; in 16th- and 17th-c. practice, the final line would be marked by the sijo-like 3-5-4-3 syllable count. The first example of kasa is Chŏng Kŭg-in's (1401–81) "Sangch'un kok" (Song to Spring), praising life in the countryside. Chŏng Ch'ŏl's two famous travelogue kasa, "Sŏngsan pyŏlgok" (Song of Sŏng Mountain) and "Kwandong pyŏlgok" (Song of Kwandong), offer an exuberant view of the Korean landscape, while Chŏng's other two kasa, "Samiin kok" (Longing for the Beautiful One) and "Sok miin kok" (Again, Beautiful One), written in the dramatic persona of a woman abandoned, are read as expressions of Chŏng's own feelings at being dismissed from office and sent into exile. The "Samiin kok" is esp. noteworthy for its dramatic structure, built around the contrast between the natural passing of the seasons and the unnatural human tendency to let warm feelings turn and then stay cold.

Hŏ Ch'o-hŭi (1563–89), better known in Korea by her pseud. Nansŏrhŏn, wrote many highly regarded hansi, as well as two kasa, "Kyuwŏn ka" (Married Sorrow) and "Pongsŏnhwa" (The Touch-Me-Not).

**D. *Later Chosŏn*.** In the 17th c., after the Japanese invasion of Korea, the change of the East Asian political map—most prominently in the demise of the Ming dynasty, which had a strong bond with Korea and the rise of the Qing—led Korea to assert its own cultural identity. Kim Man-jung (1637–92), author of two novels in Korean, declared, "Only Korean vernacular can express genuine Koreanness." Sijo, with changes in form and vernacular subjects, and kasa, as a longer form, became more widely practiced by yangban literati moving away from strictly Chinese models and by women who, confined to the house, nevertheless encouraged the circulation of vernacular Korean works.

The life of the poet Pak Il-lo (1561–1643) marks a high point in the devel. of Korean vernacular poetry. His "T'aep'yŏngsa" (Song of Peace) marked the close of the 16th c.'s final devastating decade. While many of his sijo verse compositions are unimaginative restatements of Confucian precepts, his kasa are another matter entirely. The "Sŏnsangt'an" (Lament on the Waters, 1601) returns to the theme of the naval campaign against the Japanese. "Saje kok" (The Sedge Bank, 1611) is a portrait of a rural retreat. "Nuhang sa" or "Song of a Humble Life" (1611) combines realistic plot, vividly observed setting, and strikingly mod. vernacular dialogue in a unique expression of the traditional theme of rustic retirement.

Yun Sŏn-do (1587–1671) was a brilliant innovator in the sijo form and wrote numerous individual works and sijo sequences. The most famous of the latter is his *Ŏbu sasi sa* (Fisherman's Calendar, 1651), a four-part, four-season sequence on the pleasures of the fisherman's tranquil existence. These poems are notable for their clear and flowing vernacular diction, use of an onomatopoeic refrain, and controlled easing of the usual structural patterns of the sijo.

In the 18th and 19th cs., as Chosŏn society saw significant social changes and economic growth, the new *sirhak*, or practical learning group, produced lo-

calized, realist hansi. Chŏng Yag-yong (1762–1836), a famous encyclopedic scholar who produced almost 3,000 poems, declared, "I am a Korean; I compose Korean poetry." He meant Korean poetry written in cl. Chinese. While the circulation of vernacular Korean book narratives significantly increased, poetry in the vernacular also saw diversification in form and subject matter. Perhaps most obvious was the move toward freer expression of desire and emotion, which had been tightly controlled by neo-Confucian attitudes. Some yangban scholars composed *sasŏl sijo*, a longer version of sijo and kasa, depicting blatantly erotic scenes. These devels. coincided with the emergence of *p'ansori*, a performative art of singing and narrating stories, which negotiated a controversial position between kasa and the p'ansori-novel.

The 19th c. brought fundamental transformations to the whole of Korean society. Mid-century saw the defeat of China by Eur. powers, a seismographic change in the Asian cultural sphere. Sijo and kasa continued to be performed and composed, though without notable accomplishment. The practice of hansi faded, prompted by the abolition of the state examination system with the Kabo Reform of 1894, yet it continued through the 20th c. and into the present as a practice suitable for formal occasions. Sijo and kasa, often with rhythmic patterns fitted to Western music, were written and published to accommodate the changing world.

**II. Modern Period.** Beginning in the late 19th c., rapid social change was accompanied by a fundamental transformation of the cultural system. Most revolutionary was the replacement of cl. Chinese with han'gŭl as the official script. The pursuit of a high art in vernacular Korean defined the ensuing 20th c. In the age of imperialism, many Korean literati were also national leaders, and their literary jours. functioned as instruments for cultural change. A hist. of colonial rule, liberation, and subsequent national division directed Korean lit. toward a socio-political agenda that lasted into the final decade of the 20th c.

**A. *Japanese Colonial Period (1910–45)*.** Liberation from conventional poetic form began with the *free verse imported from the West through Japan, where many Korean intellectuals studied. The beginning of a "new poetry" was announced in "Hae egesŏ Sonyŏn ege" (From the Sea to Youth, 1908) by Ch'oe Namsŏn, a poem that deploys the repeated refrain of the sea's voice urging change. Ch'oe had studied in Japan and brought back printing equipment to publish *Sonyŏn* (Youth), the first literary magazine devoted to the movement for a new Korean culture. *Onoe ŭi mudo* (Dance of Anguish), was published in 1921, an anthol. of trans. by Kim Ŏk (1895–1950) of Fr., Ir., and other poets. In 1923, Kim published the first mod. Korean poetry collection, *Haep'ari ŭi norae* (Song of Jellyfish). The trans. and poems presented a completely new voice in vernacular Korean. In 1925, one of Kim Ŏk's students, Kim Sowŏl (1902–34), published *Azaleas*, the most favored poetry book of the entire 20th c. Kim

Sowŏl's poetry, imbued with the sense of sorrowful loss, brought folk-song rhythm to mod. poetry. The title poem remains his best-known work:

> When you leave, weary
> of seeing me,
> silently I shall send you on your way.
>
> From Mt. Yak in Yŏngbyŏn,
> an armful of azaleas
> I shall gather and scatter on your way.
>
> Step by step
> on the flowers lying before you
> tread softly, deeply, and go.
>
> When you go, weary
> of seeing me,
> though I die I shall not shed one tear.

> (trans. D. McCann)

Hang Yong-un (1879–1944), a reformist Buddhist monk and a national leader in opposing Japan's colonial rule, also published a canonical poetry book, *Nim ŭi ch'immuk* (Silence of Love, 1926), evoking the absence of love as political metaphor. Many poems of the 1920s mix a nationalistic anger with sentimental tears. Yi Sang-hwa's (1901–43) "Ppaeakkin tŭl edo pom ŭn onŭka" (Will Spring Return to Stolen Fields?) and Yi Yuk-sa's (1904–44) "Chŏlchŏng" (The Summit) more directly lament the lost sovereignty.

The Korea Artista Proletaria Federatio (KAPF), organized by Marxist writers in 1925 and led by the poet and critic Im Hwa (1908–53), came to exert strong influence on the literary field. Yet political or ideological differences were accommodated in those days. Im Hwa, e.g., published his critique of Sowŏl's poems in the same jour., *Kaebyŏk* (Dawn), that had published Sowŏl's poems in the first place. Paek Sŏk (1912–95), a poet who with many others was classified in South Korea as having "gone North" after 1945, though in fact he merely stayed at his home following liberation, like So Wŏl used northern dialect and rural themes. Two poets from the modernist group *Kuinhoe* (Nine-Person Group), Chŏng Chi-yong (1902–50) and Yi Sang (1910–37), brought additional changes to Korean poetry in the 1930s. Chŏng, informed by *modernism, worked toward refining the mod. Korean lang. Yi Sang's surrealistic wit was a challenge to his contemporaries and remains so today. Yun Tong-ju (1918–45) reflected the turbulent colonial period; his works became widely popular following his death during imprisonment in Tokyo.

In 1938, Japan banned the Korean lang. in schools and, in 1941, the publication of Korean-lang. books. Writers either used the Japanese lang. or hid their works and waited.

**B.** *After the Liberation.* After liberation in 1945, accompanied by the North-South division of the country, writers occupied two positions in the political spectrum, Left or Right; but for an interval, during the two years or so known as the Liberation Space, they managed to write, publish, and engage in debate. Eventually, many of the leftists went to the communist North, the Democratic People's Republic of Korea (DPRK), while the nationalists remained in the Republic of Korea. Both states were established in 1948 and were at war with one another in 1950. Little remains known about the literary realm of the DPRK beyond its state-mandated ideology of *Juche* (self-reliance). In the South, following the Korean War's end in 1953, a new curriculum was established, built around the Korean lang., which had been banned in the late colonial period, while nationalism emerged as a guiding counterpart to the North's Juche state philosophy. Eager for work in vernacular Korean, the new generation of students welcomed the republication of books by such writers as Kim Sowŏl, Han Yong-un, and Yun Tong-ju.

During this period, Korean poetry also witnessed the arrival of two major poets, Sŏ Chŏng-ju (1915–2000) and Kim Su-yŏng (1921–68). Sŏ created an oeuvre impressive—in addition to its supple use of the Korean lang.—for its *imagery, *prosody, and vivid voice. One of his poems, "Tongch'ŏn" (Winter Sky), recaptures Kim Sowŏl's use of poetic gesture:

> With a thousand nights' dream
> I have rinsed clear the gentle brow
> of my heart's love,
> to transplant it into the heavens.
> A fierce bird knows, and in mimicry
> arcs through the midwinter sky.

> (trans. D. McCann)

Kim Su-yŏng, widely known as a political radical, opened a new imaginary space in Korean lang., urging readers to participate directly in the improvement of society. His poem "P'ul" (Grasses), pub. after his death, remains an emblematic statement of that democratic ideal:

> Grasses lie down
> Blown by the wind driving rain from the east
> grasses lie,
> at last cried
> As the day is overcast, they cried more,
> and lay again
>
> Grasses lie
> Faster than the wind they lie
> Faster than the wind they cry
> Earlier than the wind they rise
>
> The day is overcast, and grasses lie
> to the ankle
> to the sole they lie
> Later than the wind they lie
> Earlier than the wind they rise
> Later than the wind they cry
> Earlier than the wind they smile
> The day is overcast, and the grass roots lie.

> (trans. Y.-J. Lee)

Sŏ Chŏng-ju was presented as a major poet in Korean school textbooks, while Kim Su-yŏng, whose poetry was full of images of revolution mixed with Korean-lang. expression that readers found difficult, was included only after the democratizing changes of the 1980s.

During the latter half of the 20th c., South Korea experienced rapid industrialization and economic growth, accompanied by a series of repressive military dictatorships. Like their predecessors at the beginning of the century, many Korean poets committed their energies to the democratization movement, giving the 1980s the name *si ŭi sidae* (the age of poetry). The works of poets like Chŏng Chi-yong, Paek Sŏk, and others who had "gone North," banned until 1987, met with enthusiastic interest. While many poets were arrested and imprisoned, their works still managed to produce sales of several million volumes, an exceptional sales record. In this period, two major poets, both victims of repeated imprisonments, became recognized in the outer world: Ko Un (b. 1933), esp. for his *Maninbo*, (Record of Ten Thousand People), completed in 30 books over 25 years (1986–2010), and Kim Chi Ha (b. 1941) for his revival of the p'ansori form and rhythm in dissident poetry. Ko Un's *Maninbo* project, started while he was imprisoned in solitary confinement, overturned the traditional idea of the elite family genealogical records known as *chokpo*. Kim Chi Ha's long, p'ansori-style poems such as *Ojök* (The Five Bandits), received substantial international acclaim during the 1970s when he too was being held in prison.

The 1990s in Korea saw the rise of women's poetry, which had been long neglected. A few women poets such as No Ch'ŏn-myŏng (1912–57) and Kim Nam-jo (b. 1927) had achieved some reputation earlier. Kim Hyesoon's (b. 1955) poems depicted a woman's interiority amid everyday life. Her unabashedly confessional works at times took a dramatic narrative form borrowed from shamanistic trad.

With the Korean economy flourishing in the 1980s, the poetry of Hwang Chi-u (b. 1952), Yi Sŏng-bok (b. 1952), and Chang Chŏng-il (b. 1963) brought pop culture themes laced with everyday trivial into their poetic subject matter. Their focus on the present and explicit commitment to colloquial expression are to be seen and heard among new poetic voices in the 21st c., among whom are a number of women poets grappling with issues of womanhood in 21st-c. Korea.

■ **Anthologies and Translations**: *The Middle Hour: Selected Poems of Kim Chi Ha*, trans. D. McCann (1980); *Anthology of Korean Literature: From Early Times to the Nineteenth Century*, ed. P. Lee (1981); *Selected Poems of Sŏ Chŏngju*, trans. D. McCann (1989); *Modern Korean Literature*, ed. P. Lee (1990); *Sŏ Chŏngju: The Early Lyrics, 1941–1960*, trans. B. Anthony (1991); *Pine River and Lone Peak: An Anthology of Three Chosŏn Dynasty Poets*, ed. and trans. P. Lee (1991); *Selected Poems by Kim Namjo*, trans. D. McCann and H. Y. Sallee (1993); R. Rutt, *The Bamboo Grove: An Introduction to Sijo* (1998); *The Book of Korean Shijo*, trans. K. O'Rourke (2002); *The Columbia Anthology of Traditional Korean Poetry*, ed. P. Lee (2002); *The Columbia Anthology of Modern Korean Poetry*, ed. D. McCann (2004); *Everything Yearned For: Manhae's Poems of Love and Longing*, trans. F. Cho (2005); Ko Un, *Ten Thousand Lives*, trans. Y. M. Kim, B. Anthony, and G. Gach (2005); *Echoing Song: Contemporary Korean Women Poets*, ed. P. Lee (2005); D. Choi, *Anxiety of Words: Contemporary Poetry by Korean Women* (2006); S. Kim, *Azaleas: A Book of Poems*, trans. D. McCann (2007); Ko Un, *What?: 108 Korean Zen Poems*, trans. B. Anthony, G. Gach, and Y. M. Kim (2008).

■ **Criticism and History**: P. Lee, *Songs of Flying Dragons: A Critical Reading* (1975); D. McCann, *Form and Freedom in Korean Poetry* (1988); B. Myers, *Han Sŏrya and North Korean Literature* (1994); *Early Korean Literature: Selections and Introductions*, ed. and trans. D. McCann (2000); *The Record of the Black Dragon Year*, trans. P. Lee (2000); P. Lee, *A History of Korean Literature* (2003); M. Pihl, *The Korean Singer of Tales* (2003); D. Seo and P. Lee, *Oral Literature of Korea* (2005).

Y.-J. Lee; D. R. McCann

# L

**LADINO POETRY.** *See* JUDEO-SPANISH POETRY.

**LAI** (OF; Eng. *lay*; Ger. *leich*). A short narrative or lyric poem, perhaps based on Celtic material but primarily Fr., most of them secular and usually set to music. (1) In OF, the oldest narrative *lais*, almost always written in *octosyllables, are the *contes* or short romantic tales originated by Marie de France in the late 12th c. Most of them have Breton themes, chiefly love but also the supernatural. Marie's dozen lais take as their central interest true love, even if adulterous, in the face of marriages of convenience and abusive husbands. Later, the term *lai* became synonymous with *conte*. (2) The oldest lyric lais are by Gautier de Dargies, who flourished in the first third of the 13th c. The lyric lai is addressed to an earthly lady or to the Virgin, but it differs from other poems of this theme by varying the rhymes and syllable counts in its stanzas, without *refrain. One of the most interesting, by Ernoul le Vieux, has no love theme; it is the *Lai de l'ancien et du nouveau testament*. The OF lai may be related to the Occitan *descort* (discord). In the 14th c., Guillaume de Machaut standardized the form; half of this century's 57 extant lais are by him. (3) The term *Breton lay* was applied in 14th-c. England to poems set in Brittany, written in a spirit similar to that of Marie's; sometimes these poems apply the term to themselves. About a dozen Breton lays are extant in Eng., among them *Sir Orfeo*, *Sir Launfal*, *Emare*, and Chaucer's "Franklin's Tale." Since the 16th c., *lay* has been used for song; in the early 19th c., the term was sometimes used for a historical ballad, e.g. Walter Scott's *Lay of the Last Minstrel*.

*See* LEICH.

■ F. Wolf, *Über die Lais, Sequenzen, und Leiche* (1841); *Lais et descorts française du XIIIe siècle*, ed. A. Jeanroy et al. (1901); H. Spanke, "Sequenz und Lai," *Studi medievali* 11 (1938); G. Reaney, "Concerning the Origins of the Medieval Lai," *Music and Letters* 39 (1958); J. Maillard, *Évolution et ésthetique du lai lyrique* (1961); H. Baader, *Die Lais* (1966); M. J. Donovan, *The Breton Lai: A Guide to Varieties* (1969); K. W. Le Mée, *A Metrical Study of Five Lais of Marie de France* (1978); *The Lais of Marie de France*, 2d ed., trans. R. Hanning and J. Ferrante (1978); G. S. Burgess, *The Lais of Marie de France* (1987); G. S. Burgess, "Lai," *Medieval France: An Encyclopedia*, ed. W. W. Kibler (1995); C. J. Hatton, "Narrative Lai and Verse Romance: Generations and Intergeneric Play," *DAI* 65 (2004).

U. T. HOLMES; T.V.F. BROGAN

**LAISSE.** The OF epics or *chansons de geste* are divided into sections or groups of lines of no specified length called *laisses*; in the *Chanson de Roland*, they range from 5 to 35 lines. Technically, laisses are not strophic because there is no *responsion of form from one laisse to the next; the length of each depends on how much emphasis the poet wishes to give its subject. Each laisse links together its lines with terminal *assonance or—in later poems—*rhyme; the distinction between *masculine and feminine is observed. Sometimes the content of a laisse is repeated item for item in one or two following laisses, though with differing assonance or rhyme; such repetitions are called *laisses similaires*. The mod. analogue is the *verse paragraph, though this is unrhymed.

■ J. Rychner, *La Chanson de geste* (1955), ch. 4; A. Monteverdi, "La Laisse epique," *La Technique littéraire des chansons de geste* (1959); B. Schurfranz, "Strophic Structure versus Alternate Divisions in the *Prise d'Orange*," *RPh* 33 (1979); R. M. Johnston, "The Function of *Laisse* Divisions in the *Poema de mio Cid*," *Journal of Hispanic Philology* 8 (1984); E. A. Heinemann, "Measuring Units of Poetic Discourse," *Romance Epic*, ed. H.-E. Keller (1987); D. Boutet, "*Jehan de Lanson*" technique et esthétique de la chanson de geste au XIIIᵉ siècle (1988); J.-P. Carton, "A Contribution to the Study of *Laisses Similaires* in the *Chanson de Roland*: Repetition and Narrative Progression in Laisses 133–135," *Olifant* 21 (1997); E. A. Heinemann, "Toward a History of the Metric Art of the *Chanson de geste*: Laisse and Echo in the Opening Scene of the Three-Verse Version of the *Prise d'Orange*," *Echoes of the Epic*, ed. D. P. Schenck and M. J. Schenck (1998).

U. T. HOLMES; T.V.F. BROGAN

**LAKE SCHOOL,** Lake Poets, Lakers. These terms typically designate three Brit. poets of the romantic period: William Wordsworth, S. T. Coleridge, and Robert Southey. In 1802 in the *Edinburgh Review*, the hostile critic Francis Jeffery first referred to the three as a "sect" of poets, which in 1807 he coupled with "the Lakes of Cumberland" or the so-called Lake District in England. A December 1809 review calls them "The Bards of the Lake." By most accounts, the poets did not have enough in common to justify the grouping; in *Biographia Literaria*, Coleridge himself overtly objects to the identification of his work in this way, insisting on its uniqueness and originality. Fear of revolution, overshadowed by the recent revolution in France, initially inspired Jeffery's grouping of the three poets whose work he found doctrinaire and subversive. But by around 1814, the classification of the Lake school was generally accepted and no longer necessarily hostile. At first, the jibes were aimed against the new poets' political principles, but after the publication of the 2d ed. of *Lyrical Ballads* in 1800, with Wordsworth's and Coleridge's names now on the title page, the focus shifted to the innovations in poetics—simplicity in diction; novelty in meter; and, in content, the effort to focus on outsider figures of society and to naturalize the supernatural and make transcendent the natural. The association via geography was a metonym meant to imply an aesthetic of vulgar rusticity. Such a metonym, however, radically simplifies the complex concerns and poetics involved, as well as the significant differences among the philosophies, temperaments, and productions of the three poets.

*See* COCKNEY SCHOOL, ROMANTICISM.

■ D. Perkins, "The Construction of 'The Romantic Movement' as a Literary Classification," *Nineteenth-Century Literature* 45 (1990); J. Cox, "Leigh Hunt's Cockney School: The Lakers' 'Other,'" *Romanticism on the Net* 14 (May 1999), http://www.erudit.org/revue/ron/1999/v/n14/005859ar.html.

T.V.F. BROGAN; E. ROHRBACH

**LAMENT.** A poem or song of grief, frequently accompanied by instrumental music and by ritualized vocal gestures and symbolic movements such as wailing and breast-beating. As an element of ritual practices such as funerals, cultic worship, and formal rites of passage and leave-taking, and in representations of these practices in literary forms incl. epic, tragedy, and *elegy, lament reaches back to the beginnings of recorded culture: in the Mesopotamian city-laments of the 3rd millennium BCE, in Homer's *Iliad* and *Odyssey* (8th c. BCE), in the *Epic of Gilgamesh* (7th c. BCE), in the Heb. Psalms (13th–6th c. BCE) and book of Lamentations (6th c. BCE), and throughout the tragedies and pastorals of Gr. and Roman antiquity. From the Judaic trad., lament was carried over into the Christic (e.g., Christ's lament for Jerusalem in the 1st-c. gospels of Matthew and Luke) and the Islamic (e.g., in the "Lament" from Rūmī's 13th-c. poem *Masnavī*). In Sanskrit lit., "The Lament of Rati" is a celebrated passage from Kālidāsa's 5th-c. epic *Kumārasambhava*. In the Middle Ages, lament took shape in the Lat. *planctus* and in the melancholy vernacular poems of the Exeter Book poets (Anglo-Saxon), the *kharja* of Spain (Mozarabic), and the *planh* of the *troubadours (Occitan). Med. *chansons de geste* and Ren. epic poems abound in stylized laments for fallen heroes, and innumerable mod. poets have imitated the bucolic laments of Theocritus (3rd c. BCE) and Virgil (1st c. BCE) and the plangent refrain of Bion's famous "Lament for Adonis" (ca. 100 BCE). In 17th-c. Italy, the dramatic lament was popularized by Claudio Monteverdi and other composers and became an essential element of opera. Ritualized lament, with or without instrumental music, remains an important part of the mourning cultures of many societies, incl. the Druze *nabd* of Lebanon, the Irish keen, the *k'u-ko* of southern China, the Ga *adowa* of Ghana, the Setu laments of Estonia, and Af. Am. *blues.

Laments commonly figure collective as well as individual losses. They may protest the status quo, as in Tahmina's lament in Ferdowsi's 10th-c. Iranian epic *Shahnama*, or foster powerful identifications across sociopolitical divides, as in the many laments in Aeschylus's *The Persians* (472 BCE), which is as much about Athenian identification with the Persians they have destroyed as it is about Athenian joy at their defeat of the Persians at Salamis. Lament may give form to impulses of compunction, reconciliation, and forgiveness as well as despair, melancholy, and resentment. Although correspondence between representation and social practice is often obscure, archeological evidence (e.g., of Mycenaean funerary practices) and comparative anthropological evidence (e.g., of mod. Gr. ritual customs and beliefs) help supplement and clarify the literary record.

The suffering of captive women and the destruction of cities are prominent and frequently intertwined themes in ancient laments. Such laments may spur, even as they seek to manage, communal grief. The lamentations of women esp. are often marked as both dangerous and necessary—dangerous, because their public indulgence could give way to women's unchecked erotic passion or rage or exacerbate the grief of men, possibly inciting vengeance and other social disruption; necessary, because a community's potentially disabling grief requires an expressive channel, such as might be forbidden or stigmatized among men. Male lamentation abounds in ancient and mod. lits., sometimes celebrated as a masculine duty and achievement, sometimes criticized or interdicted as a feminizing practice. But in many societies, ancient and mod., women are thought to have a privileged relation to grief, and lamentation is often one of the few permissible, if constrained, forms of political expression available to them. Women tend to be the generic subjects of literary laments, even—or perhaps esp.—where the losses sustained by men and the genres (such as epic and tragedy) owned by men are thought to matter most, as in the *kommoi* shared with tragic choruses by lamenting heroines such as Electra, and in mod. instances like Britomart's Petrarchan lament in book 3 of Edmund Spenser's *The Faerie Queene* (1590, 1596). Women's losses are brought to the fore in other genres as well, incl. dramatic adaptations of Antigone's lament, from Sophocles' *Antigone* (5th c. BCE) to Griselda Gambaro's *Antígona Furiosa* (1986), and Irish poet Eileen O'Connell's (Eibhlín Dubh Ní Chonaill) literary transformation of folk mourning practices in her *Lament for Art O'Leary* (1773).

In mod. works like O'Connell's and Gambaro's, lament distinguishes itself from other poetic mourning genres, such as elegy and *epitaph, through its closer connection with ritual incantation and remains audible in Jewish and Christian psalms and in the Islamic *marthiya*. As one moves beyond poetry's religious domain, the term loses much of its distinguishing force—except in the musical trad., where lament has continued to receive distinctive formal treatment, esp. in oratorio and opera, from Monteverdi's *Lamento d'Arianna* (composed 1608) to Giacomo Carissimi's *Jephte* (ca. 1649), Henry Purcell's *Dido and Aeneas* (1689), G. F. Handel's *Agrippina* (1709) and *Saul* (1738), Modest Mussorgsky's *Boris Godunov* (1874), and Benjamin Britten's *Turn of the Screw* (1954). Mod. poems without musical settings that call themselves laments—from the late med. Scots "Lament for the Makars" by William Dunbar to the many *soi-disant* laments by Robert Burns, John Clare, Thomas Hardy, Felicia Hemans, Langston Hughes, Katharine Tynan, and W. C. Williams—may do so to reactivate the association not just with music as such but also with sung or chanted lang. as collective and communal expression, sometimes harkening back to the trads. of antiquity, sometimes using popular forms like the ballad.

*See* COMPLAINT, DIRGE, EPICEDIUM, MONODY.

■ S. Girard, *Funeral Music and Customs in Venezuela* (1980); S. Feld, *Sound and Sentiment*, 2d ed. (1990); C. N. Seremetakis, *The Last Word* (1991); P. W. Ferris Jr., *The Genre of Communal Lament in the Bible and the Ancient Near East* (1992); G. Holst-Warhaft, *Dangerous Voices* (1992); "Lament," spec. iss., *Early Music* 27.3 (1999); M. Alexiou, *The Ritual Lament in Greek Tradition*, 2d ed. (2002); N. Loraux, *The Mourning Voice* (2002); C. Dué, *The Captive Woman's Lament in Greek Tragedy* (2006); M. G. McGeachy, *Lonesome Words* (2006); R. Saunders, *Lamentation and Modernity in Literature, Philosophy, and Culture* (2007); C. Lansing, *Passion and Order* (2008); *Lament*, ed. A. Suter (2008).

M. CAVITCH

**LANDSCAPE POEM.** The term *landscape* has a variety of meanings, enfolding *nature and art, the actual world, and the world as it is seen in spatial extension and in imagination. Landscape in poetry has involved all these references. While some critics have identified a set of universal landscape values, rooted in evolutionary psychology, most agree that its meaning and organization have changed with historical changes in the social, economic, and environmental conditions of culture.

While landscape was rarely a poetic subject in its own right before the 18th c., the roots of the mod. landscape poem can be found in cl. lit. In ancient *epic, landscape played an important role in enhancing narrative, sometimes through *simile, other times through description. Landscape in Homer conveys the strategic vision of the hero, the range of terrain he experienced, or conveys the psychological and moral import of the adventure. An example of the latter is Calypso's grotto, which fans out from the hearth fire to the meadows: "it was indeed a spot where even an immortal visitor might pause to gaze in wonder and delight." Later Gr. and Roman texts introduced a dimension of scenery more concerned with the occupations, recreations, and emergent milieu of the individual. The *georgic and the *topos of the *locus amoenus* are cl. elements of landscape that would be carried forward into early mod. Eur. poetic trads.

But while cl. lit. emphasized the narrative and tonal possibilities of landscape, med. trads., distrusting the senses and materiality generally, approached landscape with a stronger analogical thrust, addressed to spiritual concerns. The wilderness of the Bible is not a place of expansive prospect, and the *hortus conclusus* of med. lit. has a strong allegorical force. Travel writing of the Middle Ages treats the landscape more as symbolic labyrinth than synoptic vista. Only with Petrarch's influential (and disputed) letter (*Familiares* 4.1) in which he describes his ascent of Mont Ventoux does the aesthetic of the single viewer's prospect really emerge, yet still in moral terms.

In the 17th c., with the conceptual and geographic divisions of space brought on by changes in science, exploration, and economics, landscape emerges as a major element of both painting and poetic description, in the case of poetry with attention to perceptual and phenomenological experience as such. While the analogical and symbolic dimension of landscape remains important, becoming increasingly ideological and moral as opposed to theological in its thrust, the principle of sensuous aliveness (*enargeia*), stirring the imagination through pleasure and struggle, is pervasive in the poetry of Jean de La Ceppède, Jean de Sponde, Luis de Góngora, John Denham, John Milton, and Andrew Marvell. The *pastoral emerges in the 17th c. as a major genre, reviving Virgilian conventions but with a greater emphasis on the harmonious order of nature. In "L'Allegro," Milton writes, "straight mine eye hath caught new pleasures / while the landscape round it measures." In *Paradise Lost*, Adam has "prospect large" and takes in a "lovely . . . landscape" of variegated colors, vernal breezes, and abundant fruits. But as Satan approaches paradise, he encounters a "steep wilderness . . . grotesque and wild" that denies access to Eden, a rugged terrain that would appeal more to later, romantic tastes. The 17th c. in England also revives the cl. praise of the country house as an expression of republican virtues. Ben Jonson's "To Penshurst" and Andrew Marvell's "Upon Appleton House" are the most admired examples of the genre (see COUNTRY HOUSE POEM). Denham's "Cooper's Hill," though little read today, was celebrated in the 18th c. and provided a model for moralizing landscape that would guide Alexander Pope in his composition of "Windsor Forest," a poem that celebrates the reign of Queen Anne. Here, as in other forms of pastoral, the rural landscape is seen as a useful retreat into the pleasures of contemplation, but with reference to the struggles of the active life. In landscape poetry, 18th-c. writers also explored political challenges by displacing them imaginatively onto the more neutral theater of nature.

In Eng., the loco-descriptive poem emerges in the 18th c. as an independent project of *taste, increasingly propelled by aesthetic over didactic impulses. During this period, a new aesthetics of the picturesque emerges, applied not only to art and lit. but to estate organization and landscape architecture. Pope's "Epistle to Bathurst" and "Epistle to Burlington" offer discourses on the well- and ill-managed estates, respectively. Joseph Addison argues in *Spectator* nos. 411 and 412 on "the pleasures of the imagination," that the description of landscape is a form of imaginary possession, opening the way further to a liberation of taste from the control of power and wealth. The picturesque aesthetic sought to cultivate the natural environment along the principles of painting. James Thomson's *The Seasons* and Thomas Gray's "Ode on a Distant Prospect of Eton College" are firmly grounded in the aesthetic of the picturesque, as is William Wordsworth's early *Descriptive Sketches*. But the aesthetic of the *sublime in landscape began to emerge in these and other late 18th c. poems, displacing harmonious landscapes in the model of painter Claude Lorrain with wild and tempestuous lines inspired by Salvator Rosa. Such poems are often called "preromantic" because they contain elements of natural description and dynamic possibilities of phenomenological perception that *romanticism would draw out to a metaphysical dimension and identify with poetic imagination itself (see PREROMANTICISM).

The prospect poem becomes increasingly important in romanticism from Wordsworth to P. B. Shelley, where the psyche reaches out to find a spatial equivalent to its sense of an interior infinite. Rather than local detail and enargeia, the impulse of the landscape poem is now toward the grand "surmise" of the supernatural truth in or beyond the natural world. Whereas neoclassical poetry introduced analogical thought in the context of a pleasing environment, romantic poetry offers a secular revelation of a sublime power.

While Victorian poets such as Alfred, Lord Tennyson and Matthew Arnold retain a romantic taste for the picturesque and even the sublime in landscape, their poetry more often turns back toward moral and social reflection. Part of their skepticism toward the visionary project comes from the increasing prominence of science and eventually Darwinian theory. Thomas Hardy's landscapes in particular seem to question the visionary power of the landscape beholder, describing instead a landscape at once infused with human memory and association yet detached from human longings, purposes, and hist. Writing after World War I, W. H. Auden would use the landscape poem to reflect both on human suffering and indifference ("Paysage Moralisé," "Musée des Beaux Arts") and on worldly beauty and pleasure ("In Praise of Limestone").

Landscape has played a special role in Am. poetry, sometimes bearing the ideology of America as nature's nation. The poetic imagination shaped the challenges and pleasures of the New World, a boundless, undomesticated "virgin land," at least by Eur. standards, and a space of self-determination. William Cullen Bryant's "The Prairies" declares, "These are the gardens of the Desert, these / The unshorn fields, boundless and beautiful, / For which the speech of England has no name—/ The Prairies."

R. W. Emerson would have a major influence on Am. prospect poetry, connecting it to the transcendentalist project in which the "each" of nature's variety is informed by the luminous "all" of divine unity. Am. prospect poetry has also been associated with imperial ambition; the power of the gaze gives the beholder the feeling of authority over the world it organizes in its sight line.

By contrast, mod. Am. poetry has been wary of idealism and solipsism. Robert Frost's landscapes are often bleak or blighted—frozen swamps, dried-up brooks, abandoned farms. Frost emphasizes the role of the human in organizing the visible scene, yet his speakers are often out walking or working in uncertain ground. W. C. Williams in *Paterson* emphasizes a destructive human hist. embedded in landscape, but, like Marianne Moore and later Hart Crane, he imagines a resilient nature beneath human abuses and ultimately seeks to reconcile the natural and the built environment. Moore's long poem "An Octopus" describes Mt. Rainier in exuberant detail, celebrating "its capacity for fact" far greater than any human prospect.

Contemp. poets have also continued to celebrate the landscape as a focus of experience and a source of *metaphor, often reimagining romantic paradigms. They have modeled poetic stances that accommodate a dynamic and changing environment and acknowledge the mediations of lang. and culture. Elizabeth Bishop's richly detailed landscape poems, ranging in their latitude from Canada to Brazil, often circle back to reveal the yearnings and presumptions of the beholder. A. R. Ammons's poetry follows an Emersonian prophetic project, treating the landscape as a site of revelation, while simultaneously insisting on the insights of science and force of quotidian reality. His long poem *Garbage* presents a new turn in landscape poetry as human excess overwhelms the natural environment. John Ashbery draws heavily on landscape *imagery to present the mind's shaping of tentative but elusive prospects. Charles Wright's landscapes, often imagined through a lens of painterly abstraction, provide a space for contemplation of "the other side" and the idea of God. Charles Tomlinson, a Brit. poet influenced by mod. Am. poetry, has concentrated on phenomenological landscape description, evoking the otherness of the natural world while contemplating the traces in it of forgotten human stories. While the forms and ideology of landscape poetry have changed, it remains, then, a vital genre in contemp. poetry.

*See* DESCRIPTIVE POETRY, PAINTING AND POETRY.

■ **Criticism and History,** *English:* M. H. Nicolson, *Mountain Gloom and Mountain Glory* (1963); R. Williams, *The Country and the City* (1973); J. Turner, *The Politics of Landscape: Rural Scenery and Society in English Poetry, 1630–1660* (1979); P. Fletcher, *Gardens and Grim Ravines: The Language of Landscape in Victorian Poetry* (1983); J. A. W. Heffernan, *The Re-Creation of Landscape: A Study of Wordsworth, Coleridge, Constable, and Turner* (1984); J. Applewhite, *Seas and Inland Journeys: Landscape and Consciousness from Wordsworth to Roethke* (1986); R. Gilbert, *Walks in the World: Representation and Experience in Modern American Poetry* (1991); *Baroque Topographies*, ed. T. Hampton (1992); C. Fitter, *Poetry, Space, Landscape: Toward a New Theory* (1995); T. Fulford, *Landscape, Liberty and Authority* (1996); R. Crawford, *Poetry, Enclosure, and the Vernacular Landscape 1700–1830* (2002); B. Costello, *Shifting Ground: Reinventing Landscape in Modern American Poetry* (2003). **French:** C. Hogsett, "On Facing Artificiality and Frivolity: Theories of Pastoral Poetry in Eighteenth-Century France," *Eighteenth-Century Studies* 4 (1971); S. Mace, "Les Mutations de l'espace pastoral dans la poésie baroque," *Études Litteraires* 34 (2002). **German:** C. Tang, *The Geographic Imagination of Modernity: Geography, Literature, and Philosophy in German Romanticism* (2008).

*Italian:* *Italian Landscape Poems,* trans. E. Alistair (1993). *Japanese:* J. T. Sorensen, "Poetic Landscapes and Landscape Poetry in Heian Japan," *PAJLS: Proceedings of the Association for Japanese Literary Studies* 6 (2005).

B. COSTELLO

**LANGUAGE POETRY.** The ensemble of consciously avant-garde aesthetic tendencies and institutional and social practices known as *Language poetry* (also known as *language-centered writing* or, more popularly but less properly, *L=A=N=G=U=A=G=E poetry*) emerged in the 1970s and 1980s among a set of writers located primarily in the San Francisco Bay area, New York, and Washington, D.C. The group included Bruce Andrews, Rae Armantrout, Tom Beckett, Steve Benson, Alan Bernheimer, Charles Bernstein, David Bromige, Abigail Child, Clark Coolidge, Tina Darragh, Michael Davidson, Alan Davies, Ray DiPalma, Ted Greenwald, Robert Grenier, Carla Harryman, Lyn Hejinian, Susan Howe, Erica Hunt, P. Inman, Bernadette Mayer, Steve McCaffery, David Melnick, Nick Piombino, Kit Robinson, Leslie Scalapino, Barrett Watten, and Hannah Weiner, among others. Spurred by coinciding aesthetic, intellectual, and social commitments, these writers founded networks of publication and mutual support outside the mainstream literary establishment—jours. (such as *Tottel's, This, Hills,* and *L=A=N=G=U=A=G=E*), presses (Roof, Potes and Poets, O Books, The Figures, Tuumba, and Sun and Moon), reading and lecture series, and collaborations. Considered together, their poems, intellectual justifications for poetry, institution-building efforts, and embodiment of an ethos of engaged writing offered an energetic response to the literary, theoretical, and social forces shaping late 20th-c. Am. poetic culture.

Aesthetically, Language poetry was a rebellion against the perceived dominance of poetic modes that emphasized the fundamentally expressive and subjective nature of the art: the so-called *confessional poets' emphasis on self-inquiry and self-disclosure, or the Deep Image poets' embrace of "inwardness" and subconscious process (see DEEP IMAGE). Even the New American Poetry (though in many ways congenial to the Language poets for its embrace of aesthetic nonconformity) was faulted for its emphasis on spontaneous utterance and natural speech. In contrast, the Language poets emphasized the arbitrariness of signification and the constructive character of meaning-making. In their hands, lang. was neither a *mimesis of life nor a vehicle for the narration of selves, the communication of messages, or the transmission of feelings. It was, rather, a *medium*: matter to be arrayed, disassembled, and reconfigured; a sign system whose material basis and social function were an object of ludic inquiry ("the pleasure of the graphic or phonic imprint . . . their value as sheer linguistic stimuli" [McCaffery]) and serious critique ("to create conditions under which the productivity of words & Syllables & linguistic form-making can be felt, & given aesthetic presence" [Andrews 1996]). The emphasis on arbitrariness, indeterminacy, and making manifest the labor of assemblage could be seen working at every level of the poem: ling., figural, rhetorical. Where a poet less programmatically oriented toward innovation or method might use *metaphor to intimate unities (actual or desired) beneath the diverse ground of experience, the Language poet tends to emphasize the metonymic accident of sheer contiguity ("metonymy maintains the intactness and discreteness of particulars" [Hejinian]; see METONYMY). Rather than situating a speaker within a scene, the Language poem produces a discourse that is multifarious and unlocatable and resists idealizations such as *voice or character ("the allure of the spontaneous & personal is cut here by the fact of wordness" [Bernstein 1984]). Where an expressive poetics may inhabit the full range of *tones available to the socially situated person, Language poetry deliberately restricts itself to tones available to the act of reflection—though these might range widely from the coolly analytical to the comic and ironic to the ferociously negating. Thus, even the most lyrical of poets influenced by the poetics of Language (e.g., Armantrout or Michael Palmer) retain a deep suspicion of the sentiment that enters into their work.

The constructedness of lang. was not a merely formal or stylistic insight. It was accompanied by the idea that persons are, in crucial ways, themselves social constructs, subject to determination by systems of knowledge and power; and that the "lyric I" as a figure of sovereign self-possession and autonomous reflection is an ideological fiction by means of which the inchoate self might be rendered coherent and the determined self naturalized. This constructivist account of persons, though available within poetic trads. both ancient and mod., was given new force by the Language poets' encounter with a variety of literary and cultural theorists and philosophers. (In this sense, Language poetry can be seen as part of the enthusiastic Am. reception of *structuralism and *poststructuralism.) From *Russian formalism, the Language poets adopted the concept of *defamiliarization to describe their efforts to jolt readers out of conventional aesthetic sensibilities and habits of mind ("poetry is like a swoon, with this difference: / it brings you to your senses" [Bernstein, "The Klupzy Girl"]). From Jacques Derrida and Jacques Lacan, they derived theoretical support for the idea that all systems of meaning-making (ling., psychological, philosophical, ethical) are subject to the endlessly displacing and decentering energies of lang. Michel Foucault provided Language poetry with a sophisticated account of discourse (incl. literary discourse) as a theater of power in which the forms of knowledge and subjectivity are created and policed ("With *afford, agree* and *arrange,* use the infinitive. / *I can't agree to die*" [Bob Perelman, "Seduced by Analogy"]); while the Marxist theorists of the *Frankfurt school confirmed their lived observation that such power could be appropriated and corrupted by mass media and the consciousness industry.

As this eclectic and sometimes contradictory collection of theorists might suggest, the Language poets' interests in theoretical accounts of lang. and subjectivity were not chiefly academic, nor were they primarily a way of justifying stylistic practices or formal concerns. Rather, such ideas seemed to suggest the possibility of integrating their aesthetic commitments with passionately held political and ethical commitments. Some of the early political rhet. of the Language poets was explicitly Marxist in its class analysis, though "unorthodoxly" so in the accompanying suggestion that the intellectual and cultural work of poetry practices could itself count as a subversion of restrictive social arrangements ("let us undermine the bourgeoisie," [Silliman 1984]). Perhaps more typical were the more restrained accounts of the role that a formally challenging poetry could play in forming or reforming political consciousness. If the Language poets' social analysis occasionally conflated opposition to the perceived conformity or conservatism of the university writing workshop (one of the centers of what Bernstein has called "official verse culture") with other forms of social opposition, it was in the interest of imagining acts of *style as strategies of cultural and institutional critique. Likewise, if Language poems deliberately eschewed some traditional poetic satisfactions and foreclosed some traditional aesthetic responses (the luxuriousness of beauty, the sturdiness of craft, the consolation of wisdom), it was in order to place an ethical obligation to *attention at the center of the act of reading. Poetry that required a high degree of attentiveness and participation on the part of readers might reasonably hope to focus their attention on the constructive choices involved in meaning-making (e.g., the exclusions entailed by acts of signification and *closure; see SIGN, SIGNIFIED, SIGNIFIER). It might also awaken readers' critical awareness of other forms of exclusion and policing taking place in and through lang. ("language control = thought control = reality control" [Bernstein 1986]). These forms of ling. idealism had particular appeal within the Vietnam-era "mediascape" in which many of the Language writers began their mature work. Even at a distance from these formative events, however, Language poetry retains a utopian strain, a sense of its political and social dissidence that no amount of mainstream success or institutional recognition has dispelled.

The forms of Language poetry have followed a similar revisionary trajectory. Some of the earlier works of Language poetry experimented with extreme ling. fragmentation—with lang. broken at the lexical or morphemic level and operating at or beyond the edges of intelligibility (examples include P. Inman, David Melnick, or Clark Coolidge). These radical experiments largely gave way to the techniques that Silliman arrayed under the label of the *New Sentence*: poems that are lexically intact and, in large measure, grammatically ordered but that, nonetheless, allow for high degrees of disjunction from sentence to sentence or element to element. With the admission of larger units of intelligibility came the possibility of staging more complex and diverse negotiations and interferences between discourses of self and of the social world. Thus, a poem like Hejinian's *My Life* (originally pub. in 1980

as 37 chapters of 37 sentences each) explores how a sense of biographical consciousness must be assembled from any number of loosely connected discursive acts and modes (concrete perception, abstract observation, recollection, meditation); while Howe's many complex negotiations with personal and historical materials dramatize both the excisions of patriarchal hist. and the reconstructive work of historical knowledge.

Language poets have historically preferred to emphasize the centrifugal nature of their practice, the diversity of the poets and styles arrayed beneath the name of the group. But they have also encouraged the perception there that exists a unified movement, through acts of collection and anthologization—Silliman's *In the American Tree* and Messerli's *"Language" Poetries*—or through retrospective narration, as in the recently completed "collective autobiography" of the West Coast Language poets, *The Grand Piano* (10 v., 2006–10). Indeed, over the last 40 years, Language poetry has undergone a dramatic transformation from a movement emphasizing numerousness and heterogeneity to one with identifiable central voices, theoretical defenses, and classic works. This transformation, so characteristic of earlier dissident artistic movements, may indeed partake in the inevitable irony of the mainstreaming of the avant-garde. But to say that Language poetry has shared the fate of other historical avant-gardes does not detract from its lasting influence. Even as its formal innovations take on a period sheen, are diverted into other channels, or are diluted into replicable gestures and motions, Language poetry's durable triumph may be seen in the increasing avant-gardism of the Am. mainstream. It may be the case that Am. poetry has always been unusually open to the renovating energies, to the new thresholds and anatomies of experimental *modernism; but the Language poets have succeeded in securing a widespread contemp. consensus that to write with a heightened awareness of lang. as medium is among the most vital currents in poetic art.

See AVANT-GARDE POETICS; POSTMODERNISM; UNITED STATES, POETRY OF THE.

■ **Anthologies**: *The L=A=N=G=U=A=G=E Book*, ed. B. Andrews and C. Bernstein (1984)—esp. C. Bernstein, "Stray Straws and Straw Men," and R. Silliman, "If by 'Writing' We Mean Literature"; *In the American Tree*, ed. R. Silliman (1986); *"Language" Poetries*, ed. D. Messerli (1987); *Onward: Contemporary Poetry and Poetics*, ed. P. Baker (1996).

■ **Criticism and History**: M. Perloff, *The Dance of the Intellect: Studies in the Poetry of the Pound Tradition* (1985); B. Watten, *Total Syntax* (1985); C. Bernstein, *Content's Dream: Essays 1975–1984* (1986); R. Silliman, *The New Sentence* (1987); S. McCaffery, *North of Intention: Critical Writings 1973–1986* (1987); G. Hartley, *Textual Politics and the Language Poets* (1989); *The Politics of Poetic Form: Poetry and Public Policy*, ed. C. Bernstein (1990); C. Bernstein, *A Poetics* (1992); B. Andrews, *Paradise and Method: Poetics and Praxis* (1996); L. Hejinian, *The Language of Inquiry* (2000); J. Ashton, *From Modernism to Postmodernism* (2005); M.-Q. Ma, *Poetry as Re-Reading: American Avant-Garde Poetry and the Poetics of*

*Counter-Method* (2008); O. Izenberg, *Being Numerous: Poetry and the Ground of Social Life* (2010).

O. IZENBERG

**LATIN AMERICA, POETRY OF.** *See* ARGENTINA, POETRY OF; BOLIVIA, POETRY OF; BRAZIL, POETRY OF; CHILE, POETRY OF; COLOMBIA, POETRY OF; ECUADOR, POETRY OF; EL SALVADOR, POETRY OF; GAUCHO POETRY; GUARANÍ POETRY; INDIGENOUS AMERICAS, POETRY OF THE; MAPUCHE POETRY; MEXICO, POETRY OF; NICARAGUA, POETRY OF; PERU, POETRY OF; SPANISH AMERICA, POETRY OF; URUGUAY, POETRY OF; VENEZUELA, POETRY OF.

**LATIN POETICS.** *See* CLASSICAL POETICS; CLASSICISM; MEDIEVAL POETICS.

## LATIN POETRY

I. Classical
II. Medieval
III. Renaissance and After

### I. Classical

**A.** *Preservation and Transmission.* Key to the understanding of ancient Lat. poetry is the issue of transmission. Most of what we have depends for its survival on mss. written in the late antique and med. (sometimes even early mod.) period in western Europe. A very modest contribution comes from ancient written texts (Roman papyri, unlike Gr. papyri, are few, and rarely preserve poetry; epigraphy offers a substantial body of texts but often by marginal or nonprofessional composers).

When compared to the remains of other ancient cultures, however, the amount of accompanying evidence is staggering: archaeology, ling., numismatics, epigraphy, prose sources, and material culture in general offer a great deal (just as for cl. *Greek poetry, while, e.g., the other great premod. corpus of written poems, Vedic poetry, offers the fascinating problem of a rich corpus of mythology and religion in a well-documented lang. being accompanied by very tenuous material evidence; see SANSKRIT POETRY).

Because of the fragility of papyrus and pergamene, only texts that have been copied at least once since the 4th c. CE had a chance to survive, i.e., to reach an age (the 14th–15th cs. in Western Europe) when the recuperation and circulation of antique texts was a major industry. The cl. Lat. texts have been sifted through a triple process of filtering:

— ancient canonization (the school system of the Roman Empire being the key, as it will be again in the mod. age when Eur. state-sponsored education is fundamental in the spread of cl. Lat. culture);
— a more occasional selection guided by med. agendas; and
— the impact of random destruction and material damage.

This has important implications: educational value was crucial to survival. Authors without an obvious support in schooling, like Petronius (ca. 27–66 CE), Catullus (ca. 84–54 BCE), and Lucretius (ca. 99–55 BCE), have been close to disappearing. On the other hand, many of the canonical works have been preserved, and there is a family atmosphere: the authors tend to create a pattern of intertextual relationship based on the practice of *imitation. Our first impression of Lat. poetry is frequently related to the striking amount of self-consciousness: the individual poet has a constant awareness of his place in the *tradition and a subtle and supple strategy for rewriting past lit. hist. and inserting himself into it. The art of writing poetry in Roman society is a form of networking. The maximum density of this approach to poetic composition and self-promotion is found in the Augustan Age (a concept explicitly used by Horace), with Virgil's (70–19 BCE) *pastoral poems, the *Bucolics* (or *Eclogues*), as a first *manifesto, and Virgil's *Aeneid* and Ovid's (43 BCE–ca. 18 CE) *Metamorphoses* as the *summae*. Not by chance, the Augustan Age has been canonized and accepted as the climax and the cl. age of Roman lit. hist.

Considering the much that survives, it is easy to forget the losses. Numerous *fragments exist of crucial works that were often quoted in prose texts (through so-called indirect transmission), for instance, Ennius's (ca. 239–169 BCE) *epic on Roman hist., the *Annales*; but other masterpieces such as Cornelius Gallus's (ca. 70–26 BCE) love *elegies (except for a tiny papyrus fragment) and Ovid's *tragedy *Medea* have been lost. Then, of course, not all the poetry recovered has been available continuously since late antiquity. It is important to study Eur. culture with an awareness of changes related to successive rediscoveries of Roman texts in the age on humanism. At the end of the first commentary made on Lucretius's Epicurean poem in the early 16th c., a postscript by an It. scholar says, "I submit everything to orthodox belief," to which a different hand has added, "Everything, then, needs revising now."

**B.** *Origins and Evolution.* During the central part of the 3d c. BCE, Rome, a mid-sized republican state in western central Italy, begins to grow at an impressive rate as a "conquest state." During the same period, inscriptions in Lat., some of them in poetic *meter, begin to rise in number and complexity (alphabetic writing already had a trad. of many centuries in Italy), and verse in Lat. appears and develops quickly into something that to us looks like a *national poetry or lit. (a double anachronism because both "literature" and "nationhood" have been shaped, in their current value, by Eur. modernity and bourgeois ideology). A local, autonomous, native Roman lit. never had a chance to surface.

Later on, the Romans—a community and an empire with a Lat.-speaking as well as a Gr.-speaking elite culture—view the generations between (roughly) the mid-3d c. and mid-2d c. BCE as "the origins." They imagined lit. hist., a concept and practice in which they were pioneers, as a process of increasingly adequate Hellenization—a far cry from romantic ideas of national lit.

The meters are all based on adaptations of Gr. originals. The "primitive" *Saturnian looks like an outlier, but it may be the result of an older process of appropriation. As a rule, the most popular *genres have a lot of metrical adaptation and "freedom," while elite verse displays a "pure Greek" metrical style. Cicero (106–43 BCE) thought that the lines of verse in comic drama were so low-key that they were not recognizable as something different from prose; Horace (65–8 BCE) avoids this style when he writes iambic poetry, and he regulates and moderates the "freedom" of comic verse. Seneca (ca. 3 BCE–65 CE) creates a sophisticated but overcontrolled template for his tragic verse, not deterred by the effect of monotony that is being imparted to the end of the lines.

The metrical forms are all quantitative (see QUANTITY) and presuppose a melodic word *accent: intensive accent is not relevant. The importance of patterns of *alliteration, linking the initial parts of adjacent words, however, points to Germanic-Celtic areas more than to Hellenism as a parallel. After the unique explosion of creativity in Plautus's (ca. 254–184 BCE) *comedies, the style tends to be regulated by ascetic elitism and separated from colloquial expression, avoiding both low-life speech and "crude" Gr. loan words: the main later exception, the mysterious and transgressive Petronius, is not by chance also the only major artist who dares to combine poetry and prose (see PROSIMETRUM).

C. *Roman Hellenism.* Being oriented on Gr. models, Roman poetry has two dominant states of mind, not mutually exclusive: submission and competition. Most of the surviving texts already belong to a stage when Rome is master of the Gr. world, so there is a constant tension and interplay between Roman domination of Greece and Hellenic intellectual colonization of Roman minds.

Between Gr. and Roman poetry, there is one main difference: Roman poetry is monocentered, centripetal, obsessed with Rome, and works on a center-periphery model (evident, e.g., in Catullus, Virgil, and Horace and in *elegy). The lang. often has an artificial feel to it, as if the writers were lifting themselves up by the bootstraps, and lit. is strongly supported and invoked by existing political unity—while Greece is a ling. community where lang., education, and culture overcome a permanent state of political fragmentation and (often) confusion and instability.

Mythology and narrative are by default Gr.-oriented, while Rome tends to supply historical examples or alternatively produces daily life, waiting to be aestheticized or criticized according to the standards of the author. The author arbitrates between the poles of Hellenization and Romanness and capitalizes on this function, drawing power from it. Most genres of Roman poetry, in *narrative and theater, are based on the assumption that the poet will not create entirely new characters: the individuals are taken from mythology (in epic and tragedy) or from hist. recorded in

prose (in historical epic and historical tragedy or *praetexta*) or from a limited repertory in stock characters (in Gr.-style comedy), and, of course, poetic skill will be evident from innovations and adaptations. In *satire, *epigram, and other less-than-elevated poetry, the assumption is that characters will be taken from daily life, although often with adaptations or pseuds.: those genres often programmatically decline "seriousness" and ambition, as if to justify their realism and direct intervention into social practice.

Other main differences are as follows: (1) Roman production is multigeneric from the start (a phenomenon rare in Gr. poetry, at least before Callimachus), so we have early Roman poets who already divide themselves among epic, theater, and other genres. (2) The Romans had prose from very early on, and there had been only a very brief time when poetry was not sharing the system with prose. (3) Thus, the Romans inherit a Gr. literary system that was already mature and ramified, the system that was in place in the 3d c. BCE, although they always have the option of going back to previous epochs and layers. (4) Roman poets are often very politicized, sometimes masters of *invective and political discourse, but they almost never inhabit a space of communal openness: there is very strong political pressure against freedom of speech of the kind practiced (and revived in Roman historical imagination) in Gr. archaic poetry or in Athenian Old Comedy. This situation favors the devel. of a rhet. of innuendo and of a tension between political control and authorial voice. Seneca addresses Nero and the opposition to Nero obliquely through a dark mythological theater; Ovid absorbs Augustan rhet. of urbanism and world domination and also criticizes Augustan bigotry and repression; Juvenal (ca. 55–127 CE) attacks the corruption of the *previous* regime; Horace sings about the impossibility of retelling the civil wars. (5) While early Gr. poetry is driven by a *performance culture and shows traces of oral composition (see ORAL POETRY), Roman poetry is from the beginning onward based on a ripe alphabetic culture: the poets show a recurring concern for "live" performance, but most of their work is oriented toward producing well-wrought scripts or scriptures. Horace's *lyric poems have an indirect and belated relationship to the issue of performance and *voice, and every single poem stands, or better, oscillates between its vocalized occasion and its inscription in the book.

What happened in Rome was not unavoidable, as we can see by contrasting the very different options of Etruscan civilization: the Etruscans invested in spectacles, like the Romans, and reveled in appropriations of Gr. images and lifestyles, but their appropriations are much less careful and respectful; moreover, they do not link the complex of leisure, art, and spectacle with the production of a systematic body of lit. in Etruscan. In Rome, the theater is a driving force during the first generations of Lat. poetry, but during the middle republic, aggressive "modernist" poets such as Lucilius (ca. 180–103 BCE) and Catullus begin to focus entirely on first-person poetry in textual format. Only one thing is clear about the origins: the initial impulse must have had to do not so much with interactions between Rome and Greece, but more with inter-Italic competition. Rome was surrounded by Italic communities that spoke incompatible langs. (Etruscan, Oscan), and "going Greek" was highly desirable to all of the emerging Italic elites. Only slightly later the phenomenon of Roman Hellenicity became entangled with the pace of conquest, first in the Gr.-speaking communities of the It. south and later all over the eastern Mediterranean. In this new phase, Lat. poems derived from Gr. models are competing not only with the Gr. models but with the furious acquisition of Gr. art, knowledge, and status symbols fueled by conquest, the slave trade, and plunder. Later, in the age of Caesar and Augustus, the Romans begin exporting a complex package of acculturation to the western Mediterranean, centered on urbanism and incl. Lat. lang. and lit. and Gr. educational values and aesthetics.

The position of Rome in relation to Gr. culture is crucial for the hist. of mod. Eur. *classicism. Roman appropriation and exploitation of Greece lives on in mod. ideas of the classics as a harmonious sum of Gr. and Lat. The primacy of Greece over Rome in the romantic imagination results in a compromise, where the Greeks are leaders in poetry and philosophy and the Romans, while lacking in the necessary originality and communal atmosphere, are role models of "mediation" and (often) imperial control. The Romans are the ones who absorb and transmit Gr. classics—as well as the Judaeo-Christian trad.—to western and northern Europe, and so ultimately to the superpowers of the 18th, 19th, and early 20th cs. *Classics* is, therefore, based on a double exceptionalism: while the miracle of Greece is self-evident and consists in absolute originality and creativity, the Roman miracle is about imitation, belatedness, and imperial opportunism. (The contingent nature of historical transmission blinded the Europeans to the fact that most of those "exceptions" were already present in Near Eastern cultures before the rise of Greeks and Romans.)

**D. Genres and Authors.** In ancient Rome, the *canon is initially formed by authors who impersonate and continue Gr. authors: only in the generation of Tibullus (ca. 55–19 BCE) and later Ovid do we begin to find authors who do not identify themselves as "new X," X being a canonical Gr. poet (e.g., Menander, Homer, Callimachus, Theocritus, Alcaeus). Ovid is also, not coincidentally, the first author who dispenses with the convention of *patronage (claiming a powerful figure as friend, protector, and, in some cases, sponsor of the work) and spreads the impression of a wide, anonymous circle of readers as a condition for his success. In a society without licensed products, copyright, and authentic mass media, this means pushing the idea of authorial independence as far as it will go until the early mod. period. Among Ovid's successors, only Martial (ca. 40–103 CE) operates on a similar scale and foregrounds the *book as his decisive medium. Before

Ovid, Catullus and Horace had offered interesting combinations of a "face-to-face" approach, addressing individual poems to recognizable persons on specific occasions (see OCCASIONAL VERSE), and of a "generalist" approach, where the same poems are being shifted away from the occasion in the direction of a general public and hedge their bets on universal fame and circulation, while still bearing traces of their primary occasion.

The Roman poets who identify themselves as "new X" are masters of ambiguity: the new work can be perceived as surrogate or continuation in another lang. but also as substitute, stand-in, and direct competitor. The poets writing in Lat. have been learning those strategies from Gr. poetry itself, esp. from the rampant *intertextuality in authors who had become "poets for poets," such as Aristophanes, Aratus, Callimachus, Theocritus, and the epigram writers.

The poets use all the resources of tact, irony, and self-fashioning in this kind of self-conscious discourse, more or less the same resources that are necessary to cultivating patronage. In the generations after Ovid, for the first time we see Roman poets who more or less implicitly declare themselves "new versions" of a *Roman*, not a Gr., model. The most famous example (esp. in the med. reception) is Statius (45–96 CE), who uses his main models—Virgil, Ovid, Seneca, and Lucan (39–65 CE)—according to the sophisticated strategies developed by the Augustan authors on their own chosen Gr. forerunners. The closure of the Lat. canon after Juvenal is a decision of great importance, and it contributes, together with the Christian revolution, to the typically introverted nature of late antique poetry: its main hero is the talented but isolated court poet Claudian (ca. 370–404 CE), while Christian poetry will slowly develop its own classicism.

Ubiquitous in Roman poetry is the relationship with prose and with *rhetoric, often too easily deplored and criticized. Important too is the strand of *didactic poetry, again nourished by Gr. prose; the genre is influenced by the gigantic and isolated Lucretius and continued by Cicero, Virgil, Ovid, Manilius (fl. 1st c. CE), and less famous poets: in this trad., still active in the Ren., the formal resources of rhythm and beauty are intertwined with more or less strong claims to science and truth. Again, the idea of Roman Hellenism is crucial here, since the acquisition of science and information was inseparable from access to definitive Gr. sources in philosophy, biology, mathematics, and cosmology. Those issues play a fundamental role in the specific ideology of Roman epic (also in narrative and heroic guise) and in its claims to encompass the world and reveal its breadth and secrets. In fact, a didactic element was never absent in any given genre of Roman poetry because every Roman poet, from the erotic Propertius (ca. 50–after 16 BCE) to the fabulist Phaedrus (15 BCE–50 CE), is more or less implicitly "teaching" his audience about the cultural capital of Hellenism, as well as realizing his own vision.

A typical breakthrough, if we focus on the later Western trad., is the reinvention of first-person poetry.

Taking some cues from Gr. trads. such as epigram and other nonpublic genres, the Roman poets develop a style related to private life and individual sentiment: hence, the many innovations in lyric, elegy, satire, and epigram, and the rise of personal voice even in the epics of Lucretius, Virgil, and Lucan. This expansion of subjectivity is combined with severe restrictions in formulating political address to the public in communal situations. The strong presence of writing throughout the Roman era and the growth of a reading public (increasingly also of women readers) created the atmosphere for the devel. of love elegy, Horatian lyric, and satire, the main contributions to the literary system initiated by the Greeks with their institutionalization of textual production in the 4th c. BCE.

The poets of ancient Rome have a fundamental role in the idea of the author and of the poetic career, as it will develop in late med. Europe and beyond. Authors such as Virgil, Ovid, Propertius, Seneca, Lucretius, and Horace are present not only with their texts but in their complex of *persona, personal *voice, and biography. Some of them, like Virgil, acquire a definitive status as the ideal of the artist. In one respect, however, the "premodern" Romans do not anticipate later devels. From the origins to late antiquity, Roman canonical verse is dominated by male authors: women poets are attested but never claim a public role or rise to the prominence of Sappho or to the almost professional status of other Gr. *poetesses. Appropriating and impersonating women's voices, therefore, is a constant preoccupation of the Roman authors: this trend is celebrated in one of the Roman texts that claim maximum influence in the Middle Ages, Ovid's *Heroides*.

**II. Medieval.** Early evidence of Christian Lat. poetry is sparse and random. If Commodian (prob. fl. mid-3d c. CE), who offers doctrine and exhortation in an accentual approximation of the cl. *hexameter, was indeed a 3d-c. African, he is an isolated phenomenon. Indicative of things to come are two short narratives, written in skillful hexameters, on Jonah and on the destruction of Sodom (ca. 300), and the beautiful *Phoenix* (ca. 310), attributed to Lactantius (240–ca. 320), wholly pagan in detail but, to the early Middle Ages, plainly a celebration of the Resurrection—a fact recognized by the later Anglo-Saxon poet who produced a vernacular adaptation of this text.

A coherent Christian Lat. trad. emerges in the 4th c., deliberately conceived as an alternative to the pagan classics on which all learned Christians had been reared but drawing principally on the metrical, stylistic, and narrative conventions of Virgilian epic. The *cento of the poetess Proba (mid-4th c.) is a mere *pastiche of tags from Virgil, carefully arranged into a biblical narrative. What is innovative in Juvencus's (4th c.) hexameter rendering of the Gospels (ca. 330) and the freer version in Sedulius's (fl. 5th c.) *Carmen paschale* (ca. 430) is their ingenuity in adapting Virgilian style to Christian purposes; and Paulinus of Nola (353–431) expresses his resolve to repudiate pagan models and write a new kind of poetry in verse richly evocative of Virgil, Ovid, and Horace. Prudentius (ca. 348–405), master of many cl. styles and genres, was a brilliant original whose complex attitude toward both Christian and pagan culture we are only beginning to fathom. Alongside his two sequences of *hymns (the *Cathemerinon* and the *Peristephanon*), he produced a number of didactic poems on theological subjects. The *Apotheosis*, which opens with a hymn on the Trinity, considers the nature of Christ, while the *Hamartigenia* deals with the question of sin. His *Psychomachia*, a short epic on the conflict of virtue and vice in the human soul, greatly influenced med. iconography and offers one of the earliest and most enduring examples of Christian *allegory.

The Christian Lat. poets were to coexist with, and even displace, the great pagans in the school curriculum of the early Middle Ages, but they had few imitators. More significant for med. Lat. poetry was the hymnody that appeared as Lat. replaced Gr. as the lang. of the liturgy. The cumbersome, dogmatic verse of Hilary of Poitiers (310–66) can hardly have had a liturgical function, and the rhythmical prose of the great *Te Deum*, despite its early and abiding popularity, was not imitated; med. Lat. hymnody begins with Ambrose (ca. 340–97), who provided his Milanese congregation with meditations appropriate to the liturgical hours and calendar couched in four-line *strophes of iambic dimeter. Psychologically profound and written in beautiful and surprisingly cl. Lat., the Ambrosian hymns were widely imitated (most famously by Prudentius and Venantius Fortunatus [ca. 530–605]) and came to form the nucleus of the med. hymnaries; and their form, four-stress lines in *quatrains, has been preserved with only minor variations down to the present day, as may be seen in the metrical index of any hymnal.

The upheavals of the later 5th c. left their mark on the Christian Lat. trad. The bookish verse of Sidonius Apollinaris (d. 480) reflects its survival in an attenuated form in Gaul; the "epic" trad. of Prudentius and Sedulius enjoys a late flowering in the *De laudibus Dei* of Dracontius (ca. 450–500); and the verse in Boethius's *De consolatione philosophiae* (early 6th c.), a prosimetrum including a range of meters imitated from Horace and Seneca, is a last manifestation of inherited familiarity with cl. culture. The *verse epistles and *occasional poems of Fortunatus (535–604), charming and often brilliantly innovative, show a marked loss of syntactic and metrical fluency, though his passion hymns *Vexilla regis* and *Pange, lingua* are among the greatest of Christian hymns. The cl. trad. is still alive in the poems of Eugenius of Toledo (fl. ca. 650) and resurfaces with the Carolingian court poets, but new devels. were also taking place. *Rhyme and accentual meters begin to appear (see ACCENTUAL VERSE), most notably in Ir. hymnody, evidently influenced by native Celtic verse forms and the rules of rhythmical prose formulated by the Lat. grammarians, culminating in the *Altus prosator* of Columbanus (d. 597). Correct Lat. verse in quantitative meters continued to be taught in schools and written by the learned past the 16th c., but accentually measured Lat. verse is the rule after the 4th c., paving the way for the accentually based prosodies of the vernaculars (Beare). The riddles of Aldhelm (d. 709), which inaugurated a popular genre, imitate the African Lat. poet Symphosius (4th or 5th c.), and the metrical life of Cuthbert by Bede (673–736) is couched in a fluent hexameter shaped by 4th-c. Christian models; but the high points of 8th-c. It. Lat. poetry are a rhythmical poem in praise of the city of Milan (ca. 738) and the accentual verse experiments of Paulinus of Aquileia (d. 802). Paulinus's somber *lament on the death of Eric of Friuli (799) is an early and influential example of the *planctus, which became a popular form and may reflect the influence of vernacular trad.

The poets who came to the court of Charlemagne brought their culture with them; much of the poetry of Paul the Deacon (d. 802) was written before he left Italy, and Theodulf (d. 821) and Alcuin (d. 804) were products of thriving schools in Spain and England. But Charles and his court inspired new poetry. *Panegyric epistles by Alcuin and Theodulf, and the Karolus Magnus et Leo Papa (ca. 800) attributed to Einhard (ca. 770–840) celebrate Charles as the champion of political and cultural renewal and Aachen as a new Rome. The poetry of the court includes charming occasional poems by Paul the Deacon and Theodulf's satire on the courts of law, but its finest product is the Christian Lat. pastoral, best illustrated by Alcuin's nightingale poems, his O mea cella, a celebration of the scholarly life at Aachen, and "Conflictus veris et hiemis," probably his, which is both a pastoral and perhaps the first example of the debate poem or Streitgedicht. This form is imitated in Sedulius Scottus's (9th c.) "Certamen Rosae Liliique" (ca. 850) and in the "Eclogue" of the pseudonymous Theodulus (9th–10th c.), and was widely popular in later periods, e.g., The Owl and the Nightingale in ME.

The later 9th and 10th cs. produced further new departures. The hexameter narrative of an anonymous "Poeta Saxo" (ca. 890) celebrates the deeds of Charlemagne as an example for the Emperor Arnulf, and Abbo of St. Germain (9th c.) combines *war poetry with moral reflections on the state of France in a poem on the Norman siege of Paris (ca. 897). The remarkable epic Waltharius, commonly attributed to Ekkehard of St. Gall (900–73) but possibly earlier, balances the impulsive and bombastic heroism of Attila against the less heroic but more sophisticated behavior of Walter of Aquitaine and his companions, providing a perspective at once sympathetic and detached on the trad. of Germanic heroism and heroic poetry that it evokes. Vernacular culture is probably reflected also in the Ecbasis cuiusdam captivi (ca. 950), a rambling beast fable in *leonine hexameters apparently written for the edification of young monks; in the mid-11th-c. Ruodlieb, the adventures of a wandering knight, based partly on an oriental tale, provide an early foretaste of chivalric romance (see MEDIEVAL ROMANCE).

This period was also a time of innovation in religious music, its most significant form being the sequence, sung at Mass between the Epistle and the Gospel, in which the emotional and dramatic scope of religious lyric is greatly expanded. The origins of the sequence are much debated, though the impulse it reflects is present in emotionally expressive poems like the Versus de Lazaro of Paulinus of Aqueliea or the O mi custos (ca. 825) of Gottschalkof Orbais (d. ca. 867). A shaping influence (formerly thought to be the originator of the sequence) was Notker of St. Gall (d. 912), whose Liber hymnorum expresses a range of spiritual feeling, often in striking dramatic *monologues and set forth in rhythmically parallel phrases designed for antiphonal singing. The later scholar of St. Gall, Ekkehard, produced a number of sequences in the same style as Notker but with few original features. Notker's work anticipates the religious poetry of Peter Damian (1007–72) and Peter Abelard (1079–1142) and the great achievements of Franciscan hymnody.

The devel. of the secular lyric is even harder to trace, but as early as the mid-10th c. the lang. of the Song of Songs was being used to celebrate an idealized beloved in a way that clearly anticipates the courtly lyric of the 12th c. (see COURTLY LOVE). The mid-11th-c. Carmina Cantabrigiensia (Cambridge Songs) ms. includes the sophisticated "O admirabile Veneris idolum," addressed to a beautiful boy; "Levis exsurgit Zephirus," which dwells on the interplay of emotion and natural setting in the manner of high med. lyric; and the magnificent "Iam dulcis amica venito," here a passionate love song but found elsewhere in a form adapted to religious use. The 12th c. saw a great flowering of secular love lyric, ranging from imitations of popular song to elaborate essays in love psychology and courtoisie by poets such as Walter of Châtillon (b. 1135) and Peter of Blois (ca. 1135–1212). Many of the best of these are gathered in collections such as the early 13th-c. Carmina Burana, which also includes drinking songs, narrative love visions like Phyllis and Flora and Si linguis angelicis (which anticipate the Roman de la Rose), and satire in the trad. of *Goliardic verse, in which poets such as Hugh Primas (fl. ca. 1150) and the anonymous Archpoet of Cologne (fl. 1160s) make their own misfortunes and dissipations, real or imagined, an occasion for discussing the ills of the world.

Religious poetry, too, appears in new forms in this period. The sequence form, now evolved into accentual verse with a regular rhyme scheme, provided a model for the powerful series of planctus in which Abelard dramatizes the sufferings of such OT figures as Samson, Dinah, and the daughter of Jepthah. In the sequences of Adam of St. Victor (d. 1177–92), subtle allegorical and theological arguments appear in forms as intricate as any lyric poetry of the period, and the sonorous rhyming hexameters of the De contemptu mundi (ca. 1140) of Bernard of Cluny (fl. 2nd c.) give a new force to religious satire.

Side by side with these new departures is a steadily evolving trad. of "learned" Lat. poetry based on cl. models. Already in the late 11th c., Marbod of Rennes (1035–1123), Hildebert of Le Mans (1056–1133), and Baudri of Bourgueil (1046–1130) had produced a new, urbane poetry, Ovidian in form and manner and devoted to such topics as friendship and the cultivation of relations with noble patrons. The broadly Virgilian biblical epic of the pseudonymous Ger. poet Eupolemius (probably 11th c.) marked a new departure in the poetic treatment of scriptural material. Though this text belongs most clearly to the trad. initiated by Prudentius, Juvencus, and Sedulius centuries earlier, Eupolemius shows little respect for convention. The topic of his lengthy hexameter poem is a battle between good and evil; but fidelity to biblical narrative is not a priority, and biblical names are used sparingly. The renewal of cl. studies in the 12th-c. cathedral schools led to more ambitious exercises. Bernardus Silvestris's (ca. 1085–1178) *Cosmographia* (ca. 1147) and the *De planctu naturae* (ca. 1170) of Alan of Lille (ca. 1128–1202), philosophical allegories in the trad. of Boethius and Martianus Capella, exhibit a new assurance vis-à-vis the great authors of antiquity. Alan's *Anticlaudianus* (1182–83), on the creation of the perfect human, announces itself as a new kind of epic; and the *Alexandreis* (1182) of Walter of Châtillon, Joseph of Exeter's (12th c.) *Ilias* (1188–90), and John of Hauville's (d. ca. 1210) virtually all-encompassing Juvenalian satire *Architrenius* (1184) reflect similar ambition, while Geoffrey of Vinsauf provided a latter-day counterpart to Horace's *Ars poetica* in his *Poetria nova* (ca. 1210). Later critics such as John of Garland (d. 1258) and Hugh of Trimberg (fl. ca. 1280) could claim these writers as mod. *auctores* worthy of the respect and study accorded the ancients. In addition, the 12th and early 13th cs. produced a range of school poetry in less ambitious but widely popular forms: topical satires like the mock-visionary *Apocalypse of Golias*, aimed at ecclesiastical corruption, and the *Speculum stultorum* of Nigel of Longchamps (fl. ca. 1190), an elaborate beast fable allegorizing monastic ambition; narrative imitations of ancient comedy such as the *Pamphilus*, which had a lasting influence on love narrative in several langs.; and a body of pseudo-Ovidian poetry, incl. the mock-autobiographical *De vetula*, which was long considered an authentic Ovidian work.

A number of the greatest examples of med. religious poetry date from the later 13th c., notably the *Philomena* of John Howden (d. 1275), a meditation on the power of love as exemplified in the lives of Christ and the Virgin; the hymns and sequence for the feast of Corpus Christi traditionally attributed to Thomas Aquinas (1229–74), the highest achievement of theological poetry in the trad. of Adam of St. Victor; and the work of a number of Franciscan poets, above all the "Dies irae" and "Stabat mater dolorosa" associated with the names of Thomas of Celano (d. 1255) and Jacopone da Todi (1230–1306). But in other areas, the great proliferation of vernacular lit. led to a decline in the production of Lat. poetry, and the typical 13th-c. works are didactic treatises, designed to systematize and compress the materials of the traditional curriculum, secular and religious, in accordance with the needs of a newly compartmentalized system of education. Examples include the *De laudibus divinae sapientiae* of Alexander Nequam (d. 1217), an encyclopedic review of Creation as a manifestation of divine wisdom; the *Aurora*, a ver-

sified biblical commentary by Peter Riga (d. 1209); and the *Integumenta Ovidii* of John of Garland. The 14th c. produces such late flowerings as the devotional verse of the Eng. mystic Richard Rolle (d. 1349) and the powerful anatomy of the social ills of England in the *Vox clamantis* (1380–86) of John Gower (ca. 1330–1408); but the most significant work of this period, the Lat. verse of Dante, Petrarch, and Boccaccio, arguably belongs to the hist. of the Ren.

**III. Renaissance and After.** Rejecting med. varieties of Lat. poetry, Ren. humanists promoted a closer study of versification and forms from cl. antiquity. The result, from the 14th to the early 17th c., was an immense output of Lat. verse in cl. meters. Petrarch (1304–74) showed the way with hundreds of hexameters on various themes in his versified *Epystole* (1333–64); a hexameter epic on the Punic Wars, *Africa* (1338–41, left incomplete after much revision); and twelve *eclogues, Bucolicum carmen* (1346–68), on poetry, politics, and contemp. hist. Further incursions into epic and pastoral marked the hist. of Lat. poetry in the 15th c., e.g., the incomplete *Sforzias* by Francesco Filelfo (1398–1481) about the rise to power of the poet's Milanese patron; a supplementary 13th book of the *Aeneid* by the humanist Maffeo Veggio (1406–58); and ten widely admired eclogues by Mantuan (Battista Spagnoli, 1447–1516) that recall cl. models while displaying a distinctive piety, humor, and satire.

Some of the best Ren. Lat. poetry appeared in cl. forms that Petrarch did not use, such as epigram, elegy, and *ode. Panormita (pseud. of Antonio Beccadelli, 1394–1471) initiated the Neapolitan Ren. with his *Hermaphroditus* (1425), two books of ribald epigrams that out-Martial Martial. His protégé, Giovanni Pontano (1429–1503), wrote *lullabies for his son (*Neniae*); Ovidian elegies for his mistresses (*Parthenopeus* and *Eridanus*), his wife (*De amore coniugali*), and deceased loved ones (*De tumulis*); and racy poems in *hendecasyllables for his male friends and their courtesans (*Biae*). At the Florentine *studium*, Cristoforo Landino (1424–98) compiled three books of *Xandra* (1443–60) in various meters about love, friendship, patriotism, and praise of the Medici. The posthumously published *Carminum libellus* of the Venetian humanist Pietro Bembo (1470–1547) offers tribute to friends and lovers in various meters.

Supremely conscious of its imitative debt to cl. texts, the finest Ren. Lat. poetry resonates with explicit echoes from ancient poetry. In Florence, Angelo Poliziano (1454–94) in five verse essays, *Silvae* (1475–86), urged poets to cultivate a cl. style. Poliziano wrought classically inspired epigrams (*Epigrammata*, 1498), as did his friend Michele Marullo (ca. 1453–1500) in poems about his exile from Constantinople and his love for his mistress Neaera. Marullo's four books of *Hymni naturales* illustrate tenets of Neoplatonic philosophy in various meters—hexameter, *alcaic, *sapphic, *iambic. The Neapolitan Jacopo Sannazaro (1458–1530) brought forth a steady flow of elegies and epigrams. His *Piscatoriae* (1526) adapts Virgilian pastoral to a seaside setting, while his short epic on Christ's nativity, *De partu virginis* (1526), appropriates formulas, expressions, and even entire lines from the epics of Virgil, Ovid, Claudian, and others.

The more Ren. humanists sought to recover the cl. past, the greater they realized their distance from it. One consequence was their effort to develop new forms and expand the repertory of Lat. poetry. The Venetian historian Andrea Navagero (1483–1529), e.g., destroyed his didactic verse but salvaged a lively experiment in pastoral epigrams, *Lusus pastoralis* (1530), which exerted great influence on later vernacular poetry. Girolamo Fracastoro (1483–1553), a professor of medicine at Padua, wrote *Syphilis* (1530), three books of hexameter verse attributing the origins of venereal disease to the New World and proposing a cure.

Amid early Reformation turmoil, a Benedictine monk at Mantua, Teofilo Folengo (1491–1544), wrote *Baldus* (1517–21), a rowdy hexameter epic in a *macaronic hybrid of Lat. and It. about an outlandish hero who hunts down witches, demons, and religious superstition. Presaging the Counter-Reformation in Rome, Marco Girolamo Vida (1485–1566) applied the principles of his versified *De arte poetica* (1527) to a six-book hexameter epic on the life of Jesus, *Christias* (1535), and a collection of Christian *Hymni* (1550). Another associate of the papal court, Marcantonio Flaminio (1498–1550), devoted himself to paraphrasing Psalms in cl. meters, *Davidis psalmi* (1546) and *Carmina sacra* (1551).

The devel. of Ren. Lat. poetry beyond the Alps followed similar patterns, confirming the stature of Lat. as a truly international lang. The Hungarian poet Janus Pannonius (1437–72) and the Ger. poet Conrad Celtis (1459–1508) wrote elegies, epigrams, hexameters, and hendecasyllables about their education in Italy and their efforts to bring humanist teachings to the North. The Dutch poet Joannes Secundus (1511–36) earned fame throughout Europe for his *Basia*, 19 erotic songs for his voluptuous mistress. The Fr. poet Salmon Macrin (1490–1557) graced the courts of Francis I and Henry II with a vast output of elegies, *epithalamia, political verse, and Christian hymns. The Scotsman George Buchanan (1506–82) issued a vast output of Lat. poetry that encompasses satire, tragedy, versified science, and trans. of the *Psalms.

With the devel. of the vernaculars and the prestige of their lits. throughout Europe in the 16th c., many poets who wrote superb Lat. lyrics turned decisively to their native langs. for important projects. Ludovico Ariosto (1474–1533) in Italy, Joachim du Bellay (ca. 1522–60) in France, and John Milton (1608–74) in England exemplify the trend. Some who wrote entirely in Lat. include two 17th-c. Jesuit poets, Maciej Kazimierz Sarbiewski (1595–1640) in Poland and Jacob Balde (1604–68) in Germany, whose religious lyrics accommodate scriptural themes to cl. meters. Though vernacular lit. gained complete ascendance, the composition of Lat. poetry survived in schools and universities well past the Ren. as an accomplishment proper to a cl. scholar.

*See* ALEXANDRIANISM, BYZANTINE POETRY, CLASSICAL POETICS, CLASSICAL PROSODY, DEVOTIONAL POETRY, GREEK POETRY, LITURGICAL POETRY, MEDIEVAL POETICS, MEDIEVAL POETRY, RENAISSANCE POETICS, RENAISSANCE POETRY.

■ **I. Classical.** *Bibliographies and Histories*: *L'Année philologique* 1—(1927–), http://www.annee-philologique.com/aph/; M. Schanz and C. Hosius, *Geschichte der römischen Literatur*, 4th ed. (1927–35); *CHCL*, v. 2; *Handbuch der lateinichen Literatur der Antike*, ed. R. Herzog and P. L. Schmidt (1989–2002); G. B. Conte, *Latin Literature: A History* (1999); *The Oxford Handbook of Roman Studies*, ed. A. Barchiesi and W. Scheidel (2010). *Hellenization*: G. Williams, *Tradition and Originality in Roman Poetry* (1968); E. Gruen, *Studies in Greek Culture and Roman Policy* (1990); D. Feeney, *Literature and Religion at Rome* (1998); R. Hunter, *The Shadow of Callimachus* (2006); A. Wallace-Hadrill, *Rome's Cultural Revolution* (2008). *Language*: J. Farrell, *Latin Language and Latin Culture* (2001); J. N. Adams, *Bilingualism and the Latin Language* (2003); *La lingua poetica latina*, ed. A. Lunelli (2011). *Poetics, Intertextuality, and Genre*: C. O. Brink, *Horace on Poetry*, 3 v. (1963–82); G. N. Knauer, *Die Aeneis und Homer* (1964); G. B. Conte. *The Rhetoric of Imitation* (1986); P. Veyne, *Roman Erotic Elegy*, trans. D. Pellauer (1988); D. C. Feeney, *The Gods in Epic* (1991); S. Hinds, *The Dynamics of Appropriation* (1998); T. Hubbard, *The Pipes of Pan* (1998); D. P. Fowler, *Roman Constructions* (2000); M. Wyke, *The Roman Mistress* (2002); F. Cairns, *Generic Composition in Greek and Roman Poetry*, 2d ed. (2007). *Primary Texts and Authors*: R. Heinze, *Virgil's Epic Technique* (1903); E. Fraenkel, *Plautine Elements in Plautus* (1922), and *Horace* (1957); W. S. Anderson, *Essays on Roman Satire* (1982); O. Skutsch, *The Annals of Quintus Ennius* (1985); M. Roberts, *The Jeweled Style* (1989); E. Courtney, *The Fragmentary Latin Poets* (1993); P. Hardie, *The Epic Successors of Virgil* (1993); D. Kennedy, *The Arts of Love* (1993); W. Fitzgerald, *Catullan Provocations* (1995); S. Braund, *Juvenal: Satires Book I* (1996); E. Gowers, *The Loaded Table* (1996); A. J. Boyle, *Roman Tragedy* (1997); M. Leigh, *Lucan: Spectacle and Engagement* (1997); C. Connors, *Petronius the Poet* (1998); E. Oliensis, *Horace and the Rhetoric of Authority* (1998); D. Sedley, *Lucretius and the Transformation of Greek Wisdom* (1998); K. McCarthy, *Slaves, Masters, and the Art of Authority in Plautine Comedy* (2000); K. Freudenburg, *Satires of Rome* (2001); P. Hardie, *Ovid's Poetics of Illusion* (2002); *Ovid: Ars amatoria*, book 3, ed. R. K. Gibson (2003); A. S. Hollis, *Fragments of Roman Poetry, c. 60 BC–AD 20* (2007); S. J. Heyworth, *Cynthia* (2009); A. Feldherr, *Playing Gods* (2010). *Roman Stage*: *The Tragedies of Ennius*, ed. H. D. Jocelyn (1967); Seneca, *Agamemnon*, ed. R. J. Tarrant (1976); R. L. Hunter, *The New Comedy of Greece and Rome* (1985); A. J. Boyle, *Roman Tragedy* (1997); F. Dupont, *The Invention of Literature* (1999); Seneca, *Thyestes*, ed. R. J. Tarrant (2000); C. Marshall, *The Stagecraft and Performance of Roman Comedy* (2006). *Social Background*: A. Richlin, *The Garden of Priapus* (1992); P. White, *Promised Verse* (1993); T. N. Habinek, *The Politics of*

*Latin Literature* (1998); J. Henderson, *Writing Down Rome* (1999); W. Fitzgerald, *Slavery and the Roman Literary Imagination* (2000); A. Keith, *Engendering Rome: Women in Roman Epic* (2000); S. Goldberg, *Constructing Literature in the Roman Republic* (2005); M. Lowrie, *Writing, Performance, and Authority in Augustan Rome* (2009). **Studies of Reception**: T. M. Greene, *The Light in Troy: Imitation and Discovery in Renaissance Poetry* (1982); L. Barkan, *The Gods Made Flesh* (1986); C. Martindale, *Redeeming the Text* (1992); D. Quint, *Epic and Empire* (1993); C. Burrow, *Epic Romance* (1993); *Classical Literary Careers and Their Reception*, ed. P. Hardie and H. Moore (2010); P. Hardie, *Rumour and Renown* (2012). **Style, Meter, and Other Formal Aspects**: L. P. Wilkinson, *Golden Latin Artistry* (1963); R.G.M. Nisbet and M. Hubbard, *A Commentary on Horace: Odes, Book 1* (1970), *A Commentary on Horace: Odes, Book 2* (1978); J. Wills, *Repetition in Latin Poetry* (1996); C. Questa, *La metrica di Plauto e Terenzio* (2007); L. Morgan, *Musa pedestris* (2010).

■ **II. Medieval**. *Anthologies and Texts*: *MGH*; Migne, *PG* and *PL*—the fullest collection of texts; *Analecta hymnica*—the fullest collections of hymns; *Carmina Burana*, ed. J. A. Schmeller, 4th ed. (1907)—the only complete text, later ed. by A. Hilka and O. Schumann, though only v. 1 (pts. 1–2), v. 2 (pt. 1), and v. 3 (pt. 1) have appeared (1931–71); *Early Latin Hymns*, ed. A. S. Walpole (1922); *Medieval Latin Lyrics*, ed. and trans. H. Waddell, 5th ed. (1948); *The Goliard Poets*, ed. and trans. G. F. Whicher (1949); F. Brittain, *The Medieval Latin and Romance Lyric*, 2d ed. (1951); *Oxford Book of Medieval Latin Verse*, ed. F.J.E. Raby (1959); *Hymni latini antiquissimi xxv*, ed. W. Bulst (1975); *More Latin Lyrics from Virgil to Milton*, ed. and trans. H. Waddell (1977); *Seven Versions of Carolingian Pastoral*, ed. R.P.H. Green (1980); *Poetry of the Carolingian Renaissance*, ed. P. Godman (1985)—long intro. **Criticism, History, and Prosody**: Keil—collects the principal med. Lat. grammarians and prosodists; Manitius—the standard lit. hist.; Meyer; H. Walther, *Das Streitgedicht in der lateinische Literatur des Mittelalters* (1920); Faral; "Mittellateinische Dichtung in Deutschen," *Reallexikon I*; Lote; Curtius; Raby, *Christian* and *Secular*; D. Norberg, *Poésie latine rythmique* (1954); Beare—good survey; M. Burger, *Recherches sur la structure et l'origine des vers romans* (1957); K. Strecker, *Introduction to Medieval Latin*, trans. and rev. R. B. Palmer (1957)—excellent intro. and bibl.; Norberg—best account of prosody; M.R.P. McGuire, *Introduction to Medieval Latin Studies* (1964); J. Szövérffy, *Annalen der lateinische Hymnendichtung*, 2 v. (1964–65); A. C. Friend, "Medieval Latin Literature," Fisher; Dronke; J. Szövérffy, *Weltliche Dichtungen des lateinische Mittelalters*, v. 1 (1970); C. Witke, *Numen litterarum* (1971); P. Klopsch, *Einführung in die mittellateinische Verslehre* (1972); Murphy—med. rhet.; F. Brunhölzl, *Geschichte der lateinischen Literatur des Mittelalters*, 3 v. (1975–2003); P. Dronke, *The Medieval Lyric*, 2d ed. (1978); *The Interpretation of Medieval Latin Poetry*, ed. W.T.H. Jackson (1980); J. Stevens, *Words and Music in the Mid-*

*dle Ages* (1980); Brogan, 720 ff.; Norden—art prose; P. Dronke, *The Medieval Poet and His World* (1985); P. Godman, *Poets and Emperors* (1987); O. B. Hardison Jr., *Prosody and Purpose in the English Renaissance* (1989)—incl. med. Lat.; J. Szövérffy, *Latin Hymns* (1989); F. Mantello and A. Rigg, *Medieval Latin: An Introduction and Bibliographical Guide* (1996)—authoritative essays and bibls.; Lausberg—rhet; *The Oxford Handbook of Medieval Latin Literature*, ed. R. Hexter and D. Townsend (2012).

■ **III. Renaissance and After**. *Anthologies*: *Poeti latini del quattrocento*, ed. F. Arnaldi et al. (1964)—with It. trans.; *Musae reduces*, ed. P. Laurens, 2 v. (1975)—with Fr. trans.; *An Anthology of Neo-Latin Poetry*, ed. F. J. Nichols (1979)—with Eng. transs.; *Renaissance Latin Verse*, ed. A. Perosa and J. Sparrow (1979); *Renaissance Latin Poetry*, ed. and trans. I. D. McFarlane (1980). **Criticism and History**: L. Spitzer, "The Problem of Latin Renaissance Poetry," *SP* 2 (1955); J. Sparrow, "Latin Verse of the High Renaissance," *Italian Renaissance Studies*, ed. E. F. Jacob (1960); W. L. Grant, *Neo-Latin Literature and the Pastoral* (1965); J. Ijsewijn, *Companion to Neo-Latin Studies* (1977); W. J. Kennedy, *Jacopo Sannazaro and the Uses of Pastoral* (1983); D. Robin, *Filelfo in Milan* (1991); S. Murphy, *The Gift of Immortality* (1997); L. Piepho, *Holofernes' Mantuan* (2001); W. Ludwig, *Miscella Neolatina* (2004); J. C. Warner, *The Augustinian Epic* (2005); *Petrarch: A Critical Guide*, ed. V. Kirkham and A. Maggi (2009). **Editions and Translations**: G. Fracastoro, *Syphilis*, ed. and trans. H. Wynne-Finch (1935); C. Celtis, *Selections*, ed. and trans. L. Forster (1948); J. Milton, *Variorum: Latin and Greek Poems*, ed. and trans. D. Bush et al. (1970); A. Navagero, *Lusus*, ed. and trans. A. E. Wilson (1973); Petrarch, *Bucolicum carmen*, ed. and trans. T. G. Bergin (1974); M. G. Vida, *De arte poetica*, ed. and trans. R. G. Williams (1976); Petrarch, *Africa*, trans. T. G. Bergin (1977); J. Secundus, *The Latin Love Elegy*, ed. and trans. C. Endres (1981); A. Poliziano, *Silvae*, ed. and trans. C. Fantazzi (2004); M. Vegio, *Short Epics*, ed. and trans. M. Putnam (2004); P. Bembo, *Lyric Poetry*, ed. and trans. B. Radice (2005); G. Pontano, *Baiae*, ed. and trans. R. G. Dennis (2006); T. Folengo, *Baldo*, ed. and trans. A. E. Mullaney (2007); C. Landino, *Poems*, ed. and trans. M. P. Chatfield (2008); M. G. Vida, *Christiad*, ed. and trans. J. Gardner (2009).

A. Barchiesi (cl.); W. Wetherbee, T.V.F. Brogan, S. Penn (med.); W. J. Kennedy (ren.)

**LATIN PROSODY.** *See* classical prosody.

**LATVIA, POETRY OF.** The roots of Latvian poetry are found in Latvian folk songs called *dainas*. A single folk meter is characteristic across the territory of Latvia: eight trochaic syllables per line, four unrhymed lines per stanza, the first two lines proposing a general situation, the last two adding a specific comment:

Viena meita Rīgā dzied,
Otra dzied Valmierā;

Abas dzied vienu dziesmu,
Vai bij vienas mātes meitas?

(One girl sings in Riga,
Another sings in Valmiera;
They both sing the same song,
Are they the same mother's daughters?)

Dainas were first celebrated by the Ger. philosophers Johann Georg Hamann and J. G. Herder, who noted that the basic form was sung, not written. Written poetic trads. began with Lutheran hymns, most notably by Christopher Fürecker (ca. 1615–85). From the Reformation to the 19th c., Lutheran pastors and the grassroots Moravian Brethren unsuccessfully urged Latvians to reject dainas in favor of Christian songs.

A 19th-c. movement of Latvian intellectuals sought subject matter in national hist., folklore, and mythology. Juris Alunāns (1832–64) inaugurated Latvian poetry with *Dziesmiņas* (Songs) in 1856. Poems by Auseklis (pseud. of Miķelis Krogzems, 1850–79) became popular in choral performances at the National Song Festivals, established in 1873; his poem "Beverīnas dziedonis" (Singer of Beverina) retells a 13th-c. chronicle account of a singer who halted a war, establishing "the power of song," as a popular theme in Latvian poetry. Andrejs Pumpurs (1841–1902) created the national epic *Lāčplēsis* (*Bearslayer*), based on folktales and dainas.

In the 1880s, Marxism precipitated a deep ideological schism in Latvian lit.; Rainis (pseud. of Jānis Pliekšāns, 1865–1929), however, synthesized national hist. and mythology with a secular love of all humanity. Aspazija (pseud. of Elza Rozenberga-Pliekšāne, 1868–1943) combined neoromantic nationalism with social conscience and feminism in her flamboyant, sensual poetry. A group led by Kārlis Skalbe (1879–1945), Jānis Akurāters (1876–1937), and Kārlis Krūza (1884–1960) published an "art-for-art's-sake" *manifesto in the 1906 literary jour. *Dzelme*. Edvarts Virza (pseud. of Jēkabs Liekna, 1883–1940) dropped a bombshell of passionately erotic poetry with *Biķeris* (1907).

After Latvian national independence in 1918, Rainis and Aspazija were greeted as national heroes when they returned from exile in Switzerland. Publications of a new artistic association, *Zaļā vārna* (Green Crow), catalyzed creative energy. Diverse content and style reflected many political and social currents. *Expressionism left an impact on Pēteris Ērmanis (1893–1969), the first Latvian poet to experiment with *free verse. Urban poet Ēriks Ādamsons (1907–46) was introspective and complex, ironic and refined, scornful of rural simplicities. The opium-laced poems of Jānis Ziemeļnieks (pseud. of J. Krauklis, 1897–1930) are hallmarks of melodic beauty. Aleksandrs Čaks (pseud. of A. Čadarainis, 1902–50) is the most original modernist, carrying a tangible legacy to subsequent generations. Forceful and iconoclastic, mocking and ironic, stressing rhythm over rhyme, he shocked the traditionalists and fascinated the young.

During World War II, many emerging poets such as patriotic bard Andrejs Eglītis (1912–2006) and

Velta Toma (1912–99) went into exile in the West. Other émigrés found their voice later, among them urban poet Linards Tauns (pseud. of Arnolds Bērzs, 1922–63), jazz-inspired Gunars Saliņš (1924–2010), nuanced master of lang. Astrīde Ivaska (b. 1926), and witty existentialist Olafs Stumbrs (1931–96). The poetry of rock music inspired Juris Kronbergs (b. 1946).

In Latvia, Stalinism and World War II left cultural life in ruins. Soviet Latvian poet Linards Laicens (1883–1938), trans. of the Finnish epic *Kalevala*, was executed during Stalin's purges in Russia. The Soviets deported Leonīds Breikšs (1908–42) from Latvia, his gravesite unknown; he is remembered for his "Prayer," sung during the Singing Revolution of 1988–91. Knuts Skujenieks (b. 1936) was arrested for political activities in 1962 and sentenced to seven years' hard labor. In the final years of Soviet rule, poet of conscience Klāvs Elsbergs (1959–87) was killed when he fell from a highrise window under suspicious circumstances.

In Soviet Latvia, socialist *realism was required. Among the best-known Stalinist praise poets were Arvīds Grigulis (1906–89) and Jānis Sudrabkalns (1894–1975). Mirdza Ķempe's (1907–74) loud political poems garnered official status, but her love poetry carried the power of truth, drawing young poets to her for mercilessly honest mentoring. Ojārs Vācietis (1933–83) was publicly ostracized for "ideological ambiguity" in his 1962 poem "Einšteiniana"; his first-person poem about Stalin's resurrection remained in ms. until 1987. Immensely popular Imants Ziedonis (b. 1933) expanded Vācietis's stylistic innovations, shaping conversational registers into musical free verse, addressing the reader directly and personally. Vizma Belševica (1931–2005) was first hailed, then silenced for eight years after her 1969 poem about a med. scribe who wrote secret notes in the margins of an official chronicle. Ārija Elksne (1928–84) likewise created islands of non-Soviet truth with her poems of gentle, feminine spirituality and love.

Most of these 20th-c. authors are also well represented in choral and pop songs; composer Imants Kalniņš (b. 1941) forged a particularly powerful combination of genres when he set to music poems by Māris Čaklais (1940–2003), multiplying political meanings hidden between the lines.

The 1970s and 1980s saw a rich influx of styles and themes through trans. by a generation of polyglot poets, among them Uldis Bērziņš (b. 1944), Leons Briedis (b. 1949), Dagnija Dreika (b. 1951), and the abovementioned Skujenieks; their poetry's transnational intertextual relations may never be fully unraveled. Others looked to native folklore. Ziedonis rediscovered the dainas' style and mythological content, while urban singing group Skandinieki revived authentic performance styles and melodies of oral poetry. Māra Zālīte's (b. 1952) simplicity and clarity echoed the powerful, grounded women's voices of folk song trad. Her librettos for musicals and rock operas resonated among the masses during and after the Singing Revolution.

Tension between censorship and honesty meant popularity for those who broke through barriers. The quirky poetry of Aivars Neibarts (1939–2001), e.g., juxtaposed words with phonetic similarities, producing playfully paradoxical, truthful statements. The loud, sometimes aggressive bravura of Māris Melgalvs (1957–2005) was a cover for sincere, vulnerable humanity; his poems were popularized by the underground rock group Pērkons. Poet Jānis Peters (b. 1939) entered politics proper as leader of the 1988 Latvian Writers' Union meeting, a public forum for free political discourse; he was later appointed independent Latvia's ambassador to Russia.

After freedom of speech was ensured by political independence, poetry was no longer needed to veil political statements; literary critic Berelis calls the 1990s a "post-prophetic era" when poets descended back to mortal life. Some lamented the sudden lack of interest in their experiments, but others such as religious poets Broņislava Martuževa (b. 1924) and Anna Rancāne (b. 1959) found broad resonance. Kornēlija Apšukrūma publishes large print runs of books popular as a source of handwritten inscriptions in greeting cards.

Poets and literary critics Māris Salējs (b. 1971) and Kārlis Vērdiņš (b. 1979) observe that poets nowadays are acutely aware of their social role. A 2005 manifesto by Gaiķu Māris (pseud. of M. Rozentāls, b. 1973) and Kikōne (pseud. of Edgars Mednis, 1984–2006) stressed respect for literary apprenticeship and the author's responsibility: "If the reader feels that the writer has wasted his time, then he reserves the right to kick, or pelt the author with rotten tomatoes."

The sense of social responsibility fosters epic, not lyrical expression, focusing on everyday experience in a larger, nonmaterial reality. Pēters Brūveris (b. 1957) sharpens perceptions through historical memory, reconstructing humanity out of the garbage of civilization. An awareness of lang. is ever present: Rūta Mežavilka's (b. 1971) grammatically crippled lines evoke deformities in life perceptions; the folksy Latgallian speech of Valentīns Lukaševičs (b. 1968) vibrates between witty rural identity and dark existentialism. For Inga Gaile (b. 1976) and Liāna Langa (pseud. of L. Bokša, b. 1960), fluid, organic images and a physical awareness of the body elicit a world of senses, not words. Latvian-Rus. poets Sergejs Timofejevs (b. 1970), Artūrs Punte (b. 1977), and Semjons Haņins (pseud. of Aleksandrs Zapoļs, b. 1970), leaders in the *Orbīta* group, publish bilingually and explore multimedia poetry.

Latvian poetry in the early 21st c. reached its largest audiences through musical performance. Heavy-metal group Skyforger and the rapper Ozols (pseud. of Ģirts Rozentāls, b. 1979) won acclaim abroad, but their success at home depended on effective poetry. Lyrics by Renārs Kaupers (b. 1974) and the popular Latvian band Brainstorm set the tone of the 2005 Youth Song Festival in Riga:

Tie ir vārdi no manas tautas, un dziesma man arī
   no tās,
un es zinu, neviens manā vietā to nedziedās.

(These are words that come from my people, and
   the song is also from them,
and I know that nobody else can sing it in my
   place.)

In contrast to images of civilization's decline and alienation that predominate in print, Kaupers projected an optimistic sense of responsibility for lang. and poetic trads., hinting at a richly multifaceted, resonant future for Latvian poetry.

■ **Anthologies:** *Latvju modernās dzejas antoloģija*, ed. A. Čaks and P. Ķikuts (1930); *Latvju sonets 100 gados 1856–1956*, ed. K. Dziļleja (1956); *Lettische Lyrik*, ed. E. Eckard-Skalberg (1960); *Contemporary Latvian Poetry*, ed. I. Cedriņš (1984); *All Birds Know This*, ed. Kristīne Sadovska (2001); *Citā gaismā*, ed. M. Lasmanis (2005)—Latvian poetry in the West; A. Pumpurs, *Bearslayer, the Latvian Legend*, trans. A. Cropley (2007); *The Baltic Quintet*, ed. E. Page (2008); *Latvian Literature*, 7 v. (2002–), http://www.literature.lv/; *Krišjāņa Barona dainu skapis*, http://www.dainuskapis.lv.

■ **Criticism and History:** E. Virza, *La Littérature lettonne depuis l'époque de réveil national* (1926); R. Ekmanis, *Latvian Literature under the Soviets: 1940–1975* (1978); *Linguistics and Poetics of Latvian Folksongs*, ed. V. Vīķis-Freibergs (1989); *Latviešu literatūras vēsture*, ed. V. Hausmanis et al., 3 v. (1998–2001); G. Berelis, *Latviešu literatūras vēsture* (1999); A. Cimdiņa, *Introduction to Modern Latvian Literature* (2001); J. Kursīte, *Dzejas vārdnīca* (2002); M. Salējs et al., *Latviešu literatūra 2000–2006* (2007).

J. SILENIEKS; G. ŠMIDCHENS

**LAUDA** (Lat., "praise"). It. genre of religious origin and content. The *lauda* was first created probably as a vernacular equivalent or adaptation of the med. Lat. *hymn, e.g., the "Stabat mater" and the "Dies irae." Its devel. is connected with a 13th-c. cult, esp. widespread in Umbria in central Italy, the confraternity of the Scourgers (*Flagellanti*). The earliest surviving example is Umbrian in origin, the *Laudes creaturarum* (Praise of the Creatures; in It., ca. 1224) of Francis of Assisi. The greatest cultivator of the lauda, Jacopone da Todi (1236?–1306), set its range of topics (from simple thanksgiving to complex multivocal dramatizations of liturgical themes) and meters of great freedom and variety; the typical form was the *ballata* with a two-line *ripresa* (*xx*) and a four-line monorhymed stanza (*aaax bbbx*, etc.) composed generally of *ottonari*, *hendecasyllables, and *heptasyllables. Jacopone's more than 100 surviving laude found no direct imitators of note, but the genre survived into the 16th c.

*See* ITALIAN PROSODY; ITALY, POETRY OF.

■ G. Ippoliti, *Dalle sequenze alle laudi* (1914); P. Dronke, *The Medieval Lyric* (1969); M. Fubini, *Metrica e poesia*, 2d ed. (1970); Wilkins; D. L. Jeffrey, *The Early English Lyric and Franciscan Spirituality* (1975), ch. 4; Elwert, *Italienische*, sect. 90–91; P. S. Diehl, *The Medieval European Religious Lyric* (1985); S. Orlando, *Manuale di metrica italiana* (1994); G. Sica, *Scrivere in versi* (2003); A. Vettori, *Poets of Divine Love: Franciscan Mystical Poetry of the Thirteenth Century* (2004).

T. WLASSICS; C. KLEINHENZ

**LAUREATE.** *See* POET LAUREATE.

**LEICH.** Poem in unequal stanzas, cultivated in Ger.-speaking areas in the 13th and 14th cs. Music survives for a few examples. The term *leich* originally designated an instrumental melody, a sense that persists in addition to that of the "nonisostrophic poem," a semantic loan on the pattern of OF *\*lai*, first attested in Ulrich von Liechtenstein (mid-13th c.). The leich has affinities with the med. Lat. sequence, Occitan and OF *\*descort*, OF lai, Occitan *\*estampida*, and OF *estampie*. Like sequence and lai (but unlike descort), the leich may be used for religious as well as secular subject matter.

There are considerably more examples of the secular leich. Its themes are mainly those of *\*Minnesang*. A new devel., not paralleled in the Romance analogues, is the introduction of a dancing section into the leich in Heinrich von Sax, Ulrich von Winterstetten, and Tannhäuser; this is associated with dactylic rhythms (*Tanzleich*). Tannhäuser is unique in introducing into the leich the didactic themes of princely *\*panegyric and lament for dead rulers.

The leich is usually considerably longer than most isostrophic poems. A high proportion of unique *\*strophes is characteristic of the religious leich and the Tanzleich. There may also be contiguous or noncontiguous repetitions of strophic patterns or partial or approximate response between sections. There is a proliferation of short rhyming units, with a high incidence of different types of rhyme. The leich is frequently divided into two halves, but in the Tanzleich, a ternary division is also found; internally, the strophes are frequently bipartite, less often tripartite. The religious leich has affinities with Lat. sequence, but in the main, the leich is more closely akin to its Romance analogues.

*See* GERMANIC PROSODY.

■ F. Wolf, *Über die Lais, Sequenzen und Leiche* (1841); O. Gottschalk, *Der deutsche Minneleich* (1908); R. J. Browne, "Stylistic and Formal History of the Middle High German Leich," Diss., Yale (1955); K. H. Bertau, *Sangverslyrik* (1964); H. Kuhn, "Leich," *Reallexikon II*; I. Glier, "Der Minneleich Im späten 13. Jahrhundert," *Werk-Typ-Situation*, ed. I. Glier et al. (1969); J. Maillard, "Lai, Leich," *Gattungen der Musik*, ed. W. Arlt et al. (1973); H. Spanke, *Studien zu Sequenz, Lai und Leich* (1977); O. Sayce, *The Medieval German Lyric, 1150–1300* (1982); *Tradition und Gattungsbewusstsein im deutschen Leich*, ed. H. Apfelböck (1991).

O. L. SAYCE

**LEONINE RHYME, VERSE.** "Once rhyme invaded the hexameter," John Addington Symonds remarked, "the best verses of the medieval period in that measure are leonine." Also the worst (Raby). Ordinarily, the term refers to internal rhyme in the med. Lat. *\*hexameter (i.e., the word at line end rhyming with the word preceding the *\*caesura); technically, it denotes an oxytonic word ending (a "feminine" rhyme; see MASCULINE AND FEMININE). Though there are examples in cl. Lat. poetry (e.g., Ovid, *Ars amatoria*) and *\*epitaph verse, leonine rhyme flourished in med. Lat. after the 9th c., being so popular it was imitated in Ir., Eng. (the OE "Rhyming Poem"), Ger., and (esp.) Fr. It is regularly mentioned in the med. prosody manu-

als of *ars metrica* and *\*séconde rhétorique*. Presumably the device came into verse from one of the clausulae of rhythmical prose, the *cursus leoninus*, though the origin of the term is uncertain: some trace it to Pope Leo the Great, others to Leoninus, a 12th-c. Benedictine canon of Paris (fl. 1135; see Erdmann).

Leonine verse refers to a hexameter-pentameter *\*couplet (not always rhymed), as in Eberhard's *Laborintus*—the meter known to antiquity as the *\*elegiac distich. Both in these couplets and in hexameter couplets, more elaborate schemes of internal rhyming quickly developed both in Occitan and OF such as rhyming the lines' first two *\*hemistichs together and last two together (Lat. *versus interlaqueati*, Fr. *rime enterlacée*, "interwoven rhyme"); or a double rhyme in the first line, a second double rhyme in the second, and a third binding the ends of the two lines—which by breaking gives the *aabccb* scheme of Fr. *rime couée*, *\*"tail rhyme." Thus, the partitioning of long-line Lat. verse via internal rhyme paved the way for a multitude of short-line lyric stanzas in the vernaculars.

■ W. Wackernagel, "Gesch. des deutschen Hexameters und Pentameters bis auf Klopstock," *Kleinere Schriften*, vol. 2 (1873); E. Freymond, "Über den reichen Reim bei altfranzösischen Dichtern," *ZRP* 6 (1882); Schipper 1.305 ff; Kastner; Meyer, 2.267; K. Strecker, "Leoninische Hexameter und Pentameter im 9. Jahrhundert," *Neues Archi für ältere deutsche Geschichtskunde* 44 (1922), 213 ff.; C. Erdmann, "Leonitas," *Corona Quernea: Festgabe Karl Strecker* (1941); Lote, 2.141 ff.; Curtius, 8.2–3; Raby, *Secular*, 1.228, 2.1; Norden.

T.V.F. BROGAN

**LESBIAN POETRY.** On the simplest level, lesbian poetry can be defined as poetry written by a self-identified lesbian poet on a clearly lesbian theme, such as erotic love for another woman. However, lesbian poetry comprises a wide field of works that may be written by self-identified lesbian poets, by poets presumed to be lesbian, by reclaimed lesbian poets whose lesbian content and themes may be "encoded," and indeed by any poet writing on themes that may be deemed lesbian. Lesbian scholars, perhaps most notably Faderman and Castle, include the vast poetry of lesbian implication—verse penned by poets known or thought to have had their primary emotional and erotic relationships with women and/or whose themes include overt or encoded references to intimate love between women. A subset of the larger field, lesbian-feminist poetry, arose from the lesbian-feminist movement of the 1970s and 1980s and is the most clearly identifiable lesbian poetry. Written by self-avowed lesbian poets with feminist political outlooks, lesbian-feminist poetry frequently takes lesbians or lesbianism as its subject matter. In the broadest sense, however, the themes of lesbian poetry range from lesbian love to feminist politics to lesbian-feminist revisionary myth-making to homophobia—or in some definitions any topic approached by the widely diverse population of lesbian poets. To limit the definition to women writing explicitly about women's same-sex love or living in cultures, eras, and situations that allow them to self-name as lesbians is an underestimation of the scope of the field.

The name *lesbian poetry* itself, and the genre, is traced by many to Sappho of Lesbos, Plato's "tenth muse." In *The Highest Apple*, Grahn traces the lineage of lesbian poetry from Sappho through an anonymous med. nun, a 19th-c. prostitute named Wu Tsao, Emily Dickinson, Amy Lowell, and Gertrude Stein, to herself and her contemporaries in the lesbian-feminist poetry movement of the 1970s and 1980s. H.D. invoked Sappho in early poems such as "Oread" and "Hermes of the Waves" in the 1910s, and Sappho's life is the central trope of Eloise Klein Healy's 21st-c. v. *The Island's Project*. Lesbians of color in the U. S. regularly look elsewhere for their points of origin and sources of inspiration. Joy Harjo (Creek/Cherokee) explicitly excludes herself from the story of "the fiery goddess in the middle of the island" in her poem "The Book of Myths" (1990). Audre Lorde looks to the women-loving trad. of her mother's Caribbean homeland, Carriacou, and to the female deities of her West Af. heritage; Gloria Anzaldúa names indigenous Mexican figures incl. Cihuatlyotl and La Malinche.

Faderman and Castle begin their anthologies of lesbian lit. with Katherine Fowler Philips (England and Wales, 1632–64) and Anne de Rohan (France, 1584–1646), respectively, flouting the Foucauldian orthodoxy that the identity "lesbian" (or "homosexual") did not exist before 1869. Both anthologists include Aphra Behn (England, 1640–89) and Sor Juana Inés de la Cruz (Mexico, ca. 1648–95). Castle traces representations of lesbian love in poetry written by men to the early 16th c. Vanita finds evidence of women's same-sex love depicted in ancient Sanskrit texts and in early verse representations of lesbianism written and performed by men who cross-dressed as women in the Indian *rekhti* poetry of the early 19th c. Faderman explains her choice of how to define *lesbian* in one instance by encouraging readers to think of lesbian as "an adjective" rather than "a noun"; Castle insists that it is possible to use the word *lesbian* in "the 'ordinary' or 'dictionary' or 'vernacular sense'," regardless of the cultural and historical specificity of the term; and Vanita argues that terms equivalent to "lesbian" and "gay" existed in various South Asian langs. long before the supposed Western invention of homosexuality as an identity in the 19th c. On the other hand, the historian Ng is "searching" among suggestive evidence rather than definitively finding lesbians in her germinal study of early 20th-c. homoerotic women's poetry in China.

Contemp. literary critics find themselves on more solid ground reading the lesbian poetry of 19th- and early 20th-c. writers such as Dickinson, Angelina Weld Grimké, and Edna St. Vincent Millay, whose "encoded" lesbian content can be understood through a combination of extant biographical evidence (such as Dickinson's letters to Sue Gilbert) and a knowledge of homoerotic tropes created by or available to the poets in their lifetimes. Many poets of the era employed natural imagery as metaphor for female genitals, e.g.,

Dickinson's "pea that duty locks"; or Lowell's "stiff, broad outer leaves; / The smaller ones, / Pleasant to touch, veined with purple; / The glazed inner leaves. / One by one I parted you from your leaves."

By fairly early in the 20th c., critics need look no further than the explicit lines of certain poets to find lesbian meaning in the contemp. sense. As early as 1919, Elsa Gidlow would "ask no man pardon" for daring to "taste with endless kisses" the "flesh, bitter and salt" of a clearly female lover. The lesbian-centered creative community of expatriate Paris in the 1920s and 1930s produced both overt and covert lesbian poetry. While Stein disguised lesbian lovemaking as "lifting belly" and orgasms as cows, her poems were explicitly sexual to those who could crack the code, esp. because she made no attempt to hide her relationship with Alice B. Toklas. At the same time, Renée Vivien (Pauline Tarn), lover of lesbian salon host Natalie Barney, employed no codes to obscure the lesbian eroticism of her work. Back in the U.S. in the same era, the lit. of the *Harlem Renaissance was replete with suggestive lesbian content, from the encoded lyric poetry of Grimké to the provocative lyrics of Ma Rainey's "Prove It on Me Blues," among the most explicit depictions of lesbianism and cross-dressing of the era: "They said I do it, ain't nobody caught me / Sure got to prove it on me / Went out last night with a crowd of my friends / They must've been women, 'cause I don't like no men / It's true I wear a collar and a tie . . . / Talk to the gals just like any old man . . ."

The 1940s and 1950s were repressive times, especially in the U.S., and much lesbian culture and lit. went underground for a time, even as World War II and its aftermath created the conditions for urban lesbian cultures in many U.S. cities. Important lesbian and bisexual women poets of the period include Elizabeth Bishop, May Swenson, and Muriel Rukeyser, the only one of the three to come out of the closet explicitly, after political tides shifted in the 1970s. Contemp. critics have noted that some of the historical figures claimed by lesbians from the pregay liberation era (before 1969), incl. writers, might more accurately be classified as bisexual or transgender (or transgender lesbian). For example, transgender author Leslie Feinberg claims Stein in addition to several prose writers. Bisexual activists point to Rukeyser, H.D., and Millay, all of whom incorporate lesbian themes in their work.

Spurred by the Women's Liberation movement and lesbian feminism of the 1960s and 1970s, a new generation began to uncover the forgotten and obscured works of earlier lesbians and to develop a clear, explicit lesbian poetry, "a whole new poetry beginning here," in the words of Adrienne Rich. Among the first salvos was Grahn's "Psychoanalysis of Edward the Dyke," which she deemed "unpublishable" in the mid-1960s, and "A Woman Is Talking to Death," chronicling her dishonorable discharge from the military for lesbianism in the early 1960s. Poetry became a major force in the lesbian-feminist movement, according to Melanie Kaye/Kantrowitz becoming as popular as "shakespeare [sic] in his own time" or "the audience for rock in the late sixties." In this, lesbian-feminist poetry resembled the politically engaged poetry of the many social and political movements of the era, such as the *Black Arts movement. The numerous feminist and lesbian periodicals of the era all published poetry, and most lesbian gatherings—political, literary, or otherwise—included poetry readings. Clausen went so far as to call feminism of that era "A Movement of Poets," many of whom were openly lesbian. Grahn, Lorde, and Rich were among the best-known lesbian poets of the period, which also saw the prominence of Pat Parker, Rita Mae Brown, Olga Broumas, Willyce Kim, Susan Griffin, and Marilyn Hacker. A larger number of lesbians of color gained visibility as they came into wider circulation in the 1980s and 1990s, among them Anzaldúa, Chrystos, Cheryl Clarke, Jewelle Gomez, Harjo, Cherríe Moraga, and Kitty Tsui.

Contemp. lesbian poetry tends to take the form of short, lyric, free verse, although some poets work in more traditional forms, and overall the category is quite heterogeneous. Grahn's poetry varies considerably in length from a few couplets to entire plays; Irena Klepfisz's "Work Sonnets" comprise a cycle of poems written in that strict form; and Hacker, notably, has utilized such demanding forms as the *sestina and *villanelle.

*See* FEMINIST APPROACHES TO POETRY, GAY POETRY, GENDER AND POETRY, LYRIC.

■ M. Kaye/Kantrowitz, "Culture Making," *Sinister Wisdom* (1980); E. Bulkin, "Introduction," *Lesbian Poetry*, ed. E. Bulkin and J. Larkin (1981); J. Grahn, *The Highest Apple* (1985); J. Clausen, "A Movement of Poets," *Books and Life* (1985); *Chloe plus Olivia*, ed. L. Faderman (1994); P. Bennett, "Lesbian Poetry in the United States, 1890–1990," *Professions of Desire*, ed. G. E. Haggerty and B. Zimmerman (1995); V. Ng, "Looking for Lesbians in Chinese History," *A Queer World*, ed. M. Duberman (1997); L. Garber, *Identity Poetics* (2001); *Queering India*, ed. R. Vanita (2002); *The Literature of Lesbianism*, ed. T. Castle (2003).

L. GARBER

**LETRILLA** (diminutive of Sp. *letra*, "letter," a short gloss). A Sp. poem generally written in short lines, often having a *refrain, and usually written on a light or satiric topic. Such poems can be found as early as the 14th c. at least but were apparently not given the name *letrilla* until much later. Famous examples are Luis de Góngora's "Ándeme yo caliente, / y ríase la gente" (As long as I am comfortable, / let people laugh) and Francisco de Quevedo's "Poderoso caballero es don Dinero" (A powerful gentleman is Sir Money).

■ Navarro.

D. C. CLARKE

**LETTER, VERSE.** *See* VERSE EPISTLE.

**LETTRISME.** A movement that first gained prominence in Paris following World War II. Founded by the Romanian expatriate Isidore Isou, who wished to reduce lang. to its constituent elements, *lettrisme* sought to displace *surrealism as the leading avant-garde movement. Since the early 1950s, Maurice Lemaître

was lettrisme's principal theorist and chief organizer; Jean-Paul Curtay introduced several innovations. Lettrisme derives from the It. futurists' *parole in libertà* (words in freedom), from the Rus. futurists' exploration of transrational lang., *zaum* (see FUTURISM), and from the Dadaists' experiments with opto-phonetic poetry. Like *Dada, lettrisme is a violently antagonistic movement that attacks the foundations of bourgeois society through the medium of the written word by reducing the letters of the alphabet to a series of phonetic or visual counters. By emphasizing the autonomy of the individual letter at the expense of the larger word, lettrisme aims to destroy signification itself. Meaning is not just fragmented but totally effaced.

In theory (and to some extent in practice), the principles underlying lettrisme may be applied to all forms of human endeavor. While letterists have become involved in such areas as politics, economics, erotology, and even pharmacy, their more significant contributions have been in the realm of the arts. Of these, poetry and the plastic arts have provided the most fertile ground for experimentation. Lettrisme originally focused on *sound poetry, combining letters in various fashions according to their phonetic values, then *visual poetry, varying the size and shape of letters to produce the graphic equivalent of drawing. Usurping the traditional prerogatives of painting, graphic conventions were placed at the service of the visual composition, and the concept of visual poetry gave way to that of visual art.

A resolutely interdisciplinary movement, lettrisme juxtaposes elements such as letters, photographs, miscellaneous signs, and pictorial images in an attempt to transcend the limits of traditional representation. The ling. sign is stripped of its ling. function. Letters are powerless to assert themselves, and the whole field of signs is reduced to the status of random marks on the page. Lacking verbal identity, the letters function exclusively as pictorial signs, with the result that their significance derives according to the rules governing abstract art.

*See* CONCRETE POETRY, VISUAL POETRY.

■ I. Isou, *Introduction á une nouvelle poésie et á une nouvelle musique* (1947); M. Lemaître, *Qu'est-ce que le lettrisme?* (1954), and *Bilan lettriste* (1955); I. Isou, *Les Champs de force de la peinture* (1964); M. Lemaître, *Lettrisme et hypergraphie* (1966); J.-P. Curtay, *La Poésie lettriste* (1974); D. Seaman, *Concrete Poetry in France* (1981); S. Foster, *Lettrisme* (1983); J.-P. Curtay, *Letterism and Hypographics* (1985); R. Sabatier, *Le Lettrisme* (1989); W. Bohn, *Modern Visual Poetry* (2001).

W. BOHN

**LIED** (Ger., "poem," "song"; pl. *Lieder*). Etymological interchange notwithstanding, the name typically applied to a musical setting of a Ger. poem minimally calling for solo voice and piano. An early fixture of the home, the genre increasingly moved into the concert hall during the later 19th c.; Gustav Mahler and Richard Strauss contributed notable examples of the *orchesterlied*. Historians have evoked a myth-laden birth for the lied, with J. W. Goethe leading the way in verse and Franz Schubert in music. Scholars now see the genre emerging in the mid-18th c. to accommodate the growing market of amateur music makers who readily responded to the tuneful primacy of *songs by, among numerous others, Johann Friedrich Reichardt and Carl Friedrich Zelter. Nineteenth-c. Ger. idealism and its absorption with absolutism and transcendence helped conscript the lied for new purposes. A good example is Schubert's "An die Musik" (To Music), which lauds song's ability to transport one to "eine beßre Welt" (a better world). Like Schubert's more than 600 lieder, Ger. song at large has served an array of cultural needs, incl. identity formation and nationalism. With its heyday in the 19th c., pivotal composers, after Schubert, are Robert Schumann, Johannes Brahms, and Hugo Wolf. Enthusiasts seek out examples in which they find a perfect union of constituent elements: variously, verse and music or the interaction of voice and accompaniment. More practically, composers have drawn on a variety of means to meet a broad continuum of expressive ends. An important subcategory is the song cycle (*Liederkreis, Liederzyklus*) in which a composer sets to music a succession of poems. Schubert again commands with *Die schöne Müllerin* (The Beautiful Maid of the Mill, 1824) and *Winterreise* (Winter's Journey, 1827).

*See* MUSIC AND POETRY.

■ D. Stein and R. Spillman, *Poetry into Song* (1996); W. Dürr, *Das deutsche Sololied im 19. Jahrhundert*, 2d ed. (2002); *Cambridge Companion to the Lied*, ed. J. Parsons (2004); *German Lieder in the Nineteenth Century*, ed. R. Hallmark, 2d ed. (2009); Y. Malin, *Song in Motion: Rhythm and Meter in the German Lied* (2010).

J. PARSONS

**LIGHT VERSE.** The term *light verse* is an *omnium gatherum*. While light verse once referred principally to *vers de société*, the Fr. term for verse reserved for one's social circle to amuse or commemorate an occasion, its meaning now includes folk poetry, *nonsense verse, ribald verse, kitsch, and more. If the earlier meaning of the term was too narrow, it has now been stretched so far that it has lost its shape. The Library of Congress cataloging system has no subject heading for "light verse"; its closest approximation is "humorous poetry," suggesting one devel. in light verse is its movement to the comic mode.

If one follows the sense of light verse as *vers de société,* one might consider Matthew Prior's *Poems on Several Occasions* (1709) the first light verse collection in Eng., but Thomas D'Urfey's *Pills to Purge Melancholy* (1719) has a valid claim if one follows the sense of light verse as verse that is light-hearted. The first serious attempt to define the term came when Frederick Locker-Lampson compiled the anthol. *Lyra elegantiarum* (1867). As the title implies, Locker-Lampson preferred verse distinguished by its wit and polish and intended to amuse polite society. A series of anthologists has broadened the term to include poetry that

is homely or comic. In *The Oxford Book of Light Verse* (1938), W. H. Auden held that light verse meant any poetry that is "simple, clear, and gay." He included performed poems, nonsense verse, and poetry of ordinary life; light verse was no longer aristocratic. While Auden was influential, however, not everyone followed his lead. In 1941, Michael Roberts explicitly distinguished between comic verse and "light verse or *vers de société.*" In 1958, Richard Armour defined light verse as "poetry written in the spirit of play," then added that light verse "can safely be limited to what is called *vers de société*: humorous or witty verse that comments critically on contemp. life. It is usually to some degree funny" (14). Such anthologists as G. Grigson and W. Harmon have extended the definition of light verse even further to include bad poetry, *epitaphs, or Cole Porter's lyrics. Matters have been further complicated by Kingsley Amis who, in the *New Oxford Book of English Light Verse* (1978), argued that the best light verse is necessarily conservative; in this, he followed a view set forth by D. Macdonald in his 1960 parody anthol.

One result of this widening and blurring of meaning is that the term is sometimes used pejoratively to mean trivial or unimportant poetry. Because some critics now include the magnificently dreadful verse of writers such as William McGonigal or Julia Moore, the term is also sometimes used as a condemnation. Yet no one would dismiss Chaucer's tales, Ben Jonson's epigrams, Alexander Pope's *Rape of the Lock*, Lord Byron's *Don Juan*, Christina Rossetti's *Goblin Market*, or T. S. Eliot's cats—all of which find a place in both standard anthologies and in collections of light verse. Thus the term seems to have retained favorable connotations for sophisticated readers who know enough about what is "weighty" to recognize and enjoy what is "light." Some critics fear this audience may be diminishing. Grigson says that nonsense verse "is in danger now because it does demand an accepted idea of the nature of verse in general, a widely shared idea of the ways in which poetry works" (*Nonsense Verse*). In a hopeful devel., the American Academy of Arts and Letters has recognized the importance of light verse with the Michael Braude Award for Light Verse, a biennial award given for light verse in the Eng. lang., regardless of the author's nationality.

Many varieties of light verse depend on technical virtuosity, such as *limericks, *clerihews, and *double dactyls. The limerick is the oldest of these; the clerihew is the most anarchic, with its formalized irregularity; the double dactyl has attracted distinguished poets. Arguably the Japanese form of *senryū* also fits in this category. If one does not insist on the comic nature of light verse, then other polished fixed-term poems would be included: *ballads, double *ballade, *rondeau, *sestina, and *triolet. Finally, there is poetry distinguished by clever use of certain techniques: verse with interlocking rhymes like Edward Lear's limericks; *acrostics like Jonson's "Argument" to *Volpone*; verse with extensive *alliteration or *assonance. A mod. example of alliterative ingenuity is the poem by Alaric Watts that begins "An Austrian army awfully arrayed / Boldly by battery besieged Belgrade" and proceeds through the alphabet (see ABCEDARIUS). There is also *visual poetry and *concrete poetry such as Lewis Carroll's "Mouse's Tail" in *Alice in Wonderland*. In all such verse, the sophistication of the craft—ingenuity, skill, and polish—is apparent, the technique serving as foil to the content. The problem with defining light verse solely on technical grounds is that it then seems to include poetry not usually considered light. George Herbert's "Easter Wings" is shaped as craftily as Carroll's "Mouse's Tail," while G. M. Hopkins's "Spring and Fall: To a Young Child" plays with words in much the same punning way as many limericks do. But neither is light verse.

If one turns from technique to content, however, other problems arise. Auden focuses on content in his three categories of light verse: "poetry written for performance, to be spoken or sung before an audience"; "poetry intended to be read, but having for its subject-matter the everyday social life of its period or the experiences of the poet"; "such nonsense poetry as, through its properties and technique, has a general sense of appeal." His first category includes folk poetry such as riddles, folk songs, or the songs of Thomas Moore or Ira Gershwin. Yet one might object that all poetry is intended to be spoken to an audience, even if the audience is the reader speaking to self. The lyrics W. S. Gilbert wrote for Arthur Sullivan's music are hardly folk songs, although clearly light verse. Furthermore, the boundary between folksongs and popular songs or between popular songs and light opera is no longer clear, as the careers of Bob Dylan and Stephen Sondheim demonstrate. Auden's category of nonsense verse, however, is uncontroversial, for nonsense is among the oldest of light verse. As Grigson points out, "The moment literature develops, nonsense literature must be expected as both a counter-genre and an innocent game" (*Nonsense Verse*).

One of the few points on which most critics agree is that light verse requires the formal confines of verse form. The poet Ogden Nash illustrates this point: he regularly stretches metrical forms with his irregular line length, yet his work depends on the reader's recognizing the rules he violates. In "Very Like a Whale," e.g., his mock-attack on the lang. of poets is made more effective by the insistent rhymes nestled among the aggressively antimetrical lines. If one transmogrifies a limerick or double dactyl into prose, one destroys part of its essence. Were the content paraphrased in prose, it would be prosaic in every sense of that word, but in verse it amuses, felicitously. To argue that a crucial characteristic of light verse is that it must be in verse is pleonastic: better to argue that light verse must be playful and that a successful game requires rules that will be observed, if not necessarily followed.

■ **Collections**: Matthew Prior, *Poems on Several Occasions* (1709); *Wit and Mirth, or Pills to Purge Melancholy*, ed. T. D'Urfey (1719); *Lyra elegantiarum*, ed. F. Locker-Lampson (1867); *Wit and Humour, Selected from the English Poets*, ed. Leigh Hunt (1882); *Speculum Amantis* and *Musa Proterva*, both ed. A. H. Bullen (1888, 1889); *A Vers de Société Anthology*, ed. C.

Wells (1900); *Oxford Book of Light Verse*, ed. W. H. Auden (1938); *Faber Book of Comic Verse*, ed. M. Roberts (1942); *What Cheer*, ed. D. McCord (1945); *The Worldly Muse*, ed. A.J.M. Smith (1951*)*; *Penguin Book of Comic and Curious Verse*, ed. J. M. Cohen (1952); *Silver Treasury of Light Verse*, ed. O. Williams (1957); *New Oxford Book of English Light Verse*, ed. K. Amis (1978); *Faber Book of Epigrams and Epitaphs* (1978), ed. G. Grigson; *Oxford Book of American Light Verse*, ed. W. Harmon (1979); *Faber Book of Nonsense Verse* (1980) and *Oxford Book of Satirical Verse* (1980), both ed. G. Grigson; *The Tygers of Wrath*, ed. X. J. Kennedy (1981); *Norton Book of Light Verse*, ed. R. Baker (1986); *The American Wits*, ed. John Hollander (2003).

■ **General**: L. Untermeyer, *Play in Poetry* (1938); R. Armour, *Writing Light Verse*, 2d ed. (1958); T. Augarde, *Oxford Guide to Word Games*, 2d ed. (2003).

F. TEAGUE

**LIMERICK.** The limerick is the most popular form of comic or *light verse in Eng., often nonsensical and frequently bawdy, but this exacting verse form existed long before it got its name in the late 19th c.

The limerick form consists of five lines of *accentual verse rhyming *aabba*, the first, second, and fifth lines having 3 stresses, the third and fourth 2; the rhythm is effectually anapestic or amphibrachic. The first syllables of each line (and unstressed syllables elsewhere in the lines, though less frequently so) may be omitted. Although the fifth line typically provides a clinching statement or twist, in the early hist. of the form and until the late 19th c., the final line simply repeated the first. A good example of this earlier pattern is the popular nursery rhyme "Hickere, Dickere Dock" (1744), a poem that shares the limerick's structure but not its traditionally bawdy subject matter.

The earliest examples of the use of this short verse form date back to the 13th c.; however, the limerick form is associated in the popular imagination with Edward Lear (*A Book of Nonsense*, 1846). J. H. Murray, writing in 1898, deemed it an error to term Lear's nonsense verse "limericks," as his use of the form did not conform to the strict pattern outlined above, and indeed the term was not used by Lear himself to describe his own verse. Undoubtedly, however, the success of Lear's variations on this form led to its widespread and enduring popularity, and it was even adopted by such authors as Alfred, Lord Tennyson, A. C. Swinburne, Rudyard Kipling, R. L. Stevenson, and W. S. Gilbert, until, by the beginning of the 20th c., it had become a fashion. The tendency in the mod. limerick of using the final line for surprise or witty reversal in place of a repeated last line has now become the norm.

The most common theory regarding the origin of the name is the form's adoption as a parlor game in which party-goers were invited to extemporize a song that ended with the line "Will you come up to Limerick?" Other theories range from the belief that it was an old Fr. form brought to the Ir. town of Limerick in 1700 by returning veterans of the Fr. war to the idea that it originated in the *nursery rhymes published as *Mother Goose's Melodies* (1791).

See CLERIHEW, NONSENSE VERSE, POULTER'S MEASURE.

■ J. H. Murray, *Notes and Queries* (1898); L. Reed, *The Complete Limerick Book* (1925); *Oxford Book of Nursery Rhymes*, ed. I. and P. Opie (1951); A. Liede, *Dichtung als Spiel*, vol. 2 (1963); G. Legman, *The Limerick* (1964, 1988); W. S. Baring-Gould, *The Lure of the Limerick* (1972); *The Limerick: 1700 Examples* (1970, 1974), *The New Limerick* (1977), both ed. G. Legman; C. Bibby, *The Art of the Limerick* (1978); G. N. Belknap, "History of the Limerick," *The Papers of the Bibliographical Society of America* 75 (1981); *Penguin Book of Limericks*, ed. E. O. Parrott (1984).

T.V.F. BROGAN; A. PREMINGER;<br>I. D. COPESTAKE

**LINE** (Sanskrit, *pāda*; Gr., *\*stichos*, Lat. *versus* "verse"). The line is fundamental to poetry itself, for the line differentiates verse from prose: throughout most of recorded history, poetry has been cast in verse, and verse is set in lines (see VERSE AND PROSE). That is, verse is cast in sentences and lines, prose in sentences and paragraphs. The sense in prose flows continuously, while in verse it is segmented to increase the density of information and the awareness of structure. It is impossible that there could be verse not set in lines. It is possible there could be poetry not set in lines, if one defines poetry as verbal composition marked by a comparatively high degree of memorability, beauty, sublimity, delightfulness, instructiveness, figurativeness, ellipticality, intensity, uncanniness, linguistic patterning, or some combination of these or other qualities. Hybrid forms such as rhythmical prose (see PROSE RHYTHM) and the *prose poem demonstrate the poetic possibilities of prose, as do many moments in short stories, novels, essays, and longer nonfictional forms throughout the world. But we must assume that the preponderance of the world's poetry has been cast in lines, whether they read from left to right (e.g., Eng., Fr., Ger.), right to left (e.g., Heb. and Ar.), or top to bottom (e.g., cl. Chinese), precisely to take advantage of those resources which verse has to offer (see PROSODY). In English, usage of "line" (etymologically descended from Lat., *līnum* "flax") to signify the "portion of a metrical composition which is usually written in one line: a verse" (*OED)* dates from the second half of the 16th c. and reflects the growth of print culture (see below).

A. *Structure.* Readers and auditors of poetry perceive the line as a rhythmical unit and a unit of structure. As a unit of *measure, it is linked to its neighbors to form higher-level structures, and as a structure itself, it is built of lower-level units. In metrical verse the line is usually segmented into elements—*hemistichs, measures or metra (see METRON), or feet (see FOOT)—but it is the line which generates these intralinear units and not vice versa. Lines are not made simply by defining some unit of measure such as a foot and then stringing units together, because the units are susceptible of differential constraint at differing points in the line. The

line, that is, has a shape or contour, and a structure as a whole, over and above the sum of its constituent elements. In various verse systems these elements are bound together in differing ways, such as structural alliteration in OE. It is true that, in the handbooks, meters are usually specified by the type of foot and number of feet per line—i.e. *monometer (a line of 1 foot), *dimeter (2 feet), *trimeter (3 feet), *tetrameter (4 feet), *pentameter (5 feet), *hexameter (6 feet), *heptameter (7 feet). But these simplistic descriptors do not capture the internal dynamics of a line, such as the Gr. hexameter.

How do readers and auditors recognize the line as a rhythmical unit? In *isometric verse, meter measures out a constant spacing, either of a certain number of events or a certain span of time (depending on one's theory of meter) which the mind's internal counter tracks in cognition; meter also provides predictable internal structure. The line can also be bound together by syntactic and rhetorical structures such as *parallelism and *antithesis which have their own internal logic of completion; these structures may or may not be threaded into meter: in biblical Heb. verse they are, in Whitman they are not.

B. *Line End.* Probably the most common strategy is to mark the *end* of the line, since without some sort of signal, we would not know where one line ended and a second one began. Traditionally the signal has been thought to be a *"pause," though not a metrical (line-internal) one but rather some kind of rhetorical or performative one. But this claim derives not from prosody (verse theory), or from claims about the nature or ontological status of poetry as *sound, but rather from assumptions put in play about *performance, about the reading aloud of verse. On this account, performers of poetry recognize the line as a unit (by seeing it as such when read from the page, for example) and mark its end in delivery with a linguistic pause or paralinguistic cue such as elongation of the final syllable. Auditors hear these cues, which cross or ignore syntax, as boundary markers.

An alternative conception of the signal, which depends rather on assumptions about the visual formatting of poetry on a page, is the stretch of empty space beyond the line, a stretch usually not aligned with the empty stretches beyond other lines, producing an appearance of jagged margining. This signal is perceived in reading and *may* be taken not only as a terminal marker but even as a part of structure (see below).

But both these answers specify phenomena *after* the line ends. A more powerful conception of the signal, not committed to any doctrine about either performance or format, would be, "some kind of marker," not after the final syllable of the line but *in* the final syllables of the line. In Gr. and Lat. poetry, where the meter is quantitative, auditors could recognize the ends of lines because they were marked by an alteration in the meter, either an increase in the formality in its closing syllables, a *cadence,* or unexpected shortening at line end, *catalexis. In the hexameter, for example, the line closes on a spondee—two heavy syllables in succession—rather than a dactyl, a closural pattern which is obligatory. In post-cl. verse, line ends have been most often marked by some distinctive sound echo, chiefly *rhyme, though important also are the several other strategies of sound-repetition that are rhyme-like or exceed rhyme: *homoeoteleuton, *assonance, *identical rhyme. Short lines in particular seem to demand the support of rhyme, or else they will be mistaken for the cola that are parts of longer lines; this is a major factor in the devel. of the *lyric. Also important are strategies for end-of-line semantic emphasis: Richard Wilbur, for example, sometimes employs the strategy of putting important words at line end, words that may offer an elliptical synopsis or ironic commentary on the argument of the poem. All these strategies, taken together as devices for end-fixing, i.e. *marking* or *weighting* line ends to foreground them perceptually, constitute one of the most distinctive categories of metrical universals, conspicuous in a wide range of verse systems.

The phenomenon of extra syllables at line end is fairly extensive and a feature of several prosodies: line endings are classified depending on whether the last stress falls on the final syllable of the line (a "masculine" ending) or the penultimate one (a "feminine" one; see MASCULINE AND FEMININE). The distinction dates from at least Occitan poetry, and may date from ancient Gr. Classifying types of line endings was also one of the central "metrical tests" that several Brit. and Ger. Shakespeare scholars of the later 19th c. hoped would yield a definitive chronology of the plays. Spedding in 1847 suggested the "pause test," which tabulated frequencies of stopped vs. enjambed lines. Bathurst (1857), Craik, and Hertzberg discussed "weak endings"; Ingram (1874) distinguished types of these as "light" endings (enjambed lines ending on a pronoun, verb, or relative bearing only secondary stress, plus a slight pause) and "weak" (enjambment on a proclitic, esp. a conjunction or preposition, allowing no pause at all—see Brogan for citations).

**C. Line and Syntax.** The syllables of the line are the arena for deploying meter or rhythm; they are also the ground of syntax and sense: these two structures, line and syntax, overwrite the same space. Some verse forms regularly align line units with sense units; such lines are known as *end-stopped. The ("closed") *heroic couplet, for example, ends the first line at a major syntactic break and the second at a full stop (sentence end). But few forms do so *every* line. Systematic contrast or opposition of line units and sense units (line end and sentence flow) is the complex phenomenon known as *enjambment. In enjambed verse, syntax pulls the reader through line end into the next line, while the prosodic boundary suggests a pause if not a stop. In reading, the mind makes projections, in that pause, based on what has come before, about what word is most likely to appear at the beginning of the next line, expectations which a masterful poet will deliberately

thwart, forcing rapid rereading: in Milton such error is the emblem of man's postlapsarian state. Certainly in modern times, at least, it has been thought that one of the chief functions of line division is to stand in tension with or counterpoint to the divisions of grammar and sense, effecting, in the reader's processing of the poem, multiple simultaneous pattern recognition. Even in enjambed verse, the word at line end, which the French call the *contre-rejet* (see REJET), receives some sort of momentary foregrounding or emphasis. This is not a matter of the word marking the end but of the end marking the word.

**D. Aural Line and Visual Line.** Since the advent of writing in Gr., ca. 750 BCE, and certainly since the advent of printing in the West, ca. 1450 CE, the line has had a visual reality in poetry, but long before that time and without interruption throughout print culture it has had an auditory one. This history gives the line—poetry itself—a fundamental duality, in the eye and ear, as both seen and heard (Hollander), a duality complicated, especially in the twentieth century and after by the ascendance of *free verse. Instances such as the ms. of the OE epic *Beowulf* (Cotton Vitellius A.xv), in which the alliterating four-stress metrical segments do not appear as individual lines, or a ms. of a Japanese haiku in which the seventeen-*mora form appears as a single vertical line, though usually represented by three lines in translation, raise interesting questions about the nature and integrity of lineation. But arguments about the historical or ontological precedence of the aural over the visual line miss the point: these forms are, for us now, both realities; the important question is how they affect each other—whether, for example, the break at line end demands a pause, performed or imagined. Two phenomena complicating discussion of the line as a visible entity are the *split line and the typographic runover. Both these phenomena force a distinction between the line as a concrete unit of printing and the line as an abstract unit of composition, which may not correspond to a single printed unit. In most modern printings of a Shakespeare play, for example, the two parts of a single iambic pentameter line split between two speakers appear on different lines on the page, the second indented to begin after the end of the one set above it. Meanwhile, in the first section of Allen Ginsberg's *Howl*, an abstract "line," which begins with the repeated, left-justified pronoun "who," may run over to many lines of print, making it unlikely that that line could ever be contained by a single line of print, even in a very large book. With the advent of *electronic poetry new possibilities arise for representing lines visually, and one can image even Ginsberg's longest line running horizontally unbroken across a screen, but the defiance of his gesture, setting two notions of "line" against one another, would be lost.

**E. Line Forms.** Up to the advent of free verse, line forms and line lengths are mainly determined by genre specification, so that poets who wish to write, say, in *elegiac distichs (hexameter plus pentameter), know or learn, by reading their predecessors, what forms have already been tried, for what kinds of subjects, with what kinds of tone, and with what success. In metrical verse, that is, line forms were mainly determined by history and convention, by the interplay of tradition and the individual talent; and the prosody which generated them was aurally based. Free verse, by contrast, foregrounded visual space and posited the line within a two-dimensional matrix where blanks, white spaces, drops, gaps, and other dislocations became possible. This is not to say that free verse abandoned aurality, for some poets, such as the Beats, Charles Olson with his "projective verse," and the proponents of *sound poetry and "text-sound," continued to speak programmatically of the line as based on the energy of the breath. It is only to say that visual prosody was made central to free verse at least in claim, and if aural prosody was at the same time not dispensed with, no poet seemed to wish or prosodist to be able, at least for the first century of free-verse practice, to give a definitive account of the relations of the one to the other.

To think, however, that the free-verse line can function solely as visual prosody, without the resources of aural prosody to aid it, is to commit what Perloff calls the "linear fallacy," making some free verse indistinguishable from prose chopped up into lines. The sonic and rhythmic devices of aural prosody offer poetry effects *not available* to prose: and if these are to be discarded, visual prosody must provide others, or else the distinction between prose and verse collapses. One might respond that several Eng. poets—Ben Jonson and Alexander Pope, to name but two—wrote out drafts of their poems first in prose before versifying them; and verse translators routinely work through intermediary prose versions. But this practice shows simply that they wished to clarify the argumentative or narrative structure first to get it out of the way, so as to concentrate on *poetic* effects.

See CLASSICAL PROSODY, FREE VERSE, METER, PROSODY, STANZA, STICHOS, VERSE AND PROSE, VERSIFICATION, VISUAL POETRY.

■ C. A. Langworthy, "Verse-Sentence Patterns in English Poetry," *PQ* 7 (1928); J. S. Diekhoff, "Terminal Pause in Milton's Verse," *SP* 32 (1935); A. Oras, "Echoing Verse Endings in Paradise Lost," *South Atlantic Studies for Sturgis E. Leavitt* (1953); C. L. Stevenson, "The Rhythm of English Verse," *JAAC* 28 (1970); D. Crystal, "Intonation and Metrical Theory," *TPS* (1971); C. Ricks, "Wordsworth," *Essays in Criticism* 21 (1971); B. Stáblein, "Versus," *MGG*, v. 13; H. McCord, "Breaking and Entering," and D. Laferrière, "Free and Non-Free Verse," *Lang&S* 10 (1977); J. Lotman, *The Structure of the Artistic Text*, trans. G. Lenhoff and R. Vroon (1977); D. Levertov, "On the Function of the Line," *Chicago Review* 30 (1979), *Epoch* 29 (1980)—symposium; M. Perloff, "The Linear Fallacy," *Georgia Review* 35 (1981), response in 36 (1982); Brogan; J. C. Stalker, "Reader Expectations and the Poetic Line," *Lang&S* 15 (1982); P. P. Byers, "The Auditory Reality of the Verse Line," *Style* 17 (1983); R. Bradford, "'Verse

Only to the Eye'?: Line Endings in Paradise Lost," *EIC* 33 (1983); S. A. Keenan, "Effects of Chunking and Line Length on Reading Efficiency," *Visual Language* 18 (1984); *The Line in Postmodern Poetry*, ed. R. Frank and H. Sayre (1988); R. Pinsky, *The Sounds of Poetry* (1998); J. Longenbach, *The Art of the Poetic Line* (2008); E. B. Voigt, *The Art of Syntax* (2009); *A Broken Thing: Poets on the Line*, ed. E. Rosko and A. Vander Zee (2011).

T.V.F. BROGAN; S. CUSHMAN

**LINGUISTICS AND POETICS.** The denotations of both *linguistics* and *poetics* are complex and contested, so their relationship depends on how each is understood. Ling. is the study of human lang.; but *language* may refer to (1) the system, incl. phonology, morphology, syntax, and semantics, that defines ling. forms, i.e., grammar; (2) the established form-meaning pairings in that system, i.e., the lexicon; or (3) ling. behavior, i.e., the use of the grammar and lexicon to compose utterances for particular purposes. What *poetics* may refer to is often elaborated and debated, but for relating ling. to poetics, there is perhaps no better starting point than Aristotle's classification of the arts—for him, all forms of *imitation—according to their media, objects, and means of imitation. The art that poetics studies, presumably "poetry," is thus, in a definition that would be useful to reclaim for contemp. use, "the art that uses words only—either in prose or verse" (*Poetics*). If in this definition "words" is taken to mean more broadly *language*, then the relationship of ling. to poetics is that of the study of lang. to the study of art that is made from it.

Exploration of this relationship is implied already in Aristotle's mention in his *Poetics* of components of grammar and, conversely, in Dionysius Thrax's mention in his *Art of Grammar* of the poetic topic of metrics. It undergirds much of the work of historical ling. reconstruction that helped define ling. as a field in its own right in the 19th c., because poetic texts provided evidence for earlier forms of langs. But in the Eur. trad. at least, it was explicitly theorized only in the 20th c., most influentially in the work of Roman Jakobson.

Jakobson cast poetics explicitly as a subfield of ling., identifying what he called "the poetic function" (see POETIC FUNCTION) as one of several functions of lang., incl. its "emotive function" of expressing the state of the speaker, its "conative function" of making the addressee do things, and, perhaps most familiarly, its "referential" or communicative function of conveying information (1960). He defined this poetic function as "a focus on the message for its own sake," meaning a focus on its lang. as opposed to its source, audience, or context, etc. In this spirit, many fields of poetic inquiry have explored how lang. shapes the functions it performs, such as *speech act theory (Pratt), *stylistics (Fowler, Verdonk), and cognitive ling. and poetics (Lakoff and Turner, Tsur). But it is perhaps those fields that have engaged most directly with grammar, a dimension of lang. it does not share with other representational systems, that show best how fruitful this conception of poetics as ling. can be and also how, as Kiparsky (1987) argues, its exploration has sometimes been hampered by inadequacies in Jakobson's own structuralist assumptions about lang. and communication.

Jakobson defined the manifestation of the poetic function, its "empirical linguistic criterion," in one of the most famous sentences in literary theory: "*The poetic function projects the principle of equivalence from the axis of selection into the axis of combination*" (1960; italics in original). "Selection" and "combination" refer to ling. behavior, as Jakobson (1960) makes clear in his description of how ordinary utterances are constituted:

> If "child" is the topic of the message, the speaker selects one among the extant, more or less similar, nouns like child, kid, youngster, tot, all of them equivalent in a certain respect, and then, to comment on this topic, he may select one of the semantically cognate verbs—sleeps, dozes, nods, naps. Both chosen words combine in the speech chain. The selection is produced on the base of equivalence, similarity and dissimilarity, synonymity and antonymity, while the combination, the build up of the sequence, is based on contiguity.

Here, the term *"equivalence," however, like the "contiguity" it displaces, refers to the ling. system itself. How Jakobson's vision of the poetic function has been and can be understood as a substantive descriptive and theoretical claim, therefore, depends on its interpretation.

For Jakobson, the structuralist assumptions manifest in the passage—that a lang. consists of a set of elements defined through relationships of mutual similarity and difference and combined sequentially to produce speech—were implemented through the formalism of distinctive features being developed by the Prague Linguistic Circle of which Jakobson was a part. That *formalism simultaneously grounds lang. in its typical functional contexts, such as the physical mechanisms and the social setting of speech, and abstracts away from these contexts to create a formal system.

In Eng. phonology, e.g., the initial consonants of *to, do, new, Sue, zoo, shoe, chew, Jew, loo* ([t, d, n, s, z, ʃ, tʃ, dʒ, l] respectively) are all similar to one another in being made with the tongue against the roof (crown) of the mouth ([+coronal]). (Here square brackets enclose representations of speech sounds in the International Phonetic Alphabet and also their formal features.) At the same time, they are different from one another in other ways—crucially different, because those differences can create meaning differences (Saussure). In [t, d, n] but not the others, where the tongue meets the roof of the mouth the passage of breath is briefly stopped entirely ([+ stop]); in [n] but not [t, d] or any of the other coronals, passage of breath is allowed through the nose instead ([+nasal]); and in [t] as well as [s, ʃ, tʃ] vibration in the vocal cords is lacking, while [d] and the other coronals maintain it ([+voice]).

In the same way, in morphology, the Eng. personal pronouns *we* and *they*, e.g., are similar to one another in being [+plural]. But they are also different from each other in that *we*, like *you* and *I* and unlike *they, he, she,* or *it*, refers to participants in the speech event itself ([+participant]), as opposed to the event(s) the speech represents. And among the pronouns referring to participants, *we* is like *I* and unlike *you* in that it expresses the subjective point of view of the speaker ([+speaker]).

These features define the kinds of equivalences that, in Jakobson's description, define the sets of possibilities from which selections are made to produce combinations, which are themselves "based on contiguity." Within a simple (unaffixed) Eng. syllable (and subject to other constraints on syllable structure), e.g., they are the only consonants that can follow an [n]: Eng. has *lent, land, lance, lens, lunch, flange*; but not *la[np], *la[nb], *la[nf], *la[nv], *la[nk], *la[ng], etc. Thus, with respect to this sequencing, all [+coronal] segments are equivalent. Similarly, since person and number features are also registered on Eng. verbs in the present tense ([-past]), Jakobson's *sleeps, dozes, nods, naps* are equivalent to each other in bearing the features [-speaker, -participant, -plural] and available for selection to follow a noun sharing these features like *child*. In syntax, many equivalences are defined directly in terms of the contiguity relationships they enter into: *sleeps, dozes, nods, naps* are all verbs partly insofar as they follow nouns but not, say, determiners (*the child sleeps*, but not *the sleeps*).

To return to the poetic function, then, and Jakobson's own example of selection and combination, if a speaker selects the particular combination *the child nods*, the poetic function may be subtly manifest in, e.g., the sequence of [d]s and more broadly of [+coronal]s; if he chooses instead *the tot nods*, it will be manifest in the sequences of [t]s and of the [+coronal +stop]s [t, n, d], and also of [a]s; and if he elaborates his utterance further to make *the tot nods and naps*, the poetic function becomes still more salient, manifest in all of the above, plus the sequence of [n]s, the extended sequence of vowels that are [+low] (the feature [a] shares with the [æ] of *naps*), and the sequence of verbs, themselves a sequence of [-speaker, -participant, -plural] forms. In this way, the sequencing of equivalents that manifests the poetic function calls attention to the resources the lang. makes available for the composition of an utterance and to their particular arrangement in that utterance.

These examples, of course, illustrate the poetic forms of *assonance, *consonance, and syntactic *parallelism; and in Jakobson's formulation, all traditional verse forms, which, following G. M. Hopkins, he terms "figures of language," imply the poetic function (1960). The very first line of Shakespeare's sonnet 12, e.g., introduces *alliteration (of *count* with *clock* and *tells* with *time*), *rhyme (of *time* with *prime*), *meter, and syntactic parallelism (of the adverbial clauses beginning with *when*), all of which can be understood as sequences of ling. equivalents calling attention to the lang. of the poem:

> When I do count the clock that tells the time,
> And see the brave day sunk in hideous night;
> When I behold the violet past prime,

And sable curls [all] silver'd o'er with white;
When lofty trees I see barren of leaves,
Which erst from heat did canopy the herd,
And summer's green all girded up in sheaves
Borne on the bier with white and bristly beard:

What is esp. innovative about Jakobson's perspective on such forms, however, is the recognition that they involve not substantive identities but grammatical equivalences. Not only do the initial [t]s of *tells* and *time* alliterate with each other in spite of any differences in their pronunciations in their different contexts because they are [+coronal, +stop, –voice, –nasal], but, more subtly, they alliterate also with the initial [k]s of *count* and *clock* because those too are [+stop, –voice]. Equivalences like the latter are codified in some trads.—in Ir. the [+stop, –voice] consonants [p, t, k] count as equivalent in rhyme, e.g., (Malone)—but Jakobson's formulation interprets such equivalences as consequences not only of poetic convention but more deeply of grammatical structure. It is, thus, an invitation to explore poetic structure and ling. structure in parallel as mutually illuminating in all langs.

Beyond the ling. substance of this invitation, there are several profound poetic insights ensconced in Jakobson's formulation and the prodigious cross-linguistic study of ling. and poetics on which it is based. It decouples the question of what is poetic from the more culturally vexed question of what is poetry. The poetic function as Jakobson defines it appears not only in such canonized works as Shakespeare's sonnets but in many kinds of writing and speaking. It appears in well-crafted prose: in an April 10, 2007, *New York Times* article headlined "Science seeks Rx for lagging female libido," Natalie Angier describes how "the age-old search continues for a simple chemical fix, Cupid encapsulated, a thrill in a pill." It appears in political slogans: Jakobson observed it in "I like Ike" (1960), and half a century later the 2008 U.S. presidential primary saw signs proclaiming "Hispanics for Hillary" and "Obama 08." It appears in conversation: Tannen documents how interlocutors repeat the form of each others' utterances. One can even repeat the form of one's own, calling daily "Where's my kitty?" then (finding him) "How's my kitty?" and finally (picking him up) "Who's my kitty?" In all these examples, the poetic function is present but dominated by others, such as the referential, conative, emotive, or even phatic; in poetry, conversely, these other functions may likewise be present, but the poetic function is dominant (Jakobson 1960).

At the same time, Jakobson's formulation defines the poetic function as an explicitly aesthetic mechanism. Prior to his displacement to Prague, Jakobson had been a founding member of the Moscow Linguistic Circle, notable not only for its close collaboration of linguists and poets but for its engagement with new ideas about art more generally. The definition of the poetic function can be understood as a statement for the particular case of lang. of Viktor Shklovsky's influential idea that "the technique of art is to make objects 'unfamiliar,' to make forms difficult, to increase the difficulty and length of perception" (see DEFAMIL-

IARIZATION). Sequences of ling. equivalents quite literally prolong attention to the lang. and invite difficult questions about it. And although Shklovsky's further claim that, in art, "the object is not important" may be far from Aristotle's concern for what makes an object suitable to be imitated in poetry, Aristotle's assumption that imitation is fundamental to art remains: Jakobson's formulation extends it from the object to the medium, since it is through imitation of itself (in the sequencing of equivalents) that lang. becomes poetic.

Jakobson's formulation also provides an empirical basis for inquiry into poetic universals and comparative poetics. One of the most exciting projects of the Prague Linguistic Circle was the search for ling. universals. In an important precursor to Noam Chomsky's influential hypothesis that the grammars of all langs. share their basic form because their possibilities are determined by an innate "language faculty" (1972), Jakobson and his colleagues explored commonalities across all langs., such as patterns of "markedness" whereby an unmarked characteristic may occur on its own but a marked one occurs only in conjunction with its unmarked counterpart. E.g., a lang. may or may not have other nasals in addition to the coronal [n], as Eng. has [m] and the final [ŋ] of *rang*; but no lang. seems to have others without [n]. A lang. may or may not have a special pronoun referring to the speaker and addressee together as Weri has *tepir*, "I and you," but no lang. seems to have such a pronoun without having one that can refer to the speaker and someone who is not the addressee; Weri also has *tenip*, "I and one other person who is not you," and Eng. allows *we* to mean that (Kiparsky and Tonhauser 2011). On this view, the equivalences whose sequencing manifests the poetic function are ling. givens not only of the particular lang. of a poetic composition but potentially of all langs.; and the otherwise surprising fact that, across unrelated and mutually unknown langs., the same figures of lang. are found in poetry—alliteration, rhyme, meter, and syntactic parallelism—begins to find an explanation. Theoretical claims about the poetic forms favored by a given lang. then also become possible: Jakobson held, e.g., that only features that are distinctive in a lang. can define the equivalences of its verse, a position with profound implications for historical devel. of verse forms across both time and place.

Finally, Jakobson's 1960 formulation relates the formal manifestation of the poetic function to the prevalence in poetry of *metaphor:

> [E]quivalence in sound, projected into the sequence as its constitutive principle, inevitably involves semantic equivalence, and on any ling. level any constituent of such a sequence prompts one of the two correlative experiences which Hopkins neatly defines as "comparison for likeness' sake" and "comparison for unlikeness' sake."

E.g., the formal equivalence in both meter and syntax of Shakespeare's lines from sonnet 12 quoted above invites the inference that these are all somehow instances of the same thing, such as experiences of noticing the passing of time. At the same time, complete equivalence of meaning is always impossible, and the differences matter too; comparisons between human-made measures of time and natural ones or between life spans briefer than a human's and longer, sharpen perception of what each phrase refers to individually, as well as what the phrases do collectively. Even the alliteration beginning with *count* and *clock*, while perhaps not inviting comparisons between those particular words, does invite comparison between the abundance of the form in the *octave and its attenuation in the *sestet, until, after the nadir of line 13 in the same sonnet, robust alliteration reappears in line 14 with *breed* and *brave*, and so with the offspring who restores at least partly the losses that time brings:

> Then of thy beauty do I question make
> That thou among the wastes of time must go,
> Since sweets and beauties do themselves forsake,
> And die as fast as they see others grow,
> And nothing 'gainst Time's scythe can make
>     defense
> Save breed, to brave him when he takes thee
>     hence.

The alliteration thus offers its own version of the sonnet's narrative; and the metaphor in that is the ultimate one of poetry, the assumption that there is similarity or even grounds for comparison between lang. and what it represents—i.e., the assumption that lang. can ever imitate the world.

Yet for all the insights entailed by Jakobson's conception of the relationship of ling. to poetics, even this brief example of thoughts it might invite about an actual poem points to obstacles to seeing it as a theoretical position at all. At a sufficient level of generality and with a little freedom in what counts as a sequence, ling. equivalents can be found almost anywhere and produced to support almost any interpretation imaginable. This objection has been influentially articulated by, e.g., Stanley Fish with reference to some of the exuberantly linguistically informed crit. that followed Jakobson under the rubric of *stylistics* (Freeman 1970, 1981); and partly because of it, literary theorists since Jakobson have mostly turned their attention elsewhere. The *Norton Anthology of Theory and Criticism* (2001), e.g., even allowing for its explicit intention to go "beyond the earlier New Critical research into the 'literariness' of literature" (see NEW CRITICISM), counts only 11 of its 140 authors as addressing "language," of whom only four postdate Jakobson and none engages seriously with grammar.

In one sense, this silence is simply the fulfillment of Jakobson's claim that poetics is a subfield of ling.: it is largely in that field that the exploration he invited has been fruitfully pursued. That does not explain, however, why the results of such exploration have been disproportionately neglected, at least in Eng.-lang. literary studies, where exploration of poetry has continued apace. Kiparsky's (1987) analysis of the intellectual dimensions of this bifurcation acknowledges the theoretical obstacles but argues that they depend on particular assumptions in Jakobson's formulation that have been superseded.

Perhaps most fundamentally, Jakobson codified the relation of ling. to poetics just ahead of major devels. in how grammar is understood. Chomsky's (1965) generative conception of grammar as knowledge of the structure of possible utterances in a lang., in contradistinction to impossible ones, set a new standard for explicitness in grammatical description. That explicitness has maintained many of Jakobson's insights, incl. a crucial role for distinctive features (Chomsky and Halle, Goldsmith), but has also shown equivalence and contiguity relations among the entities they define to be only part of a much more complex grammar, hypothesized also to include structures that are "deep" as well as "surface," hierarchical as well as linear, and imposed by the mind as well as embodied in the particular elements of a given lang.'s systems of similarity and difference (Pinker). The entities, operations, and principles of grammar, understood by historical linguists since the 19th c. to be natural forms rather than human inventions (Foucault), are in the process of being discovered. Kiparsky (1987), therefore, decouples Jakobson's description of the "empirical linguistic criterion" of the poetic function from his particular conception of grammar, retaining the assumption of the centrality to poetic form of *repetition over the equivalence classes of grammar, while leaving more open to continuing inquiry the question of what grammar and its equivalences look like.

For verse, where these repetitions are patterned in ways that can themselves be formalized—where they are traditionally called "structural" or "obligatory" as opposed to "ornamental" or "optional"—it is possible to ask what, exactly, is being repeated and whether it can be formalized in ling. terms in the predicted way (Kiparsky 1973). In Shakespeare's sonnet 12, e.g., if the end rhymes are obligatory, forming a scheme *ababcdcdefefgg*, then *beard* in line 8 supplies some structure equivalent to one in *herd* in the same way that *time* provides one equivalent to *prime*.

This raises not only the descriptive question of what equivalence in the vowel system is allowing *beard* to rhyme with *herd* in a way that *board* would not but the theoretical one of why the final vowel and the consonants following it are the locus of a required equivalence in the first place. Is it because together they form a structure that plays a role in grammar and so are attended to as a unit in a way that other sequences would not be? These are questions that may be answered through exploration of more rhymes, suitably delimited by *work, *poet, *genre, and *tradition so as to support the inference of the formalization itself (Fabb 2002), together with exploration of relevant grammatical phenomena.

And discoveries have been made along these lines. E.g., drawing on a study of the rhymes of rock songs in Eng., Zwicky showed not only how shared features may suffice to define equivalents, such as [+nasal] in the rhymes of *roam*, *grown*, and *bone* in Bob Dylan's

"The Times They Are a-Changin'," but how certain segments in certain positions in syllables may be systematically irrelevant to rhyme, such as the final [d] in the rhymes of *call, hall,* and *stalled* in the same song. Such practices, once properly attended to, turn out not only to be common to canonical poets and similar to practices in other trads. but to be explicable in the patterning of features and organization of syllables in grammar and, as suggested by Kiparsky, parallel to what is found in the grammatical phenomenon of reduplication (Holtman). Similarly, exploration of alliteration has revealed subtle practices intricately related to phonological structure, not only in the early Eng. trad. but in many other langs., and again parallel to grammatical operations.

Perhaps of all verse forms, meter has been subject to the most thoroughgoing reconceptualization, as efforts to formalize it in terms of repetitions over equivalence classes have profited from discoveries about the grammar of *rhythm. Developing Jakobson's insight that "verse design determines the invariant features of the verse instances and sets up the limits of variation" (1960), Halle and Keyser (1966, 1971) suggested that a description of meter, like a description of a lang., should make explicit the poet's knowledge, conscious or not, of the form of possible as opposed to impossible lines in the meter. How, exactly, can lines like 2 and 3 of Shakespeare's sonnet 12, with their different patterns of both syllable count and stress, be understood as repetitions of a common structure that other imaginable but unmetrical arrangements of these elements would not share? As understanding of rhythm in phonology has advanced, with explicit theories positing how it is structured cross-linguistically in ordinary lang. (Liberman and Prince, Hayes 1995), various answers have been broached not only for the Eng. *iambic *pentameter (Kiparsky 1975, 1977; Hayes 1989) but for meters of, e.g., OE, Fr., It., Sp., Rus., Gr., Ar., Sanskrit, and Finnish. Fabb and Halle suggest a unified account of many of these meters; and the theory advanced in Hanson and Kiparsky with the addendum in Hanson (2009) proposes explicitly that all traditionally recognized metrical principles of syllable count (see SYL-LABIC VERSE), stress placement (see ACCENT), *caesura and *enjambment, and *catalexis and extrametricality (feminine endings) can be modeled as parallels to phenomena in the grammar of rhythm.

Of all verse forms, perhaps the least systematically explored along these lines in the Anglo-Am. scholarly trad. has been syntactic parallelism, perhaps because it has never been obligatory in the Eng. poetic trad. But it is obligatory in some forms in many other langs., from the Heb. that Robert Lowth noted in *De sacra poesi Hebraeorum* (*Sacred Poetry of the Hebrews*, pub. in Lat. 1753, trans. 1787) and the Rus. that Jakobson (1966) himself discussed to Chinese, Finnish, and many native langs. of the Americas; and devels. in syntactic theory since Jakobson's time have offered new ways to formalize it. (See CHINA, POETRY OF; FINLAND, POETRY OF; INDIGENOUS AMERICAS, POETRY OF THE;

HEBREW PROSODY AND POETICS.) Certainly, syntactic parallelism plays a role in grammar itself: some constructions such as coordination mandate syntactic repetition, and the fact that all sentences and phrases have identical syntactic structures at some level of analysis is the basis of syntax.

If verse forms consist of repetitions of equivalences that figure in lang., then they involve imitation of lang. not only because each instance of repetition imitates another but also because all imitate their source forms in lang. This raises the question of whether repetition is necessary for the poetic function or whether what is necessary is simply imitation of lang. Nonsense literature, e.g., seems to imitate morphology not necessarily through repetition but through letting morphology run amok, creating not so much new words as imitations of old words that have lost their moorings to meaning: "The Moon was shining slobaciously from the star-bespringled sky" (Edward Lear, "The Story of the Four Little Children Who Went Round the World"; see also NONSENSE VERSE).

Similarly, the "free indirect style" found in the novel does not involve repetition but imitates fundamental aspects of lang. Expression of one point of view is demonstrably a grammatical property of any sentence (Benveniste): not only person and tense features such as [+speaker] but deictic modifiers (e.g., *this, that; now, then; here, there*—see DEIXIS) and other words and syntactic constructions that are inherently subjective must be interpreted from a single point of view established in the main clause (Kuroda, Banfield). Normally, the point of view is that of the speaker, so that an indirect report of another's speech or thought requires any first-person present tense in the original utterance to be shifted into third-person, past tense. In the "free indirect style," however, the third person and past tense of an indirect report are used without any subordinating reportive clause; and the point of view of the sentence not only can but in some cases must be taken to be that of the third-person subject: "The snail had now considered every possible method of reaching his goal without going round the dead leaf or climbing over it" (Virginia Woolf, "Kew Gardens"). As a speakerless imitation of speech and thought (Banfield), the style is certainly poetic in Jakobson's sense; as he notes with regard to fictitious speakers and addressees of poetry, "virtually any poetic message is a quasi-quoted discourse with all those peculiar, intricate problems which 'speech within speech' offers to the linguist" (1960). The novel is not distinct from poetry as Aristotle defined it, but rather one form of it; and it is to be expected that the poetic function should be somehow manifest in its characteristic lang.

A capacious view of poetics that encompasses the novel within its purview and shares important aspects of its genealogy with ling. and Rus. formalist aesthetics (see RUSSIAN FORMALISM) has also been advanced within the trad. of Fr. *structuralism (Todorov, Barthes), inspired by Propp's exploration of fairy tales to formalize narrative content in grammatical terms.

This line of inquiry's engagement with ling., however, has often been more metaphorical than substantive, seeming to contribute less to understanding literature "in its specificity" (Todorov, Eichenbaum) than to understanding elements it shares with other arts, since narrative can be represented in media other than lang.

Jakobson himself was far from uninterested in such elements of poetry. However, his conception of the poetic function of lang. distinguished it from the referential one; and alongside the devels. in theories of lang. mentioned above, devels. in theories of communication have shown that the distinction is crucial. As Kiparsky (1987) observes, under Jakobson's structuralist assumptions, meaning is treated as deriving from the same basic principles of equivalence and contiguity, similarity and difference assumed to govern ling. form, so that it may be encoded through selection and combination within the system, as can be seen in Jakobson's account of the composition of a ling. message quoted above. But for meaning, as for form, those principles have turned out to be only a small part of the picture: not only is ling. semantics itself no more reducible to them than is any other component of grammar; as Sperber and Wilson show, building on ideas of Grice, in ling. communication semantics itself contributes only one piece of information to a process of *interpretation. Far from being the decoding that a long trad. from Saussure to Jakobson himself assumed, that process is inferential, open-ended, and not specific to lang. at all.

Sperber and Wilson show, in fact, that literal representation of a thought in lang. is almost never the most efficient way to communicate it, and even the most ordinary utterances are designed to provoke a creative interpretive process. Most strikingly, the interpretive demands made by the figurative lang. esp. associated with poetry, incl. the metaphors discussed by Aristotle in his *Poetics*, *irony, and many other aspects of style, incl. repetition itself, are not fundamentally different from those made by ordinary lang. In neither case is meeting those interpretive demands a matter of ling. alone—a conclusion entirely consonant with the complexity of lang. that Jakobson sought to convey through his delimitation of poetics as ling.

*See* POETICS.

■ F. de Saussure, *Cours de linguistique générale* (1916); R. Jakobson, *Selected Writings of Roman Jakobson*, 8 v., ed. S. Rudy (1962–81)—esp. "Morphological Observations on Slavic Declension" (1959); "Linguistics and Poetics" (1960); "On the So-called Vowel Alliteration in Germanic Verse" (1963); "Grammatical Parallelism and Its Russian Facet" (1966); N. Chomsky, *Aspects of the Theory of Syntax* (1965); B. Eichenbaum, *The Theory of the "Formal Method,"* trans. L. T. Lemon and M. J. Reis (1965); *Russian Formalist Criticism: Four Essays*, ed. L. T. Lemon and M. J. Reis (1965); V. Shklovsky, *Art as Technique*, trans. L. Lemon and M. J. Rieis (1965); R. Barthes, "Introduction à l'analyse structurale des récits," *Communications* 8 (1966); E. Benveniste, *Problèmes de linguistique générale* (1966); M. Foucault, *Les mots et les choses* (1966); M. Halle and S. J. Keyser,

"Chaucer and the Study of Prosody," *CE* 28 (1966); Chomsky and Halle; *Linguistics and Literary Style*, ed. D. C. Freeman (1970)—esp. P. Kiparsky, "Metrics and Morphophonemics in the *Kalevala*" (1968); V. Propp, *Morphology of the Folktale*, trans. L. Scott, 2d ed. (1968); N. Chomsky, *Language and Mind* (1972); M. Halle and S. J. Keyser, *English Stress: Its Form, Its Growth, and Its Role in Verse* (1971); T. Todorov, *La Poétique de la Prose* (1971); P. Kiparsky, "The Role of Linguistics in a Theory of Poetry," *Daedalus* 102 (1973); S.-Y. Kuroda, "Where Epistemology, Style and Grammar Meet: A Case Study of Japanese," *A Festschrift for Morris Halle*, ed. S. Anderson and P. Kiparsky (1973); H. P. Grice, "Logic and Conversation," *Syntax and Semantics 3: Speech Acts*, ed. P. Cole and J. L. Morgan (1975); P. Kiparsky, "Stress, Syntax and Meter," *Language* 51 (1975); A. Zwicky, "Well, This Rock and Roll Has Got to Stop. Junior's Head is Hard as a Rock," *Chicago Linguistic Society* 12 (1976); P. Kiparsky, "The Rhythmic Structure of English Verse," and M. Liberman and A. Prince, "On Stress and Linguistic Rhythm," *LingI* 8 (1977); M. L. Pratt, *Toward a Speech Act Theory of Literary Discourse* (1977); Fish; *Essays in Modern Stylistics*, ed. D. C. Freeman (1981); A. Banfield, *Unspeakable Sentences: Narration and Representation in the Language of Fiction* (1982); D. Sperber and D. Wilson, *Relevance: Communication and Cognition* (1986); P. Kiparsky, "On Theory and Interpretation," *The Linguistics of Writing*, ed. N. Fabb et al. (1987); J. Malone, "Muted Euphony and Consonant Matching in Irish Verse," *General Linguistics* 21 (1987); B. Hayes, "The Prosodic Hierarchy in Meter," *Phonetics and Phonology 1: Rhythm and Meter*, ed. P. Kiparsky and G. Youmans (1989); G. Lakoff and M. Turner, *More Than Cool Reason: A Field Guide to Poetic Metaphor* (1989); J. Goldsmith, *Autosegmental and Metrical Phonology* (1990); H. Lasnik, "Metrics and Morphophonemics in Early English Verse," *University of Connecticut Working Papers in Linguistics* 3 (1990); S. Pinker, *The Language Instinct* (1994); B. Hayes, *Metrical Stress Theory* (1995); R. Fowler, *Linguistic Criticism* (1996); K. Hanson and P. Kiparsky, "A Parametric Theory of Poetic Meter," *Language* 72 (1996); A. Holtman, *A Generative Theory of Rhyme* (1996); N. Fabb, *Linguistics and Literature* (1997); A. Pilkington, *Poetic Effects: A Relevance Theory Perspective* (2000); *Norton Anthology of Theory and Criticism*, ed. V. B. Leitch (2001); N. Fabb, *Language and Literary Structure* (2002); P. Verdonk, *Stylistics* (2002); K. Hanson, "Formal Variation in the Rhymes of Robert Pinsky's *The Inferno of Dante*," *Language and Literature* 12 (2003); D. Minkova, *Alliteration and Sound Change in Early English* (2003); K. Hanson, "Meter," "Rhyme," *Encyclopedia of Language and Linguistics*, ed. K. Brown, 2d ed. (2005); D. Tannen, *Talking Voices: Repetition, Dialogue and Imagery in Conversational Discourse*, 2d ed. (2007); N. Fabb and M. Halle, *Meter in Poetry: A New Theory* (2008); D. Steriade, "The Phonology of Perceptibility Effects," *The Nature of the Word: Essays in Honor of Paul Kiparsky*, ed. K. Hanson and S. Inkelas (2008); R. Tsur, *Toward a Theory of Cognitive Poetics*, 2d ed.

(2008); K. Hanson, "Metrical Alignment," *Typologie des formes poétiques*, ed. J.-L. Aroui (2009); P. Kiparsky and J. Tonhauser, "Semantics of Inflection," *Semantics: An International Handbook of Natural Language Meaning*, ed. C. Maienborn, K. von Heusinger, P. Portner (2011).

K. HANSON

**LIPOGRAM** (Gr. *leipo*, "I leave"; *gram*, "writing"). A text in which a given letter or set of letters is deliberately left out. In contrast to the *pangram*, in which every letter of the alphabet is intentionally included (e.g., *the quick brown fox jumps over the lazy dog*), the lipogram is a form of constrained writing explicitly based on omission (see CONSTRAINT). A *pangrammatic lipogram* is a text in which all but one letter is deliberately included, as in this example where the letter *s* is excluded: *the quick brown fox jumped over the lazy dog*. If the principles of the lipogram are simple, its application may lead to intricate difficulties that vary in proportion to the frequency of the letters excluded.

The earliest examples make Lasus of Hermione (6th c. BCE) the first recognized lipogrammatist; his two *odes, now lost, excluded the sigma, probably for reasons of euphonical purism. Those odes, along with another written by Lasus's student Pindar (ca. 522–443 BCE), established the lipogram as the most ancient systemic artifice in Western lit. The oldest attested lipogram, *De aetatibus mundi et hominis*, written by the Egyptian Lat. grammarian Fabius Planciades Fulgentius (late 5th–early 6th c.), confirms the constraint's systemic possibility: the treatise is divided into 23 chapters (14 of which remain), the first written without the letter *a*, the second without *b*, and so on. Several early lipogrammatic works apply the *constraint to revise major works (the *Iliad*, the *Odyssey*, the Bible) in a similarly progressive fashion, rewriting discrete chapters without the corresponding letter. From the 17th c. to the present, a second significant trad. emerges, mostly in It. and Ger., defined by the omission of the letter *r*, which is a strong constraint in Ger., as it forbids the inclusion of any masculine relative (*er*, *der*, *dieser*, etc.). The most ambitious of these is Franz Rittler's (1732–1837) 198-page novel *Die Zwillinge* (The Twins, 1813). The third trad. of the lipogram, first developed in Spain, is the vocalic trad., where only vowels are banished. A smattering of lipogrammatic novellas was published in Spain by Félix Lope de Vega (1562–1635) and Francisco Navarrete y Ribera (1537–91), and in the anonymous novel *Estebanillo González* (1646); the Port. poet Alonso de Alcalá y Herrera (1599–1682) published *Varios effetos de amor* (Various Effects of Love, 1641), consisting of five novellas, each omitting the use of one vowel.

The difficulty of vocalic lipograms varies from lang. to lang., depending on the frequency of the vowel. E.g., Georges Perec's (1936–82) 300-page novel *La Disparition* (A Void, 1969) is a considerable feat because it omits the most common letter in Fr., the letter *e*. That novel, which recounts the mysterious disappearance of a character named Anton Voyl, has been broadly praised and translated, notably into Sp. as *El Secuestro*

(The Abduction, 1997), which omits the letter *a* instead, the most common letter in Sp.

Univocalic (or monovocalic) lipograms are texts that exclude all but one vowel, like Perec's *Les Revenentes* (The Ghosts, 1972), which uses only words spelled with *e* (thus exploiting a lexicon entirely distinct from that used in *La Disparition*). The Canadian writer Christian Bök (b. 1966) has winningly illustrated Eng. univocalism in *Eunoia* (2001), which consists of five chapters, each exclusively devoted to one vowel, frequently including commentary on the adopted rule: "Thinking within strict limits is stifling."

Additional forms of the lipogram include the *anagram and, in Oulipian constraints, the prisoner's constraint (where *d, g, h, j, k, l, p, q, t,* and *y* are disallowed to give the paper-deprived prisoner more space for his memoirs), threnodials (see HETEROGRAM), and the following apostrophic lipograms: the beautiful in-law (*belle présente*, written exclusively with the letters in an addressee's name), the beautiful outlaw (*belle absente*, written exclusively with the letters missing from an addressee's name), and the *epithalamium (written exclusively with the letters in the bride and bridegroom's names). In contrast to the more visible tautogram (in which all words begin with the same letter) and the *acrostic, a lipogram may, if unannounced in the work itself, slip by unnoticed.

*See* ARTIFICE, AVANT-GARDE POETICS, OULIPO.

■ G. Perec, "History of the Lipogram," *Oulipo: A Primer of Potential Literature*, ed. and trans. W. F. Motte (1986).

J.-J. POUCEL

**LIRA.** A Sp. stanza form of four, five, six, or, rarely, more than six Italianate *hendecasyllables and *heptasyllables, the term denoting loosely any short-strophe *canción in Italianate verse. The name was first applied to the form *aBabB* (capitals denote hendecasyllabic lines) and was taken from the end of the first line of Garcilaso de la Vega's "A la flor de Gnido." Garcilaso supposedly imitated it from Bernardo Tasso, who is credited with its invention. This form is sometimes designated the *lira garcilasiana* and has also come to be known as *estrofa de Fray Luis de León, lira de Fray Luis de León,* and *quintilla de Luis de León* for being popularized through Fray Luis de León's works and later being replaced in popularity by other forms, particularly the *lira sestina* (*aBaBcC*, also called *media estancia*).

■ Navarro.

D. C. CLARKE

**LITHUANIA, POETRY OF.** Written lit. arose in Lithuania during the Reformation and Counter-Reformation. Before that, the poetic heritage of the nation was sustained by folk songs (*dainos*), of which about 200,000 have now been recorded and which are best represented by lyrical love songs. The lyrical nature of poetic expression is characteristic of dainos in general, and it is strongly evident even in the war songs and *ballads, while mythological songs are rare and *epic narratives are altogether lacking. The most typical of the dainos exhibit numerous diminutives and employ highly developed *parallelism and a rather intricate, sometimes erotic, symbolism. Because the text and melody are integrally connected in the dainos, *rhythm is of great importance; as a result of the free stress in Lithuanian, it is variable and often mixed. Rhyme, however, is not essential. The stanzas have mostly two, three, or four lines, either with or without a *refrain. Some older songs have no stanzas at all. The earliest collection of songs, *Dainos* (1825), was by Liudvikas Rėza (Rhesa, 1776–1840), the largest (4 v., 1880–83) by A. Juškevičius (1819–80); much more extensive collections have now been assembled by the Lithuanian Academy of Science. The trad. of folk poetry became a strong factor in the formation of the distinctly national character of Lithuanian poetry.

Written Lithuanian poetry begins in the 16th c. with versions of canticles and *hymns, incl. those of Martynas Mažvydas (Mosvidius, d. 1563), who also prepared, in Königsberg, the first printed Lithuanian book, *Catechismusa Prasty Szadei* (The Plain Words of the Catechism, 1547), a trad. of the Lutheran catechism, and prefaced it with a rhymed foreword. The most outstanding 18th c. work was Kristijonas Donelaitis's (Donalitius, 1714–80) poem *Metai* (The Seasons, 1765–75, pub. 1818), a 3,000-line poem in *hexameters that exhibits in forceful lang. a keen love and observation of nature and depicts vividly the life and character of the common people. Imbued with the Pietist spirit, the poem transmits a moving sense of the sacredness of life and of the earth.

A more active literary movement appeared at the beginning of the 19th c., marked first by pseudoclassicism and sentimentalism and later by *romanticism and a growing interest in Lithuanian folklore. The latter trend was particularly evident in the poetry of Antanas Strazdas (1760–1833), who was one of the first to merge the folk song trad. with personal expression. The next peak in the devel. of Lithuanian poetry was Antanas Baranauskas (1835–1902), whose picturesque poem *Anykščių šilelis* (The Grove of Anyksciai, 1858–59) is a veiled lament for Lithuania under the tsarist Rus. regime. Baranauskas was esp. successful in creating a melodious flow of lang. using a traditional syllabic versification that is not very well suited to Lithuanian. The pre-20th c. devel. of Lithuanian poetry was concluded by Maironis (pseud. of Jonas Mačiulis, 1862–1932), the creative embodiment of the ideals of the national awakening and a foremost lyric poet (see his collection *Pavasario balsai* [Voices of Spring], 1895). His formal and structural innovations, particularly the introduction of syllabotonic versification, exerted great influence on the growth of the new Lithuanian poetry. Two other poets writing in a lyrical mode in some respects similar to that of Maironis were Antanas Vienažindys (1841–92) and Pranas Vaičaitis (1876–1901).

At the beginning of the 20th c., the general relaxation of Rus. political pressure and an ever-growing cultural consciousness increased literary production and widened its horizon. New approaches were inspired by literary movements abroad. Already evident before World War I, these trends were fulfilled during the period of independence (1918–40) when Lithuanian poetry reached high standards of creative art. *Symbolism left a strong imprint on the early period, best represented by Balys Sruoga (1896–1947), also an outstanding dramatist; Vincas Mykolaitis-Putinas (1893–1967), later a leading novelist as well; and Jurgis Baltrušaitis (1873–1944) who, after achieving distinction among Rus. symbolists, began to publish verse in his native Lithuania. In the 1920s, the more conservative trends were countered by futurist poets (see FUTURISM) who, led by Kazys Binkis (1893–1942), formed the group *Keturi vėjai* (Four Winds). Somewhat later, neoromanticism, neosymbolism, *aestheticism, and *expressionism appeared on the scene, while the group *Trečias frontas* (Third Front) advocated poetry with a leftist orientation.

These trends were transcended, however, by the achievement of the four leading poets of the second generation: Jonas Aistis (1904–73), a highly intimate poet and a master of subtle and refined expression; Bernardas Brazdžionis (1907–2002), whose poetry, sometimes stylistically innovative, sometimes rhetorical with prophetic overtones, is a synthesis of national trads.; Antanas Miškinis (1905–83); and Salomėja Nėris (pseud. of S. Bačinskaitė-Bučienė, 1904–45), both of whom transformed the best qualities of the dainos into their own personal expression. The traditional features leading to the poetry of the next generation were best reflected in the verse of Vytautas Mačernis (1920–44).

The annexation of the country by the USSR during World War II broke the natural flow of Lithuanian poetry by imposing the paralyzing specter of socialist realism; poets exiled in the West learned to use modes of Western culture to speak, above all, of the pain and virtues of exile. While some poets became eulogists of the Soviet system in Lithuania and others retreated into long silence, new authors came forth to claim the favors of the Muses. Eduardas Mieželaitis (1919–97), paradoxically a loyal communist of philosophical bent, did much to help Soviet Lithuanian poetry break through to a more mod. idiom. Justinas Marcinkevičius (1930–2011), also important as a playwright, was perhaps the most popular poet of that period, speaking with great devotion of love for his country and people. Judita Vaičiūnaitė (1937–2001) sings of love in an intimate urban setting and of myth in dreams of the past. Sigitas Geda (1943–2008) transforms both nature and myth into a single magical presence, his vision of the country and its soul. Marcelijus Martinaitis (b. 1936) mostly converses with his own and the nation's conscience about hist., myth, and the responsibility of being human. Janina Degutytė (1928–90) is an intensely personal, lyrical poet of great integrity and noble dedication to humanity.

The culturally saturated poetry of the dissident poet Tomas Venclova (b. 1937) is committed to philosophical meditations. His poetic lang. may appear direct and simple at times. It contains, though, many implicit intertextual associations with the body of world lit., political views on the life of the Soviet dictatorship, and personal experience of an emotional or intellectual nature. The bleak landscape of Europe's moribund post-war culture shaped Venclova's imagination; he began his career under Soviet occupation and was immediately confronted with its realities and art. In exile, he became the most widely known Lithuanian poet and critic, whose works and critiques of society and culture in the Eastern Bloc hold a longstanding association with the works of Czesław Miłosz and Joseph Brodsky.

A number of prominent poets belong to the second generation of writers who debuted in the 1970s. With their avant-garde orientation, they attempted to broaden literary horizons during the Soviet occupation and looked for ways of self-expression. For Nijolė Miliauskaitė (1950–2002), wife of the outstanding poet Vytautas Bložė (b. 1930), everyday reality itself is a highly poetic and leads to the revelation of metaphysical mystery. Rich in cultural allusions and inventive use of myth, the poetry of Kornelijus Platelis (b. 1951) is a medium for harmony. The meditative and compressed thoughtfulness of Donaldas Kajokas (b. 1953) evokes Eastern poetic trads. through pursuit of an ideal nirvana. Antanas A. Jonynas's (b. 1953) melodious poetry spans a range of emotions, from sentimentality to anxiety to *irony.

The generation of poets who matured during the years of independence share a postmod. worldview. Their rebellious despair and psychological distress are conveyed through polemics with traditional values, an ironic voice, and surrealistic images. Aidas Marčėnas (b. 1960) is a master of classic form, whose writings combine contexts of various cultures and lits., poetic visions and dreams that are surrealistically fused with a present reality. Related to the Eur. trad., the aesthetic works of Kęstutis Navakas (b. 1964) can best be described as a play of various combinations of time and space in search of lost time. Sigitas Parulskis's (b. 1965) attachment to the painful existential experiences during the Soviet regime is evident in his poetry.

In the West, the foremost poet was Henrikas Radauskas (1910–70). He spoke in lucid, calmly measured cl. verse of the beauty of the world seen as a carnival of love and death. His loyalty, however, is not with that world but with enchanting mysteries of poetic speech that it engenders. Kazys Bradūnas (1917–2009) looks inward and into the past to awaken the ancient spirits of his native land and engage them in an ongoing dialogue with Christianity and hist. in Lithuania. Jonas Mekas (b. 1922), one of the moving spirits of the "underground cinema" in New York, also writes nostalgic and pensive verse full of self-questioning and yearning for the truthful life. Algimantas Mackus (1932–64) found his own truth in a radical confrontation with the fact of exile that required him to transform all the images of hope and faith from the traditional cultural heritage into grim totems of death. Liūnė Sutema (pseud. of Zinaida Katiliškienė, b. 1927) chooses the opposite task of allowing the alien world to grow into the very tissue of her soul to rejuvenate both her and the land of remembrance she carries within. Her brother Henrikas Nagys (1920–96) embraces both emotional expressionism and neoromanticism. Alfonsas Nyka-Niliūnas (pseud. of Alfonsas Čipkus, b. 1919), a cosmopolitan existentialist of a deeply philosophical bent, contemplates the large and bleak presence of the cosmos through the window of Western civilization.

■ **Anthologies**: *The Daina*, ed. U. Katzenelenbogen (1935); *Aus litauischer Dichtung*, ed. and trans. H. Engert, 2d ed. (1938); *Litauischer Liederschrein*, ed. and trans. V. Jungfer (1948); *The Green Oak*, ed. A. Landsbergis and C. Mills (1962); *Lithuanian Writers in the West*, ed. A. Skrupskelis (1979); *Selected Post-war Poetry*, trans. J. Zdanys (1979); *Sigitas Geda: Songs of Autumn*, trans. J. Zdanys (1979); *The Amber Lyre: 18th–20th Century Lithuanian Poetry*, ed. J. Marcinkevičius and V. Kubilius (1983); *Four Poets of Lithuania: Vytautas P. Bložė, Sigitas Geda, Nijolė Miliauskaitė, Kornelijus Platelis*, trans. J. Zdanys (1995); *Lithuania: In Her Own Words*, ed. L. Sruoginis (1997); *Breathing Free/Gyvas atodūsis*, trans. V. Bakaitis (2001); *Voices of Lithuanian Poetry*, trans. L. Pažūsis (2001); *Five Lithuanian Women Poets*, trans. J. Zdanys (2002); *Inclusions in Time: Selected Poems by Antanas A. Jonynas*, trans. J. Zdanys (2002); *Raw Amber: An Anthology of Contemporary Lithuanian Poetry*, ed. and trans. L. Sruoginis (2002).

■ **Criticism and History**: B. Sruoga, "Lithuanian Folksongs," *Folk-Lore* 43 (1932); J. Mauclere, *Panorama de la littérature lithuanienne contemporaine* (1938); J. Balys, *Lithuanian Narrative Folksongs* (1954); A. Senn, "Storia della letterature lituana," *Storia della letterature baltiche*, ed. G. Devoto (1957); A. Rubulis, *Baltic Literature* (1970); R. Šilbajoris, *Perfection of Exile* (1970); *Baltic Drama*, ed. A. Straumanis (1981); *Lithuanian Literature*, ed. V. Kubilius (1997); T. Venclova, *Forms of Hope: Essays* (1999); *Lietuvių literatūros enciklopedija* (2001); R. Šilbajoris, *A Short History of Lithuanian Literature* (2002); *Naujausioji lietuvių literatūra*, ed. G. Viliūnas (2003).

R. ŠILBAJORIS; D. LITVINSKAITĖ

**LITOTES** (Gr., "plainness," "simplicity"). A form of *meiosis, employing (1) affirmation by the negative of the contrary ("Not half bad"; "I'll bet you won't" meaning "I'm certain you will") or (2) deliberate understatement for purposes of intensification ("He was a good soldier; say no more" for a hero). Servius, commenting on Virgil's *Georgics* 2.125, says, "non tarda, id est, strenuissima: nam litotes figura est" (not slow, that is, most brisk: for the figure is litotes). Litotes is used so frequently in *Beowulf* and other OE, ON, and Old Germanic poetry that it has become (with the *kenning) one of its distinguishing features, e.g., "ðæt wæs god cyning" (that was a good king), following a passage telling how the king flourished on earth, prospered in honors, and brought neighboring realms to pay him tribute. Chaucer's cook is described as "nat pale as a forpyned goost. / A fat swan loved he best of any roost" ("General Prologue," 205–6). John Milton has "Nor are thy lips ungraceful, Sire of men, / Nor tongue ineloquent" (*Paradise Lost* 8.18–19). Alexander Pope uses litotes as an effective satiric instrument.

Like meiosis, *hyperbole, *irony, and *paradox, litotes requires that the reader refer to the ostensive situation, i.e., to the utterance's pragmatic context, in order to perceive the disparity between the words taken literally and their intended sense. Group μ distinguishes litotes from meiosis, or "arithmetical" understatement ("one says less so as to say more") by restricting litotes to the "double" negation of a grammatical and lexical contrary. So Chimène's conciliatory remark to her lover, "Go, I do not hate you" (Pierre Corneille, *Le Cid* 3.4), negates the lexeme *hatred*, while at the same time the negative assertion posits the opposite series of statements referring to the degrees between loving and not hating. Thus, the seemingly negative construction of the litotes not only suppresses a positive seme, replacing it with the corresponding negative one, but replaces any one of a series of negative semes. Corbett illustrates how litotes may function in forensic rhet. with an example of the lawyer who assists his client "by referring to a case of vandalism as 'boyish highjinks.' A rose by any other name will smell as sweet, but a crime, if referred to by a name that is not too patently disproportionate, may lose some of its heinousness." Litotes in this instance functions like euphemism by reducing the resistance of the audience. In logic, the device corresponding to litotes is obversion.

The distinction between litotes and meiosis is that, in the former, calling a thing less than it is makes evident that it is actually larger, whereas in the latter, calling it less is meant to make it less.

■ K. Weyman, *Studien Über die Figur der Litotes* (1886); O. Jespersen, *Negation in English and Other Languages* (1917); A. Hübner, *Die "Mhd. Ironie" oder die Litotes im Altdeutschen* (1930); F. Bracher, "Understatement in Old English Poetry," *PMLA* 52 (1937); L. M. Hollander, "Litotes in Old Norse," *PMLA* 53 (1938); M. Joseph, *Shakespeare's Use of the Arts of Language* (1947); C. Perelman and L. Olbrechts-Tyteca, *The New Rhetoric*, trans. J. Wilkinson and P. Weaver (1969); Lausberg; Morier; Group μ; Corbett.

R. O. Evans; A. W. Halsall; T.V.F. Brogan

**LITURGICAL POETRY.** In the Western world, liturgical poetry has encompassed a vast array of oral and written texts, from the early Lat. *hymns of Prudentius to the Jewish *piyyutim* of Palestine and Cairo to the 12th-c. sequences of Hildegard of Bingen to the liturgical poetics of contemp. writers such as Patrick Pritchett. Within many religious trads., the liturgy consists in considerable part of poetry composed, arranged, and altered to suit the formal demands of ritual practices. Established liturgical genres (Lat. octosyllabic hymns, e.g.) may endure for centuries, though with the capacity for tremendous variations of form, style, lang., and theme. In such cases, "liturgy itself" (a quite malleable category) gives rise to its own internal habits of formal innovation by provoking its ritual makers to experiment in new poetic idioms.

As a provocation to *invention, liturgy is similarly limitless in its influence on the literary field, which can be seen in some instances as an effect of liturgical practice in the domain of ritual. In the Brit. trad. alone, liturgy has spawned myriad inventions: the anonymous *Old English Benedictine Office* (early 11th c.), with its

interspersing of Lat. doxology and alliterative lyric; John Skelton's *Philip Sparrow* (ca. 1509), which expertly parodies the Office of the Dead; and the Chester cycle's *Shepherds Play* (early 15th c.), which tropes the "Gloria in excelsis" to comic but moving effect. The Middle Scots poet William Dunbar actively poached the liturgy as part of a poetic sensibility that he shared with many vernacular writers of the Brit. Middle Ages. The polyglot literary culture of med. Britain—Ir., Welsh, Cornish, Lat., Fr., Eng., Scots—was ideally suited to formal experimentation across ling. boundaries, and it is no surprise to see poets in all these langs. consistently turning to liturgical *latinitas* as a source of ingenuity and *invention. Central to this experimentation were liturgical practices such as troping, which involved the interpolation of new ritual matter into existing liturgical. This aesthetics of insertion, dilation, and expansion became an important formal strategy for writers enlisting the liturgy as part of their poetic enterprise. Liturgical parodies (such as the "Venus Mass" attributed to John Lydgate and the Iberian trad. of the *Misa de amores*) formed an active part of this trad., and there seems little doubt that the boundaries between properly liturgical and nonliturgical poetry could be quite permeable.

The coming of a vernacular liturgy with the Book of Common Prayer (1549) instigated an equally innovative if now largely monolingual poetic trad. The metrical trans. making up *The Bay Psalm Book* (1640) are liturgical poetry of the highest order, as are many works by John Donne, George Herbert, and others. In the mod. period, poets such as W. H. Auden, David Jones, R. M. Rilke, Jerome Rothenberg, Denise Levertov, and numerous others have found deep and enduring inspiration from the text, music, and ritual forms of the liturgy, by any measure a foundational idiom for comprehending the hist. and develop. of poetry in any period or trad.

*See* COPLA; HEBREW POETRY; JUDEO-SPANISH POETRY; LATIN POETRY; PSALM; PSALMS, METRICAL; RELIGION AND POETRY.

■ J. J. Petuchowski, *Theology and Poetry: Studies in the Medieval Piyyut* (1978); B. Holsinger, "Liturgy," *Middle English*, ed. P. Strohm (2007); K. Sterlin, "Liturgical Poetry," *Oxford Handbook of John Donne*, ed. J. Shami, D. Flynn, M. T. Hester (2011).

B. Holsinger

**LOGAOEDIC** (Gr., "speech-song like" [cf., in music, *Sprechgesang*]). A term used sporadically by ancient metrists to refer to verses consisting of single long syllables in alternation first with double and then with single shorts: − ∪ − − ∪ ∪ − − x (the *alcaic decasyllable), ∪ ∪ − ∪ ∪ − ∪ − − ∪ ∪ − ∪ x (the Archebulean), etc. Some 19th-c. metrists took the term to imply actual *isochronism or durational equivalence between sequences containing single and double shorts and applied it to a much larger class of ancient forms consisting, so they believed, of metra in which the normal time values of long and short syllables were altered in such a way that *dactyl, *spondee, trochee, and a single long syllable were all durational equivalents. The *asclepiad in its Horatian form would accordingly be analyzed as a hexameter: $-- | - \cup \cup |$ $- pp | - \cup \cup | - p \cup | - pp$, where p and pp indicate pauses or lengthenings of the preceding syllable equivalent in duration to, respectively, one and two short syllables. Though now generally rejected in favor of some sort of *choriambic or *aeolic analysis of the sequences once called logaoedic, the theory continues to have occasional defenders, particularly among classicists familiar with 18th- and 19th-cs. Western music. It encourages us to find in a piece of Gr. verse the equidistant strong stresses that one might look for in trying to set it to music or that an Eng. or Ger. reader would be inclined to introduce when reciting it. (Even so staunch an opponent of isochronism as Wilamowitz was, according to Shorey's reports, a "logaoedicist" despite himself when it came to such recitations.) And it becomes, with the elimination of the spondee and the addition of the first *paeon ($- \cup \cup \cup$) to its repertory of isochronous metra, the *sprung rhythm of G. M. Hopkins. In general, however, the term has not been used by metrists in reference to mixed binary-ternary (iambic-anapestic or trochaic-dactylic) meters in mod. Eng. verse.

*See* SYNCOPATION.

■ P. Shorey, "Choriambic Dimeter and the Rehabilitation of the Antispast," *Transactions and Proceedings of the American Philological Association* 38 (1907*)*; L. Pearson, ed., *Aristoxenus. Elementa Rhythmica* (1990)—both works in favor of isochronous analysis; J. W. White, *The Verse of Greek Comedy* (1912)—against.

A. T. COLE; T.V.F. BROGAN

**LONG POEM.** The term is used almost exclusively for mod. poetry, usually in Eng. Charles Altieri notes that the mod. long poem is distinguished by a "desire to achieve epic breadth by relying on structural principles inherent in lyric rather than narrative modes." Incorporating other texts, lost voices, political speech, or bits of memory, the long poem foregrounds the writer's role in making a distinctive way through such often-resistant material.

A cluster of early 20th-c. poems put into play the tensions and possibilities that continue to mark the genre. Ezra Pound's *Cantos* (1925–72) invents a series of ling. rituals through which the poet seeks to gather and give voice to the "luminous details" of what he sees as his culture's religious, political, and literary heritage. In their eventual acknowledgment of the limits of one person's ability to make such a synthesis cohere, however, *The Cantos* made the writing of such a text its real subject, an idea that now dominates the genre. T. S. Eliot's *The Waste Land* (1922), sensing in its central figure's speechlessness before the world's "horns and motors" a way to move forward, comes to life in its own writing, weaving broken-off shards of the culture into a richly expressive inner idiom. Discovering that the nightly bombing of London during World War II opened new sources of inspiration even as it destroyed old forms, H.D.'s *Trilogy* (1944–46) attempts to "alchemize" a

new manner of thinking out of melted-down bits of once-central texts. W. C. Williams, in *Paterson* (1946–58), responds to the work of his expatriate peers with "a reply to Greek and Latin with the bare hands," turning not to the shattered forms of trads. past but to the broken words of ordinary people, shaping the voices around him into a revolutionary epic form. Finally, Hart Crane's *The Bridge* (1930) focuses even more explicitly on Am. voices and hist., attempting to draw them toward a "mystical synthesis" suggested by the "unfractioned idiom" of the arcing Brooklyn Bridge. As with all these early moderns, Crane's charged lang., though driven by a shared dream, unfolds itself in a markedly individual way.

McHale has argued that, even as a "relatively stable modernist poetics was crystallized out from the churning heterogeneity of early-modernist innovation," what fell out of this official hist. "remained available for revisiting and reappropriation by later generations of innovators." This is clearly the case with the 20th-c. long poem, as we see the work of these predecessors mined over and over again by the writers who followed them. Keller usefully sorts these reappropriations into three groups: *epic-based poems; *lyric sequences; and experimental, less representational texts. While the categories overlap, they identify ways of mapping the confrontation of an individual sensibility and larger cultural concerns that remained central to the long poem as it continued to develop.

Long poems that draw on epic models established by the first generation of modernists work toward cultural synthesis while inevitably foregrounding the presence of the writer, whose selection and arrangement of material is everywhere at issue. As Pearce, Miller, and Gardner point out, Walt Whitman's "Song of Myself" (1855) is a notable model and expression of this tension. Important long poems in this trad. include *The Maximus Poems* (1960–75) by Charles Olson, *The Anathémata* (1952) by David Jones, and *The Changing Light at Sandover* (1980) by James Merrill.

Poems shaped as lyric sequences are often more autobiographical or singular in focus than their epic-based near-relations, investigating the ways "a number of radiant centers" (Rosenthal and Gall) cluster around or grow out of a single structure or form. Important poems here include John Berryman's *Dream Songs* (1969), Robert Lowell's *Notebook 1967–68* (1969), Adrienne Rich's "Twenty-One Love Poems" (1978), and Rita Dove's *Thomas and Beulah* (1986). Wallace Stevens's "The Auroras of Autumn" (1950) and Theodore Roethke's "North American Sequence" (1964) are notable examples of sequences with meditative slants.

There has been a particularly strong flowering of innovative, lang.-based long poems, often disjunctive in form, in the years since the early modernists. Gertrude Stein's *Tender Buttons* (1914) is often acknowledged as a predecessor. These poems, while often focusing on political, philosophical, or historical themes, call particular attention to the way lang. itself, in its rhythms, silences, conventions, and expectations, offers a rich means of raising and engaging such issues. Notable poems in this category include Louis Zukofsky's *"A"* (1959–75), Robert Duncan's *Passages* (1968–87), Lyn Hejinian's *My Life* (1980, rev. and extended 1987), Michael Palmer's "Notes for Echo Lake" (1981), Rachel Blau DuPlessis's "Drafts" (begun 1985), and Susan Howe's "Souls of the Labadie Tract" (2007).

*See* MODERNISM, POSTMODERNISM.

■ R. H. Pearce, *The Continuity of American Poetry* (1961); L. S. Dembo, *Conceptions of Reality in Modern American Poetry* (1966); H. Kenner, *The Pound Era* (1971); C. Altieri, "Motives in Metaphor: John Ashbery and the Modernist Long Poem," *Genre* 11 (1978); J. E. Miller Jr., *The American Quest for a Supreme Fiction* (1979); M. A. Bernstein, *The Tale of the Tribe: Ezra Pound and the Modern Epic* (1980); C. Nelson, *Our Last First Poets* (1981); M. L. Rosenthal and S. Gall, *The Modern Poetic Sequence* (1983); M. Perloff, *The Dance of the Intellect* (1985); M. Dickie, *On the Modernist Long Poem* (1986); T. Gardner, *Discovering Ourselves in Whitman* (1989); J. Walker, *Bardic Ethos and the American Epic Poem* (1989); P. Baker, *Obdurate Brillance: Exteriority and the Modern Long Poem* (1991); J. Conte, *Unending Design: The Forms of Postmodern Poetry* (1991); R. Greene, *Post-Petrarchism* (1991); S. Kamboureli, *On the Edge of Genre* (1991); P. Quartermain, *Disjunctive Poetics: From Gertrude Stein and Louis Zukofsky to Susan Howe* (1992); L. Keller, *Forms of Expansion: Recent Long Poems by Women* (1997); M. Perloff, *21st-Century Modernism* (2002); B. McHale, *The Obligation Toward the Difficult Whole* (2004); J. Moffett, *The Search for Origins in the Twentieth-Century Long Poem* (2007); H. F. Tucker, *Epic: Britain's Heroic Muse 1790–1910* (2008).

T. GARDNER

## LOVE POETRY

I. Issues and Assumptions
II. Thematic Overview
III. Conventions and Personae

**I. Issues and Assumptions.** Love poetry is one of the oldest and most widespread types of *lyric. It has come down to us from ancient Egyptian times, been authored by male and female poets, projected through and upon different sexual personae, and developed a host of striking and sometimes globally itinerant conventions. It has etched episodes in compelling plotlines and provided an imaginative space in which to articulate and contemplate the human emotions of affection, sexual passion, and idealism as these join in what we call *love.*

Though most anthologists would acknowledge love poetry's ongoing importance in the lyric trad., it was not always so recognized by 20th-c. Eur. and Am. critics. This had to do largely with reigning theoretical and historical assumptions, as Hancock points out in "Unworthy of a Serious Song?" For instance, the notion of poetic "impersonality" often made love poetry into something of an *oxymoron. T. S. Eliot, whose *Waste Land* and individual lyrics seldom engaged

with the theme of love unless to describe its impossibility, also wrote in his critical essays of the poet's necessary "impersonality." And though many of the most appreciated mod. love poets could not easily be accommodated within this view, the position was taken up by a number of influential critics (particularly Wimsatt and Beardsley, and, more polemically, Barthes). In a commendable eagerness to emphasize poetry as lang. and text, such a critical assumption made it difficult to embrace love poetry when it dwelt, as was often the case, on seemingly "personal" themes.

Historical assumptions also hampered our understanding of love poetry. For instance, many Am. and Eur. critics of the 20th c. saw the subject of love poetry largely through the historical lens of *courtly love—a view that places the beginnings of love poetry with the 11th-c. Occitan poets. Authors such as Lewis and Rougemont provided influential hists. of Eur. love lyric, all stemming from this source. Though Dronke early pointed out the much more complex and variegated hist. of courtly love, situating it within a wider set of influences and themes, this broader view was not as often accepted as the one that saw the trad. in its more limited guise, thereby excluding a fuller hist. of love poetry.

A third problem for the study of love poetry has been the limited availability of texts from other parts of the globe. New anthols. of trans. poems have begun to remedy this gap, broadening our sense of what love poetry can be in different ling., geographical, and cultural settings. Thanks largely to this growing range of anthols., as well as fuller critical descriptions of poetry from around the world, we are beginning to gain a greater awareness of love poetry's diversity, from the earliest Egyptian love songs to the present. This article gestures toward some of this diversity, though it would be impossible to explore it fully. The list of readings included should amplify this brief discussion.

The continuing popularity of anthols. of love poetry itself bears comment. Readers have always appreciated the love lyric, even when critics have been more reticent. Perhaps readers read love poetry to reenvision their own understanding of love and, to some extent, their own sense of identity. This need not be a simple mirroring. Reading love poetry from different geographic, ling., and historical contexts expands our sense of love's possible meanings in our own lives and those of others. In this sense, love poetry is not only one of the most common types of poetry written but a type with particular audience appeal.

**II. Thematic Overview.** Love poetry imaginatively presents the vicissitudes of that human emotion we call *love.* But what is love? Is it sexual pleasure, passionate desire, religious enlightenment, joyful connection to another, a painful disruption and reconstruction of self, or a cherishing of another human being? Is it idealized or sexual, public or private, a sickness unto death or an exhilarating rebirth of the mind and the senses? If we are to believe the poets, it is all these and more. According to lang., culture, time, and individual poetic insight, love is constructed in an endless variety of ways. For love itself, as well as the poetry that represents it, is, at least in part, an imaginative construction. It may be performed in a variety of ways and with differing results.

Of the themes that have characterized love poetry across the centuries and in many cultures across the globe, the tension between ideal and earthly passion is one of the most pervasive. This is a theme sometimes supported by religious and philosophical thought and by popular poetic practice—and has varied in importance according to historical and cultural context. To generalize greatly, the love lyric in its earliest forms seems to embrace a more earthly love, while med. and early mod. poetry explore more idealizing strains. The enormously diverse love poetry of the late 19th, 20th, and 21st cs. tends again toward less idealized themes.

Our oldest known love poems from ancient Egypt reveal a frank appreciation of the earthly nature of love. Sensual themes drawn from popular song celebrate youth, nature, and the sheer pleasures—and at times, the pains—of love. These poems, existing in the oral as well as written trad., are believed to have directly influenced the Heb. Song of Songs composed centuries later. Their themes and their reliance on female as well as male speakers have persisted in African poetry to this day and assert themselves with renewed vigor in the mod. and contemp. love lyric of many cultures.

From Sappho's great love lyrics focused on erotic longing to other Gr. texts, there is a complex legacy of poetic meditations on love. Much Roman poetry—particularly that of Ovid and Catullus—while in many ways emulating the Gr. heritage, present a love poetry that is often playful and even cynical. Here, love is entertaining and sometimes dangerous—a passion to be controlled and, at times, purposely extinguished. Examples from this trad. continue over the centuries, turning to homosexual as well as heterosexual themes and later flourishing in parallel with idealizing strands.

It is not in these very early love lyrics but rather in Plato's *Phaedrus* and *Symposium* that we find the most idealizing demands of eros, as the desire for transcendence of the human for the divine. Erotic desire, often described in homoerotic or clearly homosexual terms, animates a view of love that seeks not mere earthly satisfaction so much as the continuation of passion, often until the self can fuse with the divine. It is such erotic love that Rougemont claims stands behind the courtly love trad. Death has an inevitable role to play here, often presented in love poetry through the death of the beloved (as in Dante's *Vita nuova* and *Divina commedia*), making consummation of love impossible and endless desire inevitable. But at times the death of the lover is suggested also as the outcome of ceaseless passion.

Centuries of Eur. love poetry beginning with the *troubadours in the 11th c. celebrate a love that reaches beyond the material alone to ennoble lover and beloved. But as Hamill suggests, an idealizing spirit,

with its aspiration to move from the human to a more transcendent love, is celebrated in many cultures and from very early times. In the Persian and the Ar. trads., e.g., where earthly love has a specific role in the ascent to the love of God, we find a rich vein of idealizing love poetry. Often laced with humor and irony, playing on complex ambiguities, such poetry is well known from the 9th c. onward, and its mystical aspirations reach us today through the love poetry of Andalusia as well as the powerful verses of Jalāl al-Dīn Rūmī and the *ghazals* of Ḥāfiẓ. Indian poetry from the earliest Sanskrit and *Bhakti* has made sensual love at times the figure for spiritual yearning, as well as of sexual, courtly pleasure. Poetry by figures such as the 15th-c. Kabīr and Vidyāpati have inspired generations of poets around the world. In yet another context, we find the writing of Sor Juana Inés de la Cruz, where a unique rendering of religious and earthly love emerges in a Mexico recently transformed through violent cultural encounters.

Over the centuries, these two strains of poetry have persisted and often joined forces. Later centuries mark a few thematic junctures of particular interest. The luxuries of court settings and noble rank have, for instance, often contributed to the idealizing refinement of love poetry. This occurs in a good deal of med. and Ren. Eur. court poetry, where the social status of lover and beloved itself contributes to an expected lyric decorum.

One sees very different aristocratic poetries in the long, complex hist. of both Chinese and Japanese love lyric. Associated with the courts and often with royal figures, love poetry reveals sophisticated devels. in verse forms as well as themes. Each trad. stands alone and in some ways at odds with Eur. examples, though similar in its strong dependence on an aristocratic court culture for conventions of great poetic refinement, for a poetic play within stylized themes—as well as for material survival.

In the later Eur. romantic trad., the ideal and earthly produce a very different synthesis as poets depict a love both sexual and ennobling. But unlike their med. and Ren. precursors, and corresponding to different philosophical and religious expectations, these poets did not seek a divine goal outside earthly love but rather love's innate creativity. As Singer suggests in *The Nature of Love*, the lovers become ideal because they *are* lovers, filled with the creative spirit conveyed by the joining of sensuous and spiritual aspects of love—and the expectations of 19th-c. philosophy. Its themes often depict love as a path to death and destruction, but at other times more positive views prevail. With the romantic love lyric, courtly poetry's reliance on high social station gives way to a new openness to all social ranks, and women gain greater prominence as poets and as personae (see PERSONA).

Following in the wake of these more democratic and dialogical themes, love poets of the late 19th and 20th cs. begin to describe not only the experience of "falling in love" but what Singer describes as "being in love" and "staying in love." Though the theme of death also plays a role in this more mod. poetry, it tends to quicken the senses, making present pleasures and appreciations more intense, as it amplifies the importance of memory. An awareness of the transitory infiltrates amatory experience with heightened intensity.

Of course, the 19th c. brings not only a transformed love poetry to Europe: Europe brings the political and cultural context of colonial expansion, oppression, empire, and postcolonial response to much of the world. With colonial educational systems in Africa and India, e.g., came the invasion of cultures not only with guns and tools of commercial exploitation but with the insistent contact of different literary and poetic trads. Rich legacies of original-lang. poetry experienced an often violent encounter with the lyrics of Europe. What has emerged from this impact includes waves of trans., adaptations, new verse forms, and original inspirations, as well as reactions against the poetry of the colonizing nations. The ling., formal, and thematic effects of these encounters on the poetries of all trads. deserve ongoing study. For a genre as wide-ranging and diverse as the love lyric, such study has only begun.

Partly for this reason, it is hard to generalize about the themes of 20th- and 21st-c. love poetry across many cultures. However, a few salient qualities may be noted. First, in much if not most mod. love poetry, there is a muting of interest in highly idealizing themes and a greater acceptance of sexuality and sensuality. In many cultures, though hardly all, homosexual and lesbian themes become more frequent, as does poetry composed by women. Second, there is often a turn away from universal or stylized themes to the particulars of the individual love experience. The details of everyday life and sometimes the seemingly autobiographical elements connecting lover and beloved replace the earlier, more universal themes of yearning leading to transcendence. Third, a situated, particularized memory often replaces stylized imagery with cultural, historical, stylistic, and other thematic returns to the past. Fourth, mod. and contemp. love poetry is increasingly aware of its many poetic encounters over time and geographic space. These affect both themes and formal conventions.

**III. Conventions and Personae.** The conventions of love poetry include agreed-upon elements of style, genre, and structure that restrict the poet's work yet allow him or her to communicate with the audience or reader. A few have played a role in several different cultural and historical contexts. Some of love poetry's conventions relate to its themes, outlined above, but others deal in verse forms, imagery, and personae. Who do we imagine is speaking in a poem? How private does the lang. seem—or how public and rhetorical? Though a love poem may sometimes, through its particularity and detail, give the impression of a straightforward rendition of personal experience, it is always a fashioned, indirect expression, an imaginative performance in the medium of words. It is, in short, always art. Lang., with its constructions of *diction, *figuration, and *sound, intensifies the imaginative dimensions of the poem as it mediates any direct perception of sincerity.

A. *The Secular Love Lyric: Ancient Egyptian and Hebrew.* Our earliest love songs from ancient Egypt (1305–1080 BCE) provide examples of male and female personae, in each case imagining and/or addressing lovers of the opposite sex. Some humorous, some serious in tone—all offer the earliest known love songs, still a pleasure to read. They include poems of ecstasy, despair, a listing of the beloved's qualities, and descriptions of the more physical aspects of love. The openness and variety of these poems, their oral as well as written trad., remain ongoing traits, particularly evident, e.g., in later Swahili song. Female personae reappear in many African folk trads., inspiring later poets as well.

Scholars generally believe that the early Egyptian songs, very likely used for entertainment purposes, were popular in origin, though hardly naïve. The diction remains unpretentious, not stylized, and at times humorous and ironic. Imagery evokes the pastoral with its flowers, birds, and gardens. Highly crafted poems, they were likely sung as well as written. Their lines are not metered or rhymed but have a clear rhythm. Each song has a marked end point and most belong to larger cycles.

These early Egyptian songs were part of a trad. that seems to have influenced the best-known love poem in the world: the Song of Songs. Scholars now mostly agree that this poem, long read allegorically, is a secular love lyric—or collection of them—that was created by a sophisticated poet and was likely appreciated in popular recitation as well as elite writing. The many parts (or poems) of the Song offer different personae—incl. a woman, a man, and even groups. A young woman speaker dominates much of the poem, describing her desire and pleasure in love. These are fully reciprocated in the words spoken by the man. At times, a dialogue structure of alternating voices and matching images appears, creating a sense of mutuality between male and female personae. Nature imagery, some of it conventional, some of it astonishing in its metaphorical leaps, characterizes the poem, along with imagery from art and architecture. Though the verses are not metrical or rhymed, *parallelism and, at times, direct *repetitions, shape the text. The Song as a whole celebrates young love of a joyful, openly sexual nature but also includes references to death and to separation. With its *pastoral grace and delicate shading of love with death, the poem stands alone in the Heb. and indeed in subsequent trads.

B. *Classical Greek and Latin Love Poetry.* Fundamental to the Eur. trad. of love poetry are the cl. Greeks and Romans. Most famous among them is Sappho, a woman poet from Lesbos, whose texts are spoken in a woman's voice and most often concern affection, or passion, for other women. Whether Sappho herself was lesbian is something we cannot know—neither from the fragmentary corpus of her poetry nor from biographical data. But that her poetry often spoke through and about female personae and about erotic love we do know.

Derived from a long hist. of oral poetry, the *aeolic

meter Sappho used may well go back to an IE base. With its self-conscious meditation and description of the lover's inner state, her verse may be the most famous love poetry in the Eur. trad. Bringing to the reader an interior world of love's suffering and reflection, Sappho along with Archilochus and Alcaeus ushered in the era of cl. poetry, with its quest for internal reflection. Anacreon followed. A lyric poet of great skill, whose rhythmic verse patterns were imitated by later writers, he often turned to humor rather than yearning—as he addressed both male and female lovers (see ALCAIC, ANACREONTIC).

When the Romans overcame the Greeks, the Lat. writers began to gain poetic hegemony. Yet these poets were keenly aware of their debts to the stunning Gr. trad. that came before. Catullus, whose learned and witty love poetry was addressed to Lesbia, evoking Sappho, was a case in point. Developing the Roman *elegy, based on Gr. models of alternating lines of dactylic hexameter and pentameter, Catullus's witty lyrics were followed by those of Tibullus and Propertius, with their own amatory elegies to beloved women. A poetry of high society, theirs was not a lyric of longing but of lively love affairs. But of all the Lat. love poets, Ovid was the master. His love elegies—incl. the *Heroides*, written through the personae of famous women from the cl. past—were particularly influential, as was his imagery with its martial motifs. In his *Ars amatoria* and the *Remedia amoris*, he satirically presented a view of love that influenced poets and readers for centuries to come, one in which male and female were each given new stature.

C. *"Religions of Love."* In the med. period, Eur. love poetry takes on a very different shape and distinctive set of forms as well as themes. Lewis, who in his *Allegory of Love* describes courtly love in terms of "Humility, Courtesy, Adultery and the Religion of Love," assigns its beginnings to 11th-c. Languedoc. The beloved woman, an idealized figure of high social status, inspires her male lover with a passion that ennobles him. Engaging in a sort of quest myth for union with her—but also for his own moral excellence—her lover begins a spiritual journey. A view of love shared by the troubadour poets of Occitania, then by the *trouvères* in northern France and eventually by poets throughout Europe, the convention often depended on the imagery of Ovid but joined this to an idealization of the beloved, suggesting a religion of love, reminiscent of the cult of the Virgin Mary. In this courtly context, homosexual love was rarely voiced. Apart from the *trobairity*, women seldom were poetic speakers. The early, aristocratic cult of Eur. courtly love reached its pinnacle in the *Dolce stil nuovo* and the poetry of Dante, though it continued, with important thematic variations, in Petrarch's *sonnet sequence and subsequent renditions of the Ren. love lyric. In later centuries, homosexual motifs reappeared in the works of Shakespeare and Michelangelo, for instance, and the early idealism of love was also often challenged. But these early mod. versions remained largely aristocratic, attached to court life, with its refined lang. of the developing vernaculars.

Throughout, many fixed verse forms emerged, such as the *villanelle, the *sestina, and the *canzone, though the 14-line *sonnet held the greatest appeal.

Ar. love poetry of the 7th to 10th c. developed the genre to an exquisite art form—comparable in some ways to the Eur. courtly love trad. Generally voiced by a male persona, it often described a service of love to a capricious lady. In the 9th c., such love service could take by turns idealizing and highly physical descriptions and at times included homosexual motifs. In the hands of some writers, such love poetry transformed into the fully mystical, with the poet expressing desire for a divine beloved.

Influenced by early Ar. forms and conventions, Persian poets produced similarly idealized personae and love songs. In the ghazal form, based on linked *couplets with associated imagery, a courtly love very like that of the Occitan poets appears. But in spite of its similarities to the Eur. versions, distinct differences remain. One was the greater weight given to the sensual elements of love, for earthly love was deemed a necessary step in the ladder of love. Another was the absence of adulterous love. A third difference was the acceptance of homoerotic motifs.

Throughout the Persian and much of the Ar. trad., the mystical love song remains an important form for centuries. Turning to an earthly or divine beloved, the eroticism of Rūmī and Ḥāfiz produced distinctive personae and a powerful, if highly ambiguous erotic trad.

The Indian lyric of idealized love was more varied than the Eur., Ar., or Persian, given the many langs.— such as Sanskrit, Prakrit, Tamil, Hindi, and Bengali, to mention a few—and religious motifs it expressed. Whether described as love in consummation or in separation and longing, the ancient Indian love lyric was often part of religious devotion. Poets such as Kālidāsa and Bhartṛhari address the god Śiva. In Indian religious belief, the gods can at times reciprocate. At others, the emphasis falls on the lover's continued yearning. In the Indian trad., female desire is as often celebrated as male. The 12th-c. female poet Mahādēviyakka, for instance, reveals her intense yearning and praise for Śiva, often described in very sensual terms. In more secular visions, a lover's memory may shuttle between moments of separation and consummation. Though the sensual may open out to a more mystical knowledge, it may also simply be addressed as one of the many aspects of love. The ambiguity and beauty of the verse of 15th- and 17th-c. love poetry offered by Kabīr, Bihārī Lal, and Mīrābāī remain part of the trad. in India and beyond.

D. *Court Poetries.* In Chinese and Japanese poetry of the cl. period, refined court poetries flourished. In China, early popular love poetry was widely appreciated, though sometimes later read allegorically by elite audiences. But already in the Southern Dynasties (420–589), love poetry held an important place in court culture. These poems of love were written according to specific conventions. For instance, though the poets were usually male, they took the persona of a woman in love. For the most part, these were songs of sadness, longing, and nostalgia, written from the viewpoint of the woman, left alone in her boudoir, awaiting her wandering lover. Written in series of five- or seven-character lines, the poems reveal subtle parallelisms of image and tone that unify them. The later Tang dynasty poets (618–907), particularly Li Bai and Du Fu, reached pinnacles of fame in an era when poetry had become an essential ingredient in court and professional culture. The achievement of the Tang was its establishment of regulated tone patterns within verse forms and, in terms of love poetry's themes, its exploration of the ambiguities of love. The Song dynasty (960–1295) often used a style of poetry called *ci that was tied to musical forms and particular melodies and revolved around courtesan culture. Topics of the lover's desire were often expressed in this versatile form. Late in the Ming dynasty (1368–1644), the ci was used again by the poet Chen Zilong, who exchanged lyrics with his courtesan lover Liu Shi (see SHI). Their equally passionate and talented verse reveals the devel. of female as well as male voices in poetry, one that continues into the contemp. period.

Japanese court poetry was likewise highly refined in its use of poetic form and lang. Collections of poems early presented a version of courtly love. Often a poetry of yearning, it could also at times celebrate consummation. Erotic images of tangled hair or wetness were frequently employed. And the theme of laments by passionate women was a long-lasting convention in Japanese love poetry all the way to the 20th c.

Poetry before the 13th c. was almost always associated with the courts. Compilers, who were also poets, joined short *waka* poems together in long sequences. At other times, poets gathered for *poetic contests, Some of the most famous poets of the Japanese waka period are female—incl. Ono no Komachi and Izumi Shikibu.

*Renga*, or linked poetry, existed early in the trad. but gained popularity in the Japanese Middle Ages and later in the 13th, 14th, and 15th cs. Poetry was, among other things, an art of communication—with other poets as well as the audience. Joint writing of renga was a frequent court event. When renga was composed there, women poets participated. From renga, the *haikai and eventually the *haiku developed. The 17-syllable haiku originated as the first links of renga sequences but eventually became separated for discrete appreciation. The haiku grew popular in Europe and the Americas, thanks largely to Ezra Pound. Often confined to a seasonal image from nature, it could also reflect upon love.

### E. European Romantic Poetry.

In Eur. *romanticism, when a merging of ideal and real was supported by philosophical views of the aesthetic in figures such as Immanuel Kant, Friedrich Schiller, S. T. Coleridge, and G.W.F. Hegel, the poetry of erotic love flourished. Through the work of the *imagination, feeling joined intellect as it engaged the reader with new, more "organic" (as opposed to "mechanical" and fixed) poetic form. Shakespeare, with his manifold sensibil-

ity and playful use of lang. and verse, was particularly admired. Nineteenth-c. figures such as William Wordsworth joined love with nature—and poetry with more colloquial diction. In a turn to more democratic themes, folk motifs arose. The *ballad soon finds a central place, as does the *ode, though *blank verse is often cultivated as a means to organic form. In the work of John Keats and Coleridge, the poet addresses a female beloved, though Lord Byron's poetry evokes both homosexual and heterosexual themes. Women began writing in greater number than before, and poets such as Christina Rossetti and Elizabeth Barrett Browning effectively transformed traditional forms and personae for their own purposes.

In Ger. poetry, J. W. Goethe turns to the ballad to evoke the folkloric past, as he also experiments with a number of other Eur. verse forms and the Persian ghazal. He writes *Roman Elegies* to describe a sexual awakening. At times addressing love songs to women as a source of creativity and pleasure, at others he explores homosexual themes. Schiller, in his idealizing mode, praises his beloved Laura, evoking the Petrarchan past.

In Fr. lit., the works of Jean-Jacques Rousseau sometimes inspired utopian versions of love based in marriage and virtue. But Fr. romantic poets were better known for their descriptions of the agony of love, a theme well described in Praz's book on the topic. Charles Baudelaire, with his impersonal persona and visions of sexuality and urban love, guided the love lyric toward a new realism invoking lesbians, prostitutes, and cadavers, all the while sculpting verses in traditional fixed verse forms. Arthur Rimbaud and Paul Verlaine would follow.

### F. Modern Love Poetries.

Love poetry has grown only more popular since the mid-19th c. Web sites as well as printed anthols. allow us to read lyrics from around the world and over the centuries. Poets continue to explore the genre, regularly registering its importance in the very titles of their works, as Hancock notes: Adrienne Rich ("Twenty-One Love Poems"), Anne Sexton (*Love Poems*), Pablo Neruda (*Twenty Love Poems and a Song of Despair*), Anna Akhmatova (*Forty-Seven Love Poems*), W. C. Williams (*Journey to Love*), Yehuda Amichai (*Love Poems*), Robert Graves (*Poems about Love*).

Vigorous in its production, the genre has again changed. Many poets of the 20th and 21st cs. welcome a greater openness to sexuality, while constructing a more particularized, seemingly "personal" articulation of amatory experience. Many also write with keener attention to historical, ling., and cultural situation.

More than at any time since the cl. period, the love poem embraces a new sexual frankness. Since the late 19th c., there has been an increasing inclusion of gay and lesbian poetries, as well as a less inhibited rendition of sensual love. This is clear enough in the anglophone trad. Walt Whitman, for instance, engages multitudes in his single "I," at times suggesting loves homosexual and heterosexual. Emily Dickinson brings a powerful female perspective to the erotic, Amy Lowell describes an ongoing lesbian relationship, and H.D. employs mythic figures to depict her love. W. H. Auden keeps gender uncertain in his poems.

If various renditions of earthly love have been welcome in Eur. and North Am. cultures, they have not been absent elsewhere. Latin-Am. love poetry has long embraced a warmly sensual experience of love—not only in the lyrics of Pablo Neruda, often considered the greatest love poet of the 20th c., but in those of many others as well. Gabriela Mistral, Carlos Drummond de Andrade, Octavio Paz, and younger poets such as Roberto Sosa and Coral Bracho have transformed the mod. love lyric through memory and reflection on the moment. Mod. Indian love poetry, known best through the writing of Rabindranath Tagore, imagines love in more than 20 Indian langs., often in productive exchange with Eur. and Am. styles. African poets, building on an ancient trad. of sensual love, popular song, and strong female voices, write texts in a wide variety of langs. and postcolonial contexts. From Léopold Sédar Senghor and Christopher Okigbo to Ifi Amadiume, poets join powerful imagery from Af. cultures to distinctive reflections on love. In contemp. Ar. and Persian poetry, love continues to thrive. Adūnis, writing in Ar., is one of the world's best-known poets. The astonishing poet Furūgh Farrukhzād had a transformative effect on Persian poetry, treating themes of love from a female perspective in an innovative and sometimes explicit manner. In China, love lyrics come to us from an array of male and female poets. The 19th-c. poet Wu Tsao included descriptions of lesbian love and sexual explicitness that shocked but prepared the way for later poets. Similarly, it was a woman who most transformed Japanese love poetry of the 20th c. Yosano Akiko's collection *Midaregami* changed conventional views of women's sexuality as it opened new veins of love poetry to men as well as women poets in the 20th c. Mod. Heb. showed renewed interest in secular love poetry in the 20th c., most famously in the work of Yehuda Amichai, but in later poets as well.

Exploring more earthly passions, mod. poetry also constructs more earthly, particularized descriptions—and with them a new imagination of love. No longer a vague desire for erotic fusion, love in contemp. poetry often prefers a cherishing of self and other over a longer term. Here, individual memory rather than fixed themes lends the poem depth and coherence.

Memory may invoke an image that illuminates an aspect of love, as happens, for instance, through the rural metaphors in Seamus Heaney's love lyrics addressed to his wife. But memory also inheres in poetic form and lang. The poet's very choice of such a form—Neruda's sonnets or Adrienne Rich's ghazals—elicits a conversation with poets and readers over time and space.

Other memories inhere in the lang. in which a poet writes. Lang. can evoke a postcolonial experience, or socioeconomic context, or nostalgia for a past, or an address to a particular audience. Available on the Web as well as in print form, contemp. love poetry in many cultures often turns to music for full expression, reminding us of its beginnings in the Egyptian love song. Thanks to the creativity of poets in different cultural sites, writing in varied langs. and drawing on a complex but increasingly accessible hist. of themes and conventions, fresh and exciting love poetry awaits the reader today.

*See* EROTIC POETRY, GAY POETRY, LESBIAN POETRY, PETRARCHISM.

■ **Anthologies and Primary Texts:** *A Choice of Flowers: Chaguo la Maua; An Anthology of Swahili Love Poetry*, trans. J. Knappert (1972); *A Book of Love Poetry*, ed. J. Stallworthy (1973); *Love Songs of the New Kingdom*, trans. J. L. Foster (1974—ancient Egypt); *Sanskrit Love Poetry*, trans. W. Merwin and J. Moussaieff Masson (1977); *An Anthology of Modern Persian Poetry*, trans. A. Karini-Hakkak (1978); *The Penguin Book of Hebrew Verse*, ed. T. Carmi (1981); *Chinese Love Poetry*, trans. A Birrell (1982); *Love Poems by Women*, ed. W. Mulford (1990); *The Song of Songs*, trans. M. Falk (1990); *Greek Lyric Poetry*, trans. M. West (1993); *The Arc of Love*, ed. C. Coss (1996—lesbian love poetry; *The Erotic Spirit*, ed. S. Hamill (1996); *Gay Love Poetry*, ed. N. Powell (1997); *What Sappho Would Have Said*, ed. E. Donoghue (1997); *Love Speaks Its Name*, ed. J. D. McClatchy (2001—gay and lesbian love poetry; *Music of a Distant Drum*, trans. B. Lewis (2001—Ar., Persian, Turkish, Heb.; *The Anchor Book of Chinese Poetry*, ed. T. Barnstone and C. Ping (2005); *Indian Love Poems*, ed. M. Alexander (2005); *Shambhala Anthology of Chinese Poetry*, ed. and trans. J. P. Seaton (2006); *Bending the Bow*, ed. F. M. Chipasula (2009)—African love poetry; *Islamic Mystical Poetry*, ed. and trans. M. Jamal (2009); *The Oxford Book of Latin American Poetry*, ed. C. Vicuña and E. Livón-Grosman (2009); *Love Haiku*, ed. and trans. P. Donegan and Y. Ishibashi (2010).

■ **Criticism and History:** Lewis; W. K. Wimsatt and M. C. Beardsley, "The Intentional Fallacy," *The Verbal Icon* (1954); M. Valency, *In Praise of Love* (1958)—Ren. love lyric; H. Bloom, *The Visionary Company* (1961); R. H. Brower and E. Miner, *Japanese Court Poetry* (1961); Dronke; M. Praz, *The Romantic Agony*, trans. A. Davidson (1970); J. Scott, *Love and Protest* (1972)—Chinese love lyric; R. Barthes, "The Death of the Author," *Image, Music, Text*, trans. S. Heath (1977); E. Miner, *Japanese Linked Poetry* (1979); J. Walker, "Conventions of Love Poetry in Japan and the West," *Journal of the Association of Teachers of Japanese* 14 (1979); J. Hagstrum, *Sex and Sensibility* (1980)—early mod. love; A. Perry, *Erotic Spirituality* (1980); A. Schimmel, *As Through a Veil: Mystical Poetry in Islam* (1982); D. de Rougemont, *Love in the Western World*, trans. M. Belgion, rev. ed. (1983); M. Fox, *The Song of Songs and the Ancient Egyptian Love Songs* (1985); J. Hagstrum, *The Romantic Body* (1985); R. Scheindlin, *Wine, Women and Death* (1986); G. Woods, *Articulate Flesh: Male Homo-Eroticism and Modern Poetry* (1987); P. Veyne, *Roman Erotic Elegy*, trans. D. Pellauer (1988); A. R. Jones, *The Currency of Eros* (1990)—Ren. women poets; C. Paglia, *Sexual Personae* (1991); E. Selinger, *What Is It Then between Us?* (1998)—mod. Amer. love lyric; R. Greene, *Unrequited Conquests* (1999); T. Hancock, "Unworthy of a Serious Song?" *CQ* 32 (2003);

and "The Chemistry of Love Poetry," *CQ* 36 (2007); C. Petievich, *When Men Speak as Women* (2007)—Islamic poetry; I. Singer, *The Nature of Love*, 3 v. (2009).

S. L. BERMANN

**LOW COUNTRIES, POETRY OF THE.** Dutch, which is today the native lang. of about 23 million people, originated from Germanic dialects in the delta of the Rhine river, a region in western Europe historically named the Low Countries. An uprising against Sp. sovereignty in the late 16th c. led to the independence of the Dutch- and Frisian-speaking northern provinces, which formed a new country called the Netherlands. The Dutch-, Fr.-, and Ger.-speaking southern provinces remained under Sp. rule and, with the exception of the southeastern part that became Fr. territory, they later formed Belgium (in 1830) and Luxembourg (in 1839). The term *Poetry of the Low Countries* refers to poetry written in Dutch, combining both Dutch-speaking people from the Netherlands and from Belgium. The Dutch-speaking part of Belgium is also called Flanders, and its inhabitants are called Flemish. At some points in its hist., lits. from the Netherlands and from Flanders manifest considerable differences, yet they are considered by most scholars as belonging to the same overall ling. and cultural system. Dutch is also one of the langs. in former Dutch colonies; for Surinamese and Antillean poetry in Dutch, see CARIBBEAN, POETRY OF THE. In South Africa, the descendants of Dutch colonists speak Afrikaans, a lang. similar to Dutch. For Afrikaans poetry, see SOUTH AFRICA, POETRY OF.

The oldest example of Dutch poetic production, three verses of *love poetry written in the late 11th c. to test out a new quill pen, are the most famous lines in Old Dutch. The doubts about the geographical origin of the poem's author illustrate the difficulty in distinguishing Dutch from other Germanic and Anglo-Saxon dialects in that period.

During the Middle Ages, esp. the southern part of the Low Countries witnessed the successful production of *courtly love poetry in the vernacular. In this respect, the lyrics of Hendrik van Veldeke (ca. 1150–1210), a poet who wrote in a lang. still hesitating between Dutch and Ger., remain important. His influence on Ger. poets such as Wolfram von Eschenbach (ca. 1170–1220), Hartmann von Aue (ca. 1170–1210), and Gottfried von Strassburg (ca. 1165–1210) is widely acknowledged. The poems of Veldeke and of Duke Jan I of Brabant (ca. 1253–94) deal with courtly love in a traditional, rather formulaic manner: the beloved woman is idealized yet remains untouchable; hence, the feelings of the lover hover between ecstatic joy and depression. An original religious version of this ideal of courtly love is to be found in the mystical poetry by Hadewych (ca. 1210–60), a female mystic who evoked the adoration of God (whom she addresses as Love) along similar lines. Her *Liederen* (songs) and *Visioenen* (visions) correspond to attempts by the Beguine movement to develop an authentic female expression of divine love. Next to this lyrical poetry—preserved in

the Gruuthuse Manuscript—there was also an important trad. of *epic stories in verse. Particularly popular among these were the *chansons de geste*, epic poems about heroic knights, such as the anonymous 13th-c. *Karel ende Elegast* (Charlemagne and Elegast) and the satiric beast epic *Vanden Vos Reynaerde* (Reynard the Fox, ca. 1250), an original version of some branches from the Fr. *Roman de Renart* that mocks the courtly trad. *Didactic texts were also written in verse form. Works in Lat. that had traditionally been restricted to the religious world were made available to the lay elite because of Jacob van Maerlant (ca. 1230–90), who wrote the *Spiegel historiael* (Mirror of History), a popular rhymed chronicle of world hist. based on Vincent de Beauvais' *Speculum historiale*; and Jan van Boendale (1280–1351), who presented *Der leken spiegel* (The Layman's Mirror), a moralizing encyclopedic work that compiled all knowledge a layman needed for a virtuous life.

The economic prosperity of cities such as Bruges, Ghent, and Ypres led to an increase in self-awareness among the bourgeois elite. These cities used their influence to acquire special rights—"liberties"—from their sovereigns. The Chambers of Rhetoric represent a typical reflection of this urban pride in the 15th-c. Low Countries, mainly in the county of Flanders and duchy of Brabant. These associations of literary amateurs organized all kinds of festivities and had their own *poetic contests. By the end of the Middle Ages, poetry was thus no longer written exclusively for and by the nobility but became an integral component of the literary culture in cities and within the social class of citizens. Poetry was sponsored by city authorities as a way to transmit authority, pride, and moral guidance. Popular lyrical forms were the *refrain, a strophic poem that ended with an invocation of the Prince; the *ballad; the *song; and the *rondeau. The most important rhetoricians were Anthonis de Roovere (ca. 1430–82), the first official poet of the city of Bruges, and Matthijs de Castelein (1485–1550). The poet Anna Bijns (1493–1575) also wrote in the trad. of the rhetoricians, but her verses were best known for their explicitly Catholic and vehement polemics against rising Lutheranism. Several of these texts were exported in trans. through the city of Antwerp in Brabant, which in the 16th c. became a Eur. center of book printing. The Low Countries were then ruled by the mighty Hapsburg dynasty, which had extended its power from the Ger. empire over southern Italy and Spain to the Sp. colonies in the Americas and Asia. The cosmopolitan spirit of Antwerp is reflected in the *Antwerps liedboek* (Antwerp Songbook, 1544), a collection of Dutch lyrical texts that includes several adaptations of foreign songs.

By the end of the 16th c., an increasing number of poets became fascinated by the humanist thinking and artistic ideas of the Ren. The lyrical work of Petrarch and the poets of the Fr. *Pléiade* (Joachim du Bellay, Pierre de Ronsard) became esp. influential and were imitated in various ways, resulting in the successful introduction of the *sonnet in Dutch lit. by

Lucas d'Heere (1534–84) and most notably by Jan van der Noot (ca. 1539–1600) in his volume *Het bosken* (The Forest, 1570), which combines the established trad. with Petrarchism and Ronsardian motives, making use of *alexandrines and *iambic pentameter. Of equal importance is Justus de Harduwijn's (1582–1636) later love poetry.

The combination of discontent with the increasingly centralistic policy of Hapsburg Spain that threatened old "liberties" and anger over the persecution of Protestants led to an anti-Sp. uprising in 1566 under the leadership of William of Orange. Thousands of pamphlets, lampoons, and songs functioned as war propaganda. In 1574, an anonymously edited selection of these songs was printed. Its name, *Geuzenliedboek* (Beggar Song Books), is a reference to a disparaging expression used by the Sp. authorities in reference to the Dutch rebels. The collection included the "Wilhelmus," a call of support for William's uprising, a song considered the world's oldest national *anthem.

The war against Spain ended in a stalemate. While the northern provinces gained independence in the late 16th c., the southern provinces remained under Sp. authority. As a result, the center of cultural and literary life shifted toward the north. In the 17th c., the so-called Golden Age, the Netherlands displayed enormous wealth, economically as well as culturally. Besides painting, lit. played an essential role in the cultural construction of a national identity. Poets were eager to raise the Dutch lang. to a prestige that could rival cl. Lat.; they celebrated the greatness of the Netherlands and its capital Amsterdam as the new Rome. Pieter Corneliszoon Hooft (1581–1647), who successfully applied the metrical innovations of the Ren. to his own dramas and sonnets, became one of the leading poets of the new country. In his castle Muiderslot, near Amsterdam, Hooft hosted regular meetings of writers, which included the sister poets Maria Tesselschade Visscher (1594–1649) and Anna Visscher (1584–1651). Another prestigious member of the Muider circle was the influential diplomat Constantijn Huygens (1596–1687). From erudite Neo-Lat. poetry and hermetic Dutch sonnets to vulgar farces, Huygens demonstrated remarkable literary mastery.

The relatively tolerant and economically prosperous Netherlands attracted tens of thousands of immigrants from all over Europe, incl. many religious and political refugees from the southern Low Countries, Sephardic Jews from Portugal, Ashkenazi Jews from Germany and eastern Europe, as well as Fr. Huguenots. Joost van de Vondel (1587–1679), a child of immigrants from the southern Low Countries, established himself as one of the greatest writers of his time; he is famous first and foremost for his theatrical works, but some of his poems have become classics as well. Of importance is Vondel's critical involvement with the religious and political intolerance of his time. While Vondel's work often dealt with complex theological issues, the Calvinist moral teachings of Jacob Cats (1577–1660) were intended for the common people. His poems and

emblem books became popular in Eng. and Ger. trans. The genre of the profane and religious love *emblem, which may be considered a Dutch invention, became famous all over Europe.

With the creation of the East India Company (in 1602) and the West India Company (in 1621), the Netherlands became a major participant in Europe's colonial expansion. Colonial lit. was written mostly in prose, however, and the occasional poems rarely went beyond habitual clichés about the exotic Other. Jacob Steendam (1615–72), a resident in New Netherland, is interesting insofar as he was the first to write poetry about what would later become the United States.

In the southern Low Countries, much didactic religious poetry was produced, mainly in Jesuit circles. The Catholic emblems by the Jesuit Adriaen Poirters (1605–74), who was much influenced by Jacob Cats, gained lasting success.

During the 18th c., the cosmopolitan spirit of the Enlightenment stimulated growing scientific curiosity and the analysis of humans as rational beings. This led to the elaboration of the first Dutch grammars and numerous Dutch literary spectator magazines, which combined an encyclopedic vision on the world with strong moral principles. The philanthropic side of the Enlightenment was reflected in the educational poetry for children by Hieronymus van Alphen (1746–1803).

In the winter of 1794–95, a Fr. army, aided by a Dutch contingent of pro-Fr. "patriots," conquered the Netherlands. Pasquinades, lampoons, and songs played an important role in popular protest against Fr. rule, which lasted until 1813. In verses full of *pathos, poets such as Jan Frederik Helmers (1767–1813) and Hendrik Tollens (1780–1856) expressed a mixture of pessimism about the apathy of the present generation and hope that the fervor of times past might reawaken. The most significant poetic figure in the Netherlands in the early 19th c. was Willem Bilderdijk (1756–1813). Although he continued to use traditional alexandrines, his conviction that it is the poet's task to achieve a personal voice brings him in line with nascent *romanticism. Bilderdijk's Christian fervor corresponded to that of Isaac da Costa (1798–1860), a Jewish convert who was involved in *Het Réveil*, a Christian revival movement with significant influence in Dutch cultural and political life. An exceptional voice among the many clerical poets, who tended to give preference to the (Christian) message over aesthetic quality, was François HaverSchmidt (1835–94). Under the pseud. Piet Paaltjens, he wrote poems in which *irony, *sentimentality, and cynicism alternate.

In 1830, Belgium became independent. Most Dutch-speaking writers in Belgium opposed the fact that the young Belgian state promoted its communication almost exclusively in the Fr. lang. Rather than choosing the (predominantly Protestant) Netherlands as a model, these (predominantly Catholic) writers tried to construct an authentic Dutch-speaking identity. Strongly influenced by the romantic tendency to glorify the Middle Ages, they called themselves

*Flemish* after the once-powerful med. county. At first, the objectives of the members of this emancipatory Flemish movement were almost exclusively cultural and scientific. Scholars such as Jan Frans Willems (1793–1846) and F. A. Snellaert (1809–72) collected and edited old folk songs, stories, and poetry in Dutch. Complementary to this preoccupation with the past, attempts were undertaken to establish a new, genuine "Flemish literature" within the political context of a bilingual Belgium. This resulted in a large number of poems that were destined for specific occasions: *odes, heroic and historical verses, and didactic poems. Yet, in the same period, poets became increasingly aware of their "literary" status, of the fact that lit. could no longer be reduced simply to a ready-made ethical, religious, or political message.

The greatest genius of Flemish poetry in the 19th c. was Guido Gezelle (1830–99), professionally both a Catholic priest and a teacher. His work manifests brilliantly the ongoing process of literary autonomization (see AUTONOMY). On the one hand, Gezelle was preoccupied with the didactic function of his poetry. Numerous poems were written originally for specific religious occasions: baptisms, communions, ordinations, funerals. In this respect, his work can be characterized as ideological, preoccupied with values and norms. Yet, on the other hand, Gezelle explored the possibilities of poetic lang., combining romantic themes such as religious experiences and nature with fascinating formal experiments in *rhythm and *sound, verse form, even *typography. This latter dimension has been decisive in Gezelle's canonization as a major poet, even in modernist and postmodernist circles. However, poets such as Albrecht Rodenbach (1856–80) or Hugo Verriest (1840–1922), who wrote in Gezelle's trad., never managed to achieve similar fame.

Around 1880, a major event in this shift toward autonomous poetry—in contrast to the worn-out idea that lit. is a mere vehicle for the transfer of extraliterary ideas and norms—occurred in the Netherlands with the emergence of the *Beweging van Tachtig* (Movement of the Eighties). A group of young writers incl. Willem Kloos (1859–1938), Albert Verwey (1865–1937), Frederik van Eeden (1860–1932), and Herman Gorter (1864–1927) rebelled against predominantly didactic and edifying lit. Influenced by the work of John Keats and P. B. Shelley, they rejected putting literary work at the service of any ethical, religious, or social ideal. This radical worship of beauty and of subjective experience in lit. was famously summarized by Kloos in his often-quoted adage: "Art is the most individual expression of the most individual emotion." They called their new jour. *De Nieuwe Gids* (The New Guide), copying part of the name of the most prominent literary jour. of their time. This provocation proved to have a prophetic character; in short time, *De Nieuwe Gids* outshone *De Gids* (The Guide) as the guiding voice in the Dutch literary scene.

The cult of individualism and subjectivism and the plea for an autonomous lit. by the Movement of the Eighties influenced younger generations profoundly. Yet the movement's poets themselves soon abandoned their own radical poetics. Van Eeden became a world-reformer à la H. D. Thoreau and established a communal cooperative. Gorter, who had become famous for his impressionist (see IMPRESSIONISM) and sensitive verse in the epic *Mei* (May, 1889) and in his *Liedjes* (Songs), distanced himself from the "bourgeois individualism" of the movement. His later work reveals the influence of the philosopher Baruch Spinoza and the political ideas of Karl Marx. In his poems as well as in his essays, he started to glorify socialism. In this respect, he found a prominent supporter in the socialist poet Henriëtte Roland Holst (1869–1952).

Verwey founded a new jour. in 1905, *De Beweging* (The Movement, 1905–19). Influenced by the Ger. poet Stefan George and by Dutch symbolist painters such as Jan Toorop and Floris Verster, Verwey focused on the deepening of sensual experiences and spontaneous feelings in order to combine life and art. These ideas became prominent in the transformation of impressionist into symbolist poetry. Verwey influenced many poets of a younger generation, incl. P. C. Boutens (1870–1943), Adriaan Roland Holst (1888–1976), J. H. Leopold (1865–1925), and J. C. Bloem (1887–1966), who shared a sense of unfulfilled desire. Their poetry was characterized by an archaic lang., elaborate structure, and solemn tone. Although rooted in neoclassical trads. (see NEOCLASSICAL POETICS), the emotional basis of their work was more romantic, and the influence of Charles Baudelaire is undeniable. The poetry of Leopold and Bloem is intimate, transforming sensory impressions into general emotions or a sudden revelation of harmony. Holst, on the other hand, sought his inspiration in Gr. and Celtic mythology (notably in the work of W. B. Yeats). The main representative of *symbolism in Flanders was Karel van de Woestijne (1878–1928). He started out with hypersensitive and individualist texts, in which meticulous self-analysis was formulated in periodic sentences, using many stylistic devices and ingenious symbolism. In his later work, the style is more sober and the themes are more universal: the "lyric I" considers itself a *Modderen man* (Muddy Man, 1920), a creature torn desperately between sensuous earth and transcendental spirituality.

At the beginning of the 20th c., this long-established trad. of cl. poetry and poetics was fundamentally threatened by the sudden appearance of avant-garde lit. (see AVANT-GARDE POETICS). Although traces of *futurism and *Dadaism may be found occasionally, *expressionism constituted the most important source of innovation. In Flanders, a group of young poets, pub. in the periodical *Ruimte* (Space, 1920–21), opted resolutely for *free verse and nonliterary *diction. Thematically, they incorporated explicit elements from mod. times, while advocating a general utopian solidarity among all humans. This strongly ethical "humanitarian expressionism" was put into practice by poets such as Wies Moens (1898–1982) and Marnix Gijsen (1899–1984) and for some time by Paul van Ostaijen (1896–1928), a major writer in Dutch lit. In *Het Sienjaal* (The Signal, 1918), van Ostaijen advocated a quasi-Franciscan idea of personal suffering and a social utopia in which the artist functioned as a major prophet of the ideal future. However, during World War I, he moved to Berlin and wrote *Bezette Stad* (Occupied City, 1921), which testifies to a resolutely Dadaistic and nihilistic stance. This chaotic experience of world and humankind was reflected in a fragmented style, reinforced by avant-garde typography. In his final years, van Ostaijen dismissed this "typographical expressionism" and began to write depersonalized, almost mystical verse, which demonstrated a strong musical and rhythmic awareness. This evolution toward *pure poetry or "organic expressionism," which he articulated in a number of theoretical and critical essays, was imitated by numerous younger writers, of whom Gaston Burssens (1896–1965) became van Ostaijen's main follower.

In the Netherlands, the leading Dutch poet in the 1920s was Hendrik Marsman (1899–1940), who was also thoroughly influenced by Ger. expressionism and the ideas of Friedrich Nietzsche. Marsman saw instinctive vitality, the unlimited celebration of life, as the best possible answer to desperation and degeneration. To evoke this new limitless subjectivity, he used hyperbolic lang. and cosmic imagery. However, this vital creativity concealed a strong fear of death or even a longing for destruction and an explicit death wish. In his later poetry, Marsman tried to expand this perspective of humankind into a vision of culture and the need to reconquer a natural paradise. With its prophetic message of a "vitalistic turn" and its desire for a compelling life, Marsman's *Verzen* (Verses, 1923) had an enormous impact on the younger generation.

Next to these avant-garde tendencies, however, cl. poetry remained a prominent trad. in Dutch poetry. Among the numerous adherents of this poetics, some authors gained lasting significance with their oeuvre. Richard Minne (1891–1965) opted for the observation of daily life in an ironic tone, Simon Vestdijk (1898–1971) for an elevated lang. and the principles of an established poetic trad. Gerrit Achterberg (1905–62) achieved an almost mythical status with his passionate neoromantic poems about the search for the deceased beloved and the perfect poem; his integration of non-literary elements, from journalism as well as from various sciences, became exemplary for a new lang. of lit., in which precision prevailed over aesthetic principles. The most influential figure in this respect is Martinus Nijhoff (1894–1953). His combination of trad. with elements from *modernism reinforced the idea of common speech as a genuine lang. of poetry. The influence of T. S. Eliot is crucial for Nijhoff's view of poetry, as expressed in his essays and literary reviews. Nijhoff opted for a poetry in which contemp. reality was integrated as a topic. Yet he also made abundant use of mythology and symbols from cl. lit. His epic poem *Awater* (1934) illustrates the changing literary climate due to growing political tensions in the 1930s; he refuses to continue a certain type of poetry, in which, despite "seeing the ruins," poets would still "sing about the nice weather." Whether the dream of a new human in a new society will eventually be realized remains doubtful. His modernist belief in lit. as the last resource in a decaying world has often been discussed by later Dutch poets.

During World War II, literary life became much more difficult, esp. in the Netherlands where the Ger. occupiers installed a so-called Chamber of Culture in order to push along the Nazification of Dutch lit. As a result, most writers took their work to clandestine publications. Anthols. of resistance poetry, incl. the famous *De achttien dooden* (The Eighteen Dead, 1941) by Jan Campert (1902–43), were called *Geuzenliedboeken* (Beggar Song Books) in remembrance of the rebellious 16th-c. poetry during the war against Spain. Several authors—among them Marsman and Campert—died as a result of the war, while others emigrated.

After World War II, many poets considered the restoration and a revival of the literary trad. the best way to overcome the all-encompassing political, ideological, and cultural crisis in society. Hence, they continued to write neoclassicist verses, in which formal virtuosity and the personal expression of the inner self, combined with the sensory experience of the outer world and the use of symbols, still dominated. Within this traditional poetics, many writers managed to combine public success with lasting literary prestige: Maria Vasalis (1909–98), Ida Gerhardt (1905–97), Bertus Aafjes (1914–93), Ed. Hoornik (1910–70), Jan Greshoff (1888–1971), Karel Jonckheere (1906–93), Maurice Gilliams (1900–82), Hubert van Herreweghen (b. 1920), Anton van Wilderode (1918–98), and Christine D'haen (1923–2009).

In the 1950s, however, Dutch poetry was invaded by a movement of "experimental" poetry that in an aesthetic way anticipated the profound social and political changes that would disrupt Dutch society a decade later. A group of young poets, called the *Vijftigers* (Movement of the Fifties), engaged in vehement polemics with the neoclassicist tendency to ignore traumatic historical events. Instead, they sought their inspiration in *surrealism and, above all, in the view of artistic materiality propounded by painters such as Karel Appel, Pierre Alechinsky, and Christian Dotremont linked to the CoBrA Movement. They propagated an "experimental" and "corporeal" poetics, stressing irrationality and imagery instead of rational thought, pregiven schemata and forms. They abandoned elevated literary lang. and wanted to provoke and to challenge readers, rather than providing them with familiar themes and anecdotes.

The views of the Movement of the Fifties were formulated in a number of small periodicals such as *Reflex*, *Braak*, and *Blurb*. Later, *Podium* and its Flemish counterpart *Tijd en Mens* (Time and Man, 1949–55) were particularly influential in promoting experimental poetry. The first generation of experimental poets included Hans Lodeizen (1924–50), Bert Schierbeek (1918–96), Jan Elburg (1919–92), Simon Vinkenoog (1928–2009), Leo Vroman (b. 1915)—who emigrated to the United States and became an Am. citizen—and Remco Campert (b. 1929). They were later joined by H. C. Pernath (1931–75), Paul Snoek (1933–81), and Gust Gils (1924–2002).

The main representatives of the Movement of the Fifties were Lucebert (pseud. of L. J. Swaanswijk, 1924–94), Gerrit Kouwenaar (b. 1923), and Hugo Claus

(1929–2008), who dominated Dutch poetry for several decades. Lucebert wrote rhetorical and associative poetry, using abundant imagery. His ambition was to express "the space of the entire life" in his own words. However, since human beings and the world are by no means one-dimensional entities, ambiguity and paradoxes abound in Lucebert's poetry. His work is theatrical, often inspired by his own drawings. In this respect, Lucebert may be regarded as the most radical representative of the Movement of the Fifties. In contrast, Kouwenaar transformed the poem into a "thing" of its own. To this end, the personal tone of the poet disappears in favor of a more abstract and general diction, thus creating an autonomous ling. construct. Gradually, Kouwenaar's hermetic lyrical work opened up to anecdotal and more subjective elements, resulting in a more comprehensible poetry. Claus depicts in his famous volume *De Oostakkerse gedichten* (The Oostakker Poems, 1955) a "vitalistic" world dominated by the senses and by instinctive erotic passion. However, since this primitive ideal is constantly threatened by the consciousness of the human being, Claus's later poetry integrated hist., society, and culture. Although the struggle between historical awareness and the desire for an unconscious life remains central, his later poems are characterized by the many references to Gr. mythology, the Bible, and J. G. Frazer's anthropological collection *The Golden Bough* (1890).

In the 1960s, a younger generation criticized experimental poetry for its excessively esoteric lang. and its contempt for the reading public. Instead, these writers advocated a "new realist" poetics, which took its inspiration from *Beat poets and pop art and which promoted a democratic art aimed at broad audience and explicitly related to daily life. Periodicals such as *Barbarber* and *De Nieuwe Stijl* (The New Style, a polemical reference to the modernist *The Style*) advocated this new realist view by introducing the idea of ready-mades: existing texts that were isolated and transformed into poetry (see FOUND POETRY). *Barbarber*-poets such as J. Bernlef (b. 1937) and K. Schippers (b. 1936) displayed a relativistic tone and humor in poetry that was influenced by Am. modernist poets such as e.e. cummings and Marianne Moore. New Style poets such as Armando (pseud. of H. D. van Dodeweerd, b. 1929), on the other hand, were more aggressive; they selected material about controversial themes such as sex and violence and banned any subjective interpretation. In Flanders, the poet's subjective view remained decisive in poetic diction. Whereas Roland Jooris (b. 1936) moved toward a more abstract lang., the bestselling Herman de Coninck (1944–97) adopted a melancholic tone. Myriam Van hee (b. 1952) and Luuk Gruwez (b. 1953) became known as "neoromantic" poets because of their personal and emotional involvement. Other prominent poets combine romantic motives with a profound self-analysis: Kees Ouwens (1944–2004) and Leonard Nolens (b. 1947) in a serious manner, Gerrit Komrij (b. 1944) more ironically and theatrically.

Generally speaking, Dutch poetry was dominated by two opposite trends in the 1970s. On the one hand, a number of writers opted for an autonomous, lang.-oriented poetry, taking Kouwenaar as a major example. This focus on the creative power of lang. characterized the work of Hans Faverey (1933–90) and the poets around the literary magazine *Raster*. On the other hand, many poets wrote anecdotal poems in an accessible *parlando* style. Famous representatives are Rutger Kopland (b. 1934), who later turned toward a more suggestive and abstract poetry; Jan Eijkelboom (1926–2008), Ed Leeflang (1929–2008), Judith Herzberg (b. 1934), and Eva Gerlach (b. 1948).

From the 1980s onward, Dutch poetry has been dominated by *postmodernism. Two orientations of postmod. poetry may be distinguished. Most poets opt for a rather intuitive, playful, and ironic variant of postmodernism. They articulate the problematic status of lang., world, and subject. Instead of merely expressing a fixed personality, the poet stages the "lyric I," often in a theatrical tone. The borders between high and popular culture are breached, and the fetishes of hectic mod. life become an intriguing theme. This view of lit. was promoted by a group of Dutch artists who called themselves the *Maximalen* (Maximals) as a critique of *minimalism. Although the Maximal group as such lasted only for a short period, its main representatives established a major trend in contemp. Dutch poetry. Joost Zwagerman (b. 1963) may be considered a spokesman of this generation: next to his numerous essays and novels, he writes poems that display an eagerness to show reality in a colorful and exuberant manner. The same can be said about Tom Lanoye (b. 1958), who is also praised for his novels and plays. Pieter Boskma (b. 1956) and K. Michel (pseud. of Michael Kuijpers, b. 1958) have gradually evolved toward a more abstract and philosophical poetry. A similar abundance of images dominates the poetry of Ilja Leonard Pfeijffer (b. 1968).

Next to this popular branch of postmodernism, other poets explore postmodernism more theoretically. Taking their inspiration from Jacques Derrida, Jacques Lacan, Slavoj Žižek, J.-F. Lyotard, and Paul de Man, they deconstruct the ultimate belief in lang. as an effective means of communication and a way to gain insight into the world and humanity. Instead, they propagate rupture and discontinuity, fragmentation and polyphony. *Intertextuality is used to dispel the illusion of coherence and a fixed meaning. Huub Beurskens (b. 1950), Marc Reugebrink (b. 1960), Dirk van Bastelaere (b. 1960), Erik Spinoy (b. 1960), Peter Verhelst (b. 1962), and Stefan Hertmans (b. 1951) are marked by the heritage of modernism. This is less the case for Arjan Duinker (b. 1956), Tonnus Oosterhoff (b. 1953), Nachoem M. Wijnberg (b. 1961), Peter Holvoet-Hanssen (b. 1960), and Jan Lauwereyns (b. 1969), who developed their own poetics, regardless of complex theoretical discussions. Postmodern influences can also be found in the eclectic poetry of H. H. ter Balkt (b. 1938) and Jacques Hamelink (b. 1939), who rewrite Dutch hist. in poetic *cantos.

In the early 21st c., Dutch poetry witnessed a boom of *performance poetry. Performing poets like Jules Deelder (b. 1944) and Bart Chabot (b. 1954), together with the 1960s legend Johnny van Doorn (1944–91), nicknamed the Selfkicker, influenced the slam poetry (see POETRY

SLAM) of the youngest generation around Erik Jan Harmens (b. 1970), Ingmar Heytze (b. 1970), and Tjitske Jansen (b. 1971). Phenomena like the City Poet and the Poet of the Fatherland—the Dutch variant of the *poet laureate—proved to be successful strategies to reach a broad audience.

The growing importance of the work of first- or second-generation immigrants and colonial repatriates—such as the Dutch-Indonesian Marion Bloem (b. 1952), the Dutch-Surinamese Edgar Cairo (1948–2000) and Astrid Roemer (b. 1947), the Dutch-Antillean Alfred Schaffer (b. 1973), the Dutch-Moroccan Mustafa Stitou (b. 1974), the Dutch-Iraqi Al Galidi (b. 1971), and most notably the Dutch-Palestinian poet Ramsey Nasr (b. 1974)—reflects the steady transformation of the Netherlands and Flanders into multicultural societies.

*See* BELGIUM, POETRY OF; FRANCE, POETRY OF; FRISIAN POETRY; GERMAN POETRY; INDONESIAN POETRY.

■ **Anthologies**: *Harvest of the Lowlands*, ed. J. Greshoff (1945); *Medieval Netherlands Religious Literature*, ed. E. Colledge (1965); *Reynard the Fox and Other Medieval Netherlands Secular Literature* ed. E. Colledge, trans. A. J. Barnouw (1967); *Living Spaces: Poems of the Dutch Fifties*, ed. P. Glassgold (1979); *Light of the World: An Anthology of Seventeenth-Century Dutch Religious and Occasional Poetry*, ed. C. Levenson (1982); *Fugitive Dreams: An Anthology of Dutch Colonial Literature*, ed. E. M. Beekman (1988); *Dutch Poetry in Translation: Kaleidoscope from Medieval Times to the Present*, ed. M. Zwart (1989); *From the Low Countries: Poetry from The Netherlands, Belgium, and Luxembourg*, ed. B. R. Strahan and S. G. Sullivan (1990); *Contemporary Poetry of the Low Countries*, ed. H. Brems and A. Zuiderent (1995); *Dutch and Flemish Feminist Poetry from the Middle Ages to the Present*, ed. M. Meijer (1998); *Modern Poetry in Translation 12: Dutch and Flemish*, ed. T. Hermans (1998); *In a Different Light*, ed. P. C. Evans and L. Haft (2002); *Landscape with Rowers*, ed. J. M. Coetzee (2005).

■ **Criticism and History**: T. Weevers, *Poetry of the Netherlands in its European Context* (1960); J. Snapper, *Post-War Dutch Literature* (1972); R. P. Meijer, *Literature of the Low Countries* (1978); R. Nieuwenhuys, *Mirror of the Indies: A History of Dutch Colonial Literature*, trans. F. van Rosevelt (1982); S. Schama, *The Embarrassment of Riches: An Interpretation of Dutch Culture in the Golden Age* (1987); M. A. Schenkeveld-van der Dussen, *Dutch Literature in the Age of Rembrandt* (1991); F. P. van Oostrom, *Court and Culture: Dutch Literature 1350–1450*, trans. A. J. Pomerans (1992); *Medieval Dutch Literature in Its European Context*, ed. E. Kooper (1994); M. Spies, *Rhetoric, Rhetoricians and Poets: Studies in Renaissance Poetry and Poetics* (1999); *A Literary History of the Low Countries*, ed. T. Hermans (2009); J. Dewulf, *Spirit of Resistance: Dutch Clandestine Literature during the Nazi Occupation* (2010).

D. DE GEEST; J. DEWULF

**LULLABY.** Also known as cradlesong, hush song, night song, sleep song, and *berceuse*, a lullaby is a type of *lyric in which the poet takes on the role of a singer caressing, persuading, and commanding an addressee into stillness and sleep. Lullabies imitate a spontaneous song performed by a caregiver, most often by a woman, for a young child. Yet poets frequently depart from this convention of pragmatic, simple, female-voiced song to craft deceptively complex layerings of character and voice in the guise of a sleep song.

Often in the imperative mood, lullabies typically involve a contest of wills: between the singer and the listener, between a lover and a beloved, between the hopes of the singer and the cruelty of the world. Lang. is often contractual: the song may contain promises of gifts and pleasure if the listener consents to sleep, or threats and warnings of the suffering that will ensue if the listener does not. Matter varies from the command "sleep softly now" interspersed with lulling nonsense syllables to catalogs of actions in and around the home to thoughtful meditations on loss, desire, neglect, death, and despair.

Surviving med. lullabies are frequently presented as songs performed by a lovely maiden (often the Virgin Mary) whose words have been overheard, recorded, and commented on by an unseen poet. Occasionally, the addressee will engage in dialogue with the woman, but the dominant voice in these lullabies is that of the poet, who acts as an intermediary through whom readers may glimpse the intimate moment between mother and child. These lullabies usually take the form of *carols, with the *burden repeating some variation on the soothing syllables *lullay* and *bas*. A variation on this trad. of sacred lullaby, from the early 15th-c. *Coventry Mystery Play*, depicts mothers attempting to silence their infants in order to save them from the Massacre of the Innocents by singing a lullaby lamenting the children's imminent deaths.

While religious lullabies faded following the Reformation, a secularized version of the form continued to be popular in early mod. England. Throughout the 16th and 17th cs., in addition to lyrics that continued to lull an imagined child, lullabies were written for such addressees as mistresses, lovers, kings, queens, youth, and even abstract notions, such as the wanton impulses of the poet, as in George Gascoigne's "Lullaby" (1573). They also were a popular component of plays, incl. *A Midsummer Night's Dream* (1600) and *The Play of Patient Grissell* (1603), which both use the form to emphasize an uncanny mix of pleasure, command, and danger on the edge of sleep.

With increasing commercial attention to the creation of a separate genre of lit. exclusively for the entertainment and moral instruction of children, lullabies appeared in Isaac Watts's *Divine Songs for Children* (1720) and in *Mother Goose's Melody, or Sonnets for the Cradle*, published by John Newberry (1781). William Blake's cradle songs in *Songs of Innocence* (1789) and *Songs of Innocence and Experience* (1794), while drawing on the "child's song" aspect of the popular lullaby, use the form to produce sophisticated explorations of the innocence of infancy and the ensnaring chains of adult sexuality.

Lullabies have frequently been used as an instrument of cultural and class ventriloquism. While lullaby had long been a form in which an adult lyric masqueraded as a simple song of childhood and men claimed to sing as women, in the 19th and early 20th cs. this practice expanded to explicitly cross racial, ethnic, and class boundaries. Eng. men wrote lullabies in the personae of Scottish women, white Am. men wrote lullabies in the imagined voice and dialect of Af. Am. nurses, and white Am. women wrote lullabies that ventriloquized Native Am. women. Written by members of those minorities, however, lullabies are often powerful tools of cultural reclamation and celebration, as in Langston Hughes's "Lullaby (for a Black Mother)."

Recent controversies concerning lullaby revolve around what is and is not "true" or "real" lullaby. Critics such as F. E. Budd attempt to draw distinctions between folk, or popular, lullabies (sung by caregivers to children) and those poems written in imitation of folk lullabies. The first are dismissed as vulgar, pragmatic, unpoetic, sentimental nursery rhyming, while the second are celebrated as poems inspired by and improving upon a predominantly oral form. Against Budd, Daniel Tiffany asserts that the lullabies sung to children are "true" lullabies and that the increasing formalization of lullaby is part of a hist. of literary theft by poets of the dominant trads. Still other critics, such as Anne de Vries, emphasize the complicated range of satire and social commentary present in both folk and poetic lullabies and assert that there is no great difference between the two branches of the form.

*See* ORAL POETRY.

■ A.L.J. Gosset, *Lullabies of the Four Nations* (1915); *A Book of Lullabies*, ed. E. Smith (1925); *A Book of Lullabies: 1300–1900*, ed. F. E. Budd (1930); M. Warner, "Hush-A-Bye Baby: Death and Violence in the Lullaby," *Raritan* 10 (1998); N. Orme, *Medieval Children* (2001); A. de Vries, "The Beginning of All Poetry," *Change and Renewal in Children's Literature* (2004); D. Tiffany, "Fugitive Lyric," *PMLA* 120 (2005); S. Lerer, *Children's Literature* (2008).

B. WHEARTY

**LYRIC** (Gr. *lyra*, "lyre"). In Western *poetics, almost all poetry is now characterized as *lyric*, but this has not always been the case. Over the last three centuries, *lyric* has shifted its meaning from adjective to noun, from a quality in poetry to a category that can seem to include nearly all verse. The ancient, med., and early mod. verse we now think of as lyric was made up of a variety of *songs or short *occasional poems. Since the 18th c., brevity, subjectivity, passion, and sensuality have been the qualities associated with poems called *lyric*; thus, in modernity, the term is used for a kind of poetry that expresses personal feeling (G.W.F. Hegel) in a concentrated and harmoniously arranged form (E. A. Poe, S. T. Coleridge) and that is indirectly addressed to the private reader (William Wordsworth, John Stuart Mill). A mod. invention, this idea of lyric has profoundly influenced how we understand the hist. of all poetic genres.

In the early romantic period, lit. began to be divided into three large categories, culminating in J. W. Goethe's idea of the three "natural forms of poetry": lyric, *epic, and drama. The categories were then cast as ancient distinctions, but, in fact, *lyric* was a third term added to literary description by 18th- and 19th-c. lit. crit. (Genette). This is not to say that there were no ancient or med. or early mod. or 17th- or 18th-c. lyric poems, but that these poems were not understood as *lyric* in our current sense of the term. Fowler puts the situation most succinctly when he warns that *lyric* in literary theory from Cicero through John Dryden is "not to be confused with the modern term." A persistent confusion—among verse *genres, between historical genres and natural "forms," between adjective and noun, between cognitive and affective registers, between grammar and rhet., between privacy and publicity, and among various ideas about poetry—may be the best way to define our current sense of the lyric. It is a confusion that has proven enormously generative for both poets and critics.

The etymology of *lyric* is derived from the Gr. musical instrument used to accompany the songs of poets. In the Alexandrian period, when the texts taken from Gr. songs were collected in the library, the poems once sung in *performance were grouped together and called *lyrics* (Most). Thus, *lyric* was from its inception a term used to describe a music that could no longer be heard, an idea of poetry characterized by a lost collective experience. Most of the ancient poets we refer to as the earliest lyric poets (such as Sappho, Alcaeus, Anacreon, and Pindar) would not have understood this description. Plato and Aristotle did not use the term *lyrikos* in the *Republic* and the *Poetics*; before *lyrikos* began to be used as a term for songs once sung to the lyre, the key terms were *melos* (song) and *melikos* (song-like or melodic; see MELIC POETRY). Johnson (1982) has argued that "one thing about the nature of poetry that moderns have steadily recognized and that ancients could not recognize is the significance, the importance, of the inner stories that personal lyric imitates." If we think of the personal lyric not as a mod. invention but rather as a kind of poetry that modernity has come to recognize even retrospectively, then the absence of terms and concepts to describe ancient lyrics did not mean that ancient lyrics did not exist; on the other hand, there is abundant evidence to suggest that the reason for the absence of lyric as an important category in ancient poetics is that our notion of subjectivity, *emotion, and compression in poetry—in sum, the personal lyric—did not match ideas about poetry (or persons) in antiquity.

In early Lat. verse, the performance context that characterized the Gr. sense of *lyrikos* was replaced by "the generic fluidity and self-consciousness characteristic of Roman literature" (Lowrie). Catullus experimented with various meters to "suggest epigram or incipient elegy rather than lyric proper" and brought *sapphics into Lat. in his trans. of Sappho's fragment 31, but it is Horace who claimed to have brought sapphics and *alcaics to Lat. lit. in his own poetry (Lowrie). Both Catullus and Horace understood themselves to be writing poems that referred to Gr. poems once described as *lyrikos*, but the *odes and *hymns and *epigrams they wrote belong to genres specific to ancient Rome and often to genres they created themselves. To describe all these genres as *lyric* is to gloss over the dependence of Lat. verse on an enormous range of meters (*iambic, *ionic, *aeolic, *glyconic, *elegiac distich, *hendecasyllable, iambo-dactylic, dactylic hexameters, scazons) that would not have been grouped under a single category, even if Horace esp. understood his work in various meters as faithful to the lost ideal of songs once sung to the lyre by Sappho and Alcaeus.

Thus, while it is common for mod. discussions of lyric to include Sappho and Horace among early Western lyric poets, Sappho's performance to the lyre was not referred to as *lyric* in her own time, and when Horace referred to himself in his first ode as aspiring to join the *lyrici vates* by invoking those performances several centuries later, he did so in poems that may now seem to us brief, personal, and expressive (and so congruent with our mod. definition of *lyric*) but were understood in the 1st c. BCE not as lyrics but as odes. Indeed, before the early mod. period, one often finds that *lyric* is a rather abstract term for the miscellaneous and historically specific genres that now seem to us lyrical in retrospect. Sometimes the lyric proper is thought to have arrived in *troubadour verse, but the elaborate med. distinctions among the many genres of such verse (e.g., *chanson, *tenso, *descort, *partimen, *alba, *pastourelle, *dansa, *sirventes, *cobla) are lost when we describe troubadour poems as consistently or essentially lyric (Paden). Even when medievalists such as Zumthor apply the term *lyric* retrospectively to "a mode of expression entirely and exclusively referring to an I, which, although frequently no more than a grammatical cipher, nonetheless fixes the plane and modalities of discourse to the exclusion of any narrative element," they use the mod. sense of *lyric* as poetry that is nonnarrative and personally expressive in order to characterize a variety of med. verse practices.

The problem of when to date our mod. sense of the lyric extends into the early mod. period. As Greene (1999) has written, "[A]t the beginning of the early mod. period, one finds an incommensurability between what is then labeled as lyric and what we now call by that name: the technical term as received from classical Greek and the ill-defined corpus of brief, subjective writing in verse are approaching one another, but are not yet fully joined." Through the end of the 16th c., it was common for poets and critics to think of lyric (when they thought of it at all) as a loose collection of odes, *idylls, *paeans, and celebratory compositions; but in the same period, various verse genres began to be classified as lyric not only through a nostalgia for the ancient lyre but as a contemp. mode, as when George Puttenham distinguishes heroic, lyric, elegiac, and epigrammatic verse in his *Arte of English Poesie* (1589). Although the 16th and 17th cs. are often regarded as the era in which the lyric emerged and flowered across Europe, the lyric was one of many poetic varieties (as in Puttenham's list) and was often cast as the least important, the most occasional and

ephemeral kind of poetry. Yet perhaps for this reason, Philip Sidney in his *Defence of Poesy* (pub. posthumously in 1595) responded to the marginalization of lyric verse by defending it in the strongest terms: "is it the Lyric that most displeaseth, who with his tuned lyre and well-accorded voice, giveth praise, the reward of virtue, to virtuous acts; who gives moral precepts, and natural problems; who sometimes raises up his voice to the height of the heavens, in singing the lauds of the immortal God?" Sidney's *personification of lyric attests to the personal expressive power beginning to be accorded to the idea in the later 16th c. At the same time, Sidney's personified ideal is still associated with an archaic version of lyric performance. While med. songs may have followed their own elaborate generic protocols, in the Ren., the Horatian idealization of a lost age in which the "tuned lyre and well-accorded voice" performed in concert began to do the work of genre.

With the rise of the *sonnet after Petrarch, "the early modern sonnet becomes the semi-official vehicle of contemporaneous lyric, and both theory and commentary respond to it as a given," as Greene (1999) argues. "I esteem a sonnet by Petrarch more highly than all the romances," Antonio Minturno wrote in *L'arte poetica* (1563), and it is also true that mod. critics have esteemed the Ren. sonnet more highly than the many other verse genres that circulated so promiscuously in the period. In an influential late 20th-c. argument, Fineman proposed that what we call *early modern lyric* originated out of conventions of epideixis or praise (Sidney's "lyre and well-accorded voice [that] giveth praise"; see EPIDEICTIC POETRY). In Shakespeare's *Sonnets*, Fineman argued, those early mod. notions of idealized lang. break down and are replaced by a new model of lyric subjectivity in which the divided subject of modernity "experiences himself *as* his difference from himself." The sonnet's formal qualities enable this shift, according to Fineman, since the final *couplet's turn can so aptly articulate a person at odds with himself. Surely, Greene (1999) is right to suggest that "one needs to detach Fineman's argument from the text to which it emphatically joins itself and retell the unsettling of lyric subjectivity through many more examples over a larger time-line," but it is remarkable that critics who want to find the emergence of what we have come to think of as mod. lyric tend to locate its beginnings in the Ren. sonnet and in Shakespeare's sonnets, in particular. Perhaps this is because, as Hollander has observed, "by the 1580s, a variety of poetic conventions had become assimilated to the notion of the 'lyric poem,' including 'sonnets' in both the strict and loose senses . . . epigrams, pastoral lyrics and so forth." In other words, perhaps the tendency to locate the emergence of the mod. lyric in the Ren. sonnet may be traced to the sonnet's popularity and distinction as "one of the few instances in which a genre is defined in terms of a verse form," a distinction that allowed the sonnet to stand as a concrete instance of the beginning of a historical shift in the definition of the lyric from idea to genre (Dubrow).

In the 17th c., the early moments of that historical shift in the lyric's definition proved esp. felicitous. As Saintsbury memorably rhapsodized on the Eng. trad., "in this seventeenth century of ours England was a mere nest of singing birds, a nightingale's haunt in a centennial May." He went on to remark that "it is rather a temptation to the abstract critic to inquire why it was that lyric properly so called was later than the other kinds in our Renaissance." T. S. Eliot famously answered that "the poets of the seventeenth century, the successors of the dramatists of the sixteenth, possessed a mechanism of sensibility which could devour any kind of experience. . . . [I]n the seventeenth century a dissociation of sensibility set in, from which we have never recovered" ("The Metaphysical Poets," 1921). Eliot's move to date mod. poetics from the 17th c.—a move enormously influential for the *New Criticism and perhaps not coincidentally parallel to Michel Foucault's chronology of modernity—may indeed have followed from a shift in sensibility, but it also followed from a shift in poetics, in which lyric became a more capacious category. That shift had been accomplished by the time that Eliot wrote in the 20th c., but its beginnings may be traced to the 17th c., a period in which short poems (often called *songs*) flourished in large part precisely because their marginalization as minor lit. in the 16th c. made the stakes of their composition and circulation so low. Remarkable amounts of verse circulated in ms., a practice that bound circulation to social relations and occasions. Those relations and occasions produced all kinds of poems—poems of imprisonment, poems for gift-giving, appeals for *patronage, *parodies of popular poems, *riddles for social diversion, libels or epigrams about known individuals—in all kinds of places; as Marotti remarks, such verse was written and read "not only on paper, but also on rings, on food trenchers, on glass windows (scratched with a pin or diamond), on paintings, on tombstones and monuments, on trees, and even (as graffiti) on London's Pissing Conduit." In this flourishing verse culture, the broad category of *lyric* was seldom invoked as an abstraction for such a varied array of short poems.

But, of course, (as Eliot suggested), the 17th c. was rife with anxiety about other categories, incl. (as Foucault suggested) the category of categories themselves. The promiscuous circulation of verse genres was checked and balanced by ambitious ideas about poetic genres. In Eng., John Milton's great *epic may be the most obvious instance of such ambition; if the lyric had not yet become one genre in the 17th c., the epic already seemed a belated genre in need of renewal. The 17th-c. poets that Eliot characterized (after Samuel Johnson) as *metaphysical poets were known in the period for their "strong lines," a term of disapprobation at the time. Throughout Europe and the colonial world, poets of many langs. associated with the *baroque and *mannerism made the short poem into a vehicle of philosophical speculation, a shift that sometimes demanded that the form of the verse be adapted to the argument. As John Donne wrote of the Psalms, poetry may take "such a form as is both curious, and requires

diligence in the making, and then when it is made, can have nothing, no syllable taken from it, nor added to it"—a shift in structural conception that moved poetics toward the compositional principles that Goethe later associated with the "natural form" of the lyric. While lyric still functioned more as an idea than as a genre in the 17th c., ideas later to be associated with the lyric were already doing some of the work of genre in the period. That work was crystallized in two landmark publications by Nicolas Boileau that appeared together in 1674: a trans. of Longinus's *Peri hypsous* (*On the Sublime*) and the long poem *L'Art poétique*.

The neoclassicism of Boileau had an expanding influence on ideas about poetry at the end of the 17th and the beginning of the 18th cs. (see NEOCLASSICAL POETICS). Although the term *lyric* does not appear in *On the Sublime*, the rendering of the only surviving version of Sappho's fragment 31 in the text of Longinus made an influential argument for an emerging concept of a more organic poetic form in the latter concept of a more organic poetic form in the latter part of the 17th c. After the final lines of the fragment, which Anne Carson has recently translated as

. . . tongue breaks, and thin
fire is racing under skin
and in eyes no sight and drumming
fills ears

and cold sweat holds me and shaking
grips me all, greener than grass
I am and dead—or almost
I seem to me.

(*Eros, the Bittersweet*, 1998)

Longinus turns to his reader to ask, "Are you not amazed, how at one and the same moment [Sappho] seeks out soul, body, hearing, tongue, sight, complexion as if they had all left her and were external, and how in contradiction she both freezes and burns, is irrational and sane, is afraid and nearly dead, so that we observe in her not one single emotion but a concourse of emotions? . . . [I]t is her selection of the most important details and her combination of them into a single whole that have produced the excellence of the poem" (Campbell). As Prins has argued, Longinus turns Sappho into a lyric ideal by conflating "poet and poem: in his reading, Sappho is simultaneously losing composure and composing herself, falling apart in the poem and coming together as a poem that seems to speak, with heightened eloquence, to the reader." In part because of the circulation of Boileau's trans., the personified poetic force that Longinus attributed to fragment 31 established the *sublime as a conceptual bridge from the late baroque and mannerism through neoclassicism to *romanticism. The rage for Longinus not only enhanced and furthered Horace's idealization of Sappho's lyricism but pushed it in a new direction. In Boileau's trans., the identification between Sappho and her poem represents a further step in the devel. of an idea of the lyric as a genre of personal *expression. Boileau's neoclassicism was also expressed in an *Art of Poetry* to rival Horace's, in which he repeats the

Horatian formula with the added instruction that poetry be "solide" (sound), or governed by reasonable principles:

> Qu'en savantes leçons votre muse fertile
> Partout joigne au plaisant le solide et l'utile.
> Un lecteur sage fuit un vain amusement
> Et veut mettre à profit son divertissement.
>
> (In prudent lessons everywhere abound,
> With pleasant join the useful and the sound;
> A sober reader a vain tale will slight,
> He seeks as well instruction as delight.)
>
> (4.86–89)

In Dryden's trans. as in Boileau's *alexandrines, the emphasis on the "lecteur sage" or "sober reader" speaks volumes. By insisting on the centrality of reason in the composition and consumption of poetry, Boileau resisted the 16th- and 17th-c. momentum toward making a passionate and personal lyrical idea into a mod. genre. Instead, his poetic lesson emphasized the *eclogue, the elegy, the ode, *tragedy, *comedy, *heroic verse, and epic as genres that could appeal to the decorous reader at the same time that they might prove the dictum that "Un beau désordre est un effet de l'art" (A beautiful disorder is an effect of art, 2.72). This is to say that, while the trans. of Longinus helped to further an ideal of personal lyricism, *L'art poétique* made lyricism not a genre but an intentional effect of defined verse genres that were to follow reasonable protocols rather than be swept up in flights of personal expression.

Indeed, the new neoclassical emphasis on generic *decorum led the young Alexander Pope to publish an anonymous adaptation of Boileau's treatise in his versified *Essay on Criticism* (1711). Following Boileau, Pope attributed reasonable critical *taste in verse genres to the principles of nature:

> First follow Nature, and your Judgment frame
> By her just Standard, which is still the same:
> *Unerring Nature*, still divinely bright,
> One *clear*, *unchang'd* and *Universal* Light,
> Life, Force, and Beauty, must to all impart,
> At once the *Source*, and *End*, and *Test of Art*.

It is often assumed that Pope and his Eur. contemporaries followed neoclassical prescriptions about the hierarchy of genres at the expense of the lyric, making much of the 18th c. into a nadir for lyric (excepting local trads. of *landscape, satiric, and discursive poetry) that would be redeemed only by romanticism. What Longinus meant by natural form was not what Pope and early 18th-c. poets meant by "Unerring Nature," a reasonable principle that dictated sharp distinctions among verse genres with specific social functions. The 18th-c. emphasis on "natural" social relations rather than on the transcendence of form has seemed in retrospect a marginalization or repression of the lyric. As Siskin has written (1994) with reference to England, if we think that the lyric flourished before and was repressed by the early 18th c., then "the history that results is that strange and developmental tale in which, after decades of dry reason, late 18th-c. Englishmen finally got in touch with their feelings" and revived the personal lyric as a vehicle of literary expression. One problem with that strange tale is that it supposes that, by the 18th c., the lyric had become a recognized poetic genre that could be marginalized by more decorous neoclassical verse genres. But the lyric was just emerging as a complex kind of verse, part idea and part genre, by the beginning of the century. What happened at different rates over the course of the 18th c. was that the archaic idea of poetic lyricism was pushed further away from the "just Standard" of genre, since that idea had begun to threaten to blur the lines between one category of verse and another.

In fact, it might be said that, rather than disappearing, the idea of lyric in Eng. and some other lits. had a lively career in the 18th c. precisely as a counterpoint to the hierarchy of verse genres. As Joseph Trapp wrote in his *Lectures on Poetry Read in the Schools of Natural Philosophy at Oxford* in the same year that Pope's *Essay on Criticism* circulated (1711), "As to the Nature of the Lyric Poem, it is, of all Kinds of Poetry, the most poetical; and is as distinct, both in Style, and Thought, from the rest, as Poetry in general is from Prose." On this view, the lyric became a genre that could transcend genre, both an alternative to and the realization of "all Kinds of Poetry." The kind of poetry most closely allied with this transcendent lyric ideal in the 18th c. was the *ode*, a term Trapp (like most critics in the period) uses interchangeably with *lyric* and a genre associated since the 17th c. with ancient lyricism. Abrams actually suggested in 1953 that "the soaring fortunes of the lyric may be dated to 1651, the year that Cowley's Pindaric 'imitations' burst over the literary horizon and inaugurated the immense vogue of the 'greater Ode' in England." By the middle of the century, the popularity of mod. versions of the ode (particularly those by William Collins and Thomas Gray) prompted Samuel Johnson to complain that the poets of odes modeled themselves on a primitive form of poetry written when the imagination was "vehement and rapid" and before science had been sufficiently developed to accustom the mind to close inspection and control: "From this accidental peculiarity of ancient writers, the criticks deduce the rules of lyrick poetry, which they have set free from all the laws by which other compositions are confined, and allow to neglect the niceties of transition, to start into remote digressions, and to wander without restraint from one scene of imagery to another" (*Rambler*, no. 158 September 21, 1751). Trapp had actually also suggested that Pindar "and the rest of the Grecians, receiv'd their Learning from the Nations of the East, the *Jews* and *Phoenicians*," thus not only granting the ode a transcendent lyricism but making it a transcendent vehicle of the hist. of civilization. Johnson turns that turn against itself in his complaint about the lyric's primitivism, but the notion that odes or lyrics (the terms were used practically as synonyms) were themselves vehicles of the hist. of culture would be influential for centuries to come. And perhaps the most important aspect of this turn is the symbiotic relationship between lyricism and crit.: "the criticks deduce the rules of lyrick poetry," according to Johnson, by not playing by the rules. At the same time, only a critic could understand the hist., significance, and value of that critical transgression—whether that critic valued it as did Trapp or disparaged it as did Johnson. As Siskin has written (1988), "from very early on, the English lyric has mixed with the critical, both in terms of poems being mixed with critical writing and in terms of the incorporation within those poems of critical features." But we could go further: since lyric had been an idea hovering over, among, and beneath various ideas of poetry for centuries, it rose in importance with the rise in importance of professional lit. crit. in the 18th c. Since all along the lyric had been more idea than genre, and in modernity became an idea that could transcend genre ("as distinct . . . from the rest, as Poetry is from Prose"), the idea of the lyric needed critics to understand and further it, and critics needed the slippery idea of the lyric as a field for debate.

Thus, the rise of the lyric as a mod. poetic ideal in the 18th c. went hand in hand with the lyricization of the ode and a shift in critical ideas of genre. As late as 1795, the *Encyclopaedia Britannica* defined lyric poetry by dividing it into three kinds: the Sublime ode, the Lesser ode, and the Song. Odes and songs were genres associated with specific social functions and occasions; *lyric* was an adjective that described an idea associated with those genres. Just as the sonnet was the representative genre aligned with lyric in the 16th c., and sonnets, odes, and songs were considered lyrical in the 17th c., throughout the 18th c. odes (greater and lesser, sublime or merely beautiful) and songs (set to music or as texts) were often the genres associated with an idea of lyric. Toward the end of the century, a tendency to divide lit. (itself a new category) into three distinct categories attached to large critical conceptions of generic functions rather than tied to a wide variety of actual social (or "natural") uses emerged, and these categories began to compete with the cultural work of particular genres. Although such critical division was an invention of the 18th and 19th cs., it claimed ancient origins, and later critics tend to forget that the late 18th c.'s move toward broad generic claims was not actually faithful to Aristotle or Plato or Horace or even to literary critics of early modernity (Genette). Instead, late 18th-c. poetics answered to a post-Enlightenment interest in systematic knowledge production that governed the emergence of the disciplines of natural science and economics (Poovey) and, thus, to a need to make the mobile lyric ideal into a defined genre with its own identifiable and exchangeable features and rules. So Johann A. Schlegel noted in *Einschränkung der schönen Künste auf einen einzigen Grundsatz* (1751) that a division of literary works into "lyric, epic, and drama" would correspond to the "subjective, subjective-objective, and objective" forms of representation, and Friedrich Hölderlin wrote in *Sämtliche Werke* (1790) that "in the tragic lies the completion of the epic, in the lyric the completion of the tragic, in the epic the completion of the lyric." In

a note to the *West-östlicher Divan* (1819), Goethe went further in proposing what would be an enormously influential rethinking not only of the lyric but of the system of genres that made the lyric into a new third party to a way of thinking about lit.:

> One can combine these three elements [lyric, epic, dramatic] and get infinite variations on the poetic genres; that is why it is so hard to find an order by which to classify them side by side or in succession. One can, however, extricate oneself from the difficulty by setting the three main elements on a circle, equidistant from one another, and seeking exemplary works in which each element predominates separately. Then one can assemble examples that tend in one direction or the other, until finally the three come together and the circle is completely closed.

This division into a tripartite literary system in which the parts could work dialectically to form a coherent whole that corresponded to the whole of human comprehension ("subjective, subjective-objective, objective") or the entirety of literary possibility (when "the circle is completely closed") profoundly altered the literary critical function of literary genres and radically changed the understanding of lyric. When lyric shifted from its earlier uses as nostalgic adjective or transcendent idea to become part of a generic system, the hist. of poetic genres was, in turn, revised and rewritten.

In the 19th c., the new understanding of genre as hermeneutic rather than taxonomic generated large claims for the lyric as a vehicle of personal expression, but the theoretical social relations of self and other had not yet eclipsed the actual social relations in which verse was exchanged. The lyric was gradually transformed from an idea attached to various verse genres into an aesthetic ideal that eclipsed or embraced other verse genres, but the process was uneven. When Wordsworth and Coleridge called their 1798 collection of poems *Lyrical Ballads*, they nicely captured both sides of the coin of the "lyrical" currency in their era. "It is the honourable characteristic of Poetry," the Advertisement to the book begins,

> that its materials are to be found in every subject which can interest the human mind. The evidence of this fact is to be sought, not in the writings of Critics, but in those of Poets themselves.
>
> The majority of the following poems are to be considered as experiments. They were written chiefly with a view to ascertain how far the language of conversation in the middle and lower classes of society is adapted to the purposes of poetic pleasure.

These distinctions between poets and critics and between "the language of conversation" and "poetic pleasure" speak to the direction of poetic discourse at the turn of the 19th c. On one hand, poetry is everywhere, but, on the other, it is imperative to distinguish between critical ideas about poetry and the practice of poets. On one hand, the poems this prose introduced "are to be considered experiments," not verse for particular occasions in particular genres; but, on the other, they borrow the lang. of the common people (who did exchange many particular genres on particular occasions) in order to make uncommon forms of "poetic pleasure." The *Lyrical* in the volume's title indicates the attempt to have poetics both ways—both aestheticized and common, both practical and theoretical. By 1798, then, *lyric* was coming to mean both the abstract genre that complemented the dramatic and the epic (i.e., the property of critics) and the essential poetry of the people (i.e., the original and expressive). The attempt in *Lyrical Ballads* to make both ways of understanding *lyric* work together was an index of how difficult it was to think about the lyric in both these ways at once.

As Abrams pointed out, that projection of "the lyric as poetic norm"—as the primary category for all poetry—began much earlier than Wordsworth's and Coleridge's "experiments," in the mid-18th-c. lyricization of the ode and the association of lyric with the primitive origins of civilization. According to Abrams, the 1772 publication of William Jones's *Poems Consisting Chiefly of Translations from the Asiatick Languages, to which Are Added Two Essays I) On the Poetry of the Eastern Nations, and II) Essay on the Arts Called Imitative* "deliberately set out to revise the bases of the neo-classic theory of poetry" and poetic genres. Jones did this, Abrams suggests, by weaving together "ideas drawn from Longinus, the old doctrine of poetic inspiration, recent theories of the emotional and imaginative origin of poetry, and a major emphasis on the lyric form and on the supposedly primitive and spontaneous poetry of Oriental nations." What the "Asiatick" primitive and spontaneous lyric shows, according to Jones, is that Aristotle was wrong: "poetry is not produced by *imitation*, but by a very different principle; which must be sought for in the deepest recesses of the human mind." Thus, well before *Lyrical Ballads* was published, the association of the lyric with an expressive theory of culture complemented its abstraction in the new mod. system of genres. This is why the folk *"ballads" that were actually exchanged by all kinds of people for all kinds of reasons could be rendered "lyrical" when they ceased to be ballads and became "experiments." And this is why the 19th c. was the period in which the lyric became a transcendent genre by remaining an idea that could blur the differences among specific verse genres that were actually very much in use in the same period. This is also why there was not one kind of poem in the romantic period that could be definitively named *the romantic lyric*; instead, there was still a wide range of verse genres in popular circulation that were beginning to be theorized as lyric at the same time that romantic poets were mixing popular genres (ballads and hymns, odes and songs, epistles and elegies) under the sign of the *lyric*.

Thus, rather than consolidating a sense of poetry as *lyric*, the 19th-c. definition of the lyric was deeply confused—though this state of confusion guaranteed a long and productive life for the lyric in both practical use and literary critical hist. In the first decades of the 19th c., Hegel famously elevated the lyric to the summit of his *Aesthetics*, since, in the spirit of his age, he understood the lyric as at once the least material and the most completely expressive art. But Hegel also cast the lyric as the most difficult of mod. genres, since in it the poet must become "the centre which holds the whole lyric work of art together"; and in order to do so, he must achieve a "specific mood" and "must identify *himself* with this particularization of himself as with himself, so that in it he feels and envisages *himself*." The point of such repetitive assertions for Hegel was that what was at stake in the lyric was no less than the achievement of subjectivity: "In this way alone does [the poet] then become a self-bounded subjective entity" (*Totalität*). That attainment of subjective wholeness would represent not only perfect expression but the dialectical accomplishment of historical progress, since, in his expression, the poet moves us all forward toward enlightenment. This idealist version of the lyric had the advantage of bringing together both sides of the contemporaneous ideology of lyric as aesthetic form and lyric as culturally expressive potential. Yet it resolved the potential conflict between those two ways of understanding lyricism by pushing the lyric ideal that much further away from the practice of actual poets, toward a utopian horizon.

The notion that the lyric was an ideal poetic form that no poet had yet achieved actually proved a generative model for poetics in the 19th c. In "Thoughts on Poetry and Its Varieties" (1833), Mill proclaimed that "lyric poetry, as it was the earliest kind, is also . . . more imminently and peculiarly poetry than any other: it is the poetry most natural to a really poetic temperament, and least capable of being successfully imitated by one not so endowed by nature." Here, Mill gathers the 18th-c. attribution of original or primal expression (already evident in Trapp and in Jones's antimimetic argument about "Asiatick" lyric) into the 19th-c. idealization of the lyric as subjective representation. Yet according to Mill, not even Wordsworth and P. B. Shelley, "the two English authors of our own day who have produced the greatest quantity of true and enduring poetry," could actually write lyric poetry that partook of both these qualities at once. While great, Mill laments that "the genius of Wordsworth is essentially unlyrical," and Shelley "is the reverse" in the sense that he had immense lyrical gifts but "had not, at the period of his deplorably early death, reached sufficiently far that intellectual progression of which he was capable." If for Hegel the ideal lyric poet would move civilization forward in his perfect self-expression, for Mill the ideal lyric poet would have to do two things no one had yet perfectly done: be the representative of both original nature and acquired culture. In "The Poet" (1844), R. W. Emerson echoed Mill's and Hegel's impossibly ideal characterizations of the lyric poet, casting that ideal as culturally democratic and Am., and lamenting that "I look in vain for the poet I describe." A young Walt Whitman was in the audience when Emerson gave his lecture in Brooklyn, and several years later claimed to be the poet of "lyric utterances" Emerson and Mill and Hegel and America had been looking for. To call the heroic poet of 19th-c. philosophy and Whitman's bravado *lyric* is to stretch the term very far indeed, but that is what happened to the definition of *lyric* in the second half of the 19th c. In the world of ideas, the lyric became "more imminently and peculiarly poetry than any other" verse genre, indeed, so much so that *lyric* and *poetry* began to be synonymous terms.

While the lyricization of all verse genres meant the creation of a lyric ideal in lit. crit., in the 19th-c. culture of mass print, *lyric* became a synonym for *poetry* in another sense by becoming a default term for short poems, a practical name for verse that did not obey the protocols of neoclassical genres such as the Pindaric ode or conform to the popular standards of ballads or hymns. While both neoclassical and popular genres persisted within the new print lyric, as Rowlinson has remarked, in the 19th c. "lyric appears as a genre newly totalized in print." In the titles of popular poetry volumes, *lyric* became the name for a generic alternative, as in *Lays and Lyrics* by Charles Gray (1841) or *Legends and Lyrics* by Adelaide Proctor (1863). These print uses of *lyric* shifted the sense of *Lyrical Ballads* (1798) or even of Alfred, Lord Tennyson's *Poems, Chiefly Lyrical* (1830) toward a simple noun that readers came to recognize. Both the expansion of *lyric* to describe all poetry in its ideal state and the shrinking of the term to fit print conventions and popular taste irked Poe, a writer always early to sense shifts or conflicts in the hist. of ideas. Before Whitman's "lyric utterances" stretched poetry beyond form, Poe declared in "The Philosophy of Composition" (1846) that "what we term a long poem is, in fact, merely a succession of brief ones," since "a poem is such, only inasmuch as it intensely excites, by elevating, the soul; and all intense excitements are, through a psychal necessity, brief." Poe's emphasis on an affective definition of form reached back to Longinus and echoed Coleridge, but it also proved influential for later 19th-c. theories of lyricism. To define the lyric not as the perfection of subjective representation or as primal cultural expression but as momentary sensation again made the lyric a mobile concept, adaptable to various kinds of poetry.

In practice, while there were all sorts of poems labeled *lyrics* in print and many gestures toward the lyricism associated with musical performance, there were also all sorts of self-conscious departures from "the lyric" in the poetry of the second half of the 19th c.—so much so that there were few poems critics would call purely *lyric*. Tucker has suggested that Robert Browning's dramatic *monologues have become models of what we now think of as lyric, since they represent fictional speakers, but he also suggests that the dramatic monologues "began as a dramatic response to lyric isolationism." Almost as soon as an ideal of personal lyric expression emerged in the 19th c., then, it was honored more often in the exception than as a rule.

By the end of the 19th c., the tendency to work variations on lyric in relation to social complexity moved toward an idea of lyric as a refuge from mod. life. In 1899, writing about the Fr. poets he called *The Symbol-*ist Movement in Literature*, Arthur Symons asserted that "after the world has starved the soul long enough in the contemplation of the rearrangement of material things, comes the turn of the soul" to the lyric (see SYMBOLISM). In the early 1890s, the first eds. of Emily Dickinson's poems produced an unexpected publishing sensation, since the poetry characterized in the first volume as "something produced absolutely without the thought of publication, and solely by expression of the writer's own mind" became a model of lyric expression protected from what one review called "the mass of popular print." After having been idealized in the first half of the 19th c. and reinvented in the second half, the lyric at the end of the century began to be set against a culture increasingly viewed as decadent. That shift did not mean that the idea of the lyric lost its legacy as a vehicle of cultural transmission, but it did mean that the vehicle changed character. E.g., in 1896, when Paul Laurence Dunbar's *Lyrics of Lowly Life* was published in a fancy print ed., lyrics could represent an innocent version of black culture removed from the realities of the turn into the 20th c. If Dickinson became a lyric representative by being isolated from the public in which her lyrics would circulate, Dunbar became another representative by personifying a culture imagined as less mod. than America in the last decade of the 19th c.

In the 20th c., Walter Benjamin famously suggested that, in the previous century, "Baudelaire envisaged readers to whom the reading of lyric poetry would present difficulties" ("On Some Motifs," 1939). According to Benjamin, "it is reasonable to assume that only in rare instances is lyric poetry in rapport with the experience of its readers." Benjamin's sense of the lyric in the 1930s was probably not Baudelaire's in the 1850s, but what is remarkable about Benjamin's characterization of Baudelaire's relation to his century's lyricism is his focus on the distance between modernity and the lyric. Those theories continued to reverse early 19th-c. idealizations of the lyric: rather than positioning the poet as the hero of the future, mod. theories of the lyric tended to further imagine it as a lost ideal, a kind of poetry rendered obsolete by recent hist. One early notable exception to this trend was the Am. theorist of poetics F. B. Gummere, who suggested in *The Beginnings of Poetry* (1901) that mod. lyric poets create "an imagined community" that replaces the loss of a true communal poetry in modernity. In a response to Benjamin's characterization of a mod. community out of sync with the tenor of lyric poetry, Theodor Adorno (in "Lyric Poetry and Society," originally pub. 1957, trans. into Eng. 1974) unwittingly echoed Gummere by proposing that "the universality of the lyric's substance . . . is social in nature" and suggested that since "the lyric work is always the subjective expression of a social antagonism," mod. poetry is in accord with the experience of its readers. Far from being distanced from mod. life, for Adorno the difficulties of mod. poetry could themselves be understood to represent the condition of alienation of mod. life. Gummere's, Benjamin's, and Adorno's definitions of the lyric were all essentially Hegelian, but the ways in which the lyric circulated in the 20th c. were more influenced by the messier hists. of mass print and verse experiment that had intervened since the early 19th c. than by such utopian ideas.

In the first decades of the 20th c., as in the previous century when *lyric* became an umbrella term for many different kinds of poetry, there was not one verse genre one could call *the modern lyric*; rather, there were various verse experiments in what later 20th-c. crit. increasingly cast as the alienation of the mod. lyric subject. Ezra Pound and T. S. Eliot, Robert Frost, W. C. Williams, and Wallace Stevens all wrote short poems we now call *lyric*, though they tended not to use that description of their work. As Eliot wrote in "The Three Voices of Poetry" (1957),

> The term "lyric" itself is unsatisfactory. We think
> first of verse intended to be sung . . . But we
> apply it also to poetry that was never intended
> for a musical setting, or which we dissociate from
> its music . . The very definition of "lyric," in the
> Oxford *Dictionary*, indicates that the word can-
> not be satisfactorily defined: "*Lyric:* Now the name
> for short poems, usually divided into stanzas or
> strophes, and directly expressing the poet's own
> thoughts and sentiments."
>
> How short does a poem have to be, to be called
> a "lyric"? The emphasis on brevity, and the sugges-
> tion of division into stanzas, seem residual from
> the association of the voice with music. But there
> is no necessary relation between brevity and the
> expression of the poet's own thoughts and feelings.

Eliot goes on to define *lyric* in Mill's terms, as "the voice of the poet talking to himself," but his impatience with older definitions signals another shift in the mod. sense of the term, from Mill's impossible ideal of lyricism to the normal condition of each individual's fractured private thoughts. That shift was influential for the mid-century "confessional" poets (see CONFESSIONAL POETRY), who might be thought of as pure lyric poets in Eliot's sense; but, again, by that point in the century, the term *lyric* had become very broad, as it began to be used to describe all first-person poetry.

If, in the first part of the 20th c., the notion of the lyric was still in flux, how did it become such a normative term by the middle of the century? In the hist. we have traced here, the idea of lyric began to do the work of a genre as early as the late 16th c., but it took 400 years before the lyric became synonymous with one poetic genre—or rather, 400 years before poetry was thought of as one lyricized genre. As the idea of genre itself changed in the 18th c., that shift advanced dramatically, but the discourses of poets and critics were not fully aligned in the 19th c., and the lyricization of poetry proceeded by fits and starts. It was only in the consolidation of 20th-c. lit. crit. that the process of lyricization was accomplished, and a broad idea of the lyric became exemplary for the reading of all poetry. That example emerged from and was reflected in the predominance of the *New Criticism, which took up a model of the personal lyric close to Eliot's as the object

of literary *close reading. In different ways, Am. critics such as Cleanth Brooks and Robert Penn Warren in the late 1930s, W. K. Wimsatt and M. C. Beardsley in the 1940s, and Reuben Brower in the 1950s assumed Eliot's definition of the personal lyric and used I. A. Richards's focus on individual poems in his "practical criticism" to forge a model of all poems as essentially lyric. That model was primarily pedagogical, but it became a way of reading that, in turn, influenced the way poems were written, and it remains the normative model for the production and reception of most poetry. Perhaps the most influential contemp. representative of this influential way of reading is Helen Vendler, who strongly advocates a definition of lyric as the personal expression of a fictional speaker, as "the genre that directs its *mimesis* toward the performance of the mind in solitary speech" (1997). Vendler believes that this "solitary" model of the lyric should be used to read all poetic genres at all moments in hist.

That model, while still assumed in much teaching of poetry, has since given way to poststructuralist critiques of lyric reading such as that of Paul de Man (like Vendler, a student of Brower, the New Critic who coined the phrase *close reading*), and to *postmodernism and *avant-garde poetics. When de Man wrote in "Anthropomorphism and Trope" in the late 20th c. that "the lyric is not a genre, but one name among several to designate the defensive motion of the understanding, the possibility of a future hermeneutics," he raised the question of how the lyric had become a matter of *interpretation, a way of reading. The hist. of the lyric is the hist. of the ways an idea has become a genre and the ways in which that genre has been manipulated by poets and critics alike. As in earlier centuries, the late 20th-c. reaction to the elevation of the lyric as a mode of professional reading (what Poovey has called "the lyricization of literary criticism") became a reaction-formation for and against a version of the lyric that could exist only in theory. In the 21st c., that purely theoretical sense of all postromantic personal poems as consistently lyric has prompted a critical and poetic turn away from a version of lit. hist. now retrospectively cast as consistent. In his intro. to the *Ubuweb Anthology of Conceptual Writing* (http://www.ubu.com/concept/), e.g., the poet and critic Craig Dworkin begins,

> Poetry expresses the emotional truth of the self. A
> craft honed by especially sensitive individuals, it
> puts metaphor and image in the service of song.
>
> Or at least that's the story we've inherited from
> Romanticism, handed down for over 200 years in
> a caricatured and mummified ethos—and as if it
> still made sense after two centuries of radical social
> change. . . . But what would a non-expressive po-
> etry look like?

As we have seen, the story of the lyric has hardly been "caricatured and mummified" during its long hist., nor has the hist. of the lyric precluded many "non-expressive" elements in poetry—not even, or perhaps not esp., for the last 200 years. Instead, the story of the lyric charts the hist. of poetics. The lesson of that hist. is that *lyric* has not always named the same thing, but neither has one kind of poem simply changed its name many times over the course of the many centuries the term has been in use. As of this writing, there is still an active debate in lit. crit. over the definition of the lyric. Culler has recently suggested that we try to "prevent a certain narrowing of conception of the lyric and a tendency, understandable given the realities of literary education today, to treat lyric on the model of narrative, so that the dramatic monologue becomes the model of all lyric." Instead, he urges that we retain a transhistorical definition of the lyric because "thinking of lyric as transnational and broadly historical opens up critical possibilities," particularly the possibility of comparative lit. crit. Both Dworkin and Culler tell only partial accounts of lyric as a concept. A sense of either "a caricatured and mummified ethos" or of historical and cultural continuity will not render the intricate turns in the hist. of the lyric or of ideas associated with lyric. When that hist. becomes visible behind or beneath critical and poetic fictions, it testifies to the tremendous malleability of the term, to the ways in which the lyric persists as an idea of poetry fixed at points by lit. hist., often frozen by lit. crit., but as subject to change as the definition of poetry itself.

*See* POEM, POETRY.

■ S. T. Coleridge, *Biographia Literaria* (1817); G. Saintsbury, *Seventeenth-Century Lyrics* (1892); K. Burke, "On Musicality in Verse," *The Philosophy of Literary Form* (1941); Brooks; Abrams, "The Lyric as Poetic Norm"; Frye; C. Guillén, *Literature as System* (1971); M. Foucault, *The Archaeology of Knowledge* [1969], trans. A. M. Sheridan Smith (1972); H. Gardner, *The Metaphysical Poets* (1972); W. Benjamin, *Charles Baudelaire*, trans. H. Zohn (1973); H. Friedrich, *The Structure of Modern Poetry*, trans. J. Neugroschel (1974); A. Welsh, *Roots of Lyric* (1978); S. Cameron, *Lyric Time: Dickinson and the Limits of Genre* (1979); J. Culler, "Apostrophe," *The Pursuit of Signs* (1981); A. Fowler, *Kinds of Literature* (1982); D. A. Campbell, *Greek Lyric, Volume I: Sappho and Alcaeus* (1982); W. R. Johnson, *The Idea of Lyric* (1982); G. Most, "Greek Lyric Poets," *Ancient Writers: Greece and Rome* (1982); P. de Man, *The Rhetoric of Romanticism* (1984); Hollander; *Lyric Poetry: Beyond New Criticism*, ed. C. Hošek and P. Parker (1985)—esp. H. Tucker, "Dramatic Monologue and the Overhearing of Lyric," and J. Culler, "Changes in the Study of the Lyric"; J. Fineman, *Shakespeare's Perjured Eye* (1986); J. Culler, "The Modern Lyric: Generic Continuity and Critical Practice," *Comparative Perspective on Literature*, ed. C. Koelb and S. Noakes (1988); C. Siskin, *The Historicity of Romantic Discourse* (1988); R. Greene, *Post-Petrarchism* (1991)—esp. the intro.; G. Genette, *The Architext*, trans. J. E. Lewin (1992); A. Grossman, "Summa Lyrica," *The Sighted Singer* (1992); P. Zumthor, *Toward a Medieval Poetics*, trans. P. Bennett (1992); C. Siskin, "The Lyric Mix: Romanticism, Genre, and the Fate of Literature," *Wordsworth Circle* 25 (1994); A. Marotti, *Manuscript, Print, and the English Renaissance Lyric* (1995); M. Perloff, *Wittgenstein's*

*Ladder: Poetic Language and the Strangeness of the Ordinary* (1996); H. Vendler, *The Art of Shakespeare's Sonnets* (1997); R. Greene, "The Lyric," *CHLC* v. 3, ed. G. P. Norton (1999); Y. Prins, *Victorian Sappho* (1999); "The System of Genres in Troubadour Lyric," *Medieval Lyric*, ed. W. D. Paden (2000); M. Poovey, "The Model System of Contemporary Literary Criticism," *CritI* 27 (2001); M. Rowlinson, "Lyric," *A Companion to Victorian Poetry*, ed. R. Cronin, A. Chapman, H. A. Harrison (2002); S. Stewart, *Poetry and the Fate of the Senses* (2002); H. Vendler, *Poets Thinking: Pope, Whitman, Dickinson, Yeats* (2004); V. Jackson, *Dickinson's Misery: A Theory of Lyric Reading* (2005); H. Vendler, *Invisible Listeners: Lyric Intimacy in Herbert, Whitman, and Ashbery* (2005); M. Blasing, *Lyric Poetry* (2007); J. Culler, "Why Lyric?" *PMLA* 123 (2008); H. Dubrow, *The Challenges of Orpheus* (2008); R. von Hallberg, *Lyric Powers* (2008); R. Terada, "After the Critique of Lyric," *PMLA* 123 (2008); F. Budelmann, "Introducing Greek Lyric," *Cambridge Companion to Greek Lyric* (2009); M. Lowrie, "Lyric," *Oxford Encyclopedia of Ancient Greece and Rome*, ed. M. Gargarin and E. Fantham (2010); J. Culler, "Genre: Lyric," *Genre: Collected Essays from the English Institute*, ed. R. Warhol (2011).

V. JACKSON

**LYRIC SEQUENCE.** A collocation of lyrics, the lyric sequence is generally thought to have gained its vernacular identity in the Ren. and after from Petrarch (1304–74), who wrote and arranged his sequence called *Rime sparse* (Scattered Rhymes) or, alternatively, *Canzoniere* (Songbook) over 40 years. Both titles ironically point away from the rigorous ordering of Petrarch's 366 amatory and devotional lyrics, which manifests several patterns at once (formal, fictional, calendrical) to establish a continuum—or discontinuum, considering the newfound structural importance of the white space between the lyrics—that greatly exceeds the unities of earlier lyric collections. Petrarch's diverse models included the book of Psalms; the lyric volumes of Catullus, Propertius, and other Augustan poets; Dante's prosimetric *Vita nuova* (ca. 1292–93) and his short sequence *Rime petrose* (ca. 1296); and the 13th-c. chansonniers of the Occitan *troubadours.

For two centuries after Petrarch's death, the possibilities opened by the lyric sequence—to write lyric *in extenso*, allowing each poetic integer to hold its autonomy as it participates in a larger unity—attracted the efforts of poets in all the countries of Europe; Wilkins lists most of these, an astonishing array. The lyric sequence effectively became to *lyric what tragedy was to drama or what the novel would be to narrative—not merely a "form" but a complex of generic capacities. Some particularly interesting lyric sequences are written at the margins or in the hiatuses of the convention: the 24-*sonnet sequence (1555) by the Fr. poet Louise Labé dissents from the sexual politics of *Petrarchism; the Italians Giovanni Salvatorino and Girolamo Malipiero, believing Petrarch's speaker insufficiently Christian, adapt the forms and much of the lang. of the *Rime sparse* to purely devotional experience in their respective works *Thesoro de sacra scrittura* (ca. 1540) and *Il Petrarca spirituale* (1536); and, near the end of the century, after most Eur. cultures had temporarily exhausted the sequence, a generation of Eng. sonneteers between Thomas Watson's *Hekatompathia* (1582) and Michael Drayton's *Idea* (1600) undertook a frenzy of experimentation, refinement, and superstitious imitation of Petrarch (see SONNET). While a number of poets essentially non-Petrarchan in topics and ideology are attracted by the lyric sequence (e.g., George Gascoigne, the first to use the term *sequence* in Eng., in *Alexander Nevile* [1575], and Ben Jonson in *The Forrest* [1616]), nearly every sequence in this period interprets some aspect of Petrarch's rich achievement. Even such monuments of their vernaculars as Pierre de Ronsard's *Sonnets pour Hélène* (1578, enl. 1584), Luís de Camões's *Rimas* (pub. posthumously 1595, though written as early as the 1540s), and Shakespeare's sonnets (ca. 1593–99, pub. 1609) are, in the first analysis, responses to the *Rime sparse* as a compendium of organizational strategies—formal, characterological, devotional, political, speculative.

The principal trend in the 17th-c. lyric sequence develops its religious dimensions. Virtuoso events include Jean de La Ceppède's *Théorèmes* (1613, 1622), George Herbert's *The Temple* (1633), and John Donne's *Holy Sonnets*, incl. "La Corona," a seven-unit crown of sonnets (1633; see CORONA). The first major North Am. lyric sequence, Edward Taylor's *Preparatory Meditations* (written 1682–1725), arrives near the end of this line. The 18th and 19th cs., perhaps because of an attenuation of the formal resources of Petrarchism, perhaps from ineluctable shifts in Eur. poetics and ideologies, produce little of compelling interest in the form of the lyric sequence itself (though much important poetry within the form). The romantics composed numerous lyric sequences, but the unities of these works are generally looser than those of earlier specimens; one notices the tendency, as in Novalis and William Wordsworth, e.g., to announce a lyric sequence to be, in effect, a single poem, thus affirming the idea of its unity but waiving the actual tensions generated between strong integers and an equally strong unifying structure.

The most successful 19th-c. Eur. and Am. lyric sequences tend to be like Alfred, Lord Tennyson's *In Memoriam* (1850) in that they do not imitate Petrarch's outward forms and gestures but find contemp. analogues for his inventions—which perhaps inevitably means discarding the sonnet in favor of other constituents. Noteworthy and influential examples include Charles Baudelaire's *Petites poèmes en prose* (1869) and the hand-sewn fascicles of Emily Dickinson. While in earlier eds., Dickinson's lyrics were often arranged as suited the editor's fancy (i.e., in thematic groupings), work by scholars such as R. W. Franklin, Susan Howe, and Virginia Jackson has shed light on the sequential nature of Dickinson's poems and considered the relationships among poem, fascicle page, bound fascicle, and poetic oeuvre. Walt Whitman's *Leaves of Grass* (1855 et seq.) is the most visionary of 19th-c. lyric sequences; his influence on the lyric sequence is virtually that of a New World Petrarch and has led to an extraordinary abundance of works in the mod. period, esp. in the U.S. and in Latin America. Whitman's legacy is particularly legible in Juan Ramón Jiménez's *Diario de un poeta reciéncasado* (1916), Pablo Neruda's *Veinte poemas de amor y una canción desesperada* (1924), Hart Crane's *The Bridge* (1930), Federico García Lorca's *Poeta en Nueva York* (1930), Wallace Stevens's "Notes toward a Supreme Fiction" (1942), and Frank O'Hara's *Lunch Poems* (1964), among others.

Modernist upheavals included a reinvestment in the *long poem, creating certain challenges in attempting to distinguish between long poem and lyric sequence, but the term *lyric sequence* is most accurately applied to works that maintain a sense of tension between the unity or interrelation of the whole and the independent workings of each part. The term is particularly apt when individual integers in a sequence demonstrate some level of engagement with the lyric, be this understood as subject position, level of musicality, or aim toward brevity. Some, like Conte, have insisted on a further division between the lyric sequence and the postmod. poetic series, claiming for *"serial form" a deliberate absence of the arc, progress, or devel. they deem necessary for a lyric sequence and citing projects like Robert Duncan's *Passages* (1968–87) or Robert Creeley's *Pieces* (1968) as examples. Others, like Rosenthal and Gall, speak of "poetic sequence" rather than lyric sequence and include modernist epics such as Ezra Pound's *Cantos* and W. C. Williams's *Paterson* in this category.

Mod. and contemp. poets have invented a wide range of means of sustaining continuity throughout a sequence. Pablo Neruda's *Veinte poemas* explores *persona through the use of direct address and the creation of a distinct poetic voice, while John Berryman's *77 Dream Songs* (1964) are held together by the character Henry, who both is and is not Berryman himself. O'Hara's *Lunch Poems* benefits from the conceit of the poems' spontaneous composition during his daily lunch breaks and his walks through Manhattan. The unity of Eugenio Montale's *Ossi di Seppia* (1925) derives from Montale's deep engagement with the Ligurian landscape, and that of Francis Ponge's *Le parti pris des choses* (1942) from sustained attention to commonplace objects. In *The Sonnets* (1964), Ted Berrigan breathes new life into the trad. of the sonnet sequence by combining surrealist techniques such as *collage and *aleatory procedures with epistolary address and fragmented narrative. Rosmarie Waldrop's *prose-poem sequence *The Reproduction of Profiles* (1987) derives unity from the syntactic patterning of Waldrop's intertextual engagement with Ludwig Wittgenstein, while the skillful use of repetition, the autobiographical tone, and the formal *constraint of a set number of poems with a set number of sentences make Lyn Hejinian's *My Life* (1980–87) an exemplary postmod. lyric sequence.

*See* ANTHOLOGY, CANZONIERE, RENGA.

■ E. H. Wilkins, "A General Survey of Renaissance Petrarchism," *Studies in the Life and Works of Petrarch* (1955); C. T. Neely, "The Structure of Renaissance Sonnet Sequences," *ELH* 45 (1977)—limited to Eng.; *Arethusa* 13 (1980)—five essays and bibl. on the Augustan volumes; M. L. Rosenthal and S. M. Gall, *The Modern Poetic Sequence* (1983); H. Vendler, *The Odes of John Keats* (1983)—the odes as a lyric sequence; N. Fraistat, *The Poem and the Book* (1985); *Poems in Their Place*, ed. N. Fraistat (1986)—on Eng. romantic collections; J. Freccero, "The Fig Tree and the Laurel," *Literary Theory/Renaissance Texts*, ed. P. Parker and D. Quint (1986); Hollier; T. P. Roche Jr., *Petrarch and the English Sonnet Sequences* (1989)—esp. on the religious elements of the early mod. sequence; J. M. Conte, *Unending Design: The Forms of Postmodern Poetry* (1991); R. Greene, *Post-Petrarchism* (1991); V. Jackson, *Dickinson's Misery: A Theory of Lyric Reading* (2005).

R. Greene; B. Tate

**MACARONIC VERSE.** Usually refers to the mixing of words, sometimes whole lines, of more than one lang. in a poem, most often for comic or satiric effect though sometimes (and more recently) with serious intent. Strictly speaking, a macaronic verse in its original sense entails not inserting foreign words but giving words of the poet's native tongue the inflectional endings of another lang. (Lat.), yielding a comic mock-Lat. When macaronic verse first appeared in earnest in the 12th c., vernacular (Fr.) phrases were interspersed in Lat. verses, but by far the more common practice has been the reverse, salting a poem in a vernacular lang. with Lat. or other foreign phrases (cf. abbreviations in scholarly prose and marginal glosses in med. mss., a practice to which macaronic verse may be related). Med. examples may be found in OF and It., are copious in MHG, and are more copious still in ME, though isolated earlier examples exist, notably the OE "Macaronic Poem." In Italy, the name of Tisi degli Odassi is associated with the earliest macaronics (*Carmen maccaronicum*, 1488), but Teofilo Folengo gave macaronic verse its renown through his famous mock epic *Maccaroneae* (1517–21); Folengo's anonymous Fr. translator in 1606 describes Folengo as the "prototype of Rabelais." According to Folengo, the name *macaronic verse* indicates a crude mixture—like that of flour, cheese, and butter in macaroni—and its burlesque appeal. The classic Fr. macaronic poet was Antoine de la Sablé; in Eng., some of John Skelton's verses are macaronic. But it was Ger. that maintained an affinity the longest for macaronic verse (Ger. *Nudelverse*) past the Middle Ages.

One of the rare examples of true macaronics in postmed. Eng. is the short 17th-c. *mock epic ascribed to William Drummond, *Polemo-Middinia*, in which Lat. terminations are skillfully tacked on to the Lowland Scots vernacular. Because it is multilingual and often plays on carryovers of both sound and sense from one lang. to another, macaronic poetry is most often a learned production, not a species of *nonsense verse; its comic element usually has a satiric edge. Its learned character has other import: in the ME examples, whole lines of Lat. are frequently inserted as quasi-refrains (see REFRAIN), and since the meter of both langs. often matches, macaronic poetry may have been an important vehicle for transporting the accentual rhythms of med. Lat. into Eng. Scholarly interest in the form revived in the early 19th c. (Morgan). In mod. times, both Ezra Pound (*The Cantos*) and T. S. Eliot (*The Waste Land*) have transformed the macaronic into a serious and important technique of poetic composition, allusion, and structure.

*See* XENOGLOSSIA.

■ F. W. Genthe, *Geschichte der maccaronischen Poesie* (1829); O. Delepierre, *Macaronéana ou mélanges de littérature macaronique* (1852); J. A. Morgan, *Macaronic Poetry* (1872); *Die Floia und andere deutsche maccaronische Gedichte*, ed. C. Blaümlein (1900); C. Sullivan, *The Latin Insertions and the Macaronic Verse in "Piers Plowman"* (1932); W. O. Wehrle, *The Macaronic Hymn Tradition in Medieval English Literature* (1933); U. E. Paoli, *Il latino maccheronico* (1959); B. Ristow, "Maccaronische Dichtung in Deutschland," *Reallexikon II*; L. Forster, *The Poet's Tongues: Multilingualism in Literature* (1970); P. S. Diehl, *The Medieval European Religious Lyric* (1985); T. Folengo, *Macaronee minori*, ed. M. Zaggia (1987); E. Archibald, "Tradition and Innovation in the Macaronic Poetry of Dunbar and Skelton," *MLQ* 53 (1992); S. Wenzel, *Macaronic Sermons* (1994); A. Sbraggia, *Carlo Emilio Gadda and the Modern Macaronic* (1996); M. Scalabrini, "The Peasant and the Monster in the Macaronic Works of Teofilo Folengo," *MLN* 123 (2008).

T.V.F. BROGAN; U. K. GOLDSMITH

**MACEDONIAN POETRY.** The hist. of poetry in what is now the Republic of Macedonia includes poetry composed in the Macedonian lang. and poetic trads. of other ling. groups. The focus here will be on poetry in Macedonian, with reference to other trads.

Macedonian poetry emerges from a rich heritage of folk song and folklore; the word *pesna* means both "poem" and "song." But the written trad. remained intermittent before the codification of standard Macedonian in 1945. Years of Turkish domination, followed by regional unrest and the partition of Macedonian territory in 1913, delayed the devel. of Macedonian as a literary lang. Publication in Macedonian was restricted or banned, and the lang. was dismissed as a dialect.

The lyric poem *T'ga za jug* (Longing for the South) by Konstantin Miladinov (1830–62), written in dialect and exploiting folk motifs, is recognized as foundational to mod. Macedonian poetry. Its impact is celebrated by its annual recitation at the opening of the acclaimed international festival, Struga Poetry Evenings.

The next major figure was Kočo Racin (1908–43). Considered the father of mod. Macedonian poetry, Racin expanded his ling. resources by creating a supradialect; his cycle of poems *Beli mugri* (White Dawns), written in this medium, explores the fate of impoverished Macedonians. Other poets who published in Macedonian during this period include Venko Markovski (1915–88) and Kole Nedelkovski (1912–41). Macedonia's archives contain much poetry written in Macedonian during the interwar years by writers who were unable to publish their work.

The immediate postwar period saw three outstanding writers—Blaže Koneski (1921–93), Aco Šopov (1923–83), and Slavko Janevski (1920–2000)—shape the emerging lit. of standard Macedonian. These central figures enriched the formal and generic variety of Macedonian poetry, as they ranged from the socialist realism of Koneski's lyric poetry cycle *Mostot* (The Bridge) to folkloric *ballads, narrative poems, *sonnets, and intimate lyrics.

The so-called second-generation poets, incl. Gane Todorovski (1929–2010) and Mateja Matevski (b. 1929), wrote lyrics rich in metaphor and imagery. This group, together with younger contemporaries like Radovan Pavlovski (b. 1937), Ante Popovski (1931–2003), Vlada Uroševik (b. 1934), and the internationally recognized Bogomil Gjuzel (b. 1939), devised new modes of expression enriched by contact with other poetic trads., notably Eur. *modernism.

The era of *postmodernism brought increased access to international currents. Katica Kulavkova (b. 1951) has written intimate and erotic poems pervaded by allusions to folklore, lit., and hist. Lidija Dimkovska (b. 1971) represents a new urbanism, employing lyric, narrative, and prose poetry to explore themes of science, technology, and cultural displacement. The *haiku and *haibun of Nikola Madzirov (b. 1972) and Vladimir Martinovski (b. 1974) have further expanded Macedonian poetry's formal repertoire.

Macedonia's multicultural, multiethnic society has produced acclaimed writers in Albanian, such as Salajdin Salihu (b. 1970) and Lindita Ahmeti (b. 1973); and Turkish, such as Ilhami Emin (1931), Fahri Ali (1948), and Meral Kain (b. 1976). Poetry in Romani and Aromanian is also published in Macedonia.

As this brief survey shows, Macedonian poets have participated in a wide array of literary movements, incl. *symbolism, modernism, and postmodernism. They have experimented with lang., refashioned conventional forms, and fused their rich religious and folkloric past with a variety of mod. and transnational themes.

■ **Anthologies:** *Reading the Ashes: An Anthology of the Poetry of Modern Macedonia*, ed. M. Holton and G. W. Reid (1977); *Longing for the South/Contemporary Macedonian Poetry*, ed. S. Mahapatra and J. T. Boškovski (1981); *Contemporary Macedonian Poetry*, ed. E. Osers (1991); *The Song beyond Songs: Anthology of Contemporary Macedonian Poetry*, ed. V. Andonovski (1997); *The End of the Century: Macedonian Poetry in the Last Decade of the Twentieth Century*, ed. D. Kocevski (1999); *An Island on Land: Anthology of Contemporary Macedonian Poetry*, ed. I. Čašule and T. Shapcott (1999); *20.mladi.m@k.poeti.00*, ed. L. Dimkovska (2000); *Unidentified Celestial Bosom: Anthology of Young Macedonian Poets*, ed. T. Eternijan-Jovica and Z. Ancevski (2001); *Makedonskata poezija vo svetot*, ed. V. Smilevski (2002); *Tisinata megu dva zbora: ars poetica: tematski izbor od sovremenata makedonska poezija*, ed. K. Nikolovska and D. Ahmeti (2005); *Ut pictura poesis: poezijata vo dijalog so likovnite umetnosti*, ed. V. Martinovski, N. Vinca, and D. Ahmeti (2006); *New European Poets*, ed. W. Miller and K. Prufer (2008).

■ **Criticism and History:** B. Mikasinovich, D. Milivojević, M. Dragan, *Introduction to Yugoslav Literature* (1973); *Dictionary of Literary Biography*, v. 181: *South Slavic Writers since World War II*, ed. V. D. Mihailovich (1984); M. Szporer, "Postmodernist Yugoslav Poetry in Macedonia," *World Literature Today* 62 (1988); M. Drugovac, *Istorija na makedonskata kniževnost XX vek* (1990); *Pregled na ponovata makedonska poezija*, ed. T. Jovčevski (1996); *Orpheus and Jesus: An Overview of Biblical Motifs in Contemporary Macedonian Poetry*, ed. A. Popovski (2000); J. Koteska, *Makedonsko žensko pismo: teorija, istorija i opis* (2002); E. Šeleva, *Otvoreno pismo studii za makedonskata literatura i kultura* (2003); M. Gjurčinov, *Nova makedonska kniževnost: 1945–1980* (2008); G. Stardelov, *Osnovopoložnici na sovrementa makedonska poezija: Kočo Racin, Kole Nedelkovski, Venko Markovski, Slavko Janevski, Blaže Koneski, Aco Šopov, Gogo Ivanovski*, ed. G. Stardelov (2008).

C. KRAMER

**MADRIGAL.** A name given to an It. poetic and musical form in the 14th c. and to a different form in the 16th c. and later. The early madrigal, of which Petrarch's "Nova angeletta" (*Canzoniere* 106) is an example, consisted typically of two or three three-line stanzas with no set rhyme scheme followed by a couplet or *ritornello*. The lines often comprised eleven syllables, sometimes seven. Musical settings used two or three voices, the lower of which may have been performed on an instrument. The same music was repeated for the stanzas, with different music for the ritornello.

In the 16th c., the musical madrigal used various kinds of poetic forms—the *canzone*, the *ballata*, the *sonnet—as well as the madrigal proper, which had become a very free monostrophic verse form of about a dozen seven- and eleven-syllable lines with no fixed order or rhyme scheme, although they usually ended in a *couplet. The musical settings varied considerably but usually consisted of three to six voices in a mixture of polyphonic and homophonic textures. Many 16th-c. musical madrigals, notably those by Luca Marenzio, made a point of illustrating the sense or emotion of the text by means of musical conventions, so each phrase of the text was set to its own music. The subjects tended to be pastoral and amatory. Many of these texts are anonymous, but madrigal verses by Giovanni Battista Guarini, Pietro Bembo, Antonio Alamanni, and Jacopo Sannazaro were set, as well as sonnets from Petrarch and stanzas from the narrative poems of Ludovico Ariosto and Torquato Tasso.

This later style of madrigal influenced the Sp. *villancico and was adopted by composers in Germany, Poland, Denmark, and the Netherlands. Italianate madrigals flourished esp. in England. Although madrigals were imported as early as the 1530s, the Eng. seem not to have begun composing their own until after the publication in 1588 of *Musica Transalpina*, an anthol. of It. music with words in Eng. trans. The It. models made feminine rhyme a consistent feature of these trans. The earliest Eng. poem called a madrigal appears in bk. 3 of Philip Sidney's *Old Arcadia* (written ca. 1577–80), a 15-line poem of mixed six- and ten-syllable lines with masculine rhymes.

Some later Eng. writers such as Barnabe Barnes use the term *madrigal* loosely to designate lyrics in various forms (see *Englands Helicon*, 1600). Eng. madrigal composers set verses in many forms, some of which did resemble the It. madrigal.

By the middle of the 17th c., the musical madrigal was dead in England and, in Italy, had been transformed by Caccini, Monteverdi, and others into *concertato*-style pieces with instrumental continuo that would rapidly evolve into the *baroque aria. But amateur singers in England revived some madrigals as early as the mid-18th c. They have been performed ever since.

■ K. Vossler, *Das deutsche Madrigal* (1898); *The English Madrigalists*, ed. E. H. Fellowes, rev. ed. (1956–76); E. H. Fellowes, *English Madrigal Composers*, 2d ed. (1948); A. Einstein, *The Italian Madrigal*, 3 v. (1949); A. Obertello, *Madrigali Italiani in Inghilterra* (1949); N. Pirrotta et al., "Madrigal," *MGG*; J. Kerman, *The Elizabethan Madrigal* (1962); *English Madrigal Verse*, ed. E. H. Fellowes, F. W. Sternfeld, D. Greer, 3d ed. (1967); B. Pattison, *Music and Poetry of the English Renaissance*, 2d ed. (1970); J. Roche, *The Madrigal* (1972); Wilkins; P. Ledger, *The Oxford Book of English Madrigals* (1978); A. Newcomb, *The Madrigal at Ferrara, 1579–1597*, 2 v. (1980); K. von Fischer et al., "Madrigal," *New Grove*; J. Chater, *Luca Marenzio and the Italian Madrigal*, 2 v. (1981); E. Doughtie, *English Renaissance Song* (1986); J. Haar, *Essays on Italian Poetry and Music in the Renaissance* (1986); W. Maynard, *Elizabethan Lyric Poetry and Its Music* (1986); I. Fenlon and J. Haar, *The Italian Madrigal in the Early Sixteenth Century* (1988); M. Feldman, *City Culture and the Madrigal at Venice* (1995); P. F. Cutter, "The Renaissance Madrigal: An Overview," *Recapturing the Renaissance*, ed. D. S. Wood and P. A. Miller (1995).

E. DOUGHTIE

**MAGYAR POETRY.** *See* HUNGARY, POETRY OF.

**MALAYALAM POETRY.** It is very difficult to date the earliest Malayalam poetry with precision, since there is vast disagreement among scholars on when and how to distinguish Malayalam as a separate ling. entity, different from early Tamil or emerging from a common Proto-South-Dravidian root lang. There seems to have been a variety of coexisting local langs. in the region of today's Kerala, southwestern India, all loosely labeled as *bhāṣa* (Sanskrit, "language"). Early Malayalam has also occasionally been incorrectly subsumed under the category of Tamil (sometimes being called *Kerala Tamil*), the lang. of the larger, culturally dominant neighboring state of Tamil Nadu. The complex mod. Malayalam script developed from *Vaṭṭeḷuttŭ* (round script), a descendant of the *Brahmī* script, but has incorporated *Grantha* script elements to render non-Dravidian, Sanskritic lexicon and morphology. This fusion of Tamil and Sanskritic elements is characteristic of both the ling. and literary devel. of what is today called *Malayalam*. Almost the entire extant corpus of premod. Ma-

layalam lit., i.e., the works composed between the 12th and 18th cs., is poetry, but the categorization of these works according to genres, schools, or literary trads. is still very much contested.

The 14th-c. Sanskrit grammatical treatise *Līlātilakam* distinguishes between various forms of regional langs.: the local *bhāṣa*; then *maṇipravāḷam*, which mixes bhāṣa with either Tamil or Sanskrit lexical and morphological elements, creating a blend of the two; and finally *pāṭṭŭ*, which does not conform to the Sanskritized style of maṇipravāḷam but seems rather influenced by Dravidian style and meter. Many Malayalam scholars have subsequently read maṇipravāḷam and pāṭṭŭ as a dichotomy of genres or schools, i.e., a more Sanskritized, possibly Brahminical fusion form of bhāṣa vs. a more Dravidian, Tamilized, non-Brahminical, and possibly lower-caste folk style (*nāṭan pāṭṭŭ*). However, it is not possible to distinguish clearly the existing works into either one of these categories. From a mod. critical viewpoint, the two categories of maṇipravāḷam and pāṭṭŭ might stand for a genre as much as for a distinct ling. devel., since they are both lexically and metrically different. The generic difference is important insofar as premod. Malayalam texts, esp. pāṭṭŭ, are deeply tied to various *performance trads., as Freeman argues, thus participating in a different kind of literary culture from, e.g., print poetry.

The earliest maṇipravāḷam works known today are *Vaiśikatantram*, *Uṇṇiyaccīcaritam*, *Uṇṇiccirutēvīcaritam* (all ca. 13th c.), and *Uṇṇiyāṭicaritam* (ca. 14th c.). These works are mainly concerned with courtesan culture, prostitution, the beauty of female physicality, and sexuality. The three latter works belong to the literary genre of *campu*, which blends poetry and prose. Another work named *Anantapuravarṇṇanam* (ca. 14th c.) describes the Viṣṇu temple in what is today the state capital of Thiruvananthapuram. *Candrōtsavam* (ca. 15th c.) is a love poem worshipping the moonlight in a female form. *Sandēśa kāvyas* (messenger poems), transmitting a message of love and inspired by the Sanskrit poet Kālidāsa's *Meghadūta*, were also produced during this period; some of the surviving poems are *Śukasandēśa*, *Uṇṇunīlisandēśam*, and *Kōkasandēśam* (all ca. 13th–15th cs.). Prominent examples of pāṭṭŭ are the *Rāmacaritam*, a ca. 12th-c. rendition of the Sanskrit epic *Rāmāyaṇa*, and the *Tiruniḷalmāla* (rediscovered only in 1980), which describes the social life of a temple using Dravidian meter and orthography.

A later phase in the Malayalam pāṭṭŭ trad. (14th–15th cs.) has been strongly shaped by the three so-called *Niraṇam* poets whose work is referred to as *Kaṇṇaśśan pāṭṭukaḷ* (Kanassan poetry). A blend of Sanskrit and Dravidian meters, scripts, and lexicons is characteristic of their work. Ceruśśēri's *Kṛṣṇagātha* (ca. 15th c.) is a well-known example of pāṭṭŭ that has found its way into mod. culture by being sung as a *lullaby. The 16th-c. poet Eḻuttacchan is often referred to as the founding father of mod. Malayalam. His major works include retellings of the great Sanskrit epics *Rāmāyaṇa* and *Mahābhārata* (*Adhyātma Rāmāyaṇam*,

*Śrīmahābhāratam*) in a lang. that combines characteristics of *pāṭṭŭ*, *maṇipravāḷam*, and folk lang. The Malayalam generic term for these stories told by a parrot narrator is *kiḷippāṭṭŭ* (parrot poem). It has found many subsequent imitators.

The interwoven relations between literary and performance art in Kerala are reflected in the devel. of *āṭṭakkatha* (dance story), a type of script for the dance drama *kathakaḷi*. Between the 17th and 18th cs., we find numerous āṭṭakkatha poems, some written by local rulers such as Kōṭṭayam Tamburān (ca. 17th c.), which were enacted in courts and temples. Thematically, they are often renditions of Sanskrit mythological stories (the well-known *Nalacaritam* by Uṇṇāyivāryar, *Kalyāṇasaugandhikam*, and *Gītagōvindam*). Another 18th-c. example of the performance of lit. is the *Kucēlavṛttam* by Rāmapurattŭ Vāryar, a song to be recited on a boat and written in the *Vañcippāṭṭŭ* (boat song) meter. *Tuḷḷalpāṭṭŭ*, most prominently advanced by Kuñcan Nambiyār in the 18th c., is another poetic type of dance performance that still prevails in contemp. Kerala.

During the course of the 19th c., the lang. gradually developed toward what is mod. Malayalam today. The so-called Kēraḷa Varmma and Veṇmaṇi schools of poetry were characterized by their usage of more Malayalam words as opposed to Sanskrit loans. The *pacca malayāḷam* (pure Malayalam) movement attempted to reform the lang. by avoiding Sanskrit words but did not gain wider acceptance. The 19th c. witnessed a large number of trans. from Sanskrit, Eng., and other langs. into what is now "Malayalam." Koṭuññallūr Kuññikkuṭṭan Tamburān's *Mahābhāratam* dates from this period. The early 20th c. saw a new rise of *mahākāvya* (*epic poems), again following Sanskrit models, as well as devotional *Bhakti* poetry with a new take on mythological subjects. The most famous modernists and poetic innovators were Uḷḷūr S. Paramēśvarayyar (1877–1949), Vaḷḷattōḷ Nārāyaṇa Mēnōn (1878–1958), and Kumāran Āśan (1873–1924). Vaḷḷattōḷ and Āśan were also outspoken patriots and critics of social structures and the caste system. Increasing printing and publishing activities contributed to the wider circulation and reception of these literary works at the brink of modernity, while poets began to seek inspiration in indigenous as well as Western literary trads. (e.g., Eng. *romanticism).

The mod. and contemp. periods have been immensely prolific with regard to poetry. G. Śaṅkarakkuṟuppŭ (1901–78), Iṭaśśēri Gōvindan Nāyar (1906–74), Caṅṅampuḷa Kṛṣṇapiḷḷa (1913–47), M. Gōvindan (1919–89), P. Bhāskaran (1924–2007), Ayyappappaṇikkar (1930–2006), O.N.V. Kuṟuppŭ (b. 1931), K. Saccidānandan (b. 1946), Bālacandran Cullikkāṭŭ (b. 1957), and V. M. Girija (b. 1961) are a few of the writers shaping this era. Beginning with Bālāmaṇiyamma (1909–2004) and Laḷitāmbika Antarjanam (1909–87) at the turn of the 20th c., women found their way into an otherwise male-dominated literary sphere. Sugatakumāri (b. 1934) and Kamala Das (alias Mādhavikkuṭṭi or K.

Surayya, 1934–2009) are among the best-known mod. women poets of Kerala. Twentieth-c. poetry took up virtually every aspect of mod. life, ranging from social and political issues to women's emancipation, and 21st-c. writing continues to find an engaged audience in Kerala's vibrant literary scene.

*See* INDIA, POETRY OF; RĀMĀYAṆA POETRY; SANSKRIT POETICS; SANSKRIT POETRY; TAMIL POETRY AND POETICS.

■ **Anthologies and Translations:** *Malayalam Poetry Today*, ed. K. M. Tharakan (1984); "Malayalam," *Medieval Indian Literature*, ed. K. Ayyappa Paniker, v. 3 (1999); *Unnayi Varier's Nalacaritam*, trans. S. Gopalakrishnan (2001).

■ **Criticism and History:** C. A. Menon, *Ezuttaccan and His Age* (1940); K. M. George, *Rāmacaritam and the Study of Early Malayalam* (1956); K. Chaitanya, *A History of Malayalam Literature* (1971); K. Ramachandran Nair, *Early Manipravalam* (1971); N. V. Krishna Warrior, *A History of Malayalam Metre* (1977); M. Līlāvati, *Malayāḷakavitāsāhitya caritram* (1980); E. Paramēśvaran Piḷḷa, *Malayāḷasāhityam kālaghaṭṭaṅṅaḷilūṭe* (1998); R. Freeman, "Genre and Society: The Literary Culture of Premodern Kerala," *Literary Cultures in History*, ed. S. Pollock (2003); *Sampūrṇa Malayāḷasāhityacaritram*, ed. P. Rāmacandran Nāyar (2008).

N. KOMMATTAM

## MALAY POETRY

I. Traditional Malay Poetry
II. Modern Malay Poetry

The earliest records of the Malay lang. date from South Sumatra, ca 680 CE. Over the next thousand years, Malay spread to the Malay peninsula, Singapore, East Sumatra, coastal Borneo, and the South Celebes, as well as to parts of southern Thailand and the Philippines. It was both a court lang. and a commercial lingua franca and continues in Malaysia and Indonesia to be the lang. of the state, education, and mass communications. Traditional Malay poetry was composed in the regions named above. Mod. Malay poetry comes from Malaysia, Singapore, and Brunei. The lang. is now called "Indonesian" in the Republic of Indonesia and has developed its own mod. poetry (see INDONESIAN POETRY).

**I. Traditional Malay Poetry.** This includes both oral and written genres. The best known oral form is the *pantun*, a four-line verse, with four words to a line, each verse rhyming *abab*. Each stanza consists of two couplets: the first two lines present a sound pattern and an image, usually drawn from nature, that foreshadow the sound patterns and the explicit meaning to be found in the second couplet:

Where have you gone to, where were you from?
Weeds grow taller than grain.
What year, what month, will time have spun
Around to when we meet again?

(trans. B. Raffel)

Although each stanza is self-contained, it is also possible to build "chains," in which the second and fourth lines of the first pantun become the first and third lines of the next pantun, and so on (*pantun berkait*). In this extended form, the Malay pantun has influenced Fr. and Eng. verse (*pantoum*).

The best known written form is the *syair*, a term deriving from the Ar. *syi'r*, although the Malay form is purely indigenous and has no actual connection with any Ar. or Persian form. Syair consist of long series of four-line stanzas recited to an audience, each stanza utilizing the same end rhyme. There are both narrative and nonnarrative syair. Nonnarrative syair deal with religious doctrines and practices, ethics, and such miscellaneous topics as the interpretation of dreams, astronomy, riddles, and the praise of particular people and places. The earliest extant syair are the works of the late 16th-c. religious scholar Hamzah Fansuri. Hamzah developed a mystical theology in short, terse verses, filled with Ar. and Persian words; his works were condemned and burned by antagonistic scholars in the court of Acheh. Narrative syair include romantic tales, accounts of historical events, the lives of religious figures, and moral allegories. One of the most popular romantic tales is the *Syair Ken Tambuhan*, a quest story drawn from Javanese mythology. The same motif of a prince's leaving the court and searching throughout the known world for his true love occurs in *Syair Bidasari* and many other texts as well. The syair form reached its greatest popularity in Indonesia in the late 19th c., when even contemp. murder mysteries were written in verse, thus laying the foundations for the emergence of a mod. prose fiction.

Other traditional Malay poetic forms include riddles, *proverbs, spells, the prose lyrics found in narrative tales, and the indefinite structures of the *nazam, seloka*, and *gurindam*.

**II. Modern Malay Poetry.** This is considered to have begun in 1934 with publication of a new style of poetry by Muhammad Yasin Ma'mor, in *Majallah Guru*, a magazine for village elementary-school teachers. Possibly influenced by Indonesian poetry, Yasin wrote personal works of melancholy longing provoked by the beauty of nature. Most of his poems used a four-line verse form; a few were written completely in *free verse. A more decisive break with traditional Malay verse came after World War II, with the rise of the Generation of the Fifties in Singapore. Members of the generation included teachers but also police officers and journalists. They sought a wide Malay audience and wrote in a simple, easy-to-understand style, which was particularly critical of the social breakdown they attributed to the war and the lingering effects of Brit. colonialism. A typical example is "Kami Anak Zaman Ini" (We Are the Children of This Age) by Masuri S. N., which praises past cultural glory, laments present widespread poverty, and looks forward to a time in which "full sovereignty" will be restored. Another is Usman Awang's

"Pak Utih" (Father Utih). The poem falls into two sections: in the first, Usman describes Utih, "the meritorious peasant," and his life of grinding rural poverty and disease; in the second, Utih looks at the emerging nationalist politicians, with their luxury cars and rich banquets, wondering as he "still waits in prayer, Where are the leaders going in their limousines?"

A very different movement that appeared at this same time was labeled the Obscure Poetry movement. The movement emphasized symbolism and sound patterns in a way that was sometimes reminiscent of the first two lines of the pantun. Important poets in this trad. included A. S. Amin, Noor S. I., M. Ghazali, and, occasionally, A. Samad Said, better known as a novelist.

During the 1970s, a number of younger poets reached maturity and continued to dominate Malay poetry throughout the rest of the century. They were less interested in social themes, more concerned with personal emotion, and eager to experiment with new forms. Latiff Mohidin, a painter, wrote heavily imagistic poems, extending the "obscure" trad. Baha Zain used a graphic and harsh contemp. lang. as a way of addressing current social issues.

A. Ghafar Ibrahim moved beyond meaning to pure sound in some of his work: "Tak Tun" captures the rhythm of the village tambourine, "Tak Tun / taktak Tun Taktak Tak Tun Taktak Tak Tun . . ."; "Dundun cakcak" holds the beat of the drum, "dundun / chakchak / dun / chak / dundun / chakchak . . ."; while his poem "Gagak" (Crows) is shaped like an open beak and filled with the repetitious cry "gak, gak, gak . . .".

An ongoing exploration of mystical Islamic themes has marked the work of Kemala (pseud. of Ahmad Kamal Abdullah). His poetry contains references to prayer and the scriptures; to theological ideas of God, creation, the world as a system of signs, the religious community; to historical figures, incl. the Prophet Muhammad, but also his companions, other prophets and major Middle Eastern poets; and to claims of personal religious illumination. His lang. is rich and evocative, often existing for its own sake but as a way of evoking deep resonances in the heart of the Malay reader. The long poem "Ayn" (Signs), e.g., moves effortlessly across descriptions of the early life of Muhammad, his midnight ascent to Jerusalem, the Prophet's wife Aisyah, the 8th-c. Iraqi poet Rābi'ah al-'Adawīyah, the seven sleepers of Ephesus, and various Semitic prophets.

The work of State Literary Laureate Muhammad Haji Salleh is almost the complete opposite of that of Kemala. Muhammad is a major literary scholar. Educated first in Eng. and holding a doctorate in comparative literature from the University of Michigan, he has had to struggle to gain his own Malay identity. His verse is intellectual and absolutely understated. In the poem "Intektuil" (The Intellectual), he describes himself as "the victim of the question," caught between "the pain of emotion / and the thoughts born in his head," and this theme is extensively explored throughout his work.

As in Indonesia, there are fewer women poets writing in Malay than men poets. The two most prominent are Zurinah Hassan and Siti Zainon Ismail. Zurinah's work gently explores the mysteries and uncertainties of human relationships, esp. as these are expressed (or, more often, fail to be expressed) through ordinary speech. Siti Zainon's exploration of human and religious love is more sensuous than Zurinah's work.

Although Malay is the national lang. of Malaysia and the government has provided major publishing opportunities and rewards to encourage a national lit., there are few significant poets writing in Malay from other ethnic communities. The important exception is Lim Swee Tin. Of Chinese-Thai parentage, Lim speaks Hokkien, Mandarin, and Thai but feels that he expresses himself best in Malay. However, he avoids communal references in his work, in favor of a quiet introversion and a gentle nostalgia for a culturally unspecific past.

The support of the government has perhaps ensured the steady devel. of mod. Malay poetry along a path that has maintained quality but provided few radical challenges or different directions for the past 50 years. As Salleh insists in his contemp. rewriting of the cl. hist. *Sejarah Melayu* (*Malay Annals*, composed 1535–1612)—described by Winstedt as "the most famous, distinctive and best of all Malay literary works"—the contemp. author must write "so that from the past may rise greatness, / from our history we may learn the truth" (trans. Muhammad Haji Salleh).

■ **Anthologies and Translations**: *Pantun Melayu*, ed. R. J. Wilkinson and R. O. Winstedt, 2d ed. (1955); *Modern Malay Verse, 1946–61*, ed. O. Rice and A. Majid (1963); *Selections from Contemporary Malaysian Poetry*, ed. M. H. Salleh (1978); *The Poems of Hamzah Fansuri*, ed. G.W.J. Drewes and L. F. Brakel (1986); *Malaysian Poetry 1975–1985*, ed. A. K. Abdullah, trans. H. Aveling (1987); *The Puppeteer's Wayang* (1992), and *Emas Tempawan* (2004), both ed. M. H. Salleh; *Bidasari*, ed. J. Millie (2004).

■ **Criticism and History**: R. O. Winstedt, *A History of Classical Malay Literature*, 2d ed. (1961); B. Raffel, *The Development of Modern Indonesian Poetry* (1967); M. H. Salleh, *Tradition and Change in Contemporary Malay-Indonesian Poetry* (1977); H. M. Piah et al., *Traditional Malay Literature*, trans. H. Aveling, 2d ed. (2002).

H. AVELING

**MAL MARIÉE.** An OF lyric genre, within the larger class of women's songs, in which a woman complains that her father married her to a hateful husband against her will. The poet may say he overheard her lament, or witnessed an argument between her and her husband, or saw her meet her lover, or attempted to console her himself, or heard two women confiding in one another. In a variant type, a nun wishes her lover would deliver her from the convent. The metrical form is variable, incl. motets, *rondeaux, *rotrouenges, baletes, and chansons. Numerous examples are attested among OF lyrics of the 13th c., in the 15th to 16th cs., and among mod. folk songs; the med. genre is also well represented

in It. and, more rarely, in Occitan (where it is termed the *gilozesca*), Galician, Sp., and ME. The heroine finds a counterpart in May, the young wife of January in Chaucer's "Merchant's Tale." For Bec, the origin of the *mal mariée* is to be sought among Fr. popular songs of the Middle Ages that must have coexisted with the early artistic versions.

*See* TROUVÈRE.

■ Bec; D. Evans, "Marie de France, Chrétien de Troyes, and the *mal mariée*," *Chrétien de Troyes and the Troubadours*, ed. P. S. Noble and L. M. Paterson (1984); *Chants d'amour des femmes-troubadours*, ed. P. Bec (1995); *Songs of the Women Trouvères*, ed. E. Doss-Quinby et al. (2001); S. M. Johnson, "The *Malmariée* Theme in Old French Lyric or What is a *Chanson de Malmariée*?" "*Chançon legiere a chanter*," ed. K. Fresco and W. Pfeffer (2007); H. Dell, *Desire by Gender and Genre in Trouvère Song* (2008), ch. 5.

W. D. PADEN

**MANIFESTO.** The manifesto takes, and has always taken, many forms, some deadly serious, some flip to the extreme. From the celebrated "Communist Manifesto" to Valerie Solano's SCUM manifesto with its violent antimale diatribe, the political forms are widespread, a genre unto themselves. What interests us here is the aesthetic manifesto, quite another animal, although, of course, modeled on the political. And, to the extent that such formulas as "the personal is always political" make sense, the idea that the aesthetic has always some component of the political is equally powerful.

At the heights of aesthetic movements, the manifesto is common as an insistence on what is new about the movement one wants to celebrate, what it opposes and casts off, and what it would like to do *now*. It is a necessarily revolutionary genre, in whose atmosphere there reigns the spirit of Pierre Albert-Birot's 1913 movement Nowism, the extreme casting-off rite. The manifesto must be at once declamatory, loud, dramatic, and, above all, attention-seizing, if it is to work. The work is persuasive, the tone is certain, and the conviction, entire: otherwise, forget it.

It declares some sort of "we"-speak, as opposed to an individual "I"-speak, for the manifesto is, in general, a collective statement. (Of course, the opposite is true in such spoofs as Frank O'Hara's "personism," visible and necessarily individual.) What gives it essential intensity is its own presence, intoxicating enough to keep it going. It usually takes its own position seriously, a requirement for any effort at persuading others. And the others are the ones it must persuade, not the selves already "in" the movement.

There was a great moment of manifesto-madness, stretching from 1909 and the "Futurist Manifesto" up through the excitement of *cubism in France, of the Armory Show in New York, suprematism in Russia, *Dada in Switzerland, and then *surrealism, whose impact we are still feeling. (See the most essential of the manifestos in the anthol. *Manifesto*.) But the essential quality of a manifesto remains the forward-lookingness and the quality of standing alone: it is neither prefatory nor a postlude. What it aims at is implicit in its title: at once the sense of manipulation by the hand of the creator(s), the hand or "manus" and the showing forth of the "manifest."

Among all the possible sorts of manifestos are the poem-manifesto, the painting-manifesto, and so on, up to the self-reflective metamanifesto. Some of the more exciting examples are, from the Fr. field and in the political realm, Émile Zola's "J'accuse," the "Manifesto of the 121"at the moment of the Algerian crisis, and Aimé Césaire's "In the Guise of a Manifesto." In the field of architecture, Robert Venturi's "Non-Straightforward Architecture: A Gentle Manifesto" and in the field of art, J.A.M. Whistler's "Ten O'Clock," Lucio Fontana's "White Manifesto," the performance-art piece by Carolee Schneemann called "Meat Joy," and R. B. Kitaj's "Diasporist Manifesto" are invaluable pieces, just as influential as Guy Debord's "Society of the Spectacle." Each movement has its own way of manifesting what it is about, and there abound such documents in the major anthols.

The manifesto moment made its presence felt again, after the Lillehammer Conference of Literary Critics in May of 2008 and the pub. it celebrated: an issue of *Rett Kopi* in Norway with the special "manifesto" issue of 2007, edited by Ellef Prestsaeter and Karin Nygård, full of invaluable documents and essays from the world over, including reflections on Mina Loy's "Feminist Manifesto" by Joan Retallack; on Giacomo Balla's "Futurist Manifesto" by Emily Braun; on Alison Knowles's "Word Power Manifesto" by W.J.T. Mitchell; as well as a large group of selected manifestos, incl. those by Guillaume Apollinaire, Tristan Tzara, Isidore Isou, right up through Donna Haraway's "Cyborg Manifesto." Some articles are in Norwegian, some in Eng., but all bear witness to the excitement of the genre.

■ *Theories of Modern Art*, ed. H. B. Chipp (1968); *L'Esprit Créateur* 23.4 (1983)—special issue on the "manifesto"; *Art in Theory, 1900–1990* (1993), ed. C. Harrison and P. Wood; *Theories and Manifestoes of Contemporary Architecture*, ed. C. Jencks and K. Kropf (1997); J. Lyon, *Manifestoes* (1999); *Manifesto*, ed. M. A. Caws (2001); *Rett Kopi: Documenterer Fremtiden* (2007)—special issue; M. A. Caws, "Poetry Can Be Any Damn Thing It Wants," *Poetry* 190 (2009)—intro. to eight manifestos on the centennial of the "Futurist Manifesto"; G. Yanoshevsky, "Three Decades of Writing on Manifesto: The Making of a Genre," *PoT* 30 (2009).

M. A. Caws

**MANNERISM.** Related to the Lat. *manus* (hand) but arriving in most Western vernaculars through the Lat. *manuarius* (operated by hand, pertaining to the hand), the substantive *mannerist* appears only in the second half of the 17th c. as a predominantly pejorative term to describe the excessive or affected use of style. This negative use of the term emerges against the backdrop of the classicist aesthetics of the 18th c. (see NEOCLASSICAL POETICS), and the first recorded occurrence of the concept in Eng. is in John Dryden's trans. of the Fr. painter Charles Alphonse du Fresnoy's poetic treatise on painting, *De arte graphica* (1668). In this context, the notion of mannerism comes to be regarded as a deviation from the classicist ideal of using artistic practice to perfect the imitation of reality.

The pejorative use of the term remained dominant until the late 19th c., when Heinrich Wölfflin in his influential *Renaissance und Barock* (1888) defined *mannerism* as a period between the Ren. and the *baroque characterized by a crisis of Ren. aesthetic ideals. Following a series of attempts to introduce a neutral or even positive concept of mannerism as a period style in art hist. (Dvořák, Friedlaender), Hauser's *Mannerism* claimed to see in mannerism an authentic artistic expression of the social, economic, and spiritual crisis of the 16th and early 17th cs., thus effectively establishing mannerism as an artistic response to the onset of modernity. In response, Smyth in "Mannerism and Maniera" and Shearman in *Mannerism* challenged Hauser's "anxiety-mannerism" and introduced the notion of mannerism as a "stylish style." Smyth and Shearman contended that, while Hauser's theory of mannerism was essentially a projection of modernist (particularly expressionist and surrealist; see EXPRESSIONISM and SURREALISM) aesthetic ideals into the early mod. period, their conception of mannerism was restricted to a short-lived and self-aware movement in the arts (particularly painting, sculpture, and architecture), characterized by its emphasis on the artist's *maniera* (particular manner or style) and *grazia* (grace).

Literary scholars have often followed the shifting meanings of *mannerism* in art hist. but, at times, also introduced new, specifically literary versions of it. Wylie Sypher's *Four Stages of Renaissance Style* (1955), which offered a reading of *Hamlet* and John Donne's poetry in terms of mannerism, was influenced by the work of Dvořák and Hauser. Mirollo's *Mannerism and Renaissance Poetry* followed the accounts of Smyth and Shearman in isolating a trend in Ren. poetry characterized by the aesthetic ideal of grace and *sprezzatura* (the latter term originally referring to the elegant and nonchalant manner of self-conduct in Baldassare Castiglione's *Book of the Courtier*). Meanwhile, Curtius in *Europäische Literatur und Lateinisches Mittelalter* introduced a radically different notion of literary mannerism. Calling for a complete repudiation of the notion of the baroque and of period styles more generally, Curtius theorized mannerism as a constant tendency in lit. characterized by its taste for ornate lang., particularly for such rhetorical devices as *hyperbaton and *paronomasia. For Curtius, paradigmatic mannerist authors include the Roman poet Claudian and the Sp. poet Luis de Góngora; Baltasar Gracián's *Agudeza y arte de ingenio* (1648) was regarded by Curtius as the single most important early mod. theory of mannerism.

Although in art hist. mannerism is now generally accepted as a period style, in literary studies it remains an unstable concept. It has achieved more success in certain national literary trads. than in others; thus, in It.

lit., mannerism's currency as a concept is due, at least in part, to Quondam's study of mannerism in Neapolitan poetry. For Quondam, mannerism is defined by its tendency to remain within an established trad. (in the Neapolitan case, within *Petrarchism), while simultaneously pushing this trad. and its artistic-literary conventions to their limits. Quondam's study focuses on mannerism as a period style; more recent treatments of mannerism have interpreted it as a particular, constant tendency in lit. Link-Heer (1986, 2001) has offered a detailed hist. of the notion of *maniera* as a longstanding counterpart of and alternative to style. Relying on psychological accounts of mannerism (Binswanger), Agamben also suggested revising the relationship between style and manner by defining the latter as "taking distance . . . from language through an excessive, mannered adhesion to it." These and comparable accounts of mannerism as a concept of style pushed to its limits suggest that the notion may find further application in poetics.

*See* RENAISSANCE POETICS, RENAISSANCE POETRY, STYLE.

■ H. Wölfflin, "Der Verfall," *Die klassische Kunst: Eine Einführung in die Italienische Renaissance* (1899); W. F. Friedlaender, "Die Entstehung des antiklassischen Stiles in der italienischen Malerei um 1520," *Repertorium für Kunstwissenschaft* 26 (1925); M. Praz, *Secentismo e Marinismo in Inghilterra* (1925); M. Dvořák, "Über Greco und den Manierismus," *Kunstgeschichte als Geistgeschichte* (1928); Curtius; A. Hauser, *Sozialgeschichte der Kunst und Literatur* (1953); L. Binswanger, *Drei Formen missglückten Daseins* (1956); G. R. Hocke, *Die Welt als Labyrinth: Manier und Manie in der europäischen Kunst* (1957); C. H. Smyth, "Mannerism and Maniera," *Studies in Western Art: Acts of the Twentieth International Congress of the History of Art*, ed. I. E. Rubin, 4 v. (1963); A. Hauser, *Mannerism: The Crisis of the Renaissance and the Origin of Modern Art*, trans. E. Moshbacher (1965); J. Shearman, *Mannerism* (1967); A. Quondam, *La parola nel labirinto: Società e scrittura del Manierismo a Napoli* (1975); C.-G. Dubois, *Le Maniérisme* (1979); J. V. Mirollo, *Mannerism and Renaissance Poetry* (1984); U. Link-Heer, "Maniera: Überlegungen zur Konkurrenz von Manier und Stil," *Stil, Geschichten und Funktionen eines kulturwissenschaftlichen Diskurselements*, ed. H. U. Gumbrecht and K. L. Pfeiffer (1986); J. M. Steadman, *Redefining Period Style: "Renaissance," "Mannerism," and "Baroque" in Literature* (1990); P. Sohm, "Gendered Style in Italian Art Criticism from Michelangelo to Malvasia," *RQ* 48 (1995); B. Allert, "Maniera," *The Feminist Encyclopedia of German Literature*, ed. F. U. Eigler and S. Kord (1997); L. E. Semler, *The English Mannerist Poets and the Visual Arts* (1998); G. Agamben, "Expropriated Manner," *The End of the Poem*, trans. D. Heller-Roazen (1999); U. Link-Heer, "Manier, manieristisch, Manierismus," *Ästhetische Grundbegriffe (ÄGB): Historisches Wörterbuch in sieben Bänden*, ed. K. Barck et al. (2001).

D. MARNO

**MAN'YŌSHŪ.** The oldest extant anthol. of cl. Japanese poetry (*waka*), it reached its current form in the late 8th (or perhaps early 9th) c. CE. At over 4,500 poems, it is the largest of the major waka collections and also the most varied in terms of poetic form, vocabulary, subject matter, and social position of authors. In 20 books arranged according to diverse principles, it was clearly compiled in stages by multiple editors. About half of the poems are anonymous, and named authors include early legendary and quasi-legendary figures: reliable attributions to historical individuals begin around the middle of the 7th c. The most recent poem was composed in 759, so the anthol. contains a bit more than a century's worth of dateable poetry. The title, literally "collection of ten thousand leaves," is generally taken to refer to the "myriad ages" of the future to which the work is consigned as a literary monument.

The *Man'yōshū* (*MYS*) includes a few dozen cl. Chinese-style compositions (seven-syllable *shi* poetry, prefaces, essays, and letters), but it is indisputably an anthol. of Japanese-style poetry. The primary form is that which dominated subsequent waka history: the *tanka* (short poem) in five lines of 5-7-5-7-7 syllables. But a notable feature is the prominent place of 264 chōka (long poems), of varying length but generally in lines of 5-7-5 . . . 7-5-7-7, and also the inclusion of over sixty sedōka (head-repeating poems) in six lines of 5-7-7-5-7-7—neither of which had the longevity of the shorter tanka form. Sets of poems are sequenced in various ways, perhaps most prominently the combination of chōka with subsequent tanka as *envois* (*hanka*) that amplify or transform aspects of the long poem.

The mid- to late 7th c. was a formative period during which Chinese-style statecraft and also writing and literacy were established for the first time among the elites of the Japanese archipelago. Although scholars search for signs of remnant orality in this stratum of the anthol. and also in "songs" collected in early 8th c. hists., the impression given by most early *MYS* works is of a court poetry already well engaged in synthesizing and digesting its various influences. The following period of the anthol. is dominated by its greatest poet, Kakinomoto no Hitomaro (fl. late 7th–early 8th c.), who wrote grand public poetry on topics such as royal travels, a ruined capital, and elegies for princes, as well as more personal works on parting with wives and enduring the hardships of travel. Later major figures include Ōtomo no Tabito (665–731) and Yamanoue no Okura (660–ca. 733). Tabito pioneered poetry on sinified topics such as the joys of wine and plum blossoms in early spring and, as a court-appointed governor, was central to a provincial literary circle. His friend Okura experimented with themes inspired by Buddhist thought and secular Chinese legends and depicted poverty in terms unparalleled elsewhere in the waka trad. With 473 works Tabito's son Yakamochi (d. 785) is the best-represented *MYS* poet (Hitomaro is next with 91), composing at elegant banquets and in informal exchanges (often by letter) with friends, lovers, and relations. Hundreds of works are attributed to women: roughly a fifth of those by named authors, including the important early poet Princess Nukata and Yakamochi's aunt, Lady Ōtomo of Sakanoue (who follows Hitomaro in frequency, with 84 poems). An even larger proportion of anonymous poems feature female speakers.

Earlier books, arranged by reign and by mode, appear to have been compiled independently, perhaps as an official or quasi-official anthol., by the late 7th c. This core collection was then augmented, often with material drawn from earlier, now-lost anthols. Some of the resulting books focus on particular coteries; others organize hundreds of poems (many anonymous) by topical categories; as with the subsequent waka trad., the dominant concerns are love and the seasons. Later in the editing process, the final five books were added: a long, chronologically organized collection of poetry by Yakamochi and his associates that has been likened to a poetic diary.

The anthol. is a product of capital-centered elites, filled with poetry attributed to sovereigns, other royals, and the courtiers who served them, but it is also marked by interest in socially and spatially peripheral voices. One book contains "poems of the east" (*Azuma-uta*) in nonstandard dialect, while Yakamochi collected compositions by lowly border guards. Many anonymous poems seem rooted in rustic folk song, albeit formally regularized and reworked for metropolitan tastes.

Although there were periods when it was more cited than read, the *MYS* has been an important canonical work since the 9th c. Japanese poets, scholars, and critics have repeatedly turned to it as a fount of cl. verse, for it contains early instances of much that became essential to the trad.; but they have also looked to it for heterogeneous imagery, themes, and language with which to enrich and critique the poetic mainstream.

See JAPAN, POETRY OF; JAPANESE POETICS.

■ *The Man'yōshū: The Nippon Gakujutsu Shinkōkai Translation* (1965); *The Ten Thousand Leaves*, v. 1, trans. I. H. Levy (1981); P. Doe, *A Warbler's Song in the Dusk* (1982); M. Morris, "Waka and Form, Waka and History," *HJAS* 46 (1986); *A Waka Anthology*, v. 1, trans. E. Cranston (1993); J. Robinson, "The Tsukushi Man'yōshū Poets and the Invention of Japanese Poetry," diss., Univ. of Michigan (2004); T. Duthie, "Poetry and Kingship in Ancient Japan," diss., Columbia Univ. (2005); A. Commons, *Hitomaro* (2009); H. M. Horton, *Traversing the Frontier: "Man'yōshū" Account of a Japanese Mission to Silla in 736–737* (2010).

D. B. LURIE

**MAORI POETRY.** *See* NEW ZEALAND, POETRY OF.

**MAPUCHE POETRY.** The historical territory of the Mapuche people coincides with large tracts of southern Chile and Argentina. The Mapuche lang., *Mapuzungun*, cultivated an *oral poetry in pre-Columbian times. During the early colonial period, missionaries of the Catholic Church, who were granted permission to travel through Mapuche territory, made frequent reference to the beauty and significance of the trad. of indigenous poetic song. In some cases, they studied and transcribed it in the original Mapuzungun. Shortly after Mapuche territory was colonized by the Chilean state in the late 19th c., well-known linguists, such as

Rodolfo Lenz and Felix José de Augusta, collected and translated hundreds of Mapuche poems as part of a broader anthropological endeavor to salvage what they presumed to be the last remains of a doomed culture.

In the early 20th c., educated bilingual Mapuche began to write and publish in Sp. Most notable were the works of Manuel Manquilef in the 1910s and of Guillermo Igayman, Teodoberta Neculmán, and Anselmo Quilaqueo in the 1930s. The latter published *Cancionero Araucano* (Araucanian Verses) in 1939. In it, he invoked a glorious past when his people had bravely defended their homeland against the Sp. conquistadors: "Oh Arauco! / Remember how one day you spilt / your beautiful blood upon this beloved land / refusing time and again to give in." It was not only the past he wrote of, however. "You took revenge for the way you were punished, / and for that reason you rise up again [today]." In 1966, Sebastián Queupul published the first self-authored, bilingual collection of Mapuche poetry, *Poemas mapuches en castellano* (Mapuche Poems in Spanish). A small, low-cost production, it nevertheless marked an important milestone in Mapuche literary creation. The most widely cited poem of the book was "Arado de palo" (Wooden Plough), which wistfully recalled life in the rural community before the author moved to the more hostile environment of Santiago: "I want to turn over the earth with my wooden plough / And plant my simple words in the wilderness." And yet it was also a story of the survival of indigenous culture in the capital city.

Mapuche poetry experienced a boom in the context of redemocratization (after 17 years of military dictatorship) and the newly elected Concertación government's decision to embrace the rhet. of multiculturalism. In 1989, Leonel Lienlaf published *Se ha despertado el ave en mi corazón* (The Bird Has Awakened within My Heart), the first book by a Mapuche author to be taken on by a major publishing house in Chile. Lienlaf was also the first Mapuche writer to win a national literary award, the Santiago Municipal Literature Prize of 1990. Elicura Chihuailaf was awarded the same prize in 1997 for a collection of poems titled *De sueños azules y contrasueños* (Of Blue Dreams and Counterdreams, 1995).

Born in rural southern Chile, both Chihuailaf and Lienlaf move between the rural and urban environments. They write in Mapuzungun and Sp. The rural world infuses their verses but, like Queupul, they address the problems of urban life, emphasizing the alienation and solitude felt by Mapuche migrants in Chile's urban centers. In the poem "Leyendas, visiones" (Legends, Visions, 1991), Chihuailaf writes, "in the city I am barely a rivulet / shrunken and in silence dying." Chihuailaf describes his poetry as *oralitura*: his incorporation of multiple voices, in particular, is inspired by the collective, oral trad. of his ancestors. Much of Lienlaf's poetic production is oral (recorded music, documentary film), and he addresses the limitations of the written word in one of his best-known poems "Rebelión" (1989): "My hand / told me the world / would not be written down." But his verses do not so much reject writing (after all, he has achieved a great deal by writing) as highlight the tension between the spoken and written word.

Lienlaf and Chihuailaf are the most renowned of Chile's Mapuche poets: they attend public conferences at home and abroad, and their verses—which are the subject of numerous scholarly studies—have been included in textbooks and museum exhibitions. But they are by no means the only ones to have achieved academic and popular recognition. At least 20 Mapuche writers have carved a place for themselves in national (and often international) literary circles. They are a highly diverse group, both in themselves—male and female, of different generations and territories, bilingual and monolingual, rural and urban based— and with regard to the poetry they produce. However, there are also strong links between them. They all assert their indigenous origins (making it either an explicit or implicit theme of their writings) and support the Mapuche political movement in its struggles against the Chilean state.

Since the late 1990s, the gritty, urban poetry of two Santiago-based writers—César Millahueique and David Aniñir—has attracted increasing attention. In *Profecía en blanco y negro* (Prophecy in Black and White, 1998), the former plays with a mixture of langs. and communication systems to represent the transcultural experience of the urban Mapuche population: "My codes jump from one program to another, from Word Perfect to Lotus, from Lotus to Windows; I feel the re-heated chips and the shadows staking everything to be a reality and a pacman eating the security codes." He also depicts harrowing scenes of a city dominated by the fear and repression of Augusto Pinochet's military regime. One of Aniñir's most paradigmatic poems is "María Juana la mapunky de la Pintana" (Maria Juna the Mapuche punk girl of la Pintana), in which he underscores the social exclusion of so many Mapuche in Santiago: "you are the Mapuche 'girl' of an unregistered brand / of the cold solitary corner addicted to 'that' bad habit / your dark skin is the network of SuperHyperArchi veins / that boil over with a revenge that condemns." It is a tragic story that Aniñir tells but with a strong sense of the potential for resistance.

Another recent devel. is the publication of the two-volume anthol. of Mapuche women writers: *Hilando en la memoria* (Spinning Memory, 2006–9), ed. by the Chilean scholar Soledad Falabella. These bring together 21 poets, incl. Graciela Huinao, María Isabel Millapan, Maribel Curriao, and Roxana Miranda Rupailaf. The poetry deals with recurrent themes such as orality and historic memory, but also points to the intersections between gender and race in 21st-c. Chile.

*See* ARGENTINA, POETRY OF; CHILE, POETRY OF; INDIGENOUS AMERICAS, POETRY OF THE.

■ I. Carrasco Muñoz, "Las voces étnicas en la poesía chilena actual," *Revista chilena de literatura* 47 (1995); *Ül: Four Mapuche Poets*, ed. C. Vicuña, trans. J. Bierhorst (1998); J. Park, "Ethnogenesis or Neo-indigenous Intelligentsia: Contemporary Mapuche-Huilliche Poetry," *Latin American Research Review* 42 (2007); J. Crow, "Mapuche Poetry in Post-Dictatorship Chile: Confronting the Dilemmas of Neoliberal Multiculturalism," *Journal of Latin American Cultural Studies* 17 (2008); M. E. Góngora and D. Picón, "Poesía mapuche: Actualidad y permanencias. Entrevista a Jaime Huenún," *Revista Chilena de la Literatura* 76 (2010): http://www.revistas.uchile.cl/index.php/RCL/article/viewFile/9141/9142.

J. CROW

**MARATHI POETRY.** Dnyaneshwar's (1271–96) decision to compose the *Bhavarthdeepika*, a poetic commentary on the *Bhagavad-Gītā*, in Marathi, the common lang. of Maharashtra, instead of Sanskrit, the lang. of priests and scholars, was a radical gesture that inaugurated a powerful trad. of poetry in Marathi. Although Dnyaneshwar is the first major poet in Marathi, he was not the first; the poetry of the Mahanubhava, an esoteric sect, was preserved in a coded script that was discovered in the 20th c. and probably predated Dnyaneshwar.

Dnyaneshwar belonged to the pan-Indian *Bhakti* movement (see INDIA, POETRY OF), a spiritual movement that allowed the most marginal segments of feudal, casteist, and patriarchal Indian society to articulate their identities. The Bhakti movement fueled the evolution of mod. Indian langs. and cultures. The bulk of poetry composed in Maharashtra from the 13th to the 18th c. is Bhakti poetry and mostly oral-performative in nature. Dnyaneshwar's compositions are integral to the canon of the Varkari movement, the Marathi branch of the Bhakti movement.

Other major poets in the Varkari canon are Namdev (1270–1350), Eknāth (1533–99), and Tukaram (1608–49). These poets employed folk literary forms like *abhanga*, *ovis*, and *bharud*. Even if the poetry of Ramdas (1606–82) does not belong to the Varkari movement, it can still be located in the Bhakti trad. It is notable for its nationalistic and pragmatic vision. Another trad., more elitist and influenced by Sanskrit *kāvya*, is of poets like Waman Pandit (1608–95), Mukteshwar (1574–1645), and Moropant (1729–94) in the 17th and 18th cs. They continued the trad. of *akhyana kāvya* (narrative poetry), which was popularized earlier by Eknāth. The consolidation of the Maratha Empire during this period also made *powadas* (heroic ballads) and *lavanis* (romantic songs) composed by *Shahirs* (troubadours) like Honaji Bala (1754–1844) very popular.

Nineteenth-c. Brit. colonialism brought modernity to Maharashtra, and print capitalism and Western education caused a lasting shift in poetic practice. Once primarily oral and performative, poetry now appeared predominantly in print form and bore the distinct influence of the Western intellectual and poetic trads., incl. *romanticism, social reformism, and nationalism. The major poet of this period is Keshavsut (pseud. of Krishnaji Keshav Damle, 1866–1905). Other prominent poets of the period are Balkavi (pseud. of T. B. Thombre, 1890–1918), and Bahinabai Choudhary (1880–1951), an outstanding poet whose works were unavailable in her time as they were orally composed.

In the 1920s, a group of poets called Ravikiran Mandal, led by Madhav Julian (1894–1939), rose to prominence in Pune city. The group reacted against the social reformist tone and mystical effusions of the poets like Keshavsut and wrote soft and sentimental lyrics. They cultivated poetic forms like the *ghazal and the *sonnet. In the 1930s, Anil (pseud. of Atmaram Ravji Deshpande, 1901–82) introduced *free verse in Marathi. Other notable poets of the period are B. B. Borkar (1910–84) and Kusumagraj (pseud. of V. V. Shirwadkar, 1912–99).

B. S. Mardhekar's (1909–56) *Kahi Kavita* (1947) brought about another shift in Marathi poetry. These avant-garde poems express despair resulting from World War II, growing industrialization, urbanization, and the erosion of traditional values. Mardhekar's attempt to integrate the nonconformist aspects of Bhakti poetics with international modernist aesthetics is a significant characteristic of postcolonial cultural tendencies (see POSTCOLONIAL POETICS). Important contemporaries of Mardhekar, whose *modernism avoided avant-garde excesses, are Purushottam Shivaram Rege (1910–78), Indira Sant (1914–2000), and Vinda Karandikar (1918–2010).

From 1955 to 1975, *avant-garde poetics found its expression in the "little magazine" movement. The little magazines like *Shabda*, *Vacha*, and literary periodicals like *Asmitadarsha* had a distinct antiestablishment outlook, as in the complex, experimental, and challenging poetry by Arun Kolatkar (1932–2004), Dilip Chitre (1938–2009), Vasant Dahake (b. 1942), and Namdeo Dhasal (b. 1949). Their works bear the influence of international modernist and postmodernist poetry. The Dalit poetry, or "the poetry of the oppressed," influenced by the radically reformist philosophy of Babasaheb Ambedkar (1891–1956) and Jyotiba Phule (1827–90), exploded on the scene in the same period. Poets like Dhasal straddled both avant-garde and Dalit poetics. Feminism also began to emerge in this period. Malika Amar Sheikh (b. 1957) writes vigorous poetry that combines feminism with other dissenting political ideologies. In the 1980s, tribal poets like Bhujang Meshram (1958–2007) started writing poetry that combined their quest for tribal identity with protest against the exploitative social system, while poets like Arun Kale (1954–2008) continued the trad. of Dalit poetry.

Poetic idiom was transformed in the 1990s because of the social and cultural crises caused by the processes of globalization, technological revolution, and economic reforms. New little magazines like *Shabadvedh* (1989–2009) and *Abhidhanantar* (1992–2009) played an important role by providing a platform for new voices. New poetry engages with contemp. cultural crises and shows a shift in sensibility and lang. Some of the significant voices to emerge since the 1990s are Sanjeev Khandekar (b. 1958), Mangesh Narayanrao Kale (b. 1966), Saleel Wagh (b. 1967), Hemant Divate (b. 1967), Kavita Mahajan (b. 1967), Manya Joshi (b. 1972), Santosh P. Pawar (b. 1972), and Sachin Ketkar (b. 1972).

■ *An Anthology of Marathi Poetry 1945–1965*, ed. D. Chitre (1968); S. Deo, "Twentieth-Century Marathi Literature," *Handbook of Twentieth-Century Literatures in India*, ed. N. Natarajan (1996); *Live Update: An Anthology of Recent Marathi Poetry*, ed. S. C. Ketkar (2005); D. Chitre, "The Practice of Marathi Poetry: A Survey of Seven Centuries of Interruptions," *New Quest* 175–76 (2009).

S. C. KETKAR

**MARINISM** has three basic meanings: the style of Giambattista Marino (Naples, 1569–1625), Italy's major 17th-c. poet; his numerous It. followers (*poeti marinisti*), such as Claudio Achillini, Antonio Bruni, and Girolamo Preti; and Marino's limited influence on other Eur. writers. *Marinism* is usually used as a synonym for a poetic expression that hides a scarcity of meaning behind an excessive use of rhetorical devices. Marino's poetics is founded on the concept of *meraviglia* (marvel) that, according to Emanuele Tesauro, author of *Il cannocchiale aristotelico* (The Aristotelian Telescope, 1654), is a form of "brief rapture" (*breve rapimento*) which possesses the subject and renders him "speechless" (*senza favella*). To achieve this effect of intellectual suspension, Marinism relies on two fundamental devices: the so-called metaphor of opposition, which works as a bold enthymeme, and an ingenious appropriation of cl. and mod. literary models.

Marino's diverse production in verse and prose testifies to his exceptional erudition. His collection of lyrics *La Lira* (1602, 1614) subverts the logical structure and the rarefied tone of Ren. poetry, defies traditional versification, and explores unusual and even morbid topics. In *La Galeria* (1619), he illustrates real and imaginary paintings and sculptures, whereas in *La sampogna* (1620) he recounts famous myths (e.g., the abduction of Europa, Actaeon's death) from new, unexpected narrative perspectives. The principal manifesto of It. *baroque culture is Marino's treatise *Dicerie sacre* (1614), whose three parts investigate verbal and visual lang. ("On the Shroud of Turin"); music ("On the Seven Words of Christ"); and astronomy ("The Sky"). His poem *L' Adone* (1623), three times longer than Torquato Tasso's *Gerusalemme liberata*, expands the well-known, brief "mythic fable" through narrative detours, encyclopedic *catalogs, descriptions of "marvels," and a complex and highly metaphorical *syntax.

Marino's style exerted such a pervasive influence on It. lit. that it is impossible to draw a clear distinction between his enthusiastic followers and those who, like Gabriello Chiabrera and Tommaso Stigliani, theorize a sober, more cl. form of expression. The influence of Marinism is detectable in Eng. poets such as Richard Crashaw, who trans. the first book of Marino's *La strage degli innocenti*, William Drummond of Hawthornden, and Edward Sherburne. Although it has some similarities with other Eur. baroque movements, such as *préciosité and Gongorism, Marinism is essentially an It. literary phenomenon.

In Marinism, 17th-c. pessimism finds its most effective idiom, as in the poetry of Ciro di Pers, whose verses on the image of the clock are stunning meditations on time, and in the funereal *Scintille poetiche* of the Jesuit Giacomo Lubrano. Catholic spirituality sees in Marinism a poetics accordant with the spirit of Loyolan meditation. See, for instance, Lucrezia Marinella's *canzoniere*, focused on the contemplation of sacred paintings, and Guido Casoni's *La passione di Cristo*, a visual poem divided into a series of symbolic forms, each synthesizing an essential moment of the incarnate Word's passion (e.g., the column, two scourges, the Cross, the hammer, three nails, the sponge, the spear, the stair, two dice).

*See* CONCEPTISMO; ITALY, POETRY OF.

■ B. Croce, *Lirici marinisti* (1910), and *Storia dell'età barocca in Italia* (1925); J. V. Mirollo, *The Poet of the Marvelous* (1963); H. Friedrich, *Epochen der italienischen Lyrik* (1964); M. Guglielminetti, *Tecnica e invenzione nell'opera di Giambittista Marino* (1964); C. Jannaco, *Il Seicento*, 2d ed. (1966); C. Colombo, *Cultura e tradizione nell'Adone di G. B. Marino* (1967); G. Conte, *La metafora barocca* (1972); F. J. Warnke, *Versions of Baroque* (1972); *Manierismo e letteratura*, ed. D. Dalla Valle and G. L. Zardini (1986); *Culture and Authority in the Baroque*, ed. M. Ciavolella and P. Coleman (2003); E. Ardissino, *Il Seicento* (2005); E. Russo, *Marino* (2008).

A. MAGGI

**MASCULINE AND FEMININE.** The terms *masculine* and *feminine* have to do with how prosodic units end: a masculine ending has an accented syllable at the end, while a feminine ending has an unaccented syllable at the end. The distinction is applied to how lines end, as well as to rhymes and *caesuras. The rhyme between *fount* and *mount*, e.g., is said to be masculine, that between *fountain* and *mountain* feminine.

With ordinary feminine rhyme, the accented rhyming syllable is followed by an undifferentiated unaccented syllable, so that the rhyme in both cases is between *fount* and *mount*, with the unaccented *-ain* syllable being the same in both words. In some cases, the additional syllable is some sort of functional suffix, as with *walking/talking* and *truly/duly*.

Confusingly, the feminine rhyme is sometimes called *double*, even though the actual rhyme remains an affair of single accented syllables. An authentic double rhyme, such as that between *childhood* and *wildwood*, must now be called *compound*. That sort of rhyme seems to be feminine also, except that the less-accented syllables are differentiated. Use of *double* for *feminine* does facilitate the extension of terminology to triple (*medicate/dedicate*), quadruple (*medicated/dedicated*), quintuple (*medicatedly/dedicatedly*), and so forth.

Since most Eng. verse is *iambic, most Eng. verse lines, whether rhymed or not, end with an accented syllable. Lines that happen to end with an unaccented syllable are said to have a feminine ending, but the point is hardly worth making unless such endings occur in unusual abundance, as in Hamlet's soliloquy:

> To be or not to be—that is the question:
> Whether 'tis nobler in the mind to suffer
> The slings and arrows of outrageous fortune,
> Or to take arms against a sea of troubles
> And, by opposing, end them. To die, to sleep. . . .

Some have suggested that the feminine ending is less definite, resolute, decisive, or forcible, and some likewise account for the term *feminine* on the basis of an attribution of certain qualities to women; but all that is entirely subjective, impressionistic, and conditional. With Hamlet's meditation, however, the unusual number of successive feminine endings may contribute to a slower pace and more deliberate movement.

Because of the so-called "*e* feminine" in older Fr. and in ME, many lines in Chaucer end with an unaccented syllable, which later became mute:

> As lene was his hors as is a rake,
> And he nas nat right fat, I undertake. . . .

For Chaucer, that rhyme is feminine; for us, masculine.

The commonest sort of feminine rhyme places an unaccented syllable after an accented rhyming syllable, as in *headed / breaded*. In an uncommon sort, the second syllable is undifferentiated but does carry a level of secondary stress, as with *headline / breadline*.

The distinction between masculine and feminine also applies to a midline pause or caesura. The masculine caesura falls after an accented syllable:

> Let Rome in Tiber melt, ‖ and the wide arch
> Of the ranged empire fall. ‖ Here is my space.
> Kingdoms are clay; ‖ our dungy earth alike
> Feeds beast as man; ‖ the nobleness of life
> Is to do thus; ‖ when such a mutual pair
> And such a twain can do't.

> (*Antony and Cleopatra* 1.1.34)

> The barge she sat in, ‖ like a burnished throne,
> Burned on the water: ‖ the poop was beaten
>     gold. . . .

> (*Ant.* 2.2.200)

Although much depends on a subjective response to a variable performance, the former may seem more definite and resolute, the latter indefinite and irresolute, with the possibility of a "dying fall."

Frequently in rhymed verse, a feminine rhyme will appear in an environment of mostly masculine rhymes, which are much commoner in Eng. There are very few poems that employ nothing but multiple rhymes, and all of them are humorous in one way or another. (Some suggest that the feminine rhyme is inherently paradoxical, since rhyme is defined by how a syllable ends; something after the end may seem contradictory.) Thomas Hardy's "A Refusal," on the denial of a memorial place in Westminster Abbey to Lord Byron, has no masculine rhymes. A few, such as "charity"/"clarity," are triple, but most are feminine in a variety of types. Many are ordinary ("dinner"/"sinner"); some involve *mosaic rhyme, in which one word rhymes with two ("stonework"/"own work"). A few are of the compound variety ("name mere"/"fame here").

Many poems place masculine and feminine endings in a recurrent pattern. The commonest pattern alternates feminine and masculine, as in A. E. Housman's "Epitaph on an Army of Mercenaries":

These, in the day when heaven was falling,
The hour when Earth's foundations fled,
Followed their mercenary calling
And took their wages and are dead.

Alternation of masculine and feminine is rarer and may be associated with comic syncopation:

Yankee Doodle went to town
A-riding on a pony
Stuck a feather in his hat
And called it macaroni.

Yankee Doodle keep it up
Yankee Doodle dandy
Mind the music and the step
And with the girls be handy.

G. M. Hopkins's It. *sonnet "The Windhover," with a rhyme scheme of *abbaabba cdcdcd*, uses masculine rhymes in the *a* and *c* positions, feminine in the *b* and *d*. In a small bonus, the accented syllable in the *a* rhyme ("wing," "thing," and so forth) is echoed by the unaccented syllable in the *b* ("riding"/"hiding"). A similar effect may be heard in "Epitaph on an Army of Mercenaries," where the masculine rhymes in the first stanza ("fled"/"dead") are echoed by the feminine rhymes in the second ("suspended"/"defended").

■ G. Saintsbury, *Historical Manual of English Prosody* (1919); P. W. Timberlake, *The Feminine Ending in English Blank Verse* (1931); F. Manning Smith, "Mrs. Browning's Rhymes," *PMLA* 54 (1939); Saintsbury, *Prosody*; P. Fussell, *Poetic Meter and Poetic Form*, rev. ed. (1979); W. Harmon, "Rhyme in English Verse: History, Structures, Functions," *SP* 84 (1987); P. Hobsbaum, *Metre, Rhythm and Verse Form* (1996); W. Harmon, "English Versification: Fifteen Hundred Years of Continuity and Change," *SP* 94 (1997); J. Hollander, *Rhyme's Reason* (2001).

W. HARMON

**MASNAVĪ**, also *mathnavī*. Also referred to as *muthannā* (doubled), *athnayn athnayn* (two by two), masnavī is one of the oldest poetic forms in the Persian-speaking world. Its most prevalent uses historically have been in epic-narrative, epic-romantic, epic-didactic, and homiletic expressions. It is a prosodic form (rhyme scheme) in which each *distich* (*bayt*) consists of two metrically identical rhyming *hemistichs* (miṣrā). Its Ar. counterpart, *muzdawij*, did not enjoy the general utility and thematic parameters of masnavī in Persian lit. Most masnavīs have been versified in two shorter rhyming schemes of *Baḥr-i mutaqārrib-i muthamman* and *baḥr-i khafīf*. Epic-heroic masnavīs, such as *Shāhnāma* (Book of Kings) of Firdawsī (b. 940) and *Garshaspnāma* (The Epic of Garshāsp) of Asadī Gurgānī (d. 1111), are works that aim to inspire patriotism. Sanāʾī's (d. 1130?) masnavī *Ḥadīqat al-Ḥaqīqa* (The Garden of Truth and the Path's Canon) and the voluminous *Khamsa* (Quintet) of Niẓāmī (d. 1209) best represent the mystical epic and epic-didactic, respectively. Often Niẓāmī's romantic

masnavīs examine the failings of aristocracy. Sanāʾī's other masnavī, *Sayr al-ʿibād alā al-Maʿād* (The Journey of the Pious to the Point of Return), was a poetic and generative striving of the soul for perfection that served as a model for Farīd al-Dīn Aṭṭār's (d. ca. 1221) *Manṭiq al-ṭayr* (Conference of the Birds), a series of mystical tales within an allegorical narrative of birds. Jalāl al-Dīn Rūmī's *Masnavī-i Maʿnavī* (The Masnavī of Meanings) is a mystical manifesto that is simply referred to as "the Masnavī," and the poet's inspirations for it have become folklore. Firdawsī, Sanāʾī, ʿAṭṭār, Niẓāmī, and Rūmī are models for all who followed. Amir Khusrau of Delhi (d. 1325) expanded Niẓāmī's genre to include topical materials, and Maktabī (d. 1493) responded to Niẓāmī's legend by his own *Laylī va Majnūn*. Jāmī (d. 1492) adapted themes from his predecessors to present a mystical conception of love in his massive work of lucid Sufi lessons and meanings *Haft Aurang* (Seven Thrones). Saʿdī's (d. 1292) *Būstān* (The Garden) consists of exemplary tales followed by moral glosses. Auḥadī Marāghī (d. 1338) employed an epistolary format in his *Manṭiq al-ʿushshāq* (Lovers' Converse); ʿUbayd-i Zākānī (d. 1371) used masnavī for satirical purposes. Other masnavīs of note are Hilālī Shīrāzī's (d. 1535) rhetorically rich erotic-mystic *Sihr-i Halāl* (Lawful Incantation) and *Shamʿu Parvāna* (The Candle and the Moth). Masnavī was adopted into Turkish, Ottoman, and Urdu lit., where it also acquired considerable popularity.

*See* ARABIC POETRY, PERSIAN POETRY, TURKISH POETRY, URDU POETRY.

■ "Masnawi," *Encyclopaedia of Islam*, ed. M. T. Houtsma et al. (1913–34); *The Mathnawī*, ed. and trans. R. A. Nicholson, 8 v. (1925–40); G. E. von Grunebaum, "On the Origin and Early Development of Arabic *Muzdawij* Poetry," *Journal of Near Eastern Studies* 3 (1944); M. Molé, "L'Epopée iranienne après Firdosi," *La Nouvelle Clio* 5 (1953); G. E. von Grunebaum, *Islam: Essays on the Nature and Growth of a Cultural Tradition* (1955); "Mathnavī," *Lughatnām-i Dihkhudā* (Dihkuda's Lexicon), 52 v. (1958–); J. Rypka, *History of Iranian Literature*, 2d ed. (1968); P. J. Chelkowski, *Mirror of the Invisible World* (1975); W. L. Hanaway Jr., "The Iranian Epics," *Heroic Epic and Saga*, ed. F. J. Oinas (1978); J.T.P. de Bruijn, *Of Piety and Poetry* (1983); F. al-Dīn Aṭṭār, *The Conference of the Birds*, trans. A. Darbandi and D. Davis (1984); E.J.W. Gibb, *A History of Ottoman Poetry*, v. 1, 2d ed. (1984); S. Shamīsā, *Sayrī dar Shiʿr-i Fāsī* (Assessing Persian Poetry), (1984); *Tahavvul-i Shiʿr-i Fārsī* (Generative Morphology of Persian Verse), 4th ed. (1992); M. Rastagār-Fasāʾī, *ʿAnvā -i Shiʿr-i Fārsī* (1994); W. M. Thackston, *A Millennium of Classical Persian Poetry* (1994).

J. S. MEISAMI; A. KORANGY ISFAHANI

**MASQUE.** The masque is an early mod. theatrical genre that flourished in Italy, France, and esp. England. It drew upon various kinds of entertainment that had arisen throughout Europe in the Middle Ages, and in England upon the mummings and disguisings that had become popular amusements on festive occasions, put on in the streets, as well as in halls and courts. The character of such productions took form in Italy when masked and ornately costumed figures presented as mythological or allegorical beings entered a noble hall or royal court, singing and dancing, complimenting their hosts, and, in the course of the entertainment, calling on the spectators to join them in dancing. In bringing the royal and noble personages into the company of supernatural beings, the entertainments often affirmed the relation of royalty to divinity. As a theatrical event, a masque is typically invested in *song, dance, and spectacle at the expense of plot or characters. Its performance in a courtly setting ensures that it will adopt a celebratory position toward the monarch and the aristocracy, but the mythological or allegorical nature of many masques might introduce ambiguities or equivocalities within the dominant tone. Following the transformative work of Stephen Orgel, masques have come to be regarded as complex representations of power and its tributaries. Scholars have studied how masques are connected to the pageant form, whether in the commercial theater or in civic shows; iconography; production techniques; and the relation among the elements of lang., dance, and music.

The ambitiousness of masques was taken to justify enormous expenditures for their productions. In Florence, the architect Filippo Brunelleschi and, in Milan, the younger polymath Leonardo da Vinci were called on to design scenery and to devise machines providing spectacular effects, creating heavenly and sometimes infernal vistas. Henry VIII brought the masque to England early in his reign, and it continued to play a minor but significant role in the theatrical and courtly cultures of his daughter Elizabeth I, until the Stuart kings embraced it vigorously. The It. term used for these entertainments, *maschere* (masks), was taken over by the Eng. as *maske* as early as 1513.

The poet and playwright Ben Jonson is credited with inventing the antimasque, a briefer entertainment ordinarily preceding the main one, and offering effectually the other side of the coin—comic treatment of the unruly forces and elements monarchy subdues, the grotesque persons contrasting with the gorgeous ones of the main masque.

*Circe*, a *ballet de cour* produced in Paris in 1581, helped set the mode for later Eng. masques in providing greater dramatic and thematic unity than had previously been usual. Jonson's conception of the masque as primarily the work of the poet went further in aiming for dramatic unity; in the Preface to *Hymenaei* (1606), he speaks of the theme and words of the masque as its soul, the spectacle and mime and dancing its body. The architect Inigo Jones, however, continued to stress the spectacular and, after ceasing collaboration with Jonson in 1631, was free to give full scope to the most elaborate visual effects. The Stuart kings supported his and others' work generously—James Shirley's *Triumph of Peace* (1634) was as richly produced as anything under Henry VIII. The interest in thematic and dramatic unity, however, continued, and was strengthened by the new custom of concentrating the action on a stage at one end of the hall.

The Elizabethan theater had made some place for maskings; the informal, improvised kind that was apparently very popular is briefly represented in *Romeo and Juliet*. More elaborate forms are present in *Cymbeline*, *The Winter's Tale*, and *The Tempest*. But the conventions that developed for combining music and dancing with allegory and spectacle excluded the tensions of drama; much of the controversy between Jonson and Jones concerned the question of how far the presentation of character and meaning were to challenge the choreography. In the Jacobean period, the establishment of the proscenium arch led to the devel. of a special genre that has been called the "substantive theatre masque." With the Restoration, masques were often assimilated in the new operatic works but were also sometimes offered as a special kind of opera, as one may think 18th-c. instances of John Milton's *Comus* were produced.

*See* DRAMATIC POETRY.

■ E. K. Chambers, *The Medieval Stage* (1903); A. Solerti, *Musica, ballo e drammatica alla corte medicea dal 1600 al 1637* (1905); H. Prunières, *Le Ballet de cour en France avant Benserade et Lully* (1914); *Designs by Inigo Jones for Masques and Plays at Court*, ed. P. Simpson and C. F. Bell (1924); E. Welsford, *The Court Masque* (1927); A. Nicoll, *Stuart Masques and the Renaissance Stage* (1938); J. Arthos, *On a Mask Presented at Ludlow Castle* (1954); *Songs and Dances for the Stuart Masque*, ed. A. Sabol (1959); S. Orgel, *The Jonsonian Masque* (1965); J. G. Demaray, *Milton and the Masque Tradition* (1968); A. Fletcher, *The Transcendental Masque* (1971); *Twentieth-Century Criticism of English Masques, Pageants and Entertainments*, ed. D. M. Bergeron (1972); S. Orgel and R. C. Strong, *Inigo Jones*, 2 v. (1973); R. C. Strong, *Splendor at Court* (1973); S. Orgel, *The Illusion of Power* (1975); D. J. Gordon, *The Renaissance Imagination* (1976); G.W.G. Wickham, *Early English Stages, 1300–1660*, 2d ed. (1980); M. C. McGuire, *Milton's Puritan Masque* (1983); S. P. Sutherland, *Masques in Jacobean Tragedy* (1983); R. C. Strong, *Art and Power* (1984); S. Kogan, *The Hieroglyphic King* (1986); J. Limon, *The Masque of Stuart Culture* (1990); E. T. Jordan, "Inigo Jones and the Architecture of Poetry," *RQ* 44 (1991); M. Franko, *Dance as Text: Ideologies of the Baroque Body* (1993); H. Gatti, "Giordano Bruno and the Stuart Court Masques," *RQ* 48 (1995); *The Politics of the Stuart Court Masque*, ed. D. Bevington (1998); J. M. Smith, "Effaced History: Facing the Colonial Contexts of Ben Jonson's Irish Masque at Court," *ELH* 65 (1998); T. M. Greene, "Labyrinth Dances in the French and English Renaissance," *RQ* 54 (2001); S. Orgel, "The Case for *Comus*," *Representations* 81 (2003); K. Pask, "Caliban's Masque," *ELH* 70 (2003); B. Hoxby, "The Wisdom of Their Feet: Meaningful Dance in Milton and the Stuart Masque," *English Literary Renaissance* 37 (2007); S. Orgel, "Reconstructing the Spectacles of State," *Ben Jonson Journal* 17 (2010); L. Shohet, *Reading Masques* (2010).

J. ARTHOS; F. TEAGUE; R. GREENE

**MATRIX.** In Riffaterre's semiotic system, *matrix* refers to "the structure of the given" in a poem. Unlike the *hypogram, which has a phenomenal reality, the matrix is "an abstract concept never actualized per se: it becomes visible only in its variants, the ungrammaticalities." For Riffaterre, the poem results from the "transformation of the *matrix*, a minimal and literal sentence, into a longer, complex, and non-literal periphrasis." De Man points out that Riffaterre's use of the term *matrix* is (perhaps purposefully) inconsistent.

*See* PERIPHRASIS, SEMIOTICS AND POETRY.

■ M. Riffaterre, *Semiotics of Poetry* (1978); P. de Man, "Hypogram and Inscription," *The Resistance to Theory* (1986).

H. FEINSOD

**MAYAN POETRY.** *See* INDIGENOUS AMERICAS, POETRY OF THE.

**MEASURE.** (1) Because *meter* and *measure* both derive from Gr. *metron*, which itself means measure, since the 15th c. they have been used nearly synonymously, in a general sense, to refer to the system of organization in a poem or the units that comprise that system; thus, in hymnody, *common measure* is also frequently referred to as *common meter* (see BALLAD METER). (2) In musical theories of prosody (see METER, PROSODY) that are based on the analogy of the verse measure to the bar in music, the metrical unit always begins with a stress and is usually referred to as a measure. (3) Historical meanings of measure include "tune," as early as the 14th c., and "dance," as early as the 16th.

(4) However, there is another sense in which the terms *meter* and *measure* are more divergent in reference, the latter associating itself more closely with *rhythm* in a broader and looser sense than the more precise senses that the term *meter* suggests. In a regular meter, there is but one base foot or metrical unit, variations being strictly controlled, but in loose metrical verse or *free verse, the measures may vary considerably in size and shape depending on how they are scanned. Indeed, the crucial point to recognize about all systems of *scansion that employ measures rather than feet is that the successive measures in the line are dissimilar, disparate, and frequently unpredictable, unlike the predictable regularities of foot verse. Prior to the advent of free verse in Eng., the measure was mainly associated with music or musical scansion ([2] above). It is precisely because *measure* connotes regular ordering that free-verse measures must be based on principles radically divergent from traditional prosody if they are to avoid being found simply a contradiction in terms (see VARIABLE FOOT).

(5) In other langs., however—most of the Romance-lang. prosodies, e.g. (see Scott)—the measure has long been a fundamental and constitutive element of metrical analysis. In these systems, the verse measures conform to the natural phrasal groupings of the lang., each phrase having its dominant phrase stress and being demarcated by pauses of differing degree (see FRENCH PROSODY).

(6) In the largest sense, measure is a general trope for poetic order, even poetic epistemology, acknowledged by poets and critics alike: e.g., W. C. Williams held that verse must be measured in order to be verse. Indeed, measure is the key concept in Williams's thought. It is only by the act of measuring, he insisted, that we come to know the world. When we encounter something unknown, our standard of measurement can only be what we already know; hence, the measurements of cognition necessarily entail recognition. The operations of measure in verse reflect this epistemological repetition, in that measure involves the structuring of lang. to come by reference to lang. that has already passed. I. A. Richards attributes this backward-looking aspect of verse to "the influence of past words." When poets measure lang., they allow earlier words to determine the organization of later ones. The more tightly the organization of earlier words controls that of later ones, the more regular the pattern and the more likely it is that the measure is a meter.

In any event, measuring is a fundamental principle of verse structure, and such measure in verse realizes itself in and through the *line; measurement seems to inhere in the very concept and act of lineation. Perhaps a poet's measure is a meter that, through counting syllables or stresses or both, determines structure within the line; perhaps it is something looser that, through reliance on syntactic repetitions, visual patterns, or the intermingling of end-stopped and enjambed lines, develops patterns between or among lines. Either way, no matter how tightly the influence of past words controls its own internal structure, the line itself measures out lang. in ways that are essential and unique to verse.

*See* COLON, COUPE, FOOT.

■ Richards; P. Habermann, "Takt," *Reallexikon I*; H. Nemerov, "On the Measure of Poetry," *CritI* 6 (1979); Scott; S. Cushman, *William Carlos Williams and the Meanings of Measure* (1985); J. Holden, "Poetry and Mathematics," *The Measured Word*, ed. K. Brown (2001); M. Golston, *Rhythm and Race in Modernist Poetry and Science* (2008), esp. chap 5.

T.V.F. BROGAN; S. CUSHMAN

**MEDIEVAL POETICS.** The rich trad. of med. poetics is the product of many intersections in cl. reception, education, philosophy and theology, and debates over the claims of sacred and secular writings. These fields came to shape med. literary culture through the formal procedures of learning: the trivium arts of grammar, rhet., and logic, and scriptural and philosophical commentary. The structural and intellectual interests of med. poetics in Europe grew out of engagement with cl. antiquity and, in turn, provided the grounds for early mod. and mod. poetic practices and conceptions of poetic *knowledge.

Ancient grammarians taught *ars recte loquendi* (the art of speaking correctly) or proper usage; they also taught the uses of lang. in lit. The major Lat. grammatical works of late antiquity that remained standard in the med. West were Donatus's *Ars minor* and *Ars maior* (4th c. CE) and Priscian's *Institutiones grammaticae* (6th c. CE). The Roman grammarians used cl. Lat. poetry and prose to exemplify rules and usage, but they also used poetry to illustrate deviation from rules. The third section of Donatus's *Ars maior*, known in the Middle Ages as the *Barbarismus*, treats faults or mistakes (*vitia*) that occur through ignorance: "barbarisms," which occur in single words, and "solecisms," which occur in combinations of words. But such "faults" can also be deployed deliberately by the great poets, whose mastery of lang. gives them the "license" to deviate from correct usage: in these cases, the barbarism is a metaplasm or transformation (of the form of a word), and the solecism is a "figure" (*schema*), either a figure of speech (an *ornament of lang. such as *anaphora) or a figure of thought (which involves meaning in a larger sense). A further dimension of "faults" that Donatus includes is the *trope, a purely intentional poetic device that involves transference of a word from its "proper signification" to an "improper" one based on perceived likeness between things. The Donatan treatment of figures and tropes, along with other grammatical teaching on metrical forms, was carried into Christian poetics through Bede's *De schematibus et tropis* (ca. 710) which, like other works (now mostly lost) in the trad. of the "Christianized Donatus," substituted scriptural examples for cl. Lat. poetry.

The notion that poetry was a permitted deviation from correctness extended far beyond grammar pedagogy on figures and tropes, becoming a signature definition of poetic fiction. The 4th-c. Christian apologist Lactantius formulated a surprising case for poetry (the pagan mythologists) by claiming that poets do not lie but rather are licensed to refigure truth. It is, he says, the job of poets to transpose events into other representations by means of oblique figures (*Divinarum institutiones* 1.11). Lactantius's formulation was taken up by the 7th-c. Christian encyclopedist Isidore of Seville and from here passed to many later writers, incl. Vincent of Beauvais (13th-c. encyclopedist), Pierre Bersuire (14th-c. commentator on Ovid), and Giovanni Boccaccio, whose *Genealogia deorum gentilium* (1360) gave a resounding defense of poetry against the old Platonic and Christian charges that poetry is mere falsehood. This ancient and med. notion of licensed deviation stands behind Philip Sidney's pronouncement: "the poet . . . nothing affirms, and therefore never lieth" (*Defence of Poesy*, 1595). Donatus's grammatical framing of metaplasm, figure, and trope also permeated 13th-c. scholastic thought about lang. and its ambiguities (of which poetry was seen as a perfect test case). While mod. thought about poetic lang., the figures and tropes, correctly invokes cl. authorities as the ultimate sources of such distinctions and definitions, the very habit of relying on and reformulating the ancient authorities is the direct product of med. learning.

Grammarians were also the authorities on critical matters of emending and authenticating texts and ensuring their correct interpretation. The method associated with this function was the *enarratio poetarum*

(commentary on the poet). In classroom teaching, this method incorporated *imitation of poems and similar exercises. The grammarian's enarratio formed the basis of med. textual *exegesis on both sacred and secular writings. But the practice of enarratio ranged across a continuum from gloss to schoolroom imitation to interpretive recasting, and ultimately—with the rise of vernacular lits.—trans. As the most basic critical and textual methodology, enarratio complemented the interests of cultural conservation in late Lat. antiquity and the early Middle Ages. Augustine compared Christian use of the wealth of pagan learning to the Hebrews taking the gold out of Egypt (*De doctrina christiana* 2 [397–427]), and, in general, early Christian writers recognized the necessity of conserving ancient trads. of knowledge. With the collapse of Rome, the imperative to preserve the old knowledge—for the sake of a Roman notion of "culture," as well as a fully Latinized Christianity—asserted itself in a process that the early Middle Ages conceptualized as *translatio studii* (the transference of learning, in this case from Greece and Rome to Christian Europe): along with many compendia of ancient learning, the cl. Lat. literary texts provided a benchmark of ancient authority. Virgil and later Ovid (whose popularity would burgeon in the 12th c.) were inexhaustible resources of philosophical and moral meaning, their writings the subjects of continuous exegetical reinvention. The *Expositio Virgilianae continentiae* of Fulgentius, a probably Christian mythographer and lexicographer of the late 5th c., essentially rewrites the narrative of the *Aeneid* according to its perceived philosophical content: the narrative order stays in place; but, read philosophically, it is no longer an example of artificial order (beginning *in medias res*), but of natural order, revealing the stages of the philosophical life from birth (Juno's shipwreck in book 1) through enlightenment (the journey to the underworld in book 6) and maturity. The practice of such exegetical refashioning (in Lat. and the vernaculars) is an intensified form of the grammarian's enarratio poetarum, the engine of med. poetics.

Underwriting the power of enarratio was also the rhetorical trad., which gave precepts for composing and which moved beyond the grammarian's focus on lang. and usage to questions of form and style, function, effect, and the architectonics of a work. Cicero's *De inventione* and the pseudo-Ciceronian *Rhetorica ad Herennium* were the standard curricular sources, along with Horace's *Ars poetica*, which served for over a thousand years as a classroom manual of poetic composition; all these preceptive works acquired layers of commentary through the centuries, the *Ad Herennium* only after about 1100. While the legal and political contexts for Ciceronian rhet. evaporated during the later years of the Roman Empire, the value of teaching rhetorical *invention as a habit of thought was never in doubt. Following Cicero's *De inventione* and under the influence of Boethius's exclusive focus on invention in his *De topicis differentiis* (ca. 523), commentators (among them notably the 12th-c. scholars Thierry of Chartres and Petrus Helias) elaborated the theory of invention through topics (*loci*, seats of argument in logic), thereby linking the process of composition with the process of logical or indeed legal argumentation (act, quality of the act, agent, attributes of the agent, means, motive, and so on). At the same time, the Horatian doctrine of imitating canonical models answered the question of where to look for matter to be invented. In the course of the 12th and 13th cs., Horatian and Ciceronian precepts about composition were synthesized with grammatical study of literary texts in the distinctively med. genre of the *ars poetriae*, hybrids of prescriptive rhet. and literary analysis. These texts, esp. Matthew of Vendôme's *Ars versificatoria* (ca. 1175), Geoffrey of Vinsauf's *Poetria nova* (ca. 1210), Gervase of Melkley's *Ars versificaria* (ca. 1215), and John of Garland's *Parisiana poetria* (ca. 1229), brought the full architectural significance of rhetorical thought to bear on poetic and prose composition, in ways more streamlined and practical than in Horace's allusive and subtle *Ars poetica*. Assuming that composition would begin with imitation of cl. and now also med. literary models, the artes poetriae truncated explicit inventional teaching and focused on transformation of source or given idea through the rhetorical systems of arrangement (*dispositio*) and *style (*elocutio*), and esp. in the *Poetria nova*, the stylistic techniques of *amplification and abbreviation. Some later preceptive poetics, notably Dante's *De vulgari eloquentia* (ca. 1304) and Eustache Deschamps' *L'Art de dictier* (1392), resituate the theory within particular vernacular literary cultures.

Roman rhet. also gave a vocabulary for literary analysis of *genre and the figures and tropes. The oldest model of genre, from Aristotle's *Rhetoric* and restated in the Roman rhets., was that of the three "kinds" of rhet., deliberative, forensic, and epideictic: these categories were pressed into analytical service in Cassiodorus's influential 6th-c. commentary on the Psalms. From the *De inventione* (1.19.27) and the *Ad Herennium* (1.8.13), med. writers also derived a threefold classification of narrative: *historia* (a factual account of events), *argumentum* (a realistic fiction, a plausible narrative), and *fabula* (a fantastic story made up of impossible events). The category of fabula was taken up separately in Lat. Neoplatonist thought, where it had a spectacular career, discussed below. The tripartite distinction was repeated not only by encyclopedists (e.g., Isidore of Seville's *Etymologiae* [7th c.], Dominicus Gundissalinus's *De divisione philosophiae* [12th c.], the *Speculum doctrinale* of Vincent of Beauvais [ca. 1260, printed 1624], and literary and poetic theorists, such as Conrad of Hirsau [12th c.], the artes poetriae), but by theologians such as Thomas of Chobham (13th c.), who used it to classify the narrative modes of scripture and thus resolve the status of the parable. Another contribution of rhetorical thought was to 13th-c. scholastic refinements of scriptural genres. Cicero had used the term *modus* (manner) as a category for determining the state of mind in which someone undertakes a criminal action (*De inventione* 1.27.41). In the 12th c., the term *modus* acquired an equivalence with *genus* (a "way" of doing something). In the 13th c., *modus* was extended to the notion of literary "genre" itself: the *Summa Theologica* begun by Alexander of Hales (d. 1245) and completed

by his students distinguished the "genres" of scripture in terms of the states of mind that different kinds of books produce, i.e., the "modes" of precept, example, exhortation, revelation, and prayer. Other 13th-c. commentators went on to distinguish between the narrative, admonitory, exhortative, preceptive, disputative, and epideictic modes of different books of the Bible. This can be seen as a definitive med. contribution to genre theory that looks forward to mod. conceptions of genre as a category not only of *form but of *affect.

Like grammar, rhetorical theory treated figures and tropes. But whereas grammatical thought treated them as permitted deviations from correctness, the compositional manuals of the rhetoricians approached figures and tropes as the necessary completion of the composition, the style (elocutio) that clothes or adorns naked matter that has been appropriately found (inventio) and arranged (dispositio). Thus, for the rhetoricians, style is part of the architecture of the poetic edifice (often spoken of as the decoration of the building that has been erected). Definitions of the tropes reflect not only the teaching in the lang. arts but the influence of logic and theology in the use of conceptual categories such as "transumption" (Geoffrey of Vinsauf and the 14th-c. Prague rhetorician Nicolaus Dybinus) and "similitude" (Gervase of Melkley).

Augustine's *De doctrina christiana* was a transformative influence on *hermeneutics and rhet., both sacred and secular. Its ling. thought is continuous with ancient grammar: it restates grammatical doctrines of lang. as a system of "conventional" signs by which humans make their thoughts known and further emphasizes written over spoken lang. as the object of its analysis. But in its semiotic scope, it far exceeds the grammars of its age, because it lays out a theory of sacred signs as well as human lang., incorporating an approach to the spiritual truths or "things" of scripture as the critical ground for any correct understanding of scriptural discourse. Most important, it redefines the principal part of rhet., invention or discovery (*modus inveniendi*), as a hermeneutical tool, a method of understanding or discovering what scripture means (1.1.1: the "means of discovering" what is to be understood in scripture). Since scripture is seen to have revealed all truth to be discovered, *interpretation is now the highest (indeed, the truest) form of literary activity. Thus, Augustine replaces traditional legal and logical procedures of invention with a program of close reading informed (though not limited) by Pauline notions of letter and spirit (3.5.9).

Aristotle's *Poetics* had its effect through logic and ethics. Long before it was translated into Lat. in 1278 by William of Moerbeke, it had been incorporated into Arab science as a division of logic. Arab scholars classified the parts of logic as represented by each work in Aristotle's logical works (the *Organon*), adding two further forms of logical inquiry represented by the *Rhetoric* and the *Poetics*. These last they understood as extensions of the tools of logic, each with its own particular devices of proof: the enthymeme for rhet. and the "imaginative syllogism" for poetics. This system focused on scientific method and its effects rather than on subject matter. According to the *De scientiis* of Al-Farabi (ca. 870–950), poetry constituted the weakest kind of proof when ranked against the other divisions of logic, but it was still a powerful ethical tool: "it is the property of poetics to cause, by means of its discourse, something beautiful or ugly, which does not exist, to be imagined in such a way that the hearer believes it, and despises it or desires it; for even though we are certain that it is not real, nevertheless our minds are roused to abhor or desire what is pictured forth to us" (*De scientiis secundum versionem Dominici Gundisalvi*, ed. J.H.J. Schneider [2006]). This account was transmitted to the Latin West in the 12th c. in trans. by Gundissalinus and Gerard of Cremona and was influentially restated by Thomas Aquinas in the Preface to his commentary on Aristotle's *Posterior Analytics* (1270): poetry is an "approximation [*estimatio*] through representation" that works through the device of similitude: "it is the poet's function to lead us to virtue through a fitting representation" (*Opera omnia* 1.2, Leonine ed. [1989]). Aquinas's teacher Albertus Magnus had given priority to the ethical dimension of poetry, seeing it as an instrument of moral philosophy, and his student Giles of Rome popularized the ethical argument in his *De regimine principum* (ca. 1277–80), which advised rulers to use poetic exempla as means of teaching and persuading the masses. The 12th-c. Arab philosopher Averröes extended the ethical justification of poetry in his "Middle Commentary" on Aristotle's *Poetics*, trans. into Lat. in 1256 by the Toledan translator Hermannus Alemannus. From Aristotle's suggestion that poetry originated in the genres of *invective and *panegyric (1448b25), Averröes asserted that all poetry is praise (of what is noble) and blame or censure (of what is ignoble), ethical and rhetorical categories that he equated with the genres of *tragedy and *comedy, respectively. But this is probably not the source of ideas of tragedy in works such as Dante's "Letter to Can Grande" (1321) or Chaucer's "Monk's Tale." The notion of tragedy as recitation of misfortunes is more likely to have been derived from Isidore of Seville and his partial synthesis of Lat. sources.

Philosophical commentary on poetic *myth and Christian (as well as Jewish) scriptural commentary were in some respects closely allied. Gr. divinatory exegesis had provided the essential vocabulary of *allegoria* and *symbolon*; Neoplatonist philosophers (Plotinus, Porphyry, Iamblichus, early to late 3d c.) read Plato and Homer to reveal divine and cosmological truths beneath the text. Gr. Christian commentary of the same era (esp. the writings of Origen) borrowed much of the vocabulary and shared the method of theurgic reading, discovering divine unity beneath the textual surface. For the philosopher, the textual surface—however appealing—is mere *fable, *fabula*, a vehicle of the profound and abiding truths that lie beneath. The notion of fabula was classically formulated by Macrobius (early 5th c.) in his commentary on the dream of Scipio (from Cicero's *De republica*). Here fabula is that kind of fiction that conceals a philosophical truth: these are the myths used by Plato, Cicero, and other thinkers

to keep philosophical truths undefiled by the ignorant and foolish. But for Christian exegesis, the surface or letter of the Bible is never untrue, and any apparent inconsistency or implausibility must be reconciled with deeper levels of spiritual meaning so that the true meaning may be understood. From this came the fourfold system of Christian biblical exegesis, an enduring method given its standard formulation by John Cassian in the 4th c. The Macrobian position, however, acquired new prestige in the 12th c. with the circle of Christian Platonists linked with the cathedral school of Chartres. In the vocabulary of William of Conches (ca. 1090–1154) and Bernardus Silvestris (fl. 1136–50), *fabula* is made equivalent to the term *integumentum*. According to the commentary on Martianus Capella attributed to Bernardus, figurative discourse is a "wrapping" (*involucrum*) that can be divided into *"allegory" and "integument": "Allegory is a discourse that envelops within a historical narration a meaning that is true and different from what is said on the surface, as in the story of Jacob wrestling. Integument is a discourse that encloses a true meaning under a fabulous narration, such as the story of Orpheus. . . . Allegory is appropriate to the divine page, integument to philosophy. . . . Let us note that integuments contain equivocations and multiple significations" (*The Commentary on Martianus Capella's "De nuptiis Philologiae et Mercurii" Attributed to Bernardus Silvestris*, ed. H. J. Westra [1986]). In Bernardus's own writings, the notion of the polyvalent "integument" generated inspired interpretation (his Platonizing commentary on the *Aeneid* that far outstrips its Fulgentian source in imaginative power) and cosmographical allegory (his own *Cosmographia*). The philosophical truth claimed for "integumental" writing launched further allegorical inventions, notably the cosmic visionary poetry of Alan of Lille (ca. 1116–1202) and the influential vernacular *dream vision the *Roman de la Rose* (ca. 1230, ca. 1270–80) by Guillaume de Lorris and Jean de Meun, which explicitly lays claim to philosophical authority by calling itself an "integument." The bold claims to theological authority for Dante's *Commedia* made in the "Letter to Can Grande" represent at once the most forceful extension of this secular philosophical trad. and its return to its earliest affiliations with scriptural exegesis.

A key technology of lit. crit. was the *accessus ad auctores* (introductions to the authors). These conventionalized introductions grew out of early grammatical commentary as well as rhetorical teaching of the topics and later out of Aristotelian theories of causation. They gave rise to a flexible discourse about form and meaning, but even more about authorship. In the accessus, the commentator became the voice of authorial *intention, explaining the author's motives in the belated terms of the meaning now imposed on the work. But these interpretive struggles defended the canonical value of questionable works: for instance, Ovid's erotic poems could be treated as ethical lessons because they illustrate the folly of promiscuity. These accessus, applied to any authoritative work to be studied (whether literary, theological, or scientific), also shaped the outlook of vernacular poets (e.g., Guillaume de Lorris, Jean de Meun, Dante, Chaucer, John Gower) who drew from their lang. and form to authorize their own mod. canonical ambitions.

*See* ENGLAND, POETRY OF; FRANCE, POETRY OF; GERMAN POETRY; HEBRAISM; ITALY, POETRY OF; LATIN POETRY; MEDIEVAL POETRY; MEDIEVAL ROMANCE; OCCITAN POETRY; RHETORIC AND POETRY; SPAIN, POETRY OF.

■ **Anthologies**: *Medieval Literary Theory and Criticism, ca. 1100–1375: The Commentary Tradition*, ed. A. J. Minnis and A. B. Scott (1988); *Medieval Grammar and Rhetoric: Language Arts and Literary Theory AD 300–1475*, ed. R. Copeland and I. Sluiter (2009)—both anthols. contain trans. and studies of many of the works cited.

■ **Criticism and History**: B. Smalley, *The Study of the Bible in the Middle Ages* (1941); R. McKeon, "Rhetoric in the Middle Ages," *Speculum* 17 (1942); H. de Lubac, *Exégèse médiéval* (1959–64); F. Quadlbauer, *Die antike Theorie der genera dicendi im lateinischen Mittelalter* (1962); E. Auerbach, *Literary Language and Its Public in Late Latin Antiquity and in the Middle Ages*, trans. R. Manheim (1965); W. Wetherbee, *Platonism and Poetry in the Twelfth Century* (1972); P. Zumthor, *Essai de poétique médiévale* (1972); E. Jeauneau, *Lectio philosophorum: Recherches sur l'école de Chartres* (1973); P. Dronke, *Fabula* (1974); J. J. Murphy, *Rhetoric in the Middle Ages* (1974); G. Dahan, "Notes et textes sur la poétique au moyen âge," *Archives d'Histoire Doctrinale et Littéraire du Moyen Âge* 47 (1980); J. Allen, *Ethical Poetics in the Later Middle Ages* (1983); A. J. Minnis, *Medieval Theory of Authorship* (1984); R. Copeland, *Rhetoric, Hermeneutics, and Translation in the Middle Ages* (1991); H. A. Kelly, *Ideas and Forms of Tragedy from Aristotle to the Middle Ages* (1991); D. Kelly, *The Arts of Poetry and Prose* (1991); *Lo spazio letterario del medioevo 1. Il medioevo latino*, ed. G. Cavallo et al., 5 v. (1992–98); M. Carruthers, "The Poet as Master-Builder," *NLH* 24 (1993); M. Irvine, *The Making of Textual Culture* (1994); C. Baswell, *Virgil in Medieval England* (1995); P. Mehtonen, *Old Concepts and New Poetics* (1996); B. Stock, *Augustine the Reader* (1996); *Lo spazio letterario del medioevo 2. Il medioevo volgare*, ed. P. Boitani et al., 5 v. (1999–2004); A. Butterfield, *Poetry and Music in Medieval France from Jean Renart to Guillaume de Machaut* (2002); *CHLC*, v. 2, ed. A. Minnis and I. Johnson (2005); M. Camargo, "Latin Composition Textbooks and *Ad Herennium* Glossing: The Missing Link?" *The Rhetoric of Cicero in Its Medieval and Early Renaissance Commentary Tradition*, ed. V. Cox and J. O. Ward (2006); N. Zeeman, "The Gender of Song in Chaucer," *SAC* 29 (2007); A. R. Ascoli, *Dante and the Making of a Modern Author* (2007); *The Cambridge Companion to Allegory*, ed. R. Copeland and P. Struck (2010); M. C. Woods, *Classroom Commentaries: Teaching the "Poetria nova" across Medieval and Renaissance Europe* (2010).

■ **Primary Texts**: Alexander of Hales, *Summa theologica*, ed. B. Klumper (1924–48); *Les arts poétiques du XIIe et du XIIIe siècles*, ed. E. Faral (1924); Macrobius, *Commentarii in somnium Scipionis*, ed. J. A. Willis (1994), trans. W. H. Stahl (1952); Conrad of Hirsau, *Dialogus*

*super auctores*, ed. R.B.C. Huygens (1955); Dante, *Epistle to Can Grande*, ed. and trans. P. Toynbee, 2d ed. (1966); Hermannus Alemannus, *Expositio media Averrois sive "Poetria," De arte poetica*, ed. L. Minio-Paluello (1968); Fulgentius, *Expositio Virgilianae continentiae*, ed. and trans. (in Fr.) E. Wolff (2009), trans. (in Eng.) L. G. Whitbread (1971); Alan of Lille, *Anticlaudianus*, ed. R. Bossuat (1955), trans. J. J. Sheridan (1973); Lactantius, *Institutions divines*, ed. and trans. P. Monat et al. (1973–2007); Bernardus Silvestris, *Cosmographia*, ed. P. Dronke (1978), trans. W. Wetherbee (1973); John of Garland, *Parisiana poetria*, ed. and trans. T. Lawler (1974); Bernardus Silvestris, *Commentum super sex libros Eneidos Virgilii*, ed. J. Jones and E. Jones (1977), trans. E. Schreiber and T. Maresca (1979); Alan of Lille, *De planctu Naturae*, ed. N. Häring, *Studi medievali*, 3d ser. 19 (1978), trans. J. J. Sheridan (1980); *Donat et la tradition de l'enseignement grammatical*, ed. L. Holtz (1981); Thomas of Chobham, *Summa de arte praedicandi*, ed. F. Morenzoni (1988); Cassiodorus, *Expositio Psalmorum*, ed. M. Adriaen (1958), trans. P. G. Walsh (1990–91); Dante, *De vulgari eloquentia*, ed. A. Marigo, 3d ed. (1957), trans. M. Shapiro (1990); Bede, *De schematibus et tropis*, ed. and trans. C. Kendall (1991); Eustache Deschamps, *L'Art de dictier*, ed. and trans. D. M. Sinnreich-Levi (1994); Augustine, *De doctrina christiana*, ed. and trans. R.P.H. Green (1995); Isidore of Seville, *Etymologiae*, ed. W. M. Lindsay, 2 v. [1911], trans. S. Barney et al. (2006).

R. COPELAND

## MEDIEVAL POETRY

I. Latin
II. Vernaculars

Although it is sometimes applied more widely (e.g., "medieval Japanese poetry"), the term *medieval* was coined by It. humanists to designate the period of Eur. culture between the end of Greco-Roman antiquity and the self-identified rebirth of the same in "Renaissance" Italy.

Since both the category and the historical period to which it refers are profoundly western Eur., in this article the term *medieval* refers to the period of Roman Catholic hegemony over the former western Roman Empire and its cultural productions. Terminal dates for the period vary, depending on the cultural variables under consideration (for a radical extension, see Le Goff); but in very general terms, we might place them at the definitive fall of the cl. Roman imperial system in the West (mid-5th c. CE) and the rise of It. humanism (15th c.).

Concerning the conception of *poetry*, med. verse is literary in the sense that it has been preserved in writing (for *oral poetry, see below). For its makers, performers, and audiences, poetry was an "art" in the Lat. sense of skill or craft—e.g., formal manipulation and topical recombination. It was understood in a hierarchy of arts, subsumed under grammar and rhet., and with grammar, rhet. and the rest of the seven liberal arts, set—officially, at least—in the service of (Catholic) theology.

Before the 13th c., the terms *poetry*, *poet*, and *poem* were most often reserved for writers of cl. antiquity. Before about 1050 CE, the words *poet* and *maker* were hardly ever used for a contemp. writer or versifier, even one who composed learnedly in Lat. meter; God was the sole Creator. It was applied to cl. poets somewhat pejoratively (e.g., Heloise [d. 1164] calls Ovid "poet of lust and doctor of disgrace"), though Virgil became the *Poeta* par excellence, as Aristotle eventually became *Philosophus. Auctor* was similarly affected. Versifiers were apt to designate their works as *rhythmi, versus,* or *carmina,* but not *poemata.*

Negotiations between and among the cultural hegemony of Lat. and Roman Catholicism, the emerging vernaculars, the literary langs. of the other Abrahamic religions, the authority of writing and the practices of oral composition and dissemination will characterize what we now call *medieval European poetry.* This article discusses principal trends and concepts; for med. poetry in particular langs., trads., and genres, please see the relevant entries.

**I. Latin**. Lat. is the lang. of official culture during this period; in med. usage, *letters* and *literate* almost always refer to the Lat. texts and the ability to decipher and produce them. Thus, clerical Lat. was by definition the lang. of reading and writing. From the Alps to Iceland, Lat. Christianity imposed an alphabet, writing materials, schools and libraries, and an idiom primarily developed for religious expression by a clerical class. It fused elements of Semitic and Hellenic diction, syntax, and figure with the Roman imperial lang.; it absorbed elements of the indigenous oral poetries of the empire's Celtic, Germanic, and Scandinavian peoples; it was affected, too, by the Arab world and lightly by Byzantium.

In the course of ten centuries, Western social systems changed radically, both collectively and regionally. Consequently, there were marked diversities, as literacy spread from the clerical elites to the noble and middle classes and then as the vernaculars became institutionalized in writing.

Esp. in the century following the Nicene Council (325 CE), brilliant, rhetorically trained Romans devoted themselves to developing and disseminating Christian doctrine and liturgy. They supplied the lang. of med. poetry, primarily in prose: Ambrose's *hymns and addresses, Jerome's trans. of scripture (the basis of the Vulgate Bible), and Augustine's doctrinal works expressed insensible realities in sensible terms. At the same time, Christian Roman versifiers cast Heb.-Christian poetry in traditional Lat. genres. This patristic writing, the staple of early med. schools and libraries, was popularized in sermons, liturgy, and paraliturgy as a unified body of doctrine, trad., legend, and myth that was, or might be, poetic.

**A. *Prosody and Verse Form.*** Med. Latin prosody evolved from quantitative meters (technically called "metrical verse" in the Middle Ages; see METER, QUANTITY)

to *accentual verse ("rhythmical verse," "rhythms") and *rhyme. The great influx of nonnative speakers, at first from the east and later from the north, affected Lat. meters as early as the 2d c. CE; by the end of the 4th c., when Augustine testified that his students could no longer distinguish between long and short syllables, the transition from quantity to *accent had been completed. Though learned poets continued to compose quantitative meters throughout the Middle Ages, popular poets developed patterns derived in part from Lat. art prose, which had taken on "Asian" flourishes, incl. such homophony as *alliteration, *homoeoteleuton, and rhyme.

Isosyllabism (as in Augustine's *Psalm against the Donatists*), which restricted the greater variation inherent in the quantitative system, aided memory and helped preserve the text. Emphasis on linear units of thought (as in Ambrose's hymns), partly because of choral antiphony, stimulated the growth of patterned terminal rhythms, which acquired stress in the Germanic regions. By the end of the 7th c., homoeoteleuton and *assonance were common, and as Lat. increasingly became a scholastically acquired second lang., these figures of sound increased: by the 12th c., complex di- and trisyllabic rhymes are often found.

**B. *Modes and Genres.*** At the early centers of literacy, the basic modes of Lat. verse were hymnody, hagiography, and secular verse.

Hymnody was the heart of *lyric poetry, and scriptural *psalms and canticles its muscle. Hymns, defined as songs of praise, were written and used from the patristic period, most notably by Ambrose. Later, sequences developed in the Mass from the extension of Hebraic jubilations like the *Alleluia.* Hymns were admitted into general use in the Roman Office in the 12th c.; the philosopher Peter Abelard (d. 1142) was a prolific hymn-poet of astonishing metrical inventiveness. The mendicant orders, esp. the Franciscans of the 13th c., composed some of the most moving religious lyrics ("Stabat mater," "Dies irae") of the period.

Hagiography, which had arisen in the late cl. period, combines in various proportions biblical narrative, epideictic eloquence, and Gr. romance in tales for meditation, instruction, and pious entertainment (see DIDACTIC POETRY). Because in cloisters it was employed for reading in nocturnal office and in refectory as well as for private meditation, demand and supply were high. The Eastern trad. of monasticism introduced Byzantine narrative forms and devices. These narrative structures later informed secular narrative in the vernacular: *medieval romance is often markedly hagiographical.

Secular verse was proudly antiquarian at first, a means by which members of the clerical elite displayed their learning, sophistication, and political connections. The scholars, as the only literates, composed *occasional verse—epistles, *eclogues, *epigrams, *panegyrics, and the like—usually in quantitative meters. They provided the often imaginative verse chronicles and the *specula* or "mirrors" for leaders of church and state; these ranged from manners and advice to witty trifles for amusement. Even textbooks were sometimes cast into meter, partially as models. Roman poets (esp. Virgil and Ovid) formed the core of the school curriculum (*accessus ad auctores*), and *imitation was a principal pedagogical method. Thus, from the 11th c. onward, we have skilled imitations of Roman drama, *epic, and the erotic poetry of Ovid. Such exercises in imitation shaped the style and imagination of clerically trained writers when they turned their hands to writing in the vernaculars.

Collections of med. Lat. lyric survive in mss. from the 11th c., often as part of larger codices containing ecclesiastical works in prose. The so-called Cambridge Songs (11th c.) and the 20 love poems from the Ripoll monastery in the Pyrenees (12th c.), e.g., appear in mss. also containing the core curriculum of monastic Lat. education; the *Carmina Burana* (ca. 1230), however, constitute a freestanding volume. These collections are thematically, metrically, and even linguistically varied. Their topics range from devotions and moralizations through acerbic *satire to songs in praise of drink and carnal love; poems may be *macaronic or even fully bilingual, as in the case of some of the *Carmina Burana* and Cambridge Songs. The *parodies, drinking and love songs, and scurrilities are often called *Goliardic verse; the learned literate poets who composed them introduced an ecclesiastical art to a wider public. Esp. as they located posts in civic life as chaplains or chancellors, they were prime agents in adapting the forms, imagery, idiom, and melody of Lat. verse to secular concerns and the emergent vernaculars.

## II. Vernaculars

**A. *First Surviving Poems.*** Poems and songs were composed, recited, and sung in the vernacular langs. long before they were recorded in writing.

But written texts are what we have to go by. The earliest vernacular documents are Eng. and are contemporaneous with Bede's description (*Historia ecclesiastica* 4.22) of Cædmon, the earliest identifiable Germanic poet (fl. ca. 670). According to Bede, Cædmon dreamed a hymn to the Maker of Heaven and Earth; thereafter, monastic doctors taught him scripture, which he converted to verse for their transcription.

Early Germanic verse was adapted transcription (*Widsith, Beowulf*), transference (*Genesis*), or imitation (*Phoenix*) of great poetic power. The earliest verses in the Romance vernacular (ca. 880) are a paraliturgical exaltation of an early virgin martyr, *Eulalie*, of unevenly decasyllabic assonant lines in a lang. that looks more Fr. than Lat. The same ms. contains both a Lat. *Eulalia* with lines borrowed from the Christian Lat. poet Prudentius (ca. 348–405), and the *Ludwigslied*, an OHG poem in rhyming *couplets in praise of Louis III (d. 882). Thus, the vernaculars of Western Francia are incorporated into ecclesiastical and political power structures.

Surviving mss. give evidence of a rich and varied vernacular poetic culture. As the idea of vernacular literacy takes root and becomes institutionalized, functional, practical literacy in the vernaculars spreads to the noble,

merchant, and political classes, and with it, the audience for written forms of vernacular verse. There is religious vernacular verse (devotional lyrics, hagiography, didactic verse). There is secular med. verse (panegyric, satire, parody, narrative, epic, comic, romance, and erotic lyric). There are compositions as brief as an eight-line song in a 15th-c. Castilian *songbook and as long as the 21,750 lines of the Fr. *Roman de la Rose* (ca. 1230, ca. 1270–80), and verse as uncomplicated as the octosyllabic rhyming couplet and as challenging as the *sestina.

**B. *The Troubadours.*** But within all this variety, the med. vernacular poetry best known and most profoundly influential in the West is that invented in the late 11th c. by the *troubadours (Occitan *trobadors*, "finders," "inventors") in what is now southern France. Composing in the vernacular *langue d'oc* or Occitan, the troubadours made lyric poetry of extraordinary technical sophistication that emphasized forms, enigmas, ambiguities, acuity, and surprise. New stanzaic structures for each song, within the further restrictions of rhyme and rhythm, became requisite. Though troubadour poems engaged political satire (*sirventes*), debate (*tenso, joc partit, *partimen*), and literary games (*trobar clus*), most influential in later centuries has been the love song (*canso*) and the decidedly nonclassical ideology of erotic love that the troubadours called *fin'amors* ("refined love" or *courtly love).

The earliest troubadour whose works have survived in writing is Duke William IX of Aquitaine (1071–1126); the 12th c. witnessed an outpouring of troubadour lyric, spreading into neighboring regions. As war and Crusade destabilized Occitan life in the 13th c., the emigrating poets stimulated others elsewhere. In some regions (e.g., Catalonia, Aragon, and Italy), Occitan became the authoritative lang. of vernacular lyric, regardless of the poet's native lang. Soon the troubadour ethos and the forms and conceptual vocabulary of Occitan lyric were translated into Port., Eng., It., Castilian, Fr. (the *trouvères), and Ger. (the Minnesingers; see MINNESANG). The It. lyric began at the court of Frederick II in the so-called *Sicilian school but soon burst out in the north, eventuating in the *Dolce stil nuovo* of Guido Guinizzelli and then Dante and his contemporaries— a spiritualizing and, in some ways, Platonizing of an earthbound trad. Dante's production in both Lat. and It. has the explicit aim of canonizing vernacular verse— transforming it into poetry equal in authority and prestige to that of cl. Rome. In the *Divina commedia*, Dante represents himself as apprenticing under and then superseding the ghost of Lat. epic, Virgil; Dante's *Vita nuova* (in It.) and the *De vulgari eloquentia* (in Lat.) argue for the respectability of vernacular letters (esp. in Occitan and It.).

Dante's two great Tuscan successors, Petrarch and Giovanni Boccaccio, returned his exalted vision to earth, catching in their quite different ways Dante's high conception of the poet's office. Petrarch, a multidimensional scholar but a priest of poetry, revived antiquity in receiving the laurel; his Lat. epic *Africa* was archaeology, but his *Canzoniere*, replete with feeling and perception, imposed a stamp, not always felicitous, on early mod. verse (see LYRIC SEQUENCE, PETRARCHISM). Boccaccio composed as his own epitaph *studium fuit alma poesis* (my study was nourishing poetry). *Poeta* was no longer an opprobrious word.

**C. Cross-fertilizations.** Though for the purposes of clarity we have divided med. poetry into categories including Lat. and vernacular, sacred and secular, narrative and lyric, oral and written, these categories were porous in the Middle Ages.

Marks of both oral and written composition have been observed (and debated) in the early vernacular epics, e.g., *Beowulf* (OE, preserved in a 10th-c. ms.), the *Chanson de Roland* (*Song of Roland*; Fr., 12th-c. Anglo-Norman ms.) and the *Poema del Cid* (Castilian, ms., ca. 1140). Though later written epics may adopt characteristics of oral composition (e.g., use of *formulas) as a generic marker and means of authorization, in the earliest surviving texts it is difficult to disentangle oral modes from oralizing and written modes of thought and production. References to oral trad. and to oral performance are common in vernacular narrative poetry as well, and oral folk motifs have long been identified in written vernacular lyric.

Prose and verse were far less separate literarily than they were in cl. practice. Med. writers might treat the same matter twice, once in prose for meditation and once in verse for recitation and/or memorization. Sometimes, in the model of Martianus Capella's *Marriage of Philology and Mercury* and Boethius's *Consolation of Philosophy*, they would alternate prose and verse, in the form called *prosimetrum*. A similar practice may be seen in later secular works in the vernacular—e.g., in the *chante-fable Aucassin et Nicolette* (Fr., 13th c.).

Contrast and color, more than formal unity, were desired. Thus, in the later Middle Ages, we have extensive works in verse that make a show of including multiple and contrasting metrical forms. E.g., the 14th-c. Castilian *Libro de buen amor* is mainly written in 14-syllable monorhymed quatrains characteristic of didactic and narrative verse but also includes devotional and erotic lyrics in multiple meters and, in one ms., a prose prologue in the form of a parodic sermon.

As this last example shows, sacred and secular were not mutually exclusive categories in med. poetry. The hymns mentioned above as early manifestations of med. verse spread to the marketplaces and were quickly adapted to profane use. Abelard, whose hymn production has already been mentioned, also wrote secular love poetry (whether in Lat. or the vernacular, we do not know) and, he says, took great pleasure in its popularity. Great med. Lat. poetry collections such as the Cambridge Songs and the *Carmina Burana* contain religious as well as secular and erotic verse; and vernacular (in these cases, Ger.), Lat., and plurilingual poems.

There is good evidence that "courtly love," traditionally the most Western of inventions, was constructed in part along the model of Hispano-Ar. poetry (Menocal; see AL-ANDALUS, POETRY OF).

The most striking example of the porous boundaries between langs., registers, and modes in med. Eur. poetry is a genre of secular poetry invented in Islamic Iberia, probably in the late 9th or early 10th c.: the *muwashshah*. The muwashshah is composed in cl. Ar. or Heb. on themes of panegyric, love, or wine; at its conclusion (the *kharja* or jarcha, "exit"), however, it turns from cl. to vernacular—vulgar Ar., Hispano-Ar., or Romance—and is often presented as the transcribed words of someone other than the poem's speaker, such as a woman, a member of the lower classes, or an animal.

Since the "Romance" kharjas were discovered by Samuel Stern in 1948, their interpretation has occasioned passionate debate among scholars. What is clear without a doubt is that the beginnings of Eur. lyric are profoundly hybrid, characterized by a mixture of elite and popular culture, oral and written transmission, Semitic and Romance, cl. and vernacular.

*See* CARMINA FIGURATA, CHANSON DE GESTE, FABLIAU, GAI SABER, JONGLEUR, JUDEO-SPANISH POETRY, LAI, LATIN POETRY, LITURGICAL POETRY, LOVE POETRY, MEDIEVAL POETICS, NOVAS (RIMADAS), OCCITAN POETRY, ORAL-FORMULAIC THEORY, TROBAIRITZ.

■ S. Stern, "Les vers finaux en espagnol dans les muwaššaḥs hispano-hébraïques," *Al-Andalus* 13 (1948); Curtius; E. Auerbach, *Literary Language and Its Public in Late Latin Antiquity and in the Middle Ages*, trans. R. Manheim (1965); Dronke; *Medieval Song*, ed. and trans. J. J. Wilhelm (1971)—anthol.; R. Wright, *Late Latin and Early Romance in Spain and Carolingian France* (1982); W. D. Paden Jr., "Europe from Latin to Vernacular in Epic, Lyric, Romance," *Performance of Literature in Historical Perspectives*, ed. D. W. Thompson (1983); B. Stock, *The Implications of Literacy* (1986); M. R. Menocal, *The Arabic Role in Medieval Literary History* (1987); J. Le Goff, "For an Extended Middle Ages," *The Medieval Imagination*, trans. A. Goldhammer (1988); R. Copeland, *Rhetoric, Hermeneutics, and Translation in the Middle Ages* (1991); O. Sayce, *Plurilingualism in the "Carmina Burana"* (1992); P. Zumthor, *Toward a Medieval Poetics*, trans. P. Bennett (1992); *Medieval Lyric*, ed. W. D. Paden (2000); T. Rosen, "The Muwashshah," *The Literature of Al-Andalus*, ed. M. R. Menocal, R. P. Scheindlin, M. A. Sells (2000).

C. W. JONES; T.V.F. BROGAN; P. DAMON; C. BROWN

**MEDIEVAL ROMANCE** (OF *roman*, "vernacular," versus Lat.). Such tensions mark the *genre: trans. versus invention, oral versus written, verisimilar versus marvelous, passionate versus parodic, didactic versus diverting. Texts regularly claim to be trans., but sources are used selectively and stitched together creatively (cf. Chrétien de Troyes's "bele conjointure" in *Erec et Enide*, composed ca. 1160–70), lavishly embroidered with hundreds of lines of descriptive *amplificatio*, the genre's hallmark rhetorical mode (see AMPLIFICATION). Romance has been called a secondary genre, not in importance but with regard to trans. and because it is self-reflexive, often ironic, and intellectualized. Works such as the allegorical *Roman de la Rose* (composed ca. 1230, continuation ca. 1270–80) insist on not being "fables et mensonges" (fictions and lies). Despite rhetorical downplay of *invention, romances are understood as fiction. They are furnished with recognizable details from daily life but are not mere mimetic reflections; rather, they employ the familiar in the service of debating ideals of love, politics, gender, and poetry itself.

The generic term exists for both med. readers and mod. scholars. *Intertextuality and hybridity mark this and other coexisting genres such as hagiography, *chansons de geste* (*epics), *lais, nouvelles* or *novelas*, and *fabliaux. Formally, med. romances are long narratives in written form but intended for oral performance. In earlier periods, works are composed in versified rhyming *couplets, typical of works for performance. From the 13th c. on, verse and prose coexist, with increased private reading and also the notion that prose represented truth better than verse's *artifice. Prologues, *excipits*, and interjections often indicate an author's name, views, or accomplishments; but this is often all that is known. Many works are anonymous. Thematically, romances center on characters, often a couple. Narratives are typically quests of some kind. Young knights seek a fortune through "adventure," risk-taking exploits undertaken in hope of gain. Heroines are the ultimate prize but also often are significantly cleverer than heroes. Both suffer in love's service and examine emotions through psychomachia scenes staging personified virtues in conflict. Romances, with their fictive "other worlds"—the ancient past, Arthur's court, distant Byzantium, wild forests, fairy realms—offered a locus for imagining a better world. Associatively, many romances are collected in ms. codices that demonstrate awareness of genre, grouping works by form (octosyllabic rhyming couplets, for instance) or theme (e.g., Arthurian material).

The first works using the term are the *romans d'antiquité*, from the Anglo-Norman court of Henry II and Eleanor of Aquitaine in the mid-12th c. They adapt works from Lat. antiquity, often to genealogical ends. They are adapted into many langs. in later centuries. Benoît de Sainte-Maure's *Roman de Troie* (ca. 1165) establishes Trojan ancestry for the Britons; the *Roman de Thèbes* (composed ca. 1155) adapts Statius; *Eneas* (ca. 1160) adapts Virgil, transforming political allegories into courtly love narratives. Also Anglo-Norman, Wace's *Roman de Brut* (composed ca. 1155) adapts Geoffrey of Monmouth's Lat. *Historia regum Britanniae* (ca. 1136), celebrating Britain's "Celtic" past through tales of King Arthur and offering the first mention of the Round Table. Many of the authors wrote official hists. in Lat.; by putting stories "en romanz," they sought an alternative to "history," "truth," and glorifying kings. The incestuous desire tale of Apollonius of Tyre also has many vernacular renderings.

Romance themes have been grouped under three *matières* (subjects) following Jean Bodel's formulation in the *Chanson des Saisnes* (composed ca. 1196): respectively, that of France (Charlemagne, his peers, and the Christian wars against the Saracens); Bretagne (regarding Britain and Brittany, incl. Tristan and Arthurian material); and Rome (mentioned above). He called the Breton tales "vain et plaisant" (wanton and appealing), the antique "sage et de san aprenant" (wise and instructive), and for the Fr., "their truth is confirmed every day." The wedding banquet in *Flamenca* (composed ca. 1250–80) presents a more enumerative catalog: tales of Tristan, Troy, Alexander, Thebes, Ovid's *Metamorphoses*, OT battles, the Round Table, Merlin, the Saracen Vieux de la Montagne, Charlemagne, Clovis, and Pépin. Other scholarly categories include Oriental or Byzantine (e.g., *Partonopeus de Blois*, composed ca. 1173–85, with many trans.; Chrétien's *Cligés*, ca. 1170–77; versions of the *Seven Sages of Rome*), the *roman réaliste* (e.g., those set in France by Jean Renart, Gautier d'Arras, Philippe de Beaumanoir, and others, ca. 1200–60). The 13th-c. term *roman d'aventure* refers to the Arthurian quests of Gawain, Lancelot, Percival, and other knights of the Round Table (Chrétien de Troyes's works are major exemplars: *Erec et Enide*; *Cligés*; the unfinished *Lancelot ou le Chevalier a la charette*, 1174–81; *Yvain ou le Chevalier au Lion*, 1175–81; the unfinished *Perceval ou le Conte du Graal*, 1179–91). *Allegories of love compose another subgenre, exemplified by the *Roman de la Rose*, relating the author-narrator's service to the God of Love and the 21,750-line quest to "pluck" a rose. The term is used in the *Roman de Renart*'s (composed ca. 1170) 27 branches recounting the scandalous, scatological, satirizing exploits of Renart the Fox outwitting courtly animals and laboring humans. Genealogical romances such as *Mélusine* (prose, Jean d'Arras, composed 1392–94; verse, Coudrette, 1401) recount fantastic family origins, e.g., the Lusignan line.

Med. romances flourished through the 15th c. and have been employed in establishing national identity, particularly in 19th-c. nationalist discourses. It is potentially misleading to present romances along national lines. Yet as texts in vernaculars, it is convenient to treat them by lang.

The over 200 extant OF romances had a major impact throughout Europe, with circulation, trans., and adaptations in what are now England, southern France, Italy, Spain, Portugal, Germany, the Netherlands, Scandinavia, and Greece. The predominant OF form is the octosyllabic rhyming couplet. Decasyllables appear in some branches of the *Roman d'Alexandre* (composed 1170); other versions of these exploits of Alexander the Great were also written in 12-syllable lines, whence the term *alexandrine. The vast prose cycles spurn verse and other *ornament (*Lancelot-Grail*, ca. 1215–35; *Prose Tristan*, 1235–40; *Post-Vulgate*, 1235–40).

Occitan was considered the lang. of lyric, but two rollickingly parodic romances survive: the Arthurian *Jaufre* (composed ca. 1225) and the fragmentary *Flamenca* exemplifying the *castia gilos* motif, a love triangle castigating the jealous husband.

ME works begin to appear in the 13th c. and flourish during the Hundred Years' War (1337–1453). There are some 50 works. Some use octosyllabic couplets, others use *tail rhyme (*rime couée*); a few are alliterative, in OE style. The most famous authors are the anonymous *Sir Gawain and the Green Knight* poet (fl. ca. 1375–1400), Geoffrey Chaucer, and Thomas Malory, who redacted the entire Arthurian cycle in *La Morte d'Arthur* (finished 1469).

The Germanic trad.'s 50 to 80 works flourished from the mid-12th to the 15th c., characterized by virtuoso embellishment on Fr. sources. Most are in couplets, and they are often stanzaic. Hartmann von Aue's adaptations (*Erec*, composed ca. 1180; *Iwein*, ca. 1200) amplify considerably and increase narratorial interventions. Wolfram von Eschenbach's masterpiece *Parzival* (ca. 1210) examines love service and a spiritual side of knightly prowess. Many versions of Tristan exist. The Arthurian *Widwilt* is a late med. Old Yiddish adaptation of Wirnt von Gravenburg's popular *Wigalois* (ca. 1210).

A number of It. writers composed in Fr. Prose romances in Fr. found a market in Italy; It. versions of Lancelot, Tristan, and Merlin appear in the 13th and 14th cs. Carolingian, Trojan, Arthurian, and Ovidian tales and other works such as the *Roman de la Rose* were adapted into *cantari*, verse narratives in eight-line stanzas sung in public, from the mid-13th to 15th c. The Ren. verse epics by Luigi Pulci, Ludovico Ariosto, and Matteo Maria Boiardo embroider the Carolingian material in eight-line stanzas.

In Spain, versions of Alexander and Apollonius appear in the 13th c. The first original full-length Castilian romance is the *Libro del Caballero Zifar* (composed 1310). Catalan Arthurian texts include *Curial y Güelfa* (1443–60) and Joannot Martorell's *Tirant lo Blanc* (ca. 1460). Much attention is devoted to Miguel de Cervantes's *Don Quixote* (1605, 1615), the ultimate tribute to and *parody of romance.

Although the term *romance* is originally Fr. (indeed, ME often rhymes *romaunce* with *France*), the trad. extends beyond Western Europe. Precursors in Persian and Gr. trads. should not be dismissed. One of the earliest Fr. romances, *Floire et Blancheflor* (composed ca. 1145–60), a tale of young lovers and abduction set in Babylon, claims an obscure Ar. source; it is thematically related to the Arabian tale *Neema and Noam*, the Persian *Varqa o Golšāh* by 'Ayyūqī (11th c.), and the Hellenistic abduction narratives of the 3d c. BCE. It was translated from Fr. into various vernaculars (e.g., at least five separate Ger., Dutch, and Flemish versions ca. 1170–1300); from the Tuscan *Il Cantare di Fiorio e Biancifiore* (ca. 1300–1350), it was adapted into Gr. as *Phlorios and Platzia-Phlora* using 15-syllable Gr. *political verse. Although Celtic origins of the Tristan and Iseut (or Isolde) material have long been asserted, Welsh and Ir. versions (14th c.) postdate the Fr. fragments by Thomas (composed 1170–75) and Béroul (ca. 1155–87) and the splendid rendering of Gottfried von Strassburg (ca. 1210). The Persian *Vis o Ramin* by Fakharradin Gorgani (1050–55), however, shares numerous thematic parallels, if not the tragic ending.

■ **Criticism and History:** M. Schlauch, *Romance in Iceland* (1934); E. Vinaver, *A la recherche d'une poétique*

*médiévale* (1970); A. Petit, *Naissances du roman: Les techniques littéraires dans les romans antiques du XIIe siècle* (1985); R. Dragonetti, *Le Mirage des sources* (1987); J. Bumke, *Courtly Culture* (1991); D. Kelly, *Medieval French Romance* (1993); E. Kooper, *Medieval Dutch Literature in Its European Context* (1994); R. Beaton, *The Medieval Greek Romances* (1996); P. Grieve, *"Floire and Blanchflor" and the European Romance* (1997); *Norse Romance*, ed. M. Kalinke, 3 v. (1999); F. R. Psaki, *Chivalry and Medieval Italian Romance* (2000); C. Jewers, *Chivalric Fiction and the History of the Novel* (2000); S. Kay, *The "Chanson de Geste" in the Age of Romance* (2001); D. Davis, "Greece ix. Greek and Persian Romances," *Encyclopedia Iranica*, ed. E. Yarshater (2002); K. Busby, *Codex and Context: Reading Old French Verse Narrative in Manuscript* (2002); G. Heng, *Empire of Magic* (2003); R. M. Stein, *Reality Fictions* (2006); J. Bliss, *Naming and Namelessness in Medieval Romance* (2008).

■ **Reference Works:** W. R. J. Barron, *English Medieval Romance* (1987); *The New Arthurian Encyclopedia*, ed. N. J. Lacey (1996); M. Zink, *Medieval French Literature*, trans. J. Rider (1995); *The Cambridge Companion to Medieval Romance*, ed. R. L. Krueger (2000).

S.-G. HELLER

**MEIOSIS** (Gr., "lessening"; Lat. *extenuatio*). A figure employing understatement, usually to convey that a thing is less in importance (or size) than it really is; the opposite of *auxesis. Meiosis is often confused with *litotes, which, properly understood, affirms or increases the importance, usually by negating the contrary. Litotes, however, is laudatory in intent; meiosis is derogatory. Meiosis should be considered the genus, the more general term. J. C. Scaliger (*Poetices libri septem* 3.81) says that "true *extenuatio* is a form of criticism, not mere understatement." Group μ reminds us that, as a metalogism, meiosis functions, like *hyperbole, litotes, *irony, and *paradox, by implicit reference to an ostensive situation, i.e., to the extralinguistic, pragmatic context of the utterance (132–38).

Quintilian discusses meiosis as an abuse or fault of lang. that characterizes obscure style rather than one lacking ornament but indicates that, deliberately employed, meiosis may be called a figure (*Institutio oratoria* 8.3.50). George Puttenham distinguishes the function of meiosis more particularly: "If you diminish and abbase a thing by way of spight . . . , such speach is by the figure *Meiosis* or the disabler" (*The Arte of English Poesie*). The startling simplicity of a powerful meiosis is arresting in narrative; e.g., Dante's famous "quel giorno più non vi leggemmo avante" (We read no more that day) from the Paolo and Francesca episode (*Inferno* 5.138); or the concluding lines of William Wordsworth's "Michael." Meiosis may be used as a structuring device in a poem, as in A. E. Housman's "Long for me the rick will wait, / And long will wait the fold, / And long will stand the empty plate, / And dinner will be cold" (*A Shropshire Lad* 8); or it may dominate an entire poem, as in W. H. Auden's "Musée des

Beaux Arts" and "The Unknown Citizen." Note also Shakespeare's later tragedies, esp. *King Lear*, wherein understatement often marks the most dramatic moments. In mod. times, however, what is unquestionably a valuable rhetorical device has fallen into some cultural disfavor, in part because of its abuse as a nearly obsessive Victorian locution.

■ M. Joseph, *Shakespeare's Use of the Arts of Language* (1947); L. A. Sonnino, *Handbook to Sixteenth-Century Rhetoric* (1968); Lausberg; Group μ; Corbett.

R. O. Evans; T.V.F. Brogan

**MEISTERSINGER.** Late med. Ger. burgher poets (14th–16th cs., some attested as late as the 18th c.) who traced their ancestry traditionally to twelve *Meister* among the *Minnesinger* (see MINNESANG), incl. such figures as Walther von der Vogelweide (ca. 1170–1230), Wolfram von Eschenbach (ca. 1170–1220), and Heinrich Frauenlob (ca. 1250–1318), reputedly the founder of the first *Singschule* (singing school), in Mainz; the catalog of 12 Meister was first mentioned by Lupold Hornburg around 1340. Unlike many of the earlier poets, however, whose themes were often erotic, the Meistersinger concentrated largely on didactic material, mainly moral, religious, and political themes. To some extent *Meistersang* developed from the didactic *Spruchdichtung* of the 13th and 14th cs. It was primarily intended for solo vocal performance. The Meistersang is transmitted in over 100 mss., some with melodies, incl. those ascribed to earlier poets such as Walther, but furnished with new texts.

From the end of the 14th c., Meistersinger were characterized by their organization into guilds, by their adherence to a system of rules and categories, and by the rigidly formalistic nature of their productions. Some scholars believe the guilds originated in groups of laymen organized by the Church to sing on public occasions. Before becoming a Meistersinger, an aspirant was obliged to work his way up through a series of grades from *Schüler* (pupil) through *Dichter* (poet) to the highest rank, Meister, yet even Meistersinger were restricted in their choice of material and technique. At the *Schulsingen*, or formal meetings, Meistersinger could treat only religious subjects; at the *Zechsingen*, however, informal meetings frequently held in taverns, a wider range of material was permissible, although amatory themes were not permitted for the songs until the 16th c. In technique, the Meistersinger were restricted to a certain set of *Töne*, or patterns of tune and meter; the metrical form was determined by the number of syllables and may have disregarded the natural accents of speech; often these forms display great intricacy. In fitting words to the Töne, the Meistersinger followed the *Tabulatur*, an extensive and pedantic code of rules that differed from school to school. The Meistersinger took over from the Minnesang a tripartite division of the stanza into two *Stollen* (together constituting the *Aufgesang*) followed by a third, differing section (the *Abgesang*)—structurally, *a / a / / b* (see CANSO)—which became a staple form. They called their songs *Bar* or *Par* and codified them in the *Tabulaturen*.

Famous Meistersinger include Hans Folz (d. ca. 1515), who successfully established the right of the Nuremberg Meistersinger to introduce new metrical patterns and melodies in place of the established forms; Lienhard Nunnenpeck (d. after 1515); Adam Puschmann (d. 1600); and, above all, Hans Sachs (1494–1576), the most prolific and the first to introduce *Buhllieder* (love songs). J. W. Goethe rediscovered Sachs in 1776 (see KNITTELVERS), and later Richard Wagner made him the hero of his opera *Die Meistersinger von Nürnberg*, a work that gives a generally accurate (though somewhat idealized) picture of the Meistersinger, but which incorrectly ascribes appreciation of their art to the wider public and to the ruling class, whereas in fact such appreciation was confined almost entirely to their own social sphere. Although Meistersang is predominantly didactic lyric poetry, the later Meistersinger (Folz, Sachs, Jörg Wickram [ca. 1505–before 1562], Wolfhart Spangenberg [ca. 1570–1636]) also composed short stories and Shrovetide plays.

The Meistersinger flourished for the most part in the Rhineland, Swabia, Franconia, and the Ger. lands east of the Elbe. There were some individual Meister in the north, but the characteristic guild organization seems to have existed neither there nor in Switzerland.

■ **Anthologies**: *Die Meisterlieder der Kolmarer Handschrift*, ed. K. Bartsch (1862); *Die Singweisen der Kolmarer Handschrift*, ed. P. Runge (1896), facsimile ed. U. Müller et al. (1976); H. Folz, *Meisterlieder*, ed. A. L. Mayer (1908); *Die Jenaer Liederhandschrift*, facsimile ed. H. Tervooren and U. Müller (1972); *Repertorium der Sangsprüche und Meisterlieder des 12. bis 18. Jahrhunderts*, ed. H. Brunner and B. Wachinger (1986–87).

■ **Criticism and History**: A. Taylor, *Literary History of Meistergesang* (1937); C. H. Bell, *Georg Hager, a Meistersinger of Nürnberg*, 4 v. (1947), and *The Meistersingerschule at Memmingen* (1952); B. Nagel, *Der deutsche Meistersang* (1952); R. W. Linker, *Music of the Minnesinger and Early Meistersinger* (1962); A. L. Burkhalter, *Minstrels and Masters* (1968); *Der deutsche Meistersang*, ed. B. Nagel, 2d ed. (1971); H. Brunner, *Die alten Meister* (1975); B.-F. Schultze, *Der Augsburger Meistersinger Onoferus Schwartzenbach* (1982); F. Schanze, *Meisterliche Liedkunst zwischen Heinrich von Mügeln und Hans Sachs*, 2 v. (1983–84); R. Hahn, *Die löbliche Kunst* (1984); N. Henkel, "Die zwölf alten Meister," *Beiträge zur Geschichte der deutschen Sprache und Literatur* 109 (1987); M. Galvez, "1515, Ash Wednesday: A Cobbler-Poet Becomes a Master Author," *A New History of German Literature*, ed. D. E. Wellbery (2004); *Im Wortfeld des Textes. Worthistorische Beiträge zu den Bezeichnungen von Rede und Schrift im Mittelalter*, ed. G. Dicke, M. Eikelmann, and B. Hasebrink (2006); *Aspects of the Performative in Medieval Culture*, ed. A. Suerbaum (2010).

A. Classen

**MELIC POETRY** (Gr. *melos*, "member," "song"). Later called *lyric poetry by the Alexandrians, *melic poetry* refers loosely to Gr. poetry composed from the 7th through 5th cs. BCE, exclusive of *epic, *dramatic poetry, *elegy, and *iambic. Melic poetry was sung to the accompaniment of a lyre or woodwinds or both and was divided into two broad categories, monodic and choral. Monodic melic poetry (see MONODY), whose chief representatives were Sappho, Alcaeus, and Anacreon, was sung by a solo voice and often consisted of short stanzas, the two most important of which became known as *sapphic and *alcaic. Monodic melic poetry reflected *aeolic and Ionian trads., and its lang. tended to be more conversational and personal than the monadic type (Kirkwood, Bowra). Choral melic poetry, whose chief composers were Alcman, Stesichorus, Ibycus, Simonides, Pindar, and Bacchylides, was sung and danced by a *chorus and was often arranged in triads consisting of *strophe, *antistrophe, and *epode. In contrast to monodic melic poetry, its character was more public, and it employed a highly artificial lang. with strong Doric coloring. Choral melic poetry was classified by Alexandrian eds. into various genres, the most important being *hymns, *paeans, *dithyrambs, prosodia, partheneia, *hyporchemata, *encomia, *dirges, and *epinikia. Although we have fragments from all the major choral poets (ed. Edmonds, which must be supplemented by many recent papyrological additions), the most important extant representatives are Pindar (45 epinikia) and Bacchylides (14 epinikia and 6 dithyrambs).

*See* GREEK POETRY.

■ H. W. Smyth, *Greek Melic Poets* (1900); Bowra; H. Färber, *Die Lyrik in der Kunsttheorie der Antike* (1936); J. E. Sandys, *The Odes of Pindar*, 3d ed. (1937); *Lyra Graeca*, ed. J. M. Edmonds, 3 v. (1952)—superseded by *Greek Lyric*, trans. D. A. Campbell, 5 v. (1982–93); D. L. Page, *Sappho and Alcaeus* (1955); G. M. Kirkwood, *Early Greek Monody* (1974); Trypanis; *CHCL*, v. l; R. L. Fowler, *The Nature of Early Greek Lyric* (1987); M. Davies, "Monody, Choral Lyric, and the Tyranny of the Hand-Book," *CQ* 82 (1988); C. Golston, "The Phonology of Greek Lyric Meter," *JL* 41 (2005).

W. H. RACE

**MELOPOEIA, PHANOPOEIA, LOGOPOEIA.** Three poetic modes by which, in Ezra Pound's formulation, lang. is "charged or energized." Melopoeia charges words "over and above their plain meaning, with some musical property, which directs the bearing or trend of that meaning" ("How to Read"). This charging can take the form of simple mimesis (e.g., imitation of birdsong) but is generally more abstract. Pound further distinguishes three kinds of melopoeia: "(1) that made to be sung to a tune; (2) that made to be intoned or sung to a sort of chant; and (3) that made to be spoken . . . ." Phanopoeia is "a casting of images upon the visual imagination" (see IMAGISM). Chinese poets have excelled in the use of phanopoeia, which can be readily trans. from one lang. to another. Logopoeia "employs words not only for their direct meaning, but it takes count . . . of habits of usage, of the context we *expect* to find with the word, its usual concomitants, of its known acceptances, and of

ironical play" (Pound, 170). Logopoeia relies on the reader to recognize lang. (whether from Dante, popular song, or *cliché) and to interpret the poet's (often ironical) stance toward it. T. S. Eliot's subversion of *pastoral invitation in the opening lines of "The Love Song of J. Alfred Prufrock" can be seen as an example of logopoeia.

■ E. Pound, *ABC of Reading* (1934); E. Pound, "How to Read," *Literary Essays* (1954); J. P. Sullivan, *Ezra Pound and Sextus Propertius: A Study in Creative Translation* (1964); H. N. Schneidau, *Ezra Pound: The Image and the Real* (1969); J. Hoogestraat, "Akin to Nothing But Language: Pound, Laforgue, and Logopoeia," *ELH* 55 (1988).

T. J. MATERER; P. KLINE

**MESOAMERICA, POETRY OF.** *See* INDIGENOUS AMERICAS, POETRY OF THE.

**METALEPSIS OR TRANSUMPTION** (Gr. *metalepsis*, from *metalambanein*, "to substitute"; Lat. *transumere*, "to take across"). A composite device, metalepsis involves transition from one *trope to another, where compressions of meaning are released along an associative string. The full meaning of the metalepsis may not be necessarily apparent or fully realized without the understood intermediate step. (See CATACHRESIS, mixed metaphor, where the resulting combination of tropes fails.)

As a trope, metalepsis occurs when a *metonymy is inserted into a phrase already figurative in itself. In a common example, "He is such a lead foot," *lead* is a metonymy (for *heavy*) that further charges the metaphor. While metalepsis may function to freshen a figurative use (as in R. W. Emerson's declaration that "language is fossil poetry"), an often-used metalepsis participates in the fossilization process and may speed its becoming *cliché ("an Achilles' heel").

Metalepsis has been treated somewhat dismissively by rhetoricians from antiquity to the Eng. Ren., who found it either showy or comic. In Quintilian's *Institutio oratoria* (8.6.38), it is "a trope that we give the impression of being acquainted with rather than one that we actually ever need." George Puttenham, in *The Arte of English Poesie*, calls it "the farfet [farfetched], as when we had rather fetch a word a great way off then to use one nerer hand to express the matter as well & plainer."

In contemp. poetry, its metaphorical compression has been used to offer a heightened state of *allusion. In Charles Wright's "Tattoos," the poet describes fainting as an altar boy, as "The sunlight—through St. Paul of the Twelve Sorrows—/Falls like Damascus on me." (*Damascus*, in this instance, is an allusion to the biblical story of Saul's conversion on the road to Damascus.) In Wright's "Apologia Pro Vita Sua," the phrase "Landscape's a lever of transcendence" links the speaker's attention to the natural world via the mystic Simone Weil's dictum, "Contradiction is a lever of transcendence."

The meaning of this composite trope has widened from metonymy and metaphor into any figurative substitution into another. In this sense, Heather McHugh uses a metalepsis in "Etymological Dirge" as she writes, "We get our danger from the lord"; the word *danger* has a root in *dominus*, but "lord" is a charged substitution that stands in for this entire associative string.

The theoretical reputation for metalepsis (called "the figure of interpretive allusion" by John Hollander) is broadening as well in postmodern culture and contemp. critical discourse. Harold Bloom joined Hollander and Angus Fletcher in recognizing it as "indispensable term and concept," a powerful revisionary trope that is its own style and rhetorical strategy (with Freudian defense, projection, and introjection mechanisms). In this widened sense, transumption functions in the style of R. W. Emerson, John Milton, S. T. Coleridge, and major writers whose work absorbs a trad. and transforms it.

Fr. literary theorist Gérard Genette has applied metalepsis to narratology, when the story jumps from one voice level to another, transgressing the boundaries between "the world *in* which one tells and the world *of* which one tells," finding instances in the fiction of Laurence Sterne, Denis Diderot, Julio Cortázar, and Jorge Luis Borges among others. In theater, transumption can function in breaking "the fourth wall" (Diderot), violating the invisible barrier between the audience and the players. William Nelles draws a distinction between this and characters who view other characters, as in *Hamlet*: "Properly speaking, there is no metalepsis involved in the play within a play . . . but such interplay is implicitly active in all embedded narratives."

Such transumptive strategies operate in Anne Carson's "Essay on What I Think about Most," where the poet-philologist considers how an apparent listing error from a fragment by the Gr. poet Alkman ("three seasons, summer / and winter and autumn third / and fourth spring") programs a sense of surprise into the sudden appearance of the fourth. When the speaker of the verse-essay proposes "three things I like about Alkman's poem," then supplies an unannounced fourth one, a discursive strategy of transumption is in play. The effect of transumption in discursive and narratological approaches depends less on the compression demonstrated in the trope, but the effect is similar: a sudden transport between the world of the teller and the tale.

■ A. Fletcher, *Allegory* (1964); G. Genette, *Narrative Discourse*, trans. J. E. Lewin (1972); H. Bloom, *Kabbalah and Criticism* (1975); J. Hollander, *The Figure of Echo* (1981); H. Bloom, *The Breaking of the Vessels* (1982); W. Nelles, "Stories within Stories," *Narrative Dynamics*, ed. B. Richardson (2002).

K. McFadden

## METAPHOR (Gr., "transference").

I. Critical Views
II. History
III. Recent Views
IV. Current Debates
V. Summary

A trope, or figurative expression, in which a word or phrase is shifted from its normal uses to a context where it evokes new meanings. When the ordinary meaning of a word is at odds with the context, we tend to seek relevant features of the word and the situation that will reveal the intended meaning. If there is a conceptual or material connection between the word and what it denotes—e.g., using cause for effect ("I read Shakespeare," meaning his works) or part for whole ("give me a hand," meaning physical help)—the figure usually has another name (in these examples, *metonymy and *synecdoche, respectively). To understand metaphors, one must find meanings not predetermined by lang., logic, or experience. In the terminology of traditional rhet., these figures are "tropes of a word," appearing in a literal context; in "tropes of a sentence," the entire context is figurative, as in *allegory, *fable, and (according to some) *irony.

Following Richards, we can call a word or phrase that seems anomalous the "vehicle" of the trope and refer to the underlying idea that it seems to designate as the "tenor" (see TENOR AND VEHICLE). An extended metaphor, as the name implies, is one that the poet develops in some detail. A *conceit is an intricate, intellectual, or far-fetched metaphor; a diminishing metaphor, one of its types, uses a pejorative vehicle with reference to an esteemed tenor. An extreme or exaggerated conceit is a *catachresis. Mixed metaphor, traditionally derided because it jumbles disparate vehicles together, has recently found some critical acceptance. *Dead metaphor presents fossilized metaphors in ordinary usage (e.g., "he *missed* the *point*").

What Quintilian said of tropes remains true today: "This is a subject which has given rise to interminable disputes among the teachers of literature, who have quarreled no less violently with the philosophers than among themselves over the problem of the genera and species into which tropes may be divided, their number and their correct classification." To say that metaphor is any trope that cannot be classified as metonymy, *hyperbole, etc., is to provide only a negative definition. Any attempt to define metaphor positively—e.g., "the application of a word or phrase to something it does not literally denote, on the basis of a similarity between the objects or ideas involved"—will inevitably apply to other tropes.

Some critics accept this consequence and call all tropes metaphors. But even this definition begs the question of how to distinguish the figurative from the literal or at best relegates it to accepted usage. If two species are members of the same genus on the basis of similarity, are they not "like" the genus and, therefore, like each other? Extension of this argument leads to the conclusion that all figures should be understood literally. On the other hand, every object is unique: "it is only the roughness of the eye that makes any two persons, things, situations seem alike" (Walter Pater).

Perfect literalness might be achieved by giving each object a unique name. In relation to that standard, a common noun is a metaphor because it provides a name that can be applied to different entities on the basis of a likeness between them. Hence, "literal" lang. can be considered metaphorical. Some argue that metaphor can result from grammar alone, without change of word meaning (see *Grammatical Metaphor* in biblio.). For advocates of conceptual metaphor theory, metaphors are representations of mental processes that are not revealed by ling. analysis. Others claim that metaphor is neither a ling. nor a cognitive issue but one based on the intentions of people using lang. for practical purposes. Concise treatment of the burgeoning field must exclude dozens of theories; Rolf and Leezenberg treat many that are not discussed below.

Despite these arguments and attempts to create a more satisfactory classification of figures, the definitions of the major tropes have remained unchanged since the cl. period. The most innovative attempts to clarify the status of metaphor have come from philosophers, linguists, and historians, who have explored metaphor's relation to propositional truth and meaning, to the origins of lang. and myth, to worldviews, scientific models, social attitudes, and ordinary usage. For their purposes, conventional and dead metaphors provide adequate examples for analysis. Scholars and literary critics, less concerned with theory than with practice, have usually accepted the imprecise accounts of metaphor handed down by trad. and focused their attention on its effects in particular poems. To say this is not to claim that the uses of metaphor in poetry are categorically different from those in other domains of lang. use but simply to call attention to the institutionalized character of poetry. The expectations in place when one starts reading a poem differ from those active in reading a newspaper or in conversing.

Emphasis in this discussion will be on poetics and the disciplines historically associated with that topic: rhet., philosophy, and lings. Discussion of metaphor has come full circle, reviving issues forgotten for centuries, while creating possibilities for further devels. A summary of what critics have usually said about metaphor, with some account of objections to traditional views, will provide a context for a brief discussion of historically important theories of metaphor and contemp. treatments of the subject.

**I. Critical Views.** Aristotle's discussion of *simile in the *Rhetoric* was until recently the starting point of most treatments of metaphor. In saying that Achilles "sprang at the foe as a lion," Homer used a simile; had he said "the lion sprang at them," it would have been a metaphor. In one case, according to Aristotle, the comparison is explicit (using *like* or *as*); in the other, the word *lion* is "transferred" to Achilles, but the meaning is the same. Quintilian endorsed Aristotle's view of metaphor as a condensed simile: "in the latter we compare some object to the thing which we wish to describe, whereas in the former the object is actually substituted for the thing." What Black has called the

"comparison view" of metaphor is based on the grammatical form "A is B"; metaphor is seen as a condensed simile, meaning that A is (like) B. The "substitution view," as Black says, takes "the lion sprang" as the paradigmatic form of metaphor: rather than predicating a likeness, metaphor uses a figurative word in place of a literal one. Both these views are compatible with the reductive conception of metaphor as "saying one thing and meaning another," thus implying that the poet has gone out of the way to say something other than what was meant (perhaps in the interests of decorating an ordinary thought) and suggesting that, in reading poetry, one must dismantle metaphors to find out what the poem "really means."

A different conception of metaphor is necessary to sustain Aristotle's claim, endorsed through the centuries, that metaphor is the most significant feature of poetic style: "that alone cannot be learnt; it is the token of genius. For the right use of metaphor means an eye for resemblances." New metaphors are said to spring from the poet's heightened emotion, keen perception, or intellectual acuity; their functions are aesthetic (making expression more vivid or interesting), pragmatic (conveying meanings concisely), and cognitive (providing words to describe things that have no literal name or rendering complex abstractions easy to understand through concrete analogies). Emphasis on the value of concreteness and sensory appeal in metaphor is frequent. Some mod. critics treat metaphor under the general rubric *imagery (*Bild* has a corresponding importance in Ger. crit., as does *image* in Fr. crit.).

Opposing the comparison and substitution views, 20th-c. critics and philosophers developed more intricate accounts of the verbal and cognitive processes involved in metaphoric usage. Despite their differences, the "interaction" view (Richards, Black), "controversion theory" (Beardsley), and "fusion" view (espoused by New Critics; see NEW CRITICISM) all hold that metaphor creates meanings not readily accessible through literal lang. Rather than simply substituting one word for another or comparing two things, metaphor invokes a transaction between words and things, after which the words, things, and thoughts are not quite the same. Metaphor, from these perspectives, is not a decorative figure but a transformed literalism, meaning precisely what it says. Fusion theorists argue that it unifies the concrete and abstract, the sensual and the conceptual in a *concrete universal or symbol. An entire poem, if it is organically unified, can, therefore, be called a metaphor.

A less audacious explanation of the uniqueness of metaphor is discussed in the next section; at present, let us simply note what problems this view solves and what ones it creates. Treating all tropes as metaphors, the fusion theory frees crit. from the inconsistent classification systems handed down from antiquity. Synecdoche, as a species-genus or part-whole relation, can be imputed to any comparison whatever (everything being "like" everything else in some generic respect, or part of it, if the level of abstraction is high enough). Metonymy can be an empirically observed association (cause-effect), an entailment (attribute for subject), or a contingent relation (object for possessor). Since no single principle of classification governs these distinctions, one figurative expression can exemplify two or more tropes, as Antoine Foquelin observed (*La Rhétorique françoise* [1555]). Fusion theorists eliminate this problem and seek the new meanings released by metaphor, rather than reducing them to uninformative categories.

This freedom from pedantry can, however, entail a loss of precision leading to the neglect, if not the dismissal or misperception, of many tropes. The blurring of traditional distinctions leads to changes in the ways figures are construed. *Pale death*, which would now be considered a trite metaphor involving personification, was in the Ren. a metonymy (death, not personified, is the cause of the effect paleness). The verbal vitality created by tropes other than metaphor is categorized as imagery if it is sensory and *style if it is not. Similes, otherwise identical to metaphors, are automatically accorded a lower status merely because they use the word *like* or *as*—a sign of timidity in the eyes of the fusion theorist, who may see in simile new possibilities for describing the nature of lang.

Single-minded emphasis on the meaning of metaphor, apart from the semantic and grammatical details of its realization, can lead both mod. theorists and traditionalists to questionable interpretive practices. In most textbooks, the only examples of metaphor provided are in the form "A is B," despite the fact that this is not the most common grammatical form, "the A of B" ("th' expense of spirit") and "the A B" ("the dying year") being more frequent (see Brooke-Rose). When they encounter metaphorical verbs, adjectives, and adverbs, critics who seek new meanings in poetry are tempted to transfer the figuration of these word classes over to the nouns with which they are associated. If a speaker snarls a reply or has a green thought, the critic concludes that the poet has said that the speaker is a dog or wolf and that the thought is a plant. Samuel Johnson's line in *The Vanity of Human Wishes* describing those who gain preferment—"They mount, they shine, evaporate, and fall"—may be clarified through reference to fireworks or fog and mayflies (living for a day), but its power and meaning evaporate if one concludes that the metaphoric verbs are a roundabout way of saying that the rich and famous are like insects.

The alternative assumption would be that the poet wanted to connect figurative attributes to a noun that remains literal; the nominal "A is B" equation was, after all, available to the poet, along with the other grammatical forms that create identity (apposition, demonstrative reference) and presumably would be used if that were the meaning. The tendency to think that metaphors always equate or fuse entities (nouns) reduces the varied effects of metaphor in poetry to a single register. Poets may intend their figurative renderings of process, attribute, and attitude to evoke a range of relations, from suggestiveness to total fusion. If so, they are not well served by theorists who translate every figurative inclination into a declaration

of equivalence. The affective and aesthetic functions of metaphor, usually mentioned in traditional accounts, have been emphasized by a few mod. critics who oppose the assumption that the purpose of metaphor is to convey meanings. Forrest-Thomson argues that "the worst disservice criticism can do to poetry is to understand it too soon." Mod. poets in particular try to forestall this haste by using metaphors that do not lend themselves to assimilation by the discursive elements of the text. Thus, they try to preserve poetry from reduction to paraphrastic statement. Shklovsky goes further, asserting that the purpose of new metaphors is not to create meaning but to renew perception by "defamiliarizing" the world: unlikely comparisons retard reading and force us to reconceive objects that ordinary words allow us to pass over in haste (see DEFAMILIARIZATION).

**II. History.** Four approaches have dominated all attempts to improve on the account of metaphor provided by the cl. trad. Some writers propose more logical classifications of the tropes. Others undertake semantic analysis of the ways in which features of a word's meaning are activated or repressed in figurative usage. These two modes of analysis blend into each other, but they can be distinguished from treatments of metaphor that emphasize its existential entailments—its relation to reality and to hist. rather than to logic and lang. The crudity of this fourfold classification must justify the brevity of the following discussion, which touches on only those treatments of metaphor that, from a contemp. perspective, seem crucial.

For Aristotle, metaphor has two functions and two structures. In the *Poetics*, its function is to lend dignity to style, by creating an enigma that reveals a likeness or by giving a name to something that had been nameless ("the ship *plowed* the sea"). But in the *Rhetoric*, metaphor appears as a technique of persuasion, used to make a case appear better or worse than it is. Mod. critics would say that *kill*, *murder*, and *execute* have the same denotation but differ in *connotation; for Aristotle, one of the three words would be proper in relation to a particular act, and the other two would be metaphors. From its rhetorical uses, metaphor acquires its reputation as a dangerous deviation from the truth, being for that reason castigated by Thomas Hobbes, John Locke, and other Enlightenment philosophers.

The four kinds of metaphor distinguished by Aristotle in the *Poetics* are of two structural types. One results from substitution (of species for genus, genus for species, or species for species), the two terms having a logical or "natural" relation to each other. The other type has an analogical or equational structure: A is to B as C is to D. Although only two of the four terms need be mentioned (A and D, or B and C), we must infer the other two in order to derive the meaning: "the evening of life" enables us to reconstruct "evening is to day as X is to life." Here we find the bifurcation that will henceforth characterize discussions of tropes: one type is based on accepted conceptual relationships (here, genus-species), and the other type includes all tropes that cannot be so defined. Species-genus and species-

species relations are part of common knowledge; to cross from genus to genus, we need four terms that create what might be called a hypothetical likeness, one not given by logic or nature.

The species-genus relation is one of many that make it possible to infer the tenor from the vehicle. Identification of other such relations (e.g., cause for effect, container for contents) led to the proliferation of names for the tropes in rhet. Once they separated themselves from Aristotle's generic metaphor, it was necessary to define metaphor in such a way that it would not include the other tropes. Quintilian's solution—to say that metaphor is a substitution involving any permutation of the terms "animate" and "inanimate"—is not as unreasonable as it first appears. The dividing line between these two domains, which is a fundamental feature of lang. and culture, cannot easily be crossed by species-genus, part-whole, or subject-adjunct relations. Furthermore, animate-inanimate metaphors are strikingly frequent in poetry, as are animate-animate metaphors involving humans and nature. Analysis based on meaning later gave prominence to *personification and the *pathetic fallacy, appearance and reality, or inner and outer as the quintessential forms of metaphor.

Looking back on Quintilian from the perspectives provided by Giambattista Vico, the romantic poets, and semioticians, we can see that his untidy classification (which defines metaphor by reference to its subject matter, the other tropes by reference to "categorical" relationships) reveals something about the role of metaphor that escapes notice in any purely formal analysis. But when subject matter becomes the primary basis of classification, as it is in 19th- and 20th-c. studies such as those of Brinkmann, Konrad, and Spurgeon, the specificity of the tropes dissolves in the all-embracing category "imagery."

For the Ren., Quintilian's *Institutio oratoria* (pub. 1470) provided an orderly exposition of rhet. in place of the patchwork syntheses inferrable from other cl. texts; Quintilian's renown made him one target of Peter Ramus's campaign to reform the curriculum. Ramus concluded that there were four basic tropes: metonymy (connection through cause, effect, or adjunct), irony ("a change in meaning from opposites to opposites"), metaphor ("a change in meaning from comparisons to comparisons"), and synecdoche (species and genus). In Vico's *Scienza nuova* (*New Science,* 1725), these four become the basis of a hist. of lang. and civilization. In the age of the gods, metonymy ruled: lightning and thunder were a great effect of unknown origin, and humankind imagined the agent Jove as the cause. The age of heroes was one of synecdoche: men who held themselves to be sons of Jove embodied his abstract attributes. The age of men is the age of metaphor, in which likenesses are taken from bodies "to signify the operation of abstract minds"; and philosophy gives rise to what we call "literal" meaning.

Ramus is the precursor of mod. attempts to reduce tropes to a rationale, and Vico occupies the same position in relation to mod. discussions of metaphor's importance in the devel. of lang., though their successors are not always aware of this lineage. That lang. was originally metaphorical, mythic, and poetic is a common theme in *romanticism—e.g., in Jean-Jacques Rousseau, J. G. Herder, F.W.J. Schelling, and P. B. Shelley—but there is little evidence that Vico was their source (the idea can be found in Lucretius, among others). Müller, Werner, and Cassirer exemplify the Ger. thinkers who have developed this theory; Langer and Wheelwright contributed to its popularity in Am. crit. Nietzsche's contrary thesis—that lang. was originally concrete and literal in reference and that the abstract vocabulary now considered literal is, in fact, metaphorical—has recently attracted critical attention (de Man). But as Vico pointed out, it makes little sense to speak of lang. as either literal or metaphorical before it incorporates a distinction between the two. Even Gadamer's carefully worded claims about the historical and conceptual primacy of metaphor cannot escape Vico's objection.

The theories of metaphor proposed by Richards, Black, and Beardsley, which incorporate insights into the workings of lang. and meaning derived from 20th-c. analytic philosophy, provide an alternative to traditional accounts of metaphor as a substitution, comparison, or fusion of meanings. Sentences, Richards says, are neither created nor interpreted by putting together words with unique meanings. Any ordinary word has several meanings and a number of loosely associated characteristics; often it will be both noun and verb or noun and adjective. The varied traits or semes of a word's meaning are sometimes sorted into two groups—denotations (characteristics essential to a distinct sense of the word) and connotations—but in practice, this distinction is hard to maintain (see CONNOTATION AND DENOTATION). (In his precise and revealing analysis of this issue, MacCormac describes words as "fuzzy sets.") Only when placed in a context does a word take on one or more meanings, at which time some of its traits become salient and others are suppressed. It is often difficult to decide when we have crossed the line between literal and figurative usage. In the series "green dress" (dyed), "green field" (growing), "green shoot" (alive, despite color), and "green thought," connotations shift before becoming clearly metaphorical.

Richards looked on metaphor as a "transaction between contexts," in which tenor and vehicle combine in varied ways to produce meanings. Beardsley argues persuasively that metaphor is intentional: we find it in words, not in the objects to which they refer. Black's "interaction theory" contains an important distinction between the "focus" and "frame" of a metaphor (the figurative expression and the sentence in which it occurs). The focus brings with it not just connotations but a "system of associated commonplaces"—what Eco will later call "encyclopedic knowledge"—that interact with the frame to evoke knowledge shared by a speech community. To say "the lion sprang at them," meaning Achilles sprang, makes sense only because of common lore about the lion (a hunter, not an herbivore; sociable with its own kind, unlike the tiger, but not a herd animal; monogamous; a lone hunter, unlike the wolf). The lion cannot represent courage until, through a prior mapping of culture on nature, he is the king of beasts. Black emphasizes the "*extensions* of meaning" that novel metaphors bring to lang., but his theory has proved most useful in understanding the inherited and dead metaphors that structure a society's way of thinking and talking about itself.

**III. Recent Views.** Every innovative critical theory of the later 20th c. generated a new delineation of metaphor—either as the "other" of its own conceptual domain or as the very ground of its new insights. One of the most influential innovations has been Jakobson's opposition of metaphor to metonymy. In his view, metaphor results from the substitution of one term for another; it is characteristic of poetry and some literary movements, such as romanticism and *symbolism. Metonymy, based on contiguity, appears more frequently in prose and typifies *realism. Though they often cross disciplinary boundaries, these theories of metaphor can be classified as (1) ling. or semiotic (based on intralinguistic relationships or relations between signs of any sort); (2) rhetorical or pragmatic (involving a difference between sentence meaning and speaker meaning); (3) philosophical (emphasizing relations between words and reality or sense and reference); and (4) extended (treating nonlinguistic relationships in other disciplines).

The most ambitious semiotic attempt to identify ling. features of metaphor appears in *A General Rhetoric*, produced by Group μ of the University of Liège. They treat all unexpected suppressions, additions, repetitions, or permutations of ling. elements, from phonemes to phrases, as figures, the nonfigurative being a hypothetical "degree zero" discourse from which rhet. deviates. Metaphor results from an implicit decomposition of words into their semes (lexical features), some of which will be cancelled and others added when one word is substituted for another. The natural route for such substitutions is through species and genus, as Aristotle observed, and Group μ concludes that a metaphor consists of two synecdoches, the progression being either species-genus-species (the intermediate term being a class that includes the first and last terms) or whole-part-whole (here the central term is a class formed where the first and last overlap). Levin, using a more flexible scheme for the transfer and deletion of semantic features, shows that there are six ways to interpret a metaphor (his example is "the stone died"). He points out that the grammatical structure of many metaphors allows for the transfer of features in two directions: "the brook smiled" can either humanize the brook or add sparkle and liquidity to the idea of smiling. Although he analyzes metaphor as an intralinguistic phenomenon, Levin recognizes that Aristotle's fourth type, analogy, often depends upon reference to reality—a fact that Group μ overlooked. Thus, metaphor appears to escape formalization within a system. Eco's semiotic solution to this problem is to imagine

an encyclopedia that describes all the features of reality not included in the semanticist's dictionary. For Riffaterre (1978), mimetic reference is only a feint that the literary text makes before refocusing itself in a network of semiotic commonplaces.

Proponents of *speech act theory are the most important representatives of rhetorical and pragmatic theories. They hold that metaphor cannot be explained through reference to relationships between words and their ling. contexts. They make a categorical distinction between "word or sentence meaning" and "speaker's utterance meaning." Metaphor, in their view, arises from a disparity between the literal meaning of the words used and what is intended by the speaker or writer. Words always retain their invariant "locutionary" definitions, but when used to make metaphors, there is something odd about them and the hearer infers unstated suggestions or meanings. Grice's theory of "conversational implicature" provides a set of rules and maxims for normal talk that, when violated, may alert us to the fact that someone is speaking figuratively. His theory, like Searle's, locates metaphor in a difference between utterance meaning and speaker meaning—the domain of pragmatics—and is subject to the same sorts of crit. that speech act theory has elicited (see Sadock in Ortony).

Searle and Grice are philosophers, but their theories entail empirical claims of relevance to linguists. In the work of Davidson and of Goodman, one finds more strictly philosophic treatments of metaphor. Meaning, in Davidson's view, involves only the relation between lang. and reality. He is willing to accept the pragmatic "distinction between what words mean and what they are used to do," but he denies the existence of metaphoric meaning: "metaphors mean what the words, in their most literal interpretation, mean, and nothing more." To this one might reply that if we did not realize they were patently false, we would not know they were figurative. Recognizing them as such, we may discover truths about the world, but this is not a consequence of some meaning inherent in the words. Goodman disagrees. In *Languages of Art*, he conceives of metaphor, like many other activities, as exemplification. Rather than applying a label to a thing, we use the thing as an example of the label, as when the lively appearance of the literal brook is seen as an instance of smiling. This reverses the direction of denotation: the example refers to the word, rather than vice versa, and the word may bring with it a whole schema of relationships that will be sorted anew in the metaphorical context. Goodman concludes that metaphor is "no more independent of truth or falsity than literal use."

Postponing discussion of deeper philosophical differences that divide theorists, one cannot help but note that they tend to privilege different moments in the interpretive process. At first glance, or outside time, metaphor is false (Davidson). Realizing that the creator of a metaphor means something else, one might create a theory of the difference between sentence and speaker meaning (Searle, Grice). When engaged in deciphering, a reader enacts the interaction theory—discovering new meanings—and the falsity of metaphor is forgotten. Truth usually results from testing many examples to find one rule; in metaphor, meaning emerges from repeated consideration of a single example, uncovering all its possibilities; and a hypothesis or generalization is the product of the process, not its inception. In accordance with information theory, the low probability of a word or phrase in a particular context implies that it carries a great deal of meaning.

**IV. Current Debates.** Through the work of Lakoff and Johnson, understanding of dead metaphors has been transformed. Most commonplace metaphors express a connection between a concept and a realm of experience. Among their examples of these conceptual metaphors are "argument is war" and "time is money." In their terminology, the conceptual term is the target, and the concrete term is the source. Each such "A is B" is a generic schema that can generate dozens of specific tropes, based on connections between the two domains. Their examples serve as reminders that not only nouns but adjectives, verbs, adverbs, and prepositions abound in tropes. As Searle remarked, conventional metaphors spring back to life when new aspects of the analogy are evoked (e.g., "he torpedoed my argument," "his refutation was a dud"). For Lakoff and Johnson, such interactions of the abstract and concrete are not simply analogies, and "conceptual metaphors" are not provisional aspects of lang. use. They exemplify the ways that we conceptually organize experience. War and argument cannot be separated from each other.

Poetics can certainly benefit from attention to conventional metaphors, long neglected in discussions of poetry. As Turner (1987) showed, a single domain such as kinship can generate hundreds of analogies that differ in interesting ways. He and Lakoff provide examples of how basic conceptual metaphors concerning life, time, and death occur in a wide range of traditional and contemp. poems. When metaphor is seen as a form of conceptual mapping rather than verbal expression, it has implications for psychology, anthropology, neurology, and cognitive science. If rooted in bodily experience, metaphor may reveal universal conceptual patterns; those specific to particular cultures might then be correlated with different langs. or modes of understanding (Kövecses). The cohesion of specific groups within a society may be strengthened by shared conceptual metaphors. If so, the topic is important for sociology, politics, and rhetorical studies of public relations and advertising.

When these devels. are connected with neurology and cognitive science, the scope and significance of the project become clear. What is at stake is nothing less than a unified theory of human behavior, mapping a progression from embodied experience, inscribed in neural pathways, to action, thought, and expression. This change has confirmed the relevance of earlier conceptions of metaphor. Jakobson's association of metaphor and metonymy with the right and left hemispheres of the brain, mentioned earlier, has led to numerous experiments that make use of neural imaging. The idea

that abstract thought emerged from metaphor, as suggested by Vico, Rousseau, and Herder, gained support through two centuries during which philologists traced the evolution of word meanings. Metaphor is now a topic of discussion in many disciplines, treated in hundreds of articles annually. Following the ling. turn of the 20th c., the paradigmatic shift of the 21st c. may be a tropical turn.

For poetics, the emphasis on conceptual metaphor has been immensely valuable. In both crit. and pedagogy, poetry has been rescued from the modernist overemphasis on originality and recognized as dependent on conventional cultural codes that it shares with the lyrics of popular music. The hist. of poetry suggests that innovative metaphor may be even less common than conceptual metaphor theorists suggest. They have frequently treated three examples as innovative: "man is a wolf," "that surgeon is a butcher," and "my lawyer is a shark." Dicts. and poetry anthols. confirm the impression that these have existed for centuries. The human and animal kingdoms, with the lion as the king of beasts, were mapped onto each other long ago. The names of many species—rats, snakes, skunks, foxes, weasels—have literalized meanings referring to humans. Even condensed dicts. list two literal meanings for the humans known as wolves or as sharks; a "butcher," as noun or verb, literally means a botcher or a bungler. The elaborate schemas produced to account for how we understand such usage seem beside the point, unless they are hypotheses about the neural activity of those encountering such usage for the first time or hypotheses about how we understand literal statements.

The conceptual metaphor theory of Lakoff, Johnson, Turner, and their followers treats metaphor as a cognitive, not a ling., phenomenon. The theory has prompted empirical studies of figurative lang., based on data banks such as the British National Corpus (100,000,000 words from 20th-c. pubs.). One important result of such work is evidence that metaphors commonly used in conversation and prose are quite different from those produced by theorists as examples. Often the meaning is clear even when the literal "tenor" or "target domain" is indeterminate: when a man is "gaining ground" with a woman, should we think of war, affection, or territorial encroachment? Corpus analysts conclude that there is no clear-cut boundary between literal and figurative usage. Phrases and word couplings that were once either literal or figurative are now usually or always figurative—making them, in effect, literal. E.g., "heavy blow" and "pay a high price" are rarely used literally; a search for the phrase "old fox" turns up only the (literalized) metaphorical meaning. Those who construct examples for experimental purposes sometimes mistake commonplace for original metaphors, and vice versa (Stefanowitsch, Hanks, Deignan, Hilpert). Given the lack of agreement about the difference between figurative, literalized, and literal expressions, the gap between theory and empirical studies has not been bridged.

The antithetical view of metaphor—as uncommon insight rather than an oddity reducible to literal thought and expression—has long lacked a persuasive justification. Those who have proposed this view, from Aristotle to Davidson, have not supported it with convincing arguments. Fauconnier and Turner provide the best explanation we have of connections between metaphor, insight, and ling. innovation. Each of the two entities in the traditional "A is B" metaphor has a number of features (connotations or semes). We can list the features together in a hypothetical "generic space." The traits that they share and the context will usually indicate the implied meaning. The novel or emergent metaphor does not yield its meaning through that procedure; no revealing correspondence in the generic space is evident. That leads to reconsideration of traits not shared and the creation of what Fauconnier and Turner call a "blended space," from which unanticipated meanings may emerge.

The title of Turner's book *Death Is the Mother of Beauty* (a phrase taken from a poem by Wallace Stevens) provides an example of creative metaphor. Death ends life; how can it give birth? The traditional Grim Reaper and his scythe are replaced by a maternal force that "strews the leaves / of sure obliteration on our paths." The leaves are not cut down by an untimely scythe but fall when their time has come. The lines call attention to the natural, inevitable death that makes urgent the fulfillment of desire. Paradoxically, consciousness of death gives birth—to awareness of beauty's transience. An entire stanza prompts us to make these inferences and others concerning procreation; it directs but also multiplies the potential insights. Turner and Fauconnier are sensitive to the interaction of metaphor and other tropes in contexts that limit the possible meanings in some directions but thereby expand them in others.

**V. Summary.** The figural use of "metaphor" in mod. theory, through which it assimilates not only all other tropes (as in Aristotle) but models, analogies, and narrative methods as well, leads back to the question of whether the literal and figurative can be distinguished from one another. The simplest and in some ways most logical answers are that ling. meaning is all literal (Davidson) or all figural (Nietzsche). Children do not discriminate between the two in lang. acquisition, and there is little evidence that adult comprehension of literal and metaphorical usage involves different psychological processes (Rummelhart). Some argue that tropes can be entirely literal (see *Grammatical Metaphor*). Rather than attempting to identify rules capable of accounting for literal usage and then explaining figures as transformations or deviations from this set, one can treat literalness "as a limiting case rather than a norm" and develop a pragmatic theory of meaning in which metaphors need not be considered different from other usage (Sperber and Wilson).

Figurative indirectness also seems prevalent in Chinese and Japanese poetry. Varieties of parallel structure, the Chinese stylistic figures of *bi* (comparison) and *xing* (incitation, affective image), and the tendency to imply without asserting a relation between mood and scene imply a reticence at odds with propositional assertion (Owen, Cheng, Cai). The 20th-c. confrontation

of truth and metaphor, based on the assumption that metaphor is an assertive predication, may have been misguided.

The analogies and metaphors that prompt insight do not have to appear in poetry. Many have emerged from our interactions with technology. Fauconnier and Turner call attention to the consequences of comparing a disruptive program in a computer to a virus in an organism. The analogy itself comes to life when one pursues its implications. Antibiotics will prove useless; the first line of defense would be to identify sources of the infection and methods of preventing it from entering the system. Determining the molecular structure (code) of the virus would be useful for the creation of feedback mechanisms that could neutralize its effects. Through the same kind of reasoning, the models used in scientific theories serve heuristic functions when familiar structures are used to map uncharted phenomena. Hesse and Kuhn extended Black's discussion of the subject in *Models and Metaphors*. Citing the work of Bachelard and Canguilhem, Derrida (1972) suggested that the function of metaphor in science is not merely heuristic. Hesse endorses Boyd's claim (in Ortony) that "metaphors are *constitutive* of the theories they express, rather than merely exegetical."

As the hists. of science and poetry show, metaphors and models are tools for thought that may or may not prove productive. When productive, they implant thoughts that become part of a society and culture— what we (unconsciously) think with, rather than think about. Pepper's *World Hypotheses* claims that different ways of life are based on "root metaphors" that affect every aspect of experience. For Blumenberg's philosophical anthropology, such a metaphor constitutes a worldview, a "set of institutions, customs, and expectations that maintain a life-world" and constitute its "selves" (Pavesich). The difference between creative and commonplace metaphors may be a function of the amount of consciousness they evoke.

While contributing to an understanding of its ling. features and conceptual implications, theories of metaphor show that it is not simply one critical problem among others, notable only for the number of disagreements it causes. Ricoeur finds in philosophic metaphor a potential for revealing the nature of being. But as that which lies outside the literal, normal, proper, or systematic, metaphor serves as a topic through which each theory and philosophy defines itself. Metaphor is not simply true or false but that which marks the limits of the distinctions between the two or between meaning and nonsense. As Derrida says, "Each time that a rhetoric defines metaphor, not only is *a* philosophy implied, but also a conceptual network in which philosophy *itself* has been constituted." Thus, agreement about the status of metaphor will be deferred until all other ling. and philosophic disputes have been resolved.

*See* FIGURATION, TROPE.

■ **Anthologies**: *Philosophical Perspectives on Metaphor*, ed. M. Johnson (1981); *Metaphor and Thought*, ed. A. Ortony (1993); *Aspects of Metaphor*, ed. J. Hintikka (1994); *Grammatical Metaphor*, ed. A.-M. Simon-Vandenbergen, M. Taverniers, and L. Ravelli (2003);

*Cognitive Linguistics*, ed. D. Geerarts (2006); *Corpus-Based Approaches to Metaphor and Metonymy*, ed. A. Stefanowitsch and S. Gries (2006); *The Cambridge Handbook of Metaphor and Thought*, ed. R. W. Gibbs Jr. (2008).

■ **History**: M. Müller, *Lectures on the Science of Language* (1862, 1865); F. Brinkmann, *Die Metaphern* (1878); H. Werner, *Die Ursprünge der Metapher* (1919); W. B. Stanford, *Greek Metaphor* (1936); H. Konrad, *Étude sur la métaphore* (1939); E. Cassirer, *Language and Myth*, trans. S. Langer (1946); F. Nietzsche, "On Truth and Lies in a Nonmoral Sense" [1873], *Philosophy and Truth*, ed. D. Breazeale (1979); L. Doležel, *Occidental Poetics* (1990); K.W.F. Schlegel, "Dialogue on Poesy" [1799], *Theory as Practice*, ed. J. Schulte-Sasse (1997); G. Bergounioux, "La sémantique dans le champ de la linguistique francophone jusqu' à 1916" and B. Nerlich, "La métaphore et la métonymie," *Sémiotiques* 14 (1998); B. Nerlich and D. D. Clarke, "Mind, Meaning and Metaphor," *History of the Human Sciences* 14 (2001).

■ **Texts**: C. K. Ogden and I. A. Richards, *The Meaning of Meaning* (1923); C. Spurgeon, *Shakespeare's Imagery* (1935); G. Bachelard, *La Formation de l'esprit scientifique* (1938); S. K. Langer, *Philosophy in a New Key* (1942); S. Pepper, *World Hypotheses* (1942); C. Brooke-Rose, *A Grammar of Metaphor* (1958); M. Black, *Models and Metaphors* (1962); P. Wheelwright, *Myth and Reality* (1962); I. A. Richards, *The Philosophy of Rhetoric* ([1936] 1965); V. Shklovsky, "Art as Technique" [1917], *Russian Formalist Criticism*, ed. and trans. L. Lemon and M. J. Reis (1965); M. Hesse, *Models and Analogies in Science* (1966); H. Weinreich, "Explorations in Semantic Theory," *Current Trends in Linguistics* 3 (1966): G. Canguilhem, *Études d'histoire et de philosophie des sciences* (1968); N. Goodman, *Languages of Art* (1968); K. Burke, "Four Master Tropes," *A Grammar of Motives* ([1945] 1969); M. C. Beardsley, "The Metaphorical Twist," *Philosophy and Phenomenological Research* 22 (1962); G. Vico, *The New Science*, ed. and trans. T. G. Bergin and M. H. Fisch ([1744] 1970); H. White, *Metahistory* (1973); H. Bloom, *A Map of Misreading* (1975); H.-G. Gadamer, *Truth and Method*, trans. J. Weinsheimer and D. Marshall ([1960] 1989); H. Bloom, *Wallace Stevens* (1977); P. Ricoeur, *The Rule of Metaphor*, trans. R. Czerny ([1975] 1977); D. Davidson, "What Metaphors Mean," and P. de Man, "The Epistemology of Metaphor," *CritI* 5 (1978); V. Forrest-Thomson, *Poetic Artifice* (1978); M. Riffaterre, *Semiotics of Poetry* (1978); M. Black, "How Metaphors Work," and N. Goodman, "Metaphor as Moonlighting," *CritI* 6 (1979); J. Derrida, *The Archeology of the Frivolous*, trans. J. Leavey ([1973] 1980); G. Lakoff and M. Johnson, *Metaphors We Live By* (1980); Group μ, "White Mythology," *Margins of Philosophy*, trans. A. Bass, ([1972] 1982); U. Eco, "The Scandal of Metaphor," *PoT* 4 (1983); M. Riffaterre, *Text Production*, trans. T. Lyons (1983); U. Eco, "Metaphor, Dictionary, and Encyclopedia," *NLH* 15 (1984); E. R. MacCormac, *A Cognitive Theory of Metaphor* (1985); S. Owen, *Traditional Chinese Poetry and Poetics* (1985); D. Sperber and D. Wilson, *Relevance* (1986); R. Jakobson, "Two Aspects of Language and Two Types of Aphasic Disturbances," 1956, rpt. in Jakobson, v. 2; E. F. Kittay, *Metaphor* (1987); M. Turner, *Death Is the Mother of Beauty* (1987); F. Cheng, "The Reciprocity of Subject and Object in Chinese Poetic Language," *Poetics East and West*, ed. M. Doleželová-Velingerová (1988–89); H. P. Grice, "Logic and Conversation," 1975, *Studies in the Ways of Words* (1989); G. Lakoff and M. Turner, *More than Cool Reason* (1989); *Metaphor and Thought*, ed. A. Ortony (1993)—see esp. M. Black, "More about Metaphor" (1977), R. Boyd, "Metaphor and Theory Change," T. Kuhn, "Metaphor in Science," S. Levin, "Standard Approaches to Metaphor," D. Rummelhart, "Some Problems with the Notion of Literal Meanings," J. Sadock, "Figurative Speech and Linguistics," and J. Searle, "Metaphor"; B. Indurkhya, "Metaphor as Change of Representation," and E. Steinhart and E. Kittay, "Generating Metaphors from Networks," in *Aspects of Metaphor*, ed. J. Hintikka (1994); R. M. White, *The Structure of Metaphor* (1996); G. Fauconnier, *Mappings in Thought and Language* (1997); S. Glucksberg, *Understanding Figurative Language* (2001); M. Leezenberg, *Contexts of Metaphor* (2001); G. Fauconnier and M. Turner, *The Way We Think* (2002); Z. Kövecses, *Metaphor* (2002); A.-M. Simon-Vandenbergen, "Lexical Metaphor and Interpersonal Meaning," *Grammatical Metaphor*, ed. A.-M. Simon-Vandenbergen et al. (2003); Z. Kövecses, *Metaphor in Culture* (2005); E. Rolf, *Metaphertheorien* (2005); E. Romero and B. Soria, "Cognitive Metaphor Theory Revisited," *Journal of Literary Semantics* 34 (2005); *Corpus-based Approaches to Metaphor and Metonymy*, ed. A. Stefanowitsch and S. T. Gries (2006); G. Fauconnier and M. Turner, "Conceptual Integration Networks," *Cognitive Linguistics*, ed. D. Geeraerts (2006); J. Derrida, "The *Retrait* of Metaphor," 1978, *Psyche*, ed. P. Kamuf and E. Rottenberg (2007); *The Cambridge Handbook of Metaphor and Thought*, ed. R. W. Gibbs Jr. (2008); V. Pavesich, "Hans Blumenberg's Philosophical Anthropology," *Journal of the History of Philosophy* 46 (2008); Z.-Q. Cai, "Introduction," *How to Read Chinese Poetry*, ed. Z.-Q. Cai (2008).

W. MARTIN

**METAPHYSICAL POETRY.** A term frequently applied to the poetry written by John Donne, George Herbert, Richard Crashaw, Andrew Marvell, Henry Vaughan, Thomas Traherne, and other 17th-c. Eng. poets. Metaphysical poetry is distinguished by metaphorical ingenuity, argumentative intellectuality, and stylistic obscurity. A term much less in use now than a generation ago, *metaphysical poetry* is a rubric so tainted by misogyny and misjudgment that we would surely have abandoned it if it did not still have some value. It is, moreover, a term that would have been unrecognizable to those it designates.

The hist. of the term indicates the circumspection with which it should be used. In Donne's lifetime,

William Drummond of Hawthornden writes disparagingly of poems rife with "metaphysical Ideas and Scholastical Quiddities." Later in the 17th c., John Dryden misogynistically censures Donne for violating both nature and decorum by addressing women as intellectual creatures; Donne "affects the metaphysics not only in his satires, but in his amorous verses, where nature only should reign, and perplexes the minds of the fair sex with nice speculations of philosophy." In the 18th c., Samuel Johnson in his *Life of Cowley* complains about a group he terms "the metaphysical poets," who seek out the "discovery of occult resemblances in things apparently unlike. . . . The most heterogeneous ideas are yoked by violence together." Johnson argues that the recondite philosophy and strained *metaphors of the metaphysical poets violate *decorum, a critical value of 18th-c. aesthetics (see NEOCLASSICAL POETICS).

Throughout the 18th and 19th cs., the reputation of metaphysical poetry suffers, although S. T. Coleridge expresses admiration for both Donne and Herbert. But the turn of the 20th c. ushers in a revaluation, heralded by the publication of Herbert Grierson's ed. of Donne's *Poetical Works* (1912) and his signal anthol., *Metaphysical Lyrics and Poems of the Seventeenth Century* (1921). Reviewing the latter volume, a young T. S. Eliot praises metaphysical poetry, discovering in its studied conjunction of thought and feeling a sensibility that had not suffered the *"dissociation of sensibility" afflicting neoclassical, romantic, and Victorian poetry. Eliot praises the metaphysical poets, and Donne in particular, for fusing thought and emotion, and admires their ability to "devour" "all kinds of experience." Following Eliot's cue, *modernism (ca. 1909–1950) embraces metaphysical poetry as an antidote for the disorders afflicting contemporaneous poetry. After 300 years, the metaphysical poets were again at the center of Eng. literary culture.

The New Critics of the 1930s and 1940s developed *close reading, a practice dedicated to the rigorous discovery of the formal containment of intellectual tension (Empson, Brooks; see NEW CRITICISM). This approach was well suited for metaphysical poetry, which rewards deep, ingenious, repeated readings. By emphasizing the poem as an isolated aesthetic structure, however, the New Critics sometimes elided the historical distinctiveness of this poetry. Important studies have convincingly demonstrated the links between metaphysical poetry and such phenomena as Ren. rhet., and the "new science" of the 17th c. (Tuve, Nicolson). Martz fruitfully explored the relationship between metaphysical poetry and Counter-Reformation theology, finding a model for certain metaphysical traits in the practices of formal religious meditation formulated by Ignatius Loyola. Other scholars established the importance of Reformation theology in the devel. of religious metaphysical poetry (Lewalski, Strier). And while critics focused on an imagined "school" of metaphysical poetry (Williamson, White), sometimes ignoring the distinctiveness of the various poets, studies of Herbert (Summers, Tuve, Strier, Schoenfeldt), of Crashaw (Young), of Marvell

(Friedman, Colie), and of Vaughan (Post) have established the individual accomplishments of the various metaphysical poets.

Indeed, if there is a "school" of 17th-c. poets, it would probably be comprised of the followers of Herbert, not Donne; the poetry of the 17th c. is filled with direct responses to and imitations of Herbert by Crashaw, Vaughan, and various minor poets (Stewart). Any "school of Donne," moreover, would have to include Katherine Philips, who has traditionally been left out of discussions of metaphysical poetry (although Grierson included two of her lyrics in his anthol.). Philips assimilates Donne's style as fully as any subsequent writer, and ingeniously uses Donne's imagery to articulate the passions and goals of ardent female friendship. Many predecessors and contemporaries of Donne in Europe, moreover, wrote poems in the metaphysical style, and metaphysical poetry is sometimes linked to the *baroque, famous for exaggerated aesthetic ingenuity. If the term can be applied beyond Brit. borders, then, such poets as Jean de La Ceppède in France, Constantijn Huygens and Jacobus Revius in Holland, and Francisco de Quevedo in Spain seem certainly to deserve the name *metaphysical poets*.

In England, metaphysical poetry is frequently distinguished from the work of the *Cavalier poets, a mode dedicated to the social ease and formal fluency epitomized by Ben Jonson (Miner 1971). Metaphysical poetry, by contrast, is known for rough, irregular lines and tends to flout rather than observe convention. Donne's secular poetry in particular overtly rejects the Petrarchan rhet. of idealization and distant worship (see PETRARCHISM) in favor of a celebration of the pleasures and terrors of erotic intimacy. Herbert, Crashaw, and Vaughan redirect this dramatic immediacy, along with its concomitant emotions, to God. Donne's speakers are typically in conflict with the world or with conventional poetry. A commendatory poem to the first edition of Donne's poetry (1633), written by Thomas Carew, claims Donne as the author of a major transformation of Eng. verse: "The Muses garden with Pedantique weedes / O'rspred, was purg'd by thee; / The lazie seeds / Of servile imitation throwne away; / And fresh invention planted." Carew admires Donne's deliberate refusal of affected *ornament and obsequious *convention.

The term *metaphysical poetry*, then, can help us understand the complex metaphoric and intellectual aspirations of a particular kind of tough-minded yet heartfelt poetry. It is perhaps less useful when it leads critics to value overt intellectual complexity over the hard-won simplicity of an utterance by Herbert, Vaughan, Marvell, or Philips. As one can tell from the comments of those who praise and who castigate it, metaphysical poetry is characterized by intellectual complexity and metaphorical extravagance. Interested in the tacit relations between physical and spiritual existence, metaphysical poetry is capable of developing elaborate comparisons. In one of the most justly celebrated examples, Donne likens the emotional connection of lovers separated by distance to the legs of a compass ("A Valediction: Forbidding Mourning"). In its fondness for such deliberately startling metaphors, daring rhet., and strong lines, metaphysical poetry at its best aspires to rigorous exploration of the complex continua between physical and metaphysical existence. Its sometimes rough metrics and frequently intricate metaphorics dramatize the effort and pleasure of apprehending the covert unity of apparently disparate realms of existence.

Although some scholars understandably regard the term *metaphysical poetry* as something of a misnomer (Leishman), others have argued for its continued expedience (Smith). What began as a label of inappropriate derogation, and then became a term of infelicitous evaluation, may still prove useful as a way of comprehending the remarkable accomplishment of much 17th-c. poetry.

*See* BAROQUE, CONCEPTISMO, DEVOTIONAL POETRY.

■ *Metaphysical Lyrics and Poems*, ed. H.J.C. Grierson (1921); G. Williamson, *The Donne Tradition* (1930); J. B. Leishman, *The Metaphysical Poets* (1934); H. C. White, *The Metaphysical Poets* (1936); A. Warren, *Richard Crashaw* (1939); R. Tuve, *Elizabethan and Metaphysical Imagery* (1947); Brooks; Eliot, *Essays*—"The Metaphysical Poets" and "Andrew Marvell"; R. Wallerstein, *Studies in Seventeenth-Century Poetics* (1950); R. Tuve, *A Reading of George Herbert* (1952); Empson; J. H. Summers, *George Herbert* (1954); M. Praz, *The Flaming Heart* (1958); M. H. Nicolson, *The Breaking of the Circle: Studies in the Effect of the "New Science" upon Seventeenth-Century Poetry*, 2d ed. (1960); A. Alvarez, *The School of Donne* (1961); L. Nelson Jr., *Baroque Lyric Poetry* (1961); L. L. Martz, *The Poetry of Meditation*, 2d ed. (1962); J. Bennett, *Five Metaphysical Poets*, 2d ed. (1964); H. Gardner, *The Metaphysical Poets*, 2d ed. (1967); A. Stein, *George Herbert's Lyrics* (1968); E. Miner, *The Metaphysical Mode from Donne to Cowley* (1969); R. L. Colie, *My Ecchoing Song: Andrew Marvell's Poetry of Criticism* (1970); D. Friedman, *Marvell's Pastoral Art* (1970); W. Halewood, *The Poetry of Grace* (1970); J. H. Summers, *The Heirs of Donne and Jonson* (1970); E. Miner, *The Cavalier Mode from Jonson to Cotton* (1971); B. K. Lewalski, *Protestant Poetics and the Seventeenth-Century Religious Lyric* (1979); J. Carey, *John Donne* (1981); R. V. Young, *Richard Crashaw and the Spanish Golden Age* (1982); J.F.S. Post, *Henry Vaughan* (1983); R. Strier, *Love Known: Theology and Experience in George Herbert's Poetry* (1983); S. Stewart, *George Herbert* (1986); R. Greene, *Post-Petrarchism* (1991); M. Schoenfeldt, *Prayer and Power: George Herbert and Renaissance Courtship* (1991); A. J. Smith, *Metaphysical Wit* (1992); W. Empson, *Essays on Renaissance Literature* (1993); H. Dubrow, *Echoes of Desire* (1995); J.F.S. Post, *English Lyric Poetry: The Early Seventeenth Century* (1999); R. V. Young, *Doctrine and Devotion in Seventeenth-Century Poetry* (2000); *The Cambridge Companion to Donne*, ed. A. Guibbory (2006); B. Saunders, *Desiring Donne* (2007); R. Targoff, *John Donne, Body and Soul* (2008).

M. SCHOENFELDT

**METER** (Gr. *metron*).

I. Four Categories
II. Debates About Meter
III. Functions

Meter is the *measure of sound patterning in verse, occurring when a *rhythm is repeated throughout a passage of lang. with such regularity that a base unit (such as a *foot) becomes a norm and governs poetic composition. Meter is an idealized pattern, a cultural construct understood as artistic shaping of the sound pattern of a lang. All langs. possess the makings of metrical systems. Metrical verse works the basic properties of a given lang. to a more highly regularized level. When studying meters, one focuses on their historical changes, on their cultural associations, and on describing and analyzing specific meters shaped by individual poets into metrical styles. As cultural constructs, meters are a major part of verse design. While design, like rhythm, is innate for humans desiring a sense of order, designs are made, learned, and passed on in a culture. They are open to innovation and transcend the linguistic material of which they are made (Hollander; Cushman). As a regularized organization of *sound, metrical design both uses and pulls against the speech patterning of lang. The ordinary rhythms of a lang. must rise to an unusual degree of prominence to become a meter. As a result, meter can heighten emotion and compete with sense. Aristotle noticed that a too-heightened rhythm could override sense and persuade, an effect Roman Jakobson regarded as the basis of the *poetic function (Sebeok). Julia Kristeva sees in this poetic function the argument between the rhythmic (the feminine) and the rational (the law, the masculine) dimensions of lang. (Cook).

Cultures develop particular verse trads. based on normative meters that are recognized tacitly as well formed or not, indicating that the rules are made by cultures and learned in the same way lang. competence is acquired. For this reason, meters also change; "rules" restrict what may count as metrical for a particular time and place, i.e., what linguistic situations in the verse may occur when exceptions to the norm appear in a verse meter (see individual entries for specific langs. and lit. hists., e.g., ARABIC PROSODY; CELTIC PROSODY; CHINA, POETRY OF). Measurement of verse in a given lang. may depend primarily on *quantity, *accent (stress), *syllable, tone (*pitch), or *syntax. One of these will be the dominant component of a meter, and one or more of the others may affect it, but full descriptions of the influence on metrical patterning of secondary features, such as *rhyme and sound (in all langs.; see Crystal), are still being developed by linguists.

In a stress-based lang. like Eng., two levels of stress—strong and weak—define the normative pattern that forms the idealized metrical base. Identifying the meter of a poem or part of a poem is accomplished by a process of marking stresses, called *scanning*, and yields a *scansion. In actuality, the idealized pattern is realized at three or four perceptual levels of stress. The term *scansion* has been traditionally reserved for marking the idealized pattern, but since the 1950s, theories using ling. have marked three or four levels in order to develop descriptive and explanatory "rules" (see below; see GENERATIVE METRICS, RELATIVE STRESS PRINCIPLE). Within these relative perceptual levels, the basic pattern can be perceived because the adjacent stresses remain weak or strong relative to each other (Chatman; Halle and Keyser). The actual levels of stress compose the rhythm of the passage and create sound, meaning, and expressive qualities specific to a poem. The idealized pattern gains flexibility or rigidity depending on "allowable" departures that have been built up (and continue to be built up) as a trad. of metrical composition by poets' adding new variations on the metrical base. The numbers and location of weak and strong stresses that comprise a unit define the type of meter. New meters that are devised may enter the metrical code of a literary trad. with sufficient use by poets and recognition by readers.

Four metrical categories are traditionally recognized in Eng. poetry, named for the distinguishing factor that establishes the unit of measure: accentual, accentual-syllabic (also known as accentual isosyllabic), syllabic (also known as isosyllabic), and quantitative (though this category is controversial; see below). The name of a metrical type (e.g., *ballad, *iambic *pentameter) refers variously to the poetic trad. of that meter, to an entire poem, to a section of a poem, or to the line pattern. Meter inhabits a context, as is demonstrated by lines that might be scanned as more than one meter if they occurred in different metrical contexts. E.g., this line from W. B. Yeats's "The Second Coming"—"Turning and turning in the widening gyre"—might be scanned as dactylic, except that the remainder of the poem is iambic pentameter. But the line is a quite traditional iambic pentameter, engaging an initial strong onset (*Turn*-), a strong fourth syllable, a strong (relative to the surrounding syllables) sixth syllable (*in*), and an elided weak stress (-*ening*) on the ninth syllable, which gives the line an extrametrical eleventh syllable that is weak.

The concept of measuring verse into units, called feet, and units into lines with a specified number of feet is an analytic one, originally imposed by the Greeks on poetic compositions as a way of describing the disciplining of rhythmic repetition into lines of verse when verse was written down. (Gr. prosodists were divided between the *rhythmikoi*, who measured by rhythm, as in music, and the *metrikoi*, who measured by foot.) Measuring meter in feet is known as the classical approach to meter; it was imported into Eng. during the Ren. and has prevailed as a guide to verse composition and prosodic study as influenced by Romance verse. Other approaches have been developed in the 20th c., thanks to mod. ling., scientific methods and goals of investigation, and the explosion of nonmetrical poetry. The most important of these have been systems grounded in generative metrics, linguistic

theories of the sound patterning of the Eng. phrase, and the iambic-only theory of Eng. meter. While the cl. approach is the least adequate for describing and explaining the linguistic basis of metrical occurrence and function, it is the one used in common parlance, by the majority of poets, critics, and teachers.

Although actual sound can be measured with instruments, what counts in meter, as in all *prosody, is the perception of sound pattern. Sound in poetry has physical, mental, and psychological importance. It is heard and trans. by the brain into rhythm and meaning. It is felt as vibration in the areas that produce sound, from the chest up to the mouth and nasal cavity. The psychological recognition and importance of rhythmic repetition are probably as old as human beings, a physical order felt, heard, and understood in such universal experiences as the heartbeat, walking, breathing, dance, and ritual performances, some to music and some not (Hollander, Tsur). Poets throughout hist. have asserted that they write to the paces of these rhythmic repetitions. In most meters, one measuring feature must be principal, but others may exert some constraint. The name of the unit and the number of units per line are the characteristic ways of defining metrical type.

## I. Four Categories.

**A.** *Accentual Meter* is the oldest meter in Eng., beginning with Anglo-Saxon verse; continuing into the devel. of the ballad across Great Britain, northern Europe, and Russia; and regaining prominence in the 19th and 20th cs. (see ACCENTUAL VERSE). In accentual meter, each accent (or *stress*) is felt as a strong pulse or *beat. Lines of verse typically repeat a set number of beats, but counting beats alone is not sufficient to make patterning felt with the regularity of meter, since accents are distributed over speech and prose as well. OE strong-stress meter is organized as half-lines, with two beats per half-line (*hemistich) on either side of a strong *caesura and various patterns of *alliteration governing the stresses. Over the course of the 20th c., theorists have attempted to describe OE meter, a difficult task since the nature of the Anglo-Saxon sound system must be understood from existing verse itself. Anglo-Saxon is not amenable to the cl. approach, so other systems have been developed to describe and explain the meter (see ENGLISH PROSODY, GERMANIC PROSODY). Anglo-Saxon strong-stress meter is not possible in mod. Eng. because its prosody does not have the structural patterning of the older lang. Nevertheless, poets since the Ren. have taken the four-beat alliterative characteristics of the form for verse cohesion, disregarding the other metrical restrictions. The Alliterative Revival in the late 19th and early 20th cs. saw many poets attempting alliterative accentual meter. G. M. Hopkins was inspired to write a strong accentual line with frequent alliteration, which he called *sprung rhythm. Poets such as Robert Bridges, Ezra Pound, T. S. Eliot, Wallace Stevens, W. H. Auden, Richard Wilbur, Robert Pinsky, and Seamus Heaney composed poems on the model and, on occasion, incorporated allusive, alliterative four-stress lines in free verse accentual-syllabic poems (see ALLITERATION).

The most common type of accentual poetry in Eng. is *ballad meter. The form appears to have developed from the strong-stress Anglo-Saxon meter and, in its oldest forms before the meter also developed accentual-syllabic regularity, is characterized by number of accents per line with a mid-line caesura and a variable number of syllables around accented syllables. In lines one and three of a ballad stanza, there are four stresses, two and two, on each side of a midline caesura. Lines two and four bear three stresses or, alternatively, pairings of two and two. Some argue that the number of syllables bearing weak stress and accompanying each strongly stressed syllable is restricted by a durational aspect. This restriction is likely due to musical bar-time—what can be sung or said within an isochronic perception of time (see Lehiste; ISOCHRONISM OR ISOCHRONY)—as the ballad developed as an oral form composed to music. Ballad meter is thus not a pure accentual meter for metrists who consider the pure form to be a measuring of accents only.

A pure accentual meter is rare since some regularity must be built up in order for the rhythm to be experienced as recurring with a high measure of regularity; however, the expectation trained into the ear by cultural codes for poetry may be expanded, as it has been in contemp. verse, which makes up for cohesion lost in metrical patterning with qualitative sound patterning. The five-beat line in the work of some poets (e.g., Stanley Plumly) is exemplary: positioning and grouping of units are not regular; only a norm of accents per line is. But there is leeway; some lines may bear four, six, or seven or even more beats. *Consonance and *assonance are relied on for repetition of sound. This style of metrical practice results in a "loose" accentual verse, analogous to the loose style of iambic pentameter; other critics regard this accentual style as a type of *free verse, since it only recalls, but is freed from, the accentual-syllabic constraints of traditional meters. The ten-beat line developed by C. K. Williams is another such meter: it can be viewed as a ten-beat accentual, a loose double iambic pentameter, or a free verse composition.

**B.** *Syllabic Meter* is defined by the number of syllables per line (see SYLLABIC VERSE). Simple or "pure" syllabism constitutes the basic meter of, e.g., Japanese poetry and Hungarian folk poetry. At various moments in their respective literary histories, it has also governed Polish poetry (as well as the Rus. verse based on Polish models), Slovak poetry, and Mordvinian folk songs. Complex or mixed syllabism, which combines syllabic patterning with some other obligatory linguistic feature, appears, for example, in Chinese poetry, which combines syllabism with tonal patterns, and Welsh poetry, which combines it with intricate rhyming. Sitting between these two categories, Fr. poetry presents an interesting borderline case: though usually considered syllabic, like Japanese, Fr. poetry depends heavily on rhyme to strengthen its syllabic frame in a way that Japanese poetry does not, although occasional alliteration, assonance, and consonance certainly enrich the latter. It. and Sp. versification are syllabic in their own complex ways, with a role for stress in determining the abstract pattern of the line—in general, stressed syllables must occupy certain positions—as well as rules governing the computation of syllables within and between words (see ELISION, HIATUS, DIAERESIS, SYNAERESIS); all of these factors figure in reckoning for metrical purposes the number of syllables in the line. In Eng., there is no traditional form that uses pure syllabic meter because in Eng. and other Germanic langs., accentual contour overrides the perception of syllable count. The mora-timed Japanese haiku (see HAIKAI) has been adapted to Eng., as three lines in a pattern of five, seven, and five syllables of any stress level; but what is heard foremost in Eng. are stresses, not syllables.

The limited perceptibility of the syllable in the inevitable presence of accents, however, does not mean that poets writing in Eng. do not use syllabic count as a basis for verse composition. A poet may decide to use the syllable as the compositional unit, establishing a certain number of syllables per line–either all lines having the same number of syllables or a pattern of syllables of different count for each stanza that may be quite idiosyncratic and different for each poem, such as the poems for which Marianne Moore is best known. Moore read her poems across line ends, without pause; on her printed copies, she marked the accents. Well-crafted syllabic verse may achieve a high degree of cohesion from repetition of syllable number and pattern, qualitative sound patterning, and spatial organization. As in Moore's poems, artful use of shape and space on the page, combined with repetition of phones, creates wonderful dramatic, semantic, emotional, and iconic effects (see VISUAL POETRY). On the one hand, by itself syllabic meter in poetry in a stress-based lang. is a weak device for cohesion, being aurally imperceptible or nearly so; the verse will sound rhythmic at best. On the other hand, syllabic patterning can make for strong cohesion in visual form. While some theorists maintain there can be no syllabic meter in Eng. (R. Wallace in Baker), others maintain that meter merely means measure, and the syllable-counting is one way of measuring a line, perceptible or not (Gioia in Baker). The debate about syllabic meter in Eng. turns on how meter is defined—as compositional or perceptual.

**C.** *Accentual-Syllabic Meter* is the most common by far in mod. Eng. poetry because of its synthetic devel. from Germanic and Romance langs. and poetries (see ACCENTUAL-SYLLABIC VERSE). The meter shares the structuring principles of syllabic meter and accentual meter, patterning a set number of strong and weak syllables in an idealized base. Thus, e.g., according to a cl. description, a line of iambic pentameter has five *iambs (weak/strong, weak/strong, weak/strong, weak/strong, weak/strong). Iambic pentameter is the most common Eng. meter because of the flexibility with which it can be worked for rhythmic variety. The meter began as a synthesis when med. Eng. poets adapted Fr. verse forms to the accentual system of Eng. and to established Eng. verse forms. Russom's description of Anglo-Saxon metrics suggests that Chaucer may at least in part, have been writing OE metrical patterns to a syllabic base count, as he employed a ten-syllable line with stresses that follow the romance rule of alternating stress (see Halle and Keyser; Chomsky and Halle; Russom). Although iambic pentameter has a long trad., the meter cannot be said to have been in Chaucer's time or Thomas Wyatt's or John Milton's or Alexander Pope's what it has become today. To make definition and description of the meter even more complex, what poets and critics count as "acceptable" variations on the idealized pentameter pattern is not constant, even among those within a literary period. Disagreement abounds, as it did in the Ren. with *Tottel's Miscellany* (1557), as to whether some verse is iambic pentameter if it strays too far from the idealized base. In descriptive terms, though not always in prescriptive, iambic pentameter is regarded as occurring along a range, with *strict* at one end, where the stresses fall mostly on the stressed positions of the idealized pattern, and *loose* at the other end, allowing more leeway in stress placement and in the numbers of unstressed syllables between stresses. In terms of the meter's devel., describing the line's idealized meter as five feet of iambs may be inaccurate: as Marina Tarlinskaja's statistical analysis on a large corpus of Shakespeare's verse drama shows, only the last two "feet"—the final seventh through tenth syllables—consistently take the idealized pattern of a string of weak-strong units. According to her data, the first syllable is stressed in over 42 percent of Shakespeare's lines. The cl. approach to meter calls this stressed onset a *trochaic substitution* (see SUBSTITUTION). While this may be a convenient term, the concept is inconsistent with the reality of how the meter developed or was thought of by early versifiers, since cl. scansion was imported from Lat. after iambic pentameter came into existence. What this means is that versifiers did not write by "rules" devised in the cl. poetry; rather the "rules" were a later attempt begun in the mid-Ren. to regulate the verse meter by limiting variation. The restriction on numbers of syllables per line and positions allowable for stressed syllables encouraged a stricter metrical practice, and by the 18th c., the strictest form of the meter was being written, exemplified with the greatest flexibility in the verse practice of Pope. In the early 20th c., the meter achieved its loosest form, as developed and exemplified in the loose meter used in Robert Frost's poems to sound like conversation.

D. *Quantitative Meter* measures syllabic length or duration and is the basis of ancient Gr. and Lat. prosody (see CLASSICAL PROSODY, QUANTITY). In the Ren., poets experimented with quantitative meter in imitation of cl. models, but these experiments do not sound metrical to Eng. ears (see CLASSICAL METERS IN MODERN LANGUAGES). No true quantitative meter is possible in Eng. because of its accent-based system; the Romance

langs. exhibit an alternating rhythm, like mod. Eng., but rhythm based on duration, not the relative pitch-height that is the chief component of Eng. stress.

**II. Debates About Meter.** Disagreements over meter tend to be contentious and entrenched, pitting the cl. approach against mod. ling., and linguists themselves divide over basic issues such as what is the motivation for prominence assignment; whether meter involves only measurable sound features of the foot or whether meter cannot be separated from the rhythmic influence of higher level systems and nontemporal sound structures; whether musical theory applies to meter; whether actual readers' perceptions are relevant to meter; and whether a universal theory of meter is possible (see LINGUISTICS AND POETICS).

At the opposite extreme from the cl. approach are theories that admit only one type of meter in Eng. Some theorists have asserted that meter in Eng. is trochaic, citing the pronunciations of Germanic words and compounds, which stress the onset syllable, whereas others argue that Eng. is iambic, with line onset stresses adjusted to iambs by postulating a silent uptake before the stressed onset (Wallace and essays on this debate in Baker). Latinate words, by contrast, prefer an iambic rhythm, with the two heritages mixing to comprise the two basic meters, as well as the variety seen in iambic pentameter. In the iambic-only view, *anapests are elided iambs, *dactyls are elided trochees, and *spondees are iambs as their relative stress assignments show. Debates over these issues indicate that meter in mod. Eng. combines accentual and syllabic features. From the oldest existing poetry in Eng. to mod. free verse, units are built of stressed syllables with a varying *but always limited* number of relatively weaker syllables surrounding them. This character is perhaps inevitable given the alternating stress pattern of Eng. and the regularity of repetition that makes for perception of meter.

**III. Functions.** Meter signals *genre, elicits the pleasures of musicality in expectation and surprise, imitates meaning in the content (see ICONICITY, MIMESIS), contributes to *tone (e.g., ironic, satiric, oracular, conversational), and bears social and cultural meanings. The first three of these functions were much studied by *New Criticism and *structuralism (essays in Sebeok and in Chatman and Levin). The last two of these functions have been most neglected despite their analytic potential with respect to critical and cultural studies (Hurley). Because the definitions and limits of meters are preferences of a group or a time, what is called a meter can change, and the theories and functions of meter will also change over time.

■ Saintsbury, *Prosody*; Sebeok; Chatman; M. Halle and S. Keyser, "Chaucer and the Study of Prosody," *CE* 28 (1966): 187–219; Chomsky and Halle; Wimsatt; *Essays on the Language of Literature*, ed. S. Chatman and S. Levin (1975)—historical; P. Kiparsky, "Stress, Syntax, and Meter," *Lang* 51 (1975): 576–616; M.A.K. Halliday, *Halliday: System and Function in Language*, ed. G. Kress (1976); I. Lehiste, "Isochrony Reconsidered," *JPhon* 5 (1977): 253–63; Attridge, *Rhythms*; C. Hollis, *Language and Style in "Leaves of Grass"* (1983); S. Cushman, *William Carlos Williams and the Meanings of Measure* (1985); P. Kiparsky, "On Theory and Interpretation," Fabb et al.; G. Russom, *Old English Meter and Linguistic Theory* (1987); M. Tarlinskaja, *Shakespeare's Verse* (1987); Hollander; P. Kiparsky and G. Youmans, *Rhythm and Meter* (1989); T. Steele, *Missing Measures: Modern Poetry and the Revolt against Meter* (1990); R. Tsur, *Toward a Theory of Cognitive Poetics* (1992); C. Hartman, *English Metrics: A Hypertext Tutorial and Reference* (1995); *English Historical Metrics*, ed. J. Anderson and C. McCully (1996); *Meter in English: A Critical Engagement*, ed. D. Baker (1996); C. Hasty, *Meter as Rhythm* (1997); D. Crystal, *Language and Play* (1998); R. Pinsky, *The Sounds of Poetry* (1998); J. Wimsatt, "Alliteration and Hopkins' Sprung Rhythm," *PoT* 19 (1998); T. Steele, *All the Fun's in How You Say a Thing* (1999); V. Shemtov, "Metrical Hybridization: Prosodic Ambiguities as a Form of Social Dialogue," *PoT* 22, no. 1 (2001): 165–87; Carper and Attridge; M. Russett, "Meter, Identity, Voice: Untranslating 'Christabel'," *SEL* 43, no. 4 (2003): 773–97; J. Cook, *Poetry in Theory* (2004); Y. Moriya, "Alliteration versus Natural Speech Rhythm in Determining the Meter of ME Alliterative Verse," *English Studies* 85 (2004); M. Hurley, "The Pragmatics of Prosody," *Style* 41, no. 1 (2007): 46–65.

R. Winslow

**METONYMY** (Gr., "change of name"; Lat. *denominatio*). A trope in which one expression is substituted for another on the basis of some material, causal, or conceptual relation. Quintilian lists the kinds traditionally distinguished: container for thing contained ("I'll have a glass"); agent for act, product, or object possessed ("reading Wordsworth"); cause for effect; time or place for their characteristics or products ("a bloody decade," "I'll have Burgundy"); associated object for its possessor or user ("the crown" for the king). Other kinds, previously considered *synecdoche, are now often included in metonymy: parts of the body for states of consciousness associated with them (head and heart for thought and feeling), material for object made of it (ivories for piano keys), and attributes or abstract features for concrete entities.

Because metonymy involves some literal or referential connection between *tenor and vehicle, it is often contrasted with *metaphor, in which no such relationship exists. When the effect of metonymy is to create a sense of vividness or particularity—as in Thomas Gray's "drowsy tinklings" of sheep (the sound of their bells) or John Keats's "beaker full of the warm South"—the figure is often treated as an instance of *imagery. But the metonymies "drowsy tinklings" and "South" are not concrete images. Metonymic reference can evoke entire realms of meaning concisely, as in Ezra Pound's evocation of journalism and religion: "We have the press for wafer." W. H. Auden's "the clever *hopes expire* / Of a *low* dishonest *decade*" shows that a clear surface meaning can

arise from metonymic associations of cause, attribute, and effect that are far from simple. Conversely, metonymy can create riddles, as in Dylan Thomas's "Altarwise by owl-light," which suggests facing east in the dark.

Ruwet points out that some metonymies result from verbal deletions that reduce redundancy. "A glass of Burgundy wine" becomes "a glass of Burgundy" or simply "Burgundy" or "a glass" when the sentence or context implies the rest. In "I just read [a novel by] Balzac," the phrase in brackets can be deleted because the context conveys its sense. Corpus-based studies of figurative lang. show that metonymy is often part of a ling. "collocation" in which several words always appear together. The phrase "provide [name of a country] with" produces a country-for-its-people metonymy, whereas "in [country]" is always interpreted literally. The word "heart," when preceded by a quantifier (some, few, many, all), is almost always metonymic (Hilpert).

Attempts to produce a definition of metonymy that would show what generic features its different types have in common have been part of the larger project of deriving a systematic rationale underlying *tropes. The meaning assigned to metonymy in such cases is determined by the number of tropes identified and the categorical features used to define them (ling., logical, semiotic, and/or psychological). Peter Ramus, Giambattista Vico, and their mod. followers hold that there are four basic tropes, the other three being metaphor, synecdoche, and *irony. Bloom retains six; Jakobson treats two, metonymy and metaphor. The meaning of metonymy expands as the number of tropes decreases. Among mod. adherents of fourfold classification, Burke would limit metonymy to "reduction" (incorporeal and corporeal); White defines it as part-whole reduction; Bloom treats it as a change from full to empty. In these three definitions, metonymy is not reversible: to substitute incorporeal for corporeal or empty for full would be another trope (synecdoche, for Burke and Bloom). These critics use the names of the tropes figuratively, applying them to passages or to entire texts.

In practice, it is often difficult to distinguish metonymy from the basic forms of synecdoche (part for whole, genus for species, or the reverse). Some hold that synecdoche entails a "one-many" substitution, or, in logical terms, a change of extension, whereas metonymy is a one-for-one replacement involving a change of intension (Henry). Rejecting that proposal, many critics use the term *metonymy* for both.

The opposition of metonymy to metaphor, treating these as the primary tropes, originated in Fr. *structuralism and *Russian formalism. Saussure held that there are two sorts of relationships between words: linear (syntagmatic) connections when they are used and associative (paradigmatic) connections of meaning in our minds. The Fr. psychologist Rondet referred to the linear connections as "contiguity," which sometimes evince metonymy. Paradigmatic changes, resulting from conceptual resemblance or similarity, were in his view metaphoric (Blank). Eichenbaum held that metaphor operates at a "supra-linguistic" level, that of the idea: a word is pulled from its semantic field to superimpose a second level of meaning on the literal level. Metonymy, he said, is a displacement, or lateral semantic shift, that lends words new meanings without leaving the literal plane. In "Marginal Notes on the Prose of the Poet Pasternak" (1935), Jakobson extended the dichotomy, suggesting that frequent use of metaphor unites the poet's mythology and being, separated from the world. Poets who prefer metonymy, on the other hand, project their being on an outer reality that their emotion and perception displace from the normal. The shifting, sequential character of metonymy, he said, was more common in prose than in poetry. Like Eichenbaum, Jakobson associated metaphor with poetry and metonymy with prose (Lodge).

Reworking the distinction in "Two Aspects of Language and Two Types of Aphasic Disturbances" (1956), Jakobson described metaphor as a metalinguistic operation—roughly speaking, a process through which an idea or theme is actualized in words. Metonymy, he said, was a change that operated on the hierarchy of ling. units, either affecting their order or substituting part of a word's meaning, or one associated with it, for the word itself. Both tropes can result from substitution of one word for another or from combination (the succession of words on the syntagmatic axis—see EQUIVALENCE). In metaphor, e.g., a single word can be substituted for another, or the two can be successive ("A is B"). A series of metaphors may point toward a single theme, as in Shakespeare's sonnet that successively likens old age to autumn, sunset, and a dying fire. Metonymy does not produce a metalinguistic idea unifying the chain. Jakobson held that these two tropes could be used to classify mental disorders (e.g., aphasia), literary movements (romanticism and symbolism being based on metaphor, realism on metonymy), styles in painting and cinematography, operations of the unconscious (Sigmund Freud's "identification and symbolism" being metaphor, whereas "displacement" and "condensation" are metonymy), and cultural practices (such as the two types of magic identified by J. G. Frazer—one based on similarity, the other on contiguity). Adapting Jakobson's taxonomy to his own psychoanalytic theory, Lacan treated discourse as a continuous metonymy, displaced from the real, in which metaphoric, unconscious signifiers sometimes appear (Ruegg, Vergote).

Attempts to revise or simplify the metonymy-metaphor opposition as conceived by Jakobson and Lacan have taken several forms. Henry defines metonymy as the result of a psychological focus that substitutes the name of one of a word's semantic elements (semes) for the word itself. Metaphor, in his view, is a combination of two metonymies. Le Guern argues that the "contiguity" of Jakobson's metonymy involves reference to reality, whereas metaphor is the product of a purely ling. or conceptual operation. De Man pushes this difference further, seeing metonymy not only as referential but as contingent or accidental, in opposition to the pull toward unification of essences that underlies most uses of metaphor. Bredin agrees that metonymy refers to the world and sees its "extrinsic relations" as "a kind of ontological cement holding the world together,"

not as contingencies. Metaphor is also referential in his view, both figures being opposed to the "structural" or intralinguistic relations underlying synecdoche.

The reliance of metonymy on reference to experience may account for the difficulty theorists have in defining it. To say that it depends on contiguity or the transfer of features in a single domain, scheme, or model is to admit metaphorically that it cannot be delimited. Traditional sources list 23 types of metonymy (Peirsman and Geeraerts); Radden and Kövecses identify 49. The inadequacy of referential, pragmatic, and semantic definitions has led to an analysis of tropes based on the mental operations underlying their ling. expression. For conceptual-metaphor theorists, metonymical connections between physical reality and ideas support the thesis that lang. emerged from bodily experience. Physical warmth, a red face, and high blood pressure generate metonymies related to anger; hand, heart, and head signify action, feeling, and thought. In cognitive linguistics, one finds simple verbal patterns explained as intricate configurations of metonymy. "I can see your point" becomes a metonymy for "I see your point" (potential for actual). Corporations become metonymic wholes, parts of which (company, executives, workers) are activated in different statements. Metonymy gives actions and actors the names of objects (a ski; to ski; skier). The complexity of this view, inadequately represented here, becomes apparent in the anthols. listed in the bibl. The discussion of metonymy produced by cognitive linguists and conceptual-metaphor theorists dwarfs that of the preceding two millennia. The objects of analysis are commonplace expressions that may make us aware of verbal intricacies but not of interesting variations. Poetry shares with everyday conversation a creative production of metonymy that sometimes attracts scholarly attention (Nerlich and Clarke).

Those who seek a logic underlying metonymy and other tropes are forced to redefine them, shifting some traditional meanings to other tropes and positing new conceptual entities that include the features that remain. In so doing, they often seek an explanation of tropes as rule-governed transformations of a posited conceptual literalism. The theoretical clarity thus obtained results from attempting to make the terminology of rhet. and poetics useful for philosophy, ling., and cognitive science.

*See* FIGURATION, TROPE.

■ **Primary Texts:** L. Roudet, "Sur la classification psychologique des changements sémantiques," *Journal de psychologie* 18 (1921); B. Eichenbaum, *Anna Akhmatova* (1923); K. Burke, *A Grammar of Motives* ([1945] 1969); Jakobson: v. 2 for "Two Aspects of Language" and v. 5 for essay on Pasternak (in Ger.); J. Lacan, *Écrits,* trans. B. Fink ([1966] 2006); A. Henry, *Métonymie et métaphore* (1971); M. Le Guern, *Sémantique de la métaphore et de la métonymie* (1973); H. White, *Metahistory* (1973); F. de Saussure, *Course in General Linguistics*, ed. C. Bally and A. Sechehaye, trans. W. Baskin (1974); H. Bloom, *A Map of Misreading* (1975); N. Ruwet, "Synecdoches et métonymies," *Poétique* 6 (1975); H. Bloom, *Wallace Stevens* (1977); D. Lodge, *The Modes of Modern Writing*

(1977); P. Ricoeur, *The Rule of Metaphor*, trans. R. Cz-
erny (1977); P. de Man, *Allegories of Reading* (1979); M.
Ruegg, "Metaphor and Metonymy," *Glyph* 6 (1979); G.
Lakoff and M. Johnson, *Metaphors We Live By* (1980);
J. Culler, *The Pursuit of Signs* (1981); G. Genette, *Fig-
ures of Literary Discourse*, trans. A. Sheridan (1982); U.
Eco, *Semiotics and the Philosophy of Language* (1984);
R. Jakobson, *Language in Literature*, ed. K. Pomorska
(1987); M. Hilpert, "Keeping an Eye on the Data," in
*Corpus-based Approaches to Metaphor and Metonymy*,
ed. A. Stefanowitsch and S. Gries (2006).
■ **Criticism:** A. Vergote, "From Freud's 'Other Scene'
to Lacan's 'Other,'" *Interpreting Lacan*, ed. J. Smith and
W. Kerrigan (1983); H. Bredin, "Metonymy," *PoT* 5
(1984); W. Bohn, "Jakobson's Theory of Metaphor
and Metonymy, An Annotated Bibliography," *Style* 18
(1984); J. Hedley, *Powers in Verse* (1988); Lausberg;
G. Radden and Z. Kövecses, "Towards a Theory of
Metonymy," in *Metonymy in Language and Thought*,
ed. K.-U. Panther and G. Radden (1999); A. Blank,
"Co-presence and Succession," in *Metaphor and Me-
tonymy at the Crossroads*, ed. A. Barcelona (2000);
B. Nerlich and D. Clarke, "Ambiguities We Live By,"
*Journal of Pragmatics* 33 (2001); A. Barcelona, "Clarify-
ing and Applying the Notions of Metaphor and Me-
tonymy within Cognitive Linguistics," *Metaphor and
Metonymy in Comparison and Contrast*, ed. R. Dirven
and R. Pürings (2002); *Metonymy and Pragmatic Infer-
encing*, ed. K.-U. Panther and L. Thornburg (2003);
A. Al-Sharafi, *Textual Metonymy* (2004); G. Steen,
"Metonymy Goes Cognitive-Linguistic," *Style* 39
(2005); Y. Peirsman and D. Geeraerts, "Metonymy as a
Prototypical Category," *Cognitive Linguistics* 17 (2006);
K. Allan, *Metaphor and Metonymy* (2008).

W. MARTIN

**METRICI AND RHYTHMICI** (Gr. *metrikoi*, "students
of metrics," *rhythmikoi*, "musical theorists"). Among
the ancient Greeks, there were two schools of metri-
cal theorists. The *metrici* were primarily grammarians;
they held that only long and short syllables need be
considered in *scansion and that a long syllable was
always twice the length of a short; actual variations
were ignored. The chief exemplar is Hephaestion
(2d c. CE), whose *Enchiridion*, originally in 48 books,
has survived in a one-book abridgment. In opposi-
tion to this group, the *rhythmici*, chiefly the musical
theorist Aristoxenus of Tarentum (pupil of Aristotle, fl.
4th c. BCE; see Westphal, Pearson), viewed poetry as
allied to music, maintaining that long syllables differ
greatly from one another in *quantity and that even
short syllables may differ in some degree, thus demand-
ing more complicated methods of analysis.

Certainly, much early Gr. poetry was sung to the
accompaniment of flutes or pipes (see MELIC POETRY),
as were the songs in Gr. drama, although there was
strictly recited verse such as *monody and the dialogic
portions of drama were metrical. At issue among the
theorists is not the question of performance mode but
the more fundamental issue of whether meter is in on-
tological terms a structural phenomenon or a temporal

one: essentially, metrici count the occurrence of events,
while rhythmici also insist on taking account of the
timing of those events. But on the extant evidence,
we ought not overstate the clarity or depth of ancient
theory: the metrici are mechanistic and oversimple, the
rhythmici extremely difficult.

In fact, however, this plane of cleavage between
competing theories of the nature of verse extends
through the hist. of Western *prosody up to the pres-
ent. The musical-rhythmical view is carried into the
Middle Ages by Augustine (*De musica*, ca. 389 CE); later
it is transformed into claims that quantitative verse
could be written in the Eur. vernaculars (see CLASSI-
CAL METERS IN MODERN LANGUAGES)—a vestige of
the lingering authority of Lat., which persisted until
the emergence of cl. philology in the 19th c.; and in
mod. times, it is revived in the "musical" theories of
prosody of Joshua Steele (18th c.), Sidney Lanier
(19th c.), Andreas Heusler and John C. Pope (20th c.,
for Ger. and OE), and a host of epigones, as well as in
other temporal theories not strictly musical (e.g.,
T. S. Omond, G. R. Stewart, Derek Attridge)—for
schema, see Brogan 142. Allied are those who deny that
mod. verse is metrical at all, such as G. F. Nott (1815)
and J. G. Southworth (1954). By contrast, the metrici
include Aristotle, the Lat. grammarians (texts collected
in Keil, v. 6), Bede, Philip Sidney, Samuel Daniel, Wil-
liam Mitford, Thomas Tyrwhitt, Edwin Guest, Jakob
Schipper, J. B. Mayor, and most mod. prosodists such
as W. K. Wimsatt and G. T. Wright.
■ R. Westphal, *Die Fragmente und Lehrsätze der
griechischen Rhythmiker* (1861); and "Die Tradition
der alten Metriker," *Philologus* 20 (1863); *Scriptores
metrici graeci*, ed. R. Westphal, 2 v. (1866); Keil;
J. Hadley, "Greek Rhythm and Metre," *Essays Philo-
logical and Critical* (1873); *Aristoxenos von Tarent: Melik
und Rhythmik*, ed. R. Westphal, 2 v. (1883–93)—with
commentary; T. D. Goodell, *Chapters on Greek Metric*
(1901); C. Williams, *The Aristoxenian Theory of Musical
Rhythm* (1911); Wilamowitz, pt. 1, ch. 3; H.D.F. Kitto,
"Rhythm, Metre, and Black Magic," *Classical Review*
56 (1942); Brogan; West; Aristoxenus, *Elementa Rhyth-
mica*, ed. L. Pearson (1990).

T.V.F. BROGAN

**METRON** (pl. metra). In cl. Gr. and Lat. prosody,
a unit of measurement in the metrical analysis of a
*period that is attested as early as Herodotus. Metra
are recurring and equivalent units of from three to six
long and short syllables. Verse forms that can be ana-
lyzed in terms of metra are said to be organized *kata
metron*, i.e., in *measure; such verse incl. stichic forms
such as the *iambic *trimeter and *dactylic *hexam-
eter (recitation meters); verse that is measured by cola
(see COLON), by contrast, are said to be measured *ou
kata metron* (see AEOLIC). The ancient grammarians
and metrists also analyzed metrical units in terms of
feet. In some Gr. meters—e.g., dactylic and *ionic—
a metron is equivalent to a foot, while in others—
e.g., iambic, *trochaic, *anapestic—it is equivalent
to two feet (hence, the older term dipody). Thus the

dactylic hexameter has six feet, but the iambic trimeter has three metra (scanned x – ◡ – ). It is best to measure Gr. verse in iambs, trochees, and anapests in metra primarily because verse composed in these three genres always consists of an even number of feet and certain features are restricted to the second foot. In the recited verse of Lat. comedy, however, there is no distinction between the two parts of iambic or trochaic metra; hence, these meters are measured in feet (see SENARIUS, SEPTENARIUS, OCTONARIUS). When the concepts and terms of cl. prosody were revived in the Ren. for the description of mod. meters, however, these subtleties were lost; hence, it was the foot rather than the meter that became the basis for prosodic description of intra-linear metrical units.

*See* SYSTEM.

■ Wilamowitz, 103, 441 ff.; Beare, 76–77; Maas, secs. 52, 61–66; Koster, 16–17; Dale, chaps. 1–2, and *Collected Papers* (1969), chap. 4; Allen; West, 4–6, 198, 200.

J. W. HALPORN; T.V.F. BROGAN

**MEXICAN AMERICAN POETRY.** *See* CHICANA/O POETRY.

**MEXICO, POETRY OF.** A first problem: should an article on Mexican poetry consider only the lit. written after the country became independent, in 1821? Should it include colonial times or even the pre-Columbian period? Most anthols. and critical studies on the subject have elected to trace the lit. back to the indigenous past, since that trad. has survived in art and scholarship and still has an influence on present-day authors. The lit. of Mexico is always a mixture, a hybrid texture, the mul-tiracial (*mestizo*) society, with dominant Eur. influences and suppressed indigenous elements that nonetheless arise, sometimes surreptitiously. This entry, thus, envi-sions the poetry of Mexico as inclusively as possible.

As with all ancient lit., poetry in Mexico before the Sp. conquest was associated with music, dance, and rituals. Although Mesoamerican societies (in the re-gion that roughly comprehends Mexico and northern Central America) developed "books" (known as *amox-tli*), they were used mostly to record hist., genealogies, astronomical charts, divinatory tables, calendars, and religious ceremonies. Transmitted by oral trad., poetry was captured in print by Sp. priests during the colo-nial period. Even if there were many spoken langs. in Mesoamerica, most of the materials available today come from Nahuatl and Maya, the two langs. that dominated in the region. Two of the major sources on culture at the time of the conquest are Bernardino de Sahagún's *Florentine Codex* (written 1547–69, and after 1575 partially trans. into Sp., as *Historia general de las cosas de la Nueva España* (*General History of the Things of New Spain*), a major source on Aztec life and hist., in Nahuatl with illustrations; and Diego de Landa's *Rel-ación de las cosas de Yucatán* (*Yucatan before and after the Conquest,* written ca. 1566), an important reference for Mayan life and cosmogony, written in Sp. A number of

texts would become "poems" that detail the origins of life, according to Mesoamerican beliefs.

For Nahuatl poetry, the discovery at the end of the 19th c. of two mss., the *Cantares mexicanos* (*Songs of the Aztecs,* written in the 16th c.) and the *Romances de los Señores de la Nueva España* (*Ballads of the Lords of New Spain,* written 1582), was key to its later success, thanks to the work of two prominent scholars in this field: Ángel María Garibay and Miguel León Portilla. Garibay published three volumes studying and trans-lating Nahuatl poetry (from the above-mentioned sources) in the 1950s and 1960s. León-Portilla contin-ued this work, identifying 13 poets in *Trece poetas del mundo azteca* (1967; in a later ed., he adds two more). The most important poet-philosopher known from the pre-Hispanic period was Nezahualcoyotl (1402–72), also king of Texcoco in the eastern part of the Valley of Mexico. After a war against the Tepanecs of Azcapot-zalco in 1428 (in alliance with the Aztecs), Nezahual-coyotl governed Texcoco until his death. According to Martínez (1972), 36 poems can be attributed to him. A number of themes appear in the poems: the brevity or fugacity of life, the nature of poetry, philosophical disquisitions about the creator of the world, celebra-tions of flowers and spring, praise of warriors, proph-ecies, and the afterlife. Instead of dedicating poems to known Mesoamerican gods (e.g., Quetzalcoatl, Coat-licue, Huitzilopochtli), Nezahualcoyotl addressed his poems to a god with the *epithets Ipalnemoani (Giver of Life), Moyocoyatzin (Inventor of Himself), or In Tloque in Nahuaque (Lord of the Close Vicinity), argu-ably a Toltec influence pertaining to the cl. Mesoameri-can period, before the 10th c. The conceit of the world as the creation of a book of paintings (Mesoamericans wrote books using pictograms and *ideograms; see TLA-CUILOLLI) is strikingly mod. in a Borgesian way: "Like a painting, we will be erased." Nezahualcoyotl was the first major poet of Mexico.

After the conquest, Sp. institutions were established, and most known writers followed literary currents from Spain. Although a significant number of the writings, esp. in the 16th c., were chronicles of the conquest and compilations of oral indigenous lits., poetry was much more elaborate, pertaining mainly to the court. Three Sp. poets (Gutierre de Cetina, 1519–54; Eugenio de Salazar, 1530–1602; and Juan de la Cueva, 1543–1612) traveled to New Spain, bringing the techniques, styles, and worldviews that dominated poetry of the Iberian Peninsula during the 16th c. Cetina lived his last ten years in Mexico. Like Garcilaso de la Vega before him, he practiced *Petrarchism. Although his best-known poem, "Ojos claros, serenos" (Clear, Serene Eyes), may not have been written in New Spain, it is frequently quoted in anthols. for bringing Eur. poetic style to the Sp. colonies. Francisco de Terrazas (1525–1600), born in Mexico, continued in the same Petrarchan vein as those who brought it from Spain. Parallel to love son-nets in the 16th c., a common motif is the eulogy to Mexico. The jurist and colonial administrator Salazar wrote an *epideictic poem ("Descripción de la laguna") in *ottava rima* about Tenochtitlan or Mexico City, the conquerors, and the viceroyalty of New Spain. The conquistador Bernal Díaz del Castillo's *Historia verdadera de la conquista de la Nueva España* (*True History of the Conquest of New Spain*, written after 1568) includes several passages of description that belong to this motif, notably that relating Cortés's entry into Tenochtitlan in terms of a *locus amoenus*. This trend continued with Mateo Rosas de Oquendo (b. 1559?) in "Indiano volcán famoso" (Famous Indian Volcano), a *descriptive poem about Popocatepetl, a volcano near Mexico City. And it culminates with a long poem by Bernardo de Balbuena (1561–1627), "Grandeza mexicana" (The Magnificence of Mexico, 1604), where the author describes with great detail and elaborate lang. all aspects of Mexico City, incl. its vegetation, climate, and architecture, emphasizing the splendor of what he believes is one of the greatest cities in the world. With Balbuena, Mexican poetry also moves toward the *baroque under the influence of the Sp. poets Francisco de Quevedo, Lope de Vega, Luis de Góngora, and others. *Poetic contests abounded in the 17th c. in New Spain, and many poets, often clerics, wrote elaborate and sophisticated poems for ceremonies at the court or for the church. Luis de Sandoval y Zapata (1620?–71), an honored poet of the time, was, according to some critics, a key figure who was influenced by the Sp. poets. But doubtless the most important writer of this period—and perhaps the greatest baroque poet in any lang.—was the nun Sor Juana Inés de la Cruz (ca. 1648–95), a towering intellectual to whom the convent provided an institutional setting for her poetic and philosophical work. Sor Juana's greatest poetry can be found in her sonnets and in the long poem of ideas called *Primero sueño* (*First Dream*). She uses a battery of logical, poetic, and rhetorical devices (*antithesis, *parallelism, *acrostics, *alliteration, *paronomasia, *hyperbaton, *hyperbole), employs *satire and *wit, and incorporates Lat. and Nahuatl (see XENOGLOSSIA). Fully immersed in her poetic milieu, Sor Juana responded to literary challenges, wrote poems of petition, and addressed ceremonies and special occasions. Although she adapted the rhet. of the Sp. baroque, she was able subtly to alter the male perspective. E.g., in alluding to the last line of Góngora's sonnet "Mientras por competir con tu cabello" (While to compete with your hair) with the motif of *carpe diem, she reframed the preceding lines into an *ekphrasis of a portrait representing not fleeting beauty but deceit: "This that you gaze on, colorful deceit . . . is but cadaver, ashes, shadow, void." Many mod. readers, notably Octavio Paz, see in Sor Juana a poetic program that goes beyond the baroque to anticipate *modernism.

During the wars of independence (1810–21), poets participated actively in politics. A first generation of poets celebrated Mexico with "nationalistic" poems, such as Andrés Quintana Roo's (1787–1851) *ode "16 de Septiembre" (the date commemorates Independence Day in Mexico). But Quintana Roo and others were still absorbed in *neoclassical forms, and their poetry is heavily rhetorical. A little later, two subsequent

groups emerged, the Academia de Letrán and the Liceo Hidalgo. With them, *romanticism (linked to liberalism) arrived in Mexico, e.g., with the idealized version of the indigenous past, as in "La profecia de Guatimoc" (The Prophecy of Guatimoc, written 1839, pub. 1851) by Ignacio Rodríguez Galván (1816–42). Although better known for his novels, the jurist and politician Ignacio Manuel Altamirano (1834–93), a central figure of the 19th c., also wrote poems. An important poet of the period is Manuel Acuña (1849–73), best known for the "Nocturno (a Rosario)" and also for the melancholic tendency that ended in his suicide. The transition from romanticism to *modernismo (the Sp. Am. version of Fr. *Parnassianism and *symbolism) went through Manuel Gutiérrez Nájera (1859–95), a dandy who chronicled the city in many ways, esp. in "La duquesa Job" (Duchess Job), which mocks the lifestyle of the period. He also wrote somber poems, such as "Para entonces" (When My Time Comes). Other *modernista* poets are the highly popular Amado Nervo (1870–1919), Salvador Díaz Mirón (1853–1928), Manuel José Othón (1858–1906), and Efrén Rebolledo (1877–1929; his sonnets, under the title *Caro Victrix*, use explicit sexual imagery influenced by Charles Baudelaire).

Although Enrique González Martínez (1871–1952) wrote a sonnet in 1911 about the killing of the swan (to figure the end of *modernismo*) in favor of the owl, real poetic change in the 20th c. was introduced by Ramón López Velarde (1888–1921) and José Juan Tablada (1871–1945), both of whom started as *modernistas* but persisted to write a more critical poetry. Unlike the art of the murals or the novel, a poetry of the Mexican Revolution (1910–20) was not developed as such, perhaps because many of the prevailing poets of the time looked on angrily at the violent changes in the country. There was a popular and anonymous poetry associated with the movement, through the *corridos* or *ballads that celebrated various heroes and battles. In his first phase, Tablada had been one of the key poets of *modernismo*; his poem "Misa negra" (Black Mass) used symbolist imagery. As his work evolved, he introduced the Japanese *haiku (see RENGA) into Sp. (*Un día* [One Day], 1919; and *Jarro de flores* [A Vase of Flowers], 1921) and his poetry moved toward ideographic forms in the avant-garde style of Guillaume Apollinaire's *Calligrammes* (*Li-Po y otros poemas* [Li-Po and Other Poems], 1920). In *La feria* (The Fair, 1928), written in exile, he returned to Mexican folklore, with attention to food, drinks, and typical symbols of the country. López Velarde was called the poet of the province, for having written texts reflecting the ambience of the towns of the Mexican interior. He was also a poet of eroticism fused with humor, irony, and colloquial lang. Similar to that of the Argentine Ernesto Lugones, his poetry became more self-critical. He is also known for "La suave patria" (The Gentle Homeland, 1921), a poem that commemorates the first centenary of Mexican independence, seeking a more tender and reflective motherland after the armed struggle of the preceding decade. Even though Alfonso Reyes (1889–1959) was arguably the most important Mexican writer of the first half of the 20th c., he is known more for his essays, crit., and trans. than for his poetry (see JITANJÁFORA).

Even though they were trans. of the lit. of the Eur. *avant-garde, the poets who belong to the group called *Contemporáneos* (its name comes from the literary magazine they edited between 1928 and 1931) were reticent about excessive experimentation; for instance, *euphony and *rhythm were still important elements for them. Their poetry explores topics apart from the political and social issues of the revolution; they are more interested in intimacy, solitude, death, dreams, and love (incl., for Xavier Villaurrutia and Salvador Novo, homoeroticism). Villaurrutia (1903–50) is remembered by the nocturnes of *Nostalgia de la muerte* (*Nostalgia for Death*): reflective, insomniac texts, influenced by the dreamlike imagery of *surrealism, but without arriving at automatic writing; poems that explore the space between saying and not saying and forbidden pleasures. *Muerte sin fin* (Death without End) by José Gorostiza (1901–73) is thought to be one of the most significant poems of the 20th c. Inspired by Sor Juana's *Primero sueño*, Góngora's *Soledades*, and T. S. Eliot's *The Waste Land*, it is a philosophical poem concerning the search for intangible forms—God, time, spirit, silence—and the transformation of matter, like water, lang., plants, animals, and the body. All this metamorphosis is an expression of the death that flows as a constant in life. Very different is Carlos Pellicer (1897–1977), who explores the tropics in the Latin Am. landscape. If the poetry of Villaurrutia and Gorostiza is implosive, Pellicer's is explosive. From his first book of 1921 (contemporaneous with the debut of the young Chilean Pablo Neruda), he had already demonstrated his astonishment with nature through innovative metaphors. Salvador Novo (1904–74) is perhaps the most experimental member of the Contemporáneos group, or at least the most impudent. His humor and irony play with the icons of Mexicanness: "¿Quién quiere jugar tenis con nopales y tunas / sobre la red de los telégrafos?" (Who wants to play tennis with *nopales* and prickly pears / on the network of the telegraphs? [*XX poemas*, 1925]). Later, he will explore "sexual and moral dissent" (according to Monsiváis 1979) in *Nuevo amor* (New Love, 1933), namely, the taboo of homosexuality in the Mexico of the 1930s.

*Estridentismo* was an explicit avant-garde movement in Mexico, with *manifestos and proclamations in the style of *futurism, influenced by Sp. *ultraísmo* (see ULTRAISM). The most important poet of the group, Manuel Maples Arce (1898–1981), wrote *Urbe, Superpoema bolchevique* (Urbe: Super-Bolshevik Poem, 1924), a work that links the Mexican and the Rus. revolutions and that attempts to defy poetic conventions, concentrating on movements in the streets of Mexico City. But *estridentismo* did not have a major impact on future generations, compared to how the Contemporáneos influenced Mexican poets throughout the century.

In the following generation, there are two important poets who at first share a mistrust toward the group of Contemporáneos but eventually delineate two routes for Mexican writers: the poetry of lang. of Octavio Paz (1914–98), and the colloquial and political tones of Efraín Huerta (1914–82). In Paz's *Libertad bajo palabra* (*Freedom on Parole*, 1960) two of the tenets of surrealistic ethics, freedom and poetry, are a point of reference— liberty thanks to poetry, poetry thanks to liberty. "Piedra de sol" ("Sunstone," 1957), one of the most famous poems of the second half of the century, is circular: it ends with the same lines that begin it. The title is taken from the circular Aztec stone that reveals the cosmogony of the world. In the first part of the poem, analogy helps converge nature and love: "I go among your body as among the world . . . / I go among your eyes as I swim water . . ." But soon the poetic *persona is alone, in search of a feminine subject who eludes him. In the middle of the poem, a place and a date seem to break with poetic fluency: "Madrid, 1937." Although this line in Sp. is a perfect *hendecasyllable, the numbers cut the poem in two: it is the split of the atrocities of the war that places its mark and interrupts the harmony of the beginning. But opposed to it, a couple makes love in the middle of bombs, defying everything. For Paz, historical time is the conscience that provokes anxiety. Hence, he is constantly looking for the circular time of ancient civilizations, for the paradise of the beginning (before the expulsion from the Garden of Eden), the mystical silence in which everything is annulled to enter a sacred space, where pronouns and differences are obliterated, where the lost unity is found. "Sunstone" presupposes that love, liberty, and poetry (the famous surrealist triad) can transform our reality. Several of the poems of *Ladera Este* (*East Slope*, 1969) concentrate on coitus as a way of denying differences through the rites of Tantrism. The culmination of this poetical model is "Blanco" (1967), a poem that combines readings of Stéphane Mallarmé, the theories of silence in the music of John Cage, and the ritual practice of Tantrism brought to the space of the poem. In *Pasado en claro* (*A Draft of Shadows*, 1974), an autobiographical long poem, Paz reflects on the effects of time, the role of lang., and (by the poet's standards) a more visceral tone. His childhood is seen both as troubled and as foundational to his later obsessions. In *Árbol adentro* (*A Tree Within*, 1987), poems in dialogue with painters, and the poem of love (his constant topic) "Carta de creencia" ("Letter of Testimony"), are central to the book.

Huerta is a more political and irreverent poet who uses colloquial idioms and offers paeans and diatribes to Mexico City. Late in his career, he wrote many *poemínimos*, very short sardonic poems that use any topic to make poignant observations. Alí Chumacero (1918–2010) belongs to the same generation as Paz and Huerta. His poetry (e.g., *Palabras en reposo*, [Words at Rest], 1956) uses sophisticated lang. and metaphors, sometimes with biblical and liturgical tones, to evoke people who are lonely, such as a widower, a suicidal person, or a pilgrim.

The next generation continued Huerta's use of colloquialisms and direct discourse. Jaime Sabines (1926–

1998) became the most popular poet of Mexico. His use of profanity, blasphemy, and jargon in clear, intelligible verse, and other elements ordinarily excluded from Mexican poetry, made him a celebrated poet known for poems such as "Algo de la muerte del mayor Sabines" (Something of the Death of the Elder Sabines) and "Los amorosos" (The Lovers). His readings attracted thousands of people. Rosario Castellanos (1925–74), also from the southern state of Chiapas, belongs to the same generation, although she focuses on women's role in society. After Sor Juana, she is the first poet to raise her voice against the dominant male culture in Mexican society. Tomás Segovia (1927–2011) is known for his *erotic poetry in the surrealist vein, and for *Anagnórisis* (1967), a long poem (incl., in turn, other poems invoked through a phrase or verbal image—see CENTO) that explores the ambience of the exile from different perspectives: memory, travel, and orphanhood. Homero Aridjis (b. 1940) follows this line of continuity in relation to surrealism. Informed by his ecological activism, his poems make constant reference to nature. José Emilio Pacheco (b. 1939) is a poet of daily life who observes with acuteness and pessimism the transience and the innovations of the moment. In his denunciation of the student massacre of 1968, he composed his poems using phrases and words taken from Garibay's trans. of the indigenous voices of the conquest, arranged in such a way that they become a condemnation of the events of the present. His poetry also explores the neglect and devastation of Mexico City. Gerardo Deniz's (b. 1934) poetry is cryptic, with erudite and mundane references that escape even the most avid readers. For him, every poem is an opportunity to challenge his readers and to amuse himself, sometimes with superficial themes. If the Chilean Nicanor Parra is the transparent antipoet (see CHILE, POETRY OF), Deniz is the baroque and obscure antipoet, combining multiple registers, deliberately confusing his readers. Heir of *Dada, he puts in doubt the concept of art itself. In Gloria Gervitz's (b. 1943) *Migraciones* (*Migrations*; a long poem that has grown over the years and in new eds.), a dialogue (or *monologue?) devoted to Jewish women who migrated from Eastern Europe to Mexico serves as a reinvention of the past, a reconstruction of the loss. As with Paz, Elsa Cross (b. 1946) is interested in Eastern philosophies, particularly of India. Her poetry explores the sacred as it relates to ancient cultures. David Huerta (b. 1949) has tried several different techniques. His *Incurable* (1987) is a memorable baroque poem, which combines the long verses of the Cuban poet José Lezama Lima and poststructuralist theory. Coral Bracho (b. 1951) is perhaps the most admired poet of her generation. Her first two books, intimately associated with Gilles Deleuze and Félix Guattari's concept of *rhizome*, have had a lasting influence on many younger writers. In *Tierra nativa* (Native Land, 1980), José Luis Rivas (b. 1951) recreates the tropics and his childhood in Veracruz, using long and sophisticated lines, reminiscent of the Fr. modernist Saint-John Perse. With *Ojo de jaguar* (Jaguar's Eye, 1982), Efraín Bartolomé (b. 1950) depicts the rain forest of Chiapas, in association with Mayan mythology, in a defense of nature. Although it may be difficult to point to a general characteristic of Alberto Blanco's (b. 1951) poetry, perhaps his tendency is to see the sacred in mundane situations. Myriam Moscona (b. 1955) is a Sephardic poet who employs Judeo-Sp. Her *Negro marfil* (Black Ivory, 2000) is a cubist poem of sorts, employing space, simultaneity, multiple readings, and images that resemble illegible graffiti or encoded messages (see CUBISM). María Baranda (b. 1962) combines epic dimensions with intimate feelings. Her dialogue with Dylan Thomas (*Dylan y las ballenas* [Dylan and the Whales], 2001) was enthusiastically received by the critics.

The number of contemp. poets in Mexico is very large (some would argue as many as 1,000); a diversity of themes, techniques, and poetics has been the norm since the 1970s. But despite the range, a few generalizations about its character are possible. Most Mexican poets inherited from Paz (and also from the Contemporáneos, López Velarde, Sor Juana, and others) the rigorous control of composition, sound, and words. There has tended to be a focus on craft and balance at the expense of spontaneity, even among poets who write in the idiom of the street. Ideology, politics, sentimentality, openly expressed passion, and confessionalism tend to be avoided. The idea of balance also impedes radical experimentation. Mexico lacks the unevenness—the deliberate aim of imperfection—of a poet such as the Peruvian César Vallejo or the frantic tone of the *Beat generation such as Allen Ginsberg's *Howl*. In the first decade of the 21st c., a new trend appeared: lit., incl. poetry, in indigenous langs. Mexico is returning to its roots, but with a contemp. edge. An example would be Natalia Toledo (b. 1968), a bilingual poet from Oaxaca, who writes in Zapotec and translates her work into Sp. Some of these poems reveal a world on the brink of obliteration.

*See* COLONIAL POETICS; INDIGENOUS AMERICAS, POETRY OF THE; NEOBAROQUE; SPAIN, POETRY OF; SPANISH AMERICA, POETRY OF.

■ **Anthologies:** *Antología de la poesía mexicana moderna*, ed. J. Cuesta (1928); *Poetas novohispanos*, ed. A. Méndez Plancarte (1964); *La poesía mexicana del siglo XIX*, ed. J. E. Pacheco (1965); *Poesía en movimiento*, ed. O. Paz et al. (1966; also as *New Poetry of Mexico*, ed. and trans. M. Strand, 1970); *Trece poetas del mundo azteca*, ed. M. León Portilla (1967); *Ómnibus de poesía mexicana*, ed. G. Zaid (1971); *Antología del Modernismo, 1884–1921*, ed. J. E. Pacheco (1978); *Poesía mexicana, 1915–1979*, ed. C. Monsiváis (1979); *Asamblea de poetas jóvenes de México*, ed. G. Zaid (1980); *Palabra nueva*, ed. S. Cohen (1981); *Mouth to Mouth: Poems by Twelve Contemporary Mexican Women,* ed. F. Gander, trans. Z. Anglesey (1993); *De la vigilia fértil: Antología de poetas mexicanas contemporáneas*, ed. J. Palley (1996); *El manantial latent*, ed. E. Lumbreras and H. Bravo Varela (2002); *Reversible Monuments: Contemporary Mexican Poetry*, ed. M. de la Torre and M. Wiegers (2002); *Sin Puertas Visibles: An Anthology of Contemporary Poetry by Mexican Women*, ed. and trans. J. Hofer (2003); *Words of the True Peoples: Anthology of Contemporary Mexican Indigenous-Language Writers, ed. and trans. C. Montemayor and D. Frischmann, v. 2 (2005); *Connecting Lines: New Poetry from Mexico*, ed. L. Cortés Bargalló, trans. and ed. F. Gander (2006).

■ **Criticism and History**: See prologues from anthols. above; A. M. Garibay, *Historia de la literatura náhuatl* (1953); R. Leiva, *Imagen de la poesía mexicana contemporánea* (1957); J. L. Martínez, *Nezahualcóyotl* (1972); J. J. Blanco, *Crónica de poesía mexicana* (1977); G. Sheridan, *Los Contemporáneos ayer* (1985); F. Dauster, *The Double Strand: Five Contemporary Mexican Poets* (1987); *Lugar de encuentro: Ensayos críticos sobre poesía mexicana actual*, ed. J. Fernández and N. Klahn (1987); O. Paz, *Sor Juana, or the Traps of Faith*, trans. M. Sayers Peden (1988); V. Quitarte, *Peces del aire altísino: Poesía y poetas en México* (1993); *Los Contemporáneos en el laberinto de la crítica*, ed. O. Paz, R. Olea Franco, A. Stanton (1994); O. Paz, *Obras completas*, v. 4 (1994); A. Stanton, *Inventores de tradición: Ensayos sobre poesía mexicana moderna* (1998); A. Paredes, *Haz de palabras: Ocho poetas mexicanos recientes* (1999); C. Monsiváis, *Las tradiciones de la imagen: Notas sobre poesía mexicana* (2001); E. Escalante, *Elevación y caída del estridentismo* (2002); E. Cross, *Los dos jardines: Mística y erotismo en algunos poetas mexicanos* (2003); *Poesía mexicana reciente: Aproximaciones críticas*, ed. S. Gordon (2005).

J. SEFAMÍ

**MICROPOETRIES.** *Micropoetry* refers positively to the rawness of fragmentary, ephemeral, nonliterary, unintentional, or otherwise "unviable" poetry: *doggerel, occasional verse by amateurs, and other paraliterary detritus that achieves the poetic in its effect on the *reader, audience, or recipient. Because audiences and poetic discourses vary widely, micropoetries are intensely context-specific and often arise out of the cultural practices of subcultures or informal communities with little public acknowledgment or power. E.g., graffiti, prison poetry by nonliterary inmates (as distinct from figures such as Oscar Wilde, Osip Mandelstam, et al.), slogans, private (scrapbook or diaristic) or semiprivate (correspondence, blogs, or social network) writing, poetry written by children or their strange and charming utterances, *écriture brute* (outsider writing), thieves' cants and other argots or vernaculars, and so forth, may be considered micropoetries, as might newspaper poetry, greeting-card verse, prayers, and idiolects. Intended as a capacious rather than a narrowly specific term, the category of micropoetry widens the field of the poetic by valorizing artifacts that may be considered clumsy, awkward, and inadmissible within professional poetry circles.

Introduced in the late 1990s, the term reflects the democratization of poetry and poetry scholarship in the United States. The poetic nature of micropoetries inheres as much in the critical intervention as in the artifact itself. Micropoetry scholarship draws on the Rus. formalist principle of *ostranenie* or *defamiliarization, as an index of poetic lang. but, in accordance

with insights from Rus. sociolinguists of the 1920s and Brit. cultural studies scholars of the 1970s and 1980s, aims to broaden the nature of this effect; it is also indebted to Walter Benjamin's method of combining phenomenological observation of ling. effects with social analysis and to the anthropologist Clifford Geertz's method of "thick description" as a way of making the micropoetic artifact meaningful. Micropoetry is genealogically related to ethnomusicologist Mark Slobin's term *micromusics*, musical subcultures that fall outside conventional (cl., popular, folk, and other commercial) networks of production and distribution but enjoy a relationship of productive adjacency to these mainstreams, challenging and combining with them to create new styles and otherwise to refresh popular musical culture. Micropoetry also derives from Emilie Conrad's working concept of "micro-movements," the smallest perceptible physical movements that the mover herself can detect; the practice of isolating these micromovements and inculcating awareness of them has been instrumental in working with brain- or physically injured patients. The influences of Slobin and Conrad indicate the micropoetic object's contingency and dependence on the contexts of its production and reception. In their ubiquity, micropoetries comprise a thicket of discourse and expression—quotidian, eccentric, ephemeral—that gives rise to more polished "high art" poetry and forms its background "noise," even while that elevated poetry defines itself by repudiating micropoetries in terms of complexity, craft, or taste.

*See* CULTURAL STUDIES AND POETRY, DOGGEREL.

■ M. Damon, "Post-literary Poetry, Counterperformance, and Micropoetries," *Class Issues: Pedagogy, Cultural Studies, and the Public Sphere*, ed. A. Kumar (1997); "Poetries," spec. iss. *Iowa Journal of Cultural Studies*, 8-9, ed. M. Chasar and H. Bean (2006); D. Tiffany, *Infidel Poetics* (2009).

M. DAMON

**MIME** (Gr., "imitation"). In the cl. sense of the term, a type of drama in which players rely mainly on gestures to tell a story. Found in ancient Greece and Rome, the mime probably arose, as its name implies, from the natural impulse to imitate persons or scenes from daily life. As a literary genre, however, it developed in Sicily and southern Italy, where Sophron of Syracuse (5th c. BCE) wrote, in colloquial prose, realistic scenes that border on the gross. Subsequently, Herodas (3d c. BCE) used metrics in his *mimiambi*, which, in turn, influenced the Alexandrian poetry of Theocritus; the Lat. poets Plautus, Terence, and Horace (*Epodes, Satires*); and the Roman mime writers Decimus Laberius and Publilius Syrus (1st c. BCE), of whose works only fragments survive. Lat. actors performed mime without masks and spoke in prose. Originally comic, the mime came to be closely associated with farce, which it supplanted at the ends of tragedies. Ribaldry and burlesque were its chief ingredients and its source of great popularity. The Church waged war on the mime and its actors, so that, finally in the 5th c. CE, all who took part in it fell under a ban of excommunication. As a genre, it again became popular in the commedia dell' arte of 16th-c. Italy, whence it spread to France and England. In 19th-c. France, *L'Enfant Prodigue*, a three-act mime play, culminates the hist. of the genre.

In the mod. sense of the term, which is distinct from the cl., *mime* or *pantomime* refers to a performance that relies exclusively on gesture instead of words, though it may be accompanied by music. This form was also known to the Romans, being introduced by Pylades of Cilicia in 22 BCE, but it became a sophisticated and refined form of performance with masks, in contrast to the increasingly vulgar mime described above. A famous late literary example is the dumb show in *Hamlet*; popular pantomime was revived in the 20th c.

*See* COMEDY.

■ H. Reich, *Der Mimus* (1903); O. Crusius, *Die Mimiamben des Herondas* (1926); A. Körte, *Hellenistic Poetry* (1929); A. Nicoll, *Masks, Mimes and Miracles* (1931); W. Beare, *The Roman Stage*, 2d ed. (1955); J.D.A. Oglivy, "*Mimi, Scurrae, Histriones*: Entertainers of the Early Middle Ages," *Speculum* 38 (1963); Trypanis, ch. 10; T. Leabhart, *Modern and Post-Modern Mime* (1989); D. Mann, "The Roman Mime and Medieval Theatre," *Theatre Notebook* 46 (1992); G. S. Sumi, "Impersonating the Dead: Mimes at Roman Funerals," *AJP* 123 (2002); C. Panayotakis, "Women in the Greco-Roman Mime of the Roman Republic and the Early Empire," *Ordia prima* 5 (2006); J. E. Merceron, "Pantomines dansées et jeux de rôles mimés dans les 'pastourelles assemblées,' les monologues de jongleur et les jeux carnavalesques," *Chançon legiere a chanter*, ed. K. Fresco and W. Pfeffer (2007).

R. A. HORNSBY; T.V.F. BROGAN

# MIMESIS

  I. Beginnings
  II. Plato
  III. Aristotle
  IV. Later Greek Views
  V. Legacy

**I. Beginnings.** Gr. *mimesis* is related to the noun *mimos*, which denotes both an actor of mime (in its ancient form, a subliterary dramatic genre with spoken text) and the genre itself. Performative vividness is accordingly one stratum of the semantics of *mimesis*. The cognate verb first occurs in connection with some kind of role playing by a chorus at Homeric *Hymn to Apollo* 162–64. Other early usage connects the *mimesis* word group with various kinds of depiction and expressive evocation in song, music, dance, and visual art.

In the 5th c. BCE, a trad. of poetics started to attach itself to this terminology. In Aristophanes' *Thesmophoriazusae* the tragedian Agathon, propounding a principle of creative identification between poets and their characters, says that "the qualities we do not possess ourselves must be found by mimesis" (155–56). The context here reduces to comic parody (Agathon is composing in female dress) a model of imaginative and dramatic simulation. By this date, as subsequent

evidence confirms, mimesis was becoming embroiled in theoretical debates about the workings of poetic representation and expression. Although mimesis terms are also used of behavioral imitation and emulation, *imitation* is generally an inadequate trans. for the critical and aesthetic ideas associated with this vocabulary. From the cl. period onward, mimesis is a standard Gr. way of denoting the "second life" of poetry (and other artistic media). But the word itself does not automatically bring with it any specific suppositions about the sources or ontological status of the kinds of "life" to which poetry gives form.

**II. Plato.** The lang. of mimesis has a wide range of reference in the Platonic corpus; even the cosmos itself counts as the Creator's mimetic work of art (*Timaeus*, e.g., 39e). The most concentrated account of poetic mimesis, but with important shifts of perspective, occurs in books 2–3 and 10 of the *Republic*. At *Republic* 2.373b, Socrates treats mimesis as a broad cultural category embracing poetry, visual art, music, dance, and more besides: i.e., something like a general concept of artistic representation and *figuration. Later, however, at 3.392d, he limits the term (in a typology that has influenced mod. narratologists) to the dramatic, first-person mode of narrative discourse (*diegesis*), as opposed to the descriptive, third-person mode. Socrates maintains that the inward focus of poetic mimesis in this restricted sense engenders a corresponding intensity of experience for actors and readers (reading aloud is pertinent here), encouraging a kind of psychic multiplicity: an extension of the kind of theory parodied in Aristophanes' *Thesmophoriazusae* is visible here. This part of the *Republic* belongs within a larger framework that judges poetry principally in terms of ethical "truthfulness," while nonetheless allowing for elements of invention/fiction in narrative details (e.g., 2.382d). Neither here nor elsewhere does Plato treat poetic mimesis as standing in a simple relationship to the world.

In *Republic* book 10, Socrates returns to a broader concept of mimesis, notoriously using an analogy with mirrors to set up a provocative comparison of poetry with painting. But even the mirror *simile itself (10.596d–e) is far from straightforward. Socrates applies it to the representation of objects some of which ("everything in the sky and in Hades," 596c) are *not* accessible to actual mirrors. Elsewhere in the *Republic* (e.g., 5.472d), moreover, Socrates clearly acknowledges the existence of idealized, nonrealist painting. So the critique of poetic "appearances" and "simulacra" is principally directed at the phenomenology and ethical psychology of poetic experience, not at the literal truth or otherwise of poetry's materials. Mimesis functions here as a concept with which to analyze (and question) the ways in which poetry molds its own versions of the world. It does not in itself impose a uniform paradigm of poetic representation or expression, let alone any simple notion of imitation.

Crucial to book 10's critique is the affective process by which poetry seduces its audiences into internalizing its implicit values. At the climax of the critique,

Socrates highlights the art form tragedy (incl. Homer, "teacher" of the tragedians), whose pessimistic force poses a peculiar challenge to a positive philosophical vision of reality. "Even the best of us," he says (605c–d), "surrender" to the intense emotions of such poetry: temporarily at least, tragedy makes the soul assimilate a worldview in its response to images of irremediable suffering and annihilation. The most significant aspect of mimesis, on this account, is not its use of naturalistic surfaces but its capacity to shape and imprint a whole sensibility.

Outside the *Republic*, there are many references to poetic/artistic mimesis that bear out the complexity of Plato's reflections on the subject. *Cratylus* 432a–d, e.g., advances a conception of (visual) mimesis as having a "qualitative" rather than replicatory relationship to what it represents. The *Sophist* distinguishes between two types of mimesis, "eicastic" (reliant on objective accuracy) and "phantastic" (involving a viewer-dependent perspectivism): the implications for poetry are not developed, though there are links with parts of *Republic* 10. Finally, the *Laws* contains many thoughts on mimesis, incl. an intricate analysis of the plural criteria (truth/fidelity, benefit, pleasure, beauty) by which the success of mimetic works might be judged (2.653–71). Contrary to many mod. summaries, there is no such thing as a fixed Platonic paradigm of mimesis, whether in poetry or elsewhere, only a series of attempts to define the triangular relationship between artistic expression, reality, and the minds of readers/viewers.

**III. Aristotle.** Aristotle's treatment of mimesis picks up from Plato's but gives the concept a role within a positive anthropology of human culture, whereas Plato had tended to freight it with philosophical doubts and problems. The first chapter of the *Poetics* adopts the premise, clearly assumed as familiar, that (most forms of) poetry, music, dance, and visual art are species of mimesis. Contrary to a common misunderstanding, Aristotle never says that those arts as such "imitate nature." That phrase (better translated as "follow the principles of nature") is found at, e.g., *Physics* 2.2, 194a21, referring not to artistic representations but to the teleology of human craftsmanship in imposing form on matter.

Aristotle nowhere defines mimesis. But in *Poetics* 3, he diverges from *Republic* book 3 by using mimesis rather than "narrative discourse" as the master category within which different modes of poetic representation can be distinguished. Since Aristotle distinguishes poetry, *qua* mimesis, sharply from factual discourse such as philosophy/science (*Poetics* 1) and hist. (*Poetics* 9), his notion of mimesis has affinities with later ideas of fiction. This certainly does not mean, however, that he disconnects poetic *imagination from reality. In *Poetics* 25, he states that poets, like other mimetic artists such as painters, can depict three kinds of world: actuality ("things as they are or were"), an amalgam of culturally accepted beliefs ("what people say and think"), or an ideal ("things as they ought to be"). This might seem to give poetry practically unlimited scope. Yet Aristotle's schema, while open to the operations of creative imagi-

nation (cf. *Poetics* 17), has no room for free fantasy. It presupposes that poets produce images of experience that can be grasped (both cognitively and emotionally) with implicit reference to consistent standards of human significance.

Throughout his discussion of tragedy and epic, Aristotle equates such standards with "probability and/or necessity." That formula, however, does not entail strict adherence to quotidian reality: how could it, where heroic characters and events are concerned? But it does require compelling dramatic coherence in the causality and psychology of the action portrayed. Mimesis, therefore, does not track particular features of the world. It is an exercise of emotionally engaged imagination in picturing things that "*might* happen" (*Poetics* 9). This produces a paradox in Aristotle's position: in *Poetics* 6, he calls tragedy "(a) mimesis of life," but in chs. 7–8, he stresses that the unity of a tragic/epic plot depends on narrative conditions far more rigorous than the diffuseness of life itself. Aristotelian mimesis is an artistic process that selectively reconfigures the "raw materials" of life. As such, it possesses a quasi-philosophical value: an ability to see beyond contingent particulars to a grasp of underlying structures of meaning. *Poetics* 4, which posits a human instinct for mimesis (as manifested in children's imaginative play), regards the desire to understand as a link between poetry and philosophy. *Poetics* 9 calls poetry "more philosophical" than hist., basing this judgment on poetry's capacity to convey an awareness of "universals." Unlike philosophy itself, mimesis makes this possible not through analysis and abstraction but through vivid concentration of narrative and expressive form.

**IV. Later Greek Views.** Mimesis remained a foundational concept of Gr. poetics (and philosophy of art more generally) throughout antiquity. While it always involves interpretation of the relationship between art and life/nature, its implications and nuances vary with the presuppositions of different critics and schools of thought. Broadly speaking, ideas of mimesis were divided between emphasis on fidelity (world-reflecting truthfulness) and the prioritizing of fiction (world-simulating inventiveness).

Of the two major Hellenistic schools of philosophy, the Stoics saw good poetry (like the life of Stoic virtue itself) as standing in mimetic conformity with the rational unity of the cosmos. This meant that they typically treated poetic mimesis as a medium in which philosophical ideas could be encapsulated in narrative and dramatic form: we find this, e.g., in Strabo's reading of Homer as a protophilosopher (*Geography* 1.1–2). On this account, mimesis entails true correspondence to the divine structure of reality, even if the correspondence is sometimes taken as allegorically encoded (see ALLEGORY). For Epicureanism, by contrast, mimesis is more like a superficial reflection of all the different views of life (incl. deluded beliefs) that poets and their audiences are capable of producing. This understanding of the concept makes it easy for Epicureans to see poetry as standing in no fixed relationship to truth and, accordingly, as containing space for fiction: Philodemus, in his (now fragmentary) treatise *On Poems*, appears to have occupied such a position.

Mimesis remained not only adaptable but problematic. Plutarch, in "How the Young Man Should Study Poetry," attempts to elaborate a moderate Platonism while also admitting some Aristotelian formulations. He blocks a more radical Platonic critique by equating mimesis with *invention and contrasting it sharply with (philosophical) truth. But by retaining a canon of "likeness to the truth," he struggles to reconcile the competing demands of fiction and ethical reliability in his model of poetry. A different kind of tension emerges at Philostratus's *Life of Apollonius* 6.19 (3d c. CE), where Apollonius, speaking of images of deities, contrasts mimesis as representation of "what has been seen" with *phantasia* as representation of what the artist has *not* seen but only creatively imagined. It is exaggerated, however, to claim evidence here for an entirely antimimetic aesthetic: sect. 2.22 shows that mimesis is still a basic tenet and can indeed be extended to the imaginative processes of the *recipients* of art.

Further ambiguities in the status of mimesis arise in Neoplatonism. Proclus's commentary on Plato's *Republic* fluctuates in its understanding of the concept. But it finally equates the mimetic with all poetry that works through an anthropocentric imagination and its emotions. Higher intellectual truths, according to Proclus, require poetic symbolism and allegory—or a hermeneutic that can discover these properties beneath the mimetic surface of a text. By philosophizing Homer, but also reading Plato himself as a partly mimetic writer, Proclus shows how ancient arguments over mimesis lead to deep perplexities about the resources and uses of poetry.

**V. Legacy.** Because of the variations and debates outlined above, mimesis should count not as a unitary concept but a "family" of ideas in poetic (and aesthetic) theory. Its legacy is far more complex than often suggested. Rendered by Lat. *imitatio* and vernacular equivalents, mimetic assumptions were a source of poetic theory from Ren. humanism to 19th-c. naturalism. But behind such slogans as the "imitation of nature" lurked plural conceptions of literary representation and expression. When *romanticism reacted against neoclassical canons, it did not abandon all mimetic premises, esp. since the latter could encompass (as we have seen) forms of idealism. Even in the 20th c., modified versions of mimesis remained detectable, partly in popular expectations of "truth to life" and the like, partly in more abstract theorizing. The results can be paradoxical: Bertolt Brecht, e.g., spurns the mimesis of bourgeois "illusionism" yet develops techniques for a new type of truthful realism; Roland Barthes discards belief in veridical representation but retains a "reality effect" whose credentials seem remarkably close to mimetic image-making. Despite a waning use of the older vocabulary of mimesis, many concerns associated with it have survived tenaciously in mod. poetics.

*See* COMEDY, EPIC, IMITATION, TRAGEDY.

■ G. Sörbom, *Mimesis and Art* (1966); P. Ricoeur, "Mimesis and Representation," *Annals of Scholarship* 2 (1981); R. Lamberton, *Homer the Theologian* (1986); C. Prendergast, *The Order of Mimesis* (1986); G. Gebauer and C. Wulf, *Mimesis: Culture, Art, Society*, trans. D. Reneau (1995); F. Burwick, *Mimesis and Its Romantic Reflections* (2001); S. Halliwell, *The Aesthetics of Mimesis* (2002), and "The Theory and Practice of Narrative in Plato," *Narratology and Interpretation*, ed. J. Grethlein and A. Rengakos (2009).

S. HALLIWELL

**MINIMALISM.** The principle of intentional reduction, whether formal or semantic, with respect to the size, scale, or range of a given poetic composition. The term may refer to poems that are very short and condensed, to poems that use short lines or abbreviated stanzas, or to poems that use a severely restricted vocabulary. But minimalism is not a term used to refer to just any short poem: it is not, for instance, applied to the *haiku (see HAIKAI) or *epigram. Rather, minimalism is a late 20th-c. designation for a poetics that holds that spareness, tautness, understatement, and reduction constitute poetic authenticity. As such, minimalism is an offshoot of phenomenology (see GENEVA SCHOOL), with its trust in the principle that W. C. Williams called "no ideas but in things."

The use of the term *minimalism* to designate poetic features is quite recent, having been coined originally to define specific movements in the visual arts and in music, respectively. Wollheim's 1965 essay "Minimal Art" was probably the first to define "a class of objects" that "have a minimal art-content, in that either they are to an extreme degree undifferentiated in themselves and therefore possess very low content of any kind, or else the differentiation that they do exhibit . . . comes not from the artist but from a nonartistic source, like nature or the factory." Wollheim cites the black canvases of Ad Reinhardt and the Readymades of Marcel Duchamp, but the more common reference of the term is to the primal geometric sculptures of Donald Judd, Sol LeWitt, and Robert Morris, as well as to the abstract color-field paintings of such artists as Frank Stella, Kenneth Noland, and Ellsworth Kelly.

In music, the term *minimalism* was first used to refer to compositions that use a minimum of material, such as John Cage's *4'33"* or La Monte Young's *Composition 1960 #7*, which contains only the notes B and F# with the instructions "to be held for a long time." But since the early 1970s, minimalism specifically refers to the work of Philip Glass and related composers whose tonal works restrict progression (movement from one chord to the next) so as to explore the static devel. of sonorities.

When minimalism is transferred to poetry, it thus refers to such abbreviated lyrics as Robert Creeley's "The Box" (1967):

Three sides,
four
windows. Four
doors, three
hands.

Other poets whose minimalism is often discussed are Francis Ponge (France); Ernst Jandl (Austria); Tom Raworth, Bob Cobbing, and Ian Hamilton Finlay (Britain); and, in the U.S., Williams, the early H.D., the objectivists Louis Zukofsky and George Oppen (whom Kenner calls "the geometers of minima"), David Ignatow, Gary Snyder, James Laughlin, Clark Coolidge, Aram Saroyan, and Robert Lax. Contemp. Fr. poets like Emmanuel Hocquard, Claude Royet-Journoud, and Anne-Marie Albiach have sometimes been called "minimalists," in that their tiny, fragmentary poems are surrounded by white space on an all but bare page. But the greatest practitioner of minimalism, Samuel Beckett, was primarily a writer of prose: such "residua" as *Imagination Dead Imagine*, *Ping*, and *Fizzles* permutate a rigidly circumscribed set of words and phrases in minimal units of great tension and complexity.

*See* CONCISION, CONSTRAINT.

■ J. Cage, *Silence* (1962); R. Wollheim, "Minimal Art," *Arts Magazine* 39 (1965); *Minimal Art*, ed. G. Battcock (1968); H. Kenner, *A Homemade World* (1975); C. Gottlieb, *Beyond Modern Art* (1976); R. Kostelanetz, "An ABC of Contemporary Reading," *Esthetics Contemporary* (1978); D. H. Cope, *New Directions in Music* (1981); M. Perloff, "Preface," *Contemporary Poets*, 3d ed. (1985); E. Brater, *Beyond Minimalism* (1987); R. Creeley, *Collected Essays of Robert Creeley* (1989); B. Grumman, "Mnmlst Poetry: Unacclaimed but Flourishing," (1997); K. Alexander, "The Abstract Minimalist Poetry of Robert Lax," *Interval(l)es* 1.1 (2004); A. Saroyan, *Complete Minimal Poems* (2007).

M. PERLOFF

# MINNESANG

### I. The Later 12th Century
### II. The 13th Century

The collective designation for lyrics on themes of love (*minne*), produced in Ger.-speaking areas from the 12th through the early 14th cs., the *Minnesang* is considerably influenced by the poetry of the *troubadours and *trouvères and forms part of a Eur. trad. that spread also to Sicily, north Italy, and Spain. In the 12th c., the poets were of knightly origin, but in the 13th c., there were also professional poets of lower social status. The songs (*Minnelied*, pl. *Minnelieder*) were intended for vocal performance with instrumental accompaniment before a courtly audience, but very little music survives. There is some evidence for indigenous lyric trads. in a few anonymous poems and in some poems by named Austro-Bavarian poets probably active from ca. 1150, indicating that the woman's stanza (*Frauenstrophe*), the woman's complaint of absence, desertion, or rivals (*Frauenklage*), and the indirect exchange between lovers (*Wechsel*) are native types, depicting the woman as subordinate to or equal with the man. The poems have simple structures and are predominantly monostrophic, though occasionally two, or more rarely three, stanzas may be loosely linked. (For details of the metrical structure of these and other forms described below, see GERMANIC PROSODY.) All the poets in this group whose names are known to us, and esp. Meinloh von Sevelingen, fuse native trads. with thematic features derived from knowledge of the *Romance lyric—e.g. the lover's submission to his lady, the complaint of ill-wishers—but remain uninfluenced by Romance forms.

**I. The Later 12th Century.** From ca. 1170, the thematic and formal influence of the Romance lyric, transmitted originally through a group of Rhineland and Western poets, becomes pervasive. The dominant type of poem, the equivalent of the Romance *canso*, is the first-person reflection on love, which may be combined with *apostrophe of love or the lady. Love service is presented in feudal terms as an arduous but ennobling aspiration, addressed to a lady who is a paragon of beauty and virtue but at the same time unwilling to react graciously to the man's courtship. He is, however, staying by her side with loyalty. The lady's missing approval is compensated by the devel. of courtly virtues such as loyalty (*triuwe*), consistency (*stæte*), a modest life (*mâze*), and high spirits (*hôher muot*). Often addressed is also an only vaguely defined group representing the values of society, God, or the personification of love or courtly values. A minor variant expresses the conflict between love and crusading duty (*Kreuzlied*); usually the crusader chooses his religious duty over the lady, but there are also songs that—as love is chosen—criticize the Crusades. On the pattern of the Romance lyric, polystrophic poems and tripartite stanza forms made up of short lines (see CANSO) become the norm; new types of rhyme are introduced, pure rhyme replaces *assonance, and dactylic rhythms occur for the first time. The connection between stanzas is often loose, reflecting the original predominance of the monostrophic poem.

In the period up to 1200, precise textual and formal borrowings from Occitan and OF poets may be traced in Friedrich von Hausen, Rudolf von Fenis, Bernger von Horheim, and Ulrich von Gutenburg (Frank); thereafter, direct imitation is rendered superfluous by widespread knowledge of Romance conventions and forms. However, poets such as Albrecht von Johansdorf and Reinmar, writing in areas more remote from Romance influence, those in which the lyric is first attested, also retain certain archaic features: women's stanzas and examples of the Wechsel and of long and unrhymed lines.

**II. The 13th Century.** Ger. Minnesang is written down mainly in three collective mss., known as A, B and C. A, the so-called small Heidelberg ms. (about 1265, Alsace) contains 719 stanzas, B, the Weingarten ms. (first half of 14th c., Constance), 602 stanzas. C, the so-called large Heidelberg ms. (about 1300, Zürich), also known as the Manesse ms. because of its connection to the Manesse family in Zürich, contains 5,240 stanzas. Authorship determines the order of the mss.; for each writer, a new sequence starts. The mentioning of titles in the mss. allows the quite precise allocation of different statuses to the authors such as monarchs, members of the aristocracy, or professional poets. Because the mss. were compiled at the end of the 13th or beginning of the 14th c. in southern Germany and Switzerland, the bulk of the material preserved belongs to the 13th c. and to areas close to the places of compilation. Thus, whereas there are only some 16 to 20 poets who can be assigned to the 12th c., about 130 belong to the 13th c., mostly the latter half and, on occasion, beyond. The transmission undoubtedly gives a distorted picture of the frequency and geographical distribution of poetic production at each stage but nonetheless bears witness to the immense popularity of the Minnesang over a long period.

The most original poets belong to the turn of the 12th c., when established trads. allowed scope for innovation. Walther von der Vogelweide is unique in his thematic and formal range and in his synthesis of native, Romance, and med. Lat. trads. Wolfram von Eschenbach is the first major exponent of the "dawn song" (see TAGELIED). Neidhart creates two new and formally distinct types of poem depicting summer and winter festivities and dancing, in which the poet vies with peasant rivals for his lady's favor. Both realistic details of setting, clothing, and proper names and elements of *parody and *satire are juxtaposed with Minnesang conventions. Like Walther, Neidhart is familiar with med. Lat. and probably also with the OF *pastourelle. There are other major 13th-c. poets with a substantial oeuvre, some like Walther with a wide repertoire, incl. the *leich and the didactic lyric, but also a host of minor poets.

Particularly in the first half of the 13th c., earlier features survive—single and women's stanzas, examples of the Wechsel and of crusading themes, and simple isometric forms—but in the main, the 13th c. is characterized by new devels., largely in a second wave of Romance influence. The genres of dawn song, leich, and dialogues in the manner of the Occitan *tenso are introduced; and there is a marked increase in the use of *refrains, a phenomenon very rare in the 12th c. but paralleled in the 13th-c. OF lyric. The nature introduction (see NATUREINGANG), also rare in the 12th c. except in Heinrich von Veldeke, becomes common, on the pattern both of OF and Neidhart, who uses it in virtually every poem. The schematic description of beauty, often reduced to the single symbolic feature of the red mouth, is widespread and is particularly characteristic of Gottfried von Neifen. There is a strong tendency, already present in Walther, to treat love themes didactically, which results in generalized praise of women. From Neidhart on, realism, parody, and satire form one strand in the Minnesang. Because the traditional themes had become so worn, there is increasing emphasis, particularly in the later 13th c., on formal virtuosity, manifested in complex structures, displays of rhyming skill, and combinations of alternating and dactylic rhythm, a feature first found in Heinrich von Morungen and Walther. In the middle of the 14th c., the trad. of Minnesang and *Spruchdichtung, as it is written down in the main collective mss., comes to an end. The mss. of the late 14th, 15th, and 16th cs. show a new approach to love lyrics, even if they—on different levels—still refer to the trad. of Minnesang.

*See* GERMAN POETRY.

■ **Criticism and History**: H. Kolb, *Der Begriff der Minne und das Entstehen der höfischen Lyrik* (1958); *Der deutsche Minnesang*, ed. H. Fromm, 2 v. (1963, 1985); H. Kuhn, *Minnesangs Wende*, 2d ed. (1967); *Walther von der Vogelweide*, ed. S. Beyschlag (1971); *Die deutsche Lit. des Mittelalters, Verfasserlexikon*, ed. K. Ruh et al., 2d ed. (1978–2008); P. Wapnewski, *Hartmann von Aue*, 7th ed. (1979); P. Hölzle, *Die Kreuzzüge in der okzitanischen und deutschen Lyrik des 12. Jahrhunderts* (1980); O. Sayce, *The Medieval German Lyric* (1982); *Lyrik des Mittelalters*, ed. H. Bergner et al. (1983); U. Müller, *Die mittelhochdeutsche Lyrik* (1983); *Neidhart*, ed. H. Brunner (1986); J. F. McMahon, *The Music of Early Minnesang* (1989); H. de Boor, *Die höfische Literatur*, ed. U. Hennig, 11th ed. (1991); G. Schweikle, *Minnesang*, 2d ed. (1995); E. Lienert, "*Hærâ Walther, wie ez mir stât*. Autorschaft und Sängerrolle im Minnesang bis Neidhart," *Autor und Autorschaft im Mittelalter*, ed. E. Andersen (1998); J. Bumke, *Geschichte der deutschen Literatur im hohen Mittelalter*, 4th ed. (2000); H. Haferland, *Hohe Minne* (2000); J. Bumke, *Wolfram von Eschenbach*, 8th ed. (2004); M. G. Scholz, *Walther von der Vogelweide*, 2d ed. (2005); N. Zotz, *Intégration courtoise* (2005); A. Classen, "Love of Discourse and Discourse of Love in Middle High German Minnesang," *Words of Love and Love of Words in the Middle Ages and the Renaissance*, ed. A. Classen (2008); G. Hübner, *Minnesang im 13. Jahrhundert* (2008); J. Janota, *Ich und sie, du und ich. Vom Minnelied zum Liebeslied* (2009); *Marburger Repertorium Deutschsprachige Handschriften des 13. und 14. Jahrhunderts,* http://www.mr1314.de; *Paderborner Repertorium der deutschsprachigen Textüberlieferung des 8. bis 12. Jahrhunderts,* http://www.paderborner-repertorium.de.

■ **Music**: *Kritische Ausgabe der Weisen*, ed. W. Müller-Blattau, v. 2 (1956); B. Kippenberg, *Der Rhythmus im Minnesang* (1962); *Ausgewählte Melodien des Minnesangs*, ed. E. Jammers (1963); R. J. Taylor, *Die Melodien der weltlichen Lieder des Mittelalters* (1964); U. Aarburg, "Melodien zum frühen deutschen Minnesang," *Der deutsche Minnesang*, ed. H. Fromm, 3d ed. (1966); *Deutsche Lieder des Mittelalters*, ed. H. Moser and J. Müller-Blattau (1968); R. J. Taylor, *The Art of the Minnesinger* (1968); *Litterae, Göppinger Beiträge zur Textgeschichte*, ed. U. Müller et al. (1971–)—facsimiles of mss. with music and transcriptions; *Frauenlob*, ed. K. Stackmann and K. Bertau (1981); *Die Berliner Neidhart-Handschrift c (mgf 779)*, ed. I. Bennewitz-Behr and U. Müller (1981).

■ **Primary Texts**: *Trouvères et Minnesänger*, ed. I. Frank, v. 1 (1952); *Liederdichter des 13. Jahrhunderts*, ed. C. von Kraus, 2d ed. (1978); *Des Minnesangs Frühling*, ed. H. Moser and H. Tervooren, 38th ed. (1988); *Die Schweizer Minnesänger*, ed. M. Schiendorfer, rev. ed. (1990–); *Romanisch* *beeinflusste Lieder des Minnesangs*, ed. O. Sayce (1999); *Deutsche Lyrik des frühen und hohen Mittelalters*, ed. I. Kasten (2005).

O. L. SAYCE; A. BOSTELMANN

**MINSTREL.** The general term for a professional performer of med. lyric or narrative poetry, incl. the med. Lat. *histrio* (actor) and *joculator* (jester), the OE *\*scop* and the ME *minstral*, the Fr. *\*jongleur* and the Occitan *joglar*, the Ger. *Spielmann*, and the Rus. *skomorokh*. As popular entertainers, minstrels moved in a world of traveling musicians, actors, mimes, acrobats, clowns, beggars, and others of more dubious character. Christian moralists expressed disapproval of their wicked ways from Tertullian through Thomas Aquinas, who was the first to deny that their profession was intrinsically sinful. Many minstrels traveled great distances, either as messengers or as wanderers, but others were sedentary, either because they were domestic servants or because their service had been rewarded with a gift of property.

Scholars differ over the degree of literacy that may be ascribed to the minstrels; partisans of the *\*oral-formulaic theory of *\*epic composition argue that they composed by a technique similar to that of the 20th-c. unlettered Yugoslavian *\*guslar* (Lord, Duggan). The troubadour Guiraut Riquier distinguished four classes of Occitan joglars: the lowly buffoon; the court musician and singer or *joglar* in a strict sense; the composer of melody and words or *\*troubadour; and the teacher or doctor of composition—a title Guiraut claimed for himself. Med. Lat. *ministerialis* applied to any servant active in a noble, royal, or episcopal household, or to a messenger, whether or not he performed music or poetry.

*See* GOLIARDIC VERSE, OCCITAN POETRY.

■ E. Faral, *Les Jongleurs en France au moyen âge* (1910); E. K. Chambers, *English Literature at the Close of the Middle Ages* (1945), ch. 3; R. Menéndez Pidal, *Poesía juglaresca y orígenes de las literaturas románicas* (1957)—esp. on Spain; J. Ogilvy, "Mimi, sucrrae, histriones," *Speculum* 38 (1963); J. Duggan, *The* "Song of Roland": *Formulaic Style and Poetic Craft* (1973); C. Bullock-Davies, *Menestrellorum Multitudo* (1978)—on England; R. Zguta, *Russian Minstrels* (1978); W. Hartung, *Die Spielleute* (1982)—historical sociology; W. A. Quinn and A. S. Hall, *Jongleur* (1982); K. Sutherland, "The Native Poet: The Influence of Percy's Minstrel from Beattie to Wordsworth," *RES* 33 (1982); W. Salmen, *Der Spielmann im Mittelalter* (1983)—musicians; C. Page, *The Owl and the Nightingale: Musical Life and Ideas in France, 1100–1300* (1989); J. Southworth, *The English Medieval Minstrel* (1989); P. Dronke, *The Medieval Lyric*, 3d ed. (1996); E. B. Vitz, *Orality and Performance in Early French Romance* (1999); Lord; M. Dobozy, *Re-Membering the Present: The Medieval German Poet-Minstrel in Cultural Context* (2005); M. Lawrence, "The Protean Performer: Defining Minstrel Identity in Tristan Narratives," *Cultural Performances in Medieval France* (2007); R. Schuchard, *Last Minstrels: Yeats and the Revival of the Bardic Arts* (2008).

W. D. PADEN

**MOCK EPIC, MOCK HEROIC.** The mock heroic is a literary mode, primarily satiric, in which present realities are juxtaposed to a noble and heroic past, only to be found wanting. Authors sometimes evoke the heroic past by mentioning figures or events (as in Jonathan Swift's "Battle of the Books"), but more often they do so allusively, by imitating heroic style, characterizations, actions, and so forth. Mock epic draws its heroic precedents specifically from the standard repertoire of the epic: invocations, dedications, celestial interventions, epic similes, canto divisions, and battles.

Although the mock heroic has ancient roots in the Homeric *Batrachomyomachia* (*Battle of the Frogs and Mice*) and instances can be found up to the present, the heyday of the form was the neoclassical movement of the 17th and 18th cs. Nicolas Boileau's 1674 *Le Lutrin* (The Lectern) is commonly cited as the first neoclassical mock epic. The mock heroic was common in prose (as in Henry Fielding's *Joseph Andrews* and *Tom Jones*). This period also saw other mock forms (mock odes, elegies, pastorals, romances, and others), but the mock heroic/epic most fully exemplified the tenor of the time.

In tone, neoclassical mock-heroic/epic satire is sometimes light, as in the amiable raillery of Alexander Pope's *Rape of the Lock*; in such cases, the present reality is seen as trivial, so that the contrast with the heroic point of reference is more amusing than dangerous. But more often, the satire ranges toward ridicule and humiliation of its victims (as in John Dryden's "MacFlecknoe" and Pope's *Dunciad* ). In these cases, the present reality is a matter not of amusement but of cultural, social, and moral threat. Typically, the derision is grounded in class prejudice, juxtaposing high literary form (and its noble values) and low persons pretending or, worse, acting above their station to demean the commonweal. Highborn miscreants are not exempt, however, esp. when they act below their station. Less commonly, gender roles also provide a basis for mock-heroic satire.

■ R. P. Bond, *English Burlesque Poetry, 1700–1750* (1932); G. deF. Lord, *Heroic Mockery* (1977); U. Broich, *The 18th-Century Mock-Heroic Poem* (1990); G. G. Colomb, *Designs on Truth: The Poetics of Augustan Mock Heroic* (1992); R. G. Terry, *Mock-Heroic from Butler to Cowper* (2005).

G. G. COLOMB

**MODERNISM.** For many of its protagonists, the opening phase of literary modernism signaled a decisive shift from music to painting as the privileged model for a new poetry. As the linguist Roman Jakobson observes in *Language in Literature*, "The Romantic slogan of art gravitating toward music was adopted to a significant degree by Symbolism. The foundations of Symbolism first begin to be undermined in painting, and in the early days of futurist art it is painting that holds the dominant position." This quotation is from an essay on Boris Pasternak, and Jakobson is thinking primarily of devels. in Rus. art; but the proposition is familiar as one definitive way of thinking about the evolution of modernism, as it navigates its way out of the

self-reflecting, interiorized world of fin de siècle *deca-
dence and into the light of an external world whose
vivid energies provoke lit.'s long-deferred encounter
with the definitively "modern." The It. futurist *mani-
festo of 1909 (see FUTURISM) launched this modernism
with its vociferous condemnation of the symbolist as-
sociation of music with forms of ideality and its related
poetics of memory, loss, and desire (see SYMBOLISM).
The new painting and sculpture offered the basis for a
radically different aesthetic, one for which spatiality co-
incided with the avant-garde preoccupation with mo-
dernity—with dynamism, simultaneity, and multiple
points of view. This emphasis provides one consistent
strand linking the various modernist tendencies. Even
*surrealism, famous for its fascination with the move-
ments of the unconscious, saw the historical transition
in much the same way, with the eds. of the jour. *Sur-
réalisme* observing in 1924 that "[u]ntil the beginning
of the twentieth century, the *ear* had decided the qual-
ity of poetry: rhythm, sonority, cadence, alliteration,
rhyme; everything for the ear. For the last twenty years,
the *eye* has been taking its revenge. It is the century of
the film" (quoted in Jay).

Talk of such momentous transitions has to be han-
dled with care, however, and, while, in one of his first
draft cantos, Ezra Pound would muse on the rewards
to be had "[i]f for a year man write to paint, and not
to music" ("Three Cantos. I"), his own early practice
was deeply indebted to models of verbal musicality,
from the chansons of the Occitan *troubadours to the
first volumes of W. B. Yeats, "the greatest living poet"
for Pound when he arrived in London in 1908 (Pound
1971). In many ways, of course, the idea of substitut-
ing one model for another risks blurring the dialecti-
cal relation of residual and emergent forms on which
this sort of redistribution of emphasis depends. There
had indeed been much fin de siècle speculation about,
as Arthur Symons put it in his hugely influential *The
Symbolist Movement in Literature* (1899), "shutting the
eyes of the mind, and deadening its sense of hearing,"
but the now conventional association of poems with a
dimly resonating inner world of dream was to be one of
the first casualties of modernism's emergence. Even so,
the shift was again hardly as programmatic as we might
like to assume. In Pound's case, e.g., Yeats's early con-
ception of rhythm as a hypnotic condition in which
"we are both asleep and awake" (Yeats 1961) soon began
to reveal its limitations, but to Pound's already edu-
cated ear, much could still be learned from the older
poet's practice about how a fluid rhythm might work
in counterpoint to the punctual repetitions of rhyme.

Such insights would not be wholly effaced by the
discovery of *vers libre. Indeed, as the new formal
"freedoms" became popular, Pound in *Hugh Selwyn
Mauberley* (1920) and T. S. Eliot in the quatrain poems
of *Ara Vos Prec* (1920) staged ostentatious returns to
traditional metrics (Beasley, *Theorists of Modernist Po-
etry*). In the aggressive campaigning for modernism,
however, the auditory imagination did begin to as-
sume a decidedly second place to what Pound's friend
Wyndham Lewis termed "the philosophy of the EYE,"

in his book *Men without Art* (1934). The futurist
manifesto had excoriated "the sickly, nostalgic poetry
of distance and memory," and while the painters and
writers loosely organized around Pound and Lewis as
the vorticists (see VORTICISM) pilloried F. T. Marinetti
when he lectured in London, the Italians had set the
bar high, giving substance to Arthur Rimbaud's ring-
ing phrase from the 1870s, "one must be absolutely
modern," a prescription in light of which poetry might
well now have seemed the most resistant of the arts to
modernization. Rimbaud had memorably criticized
even his radical precursor Charles Baudelaire on the
grounds that "the form which is so much praised in
him is trivial. Inventions from the unknown demand
new forms." The absoluteness of that demand for
formal innovation would be echoed many times in the
early years of the next century—in, e.g., Lewis's disap-
pointed reaction to the poems by Pound published in
*Blast*: "they 'let down,' I felt, the radical purism of the
visual contents, or the propaganda of same."

For many poets, of course, the necessity of "new
forms" was clear enough, though inevitably some, like
W. H. Auden, would continue to express a fondness for
traditional meters. Rimbaud's talk of "inventions from
the unknown" was, after all, both thrilling and discon-
certing, gesturing toward a vertiginous future in which
complex cultural hists. might be canceled at a stroke.
"Why should we look back?" Marinetti had asked, why
engage in "this eternal and futile worship of the past?"
On this issue, however, mod. poetry was to be deeply
divided, falling into often quite distinct national
groupings, themselves divisible between two broad
tendencies that some recent critics—e.g., Bürger—
have distinguished as avant-garde and modernist. For
those aligned with the former, it was indeed as if the
*aube-de-siècle* arts had suddenly opened a window on
the future, with poets such as W. C. Williams, Blaise
Cendrars, and Guillaume Apollinaire variously cel-
ebrating the dynamism of modernity as a correlative
to the energies of the *imagination. Radically new
forms were needed, as Rimbaud had foreseen: the
avant-gardist poets associated with *Dada, It. and Rus.
futurism, and with Ger. *expressionism experimented
with simultaneity, *sound poetry, and graphic effects,
inventing a dazzling array of new artistic devices, most
of which originated from experimentation in the vi-
sual arts: *collage, Marinetti's *parole in libertà* (words
in freedom), Apollinaire's *calligrammes, August
Stramm's "telegram style," **zaum'* or the "transrational"
lang. of Velimir Khlebnikov and Aleksei Kruchenykh,
Hugo Ball's *Verse ohne Worte* (Poems without Words),
and the surrealists' automatic writing, to name only a
few. Marinetti's call for the "destruction of syntax" was
being widely heeded.

*Avant-garde poetics constantly pushed at the
boundaries of art as traditionally conceived, disman-
tling its auratic structures in the name of modernity
itself. Technology and consumerism were radically re-
configuring conventional notions of time and space,
and painters and sculptors were quick to grasp the
new contours of their world as liberation from the

constraints of a tired, academic culture. When, e.g., Williams first saw Marcel Duchamp's *Nude Descending a Staircase* in the New York Armory Show of 1913, his immediate reaction was to "burst out laughing from the relief it brought me!" (1970). Rather as in Umberto Boccioni's 1911 painting *The Street Enters the House*, the everyday world was suddenly invading the poem: Apollinaire incorporated fragments of overheard dialogue in his *conversation poems; Cendrars and Valéry Larbaud hymned the pleasures of international travel and consumerism, while even the mordant balladry of Bertolt Brecht acknowledged that "In the asphalt cities I'm at home" ("Of Poor B.B.").

Yet there were also those—Eliot, Pound, R. M. Rilke, Eugenio Montale, and Umberto Saba, e.g.— who sought in the arts of modernism a kind of *defense* against what were felt to be the degenerative forces of modernity, the "sculpture of rhyme" still standing firm against the new mass-produced "mould in plaster" that the age apparently demanded (Pound, *Hugh Selwyn Mauberley*). For those representing this second, modernist tendency, the authentically new work was one rooted in a developed "historical sense . . . not only of the pastness of the past, but of its presence," as Eliot put it in "Tradition and the Individual Talent" (1919). Rimbaud's demand for the "absolutely modern" was thus qualified by a dialectical understanding of the relation of new to old according to which "[t]he poem which is absolutely original is absolutely bad; it is, in the bad sense, 'subjective' with no relation to the world to which it appeals" (Eliot, "Introduction: 1928," in Pound 1928). The "good" poem intimated here reins in the recklessly expansive gestures of avant-gardism: the tone is ironic and impersonal, the mode allusive, deliberately "difficult," and clearly controlled. Riding and Graves remarked on "the divorce of advanced contemporary poetry from the common-sense standards of ordinary intelligence," an effect produced, in part, by the allusiveness that Eliot saw as poetry's *necessary* response to the "great variety and complexity" of the mod. world ("The Metaphysical Poets," 1921). In a similar vein, Pound, in *"Noh" or Accomplishment* (1916), explained his and Yeats's enthusiasm for Japanese *Nō plays in terms of "this love of allusion in art."

The poetry of high modernism could in this respect seem somewhat lofty, aloof from the reader in its ironic projection of fictive identities and hermetically playful in its witty handling of partly hidden echoes and *allusions. The poetic "I" when it appeared at all became mercurial and deceptive, concealing itself within a shifting play of *personae or masks. In part, this was occasioned by a dissatisfaction with the transparency of the traditional *lyric, but it also reflected a self-consciously "modern" sense of poetic expression as a kind of deliberate posturing. As was clear from the earlier poetry of Jules Laforgue and Tristan Corbière— both influential precursors of modernism—the poet's awareness of his pose produced a complex mix of humor and anxiety (Eliot's "The Love Song of J. Alfred Prufrock" is the canonical example). Readers of poets as various as Yeats, Stefan George, Pound, Eliot, and Paul Valéry soon learned to be wary of poets speaking apparently *in propria persona* and began to listen attentively for ironic refractions and modulations of voice. "I banish myself," begins a poem by Salvatore Quasimodo that bears the knowingly paradoxical title "One Buried in Me Declares." Poets such as Fernando Pessoa and Antonio Machado would go further, developing various fictitious characters through whom to speak (see HETERONYM). Modernist poetry had moved far beyond John Stuart Mill's romantic opposition of "poetry" to "eloquence"—"eloquence is *heard*, poetry is *over*-heard," Mill had declared in "What Is Poetry?" (1833)—approaching more closely to Yeats's idea that "[w]e make out of the quarrel with others, rhetoric, but of the quarrel with ourselves, poetry" (*Mythologies*, 1959). Both definitions of poetry removed it from the orbit of rhet.—this would be a central tenet of modernist poetics—but Yeats's Nietzschean formulation significantly redefined subjectivity as essentially divided and potentially fictive.

The assumption that poetic "voice" was hybrid, unstable, and perhaps ultimately indeterminate had implications for modernist poetry that were at once psychological and formal. In the case of the first, this might register the poet's experienced uneasiness as expatriate or as creature of the literary salon (as in Eliot's "Portrait of a Lady" and in Pound's *Hugh Selwyn Mauberley*), or it might provide an opportunity to interrogate reflexively the nature of the aesthetic (as in Wallace Stevens's "The Comedian as the Letter C" and Marianne Moore's "Poetry"). At the formal level, the "disappearance of the poet as speaker" that Stéphane Mallarmé had predicted several decades before ("Crise de vers," 1886, 1896) governed both the stripped-down intensities of the early phase of imagist writing and the elliptical structures of the newly conceived long poem that would dominate the later phase of modernist poetry. The visual charge of the *image was intended to situate emotion in relation to clearly perceived objects, as in Pound's prototypical "one-image poem" "In a Station of the Metro," and thereby to replace literary "psychology" with a kind of painterly abstraction. Pound spoke of the image as expressing a "freedom from time limits and space limits" (1954), but perhaps the most significant freedom announced by these scrupulously poised and reduced works was a freedom from metaphorical elaboration. *Imagism made much of seeing things clearly and directly—an emphasis also prominent in Rilke's *Dinggedichte* (thing-poems) and in the productions of the acmeist poets in Russia, Osip Mandelstam, Anna Akhmatova, and Nikolai Gumilev, who were aware of the London imagists, as Painter has shown. In France, poets close to *cubism stressed in more technical fashion how the poem "situated" or "transplanted" objects from the real world to the aesthetic one; as Max Jacob put it in *Le Cornet á dès* (*The Dice-Cup*, 1917), "[O]ne recognizes that it's situated by the little shock that one gets from it or again from the margin which surrounds it, the special atmosphere where it moves."

The new "language of form and color" for which Pound called (1916) was a means by which to substitute that "shock" of encounter for the kind of periphrastic indirection he associated with the term *rhetoric*. That term haunted modernist poetics as an encoded crit. of several interconnected tendencies: thus, rhet. could allude specifically to aspects of symbolist writing (as, e.g., in Mallarmé's deliberate use of *periphrasis "to unravel the word into qualities belonging to inner realms" (Friedrich), and it could also gesture toward more general habits of literary inflation, as in Laforgue's "I find it stupid to mouth big words and play at eloquence" (quoted in Hamburger). Beyond this, rhet. as a negative counter in the discourse of modernism targeted the perceived slipperiness of lang. and its tendency to cohabit with the ideologies of power—for Yeats, "The rhetorician would deceive his neighbours, / The sentimentalist himself" ("Ego Dominus Tuus"), while for Pound, rhet. often equated directly to "any glorification of war" ("A Flock from Oxford"), similarly denoting the knowing use of abstraction to manipulate an audience. At the same time, though, commonplace denunciations of rhet. did not necessarily mean that those who criticized it foreswore it in practice: Altieri notes of Yeats and Stevens, e.g., that "despite their abiding hatred of 'rhetoric' their poetry frequently turns to the figure of the orator as a figure for the powers of idealization they project for their imaginative labors" (2004).

Indeed, certain forms of "mock-rhetoric" would play an important part in the writings of, e.g., Valéry, Saint-John Perse, Stevens, W. H. Auden, Mina Loy, and, later, John Ashbery, though this tendency was countered in part by an opposite turn to the abbreviated and the fragmentary by poets as different as Pound, H.D (Hilda Doolittle), Giuseppe Ungaretti, George Oppen, Lorine Niedecker, and Mandelstam. This strand of literary *minimalism testified to a countervailing conviction that sincerity derived from acts of local verbal precision, from the craftsman's concern with the Flaubertian *mot juste* rather than from the artfully inflated figures of the rhetorician. Technique should become "the test of a man's sincerity," a phrase of Pound's (1954) that, for a younger generation of modernist poets, would come to encapsulate the need "to objectify the poem, to make the poem an object" (Oppen)—an object in itself, i.e., rather than a vehicle for something else (a preconceived thought or moral doctrine, e.g.). The incorporation of *jazz and *blues rhythms in the work of the *Harlem Renaissance poet Langston Hughes, e.g., coupled vernacular expression with a finely tuned sense of contingent urban rhythms. Just as *free verse promised a highly mobile and *evolving* form for the *long poem, so the work's meaning would be indissolubly bound up with its emergent shape (Wallace Stevens's "Of Modern Poetry" thus conjures with "The poem of the mind *in the act of* finding / What will suffice" [emphasis added]). As Riding and Graves noted in their *Survey*, the modernist long poem no longer depended on Victorian uniformities of voice and meter as guarantors of formal order; Eliot's *The Waste Land* proceeded, they observed, not primarily by logic of narrative design but by "delicate transitions from one atmosphere to another." Such "atmospheres" were the productions of a startling array of different voices and poetic measures, "The Fire Sermon" section of the poem, e.g., modulating among formal rhymed stanza, *blank verse, and a designedly "more ragged," syncopated lyricism.

Some modernist long poems would, like *The Waste Land*, look also to the deep-lying structures of ancient mythologies and prehists. for paradigms of formal and conceptual order (Pound's *The Cantos* [1925–72], Hart Crane's *The Bridge* [1930], H.D.'s *Trilogy* [1944–46], and David Jones's *In Parenthesis* [1937] are obvious examples). Others—Valéry's *La jeune Parque* (*The Young Fate*, 1917), Rilke's *Duino Elegies* (1922), Eliot's *Four Quartets* (1936–42), Yves Bonnefoy's later *Du mouvement et de l'immobilité de Douve* (*On the Motion and Immobility of Douve*, 1953)—reinflected symbolist modes, sustaining extended meditative sequences by a subtle and insistent musicality of thought. And with a more pragmatic twist, perhaps, the poem as *"epic" could also be thought of as providing the mod. world with what Pound in an early draft of the opening of his *Cantos* called "a rag-bag to stuff all its thought in" ("Three Cantos. I"). Here was yet another version of the modernist long poem, one taking its cue in part from the capacious rhythms of Walt Whitman's *Leaves of Grass*, a model for poems with an encyclopedic scope that could weave together the life experience of the poet's self with the larger movements of hist. ("An epic is a poem including history," Pound pithily declared [1954]). The evolution of *The Cantos* was typically modernist in its rejection of a first tentative use of Browningesque dramatic *monologue in favor of a juxtapositional presentation of highly diverse materials. Pound did not now write *about* hist. but instead drew directly on its texts, incorporating them elliptically into the poem (chunks of Ren. prose here consorted with passages more patently cast in a lyric register). This paratactic method would be immensely influential, in part because of its capacity to do justice to the heterogeneity of experience, past and present, but also because it proposed a process-oriented model of writing that could be sustained over a long period of time, in Pound's case over more than 50 years.

Pound's legacy has been a powerful one, securing for poetry both public and private voices, voices expressing myriad concerns and speaking in diverse langs. This was, to borrow Scots poet Hugh MacDiarmid's words, a poetry that represented "a stand made against intellectual apathy, / Its material founded, like Gray's, on difficult knowledge" ("The Kind of Poetry I Want," 1961). In many of the long poems spawned at least in part by Pound's example—Williams's *Paterson* (1946–58), Basil Bunting's *Briggflatts* (1966), Louis Zukofsky's *"A"* (1959–75), Pablo Neruda's *Canto general* (1950), Charles Olson's *The Maximus Poems* (1960–75)—the modernist commitment to the demands of "difficult knowledge" remained firm. But that difficulty was one of both content and form: even the clearly marked structural motifs of *Four Quartets* were constantly impugned and undermined by Eliot himself as he weighed and questioned the claims of poetry to truth. In the case of *The Cantos* and its legatees, the risks in pursuit of formal "openness" were even greater. Pound acknowledged as much when he asked his readers in "Dr. Williams' Position" to "consider the number of very important chunks of world-literature in which form, major form is remarkable mainly for its absence" (1937). Perhaps, then, it is the case, as Milne states, that "[r]ather than heroically achieved structures, the poetics [of these modernist long poems] are those of baroque folly and neoclassical ruins." Yet, as Milne also notes, ruins may be hospitable where monuments are not. Like the new painting from which it so often derived its inspiration, modernist poetry situated itself quite deliberately amid the ruins of the old, its own fragmentary and unfinished shapes signaling not the absence of some idealized "major form" but rather its pursuit of a knowledge whose difficulty would continue to engage, perplex, and fascinate its readers.

*See* AVANT-GARDE POETICS, PAINTING AND POETRY, RHETORIC AND POETRY.

■ **Criticism and History**: L. Riding and R. Graves, *A Survey of Modernist Poetry* (1927); C. Brooks, *Modern Poetry and the Tradition* (1939); E. Heller, *The Hazard of Modern Poetry* (1953); F. Kermode, *The Romantic Image* (1957); J. H. Miller, *Poets of Reality* (1965); *Modern Poets on Modern Poetry*, ed. J. Scully (1966); M. Hamburger, *The Truth of Poetry: Tensions in Modern Poetry from Baudelaire to the 1960s* (1969); H. Kenner, *The Pound Era* (1971); H. Friedrich, *The Structure of Modern Poetry*, trans. J. Neugroschel (1974); D. Tashjian, *Skyscraper Primitives, Dada and the American Avant-Garde 1910–1925* (1975); G. Bornstein, *Transformations of Romanticism in Yeats, Eliot, and Stevens* (1976); *Modernism*, ed. M. Bradbury and J. McFarlane (1976); D. Perkins, *A History of Modern Poetry*, 2 v. (1976, 1987); H. Kenner, *A Homemade World* (1977); J. P. Hurston, *French Symbolism and the Modernist Movement* (1980); J. T. Gage, *In the Arresting Eye: The Rhetoric of Imagism* (1981); T. Hermans, *The Structure of Modernist Poetry* (1982); T. Diggory, *Yeats and American Poetry* (1983); S. Kern, *The Culture of Time and Space, 1880–1918* (1983); C. Christ, *Victorian and Modernist Poetics* (1984); A. M. Clearfield, *These Fragments I Have Shored: Collage and Montage in Early Modernist Poetry* (1984); M. H. Levenson, *A Genealogy of Modernism: A Study of English Literary Doctrine 1880–1922* (1984); A. Robinson, *Symbol to Vortex: Poetry, Painting, Ideas, 1885–1914* (1985); S. Schwartz, *The Matrix of Modernism: Pound, Eliot, and Early Twentieth-Century Thought* (1985); P. Bürger, *Theory of the Avant-Garde*, trans. M. Shaw (1986); M. Dickie, *On the Modernist Long Poem* (1986); M. Perloff, *The Futurist Moment* (1986); A. Ross, *The Failure of Modernism: Symptoms of American Poetry* (1986); C. K. Stead, *Pound, Yeats, Eliot and the Modernist Movement* (1986); M. Calinescu, *Five Faces of Modernity: Modernism, Avant-Garde, Decadence,*

*Kitsch, Postmodernism* (1987); M. Ellmann, *The Poetics of Impersonality: T. S. Eliot and Ezra Pound* (1987); J. Longenbach, *Modernist Poetics of History: Pound, Eliot, and the Sense of the Past* (1987); C. Altieri, *Painterly Abstraction in Modernist American Poetry* (1989); A. Eysteinsson, *The Concept of Modernism* (1992); R. Jakobson, *Language in Literature*, ed. K. Pomorska and S. Rudy (1993); M. Jay, *Downcast Eyes: The Denigration of Vision in Twentieth-Century French Thought* (1993); J. J. McGann, *Black Riders: The Visible Language of Modernism* (1993); V. Sherry, *Ezra Pound, Wyndham Lewis, and Radical Modernism* (1993); R. Emig, *Modernism in Poetry* (1995); E. Gregory, *Quotation in Modern American Poetry* (1996); C. Laity, *H.D. and the Victorian Fin de Siècle: Gender, Modernism, Decadence* (1996); J. N. Riddel, *The Turning Word: American Literary Modernism and Continental Theory* (1996); M. Bell, *Literature, Modernism and Myth* (1997); K. Tuma, *Fishing by Obstinate Isles: Modern and Postmodern British Poetry and American Readers* (1998); A. Davis and L. M. Jenkins, *Locations of Literary Modernism: Region and Nation in British and American Modernist Poetry* (2000); *The Idea of the Thing in Modernist American Poetry*, ed. C. Giorcelli (2001); M. Perloff, *Twenty-First Century Modernism: The "New" Poetics* (2002); C. Altieri, "Rhetoric and Poetics: How to Use the Inevitable Return of the Repressed," *A Companion to Rhetoric and Rhetorical Criticism*, ed. W. Jost and W. Olmstead (2004); J. Goldman, *Modernism 1910–1945* (2004); M. K. Blasing, *Lyric Poetry* (2006); S. Churchill, *The Little Magazine "Others" and the Renovation of Modern American Poetry* (2006); K. B. Painter, *Flint on a Bright Stone: A Revolution of Precision and Restraint in American, Russian, and German Modernism* (2006); D. Young, *Six Modernist Moments in Poetry* (2006); R. Beasley, *Theorists of Modern Poetry: T. S. Eliot, T. E. Hulme, Ezra Pound*; and *Ezra Pound and the Visual Culture of Modernism* (both 2007); *The Cambridge Companion to Modernist Poetry*, ed. A. Davis and L. M. Jenkins (2007); *Modernism*, ed. A. Eysteinsson and V. Liska (2007); P. Nicholls, *George Oppen and the Fate of Modernism* (2007); M. Golston, *Rhythm and Race in Modernist Poetry and Science* (2008); C. Altieri, *The Art of Twentieth-Century American Poetry* (2009); P. Howarth, *British Poetry in the Age of Modernism* (2009); P. Nicholls, *Modernisms: A Literary Guide*, 2d ed. (2009); D. Milne, "Politics and Modernist Poetics," *Teaching Modernist Poetry*, ed. P. Middleton and N. Marsh (2010); M. Whitworth, *Reading Modernist Poetry* (2010); *The Oxford Handbook of Modern and Contemporary Poetry*, ed. C. Nelson (2011).

■ **Primary Texts**: E. Pound, *Gaudier-Brzeska: A Memoir* (1916); "Three Cantos. I" and "A Flock from Oxford," *Poetry* 10 (1917); *Personae* (1926); *Selected Poems* (1928); and *Polite Essays* (1937); Eliot, *Essays*; E. Pound, *Literary Essays of Ezra Pound* (1954); W. B. Yeats, *Essays and Introductions* (1961); *Letters of Wyndham Lewis*, ed. W. K. Rose (1963); W. C. Williams, *Imaginations*, ed. W. Schott (1970); E. Pound, *Selected Letters*, ed. D. D. Paige (1971); F. T. Marinetti, *Futurist Manifestos*, ed. U. Apollonio (1973);

A. Rimbaud, *Complete Works*, trans. P. Schmidt (1976); M. Jacob, *The Dice-Cup*, trans. M. Brownstein (1979); G. Oppen, *The Selected Letters of George Oppen*, ed. R. B. DuPlessis (1990); *Modernism: An Anthology of Sources and Documents*, ed. V. Kolocotroni et al. (1994).

P. Nicholls

**MODERNISMO.** A literary movement that took shape in the 1880s in Sp. America and that has traditionally been identified with efforts to reinvigorate Sp. letters through the pursuit of formal perfection and innovation. It was, however, more than an aesthetic undertaking. *Modernismo* offered a complex response to the profound social and cultural shifts that accompanied the arrival of modernity in Sp. America. Its influence extended to both sides of the Atlantic, largely because of the artistic genius of the peripatetic Nicaraguan poet Rubén Darío (1867–1916), who selected its name and, by example and decree, came to define the movement. He established connections with the most celebrated Eur. and Am. writers of the day and, by 1896, as the sole survivor of the movement's founding members, became its creative center of gravity. While the influence of modernismo lasted well into the 20th c., its closing date is generally held to coincide with Darío's death in 1916.

Because of its pursuit of artistic freedom and its openness to different styles, the movement was viewed at first as limited in depth. Early critics, many of whom were Sp., failed to understand the sociopolitical and philosophic underpinnings of these endeavors and viewed modernismo as primarily concerned with imitation and invention at the expense of ideas. They attacked what they deemed to be an attitude of art for art's sake as well as its cosmopolitan and openly francophile perspective as escapist, often comparing it negatively with the contemporaneous and more authentic Sp. Generation of 1898, even though both groups shared certain philosophic and artistic premises. The first studies focused on tracing these diverse influences and exploring the many ways in which the *modernistas* departed from the strict rules of Sp. poetics. The modernistas made meter more flexible with the use of *enjambment, movable *caesuras, and rhythmic dislocations. They enriched their poetic arsenal with the creative use of the tetrasyllable, octosyllable, eneasyllable, hendecasyllable, hexameter (modeled on the cl. Gr. line), *alexandrine, and lines of combined verse length. They experimented with inventive rhyme schemes, *synaesthesia, *onomatopoeia, and imitation of the pictorial and musical arts.

As significant as these innovations were, they are now understood to be the outward signs of the ongoing engagement of modernismo with the multiplicity of issues related to modernization, a relationship common to Western lit. When seen from this broader perspective, characteristics of the movement that were first examined in isolation take on new meaning and reveal the basis for the impact of modernismo on later

writers. As Sp. America's first literary response to the social, political, and cultural alterations brought about by modernity, modernismo is a sophisticated encounter with concerns that continue to have an impact on intellectual life.

Throughout Sp. America, the penetration of mod. life was and, to a certain extent, continues to be uneven. Nevertheless, by the 1870s, the political independence and relative stability in the region had begun to enable increased international trade, which resulted in the importation of luxury items, books, and jours., as well as the introduction of socially progressive ideas and an increasing reliance on science and technology. The turn toward industrial capitalism, most notably in major urban centers like Santiago de Chile and Buenos Aires, where Darío lived during the 1880s and 1890s, was accompanied by an erosion of entrenched colonial arrangements. While these changes contributed to a sense of heightened well-being, prosperity, and affluence for some, for others they led to socioeconomic displacement and hardship. There developed among the writers of the period a troubled ambivalence toward what had been defined as progress.

As the poets became better acquainted with the world beyond their national borders through reading or travel or both, they recognized that many of their own anxieties had been explored in the works of others. Like the romantics, *Parnassians, and Fr. symbolists before them (and the Anglo-Am., Eur., and Brazilian modernists after them), Sp. Am. modernistas questioned the dominance of the market economy, as well as the hegemony of empiricism, technology, and pragmatism in mod. life. They offered an alternative vision that aspired to create a space for individuality, creativity, spirituality, and aesthetic values in an increasingly materialistic world. Their defense of poetry, despite its lack of a practical application, tied them to the pursuit of formal purity of the Parnassians, while their search for transcendence through musicality and evocation linked them to the symbolists (see SYMBOLISM).

At the same time, the modernistas were acutely aware of their unique place in the hist. of Sp. America, esp. their complex relationship with the national identities that were emerging from the political consolidation following the wars of independence. The resurgence of philological studies in the 19th c. provided additional support for imagining lang. as a way to understand hidden meaning and historical depth. As a result of all these factors, there developed within modernismo a belief, rooted in the legacy of *romanticism, that held to the superior epistemological power of art. Lit. was conceived as an instrument of vision and knowing that is capable of uncovering profound realities concealed by the inflexibility of empirical methods and the stultification of bourgeois concerns and values. It was also seen as a medium for addressing politics and power, one that plays an essential role in the formation of national cultures. This aspect appears most directly in the many prose pieces that make up a large part of modernista texts, but it also operates in the poetry, becoming increasingly more pronounced as the movement matures. It is no coincidence that these nationalistic concerns also play a role in Catalan *modernisme* and Anglo-Am. devels. In all its endeavors, modernismo reveals its fundamental faith in the transformative capacity of art, a characteristic that remains a strong feature of international *modernism well into the 20th c.

As the modernistas faced the complexities of mod. life free from the political and cultural domination of Spain, they formulated responses that would reverberate throughout the 20th c. They defined the poet as both visionary and outcast, at odds with the dominant social values, while striving to reveal those aspects of reality hidden by habit and convention. No longer protected by a privileged and patronized position in society, the modernistas struggled with newly commercialized social arrangements. In response, some invented refuges in premod. visions similar to those that appear in the Pre-Raphaelite paintings with which their work has been compared (see PRE-RAPHAELITISM). They sought through their poetry to fill the void left as critical reason increasingly undermined the fundamentals of religious beliefs. Their experimentation with genre, meter, and poetic structures reflected their insistence on the artistic freedom needed to capture the perceptions of the enlightened seer, the high priest of art. They pursued a lang. that was flexible enough to reflect the rhythms and harmonies they found in the natural world around them (a harmonious order linked to the Pythagorean music of the spheres), and—in a break with the conservatism of the past—in the fusion of male and female through unencumbered sexuality, a feature that lent decadent overtones to some of the poetry. In the occult sciences that were in vogue in the 19th c., they found legitimacy for their search for transcendence in the syncretic blending of diverse and, at times, highly unorthodox religious beliefs and symbols. They pursued the eternal through myth (cl., Eur., Asian, and indigenous) and addressed the present through references to fashion, to the headlines of the day, and to technological advances (such as the steamship, the railroad, the trolley, the dirigible, immunology, analytic chemistry, the telephone, the telegraph, and the phonograph). Modernity was seen in the departure from anachronistic, local reality and in the embrace of all times and all styles, a blending that made room for the autochthonous and the foreign as well as for the past, present, and future. In this way, the modernistas, like other modernists, also confronted their sense of the changing nature of time. No longer pure abstraction, time became tied to the human experience, expandable in its duration, containing traces of the past. The mod. emphasis on progress and perfectibility likewise seemed to move the utopian goals of these writers into a constantly receding future.

The most influential and famous modernista was Darío, whose skills and creativity have been compared to the greatest poets of the Sp. Golden Age and whose influence can be found in virtually all poets (and many prose writers) who followed in his wake. His work encompassed the full breadth of the movement, ranging from the sexually playful, highly decorative, dramatically iconoclastic, and politically engaged to the deeply philosophic and reflective. Believing that each poet must be free to read and decipher the universe, Darío prescribed the pursuit of individual visions and styles and rejected poetic rules. As a result, as the movement took shape and matured, the diversity of its manifestations defied easy categorization, yet inspired by the initiatives of this writer from a small town in Nicaragua, modernistas from all corners of the Sp.-speaking world envisioned themselves as sharing the same goals. The first poets to join ranks with Darío were Manuel González Prada (Peru), José Martí (Cuba), Manuel Gutiérrez Nájera (Mexico), Julián del Casal (Cuba), and José Asunción Silva (Colombia). Those who later identified themselves as modernistas included Amado Nervo (Mexico), José Juan Tablada (Mexico), Enrique González Martínez (Mexico), Ricardo Jaimes Freyre (Bolivia), Guillermo Valencia (Colombia), José María Eguren (Peru), José Santos Chocano (Peru), Leopoldo Lugones (Argentina), Julio Herrera y Reissig (Uruguay), and Delmira Agustini (Uruguay). The Sp. poets most directly associated with modernismo were Antonio Machado, Manuel Machado, Juan Ramón Jiménez, and Ramón del Valle-Inclán. The end of the movement is marked by an ever-greater loss of faith in the decipherability of the universe, a more emphatically ironic stance, and heightened rebellion against conventional poetic lang. and social structures, features that came to define the *vanguardia*, i.e., the Hispanic avant-garde.

*See* AVANT-GARDE POETICS; CATALONIA, POETRY OF; FRANCE, POETRY OF; SPAIN, POETRY OF; SPANISH AMERICA, POETRY OF.

■ **Anthologies**: *Poesía modernista 1884–1921*, ed. J. E. Pacheco (1978); *Antología crítica de la poesía modernista hispanoamericana*, J. O. Jiménez (1985); *Poesía modernista hispanoamericana y española (Antología)*, ed. I. A. Schulman and E. P. Garfield (1986); A. Acereda, *El Modernismo poético* (2001); *An Anthology of Spanish American Modernismo*, ed. K. Washbourne, trans. S. Waisman and K. Washbourne (2007).

■ **Criticism and History**: M. Henríquez Ureña, *Breve historia del modernismo* (1962); N. J. Davison, *The Concept of Modernism in Hispanic Criticism* (1966); I. A. Schulman, *Génesis del modernismo* (1968); O. Paz, *Children of the Mire*, trans. R. Phillips (1974); F. Perus, *Literatura y sociedad en América Latina* (1976); S. Yurkiévich, *Celebración del modernismo* (1976); R. Gullón, *El modernismo por los modernistas* (1980); J.-C. Mainer, *Modernismo y 98* (1980); R. Gutiérrez Giradot, *Modernismo* (1983); A. Rama, *Las máscaras democráticas del modernismo* (1985); G. Kirkpatrick, *The Dissonant Legacy of Modernismo* (1989); J. Ramos, *Desencuentros de la modernidad en América Latina* (1989); *¿Qué es el modernismo?*, ed. R. A. Cardwell and B. McGuirk (1993); C. L. Jrade, *Modernismo, Modernity, and the Development of Spanish American Literature* (1998);

A. González, *A Companion to Spanish American Modernismo* (2007).

C. L. Jrade

**MOLOSSUS.** In cl. prosody, a metrical foot consisting of three long syllables: – – –. It is found very rarely as an independent foot and never in a connected series. Sometimes it replaces an *ionic *a minore* by the contraction of the first two short syllables, and less often an ionic *a maiore* or a *choriamb. West suggests that, like the *spondee, it derived from slow, solemn chants where every syllable is fully intoned.

■ D. Korzeniewski, *Griechische Metrik* (1968); West, 55–56.

P. S. Costas; T.V.F. Brogan

## MONGOLIA, POETRY OF

I. History
II. Form

**I. History.** The origins of Mongolian poetic expression lie in shamanic *incantation and in epic. The oral culture, which prevailed up until the 1921 revolution and which still exerts a profound influence on the literary arts, was one in which the landscape, the gods, and ancestors were celebrated, propitiated, and invoked. Our principal example of early Mongolian poetry is the 13th-c. *Mongol Nuuts Tuuh*, an uneven collection of passages with lines of varying lengths and meters, presumably fashioned from different sources. Over the following centuries, poets came to write in a more sophisticated style, such as in the chronicle *Erdeniyin Tobchi*, in which regular verse forms were employed and more sophisticated devices developed. Mongolia's epic (*üliger*) trad. contains texts of up to 20,000 verses, centered around heroes such as Chinggis Haan, Erintsen Mergen, and Gesar. These are transmitted orally and are an excellent example of the standard structural form, *tolgoi süül* (see below). Despite the influence of Tibetan Buddhism, and thereby Tibetan culture, from the mid-19th c., poets such as the controversial monk Danzanravjaa (1803–56) began to fashion a specifically Mongolian style of poetry, addressing themes common to nomadic and steppe-dwelling people—livestock (esp. horses), seasonal movement, traditional culture, and ancestral lineage. Danzanravjaa's verses range from love lyrics to lengthy, although witty and entertaining, Buddhist religious instruction. The poetry scene of the 19th c. is also characterized by the preeminence of the family of the poet Vanchingbal, whose four sons (Gularansa, Sunveidanzan, Günchig, and Injinashi) each made his own significant contributions to the devel. of poetic form.

Following the revolution of 1921, Mongolian lit. was severely censored, and Mongolian writers repressed, by the government of Marshal H. Choibalsan. D. Natsagdorj (1906–37), who is generally credited with opening up Mongolian lit. (esp. the short-story form) to the West, was educated during the 1920s in Leipzig, and, following his return, became one of the most influential poets and cultural figures in Mongolia. His death, from a stress-induced heart attack, together with that of

another poet, S. Buyannemeh (1902–36), in the same year, came at the height of Choibalsan's cultural and political purges. Despite being regarded as a catalyst for postrevolutionary poetry in Mongolia, Natsagdorj's style and imagery are not esp. different from those of his contemporaries. Indeed, the Group of Revolutionary Writers (*Huvsgalin Uran Zohiolchnarin Bülgem*, founded in 1929) consisted of many of Natsagdorj's contemporaries, whose aim was to propagandize and develop revolutionary theory as it applied to lit. and its relationship to the people. Among these, poets such as B. Rinchen (1905–77), D. Chimed (1904–32), Buyannemeh, and Ts. Damdinsüren (1908–86) also made considerable contributions to the poetry from both the literary and the political point of view.

From the 1930s until Nikita Krushchev's denunciation of Josef Stalin in 1956, Mongolian poetry was very much in a state of ideological repression, with poets writing revolutionary verse to order, while prevented to some degree by their level of personal safety from writing their own poetry. In the late 1950s, B. Yavuuhulan (1929–82) started to revive the traditional poetry, that of Danzanravjaa, Vanchingbal, and his sons, and the earlier writers of epic poetry, under the general title of the New Tendency (*Shine Handlaga*). Yavuuhulan was committed to teaching and developing a poetry that brought the best of foreign lit. (he is famous for his trans. of Sergei Esenin and of Japanese *haiku) together with the Mongolian trads. His students included possibly the three most important poets of the late 20th c., D. Nyamsüren (1949–2002), O. Dashbalbar (1957–99), and G. Mend-Ooyo (b. 1952). These three can be credited for the vibrant state of Mongolian poetry at the present time, and Mend-Ooyo's Academy of Culture and Poetry (*Soyol, Yaruu Nairgin Akademi*) publishes Eng. trans. of Mongolian poetry, as well as original texts by contemp. writers. Of the younger generation, the majority is following Yavuuhulan's trad. T. Bavuudorj (b. 1969) and T- Ö. Erdenetsogt (b. 1974) use Buddhist imagery alongside the ideas of landscape and hist. to develop new ways of working with ancient ideas and forms. Although there are very few writers actively involved with formal experimentation, there is some interest in postmodernism and the Rus. OBERIU movement among poets such as B. Odgerel (b. 1967), G-A. Ayurzana (b. 1970) and B. Galsansuh (b. 1972).

**II. Form.** There is one standard form of Mongolian poetry, which goes back to the epic and which was clearly a mnemonic device for recitation. This is the head/tail (*tolgoi/süül*) form, where the first letter (occasionally syllable) of every line (whether of a poem, a couplet, or a verse) is the same and where (now less frequently) the last word of every line is the same.

■ W. Heissig, *Geschichte der Mongolische Literatur* (1972); Danzanravjaa, *Perfect Qualities*, trans. S. Wickham-Smith (2006); O. Dashbalbar, *The River Flows Gently*, trans. S. Wickham-Smith (2008); *Anthology of Mongolian Literature*, ed. S. Wickham-Smith and Sh Tsog (2008); B. Yavuuhulan, *Mongolian Verse*, trans. S. Wickham-Smith (2009).

S. Wickham-Smith

**MONK'S TALE STANZA.** An eight-line stanza derived by Chaucer from the Fr. *ballade* octave, a stanza first used in OF for narrative verse by Oto de Graunson. The monk's rhyme scheme, *ababbcbc*, is found as well in Chaucer's "ABC," and several of his ballads: "To Rosamounde," "The Former Age," "Fortune," and "Lenvoy de Chaucer a Bukton." His "Complaint of Venus" follows a slightly different pattern: *ababbccb*. The line itself, called iambic pentameter by some, contains five metrical stresses; most lines are decasyllabic.

■ H. Braddy, *Chaucer and the French Poet Graunson* (1947); J. Scattergood, "Chaucer's Complaint of Venus and the 'Curiosite' of Graunson," in *Essays in Criticism* 44, no. 3 (1994); Helen Phillips, "The Complaint of Venus: Chaucer and de Graunson," *The Medieval Translator* 4 (1994).

L. L. Howes

**MONODY.** Early Gr. *melic poetry is divided into two general classes: the choral *ode, sung to flute accompaniment with a dancing chorus—e.g. *threnodies, *paeans, maiden songs, wedding songs, expressive dances (*hyporchemata*), processional songs (*prosodia*), *dithyrambs, praises of great men (*enkomia*), and victory songs (*epinikia*)—and the solo song or monody—originally an ode sung by a single voice, e.g., by one of the characters in a tragedy, or to a more private audience, as at a symposium. The *sapphic and *alcaic are the principal subgenres. Its themes were wider in scope than those associated with mod. lyric—they include politics and satire—but it came to be associated with the lamentation of a single mourner and, hence, came to refer to a *dirge or funeral song. In metrical form, the *strophes are *isometric, i.e., repeated without variation. In Eng. poetry, John Milton's "Lycidas" is referred to (in the epigraph) as a monody, though it is written in irregular Eng. *canzoni rather than in regular strophes. Matthew Arnold titled his *elegy on A. H. Clough "Thyrsis, A Monody"; likewise, S. T. Coleridge elegizes Thomas Chatterton in "Monody on the Death of Chatterton"; Herman Melville's "Monody" is either for his own son Malcolm or for Nathaniel Hawthorne.

*See* GREEK POETRY, LAMENT.

■ J. H. Baron, "Monody," *Musical Quarterly* 54 (Oct. 1968); G. M. Kirkwood, *Early Greek Monody* (1974); Trypanis; *CHCL*, v. 1; M. Davies, "Monody, Choral Lyric, and the Tyranny of the Hand-Book," *CQ* 82 (1988).

T.V.F. Brogan; R. A. Hornsby

**MONOLOGUE.** In the widest sense, a sustained first-person utterance for which, whether or not an audience is expressly evoked, rhetorical motives outweigh meditative or deliberative ones. Orations, petitionary prayers, and *laments are often monologues; so are many *lyric poems. Thus, monologue is less a genre than a device many genres employ. Arising from the implied circumstances that shape it, monologue has a clearly dramatic element: it characteristically defines elements of subjectivity and personality against pressures—destiny, hist., other people—whose resistance gives those elements

shape. The term may refer to sections within a longer work that privilege a single voice and unitary standpoint. The technical, literary sense of monologue is not inconsistent with more ordinary usage: speech that monopolizes conversation, or the patter of a stand-up comic.

In poetry, monologue has clear connections to drama. *Soliloquy* refers to a form of monologue in which an actor speaks alone on stage, whether overheard in the act of formulating private thoughts and feelings (Hamlet) or addressing the audience directly (Iago). Sometimes a work opens like Christopher Marlowe's *Doctor Faustus* or Lord Byron's *Manfred* with a soliloquy by the main character. Heard or overheard, monologue invites complex interplay between character and audience. Some of the most powerful passages in dramatic poetry are written as monologue.

The technique is ancient and so entwined with the ritual roots of drama that no distinct origin may be specified. Significant biblical examples occur in the Psalms and the prophets, where utterances cast in monologic form riveted the connection between vatic inspiration and impassioned verse. Lengthy speeches couched in refined rhet. and articulating an individual position appear in cl. epics and odes as well as dramas. Some miming included single-voiced speech, although dialogue was preferred there.

The cultivation of first-person speakers in Theocritus's idylls produced admirable examples of monologue, as did elegiac poems by Propertius. Elegies, diatribes, and comic harangues often display strong monologic elements; philosophical poems seldom do; verse epistles, while meant to be read rather than declaimed, still are monologic in their emphasis on the written performance of character. *Prosopopoeia, a cl. rhetorical form feigning speech by a personage of note (Athena, Hector), held an important place within pedagogy. It also influenced the female impersonations comprised by Ovid's *Heroides*, a work strikingly analogous to the independent Chinese trad. wherein courtiers sought preferment by addressing to the emperor poems in the guise of an abandoned woman.

Monologue like other devices stemming from drama remains open to ironies of context, although in some historical phases these may lie dormant. Germanic lit., incl. OE derivatives like "The Wanderer" and "The Wife's Lament," employs the monologue to valorize subjectivity. Devotional poetry tends to canonize monologue: in the later Middle Ages, e.g., speeches addressed by the Virgin to the Cross became a fixed subgenre. The dramatic element incubated within med. religious verse emerged in early mod. variations on the cl. epistle and *complaint. Poets from William Dunbar to Thomas Wyatt bred out of Chaucer's stock, with grafts from Ovid and Horace, a precedent emulated throughout the later 16th c. by George Gascoigne, Walter Ralegh, and others. These Elizabethans, like their dramatist counterparts, exploited monologic effects ranging from uncompromising rhetorical directness to the self-anatomy of a divided mind. Satan's monologue at the start of John Milton's *Paradise Lost*, book 4, culminates this development; Milton's complementary

"L'Allegro" and "Il Penseroso" point up the tendency for monologue to solicit, or preempt, response.

Retreating in the face of socially preoccupied Restoration and Augustan verse, monologue remained essential to Alexander Pope's self-fashioning, most subtly in "Eloisa to Abelard," a poem that inspired many successors during the *sensibility era. In the romantic period, the normative identity of poet with speaker elevated monologue to stardom as a vehicle for heroic recuperations of creative selfhood as performed in elegy and ode. Yet, at the same time, the ironic potential suppressed under high romanticism flourished in the comedy routine that was Byron's *Don Juan*. Even in more sober productions like William Wordsworth's "Tintern Abbey," monologue so winnowed consciousness as to render the confessing mind an object of curiosity to itself. S. T. Coleridge's term for the lyric genre thus produced, *conversation poem*, expresses a paradox that resided within monologue all along.

Lineally descended from this romantic genre, the Victorian dramatic monologue represents the most significant generic flowering of the device in postromantic poetry. Robert Browning called "My Last Duchess" and its congeners "dramatic lyrics," a name that emphasizes the genre's hybridity. Browning preeminently, but in tandem with Alfred, Lord Tennyson and Elizabeth Barrett, drove to new intensity monologue's constitutive tension between speakers' psychological complexity and the web of ambient circumstance in which they are enmeshed. Formally, the Victorian dramatic monologue embraced both the legacy of stage monologue in blank verse and also the trad. of the *ballad, with adapted stanzaic forms whose artifice figures the genre's oblique but persistent link to narrative. In *Maud: A Monodrama*, Tennyson took monologue where a prosopopoeia like his "Ulysses" had pointed, toward a serial tableau portraying mercurial moods of a single mind rather than a dramatic situation powerfully conceived. Later Victorian and Edwardian poets developed these overtures, most notably William Morris, D. G. Rossetti, Christina Rossetti, A. C. Swinburne, and Augusta Webster.

Affinities between these 19th-c. devels. and *closet drama show the dramatic monologue anticipating modernist playwriting by August Strindberg, Luigi Pirandello, and Samuel Beckett. Browning's conception flows through modernist poetry via Ezra Pound, Tennyson's via T. S. Eliot, whose doctrine of impersonality adjoined W. B. Yeats's doctrine of the mask or *persona to provide the mod. poetic monologue with theoretical support. Among Am. poets E. A. Robinson, Edgar Lee Masters, Robert Frost, and Langston Hughes worked regional or ethnic variations on monologue's capacity to project a representative identity, while in later generations Robert Lowell, Sylvia Plath, Elizabeth Bishop, and John Ashbery renewed the discrepancy between poet and speaker by spinning the psychological thread of monologue to a virtually clinical fineness. To rehistoricize this trad. and highlight its political subtexts has been the achievement of such contemp. poets as Richard Howard, Frank Bidart, Ai, and Carol Ann Duffy.

*See* DIALOGUE, DRAMATIC POETRY.

■ F. Leo, *Der Monolog im Drama* (1908); E. W. Roessler, *The Soliloquy in German Drama* (1915); I. B. Sessions, "The Dramatic Monologue," *PMLA* 62 (1947); H. Schauer and F. W. Wodtke, "Monolog," *Reallexikon II*, v. 2; R. Langbaum, *The Poetry of Experience* (1957); A. D. Culler, "Monodrama and the Dramatic Monologue," *PMLA* 90 (1975); R. W. Rader, "The Dramatic Monologue and Related Lyric Forms," *CritI* 3 (1976); A. Sinfield, *Dramatic Monologue* (1977); J. Blundell, *Menander and the Monologue* (1980); K. Frieden, *Genius and Monologue* (1985); L. D. Martin, *Browning's Dramatic Monologues and the Post-Romantic Subject* (1985); A. Rosmarin, *The Power of Genre* (1985); W. Clemen, *Shakespeare's Soliloquies* (1987); J. T. Mayer, *T. S. Eliot's Silent Voices* (1989); W. D. Shaw, *Origins of the Monologue* (1999); G. Byron, *Dramatic Monologue* (2003).

B. A. NICHOLS; H. F. TUCKER

**MONOMETER.** A metrical line consisting of one measure, either a *foot (in the mod. langs.) or a *metron (in cl. verse). Poems in monometer are rare, the shortness of the lines making for severe segmentation of syntax. The best known Eng. example is Robert Herrick's "Upon his Departure Hence," an epitaph of 15 lines beginning "Thus I /; Passe by /; And die. . . ."

T.V.F. BROGAN

**MONORHYME** (Ger. *Reimhaufung*). Refers to a passage, stanza, or entire poem in which all lines have the same end rhyme, i.e., the rhyme scheme *aaa* . . . Although monorhyme may seem singularly limited in its expressive capabilities, its distinguished use in Eng., Lat., Ar., Fr., Ger., Sp., and Filipino poetry suggests the opposite. Monorhyme has a rich hist. in med. Lat. poetry (Commodian, St. Augustine, Notker, and Gottschalk). It was also used by the Goliards in stanzas of four 13-syllable lines (see GOLIARDIC VERSE). Monorhyme couplets appear in 12th-c. Fr. narrative poetry; Warren argues that their frequency derives from the epic *strophe, which was also written in monorhyme. In mod. Fr., monorhyme has been employed by Voltaire, Jean-Jacques Lefranc de Pompignan, and Théophile Gautier. Ger. examples of monorhyme (*gehäufter Reim*) are rare, but an early 13th-c. *lied* by Walther von der Vogelweide has stanzas monorhymed on the vowels *a, e, i, o,* and *u* (Richardson). In Sp., Julián del Casal's monorhymed *tercets are notable for their influence on his modernist successors (Nunn). The Ar. *ghazal and *qaṣīda sustain monorhyme across hundreds of lines: when performed at the *musha'arah*, the dramatic monorhymes of the ghazal keep the listener in a constant state of suspense. Monorhyme is also common in some Tagalog oral poetry such as the *tanaga*, for which a single rhyme facilitates memorization and transmission (Lumbera), and in the heptasyllabic Mangyan *ambahan* (Postma).

Monorhyme conjures a variety of moods, from comic to reverent. Calin notes the "solemnity and sonority" that monorhyme couplets can provide in Fr., and this is certainly true in Eng. examples by William

Blake ("Silent, Silent Night") and D. G. Rossetti ("The Woodspurge"). Although monorhyme in Eng. is uncommon, it is hardly unknown; other prominent examples are found in John Skelton, Robert Herrick ("Upon Julia's Clothes"), Edward Lear ("To Miss Lear on her Birthday"), Thomas Hardy ("The Respectable Burgher"), and Robert Frost ("The Rose Family"). Hardy seizes on monorhyme's potential for biting satire, Herrick and Frost on monorhyme's playfulness. One of the longest and most virtuosic examples of monorhyme in Eng. belongs to the 13-year-old Lear (112 lines ending in "-tion").

■ F. M. Warren, "Some Features of Style in Early French Narrative Poetry," *MP* 4 (1907); C. F. Richardson, *A Study of English Rhyme* (1909); M. Nunn, "Julián del Casal, First *Modernista* Poet," *Hispania* 23 (1940); W. Calin, "Cain and Abel in the 'Mystère d'Adam,'" *MLR* 58 (1963); C. Lyons, "The Effect of Monorhyme on Arabic Poetic Production," *Journal of Arabic Literature* 1 (1970); A. Postma, *The Concept of Time among the Mangyans* (1985); B. Lumbera, *Tagalog Poetry, 1570–1898* (1986).

T.V.F. BROGAN; W. HUNTER

**MONOSTICH.** A poem consisting of a single line. Before the advent of mod. *free verse, a single line would have to have been metrical to be recognized as verse; and there are certainly a considerable number of metrical gnomes, *epigrams, proverbs, and funerary inscriptions of the ancient world, both in cl. Gr. and Celtic, that presumably were thought of as, in some sense, poetic. The Delphic Oracle spoke thus. The several collections of monostichs attributed to Menander, who used them both seriously and ironically in his plays, fall into this category, too, though probably few of the 800-odd extant lines are genuinely his. Cf. the *Greek Anthology*, 11.312. Although most mod. monostichs lack meter, and hence may be viewed by some as jokes or *aperçus* rather than poems, the more effective ones operate as other very short poems do. Some offer descriptive vignettes in the manner of *imagism or of pared-down *haiku. Others are humorous or satirical, epigrams as compact as a comedian's one-liner, or deploy puns to suggest figures.

The most famous mod. example, entitled "Chantre" ("Singer"), was composed by Guillaume Apollinaire in 1913:

Et l'unique cordeau des trompettes marines
(And the single string of the marine trumpets)

Appended to the proofs of *Alcools* at the last moment, this little poem is a dense cord of puns. In addition to its primary meaning, e.g., "cordeau" evokes a conch (*cor d'eau*) and the sea (*corps d'eau*). The *trompette marine* was a single-stringed med. instrument, played with a bow. The poem itself is divided into two units of equal significance, the title and the monostich proper. Read this way, it counterposes the poet and the instrument, or—in cosmological terms—God and the source of the divine music that governs existence. (In the Middle Ages, the Pythagorean concept of universal harmony was often illustrated by drawings of an instrument with a single string.) Together the two units constitute an *alexandrine, the traditional building block of Fr. poetry.

As in Apollinaire's case, many monostichs would be pointless or obscure without the context provided them by titles. In the mod. period and beyond, the form has remained infrequent, although notable examples have been created by Yvor Winters, A. R. Ammons, W. S. Merwin, Howard Nemerov, and others.

*See* GNOMIC POETRY, STICHOS.

■ W. Görler, *Menandrou gnomai* (1963); G. Apollinaire, *Alcools*, trans. A. H. Greet (1965); A. Fongaro, "Un Vers univers," *Revue des Lettres Modernes* (1976); rpt. in *Apollinaire poète* (1988); M. Poupon, "Un Parangon de poésie apollinarienne 'Chantre'," *Revue des Lettres Modernes* (1976); D. Gullentops, "Lecture de 'Chantre'," *Revue des Lettres Modernes* (1996).

T.V.F. BROGAN; R. B. SHAW; W. BOHN

**MORA** (pl. morae or moras; Lat. *mora*, "delay"; cognate with Old Ir. *maraim*, "remain" [*OED*]). A short syllable, as measured in langs. (e.g., Gr., Hawaiian, Slavic, Japanese) where duration is an aspect of meaning and/or *rhythm. While the short syllable is one mora (monomoraic), the long syllable may consist of two moras or a duration midway between one and two moras (bimoraic) or as many as three moras (trimoraic). In Eng., mora appeared as early as 1569 in Scottish legal texts and continues to the present as a legal term meaning unnecessary delay in bringing forth a claim. In prosody, the earliest use appears in the *Encyclopedia Americana* and is used thereafter in rhythmic and metric studies of cl. langs. The term was adopted by Leonard Bloomfield in 1933 to refer to a relative quantity of sound structure (*OED*) and was taken up by George Trager several years later to denote a segment of a syllabic unit that functions to mark prominence when the entire syllable is not the marker. The mora is important as a unit of durative measure in langs. with relative durations (lengths of time) on vowels, such as Japanese, which counts moras instead of syllables. The haiku is measured by moras, not syllables: thus, the three lines of the form consist of five, seven, and five moras, respectively. A syllable may have more than one mora, depending on the length of time required for pronunciation. So, the haiku, or any Japanese word, may have an identical number of mora but not the same number of syllables. Langs. differ as to the relation of moras to syllables as prosodic markers of prominence. Linguists do not agree on the nature and occurrence of moras in stressed langs. such as Eng., where duration may vary with individual or dialect as length of time is always one of three features for marking prominence, the most important being *pitch change.

*See* HAIKAI, METER, PROSODY, QUANTITY.

■ L. Bloomfield, *Language* (1933); G. Trager, "The Theory of Accentual Systems," *Language, Culture and Personality*, ed. L. Spier et al. (1941); J. Clark, C. Yallop, and J. Fletcher, *Introduction to Phonetics and Phonology*, 3d ed. (2007).

R. WINSLOW

**MORALE ÉLÉMENTAIRE** (Fr., "elementary morality"). The generic name for a poem in fixed form invented by Raymond Queneau (1903–76), first presented in his last book *Morale élémentaire* (1975). Almost exclusively practiced by members of the *Oulipo group, it is a 15-line poem in three parts: the opening consists of 12 noun-adjective couplings (or biwords) presented over six lines, or three *couplets containing 3-1, 3-1, 3-1 adjective-noun pairings; the interlude consists of six lines, varying in length from one to five syllables; and, the concluding couplet repeats the 3-1 structure of the opening, possibly repeating words previously used. Queneau explicitly defined the form in a note accompanying the publication of several early morales élémentaires (1974), at which time Georges Perec (1936–82) directly borrowed words from that definition to write "Roubaud's Principle," a poetics written in the form and pattern of a morale élémentaire. The form has received keen attention by members of the Oulipo because of both Queneau's influence and the form's flexibility. Ian Monk's bilingual "Morale élémentaire/Elementary Morality" (2003) plays on the difference in Fr. and Eng. word order, the noun-adjective/adjective-noun sequences, while exploiting true and false cognates:

| Roman court | bled rose | mobile suspect |
|---|---|---|
| | double grave | |
| Main plate | pied fin | smoking orange |
| | dire nature | |
| Dancing trouble | instant rose | vague future |
| | base promise | |
| | court | |
| | comment | |
| | on | |
| | court | |
| | comment | |
| | on | |
| | court | |
| Base double | main alternative | vague promise |
| | double content | |

■ P. Fournel, *Élémentaire morales* (1978); J. Roubaud, *Autres morales élémentaires* (1992), and *Trois ruminations* (1996); F. Forte, *Petite morale élémentaire portative* (2008); "Morale Élémentaire: Aventures d'une forme poétique," *La Licorne* 81 (2008)—spec. iss.; M. Grangaud, *Les temps traversés* (2010).

J.-J. POUCEL

**MOSAIC RHYME.** (Occitan *rim trencatz*, Ger. *gespaltener Reim*, It. *rime composte*), sometimes *broken rhyme*, *split rhyme*, rarely *heteromerous rhyme*. The "piecing together" of two or more short (often monosyllabic) words to rhyme with one longer (usually polysyllabic) one. Cases where both the rhymes are made out of more than one word, e.g., "pray thee / slay thee," "greet me / meet me" (J. G. Whittier), are viewed by some as mosaic but by most as simply double or feminine rhymes (see MASCULINE AND FEMININE). Traditionally, *rhyme concerns the phonological structure of one or more syllables but respects morphological categories; mosaic rhymes, by contrast, transgress word boundaries in order to effect the rhyme, highlighting that fact in the rhyme by the contrast between the rhyme fellows. Thereby, they expand the range of the rhyme device. Lord Byron has the famous mosaic rhyme "intellectual / hen-peck'd you all." J. R. Lowell has "Unqualified merits, I'll grant, if you choose, he has 'em, / But he lacks the one merit of kindling enthusiasm." Robert Browning, who was partial to the device, has 16 out of a possible 37 in "A Grammarian's Funeral," incl. such novelties as "fabric / dab brick," "far gain / bargain," "all meant / installment," "failure / pale lure," "soon hit / unit," "loosened / dew send." G. M. Hopkins has "I am and / diamond."

Since polysyllables are, despite greater commonality of endings, more difficult to rhyme and since Eng. as a Germanic lang. has a greater stock of monosyllables than the Romance langs., one might think that this sort of rhyming would be limited in scope and confined mainly to Eng. But the effect is striking, and this is not the case: the mosaic technique, which takes advantage of compounding in morphology and which can be combined with other strategies, has been popular in other langs. Occitan, Fr., and Ger. developed a variety of mosaic rich or *identical rhyme in which two words rhyme with one, both members having the same spelling and sound but different senses, e.g., *a roi / aroi, des cors / descors*. This is known in Fr. as *rime équivoque*; first attested in Gautier de Coincy (13th c.), it was very popular among the *rhétoriqueurs* of the late 15th and early 16th cs., e.g., the brothers Badouin and Jean de Condé, and even Clément Marot in some *épitres*. Guillaume Apollinaire rhymes "Ah, Dieu" with "adieu"; Louis Aragon develops the technique, which he calls *rime complexe*. Cognate is Ger. *rührende Reim*, in which one of the rhyming words is a compound of the other, e.g. Ger. *zeigen / erzeigen* or Eng. *mortal / immortal*, though these are not, strictly, mosaic.

*See* TRIPLE RHYME.

■ A. Tobler, *Le Vers français ancien et moderne* (1885); Patterson, 168–69 and index; L. Schourup, "Mosaic Rhyme," *Lang&S* 21 (1988).

T.V.F. BROGAN

**MOSCOW-TARTU SCHOOL.** *See* STRUCTURALISM.

**MOTE.** A Sp. poem consisting of a single line or *couplet, rarely more, containing a complete thought. Usually, but not always, this thought is glossed in verse, the whole composition then being called either *mote* or *glosa*, occasionally *villancico* or *letra*. One mote may be glossed by several poets or by the same poet in several versions. The mote was particularly popular in the 15th c.

■ Le Gentil; Navarro.

D. C. CLARKE

**MOTIF.** (Fr. *motif*, an overarching theme, often a color scheme within the visual arts; It. *motivo*, "motive," theme, or pattern). *Motif* often refers to a melodic phrase that provided structure and unity to a musical work. It has been used in lit. since the 19th c. to mean a salient and recurrent feature, theme, character, subject, or image within a work. A poetic motif may also occur as reiterated words or patterned phrases such as in a *refrain at the conclusion of stanzas.

*See* ORAL-FORMULAIC THEORY, THEMATICS, TOPOS.

■ A. Dundes, "The Motif Index and the Tale-Type Index: A Critique," *Journal of Folklore Research* 34 (1997).

A. M. GUGLIELMO

**THE MOVEMENT.** A group of Eng. poets who came to prominence in the 1950s: Philip Larkin, Kingsley Amis, Thom Gunn, Donald Davie, John Wain, Robert Conquest, D. J. Enright, Elizabeth Jennings, and John Holloway. They were originally publicized as a distinct phenomenon in a series of BBC radio broadcasts in 1952–53, which emphasized the group's "dry anti-romantic flavor." A year later the London *Spectator* coined the term *the Movement* to label this new generation, dubbing it skeptical, robust, and ironic. Alternative names for the group included the University Wits, Empsonians, and New Augustans, but it is the vaguer *Movement* that persisted. Subsequently, the Movement was represented by two anthologies: Enright's *Poets of the 1950s* and Conquest's *New Lines*.

While the poets belonging to the Movement denied an intention to form a unified group, their anthols. and other publications presented a distinctive aesthetic program that championed lucidity, moderation, and, in Enright's words, "chastened common sense." Turning away from *free verse and other modernist experiments, the Movement poets often used traditional *prosody, rhyme, and stanzaic patterns, which they admired as a sign of stability and order. In *Purity of Diction in English Verse* (which Davie later described as the *manifesto the group might have adopted, if they had agreed to adopt one), Davie lauded poetry with "pure diction," "prosaic strength," and economy of metaphor. In their subject matter, the Movement poets gravitated toward the ordinary rather than the grandiose, exemplified by Larkin's "Born Yesterday" (1954). Larkin, who became the most prominent poet of the Movement, suggests that being average, ordinary, and even dull is preferable to clichéd notions of beauty and love, because an excess of anything might "pull you off your balance." As a counterweight to the unbridled, exalted sentiment of *romanticism and neoromanticism, Larkin's poem takes a characteristic Movement stance in its advocacy of equilibrium and restraint and offers an alternative form of emotion that finds its power in subtlety and attentiveness: a "flexible, / Unemphasised, enthralled / Catching of happiness." The hesitant, skeptical, unsentimental poetic *persona often found in Movement poems was intended as an antidote to the "heavy dramatization of the poet's personality," as Wain termed it, that the group saw in some of their predecessors. Not limited to an aesthetic program, the Movement also embodied a social rebellion: most of its members were provincial university lecturers from lower- or middle-class backgrounds who saw their work as a protest against an urban, upper-class, literary establishment.

Historically, the Movement's members positioned themselves simultaneously against the neoromantic, neoapocalyptic, symbolist tendencies of 1940s poets (particularly Dylan Thomas, whom they regarded as emotionally excessive and self-indulgent) and the *modernism of T. S. Eliot and Ezra Pound. As Enright put it, they "steered between the rock of Wastelanditis and the whirlpool of Dylanitis." They modeled themselves after figures such as Thomas Hardy, Robert Graves, William Empson, and F. R. Leavis. Yet in the broader context of 20th-c. poetry, the Movement represents less of a rejection of modernism than is commonly supposed. Their poetic stance returns not just to premodernist and preromantic poetry but to an early, tempered version of modernism itself, embodied in Pound's and H.D.'s Anglo-Am. *imagism of the 1910s. Both the Movement poets and the imagists positioned themselves as antisymbolist (see SYMBOLISM); rejected grandiose themes, *sentimentality, and *obscurity; called for sobriety, hardness, and precise craftsmanship; and similarly proffered "good prose" as a model for poetry. While in practice the two groups produced very dissimilar works, the coincidence of their aims exemplifies the recurring impulse toward clarity and moderation that often follows a generation regarded as extreme, obscure, or outrageous.

In later years, the Movement poets moved apart from each other, and, as a clearly demarcated phenomenon, the Movement is thought to have ended with the 1950s. Davie's essay "Remembering the Movement" has been regarded by some critics as its epitaph. Several of the individual poets continued to pursue the Movement's aesthetic principles for the rest of their careers, however, and the term *Movement* has come to indicate a broader aesthetic, found not only in the original nine poets but in later poets. For a retrospective essay on the Movement published in 2009, Conquest wrote a new poem that aptly celebrates the "Movement spirit": "Neither too mad nor too mild, / Neither too tame nor too wild."

■ D. Davie, *Purity of Diction in English Verse* (1952); A. Hartley, "Poets of the Fifties," *Spectator* no. 193 (August 27, 1954); J. Scott, "In the Movement," *Spectator* no. 193 (October 1, 1954); *Poets of the 1950s*, ed. D. Enright (1955); *New Lines*, ed. R. Conquest (1956); W. O'Connor, *The New University Wits and the End of Modernism* (1963); D. Davie, "Remembering the Movement" (1959), *The Poet in the Imaginary Museum* (1977); B. Morrison, *The Movement* (1980); J. Bradley, *The Movement* (1993); *The Movement Reconsidered*, ed. Z. Leader (2009).

K. B. PAINTER

**MOZARABIC POETRY.** *See* AL-ANDALUS, POETRY OF; SPAIN, POETRY OF.

**MUSE** (Gr. *mousa*, pl. *mousai*, related to *mnaomai*, "I remember" and "I remind"). The ancient Gr. goddesses of artistic *inspiration were the daughters of Zeus and Mnemosyne. Hesiod states in the *Theogony* (ca. 700 BCE) that Zeus lay with Mnemosyne for nine nights and thus conceived nine daughters: Clio, Euterpe, Thalia, Melpomene, Terpsichore, Erato, Polymnia, Urania, and Calliope. It was not until the Roman period that the Muses were linked with discrete activities; we now generally associate Calliope with poetry, Clio with hist., Thalia with comedy, Melpomene with tragedy, Euterpe with music, Terpisichore with dance, and Urania with astronomy. In various times and places since antiquity, the word *muse* refers to that mysterious place, either outside or within the *poet, from which artistic inspiration emanates.

If the Muses were born from Mnemosyne, the personification of memory, then part of their work, as Hesiod demonstrates, is to inspire artists to sing of the past. In the *Odyssey*, the *Iliad*, and the *Theogony*, Homer and Hesiod emphasize the Muses' status as active bearers of stories, truth, knowledge, and wisdom. The invocation by which the Muses are called discretely or as a group to speak through or for the poet was a standard introduction in the ancient literary trad. And yet the Muse is not simply a formality with which the Gr. poets quickly dispensed. Not only do the Muses tell Hesiod what to sing, but they give him the structure of the verse, the arrangement of the song, the poem itself. In Plato's *Ion* (ca. 380 BCE), Socrates explains the importance of the figure of the Muse: art emanates directly from the Muses, who spin a web of influence that extends through the ages.

As the Common Era began, two different meanings of the word *muse* evolved. The first refers to the Gr. deities who tell the rather passive poet what to write—the Muse of *epic. The importance of the epic Muse begins to ebb with the decline of Roman antiquity, exemplified by a satirical reference in the first book of Horace's *Satires* (ca. 35 BCE). Curtius explains that the dwindling references signal med. poetry's rejection of the cl. Muse in view of her pagan associations. At this point, what we might call the personal muse begins her ascendance. Med. vernacular lyric poetry e.g., by Bernart de Ventadorn, Dante, and Petrarch, is rife with references to the beloved *dame* or *donna*, the object of the poet's love, the inspiration of his verse. During the Ren., the epic Muse once again becomes an important symbol for poetic inspiration: Edmund Spenser calls to his patron, Queen Elizabeth, "holy virgin chief of mine," for inspiration (*The Faerie Queene*, 1590, 1596), while Shakespeare intends *Henry V* (1600) to take its place as one of Britain's foundational epics when the Chorus invokes the Muse in the first lines of the play. John Milton in *Paradise Lost* (1667, 1674) addresses three invocations to the Muse, in books 1, 3, and 9, inflected with his ambition to "soar / Above th' *Aonian* Mount," the traditional home of the Muses on Mount Helicon, as well as his Puritan faith ("O Spirit, that dost prefer / Before all Temples th' upright heart and pure." But some of these poets may also call to a personal muse, as Shakespeare does in the sonnets when he addresses both an epicene young man and a sexually experienced dark woman. Eighteenth-c. France is known for rational, well-ordered writings such as political tracts and encyclopedias, and in Britain, William

Blake bids the Muse adieu in "To the Muses" (1783). Enlightenment writers and philosophers mention "enthusiasm," a creative furor that is associated with poetic inspiration, but they generally do not refer to divine forces. Eighteenth-c. thinkers saw poetry as a spiritual exercise that combined *imagination, sentiment, and reason, not as divinely inspired by a being or force outside the mind of the poet. The romantic period witnessed a resurgence in references to the Muse, although often she is associated with *nature, a more profound source of inspiration for poets such as William Wordsworth or Alphonse de Lamartine (although the latter, like Dante, has a decidedly personal muse named Elvire, who inspired "Le Lac" [1820], one of the most famous poems in Fr.).

Like the corresponding poets, who may be socially marginal figures, the symbolist and modernist muse is knocked off her pedestal (see SYMBOLISM, MODERNISM) and suffers the humiliations of urban, quotidian experience. Arthur Rimbaud writes in *Illuminations*, "One evening I took Beauty in my arms—and I thought her bitter—and I insulted her," while in "N.Y." Ezra Pound exclaims,

> My City, my beloved,
> Thou art a maid with no breasts.
> Thou art slender as a silver reed.
> Listen to me, attend me!
> And I will breathe into thee a soul,
> And thou shalt live for ever.

Because most references to the muse involve a male poet and a female muse and because the mod. muse is often a passive female figure inspiring an active male poet, the issue of gender has been a fruitful one in scholarly discussions. Plato is credited with calling Sappho "the tenth muse," and the epithet has been applied to several women poets such as Anne Bradstreet (*The Tenth Muse Lately Sprung Up in America*, 1650) and Sor Juana Inés de la Cruz. In fact, through the ages, women poets were often referred to as muses, perhaps as a way of containing their literary power; cast as muses instead of acknowledged as creators, they are relegated to the passive role that the inspirer generally inhabits. Contemp. literary critics have theorized what the traditional figure of the muse means for women poets, incl. (as DeShazer has it) mother-muses, female lover-muses, and muses that are "complex multiplicities of selves in communion with others." However, for the most part, the muse is an antiquarian rather than an immediate reference for contemp. poets, even while many of them acknowledge other unconscious forces at work in the act of literary creation. The literary figure of the muse touches on many issues central to discussions of poetry and art in general: inspiration, creation, *genius, gender, power, and *influence.

*See* COURTLY LOVE, DANCE AND POETRY, GENDER AND POETRY, GREEK POETRY, MYTH, ORAL POETRY, SAPPHIC.

■ Curtius; J. F. Diehl, "'Come Slowly—Eden': An Exploration of Women Poets and Their Muse," *Signs* 3 (1978); P. Murray, "Invocation to the Muses," *Greece Old and New*, ed. T. Winnifrith and P.

Murray (1983); M. K. DeShazer, *Inspiring Women: Reimagining the Muse* (1986); A. Becq, *Genèse de l'aesthétique moderne française* (1994); G. Levy, *Refiguring the Muse* (1999); *Figures modernes de la muse*, ed. J.-M. Maulpoix (2002); R. Hard, "Lesser Deities and Nature-Spirits," *The Routledge Handbook of Greek Mythology*, 7th ed. (2003).

G. LEVY

**MUSIC AND POETRY** (Gr. *mousikē*, "the art of the Muses"). Our best evidence about primitive song suggests that melodies and rhythms precede words, that the first step toward poetry was the fitting of words to preexistent musical patterns. Primitive cultures did not make the distinctions we now make between music and poetry: the Egyptian "hymn of the seven vowels," e.g., appears to have exploited the overtone pitches present in the vowels of any lang. The ancient Gr. ling. system of pitch accents was strikingly similar to the tetrachordal system of ancient Gr. music. Spoken Gr. moved between two stable pitches, a high pitch (indicated in post-Alexandrian texts by the acute accent) and a low pitch (indicated by the absence of accent); these pitches framed an area from which the sliding pitch indicated by the circumflex accent arose; the grave accent may also indicate such a medial pitch. Gr. music also moved between two fixed pitches; these tones, a perfect fourth apart, framed a middle area containing two sliding microtonal pitches. The ling. pitch system operated independently from the rhythmic system we now call quantitative meter; high-pitched syllables did not necessarily correspond with long positions in the meter. But the scraps of ancient music we possess do show a general correspondence between pitch accent and melodic shape, and studies of "accentual responsion" in the lyrics of Sappho and Pindar suggest that the poet's choice of words in an *antistrophe may have been constrained by an attempt to have those words correspond to the melodic pitch pattern established in the *strophe.

The Greeks used the same word, *mousikē*, to describe dance, music, poetry, and elementary education. Mousikē was essentially a "mnemonic technology," a rhythmic and melodic way of preserving the wisdom of the culture; alphabetic writing, the next advance in mnemonic technology, forced changes. It was adopted as a musical notation soon after its introduction, with letters of the alphabet written above the vowels in a poetic line to indicate pitches. Thanks to the quantitative conventions of Gr. meter, no separate rhythmic notation was necessary. The visual separation of pitches and words in the new notation began to separate the once unified arts; alphabetic writing led to both rhetorical and musical theory, the latter of which, thanks to Pythagorean mysticism, quickly became concerned with advanced theoretical and mathematical problems virtually divorced from performance.

Roman poetry, in which the normal word accents of Lat. words were arbitrarily distorted as those words were wedged into what had once been the rhythms of Gr. music, was another step in the separation. What began as mousikē, an organically unified art, had now become not two but four elements: performed music, music theory, poetry, and rhetorical theory. Christian thought altered the relative prestige of the four elements: the Church fathers embraced the elaborate mathematical music theory of the ancient world and allegorized its numbers; they banished instrumental music from the Church and sought to alter and control vocal music; on the literary side, by contrast, pagan poetry itself had to be saved by *allegory, while rhetorical theory was treated with suspicion. The drift in Lat. poetry away from quantitative verse toward *accentual-syllabic verse, in which the hymns of Ambrose and Augustine are important documents, was a motion away from writing Lat. words to Gr. tunes toward writing Lat. words to Christian tunes whose origin was probably Heb.

In the early Middle Ages, liturgical chant became longer, more complex, and more ornate, despite attempts by Charlemagne and Pope Gregory I to arrest its devel. When the lengthy melismatic passages sung to the last *a* of the word *alleluia* proved hard to memorize because church singers had a much less accurate notational system than the now-forgotten letters of the ancient Greeks, monks began writing words for them; the resulting works were called sequences or proses, though they employ many devices we would call poetic. By fitting new words to a preexisting melody, such sequence poets as Notker Balbulus (ca. 840–912) again altered poetry, moving it still closer to mod. stanzaic form, including *rhyme. The *troubadours and *trouvères, composer-poets writing in the vernacular, took over and extended the formal innovations of the sequence, producing increasingly complex stanzaic forms with elaborate rhyme schemes. In their art, poetic form was more complex than musical form, and by the time Dante defined poetry as a combination of music and rhet., *music* had become a somewhat metaphorical term. Not only were the It. poems in forms derived from the troubadours normally written without a specific tune in mind, but poetic form itself had become sufficiently demanding to occupy the attention once devoted to making words fit a preexisting tune.

Musicians, who were now increasingly called on to compose settings of preexisting words, made an important technical advance in the invention of polyphony. They may have gotten the idea of combining two or more melodies from the literary notion of allegory, realizing that the mystical simultaneity of an OT story and its NT analogue could become, in music, actual simultaneity. One result, oddly parallel to the dropping away of music from the troubadour trad., was that texts became less audible in polyphonic vocal music than in the monodic singing of all previous music. In early polyphony, the *tenor* or lowest part often sustained one vowel for many long notes, while the more rapidly moving upper parts sang as many as 40 short notes on one vowel. Predictably, these upper parts often picked up new texts, including Fr. texts glossing or commenting ironically on the liturgical Lat. text being sustained in the lower part.

Influenced by Christian versions of the ancient Gr. numerological theory, in which the universe was conceived as created and ordered by numbers, med. poets and composers frequently constructed their pieces by complex, mystical, mathematical formulas. Fr. isorhythmic motets, tricky crab canons in which one line is the other sung backward, *anagram poems concealing the names of mistresses—all elaborate forms whose principles of construction cannot be heard in performance—flourished as representations of the numerical mystery of the universe or (for adepts in both arts) as secret displays of technical ingenuity. In the service of such causes, musicians treated texts as a tailor treats cloth: they cut them up, stretched them out, redistributed their rhythms in ways that entirely destroyed the original poetic form, obscured the rhyme scheme, and made the content impossible to hear—esp. in motets, where three different texts in two different langs. were sung simultaneously. Guillaume de Machaut (ca. 1300–77), who was at once the leading composer and the leading poet of his period, wrote such motets but also simpler monodic songs such as chansons, *virelais, and *lais in which expression of the text was an artistic concern.

In Ren. poetry and music, techniques initially developed as virtuoso modes of construction, such as rhyme in poetry and chordal harmony in music, began to acquire expressive values. A new rereading of the ancient poets and rhetoricians, with fresh interest in persuasion, emotion, and the moral force of sounds, was an important factor. Med. composers had often worked out their music before pasting in a text, but Ren. composers normally started with a text and worked in various ways at animating or expressing it. Josquin des Prez (ca. 1450–1521), who used dissonant harmonies at painful moments in the text, pointed the way toward the witty rhetorical musical expression of the It. *madrigal school, which developed a number of harmonic and melodic "word-painting" conventions for setting words dealing with running, weeping, dying, and so forth. When Cardinal Bembo's edition of 1501 restored Petrarch as a model for *lyric poetry, composers of secular songs were compelled to increase the musical sophistication of their settings, and in searching for musical equivalents of Petrarchan *oxymorons—"freezing fires" or "living deaths"—they developed a more expressive use of harmony. Despite this general motion toward expression, however, the highly elaborate methods of construction typical of med. art survived, as virtuosity or mysticism, in both arts, esp. in England, where the hidden numerical schemes of Edmund Spenser's poetry and the abstract patterns of John Bull's keyboard fantasias provide extreme examples.

The increased attention to the rhet. and meaning of poetry on the part of composers did not satisfy the literary reformers now called the "musical humanists" (the *Camerata* of Giovanni de' Bardi in Florence and the *Académie* of Jean-Antoine de Baïf in Paris). Fired by ancient myths concerning the capacity of music to arouse various passions, these men concluded that it would do so most effectively by submitting to the rule of the text: they opposed independent musical rhythm, arguing that music should exactly follow the rhythm of the poem; they opposed the staggered declamation typical of the madrigal, favoring homophonic, chordal singing or *monody. Such composers as Claudio Monteverdi paid lip service to the aims of this reform program but did not allow it to deprive their art of the techniques it had developed since the Middle Ages. Operatic recitative is the most familiar legacy of musical humanism, but Monteverdi's operas show as much attention to musical construction as to literary expression. By the later 17th c., opera singers had become more important in the public view than either composers or librettists, and arias designed for vocal display became a central part of operatic practice.

While most Ren. poets possessed some technical understanding of music, thanks to the importance of music in the traditional school curriculum, poets in later centuries often lacked such knowledge, and their mimetic theories of musical expression proved increasingly inadequate. In 18th-c. vocal music, such composers as J. S. Bach continued to employ versions of the mimetic word-painting techniques of the madrigal; Alexander Pope's witty lines on "sound and sense" in the *Essay on Criticism* are a poetic analogy. But composers, unlike poets, were able to use materials that originated in such local *mimesis as building blocks from which to construct a larger structure. Trained by such rhetorically organized texts as Johann Fux's *Gradus ad Parnassum* (1725), a treatise on counterpoint praised by Bach, they were also learning to combine canonic procedures with an increasingly stable tonal grammar; these devels. liberated instrumental music, which could now embody several kinds of purely musical meaning. The willingness of later 18th-c. concertgoers to attend purely instrumental performances demonstrated once and for all the inadequacy of Ren. theories that had maintained that music's only legitimate function was to animate texts. Mimetic theorists, however, shifted their ground. No longer able to maintain that composers were imitating words, they now insisted that they were imitating or expressing feelings, a doctrine that led to the *Affektenlehre*, a systematic catalog of musical formulas for expressing passions.

Two fundamentally opposed conceptions of music were now coexisting uneasily: poets and philosophers continued to insist on the mimetic function of music, now calling it a lang. of the passions, but composers and some theorists, by developing the tight musical syntax we now call the tonal system, had given music a grammar of its own, a meaning independent of imitation that made possible such larger forms as the *sonata-allegro*. The romantic poets, just as ignorant of musical technique as their Augustan predecessors, now embraced music for the very qualities that had made it unattractive to those older poets, its supposed vagueness, fluidity, and "femininity." They sought in their poetry to imitate these myths about music, not the logical, witty music actually being written by such composers as Franz Joseph Haydn. In the cause of a more "musical" poetry, the romantics loosened Eng. syntax, while Haydn and W. A. Mozart were tightening and refining musical syntax. But eventually these romantic and literary myths about music began to affect composers, and in the music of Hector Berlioz, Franz Liszt, and Richard Wagner, all of whom acknowledge literary influences, a similar loosening of musical syntax takes place. Later 19th-c. composers frequently embraced poetic aims: "program" music, the idea of the leitmotif, the revived claim that music could express emotions and tell stories.

Wagner's opponent Eduard Hanslick insisted on the autonomy of music, espousing the revolutionary idea that musical structure itself was the real subject of music. Contemporaneous poetic theories of *autonomy were somewhat similar in their drive to separate poetry from its subject matter. But while Hanslick rejected all attempts to describe music as a lang., the poetic autonomists (E. A. Poe, Oscar Wilde, Walter Pater) claimed to want to make poetry more like music. Fr. symbolist poetry (see SYMBOLISM), in its fascination with sound and its attempt to maximize the extent to which words in a poem acquire their meaning from that particular poetic context alone, attempts to realize the program announced in Paul Verlaine's familiar declaration *de la musique avant toute chose* (music before everything). Still, the waning of the tonal system in 20th-c. music and Arnold Schoenberg's success in devising a new system for composition suggested again the limitations of attempts to describe music in ling. terms. Twentieth-c. relations between the arts often followed the old axes of numerical construction: Schoenberg was profoundly influenced by the mathematical constructive procedures in the poetry and music of Machaut; in his "expressionist" period, he used poetic line lengths to determine musical structure. Alban Berg organized his *Lyric Suite* on a sonnet by Stéphane Mallarmé but suppressed the text; W. H. Auden, in seeking a musical sophistication of technique, invented poetic forms closely related to the serial techniques of mod. music. Despite the large differences in the way music and poetry are practiced in the mod. world, Ezra Pound's cranky insistence that "poets who will not study music are defective" acknowledges the advantages of a long and fruitful partnership.

*See* AIR, BALLAD, BLUES, CACOPHONY, DITTY, EUPHONY, JAZZ POETRY, SONG, SOUND.

■ **Bibliographies**: Modern Language Association of America, *A Bibliography on the Relations of Literature and the Other Arts 1952–1967* (1968); S. P. Scher, "Literatur und Musik: Eine Bibliographie," *Literatur und Musik: Ein Handbuch zur Theorie und Praxis*, ed. S. P. Scher (1982); M. L. Switten, *Music and Literature in the Middle Ages: An Annotated Bibliography* (1990).
■ **Criticism**: G. Reese, *Music in the Middle Ages* (1940); T. S. Eliot, *The Music of Poetry* (1942); C. S. Brown, *Music and Literature* (1948); B. Pattison, *Music and Poetry of the English Renaissance* (1948); *Source Readings in Music History*, ed. O. Strunk (1950); G. Reese, *Music in the Renaissance*, 2d ed. (1954); A. Einstein,

*Essays on Music* (1956); J. Hollander, "The Music of Poetry," *JAAC* 15 (1956); J G. Springer, "Language and Music: Parallels and Divergencies," *For Roman Jakobson*, ed. M. Halle (1956); *Sound and Poetry*, ed. N. Frye (1957); D. Feaver, "The Musical Setting of Euripides' *Orestes*," *AJP* 81 (1960); J. Hollander, *The Untuning of the Sky: Ideas of Music in English Poetry, 1500–1700* (1961); J. Stevens, *Music and Poetry in the Early Tudor Court* (1961); C. M. Bowra, *Primitive Song* (1962); K. G. Just, "Musik und Dichtung," *Deutsche Philologie im Aufriss*, ed. W. Stammler, v. 3, 2d ed. (1962); A. Wellek, "The Relationship between Music and Poetry," *JAAC* 21 (1962); F. W. Sternfeld, *Music in Shakespearean Tragedy* (1963); D. T. Mace, "Musical Humanism, the Doctrine of Rhythmus, and the St. Cecilia Odes of Dryden," *Journal of the Warburg and Courtland Institutes* 27 (1964); H. Petri, *Literatur und Musik: Form- und Strukturparalleln* (1964); W. Mellers, *Harmonious Meeting* (1965); G. Reichert, "Literatur und Musik," *Reallexikon II*, v. 2; M. Pazzaglia, *Il verso e l'arte della Canzone nel De vulgari Eloquentia* (1967); S. P. Scher, *Verbal Music in German Literature* (1968); C. S. Brown, "Musico-Literary Research in the Last Two Decades," *Yearbook of Comparative and General Literature* 19 (1970), ed., spec. iss. of *CL* 22 (1970); L. Lipking, *The Ordering of the Arts in Eighteenth-Century England* (1970); E. Wahlström, "Accentual Responson in Greek Strophic Poetry," *Commentationes Humanarum Litterarum* 47 (1970); J. M. Stein, *Poem and Music in the German Lied from Gluck to Hugo Wolf* (1971); P. Johnson, *Form and Transformation in Music and Poetry of the English Renaissance* (1972); H. Van der Werf, *The Chansons of the Troubadours and Trouvères* (1972); D. J. Grout, *A History of Western Music*, 2d ed. (1973); R. Hoppin, *Medieval Music* (1978); Michaelides; *Dichtung und Musik*, ed. G. Schnitzler (1979); D. Hillery, *Music and Poetry in France from Baudelaire to Mallarmé* (1980); J. A. Winn, *Unsuspected Eloquence: A History of the Relations between Poetry and Music* (1981); E. B. Jorgens, *The Well-Tun'd Word* (1982); W. Mullen, *Choreia: Pindar and Dance* (1982); S. P. Scher, "Literature and Music," *Interrelations of Literature*, ed. J. P. Barricelli and J. Gibaldi (1982); L. Kramer, *Music and Poetry: The Nineteenth Century and After* (1984); L. Schleiner, *The Living Lyre in English Verse from Elizabeth through the Restoration* (1984); B. Stimpson, *Paul Valéry and Music* (1984); Hollander, esp. chs. 1, 2, 4; E. Doughtie, *English Renaissance Song* (1986); J. Neubauer, *The Emancipation of Music from Language* (1986); J. Stevens, *Words and Music in the Middle Ages* (1986); J. P. Barricelli, *Melopoiesis* (1988); D. M. Hertz, *The Tuning of the Word* (1988); G. Comotti, *Music in Greek and Roman Culture*, trans. R. V. Munson (1989); C. O. Hartman, *Jazz Text* (1991); *The Jazz Poetry Anthology*, ed. S. Feinstein and Y. Komunyakaa (1991); *Music and Text*, ed. S. P. Scher (1992); D. K. McColley, *Poetry and Music in Seventeenth-Century England* (1997); International Assoc. for Word and Music Studies, *Word and Music Studies* (1997–)—annual pub.; D. Albright, *Untwisting the Serpent* (2000); S. Bruhn, *Musical Ekphrasis* (2000);

*Musico-poetics in Perspective*, ed. J.-L. Cupers and U. Weisstein (2000); P. Kivy, *Antithetical Arts* (2009).

J. A. WINN

**MUWASHSHAḤ.** *See* AL-ANDALUS, POETRY OF; ARABIC POETRY; HEBREW POETRY.

# MYTH

  I. Myth and Society
 II. Myth and Metaphor
III. Mythological Tradition
IV. "The Mythical Method" in High Modernism
 V. Mythological Allusion

**I. Myth and Society.** Everyone knows what a myth is, but perhaps nobody can arrive at a foolproof definition. Myths are universal and ubiquitous, like Pan, but elusive and variable, like Proteus. A myth is a generally received, quasi-authoritative, widely known and relied-upon story, generally independent of a specific author or text, in some sense deathless, unique, tenacious, and recurrent: often a somewhat fabulous or fantastical narrative or account of events in which at least some of the agents are supernatural beings, or lack the natural limitations of ordinary humans or other sentient creatures, and/or are marked for special and distinguished destinies, and in which the occurrences or story events are miraculous, unprecedented, charged with archetypal or generic significance, and have enduring consequences or abiding influence in the human world and experience. Any given myth is also a constituent unit within a mythology. And—almost by definition—a myth is a story that is *re*told (and reworked) for the lifetime of a given culture. It is more or less unauthored. From this, it follows that the word *myth* may be more loosely applied to any accepted or received story that typifies or illustrates widely diffused ideas, principles, or concepts by means of a narrative (e.g. the Horatio Alger myth that hard work pays off in success for the enterprising individual in a capitalistic society). Myths belong to societies and define them, and they are propagated there, so long as the particular society itself survives or is conserved in a subsequent culture's memory (e.g., "the myth of the French Revolution" as popularly received by the contemp. French).

**A.** *Myth Criticism.* In both society and lit., myth has little independent existence, insofar as it tends to appear in compound form, i.e., with ritual, cult, drama, theogony, heroic *saga, folktale, romance, legend, *archetype, psychological "complexes," primordial hist., historical reminiscence, aristocratic and tribal pedigrees, totemism, etiological tale and beast fable ("just so stories"), hearsay, hagiography, miracle stories, the practice of magic, magical thinking, animism, dream psychology, fantasy, *allegory, *personification, *metaphor, and lit. Mod. myth crit. can divide along these lines, but as often it crossbreeds them.

Although Aristotle's *Poetics* (ca. 384–322 BCE) uses *mythos* narrowly to mean the ground plan for the main action imitated by a drama ("by myth I mean the arrangement of the incidents," presumably originally a sequence of ritual reenactments), the dramatic plots Aristotle cites are mythic in the sense eventually found in the word's wider application in various typologies for the social sciences. While myth's use to mean the archetypal aspect of any dramatic plot *in lit.* is prominent in the work of Northrop Frye, the most articulate exponent of this usage, he also writes about myth as a kind of ineradicable anthropological and ideological substrate in humanity's self-understanding and self-representation.

**B.** *Myth and Culture.* Figuring prominently in earlier mod. psychology, myths have been read there as projections of infantile or regressive fantasies, as the return of socially repressed or prohibited impulses and practices in fantasy form, or as paradigms for the devel. of personalities or character traits. In the psychoanalytic lit., as Alfred Adler puts it, "'analogical thinking,' that is, the attempted solution of problems according to the analogy of former experiences, is more strongly and distinctly expressed in him [the neurotic] than in normal individuals." Moderns have indeed perceived their contemporaries' lives as individually determined by Jungian archetypes of the collective unconscious, Freudian complexes, parental *imagos*, narcissistic and histrionic personality disorders, and so forth, all as if myth were alive and well among the remains of the "old brain" and old culture, dwelling among the foundations of experience. In the *Dictionary of the History of Ideas* (1973), Mircea Eliade notes that Freud's *Totem and Taboo* "insists that the beginnings of religion, morals, society, and art converge in the Oedipus complex"; and under the strong influence of psychoanalysis's heavy father figure, there are recent literary critics (such as Harold Bloom and William Kerrigan) who have seemed eager to agree.

Prominent in much social anthropology from the last century, the study of a society's myths as foundational also belongs to academic work on ritual, ceremonial, and religious practices, originally those deemed "primitive" or belonging to "natives" and their characteristic thought processes. J. E. Harrison cites Gr. definitions of myth as "the things that are spoken in ritual acts" (in her 1927 *Thespis* and her 1922 *Prolegomena to the Study of Greek Religion*: after Pausanius 2.37.2, with Galen, *de usu part.* 6.14). Thus, the Bible's recital of the first week in Genesis ("things spoken") inculcates Sabbath keeping ("things done"). Therefore, things reported as done in the mythic past can explain things done in the social present, as Harrison notes in *Themis* (1927): "The outrageous myth of the birth of Athena from the head of Zeus is but the religious representation . . . of a patrilinear social structure." Anthropological approaches study mythic narratives and cultic practice among indigenous peoples as reflecting their socioeconomic realities, local livelihoods, ecological niches, and institutions of clanship and connubium. The book of Genesis advances ethnological explanations for Israel's relations with its near neighbors in foundational tales of divided brothers. (In the latter day, the two characters in Robert Frost's "Mending Wall" reerect some of these same mythic divisions between them—and/or between their properties. Pine trees host parasites fatal to apple orchards—hence, the neighbors' breached defenses.)

The analogical thinking characteristic of myth-making and magic typically coordinates divine or sacral practice with social or secular practice or asserts a likeness between them—or between culture and nature. *Sir Gawain and the Green Knight* implicitly underwrites the ordeal undergone by its protagonist with initiation into an esoteric fertility or virility mystery; Gawain subjects himself to a ritual bloodletting on the feast of the Circumcision—as Christ submitted to pangs to redeem humankind from the Old Law (and Adam's ancient contract with the devil), so the New Year delivers the Old North from the bondage of winter.

In Frazer's influential *Golden Bough* (1890) and the allied Cambridge School, myths are read backward, as ancient scripts for ritual practices concerned with the political and economic well-being of a community and its food supply. Folklorists have found mythic material and practice surviving in concealed form in fairy tales for children. The enchanted Brunhilde becomes Briar-rose or Snow White—or Little Red Riding Hood's grandmother dissimulates a shaman garbed in wolf skins. In this vein, it is notable that the Eng. church's hymn "We Plough the Fields and Scatter" is sung to the tune of the old Eng. folk song "John Barleycorn"—here, the title character may go back to Beowa (barley) in Anglo-Saxon genealogies and *Beowulf*. The old verses relate Barleycorn's suffering, murder, *sparagmos* (dismemberment), and resurrection, and the reviving effects of consuming his blood: he dies so others, eating bread made from his body, may live. A rhythm of cyclic recurrence or redoing seems to underlie both the action and telling of myth, as in William Blake's "monomythic" epitome "The Mental Traveller."

Despite the scholarly propensity to allegorize myths to overcome irrationality or contradiction in them, myths are also seen (as by Claude Lévi-Strauss) as originally helping to define, classify, rationalize, and regulate the initiate's and the native's conduct and his or her material world, elements in a tale dividing variously between such polarizations as vital and moribund, safe and lethal, palatable and inedible, pure and defiled, licit and proscribed, sacred and profane, seemly (or *comme il faut*) and taboo (or transgressive), couth and uncouth, advantageous and detrimental, incorporable and excommunicable. In Francis Bacon's *Wisdom of the Ancients*, however, myths are not connected backward to the natural cycle and the circulation and supply of food and water but forward to the supply of *knowledge*: i.e., they are read as protoscientific thinking and conjecture in the poetic, parabolic, and riddling disguise of the cl. gods.

Crit. of myth must mediate between opposed conceptions of a mythic world, in which nearly everything possible to be believed is true, and a mythical one, where those same possibilities are regarded as mainly false, fabulous, and superstitious—the age of

their childish miracles, bad science, and old wives' tales being quite past. The rationalization of myth takes two prominent forms. Early in the 18th c., Giambattista Vico asserted that every culture invents its own Hercules, while Euhemerus, in the late 4th c. BCE, believed that myths merely deified the deceased rulers and other prominent and venerable or notorious personages of the historical past ex post facto. From the point of view of the comparative folklorist in the democratic age of the "common man," Vico's observation applies to the promulgation of legendary stories like those of Paul Bunyan and John Henry. Euhemerus's theory, on the other hand, might help explain Bram Stoker's conflation of the vampire myth with the name of Dracula, the patronymic of the 13th-c. Wallachian dynast whose savage practices also earned him the name Vlad the Impaler.

Myth has often been rationalized as encrypted knowledge by reading its fabulous stories as allegories of moral and historical or natural, physical, calendrical, and astronomic phenomena: solar allegories have been particularly popular. They have been found ingeniously dissimulated throughout Odysseus's adventures and likewise in the ursine year cycle for Beowulf's occultations. Although the determination of any given myth's meaning, reference, or original "site-in life" is the somewhat ineffable Holy Grail of myth's mod. study (Mircea Eliade, *Cosmos and History* [1952]), presumably the more esoteric the significance—psychological, ethnographic, cultural, religious, anthropological, ideological, historical, protoscientific—the more investigators must be *initiated* into it (Radin) and, thus, themselves become its referent by some reenactment of it.

**II. Myth and Metaphor.** Following Jacob Grimm's *Deutsche Mythologie* (1812–15), Max Müller and Adalbert Kuhn traced the origins of mythology to a "disease of language." "Myth," by these lights, substitutes Odysseus's Calypso for solar eclipses and gold-recovering Beowulf (bee hunter) for the ursine seeker of honey. Anglo-Saxon *kennings such as *whale-road* for sea are condensed metaphors, and an analogous process appears in the constructions of mythical thought: the hyphenation of earth-goddess or sun-god (Helios Hyperion, Phoebus Apollo) or the personification in Mother Nature or Father Time. The connection between myth and metaphor is apparent when Emily Dickinson writes, "The lightning is a yellow fork / from tables in the sky / By inadvertent fingers dropped": the "awful cutlery" once belonged to a sky-god like the Jehovah who sends lightning in Job 38:35 or the earth-shaker Poseidon with his trident. But submitted to philological and etymological study, langs. are themselves revealed as cemeteries of moribund metaphors and lost connections (hospital/hospitality), quasi-mythic links of the pathic kind included: *the bowels of the earth, an act of God, a devil of a time, at the height of his powers, fatalities, disasters, dismal (dies malae), influence*, etc. Capitalizing on lang.'s natural process but reversing its direction, poetry activates and mythicizes natural objects and phenomena by crediting them with intentions and psychopathies. According to Lucien Lévy-Bruhl's widely accepted theory, indigenous people think *participatively*, i.e., they do not sharply divide between subject and object. Ernst Cassirer (*Mythical Thought*) on Mother Earth is instructive: "In Plato's *Menexenos*, we . . . find it said that it is not the earth which imitates women in conceiving and giving birth but women who imitate the earth. But for the original mythical intuition there is here no before or after, nor first or second, only the complete and indissoluble involvement of the two processes." Amphion's lyre raises cities, and a comparable *furor poeticus* aligns the lyre-like cables of Hart Crane's Brooklyn Bridge.

But myth in poetry and story, as in thought, has both a participatory and departicipatory aspect, the first turning on homeopathic and sympathetic operations as found in magical and folkish thinking and practice and the second on these operations' suspension or rejection as a *pathetic fallacy. When the Chorus asks Sophocles' Oedipus what drove him to blind himself, he answers: "It was Apollo, friends, it was Apollo. He brought on these troubles, the awful things I suffer. But the hand which stabbed out my eyes was mine alone." Even the Azande rule out sorcery in suicide.

**III. Mythological Tradition.** The collecting, recording, cataloguing, and archiving of myth begins with the Vedas, the *Homeric Hymn* collection, and Hesiod; and it continues in the renarrating of Pausanius, Apollodorus, Plutarch, Ovid, and Hyginus, and in the age of print from Natale Conti right down to the elephants' graveyard of mythic story in William Morris's *The Earthly Paradise*. Following in med. mythographers' and Giovanni Boccaccio's academic line, a considerable branch of subsequent literary culture in the West has been devoted to the expounding of cl. myths and cults and their symbology in pantheonlike wholes. Often this work of *taxis* has been governed by a unifying or universalizing thesis, such as Pythagorean doctrine in Ovid, Christian typology in Ovid moralized, sacred kingship and the life-story of the year-spirit in Frazer, and calendrical symbolism in Max Müller (solar) and Robert Graves (lunar).

Thomas Mann said time is the medium of narration, and myths are stories; but if everybody knows them, then the storyteller is deprived of the attention-getting devices of suspense and surprise, which are the product of the dynamic way in which a story is told, by means of a specific, fixed temporal arrangement of incidents and information in relation to evolving states of knowledge—or a plot. Myths can be characterized as "curious" by a cultural outsider; but, being also "timeless," they are not organized around the novelistic or dramaturgical disclosure of a secret episode located in a story's "past" or temporal background—contra the hero's very existence in *Oedipus Rex*. A variation on the timelessness or static character of myth appears in the myths of historical priority and/or origins: the first human, the first sin, clothes, murder, voyage, evil

(Pandora's box), and the variants of absented civilizations (Babel, Atlantis, Utopia), and a lost golden age, time of innocence, or paradisal or antediluvian state.

**A. *Mythic Story Cycles and Cyclical Stories.*** Myth's seemingly synoptic or universal nature leads to Joseph Campbell's coinage *monomyth* for the overall career of the divine or godlike hero. Works such as Robert Graves's *The White Goddess* and W. B. Yeats's *A Vision* show individual authors constructing their own monomyth out of the common stock. On the one hand are omnibus-like cycles in which myths agglomerate—e.g., the *Mahābhārata*, the Volsung saga, etc.—on the other hand, the abbreviated, single-author treatments or reinventions of mythic material in such works as Blake's *Four Zoas*, John Keats's *Endymion*, P. B. Shelley's *Prometheus Unbound*, Richard Wagner's *Ring* cycle, Henrik Ibsen's *Peer Gynt*, Thornton Wilder's *The Skin of Our Teeth*, and J.R.R. Tolkien's *Lord of the Rings*. The single-author works all seem haunted by tasks of the first half of life found in the mythologem of the hero, whose birth, childhood adventures, and visits to the realm of the dead are sometimes thought to be late in the devel. of any given avatar's or hero's life story: "products of a phase when the hero is passing into myth," according to H. M. and N. K. Chadwick in *The Growth of Literature* (1940). In mythic plots, birth often betokens rebirth, incl. the regeneration of a given myth. The birth of Rabelais's Dionysian Pantagruel, e.g., can symbolize the advent of the Ren. itself—with its "myth of learning's rebirth."

The monomyth's most salient feature, in Campbell's Frobenius-influenced version of it ("separation-initiation-return"), is the mythicized hero's otherworld or underworld quest-journey (interior or distant) for the sake of unrevealed knowledge, esp. that of death or the afterlife; as found in the *Epic of Gilgamesh*, Orphic underworld visits in Roman narratives, the pilgrimage in Dante's *Divina commedia*, the Menippean lunar journey of Ludovico Ariosto's Astolfo, Edmund Spenser's Guyon's three days in Mammon's Plutonian Cave, John Milton's Satan traversing Chaos in *Paradise Lost*, the descent of J. W. Goethe's Faust to "the Mothers," Marlow's passage up the Congo in Joseph Conrad's *Heart of Darkness*, and Bloom's visit to Nighttown in Joyce's *Ulysses*. On the female side—anciently that of the Sumerian goddess Inanna—mod. yet Inanna-like examples are Jean Cocteau's movie of *Beauty and the Beast* and, more obliquely, James Agee's short story "A Mother's Tale."

The most important myth in the lit. of the Middle Ages is that of Christ's harrowing of hell, as found in Dante and William Langland and on many church walls; it has, of course, both cl. antecedents and Ren. successors. E.g., the late med. prose *Ovid Moralisé* explains Perseus as Christ, Andromeda as Eve, the sea monster as the gulf of hell, the espoused bride as Holy Church, and the marriage feast as paradise. This approximates Spenser's allegorical St. George legend, which begins with the Redcrosse Knight escaping the Laocoön-like coils of a monstrous Error, who has stabled and whelped deep in the *selva oscura* of a wandering wood.

**B. *Mythic Templates.*** Like the fable or ground plot in Ren. theories of fiction, a *mythical analogate* can function in Ren. poetry as an internalized blueprint or the skeletal or structural armature around which a sculpture gets molded: Apollo's *enfance* (infancy; from Gr. hymns and choruses) in Milton's Nativity ode (see NATIVITY POEM), or the Mediterranean Adonis-lament (as inherited by Virgil's "Daphnis" and Luigi Alamanni's first *eclogue) in the same poet's pastoral *elegy "Lycidas." The cl. myth of Proserpina, which illustrates and embodies, by means of an explanatory fable, the annual polarization of seasonal change by the death and rebirth of vegetation, flowering and going to seed, when taken with the comparable Adonis myth, informs Spenser's interlaced tales of Florimell and Marinell, with his Proteus standing in for Old Man Winter. In Milton's *Paradise Lost*, Adam and Eve's courtship and congress are hedged with allusions to Echo and Narcissus, Daphne and Apollo, Helen and Paris, Dido and Aeneas, and Zeus and Hera—plus the poet's own mythic prodigies Sin and Death. While the primal scene of our first parents' pairing reverses the moral tenor and immediate outcome of the others cited (i.e., delusion and drowning, erotic frustration, marital breakdown, the Punic Wars, wifely deception, and incestuous rape), it is nonetheless gendered along the ominous lines of the myths and tales it departs from.

The Enlightenment's dismissals of myth as an archaic, primitive, childish, irrational kind of magical thinking are somewhat contradicted by the views of J. G. Herder, who saw myth as an essential part of the inherited code of any culture, no less expressive of its genius than lang., customs, beliefs, and poetry: understanding any nation's or gens' character required immersion in its mythology. Artistic and revisionary re-creations of myths, esp. in poetry, from Herder's time on, likewise react to the Enlightenment view. We find the literary redeployment and reassertion of myth in major individual authors as themselves mythmakers: Fall and Gnostic myths in Blake's "prophecies," the Prometheus myth in Shelley's "unbound" drama and Mary Shelley's *Frankenstein*, Don Juan's myth of the seducer in Lord Byron's epic jeu d'esprit and G. B. Shaw's protofeminist play, the rescripted compact of Faust's myth in Goethe's masterwork, and the Sinaitic revelation in Friedrich Nietzsche's *Thus Spoke Zarathustra*. These more mod. treatments revise their heroes' stories under the inspiration and pressure of unprecedented historical changes. Traditionally, myths endow supernatural agents with powers that humankind lacks yet has since acquired; thus, Prometheus's theft of fire is as crucial for the industrializing era as the technological myth of Daedalus may prove for ours. James Joyce's would-be writer Stephen Dedalus, pursuing arts, escaped from an island to a continent. Within six months of the fictive date of Stephen's Icarian descent in *Ulysses*, the Wright brothers had achieved flight, and humankind had begun to slip the surly bonds of earth on wings of its own manufacture.

**IV. "The Mythical Method" in High Modernism.** When cross-referenced with either a realistic or contemp. alternative, an older myth accommodates a two-way traffic: a legendary story can be demythicized by a mod. or historicizing treatment of it, but it can also be reinstated this way, by allusions to it as governing precedent and archetype. In Yeats's "Leda and the Swan," Leda's mythic rape and impregnation recasts Luke 1:35: "The power of the Highest shall overshadow thee." In the same poet's "The Second Coming," the migration of the unborn, sphinxlike "rough beast" to the site of the Nativity reanimates Matt. 2:15: "Out of Egypt have I called my son" (followed by "Then Herod . . . slew all the children that were in Bethlehem"). Each of Yeats's poems ends with a rhetorical question addressing the re-aborning myth of the Annunciation: one that violently *un-*begins Christian hist.

In " 'Ulysses,' Order and Myth" (1923), T. S. Eliot called attention to both Yeats and the literary impact of *The Golden Bough* in his influential notice of "the mythical method" of Joyce's *Ulysses*. Eliot's declaration that "instead of narrative method, we may now use the mythical method" might also be applied to the poetics of Joyce's *Finnegans Wake*. The satirical hash resulting from the multiple crossovers among mythic, historic, and more local parallels in that work, as continuously afforded by the unprecedented lexical density of its puns, portmanteau words, polyvocality, and running fantasia of the unconscious, seems appropriate to a scandalous story that is also a garbled one—one way of understanding myths themselves. Closer to Eliot's method in *The Waste Land*, Ezra Pound's Cantos 39 and 47 shore lyric fragments of mythic and Frazer-like rites of spring against the ruins of an Odyssean cultural peripatetic. "[B]earing the golden bough of Argicida" (Argus-killer) at the end of Canto 1, Pound's *persona presents his Frazerian passport to a land of the dead—the poem's archival bricolage of texts, myths, cultures, and historical records. Cubism and related movements brought the abstract geometry underlying visual art into prominent view, and high modernist literary practice gave an analogous prominence to the mythic elements underlying the arts of literature.

**V. Mythological Allusion.** Older lit. lacks a firm distinction between itself and the retailing of myths, legends, and tales of humans patronized by gods or performing superhuman or miraculous acts. Newer lit. does not necessarily dispense with a mythical story, but it does tend to exploit or capitalize on ironic differentia. Shakespeare's Hotspur, or Percy, is a warrior and a horseman, his names suggesting he's "hot as Perseus" and as bent on rescuing a gorgonion-like honor from drowning in the deep. But his mythical identification with March-Mars finds him competing to distinguish himself from his princely rival Hal, who is figuratively mounted, with the Ren. Perseus, on Pegasus, as a May-Mercury. These mythic twins prove one too many to occupy the same sphere. More ironic authors may well disavow such comparisons, even while covertly bruiting them: "He was not the hero descending from heaven bright-sworded to smite a woman's fetters off her limbs and deliver her from the yawning mouth-abyss," George Meredith reports of Vernon Whitford, the eventual rescuer of Clara Middleton from an unwanted engagement to marry *The Egoist*'s title character—who is a kind of monster in human disguise, as Sir Willoughby Patterne. But Patterne's name and story encrypt the villain of the cold pastoral locked into the story on willow-pattern china. Myths *are* patterns.

More recent mytho-heroic identifications have obviously made a mod.-day comeback, esp. in crit.: the art critic Robert Hughes, when he was a reviewer for *Time*, once identified Mick Jagger performing in a gap-ridden bodysuit as the Apollo-skinned Marsyas, and he recognized a pitiless Mithraic sun fixed over a tragic bullring in the lightbulb hanging over the fallen swordsman in Picasso's *Guernica*. The annual rite in which an American president spares a Thanksgiving turkey renews, mythically speaking, Pilate's release of Barabbas ("Son of the Father") to the people: a NT scenario that recreated the original scapegoat ritual from the OT.

Such artful mythological allusions have often been indistinguishable from the very substance of a *lyric poem, as in Petrarch's *sonnets depending on his protracted reference to Laura worshipped as Apollo's sacred tree. R. M. Rilke's sequence *Sonnets to Orpheus* locates the title character's *Sagenkreis* (1.20) in the aesthetic, perceptive, and sensual receptivities that survive, re-embody, and hallow Orpheus's existence in the poet's own psyche, despite his living in the age of machines: like "the singular twig that instead of breaking bends itself into a lyre" (1.17) or the transformed Daphne that "feels laurel" and wants the pursuing Apollo to turn into the breeze (2.12)—or the breath of praise (Lat. *laurus*)—passing through her leaves as if through the text's own pages. Rilke thus revisits Europe's most celebrated sonneteer's principal mythic allusion and shows poetry's eloquent recuperation of the old gods while approaching a virtual theophany. Whether a myth is implanted subliminally or acknowledged in full flourish, its presence is conservative, implicitly and inevitably perpetuating "reverence for the archetype" (Herman Melville, "Greek Architecture")—even where ingenious mythopoeia is at work recasting and reenshrining our deepest intuitions, apprehensions, and customary practices in more local habitations and newly evocative names.

■ O. Rank, *The Myth of the Birth of the Hero*, trans. F. Robbins and S. E. Jeliffe (1914); L. Lévy-Bruhl, *How Natives Think*, trans. L. A. Clare (1926); M. Bodkin, *Archetypal Patterns in Poetry* (1934); F. M. Cornford, *The Origin of Attic Comedy* (1934); J. G. Frazer, *The Golden Bough*, 3d ed., 12 v. (1905–15); P. Radin, *Primitive Religion: Its Nature and Origins* (1937); J. Seznec, *The Survival of the Pagan Gods: The Mythological Tradition and its Place in Renaissance Humanism and Art*, trans. B. F. Sessions (1953); E. Cassirer, *Mythical Thought*, v. 2 of *The Philosophy of Symbolic Forms*, trans. R. Manheim (1955); *Myth: A Symposium*, ed. T. Sebeok (1958); D. Bush, *Mythology and the Renaissance Tradition in English Poetry*, new rev. ed. (1963); C. Lévi-Strauss, *The Savage Mind* (1966); N. Frye, "Literature and Myth," *Relations of Literary Study*, ed. J. E. Thorpe (1967); *Myth and Cosmos: Readings in Mythology and Symbolism*, ed. J. Middleton (1967); D. Bush, *Mythology and the Romantic Tradition in English Poetry*, 2d ed. (1969); *The Rise of Modern Mythology, 1680–1860*, ed. B. Feldman and R. D. Richardson (1972); F. M. Cross, *Canaanite Myth and Hebrew Epic* (1973); M. Eliade, *Patterns in Comparative Religion*, trans. R. Sheed (1974); J. Campbell, *The Masks of God*, 4 v. (1976); H. Blumenberg, *Work on Myth*, trans. R. M. Wallace (1985); *Jung on Mythology*, ed. R. M. Segal (1995); *The Myth and Ritual Theory*, ed. R. M. Segal (1998); N. Conti, *Mythologiae*, trans. J. Mulryan and S. Brown (2006).

J. NOHRNBERG

**NAHUATL, POETRY OF.** *See* INDIGENOUS AMERICAS, POETRY OF THE.

**NAÏVE-SENTIMENTAL.** An antinomy developed by Friedrich Schiller in the last of his aesthetic philosophical essays, "Über naive und sentimentalische Dichtung" (1795–96). The naïve was already an established category, having been treated recently by Moses Mendelssohn, Denis Diderot, J. G. Sulzer, and Immanuel Kant, but by opposing it to the sentimental, Schiller insisted on the relative or perspectival character of both conceptions. The natural becomes naïve only when it is contrasted with art or artifice. The naïve is, thus, a moral, not an aesthetic, pleasure (as Kant defined the terms) since it is mediated by a concept. In the first installment of Schiller's essay, the naïve seems closer to the sentimental than to traditional ideas of the naïve, in effect because he focuses on our interest in the naïve, not on how things would seem to a naïve poet. The difference is that, viewed as naïve, *nature puts art to shame, while from the sentimental perspective (which is only introduced in later installments), artificiality and culture have a value of their own that compensates for a loss of naturalness. When Schiller in the first installment contrasts the Greeks, who felt or experienced naturally, to the moderns, who experience nature, offering Werther's response to Homer as an example, it is an instance of being moved by the naïve, but it is not what Schiller means by sentimental.

When he comes to contrast naïve and sentimental types of poets, Schiller levels his conception of naïve, as in this statement: the naïve poet *is* nature, while the sentimental poet *seeks* it. This has led to a common reductive understanding of his intentions in drawing the contrast. He did not characterize J. W. Goethe as a naïve poet in the sense Homer was (or is now for us) but as a mod. poet drawn to imitate the manner if not the mentality of the Greeks, in contrast to his own poetic stance, which acknowledges the reflective break with nature and the resulting mod. tension between feelings and principles but which seeks its strength in that tension and in the "abstract" ideas and ideals that perpetuate it (see his letters to Goethe, Aug. 23, 1794; to Wilhelm von Humboldt, Oct. 26, 1795; and to J. G. Herder, Nov. 4, 1795). In a later installment of the essay, Schiller remarks that in much of *Sorrows of Young Werther, Tasso, Wilhelm Meister's Apprenticeship*, and in the first part of *Faust*, Goethe is clearly a sentimental poet. Given Schiller's complex and changing devel. of these ideas, it was perhaps inevitable that their influence would proceed from a reduced version. His comments on *genius as a property of the naïve resonated throughout *romanticism, while on a deeper level his (scrupulously qualified) contrast of the cultural situations of the cl. (Gr. but not Roman) and the mod. poet

subsequently proved important for Friedrich Hölderlin, K.W.F. Schlegel, A. W. Schlegel, G.W.F. Hegel, Matthew Arnold, and others. The essay has received recent attention as an early definition of *das Moderne* (Hinderer), yet Sharpe concludes a review of the critical reception of Schiller's aesthetics saying this last essay is "still a neglected work," and this holds true.

*See* PRIMITIVISM, ROMANTIC AND POSTROMANTIC POETRY AND POETICS, SENTIMENTALITY.

■ U. Gaede, *Schillers Abhandlung "Ueber naive und sentimentalische Dichtung"* (1899); H. Meng, *Schillers Abhandlung ueber naive und sentimentalische Dichtung* (1936); H. Cysarz, "Naive und sentimentalische Dichtung," *Reallexikon II*; O. Sayce, "Das Problem der Vieldeutigkeit in Schillers Ästhetischer Terminologie," *Jahrbuch der deutschen Schillergesellschaft*, ed. F. Martini, W. Muëller-Seidel, and B. Zeller (1962); H. Jäger, *Naïvität* (1975); H. Koopmann, *Friedrich Schiller*, v. 2 (1977)—overview of the secondary lit.; L. Sharpe, *Schiller's Aesthetic Essays: Two Centuries of Criticism* (1995); W. Hinderer, "Schiller's Philosophical Aesthetics," *A Companion to the Works of Friedrich Schiller*, ed. S. D. Martinson (2005).

J. BARNOUW

# NARRATIVE POETRY

I. History
II. Poetic Form and Narrative Poetry
III. Criticism

Narrative turns the raw material of story—the "telling" of a concatenation of events unfolding in linear time—into a (more or less) artful organization of those events that may complicate their chronology, suggest their significance, emphasize their affect, or invite their interpretation. Narrative *poetry* heightens this process by framing the act of telling in the rhythmically and sonically constructed lang. of verse. Although particularly monumental and foundational works from many cultures (e.g., the Mesopotamian *Epic of Gilgamesh*, the Sanskrit *Mahābhārata* and *Rāmāyaṇa*, the Homeric epics, the OE *Beowulf*, the MHG *Nibelungenlied*) and certain poetic genres (e.g., *epic, metrical *romance, *ballad) are particularly associated with narrative poetry, poetic narrative is a capacious category and also embraces beast *fable, *satire, the dramatic *monologue, reflective spiritual autobiography (e.g., William Wordsworth's *The Prelude*), allegorical anatomy (*Roman de la Rose, Piers Plowman*), some elegies (e.g., Walt Whitman's "When Lilacs Last in the Dooryard Bloom'd" and G. M. Hopkins's "The Wreck of the Deutschland"), and, albeit in fragmented or subverted form, the modernist *lyric sequences of Hart Crane, T. S. Eliot, Ezra Pound, and W. C. Williams (see LONG POEM). Furthermore, the boundaries between narrative and lyric verse are always fungible: poems usually classified as *lyric may supply a significant amount of narrative context for an act of reflection unfolding in arrested time (as in the work of Elizabeth Bishop, Robert Lowell, and Seamus Heaney).

Although theories of narrative tend to focus primarily, if not exclusively, on the novel, narrative poems vigorously exploit and in many cases anticipate the literary practices we find in sophisticated prose fictions. Traditional ballads like "Tam Lin" often make telling use of *ellipsis and parataxis (see HYPOTAXIS AND PARATAXIS). The late 14th-c. alliterative romance *Sir Gawain and the Green Knight* interlaces and eventually fuses its multiple plot motifs with great elegance and power. Chaucer's *Troilus and Criseyde* presents its characters with a degree of verisimilitude and a detailed attention to their physical surroundings and speech that has provoked some readers to praise its "novelistic" qualities. The epic narrative of John Milton's *Paradise Lost* elaborately reorders linear chronology and interrupts narrative sequence with prolepsis and flashback. Robert Browning's well-known dramatic monologue "My Last Duchess" makes use of a framed narration and an unreliable narrator. Many of Robert Frost's narrative poems advance action and develop character through the careful unfolding of dialogue.

The heightened, ordered lang. of pre-20th-c. narrative poetry does mean, however, that the illusion of transparent representation of experience so valued in the realist novel will be adumbrated by the visible and sometimes elaborate *artifice of poetic form. Indeed, major narrative poems become the occasion for the invention of new stanzaic vehicles, fresh rooms for the creation of a particular imaginative universe (e.g., the nine-line stanza developed by Edmund Spenser for *The Faerie Queene*, the *terza rima* of Dante's *Divina commedia*, and the sonnet-like stanzas of Alexander Pushkin's *Evgenij Onegin*). Complex internal patterning can produce its own order of *mimesis: the evocation of a particular kind of experience may be achieved through metrical design or the structures of rhyme (as we see in the use of *enjambment and *caesura to organize meaning across Milton's blank verse paragraphs or in the deployment of Chaucer's hypnotic repetition and recontextualization of semantically loaded rhyme pairs—*routhe / trouthe, herte / smerte, Troye / joye*—across the narrative arc of *Troilus and Criseyde*). Poetic fictions can, moreover, draw on the dynamics of lyric to interrupt linear narrative drive, sometimes offering pauses, reflection, and dilation by way of a shift in the genre of represented utterance (e.g., the elegiac digressions within the later stages of *Beowulf*), sometimes embedding songs within the action (as in Alfred, Lord Tennyson's *The Princess*), sometimes by way of a larger hybridization produced by the fusion of "lyric" and "narrative" (or synchronic and diachronic) possibility.

**I. History.** The hist. of narrative poetry suggests that different poetic modes speak to the needs of particular historical moments; at the same time, it is one of perpetual return as genres are reclaimed and revised. In preliterate cultures, the protocols of orally composed poetry—formulaic diction, the rhythmic patterning of elevated utterance, the deployment of traditional themes and episodes—help to bind and fix important narratives: stories of origin (etiologies, theodicies, genealogies), cultural hists., hero tales, national myth. Homeric epic also foregrounds, in the *Odyssey*, the narrative capacity of the individual as well as the tale of the tribe: Odysseus, the man of many turns and many stories, repeatedly refashions himself in narrative. The later hist. of epic reveals that monumental poetic acts of storytelling are always in dialogue with other narrative poems. Virgil's *Aeneid* (29–19 BCE) adapts Homeric epic to celebrate the values of Augustan Rome; his appropriation of Homer's characters and his repositioning of Trojan refugees as the founders of his own city fuse the wars of the *Iliad* and the wanderings of the *Odyssey* within a single work that translates the Homeric warrior code into the civic duty and stoicism of the virtuous Aeneas. The *Aeneid* discloses, furthermore, the time-bending capacity of poetic narrative: the Trojan past and the events of Virgil's own historical moment are folded into the struggles of his hero.

Ovid's *Metamorphoses* (1–8 CE) reimagines epic, inserting idiosyncratic and selective coverage of events from the *Iliad*, *Odyssey*, and *Aeneid* in books 12–14 of its ambitious compendium of myth and hist. The work's narrative technique is strikingly inventive and even experimental, incl. complex framings of embedded episodes and acts of internal storytelling, formal virtuosity (as in the phrases reflecting across line endings in book 3's account of Narcissus at the pond), and stylistic play (extending at times into *parody, as in the hyperbolic pastoral lyric of the giant Polyphemus).

The vernacular long poems of the Eur. Middle Ages include heroic narratives (e.g., the *Chanson de Roland* and the *Poema del Cid*) but more notably fuse chivalric and courtly ideals in the romances that flourished in the wake of Chrétien de Troyes's 12th-c. Arthurian narratives, whose octosyllabic rhymed *couplets frame courtly dialogue and explorations of interiority as well as knightly adventure. Romance slides toward lyric in the *Lais* of Chrétien's near-contemporary, Marie de France, whose tales include short evocative mood pieces (e.g., *Chevrefoil*). In Eng., the author of *Sir Gawain and the Green Knight* demonstrates the power of sophisticated alliterative verse to frame a quest narrative that is also a moral journey, although it is metrical romance (*King Horn, Sir Orfeo, The Squire of Low Degree*) that constitutes the predominant popular narrative mode. Chaucer's late 14th-c. narrative poems are remarkable for their modal range (they include *fabliaux, *dream visions, saint's lives, beast fables, Ovidian adaptations, the sophisticated romance of the aforementioned *Troilus and Criseyde*), and the lively frame of the storytelling competition between the pilgrims of the *Canterbury Tales* embraces numerous carefully imagined alternative narrators who variously present their tales in protoheroic couplets or formal stanzas.

The most ambitious experiments of med. narrative poetry are notably evident in Italy. Dante's *Commedia* (written 1307–21) offers religious epic focused through a first-person narrator; his introduction of Virgil as the narrator's guide through hell and purgatory puts his work in quite literal conversation with cl. epic. The recursive rhymes of the *Commedia*'s terza rima afford a particularly striking medium for the descriptive, meditative, and visionary passages that interweave its protagonist's three-part journey. The innovative lyric sequence of Dante's near-contemporary. Petrarch, the *Canzoniere*, while not strictly a narrative project, demonstrates the potential for a congeries of lyric moments to provoke or suggest a narrative dynamic; subsequent lyric sequences (most notoriously Shakespeare's *Sonnets*) have continued to provoke narrative interpretation.

The great narrative poems of the Ren. fuse multiple genres even as they stake their claims for vernacular national poetries. Ludovico Ariosto's *Orlando furioso* (1516) and Torquato Tasso's *Gerusalemme liberata* (1581) interlace erotic quests with heroic matter, and Ariosto marshals a striking mixture of tones in his cheerfully errant and digressive storytelling. Both use the intricate *ottava rima* stanza developed by Giovanni Boccaccio in his *Teseida* and *Il Filostrato* two centuries previously. Spenser's *The Faerie Queene* (1590, 1596) complicates epic-romance with sophisticated allegorical anatomy; although influenced by Ariosto, the author replaces ottava rima with his own nine-line stanza. The *Faerie Queene*'s mythopoesis often draws on and revises the *Metamorphoses*; lighter ventures into Ovidianism appear in the shorter *epyllion (or "short epic") form, most notably Christopher Marlowe's *Hero and Leander* (1593) and Shakespeare's *Venus and Adonis* (1593). Marlowe's poem offers a striking example of the narrative possibilities of the *heroic couplet, not only in its passages of rapid action but also in elaborate rhetorical set pieces and ekphrastic digressions.

Milton's *Paradise Lost* (1667, 1674) breaks with what he termed the "bondage" of rhyme and offers the first Eng. blank-verse epic. In the poet's ambitious retelling of the origins of the human condition, lengthy *verse paragraphs elaborate meaning and complicate the sequential unfolding of thought through sustained enjambment, mirroring on the small scale the work's challenging representation of a timeline that encompasses both genesis and apocalypse. In the century after Milton, the long satirical narratives and *mock epics of John Dryden and Alexander Pope eschew *blank verse in favor of the more aphoristic possibilities of the heroic couplet; in the later 18th c., George Crabbe discloses the quieter and more naturalistic capacities of that particular form in the rural narratives of *The Village* (1783).

The romantics appropriate and revise the blank-verse epic (most obviously in the spiritual autobiography of Wordsworth's *The Prelude* [1805, pub. 1850], although Wordsworth also employs blank verse in shorter narrative works such as "Michael"). Their poetry also reworks other narrative forms. The traditional ballad's effective use of simple, charged diction, minimalist but telling description, and a narrative dynamic heavily reliant on repetition with variation had attracted more literary treatments in earlier centuries (e.g., in Walter Ralegh's "Walsingham"); the very title of Wordsworth and S. T. Coleridge's *Lyrical Ballads* (1798) suggests an interest in appropriating the form in a more reflective manner (both Wordsworth and Coleridge experiment with a more dilatory six-line stanza in, e.g., the former's "The Idiot Boy" and the latter's *The Rime of the Ancient Mariner*). Elsewhere, John Keats's use of an abbreviated final line in the quatrains of "La Belle Dame sans Merci" (1820) modifies the conventional ballad stanza to create a powerful sense of loss, diminishment, and melancholy.

Keats borrows the recursive *Spenserian stanza for the leisurely sensuous romance narrative of "The Eve of St. Agnes" (1820); Lord Byron deploys its capacity for digression and interruption to very different effect in his satirical epic *Don Juan* (1819–24). As the 19th c. unfolds, a continuing interest in the long narrative poem diverges, on the one hand, into nostalgia and neomedievalism (Tennyson's *Idylls of the King*, the poems of D. G. Rossetti, and, eventually, W. B. Yeats's Celtic mythologies) and, on the other, into something not dissimilar to the verisimilitude of the realist novel. Pushkin's *Evgenij Onegin* (1825–32) makes a complex and artful stanzaic form the vehicle for representing colloquial description and dialogue and reflections on contemp. life (see ONEGIN STANZA). Robert Browning's multipart blank-verse narrative *The Ring and the Book* (1868–69) brings together a sequence of idiosyncratic dramatic monologues retracing the same set of events in Ren. Italy; Elizabeth Barrett Browning's account of the travails of a female artist in *Aurora Leigh* (1856) offers a contemp. blank-verse Bildungsroman. George Meredith's *Modern Love* (1862) co-opts the lyric sequence for quasi-novelistic purposes. Moving into the 20th c., one finds a sparser, starker version of romantic blank-verse narrative in the snapshot rural narratives (e.g., "The Death of the Hired Man," "Home Burial") of Robert Frost's *North of Boston* collection (1914).

With the particular valorization of the lyric (and the lyric sequence) in the 20th c., poetic storytelling tends to fall out of favor and becomes associated with middlebrow "parlor poetry" (like some of the highly recitable works of Rudyard Kipling and H. W. Longfellow) or with the Victorian *light verse of Lewis Carroll and W. S. Gilbert. Its early 20th-c. exponents are little read, although they too can revisit older modes, as in John Masefield's beast fable *Reynard the Fox* (1919) or G. K. Chesterton's melodramatic take on Ren. heroic poetry in "Lepanto" (1911). Narrative poetry does not, however, disappear. The accessible vignettes of Edgar Lee Masters's *Spoon River Anthology* (1916) have a more sophisticated modernist counterpart in Melvin B. Tolson's lyric sequence *Harlem Gallery* (1965). T. S. Eliot's structural use of the Grail quest myth and his fragmentary and fragmented quotation of earlier narrative poetry and familiar forms (dramatic blank verse, the narrative quatrain) in *The Waste Land* (1922) work in tension with the ellipses and discontinuities of a poem that keeps entertaining narrative possibilities only to frustrate them.

The ballad has continued to attract mod. and contemp. practitioners (see, e.g., W. H. Auden's "As I Walked Out One Evening" and Dudley Randall's "Ballad of Birmingham"). An almost Ovidian interest in rewriting old stories in new terms characterizes the work of Carol Ann Duffy ("Mrs. Midas," "Little Red Cap"). The Caribbean poet Derek Walcott's expansive postcolonial epic *Omeros* (1990), composed in a modified version of terza rima, embraces extended allusions to Homeric and Dantean journeyings (and exiles) as it both retraces the horrors of the middle passage and slides into metapoetic reflections. Rather less monumentally, Vikram Seth's *The Golden Gate* (1986) attempts a Pushkinesque narrative in tetrameter sonnets set in contemp. California. Narrative poetry has been championed by some New Formalists (such as Annie Finch and Mark Jarman—see NEW FORMALISM), but less conservative artists have also worked in this territory. The experimentalist Ronald Johnson creates a new story by selectively erasing much of the text of the first four books of *Paradise Lost* in *RADI-OS OI-OIV* (1976); the classicist Anne Carson offers a postmod. spin on the Geryon/Hercules myth in *Autobiography of Red* (1998); Lyn Hejinian's at once highly structured and paratactic sequence of prose poems *My Life* (1980–87) might be seen as a contemp. (and differently gendered) response to *The Prelude*.

## II. Poetic Form and Narrative Poetry.

In narrative poetry, the resources of poetic form have always been thoroughly entangled with the fiction-making process. At the conclusion of each long stanza of alliterating lines in *Sir Gawain and the Green Knight*, an isolated line with a single stress is followed by a rhymed quatrain, and this five-line *bob and wheel presents new information in a particularly emphatic manner. A stanza detailing the hero's lonely quest is followed by the miniature line "al one" (all alone), whose very isolation emphasizes the protagonist's condition; after an extended description of the alien warrior who invades King Arthur's court, the information that he is not only mysterious but entirely *green* is delayed to the final emphatic rhyme word of the quatrain. The wandering romance narratives and perpetual self-complication of Spenser's *Faerie Queene* are complemented by its stanzaic design whose *ababbcbcc* rhyme scheme encourages recapitulation, a small-scale doubling back that augments or reexamines what has already been said; at the same time, Spenser's switch from iambic pentameter to a longer *alexandrine in the ninth lines of each stanza produces repeated (and repeatedly superseded) moments of summary, gloss, or provisional closure that complement the larger narrative's own insistent swerves from any final ending. Spenser's additional predilection for allowing sonic effects to heighten narrative action is evident in the following description of his Red Cross Knight's encounter with the female monster Errour:

> Yet kindling rage, her selfe she gathered round,
> And all attonce her beastly body raizd
> With doubled forces high above the ground:
> Tho wrapping up her wrethéd sterne arownd,

> Lept fierce upon his shield, and her huge traine
> All suddenly about his body wound

The repeated rhymes on "wound" encourage the stanza to wind about the reader even as the monster entangles the knight.

Repetition with variation, a favorite strategy of both the traditional and the literary ballad, can be deployed with powerful narrative force. In "She Moved through the Fair," a poignant folk lyric collected by the Ir. poet Padraic Colum, the words of the narrator's lost beloved, "It will not be long, love, / 'Til our wedding day," take on a quite different meaning when, as a ghost, she reiterates her promise in the work's concluding stanza. In *The Rime of the Ancient Mariner*, Coleridge's occasional expansion of the traditional four-line stanza into six lines, repeating with minimal variation the fourth line in the sixth, enhances the obsessive and incantatory nature of the tale told by the Mariner to the Wedding Guest. Meter can also powerfully shape narrative tone and mood: in Christina Rossetti's *Goblin Market* (1862), the steady accretion of lines beginning with trochaic and dactylic feet not only emphasizes the feverish quality of the fable but heightens, in its climactic stanzas, the assault on all the senses endured by its heroine. G. M. Hopkins's innovative *sprung rhythm in "The Wreck of the Deutschland" (1918) evokes the turbulence and uncertainty of tempest and shipwreck.

Narrative poems in rhymed couplets offer in each rhyme's completion temporary gestures toward containment and *closure that may operate in tension with the forward drive of plot and foster the witty and epigrammatic quality of poets as disparate as Chaucer, Marlowe, and Pope. In satiric narrative, they can also offer exquisitely controlled moments of comic *anticlimax, as in the following from Pope's *Rape of the Lock* (1714): "The skilful nymph reviews her force with care / 'Let spades be trumps!' she said, and trumps they were." (Wilfred Owen's World War I dream narrative "Strange Meeting" [1918] poignantly unbalances the confident pace of couplet narrative in its employment of half- and slant rhymes throughout.) Blank-verse narrative removes sonic closure, and its enjambments can open up line endings to a powerful sense of semantic uncertainty, vigorously exploited by Milton in *Paradise Lost*, whose extended and flexible verse paragraphs regularly qualify meaning and create surprise, as in the retrospective reinflection of the word "merit" by the enjambed line that follows in the poet's description of how, in imperial splendor,

> Satan exalted sat, by merit raised
> To that bad eminence.

The mere absence of rhyme does not preclude, of course, the heightened effects of poetic diction and meter: in the following description of Satan's voyage through Chaos, the accumulation of monosyllables and *spondees in the second and third lines and the pounding *iambs that place strong stress on verbs of movement in the fourth powerfully evoke a laborious, scrabbling, almost animal journeying:

> . . .the Fiend
> O'er bog or steep, through strait, rough, dense, or
>   rare,
> With head, hands, wings, or feet pursues his way,
> And swims or sinks, or wades or creeps or flies.

The deployment of strong caesurae in both blank and rhymed verse also contributes to strong narrative effects; a metrical pause can allow discourse to change direction or create a space for the reader to fill. Browning uses these tactics simultaneously when the murderous narrator of "My Last Duchess" offers self-revelation at the very moment that he swerves from full confession:

>                                I gave commands;
> Then all smiles stopped together. There she stands
> As if alive. Will't please you rise? We'll meet
> The company below.

Narrative poetry can, furthermore, deploy the resources of *typography to reinforce the work of form in shaping the unfolding of a fiction. In Frost's "Death of the Hired Man," a final *split line packs a climactic punch:

> "Warren?" she questioned.
>                          "Dead," was all he answered.

In Eliot's *The Waste Land*, by contrast, typography repeatedly shatters the formal containment of putative plot: teasing fragments of narrative are interrupted by white space; new beginnings or fruitless returns erupt out of nowhere.

**III. Criticism.** Little critical work has focused specifically on narrative poetry, although the critical taxonomies and terminologies developed by narrative theorists such as Chatman, Genette, and Ricoeur may be usefully applied to narrative in verse. This is, to a large extent, the result of a critical tendency to rely on a poetry/prose binary that reduces poetry to lyric and elides the presence and work of poetic narrative; the influential stylistic poetics of Jakobson, e.g., associates epic with the "metonymical" capacity of prose fiction as opposed to the "metaphoric" nature of lyric. Scholes, Kellogg, and Phelan's *The Nature of Narrative* pays more sustained attention to narrative poetry than any other work in this field, although the authors' interest in the historical develop. of narratives allows relatively little space for discussion of the particular shaping capacities of poetic form. Among crit. not strictly aimed at narrative poetry, McHugh's rich essay on the linear unfolding of meaning in lyric and the pivotal force of the line ending in "making and breaking" sense might be equally well applied to the workings of narrative poetry. Among works on particular narrative poets or particular narrative genres, the crit. of Boitani (on med. poetic narrative), Greene (on the epic trad.), Berger (on Spenser's *Faerie Queene*), Crosman (on Milton's *Paradise Lost*), Fischer (on romantic verse narratives), and Tucker (on the Victorian *long poem) offer particularly useful insights.

See DRAMATIC POETRY; FICTION, POETRY AS; MEDIEVAL ROMANCE; ORAL POETRY.

■ R. Jakobson, "Linguistics and Poetics," *Style in Language*, ed. T.A. Sebeok (1960); T. M. Greene, *The Descent from Heaven: A Study in Epic Continuity* (1963); F. Kermode, *The Sense of an Ending* (1967); S. Chatman, *Story and Discourse: Narrative Structure in Fiction and Film* (1978); R. Crosman, *Reading "Paradise Lost"* (1980); G. Genette, *Narrative Discourse*, trans. J. Lewin (1980); F. G. Andersen, O. Holzapfel, and T. Pettitt, *The Ballad as Narrative* (1982); P. Boitani, *English Medieval Narrative in the Thirteenth and Fourteenth Centuries*, trans. J. K. Hall (1982); *The Oxford Book of Narrative Verse*, ed. I. Opie and P. Opie (1983); P. Ricoeur, *Time and Narrative*, trans. K. McLaughlin and D. Pellauer (1984); H. Berger Jr., *Revisionary Play: Studies in the Spenserian Dynamic* (1988) P. Zumthor, *Oral Poetry*, trans. K. Murphy-Judy (1990); H. Fischer, *Romantic Verse Narrative* (1991); C. R. Kinney, *Strategies of Poetic Narrative: Chaucer, Spenser, Milton, Eliot* (1992); H. McHugh, "Moving Means, Meaning Moves: Notes on Lyric Destination," *Poets Teaching Poets*, ed. G. Orr and E. B. Voigt (1996); *After New Formalism: Poets on Form, Narrative and Tradition*, ed. A. Finch (1999); N. Roberts, *Narrative and Voice in Postwar Poetry* (1999); P. Cobley, *Narrative* (2001); R. Scholes, R. Kellogg, and J. Phelan, *The Nature of Narrative*, 2d ed. (2006); H. F. Tucker, *Epic: Britain's Heroic Muse, 1790–1910* (2008).

C. R. KINNEY

**NARRATOR.** *See* PERSONA; VOICE.

**NATIONAL POETRY.** Although poetry as a form of human expression is ancient, national poetry is a mod. phenomenon, a product of nationalism and the institutionalization of lit. It manifests two different conceptions of sovereignty, that of a people as a unique ethnic group and that of lit. as a discrete aesthetic category. In order to understand national poetry, therefore, we have to grasp these two mod. forces: the will to unite an ethnic group and endow it with political independence and the impulse to create an autonomous lit. to express the new national reality.

While the *Epic of Gilgamesh*, the verses of Sappho, or Aztec poetry were composed and rooted in their respective langs. and societies, they were neither considered a reflection of their cultures nor regarded as autonomous aesthetic artifacts. National poetry, on the other hand, is a paradoxical entity, both a self-conscious aesthetic form and a participant in social life.

Nationalism arose as a powerful ideology in Europe during the latter part of the 18th and early 19th cs. A complex manifestation of social, political, cultural, and economic factors, nationalism molded ancient ethnicities into mod. nations. Although people had always organized themselves into separate groups, dividing those inside from those outside, nationalism gave this tendency a political foundation. In other words, nationalism politicized the human practice of distinguishing the self from the other, making ethnicity the basis for self-government. It made culture, the identity of the ethnic group, the foundation of the new state, bringing about a marriage between culture and politics, nation and state.

This new nation-state was to have its own apparatus (e.g., army, bureaucracy, borders) and symbols (lang., flag, *anthem). Lit. emerged as one of the most characteristic signs of the nation, both giving voice to and promoting national uniqueness. Literary figures were often determined supporters of national independence and in some cases became political figures. The rise of national lit. demonstrates the public nature of poetry—that it partakes in the daily life of the community.

This could only have taken place because lit. itself was gradually emerging as a partitioned phenomenon, manifesting a far grander process of social compartmentalization or what sociologists refer to as functional differentiation—the division of society into separate spheres of human activity such as the economy, culture, law, medicine, and so on. Lit., in other words, was taking shape as an institution unto itself, with its own regulations (to separate "good" from "bad" writing, the high from the low), social sites (publishing houses, newspaper book reviews, university curricula), and modes of consumption (leisure, serious, academic, and pedagogic reading). Residing within the greater institution of art, lit. was constituted by the *genres of poetry, the novel, short stories, drama, and nonfiction and necessitated a particular way of interpreting texts, both oral and written. In short, it unified diverse types of texts and of approaches.

Thereafter, poetry would belong to this institution of lit. and to the cultural trads. of nations. Indeed, with the exception of a few supranational figures such as Rubén Darío (1867–1916) in Sp. America (see MODERNISMO), most poetry would henceforth be considered national, i.e., it would indisputably belong to one people, helping this people differentiate itself from the cultural productions of its neighbors. That poetry turned inward and looked back to its indigenous ling. and literary roots does not mean, however, that it somehow became backward. On the contrary, to the extent that it was national lit., it lit the path to modernity. National poetry was as much a sign of modernity as capitalism, industrialization, the train, or the jet engine. Indeed, it promoted modernization by asking people to see themselves as members of nation-states and consumers of self-consciously aesthetic products.

National poetry manifested wider cultural tensions between *tradition and modernity, *mimesis and *originality, locality and universality, homogeneity and heterogeneity. While in theory poetry seemed to push toward the old, the regional, and the standardized, in all these cases, it was actually created, and it encouraged the interaction between the individual and the general, the self and the other. It was syncretic while all the time claiming to be monocultural.

The mod. Gr. poet Dionysios Solomos (1798–1857) exhibits the hallmarks of the national poet: he is now celebrated as a *bard, representative of Greece, the inventor of the mod. lyric trad., the composer of its national anthem, and the manifestation of excellence in poetic craft (see GREEK POETRY). Yet, in both his life and his work, he typified the contradictions of writers of 19th-c. Europe and of 20th-c. postcolonial societies.

Born on the Ionian island of Zakynthos, then a Venetian possession and later to be taken over by Great Britain, Solomos grew up speaking Gr. and It. After spending ten years studying in Italy, he returned to his place of birth, more at home in It. than in Gr. His first poems were composed in It.; indeed, his later mature work was originally written in the lang. of the colonizer and then translated into demotic. What is now hailed as supremely Gr. lyric had originally been composed in It. and suffused with Ger. idealist philosophy. National in name, his work was federative in practice—which is what makes it so national in the first place. Solomos's genius lay in fashioning a synthesis between the vernacular tongue and the work of Friedrich Schiller, folk poetry and cosmopolitan romantic discourse, the lang. of the occupier and the idiom of the freedom fighter. This makes his oeuvre, and that of any other poet, national and transnational at the same time, a paradox much like the title of his well-known poem *The Free Besieged*.

Mod. writers, Solomos himself noted, differ from village poets in being conscious of their place in the institution of national lit.: "the nation asks us that the treasure of our individual intelligence be dressed in national garments." The mod. poet often reflects on the aesthetic and political task ahead, which makes him feel socially engaged and alienated at the same time. On the one hand, this self-reflexivity brings about a distance between artist and society, as G.W.F. Hegel well understood; but on the other, it fosters a common, public sense of purpose. Solomos manifested both tendencies. Tortured by the romantic theory of the absolute, he slaved away at various versions of his poems, rarely publishing final drafts in his lifetime. In fact, most of his corpus exits in fragmentary form. Yet in aspiring toward the aesthetic *sublime, Solomos also understood that poets were living in transitional times, which demanded that they engage in the creation of new social systems and novel poetic trads. Solomos, like Ger. poets before him and many after him all over the world, profoundly experienced the belatedness of his society. His studies in Italy forced him to confront the gap between his own colonized, economically backward country and the progress and enlightenment of metropolitan Europe.

His work is paradigmatic of how poets in modernizing societies see themselves as agents of change. The comparisons these poets and intellectuals make between advanced and developing societies prompt them to initiate and promote projects of modernization and nationalism. In assisting the creation of national cultures and national lits., these writers participate in a mod. act, pushing their populations toward a globalized modernity, toward engagement with the outside world rather than retrenchment.

On his own return home, Solomos discovered the

absence of an institution of lit.: the lack of a literary ling. medium, of genres beyond lyric, and the social network required to support a national lit. So he set out to create it with his verse, bending romantic theory into the *ballad form, translating metaphysical philosophy into the vernacular, modernizing traditional rhythm for a new purpose. He combined, in other words, the principles of aesthetic and national consolidation. This double dance ensured that his poetry would remain lit. above all, rather than a sheer reflection of the nation. Although his *Free Besieged* deals with the revolutionaries of Missolonghi—the place where Lord Byron met his death in the struggle for Gr. independence from Ottoman rule—the poem is not a *panegyric, cheering the warriors to victory, but about military and aesthetic failure. Just as the warriors are defeated by the Ottomans, the poem too is crushed by the contradictions of the poet's task to express absolute "form with the demotic language."

The contradictions inherent in poetic lang. render national poetry an unsettled and unsettling medium, never sliding into one-dimensional portrayal of social reality. Moreover, the tensions of the entire modernizing project also ensure that such poetry is a syncretic phenomenon, fitting imported institutions to local needs. As such, national poetry is another manifestation of the human negotiation between the local and the universal, between aboriginal realities and imported ideologies and institutions.

One of the abiding dreams of national poetry is the search for and depiction of the unique ethnic self. If national poetry is born out of comparisons between self and other, colonizer and colonized, the indigenous and the transnational, it is to be expected that the local defines itself always with respect to external agents and forces. Yet again, even if this project resembles an ontological hunt for truth, it comes to be through a confrontation with difference. This dialogue with the other prevents national poetry from becoming merely a celebration of the nation. That a national culture is established does not mean that all differences are extinguished in the new foundation, much as standardization of lang. within the nation does not erase all ling. diversity. The Brazilian poet and critic Haroldo de Campos (1929–2003), observing the context around the avant-garde movement of the 1920s and after known as *antropofagia*, proposes to replace "ontological nationalism" ("a model which inspires and underlies any literary historiography which seeks to identify a 'national classicism,' a moment of perfection of a slow blossoming") with "a modal, differential nationalism," which considers "nationalism as a dialogical movement of difference": "the dis-character, instead of the character, the rupture instead of the linear course." The "great and unclassifiable" novelist Machado de Assis, Campos remarks, has swallowed Laurence Sterne and "innumerable others"; he "is national because he is not national." At the very core, lit. always maintains a negotiation between the local and the global, the national and the transnational.

Authenticity, moreover, becomes a rallying call for innovation and *invention. This insight is confirmed by the experience of Germany, the country where so much thought about nationalism originally took shape. Toward the end of the 18th c., many bourgeois intellectuals found themselves shut out from the public sphere by an aristocracy beholden to Fr. culture. To a certain extent, these intellectuals devised the notion of an authentically Ger. identity to displace the privileged position of Fr. lit. in Ger. society. In a quintessential class struggle against the aristocracy, they tried to imagine a unified Ger. nation before it had been achieved politically, using culture as a weapon to augment their social position. G. E. Lessing (1729–81) gave voice to this cultural and social exclusion in *Hamburg Dramaturgy* (1767): "[W]e are the sworn copyists," he argued, "to all that is foreign; especially, are we still the obedient admirers of the never sufficiently admired French?" J. G. Herder (1744–1803) similarly wondered whether the Ger. people were fated to remain translators and imitators. Why, he asked, did young Germans prefer It., Fr., and Eng. writers?

This disquieting question has since been posed countless times in modernizing societies by writers who have to confront the avowed supremacy of their more powerful neighbor or their colonizing state. We have heard it from Herman Melville in the U.S., Antonio Gramsci in Italy, José Rizal in the Philippines, Ngũgĩ wa Thiong'o in Kenya, José Carlos Mariátegui in Peru, and Margaret Atwood in Canada. The question "where are our great authors?" indicates how far-reaching the discourse of nationalism has been in promulgating the belief that each nation needs its own lit., incl. poetry. In the age of nationalism, the act of copying foreign models is supremely humiliating because it places the home culture in a derivative situation, seemingly secondary and inauthentic. The belief that all nations are products of and capable of originality is a powerful message against the universality of imperialism. Based on the Herderian notion of the incommensurability of cultures, it is a driving force against foreign rule, emboldening people to look for the center of their creativity in indigenous models.

In the case of Germany, this theory was tested by the Napoleonic invasions of Germany in 1800. Although Ger. intellectuals and poets were supportive, often enthusiastically, of the Fr. Revolution, this attack forced them to look to their own trads. J. G. Fichte (1762–1814) gave voice to this resistance in a series of lectures he gave in a vanquished Berlin during the years 1807–8, lectures that would become important nationalist documents. He tried to rouse the Germans to look at the cultural ties binding them together against a common foe. Each separate nation, he asserted, "has the right to take independent charge of its affairs and to govern itself." Culture becomes, then, the basis for self-governance. Unity by culture leads to unity by citizenship. This remains a potent political message to this day.

If we often think that lit. is itself a secondary agent in society, lit.'s role in nationalizing societies shows its relevance in great political struggle. National poetry does not by itself lead to revolution. It cannot overthrow the aggressor or build a new society. But it provides the arguments, figures, and lang. for the assertion of national independence and self-governance. Indeed, poets often offer images of national unification years before the actual consolidation of the state.

That poetry engages in such a mission does not make it into a positivistic discourse, a mouthpiece for the general and the bureaucrat. We have to keep in mind that the very label *national poetry* identifies it as a partly political and partly aesthetic enterprise. The *tropes of poetic lang. remind readers that the text before them is primarily a literary document rather than a political tract; it transmits representations, images, and fictions. These tropes themselves oppose nationalization, playing havoc with the very idea of one single, unitary identity.

The Gr. case demonstrates this well. Solomos may have helped found a trad. of national poetry on the basis of the demotic lang., but a half century later, C. P. Cavafy (1863–1933) resisted this nationalization of Gr. letters. Although hailed as a canonical figure today, Cavafy was marginalized in his time. He lived most of his life in Alexandria, outside the borders of the Gr. kingdom, having visited Greece only a few times. Moreover, he felt at home in Eng., the lang. of the colonial power in Egypt, even as he ignored contemp. Egypt in his verse. In so many ways, his writing does not fit comfortably within the walls established by Solomos and his followers, pointing in this way to the different, often conflicting schools that can form within the national *canon.

First of all, mod. Greece, as a sociopolitical reality, rarely enters Cavafy's work. Second and more important, Cavafy gave voice to the ling. variety of the Gr. trad. Rather than adopting demotic, the lang. of national lit., he wrote in a hybrid of vernacular and learned registers. What is more, he also incorporated the vast historical range of Gr. His poems often contain words, phrases, or entire passages from cl., late antique, and Byzantine Gr., demonstrating poetically the ling. heterogeneity that made his work possible.

Moreover, Cavafy offered an unorthodox view of Gr. hist. While his contemporaries were celebrating the glories of 5th-c. BCE authors, representing themselves implicitly and explicitly as the heirs of that period, Cavafy wrote of decline, the Hellenistic epoch, and the time of late antiquity when the Gr. world had been conquered by Rome. Cavafy spoke of barbarians at the walls of the city, of imperial expansion and a great mixing of peoples, langs., and religions: "We the Alexandrians, the Antiochians, / the Celeucians and the many / other Greeks of Egypt and Syria, / and those of Media and Persia" ("In the Year 200 BC"). His historical figures are often people who find themselves on the wrong side of glory, provincial types trying to ape the ways of elites in Rome. Cavafy shares an ironic view of Gr. hist., showing tarnished accomplishments and shabby realities. He writes about when Greece was in decline and when Gr. culture, spread throughout the eastern Mediterranean, was characterized by a proud multiculturalism.

This ironic interpretation of the past is enhanced by Cavafy's frank treatment of homosexuality and his implicit critique of virile nationalism. The poems set in both mod. and ancient Alexandria feature men adoring other men: "Lines of the body. Red lips. Erotic limbs. / Hair as if taken from Greek statues" ("Much I Observed"). The "faultlessly beautiful" young men of Alexandria, so enamored of their own masculine attraction, seem distant from the fighters in Missolonghi. Yet they constitute part of the same canon, which goes to show that no national poetry is monolithically national. The canon contains diverse styles, trads. and interpretations often in conflict with one another. These trads. give voice to a diversity of lang. and historical experience that the title *national poetry* seems to occlude. National poetry is as much about the other as it is about the self.

The trajectory of national poetry in the 19th and 20th cs. was made possible by the privileging of the powers of narrative and of lit. to express identities. In the 21st c., however, poetry outside mass culture is no longer considered a dominant literary form. We cannot be sure, therefore, that national poetry will continue to signify in the 21st c. what it did in the previous two. What is certain, however, is that people still organize themselves into distinct ethnic and national groupings. They still have to negotiate between transnational economic and cultural flows and their own lives. Poetry, perhaps in association with other aesthetic forms and new media, may still adapt to express this dialectic between self and other.

*See* AUTONOMY, POET LAUREATE, POLITICS AND POETRY.

■ J. G. Fichte, *Addresses to the German Nation* (1835); J. G. Herder, *Reflections on the Philosophy of the History of Mankind*, ed. F. E. Manuel (1968); J. C. Mariátegui, *Seven Interpretive Essays on Peruvian Reality*, trans. M. Urquidi (1971); Ngũgĩ wa Thiong'o, *Homecoming: Essays on African and Caribbean Literature, Culture and Politics* (1972); B. Anderson, *Imagined Communities* (1983); B. Harlow, *Resistance Literature* (1987); P. U. Hohendahl, *Building a National Literature: The Case of Germany 1830–1870* (1989); J. G. Herder, *Against Pure Reason: Writing on Religion, Language, and History*, trans. M. Bunge (1989); *Nation and Narration*, ed. H. Bhabha (1990); G. Jusdanis, *Belated Modernity and Aesthetic Culture: Inventing National Literature* (1991); D. Sommer, *Foundational Fictions: The National Romances of Latin America* (1991); R. Helgerson, *Forms of Nationhood: The Elizabethan Writing of England* (1992); G. Jusdanis, *The Necessary Nation* (2001); D. Damrosch, *What Is World Literature?* (2003); H. de Campos, "The Rule of Anthropophagy: Europe under the Sign of Devoration," *Novas*, ed. A. S. Bessa and O. Cisneros (2007).

G. JUSDANIS

**NATIVE AMERICAN POETRY.** *See* INDIGENOUS AMERICAS, POETRY OF THE; INUIT POETRY; NAVAJO POETRY.

**NATIVITY POEM.** Though it might seem a minor occasional genre associated with *lauda*, *carols, and *hymns, the nativity poem has closely tracked literary, religious, and political changes since the 4th c. The nativity poem emerged in early med. culture as a liturgical practice wary of echoing pagan and Roman natal celebrations. Thus, the hymns and poems of Prudentius and Ephrem in the 4th c. typically offer typological reflections or theological explorations of the Incarnation.

Within the literary vernaculars of the 14th c., the nativity poem became less strictly liturgical as the influence of the Franciscans and the popularity of mystery plays encouraged a more participatory, affective spirituality. The *courtly love trad. inspired visions of the maiden Mary, while naturalistic depictions thrived as lower classes found their struggles dignified by the humble setting of Christ's birth. Chaucer's Marian verse is exemplary among the numerous Nativity-themed lyrics through the 15th c.

In the 16th and 17th cs., the genre grew increasingly complex, incorporating *epic and *pastoral *tropes and *baroque *conceits while negotiating the religio-political tensions engendered by the Reformation and Counter-Reformation. Luis de Góngora is important here, as is John Milton, whose "On the Morning of Christ's Nativity" balances Puritan disdain for Catholic imagery with subtle reverence for Christ's birth scene. After the mid-17th c., more conventionally pious nativity poems predominated even as the diminishing numbers of the genre reflected the rise of the new science, deism, and other challenges to traditional pieties.

While meditative and innovative nativity poems continued to thrive across the last two centuries (e.g., S. T. Coleridge, Christina Rossetti, W. H. Auden, and Joseph Brodsky), *romanticism opened a new relationship with the Nativity, which became an allusive presence in works addressing broader ontological concerns, as in William Wordsworth's "Ode: Intimations of Immortality." In the 20th c., the genre grew increasingly ironic and reflexive. Consider T. S. Eliot's oblique Nativity reference in "Gerontion" to a time "swaddled in darkness" or the insinuating Nativity theme in postcolonial poets such as Christopher Okigbo.

*See* DEVOTIONAL POETRY, LITURGICAL POETRY, RELIGION AND POETRY.

■ L. C. Sledge, *Shivering Babe, Victorious Lord: The Nativity in Poetry and Art* (1981); "Nativity," *A Dictionary of Biblical Tradition in English Literature*, ed. D. L. Jeffrey (1992); *Divine Inspiration*, ed. R. Atwan, G. Dardess, and P. Rosenthal (1998); *Middle English Marian Lyrics*, ed. K. Saupe (1998); A. Vander Zee, "Milton's Mary: Suspending Song in the *Nativity Ode*," *MP* 108 (2011).

A. VANDER ZEE

**NATURALISM.** There are two principal ways in which this multivalent term is used in the study of poetry: one emphasizes (esp. in Eng. poetics) a set of romantic principles concerning the "lyrical" evocation of *nature and their prevalence throughout most of the Victorian era, while the other, more narrowly, identifies an aesthetic program that is based on an aggressively antiromantic system of philosophical-scientific doctrines. Walter Pater has the former concept in mind when, in the Preface to *The Renaissance* (1873), he mentions William Wordsworth's naturalistic vision as "that strange, mystical sense of a life in natural things, and of man's life as a part of nature." *Naturalism* here refers to the poetic representation of a vital reciprocity between the human being and his living (natural) environment, an experience that may allow intimations of a transcendent reality to emanate from this close sympathy between private sensibilities and the domain of organic life. Alfred, Lord Tennyson's view of nature as "red in tooth and claw," on the other hand, is predicated on the contrary notion that a person's existence is a constant "struggle for life," dominated by morally indifferent compulsions and subject to a blind dynamism of regeneration undone by destruction. The Am. novelist Frank Norris called it "the primal instinct of the brute struggling for its life." Nature here is an impediment to virtuous self-fulfillment, to humane civilization, and to ennobling vision. In either case, whether nature is perceived as a benign source of value or as an agent of rapacious biological and environmental destiny, the term *naturalism* refers to an abiding preoccupation with nature, usually equated with objective reality, as the essential determinant of life.

More restrictively, however, the term *naturalism* in poetics is closely associated with the mechanistic and deterministic principles developed by late 19th-c. science. In this context, the term refers to the programmatic systematization of a literary aesthetic that sought to reconcile the aims of art with the all-pervasive authority of the natural sciences. This meant subordinating an "antimodern" insistence on creative individualism to nomological methods of construction that reflect the techniques of advanced scientific specialization. In consequence, the categorical difference between art and reality was being blurred, and lit., esp. poetry, began to circulate widely as merely one of many forms of popular entertainment. Its challenge was to stay up to date ("experimental").

Use of the term *naturalism* to designate a style or a movement is infrequent in Eng. literary scholarship, while the Era of Naturalism in Am. writing (1900–15) is applied only to distinctive prose fiction (by Norris, Stephen Crane, later by Theodore Dreiser and J. T. Farrell). An exception may be the socially conscious verse of William Vaughn Moody (1869–1910). In Europe, where naturalism was generally identified with Émile Zola's programmatic essays and his novels, critics and readers often reacted with vituperative derogations. Most of the poets from the naturalistic generation (incl. Zola's *groupe de Médan* of 1880, which produced no distinctive verse in their master's vein) therefore preferred to call themselves realists or modernists. The reason for this was twofold: while many "naturalists" were engaged with social and political issues as partisans of working-class aspirations, they needed the bourgeoisie as their readers and thus had to accommodate themselves to bourgeois preferences that considered art a domain independent of and above the conflicts of politics and labor. At the same time, the cultural program, e.g., of social democracy (or any other nonrevolutionary workers' organization) rejected all naturalistic art for its choice of "sordid milieus" and "depraved characters" as an offense to the industrial workers' self-esteem.

This holds true esp. for Germany, where Otto von Bismarck's *Sozialistengesetz* of 1878 (an emergency measure that also protected official Prussian culture against "socialist subversion") was not repealed until 1890. Even so, naturalism had come into its own by 1885, earlier in France and later in Britain, with *manifestos and poetry anthols., both proclaiming group solidarity. But, in fact, diffuse thematic and stylistic orientations prevailed, and no poet practiced what his or her stated purposes postulated. A good example of this discrepancy between the pathos of revolutionary aims and, all in all, an eclectically epigonous, though technically accomplished, style is the collection *Moderne Dichter-Charaktere* (1885), ed. by W. Arent, H. Conradi, and K. F. Henckell, that offers a sampling of work by 22 contributors. The only poet in Germany (and perhaps anywhere) who philosophically justified (in *Die Kunst und ihre Gesetze*, 2 v., 1891–93; and in *Revolution der Lyrik*, 1899) and practiced (in *Das Buch der Zeit: Lieder eines Modernen*, 1886) what he called "konsequenter Naturalismus" (consistent naturalism) was Arno Holz (1863–1929). But this naturalism soon turned into a method, a virtuoso's purely formal concern, rather than the poetically realized expression of an engagement with social issues. His chef d'oeuvre, the prose poem *Phantasus* (first version 1898–99), depicts the poet in an ever-expanding variety of even cosmic metamorphoses. The poet's soul is part of a hypertrophic growth and subsequent dissolution of the world of objects, kaleidoscopic but totally arbitrary. The lang. of this "gigantic-Phantasus-nonplusultra poem" (Holz) has abandoned all but one formal *constraint: it is arranged along an imaginary central axis as symmetrical half lines. The attempt, finally, to turn art back into nature (reality), reflecting a subjectivistic conception of nature, has produced a hypernaturalism that is an excessive impressionism.

■ St. A. Brooke, *Naturalism in English Poetry* (1920); F.W.J. Hemmings, "The Origins of the Terms *Naturalisme, Naturaliste*," *FS* 8 (1954); C. C. Walcutt, *American Literary Naturalism* (1956); *Literarische Manifeste des Naturalismus 1880–1892*, ed. E. Ruprecht (1962); W. R. Maurer, *The Naturalistic Image of German Literature* (1972); J. Schutte, *Lyrik des deutschen Naturalismus, 1885–1893* (1976); *Naturalismus, Ästhetizismus*, ed. C. Bürger, P. Bürger, J. Schulte-Sasse (1979); R. C. Cowen, *Der Naturalismus*, 3d ed. (1981); W. B. Michaels, *The Gold Standard and the Logic of Naturalism: American Literature at the Turn of the Century* (1987); G. Mahal, *Naturalismus*, 2d ed. (1990); F. Caudet, "Clarín y el debate sobre el naturalismo en España," *Nueva revista de filolgía Hispánica* 42 (1994); *The Cambridge Companion to American Realism and Naturalism*, ed. D. Pizer (1995); *Spectacles of Realism*, ed. M. Cohen and C. Prendergast (1995); G. Nouzeilles, "Pathological Romances and National Dys-topias in Argentine Naturalism," *Latin American Literary Review* 24, no. 47 (1996); Y. Chevrel, "Poétique du naturalisme," *Histoire des poétiques*, ed. J. Bessiere et al. (1997); *Documents of American Realism and Naturalism*, ed. D. Pizer (1998); G. Finney, "Poetic Realism, Naturalism, and the Rise of the Novella," *The Camden House History of German Literature*, v. 9 (2005).

M. WINKLER

**NATURE.** In their classic study of the term, Lovejoy and Boas teased out 61 categories of meaning for our word *nature*. Given the term's vast breadth and cultural significance, Williams's observation, which has been repeatedly echoed (often in exasperation) by literary critics, is hardly surprising: "any full history of the uses of 'nature' would be a history of a large part of human thought." Complicating matters, our concept of nature was influenced not only by the Lat. *natura*, from whence our word derives, but by the Gr. *physis* and OE *cyn*. Nonetheless, while their hists. are intricate and circuitous, behind each of these words lies a single, shared meaning.

*Physis, natura,* and *cyn* each originally denoted birth and growth. This core meaning is so old that it predates the first Gr., Lat., and OE utterances, having its origin in two IE words: *bheue* (from which we get *physis*) and *gen* (which gave us *natura* and *cyn*). Although the ancient IE sense of birth and growth is rarely invoked when we use the word *nature* today, this meaning was still available to Heraclitus and his student Cratylus: to both philosophers, *physis* signals birth, growth, and passing away, the endlessly reoccurring process of becoming, whereby everything everywhere is ever coming into and out of existence. Because Cratylus observed that such change happens quickly, he criticized (as Aristotle noted) "Heraclitus for saying that one cannot step twice into the same stream, for he himself thought it could not be done even once." Doubting that lang. could successfully represent nature, which he saw as manifestly and wildly in flux, Cratylus chose to communicate only by gesturing, silently pointing to nature endlessly in flux.

Because he argued that lang. failed to represent nature successfully, the mute and gesturing Cratylus was profoundly worrisome to Plato. Fortunately for Plato, he found a teacher, Socrates, who promised to save lang. from the relentless flux of nature by postulating a fixed and immutable realm securely "beyond nature" (*metaphysikē*), which, he reasoned, is what lang. must refer to, or at least should represent, if uttered truthfully by a knowledgeable person. Not content with merely theorizing this supersensory realm, in his dialogue *Cratylus* (389c), Plato triumphantly underscored this achievement by redefining *physis* as equivalent to his changeless *Ideas* (which he postulated as existing only in the metaphysical realm), thereby turning the old definition, which Cratylus still echoed, on its head.

Plato thus marks a turning point in the hist. of the concept of nature, which resulted in nature's being locked into (and seen as the inferior member of) a binary structure with the metaphysical. As a result, after

Plato, "true nature" is often imagined as that which lies firmly beyond the flux of nature. This dualistic view quickly came to dominate Western thinking, first through Plotinus and the Neoplatonists, then in Christian thinking, esp. with the Scholastics, with heaven imagined as the superior, metaphysical realm and the soul actually at risk of contamination from the earthly environment. By the Ren., this view had become a commonplace.

Shortly after Plato, the poet Theocritus, by way of the pastoral mode of writing he largely inaugurated, imagined nature as entangled with other concepts. A member of Ptolemy's court in Alexandria, Theocritus wrote of country places (fondly recalled from his youth in rural Sicily) from the perspective of city and court, praising the country at the expense of the latter (see ALEXANDRIANISM). Thus, the dyad that Theocritus explored, which Plato had already taken up more generally, was one in which culture opposed nature. In *pastoral poetry, built environments (like cities) and strongholds of human culture (like courts) often stand in opposition to places where nature is imagined to still be unfolding freely, unimpeded by human interaction. Of course, as we now know, the pastures depicted in pastoral poetry were themselves highly modified environments, the result of wholesale deforestation maintained by the constant grazing of livestock (as Harrison and others have observed). Nonetheless, pastoral poetry, which is nearly always written from an urban vantage point, generally, and often wistfully, portrayed these places as the refuge of nature, even as it acknowledged and lamented their passing as a result of human action.

The manner by which Plato and Theocritus (along with a range of other Gr. thinkers) reconceived of nature had profound consequences. First, because nature was imagined in opposition to certain places, such as cities, it became more a spatial than a temporal category. Having inherited this view, we often think of nature as a place (such as a rural locale, following Theocritus), rather than that by virtue of which all places—and everything else, for that matter—are changed over time. Moreover, in setting up nature in opposition to culture, these Gr. thinkers presaged an enormously influential distinction, often first attributed to Cicero, between "first nature," existing separately from human intervention, like an untouched forest, and "second nature," which references human culture and works, such as a table made from the forest's trees. This is an important distinction that is still very much alive today, as we often judge "naturalness," be it of a place or a consumer product, on the extent of its human modification. The first/second nature dyad echoes a similar distinction that emerged with the Greeks, between nature and art, with the latter often being seen (such as in the close of Plato's *Republic*) as an inferior reflection of nature

Not surprisingly, the question of the relation of nature to art is one to which writers from Aristotle through Edmund Spenser and into the 21st c. have repeatedly turned. Moreover, as Watson has recently argued, the issue of whether writers and artists could truly be successful in their efforts to represent nature caused a great deal of anxiety even in the late Ren. More recently, poststructural thinkers (such as Derrida), following the phenomenologists of the first half of the 20th c., have reopened this question.

In both his *Eclogues* and *Georgics*, Virgil took up the question of first and second nature. In his first *eclogue, which both Alpers and Patterson argue established the paradigm for nearly all subsequent pastoral, Virgil reflected on the pastoral mode he inherited by considering how culture (by way of political decisions) can affect nature (i.e., first nature, in the form of a rural locale). Following Hesiod, Cato, and Varro, and postulating, like the authors of Genesis, that human beings once lived at peace with nature in a golden age but lost that perfect state through human folly, in his *Georgics* Virgil focused on the necessary creation of second nature through agriculture. In general, as ecocritics have repeatedly made clear, in Gr., Roman, Heb., and Christian thinking, human beings are frequently imagined as living in an adversarial relationship with nature, mandated to convert an inhospitable (in Genesis "fallen") first nature into second through backbreaking labor.

With nature understood in so many ways, its value was drawn into question for future writers. E.g., conceiving of nature as locked into two binaries (nature vs. the metaphysical, nature vs. city; being marginalized in the first, privileged in the second) raised a key question: is nature evil or good? The Ren. poet Petrarch, who wrote of his "hate . . . of Town, and love of the woods" in his letters, nonetheless related that he became "enraged" with himself for "admiring earthly things" (a beautiful mountaintop) when his mind's eye should have been turned toward God and heaven. In some sense, this dilemma was resolved by thinkers after Petrarch, such as Baruch Spinoza, who, rejecting metaphysical dualism, saw God as not separate from but rather immanent in nature. This approach paved the way for the romantics, many of whom saw nature as a manifestation of deity.

Not everyone, however, would see God as immanent in nature. Francis Bacon, e.g., who inherited the Gr. and med. trad. of imagining nature as a goddess, saw her not only as the most elemental and important object of scientific inquiry but (as Merchant, following Adorno and Horkheimer, has stressed) as desperately in need of control. To facilitate this project of gaining power over nature by way of knowledge, Bacon favored terse aphoristic prose, which has given birth to mod. scientific and technical writing. In contrast, as Fletcher has argued, from the late Ren. onward, writers took up the daunting challenge of developing poetic lang. that could describe and praise nature without making it an object of scientific enquiry. To Fletcher, this project culminates with the poetry of John Ashbery.

With the advent of technological modernity and the so-called Industrial Revolution, the second nature of industrial cities and suburbs was often seen in opposition to areas least altered by human beings—which were becoming a rarity throughout Europe by the close of the Ren. Thus, as it was increasingly understood spatially, first Nature (now often capitalized) soon became a near synonym for wilderness. In order to understand the emotional response that wilderness was increasingly invoking, in the 18th c., Immanuel Kant and Edmund Burke (and others) revised Longinus's cl. notion of the *sublime as a way of expressing the simultaneous awe and attraction that human beings were developing toward wilderness. By the 19th c., first nature/wilderness not only was often seen as a manifestation of deity but became a fetish object for a broad range of writers and artists across Europe and America, incl. J. W. Goethe, William Wordsworth, H. D. Thoreau, Walt Whitman, and Thomas Hardy. This strain of broadly romantic reverence for nature continued into the 20th and 21st cs. with writers such as Dylan Thomas, Robert Frost, Seamus Heaney, and Wendell Berry. However, as untouched wilderness was quickly being domesticated throughout the Northern Hemisphere, benign areas imagined as wilderness, which had in fact already been extensively modified by human beings, such as the Lake District of 19th-c. England and Thoreau's Walden Pond, soon began to stand for wilderness in much nature writing.

Thus, an inversion in the way that nature (as wilderness) was looked on took place in modernity, insofar as earlier representations of nature, such as in the med. period (i.e., *Beowulf*, "The Seafarer"), often portrayed it as dangerous and menacing, while in the mod. period domesticated wilderness was frequently romanticized as welcoming, even if invoking sublime awe. John Milton is a pivotal figure here insofar as *Paradise Lost* contains both a foreboding wilderness and a hospitable garden that it surrounds. Yet even in Milton's time, there was an anxiety over the domestication of wilderness (see, e.g., Justus Lipsius, Andrew Marvell, and George Herbert). Nonetheless, because domesticated wilderness was increasingly represented by a range of poets and artists as intensely appealing, this essentially pastoral impulse resulted in the romanticizing of earlier periods as environmental golden ages, which were imagined as eradicated by extensive changes in mod. agricultural and industrial practices, as well as by the expansion of cities and their suburbs. Examples of this impulse include Wordsworth's "Michael" and even T. S. Eliot's *The Waste Land*. Supporting this pastoralization of the past were works such as George Marsh's *The Earth as Modified by Human Action* (1884), a sweeping reassessment of human hist. as bringing environmental devastation to vast regions of the globe.

Critically, nature has received a great deal of attention in recent decades. In the 1980s, the deep ecology movement, which was preoccupied with wilderness and its preservation, spawned interest in texts that celebrated first nature, such as by Arne Næss, Bill Devall, and George Sessions. While interest in such texts continued in the 1990s, with notable works by Buell on Thoreau and Bate on Wordsworth, at the same time Latour and Haraway largely deconstructed the binary of first and second nature, which contributed to interest in both the liminal space between first and second

nature and places where nature has been significantly altered by human beings, such as cities and suburbs. As the 21st c. dawned, works such as *The Environmental Justice Reader* drew attention to the fact that class, race, gender, colonialism, and other factors significantly influence perceptions of nature. Complex visions of nature have recently influenced a range of writers, incl. Barbara Kingsolver, Michael Pollan, and Bill McKibben, to name but a few.

*See* ENVIRONMENT AND POETRY, GEORGIC, LANDSCAPE POETRY.

■ A. O. Lovejoy and G. Boas, *Primitivism and Related Ideas in Antiquity* (1935); L. White Jr., "The Historical Roots of Our Ecological Crisis," *Science* 155 (1967); T. W. Adorno and M. Horkheimer, *Dialectic of Enlightenment*, trans. J. Cumming (1972); C. Merchant, *The Death of Nature: Women, Ecology, and the Scientific Revolution* (1980); R. Williams, *Keywords*, 2d ed. (1983); B. Devall and G. Sessions, *Deep Ecology* (1985); A. Patterson, *Pastoral and Ideology: Virgil to Valéry* (1987); A. Næss, *Ecology, Community and Lifestyle: Outline of an Ecosophy*, trans. D. Rothenberg (1989); J. Bate, *Romantic Ecology: Wordsworth and the Environmental Tradition* (1991); D. J. Haraway, *Simians, Cyborgs, and Women: The Reinvention of Nature* (1991); R. P. Harrison, *Forests: The Shadow of Civilization* (1992); B. Latour, *We Have Never Been Modern*, trans. C. Porter (1993); L. Buell, *The Environmental Imagination: Thoreau, Nature Writing, and the Formation of American Culture* (1995); P. Alpers, *What is Pastoral?* (1996); *The Environmental Justice Reader: Politics, Poetics, and Pedagogy*, ed. J. Adamson, M. M. Evans, and R. Stein (2002); A. Fletcher, *A New Theory for American Poetry: Democracy, the Environment, and the Future of Imagination* (2004); R. N. Watson, *Back to Nature: The Green and the Real in the Late Renaissance* (2006).

K. HILTNER

**NATUREINGANG** (Ger., "nature opening" or "nature introduction"). The term is traditionally used by philologists for the seasonal opening or nature exordium of a *troubadour *canso* or *sirventes* in *Occitan poetry; it is also applied to similar situations in vernacular lyric genres of the noble register. Occurring in the beginning of the lyric text, usually in but not limited to the first stanza, the *Natureingang* is an abbreviated form of cl. *topoi* such as the invocation to nature and the ideal landscape (*locus amoenus*). In contrast to cl. precedents and to a certain extent the Middle Lat. love lyric that contain seasonal exordia (see GOLIARDIC VERSE), the troubadour Natureingang adapts the cl. topography or harmonious description of a pleasant place within a highly developed declaration of self-referentiality and poetic activity. The opening lyric stanza in troubadour texts stages a turning away from this place, even if limited to only a few elements of the cl. topos. Once thought to be a determinant feature of a canso, the Natureingang is now considered an expansion of the invariant opening of the speaker's admission of the here-and-now engagement of verbal or musical activity and the final result of the poem (Ghil). A typical example consists of temporal elements (usually of spring-time), such as descriptions of vegetation or scenery characteristic of the season (foliage, birdsong, water), positively qualified as pleasant or sweet and producing joy. After the description, the speaker adapts these seasonal elements to his or her needs. The season may move the speaker to think about love and sing, or the song may emerge from the contradiction between the joy of spring and the lover's despair over separation from the loved one (see Bernart de Ventadorn, "Can l'erba fresch'e·lh folha par" [When the new grass and leaves come forth] and Jaufré Rudel, "Lanquan li jorn son lonc en may" [When days grow long in May]). Other notable versions include sophisticated seasonal descriptions that foreground the poet's rhetorical artistry using a floral or vegetal lexeme (Arnaut Daniel) and inversions of the conventional nature opening (Raimbaut d'Aurenga, Bernart de Ventadorn) in which the lover takes the effects of the season for its contrary or the speaker states his joy in spite of the season's dreariness: "Ar resplan la flors enversa / Pels trencans racx e pels tertres / Cals flors? . . . Quar enaissi m'o enverse / Que bel plan mi semblon tertre" (Now the reversed flower / shines among the sharp cliffs and among the hills. / What flower? . . . For I reverse things in such a way that now hills seem a beautiful plain to me [Pattison 39.1–3, 9–10]) and "Tant ai mo cor ple de joya / tot me desnatura" (My heart is so full of joy that she transforms everything for me).

*See* LANDSCAPE POEM, NATURE; REVERDIE.

■ **Primary Texts**: *The Life and Works of the Troubadour Raimbaut d'Orange*, ed. W. T. Pattison (1952); *Canzoni*, ed. G. Toja (1960)—Arnaut Daniel; *Bernart de Ventadorn: Chansons d'amour*, ed. and trans. Moshé Lazar (1966); *The Songs of Jaufré Rudel*, ed. R. T. Pickens (1978).

■ **Criticism and History**: Curtius; E. Schulze-Busacker, "En marge d'un lieu commun de la poésie des troubadours," *Romania* 99 (1978); E. M. Ghil, "The Seasonal Topos in the Old Provençal *canzo*: A Reassessment," *Studia Occitanica*, ed. H.-E. Keller (1986); S. Bianchini, "Guglielmo IX, *Pos vezem de novel florir* (BdT 183, 11): esordio stagionale o invocazione alla natura?" *Annali dell'Istituto Universitario Orientale–Sezione Romanza* 41 (1999).

M. GALVEZ

**NAVAJO POETRY.** In the late 1890s, Dr. Washington Matthews, an army surgeon who had an interest in Navajo ceremonial ways, described Navajo oral storytellers and singers as "poets" and their songs as "poems." He argued that, if the Navajo lang. (*Diné bizaad*) were written, one would find that Navajo poets had as many poetic devices as their Eng. counterparts, if not more. Written poetry by Navajos, however, began not in the Navajo lang. but in Eng., and, indeed, the impetus for writing poetry came from the Bureau of Indian Affairs (BIA) and the school system of the time. E.g., in 1933, a short, eight-line poem was published in *Indians at*

*Work*, a U.S. government publication (Hirschfelder and Singer). The poem was composed by Navajo students at Tohatchi School in New Mexico, on the Navajo Nation. This poem, "If I Were a Pony," is one of the first published poems by a Navajo; it is written entirely in Eng.

The BIA schools, through their Creative Writing project, encouraged the writing of poetry by young Navajos as a way to teach them Eng., which led to the publication of the annual jour. *Arrow* from 1968 to 1974, a venue for many young Native American poets, incl. Navajos. Some pub. poetry included Navajo vocabulary such as *mą'ii* (coyote) and *shicheii* (my grandfather), here written in the current orthography of the Navajo Nation. Poems often addressed contemp. issues facing Navajos, such as siblings at war in Vietnam or the poverty on the Navajo Nation. The poet and artist Gloria Emerson published politically engaged poetry in the overtly political *The Indian Historian* out of San Francisco. In 1977, as Eng.-lang. Navajo poetry became more visible, Nia Francisco published a poem in Navajo in the journal *College English*. In the 1980s, even more poetry would be published by Navajos. By the mid- to late 1980s, individually authored books of Navajo poetry were appearing more frequently. In 1989 and 1995, Rex Lee Jim published two collections of poetry through the Princeton University Library, *Áhí Ni' Nikisheegiizh* and *saad*, that were written entirely in Navajo; and in 1998, Jim published *Dúchas Táá Kóó Diné*, a trilingual collection of poetry in Navajo, Gaelic, and Eng. Alyse Neundorf, a poet and linguist, published poetry in both Navajo and Eng. during the 1990s. In 1993, the Navajo Community College Press published *Storm Patterns*, a collection of poetry by two Navajo women, Della Frank and Roberta Joe–one of the only examples of a book of Navajo poetry published on the Navajo Nation. Most Navajo poetry is published either by university presses in the southwestern U.S. or by independent poetry publishers off the reservation.

Recognized Navajo poets in addition to the figures mentioned above include Tacey Atsitty, Rutherford Ashley, Shonto Begay, Esther Belin, Sherwin Bitsui, Norla Chee, Hershman John, Blackhorse Mitchell, Luci Tapahonso, Laura Tohe, Orlando White, and Venaya Yazzie. Some, like Jim, Tapahonso, and Tohe, are recognized both on and off the Navajo Nation, while others, like Belin, are better known outside the Nation.

Contemp. Navajo poetry is primarily written in Eng. While Navajo is spoken by many residents on the Navajo Nation, literacy in Navajo is not widespread (McLaughlin). Indeed, poets such as Tohe—whose Navajo was almost entirely oral—have actively begun to learn the written lang.

Navajo poets often write about topics and themes connected with home and history. Most Navajo poets have written about the Long Walk (1864–68), when many Navajo were forcibly relocated from their homeland for four years, and connected it with contemp. concerns about identity and homeland. Poets have also written about such topics as the loss of the lang., what it means to be a Navajo in a Western world, and economic and environmental inequalities. Some Navajo poets employ poetry as a way to educate non-Navajos about important cultural, spiritual, and philosophical issues. The themes of growing up on the Navajo Nation and experiencing government-operated boarding schools continue to be central in Navajo poetry. In these examples, Navajo poets present their writing as a historical and cultural supplement to the Westernized education received by young Navajos. The awareness and confirmation of Eng. as a tribal (*Diné*) lang. emerge as intriguing themes in the writing of contemp. Navajo poets.

Sound symbolism (and *iconicity more broadly), *parallelism, quoted speech, and a variety of poetic devices found in traditional Navajo oral poetry have been actively incorporated into some contemp. written poetry as well. Navajo poets have also experimented with *free verse, *sestinas, *limericks, *concrete poetry, *haiku (see RENGA), and other poetic trads.

Contemp. poets in *performance have taken on the roles of tribal storyteller and *hataali* (traditional Navajo chanter who performs healing through singing). Narrative remains very popular. In many Navajo narrative genres—Coyote stories, e.g.—there can be a sung portion within the narrative (Webster), and two poets in particular, Mitchell and Tapahonso, have incorporated song into their poetry readings. While the strong influence of Eng. literacy and education has thwarted many traditional Navajo practices, the visibility of poets in cultural celebrations indicates the transformation of poetry into an essential factor for Navajo cultural survival.

*See* INDIGENOUS AMERICAS, POETRY OF THE; ORAL POETRY.

■ **Anthologies and Primary Texts**: W. Matthews, *Navaho Legends* (1897)—reissued 1994; T. D. Allen, "Please Read Loose," in B. Mitchell, *Miracle Hill*, (1967)—2d ed. (2004) omits Allen's intro.; J. Milton, *The American Indian Speaks* (1969); G. Emerson, "The Poetry of Gloria Emerson," *The Indian Historian* 4 (1971); and "Slayers of the Children," *The Indian Historian* 5 (1972); S. Allen, *Yei* (1972); *The Whispering Wind*, ed. T. Allen (1972); J. Milton, *Four Indian Poets* (1974); N. Francisco, 'táchééh,' *CE* 39 (1977); *The South Corner of Time*, ed. L. Evers (1980); L. Tapahonso, *Seasonal Woman* (1982); L. Tohe, *Making Friends with Water* (1986); L. Tapahonso, *A Breeze Swept Through* (1987); N. Francisco, *Blue Horses for Navajo Women* (1988); R. L. Jim, *Áhí Ni' Nikisheegiizh* (1989); D. McLaughlin, *When Literacy Empowers: Navajo Language in Print* (1992); *Rising Voices: Writings of Young Native Americans*, ed. A. Hirschfelder and B. Singer (1992); D. Frank and R. Joe, *Storm Patterns: Poems from Two Navajo Women* (1993); L. Tapahonso, *Sáanii Dahataał: The Women are Singing* (1993); N. Francisco, *Carried Away by the Black River* (1994); S. Begay, *Navajo Visions and Voices across the Mesa* (1995); R. L. Jim, *saad* (1995); L. Tapahonso, *Blue Horses Rush In* (1997); R. L. Jim, *Dúchas Táá Kóó Diné* (1998); E. Belin, *From the Belly of My Beauty*

(1999); A. Neundorf, "Dííjį́ Nánísdzá, I come home today," "Diné Hosiidlį́į́'gi," "Hayííłką́, At Dawn," "Hóyéé," *Red Mesa Review* 6 (1999); L. Tohe, *No Parole Today* (1999); V. Browne, *Ravens Dancing* (2000); R. Ashley, *Heart Vision 2000* (2001); N. Chee, *Cedar Smoke on Abalone Mountain* (2001); *Sister Nations*, ed. H. Erdrich and L. Tohe (2002); S. Bitsui, *Shapeshift* (2003); G. Emerson, *At the Hems of the Lowest Clouds* (2003); L. Tohe, *Tséyi': Deep in the Rock* (2005); V. Yazzie, *Livin Matriarchal: Chapbook I* (2006); H. John, *I Swallow Turquoise for Courage* (2007); L. Tapahonso, *a radiant curve* (2008); T. Atsitty, *amenorrhea* (2009); S. Bitsui, *Floodsong* (2009); O. White, *Bone Light* (2009).

■ **Criticism and History**: E. G. Belin, "Contemporary Navajo Writers' Relevance to Navajo Society," *Wicazo Sa Review* 22 (2007); All by A. K. Webster—"Coyote Poems: Navajo Poetry, Intertextuality, and Language Choice," *American Indian Culture and Research Journal* 28 (2004); "The Mouse That Sucked: On 'Translating' a Navajo Poem," *Studies in American Indian Literature* 18 (2006); *Explorations in Navajo Poetry and Poetics* (2009); "Imagining Navajo in the Boarding School," *Journal of Linguistic Anthropology* 20 (2010)—ling. analysis of Tohe's *No Parole Today*; "Towards a History of Navajo English in Navajo Poetry," *World Englishes* 29 (2010); "'Please Read Loose': Intimate Grammars and Unexpected Languages in Contemporary Navajo Literature," *American Indian Culture and Research Journal* 35 (2011).

E. G. BELIN; A. K. WEBSTER

**NEAR RHYME,** generic rhyme, half rhyme, imperfect rhyme, oblique rhyme, off-rhyme, pararhyme, partial rhyme, slant rhyme. There is no standard term in Eng.; *near rhyme* will be used here as a cover term for several varieties of rhyming practice that are related to yet do not fulfill the canonical definition of *rhyme nor exceed it, as in *rich rhyme. Judgmental adjectives were better avoided, for they carry the pejorative implication that a near rhyme is a failure to achieve true rhyme, either on account of deficiency of lang. resources or incompetence of the poet—equally dubious assumptions, both. *Near* must be taken, therefore, not in the sense of "imperfect" but rather of "approximate," i.e., close to the narrow band of instances qualifying as canonical end rhyme but outside it, in the wider field of "related but alternative forms of sound correspondence" (Scherr). Within the Eng. taxonomy, most forms of near rhyme, of which there are several, amount to various complex types of *consonance and produce such rhymes as "justice" / "hostess" (Jonathan Swift), "port" / "chart" (Emily Dickinson), or word such as *grope / cup, maze / coze, drunkard / conquered*. Zirmunskij distinguishes the forms of rhyme as "exact," "augmented" (by deletion or addition), and "altered" (by both, meaning substitution), a typology accepted and extended by Gasparov.

In judging rhymes, it is important not to be misled by shifts in historical phonology, whereby rhymes that now seem only near were actually true rhymes in their day, e.g., Alexander Pope's "obey" / "tea." Further, it is important that near rhyme be conceived not solely in terms of Eng. practice; for since the early 20th c., the status of near rhyme in Eng. has been problematized, while in Rus., e.g., prosodists since Zirmunskij have recognized both "approximate" and "inexact" rhyme as part of the standard definition of *rhyme* (see Scherr). In *Celtic prosody, too, esp. Ir. and Welsh, near rhyme has been recognized and approved as an important and constructive element of rhyming technique since the Middle Ages under the rubric of *generic rhyme*; and indeed, near rhyme first appears in Eng. deliberately in Henry Vaughan, in imitation of Welsh prosody. In Fr. prosody of the early 20th c., the term *accord* was proposed by Jules Romains (pseud. of Louis Farigoule, 1885–1972) and Georges Chennevière (1884–1927), poets and theorists of the movement known as unanimism, for a variety of forms of consonance and near rhyme. The accords of Romains were attacked by Maurice Grammont but may have influenced the *pararhyme* of Wilfred Owen.

In fact, near rhyme has played an important role in most of the major Western prosodies of the late 19th and early 20th cs.—not only Brit. (G. M. Hopkins, W. B. Yeats, Owen, W. H. Auden, Cecil Day-Lewis, Stephen Spender, Louis MacNeice, Dylan Thomas) and Am. (Dickinson—from whom much of the later Am. practice derives), but Rus. (Alexander Blok, Valery Bryusov, Vladimir Mayakovsky, Boris Pasternak). In Eng., the trad. of canonical rhyme was old but not deeply established, having always had to contend with the enormous force of Shakespearean and Miltonic *blank verse and, after 1855, *free verse. But Rus. never developed extensive trads. of either blank or free verse, so that, in the 20th c., Rus. modernist poets experimented extensively with new and variant rhyme forms—as many as 50% of Mayakovsky's rhymes are noncanonical. In the West, the avant-garde prosodies sought to dispense with both meter and rhyme, but, in Russia, it was only the former: rhyme practice was not abandoned but expanded. Experiments with the one went hand in hand with experiments with the other, but renunciation of the one did not necessarily entail the other as well. In Eng., free verse, of course, dropped rhyme, but several major poets who retained traditional verse forms and meters, e.g., Yeats and Auden, also chose to explore near rhyme: Yeats's practice includes rhymes such as "push"/"rush" and "up"/"drop" in a sonnet, e.g., ("Leda and the Swan"). Owen developed what he called *pararhyme*, a kind of frame rhyme in which the initial and final consonants are repeated while the vowel is varied—e.g. "killed"/"cold," "mystery"/"mastery," "friend"/"frowned"—deliberately to express the wrenching sensation of war. This sort of effect is explored also by Dickinson and Hopkins, as it had been by Vaughan.

In much late Victorian and Edwardian crit., one finds frequent attacks by reactionary prosodists on all less-than-correct rhyming as decadent, degenerate, and incompetent, attacks epitomized in George Saintsbury and Brander Matthews. But in retrospect, such practice is to be seen not as a falling away from a standard but as a redefinition of that standard. In a radical age, the breaking of conventions is an expansive and creative act. Near rhyme is, in this sense, not an abandonment of rhyme in defeat but an opening up of possibilities, not supplanting rhyme but enriching it.

There is evidence from Rus., if any were needed, that each poet develops his or her own distinctive idiolect in near rhyme, preferring to explore not the entire range of possibilities but rather only certain types. But no extensive and reliable set of data on rhyme has yet been collected. The practice of near rhyme in art verse is, of course, the primary interest, but it has also been used extensively and probably for much longer in *light verse, *satire, and (perhaps) *dialect poetry.

■ K. Meyer, *Primer of Irish Metrics* (1909); V. Zirmunskij, *Rifma* (1923), ch. 3; J. Romains and G. Chennevière, *Petit traité de versif* (1923); J. Hytier, *Les techniques modernes du vers français* (1923), reviewed by M. Grammont in *Revue des langues romanes* 62 (1923); T. W. Herbert, "Near-Rimes and Paraphones," *SR* 14 (1937); L. Pszczolowska, *Rym* (1972); B. P. Goncarov, *Zvukovaja organizatsija stixa i problemy rifmy* (1973); M. Shapiro, *Asymmetry* (1976), ch. 4; W. E. Rickert, "Rhyme Terms," *Style* 12 (1978); M. L. Gasparov, "Towards an Analysis of Russian Inexact Rhyme," *Metre, Rhythm, Stanza, Rhyme*, ed. G. S. Smith (1980); Scott, 233–36; W. Frawley, "A Note on the Phonology of Slant Rhyme," *Lang&S* 17 (1984); Scherr, ch. 4; B. J. Small, *Positive as Sound* (1990)—Dickinson.

T.V.F. BROGAN

**NEGATIVE CAPABILITY.** In an 1817 letter to his brother and sister-in-law, the Brit. romantic poet John Keats coined the term "*Negative Capability*, that is when man is capable of being in uncertainties, Mysteries, doubts, without any irritable reaching after fact & reason" (*Letters*). Keats begins by defining the quality broadly as that which informs "a Man of Achievement" but also specifies it as an urgent literary principle with Shakespeare as the primary model.

This single letter is the only remaining record of Keats's use of the term, but the concept deeply informs the poet's thought and poetic works. In a letter of 1818, for instance, Keats's definition of the "poetical Character" as having "no character" appears consistent with the protean mobility of mind that the quality of negative capability entails: the ability not to insist on a conclusion or decision that would eliminate alternate possibilities. Unlike the "wordsworthian or egotistical sublime" that "stands alone," the poetical character "has no self—it is everything and nothing—It has no character—it enjoys light and shade; it lives in gusto, be it foul or fair, high or low, rich or poor, mean or elevated—It has as much delight in conceiving an Iago as an Imogen." As an aesthetic principle, negative capability becomes visible in the blurring of the line between subject and object in "Ode to Psyche" and "Ode to a Nightingale" and in the absence altogether of the pronoun "I" in "To Autumn."

Negative capability enables, moreover, the pursuit of the twin concepts of beauty and truth. "[W]ith a great poet," Keats writes, "the sense of Beauty overcomes every other consideration, or rather obliterates all consideration." Keats criticizes his friend's inability to arrive at a truth as stemming from a lack of negative capability: this friend, Charles Dilke, "cannot feel he has a personal identity unless he has made up his Mind about every thing. The only means of strengthening one's intellect is to make up ones [sic] mind about nothing—to let the mind be a thoroughfare for all thoughts. Not a select party." While the self-containment of individual "identity" limits the imaginative capacity, negative capability embraces the values of uncertainty and doubt that open the mind to multiple possibilities, thereby expanding the imagination so as better to approximate beauty and truth.

See EMPATHY AND SYMPATHY.

■ J. Keats, *Letters of John Keats*, ed. H. Rollins, 2 v. (1958); N. Roe, *Keats and the Culture of Dissent* (1997)—230–67 on politics of negative capability; S. Wolfson, "Keats and Gender Criticism," *The Persistence of Poetry*, ed. R. Ryan and R. Sharp (1999); R. Kaufman, "Negatively Capable Dialectics: Keats, Vendler, Adorno, and the Theory of the Avant-Garde," *CritI* 27 (2001).

E. ROHRBACH

**NEGRITUDE.** Negritude began as an aesthetic and literary movement in the 1930s, centering on black consciousness and black creativity. While the movement has no single founding text, it was led by the writings of two black scholars from Fr. colonies, Aimé Césaire of Martinique and Léopold Sédar Senghor of Senegal.

The Fr. term *négritude* had both a cultural and a political dimension. It gained international recognition as a literary movement with the publication of Césaire's book-length poem *Cahier d'un retour au pays natal* (*Notebook of a Return to the Native Land*) in 1939. Césaire and Senghor met as colonial scholarship students in Paris. Both had been strongly influenced by recent movements rehabilitating black hist. and culture like the *Harlem Renaissance and such Haitian literary movements as *indigénisme* and *noirisme*, and admired greatly the work of such poets as James Weldon Johnson and Claude McKay. The *Revue du monde noir* (Review of the Black World, 1931–32), introduced them to the work of such thinkers as Langston Hughes and Alain Locke; they were also influenced by the presence in Paris of the Fr. Guyanese author René Maran, the author of *Batouala*, which had won the Fr. Prix Goncourt in 1921 and had subsequently been banned in Fr. Af. colonies. Together with a group of fellow students, they launched a literary magazine, *L'Etudiant noir* (The Black Student), which took a militant stand against black cultural assimilation by actively seeking to explore the singularity of the black cultural experience; the publication inaugurated the use of the word *Negritude*, managing roughly a half-

dozen issues before closing in 1936. It contained the work of writers from both Africa and the West Indies, incl. Césaire, Léon Damas, Léonard Sainville, Senghor, and Birago Diop. Together, these publications created the intellectual ferment that gave birth to Negritude. The movement became a framework for the articulation of black consciousness and its attendant cultural expression, esp. important given the context of colonialism and racism.

Initially, Negritude drew heavily on Fr. *surrealism, which first made its appearance in postwar France and influenced greatly recent arrivants like Césaire. To this liberating vein must be added the work of Leo Frobenius, particularly his groundbreaking *History of African Civilization*, which exploded the myth of Negro barbarity. Negritude's writers inscribed art, emotion, intuition, and rhythm as intrinsic opposites to supposedly Western characteristics of order, reason, and logic.

Negritude embodied an assertion of pride, reversing the traditional denigration of black subjectivity. Through the *Cahier*'s voicing these sentiments, poets rediscovered empathy with their African ancestry, enabling them to join lyricism to self-revelation. Negritude became a framework for creative cultural expression that valorized black civilizations past and present and, thus, at least in the *Cahier*, challenged the static acceptance of colonial inferiority by actively asserting an alternative historical viewpoint.

Senghor differed from Césaire in both his vision and his practice of Negritude; uncovering the values of the Af. world led him to affirm basic life forces as the enabling framework for a *poiēsis* of Af. civilization. Senghor promulgated a return to historical and cultural sources through the cultivation of indigenous langs. and trads., reflected in the themes and symbolism of his published poetry.

In his *Hosties noires* (*Black Hosts*) and the collection *Anthologie de la nouvelle poésie nègre et malgache de langue française*, Senghor celebrates the culture and trad. of his Af. homeland. In contrast to Césaire's, his writing stresses a particular black emotional and psychological experience, drawing on a specifically Af. relationship to the forces of the universe that is strongly non-Western. For Senghor, the black African perceives and internalizes external stimuli primarily in an emotional way, while the Westerner, in her turn, comprehends the world through analysis and reason. This argument extended a particular ontology to the concept of Negritude, engendering a sense of difference that allowed it to provide an enabling framework for a growing number of Af. and Caribbean writers to express their vision of their own cultural and historical experience, ultimately turning these cultural ends to a politics of liberation.

Negritude was above all a product of its time, one whose primary shortcoming was that it drew unconsciously on the binaries of the colonial era. It gave rise to a flood of creative black expression, but alternative approaches to black identity eventually took its place. Ultimately, it put into practice a discourse of cultural and colonial contestation that led to Caribbean literary movements like *antillanité* and *créolité*, as well as independence movements across francophone Africa. Negritude gave value to the black world by embodying the antithesis of the West and by emphasizing an incendiary, if not indeed an insurrectional, vocabulary.

See AFRICA, POETRY OF; CARIBBEAN, POETRY OF THE.

■ J-P. Sartre, "Orphée Noir," *Anthologie de la nouvelle poésie nègre et malgache de langue française*, ed. L. S. Senghor (1948); L. S. Senghor, *Liberté 1: négritude et humanisme* (1964); S.W. Bâ, *The Concept of Negritude in the Poetry of Léopold Sédar Senghor* (1973); B. Cailler, *Proposition poétique: une lecture de l'oeuvre d'Aimé Césaire* (1976); R. Scharfman, *Engagement and the Language of the Subject in the Poetry of Aimé Césaire* (1980); A. J. Arnold, *Modernism and Negritude: The Poetry and Poetics of Aimé Césaire* (1981); *Aimé Césaire: The Collected Poetry*, trans. C. Eshleman and A. Smith (1983); P. Taylor, *The Narrative of Liberation: Perspectives on Afro-Caribbean Literature, Popular Culture, and Politics* (1989); R. Confiant, *Aimé Césaire: une traversée paradoxale du siècle* (1993); M. Richardson, *Refusal of the Shadow: Surrealism and the Caribbean*, trans. K. Fijalkowski and M. Richardson (1996); G. Davis, *Aimé Césaire* (1997); C. Filostrat, *Negritude Agonistes: Assimilation against Nationalism in the French-Speaking Caribbean and Guyane* (2008).

H. A. MURDOCH

**NEOBAROQUE.** A style of poetry common in the late 20th c. in Latin America, in which *artifice, *figuration, and a consciousness of *textuality are highly developed, often with explicit or covert reference to the *baroque poetry of the early mod. period. The term *neobarroco* as applied to Latin Am. lit. was arguably coined by the Brazilian poet Haroldo de Campos (1929–2003), writing about Umberto Eco's *opera aperta* (open work), to refer to the unconventional nature of contemp. writing. As Campos was to insist on several occasions, Latin Am. cultures share a genealogy from the time of their cultural formations under the auspices of the Eur. baroque; they contributed their own inflections to what came to be called the *Barroco de Indias* (Baroque of the Indies), a major devel. that included the work of perhaps the greatest baroque poet in the Americas, the Mexican nun Sor Juana Inés de la Cruz (ca. 1648–95). Through Paul Verlaine and Stéphane Mallarmé, several of the poets of Sp. Am. *modernismo (the Nicaraguan Rubén Darío [1867–1916], the Uruguayan Julio Herrera y Reissig [1875–1910], and the Argentinian Leopoldo Lugones [1874–1938], among others) revisited the poets of the 17th-c. baroque, rereading Francisco de Quevedo, Luis de Góngora, and Félix Lope de Vega in a spirit of appropriation and transformation. In 20th-c. Spain, Federico García Lorca (1898–1936) and his fellow poets belonged to the Generation of 1927, which refers to the tercentenary of Góngora's death (1627). The Mexican poet and critic Alfonso Reyes (1889–1959) and the Cuban José Lezama Lima (1910–76) dedicated influential essays to the Sp. poet. All this is to say that, when Campos first articulated the epithet *neobaroque*,

he was reaching into a complex relation between Latin Am. cultures, mod. as well as colonial, and the early mod. baroque.

In 1972, the seminal essay "El barroco y el neobarroco" by the Cuban writer Severo Sarduy (1937–93) oriented the discussion of the baroque and its outcomes in Latin Am. lit. to the Fr. structuralist and poststructuralist poetics of the *Tel Quel* group (see STRUCTURALISM, POSTSTRUCTURALISM). Pointing to writing strategies, Sarduy referred to *intertextuality and intratextuality as signs of the heavily textual fabric of the neobaroque (which extends from lit. to other media, such as film, the visual arts, music, and popular culture). By substitution, proliferation, or condensation of signs, this lit. involves an unusual degree of artifice in lang., esp. the recirculation of *metaphors from all epochs (see SIGN, SIGNIFIED, SIGNIFIER). Sarduy referred to various Latin Am. novels that had appeared a few years before his essay, such as Lezama Lima's *Paradiso*, Gabriel García Márquez's *Cien años de soledad* (*One Hundred Years of Solitude*), Guillermo Cabrera Infante's *Tres tristes tigres* (*Three Trapped Tigers*), and Alejo Carpentier's *El siglo de las luces* (The Century of Lights). Following Sarduy, many articles and books on Latin Am. narrative describe a neobaroque poetics and invoke the nomenclature, sometimes as a replacement for *lo real maravilloso* (usually translated into Eng. as *magic realism*). But Sarduy also referred in his essay to Pablo Neruda and to a new type of poetry that Campos developed in *Galáxias* (pub. as individual poems after 1963, collectively in 1984 and 2004), a series of 50 "texts" that play on the border between prose and poetry, between *semantics and *sound. Using *paronomasia as a major technical device, the book is a metonymic adventure in search of the materiality of lang.

Lezama Lima's poetry, Sarduy's essays, the Poundian style of the Peruvian poet Rodolfo Hinostroza's (b. 1941) *Contranatura* (1970), the erudite new antipoetry of the Mexican Gerardo Deniz (b. 1934), and, in Brazil, the work of Campos and the *concretistas* served as the background for a new generation of poets that could be loosely linked to the neobaroque. Néstor Perlongher (1949–92) coined the term *Neobarroso* in order to link it to the dirt or mud of the River Plate. Eduardo Espina (b. 1954) spoke in the same playful tone of *barrococó* (obviously a play with *baroque* and *rococo). In 1996, *Medusario*, a major compilation of neobaroque poetry, circulated widely in Latin America, and this type of poetry became one of the dominant trends in Latin Am. lit. at the end of the 20th c. In addition to the above, other Latin Am. poets commonly associated with the neobaroque are José Kozer (Cuba, b. 1940), David Huerta (Mexico, b. 1949), Coral Bracho (Mexico, b. 1951), Mirko Lauer (Peru, b. 1947), Arturo Carrera (Argentina, b. 1948), Raúl Zurita (Chile, b. 1950), Eduardo Milán (Uruguay, b. 1952), Marosa di Giorgio (Uruguay, 1932–2004), and Reynaldo Jiménez (Peru, b. 1959).

■ J. Lezama Lima, "La curiosidad barroca," *La expresión americana* (1957); A. Carpentier, "Lo barroco y lo real maravilloso," *Razón de ser* (1976); H. de Campos,

"The Open Work of Art," trans. M. L. Santaella Braga, *Dispositio* 6 (1981); S. Sarduy, *Ensayos generales sobre el barroco* (1987); E. Milán, *Una cierta mirada* (1989); J. Sefamí, "El llamado de los deseosos: poesía neobarroca latinoamericana (1970–?)," *Siglo XX/20th Century* 12 (1994); *Caribe transplatino*, ed. N. Perlongher (1991); *Medusario*, ed. R. Echavarren, J. Kozer, J. Sefamí (1996); N. Perlongher, *Prosa plebeya* (1997); J. Sefamí, "Los poetas neobarrocos y el modernismo," *Todo ese fuego*, ed. Mara García (1999); H. de Campos, "Anthropophagous Reason: Dialogue and Difference in Brazilian Culture" (1982), trans. O. Cisneros, *Novas*, ed. A. S. Bessa and O. Cisneros (2007); R. Greene, "Baroque and Neobaroque: Making Thistory," *PMLA* 124 (2009).

J. SEFAMÍ

## NEOCLASSICAL POETICS

I. General Survey
II. National Literatures

**I. General Survey.** Neoclassical poetics concerns the literary aspect of that broad movement in Eur. culture and the arts extending from the early 17th c. to approximately the mid-18th c. Separate literary cultures offer discrete attitudes and varying emphases, but in terms of what is more widely shared, neoclassical poetics is first of all a set of interests deriving from an effort to imitate and reconstitute the literary values of ancient Greece and Rome, continuing the attention of humanism to those values (see RENAISSANCE POETICS) but doing so in reaction against what were thought the stylistic indiscipline and excessive *invention of Ren. poets, esp. the *concettismo* of the Romance poetries and the Eng. metaphysical mode (see CONCEPTISMO; METAPHYSICAL POETRY). This reactive mood also sets neoclassical poetics against other artistic tendencies in the late 17th and early 18th cs., esp. efforts at verbal *wit, exotic fiction, and contemp. realism. Two general criteria influenced neoclassical crit. with respect to its championing of the ancients: first, the belief that their poems were a more direct and faithful representation of *nature, esp. human nature, than has usually been achieved since; and second, the conviction that the restraint, simplicity, and impersonality in style observable in the best Roman poets were more likely to please an audience. These two values were the principal grounds for an embattled polemic mounted against what was called a barbaric or "gothic" taste (Dominique Bouhours, *Conversations of Aristo and Eugene*, 1671; Joseph Addison, *Spectator* nos. 58–63 [1711]).

Influenced by the Renaissance practice of *commonplace collection, Ben Jonson (1572–1637) considers properly exercised *imitation as the assimilation of the best of ancient poetic forms and style to a personal idiom, "to draw forth out of the best and choisest flowers, with the Bee, and turne all into Honey" (*Timber* [1641]). This concept developed into an adherence to cl. ideas of *decorum and *genre, but there are various shadings of opinion. Bouhours (1628–1702) warns against "larceny" and limiting oneself to cl. models,

while Jean de La Bruyère (1645–96) gloomily announces that the ancients have already said everything worth saying (*Caractères*, 1688). Samuel Johnson (1709–84), on the other hand, recommends caution on the grounds that a copy is almost always inferior to its model (*The Rambler* no. 121 [1751]).

The cult of imitation, however much its partisans might insist on assimilation and adaptation, nevertheless tended to imply the inimitable mastery of Homer and Virgil, and to a lesser extent of the Gr. and Roman dramatists and lyric poets. It thus gave rise to debates over the relative worth of ancient and mod. writers (see QUERELLE DES ANCIENS ET DES MODERNES) that often took the form of quarreling over which group had the better contact with nature. Nicolas Boileau (1636–1711), e.g., mocks the literal realism of Marc-Antoine Girard de Saint-Amant, who has the fish watching the Israelites marching between the parted waters of the Red Sea (*Art poétique* [1674], canto 3), and Jonathan Swift (1667–1745) in "The Battle of the Books" (1710) charges the mods. with spinning matter out of their own entrails, like spiders. The ancients, having discovered the natural "laws" governing literary genres, which, in turn, realize the various forms of human social organization and universal (as opposed to particular) experience, thereby stood as a model to be followed by all but the most exceptionally imaginative *genius (Alexander Pope, *Essay on Criticism* [1711]). This argument depends on a view that associates the ancients with common sense, nature, and the rules of composition, though it must be noted that the rules were often understood as practical guides. Such is the lesson Pierre Corneille (1606–84) hoped to teach in his three "Discours" introducing the 1660 ed. of his works. These essays, his belated answer to the French Académie's adverse judgment of *Le Cid* (1637), set common sense and the artistic judgment of the poet against the arbitrary authority of the state and trad. At the same time, the natural, far from being the detailed recording of current actuality, is seen as manifested in the typical and in that which transcends temporal and cultural difference (Wellek). The value of such imperatives is that they help to make the works of the past in some sense contemp. The disadvantage, as the partisans of the mod. pointed out, is the discouraging of contemp. talent, the elimination of freshness and variety, and the hardening of poetic forms into fixed genres. One result is the paradox that the most conventional literary forms are considered the closest to nature.

The concept of probability, which for Aristotle had governed the structure of *plot and guaranteed the universality of poetry, formed the heart of this system and was justified on the grounds that inventions that were fantastic or divergent from common experience would be unwelcome to an audience. The unities are defended by many critics on the grounds that they encourage the audience's sense of the correspondence between stage events and likely events. As Crites in John Dryden's *Essay of Dramatic Poesy* (1668) remarks, "that play is thought to be the nearest imitation of nature, whose plot is confined within [24 hours]." The rules had the effect of imposing strict limitations on poetic invention or exuberance, but their implications in neoclassical poetics go well beyond their apparent status as arbitrary, conventional, and restrictive. Appealing to *doxa*, what neoclassical critics call probability is closer to what we call public opinion. Poets were given license to modify the details of ancient works to adapt the ancient texts to current stereotypes and social mores. Theories assumed that the contemporary spectator sought the reflection of her own, present-day beliefs and experiences in ancient works. Even so, it escaped no one's notice that, from Homer to John Milton, there were a few exceptional figures whose works could be seen to exemplify the very faults of logic or sense that neoclassical critics liked to enumerate or whose genius seemed to have nothing to do with the observance of established conventions. Moreover, the general neoclassical preference for the *epic as the first among genres is evident in comments testifying to its scale and abundance, e.g., Boileau's approval of its lavish use of trope and myth (*L'Art poétique*), René Le Bossu's (1631–80) insistence on the greatness and importance of its action (*Traité du poème épique*, 1675), Thomas Hobbes's (1588–1679) seconding of the "majesty" of the heroic style (*Answer to Davenant's Preface to "Gondibert*,*"* 1650), and John Dennis's (1657–1734) enthusiastic endorsement of Milton's *Paradise Lost* as "the greatest poem ever written" (*The Grounds of Criticism in Poetry*, 1704). And despite Le Bossu's position that epic poems are rationally planned, tightly structured, and basically didactic works, what Alexander Pope (1688–1744) called "a grace beyond the reach of art" and the Fr. termed *je ne sais quoi*, the inexplicable, was widely acknowledged. Some 20th-c. scholars argued that this acknowledgment in critics such as Dryden (1631–1700) or Boileau or Johnson reflects a commendable effort to offer a balanced theory of poetics (e.g., Mahoney, Engell), but it can also be seen as a reflection of a profound distrust of the contemp. and of the subjective, a view bolstered by the tendency in 17th- and 18th-c. critical theory to subordinate the writer to his task and his audience, to caution him against vanity and self-indulgence, charges from which Johnson does not exempt Shakespeare, however generous his praise. Nevertheless, contemp. poetry had strong defenders, e.g., Dryden early in his career (*An Essay of Dramatic Poesy*), Charles Perrault ("Le Siècle de Louis Le Grand," 1687), and Addison (*Spectator* no. 160 [1711]).

If it is to offer its audience images of nature, then, as John Dennis asserted, "the speech by which poetry makes its imitation must be pathetic" (*The Advancement and Reformation of Poetry*, 1701). For all the neoclassical claims to a rational, commonsensical, orderly poetic system, it is nevertheless the case that the prerogatives of form exist side by side with a firm belief that the central appeal of poems, plays, and works of fiction is their *representation of human emotion or their providing the audience with an emotional rendering of human events. The rules of verisimilitude were formulated to maximize the likelihood of cathartic response by minimizing the awareness of *artifice. This means that neoclassical poetics invests in the passions as the objects of representation and in emotional response as the portion of the audience, though such orthodox thinkers as Corneille and René Rapin (1621–87) also suppose that, by the end of a *tragedy, the spectator's mind must be, as Corneille remarks, "serene."

Neoclassical and 18th-c. attention to *emotion has further implications. Aristotle proposed as the source of the audience's emotion the movement of tragic action from ignorance to knowledge. This gives way to a mode of action as conflict between irreconcilable claims, and the audience is prompted to respond to the drama of inner conflict, moving away from Aristotle's priority of action to that of character (Corneille, "Essay on Tragedy," 1660). Two separate but related lines of thought about the impact of *tragedy may be noted. On the one hand, there is a reiteration and partial rethinking of the Aristotelian notion of tragic pleasure. *Catharsis, according to Rapin (*Réflexions sur la Poétique d'Aristote*, 1674), is the spectator's total absorption into the feelings of tragic characters, so that the soul is "shaken" and the mind is cured of its fears; earlier, Boileau had simply required strong emotionalism, and Corneille had seen the tragic emotions as a kind of warning to the audience. Dryden argues that emotions other than pity and fear are common in mod. tragedies ("Heads of an Answer to Rymer," 1677), and Thomas Rymer (1641–1713) himself assents that the effectiveness of tragedy lies in its management of poetic justice ("Tragedies of the Last Age Considered," 1678). Generally, in the early 18th c., there is an increasing emphasis on sympathy or compassion (see EMPATHY AND SYMPATHY) as the spectatorial response to suffering; this is perhaps a reaction to the partial displacement of strictly cl. forms by domestic *pathos. Neoclassical theories of how poetry can engage the emotions to promote moral education prepares a vocabulary that, combined with the etiquette protocol of court society, eventually migrates to shape the discourse of ethics (e.g., Adam Smith's *Theory of Moral Sentiments*, 1767).

The second feature of tragic crit. is what has been called the "Lucretian return upon ourselves," the argument that spectacles of distress and suffering are tolerable and pleasurable because the spectators are themselves exempt, onlookers only (Hathaway). Such a view often equates spectacles such as public executions, in which people actually suffer and die, with theatrical representations. But Jean-Baptiste Du Bos (1670–1742), for one, argued that no one ever mistook a play for real events (*Réflexions critiques sur la poésie et la peinture*, 1719–33). Perhaps the most sophisticated (though not an influential) theory is David Hume's (1711–76) proposal that the formal properties of the tragedy as a work of art transform and shape events and emotions so that the responses of spectators are themselves different from what they would be to an actual event: "the fiction of tragedy softens the passion, by an infusion of new feeling" ("Of Tragedy," 1757; cf. Cohen).

Interest in kinds of audience response also centers in the *sublime. The term had been used in the Ren. to characterize the grand style (see STYLE), which was thought to prompt the strongest emotion. Boileau's trans. of Longinus's *Peri hypsous* (*On the Sublime*, 1674), and esp. his introduction and subsequent comments ("Réflexions"), served to promote an entirely different concept, emphasizing grandness of conception translated by simple and understated lang. The sublime rapidly became a popular subject of critical thought in England and Germany (less so in France and Italy), eventually extending well beyond theories of style or literary representation to include the arts and the experience of landscape, esp. features of overwhelming grandeur such as the Alps (Monk, Nicolson). As a theory of emotional experience, the sublime served neoclassical poetics precisely because it envisaged a transcendence of the limits, visual and imaginative, central to neoclassical aesthetics, offering a contrast of scale by which to differentiate types of aesthetic experience. Artistic representations observing human scale and clearly perceived limits were the province of *beauty*, a difficult term in that it evoked debate over whether aesthetic experience was entirely subjective or was the consequence of particular properties in the viewed object (Jean-Pierre de Crousaz, *Traité du beau*, 1685; Francis Hutcheson, *Inquiry into the Origin of Our Ideas of Beauty and Virtue*, 1725). Implicated in the debate over the nature of beauty, which was usually defined as unity in multiplicity and as symmetry or its perception, was the troubled question of *taste*. Apart from the rather obvious effort of late 17th- and 18th-c. critics to argue for a universal standard of taste, based either in the authority of cl. models or the theories of Johnson and Hume that time reveals universal excellence, taste reveals the neoclassical hunger for an experience of art as spontaneous and uncalculated as possible, joined to a recognition that a superior taste requires study, experience, and civilized company (Edmund Burke, *A Philosophical Enquiry into the Origin of Our Ideas of the Sublime and the Beautiful*, 1757; Hume, "Of the Standard of Taste," 1757).

The neoclassical interest in measurable limits shows in a concern for the sensory, and esp. the visual, as a component of lang. New significance was given in 17th- and 18th-c. theory to the ancient rhetorical notion of *evidentia*, which held that lang. could render objects as if present to the sight. John Locke's (1632–1704) theory that lang. represents "ideas" (i.e., mental images) of objects, rather than objects themselves, results in an emphasis on mental "seeing" as a process, as opposed to a static, quasi-pictorial representation (Burke; cf. Hagstrum 1958). A word may prompt us to recall an object, or more properly the idea of an object, but our individual experience, as described by associationist psychology, entails that what we recall is a context. This complicated the neoclassical desire for clarity of representation by suggesting variability of meaning, a problem intensified by the post-Lockean doctrine that words have arbitrarily, not naturally, assigned meanings or referents. It was also eventually to trouble the effort to establish a universal standard of taste, as well as the persistent effort to discover in lang. a means to reconnect the mind with essential nature, i.e., with states of sympathetic feeling.

These tendencies combine in the neoclassical interest in the Horatian formula *ut pictura poesis*. This emerged at first in efforts to make fairly simple parallels between the plastic and verbal arts (Dryden, "A Parallel of Poetry and Painting," 1695), and then, beginning with Du Bos's *Réflexions* and culminating in G. E. Lessing's (1729–81) *Laokoön* (1766), developed into a countermovement concentrating on the psychological and aesthetic consequences of the radical differences between these media. Poetry was seen to be conditioned by the temporal linearity of lang., and painting and sculpture were understood to represent frozen moments in a narrative—notions that for both Du Bos and Lessing guarantee the superiority of poetry. At the same time, the critical effort involved in these and similar discussions continued to regard words as vehicles rather than objects. In moving from a debate over style to theories of perception and *affect*, the attention to lang. also produced extensive efforts, such as those of Étienne Bonnot de Condillac (1715–80), to establish the origins of lang., an activity continued in preromantic and romantic critical theory (see ROMANTIC AND POSTROMANTIC POETRY AND POETICS). Yet behind the awareness of lang. as a dynamic system of representation, there lingers the neoclassical desire for a vision of universal and permanent forms and fixed truths (Aarsleff), a desire suggested by the wide interest in the visual and also by the efforts in 17th- and 18th-c. crit. to refine and settle vernacular styles into enduring modes.

## II. National Literatures

A. *France.* France is generally conceded to have established the main outlines of neoclassical poetics to which the rest of Europe responded and referred. One of the earliest critics to offer prescriptive standards for poetry, Jean Chapelain (1595–1674), censures Giambattista Marino's *Adone* (1623), for its lack of verisimilitude (what ought to be) and its promotion of the marvelous in excessive *ornament*: both, he argues, distract the reader to secondary and inessential features of the poem. His approach is neo-Aristotelian and Horatian: he prescribes utility joined to pleasure, proclaims the natural origin of the rules and conventional genres, and insists on a style limited to what the subject matter dictates ("Letter . . . Conveying His Opinion of *Adone*," 1623). Chapelain is famous for having attacked Corneille's handling of the unities in his *Les Sentiments de l'Académie française sur la tragi-comédie du Cid* (1638), which eventually prompted Corneille's *Trois Discours sur le poème dramatique* (*Three Discourses on Dramatic Poetry*, 1660), in which the playwright generally adhered to a version of cl. rules while significantly modifying them. Jean Racine (1639–99) offered a more strictly correct dramatic practice, one that combined severe formal restraint enclosing powerful emotional conflict. The 17th c., which saw the appearance of the major writers of Fr. *classicism—Corneille, Racine, Molière, and Jean de La Fontaine—has been described as a time when poetry achieved an esp. concentrated analysis of the human character (Peyre), but it should also be understood as a period of primary critical attention to the impact of poetry on its audience.

Strictness of generic form and prescriptions for style are the twin poles of Fr. classicism as urged by the two most influential critics of the later 17th c., Bouhours and Boileau. Bouhours crystallized the reaction against *concettismo* and *baroque support of verbal ornament, arguing for restraint in *metaphor and a congruity of subject matter and expression. He thus established the influential view that verbal ornament by itself is vain, that it can be tolerated only by logical indebtedness to a prior and authorizing concept. Boileau expressed similar views in arguing for a reasoned and calculated exercise of the established poetic genres, though his comments on the sublime propose less obvious relationships, and his instructions for tragic drama, in contrast to the pedantic Abbé d'Aubignac (1604–76), allow room for elevated diction and strong metaphor as agencies of powerful emotional effect. Generally the tone of Boileau's treatise is reasonable, but his critical procedure accepts the inevitability of genres and the aim of pleasing as requiring the knowledgeable artist, i.e., a man of taste (Brody 1958). Some mod. crit. tends to emphasize the sanity, rational freedom, even the wise conformity of the major Fr. classicist critics and poets (Borgerhoff, Peyre). Although there is a tendency to see classicism as dissipated in the early 18th c. under pressure from Enlightenment thinking (Peyre), Voltaire (1694–1778) continues the standard views of tragic form, and Du Bos, who explores the topic of pleasure, can be seen as extending neoclassical interests in theatrical spectacle. Rapin's neo-Aristotelian writings were widely echoed, among other things in maintaining the doctrine of illusion in conformity with "bienséance" (decorum), and verisimilitude. Denis Diderot's (1713–84) dramatic crit. (*Entretiens sur le fils naturel*, 1757; *De la poésie dramatique*, 1758; *Le Paradoxe sur le comédien*, 1770–77), shifts away from neoclassical orthodoxy, arguing against the maneuvers of illusionism and the theatricality of rules and poetic lang. Nevertheless, the triumph of Fr. classicism lies in its concern for the theatrical both as genre and as a basis for theoretical speculation.

**B. Britain.** Here neoclassical poetics has its foreshadowings in Jonson and extends nearly to the end of the 18th c. (Crane), but its maturity owes much to the Fr. example, however often Eng. critics deplore Fr. pedantry and rigidity. Dryden translated Boileau's *Art poétique*, and though he was sensitive to a variety of critical views, the burden of his dramatic crit. is to argue with Fr. theories with Fr. examples in mind. Rymer, the translator of Rapin, is the most obviously orthodox of the Eng. neoclassical critics, demanding strict attention to the unities and rigid probability, as his negative account of *Othello* indicates ("A Short View of Tragedy").

Addison's view of Eng. tragedy is scarcely more generous, measuring the local taste for "butchery" on stage against superior continental delicacy (cf. *Spectator* no. 42, 44). Many critics in spite of their allegiance to classicist standards accepted what were considered the obvious deviations of Shakespeare—Dryden, Pope, and Johnson are the critics most often cited—while others, such as Addison, sought to accommodate Milton to neoclassical standards (*Spectator* no. 279).

More broadly viewed, Eng. neoclassical poetics is a continuing effort to reduce lit. and its crit. to a system governed by a theory of pleasure derived from empirical psychology and responsive to what Addison calls a "polite" imagination (*Spectator* nos. 409–10). On the one hand, this disposition shares in the Fr. distaste for excesses of stylistic ornament and penchant for powerful emotional affect; on the other hand, it anticipates the extensive Eng. and Scottish interest in aesthetics. Addison, though himself most unsystematic, with the help of Anthony Ashley Cooper, the third Earl of Shaftesbury (1671–1713), is the key figure, raising the issues of taste, *imagination, and visual and verbal affect that were taken up by Hutcheson, Burke, Hume, Alexander Gerard (1728–95), and Lord Kames (Henry Home, 1696–1792), to name the more obvious.

Dennis's interest in emotionalism (*The Grounds of Criticism in Poetry*, 1704), Addison's discussion of the sublime in *Spectator* no. 412, and Mark Akenside's incoherent but immensely popular poem *The Pleasures of Imagination* (1774) helped make the sublime a central topic of Eng. crit. throughout the 18th c. Burke's definition of the sublime as terror of the unseen links it to tragedy, and it has from the time of Hobbes been tied to heroic poetry, esp. by Dennis and Addison. Although the sublime was generally supposed as a result of Boileau's theory to be a category of experience and thought beyond lang., it was nevertheless seen to result in the lang. of transport. At the same time, its devel. in Eng. was closely linked to an interest in landscape (see LANDSCAPE POETRY).

For many mod. critics, Samuel Johnson represents the most mature and flexible representative of neoclassical thought in his insistence on a timeless, universal critical standard ("Preface to Shakespeare" [1765]), his belief that the poet's task is to record the typical (*Rasselas*, ch. 10 [1759]), and his dislike of romance. Consistently, he censures the metaphysicals for a lack of logic, while conceding their learning, and praises Shakespeare while depriving him of everything local, Elizabethan, and idiosyncratic (*Life of Cowley* [1779], "Preface to Shakespeare").

**C. Germany.** German neoclassical poetics has two phases. The first, exemplified by J. C. Gottsched's (1700–66) *Versuch einer kritischen Dichtkunst* (1730), is deeply indebted to Boileau and Fr. classicism and characterized by their doctrines of imitation, style, and genre. The second and aesthetic phase, which owes something to Gottsched's concept of beauty as the perfection of the poem, begins in Johann Winckelmann's

(1717–68) *Gedanken über die Nachahmung der griechischen Werke in der Malerei und Bildhauerkunst* (*Thoughts on the Imitation of the Painting and Sculpture of the Greeks*, 1755) and culminates in the critical reflections and early work of J. W. Goethe (1749–1832). Ger. neoclassicism overlaps substantially with *romanticism, sometimes in the same writer. Both strains are powerfully philosophical, neoclassical poetics being grounded in the rationalism of G. W. Leibniz (1646–1716) and the Cartesian psychology of Christian Wolff (1679–1754). There is a consistent and conscious line of critical theorizing from A. G. Baumgarten (1714–62), G. F. Meier (1718–77), and Moses Mendelssohn (1729–86) to Lessing that argues for a poetics following the general laws of reason, probability, and internal consistency deduced from the nature of the representational faculties. This theory links the poem to beauty as a relation between the object, its representation, and the effect in the soul. Since the relationship is all important, the verbal sign must be transparent (see SIGN, SIGNIFIED, SIGNIFIER). Lessing develops this theory by proposing that the object of aesthetic enjoyment is not the words of the poetic text but the imaginative concepts they prompt (*Laokoön*, ch. 17). Ger. neoclassical aestheticism flourished in the context of the Hellenism popularized by Winckelmann, for whom the Gr. concept of beauty was its supposed "noble simplicity and tranquil grandeur," a view challenged by Lessing's theory of narrative and dramatic dynamism.

The classicism of Friedrich Schiller (1759–1805) and Goethe proposes a new direction, beginning with Schiller's idea of an absolute value for the work of art independent of its effect on the reader or spectator. Schiller opposes mimetic emotional immediacy and requires an artistic idealizing (review of Bürger's poems, 1791; Hohendahl). Goethe supplements Schiller by a concept of style that universalizes and objectifies, producing the cl. symbolic form as a cognition of essences; thus, he moves toward a concept of lit. as autonomous (Hohendahl; see AUTONOMY).

**D. Italy.** It. neoclassical poetics is complicated by the 17th-c. Fr. attack on Ren. It. poets, esp. Torquato Tasso and Giambattista Marino, which divided the sympathies of It. critics drawn to neoclassical doctrine. With the arrival of G. V. Gravina (1664–1718), however, a spirit of undivided neoclassicism took over, a reaction against Marino having taken root in the founding of the academy Arcadia at Rome in 1690. Dedicated to the propagation of *buon gusto* (good taste) and the establishment of the laws of poetry manifested in generic orthodoxy and simplicity of style and feeling, the influence of the Arcadian academy reached well into the 18th c. Gravina's attention to the ties between science and art included an interest in the early hist. of poetry, esp. the Homeric poems, but unlike Giambattista Vico (1668–1744), who looked on early poetic expression as a necessary feature of barbaric humanity, Gravina finds in them an expression of Gr. life. Another Arcadian, G. M. de'Crescimbeni (1663–1728), links the vernacular to Gr. poetry and prescribes

an internal spiritual beauty against external, superficial ornament. Somewhat differently, the familiar topics of the beautiful and the true as the objects of imitation, as well as the problem of taste, appear in Giuseppe Spalletti's (fl. 1746) *Saggio sopra la bellezza* (1765). An empiricist, Spalletti contends that beauty is determined by repeated sensory observation and that aesthetic pleasure has its source in human *amour propre* (self-regard). The Enlightenment interest in lit. hist. emerges in the extensive antiquarian studies of L. A. Muratori (1672–1750), who with Gravina sought in promoting visual representation and probability to recover the best elements of It. Ren. poetry from the indiscipline of the baroque. A different side of It. neoclassicism appears in the work of Melchiorre Cesarotti (1730–1808). An admirer of Gravina, he was familiar with Brit. empiricism, argued against Du Bos and Hume about tragic emotion, praised Lucian over Homer, and produced important essays on the philosophy of linguistic change.

**E. Spain.** The effects of Eur. neoclassical poetics and of neoclassicism in general are belated in Sp. culture and coexist with vestiges of baroque styles during the early 18th c. and with sentimental and preromantic impulses somewhat later. As elsewhere, Fr. classicist doctrine was imported to combat what some saw as excessive and lawless habits of expression. A beginning is illustrated in the Real Academia Española's effort to regularize the vernacular in its dictionary (1714) and the attempt at encouraging a standard marks the *Poética* (1737) of Ignazio de Luzán (1702–54), a Boileau-like manifesto urging moral purpose in lit. by means of common sense, clarity, and simplicity of style, restraint of the imagination, verisimilitude, and the imitation of nature. A member of the symptomatically named Academia del Buen Gusto (Academy of Good Taste), Luzan belonged to an anti-Góngora set in reaction to baroque style, much as had their Fr. predecessors Bouhours and Boileau. The Benedictine essayist B. J. Feijoo (1676–1764) was perhaps the most instrumental figure in urging northern Eur. culture on Spain. His volumes *Teatro critico universal* (1726–39) and *Cartas eruditas y curiosas* (1742–60) involved every conceivable subject while focusing on ignorance and superstition, encouraged literary rules, but conceded the exemption of genius (*no sé qué*).

Later 18th-c. Sp. neoclassical poetics is exemplified by Nicolás Fernández de Moratín (1737–80), ed. of the periodical *El Poeta* (est. 1764) and a tragedian. His work argued for traditional values and historical and patriotic subjects, but like much Sp. neoclassical tragedy at this time, it reflected the taste of the court rather than the theater-going population at large. His son, Leandro Fernández de Moratín (1760–1828), produced comedies and within a neoclassical framework developed a form of *comedy featuring contests between the forces of reason and unreason. Besides the obvious influence of writers such as Boileau, Voltaire, and Jean-Jacques Rousseau, educated Sp. taste was conversant with the works of André, Charles Batteux, Du

Bos, Diderot, and Jean-François Marmontel, as well as Hutcheson, Addison, Pope, Shaftesbury, Burke, and Blair. And as in the countries from which Sp. neoclassical crit. drew its examples, it gave way at the end of the century to preromantic and romantic tendencies with which it had coexisted in its later stages, tendencies that in various ways dissipated concerns for critical rationalism, rules, imitation, stylistic moderation and simplicity, and various forms of restraint.

**F. Russia.** Almost entirely derivative from Fr. and Eng. models, Rus. neoclassical poetics was encouraged by Peter the Great's efforts to modernize Rus. culture. It largely took shape as an interest in the standard litzerary genres and their rules or features, as presented in Boileau's *Art poétique*. Much translated into Rus. in the 18th c., this work was seminal in encouraging judgment, discrimination, and simplicity of style, though Mikhail Lomonosov (1711–65), with some affinity for the strain of *\*préciosité* in 17th-c. Fr. lit., and influenced in part by Ger. baroque aesthetics, in part by the work of the Jesuit Nicolas Caussin, offered a more emotive and rhetorically ornamental version of the *\*ode.* At the same time, he accepted the cl. rhetorical doctrine of three levels of style. A more thoroughly conventional adaptation of Fr. doctrine informs the Kiev Academy lectures of Feofan Prokopovich (1681–1736) on poetics and rhet. (1705–7). These insisted on imitation of Gr. and Lat. models for style and repeated the usual Horatian imperatives of delight and utility.

The central figure in Rus. neoclassicism is A. P. Sumarokov (1717–77). Using Boileau to propagate the concept of dramatic rules, Sumarokov wrote in some detail on the genres and unities and discussed the major figures in Fr. classicism, as well as exhibiting some acquaintance with Shakespeare, Milton, Tasso, and Luís de Camões. In all, he wrote nine tragedies, imitating Racine, Corneille, and Voltaire, a practice that indicates that neoclassical imitation was as much an effort to adapt nearly contemp. models as it was a conformity to Gr. or Roman originals (Brown). Other features of the Rus. movement may be seen in the ode on taste of V. I. Maikov (1728–78), a follower of Sumarokov's, and in the didacticism of G. R. Derzhavin (1743–1816). Although the dominance of neoclassicism in Rus. lasted only a brief time (ca. 1747–70), when the drift toward romanticism begins, it is important in Europeanizing and modernizing Rus. lit. and critical thinking and in providing examples and concepts that significantly broadened and sophisticated Rus. letters.

*See* NAÏVE-SENTIMENTAL, PREROMANTICISM, SENSIBILITY, SENTIMENTALITY.

■ **General Studies:** K. Borinski, *Die Antike in Poetik und Kunsttheorie*, 2 v. (1914–23); S. H. Monk, *The Sublime: A Study of Critical Theories in XVIII-Century England* (1935); B. Hathaway, "The Lucretian 'Return upon Ourselves' in 18th-Century Theories of Tragedy," *PMLA* 62 (1947); J. Hagstrum, *Samuel Johnson's Literary Criticism* (1952); R. S. Crane, *The Languages of Criticism and the Structure of Poetry* (1953); Wellek; Wimsatt and Brooks; J. Hagstrum, *The Sister Arts* (1958); M. H. Nicolson, *Mountain Gloom and Mountain Glory* (1959); R. Cohen, "The Transformation of Passion: A Study of Hume's Theories of Tragedy," *PQ* 41 (1962); L. Lipking, *The Ordering of the Arts in 18th-Century England* (1970); Saisselin; T. Jones and B. Nicol, *Neoclassical Dramatic Criticism, 1560–1770* (1976); H. Aarsleff, *From Locke to Saussure* (1982); D. L. Patey, *Probability and Literary Form* (1984); J. Mahoney, *The Whole Internal Universe: Imitation and the New Defense of Poetry* (1985); J. Engell, *Forming the Critical Mind: Dryden to Coleridge* (1989); J. Levine, *The Battle of the Books: History and Literature in the Augustan Age* (1991); R. L. Montgomery, *Terms of Response* (1992); R. Habib, *A History of Literary Criticism* (2005); *A Companion to Eighteenth-Century Poetry*, ed. C. Gerrard (2006); P. Shaw, *The Sublime* (2006); *The Classical Tradition*, ed. A. Grafton, G. Most, S. Settis (2010).

■ **National Literatures.** *France*: R. Bray, *La Formation de la doctrine classique en France* (1931); P. Bénichou, *Morales du Grand Siècle* (1948); H. Peyre, *Qu'est-ce que le classicisme?*, rev. ed. (1965); B. Tocanne, *L'idée de nature en France dans la seconde moitié du XVII siècle* (1978); G. Pocock, *Boileau and the Nature of Neo-Classicism* (1980); M. Hobson, *The Object of Art* (1982); Hollier; P. Dandry, "Les deux esthétiques du classicism français," *Littératures classiques* 19 (1993); B. Beugnot, *La Mémoire du texte: essais de poétique classique* (1994); P. Dandry, "Qu'est-ce que le classicisme?," *L'état classique, 1652–1715*, ed. H. Méchoulan and J. Cornette (1996); N. Cronk, *French Neoclassicism and the Language of Literature* (2003); B. Craveri, *The Age of Conversation* (2005); L. Norman, *The Shock of the Ancient: Literature and History in Early Modern France* (2011). *Britain*: J.W. H. Atkins, *English Literary Criticism: Seventeenth and Eighteenth Centuries* (1951); R. Cohen, "The Augustan Mode in English Poetry," *Eighteenth-Century Studies* 1 (1967); P. Stone, *The Art of Poetry: 1750–1820* (1967); J. Johnson, *The Formation of English Neoclassical Thought* (1967); E. Marks, *The Poetics of Reason* (1968); R. Stock, *Samuel Johnson and Neoclassical Dramatic Theory* (1973); E. Pechter, *Dryden's Classical Theory of Literature* (1975); *Horace Made New*, ed. D. Hopkins and C. Martindale (1993); *The Sublime: A Reader in British Eighteenth-Century Aesthetic Theory*, ed. A. Ashfield and P. De Bolla (1996); *Augustan Critical Writing*, ed. D. Womersley (1997); B. Parker, *The Triumph of Augustan Poetics* (1998); *Eighteenth-Century British Aesthetics*, ed. D. Townsend (1999); *A Companion to Hume*, ed. E. Radcliffe (2011). *Germany*: E. Cassirer, *The Philosophy of the Enlightenment*, trans. F.C.A. Koelln and J. P. Pettegrove (1951); A. Nivelle, *Les théories esthétiques en Allemagne de Baumgarten à Kant* (1955); H. Allison, *Lessing and the Enlightenment* (1966); K. Scherpe, *Gattungspoetik im 18. Jahrhundert* (1968); D. Wellbery, *Lessing's "Laocoön": Semiotics and Aesthetics in the Age of Reason* (1984); K. Berghan, "From Classicist to Classical Literary Criticism, 1730–1806," *A History of German Literary Criticism, 1730–1980*, ed. P. Hohendahl (1985); H. Nisbet, "Introduction," *German Aesthetic and*

*Literary Criticism*, ed. H. Nisbet (1985); B. Bennett, *Goethe's Theory of Poetry* (1986); F. J. Lamport, *German Classical Drama* (1992); P. Mitchell, *Johann Christoph Gottsched (1700–1766)* (1995); S. Marchand, *Down from Olympus: Archaeology and Philhellenism in Germany, 1750–1970* (1996); *A New History of German Literature*, ed. D. Wellbery, J. Ryan, and H. U. Gumbrecht (2004). **Italy:** H. Quigley, *Italy and the Rise of a New School of Criticism in the Eighteenth Century* (1923); M. Fubini, *Dal Muratori al Baretti* (1946); B. Croce, *La letteratura italiana del Settecento* (1949); J. Whitfield, *A Short History of Italian Literature* (1960); *Antologia della critica letteraria*, ed. G. Petronio, v. 2 (1967); G. Petrocchi, *Questioni di critica letteraria* (1970); G. Natali, *Il settecento*, 4th ed., ch. 6 (1973). **Spain:** J. Cook, *Neoclassical Drama in Spain: Theory and Practice* (1959); N. Glendinning, *A Literary History of Spain: The Eighteenth Century* (1972); J. Stamm, *A Short History of Spanish Literature* (1979); F. Aguilar Piñal, *Introducción al Siglo XVIII* (1991); R. Sebold, *La perduración de la modalidad clásica* (2001); J. Berbel, *Orígenes de la tragedia neoclásica española (1737–1754)* (2003); *Cambridge History of Spanish Literature*, ed. D. Gies (2004). **Russia:** D. Cizevskij, *History of Russian Literature from the Eleventh Century to the End of the Baroque* (1970); *The Eighteenth Century in Russia*, ed. J. G. Garrard (1973); R. Neuhauser, *Towards the Romantic Age: Essays on Sentimental and Preromantic Literature in Russia* (1974); *Russian Literature in the Age of Catherine the Great*, ed. A. Gross (1976); W. E. Brown, *A History of Eighteenth-Century Russian Literature* (1980); *Cambridge History of Russian Literature*, ed. C. A. Moser (1989).

R. L. Montgomery, K. Hume

**NEO-GONGORISM.** A term used to designate a brief but significant 20th-c. Sp. poetic trend stemming from a revival of the 17th-c. *baroque poet Luis de Góngora (1561–1627) on the tricentennial of his death. Góngora's style, characterized by brilliant if extravagant *metaphors and convoluted or Latinate syntax, created a new interest in the formal possibilities of lang. that led to the publication of mod. eds. of his work and important stylistic studies of his poetry. Among contributors to this vogue were Dámaso Alonso, Gerardo Diego, and José Maria de Cossío. Renewed enthusiasm for Góngora was esp. reflected in the poets of the Generation of 1927, whose name may be attributed to the commemoration they organized in that year. The group carried out a conscious revision of baroque lit., which affirmed its own difficulty. The first rediscovery of Góngora's writing has also been attributed to the poetic revisions by Sp. Am. writers José Martí and Rubén Darío, and later Alfonso Reyes, prior to the Generation of 1927. The *Novísimos* generation of 1968 again paid homage to Góngora.

The selection of baroque art as a basis for renovation has been explained by the lack of a strong romantic movement in Sp. In part, the 20th c.'s interest came from Góngora's identity as an unassimilated or "different" poet; his techniques of ling. structure sought a fundamental renovation of creative expression in a

way paradoxically similar to the *avant-garde poetics emerging at the same time. While the avant-garde rejected Western high culture and was antiacademy, Góngora was accepted because he signified the reworking of syntax and the creation of neologisms. Important works by this movement include Rafael Alberti's *Cal y canto*, Gerardo Diego's *Fábula de Equis y Zeda*, Miguel Hernández's *Perito en Lunas*, and Federico García Lorca's remarkable lecture on poetic imagery in Góngora's work.

*See* CREATIONISM; SPAIN, POETRY OF; ULTRAISM.

■ H. Friedrich, *Die Struktur der modernen Lyrik* (1956); P. Salinas, *Reality and the Poet in Spanish Poetry* (1966); C. B. Morris, *A Generation of Spanish Poets, 1920–1936* (1969); J.-C. Mainer, *La edad de plata (1902–1939)* (1981); J. L. Bernal, *Gerardo Diego y la vanguardia hispánica: Actas del Congreso Internacional Iberoamérica y España en la Génesis de la Vanguardia Hispánica* (1993); R. González Echevarría, *Celestina's Brood: Continuities of the Baroque in Spain and Latin America* (1993); N. Palenzuela, "Cubismo y neogogorismo en las poéticas narrativas de los años veinte" (1994); J. Delgado Casado and P. Canelo, *Gerardo Diego y la poesía española del siglo XX* (1996); *Hispanic Baroques: Reading Cultures in Context*, ed. N. Spadaccini and L. Martín Estudillo (2005).

A. W. Phillips; K. N. March

**NEOTERICS** (Gr. *neoteroi*, "new poets"). In Roman antiquity, the term and its cognates (Lat. *poetae novi* and *cantores Euphorionis*; Gr. *neoteroi*) are applied by Cicero to the members of the fashionable trend in Roman poetry to which he belonged himself in his younger period, influenced by Alexandrian Gr. poetry and its later devels. The most famous example is Catullus, but others whose work survives in fragments are Laevius, Calvus, Cinna, Cornificius, Furius Bibaculus, and Ticidas. The Alexandrian poets who served as antecedents included Callimachus and Theocritus. The term *neoteric* has been extended to later cohorts in the Roman trad.—a notable instance is a group, often called the *poetae novelli*, flourishing in the 2d c. CE—and to postclassical vernacular poets in Europe who styled themselves (or were retrospectively designated) as *new poets*.

*See* ALEXANDRIANISM, LATIN POETRY.

■ J. de Ghellinck, "Neotericus, neoterics," *Archiuum Latinatis Medii Aevi* 15 (1940); B. Otis, *Virgil* (1963); E. Castorina, *Questioni Neoteriche* (1968); R. Helgerson, "The New Poet Presents Himself: Spenser and the Idea of a Literary Career," *PMLA* 93 (1978); R.O.A.M. Lyne, "The Neoteric Poets," *CQ* 28 (1978); W. V. Clausen, "The New Direction in Poetry," *CHCL*, v. 2; J. K. Newman, *Roman Catullus* (1990); R. D. Brown, *"The New Poet": Novelty and Tradition in Spenser's "Complaints"* (1999); R. Greene, "Spenser and Contemporary Vernacular Poetry," *Cambridge Companion to Spenser*, ed. A. Hadfield (2001).

J. K. Newman

**NEPĀL BHĀṢA.** *See* NEWAR POETRY.

**NEPALI AND PAHARI POETRY.** The Pahari langs. form a band along the Himalayan range from Kashmir through Nepal. By the early 19th c., the entire region was divided among small principalities in the west, territory under the control of the Brit. Empire in the center, and the newly consolidated kingdom of Nepal in the east. Of the various langs., Nepali came to serve as the vehicle of a national lit. of the mod. type, while Dogri has been named one of the official langs. of the Indian state of Jammu and Kashmir. Between these extremes, the territory now forming the Indian states of Himachal Pradesh and Uttarakhand adopted Hindi as the official lang., with Pahari langs. persisting as the tongues of household and of oral lit. and ritual.

One of the striking characteristics of all Pahari-speaking territories is the richness of oral poetic trads. Noteworthy are *ballad singing (cf. the Gaine of central Nepal), humorous and satiric poetry and song, and the role of mythic narrative as part of rituals, sometimes of shamanic healing. Throughout, poets have maintained what is probably an ancient office of praising kings (see EPIDEICTIC POETRY, PANEGYRIC). In particular, the Central Himalayan region, incl. Uttarakhand and far western Nepal, shows a distinctive devel. of *narrative poetry performed by singer-drummers. These bards perform *epics, heroic ballads, vernacular renditions of Hindu epics and myths, and narrative *hymns to the regional gods, in a variety of styles.

Throughout the Himalayas, the last centuries have also seen the devel. of vernacular written lits. inspired both by Sanskritic and North Indian models and by local trads.

Western Pahari courtly langs. served for the trans. of religious poetry, while Dogri has had an established literary trad. since the 18th c. In the Central Himalayas, poetry has been written in the two main langs., Garhwali and Kumaoni, since the early 19th c. Lok Ratna Pant "Gumāni" (1791–1846) is said to have established Kumaoni as a literary lang., while Gaurī Datt Pāṇḍe "Gaurdā" (1872–1939) is remembered for sensitive and sometimes satirical poetry, often in the cause of social reform and Indian independence. In the Indian Himalayas, efforts to valorize regional langs. have continued, and there has been a renaissance of topical and popular song, often with a political edge.

In Nepal, the earliest written poetry, dating from the late 18th c., consists of martial epics praising the king. But the foundational text of Nepali lit. is usually considered Bhānubhakta's (1814–68) rendition of the *Rāmāyaṇa*, composed in something close to spoken Nepali. This work was rediscovered by Motīrām Bhaṭṭa (1866–96), another major poet. Three great names dominated the 20th c.: the master craftsman Lekhnāth Pauḍyāl (1884–1965), who was influenced by oral poetic forms; Bālkṛṣṇa Sama (1902–81), known primarily for his dramas; and the neoromantic Lakṣmīprasād Devkoṭa (1909–59; see Rubin), who composed his ballad *Munā Madan*, still sung today, in folk meters. From the 1940s, traditional verse forms were challenged, and from the 1960s, with the *Tesro Āyām* (Third Dimension) poets, there was an opening to personal expression. Since then, Nepali poetry has gone through a series of movements, all related, as elsewhere in the Pahari-speaking region, to political struggles. The ten-

sion here is among poetry as a self-referential craft of lang., as a vehicle of sometimes subtle self-expression, and as a tool for social transformation.

See HINDI POETRY; INDIA, POETRY OF; KASHMIRI POETRY; RĀMĀYAṆA POETRY; SANSKRIT POETICS; SANSKRIT POETRY.

■ D. Rubin, *Nepali Visions, Nepali Dreams: The Poetry of Laxmiprasad Devkota* (1980); K. Pradhan, *A History of Nepali Literature* (1984); K. Meissner, *Malushahi and Rajula: A Ballad from Kumaun* (1985); M. Hutt, *Himalayan Voices: An Introduction to Modern Nepali Literature* (1991); C. C. Pande, *Echoes from the Hills: Poems of Gaurda* (1997); G. Maskarinec, *Nepalese Shaman Oral Texts* (1998).

J. LEAVITT

**NETHERLANDS, POETRY OF THE.** See LOW COUNTRIES, POETRY OF THE.

**NEWAR POETRY.** Nepāl Bhāṣā (Kathmandu Newar), the lang. of the Newars, is a Tibeto-Burman lang. spoken primarily in the Kathmandu Valley. The term *Nepāl Bhāṣā* is the traditional and preferred term, although *Newar* and *Newari* are often used. Written sources from the med. period date back as early as 1114 CE. Of the approximately 350 Tibeto-Burman langs., only three others have literary trads. of comparable historical depth.

In the Malla era (1400–1769), the cl. literary lang. was highly Sanskritized, with much of the vocabulary from Indic sources. Verse forms imitating Sanskrit models appeared in the 15th c., sometimes authored by royalty, often anonymous. These sung verse forms (*mye*) were primarily religious, with the exception of the *bākhā mye* (ballad songs) and *sinhājyā mye* (rice-planting songs). Characteristically, in Newar, the *sinhājyā mye* invoke the spring passions of men and women working together during planting season. Many continue to be sung in the mod. period.

With the Gorkha conquest of the Kathmandu Valley in 1769 and the promotion of Nepāli, an Indic lang., under the Shah regime (1769–1847), Newar cultural institutions began to suffer. During the Rana period (1905–51), Newar-lang. publications were banned outright, writers and activists jailed. Shaped by this oppression, the mod. era also contains the seeds of resistance and a literary renaissance. Among the poets of this period, Siddhi Dās Āmātya (1867–1930) and Yogbir Singh Kansākar (1885–1941) were foundational influences.

The iconic poet of the 20th c. Nepāl Bhāṣā movement is Chittadhar Hṛdaya (1906–82). Jailed five years for literary activism, Chittadhar withstood confinement by writing his masterpiece *Sugata Saurabha* and having the chapters smuggled out of prison. The epic poem (19 chs.) is a deeply erudite Nepāl Bhāṣā redaction of the Buddha's life in rhymed *couplets, employing Sanskrit meters and allusions to canonical Buddhist biographical and philosophical trads. More significant where the canonical sources lacked narrative detail, the poet localizes the Buddha's story, weaving in details unique to Newar culture: food, domestic life, clothing and jewelry, music, rites of passages, marriage customs, rituals, festivals, even local architecture. The chapters teem with allusions to contemp. social concerns. Similarly, the vocabulary ranges from esoteric religious terms to colloquial, onomatopoeic expressions ubiquitous in Newar conversation. This complex intertextuality brings Nepāl Bhāṣā poetry into the mod. period. Others of Chittadhar's poems reflect contemp. themes and greater formal flexibility. In *TB*, a recovering wife in a sanitarium finds her husband has taken a second wife. *Pragati* is an allegorical critique of the mod. concept of progress.

With the onset of a fragile democracy in 1951, contemp. poets exhibit increased formal freedoms, political awareness, and secularization. Durga Lāl Shresta (b. 1937), a prolific composer of songs, plays, and poems, writes richly melodic lines: imagistic, deeply personal and political. Purna Vaidya (b. 1941) brings introspective *free-verse sensibilities to contemp. Newar poetry. With the increasing influence of Eng. and the educational system's emphasis on Nepali as a national lang., today's poets face the challenge of sustaining the Nepāl Bhāṣā literary community.

*See* INDIA, POETRY OF; NEPALI AND PAHARI POETRY; SANSKRIT POETICS; SANSKRIT POETRY.

■ K. P. Malla, *Classical Newari Literature* (1982); *Songs of Nepal*, ed. S. Lienhard (1984); C. Hṛdaya, *Dega* (Pagoda), trans. V. P. Lācoul, M. Karmācārya, U. Malla (1996); *A Representative Collection of Nepal Bhasa Poems,* ed. K. C. Pradhan, trans. T. L. Tulādhar and W. Amtis (1997); D. L. Śhresta, *Twists and Turns,* trans. T. T. Tulādhar (2000); *Contemporary Writing in Nepāl Bhāṣā,* ed. B. P. Śhresta and P. S. Tulādhar (2000); C. Hṛdaya, *Sugata Surabha,* trans. T. T. Lewis and S. M. Tulādhar (2007).

D. HARGREAVES

**NEW CRITICISM.** A term used to designate the work of a wide variety of Anglo-Am. critics writing between the 1920s and 1960s. It was first coined by John Crowe Ransom in his 1941 book by the same name, a critical study of the work of I. A. Richards, William Empson, T. S. Eliot, and Yvor Winters. At various times, the label has also been applied to critics as diverse as Kenneth Burke, R. P. Blackmur, and René Wellek. However, as most commonly used, the term refers to the movement to reform Am. literary scholarship and pedagogy spearheaded by Ransom and a group of his former students: Cleanth Brooks, Allen Tate, and Robert Penn Warren. These writers advocated a formalist approach to practical crit., a distillation of modernist ideas about lit. that had circulated among the literary avant-garde since the 1910s and 1920s.

As an institutional movement, the New Criticism originated at Vanderbilt University in the early 1920s. Ransom, a lecturer at the university, introduced the method of *close reading into his classes. An accomplished poet, he also became the central figure in a modernist literary coterie called the *Fugitives, which encompassed several of Ransom's most gifted students, incl. Tate and Warren. This group evolved into a regionalist political movement known as the Agrar-

ians and published their key manifesto, *I'll Take My Stand*, in 1930. This text argued for the preservation of a distinctive southern U.S. culture and economics against the intrusion of the industrial North. By the mid-1930s, Ransom and many fellow Agrarian writers had become disenchanted with regional politics and instead focused their energies upon the reform of literary studies. Ransom became the ed. of the influential critical jour. *The Kenyon Review*. Warren and Brooks joined *The Southern Review* and also published a series of undergraduate textbooks that reshaped Am. literary pedagogy: *Understanding Poetry* and *Understanding Fiction*. The resulting New Criticism was less an abandonment of the Agrarians' anti-industrial, conservative ideology than a reconstitution of it on other grounds. The New Critics viewed lit. as a repository of the anti-scientific rationality that they had previously associated with the traditional culture and agricultural economy of the southern U.S. In Ransom's terms, poetry embodies an experience of preconceptual particularity, what he called the "world's body," otherwise inaccessible to the mod., Western mind. The New Critics hoped to transform literary studies into a discipline capable of tracing the ontological maneuver by which the lang. of poetry evades the rationalism of scientific thought.

Most of the New Critics contrasted this approach to crit. to two types of literary scholarship predominant in the 1930s academy. First, they distanced themselves from biographical and historical studies of lit. Second, they rejected the impressionistic crit. of humanists such as Irving Babbitt. Like the Rus. formalists of the 1920s, they instead argued for an objective crit. that would identify the literariness of literary lang.—the structural and linguistic features that distinguish it from other types of writing. These features are esp. evident in poetry—for the New Critics, the quintessential literary art. In particular, the New Critics highlighted the pervasiveness of *irony and *paradox in poetry, which disrupted the denotative clarity of ordinary prose.

This emphasis upon the literariness of literary lang. led the New Critics to develop a set of rules and injunctions that they hoped would henceforth guide practical crit. Chief among these was the "heresy of paraphrase," a term coined by Brooks. Because of their semantic complexity, works of lit. could not be summarized or redacted without effacing their distinctive literary qualities. Nor could critics uphold commonsense distinctions between literary form and content; a poem's form is not a mold or container that can be separated from its content. W. K. Wimsatt and M. C. Beardsley added two more injunctions: the *intentional fallacy held that poems should be read without appeal to the poet's biographical intent, which is inaccessible to the critic and meaningless given literature's semantic irreducibility, while the *affective fallacy held that poems should be read without appeal to the emotions or responses that they potentially evoke in the reader. Both fallacies, Wimsatt and Beardsley argued, distract critics with empirical considerations that take them away from the poem itself. Both also threaten to dissolve literary study into one of several rival disciplines that had been colonized by scientific positivism: sociology, hist., and psychology.

The New Critics also advanced an organicist account of lit.; they imagined the successful poem as a complex unity, with its inner semantic tensions held in balance by its overarching structure. In Brooks's terms from *The Well Wrought Urn*, this structure should be understood in dramatic terms, as a series of statements and counterstatements unfolding in time. The resulting organic unity could be experienced but never described, which lent an abstruse cast to many New Critical pronouncements about poetry. In Archibald MacLeish's terms, a poem must not "mean" but "be." This emphasis upon complex unity also led the New Critics to disparage didactic and overly prosaic lit.—notably much of the *protest poetry and naturalist fiction produced by left-wing writers in the 1930s.

In the U.S., the New Criticism profoundly reshaped literary studies. As Gerald Graff details in *Professing Literature*, the Am. New Critics began to popularize their ideas shortly before the rapid expansion of the university system after World War II. Close reading, which eschewed biographical and historical research, seemed ideally suited to the postwar influx of first-generation university students, many of whom did not share any common cultural background. At the same time, close reading enabled critics to conceive of literary studies as a professional discipline, capable of competing with while remaining distinct from the sciences and social sciences in the postwar multiversity. Ransom outlined this ambition in his aptly titled 1937 essay, "Criticism, Inc.," which called for formalist critics within the university to institutionalize a rigorously systematic approach to lit. that would rival the positivist techniques of the hard sciences. The New Criticism was thus part of the more general movement toward disciplinary specialization that characterized the post–World War II academy. At the same time, the New Critics transformed high and middlebrow literary tastes. They disseminated previously neglected works of modernist lit. to a generation of students and more generally helped elevate linguistic and structural complexity into the chief criteria of literary value. Indeed, as John Guillory argues, the New Criticism's principal disciplinary effect was to transform literary interpretation into an advanced form of cultural capital.

The New Critical hegemony began to dissolve in the 1960s, with the emergence of alternative approaches such as the archetypal crit. of Northrop Frye and various strands of Fr. structuralist and poststructuralist thought. In particular, the generation of politically oriented students and young professors who disrupted the 1968 Mod. Lang. Assoc. convention chafed against the New Criticism's ostensibly apolitical *formalism, which they associated with cold-war consensus and the technocratic rationalism of the postwar university. Most subsequent trends in literary theory were oriented against some key tenet of the New Criticism. Deconstructive critics, while retaining the New Critics' emphasis upon literature's semantic irreducibility, rejected their notion of organic unity. *Reader-response critics

abandoned the affective fallacy, while New Historicists revitalized the context-based crit. that the New Critics had banished to sociology and hist.

Nevertheless, many of the changes wrought by the New Criticism proved to be enduring. While most critics reject the ontological assumptions that once underlay close reading as a disciplinary practice, they continue to rely upon it in their scholarship and pedagogy. The New Critics' valuation of interpretive complexity also seems self-evident to most literary critics, as does their tendency to imagine lit. as an antipositivistic discipline. For better or for worse, the institutional effects of the New Criticism outstripped its founders' ideological intentions and established a paradigm for literary professionalism still influential in the present day.

*See* NEW HISTORICISM, READER, RUSSIAN FORMALISM.

■ J. C. Ransom et al., *I'll Take My Stand* (1930); J. C. Ransom, "Criticism, Inc.," *The World's Body* (1938); J. C. Ransom, *The New Criticism* (1941); C. Brooks and R. P. Warren, *Understanding Fiction* (1943); Brooks; W. K. Wimsatt and M. C. Beardsley, "The Intentional Fallacy" and "The Affective Fallacy," *The Verbal Icon* (1954); Brooks and Warren; G. Hartman, *Beyond Formalism* (1970); T. D. Young, *Gentleman in a Dustcoat* (1976); F. Lentricchia, *Beyond the New Criticism* (1981); G. Graff, *Professing Literature* (1987); J. Guillory, *Cultural Capital* (1993); M. Jancovich, *The Cultural Politics of the New Critics* (1993); S. Schryer, "Fantasies of the New Class," *PMLA* 122 (2007).

S. SCHRYER

**NEW FORMALISM.** A movement, largely in the U.S., that promoted the use of metrical verse technique and rhyme. The group emerged during the 1980s, consisting (in Jarman and Mason's account) of poets born after 1940. The group's forceful prose gained wide attention. Prominent statements include Dana Gioia's "Notes on the New Formalism" (*Can Poetry Matter?*, 1992) and Timothy Steele's *Missing Measures*. Following the trend of Am. poets claiming outsider status, Gioia described "formal verse" as "the unexpected challenge [to] the long-established, ruling orthodoxy" of *free verse. As in his other crit., Gioia described New Formalism as a populist movement that rejected academic specialization and emphasized poetry's aural pleasures.

While Gioia dismissed "metrical versus nonmetrical verse" as "a tired argument," others insisted on this distinction, arguing for the former's superiority. In *Missing Measures*, Steele traces why free-verse technique attracted mod. poets. In the book's polemical conclusion, Steele argues that metrical verse uniquely "nourishes" virtues such as "a love of nature, an enthusiasm for justice, a readiness of good humor." At such moments, Steele argues for metrical verse's essential goodness.

New Formalism also gained attention by publishing anthologies: most notably, Richman's *The Direction of Poetry* and Jarman and Mason's *Rebel Angels*. Annie Finch's *A Formal Feeling Comes* attempted to "contradict the popular assumption that formal poetics correspond to reactionary politics and elitist aesthetics," a charge often made by critics of New Formalism. (The term *New Formalism* was first used by Ariel Dawson in her attack upon "The Yuppie Poet" [*AWP Newsletter*, May 1985].) Figures associated with New Formalism developed publishing venues, incl. Story Line Press, and jours. such as *The Formalist* (1990–2004) and *The Reaper* (1980–89). In 1995, Gioia and Michael Peich, publisher of Aralia Press, founded the annual Exploring Form and Narrative Conference, held at West Chester University.

Like other movements, New Formalism sought to distinguish its work from that of its predecessors and perceived competitors, often at the cost of simplifying lit. and cultural hist. The distinction of "free" and "metrical" verse remains crude. The specific forms and meters that the poets employ and those they avoid more tellingly suggest the poet's aesthetic commitments. For instance, many New Formalist poets use *iambic verse, a meter amenable to the conversational tones they favor. While many observers describe a "return" to "traditional forms," it is more accurate to observe that the movement promotes a selective reclamation of a particular aspect of Eng.-lang. poetic trad. Continuing previous debates between "innovative" and "traditional" poets, critics often distinguish the New Formalists from the Language poets (see LANGUAGE POETRY), casting the two groups as opponents. Yet this vision of the "poetry wars" neglects the many distinguished writers of metrical verse—ranging from Donald Justice to Thom Gunn to H. L. Hix—who show a familiarity with self-professed avant-garde writers and their work, sharing perhaps more than their admirers care to admit. New Formalism's influence may be observed in the next generation of poets, who draw from different verse trads. without necessarily pitting one against the other.

As in the wake of other literary movements, the challenge that critics face after New Formalism is to identify the major figures' distinctive achievements, whether R. S. Gwynn's light verse, B. H. Fairchild's narrative poetry, or Marilyn Hacker's dexterous handling of intricate verse forms.

■ A. Shapiro, "The New Formalism," *CritI* 14 (1987); D. Wojahn, "Yes, But: Some Thoughts on the New Formalism," *Crazyhorse* 32 (1987); D. Gioia, "Notes on the New Formalism," *HudR* 40 (1987); R. Richman, *The Direction of Poetry* (1988); *Expansive Poetry*, ed. F. Feirstein (1989); T. Steele, *Missing Measures: Modern Poetry and the Revolt Against Meter* (1990); *A Formal Feeling Comes*, ed. A. Finch (1994); *Rebel Angels: 25 Poets of the New Formalism*, ed. M. Jarman and D. Mason (1996); *After New Formalism*, ed. A. Finch (1999); *New Expansive Poetry: Theory, Criticism, History*, ed. R. S. Gwynn (1999).

D. CAPLAN

**NEW HISTORICISM** was less a specific interpretive methodology than a particular historical moment, a constellation of critics, institutions, and events over a 25-year period. The label was partially a revision of *New Criticism, the interpretive mode that had dominated Eng. departments for the previous 30 years. New Historicism argued that the most interesting thing about poetry and lit. generally was its embodiment of hist. Instead of celebrating a poem's articulation of transhistorical truths or its capacity to be "an instance of the doctrine which it asserts" (Brooks), New Historicism saw the poem as an example of the operation of hist.—of a particular society's ability to do what it could not otherwise say (Adorno). New Historicism often retained the minute attention to detail associated with New Criticism. What changed was the ultimate point of that attention. As Montrose argued, New Historicism focused on both the "historicity of texts" and the "textuality of history." Hist. itself became the object of *close reading, and New Historicism began to read closely everything from Edmund Spenser's participation in Eng. imperialism in Ireland to the homeless living around Tintern Abbey on July 13, 1798 (Greenblatt 1980, Levinson).

Though the turn to a New Historicism was in many respects an extension of New Criticism, it also set in motion an extremely wide range of materials. New Historicism closely resembled the critical practices of the mid-20th-c. critics Erich Auerbach, Kenneth Burke, Leo Spitzer, and William Empson. It also drew heavily on the structuralist arguments of Claude Lévi-Strauss; the Fr. historiography by Michel Foucault and Michel de Certeau; the Marxism of the *Frankfurt school, E. P. Thompson, and Louis Althusser; Lacanian psychoanalysis; the sociology of Max Weber and Pierre Bourdieu; and the anthropology of Victor Turner and Clifford Geertz. The methods of these fields were deployed in a self-consciously eclectic fashion, but they also supplied new subjects to which many of the skills of a literary critic could be applied. The jour. founded at the University of California, Berkeley, in the early 1980s was named *Representations* in part because it meant that textual representations of any sort were ripe for close analysis (Gallagher and Greenblatt).

Two characteristic features of New Historicism are worth isolating from its heterogeneous methods: the use of the *anecdote and a concern with structural totality. New Historicist analyses frequently began with a historical anecdote, a short narrative out of which the rest of the essay developed. The anecdote was meant to provide a historical scene, a "touch of the real," without necessarily subscribing to a grand historical narrative as an explanatory frame (Fineman 1989, Gallagher and Greenblatt). The anecdote also functioned to delimit a specific area of hist. in order to bring a momentary end to the otherwise endless flux of hist. (Simpson 1995, Liu 1990). However, the anecdote was caught up in a more general question of postmodern understandings of hist.; despite its name, New Historicism's anecdotes often also simultaneously participated, however complexly, in the general absence of hist. that is also a feature of *postmodernism (Jameson, Thomas).

Some of the advantages of and difficulties with this use of anecdotes were esp. apparent in New Historicism's vexed relation with the legacy of New Critical emphasis on poetic *closure and the question of *structure. The explicit turn to hist. was, in one sense, a clear rejection of poetic closure; the poem was seen as working within a historical world, rather than insulated from or transcending it. Yet New Historicism often ended up treating that historical world much as a New Critical lyric. Whereas for New Criticism the poem might be treated as a self-referential unit, for New Historicism that unit was often culture more broadly conceived. In this light, Foucault's conceptions of knowledge and power became crucial terms. Like the structure of a poem, the *epistemē* or discourse of knowledge of a society seemed to control all circulation of cultural energy within it. Out of this latent *structuralism emerged a sometimes acrimonious debate about whether works could subvert, or were contained by, the power structures they expressed (Dollimore, Greenblatt 1985). At the same time, this tacit structuralism also made possible striking homologies between texts as seemingly diverse as, e.g., Frank Norris's *McTeague*, Georg Simmel's *The Philosophy of Money*, and Thomas Nast's political cartoons, by understanding them all as part of an elusive "gold standard" (Michaels, Jameson).

The stress on political readings led many practitioners of New Historicism to imagine themselves as inaugurating a break with a formalist, ahistorical, and elitist past (Greenblatt 1990). New Historicism was a prime participant in the culture wars of the 1980s and 1990s (Guillory). Esp. influential were Williams's critiques of the class politics of literary classics and Althusser's critique of humanism. Nevertheless, what a "political reading" meant was often unclear. Sometimes it meant something as specific as the reinforcement of class oppression in questions about Shakespeare on Brit. school examinations (Sinfield); sometimes it meant reading Jacobean poems under a Foucauldian rendering of monarchical absolutism (Goldberg); sometimes it meant revising the Wordsworthian imagination as a specific historical dilemma (Liu 1989, Simpson 1987). A frequent target of such political crit. was the sovereign subject or individual. Whereas previous generations of critics had sometimes celebrated a poem as the private utterance of an autonomous *poet or *persona, New Historicism tended to see not only the poem but the very concept of individuality as a component in a broader historical movement (Fineman 1986). Hist. made individuals and poems subjectivities—rather than the other way around.

Notwithstanding its sophisticated deployment of a broad range of critical theory, New Historicism had one paradoxical outcome to its methodological heterogeneity: a deep-seated antitheoretical bent. New Historicism was as often as not "Against Theory," as one highly influential article was titled (Michaels and Knapp), and it bore a great deal of similarity to Am. pragmatism (Poirier). Great stress was placed on "practice" rather than on abstract theoretical principles: Gal-

lagher and Greenblatt titled their 2000 book *Practicing New Historicism*, and the bulk of the book consists of examples of particular readings rather than an abstract account of a method.

*See* HISTORICISM, HISTORY AND POETRY.

■ Brooks; L. Althusser, "Ideology and Ideological State Apparatuses (Notes towards an Investigation)," *Lenin and Philosophy and Other Essays*, trans. B. Brewster (1971); R. Williams, *The Country and the City* (1973); S. Greenblatt, *Renaissance Self-Fashioning* (1980); J. Goldberg, *James I and the Politics of Literature: Jonson, Shakespeare, Donne and Their Contemporaries* (1983); *Political Shakespeare: New Essays in Cultural Materialism*, ed. J. Dollimore and A. Sinfield (1985)—esp. J. Dollimore, "Transgression and Surveillance in *Measure for Measure*," S. Greenblatt, "Invisible Bullets: Renaissance Authority and Its Subversion, *Henry IV* and *Henry V*," and A. Sinfield, "Give an account of Shakespeare and Education, showing why you think they are effective and what you have appreciated about them. Support your comments with precise references"; W. B. Michaels and S. Knapp, "Against Theory," *Against Theory: Literary Studies and the New Pragmatism*, ed. W.J.T. Mitchell (1985); J. Fineman, *Shakespeare's Perjured Eye: The Invention of Poetic Subjectivity in the Sonnets* (1986); M. Levinson, *Wordsworth's Great Period Poems* (1986); L. Montrose, "The Elizabethan Subject and the Spenserian Text," *Literary Theory/Renaissance Texts*, ed. P. Parker and D. Quint (1986); D. Simpson, *Wordsworth's Historical Imagination* (1987); W. B. Michaels, *The Gold Standard and the Logic of Naturalism: American Literature at the Turn of the Century* (1988); J. Fineman, "The History of the Anecdote," *The New Historicism*, ed. H. A. Veeser (1989); A. Liu, *Wordsworth and the Sense of History* (1989), and "Local Transcendence: Cultural Criticism, Postmodernism, and the Romanticism of Detail," *Representations* 32 (1990); S. Greenblatt, *Learning to Curse: Essays in Early Modern Culture* (1990); T. W. Adorno, "On Lyric Poetry and Society," *Notes to Literature*, ed. R. Tidemann, trans. S. W. Nicholsen (1991); F. Jameson, *Postmodernism or, The Cultural Logic of Late Capitalism* (1991); B. Thomas, *The New Historicism and Other Old-Fashioned Topics* (1991); R. Poirier, *Poetry and Pragmatism* (1992); J. Guillory, *Cultural Capital* (1993); D. Simpson, *The Academic Postmodern and the Rule of Literature* (1995); C. Gallagher and S. Greenblatt, *Practicing New Historicism* (2000).

C. WARLEY

**NEW NORSE (NYNORSK).** One of the two official written langs. of Norway, Nynorsk was reconstructed in the mid-19th c. by the philologist Ivar Aasen (1813–96) from rural dialects that were directly descended from ON. Aasen wanted to give his country a literary lang. less influenced by Danish, and he demonstrated the viability of *landsmaal*, as it was called at the time, by translating foreign poetry and writing his own literary works of national romanticism in various genres. The first important poet to write in Nynorsk was Aasmund Vinje (1818–70), who established the combination of cosmopolitan intellectual engagement and regional consciousness that can be seen in many later Nynorsk writers. Around the turn of the 20th c., Arne Garborg (1851–1924) and Olav Aukrust (1883–1929) demonstrated the remarkable power and rich melody of the new medium. Since then, many of Norway's most innovative literary figures have used Nynorsk, incl. the expressionist Kristofer Uppdal (1878–1961), the novelist and poet Tarjei Vesaas (1897–1970), and the revered poet Olav H. Hauge (1908–94), who translated many key 20th-c. writings to the lang. Contemp. lit. in Nynorsk boasts some artistically brilliant figures, such as the novelist Kjartan Fløgstad (b. 1944) and the widely acclaimed dramatist and poet Jon Fosse (b. 1959).

*See* NORWAY, POETRY OF.

■ O. J. Falnes, *National Romanticism in Norway* (1933); L. S. Vikør, *The New Norse Language Movement* (1976); *Twenty Contemporary Norwegian Poets*, ed. T. Johanssen (1984); S. Walton, *Farewell the Spirit Craven: Ivar Aasen and National Romanticism* (1987); T. Vesaas, *Through Naked Branches*, ed. and trans. R. Greenwald (2000); O. H. Hauge, *The Dream We Carry*, trans. R. Bly and R. Hedin (2008).

S. LYNGSTAD; D. KROUK

**NEW YORK SCHOOL.** Among the several closely related strands of the New American Poetry during the decades following World War II, the New York school is distinguished for its affinity with Eur. (esp. Fr.) *modernism and the visual arts. John Ashbery, Barbara Guest, Kenneth Koch, Frank O'Hara, and James Schuyler are most commonly identified as founders of the "school," so named by a gallery director, John Bernard Myers, who sought to lend the poets some of the glamour that the New York school of painting ( Jackson Pollock, Willem de Kooning, et al.) had recently acquired as rival to the school of Paris (Pablo Picasso, Henri Matisse, et al.). *Abstract expressionism*, an alternative term for the new Am. painting, further distinguishes the New York school poets from their literary contemporaries, the Beats (see BEAT POETRY). Although expressionist, like the Beats, New York school poets tended to be more abstract in their emphasis on the verbal medium. Words could assume their own expressive quality independent of representational meaning.

New York City, the scene that brought the poets together during the 1950s, is often depicted in vivid detail in their work, esp. that of O'Hara, but city life informs the New York school aesthetic most profoundly in abstract qualities of scale and dynamics. O'Hara admired the painters for producing "works as big as cities," and the *long poem became a New York school specialty. However, in examples such as Koch's *Ko, or a Season on Earth* (1959), O'Hara's *Second Avenue* (1960), Schuyler's *Hymn to Life* (1974), Guest's *The Countess from Minneapolis* (1976), and Ashbery's *Flow Chart* (1991), the individual voice stands out, rather than any common

style. Ashbery in particular is noted for the meditative pace of his expansive verse, a quality that might seem to set it at a distance from the frenzy often associated with urban experience. But at the core of New York school poetry is a "quietness," as O'Hara called it, reflecting a human angle even on experience that many contemporaries found alienating. In the "urban pastoral" mode that several critics have identified with O'Hara, the poet is usually walking the city streets, rather than racing through them in a car like the Beats.

During the 1960s, the Lower East Side of Manhattan provided a laboratory for a "second generation" to extend the experimental spirit of the New York school into an experiment in community. Attracted by cheap rents, younger poets such as Bill Berkson, Tony Towle, Frank Lima, Ted Berrigan, Anne Waldman, Lewis Warsh, Ron Padgett, and Larry Fagin found themselves living in proximity. Accustomed to sharing work with one another, they readily took the next step of sharing in public, through readings at coffee houses such as Les Deux Mégots and Le Metro, and through mimeographed magazines published by the poets themselves, such as *Adventures in Poetry*, *Angel Hair*, and *C*. In 1966, such activities inspired the formation of the Poetry Project at St. Mark's Church in the Bowery, which for many years published its own magazine, *The World*. As an enduring institution, the Poetry Project has kept alive the spirit of the New York school despite the passing of the first generation, starting with O'Hara's untimely death in the year of the project's founding. Meanwhile, second-generation poets carried that spirit far beyond the confines of New York City. For instance, during the 1970s, Berkson and Warsh were among several New York poets who developed a rural version of the Lower East Side community in the hamlet of Bolinas on the northern California coast. In 1975, while still officially director of the Poetry Project, Waldman collaborated with Allen Ginsberg in founding the Jack Kerouac School of Disembodied Poetics at the Naropa Institute in Boulder, Colorado.

Collaboration among two or more poets (or among poets and artists) is one of the experimental techniques that reflect the New York school sense of community. Other reflections include prominent attention to the details of daily life, frequent use of personal names (friends of the poet, often otherwise left unidentified), various adaptations of diary or jour. form, and the projection of an intimate tone or voice. The term *personism*, also the title of an essay by O'Hara (1959), has come to stand for this constellation of features. During the 1960s, when protest against the Vietnam War put pressure on poets to assume a public voice, the apparent privacy and self-absorption of New York school poetry threatened to render it irrelevant. In subsequent decades, identity politics has given personism a political spin, particularly in the direction of gay liberation. O'Hara, Schuyler, and (much more cryptically) Ashbery wrote from their experience as gay men, as have later poets associated with the New York school (John Giorno, Tim Dlugos, David Trinidad). After

Guest, younger women such as Waldman, Alice Notley, and Eileen Myles have shown special concern for the female voice in this trad., Myles speaking explicitly for "The Lesbian Poet" (1994).

Within the politics of poetry, personism has been regarded with suspicion by the Language poets, who reject the "I" of traditional lyric and emphasize instead the social forces that construct the subject position in and through lang. (see LANGUAGE POETRY). On the East Coast, the New York school nurtured the devel. of Language poets such as Charles Bernstein, Nick Piombino, and Hannah Weiner, all of whom participated in Bernadette Mayer's workshops at the Poetry Project in the early 1970s. As a result, Language poets' critiques often aimed at saving the New York school from itself, praising textual appropriation and *collage in Ashbery's *The Tennis Court Oath* (1962), e.g., while regretting the regression into romantic subjectivity in *Self-Portrait in a Convex Mirror* (1975), the volume that secured Ashbery's place in the mainstream of Am. poetry. However, doctrinaire distinctions have yielded to the pressure of poetic practice. Poets emerging since the 1990s have drawn on the practice of lyric in the New York school as a rich resource for further experiment.

*See* AVANT-GARDE POETICS; EXPRESSIONISM; GAY POETRY; UNITED STATES, POETRY OF THE.

■ *The Poets of the New York School*, ed. J. B. Myers (1969); *An Anthology of New York Poets*, ed. R. Padgett and D. Shapiro (1970); *Out of This World*, ed. A Waldman (1991); D. Lehman, *The Last Avant-Garde* (1998); *A Secret Location on the Lower East Side*, ed. S. Clay and R. Phillips (1998); G. Ward, *Statutes of Liberty*, 2d ed. (2001); W. Watkin, *In the Process of Poetry* (2001); *The Scene of My Selves*, ed. T. Diggory and S. P. Miller (2001); D. Kane, *All Poets Welcome* (2003); M. Nelson, *Women, the New York School, and Other True Abstractions* (2007); M. Silverberg, *The New York School Poets and the Neo-Avant-Garde* (2010).

T. DIGGORY

## NEW ZEALAND, POETRY OF

I. Maori Poetry
II. Maori Poetry in English
III. Poetry in English

**I. Maori Poetry.** Maori poetry is a *song and *chant trad. beginning more than 800 years ago with the Polynesian settlement of Aotearoa, now New Zealand; it retains many of its oral features such as adept manipulation of lang., *repetition, and patterning accompanied by illustrative gestures by performers (see ORAL POETRY). Poetry was recited or sung during everyday activities and group occasions. An orator was supported at the end of a speech by a relevantly themed song or *waiata*. Highly structured musically and thematically, some of the many song types include *waiata aroha* or love lyrics often addressing loss and longing; *pao* or topical, linked *epigrams (McLean and Orbell 1979); *poi* or performance art incl. swinging poi-ball actions;

*oriori* or educational compositions sung at the birth of children; *waiata tangi* or *laments concerning the dead or misfortunes; and *karanga* or ceremonial calls of welcome, encouragement, or farewells to the departed.

Recited types include the *haka* (assertive posture-dance with or without weapons, with vocals akin to "stylized shouting" [McLean and Orbell 1979], "hair-raising blood-curdling shouts" [Ngata] designed "to stiffen the sinews, to summon up the blood" [Kāretu]). *Kaioraora* (cursing chants) are noted for their fury in venting past wrongs. *Karakia* are *incantations, *charms, and invocations; because of their sacerdotal function, they are rarely recorded. *Whakaaraara pā* were cried by sentinels as they watched fortresses.

Nationally known composers of the past included tribal and pan-Maori nobility, community leaders, and educators. The famed Rihi Puhiwahine's (1816?–1906) lyrics are colorful and deeply felt. In "Kāore Hoki Koia Te Rangi Nei" ("Oh What a Day"; Orbell), she wittily catalogs her aristocratic lovers while making reassuring asides to their spouses and incorporates the symbolic landmarks of her adventures with them. Noted compositions by others include the 19th-c. haka "Ka mate ka mate" (I Die, I Die) by the chief Te Rauparaha (ca. 1760–1849); "Poia atu taku poi" (Swing Out My Poi) by Erenora Taratoa (fl. 1850s), which was composed in response to Puhiwahine's disapproval of Taratoa's affair with Puhiwahine's brother (Royal); and the early 20th-c. songs "Po Atarau" (Moonlit Night) by Maewa Kaihau (b. 1879), popularized overseas as "Now Is the Hour" by Gracie Fields and later by Bing Crosby, and "Pokarekare ana" ([The Waves] Are Breaking) by Paraire Tomoana (1874?–1946). In the 20th c., composers adapted lyrics to popular tunes; for instance, Tuini Ngāwai's (1910–65) Maori battalion farewell "Arohaina Mai" (Bestow Your Love) was set to George Gershwin's "Love Walked In." These well-known tunes aided the recall of concert groups who performed on occasions such as the opening of meeting houses, anniversaries, and welcomes (*Dictionary of New Zealand Biography*, Spittle). Ngāwai wrote many popular songs. Ngoi Pēwhairangi (1922–85) composed the lyrics for the very popular "Poi E" (Swing) which was turned into a music video featuring break dancers with the Pātea Maori Club; the Prince Tui Teka hit song "E Ipo" (Beloved); and the waiata "Whakarongo" (Listen), exhorting listeners to retain and speak the Maori lang. Nontraditional Maori lang. poetry is continually evolving, while traditional forms are relatively fixed vocally and musically in performance.

With the continuing revival of Maori culture and lang., there are many performances of both contemp. and traditional waiata and haka in concert parties; tribal, regional, and national events and competitions; televised performances; and musical albums. The most prominent published collections are by George Grey (1802–98), who compiled *Ko nga moteatea me nga hakirara o nga Maori* (Poems, Chants and Traditions of the Maoris, 1853), and Apirana Ngata (1874–1950), whose four-volume collection *Ngā Moteatea* (The Sung

Poems) was completed posthumously by other scholars. There are numerous other book, audiovisual, and ms. collections as well as contemp. composers and performers. Hirini Melbourne (1950–2003) did much to popularize the waiata and traditional Maori music within wider contemp. culture.

**II. Maori Poetry in English.** The critically and popularly acclaimed Hone Tuwhare (1922–2008) was the first Maori to publish a single-authored literary collection. His oeuvre of 13 books began in 1964 with *No Ordinary Sun*. His poetry is imbued with affective significance, a term coined by the Marxist aesthetician Christopher Caudwell, whose work influenced Tuwhare, and code switching (Manhire) from hieratic to demotic modes. Mitcalfe's term *hotu* (heart notes), used to describe sung feelings in Puhiwahine's Maori-lang. poems, is apt for Tuwhare's complete oeuvre. Naturalistic and sensual, Tuwhare also wrote political verse centered on Maori land-rights struggles from the mid-1970s. Many scholars (Keown, DeLoughrey, Battista, Sullivan) note Tuwhare's mythological symbolism, such as the tree-deity Tāne Mahuta appealing to humanity, in his antinuclear poem "No Ordinary Sun": "O tree / in the shadowless mountains/ the white sea plains and / the drab sea floor / your end at last is written." Tuwhare's animation of natural elements perhaps extends from Maori-lang. poetics, as do repetition of words and musical and incantatory phrasing. His appetitive poetry enjoys sexual themes and humor. Tuwhare was a national icon and influenced many New Zealand poets.

The Booker Prize–winning author Keri Hulme (b. 1947) refers to place names, close observations of the natural environment, "living time" rather than "calendar time," and Maori female deities to indicate indigenous alterities and worldview. Like Tuwhare, Hulme is a connoisseur of land and sea who brings the natural world into the body of her writing ("pink flesh of smoked eels, then tiny succulence of oysters . . . ," [*Strands*, 1992]) and delivers a feminist poetics that easily aligns with the earth-mother. Identity is a key issue for the writer in her collection *The Silences Between Moeraki Conversations*, 1982).

The pioneer author J. C. Sturm (1927–2009) began publishing poems in 1947. In *Dedications* (1996) and *Postscripts* (2000), Sturm writes on intimate and larger scales about family, death, public occasions, race relations, the contemp. and historical effects of colonization, and life's vicissitudes. Her lines favor a three- or four-stress meter, reminiscent of Maori-lang. poetry. Sturm was married to the eminent New Zealand poet James K. Baxter (1926–72), who was esp. influenced by Maori poetics in his later work.

Robert Sullivan's (b. 1967) collections *Star Waka* (1999), *Captain Cook in the Underworld* (2002), and *Voice Carried My Family* (2005) traverse Eur., Polynesian, and Maori historical figures, as well as personal, family, and tribal narratives. Roma Potiki's (b. 1958) collection, *Oriori: A Maori Child Is Born* (1999), a collaboration with the painter Robyn Kahukiwa, is a series of meditations on birth centered on the tradi-

tional book-title form. In *Stones in Her Mouth* (1993), she confronts and negotiates the masculine workings of power within Maori society. Many poems focus on motherhood, its joys and challenges. Apirana Taylor (b. 1955) emerged in the late 1970s as a playwright and poet. His work emphasizes sound qualities and is often performed with musical accompaniment such as with the *koauau* or bone flute and the guitar. Taylor's 1996 poem "Te Ihi" (The Essential Force or Awe) explores the multidimensionality of a Maori word within a repetitive soundscape that directly evokes the haka form. Rangi Faith's (b. 1949) two collections show a concern for the environment within traditional and recreational contexts, excavations of tribal memories, and the impact of war on friends and families. The poet and musician Hinemoana Baker's (b. 1968) opening title poem in her collection *Mātuhi/Needle* (2004) alludes to an oratorical chant used at the beginning of speeches and interlaces Maori phrases throughout that collection while song elements such as the nose-flute also feature. Trixie Te Arama Menzies (b. 1936) belongs to the collective of women writers and artists Waiata Koa. She draws on traditional arts such as weaving by master craftswomen for inspiration. Vernice Wineera Pere, domiciled in Hawai'i, writes from a Maori and Polynesian perspective in nuanced and lyrically adept poems that explore mixed-race identity and spirituality, among other issues. The pioneer playwright Rore Hapipi (b. 1933) has composed many poems often sung in dramatic performance, as does Brian Potiki (b. 1953), whose collection *Aotearoa* (2003) is a mixture of songs and poetry influenced by the *Beat movement, the hist. of 19th-c. Maori pacifist resistance, and fellow writers and artists. Arapera Blank (d. 2002) deploys rich cultural symbolism in both langs., such as a garden of sweet potatoes representing the abundance of families and flax representing womankind. Michael O'Leary (b. 1950) writes on a wide range of Irish-Maori, personal, literary, satirical, and historical themes. Phil Kawana's (b. 1965) first poetry collection, *The Devil in My Shoes* (2005), ranges from ostensibly cultural to urban themes. Many poets have yet to achieve book publication.

**III. Poetry in English**

**A.** *The Nationalist Era.* To understand the hist. of New Zealand poetry in Eng., it is best to begin in the middle. In 1945, Allen Curnow (1911–2001) published the single most influential anthol. of New Zealand poetry, *A Book of New Zealand Verse, 1923–1945*. In a trenchant introduction, Curnow declared his own generation to be the first to see the true purpose of a distinctly New Zealand poetry: "a real expression of what the New Zealander is and a part of what he may become." He was withering in his crit. of the poetry of the first quarter of the 20th c., which he saw as marked by a "lack of any vital relation to experience [and] a fanciful aimlessness." *Kowhai Gold*, the unfortunately twee title of Quentin Pope's 1930 anthol. (referring to the beautiful yellow flowers of the native kowhai tree), became the generic term for these self-consciously "exoticizing" approaches to the New Zealand landscape, and the reputation of the poets from this period has never really recovered from Curnow's attack.

Curnow's unifying account of a generation of poets dedicated to "forms as immediate in experience as the island soil under [their] feet" both relied on and helped foster a certain selectivity of focus. When R.A.K. Mason (1905–71) wrote in "Sonnet of Brotherhood" of "this far-pitched perilous hostile place," he was referring to the planet earth "fixed at the friendless outer edge of space," but the nationalist paradigm made it difficult not to read this alongside Charles Brasch's (1909–73) "Remindingly beside the quays, the white / Ships lie smoking . . . distance looks our way" ("The Islands"); Curnow's own "In your atlas two islands not in narrow seas / Like a child's kite anchored in the indifferent blue" ("Statement from *Not in Narrow Seas*"); or A.R.D. Fairburn's (1904–57) vision of the colonists "sprouting like bulbs in warm darkness, putting out / white shoots under the wet sack of Empire" ("Dominion").

The title of Ursula Bethell's (1874–1945) first England-pub. collection, *From a Garden in the Antipodes* (1929), suggested an anglocentric approach to her New Zealand experience; but in Curnow's anthol., her universally comprehensible lament for the transience of "our small fond human enclosures" and prayer that her garden "become established quickly, quickly . . . For I am fugitive, I am very fugitive" ("Pause") seemed of a piece with Robin Hyde's (1906–39) account of a "young crude country" forging a new identity and Denis Glover's (1912–80) iconic story of the magpies indifferently singing "Quardle oodle ardle wardle doodle" as a local farm fails and falls to "the mortgage-man" ("The Magpies").

Curnow's own poetry in the anthol. adopts a less confident stance than his introduction. New Zealand's hist. appears marred by violence—"The stain of blood that writes an island story"—and radically ungraspable:

> It is something different, something
> Nobody counted on.
>
> ("The Unhistoric Story")

In a much-quoted meditation on the skeleton of an extinct native bird, Curnow declared that it would not be him or his generation, but rather "some child, born in a marvelous year" who "will learn the trick of standing upright here" ("The Skeleton of the Great Moa in the Canterbury Museum, Christchurch").

**B.** *The Wet Sack of Empire.* This sense of a hist. evolving too rapidly to be understood would have been familiar to the colonial forebears of the nationalist poets. Eng.-lang. poetry first finds New Zealand as a remote and none-too-welcoming coast; in the brief precolonial period of Eur. contact, Brit., Australian, and Am. seamen, sealers, and whalers work their hard-won New Zealand experience into their shanties and work-songs:

> We cured ten thousand skins for the fur, for the fur,
> Yes we cured ten thousand skins for the fur.

> Brackish water, putrid seal,
> We did all of us fall ill,
> For to die, for to die, for to die.
>
> (Anonymous, "David Lowston," ca. 1810–15)

After the Treaty of Waitangi in 1840 ceded sovereignty from the Maori chiefs to the Brit. Crown, a steady stream of Brit. colonists, the usual mixture of the adventurous and the desperate, began to arrive (and, often, depart again), with many using poetry to make sense of their experience. The prototype of the colonial poet is Alfred Domett (1811–87), the model for Robert Browning's "Waring," who, aged 20, "gave us all the slip . . . With no work done, but great works undone" to build a life "where whole new thousands are." Domett, briefly New Zealand's premier, produced a bloated epic, *Ranolph and Amohia: A South-Sea Day-Dream* (1872), designed to present an exotic world that is readily legible in familiar conceptual frames. Whether as edenic rebuke to our supercivilized world or savage reminder of a primitive past, Domett's poem works to cast the New Zealand landscape and the Maori inhabitants into familiar conceptual templates.

Nonetheless, the poem also registers the "unhistoric" drift that is making a nation "nobody counted on." At the end of the poem, Ranolph, a white adventurer, returns to Britain with Amohia, his Maori princess bride, fully conscious of the shock such a union will create in Brit. drawing rooms but determined "from the ebon-ivory range / Of chequered days and chance and change, / [to] Draw symphonies serene and strange." This same utopian sense of the possibility of a radical reconfiguration of national and racial identity in the fluid colonial environment can be found in David McKee Wright's (1868–1928) "Our Cities Face the Sea" (1900):

> Cousin Jack and Cockney, Irishman and Scot,
> And the native is a brother to the whole blooming
>    lot.
> Pulling, pulling on the one rope strong
> Bringing up the future with a shout and a song.

Colonial plasticity could also offer the possibility of deliberate reinvention. William Pember Reeves (1857–1932), another colonial politician, proclaimed himself "rooted. Firm and fast" in a New Zealand whose apparent crudity masked a vital creative opportunity ("A Colonist in His Garden," 1904):

> "No art?" Who serve an art more great
> Than we, rough architects of State
> With the old Earth at strife?

In "The Passing of the Forest" (1898), though, Reeves acknowledged the "bitter price" of "beauty swept away" that the art of nation building exacted. The "Burnt bush" appeared as a rebuke in Blanche Baughan's (1870–1958) "A Bush Section" (1908), too. Of the Maori inhabitants of that bush and the bloody price they paid for New Zealand's transformation, few

Eng.-lang. poets made explicit mention. Jessie Mackay (1864–1938), however, the ardent proponent of Ir. and Scottish Home Rule, universal suffrage, and temperance, wrote scathing satires on the settler government's belligerent and self-serving approach to the Maori.

**C. *The Maori Renaissance.*** The emergence of a Maori voice in New Zealand poetry in Eng. was one of the principal devels. of the post–World War II years. Beginning in the 1950s with the Cook Islands Maori writer Alistair (later Alistair Te Ariki) Campbell (1925–2009), whose first, intensely lyrical, collections made no mention of the ethnic origins that would later become an abiding concern, continuing in the 1960s with Rowley Habib (b. 1933) and with Tuwhare, whose "No Ordinary Sun" drew on a deep Maori reverence for the forests to voice a moving lament for the effects of nuclear testing, and flourishing in the later work of poets such as Taylor, Hulme, Sturm, and Sullivan, Maori poets have in one sense fulfilled the utopian hopes of Wright, while forcing a radical reexamination of the outright racism and blithely paternalistic ethnocentrism that New Zealand's official myth of racial harmony too often belied.

**D. *Marvelous Children.*** Elsewhere, the synthetic power of Curnow's nationalist thesis was challenged almost immediately in the 1950s. The so-called Wellington Group, a loosely affiliated group of poets incl. James K. Baxter (1926–72), W. H. Oliver (b. 1925), Alistair Campbell, and Louis Johnson (1924–88), attacked Curnow's localism as a historical dead end and declared themselves to be internationalists. By the 1960s, both sides in this once heated debate had come to seem old hat. Charles Doyle's 1965 anthol., *Recent Poetry in New Zealand*, features self-descriptions from poets such as Doyle (b. 1928), Fleur Adcock (b. 1934), Kendrick Smithyman (1922–95), and C. K. Stead (b. 1932) that proclaim a rigorously decontextualized commitment to "craft" as their highest ideal.

The 1970s saw an explosion of new voices in New Zealand poetry. The jour. *The Word Is Freed* (1969–72) was the epicenter of the new poetry, and its title gestured toward the formal experimentation that would become the rallying cry of the new generation, incl. poets such as Ian Wedde (b. 1946), Alan Brunton (1946–2002), Jan Kemp (b. 1949), and Murray Edmond (b. 1949). *Open form was the shibboleth of the movement, and the championing of Am. models such as Charles Olson and Robert Creeley seemed to mark a turn away both from any last holdovers of colonial fealty to Britain and from the old obsession with "what the New Zealander is."

In the ensuing decades, New Zealand poetry has become at once more popular and widespread than it ever was before (a vibrant culture of poetry *performance—owing much to the tireless troubadouring of Sam Hunt [b. 1946]—helps see to that) and far less bold in its claims to public significance. The dominant figure in New Zealand poetry from the late 1970s to the present day is Bill Manhire (b. 1946), a poet of cool ironies and oblique wit. His wry take on Curnow's nationalist isolationism neatly punctures the idea of "New Zealandness" as special burden or heroic challenge: "I live at the edge of the universe, / like everybody else" ("Milky Way Bar").

The work of the best poets of this period—Manhire, Elizabeth Smither (b. 1941), Andrew Johnston (b. 1963), Jenny Bornholdt (b. 1960), Brian Turner (b. 1944), Michele Leggott (b. 1956), Lauris Edmond (1924–2000), and Fiona Farrell (b. 1947), to name a few—tends to be small-scaled, often domestic or autobiographical and, if formally sophisticated, not overtly experimental. Whether that is "a real expression of what the New Zealander is" is a question for a later, more marvelous, year.

*See* POLYNESIAN POETRY.

■ **Maori.** *Anthologies*: *Te Ao Marama: Contemporary Maori Writing*, ed. W. Ihimaera, v. 1 (1993); *Kāti Au i Konei: A Collection of Songs from Ngāti Toarangatira and Ngāti Raukawa*, ed. T.A.C. Royal (1994); H. Melbourne and R. Nunns, *Te Kū Te Whē* (1994)—music CD; *Whetu Moana: Contemporary Polynesian Poems in English*, ed. A. Wendt, R. Whaitiri, and R. Sullivan (2003); *Ngā Moteatea: The Songs*, ed. A. T. Ngata, et al., rev ed., 4 v. (2004–7); ***Criticism and History***: P.T.H. Jones, "Puhiwahine: Maori Poetess," *Te Ao Hou* 28–33, 6 parts (1959–61), http://www.teaohou.natlib.govt.nz/; B. Mitcalfe, *Maori Poetry: The Singing Word* (1974); A. Salmond, *Hui: a Study of Maori Ceremonial Gatherings*, 2d ed. (1976); *Traditional Songs of the Maori*, ed. M. McLean, trans. M. Orbell (1979); R. Oppenheim, "Internal Exile: Continuity and Community in Maori Poetry," *Journal of the Polynesian Society* 92 (1983); *Dictionary of New Zealand Biography* (1990–), http://www.dnzb.govt. nz/; B. Manhire, "Dirty Silence: Impure Sounds in New Zealand Poetry," *Dirty Silence: Aspects of Language and Literature in New Zealand*, ed. G. McGregor and M. Williams (1991); M. Orbell, *Waiata: Maori Songs in History* (1991); T. Kāretu, *Haka! The Dance of a Noble People* (1993); M. McLean, *Maori Music* (1996); G. Spittle, *Counting the Beat: A History of New Zealand Song* (1997); J. Hunt, *Hone Tuwhare: A Biography* (1998); A.T.P. Somerville, "Nau Te Rourou, Nau Te Rakau: The Oceanic, Indigenous and Postcolonial and New Zealand Comparative Contexts of Maori Writing in English," diss., Cornell University (2006); M. Keown, *Pacific Islands Writing: The Postcolonial Literatures of Aotearoa/New Zealand and Oceania* (2007); E. DeLoughrey, "Solar Metaphors: *No Ordinary Sun*," *Ka Mate Ka Ora* 6 (2009).

■ **English.** *Anthologies*: *New Zealand Verse*, ed. W. Alexander and A. Currie (1906)—for colonial verse; *An Anthology of New Zealand Poetry in English*, ed. J. Bornholdt, G. O'Brien, and M. Williams (1997); A. Curnow, *Early Days Yet: New and Collected Poems, 1941–1997* (1997); *Big Smoke: New Zealand Poems, 1960–1975*, ed. A. Brunton, M. Edmond, and M. Leggott (2000); *Twenty Contemporary New Zealand Poets: An Anthology*, ed. R. Marsack and A. Johnston (2009). ***Criticism and History***: E. H. McCormick, *Letters and Art in New Zealand* (1940); K. Smithyman, *A*

*Way of Saying: A Study of New Zealand Poetry* (1965); C. K. Stead, *In the Glass Case: Essays on New Zealand Literature* (1981); H. Ricketts, *Talking about Ourselves: Twelve New Zealand Poets in Conversation with Harry Ricketts* (1986); A. Curnow, *Look Back Harder: Critical Writings, 1935–1984*, ed. P. Simpson (1987); P. Evans, *The Penguin History of New Zealand Literature* (1990); S. Murray, *Never a Soul at Home: New Zealand Literary Nationalism and the 1930s* (1998); *Oxford History of New Zealand Literature in English*, ed. T. Sturm (1998).

R. SULLIVAN (MAORI); H. ROBERTS (ENG.)

**NIBELUNGENSTROPHE** (*Kürenbergstrophe*). The most important stanza of MHG epic poetry. The *Nibelungenstrophe* is named from its use in the *Nibelungenlied* (ca. 1200–10), although its earliest recorded use is by Der von Kürenberg (fl. 1150–70). It is composed of four long lines (*Langzeilen*) in which each pair is bound by end rhyme. The long lines are divided by a clear *caesura into pairs of *hemistichs. Occasionally, there is also rhyme at the caesura.

Mod. prosodists confine themselves to a descriptive formula, according to which hemistichs 1 to 7 contain three stresses each, and the eighth 4; further, 1, 3, 5, and 7 as a rule show feminine and 2, 4, 6, and 8 masculine endings (see MASCULINE AND FEMININE). A recent study (Wakefield) rejects the "performance based" metrics of Andreas Heusler and most of his successors with its concomitant notion that the verse of Ger. poetry is essentially four-stressed. Basing his description on a statistical study of the distribution of syllables in the strophes in the St. Gall ms. (usually called Ms. B), Wakefield describes verses 1, 3, 5, and 7 of the Nibelungenstrophe as belonging to a long realization of the verse and verses 2, 4, and 6 as belonging to a short realization. Both realizations tend to show an alternation of stressed and unstressed syllables, particularly toward the cadence. Verse 8, however, follows a quite different pattern, called "dipodic" by Wakefield, which exhibits two cadential structures rather than one.

The Nibelungenstrophe is one of a family of strophes built on the simpler model of the Hildebrandston, which is identical to the Nibelungenstrophe except that it lacks the extra stress in the final hemistich—i.e., hemistich 8 is identical to hemistichs 2, 4, and 6. Some later heroic epics in MHG (e.g., *Ortnit, Wolfdietrich, Alpharts Tod*) are composed in this strophe. The Hildebrandston was replaced in later poetry by the Heunenweise, which requires rhymes at the caesura throughout. Poems in the Heunenweise are often printed in alternating rhyme-pairs that obscures their derivation from the Hildebrandston.

The use of the Nibelungenstrophe has continued over the centuries in many variants, e.g., among the *Meistersinger as the "Hönweise," in the church hymn (P. Gerard, *O Haupt voll Blut und Wunden*); in the mod. secular lied, esp. among the romantics (L. Uhland, *Des Sängers Fluch*); and even in the drama (Z. Werner, *Die Söhne des Thals* [1803]).

*See* GERMAN POETRY.

■ A. Heusler, *Deutsche Versgesch.*, 3 vols. (1925–29, rpt. 1956); P. Habermann, "Nibelungenstrophe," *Reallexikon I*; F. Panzer, *Das Nibelungenlied* (1955); U. Pretzel and H. Thomas, "Deutsche Verskunst," *Deutsche Philologie im Aufriss*, 2d ed., ed. W. Stammler, vol. 3 (1957); H. de Boor, "Zur Rhythmik des Strophenschlusses im Nibelungenlied," *Kleine Schriften*, ed. R. Wisniewski and H. Kolb (1966); S. Beyschlag, *Altdeutsche Verskunst in Grundzügen* (1969); H. de Boor, "Die 'schweren Kadenzen' im Nibelungenlied," *BGDSL (T)* 92 (1970); R. M. Wakefield, *Nibelungen Prosody* (1976); E. Stutz, "Die Nibelungenzeile: Dauer und Wandel," *Philologische Studien: Gedenkschrift R. Kienast*, ed. U. Schwab and E. Stutz (1978); G.J.H. Kulsdom, *Die Strophenschlüsse im "Nibelungenlied"* (1979).

U. K. GOLDSMITH; E. R. HAYMES

## NICARAGUA, POETRY OF

   I. Rubén Darío and Modernismo
   II. Post-modernistas
   III. The Vanguard Movement
   IV. Generation of the 1940s
   V. The Frente Ventana and the Betrayed
      Generation, New Voices
   VI. Women Poets of the 1970s to the Present
   VII. Caribbean Coast Writers

**I. Rubén Darío and Modernismo.** Although Nicaragua is a poor country of only five million inhabitants with scarce resources for education, poetry is important to its cultural identity. This condition is due in large part to the internationally renowned Nicaraguan poet Rubén Darío (1867–1916). Much as Simón Bolívar is associated with Hispanic America's political independence from Spain, Darío initiated—via poetry—the cultural freedom of Sp. America. He championed *modernismo, a late 19th-c. Hispanic Am. literary movement involving poets of several nationalities, incl. the Cuban nationalist José Martí. Darío transformed the Sp. lang. by creating new rhythmic patterns based on the poetry of Victor Hugo and Walt Whitman, esp. in the extravagant musicality of his poem "Marcha triunfal." He enriched his mother tongue by incorporating a vocabulary and a thematic panorama from indigenous America. Darío's poem to the volcano Momotombo in Nicaragua is a geographical rebellion against Spain, an assertion of identity that contains the ancient force of toponymy. Darío encountered supremacist, racist thinking in Spain during his first visit there in 1892 but insisted on asserting with pride his heritage as a *mestizo*. In *Prosas profanas*, he famously declares, "If there is poetry in our America, it can be found in the old things: in Palenque and Utatlán, in the legendary Indian and the sensual, refined Inca, and in the great Moctezuma on his throne of gold." The indigenous figures in Darío's poems "Caupolicán" and "Tutecotzimí" are a source of liberating and audacious originality that deeply influenced future generations of his literary compatriots.

The magnitude of Darío's major works of poetry, which include *Azul . . .* (1888), *Prosas profanas y otros poemas* (1896 and 1901), *Cantos de vida y esperanza, los cisnes y otros poemas* (1905), *El canto errante* (1907), *El viaje a Nicaragua e intermezzo tropical* (1908), *El poema del otoño y otros poemas* (1910), and *Canto a la Argentina y otros poemas* (1914), gave the country a respected place on the world's literary map. The cosmopolitan Darío spent most of his life outside his homeland, preferring Europe and Europeanized cities such as Buenos Aires, though he traveled constantly, sometimes to far-flung places such as North Africa, to produce the articles for the Argentine newspaper *La Nación* that allowed him to eke out a living.

As a *modernista*, Darío is a poet of conflicting ideals. E.g., in his famous poem "A Roosevelt" ("To Roosevelt"), he portrays the United States as a future invader of Nicaragua, while in "Salutación al águila" ("Saluting the Eagle"), he praises the work ethic and entrepreneurial spirit of his country's northern neighbor. Darío wrote escapist poems, such as the often-recited "A Margarita Debayle," celebrating journeys to exotic places inhabited by mythological creatures. But he is also the author of "Lo fatal" ("Destined to Die"), one of the most famous poems in the lang., revered for its existential anguish and fatalistic pessimism. Each generation of readers has found something new and provocative in the modernismo of Darío.

**II. Post-modernistas.** Nicaragua's three exemplary postmodernista writers, Azarías H. Pallais (1885–1954), Alfonso Cortés (1893–1969), and Salomón de la Selva (1893–1959), maintain a literary dialogue with their great predecessor but also forge a new poetics. While they shared Darío's passion for cl. lit. and mythology, they grew tired of the legions of his superficial imitators. A rebellious, impoverished priest guided by the teachings of the Gospel, Pallais sided with the poor in his poetry; his volumes include *A la sombra del agua* (1917), *Espumas y estrellas* (1918), *Caminos* (1921), *Bello tono menor* (1928), *Epístola católica a Rafael Arévalo Martínez* (1947), and *Piraterías* (1951). Cortés, a metaphysical poet concerned with the relativity of time and the preeminence of space, used his severe mental illness to create a therapeutic art to assuage his isolation and lack of intimate human contact. Some of Cortés's best poetry (such as the deeply enigmatic "Yo," "La gran plegaria," "Pasos," and "La canción del espacio") was anthologized by the poet Ernesto Cardenal and translated into Eng. by the Catholic writer Thomas Merton at the Trappist monastery in Gethsemani, Kentucky, in the late 1950s. Cortés's most accomplished collections of poetry are *Poesías* (1931), *Tardes de oro* (1934), and *Poemas eleusinos* (1935). De la Selva's *Tropical Town and Other Poems* (1918) appeared in Eng. in the U.S., where the poet lived and worked, publishing his poems in important jours., corresponding with noted poets such as Edna St. Vincent Millay, and teaching at Williams College. His second book, *El soldado desconocido* (1922), is a testimonial work about his experiences as a soldier in World War I. By this time, for ideological reasons that had to do with the interventionist policies of the U.S. in Latin America,

the bilingual poet had made the decision to publish his work almost exclusively in Sp. His books, which draw on a deep knowledge of Greco-Roman myth and hist. (occasionally mixed with themes from the Aztec world), include *Evocación de Horacio* (1949), *La ilustre familia* (1954), *Canto a la independencia nacional de México* (1956), *Evocación de Píndaro* (1957), and *Acolmixtli Netzahualcóyotl* (1958).

**III. The Vanguard Movement.** The writers associated with Nicaragua's Vanguard Movement, notably José Coronel Urtecho (1906–94), Pablo Antonio Cuadra (1912–2002), and Joaquín Pasos (1914–47), were young provocateurs who burst onto the literary scene in the city of Granada in the late 1920s by challenging upperclass values and attacking the derivative followers of Darío. The nationalistic, conservative stance of the *vanguardistas* and their fervent belief in *Hispanidad* (Hispanicity) as a bulwark against Communism led them to give moral support to dictators such as Anastasio Somoza García in Nicaragua and Francisco Franco in Spain. Much of the material they used to renovate Nicaraguan lit. was based on new poetry of the U.S. and France that the vanguardistas translated and incorporated in their own work, as well as Nicaraguan folklore and traditional culture.

Coronel Urtecho's poetry (as well as his Sp. versions of poems by Marianne Moore and T. S. Eliot) is collected in a volume with a title taken from the Greek of the *Odyssey: Pol-la d'ananta katanta paranta* (1970, rev. 1993). This book contains Coronel Urtecho's classic narrative poem "Pequeña biografía de mi mujer," a homage to his wife María Kautz. His *Paneles del infierno* (*Panels of Hell*, 1981) is an extensive historical poem that takes its rhetorical point of departure in support of the 1979 Sandinista revolution from the opening poem of Edgar Lee Masters's *Spoon River Anthology*.

Taken as a whole, the poetry of Cuadra provides deep insights into Nicaraguan culture, esp. when it is collated with his essential book-length essays *El nicaragüense* and *Muestrario del folklore nicaragüense*. In addition, no writer has more vividly portrayed Nicaragua's geographical and biological diversity. Cuadra's major works include *Poemas nicaragüenses* (Nicaraguan Poems), first published in 1934, but revised extensively throughout the poet's life; *El jaguar y la luna* (The Jaguar and the Moon, 1959), poems based on ancient designs of Nahuatl ceramics; *Cantos de Cifar* (*Songs of Cifar*, 1971), narrative verse in clipped lyrical lines about the people who navigate the dangerous Homeric waters of Lake Nicaragua; *Siete árboles contra el atardecer* (*Seven Trees against the Dying Light*, 1980), in which seven different species of Nicaraguan trees store a country's myths, hist. and collective memory; and *La ronda del año* (written primarily between 1984 and 1986), twelve poems that reflect a year's natural cycle in Nicaragua.

Pasos, who died prematurely in 1947, is nearly unknown outside Nicaragua. His collected poetry, *Poemas de un joven* (1962), edited by Cardenal, contains the apocalyptic long poem "Canto de guerra de las cosas"

(War Song of the Things), perhaps the most important overlooked masterpiece in 20th-c. Latin Am. poetry.

**IV. Generation of the 1940s.** Ernesto Mejía Sánchez (1923–85), Carlos Martínez Rivas (1924–98), and Ernesto Cardenal (b. 1925), the three most noted writers who followed the Vanguard Movement, looked toward Nicaraguan vanguardistas as mentors, not figures whose work needed to be openly questioned as Coronel Urtecho had done in his iconoclastic "Oda a Rubén Darío" in the late 1920s—a continuation rather than a rupture in the dialogue between literary generations.

Mejía Sánchez was educated in Mexico and is widely recognized as the most gifted scholar of Darío's poetry. His own verse is collected in the anthol. *Recolección al mediodía* (1972). One of his lasting contributions is *prosemas*, short *prose poems.

Martínez Rivas produced the single most influential book of poetry in Nicaraguan lit. for several generations, *La insurrección solitaria*, first published in Mexico in a limited ed. in 1953 after his formative years in Madrid and Paris in the late 1940s that enabled him to work with Octavio Paz and Julio Cortázar. Conceived in the French tradition of the *poète maudit*, his poetry creates new, almost impossible, standards for verbal perfection.

Cardenal is Nicaragua's most internationally recognized poet of recent decades. He served as minister of culture during the 1980s; as both a poet and a government official, he has traveled the globe, giving readings to enthusiastic audiences. With Coronel Urtecho, Cardenal translated an influential anthol. of U.S. poetry (which included a selection of Native Am. texts) and formulated what has come to be known as *Exteriorismo*, emphasizing a *collage of factual data in prosaic *free verse stripped of metaphor and the incorporation of original historical sources. Exteriorista poetry was a defining, albeit controversial, characteristic of Nicaraguan poetry from the 1970s through the mid-1990s.

Cardenal's poetry has a pronounced political trajectory that corresponds in part to his own life. E.g., his peripheral involvement in the 1954 April Rebellion against the government of Somoza García resulted in his poem *Hora cero* (*Zero-Hour and Other Documentary Poems,* 1960). His religious vocation led him to a spiritual friendship with Merton as well as an exploration of the tenets of liberation theology. Merton encouraged Cardenal to become ordained as a priest and, later, to establish a contemplative community called Solentiname on an island in Lake Nicaragua in the mid-1970s. When the repression of Anastasio Somoza Debayle's National Guard destroyed the community, Cardenal went into exile in Costa Rica, where he became a voice of the revolution that finally toppled the dictatorship in July of 1979.

Other works by Cardenal include *Epigramas* (1961), which imitates the cl. style of Martial and Catullus; *Salmos* (Psalms, 1964), modeled on the *Psalms of the OT in their poetic indictment of wars, capitalism, and repressive governments; the long historical narrative poem *El estrecho dudoso* (*The Doubtful Strait,* 1967); *Canto nacional* (1972); *Oráculo sobre Managua* (1973), pub. the year after the earthquake that destroyed Nicaragua's capital; and *Vuelos de victoria* (*Flights of Victory,* 1985), a collection of poems that praise the Sandinista Revolution. In *Homenaje a los indios americanos* (*Homage to the American Indians,* 1969) and *Los ovnis de oro* (*Golden UFOs,* 1985), Cardenal proposes models for contemp. ethical behavior based on ancient civilizations. In his more recent poetry, he has been looking into the far reaches of the universe, exploring the big-bang theory and quantum physics in *Cántico cósmico* (*Cosmic Canticle,* 1989) and, in a more streamlined style in keeping with his monastic poems, *Telescopio en la noche oscura* (Telescope in the Dark Night, 1993).

**V. The Frente Ventana and the Betrayed Generation, New Voices.** Although there are important Nicaraguan writers of the 1950s such as Guillermo Rothschuh Tablada (b. 1926), Raúl Elvir (1927–98), Ernesto Gutiérrez (1929–88), Mario Cajina-Vega (1929–95), Eduardo Zepeda-Henríquez (b. 1930), Octavio Robleto (b. 1935), Horacio Peña (b. 1936), and esp. Fernando Silva (b. 1927), it was during the 1960s that two divergent literary groups engaged in a debate on poetics that changed the course of Nicaraguan lit. hist. The Frente Ventana (Window Front), based at the university in León and headed by Fernando Gordillo (1940–67) and Sergio Ramírez (b. 1942—now Nicaragua's most prominent novelist), sought ways to link art with a revolutionary struggle in keeping with the idealism, commitment, and sacrifice that attended the birth of the Frente Sandinista de Liberación Nacional (FSLN) in 1963, in conjunction with the influential political writings of Carlos Fonseca Amador (1936–76). One highly promising writer martyred in the armed political struggle of that era was Leonel Rugama (1949–70), whose poetry was published posthumously in the volume *La tierra es un satélite de la luna* (*The Earth Is a Satellite of the Moon,* 1983). The other main literary group from the 1960s, *La Generación Traicionada* (The Betrayed Generation), was based in Managua and founded by Roberto Cuadra (b. 1940), Edwin Yllescas (b. 1941), Iván Uriarte (b. 1942), and Beltrán Morales (1944–86). They tended to identify themselves more with the freewheeling *Beat poets of the U.S. than with Marxist struggles for social equality in their own country.

New voices that constitute the Nicaraguan literary scene in recent decades include those of Luis Rocha (b. 1942), former ed. of the literary supplement *El Nuevo Amanecer Cultural*; the surrealist poet Francisco Valle (b. 1942), author of the collection of prose poems *Laberinto de espadas* (1974 and 1996); and Francisco de Asís Fernández (b. 1945), co-organizer with the poet Gloria Gabuardi of the International Poetry Festival in Granada. Three contemp. poet-critics are worthy of mention: Álvaro Urtecho (1951–2007), whose works of poetry include *Cantata estupefacta* (1986), *Esplendor de Caín* (1994), *Tumba y residencia* (2000), and *Tierra sin tiempo* (2007); Julio Valle-Castillo (b. 1952), one of Nicaragua's premier literary scholars and art historians and the author of *Materia jubilosa* (1986) as well as *Lienzo del pajaritero* (2003), a series of poems that document the myths and folk dances of Masaya; and Nicasio Urbina (b. 1958), most recently the author of *Viajemas* (2009).

**VI. Women Poets of the 1970s to the Present.** Perhaps the most important literary phenomenon of the 1970s was the emergence of a new generation of women authors, transforming a literary world that had been dominated by men. Two poets who began publishing in the 1970s are esp. accomplished: Ana Ilce Gómez (b. 1945), author of *Las ceremonias del silencio* (1975) and *Poemas de lo humano cotidiano* (2004), and Gioconda Belli (b. 1948), who published *Sobre la grama* (1973); *Línea de fuego* (1978), which explores themes of sexual and political liberation and won Cuba's Casa de las Américas prize; *Truenos y arco iris* (1982); *Amor insurrecto* (1985); *De la costilla de Eva* (1987); *El ojo de la mujer* (1991); *Apogeo* (1997); and *Fuego soy apartado y espada puesta lejos* (2007).

There were some important precursors to these writers, such as María Teresa Sánchez (1918–94), Mariana Sansón Argüello (1918–2002), and the internationally recognized Claribel Alegría, who was born in Nicaragua in 1924, lived for most of her life in El Salvador and Europe, then returned to Nicaragua, where she currently resides. Alegría's work was translated into Eng. by the U.S. poet Carolyn Forché as *Flowers from the Volcano* (1982).

Other notable women poets who remain active in Nicaragua's literary life include Vidaluz Meneses (b. 1944), Gloria Gabuardi (b. 1945), Michéle Najlis (b. 1946), Daisy Zamora (b. 1950), and Rosario Murillo (b. 1951), author of *Las esperanzas misteriosas* (1990), founder of the group *Gradas*, director in the 1980s of the Sandinista Association of Cultural Workers, and the wife of president Daniel Ortega.

Additional recent women's voices in Nicaraguan poetry include Yolando Blanco (b. 1954); Isolda Hurtado (b. 1957); Blanca Castellón (b. 1958); Carola Brantome (b. 1961); Esthela Calderón (b. 1970), who published *Soledad* (2002), *Amor y conciencia* (2004) and *Soplo de corriente vital* (2008), a remarkable collection of ethnobotanical poems that recovers traditional knowledge about plants indigenous to Nicaragua's Occidental region; and Marta Leonor González (b. 1972), editor of *La Prensa Literaria*, cofounder of Nicaragua's most important new literary group *400 Elefantes*, and author of *Huérfana embravecida* (1999) and *Casa de fuego* (2008).

**VII. Caribbean Coast Writers.** Given the Pacific Coast literary establishment's refusal to recognize multilingual Atlantic Coast writers, one esp. welcome recent develop. is the attention that the Nicaraguan Association of Women Writers (ANIDE) has paid to the country's Caribbean women authors. In the jour. *Anide*, editor Vilma de la Rocha has published the work of such poets as June Beer (1935–86), the Atlantic Coast's first woman poet, who wrote her work in both Eng.-Creole and Sp.; Gloriantonia Henríquez (b. 1948), author of *Primera vigilia* (2004); Andira Watson (b. 1977), who published the collection *Más excelsa que Eva* (2002) and won the Mariana Sansón National Poetry Prize in 2009; Brígida Zacarías Watson, whose poetry written in the Miskitu lang. appears in *Miskitu tasbaia (Tierra miskita,* 1997); Erna Narcisso Walters, who writes in both Eng. and Sp, and whose work was anthologized in *Antología poética de la Costa Caribe de Nicaragua*; Isabel Estrada Colindres, a Garífuna woman who lives in Bluefields and writes in Eng., Sp., and Creole; and Ana Rosa Fagot Müller (b. 1944), who writes in Miskitu and coedits the jour. *Tininiska*. Some of the work included in this selection published in *Anide* was translated into Sp. by Carlos Rigby, who was born in Laguna de Perlas in 1945 and has been a peripheral part of Nicaraguan poetry for decades. Rigby is the most prominent Nicaraguan Caribbean Coast poet, together with David MacField, who was born in Ciudad Rama in 1936 and who published *Dios es negro* (1967), *En la calle de enmedio* (1969), *Poemas para el año de elefante* (1970), *Poemas populares* (1972), and *Los veinticuatro: poemas y canciones* (1975). Given the lang. barriers, the extreme poverty, and the general isolation of the Atlantic Coast in relation to the western side of Nicaragua, more work is needed to establish greater understanding and cultural respect between the two regions.

*See* INDIGENOUS AMERICAS, POETRY OF THE; SPANISH AMERICA, POETRY OF.

■ E. Torres, *La dramática vida de Rubén Darío* (1966); E. Mejía Sánchez, *Estudios sobre Rubén Darío* (1968); K. Ellis, *Critical Approaches to Rubén Darío* (1974); J. Concha, *Rubén Darío* (1975); *Poets of Nicaragua: 1918–1979*, ed. S. White (1982); C. L. Jrade, *Rubén Darío and the Romantic Search for Unity* (1983); S. White, *Culture and Politics in Nicaragua: Testimonies of Poets and Writers* (1986); *Modern Nicaraguan Poetry: Dialogues with France and the United States*, ed. S. White (1993); J. E. Arellano, *"Azul . . ." de Rubén Darío: Nuevas perspectivas* (1993); J. E. Arellano, *Literatura nicaragüense* (1997); S. White, *La poesía más que humana de Pablo Antonio Cuadra: un estudio ecocrítico* (2002); *El siglo de la poesía en Nicaragua*, ed. J. Valle Castillo, 3 v. (2005); P. A. Cuadra, *Seven Trees against the Dying Light*, trans. G. Simon and S. F. White (2007); S. White, *Arando el aire: la ecología en la poesía y la música de Nicaragua* (2011).

S. F. WHITE

**NIL VOLENTIBUS ARDUUM** (Nothing Is Difficult to the Willing). A society of Dutch poets founded in Amsterdam in 1669. The main concerns of the society were the improvement of the artistic quality and moral standard of the plays presented at the Amsterdam City Theater, which was dominated at the time by the spectacular horror drama of Jan Vos. Nil Volentibus Arduum strove to apply Fr. neoclassical artistic principles, such as rationality, simplicity, and clarity, to Dutch *dramatic poetry and strongly condemned the use of religious and political subject matter. The founding and most influential members of the society were the physician Lodewijk Meyer and the jurist Andries Pels, both of whom also wrote dramatic poetry. In 1681, after the death of Meyer and Pels, the society began to decline in influence. Important writings by Nil Volentibus Arduum include Pels's *Gebruik én misbruik des tooneels* (Use and Abuse of the Theater, 1681) and the *Nauwkeurig onderwys in de tooneel-poëzy* (Precise Instruction in Dramatic Poetry), a collection of lectures by the members of the society pub. in 1765.

■ T. Harmsen, "26 november 1669: Oprichtings-vergadering van Nil Volentibus Arduum: Het Frans-classicisme verovert de Schouwburg," *Nederlandse literatuur*, ed. M. A. Schenkeveld-van der Dussen (1998); K. Porteman and M. Smits-Veldt, *Een nieuw vaderland voor de muzen* (2008).

F. J. WARNKE; S. MAREEL

**NŌ.** A form of traditional Japanese drama. Its precise origins are unknown, but it was refined in the 14th and 15th cs. during Japan's med. era and has been performed continuously ever since. *Nō* (also written *noh*) means "ability" and was originally known as *sarugaku* (monkey music). The plays include extensive passages in verse. They are sung and recited by masked and unmasked actors wearing elaborate costumes, accompanied by a chorus and three or four musicians playing drums and a bamboo flute. Almost every play includes a dance or other choreographed movement and is performed on a roofed stage built of polished Japanese cypress.

Although thousands of plays are extant and new ones continue to be written, the repertory of plays currently performed by professional troupes includes only about 240 works. Nō plays are conventionally classified by theme into five categories: god plays, warrior plays, "wig" plays (i.e., those in which the principal character is a woman; traditionally, all roles were played by male actors); miscellaneous plays; and demon plays. In a classic one-day program, one play would be performed from each category in the above order.

The plays may alternatively be classified by method of depiction into two categories: dream (*mugen*) plays and contemp. (*genzai*) plays. In dream plays, the principal characters are ghosts, spirits, demons, or deities. In *Shigehira*, e.g., a traveling Buddhist monk reaches a hill in the town of Nara and meets an old man who points out some of the temples nearby, then vanishes. In the second act, the old man shows his true form, the suffering ghost of the commander whose troops burned down two of the largest temples, killing thousands, during a 12th-c. war. Some ghosts attain enlightenment thanks to the monk's prayers; others return to the afterworld. Contemp. plays enact dramatic encounters between living human beings. In *Yuya*, e.g., a general forbids his mistress to visit her ailing mother because he wants her by his side to view the cherry blossoms; distraught, she expresses her sadness in a dance and a poem, and he finally assents.

The great med. playwrights—Zeami Motokiyo (?1363–1443), his son Kanze Motomasa (d. 1432), and son-in-law Komparu Zenchiku (b. 1405)—adapted plots from a variety of sources. These included works of literary fiction (such as *The Tale of Genji*); war epics; cl. poems (see WAKA) and the lore surrounding them; folk tales; Chinese hist. and lit.; Buddhist scriptures, sermons, and anecdotes; and Shinto mythical narratives. The lines of nō plays frequently contain allusions to other literary works. The playwrights' methods of imagistic association draw on techniques used in the Japanese art of linked verse (see RENGA).

Nō prosody and poetics have much in common with other genres of cl. Japanese poetry. Verse passages are composed of sequences of fixed numbers of syllables, unrhymed and unaccented. The most common meter is the traditional one of seven- and five-syllable units used in alternation, but pairs of eight- and four-syllable "lines" are also used. Rhetorical devices include the "pivot word," a type of *syllepsis.

Originally, handwritten vocal scores were circulated exclusively among professional actors. Amateurs began learning how to perform nō plays and individual songs in the 16th c., creating a need for printed texts. The commentary *Utaishō* was commissioned in 1595 to explicate allusions and other difficult aspects of the plays. Nō libretti were included in the national literary canon established during the 19th c. and, validated in part by its prestige in the West, nō became the object of serious scholarly inquiry in Japan and abroad. The study of nō also extends to its hist., aspects of performance, and the theoretical treatises on acting, stagecraft, and dramaturgy that were written by Zeami, Zenchiku, and their successors.

Little was known or understood outside Japan about nō until the mid-19th c., when the country opened to trade and broad cultural contact with the West. As the official state entertainment of the Tokugawa shogunate, nō fell into disfavor when the shogunate collapsed in 1868 but was revived under the new Meiji state, partly because it was a suitable equivalent to Eur. opera that could be performed before visiting foreign dignitaries. Nō was performed for the former U.S. president Ulysses S. Grant during his tour of Japan in 1879.

In the early 20th c., a number of books by prominent authors and trans. introduced nō to the Eng.-speaking world. These works included *"Noh" or Accomplishment: A Study of the Classical Stage of Japan* by Ernest Fenollosa and Ezra Pound (1916) and *The Nō Plays of Japan* by Arthur Waley (1921). W. B. Yeats contributed an intro. to Fenollosa and Pound's volume and wrote plays, such as *At the Hawk's Well*, that were shaped by his understanding of nō. Other writers influenced by nō include Pound himself, who saw similarities between *imagism and the insistence on key visual images characteristic of nō; Bertolt Brecht, who adapted the nō play *Taniko* (*The Valley Rite*) into two plays, *Der Jasager* (*The Yes-Sayer*) and *Der Neinsager* (*The Nay-Sayer*); and Benjamin Britten, whose opera *Curlew River* is based on the nō play *Sumidagawa* (*The Sumida River*).

See DRAMATIC POETRY; JAPAN, POETRY OF.

■ *Twenty Plays of the Nō Theatre*, ed. D. Keene (1970); *Yōkyokushū*, ed. M. Itō, 3 v. (1983–88); T. B. Hare, *Zeami's Style* (1986); M. J. Smethurst, *The Artistry of*

*Aeschylus and Zeami* (1989); J. Goff, *Noh Drama and "The Tale of Genji"* (1991); *Japanese Nō Dramas*, trans. R. Tyler (1992); S. T. Brown, *Theatricalities of Power* (2001); E. Terasaki, *Figures of Desire* (2002); P. S. Atkins, *Revealed Identity* (2006); Zeami, *Performance Notes*, trans. T. Hare (2008).

P. S. ATKINS

**NOIGANDRES.** Title of a Brazilian avant-garde poetry jour. founded and ed. by Augusto de Campos, Haroldo de Campos, and Décio Pignatari, leaders of Brazil's *concrete poetry movement. These poets emerged from the atmosphere of postwar poetic renewal spearheaded by João Cabral de Melo Neto, adding to that the influences of the international literary avant-garde, especially Ezra Pound, James Joyce, Guillaume Apollinaire, Vladimir Mayakovsky, and Stéphane Mallarmé; and of Brazilian modernists, esp. Oswald de Andrade and his *antropofagia*. The title of the jour. refers to a mysterious word in a song by the Occitan *troubadour Arnaut Daniel mentioned in one of Ezra Pound's *Cantos*. The *Noigandres* poets were also influenced by constructivist art and design and concrete or serial music. Having previously brought out discrete chapbooks, they decided to publish together in a jour., thus creating a sense of intellectual kinship. Five issues in total came out in November 1952, February 1955, December 1956, March 1958, and November 1962. At first, only work by both de Camposes and Pignatari appeared in the jour., but *Noigandres* 3 also features work by the nonlinear experimentalist Ronaldo Azeredo (the brother-in-law of both the poets A. de Campos and José Lino Grünewald) and includes, for the first time, the label *concrete poetry*. The 210-page *Antologia Noigandres 5—Do Verso à Poesia Concreta* includes poetry by the de Campos brothers, Pignatari, Azeredo, and Grünewald.

*See* AVANT-GARDE POETICS; BRAZIL, POETRY OF; CONSTRUCTIVISM; MODERNISM; MUSIC AND POETRY; SERIAL FORM; VISUAL POETRY.

■ D. Pignatari and J. M. Tolman, "Concrete Poetry: A Brief Structural-Historical Guideline"; J. M. Tolman, "The Context of a Vanguard: Toward a Definition of Concrete Poetry"; C. Clüver, "Reflections on Verbivocovisual Ideograms," all in *Poetics Today* 3 (1982); "From Dante to the Post-Concrete: An Interview with Augusto de Campos," *Material Poetry of the Renaissance/The Renaissance of Material Poetry*, ed. R. Greene, *Harvard Library Bulletin* n.s. 3.2 (1992), UbuWeb, http://www.ubu.com/; L. de Barros and J. Bandeira, *Grupo Noigandres* (2002); H. de Campos, *Novas*, ed. A. S. Bessa and O. Cisneros (2007); C. Clüver, "The *Noigandres* Poets and Concrete Art" and W. Bohn, "Exploring the Concrete Labyrinth," both in *Ciberletras* 17 (2007).

O. CISNEROS

**NONSENSE VERSE.** Some consider *nonsense* a wide category that includes almost any verse that creates a fantastical world with its own rules, while others consider it a narrow category that includes only verse that disrupts the operations of lang., typically by employing an abnormal syntax or invented words. Both these formulations describe many aspects of *nonsense*, and the two often overlap. E.g., Lewis Carroll's "Jabberwocky," an instance of nonsense verse that uses a largely invented vocabulary, is introduced in the context of Carroll's fantastical Looking-Glass world:

> 'Twas brillig, and the slithy toves
>     Did gyre and gimble in the wabe:
> All mimsy were the borogoves,
>     And the mome raths outgrabe.

Neither of these formulations, however, suffices to describe the broad scope of what authors, anthologizers, and critics have called *nonsense verse*. Nonsense verse is the versified instance of nonsense lit., a category of writing that transforms into virtues the vices associated with the pejorative term *nonsense*: silliness, incomprehensibility, childishness, pointlessness, and triviality, among others.

Critics have disagreed over whether nonsense is a genre, as Tigges believes, or something more nebulous, "less a genre than a possibility, a dimension, a boundary which poetry touches more frequently than we usually imagine," as Haughton does. In either approach, critics treat the works of Edward Lear and Carroll as the foremost exemplars of the category in Eng. Nevertheless, Malcolm has found the origins of Eng. nonsense not in the mid-19th c. but earlier, in the 17th. A Fr. nonsense trad. dates to the Middle Ages. While some critics warn against tendencies to universalize nonsense, it exists in a wide spectrum of trads., whether Eur., Chinese, Indian, or Ar.

Despite its name, nonsense does not wholly escape sense, and critics draw a sharp distinction between nonsense and mere gibberish. Nonsense remains rule-based, even if the rules are different from those of our world, and Lecercle has urged readers to dispel the notion that nonsense "presents us with the charming disorder of freedom." Rather, nonsense deals in a complex interplay of order and disorder, of meaning and nonmeaning. Even the most gibberish-like instances of verse engage a reader's impulse toward meaning, "the mind's force toward order" (Sewell). Tigges argues that such interplay is the central characteristic of nonsense, which he considers "a genre of narrative literature which balances a multiplicity of meanings with a simultaneous absence of meaning."

Nonsense is not just light but willfully unserious: its very point often seems to be pointlessness. Nevertheless, some critics have rejected a connection between nonsense and the comic, arguing that much of what happens in nonsense is serious indeed. Even when deeply serious or troubling events happen in nonsense, however, they tend to be deployed for comic effect. Lear's *limericks, e.g., feature heinous acts of violence and tragedy, but the reader is meant to delight in those acts:

> There was an Old Man of Peru,
> Who watched his wife making a stew;
> But once, by mistake, in a stove she did bake
> That unfortunate Man of Peru.

Understood realistically, this event would be tragic. In the context of nonsense, it is funny and even silly, as the prominent grin on the face of the woman in Lear's accompanying illustration confirms.

Writers of nonsense often adopt a poetics of formal excess that values improbability more than precision. Nonsense rhymes, often polysyllabic, jarring, and repeated over and over again, are regularly played for laughs. Like Lear's limericks, most instances of nonsense verse feature four- and three-beat rhythms.

Critics have identified a number of characteristic devices through which nonsense disrupts common sense. Sewell, Stewart, and Tigges catalog many of these devices, incl. mirroring, reversals, and inversions, as in Carroll's Looking-Glass world; the simultaneous juxtaposition of improbable elements; and the adoption of and strict adherence to seemingly arbitrary rules. These devices create an alternative to the ordinary world, but they also reflect it. By creating a nonsensical alternative world order, they reveal the rules of the ordinary world to be arbitrary as well. As Wittgenstein once wrote, "[T]he negation of nonsense is nonsense" rather than normative sense.

Even when nonsense does not disrupt syntax or vocabulary, it tends to have a special relationship to lang. in which the metaphorical mechanisms of lang. are taken literally or in which lang. is treated as a tangible material object. Stewart cites the expression "he thought that the sun rose and set on her," noting that in nonsense "the person is likely to get very hot or, at least, very tired from such a burden."

The relationship of nonsense to satire and parody has been a source of significant critical disagreement. Some, like Chesterton, Cammaerts, and Sewell, argue that nonsense should be disconnected from real-world concerns, that satire and parody would taint "that state of security, freedom, and purely mental delight that is proper to the [nonsense] game" (Sewell). Others, incl. Amis and Lecercle, associate parody and satire closely with nonsense, arguing that "a great deal of what passes for nonsense is or was generic parody" (Amis), that "parodies . . . are very frequent in nonsense texts, . . . and they are the privileged locus for the dialogue between the author and his child readers" (Lecercle).

The assumption that the audience of nonsense is children, however, proves equally vexed. While much nonsense is aimed directly at children, much is intended for the delight of adults, incl. the 17th-c. examples explored by Malcolm. These poems do not aim for a juvenile readership at all but instead take the adult lang. of reason to hyperbolic extremes, so forcefully embracing the sophistication of academic lang. as to render it utterly silly.

Though nonsense verse includes a great deal of verse that does not disrupt the operations of lang., Carroll's archetypal example of nonsense verse remains the best of what does. Many of the words in "Jabberwocky" are Carroll's inventions, and ling. textbooks regularly cite the stanza as an example of the power of ling. structure to produce meaning despite the absence of stable meanings for much of its vocabulary. As important to what makes "Jabberwocky" nonsense as the lang. itself, however, is the context in which the poem appears, in *Through the Looking-Glass*. Alice encounters the poem and is baffled by it, and Humpty Dumpty later confidently but dubiously explains the meanings of various of Carroll's invented words: "'Well, 'TOVES' are something like badgers—they're something like lizards—and they're something like corkscrews.'" Humpty Dumpty, it becomes clear, provides few actual solutions to the problems of meaning in the poem. In part, readers are meant to laugh at his confident analysis. The silliness of these reactions to the poem, and not just its disruption of lang., makes it fit into the same category of nonsense verse as Lear's limericks. Carroll's original version of the first stanza of the poem falsely posited it as a newly discovered "Stanza of Anglo-Saxon Verse" and glossed every single unfamiliar term in a straight-faced mockery of academic discourse, suggesting that the joke was in place all along. It is not just that "Jabberwocky" is written in invented lang. but that we understand it as invented and are in on Carroll's joke that allows us to categorize it as nonsense.

*See* CLERIHEW, LIGHT VERSE, NURSERY RHYMES.

■ G. K. Chesterton, *The Defendant* (1902); *A Nonsense Anthology*, ed. C. Wells (1902); E. Cammaerts, *The Poetry of Nonsense* (1926); L. E. Arnaud, *French Nonsense Literature in the Middle Ages* (1942); E. Partridge, *Here, There and Everywhere* (1950); E. Sewell, *The Field of Nonsense* (1952); G. Orwell, *Shooting an Elephant* (1954); *Anthologie du nonsense*, ed. R. Benayoun (1957); W. Forster, *Poetry of Significant Nonsense* (1962); A. Liede, *Dichtung als Spiel*, 2 v. (1963); G. Deleuze, *Logique du sens* (1969); R. Hildebrandt, *Nonsense* (1970); *The Nonsense Book*, ed. D. Emrich (1970); A. Schöne, *Englische Nonsense und Gruselballaden* (1970); D. Petzolt, *Formen und Funktionen der englischen Nonsense Dichtung im 19* (1972); K. Amis, "Introduction," *The New Oxford Book of Light Verse*, ed. K. Amis (1978); S. Stewart, *Nonsense: Aspects of Intertextuality in Folklore and Literature* (1979); P. Cachia, "An Uncommon Use of Nonsense Verse in Colloquial Arabic," *Journal of Arabic Literature* 14 (1983); H. Haughton, "Introduction," *The Chatto Book of Nonsense Poetry*, ed. H. Haughton (1988); W. Tigges, *An Anatomy of Literary Nonsense* (1988); J.-J. Lecercle, *Philosophy of Nonsense* (1994); M. Parsons, *Touch Monkeys* (1994); L. Wittgenstein, *Cambridge Letters*, ed. B. McGuinness and G. H. von Wright (1995); N. Malcolm, *The Origins of English Nonsense* (1997); *The Penguin Book of Nonsense Verse*, ed. Q. Blake (2001); E. Lear, *The Complete Verse and Other Nonsense*, ed. V. Noakes (2002); R. McGillis, "Nonsense," *A Companion to Victorian Poetry*, ed. R. Cronin, A. Chapman, and A. H. Harrison (2002); *The Everyman Book of Nonsense Verse*, ed. L. Guinness (2005); *The Tenth Rasa: An Anthology of Indian Nonsense*, ed. Michael Heyman (2008).

E. RETTBERG

**NORSE POETRY.** The vernacular poetry of the Viking Age and med. West Scandanavia. Norse poetry is related to the poetic trads. of OE, Old Saxon, and OHG and is, therefore, based on a structural principle of *alliteration, although features such as internal rhyme and the counting of syllables were also important (see SYLLABIC VERSE). Norse poetry differs from alliterative poetry in other Germanic langs. in that it is stanzaic rather than stichic. A handful of Viking Age (ca. 800–1100) runic inscriptions contain verse, and scholars believe that poets whose work has survived lived as long ago as the end of the 9th c. and that some anonymous verse may have had an oral prehist. However, virtually all the evidence for Norse poetry is found in mss. from the 13th c. and later. There is ample med. evidence of the analysis of poetics from the Middle Ages: the poem *Háttalykill* (apparently a loan trans. of *clavis rhythmica*) of the Icelander Hallr Þórarinsson and the Orkney Jarl Rǫgnvaldr in the 1140s; four grammatical treatises; and, most important, the *Edda* (composed ca. 1178–1241; see EDDA) of the poet and chieftain Snorri Sturluson. *Edda* probably means "poetics," and the work contains, besides a prologue, sections devoted to the mythology (*Gylfaginning*, "Deluding of Gylfi"), poetic vocabulary (*Skáldskaparmál*, "Poetic Diction"), and *Háttatal* ("Enumeration of Meters"), a poem exhibiting 100 metrical or lexical variations, equipped with a metrical commentary.

Snorri named the most commonly used form *dróttkvæðr háttr* (meter recited before the retinue) or *dróttkvætt* (recited before the retinue). In the beginning of *Háttatal*, he presented this verse to exemplify the use of alliteration, rhyme, and syllable-counting:

> Lætr, sás Hákun heitir
> (hann rekkir lið) bannat,
> jǫrð kan frelsa fyrðum
> friðrofs konungr ofsa;
> sjálfr ræðr alt ok Elfar,
> ungr stillir sá, milli
> (gramr á gipt at fremri)
> Gandvíkr jǫfurr landi.

Snorri explains that there are 12 "staves" (alliterating sounds) in the verse, two in odd lines and one in even lines, and that they link "quarter-stanzas," i.e., pairs of lines. The staves that appear initially in the even lines he calls "head-staves," and, he says, they control the alliteration. The other staves, in the odd lines, are "props." Thus, in the above verse, the head staves are the initial sounds of the syllables *hann*, *frið-*, *ungr*, and *Gand-*, and the alliterations require either identical consonants (e.g., *Hák-* and *heit-* in the first pair of lines) or, when a vowel begins the "head-stave," any other vowel (*ungr*, *alt*, *Elf-*). Besides this principle of alliteration, each line is to contain six syllables (a sequence like *Lætr* or *ungr* is one syllable). In addition, there is a requirement for half rhymes in odd lines (*Lætr/heit-*, *jǫrð/fyrð*, *sjálfr/Elf-*, *gramr/frem-*) and full rhyme in even lines (e.g., *hann/bann-*). Finally, although Snorri does not articulate it here, every line ends in a trochee, and the basic poetic unit is actually the half-stanza (Norse *helmingr*, "half").

Word order is very free. A literal trans. following the word order of the above verse would look something

like this: "Causes, the one who is named Hákun (he emboldens an army) to be banned, earth can free for men breaking of the peace the king arrogance; himself rules all Elfr [the Göta River] young prince that between (the prince has fortune the greater) Gandvík [the White Sea] the land." There are three clauses in the first *helmingr*: Hákun causes the arrogance of war to be banned for men; he emboldens an army; the king can free the earth. The second has only two, but, in characteristic skaldic complexity, the object of the verb in the fifth line is found only in the eighth, and a prepositional phrase has parts in three of the four lines: "That young prince himself rules the land between Elfr and Gandvík; the prince has fortune the greater." Because Norse was a far more inflected lang. than Eng., unraveling the strands is easier than it appears in trans., but it is still tricky enough that many eds. routinely recast verses into normal prose word order, if only to make clear their interpretations.

Later in *Háttatal*, Snorri discusses variations within this 24-syllable scheme with its alternating alliterative staves and alternating half and full rhymes for the *helmingr*; these concern primarily the syntax and arrangement of the clauses. He also discusses variations from the scheme: changing the syllable count, changing or moving the alliterations, changing or moving the rhymes. To most of these variations, he assigns a name; these terms are still used in the discussion and analysis of Norse poetry.

Snorri used the verse cited above to exemplify the poetic structure. His next order of business, begun in the very next stanza he presented and discussed, was to explain poetic vocabulary. Although he distinguished between a number of concepts, later scholarship names them all *kennings: substitution for a single noun of some other term that is "made known" (*kennd*) by another noun. Thus, e.g., *battle* may be expressed with "spear-din." Kennings may, however, be extended: the "fire of battle" is a sword, as is, therefore, "fire of spear-din."

Here is a *helmingr* from the second stanza of *Háttatal*, with the alliterating staves in bold and rhymes italicized:

> **H**ol*t* felr **h**ildige*lt*i
> **h**ei*l*a bœs ok dei*l*ir
> **g**ul*l*s í **g**elmis sta*ll*i
> **g**unnsei*ð* skǫrungr rei*ð*ir.

The *helmingr* contains two clauses, whose verbs are *felr* (covers) in line 1 and *reiðir* (brandishes) in line 4. The subjects are *deilir gulls* (distributor of gold), a kenning for a king based upon his supposed generosity (such references are common; poets may have wished to remind kings of their obligation to reward them) and *skǫrungr* (prominent man) in line 4, also referring to the king. What he covers and brandishes are his head and his sword. "Head" is rendered here with *holt bœs heila* (forest of the inhabited place of the brain): the brain lives in the skull, and its forest is hair, which here functions as a metonym for the head (see METONYMY). "Sword" is *gunnseið[r]* (battle fish), a kenning that sounds unlikely to our ears but is based on the similarity in shape. Technically, a *seiðr* is a pollack, but any fish will do for the kenning, and *seið[r]* enables the required full rhyme. The king covers his head with a *hildigǫltr*—the form in line 1 is a dative instrumental—(battle-boar). Although this kenning might conceivably have originated in pagan-cult practice suggested by the archaeological record, it is most easily explained by reference to a helmet with this name in heroic trad. This explanation demonstrates that some kennings required knowledge of traditional narratives from heroic legend and myth.

For nearly all the hist. of Norse poetry, kennings were as important a poetic feature as the strict requirements for alliteration, rhyme, and number of syllables. However, in the high Middle Ages, some Christian poets objected to kennings as obscuring their message and turned away from using them; the most famous manifestation of this objection is the Icelandic monk Eysteinn's mid-14th-c. *Lilja* (Lily), a hist. of Christian salvation. He composed it in a meter called *hrynhent* ("falling" or "floating meter"), which varies from *dróttkvætt* in that it adds another trochee to each line; the result is quite stately.

A poet was called a *skáld*. If, as some scholars argue, the word is etymologically related to verbs like the Ger. *schelten* (reproach) or was the source of the Eng. verb *scold*, we have some indication of the power of poetry in Old Scandinavian society. Further indication of such power is found in narratives about the impact of insult poetry and laws prohibiting insult poetry and certain kinds of erotic verse. We know that skalds were active in the retinues of powerful men and the courts of kings; one text, *Skáldatal* (enumeration of skalds), links known skalds to known kings of the Viking Age. Throughout the Viking Age, at least, skalds functioned as eyewitnesses to kings' deeds, mostly perhaps in battle, but we also have an old trad. of ekphrastic poetry (see EKPHRASIS), as well as a large collection of individual occasional verses. Later commentators distinguished a poem equipped with a refrain and other structural features, which they called a *drápa* (etymology unknown), from a more simple grouping, a *flokkr* (flock). Occasional stanzas are called *lausavísur* (unbound verses).

Trad. names the first skald Bragi Boddason, who was probably active in Norway in the late 9th c. Some scholars have imagined that Bragi himself created *dróttkvætt*, and although no evidence can be brought to bear, it is undeniable that the first skalds use the form with great facility. The mythology also has a Bragi, god of poetry, and it is not difficult to link the two. But the form adapted easily to Christian subjects as well, and there are poems on all manner of Christian themes. The first great Christian *drápa* was *Geisli* (Sunbeam) by the Icelander Einarr Skulason, an *encomium to St. Olaf recited more than a century after his death, when the see of Niðaróss in western Norway was elevated to an archdiocese in 1153–54. By then, skaldic poetry already was an Icelandic monopoly, and in Iceland, the form lived on throughout the Middle Ages. Its metrical complexities were taken up in a new form of long narrative poem, the *rímur* (from OF *rime*).

One ms. contains a collection of poems on mythological and heroic topics in the far simpler alliterative form of other Germanic trads. (but still stanzaic), and the type of poems in it were named "eddic" following an Enlightenment surmise. Other such poems are known as well, many in Icelandic sagas set in the heroic age. Unlike *dróttkvætt* poetry, these poems are transmitted without the name of a composer, perhaps because they are set in a prehist. about which Icelanders had no information. Because of its Germanic context, eddic poetry has received a great deal of scholarly attention, but it represents only a tiny portion of Norse poetry.

■ L. M. Hollander, *A Bibliography of Skaldic Studies* (1958).

■ **Editions**: *Eddica Minora*, ed. A. Heusler and W. Ranisch (1903); *Den norsk-islandske skjaldedigtning*, ed. F. Jónsson, 4 v. (1912–15); *Íslenzkar miðaldarímur*, ed. Ó. Halldórsson, 4 v. (1973–75); *Snorri Sturluson, Edda*, ed. A. Faulkes (1982–98); *Skaldic Poetry of the Scandinavian Middle Ages*, ed. M. Clunies Ross et al. (2007–)—in print as of 2009 are v. 2, *Poetry from the Kings' Sagas*, ed. K. E. Gade (2009); and v. 7, *Poetry on Christian Subjects*, ed. M. Clunies Ross.

■ **Translations and Commentaries**: *Snorri Sturluson, Edda*, trans. A. Faulkes (1987); *The Poetic Edda*, trans. C. Larrington (1996); K. von See et al., *Kommentar zu den Liedern der Edda* (1997–); M. Clunies Ross et al., *Skaldic Poetry of the Scandinavian Middle Ages* (see above).

■ **Critical Studies**: R. Meissner, *Die Kenningar der Skalden* (1921); G. Kreutzer, *Die Dichtungslehre der Skalden*, 2d ed. (1977); R. Frank, *Old Norse Court Poetry* (1978); K. von See, *Skaldendichtung* (1980); E. Marold, *Kenningkunst* (1983); M. Clunies Ross, *Skáldskaparmál* (1986); K. E. Gade, *The Structure of Old Norse Dróttkvætt Poetry* (1995); G. Nordal, *Tools of Literacy* (2001); M. Clunies Ross, *A History of Old Norse Poetry and Poetics* (2005).

J. LINDOW

**NORSKE SELSKAB.** *Det norske Selskab* (The Norwegian Society) was a literary and patriotic club of Norwegian writers and students who gathered at a coffeehouse in Copenhagen in the late 18th c. Founded in 1772, the group fostered a form of cultural conservatism based on Fr. neoclassicism and Eng. empiricism and opposed to F. G. Klopstock and the influential Danish sentimentalist Johannes Ewald (1743–81). The club had more than 100 members in its prime; some of the important poets among them were Johan Nordahl Brun (1745–1816), Claus Frimann (1746–1829), Johan Herman Wessel (1742–85), and Jens Zetlitz (1761–1821). The literary endeavors of the members ranged over most of the neoclassical genres, from heroic drama and *fables in verse to *elegy and *epigram. Wessel, the most admired member, was a master of witty and elaborate *satire. The society published three *Poetiske Samlinger* (poetic collections) during the final decades of the century. Worthy of note as Norway's first national historical play is Brun's *Einar Tambeskielver* (1772). By cultivating a national identity and lit., the society laid the foundations for the Norwegian romantic cultural revival that came in the 1830s.

See DENMARK, POETRY OF; NEOCLASSICAL POETICS; NORWAY, POETRY OF.

■ A. H. Winsnes, *Det norske Selskab, 1772–1812* (1924); C. F. Engelstad, *Norske Selskabs Blomst og Krone* (1992); L. Bliksrud, *Den smilende makten* (1999).

S. LYNGSTAD; D. KROUK

**NORWAY, POETRY OF.** For a small nation on the fringes of Europe, Norway has an exceptional collection of mod. and contemp. poets. Over large stretches of its hist., however, poetry in Norway has not enjoyed such an auspicious climate, and it was not until the late 18th c. that the national trad. began to distinguish itself from that of Denmark.

The story of Norwegian poetry begins in the late Middle Ages, after the eddic and skaldic verse of ON lit. The first major works were folk *ballads, which derived their new style from *troubadour verse. Of particular interest is *Draumkvæde* (The Dream Ballad), a remarkable visionary poem that blends elements of pagan and Christian myth. The first significant Norwegian poet was Petter Dass (1647–1707), whose *Nordlands Trompet* (The Trumpet of Nordland, composed ca. 1700, pub. 1739) combines a *baroque style with descriptions of the life and landscape of northern Norway. Dass's contemporary and Norway's first recognized female author, Dorothe Engelbretsdatter (1643–1716), expressed powerful religious emotions in her *hymns and poems, which were published in *Sielens Sang-offer* (The Soul's Offering of Songs, 1678).

The Norwegian-born dramatist and Enlightenment polymath Ludvig Holberg (1684–1750) was the major figure of the joint lit. of Denmark-Norway, a political entity that lasted over 400 years until it was dissolved in 1814. Before writing his well-known comedies and epistles, Holberg published the verse epic *Peder Paars* in 1720. Another high point in 18th-c. Dano-Norwegian verse is the *pastoral description of spring in "Majdagen" (1758) by Christian Braunman Tullin (1728–65), which offers a somewhat Rousseauian critique of the corrupting influence of urban culture. In the late 1700s, a group of writers belonging to *Det *norske Selskab* (The Norwegian Society) in Copenhagen sought to create poetic tragedy in the Fr. neoclassical style while cultivating a national identity. Though they produced work in many genres, they are remembered chiefly for the ironic satire *Kierlighed uden Strømper* (Love without Stockings, 1772), written in graceful *alexandrines by the most talented among them, Johan Herman Wessel (1742–85).

*Romanticism reached Norway in the 1830s, when a cultural debate took place between those who followed Danish models and those who wanted to reject Danish cultural hegemony and build a national lit. Henrik Arnold Wergeland (1808–45), leader of the nationalist Patriots, possessed enormous talents and inexhaust-

ible energy, which he directed to politics and popular education in addition to literary creation. Wergeland's production includes the vast lyric drama *Skabelsen, Mennesket og Messias* (Creation, Man, and Messiah, 1830), and narrative poems such as *Jøden* (The Jew, 1842) and *Den engelske Lods* (The English Pilot, 1844). His inventive lyric poetry reached its apex as he neared death, in poems like "Til min Gyldenlak" (To My Wallflower) and "Til Foraaret" (To Spring), the latter in *free verse. Whereas lit. meant rapture and organic form to Wergeland, it meant the opposite to the leader of the Intelligentsia Party, Johan Sebastian Welhaven (1807–73), a poet of quiet reflection and chiseled form who adopted the conservative aesthetic ideology of the influential Danish figure J. L. Heiberg. Welhaven represented a more understated and sober strand of romanticism; he attacked Wergeland's artistic excesses in *Norges Dæmring* (The Dawn of Norway, 1834), a series of epigrammatic *sonnets that also mocked the Patriots' nationalism and advocated a broadly Eur. cultural orientation. Wergeland and Welhaven can be seen as establishing two models of influence within Norwegian lit.: one protean, passionate, progressive, and nationalistic; the other modest, melancholy, moderate, and Eur.

The 1840s saw the rise of National Romanticism, when the scholars Peter Christen Asbjørnsen (1812–85), Jørgen Moe (1813–82), and M. B. Landstad (1802–80) collected folk culture and lit. While Asbjørnsen and Moe transformed Norwegian lit. with their folktales, Landstad's *Norske Folkeviser* (Norwegian Folk Ballads, 1853) exerted a broad influence on poetry. Another manifestation of National Romanticism was the work of the philologist Ivar Aasen (1813–96), who created *landsmaal*, the lang. now called *nynorsk*. Aasmund Vinje (1818–70) was the first important poet to use this lang. as a medium of literary expression, in works such as the well-known poem "Ved Rundarne" (1861). Since that time, the poetic trad. in Norway has been enriched by the presence of two literary langs.

Before writing his world-famous prose dramas, Henrik Ibsen (1828–1906) demonstrated the strengths of Norwegian as a medium for dramatic poetry in his many verse dramas, such as the National-Romantic *Gildet paa Solhaug* (The Feast at Solhaug, 1856), a historical *idyll based on a folk ballad. *Kjærlighedens Komedie* (Love's Comedy, 1862) marks the beginning of Ibsen's realism; its variously rhymed, skipping iambic *pentameters abound in caricature and paradox. In the masterpieces *Brand* (1866) and *Peer Gynt* (1867), Ibsen both exposes the faults of the Norwegian national character and offers a romantic depiction of the mountains and fjords of the country's landscape. The metrical variety of *Peer Gynt*, in contrast to the *Knittelvers used in *Brand*, produced a vast range of effects, from idle daydreaming to physical abandon, from the lightest banter to funereal solemnity. Ibsen also published a single collection of lyric poetry, *Digte* (Poems, 1862), which included the popular narrative poem "Terje Vigen."

While Ibsen's poetry was written in the manner of

Welhaven, the 1903 Nobel Prize laureate Bjørnstjerne Bjørnson (1832–1910) saw himself as literary heir to Wergeland, and he was similarly vocal about left-wing political causes. His National-Romantic saga dramas *Kong Sverre* (1861) and *Sigurd Slembe* (1862) were meant to give Norway a gallery of heroes matching those of the other Eur. nations. Bjørnson published the narrative romance cycle *Arnljot Gelline* (1870) and a collection of lyric poems, *Digte og Sange* (Poems and Songs, 1880), and he later became a central figure of socially and politically engaged critical realism during the Modern Breakthrough era of Scandinavian lit.

Poetry in the 1890s acquired a more personal tone, one attuned to nature, mysticism, and fantasy. Friedrich Nietzsche, Edvard Munch, and Fr. *symbolism were important sources of inspiration for the fin de siècle poets Vilhelm Krag (1871–1933) and Sigbjørn Obstfelder (1866–1900). Krag expressed a world-weary melancholy, while Obstfelder evoked bizarre moods of angst and wonder in a highly original form marked by pauses, repetitions, abrupt transitions, and incompleteness. Though symbolist in conception, Obstfelder's poetry, with its free verse and urban imagery, anticipates Scandinavian *modernism. Arne Garborg (1851–1924) continued the nynorsk trad. with *Haugtussa* (The Elf Maiden, 1895) and *I Helheim* (In Hel's Home, 1901), which give voice to the dark, uncanny forces in humankind and nature while expressing a profound religious nostalgia. Another important writer, the 1920 Nobel laureate Knut Hamsun (1859–1952), published the exquisite mystical poem "Skjærgaardsø" in his influential collection *Det vilde Kor* (The Wild Chorus, 1904).

Hamsun's verse was a source of inspiration for a lyric revival that occurred around 1910, with the work of Herman Wildenvey (1886–1959) and Olaf Bull (1883–1933). Wildenvey's *Nyinger* (Bonfires, 1907) alternates between seductive love lyrics and pantheistic nature poetry, mixing biblical and ballad idioms with jargon and slang. For Bull, as for fellow symbolists such as R. M. Rilke and Paul Valéry, the purpose of poetry was to transmute fugitive moments of experience into what W. B. Yeats called the "artifice of eternity." Bull's masterpiece "Metope" (1927) is a formally perfect and moving meditation on love and the destructiveness of time. Around this time, the nynorsk trad. was also enriched with the work of Olav Aukrust (1883–1929) and Tore Ørjasæter (1886–1968), who treated religious and philosophical themes in a national spirit using forms derived from the *edda and the *ballad. Aukrust's main work, *Himmelvarden* (The Cairn against the Sky, 1916), is a visionary poem based on a quasi-mystical experience.

The interwar period brought new themes and original voices, incl. some early signs of modernism, which would become dominant after World War II. The work of Emil Boyson (1897–1979) was influenced by the poetics and preoccupations of Fr. symbolism, while Claes Gill (1910–73) followed the Anglo-Am. modernists to create ecstatic imagist verse that disregards ordinary syntax and logic. Apart from the captivat-

ing expressionist poets Kristofer Uppdal (1878–1961) and Åsmund Sveen (1910–63), nynorsk poetry in the early 20th c. was formally traditional. One of the major Scandinavian poets of the century, Rolf Jacobsen (1907–94), debuted in the 1930s with *Jord og jern* (*Earth and Iron*, 1933) and *Vrimmel* (*Swarm*, 1935). In these collections, he used *free verse and technological imagery in an ambivalent encounter with industrial modernity. In the postwar period, Jacobsen began to see technology as an unstable and sinister force, and he adopted an ecological stance that was highly critical of consumerist culture, for instance, in *Hemmelig liv* (*Secret Life*, 1954) and *Headlines* (1969). Jacobsen's poetry presents a kaleidoscope of contrasting moods, effects, and angles of vision—pathos and humor, the commonplace and the cosmic, sensory vividness and symbolic resonance. The love poems to his deceased wife in Jacobsen's final collection, *Nattåpent* (*Night Open*, 1985), are some of the best in Norwegian lit.

Politically and socially oriented poetry in traditional form was also quite significant in the decades before World War II. The two leading leftist poets were Arnulf Øverland (1889–1968) and Nordahl Grieg (1902–43), both of whom became active in the resistance movement during the Nazi occupation. Øverland survived imprisonment in the Sachsenhausen concentration camp, but Grieg died as a war correspondent in Germany. Much of Øverland's work springs from a religiously conceived socialist ideal, often presented in biblical symbols. *Den røde front* (The Red Front, 1937) is devoted to proletarian songs and other texts with a political message. Notable monuments to the 1930s are the poems "Guernica," inspired by Picasso's famous painting, and the antifascist "Du må ikke sove" (You Must Not Sleep). Øverland's laconic form and austere diction place him decidedly in the formal trad. of Welhaven; he was later a vocal traditionalist opponent of modernist formal experimentation in the poetic debates of the 1950s. Grieg, who was also a novelist and playwright, wrote socially oriented patriotic lyrics in a style of impassioned eloquence. His greatest success was the collection of war poems titled *Friheten* (*Freedom*, 1943). Another mid-century socialist poet, Inger Hagerup (1905–85), wrote condensed love lyrics as well as eloquent war poems (e.g., *Aust-Vågøy*, 1941). Also worthy of mention is Gunnar Reiss-Andersen (1896–1964), who combined a brooding introspection with sensitivity to a world in crisis. During the war he was an important spokesman for his country while in Swedish exile, after which he published *Dikt fra krigstiden* (Wartime Poems, 1945).

The leading postwar modernist was Paal Brekke (1923–93), whose Swedish exile during the war had exposed him to the modernist authors called *Fyrtiotalisterna*. Brekke published his trans. of *The Waste Land* and other poems of T. S. Eliot, as well as his own first collection, *Skyggefektning* (Shadow Boxing), in 1949. Brekke's poetry employs a richly allusive, fractured lang., with abrupt shifts in register, mood, and rhythm—pathos alternates with black humor, personal recollection with glimpses of a world falling apart, quotidian banality with the mythic sublime. His best work, *Roerne fra Itaka* (The Oarsmen from Ithaca, 1960), is a poetic cycle in which Brekke, like Eliot, juxtaposes contemp. actuality with ancient myth. Another distinctive postwar modernist is Gunvor Hofmo (1921–95), whose work deals with the extreme experience of trauma and loss at a personal and historical level; her best friend was murdered at Auschwitz. Hofmo's first collection, *Jeg vil hjem til menneskene* (I Want to Go Home to the People, 1946), contains the starkly powerful poem "Det er ingen hverdag mer" (There Is No Everyday Anymore). Tarjei Vesaas (1897–1970), a key nynorsk novelist, also adopted a moderate modernism in his poetry, which has been collected in Eng. trans. His wife, Halldis Moren Vesaas (1907–95), was also an accomplished poet whose nonmodernist work explores women's lives and perennial themes of nature, love, life, and death.

By 1960, modernism in poetry was taken for granted, and many new voices were heard. Chief among them were Stein Mehren (b. 1935) and Georg Johannesen (1931–2005). Mehren is a novelist, playwright, and cultural critic as well as poet. His entire oeuvre forms an existential quest for authenticity and an engagement with philosophy of lang. By way of contrast, the work of Johannesen is social and political; he was deeply influenced by Bertolt Brecht, and his style is condensed and elliptical, characterized by bizarre contrasts and mordant irony. *Ars Moriendi eller de syv dødsmåter* (*Ars Moriendi* or the Seven Ways of Death, 1965), his main collection, treats the seven deadly sins within a strict, semischolastic format, a style at odds with the often surrealist imagery.

In the late 1960s, new political and poetic tendencies became evident in the work of Jan Erik Vold (b. 1939), who was associated with the influential left-wing modernist literary magazine *Profil*. Vold began as an experimentalist preoccupied by solipsism, and his early work includes forays into emblematic verse (see EMBLEM) and *concrete poetry. *Hekt* (Verge, 1966), framed by a document from the Vietnam War, creates a world poised on nightmare through grotesque imagery that evokes the uncanny. Subsequently, under the influence of W. C. Williams and contemp. Swedish poets, Vold moved toward a "new simplicity," anecdotal and confessional in *Mor Godhjertas glade versjon. Ja* (Mother Goodheart's Glad Version. Yes, 1968), almost purely visual and objective in *spor, snø* (tracks, snow, 1970), where he adapts *haiku form. The antisymbolist style of "new simplicity" was also perfected by an important older nynorsk poet, Olav H. Hauge (1908–94), who progressively simplified his style until, with *Dropar i austavind* (Drops in the East Wind, 1966), he was writing about everyday things in an unadorned idiom akin to his Chinese and Japanese models. Hauge, who lived his whole life in an orchard in western Norway, was also active as a translator of many foreign poets, such as W. B. Yeats, Arthur Rimbaud, Georg Trakl, and Paul Celan. Hauge's sober and minimal style has had an enormous influence on contemp. Norwegian lit., and, with Jacobsen, he is the most revered and most translated 20th-c. Norwegian poet.

In the final decades of the 20th c., after the politicized lit. of the 1970s, Norwegian poetry showed a variety of tendencies, from lyrics influenced by ballads and folk songs to continued late modernist minimalism to new forms of multimedia and genre-crossing experimentalism. Two significant contemp. poets are also celebrated dramatists: Jon Fosse (b. 1959) and Cecilie Løveid (b. 1951). Other figures who may be seen as vital to the landscape of contemp. poetry are Eldrid Lunden (b. 1940) and Paal-Helge Haugen (b. 1945), both of whom emerged from the *Profil* group of 1960s radicals. Like Hauge, Haugen's terse and concrete form of expression was influenced by Chinese and Japanese poetic forms. Perhaps the most fascinating late-20th-c. Norwegian poet is Tor Ulven (1953–95), who crafted a distinctively pessimistic voice with an astonishing use of archaeological motifs, from *Etter Oss, Tegn* (After Us, Signs, 1981) to the *prose poems of *Stein og speil* (Stone and Mirror, 1995). In 2004, Øyvind Rimbereid (b. 1966) won the prestigious Kritikerprisen (The Norwegian Critics' Prize for Literature) for *Solaris korrigert* (Solaris Corrected), which contains an epic science-fiction poem written in a futuristic hybrid composed of dialectal Norwegian, Eng., ON, and other langs. Poetic creativity continues to thrive in contemp. Norway, in part because of generous support from the government's Arts Council.

*See* DENMARK, POETRY OF; ICELAND, POETRY OF; NEW NORSE (NYNORSK) POETRY; SWEDEN, POETRY OF.

■ **Anthologies and Primary Texts:** *Oxford Book of Scandinavian Verse*, ed. E. W. Gosse and W. A. Craigie (1925); H. Wergeland, *Poems*, trans. G. M. Gathorne-Hardy et al. (1929); *Anthology of Norwegian Lyrics*, trans. C. W. Stork (1942); T. Vesaas, *30 Poems*, trans. K. G. Chapman (1971); *Modern Scandinavian Poetry 1900–1975*, ed. M. Allwood (1982); *20 Contemporary Norwegian Poets*, ed. T. Johanssen (1984); H. Ibsen, *Poems*, trans. J. Northram (1987); T. Vesaas, *Through Naked Branches*, ed. and trans. R. Greenwald (2000); R. Jacobsen, *North in the World*, ed. and trans. R. Greenwald (2002); H. Wergeland, *The Army of Truth*, trans. A. Born (2003); O. H. Hauge, *Leaf-Huts and Snow-Houses*, trans. R. Fulton (2004), and *The Dream We Carry*, trans. R. Bly and R. Hedin (2008); *New European Poets*, ed. W. Miller and K. Prufer (2008); H. Wergeland, *Jan van Huysum's Flower Piece*, trans. J. Irons (2009).

■ **Criticism and History:** *Norges litteraturhistorie*, ed. E. Beyer, 6 v. (1974–75); M. K. Norseng, *Sigbjørn Obstfelder* (1982); A. Aarseth, "The Modes of Norwegian Modernism," *Facets of European Modernism*, ed. J. Garton (1985); H. Naess, *A History of Norwegian Literature* (1993); *Etterkrigslitteraturen*, ed. Ø. Rottem, 3 v. (1995–98); L. Bliksrud, *Den smilende makten* (1999); P. T. Andersen, *Norsk litteraturhistorie* (2001); I. Havnevik, *Dikt i Norge* (2002); J. Brumo and S. Furuseth, *Norsk litterære modernisme* (2005); *Lyrikkhåndboken*, ed. J. M. Sejersted and E. Vassenden (2007).

S. LYNGSTAD; D. KROUK

**NOVAS (RIMADAS).** A term used in the plural, even for a single composition. Occitan nonlyric poems (verse narratives) ordinarily written in rhymed octosyllabic *couplets. Although the term was sometimes applied to poems with a strong didactic element, it normally designated some kind of narrative, the most famous examples being the verse fictions *Jaufré* and *Flamenca*; the latter in particular is one of the gems of Occitan lit.

■ Chambers; E. W. Poe, "'No volc aver nom Raÿmbaut!': Names and Naming in *So fo el tems*," *Tenso* 22 (2007).

F. M. CHAMBERS

**NOVEL, POETRY IN THE.** Some novelists aspire to the poetic; others conspire against it. If a novel is itself poetic, like Boris Pasternak's *Doctor Zhivago*, poems extend the work's themes and enhance its sensibility. Thus, Pasternak's book ends with its hero's verse "The Poems of Yuri Zhivago," which are arguably the book's greatest achievement.

From antiquity on, a quite different possibility has also tempted prose writers: *satire. Rather than coexisting harmoniously, poetry and prose may form what Mikhail Bakhtin (1968) called "an oxymoronic combination" in which the sublime is brought low by an "inappropriate word." In such combinations, poetry can be used to signal a "poetic" view of life, which the surrounding prose then subjects to scrutiny and *parody. The "poetic" signifies the limit to which poetry supposedly tends, the way in which terms like "the dramatic" and "the operatic" point to extremes or an alleged essence. Satiric combinations represent the "poetic," so understood, as ridiculous. The "prosaic" usually has the last word.

Ancient Menippean satire was sometimes defined as a combination of prose and poetry, but not in a way that would have applied to *Doctor Zhivago*. Rather, the prose of Menippean satire does not just lie alongside the poetry but subjects it, and everything "poetic," to parodic debasement. The Menippean mixture of prosaic and poetic broadened over the centuries. The "poetic" came to include any number of "uplifting" attitudes: the view of life as exalted and humanity as noble, as well as all idealism, utopianism, and transcendence of the mundane. In Lucian's *Philosophies for Sale* and Erasmus's *Praise of Folly*, philosophers, with their sense of rising above ordinary concerns, are treated as another sort of absurd poet. When, in *Le rire*, Henri Bergson identifies laughter with the subversion of soul by body and of the spiritual by the mechanical, he expresses how Menippean satire treats anything "poetic." Whatever pretends to soar falls to earth, usually into mud or excrement, the way Gulliver, in a state of poetic dreaminess, falls into a giant Brobdingnagian turd.

The mod. novel is often traced to the Ren., whose greatest novelistic masterpieces juxtapose the prosaic and poetic in this way. The 13th ch. of François Rabelais's *Gargantua* contains a *rondeau about orifices ("Yesterday shitting, I did know / The profit to my arse I owe.") Of course, *Don Quixote* represents various "poetic" ideals as mad. In bk. 1, ch. 5, the hero repeats verses from a tale "no more authentic than the miracles of Mohammed" beginning: "Where art thou, lady of my heart, / That for my woe thou dost not grieve?" When the barber and curate examine Don Quixote's library, the niece tells them to burn the pastorals as well, lest he "suddenly take it into his head to turn shepherd and roam through the woods and fields, singing and piping, and what is worse, turning poet, for it is said that disease is incurable and catching."

Some 19th-c. realist novels advocated a "prosaic" view of life, which set the highest value on how ordinary moments are lived and everyday decisions made. In these works, the opposite view was often represented by poetry, esp. romantic poetry. The scheming heroine of Anthony Trollope's *The Eustace Diamonds* sings, plays the harp, and quotes poetry: "She had learned much poetry by heart, and could apply it." "Applied poetry" deceives others, but self-deception is still more likely in these novels advocating the prosaic. In Jane Austen's *Persuasion*, Anne detects the overwrought quality of Captain Benwick's love of Walter Scott and Lord Byron. Discoursing on "whether *Marmion* or *The Lady of the Lake* were to be preferred, and how ranked the *Giaour* and *The Bride of Abydos*; and, moreover, how the *Giaour* was to be pronounced, he shewed himself acquainted with all the tenderest songs of the one poet, and all the impassioned descriptions of hopeless agony of the other." Anne hopes that "he did not always read only poetry" and says "that she thought it was the misfortune of poetry, to be seldom safely enjoyed by those who enjoyed it completely." In such metaliterary passages, Austen and Trollope point to the prosaic values of their own prose.

Fyodor Dostoevsky repeatedly quotes or paraphrases "poetic" poetry, not only to mock naïve idealism but to counter naïve psychology. *Notes from Underground* and *The Brothers Karamazov* contain endless references to Dostoevsky's symbol of both kinds of naiveté, Friedrich Schiller. In *The Idiot*, Aglaia quotes Alexander Pushkin's poem about a "poor knight" both to mock and praise Myshkin for his quixotic spirit. In *Demons* (*The Possessed*), the narrator paraphrases Stepan Trofimovich's absurdly romantic poem. It is "some sort of allegory, recalling the second part of *Faust*," which opens with "a chorus of incorporeal figures of some sort" and "a chorus of spirits not yet living but very eager to live" who sing "about something indefinite, for the most part about somebody's curse." Everything displays "a tinge of higher meaning" until a young man tells a fairy "that his greatest desire is to lose his reason at once (a desire possibly superfluous)." We get the poem only through its satiric rendition in prose.

The narrator of *Demons* does much the same to the poetic prose of Karmazinov (a *parody of Ivan Turgenev). Karmazinov, we are told, may describe a drowned woman and a dead child, but "one seemed to read between the lines . . . Look rather at *me*, see how I was unable to bear that sight and turned away from it. . . . I blinked my eyes—isn't that interesting?" Unexpectedly enough, this novel also uses poetry to mock even the prosaic lang. of ordinary society life with lang. that is the very opposite of "poetic." Extremely unpoetic verse does to prose what prose does to "the poetic" when the drunken Lebyadkin recites his poem "The Cockroach," at the end of which a servant empties a jar full of insects, "the whole stew, flies, beetles and all, into the pig pail . . . but observe, madame, observe, the cockroach doesn't complain."

The two greatest novels in verse—Byron's *Don Juan* and Pushkin's *Evgenij Onegin*—follow the Menippean procedure with a twist. Both "the poetic" and "the prosaic" appear in verse, yielding to each other in a complex sequence. Byron's "pedestrian muse" manages to inspire digressions from digressions that somehow still fit the verse pattern. So do vulgarities, phrases from foreign langs., and rhymes so bad they are good: "But— Oh! Ye lords of ladies intellectual, / Inform us truly, have they not hen-pecked you all?" Beginning with his verse dedication, Byron repeatedly targets William Wordsworth, S. T. Coleridge, and Robert Southey. Canto 1 ends by working four appalling—but not appalling enough—lines of Southey into the *Juan* stanza:

> "Go, little Book from this my solitude!
> I cast thee on the waters—go thy ways!
> And if—as I believe, thy vein be good,
> The World will find thee after many days."
> When Southey's read, and Wordsworth
>     understood,
> I can't help putting in my claim to praise—
> The four first rhymes are Southey's every line:
> For God's sake, reader! take them not for mine!

Pushkin's 14-line *Onegin stanza—well imitated in Vikram Seth's novel in verse *The Golden Gate* (1986)— allows for still more digression, variety in tone, and *macaronic rhymes across alphabets as well as langs. Once the parodic and always ironic tone is established, Pushkin introduces the romantic poet Lensky by quoting his verse, which just happens to fit the Onegin stanza. Like an elegy put into *limerick form, mockery is inevitable even when not otherwise expressed.

The all-consuming "prosaic" irony of *Onegin* turns on itself, so that it too becomes the subject of its own parody. In the end, it is hard to say whether *Onegin* ultimately mocks the poetic with the prosaic, or vice versa, or both. However shrewd the prosaic may be, the poetic can sometimes rise above it.

■ R. Colie, *Paradoxia Epidemica* (1966)—Ren. paradox; M. M. Bakhtin, *Rabelais and His World*, trans. H. Iswolsky (1968); G. S. Morson, *The Boundaries of Genre* (1981)—Dostoyesky's "Diary of a Writer"; M. M. Bakhtin, *Problems of Dostoevsky's Poetics*, ed. and trans. Caryl Emerson (1984); R. B. Branham, *Unruly Eloquence* (1989)—Lucian.

G. S. MORSON

**NUMBER(S).** From the cl. era through the romantic, number was a *synecdoche for metrical verse, since meter was conceptualized as the *number* of syllables in each line. Sometimes, number referred to rhyme and more rarely to stress or *accent. More important, in each of these periods, number indicated poetry's participation in the divine order. After ca. 1820, number became a quaint archaism.

In *classical prosody, Cicero and Quintilian discussed number, as did Augustine and Bede in med. prosody. The biblical book of Wisdom famously claimed that God "ordered all things by measure, number, and weight," and Plato's *Timaeus* also found universal order in music and number. Of a piece with music, harmony, and the universe, meter was only one of several kinds of *numerology that determined the line, the stanza, and other formal features. In *Paradise Regain'd*, John Milton describes cl. Athens: "There thou shalt hear and learn the secret power / Of harmony in tones and numbers hit / By voice or hand, and various measured verse." Vocal and instrumental music as well as "*measured* verse" use "tones and numbers" to create "harmony," unlocking a "secret power."

Because number meant harmony, regularity was prized over *variation or *substitution. In *An Essay on Criticism*, however, Alexander Pope articulated an emerging aesthetic: "But most by numbers judge a poet's song, / And smooth or rough with them is right or wrong." "Smooth" numbers meant little variation, while "rough" numbers took liberties with the meter. Nudging harmony aside, Pope valued expression more: "The sound must seem an echo to the sense."

Over the 19th c., number fell from being a synecdoche for poetry and, beyond it, for the divine order to become a synecdoche merely for metrical verse. In *Of Human Bondage*, when W. S. Maugham described the "exquisite numbers" of "old Herrick," the term no longer implied the "order of all things."

*See* MUSIC AND POETRY.

■ P. Fussell, *Theory of Prosody in Eighteenth-Century England* (1966); J. Hollander, *The Untuning of the Sky* (1970); D. Attridge, *Well-Weighed Syllables* (1974); J. Stevens, *Words and Music in the Middle Ages* (1986); O. B. Hardison, *Prosody and Purpose in the English Renaissance* (1989); S. K. Heninger, *The Subtext of Form in the English Renaissance* (1994).

M. L. MANSON

**NUMEROLOGY.** A theory of composition whereby authors order their works according to numerical patterns—when number itself becomes, in Roman Jakobson's phrase, a "constitutive device of the sequence." The items arranged may be almost anything countable, whether substantive (events of a narrative, days of its action) or formal (chapters, stanzas, lines). Equally various are the possible patterns: they range from complex arrays of Platonic numbers or numbers bearing special religious significance—such as the number three in Christianity—to simple round-number counts or mere allusions—like the 200s that refer to Carolus Calvus (CC in Roman numerals). The art of intricate numerology (as of its concealment) can achieve effects of great subtlety.

Much med. and Ren. numerology derived from the Bible, which itself offered models for such organization, notably in Lamentations and the *acrostic Psalms.

These examples exerted immense authority through the trads. of biblical poetics and of Heb. poetics (see HEBREW POETRY, HEBREW PROSODY AND POETICS): the letter total of the Heb. alphabet, e.g., used in Psalm 119, became a favorite compositional number. Indeed, handbooks of number symbolism (arithmology), such as Pietro Bongo's *Numerorum mysteria* (1591), most often based a number's symbolisms on the contexts of its biblical occurrences. But it is important to recognize that numerology could nevertheless be mimetic, since creation itself was thought to reveal patterns of number symbolism. A much-quoted authority was Wisdom of Solomon 11:20: "Thou hast ordered all things by measure, number, and weight."

Philo Judaeus gave a decisive turn to number symbolism when he interpreted Genesis in terms of Pythagorean number theory (e.g., the six days of creation made a perfect number). Subsequently, biblical numbers mingled with Pythagorean-Platonic symbolisms like the *tetraktus* (1 + 2 + 3 + 4 = 10) and the *lambda* series (1, 2, 4, 8; 1, 3, 9, 27). Such principal symbolic numbers informed patterns throughout Western culture: they appear in early med. Celtic romances and 17th-c. ecclesiastical music, in biblical commentaries and lyric poems, in *masque dances and cathedral architecture.

Ren. poets emulated the symmetries and Pythagorean proportions of architecture fairly directly, so that a doctrine of *ut architectura poesis* developed, comparable with the more familiar *ut pictura poesis. Poets esp. liked to form symmetries emphasizing an array's central position, which carried associations of sovereignty or dignity. Thus, Dante treats divine love in the central canto of the *Divine Comedy* at the center of a symmetrical array of line totals: 151/145/145/139/145/145/151. Texts like Gen. 3:3 and Exod. 8:22 ("I am the Lord in the midst of the earth") authorized such procedures. Consequently, in approaching a late med. or Ren. poem, it is worth counting to find what lies at its center: in John Milton's *Paradise Lost*, e.g, Messiah ascends his throne in the central lines of the first edition's 10,550 lines (exact numerology was often confined to the *editio princeps*).

Another common sort of numerology is calendrical. Here, again, there was biblical authority in texts like Ps. 90:12 ("teach me to number my days"). Petrarch took these to heart, structuring his *Canzoniere* as a calendar and noting the astrological circumstances of composition of individual poems. In the Ren., Edmund Spenser perhaps followed this trad. most extensively: his *Epithalamion* represents a celebrated instance of numerology, rediscovered by Hieatt. Many Elizabethan *sonnet sequences have calendrical numerology, e.g., Spenser's *Amoretti*. Alternatively, they may use allusive numbers such as the 108 of the Penelope Game in Philip Sidney's *Astrophil and Stella* and Alexander Craig's *Amorous Songs, Sonnets and Elegies*.

Many Ren. poems of any formal pretensions are organized numerologically. And certain mannerist poets (such as George Chapman) reach a ne plus ultra if not a reductio ad absurdum of self-conscious intricacy in this regard by continual references to their own numerology. But this is far from obvious, since they assiduously

finesse by "concealing" their secrets—e.g., by using totals one more or one less than the significant number.

In the Middle Ages and the Ren., numerical composition was taken for granted; it formed part of the poetic craft or "mystery"—like that whereby the rules of prosody are still handed down. Few Ren. writings about numerology have survived, and these are not on a high plane of critical interest. In the 18th c., with the spread of a new worldview, numbers came to be assigned a less symbolic function, and interest in numerology declined. The romantic movement brought a rupture with the older compositional trad., so that numerology had to be rediscovered by the Pre-Raphaelite D. G. Rossetti, by devout students of med. Catholicism, by early 20th-c. Dante scholars, and by hermetic modernists such as James Joyce. Numerology is, after all, a form of *constraint and has affinities with the procedures of *Oulipo and other experimentalists. In the 1960s and early 1970s, numerology enjoyed something of a vogue among a set of critics, principally medievalists and early modernists, who found in it an alternative to both an exhausted *formalism and *historicism (in the pause before a resurgent, i.e., *New, Historicism); in that era, the claims made for numerological structures were sometimes extravagant, and (except for Hieatt on Spenser and a few others) seldom made a lasting mark on the critical conversation around major works. Still, numerology can be indispensable to a full appreciation of earlier poetry, and sometimes (particularly where allusive numbers are involved) it can aid inferential crit. decisively. There is still no comprehensive study of the subject.

■ Curtius, Excursus 15; A. K. Hieatt, *Short Time's Endless Monument* (1960); A. Fowler, *Spenser and the Numbers of Time* (1964); W. Haubrichs, *Ordo als Form* (1969); C. Butler, *Number Symbolism* (1970)—wide-ranging primer; A. Fowler, *Triumphal Forms* (1970); *Silent Poetry*, ed. A. Fowler (1970); M. Hardt, *Die Zahl in der Divina Commedia* (1973); E. Hellgardt, *Zum Problem symbolbestimmter und formalästhetischer Zahlenkomposition in mittelaltericher Literatur* (1973); *Fair Forms*, ed. M.-S. Rostvig et al. (1975); R. G. Peterson, "Critical Calculations," *PMLA* 91 (1976); *Essays in the Numerical Criticism of Medieval Literature*, ed. C. D. Eckhardt (1980); J. MacQueen, *Numerology* (1985)—the best intro., esp. valuable for the earlier periods; J. J. Guzzardo, *Dante: Numerological Studies* (1988); T. P. Roche Jr., *Petrarch and the English Sonnet Sequences* (1989); A. Dunlop, "Number Symbolism, Modern Studies in," and M.-S. Røstvig, "Number Symbolism, Tradition of," *The Spenser Encyclopedia*, ed. A. C. Hamilton et al. (1990); *Medieval Numerology*, ed. R. L. Surles (1993); G. Alexander, "Constant Works: A Framework for Reading Mary Wroth," *Sidney Newsletter and Journal* 14 (1996–97); C. Andrews, "Numerology and Mathematics in the Writing of Raymond Queneau," *Forum for Modern Language Studies* 40 (2004).

A. FOWLER; R. GREENE

**NURSERY RHYMES.** Verses, either spoken or sung, often originating in oral trad. and adult sensibilities but preserved in the world of young children. The definitive study of these perennially popular verses ("London Bridge is broken down,/Broken down, broken down . . ." e.g., or "Mary, Mary, quite contrary,/How does your garden grow? . . .") remains *The Oxford Dictionary of Nursery Rhymes*, ed. and introduced by Iona and Peter Opie. The term *nursery rhyme* was not coined until the early 19th c.; before then, these verses were known in England as "songs" or "ditties" and in America as Mother Goose rhymes. Although the Opies, Robert Jamieson (1806), James Orchard Halliwell (1842), Morag Styles (1998), and others acknowledge that similar rhymes for young children have existed across cultures for centuries, often with striking resemblances to each other, *nursery rhyme* has come to refer to these traditional Anglo-Am. verses and their variants, which "enter the nursery through the predisposition of the adults in charge of it" (Opie) and which are distinct from playground and school verses for older children (J. Ritson's *Gammer Gurton's Garland* is dedicated to "all good little children who can neither read nor run"). Nursery rhymes tend to be in accentual verse, often in *ballad meter; in trans., the Opies assert, "the English nursery rhyme has probably been carried into every country in the world."

Nursery rhymes have retained remarkable integrity and appeal over time, a phenomenon the Opies attribute to the tenacity of children and to the vitality of oral culture in the world of the young and their caretakers. Nursery rhymes have also been admired for their literary value. "The best of the older ones," according to Robert Graves, "are nearer to poetry than the greater part of *The Oxford Book of English Verse*." Walter de la Mare wrote that "they have their own complete little beauty if looked at closely," and a number of well-known poets—Christina Rossetti, Robert Louis Stevenson, Randall Jarrell, John Ciardi, Robert Frost, Theodore Roethke, and others—have composed poems for children. However, Styles distinguishes as "two quite separate traditions" the nursery rhyme, which comes out of "the disorderly, casual, robust world of the oral tradition; and poetry consciously composed with children in mind by writers who wish to communicate with young readers."

With sources as variant as riddles, alphabet primers, ciphers, prayers, proverbs, tavern songs, barrack-room refrains, seasonal chants, street ballads, tongue twisters, monger cries, mummers' plays, and theatrical productions, the Opies assert that "the overwhelming majority of nursery rhymes were not in the first place composed for children." Ten percent of the rhymes in *The Oxford Dictionary of Nursery Rhymes* date back to 1650 or earlier, with nearly half at least 200 years old and a few hearkening back to the Middle Ages and earlier (the cradle song "Lullay, lullay, litel child,/Softë slep and faste" dates from a ms. of 1372, and "White Bird Featherless" appears in Lat. in the 10th c.). The Opies suggest that "of these pieces which date from before 1800, the only true nursery rhymes (i.e., rhymes composed esp. for the nursery) are the rhyming alphabets, the infant amusements (verses which accompany a game), and

the lullabies. Even the riddles were in the first place designed for adult perplexity." Attitudes toward children in 17th- and 18th-c. England, when the majority of traditional nursery rhymes originated, were permissive, with children treated as miniature adults, perhaps accounting for the often bawdy, profane, and even violent content of some of the verses ("Here comes a candle to light you to bed,/Here comes a chopper to chop off your head," for instance, from "Oranges and Lemons").

The Opies and subsequent scholars have taken care to explore and, when necessary, debunk as apocryphal attempts over the centuries to vest with social, psychological, and political import many nursery rhymes, such as "Sing a Song of Sixpence," which has been wrongly interpreted as alluding to the choirs of Tudor monasteries, or to attribute the identity of "Mother Goose" to an actual person, when in fact her persona was introduced in Europe by a Frenchman, Charles Perrault, in *contes de ma mère l'Oye* in 1697.

Interest in nursery rhymes remains vital in the late 20th and early 21st cs. Any visitor to the Internet will find that fresh print and musical, MP3 downloadable versions of nursery rhymes appear often. Traditional nursery rhymes continue to find their way into contemp. adult work as well, in forms ranging from Anne Carson's long poem *The Glass Essay* (1995) ("Violante in the pantry/Gnawing at a mutton bone") to Michael Franti and Spearhead's spin on "Mary, Mary, Quite Contrary" in their anthem "Ganja Babe" (2002). It seems likely that traditional nursery rhymes will survive largely intact, though with fresh contexts and applications, in oral and print cultures for generations to come.

*See* ACCENTUAL VERSE, BALLAD, CHANT, LULLABY, ORAL POETRY.

■ J. Ritson, *Gammer Gurton's Garland: or, the Nursery Parnassus* (1784); R. Jamieson, *Popular Ballads and Songs from Tradition, Manuscripts, and Scarce Editions* (1806); J. O. Halliwell, *The Nursery Rhymes of England*, rev. ed. (1843); *The Authentic Mother Goose Fairy Tales and Nursery Rhymes*, ed. J. Barchilon and H. Pettit (1960); L. Rollin, *Cradle and All* (1992); *Oxford Dictionary of Nursery Rhymes*, ed. I. and P. Opie (1951; 2d ed. 1997); M. Styles, *From the Garden to the Street* (1998); J. Thomas, *Poetry's Playground* (2007).

L. R. SPAAR

**NUYORICAN POETRY.** *Nuyorican* is a portmanteau word that brings together *New York* and *Puerto Rican*, as well as *neo-* and *Rican*; it represents an identity of Puerto Ricans and people of Puerto Rican descent who live in New York City. Historically, the Nuyorican experience over the 20th and 21st cs. has been shaped by poverty, racial discrimination, crime, migration, bilingualism, and labor exploitation. Nuyorican poetry typically gives voice to these issues, although the roots of its aesthetics and concerns reach back much further.

Nuyorican poetry is largely characterized by qualities of orality, *performance, and ling. self-awareness, aspects grounded in Puerto Rican antecedents. Early

Puerto Rican poetics syncretized the prehistoric, indigenous Taíno *areyto*, a ceremony in which songs of secular wisdom were performed communally; the West African role of the *griot*, a *bard responsible for preserving cultural hist. and interpreting new challenges in an aesthetic, spoken form; and the Sp. lang., the lingua franca of the colonized island. Many Nuyorican poets invoke this multicultural amalgam in justifying the contemp. aesthetic of Nuyorican poetry.

Several historical events contributed to the vast migration of Puerto Ricans to New York City in the 20th c. As an outcome of the Sp.-Am. War, Spain ceded Puerto Rico to the U.S. with the passage of the Treaty of Paris in 1898. The Foraker Act of 1900 established a popularly elected House of Representatives for Puerto Rico, an achievement that added to a communal sense of Puerto Rican sovereignty and political self-determinism. In 1917, the Jones-Shafroth Act established for Puerto Rico a popularly elected Senate and granted U.S. citizenship to Puerto Ricans, a right freely exercised by tens of thousands in the 1940s and 1950s, partially in response to the Puerto Rican politician Teodoro Moscoso's Operation Bootstrap, a program that encouraged U.S. industrial investment in post–Depression-era Puerto Rico at the expense of thousands of agricultural jobs. Many Puerto Ricans were motivated to seek employment in the U.S., which had tightened immigration laws during World War I but experienced a growing economy during and after World War II. New York City, esp. under Mayor Robert Wagner, was the most popular and inviting destination for Puerto Rican migrants in the mid-20th c. Given that Puerto Ricans were U.S. citizens, a phenomenon arose after the Great Migration of the 1940s–60s: the so-called Revolving Door, a tendency for Puerto Ricans in New York City to return periodically to the island and then return again to New York for economic, familial, and educational reasons.

By the 1960s, Puerto Rican communities in New York City had become firmly established. Many Nuyoricans, as well as Puerto Ricans who had migrated to New York City as children or young adults (esp. after service in the U.S. military), had native fluency in Eng. and, motivated by the atmosphere of multiculturalism and liberalism in the 1960s and 1970s, some began to explore a new artistic consciousness, one that expressed the images and emotions of their poor immigrant communities. Jesús Colón, Esmeralda Santiago, Piri Thomas, and Nicholasa Mohr were among the first Nuyorican writers, composing in various genres, esp. fiction, the essay, and the memoir. One neighborhood in New York City of particular importance to the Nuyorican poetry movement was the Lower East Side, an area so largely Nuyorican that it is commonly known also as *Loisaida*; it could be said that the movement was born there. Among the first Nuyorican poets were Sandra María Esteves, Pedro Pietri, Bimbo Rivas, Shorty Bón Bón, and Américo Casiano, who established a community of Nuyorican poets in the Lower East Side by collaborating on poetry readings at the home of Miguel Algarín, a poet and scholar who taught at

Rutgers University. By 1973, these events became regular occurrences that attracted a diverse following, and in 1975, Algarín established the *Nuyorican Poets Café, which has remained a fixture in the Lower East Side and a world-renowned beacon for urban poets.

One of the early and most popular volumes of Nuyorican poetry was Pietri's *Puerto Rican Obituary* (1973), whose title poem became an anthem of sorts among Nuyorican audiences. In 1975, William Morrow published *Nuyorican Poetry: An Anthology of Puerto Rican Words and Feelings*, ed. by Algarín and Miguel Piñero. The poems collected in these pages oscillate between Eng. and Sp., happy and angry, urban landscapes and nostalgia, encapsulating a range of frustrations and epiphanies endemic to Nuyorican experiences of the time. A hallmark of this early poetry is its bilingualism; central to the Nuyorican poetic consciousness is the anxiety caused by inhabiting two ling. identities, Eng. and Sp., and the hybrid speech it breeds. In his introduction to *Nuyorican Poetry*, "Nuyorican Language," Algarín claims that "the experience of Puerto Ricans on the streets of New York has caused a new language to grow: Nuyorican. . . . The mixture of both languages [Eng. and Sp.] grows. The interchange between both yields new verbal possibilities, new images to deal with the stresses of living on tar and cement." Thus, code switching becomes a salient feature of the poetic form, often echoing ironies of the racial or political complexities of Nuyorican identity. Among many examples in *Nuyorican Poetry*, Martita Morales's "The Sounds of Sixth Street" and "Teatro" demonstrate this verbal play across languages, often highlighting the position of slang in registers of speech.

This play between Eng. and Sp. (and "Spanglish"), as well as between standard expressions and slang derivations, was vital to early Nuyorican poetry in its assertion of a new poetic lang.—as was a potent sympathy for the working class and the urban poor, as captured in Pietri's "Puerto Rican Obituary."

The concerns of reconciling ling. duality and social injustices run seamlessly through the production of Nuyorican poetry from its earliest appearance in the 1970s through the 1980s and 1990s, expressed in works such as Pietri's *La Bodega Sold Dreams* (1980) and Tato Laviera's *La Carreta Made a U-Turn* (1992), whose poem "my graduation speech" seems to sum up the pathos of Nuyorican poetry.

In 1982, the Nuyorican Poets Café closed for renovations and remained closed until 1989, when it reopened—but with a noticeably changed purpose. Bob Holman, a Columbia University graduate from Kentucky who had performed at the café on numerous occasions, assumed its leadership and brought with him a new agenda: the *poetry slam. It was Holman's intention to popularize poetry and to make the Nuyorican Poets Café a primary site for open-mike performances and scored poetry competitions. Since 1990, and because of the reputation of the new café, Nuyorican poetry has increasingly been associated with the slam movement and, in reciprocal fashion, Nuyorican poetry's connection to Puerto Rican cultural issues and ideas has diminished, rendering the category—once a response to a turbulent era of political relations between the U.S. and Puerto Rico—more a historical designation than a living phenomenon. Nevertheless, some poets today, such as Willie Perdomo and Caridad "La Bruja" de la Luz, still compose and publish poems in the original Nuyorican trad.

■ E. V. Mohr, *The Nuyorican Experience: Literature of the Puerto Rican Minority* (1982); F. R. Aparicio, "La vida es un Spanglish disparatero: Bilingualism in Nuyorican Poetry," *European Perspectives on Hispanic Literature of the United States*, ed. G. Fabre (1988); W. Perdomo, *Where a Nickel Costs a Dime* (1996); Z. A. Cintrón, *Salsa y control: Codeswitching in Nuyorican and Chicano Poetry* (1997); M. Brown, *Neither Here nor There: Nuyorican Literature, Home, and the "American" National Symbolic* (1998); J. Flores, "Life off the Hyphen: Latino Literature and Nuyorican Traditions," *From Bomba to Hip-Hop: Puerto Rican Culture and Latino Identity* (2000); L. Sánchez-González, *Boricua Literature: A Literary History of the Puerto Rican Diaspora* (2001); *Piñero*, dir. León Ichaso (2001); D. Kane, *All Poets Welcome: The Lower East Side Poetry Scene in the 1960s* (2003); *Writing off the Hyphen: New Critical Perspectives on the Literature of the Puerto Rican Diaspora*, ed. J. L. Torres-Padilla and C. Haydée Rivera (2008).

D. A. Colón

**NUYORICAN POETS CAFÉ** (NPC) is a nonprofit organization that sponsors cultural events and *poetic contests, located at 236 East Third Street on the Lower East Side of Manhattan.

The NPC began in 1973 as a series of informal gatherings hosted by the poet Miguel Algarín, then teaching at Rutgers University. In Algarín's home, local poets of Puerto Rican heritage would give readings in an effort to establish a new art community of Puerto Rican New Yorkers and to express their cultural experience in the mainland U.S. through their emergent, urban, and often bilingual lang. Participants in these early poetry events included Tato Laviera, Miguel Piñero, Pedro Pietri, Sandra María Esteves, Lucky Cienfuegos, Richard August, Belle Starr, Diane Burns, and Eddie Figueroa. In 1974, Piñero's play *Short Eyes* was performed on Broadway, was nominated for six Tony Awards, and won the New York Drama Critics' Circle Award and the Obie Award for best play, drawing general attention to the Nuyorican literary community. In 1975, William Morrow's publication of the anthology *Nuyorican Poetry*, ed. by Piñero and Algarín, added to this burgeoning interest, and the popularity of Algarín's poetry events grew further. To accommodate more people, Algarín in 1975 rented the Sunshine Bar, 505 East Sixth Street, and renamed it the Nuyorican Poets Café. *Beat poets Allen Ginsberg, William Burroughs, and Gregory Corso were among the Sixth Street NPC's guests. In 1980, the NPC moved to the larger Third Street location, where it continues to operate.

After 1989, Bob Holman reconceived the NPC as a site for *poetry slam competitions, marketing the NPC as a multicultural (rather than exclusively Puerto Rican) community of urban lyricists. Since 1990, the NPC has hosted regular poetry slams, where teams compete in a form of stylized urban *performance poetry and are judged by a panel. The NPC has garnered an international reputation for its slams; notable participants have included Paul Beatty, Reg E. Gaines, Saul Williams, Mahogany Browne, and Karen Jaime. The NPC now hosts a range of artistic events, incl. jazz performances, theatrical productions, *hip-hop shows, and open-mike sessions.

*See* NUYORICAN POETRY.

■ D. Vidal, "'Nuyoricans' Express Pain and Joy in Poetry," *New York Times* (May 14, 1976); E. Nieves, "Again, Clubs for Poets to Read and Rage," *New York Times* (Nov. 19, 1990); *Aloud: Voices from the Nuyorican Poets Cafe*, ed. M. Algarín and B. Holman (1994); *Action: The Nuyorican Poets Cafe Theater Festival*, ed. M. Algarín and L. Griffith (1997); *Burning Down the House: Selected Poems from the Nuyorican Poets' Café National Slam Champions*, ed. R. Bonair-Agard et al. (2000); M. Navarro, "The Poetry of the Nuyorican Experience: Writers Following in the Literary Tradition of Miguel Piñero Thrive in a Poets Café," *New York Times* (Jan. 2, 2002); *The Spoken Word Revolution: Slam, Hip-Hop and the Poetry of a New Generation*, ed. M. Eleveld (2003); Nuyorican Poets Café, http://www.nuyorican.org/.

D. A. Colón

# O

**OBJECTIVE CORRELATIVE.** The term is defined in T. S. Eliot's essay "Hamlet and His Problems" (1919): "the only way of expressing emotion in the form of art is by finding an 'objective correlative'; in other words, a set of objects, a situation, a chain of events which shall be the formula of that *particular* emotion; such that when the external facts, which must terminate in sensory experience, are given, the emotion is immediately evoked." Eliot used the formula to pronounce *Hamlet* "an artistic failure," on the grounds that Hamlet suffers from an emotion "he cannot objectify." (The judgment derived from one of the books Eliot was reviewing, J. M. Robertson's *The Problem of "Hamlet,"* [1919], where the play is called "an aesthetic miscarriage.") Eliot went on to speculate that this difficulty is a "prolongation" of Shakespeare's inability to express his own feelings satisfactorily. Hamlet's "disgust" exceeds its object (his mother's incestuous remarriage), just as the Hamlet story is an inadequate vehicle for the emotion ("by hypothesis unknowable") that prompted Shakespeare to write the play.

Eliot's essay did not convince many to judge *Hamlet* a failure, but the phrase *objective correlative* passed into general usage. Between 1980 and 2011, long after the heyday of Eliot's critical influence, the term appeared in more than 350 scholarly articles. When we feel that an image (or any other element) in a work fails to embody the "*particular* emotion" required or that an emotion is being described rather than "presented," we say that the artist has not found an objective correlative. And when we suspect that some emotion of the artist's has not been fully expressed, we say that the work itself is an inadequate objective correlative.

Eliot's technical-sounding formula has a modernist flavor, but the idea that poems evoke emotions by the representation of sensory experience was conventional in the 19th c. Antecedent instances have been identified in Walter Pater (DeLaura); Washington Allston, in whose *Lectures on Art* (1850) the phrase appears (Stallman); S. T. Coleridge (DiPasquale); and Friedrich Schiller (Wellek), among many others. The concept has also been connected with the philosopher F. H. Bradley, on whom Eliot wrote his Harvard diss. (Habib). In fact, Eliot's formula is standard in 20th-c. *imagism. Ford Madox Ford, reviewing Pound's *Cathay* (1915), cited "the theory that poetry consists in so rendering concrete objects that the emotions produced by the objects shall arise in the reader"—a phrase Eliot quoted in *Ezra Pound: His Metric and Poetry* (1917). And there are other instances contemporaneous with Eliot's essay (Menand). In "Tradition and the Individual Talent" (1919) and elsewhere, Eliot suggests that the artistically successful construction of the poem relieves the poet of a psychic distress—a "personal" emotion that need have no connection with the emotions expressed in the poem. This psychobiographical aspect of the objective correlative has no necessary relation to its imagist aspect; Eliot's yoking of the two in the *Hamlet* essay—Hamlet's "problem" reproduces Shakespeare's—represents his own psychologizing of imagist doctrine.

Although the objective correlative has proved useful for sympathetic readings of Eliot's own poetry (e.g., Matthiessen), Eliot's formulation verges on tautology— "the emotions evoked by a work of art must be the product of elements in that work" is a possible paraphrase. But because it names something intuitively felt about art, *objective correlative* seems one of those terms that are destined to survive their theoretical supersession.

■ F. M. Hueffer [Ford], "From China to Peru," *The Outlook* 35 (1915); F. O. Matthiessen, *The Achievement of T. S. Eliot* (1935), ch. 3; T. S. Eliot, *Ezra Pound* (1917); "Hamlet and His Problems" in *The Sacred Wood* (1920)—rev. as "Hamlet" in *Essays*; "Tradition and the Individual Talent" (1919)—rpt. in *Essays*; and "Modern Tendencies in Poetry," *Shama'a* (1920); E. Vivas, "The Objective Correlative of T. S. Eliot," *The Critic's Notebook*, ed. R. W. Stallman (1950); Wellek, v. 1; G. Hough, *Image and Experience* (1960); D. J. DeLaura, "Pater and Eliot: The Origin of the Objective Correlative," *MLQ* 26 (1965); P. DiPasquale Jr., "Coleridge's Framework of Objectivity and Eliot's Objective Correlative," *JAAC* 26 (1968); L. Brisman, "Swinburne's Semiotics," *Georgia Review* 31 (1977); L. Menand, *Discovering Modernism* (1987), ch. 6; M.A.R. Habib, *The Early T. S. Eliot and Western Philosophy* (1999), ch. 5.

L. MENAND

**OBJECTIVISM.** A term used to designate what some have regarded as a movement in 20th-c. Am. poetry, initiated by the February 1931 issue of *Poetry*, guest-edited by Louis Zukofsky, and further represented in *An "Objectivists" Anthology*, ed. by Zukofsky and pub. by George Oppen's TO Publishers, in 1932, and in books issued by the cooperative Objectivist Press from 1933 to 1936. In wider application, the part of mod. and postmod. Am. poetry that has developed out of *imagism as opposed to *symbolism. Poems in this trad. tend to use lang. more literally than figuratively, presenting concrete objects for themselves rather than as embodiments of abstract ideas. They may also reflect a greater interest in composing apprehensible structures of relationships than in offering interpretations of experience, and show awareness of lang. itself as a structure interposed between the I/eye and the world.

The poets most frequently associated with objectivism are the Ams. Charles Reznikoff (1894–1976), Zukofsky (1904–78), Oppen (1908–84), Carl Rakosi

(1903–2004), and Lorine Niedecker (1903–70), as well as the Eng. poet Basil Bunting (1900–85). Their work was championed by the older Am. modernists Ezra Pound, who put most of them in contact with one another and recommended Zukofsky as a guest editor for *Poetry*, and W. C. Williams, who published with the younger objectivists and reviewed their work, as well as corresponding with Zukofsky, who critiqued and influenced his own work.

Critics have been divided as to whether objectivism was a movement with a particular poetics. Some have taken Zukofsky's "Sincerity and Objectification" as an articulation of its principles. In that essay, Zukofsky argues that sincerity is manifested in details of seeing and wording and that perfected poetic structure can achieve objectification of the poem. To Reznikoff and Rakosi, however, the goal of poetic craft was, more simply, a clear, precise naming of things, serving to evoke emotion. The objectivists produced a considerable diversity of styles, ranging from the nearly transparent sentences of Reznikoff to the intricate sound play of Zukofsky, Niedecker, and Bunting, from the sharp satire of Rakosi to the fluid meditation of late Oppen. Zukofsky himself denied the existence of objectivism as a movement; the term he coined was *objectivist*, which he meant to designate only individual poets. If any generalization can be made about the aesthetic values of all the poets dubbed objectivists, it might be that they sought to "think with things as they exist" (Zukofsky's phrase), to extend the range of imagism while retaining its respect for things and for craft, and to open the poem to contemp. realities and historical context.

Though these poets differ widely from each other and never worked together as a group, they were bound by a loose network of affiliations that has been usefully characterized as a nexus. Reznikoff, Zukofsky, Oppen, and Rakosi were all Jewish; Reznikoff and Zukofsky grew up in immigrant households in New York and spent their lives in that city. Oppen lived there in the 1930s, and the three poets met and talked regularly. Niedecker, who spent her life in rural Wisconsin, wrote Zukofsky after reading the "Objectivists" issue of *Poetry*, and the two maintained an intense correspondence and exchange of mss. and critiques until Niedecker's death. Bunting corresponded regularly with both of them. Oppen, Rakosi, and Bunting stopped writing for several decades, returning to poetry in the 1960s. All these poets were highly educated but made modest livings, were leftist in their political views, and identified with the poor. The Depression, the Holocaust, and World War II made a deep impact on them.

Though the objectivists worked largely in obscurity, their poetry influenced a number of their younger contemporaries associated with Black Mountain College (see BLACK MOUNTAIN SCHOOL) and *projective verse, notably Robert Creeley and Robert Duncan, and some of the principal practitioners of *Language poetry, including Charles Bernstein and Ron Silliman.

*See* AVANT-GARDE POETICS, CREATIONISM.

■ *Poetry* 37.5 (1931) and *An "Objectivists" Anthology* (1932), both ed. L. Zukofsky; W. C. Williams, *Autobiography* (1951); L. S. Dembo, "The Objectivist Poet: Four Interviews," *Contemporary Literature* 10 (1969); S. Fauchereau, "Poetry in America: Objectivism," *Ironwood* 6 (1975); H. Kenner, *A Homemade World* (1975); R. Schiffer, "Die Poetik und Lyrik der Objektivisten," *Die amerikanische Literatur der Gegenwart*, ed. H. Bungert (1977); C. Altieri, "The Objectivist Tradition," *Chicago Review* 30 (1979); *Louis Zukofsky* (1979) and *Basil Bunting* (1980), both ed. C. F. Terrell; *George Oppen*, ed. B. Hatlen (1981); R. Silliman, "Third Phase Objectivism," *Paideuma* 10 (1981); L. Zukofsky, "An Objective," *Prepositions*, 2d ed. (1981); *Charles Reznikoff*, ed. M. Hindus (1984); N. M. Finkelstein, "What Was Objectivism?" *American Poetry* 2 (1985); "George Oppen: A Special Issue," *Ironwood* 26 (1985); M. Heller, *Conviction's Net of Branches* (1985); P. Makin, *Bunting* (1992); *Carl Rakosi*, ed. M. Heller (1993); *Niedecker and the Correspondence with Zukofsky* and *Lorine Niedecker*, both ed. J. Penberthy (1996); *The Objectivist Nexus*, ed. R. B. DuPlessis and P. Quartermain (1999); S. Fredman, *A Menorah for Athena* (2001); P. Nicholls, *George Oppen and the Fate of Modernism* (2007).

E. BERRY

**OBSCURITY.** *Obscurity* has a long hist. in poetry, but its causes have varied at different historical moments. One of the earliest and most significant forms of obscurity appears in med. *allegory. The impulse behind allegorical obscurity in the Middle Ages lies in the recoding of the OT in a modified figural system that could be used by readers of the NT, based on the premise that the subject matter of OT texts held a second, concealed meaning to be fulfilled in the future (see EXEGESIS). Characteristically, med. theorists did not always foreground the intrinsic elements of the text in a discernible formal arrangement but rather interpreted the fragmentary signs and traces embedded in the OT as veiled disclosures of a mysterious God's half-illuminated message. Because the subject matter was obscure, the deeper meaning of OT texts was assumed to be still hidden and subject to interpretation. Dante's *Divina commedia* is perhaps the best example of allegorical obscurity in med. lit. To the same category belongs the esoteric and obscure poetry of the *Dolce stil nuovo* of Guido Guinizzelli and Guido Cavalcanti. To be sure, obscure poetry was attacked in the 14th c. because it was thought to be unnecessarily incomprehensible and opaque. Nevertheless, Giovanni Boccaccio defended poetry in his *Genealogia deorum gentilium* (1360), where he argued that the value of a poem is heightened by the obstacles that stand in the way of its decipherment.

In Ren. Europe, disguised political commentary and theories were often concealed in a double-voiced allegorical obscurity whose meaning was hard to formulate—e.g., in Eng., Edmund Spenser's *Shepheardes Calender* (1579) and Philip Sidney's *Arcadia*

(1590, 1593). The devel. of obscurity in Ren. poetry was also influenced by the writings of Hermes Trismegistus (2d c. CE), disseminated in western Europe by Giordano Bruno. The exceedingly complex and intricate occult symbolism that the hermetic trad. brought to poetic lang. clearly contributed to the power and richness of Ren. poetry. In *The Faerie Queene* (1590, 1596), e.g., Spenser uses stellar symbolism and cosmology adapted from hermetic iconography. Other surviving remnants of hermetic obscurity are evident in a large number of Ren. works such as the poetry of Pontus de Tyard and Sor Juana Inés de la Cruz, Ben Jonson's *masques, John Milton's "L'Allegro" and "Il Penseroso," and the lyrics of Henry Vaughan and Thomas Traherne. Obscurity can also be found in 17th-c. *metaphysical poetry, where several heterogeneous elements combine to produce obscurity: *hyperbole and *conceit; deliberate syntactic inversions; and abstruse *diction employing terminology from alchemy, scholastic philosophy, astronomy, mathematics, and geography.

The obscurity of much 20th-c. poetry is characterized by a number of distinctive features: disjointed *syntax, broken lines, rupture, and *dissonance—a renunciation of the referential and communicative functions of lang. The intricate wordplay of poetry that developed under the influence of *symbolism, *futurism, *Dada, and other avant-garde movements is strange, unfamiliar, and esoteric in order to subvert conventional reading strategies. Instead of evoking the obscurity of spirit, the unconscious, or the distant past, Rus. modernist poets explore the effects of loosening the connections of lang. and meaning. In the years following the 1917 revolution, the futurist poets Vladimir Mayakovsky and Velimir Khlebnikov sought to open up lang. by separating out its basic building blocks (morphemes, syllables). *Zaum'* or "transsense" poetry does not so much abandon meaning as push the emphasis toward *sound and *rhythm (see SOUND POETRY). Khlebnikov's poem "Incantation by Laughter" repeats a series of neologisms generated from the Rus. word *shmekhat* (laughter). The series—*laughicate, laugherino, laughify*—imitates the repetitive sounds of laughter, in addition to foregrounding how nouns and verbs are constructed.

The formal devel. of obscurity has been accompanied by a proliferation of programmatic and justificatory statements: "There is a certain glory in not being understood" (Charles Baudelaire); "I utter the word in order to plunge in back into its inanity" (Stéphane Mallarmé); "I have no language, only images, analogies, symbols" (W. B. Yeats). Schwartz locates the obscurity of mod. poetry in the *"dissociation of sensibility" that T. S. Eliot argued took place in the 17th c. when emotions and sensibilities became subordinate to the instrumental categories of science. There thus emerges a mechanistic rationality that reaches its full devel. in the sterile classificatory schemas of 19th-c. science. A poetic sensibility rooted in a common lang. can no longer exist in such a society, and unable to express himself or herself in shared ling. usage, a poet must slip into an idiosyncratic and specialized discourse.

In the late 20th c., discussion focused less on social diagnoses than on the interpretive codes through which the critic tries to decipher the poem. Riffaterre suggests that a "hermeneutic model" is at work within the poem, helping readers to unravel the peculiarities of the text. Such a model offers readers "a frame of thought or a signifying system that tells the reader how or where to look for a solution, or from what angle the text can be seen as decipherable" (see HYPOGRAM, SEMIOTICS AND POETRY). Significantly, Riffaterre emphasizes words or phrases that "resist deciphering or whose reason for being is hard to judge." Hence, *interpretation is encoded within the site of obscurity in the poem.

In the last decades of the 20th c., poets associated with the Language group and the jour. of the same name sought to free poetry from the burden of meaning and the hierarchy of the sentence (see LANGUAGE POETRY). Drawing on the structuralist observation of the arbitrary relationship between ling. signifier (word or sound) and the signified (the concept designated) and on the poststructuralist insights into the instability within any ling. sign (see SIGN, SIGNIFIED, SIGNIFIER), Language poetry attempted to detach words from meaning by foregrounding their materiality: the shape and density of letters, relations to other words and to the page. Charles Bernstein's poem "Veil," lines of overtyped text forming a "technical palimpsest" (Dworkin), an intricate veil of effaced words; Susan Howe's "Melville's Marginality," constructed from vertical and slanted overwritten blocks of text; Christian Bök's *Eunoia*, built out of prose sections each focused on only one of the five vowels; David Melnick's "Pcoet," formed with intrusive consonants rendering words unreadable—all these practices demonstrate a self-reflective use of lang. to interrupt deliberately the conventional action of horizontal reading and highlight the poem as printed artifact. In Bernstein's poetics (1992), the unreadable text is situated at the cusp of "the field of human language and the inhumanness of sheer materiality." Similarly, for Silliman, Language poetry does not turn away from meaning but instead situates it as "a construct built from the determinate code of language," compelling readers to attend to the conflicted social processes that shape a poem, incl. the ink, markings, and paper, the disposition of material units. These new practices echo Ludwig Wittgenstein's entreaty: "don't think, but look" (quoted in Dworkin).

In the 21st c., the technological capacities of computers have been used by cyberpoets to produce dynamic, mobile forms of poetry (see CYBERTEXT, ELECTRONIC POETRY). Letters circulate across the screen, sometimes forming words, sometimes not; words appear and move into different configurations; the entire poem may disappear, leaving a blank screen, perhaps the ultimate form of obscurity in poetry (see, e.g., Brian Kim Stefans's "The Dreamlife of Letters"). Because the electronic text brings movement to what was a static page, Stefans compares the poet to a choreographer and the poem to a ballet. Perloff, however, cautions not to "fetishize digital presentation" and urges readers and viewers to consider Stefans's reconstruction of a commentary by Rachel Blau DuPlessis, a very traditional intertextual engagement embedded within the cybertext but made obscure by the constant movement of the letters and words. As in modernist poetry, obscurity in Language poetry and cyberpoetry initiates a process of *defamiliarization, provoking readers to approach the poem with new and different strategies of comprehension.

Discussions about the obscurity of mod. and contemp. poetry are not limited to Western crit. Tay has shown that controversy about obscurity (*menglong*) in poetry extends to post-Maoist China. In the 1970s and 1980s, poets such as Gu Cheng, Wang Xiaoni, and others created a corpus of work whose expression resembles imagist poetry. More recently, Wang comments that the experimental writings of the Feifei school of poetry (Daozi, Zhou Lunyou, and others) challenge canonical modernist writings with a style influenced by Western avant-garde poets.

*See* CLOSE READING, DIFFICULTY, EXPLICATION.

■ E. Holmes, *Henry Vaughan and the Hermetic Philosophy* (1932); D. Schwartz, "The Isolation of Modern Poetry," *KR* 3 (1941); R. Daniells, "English Baroque and Deliberate Obscurity," *JAAC* 5 (1946); Eliot, "The Metaphysical Poets"; Auerbach, ch. 8; E. J. Brown, *Mayakovsky: A Poet in the Revolution* (1973); D. C. Allen, *Mysteriously Meant* (1979); F. Yates, *Giordano Bruno and the Hermetic Tradition* (1978), and *The Occult Philosophy in the Elizabethan Age* (1979); D. Brookes-Davis, *The Mercurian Monarch* (1983); *The L=A=N=G=U=A=G=E Book*, ed. B. Andrews and C. Bernstein (1984)— esp. R. Silliman, "If by 'Writing' We Mean Literature"; M. Riffaterre, "Hermeneutic Models," *PoT* 4 (1983); A. Patterson, *Censorship and Interpretation* (1984); *In the American Tree*, ed. R. Silliman (1986)—anthol. of Language poetry; G. Hartley, *Textual Politics and the Language Poets* (1989); M. Perloff, *Radical Artifice: Writing Poetry in the Age of Media* (1991); C. Bernstein, *A Poetics* (1992); C. Dworkin, *Reading the Illegible* (2003); *New Media Poetics: Contexts, Technotexts, and Theories*, ed. A. Morris and T. Swiss (2006)—esp. B. K. Stefans and D. Wershler-Henry, "Toward a Poetics for Circulars"; W. Tay, "Obscure Poetry," *After Mao: Chinese Literature and Society, 1987–81*, ed. J. C. Kinkley (1985); N. Wang, *Translated Modernities* (2010); UbuWeb, http://ubuweb.com/.

P. McCallum

**OCCASIONAL VERSE.** All literary works are occasioned in some sense; occasional verse differs in having not a private but a public or social occasion. From Pindar's *odes to Walt Whitman's "When Lilacs Last in the Dooryard Bloom'd," poets have found public occasions for writing: e.g., the memorial pieces in honor of Edward King, among which John Milton's "Lycidas" was one; the odes expected of a *poet laureate; tributes to a poet placed at the beginning of his volume, esp. in the 16th and 17th cs.; *epithalamia, such as those

by Edmund Spenser and John Donne; funeral *elegies, respectful or ironic; *sonnets or odes memorializing some state occasion or historic event; or the prologues and epilogues to 17th- and 18th-c. plays. Counterparts abound in modernist and contemp. poetry; W. B. Yeats, Ezra Pound, and W. C. Williams wrote a good deal of occasional verse. Some mod. occasional poems are Thomas Hardy's "On an Invitation to the United States," Yeats's "Easter, 1916," and W. H. Auden's "September 1, 1939." Although occasional verse is often associated with poets from the Ren. through the Enlightenment, that is too narrow a view, as is also the restriction to Eur. writers. Islamic poetry is rich in *panegyrics founded on occasion, as is Korean. With their strong assumption of the historical purchase of poetry, Chinese poets typically write occasional verse. Japanese poems of the court period specify occasions, if only fictional, in their headnotes. In short, although occasional verse is often taken to be ephemeral or trivial or public, it is difficult to devise theoretical terms to distinguish rigorously among "Lycidas," Emily Dickinson's imaginary occasions of her own death, Robert Lowell's "For the Union Dead," and various Asian examples. On the other hand, to be dismissive is to violate the most serious conceptions of much of the world's lyric poetry, and even narrative and drama may arise from occasion.

*See* ENCOMIUM, EPIDEICTIC POETRY, EPINIKION.

■ R. Haller, "Gelegenheitsdichtung," *Reallexikon*; P. Matvejevic, *La poésie de circonstance et l'engagement en poésie*, diss., Univ. of Paris (1967); E. M. Oppenheimer, *Goethe's Poetry for Occasions* (1974); W. Segebrecht, *Die Gelegenheitsgedicht* (1977); M. Z. Sugano, *The Poetics of the Occasion* (1992); *Theorie und Praxis der Kasualdichtung in der Frühen Neuzeit*, ed. A. Keller et al. (2010).

E. MINER; A.J.M. SMITH; T.V.F. BROGAN

**OCCITAN POETRY.** The root of the term *Occitan* is the word *oc* (yes) in the lang. of med. southern France, in contrast to OF *oïl* (stressed like mod. Fr. *oui*) and It. *si*; Dante made this triple distinction in his *De vulgari eloquentia* (*On Vernacular Eloquence*, ca. 1304). The Occitan lang. has been called *langue d'oc*, Provençal, and other names since the 12th c. The term *Provençal* was long preferred but has the disadvantage that it seems to refer specifically to Provence (Lat. *Provincia Romana*, the region of Gaul nearest to Rome), which is the area east of the Rhône and home of the 19th-c. poet Frédéric Mistral (1830–1914; see below), but only one part of the larger area from the Atlantic to the Alps where the lang. is or was spoken. As a geographical term, *Languedoc* refers to the territory west of the Rhône. *Occitan* is free from misleading specificity and enjoys increasing acceptance, although it was introduced only recently in both Fr. (1886) and Eng. (1940).

From the time before the *troubadours, who appeared ca. 1100, we have a handful of very short poetic texts, most of them fragmentary, that date from the 10th and 11th cs. The oldest one appears to be a birthing *charm; another is a fragment of a passion narrative, yet another a religious *alba in Lat. with a refrain in Occitan. A fragmentary proto-*canso (see below) evokes the lover as a hawk, while a fragmentary and obscure proto-*sirventes seems to criticize amorous nuns. Narrative verse begins with the *Boeci*, a longer but incomplete paraphrase of Boethius's *Consolation of Philosophy* that was written about 1000 and continues with the *Chanson de Sainte Foy*, a life of the child saint from about 1050.

In their halcyon days, the troubadours sang of *courtly love (which they called *fin'amor* or "true love") and a range of other subjects. Scholars debate whether William IX, Duke of Aquitaine and Count of Poitiers (1071–1126), was the first troubadour who composed or merely the first whose compositions have been transmitted to us. Among William's 11 (or 10) extant poems, some describe the humility and devotion of the courtly lover, but others express explicit eroticism: in one, sometimes called a *fabliau,* the narrator is a sexual athlete and far from humble. In another, William takes leave of earthly power, perhaps because of an imminent departure on crusade or because he believed he soon would die. In the next generation, the moralist Marcabru (fl. 1130–49) scourged the sexual license of married men and women but also retold encounters of a first-person narrator with a young girl. In one of these, the prototypical *pastorela* (see PASTOURELLE), the narrator attempts to seduce the girl, but she steadfastly refuses; in another, a girl curses the king who called her lover away on crusade. In the middle years of the 12th c., Peire d'Alvernhe (fl. 1149–68) developed a theory of difficult style, or *trobar clus* (closed composition), which involved elaborate sound patterns, unexpected rhymes, obscure vocabulary, and difficult syntax. Raimbaut d'Aurenga (ca. 1144–73) advocated such an abstruse manner in a debate with Giraut de Bornelh (fl. 1162–99), who defended *trobar leu* or the easy style. Bernart de Ventadorn (fl. 1147–70 or perhaps somewhat later), considered one of the greatest love poets among the troubadours, sang with an air of deceptive simplicity about his adoration for his lady, the joy of love and the grief of yearning, and less frequently about his ecstasy in sexual fulfillment.

By about 1170, the troubadours had developed a set of generic concepts. In terms of this system, their 2,500-odd extant poems comprise about 1,000 cansos or love songs, about 500 sirventes or satires, and about 500 *coblas* or individual stanzas, while those remaining include the pastorela or pastourelle, the alba or dawn poem, debate poems such as the *tenso* and the *partimen*, the *planh* or funeral lament, and minor genres. Bertran de Born (ca. 1150–1215), whose castle of Altafort was besieged and taken by Richard Lionheart, sang sirventes of political passion with the commitment of a lord who regarded warfare as a source of moral stature. The male aristocratic mentality also informs the *chanson de geste* of Giraut de Roussillon (ca. 1150), written in an artificial blend of Occitan and Fr., and the parodic romance *Jaufre* (late 12th c.; see MEDIEVAL ROMANCE).

In the early 13th c., the Occitan region was the scene of the Albigensian Crusade, waged at the invitation of the pope by a Fr. leader, Simon de Montfort, against the heretical Cathars who were centered at Albi. According to a long-standing interpretation, the crusade destroyed the courtly society that had nourished the troubadours and so destined Occitan poetry to inevitable decline. However, it is doubtful that this conflict, which was one among many, played so decisive a role. Peire Cardenal (fl. 1205–72) criticized the Church for the failings of unworthy priests, incl. members of the Inquisition, while expressing his own orthodox piety. Perhaps the mid-13th c. saw the composition of the delightful romance of *Flamenca*, whose heroine succeeds, despite the cruelty of her jealous husband, in enjoying the love of a perfect knight. Late in the century, Guiraut Riquier (fl. 1254–92) complained of the insecurity of the courtier's life and lamented that he had come among the last of the troubadours. In the early 14th c., poets of the school of Toulouse turned to increasingly religious themes, esp. the praise of the Virgin. Only one poet of this period, Raimon de Cornet (fl. 1324–40), has left an extensive body of work incl. lyrics, verse letters, didactic texts, and two poems in Lat. Both priest and friar, Raimon de Cornet indulged in a ribald tale of his mistress's revenge for his infidelity, but in another mood, he seriously defended the value of poetry.

Though we have the melodies of only one-tenth of the troubadour poems, it has often been assumed that virtually all of them were set to music. The troubadour wrote both text and melody, which were performed by the *joglar* (see JONGLEUR). Joglars and troubadours traveled widely: William IX on crusade to Syria, Marcabru and Guiraut Riquier to Spain, Bertran de Born to northern France. Peire Vidal (fl. 1183–1204) ventured as far as Hungary. These travels contributed to the diffusion of the art form into other langs. starting at the end of the 12th c. in Fr. (see TROUVÈRE) and Ger. (see MINNESANG), and continuing in the 13th c. in It. at the court of the Emperor Frederick II (see SICILIAN SCHOOL), and in Galician-Port. (see GALICIA, POETRY OF). The heritage of the troubadours was acknowledged by Dante and Petrarch, who extended their indirect influence throughout the Europe of the Ren. (see PETRARCHISM) and beyond. Poets of the 20th c. who returned to the troubadours include Ezra Pound, Paul Blackburn, and W. D. Snodgrass in Eng., Jacques Roubaud in Fr., and Augusto de Campos in Port.

A trad. of commentary on the troubadours and their songs began in the early 13th c. with Raimon Vidal's prose *Razos de trobar* (Principles of Composition) and continued with the *Donatz proensals* (Provençal Grammar) of Uc Faidit. Uc and other writers compiled the *razos*, brief prose commentaries on individual songs, and the *vidas*, or lives of the troubadours. Around 1290, Matfre Ermengau (fl. 1288–1322) attempted to reconcile the love sung by the troubadours with love of God in his encyclopedic verse *Breviari d'amor* (Breviary of Love).

During the 14th and 15th cs., Occitan poetry fell into decline. The trad. was maintained at Toulouse by the *Consistori de la Sobregaia Companhia del Gay Saber* (Consistory of the Merry Band of the Gay Knowledge—see GAI SABER), which awarded prizes for the best compositions in various troubadour genres (see POETIC CONTESTS). The regulations of these contests were codified in a taxonomy of troubadour practice called *Las Leys d'amors* (ca. 1341), understood as equivalent to a code of poetry. We are still indebted to *Las Leys d'amors* for definitions of the genres and for prosodic distinctions such as those among *coblas unissonans*, in which all the stanzas of a song have the same rhyme sounds; *coblas singulars*, in which the rhyme sounds change with every stanza; *coblas doblas*, in which given rhyme sounds are maintained for two stanzas; *coblas ternas*, in which they are maintained for three stanzas; and *coblas quaternas*, in which they are maintained for four. In *coblas capcaudadas*, the first line of one stanza uses the rhyme sound of the last line of the preceding stanza, whereas in *coblas capfinidas*, the first line of one stanza repeats a key word from the last line of the preceding one. In *coblas retrogradadas*, the rhymes of a stanza repeat those of the preceding one but do so in reverse order. In all these permutations of concrete rhyme sounds, the abstract rhyme scheme remains constant. On the other hand, the authority of the *Leys* has obscured evolutionary devels. in troubadour practice. We are only beginning to realize the implications of the fact that the earliest troubadours used no generic distinctions among types of song, hence that the devel. of the generic system requires explanation. Another fundamental evolution occurred in the practice of metrical imitation, or *contrafacture*, which gradually became characteristic of the sirventes but was adopted in the *Leys* as its timeless defining trait. The elaborate rhyme patterns of the troubadours analyzed by the *Leys* are only a few of the endless variations of their technique.

The fate of Occitan may be illustrated in the career of Gaston Fébus, the powerful Count of Foix (1331–91). Although he requested that the Lat. encyclopedia by Bartholomaeus Anglicus, *De Proprietatibus Rerum* (On the Properties of Things), be translated into Occitan, in which it became the *Elucidari de las proprietatz de totas res naturals* (Elucidarium of the Properties of All Natural Things), Gaston Fébus chose to use Fr. for his own treatise on hunting and Fr. and Lat. for his collection of prayers. In Occitan, he composed only a single love song. The 14th-c. *Jeu de Sainte Agnès* shows verve in its elaboration of the traditional story and in its use of music, but two cycles of mystery plays from the 15th and 16th cs. are less successful. When, in the edict of Villers-Cotterêts (1539), Francis I decreed that Fr. (and not Lat.) must be the lang. of administration throughout his kingdom, he laid royal claim on the practice of law, against the claim of the Church. Occitan was gradually excluded from usage in law and in other areas.

Historians of Occitan poetry speak of a first Ren. in the 16th c., illustrated by the Gascon Protestant Pey de Garros (ca. 1525–81), the Provençal Bellaud de la Bellaudière (ca. 1543–88), and Pierre Godolin of Toulouse

(1580–1649). A second Ren. in the 19th c. was marked by the group of seven poets called the *\*Félibrige*, led by Mistral. Despite continuing factional disputes, Occitan poetry grew broader in appeal during the 20th c. with the work of poets such as Max Rouquette (1908–2005) and Bernat Manciet (1923–2005). A number of figures such as René Nelli (1906–82), Charles Camproux (1908–94), Pierre Bec (b. 1921), and Robert Lafont (1923–2009) are both troubadour scholars and practicing poets. The composer and singer Claudi Martí (b. 1940), who recorded troubadour songs, allied Occitan poetry with the regionalist movement during the 1970s.

*See* AL-ANDALUS, POETRY OF; FRANCE, POETRY OF; TROBAIRITZ.

■ **Anthologies**: *Trouvères et Minnesänger*, ed. I. Frank (1952); *Les Troubadours*, ed. R. Lavaud and R. Nelli, 2 v. (1960–66); *Anthologie de la poésie occitane 1900–1960*, ed. A. Lafont (1962); *Anthology of Troubadour Lyric Poetry*, ed. A. Press (1971); *La lírica religiosa en la literatura provenzal antigua*, ed. F. J. Oroz Arizcuren (1972); *Anthology of the Provençal Troubadours*, ed. R. Hill and T. Bergin, 2d ed., 2 v. (1973); *Lyrics of the Troubadours and Trouvères*, ed. F. Goldin (1973); *Los Trovadores*, ed. M. de Riquer, 3 v. (1975); *Anthologie des troubadours*, ed. P. Bec (1979); F. Hamlin et al., *Introduction à l'étude de l'ancien provençal*, 2d ed. (1985); M. Switten et al., *The Medieval Lyric*, 3 v. (1987–88); *Trobairitz*, ed. A. Rieger (1991); *Chants d'amour des femmes-troubadours*, ed. P. Bec (1995); R. Lafont and P. Gardy, *Histoire et anthologie de la littérature occitane*, 2 v. (1997)—to 1789; W. D. Paden, *An Introduction to Old Occitan* (1998); *Songs of the Troubadours and Trouvères*, ed. S. N. Rosenberg et al. (1998); *Songs of the Women Troubadours*, ed. M. Bruckner et al. (2000).

■ **Bibliographies**: A. Pillet and H. Carstens, *Bibliographie der Troubadours* (1933); C. A. Knudson and J. Misrahi in Fisher; F. Pic, *Bibliographie des sources bibliographiques du domaine occitan* (1977); R. Taylor, *La Littérature occitane du moyen âge* (1977); F. Zufferey, *Bibliographie des poètes provençaux des XIVe et XVe siècles* (1981); M. L. Switten, *Music and Poetry in the Middle Ages: A Guide to Research on French and Occitan Song, 1100–1400* (1995); P. Ricketts, *Concordance de l'Occitan Médiéval: COM2, Les troubadours, Les textes narratifs en vers* (2005)—electronic resource with complete texts, bibl., and concordance program.

■ **Criticism and History**: Jeanroy; Patterson; C. Camproux, *Histoire de la littérature occitane* (1953); H.-I. Marrou (pseud. H. Davenson), *Les Troubadours* (1961); M. Lazar, *Amour courtois et "fin'amors" dans la litt. du XIIe siècle* (1964); R. Lafont and C. Anatole, *Nouvelle Histoire de la littérature occitane*, 2 v. (1970); J. J. Wilhelm, *Seven Troubadours* (1970); L. M. Paterson, *Troubadours and Eloquence* (1975); L. Topsfield, *Troubadours and Love* (1975); R. Boase, *The Origin and Meaning of Courtly Love* (1976); D. Rieger, *Gattungen und Gattungsbezeichnungen der Trobadorlyrik* (1976); N. B. Smith, *Figures of Repetition in the Old Provençal Lyric* (1976); P. Makin, *Provence and Pound* (1978); *GRLMA* v. 2.1 (1979–90); U. Mölk, *Trobadorlyrik*

(1982); J. J. Wilhelm, *Il Miglior Fabbro: The Cult of the Difficult in Daniel, Dante, and Pound* (1982); J. Gruber, *Die Dialektik des Trobar* (1983); J. Roubaud, *La fleur inverse: essai sur l'art formel des troubadours* (1986); M. R. Menocal, *The Arabic Role in Medieval Literary History* (1987); L. Kendrick, *The Game of Love* (1988); C. Di Girolamo, *I Trovatori* (1989); S. Gaunt, *Troubadours and Irony* (1989); Hollier; S. Kay, *Subjectivity in Troubadour Poetry* (1990); A. E. van Vleck, *Memory and Re-Creation in Troubadour Lyric* (1991); L. M. Paterson, *The World of the Troubadours* (1993); P. Cherchi, *Andreas and the Ambiguity of Courtly Love* (1994); *Handbook of the Troubadours*, ed. F.R.P. Akehurst and J. M. Davis (1995); G. A. Bond, *The Loving Subject* (1995)—troubadours and med. Lat.; S. Gaunt, *Gender and Genre in Medieval French Literature* (1995); W. D. Paden, "The Troubadours and the Albigensian Crusade: A Long View," *RPh* 49 (1995); P. Dronke, *The Medieval Lyric*, 3d ed. (1996); G. Brunel-Lobrichon and C. Duhamel-Amado, *Au temps des troubadours* (1997)—external hist.; M. Winter-Hosman, "Domna et dame: Images différentes?" *Le Rayonnement des troubadours* (1998); *Troubadours*, ed. S. Gaunt and S. Kay (1999); W. Calin, *Minority Literatures and Modernism: Scots, Breton, and Occitan, 1920–1990* (2000); O. Holmes, *Assembling the Lyric Self* (2000)—authorship from troubadours to It. poets; D. Vitaglione, *The Literature of Provence* (2000), and *A Literary Guide to Provence* (2001)—east of the Rhône; A. Callahan, *Writing the Voice of Pleasure* (2001); F. L. Cheyette, *Ermengard of Narbonne and the World of the Troubadours* (2001); L. Lazzerini, *Letteratura medievale in lingua d'oc* (2001); D. P. Bec, *Per un païs . . . : Écrits sur la langue et la littérature occitanes modernes* (2002) and "Prétroubadouresque ou paratroubadouresque? Un Antécédent médiéval d'un motif de chanson folklorique Si j'étais une hirondelle," *Cahiers de civilisation médiévale* 47 (2004); W. D. Paden, "Before the Troubadours: The Archaic Occitan Texts and the Shape of Literary History," *De Sens Rassis*, ed. K. Busby et al. (2005); S. Gaunt, *Love and Death in Medieval French and Occitan Courtly Literature* (2006); W. D. Paden, "Provençal and the Troubadours," *Ezra Pound in Context*, ed. I. B. Nadel (2010); W. D. Paden and F. F. Paden, "Swollen Woman, Shifting Canon: A Midwife's Charm and the Birth of Occitan Poetry," *PMLA* 125 (2010).

■ **Translations**: *Personae*, trans. E. Pound (1926); *Songs of the Troubadours*, trans. A. Bonner (1972); *Six Troubadour Songs*, trans. W. D. Snodgrass (1976); *Proensa*, trans. P. Blackburn (1978); *Mais provençais: Raimbaut e Arnaut*, trans. A. de Campos, 2d ed. (1987); *Lark in the Morning*, trans. R. Kehew et al. (2005); *Troubadour Poems from the South of France*, trans. W. D. Paden and F. F. Paden (2007).

■ **Versification and Music**: Patterson, v. 1.1.2; Lote; F. M. Chambers, "Imitation of Form in the Old Provençal Lyric," *RPh* 6 (1952–53); I. Frank, *Répertoire métrique de la poésie des troubadours*, 2 v. (1953–57); F. Gennrich, *Das musikalische Nachlass der Troubadours*, 3 v. (1958–65); F. Gennrich, "Troubadours, trouvères," *MGG*, v. 13 (1966); H. van der Werf, *The Chansons of the Troubadours and Trouvères* (1972); *Las cançons dels trobadors*, ed. I. Fernandez de la Cuesta (1979); U. Mölk, "Zur Metrik der Trobadors," *GRLMA*, v. 2.1 (1979–90); P. Bec, "Le problème des genres chez les premiers troubadours," *Cahiers de civilisation médiévale* 25 (1982); *The Extant Troubadour Melodies*, ed. H. van der Werf and G. Bond (1984); Chambers; F. A. Gallo, *Music in the Castle* (1995)—Occitan troubadours in Italy; E. Aubrey, *The Music of the Troubadours* (1996), and "Genre as a Determinant of Melody in the Songs of the Troubadours and the Trouvères," *Medieval Lyric*, ed. W. D. Paden (2000); J. Haines, *Eight Centuries of Troubadours and Trouvères* (2004); W. D. Paden, "What Singing Does to Words: Reflections on the Art of the Troubadours," *Exemplaria* 17 (2005).

W. D. PADEN

**OCTAVE** (rarely, octet). A *stanza of eight lines. Octaves appear as isolable stanzas, such as the It. *ottava rima* (rhyming *ababbcc*) and the Fr. *ballade* (*ababbcbc*), as well as the single octave in Fr. called the *huitain* and the single *ballade* stanza in Eng. called the *monk's tale stanza after Chaucer's usage. The octave is the stanza of the first rank in *Occitan poetry, a favorite of the *troubadours; and although the *trouvères* of northern France are less exclusive, they still show a preference for the octave: roughly a third of all extant OF lyrics are set in one form or another of octave. In Sp., the octave of octosyllables rhyming *abbaacca*, less often *ababbccb* or *abbaacac*, is called the *copla de arte menor*; that of 12-syllable lines, the *copla de arte mayor*. In It., the Sicilian octave in hendecasyllables rhyming *ababababab* first appears in the 13th c. In ON skaldic poetry, the most important stanzas are *drottkvætt* and *hrynhent*, octaves of six- and eight-syllable lines, respectively. In Rus. poetry, which favors *quatrains, poets frequently connect two quatrains to form octaves, as in Alexander Pushkin, or vary rhyme schemes; e.g., Fyodor Tiutchev and Marina Tsvetaeva formed their own octaves with uneven rhyme schemes (*aabccbba* and *ababacac*, respectively).

Octaves are also important components of larger stanzas: the first eight lines of the *sonnet are called the octave. P. B. Shelley uses octaves for "The Witch of Atlas," as does John Keats for "Isabella." "I have finished the First Canto, a long one, of about 180 octaves," says Lord Byron in a letter apropos of *Don Juan*. G. M. Hopkins uses the scheme *ababcbca* for "The Wreck of the Deutschland." Osip Mandelstam composed a famous set of varying octaves in the early 1930s, the "Vos'mistishiia." John Berryman uses heterometrical octaves in *abcbddba* for "Homage to Mistress Bradstreet" (1953). Louis Zukofsky's *80 Flowers* is a sequence of 81 octaves.

■ Schipper; R. Beum, "Yeats's Octaves," *TSLL* 3 (1961); R. Moran, "The Octaves of E. A. Robinson," *Colby Quarterly* 7 (1969).

T.V.F. BROGAN; K. M. CAMPBELL

**OCTONARIUS.** The Lat. equivalent of the Gr. acatalectic *tetrameter, iambic, trochaic, or anapestic, used in Roman comedy, and of which the units are feet, not metra (see METRON). The iambic octonarius of Plautus has two forms: the first with a medial *diaeresis, with the seventh position short, and with the eighth allowing *brevis in longo* (see ANCEPS), having the effect of creating two iambic *quaternarii*; the second with a *caesura after the ninth position. This meter is rarely used as stichic verse but often in cantica (see CANTICUM AND DIVERBIUM). The trochaic octonarius is only a meter of cantica. Having medial diaeresis, it too might be regarded as a system of trochaic *quaternarii*, as might the anapestic. ■ Beare, 137–40; Crusius; C. Questa, *Introduzione alla metrica di Plauto* (1967); Halporn et al.

J. W. HALPORN

**OCTOSYLLABLE.** A line of eight syllables, one of the two most popular line forms in the Eur. vernaculars: the chief line form in Sp. poetry, the oldest in Fr., and the second most important in Eng. It derives presumably from the iambic *dimeter line of med. Lat. hymnody, established by Ambrose in the 4th c. and pervasive in the later Middle Ages. In Fr., the octosyllable first appears in the 10th c. in the *Vie de Saint Léger* (40 sixains in *couplets) and is the most popular meter of OF and Anglo-Norman narrative poetry (excluding the *chansons de geste*, which adopted first the *decasyllable, then the *alexandrine) of the 12th through 15th c.—i.e., chronicles, romances (e.g., Wace), saints' lives, *lais*, *fabliaux*, and *dits*—and was esp. favored (along with the decasyllable) for the *courtly love lyric (esp. *ballades and *rondeaux) and popular lyric genres (*chansons de toile*, *pastourelles*) from the 14th to the mid-16th c. It is also common in med. drama. Finally, it is the staple meter of folk verse, of poetry of the oral trad., as in the late med. ballads. In succeeding centuries, the octosyllable never lost the close connections thus established to hymnody, song, and orality, and (esp. in couplets) to narrative.

After 1500, Pierre de Ronsard and François de Malherbe made it the meter of the *ode, but in post-Ren. Fr. poetry, the octosyllable became associated with *light verse: even as late as the 18th c., Alain René Le Sage, Alexis Piron, and Voltaire used it for popular appeal. Its lability and the swift return of its rhymes have given it a reputation for alertness, impertinence, and zest. In rhythmical structure, the *octosyllabe* is mercurial and often ambiguous: it has only one fixed accent, on the eighth syllable, either one or two secondary accents, and no *caesura. This ambiguity derives from the fact that it is caught uneasily between the three-accent norm of the decasyllable and the two-accent norm of the hexasyllable, thus frequently inviting both a two-accent and a three-accent reading, e.g., Théodore de Banville: "Quand je baise, pâle de fièvre" (3 + 5 syllables or 3 + 2 + 3). Whereas the alexandrine is the line of sustained discourse, usually enjoying a certain syntactic completeness, the octosyllable parcels syntax into a series of fragmentary tableaux or near-autonomous images that can stand in a variety of potential relationships with each other. These are the qualities that attracted Théophile Gautier (*Émaux et camées*, 1852) and the symbolist poets to octosyllabic verse.

Spain received octosyllables (normally in varied *rhyme schemes rather than couplets) in the 14th c. (Juan Ruiz, *Libro de buen amor*) from the Occitan *troubadours by way of Galician-Port. sources; these reinforced a native tendency toward the octosyllable in earlier Sp. poetry. By the 15th c., the Sp. *octosílabo* was firmly established through collections of courtly lyrics (e.g., the *Cancionero de Baena*) and since that time has come to be the national meter par excellence in Spain (see SPANISH PROSODY). There is no set rhythmical pattern: the only requirement is that the line contain from seven to nine syllables (endings vary) with stress on the seventh.

In Eng., the octosyllable is, in the Latinate terminology of foot metrics, commonly called iambic *tetrameter; in Ger., it is called the *Kurzzeile* or *Kurzvers*. Occasionally, it is trochaic, and when so, often catalectic (see CATALEXIS), the "8s and 7s" giving a special (and powerful) effect, as in the stanzas of W. H. Auden's elegy to W. B. Yeats beginning "Earth receive an honored guest." It forms the staple line of several stanzas, such as the long meter of the ballads (see BALLAD METER) and the *In Memoriam stanza but is more commonly associated with couplets. Lord Byron's reference to "the fatal facility of the octo-syllabic meter" alludes to the danger of singsong monotony, a danger offset, however, by the rapid movement of the line, which makes it an excellent medium for narrative verse. But in the hands of a skilled craftsman, monotony is not difficult to avoid, as evidenced by John Milton's "Il Penseroso" and J. W. Goethe's "Selige Sehnsucht."

In England, the influence of the Fr. octosyllable in the 12th and 13th cs. through Anglo-Norman poets such as Geoffrey Gaimar, Wace, and Benoît de Sainte-Maure led to a refinement in the syllabic regularity of the indigenous ME four-stress line used for narrative verse (Layamon; *The Owl and the Nightingale*; *Sir Orfeo*; John Barbour's *Bruce*). Chaucer translated part of the *Roman de la Rose*, which is in octosyllabic couplets, from which, according to the received theory, he learned to adapt, *mutatis mutandis*, the metrical structures of the OF line to the exigencies of the Eng. lang. The octosyllables of *The Book of the Duchess* and *The House of Fame* yield to the decasyllables of the *Canterbury Tales*. Chaucer's successors, esp. John Gower (*Confessio amantis*), could not equal his flexibility. The octosyllable finds heavy use in the miracle and morality plays but a lessening use in the 16th c. (chiefly songs). After 1600, the tetrameter becomes the vehicle of shorter poems, descriptive or philosophical, by Ben Jonson, Milton ("L'Allegro" and "Il Penseroso"), Andrew Marvell ("To His Coy Mistress"), John Gay, Matthew Prior, Jonathan Swift (his favorite meter, e.g., "Verses on the Death of Dr. Swift"), William Collins, and others; the jogging, satiric octosyllables and polysyllabic rhymes of Samuel Butler's *Hudibras* (1663–78) canonized the name—*hudibrastic verse. In the

19th c., narrative verse both serious and whimsical was again written in the "8s" as Robert Burns, William Wordsworth, and S. T. Coleridge ("Christabel," in couplets), but esp. Lord Byron, Walter Scott, John Keats, and William Morris ("The Earthly Paradise") brought the tetrameter couplet to a height it had not seen since ME.

However, it is dangerous to treat all eight-syllable lines as a class, without due adjustment for the differences in metrical systems of each national poetry. One cannot treat the Sp. *octosílabo*, the Fr. *octosyllabe*, the Lat. *octonarius*, and the Eng. iambic tetrameter, e.g., as necessary equivalents—i.e., as having the same structure or effects. Each resides within a distinctive verse system dependent in part on the lang. in which it operates. As Michel Grimaud has put it, "eight is a different number" in langs. such as Fr. and Eng.

■ C. M. Lewis, *The Foreign Sources of Modern English Versification* (1898); E. P. Shannon, "Chaucer's Use of the Octosyllabic Verse," *JEGP* 12 (1913); Thieme, 373 ff.; P. Verrier, *Le Vers français*, 3 v. (1931–32); P.-A. Becker, *Der gepaarte Achtsilber in der französischen Dichtung* (1934); E.N.S. Thompson, "The Octosyllabic Couplet," *PQ* 18 (1939); D. C. Clarke, "The Spanish Octosyllable," *HR* 10 (1942); Lote; J. Saavedra Molina, *El octosílabo castellano* (1945); M. D. Legge, *Anglo-Norman Literature and Its Background* (1963); F. Deloffre, *Le Vers français* (1969); Elwert; Navarro; C. Scott, *A Question of Syllables* (1986); E. B. Vitz, "Rethinking Old French Literature: The Orality of the Octosyllabic Couplet," *RR* 77 (1986); J. Kittay, "On Octo," *RR* 78 (1987); S. R. Guthrie, "Machaut and the Octosyllabe," *Chaucer's French Contemporaries*, ed. R. B. Palmer (1999); R. Noyer, "Generative Metrics and Old French Octosyllabic Verse," *Language Variation and Change* 14 (2002).

T.V.F. BROGAN; C. SCOTT

**ODE** (Gr. *aeidein*, "to sing," "to chant"). In mod. usage, the term for the most formal, ceremonious, and complexly organized form of *lyric poetry, usually of considerable length. It is frequently the vehicle for public utterance on state occasions, e.g., a ruler's birthday, accession, or funeral, or the dedication of some imposing public monument. The ode as it has evolved in contemp. lits. generally shows a dual inheritance from cl. sources, variously combining the measured, recurrent stanza of the Horatian ode, with its attendant balance of *tone and sentiment (sometimes amounting to a controlled ambiguity, as in Andrew Marvell's "Horatian Ode" on Oliver Cromwell), and the regular or irregular stanzaic triad of Pindar, with its elevated, vertiginously changeable tone (as in William Collins's "Ode on the Poetical Character"), in interesting manifestations as late as Robert Bridges and Paul Claudel. Both forms have frequently been used for poems celebrating public events, but both have just as frequently eschewed such events, sometimes pointedly, in favor of private occasions of crisis or joy. Nonetheless, of all poetic forms, the ode has continued since Pindar to be the mostly likely choice of poets reimbursed as laureates or other spokespersons. The serious tone of the ode calls for the use of a heightened diction and enrichment by poetic device, but this lays it open, more readily than any other lyric form, to burlesque.

In Gr. lit., the odes of Pindar (ca. 522–443 BCE) were designed for choric song and dance (see MELIC POETRY). The words, the sole surviving element of the integral experience, reflect the demands of the other two arts. A *strophe, a complex metrical structure whose length and pattern of heterometrical lines vary from one ode to another, reflects a dance pattern, which is then repeated exactly in an *antistrophe (the dancers repeating the steps but in the opposite direction), the pattern being closed by an *epode, or third section, of differing length and structure. The ode as a whole (surviving examples range from fragments to nearly 300 lines) is built up by exact metrical repetition of the original triadic pattern. These odes, written for performance in a Dionysiac theater or perhaps in the Agora to celebrate athletic victories, frequently appear incoherent in their brilliance of imagery, abrupt shifts in subject matter, and apparent disorder of form within the individual sections. But mod. crit. has answered such objections, which date from the time of Pindar himself, by discerning dominating images, emotional relationships between subjects, and complex metrical organization. The tone of the odes is emotional, exalted, and intense; the subject matter, whatever divine myths can be adduced to the occasion.

Apart from Pindar, another pervasive source of the mod. ode in Gr. lit. is the cult *hymn, which derived from the *Homeric Hymns* and flourished during the Alexandrian period in the work of Callimachus and others. This sort of poem is notable not for its form but for its structure of argument: an invocation of a deity (later of a personified natural or psychological entity), followed by a narrative genealogy establishing the antiquity and authenticity of the deity, followed by a petition for some special favor, and concluding with a vow of future service. A complete mod. instance of this structure is John Keats's "Ode to Psyche." Yet another source of the mod. ode's structure of prayerful petition is the Psalms and other poems of the Heb. Bible (see HEBREW POETRY, PSALM), which increasingly influenced Eng. poetry by way of John Milton, the crit. of John Dennis, the original and translated hymns of Isaac Watts, and Robert Lowth's *De sacra poesi Hebraeorum* (*Sacred Poetry of the Hebrews*, 1753; see HEBREW PROSODY AND POETICS).

In Lat. lit., the characteristic ode is associated with Horace (65–8 BCE), who derived his forms not from Pindar but from less elaborate Gr. lyrics, through Alcaeus and Sappho. The Horatian ode is tranquil rather than intense, contemplative rather than brilliant, and intended for the reader in private rather than for the spectator in the theater. Horace also wrote commissioned odes, most notably the "Carmen saeculare" for Augustus, all of which more closely approximated the Pindaric form and voice; but his influence on mod. poetry is felt more directly in the trad. of what might be called the sustained *epigram, esp. in the period between Ben Jonson and Matthew Prior. Among the

Eng. poets of note, only Mark Akenside habitually wrote odes in the Horatian vein, but in the 17th c. poets as diverse as Robert Herrick, Thomas Randolph, and—most important among them—Marvell with his Cromwell ode wrote urbane Horatians.

The third form of the mod. ode, the *anacreontic, is descended from the 16th-c. discovery of a group of some 60 poems, all credited to Anacreon, although the Gr. originals now appear to span a full thousand years. In general, the lines are short and, in comparison with the Pindaric ode, the forms simple, the subjects being love or drinking, as in the 18th-c. song "To Anacreon in Heaven," whose tune was appropriated for "The Star-Spangled Banner."

Throughout Europe, the hist. of the ode commences with the rediscovery of the classic forms. The humanistic ode of the 15th and earlier 16th c. shows the adaptation of old meters to new subjects by Francesco Filelfo, in both Gr. and Lat., and by Giannantonio Campano, Giovanni Pontano, and Marcantonio Flaminio in Neo-Lat. The example of the humanistic ode and the publication in 1513 of the Aldine edition of Pindar were the strongest influences on the vernacular ode in Italy; tentative Pindaric experiments were made by Giangiorgio Trissino, Luigi Alamanni, and Antonio Minturno but without establishing the ode as a new genre. More successful were the attempts in France by members of the *Pléiade: after minor trials of the new form by others, Pierre de Ronsard in 1550 published *The First Four Books of the Odes*, stylistic imitations of Horace, Anacreon, and (in the first book) Pindar. Influenced by Ronsard, Bernardo Tasso and Gabriello Chiabrera later in the century succeeded in popularizing the form in Italy, where it has been used successfully by, among others, Alessandro Manzoni, Giacomo Leopardi (in his *Di canzone*, 1824), Giosuè Carducci (*Odi barbare*, 1877), and Gabriele D'Annunzio (*Odi navale*, 1892). In France, the example of Ronsard was widely followed, notably by Nicolas Boileau in the 17th c. and by Voltaire and others in formal *occasional verse in the 18th. The romantic period lent a more personal note to both form and subject matter, notably in the work of Alphonse de Lamartine, Alfred de Musset, and Victor Hugo. Later, highly personal treatments of the genre may be found in Paul Verlaine's *Odes en son honneur* (1893) and Paul Valéry's *Odes* (1920). Claudel's *Cinq grandes odes* (1907), finally, shows a tendency in many odes of the 20th c. to explore traditional forms of experience, in this case Catholic devotion. In Sp., odes have figured in the work of Pablo Neruda (1904–73), who wrote three volumes of them: *Odas elementales* (1954), *Nuevas odas elementales* (1956), and *Tercer libro de las odas* (1957).

The ode became characteristically Ger. only with the work of G. R. Weckherlin (*Oden und Gesänge*, 1618–19), who, as court poet at Stuttgart, attempted to purify and refashion Ger. letters according to foreign models. In the mid-18th c., F. G. Klopstock modified the cl. models by use of free rhythms, grand abstract subjects, and a heavy influence from the Lutheran psalms. Later, J. W. Goethe and Friedrich Schiller returned to cl. models and feeling, as in Schiller's "Ode to Joy," used in the final movement of Ludwig van Beethoven's Ninth Symphony. At the turn of the 19th c., Friedrich Hölderlin in his complex, mystical, unrhymed odes united cl. themes with the characteristic resources of the Ger. lang. Since Hölderlin, few noteworthy odes have been written in Ger., with the possible exception of those of Rudolph Alexander Schröder (*Deutsche Oden*, 1912).

The few attempts at domesticating the ode in 16th-c. England were largely unsuccessful, although there is probably some influence of the cl. ode on Edmund Spenser's *Fowre Hymnes*, *Prothalamion*, and *Epithalamion*. In 1629 appeared the first great imitation of Pindar in Eng., Jonson's "Ode on the Death of Sir Lucius Cary and Sir H. Morison," with the strophe, antistrophe, and epode of the cl. model indicated by the Eng. terms "turn," "counter-turn," and "stand." In the same year, Milton began the composition of his great ode, "On the Morning of Christ's Nativity," in regular stanzaic form. The genre, however, attained great popularity in Eng. only with the publication of Abraham Cowley's *Pindarique Odes* in 1656, in which he attempted, like Ronsard and Weckherlin before him, to make available to his own lang. the spirit and tone of Pindar rather than to furnish an exact transcription of his manner. Cowley was uncertain whether Pindar's odes were regular, and the matter was not settled until 1706, when the playwright William Congreve published with an ode of his own a "Discourse" showing that they were indeed regular. With the appearance in 1749 of a scholarly trans. of Pindar by Gilbert West, the fashion for Cowleyan Pindarics died away. With John Dryden begin the great formal odes of the 18th c.: first the "Ode to the Memory of Mrs. Anne Killigrew" and then, marking the reunion of formal verse and music, the "Song for St. Cecilia's Day" and "Alexander's Feast." St. Cecilia's Day odes by many authors had long been written, but the trad. ended with "Alexander's Feast." For the 18th c., the ode was the perfect means of expressing the *sublime. Using *personification and other devices of *allegory, Thomas Gray and William Collins in the mid-18th c. marshal emotions ranging from anxiety to terror in the service of their central theme, the "progress of poetry," making the ode a crisis poem that reflects the rivalry of mod. lyric with the great poets and genres of the past. The romantic ode in Eng. lit. is a poem written on the occasion of a vocational or existential crisis in order to reassert the power and range of the poet's voice. It is the romantic ode that best suits the remark of Susan Stewart that "[o]des give birth to poets." The Eng. romantic ode begins with S. T. Coleridge's "Dejection: An Ode" (1802) and William Wordsworth's pseudo-Pindaric "Ode: Intimations of Immortality" (1804, pub. 1807). Wordsworth's "Intimations" ode, with its varied line lengths, complex rhyme scheme, and stanzas of varying length and pattern, has been called the greatest Eng. Pindaric ode. Of the other major romantic poets, P. B. Shelley wrote the "Ode to the West Wind" and Keats the "Ode on a Grecian Urn,"

"Ode to a Nightingale," and "To Autumn," arguably the finest odes in the lang. These odes were written in regular stanzas derived not from Horace but from Keats's own experiments with the *sonnet form. Since the romantic period, with the exception of a few brilliant but isolated examples such as Alfred, Lord Tennyson's "Ode on the Death of the Duke of Wellington" and G. M. Hopkins's "The Wreck of the Deutschland," the ode has been neither a popular nor a really successful genre in Eng. Among mod. poets, the personal ode in the Horatian manner has been revived with some success, notably by Allen Tate ("Ode to the Confederate Dead") and W. H. Auden ("In Memory of W. B. Yeats," "In Praise of Limestone").

*See* EPINIKION, GREEK POETRY (CLASSICAL), LATIN POETRY (CLASSICAL), STANCES, STASIMON.

■ Schipper, v. 2, sects. 516–25, and *History*, 366 ff.—on the Pindaric; G. Carducci,"Dello svolgimento dell'ode in Italia," *Opere*, v. 16 (1905); E. R. Keppeler, *Die Pindarische Ode in der dt. Poesie des XVII und XVIII Jhs.* (1911); R. Shafer, *The English Ode to 1660* (1918); I. Silver, *The Pindaric Odes of Ronsard* (1937); G. N. Shuster, *The English Ode from Milton to Keats* (1940); G. Highet, *The Classical Tradition* (1949); N. Maclean, "From Action to Image: Theories of the Lyric in the Eighteenth Century," in Crane; C. Maddison, *Apollo and the Nine: A History of the Ode* (1960); Bowra; K. Viëtor, *Gesch. der deutschen Ode*, 2d ed. (1961); A. W. Pickard-Cambridge, *Dithyramb, Tragedy and Comedy*, 2d ed. (1962); S. Commager, *The Odes of Horace* (1962); K. Schlüter, *Die englische Ode* (1964); H. D. Goldstein, "*Anglorum Pindarus*: Model and Milieu," *CL* 17 (1965); P. Habermann, "Antike Versmasse und Strophen-(Oden-) formen im Deutschen," and J. Wiegand and W. Kohlschmidt, "Ode," *Reallexikon II*; J. Heath-Stubbs, *The Ode* (1969); G. Hartman, "Blake and the Progress of Poetry," *Beyond Formalism* (1970); G. Otto, *Ode, Ekloge und Elegie im 18. Jahrhundert* (1973); J. D. Jump, *The Ode* (1974); Wilkins; M. R. Lefkowitz, *The Victory Ode* (1976); P. H. Fry, *The Poet's Calling in the English Ode* (1980); J. Culler, *The Pursuit of Signs* (1981), ch. 7; K. Crotty, *Song and Action: The Victory Odes of Pindar* (1982); W. Mullen, *Choreia* (1982); H. Vendler, *The Odes of John Keats* (1983); M. H. Abrams, *The Correspondent Breeze* (1984), ch. 4; J. W. Rhodes, *Keats's Major Odes: An Annotated Bibliography of Criticism* (1984); A. P. Burnett, *The Art of Bacchylides* (1985); D. S. Carne-Ross, *Pindar* (1985); N. Teich, "The Ode in English Literary History," *Papers on Language and Literature* 21 (1985); Terras; S. Curran, *Poetic Form and British Romanticism* (1986), ch. 4; W. Fitzgerald, *Agonistic Poetry: The Pindaric Mode in Pindar, Horace, Hölderlin, and the English Ode* (1987); Hollier, 198 ff.; *Selected Odes of Pablo Neruda*, ed. and trans. M. S. Peden (1990); G. Davis, *Polyhymnia* (1991); J. D. Kneale, "Romantic Aversions: Apostrophe Reconsidered," *ELH* 58 (1991); L. Kurke, *The Traffic in Praise: Pindar and the Poetics of Social Economy* (1991); J. Ygaunin, *Pindare et les poètes de la celebration*, 8 v. (1997); S. P. Revard, *Pindar and the Renaissance Hymn-Ode, 1450–1700* (2001); S. Stewart,

"What Praise Poems Are For," *PMLA* 120 (2005); N. Dauvois, *Renaissance de l'ode: l'ode française au tournant de l'année 1550* (2007); M. Koehler, "Odes of Absorption in the Restoration and Early Eighteenth Century," *SEL* 47 (2007).

S. F. FOGLE; P. H. FRY

**ODL** (Welsh, "rhyme"). Both end rhyme and *internal rhyme are features of *Welsh poetry from its origins in the 6th c. to the present day, with internal rhyme reaching its highest levels of complexity in the *cynghanedd that has been a required component of Welsh "strict-meter" poetry since the 14th c. Rhyme in Welsh is purely syllabic, and Welsh poetry recognizes rhymes between two unstressed syllables (as in Eng. *singing* : *dáncing*) and between stressed and unstressed syllables (as in Eng. *king* : *dáncing*), the latter pattern being an obligatory feature of some verse forms (*englyn and *cywydd*). This type of syllabic rhyme arose because, unlike Eng., Welsh does not have a strong stress accent, and vowel quality remains distinct even in unstressed syllables. Furthermore, the rhyming of final syllables was likely established before the shift of accent from final to penultimate syllables, which had the effect (once the shift was completed) of making rhyme independent of stress accent.

In addition to true rhymes, Welsh poetry also recognizes two kinds of partial rhyme. In *generic rhyme, known to Welsh poets as *odl Wyddelig* (Ir. rhyme) because of its widespread use in Ir. poetry, the vowels are identical, while the consonants following them need only belong to the same phonetic group (as in Eng. *cat* : *nap*, where both words end with voiceless stops). In *proest*, the consonants following the vowel correspond exactly, but the vowels or diphthongs preceding them need only be of the same class: short vowels (*cat* : *pot*); long vowels (*eel* : *fool*); diphthongs ending in *w* (*south* : *growth*); or diphthongs ending in *i, e*, or *y* (*day* : *boy* or *main* : *coin*). Wilfred Owen made much use of *proest* in Eng., which he called "pararhyme."

*See* CELTIC PROSODY.

■ Morris-Jones; Parry, *History*; Myrddin ap Dafydd, *Clywed Cynghanedd* (2003); A. Llwyd, *Anghenion y Gynghanedd* (2007).

D. M. LLOYD; B. BRUCH

**OMAR KHAYYÁM QUATRAIN** or *Rubaiyat* stanza (from Persian, originally Ar. *rubāʿiyyāt* [pl.], "quatrains"). In Eng. poetry, a quatrain of decasyllabic lines rhyming *aaba* (rarely *aaaa*). The term is taken from Edward FitzGerald's famous collection *Rubáiyát of Omar Khayyám* (1859), which is a free adaptation of a selection of poems by the Persian poet ʿUmar Khayyām (d. 1122), whose major reputation within the cl. Ar. trad. is as an algebraist. There is considerable doubt as to the attribution of a large part of Khayyām's poetry, but about 50 poems are clearly authentic, while a large number of others are also thought to be so. The wide popularity of FitzGerald's versions must be seen in the context of an extraordinary vogue in the 19th c. for Oriental *exoticism. While many

of the subtleties of *imagery and lang. in the original
Persian escaped FitzGerald, his renderings clearly pre-
sented a new and different poetic voice. Whereas Ar.
and Persian poetry in *qaṣīda form uses *monorhyme,
the rubā'iyyāt break the rhyme in the third line of
each stanza, and FitzGerald follows this rhyme scheme
in his versions: "I sometimes think that never blows so
red / The rose as where some buried Caesar bled; / That
every hyacinth the Garden wears / Dropt in its Lap
from some once lovely Head." *Enjambment is com-
mon in the initial *couplet. A. C. Swinburne's imita-
tion in "Laus Veneris" links third lines in pairs.

*See* PERSIAN POETRY.

■ *Reallexikon II* 2.824; W. Cadbury, "FitzGerald's
*Rubáiyát* as a Poem," *ELH* 34 (1967); W. L. Hana-
way Jr., "Persian Literature," *The Study of the Middle
East,* ed. L. Binder (1976); V.-M. D'Ambrosio, *Eliot
Possessed* (1989); D. Davis, "Persian," *The Oxford History
of Literary Translation in English, Vol. 4: 1790–1900,* ed.
P. France and K. Haynes (2006); *VP* 46.1 (2008)—
spec. iss. on the *Rubáiyát.*

R.M.A. ALLEN

**ONEGIN STANZA.** The vehicle the Rus. poet Alex-
ander Pushkin created for his masterpiece *Evgenij One-
gin* (1825–32). A variation on the *sonnet, the Onegin
stanza has the rhyme scheme *AbAb CCdd EffE gg* (upper-
case letters represent feminine rhymes, lowercase mascu-
line), where all three quatrain structures are different—
alternating, adjacent, and embracing. According to B. V.
Tomaševskij, the first quatrain presents the main idea,
the next two develop it, and the witty *couplet rounds
it out. The Onegin stanza is admirably suited for the
varying tone of the ironic and playful author-narrator,
who frequently indulges in urbane chatter, lyrical di-
gressions, and professional comments. Later imitations
of the Onegin stanza by poets such as Mikhail Lermon-
tov ("Tambovskaia kaznacheisha," 1837–38), Dmitrii
Minaev ("Evgenii Onegin nashego vremeni," 1865–77),
Viacheslav Ivanov ("Mladenchestvo," 1913–18), and
Valerii Pereleshin, ("Poema bez predmeta," c. 1972–76)
are interesting but lack the brilliance of the master.

■ B. V. Tomaševskij, *Stix i jazyk* (1959); K. Post-
outenko, *Oneginskij tekst v russkoj literature* (1998).

J. O. BAILEY; I. K. LILLY

**ONOMATOPOEIA** (Ger. *Klangmalerei, Lautsym-
bolik*). The traditional term for words that seem to imi-
tate their referents. In the strict sense, onomatopoeia
refers to words that imitate sounds (e.g., *dingdong,
roar, swish, murmur, susurrus*), but other qualities such
as size, motion, and even color may be suggested; the
term is often used to denote any word whose sound is
felt to have a "natural" or direct relation with its sense.
Since their phonetic shapes seem motivated rather than
arbitrary, onomatopoeic words exert significant limita-
tions on Ferdinand de Saussure's doctrine of the arbi-
trariness of the sign. Both Otto Jespersen and Edward
Sapir showed evidence that Saussure greatly overstated
his case.

Onomatopoeia is one of four verbal effects often
called "expressive" or "mimetic" but known in ling. as
"phonetic symbolism" or "sound symbolism." None of
these descriptors is wholly satisfactory, and, in fact,
onomatopoeic words are, per the terminology of Char-
les S. Peirce, *icons* rather than *symbols*; they are not
symbolic in the way ordinary words are, for their semi-
otic approach to representation is a highly motivated
attempt at direct identity, rather than an arbitrary or
relatively motivated form of indirect analogy. Beyond
(1) onomatopoeia itself (words that imitate sounds in
nature), three other interrelated iconic verbal effects
include (2) articulatory gestures or kinesthesia (predi-
cated on movements of the vocal or facial muscles; see
SOUND); (3) *synaesthesia, *phonesthemes, and other
associative phenomena (wherein heard sounds trigger
other sensory impressions); and (4) morphosymbolism
and iconic syntax (see below).

It has long been fashionable among literary critics to
disparage onomatopoeia as a crude and over-obvious
poetic device, but there is considerable ling. evidence
for *iconicity as an important process in lang.; indeed,
certain iconic effects operate across a wide spectrum of
langs. and so may be linguistic universals. Jespersen's
astonishingly long list of words having the unrounded
high front vowel /i/, with all connoting "small, slight,
insignificant, or weak," is famous; in Eng., this *pho-
neme is used almost universally as a suffix for small,
familiar, or comforting things (e.g., *mommy, daddy,
baby, doggie, kitty*). Woodworth's analysis of *deixis in
26 langs. revealed a "systematic relationship between
vowel quality and distance," namely, that a word hav-
ing proximal meaning has a vowel of higher pitch than
one having distal meaning.

Furthermore, iconic effects in lang. are not merely
phonological but morphological and syntactic. Ono-
matopoeia is, therefore, simply the most conspicuous
instance of a broad range of natural linguistic effects,
not a merely "poetic" device. In ordinary speech, sound
is motivated by sense: once sense is selected, sound
follows. But in iconic speech, sense is motivated by
sound: words are chosen for their sound, which itself
determines meaning. In the case of onomatopoeia,
the sound of the word may imitate a natural phenom-
enon in the world, but the sound of the word is not
often precisely the sound of the thing. As Seymour
Chatman shows, the connection is not exact, and
most onomatopoeic words are only approximations
of the natural sounds. Even words for animal sounds
are highly conventionalized in every lang.: the Eng.
speaker styles the dog's bark as *bow wow* or *arf arf*
or *woof*, whereas the Mandarin Chinese speaker has
it as *wang wang*. Meanwhile, in Eng., the pig's grunt
is styled *oink, oink*, whereas the Brazilian Portuguese
speaker has it as *croinh croinh*.

All of this suggests that sound-symbolic effects do
not operate without words to trigger them: words that
are primary in establishing the semantic field. Sounds
can never precede meaning: they can only operate on
meanings already lexically created. Nevertheless, ono-

matopoeia generally aims to approximate the physical properties of its sounds to the physical properties of its real objects. From the wider perspective of sound symbolism or iconicity, onomatopoeia is part of a much larger set of associative relations between word-sounds and meanings. Associative processes operate extensively among words themselves, particularly in morphology, though also in syntax. The sound shape of a word is almost never created from nothing: it is usually formed in relation to some existing word. After it comes into existence, it is continuously subject to diachronic and synchronic influence from other words in the lang. system. Any entity, no matter how arbitrary upon its entry into the system, is thereafter subject to continuous accommodation to and influence by other entities in the system.

It should be noted that many writers use the term *onomatopoeia* for something that amounts to what Dwight Bolinger has termed "reverse onomatopoeia": here "not only is the word assimilated to the sound, but the sound is also assimilated to the 'wordness' of the word." Bolinger identifies a series of morphosemantic processes based mainly on association whereby the form influences the meaning or the meaning influences the form of words. In this way, constellations of words form over time, all having similar meanings and similar sounds: one example is the series of Eng. words beginning with *gl-* which have to do with light; another is the set of words ending in *-ash*. Consequently, as Bolinger explains, "when we speak of sound-suggestiveness, we speak of the entire lang., not just of a few imitative or self-sufficient forms."

The subject of iconicity in lang. has always been a significant issue for linguists and stood as a topic of lively interest to the ancients. It is central to Plato's *Cratylus*, and also appears in Aristotle (*Rhet.* 3.9), Demetrius (*On Style*), Dionysius of Halicarnassus (*On Literary Composition*), and Quintilian (*Institutio oratoria* 9.3, 9.4). Saussure impressed indelibly upon the mind of the 20th c. the idea that the relation between word and thing is arbitrary. But of course, desire cuts so much deeper than fact. Poets continually desire to make lang. appropriate, so that words partake of the nature of things. And the agency is the fact that words *are* things, have physical bodies with extension in space and duration in time. For fuller discussion of the several types of expressive sound in poetry, see CACOPHONY, DISSONANCE, EUPHONY, MIMESIS, REPRESENTATION, TIMBRE.

■ O. Jespersen, "Sound Symbolism," *Language* (1922); J. R. Firth, *Speech* (1930); C. S. Peirce, *Collected Papers*, ed. C. Hartshorne and P. Weiss, 8 vols. (1931–58); O. Jespersen, "Symbolic Value of the Vowel *I*," *Linguistica* (1933); E. Sapir, *Selected Writings* (1949); J. R. Firth, "Modes of Meaning," *E&S* 4 (1951); D. T. Mace, "The Doctrine of Sound and Sense in Augustan Poetic Theory," *RES* 2 (1951); Wellek and Warren, chap. 13; W. T. Moynihan, "The Auditory Correlative," *JAAC* 17 (1958); Z. Wittoch, "Les Onomatopées forment-elles une système dans la langue?" *AION-SL* 4 (1962); D. Bolinger, *Forms of English* (1965), esp. "The Sign

Is Not Arbitrary," "Word Affinities," and "Rime, Assonance, and Morpheme Analysis"; Chatman; M. B. Emeneau, "Onomatopoetics in the Indian Linguistic Area," *Lang* 45 (1969); J. D. Sadler, "Onomatopoeia," *CJ* 67 (1972); J. A. Barish, "Yvor Winters and the Antimimetic Prejudice," *NLH* 2 (1970); G. L. Anderson, "Phonetic Symbolism and Phonological Style," *Current Trends in Stylistics* (1972); W. K. Wimsatt, "In Search of Verbal Mimesis," *Day of the Leopards* (1976); P. L. French, "Toward an Explanation of Phonetic Symbolism," *Word* 28 (1977); Y. Malkiel, "From Phonosymbolism to Morphosymbolism," *Fourth LACUS Forum* (1978), supp. by D. B. Justice, "Iconicity and Association," *RPh* 33 (1980); R. Jakobson and L. Waugh, "The Spell of Speech Sounds," *The Sound Shape of Language* (1979), also rpt. in Jakobson, vol. 8; L. I. Weinstock, "Onomatopoeia and Related Phenomena in Biblical Hebrew," *DAI* 40 (1979): 3268A; D. A. Pharies, "Sound Symbolism in the Romance Languages," *DAI* 41 (1980): 231A; R. A. Wescott, *Sound and Sense: Essays on Phonosemic Subjects* (1980); M. Borroff, "Sound Symbolism as Drama in the Poetry of Wallace Stevens," *ELH* 48 (1981); Brogan, 97–108— survey of studies; Morier; R. Lewis, *On Reading French Verse* (1982), chap. 7; N. L. Woodworth, "Sound Symbolism in Proximal and Distal Forms," *Linguistics* 29 (1991); M. Borroff, "Sound Symbolism as Drama in the Poetry of Robert Frost," *PMLA* 107 (1992); H. Bredin, "Onomatopoeia as a Figure and a Linguistic Principle" *NLH* 27 (1996); E. R. Anderson, *A Grammar of Iconism* (1998).

T.V.F. BROGAN; J. M. COCOLA

**OPEN FORM.** An "open" term encompassing a variety of overlapping poetic programs. While *free verse tends to be the technical norm, open form is justified as part of a general imperative to respond to the particulars and emergencies of the historical moment, politics, psychology, physiology, and so on. If 19th-c. ideas of organic form are in the background of the concept of open form, the figure of Ezra Pound looms in the foreground. The term gained currency as part of a politically charged reaction against New Critical formalism (see NEW CRITICISM). In the essay "Projective Verse" (1950), Charles Olson made his bold statement, courtesy of "one Robert Creeley," that "FORM IS NEVER MORE THAN AN EXTENSION OF CONTENT." Olson's open or *projective verse, which he also calls *composition by field, rejects the "inherited line, stanza, over-all form"—the "old" bases of "closed verse" or "verse that print bred"—and turns, instead, to the "laws and possibilities of breath," the "speech-force of language," and the "kinetics" of the poem as a "high-energy construct."

The organicist basis of Olson's open verse—which actually relies on *typography—points to a "stance toward reality" that is "larger than" or goes "beyond" technical matters. Allen's influential 1960 anthol. *The New American Poetry 1945–1960*—expanded and retitled *The Postmoderns* in 1982—promoted an aesthetic of *presence, *spontaneity, and openness to experience and considered open-form poets to be "the most truly authentic, indigenous American writers." The *Poetics of the New American Poetry*, a collection of essays by open-form poets, traced these values back to Walt Whitman. Berg and Mezey, opting for "open form" over "free verse" and "organic" form, in their 1969 anthol. *Naked Poetry* confirmed the thematic bias of the term as distinct from the strictly technical designation of *free verse*. In the editors' words about their selection of poets, "formal qualities" came "to seem more and more irrelevant, and we find we are much more interested in what they say, in their dreams, visions, and prophecies. Their poems take shape from the shapes of their emotions, the shapes their minds make in thought, and certainly don't need interpreters."

In general, open form appeals to a higher authority than that of poetic trads., incl. trads. of free verse, in order to render "openness" somehow necessary and thus meet one criterion of verse. *Open* both describes improvisational forms and appropriates the formal revolution of free verse for nonformal purposes, authorizing such forms by invoking larger "freedoms." Ramifying by analogy, open form promotes other kinds of openness considered morally desirable: openness to natural rhythms and processes, "dreams, visions, and prophecies," nonconformist social values, and reformist or revolutionary politics. The sociopolitical valence of the term enables open forms that would "naturalize" poetic lang. to turn around and also naturalize certain social and political arrangements and values.

Moreover, open form also takes "a new stance toward the reality of a poem itself" (Olson), and the practice of writing now becomes part of the content of a verse that registers the processes of the composition of its sonic form, its evolving thought, and the shaping of its page by the typewriter. *Language poetry develops some of these principles. The term calls for a readjustment of the form/content hierarchy and is best understood in the politicized contexts of literary, critical, and philosophical develops.: *historicism as opposed to *formalism, self-referential practices that address their own procedures, and a politicization of poetic form.

■ *The New American Poetry 1945–1960,* ed. D. Allen (1960)—contains Olson's essay; *Naked Poetry: Recent American Poetry in Open Forms*, ed. S. Berg and R. Mezey (1969); *Poetics of the New American Poetry*, ed. D. Allen and W. Tallman (1973); *The Postmoderns*, ed. D. Allen and G. Butterick (1982).

M. K. Blasing

**ORAL-FORMULAIC THEORY.** Also known as the Parry-Lord theory of oral composition, oral-formulaic theory is an approach to oral and oral-derived texts that seeks to explain the performance and transmission of folkloristic and literary material through a series of structural units: *formula, theme, and story pattern*. The formula is a substitutable phrase that provides the performer with a malleable, ready-made idiom that simplifies the task of oral composition in

performance; the theme and story pattern amount to formulas at the higher levels of the typical scene and tale type, respectively. All three of these units are characterized as single "words"—integral bytes of structure and meaning—by South Slavic oral epic singers (*guslari*; see GUSLAR) and their counterparts in other oral trads. (Foley 2002). The theory evolved from its original derivation in ancient Gr. and South Slavic epic to more than 150 lang. trads. It flourished during the period 1950–90 and, after that point, began to dovetail with other approaches such as performance theory, *ethnopoetics, and traditional referentiality.

Anticipators of oral-formulaic theory were many, starting from the Jewish priest Josephus in the 1st c. CE through the amateur classicists François Hédelin and Robert Wood in the 18th c., but the true antecedents were the Ger. philologists and Rus. and other Slavic ethnographers, chiefly of the 19th c. Of the former, the most significant are Friedrich Wolf (1795), who offered archaeological proof that writing was not available to Homer, and the linguists Johann-Ernst Ellendt (1861), Heinrich Düntzer (1872), and others, all of whom studied the relationship of Homeric phraseology to its meter. As for the ethnographers, Wilhelm Radlov's report (1885) of fieldwork among the central Asian Kara-Kirghiz, which treated the questions of improvisation versus memorization, the units of composition, the role of the audience, and the multiformity of tales, had special interest for Milman Parry. Also extremely influential were Matija Murko's accounts (1929 and the posthumous masterwork of 1951) of his experiences among the South Slavic epic singers. It was to this "living laboratory" in the former Yugoslavia that Parry and Albert Lord were eventually to travel in order to confirm the discoveries made through analysis of the Homeric texts.

As early as his 1923 master's thesis, one can glimpse Parry's vision of a long-standing trad. of ancient Gr. singers that led eventually to Homer. His explanation, which superseded the contemp. debate in cl. philology between Unitarians and Analysts over the authorship of the Gr. epics (one or many Homers), was a radical proposal: in his 1928 thesis, Parry showed that the lang. and style of Homer were neither an original creation nor the composite work of redactors, but rather the bequest of traditional poets who, over generations, had assembled an adaptable *diction and a flexible narrative repertoire. Thus, Parry conceived of the formula as "a group of words which is regularly employed under the same metrical conditions to express a given essential idea"; the "formulaic system" consisted of a set of formulas that shared a common pattern of phraseology. A singer's formulas and systems together comprised something akin to a set of phraseological equations, some of them constant and others with variables, that could be called upon to solve whatever compositional problem arose. According to this theory, there simply was no narrative situation that could not be handled by recourse to this plastic, generative diction. Parry also showed that the noun-epithet phrases (e.g., "swift-footed Achilles" or "wily Odysseus"), a species of formula, exhibit a kind of *thrift*, in that each hero or god is customarily assigned only one such phrase for a given part of the \*hexameter verse and that Homer tended to avoid \*enjambment, his thought being either complete in a single hexameter line or optionally (rather than necessarily) continued to the next line. These and other findings led Parry to posit a formulaic diction in which individual aesthetic choice is subservient to metrical expediency and in which the kind of creative artistic effect so cherished by mod. crit. was considered much less likely than traditional values epitomized through traditional structures.

From the hypothesis of trad., Parry moved, at the suggestion of Murko and Parry's mentor Antoine Meillet, to the further and complementary hypothesis of *orality*. In his studies of 1930 and 1932, Parry argued that Homer's formulaic diction must also have been oral, since nothing less than the ongoing pressure of composition in performance could have stimulated the production and maintenance of this special verse idiom. Parry's field trips to the former Yugoslavia in 1933–35, with Lord, were intended to provide a comparison between the ms. texts of Homer and the living oral trad. of the South Slavs. With the discovery of formulaic diction in the Yugoslav songs, as recorded in Parry's partially published field notes, "Ćor Huso," the oral-formulaic theory as a comparative approach was born.

With Parry's premature death in 1935, the completion and extension of his work were undertaken by Lord, who made trips to the former Yugoslavia and Albania in 1950–51 and, with David E. Bynum, in the 1960s. First in importance among Lord's works, and in the field at large, stands *The Singer of Tales*, in which he brings the Yugoslav analogy to bear on ancient Gr., OE, OF, and Byzantine Gr. narrative. This volume also saw the elaboration of the concepts of theme (e.g., arming the hero, feasting, boasting) and story pattern (e.g., the Return Song, the Wedding Song), which together with formula offered an explanation of oral-traditional multiformity at all levels of epic verse. Crucial to the extension of oral-formulaic theory to other trads. was Lord's concept of "formulaic density," through which, following Parry's famous analyses of passages from the *Iliad* and the *Odyssey*, he claimed that one could determine whether a text was orally composed by calculating its percentage of formulas and systems. Also important has been the publication of the South Slavic songs (Parry et al., 1953–) gathered during fieldwork, particularly the 13,000-line *The Wedding of Smailagić Meho* by Avdo Medjedović (see also Foley 2004). His later comparative research treated Rus., Latvian, Finnish, Ukrainian, Bulgarian, and other oral trads. As the two "Perspectives" articles (1974, 1986) illustrate, Lord brought the oral-formulaic theory from a revolutionary but narrowly applied method to a discipline of broad comparative importance.

This hist. and rapid expansion during the period 1950–90 are chronicled in Foley (1988) and bibliographically surveyed in Foley (1985, with updates). Among the most significant issues and points of disagreement were (1) the question of how far the comparative method can be extended and how binding are proofs by analogy (e.g., Kirk, Watts); (2) the problem of the seemingly mechanistic nature of oral-formulaic theory and its impact on aesthetic crit. of the works involved (e.g., Vivante); (3) the legitimacy of the "formulaic density" criterion (e.g., Benson); (4) the phenomenon of "transitional texts" that reveal signs of both oral and written provenance (Lord 1974); and (5) the respective roles of fieldwork and textual analysis in the study of oral trads. (e.g., Finnegan). A number of related and parallel areas took on considerably greater prominence, among them philosophical and historical treatments of oral trad. (e.g., Havelock; Ong 1967, 1982). In order to provide a central forum for the interdisciplinary debate surrounding the area, the jour. *Oral Tradition* (1986–) and the Lord monograph series (1987–) were established.

Over the last 20 years, oral-formulaic theory has combined with other approaches as scholars seek to understand better the aesthetics of oral and oral-derived poetry (Foley 1995). Attention has been focused not only on the structural rules for generation of traditional units (Foley 1990) but on the connotative meaning of these units and patterns. The principle of *traditional referentiality* (Foley 1991, 2002), whereby formulaic phrases, scenes, and story patterns idiomatically engage the larger implied trad., has directed attention beyond mechanics and structure toward the fundamental issue of poetic artistry. Digital and Internet media have also been harnessed to represent more faithfully the dynamic, patterned, performative nature of oral poetry (Foley 2004, 2010–).

*See* ANTHROPOLOGY AND POETRY, ORAL POETRY.

■ J. Ellendt, *Über den Einfluss des Metrums* (1861); H. Düntzer, *Homerische Abhandlungen* (1872); W. Radlov, *Der Dialect der Kara-Kirgisen* (1885); M. Murko, *La Poésie populaire épique en Yougoslavie au début du XXe siècle* (1929); and *Tragom srpsko-hrvatske narodne epike* (1951); *Serbo-Croatian Heroic Songs (Srpskohrvatske junačke pjesme)*, coll., ed., and trans. M. Parry, A. B. Lord, D. Bynum (1953–); G. S. Kirk, *The Songs of Homer* (1962); E. Havelock, *Preface to Plato* (1963); L. Benson, "The Literary Character of Anglo-Saxon Formulaic Poetry," *PMLA* 81 (1966); W. Ong, *The Presence of the Word* (1967); A. C. Watts, *The Lyre and the Harp* (1969); Parry; A. B. Lord, "Perspectives on Recent Work on Oral Literature," *Forum for Modern Language Studies* 10 (1974); R. Finnegan, *Oral Poetry* (1977); W. Ong, *Orality and Literacy* (1982); P. Vivante, *The Epithets in Homer* (1982); J. M. Foley, *Oral-Formulaic Theory and Research* (1985)—updates in *Oral Tradition* 3 (1988) and 12 (1997); F. Wolf, *Prolegomena to Homer* (1795), trans. A. Grafton, G. W. Most, J.E.G. Zetzel (1985); A. B. Lord, "Perspectives on the Oral Traditional Formula," *Oral Tradition* 1 (1986); *Oral Tradition* (1986–), http://journal.oraltradition.org; Albert Bates Lord Studies in Oral Tradition monograph series (1987–), http://www.oraltradition.org/about/abl; A. Renoir, *A Key to Old Poems* (1988); J. M. Foley, *The Theory of Oral Composition*

(1988); *Comparative Research on Oral Traditions*, ed. J. M. Foley (1989); J. M. Foley, *Traditional Oral Epic* (1990); *Immanent Art* (1991); *The Singer of Tales in Performance* (1995); *Homer's Traditional Art* (1999); and *How to Read an Oral Poem* (2002); Lord; *The Wedding of Mustajbey's Son Bećirbey: As Performed by Halil Bajgorić*, ed. and trans. J. M. Foley (2004), http://oraltradition. org/zbm); The Pathways Project (2010–), http://path waysproject.org.

J. M. FOLEY

**ORAL POETRY.** Oral poetry encompasses two general types of verse: oral traditional poetry and oral textual poetry. Oral traditional poetry includes songs that are, for the most part, both orally composed and orally performed. They are primarily ritual, lyric, and narrative poems. By contrast, oral textual poetry is often written down but presented orally in *performance. It includes popular songs as well as more contemp. genres such as spoken-word poetry. Oral performance is a fundamental, defining characteristic of both oral traditional and oral textual poetry.

Oral poetry functions in many different ritual and social contexts and assumes a wide variety of forms. The meaning of *oral poetry* is complicated by the fact that oral poetry is rarely, if ever, entirely oral because of the inevitable intersections between oral and written culture. Questions regarding the parameters and nature of oral poetry have engendered much scholarly debate. The dynamics of oral composition and performance are addressed by the major theoretical approaches in the field (*oral-formulaic theory, performance studies, and *ethnopoetics).

In preliterate societies, all poetry is unambiguously oral traditional—composed and transmitted in performance by people who do not read or write. In literate or partially literate societies, however, the situation is far more complicated since orality and literacy naturally interact, resulting in overlapping forms of oral and written poetry. It follows that rigid categories of oral and literary verse and the insistence on an explicit divide between them are untenable.

Ritual, lyric, and narrative song are the principal categories of oral traditional poetry. *Ritual verse* is rooted in an ancient past; indeed, all poetry begins with oral poetry, the origins of which are found in the rhythms, sound patterns, and repetitive structures that reinforce and empower the words and actions of ritual. Ritual poems are short, nonnarrative songs that include *lullabies, ritual wedding songs, *laments, praise poems (see EPIDEICTIC POETRY), songs for special festivals and ceremonies, and *incantations. Most ritual poetry is performed at either life- or calendrical-cycle celebrations.

Life-cycle ritual poetry marks primarily birth, marriage, and death. Associated with birth, lullabies are short songs with repetitive verses and sounds (often nonsense syllables) and are sung to lull babies to sleep. Wedding songs are among the richest ritual genres and commemorate the most celebrated life-cycle passage in traditional society, marriage. Many wedding songs

articulate the bride's emotional and often painful separation from her childhood and incorporation into adult status as a wife, esp. in patrilocal societies; some are termed wedding laments. Death lament—poetry that is often chanted or declaimed—is the genre of death rites, frequently performed by women. It typically includes direct discourse to the deceased by the mourner(s) as well as imagined dialogues between them.

While death laments performed by mourners eulogize the deceased, praise poems or *panegyric odes composed by praise singers declaim and glorify the living, typically elite members of society. At one time attested throughout the world, this genre now figures most conspicuously in Africa and Oceania.

Songs for calendrical festivals and ceremonies are performed at key times in the year, both secular and religious. In agricultural societies, these oral poetic forms are frequently associated with the solstices. Songs at these junctures are often stanzaic and sung in groups, e.g., *carols, performed at Christmas and New Year's. Seasonal songs sometimes express religious messages. More often they convey wishes for fertility, good health, and fortune and express the eternal hope of new beginnings (the new year, springtime); they also accompany rituals of divination.

Incantations are verbal charms that are sung as part of magic rituals. Most common are healing charms, curses, spells, and exorcisms. Sound patterns (*alliteration, *assonance, and repetition of certain syllables, words, and word combinations) are conspicuous in incantations since it is often believed that the "exact" repetition of specific sounds and words is necessary to effect the desired magic.

*Oral lyric poems* are short, informal, nonnarrative songs and are universal. They are melodic and often stanzaic. *Lyric poetry covers a great variety of topics, the most common being love and longing; many are also about suffering. Dancing and drinking songs, as well as work, war, or political songs, among many others, also figure in lyric poetry. These forms are usually ephemeral. Words and ideas are perpetually repeated and paraphrased in oral lyric since songs typically dwell on single ideas and the emotional responses that they engender.

The two principal genres of oral traditional *narrative poetry* are *epic and *ballad. Oral epic poems are songs of considerable length and complexity that recount deeds of significance—both heroic and mythic—to the community or nation. The epic tells a story from beginning to end, often with a fullness of detail. As a result, epic performances sometimes last for many hours, even days. Epic poetry is usually stichic (see STICHOS); the same metric line—with some variation—is repeated in a linear fashion. The melodies of epic poetry are typically repetitive; verses, however, are sometimes chanted instead of sung. Sometimes epic is a combination of poetry and prose, e.g., the Congolese *Mwindo* epic, West African *Sunjata*, and Turkic *Book of Dede Korkut*. While some epics such as the *Iliad* or the *Chanson de Roland* have tragic overtones, oral epic is by and large optimistic. The hero generally triumphs gloriously over the enemy (as in Rus., Armenian, South Slavic, or Af. trads.). Oral epic has circulated since antiquity. The genre in the pre-20th-c. world is known to posterity because the poetry was written down, presumably when it was still being performed. Orally composed and performed but surviving only in textual form are epics such as the *Epic of Gilgamesh*, the *Mahābhārata*, the *Rāmāyaṇa*, the *Odyssey*, the *Iliad*, the Persian *Shâh-nâma*, *Beowulf*, OF *chansons de geste*, the *Kalevala*, and numerous others. Termed "oral-derived" poetry, many of these epics were perpetuated both orally and in textual transcriptions, exemplifying how oral and literary forms mingle and overlap over time. Some epics have continued to be performed up to the present day or at least until the late 20th c. (the Kyrgyz *Manas*; South Asian, Ar., and Romanian epics).

Ballads are relatively short, narrative, nonheroic poems that focus on single episodes—usually sensational domestic dramas. Although there are comic ballads, the genre as a whole has an elegiac tone. The tempo of narration is more leisurely than in epic; some ballads consist entirely of dialogue. Ballads are generally stanzaic and their musical forms lyric. Eng. and west Eur. ballads as a genre date from at least the 13th c. and flourished until relatively recently. Anglo-Am. ballads are among the best known (e.g., "Lord Lovel," "Barbara Allen," "Fair Margaret and Sweet William"). Many ballads are also oral-derived.

*Oral textual poetry* refers to oral poems that are composed in writing but performed orally. Many are popular songs that first circulate as written texts and subsequently enter oral trad. Typical of this category are Eng. *broadside or street ballads, which were sold in printed form to the public and then spread orally. *Blues, contemp. popular, and "folk" songs fit here as well. Some songs travel back and forth between printed and oral forms, illustrating again the complex interplay between oral and written poetry.

Oral textual poetry also refers to a widespread contemp. urban genre termed *spoken-word poetry*. Spoken-word poems are original compositions written by poets who perform them orally at *poetry slams. The poems are typically nonmetrical and are accompanied by gestures and dramatic vocal and facial expressions. They convey personal and social concerns such as poverty, injustice, racism, and sexism; the genre is heavy with pain and biting social commentary. Although *poetic contests have been staged since antiquity, poetry slams date from the mid-1980s in the United States. They have since spread throughout the world.

Performers of oral poetry learn their repertoires from other performers or printed texts. "Learning" poetry can be a process of explicit (intentional) or implicit (internalized or passive) imitation. The former is typical of longer and more complex genres (such as epic), while the latter usually occurs in genres that are shorter and more frequently performed (ritual, lyric, and popular songs).

The most distinctive characteristic of oral poetry is its variability and fluidity of form, in words and, when singing is involved, music. Multiple performances of the "same song" are invariably different, even in oral textual poetry. There is more variation in different performances of lengthier poems and conversely sometimes verbatim reiteration in shorter poetic forms. Perhaps the most significant mechanism of orality is repetition—from sounds and words to verses, passages, and, in epic and ballad, narrative patterns. The use of *parallelism in sound, syntax, and rhythm aids oral poets in moving from one verse to another. Thus, lines and clusters of lines are formed and held together by sound, structure, and association of meaning. Oral poetry is characteristically paratactic: verses are "added" to what precedes them. Other rhetorical devices of repetition include *anaphora, epistrophe, *anadiplosis, and *ring composition. Figures of speech such as *similes and *metaphors are also part of the compositional stylistics of oral poetry. On the level of content, *multiform* refers to the existence of narrative ideas in multiple forms and is key to understanding the structure of oral poetry.

Several major approaches guided the research on oral poetry in the 20th c. In the 1930s, both Parry and Lord explored compositional style in oral epic in the former Yugoslavia in order to shed light on the art of oral epic verse-making in Homer. Formally presented in the 1960 publication of Lord's *Singer of Tales*, their findings became known as the oral-formulaic theory. Lord argued that, in preliterate cultures, oral-epic poets learn a special technique of composition by "formula" and "theme." The formula is "a group of words which is regularly employed under the same metrical conditions to express a given essential idea." The most commonly sung phrases, lines, or *couplets—those that a singer hears most frequently when learning—establish the patterns for the poetry, its syntactic, rhythmic, metric, and acoustic molds and configurations. In time, the poet can form new phrases or create formulas by analogy and become proficient in thinking in these traditional patterns, the special lang. of oral epic. A theme is a repeated passage that functions in much the same way; it has a more or less stable core of lines or parts of lines, surrounded by various elements adapting it to its context. The oral-formulaic theory has been employed in countless investigations of composition in oral poetry and has dominated the field and profoundly influenced the study and understanding of oral epic for over 50 years.

The most significant devel. in the field of oral poetry since the oral-formulaic theory is performance studies, an appreciation and detailed investigation of oral verbal art in the context of performance. In response, in part, to what was viewed by some as an overly narrow understanding of oral poetry by Lord, Finnegan and others in the 1970s and 1980s began to advocate a broader understanding of the "oral" in oral poetry, an increased appreciation of the significant intersection between oral and literary poetry, and a greater recognition of the critical role of performance. Key in developing the theoretical framework for performance studies, Bauman (1977, 1986) argued that performance is critical to an understanding of oral poetry (and folklore in general). He and others suggested that oral trads. be viewed as communicative events that involve both verbal artist(s) and audience as participants. Moreover, they proposed that performance stylistics be recognized as verbal and nonverbal alike.

Related to performance studies, ethnopoetics was first formulated in the 1980s and 1990s by Hymes and by Tedlock, who recommended that transcriptions of oral verbal art reflect the dynamics of performance through detailed prompts in the text. In this way, readers can "reperform" oral texts as they experience them. Foley (1991) also brought depth to comparative textual readings of oral poetry (esp. epic) by seeking to appreciate the idiomatic lang. of oral verse and its traditional register.

Other recent devels. in the study of oral poetry include an increasing globalization of the field as primary source materials expand and research encompasses broader areas of inquiry. The Internet, information-filled Web sites, and other media technologies are also progressively employed to provide ever more detailed "performances" and thus fuller and more nuanced understandings of the mechanics and meanings of oral poetry.

■ **Anthologies:** *Heroic Epic and Saga*, ed. F. J. Oinas (1978); *Oral Tradition in Literature* (1986), *Comparative Research on Oral Traditions* (1987)—both ed. J. M. Foley; *Oral Epics in India*, ed. S. H. Blackburn (1989); *Oral-Formulaic Theory* (1990), *De gustibus* (1992)—both ed. J. M. Foley; *Aloud: Voices from the Nuyorican Poets Cafe*, ed. M. Algarín and B. Holman (1994); *A Beowulf Handbook*, ed. J. D. Niles and R. E. Bjork (1997); *A New Companion to Homer*, ed. I. Morris and B. Powell (1997); *Prosimetrum*, ed. J. Harris and K. Reichl (1997)—cross-cultural perspectives; *Songs of the Serbian People: From the Collections of Vuk Karadžiç*, ed. M. Holton and V. Mihailovich (1997); *Teaching Oral Traditions*, ed. J. M. Foley (1998); *Epic Traditions in the Contemporary World*, ed. M. H. Beissinger et al. (1999); *In Search of Sunjata*, ed. R. A. Austen (1999); *Nuyorican Poets Café Slambook*, ed. K. Roach (2000); *The Oral Epic*, ed. K. Reichl (2000); *Textualization of Oral Epics*, ed. L. Honko (2000); *Epea and Grammata*, ed. J. M. Foley (2002)—ancient Greece; *Oral Performance and Its Context*, ed. C. J. Mackie (2004); *A Companion to Ancient Epic*, ed. J. M. Foley (2005); *Heroic Poets and Poetic Heroes in Celtic Tradition*, ed. F. Nagy and L. E. Jones (2005).

■ **Bibliographies:** *The Index of the Milman Parry Collection 1933–1935*, ed. M. Kay (1995); *Oral Formulaic Theory and Research*, ed. J. M. Foley, rev. ed. (1995)—updated electronic version, http://www.oraltradition. org/bibliography.

■ **Criticism and History:** Parry; D. Tedlock, *Finding the Center: Narrative Poetry of the Zuñi Indians* (1972); R. Bauman, *Verbal Art as Performance* (1977); D. Biebuyck, *Hero and Chief: Epic Literature from the Banyanga Zaire Republic* (1978); S. Koljević, *The Epic in the Making* (1980); D. H. Hymes, *In Vain I Tried to Tell You: Essays in Native American Ethnopoetics* (1981); C. J. Clover, *The Medieval Saga* (1982);

Y. R. Lockwood, *Text and Context: Folksong in a Bosnian Muslim Village* (1983); D. Tedlock, *The Spoken Word and the Work of Interpretation* (1983); R. Bauman, *Story, Performance, and Event* (1986); E. A. Havelock, *The Muse Learns to Write* (1986); J. Goody, *The Interface between the Written and the Oral* (1987); S. Slyomovics, *The Merchant of Art: An Egyptian Hilali Oral Epic Poet in Performance* (1987); R. H. Finnegan, *Orality and Literacy* (1988); R. P. Martin, *The Language of Heroes: Speech and Performance in the "Iliad"* (1989); J. S. Kolsti, *The Bilingual Singer: A Study in Albanian and Serbo-Croatian Oral Epic Poetry* (1990); W. B. McCarthy, *The Ballad Matrix* (1990); J. T. Titon, *Downhome Blues Lyrics* (1990); M. H. Beissinger, *The Art of the "Lǎutar": The Epic Tradition of Romania* (1991); J. B. Flueckiger, *Boundaries of the Text: Epic Performances in South and Southeast Asia* (1991); J. M. Foley, *Immanent Art: From Structure to Meaning in Oral Traditional Epic* (1991); S. A. Mitchell, *Heroic Sagas and Ballads* (1991); R. H. Finnegan, *Oral Traditions and the Verbal Arts* (1992); R. Keeling, *Cry for Luck: Sacred Song and Speech among the Yurok, Hupa, and Karok Indians* (1992); J. E. Limón, *Mexican Ballads, Chicano Poems* (1992); I. Okpewho, *African Oral Literature* (1992); K. Reichl, *Turkic Oral Poetry* (1992); *Russian Folk Lyrics*, intro. V. Propp, trans. R. Reeder (1993); T. A. DuBois, *Finnish Folk Poetry and the "Kalevala"* (1995); J. M. Foley, *The Singer of Tales in Performance* (1995); A. B. Lord, *The Singer Resumes the Tale* (1995); D. F. Reynolds, *Heroic Poets, Poetic Heroes: The Ethnography of Performance in an Arabic Oral Epic Tradition* (1995); D. C. Rubin, *Memory in Oral Traditions* (1995); P. G. Zolbrod, *Reading the Voice: Native American Oral Poetry* (1995); G. Nagy, *Homeric Questions* and *Poetry as Performance: Homer and Beyond* (both 1996); S. Niditch, *Oral World and Written Word: Ancient Israelite Literature* (1996); *Oral Epics from Africa*, ed. J. W. Johnson et al. (1997); D. Brown, *Voicing the Text: South African Oral Poetry and Performance* (1998); T. A. Hale, *Griots and Griottes* (1998); M. Levin, *Slam* (1998); J. Opland, *Xhosa Poets and Poetry* (1998); J. Sherzer, *Verbal Arts in San Blas* (1998); S. P. Belcher, *Epic Traditions of Africa* (1999); J. D. Niles, *Homo Narrans: The Poetics and Anthropology of Oral Literature* (1999); R. H. Kaschula, *The Bones of the Ancestors are Shaking: Xhosa Oral Poetry in Context* (2000); Lord; J. H. McDowell, *The Ballad Tradition of Mexico's Costa Chica* (2000); K. Reichl, *Singing the Past: Turkic and Medieval Heroic Poetry* (2000); B. J. Reagon, *If You Don't Go, Don't Hinder Me: The African-American Sacred Song Tradition* (2001); J. M. Foley, *How to Read an Oral Poem* (2002); D. Atkinson, *The English Traditional Ballad* (2002); M.-A. Constantine and G. Porter, *Fragments and Meaning in Traditional Songs* (2003); L. Goodman, *Singing the Songs of My Ancestors* (2003); L. Honko, *The Maiden's Death Song* and *Textualising the Siri Epic* (both 2003); A. Vidan, *Embroidered with Gold, Strung with Pearls: The Traditional Ballads of Bosnian Women* (2003); *The Wedding of Mustajbey's Son Bećirbey*, ed. and trans. J. M. Foley (2004); T. A. DuBois, *Lyric, Meaning, and Audience in the Oral Tradition of Northern*

*Europe* (2006); R. H. Finnegan, *The Oral and Beyond* (2007)—on Africa.

M. H. BEISSINGER

**ORGANICISM.** Organicism is neither strictly a theory of poetry nor a comprehensive methodology but a set of concerns derived from the analogy between a work of art and a living thing. The term often serves as a placeholder for thinking about the conditions of poetic *unity and the nature of *form, as well as about the inextricability of form from meaning. Although the hist. of organic *metaphors in general can be traced back to Plato (who first articulated the problem of unity in terms of the relation of the parts to the whole) and Aristotle (who consolidated the idea of the interdependence of form and matter in the concept of substantial form), the conceptual thrust in the organicist story was provided by 18th-c. Ger. philosophers and poets (J. W. Goethe, Immanuel Kant, A. W. Schlegel, and Friedrich Schiller). Kant's characterization of works of art, as seemingly endowed with the kind of purposiveness we assign to natural things, revolutionized thinking about aesthetic objects. In the metaphysics of the Ger. romantics, poems not only behave *like* natural things (i.e., develop into their complete form according to an inner principle of growth, display a strict interdependence of parts and whole, with the whole having an a priori existence to the parts) but *are* nature's ultimate product, the apotheosis of its vital and organizing powers realized through the artist's creativity. S. T. Coleridge imported many of these ideas to England, the most prominent being A. W. Schlegel's opposition between organic form (innate and self-evolved) and mechanical form (imposed from the outside). However, it remains a question how useful biological analogies derived from a metaphysical system are for modern poetics. The early organicists did not, in fact, offer any but figurative clues to the kind of structure an "organic" poem might actually have.

It remained for 20th-c. critical movements (mainly *Russian formalism, *New Criticism, and the *Chicago school) to give new life to these notions. As the most prominent proponents of organicism, the New Critics derived their concepts of tension and internal coherence from Coleridge's "unity in multeity." The poem thus became for them a special kind of thing: an intricate, highly organized autonomous structure that requires intense, close analysis of the dynamic relations between its parts. As a result of a close study of lang., most formalists asserted the absolute and organic interdependence of form and content.

With its roots in a monistic philosophy, organicism always had a moral inflection and was thus suspect to some critics. Values such as coherence, completeness, and *autonomy were not only appraisals of poetic merit (the more highly integrated a poem, the better and the closer to the ideal of beauty) but judgments against forms of *realism that were "merely" mimetic and thus inadequately universal. Consequently, organicism was not well received by postmodern critics. Deconstruction undid organicist notions of coherence by pointing to the endless possibilities for discontinuity and difference (see POSTSTRUCTURALISM); *New Historicism did the same by reestablishing the irreducibility of external context as the poem's environment.

While critiques of the privileged status of the aesthetic object reestablished the dialectical nature of aesthetic experience, they never quite deflated the power of the organic *trope. On the one hand, aesthetic experience continues to call for animate lang. to illuminate its workings, and on the other, ever-elusive questions about poetic structure regularly return to the indissoluble bond between form and content. Organicism, as it is known today, emerged as a result of the paradigm shift in the late 18th c. but was never (for its early advocates) solely a totalizing process. The variety of questions organicism has generated over the years points to its relevance for the study of poetry. In many ways, it remains a reference point for basic questions about poetic structure, questions that remain constant at the intersection of life and art, even as answers change over time.

*See* NATURE, ROMANTIC AND POSTROMANTIC POETRY AND POETICS.

■ C. Brooks, "The Poem as Organism," *English Institute Annual 1940* (1941); J. Benziger, "Organic Unity: Leibniz to Coleridge," *PMLA* 66 (1951); Abrams; C. Brooks, "Implications of an Organic Theory of Poetry," *Literature and Belief,* ed. M. H. Abrams (1958); C. Lord, "Organic Unity Reconsidered," *JAAC* 22 (1964); G.N.G. Orsini, "The Organic Concepts in Aesthetics," *CL* 21 (1969); *Organic Form: The Life of an Idea,* ed. G. S. Rousseau (1972); G.N.G. Orsini, "Organicism," *Organic Unity in Ancient and Later Poetics* (1975); E. Rothstein, "'Organicism,' Rupturalism, and Ism-ism," *MP* 85 (1988); J. Neubauer, "Organicist Poetics as Romantic Heritage?" *Romantic Poetry,* ed. A. Esterhammer (2002); C. I. Armstrong, *Romantic Organicism: From Idealist Origins to Ambivalent Afterlife* (2003); F. Beiser, *The Romantic Imperative: The Concept of Early German Romanticism* (2004).

H. JANISZEWSKA

**ORIGINALITY.** Usually denotes the quality of novelty or creativity inherent in an artistic work relative to other works. Behind this seemingly self-evident notion lie substantial interpretive problems that have occupied artists at least since the Romans wrote in the shadow of the Greeks. The most interesting of these is what McFarland has termed "the originality paradox," in which those writers most concerned with their own originality will insist elsewhere, in equally strong terms, that all writing is *imitation. Thus, R. W. Emerson, who warned that "imitation is suicide" ("Self-Reliance," 1841), also wrote, "Every book is a quotation; and every house is a quotation out of all forests, and mines, and stone quarries; and every man is a quotation from all his ancestors" (*Representative Men,* 1850). Often the strongest declarations of originality are themselves imitations or trans.: Ezra Pound's exhortation to "make it new," which has come to encapsulate the 20th c.'s emphasis on innovation, is itself a deliberate mistrans. of an ancient Chinese inscription, as Heinzelman has argued. The counterintuitive relation of originality to imitation is where any serious discussion of the term must begin.

From the Roman period, writers have often insisted on ownership of their own words or attacked others for stealing them. Martial first employed the term *plagiarius* (*Epigrams* 1.52), meaning "kidnapper," to describe literary theft (plagiarism), and poets up through the Ren. frequently defended the uniqueness of their work. John Donne wrote in his second satire that of all poets, "he is worst, who (beggarly) doth chaw / Others' wits' fruits." Certainly, a writer's sense of ownership over his or her own works, and a concomitant belief that those who copy them are stealing the writer's words or ideas, seems a necessary if not a sufficient criterion for the mod. concept of originality.

Yet for much of the hist. of Western poetry, as well as that of most Eastern trads., writerly creativity was judged more by the artful imitation of other writers than by the quality of novelty. Put more strongly, imitation was viewed as the most effective path to originality. Writers went forward by looking backward. Horace, whose *Odes* were themselves modeled on earlier Gr. lyrics, enjoined poets in his *Ars poetica* to "review the Greek models night and day" and, by doing so, to produce creatively challenging work. In fact, a better term than *originality* for pre-18th-c. attitudes might be what Greene and others have called "creative imitation," the imitation and strategic revision of prior authors in order to create a mingling of (in Greene's words) "filial rejection with respect." Such a work responds to and struggles against the great works of the past to engage more fully with the present. Most folk trads., as well as Eastern literary and artistic trads. (which, in general, are less concerned than Western art about the question of originality), have also underlined the primacy of imitation; Confucius's statement "I transmit rather than create" remains influential, though not universal, in Chinese artistic practice.

Through the end of the 17th c., in England as well as throughout Europe, most literary writers exercised some form of creative imitation. Indeed, writing that announced itself as sui generis was viewed with suspicion. Three major aspects of med. and early mod. culture—one theological, one literary, and one technological—help account for this view of originality. The first derives from the pervasive Christian notion of *imitatio Christi*, which held that human beings should imitate God, the only original. Originality might thus be considered as a sin of pride, a view that John Milton underscores in *Paradise Lost* by associating the concept exclusively with Satan, Chaos, and, of course, "original" sin. The second involves the importance of cl. authorities, esp. Homer and Virgil, whom the Middle Ages saw as crucial models for literary achievement. The Ren. humanists, who in many ways broke from med. paradigms, in this regard heightened the importance of cl. models, viewing Gr. and Roman antiquity as a kind of summit that could be imitated but probably not attained. Third, ms. writing practices (the printing press was invented in the mid-15th c.),

with their reliance on anonymity, collaborative authorship, trans., and commentary, resisted the centralizing "author function," in Michel Foucault's phrase ("What Is an Author?," 1979), which contributed to mod. originality by associating a given creative production with a singular individual.

The term *originality* and its emphasis on ex nihilo newness, rather than the imitation of past writers, appeared only in the mid-18th c. An ideal of intrinsic, organic creativity began to displace the earlier ideal of imitation—now defined as a mechanical, extrinsic process derived from the assiduous copying of earlier and better writers. In one of the first essays to address the topic at length (*Conjectures on Original Composition*, 1759), Edward Young set the mod. terms of the debate: "An *Original* may be said to be of a *vegetable* nature; it rises spontaneously from the vital root of Genius; it *grows*, it is not *made*: *Imitations* are often a sort of *Manufacture* wrought up by those *Mechanics*, *Art*, and *Labour*, out of pre-existent materials not their own." The romantic poets, with whom the notion of originality is most closely identified, roughly equated originality with the *imagination. For S. T. Coleridge, the poet is like a lute lying open to the natural breezes of *inspiration. (Yet Coleridge, in his letter to Thomas Curnick of April 9, 1814, also described even the best poetry as "a cento of lines that had pre-existed in other works" [see CENTO].) William Wordsworth and Coleridge's famous definition of poetry (in the Preface to the second ed. of *Lyrical Ballads*, 1800) as "emotion recollected in tranquility" likewise encourages an identification of originality with the poet's authentic, expressive self. For Woodmansee and others, the rise of originality coincides roughly with the devel. of copyright and a strong conception of authorship: originality makes the most sense only when an identifiable author can lay claim to legal ownership of his or her writing. It is probably no accident that Wordsworth advocated vociferously to extend the term of copyright under Brit. law.

After the romantics, ideas of originality found their strongest focus in three contrasting dicta of modernist poetics. The most famous, Pound's "make it new," has been used as a rallying cry for avant-garde innovation in the form of radical breaks with the past (see AVANT-GARDE POETICS, MODERNISM). But this belies Pound's actual poetic practice, which relied heavily on the imitation, trans., and renovation of earlier poets and poetic forms. The second dictum is T. S. Eliot's subtle plea for the value of imitation in "Tradition and the Individual Talent" (1919): "we shall often find that not only the best, but the most individual parts of [a poet's] work may be those in which the dead poets, his ancestors, assert their immortality most vigorously." As Frye argues in *Anatomy of Criticism*, "any serious study of literature soon shows that the real difference between the original and the imitative poet is simply that the former is more profoundly imitative." Pound and Eliot are closer than they might appear; scholars have suggested that both poets think of originality as the calculated infusion of the moribund present with the immediacy of the past. "Innovation," writes Hollander, "is itself an innovation of periods in our hist. that were aware of their forerunners."

The third poet whose rethinking of originality in the beginning of the 20th c. most influenced later poets is Gertrude Stein, whose deceptively casual assertions such as "I am inclined to believe there is no such thing as repetition" ("Portraits and Repetition," 1935) paved the way for postmodernist challenges by asking whether there is such a thing as originality at all and, if it exists, whether it is desirable. If there is no *repetition—i.e., if every repetition is actually in some sense a new creation—then there can also be no originality because every new instance of lang. is as original as every other. The use of repetition, a central feature of Stein's poetic practice, has since been explored most pointedly in visual art, from Marcel Duchamp's *Fountain* to Andy Warhol's Campbell's Soup experiments to Sherrie Levine's "Appropriation Art." Coming at the problem from the opposite direction, Baudrillard argues that "a truly unique, absolute object . . . is unthinkable," because objects draw their meaning from their relation to other objects, to the series of which they are always a part.

In the late 20th c., *innovation* and *experiment* largely replaced *originality* as the terms of art in Eng., with subtle differences in emphasis. Although poetry that refers to itself as innovative often explicitly rejects romantic poetic practice, this rejection takes form more often against the romantic conception of the authentically expressive speaker than against the originality of individual *genius per se. In the 21st c., however, poets and theorists have addressed the paradox of originality more directly. Schwartz posits that, under the pressures of digital replicating technologies, the Internet, and postmod. approaches to copyright and intellectual property, "creation and imitation, invention and repetition may become as indistinct as knowing is from copying." *Oulipo has rethought originality by emphasizing techniques of randomness and collaboration and by emphasizing process and "potential" over the finished products of identifiable genius. (Perhaps the most radical challenge to originality, Oulipo suggests, is nonchalance.) Recent experiments in textual appropriation, such as the *Flarf movement's use of lang. culled from Google searches, have sought to redraw the boundaries between plagiarism and originality. *Conceptual poetry often uses techniques of plagiarism, copying, and appropriation, leading Kenneth Goldsmith to declare in "Conceptual Poetry/Conceptual Interview," an interview with Anne Guthrie (2008), that "[c]onceptual writing obstinately makes no claims on originality." One of the most sustained interrogations of originality has emerged from feminist poets who, harkening back to Jackson Mac Low's Buddhist-influenced experiments with *aleatory poetics, see originality as "an ego project," and seek to reconceive the act of creation through other patterns of *influence and generation. Hillman, for instance, considers creation via the mysteries of alchemy: "an inventor is subsumed in

her process but a style makes an original thing. How? Can't help you there."

See AGUDEZA, CONCEPTUAL POETRY, EXPRESSION, INVENTION, WIT.

■ Frye; H. White, *Plagiarism and Imitation during the English Renaissance* (1965); W. J. Bate, *The Burden of the Past and the English Poet* (1970); H. Bloom, *The Anxiety of Influence* (1973); E. Eisenstein, *The Printing Press as an Agent of Change* (1980); S. Orgel, "The Renaissance Artist as Plagiarist," *ELH* 48 (1981); T. M. Greene, *The Light in Troy: Imitation and Discovery in Renaissance Poetry* (1982); S. Sargent, "Can Latecomers Get There First?: Sung Poets and T'ang Poetry," *Chinese Literature* 4 (1982); D. Quint, *Origin and Originality in Renaissance Literature* (1983); R. Krauss, *The Originality of the Avant Garde and Other Modernist Myths* (1985); T. McFarland, *Originality and Imagination* (1985); A. Plaks, "The Aesthetics of Irony in Late Ming Literature and Painting," *Words and Images*, ed. A. Murck and W. Fong (1991); M. Woodmansee, *The Construction of Authorship* (1994); W. Alford, *To Steal a Book Is an Elegant Offense* (1995); H. Schwartz, *Culture of the Copy* (1996); J. Hollander, *The Work of Poetry* (1997); B. Hillman, "Twelve Writings toward a Poetics of Alchemy, Dread, Inconsistency, Betweenness, and California Geological Syntax," *American Women Poets in the 21st Century*, ed. C. Rankine and J. Spahr (2002); J. Loewenstein, *Ben Jonson and Possessive Authorship* (2002); *Plagiarism in Early Modern England*, ed. P. Kewes (2003); *Make It New: The Rise of Modernism*, ed. K. Heinzelman (2004); J. Baudrillard, *The System of Objects*, trans. J. Benedict (2005); *The Consequence of Innovation: 21st-Century Poetics*, ed. C. Dworkin (2008); M. Boon, *In Praise of Copying* (2010).

D. GOLDSTEIN

**ORIYA POETRY.** The Oriya-speaking area of India, now called Odisha—a state on the country's eastern coast, between Bengal and Andhra Pradesh—was known as Udra, Kalinga, Kangod, Koshala, and Utkala during different historical periods since the composition of the *Mahābhārata*, ca. 2500 BCE. The ancient form of the lang., now the mother tongue of more than 30 million people, incl. 62 different tribes (which speak various dialects) and the diasporic population, is mentioned in the Sanskrit grammarian Panini's *Astādhyāyi* (5th c. BCE), where he refers to it as "Udra Bibhasha." However, written lit. in Oriya began only in the 10th c. CE. The major poets of that era—such as Sabaripa, Kanhupa, and Luipa—were Buddhist Sahajayana mystics. Their poems, called *Charyapada*, are artistic records of the lives of disciplined spiritual practitioners. They can be read at different levels: they simultaneously evoke the terrestrial and transcendent realms; they also cloak the sublime under a seemingly erotic surface. Poetry seems for them to be the locus in which the natural world and intimations from beyond come together.

This foundational notion that a poet's consciousness is intimately in touch with a subtle, unseen, and all-controlling force, even as the poet remains firmly planted in the visible world of objects, seems to permeate the entire oeuvre of Oriya poetry. Although between the 12th and 19th cs. Sahajayana Buddhism gave way to spiritual practices such as Shakti worship, Shaivism, the Jagannath cult, and Vaishnavism as the dominant belief systems informing poetic art, poetry in Oriya was always seen as an intermediate space between the immanent and the transcendent, an inevitable part of the spiritual practice leading to *Moksha* or liberation. Depending on the methods adopted for such liberation, poet-seekers can be divided mainly into two categories: *Yogis*, who perceive the sensory world as *Maya* or illusion and seek to withdraw from it, and *Bhaktas*, or poets of devotion, who represent the world of objects as a legitimate means by which to transcend it. The poets Achyutananda Das (early 17th c.), Yasobanta Das, and Ananta Das (both later 17th c.) belong to the first category, while Banamali (1729–90), Baladeva Ratha (1789–1845), Gopalakrishna Patnaik (1785–1862), and Gourahari (1814–90) represent the latter. Bhimabhoi (1845–95) dares to embrace hell eternally so that the rest of the world can obtain deliverance. From the margins of society, this poet-activist challenged all forms of the status quo and created a political and poetic idiom that pleaded for an egalitarian social order. He represents the acme of Oriya poetic genius.

The 1,000-year span between the beginnings of Oriya written lit. and the 19th-c. poets includes a number of humanistic poems in various subgenres, such as *bhajans* (devotional songs), *jananas* (songs of supplication), *chaupadis* (rhyming quartrains), *chitaus* (epistolary poems), *chautishas* (poems in 34 *couplets, each beginning with a consonant), *koilis* (odes addressed to a cuckoo), *samhitas* and *patalas* (two forms of discursive poetry), and *champus* (chaupadis in chautisha form). In these, poets translate their particular experiences into a universal idiom.

A parallel trad. of *puranas*, *epics, and *kavyas* existed as well during this period, originating with Sarala Das's 15th-c. trans. of the *Mahābhārata*, *Saptasati Chandi*, *Devi Māhātmya*, and *Bichitra Rāmāyana* and bolstered by 16th-c. trans. of the *Rāmāyana* and the *Bhāgabata* by Balaram Das (1465–1546) and Jagannath Das (1470–1542), respectively. These trans. were radical attempts at vernacularization and coincided with the founding of a powerful Oriya empire by Kapilendra Dev and its subsequent consolidation by his inheritors. The aesthetic evident in these works can be said to mirror the sociopolitical by subverting the dominant pan-Indian Sanskritic-Brahminical hegemony. The trans. violated the hitherto inviolable purity of the so-called holy texts, producing syncretic works that brought 1,000 years of local hist. and quotidian concerns into confrontation and reconciliation with what was perceived to be universal. These pioneers mediated elite ideas in plebeian lang., humanized the epic characters, and set a model for the subsequent 200 noniconic trans. that constitute the bulk of med. Oriya poetry.

After securely establishing its identity, Oriya poetry began in the 18th c. to compete directly with the Sanskrit master texts. In the isolation and elegance of the royal courts, an ornate poetic trad. was developed by the court poets, who dared to surpass the stylization, verbal artistry, technical elegance, and erudition hitherto available only in Sanskrit poetics. This attempt to valorize Oriya over Sanskrit, at least in the limited and arid realm of stylized expression, by poets like Arjuna Das (16th c.), Dhananjaya Bhanja (1611–1701), Dinakrishna Das (ca. 1670–1740), Upendra Bhanja (ca. 1685–1750), and Abhimanyu Samantasinghar (1757–1806), can be considered an aesthetic recompense in the face of a larger sociopolitical malady. The Gajapati empire, which had held the Oriya people and their pride together, had collapsed. First under the Muslims and then under the Marathas, the Oriyas suffered greatly. The artistic poise that Oriya ornate poetry achieved was absolutely disconnected from the turmoil and uncertainty experienced by the population.

A semblance of order seems to have been restored with the advent of the British in the early 19th c. Oriya poetry now rarely considered Sanskrit to be a competing discourse but rather looked westward for inspiration. The impact of Europe created a Janus-faced poetic consciousness that demonstrated alternately subservience and hostility toward colonial cultural structures. On the one hand, the poets searched for their roots so as to reinvent themselves authentically; on the other, they eagerly appropriated the innovations available in the hegemonic culture. The contributions of Radhanath Ray (1848–1908), Madhusudan Rao (1853–1912), Fakirmohan Senapati (1843–1918), and their 20th-c. inheritors reflect this divided allegiance.

Western contact transformed Oriya poetry in many other ways. Eur. *romanticism, democratic ideals, and liberal thought galvanized nationalist consciousness. Quotidian social, economic, political, cultural, and epistemic issues found expression and legitimacy. Major intellectual currents as well as thematic and stylistic innovations tried out in the West found an echo in Oriya poetry. It can be argued that Oriya poetry in the 20th c. once again became dependent, as ornate poetry in the 18th and 19th cs. had been, through its replication of *Sanskrit poetics. But there is an important difference. While the earlier mode had been more inward and exclusive, cutting itself off from the life of ordinary people, contemp. poetry has been more outward and inclusive, truly global in its aspirations, even as it tries to represent the local faithfully.

The journey of Oriya poetry seems to have come full circle. The genre used by Sarala Das, Balaram Das, and others to shake off intellectual dependence on the elite Sanskrit *epistemē* and assert Oriya regional identity and by the saint-poets of the *Bhakti* movement to articulate indigenous philosophical ideas could not maintain its distinct identity. Sociopolitical conditions created new dependencies in the 18th c. and after. Since literary trends are not immune to economic and political pressure, such dependencies were in a way inevitable. What is significant, however, is that Oriya poetry has profitably negotiated changing conditions. It remains to be seen how Oriya poetry responds to the facts of today's global world, with its threats of monolingualism and monoculturalism.

■ S. Dash, *Odia Sahityara Itihasha* (History of Oriya Literature, 4 v., 1963–68); G. Nandasharma, *Sribharata Darpana* (The Mirror of the Mahābhārata, 1964); N. Samantaraya, *Odia Sahityara Itihasha* (History of Oriya Literature, 1964); K. Kar, *Ascharya Charyachaya* (Wonderful Art of Charya Poetry, 1969); S. Acharya, *Odia Kavyakaushala* (Oriya Aesthetics and Stylistics, 1983); S. Mishra, *Atitara Barnabodha* (The Primer of the Past, 2002).

D. R. Pattanaik

**ORNAMENT.** The poetic notion of ornament was shaped by the rhetorical trad. in which it originated. In cl. rhet., ornament (Gr. *kosmos*, Lat. *ornatus*) is the third major component of *style, after grammatical correctness and clarity of expression (see, e.g., Quintilian, *Institutio oratoria* 8.3). Figures and *tropes but also the twin arts of choosing the best words and combining them for effect (with respect to *syntax, *sound, and *rhythm) all pertain to ornament. While correctness and clarity define an orator's basic stylistic competence, ornament makes the speech elegant or brilliant, causing pleasure and admiration in the listener or reader and preventing boredom in the process. There are cases in which ornament does not seem to exceed the requirements of correctness and clarity: in *plain style, the apparent absence of ornament functions in fact as one. More generally, from a rhetorical perspective, it is through ornament that style or "elocution" (alongside the *"invention" and "disposition" of arguments) contributes to the orator's persuasive task, notably by amplifying or diminishing what is being discussed. One key condition is that ornament be also apt, proper, and appropriate: all aspects of the speech having to "fit" one another, ornament must be well suited to subject and context, even though its core function is to transform what we perceive of them. It follows that ornament varies with the genre of the speech.

In epideictic rhet. (praise and blame—see EPIDEICTIC POETRY), which is not supposed to have an immediate persuasive purpose, ornament is freer to draw attention to itself as something to be enjoyed, whereas such aesthetic relish can hinder persuasion in forensic or deliberative (political) eloquence: there the beautiful must never be separated from the useful, and ornament must not be perceived as superfluous or excessive in any way. Successful ornament, in this view, is absorbed in the energy it generates. Thus, a forensic speech may not be less prone to figurative lang., nor give less attention to rhythm, than a demonstrative one; but in the former, the very effectiveness of ornament is supposed to preclude its perception as a distinct source of enjoyment. This contrast is often set between two qualities of style—force versus grace, dignity versus loveliness—and enhanced by heavily gendered metaphors: true orators must not indulge in effeminate, overly sweet ornaments but favor brisk, virile ones; the glint of speech must be that of steel, not gold; its color, that of flesh and blood, not makeup.

From this perspective, poetry tended to be seen as an art designed primarily for pleasure, in which ornament could be deployed for its own sake (although Lat. rhetoricians, while warning orators against the toxic wiles of poets, relied on Virgil as often as Cicero to provide examples of "effective" ornament). Thus, rhythm is more perceptible in verse than in prose; poetic comparisons and metaphors can afford to be obscure or distracting instead of having to sharpen an argument; ornaments of all kinds, flaunting their own charm, may even reflect themselves in the poem's subject matter, presented as worthy of aesthetic contemplation (such as a beautiful woman, a flowery landscape, a work of art)—hence, e.g., the central role of description in late Lat. and med. poetry, in which the poetic tended to merge with the epideictic, while treatises of poetics, for their part, mined the catalog of rhetorical ornaments, split between *ornatus difficilis* (tropes, involving a mutation of meaning) and *ornatus facilis* (other figures).

Yet practitioners of ostentatious ornament did not necessarily see it as lessening a speech's persuasive vigor: the norm that defined excess was never stable. What a particular era deemed too flamboyant and "poetic" to be effective in political speech could strike other tastes—during Rome's late imperial period, e.g., or among 15th-c. *rhétoriqueurs*—as the height of rhetorical power. Conversely, while excessive ornament was often attacked, within the rhetorical trad., in the name of appropriate eloquence, it was destined to become the hated symbol of this very trad. in the eyes of later times (such as the 18th and 19th cs.), which endeavored to free "natural" eloquence (incl. poetry) from all the conventions of rhet. itself.

In truth, while pondering its debt to rhetorical models, poetry had never ceased to reflect (and feel ambivalent) about ornament; it had issued its own warnings against excess and enacted its own version of the rhetorical contrast between force and grace. Ren. poetry, in particular, was caught between a renewed cult of beauty and a renewed obsession with oratory's persuasive impact. Sixteenth-c. poets and poeticians often tried to fuse the two in one specific idea of poetic eloquence, notably in the grander genres (such as the *epic), which cast elevated public matters in a sublime light without obeying the strictures of utilitarian persuasion. A key figure in this respect was *enargeia* (or *evidentia*, i.e., "showing" vividly with words), which helped attach rhet.'s culture of heightened emotion to the idea of representation (*mimesis), increasingly understood as poetry's defining task, following Aristotle. Yet the art of verbal "painting" could also be used, in lighter poems, to aestheticize objects for enjoyment, and to cultivate poetic admiration as a self-referential experience (see UT PICTURA POESIS).

Thus, the notion of poetic ornament, of poetry *as* ornament, remained ambiguous throughout the successive rhetorical ages: while ornament could always be understood as decoration (and be dismissed, or savored, as such), it also suggested a splendid fusion of the convincing and the beautiful, transcending their respective limits. The nature, means, and goals of such an effect were as varied and problematic as the definition of poetry itself. However, when romantic poetics sought to break away from the rhetorical paradigm and refused altogether to view beauty as something "added" to thought by way of words, ornament became a foil to mod. concepts of lit.—and, in particular, of *pure poetry as subjective expression and ling. creation. Yet mod. poets often circled back to it, metaphorizing ornament as a paradoxical, mysterious emblem of their art: thus, in 19th-c. France, e.g., from Charles Baudelaire's "flowers of evil" and "sonorous jewels" to Stéphane Mallarmé's "abolished bauble of sonorous inanity," the problem of ornament's power and substance (or lack thereof) proved central to the very sense of what the poetic form hoped to accomplish.

See ARTIFICE, RENAISSANCE POETRY, RHETORIC AND POETRY, ROMANTIC AND POSTROMANTIC POETRY AND POETICS.

■ Curtius; A. Michel, *La parole et la beauté* (1982); J. Lecointe, *L'idéal et la différence* (1993); P. Galand-Hallyn, *Le reflet des fleurs* (1994), and *Les yeux de l'éloquence* (1995).

F. CORNILLIAT

**OTTAVA RIMA.** Though now widely dispersed in various Western langs., largely because of the fame of Lord Byron's masterpiece *Don Juan*, ottava rima (or *ottava toscana*; Ger. *stanze*; Rus. *oktava*) originated as an *Italian prosody, an *octave stanza in *hendecasyllables rhyming *abababcc*. Though its origin is obscure, it is clearly a form that evolved in an oral poetic culture. Scholars relate the form to the stanza of the *canzone or the *sirventes, perhaps in imitation of the Sicilian *strambotto that emerged in the 14th c. for long poems (*cantari*) of less than epic length. It was in use in religious verse of late 13th-c. Italy, but only received definitive artistic form in Giovanni Boccaccio's *Filostrato* (1335?) and *Teseida* (1340–42?). It soon became the dominant form of It. narrative verse, being developed in the 15th c. by Politian, Luigi Pulci, and Matteo Maria Boiardo and reaching its apotheosis in the *Orlando furioso* (1516) of Ludovico Ariosto, where its potentialities for richness, complexity, and variety of effect are brilliantly exploited. Torquato Tasso (*Gerusalemme liberata*) showed his mastery of the form later in the century, and it was subsequently employed in Italy by Giambattista Marino (*Adone*), Alessandro Tassoni (*La secchia rapita*), Vittorio Alfieri (*Etruria vendicata*), Niccoló Tommaseo (*Una serva, La Contessa Matilde*), and Giovanni Marradi (*Sinfonia del bosco*).

In the broader Eur. context, the poets of Ren. Spain and Portugal followed the It. example in adopting the form for narrative purposes. Notable *epics in ottava rima are Alonso de Ercilla's *La Araucana* in Sp. and Luís de Camões' *The Lusíads* in Portuguese. The form was explored by Eng. Ren. poets like Thomas Wyatt (some 15 poems, most monostrophic), Philip Sidney (*Old Arcadia*), Edmund Spenser, Samuel Daniel (*Civil Wars*), Michael Drayton, and Fulke Greville; and it was followed as well in the great trans. by John Harington (Ariosto) and Edward Fairfax (Tasso). John Milton uses it for the coda of "Lycidas."

The form did not find its true non-It. master until Byron, whose trans. of a portion of Pulci's *Morgante Maggiore* (inspired by J. H. Frere's *The Monks and the Giants*) launched him into a deep exploration of the stanza's poetic resources. After a brief use of the form in an epistle to his sister in 1816, he began using the stanza extensively in 1817, first in *Beppo* and then, with astonishing panache, in *Don Juan* and *The Vision of Judgment*. P. B. Shelley used it after 1820, chiefly for "The Witch of Atlas," and John Keats uses it earlier for "Isabella." It was popularized in Rus. poetry by Alexander Pushkin on the model of Byron.

The work of the great masters of the stanza—Boccaccio, Pulci, Ariosto, Byron—suggests that ottava rima is most suited to work of a varied nature, blending serious, comic, and satiric attitudes and mingling narrative and discursive modes. Referring to Pulci, Byron calls it "the half-serious rhyme" (*Don Juan* 4.6). Its accumulation of rhyme, reaching a precarious crescendo with the third repetition, prepares the reader for the neatsummation, the acute observation, or the epigrammatic twist that comes with the final couplet:

> And Julia's voice was lost, except in sighs,
>   Until too late for useful conversation;
> The tears were gushing from her gentle eyes,
>   I wish, indeed, they had not had occasion;
> But who, alas! can love, and then be wise?
>   Not that remorse did not oppose temptation:
> A little still she strove, and much repented,
> And whispering "I will ne'er consent"—
>   consented.
>
> (*Don Juan* 1.117)

At eight lines (cf. the Spenserian of nine), the ottava rima stanza is long enough to carry the thread of narrative but not so long that it becomes unmanageable, and it allows much greater room for exposition and elaboration than do *quatrains.

Although A. C. Swinburne remarked that Byron's achievement had spoiled the chances for later poets, he himself employed the form to wonderful effect in his seriocomic narrative "Arthur's Flogging." W. B. Yeats, a mod. master of the form, uses it for some 15 of his poems, incl. "Sailing to Byzantium," "Among School Children," and "The Circus Animals' Desertion." Significantly, Yeats develops the form precisely at the same time (1910–19) that the dreamy style of his early period is evolving into the more realistic, colloquial style of the great poems of his middle period. After Yeats, the form is brilliantly used by A. D. Hope, James Merrill, Kenneth Koch (*The Duplications*, 1975), Anthony Burgess (*Byrne*, pub. posthumously in 1995), Alan Wearne (*The Lovemakers*, 2001), and by various other late 20th-c. Eng.-lang. poets.

See SICILIAN OCTAVE.

■ Schipper; P. Habermann, "Stanze," *Reallexikon I*; G. Bunte, *Zur Verskunst der deutschen Stanze* (1928); V. Pernicone, "Storia e svolgimento della metrica," *Problemi ed orientamenti critici di lingua e di letteratura italiana*, ed. A. Momigliano, vol. 2 (1948); G. M. Ridenour, *The Style of "Don Juan"* (1960); A. Limentani,

"Storia e struttura dell'ottava rima," *Lettere italiane* 13 (1961); A. Roncaglia, "Per la storia dell'ottava rima," *CN* 25 (1965); R. Beum, *The Poetic Art of W. B. Yeats* (1969), chap. 10; E. G. Etkind, *Russkie poety-perevodchiki ot Trediakovskogo do Pushkina* (1973), 155–201; Spongano; Wilkins; Elwert, *Italienische*; I. K. Lilly, "Some Structural Invariants in Russian and German Ottava Rima," *Style* 21 (1987); F. Calitti, "L'ottava rima: stile pedestre, umile, moderno," *Anticomoderno* (1996); L. Bartoli, "Considerazioni attorno ad una questione metricologica. Il Boccaccio e le origini dell'ottava rima," *Quaderns d'Italià* 4–5 (1999–2000); C. Addison, "*Ottava Rima* and Novelistic Discourse," *Journal of Narrative Theory* 34.2 (2004).

A. Preminger; C. Kleinhenz; T.V.F. Brogan.; J. McGann

**OULIPO**, an acronym for *OUvroir de LIttérature POtentielle* (Workshop of Potential Literature), is a Paris-based group of writers and mathematicians who explore and extend the field of lit. through the practice of "writing under constraint" (see CONSTRAINT). Founded in 1960 by François Le Lionnais (1901–84) and Raymond Queneau (1903–76), the Oulipo has come to occupy a singular position among international avant-gardes and contemp. literary research groups, partly because, for more than 50 years, its three generations of members have managed to sustain a distinctive and coherent agenda. At its inception, the Oulipo was a scientific seminar adhered to by a small group of writers, linguists, and mathematicians united by friendship and their common predilection for literary humor, wordplay, and the peculiar rigorous virtuosity of authors such as Alphonse Allais, Lewis Carroll, and Raymond Roussel. Renowned members of the Oulipo include Marcel Duchamp, Georges Perec, Jacques Roubaud, Marcel Bénabou, Jacques Jouet, Anne Garréta (all Fr.), Italo Calvino (It.), Harry Mathews (Am.), and Oskar Pastior (Ger.).

In its early years, the Oulipo adopted programmatic principles in direct contrast to those espoused by *surrealism: instead of celebrating automatism, where inspiration purportedly springs from the artist's unconscious, the Oulipo wagered that innovation and change in literary form may be best accessed through the intentional elaboration of literary forms by way of volitional writing practices. The practice of writing under constraint consists of obeying self-imposed and explicit rules of composition. These constraints are rules or axioms with varying degrees of difficulty that determine the making of the text. While they are not always immediately visible; in principle, they remain verifiable by the *reader, who is often invited, by clues in the text, to observe the procedures involved in its making; as such, Oulipian works are available to conventional readings as well as to those that engage in puzzle-solving.

Broadly speaking, Oulipian constraints fall into two categories: those gleaned and elaborated from constraints already present in lit. and those devised independently, often based on models borrowed from mathematics, for the explicit purpose of testing their productivity. The Oulipian poetics of constraint accounts alike for forms available to verse, the *prose poem, prose fiction, and theater.

The earliest seminal Oulipian work is Raymond Queneau's *Cent mille milliards de poèmes* (*Hundred Thousand Billion Poems*, 1961). In this collection of ten *sonnets, each line of each sonnet may be transposed to replace the corresponding line in the other nine primary sonnets. This interchangeability of lines, highlighted in the volume's presentation, produces a vertiginous number of poems, 100 trillion, or $10^{14}$. In addition to rendering accessible in one slim volume more sonnets than all the sonnets ever written, or, for that matter more text than had ever been written by all humans at that time, Queneau's *sonnet sequence demonstrates how the intentional use of constraints can add dimension to long-established fixed forms, esp. those (like the sonnet) that elaborate a poetics of constraints in their own right.

Another historic constraint practiced by the Oulipo is the *lipogram, illustrated in Georges Perec's (1936–82) *La disparition* (*A Void*, 1969), a 300-page mystery novel written without the letter *e*. *La disparition* illustrates key points about writing under constraint. First, constraints establish obstacles, eliminate possibilities, and elaborate an aesthetic of restraint. Deprived of the letter *e*, Fr. becomes significantly smaller; this radically affects how the story can be told. Second—and this aesthetic principle remains central to constrained writing—the difficulty of a constraint is proportional to its value. *La disparition* was extraordinarily difficult to write, both because of its length and because it omits the most common letter in Fr. (a lipogram in *z* would pose comparatively little difficulty). Third, Oulipian constraints are metapoetic. Because it stages the mystery of a missing person (Anton Voyl, whose name sounds like *vowel*), constraint in *La disparition* is given a thematic status. In this and other Oulipian works, form is thematized. The degree to which authors in the Oulipo employ constraints as a metapoetic code varies considerably, though referring to the craft of constraint is elementary in paradigmatic Oulipian works; for some, the elegance with which a work encodes and alludes to its axiomatic principles contributes to its literariness.

The invention of new constraints by the Oulipo has evolved from simple compositional techniques, such as S + 7 (where a writer rewrites a text by replacing all the nouns in a chosen text with the seventh noun following it in a chosen dictionary), toward the use of multiple constraints in a single work, and more recently, toward performative or conceptual forms of constraint. The use of the "knight's tour" in Georges Perec's *La vie mode d'emploi* (*Life: A User's Manual*, 1978) is a representative example of a new form deployed, along with others, in the composition of a novel. Based on a 10 × 10 grid corresponding to the cross-section of a Parisian apartment building, each chapter of this novel traces the action from room to room, moving from one to the other in the same way a knight moves on the chess board, without twice landing in the same box. Jacques Jouet's *Poèmes de métro* (2000) illustrates a turn toward an experiential *formalism: these poems were composed in the metro, strictly limiting the act of writing itself to the moments the train has stopped, beginning new stanzas with connecting trains, and composing the concluding line on arrival. In this work, the longest poem attempts, in a drive that is similar to that of the knight's tour, to pass through every station of the Paris Métro in as direct and least repetitive a fashion as possible. The aesthetic values present in these examples, principles of exhaustion and efficiency, are found elsewhere in Oulipian works.

Exactly what is meant by "potential literature" remains strategically undefined. For the Oulipo, constrained writing does not necessarily aspire to the creation of a literary work; rather, it participates in a general research program invested in interdisciplinary *invention, collaborative innovation, ludic approaches to writing and reading, and the elaboration of new economies of expression, complex literary forms that become the springboard for a speculative lit. Constraints are not, for the Oulipo, an end in themselves, but rather, as Le Lionnais would insist, a means for exploring new possibilities in human expression. In this context, the figure of the clinamen, or swerve, takes on special dimensions: in specific instances when the rule can be obeyed, it is intentionally broken for the purpose of drawing attention to the form as a mere code and to encourage readers to consider the sense of the work beyond its palpable formalisms.

The Oulipo remains active to this day, meeting monthly in private to discuss current research horizons. The group publishes new findings in the form of short texts in the *Bibliothèque Oulipienne*, gives regular public readings in Paris, and leads creative-writing workshops worldwide.

*See* ALEATORY POETICS, AVANT-GARDE POETICS, CONCEPTUAL POETRY, MODERNISM, MORALE ÉLÉMENTAIRE, PERFORMANCE.

■ Oulipo, *La Littérature potentielle* (1973); P. Fournel, *Clefs pour la littérature potentielle* (1978); J. Bens, *Oulipo, 1960–1963* (1980); Oulipo, *Atlas de littérature potentielle* (1981); *Oulipo: A Primer of Potential Literature*, ed. and trans. W. F. Motte (1986); Oulipo, *Oulipo Compendium* (1998), and *Anthologie de la l'OuLiPo* (2009); D. L. Becker, *Many Subtle Channels: In Praise of Potential Literature* (2012).

J.-J. POUCEL

**OXYMORON** or *synoeciosis* (Gr., "pointedly foolish"; Lat. *contrapositum*). A figure of speech that yokes together two seemingly contradictory elements. Oxymoron is, thus, a form of condensed *paradox. Shakespeare has "O heavy lightness! serious vanity! / Mis-shapen chaos of well-seeming forms! / Feather of lead, bright smoke, cold fire, sick health!" (*Romeo and Juliet* 1.1.178–80). Although oxymoron has been a recurrent device in poetry at least since the time of Horace ("*concordia discors rerum*"—the jarring harmony of things [*Epistulae* 1.12.19]), it was an important device in the poetry of *Petrarchism and was the *trope of the *baroque era par excellence. Such poets as Giambattista Marino in Italy, Luis de Góngora in Spain, and Richard Crashaw in England made it a primary vehicle of the 17th-c. sensibility:

Welcome, all wonders in one sight!
Eternity shut in a span,
Summer in winter, day in night,
Heaven in earth, and God in man!

As this quotation shows, oxymoron is particularly effective in evoking religious mysteries or other meanings that the poet feels to be beyond the reach of logical distinction or ordinary sense. Its popularity in the late Ren. owes something to the heightened religious concerns of that period and something, too, to the revival of the habit of analogical thinking. John Milton uses the figure often in the early books of *Paradise Lost*, in part to evoke the unimaginable glories of God. Note, however, that oxymoron, which reveals a compulsion to fuse all experience into a unity, is to be distinguished from *antithesis, which tends to divide and categorize elements of experience. Significantly, the latter figure, with its basis in rationality, dominates the poetry of the 18th c., a period that regarded the figures of the baroque poets as examples of "bad taste" and "false wit." But oxymoron returns in many passages in John Keats, who also uses it to express the paradoxes of man's sensuous experience.

Oxymoron is a complex figure best understood by placing it in the group formed by the other related figures of contrast such as antithesis, antiphrasis, and paradox; Ren. rhetoricians distinguished 11 of these. Ducrot and Todorov define oxymoron as the "establishment of a syntactic relationship between two antonyms." Group μ attempts (with only partial success) to distinguish oxymoron from the other complex figures of contrast by analyzing the semantic elements in the oxymoric conjunction: "the contradiction is absolute because the negation takes place in an abstract vocabulary: 'harmonious discord,' 'black sun.' We have, therefore, a figure in which one term is a nuclear seme (semantic trait, element of meaning) negating a classeme (the generic element indicating the class to which individual semes belong, e.g. the same *color* for the word *red*) of the other term." E.g., in the well known Miltonic oxymoron "darkness visible," "'darkness' imposes the classeme *obscure*, which is cancelled by *visible*." Thus, oxymoron is a "*coincidentia oppositorum*" in which the antithesis is denied and the contradiction fully assented to." Oxymoron differs from antiphrasis, a "metalogism [figure of thought] by repetition (*A* is not *A*)," because oxymoron "violates the code and belongs *de facto* to the class of metasememes [tropes]." Group μ does not discuss the difference between oxymoron and paradox. Dupriez distinguishes between oxymoron (words), oxymoric sentences, and oxymoric sentiments and ideas.

Oxymoron is by no means reserved, however, for religious experience or even love's contradictions; the mod. world abounds in it even for quotidian existence—e.g., "sight unseen"—and G.W.F. Hegel has, we recall, *"concrete universal." Finally, one may note that in the novel *1984*, oxymoron is the very basis of "doublethink," that process of holding two opinions simultaneously, "knowing them to be contradictory and believing in both of them." This way not higher unification of opposites but madness lies.

*See* CATACHRESIS, SYNAESTHESIA.

■ H. J. Büchner, "Das Oxymoron in der griechischen Dichtung von Homer bis in die Zeit des Hellenismus mit einem Überblick Über seine Entwicklung," diss., Univ. of Tübingen (1950); E. McCann, "Oxymora in Spanish Mystics and English Metaphysical Writers," *CL* 13 (1961); E. Weber, "Das Oxymoron bei Shakespeare," diss., Univ. of Hamburg (1963); W. Freytag, *Das Oxymoron bei Wolfram, Gottfried und andern Dichtern des Mittelalters* (1972); Lausberg; O. Ducrot and T. Todorov, *Encyclopedic Dictionary of the Sciences of Language*, trans. C. Porter (1979); B. Dupriez, *Gradus* (1980), under "alliance"; Group μ; Morier; W. Blumenfeld, *Jumbo Shrimp* (1986); Y. Shen, "On the Structure and Understanding of Poetic Oxymoron," *PoT* 8 (1987); Vickers; Corbett.

F. J. WARNKE; A. W. HALSALL; T.V.F. BROGAN

# P

**PAEAN.** A type of Gr. *hymn whose name derives from *ié paián*, a cry addressed to Apollo as the god of healing that often forms the *refrain (cf. Homer, *Hymn to Apollo* 517). Paeans were sung on numerous occasions: to Apollo in his role as healer or protector (e.g., *Iliad* 1.473); as a song of hope before going into battle (Pindar, *Paeans* 2) or of joy after victory (*Iliad* 22.391); and at the beginning of a symposium (Alcman, frag. 98; Ariphron, "Paean to Health"). Paeans were addressed to gods other than Apollo (e.g., Zeus, Poseidon, Dionysus, and Hygeia) and even, in the late 5th c. and Hellenistic period, to victorious generals (e.g., Lysander and Titus Flamininus). Composed for both choral and monodic performance, paeans were accompanied by lyres or woodwinds or both. The ancient debate whether Aristotle's poem to Hermias was a paean or a *skolion shows that the distinctions between paean and other lyric genres were not precise (Harvey).

Although many early Gr. lyric poets wrote paeans, the only substantial remains are papyrus fragments of 22 paeans by Pindar, of which *Paeans* 2, 4, and 6, written for Abderitans, Ceans, and Delphians, respectively, are the best preserved. A number of Hellenistic paeans surviving as inscriptions are collected in Powell. Although some poems of Horace (e.g., *Odes* 4.5) resemble paeans, the genre was moribund by his time, and in mod. usage, *paean* refers loosely to any song of joy or triumph.

See GREEK POETRY.

■ Pauly-Wissowa; A. Fairbanks, *A Study of the Greek Paean* (1900); H. W. Smyth, *Greek Melic Poets* (1900); J. U. Powell, *Collectanea Alexandrina* (1925); H. Färber, *Die Lyrik in der Kunsttheorie der Antike* (1936); J. E. Sandys, *The Odes of Pindar* (1937); A. E. Harvey, "The Classification of Greek Lyric Poetry," *CQ* 5 (1955); Michaelides; I. Rutherford, "Apollo in Ivy: The Tragic Paean," *Arion* 3 (1995), and "Apollo's Other Genre: Proclus on Nomos and His Source," *CP* 90 (1995); M. Depew, "Enacted and Represented Dedications: Genre and Greek Hymn," *Matrices of Genre*, ed. M. Depew and D. D. Obbink (2000); I. Rutherford, *Pindar's Paeans: A Reading of the Fragments with a Survey of the Genre* (2001)—incl. trans.; A. Ford, "The Genre of Genres: Paean and 'Paian' in Early Greek Poetry," *Poetica* 38 (2006).

W. H. RACE

**PAEON.** In *cl. prosody, a metrical unit that is formed of one of the four permutations of one long and three short syllables: these are called *first paeon* (– ◡ ◡ ◡), *second paeon* (◡ – ◡ ◡), *third paeon* (◡ ◡ – ◡), and *fourth paeon* ◡ ◡ ◡ –). The first and the fourth paeons are, in effect, *cretics (– ◡ –) by resolution of their last and first syllables, respectively. The second and the third, however, are to be found

only in ancient metrical theory, and the fourth is quite rare. But the first paeon, esp., is found in Gr. poetry and drama (more frequently in comedy than in tragedy). Cretics and paeons may occur in combination (cf. Aristophanes, *Acharnians* 210 ff.). Forms of paeons are also common as clausular cadences in Gr. rhythmical prose. But only the most resolutely classicizing of metrists would find these Gr. rarities in Eng. meter, which is founded on a different basis.

■ J. W. White, *The Verse of Greek Comedy* (1912); Wilamowitz, pt. 2, ch. 8; B. Ghiselin, "Paeonic Measures in English Verse," *MLN* 57 (1942); Dale, ch. 6; West; Norden.

D. S. PARKER

**PAINTING AND POETRY.** The hist. of the relation of poetry to painting might be construed as an account of the innumerable contacts between these arts since cl. antiquity; it might be taken to concern poets such as R. M. Rilke (1875–1926) who adapt values and conventions from painting to poetry; it might treat figures who were both artists and poets, notably Michelangelo Buonarroti (1475–1564). This entry, with a focus on Europe, approaches the topic through several questions that shadow the hist. of this relation.

In antiquity, the two arts were often defined against one another or invoked together to discuss the nature of *representation. In the *Phaedrus*, Plato shows Socrates commenting with wonder and frustration that poetry and painting both offer the same pleasure in delusion. Like poetry, Socrates argues, when a painting is interrogated, it tells us only the same thing that we first saw, the living quality of things and people. Like painting, the words of poetry talk to us as though they were alive in the voice of the person before us. But the more we listen, the more they repeat the knowledge we already have, for only the appearance of *voice is presented to us, not the bodily dialogue that is the mark of living, illuminating thought. Aristotle looked further into *mimesis in the context of literary representation and, in giving poetry a more or less systematic rationale of its own, largely dismissed the comparison with painting. But the productive friction between the two arts was to reappear often, for instance, in the work of the Gr. rhetorician Dionysius of Halicarnassus (ca. 60–7 BCE), the first to use the term *ekphrasis for the representation, trans., or transposition of one work into another art form. Contemporaneously, Horace's celebrated dictum in his *Ars poetica* (ca. 18 BCE) *ut pictura poesis (as is painting, so is poetry) is a statement of the ambition of both art and poetry. It suggests a competition between the arts that is also a coming together: imaginative texts deserve the same merit and attention as paintings and frescos. Still, the competitiveness in ekphrasis might imply the supremacy of either the source art form or the target one. Is there room for a more liberated, if more uncomfortable, understanding of the way the verbal and the visual arts illuminate one another?

A celebrated example of this tense partnership is Nicolas Poussin's *Et in Arcadia Ego* (1637–39). The title is taken from Virgil, and its meaning is that, even in pastoral world of blissful unity with nature, death (the I or ego) is ever present. Poussin's two versions of the painting are not only ekphrastic but intertextual within the domain of painting (see INTERTEXTUALITY). Poussin omits the skull that often provides mortality with a conventional symbolization. Instead, the concept of death has been made something that is literally being read; the Arcadian shepherds are reading and discussing the inscription on the side of the tomb that occupies the center of the composition. The message from antiquity, *et in arcadia ego*, is made a matter of visual interpretation and of trans. into present knowledge. Not only has Socrates' doctrine in the *Phaedrus* of the migration of souls been translated into a humanist one, by which humankind forges knowledge on the basis of its own mortality and a Christian afterlife, but the conventions of present reading and present dialogue are given the foreground. The Arcadian setting, composed in the mode of Eur. neoclassicism, provides the light in which the Socratic pursuit of truth beyond the forms of its revelation is lost, found, and lost again. Thus, ekphrasis, rather than compounding *imitation with imitation, might also allow for an open-ended process of adaptation in which the arts enter into a dialogue about their own hist. and purpose.

Is each art bound to represent the ambitions of another art? In what ways is the relation of art to art speculative? Does it involve convergence or divergence? In her seminal book *The Colors of Rhetoric* (1982), Wendy Steiner writes that G. E. Lessing's *Laocoön: An Essay on the Limits of Painting and Poetry* (1766)—a key Enlightenment statement on the nature of art, which is discussed once again through the relation *between* the arts—sends a loud message of divergence. Although the arts are similar in being imitations, this is a "relational rather than a substantive similarity." Both are symbolic in relation to reality, but each expresses in different ways its own detachment from the objects of its mimesis. In a romantic light and beyond, this detachment among the arts—the sense that they are different in ways that make fresh perspectives available when one art comes into sustained contact with another—is a source of symbolic enrichment.

In *romanticism and after, as M. H. Abrams shows in *The Mirror and the Lamp* (1953), the purpose of art turns from imitation to the expression of emotion. Norman Bryson in *Tradition and Desire* (1984) shows Eugène Delacroix's (1798–1863) art developing the romantic desire to account for opposing tendencies in the psyche into a vision "which exceeds the fixities of representation" altogether, and which presents the "existence of the body beyond representation." In turn, Charles Baudelaire (1821–67) develops his poetics as a response to the developing modernity of his time, and

its painting in particular. Delacroix, as well as Francisco Goya (1746–1828) from the previous generation, is a key beacon in his aesthetic thought, with Jean-Auguste-Dominique Ingres (1780–1867) acting as an aesthetic foil.

By means of his celebrated challenges to the morality of his day, encapsulated in the title of his book of verse *Les Fleurs du mal* (*The Flowers of Evil*, 1857, 1861), Baudelaire systematically cajoles his reader into questioning his or her modes of recognition and response. In his *Salon de 1845*, Baudelaire suggests that Delacroix's aesthetic of excess is dramatized in his use of color which extends the lines of drawing and creates an art showing "the ungraspable and trembling character of nature." Color is thus removed from its mimetic connection with the material world and with received *taste and morality. In this, Baudelaire and Delacroix together anticipate the postimpressionism of Paul Gauguin (1848–1903), the fauvism of the early 1900s, and the orphism of Guillaume Apollinaire (1880–1918) and Robert Delaunay (1885–1941).

Baudelaire's classic essay "Le Peintre de la vie moderne" ("The Painter of Modern Life," 1863) is an exercise in ekphrasis on the grandest scale. The position of the poet Baudelaire in relation to his art is rhetorically translated into that of the painter and draftsman Constantin Guys (1802–92) in relation to his own. But equally, the art of Guys is swamped by Baudelaire's elusive evocation of it, which evokes a style of painterly brushwork in conjunction with a mode of thought, rather than comparing particular works of painting and writing. Rapid execution and the unfinished product emerge as core indicators of a dynamic art able to respond to the hist. of its own time, and to the complexity of the relations between attachment to circumstance and the demand for synthesis.

What is at stake is the capacity of the poetic sign in general to give a total account of human experience: life as we understand it systematically, as well as life lived in the moment. Penny Florence's *Mallarmé, Manet and Redon* (1986) is devoted to reading the relations between *impressionism (1870s and 1880s) and *symbolism (1880s to the turn of the century) dramatized in the works of the artists in her title. Her readings of these works explore the power of form to change the way visual and verbal signs make sense. Florence describes the perfect sign as "a kind of poise," offering an understanding of how it works but also an ability to alter rather than repeat the patterns of recognition it prompts. Florence takes the example of the decadent poet Jules Laforgue, who was born in Montevideo in 1860 and died in Paris in 1887. As Florence describes it, Laforgue's ambition for *versification, developed in large part through his engagement with impressionist painters from 1881 onward, is the desire to convey "reality in the living atmosphere of forms."

But once again, this is not purely a matter of poetry imitating art, and Laforgue's verse in *Les Complaintes* (The Laments, 1885) exceeds a literal ling. trans. of the retinal impressionism of the works of Claude Monet (1840–1926) and others from the 1870s and 1880s. In

Laforgue's verse as Florence characterizes it, an impressionist optics of the moment is transformed into a poetic space in which the various elements involved fail to cohere. An exploration by critics and practitioners alike of the interaction between the arts certainly frees each art individually from the incapacity to account for its own hist. But on the other hand, relations of visual and verbal aesthetics resist synthesis since they do not share the same perceptual space or the same time of reading or viewing.

In Mallarmé's *Un coup de dés* (*A Throw of the Dice*, 1897), the words of the poem and its syntax are scattered across a series of open-book pages in patterns that are indeterminately verbal and visual. The text exemplifies self-critical thought: it creates a partnership of meaning in a composition that resolutely preserves the disparate nature of the elements involved (see BOOK, POETIC; VISUAL POETRY). Such an anticoalescent approach to knowledge may not be appropriate to finding solutions to practical problems. But a disciplinary partnership that refuses appropriation might provide the basis for developing meaningful cultural dialogue rather than conflict.

A desire to respond to the events and calamities of their time drove the practice of artists in the Eur. avant-garde from 1907, the year of Pablo Picasso's *Les Demoiselles d'Avignon*, to the start of World War II in 1939. This new aesthetic renaissance is once again characterized by the interart dialogues of *cubism, *vorticism, It. *futurism, Rus. futurism, *expressionism, and *surrealism. The resolution of apparently opposing ideas and practices is the battle cry of André Breton (1896–1966) and his ambition for surrealism. Resolution is the only response possible for artists concerned to make a stand against the shocking reality of World War I. Unlike Sigmund Freud, Breton envisages a society harnessing the psychic energy displayed by dream, rather than regarding all unconscious activity as available only as symptom, a sign of what the socializing process will grudgingly allow into the public space. A creative resolution of subjective and objective experience is the aim of all authentic thought, for Breton, and of creative art in particular.

But while the arts come together, the avant-gardist radicalizing mission itself, examined by Peter Bürger in *Theory of the Avant-Garde* (1976, trans. 1984), is again articulated in the asymmetry of their interaction. In his 1928 text *Le Surréalisme et la peinture* (*Surrealism and Painting*, 1928), Breton promotes two related objectives: seeing in its precivilized state and a purely interior model for art. Both are inherently paradoxical. The uncivilized can only be conceived from the point of view of civilization—Picasso's *Les Demoiselles d'Avignon* explores that drama; and an interior *model* is as much a public or external concept as a uniquely subjective one. Such tensions are manifest in Breton's readings of individual painters. He presents Salvador Dalí's painting as enabling a realignment of the reality and pleasure principles, releasing creativity from inhibition and conformity. Yet Dalí, in works such as *Soft Construction with Boiled Beans (Premonition of War)* (1936), which is a now-iconic response to the Spanish

Civil War (1936–39), suggests a more horrified investigation of subjective desire and its devastating involvement with authority.

In *S/Z* (1970, trans. 1974), Roland Barthes examines the lure of the holistic in the postromantic realism of Honoré de Balzac (1799–1850): his aspiration to a holistic account of the human psyche and social causality, as well as the failure to achieve it. An avatar of poststructuralist methodology, *S/Z* is far more a work of original critical writing, in the form of a reading of a literary text responding to visual art, predominantly sculpture on this occasion but also portraiture (see POSTSTRUCTURALISM). In Barthes's reading of Balzac's *Sarrasine* (1830), the Enlightenment aspiration to complete classification, as well as the Romantic aspiration to organic understanding, both come to a traumatic halt. But such aspirations, however fantastic, cannot simply be modified or dispensed with. Barthes communicates with increasing alarm his sense that a mad and aggressive pursuit of wholeness and oneness, in the arts as in all forms of knowledge, is produced in the narrative structures designed to expose it, as well as in the social and cultural laws designed to prohibit it.

In opening out to the aesthetic forms with which it engages, critical writing creates various ways of understanding not only seeing but understanding *through* seeing—in human time and in gendered time. Here are three further examples of ways in which critical writing is creatively advanced by its engagement with painting.

In *Reading "Rembrandt"* (1991), Mieke Bal explores how her engagements with pictures variously attributed to Rembrandt are driven by the existential wounds of gender. These are wounds coexistent with birth and death, and as such, we understand them through narrative. Not only thematically but *formally*, Bal suggests, in readings that create an interplay among narratology, *speech act theory, and psychoanalytic theory, word-image oppositions are held in creative suspension, just like the seeming opposition of movement and immobility. Gender difference, however violent, finds new voice. On the other hand, Jean-Luc Nancy's writing on touch with regard to Rembrandt in *Noli me tangere* (2003, trans. 2008) predicates mimetic understanding on touch as we know it but cannot feel it in the image. At a simple and fundamental level of encounter with painting, viewers are looking at what lies beyond their own seeing; and Nancy finds a lang. of poetic and philosophical simplicity with which to express the enigma of aesthetic form. Finally, in *The Sight of Death: An Experiment in Art Writing* (2006), T. J. Clark illuminates Poussin's painting by addressing his own material and personal situation as critic. Questions of dimension in Poussin's works are explored in terms of the specific places in which Clark is viewing them and writing about them. The existential dimension of reading painting is given new form in this experiment in writing art intransitively. In such works, an open-ended argument emerges on the relation of painting to writing, renewing the possibilities of art writing and its ability to understand the frames of seeing and knowing.

*See* CONCRETE POETRY.

■ E. Cassirer, *The Philosophy of the Enlightenment*, trans. F. Koellin and J. Pettegrove (1951); A. Blunt, *Poussin* (1967); W. Benjamin, *Charles Baudelaire*, trans. H. Zohn (1973); R. E. Krauss, *Passages in Modern Sculpture* (1977); *Image and Code*, ed. W. Steiner (1981); J.-F. Lyotard, *Discours, Figure* (1985); C. Prendergast, *The Order of Mimesis* (1986); B. Thomson, *Gauguin* (1987); R. Wollheim, *Painting as an Art* (1987); D. Scott, *Pictorialist Poetics* (1988); W. Steiner, *Pictures of Romance* (1988); E. Kelly, *The Mallarmé Suite* (1993); R. E. Krauss, *The Optical Unconscious* (1993); W.J.T. Mitchell, *Picture Theory* (1994); M. Bal, *The Mottled Screen: Reading Proust Visually*, trans. A.-L. Milne (1997); Y.-A. Bois and R. E. Krauss, *Formless: A User's Guide* (1997); R. E. Krauss, *"A Voyage on the North Sea": Art in the Age of the Post-Medium Condition* (2000); T. Mathews, *Literature, Art and the Pursuit of Decay in Twentieth-Century France* (2000); *The Dialogue between Painting and Poetry: Livres d'artistes 1874–1999*, ed. J. Khalfa (2001); G. Deleuze, *Francis Bacon*, trans. D. W. Smith (2003); E. Karpeles, *Paintings in Proust* (2008); *One Poem in Search of a Translator*, ed. E. Loffredo and M. Perteghella (2008); S. R. Harrow, *The Body Modern: Pressures and Prospects of Representation* (2010).

T. MATHEWS

**PALINDROME** (Gr., "running back again"). A word (*Eve* or *madam*), sentence, or verse (whence *versus cancrinus*, "crab verse") that reads alike backward or forward. Ben Jonson invented the Eng. word *palindrome* (*Under-woods*). George Puttenham's example (*Arte of English Poesie*, bk. 1, ch. 7), which he calls *Verse Lyon* (from the Fr.), reverses merely the order of the words. Several varieties exist: (1) in the canonical form, the sentence or verse reads alike in either direction letter by letter; (2) in another variety, the reversal is word by word; (3) a third variety reverses line by line. Outside of the Eng. and Nordic langs., diacritical marks need not be preserved in both directions to have the palindrome be considered correct. In addition to their appearances in literary texts, palindromes exist in fields such as music, medicine, and mathematics. Palindromes have influenced composers such as Ned Rorem.

The reputed inventor of the palindrome was Sotades, a minor Alexandrian poet of the early 3d c. BCE who wrote virulent *invective and obscene verses (see SOTADEAN); no examples are extant from the cl. Gr. period. The best-known palindrome in post-cl. Gr. is "nipson anomemata me monan opsin" (wash my transgressions, not only my face), attributed to Gregory of Nazianzus (4th c.) and often inscribed on fonts in monasteries or churches. Other familiar ones in Lat. are "Roma tibi subito motibus ibit amor" (Sidonius Apollinaris *Epistulae* 9.14) and the so-called devil's verse, "Signa te, signa, temere me tangis et angis." Camden illustrates type (2) with this "perfect Verse": "Odo tenet mulum, madidam mappam tenet Anna / Anna tenet mappam madidam, mulum tenet Odo." One masterly shaped palindrome contains one word per line and can be read in four directions: "Sator arepo tenet opera rotas." Palindromes

were esp. popular in Byzantine times, and we possess several written by Emperor Leo the Wise (10th c.). The Sp.-Heb. poet Judah Alharizi (late 12th–early 13th c.) inserted "Palindrome for a Patron" into his *māqāmat The Book of Tahkemoni*. Purportedly, an Elizabethan aristocrat defended her honor with a palindromic motto: "ablata at alba" (retired I am pure). Preceding Jonson's definition, John Taylor the Water Poet wrote the first palindrome in Eng.: "lewd did I live & evil I did dwel." Ger. palindromes were written by J. H. Riese in the 17th c.; and in 1802, Ambrose Pamperis published in Vienna a pamphlet containing 416 palindromes recounting the campaigns of Catherine the Great. Among the best-known examples of palindromes are *Madam, I'm Adam* and *Able was I ere I saw Elba*, the latter attributed to Napoleon. More recent poets including W. H. Auden; Jeff Grant, author of the longest palindrome in Eng. with over 10,230 words (New Zealand); Petar Preradović (Croatia); and Velimir Khlebnikov (Russia) have written them; *Oulipo members wrote and inspired palindromes (go to http://graner.net/nicolas/salocin/ten.renarg//:ptth. to see a palindrome in French by Oulipo member Georges Perec [note that the URL is also a palindrome]); Susan Stewart's "Two Brief Views of Hell" (*Columbarium*) and James Linton's "Doppelganger" employ type (3).

The metrical analogue of the palindrome is *reciprocus versus*, a line that scans identically forward and backward, either letter by letter or word by word. Sidonius Apollinaris (5th c. CE) mentions *versus recurrentes* (*Epistulae* 9.14) which, when read backward, retain the same order of letters and meter ("Roma tibi . . .," above): this is a palindrome both in sense and meter. And Virgil's *Aeneid* 1.8 is still a dactylic hexameter when the order of the words is reversed. For examples, see Keil 1.516.24–517.14, 6.113.11–114.10.

■ W. Camden, *Remains concerning Britain* (1870); G. R. Clark, *Palindromes* (1887); K. Krumbacher, *Geschichte der byzantinische litteratur*, 2d ed. (1897); H. T. Peck, *Harpers Dictionary of Classical Antiquities* (1898); K. Preisendanz, "Palindrom," in Pauly-Wissowa; A. Liede, *Dichtung als Spiel*, 2 v. (1963); H. Bergerson, *Palindrones and Anagrams* (1973); West, 65; P. Dubois, "(Petite) histoire des palindrones," *Littératures* 7 (1983); T. Augarde, *Oxford Guide to Word Games* (1984); W. Irvine, *Madam I'm Adam* (1987).

T.V.F. BROGAN.; R. J. GETTY; J. LEWIN

**PALINODE.** A poem or song of retraction; originally a term applied to a lyric by Stesichorus (early 6th c. BCE) in which he recanted his earlier attack upon Helen as the cause of the Trojan War. The palinode became common after Ovid's *Remedia amoris*, supposedly written to retract his *Ars amatoria*. It is a frequent device in med. and Ren. love poetry, incl. the *Roman de la Rose*. Chaucer's *Legend of Good Women* is a palinode retracting *Troilus and Criseyde*, and a character called Palinode appears in Edmund Spenser's *The Shepheardes Calender*. Any ritualistic recantation may loosely be called a palinode, even one in prose, but the term *palinodic form* denotes a particular pattern in which two metrically corresponding elements are interrupted by another pair of similarly corresponding elements. The palinodic form may be represented as *a b b' a'* where the letters refer to lines, stanzas, or strophes, and where *a b* makes a statement that *b' a'* recants.

*See* RECUSATIO.

■ U. von Wilamowitz-Moellendorff, *Sappho und Simonides* (1913); P. Philippy, *Love's Remedies* (1995); M. Demos, "Stesichorus' Palinode in the 'Phaedrus,'" *CW* 90.4 (1997); C. Gutleben, "Palinodes, Palindromes and Palimpsests: Strategies of Deliberate Self-Contradiction in Postmodern British Fiction," *Miscelánea* 26 (2002).

R. A. HORNSBY; A. L. FRENCH

**PANEGYRIC** (Gr. *panegyricos*, "for a festival assembly") originally denoted an oration delivered at one of the Gr. festivals; later it came to designate a speech or poem in praise of some person, object, or event. As such, panegyric is rhetorically classed as a type of *epideictic poetry or oratory, the major branches of which are praise and *invective. Panegyrics praising heroes, athletes, armies, and dynasties are present in most cultures, incl. in *oral poetry, though Western scholarship generally borrows the terminology for panegyric and its particular subgenres and specific occasions from the Gr., such as *epinikion, a victory *ode; *epithalamium, a marriage song; *encomium, presumably praise of the host at the *komos* revel; and eulogy, a speech or poem in praise of the dead. In med. China, however, panegyric, for which a technical term is lacking, was not conceived as a separate genre but rather as poetry (*shi*) "written at imperial command" (*yingzhao* or *yingzhi*), an effect of the commission by or dedication to a reigning monarch. With its morphological elasticity, the Ar. root for "praise," *m-d-ḥ*, produces an extensive terminology for the relations involved in panegyric: praise or a mode of poetry (*madḥ*), the praised one or patron (*mamdūḥ*), the panegyrist (*mādiḥ*), a panegyrical poem or section of a poem (*madīḥ, midḥa*), and self-glorification (*tamadduḥ*).

The cl. rules of panegyric are given in the rhetorical works of Menander and Hermogenes; famous examples include the *Panegyricus* of Isocrates, the panegyric of Pliny the Younger on Trajan, and the 11 other *XII Panegyrici latini* (4th c. CE). Pindar's odes have sometimes been described as panegyrics. After the 3d c. BCE, when much of rhetorical theory was appropriated for poetics, panegyric was accepted as a formal poetic type, and its rules were given in handbooks of poetry. Significant Western examples of panegyrics include Sidonius Apollinaris's poems on the Emperors Avitus, Majorian, and Anthemius; Claudian's on the consulships of Honorius, Stilicho, Probinus, and Olybrius; the panegyric on the death of Celsus by Paulinus of Nola; Aldhelm's *De laudibus virginitatis*; and innumerable Christian Lat. poems in praise of Mary, the Cross, and the martyrs, though hagiographical or devotional praise might well constitute a distinctly different type of praise from panegyric, since the author is not engaged with the social exchange inherent in a patron-poet relationship. J. C.

Scaliger (*Poetices libri septem*, 1561) distinguishes, e.g., between panegyric, which tends to deal with present men and deeds, and encomium, which deals with those of the past; but, in general, the two are indistinguishable. Menander I, however, categorizes epideictic according to the object of praise, incl. praise of the gods (*hymnos*), praise of countries or cities, and praise of people or animals.

In Ar. and early Persian trads., the *qaṣīda was the primary verse form for panegyric, though it contained other sections, as well. In later centuries, esp. in Persian, the *ghazal and *rubāʿī forms were sometimes used as vehicles of panegyric. In addition to praising the justice, wisdom, power, and victories of the ruler, a Persian panegyric often closes with two lines of prayer for him. Most Persian works of *epic and romance open with a section of praise, sometimes several hundred lines long and organized hierarchically, first to God, then the Prophet, possibly the caliphs or saints, followed by the ruling patron, and often the crown prince. The basic system of *patronage that developed for Ar. at the caliphal court in Damascus, Baghdad, and Cordoba was replicated throughout the Middle East, South and Central Asia, North Africa and Andalusia, and for other lits., Persian, Turkish, and Urdu, etc. Kings, sultans, and military potentates, whether of local dynasties or major empires (Timurid, Safavid, Ottoman, Mughal) felt the need to retain poets, one of whom often served as *poet laureate, and to encourage recitation of panegyric poems on state, religious, and other ceremonial occasions. Al-Mutanabbī (d. 965), e.g., made Sayf al-Dawla and his court in Aleppo famous through his successful panegyrics. Persian poetry reemerged as a literate trad. in the 10th and 11th cs. largely because the Samanid and Ghaznavid courts decided actively to patronize and encourage Persian poets. Maḥmūd of Ghazna (d. 1030), the Maeceneas of Persian poetry, gathered major panegyric poets around his court (e.g., Farrukhī and ʿUnṣurī) and established the expectation that other sultans and shahs would do likewise. Panegyric poets at the Arabo-Persian courts frequently served as courtiers and boon companions, occasionally coming under political suspicion and suffering imprisonment or execution. The inherent threat of revenge in verse, however, balanced the power relation to some extent; some patrons' reputations were forever tarnished by satires from disgruntled former panegyric poets, e.g., al-Mutanabbī's wicked invective on Kāfūr in the 10th c.; and Firdawsī's satire on Maḥmūd of Ghazna in the 11th c. The complex dynamics of these patronage relationships led rhetoricians to analyze the poetics of *sincerity under rubrics like "praise that sounds like blame" and "blame that sounds like praise."

Panegyric remained popular through the Eur. Middle Ages both as an independent poetic form and as an important *topos in longer narrative poems, esp. epic and, like other such forms, it persisted into the Ren., with perhaps more emphasis on the praise of secular figures and institutions. The panegyric underwent a brief revival in 17th-c. encomiastic *occasional verse, e.g., Edmund Waller's "Panegyrick to My Lord Protector" (1655). The Eng. subgenre known as the *country house poem is a variety of panegyric.

■ Pauly-Wissowa 5.2581–83, 18.2340–62; T. Burgess, *Epideictic Literature* (1902); Curtius; R. Haller, "Lobgedichte," *Reallexikon II*; *XII Panegyrici latini*, ed. R.A.B. Mynors (1964); T. Viljamaa, *Studies in Greek Encomiastic Poetry of the Early Byzantine Period* (1968); J. Stuart, *Izibongo: Zulu Praise-Poems*, ed. T. Cope (1968); A. Georgi, *Das lateinische und deutsche Preisgedicht des Mittelalters* (1969); F. Cairns, *Generic Composition in Greek and Roman Poetry* (1972); B. K. Lewalski, *Donne's "Anniversaries" and the Poetry of Praise* (1973); J. D. Garrison, *Dryden and the Tradition of Panegyric* (1975); S. Sperl, "Islamic Kingship and Arabic Panegyric Poetry in the Early Ninth Century," *Journal of Arabic Literature* 8 (1977); A. C. Hodza, *Shona Praise Poetry*, ed. G. Fortune (1979); J. O'Donnell, *Cassiodorus* (1979); *Leaf and Bone: African Praise-Poems*, ed. J. Gleason (1980); S. MacCormack, *Art and Ceremony in Late Antiquity* (1981); R. S. Peterson, *Imitation and Praise in the Poems of Ben Jonson* (1981); A. Hardie, *Statius and the Silvae* (1983); R. Helgerson, *Self-Crowned Laureates: Spenser, Jonson, Milton and the Literary System* (1983); G. W. Most, *The Measures of Praise* (1985); J. Altieri, *The Theatre of Praise: The Panegyric Tradition in Seventeenth-Century English Drama* (1986); B. Gold, *Literary Patronage in Greece and Rome* (1987); J. S. Meisami, *Medieval Persian Court Poetry* (1987); W. Portmann, *Geschichte in der spätantiken Panegyrik* (1988); *Patronage in Ancient Society*, ed. A. Wallace-Hadrill (1989); L. Kurke, *The Traffic in Praise* (1991); S. P. Stetkevych, *Abū Tammām and the Poetics of the Abbasid Age* (1991); A. Hamori, *The Composition of Mutanabbi's Panegyrics to Sayf al-Dawla* (1992); J. T. Rowland, *Faint Praise and Civil Leer: The "Decline" of Eighteenth-Century Panegyric* (1994); *Reorientations: Arabic and Persian Poetry*, ed. S. P. Stetkevych (1994); *Qasida Poetry in Islamic Asia and Africa*, ed. S. Sperl and C. Shackle, 2 v. (1996); *The Propaganda of Power: The Role of Panegyric in Late Antiquity*, ed. M. Whitby (1998); *Greek Biography and Panegyric in Late Antiquity*, ed. T. Hägg and P. Rousseau (2000); P. L. Bowditch, *Horace and the Gift Economy of Patronage* (2001); S. P. Stetkevych, *The Poetics of Islamic Legitimacy* (2002); B. Gruendler, *Medieval Arabic Praise Poetry: Ibn al-Rūmī and the Patron's Redemption* (2003); H. Mackie, *Graceful Errors: Pindar and the Performance of Praise* (2003); D. Fearn, *Bacchylides: Politics, Performance, Poetic Tradition* (2007); *Pindar's Poetry, Patrons, and Festivals*, ed. S. Hornblower and C. Morgan (2007); F. Wu, *Written at Imperial Command: Panegyric Poetry in Early Medieval China* (2008); *A Companion to Horace*, ed. G. Davis (2010). F. Lewis, "Sincerely Flattering Panegyrics: The Shrinking Ghaznavid Qasida," *Necklace of the Pleiades*, ed. F. D. Lewis and S. Sharma (2010).

O. B. HARDISON; T.V.F. BROGAN; F. LEWIS

**PANTUN** (Eng. and Fr. *pantoum* or *pantoun*). In contemp. poetry, the pantun is a poem of indeterminate length composed of *quatrains in which the second and fourth lines of each stanza serve as the first and third lines of the next. This pattern breaks in the final stanza, whose second and fourth lines are recurrences of the first and third lines of the first stanza; thus, the pantun begins and ends with the same line. Nineteenth-c. pantuns were often written in *cross rhyme, but contemp. examples by such poets as John Ashbery, Carolyn Kizer, Donald Justice, and the Ger. *Oulipo poet Oskar Pastior are often unrhymed; similarly, there is no established meter.

The schematic pantun, like the schematic *villanelle, was invented by 19th-c. romantics and *Parnassians as part of a programmatic promotion of fixed forms. The first original schematic pantuns in the Occident are probably those published in 1822 by the Ger. botanist Adelbert von Chamisso, but 19th-c. Fr. poets practiced the pantun most. In the notes to his 1829 *Les Orientales*, Victor Hugo included orientalist Ernest Fouinet's Fr. trans. of a pantun from William Marsden's 1812 *Grammar of the Malayan Language*; the form of this poem influenced the pantuns of Théodore de Banville and Charles-Marie Leconte de Lisle as well as Charles Baudelaire's pantun "Harmonie du Soir" (rhymed *abba*).

The pattern that Westerners associate with the pantun is highly atypical of the Malay-lang. verse form (see MALAY POETRY). The Malay-lang. pantun can have six to twelve lines, but it is usually in four lines consisting of two end-stopped cross-rhyme couplets. The first couplet, the *sampiran*, tends to be highly charged and evocative, while the second couplet soars, sometimes obscurely, on the basis of the first: a Malay-lang. proverb declares, "A pantun is like a hawk with a chicken; it takes its time about striking."

■ Kastner; P. G. Brewster, "Metrical, Stanzaic, and Stylistic Resemblances between Malayan and Western Poetry," *RLC* 32 (1958); R. Etiemble, "Du 'Pantun' malais au 'pantoum' à la française," *Zagadnienia rodzajow literackich* 22 (1979); G. Voisset, *Histoire du genre pantoun* (1997); J. Jouet, *Échelle et papillons* (1998); F. R. Daillie, *La lune et les étoiles* (2000).

T.V.F. BROGAN; A. PREMINGER;
B. RAFFEL; A. L. FRENCH

**PARABASIS.** A formal part of Athenian Old Comedy, *parabasis* signifies a transgression or digression that interrupts the dramatic action of the play. Stemming from the Gr. verb *parabaino* (to overstep or pass over), it suspends the make-believe of theater. In the parabasis, usually made up of seven parts, each following prescribed rules of Gr. meter, members of the chorus stepped off the stage, removed their masks and costumes, and addressed the audience on matters of social, cultural, and political import. They often pointed directly to Athenian politicians and personalities sitting in front, mocking them while chastising the audience for having elected such idiots. These episodes often constituted unbridled ad hominem attacks on public figures. The parabasis accomplished its critique by violating the boundary between stage and viewer, thereby affirming to the spectators that the work before them was both illusion and reality. It went beyond Bertolt Brecht's notion of alienation in refusing to allow members of the audience to identify with the illusion.

Today, the parabasis is largely associated with the work of Aristophanes because, of all the ancient comedians, his work has largely survived. Even though his plays have socially relevant topics, such as peace and war in *The Acharnians*, peace and women in *Lysistrata*, and education in *The Clouds*, the parabasis punctures the curtain of fantasy to speak about the here and now. By breaking down the illusion of art, it paradoxically makes the spectators part of the spectacle.

■ E. Burkardt, *Die Entstehung der Parabase des Aristophanes* (1956); G. M. Sifakis, *Parabasis and Animal Choruses* (1971); T. K. Hubbard, *The Mask of Comedy* (1991); G. W. Dobrov, *Figures of Play* (2001); G. Jusdanis, *Fiction Agonistes* (2010).

G. JUSDANIS

**PARACLAUSITHYRON** (Gr., "sung by a locked door"). While the term itself occurs only in a late source, Plutarch's *Moralia* 753B, it is now generally applied to the lover's futile *lament outside his beloved's house. The *paraclausithyron* may have originated from the *komos*, the rowdy procession through the street after a night's drinking at the symposium, culminating in songs spurring youthful assaults on a brothel; but in the developed form, the lover must break his beloved's will, not the door (James). Key elements of the paraclausithyron are the urban setting, night, the lover's drunkenness, the refusal of the door to open, tears, and a festive garland left on the threshold. The paraclausithyron epitomizes the frustrations and sufferings of love. It is not a separate genre (Cairns) but has a long literary hist., appearing within ancient *lyric, *comedy (e.g., Alcaeus, frag. 374, the first attestation of the paraclausithyron; Aristophanes, *Ecclesiazusae* 952–75), *epigram, and *elegy. In Roman lit., the door plays a particularly prominent role as *metonymy for the unyielding beloved, perhaps because the door for the Romans was sacred (Copley, Yardley); in the first appearance of the paraclausithyron in Roman lit., at Plautus's *Curculio* 147–55, the lover addresses the door bolts. Roman love elegy developed the paraclausithyron as a prime example of male amatory persuasion (Yardley). The lover's immediate goal, to spend the night with the beloved, fails; yet, overall, his lament has the strategic advantage of revealing his devotion. Themes associated with the paraclausithyron occur throughout Catullus and the Augustan elegiac poets, all of whom also wrote a formal paraclausithyron (Catullus 67; Tibullus 1.2; Propertius 1.16; Ovid, *Amores* 1.6). Ovid claimed that the paraclausithyron was the beginning of all poetry (*Fasti* 4.109–12). Though Ovid has been accused of exhausting the *topos (Canter, Copley), later poets exploit its dramatic potential in various contexts; e.g., Bottom's address to the "sweet, o lovely Wall . . . wicked Wall" (Shakespeare, *A Midsummer Night's Dream* 5.1.174–81); John Donne's "Batter my

Heart" (*Holy Sonnets* 14) adapts the motifs of the paraclausithyron to a religious context; Alfred, Lord Tennyson's *In Memoriam* 7 and 119 use the convention to express the pain of bereavement.

The paraclausithyron has a vivid presence in popular music of all genres: rhythm and blues (Jack McVea's "Open the Door, Richard"), doo wop (The Genies' "Who's That Knocking"), soul (Otis Redding's "Open the Door"), rock and roll (The Beatles's "No Reply"), psychedelia (Jefferson Airplane's "Let Me In"), *fado* (Amalia Rodrigues's "A Chave da Minha Porta"), country (George Jones's "The Door"), and samba (Jamelão's "Fechei a Porta"), among others.

■ H. V. Canter, "The *Paraclausithyron* as Literary Theme," *AJP* 41 (1920); O. Copley, *Exclusus Amator* (1956); F. Cairns, *Generic Composition in Greek and Roman Poetry* (1972); J. C. Yardley, "The Elegiac Paraclausithyron," *Eranos* 76 (1978); S. James, *Learned Girls and Male Persuasion: Gender and Reading in Roman Elegy* (2003).

C. E. NEWLANDS

**PARADOX.** A daring statement that unites seemingly contradictory words but that on closer examination proves to have unexpected meaning and truth ("The longest way round is the shortest way home"; "Life is death and death is life"). The structure of paradox is similar to the *oxymoron, which unites two contradictory concepts into a third ("heavy lightness"), a favorite strategy of *Petrarchism. Paradoxes are esp. suited to an expression of the unspeakable in religion, mysticism, and poetry. First discussed in its formal elements in Stoic philosophy and cl. rhet., the paradox became more widely used after Sebastian Frank (*280 Paradoxa from the Holy Scriptures*, 1534) and has always retained an appeal to the Christian mode of expression, as in Martin Luther and Blaise Pascal. In the *Concluding Scientific Postscript* (1846), Søren Kierkegaard considered God's becoming man the greatest paradox for human existence.

The most famous literary example of sustained paradox is *The Praise of Folly* by Erasmus (1511). In the *baroque period, paradox became a central figure; it is particularly important in *metaphysical poetry, esp. the poetry and prose of John Donne, who makes frequent use of paradox and paradoxical lang. in the *Paradoxes and Problems* and *Songs and Sonnets* (both 1633). The paradox is manifest in the lit. of the 17th and 18th cs. in its antithetical verbal structure rather than as argument. Denis Diderot in his late dialogue *Le Paradoxe sur le comédien* (1778)—on the art of acting but with far-reaching implications for poetry—holds that an actor should not feel the passion he expresses but should transcend direct imitation and rise to the conception of an intellectual model. Everything in him should become a controlled work of art, and the emotional state should be left to the spectator. In the romantic period, Friedrich Schlegel (*Fragments*, 1797) called the paradox a basic form of human experience and linked it closely with poetry and *irony. Thomas De Quincey in his *Autobio-

*graphical Sketches* (1834–53) argued that the paradox is a vital element in poetry, reflecting the paradoxical nature of the world that poetry imitates. Friedrich Nietzsche made paradox a key term of human experience and of his own literary expression. In the lit. of the 20th c., paradox often fuses with the absurd, which can be interpreted as an intensified, often existential expression of the paradox.

The term *paradox* is widely employed in 20th-c. crit., esp. in the work of the *New Criticism. Cleanth Brooks discusses it in *The Well Wrought Urn* (esp. chap. 1) as a form of indirection that is distinctively characteristic of poetic lang. and structure. As his example from William Wordsworth ("Composed Upon Westminster Bridge") illustrates, Brooks does not use paradox in the strict antithetical sense but gives it an unusually broad range by showing that good poems are written from insights that enlarge or startlingly modify our commonplace conceptions and understandings, esp. those residing in overly simplistic distinctions; this disruptive function of poetic lang. is precisely what Brooks calls paradoxical. Since the degree of paradoxical disruption is an index of poetic meaning, paradox and poetry assume a very close affinity with one another. Subsequently, this New Critical emphasis on paradox was taken up in deconstruction. Paul de Man argued that the insistence by the New Critics on the unity, harmony, and identity of a poetic work was irreconcilable with their insistence on irony, paradox, and ambiguity—or, rather, that the insistence on unity was the "blindness" of the New Criticism, whereas the insistence on irony and paradox was its "insight."

*See* ANTITHESIS.

■ Brooks; A. E. Malloch, "Techniques and Function of the Renaissance Paradox," *SP* 53 (1956); W. V. Quine, *The Ways of Paradox and Other Essays* (1966); R. L. Colie, *Paradoxia Epidemica: The Renaissance Tradition of Paradox* (1966), "Literary Paradox," *DHI*; de Man; *Le Paradoxe au temps de la Renaissance*, ed. M. T. Jones-Davies (1982); J.J.Y. Liu, *Language— Paradox—Poetics: A Chinese Perspective*, ed. R. J. Lynn (1988); W. D. Shaw, *Elegy and Paradox* (1994).

E. H. BEHLER

**PARALIPSIS** (Gr. *paraleipsis*, "a leaving aside"). The device by which a speaker draws attention to a topic by claiming not to speak of that very same topic (e.g., "I'm not going to tell you what I heard, but . . ."). A narrower term than *apophasis* (*OED*: Gr. "denial," from "to speak off"), which includes other methods of argument or representation by denial (such as the apophatic or negative theology of denying or negating positive statements about what God is), paralipsis should not be confused with *occupatio,* the anticipating and answering of an opponent's arguments (Kelly). Paralipsis is also known as preterition (Lat. *praeteritio*). Paralipsis has been used as synonymous with *paralepsis* (Gr., "a taking aside"), though the precision of this use is questionable. *Aposiopesis* (Gr., "a becoming silent")

is different from paralipsis since it refers to the speaker's coming to an abrupt halt in speech, as if overwhelmed with emotion by the unexpressed thought. The Lat. *occultatio* is also related to paralipsis because *occultatio* is used to present evidence that is exaggerated, cannot be proved, or does not stand up against scrutiny by passing over such information as if it were unimportant to the argument. In narrative theory, paralipsis refers to a homodiegetic narrator's omitting or suppressing information that he or she is fully cognizant of from the temporal point of narration; *paralepsis* is the opposite of paralipsis. Paralipsis is related to—but should not be confused with—*analepsis* (a flashback) and *prolepsis* (a flash-forward). James Phelan identifies some examples of paralipsis as paradoxical (e.g., when a narrator unselfconsciously appears to be as naïve as his or her narrated self). Alison Case suggests that Phelan's vision of paralipsis is a convention of 20th-c. fiction rather than a perennial aesthetic.

■ *Rhetores Graeci*, ed. C. Walz, 9 vols. (1832–36); S. Usher, "*Occultatio* in Cicero's Speeches," *AJP* 86, no. 2 (April 1965); H. A. Kelly, "*Occupatio* as Negative Narration," *MP* 74, no. 3 (1977); J. Phelan, *Narrative as Rhetoric* (1996); *A Companion to Narrative Theory*, ed. J. Phelan and P. J. Rabinowitz (2005)—chap. 20 and glossary.

D. VERALDI; S. CUSHMAN

**PARALLELISM** (Gr., "side by side"). Parallelism is widely understood as a repetition of structure or pattern in adjacent phrases, clauses, or sentences within discourse in general and poetry in particular, e.g., "When the eye is cleared of obstacles, it sees sharply. When the ear is cleared of obstacles, it hears well" (*Wisdom of Lao-Tse*). The repeating structure is often syntactic in nature, as in the present example and in general in Chinese poetry (Plaks). However, the repetition may entail other ling. components such as lexicon, phonology, morphology, and rhythm (Jakobson, Hrushovski). A repetition in structural form serves, like rhyme, to associate the semantic content of the phrases or lines that share the common feature. Sometimes formally parallel propositions are roughly synonymous, e.g., "I will knock a boy into their wombs, / a baby into their embrace" (*Kalevala*; Finnish); but sometimes the coupled lines express different, though related, notions, e.g., "He wept evenings, he wept mornings, / most of all he wept nights" (*Kalevala*). Here the contrast between daytime and nocturnal behavior is crucial. Psycholinguistic investigations suggest it is natural, or at least conventional, to correlate similarity of structure and similarity of meaning. Thus, a subject in an experiment, when presented with the stimulus sentence "The lazy student failed the exam," responded with "The smart girl passed the test," a sentence parallel in structure and related in meaning.

Parallelism is characteristic of popular and formal poetry in many cultures, from ancient to mod. times, but it may function as an only occasional *trope within a work. The Babylonian creation myth *Enuma Elish* (ca. 1200 BCE) begins with a couplet in parallelism: "When on high the heaven was not yet named, / [and] below the earth was not called by name [i.e., created]" (trans. Greenstein; cf. Foster 439). Although parallelism frequently recurs in this lengthy text, it is not continuous. In such works as biblical Heb. poetry and the *Kalevala*, most couplets exhibit parallelism. Consider, e.g., this typical sequence from the prebiblical epic poetry of North Syria (Ugarit):

> Pour wine into a silver basin, / Into a gold basin, honey.
> Ascend to the top of the lookout; / Mount the city-wall's shoulder.
> Raise your hands toward the sky. / Sacrifice to Bull El, your Father.
> Adore Baal with your sacrifice, / Dagon's Son with your offering.
> > (*Kirta*; trans. Greenstein in Parker 14)

In each couplet, the second line essentially elaborates the content of the first. Kugel and Alter in their studies of biblical parallelism indicate that the second line in parallelism often intensifies or extends the sense of the first; compare:

> The new-wed groom will go forth;
> To another man he'll drive his wife; / To a stranger his own true love.
> > (*Kirta*; trans. Greenstein in Parker 15)

In this example, as in many others, the syntax of the parallel line is identical in the underlying pattern, in the deep structure, while there are variations, such as deleting (gapping) the verb ("he'll drive") in the surface structure. Parallelism in syntactic structure must accordingly be sought in the deep structure as well as in the surface form (Kiparsky, Greenstein). In the Heb. Psalm 105:17, the line "He [God] sent ahead of them a man" is followed by "Joseph was sold as a slave." Though on the surface the syntax of each line seems different, in generative theory the second line, formulated in the passive voice, is underlyingly active— "[Someone] sold Joseph as a slave." The sentence in the deep structure is transformed in the surface structure into a concrete passive sentence. On the deep or abstract level, the syntactic structures are identical (subject noun-phrase, verb-phrase, adverbial phrase). The fact that parallelism obtains fundamentally on the abstract level is clear from instances in which a word or phrase in the surface structure of the first line is gapped in the second line, even when it lacks grammatical agreement. E.g., in the following Ugaritic (N. Syrian, 13th c. BCE) couplet—"Her father sets the stand of the balance, / Her mother the trays of the balance" (*Nikkal and Yarikh*)—the verb "sets" is masculine; if it were to appear in the surface structure of the second line, it would have to be feminine in form (trans. Greenstein; cf. D. Marcus in Parker 217).

When a word or phrase is deleted in the parallel line, it is routine to compensate for the syllables lost by expanding one of the parallel elements, e.g., "I will certainly stop the women's laughter, / the daughters' peals of laughter" (*Kalevala*). In the Heb. couplet, "Why is light given to one-who-suffers, / and life to those-bitter-of spirit?" (Job 3:20), the verb "is given" is gapped in the second line and the single word "one-who-suffers" is paralleled by the two-word phrase "those-bitter-of spirit," which is an extension in sense as well as form, as Job extrapolates from his own instance of suffering to that of others, perhaps even all others, as well.

In biblical Heb. verse, the first line of a couplet nearly always comprises a complete clause, if not a complete sentence, and the second line ordinarily reiterates it in parallelism, at least in part. The second line, however, may extend the first line without repeating any of its syntactic structure. The result is a sort of *enjambment, e.g., "He called up against me a holiday / for breaking down my young men!" (Lam. 1:15; see Dobbs-Allsopp). In such cases, we may either understand the entire first line to be repeated in the deep structure of the second line—and deleted; or we may understand that, in this parallelism, balance of line length, rather than repetition of syntactic structure, is determinative (see below).

Biblical Heb. is the best-known system of parallelism, first described in depth by Bishop Robert Lowth in 1753 (see HEBREW POETRY, HEBREW PROSODY AND POETICS). Jewish exegetes of the Middle Ages had expressed a less elaborate understanding of parallelism according to which "it is a doubling of the meaning using different words" (David Kimḥi, Provence, ca. 1200). Lowth, too, laid emphasis on semantic reiteration alongside syntactic repetition: "When a Proposition is delivered, and a second is subjoined to it, or drawn under it, equivalent, or contrasted with it in Sense; or similar to it in the form of Grammatical Construction; these I call Parallel lines; and the words, or phrases, answering one to another in the corresponding Lines, Parallel Terms" (*Isaiah: A New Translation*, 1778).

In the 1980s, both O'Connor and Greenstein suggested that parallelism be regarded as the rhetorical structuration of propositions, whose meanings are brought into conjunction by their formal similarities. Consider Psalm 23:1: "The Lord is my shepherd, / I shall not want." The two propositions have no inherent link semantically. Bringing the two clauses together through parallelism, however, establishes a meaningful connection: the speaker will lack nothing because the Lord is, metaphorically, a shepherd who protects, guides, and cares for him or her. Note as well that the two lines of the couplet have different syntactic structures. They display above all a quasi-metrical balance. A minority view holds that there is a strictly recoverable metrical component to the poetry of the Heb. Bible (e.g., Sievers), but in the absence of any convincing theory, it is more generally maintained that there is an unrecoverable or vague metrical element in the verse.

Biblical parallelism, as J. G. Herder first observed in 1783, is primarily characterized by a balance of line length. Secondarily, it may feature a repetition of syntactic structure and the distribution of conventionally paired words (silver-gold, heaven-earth, father-mother, slave-son of a maidservant, wine-blood of grapes, listen-give ear, etc.) between the parallel lines. Accordingly, the couplet immediately following Psalm 23:1 is "In grassy meadows he lays me down (*yarbitséni*), / By still waters he leads me (*yenahaléni*)." Here we find a quasi-metrical balance, full repetition of syntactic structure, the distribution of the word pair "meadow-waters" (cf. Joel 1:20) between the two members of the parallelism, and on top of that a phonetic echo of the verb from line to line.

In Chinese verse and rhet., as was said, it is typical to formulate full lines in complete syntactic parallelism, e.g., "In the vast desert a solitary column of smoke rises straight, / Over the long river the setting sun looms round" (Wang Wei; quoted in Plaks 536). In Eng. Ren. poetry, by contrast, it is common to pattern phrases in sequence in parallelism, e.g., "Light of my life, and life of my desire"; "Oft with true sighes, oft with uncalled teares, / Now with slow words, now with dumbe eloquence" (Philip Sidney, *Astrophil and Stella* 68, 61). Such sequences can be extended, e.g., "My mouth doth water, and my breast doth swell, / My tongue doth itch, my thoughts in labour be" (37). In more complex structures, the individual entities are themselves likely to be more complex, forming full sentences in parallelism:

> Let Fortune lay on me her worst disgrace,
> Let folke orecharg'd with braine against me crie,
> Let clouds bedimme my face, breake in mine eye,
> Let me no steps but of lost labour trace,
> Let all the earth with scorne recount my case.
> (*Astrophil and Stella,* 64)

In Eur. poetry since the Ren., biblical influence has reinforced the use of parallelism to the point that few major verse texts are without some parallelism. William Blake and Christopher Smart both use quasi-biblical parallelism extensively. This tendency reaches a turning point when Walt Whitman makes use of biblical structures to supplant the metrical basis of Eng. prosody itself:

> The prairie-grass accepting its own special odor breathing,
> I demand of it the spiritual corresponding,
> Demand the most copious and close companionship of men,
> Demand the blades to rise of words, acts, beings.
> ("Calamus," *Leaves of Grass*)

Full, indeed extraordinarily long, lines can be formulated in parallelism, as in Dylan Thomas's opening affirmation, "The force that through the green fuse drives the flower / Drives my green age" and its (nonadjacent) parallel, "The force that drives the water through the rocks / Drives my red blood." Similarly in the well-known opening of Allen Ginsberg's *Howl* (1955), the second line refers back to the syntax of the latter part of the first line (beginning "I saw the best minds of my generation . . ."), reduplicating and elaborating it. The underlying structure of the second line is, accordingly, "[I saw the best minds of my generation . . .], dragging themselves through the negro streets at dawn looking for an angry fix." Essentially, the form we find here is the same as that of ancient Ugaritic and Heb. verse, in which the deletion of an element in the second line is accompanied by an extension of an ungapped element.

Ginsberg's poem captures the cadences of oral discourse, bringing the historical trajectory of parallelism full circle, for while parallelism becomes a convention of formal, literate composition, its beginnings are unquestionably in an oral context. Many poetries featuring parallelism tend to be either oral or early literate. The later typological category is important: the poetry of the Heb. Bible began to be written down over two and a half millennia ago, while Finnish folk poetry has been recorded for only a century and a half, but cl. Heb. and Finnish poetry are comparably close to the oral poetic situation and comparably far from the literate setting (see ORAL POETRY).

Parallelism is well represented in traditional poetry in Chinese (and its literary offspring, Vietnamese), in Toda (but not in the other Dravidian tongues), in Semitic langs. (see above and cf. several types of "parallel prose" in Ar.), in the Uralic langs. (incl. Finnish), in the Austronesian langs. (Rotinese is the best known), and in the Mayan langs. Both med. and mod. Rus. folk poetry is parallelistic, as is some Altaic (Mongol and Turkic) verse.

*See* HYPOTAXIS AND PARATAXIS.

■ R. Lowth, *De sacra poesi Hebraeorum, Lectures on the Sacred Poetry of the Hebrews*, trans. G. Gregory (1753); J. G. Herder, *Vom Geist der hebräischen Poesie* (1753), trans. *The Spirit of Hebrew Poetry* (1833); E. Sievers, *Metrische Studien I–II* (1901–7); *The Wisdom of Laotse*, trans. and ed. Lin Yutang (1948); Jakobson, esp. v. 3; *The Kalevala*, trans. F. P. Magoun Jr. (1963); B. Hrushovski, "Prosody, Hebrew," *Encyclopedia Judaica* (1971); P. Kiparsky, "The Role of Linguistics in a Theory of Poetry," *Daedalus* 102 (1973); J. J. Fox, "Roman Jakobson and the Comparative Study of Parallelism," *Roman Jakobson*, ed. D. Armstrong and C. H. Van Schooneveld (1977); J. M. Lotman, *The Structure of the Artistic Text*, trans. G. Lenhoff and R. Vroon (1977); S. A. Geller, *Parallelism in Early Biblical Poetry* (1979); M. O'Connor, *Hebrew Verse Structure* (1980); J. L. Kugel, *The Idea of Biblical Poetry* (1981); E. L. Greenstein, "How Does Parallelism Mean?" *A Sense of Text* (1983); R. Alter, *The Art of Biblical Poetry* (1985); A. Berlin, *The Dynamics of Biblical Parallelism* (1985); Terras; M. R. Lichtmann, *The Contemplative Poetry of G. M. Hopkins* (1989); A. H. Plaks, "Where the Lines Meet: Parallelism in Chinese and Western Literature," *PoT* 11 (1990); *Ugaritic Narrative Poetry*, ed. S. B. Parker (1997); F. W. Dobbs-Allsopp, "The Enjambing Line in Lamentations: A Taxonomy (Part 1)," *Zeitschrift für die alttestamentliche Wissenschaft* 113 (2001); B. R. Foster, *Before the Muses* (2005)—anthol. of Akkadian lit.

M. P. O'CONNOR; E. L. GREENSTEIN

**PARAPHRASE, HERESY OF.** The Am. New Critic Cleanth Brooks describes "the heresy of paraphrase" in the concluding chapter of his widely read and important book *The Well Wrought Urn* (1947). Following the Brit. critic I. A. Richards's *Science and Poetry* (1926), he insists on the essential difference between scientific statements (which are paraphrasable) and poetic statements (not paraphrasable; see PSEUDO-STATEMENT). In the former, the same content can be expressed in other words; in the latter, form and content work together to produce meaning so that a poem cannot be reduced to a prose précis.

In analyzing a poem, a critic must sometimes resort to a discursive summary statement about its meaning. However, such plain statements are always put into question by the formal structure of the poem itself. As Brooks puts it, "[W]hatever statement we may seize upon as incorporating the 'meaning' of the poem, immediately the imagery and rhythm seem to set up tensions with it, warping and twisting it, qualifying and revising it." This process is the indispensable structural principle from which the meaning of a poem derives. For Brooks, a poem is never a clear-cut scientific proposition. It is a structure of "gestures and attitudes" that constitutes an autonomous poetic universe. These ideas draw on the poetry and poetics of *modernism. T. S. Eliot describes a poem as "heterogeneity compelled into unity," suggesting a process similar to Brooks's "warping and twisting." The final lines of Archibald MacLeish's "Ars Poetica" (1926) are "A poem should not mean / But be."

Brooks writes in *The Well Wrought Urn* that a poem resembles drama: "the poem does not merely eventuate in a logical conclusion. . . . It is 'proved' as a dramatic conclusion is proved: by its ability to resolve the conflicts which have been accepted as the *données* of the drama." Thus, a poem has a meaning because a dramatization of experience is enacted structurally within the poem: tensions are set in motion; elements are played against one another; conflicts are embodied in metrical patterns and figurative lang. Through this process of internal dynamism, putting in motion *irony, *ambiguity, and *paradox, Brooks argues, a poem creates meaning.

The heresy of paraphrase, with its implications about the implicit inner coherence of a poem, was an influential contribution to the formalist analysis of poetry. Situating *New Criticism within intellectual hist., Herbert argues that 19th-c. scientific thought (Charles Darwin, Karl Pearson, Herbert Spencer) and 20th-c. aesthetics and ling. (Benedetto Croce and Ferdinand de Saussure) generated key ideas about coherence that received their fullest explication for lit. crit. in Brooks and Robert Penn Warren's *Understanding Poetry* (1938). In a different historicizing analysis, Jancovich points out that Brooks's *formalism, his stress on the internal workings of a poem, moves away from the more socially rooted values of the first-generation New Critics John Crowe Ransom and Allen Tate, who celebrated what they saw as the organic communities of preindustrial agricultural societies.

■ M. Krieger, *The New Apologists for Poetry* (1956); T. S. Eliot, "The Metaphysical Poets," *Selected Prose,* ed. F. Kermode (1975); M. Jancovich, *The Cultural Politics of the New Criticism* (1993)—esp. ch. 14; C. Herbert, "The Conundrum of Coherence," *NLH* 35 (2004).

P. McCallum

**PARENTHESIS** (Gr., "to put in beside"). In Eng., *parenthesis* has two meanings: a rhetorical figure that inserts a word, phrase, or sentence into a sentence already complete in itself; and the rounded brackets (sometimes called "half moons") used to mark that insertion. The figure dates from antiquity, while the graphic signs that enclose the figure were first used by humanist writers in the late 14th c. (Lennard). Reflecting its etymology, parenthesis is usually defined by its status within a larger, more important unit of discourse. The content of the figure varies, but a parenthesis commonly inserts speech attributions, sententiae, relative and conditional clauses, or figurative comparisons. The contents of a parenthesis may or may not relate to the subject of the larger sentence, which retains its sense with or without the parenthetical insertion. Definitions of parenthesis from the cl. period forward emphasize its structural independence from the host sentence, insisting that its removal would leave a "whole," "full," or "entire" sentence behind. Thus, in parenthesis we see the operations of not only a spatial logic (it is "in between") but a temporal logic (it is a belated addition to an already complete text, an addition that may be subsequently removed). As this formulation suggests, definitions of parenthesis tend to be self-instantiating, using the figure to exemplify its own status as unnecessary interruption.

Cl., early mod., and neoclassical rhetorical handbooks often conclude their definitions of parenthesis with a warning; as Pierre Fontanier explains, "[B]y the very fact that [parentheses] interrupt the discourse and draw attention away from its principal object, they tend to produce encumbrance, obscurity, and confusion" (*Les Figures autres que les tropes*, 1827). A parenthesis distracts the reader from the text's primary idea or narrative, and if it goes on too long without a return to that primary subject, it may confound meaning. Because the figure disrupts syntactical flow and may even fragment the narrative line, uses of parenthesis often belie definitions that insist on its accessory function within the sentence. A passage from Philip Sidney's *Arcadia* (1590, 1593) indicates the tension between definition and use: "He, swelling in their humbleness (like a bubble swollen up with a small breath, broken with a great), forgetting (or not knowing) humanity, caused their heads to be struck off." The removal of these parentheses would leave the sentence grammatically intact, yet its meaning would be substantively altered. As in this instance, literary uses of parenthesis often disturb distinctions between necessary and expendable textual matter. The figure instantiates what Derrida describes in *Of Grammatology* as the conundrum of the supplement: it adds an inessential piece of text to something already complete, yet the very presence of the figure exposes a lack in what was supposed to be complete in itself.

*See* FIGURATION, ORNAMENT, SCHEME.

■ Lanham; J. Lennard, *But I Digress* (1991); R. G. Williams, "Reading the Parenthesis," *SubStance* 22 (1993); Derrida; *Parentheticals*, ed. N. Dehé and Y. Kavalova (2007).

J. C. MANN

**PARNASSIANISM.** The *Parnassiens* (in Eng., Parnassians) were a loose cohort of Fr. poets born from 1840 to 1850 who were influenced by Théophile Gautier (1811–72) and gravitated around Charles-Marie Leconte de Lisle (1818–94). They treated a number of themes taken from hist., science, philosophy, nature, or contemp. life according to an aesthetic of unsentimental craftsmanship. They were generally classicist in outlook, used traditional verse forms, and regarded the cult of poetry as a religion. *Le prémier Parnasse contemporain* (1866) was followed by other *recueils* in 1871 and 1876, but the works of Parnassians covered the period from 1865 to the end of the century, representing an important trend in Fr. poetry between the romantics and the symbolists. Parnassianism had an international reach, influencing the Sp. Am. *modernismo* of Rubén Darío and his contemporaries as well as several Eur. poetry movements predicated on *symbolism, *aestheticism, and *decadence, and serving as an often negative point of reference for many 20th-c. modernists in the U.S., Brazil, and elsewhere.

The movement was initiated by Catulle Mendès (1841–1909) and L.-X. de Ricard (1843–1911) in the early 1860s, when the Parnassians first met in Lemerre's bookshop and in the salon of the Marquise de Ricard; later they gathered in the salon of Mme. Leconte de Lisle, whose formidable husband was regarded as a kind of oracle. Of the 50 or more poets called Parnassians only a few can be mentioned here. Among the more independent, Albert Glatigny (1839–73) was a wit and virtuoso who took his cue from Théodore de Banville (1823–1891). F.R.A. Sully-Prudhomme (1839–1907) explored the secrets of the inner life in verses as poignant as Heinrich Heine's but without Heine's bitterness. He wrote philosophic poems using a delicate imagery drawn from the natural sciences. François Coppée (1842–1908) described the life and problems of humble folk and, like Sully-Prudhomme, was sensitive to the writer's moral responsibilities. The followers of Leconte de Lisle respected traditional morals but worshipped Art. Gautier as well as Banville remained a potent influence. Léon Dierx (1838–1912) wrote tragic poems on historical themes and struck a note of despair. Jean Lahor (1840–1909) exhaled his melancholy in Buddhistic verses. J.-M. de Heredia (1842–1905) drew inspiration from the Gr. myths, from the *epigrams of the *Greek Anthology*, and from the Lat. poets. He was something of a scholar and paleographer but above all a finished artist. Most of his *Trophées* (1895) are *sonnets, and he is one of the outstanding sonneteers of late 19th-c. France. Anatole

France (1844–1924) was more independent: although a versatile neo-Hellenist, he was also, in his *Poèmes dorés*, an able nature poet. Jules Lemaître (1853–1914), the critic and literary historian, was a *conteur* and poet who achieved formal eloquence.

Though some of them underwent the influence of Louis-Nicolas Ménard (1822–1901), the Parnassians were not primarily Hellenists, nor were they as a whole impassive or impersonal. If they had anything in common, it was a love of precision, a devotion to formal beauty and the cult of *rhyme, and, beyond that, "un romantisme assagi et mitigé" (Henri Peyre), which left a mark on such great poets as Stéphane Mallarmé and Paul Verlaine and, to a lesser extent, on a few figures of the following generation such as Paul Valéry in his *Album de vers anciens*. In England, the work of Banville and others inspired a vogue for Fr. fixed forms such as the *villanelle, *sestina, and *triolet.

■ C. Mendès, *La Légende du Parnasse contemporain* (1884); R. Canat, *La Renaissance de la Grèce antique* (1911); M. Ibrovac, *J. M. de Heredia: Sa vie, son oeuvre* (1923); T. Martel, *Le Parnasse* (1923); F. Desonay, *Le Rêve hellénique chez les poètes parnassiens* (1928); E. Estève, *Le Parnasse* (1929); A. Therive, *Le Parnasse* (1929); A. Schaffer, *Parnassus in France* (1930); M. Souriau, *Histoire du Parnasse* (1930); H.-M. Peyre, *Louis Ménard (1822–1901)* (1932), and *Bibl. critique de l'hellénisme en France de 1843 à 1870* (1932); F. Vincent, *Les Parnassiens* (1933); M. G. Rudler, *Parnassiens, symbolistes et décadents* (1938); Z. Rosenberg, *La persistance du subjectivisme chez les poètes parnassiens* (1939); A. Lytton Sells, "Heredia's Hellenism," *MLR* 37 (1942); A. Schaffer, *The Genres of Parnassian Poetry* (1944); V. Errante, *Parnassiani e simbolisti francesi* (1953); M. Decaudin, *La Crise des valeurs symbolistes* (1960); P. Martino, *Parnasse et Symbolisme* (1964); A. Racot, *Les Parnassiens* (1968); R. T. Denommé, *The French Parnassian Poets* (1972); H. Peyre, *Qu'est-ce le Symbolisme?* (1974); L. Decaune, *La Poésie parnassienne* (1977); *The Symbolist Movement in the Literature of European Languages*, ed. A. Balakian (1982); Hollier; R. J. Kaliman, "La carne y el mármol: Parnaso y simbolismo en la poética modernista hispanoamericana," *Revista Iberoamericana* 55 (1989); M. Rubins, *Crossroad of Arts, Crossroad of Cultures: Ecphrasis in Russian and French Poetry* (2000); S. Murphy, "Logiques du Bateau Ivre," *Littératures* 54 (2006); S. Whidden, *Leaving Parnassus: The Lyric Subject in Verlaine and Rimbaud* (2007).

A. L. SELLS

**PARODY.** Derived from the Gr. roots *para* (alongside, counter) and *odos* (song), parody as a form of ironic *imitation has been with us since ancient times. It changes with the culture, however, so no transhistorical definition is possible: its forms, its relations to the parodied text, and its intentions are not the same in North America today as they were in 18th-c. England or Aristotle's Greece. Theories of parody have changed along with the form's aesthetic manifestations, but two major views have emerged, both derived, though in different ways, from the word's etymology. In the age of Alexander Pope and John Dryden, e.g., parody was seen as a "countersong"—a biting, often satiric, imitation intended to wittily "counter" (i.e., to mock or ridicule) what really was an intended "target." In our mod. and postmod. times, parody has come to mean more of an intimate "song beside"—an ironic but not necessarily disrespectful revisiting and recontextualizing of an earlier work.

In formal terms, parody is a doubled structure, incorporating backgrounded aspects of the parodied text of the past into the foreground of its present self. The two texts neither merge nor cancel each other out; they work together, while remaining distinct. From either of its historically defined perspectives, parody involves opposition or contrast: it is a form of repetition with ironic critical difference, marking difference rather than similarity (Gilman 1974, 1976; Hutcheon). Therein lies the difference between parody and *pastiche. Though both are forms of acknowledged borrowing (and in that acknowledging, they differ from the hoax, the plagiarism, or the forgery), pastiche does not aim at ironic inversion leading to difference. Neither does *allusion or quotation in itself, though both can be used ironically. To continue with distinctions, both burlesque and travesty by definition involve ridiculing humor, but parody does not necessarily—neither now nor in its cl. uses (Householder). It can range in its tones and moods from the seriously respectful to the playful to the scathingly critical because that is the range of *irony, its major rhetorical strategy.

But it is parody's defining critical distance that has always permitted *satire to be so effectively deployed through parodic textual forms. From Catullus to Wendy Cope, satirists have used and continue to use the pointed and effective doubling of parody's textual voices as a vehicle to unmask the duplicities of human society. Pope's *mock epics *The Rape of the Lock* and *The Dunciad*, the latter with its ironic use of Virgil's *Eclogues*, stand as fine examples of the complexity of the interrelationship of parody and satire: the mock epic did not mock the epic but satirized the pretensions of the contemporary as set against the ideal norms implied by the parodied text or set of conventions. This is not to say that the literary forms themselves could not be critiqued: John Milton's *Paradise Lost* uses epic conventions but also critically parodies those conventions and the whole cl. heroic ethos, by consistently associating them with Satan and his legions; and Chaucer's "The Tale of Sir Thopas" ridicules the clichés of med. verse romance.

A form of what has been called *intertextuality (Kristeva, Genette) or interart discourse, parody can also involve a self-reflexive (Rose 1979) and critical act of reassessment and acclimatization. But there is often a tension between the potentially conservative effect of repetition and the potentially revolutionary impact of difference. These contradictory ideological implications of parody took center stage in the postmod. 1980s and the years after, in both the lit. itself and the critical theorizing. And yet despite the complicity that post-

mod. parody implied, it was the more critical dimension that would come to dominate because of changes in political contexts. Parody's echoing repetition has always implicitly contested romantic concepts of creative *originality and singularity, as well as capitalist notions of individual ownership and copyright, but it clearly was seen to challenge (or, more accurately, to be *used* to challenge) many other dominant political positions. Parody came to be reinterpreted through what Rich called women's "re-visioning," a looking back with new eyes on a literary trad. dominated by male perspectives and a subsequent rewriting of it in a differently gendered key. This echoing contestation was mirrored in what Gates and others historicized as Af. Am. *"signifying"—another kind of double-voiced repetition and inversion, but this time one that responds to both dominant and vernacular discourses. Postcolonial crit.'s focus on how formerly colonized writers could "write back" to empire through critically rewriting or even (in Bhabha's refigured sense of the word) mimicking its canonical texts coincided with the work of indigenous writers in the Americas to adapt dominant discourses to create new and highly critical hybrid forms (Powell). Queer writing and theory politicized Sontag's notion of "camp" to make ironic repetition the device of choice for challenging homophobia.

In short, whatever the political contestation, parody proved a useful rhetorical strategy, a counter-discourse (Terdiman), to confront the past and potentially to move beyond it. For example, Thylias Moss's various parodies that recode poems racially ("Interpretation of a Poem by Frost" or "A Reconsideration of the Blackbird") are typical of all these manifestations, in both theory and practice, in that the parodies' situation in the world, so to speak, becomes the focus of attention: the time and the place, the ideological frame of reference, the personal and social context—not only of parodist but also of readers of the work. What has also become clear through this new politicized context, however, is that parody is fundamentally ambivalent or paradoxical; it is doubled and divided because of that defining mix of repetition and difference. If it is transgressive, it is only as a form of authorized transgression, like Bakhtin's carnivalesque (1973). It cannot help inscribing and granting authority to what it parodies, even if it aims to challenge it. Parody enacts both continuity and change.

That unavoidable ambivalence may help explain why, depending on the time and place, parody has been either prized or derided, called both noble and vile. On the negative end of the evaluation scale, it has been called parasitic and derivative, esp. within a romantic aesthetic. With the inauguration of copyright laws came defamation suits against parodists. Yet, early in the 20th c., the *Russian formalists prized works like Lord Byron's *Don Juan* because their parodic form coincided with their own theory of the essential conventionality of literary form and the role of parody in its denuding or laying bare (Erlich). Read in contexts ranging from T. S. Eliot's valorizing of what he called the historical sense to Bakhtin's privileging of dialogism or double voicing, parody has been welcomed as a form of textual appropriation that self-reflexively foregrounds both the formal and the ideological dimensions of lit. It has become one mode of coming to terms with the texts of that rich and, for some, intimidating legacy of the past (Bate), offering a model, however ironized, for the process of transfer and reorganization of that past—whether such recycling be of literary conventions or individual works.

Parodies must be recognized as double-voiced discourses in order for their ironic inversion to function; if they are not, they will simply be naturalized and their doubling ignored. That is why some parodists resort to overtly revealing titles: Anthony Hecht's famous ironic take on Matthew Arnold is dubbed "The Dover Bitch"; P. B. Shelley's parody of William Wordsworth is titled "Peter Bell the Third," while William Maginn's of S. T. Coleridge is called "The Rime of the Auncient Waggonere." For parody to be recognized and interpreted, there must be (cultural, ling., literary) codes shared between the encoder and the decoder, the parodist and the reader, or the structural superimposition of texts will be missed. The potential for elitism inherent in the need for shared codes has been frequently pointed out, but less attention has been paid to the didactic value of parody in teaching or in positively co-opting the art of the past by textual incorporation and ironic commentary. Forrest-Thomson has argued that the mod. poet manages to mediate between the ling. codes we normally recognize and use and those that emerge from an assimilation and transformation of those codes. Parodic poetry in particular can function overtly as this kind of link. Parody is a way to preserve continuity in discontinuity—without the Bloomian anxiety of *influence.

■ **Anthologies**: *A Book of Parodies*, ed. A. Symons (1908); *A Century of Parody and Imitation*, ed. W. Jerrold and R. M. Leonard (1913); *A Parody Anthology*, ed. C. Wells (1919); *Apes and Parrots*, ed. J. Collings Squire (1928); *American Literature in Parody*, ed. R. P. Falk (1955); *Parodies*, ed. D. Macdonald (1960); *The Brand X Anthology of Poetry*, ed. W. Zaranka (1981); *The Faber Book of Parodies*, ed. S. Brett (1984); *Unauthorized Versions*, ed. K. Baker (1990); *Romantic Parodies, 1797–1831*, ed. D. A. Kent and D. R. Ewen (1992).

■ **Criticism and History**: S. Martin, *On Parody* (1896); C. Stone, *Parody* (1914); G. Kitchin, *A Survey of Burlesque and Parody in English* (1931); F. W. Householder, "Parodia," *CP* 39 (1944); F. J. Lelièvre, "The Basis of Ancient Parody," *Greece and Rome* 1 (1954); E. Courtney, "Parody and Literary Allusion in Menippean Satire," *Philologus* 106 (1962); G. Highet, *Anatomy of Satire* (1962); V. Erlich, *Russian Formalism*, 2d ed. (1965); J. G. Riewald, "Parody as Criticism," *Neophilologus* 50 (1966); U. Weisstein, "Parody, Travesty, and Burlesque," *Proceedings of the 4th Congress of the ICLA* (1966); S. Sontag, "Notes on Camp," *Against Interpretation* (1967); S. Golopentia-Eretescu, "Grammaire de la parodie," *Cahiers de linguistique théorique et appliquée* 6 (1969); G. D. Kiremidjian, "The Aesthetics of Parody," *JAAC* 28 (1969); W. J. Bate, *The Burden of the Past and the English Poet* (1970); G. Lee, *Allusion,*

*Parody and Imitation* (1971); M. M. Bakhtin, *Rabelais and His World*, trans. H. Iswolsky (1973); H. Bloom, *The Anxiety of Influence* (1973); T. Verweyen, *Eine Theorie der Parodie* (1973); O. M. Friedenberg, "The Origin of Parody," *Semiotics and Structuralism*, ed. H. Baran (1974); S. L. Gilman, *The Parodic Sermon in European Perspective* (1974); L. Dällenbach, "Intertexte et autotexte," *Poétique* 27 (1976); S. L. Gilman, *Nietzschean Parody* (1976); W. Karrer, *Parodie, Travestie, Pastiche* (1977); V. Forrest-Thomson, *Poetic Artifice* (1978); Z. Ben-Porat, "The Poetics of Literary Allusion," *PTL: A Journal for Descriptive Poetics and Theory of Literature* 1 (1979); A. Rich, *On Lies, Secrets, and Silence* (1979); M. A. Rose, *Parody//Meta-Fiction* (1979); M. M. Bakhtin, *The Dialogic Imagination*, ed. M. Holquist, trans. C. Emerson and M. Holquist (1981); W. Freund, *Die literarische Parodie* (1981); H. Bhabha, "Of Mimicry and Man," *October* 28 (1984); E. Cobley, "Sameness and Difference in Literary Repetition," *Semiotic Inquiry* 4 (1984); R. Terdiman, *Discourse/Counter Discourse* (1985); J. Kristeva, "Word, Dialogue and Novel," *The Kristeva Reader*, ed. T. Moi (1986); J. A. Dane, *Parody* (1988); H. L. Gates Jr., *The Signifying Monkey* (1988); M. A. Rose, *Parody* (1993); G. Genette, *Palimpsests*, trans. C. Newman and C. Doubinsky (1997); *Parody*, ed. B. Müller (1997); S. Dentith, *Parody* (2000); L. Hutcheon, *A Theory of Parody*, 2d ed. (2000); M. Powell, "Rhetorics of Survivance: How American Indians *Use* Writing," *CCC* 53.3 (2002), http://www.inventio.us/ccc/; R. L. Mack, *The Genius of Parody* (2007).

L. Hutcheon and M. Woodland

**PAROEMIAC** (Gr., "proverbial"). In cl. prosody, the term for an anapaestic dimeter catalectic, common in *proverbs and popular expressions: it has the metrical form ‿ ‿ – ‿ ‿ – ‿ ‿ – – and was used in series as a march rhythm and as a close to anapestic systems. It finds related use in the cantica of Plautus (see CANTICUM AND DIVERBIUM) and was used later as a stichic line by med. Lat. poets such as Boethius.

■ Crusius; Dale; *Oxford Classical Dictionary* (1970), "Paroemiographers"; Halporn et al.; West 53.

J. W. Halporn

**PARONOMASIA** (Gr., occasionally in Lat. [pure Lat. *agnominatio*], Eng. from 1577, *OED*). Wordplay based on like-sounding words, e.g., a pun. In rhet., often one type of pun only, as against, e.g., *antanaclasis* (Lanham). *Pun*, a later word (from 1644, *OED*), has come to include earlier rhetorical figures for wordplay (Spitzer).

Rhetoricians from Aristotle onward are mostly cautious about paronomasia, chiefly about its overuse, while noting its effectiveness when used appropriately (*Rhetorica ad Herennium*, early 1st c. BCE; Geoffrey of Vinsauf, *Poetria nova*, ca. 1210). Some stress its low status (Henry Peacham, *The Garden of Eloquence*, 1593; Ben Jonson, *Timber*, 1641; César Chesneau Dumarsais, *Traité des tropes*, 1730). Overuse is a question of competence, but status is simply a question of *taste and fashion, which may vary from one era to another. From cl. through med. to Ren. writing, the functions of paronomasia were not confined to comic, let alone trivial, purposes. But 18th-c. neo-classical writers disliked it (Joseph Addison, *Spectator* no. 61, 1711, where it is called "false wit"; Alexander Pope, *Peri Bathous* [Bathos], 1727). Poets in the 19th c. made little use of paronomasia compared with their 17th-c. predecessors, though some enjoyed it in prose writing (S. T. Coleridge, Charles Lamb). Among major poets, Emily Dickinson and G. M. Hopkins are exceptions. In general, the 19th c. assigned it to comic verse (Thomas Hood, Lewis Carroll, Edward Lear, W. S. Gilbert). Modernist poets (e.g., T. S. Eliot, Wallace Stevens) used paronomasia for serious effects, reviving the concept of *serio ludere*. But it is still a question whether paronomasia has regained its earlier status as a figure, lost when 18th-c. rhet. downgraded the pun.

Paronomasia may occur in all types of poetry, from comic to sublime. The Heb. Bible uses it (*Moses* means both one "drawn out" of the water [Heb. *mosheh*] and one who "draws out" Israel from bondage [Heb. *mashah*]; Marks); so does the Christian Bible (Jesus puns on the name *Peter* and *petra*, rock, Matt. 16:18). Cl. Gr. writers enjoyed it (Stanford), as did some Lat. writers, such as Virgil (Ahl, Spence). Augustine records the delight of contemp. North African congregations in *hilaritas*, incl. wordplay (Brown). Shakespeare is fertile in the deployment of paronomasia for both comic and serious effects. Mercutio's dying pun is well known: tomorrow he will be "a grave man" (*Romeo and Juliet* 3.1.98); Hamlet puns on "sun" and "son" (*Hamlet* 1.2.64 and 67), a pun sometimes extended to Christ, as in George Herbert's "The Son." John Milton puns in the first line of *Paradise Lost* on "fruit" of a tree and "fruit" as result. *Limericks delight in outrageous witty puns.

Paronomasia runs from *piano* to *forte* effects. Edmund Spenser's is quiet and often builds slowly, as does the paronomasia in poetry by Herbert through Elizabeth Bishop and beyond. John Donne's likes to display itself ("A Hymn to God the Father," 1633: "done" and "Donne").

In the analysis of puns, the most familiar division is between homophonic puns (like-sounding, as in "done" and "Donne") and homonymic or semantic puns (different meanings in one word, as in railroad "ties" and "ties" of the heart in Bishop's "Chemin de Fer"). In poetry, it is useful to distinguish paronomasia as a *scheme and paronomasia as a *trope. A simple homophonic pun without further reverberation beyond sheer pleasure would be classified as a scheme (Hood's "Faithless Sally Brown": "They went and told the sexton / And the sexton tolled the bell.") But puns can move toward trope, when they begin to generate fables about themselves (Fried), as seen with Virgil or Stevens above.

Multilingual puns also flourished over the centuries, esp. when Lat. was commonly known. Ludovico Ariosto used an ancient one, newly rediscovered, in his hippogryph or horse-griffin (*gryphus* puns on the griffin and a type of playful riddle, *griphos*, a pun that Car-

roll also used for his Gryphon in *Alice in Wonderland* [Cook 2006]). James Joyce's *Finnegans Wake* is rich in such puns, and the art is not lost in poetry: witness Stevens's brilliant paronomasia on "selvages / salvages" in "Esthétique du Mal," sect. 5, echoing Dante's *selva oscura* and Eliot's "The Dry Salvages."

Most paronomasia in poetry is verbal, but visual puns are possible, as in James Merrill's "The owlet umlaut peeps and hoots / Above the open vowel" ("Lost in Translation") or Tony Harrison's "blank printer's ems" that duly appear in the next line, resulting in a justified right margin ("Self-Justification"). So are oral puns, as in "Crows in Winter" by Anthony Hecht: "the wind, a voiceless thorn" (punning on the OE letter *thorn*, the unvoiced *th*).

A few words have a hist. of paronomasia in poetry and invite special attention, e.g., *turn, leaves, room*. *Turn* is the root meaning of Gr. *trope* and may also refer to the turning of the end of a poetic line (cf. Fr. *verser*). Seamus Heaney, following an old trad., extends this to the lines made by a ploughman (*Preoccupations*). *Leaves* is a longstanding trope for the souls of the dead, from Homer through Virgil, Milton, P. B. Shelley, Stevens, and others; a pun on the Eng. verb *leave* is a given. *Stanza* means "room."

As with *riddle and *charm, the pun is associated with very early writing. Possibly it gave birth to Western writing itself in the Sumerian alphabet of pre-3000 BCE Mesopotamia, to follow Jared Diamond in *Guns, Germs and Steel* (1997): *ti* as "life" and as "arrow." As Frye says, "Paronomasia is one of the essential elements of verbal creation."

■ S. Freud, "The Technique of Jokes," *The Standard Edition of the Complete Psychological Works*, ed. and trans. J. Strachey, v. 8 (1905); W. B. Stanford, *Ambiguity in Greek Literature* (1939); L. Spitzer, "Puns," *JEGP* 49 (1950); Frye; M. M. Mahood, *Shakespeare's Wordplay* (1957); P. Brown, *Augustine of Hippo* (1967); F. Ahl, *Metaformations: Soundplay and Wordplay in Ovid and Other Classical Poets* (1985); E. Cook, *Poetry, Word-Play and Word-War in Wallace Stevens* (1988); J. Culler, "The Call of the Phoneme: Introduction," and D. Fried, "Rhyme Puns," *On Puns: The Foundation of Letters*, ed. J. Culler (1988); Lanham; *Connotations* 2.1–3 (1992) and 3.1–2 (1993–94)—largely on paronomasia; H. Marks, "Biblical Naming and Poetic Etymology," *Journal of Bible Literature* 114 (1995); E. Cook, *Enigmas and Riddles in Literature* (2006); S. Spence, "Avian Ways: Influence and Innovation in Lucretius and Vergil," *L'Esprit Créateur* 49 (2009).

E. COOK

**PARTIMEN** (also *joc partit*, Fr. *jeu parti*). In Occitan, a specialized variety of *tenso in which one poet proposes two hypothetical situations (e.g., whether it is better to love a lady who does not love you or to be loved by a lady whom you do not love). The second poet chooses and defends one of these alternatives, while the first poet upholds the other. After each has had his say in the same number of stanzas (usually three), all identical in structure, the poets commonly refer the debate to one or more arbiters for settlement. There are also partimens involving three poets and three choices, but these are far less frequent. It seems certain that these partimens really represent the cooperative work of two or more poets; but in view of the difficulties involved, it is unlikely that they were actually improvised, as they purport to be. Sometimes it is even clear from the poem itself that the poets were writing back and forth over a considerable distance.

■ A. Långfors, *Recueil général des jeux-partis français*, 2 v. (1926); S. Neumeister, *Das Spiel mit der höfischen Liebe* (1969); E. Köhler, *GRLMA* 2.1B.16 ff.; D. Billy, "Pour une réhabilitation de la terminologie des troubadours: *Tenson, partimen* et expressions synonymes," *Il genere 'tenzone' nelle letterature romanze delle Origini*, ed. M. Pedroni, A. Stäuble, G. A. Papini (1999).

F. M. CHAMBERS

**PASTICHE.** Describes a work of art that imitates the style, gestures, or forms of an older work or antique model. As a formal descriptor of literary works, the word *pastiche* dates back centuries; as an evaluative term, its usage gradually acquired a hint of negative or dismissive connotation. The word implies a lack of *originality or coherence, an imitative jumble. It was only in the latter half of the 20th c.—and most esp. in the context of theories of postmod. narrative—that *pastiche* acquired its current critical purchase.

While the term is almost unthinkable today outside the umbrella of *postmodernism, its etymological root is instructive. *Pastiche* comes from *pasticcio*, the It. word for a hodge-podge of a pie containing both meat and pasta. The food analogy offers a useful image for conceiving of pastiche as both an artistic form and compositional technique. Like its close cousins *collage and *parody, pastiche involves mixing available elements into a new pie. A pastiche uses recognizable ingredients but offers no new substance.

It was precisely this resolute—even mechanical—referentiality and copy that marked pastiche as a signature mode of postmodernism. Jameson identifies pastiche as a "well-nigh universal" discursive practice of late capitalism. In this account, the ascendance of pastiche seems inevitable and is best understood through its new distinction from the term *parody*. All lang. having been flattened out into a kind of Orwellian mediaspeak, Jameson writes, "pastiche is, like parody, the imitation of a peculiar or unique, idiosyncratic style, the wearing of a linguistic mask, speech in a dead language. But it is a neutral practice of such mimicry, without any of parody's ulterior motives, amputated of the satiric impulse, devoid of laughter and of any conviction that alongside the abnormal tongue you have momentarily borrowed, some healthy linguistic normality still exists. Pastiche is thus blank parody."

In postwar poetry, a key early example of deliberate, systematic pastiche is W. H. Auden's long poem *The Age of Anxiety: A Baroque Eclogue* (1947). The subtitle already names the style (*baroque) and genre (*eclogue) that the poem will combine and replicate.

But in Auden's adoption of an OE alliterative line, one hears most clearly how pastiche—at times a pastiche of Auden's own distinctive 1930s voice—drives this poem. One radio news report, e.g., applies the sonic imperative of alliterative verse to callow, euphemistic wartime media-speak: "Now the news. Night raids on / Five cities. Fires started."

Edward Dorn's *Gunslinger* (1968–75) offers a powerful later example of poetic pastiche. This pop epic centers on the western United States—or rather, on the Technicolor version of it. Thus, the very landscape, as much as the discursive modes of the poem, is a replication of a mediated replication. In Perloff's introductory description of *Gunslinger*, Dorn's work provides a "poetic Sourcebook on postmodern discourses—the discourses of atomic science and cybernetics, pop song and media-speak, Heideggerianism and high finance"; further, *Gunslinger* is a definitive late 20th-c. "parapoem . . . with its amalgam of 'theory' and lyric, of prose narrative and sound-text, and especially of citation embedded in or superimposed on the speech of a particular self." Pastiche here, preeminent among those "postmodern discourses," has become an accomplishment rather than a symptom—an achievement rather than a deflated imitation. To this point, the buoyancy of Kenneth Koch's imitations of other poets offers perhaps the preeminent example of pastiche positively constructed—as deliberate, witty homage or playful imitation.

■ E. Dorn, *Gunslinger*, intro. M. Perloff (1989); F. Jameson, *Postmodernism, or the Cultural Logic of Late Capitalism* (1991); L. Bliss, "Pastiche, Burlesque, Tragicomedy," *English Renaissance Drama*, ed. A. R. Braunmuller and M. Hattaway (2003); R. Dyer, *Pastiche* (2007); P. Aron, *Histoire du pastiche: le pastiche littéraire français, de la Renaissance à nos jours* (2008).

C. BOWEN

# PASTORAL

I. Ancient
II. Modern

**I. Ancient.** Ancient pastorals are poems in *hexameters, either dramatic in form or with minimal narrative framing, in which fictional herdsmen sing songs to one another or to an absent beloved, in a stylized natural setting. The poems are short, typically less than 150 lines long, and plot and character devel. are minimal: pastoral's major innovation is to make the performance of an internal poetic event—the pastoral song—and the fictional world in which this performance takes place—a *locus amoenus*, or peaceful rural location with flowing water and shady trees—the chief attractions of a literary genre.

Models for the centrality of performance and the herdsman as a poetic subject can be found in earlier lit.: the songs of the fictional bard Demodocus and the pastoral life of the Cyclops in Homer's *Odyssey* are esp. important. However, pastoral owes its existence as a genre to Theocritus, a Sicilian Greek of the early 3d c. BCE who synthesized these elements of Panhellenic literary *myth with mythical and performance trads. of his native country, making the legendary herdsman

Daphnis the prototypical pastoral singer and adapting the mime trad. known to us through the fragments of the Syracusan Sophron (late 5th to early 4th c. BCE) to his own poetic purposes.

The fictional world Theocritus fashioned from these diverse materials is highly resistant to epistemological reduction: mythical trads. are blatantly contradicted, mimetic and mythical registers are superimposed, and characters with the same name do not resemble one another from one poem to the next. The herdsmen speak hexameters, but in a Doric dialect—a strange conflation of rusticity and heroic *epic—and there is no attempt to distinguish metrically between the spoken and sung portions of the poems (unlike in, e.g., Edmund Spenser's *Shepheardes Calender*). The unifying *trope is the pastoral singer's self-identification with an imagined predecessor: a would-be herdsman-singer proves his mastery by merging with his own archetype in performance (*Idyll* 1, 5, 7) or fails conspicuously in his attempt to do so (*Idyll* 3).

*Imitation of Theocritus began early, and the collections of Gr. pastoral poetry that have survived contain spurious poems that expand the genre's formal and characterological range: the songs of *Idyll* 8 are set off as elegiacs, *Idyll* 21 is about fishermen, and the consummated teen romance of *Idyll* 27 contrasts with the unrequited desire that defines the Theocritean lover. More ambitious devels. can be seen in two poems that marry the setting of Theocritean pastoral with Near Eastern *lament trads.: the "Lament for Adonis" of Bion (probably late 2d c. BCE) and the "Lament for Bion," erroneously ascribed to Moschus (mid-2d c. BCE). The former is distinguished by an affective intensity, particularly in its use of *pathetic fallacy, alien to Theocritus; the latter portrays a historical poet lamented by his own characters, boldly foregrounding the possibility that the poet might include himself within his pastoral fiction that is merely hinted at in Theocritus's *Idyll* 7.

The supreme achievement of ancient pastoral and the one that ensured the genre's survival in later Eur. lit. is Virgil's *Eclogues* (between 42 and 35 BCE). Virgil had no literary dialects to play with, and what distinguishes his herdsmen as speakers and singers is an exquisitely wrought *diction that exploits all the resources of Lat. phonology, word order, and verbal *rhythm to create a richly textured art lang., inviting recognition as the first great achievement of an ambitious young poet. Virgil himself moves in and out of his collection as he merges with and withdraws from his fictional singers: in *Eclogue* 5 and 9, Menalcas is closely identified with the authorial voice, while the narrator of *Eclogue* 6 cites words of Apollo that refer to him as Tityrus, an identification of poet and character that gains additional credence from the argument of Virgil's 4th-c. commentator Servius, that Tityrus represents the poet in *Eclogue* 1 because he too had his land saved from appropriation by military veterans through the intervention of a powerful figure at Rome.

No single identification of poet and character can be easily maintained over the entirety of the *Eclogues*. However, the possibility of such an identification, which is adopted intermittently as an interpretive possibility by ancient commentators on Theocritus's *Idylls*, in Virgil's book becomes pastoral's founding fiction: authorial self-disguising is what allows the pastoral world to be recognized as contemp. hist. in herdsman's clothing. Conversely, as the *Idylls* stage the emergence of consolatory forms of fictional self-projection, the *Eclogues* show how such self-projection is constrained by historical circumstance. The songs of the *Eclogues* are sung in a cultural landscape, and the transactions of pastoral identity that occur in them are subject to cancellation from without.

The *Eclogues* of Calpurnius Siculus (mid-1st c. CE) make the conditions of pastoral dependence an occasion of praise for the Emperor Nero. Reading Virgil's Tityrus as a figure of poetic gratitude, Calpurnius presents himself as Corydon, a cowherd who has seen the wonders of Rome and returned to proclaim a new Golden Age to his fellow herdsmen. Calpurnius dispenses with the ambiguities of Virgil's identifications, using a single herdsman to develop a sustained vision of poetry's dependence on imperial *patronage, and of the pastoral fiction in which this dependency is figured. Calpurnius is a master of court pastoral; the same cannot be said of the author of the two Einsiedeln Eclogues, named after the Swiss monastery in which their ms. was discovered: even in their incomplete state, the turgidity of their poetic lang. and the poverty of invention with which they attempt to emulate Calpurnius's courtly dramas are painfully apparent.

The final flowers of the ancient pastoral trad. are the four *Eclogues* of the 3d-c. Carthaginian Nemesianus, the last of which provided the epigraph to Ezra Pound's *Hugh Selwyn Mauberley*. Nemesianus evinces no interest in the metapoetic potential of the herdsman-singer, fashioning instead a sequence of brief *bucolic dramas that, while classicizing in their lang., are innovative in landscape and character. *Eclogue* 2 is particularly noteworthy: two adolescent shepherd boys recall the intensity of the desire that led them to rape a young girl as she was gathering flowers in the countryside. In its mixture of erotic violence, mythic depth, and social realism, the poem points to the continuing vitality of the genre of which Nemesianus's *Eclogues* are our last ancient example.

**II. Modern.** From the Ren. to *romanticism, Europe and its overseas territories hosted a great flowering of pastoral lit., accompanied by ubiquitous representations of idyllic *nature in the visual arts and music. Propelled by humanism and increasing secularization, mod. pastorals rehearse the *kind's signature themes of natural harmony, love, friendship, virtue, and poetry itself, using a coded set of names, locales, and poetic commonplaces associated with ancient literary shepherds. Its predictable artifice notwithstanding, the resilient *convention proved an apt mirror for dramatic changes in early mod. experience—rising nations, growing cities and courts, rural depopulation, religious tensions, territorial expansion, new human encounters—as trans-Atlantic Edens and New Arcadias attest. Naturally capacious in form and subject, mod. pastorals experiment energetically with hybridity and polyphony, recombining inherited materials while reaching into new discursive territories.

In the early 14th c., eclogues modeled on Virgil appear first in Italy, where Dante, Petrarch, and Giovanni Boccaccio prepare the way for more Lat. eclogues by Mateo Boiardo, Baptista Spagnuoli (known as Mantuan), Jacopo Sannazaro, and numerous other Eur. poets. Widespread trans. of Virgil, among them those of Bernardino Pulci in 1482 and Luis de León, ca. 1580, parallel cultivation of vernacular eclogues by leading 16th-c. poets, incl. Garcilaso de la Vega, Fernando de Herrera, Francisco de Figueroa, Luís de Camões, Clément Marot, Pierre de Ronsard, and Edmund Spenser. Some prove enormously influential for the course of *national poetry: Garcilaso's three eclogues (1543) reinvent *lyric lang. in Sp.; Spenser's Shepheardes Calender (1579), composed of 12 eclogues, is often considered the first great Eng. Ren. poem (Kermode). As an umbrella for diverse prosodic and rhetorical types, vernacular eclogues welcome *panegyrics, *poetic contests and disputes, *elegies, laments and quarrels, *songs, *epithalamia, narrative *anecdotes, *satires, and philosophical meditations. Verse on pastoral themes is ubiquitous: virtually every significant early mod. poet (among them John Milton, Luis de Góngora, and Giambattista Marino) uses the mode to treat themes of love and loss, often borrowing *tropes and sentimental postures from *troubadour lyric, Petrarch's Canzoniere, oral lyric and *ballad trads., and rustic vernacular dialects. But the kind makes room for Christian themes, as in Sannazaro's short Lat. epic De partu virginis (On the Virgin Birth, 1526), Luis de León's contemplative vernacular odes, and the mystical Cántico espiritual (Spiritual Canticle, 1584; 1586–91) of St. John of the Cross.

Pastoral dramas offer imaginary rustic diversions to audiences in cities and aristocratic courts, using the kind's stylized settings as backdrop for staging such concerns as the workings of *affect, temperament, passions, virtues, and good government. With precedent in Boccaccio's allegorical Ameto (1341–42), Giambattista Giraldi Cinthio's satyr play Egle (1545), Torquato Tasso's Aminta (1581), and Giovanni Battista Guarini's Il pastor fido (written 1583, pub. 1590) dramatize for court audiences at Ferrara period debates about the nature of virtuous love. A vogue of pastoral-mythological plays (30 in 1580s Italy alone) established pastoral *tragicomedy as a legitimate third dramatic genre along with *comedy and *tragedy and made It. plays models for international imitation. In France, Honorat de Bueil, seigneur de Racan's Les Bergeries (1625) spawned a school of courtly shepherds' plays; John Lyly's Gallathea (1592), George Peele's Arraignment of Paris (1584), John Fletcher's Faithful Shepherdess (1610), Ben Jonson's Sad Shepherd (1641), and Allan Ramsay's Gentle Shepherd (1725, in lowland Scots dialect), parallel pastoral scenes in Shakespeare and other Eng. dramatists. In Spain, building on med. trads. (oral lyric, pastorela; see PASTOURELLE, SERRANILLA), early 16th-c. performable eclogues by Gil Vicente, Juan del Encina,

and Lucas Fernández treat secular and sacred subjects, perfecting the comic type of the rustic shepherd. Pastoral episodes, courtly and rustic, are common in 17th-c. historical comedies, mythological palace dramas, and *autos sacramentales on eucharistic themes, notably in Sor Juana Inés de la Cruz's Auto del divino Narciso (1590).

Anticipated in Boccaccio's Ameto, the hybrid pastoral romance takes hold in Eur. imagination following publication of Sannazaro's Arcadia (1502, 1504), which frames 12 eclogues in prose narrative, and Jorge de Montemayor's Diana (1559), whose looser alternation of *verse and prose subsequently prevails. Both inspire many imitations, incl. Gaspar Gil Polo's Diana enamorada (1564), Miguel de Cervantes's La Galatea (1585), Philip Sidney's Arcadia (1590, 1593), Félix Lope de Vega's La Arcadia (1598) and the sacred Pastores de Belén (Shepherds of Bethlehem, 1612), and Honoré d'Urfé's L'Astrée (1607–28). In contrast with much ancient and early mod. pastoral verse, these romances accord central roles and the privilege of lyric expression to their female characters. By displacing refined courtiers into edenic settings where they meet savages (as in Montemayor, Cervantes, and Spenser's Faerie Queene, [1590, 1596]), their fictions resonate with experiences of exile (Sephardic diaspora, forced conversions), utopian dreaming, and New World wanderings. Ties to epic, court *masque, early mod. opera, the long mythological poem, and dialogues such as Luis de León's De los nombres de Cristo (The Names of Christ, 1583) bespeak pastoral romance's seminal importance in early mod. generic experiments. Pastoral material (idyllic interludes, poems, dialogues) turns up regularly in Ren. romance (chivalric, Moorish, sentimental, Gr., historical), fostering mergers among those kinds and creating a laboratory for the representation of subjectivity in prose. Though gradually stripped of conventional trappings, pastoral's motifs and sentimental discourses are steadily integrated into the central business of prose fiction, making it a fundamental building block of the mod. novel.

Emphasis on lang. and place makes pastoral a natural home for discussions on the role of vernaculars and lit. in mod. civilizations. The simple, rustic diction that purist decorum assigns to shepherds is redefined as an aesthetic of melodic eloquence, an ethics of truthful speech, and the badge of cultural distinction. Numerous pastoral poets (Dante, Pietro Bembo, Joachim du Bellay, Fernando de Herrera, Cervantes, Sidney) publish defenses of mod. langs. and poetry. Foundational in discourses of nationhood as verbal incarnation of place, cultivated lang. elevates pastoral's historical geographies and precious verbal artifacts to the status of national treasure.

Although courtly pastoral, exhausted by overuse and the extreme stylizations of *préciosité and *rococo, went the way of Europe's absolutist courts and aristocratic estates, the kind's humanistic engagement with philosophical and political questions gave it a long hold on the literary imagination. Antonio de Guevara's double-edged satire and international best seller Menosprecio *de corte y alabanza de aldea* (Dispraise of the Court and Praise of the Village, 1539) earned centuries of trans., imitations, and adaptations. The mode's strategy, suggestive of its links to neo-Stoic thought, of apparently retreating from the world, then reflecting on it, has made it useful in very diverse contexts. In the face of absolutist and ecclesiastical censorship, as in late 16th-c. Spain, pastoral's affinity for masking, displacement, and *allegory provides a vehicle for political and cultural critiques certain to be suppressed in more direct discourses. Pastoral's interest in the relation of humans to the natural world and to each other accounts for its tendency to surface in contexts like anticonquest discourse (Bartolomé de Las Casas's vision of wolves, sheep, and good shepherds in the Americas), Enlightenment philosophy (Jean-Jacques Rousseau's natural man), and romantic poetry (the "precious boon" of nature that William Wordsworth accused humans of giving away). Giamatti finds ubiquitous earthly paradises in early mod. Eur. epics; New World sagas such as Alonso de Ercilla's *Araucana* (3 parts: 1569, 1578, 1589) make frequent political use of the same trope and particularly of the feminine voices of pastoral romance.

See ALEXANDRIANISM, DRAMATIC POETRY, ECLOGUE, IDYLL, LATIN POETRY, PETRARCHISM, ROTA VIRGILIANA.

■ **I. Ancient**: P.-E. Legrand, *Etude sur Théocrite* (1898); U. von. Wilamowitz-Moellendorf, *Hellenistische Dichtung in der Zeit des Kallimachos.* 2 v. (1924); W. Arland, *Nachtheokritische Bukolik* (1937); B. Otis, *Virgil: A Study in Civilized Poetry* (1963); M.C.J. Putnam, *Virgil's Pastoral Art* (1970); E. A. Schmidt, *Poetische Reflexion: Vergils Bukolik* (1972); W. Elliger, *Die Darstellung der Landschaft in der griechischen Dichtung* (1975); J. Van Sickle, *The Design of Virgil's Bucolics* (1978); P. Alpers, *The Singer of the Eclogues* (1979); C. Segal, *Poetry and Myth in Ancient Pastoral* (1981); D. M. Halperin, *Before Pastoral* (1983); E. Bowie, "Theocritus' Seventh *Idyll*, Philetas and Longus," *CQ* 35 (1985); C. Newlands, "Urban Pastoral: The Seventh Eclogue of Calpurnius Siculus," *Classical Antiquity* 6 (1987); A. Patterson, *Pastoral and Ideology* (1987); K. J. Gutzwiller, *Theocritus' Pastoral Analogies* (1991); *Theocritus*, ed. M. A. Harder, R. F. Regtuit, G. C. Wakker (1996); *Cambridge Companion to Virgil*, ed. C. Martindale (1997); T. K. Hubbard, *The Pipes of Pan* (1998); M. Fantuzzi, "Theocritus and the Bucolic Genre," *Tradition and Innovation in Hellenistic Poetry*, ed. M. Fantuzzi and R. L. Hunter (2004); B. Breed, *Pastoral Inscriptions: Reading and Writing Virgil's "Eclogues"* (2006); *Brill's Companion to Greek and Latin Pastoral*, ed. M. Fantuzzi and T. D. Papanghelis (2006); *Pastoral Palimpsests*, ed. M. Paschalis (2007); M. Payne, *Theocritus and the Invention of Fiction* (2007).

■ **II. Modern**:W. Empson, *Some Versions of Pastoral* (1935); M. I. Gerhardt, *La Pastorale* (1950); *English Pastoral Poetry from the Beginnings to Marvell*, ed. F. Kermode (1952); R. Poggioli, *The Oaten Flute* (1957); J.-B. Avalle-Arce, *La novela pastoril española* (1959); A. B. Giamatti, *The Earthly Paradise and the Renaissance Epic* (1960); E. L. Rivers, "The Pastoral Paradox of Natural Art," *MLN* 77 (1962); T. G. Rosenmeyer, *The Green Cabinet: Theocritus and the European Pastoral Lyric* (1969); P. V. Marinelli, *Pastoral* (1971); C. McDonald Vance, *The Extravagant Shepherd* (1973); F. López-Estrada, *Los libros de pastores en la literatura española* (1974); A. Solé-Leris, *The Spanish Pastoral Novel* (1980); M. Y. Jehenson, *The Golden World of the Pastoral* (1981); P. Fernández-Cañadas de Greenwood, *Pastoral Poetics: The Uses of Conventions in Renaissance Pastoral Romance* (1983); W. J. Kennedy, *Jacopo Sannazaro and the Uses of Pastoral* (1983); P. Alpers, *What Is Pastoral?* (1996); *Cambridge History of Italian Literature*, ed. P. Brand and L. Pertile, 2d ed. (1999); L. Sampson, *Pastoral Drama in Early Modern Italy* (2006).

M. PAYNE (ANCIENT); M. M. GAYLORD (MOD.)

**PASTOURELLE.** A genre of med. *lyric poetry most frequently found in OF. In the "classical" type, the narrator, sometimes identified as a knight, recounts his meeting with a shepherdess and his attempt to seduce her. Sometimes he says he was humiliated, even beaten, or the shepherdess made a clever escape; in other poems, he says they made love, either by consent or by force. In the "augmented" *pastourelle*, a shepherd lover joins the cast (e.g., the girl quarrels with Robin, and the poet takes her away); in the *bergerie*, the poet recounts his meeting with a group of peasants who dance or quarrel; in the *pastoureau*, the poet meets a shepherd and talks with him.

The genre originated in Occitan; the Fr. term shows influence of the Occitan word *pastorela* in the retention of the *s* and in the treatment of the vowel spelled *ou*. Following antecedents in med. Lat., among the Romance *kharjas*, and in Chinese around the 2d c. CE, the cl. pastourelle appeared in the early 12th c. with the *troubadour Marcabru and was imitated in Occitan, Lat., and Fr. In the 13th c., it flowered in Fr. and continued in Occitan, with a hiatus around mid-century after which it was reintroduced, perhaps under Fr. influence; it was practiced in Lat. until the *Carmina Burana* (ms. ca. 1230) and was introduced into Ger., It., and Galician-Port. Fourteenth-c. Fr. poets lost interest in the pastourelle, but it inspired the invention of the *serranilla* in Sp.; more were written in Ger. and It., and a few in Gascon, Eng., and Welsh. We have 15th-c. pastourelles in Fr., Ger., and Franco-Provençal, and more serranillas in Sp. After the Middle Ages, the pastourelle has been cultivated by poets and folksingers in Fr., Gascon, Catalan, Sp., and Eng.

As a genre, the pastourelle influenced other forms such as the theatrical *Jeu de Robin et Marion* (ca. 1283) by Adam de la Halle, Mahieu le Poirier's narrative *Court d'amours* (ca. 1300), and the *Dit de la pastoure* (1403) by Christine de Pizan. A shepherdess named Pastorella figures in an episode of Edmund Spenser's *Faerie Queene* (6.9–12) that is reminiscent of an augmented pastourelle. In Shakespeare's *Tempest*, the wooing of Ferdinand and Miranda recalls the cl. pastourelle, and the masque of reapers recalls the bergerie. Molière's Dom Juan seduces two country girls in the med. manner. The shepherdess in the pastourelle is a female character in contrast to the lady sung by the troubadours and the *trouvères*; as a representation of a woman who speaks, she relates to women poets such as the *trobairitz in Occitan and the female trouvères in Fr.

See FRANCE, POETRY OF; OCCITAN POETRY.

■ **Anthologies**: *Romances et pastourelles Françaises des XIIe et XIIIe siècles*, ed. K. Bartsch (1870); *La Pastourelle dans la poésie occitane du moyen âge*, ed. J. Audiau (1923); *Pastourelles*, ed. J.-C. Rivière, 3 v. (1974–76)—anonymous OF works; *The Medieval Pastourelle*, ed. and trans. W. D. Paden, 2 v. (1987)—the cl. pastourelles in 16 langs.; C. Franchi, *Pastorelle occitane* (2006).

■ **Criticism and History**: M. Zink, *La Pastourelle* (1972); Bec—study and texts; E. Köhler in *GRLMA*, v. 2.1.5 (1979); K. Bate, "Ovid, Medieval Latin, and the Pastourelle," *Reading Medieval Studies* 9 (1983); S. C. Brinkmann, *Die deutschsprachige Pastourelle* (1985); K. Gravdal, "Camouflaging Rape: The Rhetoric of Sexual Violence in the Medieval Pastourelle," *RR* 76 (1985); W. D. Paden, "Reading Pastourelles," *Tenso* 4 (1988), and "Rape in the Pastourelle," *RR* 80 (1989); K. Gravdal, *Ravishing Maidens: Writing Rape in Medieval French Literature and Law* (1991); M. Sichert, *Die mittelenglische Pastourelle* (1991); W. D. Paden "Christine de Pizan as a Reader of the Medieval Pastourelle," *Conjunctures*, ed. K. Busby et al. (1994); C. Edwards, "Von Archilochos zu Walther von der Vogelweide: Zu den Anfängen der Pastourelle in Deutschland," *Lied im deutschen Mittelalter* (1996); I. Kasten, "Die Pastourelle im Gattungssystem der höfischen Lyrik," *Lied im deutschen Mittelalter* (1996); W. D. Paden, "Flight from Authority in the Pastourelle," *The Medieval Opus* (1996); S. Hartung, "Stilnovismus und Pastourelle bei Cavalcanti: Konfrontation inkompatibler Liebesdiskurse vor Dante," *Romanistisches Jahrbuch* 49 (1998); W. D. Paden, "The Figure of the Shepherdess in the Medieval Pastourelle," *Medievalia et Humanistica* n.s. 25 (1998), and "New Thoughts on an Old Genre: The Pastorela," *RLA: Romance Languages Annual* 10 (1998); A. Petrina, "Deviations from Genre in Robert Henryson's 'Robene and Makyne,'" *Studies in Scottish Literature* 31 (1999); S. Huot, "Intergeneric Play: The Pastourelle in Thirteenth-Century French Motets," *Medieval Lyric*, ed. W. D. Paden (2000); L. C. Jones and J. J. G. Alexander, "The Annunciation to the Shepherdess," *Studies in Iconography* 24 (2003); L. O. Vasvari, "Women Raping Men: The Sexual-Textual Violence of the Anti-Pastourelle," *'Entra mayo y sale abril': Medieval Spanish Literary and Folklore Studies in Memory of Harriet Goldberg* (2005); C. Franchi, *Trobei pastora* (2006); C. Callahan, "Tracking Robin, Marion and the Virgin Mary: Musical/Textual Interface in the Pastourelle Motet," *Chançon legiere a chanter*, ed. K. Fresco and W. Pfeffer (2007); H. Dell, *Desire by Gender and Genre in Trouvère Song* (2008), ch. 3; G. L. Smith, *The Medieval French Pastourelle Tradition* (2009).

W. D. PADEN

**PATHETIC FALLACY.** A phrase coined by John Ruskin in volume 3, chapter 12 of *Modern Painters* (1856) to denote an enduring practice in Western lit.: the tendency of poets and painters to imbue the natural world with human feeling. For Ruskin, it becomes an important criterion of artistic excellence. The fallacy, due to "an excited state of the feelings, making us, for the time, more or less irrational," creates "a falseness in all our impressions of external things." The offending example is taken from a poem in Charles Kingsley's novel *Alton Locke*: "They rowed her in across the rolling foam— / The cruel, crawling foam." Ruskin declares that "the foam is not cruel, neither does it crawl," the author's state of mind being "one in which the reason is unhinged by grief."

For Ruskin, there are two classes of poets, "the Creative (Shakspere [sic], Homer, Dante), and Reflective or Perceptive (Wordsworth, Keats, Tennyson)"; it is one of the faults of the latter group that it admits the pathetic fallacy. But Ruskin was unconcerned with the psychological origins of the pathetic fallacy, and his ideas should not be applied indiscriminately to other lits. B. F. Dick contends that the "origins of the pathetic fallacy probably lie in a primitive homeopathy . . . wherein man regarded himself as part of his natural surroundings." In older lits., the pathetic fallacy does not always have the pejorative implications that Ruskin's definition established. Dick considers the Babylonian *Epic of Gilgamesh* an early and important source of the pathetic fallacy: in a climactic passage, all of nature weeps for the death of the warrior Enkidu; since Enkidu embodies the ideals of the natural man, nature as the universal parent must reflect the joys and sorrows of her children. Homer, for Ruskin one of the first order of poets, occasionally employs the pathetic fallacy, but he characteristically attributes human feelings to weapons instead of the natural world—a standard convention of the war epic. It is generally agreed that in the *Iliad* Homer falls prey to Ruskin's censures only once, when the sea rejoices as Poseidon passes overhead in his chariot (13.27–29). Yet even in this case, Homer strictly curtails the passage, avoiding the indulgences Ruskin would later criticize.

Based on various cl. models, the *pastoral elegies of the 16th and 17th cs. provided Eng. poetry with a natural arena for the pathetic fallacy. The early Eng. translators—e.g., Sir William Drummond, who trans. the sonnets of the It. poet Jacopo Sannazaro in 1616—were among the first poets to provide the Eng. trad. with flowers, lilies, and columbine that would bow their heads in sympathetic response to the poet's grief; the pathetic fallacy's earliest appearance is, thus, not the result of native invention but of the preservation of a pastoral convention.

Although he was unconcerned to invent a name for it, Samuel Johnson recognized the phenomenon in the 18th c. and complained 100 years earlier than Ruskin that the phrase "pastoral verse" referred simply to poetry in which, among other things, "the clouds weep." Johnson was reacting to the excesses of *sentimentality in 18th-c. verse, but the device continued to be employed: it appears with varying frequency throughout the work of William Collins, William Cowper, Robert Burns, William Blake, William Wordsworth, P. B. Shelley, John Keats, Alfred, Lord Tennyson, and G. M. Hopkins. Wordsworth, justifying its usage, argued that "objects . . . derive their influence not from properties inherent in them . . . , but from such as are bestowed upon them by the minds of those who are conversant with or affected by these objects." Tennyson, on the other hand, was well schooled in the scientific issues of his day, and his descriptions of natural objects are often clinically precise: after 1842, his verse reveals a markedly less frequent usage of pathetic fallacy (Miles), and *In Memoriam* offers a striking revision of the device by evoking its essential effect without indulging its excesses ("Calm is the morn without a sound. / Calm as to suit a calmer grief" [11.1–2]).

During the 20th c., the most vigorous applications of the pathetic fallacy have been self-consciously designed to explore the epistemological issues implied by the technique. Mod. usage of the pathetic fallacy ironically emphasizes the loss of communion between the individual and the natural world; and in its implied envy of an older world where such communion once existed, it resurrects yet another remnant of its ancient origin, pastoral nostalgia. Recent attempts to deploy the concept have not advanced the discussion in significant ways; at best, the pathetic fallacy has migrated into more subjective renderings of individual perception that privilege a kind of "middle ground" between the object we perceive and the act of perception itself. Mervyn Sprung argues in his discussion of the pathetic fallacy in *After Truth* that "to treat outer objects either as possessing nothing but their spatial properties . . . or as naturally possessing all qualities we give them in the everyday . . . is to fail to grasp the symbiosis of the inner and outer." Clearly, Ruskin was not concerned about achieving the "symbiosis of inner and outer"; the central confusion here speaks, among other things, to the overall weariness of the concept in contemp. usage.

*See* NATURE, PERSONIFICATION, SENTIMENTALITY.

■ F. O. Copley, "The Pathetic Fallacy in Early Greek Poetry," *AJP* 58 (1937); J. Miles, *Pathetic Fallacy in the 19th Century* (1942); B. F. Dick, "Ancient Pastoral and the Pathetic Fallacy," *CL* 20 (1968); J. Bump, "Stevens and Lawrence: The Poetry of Nature and the Spirit of the Age," *Southern Review* 18 (1982); D. Hesla, "Singing in Chaos: Wallace Stevens and Three or Four Ideas," *AL* 57 (1985); A. Hecht, "The Pathetic Fallacy," *Yale Review* 74 (1985), M. Sprung, *After Truth* (1994).

S. BURRIS

**PATHOS** (Gr., "suffering," "passion"). Evoking an audience's emotions in order to use them as a means of persuasion. In the *Rhetoric* (1:1356a), Aristotle distinguishes three types of persuasive appeal: ethical (*ethos*); emotional (*pathos*), which depends on putting the audience into a fit state of mind; and logical (*logos*), which depends on the forms of proof or apparent proof. The orator has to study the emotions to know how to arouse them. Toward that end, Aristotle provides one of the first systematic treatments in the West of emotions and of the types of audience members with which they are associated and, consequently, in which they are most readily aroused. As should be evident, there is a close relation between ethos and pathos, which continued to be exploited in the

long trad. of writing "characters"—brief moral-psychological essays usually meant to assist orators with audience analysis (see CHARACTER, THEOPHRASTAN). Too, the study of pathos, as seen in Aristotle and in later writers on religion and "physics," is relevant to discussions not only of the "soul" (*psyche*) but of medicine; in the latter, the subject became assimilated to the "humors"—mainly physical elements that gave a character or personality type a propensity toward certain behaviors. With the rise of 18th-c. science, the newly established discipline of psychology began drawing to itself these formerly dispersed treatments of the emotions and contributed to the narrowing of the sense of the term *pathos* to merely the pitiable or sad. This abuse of the original sense of *pathos* is more properly linked to *sentimentality. The importance of pathos as a means of persuasion—or as it is commonly referred to today, *audience appeal*—has never diminished in the study of rhet. or in rhetorical approaches to poetry. In the latter study, the traditional link between pathos and the figures of speech—Aristotle, e.g., claims that anger demands *hyperbole (3:1413a)—undergirds such mod. stylistic approaches as reader-response crit. (see READER). The *locus classicus* of the general link between poetry and pathos remains the Aristotelian theory of *catharsis, but here it is theorized that the arousing of emotions (pity and fear) in the audience of a *tragedy is aimed not so much at persuasion toward an argumentative point as at purgation of the emotions themselves.

*See* EMOTION, RHETORIC AND POETRY.

■ M. Joseph, *Shakespeare's Use of the Arts of Language* (1947), ch. 5, 9; J. de Romilly, *L'évolution du pathétique d'Eschyle À Euripide* (1961); B. R. Rees, "Pathos in the *Poetics* of Aristotle," *Greece and Rome* (1972); S. Fish, *Self-Consuming Artifacts* (1972); H. Plett, *Rhetorik der Affekte—Englische Wirkungsästhetik im Zeitalter der Renaissance* (1975); C. Gill, "The Ethos/Pathos Distinction in Rhetorical and Literary Criticism," *CQ* 34 (1984); S. Fish, *Doing What Comes Naturally* (1989); Corbett, esp. 86–94; Lausberg; R. Terada, "Pathos (Allegories of Reading)," *Studies in Romanticism* 39 (2000)—on P. de Man; J. Walker, "*Pathos and Katharsis in 'Aristotelian' Rhetoric: Some Implications," *Rereading Aristotle's Rhetoric*, ed. A. G. Gross and A. E. Walzer (2000); R. Buch, "The Resistance to Pathos and the Pathos of Resistance: Peter Weiss," *Germanic Review* 83 (2008).

T. O. SLOANE

**PATRONAGE**

I. Noble Patronage
II. Subscriptions
III. Printing and the Market
IV. Twentieth- and Twenty-First-Century Patronage

The word *patronage* entered the Eng. lang. around the end of the 13th c. and was used mainly in the context of the Church, denoting assistance offered to a member of the clergy who sought a living or benefice.

By the 16th c., *patron* was applied to a person who supported poets and the arts, yet poetic patronage as a cultural concept comes in many guises and is difficult to quantify. Holzknecht, writing about med. forms of patronage, usefully suggests that the phenomena may be understood as "the employment of favor, protection, and influential support to advance the interests of art, limited generally to the habit of subsidizing authors." Nevertheless, while patronage may narrowly be defined as the support of a writer or artist by a benevolent protector, this is not always the case. Holzknecht notes, therefore, that when monetary wealth is concentrated in small social groups, particular patrons become a necessity but when wealth is widely distributed through society, poetry is generally patronized by the public (as was the case for Pindar and Herodotus, who received gifts from the Athenian people). Poetic patronage more broadly, then, is a social and economic exchange that directly or indirectly works to support or encourage poets and presents different aspects in various historical moments and circumstances. At times, it might manifest itself as personal financial support or subsidy; at others, it can be perceived in more social or institutional encouragements of poetic endeavor. It is intrinsically bound up with questions about the nature and function of poetry in society per se and with the perceived status and social role of the poet.

**I. Noble Patronage.** The Roman Gaius Cilnius Maecenas (ca. 70–8 BCE), an adviser of the emperor Augustus Caesar before and during his reign, is the archetype of a noble patron. His support of Virgil, Horace, and Propertius was the envy of later poets such as Petrarch, who, at his coronation as poet laureate in 1341, explicitly linked poetic endeavor to national glory and placed himself in a trad. of Roman poets who had "attained to the highest and most illustrious mastery of their art." Patronage, manifested here in prize giving, created the poet as a loyal servant to the state and defined poetry as nationally advantageous: Petrarch, as if to bolster this view, explicitly asserted that he wrote poetry above all for "the honor of the Republic."

It is often difficult to ascertain, however, whether a med. or early mod. poet received assistance or subventions from a patron because of his poetry or for other services. The 14th-c. poet Chaucer is known now as a literary figure, but during his lifetime, he was an esquire of the royal household, controller of customs in London, and clerk of the king's works. He received regular stipends from his court offices, being valued, as Pearsall (1999) notes, for his accounting and secretarial skills, not his poetry. Chaucer's compatriot Thomas Hoccleve, a scribe in the office of the Privy Seal, used his poetic talents to write begging poems to his paymasters but was repeatedly unsuccessful in his quest for patronage, even though he wrote a series of poems that were, in Pearsall's words, "almost 'policy statements' " for the new reign of Henry V. He never received the kind of noble patronage offered to the more successful John Lydgate, who captured Henry's attention before the latter's accession and embarked on a remunerative

career as "a Lancastrian poet-propagandist" (Pearsall 1999).

The Maecenian model of a noble patron also brought with it fears about the loss of artistic freedom. Although a noble patron's support of a poet might involve an apparently mutual exchange of benefits or goods, the proffer of such support could engender an expectation in the patron of certain laudatory or politically inflected forms of writing. Nowhere is the ambivalent position of a poet in relation to his patron more apparent than in the work of the It. Ludovico Ariosto, whose famous romance epic *Orlando furioso* (1516) was dedicated to the Este family of Ferrara. At the same time that the poet wrote entertainments and traveled on diplomatic missions for Cardinal d'Este, his ms. satires expressed dissatisfaction with the patronage system. Imitating the Roman Horace's laments about poetic patronage, he advised prospective poets to "Toss your verses into a privy and your lyre after them, and learn a more acceptable skill if you desire to earn benefices," continuing ominously: "But as soon as you have received them, remember you have lost your precious liberty no less than if you had gambled it away with dice."

Fears about the loss of liberty continued to haunt more traditional forms of noble patronage, sometimes leading, in the early mod. period, to the representation of patronage as a form of mutual gift giving, rather than a system of reward or payment. This emphasis on the gift is exemplified in Ben Jonson's epigram 84, "To Lucy, Countess of Bedford," which celebrates the countess's promise to send Jonson a haunch of venison. The poem commemorates the promise of a gift, rather than the gift itself, thereby allowing Jonson to praise the countess from a position of semi-equality, unencumbered by gratitude or indebtedness. Moreover, his ten-line *epigram (which is an incomplete *sonnet, comprising two, rather than three, quatrains, and a rhyming *couplet) joins poet and patron together in mutual awareness of a literary joke that celebrates the intelligence of each party and looks forward to the time when Jonson will receive his gift and complete his imperfect poem.

Jonson provides a forceful example of a poet who presented writing as a vocation and who exploited the possibilities not only of ms. circulation but of the medium of print. The 1616 folio edition of his *Workes* collected his literary production into one volume in a manner that marks a distinctive moment in the hist. of professional writing. Indeed, as Bergeron has noted, the quest for patronage is inseparable from Jonson's emerging vocation of authorship. The printed dedications to his work, such as the epistle to the universities of Oxford and Cambridge that prefaces his play *Volpone*, reveal a wide-ranging attitude toward patronage and patrons. The *Volpone* epistle also demonstrates Jonson's advocacy of poetry as a socially beneficial activity: in many ways, he presents himself as poetry's own patron, noting that "the principal end of poesy" is "to inform men in the best reason of living" and forcefully asserting "the impossibility of any man's being the good poet, without first being a good man." Emphasizing the hard-won skill and mature judgment of the learned and socially responsible poet, he excoriates those who in their "manifest ignorance" have adulterated poetry's form, positioning the good poet as of intrinsic value to a well-functioning society.

Jonson was arguably the most successful poet at attracting patronage in early Stuart England. He received commissions to write entertainments from two kings, from a host of noblemen, and from the city of London guilds and trading companies; and he did much to open for later generations the possibility that writing might be a professional choice rather than a rich man's leisure activity. He also exploited a diverse range of patronage opportunities at the same time as he explored the possibilities of the burgeoning market for printed works. Nevertheless, his works, both dramatic and poetic, constantly negotiate between crit. and compliment. Montrose has noted that noble gift-giving in the early mod. period was really "a tacitly coercive" process, and nowhere is this more apparent than in Jonson's career: he fell from royal favor in 1631 after a dispute about artistic precedence with the king's surveyor, Inigo Jones, and ended his life under the partial patronage of the Earl of Newcastle.

Despite the pitfalls attendant on this Maecenan model, the patronage of poets by the nobility continued well into the 18th c. As Kord observes, however, the class distribution of patronage shifted progressively "down the ranks" to the middle and lower classes. The Suffolk-born 18th-c. poet Ann Candler, e.g., spent time in a workhouse and was supported by a local minister who helped increase her readership by promoting her work, while Elizabeth Hands, the wife of a blacksmith, was encouraged to publish her poems by some of the Rugby School's masters and attracted 1,200 subscribers for her 1789 book *The Death of Amnon*. Increasingly, then, the availability of printed books opened up new avenues for the distribution of poetry at the same time that it helped refashion the poet's social status, audience, and professional identity.

**II. Subscriptions.** Publication by subscription gained in popularity during the 18th c., bringing to the forefront a new form of literary patronage that, while it involved the nobility, did not rely exclusively on them. The 16th-c. poet George Wither was probably the first to gather subscriptions for a poetry collection and presented this method of funding his publication as a means of freeing himself from the patronage system. Although he eventually did not collect his money, the preface to his *Fidelia* (1615) noted, "by this means also I shall be beholding to none, but those that love Virtue or Me, and preserve the unequalled happiness of a free spirit." For Wither at least, subscription offered political and artistic freedom.

Publication by subscription in the 18th c. provides clear evidence that patronage models were changing. Christopher Smart's *Poems on Several Occasions* (1752), e.g., had over 800 subscribers and was dedicated to the Earl of Middlesex but failed to secure the latter's

patronage. A year later, the Ir. writer Arthur Murphy observed wryly it was "an indelible Reproach to the Age" that Smart had not "found a *Maecenas*," adding, "a bookseller is his only friend, and for that bookseller, however liberal, he must toil and drudge." More fortuitously, Robert Burns published 600 copies of his *Poems, Chiefly in the Scottish Dialect* by subscription in 1786, aided by the Scottish lawyer Robert Aiken, who signed up 145 subscribers and to whom Burns subsequently dedicated his poem "The Cotter's Saturday Night." The work was well received, and within a month, Burns was dining with the noble Lord Daer but was also being courted by professors, editors, and the Edinburgh literati.

Literary patronage, then, was not dying out at the end of the 18th c. but was spreading to the literate middle classes. Middle-class subscribers appreciated the social cachet they gained when their names were printed in subscription lists alongside those of the nobility, but there was also a genuine interest in poetry for its own sake, esp. as advances in printing technology meant that books became more widely available. Indeed, by the 19th c., poetry had begun to participate in the phenomenon of mass-market publication.

**III. Printing and the Market.** The arrival of printing changed poetry patronage because it facilitated a move from small-scale ms. circulation among friends to the commercial book trade. A growing leisure class and rising literacy rates increased the audience for printed materials, and, by the start of the 19th c., a mass demand developed for works of poetry. Sir Walter Scott's *Marmion* (1808) sold 2,000 copies in the month after its publication, and Lord Byron became an overnight sensation in 1812 when the first two cantos of *Childe Harold's Pilgrimage* sold out within two days. His *Bride of Abydos* (1813) sold 6,000 copies in a month, while his *Corsair* (1814) set a record when it sold 10,000 copies on the day it was published.

The rise in printing accorded greater influence to publishers, editors, and critics, with *The Publishers' Weekly* of April 19, 1890, asserting that the publisher was "or ought to be, the Maecenas of the nineteenth century." Some publishers helped poets with royalty agreements and profit-sharing and made use of newspapers to advertise and raise interest in poetry books. Meanwhile, magazines such as *Blackwood's Edinburgh Magazine*, the *London Magazine*, and the *North American Review* acted as arbiters of public taste, promoting the poetry of P. B. Shelley and John Keats and crit. concerning their work. Similar magazines appeared throughout Europe: in France, e.g., the weekly literary magazine *La république des lettres* published reviews of poetic works such as Stéphane Mallarmé's "L'Après-midi d'un faune" (April 20, 1876), while *La nouvelle revue française*, founded in 1908 by André Gide, became, for a time, the country's premier literary jour.

The benefits of literary patronage continued to be discussed as the century progressed, with the Eng. periodical *The Academy* reporting on October 5, 1901 that "honest and aspiring literature" was made possible by support of the public. Forcefully stating that the patronage of wealthy gentlemen was no longer necessary nor desirable, the paper made it clear that poetry was to be appreciated and patronized by the many, rather than a few.

**IV. Twentieth- and Twenty-First-Century Patronage.** Twentieth-c. magazines and poetry publishers retained their important influence on the dissemination and promotion of poetry. In 1912, e.g., the Chicago editor and critic Harriet Monroe founded *Poetry*, a magazine that revolutionized the poetry scene of the U.S. by publishing the modernist experiments of Ezra Pound and T. S. Eliot. The magazine garnered a loyal following that included Ruth Lilly, great-grandchild of Eli Lilly, founder of the pharmaceutical firm. In 2002, she bequeathed $100 million to the magazine, turning it into one of the world's richest publications.

In Europe, too, poetry magazines such as France's *Action poétique* (established in 1950 and one of France's longest-standing poetry jours.) or the United Kingdom's *PN Review* (a literary jour. edited by the influential scholar Michael Schmidt) provide forums for the publication of new poetry, both national and international, as well as the lively evaluation of more established poets and their works. At the same time, Eur. states have tended, superficially at least, to support poetic endeavor. The UK's Poetry Library on the South Bank in London is funded by the state-backed Arts Council, while, in France, the Académie française, established by Cardinal Richelieu in the 17th c. for the greater glory of the Fr. state and operating under the umbrella of the Institut de France, promotes itself as "un prestigieux mécénat" and distributes thousands of euros in prizes and grants to support literary activities.

Poetry prizes and fellowships have a useful role to play in contemp. poetic patronage, as they provide recognition and validation of a poet's work. Since 1901, the Sweden-based Nobel Prize in Literature has been awarded to numerous poets, incl. W. B. Yeats and Eliot, while the Am. Pulitzer organization has recognized poets since 1918, when a poetry prize was established with the help of the Poetry Society of America. The U. S. Library of Congress instituted the Bollingen Prize in Poetry in 1948; controversially, it was awarded to Pound for his *Pisan Cantos* in 1949. Later administered by Yale University's Beinecke Library, the prize is now supported by an endowment from the Andrew W. Mellon Foundation.

As in the 18th and 19th cs., journalists, professors, and critics still play a role in patronage; but since the mid-20th c. academic programs in creative writing and writers' colonies (such as Yaddo and MacDowell in the U.S.), retreats (such as Cave Canem for Af. Am. poets—see AFRICAN AMERICAN POETRY), and workshops have been increasingly important.

Nomination for prizes, fellowships, or even acceptance into a colony often requires a certain amount of patronage, making these institutions both a source of patronage and a function of it. Nevertheless, in the mod. Western world, the old model of a single Maece-nas figure has largely disappeared, perhaps supporting Holzknecht's contention that where wealth is distributed widely through society, poetry is patronized by the public. When extraordinary personal acts of patronage do occur, they are directed less at poets and more toward poetry itself as an art form. Nowadays, then, the most overwhelming support for poets and poetry comes not from state grants and charitable funds but from the people who write, read, criticize, and enjoy it.

*See* BOOK, POETIC; POET; TECHNOLOGY AND POETRY.

■ K. Holzknecht, *Literary Patronage in the Middle Ages* (1923); J. Buchan, *Augustus* (1937); R. P. Basler, *The Muse and the Librarian* (1974); D. Pearsall, *Old English and Middle English Poetry* (1977); L. A. Montrose, "Gifts and Reasons: The Contexts of Peele's *Araygnement of Paris*," *ELH* 47 (1980); *Patronage in the Renaissance*, ed. G. F. Lytle and S. Orgel (1981); E. Rothstein, *Restoration and Eighteenth-Century Poetry* (1981); R. P. Saller, *Personal Patronage under the Early Empire* (1982); R. Helgerson, *Self-Crowned Laureates* (1983); D. Pearsall, *The Life of Geoffrey Chaucer* (1992); D. Griffin, *Literary Patronage in England, 1650–1800* (1996); *The Cultural Patronage of Medieval Women*, ed. J. H. McCash (1996); *Chaucer to Spenser*, ed. D. Pearsall (1999); *Romantic Period Writings, 1798–1832*, ed. I. Haywood and Z. Leader (1998); E. Knapp, *The Bureaucratic Muse* (2001); R. R. Nauta, *Poetry for Patrons* (2002); H. Bloch, *The Anonymous Marie de France* (2003); S. Kord, *Women Peasant Poets* (2003); *Women and Poetry, 1660–1750*, ed. S. Prescott and D. E. Shuttleton (2003); D. Bergeron, *Textual Patronage in English Drama, 1570–1640* (2006).

K. BRITLAND

**PATTERN POETRY.** *See* CALLIGRAMME; CONCRETE POETRY; TECHNOPAEGNION; VISUAL POETRY.

**PAUSE.** The question of pause in poetry is one of unexpected complexity because any answer implies far-reaching assumptions. In general, temporal theories of *meter are amenable to including pause as a structural feature, while stress theories are more likely to relegate pause to *performance. Some 20th-c. descriptions of Old Germanic meter posited a regular pause in alliterative verse (see ALLITERATION), but few current approaches to the older poetry have found a justification for it.

There are essentially three kinds of pause, the first being perhaps a universal feature of poetry across langs., the other two being confined to *accentual-syllabic verse. The first type, the pause that often accompanies a *caesura, is an epiphenomenal element and is not our concern here. It is dependent on word boundaries and syntactic breaks, which may themselves be specified as part of the metrical structure. The question of whether the pause is an element of design or of performance is a matter of debate.

Much clearer are the *beats and offbeats that occur where syllables are missing in template meters. Template meters include accentual-syllabic meters that specify a preexisting, platonic configuration of beats and offbeats. The beats and offbeats are usually realized as accented and unaccented syllables; thus, they figure in langs. like Eng. and Ger., which incorporate accent or stress as an element of the meter. Once a pattern of expectation has been established, a beat or an offbeat can occur even without a syllable. The most salient examples might be those that Attridge calls "virtual beats," as in *limericks, some *nursery rhymes ("Hickory, dickory, dock"), and the ends of even lines in both popular and literary four-beat meters: e.g., the various *ballad meters and the following stanza from Robert Herrick:

> Gather ye rosebuds while ye may,
>   B      B        B      B
>
> Old time is still a-flying;
>   B      B    B  [B]
>
> And this same flower that smiles today
>   B        B       B          B
>
> Tomorrow will be dying.
>   B        B   B [B]

The second kind of pause that occurs without a syllable is the offbeat that spaces two consecutive beats, as in this line from P. B. Shelley ("Alastor" 362):

>                     x   x   /   /
> Suspended on the sweep of the smooth wave
>                    o   o  B  ô  B

There is no syntactic break between "smooth" and "wave," and there may be no silent moment or cessation of vocalization. However, we feel a pulse between the two consecutive stressed syllables, and this we can call with Attridge "an implied offbeat." It is a part of the phonology of Eng. and of other "stress-timed languages" (see ISOCHRONISM OR ISOCHRONY). It is what Selkirk calls "silent demibeat addition."

If the two consecutive stressed syllables happen to occur on either side of a syntactic break, the pulse is even more obvious, although the important point is that this kind of pause does not depend on any particular level of phrase structure (*King Lear* 4.6.172):

> Pull off my boots; harder, harder—so.
>  o  B  o  B [o] B  o   B   o   B

The brackets indicate that the "virtual offbeat" coincides with a syntactic pause.

Clearly, the problems of pause raise questions about the ontology of the line and the locus of existence of the poetic text. If one's view (common among "stressers") is that the "line" of poetry consists entirely of syllables, then the virtual and implied pauses noted here are not part of the line. If one's view is that the "line" of poetry includes temporal elements as well as syllables (common among "timers," some of whom load up the line with musical notation in excess of the limited contexts described here), then the beats and offbeats without syllables, indicated by [B] and ô, respectively, are as much a part of the line as the words "smooth" and "wave."

■ T. S. Omond, *A Study of Metre* (1903); A.L.F. Snell, *Pause* (1918); E. Smith, *Principles of English Metre* (1923); W. Thomson, *The Rhythm of Speech* (1923); G. R. Stewart Jr., *The Technique of English Verse* (1930); *Coventry Patmore's Essay on English Metrical Law*, ed. M. A. Roth (1961); E. K. Schwartz et al., "Rhythm and Exercises in Abstraction," *PMLA* 77 (1962); D. Abercrombie, "A Phonetician's View of Verse Structure," *Linguistics* 6 (1964); Michaelides—see *chronos, parasemantike*; D. Attridge, *Rhythms*; E. Selkirk, *Phonology and Syntax* (1984); Carper and Attridge.

T. CABLE

**PAYADA.** An Argentinian *song or *ballad, generally anonymous, in simple *meter, sung by popular poets who wandered the pampas. These mod. *troubadours were called *payadores*, and their improvisations were generally accompanied by the guitar. Its types included *vidalitas, cielitos, tristes*, and *milongas*. They began to appear in print in the 18th c. As in the Middle Ages, the *payada* was most often a poetic debate in the form of questions and answers, known as *contrapunto*, played before an audience that was both witness and judge. The famous mythical payador Santos Vega, so legend tells us, conquered the Devil in such a contest. The most celebrated payada takes place in the second part of *Martín Fierro* (*The Return*, Canto 30, 1879), a long narrative *gaucho poem by José Hernández and one of the masterpieces of Argentinian lit. This competition has highly dramatic overtones, as Martín Fierro is challenged by El Moreno, a man wishing to avenge the murder of his brother. This payada in contrapunto is not an improvisation but an integral episode of the poem (itself highly realistic) wherein the two contestants forget their rustic antecedents and sing of abstract ideas and supernatural themes.

As a sung, improvised poetic text, the payada is also found in other regions. The performances have guitar accompaniment and are often an exchange between payadores. Similar musical debates are the *peleja* and *desafío* of Brazil. Hernández compares his payada to a game of cards called *truco*; both require wit and speed. As a poetic combat, the payada is an expression of manliness, but the "conquest" is of words. The *criollismo* of the nonstandard, marginalized speech used in the payada is relevant to the sense of national identity as well.

*See* POETIC CONTESTS.

■ F. Page, *Los payadores gauchos* (1897); L. Lugones, *El payador* (1916); F. de Onís, "El 'Martín Fierro' y la poesía tradicional," *Homenaje ofrecido a Menéndez Pidal* (1925); R. Porter de la Barrera, "Los payadores de antaño," *En viaje* (1941); E. F. Tiscornia, "Orígenes de la poesía gauchesca," *Boletín de la Academia Argentina de Letras* 12 (1943); I. Guerrero Cárpena, "Santos Vega y Poca Ropa, payadores ríoplatenses," *Boletín de la Academia Argentina de Letras* 13 (1946); J. Ludmer, "Oralidad y escritura en el género gauchesco como núcleo del nacionalismo," *Revista de crítica literaria latinoamericana* 33 (1991); A. C. Cara, "The Poetics of Creole Talk: Toward an Aesthetics of Argentine Verbal Art," *Journal of American Folklore* 116 (2003); R. Campra, "En busca del gaucho perdido," *Revista de crítica literaria latino-*

*americana* 60 (2004); R. Dorra, "El Arte del Payador," *Revista de literaturas populares* 8 (2007).

A. W. PHILLIPS; K. N. MARCH

**PENITENTIAL PSALMS.** Since at least Cassiodorus in the 6th c., Psalms 6, 32, 38, 51, 102, 130, and 143 according to the Masoretic numbering adopted by Protestants (6, 31, 37, 50, 101, 129, and 142 in the Septuagint) have been regarded as a group and recommended to penitents seeking forgiveness. Augustine had these seven psalms placed around his deathbed; in the later Middle Ages, after Innocent III, they became part of the Roman Catholic liturgy during Lent and at funerals. Although Protestants officially rejected their use in the sacrament of Penance, they continued to be popular in devotional practice, and Psalm 51 remains central to the Church of England's Ash Wednesday liturgy. Verse paraphrases of the penitential psalms (Richard Maidstone, ca. 1390–96; Thomas Brampton, ca. 1414) are among the earliest surviving metrical psalms in Eng., perhaps because of the prominence of these psalms in devotional primers (see PSALMS, METRICAL). Even after the Reformation, the general popularity of metrical psalms in worship and devotions ensured the continuing production of versions of the penitential seven. The most famous of these was written by Thomas Wyatt, perhaps during one of his periods of imprisonment in the Tower (1536, 1541). Wyatt's long paraphrase intersperses nonbiblical verse narratives among the seven penitential psalms to create one long poem describing the penitence of King David after his adultery with Bathsheba and his effective murder of her husband Uriah (2 Sam. 11–12). The association of the penitential psalms with David has a long hist., encouraged by the biblical headnote to the central Psalm 51. Wyatt's psalms (pub. 1549) were a relatively free trans. from the It. prose version of the penitential psalms by Pietro Aretino (1534), but Wyatt's choice of *terza rima* (not used in Eng. since Chaucer) derived from an It. metrical version by Luigi Alamanni (1532). Metrical versions of the penitential psalms were also produced during the Middle Ages and the Ren. in Fr. (by Christine de Pizan and Jean de La Ceppède), Sp. (by Luis de Léon and Diego Alfonso Velázquez de Velasco), and other Eur. langs.

Among Martin Luther's early works were a trans. and commentary on the penitential psalms, as well as his metrical version of Psalm 130, "Aus tiefer Not." Other Eng. versions were written by Edmund Spenser (not extant), William Hunnis (*Seven Sobbes of a Sorrowfull Soule*, 1583), and John Davies of Hereford (*The Dolefull Dove*, 1612). The Eng. verse paraphrase of the Catholic activist Richard Verstegan or Rowlands (1601) was included in Elizabeth Grymeston's *Miscelanea* (1604), a collection of advice to her children. Apart from Wyatt's, these metrical paraphrases are unaccomplished, written in variations on the popular *ballad meters of the psalms adapted by Thomas Sternhold and John Hopkins. However, some sophisticated verse paraphrases were fashioned from particular psalms from the penitential set. George Gascoigne's "Gas-

coigne's *Deprofundis*" (Psalm 130) was included in his *Posies* (1575), and Anne Lock's extended paraphrase of Psalm 51 (*A Meditation of a Penitent Sinner*, 1560) may be the first *sonnet sequence in Eng. The form and mode of the penitential psalms had an influence beyond strict trans. and paraphrases. Francis Bacon's "Penitential Psalms," dedicated to George Herbert, included seven biblical psalms that were not the traditional seven. George Chapman's "Penitential Psalms" (1612) were a loose verse trans. from the Lat. prose of Petrarch's seven psalm-like but nonbiblical "Penitential Psalms" (ca. 1355). Thomas Campion's *Songs of Mourning* (1613) for Prince Henry consisted of seven original poems modeled on the seven-part penitential structure, while the seven mournful instrumental pieces of John Dowland's *Lachrimae, or Seven Tears* (1604) abandoned text altogether. Since the 17th c., poets have shown little interest in the penitential psalms.

*See* DEVOTIONAL POETRY; LITURGICAL POETRY; PSALMS, METRICAL.

■ W. Drumm, "Psalms," *Catholic Encyclopedia* (1911); B. Ó Cuiv, "The Penitential Psalms in Irish Verse," *Éigse* 8 (1955); R. G. Twombly, "Thomas Wyatt's Paraphrase of the Penitential Psalms of David," *TSLL* 12 (1970); S. Greenblatt, *Renaissance Self-Fashioning* (1980), ch. 3; R. Zim, *English Metrical Psalms* (1987); A. Halasz, "Wyatt's David," *TSLL* 30 (1988); E. Duffy, *The Stripping of the Altars* (1992); E. M. Heale, *Wyatt, Surrey, and Early Tudor Poetry* (1998); C. Costley, "David, Bathsheba, and the Penitential Psalms," *RQ* 57 (2004); H. Hamlin, *Psalm Culture and Early Modern English Literature* (2004).

H. HAMLIN

**PENTAMETER.** In cl. prosody, this term should denote a meter of five measures or feet, as its name says, but, in fact, the Gr. pentameter, which is dactylic, does not contain five of any metra (see METRON): it consists of two *hemiepes with an invariable *caesura: –
∪ ∪ – ∪ ∪ – | – ∪ ∪ – ∪ ∪ – . Contraction of the shorts in the first half of the line is common; the second half runs as shown. It is the conventional name for the second verse in the couplet form called the *elegiac distich, though this is probably a hexameter shortened internally. The cl. Gr. and Lat. pentameter should not be confused with the Eng. "iambic pentameter," despite the fact that the Ren. prosodists derived that name from cl. precedent, for the Eng. line had been written in great numbers for two centuries (since Chaucer) before it was given any cl. name, and the internal metrical structures of the two meters are quite distinct—this follows from the deeper and more systematic differences between quantitative and accentual verse-systems (see ACCENTUAL VERSE, METER, QUANTITY). Other terms lacking cl. connotations that were formerly and are sometimes still used for the staple line of Eng. dramatic and narrative verse include *heroic verse and *decasyllable (see BLANK VERSE, HEROIC COUPLET); which term of these three one chooses depends on what genealogy one assumes for the Eng. line (cl., native, romance, mixed) and what features of

the line one takes as constitutive—feet, stress count, syllable count, or the latter two, or the latter two as creating the first one (feet). Despite the fact that trochaic tetrameters (see TETRAMETER, RISING AND FALLING RHYTHM) are fairly frequent in Eng., trochaic pentameters are extremely rare—Shakespeare's line "Never, never, never, never, never" (*King Lear* 5.3.365) notwithstanding; virtually the only sustained example is Robert Browning's "One Word More."

■ Wilamowitz; Crusius; Halporn et al.; Snell; West; P. Groves, *Strange Music* (1998); D. Keppel-Jones, *The Strict Metrical Tradition* (2001).

J. W. HALPORN; T.V.F. BROGAN

**PENTHEMIMER** (Gr., "of five halves," i.e., 2½ *feet). In cl. poetry, a *colon of the form x – ⏑ – x, which is the first half of the line in the iambic *trimeter when the main *caesura occurs after the fifth position. The corresponding first half of the dactylic *hexameter with caesura also after the fifth position (– ⏑ ⏑ – – ⏑ ⏑ –) is called *hemiepes. In both meters, this caesura after the first half of the third foot is known as penthemimeral, while caesura amid the fourth foot (much rarer) is known as hephthemimeral.

■ West.

T.V.F. BROGAN

**PERFORMANCE** (Lat. *recitatio*; Ger. *Vortrag, Rezitation*).

I. Theory
II. History
III. Practice

**I. Theory.** Performance refers to the recitation of poetry by its author, a professional performer, or any other reader either alone or before an audience; the term normally implies the latter. The performance of poetry also entails a setting and a performance style. Though poets naturally seem the most likely performers, from ancient times to at least the Ren., a class of professional performers or singers has usually been available for performance (see JONGLEUR, MINSTREL, SCOP, GUSLAR). The setting for performance may be a literary salon, a ceremonial civic or state occasion, or a quasi-theatrical performance at which a poet, poets, or performers address a public. By extension to electronic audio and visual media, performances also have been disseminated via radio or television broadcasts; phonograph records, audio tapes, or compact disks; and videotapes, DVDs, and films. A distinction should be made here between performances that are live and static recordings thereof: the latter are fixed copies of but a single performance reduced in form and recoded into some machine lang.

It is also essential to distinguish between the performance of a poem and its composition. These two processes may or may not coincide. In the first case, the poetry presented in performance has already been transcribed as a written text, whether ms., scribal copy, or pub. book. This is the condition of nearly all mod., literary poetry: composition has been completed, and the work has passed into *textuality. Here performance and composition are separated in temporal sequence.

In the second case, namely, *oral poetry, no distinction is made between composition and performance: the "text" is spontaneously composed during performance by illiterate *bards. Such a "text" is unique in every performance. Successive recitations by even the same bard may draw upon the same story pattern, but the construction of scenes and selection of verbal details are different in every case; the choice of wording and phrasing is both controlled by, and assists, a stock of relatively fixed *"formulas." These are at once both narrative and metrical building blocks, serving to construct metrical lines and a coherent story. It should be noted that, in historical terms, the second class preceded the first—i.e., orality preceded the invention of writing, print technology, and the spread of literacy (reading). But even in mod. literate cultures where written texts are widely pub., spontaneous composition has reemerged as a species of what Walter Ong terms "secondary orality."

The audience is one of the least understood components of all performative arts: Western poetics has taken virtually no interest in this subject. It is obvious, however, that audiences often bring with them significant sets of expectations about subject, diction, tone, and versification. As William Wordsworth remarked, the poet who would write in a new style must create the audience by which it will be appreciated—or perish. Some audiences are trained, but most are not. Audience comprehension of oral texts is unknown: some verse trads., such as OE, apparently helped auditors recognize meter with musical chords, e.g. In general, it would seem reasonable to assume that audiences cannot quickly process archaisms or unusual words, complex meters or heterometric stanza forms, or distanced rhymes or elaborate sonal interlace. On the other hand, sound patterns are very much obscured by orthography, particularly in a lang. such as Eng. Sound patterning can certainly be recognized *as* elaborate in performance even when it is not evident *how*, exactly, the sounds are structured. It is a question just how much of poetic form is perceived in oral transmission.

In one respect, however, audiences have an easier time with the recognition of meaning in oral texts. Seymour Chatman isolates a central difference between the reading and *scansion of poems on the one hand and their performance on the other: in the former two activities, ambiguities of interpretation can be preserved and do not have to be settled one way or the other ("disambiguated"). But in performance, all ambiguities have to be resolved before or during delivery. Since the nature of performance is linear and temporal, sentences can be read aloud only once and must be given a specific intonational pattern. Hence, in performance, the performer is forced to choose between alternative intonational patterns and their associated meanings.

Performance styles are one of the most interesting subjects in *prosody and have direct connections to acting and articulation in the theater. Jakobson has distinguished between "delivery design" and "delivery instance," the former set by verse form, the latter representing the features that are specific to each performance. But between these lies the realm of expressive style. The two general classes of styles are realistic (naturalistic) and oratorical (declamatory, dramatic, rhapsodic, incantatory). C. S. Lewis once identified two types of performers of metrical verse: "minstrels" (who recite in a singsong voice, letting scansion override sense) and "actors" (who give a flamboyantly expressive recitation, ignoring meter altogether). And early in the 20th c., Robert Bridges argued that verses should be scanned in one way but read aloud in another, tilting toward minstrelsy.

The triumph of naturalistic technique in mod. drama has obscured the fact that artificial modes of delivery are well attested in antiquity, as reported by the grammarian Sacerdos (Keil 6.448). The evidence adduced by W. S. Allen for "scanning pronunciation" and the demonstration of Ren. pedagogy by Attridge suggest that the practice of reciting verses aloud in an artificial manner has been more the rule than the exception in the West. E.g., the romantic poets usually chanted their poetic texts when reading aloud, differentiating their lang. from natural speech by moving it closer to music (Perkins). For dramatic verse that is metrical, particularly Shakespeare's, actors learn that attention to scansion will elucidate nuances of meaning in lines that a literal or natural delivery style will not manifest (Hardison). Consequently, great actors learn how to convey both sense and meter together, so that each supports the other.

**II. History.** In Asian poetry, the trad. of poetry presentation is esp. important in Chinese and Japanese poetry (see CHINA, POETRY OF; JAPAN, POETRY OF) and continues in 20th-c. Japan. Western poetry readings from the Greeks to the 19th c. have mainly favored invitational performances in courtly settings. It is likely that performances of poetry took place at the Alexandrian court of the Ptolemies (ca. 325–30 BCE) and, at Rome, in the aristocratic residences of Gaius Cilnius Maecenas (d. 8 BCE), who encouraged the work of Virgil, Horace, and Propertius. In Petronius's *Satyricon*, Trimalchio first writes, then recites, his own "poetry" to the guests at his banquet.

The fifth of the five great divisions of cl. rhet.—after *inventio* (discovery), *dispositio* (arrangement), *elocutio* (style), and *memoria* (memorization)—was *pronuntiatio* or delivery. This was less developed in antiquity than the first four subjects, though Aristotle discusses it, as do Cicero (*De Inventione* 1.9) and the *Rhetorica ad Herennium* (3.9), treating, like most subsequent rhetoricians, voice control and gesture. Quintilian devotes a lengthy chapter to the subject (*Institutio oratoria* 11.3). The practice of reciting Lat. verses was encouraged by all the med. Lat. grammarians and central to Ren. education (see PRONUNCIATION).

The Occitan *troubadours retained professional performers, *joglars,* to recite their verses, though the poets of the *Minnesang did not; other itinerant minstrels maintained themselves by recitation throughout the Middle Ages. Written poetry was recited at the 13th-c. court of Frederick II (see SICILIAN SCHOOL), in the Florentine circle of Lorenzo de' Medici (late 15th c.), and in the late 17th-c. *salons* of the Princes de Condé. In the 18th c.,

however, the patronage system gave way to one of public consumption of published books, and performance accordingly changed from a courtly to a public function. As a young poet of the late 1770s, J. W. Goethe read his work at the Weimar court; on the occasion of a production of *Faust* to commemorate his 80th birthday in 1829, he personally coached the actors in the delivery of their lines. The 18th c. also witnessed the emergence of elocution as an important part of the theory of rhet. In the U.S., before the flourishing of printing presses, the typical mode of disseminating poetry was through handwritten ms. and oral performance, increasingly in forums such as clubs and literary circles.

In the 19th c., public recitations by both poets and their admirers became commonplace (see RECITATION). The work of Robert Browning was recited in meetings of the Browning Society (founded 1881), an organization that produced hundreds of offshoots in the U.S. in the 1880s and 1890s. A *Goethe Gesellschaft* (founded 1885) held readings in places as distant as St. Petersburg and New York. Elocution was even further popularized in the 19th c.; the practice of reading aloud from lit. after dinner in Victorian households was widespread. The work of treasured poets was memorized and declaimed regularly in schools and churches, and some famous late 19th-c. poets, incl. Alfred, Lord Tennyson and a reader believed to be Walt Whitman, were recorded on wax cylinder. Elocution led to the emergence in the 20th c. of "oral interpretation" as a formal activity in Am. university departments of speech.

The performance of poetry is central to symbolist poetics (see SYMBOLISM). Stéphane Mallarmé read his poetry to a select audience on designated Tuesdays at which the poet himself played both host and reader in oracular style. While Mallarmé's poetry was anything but spontaneously written, his performances both personalized and socialized the work. Stefan George's mode of delivery was consciously influenced by Mallarmé: the audience was restricted to the poet's disciples (*Kreis*), and the occasion was perceived as cultic and sacral. George read from ms. in a strictly rhapsodic style that disciples were required to follow.

In the 20th c., naturalistic or realistic delivery styles gradually have gained the upper hand over a more artificial, vatic performance style. W. B. Yeats was much concerned with having his work sound spontaneous and natural, though his delivery style, like Ezra Pound's, was dramatic and incantatory. By contrast, T. S. Eliot's performances were aristocratic in style and tonally flat. The Wagnerian prescription of having the performer seem spontaneous in expression but personally remote had its best 20th-c. exemplar in Dylan Thomas, whose dramatic, incantatory style contrasted sharply with the plain, conversational style of Robert Frost and W. H. Auden. Frost's "sentence sounds" are the intonational patterns of colloquial speech, esp. as frozen into idioms—precisely the kind of speech effects that would be likely to come across well to audiences on Frost's frequent reading tours.

Politically motivated poetry readings early in the 20th c. served as models for others to come in the second half of the century. In postrevolutionary Russia, Vladimir Mayakovsky sang the praises of the October Revolution in lyrics written to be read aloud; his dramatic performances attracted mass audiences both in western Europe and the U.S. Avant-garde movements of the 1920s and 1930s such as *Dada and *surrealism generated performances of poetry staged simultaneously with music, dance, and film, and so anticipated the intermedia performances later in the century. *Poetry readings of the 1950s and 1960s often took the form of multimedia presentations and random artistic "happenings." Prominent innovators of the poetry performance in the 1950s were the *Beat poets, notably Allen Ginsberg, Gregory Corso, and Lawrence Ferlinghetti, all instrumental figures in the movement now known as the *San Francisco Renaissance. Orality and performance were foregrounded in the poetics of Charles Olson, who conceived of the poem as a "field of action" and made his unit of measure the "breath group." Olson's *"projective verse" found followers in Robert Duncan, Robert Creeley, and Denise Levertov. Af. Caribbean dub poetry, a form that originated in Jamaica in the 1970s where poetry is spoken over reggae rhythms, has been important to a range of diasporic artists, like Linton Kwesi Johnson, who intervene in an evolving cultural politics through performance.

Since 1960, New York, Chicago, and San Francisco have been the major Am. poetry performance centers, with London, Amsterdam, and West Berlin their Eur. counterparts. In New York, the poetry-reading movement of the 1960s generally associated with the name of Paul Blackburn served as a stimulus for a new vogue of poetry readings in other parts of the country, esp. in Chicago and on the West Coast. Further experimentation with elements of recitation, music, song, digitized or synthesized sound, drama, mime, dance, and video, which are mixed, merged, altered, choreographed, or improvised in seriatim, simultaneous, random, or collage order, characterized the phenomena variously called *sound poetry, multimedia, or sometimes "performance art" of the 1970s and 1980s. David Antin called his improvisations "talk poems." Jerome Rothenberg's interest in tribal poetry led to his reconstruction in print of sound poetry along with notation of the ritual contexts that surround it. The anthropologist Dell Hymes, with Rothenberg a proponent of *ethnopoetics, devised a method of transcribing and analyzing folklore and oral narrative that pays attention to poetic structures within speech.

Since the 1950s, then, the performance of poetry in America has undergone a resurgence, becoming a standard element in the practice of poetry in the Eng.-speaking world. Its tone ranges from conversational idioms to street lang. Jazz or rock music, electronic audio and visual effects, and spontaneous dramatic presentations sometimes accompany recitation, esp. outside of universities, where, it has been argued, an aesthetic narrowness prevails (Lazer). The ethos in intermedia events such as these is one of experimentation, liberation, and spontaneity. Like other contemp. literary genres, postmod. poetry maintains a strong inter-

est in performance as a reaction to academic interpretation and its fixation on the text.

Dana Gioia has noted the decline of print culture in the late 20th and 21st cs. and the rise of a new oral poetry, encompassing rap (see HIP-HOP POETICS), *cowboy poetry, and *poetry slams, that recalls poetry's origins in preliterate cultures and is overwhelmingly formalist and populist. While some of the new performance poetry is performed live and subsequently disseminated in traditional print form, other work is delivered to audiences through electronic media, incl. radio, recordings, and television, as in the PBS series *The United States of Poetry*, HBO's *Def Poetry Jam*, and MTV's *Spoken Word Unplugged*. Sound files on the Internet, through such archival sites as UbuWeb and PennSound, enable anyone with access to a computer to hear the voice of mod. and contemp. poets reading aloud from their work. Former U.S. Poet Laureate Robert Pinsky's Internet-based Favorite Poem Project, launched in 1998, includes videos of ordinary Americans reading their favorite poems.

The heritage of all the various forms of postmodernism in America has been a turning away from the autonomy of the text and the presumption that a text presents one determinate meaning (see INDETERMINACY) or its author's intended meaning (see INTENTION) toward the more fluid, less determinate, free play of readerly responses to texts. Hence, critical interest has shifted from written documents to performances as experiences. Many audiences still consider the performance of poetry a communal, nearly sacral event for heightened speech, investing the poet with the transformative powers of the *vates. And many readers and teachers of poetry continue to believe that poetry achieves its body only when given material form, as sound, in the air, aloud. See also BOUTS-RIMÉS, EISTEDDFOD, POETIC CONTESTS.

**III. Practice.** Discussions of poetic performance from earliest times to the present focus mainly on bards', actors', and poets' oral presentations, rather than the inner performances that precede and shape our vocalizations. But before a person recites a poem, particularly a metrical poem, he or she has already made decisions about which words in the lines invite special emphasis. Largely the decisions are determined by characteristics of the lang. being spoken and the meter, if any, being used: these will lead the reader familiar with the lang. and its poetic forms to observe mid- and end-line pauses and to emphasize particular syllables. But further refinements and judgments are personal.

The notion that there is, or should be, an entirely "correct" performance of any given line is put in doubt when highly regarded scholars insist on differing rhythmic performances of well-known lines from esteemed poets. Every reader/performer of Shakespeare's sonnet 116, which begins "Let me not to the marriage of true minds/Admit impediments," must come to a conclusion about how to respond to and produce that opening line either in mind or out loud. George T. Wright hears the poem opening with the "quiet, confidential tones" he finds characteristic of the sonnet as a whole, so he begins his commentary by suggesting that "Let" is the line's first emphasized word and that while "not" carries the second beat, it is relatively unemphasized: "*Let* me not." Helen Vendler hears the sonnet's opening differently. Experiencing the poem as a rebuttal of another's claims (the young man's), she feels that "the iambic prosody" brings "the pressure of rhetorical refutation" into the poem's first line, requiring an emphasis on "me": "Let *me* not."

However much one may insist on the correctness of either performance, each is right in its own way and worthy of consideration. And it is by adding one's own experience with the line to such efforts of judgment that a deeper involvement with Shakespeare's memorable sonnet can be achieved.

Lines in many poems have a variety of linguistically and metrically permissible emphases, but there are instances when established metrical patterns limit the possibilities of alternative performances. E.g., John Donne, in "The Canonization," creates metaphors for his love in five stanzas whose second lines can be felt as four beats, even though the third stanza's second line could be experienced as having three beats ("Call her *one*, mee an*oth*er *flye*") or even five beats ("*Call* her *one*, *mee* an*oth*er *flye*"). However, the performance that gives emphasis to both "her" and "mee" not only satisfies metrical expectation ("Call *her* one, *mee* an*oth*er *flye*") but heightens the sense of the lovers' unity. Likewise, in the same poet's "The Sun Rising," the fifth lines in the poem's three stanzas ("Sawcy pedantique wretch, goe chide," "If her eyes have not blinded thine," and "Thou sunne art halfe as happy'as wee") are easily experienced as having four beats. Although a prose-like performance of the second-stanza line is possible ("If her *eyes* have not *blind*ed *thine*"), it is the four-beat performance ("If *her* eyes *have* not *blind*ed *thine*") that both realizes the metrical norm and dramatizes the loved one's eyes whose brightness challenges the sun's.

Performing the various rhythmical possibilities of even the most familiar poems can extend their ranges of implication and meaning. Two quite different notions about the personalities of the speaker in Robert Frost's "Stopping by Woods on a Snowy Evening" and the landowner whose "house is in the village" can emerge from slightly different choices among the permissible emphases of the poem's third line, "He will not see me stopping here." One likely performance of the line would follow the steady iambic, or offbeat-beat, pattern clearly established at the poem's opening: "He *will* not *see* me *stop*ping *here*." But on reimagining, and reperforming, a linguistically permissible emphasis on "He" would more strongly evoke a sense of difference that is central to the poem—the difference between a villager who regards his woods as a possession and the poet-speaker who regards them as a place for experiencing things "lovely, dark and deep." And with the new performance taken into account, other words take on new significance: "He will not see me stopping here" becomes more apprehensive, perhaps even threatening,

than something like "He will not mind my stopping here." An alternate performance again enlarges possibilities of feeling and the poem's pleasures.

■ **Theory and History:** JOURNALS: *Literature in Performance* (1980–88) and continued as *Text and Performance Quarterly* (1989–); *Oral Tradition* (1986–). STUDIES: Bridges; R. C. Crosby, "Oral Delivery in the Middle Ages," *Speculum* 11 (1936); W. B. Nichols, *The Speaking of Poetry* (1937); R. C. Crosby, "Chaucer and the Custom of Oral Delivery," *Speculum* 13 (1938); S. F. Bonner, *Roman Declamation* (1950); D. Whitelock, *The Audience of Beowulf* (1951); K. Wais, *Mallarmé*, 2d ed. (1952); E. Salin, *Um Stefan George*, 2d ed. (1954); F. Trojan, *Die Kunst der Rezitation* (1954); S. Chatman, "Linguistics, Poetics, and Interpretation," *QJS* 43 (1957); Y. Winters, "The Audible Reading of Poetry," *The Function of Criticism* (1957); C. S. Lewis, "Metre," *REL* 1 (1960); Jakobson, "Linguistics and Poetics," *Style in Language*, ed. Sebeok (1960); F. Berry, *Poetry and the Physical Voice* (1962); S. Chatman, "Linguistic Style, Literary Style, and Performance," *Monograph Series Languages & Linguistics* 13 (1962); S. Levin, "Suprasegmentals and the Performance of Poetry," *QJS* 48 (1962); D. Levertov, "Approach to Public Poetry Listenings," *VQR* 41 (1965); K. T. Loesch, "Literary Ambiguity and Oral Performance," *QJS* 51 (1965); D. Norberg, "La Récitation du vers latin," *NM* 66 (1965); *The New Russian Poets, 1953–1968*, ed. G. Reavey (1966); W. C. Forrest, "The Poem as a Summons to Performance," *BJA* 9 (1969); G. Poulet, "Phenomenology of Reading," *NLH* 1 (1969); H. Hein, "Performance as an Aesthetic Category," *JAAC* 28 (1970); P. Dickinson, "Spoken Words," *Encounter* 34 (1970); *The East Side Scene*, ed. A. De Loach (1972); S. Massie, *The Living Mirror: Five Young Poets from Leningrad* (1972); Allen; D. Attridge, *Well-Weighed Syllables* (1974); *Performance in Postmodern Culture*, ed. M. Benamou et al. (1977); Ruth Finnegan, *Oral Poetry* (1977); M. C. Beardsley, "Right Readings and Good Readings," *Literature in Performance* 1 (1980); D. Hymes, *"In Vain I Tried to Tell You"* (1981); M. L. West, "The Singing of Homer," *JHS* 101 (1981); W. Ong, *Orality and Literacy* (1982); *The Poetry Reading*, ed. S. Vincent and E. Zweig (1981); B. Rowland, "*Pronuntiatio* and its Effect on Chaucer's Audience," *SAC* 4 (1982); O. B. Hardison, "Speaking the Speech," *ShQ* 34 (1983); D. A. Russell, *Greek Declamation* (1983); W. G. Thalmann, *Conventions of Form and Thought in Early Greek Epic Poetry* (1984), chap. 4; D. Wojahn, "Appraising the Age of the Poetry Reading," *NER/BLQ* 8 (1985); J.-C. Milner and F. Regnault, *Dire le vers* (1987); E. Griffiths, *The Printed Voice of Victorian Poetry* (1988); R. Schechner, *Performance Theory*, 2d ed. (1988); G. Danek, "Singing Homer," *WHB* 31 (1989); M. Davidson, *The San Francisco Renaissance* (1989); D. Oliver, *Poetry and Narrative in Performance* (1989); H. M. Sayre, *The Object of Performance* (1989); "Performance," *Critical Terms for Literary Study*, ed. F. Lentricchia and T. McLaughlin (1990); D. Cusic, *The Poet as Performer* (1991); S. G. Daitz, "On Reading Homer Aloud," *AJP*

112 (1991); D. Perkins, "How the Romantics Recited Poetry," *SEL* 4 (1991); *Performance*, spec. iss. of *PMLA* 107.3 (1992); H. Lazer, "Poetry Readings and the Contemporary Canon," *Opposing Poetries: Volume One* (1996); M. Morrisson, "Performing the Pure Voice: Elocution, Verse Recitation, and Modernist Poetry in Pre-War London," *Modernism/Modernity* 3 (1996); *Sound States*, ed. A. Morris (1997); *Close Listening*, ed. C. Bernstein (1998); Lord; J. M. Foley, *How to Read an Oral Poem* (2002); D. Gioia, *Disappearing Ink* (1994), chap. 1; M. Loeffelholz, *From School to Salon* (2004); P. Middleton, *Distant Reading* (2005); J. S. Rubin, *Songs of Ourselves* (2007).

■ **Practice:** Attridge, *Rhythms*; G. Wright, *Shakespeare's Metrical Art* (1988); Attridge, *Poetic Rhythm*; H. Vendler, *The Art of Shakespeare's Sonnets* (1997); Carper and Attridge.

T.V.F. Brogan, W. B. Fleischmann, T. Hoffman (theory and history); T. Carper (practice)

# PERIOD

I. Prosody
II. Rhetoric

**I. Prosody.** In *classical prosody, a term used to refer to (1) any rhythmic sequence that is whole and complete in itself—i.e., capable of constituting an entire poem but also of being used as one element alongside others in some higher-order rhythmic structure or (2) any sequence separated from what precedes and follows by a break in *synapheia—i.e., some sort of *pause. Form (1) is thus what mod. metrists would call a *verse paragraph* or a poetic sequence ending in *closure and seems a much narrower category than (2). The latter includes not only *stanzas and their major subdivisions, in stanzaic verse, but the individual lines in stichic verse (see STICHOS), as well as sequences such as the *pentameter in the *elegiac distich and a number of even shorter lyric segments that, unlike stichic units such as *hexameter and *trimeter, are never found as isolated, independent poetic utterances. The nature of the pauses to which such breaks in synapheia correspond and the reasons for their distribution within a composition are imperfectly understood: reinforcing closure is obviously one purpose but probably not the only one. Caution in the use and interpretation of the term *period* is, therefore, in order. Dale distinguishes (1) and (2) as "major" and "minor" periods, Rossi as *period* and *verse*. But not all metrists are so careful.

**II. Rhetoric.** The term was taken over into rhet. from prosody for discussion of prose style. Cicero (*Orator* 174 ff.) credits Thrasymachus with the introduction of poetic rhythms into prose, Gorgias with the devel. of the figures or schemes, and Isocrates with combining the two, so that a rhetorical period came to have both metrical and schematic form. Aristotle (*Rhetoric* 3.9) differentiates between "periodic" or "rounded" style and nonperiodic or "continuous," the latter the more sophisticated form. He defines the period in both structural (logical) and rhythmical terms, as a sentence "which has a beginning and end in itself, and a size which can be seen as a whole." Periodic style is pleasing because "the hearer thinks always he has a grip on something, because there is always a sense of completion," and comprehensible "because it is easily remembered; this is because the periodic style has number. . . . The period must be completed also with the sense. . . . The period may be either composed in cola or simple. A sentence in cola is one which is complete, has subdivisions, and is easily pronounced in a breath" (trans. Fowler). The end of the period, thus, completes at once the sense and the metrical figure, but more the former than the latter, apparently; Aristotle recommends marking the beginning and end with a distinct *metron such as the *paeon, but he discourages extensive use—even the paeon he thinks obtrusive—and none of his examples uses paeons at both ends. Aristotle permits only two *cola per period—this too came from metrics—perhaps because he emphasizes structures of antithesis, but later writers such as Demetrius quite reasonably allow more; and Aristotle allows periods of only one colon, denied by most later writers. The crucial point, however, is that good style is rhythmic and that these rhythms flow either continuously or in periods, segments that are short enough to be perceived as a whole, complete themselves in sense, and are marked rhythmically as distinct segments. This segmenting and shaping allow auditors to perceive structure. As Theophrastus puts it (Cicero, *De oratore* 3.184), one can count falling drops of water, but a flowing stream cannot be measured.

*See* FOOT, PUNCTUATION, SYSTEM.

■ **I. Prosody:** Wilamowitz, esp. 441 ff.; Maas, sect. 52; Dale, 11–13; L. E. Rossi, "Verskunst," *Der kleine Pauly*, v. 5 (1975); T.C.W. Stinton, "Pause and Period in the Lyrics of Greek Tragedy," *CQ* 71 (1977); Halporn et al., esp. 6, 66; West, esp. 4–6, 198.
■ **II. Rhetoric:** J. Zehetmeier, "Die Periodenlehre des Aristoteles," *Philologus* 85 (1930); R. L. Fowler, "Aristotle on the Period," *CQ* 32 (1982); Norden.

T. Cole (prosody); T.V.F. Brogan (rhet.)

**PERIPHRASIS.** A circumlocution, a roundabout expression that avoids naming something by its most direct term. Since it is constituted through a culturally perceived relationship to a word or phrase that it is *not*, periphrasis has no distinctive form of its own but articulates itself variously through other figures, esp. *metaphor. Quintilian (*Institutio oratoria* 8.6.59) subdivides it by function into two types: the euphemistic or "necessary," as in the avoidance of obscenity or other unpleasant matters (Plato's "the fated journey" for "death"—cf. the mod. "passing away"); and the decorative, used for stylistic embellishment (Virgil's "Aurora sprinkled the earth with new light" for "day broke"). The descriptive kind includes most periphrases that approximate a two-word definition by combining a specific with a general term ("the finny tribe" to signify fish). Longinus considered it productive of sublimity but, like Quintilian, warned against its excesses, such as preciosity or pleonasm (28–29). Later writers have characterized it as representing a term by its (whole or partial) definition, as in the expression "pressed milk" for "cheese." Periphrasis also appears in poetry that tries to translate culture-specific concepts from one lang. to another without neologism.

Though it is unlikely that any movement or era in poetry has succeeded in suppressing periphrasis altogether, some styles favor it more than others. Curtius associates it, like other rhetorical ornaments, with *mannerism and marks stages in its use and abuse. Oral traditions frequently build formulas around periphrases, as in the patronymic "son of Tydeus" for "Diomedes"; these have important metrical functions and are not ornament (see FORMULA, ORAL POETRY).

While widely used in biblical and Homeric lit. and by Hesiod, the devel. of periphrasis as an important feature of poetic style begins with Lucretius and Virgil, and through their influence, it became a staple device of *epic and *descriptive poetry throughout the Middle Ages and into the Ren. Classified by med. rhetoricians as a trope of *amplification, periphrasis suited the conception of style that emphasized *copia* and *invention. The OE poetic device of *variation typically employs multiple periphrastic constructions, as does the *kenning, the characteristic device of Old Germanic and ON poetry, which, in its more elaborate forms, illustrates the connection between periphrasis and *riddle.

Given new impetus through the work of the *Pléiade*, periphrasis proliferated in 17th-c. diction, particularly as influenced by the scientific spirit of the age, and even more so in the stock poetic diction of the 18th c., where descriptive poetry often shows periphrastic constructions (Arthos). Since the 18th c., the form has lost much of its prestige in the romantic and mod. reaction against rhetorical artifice; more often than not, it survives only in inflated uses for humorous effect, as in Charles Dickens. Yet its occasional appearance in the work of modernists such as T. S. Eliot ("white hair of the waves blown back" for "foam") suggests that, insofar as directness of locution is not always the preferable route (direct speech being, most often, shorn of semantic density and allusive richness), periphrasis has an enduring poetic usefulness.

*See* DICTION.

■ P. Aronstein, "Die periphrastische Form im Englischen," *Anglia* 42 (1918); J. Arthos, *The Language of Natural Description in Eighteenth-Century Poetry* (1949); Curtius; D. S. McCoy, *Tradition and Convention: A Study of Periphrasis in English Pastoral Poetry from 1557–1715* (1965); Lausberg—compendium of citations; A. Quinn, *Figures of Speech* (1982); J. P. Blevins, "Periphrasis as Syntactic Exponence," *Patterns in Paradigms*, ed. F. Ackerman, J. P. Blevins, and G. S. Stump (2008).

W. W. PARKS; J. ARTHOS

# PERSIAN POETRY

**I. Scope.** Evidence for poetic practice in Old and Middle Persian is scanty and reveals little of its prosody,

forms, or themes. The substantive hist. of Persian poetry begins in the 9th c. with the emergence of New Persian written in modified Ar. script. Three dialects of Persian now serve as the national lang. of Iran (*Fārsī*), Afghanistan (*Darī*), and Tajikistan (*Tājīk*). Using Farsi to refer to Persian in Eng. sows confusion and obscures two important features of the trad. First is its continuity: the earliest works of Persian poetry from the 10th c. are probably more readily comprehensible to mod. speakers of the lang. than Shakespeare's works are to mod. speakers of Eng. Second is the geographical extent of the trad. Farsi is spoken only in Iran (and the Iranian diaspora), but for centuries Persian poetry was written and read throughout much of Asia. Literary centers in regions that are now part of the nations of not only Iran, Afghanistan, and Tajikistan but also of Turkey, Azerbaijan, Georgia, Pakistan, India, Turkmenistan, and Uzbekistan were in constant communication and unified by common poetic practices and values.

**II. Prosody, Forms, and Rhetoric.** Traditional verse forms employ quantitative metrics. The system of meters was conceptualized according to models laid down for the *'arūḍ* system of *Arabic prosody. But because of phonetic differences and perhaps Middle Persian prosody, Persian metrics diverges significantly in practice from its Ar. counterpart. Some of the most frequently used meters in Persian are rare in Ar. Persian does not permit the substitution of long and short syllables found in most Ar. meters and adds a third category of "overlong" syllables (long vowel-consonant) to the Ar. system. Several common words and particles may be counted either short or long, and word-initial vowels may be elided with the final consonants of preceding words. In Persian, repeated, refrain-like syllables, known as the *radīf*, often follow the rhyme, a feature rarely found in Ar. Persian also adopted formal genres of Ar. poetry such as the *qaṣīda, *ghazal, and *qiṭ'a but added new forms, such as the *rubā'ī, the *masnavī, and the strophic *tarkīb-band*. The rhymed *couplets of the masnavī enable the composition of long narrative poems, which have significantly shaped the hist. of Persian poetry.

Drawing again on Ar. models, Persian writers have cataloged an extensive array of rhetorical devices, from types of puns and verbal figures to varieties of *similes, *allusions, and *metaphors. Traditional lit. crit. in Persian is generally limited to prosody, form, and rhet., but incidental critical comments found in biographies of poets, historical writing, and metapoetic reflections can tell us much about how poetry was read, utilized, and evaluated.

**III. Historical Overview.** Until the mod. period, poetic novelty was rarely prized for its own sake. Apprentice poets were expected to memorize thousands of verses by their predecessors and contemporaries. Poets drew on a well-established stock of themes, settings, images, and similes; certain poetic metaphors even came to be lexicalized, like the word *la'l* (ruby) which acquired the definition "beloved's lips." Innovation took place against the background of authoritative models, and poets would often write responses to the work of earlier masters, using the same meter and rhyme scheme or rewriting the same story. Poetic practice, however, changed gradually over the course of generations. Since the early 20th c., the hist. of Persian poetry has been loosely divided into four broad period styles or *sabk*. New Persian poetry emerged in the region of Khorasan (now divided among Iran, Afghanistan, and Uzbekistan), whence the name of the *sabk-i Khurāsānī* to characterize Persian poetry from the 10th to the middle of the 12th c. It is marked by a number of archaic grammatical features; *diction tends to be simple and measured, and metaphors and similes are usually explicit and concrete. During the 12th c., Persian poetry began to expand south toward the subcontinent and west across the Iranian plateau, and an esp. significant school of poetry emerged in Azerbaijan. As populations and poets scattered before the Mongol invasions of the early 13th c., Persian poetry spread past the Hindu Kush into India, to the Persian Gulf in southwestern Iran, and westward into Anatolia. This movement marks the emergence of the *sabk-i ʿIrāqī* (Iraq here referring to western Persia). Poetic lang. was standardized and greater use made of words borrowed from Ar. Rhetorical figures of speech are deployed with more frequency and sophistication, as poetic conventions and genres (esp. the ghazal) are crystallized. At the end of this period, the trad. is consolidated and codified in the literary school of Herat, and the end of the 15th c. it has sometimes been considered the end of the high cl. period of Persian poetry. But with the foundation of the centralizing dynasties of the Safavids in Persia and the Mughals in India in the early 16th c., Persian became the authoritative lang. of administration and high culture across western, south, and central Asia and served as a cl. reference point for poets writing in Ottoman Turkish. This innovative period first witnessed the emergence of the relatively short-lived *maktab-i vuqūʿ* (phenomenalist school), which used a plain diction to explore the psychology of amorous encounters. Of much more lasting significance was a style known to its practitioners as the Fresh Style, but later called the *sabk-e Hindī* or Indian style. Despite its name, this style was transregional in its devel. and practice, and poets traveled freely between major literary centers in Persia, India, and central Asia. Emphasis on the fresh is manifest particularly in the use of colloquial idioms and the cultivation of conceptual metaphors, subtle *conceits, and other figures of thought. While this style held sway in India and central Asia until the early 20th c. and helped shape emerging vernacular lits. in these areas, in Persia proper, a reaction to the perceived obscurities of this *baroque-like style took shape as the Literary Return movement (*sabk-i bāzgasht-i adabī*), which sought to return to the norms of the Khurāsānī and ʿIrāqī styles. Though poetry in the traditional forms continues to be written today, the economic and cultural impact of the West had far-reaching effects on Persian poetry in the 20th c.,

weakening the authority of the trad. and leading to wholesale changes in poetic norms.

**IV. Genres.** There is no strict correlation between theme and form in Persian poetry. *Panegyric, e.g., is most commonly associated with the qaṣīda but can also be found in the masnavī, rubāʿī, and even ghazal forms; conversely, the qaṣīda often contains lyrical elements and can be used for didactic purposes or for the praise of religious figures, either living or dead. The discussion below is thus organized around four broad thematic categories: (1) didactic, homiletic, and gnomic, (2) *epic and romance, (3) panegyric and eulogy, and (4) *lyric.

Poetry is traditionally the privileged form of verbal discourse and the preferred vehicle for the transmission of wisdom and knowledge. Poetry can teach subjects from the mundane to the esoteric. Two early masnavīs indicate the range of possible didactic topics: the *Dānishnāma* (Book of Knowledge, completed in 980) by Ḥakīm Maysarī presents a compendium of medical science, while the *Ḥadīqat al-ḥaqīqa* (Garden of Truth) by Sanāʾī (d. ca. 1131) uses short anecdotes to preach on a wide range of ethical and religious issues. Sanāʾī's model acquires a more distinctively mystical or Sufi content in the masnavīs of Farīd al-Dīn ʿAṭṭār (d. ca. 1221), such as *Manṭiq al-ṭayr* (*Conference of the Birds*), and the *Masnavī-yi Maʿnavī* (Spiritual Couplets) by Jalāl al-Dīn Rūmī (d. 1273). Even in the 20th c., the Indo-Persian poet Muḥammad Iqbāl (d. 1938) used the masnavī to present his revision of Islamic philosophy. Works like these can consist of several thousand verses and contain dozens of anecdotes and exempla, but homiletic themes also appear in gnomic, aphoristic form, as in the rubāʿī or quatrains of ʿUmar Khayyām (d. 1122), which draw on the ancient Near Eastern trad. of wisdom lit. (See DIDACTIC POETRY, GNOMIC POETRY.) Didactic passages also occur frequently in epic and romance, and panegyrics often include injunctions to the patron to adhere to rules of proper conduct and rule. Even the ghazal, the preeminent lyrical form, may be used as the medium for reflections on theosophy, human nature, and ethics. Throughout Persian poetry, nature and hist. tend to be viewed as *ʿibrat*, as instructive or admonitory manifestations of general laws of existence and behavior, and the wisdom of poetry is to teach its audience to interpret these phenomena. Objects, persons, and events are typically represented as exemplars of ideal, transcendental forms; the particular is of interest insofar as it represents the type. This principle helps explain why mystical Sufism found such a congenial home in Persian poetry, but it holds true for secular as well as explicitly religious lit.

A preexisting oral and written trad. on the pre-Islamic kings of Persia formed the basis for the first great work of New Persian poetry, the *Shāhnāma* (*Book of Kings*) by Abū al-Qāsim Firdawsī (d. 1025). This vast epic tells the story of Persia from the creation of the world and dawn of civilization to the collapse of the

Sasanian dynasty and the coming of Islam. The epic is built around the reigns of 50 kings from the legendary Jamshīd to the historical Yazdigird, but some of its most famous stories deal with noble paladins like Rustam, who play major roles in the battles between Īrān and the rival kingdoms of Tūrān and Rūm. Stories of feasting and fighting often give the narrator cause to reflect on the tragic nature of hist. and problems of loyalty, authority, and proper rule. Following on Firdawsī's example, other figures from Persian heroic lore became subjects of a subsidiary epic lit., such as Asadī Tūsī *Garshāspnāma* (Book of Garshāsp, composed 1066). Episodes from the *Shāhnāma* also served as the basis for the devel. of romance narratives focusing on the adventures and loves of noble heroes, most notably *Khusraw va Shīrīn* (Khusraw and Shirin) and *Haft Paykar* (The Seven Beauties) by Nizāmī of Ganja (d. 1209). But Nizāmī also drew on the legends of neighboring cultures. His two-part work on Alexander the Great (*Iskandarnāma*) follows Firdawsī in integrating this Gr. hero into the Persian trad., and for his story of the star-crossed lovers Majnūn and Laylā, Nizāmī turned to the tribal lore of Arabia. These works, together with his collection of didactic tales *Makhzan al-asrār*, would serve as models for poets as late as the 19th c. The first poet to attempt to match Nizāmī's achievement, Amīr Khusraw of Delhi (d. 1325), initiated two trends that would shape the hist. of the genre. First, he turned to Indian legend and fable for some of his stories, providing a precedent for later poets of the Mughal period to look to Sanskrit sources for their stories; Fayzī (d. 1596), e.g., adapted his story of Nal and Daman from a tale in the *Mahābhārata*. Second, Amīr Khusraw composed epic-like narrative poems based on contemp. events. Masnavīs modeled on the *Shāhnāma* celebrating the deeds of living monarchs and patrons served to legitimize their rule by integrating it with the epic trad., and an imperial office for the writers of such Persian-lang. *Shāhnāma*s existed for a time even in the Ottoman Empire.

In such poems, the epic masnavī merges with courtly panegyric, but the principal form for eulogistic poetry was the qasīda. This genre drew heavily on the long trad. of Ar. court poetry and was the most prestigious literary form in the first period of Persian poetry. From Farrukhī (d. 1038) and Anvarī (d. 1189) in Khorasan to Qatrān (d. 1072) and Khāqānī (d. 1199) in Azerbaijan, the most accomplished poets throughout the Persian world earned their living by singing the praises of rulers, soldiers, viziers, and government officials. Qasīdas often opened with lyrical descriptions of gardens, the beauties of the season, festival celebrations, or the speaker's experiences in love before turning to ritualistic praise of the patron's victories, prowess in battle, justice in civic administration, or building projects. Generosity was paramount among the noble virtues, and the praise poem served as a social contract among the patron, the poet, and society: the patron was expected to live up to the idealized portrait presented in the poem and to reward the poet for his labors. Failure to do so could unleash the panegyric's dark opposite, the *invective or lampoon (hajv), in which the object of the speaker's wrath was subjected to public vilification and abuse. Though praise poetry was a product of cultural economics and political interests, it was informed by a system of social, ethical, and religious ideals. These come to the fore in the poetry of Nāsir Khusraw (ca. 1004–72), whose praise for the distant Fatamid rulers of Egypt and North Africa is sometimes overwhelmed by his critique of the society in which he lived in Badakhshan. Panegyric themes are also often found in elegies, as the deceased is praised for virtues and accomplishments that his successor will be expected to preserve. Esp. after the rise of the Shiʾite Safavid dynasty, eulogistic elegies are also composed for the Prophet Muhammad and his descendants, in which the responsibility for preserving their heritage falls to the current temporal rulers and the larger community of believers.

After the Mongol invasions of the 13th c., the qasīda lost much of its prestige, and literary patronage spread from the royal court to local lords and landholders, wealthy merchants, and Sufi lodges. The ghazal, which began as amatory lyric for courtly song and entertainment, gradually emerged as the preeminent short poetic form. It occupied an increasingly prominent place in the oeuvre of 12th-c. poets, such as Sanāʾī, ʿAttār, Anvarī, and Khāqānī, and it became the genre of choice of the major 13th-c. poets Rūmī and Saʿdī (ca. 1184–1292), in whose hands it achieved its cl. form. The ghazal is defined by the first-person *voice of the lover who describes, praises, cajoles, or complains of his aloof and idealized beloved. Persian pronouns give no indication of the gender, and the beloved was frequently a young male *ephebe*. The ghazal was composed for and performed in a wide range of contexts, and the beloved could take on various identities. While often an object of amorous passion, the beloved could also merge with the patron and the poem serve as a veiled courtly negotiation. In religious and mystical circles, the beloved could stand as a witness to divine grace or a symbol of God. Deciding on the most apt interpretation of this richly polysemous object of desire can be difficult, and the acknowledged master of the genre, Hāfiz (ca. 1325–89) took full advantage of this ambiguity, his poems sometimes allowing readings in all three registers at once. While it never lost its grounding in the experience of love, the ghazal in the works of fresh-style masters such as Sāʾib (ca. 1601–76) and Bīdil (d. 1725) could serve as a vehicle for wide-ranging existential, theosophical, and ethical ruminations, as conventional lyrical images of flowers, wine, gardens, music, and the beloved's physical features took on increasingly subtle, far-ranging metaphorical and symbolic meanings.

Genres in Persian poetry are frequently mixed. Ghazals and first-person lyrical passages, e.g., are often integrated into the romance, as lovers write to one another or lament their disappointments. Elegies on friends or family members praise the deceased but also explore the speaker's feelings of loss and bereavement and meditate on the transitoriness of human life. The 16th c. witnessed the emergence of the genre *sāqīnāma* (cupbearer's song) in rhymed couplets, in which the lyrical repertoire of wine and intoxication is used to represent a psychological crisis that is often resolved by an affirmation of religious belief or political affiliation. Khāqānī composed the masnavī *Ṭuhfat al-ʿIrāqayn* (Gift of the Two Iraqs) in 1157 as an account of his pilgrimage to Mecca, and poets of the 16th and 17th cs. revived this model in versified travelogues and other topographic poetry that cover the vast geographical expanse of the Persian cultural sphere in the early mod. period. The autobiographical narrator describes the natural and manmade environment in terms drawn from epic, romance, and panegyric poetry; praises those who offer sustenance and guidance; censures those who do not; and often pauses to reflect on the lessons of his experience.

**V. Modern Developments.** Western economic power, political thought, and cultural dominance have had a profound impact on Persian poetry. The transregional cultural continuum of Persian poetry was divided along new national boundaries, and local vernaculars came to replace Persian as a lang. of administration and culture across much of its former range. Economic and political changes destroyed old systems of patronage, and the quest for modernization called into question authoritative trads. and well-established poetic conventions. Proponents of new and *free verse challenged the rules of prosody, but the flexible forms and genres of traditional Persian poetry have nevertheless proven remarkably resilient. Questions of political order and authority had long been a concern of epic and panegyric poetry, and this trad. helped inform a new lit. of nationalism and constitutional rule in the poetry of Adīb al-Mamālik (1860–1917) and Muḥammad Taqī Bahār (1884–1951). After World War II, new and free verse forms served as the vehicle for a politically engaged, oppositional poetry in the work of poets such as Nīmā Yūshīj (1896–1960), Siyāvush Kasrāʾī (1927–96), and Aḥmad Shāmlū (1925–2000). The painter and poet Suhrāb Sipihrī (1928–80) dispensed with formal prosody altogether but drew inspiration from the mystical strain of traditional Persian poetry. Even a form as weighted with trad. as the ghazal has found a mod. relevance in the poetry of Sīmīn Bihbihānī (b. 1927), even if her drive for inner authenticity and sexual frankness do not match those of mod. Iran's foremost woman poet, Furūgh Farrukhzād (1935–67). The dust has largely settled on the debate between proponents of free verse and traditional forms, and it is not unusual to find poets today producing work in both idioms.

**VI. Poetry and Other Arts.** As the most prestigious form of verbal discourse and artistic expression in Persian culture, poetry has exerted a tremendous influence on other art forms. Histories, philosophical and theosophical treatises, and other prose writings are often studded with verses that summarize, elaborate, or comment on their message. Even today, quoting apropos verses of cl. poetry enlivens daily conversation. The highly regarded art of calligraphy has often employed poetry as its subject matter. Miniature painting evolved as the art of illustrating poetic texts, most notably the *Shāhnāma* and the works of Niẓāmī and presents the same idealized vision of the world as poetry itself. Verses of poetry also decorate metalwork and ceramics, and public buildings are often embellished with poetry, sometimes composed esp. for its placement on the structure.

■ E. G. Browne, *Literary History of Persia*, 4 v. (1902–24); Z. Ṣafā, *Tārīkh-i adabiyāt dar Īrān*, 8 v. (1956–90); A. J. Arberry, *Classical Persian Literature* (1958); A. Pagliaro and A. Bausani, *Storia della letteratura persiana* (1960); J. Bečka, "Tajik Literature from the Sixteenth Century to the Present," and J. Rypka, "History of Persian Literature up to the Beginning of the Twentieth Century," *History of Iranian Literature*, ed. K. Jahn (1968); C.-H. de Fouchécour, *Moralia: Les notions morales dans la littérature persane du 3e/9e au 7e/13e siècle* (1968); J. Meisami, *Medieval Persian Court Poetry* (1987); R. Zipoli, *Encoding and Decoding Neopersian Poetry* (1988); D. Davis, *Epic and Sedition: The Case of Ferdowsi's "Shahnameh"* (1992); A. Schimmel, *A Two-Colored Brocade: The Imagery of Persian Poetry* (1992); A. Karimi-Hakkak, *Recasting Persian Poetry: Scenarios of Poetic Modernity in Iran* (1995); F. Lewis, "Reading, Writing and Recitation:Sanāʾī and the Origins of the Persian Ghazal," diss., Univ. of Chicago (1995); J.T.P. de Bruijn, *Persian Sufi Poetry: An Introduction to the Mystical Use of Classical Persian Poems* (1997); G. Doerfer, "The Influence of Persian Language and Literature among the Turks," *The Persian Presence in the Islamic World*, ed. R. Hovannisian and G. Sabagh (1998); P. Losensky, *Welcoming Fighānī: Imitation and Poetic Individuality in the Safavid-Mughal Ghazal* (1998); J. Meisami, *Structure and Meaning in Medieval Arabic and Persian Poetry* (2003); *A History of Persian Literature*, ed. E. Yarsharter, v. 1: *General Introduction to Persian Literature*, ed. J.T.P. de Bruijn (2006).

P. LOSENSKY

**PERSONA.** Denotes the speaker (or more generally, the source) of any poem that is imagined to be spoken in a distinctive *voice or narrated from a determinate vantage—whether that speaker is presumed to be the poet, a fictional character, or even an inanimate object. But the *idea* of persona carries in it all the complexity of the hist. of the word. Originally used to denote the mask worn by an actor in Roman drama, *persona* has been offered as a trans. of the Gr. *prosopon* (face), though the idea of their synonymy antedates both terms; and also (suggestively but mistakenly) as a derivation from *per sonare* (to sound through). This pair of false etymologies recapitulates a tension apparent in the term's use: in Cicero's theory of *personae*, the public roles that an adult is called on to play were understood to be aspects, rather than concealments, of the self. For Seneca, the performance of a public persona represented a falsification of the true self that lies beneath.

Early in its hist., then, we find *persona* referring to both performance and actor, to the public trapping and suits of feeling, and also to that within that passes show.

*Persona* becomes an important term for poetry precisely because so much of it speaks in the first person—seemingly disclosing private or hidden aspects of self and subjective experience—but does so in highly shaped and mediated ways, in lang. that bears the stamp of artifice and form. Thus, persona is a conceptual peg on which to hang the distinction between the idea that poems are the sincere expression of the person who makes them and the idea that poems are constructions that use lang. in some other, estranging or objectifying way. Accounts of what that way is—and what function it serves—vary; a poetic persona may be a transparent impersonation, as in dramatic *mono-logue. Creating a morally compromised or troubling speaker like Robert Browning's Duke of Ferrara or Ai's Joseph McCarthy puts the poet in an ironic relation to his or her own words and places readers in a critical relationship to the idea of sincere expression and literal lang. But the use of a persona need not identify a poem as a "mere" fiction. A poetic persona may stand in a complex rhetorical and performative relation to the poet, as in Juvenal's satires or Jonathan Swift's, making the identification of propositions and attitudes into a puzzle or a hall of mirrors (in John Berryman's *Dream Songs,* Henry, the poet's alter ego, has his own alter ego and interlocutor, Mr. Bones). Persona may function in a universal or representative capacity, as does Dante's questing protagonist ("Dante") in the *Divine Comedy.* *Persona* may also refer to the idea that a poem puts forward beliefs, attitudes, or feelings in hypothetical form—as a way of inquiring into what it is to be a self or as a means of operating on oneself. This sense may be in operation when a speaker is obviously an invention (as in Frank Bidart's "Herbert White," which refracts the poet's desperate desire to animate the world outside the self with sense through the persona of a child-murdering necrophiliac); but even "I" may be a persona in this sense, as Emily Dickinson suggests: "When I state myself, as the Representative of the Verse—it does not mean—me—but a supposed person."

The recent hist. of the concept of persona focuses on the tension between person and supposition and exacerbates it. If persona becomes a *theoretical* issue in the wake of the explicit articulation of the idea that the poet speaks *in propria persona,* and speaks so truly and sincerely, then the theoretical *problem* of persona is a postromantic one—and even more acutely, a modernist one. Paul Valéry's "sieved" and "filtered" inspiration, W. B. Yeats's daemons and masks, T. S. Eliot's doctrine of "impersonality," Ezra Pound's *Personae,* and Fernando Pessoa's *heteronyms all in their various ways cultivate persona as a reaction against the idea of romantic poetics.

Translating these modernist experiments into interpretive principles, the New Critics theorized the gap between a thought or feeling and its objectification (see NEW CRITICISM). The idea of a poem as a "verbal icon" (Wimsatt) or "a dramatic fiction" (Brower) may have been initially intended to block inquiry into the poet's expressive intention in order to focus attention on the dynamics of lang. and form; its effect was to make persona seem an entailment of the very idea of verbal art. Thus, the *obligation* to treat poetic speakers as personae carries over into postmodernity in ever-more extreme forms, both as a theory of poetry (Berryman, speaking even of Robert Lowell's ostensibly *confessional "Skunk Hour": "The necessity for the artist of selection opens inevitably an abyss between his person and his persona") and as a general problematic for life in lang. (Paul de Man's claim that autobiography is both a characteristic of every text and "a defacement of the mind" is, in effect, an argument for the inescapability of persona, as is Barthes's notion that "all writing" partakes of a "special voice" of which lit. "is precisely the invention").

*See* ADDRESS.

■ R. P. Blackmur, "The Masks of Ezra Pound," *The Double Agent* (1935); Richard Ellmann, *W. B. Yeats: The Man and the Masks* (1948); R. Brower, *Fields of Light* (1951); M. Mack, "The Muse of Satire." *Yale Review* 41 (1951); W. K. Wimsatt and M. C. Beardsley, "The Intentional Fallacy" and "The Affective Fallacy," *The Verbal Icon* (1954); T. S. Eliot, "The Three Voices of Poetry," *On Poetry and Poets* (1957); G. Wright, *The Poet in the Poem* (1960); I. Ehrenpreis, "Personae," *Restoration and Eighteenth-Century,* ed. C. Camden (1963); L. Trilling, *Sincerity and Authenticity* (1971); *The Author in His Work,* ed. L. L. Martz and A. Williams (1978); R. Elliott, *The Literary Persona* (1982); C. Altieri, *Self and Sensibility in Contemporary Poetry* (1984); P. de Man, "Autobiography as De-facement," *The Rhetoric of Romanticism* (1984); R. Barthes, "The Death of the Author," *The Rustle of Language,* trans. R. Howard (1989); C. Park, "Talking Back to the Speaker," *Rejoining the Common Reader* (1991); M. Perloff, "Language Poetry and the Lyric Subject: Ron Silliman's Albany, Susan Howe's Buffalo," *CritI* 25 (1999); S. Bartsch, *The Mirror of the Self* (2006); O. Izenberg, *Being Numerous: Poetry and the Ground of Social Life* (2011).

O. IZENBERG

**PERSONIFICATION.** A device that brings to life, in a human figure, something abstract, collective, inanimate, dead, nonreasoning, or epitomizing: Oiseuse, the porter at the gate of the walled garden of the *Roman de la Rose,* and her porter-colleagues—both named Genius—in two gardens of *The Faerie Queene*; Mankind in his morality play; Love, Lady Mary Wroth's ever-crying child; Honour, William Collins's gray pilgrim; Autumn at the cider-press in John Keats's *ode; W. B. Yeats's Quiet, who "wanders laughing and eating her wild heart"; Patrick Pearse's lonely mother Ireland; and Clumsy, Mrs. Clumsy, and No-No in Gjertrud Schnackenberg's parlor *allegory. A prominent strategy for poets, personification also appears in ordinary speech, prose, painting, sculpture, architecture, cartoons, film, and other media.

Familiar in antiquity, personification becomes esp. important and complex in the aesthetic programs of the Eur. Middle Ages and Ren., which exploited its capacity for philosophy and enlisted its predilection for hiding the arcane or even dangerous proposition in plain sight. Though often instigated by something as simple as grammatical gender, personification is a way of thought that can generate a wide range of effects and consequences: from folkloric characters such as Jack Frost to the "persons" accorded rights in the medical, civil-rights, and corporate-law decisions of contemp. high courts. Thus, it can act as a figure of speech and as a form of social or political acknowledgment.

In lit., personification is a mode of characterization that, when pervasive, may grow into personification allegory (e.g., Prudentius's *Psychomachia*, William Langland's *Piers Plowman*, John Bunyan's *The Pilgrim's Progress*). Yet it may also make an isolated appearance as a person when a character becomes symbolic in a nonallegorical work. Allegorical personifications are notable for their slippery qualities. In a psychologically revealing yet not naturalistic canto by Edmund Spenser, the beleaguered husband Malbecco transforms into Jealousy itself. Rarely do personifications remain static; even the deadly sins of *Piers Plowman* repent, belying their nomination. Personification is sometimes unjustly regarded as a badly wrought or primitive kind of characterization because of its abstraction. Such a view fails to notice that the purpose of literary character is not always to render an individual person one might wish to be or to love. In its abstraction, personification is capable of considering personhood over the scope of the entire fiction, past the bounds of character. In this role, personification should be seen as a device for distributing agency, emotion, cognition, gender, and the like.

The notions of quintessence and epitome are conveyed by the ordinary expression "to personify": when we say, "she personifies grace and beauty," for instance, we take an already human figure and regard it as a personification. The canonical personifications Christian (the hero of *Pilgrim's Progress*) and Everyman (he of the 15th-c. morality play) suggest that fiction does personify humans (the Christian, the ordinary man), though definitions have specified the nonhuman as the material of personification. Similarly, it is profitable to see the conventional persons that dominate the thought of disciplines (legal person, economic man, the reasonable person, the soul, the object of figurative painting, and so forth) as personifications too, in that they embody notions of personhood that entail complex argument. Considered in this way, all characterization involves a degree of personification. But it must be understood that to say so is to apply personification as an analytic tool (in a way analogous to the practice of allegoresis on a work that is not allegorical) without regard to whether we have received cues from the lang. that fit the work to the primary definition of *personification*. Such a move should not be allowed to erode *personification*'s specificity as a technical term that can identify examples of a poetic device.

Like other devices, personification has many near neighbors and collaborators that help to distinguish it. *Apostrophe is closely associated with personification because *address can be part of the process, conjuring *presence and agency. Personification appears frequently in dialogue and debate: for instance, Boethius's *De consolatione philosophiae* (*Consolation of Philosophy*) fashions its complaints and inquiries in the form of a conversation between the author and Lady Philosophy; and, in *Piers Plowman*, Will's interlocutors are often drawn from faculty psychology—Conscience, Imagynatif, Kynde Wyt, and so forth. Similarly, the late med. morality play involves its protagonist in dialogue with a series of allegorical personifications. When a poet gives speech to an animal or object (such as the speaking Cross in the OE "Dream of the Rood"), the resulting personification may be called *prosopopoeia. In practice, this term is nearly synonymous with personification, though *prosopopoeia* is more a term of rhet. than of lit. crit. *Personification* is best reserved for personhood: in cases like Emily Dickinson's "I like to see it lap the miles," where a train acts like a horse, perhaps we need a word like "beastification." Such a term might also cover beast fables, in which animals are given human motivations and capacities without becoming human figures. Are they humans turned into beasts or beasts into part-humans? A glimmer of personification that does not develop into a recognizably human figure (like Katherine Philips's "courteous Tree") is better identified as an example of *pathetic fallacy.

William Wordsworth abjured personification. Ernst Cassirer saw personification as a regime in the hist. of human intellectual devel., a mode of thought that replaced *myth when, with the waning of the premod. era, human consciousness became more skeptical and less primitive. These mod. slights seem to underestimate the sophisticated ontological theses of ancient and med. personification and falsely to impute a mature rationality to mod. thought. When in "The Knight's Tale" Chaucer moves with subtlety among the many possible shapes of Venus, it is exquisitely effective, amounting to a psychology, an astronomy, a theology, an anthropology, a literary feat, and a theory of art, by turns. She is a personification of love and of the influence of the planet Venus; she is a goddess worshiped by Palamon and his culture; she is a literary character, an *allusion, and part of the epic machinery; she is feminine beauty and its abstract force. Personification is influentially discussed by the cognitive linguists Lakoff and Johnson as "entity" *metaphor, a species of ontological metaphor; yet personification's epistemological functions can be comically overstated, as is suggested by the voyeuristic glimpse of Venus disporting with Riches, her porter, in the back corner of the temple in Chaucer's *Parliament of Fowls*. That the device has important, noncognitive appeals to sensual response is made esp. clear there and in the many erotic portraits of personified love produced by artists in words, paint, and other media over the centuries.

■ R. W. Frank, "The Art of Reading Mediaeval Personification Allegory" *ELH* 20 (1953); A. Fletcher, *Allegory* (1964); R. Tuve, *Allegorical Imagery* (1966); N. D. Isaacs, "The Convention of Personification in *Beowulf*,"

*Old English Poetry*, ed. R. P. Creed (1967); A. D. Nuttall, *Two Concepts of Allegory* (1967); M. W. Bloomfield, "Allegory as Interpretation" *NLH* 3 (1972); M. Quilligan, *The Language of Allegory* (1979); S. Barney, *Allegories of History, Allegories of Love* (1979); G. Lakoff and M. Johnson, *Metaphors We Live By* (1980); D. Davie, "Personification," *Essays in Criticism* 31 (1981); P. de Man, *The Rhetoric of Romanticism* (1984); L. Griffiths, *Personification in "Piers Plowman"* (1985); S. Knapp, *Personification and the Sublime* (1985); D. A. Harris, *Tennyson and Personification* (1986); J. Whitman, *Allegory* (1987); J. H. Miller, *Versions of Pygmalion* (1990); J. J. Paxson, *The Poetics of Personification* (1994); F. Ferguson, "Canons, Poetics, and Social Value: Jeremy Bentham and How to Do Things with People" *MLN* 110 (1995); G. Teskey, *Allegory and Violence* (1996); M. Loeffelholz, "Poetry, Slavery, Personification," *SIR* 38 (1999); E. Fowler, *Literary Character* (2003); A. Hungerford, *The Holocaust of Texts* (2003); F. Kiefer, *Shakespeare's Visual Theater* (2003); S. Tolmie, "Langland, Wittgenstein, and the End of Language," *YLS* 20 (2006); A. Escobedo, "Allegorical Agency and the Sins of Angels," *ELH* 75 (2008); H. Keenleyside, "Personification for the People: On James Thomson's *The Seasons*" *ELH* 76 (2009).

E. FOWLER

**PERU, POETRY OF.** Peru can claim one of the richest and most complex poetic trads. of any Sp. Am. nation. With César Vallejo (1892–1938), it can also take pride in a major 20th-c. poet. Even though there are many splendid anthols. of Peruvian poetry, the sheer volume of Peruvian poetry makes its synthesis a daunting task. Most monographs, like Higgins's *The Poet in Peru*, limit themselves to a handful of poets. In 1964, when the Argentine literary jour. *Sur*, whose editorial board included Victoria Ocampo and Jorge Luis Borges, asked José Miguel Oviedo to prepare a representative anthol. of contemp. Peruvian poetry, the distinguished literary critic found himself in a challenging situation. He regretted the exclusion of many poets, even as he limited his selection to those whose ages ranged from 25 to 40 and who were active as poets in the 1950s and the 1960s. Since the 1950s, it has been customary in Peru to discuss and organize the poetic production of national poets with the convenient and yet anachronistic criterion of generations; and since the late 19th c., a significant share of critical discussion of Peruvian poetry has focused on the tensions between aesthetic and political imperatives informed by the social and historical dilemmas of the moment.

After the seminal *Antología General de la Poesía Peruana* (General Anthology of Peruvian Poetry, 1957) by Alejandro Romualdo (1926–2008) and Sebastián Salazar Bondy (1924–65)—major Peruvian poets in their own right—comprehensive accounts of Peruvian poetry cannot neglect the poetic trads. of the indigenous peoples of Peru. Aboriginal Peruvian peoples did not have a written lang., and their rich and variegated oral trads. came to the attention of most literary critics through transcriptions and trans. Some of the most

important sources of the old lits. were unearthed in the 20th c., such as the poetry transcribed from the Quechua by Felipe Guáman Poma de Ayala (ca. 1535–1616) in *El primer nueva corónica y buen gobierno* (*The First New Chronicle and Good Government*, ca. 1615), a fundamental book of Andean culture. These poems include love poetry of seduction and of parental obstacles to the union of star-crossed lovers, which resonate with the concerns of early mod. Eur. lit.

The recognition of indigenous poetry as lit., as opposed to folklore, was made possible by the pioneering work of 20th-c. anthropologists and writers, in particular by José María Arguedas (1911–69), who argued that the belated acknowledgment of this literary corpus was due to the willful repression of indigenous cultures by the descendants of Eur. colonizers. Arguedas was also the ed. and translator of influential anthols. of ancient Peruvian poetry and one of the first Peruvians whose own Quechua poetry was drafted in writing. One of the high points of Arguedas's literary career, his trans. of the anonymous 18th-c. *elegy "Apu Inca Atawallpaman" (To the Inca Atahuallpa), expresses "the collective vulnerability of a people suddenly stripped of a destiny," as Ortega has underscored.

The interest in indigenous Quechua poetry also sparked curiosity about the poetry of indigenous peoples from the Andes who spoke Aymara and of the peoples of the Peruvian Amazonian region. It emboldened some to celebrate popular and refined trads. by other neglected groups. Nicomedes Santa Cruz (1925–92) wrote poetry evoking the Af. rhythms of his own Peruvian speech and made considerable efforts to disseminate Afro-Peruvian trads., showing how some of them had synthesized popular improvisation and venerable Sp. forms. No literary critic made a more ardent plea in favor of inclusiveness than Cornejo Polar, yet he painfully acknowledged, in his own hist. of Peruvian lit., that he could not "offer an alternative to the traditional typologies of our literary hists. because we lack the critical and historical groundwork to introduce Indigenous and popular contributions into an overview of this kind."

The acknowledgment of Andean pre-Columbian langs. in Peru's literary heritage would have felt extraneous to Peruvian poets in the first few decades following the independence of 1821. Not even the Sp.-lang. poetry written during the times of the conquistadors and the Sp. viceroyalty was considered germane to Peruvian lit. until the second half of the 19th c., in a process Cornejo Polar aptly labeled the "nationalization" of the colonial past. Today, no one would exclude the satirical poetry of Juan del Valle y Caviedes (1652–97), who invented a first-person poetic *persona to expose the shortcomings of Peruvian colonial society; the *epic poetry of Pedro de Peralta Barnuevo (1664–1743); or the *baroque poetry of Juan de Espinosa Medrano (1632–88) from the *canon of Peruvian lit.; and acute scholarship in the first decade of the 21st c., by Lasarte and others, has shown the extent to which these writers are central to understanding the gestation of a distinctly Peruvian ethos that precedes the creation of the mod. state. Refined poetry in the Petrarchan style (see PETRARCHISM) was also cultivated in the viceregal court of Peru, and the "Epistola a Belardo" (Letter to Belardo, 1621) by the mysterious Amarilis (an exquisite local poet or a Spanish invention, perhaps by Félix Lope de Vega) stands out as a captivating poetic evocation in the voice of a female descendant of Sp. conquistadors.

To understand the hist. of Peruvian poetry, it is necessary to keep in mind that the late 19th c. laid a claim to the legacy of poetry written in Sp. by Spaniards in the geographical region that today encompasses the Peruvian state and that the legacy of the indigenous world (and of other non-Western cultures, incl. those of Asian immigrants) was claimed in the 20th c. The earliest poets of the Andean region considered themselves to be people of Sp. descent who had made a political break with Spain, and in the case of Peru, the majority of its representative poets had sympathized with the Sp. crown until after the Peruvian nation was established. An exception is Mariano Melgar (born in Arequipa, 1790–1815), best known for his *yaravíes*, which draw on indigenous forms and themes in his Sp.-lang. poetry of melancholy longing.

Sp. royal forces executed Melgar during the wars of independence. The case of José Joaquín de Olmedo (1780–1847) is more representative of the nationalistic ethos of poets who, until the independence period, were fully committed to Spain. Born in Guayaquil and educated in Lima, Olmedo had written poems deploring the Napoleonic invasion of Spain. Years later he was a member of the constitutional assembly as the nation of Peru was being established; but when Ecuador came into being, he actively participated in its political life and became one of its first heads of state. Peruvians and Ecuadorians both claim him as a national poet, and his "La victoria de Junín: Canto a Bolívar" (The Victory of Junin, Ode to Bolívar, 1825), is the single most important poem about the Sp. Am. wars of independence.

Most hists. of Peruvian poetry stress the significance of the liberal Manuel Ascencio Segura (1805–71) and the conservative Felipe Pardo y Aliaga (1806–68). Inspired by the Sp. trad. of *costumbrismo* (the depiction of local manners and customs), they wrote satirical poems about Peruvian life. These foundational poets of the Republican period, like Olmedo before them, had been previously aligned with Spain during the wars of independence. Ricardo Palma (1833–1919), the greatest Peruvian literary figure of the 19th c., created a hybrid literary genre, the *tradición peruana*, which combined poetry, fiction, local color, and historical anecdotes, presupposing the fluid continuity of a Peruvian culture since pre-Columbian times. The most celebrated Peruvian romantic poet, Carlos Augusto Salaverry (1830–91), expressed intense feelings of sexual longing matched by misogynistic anger and an uneasy relationship with the Christian god.

A positivist and the premier Peruvian political essayist of the 19th c., Manuel González Prada (1848–1918) was also a poet whose clear, sober, and atheist poetry was an affront to the prevailing Christian sensibility of the epoch. González Prada's work was contemporaneous with the rise of *modernismo*, but his poetic search was more in line with a sober romantic sensibility, as he worked with discrete meters, some of his own invention. Restraint was not the hallmark of José Santos Chocano (1875–1934), Peru's most famous and colorful literary figure in his own lifetime. Within the *modernista* idiom of the Nicaraguan poet Rubén Darío, Chocano attempted a sweeping lyrical vision aiming to transcend the Andean world and to encompass all of Sp. America.

A contemporary of Chocano, José María Eguren (1874–1942) emerged out of the modernista trad. but was understated where Chocano was loud. Some dismissed him for his apparent simplicity and for themes evocative of childhood songs and adolescent concerns, but Eguren is one of the Peruvian poets most revered by other Peruvian poets. Ricardo Silva-Santisteban (b. 1941), e.g., considers him to be Peru's first mod. poet. Eguren produced a pristine poetic lang. with a wide but carefully chosen vocabulary, attentive to the emotional resonances of words, with which he creates an alternative reality based on visions and dreams. Abraham Valdelomar (1888–1919) moved away from the mellifluous style of Darío, into dignified meditations about the Peruvian provinces and the family home, with a sense of rueful melancholy. He empowered poets throughout Peru to express regional pride. He also established and edited *Colónida* (1916). The bohemian and groundbreaking literary jour. paved the way for the reception of *Amauta* (1926–30), a jour. founded by José Carlos Mariátegui (1894–1930) that promoted the socialist vindication of the indigenous populations and the reception of a decided avant-garde aesthetic (see AVANT-GARDE POETICS).

This is the context in which Vallejo, one of the greatest poets of the Sp. lang., came into his own. González Prada, Valdelomar, Eguren, and Mariátegui recognized Vallejo's talent from the outset and warmly encouraged his literary career. The emotional rawness of Vallejo's poetry stretched the Sp. lang. beyond grammar and lexicon into compelling dissonances and asymmetries, unprecedented and unsurpassed in the hist. of Hispanic poetry. His affecting directness makes him immediately accessible, even while his poems can defy interpretation. Like Paul Celan, Vallejo has presented daunting perplexities to his readers and translators: his lang., fraught with inner tensions, generates fragmentations, silences, and paradoxes. His poetry cannot be analyzed within a single register because he writes in multiple ones and can shift from one to another or operate simultaneously within several in the same poem. In Vallejo, oral expression and the conventions of written lang. are often in conflict, but his distortions can be moving, and his visual configurations are often emotionally arresting, as are his auditory effects. His ambiguities and ambivalences, made up of embers and auras of meaning, constitute an affront to reductive paraphrase. He managed to reorient the local and cosmopolitan literary trads. on which he drew. His poetry is imbued with feelings of guilt, uncertainty, and intimations that the satisfaction of one's own needs can feel shameful when confronted with the suffering of others. In *Los heraldos negros* (*The Black Heralds*, 1919), his first book of poems, Vallejo faces his theological demons, expressing a tragic vision in which sexuality and sin are one and the same. With *Trilce* (1922), he still longs for attachment and is nostalgic for family bonds but no longer relies on the rhet. of religion to address his angst, reaching his most persuasive experimental heights. In his posthumous books *España, aparta de mí este cáliz* (*Spain, Take This Cup from Me*, 1937), and *Poemas humanos* (*Human Poems*, 1939), his poetry of collective anguish and compassion is expressed with a keener historical awareness and a nettled attentiveness to cosmopolitan concerns. While some have branded Vallejo's most difficult poetry as densely hermetic or as a challenge to the logos of Western culture, others have argued that his difficulties are an aperture into the indigenous soul of the Andean peoples. Vallejo's complete poetry exists in a trans. that the Am. poet Clayton Eshleman took five decades to complete.

As with the poetry of Vallejo, the Peruvian avant-garde made serious attempts to engage with the indigenous. The tensions and contradictions between modernity and trad. informed urgent intellectual discussions of the time. In addition to *Amauta*, the most influential jour. in Peruvian lit. hist., it is important to cite the *Boletín Titikaka* (1926–30), ed. by the brothers Arturo (1897–1969) and Alejandro Peralta (1899–1973). Both jours. made efforts to engage the integration of popular culture and avant-garde cosmopolitanism, giving way to the poetic impulses that were to follow in authors such as César A. Rodríguez (1889–1972), Alberto Hidalgo (1897–1967), Guillermo Mercado (1906–83), Xavier Abril (1905–90), Alejandro Peralta, and most notably Arguedas. There was also an avant-garde current oriented to the populist Alianza Popular Revolucionaria Americana or APRA, the most enduring of all political parties in 20th-c. Peru, which produced important poets such as Magda Portal (1900–89).

In a period concerned with the impact of new information technologies, the star of Carlos Oquendo de Amat (1905–36) has been rising. His *5 metros de poemas* (5 Meters of Poetry, 1927) is considered the first Peruvian multimedia poem in which the written word plays with the conventions of x-ray photography, cinema, and advertising. Its 28 pages unfold into a single continuous sheet over four meters long, and some of its pointed effects depend on the visual disposition of the type (see CONCRETE POETRY, TYPOGRAPHY, VISUAL POETRY). Two major poets brought *surrealism to Peru, César Moro (1903–55) and Emilio Adolfo Westphalen (1911–2001). Moro, who signed one of the surrealist manifestos, wrote poetry of unbound desire, unrestrained transgression, and pain. *La tortuga ecuestre* (The Equestrian Turtle, 1938–39) is his most important book in Sp. He also wrote poetry in Fr. now included in Eur. anthols. of surrealistic poetry. Westphalen has summarized the gist of his poetic appeal: "After reading

Moro one feels trampled under foot and crushed by the beasts of love—inconsolable from the infernal breath that spews out of love and beauty. These demented extremes unleash the lightning that unites, destroys and regenerates." Westphalen's best known books are *Las ínsulas extrañas* (Strange Islands, 1933) and *Abolición de la muerte* (Abolition of Death, 1935). More measured than Moro's, his poetry is concerned with death as it delves into the painful obscurities of love, silence, and the unconscious. Another major figure, Martín Adán (1908–85), was a master of traditional poetic forms as well as *free verse. A hermetic poet with mystical urges (see HERMETICISM), he was skeptical that lang. could give relief to the quiet anguish of an introverted poetic persona who struggles with mundane desires against the deterioration of the body and the fragility of the mind.

In the second half of the 20th c., one of the great figures of Peruvian poetry is Carlos Germán Belli (b. 1927), best known for his remarkable mastery of the traditional forms of Sp. and It. poetry, as he addresses the anguish and alienation of contemp. urban life. Jorge Eduardo Eielson (1924–2006) began his career as a poet deconstructing Western myths and Christian images, but he purified his poetry, divesting it of its engagements with trad., in a dialogue with his activities as a visual artist. In the 1960s, Eielson became intrigued with the *quipu*, a pre-Columbian object made of strings and knots whose purpose is the stuff of speculation. Eielson reduced the quipu to a single knot, which became the central object of his most important paintings, installations, and final poems. As Padilla has pointed out, Eielson aimed to deconstruct lang. in order to reconnect with matter, and the knot suggests his lingering attachments to Peru.

Blanca Varela (1926–2009) was a major literary figure. In meticulous poems, her secure lyrical voice explores intense emotions without a hint of sentimentalism but with a tone that can sometimes be playful and even parodic. Her poetry converses with sights and sounds, music and the visual arts, and is often set in a nondescript urban context; but she has also created a lyrical geography that loosely evokes the coast of Lima as it is situated between the sky and the sand, near the sea. Her lyrical world abounds with homes and gardens populated by flowers, animals, insects, and ghosts. Varela transgresses the semantic conventions of the lang., and to some commentators, these transgressions have suggested the disjointedness of surrealism. Her images, however, are neither surrealistic nor impenetrable. Her poetry is not hermetic. She fashioned distinct patterns of signification. Images like "hacer la luz aunque cueste la noche" (to make light even if it costs the night) are paradoxes that reflect one of the central themes of her poetry: the relationship between the light of perception and the dark force of memory. Among Varela's contemporaries one could cite Javier Sologuren (1921–2004), Raúl Destua (1921–2005), José Ruiz Rosas (b. 1928), Pablo Guevara (1930–2006), Juan Gonzalo Rose (1928–83), and Washington Delgado (1927–2003).

Javier Heraud (1942–63) is the legendary poet killed as a guerrilla fighter before he could fulfill the promise of his flowing, seductive lyrical style. With a post-Whitmanesque ease, the poetry of Antonio Cisneros (b. 1942) addresses social concerns and hist. and brings a sense of presence through the sensual evocation of taste and smells. With the publication of his *El libro de Dios y de los húngaros* (The Book of God and the Hungarians, 1978), Cisneros surprised some readers by his conversion to Catholicism, without renouncing his socialist convictions. Rodolfo Hinostroza (b. 1941) captures the esoteric and occultist bent of Peruvian poetry of the 1960s with a New Age embrace of Eastern cultures and of Sigmund Freud. César Calvo (1940–2000) was admired for his love of beauty, compassion for the bereft, exploration of intense experiences, and idealization of the Amazon region. Other significant poets of this period are Luis Hernández (1941–77), Julio Ortega (b. 1942), Mirko Lauer (b. 1947), and Marco Martos (b. 1941).

Toro Montalvo's anthol. *Poesía Peruana del 70* (Peruvian Poetry of the 70s, 1991) underscores the impact for poetry of the 1968 military coup by General Juan Velasco Alvarado and of a new cultural sensibility informed by pop music, *chicha* (a fusion of the indigenous *huaino* and the *cumbia*), and salsa. An influential group in the 1970s was the *Hora Zero* movement, which brought together Enrique Verástegui (b. 1950), Jorge Pimentel (b. 1944), Jorge Nájar (b. 1946), Carmen Ollé (b. 1947), and Tulio Mora (b. 1948). Other significant poets of that moment are Abelardo Sánchez León (b. 1947), Elqui Burgos (b. 1946), José Watanabe (1946–2007), and Mario Montalbetti (b. 1953).

In the 1980s, the belated feminist movement of Peru made decisive inroads in poetry. Giovanna Pollarolo (b. 1952) and Mariela Dreyfus (b. 1960) confronted Peruvian machismo with a sense of freshness and irony. Patricia Alba (b. 1960), Rosella de Paollo (b. 1960), and Rocío Silva-Santisteban (b. 1963) explored dimensions of female sensuality that Peruvian poetry had previously shunned. It was also a period marked by the impact of the Shining Path terrorist movement and by the dirty war that ensued. Among the most notable poets of this time, one could cite Oswaldo Chanove (b. 1953), Carlos López Degregori (b. 1952), Alonso Ruiz Rosas (b. 1959), Eduardo Chirinos (b. 1960), José Antonio Mazzotti (b. 1961), Roger Santiváñez (b. 1956), and Magdalena Chocano (b. 1957).

The anthol. of Peruvian poetry *Los relojes se han roto* (The Clocks Are Broken, 2005) includes poets who grew up in a climate of terrorism followed by the corruption of President Alberto Fujimori's regime. These poets include José Carlos Yrigoyen (b. 1976), Montserrat Álvarez (b. 1969), and Chrystian Zegarra (b. 1971), who stands out for his renewal of Vallejo's jagged undertones to express the despair of a society unable to process psychological and physical trauma in the uncertain cosmopolitanism of the mod. world.

*See* INDIGENOUS AMERICAS, POETRY OF THE; SPANISH AMERICA, POETRY OF.

■ **Anthologies and Primary Texts**: *Poesía peruana: Antología general.* v. 1: *Poesía aborigen y tradicional popular*, ed. A. Romualdo; v. 2: *De la conquista al modern-*ismo, ed. R. Silva-Santisteban; v. 3: *De Vallejo a nuestros días*, ed. R. González Vigil (1984); *Antología general de la poesía peruana*, ed. R. Silva-Santisteban (1994); *El bosque de los huesos: Antología de la poesía peruana (1963–1993)*, ed. M. Zapata and J. A. Mazzotti (1995); *Poesía peruana: Siglo XX. Vol. I: Del modernismo a los años '50; Vol. II: De los años '60 a nuestros días*, ed. R. González Vigil (1999); *La poesía del siglo XX en el Perú: Antología esencial*, ed. J. M. Oviedo (2008); *Poesía vanguardista peruana I and II*, ed. L. F. Chueca (2009).

■ **Criticism and History**: J. Higgins, *The Poet in Peru: Alienation and the Quest for a Super-Reality* (1982); E. A. Westphalen, *La poesía los poemas los poetas* (1995); A. Cornejo Polar, *Literatura peruana: Siglo XVI a siglo XX* (2000); *En Nudos Homenaje a J. E. Eielson*, ed. J. I. Padilla (2002); J. Ortega, "Transatlantic Translations," *PMLA* 118 (2003); R. Silva-Santisteban, *Escrito en el agua II* (2004); P. Lasarte, *Lima satirizada (1598–1698): Mateo Rosas de Oquendo y Juan del Valle y Caviedes* (2006).

E. KRISTAL; M. ORTIZ CANSECO

**PETRARCHISM.** The term *Petrarchism* refers to the *imitation—whether in verse or prose, directly or indirectly—of features in the It. poetry of Francesco Petrarca (in Eng., Francis Petrarch, 1304–74), who derived his style from cl. Lat. verse, Occitan *troubadour poetry, the It. *Dolce stil nuovo*, and his immediate predecessor Dante. Its rhetorical features include metaphorical descriptions of the beloved's (whether male or female) shining eyes, radiant smile, and physical beauty (see BLASON); exuberant wordplay and figurative *conceits; and expressive *paradoxes and *oxymorons, e.g., "fire and ice" to express the beloved's countervailing allure and resistance. Its representational features include avowals of unrequited love and psychological alternations between fleshly desire and forced abstinence. Its structural features include a saturation of forms such as *sonnet, *canzone (*ode), *madrigal, and *sestina and the placement of poems in a sequence with narrative, emotional, or ritual implications.

Many who embraced Petrarchism were amateur writers who used its features to express amatory travail. Others were professional poets who used it to advertise their writerly ambitions to initiate high-minded literary projects. Still others were major poets who associated Petrarchism with a refined and cultivated style, providing a vehicle to catalyze a *national poetry. Poetic borrowing from Petrarch began even during his lifetime in the 14th c. (e.g., Giovanni Boccaccio, Cino da Pistoia, Chaucer), reached considerable proportions in the last half of the 15th c. (Ausiàs March, Angelo Poliziano, Lorenzo de' Medici, Matteo Maria Boiardo), and became the predominant mode of poetic expression in the 16th c. not only in Italy but throughout most of western Europe, with survivals even into the age of *romanticism.

Lyric poets of the later Ren. approached Petrarch in printed eds. of his *Rime sparse* (Scattered Rhymes) or *Canzoniere* (Songbook) that appeared with biographies of the author and commentaries projecting various—and often competing—views of his achievement. The earliest include antipapal, proimperial glosses composed by the humanist scholar Francesco Filelfo at the despotic Visconti court in Milan during the 1440s (pub. 1476); by the Ghibelline lawyer Antonio da Tempo at Padua (pub. 1477); and by the Veronese entrepreneur Hieronimo Squarzafico (1484). At Venice in 1501, Aldus Manutius published a carefully prepared ed. of Petrarch's poetry, for which he recruited the skills of the humanist scholar Pietro Bembo. The latter then wrote a full-length critical defense of Petrarch in *Prose della volgar lingua* (Writing in the Vernacular, 1525), authorizing the poet's archaic Tuscan style with its Sicilian turns of phrase and its Lat. neologisms as the supreme norm for lyric composition in the It. vernacular.

Later eds. presented Petrarch from still different perspectives. At Venice in 1525, Alessandro Vellutello rearranged the sequence to recount a coherent narrative about Petrarch's love for Laura. Giovanni Andrea Gesualdo and Sylvano da Venafro, both at Naples in competing eds. of 1533, emphasized Petrarch's rhetorical techniques in his deployment of literary and historical *allusion, cl. *myth, and rhetorical *figuration. In 1536, the Paduan scholar Bernardino Daniello related the *Rime sparse* to ancient Lat. and Gr. models. Hospitable to Lutheran reform, Fausto da Longiano at Modena (1532), Antonio Brucioli at Ferrara (1548), and Lodovico Castelvetro at Modena (pub. posthumously 1582) identified scriptural and doctrinal allusions in the *Rime sparse* and iterated Petrarch's crit. of the Avignon papacy.

The result was an accumulation of ideas about Petrarch that influenced his imitators in different ways at different times. In Italy alone, the range is vast, from Bembo's amatory sonnets (1530) to Torquato Tasso's "heroic" sonnets celebrating great men and public deeds (written 1567–93). It includes sonnets written by noblewomen such as Vittoria Colonna and Veronica Gambara about their virtuous widowhood, and others written by professional courtesans such as Tullia d'Aragona and Gaspara Stampa about their worldly amours. Writers famous for accomplishments in other pursuits made notable contributions. Michelangelo Buonarroti, e.g., wrote scores of Petrarchan sonnets and madrigals (unpub. until 1634) about *patronage, art, and religious faith.

In Spain, the prestige of Petrarchism blossomed with the publication of *Las obras* (1543) by Juan Boscán and his aristocratic friend Garcilaso de la Vega, whose imitations of Petrarch augured a literary standard for Charles V's expansive empire. A century and a half of Petrarchism in Iberia prompted experimentation and refinement by Castilian poets such as Fernando de Herrera, Félix Lope de Vega, and Francisco de Quevedo, with Port. contributions by Francisco Sá de Miranda, António Ferreira, and Luís de Camões. The publication at Madrid in 1692 of philosophical, religious, and amatory poetry by Sor Juana Inés de la Cruz, a *criolla* nun in Mexico City, marked its end.

During the 1530s and 1540s, Petrarchism emerged in France with trans. of Petrarch by Clément Marot

and Jacques Peletier and creative imitations by Mellin de Saint-Gelais and Maurice Scève, whose *dizains in *Délie* (1544) echo the It. poet's amatory obsession. Joachim du Bellay designed his sonnet collection *Olive* (1549) as an embodiment of literary tenets proposed in his contemporaneous *La Deffence et illustration de la langue françoyse* (*Defense and Enrichment of the French Language*) to advance a cultural agenda for Henry II's monarchy. His *Les Regrets* (1558) deployed Petrarchism in a satiric vein to express patriotic nostalgia for France while serving the Crown in corrupt Italy. His friend Pierre de Ronsard, meanwhile, presented himself to the king as a professional poet advertising career-centered ambitions in *Les Amours* (1552). For the rest of his life, Ronsard revised and amplified this collection about his love for Cassandre, adding sonnets for Marie, Sinope, and other women; and in 1578, he extended his skills in two volumes of *Sonnets pour Hélène*. Among poets who embraced his program, Louise Labé challenged the women of her native Lyon to follow her example in the Petrarchan sonnets of her *Oeuvres* (1555).

Petrarchism entered England at the court of Henry VIII during the late 1520s with the amateur sonnets of the knightly adventurer Thomas Wyatt and his friend Henry Howard, the Earl of Surrey. The spoils and perils of a gallant life received definitive Petrarchan treatment in Philip Sidney's *Astrophil and Stella* (1591), which inaugurated a vogue for Petrarchism among aspiring professionals such as Samuel Daniel (*Delia*, 1592) and Michael Drayton (*Idea's Mirror*, 1594). Late in his career, Edmund Spenser published a *sonnet sequence about marriage (*Amoretti*, 1595), ostensibly to honor his new bride but also to assert his claims as England's *poet laureate. Fifteen years later, Shakespeare published his *Sonnets* (1609) to complement his career as a successful dramatist. In 1621, Philip Sidney's niece, Mary Wroth, brought Eng. Petrarchism to an end with her sonnet sequence, *Pamphilia to Amphilanthus*, appended to her prose romance *Urania*.

Early 17th-c. Europe resuscitated Petrarch's use of *conceits and *ingenio* (see WIT) in such movements as It. *concettismo*, Sp. Gongorism (see CONCEPTISMO), Fr. *préciosité*, and Eng. *metaphysical poetry. John Donne, e.g., tapped deep springs of Petrarchism that flow from his love poems into his *Holy Sonnets* (1633). On the whole, even in its decadent phase, Petrarchism motivated poets who valued the inventiveness and the lyric value of Petrarch's style. For these reasons, it represents one of the most dynamic stages in the hist. of early mod. poetry.

*See* COURTLY LOVE, LOVE POETRY, LYRIC SEQUENCE.

■ E. H. Wilkins, "A General Survey of Renaissance Petrarchism," *CL* 2 (1950); L. Forster, *The Icy Fire: Five Studies in European Petrarchism* (1969); J. G. Fucilla, *Oltre un cinquantennio di scritti sul Petrarca (1915–1973)* (1982); T. M. Greene, *The Light in Troy: Imitation and Discovery in Renaissance Poetry* (1982); F. Rigolot, *Le Texte de la Renaissance* (1982); C. Kleinhenz, *The Early Italian Sonnet* (1986); T. P. Roche Jr., *Petrarch and the English Sonnet Sequences* (1989); A. R. Jones, *The Currency of Eros* (1990); R. Greene, *Post-Petrarchism* (1991);

W. J. Kennedy, *Authorizing Petrarch* (1994); I. Navarrete, *Orphans of Petrarch* (1994); H. Dubrow, *Echoes of Desire* (1995); G. Braden, *Petrarchan Love and the Continental Renaissance* (1999); R. Greene, *Unrequited Conquests* (1999); W. J. Kennedy, *The Site of Petrarchism* (2003); C. Warley, *Sonnet Sequences and Social Distinction in Renaissance England* (2005); C. Alduy, *Politique des "Amours"* (2007); J. DellaNeva, *Unlikely Exemplars* (2010).

W. J. KENNEDY

**PHALAECEAN.** In *classical prosody, a hendecasyllabic line that has the pattern x x – ∪ ∪ – ∪ – ∪ – x, so called after the Gr. poet Phalaikos (4th c. BCE?). It is used at times by Sophocles (*Philoctetes* 136, 151) and Aristophanes (*Ecclesiazusae* 942 ff.); the Alexandrian poets employed it for whole poems, e.g., Theokritos (*Epode* 20), Phalaikos (*Anthologia Palatina* 13.6). In Lat., it is attempted by Laevius and Varro but finds its deepest roots in Catullus, e.g., Ādēste ēndĕcăsyllăbĭ, quŏt ēstĭs. Forty of his 113 extant poems are in *hendecasyllables, ranging from *love poetry to *invective. These have been imitated in mod. accentual form in Ger. by Conrad Gesner (*Mithridates*, 1555) and in Eng. by Philip Sidney (*Arcadia*, "Reason, tell me thy mind, if here be reason"), S. T. Coleridge (who makes [intentionally?] the opening trochee a *dactyl) in "Hear, my beloved, an old Milesian story"; W. S. Landor; Alfred, Lord Tennyson in "O you chorus of indolent reviewers" and "All composed in a meter of Catullus" ("Enoch Arden," 1864); A. C. Swinburne in "In the month of the long decline of roses" (*Poems and Ballads*, 1866), and Thomas Hardy ("The Temporary the All," "Aristodemus the Messenian"). The rhythm is basically that of a trochaic pentameter. Nearly all these examples fall within the Catullan strain of cl. imitations. ■ Hardie, pt. 1, ch. 8; Wilamowitz, pt. 2, ch. 1; Halporn et al.; West.

T.V.F. BROGAN; R. A. SWANSON

**PHILIPPINES, POETRY OF THE**

I. Tagalog
II. English

**I. Tagalog.** The lang. of the Tagalogs, the largest ethnic group in the Philippines, is spoken in at least eight countries, but most Tagalog poems were and are written by poets living in the central part of Luzon island, where the lang. is the mother tongue.

The earliest poems were handed down orally. These monorhyming poems were *riddles, *proverbs, and short lyrics (mostly in *quatrains). Although other societies have preserved longer poems in the form of oral heroic *epics, no precolonial Tagalog long poem has yet been discovered.

Early poems established the three key features of Tagalog poetry: syllabic meter (see SYLLABIC VERSE), *rhyme based on identity of vowels and *equivalence of consonants, and *talinghaga* (a cross between mod. *metaphor and med. anagogy, but without the latter's religious context; see EXEGESIS). The second feature is best known in its formulation by José Rizal (1861–96):

for purposes of end rhyme, there are only two consonant "sounds" in Tagalog, that of *b, d, g, k, p, s,* and *t*; and that of *l, m, n, ng, r, w,* and *y*. Words ending with the same vowel but different consonants, as long as the consonants belong to the same set, are considered rhyming.

Printing was introduced into the islands in 1593 by Sp. colonizers. The first pub. poems in Tagalog were written by missionaries who learned the lang. for evangelization or by translators of Sp. texts in the early 17th c.; these poems followed Eur. rather than Tagalog prosody. The first pub. poem that strictly followed the oral trad. was "May Bagyo Ma't May Rilim" ("Though It Is Stormy and Dark," 1835), a 30-line poem in six monorhyming stanzas.

Their encounter with Sp. lit. led Tagalog poets to adapt Eur. genres such as the metrical *romance to the native trad. Considered masterpieces are *Ang Mahal na Pasion* (The Passion [of Jesus], 1704) by Gaspar Aquino de Belen (fl. 17th c.) and *Florante at Laura* (1838) by Francisco Baltazar (1788–1862). Baltazar, writing under the pen name Balagtas, is considered the greatest Tagalog poet, having brought the spoken lang. to a high literary level, much as Chaucer did with Eng. and Dante with It.

Balagtas was such a strong influence on subsequent poets that the modernist movement in the 20th c. was characterized as a battle between his disciples and his detractors (see MODERNISM). Ranged among his disciples were political poets such as Andres Bonifacio (1863–97), Marcelo H. Del Pilar (1850–95), and Amado V. Hernandez (1903–70); and romantic poets such as José Corazon de Jesus (1896–1932). Among those who consciously moved away from his trad. were experimental poets such as Alejandro G. Abadilla (1906–69) and Rolando S. Tinio (1937–97).

Working with traditional forms such as the *tanaga* (a quatrain of heptasyllabic lines), the *dalit* (a quatrain of octosyllabics), and the folk epic or ethnoepic, as well as with Eur. forms, Virgilio S. Almario (b. 1944), considered the major poet of the 20th c., integrated the best features of the oral trad., the Balagtas trad., and modernism. Twenty-first-c. poems have extended the trad. to include the *prose poem and *electronic poetry, but traces of syllabic count, consonant equivalence, and talinghaga remain strong.

**II. English.** On the rocky isle of Corregidor, soon after Commodore George Dewey effectively ended Sp. colonial rule in the Philippines on May 1, 1898, the first makeshift Am. public school was established by U.S. soldiers. In 1901, 600 teachers from the U.S. arrived aboard the transport *Thomas* to serve as principals, superintendents, and teachers in the highly centralized public-school system. Since there are more than 170 Philippine langs., Eng. was employed as the medium of instruction and communication; pupils who dared speak their native langs. in the school premises were punished. The Am. colonial government also began sending Filipino students and professionals to various colleges and universities in the U.S., and in 1908, the Philippine legislature established the University of the Philippines (UP). The Philippine Commonwealth was established by the U.S. in 1935, to be interrupted during World War II by the Japanese occupation from 1942 to 1944, and the independent Republic of the Philippines was founded in 1946.

Through the influence of Am. educators after 1898, Eng. effectively became the country's first national lang. or lingua franca. It became not solely the chief instrument for the acquisition of new learning, not only a favored medium by which to represent the Filipinos to themselves and to the world, but a principal means to employment, social status, prestige, and power. The country's lit. in Eng., like its scholarship, was bred in the university, and UP may justly claim to be the cradle of Philippine letters in Eng. through its literary organs *The College Folio* (1910–13) and *The Literary Apprentice* (since 1928) of the UP Writers' Club and through its national writers' workshop every summer since 1964.

In only half a century after the first Eng.-lang. literary endeavors pub. in *The Filipino Students' Magazine* in Berkeley, California, in 1905, the country already possessed a significant body of fiction, poetry, drama, and essays in Eng. It may be said that, if at first the writers wrote *in* Eng., later they wrought *from* it because its use in lit. had been chiefly toward affirming, within the adopted lang., a Filipino sense of their world. By the mid-1950s, "Philippine Literature in English" was already offered as a formal course at the UP.

Philippine poetry in Eng. may be regarded as having passed through three overlapping transformative phases: a romantic era during the first 40 years or so since 1905, a New Critical phase from the 1950s to the 1970s, and a poststructuralist period from the 1980s to the present.

Because the country already had accomplished writers in Sp., Tagalog, and other native langs., the literary apprenticeship during the romantic phase was ling. and cultural rather than literary or poetic. The tension that inevitably emerged between poets' creative struggle with the adopted lang. and their responses to the new historical situation cleared the poetic terrain for their own sensibility and perception of their circumstances. Such engagement with their own cultural and social milieu is already signaled in Ponciano Reyes's "The Flood" in 1905, a narrative poem that addresses the plight of the working class during a natural disaster. Among the romantic poets of note are Fernando M. Maramág (1893–1936), Luis G. Dato (1906–83), Angela C. Manalang Gloria (1907–95), Jose Garcia Villa (1908–97; known in the U.S. for his experiments such as *reversed consonance and *comma poems—he appears in a famous photo taken in the Gotham Book Mart on November 9, 1948), Carlos Bulosan (1913–56; author of the influential, partly autobiographical novel *America Is in the Heart* [1943]), Trinidad L. Tarrosa Subido (1912–94), Amador T. Daguio (1912–66), Rafael Zulueta y da Costa (1915–90), and Nick Joaquin (1917–2004), the latter an esp. prolific poet, historian, and journalist.

In the 1950s, the Am. *New Criticism began to hold critical sway: Cleanth Brooks, John T. Purser, and Robert Penn Warren's *Approach to Literature* (1936) was the standard textbook for the collegiate introductory course in lit. from the 1950s to the early 1980s; noteworthy also is the series of formalist studies of Philippine lit. in Eng. by the Am. critic Leonard Casper following his anthol. *Six Filipino Poets* (1954), incl. *The Wayward Horizon* (1961) and *The Wounded Diamond* (1964). Indeed, the New Criticism is to the present still conspicuous in writers' workshops, book reviews, and judgments in *poetic contests (see BALAGTASAN). Of the six poets in Casper's anthol., three—Dominador I. Ilio (1913–2006), Edith L. Tiempo (1919–2011), and Ricaredo Demetillo (1919–98)—were graduates of the University of Iowa Writers' Workshop. Among other poets during this period are Carlos A. Angeles (1921–2000), Virginia R. Moreno (b. 1925), Alejandrino G. Hufana (1926–2003), Emmanuel Torres (b. 1932), Ophelia Alcantara Dimalanta (1932–2010), and Cirilo F. Bautista (b. 1941).

Yet even among these later poets, the transformation of both lang. and sensibility owes more to the poet's creative toil with lang. in response to his or her historical circumstances than to the influence of New Critical formalism. Political activism in the mid-1960s and the martial-law regime under President Ferdinand Marcos from 1972 to 1986 compelled poets to connect with their social reality, even as they recognized a formalist imperative. There are many more contemp. poets of note, among whom are Alfred A. Yuson (b. 1945), Ricardo M. de Ungria (b. 1951), Marne L. Kilates (b. 1952), Eric T. Gamalinda (b. 1956), Luis Cabalquinto (b. 1935), J. Neil C. Garcia (b. 1969), Merlie M. Alunan (b. 1943), Rowena Tiempo Torrevillas (b. 1951), Marjorie M. Evasco (b. 1953), and Luisa Igloria (b. 1961, formerly Maria Luisa B. Aguilar Cariño). Of these, significantly, four—Gamalinda, Cabalquinto, Torrevillas, and Igloria—now reside in the U.S.

■ **Tagalog.** V. Almario, *Balagtasismo versus Modernismo* (1984); B. Lumbera, *Tagalog Poetry, 1570–1898* (1986); V. Almario, *Taludtod at Talinghaga* (1991); V. Almario, *Poetikang Tagalog* (1996); V. Almario, *Pag-unawa sa Ating Pagtula* (2006); V. Almario, *Sansiglong Mahigit ng Makabagong Tula sa Filipinas* (2006).

■ **English.** *Anthologies*: *Man of Earth*, ed. G. H. Abad and E. Zapanta-Manlapaz (1989); *A Native Clearing*, ed. G. H. Abad (1993); *Brown River, White Ocean*, ed. L. H. Francia (1993); *Returning a Borrowed Tongue*, ed. N. Carbó (1995); *A Habit of Shores*, ed. G. H. Abad (1999); *At Home in Unhomeliness*, ed. J.N.C. Garcia (2007). *Criticism and History*: *A Passionate Patience*, ed. R. M. de Ungria (1995); J.N.C. Garcia, *Postcolonialism and Filipino Poetics* (2004); *Pinoy Poetics*, ed. N. Carbó (2004); E. L. Tiempo, *Six Poetry Formats and the Transforming Image* (2007); G. H. Abad, *Our Scene So Fair* (2008).

I. R. CRUZ (TAGALOG); G. H. ABAD (ENG.)

**PHILOSOPHY AND POETRY.** In his *Republic* (ca. 380 BCE), Plato (427–347 BCE) deepened a divide that had already emerged in 4th-c. Athens between two powerful civic discourses, poetry and philosophy, setting them literally apart from each other. In this, his best-known dialogue, Plato thus imagined it necessary to expel most *poets from the ideal, philosopher-ruled city he envisaged, retaining only those poets who would be virtuous tools of the state. At this moment in the evolution of Gr. culture, poetry offered a view of the world that was still widely esteemed as a source of wisdom, albeit in an idiom distinct from that of philosophical reflection and disputation. However, Plato radically questioned the grounds of this popular estimation of poetry, finding in it instead a dangerously seductive avatar of deception, dissimulation, and irrational persuasion. Put to the test of Socrates' interrogative skepticism, the claims of poets to possess a deep relation to truth were exposed in Plato's dialogues as little more than an amalgam of bluster, error, and confusion. Like the dark, gnomic pronouncements of pre-Socratic philosophy, the statements of poetry were too closely bound to the prephilosophical pragmatics of *myth, popular wisdom, and divination to earn the respect of this leading practitioner and advocate of philosophical thought.

As Detienne suggests, Plato's arguments against poetry express particular historical and political objections to a preceding archaic organization of Gr. society in which the functions of poet, priest, and ruler were not yet clearly distinguished. Three social types, Detienne explains, converged in the earliest Gr. culture: the poet, the diviner, and the king, each of whom has a special relation to truth mediated by practices and institutions of effective speech. Each, he suggests, was a "master of truth," whose authority came from performances of lang. that also produced effects in the real world, bonding the social community in ritual observance and commemoration, communicating between the human world and the divine, and instituting the cosmic rule set out by the gods. Detienne goes on to trace a process of secularization, parallel to the rise to the cl. Gr. civic order, in which a new, more differentiated mentality and understanding of truth emerged. Only in the latter social order, he suggests, do "poetry" and "philosophy," along with "politics" and "religion," achieve their relatively autonomous existence. Only in the city-state order does the poet's speech begin to be sharply—often polemically—distinguished from the "prose" rhet. of other, competing social types: philosophers, physicians, historians, and political orators.

The Gr. historical trajectory from "masters of truth" to specialized discourses such as philosophy and poetry, which possess their own partial and problematic relations to truth, was decisive for later Eur. and perhaps even global intellectual hist. Nevertheless, it was also a culturally particular devel., and it can be compared with analogous, though different devels. in other cl. civilizations with powerful bodies of poetic and philosophical work, such as in India and China. In these civilizations, too, we can observe how poetry, philosophy, and statecraft form an intertwined matrix of concepts, practices, and mentalities, which, in the course of their historical devel., grow more autonomous and elaborately differentiated. Although India, as Sreekantaiya points out, possessed a vast and ancient body of poetry and thought, *poetics was not originally distinguished among the "limbs" of Vedic study (as was, e.g., grammar), nor was it named as one of the 14 branches of learning. It is only relatively late that poetics as such emerges as a distinct topic in Sanskrit rhet. From the outset of the Common Era, however, rhetoricians began elaborating three categories through which written texts could be distinguished: *veda* (scripture), *śāstra* (philosophy, hist., and myth), and *kāvya* (poetry). Each category of text related lang. to truth in a distinct fashion. In scripture, the very sequence of letters must remain inviolate. In being written just so, the scriptural text discloses the transcendent, divine truth that was its origin and essence. The "prosaic" realm of *śāstra*, by contrast, relates to truth through the overall meaning of the text and, by this means, sets out rules and guidelines for right action. Poetry, finally, is primarily a means to bring about a special experience of mind called *rasa*, which relates to a particular ordering of musical notes or words, although rasa is not the order itself but the state of delight that perceiving this order brings about. In analogy to the Gr. devel. traced by Detienne, Indian society showed a similar though differently mapped differentiation of mental orientations to truth, each of which reflected specialized skills and disciplines, social roles, and practitioners (see SANSKRIT POETICS).

In Confucianism, with its strong ethical orientation, poetry was esp. situated as a means of inculcating virtue, and the *Shijing* (*Classic of Poetry*, also known as the *Book of Songs*; usually dated ca. 1000–600 BCE) was included among the four books and the five classics comprising the *canon of Confucian study, along with the growing body of commentary on them. Confucianism consistently associated the arts with moral cultivation. The refinement of one's sense of beauty is one among other forms of ethical discipline that may communicate and reinforce each other analogously from domain to domain. Even political statecraft ultimately may be aided by this cultivation of aesthetic justness manifested in the beauty of poetry and music. A primary focus of Confucian political thought was the idea of the "rectification of names," the appropriate relating of lang. to the truth of things. Other complementary forms of rectification could help foster in the governing elite the ethical virtues that would avoid social disorder and preserve justice. Poetry in cl. Chinese civilization was, thus, highly refined as a specific activity the intellectual elite should practice and, at the same time, thoroughly integrated into the larger, comprehensive system of ethical cultivation mobilized by Confucian philosophy and political thought (see CHINA, POETRY OF).

If Aristotle's (384–322 BCE) work in its entirety can justifiably be seen as the culmination of philosophy as an intellectual practice in Gr. society, so too his *Poetics* (ca. 335 BCE) represents a high point in Gr. philosophy's reflection on poetry, in turn influencing a wide range of thinkers through the Hellenic world and later in Europe, Byzantium, and the Ar. world as well. Surpassing and partially refuting Plato's ontological crit. of poetry, Aristotle's *Poetics* offers the first fully philosophical theory of poetry in Gr. antiquity, as can be seen by three major features of its argument. First, Aristotle grounds his theory of poetry ontogenetically in basic capacities of human nature, esp. in the natural pleasure human beings take in finding things out, their natural inclination to imitate, their ability to think in terms of analogy, and their ability to create patterns of rhythm and emphasis related to the basic motility of living bodies. He extends this "philosophical anthropology" underlying the possibility of poetry into further reflections on more complex structures of human experience such as the organization of events into meaningful narrative sequences ("plots"), character types correlated with social codes of action, and the types of emotion appropriate to different types of characters and plots. Second, he formulates a philosophical semantics of poetry that distinguishes poetry from other sorts of textual production such as the writing of hist., a competing "prose" form for narrating human events. Whereas hist., Aristotle argues, focuses on how things actually were, poetry addresses the question of how things could or should be. This modal character of poetry, which orients it toward the possible and the general, makes poetic statements akin to the conceptual. Oriented toward generality, toward what could happen, Aristotle concludes, poetry is more philosophical than is hist., which remains bound to the concrete happening. Finally, Aristotle valorizes the genre of *tragedy not solely as a prestigious literary form with an important place in the civic life of Athens. In its structured turns and surprises, he suggests, in its interplay of error and disclosure of truth, tragedy also puts on display fundamental aspects of human motivation, knowledge, and experience. Even in the fragmentary form in which it has been preserved, Aristotle's treatise is not simply a technical manual for tragic poets but rather a full-scale philosophical exposition of tragedy as a framework for understanding human existence.

In his philosophical emphasis on tragedy, Aristotle anticipates the analogous and even richer philosophical treatment of the tragic, centuries later, in Ger. idealism; for G.W.F. Hegel, F.W.J. Schelling, Arthur Schopenhauer, and Friedrich Nietzsche, beyond its status as a literary genre, tragedy related basic truths of dialectical epistemology, psychology, ethics, and the philosophy of hist.

Aside from Aristotle's imputation to poetry of a special ability to isolate and dramatize situations of fundamental human import, poetry's historical roots in the "truth-saying" functions of archaic society and its special semantic status may equip it with the expressive means to formulate "philosophical" wisdom of many sorts, from moral epigrams to full-scale metaphysical speculation. Thus, e.g., a long trad. viewed Horace (65–8 BCE) as a poet dedicated to philosophy and capable of subordinating poetry's flights to the ethical

task of educating men in basic wisdom, such as that of the fleeting of mortal time:

> Sapias, vina liques, et spatio brevi
> spem longam reseces. Dum loquimur, fugerit invida
> aetas: carpe diem, quam minimum credula postero.

(Be wise, decant the wine, and trim back your hopes for the long run. Even as I speak envious time is fleeing: seize this day, and trust not in the next.)

Yet as Mayer has suggested, to align Horace's concern with "philosophy," at least in the sense in which that was understood in the Roman society of his day, is a misunderstanding. Philosophy, as a civic practice of truth-seeking, was defined by clear professional specialization and by subscription to one of the highly competitive sects, with jealous claims to special ways of thinking and signature vocabularies. Precisely these features of Roman philosophy, Mayer argues, are signally missing from Horace's writing, despite his engagement with wisdom and ethical conduct. One might see an analogous relation of poetry and philosophy in another poet who, because of his ethical and reflective depth, is loosely characterized as "philosophical": J. W. Goethe (1749–1832). Like Horace, Goethe poetically engages in reflections that are of a high conceptual content resembling the contemp. discourse of idealist philosophy, as in his poem "Dauer im Wechsel" ("Permanence in Change," 1803):

> Laß den Anfang mit dem Ende
> Sich in Eins zusammenziehn!
> Schneller als die Gegenstände
> Selber dich vorüberfliehn!
> Danke, daß die Gunst der Musen
> Unvergängliches verheißt,
> Den Gehalt in deinem Busen
> Und die Form in deinem Geist.

(Let beginning and end contract into one, more swiftly still than these objects fly by! Give thanks that the favor of the Muses promises an imperishable thing: the meaning in your heart and the form in your mind.)

Yet here, too, there is a subtle competition, even a polemical relation of poetry to philosophy implicit in Goethe's stance. The poet does not merely borrow from the philosopher or challenge him in the formulation of truth. Through poetry's stylization of lang., *rhythm, and *sound, the poet surpasses the philosopher in a way that implicitly criticizes philosophy's specialization, its scholastic limitations, its separation of the mind from sensual life, and the gray abstraction of its discursive idiom.

In contrast, Lucretius (ca. 99–55 BCE), in *De rerum natura*, established a more genuine hybrid of philosophy and poetry, imbuing his verse with both the content and the logical sequencing of Epicurean philosophical argumentation. Moreover, he intends manifestly to reveal "the nature of things" in a philosophical exposition of the natural world, which, in turn, as a therapeutic medicine against fear and superstition, may also have ethical benefits for his reader. "Now," he exhorts, "apply your mind to true reasoning. For a mightily new thing is labouring to fall upon your ears, a new aspect of creation to show itself." Lucretius in this way defined the type of "philosophical poetry" for centuries to come. The late Goethe, in the second part of *Faust*, e.g., may be thought to reside within this trad. of versified conceptual thought, along with other mod. writers from Erasmus Darwin's natural historical poetry in the 18th c. to P. B. Shelley's and Robert Browning's in the 19th to Wallace Stevens's and Louis Zukofsky's in the 20th.

Christian late antiquity and the high and late Middle Ages saw a vast and diverse devel. of both poetry and philosophy, but, in general in these social formations, they were both subordinated to the aims and authority of theology. In his *Confessions* (397–98 CE), e.g., Augustine of Hippo (354–430) famously unpacked the mysterious nature of time and memory according to the *metaphor of the recitation of a *psalm. Expectation and memory pervade the entire act of unfolding the poem as the mind passes from sign to sign, just as these two faculties also act at other scales of duration: the extent of a human life or of the whole hist. of humanity. However, the human temporality that derives from moving from sign to sign of the created world and is comprehensible by analogy to acts of synthesizing ling. signs through reading or reciting stops short before the mystery of God, who is outside time and cannot be comprehended by any sign (see SIGN, SIGNIFIED, SIGNIFIER). Nevertheless, in the Augustinian trad., as well as in the later Scholastic and Neoplatonic tendencies, poetry and philosophy are both seen as complementary, partial means toward the mind's ascent to God, who can only be approached more nearly through a mystical leap or the experience of conversion. Dante's (1265–1321) *Divina commedia* (1307–21) offers a topology of ascent up the rungs of spiritual experience through the various domains of mythology, hist., politics, poetry, philosophy, and theology. His *Paradiso*, however, is above all populated by saints and theologians, while poets are mostly found in the lower and middle canticles, incl. the esteemed Virgil, who as "guide" cannot accompany the pilgrim to the highest levels of divine vision.

The most consequential relation of poetry and philosophy in late antiquity and the Middle Ages, however, resided in the practices of *interpretation that could allegorically derive moral, philosophical, and mystical senses from written texts, incl. the poetic works of pagan antiquity. In Byzantine culture, the *epics of Homer were considered to be cryptic Christian allegories or to contain general moral and philosophical truths consonant with Byzantine political theology. In the Latin West, the fourfold model of interpretation developed by Origen (ca. 185–254) in *Peri archōn* (On

*First Principles*, before 231) and Augustine in *De doctrina christiana* (*On Christian Doctrine*, 397; bk. 4, 426) was originally applied only to biblical interpretation; the texts of the Bible were seen to possess simultaneously a literal sense, a typological sense, a moral sense, and an "anagogical" or mystical sense related to the things of the afterlife (see EXEGESIS). Eventually, however, the fourfold method was extended to vernacular literary texts as well, most notably by Dante to his own *Commedia*, as he expounded in his letter to Can Grande, dedicating the *Paradiso* to this lord of Verona and explaining his overall allegorical design. Moreover, because med. sign theory distinguished between two levels of signification—the human, in which words referred to created things, and the divine, in which created things referred to moral and spiritual meanings deriving from their sacred origins—even the most humble description or *catalog of things in verse could take on a variety of conceptual and spiritual resonances.

Much *medieval poetry, admittedly, treats relatively secular historical and political issues or rehearses popular beliefs and stories or is intended primarily to amuse and entertain; highly spiritual or philosophical poetry is a restricted, elite phenomenon, as might be expected. On the other hand, however, allegorizing interpretation was available as a means for elite readers to distinguish themselves intellectually and spiritually from more popular modes of understanding texts, and the method could elicit more profound philosophical and spiritual dimensions of a wide range of texts, incl. those not immediately sacred in character. Within this interpretive outlook, any purely "philosophical" or "poetic" realm thus necessarily blurs over into the broader spiritual, theological domain, with ultimate mystical reference to an ineffable God and the kingdom of heaven to come. In Canto 4 of *Paradiso*, e.g., Dante converses with Beatrice about various philosophical and theological conundrums that trouble his ascent in understanding, one of which is Plato's doctrine of the return of the souls to the stars from which they originated. Beatrice offers Dante this consolation of spiritual allegory to still his doubt:

> Quel che Timeo de l'anime argomenta
> non è simile a ciò che qui si vede,
> però che, come dice, par che senta.
>
> Dice che l'alma a la sua stella riede,
> credendo quella quindi esser decisa
> quando natura per forma la diede:
>
> e forse sua sentenza è d'altra guisa
> che la voce non suona, ed esser puote
> con intenzion da non esser derisa.
>
> (That which Timaeus argues of souls is unlike that
> which you see here, for seemingly he speaks as he
> truly thinks. He says the soul returns to the same
> star from which—he believes—it had been severed
> when nature gave it form; but perhaps his opinion
> is to be taken in another way than his words profess, with a meaning not to be derided.)

Precisely thus, in this allegorical subsumption of poetic, philosophical, historical, and moral concerns into theology, poetry and philosophy could stand in productive, coeval communication in the Eur. Middle Ages.

The It. humanists, starting with Petrarch (1304–74) and Giovanni Boccaccio (1313–75) in the 14th c. and continuing as late as the 18th-c. "new science" of Giambattista Vico (1668–1744), challenged the subordinate place occupied by poetry in med. worldviews, which, in many cases, had been complemented by the denigration of the pagan gods and heroes of pre-Christian cl. poetry. Arguing that the cl. poets hid their deeper intentions from ready popular access, humanists utilized allegorical interpretation to decode philosophical and religious meanings underlying poetic characters and actions, which they also took as distorted figures of real places, persons, and events in universal hist. Petrarch and Boccaccio, e.g., both defended poetic polytheism as the allegorical mask of an ancient monotheism. The gods of cl. mythological poetry had to be seen, they argued, as attributes of a single sublime divinity, with a status reconcilable with the "One" of Platonist and Neoplatonic philosophy and with the God of Heb. and Christian theology. In the process of transmission across time through poetically figured texts, the wisdom of the ancients had been, at once, preserved for posterity and subjected to misunderstanding. This theory thus boldly set poetry at the center of a process of communication across historical epochs and established its equal rights with historical discourse, philosophical truth, and theological revelation.

Though innovative in his powerful identification of hist. with the transformation of poetic figures across civilizational time, Vico's *Scienza nuova* (*New Science*, 1725), written in the early decades of the Eur. Enlightenment, exhibits strong continuities with the thinking of much earlier humanism. Vico conceived of an originary "poetic metaphysics" proper to the primitive gentiles out of which grew all the more sophisticated branches of knowledge. From the crude poetic wisdom of the ancients, Vico wrote, "as from a trunk, there branch out from one limb logic, morals, economics, and politics, all poetic; and from another, physics, the mother of cosmography and astronomy, the latter of which gives their certainty to its two daughters, chronology and geography—all likewise poetic." He thus situates poetry in a complex dialectical relation with the other disciplines of knowledge, political organization, and rational human practice. Poetry stands at the ontogenetic and phylogenetic origins of all forms of knowledge, and more advanced forms of knowledge develop precisely through the gradual clarification of the figurative, imaginatively and emotionally charged topoi of poetic wisdom, the poetic universals that constitute the anthropological constants of gentile world hist. Vico thus sets poetry on a footing equal or even superior to that of the "prose" disciplines in the sciences and humanities, with one possible exception: philosophy as the New Science, which can encompass both poetry and its rational offshoots in a single con-

ceptual framework. Vico's philosophy stands above the whole of human knowledge, unfolding its developmental logic in hist. He offers his readers a poetic philosophy of world hist., understood as the cyclically enacted, rationalizing transmission of imaginative universals from epoch to epoch.

*Romanticism lent further impetus to this elevated view of poetry as a comprehensive form of thought closely related to philosophy, which in the hands of systematic philosophers such as Immanuel Kant, J. G. Fichte, Hegel, and Schelling was seeking to encompass society, nature, science, hist., theology, and art in a single, total conceptual framework. In one of his *Athenäum* fragments, Friedrich Schlegel (1772–1829) compared poetry to transcendental philosophy, which not only expressed philosophical truths but reflected critically on the conditions of philosophy itself. By analogy, he suggested, one could speak of a "transcendental poetry," a "poetry of poetry," that was at once poetry and the outlines of a theory of the poetic faculty, an exploration of the conditions, nature, and limits of the poetic *imagination. Poetry (and more broadly for Schlegel, art) should occupy that medium of the absolute, which is no longer the self-reflection of a subject, as in the philosophy of Fichte, but the self-reflection of poetic form on poetry's own capacities for evolution and transcendence. In light of Schlegel's fragment, one might accordingly observe in the verse of romantic poets such as William Wordsworth, S. T. Coleridge, and P. B. Shelley, a typical shuttling between "primary" presentations of poetic episodes or other subject matter and reflective passages that offer philosophical views of the imaginative or other subjective faculties. Thus, e.g., Coleridge's 1795 poem "The Eolian Harp" dramatizes the ontological dynamics of its own becoming: "O! the one Life within us and abroad, / Which meets all motion and becomes its soul, / A light in sound, a sound-like power in light, / Rhythm in all thought, and joyance every where—." It reflects on the mental and emotional process by which an external impetus is transformed into the poem one is reading. In many cases, one can find in the poem complementary hints about how the act of reading apprehends and reiterates the original imaginative production that first took place in the poet's mind.

*Modernism and the avant-garde poetries of the 20th c. called into question the formal and communicative conventions of earlier poetry and substituted for them various reflexive features of *style, *form, and lang. use; these postconventional poetic means were often reinforced by an implicit armature of philosophical or theoretical ideas. Philosophers, thus, often play an important role for the work of major modernist and postmodernist writers: e.g., Hegel for Stéphane Mallarmé, Henri Bergson and F. H. Bradley for T. S. Eliot, Nietzsche and Oswald Spengler for Hart Crane, R. W. Emerson and George Santayana for Wallace Stevens, William James for Gertrude Stein and Lyn Hejinian, John Dewey for W. C. Williams, Martin Heidegger for George Oppen and Paul Celan, and Ludwig Wittgenstein for a number of avant-garde writers ranging from

Ingeborg Bachmann, Thomas Bernhard, and Friedrich Achleitner to Rosmarie Waldrop, David Shapiro, Michael Palmer, and Ron Silliman. The poets' use of philosophy, however, tends to be quite variable and intermittent, pragmatic and eclectic in its treatment rather than systematic. Philosophical ideas form only one set of materials among others that the poet may draw on in constructing the poem. One finds in Wallace Stevens (1879–1955), e.g., conceptual *imagery that, at least metaphorically, figures the philosophical activity of the mind reflecting on its own processes and powers:

> We feel the obscurity of an order, a whole . . .
> We say God and the imagination are one . . .
>
> ("Final Soliloquy of the Interior Paramour," 1950)

Yet to reduce Stevens's poetry to a philosophical—i.e., a conceptual or discursive impulse—not only ignores the extent to which concepts serve the poet as mere "occasions" for flights of poetic invention but forgets Stevens's poetic agon with philosophy in the name of sensual life, a polemic that we have also seen, e.g., in the poetic stance of Goethe. Thus, as Stevens writes of this invigorating, nonconceptual richness of sensual life in his elegy for Santayana, "To an Old Philosopher in Rome" (1952):

> The sounds drift in. The buildings are
>   remembered.
> The life of the city never lets go. . . .

The poet, in Stevens's view, is not only an acolyte of thought's transcendence but the guardian of the phenomenal world in its sheer, gaudy, vital being-there. More generally, we may conclude, merely on account of their use of heightened conceptual material, such "philosophical" lyrics cannot truly fulfill Schlegel's ideal of "transcendental poetry" or justify the often extravagant claims about the so-called conceptual nature of modernist and avant-garde poetry.

From the side of philosophy, two very consequential mod. defenses of poetry should be mentioned in conclusion: the studies of poetry and "lived experience" by the neo-Kantian philosopher and hermeneutic theorist Wilhelm Dilthey (1833–1911) and the lectures on Friedrich Hölderlin and other poets by the existential phenomenologist Martin Heidegger (1889–1976). In his 1905 collection *Das Erlebnis und die Dichtung* (*Poetry and Experience*) along with other studies of poetry, Dilthey developed a nuanced view of how intense personal experiences of the poet are crystallized through acts of poetic objectification and how, in turn, expressive features of the poem foster analogous acts of poetic understanding in the *reader, who reproduces and reactivates the lived experience that gave rise to the poem. Heidegger, in numerous lectures and seminars on poetry from the 1930s until his death in 1976, wholly recasts his earlier existential phenomenology, originally articulated in *Sein und Zeit* (*Being and Time*) in 1927, in terms of the world-making and ontologically primordial character of poetry. The Ger. romantic poet Hölderlin played an esp. important role in this turn in Heidegger's later thought. From Hölderlin, Heidegger borrowed the motif of the fourfold division of the world as a historically specific relating of earth, sky, gods, and the mortals; and he sees poetry as the means by which this fourfold apportioning of being is brought to lang., disclosed, and lent historical endurance. In one sense, Heidegger's claims for poetry represent one of the strongest philosophical visions of poetry in the Western trad., rivaling that of Aristotle. In the seminars on Hölderlin, the poet no longer appears as a mere mod. specialist in a particular practice of thinking and writing. Rather, he is a visionary thinker standing above social division and pointing a people toward a historical future he alone discerns and articulates. As Heidegger's etymological pun would have it, the authentic poet must ultimately be nothing less than the authoritative *Sager* (sayer) of a "world," an order of being underlying the historical *Sage* (saga) of a people or civilization. Yet despite profound insights into the nature of poetic lang. and esp. into Hölderlin's difficult texts, Heidegger also closes the circle of the long trajectory of Western philosophy and poetry with a regression to the myth of their reunification in a reemergent, postscientific "master of truth," a "leader-poet-priest" figure with disquieting resonances with the *Führer* myth of National Socialism.

*See* ALLEGORY; AUTONOMY; AVANT-GARDE POETICS; CHINESE POETICS; CLASSICAL POETICS; CONCEPTUAL POETRY; HERMENEUTICS; NEOCLASSICAL POETICS; RENAISSANCE POETICS; ROMANTIC AND POSTROMANTIC POETRY AND POETICS.

■ K.W.F. Schlegel, *Kritische Schriften und Fragmente* (1798–1801); J. Seznec, *The Survival of the Pagan Gods*, trans. B. F. Sessions (1953); R. Mayer, "Horace's *Epistles* I and Philosophy," *AJP* 107 (1986); R. Lamberton, *Homer the Theologian* (1989); M. Detienne, *The Masters of Truth in Archaic Greece*, trans. J. Lloyd (1996); M. Heidegger, *Hölderlin's Hymn "The Ister,"* trans. W. McNeill and J. Davis (1996); M. Heidegger, *Elucidations of Hölderlin's Poetry*, trans. K. Hoeller (2000); T. N. Sreekantaiya, *Indian Poetics*, trans. N. Balasubrahmanya (2001); Friedrich Ohly, *Sensus Spiritualis*, ed. S. P. Jaffe, trans. K. J. Northcott (2005).

T. MILLER

**PHONESTHEME.** Apparently coined by J. R. Firth (1930) for a phenomenon related to or included in *onomatopoeia and sound symbolism, *phonestheme* signifies a specific *sound that seems to be "shared by a group of words which also have in common some element of meaning or function" (Firth). Although many students of lang. consider such a theory tentative, others agree on the existence of phonesthemes but warn against excesses in discovering them. That is, since a given phone or combination of phones does not always force a given cognitive reaction, a phonestheme to be effective as a stimulant to the mind or the emotions must be aided by lexical associations in context.

Nearly every phonestheme so far discovered by count or by psychological tests is an initial or final consonant or consonant cluster and—it is claimed—aids cognition when employed in *alliteration or *consonance. A convincing argument has been made by Dwight Bolinger for the morpheme *-ash*, which in stressed syllables of 21 of 48 possible forms signifies "headlong," "hit," or the result of hitting, as in *splash, lash*. The cluster *st* often begins words suggesting firmness or arrest in Germanic langs., e.g., *stand, stable*, or *Stark, stecken*, and has been a favorite of poets wishing to stress those notions, as in G. M. Hopkins's "underneath him steady air and striding / High there." Other consonantal phonesthemes argued for are *gl-* for visual phenomena (*glare, gleam, glow, glitter*); *sk-* for swiftness; *l-* for softness; and *tw-* for twisting motions—e.g., John Dryden's "twine / The sallow twigs." Perhaps more convincing are theories about *s* and *z* for whistling or buzzing; the Grs. and Romans, L. P. Wilkinson says, "thought an excess of sibilants cacophonous" (see CACOPHONY).

Although less has been claimed for vowels, Grammont, Chastaing, and other Fr. prosodists offer theories about vowel symbolism, while Jespersen and others in Eng. conclude that the vowel in Ger. *licht* and Eng. *bit* universally reflects lightness and smallness. In Eng., the vowel in *no* has been popular for death and melancholy, not just with E. A. Poe in the theory about "nevermore" and throughout "Lenore" but with Alexander Pope in "Eloisa" and "Elegy to . . . an Unfortunate Lady" and with Alfred, Lord Tennyson in "Ballad of Oriana" and the song of "The Dying Swan," whose voice "With a music strange and manifold / Flow'd forth on a carol free and bold." The Am.-Eng. low mid-vowel of *dull* and *blood* is, David I. Masson claims, Wilfred Owen's "great discovery in assonance" and presents "the sensuous and spiritual desert of war," but Masson also states that phonesthemes were employed by Shakespeare, Dryden, P. B. Shelley, and others to suggest ugliness, disgust, clumsiness, and sulky states of mind, as in Pope's attack on Lady Mary in *Epistle II* and, again and again, in *The Dunciad*. But in identifying phonesthemes, one must remember the cautions of Roman Jakobson and others (incl. Pope) that the thought or emotion must fit the sound.

■ M. Grammont, *Le Vers français* (1913); O. Jespersen, "Sound Symbolism," *Lang* (1922); E. Sapir, "A Study in Phonetic Symbolism," *Journal of Experimental Psychology* 12 (1929); J. R. Firth, *Speech* (1930); O. Jespersen "Symbolic Value of the Vowel I," *Linguistica* (1933); M. M. McDermott, *Vowel Sounds in Poetry* (1940); W. B. Stanford, *Aeschylus in His Style* (1942); J. R. Firth, *Sounds and Prosodies*, (1948); D. L. Bolinger, "Rime, Assonance, and Morpheme Analysis," *Word* 6 (1950); L. P. Wilkinson, *Golden Latin Artistry* (1963); M. Chastaing, "Dernières Recherches sur le symbolisme vocalique de la petitesse," *Revue philosophique* 155 (1965); W. B. Stanford, *The Sound of Greek* (1967); G. M. Messing, "Sound Symbolism in Greek and Some Modern Reverberations," *Arethusa* 4 (1971); P. G. Adams, *Graces of Harmony: Alliteration, Assonance, and Consonance in Eighteenth-Century British Poetry* (1977); Brogan, esp. 97–108; P. Delbouille, *Poésie et sonorités, II* (1984); J. B.

Nuckolls, "The Case for Sound Symbolism," *Annual Review of Anthropology* 28 (1999); E. R. Anderson, *A Grammar of Iconism* (1999).

P. G. ADAMS; D. VERALDI

**PIE QUEBRADO** (Sp., "broken foot"). Although this Sp. metrical term may occasionally mean any half line used with its corresponding whole line (as the *heptasyllable or the pentasyllable with the *hendecasyllable, the hexasyllable with the dodecasyllable), *pie quebrado* usually denotes the tetrasyllable (or equivalent) used in combination with the octosyllable, particularly in the *copla de pie quebrado* (see COPLA). The use of the pie quebrado has been common in Sp. poetry since at least the early 14th c., when it appears in the *Libro de buen amor*.

■ Le Gentil; Navarro.

D. C. CLARKE

**PITCH.** The frequency of a sound, represented on an oscilloscope by the number of sound waves in a given duration and perceived by auditors as higher vs. lower. Pitch is one of the three elements of sound relevant to signaling meaning and prominence in speech, the others being loudness and length. (A fourth component, *timbre, is not relevant to meaning focus in speech.) Sound frequency is measured in number of sound waves or cycles per second (quantified in acoustics as Hertz [Hz; 1000 Hz = 1 Millihertz (Mhz)]; though medians for the human voice vary from study to study, the median frequency for the male voice is ca. 125 to 150 Hz and for the female voice is ca. 200 to 220 Hz; the range of the human ear is ca. 20–20,000 Hz). Research in articulatory phonetics and acoustics has shown that the sound produced by human vocal cords is actually not single but a complex band or bands of vowel frequencies called "formants"; pitch is, therefore, often represented in ling. as "fundamental frequency," the lowest frequency in a sound wave.

Prior to 20th-c. technologies for recording, graphing, and analyzing sound (e.g., the sound spectrograph, developed in the 1940s), pitch was not clearly differentiated from stress because the three components of stress co-occur. Stress on syllables correlates highly with changed pitch level (and increased length as well); indeed, stress itself seems to be mainly a function of pitch change, where pitch level is raised or lowered from a mid-range pitch where the most weakly stressed syllables are voiced. The precise nature and relations of pitch and stress are still being investigated, a slow process given the number of langs. in the world and the various relations of the two aspects even within the same lang. Ren. grammarians and prosodists, who drew their concepts from antiquity, speak of "tone" as a raising or lowering of the voice. It is not until the 18th c., in the work of prosodists such as Sir Joshua Steele, that real advances began to be made in developing a terminology that accurately described what critics and readers of poetry had heard for centuries but could not adequately explain. Steele's work is based on music, following the understanding of prosody imported from cl. langs. during the Ren. and is, therefore, of historical interest more than linguistic pertinence. In the West, an important pitch-based lang. was cl. Gr., which, according to the ancient grammarians and their mod. successors (though see Allen), used pitch for accentuation but syllabic length or quantity for metrical patterning, making Gr. prosody inherently more complex than the mod. prosodies, which use the same sound features for meter as are used in the lang.

In Germanic langs. like Eng., stress indicates prominence of syllable in the word and of word in the phrase; pitch change is present in more than 99 percent of occurrences of prominence and is, therefore, the component of sound that most accurately indicates prominence. In 1900, Otto Jespersen first devised a method of marking four degrees of stress, from one (lowest). Degree of pitch change from the lowest level (unstressed) largely determines the degree of stress (still today given usually in four, but for some researchers three, levels of perceptual capacity). In single words, stress assignment is regulated by the lang. system and is specified as ling. rule because of the high degree of regularity. In passages of lang. longer than words, stress is distributed over the phrase in a suprasegmental pattern called an intonational contour or an accentual contour, depending on one's orientation to tone or to information focus. In addition, certain intonational contours that rely on tonal shifts indicate questions, statements, *irony, *emotion, and so on. E.g., in Eng., pitch patterns are used to differentiate questions (rising contour at the end) from statements (falling), as in "You need help," which can either confirm or query depending on how inflected. Pitch can even change within a word: every child knows the difference between a "no" that is a "no!" and one that is a "maybe." This example shows that pitch can counter lexical meaning—or, more precisely, that a word can have more than one pitch pattern, hence more than one meaning since intonation is one indicator of meaning. But for the most part in stress-based langs., pitch applies more to the entire utterance than the word. In tonal langs., like Chinese, the pitch itself (i.e., not the level with respect to surrounding syllables) often indicates a different word, hence a different meaning.

At present, pitch, whether tone or pitch change, is regarded as a principal feature of sound structure and therefore of rhythm and meter in the world's major langs. Recent and current research on pitch is concerned with detailed study of where pitch occurs and how it functions in the various langs. and poetries.

*See* ACCENT, DURATION.

■ J. Steele, *Prosodia rationalis*, 2d ed. (1775); K. L. Pike, *Tone Languages* (1948); D. L. Bolinger, "A Theory of Pitch Accent in English," *Forms of English* (1965); I. Lehiste, *Suprasegmentals* (1970); D. Crystal, *Prosodic Systems and Intonation in English* (1969), esp. the hist. in chap. 2; Allen, esp. chap. 6; I. Maddieson, "An Annotated Bibliography of Tone," *UCLA Working Papers in Phonetics* 28 (1974)—551 items; D. Crystal, "Intonation and Metrical Theory" in *The English Tone of Voice* (1975); *Studies in Tone and Intonation*, ed. R. M. Brench (1975); J. Mukarovski, "Intonation as

the Basic Factor of Poetic Rhythm," *The Word and Verbal Art*, ed. and trans. J. Burbank and P. Steiner (1977); *Tone: A Linguistic Survey*, ed. V. A. Fromkin (1978); D. R. Ladd Jr., *The Structure of Intonational Meaning* (1980); J. J. Ohala, "Cross-language Use of Pitch: An Ethological View," *Phonetica* 40 (1983); D. L. Bolinger, *Intonation and Its Parts* (1986), esp. chap. 1; and *Intonation and Its Uses* (1989); Attridge, *Poetic Rhythm*; "Special Issue: Intonation in Language Varieties," *L&S* 48, no. 4 (2005); C. Gussenhoven and T. Riad, ed., *Tones and Tunes, Vol. 2: Experimental Studies in Word and Sentence Prosody* (2007).

T.V.F. BROGAN; R. WINSLOW

**PLAIN STYLE.** For several millennia, writers have used the plain style to communicate meaning or intention without stylistic distractions. In absolute terms, this may be impossible, but a *style is plain in relation to other styles of its time and place, not absolutely. A plain style usually aims to eschew the characteristics of other styles, so it may be defined negatively, as a paradoxically styleless style: it does not employ specialized or unusual *diction, it does not highlight obvious *sound patterns or vary greatly from everyday *syntax, it is not highly metaphorical, and it contains few other rhetorical figures. At different times, it has been regarded as antirhetorical, anticourtly, and anti-Ciceronian. Positively, it is clear, simple, bare, functional, direct, and brief. Such stylistic qualities have often been seen as ethical and political virtues.

As a category, however, the plain style is surprisingly lacking in clarity and simplicity. Although its presence generally attests to a writer's desire for truth, the plain style has proven to be as various as truth itself. It has been linked most often to dialectical, religious, and scientific truth; and frequently identified plain styles include the cl., the Christian, the passionate, (and in Eng.) the native, the Puritan, the Anglican, and the Augustan. This proliferation of plain styles implicitly calls into question both the epistemological and the ethical claims made for the style, which have been challenged by those who find the end of transparency naïve and by those who suspect, like *King Lear*'s Cornwall, that the claim to honesty may hide craft and corruption. Both these objections and the long-standing association of the plain style with true counsel, friendship, and free speech (*parrhesia*) are inescapable parts of the plain-style trad.

Two main species of plain style in antiquity have influenced later poetry. The first originated in cl. rhet., which distinguishes three levels of style: the high, the middle, and the low or plain. The cl. plain style, or *genus tenue*, was originally associated with teaching and forensic oratory; it came to be seen as well as a style of conversation and self-revelation and acquired the name Attic. Perhaps the best-known description of this prose style is in Cicero's *Orator* 75–90; among its most important defenses is letter 40 of Seneca's *Epistulae Morales*, which declares that "speech that deals with the truth should be unadorned and plain." The cl. poets who embraced the principles of the plain style include Horace, Persius, and Martial. They used a plain style to achieve the brevity and sententiousness of the *epigram, the familiarity and flexibility of the letter, the sharpness and candor of *satire, and the freedom and *wit of *comedy. The ideals of the cl. plain style were again articulated in the anti-Ciceronian movement of the Ren. by such writers as Justus Lipsius, Juan Luis Vives, Michel de Montaigne, and Francis Bacon and are among the foundations of mod. prose style in the West.

The second type of plain style is the Christian plain style. Also known as *sermo humilis*, it developed from the Christian response to the form and substance of the Bible, particularly the Gospels and Paul's letters. To classically trained church fathers such as Origen, Jerome, and Augustine, the biblical style seemed low and artless, but this quality could be explained by the lowliness of Christ's origins and by the needs of the uneducated audience to whom much of the Bible was addressed. Christ's subversion of cl. hierarchies, incl. the levels of style, showed that sublimity and plainness may coexist: for Augustine, as Auerbach writes, "the highest mysteries of the faith may be set forth in the simple words of the lowly style which everyone can understand." A plain style defined by its humility, modesty, and brevity consequently came to be seen as a way to express the sincerity and passion of religious conviction and a spiritual truth inaccessible to the senses and to sensuously richer styles. Like its cl. counterpart, the Christian plain style typically addresses its audience in a familiar, even intimate manner, includes an introspective and confessional dimension, and encompasses a wide range of subject matter. But the differences are substantial. In Matthew Arnold's terms (*Culture and Anarchy*, 1869), the Christian plain style is a somewhat loosened *Hebraism to the Hellenism of the cl. plain style: one seeks above all to proclaim the truth it knows with zeal and ardor in order to make it prevail, while the other wishes to increase its store of knowledge through the free play of the urbane intellect. One is a style more of conviction, the other of discovery.

Later poetry has drawn periodically on one or both of these stylistic trads. In some med. Eng. poetry, the influence of the Christian plain style predominates; this poetry is public, didactic, moralistic, and aphoristic. Poets such as Thomas Wyatt, George Gascoigne, Isabella Whitney, and Walter Ralegh continued this style into the 16th c., where it is sometimes referred to as the *native plain style*; it became an aspect of Protestant poetics in poets as different as Robert Crowley, Fulke Greville, and George Herbert. Am. poets from Anne Bradstreet to Emily Dickinson were influenced by a Protestant version of the Christian plain style, the so-called Puritan plain style. The Ren. revitalized the cl. plain style, which Ben Jonson described in *Discoveries* and practiced particularly in his epigrams and verse letters and which continued to inspire Restoration and 18th-c. verse. Exemplified by the poetry of Alexander Pope, the Enlightenment plain style exhibits a conversational ease and flexibility that is both familiar and performative and that has been seen as an element of the emerging public sphere.

In the last two centuries, invocations of the plain-style trad. have tended to be less overt. When late 18th-c. poetry saw a vogue for poetic diction, William Wordsworth called for "a plainer and more emphatic language," a "language really used by men," in the Preface to the 2d ed. of *Lyrical Ballads* (1800). Similarly, in its response to Edwardian poetics, some modernist poetry can be seen as seeking a plain style of true perception. But *modernism generally associated the plain style with individualism and Enlightenment rationalism, as exemplified by the Royal Society's support of a scientific plain style, and rejected it. Nevertheless, the plain style has continued to find exponents and practitioners, from Donald Davie, Philip Larkin, and the *Movement poets in England to Yvor Winters and J. V. Cunningham in the U.S., and remains part of the conversation about poetry, lang., and truth.

*See* RENAISSANCE POETRY, SINCERITY.

■ W. Trimpi, *Ben Jonson's Poems* (1962); E. Auerbach, "*Sermo Humilis*," *Literary Language and Its Public in Late Latin Antiquity and in the Middle Ages*, trans. R. Manheim (1965); M. Croll, *"Attic" and Baroque Prose Style*, ed. J. M. Patrick, R. O. Evans, J. M. Wallace (1966); D. L. Peterson, *The English Lyric from Wyatt to Donne* (1967); Y. Winters, "The Sixteenth Century Lyric in England," *Elizabethan Poetry*, ed. P. J. Alpers (1967); J. Baxter, *Shakespeare's Poetic Styles* (1980); K.J.E. Graham, *The Performance of Conviction* (1994); P. Auksi, *Christian Plain Style* (1995); T. Stojković, *"Unnoticed in the Casual Light of Day": Philip Larkin and the Plain Style* (2006).

K.J.E. GRAHAM

**PLANCTUS.** The mod. generic term encompasses laments of many kinds, often in the form of a *dirge (esp. for a royal or otherwise distinguished figure, whether fictional or historical) but also expressions of grief in exile or as a result of the destruction of a city, amorous *complaintes*, or laments of the Virgin Mary for the deceased Christ (the *planctus Mariae*). The genre, which was not conceived so broadly in the Middle Ages, flourished from the 9th to the 15th cs. and was practiced in Lat., Fr. (*plaint, complainte*), Eng., Ger. (*Klage*), It. (*pianto, lamento*), Occitan (*planh*), Catalan, and Galician-Port. It was most frequently freestanding, but mod. scholars sometimes describe as *planctus* expressions of grief in narratives such as *Beowulf* or the *Chanson de Roland*. Formal characteristics of the planctus were not fixed, but some are related to the sequence and the *lai*. The earliest extant planctus with music notation are compiled in mss. associated with Saint Martial at Limoges. Some of the most famous examples include Peter Abelard's 12th-c. planctus on biblical themes and Gaucelm Faidit's planh for Richard the Lionhearted. Religious planctus were nonliturgical, but there is evidence they were performed in churches, particularly as part of Passion plays.

*See* COMPLAINT, ELEGY, LAMENT.

■ P. Zumthor, "Les *Planctus* épiques," *Romania* 84 (1963); P. Dronke, *Poetic Individuality in the Middle Ages* (1970)—esp. 27–31; J. Yearley, "A Bibliography of Planctus in Latin, Provençal, French, German, English, Italian, Catalan and Galician-Portuguese from the Time of Bede to the Early Fifteenth Century," *Journal of Plainsong and Medieval Music Society* 4 (1981); J. Stevens, *Words and Music in the Middle Ages* (1986)—esp. 119–40; J. Stevens, "Planctus," *Grove Music Online, Oxford Music Online,* http://www.oxfordmusiconline.com/subscriber/article/grove/music/21905.

E. ZINGESSER

**PLANH.** Occitan funeral *lament. In form, it may be considered a specialized variety of *sirventes. Of the 40-odd *planhs* preserved, three-fourths bewail the death of some distinguished person, normally a patron or patroness; only ten are laments for close friends and loved ones. The poem ordinarily consists of conventional and hyperbolic eulogies of the departed (he was generous, hospitable, gracious, chivalrous, well-mannered, wise, brave, all to a supreme degree), a prayer for his soul, and a statement of the poet's sense of loss, the sincerity of which is sometimes open to question.

*See* DIRGE, ELEGY, PLANCTUS.

■ S. C. Aston, "The Provençal Planh, I, II," *Mélanges offerts À Rita Lejeune,* v. 1 (1968); P. H. Stä, *GRLMA* 2.1B.83 ff.; S. C. Aston, *Mélanges de philologie romane . . . Jean Boutière* (1971); D. Rieger, *Gattungen und Gattungsbezeichnungen der Trobadorlyrik* (1976); P. H. Stäblein, "New Views on an Old Problem: The Dynamics of Death in the 'Planh,'" *RPh* 35 (1981); V. Pollina, "Word/Music Relations in the Work of the Troubadour Gaucelm Faidit: Some Preliminary Observations on the *Planh*," *Cultura Neolatina* 48 (1988).

F. M. CHAMBERS

**PLÉIADE.** Although lit. hist. has used this term to designate a group of 16th-c. Fr. poets, it is a misnomer. Pierre de Ronsard (1524–85), the leader of the group, used it once, in 1556, to welcome a new member by referring to the name chosen by well-known Alexandrine poets who had themselves borrowed it from the constellation in the northern sky. Ronsard's friends, however, preferred the term *Brigade*, with its more militant connotation, whenever they referred to their intellectual circle. Ten years after its first and last mention by Ronsard, Henri Estienne used it in his *Apologie pour Hérodote* in confident expectation that it would be understood to refer to the contemp. group of Fr. poets. Yet only in the early 19th c. did the term *Pléiade* become associated with a mythical school whose agenda was then viewed as exemplary and prefiguring the profound literary aspirations of *romanticism.

Although membership in the Pléiade varied with the years, it did not at any time exceed seven. Four major poets had lifetime status: Joachim du Bellay (ca. 1522–60), Jean-Antoine de Baïf (1532–89), Étienne Jodelle (1532–73), and Pontus de Tyard (1521–1605). In 1555, two early members, Guillaume Des Autels (1529–81) and Jean de La Péruse (1529–54), were replaced by Jacques Peletier (1517–82) and Remy Belleau (1528–77). According to Ronsard's first biographer, Claude Binet, the name of Peletier was eventually replaced by that of the poet's teacher, Jean Dorat (1508–

88), one of the great Hellenists of the Fr. Ren. Three members of the Pléiade were influential contributors to Fr. poetic theory of the Ren.: Peletier, du Bellay, and Ronsard himself. As early as 1541, Peletier had published a trans. of Horace's *Ars poetica* prefaced by remarks of his own that enunciated the fundamental principle later adopted by Ronsard and his associates: that Fr. writers should *defend* and *illustrate* (i.e., render illustrious) their own lang. by writing in Fr., not Lat. or Gr. In 1555, Peletier published his *Art poétique* in which he reaffirmed the position he had adopted in the 1541 preface to *Ars poetica*, insisted on the divine nature of poetry, and discussed the relationship between technique and native endowment, the function of imitation, the varieties of poetic subjects, and genres (Patterson; see RENAISSANCE POETICS).

In matters of theory, both du Bellay and Ronsard may be called disciples of Peletier. The former published in 1549 the renowned *Deffence et illustration de la langue françoyse*, which, though it followed by eight or more years Peletier's preface, became, because it arrived precisely at the right moment and because of the intensity of its lang., the *manifesto of the new "school." Du Bellay blames the alleged poverty of the Fr. lang. of his time on the unwillingness of earlier generations of Frenchmen to devote their energies to its cultivation. Intrinsically, he says, it is capable of the highest reaches of poetic and philosophic expression and need not bow in these respects before any of the langs. of antiquity or mod. times. This is the essence of his *deffence*. As for the *illustration*, du Bellay rejects the position that trans. of the great classics into Fr. can of itself suffice to raise Fr. literature to a status of equality with Gr., Lat., or It. The Fr. poet needs so intimate a knowledge of the classics and of the more important mod. lits. that their substance will become part of his own and that ideally his imitation of them will result in a natural assimilation and transformation.

The *Abrégé de l'art poétique françois* of Ronsard (1565) is a brief practical handbook intended for the young beginner in poetry. Like Peletier and du Bellay, Ronsard's fundamental premise is that the poet must write in Fr., although he too demands that the would-be writer possess as profound a cl. instruction as possible. He demands that the poet, who for him is the inspired prophet of the Muses, should hold them "in singular veneration and never reduce them to a position of dishonorable servitude" (*Œuvres complètes,* 1993).

To form a clear idea of the contribution of the Pléiade in the area of poetic practice, it is useful to consider each member's accomplishments and, in the works of these poets, which features proved to be the most creative and enduring. Baïf, although innovative in many ways (he founded the Fr. Academy of Poetry and Music in 1570), unsuccessfully tried to adopt a Greco-Lat. quantitative meter (see CLASSICAL PROSODY, METER, QUANTITY), which proved unfit to Fr. ears. Belleau, a gifted trans. of Anacreon, obtains striking effects in praising natural objects like the cherry, the oyster, or the snail (what he calls "petites inventions") and the mystical virtues of precious stones (1576). Tyard, Leone Ebreo's able trans. and a theorist of Neoplatonism, makes a powerful case for poetry as "divine fury" (see FUROR POETICUS). Jodelle's stand against *Petrarchism makes him the most unruly member of the group. He is also the author of *Cléopâtre captive*, the first *tragedy of the Fr. repertory. With the exception of Ronsard, du Bellay outstripped the other members of the Pléiade in his mastery of the *sonnet, in the music of his syllables (see SYLLABIC VERSE), and in expressiveness of inner feeling, esp. the nostalgia of his Roman poetry in his *Antiquités*, imitated by Edmund Spenser, and the satire of It. mores in his *Regrets*. The range and the quality of the poetic activity of Ronsard, however, place him unquestionably above his colleagues.

Ronsard's sense of the dignity of his poetic calling is reflected in the cl. and It. forms that he chose: the *ode, the sonnet, the *elegy, the *eclogue. The technical mastery that he amply demonstrates in these is matched by sound placement, concrete *diction, grace of expression, and rhythm in a wide variety of metrical forms. His sure taste seized on the *alexandrine and demonstrated for all time its peculiar suitability to the Fr. tongue. To embellish his verse, Ronsard made bold and broad use of the abundant resources of cl. mythology. He imparted renewed validity to the legends of antiquity by adopting them as his principal mode of figurative expression, at a time that these myths were still perceived by some with mistrust. In his hands, myth became the means of exploring the many facets of human experience.

If Ronsard's leadership of the Pléiade springs from the wider range of form and theme that he deploys, it is, nevertheless, as a poet of love that he excels. In this key area, he seeks and finds originality by adroit exploitation of both Petrarchan and Neoplatonic *topoi* (see TOPOS), through which devices he expresses his sufferings on the one hand and idealizes the object of his love on the other. Yet over and above the traditional erotic imagery, Ronsard weaves into his *love poetry a perception of *nature that is at once fresh and intimate. Few poets have been able to capture the exquisite mingling of beauty and ephemerality that haunts the celebrated *Ode à Cassandre*. At this level, Ronsard achieves his goal of rivaling the ancient poets, while leaving for posterity a practical aesthetic.

Soon after Ronsard's death (1585), François de Malherbe (1555–1628) campaigned against the Pléiade's aesthetic inadequacies (lack of regularity, excessive imagery, uncontrolled ling. creation) as the idea of "progress" developed in the arts and sciences. For the next two centuries, Ronsard and his friends were lumped together as representatives of pedantic erudition and bad taste. They finally rose from the grave where the Enlightenment had buried them with C. A. Sainte-Beuve's polemical efforts in his *Tableau de la poésie française* (1828). As the romantic period begins, qualities of subjective lyricism, equally present in the poets of the Pléiade but neglected during the period of Fr. *classicism, came once more to the fore. The influence of the Pléiade was thus durable and pervasive, and it is fair to

say that the principles laid down by Peletier, du Bellay, and Ronsard have not lost their vigor, except among poets for whom harmony and sonority take precedence over communication.

*See* FRANCE, POETRY OF; FRENCH PROSODY; RENAISSANCE POETRY.

■ C. A. Sainte-Beuve, *Tableau historique et critique de la poésie française* (1828); Patterson; H. Chamard, *Histoire de la Pléiade*, 4 v. (1939–41); R. J. Clements, *The Critical Theory and Practice of the Pléiade* (1942); *Critical Prefaces of the French Renaissance*, ed. B. Weinberg (1950); F. Desonay, *Ronsard, poète de l'amour*, 3 v. (1952–59); H. Weber, *La Création poétique au XVIe siècle en France* (1956); I. Silver, *Ronsard and the Hellenic Renaissance in France*, v. 1: *Ronsard and the Greek Epic*, (1961); v. 2: *Ronsard and the Grecian Lyre*, Part I (1981), Part II (1985), Part III (1987); *The Intellectual Evolution of Ronsard*, v. 1: *The Formative Influences* (1969); v. 2: *Ronsard's General Theory of Poetry* (1973); v. 3: *Ronsard's Philosophic Thought* (1992); G. Castor, *Pléiade Poetics* (1964); D. Stone, *Ronsard's Sonnet Cycles* (1966); F. Gray, *Anthologie de la poésie française au XVIe siècle* (1967); E. Armstrong, *Ronsard and the Age of Gold* (1968); H. W. Wittschier, *Die Lyrik der Pléiade* (1971); G. Demerson, *La Mythologie dans l'œuvre de la Pléiade* (1972); *Ronsard the Poet*, ed. T. Cave (1973); I. D. McFarlane, *Renaissance France, 1470–1589* (1974); F. Rigolot, *Poétique et onomastique* (1977); M. Quainton, *Ronsard's Ordered Chaos* (1980); M. McGowan, *Ideal Forms in the Age of Ronsard* (1985); Y. Bellenger, *La Pléiade* (1988); *A New History of French Literature*, ed. D. Hollier (1989); *Traités de poétique et rhétorique de la Renaissance*, ed. F. Goyet (1990); G. H. Tucker, *The Poet's Odyssey* (1990); F. Rouget, *L'Apothéose d'Orphée* (1994); H. Campangne, *Mythologie et rhétorique aux XVe et XVIe siècles* (1996); C. Faisant, *Mort et résurrection de la Pléiade* (1998); *CHLC*, v. 3, ed. G. P. Norton (1999); *Poétiques de la Renaissance*, ed. P. Galand and F. Hallyn (2001); *Lyrics of the French Renaissance*, ed. N. Shapiro and H. Glidden (2002); F. Rigolot, *Poésie et Renaissance* (2002); C. Alduy, *Politique des "Amours"* (2007); D. Maira, *Typosine, la dixième Muse* (2007).

F. RIGOLOT

**PLOCE,** ploche (Gr., "plaiting"; Lat. *iteratio*). The genus of figures for word repetition, with or without intervening words, generally in proximity in the clause or line; commonly conflated with *epizeuxis*. Quintilian and Herodian define *epizeuxis* as repetition with no words intervening, while George Puttenham in the *Arte of English Poesie* (1589) defines *ploce* as "speedy iteration of one word but with some little intermission by inserting one or two words between." Examples of ploce include Euripides' "O mortal man, think mortal thoughts" (*Alcestis* I), Philip Sidney's "Even those sad words in sad me did breed" (*Astrophil and Stella* 58.14) and Alexander Pope's "Where Wigs with Wigs, with Sword-knots Sword-knots strive, / Beaus banish Beaus, and Coaches Coaches drive" (*The Rape of the Lock* 101–2). Examples of epizeuxis are Shakespeare's "Never, never, never, never,

never" and "Then kill, kill, kill, kill, kill, kill" from *King Lear*, and "Tomorrow, and tomorrow, and tomorrow" and "O horror, horror, horror" from *Macbeth*. Representative examples from the 19th c. include Alfred, Lord Tennyson's poem "Break! Break! Break!" and many of G. M. Hopkins's poems, e.g., "The Leaden Echo and the Golden Echo," which includes both "to despair, to despair, / Despair, despair, despair, despair" and "We follow, now we follow.—Yonder, yes yonder, yonder, yonder, / Yonder." Twentieth-c. Am. poet Stephen Crane employs both ploce and epizeuxis in his poem "In the Desert." Both poetic figures are widespread in 20th- and 21st-c. poetry. Epizeuxis is common in hip-hop lyrics (e.g., Flo Rida's "Low").

Johannes Susenbrotus writes in *Epitome troporum ac schematum* (1563) that epizeuxis is valuable "for the sake of greater vehemence" in speech, imitating the iterations natural to moments of great emotion. Sometimes the meaning of the word may be altered by its repetition. Some scholars argue that vehement repetition indicates avoidance or repression, while others believe that ploce concerns simple iterations of a word without a shift in its grammatical form or meaning.

More complex rhetorical figures that deploy word repetition in syntax are *anaphora (word-repetition at beginnings), epistrophe (at ends), symploce (a combination of the two preceding, i.e., one word repeated at beginnings), *epanalepsis (same word repeated at beginning and at end), and *anadiplosis (word at end of one line repeated at beginning of the next). In written poetic forms, these figures take advantage of the heightened visibility offered by the special status of boundaries in the flow of discourse; in performance poetry, these repetitions often provide formal structure in the absence of a visible poem. Hip-hop lyrics often employ repetitive wordplay to emphasize *syncopation with the musical beat.

*See* POLYPTOTON.

■ A. Smith, "The Philosophy of Poetry," *Blackwoods* 38 (1835); C. Walz, *Rhetores Graeci*, 9 v. (1832–36); M. Joseph, *Shakespeare's Use of the Arts of Language* (1947); L. A. Sonnino, *Handbook to Sixteenth-Century Rhetoric* (1968); A. Quinn, *Figures of Speech* (1982); Vickers, *Defence*; Corbett; A. Pilkington, *Poetic Effects* (2000); P. Hammond, *Figuring Sex between Men from Shakespeare to Rochester* (2002); A. Ribeiro, "Intending to Repeat: A Definition of Poetry," *JAAC* 65 (2007); M. Cavitch, "Stephen Crane's Refrain," *ESQ* 54 (2008).

T.V.F. BROGAN; M. MARTIN

**PLOT** may be defined as the pattern or structure of textual events. Conceptions of plot vary, but common to most of them is the notion of a sequence of actions related by chronology and perhaps also by causality. While some theorists use the term to designate any textual design, plot is more commonly considered a feature of temporal structures. Although plot has traditionally been associated with drama, epic, and prose fiction, it may figure in any genre, from sonnet (e.g., John Milton's "Methought I saw my late espousèd Saint") to painting (e.g., William Hogarth's "Rake's

Progress"). Though technically plot may refer to any sequence of actions in a text, it is also usually associated with event structures that can be related to textual themes. As Frye conceives it, e.g., plot is theme in movement; theme is plot at rest. Most narrative theorists consider plot an element of a text's deep structure, independent of the precise lang. or surface form of a work, and thus able to be translated, summarized, or transposed to another medium: thus, a single plot—say, Figaro's marriage—can be represented as a drama, opera, verse narrative, film, or summary. Some theorists (e.g., Smith) maintain, however, that these different retellings are necessarily distinct versions and thus arguably different plots.

Until the 20th c., analyses of plot were framed almost entirely within the terms given by Aristotle, for whom plot is the most essential element of dramatic art. Aristotle's *Poetics* defines plot (*mythos*) as "the imitation of the action" and "the arrangement of the incidents," stressing at once the content and its representational form. Aristotle favors "whole and complete" plots that include a "beginning, a middle, and an end"; involve a change of fortune that seems probable or inevitable rather than accidental or mechanical; and retain a strict unity of action, "so that, if any part is displaced or deleted, the whole plot is disturbed and dislocated." The best plots develop through recognition (*anagnorisis*, a change from ignorance to knowledge) and reversal (*peripeteia*, a corresponding change of situation to its opposite). Particularly when events are "unexpectedly interconnected," the well-wrought tragic plot creates the experience of pity and terror that Aristotle considers the project of tragedy (see CATHARSIS). Aristotle also believes that different genres necessitate different forms of plot: a "double" plot is appropriate to *comedy, in which "the good are rewarded and the bad punished," while in *tragedy, a "single" plot represents a hero's suffering.

Although plot does indeed dominate the literary works that Aristotle analyzes, his privileging of plot over character and his strictures for good plotting have been challenged as historically and culturally contingent. Esp. in explorations of mod. lit., with its focus on individual psychology and inner life, character has been considered more important than plot, and a focus on plot has sometimes been seen as a deterrent to the representation of character. Henry James's "The Art of Fiction" (1884) mediates the argument by asking, "What is character but the illustration of incident? What is incident but the revelation of character?" Other theorists have argued that the tightly wrought, logical plot, with its corresponding aesthetic of closure and unity, assumes a deterministic universe. Some theorists have likewise challenged Forster's cl. distinction between plot—a causal sequence of events—and story—a mere temporal succession—rejecting the association of plot with causality and even arguing (e.g., Richardson) that textual sequence suffices to constitute a plot. Some feminist and queer theorists (e.g., de Lauretis, Miller, Lanser, and Farwell) suggest that plots may be structured through (hierarchical) distinctions of gender and sexuality attendant upon social practices, while postcolonial and race critics (e.g., Gates) have described hybrid plot forms born of cross-cultural contact and conflict. Under such reconceptions, narratives that Aristotelian poetics might have deemed "plotless" or "poorly plotted" become signs of social difference, cultural resistance, or literary diversity.

During the early decades of the 20th c., critical attention both to character and to the *"close reading" of texts led some scholars to deem plot scarcely worth critical analysis. At the same time, however, formally oriented theorists, less interested in prescribing and evaluating plots than in identifying their distinguishing features and potential dynamics, began to give plot a renewed prominence. Propp broke new ground in identifying 31 "functions," or actions defined "from the point of view of [their] significance for the course of action of the tale as a whole," that occur in invariant order (though not invariant number) in every Rus. tale. Viktor Shklovsky proposed in 1919 what became a widely accepted understanding of plot by distinguishing between events as ordered in the content of the story (*fabula*) and events as the text arranges and presents them (*sjuzet*), a distinction that Fr. *structuralism more or less replicates in the terms *histoire* and *récit*. The work of these early analysts was continued in the Fr. *structuralism of the 1960s as scholars of narrative (often called "narratologists") sought to identify the specific mechanisms or "grammar" of plot. Genette influentially analyzed the relationship through his exploration of narrative *order*, attending in particular to temporal features that reshape story into plot. Within this framework, plot comes to be a function of the relationship between the story's chronological events (*histoire*) and the order and manner in which they are revealed in the temporality and spatiality of the text (*récit*).

Abstracting from Propp's notion of functions, other narrative theorists have explored the "verbal" position of action within a narrative "grammar" (e.g., Todorov) and the interrelated temporal and thematic reversals that plot effects (Greimas). Bremond's "logic of narrative" proposes that every event sequence opens a binary of actualization vs. nonactualization, which can open a further binary of success or failure, so that all plot relies on a continual tension between contrary forces. Pavel likewise formulates plot in terms of "moves," each of which is defined as "the choice of an action among a number of alternatives" in a rule-governed situation. Ryan's influential concept of "possible worlds" extends Bremond's notion to see plot as the "network of possibilities" that readers of narrative anticipate; by incorporating virtual domains that reside only in the minds of characters, Ryan sees plot as emerging from the interaction between actual and virtual realities. Bakhtin has usefully added the concept of *chronotope*, through which narratives plot along time-space trajectories, which are deployed differently in different genres and historical contexts. Within these various models, plot becomes a complex structure in which multiple textual elements (order, pacing, point of view) participate.

Although such investigations of plot seem to assume a set of structures inherent in the text, many mod. critics see plot as a construction undertaken by readers according to a set of conventions learned through the practice of reading. As Culler puts it, "the reader must organize the plot as a passage from one state to another and this passage or movement must be such that it serves as a representation of theme. The end must be made a transformation of the beginning so that meaning can be drawn from the perception of resemblance and difference." Plot thus becomes a reading effect that may be imposed upon the most unconventional narratives to render them intelligible and orderly. When understood as constituted by and constituting the interrelationship among all textual elements, plot becomes, phenomenologically, "the intelligible whole that governs a succession of events in any story" (Ricoeur). Taking impetus from dynamic, reader-oriented narrative inquiries, cognitively oriented narratologists (e.g., Herman, Fludernik, Dannenberg) have begun to explore the mental operations by which readers process plots and the ways in which narrative capacities and plot forms have intersected with human social devel. (Zunshine, Flesch).

Distinguishing among types of plot is a continuing critical project that dates from Aristotle's distinctions between tragedy and comedy. Frye's *Anatomy of Criticism*, attempting to classify the whole of lit. through intersecting typologies, names four *mythoi* or generic plots: comedy, which typically involves movement from one society to another, usually through marriage; romance, which carries forth the adventure or quest plot; tragedy, which emphasizes the individual whose fall brings about the disintegration of family or society; and irony or satire, which represent struggles between societies or social norms. Categorizations of plot are famously myriad: Crane categorizes plots by subject matter and Ryan by narrative world types, while Todorov looks within a seemingly unified genre—the detective novel—to distinguish the formal dynamics of the "whodunit" from those of the "thriller."

Psychoanalytic theorists, often synthesizing cl. and postmod. notions of plot, have added a further dimension to our understanding of the term in arguing that plot forms articulate unconscious as well as conscious desires. Sophocles' *Oedipus Rex*, e.g., exposes human psychodynamics as Oedipus is taken over by the discourse of the oracle and not only lives out but fails to recognize the horror of his deeds until his need to know becomes imperative. *Oedipus* thus exposes a plot beneath the plot: a chaotic story that threatens to disturb the coherence of the traditional plot, which becomes, in turn, an effort both to repress and to articulate desire. The reader's construction of plot may then be seen as a response not simply to learned conventions but to deeper needs for certain kinds of revelation, repetition, and control. Thus, in ways that evoke Aristotle's notion of catharsis, psychoanalytic critics (e.g., Brooks) see plot not only as inscribing structures of desire but as drawing readers into displaced engagements with their own desires, incl. the wish, already apparent in

*Oedipus*, for a mastery that cannot be attained. And as it is in the nature of desire that it will be endlessly repeated, never completely fulfilled or understood, people will always be "reading for the plot."

See ARGUMENT, NARRATIVE POETRY, STRUCTURE.

■ *Aristotle on the Art of Poetry*, trans. L. Cooper (1913); E. M. Forster, *Aspects of the Novel* (1927); V. Propp, *Morphology of the Folktale,* trans. L. Scott ([1927] 1958); R. S. Crane, "The Concept of Plot and the Plot of *Tom Jones*" in *Critics and Criticism* (1952); Frye; R. Scholes and R. Kellogg, *The Nature of Narrative* (1966); R. Barthes, *S/Z*, trans. R. Miller (1970); A. J. Greimas, *Du Sens* (1970); C. Bremond, *Logique du récit* (1973); S. Chatman, *Story and Discourse* (1978); T. Todorov, *The Poetics of Prose,* trans. R. Howard (1978); G. Genette, *Narrative Discourse,* trans. J. E. Lewin (1980); B. H. Smith, "Narrative Versions, Narrative Theories," *CritI* 7 (1980); J. Culler, *The Pursuit of Signs* (1981); M. M. Bakhtin, *The Dialogic Imagination*, ed. M. Holquist, trans. C. Emerson and M. Holquist (1981); S. Rimmon-Kenan, *Narrative Fiction* (1983); P. Brooks, *Reading for the Plot* (1984); P. Ricoeur, *Time and Narrative*, trans. K. McLaughlin and D. Pellaver (1984); N. Miller, "Emphasis Added: Plots and Plausibilities in Women's Fiction," *PMLA* 96 (1981); T. Pavel, *The Poetics of Plot* (1985)—Ren. drama; T. de Lauretis, *Alice Doesn't* (1986); S. S. Lanser, "Toward a Feminist Narratology," *Style* 20 (1986); H. L. Gates, Jr. *The Signifying Monkey* (1988); J. Phelan, *Reading People, Reading Plots* (1989); M.-L. Ryan, *Possible Worlds, Artificial Intelligence, and Narrative Theory* (1991); M. Farwell, *Heterosexual Plots and Lesbian Narratives* (1996); M. Fludernik, *Toward a "Natural" Narratology* (1996); D. Herman, *Story Logic* (2002); P. Jani, *Postcolonial Narrative and the Work of Mourning* (2004); B. Richardson, "Beyond the Poetics of Plot," *A Companion to Narrative Theory*, ed. J. Phelan and P. J. Rabinowitz (2005); A. Quayson, "Fecundities of the Unexpected," *The Novel*, ed. F. Moretti, v. 1 (2006); L. Zunshine, *Why We Read Fiction* (2006); W. Flesch, *Comeuppance* (2007); H. Dannenberg, *Coincidence and Counterfactuality* (2008).

S. S. LANSER

**POEM.** A composition, often in *lines, that draws on some or all of the following common features: *rhythm, *meter, *figuration (incl. rhetorical *schemes and *tropes), and *artifice (incl. *diction and *syntax). Poems of different times and places do not necessarily resemble one another so much as they share a recognition from their respective cultures that they embody poeticity or what the Rus. linguist Roman Jakobson called the *poetic function: "Poeticity is present when the word is felt as a word and not a mere representation of the object being named or an outburst of emotion, when words and their composition, their meaning, their external and inner form acquire a weight and value of their own instead of referring indifferently to reality." The poem comes into existence when an actual set of elements such as those named above is attached to the relevant cultural category (e.g., Fr. *poème*, Ger. *Gedicht*, Hungarian *vers*, Polish *wiersz*, or Chinese

*shi*). Not only is a poem both made and recognized as such by its maker or others, but the network of related concepts, most manifestly *poetry and *poet, is potentially modified by the admission of the new poem. *Poem* is not a universal concept: sometimes, as in the Occitan *vers*, the relevant term means "verse" (in the sense of a single line or several lines, a strictly technical meaning) and only implies *poem* (in the culturally recognized sense).

As the integer or complete constitutive unit of poetry, the poem displays some of the generative principles theorized in poetics such as *equivalence, *unity, *intertextuality, or *defamiliarization. In principle, it is often a statement in little of a poetics (derived from, e.g., *classical poetics, *futurism, *objectivism, or other established or ad hoc principles). However, in practice—i.e, under reading or *interpretation—the character of the poem, like that of any work of lit., is often autonomous, equivocal, or ambiguous. If poems are made by their creators, they are often remade in interpretation by each generation of readers.

Theorists, poets, and observers have more often defined *poetry* than the term *poem*. Unlike the *genre or medium we call *poetry*, which maintains a theoretical and practical discourse going back to Plato, the object into which poetry is usually resolved, the poem, is notoriously hard to isolate and discuss. Theories of poetry may be classified in a number of ways, notably according to the scheme advanced by M. H. Abrams in the 1950s and developed since, which considers four kinds of theories: mimetic, expressive, pragmatic, and objective.

The first two categories, which are concerned with *mimesis and *expression, respectively, and thus are associated with cl. and romantic doctrines, while they often address the nature of the poem, tend to give more attention to other factors, such as the nature of poetry or the power of the poet; in contrast, theories of the latter two categories often have a great deal to say about the poem in the context of their propositions about poetry. Pragmatic theories in the West, as Abrams shows, derive from ancient rhetorical theory and esp. from Horace's *Ars poetica* (1st c. BCE), which emphasizes the effects produced in the reader who is taught and moved. Much poetic theory of the Ren. and the Enlightenment is largely pragmatic, but this approach belongs to no age; it may appear in any time or place in which the ends or effects of poetry are in focus (see NEOCLASSICAL POETICS, RENAISSANCE POETICS). Abrams argues that, in Europe, objective theories develop in the 18th c. out of two models for the poem: the "heterocosmic model," which grants each poem the status of a "unique, coherent, and autonomous world," and the "contemplation model," which emphasizes the disinterested study of the poem. Notions of the poem as world are esp. prevalent in the work of Ren. thinkers such as Torquato Tasso, J. C. Scaliger, and Philip Sidney; but one might argue that they proceed from a certain understanding of poetry as world-making and the poet as a godlike creator rather than from a speculative attention to the nature of the poem per se. Alexander Baumgarten's dictum in *Meditationes Philosophicae de Nonnullis ad Poema Pertinentibus* (*Reflections on Poetry*, 1735)—"the poet is like a maker or creator, so the poem ought to be like a world"—indicates his prior assumptions about the poem. Likewise, the contemplative approach often has more to do with valorizing the role of the perceiver or reader—augmenting his or her office with a moral and even theological dimension—than with a new idea of the poem itself as somehow suitable for contemplation.

Romantic and decadent thinkers such as John Keats and E. A. Poe bring a new measure of concern to the nature of the poem as such: any hist. of ideas about the poem must take account of Poe's famous statement that "a poem is such, only inasmuch as it intensely excites, by elevating, the soul, and all intense excitements are through a psychal necessity, brief" ("The Philosophy of Composition," 1849). Charles Baudelaire repeats this observation: "anything that exceeds the period of attention which a human being can give to the poetic form is no longer a poem" (see ROMANTIC AND POSTROMANTIC POETRY AND POETICS). But it is really under the auspices of *modernism—when poems were very long as often as very short—that a concentration of speculative power attaches to the poem itself, perhaps through an exhaustion with general and idealist theories of poetry, perhaps through a new awareness of the social and cultural lives of poems as objects in the world, like paintings and sculptures.

Observations about the nature of the poem by poets and critics of the 1900s and after tend to be not only object- rather than genre-oriented but openly prescriptive and empirical rather than theoretical, and may be nakedly ideological as well: after all, this is a question that lends itself to pronouncements and dicta more readily than does the nature of the genre. For instance, Ezra Pound's famous "A Retrospect" about *imagism (1918) is a set of prescriptions at the level of the poem rather than of poetry (e.g., "to use absolutely no word that does not contribute to the presentation"); in Pound's assessment of the preceding six years of imagism, "perhaps a few good poems have come from the new method, and if so it is justified." Emphasizing craft, procedure, and values, many such modernist observations seem intended to shed the idealisms and mystifications that had accumulated around the idea of poetry since at least the Ren. Even the gnomic "Ars Poetica" (1926) by Archibald MacLeish, composed during his sojourn in the community of Am. expatriates in Paris, restates these premises while perhaps inadvertently reintroducing mystification: "A poem should not mean / But be."

To be precise, notions about the poem are articulated on a different plane than theories about poetry itself. The assumptions and practices of a reader confronted with an actual poem are often ideological and experiential rather than theoretical; practical and object-oriented instead of abstract. The question "How do I go about understanding this poem?" is not fully answered by Abrams's four doctrines, which provide broad principles for the nature of poetry; operating

within those doctrines, readers in empirical practice tend to follow procedures that reflect their education, interests, or inclinations. These reading and writing practices belong to at least four categories: the assimilationist, the integrationist, the artifactualist, and the irreducibilist. While any of these may coincide with the kinds of theories of poetry that Abrams and others describe, they are more ad hoc than those theories, often more assumed or felt than reasoned. Moreover, they are not radically separate from one another; rather, these positions are often in conversation with one another, so that traces of one become visible even in what appears to be an uncompromising statement of the other.

Assimilationist accounts of the poem emphasize its continuity with other literary and cultural *genres and forms. From this standpoint, poetry may be close to narrative and drama (for instance, it may be fundamentally dramatic, as in Kenneth Burke's theory of dramatism), or the poem may deeply resemble other sorts of art objects or events such as painting, sculpture, or dance. Perhaps Horace, with his dictum *ut pictura poesis*, is the original assimilationist, but many other critics and readers of the postclassical era, from Sidney to Ezra Pound to the textual artist Kenneth Goldsmith, subscribe to this notion.

Integrationists take seriously the notion that poems rarely exist in isolation from other poems and, thus, seek to absorb them into larger wholes such as *anthologies, *books, *songbooks, *lyric sequences, genres, schools, and movements. Implicitly or directly, they may challenge the premise that the poem is the relevant integer of analysis. Much scholarship on *medieval poetry, of Asia as well as Europe, is of this sort, reflecting the conditions in which many premod. poems were performed or written, with little or no investment in the idea of the individual poem; likewise, a great deal of crit. concerning Ren. sonneteers from Petrarch through the early 17th c. The genre crit. of Eur. poetry that was current from the late 1950s (prompted by Northrop Frye's "Theory of Genres" in *Anatomy of Criticism*, 1957) to about 1980 followed an integrationist paradigm.

The artifactualist position does not always entail an understanding of the poem's nature different from that of the two categories already mentioned; in fact, it may serve as the adjunct to any of the other positions, relating to any and all of them in some measure. An artifactualist statement describes a poem as the expression of some abstract principle—*form, *structure, *texture, artifice, hist.—and describes or narrates how such a principle becomes manifest in the poem we have. It is tempting to think of artifactualism as the default position of mod. poetics because its reliance on formal description in the service of various possible ends strikes many contemp. readers as natural and inevitable. To put it another way, from the mid-20th c. on, nearly any other position from *historicism to *formalism to personalism (the construal of poems according to one's own poetic practice) may compromise with artifactualism without incurring the charge of inconsistency; on the contrary, the neglect of artifactualism may be reproached as insufficiently attentive to the poem itself. Many poets who do not articulate an explicit poetics but discuss the making of their and others' poems are loosely artifactualist (e.g., W. B. Yeats, Pablo Neruda, Cid Corman), as are many critics who give their attention to the sources, genesis, and reception of particular poems (e.g., Hugh Kenner on Pound's career) and many critics who are also poets, such as Veronica Forrest-Thomson. Readers of Anglo-Am. poetry who are accustomed to thinking of historicism and formalism as opposed positions may think it odd to find both standpoints in the same category. Nonetheless, it is the nature of a default position to stand invisibly behind views that ostentatiously stage a competition even as they agree in fundamental matters.

Finally, the irreducibilist view is that every poem is a unique event unassimilable to genres and the other arts and only minimally responsive to general values such as form, craft, or period. Octavio Paz asks, "How can we lay hold on poetry if each poem reveals itself as something different and irreducible? . . . Poetry is not the sum of all poems. Each poetic creation is a self-sufficient unit. The part is the whole." Irreducibilists may be at once the ultimate historicists (not only every period but every poem—its own period—must be read on its terms) and the ultimate formalists (each poem generates a unique formal protocol that must be recovered and explained); and while irreducibilism may accept something like an artifactualist position in practice, its logical outcome is properly spoken by Paz when he asserts that "each poem is a unique object, created by a 'technique' that dies at the very moment of creation." A strict irreducibilism would hold that, when poems are susceptible to analysis under rubrics such as genre or form, they have failed as poems ("when a poet acquires a style, a manner, he stops being a poet and becomes a constructor of literary artifacts"). A further step in this doctrine notes that most critics and readers, fixated on constants in poetry such as form or style, are unable to recognize what is properly poetic in the objects they address or the creators who made them. While the irreducibilist strain runs through a great deal of historical and contemp. discourse on poetry, uncompromising (as opposed to merely nominal or superstitious) irreducibilists are rare. The It. philosopher Benedetto Croce was one. The kind of experimental poet who produces poems and perhaps manifestos but not crit. or who is uninterested in formulating an explicit poetics is often an irreducibilist; the Brazilian modernist Oswald de Andrade sometimes expresses such views, and several well-known poems of the later modernist era in Brazil (Manuel Bandeira's "O Último Poema" ["The Last Poem," 1968] and Carlos Drummond de Andrade's "Procura da Poesia" [Search for Poetry, 1945]) take this stance. Some of the less discursive, more atomistic work associated with the era of *Language poetry in the U.S. belongs to an irreducibilist impulse (e.g., Bruce Andrews, P. Inman). Paz is among the most prominent poet-critics to embrace the position without equivocation; it does not impede but curiously enlivens his most important work of crit.,

concerning the Mexican *baroque poet Sor Juana Inés de la Cruz.

As object and event, an inalienable element of lives and societies, the poem responds as much to cultural and personal notions as to theories and doctrines of poetry. It may seem so ubiquitous as to be invisible, so firmly possessed as to be ours alone, so natural as to resist abstraction. To take these conditions into account while explaining the poem in principle is one of the continual challenges of poetics.

*See* ARTIFACT, POETRY AS; AUTONOMY; FICTION, POETRY AS; INFORMATION, POETRY AS; KNOWLEDGE, POETRY AS.

■ C. Brooks, "The Poem as Organism," *English Institute Annual* 1940 (1941); Abrams; A. Baumgarten, *Reflections on Poetry*, trans. K. Aschenbrenner and W. B. Holther (1954); W. K. Wimsatt, "The Concrete Universal" (1947) and with M. C. Beardsley, "The Intentional Fallacy" (1946), both in *The Verbal Icon* (1954); Jakobson, "What Is Poetry?" v. 3; O. Paz, *The Bow and the Lyre*, trans. R.L.C. Simms (1973); C. Baudelaire, *Oeuvres complètes*, ed. C. Pichois, 2 v. (1975–76); B. Croce, *Poetry and Literature*, trans. G. Gullace (1981); M. H. Abrams, "Poetry, Theories of (Western)," *New Princeton Encyclopedia of Poetry and Poetics*, ed. A. Preminger and T.V.F. Brogan (1993).

R. GREENE

**POET.** The Greeks called the poet a "maker"—*poiētēs* or *poētēs*—and that word took hold in Lat. and other Eur. langs., incl. It., Fr., and Eng. But what precisely does the poet make? The obvious answer is *poems, the arrangements of words that he or she composes. Yet poets have often been given credit for bolder kinds of making. According to ancient Gr. fables, Amphion built Thebes from stones his songs called into place, and Orpheus's songs drew trees and beasts and stones to follow him. Ren. critics allegorized these stories as the harmonious beginning of civilization: poets had tamed the wilderness and softened the hearts of men. In the *Defence of Poesy*, Philip Sidney thought that the poet delivered a golden world, "in making things either better than Nature bringeth forth, or, quite anew, forms such as never were in Nature." Potentially that power of creation resembles, at one remove, the power of the Creator who first made the world. Other cultures have also regarded poets as godlike. Vyasa, who is both the putative author of the Indian *Mahābhārata* and a character in the epic, sometimes seems to be an avatar of the god Krishna. And even those who find such exalted views of the poet presumptuous or absurd concede that poets are capable of making fabulous fictions or myths (see FICTION, POETRY AS). Historically, most nations and societies have preserved poems, usually attributed to a specific maker, that embody their trads. and values. The works of Homer were so revered in ancient Greece that they supplied the basis of education. In this way, the poet can represent a whole community bound by a common lang. and stories that everyone knows.

The ideal of the poet as maker of golden worlds and founding myths tends to lose sight of the maker of poems, however, who dwindles to a mere name or legend. No one knows with any certainty who Homer was or where or when he lived or whether he was blind or even whether any one person composed the works attributed to him. Thus, "Homer" signifies a stamp of authenticity, a name that certifies the greatness of the poems. The effort to trace a particular person seems incidental to the aura of the maker. The first poet recorded by hist., Enheduanna of Ur (ca. 2400 BCE), was the daughter of King Sargon and priestess of Inanna (Ishtar), whom she magnifies in hymns that also refer to herself. Yet the goddess, the historical figure, the poet, and the legend are hard to separate, esp. since mss. of these poems date from centuries later. Similar problems veil the identities of virtually all early poets. In works preserved through oral trads. or scattered tablets, it is generally impossible to single out the original maker or to determine whether such an individual ever existed. Often the title of author falls to the scholar who first put a standard text together or wrote it down. Thus, the Mesopotamian *Epic of Gilgamesh* is supposed to have been revised and codified by Sîn-liqe-unninni (ca. 1200 BCE), a priest and scribe who lived more than a millennium after the work began and who inherited the honor of being its poet. Mod. ideas of authorship are challenged by these attributions. Nevertheless, the name of the poet casts a spell, as "Sappho" lends luster to every scrap or fragment of verse ascribed to her. It is as if the power of wonderful poems compelled their audiences to imagine the wonder-workers or divine spirits who made them. In the Heb. Bible, great hymns and songs are traditionally associated with inspired leaders and kings such as Moses (Deut. 32, 33), David (Ps.), and Solomon (Song of Sol.). Here the maker of nations absorbs the maker of verses; only someone anointed by God seems worthy of this sublime lang.

From this point of view, the poet is someone chosen, not someone who willfully tries to make poems. Hesiod, the poet of the *Theogony* (ca. 700 BCE), introduces himself as a shepherd tending his flock on Helicon when the *Muses descended on him, gave him a staff of bay, breathed a voice into him, and instructed him to spend his life singing their praises. Variations on this theme recur in many other times and places. In a prologue attached to some versions of the *Rāmāyana*, when the illiterate Vālmīki sees a hunter shoot a crane, the cries of its grieving mate inspire him to invent the meter (*sloka*) in which, at the bidding of Brahma, he will compose the epic that follows. Another illiterate, Cædmon, was sleeping in a cowshed, according to the Venerable Bede (ca. 731 CE), when a mysterious voice taught him to sing in praise of God. Sophisticated poets of later eras have also felt themselves to be chosen—sometimes, as with Friedrich Hölderlin, almost against their will. John Keats's *Fall of Hyperion* (1856) begins with a vision in which the narrator, in mortal peril, confronts the possibility that he might be an idle dreamer rather than a chosen poet; the issue was unresolved, and the poem remained unfinished. But many lovers of poetry still contend that no one can resolve to be a poet or learn the trade because poets are born—or chosen—not made.

To call someone a true poet, therefore, is frequently less a description than a glorification. The word itself implies a superior talent, if not a touch of *genius. In many fields, as Horace famously advised, mediocrity is quite acceptable—a second-rate lawyer can still do useful work—but neither men nor gods nor booksellers can abide a would-be poet. A number of terms distinguish poets from pretenders, who are called versemongers and versifiers, poetasters and rhymers. Even in mod. times, when canonizing a chosen few might be regarded as judgmental or elitist, it seems important to decide who qualifies as a poet and who does not. Verdicts like these apply to every kind of verse maker, to lyricists and *troubadours as well as *poets laureate; not every candidate can be the real thing. Perhaps a lingering sense of the role of those poets who once functioned as priests and prophets or as the living memory of their people accounts for the claims still made for poets, even in societies that do not award them much status or financial support. Yet secular eras have also reserved a special place for those who seem to be born to the calling. Cædmon's story set a pattern that has been often repeated. A fascination with "natural," uneducated makers of verse grew esp. strong in 18th- and 19th-c. Britain, when working-class or peasant geniuses appealed to the reading public; and at least two, Robert Burns and John Clare, eventually came to be recognized as major poets. Nature, not art, was supposed to have formed them and blessed them with inspiration. More recently, in 1955, Minou Drouet, just eight years old, became a best-selling Fr. poet (despite suspicions that her mother had written the poems). Apparently, children too can be struck by the muse.

A rival view of the poet, however, would stress the importance of learning a craft. From that perspective, poets are made, not born. As a demanding vocation, poetry requires unceasing study, a knowledge of what other poets have done, a mastery of *prosody and all the tools of verse, and lifelong practice. Such study is needed still more as the poet ages. Almost everyone is capable of writing one heartfelt poem, it is sometimes said, but only someone devoted to the craft of poetry can continue to write and to grow (Drouet stopped writing poems when she was 14). Moreover, the poet must understand the world in order to write well about it. Through much of hist., poetry was considered a type of learning, and "the learned poet" furnished an example to be followed. Scholars and critics often looked down on writers who were unacquainted with cl. texts. In *The Wisdom of the Ancients* (1609), Francis Bacon interpreted Orpheus as "a representation of universal Philosophy"; the archetypal poet was also the archetypal sage. The association of poetry with wisdom spans many cultures. It has been esp. powerful in early societies around the world, from the Americas to Africa to Iceland to Java, where native poets have supplied some basic models of how to live. But cl. trads. in the West have asked the poet for supreme craftsmanship as well as universal knowledge. In this respect, the exemplary figure is Virgil, who in late Roman times and in the Middle Ages came to be known simply as "the Poet." Virgil excelled in each of the genres most admired in his time: *eclogues, *georgics, *epic; he absorbed and improved on the best poems of the past;

in search of perfection, he wrote only a few lines a day and constantly revised them; he created not only individual poems but the pattern of a full poetic career, in which the poet progresses through stages until each work seems part of one great whole, the lifework of the poet. Yet, in addition, Virgil was renowned as a *vates or seer who had foreseen the coming of Christ and learned the secrets of the dead and whose works could be consulted to divine the future (the *sortes Virgilianæ*). Hence, "the Poet," both craftsman and magus, guides Dante through hell and purgatory in the *Divine Comedy* until, at the earthly paradise, they reach the limits of pagan and earthly knowledge. The poet Dante acknowledges his master and at the same time asserts the superiority of a Christian worldview. But together the two great poets affirm the value of their vocation, a craft that, pursued through a lifetime, culminates in understanding and bringing word of first and last things through art.

In such works, the master craftsman mounts above any mere human being. "The Poet" may take the name of Virgil, but he has gone far beyond the particular person who once lived and behaved as other people do. As characters in the *Divine Comedy*, both "Virgil" and "Dante" are useful fictions, filling the roles they play in the grand scheme of the poem. To be sure, the fictional Dante does draw on the memories and opinions of the poet who has created him and whose name he shares. But the relation between the character and his creator can never be taken for granted. In the past few centuries, many poets have tried to close that gap; they insist that the voice that speaks in a poem should be the same as that of the man or woman who made it. The romantics often regarded a capacity for deep feeling as the mark of a poet and direct expression of feeling as the mark of a good or authentic poem. In *The Prelude*, William Wordsworth gave epic scope to the story of how he had realized himself as a poet; and later poets, such as Walt Whitman and Vladimir Mayakovsky, liked to imply that their work had exposed the naked truth of who they were. Rhetorically, that open self-presentation can help to establish a sense of intimacy between writer and reader. Older poets had also recognized its power. Sappho seems to hold nothing back; Catullus and Ovid seem adept at revealing themselves; Petrarch and Dante confess their personal faults and obsessions. Moreover, even those who are ordinarily more reserved can flash forth at crucial moments. Many readers cherish the passages in *Paradise Lost* when John Milton, in the first person, thrusts his own struggles and feelings into the story.

It is tempting to view such disclosures as a transparent kind of autobiography, encompassing not only the situation of the poet but his or her inner life. Yet the image of the poet within the poem, like a painter's self-portrait, reveals only as much as will serve an artistic effect. Quite often a glimpse of the person behind the lines may function to tease or intrigue the reader, provoking a curiosity forever invited and yet evaded. T. S. Eliot, for instance, mastered that art, despite his advocacy of "impersonality." Good craftsmen know

what to withhold as well as what to divulge. These strategies can be very complex. Hence, self-portraits of poets cover a wide range of forms and purposes, from Li Ch'ing-chao's *tz'u* to Allen Ginsberg's *Howl*. In the Japanese genre of the poetic diary (*uta nikki*) (see JAPANESE POETIC DIARIES), prose and verse combine in a personal journal enriched by an anthol. of poems. Thus, Matsuo Bashō's *Narrow Road to the Interior* (1689) offers a travelogue sprinkled with haiku in which exquisite descriptions of nature convey the inner landscape of the poet. The diary documents spontaneous impressions of a historical journey into perilous regions. Yet it was carefully revised to accommodate both the facts and the person to a series of moods woven together, as if the writer himself were a work of art. Other poetic genres also insinuate that they are revealing the private life of the poet. The *sonnet sequences of Petrarch, Pierre de Ronsard, and Shakespeare, e.g., have often been combed like diaries for evidence of whom and how the poet loved. But such evidence is untrustworthy at best. The sonnets of Louise Labé offer a famous, searing case hist. of a passionate woman in love; but lately some scholars have argued that Labé never existed and that a group of men concocted those sonnets. Whatever the truth may be, it cannot be determined solely by the testimony of the poems, whose personal voice often echoes the voices of many earlier works. In this way, the poet seems constructed or pieced together from expectations about what a poet should be.

Those expectations also keep changing over time. Perhaps, in the distant past, poets knew just what societies wanted from them. The shaman, the *bard, the court poet all were rewarded for doing their duty, whether as oracles, entertainers, or eulogists of their patrons. Even in those days, they tended to complain about the difficulty of making verses to make a living. Yet their way of life was accepted. In some societies, everyone recognized the value of poetry, which seemed as indispensable as breathing. During most of Chinese hist., from the earliest emperors until the era of Mao Zedong, all educated people could and did write verse, catching fleeting emotions or memorializing special occasions. The practice was so familiar that Chinese has no word that designates "the poet," although great writers like Li Po and Tu Fu were honored as masters or "teachers." In lesser hands, a skillful piece of verse might function to impress superiors or advance a career; a courtier who could not ask a favor from the emperor directly could appeal to him with a poem. But in most mod. societies, poets can seldom rely on being valued or noticed. Since the rise of print culture and the decline of *patronage, they have largely depended on selling their wares to the public, and very few have found that profitable. Nor does poetry seem quite respectable as a profession or job description. The vast majority of poets earn their keep by doing other kinds of work, most often (in the U.S.) by teaching. There is little agreement, moreover, about what they contribute to society or about what society owes them. Poets and lovers of poetry continue to feel that poems provide something essential, whether by revitalizing lang., by noticing things that daily routines pass over, or by reminding readers of what it means to be alive. But much of the public seems content with a world in which the poet has no place at all.

The lack of any well-defined social role might be regarded, even so, as a peculiar advantage. If poets are outsiders, they are free to examine and challenge all the assumptions that other people usually take for granted. One model of the poet was put forward in the 15th c. by François Villon, whose popular ballads traded on his exploits as a ruffian and thief. Four centuries later Charles Baudelaire explored the creative possibilities of evil, Paul Verlaine and Arthur Rimbaud devoted themselves to breaking rules and laws in poems, and Oscar Wilde linked criminals and poets—an association that rappers and other performing rebels still make the most of. But the freedom of poets from social constraints and conventions can also inspire a more positive mission, a resistance to the empty formulas of those in power. When others are afraid to speak, the poet sometimes bears a special burden. In the former Soviet Union, when the government brooked no opposition and suppressed any unauthorized publication—"Poets, we are—and that rhymes with pariahs," Marina Tsvetaeva wrote in "Poets"—a small core of outcast writers, whose poems circulated in secret or by word of mouth, seemed to represent the conscience of the nation. Osip Mandelstam paid with his life for "anti-Soviet" verse, and Anna Akhmatova bore witness to the suffering of her people. Such poetry broke a terrible silence; many readers knew those poems by heart. And poets have seldom been more revered. (In the relative freedom of Russia today, some writers complain, poetry matters less.) Yet the mandate to serve as watchman and witness has not lost its force. Amid the troubles of times and places where free speech is throttled, dissident poets around the world have managed to defy authority and scorn injustice. That social or antisocial role has honored the name of the poet.

Yet most countries tolerate poets. Insofar as the mod. poet does have a voice, it tends to be the still, small voice that lingers in the mind when someone has turned off the busy hum of mass-market diversions. A memorable phrase or two—"the still small voice," "the busy hum"—can alter perceptions. Hence, poets take on the special task of ministering to lang., refining its rhythms, preserving or transforming its stock of words and expressions. Ever since Stéphane Mallarmé, some theorists have claimed that the poet is foremost a maker of lang., giving "a purer sense to the words of the tribe" ("The Tomb of Edgar Poe"). The power of poetic lang. to mold ideas, or even to inspire fresh ways of thinking, had earlier moved P. B. Shelley to declare that "poets are the unacknowledged legislators of the World"; they create the words and ideals that will govern the future. Lately, more skeptical theorists have sometimes reduced the poet to a captive or special effect of lang., a medium in which all human beings are submerged and that dissolves any illusion of a unique personality. Yet somehow that special effect of lang. has

survived long after the tongues that first gave rise to it have passed away. The maker of golden worlds and the maker of poems still represent the possibility of making something new. The poet, as R. W. Emerson said, is "the Namer, or Language-maker" who converts the world into words, and that process links the distant past to those who make poems today.

*See* INFLUENCE, ORIGINALITY, POÈTE MAUDIT, POETESS.

■ Curtius; T. S. Eliot, *On Poetry and Poets* (1957); W. H. Auden, *The Dyer's Hand* (1962); *Japanese Poetic Diaries*, trans. E. Miner (1969); W. J. Bate, *The Burden of the Past and the English Poet* (1970); M. Heidegger, *Poetry, Language, Thought*, trans. A. Hofstadter (1971); M. Foucault, *Language, Counter-Memory, Practice*, trans. D. F. Bouchard and S. Simon (1977); R. Hingley, *Nightingale Fever: Russian Poets in Revolution* (1981); L. Lipking, *The Life of the Poet* (1981); R. Helgerson, *Self-Crowned Laureates* (1983); R. Alter, *The Art of Biblical Poetry* (1985); M. W. Bloomfield and C. W. Dunn, *The Role of the Poet in Early Societies* (1989); C. Bernstein, *A Poetics* (1992); C. Watkins, *How to Kill a Dragon: Aspects of Indo-European Poetics* (1995); P. Bourdieu, *The Rules of Art*, trans. S. Emanuel (1996); J. Brockington, *The Sanskrit Epics* (1998); J. Black, *Reading Sumerian Poetry* (1998); A. Hiltebeitel, *Rethinking the Mahābhārata* (2001); M. Huchon, *Louise Labé* (2006); G. M. Sanders, *Words Well Put: Visions of Poetic Competence in the Chinese Tradition* (2006); A. R. Ascoli, *Dante and the Making of a Modern Author* (2008); J. Ramazani, *A Transnational Poetics* (2009).

L. LIPKING

**POÈTE MAUDIT.** A phrase that reflects the widening gulf in 19th-c. France between the gifted poet and the public on whom his survival might depend. It was given currency by Paul Verlaine's *Les Poètes maudits* (1884), a collection of essays on poets hardly known at the time, such as Tristan Corbière, Arthur Rimbaud, and Stéphane Mallarmé. A half century earlier, Alfred de Vigny's *Stello* (1832) had developed, in successive tales about Nicolas-Joseph Gilbert, Thomas Chatterton, and André Chénier, the idea that poets ("the race forever accursed [*maudite*] by those who have power on earth") are envied and hated for their superior qualities by society and its rulers who fear the truths they tell. Thereafter, a sick, impoverished, or dissolute poet of significant but generally unrecognized talent came to be seen in these terms as doubly victimized by a hostile and insentient society.

■ F. F. Burch, "Paul Verlaine's 'Les Poètes Maudits': The Dating of the Essays and Origin of the Title," *MLN* 76 (1961); M. Perloff, "*Poètes Maudits* of the Genteel Tradition: Lowell and Berryman," *Robert Lowell*, ed. S. G. Axelrod and H. Deese (1986).

A. G. ENGSTROM

**POETESS.** The Poetess is a generic figure with a long and various hist., often connected to popular poetry with broad national and international circulation and reaching its height in the 19th-c. verse culture of Europe and the U.S. Tracing the use of *poetess* back to the 16th c., the *OED* defines the term simply as "a female poet; a woman who composes poetry," but it has also been used in more complex ways since the 18th c. to celebrate or denigrate popular women poets writing within a Poetess trad. (hence, the capital letter, to indicate that trad. at work). After rising to fame, the figure fell into obscurity in 20th-c. crit. until the emergence of second-wave feminism (ca. 1960–90), producing several generations of feminist critics who have contributed to the recovery of "lost" women poets and the reconstruction of "Poetess poetics" from different historical and theoretical perspectives. The Poetess is now understood to be an important figure within lit. hist., as a shifting aesthetic category that is closely linked to historical transformations in mod. reading practices.

In the Middle Ages, the *trobairitz* of Occitania and the female *trouvères* of France were women poets associated with *song, but they were not Poetesses in the mod. sense of the term, nor were Christine de Pizan, Louise Labé, or most other med. or early mod. female poets. We should not assume that all women poets wrote in a Poetess trad. Rather, such a trad. is highly selective and often involves poets and readers of one era celebrating both antecedents and contemporaries in an act of identification. One recurring prototype for the Poetess is Sappho (fl. ca. 600 BCE), the ancient Gr. poet invoked as "the tenth muse" in antiquity and idealized over the centuries as a woman singing her poems at the origins of a *lyric trad. Educated women poets were often named "a Sappho" or "the Sappho" of their era: Katherine Philips (1632–64) was celebrated as the English Sappho in the 17th c., and by the 18th c., the compliment could also be reversed, as it was by Alexander Pope in a poem addressed to Anne Finch (1661–1720): "In vain you boast Poetick Dames of Yore, / And cite those Sapphoes wee admire no more." Looking toward the future rather than the past, Mary Robinson (1757–1800) sought to legitimize women's poetry in the name of Sappho: in 1797, she published "Sappho and Phaon: A Series of Legitimate Sonnets" with a preface urging her "illustrious country-women" to write for posterity like Sappho, who "knew that she was writing for future ages."

As a detachable figure that exceeded the work of any actual woman poet, the Poetess became a repeatable *trope, a *personification, performed by female poets (and indeed by some male poets, as in the early poetry of Alfred, Lord Tennyson, or E. A. Poe's mimicry of poetesses in his circle). Available for occupancy but also advertising its vacancy, this personification was used for multiple and often contradictory purposes, determined by particular historical contexts but also overdetermined by larger cultural patterns of production and reception in an expanding literary market. The Poetess became common currency in early 19th-c. England and the U.S., when women's verse was increasingly commodified through publication in newspapers, periodicals, musical broadsides, anthols., annuals, decorative eds., and other forms of print.

Among the first to capitalize on this market were Felicia Hemans (1793–1835) and L.E.L. (Letitia Elizabeth Landon, 1802–38). Through the frequent reprinting of poems in *Records of Woman* (1828) and *Songs of the Affections* (1830), Hemans became the very type of the popular Brit. Poetess whose character seemed "strongly impressed upon her writing," as noted by L.E.L. in "On The Character of Mrs. Hemans's Writings" (1835). What made Hemans a vivid figure was less an individual self than an idea of national character defined through the domestic ideology of her poetry. The poetry of L.E.L. was an even more elaborate print production, so broadly marketed that it caused speculations about the promiscuous circulation of her literary character. Laman Blanchard's poem "On First Seeing the Portrait of L.E.L." (1841) recalls how she was revealed to the curious public, an anonymous figure first identified only by three magical letters and then transformed into "this dainty little picture" that encouraged readers to read L.E.L. as a personification of the Poetess.

Projecting the Poetess simultaneously into and out of her writing is a convention at the heart of 19th-c. sentimental reading (see SENTIMENTALITY). According to a review of nine "Modern English Poetesses" in the *Quarterly Review* (1840), the difference between the "I" who writes and the "I" who reads is blurred as "the eye swims too deep in tears and mist over the poetess herself in the frontispiece." Yet what seems most personal in this moment of sympathetic identification proves most abstract, as the poetess in the frontispiece (so often glimpsed in 19th-c. volumes of women's verse) is not "the poetess herself" but a reflection on her personification: not a person but the figure of a figure. The recognition of the figurality of this figure, simultaneously empty and infinitely productive, is a characteristic feature of Poetess poetics, played out in many different versions that proliferated in the course of the century. The anthologizing of women poets was a logical extension of Poetess poetics, in numerous 19th-c. anthols., ranging from Alexander Dyce's *Specimens of British Poetesses* (1825) and Rufus Griswold's *The Female Poets of America* (1848) to Eric Robertson's *English Poetesses* (1883) and Alfred H. Miles's *The Women Poets of the Nineteenth Century* (1907).

The paradigmatic career of the Poetess embodied in her verse was sufficiently familiar for Elizabeth Barrett Browning (1806–61) to narrate in *Aurora Leigh* (1856). Beginning with the tautology of "I, writing thus," the character of Aurora develops as a reflection both of and on the poetic conventions that make her into a Poetess. This generic autobiography could be read back into the poetic career of Browning, whose "novel poem" consolidated her reputation as exemplary Poetess for other women poets to imitate, on both sides of the Atlantic. The Poetess had already become a vehicle for transnational circulation, esp. through Hemans who served as model for the French *poétesse* Amable Tastu (1798–1885), the German *Dichterin* Annette von Droste-Hülshoff (1797–1848), Lydia Sigourney (1791–1865) who was widely known as the American Mrs. Hemans, and the Af. Am. Frances Harper (1825–1911), who performed a complex relation to the racial politics of this cultural category. Later, Mrs. Browning took the place of Mrs. Hemans for aspiring Poetesses, as Emily Dickinson (1930–86) famously wrote: "I think I was enchanted / When first a somber girl / I read that Foreign Lady."

By the end of the century, the Poetess went into global circulation as a domesticated version of "that Foreign Lady," carrying a wide range of ideological implications within different national discourses. Even before the 19th-c. consolidation of the Poetess for the identification of (and with) white bourgeois femininity, Phillis Wheatley (1753–84) had already been read as America's "African Poetess," demonstrating the malleability of a category that could signify what was both familiar and foreign, performing "whiteness" as well as racial "otherness." The "Indian Poetess" Toru Dutt (1856–77) came to be read in England as an exotic figure, celebrated by the critic Edmund Gosse to represent an alien homeland. Later, Gosse also introduced Sarojini Naidu (1879–1949) to Eng. readers who identified (with) the poetess in the frontispiece of her early volumes of verse, pub. in London before she returned to India to become their new "national" poetess (see INDIA, ENGLISH POETRY OF). The international circulation of the Poetess is evident as well in the work of Pauline Johnson (1861–1913), who moved between England and Canada to perform the role of a "Mohawk Indian Princess" identified with a lost nation. The words of the Jewish Am. writer Emma Lazarus (1849–87), famously inscribed on the Statue of Liberty as a personification of a homeland calling out to all immigrants, is another performance of the Poetess as a generic figure.

While the Poetess may seem an obsolete designation (and according to some, a denigration) of the mod. woman writer, we encounter permutations of Poetess poetics well into the 20th c. In 1922, Amy Lowell (1874–1925) published "The Sisters" to reflect on a poetic lineage that includes Sappho, Dickinson, and Browning ("we're a queer lot, / We women who write poetry"), thus acknowledging the Poetess as a vehicle for women's poetry. The Poetess continued to be a mobile figure for mod. women poets (e.g., Angelina Grimké [1880–1958], Edna St. Vincent Millay [1892–1950], Gertrud Kolmar [1894–1943], Marina Tsvetaeva [1892–1941], Bing Xin [1900–99], Sylvia Plath [1932–63]), and this generic category also mobilized critical reading, perhaps most obviously in a renewed impulse to anthologize women's poetry toward the end of the 20th c. Along with selected trans. of women's poems from many langs. for the Defiant Muse series (pub. by The Feminist Press), and popular collections such as Cora Kaplan's *Salt and Bitter and Good: Three Centuries of English and American Women Poets* (1977), anthols. organized by historical period or nationality are part of an ongoing project to recover women poets, not only in books but in digital archives and other technologies for making their poetry available on line.

Yet, as Lootens argues in her ongoing account of the Poetess trad., the more we try to make the Poetess visible the more she seems to dissolve before our eyes. The primary challenge for the emerging field of Poetess studies is not to treat the figure as a stable object of recovery but to trace the loss of the Poetess as the very means of its literary transmission. One reason for the disappearance and reappearance of the Poetess is that she is not the content of her own generic representation: not an "I," not a consciousness, not a subjectivity, not a *voice, not a *persona, not a self. This has proved a controversial claim among critics whose rhetorical reading of poems as the personal testimony of women poets comes into conflict with the historical recognition that they cannot be recovered from the idealized abstraction of the Poetess that is performed again and again in their poetry. Rather than reading the Poetess expressively, as the expression of a female subject, a more productive approach would be to read the figure even more rhetorically as historical reflection on the very conventions that made it possible for the Poetess to circulate so widely.

*See* FEMINIST APPROACHES TO POETRY, GENDER AND POETRY, POET.

■ A. Leighton, *Victorian Women Poets: Writing against the Heart* (1992); V. Blain, "Letitia Elizabeth Landon, Eliza Mary Hamilton, and the Genealogy of the Victorian Poetess," *VP* 33 (1995); G. Greer, *Slip-Shod Sibyls: Recognition, Rejection and the Woman Poet* (1995); I. Armstrong and J. Bristow, "Introduction," *Nineteenth-Century Women Poets*, ed. I. Armstrong and J. Bristow (1996); T. Lootens, *Lost Saints: Silence, Gender, and Victorian Literary Canonization* (1996); A. K. Mellor, "The Female Poet and the Poetess: Two Traditions of British Women's Poetry, 1780–1830," *SIR* 36 (1997); L. Peterson, "'For My Better Self': Auto/biographies of the Poetess," *Traditions of Victorian Women's Autobiography* (1999); M. E. Leighton, "Performing Pauline Johnson: Representations of 'The Indian Poetess' in the Periodical Press, 1892–95," *Essays on Canadian Writing* 65 (1998); M. Linley, "Dying to Be a Poetess: The Conundrum of Christina Rossetti," *The Culture of Christina Rossetti*, ed. M. Arseneau, A. Harrison, L Kooistra (1999); V. Jackson and Y. Prins, "Lyrical Studies," *Victorian Literature and Culture* 27 (1999); T. Lootens, "Hemans and Her American Heirs," *Women's Poetry: Late Romantic to Late Victorian*, ed. I. Armstrong and V. Blain (1999); Y. Prins, *Victorian Sappho* (1999); *Romanticism and Women Poets*, ed. H. K. Linkin and S. C. Behrendt (1999); S. Brown, "The Victorian Poetess," *The Cambridge Companion to Victorian Poetry*, ed. J. Bristow (2000); P. Bennett, *Poets in the Public Sphere: The Emancipatory Project of American Women's Poetry, 1800–1900* (2003); M. Thain, "What Kind of a Critical Category Is 'Women's Poetry'?" *VP* 41 (2003); A. Chapman, "The Expatriate Poetess," *Victorian Women Poets*, ed. A. Chapman (2003); L. Mandell, "Introduction: The Transatlantic Poetess," *Romanticism and Victorianism on the Net* 29–30 (2003)—http://www.ron.umontreal.ca; M. Loeffelholz, *From School to Salon: Reading Nineteenth-Century American Women's Poetry* (2004); E. Richards, *Gender and the Poetics of Reception in Poe's Circle*

(2004); J. Fernandez, "Graven Images: The Woman Writer, the Indian Poetess, and Imperial Aesthetics in L.E.L.'s 'Hindoo Temples and Palaces at Madura,'" *VP* 43 (2005); A. Finch, *The Body of Poetry: Essays on Women, Form and the Poetic Self* (2005); V. Jackson, *Dickinson's Misery: A Theory of Lyric Reading* (2005); T. Lootens, "Bengal, Britain, France: The Locations and Translations of Toru Dutt," *Victorian Literature and Culture* 34 (2006); P. Backscheider, *Eighteenth-Century Women Poets and Their Poetry* (2007); T. Lootens, "States of Exile," *The Traffic in Poems: Nineteenth-Century Poetry and Transatlantic Exchange* (2008); V. Jackson, "The Poet as Poetess," *The Cambridge Companion to Nineteenth-Century American Poetry*, ed. K. C. Larson (2011); T. Lootens, *Haunted Spheres: Anti-Slavery Afterlives and Transatlantic Poetess Writing* (2013).

Y. Prins

**POETIC CONTESTS** are formal, agonistic exchanges in verse that display some or all of the following characteristics: (1) two or more poet contestants, (2) physically present to each other, (3) in a public setting before witnesses, (4) engaging in a verbal duel or debate that (5) treats a conventionalized or stipulated subject matter (often of an ad hominem variety), (6) undertaken for the sake of a prize, material or spiritual, and (7) resolved through appeal to external judgment. Since all seven elements seldom obtain in a single work, the class of poetic contests is heterogeneous, encompassing several subgenres and defying precise circumscription. Indeed, the poetic contest itself is not a *genre at all but rather the verbal expression of a general mode of human interaction—the aggressive and agonistic—whose roots extend deep into biology and psychology. The distinction between "real" and "imaginary" (or, more precisely, extratextual and intratextual) poetic contests is fundamental though not inviolable. Historically, actual contests (such as the Athenian *dionysia*) may occasion the composition of poems that contain no contestual elements; fictional contests (such as the *Canterbury Tales*), on the other hand, may be dramatized in poems that were not themselves products of a contest. Yet the line may be blurred, as when a real poetic contest results in poetic works with contestual elements recognizable only by audiences who knew the original *performance setting. Poetic contests are usually rooted in the world of orality that assumes greater interdependence between poem and presentational context than is customary in the poetries of highly literate societies. When speaking of a poetics of poetic contests, scholars note the various thematizations of competition, such as reference to *metaphors, *riddles, and puzzles, and religious vs. lay discourses. In these versions of the contest, the poet defines himself or herself through a conflict-based literary structure, which can include metaphors of war and violence as a mode of self-expression. In this sense, one might view poetic contests as producing an agonistic aesthetics bound up with a bodily performance against a competitor and before a judge and audience (Kellner and Strohschneider).

Verbal contest forms akin to poetic contests flourished in ancient civilizations. Ancient Gr., Ar., and Celtic legends feature poet-magicians whose satirical verses could produce a range of woes from the raising of blisters to death; occasionally, such versifiers match off in supernatural contests. In heroic poems such as the *Iliad*, *Mahābhārata*, *Beowulf*, and the *Chanson de Roland*, warrior pairs hurl boasts and insults before battle. In such exchanges, the spoken word poetically cast is perceived as an extension of the vital energy, martial prowess, or moral worth of the speaker. The poetic contest emerges spectacularly into the foreground of Western lit. hist. in the great dramatic festivals of cl. Athens (5th c. BCE). While this contest setting is not directly reflected in the content of Gr. *tragedy, Aristophanes made it the subject of *The Frogs*, where Aeschylus and Euripides compete posthumously before Dionysus for the laurel crown. From Hellenistic times, singing matches begin to make their appearance in *pastoral poetry, first in Theocritus's *Idylls*, later in the *eclogues of Virgil and Ren. Eur. poets. Some of the verse *satires of Horace and later writers in the satiric trad. are cast in argumentative, dialogic frames.

It is in the Middle Ages, however, that contests both fictive and actual are most abundantly represented. Med. Lat. poems of *conflictus* feature altercations between character types or allegorical *personifications such as summer and winter; wine and water; body and soul; rustics and clerics; or among a Muslim, a Jew, and a Christian, subjects that recur in several vernacular lits. In the 12th c., love emerges as a major topic, as in the *Altercatio Phyllis et Florae*. In the same period in Fr. and Occitan lit. emerges the *tenso*, in which *troubadours debate in alternating *strophes on matters of politics, morality, poetics, or, above all, love and women. Perhaps derived from the *sirventes*, a political or satirical diatribe, and incorporating such subgenres as the *partimen*, the tenso is the dominant med. verse debate form, although debate elements appear in other genres as well, such as the *pastourelle*, the It. *lauda* and *contrasto*, and the 13th- to 15th-c. Galician-Port. *cantigas d'escarnho e de mal dizer* and the Sp. *pregunta*. The purest and most dramatic med. poetic contest is the 13th-c. MHG *Wartburgkrieg*, in which five poets are pitted against a magician in a riddle competition with death as the penalty for losing. Several Eddic poems feature verbal contest between such adversaries as Thor and Odin. ME produced a classic *débat* in the late 12th- or early 13th-c., *The Owl and the Nightingale*; Chaucer's *Canterbury Tales* represents a full-blown peregrine contest with some 30 contestants, a judge, and a prize. The flamboyant *flytings of 15th- to 16th-c. Scotland feature volleys of fantastic *invective and abuse between noted contemp. poets, possibly as court entertainment.

The scope and longevity of these forms should be taken as an index of the wide popularity of verbal contesting in the Middle Ages in circles both courtly and popular. Rival troubadours and *Minnesingers* such as

Gottfried von Strassburg and Wolfram von Eschenbach traded barbs by alluding to each other, by name or epithet, in their works. Cultivating independence from courtly *patronage, Fr. poets and *minstrels in the 13th c. began to form associations (*puys*) that trained apprentices in the craft and sponsored competitions for prizes. *Meistersinger guilds in 14th- to 16th-c. Germany served similar functions. Several such associations and annual festivals still survive, such as the *Jocs florals* in Toulouse (see GAI SABER) and the National *eisteddfod in Wales (see WELSH POETRY). In these cases, poetic contests reflect the transformation of lyric reception in late med. urban environments, as the transmission and practice of poetry moved from aristocratic courts to municipal institutions. For instance, in the 14th c., laymen founded the *Consistori de la Sobregaia Companhia del Gay Saber* (Consistory of the Merry Band of the Gay Knowledge) to maintain the practice of *courtly love and the knowledge of how to write poetry. The founders modeled their activities on the ceremonies of the city's university, awarding degrees and treating the competition as a public examination. The ritualization and codification of lyric poetry through contests were a means of civic identity and self-representation. The creation of poetic institutions—incl. the compilation of *songbooks and poetic manuals that contained the rules and procedure for such competitions—maintained the prestige of an earlier vernacular trad. while transforming this trad. into an accessible craft.

After the Ren., poetic contests witnessed a decline both as poetic topic and social custom. Despite its allusion to the laurel crown of cl. contests, the status of *poet laureate became a reward more for political loyalties than for poetic skill—although debate features persisted in the pastoral, Ren. and neoclassical drama, and other genres. Jean Racine, Pierre Corneille, and Voltaire asserted their superiority over their rivals in the prologues of their plays, and John Dryden's "MacFlecknoe" and later Augustan satires register through thinly veiled fictions real social and poetic rivalries. Still, students of poetry looked to the prestige of the contest to revivify native literary trads. In the 18th c., the Swiss poet and critic Jakob Bodmer used the poetic contest as a figure for cultivating a philological and romantic connection to the med. past. In his allegorical tale *Das Erdmännchen*, e.g., a *Wettgesang* or singing match ensues between a med. and a contemp. poet, as *anacreontic verses are antiphonally juxtaposed with those from the main *Minnesang* songbook, which Bodmer had transcribed. This contest represents how Bodmer believed that the study of MHG lyric could revitalize Ger. literary lang.

In Asia, Japanese poetic contests are perhaps the most elaborate in the world. They began in the late 9th c. as one of a variety of matches on objects ranging from iris roots to paintings and were largely social; the low-ranking nobility commonly writing the poems did so for presentation by their betters. But in time, social distinctions became less important and competition keener, often bitter. To facilitate judgment, topics were increasingly given out in advance and became more detailed as well as fictionalized, e.g., "Cherry Blossoms at a Mountain Temple," "Love Consummation Unconsummated." Because poetic contests were a major form of publication and because of increasing rigor, standards of judgment were conservative, being based on precedent. But standards altered, and the judgments at contests provide important insights into poetic theory as well as praxis. At the Japanese court, two of the most important contests were *The Poetry Contest in 600 Rounds* (i.e., 1,200 poems, 1193 CE) and *The Poetry Contest in 1500 Rounds* (3,000 poems, 1202). There were also poetic contests by one person, pitting poems on the same topic against each other for judgment by an esteemed critic, e.g., Monk Saigyō's *Mimosusogawa Poetry Match* (1187). There were numerous other variants. Closest to the kind, and indeed often part of it, 100-poem sequences were often the unit of competition. Subsequently, other kinds of matches occurred, chiefly those of linked poetry (*renga*) and *nō. Contests of various kinds are a major feature of Japanese lit. until about 1600, after which only modified and attenuated versions exist. But during these six or seven centuries, poetic contests are a more important feature of Japanese lit. than of any other.

In the contemp. era, while real poetic contests are a regular feature of the literary landscape, the resultant poetry is seldom agonistic in style or subject. Yet poetic contests remain vital in the developing world and everywhere in popular culture. Such poetic or semipoetic modes as playing the *dozens, *toast, *signifying, and rapping, widely in evidence among contemp. Af. Americans and often realized as verbal duel, feature rhetorical pyrotechnics and a marked facility for extemporization. Other instances of contests attest to their cross-cultural popularity and diversity: Greenland Inuit resolved quarrels through poetic duels (called *Iviutiit*) adjudicated by the tribe (see INUIT POETRY); obscene dueling genres flourish among Turkish and Guatemalan adolescents; and Eur. television broadcasts an annual *Saengerkrieg*, taking its title from the "war of singers" at the Wartburg.

*See* POETRY SLAM.

■ H. Knobloch, *Die Streitgedichte im Provenzalichen und Altfranzösischen* (1886); H. Jantzen, *Geschichte des deutsches Streitgedichtes* (1896); B. Petermann, *Der Streit um Vers und Prosa in der französischen Literatur des XVIII Jarhunderts* (1913); H. Walther, *Das Streitgedichte in der lateinischen Literatur des Mittelalters* (1920); Jeanroy; H. Pflaum, *Die religiöse Disputation in der europäischen Dichtung des Mittelalters* (1935); J. Huizinga, *Homo Ludens* (1938); R. Elliott, *The Power of Satire* (1960); R. H. Brower and E. Miner, *Japanese Court Poetry* (1961); J. G. Cummins, "Methods and Conventions in Poetic Debate," *Hispanic Review* 31 (1963); W. Labov, *Language in the Inner City* (1972); G. Bebermeyer, "Streitgedicht," *Reallexikon II* 4.228–45; C. Lindahl, *Earnest Games* (1987); *Medieval Debate Poetry: Vernacular Works*, ed. and trans. M.-A. Bossy (1987); A. W. Pickard-Cambridge, *The Dramatic Festivals of Athens*, 2d ed.

(1989); R. Osmond, *Mutual Accusation* (1990); W. Parks, *Verbal Dueling in Heroic Narrative* (1990); T. L. Reed, *Middle English Debate Poetry and the Aesthetics of Irresolution* (1990); M. Galvez, "Ash Wednesday, 1515: Hans Sachs is accepted into the guild of Mastersingers at Würzburg," *A New History of German Literature*, ed. D. E. Wellbery et al. (2004); B. Liu, *Medieval Joke Poetry: The "Cantigas d'escarnho e de mal dizer"* (2004); B. Kellner and P. Strohschneider, "Poetik des Krieges: Eine Skizze zum Wartburgkrieg-Komplex," *Das fremde Schöne: Dimensionen des Ästhetischen in der Literatur des Mittelalters*, ed. M. Braun and C. Young (2007); C. Léglu, "Languages in Conflict in Toulouse: *Las Leys d'Amors*," *MLR* 103 (2008); M. Galvez, "From the *Costuma d'Agen* to the *Leys d'Amors*: A Reflection on Customary Law, the University of Toulouse, and *the Consistori de la sobregaia companhia del gay saber*," *Tenso* 26 (2011).

W. Heaton; W. W. Parks; E. Miner; M. Galvez

**POETIC FUNCTION.** As defined by Rus. formalist linguist and literary theorist Roman Jakobson, the poetic function is "[t]he set (*Einstellung*) toward the message as such, focus on the message for its own sake." The context for this definition is his analysis of the act of verbal communication, formulated at an international conference on style held at Indiana University in 1958. According to this formulation, every such act involves six elements: an *addresser*; an *addressee*; a *context* referred to; a *code* common to addresser and addressee as encoder and decoder of the message; a *contact*, i.e., "a physical channel and psychological connection between the addresser and the addressee"; and the *message*, i.e., the actual spoken or written discourse in all its linguistic particulars. Each element corresponds to one of six functions of lang.: the *emotive* or expressive (oriented toward the addresser, aiming at a direct expression of his or her attitude); the *conative* (oriented toward the addressee and often expressed grammatically through the vocative case of a noun designating the addressee and the imperative mood of verbs); the *referential* (toward the context); the *metalingual* (toward the code); the *phatic* (toward the contact, aimed at establishing, maintaining, or prolonging communication); and the *poetic* (toward the message). What Jakobson here calls the poetic function, he sometimes elsewhere refers to as the aesthetic function.

This notion of the poetic function was adumbrated by Jakobson as early as 1928, in a study of the Rus. futurist poet Velimir Khlebnikov, and elaborated over the intervening 30 years in a series of analytical articles and theoretical papers through which he sought to establish an appropriate focus for literary studies. The poetic function of lang., Jakobson stressed, is not restricted to poetry, nor are the other functions absent from poetry. In any act of verbal communication, several functions, having different degrees of importance, may be realized, one being predominant. A poetic work, then, is a verbal message whose aesthetic function is dominant.

The predominant function is, for Jakobson, the primary determinant of the verbal structure of the message. Where the poetic function is predominant, the principle of *equivalence is projected "from the axis of selection into the axis of combination." That is, words in the text are related to each other not only syntagmatically, by contiguity, but also paradigmatically, i.e., as they are related to other words that could be substituted for them. Where the poetic function is predominant, the words present in the text will have the same kinds of linguistic relations to each other as they do to the words from among which they were chosen. These relations include phonological identity (whence meter and rhyme), grammatical parallelism, and semantic synonymy or antithesis.

This definition of the poetic function of lang. has important implications for *stylistics; the task of the stylistician becomes that of analyzing exhaustively the linguistic structure of a text and thereby discovering patterns of equivalences. Jakobson himself practiced such stylistic analysis on poems in many langs. and of periods from med. to mod. Among these analyses, one, with Claude Lévi-Strauss, of Baudelaire's "Les Chats" and one, with Lawrence Jones, of Shakespeare's sonnet 129 are esp. notable for the controversy they have stirred. In each, different parts of the poem are contrasted in terms of the presence or absence of features in binary opposition, revealing multiple symmetries.

Jakobson's methodology and results have been challenged by Michael Riffaterre, who has argued that a given linguistic equivalence is not necessarily stylistically relevant unless or until it becomes perceptible to readers (other than trained linguists). Similarly, Paul Werth has argued that recurrence will be found in any text, that its perceptibility and effects depend in part on the nature of the repetition and of the units involved (whether phonological, lexical, or syntactic), that binary oppositions can be generated at the whim of the analyst, that it is pointless if not impossible to attempt an analysis that is exhaustive at all levels, and that semantic analysis is properly a prerequisite to analysis of other aspects of text structure. Countering such objections, Paul Kiparsky has pointed to Jakobson's stipulation that only linguistically relevant categories can enter into the patterning of poetry and noted that his idea of poetic function "opens the way to an understanding of the *grammatical* texture of poetry."

Jakobson was not the only 20th-c. scholar to discriminate functions of lang. use in a way that bears on the analysis of poetry. As early as 1925, I. A. Richards distinguished between the scientific use of lang., for the sake of reference, and the emotive use, for the sake of the emotion produced. Richards's emotive function, being concerned with production of attitudes in the audience, is different from Jakobson's, which involves expression of emotion by the addresser. Whereas Jakobson derived his functions from an analysis of the act of communication, Richards simply attempted to categorize the kinds of work a sentence can do. By 1949, he was distinguishing six such jobs: *indicating, characterizing, realizing, appraising, influencing,* and *structuring*. In Jakobson's terms, the first three jobs seem to be referential; the fourth and fifth, emotive. Only the sixth resembles Jakobson's poetic function.

*See* interpretation, pseudo-statement.

■ Richards; R. Jakobson and J. Tynjanov, "Problems

in the Study of Literature and Language" (1928), rpt. in Jakobson, vol. 3; R. Jakobson, "The Dominant" (1935); and "Linguistics and Poetics" (1958), both rpt. in Jakobson, vol. 3; R. Jakobson and C. Lévi-Strauss, "*Les Chats* de Charles Baudelaire," *L'Homme* 2 (1962); R. Jakobson and L. G. Jones, *Shakespeare's Verbal Art in "Th'Expense of Spirit"* (1970); M. Riffaterre, "Describing Poetic Structures," *Structuralism*, ed. J. Ehrmann (1970); Culler, chap. 3; E. Holenstein, *Roman Jakobson's Approach to Language*, trans. C. and T. Schelbert (1976); P. Werth, "Roman Jakobson's Verbal Analysis of Poetry," *JL* 12 (1976); T. J. Taylor, *Linguistic Theory and Structural Stylistics* (1980), chap. 3; L. R. Waugh, "The Poetic Function in the Theory of Roman Jakobson," *PoT* 2, 1a (1980); P. Kiparsky, "The Grammar of Poetry," *Roman Jakobson: What He Taught Us*, ed. M. Halle (1983); J. P. Russo, *I. A. Richards* (1989).

E. BERRY

**POETIC LICENSE.** This phrase originally referred to the freedom allowed the poet to depart in diction, grammar, or subject matter from the norms of prose discourse or, later, from poetic "rules." *Poetic license* is still a popular phrase in common usage, but in crit., it is now chiefly a term used to describe the creative management of historical fact—Virgil's decision to make Dido the contemp. of Aeneas, e.g. But many other rhetorical ploys once fell under its aegis, among them the use of archaic words or pronunciations (see ARCHAISM) and inversions of syntax (see HYPERBATON). Both Aristotle and Horace thought it feasible for poets to coin, lengthen, shorten, alter, or import words that might distinguish their lang., and Aristotle even encouraged poetic license to enhance verisimilitude: "for poetic effect a convincing impossibility is preferable to that which is unconvincing but possible" (trans. Butcher). The notion of a license itself implies, however, a fairly strict set of rules or norms of generic or structural specification that the poet is given permission to ignore, and mod. critical theory has refined and altered considerably the ideas that pertain to the nature of literary genres and the authority of *convention. Genre studies have questioned the integrity of the various rules that once governed the assignment of a text to the ranks of poetry or prose; and the confidence that once allowed a critic to identify an instance of poetic license is of very limited use in describing the *prose poem, as Arthur Rimbaud implicitly demonstrated in *A Season in Hell*. In conceptualizing poetic making as either deviation from strictly defined "rules" (that do not exist) or as lawless freedom to create, the phrase distracts attention from the specific and important functions that innovation and *invention can serve. Paul Celan was one of the most innovative poetic neologists of the 20th c., but his coinages are very poorly served by being described as poetic license because they were not designed to create effects simply by violating standard Ger. vocabulary. Rather, by taking advantage of the natural affinity of Ger. for making compounds, Celan was able to combine neology and etymology for constructing a critique of lang. and its influence on perceptions of reality.

In mod. *stylistics, similar characterizations of unusual lexical and syntactic constructions are occasionally found; these, too, are unfortunately cast in negative rather than positive terms. In *prosody, it was sometimes said that poetic license allowed the poet freedom to alter *diction or *syntax so as to meet the stricter requirements of *meter, but this amounts to an indictment of the competence of the poet, who on this account is not master of the meter for his or her own purposes but is mastered by it. This too is inept: prose norms of diction or order have no precedence or authority such that poetry should be judged against that standard. The concept has proved only minimally useful in discussions of contemp. poetics. Most notably, Marjorie Perloff's *Poetic License* uses the phrase to set up a traditional discussion of the two senses of *license*—and of the two poles between which poetry operates aesthetically—as "permission from an outside authority" or as "defiance of authority."

■ M. Perloff, *Poetic License* (1990).

T.V.F. BROGAN; S. BURRIS

**POETIC MADNESS** (Gr. *mania* or *enthousiasmos*; Lat. *\*furor poeticus*). Up to the Ren., the central component of the Western conception of poetic composition was that of divine *inspiration—literally, a "breathing in." The notion that the *poet may become "possessed" by a frenzy or ecstasy bequeathed by a god in order to create poetry descends from the Greeks. In the earliest Gr. poetry, the *voice of the poet is simply the stringed instrument of the *Muses, who impart information that he either could not know himself or is not able to remember. Homer several times appeals to the Muses for factual information, though the notion of divine inspiration for poetic *form*, by contrast, is nonexistent in his works. The first extant reference to poetic madness is by Democritus (frag. 17, 18), who says that no one can be a poet without "divine breath."

Plato in the *Phaedrus* (244a–245a, 265a–b) identifies four types of madness—prophetic, ritual (Dionysiac), poetic, and erotic—a formulation surviving from archaic times, when the boundaries among religious ecstasy, drunkenness, mystical prophecy, and poetic creation were blurred, if existing at all. But in the *Laws*, where Plato defines poetic madness best, the distinction between ecstasy (see ECSTATIC POETRY) and the capacities of the poet is more clearly drawn. Here too, as is the case with *enthousiasmos*, there is no definitive evidence in early Gr. documents that the Greeks believed the poet acted without some form of agency in the act of "making" (i.e., *poeien*, to make).

Subsequently, Plato's four types were reduced to three, which appear two millennia later in Shakespeare (*Midsummer Night's Dream* 5.1), when the Duke confirms that "the lunatic, the lover, and the poet / Are of imagination all compact." Socrates asserts that poets cannot succeed without poetic madness. In the *Ion*, both poet and critic are described as so possessed that they no longer consciously control their words—clear evidence of the Platonic denigration of craft, for, in fact, Plato's purpose is to show that poetry, being wholly *given*, is no art at all. The Roman poets and critics also accepted poetic madness: Horace says that drink improves poetic creation; Cicero says that no one can be a poet "who is not on fire with passion and without a certain touch [*afflatus*] of frenzy" (*De oratore* 2.46); Ovid remarks that "a god is within us; when he urges, we are inspired." Thereafter, the idea was appropriated by Neoplatonism.

All these references amount to claims that (1) a heightened state of consciousness or intensity of experience is the necessary condition or effect not only of genuine madness (insanity) but of artistic creativity and erotic transport and that (2) category divisions between these states are largely immaterial. "Great wits are sure to madness near allied," says John Dryden in *Absalom and Achitophel*, "And thin partitions do their bounds divide." The belief that the *genius ("spirit") and lunatic ("driven by the Moon") are fed from the same springs has never departed Western culture.

In the subsequent hist. of Western *poetics, major alterations in this conception are but two: with the advent of Christianity, transfer of the locus of generation from pagan gods to a Christian God and, with the advent of secular psychology, from external inspiration to internal creation. And while Plato clearly distinguishes between madness that is divinely inspired and that caused by physical disease ("our greatest blessings come to us by way of madness," says Socrates, "provided the madness is given us by divine gift" [trans. Dodds]), the subsequent devel. of the concept of madness has served mainly to call the very notion into question. Many Ren. poets and critics (e.g., Pierre de Ronsard and Michel de Montaigne) embrace it, while others are ambivalent: Philip Sidney in the *Defence of Poesy* mouths the traditional (Neoplatonist) line but also insists on the power of the poet as maker; and in *Astrophil and Stella* (e.g., 74), he rejects poetic madness outright. The notion of divine origination and control of poetic creation ran counter to the emergent Ren. spirit of scientific rationalism, as well as to the profound humanist distrust of the irrational and immoral. To a humanist, it would be sacrilege to assign to mere mortals qualities of the divine.

But in romantic poetics, the role of the poet is given new primacy as both visionary and tormented outcast (see POÈTE MAUDIT, ROMANTICISM). And though inspiration is now dissociated from divinity for some of the romantics, or else transferred to a pantheistic source, the aesthetics of *spontaneity, *originality, and *imagination all affirm intensified consciousness. To poems that are the result of intoxication or hallucination are now added poems given in a dream or reverie—S. T. Coleridge's "Kubla Khan," E. A. Poe's "The Raven"— though Coleridge himself calls "Kubla Khan" a "psychological curiosity."

Mod. reformulations of the idea of poetic madness derive almost entirely from the emergence of psychology in the late 19th c. The connection to the concept in antiquity is simply the new belief that creativity is the work of the id, not the ego. To Sigmund Freud (in his essay "The Relation of the Poet to Day-Dreaming" and elsewhere), the artist is neurotic, and the artist's work is a by-product and a symbolic statement of his or her disturbance, particularly so in that, for Freud, the unconscious itself works by processes that are tropological. But for Carl Jung, creative activity puts the poet in touch with the primal source of human vitality, the energy welling up from the collective unconscious; it synthesizes id as eros and ego as will to power in a productive act. This is only to say that poets who really were mad—such as Lucretius, François Villon, Christopher Marlowe, William Collins, Christopher Smart, William Blake, Gérard de Nerval, Friedrich Hölderlin, Friedrich Nietzsche, and Ezra Pound—or, at the very least, exhibit marked personality disorders, nevertheless seemed able, thereby, to access regions of creativity not available to others. The question of who is mad, thus, begins to seem really the question of who gets to define the criteria: on aesthetic criteria, it is bourgeois materialism and philistinism that seem mad.

The issue of whether art is neurotic or an emblematic of deeper health has been explored by Thomas Mann, Kenneth Burke, Lionel Trilling ("Art and Neurosis"), and esp. Edmund Wilson: in *The Wound and the Bow* (1941), "wound" refers to the artist's neurosis and "bow" to the art that is its compensation. Now, poetry like all art is a *catharsis for the poet, whereas, for the Greeks, it was one for the audience. Even I. A. Richards's theory of poetry was originally neurologically based, emphasizing interinanimations, synergism, and wholeness.

■ G. E. Woodberry, "Poetic Madness," *The Inspiration of Poetry* (1910); F. C. Prescott, "Poetic Madness and Catharsis," *The Poetic Mind* (1922); R. Graves, *Poetic Unreason* (1925); A. Delatte, *Les Conceptions de l'enthousiasme chez les philosophes présocratiques* (1934); L. Trilling, *The Liberal Imagination* (1950); E. R. Dodds, *The Greeks and the Irrational* (1951); Curtius, excursus 8; J. C. Nelson, *Renaissance Theory of Love* (1958); Weinberg, "Furor" in the index; B. Hathaway, *The Age of Criticism* (1962); G. Bruno, *The Heroic Frenzies*, trans. P. E. Memmo Jr. (1964); *Intoxication and Literature*, ed. E. R. Peschel (1974); E. Fass, *Shakespeare's Poetics* (1986); J. Britnell, "Poetic Fury and Prophetic Fury," *Renaissance Studies* 3 (1989); A. Rothenberg, *Creativity and Madness* (1990); F. Burwick, *Poetic Madness and the Romantic Imagination* (1996).

T.V.F. BROGAN

# POETICS, WESTERN

Poetics is the branch of lit. crit. devoted to poetry, esp. to the study of its characteristic techniques, conventions, and strategies. The word can also refer to theoretical texts on the topic, above all to Aristotle's famous philosophical treatise. Sometimes *poetics* is used in both a narrower and a more expansive sense. On the one hand, it can designate the compositional principles to which a particular *poet subscribes. These principles may remain implicit, or they may be made overt in a variety of ways, ranging from the occasional and casual, such as John Keats's famous discussion of *"negative capability" in a letter to his brother on December 21, 1817, to the serious and scholarly, such as Czesław Miłosz's Charles Eliot Norton Lectures, published as *The Witness of Poetry* (1984). On the other hand, *poetics* may be used as a label for any formal or informal survey of the structures, devices, and norms that enable a discourse, genre, or cultural system to produce particular effects. Prominent examples would include Gaston Bachelard's *La Poétique de l'espace* (1958; trans. as *The Poetics of Space*, 1964), Linda Hutcheon's *A Poetics of Postmodernism* (1988), and Tzvetan Todorov's *Poétique de la prose* (1971; trans. as *The Poetics of Prose*, 1977), none of which places poetry at the center of its argument. When employed in this expanded sense, *poetics* is often implicitly opposed to *hermeneutics, i.e., the practice of *interpretation. In other words, one explains how something works, not what it means.

**I. Classical.** In the West, the discipline of poetics has its origins in Gr. antiquity. Although he never wrote a single extended work on the subject, Plato's scattered comments on poetry have served as a standard starting point for understanding the art form. His dialogue *Ion*, for instance, argues that poetry is written in a state of divinely inspired madness (see FUROR POETICUS). The thesis that poetry comes to a poet from outside, from some higher or alien authority, has had a long and surprising hist. in the millennia since, down to 20th- and 21st-c. experiments with automatic writing (see ALEATORY POETICS), *computational poetry, *cybertext, and *found poetry.

Plato is best known for a set of related arguments made in the *Republic*. He maintains that poetry addresses itself to the emotions. Instead of encouraging rational thought, it stirs the passions of its audience. Such manipulation may be acceptable in a few limited cases, such as *hymns to the gods or *encomia celebrating illustrious heroes, which encourage people to live better lives. Otherwise, poetry is an inferior art. It is no more than a crude attempt to reproduce in words ideas that transcend lang. (see IMITATION, MIMESIS).

Again, these propositions have cast a long shadow. Statements on poetics have conventionally taken a stand on whether poetry's propensity to provoke strong feelings is to be celebrated, as Longinus (see SUBLIME for the author and dating controversy) does in *Peri hypsous* (*On the Sublime*, 1st c. CE), or to be handled carefully, as in William Wordsworth's Preface to the 2d ed. of *Lyrical Ballads* (1800), which advocates tempering *emotion through the use of regular *rhyme and *meter. Similarly, the question of poetry's relation to truth has been a leitmotif in writings on poetics, with fascinating consequences, such as Pierre de Ronsard's insistence in *Abrégé de l'art poétique françois* (A Summary of the French Art of Poetry, 1565) that poets must study as many occupations as possible, incl. blacksmithing, falconry, and sailing, if they are to gain the experiential knowledge necessary for fine writing—or W. H. Auden's public confession in "Dichtung and Wahrheit" (1959) that he was sexually attracted to someone other than his long-term companion Chester Kallman.

Aristotle's *Poetics* made the problems of *affect and representation fundamental to Western discussions of poetry. In response to Plato, he maintains that imitation is not the same thing as producing a flawed, degraded copy. Children, he notes, spontaneously enjoy imitating others; it is a natural human faculty, as well as a technique fundamental to all learning. Moreover, poets do not slavishly repeat what they witness, know, or have heard. When they compose poetry they invent scenes, characters, and actions. Historians might find themselves constrained by the arbitrariness of actual events; poets, in contrast, present their audiences with pretend but "probable" scenarios that are better suited to moving them in appropriate ways. *Tragedy, for instance, relies on the spectacle of heroic men and women undergoing apt suffering to cause people to feel intense fear and pity. After being "purged" of these troublesome emotions (*catharsis), they will then, presumably, be prepared to act more rationally and hence make better decisions in the future.

It can be surprising to encounter mention of tragedy in the middle of a broader discussion of poetics. In the course of his rebuttal of Plato, Aristotle pursues his usual strategy of argument by classification. He identifies and differentiates two poetic *genres, *epic and tragedy (with a third genre, *comedy, apparently covered in the lost second half of the *Poetics*). This taxonomic project stands at the head of a long series of similar endeavors with great influence on later writers. E.g., Pierre Corneille's *Trois Discours sur le poème dramatique* (Three Discourses on Dramatic Poetry, 1660) formalizes the Aristotelian doctrine of the three unities of place, time, and action that later governed not only neoclassical drama but modernist works such as James Joyce's *Ulysses* (1922). Torquato Tasso reverses Aristotle by elevating epic above tragedy in *Discorsi del poema eroico* (*Discourses on the Heroic Poem*, 1594), an argument that had a profound effect on John Milton as he mulled his literary future. Northrop Frye's *Anatomy of Criticism* (1957) takes Aristotle's arguments about genre and uses them as a starting point for proposing a sweeping model for understanding all of literary hist.

For many, a second surprising aspect of Aristotle's *Poetics* is its relative lack of attention to *prosody. Although he does twice discuss meter (books 4.14 and 24.5–6), he does not directly and intimately connect the act of making (*poiēsis) that defines poetry with the patterning of *sound. Like Plato, he can often appear more concerned with what a poem relates—its content—than the specific words, and the specific word ordering, that a poet selects. There are instances of such analysis in antiquity—above all Dionysius of Halicarnassus's *Peri syntheseos onomaton* (On the Arrangement of Words, 1st c. BCE), but already one can begin to see the possibility of what later critics will consider to be a distinction between *verse* and *poetry*.

Francis Bacon's *The Advancement of Learning* (1605), for instance, acknowledges that some critics might consider poetry distinguishable by its *style but rejects such a definition as superficial and prefers the argument that poetry is "feigned history." By the time of P. B. Shelley's *Defence of Poetry* (1840), it was possible to argue that, as long as they display Aristotelian virtues such as harmony, order, and *unity, artworks of any kind (music, sculpture, dance) deserve the label *poetry*.

**II. Medieval and Early Modern.** In general, cl., med., and early mod. authors worry less about *form and more about poetry's ability to educate readers, esp. young people. Plato's *Protagoras* and Aristotle's *Politics* both argue that the purpose of poetry is to edify its audience, and Plutarch's "Quomodo adolescens poetas audire debeat" ("How the Young Man Should Study Poetry," 1st c. CE) goes so far as to recommend that one should emend poets' writings to guarantee their probity. Often treatments of poetry's instructional potential also contemplate its seductive qualities. Horace's *Ars poetica* (1st c. BCE) famously asserts that poets are "those who mix the useful with the sweet," and he prescribes such a mixture as the best means of "mold[ing] a child's young lips." While in later centuries there are dissenters such as Lodovico Castelvetro—whose *Poetica d'Aristotele vulgarizzata e sposta* (Aristotle's *Poetics* Translated and Expounded; 1570, 1576) endorses pleasure as the primary motivation for reading or writing poetry—until the 19th c. it remained conventional to defend poetry's capacity for moral instruction, as well as to justify any by-the-by enjoyment as a means of enticing the weak and impressionable to start on the path toward virtue and goodness. Indeed, given that the primary text on poetics available during the Middle Ages, a commentary on Aristotle's *Poetics* by the Ar. philosopher Ibn Rushd (Averroës), emphasizes poetry's moral purpose and civic-mindedness, one could track an unbroken lineage in the West of moralizing statements on poetics from Plutarch to late 20th-c. works such as Adrienne Rich's "When We Dead Awaken: Writing as Re-Vision" (1971) and Cary Nelson's *Repression and Recovery* (1989).

Significantly, this trad. rarely embraces straightforward didacticism. Dante's *Convivio* (ca. 1304–7), e.g., argues that, in a good poem, the literal, denotative meaning is supplemented by other, "allegorical" strata that touch on matters such as ethics and theology. In his *Difesa della Commedia di Dante* (*On the Defense of the Comedy of Dante*, 1587), Giacopo Mazzoni further explains that *allegory is necessary because poets must use concrete and credible images to communicate with a wide audience, many of whom are ill-suited to abstract thought. Poetry might, therefore, resemble a game in certain respects; but as long as poets play such word games in the service of public virtue, then, *contra* Plato, they perform a useful function in society. Such gaming could, in fact, Giambattista Giraldi Cinthio contends in his *Discorso intorno al comporre dei romanzi* (Discourse on the Composition of Romances, 1554), lead poets to innovate boldly, even

creating entirely new and unprecedented kinds of poetry, such as Ludovico Ariosto's long, self-interrupting narrative poem *Orlando furioso* (1516), which departs from Aristotelian prescriptions on almost every count. Even if the purpose of poetry remains constant across the ages—to praise the good and condemn the bad—to remain effective, poets must vary the means by which they pursue those ends.

The republication of Aristotle's *Poetics* in 1508 and its trans. into Lat. in 1536, plus the ready availability of Horace's *Ars poetica* in significant eds. such as the one pub. in Paris in 1500, ensured that the questions of seeming, pleasure, truth, and utility remained central to Western discussions of poetics during the Ren. and into the Enlightenment. Landmark works such as Philip Sidney's *Defence of Poesy* (1595), John Dryden's *Essay of Dramatic Poesy* (1668), and Alexander Pope's *Essay on Criticism* (1711) devote themselves to reprising and revising cl. stands on these subjects. When Samuel Johnson states that "the greatest excellency of art" is to "imitate nature; but it is necessary to distinguish those parts of nature, which are most proper for imitation" (*Rambler*, no. 4), or when Matthew Arnold claims that "truth and seriousness" are the *sine qua non* of good verse ("The Study of Poetry," 1880), one can hear echoes of Aristotle on *mimesis as well as two millennia of debates concerning the most compelling, improving, and expedient means of representing humans and the world. Even treatises such as Baltasar Gracián's *Agudeza y arte de ingenio* (*Cleverness and the Art of Wit*, 1642, rev. ed. 1648) that defend what might appear to be disruptively antimimetic devices—in particular, wild punning and exaggerated uses of figurative lang.—nevertheless continue to justify such obstructive *artifice by crediting pyrotechnic displays of *wit with the power to render poetry's lessons more sensuously and intellectually appealing.

Variations within this overall pattern do exist. E.g., George Puttenham's *Arte of English Poesie* (1589) distinguishes itself by blurring the boundaries between *rhetoric and poetics. He borrows terms pell-mell from rhetorical manuals in the trad. of Cicero's *De inventione* (ca. 86 BCE), the *Rhetorica ad Herennium* (early 1st c. BCE), and Quintilian's *Institutio oratoria* (ca. 93–95 CE) to anatomize Eng. verse. Surprisingly, he also attends closely to sound, distinguishing Elizabethan stress-based meters from cl. quantitative prosody. Puttenham's emphasis on poetry as, first, a discursive system susceptible of formal analysis and, second, a means of stirring an audience can make him sound unusually contemporary. In fact, New Historicists in the 1980s and 1990s such as Jonathan Goldberg, Stephen Greenblatt, and Patricia Parker looked to Puttenham as a touchstone and precursor, someone who pioneered the exploration of the dynamic relationship between literary texts and cultural contexts (see NEW HISTORICISM). One could also, however, construe Puttenham as engaged in a variant on the *querelle des anciens et des modernes* (quarrel of ancients and moderns), seeking to prove that a vernacular lang. and lit. can achieve excellences similar to but distinct from Lat. and Gr.

precursors. In this regard, the *Arte of English Poesie* deserves comparison to works such as Vasily Trediakovsky's *Novyi i kratkii sposob k slozheniiu rossiiskikh stikhov* (New and Brief Method for Composing Russian Verse, 1735) and Mikhail Lomonosov's *Pis'mo o pravilakh rossiiskogo stikhotvorstva* (Letter on the Rules of Russian Prosody, 1739), which similarly turn to the study of rhet. to help codify the *conventions, devices, and forms characteristic of an emergent *canon of vernacular poetry.

Another prominent strand within early mod. and Enlightenment poetics concerns comparisons between poetry and the other arts. Sometimes this discussion takes the form of a *paragone*, a mock-combat reminiscent of the duels between singing shepherds in the cl. *pastoral, as in the first act of Shakespeare's *Timon of Athens* (1623). At other times, the exercise leads to an extended philosophical reflection, as in Leonardo da Vinci's jours., or most famously in G. E. Lessing's *Laokoön* (*Laocoön*, 1766). Lessing maintains that Horace's injunction *ut pictura poesis*—that a poem should resemble a painting—was mistaken. Poetry, he believes, unfolds over time, whereas painting extends across space but can be taken in by the eye in an instant. Devices suitable to one art simply cannot be transposed effectively into the other. These arguments concerning what might now be called *medium specificity* have haunted poetics ever since. Is poetry distinguished from other art forms simply because it uses lang. to communicate, as Clement Greenberg contends in "Towards a Newer Laocoön" (1940)? Or is it at its core something more precise, as Nathaniel Mackey argues in *Paracritical Hinge* (2005), an art that showcases the "occult clamor" audible in speech and song?

**III. Romanticism to Modernism.** Around the year 1800, poets, literary critics, and philosophers began not simply to question or revise but to break with the Aristotelian legacy. As M. H. Abrams recounts in *The Mirror and the Lamp* (1953), mimetic theories of poetry started to give way to an emphasis on *expression. In the West, people took to describing and evaluating poetry based on its success or failure in eloquently and accurately communicating a writer's innermost thoughts, feelings, experiences, fantasies, and dreams, esp. as they touch on abstractions, spiritual matters, and historical causes that transcend the merely personal and arbitrary. From this vantage point, fidelity in *representation and seriousness of moral purpose matter less than a given writer's *intensity, *sincerity, passion, and ingenuity. Indecorous or lowly content and mannered or otherwise distorted depictions of the external world are excusable as long as poets obey the dictates of their *imagination and conscience. In doing so, moreover, they are free to dispense with received guidelines and models concerning proper poetic form. A poem's *structure, *diction, *rhythm, and other organizing traits should arise *organically*, i.e., in tight, close conjunction with the unfolding of its denotative meaning and its connotative associations (see CONNOTATION AND DENOTATION).

These precepts are all well known, of course, as aspects of romantic poetics. Key texts include A.W. and Friedrich Schlegel's jour. the *Athenaeum* (1798–1800), S. T. Coleridge's *Biographia Literaria* (1817), Wordsworth's Preface, and Shelley's *Defence*. Philosophically, the most important contributions were by Immanuel Kant and G.W.F. Hegel. In different but complementary ways, they assert that the mind plays an active role in the constitution of the external world. Later writers and thinkers became enamored of the power and the possibilities that this idea makes available. In the extreme formulation of this argument, poets do not reflect existing realities. Through the agency of the imagination, they, in fact, can create new ones ex nihilo—and might even be responsible for generating and sustaining the current actuality that they inhabit. Wallace Stevens's *The Necessary Angel* (1951) represents perhaps the most rigorous, sober, yet also far-reaching formulation of this romantic doctrine.

Kant deserves mention here for a second, additional reason. His *Kritik der Urteilskraft* (*Critique of Judgment*, 1790) holds that aesthetic judgments belong to a category independent of moral judgments and judgments that convey information or knowledge. To read a poem and expect to come away with moral instruction or other kinds of useful data is to make a logical mistake, i.e., to treat it as something other than a work of art. (As Ludwig Wittgenstein's *Zettel* [1967] puts it, "Do not forget that a poem, although it is composed in the language of information, is not used in the language-game of giving information.") Kant, in effect, makes the first sustained case for art's *autonomy, its separation from other spheres of human activity; the next two centuries would see many restatements and revisions of this thesis. Friedrich Schiller's *Ästhetische Erziehung des Menschen* (*On the Aesthetic Education of Man*, 1795), e.g., stakes out a position that would later be summed up as "art for art's sake" (see AESTHETICISM). Theodor Adorno's "Rede über Lyrik und Gesellschaft" ("Lyric Poetry and Society," 1957) claims that, insofar as Western aesthetics from Kant onward has provided poets an illusion of refuge from hist. and politics, they are thereby granted an opportunity to imaginatively negate the world they inhabit and dream of living free of capitalist necessity.

The expressive school of poetics found its last great expositor in Benedetto Croce. In *Ariosto, Corneille e Shakespeare* (1919), he states that "style is nothing other than the expression of the poet and his very soul." He believes that one should approach a poem as an aesthetic whole and trace its tone and other formal features in order to elucidate the mind and spirit that prompted its composition. Of course, such an approach presupposes that a given author's internal life is worth reconstructing and appreciating, an assumption that would come under attack from many quarters over the course of the 20th c. One set of writers expressed strong reservations regarding whose subjectivities and experiences are presumed to be normative within Western expressive poetics. They also questioned whether poetry could or should address a generic reader. These opponents of unreflective universalism include Gloria Anzaldúa, Amiri Baraka, Audre Lorde, M. NourbeSe Philip, and Denise Riley.

Other critics wondered whether poetry ought to place any priority at all on individual expression. In *Towards the Decolonization of African Literature* (1980), Chinweizu, Onwuchekwa Jemie, and Ihechukwu Madubuike argue that the anglophone poetic canon is excessively inward-directed and protective of privacy. They contrast it to the "public language" exemplified by oral Af. poetries, which emphasize direct, performative connections between poet and audience. Léopold Sédar Senghor, in his *Dialogue sur la poésie francophone* (Dialogue on Francophone Poetry, 1979), goes further, suggesting that the mod. Eur. has entirely lost touch with *myth, the shared collective system of stories and symbols that elevate poetry above self-indulgent coos and complaints. On the other side of the Atlantic, Édouard Glissant, in *L'intention poétique* (*Poetic Intention*, 1969), makes a parallel argument, disparaging Crocean creative *genius in the name of a poetry that could embody and perpetuate a healthy group consciousness.

Early in the 20th c., the Rus. formalists proposed a fundamental reorientation of poetics away from expression altogether (see RUSSIAN FORMALISM). Beginning with Viktor Shklovsky's "Voskreshenie slova" ("Resurrection of the Word," 1914), they polemically minimized the status of the author in favor of attending to the *priemy* (devices) in a work of lit. A poem does not convey a message; it draws attention to itself, more specifically, to its construction and function. Poetry in the aggregate, too, is not a gallery of brilliant achievements. It is a self-generating system of texts. New poems are not the product of *inspiration and brilliant execution. Rather, as Yuri Tynianov says in "Literaturnyi fakt" (Literary Fact, 1924), they are "mutations" that receive attention (instead of vanishing into historical oblivion unnoticed) because they depart in unusually striking ways from once-popular but now overly familiar, commonplace ways of assembling poetic devices.

Anglo-Am. *New Criticism also sharply differentiated between poet and poem. E.g., even when written in the first person and offering seemingly autobiographical details, a *lyric, New Critics such as John Crowe Ransom, Allen Tate, and Robert Penn Warren would assert, remains a thing apart, voiced by an implied "speaker" who, whatever overlap might exist with the poet, never coincides entirely. Studies such as Cleanth Brooks's *The Well Wrought Urn* (1947) and William Empson's *Seven Types of Ambiguity* (1930) demonstrate the virtues of *close reading, the intensive scrutiny of a poem's lang. and prosody that proceeds with limited or no reference to the original historical context in which it was written or to its poet's biography or psychology. If a poem is worthwhile, close reading can proceed almost indefinitely, since its paradoxes, convoluted figures of speech, and many levels of meaning reward intense prolonged interpretation. As promoted via arguments such as W. K. Wimsatt and M. C. Beardsley's essays *"The Intentional Fallacy" (1946) and *"The Affective Fallacy" (1946), close read-

ing amounts to a somewhat peculiar variant on cl. rhet. that limits itself to the formal analysis of texts while neglecting their intended or observed effects on *readers.

**IV. Postmodernism and Beyond.** Although strong pedagogically, New Criticism did not happen to offer a consistent theory of poetry as a literary system. It preferred to examine poems, not to generalize about poetry as a whole. *Structuralism, as developed and practiced in France in the decades after World War II, reverses this privileging of *texts over *textuality—i.e., instead of focusing on the appreciation of singular artworks, it seeks to elucidate cultural sign systems in toto. As Gérard Genette explains in "Structuralisme et critique littéraire" ("Structuralism and Literary Criticism," 1966), discrete literary objects should be conceived not as unitary and stand-alone but as relational entities, explicable only with reference to the larger system of themes, motifs, and keywords that constitute the literary system out of which the work has been assembled. Michael Riffaterre's *Semiotics of Poetry* (1978) asserts that, as a consequence, it is a mistake to read literary works such as poems as if they were primarily referential or mimetic. A poem's sentences, images, themes, and rhetorical devices signify—convey meaning—only insofar as they participate in *semiotic structures*, the sign configurations that make up poetry as a system that readers have learned to recognize. Jonathan Culler's *Structuralist Poetics* (1975) summarizes this approach to reading by stating that it privileges poetics over interpretation. In other words, instead of seeking to restate a poem's meaning in new words, it engages in description intended to locate a poem within an array of relevant categories. E.g., if a critic recognizes that Jan Kochanowski's *Treny* (Threnodies, 1580) is a collection of elegies for his daughter Urszula, she cannot straight away begin by pondering whether the poet is being overly sentimental, nor can she start expounding on the blend of Ren. humanism and staunch Catholicism that the lyrics exhibit. She must first ask what is an *elegy, how *Treny* relates to other elegies, and where elegy fits within literary production as a whole in the early mod. Polish-Lithuanian Commonwealth.

Structuralism quickly gave way to a variety of *poststructuralisms that then had widespread impact in Western academies during the 1970s and 1980s. Structuralism, critics quickly discovered, has a fatal flaw. It requires people to agree that it is possible to create ling. descriptions that can analytically stand in for actual cultural systems. Roland Barthes's book *Système de la mode* (*The Fashion System*, 1967), for instance, has to be understood as offering *in words* a sufficient mapping and explanation of how fashion itself operates in Fr. society. Poststructuralists attack this assumption from many different angles. Can any use of lang. ever accurately depict what happens in the ever- and swiftly changing external world? Are systems ever intelligible in their entirety? Do they even exist as wholes, or are they, in fact, made up of myriad competing interlinked ephemeral partial systems?

One philosopher who helped poststructuralists

address these issues is Martin Heidegger, whose later essays such as "Der Ursprung des Kunstwerkes" ("The Origin of the Work of Art," 1935) and ". . . dichterisch wohnet der Mensch . . ." ("Poetically Man Dwells," 1951) propose that Truth and Being never entirely reveal themselves. They can be approached only sidelong, and each revelation, by spotlighting one aspect of what people seek to know, often distracts them from or even blinds them to other facets. What is one to do? Poetry, Heidegger contends, is the art in which lang. most overtly stages its own emergence from nothingness, thus making it the best vehicle for pondering how and why the world exists.

The intellectual ferment in poststructuralist circles gave rise to numerous provocative arguments about poetics. The Yale School—which includes Harold Bloom, Paul de Man, Barbara Johnson, Geoffrey Hartman, and J. Hillis Miller—concentrated on showing that poetry always resorts to misnaming and misrecognition in its perpetual quest to affirm truths and essences that, in reality, are never self-evident or fully apprehensible. In essays such as "Shibboleth. Pour Paul Celan" (1986), Jacques Derrida suggests that a poem can best be read by launching off from particular details (such as an appended date of composition) and exploring its many ramifications as far as one may go. On this view, a poem is neither a self-enclosed *artifact nor a gateway to systemic verities but a starting and ending point for a voyage into ling. possibility. Marjorie Perloff's *The Poetics of Indeterminacy* (1978) agrees that poems open outward into vertiginous anarchic free play and speculation, but she also underscores that such moments of *indeterminacy remain constricted or counterbalanced by convention, context, and what else appears in a text. A poem cannot mean "just anything." Julia Kristeva's *La révolution du langage poétique* (1974, trans. as *Revolution in Poetic Language*, 1984) associates the infinite suggestiveness in good poetry with its nonsemantic components, esp. its rhythm and sound play, which she believes are traces of the profound, embodied communicative ties between child and mother that precede the forced imposition of patriarchal grammar and logic.

Poststructuralism's near-exclusive focus on lang., texts, and *intertextuality quickly produced its own countermovement, a push toward relocating poetry's meaning in social, cultural, economic, and political institutions and discursive practices. Indispensable have been philosophers such as Michel Foucault, whose *Surveiller et punir* (1975, trans. as *Discipline and Punish*, 1979) presents all texts as implicated in networks of power and knowledge, and Antonio Gramsci, whose *Quaderni del carcere* (1964, trans. as *Prison Notebooks*, 1971) maintains that texts acquire meaning and social significance not so much through what they say but through the links made between different spheres of activity. (An antiwar poem, for instance, can have no impact on a nation's war effort unless poetry is "articulated with," considered vitally connected to, other forms of effective political speech. Otherwise, it might as well celebrate May flowers or the *Mayflower*.)

*New Historicists present poetry as a mode of cultural production that has unacknowledged connections to other varieties. It can, Stephen Greenblatt argues in *Renaissance Self-Fashioning* (1980), serve as a means of drawing attention from patrons and heightening one's social status. Louis Montrose's *The Purpose of Playing* (1996) isolates "theatricality" as a shared attribute and value in Ren. Eng. religion, courtly society, and verse drama. More recent *cultural studies approaches to poetics—as Maria Damon and Ira Livingston recount in their introduction to *Poetry and Cultural Studies* (2009)—define themselves by setting aside any conventional distinctions between high/elite and low/mass/popular culture, by suspending evaluative distinctions between good/bad, and by denying the autonomy of aesthetics. The composition and the interpretation of poetry are often related to, and grounded in, contemp. activist projects, and a critic should not prejudge which humanities, social sciences, or other disciplines will prove best suited to illuminating a poem's "cultural work," its particular contribution to society, economics, and politics on behalf of what particular constituency.

Dissatisfaction with disciplinary limits characterizes other continuing conversations within the field of poetics. Many scholars have grown uneasy with the national, geographic, and ling. divisions that all too often artificially seal off different corpora of poetry from one other. In response, they have started surveying ways in which poetry takes shape and operates *transnationally*, i.e., across and despite nation-state boundaries. Indeed, studies such as Yunte Huang's *Transpacific Displacements* (2002) trouble the East/West divide. Another set of boundary-crossing scholars have attempted to supplement the humanistic analysis of poetry with methods and insights drawn from ling., psychology, neuroscience, and philosophy of mind. In *Toward a Theory of Cognitive Poetics* (1992), Reuven Tsur describes the enterprise of *cognitive poetics as an inquiry into how mental processes shape and constrain literary response and poetic structure. Crit. in this vein meticulously examines patterns in texts while simultaneously paying close attention to the cognitive states and dynamics involved in acts of interpretation.

A final important point: one should not assume from this overview that, by the year 2000, poetics had become solely an academic or university-based pursuit. As the new millennium approached, poets, too, continued to show themselves as capable as ever of making pioneering provocative arguments about the nature and function of their chosen art form. One recurrent ambition was to define poetry as a special kind of rhet. whose antimimetic and nonsemantic aspects enable it to serve liberatory political ends. The Moscow Conceptualists, e.g., among them Andrei Monastyrsky, Vsevolod Nekrasov, and Lev Rubinshtein, hold that poetry can provide an escape from oppressive ideologies and state surveillance. They believe that attending to the empty unmeaning clichés, errors, repetitions, and other verbal "junk" pervasive in everyday lang. use grants access to a blissful nothingness external to officially sanctioned truths and values. Halfway around the globe, another literary movement, *Language poetry, challenged the liberal democratic faith in the autonomy of the individual in the name of alternative, revolutionary modes of being in the world and being with others. Am. and Canadian writers affiliated with the movement such as Charles Bernstein, Lyn Hejinian, and Steve McCaffery frequently characterize their readers as "co-creators" of a poem, completing or continuing the process of meaning production initiated by its author. In Latin America, the publication of Haroldo de Campos's *Galáxias* (1984) helped to catalyze the emergence of a self-consciously *neobaroque poetics that is assertively, foundationally "postcolonial" and "antimodern." Coral Bracho, Eduardo Milán, Néstor Perlongher, and Raúl Zurita celebrate *archaism, *ornament, excess, inconsistency, asymmetry, and other disruptive, striking, and fanciful devices as means of seducing readers away from what they perceive as the misleading clarity and unearned rectitude of Western rationalist thought. They seek, as John Beverley puts it in "Nuevas vacilaciones sobre el barroco" (New Vacillations on the Baroque, 1988), a "possible culture and society starting from the mutilation that imperialism has inflicted on its people."

While all these figures might polemically oppose the centrality that mimesis has played in Western poetics since the days of Plato and Aristotle, they nonetheless recognizably operate within that same trad.: i.e., they focus their attention on whether and how lang. touches on the world, and they inquire into poetry's capacity to improve human behavior. And these concerns, too, more broadly typify the best contemp. writing on poetry by poets, whether represented by, say, the exilic musings of Agha Shahid Ali, the affirming feminism of Nicole Brossard, or the probing postapartheid meditations on justice and ethics by Ingrid de Kok. In the 21st c., the word *poetics* will surely continue its curious ambiguity, signifying, on the one hand, something institutional and perduring—a branch of lit. crit.—and, on the other hand, something altogether more changeable, porous, and unpredictable, namely, the compositional principles that poets themselves discover and apply during the writing process.

*See* POEM, POETRY, REPRESENTATION.

■ T.S. Eliot, *The Sacred Wood* (1920); E. Pound, *ABC of Reading* (1930); E. Drew, *Discovering Poetry* (1933); J. C. Ransom, "Criticism, Inc.," *Virginia Quarterly Review* 13 (1937); A. Tate, "Tension in Poetry," *Southern Review* 4 (1938); Y. Winters, *In Defense of Reason* (1947); R. P. Blackmur, *Language as Gesture* (1952); J. Lezama Lima, *La expresión americana* (1957); Weinberg; B. Hathaway, *The Age of Criticism* (1962); G. Stein, "Composition as Explanation" [1926], *What Are Masterpieces?* (1970); F. Kermode, *Renaissance Essays* (1971); H. Bloom, *The Anxiety of Influence* (1973); R. Barthes, *The Pleasure of the Text*, trans. R. Miller (1975); J. M. Lotman, *The Structure of the Artistic Text*, trans. G. Lenhoff and R. Vroon (1977); V. Forrest-Thomson, *Poetic Artifice* (1978); P. N. Medvedev and M. M. Bakhtin, *The Formal Method of Literary Scholarship*, trans. A. Wehrle (1978); de Man; A.

Easthope, *Poetry as Discourse* (1983); J. J. McGann, *The Romantic Ideology* (1983); T. Todorov, *Introduction to Poetics*, trans. R. Howard (1983); *Lyric Poetry*, ed. C. Hošek and P. Parker (1985); A. Carson, *Eros the Bittersweet* (1986); S. McCaffery, *North of Intention* (1986); C. Bernstein, *Artifice of Absorption* (1987); B. Johnson, "Apostrophe, Animation, and Abortion," *A World of Difference* (1987); R. B. DuPlessis, *The Pink Guitar* (1990); M. Brown, *Preromanticism* (1994); H. de Campos, *Ideograma* (1994); H. Meschonnic, *Politique du rythme, politique du sujet* (1995); J.-L. Nancy, *The Muses*, trans. P. Kamuf (1996); G. Agamben, *The End of the Poem*, trans. D. Heller-Roazen (1999); R. Jakobson, "The Newest Russian Poetry" ("Noveishaia russkaia poeziia," 1921), *My Futurist Years*, ed. B. Jangfeldt and S. Rudy, trans. S. Rudy (1999); P. Lacoue-Labarthe, *Poetry as Experience*, trans. A. Tarnowski (1999); M. Perloff, *Wittgenstein's Ladder* (1999); L. Hejinian, *The Language of Inquiry* (2000); S. Stewart, *Poetry and the Fate of the Senses* (2002); *Poetry in Theory*, ed. J. Cook (2004); M.A.R. Habib, *A History of Literary Criticism from Plato to the Present* (2005); R. von Hallberg, *Lyric Powers* (2008); B. Groys, *History Becomes Form* (2010).

B. M. REED

**POET LAUREATE.** The term derives from the med. university practice of crowning with laurels a student admitted to an academic degree in grammar, rhet., and poetry. In time, it grew in application to denote any significant poetic attainment, in accordance with Apollo's declaration that a branch or bay from his emblematic plant should become the prize of honor for poets and victors (Ovid, *Metamorphoses* 1). Paralleling the traditional role of poetic entertainer to the ruling court in other cultures (the Scandinavian *skald*, the Welsh *bard*, the Anglo-Saxon *scop*, and the Scots *makar*), the Eng. poets laureate were required to sing the glories of kings and chieftains. *Poet laureate* was used as a term of respect to compliment poets such as Chaucer and Petrarch and became a title informally bestowed on John Gower, John Lydgate, John Skelton, and Bernard Andreas (the Augustinian friar at Henry VII's court) for their work undertaken at royal courts. Official recognition of poetic court duties increased for Edmund Spenser, Michel Drayton, and Samuel Daniel; and Ben Jonson considered himself poet laureate in light of his two pensions and popular acclaim. Apollo's founding convergence of poetic expression with ruling power was then secured when John Dryden became the first authorized appointment to the office of poet laureate in 1668 and royal historiographer in 1670. The roles were separated in 1692, but the office continued to be associated with the writing of officially sanctioned poetry, as illustrated by Dryden's *Absalom and Achitophel* (1681), which allegorizes its support of the royal cause during the turbulence that accompanied Charles II's restoration to the throne.

Subsequently, the office was held in Britain by Thomas Shadwell, 1689–92; Nahum Tate, 1692–1715; Nicholas Rowe, 1715–18; Laurence Eusden, 1718–30;

Colley Cibber, 1730–57; William Whitehead, 1757–85; Thomas Warton, 1785–90; Henry James Pye, 1790–1813; Robert Southey, 1813–43; William Wordsworth, 1843–50; Alfred, Lord Tennyson, 1850–92; Alfred Austin, 1896–1913; Robert Bridges, 1913–30; John Masefield, 1930–67; C. Day-Lewis, 1968–72; Sir John Betjeman, 1972–84; and Ted Hughes, 1984–98. At his appointment in 1999, Andrew Motion negotiated the terms of the office such that it was held for ten years, rather than for life. The honorarium was also increased to around £5,000, replacing the previous arrangement of £200 plus a "butt of canary" (container of a Spanish wine). Trad. was further overhauled with the appointment in 2009 of Carol Ann Duffy, the first female poet laureate.

For a time during the 18th c., holders were required to become a member of the royal household and to compose a New Year's and birthday *ode to the king; this custom was dropped in order to preserve the dignity of the office, and the poet laureate became more regularly required to write eulogies, *elegies, and other *occasional verse. The longest serving poet laureate, Tennyson composed his "Ode on the Death of the Duke of Wellington" (1852) for this purpose, and the office's stately requirements may be appreciated by comparing this with the poet's other more personal elegiac compositions. In the 21st c., the poet laureate's role has been officially demarcated from the business of the royal court, and it is now an honorary title awarded to a poet whose work is of national significance. Accordingly, the poet laureate continues to provide poetic compositions on occasions of royal significance, such as for jubilee celebrations, but the honor and responsibility of speaking for and to a nation has seen the poet address issues of collective memory (such as for war losses) and collective hopes and disappointments (in the sporting arena, e.g.).

In accordance with changes to the Brit. political landscape, comparable roles of Scots Makar (established 2004) and National Poet for Wales (established 2005) are now recognized alongside the Brit. poet laureate. In America, the unofficial role of poet laureate (in existence since 1937) was established as the honorific title Poet Laureate Consultant in Poetry. Holders of this year-long position include (among others) Elizabeth Bishop, Joseph Brodsky, Billy Collins, Rita Dove, Robert Frost, Louise Glück, Donald Hall, Robert Hass, Ted Kooser, Maxine Kumin, Stanley Kunitz, Philip Levine, W. S. Merwin, Robert Pinsky, Kay Ryan, Karl Shapiro, Charles Simic, Mark Strand, Allen Tate, Robert Penn Warren, and Richard Wilbur. Its duties include one poetry reading and a public lecture. Such parallel institutions illustrate how the poet laureate's role continues to develop and change in its accommodation of a conservative heritage and a unique engagement with the life of national politics.

See PATRONAGE.

■ W. S. Austin Jr. and J. Ralph, *The Lives of the Poets Laureate* (1853); W. Hamilton, *The Poets Laureate of England* (1879); K. West, *The Laureates of England from Ben Jonson to Alfred Tennyson* (1895); W. F. Gray, *The Poets Laureate of England* (1914); E. K. Broadus, *The Laureateship* (1921); E. H. Wilkins, "The Coronation of Petrarch," *The Making of the "Canzoniere" and other Petrarchan Studies* (1951); K. Hopkins, *The Poets Laureate*, 3d ed. (1973); R. Helgerson, *Self-Crowned Laureates* (1983); R. J. Meyer-Lee, *Poets and Power from Chaucer to Wyatt* (2007); M. Nolan, "The New Fifteenth Century: Humanism, Heresy, and Laureation," *PQ* 87 (2008); *The Poets Laureate Anthology*, ed. E. H. Schmidt (2010).

B. N. SCHILLING; R. WILLIAMS

**POETRY.** Accounts of *poetry* as a category tend to outline essential features in an argument that might claim general assent. The range of past and present usage of the word, however, eludes such unifying accounts and invites us to think of *poetry* as a word of ancient Gr. origin, with a long and rich hist. One part of that hist. is the assumption that the word refers to something that transcends its hist. or has a conceptual core that runs through all the variations in its use. That hist. has been driven by acts of calling certain representations or classes of *representation poetry*.

The hist. begins with a set of Gr. terms: *poiēsis*, making; *poiēma*, a thing made, a work; *poiētēs*, a maker, *poet; *poiētike* (*technē*), the making (art/technique), *poetics. None of these words quite corresponds to the later categorical term *poetry*. The first attempt to give a comprehensive account, Aristotle's *Poetics*, set this hist. of change in motion by incl. the Socratic dialogues in prose but excluding Empedocles's versified natural philosophy. Prior to Aristotle, the Greeks had roughly assumed that *poetry*, when applied to discourse, referred to making verse. By excluding metrical composition as the defining criterion, Aristotle turned the object of "making" into a problem. Combined with Plato's critique of the conceptual value of poetry (for which Aristotle had an answer), Aristotle's question of what poetry "is" and, no less important, what poetry "is not" initiated a process of redefining and extending the categorical term. That process had a weight that was lacking in more specific questions: what is a *sonnet or a play or even a debated term like *epic?

Aristotle, thinking primarily of *drama and epic, answered the question he posed with the claim that the object of "making" was a *plot (*muthos*), an old term redefined and transformed into a set of internally necessary relations by the logic of Aristotle's argument. Although we now identify poetry primarily with *lyric, it is not at all clear how well Gr. lyric would have satisfied Aristotle's definition. Thereafter, poetry, in its mutations through various Eur. langs., was destabilized, in natural lang. referring to a set of metrical genres and in theory referring to some idea realized in only a subset of texts.

In the wholesale borrowing of Gr. literary vocabulary by the Romans, the conceptual morphology of *poiēsis* was Latinized and used for general terms covering a range of metrical discursive forms more commonly referred to by specific genre names, some borrowed from Gr. but others such as *carmina* (oddly trans. as *odes) from native Lat. We will call these Latinized and later vernacularized variations of the Gr. *poiēsis* "poetry words," the borrowed terms that helped create the impression of a universal concept that transcended its instantiation in any particular lang. Until the late Middle Ages, *poema, poetica* (*ars*), and *poeta* remained Lat. terms. The *bards, *scops, and *skalds*, *troubadours*, *trouvères*, *rimatori*, and *Minnesänger* came to be called *poets* in the vernacular only later. If such rhymers were referred to in Lat., the poetry words were sometimes used. In Dante, the poetry words were firmly established for vernacular composition. Indeed, in the *Vita nuova* and the *Convivio,* we have *poetria*, a categorical term roughly corresponding to *poetry*. The term was borrowed from med. Lat. but used in an apparently new way. Petrarch, who so profoundly aspired to be a "poet" in the Lat. sense, still termed his vernacular verse *Rime sparse* (or *Rerum vulgarium fragmenta*)—even though he calls what he does in the vernacular lyrics *poetando*, "making poems." The term *poetry*, in its variations, gradually came into use in the Eur. vernaculars; there it appears as a general term, covering a wide range of metrical discourses in the vernacular and implicitly linking recent vernacular metrical writing to Gr. and Lat. trads.

On a certain level of theoretical discourse, the vernacular derivatives of the Lat. continued to carry the full range of the Aristotelian usage, referring to epic (and verse *narrative), drama (in verse), and even lyric (although Ren. It. critics rarely considered lyric in their treatises on poetics). This range continued well into the 19th c., esp. in Germany, which came to favor the native term *Dichtung* for metrical composition, as opposed to the general term (derived from Fr.), *Poesie*, for lit. in a larger sense, incl. the novel. In popular usage, however, *epic* and *drama* increasingly appeared as marked terms (such as John Dryden's *An Essay of Dramatic Poesy*), while the unmarked term *poetry* came to refer primarily to lyric. In the 19th c., variations on the term *literature* eventually supplanted this larger sense of "poetry."

As the meaning of *poetry* was becoming increasingly centered on lyric and shorter *narrative verse, the range of discursive forms called *poetry* was broadening in the late 18th and 19th cs. In part, this broadening followed from renewed interest in and the recovery of earlier lit. from the Middle Ages, whose vernacular lyrics were now conventionally called *poetry*. Anonymous oral verse such as *ballads and folk songs became *poetry*. *Poetry* was also used to describe a variety of metrical genres from the old, literate cultures of Asia, genres that were sometimes very far from the sense of the term that we find in Aristotle. *Shi'ir*, the categorical term for strict metrical lyric genres in the Islamic world, was called *poetry*. *Kāvya*, with a range that included prose and was centered, like Aristotle, on epic and drama, was called *poetry*. The lyric form *shi*, in its East Asian variations, was, like *poetry*, a concept going beyond formal definition (by this period in Chinese one could say that there was no "shi" in something that was formally a "shi"); this too was called *poetry*. In the latter part of the 19th c., protoanthropologists found *poetry* in the verse of preliterate societies. Eventually in the 20th c., Homer, once the prime example of the poet as maker, became

the name attached to the record of a collective practice of oral composition, which was called *oral poetry*. Such a radically extended corpus of what might be considered poetry, combined with the evolving practice of Eur. writers who called themselves *poets*, required a new and far broader understanding of the term.

Some basic transformations in the idea of poetry occurred in the early 19th c. These transformations have come to be so taken for granted that they are now seen as essential to poetry rather than as historical phenomena.

Aristotle's claim that a poet made "plots" was no longer appropriate for the new ways in which the word *poetry* was used. G.W.F. Hegel proposed in the *Aesthetics* that the material of poetry was "inner representations" (*innere Vorstellen*) to which the poet gave form and that lang. was merely an accidental means of manifestation. From this, Hegel concluded that poetry could be translated from one lang. to another without essential loss. Only a few decades separated Hegel's lectures on aesthetics from P. B. Shelley's memorable comparison of translating poetry to casting a violet into a crucible (*A Defence of Poetry*). The differences among discursive forms called *poetry* were the companion of the nationalization of poetry. Even Hegel insists that there are different poetries of different nations or areas, each distinct in "spirit, feeling, outlook, expression." The idea that poetry appears through particular words in a unique national lang. and is thus untranslatable was very much a product of the 19th c. It went with the idea of a distinctly national culture, the unprecedented dissemination of a normalized national lang. and the suppression of regional variation through a new school system based on the authorized vernacular. It was an idea that served the mythology of the ethnic unity of the nation-state (see NATIONAL POETRY).

We see yet another important transformation in poetry in Hegel's *Aesthetics*: the rejection of *occasional poetry, which is made to answer social needs and demands. Through much of its hist., lyric poetry in particular was socially grounded—it served to praise, blame, petition, insult, and seduce. Such contingency in poetry violated the freedom that Hegel saw at the heart of poetry. The idea that poetry should be an end in itself was to have profound consequences later in the century.

In the 19th c., a few poets could still make a living by writing poetry (Victor Hugo may have been the last), but by and large, poetry came to be seen as an exercise of pure art detached from any pragmatic social ground. Mod. theorists from Theodor Adorno to Pierre Bourdieu have argued that valorizing poetry's disengagement from social utility was itself socially grounded. The putative social *autonomy of the poet has remained, however, the general assumption, with the only serious exception being the subordination of poetry to the needs of socialist revolution. Nonsocialist critics consider such poetry potentially propaganda, thus, not true poetry.

Like other cultural products of Europe, this new version of poetry traveled with colonialism and the display of Eur. technological power. The Eur. diasporic cultures of the New World, Africa, and the Pacific kept up by reading and sometimes sending aspiring young poets back to Europe—most often to Paris. From the mid-19th through the early 20th c., Fr. and Eng. poetry was exported to the literate cultures of Asia. In Asia, these imported Eur. trads. competed with and sometimes entirely replaced established literary trads. There was usually a stage during which writers tried to accommodate new Eur. ways of writing in traditional forms, beginning with *Tanzimat* (Transformation) in Ottoman Turkey in the 1840s. Similar phases came later in Japan, China, South Asia, and the Persian and Ar. world. In some cases, as with the destruction of the culture of Mughal Dehli following the Sepoy Rebellion, political upheaval destroyed the community on which continuity depended. In other cases, the dissatisfaction of young writers with traditional poetic forms led to what was often termed *new poetry*, essentially on a Eur. model (ranging from *romanticism to the avant-gardes of the early 20th c.; see AVANT-GARDE POETICS).

In Japan, China, South Asia, and the Islamic world, these versions of *new poetry* entered a tense relationship with the existing older poetry. The later represented cultural trad., a conservatism that, through the course of the 20th c., increasingly represented nationalism. The former began with its eyes fixed firmly on Western Europe but gradually saw itself as representing an international community of poetry. Both the *new poetry* and the various forms of older poetry were, however, understood as different versions of some universal thing now called *poetry*. Although the terms used for *poetry* were regional and thus asserted continuity with older trads., the semantic range of such terms expanded to accommodate the vague universalism of *poetry*, as used in the various Eur. vernaculars.

Through the 19th c. and early 20th c., Western Eur. poetry was being diffused through the Eur. diaspora, through Eastern Europe and Russia and through the colonies and independent states feeling the weight of Eur. technological power. During this same period, poetry was changing rapidly, primarily in France. One could easily argue that the technology of distribution had become so rapid that, in order to retain their cultural advantage, Fr. poets had continuously to supersede their recent predecessors; they had, in effect, entered a mod. self-conscious fashion system.

It is important to understand the differences in cultural power at this long moment in hist. The Rus. elite visited and stayed in Paris; the Fr. elite by and large did not stay in Moscow or St. Petersburg. If Rus. books were imported to France, they were purchased by Russians; if Fr. books were imported to St. Petersburg, they were purchased by Russians. Rubén Darío went to Paris and brought back a new poetry that began a transformation of Latin Am. poetry; although the Fr. would eventually become interested in the new Latin Am. poetry, they did not go to Mexico City at the turn of the 20th c.—much less to León, Nicaragua, where Darío became a poet—to get literary inspiration. Orientalists in England, France, and Germany studied cl.

Ar., Persian, and Ottoman poetry; their trans. were widely read and appreciated, giving us J. W. Goethe's *West-östlicher Divan* (*West-Eastern Divan*; see DIVAN) and Edward FitzGerald's trans. of ʿUmar Khayyām (see OMAR KHAYYÁM QUATRAIN). But (somewhat later), young Ar. and Turkish intellectuals frequented the Fr. bookstores in Alexandria and Istanbul for the latest shipments from Paris. In Alexandria (and often in Paris), C. P. Cavafy was arguably not a "Greek poet," but a very innovative "Western European poet" who wrote in Gr.

An essay by the Am. poet E. A. Poe, "The Poetic Principle," had an immense impact in France. Poetry was to aspire to the condition of music, a pure aesthetic experience of concentrated intensity. Although still tied to the ideology of national lang. in its untranslatability, the lang. of *pure poetry was distinct from lang. elsewhere, which was seen as based on utility and social engagement.

From the middle of the 19th c., there was an ever-increasing diversity in the kinds of discourse that were called *poetry*. Paris attempted to assert hegemony in successive versions of an avant-garde and, for much of the world, succeeded until World War II. Such hegemony, however, could be contested from the very beginning of poetic modernity in figures such as Walt Whitman and Emily Dickinson.

Changes in technology and the structures of cultural authority in the second half of the 20th c. and into the 21st c. have profoundly changed the world of poetry. Improvements in the technology of printing and dissemination made the production of poetry less dependent on large publishers with established structures of distribution. The shrinking readership for contemp. poetry simultaneously made publishing poetry less desirable for large publishers. By the end of the 20th c., the Web became an important venue for poetry, with communities of readers no longer in any common physical location but able to communicate with each other—and sometimes with the poets—with great ease.

The literary reviews of an earlier era, in which the judgment of established cultural figures exerted a profound influence on the careers of younger poets, became less important. The rapid expansion of the university system in the second half of the 20th c. made the academy a central force in the evolution of poetry, with a proliferation of critics recovering and publicizing older poetry, passing judgment on contemp. poetry, offering venues for poets giving readings and lectures, and often providing regular employment for poets. The sheer number of such colleges and universities in the New World, Europe, and much of Asia has led to a radically decentered world of poetry. The poetry communities on the Web have increasingly offered challenges to such academic authority.

What is the understanding of poetry that unites diverse practices from *concrete poetry to computer-generated poems to *waka that follow the sentiments and rules of propriety from a millennium earlier to a traditional Chinese poem in which a father admonishes his son who has asked for money to buy a tape recorder? In each case, a cultural authority of one sort or another can step in and say, "That is *not* poetry." Yet each of the diverse practices of poetry in the early 21st c. derives from some moment in the hist. of the word, and each stakes a claim that excludes some practice of poetry elsewhere.

*See* POEM.

■ J. W. Mackail, "The Definition of Poetry," *Lectures on Poetry* (1911); J. C. Ransom, "Poetry: A Note in Ontology," *The World's Body* (1938), and "Wanted: An Ontological Critic," *The New Criticism* (1941); M. T. Herrick, *The Fusion of Horatian and Aristotelian Literary Criticism, 1531–1555* (1946), esp. ch. 4; J. J. Donohue, *The Theory of Literary Kinds*, v. 2 (1949); E. C. Pettet, "Shakespeare's Conception of Poetry," *E&S* 3 (1950); Abrams; Curtius, 152–53; R. Wellek, "The Mode of Existence of the Literary Work of Art," Wellek and Warren; C. L. Stevenson, "On 'What Is a Poem?'" *Philosophical Review* 66 (1957); S. Hynes, "Poetry, Poetic, Poem," *CE* 19 (1958); R. Jakobson, "Linguistics and Poetics," Sebeok, rpt. in Jakobson, v. 2; N. A. Greenberg, "The Use of *Poiēma* and *Poiēsis*," *Harvard Studies in Classical Philology* 65 (1961); V. M. Hamm, "The Ontology of the Literary Work of Art," *The Critical Matrix*, ed. P. R. Sullivan (1961)—trans. and paraphrase of Ingarden, continued in *CE* 32 (1970); R. Fowler, "Linguistic Theory and the Study of Literature," *Essays on Style and Language* (1966); J. Levy, "The Meanings of Form and the Forms of Meaning," *Poetics—Poetyka—Poetika*, ed. R. Jakobson et al. (1966); E. M. Zemach, "The Ontological Status of Art Objects," *JAAC* 25 (1966–67); J. A. Davison, *From Archilochus to Pindar* (1968); R. Harriott, *Poetry and Criticism before Plato* (1969); R. Häussler, "Poiema und Poiesis," *Forschungen zur römischen Literatur*, ed. W. Wimmel (1970); D. M. Miller, "The Location of Verbal Art," *Lang&S* 3 (1970); R. Ingarden, *The Literary Work of Art*, trans. G. G. Grabowicz (1973), and *The Cognition of the Literary Work of Art*, trans. R. A. Crowley and K. R. Olson (1973); T. McFarland, "Poetry and the Poem," *Literary Theory and Structure*, ed. F. Brady et al. (1973); J. Buchler, *The Main of Light* (1974); E. Miner, "The Objective Fallacy and the Real Existence of Literature," *PTL* 1 (1976); ); M. P. Battin, "Plato on True and False Poetry," *JAAC* 36 (1977); J. Margolis, "The Ontological Peculiarity of Works of Art," *JAAC* 36 (1977); Fish, "How to Recognize a Poem When You See One"; E. H. Falk, *The Poetics of Roman Ingarden* (1981); A. L. Ford, "A Study of Early Greek Terms for Poetry: 'Aoide,' 'Epos,' and 'Poesis,'" *DAI* 42 (1981); J. J. McGann, "The Text, the Poem, and the Problem of Historical Method," *NLH* 12 (1981); W. J. Verdenius, "The Principles of Greek Literary Criticism," *Mnemosyne* 4 (1983); R. Shusterman, *The Object of Literary Criticism* (1984), ch. 3; G. B. Walsh, *The Varieties of Enchantment: Early Greek Views of the Nature of Poetry* (1984); Hollander; T. Clark, "Being in Mime," *MLN* 101 (1986); P. Fry, *A Defense of Poetry: Reflections on the Occasion of Writing* (1995); G. Agamben, *The End of the Poem*, trans. D. Heller-Roazen (1999); D. Heller-Roazen, *Echolalias: On the Forgetting of Language*

(2008); A. Grossman, *True-Love: Essays on Poetry and Valuing* (2009).

S. OWEN

**POETRY READING.** Although oral poetry *performance is coextensive with the hist. of poetry, the poetry reading is a relatively recent type of such performance, a cultural category of a discrete live event at which an author reads aloud from a written text of his or her own poetry to a public audience. Text-based performance by the author has become central to mod. poetry trads. since the middle of the 20th c. and performs a number of functions: it provides publicity and financial support for the careers of poets; it promotes the dissemination of poetry in societies whose mass media pay little attention; it makes possible the borrowing of cultural capital from other events such as conferences, rallies, and social campaigns; and it generates new modes of poetry. Almost all poetry since the 1950s anticipates both silent reading and aural reception, and this duality of reception gives impetus to poetic forms well suited to public authorial projection, such as first-person confessional lyrics, oratorical and highly rhetorical styles, and even disjunctive, paratactic verse (purely *oral poetry is heavily paratactic; see HYPOTAXIS AND PARATAXIS). The growing dominance of the poetry reading has also enabled many other performance trads.—incl. performance art, live comedy, praise poetry, the griot, the *phalène*, the *eisteddfod, the *mushaira*, and pop-music lyrics—to influence the poetry reading and has led to speciation into spoken word, *poetry slam, hip-hop, experimental performance, *sound poetry, and crossovers with music, visual art, and theater. This intense activity around the poetry reading continues to drive devels. in poetic form.

The public reading aloud of written poems has diverse origins. Although poets have always recited their work aloud privately to family, friends, and patrons, most oral reading of poetry was done not by the author but by professionals, priests, courtiers, officials, and others at religious or ceremonial occasions or by actors in public entertainments. A few 19th-c. authors, notably Walt Whitman, gave public readings in the wider context of popular lectures. In the early 20th c., avant-garde venues and universities in particular provided intermittent opportunities for poets to give poetry readings; but with a few exceptions, poetic composition was not directed at authorial public performance, and there was no defined cultural category of poetry reading. Until the mid-20th c., the majority of occasions when poetry was read aloud were everyday private gatherings, where ordinary readers entertained a circle of listeners by reading aloud, a commonplace oralcy that deeply shaped both the composition and reception of poetry until the early 20th c.

Rapid decline of such homemade entertainment from the 1920s onward in the face of new leisure opportunities provided by the automobile, the cinema, and radio ended this hist. of self-reliant communal entertainment and, in the process, removed the experience of hearing poetry from most readers. After

World War II, demand for radio broadcasts of poems by their authors, a continuing minor trad. of poetry readings in universities, the success of Dylan Thomas's tour of America, new affordable recording technology, and perhaps a felt lack of live poetry in everyday life all contributed to the emergence of the poetry reading as a major force in the 1950s, a devel. symbolized by notable events such as the Six Gallery reading at which Allen Ginsberg premiered *Howl* and by Evgenii Evtushenko's performances of "Babi Yar." Most poetry pub. since the 1960s is intended to be both read silently on the page with the sharpened attention to semantic, visual, and sonic cues made possible by rereading and heard and remembered as a performed work.

Poetry readings are easily thought of as no more than live public entertainments at which audiences can see and listen to poets in action. Critics of the poetry reading have deplored their popularity as pandering to a taste for vaudeville or at best no more than a mutual celebration of cultural capital; scholars have sometimes assumed that, despite apparent parallels between the texts of poems and musical scores or drama scripts, performance of a written text adds nothing to the value and meaning of a poem that could not be had by silent reading. Now that performance is an essential component of the public culture of poetry, researchers have begun to ask whether the poetry reading affects any of the core conceptual issues of literary interpretation, and several areas of investigation have been proposed.

Many poets argue that *sound is the primary carrier of meaning in the poem through the *iconicity of phonemes, the affective coloration of phonetic articulation produced by the body's vocal organs, and associations between the sound of the poem's lang. and the sensory complexity of the world's soundscapes. Researchers have investigated whether the poetry reading offers opportunities similar to those of musical performance to explore these possibilities of the poetic acoustic in ways to which the inner mental theater can do only limited justice and to study the intersections of physical and metaphorical voice in texts and performance. Others note that poetic movements tend to adopt speaking styles that could be studied like hegemonic singing styles; that performance can elicit intersubjective dynamics of *address; that poetry performance is interdependent with recording and mediating technologies; that many poetry readings are site-specific; and finally that poetry readings frequently stage existential and institutional issues of authorship, as an audience witnesses what it means to embody and affirm these particular words in a poem in public.

Charles Bernstein writes that he "would add the poet's own performance of the work in a poetry reading, or readings, to the list of variants that together, plurally, constitute and reconstitute the work." Until the end of the 20th c., lit. crit. wrote little about this possibility (even poets had little to say) and left the field to ethnographers of oral lit., but researchers increasingly agree with Bernstein's claim. In addition to a rapidly growing critical lit., many Web sites now present audio and video recordings of poetry readings, and major archiving projects of a hist. at risk of disappearance are also underway both online and in national libraries.

See HIP-HOP POETICS, NUYORICAN POETS CAFÉ, RECITATION.

■ **Criticism and History**: E. Fogerty, *The Speaking of English Verse* (1923); J. Masefield, *With the Living Voice* (1924); M. M. Robb, *Oral Interpretation of Literature in American Colleges and Universities* (1941); Y. Winters, "The Audible Reading of Poetry," *HudR* 4 (1951); F. Berry, *Poetry and the Physical Voice* (1962); *Poets on Stage*, ed. A. Ziegler et al. (1978); S. McCaffery, "Sound Poetry," *L=A=N=G=U=A=G=E* 7 (1979); D. Levertov, "An Approach to Public Poetry Listenings," *Light Up the Cave* (1981); *The Poetry Reading*, ed. S. Vincent and E. Zweig (1981); G. Economou, "Some Notes towards Finding a View of the New Oral Poetry," *Boundary 2* 3 (1985); D. Hall, "The Poetry Reading," *American Scholar* 54 (1985); D. Oliver, *Poetry and Narrative in Performance* (1989); G. Stewart, *Reading Voices* (1990); F. C. Stern, "The Formal Poetry Reading," *Drama Review* 35 (1991); R. Finnegan, *Oral Poetry* (1992); A. T. Gaylord, "Reading Chaucer," *Chaucer Yearbook* 1 (1992); K. H. Machan, "Breath into Fire: Feminism and Poetry Readings," *Mid-American Review* 12 (1992); R. Tsur, *What Makes Sound Patterns Expressive?* (1992); C. Habekost, *Verbal Riddim* (1993); P. Finch, *The Poetry Business* (1994); H. Lazer, *Opposing Poetries* (1996); M. Davidson, *Ghostlier Demarcations* (1997); A. Morris, *Sound States* (1997); C. Bernstein, *Close Listening* (1998); D. Brown, *Voicing the Text* (1998); B. Cobbing and L. Upton, *Word Score Utterance Choreography* (1998); F. P. Brown, *Performing the Word* (1999); T. Hoffman, "Treacherous Laughter," *Studies in American Humor* 3 (2001); V. Stanton and V. Tinguely, *Impure/Reinventing the Word* (2001); *Writing Aloud*, ed. B. LaBelle and C. Migone (2001); *Additional Apparitions*, ed. D. Kennedy and K. Tuma (2002); J. M. Foley, *How to Read an Oral Poem* (2002); A. Hoyles and M. Hoyles, *Moving Voices* (2002); M. Robinson, *Words Out Loud* (2002); *The Spoken Word Revolution*, ed. M. Eleveld (2003); N. Murr, "Poetry Readings," *Poetry* 184 (2004); P. Middleton, *Distant Reading* (2005); and "How to Read a Reading of a Written Poem," *Oral Tradition* 20 (2005); A. Lopez, *Meaning Performance* (2006); N. Marsh et al., "Blasts of Language," *Oral Tradition* 21 (2006); H. Meschonnic, *La rime et la vie* (2006); J. S. Rubin, *Songs of Ourselves* (2007); C. Graebner, "The Poetics of Performance Poetry," *World Literature Today* 82 (2008); H. Gregory, "(Re)presenting Ourselves," *Oral Tradition* 23 (2008); L. Wheeler, *Voicing American Poetry* (2008); *The Sound of Poetry/The Poetry of Sound*, ed. M. Perloff and C. Dworkin (2009); *Performing Poetry*, ed. A. Casas and C. Graebner (2010).

■ **Web Sites**: Archive of the Now, http://www.archiveofthenow.com/; Penn Sound, http://writing.upenn.edu/pennsound/; Poets.Org, http://www.poets.org/; The Poetry Archive, http://www.poetryarchive.org/poetryarchive/home.do. See also holdings of audio and video at the Library of Congress, the British Library, and other national libraries. YouTube contains a large, changing collection of video and audio recordings.

P. Middleton

**POETRY SLAM.** A contest in which poets compete against each other with judges (chosen at random from the audience) assigning a score to each performance on a scale of one to ten to determine the winner. The entertainment is characterized by a high level of participation between poet and audience and is often held at a bar or café, with the intent of drawing a paying crowd. Typically, no props or costumes are allowed, and performances are limited to three minutes. Many slams are open to the public, though some are by invitation only. The poetry slam has been credited as a factor in returning poetry to the people.

The poetry slam is part of a broad late 20th-c. resurgence of the spoken word, incl. in music (rap and *hip-hop), and has been likened to ancient trads. of competitive and/or linked rhymes between orators—from the Gr. mythological tale of Apollo and Marsyas to the Af. griots, from the Sanjurokunin sen, or imaginary poetry team competitions, of 10th-c. Japanese court poet Fujiwara no Kinto to the Af. Am. *dozens. Its rise in the U.S. in the early 1980s is traceable to a poetry "bout" between poets Ted Berrigan and Anne Waldman—both decked out as boxers—in 1979. (Future bouts moved to New Mexico and became the Taos Heavyweight Poetry Championship.) The next year, in an unrelated occurrence, the Chicago poet Jerome Salla and the musician Jimmy Desmond, who previously had gotten drunk and created a disturbance at one of Salla's readings, engaged in what was billed as "a ten-round poetry fight to the death." The fight was inspired by professional wrestling, which was enjoying immense popularity in the U.S. at the time, as well as punk rock, which came to the U.S. in the late 1970s, with the erosion of the boundary between artist and spectator informing the dialogic relationship between audience and poet that is central to the poetry slam. The poetry slam also has links to earlier trads. of U.S. performance poetry, perhaps most notably the *Beat poets and the carnival culture that prevailed at their readings.

Marc Smith started the poetry slam in Chicago in 1986 at a club called the Green Mill. In New York, Bob Holman introduced the poetry slam at the *Nuyorican Poets Café in 1989, one of the original venues to host such competitions. In San Francisco in 1990, Gary Mex Glazner organized the first National Poetry Slam, where competitors from across the U.S. came to compete. The poetry slam has become a widespread cultural phenomenon, regularly convening ordinary people either weekly or monthly in many North Am. cities. The National Poetry Slam is an international event, with championships taking place in England, Germany, Israel, and Sweden.

Styles of slam poetry range from the searingly funny to the wrenchingly confessional. Through strategies of counteridentification and even disidentification, slam poets often seek to transcend the boundaries of socialized roles, and the poetry slam itself becomes a site for the ritual enactment of *communitas*. Much of the poetry performed at the poetry slam is fueled by identity politics, and the poetry slam itself has been hailed as both democratic and multicultural, featuring a pluralist cast of poets who are tied up in powerful social movements that have reframed—and validated—cultural identities of minority citizens, particularly as those identities are informed by race, ethnicity, class, gender, and sexuality. The poetry slam thus has given a voice to subaltern groups and their resistant, sometimes subversive, politics. On the other hand, the poetry slam also has sought to harness the energies and strategies of late market capitalism in an effort to compete for consumers' attention, complicating for some its claims to alterity.

Concern has been expressed about the commodification of the poetry slam—its trendiness and gimmickry—as by the poet Amiri Baraka, who likens it to a "strong-man act," a sideshow spectacle that relies too much on the personality of the poet and not enough on the intrinsic quality of the poem. Some have condemned the slam as "anti-art," with the literary critic Harold Bloom proclaiming it "the death of art." Others have questioned in more subdued tones whether slam poetry can operate successfully on the page.

A number of slam poets have published work in traditional print form; others have released cassettes and compact discs in addition to, or in the place of, books. Many of the most popular performance poets in the U.S. in the early 21st c. got their start in the arena of the poetry slam, among them Staceyann Chin, Reg E. Gaines, Bob Holman, Tracie Morris, Patricia Smith, and Saul Williams.

*See* PERFORMANCE, POETIC CONTESTS, POETRY READING.

■ *Aloud: Voices from the Nuyorican Poets Cafe*, ed. M. Algarin and B. Holman (1994); *SlamNation*, dir. Paul Devlin (1998); G. M. Glazner, *Poetry Slam: The Competitive Art of Performance Poetry* (2000); T. Hoffman, "Treacherous Laughter: The Poetry Slam, Slam Poetry, and the Politics of Resistance," *Studies in American Humor* 3 (2001); Julie Schmid, "Spreading the Word: A History of the Poetry Slam," *Talisman* (2001–02); Kurt Heintz, "An Incomplete History of Slam," http://www.e-poets.net/library/slam.

T. Hoffman

**POETRY THERAPY.** *See* THERAPY AND POETRY.

**POIĒSIS** (from the Gr. verb *poieō*, infinitive *poiein*, "to make form"). The verb, not the noun, was prominent in usage first. In the context of poetry, the substantive *poiētēs* (*poet) was long more common than the abstract noun *poiēsis*. Indeed, the art of poetry as such was often denoted as *poiētikē*, from which the discipline of *poetics obtains its name.

In general usage, the verb form *poiein* retained as primary meaning an act of formation and transformation of matter in the cosmic sphere in relation to time. Though ultimately, as a social practice, it involves *technē* (art) and thus belongs to the world of art, *poiēsis* in the sense of making form is still present in the lang. of biology and cybernetics (as in *autopoiesis*, the self-generation of living organisms) or medicine (as in *hematopoiesis*, the process by which bone marrow produces red blood cells).

It is important to observe this primary sense of making form when discussing the term *poiēsis* in the context of poetry and poetics. The poet as *homo faber* (man, the maker) and the poem as the made thing are commonplaces that persist throughout the hist. of Western poetics, often in tension with other formulations that identify the poet as prophet or seer (Lat. *vates*), as a vessel of divine *inspiration, or as the transcendent voice of the age.

Esp. when the complement or alternative has been an idealist program for poetry—for instance, the Aristotelian notion of poetry as *mimesis* as adapted in the Eur. Ren.—the notion of poetry as poiēsis has held an undiminished power, perhaps because it explains what other programs often cannot: how we encounter a poem as object, how a poem radically alters reality, how a poem is actually made. The hist. of Western poetics includes many episodes in which idealist or even metaphysical claims for poetry are answered (and not necessarily contradicted) by corresponding claims that proceed from poiēsis: e.g., Philip Sidney's fusion of Platonism and Aristotelianism in his *Defence of Poesy* (written ca. 1580, pub. 1595) meets its counterpart in George Puttenham's contemporaneous *Arte of English Poesie* (1589), which begins with this statement: "a poet is as much to say as a maker." A reductive but not inaccurate thesis would have it that this tension between idealist creating and materialist making permeates the entire hist. of signification of the term *poiēsis*.

In the 20th c., renewed attention to poiēsis was the outcome of a modernist aspiration to shake off the burden of the romantic *genius. Modernist poetry and crit. often named the poem not as fiction, ideation, or reflection but as new reality in itself; described the poetic act as the making of a new thing; and—in the spirit of Dante's praise of Arnaut Daniel as "miglior fabbro del parlar materno" (a better craftsman of the mother tongue; *Purgatorio* 26.117), echoed in T. S. Eliot's dedication to *The Waste Land* (1922)—celebrated the poet as agent of creation rather than instrument of *representation (see MODERNISM). Crucial here would be the early theoretical texts of Paul Valéry: "The Introduction to the Method of Leonardo da Vinci" (1894) and "Poetry and Abstract Thought" (1939).

In this specific sense, one might discern in modernist thinking something of the emergent notional frame of *poiēsis*. Its most ancient appearance in Homeric Gr. (as *poiein*) pertains primarily to working on matter, shape, or form and only secondarily to abstraction, whereby it might suggest availing or producing forms. As philosophy takes over in the cl. Gr. imaginary, this primary materialist notion of *poiēsis* becomes degraded relative to *praxis* (action) or *dēmiourgia* (creation). Yet it is interesting to note that, in strict etymology, the root reference of *dēmiourgia* bears a sort of communal

instrumentalism. As opposed to poiētēs, who encounters form as object, dēmiourgos is one whose work derives its primary meaning from the public sphere, as the word itself shows: *dēmos + ergon*. This ergon (work) covers a range of action: a dēmiourgos can be a seer as much as a doctor.

Arguably because of the Christian investment in the notion of creation out of the absolute, but no doubt also because of the epistemological permutations of Platonism from the Hellenistic era onward, the referential framework that comes to measure the genius of a poet is drawn not from *poiēsis* but from *dēmiourgia*. In Plato, one might say (though in *Timaeus* both notions are intertwined) that dēmiourgos is still in effect a worker who commits an ergon, even if this ergon is the universe itself, while the poet is a shaper who shapes forms. But for Plato, shaping forms is, in the last instance, inevitably misshaping, de-forming—hence, his alarm for the poet as a shaper who *transforms* morals, essentially a political, not ethical, act that leaves no place for the poet but exile from the city. Plato's concern is warranted from the standpoint of what will become the philosophical (and later, theological) desire to harness an unalterable, inalienable truth. This is because shaping is always altering; thus, to form is always to *transform*, conceived, in a materialist way, as the process of bringing otherness to bear on the world, as opposed to receiving otherness as external authority. In this respect, inherent in the infinitive *poiein* is also an element of destruction, and there is no external guarantee that would absolve any poiēsis of the destructive elements of the alteration it performs.

The mod. viewpoint sustains this creative and destructive action in *poiein*. The struggle between what we can abusively call "private" and "public" poetics has not resolved, historically, the social demands posed by the idea of the poet as a shaper of forms. Astonishingly long lasting, the force of Plato's political prejudice has been crucial in the formation of modernity. Discussions of the Platonic dimensions of the term *poiēsis* often restrict themselves to its central invocation in the *Symposium*, where the notion is infused with various permutations of eros. There too, however, the ultimate power of poiēsis consists not in the shaping of form or even the erotic creation and production of life but in the transformation of the soul by virtue of philosophical practice. In the usurpation of poiēsis, philosophy defeats poetry yet again.

It is no surprise that, in the long precession of Western thought, whereby the quarrel between poetry and philosophy is relentlessly conducted, the advocates of poiēsis as material (trans)formation are those who resist the seductions of Platonism and its derivatives. Few, however, explicitly name poiēsis as such to be the matrix of their philosophical pursuit. One such thinker would surely be Giambattista Vico, whose *Scienza nuova* (*New Science*, 1725) extends the Ren. rendition of poiēsis beyond the task of *imitatio natura* and indeed inaugurates thinking of hist. as a poetic project. While it is difficult to speak of Vico's direct philosophical descendants, in retrospect a vast trajectory of strains of thought either in *avant-garde poetics (from the 19th c. on) or political aesthetics (esp. heterodox tendencies unfolding out of Hegelian Marxism) engages with similar views of hist. as poiēsis.

However, of all mod. philosophical encounters with poiēsis specifically, Martin Heidegger's engagement remains most influential. Although Heidegger's claim to discover the originary meaning of *poiēsis* should be taken lightly, nonetheless his explicit decision to out-maneuver the vast Platonic legacy by turning to the pre-Socratics lends a new aspect to the notion. In Heidegger's texts, poiēsis is invoked as the overcoming of the ancient quarrel between poetry and philosophy by standing for the disclosure (*a-lētheia*) of Being. Already in the *Einführung in die Metaphysik* (*Introduction to Metaphysics*, 1936), Heidegger forwards what will eventually become the central focus of his work: poetry is thought itself (*dichten ist denken*), and thereby all philosophical thinking is truly poetic and vice versa. Even if one can trace theological elements in Heidegger's invocation of poiēsis as radical creation, his gesture does, in part, return to the Gr. *poiein* its radical formative force.

This force resonates in discourses of modernity, both aesthetic and political. An entire society can be said to engage in poiēsis in its radical moments of self-determination. In this sense, and bearing reference to Vico, poiēsis can be linked to hist. in the making. This making cannot be said to have a precise temporality; hence, traditional methods of historiography cannot grasp it. Its working is a perpetual re-working that would not spare even itself as an object of that work. (The commonplace notion of a poem always being at work on itself, on making itself into a poem, should be understood here as an elemental force of poiēsis.) The duration of shaping matter into form, as Henri Bergson would have it, occurs in (or as) a radical present. This is a paradoxical condition, which is why its boundaries exceed the capacity of both narration and symbolization and can only be grasped in a performative vein. The energy of poiēsis is dramatic: literally, to form is to make form happen, to change form—incl. one's own. The social and political substance of poiēsis is thus signified not only by its constitutively transformative power, which would be a mere abstraction, but by the fact that, since its ancient Gr. meaning, it pertains to humanity's immanent (even if perpetually self-altering) encounter with the world.

*See* ARTIFACT, POETRY AS; CLASSICAL POETICS; MEDIEVAL POETICS; PHILOSOPHY AND POETRY; RENAISSANCE POETICS.

■ H. Bergson, *The Creative Mind*, trans. M.L.C. Addison (1946); M. Heidegger, *Introduction to Metaphysics* (1936), trans. R. Manheim (1959); H. Maturana and F. Varela, *Autopoiesis and Cognition* (1974); M. Heidegger, *Poetry, Language, Thought*, trans. A. Hofstadter (1976); H.R. Jauss, "Poiesis," trans. M. Shaw, *CritI* 8 (1982); D. W. Price, *History Made, History Imagined: Contemporary Literature, Poiesis, and the Past* (1999); W. V. Spanos, "The Question of Philoso-

phy and Poiesis in the Posthistorical Age: Thinking/Imagining the Shadow of Metaphysics," *Boundary 2* 27 (2000); T. Martin, *Poiesis and Possible Worlds: A Study in Modality and Literary Theory* (2004); J. Hölzl, *Transience: A Poiesis, of Dis/appearance* (2010); S. K. Levine, *Poiesis: The Language of Psychology and the Speech of the Soul* (2011).

S. GOURGOURIS

**POINT OF VIEW.** *See* PERSONA; PLOT; VOICE.

## POLAND, POETRY OF

  I. The Middle Ages to the Fourteenth Century
  II. The Fifteenth Century
  III. The Sixteenth Century
  IV. The Seventeenth Century
  V. The Eighteenth Century
  VI. The Nineteenth Century
  VII. The Twentieth Century
  VIII. The Twenty-First Century

**I. The Middle Ages to the Fourteenth Century.** Pre-Christian oral poetry in Polish dialects has not been uncovered, but its traces may be found in folk lit. Christianity in Western form was adopted in Poland in 966. The result was sustained literary activity in Lat. until the 17th c. Among the numerous liturgical songs of the med. period, the hymn *Gaude Mater Polonia* devoted to St. Stanislaus was esp. important. The anonymous song "Bogurodzica" (Mother of God) is the oldest poem preserved in the Polish lang. The only two copies date from the beginning of the 15th c., but it was most likely composed in the 13th c. It was sung throughout the country in various versions and was even considered an *anthem of the Polish kingdom. Consisting of two stanzas and the refrain "Kyrie eleison," the equivalent of the iconographic theme of deesis (Christ Pantocrator, Mary, and St. John the Baptist) is visible in its sophisticated construction. Only fragments of other Polish poems of the Middle Ages have been preserved, but Christian literary production (both oral and written) was probably much more extensive. The first trans. of the Psalms at the end of the 14th c. (the so-called Psałterz floriański) had a lasting impact on the devel. of Polish poetry.

**II. The Fifteenth Century.** Religious literary activity of this period was very rich; some Christmas *carols and Lenten and Easter songs are still sung in Polish churches. The song "Żale Matki Boskiej pod krzyżem" (Lament of the Mother of God at the Foot of the Cross) is the most innovative work of the time. The monologue, expressing Mary's powerful emotions, is likely a part of a missing Passion mystery play. *Epic poetry is poorly represented. *Legenda o świętym Aleksym* (The Legend of Saint Alexis) is an example of verse hagiography, drawing on foreign sources. Only a few fragments of secular poems have been preserved. The most impressive is "Rozmowa Mistrza Polikarpa ze Śmiercią" (A Dialogue between Master Polycarpus and Death), a form of med. dialogism or perhaps part of a morality play. Opulent in lang., imagery, black humor, and even grotesque elements, it constitutes a reflection on the topos of the *danse macabre*. The verse structure of Polish poetry at that time was based on a system of relative syllabism with approximate rhymes (see SYLLABIC VERSE).

**III. The Sixteenth Century.** Humanist influences are pronounced in Lat. poetry in the first part of the century. In describing Polish landscapes and recounting Polish hist., Janicíus (pseud. of Klemens Janicki, 1516–43) imitated the forms of ancient poetry. Some poets—among them, Jan Kochanowski (1530–84) and Szymon Szymonowic (1558–1629)—cultivated bilingual (Lat. and Polish) poetry.

Poetry in vernacular came into prominence. Mikołaj Rej (1505–69, called the father of Polish poetry) used Polish exclusively in his didactic or satiric poetry expressing the ideology of the Reformation; his verse structure is close to syllabism.

Jan Kochanowski was the most eminent poet of the Polish Ren. He imported the forms of ancient poetry and established a strictly syllabic system of Polish verse, incl. exact rhyme, stabilized *caesura, paroxytonic *cadence and *enjambment, thus making possible an interplay between syntax and verse structure. His poetry consists of the collections *Psałterz Dawidów* (an adaptation of the Psalms, 1578), *Treny* (Laments, 1580), *Fraszki* (Trifles, written throughout his life, ed. 1584), *Pieśni* (Songs, ed. 1586), some epic poems, and the cl. verse tragedy *Odprawa posłów greckich* (*The Dismissal of the Greek Envoys*, 1578). The anacreontic trifles and Horatian songs he composed from his early years until his death express an enjoyment of everyday life and acceptance of nature: they are inspired by Stoic and Epicurean philosophy. In his *laments, written after the death of his four-year-old daughter, the poet expresses a wide range of shifting emotions, from despair to final reconciliation with God's will.

Mikołaj Sęp Szarzyński (1550?–81?) was a profoundly metaphysical poet whose work expressed impassioned spiritual experience. He converted from Calvinism to Catholicism (as was typical for Polish nobles during the Counter-Reformation). His work foreshadowed the emerging poetics of the early *baroque (or *mannerism): oxymoronic imagery, abundant inversions, ellipses, and enjambments. Sęp Szarzyński was the author of only one volume of poems, ed. posthumously: *Rytmy abo wiersze polskie* (Rhythms or Polish Verses, 1601). Another metaphysical poet of the period was Sebastian Grabowiecki (ca. 1543–1607), who expressed quietism through his refined, sophisticated lyricism.

**IV. The Seventeenth Century.** Szymon Szymonowic was a poet of the late Ren. who followed Kochanowski in his poetics but also imitated the Alexandrian poet Theocritus in his *Sielanki* (Idylls, 1614). His semirealistic *pastorals became the model for the genre in the 17th and 18th cs. Maciej Kazimierz Sarbiewski (1595–1640), known as the Christian Horace, vaulted to Eur. fame as an intellectual poet writing in Lat. and

the author of a theory of baroque poetry. The Protestant Daniel Naborowski (1573–1640) continued "the metaphysical line" in Polish poetry. His oxymoronic poetry, full of contradictions, expressed the uncertainty of human existence in the world.

Another kind of Polish baroque poetry, court poetry, was inspired by Giambattista Marino (see MARINISM) and Luis de Góngora (see CONCEPTISMO). It was more cosmopolitan, close at times to Fr. libertinism. The premier author in this mode was Jan Andrzej Morsztyn (1621–93); his poetry, full of *wit and *conceits, constituted a kind of verbal game. Its main theme was love and its *paradoxes.

The dominant strain in 17th-c. Polish culture was the Sarmatian baroque. Ancient Sarmatia was a founding myth of the Polish nobility, and many poets subscribed to the ideology this myth embodied. Their poetry employed various forms, both epic and lyric. Wacław Potocki (1621–96) composed the epic poem *Wojna chocimska* (War of Chocim, 1670) and the series of "Moralia" (1688). Wespazjan Kochowski (1633–1700) was the author of the collection of lyrics and epigrams *Niepróżnujące próżnowanie* (Unleisurely Leisure, 1674) and of a long poem in biblical prose *Psalmodia polska* (Polish Psalmody, 1695), a messianic interpretation of Polish hist.

**V. The Eighteenth Century.** Polish poetry in the 18th c. remained under the strong influence of the Sarmatian baroque. In 1766, an epigone of the style, Józef Baka (1707–80), published his devotional and moralistic poems, full of paradoxes and a very particular black humor. A vast wave of anonymous patriotic and religious poetry appeared after the gentry rebellion called Konfederacja Barska (the Confederacy of Bar, 1768). The 1760s marked a significant turn in Polish poetry, in response to the political changes following the election of the last king of independent Poland, Stanisław August Poniatowski (r. 1764–95). The ideology of the Enlightenment gained currency in intellectual circles surrounding the royal court and other aristocratic courts. Didactic poetry propagating the new philosophy and worldview emerged; and the baroque style was replaced by Fr. *classicism, *rococo, and preromantic sentimentalism. The new tendencies intermingled with older Sarmatian models in the work of Adam Naruszewicz (1733–96). In his poetry, didactic and rhetorical, he employed cl. genres such as the *ode or *satire. At the same time his lang. was crude and abounded in *antitheses.

Ignacy Krasicki (1735–1801) was the most magnificent poet of the Polish Enlightenment. His poetic production encompassed *fables, satires, and a *mock epic (*Monachomachia*, 1778). His works were full of irony and sophisticated humor, marked by precise lang., brilliant dialogues, innovative rhymes and cl. forms. Krasicki ridiculed contemp. morals, incl. the life of the clergy; his skepticism about human nature shows his affinities with the philosophy of Voltaire. His poetry was didactic without intrusive rhet. Stanisław Trembecki (1739?–1812) and Tomasz Kajetan

Węgierski (1756–87) represented the libertine poetry of the rococo. Trembecki composed both political odes and obscene *erotic poems; his highest achievements, however, were his anacreontics and the *descriptive poem *Sofiówka* (Sophie's Garden, 1806). Węgierski was far more radical in his libertinism, writing not only erotic poems but antireligious poetic pamphlets and harsh moral satires as well. Another stream of rococo verged on sentimentalism. Franciszek Dionizy Kniaźnin (1750–1807) produced anacreontics, fables, and *bucolic verse. Franciszek Karpiński (1741–1825) wrote erotic poems, sentimental rather than libertine, *idylls, and religious songs (among them one of the most refined Polish Christmas carols, "Bóg się rodzi" (God Is Born).

After several years of political upheaval (a profound crisis in the government, efforts to rectify it, internal tensions, foreign political interference), Poland was partitioned among its neighbors—Russia, Prussia, and Austria—and disappeared as an independent nation in 1795. In Polish lit. and esp. in poetry, an entirely new situation emerged. From this time on, poetry became a substitute for other means of shaping national ideology and culture (see NATIONAL POETRY).

## VI. The Nineteenth Century

A. *The Classical and Preromantic Period.* The beginning of the century was marked by the continued domination of cl. poetry, but new tendencies also developed. Apart from Trembecki's work, another significant descriptive poem—influenced by Virgil—was *Ziemiaństwo polskie* (Polish Landed Gentry, 1839), which occupied the poet Kajetan Koźmian (1771–1856) for almost three decades. Kazimierz Brodziński (1791–1835) composed a series of sentimental bucolics. Alojzy Feliński (1771–1820) authored a cl. tragedy in syllabic verse inspired by Polish hist., *Barbara Radziwiłłówna* (1811, staged in 1817). Jan Paweł Woronicz (1757?–1829) was the author of *Hymn do Boga* (Hymn to God, 1805), a messianic explication of Polish hist. (the romantics were later inspired by this vision). The *Śpiewy historyczne* (Historic Songs, 1816) of Julian Ursyn Niemcewicz (1758–1841) were written in the style of James Macpherson's Ossianic songs and told of Poland's heroic past. Aleksander Fredro (1793?–1876) was the author of comedies inspired by cl. forms (Molière, Marivaux) but dealing with the Sarmatian trad. (*Zemsta*, Vengeance, staged 1834) or the new romantic sensibility (*Śluby panieńskie*, Maidens' Vows, staged 1839). Fredro's raillery was rooted in both a libertine outlook and rational common sense. He was inventive in his poetics and lang.; wit and play with various styles were the main sources of his humor.

B. *The Romantic Period.* The period between 1818 and 1822 was marked by "the battle between the Classicists and the Romantics." The dispute was settled by the debut of Adam Mickiewicz (1798–1855), with his volume *Ballady i romanse* (Ballads and Romances, 1822). Mickiewicz, the greatest Polish poet since Kochanowski, was the first Polish romantic. He had read J. W. Goethe, Friedrich Schiller, Lord Byron, and other Eur. romantic authors; but, educated in the spirit of the Enlightenment, he knew cl. lit. as well. In his work, both tendencies are visible. *Oda do młodości* (Ode to Youth, 1820) is an example of combining cl. rhet. with the new romantic ideology of youth as a divine power creating a new world. Mickiewicz was a master of Polish verse. He experimented with forms of rhythm, sought out revealing rhymes, and played with multiple genres. Above all, he took full advantage of the possibilities of the Polish lang., esp. its syntax and vocabulary. Mickiewicz's ballads refer to native folklore, though they are more frequently Belarusian or Lithuanian than ethnically Polish. This helped him maintain distance from the described world, full of fantasy and supernatural phenomena but, at the same time, made it possible to oppose rationalist philosophy and express the heart's "living truth." His poetic drama *Dziady* (Forefather's Eve, two parts, 1823; third part, 1832) has the structure of a mystery play; while it refers to folk commemorative ceremonies, its construction and versification are innovative. The sequence of *Sonety krymskie* (Crimean Sonnets, 1826) linked precise cl. form with a romantic way of describing exotic landscapes. His Byronic tale in verse *Konrad Wallenrod* (1828) introduced the political and ethical topic of a secret struggle against the nation's powerful enemies. After the collapse of the November Insurrection of 1830–31, when many Polish intellectuals went into exile in Western Europe (esp. France), Mickiewicz became far more than an eminent poet; he was considered a *wieszcz* (prophet, bard) and gained moral and political prestige through his metaphysical (messianic) interpretation of Polish hist.

In 1834, Mickiewicz published *Pan Tadeusz* a long poem recognized as the Polish national epic. From one point of view, it constitutes a Homeric epic on the poet's homeland (a province at the border between Poland, Lithuania, and Belarus) during the time of the Napoleonic wars (1811–12). But one can also find attributes of other genres, e.g., the descriptive poem, bucolic, mock epic, sentimental novel, and *gawęda* (a kind of tale, often oral, peculiar to Sarmatian culture). The work mixes nostalgia with humor and irony. In subsequent years, Mickiewicz grew absorbed in mystical soul-searching and political activity and virtually stopped writing poetry. His last sequence of poems (the so-called Lausanne lyrics, written in 1839) could have opened a completely new path in Mickiewicz's work. Ascetic, concise, focused on the word rather than syntax or syllabic rhythm, they violated the romantic paradigm.

A number of young poets followed Mickiewicz in the 1820s and 1830s, but they were much more typically romantic: Antoni Malczewski (1793–1826), Józef Bohdan Zaleski (1802–86), Seweryn Goszczyński (1801–76). The truly distinctive talent among them was Juliusz Słowacki (1809–49). Inventive in his poetics, esp. in his breathtakingly innovative rhymes, he experimented with many genres: lyric poems, tales in verse, visionary epics, and poetic dramas. He opposed Mickiewicz (his play *Kordian*, 1834, was a polemic against Mickiewicz's play *Dziady*) in his interpretation of Polish hist. and his philosophy of existence. Tragedy intermingled with bitter humor and deep romantic irony in his work. He was masterful in his range of emotional expression. In his dramas, inspired by Shakespeare, he experimented with versification, dramatic construction, and the creation of an inner world—realistic, fantastic, dreamlike, symbolic, and ambivalent (e.g., *Balladyna*, written 1834, pub. 1839). In his poems, Słowacki employed complex stanzaic forms, *ottava rima*, and biblical prose, inter alia. His "poem of digression" *Beniowski* (1841), resembling the narrative poems of Byron or Pushkin, is a recapitulation of the author's poetic path and a reckoning with himself, his enemies, poetry, and the world. It was a turning point in Słowacki's work, initiating a mystical period in his life and work. *Król-Duch* (King-Spirit, 1847), a mythopoetic vision of the incarnation of the nation's spirit in the great personalities of hist., was an expression of the poet's new convictions.

Zygmunt Krasiński (1812–59) was considered the third *wieszcz*, or bard (after Mickiewicz and Słowacki). However, his poetics lack the force of the others' work. In contemp. times, he is appreciated not so much for his poems as for his political dramas, which express a conservative vision of the crisis of Christian civilization, and his fascinating letters.

In his lifetime, Cyprian Norwid (1821–83) was isolated from the mainstream of Polish poetry. Forgotten for several decades, he was rediscovered in the 20th c. and is considered a precursor of mod. Polish poetry. In his poetics, he developed and even violated romantic rules. He was a master of the brief lyric (*Vade-mecum*, a collection of poems written before 1866, pub. posthumously), but he also wrote long poems, dramas, and stories. He was a magnificent epistolary writer as well. His works are verbally precise; many phrases—pointed and laconic—sound like aphorisms. A poetics of *ellipsis and even of silence plays a crucial role in his work. Subtle irony and ambivalence are his key methods of presenting the world; his use of parable, *allegory, and *symbolism convey an ambiguous vision of reality. Rhythm and rhyme are subordinate to sense in this intellectual poetry. Norwid called into question central tenets of romanticism; he was a humanist or personalist in a mod. sense.

All four great poets lived in exile in Western Europe. The domestic poetry of the time was less interesting. Kornel Ujejski (1823–97) wrote ardent patriotic poems; Teofil Lenartowicz (1822–93) based his lyric style on the folklore of Mazovia (the region where Warsaw is located), while Władysław Syrokomla (1823–62) gave voice to the worldview of the nobility.

**C. *The Postromantic Period.*** The epoch following the exhaustion of high romanticism—the collapse of the insurrection of 1863 marked a decisive shift—was programmatically antipoetic; the ideology of positivism dominated intellectuals. Though poetry generally continued under the influence of romanticism, a few poets transcended mere epigonism. Adam Asnyk (1838–97) wrote erotic and intellectual lyrics. Apart

from her abundant work in prose, Maria Konopnicka (1842–1910) composed numerous poems inspired by folklore; they described landscapes and often expressed social or metaphysical rebellion.

The last decade of the 19th c. saw new trends in poetry: this period was called Young Poland. Poets were inspired by Fr. symbolism and the philosophy of Arthur Schopenhauer and Friedrich Nietzsche: they rediscovered and reinterpreted high Polish romanticism ("neoromanticism"). This signaled the early beginnings of *modernism. The most influential poet of the time was Kazimierz Przerwa Tetmajer (1865–1940). He expressed the decadent mood of the generation through his erotic lyrics and descriptive poems employing impressionist methods.

## VII. The Twentieth Century

**A. *The Modern Period.*** The lyric production of Jan Kasprowicz (1860–1926) opened new horizons for poetry. He began with naturalistic poems depicting peasant poverty, while in the 1890s he focused on symbolist, descriptive works. The publication of a sequence of hymns (1898–1901) marked a turning point in his creation: they convey an expressionistic, deeply pessimistic, almost blasphemous representation of the world in Satan's power. He finds reconciliation with God in the sequence's final hymns. In his late works, he invented "tonism," a system of accentual versification based on an equal number of stresses, not of syllables (see ACCENTUAL VERSE). The way to *vers libre was open. Stanisław Wyspiański (1869–1907) was a painter, poet, and author of verse dramas. *Wesele* (Wedding, 1901) is a symbolic play inspired by romantic drama and Richard Wagner's idea of the theater as a synthesis of the arts. Poetic lang. is subordinated to the hypnotic rhythm of folk music. The play, full of symbols and ambiguity, is a kind of psychoanalysis of Polish national and social traumas. Leopold Staff (1878–1957) began his career as a "decadent," but after reinterpreting Nietzsche and finding inspiration in Stoicism and Franciscan Christianity, he became a poet of mental equilibrium, joie de vivre, and spiritual power. He was inspired by neoclassicism, *Parnassianism, and symbolism, and served as a mentor to young poets in the 1920s. He incorporated *avant-garde poetics into his late work, in the 1950s.

Bolesław Leśmian (1878–1937) was the greatest poet of the first half of the century. A symbolist, he explored the impossibility of adequately describing a world in constant motion. Following the philosophy of Henri Bergson, he conveyed the instability of a reality always in *statu nascendi*. In his opinion, only poetry could truly articulate élan vital; hence, rhythm (*accentual-syllabic verse) was key to his poetics. He wrote *ballads in stylized folk forms, which he turned to intellectual, existential, and metaphysical purposes. He was distinguished by the extraordinarily inventive verbal coinages he developed to convey the nuances of his philosophy. Leśmian's first poetic volume was published only in 1912; three subsequent volumes were edited in the 1920s and 1930s.

After World War I and the rebirth of an independent Poland in 1918, new tendencies in Polish poetry appeared. Reinterpretations of trad. were confronted by avant-garde movements on the one hand and a quest for inspiration in folk culture on the other. Many programs were proclaimed, and a wide range of groups and periodicals (most of them ephemeral) came into being. The group Skamander, established in 1918, played a central role in the literary life of the period. Jan Lechoń (1899–1956) reinterpreted the romantic trad. Antoni Słonimski (1895–1976) linked *Parnassianism with *expressionism and radical political ideas. Jarosław Iwaszkiewicz (1894–1980) created personal, introspective poetry; he chose *aestheticism as his principal attitude and was inspired by expressionism, neoclassical and other, sometimes exotic, trads., such as Persian; sensitive to the musical aspects of verse, he discovered the possibilities of *dissonance in poetry. Kazimierz Wierzyński (1894–1969) began as a neoclassicist; in his later works, he was inspired by expressionism, romanticism (esp. during World War II), and even the avant-garde (beginning in the 1950s). Julian Tuwim (1894–1953) was the most inventive poet of the group. He played with lang., discovering a new colloquial idiom. He experimented with the sounds and senses of words and sought inspiration in *classicism as well. He also composed popular songs, cabaret songs, and children's poetry. In the 1920s, the poets of Skamander focused on ordinary existence; they expressed joy in daily life and discovered popular culture for poetry (Wierzyński, e.g., dedicated a sequence of poems to sports). In the 1930s, their poetic tone grew increasingly dark. Iwaszkiewicz's poems expressed existential fears; Wierzyński became a harsh judge of mod. civilization; Tuwim grew more and more radical politically.

Skamander marked the more traditional wing in Polish poetry of the time. Other poets were close to their orientation. In her refined poems, Maria Jasnorzewska-Pawlikowska (1891–1945) employed paradoxes, *oxymorons, and ellipses to express the experience of the mod. woman, esp. her eroticism. Władysław Broniewski (1897–1962) wrote impressive political poems (he was a fellow traveler of the Communist Party) making the most of the new system of versification (tonism) and appealing to the romantic trad. Jerzy Liebert (1904–31) was a poet of dramatic religious experience (in Blaise Pascal's spirit); influenced by classicism, he pursued lucidity in his poetics. Konstanty Ildefons Gałczyński (1905–53) linked grotesquery and mockery with emotional lyricism in his work.

The experimental wing in Polish poetry was represented by *futurism and the avant-garde. The futurists were radical in their views on poetics and politics (Communism); in their practice, they came close to *Dada. The most important poets of this movement were Bruno Jasieński (1901–39) and Aleksander Wat (1900–67); in his late poetry, Wat changed his aesthetics, reflecting on the experience of pain. The avant-garde program was announced in the 1920s: its most prominent representatives were Tadeusz Peiper (1891–69) and Julian Przyboś (1901–70). The avant-garde reformed poetics: *syntax or even the *line constituted a poem's rhythm, not equal numbers of syllables or stresses. They proclaimed and practiced economy in lang., leading to their preference for *metaphor and ellipsis as basic figures. The avant-garde affirmed mod. civilization: its poetry exuded dynamism and belief in creative potency. The avant-garde of the 1930s was a different matter. Józef Czechowicz (1903–39) linked his experience of these new tendencies with the trads. of folk poetry; in his poems, the bucolic collides with visions of historical catastrophe.

The most eminent poet of this movement was Czesław Miłosz (1911–2004, winner of the Nobel Prize in Literature, 1980). In his early poems, the poetics of neosymbolism and *surrealism conjoined with romantic or biblical ways of constructing visions and a cl. rigor of form: it expressed a sense of the eminent metaphysical catastrophe of civilization. During World War II, Miłosz altered his poetics. In his search for the "proper form," he appealed to various trads., from the Bible to Far Eastern poetry, from the Middle Ages to the avant-garde. His poetry is polyphonic, often ironic. In spite of its intellectual and metaphysical character, the poetry is focused on the concrete particulars of reality. Among themes of the Miłosz's works are ethics, hist., God, nature, and the purpose of existence. It is difficult to overestimate Miłosz's influence on Polish poetry of the 20th c.

**B. *Era of War and Totalitarianism.*** A turning point in Polish hist. and culture came in 1939: World War II, which divided Poland between totalitarian regimes (Nazi and Soviet), led in turn to the Holocaust, mass exterminations, displaced peoples, the destruction of cities (esp. Warsaw), and the installation of a Communist regime following the war. Numerous poets lost their lives during the war, and the wartime and postwar years saw waves of emigration among poets, continuing until the 1980s. Under Nazi occupation, official literary life was virtually nonexistent; important works were produced and published only underground. Under Soviet occupation and later in Communist Poland until Stalin's death, all lit. was subordinated to ideology, in the form of socialist realism. Even after the liberalization of 1956, the harsh state censorship controlled and deformed all poetic production. At the same time, numerous authors played games with their readers, conveying indirect meanings through *allusions and special codes. From the mid-1970s until the collapse of Communism in 1989, alternative underground publishing houses published many major volumes of poetry.

Poets of the generation born in the 1920s, who came to maturity during the war, chose a variety of aesthetics. For many of them, the experience of war, evil, fear, pain, and death played a crucial role. Krzysztof Kamil Baczyński (1921–44) followed Miłosz in his neosymbolic poetry of visions. Tadeusz Gajcy (1922–44) drew upon the poetics of the baroque and the avant-garde (esp. surrealism). Tadeusz Różewicz (b. 1921), as a descendant of the avant-garde, invented new forms of ascetic verse. Julia Hartwig (b. 1921) was inspired by early

Western avant-garde artists such as Walt Whitman and Guillaume Apollinaire. Miron Białoszewski (1922–83) was extremely inventive in his ling. play and imitation of spoken lang.; he crossed the borders between verse and prose in his "ling. poetry." In her intellectual and conceptual poetry, Wisława Szymborska (1923–2012; winner of the Nobel Prize in Literature, 1996) uses irony and exploits ling. ambiguity (in the meanings of words and even in grammar). Zbigniew Herbert (1924–98) linked the inspiration of the avant-garde (esp. in his use of metaphor and ellipsis) with appealing topoi and a stoic philosophy derived from neoclassicism: *irony plays a special role in his poetry. Their poetry articulates a sense of deep cultural crisis as it searches for ways to preserve human values—in ethics, in ordinary life, or in poetry itself.

Some older figures found their original poetic ways during this period. For instance, in her late, ascetic poems, Anna Świrszczyńska (known as Anna Swir, 1909–84) candidly described the specifics of women's lives, esp. during wartime. The current of metaphysical or religious poetry continued in the work of Jan Twardowski (1915–2006), a Catholic priest who wrote Franciscan poems full of humor and paradoxes about the "unfinished" Creation. Karol Wojtyła (Pope John Paul II, 1920–2005) composed mystical and intellectual meditations: the best known of these is his late, long poem *Tryptyk rzymski* (Roman Triptych, 2003).

Younger poets looked for inspiration in various aesthetics. In his poetry inspired by folk culture, Tadeusz Nowak (1930–91) expressed the moral and metaphysical unrest of the individual endangered by mod. civilization. Krystyna Miłobędzka (b. 1932) in her minimalistic poetry searches for the exact words in the world's description. Stanisław Grochowiak (1934–76) used a surreal aesthetic of ugliness to demonstrate the crisis of traditional codes of beauty. Jarosław Marek Rymkiewicz (b. 1935) propounds a program of mod. neoclassicism: he appeals to trad., esp. to the late, Sarmatian Polish baroque.

For poets of the Generation of '68 (also called the New Wave) the crucial problem is finding an adequate lang. for describing the contemp. world. In their early poetry, these poets appealed to the experience of the avant-garde (esp. "linguistic poetry"): later, they began to seek out inspiration in various trads. In his ascetic poetry, Ryszard Krynicki (b. 1943) follows the Asian trad. of playing with a minimal number of words and with silence to express his ethical and metaphysical meditations. Using enumerations and inventive metaphors, Adam Zagajewski (b. 1945) tries to represent the world in its opulence and abundance. Ewa Lipska (b. 1945) links sophisticated metaphors with irony to reveal the paradoxes of existence. Rafał Wojaczek (1945–71) used an expressionistic aesthetic of shock to overcome mental and moral taboos. Bohdan Zadura (b. 1945) in his recent works invents a poetics of paradox in the daily lang. Stanisław Barańczak (b. 1946) exposes the ambiguities of lang., esp. of propaganda; in his later work, he draws inspiration from Eng. *metaphysical poetry to ask basic questions about life's mean-

ing. Piotr Sommer (b. 1948) follows mod. Eng.-lang. poetry; he describes reality by using words intended to stick as closely as possible to the things themselves. Bronisław Maj (b. 1953) develops Miłosz's poetics of epiphany, representing the world in its moments of beauty and sense.

**C. *Post-Communist (Late Modern) Period.*** In 1989, Communism in Poland collapsed, and the situation of lit. consequently changed completely. Censorship disappeared; borders were opened; and a new context was shaped by pop culture, mass media, a free market, and democracy. The 1990s were marked by a poetry in evident flux. Apart from the continued activity of older poets (incl. Miłosz), young poets were expansive in their quest for a new and varied poetics. Andrzej Sosnowski (b. 1959) writes intellectual poems, using complicated metaphors to reveal the glimmerings of equivocal words. Marcin Świetlicki (b. 1961), the icon of his generation, is close to the ideology of counterculture and focuses on the experience of ordinary life: as the leader of a rock band, he revolts against traditional forms of poetry. Eugeniusz Tkaczyszyn-Dycki (b. 1962) uses forms of baroque poetry to express the fears and doubts arising from the mod. world. Krzysztof Koehler (b. 1963) is a representative of the cl. tendency in poetry: inspired by various trads. (esp. the baroque), he focuses on metaphysical problems. Jacek Podsiadło (b. 1964) plays with different poetics, between an aesthetic of paradox and shock and an aesthetic of "classical," refined verse. Miłosz Biedrzycki (b. 1967) is inspired by the poetics of surrealism and the "liberated imagination."

**VIII. The Twenty-first Century.** The beginning of the century was a time of change. The turning point for traditional poetry was Miłosz's death in 2004. Young poets have chosen a variety of aesthetics. Tomasz Różycki (b. 1970) tries to revive cl. forms that clash with the poetics and consciousness of the contemp. individual and experience of avant-garde. Tadeusz Dąbrowski (b. 1979), describing metaphysics in postmod. life, plays with paradox. A radical appeal to the avant-garde is visible among the "neolinguistic" poets (incl. Maria Cyranowicz, b. 1974; Jarosław Lipszyc, b. 1975; and Joanna Mueller, b. 1979).

■ **Anthologies:** *Od Kochanowskiego do Staffa,* ed. W. Borowy (1930); *Poeci renesansu,* ed. J. Sokołowska (1959); *Zbiór poetów polskich XIX wieku,* ed. P. Hertz, 7 v. (1959–75); *Poeci polskiego baroku,* ed. J. Sokołowska and K. Żukowska (1965); *Poezja Młodej Polski,* ed. M. Jastrun (1967); *Poezja polska,* ed. S. Grochowiak and J. Maciejewski, 2 v. (1973); *Kolumbowie i współcześni,* ed. A. Lam (1976); *Poezja polska XVIII wieku,* ed. Z. Libera, 2d ed. (1976); *Antologia polskiego futuryzmu i Nowej Sztuki,* ed. Z. Jarosiński and H. Zaworska (1978); *Five Centuries of Polish Poetry,* ed. J. Peterkiewicz and B. Singer, 3d ed. (1979); *Średniowieczna pieśń religijna polska,* ed. M. Korolko, 2d ed. (1980); *Ze struny na strunę,* ed. A. Lam (1980); *Postwar Polish Poetry,* ed. C. Miłosz, 3d ed. (1983); *Poeta pamięta,* ed. S. Barańczak (1984); *Poezja polska 1914–1939*, ed. R. Matuszewski and S. Pollak, 3d ed. (1984); *Monumenta Polonica: The First Four Centuries of Polish Poetry: A Bilingual Anthology*, ed. B. Carpenter (1989); *Polish Poetry of the Last Two Decades of Communist Rule*, ed. S. Barańczak and C. Cavanagh (1992); *Antologia polskiej poezji metafizycznej epoki baroku*, ed. K. Mrowcewicz (1993); *Young Poets of a New Poland*, ed. D. Pirie (1993); *Określona epoka—Nowa Fala 1968–1993*, ed. T. Nyczek, 2d ed. (1995); *Polish Renaissance*, ed. M. J. Mikoś (1995); *Ambers Aglow: An Anthology of Polish Women's Poetry*, ed. R. Grol (1996); *Macie swoich poetów: liryka polska urodzona po 1960 roku*, ed. P. Dunin-Wąsowicz, J. Klejnocki, and K. Varga (1996); *Międzywojenna poezja polsko-żydowska*, ed. E. Prokop-Janiec (1996); I. Krasicki, *Polish Fables*, trans. G. T. Kapolka (1997); *Poezja polska okresu międzywojennego*, ed. M. Głowiński and J. Sławiński, 2d ed. (1997); *Współcześni poeci polscy: poezja polska od 1956 roku*, ed. K. Karasek (1997); *Panorama literatury polskiej XX wieku*, ed. K. Dedecius (2001); B. Leśmian, *Magic and Glory of Twentieth-Century Polish Poetry*, trans. J. Langer (2000); *Antologia poezji polskiej na obczyźnie*, ed. B. Czaykowski (2002); *Antologia poezji sarmackiej*, ed. K. Koehler (2002); *Literatura staropolska*, ed. P. Borek and R. Mazurkiewicz (2002); *Polska poezja rokokowa*, ed. R. Dąbrowski (2003); *Świat poprawiać—zuchwałe rzemiosło*, ed. T. Kostkiewiczowa and Z. Goliński, 2d ed. (2004); *Gada !zabić? Pa(n)tologia neolingwizmu*, ed. M. Cyranowicz and P. Kozioł (2005); *Poza słowa: Antologia wierszy 1976–2006*, ed. T. Dąbrowski (2006); Z. Herbert, *The Collected Poems*, trans. A. Valles, C. Miłosz, P. Dale (2007); *Poezja drugiej połowy XIX wieku*, ed. J. Bajda (2007); *Poezja pierwszej połowy XIX wieku*, ed. E. Grzęda (2007); *Selected Masterpieces of Polish Poetry*, trans. J. Zawadzki (2007); *Solistki: Antologia poezji kobiet (1989–2009)*, ed. M. Cyranowicz, J. Mueller, J. Radczyńska, (2009); *Poeci na nowy wiek*, ed. R. Honet (2010).

■ **Criticism and History**: W. Weintraub, *The Poetry of Adam Mickiewicz* (1954); M. Kridl, *A Survey of Polish Literature and Culture* (1956); M. Giergielewicz, *Introduction to Polish Versification* (1970); T. Kostkiewiczowa, *Klasycyzm, sentymentalizm, rokoko* (1975); A. Witkowska, *Adam Mickiewicz* (1975); S. Jaworski, *Między awangardą a nadrealizmem* (1976); J.M.G. Levine, *Contemporary Polish Poetry, 1925–1975* (1981); B. Carpenter, *The Poetic Avant-Garde in Poland, 1918–1939* (1983); C. Miłosz, *The History of Polish Literature*, 2d ed. (1983); M. Zaleski, *Przygoda drugiej Awangardy* (1984); *Poznawanie Miłosza*, ed. J. Kwiatkowski (1985); S. Barańczak, *A Fugitive from Utopia* (1987); G. Gömöri, *Cyprian Norwid* (1988); F. W. Aaron, *Bearing the Unbearable: Yiddish and Polish Poetry in the Ghettos and Concentration Camps* (1990); S. Barańczak, *Breathing under Water and Other East European Essays* (1990); R. Sokoloski, *The Poetry of Mikołaj Sęp Szarzyński* (1990); M. Inglot, *Cyprian Norwid* (1991); A. Kowalczykowa, *Słowacki* (1992); J. Dudek, *Poeci polscy XX wieku* (1994); E. Hurnikowa, *Natura w salonie mody: O międzywojennej liryce Marii Pawlikowskiej-Jasnorzewskiej* (1995); S. Stabro, *Poezja i*

*historia: Od Żagarów do Nowej Fali* (1995); R. Nycz, *Sylwy współczesne*, 2d ed. (1996); *Radość czytania Szymborskiej*, ed. D. Wojda and S. Balbus (1996); T. Venclova, *Aleksander Wat: Life and Art of an Iconoclast* (1996); K. Wyka, *Rzecz wyobraźni* (1997); J. Kwiatkowski, *Magia poezji: O poetach polskich XX wieku* (1997); J. Błoński, *Miłosz jak świat* (1998); W. Bolecki, *Pre-teksty i teksty* (1998); M. Głowiński, *Zaświat przedstawiony: Szkice o poezji Bolesława Leśmiana*, 2d ed. (1998); J. Sławiński, *Koncepcja języka poetyckiego Awangardy Krakowskiej* (1998); *Poznawanie Herberta*, ed. A. Franaszek, 2 v. (1998–2000); P. Czapliński, P. Śliwiński, *Literatura polska 1976–1998* (1999); Z. Jarosiński, *Literatura lat 1945–1975*, 3d ed. (1999); H. Markiewicz, *Pozytywizm*, 4th ed. (1999); G. Gömöri, *Magnetic Poles: Essays on Modern Polish and Comparative Literature* (2000); A. Hutnikiewicz, *Młoda Polska*, 6th ed. (2000); *Poznawanie Miłosza 2*, ed. A. Fiut, 2 v. (2000–2001); J. Błoński, *Mikołaj Sęp Szarzyński a początki polskiego baroku*, 2d ed. (2001); M. Dłuska, *Odmiany i dzieje wiersza polskiego* (2001); R. Nycz, *Literatura jako trop rzeczywistości: Poetyka epifanii w nowoczesnej literaturze polskiej* (2001); J. Pelc, *Kochanowski: Szczyt renesansu w literaturze polskiej*, 3d ed (2001); M. Podraza-Kwiatkowska, *Literatura Młodej Polski*, 4th ed. (2001); J. Prokop and J. Sławiński, *Liryka polska: Interpretacje*, 3d ed. (2001); R. Nycz, *Język modernizmu: Prolegomena historycznoliterackie*, 2d ed. (2002); K. Barry, *Skamander: The Poets and Their Poetry, 1918–1929* (2004); B. Kaniewska, A. Legieżyńska, P. Śliwiński, *Literatura polska XX wieku* (2005); J. Święch, *Literatura polska w latach II wojny światowej*, 6th ed. (2005); T. Michałowska, *Średniowiecze*, 8th ed. (2006); J. Ziomek, *Renesans*, 11th ed. (2006); C. Hernas, *Barok*, 8th ed. (2006); M. Klimowicz, *Oświecenie*, 9th ed. (2006); A. Nasiłowska, *Literatura okresu przejściowego 1975–1996* (2006); M. P. Markowski, *Polska literatura nowoczesna: Leśmian, Schulz, Witkacy* (2007); A. Witkowska, R. Przybylski, *Romantyzm*, 8th ed. (2007); J. Kwiatkowski, *Dwudziestolecie międzywojenne*, 3d ed. (2008); R. Koropeckyj, *Adam Mickiewicz* (2008); S. Barańczak, *Etyka i poetyka*, 2d ed. (2009); C. Cavanagh, *Lyric Poetry and Modern Politics: Russia, Poland, and the West* (2009); *Nowa poezja polska: Twórcy—tematy—motywy*, ed. T. Cieślak (2009); A. Kałuża, *Bumerang: Szkice o poezji polskiej przełomu XX i XXI wieku* (2010); *Nowe dwudziestolecie (1989–2009): Rozpoznania. Hierarchie. Perspektywy*, ed. H. Gosk (2010); J. Fiedorczuk et al., *Literatura Polska 1989–2009: Przewodnik* (2011).

K. Biedrzycki

**POLITICAL VERSE** (Gr. *politikos stichos*, "the verse of the polis and its citizens"). A Byzantine meter of 15 syllables, accentually based and *iambic. Political verse first appears in the 10th c. CE and is the standard meter for mod. Gr. poetry from at least the 12th c. to the present day. It consists of two cola of eight and seven syllables with a *caesura after the eighth syllable, each *colon having one main accent, on the eighth or sixth syllable in the first and on the fourteenth in the second. Maas gives the *scansion xx/xxx/x/ x/x/x/x as common. The origin of the verse is uncertain; some imperial *dirges of ca. 912 CE are in political verse, and the *hymns of Symeon the New Theologian (fl. 1000 CE) include some 5,000 lines of it. The Byzantine grammarian Eustathios thought it originated in the cl. trochaic tetrameter, Krumbacher in a mixture of the cl. iambic and trochaic tetrameter; but all such hypothesized connections to antiquity seem remote. From the beginning, it is a medium of *oral poetry and popular verse.

*See* GREEK POETRY.

■ K. L. Struve, *Ueber den politischen Vers der Mittelgriechen* (1828); K. Krumbacher, *Geschichte der byzantinischen Litteratur*, 2d ed. (1897), 651 ff.; P. Maas, *Byzantinischen Zeitschrift* 18 (1909); Maas; I. Sevcenko, "Poems on the Death of Leo VI and Constantine VII in the Madrid Manuscript of Scylitzes," *Dumbarton Oaks Papers* 23–24 (1969); H. G. Beck, *Geschichte der byzantinischen Volkslitteratur* (1971), 15 ff.; M. J. Jeffreys, "The Nature and Origins of the Political Verse," *Dumbarton Oaks Papers* 28 (1974); Trypanis, 454 ff.

T.V.F. BROGAN

**POLITICS AND POETRY.** In 1968, the poet James Merrill was asked about the relationship between poetry and "political realities." "Oh dear," he answered, "these immensely real concerns do not produce *poetry*." *L'art pour l'art* (art for art's sake) was at that moment more a posture than a tenable position, though 20 years earlier many Western poets and critics had operated on the assumption that poetry suffers from contact with political subjects. Skepticism about political subjects derived then largely from a strong postwar anti-Stalinist impulse among Western literary intellectuals, who had been sympathetic to Soviet Marxism until the Nazi-Soviet pact of 1939. Am. and Western Eur. critics perceived the major controversy among Rus. poets as the role of private rather than public subject matter: Vladimir Mayakovsky, in their view, was the state's eager propagandist, while the quintessentially lyrical Anna Akhmatova, attacked by Soviet critics for her suspiciously individualist love lyrics, directed her greatest political poem, *Requiem* (written 1935–40, pub. 1963), against Stalin's terror (it remained unpublished in the Soviet Union during her lifetime). In fact, Soviet politicians and critics had castigated Mayakovsky and Akhmatova alike early on for excess "lyricism," pointing to the schism that divides Eastern and Western Eur. perceptions of poetic politics. Still, the devel. of an exalted *lyric, antipolitical poetic in the West after World War II was one literary aspect of the cold war. The political record of the high modernist poets was also discouraging to Western intellectuals: from 1945 to 1958, Ezra Pound was incarcerated in a Washington mental hospital because of charges of treason (see MODERNISM).

The hist. of poetry, as Paulin demonstrates, abounds in successful political poems: med. peasant's songs, the *Divine Comedy*, Andrew Marvell's Horatian *ode, Milton's political *sonnets, Egan O'Rahilly's Gaelic *la-

ments, John Dryden's *Absalom and Achitophel*, William Blake's "London," André Chénier's "Iambes VIII," William Wordsworth's *Prelude*, W. B. Yeats's "Easter, 1916," Marina Tsvetaeva's "André Chénier," Akhmatova's "Voronezh," Pablo Neruda's "The United Fruit Co.," Zbigniew Herbert's "Elegy of Fortinbras," Seamus Heaney's "Punishment." The lineaments of heroism, the limits of national or tribal solidarity, the power of persuasion, the forceful imposition of authority, and war—these homeric themes have long been central to poetry. Toward the periphery the lesser genres—seduction songs, *epithalamia, nature poems—now seem, though less obviously, still fascinatingly political.

What counts as a political subject—or a political form—is a question of audience. Poems like Bertolt Brecht's "The God of War" seem only vaguely political in peacetime, but in time of war, such a poem would be understood to be insistently partisan. Therefore, we may say, all that can be changed by social consensus or external authority is properly called *political*. The possibility of change itself, certainly not the state, is, after all, the source of political passion. Political poems concern situations that might be otherwise—and this links them with the "dream of a world in which things would be different" that Theodor Adorno sees at the heart of the lyric particularly.

The boundaries dividing overtly political from "apolitical," and even "antipolitical," poetry are fluid. "So long as the poet, East or West, appears before the public only as a lyrist, banking on the irresponsibilities traditionally associated with that role, he will be tolerated by the governing class and allowed to communicate with his readers," Davie asserts. But the programmatically collectivist states of the former Eastern Bloc considered the "lyric I" ideologically suspect. Even the most seemingly introspective poems may reveal their subversive potential in such contexts.

Wordsworth's "Tintern Abbey" is a case in point. Many recent critics have seen the poem as marking Wordsworth's rejection of a revolutionary politics that engages the world in favor of a subjective, internal transformation that elides it. It thus becomes emblematic of a romantic and postromantic poetry that "typically erases or sets aside its political and historical currencies" in its embrace of the quasi-autonomous individual subject (McGann). The Polish poet Czesław Miłosz experienced Wordsworth's lyric differently. His trans. of the poem, completed shortly after the postwar Soviet takeover, could not be published in the Polish People's Republic. Under the Communist regime, Miłosz warns, the poet who feels "that boundless exaltation in the face of nature that seized Wordsworth on his visit to Tintern Abbey is at once suspect." Such raptures were reserved for state occasions and officially approved topics alone. Conversely, young Eastern Eur. writers of the post-Stalinist cultural "thaw" embraced Mayakovsky's officially sanctioned poetry—imposed under Stalin "like potatoes under Catherine the Great," as Boris Pasternak said—not for its revolutionary sentiments but for its subversively lyrical tendencies.

"In Western Europe," A. Alvarez comments in his

introduction to Zbigniew Herbert's *Selected Poems* (1968), "we take for granted that there is a fundamental split between poetry and politics. The problem is not that the twain can never meet but that they can do so only at a great cost. The complexity, tension and precision of modern poetry simply does not go with the language of politics, with its vague rhetoric and dependence on clichés." From the mid-1960s on, anglophone poets turned increasingly, like Alvarez, to writing in trans. to counteract what they saw as the political and social marginality of mod. poetry in the West. The writers of Latin America and Eastern Europe particularly invited emulation through their socially engaged verse. "Poets such as Zbigniew Herbert, Różewicz, Holub remind us," Paulin comments, "that in Eastern Europe, the poet has a responsibility both to art and to society, and that this responsibility is single and indivisible": 'In this authoritarian or totalitarian reality there is no private life, no domestic sanctuary, to retire into. Here, any and every action has a political significance which cannot be evaded' " (1986). The "impact of translation" (Heaney) has been profound in recent decades. But it has often led anglophone poets to underestimate, as Paulin does, the shifting relationship between public and private in trads. whose political and cultural complexities are veiled, if not lost, in trans.

Critics of the 1970s and 1980s demonstrated repeatedly how subjects formerly thought not to be political are, in fact, importantly so, partly because the range of imaginable social change has expanded. The literary representation of women is an obvious example. The description of landscape is a less obvious one: Williams showed that the landscapes of Eng. poetry are political figurations of the prerogatives of wealth and class (see LANDSCAPE POEM). Other critics focused on all that is taken for granted in poetry, for that is where political issues are treated as already somehow settled. Empson argues that figurative lang. can shut off inquiry by suggesting that some political or historical event is natural, no more in question than an ocean or mountain. Neo-Marxist interpreters set themselves the task of counteracting the alleged effort of poets to render politics invisible: "Even apolitical poetry is political," as Wisława Szymborska notes mockingly in "Children of Our Age." One weakness of this approach is the presupposition that, once political intent has been unveiled, a critic's job is done, as though the revelation that poetry is politically motivated were itself a critical achievement. Another is the dismissal of poetic *form as inherently apolitical. Poetry's "very formality is social," Pinsky comments. The ostensibly ahistorical bent of Anglo-Am. *New Criticism and *Russian formalism has been much overstated: both movements imbedded their readings in a shifting range of political and cultural contexts. As Wolfson has argued, close attention to form, by writers and critics alike, may, in fact, reveal the complexity of the lyric's social and political concerns.

Mythological figures are more obviously political than natural ones, since they bear both a weight of her-

meneutical trad. and explicit cultural authority. When Dryden characterized Charles II as King David, the Duke of Monmouth as Absalom, and the first Earl of Shaftesbury as Achitophel, the political significance of the poem was set forth explicitly. Invocations of myth, hist., or scripture to structure contemp. political events are different from other sorts of figures, however, in that the criterion of aptness is counterbalanced by one of audacity. The choice of a framing myth, esp. in satire, is usually outrageous: Charles II as David? Lenin as Christ, in Hugh MacDiarmid's "First Hymn to Lenin"? Dwight Eisenhower as Satan, in Robert Duncan's "The Fire"? But that is where the controversial aspect of these poems is sharpest; what David, Absalom, and Achitophel are made to say is much less tendentious. The pleasure and success of such poems depend on the framing myth seeming audaciously afield yet, finally, acute. The mythological bent of poets such as C. P. Cavafy and Herbert has exerted particular influence on contemp. writers: Herbert's Procrustes, with his murderous bed, clearly evokes the mod. world's most infamous experiments in the engineering of bodies and souls alike.

The supposed strain between politics and poetry is actually more a strain between politics and the evaluative criteria of crit. Mod. crit. has only limited access to a didactic view of poetry (see DIDACTIC POETRY). Didactic poems are esteemed according to a universality or generality criterion, whereby a poem succeeds insofar as it speaks to the conditions of life in different historical contexts. By this measure, either *satire derives from an overall moral norm, or it counts as a minor genre because it names names and deeply loves its historic moment. Samuel Johnson's "Preface to Shakespeare" blocks the access of mod. critics to a contemporaneity criterion that can treasure the minute particulars of a local social milieu. Dryden, Alexander Pope, the Pound of *Cantos* 14 and 15, and among contemporaries, Turner Cassity, express a kind of curiosity and, beyond the satire, a fondness for very specific details of their time. Crit. needs a way of appreciating this poetry, not because the details are heterogeneous but because they are thorny and abundant evidence of a citizen's passionate engagement less in a party than in a particular moment.

McKeon argues that ideological comprehensiveness is the apt criterion for political poetry: political poets succeed by comprehending a wide range of the demands and conflicts of their time, not by rising above their historical moment. This view addresses the apprehensions of New Critics, such as Cleanth Brooks, in the face of partisan leftist poetry of the 1930s: leftist poems employed, in Burke's terms, a rhet. of exclusion. Those circumstances or considerations that did not fit a leftist ideological perspective were ignored, not incorporated into the poem as a sign of faith with the historical moment. The result, Brooks argues, was a sentimental appeal to a reader's political beliefs.

Pindar's songs in praise of Gr. tyrants provide the most obvious archaic example of Western political poetry (the political significance of the *Iliad* is more abstract). Although Robert Lowell wrote praise poems for Senators Eugene McCarthy and Robert Kennedy during the 1968 Am. presidential campaign and Gary Snyder wrote sympathetically about California Governor Jerry Brown in the late 1970s, mod. poets have been generally disinclined to employ their art to praise the state in any form. What we now appreciate in Pindar is less his capacity to praise, which Pound dismissed as a big bass drum, than the back of his hand: his clever management of myths to warn the tyrants against the abuses of power. The most admired praise poem in Eng., Marvell's Horatian ode, is esteemed for its mix of praise and blame (see EPIDEICTIC POETRY, PANEGYRIC). Mod. poems of sheer blame, such as Robert Bly's "Asian Peace Offers Rejected without Publication" and Adrienne Rich's "Rape" have been far more widely appreciated. But poems of true praise are much harder for critics to admire. More important, the middle ground between praise and blame has been badly eroded by an oversupply of extremist crit. Edwards argues that the best political poems express mixed feelings: if outrage then also complicity, if contempt then also sympathy. This view draws support from two considerations: (1) an ambitious poem should do more than gild the monolith of an ideology, and (2) political issues are generally more complicated than one or another party suggests. Osip Mandelstam's longest poem, "The Horseshoe Finder: A Pindaric Fragment," exemplifies the complexities of the mod. praise poem. The speaker seeks to follow Pindar in praising the unnamed captain of a mod. ship of state but falters both through his own ambivalence and because his lyric gifts apparently no longer answer the needs of a new revolutionary regime.

However, mod. poets and critics tend to admire, even more than mixed feelings, frankly oppositional poems: hence, the burgeoning in recent decades of anthols. celebrating an international "poetry of witness," through which Anglo-Am. poets are invited to identify with writers whose work emerges under the very real threat of political persecution. Indeed, political poetry, if not poetry in general, is commonly (and too narrowly) understood now to be oppositional by definition. Even a centrist critic like Kermode has argued that "literature which achieves permanence is likely to be 'transgressive'. . . [the art] of the stranger in conflict with the settled order." Most contemp. political poems, however offensive they would be to those who do not read them, are consoling to those who do. Am. poets write about the possibility of civic change, but their poems are—quite rightly—no longer of interest to politicians, statesmen, and political administrators, because few Am. poets begin from a belief in political processes or agents as worthy of sustained scrutiny. They rarely take politics seriously enough in political terms, nor do they present political problems as difficult to solve or as ethically problematic. Am. poets such as Bly, Duncan, and Allen Ginsberg attribute mean motives and low intelligence to their political adversaries, as though virtue or cleverness could make a great difference. When Am. poets now attempt to extend sympathy to politicians, they invoke a psycho-analytic frame, in which no one is really guilty, but the sympathy is clinical and well outside of politics. Critics might credit as oppositional only that political poetry that challenges the political opinions of its audience and condemn those poems that extend the blunt discourse that is routine in political controversy.

Probably well before Milton's prefatory note to *Paradise Lost* readers sensed an analogy between social and prosodic order. Departure from prosodic norms has been loosely likened to political liberty, and discussions of poetic form have thereby been burdened by political polemics. One of the paradoxes of such thinking is that the modernist poets responsible for breaking the force of metrical convention were not champions of political liberty. F. T. Marinetti, Ezra Pound, and T. S. Eliot were staunchly on the political right, though their efforts in *free verse made it difficult for younger poets to continue writing in *meter. Pound, Eliot, and other modernists felt unconstrained by the pressure of immediate poetic precedent, by the desire of readers to find continuity from one generation to the next, or by the daily secular experiences of their readers. These poets made a radical break with the conventions of late 19th-c. Brit. and Am. verse. They dealt with historical subject matter very selectively and from a bird's-eye view, skipping over that which did not engage them. And together with Yeats, they asserted claims to suprarational revelations. The willfulness that Pound displayed in lit. crit. and admired in the poetry of Dante he also admired in totalitarian politics of the right.

Under the influence of continental theory, academic critics in England and America have begun to locate the oppositional effort of poetry not in ideas or statements so much as in technical expressions of noncompliance with the referential and discursive features of descriptive, narrative, and expository prose—all of which supposedly underwrite the prevailing capitalist economic and social order. For many critics, a poet's breaking of genre conventions is itself an admirable act of political defiance. The Am. Language poets of the 1970s (see LANGUAGE POETRY) argued that the undermining of narrative structure and the disruption of syntactic expectations are the most responsible ways in which poets can contribute to large-scale social change: "language control = thought control = reality control," Charles Bernstein has said. "Poetry, like war," his collaborator Ron Silliman writes, "is the pursuit of politics by other means." These poets see their writing as a poetic and expressly Marxist part of a broad intellectual movement in literary theory and philosophy that includes Jacques Derrida, Roland Barthes, Fredric Jameson, and Richard Rorty. One major objection to this approach to the nexus of politics and poetry is that it appeals only to academics who see it as a demonstration of the practical implications of literary theoretical texts that have achieved currency, as well as one way of reconciling these theories with neo-Marxism.

New Historicist critics have pushed well beyond broad analogical arguments by identifying ways in which political motives determine the writing of poets and other writers within a culture; they discover intentional connections between particular discursive practices and specifiable political positions (see NEW HISTORICISM). Helgerson has shown how the controversy of the 16th and 17th cs. about quantitative verse in Eng. was understood then to be part of a debate about the kind of nation England would become, the kind of civil laws it would establish (see CLASSICAL METERS IN MODERN LANGUAGES). Barrell has argued that conditions of *patronage fostered a particular kind of periodic structure in Ren. Eng. praise poems. In reconstructing the political significance of poetic forms, this devel. in lit. crit. is restoring continuity to a view of poetry that was distinguished until very recently by the work of poet-critics such as Empson, who insisted always that a poet's formal choices expressed political considerations alive at the time of writing.

The Marxist or neo-Marxist thought that shapes much New Historical crit. has led to some surprising historical blind spots, though. Like contemp. postcolonialist critics, the New Historicists largely omit discussion of the former "second world," with its troublesome hist. of Marxist imperialism. They thus overlook a crucial link between current historically inflected crit. of the lyric particularly and early Soviet discussions on the proper place of poetry in the new state. "Our epic is not lyric," Leon Trotsky proclaimed in 1924. Nikolai Bukharin echoed Trotsky's comments a decade later in a collectively authored, programmatic speech on "Poetry, Poetics, and the Problems of Poetry in the U.S.S.R." given at the First All-Soviet Writers' Congress of 1934: he extolled the "synthetic poetry" of the future to which he opposes outmoded the "'antirealist'" . . . lyric seeking for a 'world beyond.'" Mikhail Bakhtin was very much Bukharin's comrade-at-arms in this, if little else. The poet, he charges in "The Word and Culture" (1934–35), destroys "all traces of social heteroglossia and diversity of language" in its efforts to achieve "a purely poetic, extrahistorical language": hence, the tendency of all poetic speech to become "authoritarian, dogmatic and conservative."

New Historicist critics of romantic poetry particularly have embraced Bakhtin's ideas without recognizing their historical genesis in the political and theoretical battles between formalists and Marxists that led finally to the literary policies articulated by Bukharin and others. In official Soviet culture, with its cult of the collective, the "'lyric I' became almost 'taboo'" (Eikhenbaum), along with the retrograde ideology it represented. And this, in turn, constituted its distinctive, disruptive power. Under such circumstances, "the attempt to save or defend one's own personality and the right to individuality is the most subversive public act" a poet can commit, the erstwhile Polish poet-dissident Stanisław Barańczak insists. Wordsworth and his descendants, Bromwich argues, likewise oppose "the abstracting tendency of modernization" with the capacity, cultivated through poetry, "to feel as an individual being rather than as a member of an aggregate being."

Critics must maintain a broad range of interpretive and, esp., evaluative principles for analyzing the relations of politics to poetry, so that the political significance of poetry will not be confined to prophecy, invective, or satire. More than this, they must remain alert to the shifting functions and possibilities of poetry, lyric, and otherwise, in multiple trads. as well as modes. Mod. poetry tests the profoundly social issue of "human belonging or not belonging" by continuously tracing and retracing "the boundaries that define inclusion and exclusion" as it crosses "back and forth between an inner self and a world out there," Fletcher has argued. As such, it speaks, at least potentially, "of subjects of interest to all the citizens" (Miłosz 1953).

■ **Anthologies**: *Political Poems and Songs Relating to English History*, ed. T. Wright (1859); *Poems on Affairs of State*, ed. G. deF. Lord et al., 7 v. (1963–75); *Postwar Polish Poetry*, ed. C. Miłosz (1970); *Marx and Engels on Literature and Art*, ed. L. Baxandall and S. Morawski (1973); *Another Republic*, ed. C. Simic and M. Strand (1976); C. Miłosz, *The Witness of Poetry* (1983); *Poeta pamięta*, ed. S. Barańczak (1984); *Carrying the Darkness: The Poetry of the Vietnam War*, ed. W. D. Ehrhart (1985); *Poetry and Politics*, ed. R. M. Jones (1985); *Faber Book of Political Verse*, ed. T. Paulin (1986); *Politics and Poetic Value*, ed. R. von Hallberg (1987); *Unaccustomed Mercy: Soldier Poets of the Vietnam War*, ed. W. D. Ehrhart (1989); *Against Forgetting*, ed. C. Forché (1993); *From the Republic of Conscience*, ed. K. Flattley (1993); *Poetry and Politics*, ed. K. Flint (1996).

■ **Criticism and History**: W. Empson, *Some Versions of Pastoral* (1935); K. Burke, *Attitudes toward History* (1937); C. Brooks, *Modern Poetry and the Tradition* (1939); A. P. d'Entrèves, *Dante as a Political Thinker* (1952); C. Miłosz, *The Captive Mind*, trans. J. Zielonko (1953); D. V. Erdman, *Blake: Prophet against Empire* (1954); C. V. Wedgwood, *Poetry and Politics under the Stuarts* (1960); L. Trotsky, *Literature and Revolution*, trans. R. Strunsky (1960); B. Snell, *Poetry and Society in Ancient Greece* (1961); V. Erlich, *The Double Image: Concepts of the Poet in Slavic Literatures* (1964); M. Adler, *Poetry and Politics* (1965); C. M. Bowra, *Poetry and Politics, 1900–1960* (1966); P. Demetz, *Marx, Engels, and the Poets*, trans. J. L. Sammons (1967); M. Mack, *The Garden and the City: Retirement and Politics in the Later Poetry of Pope* (1969); C. Woodring, *Politics in English Romantic Poetry* (1970); T. R. Edwards, *Imagination and Power* (1971); K. W. Klein, *The Partisan Voice: A Study of the Political Lyric in France and Germany, 1180–1230* (1971); V. J. Scattergood, *Politics and Poetry in the Fifteenth Century* (1971); L. C. Knights, *Public Voices* (1972); S. N. Zwicker, *Dryden's Political Poetry* (1972); E. J. Brown, *Mayakovsky, A Poet in the Revolution* (1973); T. Adorno, "Lyric Poetry and Society," *Telos* 20 (1974); J. F. Mersmann, *Out of the Vietnam Vortex* (1974); N. Reeves, *Heinrich Heine: Poetry and Politics* (1974); M. McKeon, *Politics and Poetry in Restoration England* (1975); R. Williams, *The Country and the City* (1975); *Geschichte der politischen Lyrik in Deutschland*, ed. W. Hinderer (1978); N. Bukharin, "Poetry, Poetics, and the Problems of Poetry in the U.S.S.R.," *Problems of Soviet Literature*, ed. H. G. Scott (1980); M. M. Bakhtin, *The Dialogic Imagination*, ed. M. Holquist, trans. C. Emerson and M. Holquist (1981); W. Mohr and W. Kohlschmidt, "Politische Dichtung," *Reallexikon I*, 3.157–220; M.

Calinescu, "Literature and Politics," *Interrelations of Literature*, ed. J. P. Barricelli and J. Gibaldi (1982); J. J. McGann, *The Romantic Ideology* (1983); R. Pinsky, "The Idiom of a Self," *Elizabeth Bishop and Her Art*, ed. L. Schwartz and S. Estess (1983); C. G. Thayer, *Shakespearean Politics* (1983); J. K. Chandler, *Wordsworth's Second Nature* (1984); D. Norbrook, *Poetry and Politics in English Renaissance* (1984); T. Olafioye, *Politics in African Poetry* (1984); *Poetry and Politics in the Age of Augustus*, ed. T. Woodman and D. West (1984); S. N. Zwicker, *Politics and Language in Dryden's Poetry* (1984); R. von Hallberg, *American Poetry and Culture, 1945–1980* (1985); D. Davie, *Czesław Miłosz and the Insufficiency of Lyric* (1985); C. Bernstein, *Content's Dream* (1986); P. Breslin, *The Psycho-Political Muse* (1987); J. Montefiore, *Feminism and Poetry* (1987); R. Silliman, *The New Sentence* (1987); B. Eikhenbaum, *O literature* (1987); P. S. Stanfield, *Yeats and Politics in the 1930s* (1988); T. Des Pres, *Praises and Dispraises* (1988); B. Erkkila, *Whitman the Political Poet* (1988); R. Helgerson, "Barbarous Tongues," *The Historical Renaissance*, ed. H. Dubrow and R. Strier (1988); *"The Muses Common-Weale": Poetry and Politics in the 17th Century*, ed. C. J. Summers and T-L. Pebworth (1988); A. Patterson, *Pastoral and Ideology* (1988); S. Birkerts, *The Electric Life* (1989); S. Heaney, *The Government of the Tongue* (1989); F. Kermode, *History and Value* (1989); L. Fleishman, *Boris Pasternak: The Poet and His Politics* (1990); A. Zagajewski, *Solidarity, Solitude*, trans. L. Vallee (1990); T. Paulin, *Minotaur: Poetry and the Nation-State* (1992); M. Edmundson, *Literature against Philosophy* (1995); P. G. Stanwood, *Of Poetry and Politics* (1995); D. Bromwich, *Disowned by Memory: Wordsworth's Poetry of the 1790s* (1998); S. Wolfson, *Formal Charges* (1999); S. Zimmerman, *Romanticism, Lyricism, and History* (1999); J. Bate, *The Song of the Earth* (2000); T. Hoffman, *Robert Frost and the Politics of Poetry* (2001); N. Roe, *The Politics of Nature* (2002); J. Cox, *Poetry and Politics in the Cockney School* (2004); A. Fletcher, *A New Theory for American Poetry* (2004); J. Longenbach, *The Resistance to Poetry* (2004); G. Dawes, *Verses against the Darkness: Pablo Neruda's Poetry and Politics* (2006); P. Lacoue-Labarthe, *Heidegger and the Politics of Poetry*, trans. J. Fort (2007); D. Orr, "The Politics of Poetry," *Poetry* July/Aug. (2008), http://www.poetryfoundation.org/poetrymagazine/article/181746; J. Paulhan, *On Poetry and Politics*, trans. J. Bajorek and E. Trudel (2008); C. Cavanagh, *Lyric Poetry and Modern Politics: Russia, Poland, and the West* (2010).

R. von Hallberg; C. Cavanagh; Y. Lorman

# POLYNESIAN POETRY

I. Poetry In Polynesian Languages
II. Poetry In English

**I. Poetry In Polynesian Languages.** Polynesia is a vast triangle of thousands of islands, with apexes at Hawai'i to the north, Easter Island to the southeast, and New Zealand to the southwest; Tuvalu and enclaves are farther west in Melanesia and Micronesia. Each of the archipelagoes has majority populations of Polynesian descent, except for New Zealand and Hawai'i, where Maori and Kanaka Maoli remain substantial groups. Before Eur. contact, knowledge was mainly transmitted by oral presentation and by demonstration, which are both of continuing importance. Polynesia elevated oral art to a high level of beauty and subtlety. Poets use numerous homonyms, puns, and repetitions, along with reduplication and *alliteration, as they enjoy frequent reiterations of sound.

Western culture introduced by 19th-c. missionaries, settlers, colonial officials, and voyagers stimulated poetic creativity by adding new concepts and symbols without, however, the traditional art's losing its indigenous identity. Poetry's social function, however, has altered with Westernization. Traditional poetry, integral to personal life from birth to death and to both religion and entertainment, was frequently entwined with ritual, vocalization, and dance to express values, give aesthetic pleasure, transmit knowledge, and affirm the connection of human beings to nature and the supernatural. Poetic strategies across introduced and indigenous langs. include personifying nature with gods and spirits (many regarded as ancestors) and reacting emotionally to changing aspects of landscape with minute observation, vivid description, and extensive naming of places and natural forces.

Since traditional poetry and music are inseparable, each adding power to the other, a poet composed text and melody at the same time. Each category of poetry had its characteristic modes of rhythmic oral delivery, the principal modes being song or recitative, with variations and combinations of each. Hawaiians, e.g., distinguished between an *oli* and a *mele* but adapted a poem to either. An *oli* was a dignified recitative, most often a solo, with limited gestures and occasional percussion accompaniment, for *dirges, prayers, eulogies, and genealogies, each class with its special *oli* style. The basic style was a rapid, guttural, vibrating monotone on a single pitch that required a strong, deep voice trained to hold the breath through long phrases often ending with a trill. Continuity of sound was essential because breath carried the words filled with *mana* (supernatural power), and a break or hesitation, except at appropriate places, was believed unlucky in a secular poem and fatal in a sacred. A *mele* was sung or chanted to the accompaniment of dance (*hula*), pantomime, and instruments (not always the three together); a subtype was performed either with or without dance for love songs, name songs honoring individuals, or genital chants celebrating generative powers. A *mele*, customarily performed with a chorus whose leader sang solo parts, had marked, repeated rhythmic patterns if danced and a wider range of *pitch and freedom than the *oli*. Missionary hymns brought melody, which Polynesians called *hīmeni* and combined with old styles of delivery for new poems, not necessarily sacred, but not danced. While music changed as Westerners introduced their folk and work songs, texts retained many traditional themes and devices. The same was the case in other archipelagos beside the Hawaiian.

A new poem that met an audience's approval was performed repeatedly and might become a classic passed on for generations. In New Zealand, compositions by Kingi Tahiwi, Te Rauparaha, Paraire Tomoana, Sir Apirana Ngata, Te Ari Pitama, Te Arikinui Te Atairangikaahu, Kingi Tawhiao, Ngoi Pewhairangi, Tuini Ngawai and many others are still sung and performed. Their genius lay in fresh and innovative rearrangement or reinterpretation of recurrent themes, images, phrases, and lines.

Samoan chiefs (but not commoners) could sing a *solo* (the Samoan term for a recitative epitomizing a myth or legend) of the subcategory *fa'ali'i*, meaning "royal" and concerning a royal lineage. A politically important trad., e.g., centered on Sanalālā: when his canoe was swept to sea from Tonga to Samoa, his father's land, his Tongan mother, Chieftess Fitimaupaloga, composed a 21-line *solo fa'ali'i* considered "exceedingly beautiful." A chief was much admired when he sang it with a plaintive *cadence while accompanying himself on a type of drum only certain chiefly families could use (Freeman).

The *solo* uses common Polynesian poetic devices of inspiration from nature and place; irregular but rhythmic lines; repetition of sounds, words, and syllables; and (peculiarly western Polynesian) deliberate rhyming and termination of sets of lines with a certain sound. Many traditional Maori song poems (*waiata*) follow a quantitative meter where eight or 12 vowels are contained in each half line of text corresponding to a musical phrase. A whole line corresponds to a musical *strophe.

Sacred creation and genealogical *chants were intoned by senior males and high priests in consecrating a chief's primary wife's firstborn son and on other occasions. Numerous resemblances with other chants elsewhere prove the chants share the same Polynesian heritage. Their fundamental function concerned procreation and the continuity of life through the chief, on whom, as the closest link to the gods, the fertility of nature and people depended. Starting with creation, a chanter connected the infant to his divine and earthly kin and thereby confirmed his rank, privileges, taboos, territory, and power. Because words had power to produce action, an error or hesitation negated a sacred chant.

An example is the Hawaiian *Kumulipo* (Origin in Deepest Darkness), a 2,102-line masterpiece of the type called *ku'auhau*, pathway lineage, property of the family of Kalākaua and his sister Lili'uokalani, the last rulers in the 19th c. of the monarchy established by Kamehameha I in 1795. When priests ca. 1700 CE chanted the *Kumulipo*, each name activated the latent *mana* of High Chief Keawe's son and heir, named Lono-i-ka-makahiki because he was born during the annual Makahiki festival for Lono, god of peace and prosperity. It may have been recited in 1779 over Captain James Cook as the returned god Lono. It also establishes linkages to pan-Polynesian deities such as Maui.

Eastern Polynesian chiefs and priests, who were educated in sacred houses of learning, excelled in technical skill at composition and erudition. Marquesan and Mangarevan masters served rulers as organizers and directors of ceremonies, determined official versions of sacred chants and hist., and recited the most sacred parts of chants. A Marquesan tribal master of chants, outranked only by the ruler and the inspirational priest, might be deified at death. Nonetheless, if another tribe's master challenged him, he had to compete successfully before an audience, exhibiting his learning, quickness in composition, and ability in other oral arts at the risk of losing his title or even his life. Many Polynesian islands had such contests of wit and learning.

A Samoan chief's talking chief, also a master of ceremony and subject to challenges from a rival, upheld his chief's and village's prestige, esp. on official visits to other villages, by his command of the complex art of oratory, learning, composition, and knowledge of procedure and etiquette due each titled man present. Tonga, by contrast, had a class of professional poets, generally untitled but with status roughly equivalent to a ruler's ceremonial attendants. A poet, though honored, was entirely dependent on his patron chief and usually insecure even as to his life. At one time, contests between poets became so bitter they had to be discontinued. Like other members of ruling families of Polynesia, Queen Salote of Tonga was famed for her compositions.

In New Zealand, Maori women, who as a group predominated as composers, were more likely than men to compose songs about frustrated love or *waiata aroha* ("Would I were a broken canoe that might be mended") and short, informally arranged, intensely personal *laments (*waiata tangi*) often for those slain in tribal or anticolonial wars, coupling frank emotion and natural imagery ("Like the tides within Tirau forever rising and falling / Is my wild lamentation within Houhangapa"). Maori men were more likely to compose longer, more formally structured laments, filled with elaborate metaphors to emphasize that the whole tribe had lost a great man ("like a star shining apart in the Milky Way" or "a sheltering rata tree from the north wind"). There are many thematic categories of Maori song poem, or *waiata*, and oratorical chant, or *tauparapara*. The *haka* is a form of assertive or war dance poetry in New Zealand, widely popularized by the national rugby team who perform and chant a *haka* before international matches. Experts of the form have criticized the team's bowdlerized versions, while there has been a general resurgence in the variety and quality of haka performed by many Maori groups (Karetu, Ngata, Mead).

**II. Poetry in English.** Many of the contemp. Eng.-lang. poets are resident in New Zealand and Hawai'i, while Eng.-lang. poets of Melanesia (e.g., John Kasaipwalova, Steven Winduo, Jully Makini, Grace Molisa) and Micronesia (Teresia Teaiwa, Emelihter Kihleng, Craig Santos Perez) highlight the porosity of cultural boundaries as they are influential in the region. The following selected poets have books published.

**A. *Cook Islands.*** *Mine Eyes Dazzle* (1950), by the New Zealand-based Cook Islands (Tongareva) poet Alistair Te Ariki Campbell (1925–2009), was the first book of poetry by a Polynesian to be published in Eng.

Campbell's early work referenced New Zealand and Eng. romantic modes, while his work from the 1960s on is infused by his Tongarevan and broader Polynesian heritage, incl. *Sanctuary of Spirits*, *The Dark Lord of Savaiki*, *Soul Traps*, and *Maori Battalion*. His *lyric poetry, incl. the littoral and the oceanic, fuses a personal desire to belong to a familial collective in dialogue with personae from the historical and mythological past, and always has an elegiac edge. It includes direct trans. of Tongarevan chant and genealogy (see NEW ZEALAND, POETRY OF). Campbell's prolific Cook Islands compatriot Kauraka Kauraka (1951–1997) wrote *tateni* style poetry in praise of persons in Eng. and Cook Islands Maori.

**B. *New Zealand (Maori).*** Former New Zealand poet laureate Hone Tuwhare (1922–2008) was an arts icon and the first Maori poet in Eng. to be published. His *No Ordinary Sun* (1964) has been reprinted ten times (he published 13 poetry books in all); the title poem was a protest at nuclear testing in the Pacific, reflecting his socialist ideology and environmentalism. His work code shifted between multiple vernacular and chiefly oratorical registers and featured a strong relationship between myth and nature, romance, a panegyric sensibility, and a cultural relationship to the land. Many Maori poets have followed in Tuwhare's wake, incl. multigenre author Apirana Taylor, who combines the qualities of orature with text—namely, repetition, Maori names and words, short lines composed for the breath, and music in live performance. Roma Potiki employs traditional forms such as the *oriori* or instructional *lullaby, while Trixie Te Arama Menzies directly borrows from famous *waiata tangi* (laments), such as *E pā tō hau*. Arapera Blank composed in Maori and Eng., relying on such chiefly symbolism as the *kokako* (a cousin of the highly prized and extinct *huia* wattlebird). J. C. Sturm, a poet of Tuwhare's generation like Blank and Menzies, imbues her poetry with *karanga* (initial call of welcome in greeting ceremonies) and *tangi* (lament). Keri Hulme's poetry is infused with humor, mythological shapes, natural and spiritual omens, gods, and songs. Robert Sullivan's six books of short poems and extended sequences range from personal to cultural subjects, incl. oceanic exploration in *Star Waka*. Rangi Faith also incorporates Maori symbolism in his collections. Hinemoana Baker's first collection draws on traditional models such as the *waiata tangi*, Michael O'Leary is influenced by Pakeha (Eur.) poet James K. Baxter, who borrowed from Maori trads., and Brian Potiki's collection *Aotearoa* studs his texts with praise for artist-heroes such as Tuwhare.

**C. *Samoa.*** Albert Wendt, the influential and prolific Samoan author and poet, anthologized wider Oceanic (Melanesia, Micronesia, Polynesia) lit. in *Lali*, and *Nuanua* and Polynesian poetry in *Whetu Moana* with Reina Whaitiri and Robert Sullivan. His early elegiac sequence "Inside Us the Dead" incorporates high rhetorical flourishes grounded in immediate referents, as well as elements of genealogical recitations (*gafa*) and formal oratorical codes (*fa'alupega*), while providing a

family and social hist. as he recounts the death of his brother. A verse novel, *The Adventures of Vela*, is a contemp. myth-saga featuring a contest between poets. *The Book of the Black Star* merges images with text ranging from relaxed to heightened modes. Tusiata Avia's *Wild Dogs under My Skirt* underscores her work by referring to the Mau Samoan resistance movement and myths, and uses Samoan words. Her contemporary, Sia Figiel, also richly weaves Western with Samoan concepts of the self. Momoe Malietoa Von Reiche uses her relationship with the land as a refuge and source of nourishment (Marsh). Selina Tusitala Marsh's first book, *Fast-talking PI*, pays homage to many poets of the region. Tutuila (Am. Samoan) poet Caroline Sinavaiana negotiates Am. colonialism and indigeneity through the lens of the warrior goddess Nafanua and the power of *tagi* (lament).

**D. *Tonga.*** Tongan poet Konai Helu Thaman draws on traditional symbolism in her popular work, such as the association of the sun with monarchs, the contrast of *langakali* flowers (symbolizing fertility and regeneration) against corrupting Westernization, as well as other botanical references significant within Tongan lang. compositions. She composes in Tongan and translates her compositions into Eng. (Marsh). Karlo Mila's *Dream Fish Floating* summons her family genealogy to rationalize first-generation Tongan-Samoan-Palagi (Eur.) life in New Zealand and adeptly pays homage to poets of the older generation (*tuakana*).

**E. *Hawai'i.*** Political leader and scholar Haunani-Kay Trask's minimalist *free-verse *strophes are focused on sovereign justice, dignity in the face of cultural denigration, and recovery. She draws on places, figures, and protocols important to the volcanic goddess Pele, who represents overwhelming indigenous power and who features in traditional poetry cycles. Wayne Kamuali'i Westlake (1947–1984), whose poetry included *Dadaist and Confucian ideas, wrote *concrete poems using Hawaiian words to inflect his anger at Am. colonialism, such as *pupule* (Hawaiian for "crazy"). The scattered letters in pupule also form words for prayer (*pule*), guns (*pu*), appetizers (*pupu*), and a letter-jumble similar to the litter on the sidewalks of Waikiki (the subject of a sequence), forming random words in multiple langs. Mahealani Perez-Wendt references the last monarch, Queen Lili'uokalani, in the title of her collection *Uluhaimalama*, which was the queen's garden. The hidden meaning of that name refers to growth into the light, both for the plants in the garden and the Hawaiian nation. Imaikalani Kalahele juxtaposes illustrations and poems, using the rhythms of jazz and Hawaiian lang. Joseph Balaz is one of the most accomplished Hawaiian poets, who writes in standard and pidgin Eng. He produced the first spoken-word album, *Electric Laulau*, in 1998. Sage U'ilani Takehiro's *Honua* was published with the assistance of indigenous publisher Kuleana 'Ōiwi Press, also the publisher of skilled lyric poet Brandy Nālani McDougall. Takehiro passionately braids natural elements into a literary shelter (or *honua*).

**F. *Rotuma and Niue.*** David Eggleton, of Rotuman descent, is one of the most successful New Zealand performance poets of his generation, preceding the spoken-word poets who most obviously link to techniques of orature. When in contemplative mode, he occasionally explores Maori and colonial history. John Puhiatau Pule, who was born in Niue but spent most of his life in New Zealand, incorporates hist., mythology, nature, and love poetry in his novel *The Shark That Ate the Sun* in a 30-poem reconstructed sequence by a fictional 19th-c. poet.

**G. French Polynesia/Te Ao Mā'ohi.** The anthol. *Varua Tupu* has made an extensive selection of Fr. Polynesian writing available in Eng. Notable poets include cultural leader Henri Hiro, Flora Devatine, Patrick Arai Amaru, and Rai a Mai (Michou Chaze). These poets compose in Tahitian and Fr.

■ **Special Publications:** Bishop Museum *Bulletin* 8, 9, 17, 29, 34, 46, 48, 95, 109, 127, 148, 158, 183; Bishop Museum *Memoirs* 4, 5, 6; Bishop Museum *Special Publications* 2, 51, 61; Polynesian Society *Memoirs* 3, 4, 5, 41; *Maori Texts*: A. T. Ngata, ed., trans., and comp., *Nga Moteatea*, pt. 1 (1959), and A. T. Ngata and P. Te Hurinui, ed., trans., and comp., pt. 2 (1961); *MANA*, South Pacific Creative Arts Society (1973– 1977).
■ **Studies:** W. W. Gill, *Myths and Songs from the South Pacific* (1876), and *Historical Sketches of Savage Life in Polynesia* (1880); N. B. Emerson, *Unwritten Literature of Hawaii: Sacred Songs of the Hula* (1909; rpt. 1977), and *Pele and Hiiaka, a Myth from Hawaii* (c. 1915; rpt. 1978); M. W. Beckwith, "Introduction," *The Hawaiian Romance of Laieikawai* (1919); S. H. Elbert, "Chants and Love Songs of the Marquesas, Fr. Oceania," *Jour. P. Society* 56 (1947); J. D. Freeman, "The Tradition of Sanalāla," *Jour. P. Society* 56 (1947); M. K. Pukui, "Songs (Meles) of Old Ka'u, Hawaii," *JAF* 62 (1948); M. W. Beckwith, *The Kumulipo, a Hawaiian Creation Chant* (1951; rpt. 1972); S. H. Elbert, "Hawaiian Literary Style and Culture," *American Anthropologist* 53 (1951); D. Christensen and G. Koch, *Die Musik der Ellice-Inseln* (1964); S. M. Mead, "Imagery, Symbolism, and Social Values in Maori Chants," *Jour. P. Society* 78 (1969); M. Pukui and A. Korn, *The Echo of Our Song: Chants & Poems of the Hawaiians* (1973); M. McLean and M. Orbell, *Traditional Songs of the Maori* (1975); M. McLean, "Text and Music in 'Rule of Eight' Waiata," *Studies in Pacific Languages & Cultures*, ed. J. Hollyman et al. (1981); K. Luomala, *Voices on the Wind: Polynesian Myths and Chants*, rev. ed. (1986); T. Karetu, *Haka: The Dance of a Noble People* (1993); *Te Ao Marama: Contemporary Maori Writing*, 5 vols., ed. W. Ihimaera (1993–96); *Whetu Moana: Contemporary Polynesian Poems in English*, ed. A. Wendt, R. Whaitiri, and R. Sullivan (2003); S. T. Marsh, " 'Ancient Banyans, Flying Foxes and White Ginger': Five Pacific Women Writers," diss., Univ. of Auckland (2004); K. Ho'omanawanui, "He Lei Ho'oheno no nā Kau a Kau: Language, Performance, and Form in Hawaiian Poetry," *Contemporary Pacific* 17, no. 1 (2005); F. Stewart, K. Mateatea-Allain, A. Dale Mawyer, *Vārua Tupu: New Writing from French Polynesia* (2006);

R. Sullivan, "Hone Tuwhare Memorial Issue," *Ka Mate Ka Ora* 6 (2008), http://www.nzepc.auckland.ac.nz/kmko/.

R. Sullivan; K. Luomala

**POLYPTOTON** (Gr., "word in many cases"; Lat. *traductio*). Related to the varieties of simple word repetition or iteration, which in cl. rhet. are treated under the genus of *ploce, is another class of figures that repeat a word or words by varying their word class (part of speech) or by giving different forms of the same root or stem. Shakespeare takes great interest in this device; it increases patterning without wearying the ear, and it takes advantage of the differing functions, energies, and positionings that different word classes are permitted in speech. Schaar says that Shakespeare uses polyptoton "almost to excess," "using derivatives of more than a hundred stems" in the sonnets. Some of these are but natural in the amplification of any theme, e.g., *love— lov'st—beloved—loving—love's—lovers*, though it is obvious in other cases that the figuration is intentional, as in sonnet 43:

> And darkly bright, are bright in dark directed.
> Then thou, whose shadow shadows doth make
>   bright—
> How would thy shadow's form form happy show
> To the clear day with thy much clearer light.

To Shakespeare's hundred forms in 154 sonnets, compare Philip Sidney's 45 in the 108 of *Astrophil and Stella*, Edmund Spenser's 27 in the 89 *Amoretti*, and Pierre de Ronsard's 63 in the 218 of *Amours* I.

Transferred to prosody, polyptoton at line end becomes, mutatis mutandis, a type of rhyme that also avails itself of grammatical categories, which was known to the *rhétoriqueurs* as *rime grammaticale* (see GRAMMATICAL RHYME; RHÉTORIQUEURS, GRANDS). To us now, this does not seem true rhyme, but standards for acceptability in rhyming have varied from age to age (see IDENTICAL RHYME).

Very similar to polyptoton is antanaclasis, repetition of a word with a shift in meaning. By using two forms of a word, antanaclasis can play on two senses of it and thereby generate homonymic puns. Shifting the meaning of the word without repeating it, the shift being entailed by a second predicate or modifier, is the function of the elusive *syllepsis. Recognition of all these forms suggests that we should construct a taxonomy of the varieties of word repetition as given (albeit often confusedly) in cl. and Ren. rhet. Four types seem distinguishable: repetition of the same word, in the same grammatical form, with the same meaning (ploce and epizeuxis); same word, same form, different meaning (antanaclasis); same word, different form, same meaning (polyptoton); same word, different form, different meaning (sometimes called antanaclasis, sometimes polyptoton). Here, however, one must define *word* and *form* carefully. Also related is *anthimeria—another favorite of Shakespeare's—the turning of one part of speech into another, particularly the making of verbs out of nouns.

Some rhetoricians have used *traductio* in the sense not of polyptoton but of ploce, or direct word repetition (see Quintilian, *Institutio oratoria* 9.3.68–73); one should, therefore, be explicit about definitions when using any of these terms.

■ M. Joseph, *Shakespeare's Use of the Arts of Language* (1947); C. Schaar, *An Elizabethan Sonnet Problem* (1960); L. A. Sonnino, *Handbook to Sixteenth-Century Rhetoric* (1968); Group μ, 124–26; A. Quinn, *Figures of Speech* (1982); Vickers; B. Vickers, *Classical Rhetoric in English Poetry*, 2d ed. (1989)—esp. 129–30, 146–48; Corbett; M. E. Auer, "'Und eine Freiheit macht uns alle Frei!' Das Polyptoton in Schillers Freiheitsdenken," *Monatshefte für Deutschsprachige Literatur und Kultur* 100 (2008); V. Langer, "De la métamorphose," *Esprit généreux, esprit pantagruélique*, ed. R. Leushuis and Z. Zalloua (2008).

T.V.F. Brogan

**POLYSEMY.** Denotes a plurality of meanings in a given sign, statement, or text, referring at once to multiple contexts for *interpretation. Perhaps the most inclusive category of its kind, polysemy indicates the coincidence of multiple and sometimes contradictory meanings under the same sign, as opposed to *irony, a discrepancy between two meanings or interpretations; *aporia, a logical impasse; or *indeterminacy, an indecision with regard to meaning.

There are two fundamental paradigms by which one can think about the occurrence of polysemy in literary lang.: referential and differential. The referential paradigm assumes that lang. has the basic function of referentiality, i.e., it points to things that exist outside it; accordingly, polysemy would be understood as a trait of certain texts in which signs do not function ordinarily (having one or two referents at most) but bear multiple relational associations, so that such a text becomes, as Perloff calls it, "a reverberating echo chamber of meanings." Nevertheless, these intricate webs of meanings and associations do not occur spontaneously but are aligned along the same axis of figurative associations (see METAPHOR, METONYMY). A sign in a given polysemous text will bear multiple relational meanings, while certain unassociated meanings will remain excluded from consideration. Even though each signifier will have more than two signifieds, polysemy under the referential paradigm will always remain a polysemy of controlled meanings—confined, as it were, to the rule of association (see SIGN, SIGNIFIED, SIGNIFIER).

The second, differential paradigm assumes that polysemy is not a property of *texts but a function of lang. itself. According to this paradigm, lang. is not a naming operation but is instead a closed system of interdependent terms in which the value of each term results solely and arbitrarily from the simultaneous presence of all others. The meaning of each given term emerges by virtue of its differentiation from all other meaningful terms in lang. and remains fixed only with respect to the simultaneous concurrence of every meaning that exists outside it. Likewise, the literary text does not have a single fixed meaning or even several meanings, but its meaning is always constituted by virtue of its differentiation from all other texts that exist in lang. Thus, a text is infinitely polysemous, connoting endless other contexts for interpretation. In fact, one can really speak only of a single text, since its limits are the limits of lang. itself. Therefore, the polysemy of a given text does not consist of an enumeration of different meanings or interpretations because those meanings can never be closed off or constructed hierarchically; as Barthes claims, "everything signifies ceaselessly and several times, but without being delegated to a great final ensemble, to an ultimate structure."

For critics working under the differential paradigm, polysemy represents a case of *intertextuality in which an expression, while signifying one thing, always signifies another thing without ceasing to signify the first, whereas, for critics working under the referential paradigm, polysemy is a property of particular texts that explore and bring to light the multiple associative relations that a sign carries, relations that usually remain submerged or repressed in ordinary use of lang. One noteworthy case in which these two paradigms converge is T. S. Eliot's *The Waste Land*. In terms of the differential paradigm, the poem contains numerous intertextual references to such sources as Dante's *Inferno*, the Bible, Charles Baudelaire's *Fleurs du mal*, Richard Wagner's *Tristan und Isolde*, Shakespeare's *The Tempest*, Ovid's *Metamorphoses*, and so on. These textual references are so thoroughly embedded into the fabric of the text that one cannot detach from the poet's own voice, effectively bringing about the "death of the author" as a singular voice to which a specific origin can be assigned. In terms of the referential paradigm, *The Waste Land* maintains referential unity between signifier and signified. Thus, as Perloff argues, Eliot's "Unreal City" is a real fog-bound London, and one can find numerous references to locales such as the London Bridge, the Cannon Street Hotel, the Metropole, the Strand, and Queen Victoria Street. Yet, at the same time, Eliot's London also bears multiple relational meanings as it echoes Dante's hell and Baudelaire's Paris. Along the same lines, various figures and locales are related along an axis of metaphoric and metonymic associations. Thus, e.g., the Church of St. Magnus Martyr brings to mind the martyrdom of Christ, and its "Ionian white and gold" is an *allusion both to liturgy and cl. Greece, symbolically opposed to the decayed London of brown fog and winter.

*See* AMBIGUITY.

■ Empson; R. Barthes, "The Death of The Author," *Image, Music, Text*, trans. S. Heath (1977); R. Barthes, *S/Z*, trans. R. Miller (1974); M. Perloff, *The Poetics of Indeterminacy* (1981); U. Eco, "History and Historiography of Semiotics," *Semiotik/Semiotics, Ein Handbuch zu den zeichentheoretischen Grundlagen von Natur und Kultur/A Handbook on the Sign-Theoretic Foundations of Nature and Culture*, ed. R. Posner, K. Robering,

T. A. Sebeok, v. 1 (1996); P. Ricoeur, "The Problem of Double Meaning as Hermeneutic Problem and as Semantic Problem," *The Conflict of Interpretations: Essays in Hermeneutics*, ed. D. Ihde, trans. K. McLaughlin (2007).

N. Pines

**POLYSYNDETON** (Gr., "much compounded"). The repetition of conjunctions, normally *and*; the opposite of *asyndeton, which is the omission of conjunctions; common in all kinds of poetry. Quintilian (*Institutio oratoria* 9.3.51–54) remarks, however, that "the source of [both figures] is the same, as they render what we say more vivacious and energetic, exhibiting an appearance of vehemence, and of passion bursting forth as it were time after time," citing, as an illustration, "Both house, and household gods, and arms, and Amyclaean dog, and quiver formed of Cretan make" (Virgil, *Georgics* 3.344–45). Longinus discusses both figures, differentiating them. Mod. rhetorical theorists point out that, in addition to a sense of breathlessness, polysyndeton may add emphasis to the items in an enumeration or may represent the "flow and continuity of experience" (Corbett). Conversely, Quinn observes that by slowing down a sentence, polysyndeton may add "dignity" to it or produce an incantatory effect. The latter usage may explain the numerous examples of polysyndeton often cited in the Bible (e.g.,Gen. 1:24–25; Rev. 13:1). Examples may be found in Horace, *Odes* 15; in Petrarch, *Canzoniere* 61 (polysyndeton is a major structuring device in Petrarch's poetry); in Shakespeare, sonnet 66; in Walt Whitman; and in T. S. Eliot's "Journey of the Magi" (11–15). Group μ, which classifies polysyndeton among metataxes, i.e., as a figure of repetitive addition affecting syntax, explains the effect in the Eliot passage as "responsible for the harmony of the sentence and the metrical scheme of the verse. This is not by chance, since . . . harmony and metrics are systematic groups of practices and rules, two vast syntactic figures that proceed by addition and repetition." In some cases, then, the polysyndeton may contribute to rhythm. Although polysyndeton in Eng. poetry mainly involves the repetition of *and*, examples occur in which other conjunctions repeat, as in Eliot's "The Love Song of J. Alfred Prufrock" (101–2), though these are disputed, since they do not give the same effect; cf. Milton, whose Satan "pursues his way/And swims or sinks, or wades, or creeps, or flies" (*Paradise Lost* 2.949–50) or *Othello* 3.3.77–80, where a series of *or*s offer logical alternatives.

*See* HYPOTAXIS AND PARATAXIS.

■ Group μ; A. Quinn, *Figures of Speech* (1982); J. P. Houston, *Shakespearean Sentences* (1988); Corbett.

T.V.F. BROGAN; A. W. HALSALL

**PORTUGAL, POETRY OF.** Port. poetry originates in the med. (12th–14th cs.) Galician-Port. *cantiga. The cantigas are generally divided into three major genres: *cantigas de amigo* (songs in the voice of women), *cantigas de amor* (courtly love songs in the voice of men), and *cantigas de escarnho e mal dizer* (joke and insult poetry). Galician-Port. poetry circulated orally and through *performance. The cantigas de amigo are unique to Portugal and Iberia and constitute the largest corpus of woman-voiced poetry in Europe, although all extant compositions are attributed to male poets. The cantigas de amor tend to follow the model of *Occitan poetry and in that regard are more conventional. The joke poetry is accomplished in *polysemy, revels in transgressive *imagery and bawdy humor, and presents ludic constructions of sexuality, gender, and cultural and religious orthodoxies. Many of the cantigas, esp. the cantigas de amigo, invoke the sea and ships as motifs in amatory complaint and yearning and thus establish a trad. of maritime poetry in Portugal. Some salient poets are Pero da Ponte (fl. 1235–60), who composed in all three major genres; Johan Zorro (fl. late 13th c.); Martim Codax (fl. mid-13th c.); Pai Gomez Charinho (ca. 1225–95); and Pero Meogo, whose sea-inspired love songs stand as examples of med. poetic virtuosity. The work of over 150 poets represents the Galician-Port. lyric school.

Following the cantigas, the poetic record is silent for a century until 1516 when Garcia de Resende (ca. 1470–1536) published the bilingual (Port.-Castilian) *Cancioneiro Geral* (General Songbook), a collection of erudite, courtly verse that testifies to the shift from oral to written poetic culture. These poems were intended as palace entertainments. Resende, himself one of the *Cancioneiro* poets, assembled compositions on aristocratic themes (such as the formalities of love and courtship) that are usually structured as the popular *redondilha maior* or line of seven syllables. A common format is an initial refrain (*mote*) that is then glossed (*glosa*). Petrarchan ideas on love first appear here (e.g., love that delights in suffering and contradiction; see PETRARCHISM), but some poems take on humorous and satirical topics or reveal the social realities of 15th- and 16th-c. Portugal with personages such as the sorceress, the Jew, and the Moor. Resende's stanzas on the tragic death of Inês de Castro, João Rodrigues de Castelo Branco's "Cantiga sua partindo-se" (Song of Parting), and Jorge da Silveira's contemplation on love are notable examples. The verses of the first known woman poet, Filipa de Almada, appear in this *Cancioneiro*. Other poets include Jorge de Aguiar, Duarte de Brito, Francisco Sá de Miranda, Anrique da Mota (d. after 1544), Francisco de Sousa, and Gil Vicente (ca. 1465–1536), the first major figure of Port. theater who composed his plays in verse and included lyrical passages and interludes in them. Much of his poetry is inspired by traditional forms and subject matter that were reworked to theatrical ends. In this, Vicente's plays are a repository of Port. poetry but one that rewrites and reformulates the trad. through the playwright's acute literary sensibilities. Vicente's command of poetry is apparent across the genres he cultivated, namely, religious plays, comedy, and farce. Later in the 16th c., Joana da Gama (d. 1586) employed the popular verse forms characteristic of Resende's collection to express an anguished vision of life in *Ditos da freyra* (Sayings of the Nun).

After a sojourn in Italy, Sá de Miranda (1481–1558) brought It. Ren. genres to Portugal, incl. the Petrarchan *sonnet that would dominate Port. poetry from then on. He would, however, continue to cultivate the old style of poetry even after the introduction of Italianate forms. His *Trovas à maneira antiga* (Stanzas in the Old Style), e.g., are largely composed in the traditional redondilha and explore their topics in learned and erudite lang. and *conceits. Alongside his friend Bernardim Ribeiro (1490?–1536?), Sá de Miranda is credited as the first to compose *eclogues in Port. following Virgil's example. Sá de Miranda's moralistic poetry is technically proficient and often conceptually difficult, and its Port.-Castilian bilingualism bears evidence, as does other poetry of the time, of the interconnected literary cultures of Portugal and Spain. Ribeiro is the author of five eclogues, and some of his poetry first appears in Resende's *Cancioneiro*. Ribeiro develops a sentimental vein in his work turning on love and its psychological contours that is also reflected in Cristóvão Falcão's *Écloga Crisfal* (Crisfal Eclogue, first pub. anonymously then reprinted together with Ribeiro's works in 1554). Ribeiro's sentimental pastoral fiction *História de Menina e Moça* (Story of a Young Girl, 1554, 1557), which is interspersed with verse, elaborates a psychology of love, nostalgic yearning (*saudade*), and a fatalistic sense of life. Saudade is a cornerstone of Port. literary and cultural identity, beginning with the med. cantigas, and is the basis of the 19th- and early 20th-c. poetic movement known as *saudosismo*. *Menina e Moça* includes literary motifs on the dimensions and characteristics of amorous sentiment and consciousness that will be further elaborated and explored in the widely influential verses of Luís de Camões.

The poetry of António Ferreira (1528–69) and Luís de Camões (1524?–80) stands out as representative of lyric verse in Ren. Portugal, with Camões as the culminating figure now at the heart of the Port. literary canon. Ferreira, an admirer of Sá de Miranda, wrote poems based on It., Lat., and Gr. models and eschewed the Port.-Castilian bilingual practice in favor of Port. alone. His poems were published under the title *Poemas Lusitanos* (Lusitanian Poems, 1598) and rehearse topics important to humanism. (Neo-Lat. humanist poets, such as André de Resende [1500?–73], revived Lat. as a poetic lang.; see LATIN POETRY.) Camões's poetry earned him international renown. He wrote in the Ren. genres of the sonnet, eclogue, *song, *ode, *elegy, and *epic. The lyrics were published posthumously under the generic title of *Rimas* (Rhymes, 1595, 1598); they often express their topics through the prevailing lens of Petrarchism. But they also characteristically inflect intense, personal experience with a melancholic tone and perspective and address such universal themes as love, hope, happiness, and death. Maritime expansion and travel, the historical backdrop of 16th-c. Portugal, exercise an influence on the metaphors and the real and imagined experiences of the Camonian poetic subject. As a virtuoso sonneteer, Camões shapes a philosophy of existence informed by the contradictory nature of love,

melancholy, sadness, and the "desconcerto do mundo" (disorder of the world) or the dissonance between the world as it should be and as it actually is. He charts the workings of *affect in all its contradictions. His epic *Os Lusíadas* (*The Lusiads*, 1572), modeled in large part on Virgil and Ludovico Ariosto, takes as its story the 1497–99 voyage of Vasco da Gama to India. While *The Lusiads* is, on one level, an expression of Christian imperialist ideology, it is also fraught with contradiction and failure and expressed in a rhet. that frequently enters the realm of the lyrical. The poem is an exploration of the Port. Ren. imagination and joins hist., myth, and literary culture into a vibrant cohesiveness. Camões is one of the Ren.'s most influential mythographers and psychologists of love. *The Lusiads* quickly achieved international currency and, along with the *Rimas*, establishes connections to other poets of early modernity writing in the contexts of (maritime) exploration, literary creation, and subjectivity.

Camões's epic initiative was continued and imitated in the 16th and 17th cs. by poems based on other imperial figures or events in Africa, Asia, and Brazil. Jerónimo Corte-Real (1533–88) wrote the *Naufrágio e lastimoso sucesso da perdiçam de Sepúlveda* (Shipwreck and Sorrowful Loss of Sepúlveda, 1594), based on the famous shipwreck off the coast of East Africa in 1552. Bento Teixeira's *Prosopopéia* (1601) tells of Jorge de Albuquerque Coelho's shipwreck off Recife, Brazil, in 1565. Other epic poems in this trad. are Francisco de Andrada, *O primeiro cerco de Diu* (The First Siege of Diu, 1589), Vasco Mouzinho de Quevedo Castel-Branco, *Affonso africano* (Afonso the African, 1611), Francisco de Sá de Meneses, *Malaca conquistada* (Malacca Conquered, 1634), and João Franco Barreto, *Eneida portuguesa* (Portuguese *Aeneid*, 1664), a Port. trans. of the *Aeneid* that often incorporates verses taken directly from *The Lusiads*.

Francisco Rodrigues Lobo (1574?–1621), probably best known for his dialogues on court life (*Corte na Aldeia*, 1619), is an important voice in late Ren. *bucolic poetry on the eve of the *baroque. In 1596, Rodrigues Lobo imported the genre of the *romance into Portugal from Spain with his *Romanceiro*. The *Éclogas* (1605) are polished examples of bucolic verse in which the motifs of *desengano* (disillusion) and melancholy are present; the poems also display Sá de Miranda's moralizing influence. Camões and Spain's Luis de Góngora will remain the two major poetic influences throughout the century. Góngora's *conceptismo* and *cultismo* are evident in Sóror Violante do Céu (1601–93), a Dominican nun whose religious and accomplished *Rimas Várias* (Diverse Rhymes, 1646) establishes *devotional poetry as a terrain for women poets. Another nun, Sóror Maria do Céu (1658–1753), also composed religious poetry. The multilingual Bernarda Ferreira de Lacerda (d. 1645?) wrote verse on epic (*España libertada*) and bucolic (*Soledades de Buçaco*) themes.

Francisco Manuel de Melo (1608–66), while known more for his prose works, typifies in his poetry the aristocratic and learned peninsular culture in the final years of the Sp. annexation of the Port. crown (1580–1640).

His *Obras Métricas* (Metrical Works, 1665) encompass all poetic genres cultivated at the time. They are arranged according to the nine Muses. Satirical poetry flourishes at the end of the century and is to some extent a reaction against Gongorism. This satirical poetry is collected in anthols. of the early 18th c., such as *Fénix Renascida* (Phoenix Reborn, 1715–28), and includes Tomás de Noronha (d. 1651), the Coimbra-educated Brazilian Gregório de Matos (1636–96), and Tomás Pinto Brandão (1664–1743).

The 18th c. witnessed a continuation of baroque practices in its first decades and a neoclassical period (see CLASSICISM, NEOCLASSICAL POETICS) beginning roughly in mid-century with the renovation of Port. culture and society under the enlightened despotism or rationalism of the Marquis of Pombal. The distinction between these two periods is approximate, since, despite rationalist arguments against the excesses of the baroque and Gongorism, some aspects of the baroque (such as the reliance on cl. mythology) continued throughout the century. Academic neoclassicism was initiated with the creation of the Arcádia Lusitana or Olissiponense (Lusitanian or Lisbon Arcadia) in 1756 and reaffirmed in 1790 with the Nova Arcádia (New Arcadia). Neoclassical Port. intellectuals (e.g., Luís António Verney [1713–92] and Cândido Lusitano [1719–73]) debated the didactic and learned status of poetry and its social functions and developed dogmatic precepts of lang., grammar, and phonetics guided by the motto "inutilia truncat" (eliminate that which is useless). Unrhymed (*blank) verse was widely adopted as appropriate for the imitation of Greco-Roman poets and their numerous genres and subgenres. Arcadian poets, inspired by Fr. authors, adopted literary pseuds. under which they wrote and published, a gesture meant to erase social distinctions and promote a literary form of aristocracy. The realities of daily bourgeois life were a favorite theme. The best-known lyrics on love and the domestic life were the collection titled *Marília de Dirceu* (1792, 1799) by Tomás António Gonzaga (1744–1810). Born in Portugal but sent to Minas Gerais in Brazil and eventually exiled to Mozambique, Gonzaga composed this poetry to his lover Marília under the Arcadian pseud. Dirceu. Like some of the poetry of António Diniz da Cruz e Silva (1731–99), he brought Brazilian nature and landscapes into Port. poetry, and *Marília de Dirceu* was one of the most popular books in Portugal and Brazil at the time. Other lyric poets include Pedro António Correia Garção (1724–72), Domingos dos Reis Quita (1728–70), and Cruz e Silva, who also wrote a comic epic *O Hissope* [The Hyssop]). Nicolau Tolentino de Almeida (1740–1811) was a major figure of the century whose satires target the sordid and vice-laden aspects of Port. society and class structure, while also treating general themes such as war. Social types and manners also frequently appear in his poetry. Tolentino characteristically employs a prosaic idiom in his poems. Manuel Maria Barbosa du Bocage (1765–1805, Elmano Sadino of the Nova Arcádia), like Tolentino, wrote of bohemian life and composed sonnets of considerable accomplishment, many of them engaging motifs that became mainstays of *romanticism such as the obsession with death and the tenebrous. António Lobo de Carvalho (ca. 1730–87) was a satirist noted for his scabrous and obscene poems in the spirit of med. joke poetry. Bocage's contemporary, José Agostinho de Macedo (1761–1831), was a lyric poet but is better known for his pamphleteering and virulent crit. of Camões who, in Macedo's opinion, grossly contravened verisimilitude in *The Lusiads*. Macedo countered *The Lusiads* with his poem *O Oriente* (The Orient) and wrote a heroic-comic poem titled *Os Burros* (The Asses). Leonor de Almeida (1750–1839), later the Marquesa de Alorna, also heralds romanticism; her lyrics oscillate between religious devotion and an acute sense of melancholy and, like the work of Reis Quita, present a poetic voice that often turns on saudade. Two friends of the marquesa participate in moving Port. poetry toward the early romantic sensibility: Catarina de Lencastre (1749–1824) expresses a conflict between reason and sentiment, and Francisca de Paula Possolo (1783–1838), the Arcadian "Francília," rejects reason and acknowledges the irrational powers of the imagination.

Romanticism is rooted in the poetry of the later Arcadians but became solidified as a movement with the sociopolitical changes of the liberal revolution of 1832–34 and the new, secular society formed after the abolition of the religious orders in Portugal. Almeida Garrett (born João Baptista da Silva Leitão, 1799–1854) is credited with introducing romanticism in Portugal after a stay in England and exposure to the works of Walter Scott and Lord Byron with the narrative poem *Camões* (1825). A novelist and playwright, Garrett fueled the Port. romantic desire for a national theater. Garrett's contemporary Alexandre Herculano (1810–77), mostly a prose writer, inaugurates religious-themed romantic poetry. Herculano, who believed that social and political revolution should find literary expression, expounds a theory of romantic lit. as anti-Arcadian, popular, and of the masses but in alignment with current philosophical currents and in which a return to med. roots would displace classicism and absolutism. Garrett, an admirer of the Arcadian Filinto Elísio, first composed neoclassically inspired poetry but moved definitively into the romantic mode with *Adosinda* (1828) and the publication of his *Romanceiro* (1851), a collection of *romances* or popular poetry with med. themes inspired by Madame de Staël and the Ger. interest in folkloric lit. Garrett's best-known book of poetry is *Folhas Caídas* (Fallen Leaves, 1853), which directly expresses states of passion; his belief that lit. should manifest a national character, based on folklore and trad. as the most authentic expressions of *lusitanidade* (Lusitanianness), is adopted by late 19th-c. writers and is known as *neogarrettismo* (neo-Garrettism). António Feliciano de Castilho (1800–75) adheres to a conservative, neoclassical mindset in terms of ling. discipline, though his poetry is regarded as romantic. Poets whose work appeared around 1838 are called the *ultraromantics* (notionally the representatives of the final phase of romanticism, though ultraromantic themes and lang. are present earlier, such as in the poetry of Castilho) and include Maria Browne (1797–1861), António Augusto Soares de Passos (1826–60), and Tomás Ribeiro (1831–1910).

In 1865, a group of students at the University of Coimbra rebelled against romanticism and called for social, political, and scientific reforms that, in the domain of lit., led to *realism. This ideological polemic came to be known as the Questão Coimbrã and its adherents as the Generation of 1870, headed by the poet Antero de Quental (1842–91). Antero's poetry culminated in a collection of masterful *Sonetos* (1886), which are, at turns, pessimistic, religious, and philosophical, and borrow concepts from thinkers such as G.W.F. Hegel. Guerra Junqueiro (1850–1923) wrote political poetry and at the time was considered a major exponent of contemporary reality. Toward the end of the century, Port. *Parnassianism was briefly practiced by poets such as Gonçalves Crespo (1846–83) and António Feijó (1859–1917). Realist poetry is most accomplished in the work of Cesário Verde (1855–86), whose posthumously published *O Livro de Cesário Verde* (The Book of Cesário Verde, 1901) depicts the concrete realities of Lisbon and the oppressive life of the working class. As one of the most remarkable poets of city life and its sensorial aspects, Verde rejected romantic rhet. with a vividness of description that includes market stalls, the sounds and rhythms of daily living, the squalor of the streets, and yellow fever.

Apart from Verde, Port. *symbolism, with its emphasis on the impalpable, autumnal, nostalgic, and distance from the real, characterizes fin de siècle poetry. Eugénio de Castro's (1869–1944) *Oaristos* (1890) formally initiated Port. symbolism, which lasted until 1915. Though not published until 1920, Camilo Pessanha's (1867–1926) *Clepsidra* (Water Clock) constitutes an important moment in symbolist poetry. Other poets of the time are António Nobre (1867–1900) and Teixeira de Pascoaes (1877–1952). Pascoaes is the main proponent of saudade or nostalgia as the basis of the pantheistic, messianic philosophy and literary movement known as saudosismo. Saudosismo promoted a certain neoromantic lexicon and sensibility that appear in the early work of some modernist poets.

At the end of the first decade of the 20th c., a group of artists and writers who came together in Lisbon, would usher in *modernism, a movement that broke with the past with iconoclastic force, often incorporating ideas on lit. and art brought to Portugal from Paris and expressed through a variety of print and other artistic media. It included movements such as *paulismo*, *interseccionismo*, *sensacionismo*, and *futurismo*. The first group of modernists include Fernando Pessoa (1888–1935), Mário de Sá-Carneiro (1890–1915), and José Sobral de Almada-Negreiros (1893–1970), the latter known more for his paintings and designs but whose *Manifesto Anti-Dantas* stands out as a main text of the new movement. This group published several literary magazines; its first publication, *Orpheu* (1915), provided the name to this first wave of the new, revolutionary aesthetic. A divided, fragmented self, frequently the result of the irreconcilability of thought and emotion, achieves lasting expression in the poetry of Pessoa, by far Port. modernism's preeminent representative and perhaps the greatest mod. poet in any language. The nature of the (lyric) self in its many textual and philosophical aspects is also evident in Sá-Carneiro (*Dispersão* [Dispersion, 1914], and *Indícios de ouro* [Traces of Gold, 1937]). Pessoa created literary personae or *heteronyms—discrete personalities with distinctive styles and poetic attitudes often antithetical to one another. The heteronyms testify to the fluctuation between plurality and unity consistently found as a sort of existential statement in Pessoa's work. Pessoa's three main heteronyms are the pantheistic Alberto Caeiro, the neoclassical Ricardo Reis, and the modernist/futurist Álvaro de Campos. Pessoa also signed poetry under his own name, work that uses the meters and phrasings of traditional verse. Other poets of the first wave of modernism include Ronald de Carvalho (1893–1935), Ângelo de Lima (1872–1921), Luís de Montalvor (1891–1947), Alfredo Pedro Guisado (1891–1975), and Mário Saa (1893–1971). Port. modernism's second moment centers on the magazine *Presença* (1927–40) whose collaborators include Branquinho da Fonseca (1905–74), Adolfo Casais Monteiro (1908–72), José Régio (1901–69), João Gaspar Simões (1903–87), and Miguel Torga (1907–95). While not as subversive as the Orpheu group, *presença* capped the modernist movement as a whole. It validated the Orpheu poets while also seeking to promote pure aesthetic values and extract artistic creation from political concerns as much as possible. It includes a significant amount of prose writing and lit. crit., and the members of the *presença* group (or *presencistas*) experienced moments of ideological dissidence among themselves.

The experimentation with subjectivity, poetic *sincerity, and plurality of being typical of the first moment of modernism and the heteronyms extend to the realm of gender and sexual orientation. One of the Orpheu poets, Armando Côrtes-Rodrigues (1891–1971), composed a series of poems under the female identity of Violante de Cysneiros. Poems or parts of poems in Pessoa's work express homoerotic desire, feminized passivity, or masochistic tendencies. António Botto (1897–1959) and Judith Teixeira (1873–1959) were gay and lesbian poets whose work appeared during the first moment of modernism. Pessoa was a friend and literary collaborator of Botto and translated his *Canções* (1920 and subsequent eds.) into Eng. as *Songs*. Unlike Botto's candid homoeroticism, Teixeira's poetry tends toward the ambiguous and the symbolic and often employs a decadent idiom (see DECADENCE). Other important women poets emerged in the 20th c., such as Irene Lisboa (1892–1958), who published under the male pseud. João Falco, and Florbela Espanca (1895–1930). Espanca's sonnets, with their emphasis on female eroticism and an awareness of a patriarchal literary trad., are precursors to the fully developed feminist consciousness later in the century.

Following the publication of *Presença*, a series of *Cadernos de Poesia* (Poetry Notebooks) were published beginning in the 1940s, a period in which the socially and politically committed agendas of neorealism had already appeared in the 1930s and lasted to the 1950s. Mostly a prose fiction movement, neorealism included the poets Manuel da Fonseca (1911–93) and Fernando Namora (1919–89). After World War II, Port. surrealist poetry emerged, characterized by the automatic workings of the subconscious, black humor, and verbal associations (see SURREALISM). António Pedro (1909–66) ranks as a major surrealist artist and poet and was a founding member of the first surrealist group in Portugal. Pedro was also a prose writer and cultivated a multimedia oeuvre, incl. ceramics, and exalted the plastic arts. Mário Cesariny de Vasconcelos (1923–2006) became Port. surrealism's best-known figure with poetry that is sarcastic, explosive, and often erotic. It employs the technique of the surrealist inventory, as does the poetry of another of the surrealist writers, Alexandre O'Neill (1924–86).

Jorge de Sena (1919–78), who pursued a career as a professor in the U.S., claims a place among mid-20th c. poets. Eugénio de Andrade (1923–2005) wrote verses of a lyrical musicality that exist outside of movements and schools. Andrade is associated with the Generation of 1927 in Spain, since he admired and translated Federico García Lorca as a young man. Sophia de Mello Breyner (Andresen, 1919–2004) is an important voice of the 20th c.; her prolific work roots itself in limpid lang. and metaphors that extol the Port. maritime landscape and human habitation in it, expressed in a refined poetic diction. Later 20th-c. experimental and concretist poets, who bring visual aspects to poetry and reimagine the poetic or textual sign (see CONCRETE POETRY, VISUAL POETRY), include Ana Hatherly (b. 1929), Herberto Hélder (b. 1930), E. M. de Melo e Castro (b. 1932), and Gastão Cruz (b. 1941).

Port. lit. in general was brought definitively in line with feminist concerns with *Novas Cartas Portuguesas* (New Portuguese Letters, 1972) by Maria Isabel Barreno (b. 1939), Maria Teresa Horta (b. 1937), and Maria Velho da Costa (b. 1938). This book intersperses prose with poetry and further solidifies a female literary subjectivity announced earlier with poets like the Marquesa de Alorna and Espanca. The work of Natália Correia (1923–93) participates in the movement represented by the *Cartas*. (Correia also edited an important anthol. of satiric and erotic poetry in Port.) Other contemp. women poets of note are Luísa Neto Jorge (1939–89), Ana Luísa Amaral (b. 1956), and Adília Lopes (b. 1960).

*See* ÉVORA CRITICS; SPAIN, POETRY OF.

■ **Anthologies and Translations**: *Poems from the Portuguese*, trans. A.F.G. Bell (1913); *Antologia da poesia feminina portuguesa*, ed. A. Salvado (1973); *Contemporary Portuguese Poetry*, ed. H. Macedo and E. M. de Melo e Castro (1978); *Líricas portuguesas*, ed. J. de Sena, 2 v. (1984); *Songs of a Friend*, trans. B. H. Fowler (1996); S. de M. Breyner, *Log Book*, trans. R. Zenith (1997); *The Lusíads*, trans. L. White (1997); *Antologia de poesia portuguesa erótica e satírica*, ed. N. Correia, 3d ed. (2005); *Luís de Camões*, trans. W. Baer (2005);

F. Pessoa, *A Little Larger Than the Entire Universe*, trans. R. Zenith (2006); *Poets of Portugal*, trans. F. G. Williams (2007); *The Songs of António Botto*, trans. F. Pessoa (2010).

■ **Criticism and History**: T. Braga, *História da litteratura portugueza* (1896)—includes summaries of poetic schools and periods; A.F.G. Bell, *Studies in Portuguese Literature* (1914); J. G. Simões, *História da poesia portuguesa das origens aos nossos dias* (1955); *Presença da literatura portuguesa*, ed. A. Soares Amora, 5 v. (1971–74); *Dicionário de literatura: brasileira, portuguesa, galega, estilística literária*, ed. J. P. Coelho, 3d ed. (1985); T. F. Earle, *The Muse Reborn* (1988); A. J. Saraiva and O. Lopes, *História da literatura portuguesa*, 17th ed. (1996); S. Reckert, *From the Resende Songbook* (1998); M. Sousa Santos, "Re-inventing Orpheus: Women and Poetry Today," *Portuguese Studies* 14 (1998); *A Revisionary History of Portuguese Literature*, ed. M. Tamen and H. C. Buescu (1999); K. D. Jackson, *As primeiras vanguardas em Portugal* (2003)—biblios. of poets and critical studies; A. J. Saraiva, *Initiation into Portuguese Literature* (2006); *Embodying Pessoa*, ed. A. Klobucka and M. Sabine (2007); C. C. Stathatos, *A Gil Vicente Bibliography, 2000–2005* (2007); V. Aguiar e Silva, *A lira dourada e a tuba canora* (2008); *A Companion to Portuguese Literature*, ed. S. Parkinson, C. Pazos Alonso, T. F. Earle (2009).

J. BLACKMORE

**POSTCOLONIAL POETICS.** Postcolonial literary studies is often seen as having been launched by the publication of Edward Said's critique of Western constructions of the East in *Orientalism* (1978) and as having been academically institutionalized by the publication of *The Empire Writes Back* (1989) by Ashcroft, Griffiths, and Tiffin. As a field, it has emphasized many of the so-called third-world writers explored by Commonwealth studies before it, but postcolonial studies supplanted that earlier field with a style of critical work more theoretically inflected and politically urgent.

Widely debated, the term *postcolonial* (often hyphenated) has several different meanings. "Occurring or existing after the end of colonial rule; of or relating to a former colony" is the *OED*'s definition. In this sense, postcolonial poetry is postindependence poetry—written, i.e., by peoples liberated after the ending of Eur. colonial rule and the establishment of sovereignty over their lands. Accordingly, the term has been applied primarily to parts of Asia, Africa, Oceania, the Caribbean, and elsewhere in the third world after decolonization, particularly from the time of Indian and Pakistani independence in 1947 through the 1970s, when the Brit., Fr., Dutch, Port., Ger., Sp., and other mod. Eur. colonial powers relinquished control over most of the earth's surface. The assumption of a sharp dividing line often does not coincide, however, with lit. hist., since works written by many poets publishing before independence do not diverge essentially from those published afterward—e.g., Derek Walcott's poetry published before and after his natal island of Saint Lucia's formal independence from the United Kingdom in 1979.

A broader use of the term *postcolonial* has involved its application to postcolonization lit. In this sense, all poetry produced after Sp., Brit., Fr., and Dutch colonization of the Caribbean, e.g., is "postcolonial." But this usage raises still other problems, such as whether highly imitative or derivative "colonial" poetry is postcolonial in the same way that later poems often more resistant to aesthetic and political domination are postcolonial.

Hence, *postcolonial* is sometimes used in a third sense, closer to *anticolonial*: poems that exemplify or enact the struggle against Eur. colonial rule. This usage raises further questions, since many poems produced both before and after independence exhibit varying degrees of anticolonialism and anti-anticolonialism and cannot be flattened into a teleological political program. In sum, no one of these three senses of *postcolonial* seems entirely satisfactory, so perhaps they can be combined to mean something like the following: poetry written by non-Eur. peoples in the shadow of colonialism, both after independence and in the period leading up to it, particularly works that engage, however obliquely, issues of living in the interstices between Western colonial and non-Eur. cultures.

Another issue in postcolonial studies is whether the term should be extended from the third world to white settler colonies, or dominions, such as Australia and Canada. The commonalities are often acknowledged. But some critics would not wish the distinctions lost between white settler colonies, where majority populations of Eur. descent extended and adapted Western cultural resources to local circumstances and colonized indigenous populations, and other colonies, where the majority populations were not of Eur. descent and the discrepancies between local cultural resources and those of the colonizer were vast.

In conceptualizing postcolonial poetics, two primary paradigms stand out. The first is decolonization. The poets affiliated with Fr.-lang. *Negritude in the 1930s and after, such as Aimé Césaire of Martinique and Léopold Sédar Senghor of Senegal, exemplify the quest to reclaim a precolonial blackness: an Af. and Af. diaspora sensibility and culture that Eur. colonialism suppressed and degraded. Physical and cultural attributes once seen as negative—blackness, rhythm, instinct—are transvalued. Senghor urges, in his poem "Nuit de Sine" (Night of Sine), "listen to the beating of our dark blood, listen / To the beating of the dark pulse of Africa in the mist of lost villages." Césaire, who coined the Fr. term *négritude*, titled his magnum opus *Cahier d'un retour au pays natal* (*Notebook of a Return to the Native Land*, 1939), a title suggestive of poetry's role in returning to and reclaiming native land from colonization. Similarly, lusophone poet José Craveirinha of Mozambique celebrates attributes once disparaged: "My beautiful short kinky hair / and my black eyes / great moons of wonderment on the most beautiful night" ("Manifesto").

Such nativist and nationalist reclamation is a strong impetus as well in much anglophone poetry. To the extent that Ireland, though Eur., resembles non-Eur. nations undergoing decolonization (Ireland having once been conceived as England's racial and religious "other"), a poet such as W. B. Yeats may be considered postcolonial in seeking to construct a national imagination based in pre-Christian and precolonial myths and to reclaim Ireland for the Ir. by renaming and remythologizing it. Later examples of postcolonial poets for whom poetry has been a tool of decolonization include the Ugandan Okot p'Bitek, one of East Africa's most celebrated poets, who brought into literary verse indigenous Acoli *songs, *proverbs, and *metaphors; and the Jamaican Louise Bennett, popular disseminator of her Creole poems on the stage, radio, television, and Jamaica's national newspaper, who helped free West Indians from a Eur.-imposed sense of inferiority about oral customs, lang., and folklore. Following Bennett and Césaire, an influential poet from Barbados, Kamau Brathwaite, emphasized the importance of returning Af. diasporic cultures to their oral roots and throwing off the "tyranny of the pentameter," the *sonnet, and other Eur. literary forms ("History of the Voice"). Just as culture played a significant role in colonization, so too, for many postcolonial poets, the retrieval of native cultural resources and the indigenization of poetic forms were seen as essential to decolonization.

The nativist and nationalist models of postcolonialism have proved to be limited, however, in various ways. An obvious danger is the reduction of poetry to platform politics, despite the differences between much poetry and more expository forms. Another risk is underestimating the extent to which even nativist poetry is implicated in what it resists: as Frantz Fanon observed in *Les damnés de la terre* (*The Wretched of the Earth*), Negritude and other nativisms replicate in reverse the Eur. values against which they are pitted. Finally, even the most nativist poets, such as the Paris-based leaders of Negritude, draw on transnational influences, tropes, forms, and resources, paradoxically, in reclaiming indigeneity.

A second paradigm for postcolonial poetics is hybridity. Drawing on both indigenous cultural resources and those of Eur. colonizing powers, postcolonial poetry is richly syncretic, layered, and transnational. Revalorizing Cuba's Af. roots, Nicolás Guillén combined modernist and surrealist elements, as well as Sp. ballads, with Af. Cuban musical forms such as the *son* (sound) and street vernacular to create a poetic *mestizaje* (mixture). Through hybridization, poets create forms that embody their experience of living between the discrepant cultural worlds of global North and South. The Indian poet A. K. Ramanujan synthesized influences from Eur. modernist poets such as Yeats, T. S. Eliot, and Ezra Pound with literary techniques and tropes in the Dravidian poetry of South India, bringing into poetic expression a South Asian experience of modernity. A poet from Kashmir, Agha Shahid Ali, similarly fused Eliot's fragmentary and apocalyptic poetics and James

Merrill's *formalism with Urdu-Persian genres such as the **ghazal*. Walcott, who ironically dubbed himself a "fortunate traveller" in a poem by that name, combines in *Omeros* Western *epic and *terza rima* with Af. Caribbean myths, rhetorical forms, and landscapes. Creating cross-cultural poetic rituals that answered to his interstitial experience, the Igbo poet Christopher Okigbo delicately interlaced Af. praise song, drumming, local botanical names, and Nigerian place-names with biblical echoes from his Catholic education, syncretic strategies from Eliot and Pound, and formal lyric devices from Lat. verse.

While such overtly cosmopolitan poets obviously hybridize discrepant trads., even strongly nativist poets, such as those already mentioned, often practice a transnational poetics: they yoke together tropes, idioms, and ideologies across hemispheres, while working toward decolonization. Césaire is both a Caribbean poet and a Fr. surrealist; Yeats fuses Ir. place names and myths with anglophone orthographies and lyric trads.; Bennett writes Creole poetry in the Brit. *ballad stanza; Okot p'Bitek draws on H. W. Longfellow and Western dramatic monologue as well as Acoli oral trads.; Brathwaite combines West Indian landscapes and tropes with a creolized Caribbean idiom made available to him by Eliot's conversational style.

The hybridity model, however, also has drawbacks. It has been criticized for naturalizing aesthetic processes, reinforcing formulaic dualities of Western and non-Western influences, glossing over uneven power relations between colonizer and colonized by its false symmetries, depoliticizing postcolonial studies, recycling a term (*hybridity*) contaminated by earlier racist usages, and oversimplifying as homogeneous the always already heterogeneous trads. fused in hybridization. Given the limitations and capabilities of both the hybridity and decolonization models, one solution (albeit imperfect) is to use them in tandem as mutual correctives, without forsaking either the aesthetic traction of "hybridity" or the political thrust of "decolonization."

Another way of exploring postcolonial poetics is to delineate a few of the poetry's recurrent preoccupations. First, because of the distortion and effacement of local trads. by Eur. colonialism, many postcolonial poets, such as the aforementioned Negritude poets, seek through poetry to nurture collective historical memory. Af. Caribbean poets write with an acute consciousness of the devastations of slavery and colonialism, recuperating Af. rituals, gods, and names lost in the Middle Passage. Redeploying oral trads., Lorna Goodison, e.g., thinks back through the lives of her Jamaican female ancestors to oral tales of her slave progenitors in poems such as "Guinea Woman." Af. poets sometimes summon the powers of precolonial gods: in Wole Soyinka's long poem *Ogun Abibiman* (Ogun of the Land of the Black Peoples), the Yoruba god of roads, iron, creativity, and war is extolled in the service of the antiapartheid struggle. Occasionally recalling the violence of Brit. colonial rule, South Asian writers reach back to earlier literary and cultural trads. Ali, whose poem "The Dacca Gauzes" recalls how the Brit.

severed Indian weavers' thumbs to prevent competition with Brit. muslins, poetically reinstantiates aspects of Moghul-era Muslim Indian culture. Ramanujan builds the poetic sequence "Prayers to Lord Murugan" on the example of a 6th-c. Tamil devotional poem.

Second, poets writing in Eur. langs. must grapple with the alienating effects of working in a lang. imposed under colonialism. The Indian poet R. Parthasarathy laments his imprisonment in an oppressive lang.: "My tongue in English chains." Recalling that slaves were sometimes prohibited from speaking in Af. langs. and even had their tongues removed in punishment, M. NourbeSe Philip from Trinidad and Tobago plays revealingly on the Eng. "language" as a "foreign lan" and "foreign anguish" in her poem "Discourse on the Logic of Language." But many poets attempt to remake Eur. langs. for their local circumstances. Anglophone poets sometimes stud Eng. with indigenous words, place names, and names of flora and fauna; and sometimes they write in dialect, despite the stigma of inferiority that has attached to it, esp. in the former Brit. colonies. Guyanese poet John Agard half-humorously writes in "Listen Mr Oxford don" of "mugging de Queen's English" and "slashing suffix in self-defence."

Third, poetry often serves efforts of self-definition in relation to nation and world, colonizer and colonized, place and displacement. In "Balada de los dos abuelos" ("Ballad of the Two Grandfathers"), Guillén dramatizes his mixed lineage: he imagines his white and black grandfathers embracing and interfusing in his poem across differences of power. Walcott famously agonizes over his mixed inheritances: "I have Dutch, nigger, and English in me, / and either I'm nobody, or I'm a nation." With its layers and ambiguities, poetry seems esp. well suited, for poets such as Walcott and Guillén, to holding discrepant inheritances in tension with one another—Eur. *modernism and Af. Caribbean orality, Gr. *archetypes and black fishermen. Sometimes in postcolonial poetry this in-betweenness or interstitiality is a tragic condition, as when Walcott declares himself "divided to the vein" and "poisoned with the blood of both" his Eur. and his Af. ancestors ("A Far Cry from Africa"). Bleakly self-descriptive, the Indian poet Eunice de Souza states, "my name is Greek / my surname Portuguese / my language alien," and concludes of these disparate "ways / of belonging": "I belong with the lame ducks" ("Ways of Belonging"). But sometimes these disparate inheritances are celebrated for the powerful new possibilities they unleash, despite the lingering wounds: Brathwaite ends his epic trilogy *The Arrivants* announcing his aspiration to make "some- / thing torn // and new"—presumably, in part, the creolized epic that these very lines complete.

*See* COLONIAL POETICS.

■ K. Brathwaite, *History of the Voice* (1984); B. Ashcroft, G. Griffiths, H. Tiffin, *The Empire Writes Back: Theory and Practice in Post-Colonial Literatures* [1989], 2d ed. (2002); J. Ramazani, *The Hybrid Muse: Postcolonial Poetry in English* (2001); R. Patke, *Postcolonial Poetry in English* (2006); J. Ramazani, *A Transna-*

*tional Poetics* (2009), and "Poetry and Postcolonialism," *The Cambridge History of Postcolonial Literature,* ed. A. Quayson (2011).

J. RAMAZANI

# POSTMODERNISM

I. Definition and History
II. Self-Reflexivity
III. Subjectivity
IV. Language and Form

**I. Definition and History.** The definition and hist. of postmodernism have both been highly contested; postmodernism was declared dead shortly after it came into being, yet it appears to be still with us. Its very name embodies its fundamentally paradoxical or ambivalent nature. The *post* in relation to *modernism* is at once temporal (after), causal (because of), and directional (beyond). The postmod. marks both continuity with and rupture from the mod.; it is both critical of and complicit with the aesthetic of modernism (Hutcheon 1988, 1989). Over the years, however, *postmodernism* has become a convenient label for a broad artistic movement related to the general philosophical, social, and cultural condition called postmodernity. Arising after the grand ideological failures of World War II and provoked and nourished by the civil rights and women's movements and by *poststructuralism, it developed in mid- to late 20th-c. Europe and the Americas before spreading around the world. Despite this dispersion, certain impulses persisted in the specifically postmod. poetries that emerged: a marked self-reflexivity, often combined with a certain, sometimes parodic, intertextual exuberance and a critical engagement with hist. and historiography; an in-depth exploration of subjectivity's construction in lang.; and a contesting of the transparency of lang. itself as well as of the "naturalness" of the relationship between form and content through a simultaneous use and abuse of poetic convention.

Though the term itself has existed for some time, this particular sense of postmodernism first arose in architecture to signal a building's "double-coding": both new/modernist and old/historical (though often ironically or parodically so) and, thus, accessible and popular at once to art-world insiders and the general public. The other arts—from visual appropriation art to film, from music to dance and theater—developed related, yet differing, ways to double-code and challenge restrictive *either/or* thinking. Over time, postmodernism's persistent *both/and* inclusive logic came to undercut Hassan's early attempt to define it through rigid binaries, in which modernism meant form, purpose, and hierarchy and postmodernism was associated only with antiform, play, and anarchy.

McHale (2007) has convincingly argued that postmodernism developed differently and unevenly across the art forms. Such differences and unevenness also emerged *within* each specific art form, thus rendering historical delimitation as difficult as definition. For example, Am. poetry in the 1950s and 1960s re-acted *against* modernism in widely divergent ways. The countercultural *Beat poets insisted on immediacy of expression, rejecting traditional form in favor of "spontaneous" prosody. The poets of the *New York school responded to the "seriousness" of high modernism by blurring "high" and "low" culture. *Confessional poetry replaced modernist impersonality with a focus on the dramas of private life. *Black Mountain school poet Charles Olson maintained Ezra Pound's experimental, intertextual, and historiographic poetics, while adopting a more openly exploratory stance, a more democratic politics, and a greater devotion to the merely local rather than universal. Out of all these diverse responses emerged that series of persisting poetic impulses that characterized postmod. (plural) poetries.

**II. Self-Reflexivity.** Postmodernist self-reflexivity can be found in many different forms and tones: e.g., in the self-undermining narrative play of Mark Strand and James Merrill, in John Ashbery's "Paradoxes and Oxymorons," and in Susan Howe's *My Emily Dickinson,* a self-conscious poetic meditation on Dickinson's philosophical, literary, and historical contexts and their influence on Howe's writing. Another entire dimension of the self-reflexive further complicated the postmod. challenge to modernist historiography. While theorist Jameson saw a loss of what he called genuine historicity in the postmod. logic of late capitalism, poets were busy struggling with the concepts of both the "genuine" and the "historical." Cultural assumptions about totalities and coherent unities, logic and reason, consciousness and subjectivity, representation and truth(s) all came under scrutiny. Manifesting what Lyotard famously dubbed the postmod. incredulity toward master narratives, both narrative and lyric poetry placed hist.—modernism's Joycean nightmare—and its writing under the microscope, posing new questions that echoed those of contemporaneous historians. Together they asked: Whose story got told in the official histories? Whose did not? Who was allowed to tell it? What did the archive omit? The lingering positivist and empiricist assumptions of the discipline of hist., inherited from the 19th c., came under fire: historical events, it was argued, were made into historical facts (i.e., were constructed as facts) by the historian's act of putting them into a narrative (White).

Suddenly the individual (and even lyric) voice was no longer banned from historical discourse, as even historians sometimes refused to hide behind the third-person mask of putative objectivity and instead called attention to the ideological positioning inevitable in any historical account. In poetry, Margaret Atwood retold a personalized and feminist version of the story of a 19th-c. Canadian pioneer woman of letters in *The Journals of Susanna Moodie;* Geoffrey Hill's lyrics (e.g., *The Mystery of the Charity of Charles Péguy*) reflected on historical events *and* on his own reflections on and writing about them. The historical record might be unreliable, but Hill questioned too his own motives in writing about hist. and how these shape the results. Writers of the postmod. long poem as well as the lyric often chose to recount not the master narratives of hist. but smaller, more local (and conflicted) hists. Here the postmod. dovetailed with the feminist and postcolonial in the work of writers like Kamau Brathwaite, Lorna Goodison, Simon Ortiz, Paul Muldoon, and Derek Walcott.

**III. Subjectivity.** The radical postmod. challenges to the humanist notion of the self as coherent, unified, and centered that were undertaken by contemp. psychoanalysis and philosophy found their echo also in postmod. poetry, though not without a particularly poetic twist or two. The reasons for the poststructuralist refusal of any deep, single, stable, autonomous identity were bound to have repercussions for poetry—and for poets, whether narrative or lyric: if human consciousness is not the source of lang. but is constructed in and by lang., poets would have to think differently about both their work and their identity. The postmod. adoption of the idea of the "subject" to replace that of either "self" or "identity" was intended to suggest both the "subject" of a sentence (the agent of a verb) and the condition of being "subjected to" the lang. that constructs one's identity. Thus, poets and theorists saw in postmod. poetry evidence that lyric consciousness does not exist prior to or aside from lang. (Bernstein). The subject is entirely constituted by and knowable through a heterogeneous field of ling. and real-world engagements (Altieri 1973).

This understanding of subjectivity was embodied in a wide range of poetic styles and modes. Confessional postmod. poets Robert Lowell and Sylvia Plath used the lessons of psychoanalysis to expose their own hists. of mental illness, sexuality, infidelity, and parenthood. Frank O'Hara's "I do this, I do that" poems presented the quotidian details of his movements through New York City. The postmod. tendency to blur the boundaries between high and low culture and to incorporate a wide range of popular reference showed how subjectivity is culturally constituted. Ashbery's "Farm Implements and Rutabagas in a Landscape," e.g., is a sestina involving characters from Popeye; Amiri Baraka and other members of the *Black Arts movement drew on the rhythms of jazz and popular music; and *Asian Am. poets such as John Yau showed how Hollywood stereotypes of Asians influence Asian Am. subjectivity. *Flarf poets such as K. Silem Mohammad have used Google searches to generate material for lyric poems. Diverse as these poetries are, each in its own way articulated the speaking/writing subject more as product or process than as producer.

**IV. Language and Form.** Many postmodernist poets, from Olson to bpNichol to Charles Bernstein, have challenged the concept of individual, coherent *"voice" that has been central to the hist. of lyric poetry, and this challenge has had implications for the forms that poetry takes. *Language poetry, which epitomized the postmodernist concern with how lang. shapes subjectivity, took an explicit position against the idea that speech is the basis of poetry and often foregrounded the materiality of the page and text. Rejecting the idea of lang. as a transparent medium of communication, Language poetry called attention to and problematized the role of ling. structures and conventions in generating meaning. Formal fragmentation at the level of the word, phrase, or line marked the ling. version of this contestation. Some poems prohibited us from deploying the usual interpretive codes (always as ideological as they are formal) we need to make meaning, sometimes through the physical *textuality of the page, as noted above (see BOOK, POETIC; TYPOGRAPHY).

There was at the same time a paradoxical impulse in postmodernism in all the arts to both exploit and explode the conventions upon which it depended; poetries were no different. One means of contesting, while provoking, our readerly impulses toward coherence and meaning could be found in the deliberately arbitrary use of formal *constraint. A tour de force of the *Oulipo-esque genre, Christian Bök's *Eunoia*, e.g., uses only one vowel per short section; every line in Ashbery's "Into the Dusk-Charged Air" mentions the name of a river; John Cage famously deployed intricate but *aleatory methods to generate poems; Lyn Hejinian's *My Life*, composed when the poet was 37, contains 37 sections of 37 sentences each, while Ron Silliman's *Tjanting* expands according to a Fibonacci mathematical sequence. Conte has perceived a distinctly postmod. manner of using strict, traditional forms, particularly ones involving *refrain. Rather than carefully shaping form and content to communicate the poet's intentions, the poet let the form generate the poem. Such works used strict patterning on a "micro" level to undermine coherence on the more "macro" semantic and thematic levels, but with the postmod. extremes of such patterning, there was an implied critique of the very form/content separation.

A slightly different set of problems emerged on the larger scale of the *long poem. The modernist *collage form of Pound, T. S. Eliot, W. C. Williams, or the early Louis Zukofsky could be made to cohere, often through the poet's subjectivity. But in keeping with its challenges to any sense of coherent identity, postmodernism made this sense of formal wholeness problematic. For Conte, the postmod. long poem used an open-ended *"serial form" that contested the narrative and thematic coherence of classic long poems, while still gesturing toward the scale and importance of *epic and its modernist reincarnations. Jack Spicer's "book" compositions, A. R. Ammons's *Tape for the Turn of the Year*, or Ashbery's *Flow Chart* exemplified this kind of work. Kroetsch saw the long poem as allowing a kind of Foucauldian "archaeology" to replace the continuous, totalizing, teleological narrative form of hist.

Even given the persistent suspicion of the rhet. of periodization, esp. by poets themselves (McCaffery), the complex relationship of the *post* to the *modern* has clearly been one of critical rethinking, leading either to a continuation and often intensification or a rejection. If modernist poets broke with traditional forms and pioneered techniques of fragmentation and collage, it was often in the service of finding a new order. Postmodernist poets adapted, rather than adopted, many modernist techniques but were far more skeptical about the prospect of ultimate coherence. What Perloff (1991) has called the poetics of *indeterminacy emerged from some of modernism's most radical gestures, which existed in tension with a drive toward order; for much postmod. poetry, representing such indeterminacy was precisely the goal.

See AVANT-GARDE POETICS, CONCRETE POETRY, FEMINIST APPROACHES TO POETRY, HISTORY AND POETRY, INTERTEXTUALITY, SOUND POETRY.

■ **Anthologies**: *The New American Poetry 1945–1960*, ed. D. Allen (1960); *In the American Tree*, ed. R. Silliman (1986); *"Language" Poetries*, ed. D. Messerli (1987); *Postmoderne*, ed. C. Bürger and P. Bürger (1987); *Past the Last Post*, ed. I. Adam and H. Tiffin (1990); *Postmodernism*, ed. P. Waugh (1992); *The Post-Modern Reader*, ed. C. Jencks (1992); *Essays in Postmodern Culture*, ed. E. Amiran and J. Unsworth (1993); *Postmodernism*, ed. T. Docherty (1993); *A Postmodern Reader*, ed. J. P. Natoli and L. Hutcheon (1993); *Feminism and Postmodernism*, ed. M. Ferguson and J. Wicke (1994); *From the Other Side of the Century*, ed. D. Messerli (1994); *Postmodern American Poetry*, ed. P. Hoover (1994); *The Postmoderns*, ed. D. Allen (1994); *Early Postmodernism*, ed. P. Bové (1995); *The Postmodern Arts*, ed. N. Wheale (1995); *From Modernism to Postmodernism*, ed. L. E. Cahoone (1996); *International Postmodernism*, ed. H. Bertens and D. Fokkema (1997); *Poems for the Millennium*, ed. J. Rothenberg and P. Joris, v. 2 (1998); *Postmodern Times*, ed. T. Carmichael and A. Lee (2000); *Norton Anthology of Modern and Contemporary Poetry*, ed. J. Ramazani, R. Ellmann, and R. O'Clair, v. 2 (2003); *Lyric Postmodernism*, ed. R. Shepherd (2008).

■ **History and Theory**: M. Foucault, *The Order of Things* (1970); C. Altieri, "From Symbolist Thought to Immanence: The Ground of Postmodern American Poetics," *Boundary 2* 1 (1973); G. Graff, "The Myth of the Postmodernist Breakthrough," *TriQuarterly* 26 (1973); H. White, *Metahistory* (1973); G. Hoffmann, A. Hornung, and R. Kunow, "'Modern,' 'Postmodern' and 'Contemporary' as Criteria for Analysis of Twentieth-Century Literature," *Amerikastudien* 22 (1977); C. Jencks, *The Language of Post-Modern Architecture* (1977); V. Forrest-Thomson, *Poetic Artifice* (1978); M. Perloff, *The Poetics of Indeterminacy* (1981); I. Hassan, *The Dismemberment of Orpheus*, 2d ed. (1982); J. Baudrillard, *Simulations*, trans. P. Foss, P. Patton, and P. Beitchman (1983); R. Kroetsch, "For Play and Entrance: The Canadian Long Poem," *Open Letter* 4 (1983)—spec. iss. "Robert Kroetsch: Essays"; J.-F. Lyotard, *The Postmodern Condition*, trans. G. Bennington and B. Massumi (1984); C. Russell, *Poets, Prophets and Revolutionaries* (1985); R. von Hallberg, *American Poetry and Culture, 1945–1980* (1985); C. Bernstein, *Content's Dream* (1986); A. Huyssen, *After the Great Divide* (1986); L. Hutcheon, *A Poetics of Postmodernism* (1988); J. Collins, *Uncommon Cultures* (1989); D. Harvey, *The Condition of Postmodernity* (1989); L. Hutcheon, *The Politics of Postmodernism* (1989); *Postmodern Genres*, ed. M. Perloff (1989); T. Docherty, *After Theory* (1990); A. Gelpi, "The Genealogy of Postmodernism: Contemporary American Poetry," *Southern Review* 26.3 (1990); J. M. Conte, *Unending Design* (1991); F. Jameson, *Postmodernism* (1991); J. McGowan, *Postmodernism and Its Critics* (1991); M. Perloff, *Poetic License* (1991), and *Radical Artifice* (1992); C. Norris, *The Truth about Postmodernism* (1993); N. Zurbrugg, *The Parameters of Postmodernism* (1993); H. Bertens, *The Idea of the Postmodern* (1995); M. Blasing, *Politics and Form in Postmodern Poetry* (1995); T. Eagleton, *The Illusions of Postmodernism* (1996); C. Jencks, *What Is Postmodernism?* (1996); V. Leitch, *Postmodernism* (1996); S. Morawski, *The Troubles with Postmodernism* (1996); A. L. Nielsen, *Black Chant* (1997); S. Ahmed, *Differences That Matter* (1998); C. Altieri, *Postmodernisms Now* (1998); M. Perloff, *Poetry on and off the Page* (1998); Z. Sardar, *Postmodernism and the Other* (1998); S. Malpas, *Postmodern Debates* (2001); B. McHale, "Weak Narrativity: The Case of Avant-Garde Narrative Poetry," *Narrative* 9 (2001); C. Altieri, *The Art of Twentieth-Century American Poetry* (2006); S. McCaffery, "Autonomy to Indeterminacy," *Twentieth Century Literature* 53 (2007); B. McHale, "What Was Postmodernism?" *Electronic Book Review* (2007), http://www.electronicbookreview.com/thread/fictionspresent/tense.

L. HUTCHEON, M. WOODLAND,
T. YU, A. DUBOIS

**POSTSTRUCTURALISM.** *Structuralism—associated with early 20th-c. thinkers such as the linguist Ferdinand de Saussure (1857–1913) and the anthropologist Claude Lévi-Strauss (1908–2009)—was a methodology as well as a theory of existence. It claimed that we can study cultural phenomena only as full systems, not as single terms, *and* that human beings experience their worlds according to structures (such as myths, symbols, and lang.). Structuralism placed more value on relations and differences than identities. In ling. terms, it insisted that langs. do not consist of signs that label a distinct reality but that differences among sounds enable minds and cultures to distinguish and differentiate within an otherwise meaningless reality. (If we want to understand a word, e.g., we need to know the position it takes in a lang.; there is no such thing as a direct trans. from one lang. to another.) In anthropology, structuralism regarded *myths as functions rather than meaningful stories; myths allow for the distinction between good and evil, pure and impure, inside and outside, male and female, even self and other. To understand a myth is to analyze it as an organizing system. In poetics, structuralism could look at the way literary works created distinctions, oppositions, and categories through the production of contrasting terms. Structuralism focused on relations among terms (how langs. produce distinctions) and situated those relations within a relatively closed system (a lang., a culture, a practice or a network—such as fashion systems or tribal markings).

Poststructuralism follows from, and overturns,

structuralism. One of the key historical markers for poststructuralism—which is often associated with philosophies of postwar France—was the May 1968 student protests. Traditional leftist political movements were grounded on so-called material conditions: the real role of workers in hist. and production. But when students protested across Europe and the Communist parties failed to support the revolution because it was deemed not to be properly political or economic, there emerged a need to rethink the problems of intellectual or cultural resistance. If systems are the means through which we think and act, how can those systems be destabilized, opened, or ruptured? How do they come into being and pass away? These were political and material questions, but they also concerned the politics and matter of sign systems. If we accept the premises of structuralism—that identity is created through differentiation—then we open up a new problem concerning the closure of structures. Can we think outside the structures that produce identity? What position of knowledge do we occupy when we examine differences among structures and the emergence of structures? Jacques Derrida (1930–2004), beginning in the late 1950s, in a series of essays that radicalized the premises of structuralism, argued that any thought or concept of a structure (such as lang. or culture) would itself be dependent on structures; we would always be caught up in relations of difference, never capable of stepping outside the tracing of relations of difference that we are trying to explain. Structuralism, like all Western thought, relied on positing a founding presence, such as the explanatory concept of culture or lang. (even though these terms are themselves effects of lang. and culture). Any thought of some origin, any account of the genesis of structures, would itself be an effect of structuring differences. Further, even if we accept that we are always within networks of difference and, therefore, never capable of grasping a pure unmediated truth outside of difference, we cannot avoid the *effect* of presence. If we claim that langs., cultures, myths, or texts create the differences through which we conceptualize the world, then we are bringing in another foundation, and we avoid the ways in which foundational terms are also made possible only by difference and relation. Derrida, therefore, argued for a deconstruction of textual relations and forces; texts are "scenes of writing" in which oppositions are produced. *Literary texts* tend to foreground writing and inscriptive processes and, in so doing, allow for a continuing disturbance of the seemingly self-present nature of identity.

Poststructuralism also had implications for the ways in which human consciousness and the unconscious could be approached. Jacques Lacan (1901–81) argued for what he referred to as the "agency of the letter" in the unconscious. There are not self-present minds or egos that have experiences, some of which are repressed to produce an unconscious. Rather, from differential processes—such as the symbolic order of lang. that allows us to speak and think of ourselves as subjects—we imagine that there is both a world of fixed identities, an ultimate reality beyond the vagaries of perception,

and an original subject who is the origin of all speech and meaning. What we *cannot think*—what constitutes a necessarily and radically absent unconscious—is the differential system through which we are able to think of ourselves as unified subjects. For Lacan, there is a special value to lit. in its presentation of the sign as such—the *letter* that we always imagine to be the *sign of* some ultimate presence.

Despite psychoanalysis and its Oedipal theories being ostensibly disastrous for women's identity, Lacanian psychoanalysis was crucial for poststructuralist feminist literary theory (see FEMINIST APPROACHES TO POETRY). Poststructuralist feminism, in general, rejected the notion of a natural femininity that would be masked or belied by culture: the very notion of a pure nature overlaid by culture is itself an effect of structure (and one that had helped sustain the figure or image of a mother nature outside signs and hist.). Poststructuralism in its psychoanalytic form enabled some explanation of why there had always been some presupposed maternal origin or plenitude that we now regard as lost. Because we are speaking beings, produced through structure, we also imagine some prestructural origin. We presuppose an ultimate "beyond" or plenitude that exists in excess of the social order of the symbolic. Lacan suggested that Woman (or the figure of that which lies beyond the differentiating laws of the symbolic order) *does not exist* and that ethics would only begin if we could—in a mode of poststructuralist affirmation—relinquish the imagination of the feminine "beyond." Feminists who followed Lacan took a different path and suggested a new way of reading texts. For Julia Kristeva (b. 1941), *poetic* lang. would be directly revolutionary because it does not accept the terms of a structure (such as lang.) and work within its terms but draws on sonorous, rhythmic, and tonal matters from which logical systems emerge. In poetry, it is as though the subject of logic, judgment, and identity is drawn back to some pre-Oedipal moment of emerging differentiation (what Kristeva referred to as the "chora"). For Luce Irigaray (b. 1932), the Lacanian theory of the subject is only half the story. The notion that we are subjected to a symbolic order of law *from which* we must presuppose a lost and desired prohibited feminine that is nothing more than an effect must be coupled with another sexed subject. For Irigaray, this other subject would be feminine, and her mode of existing and speaking would not be negative and mournful—imagining a lost fantasized feminine—but creatively *different*. In the male-female relation, one recognizes an other or otherness beyond the system of signs that would structure reality in advance. There is at least one other sexed subject—woman—whose modes of speech, touch, and experience are not those of a differentiating subject faced with an undifferentiated object or matter. Irigaray argues that, in relations of sexual difference, we encounter others as desiring relations, not as differentiated objects. Her theory of sexual difference is also a theory of textual difference, in which we experience the world not as blank matter to be represented by an active subject but as a living world that has its own dynamism. In certain mythic or spiritual modes of writing, contact is made with an "elemental" aspect of existence that is neither brute unstructured reality nor constructed objectivity but a process of relation that produces differences.

Poststructuralism, though diverse in the disciplines from which it drew (incl. philosophy, ling., anthropology, psychoanalysis, and poetics) was nevertheless united in being a complex mode of antifoundationalism. Like structuralism, it argued that one could not grasp a foundation or origin outside the system of differences through which identities and relations are made possible. Unlike structuralism, though, poststructuralism maintained that the terms used to describe structures are themselves effects of difference *and* that the *effects* or *illusions* of an ultimate presence could not simply be avoided. In other words, we at once acknowledge that all terms or identities can only be known through some mediating structure, yet any term used to describe that structure will nevertheless appear as one more privileged foundation. The idea that all concepts are effects of lang. posits lang. as some ultimate and single ground, but lang.'s differential system is never a full presence and is only known and experienced differentially. Derrida referred to this as a "necessary impossibility": the idea of truth or some presence beyond relative differences is necessary for all thinking (for we always take signs to be signs *of* something signified, something that *will be* present). But that presence can never arrive. In his later work, Derrida referred to a "future to come" or messianism without messiah. P. de Man (1919–83), lit. crit.'s most audacious poststructuralist and one of the Yale school of theorists who transposed poststructuralist Fr. philosophy into lit. crit., diagnosed what he referred to as the continual "relapse" of meaning effects. Lit. offers us nothing more than traces and marked-out oppositions, yet we always posit some nature or ground (or meaning) from which some effects have supposedly emerged. De Man argued that *allegory—seeing signs as doubles of some prior nature, or foundational meaning—is what reading ought to aim to destroy, yet any destroyed allegory could never arrive at a degree zero and would always lapse back into seeing texts and relations as having derived from some prior and fruitful ground. In this respect, de Man—despite his manifest association with Derrida and deconstruction—was closer to the insistently immanent poststructuralism of Gilles Deleuze (1925–95) and Michel Foucault (1926–84): i.e., he rejected a future or messianism that might be intimated but never known; instead, he insisted on the labor of *reading* that would always focus on the textual differences themselves (and not some imagined presence of which they were effects). De Man, therefore, rejected transcendence or a presence beyond the differences and relations of textual traces, and, in this sense, he—like Deleuze and Foucault—was more insistently a theorist of immanence, taking up Friedrich Nietzsche's (1844–1900) *nihilist* project of positively destroying or annihilating any supposed "higher" world or value.

Deleuze, who coauthored a series of works with the Fr. psychoanalyst Félix Guattari (1930–92), aimed to liberate thought from transcendence or the idea that perceptions, images, signs, desires, and identities are grounded on some ultimate or transcending "plane." Unlike Derrida, whose work increasingly insisted on a "to-come" that might be thought but never known, Deleuze embraced the deep interior of thinking—phenomena such as stupidity, malevolence, and nonsense—in which life would appear as such and not indicate any logic or rationale beyond itself. He insisted that relations were external to terms: there are not identities that then explain how the world unfolds; nor is there a general law that explains and orders all identities. Relations—or the terms and systems we know—are effects of contingent encounters that could always have been otherwise. Deleuze's work was close to Foucault's, although Foucault was less explicitly philosophical. Like all poststructuralists, Foucault was indebted to Nietzsche and the genealogical approach: one does not assume identities that come to realization through time. Genealogy traces wayward and awkward connections and mappings of vastly different and disjoined phenomena. The very idea of "man," for Foucault, was only possible after certain spatial redistributions, knowledge practices, sociopolitical procedures, and different styles of perceiving and knowing. The human being is an effect of knowledge, and knowledge is enabled by distributions of knowledge: "man" is produced as an object of study by (e.g.) mod. penal practices of analysis and interpretation, which, in turn, enable criminology and the project of the human sciences.

In this respect, Foucault, like all poststructuralists, produced a corpus that was an antidote to what has come to be known as *postmodernism. The idea that the world is an effect of signs and that everything is relative (esp. relative to human knowledge) is one more foundational idea that puts the human being at the center. Poststructuralists insisted that there would always be hierarchies, disjunctions, systems that do not cohere, and ongoing mutations and distortions that would preclude a general relativism. The one poststructuralist who did use the term *postmodernism* in his work, Jean-François Lyotard (1924–98), defined the postmod. condition as one of an "incredulity towards metanarratives": there could be no general account capable of subsuming all phenomena. The idea that "everything is simulation" or that "the world is the effect of representation" would be just as totalizing as a fundamental religion or metaphysical schema. Lyotard, therefore, drew attention to what he referred to as the "postmodern sublime"—purely sensible events that could not be reduced to already given or commanding concepts.

Overall, then, the poststructuralist legacy is still to be played out and still presents a challenge to many current modes of thought—such as the attempt to account for differences through a single overarching system, such as culture, hist., lang., or "life."

■ M. Foucault, *Les Mots et les choses* (1966), and *L'archéologie du savoir* (1969); *The Languages of Criticism and the Sciences of Man: The Structuralist Con-

*troversy*, ed. R. Macksey and E. Donato (1970); J. Derrida, *Writing and Difference*, trans. A. Bass (1978); *Structuralism and Since: From Lévi-Strauss to Derrida*, ed. J. Sturrock (1979); de Man; J. Kristeva, *Revolution in Poetic Language*, trans. M. Waller (1984); J.-F. Lyotard, *The Postmodern Condition*, trans. G. Bennington and B. Massumi (1984); L. Irigaray, *Speculum of the Other Woman*, trans. G. C. Gill (1985); E. A. Grosz, *Sexual Subversions: Three French Feminists* (1989), and *Jacques Lacan: A Feminist Introduction* (1990); R. Braidotti, *Patterns of Dissonance: A Study of Women in Contemporary Philosophy*, trans. E. Guild (1991); G. Deleuze, *Difference and Repetition*, trans. P. Patton (1994); M. McQuillan, *Paul de Man* (2001); J. Culler, *The Pursuit of Signs*, rev. ed. (2002); J. Lacan, *Ecrits: A Selection*, trans. B. Fink (2002); S. Mills, *Michel Foucault* (2003); N. Royle, *Jacques Derrida* (2003); C. Colebrook, *Philosophy and Post-Structuralist Theory: From Kant to Deleuze* (2005); J. Williams, *Understanding Poststructuralism* (2005).

C. COLEBROOK

**POULTER'S MEASURE.** A rhymed *couplet, the first line having 12 syllables and the second 14: "What length of verse can serve brave Mopsa's good to show, / Whose virtues strange, and beauties such, as no man them may know?" (Philip Sidney, "What Length of Verse?"). After confessing ignorance of its name, George Gascoigne called it a "poulter's measure" since the poultry man gives 12 eggs for the first dozen and 14 for the second. Although the definition refers to the number of syllables, poets understood that the meter was *iambic and that the first line had six beats and the second seven.

One of the few native poetic forms created in Eng. during the Ren., poulter's measure peaked early, in the 1560s and 1570s, as Gascoigne, Fulke Greville, Nicholas Grimald, Sidney, the Earl of Surrey (Henry Howard), Thomas Wyatt, and others sought the right meter for *heroic verse. By the 1590s, poets turned away, mocking it as Sidney does above for its singsong and supposedly uncouth qualities. Soon, iambic *pentameter dominated, and poulter's measure disappeared.

The appeal and demise of poulter's measure stem from its rhythmic similarity to *short meter. The beat pattern of poulter's measure is 6 and 7, and the Ren. practice of placing a *caesura in the middle of each line meant that the rhythm often sounds like 3-3-4-3, echoing the beat pattern of short meter. As Malof, Thompson, and Attridge explain, short meter (and its relative the *limerick, which breaks the 4-beat line in half, creating a 3-3-2-2-3 beat pattern) creates an insistent rhythm, the singsong that appealed to the Ren. love of *ornament but also doomed poulter's measure for long poems. By contrast, iambic pentameter has structural advantages that prevent the devel. of a rollicking rhythm.

*See* BLANK VERSE, FOURTEENER, HEROIC COUPLET.

■ G. Gascoigne, *Certayne Notes of Instruction* (1575); J. Malof, *A Manual of English Meters* (1970); Attridge,

*Rhythms*; S. Woods, *Natural Emphasis* (1984); O. B. Hardison, *Prosody and Purpose in the English Renaissance* (1989); J. Thompson, *The Founding of English Metre*, 2d ed. (1989).

M. L. MANSON

**PRAGUE SCHOOL.** *See* STRUCTURALISM.

**PRAKRIT POETRY.** The term *Prakrit* refers in its broadest sense to a wide range of Middle Indo-Aryan langs., related to but different from Sanskrit. Although the name is drawn from a Sanskrit word referring to these langs. as "original" or "natural" in contrast to the "refined" status of codified Sanskrit, a description pointing to a recognition of their status as vernaculars, several of the Prakrit langs. had standardized forms of their own and enjoyed a long hist. of use both as court langs. in South Asia and by groups such as the Buddhists and Jains, who opposed the claims of authority made by Brahmanical users of Sanskrit. The oldest surviving written examples of Middle Indo-Aryan langs. are from the 3d c. BCE, in the inscriptions of the Buddhist emperor Aśoka, and a very large corpus of Buddhist texts survives both in the Pali lang. and in various Prakrit langs. An unknown portion of Prakrit lit. has been lost; in only the last 15 years, e.g., excavations in Central Asia have increased the numbers of known mss. in Gāndhārī Prakrit from one example to hundreds. In addition to the Buddhist texts, Jain canonical works are preserved in Prakrit langs. such as Ārdhamāgadhī and Jain Māhārāṣṭrī. Alongside these uses, several Prakrit langs. were used for literary purposes by Brahmanical authors as well. In mod. usage (continuing the practice of Sanskrit authors) the term *Prakrit* generally excludes the Pali lang. as well as the later stages of Middle Indo-Aryan known as Apabhraṃśa, despite the literary uses of these langs.

Sanskrit writers on poetics treat Prakrit as a ling. option for poetic purposes alongside Sanskrit and Apabhraṃśa, sometimes incl. as well the "goblin language" or Paiśācī, in which was composed a famous collection of stories called *Bṛhatkathā* (The Great Story), now lost in the original but surviving in several versions in Sanskrit dating from the 6th c. onward. In addition to the use of Prakrit as the lang. in which entire works are composed, in Sanskrit dramaturgy the use of several Prakrit langs. is assigned by rule to characters of certain classes: in the plays, it is generally only educated upperclass men who speak Sanskrit, while women speak in Śaurasenī Prakrit and sing in Māhārāṣṭrī Prakrit, and less refined men speak other forms of Prakrit such as Māgadhī. Prakrit grammars written in Sanskrit described these langs. largely by giving rules for converting Sanskrit into Prakrit, and from early med. times onward, it became increasingly clear that most Sanskrit playwrights were thinking in Sanskrit and employing such conversions to produce their Prakrit sentences. It is perhaps for this reason that the great poet Bhavabhūti, author of three plays in the 8th c., wrote prose in both Sanskrit and Prakrit but composed verses only in Sanskrit. It is also clear that readers as well were less able over time to understand Prakrit directly, as shown in the fact that commentaries on the plays regularly provide Sanskrit trans. of the Prakrit passages and in the widespread corruption of Prakrit passages in mss.

Māhārāṣṭrī Prakrit, associated with the region in which mod. Marathi is spoken (see MARATHI POETRY), played an esp. important role in poetry and is treated as the fundamental Prakrit in written grammars. The oldest collection of verses is the anthol. named *Sattasaī* (Seven Hundred), attributed to the 1st-c. king Hāla but containing *couplets mostly from the 3d to 5th c. and from as late as the 7th c. The verses, called *gāthā*s, are couplets, syntactically independent like Sanskrit couplets but composed in freer meters of the *āryā* pattern, a type apparently related to regional folk songs, not allowed in the most prestigious form of Sanskrit poetry but adopted with enthusiasm in other forms of Sanskrit composition. The verses deal esp. with the psychological aspects of love and were influential in providing the model for similar collections in Sanskrit such as the *Amaruśataka* (The Hundred Verses of Amaru, ca. 7th c.), an anthol. of verses offering psychological vignettes of life in an aristocratic polygamous society, using techniques of poetic suggestion similar to those found in many of the Prakrit gāthās. Such poetry was the impetus for the devel. of the theory of poetic suggestion that looms large in Sanskrit poetics beginning with the 9th-c. *Dhvanyāloka* (Light on Suggestion) treatise of Ānandavardhana, which uses as examples not only Sanskrit verses from Amaru's collection but many Prakrit verses from the *Sattasaī*. Later Sanskrit poetic works such as the 12th-c. *Āryāsaptaśatī* (Seven Hundred Āryā Verses) imitate the *Sattasaī* not only in flavor but in meter as well. Commentaries in Sanskrit were written on many of the Prakrit poems.

In addition to the gāthā lit., Prakrit poets also composed in most of the standard genres of Sanskrit poetry or in related Prakrit genres. Examples are the 7th-c. *sargabandha* (composition in *cantos, the ornate *epic also called *mahākāvya* or great poem in Sanskrit) of Pravarasena titled *Setubandha* (The Forming of the Bridge), the 8th-c. *campu* (poem in mixed prose and verse) of Uddyotana Sūri titled *Kuvalayamālā* (The Garland of Water Lilies), and the long 8th-c. poem *Gaüḍavaha* (The Slaying of the Gauda) of Vākpatirāja, who was also among the latest of the authors included in Hāla's collection. Several distinctive Prakrit genres are defined in early Sanskrit treatises on poetics, but examples have survived only sporadically. Other authors used Sanskrit and Prakrit together, as in works with Sanskrit verses and Prakrit prose, in *macaronic verses with one half in Sanskrit and the other in Prakrit, and even in verses designed to sound the same in both langs.

A considerable portion of these poetic works in Māhārāṣṭrī Prakrit was composed by Jain authors, many of whom continued to use distinctively Jain forms of Prakrit for literary as well as expository and philosophical uses.

Extensive treatment of the differences in effect between Sanskrit and Prakrit, of the distribution of Prakrit langs. geographically and socially, and of the social milieu of the Prakrit court poets is provided in the 9th-c. *Kāvyamīmāṃsā* (Exegesis of Poetry), an encyclopedic work on lit. by Rājaśekhara, who was the most prolific of Sanskrit court poets and prided himself on his abilities in Prakrit, as evidenced in his play titled *Karpūramañjarī* (Camphor Cluster), which is composed entirely in Prakrit langs.

*See* INDIA, POETRY OF; SANSKRIT POETICS; SANSKRIT POETRY.

■ A. C. Woolner, *Introduction to Prakrit*, 2d ed. (1928); M. A. Selby, *Grow Long, Blessed Night: Love Poems from Classical India* (2000); S. Pollock, *The Language of the Gods in the World of Men: Sanskrit, Culture, and Power in Premodern India* (2006); *Poems on Life and Love in Ancient India: Hāla's "Sattasaī,"* trans. P. Khoroche and H. Tieken (2009).

G. TUBB

**PRÉCIOSITÉ.** Deliberate pursuit and "prizing" of refinement in manners, dress, lang., and lit. Bray (among others) has traced the hist. of *préciosité* from med. *courtly love to the present (via Stéphane Mallarmé and Jean Giraudoux), but as a significant cultural phenomenon, it is most pertinently applied to 17th-c. Fr. salons and polite society (1630–60). In 1608, the Marquise de Rambouillet, disgusted by the licentious court of Henri IV, retired to her Parisian manor, noted for its *chambre bleue*; as a salon, it reached its height from 1630 to 1645. Elegance in clothing and manners, decorum and modesty in behavior, and witty conversation were cultivated. Love and lit. were the topics of discussion. Honoré d'Urfé's pastoral novel *L'Astrée* (1607–28) was analyzed and imitated; authors (incl. Pierre Corneille) read aloud their works. The poet and epistolist Vincent Voiture (1597–1648) animated the group and epitomized the delicate, ludic tone of the *précieux* style. In the 1650s, préciosité appeared in several salons, most notably that of Mlle. de Scudéry, renowned for her lengthy novels. Préciosité became widespread and fashionable in polite (*mondaine*) society. Some critics (Lathuillère) consider this decade the only period of true préciosité. By the time of Molière's satiric attack in *Les Précieuses ridicules* (1659), the episode was already beginning to wane.

As an attitude and endeavor, préciosité is characterized by reductionism, purity, artifice, and abstraction. In terms of lang., it continued François de Malherbe's task of rejecting the cacophonous Latinate neologisms of the Ren. The précieux lang. of the *ruelle* (an alcove in the salon) stressed exaggerated metaphors, clever *pointes* (puns, witticisms), and paraphrase. Objects could not be crudely designated by their vulgar, common names: in Antoine Baudeau de Somaize's *Dictionnaire des précieuses* (1660), a mirror is a "counselor of the graces," cheeks are the "thrones of modesty." Platonic love interests were encouraged, which gave rise to the literary forms valued by préciosité: the epistle, *ode, *sonnet, *rondeau, *epigram, and *madrigal. But the more popular préciosité became, the clearer and more frequent were the abuses of extravagance and pretension (esp. among the bourgeois). Burlesque poetry and realistic novels were linked, inversely, to précieux thought.

An element of the Fr. *baroque, préciosité had several earlier Eur. analogues of idealized refinement: Euphuism, Gongorism, *Marinism. Yet it did not seek the periodic style of Euphuism, the Latinate vocabulary of Gongorism, or the rambling syntax of Marinism. The influence of préciosité, restricted to Fr. lit., was considerable, since the psychological analysis of love, expressed by *galant* terms (but without florid images or an excessive style) is evident in Mme. de Lafayette, the *Lettres portugaises,* and François de La Rochefoucauld.

*See* BOUTS-RIMÉS.

■ R. Bray, *La Préciosité et les précieux* (1948); O. de Mourgues, *Metaphysical, Baroque and Precious Poetry* (1953); G. Mongrédien, *Les Précieux et les précieuses* (1963); Y. Fukui, *Le Raffinement précieux* (1964); R. Lathuillère, *La Préciosité* (1966); J.-M. Pelous, *Amour précieux, amour galant* (1980); R. Lathuillère, "La Langue des précieux," *Travaux de Linguistique et de Littérature* 25 (1987); J. Campbell, "La 'Modernité' de *La Princesse de Clèves,*" *Seventeenth-Century French Studies* 29 (2007).

A. G. WOOD

**PREGUNTA.** The *pregunta* or *requesta* (question) with its corresponding *respuesta* (answer) was a form of poetic debate practiced principally by Sp. court poets of the late 14th and 15th cs. One poet presented his question—often on such themes as morals, love, philosophy, or religion—in a poem, and another poet gave the answer in a poem of identical form, incl. the rhymes. Sometimes answers in identical form were given by more than one poet. Occasionally, an answering poet was unable to follow the rhymes of the pregunta and might excuse himself for his substitutions.

■ Le Gentil; J. G. Cummins, "Methods and Conventions in Poetic Debate," *HR* 31 (1963); J. J. Labrador Herraiz, *Poesía dialogada medieval: La "pregunta" en el "Cancionero de Baena"* (1974); Navarro.

D. C. CLARKE

**PRE-RAPHAELITE BROTHERHOOD.** Arguably the first mod. avant-garde movement, the Pre-Raphaelite Brotherhood (PRB) exercised an influence disproportionate to its short life. Three young Brit. art students banded together in London in 1848 to protest academic conventionalism in Eng. art. W. H. Hunt, J. E. Millais, and D. G. Rossetti were the most important figures in a group that eventually numbered seven (plus associated artists and writers F. M. Brown, W. B. Scott, and Christina Rossetti) before dispersing in the early 1850s. The PRB sought to lead Eng. art and lit. back to a studied simplicity, what Ruskin, writing in their defense, called "archaic honesty," taking inspiration from the work of northern Eur. and It. "primitive" art and lit. of the late Middle Ages and early Ren.: i.e., before Raphael. In 1850, the group launched an

ambitious small magazine of poetry, crit., and original designs, *The Germ: Thoughts toward Nature in Poetry, Literature and Art,* which sold few copies but survived four issues.

Paintings signed "PRB," first appearing publicly in 1849, accumulated sharply observed details in bright, local color to render scenes of socially or sexually charged encounters from lit., the Bible, and mod. life (e.g., Millais's *Christ in the House of His Parents, Isabella, Mariana, Ophelia;* Hunt's *The Light of the World, Claudio and Isabella, The Hireling Shepherd, The Awakening Conscience;* D. G. Rossetti's *Mary's Girlhood, Ecce Ancilla Domini!,* and *Found* ). PRB artists used minimal chiaroscuro, avoiding lights and shadows conventionally used for dramatic or narrative simplification and illusions of depth; employed colors that struck contemporaries as jarringly vivid, and rendered their subjects with scrupulous fidelity, painting outdoor backgrounds in situ under often-trying conditions and refusing to idealize their working-class subjects. Eliminating depth of field, they labored minutely on visual detail across their canvases. Preternaturally focused visual attention, overriding ordinary conventions for organizing pictorial and narrative scenes, created formal patterns and suggested heightened states of mind.

Rossetti preferred imagined scenes, using one figure as what he termed an "inner standing point" for states of mind rendered through concrete sensory details— a process that shaped both his two exhibited oils and poems first pub. in *The Germ:* "The Blessed Damozel," "My Sister's Sleep," and "Sonnets for Pictures" by Andrea Mantegna, Giorgione, Leonardo da Vinci, and Hans Memling. Rossetti's prose tale "Hand and Soul" in the *Germ's* inaugural issue captures the group's interest in intensely "seen" psychohistories taking inspiration from earlier (and then-unpopular) moments in the hist. of art revisited through mod. sensibilities. Subsequent issues published C. Rossetti's strange, beautifully crafted short lyrics ("Dream Land," "An End," "A Pause of Thought," "Song: Oh! Roses for the flush of youth," "A Testimony," "Repining," and "Sweet Death") under the pseud. Ellen Alleyn. As in painting, so in poetry PRB contributors experimented with a spare, antirhetorical style and cultivated sensory and emotional intensity.

*See* AVANT-GARDE POETICS, PAINTING AND POETRY, PRE-RAPHAELITISM.

■ J. Ruskin, *Pre-Raphaelitism* (1851), and "Letters on the Pre-Raphaelite Artists" (1851, 1854), *Works of J. Ruskin,* ed. E. T. Cook and A. Wedderburn, v. 12 (1904); W. H. Hunt, *Pre-Raphaelitism and the Pre-Raphaelite Brotherhood,* 2 v. (1905–6); A. Staley, *The Pre-Raphaelite Landscape* (1973); *Pre-Raphaelitism,* ed. J. Sambrook (1974); W. M. Rossetti, *The P.-R.-B. Journal,* ed. W. E. Fredeman (1975); Tate Gallery, *The Pre-Raphaelites,* exhibition catalog (1984); J. Marsh and P. G. Nunn, *Women Artists and the Pre-Raphaelite Movement* (1989); *Pre-Raphaelites Re-viewed,* ed. M. Pointon (1989); *Pocket Cathedrals,* ed. S. Casteras (1995); *Re-framing the Pre-Raphaelites,* ed. E. Harding (1996); T. Barringer, *Reading the Pre-Raphaelites* (1998); J. B. Bullen, *The Pre-Raphaelite Body* (1998); E. Prettejohn,

*The Art of the Pre-Raphaelites* (2000); *Ruskin, Turner and the Pre-Raphaelites*, ed. I. Warrell and S. Wildman, exhibition catalog (2000); *Pre-Raphaelite Vision*, ed. A. Staley and C. Newall, exhibition catalog (2004).

E. K. HELSINGER

**PRE-RAPHAELITISM.** The term is loose but useful to describe shared ideals and practices in circles around D. G. Rossetti and William Morris in the later 1850s and 1860s, after the dissolution of the original *Pre-Raphaelite Brotherhood. Pre-Raphaelitism was a site of poetic innovation and experiment, beginning with Morris's 1858 *The Defense of Guenevere*; D. G. Rossetti's trans. from Dante and his circle, *The Early Italian Poets* (1861); Christina Rossetti's *Goblin Market* (1862); A. C. Swinburne's *Atalanta in Calydon* (1865) and *Poems and Ballads, First Series* (1866); and D. G. Rossetti's *Poems* (1870). The influence of poetic Pre-Raphaelitism affected contemporaries (e.g., George Meredith's *Modern Love*, 1862; G. M. Hopkins; Thomas Hardy) and extended to later devels. it nurtured or partly inspired (*aestheticism, *symbolism, *decadence, and significant aspects of *modernism and *postmodernism, particularly *Language poetry).

Poetic Pre-Raphaelitism is characterized by sharpened attentiveness to sensory perception valued as a mode of knowledge, giving access to heightened states of psychological and visionary intensity, particularly as provoked by passion or desire. Sensuous figuration and formal design evoke affective moods and psychological conditions to explore social, sexual, political, and metaphysical ideas. Pater was probably the first and best critic of this aspect of Pre-Raphaelitism, but the poets themselves were significant critics in prose as well as verse (e.g., Swinburne, *Notes on Poems and Reviews* [1866], *William Blake* [1868], *Notes on Some Pictures of 1868*; and D. G. Rossetti, *The Stealthy School of Criticism* [1871]). Pre-Raphaelite crit. vigorously resisted Victorian strictures on style and subject matter, insisting on "poetry for poetry's sake" (Swinburne, *William Blake*).

The poets' fundamental commitment to the seriousness of their subjects was pursued through formal innovation. While looking back to Blake; P. B. Shelley; John Keats; the early Alfred, Lord Tennyson; and Robert Browning, Pre-Raphaelitism drew on a much wider range of foreign and intermedial material. As a poetic practice, Pre-Raphaelitism was distinctively arts-inflected, emphasizing verbal rhythm, texture, and design in a variety of lyric forms and skillfully working the interplay of graphic and aural patterns to produce meaning. The four major poets of Pre-Raphaelitism paid unusual attention to poetry's material forms in page and book design (see BOOK, POETIC). They made frequent use of trans. (from Fr., It., Icelandic, Gr.), turning for fresh ideas to earlier historical periods, particularly the Eng. and Eur. Middle Ages and the Ren. (as noted appreciatively by Ezra Pound), but also to painting, drawing, the decorative arts, and music, challenging contemp. attitudes (toward love, desire, religion, politics) while expanding the ling. and formal possibilities for Eng. poetry. C. Rossetti drew on market

cries, *nursery rhymes, and *ballads as well as Tractarian poetics and other religious poetry and commentary. Morris, D. G. Rossetti, and Swinburne brought med. continental lyric forms back to Eng. poetry with brilliant experiments in the *carol, *sestina, *ballade, and *rondeau. D. G. Rossetti and Swinburne wrote exemplary terse *ballads (Rossetti, "Sister Helen" [1870]; Swinburne, "The Tyneside Widow," "The Lyke-Wake Song" [1889]), while both Rossettis composed innovative *sonnet sequences (D. G. Rossetti, "The House of Life" [1870, 1881]; C. Rossetti, "Monna Innominata" and "Later Life: A Double Sonnet of Sonnets" [1880]).

Individually distinctive, Pre-Raphaelitism's poets shared aspirations, practices, and spaces; their impact was enhanced by relationships at once social and professional. Poets worked with artists (e.g., Edward and Georgiana Burne-Jones, Philip Webb, J. M. Whistler, Elizabeth Siddall, Jane Burden Morris, Simeon Solomon, Frederick Sandys) in Red Lion Square in the late 1850s; Morris's Red House in Bexleyheath, Kent (1860–65); and from 1862, Rossetti's Tudor House, Chelsea (Swinburne, Meredith, and W. M. Rossetti were occasional tenants). Collaborative projects included the *Oxford and Cambridge Magazine* (1856), ed. by Morris and Burne-Jones; decoration of the Oxford Debating Society's rooms in the Oxford Union under the charismatic Rossetti (1857); design and decoration of Red House; a decorative-arts business (Morris, Marshall, Faulkner and Co.; after 1875, Morris and Co.); painting exhibitions; and extensive shared editorial labor (e.g., D. G. Rossetti's contributions to C. Rossetti's books of 1862 and 1865 and the collaborative work on his *Poems*, 1870; Morris and Burne-Jones's "big book" project, 1865–68, for an illustrated ed. of Morris's *The Earthly Paradise*; and in the 1890s, Morris's Kelmscott Press).

*See* AVANT-GARDE POETICS, FLESHLY SCHOOL OF POETRY.

■ W. Pater, "Aesthetic Poetry" and "Dante Gabriel Rossetti," *Appreciations* (1889); T. S. Eliot, "Imperfect Critics" (1919) and "Swinburne as Poet" (1920), *The Sacred Wood* (1920); G. Hough, *The Last Romantics* (1949); E. Pound, "Swinburne versus His Biographers" (1918) and "How to Read" (1919), *Literary Essays of Ezra Pound*, ed. T. S. Eliot (1954); W. E. Fredeman, *Pre-Raphaelitism* (1965); J. D. Rosenberg, "Swinburne," *Victorian Studies* 11 (1967); J. D. Hunt, *The Pre-Raphaelite Imagination* (1968); J. J. McGann, *Swinburne* (1971); L. Stevenson, *The Pre-Raphaelite Poets* (1972); *Pre-Raphaelitism*, ed. J. Sambrook (1974); R. L. Stein, *The Ritual of Interpretation* (1975); J. Dunlap and J. Dreyfus, *William Morris and the Art of the Book* (1976); J.M.S. Tomkins, *William Morris* (1988); J. Hollander, "Arduous Fullness: On D. G. Rossetti," *The Work of Poetry* (1989); C. Bernstein, "Artifice of Absorption," *A Poetics* (1992); J. J. McGann, *Black Riders* (1993); *The Whole Music of Passion*, ed. R. Rooksby and N. Shrimpton (1993); Y. Prins, "Swinburne's Sapphic Sublime," *Victorian Sappho* (1998); *After the Pre-Raphaelites*, ed. E. Prettejohn (1999); J. J. McGann, *Dante Gabriel Rossetti and the Game That Must Be Lost* (2000); C. Maxwell, "Swinburne's Metamorphoses,"

*The Female Sublime from Milton to Swinburne* (2001); L. J. Kooistra, *Christina Rossetti and Illustration* (2002); C. Hassett, *Christina Rossetti* (2005); E. Helsinger, *Poetry and the Pre-Raphaelite Arts* (2008); E. Prettejohn, *Art for Art's Sake* (2008).

■ **Journal:** *Journal of Pre-Raphaelite Studies* (founded in 1977), http://www.yorku.ca/jprs.

E. K. Helsinger

**PREROMANTICISM** (Fr. *Préromantisme*, Ger. *Vorromantik*). An umbrella term, introduced by the comparative lit. scholar van Tieghem in 1924 to denote all the various forms of "dissent" from the prevalent neoclassical system of rules and from the hegemony of the cl. trad. in 17th- and 18th c. Europe. They ultimately combined to form high romanticism. Changes of paradigm included the substitution of imaginative *originality for cl. *imitation (Edward Young); the preference for solitude and night over society and daylight (Anne Finch, Countess of Winchilsea) or the withdrawal from metropolitan salons into small sympathizing family circles (Anna Letitia Barbauld); the replacement of "artisan poetry" composed according to rule and reason by *inspiration, enthusiasm, and *poetic madness (William Blake); opposition to academic crit. according to rules (Nicholas Rowe); the growth of original genius in *nature rather than schools (James Beattie); introspective individualism in the lyrical revival (Joseph and Thomas Warton, the Bluestocking Circle, the Eng. Della Cruscans); the med. revival (Richard Hurd); the preference for simple vernacular diction and the native countryside (William Cowper); the literary revindication of regional dialects (Robert Anderson, Robert Fergusson, Robert Burns, Susanna Blamire); a preference for the child of nature and noble savage over against the cultivated Augustan (Jean-Jacques Rousseau, Lord Monboddo), as well as for wild poetic ecstasy (William Collins); a passion for the rights of man and abolition of feudal society and institutions (William Godwin, Thomas Paine); the inclusion of animals in natural egalitarian human sympathy (Joseph Ritson); the revival of "primitive and oriental" poetry such as Heb., Ar., Germanic, Celtic, Indian, and Chinese, as opposed to cl. Gr. and Lat. lits. and myths (Robert Lowth, J. G. Herder, Hugh Blair); the sentimental movement with its egalitarian tendency, as well as its repudiation of *satire and punitive ridicule; and the substitution of music for painting (see UT PICTURA POESIS) in the ordering of the arts: *ut musica poesis*. Changes of genre included the *sonnet revival (Charlotte Smith, William Lisle Bowles); the *ballad and romance revival (Allan Ramsay, Thomas Percy); *graveyard poetry (Young, Thomas Gray, James Hervey, Robert Blair); topographical and regional poetry (James Thomson, John Dyer); the sensational melodrama (Guilbert de Pixerécour, Thomas Holcroft); the sentimental comedy with its preference for touching positive examples of virtue as opposed to derided examples of vice and folly (Colley Cibber, Richard Steele, Hugh Kelly); the sentimental or domestic tragedy with its desertion of the classical rules of *Fallhöhe* and *Ständeklausel*, as well as its rank-ing of pity above objectifiable fear in the tragic *catharsis (George Lillo, Edward Moore); the sentimental novel with its "romantic triangle" engaging the reader's emotions in favor of rebellious marriages of love against feudal marriages of rank and riches (Samuel Richardson, Rousseau, Henry Mackenzie, J. W. Goethe, Laurence Sterne); the Gothic novel with its return of the suppressed unconscious as a "sublime" offshoot of the sentimental novel (Horace Walpole, Clara Reeve, Matthew Gregory Lewis, Mary Robinson, Charlotte Dacre, Ann Radcliffe) and the Radical or Jacobin novel as the Gothic novel's transposition into the real present-day horror of political persecution by the *ancien régime* (Robert Bage, Holcroft, William Godwin); the Gothic drama (Walpole, Joanna Baillie); and the Gothic or oriental tale as forerunner of the short story (Walter Scott, Washington Irving, William Beckford). In philosophy, these devels. were paralleled by inquiries into an innate prerational moral and aesthetic sense (Anthony Ashley Cooper, the third Earl of Shaftesbury interpreted by Francis Hutcheson); doubt about the cognitive faculty of reason (David Hume, Immanuel Kant); exploration of the origins of the incomprehensible and dark Longinian *sublime as a core of the Gothic (Edmund Burke); and concern with interiority, the human psyche, *sensibility, and innate *taste (Adam Smith, Alexander Gerard). The direction of all these devels. was retrospective, primitivist, and nostalgic, because of a growing fatigue with the "tyranny of reason" in Enlightenment philosophy, neoclassical art, and the Church, as well as the state embodied in the ancien régime. Thus, philosophy and poetry began to clash long before John Keats praised the poet's *"negative capability."

In Britain, the call for "liberation" in favor of *imagination, *fancy, passion, and *wit was the earliest of all, beginning even before the year of the Restoration (1660). This developing awareness was due to the Eng. self-reinvention as a nation of liberty against the French as a "nation born to serve" (Alexander Pope), the tenacity of Scottish primitivism (Ramsay), the Protestant Nonconformist call for variety in contradistinction to the Anglican ideal of uniformity, and the disastrous consequences of the Agricultural and Industrial Revolutions, such as deserted villages, destroyed landscapes, and overpopulated slum cities. The Dissenters were a driving force both of preromantic poetry (as in the Bluestocking Circle), women's liberation (Mary Wollstonecraft, Mary Hays), and the Radical or Jacobin demand for *liberté, égalité, fraternité* (Anna Seward, Helen Maria Williams, Amelia Opie, Joseph Priestley). In their Radical youth, even high romantic poets of Anglican origins were deeply influenced by the culture of Dissent (William Wordsworth, S. T. Coleridge). In its growing recognition of its own limitations, Enlightenment rationalism and neoclassicism (see NEOCLASSICAL POETICS) unwittingly advanced the cause of romanticism. Thus, Shaftesbury opposed his teacher John Locke by pleading for an innate moral and aesthetic sense in unison with reason, a sudden sense of virtue and beauty in an elegant, sensitive "virtuoso," later interpreted as "man and woman of feeling" in the Scottish Enlightenment "moral sense school" (Hutcheson, Smith, Hume, Adam Ferguson). Dominique Bouhours and Pope admitted the existence of \*"je ne sais quoi de beau," graces "beyond the reach of art." Thus, Nicolas Boileau translated and wrote a commentary on Longinus's *Peri hypsous* (*On the Sublime*). Lowth's and Burke's subsequent insistence on the indispensability of a sensitive poet's "sublime sentiments," inspired by infinity and incomprehensibility, shifted the distinction of poetry and prose from a formally manufactured sublime style (*genus sublime*) to what Wordsworth was to call "the spontaneous overflow of powerful feelings." *Entgrenzung*, breaking the narrow limits of reason and artifice in favor of imagination and spontaneity, promoted religious enthusiasm and Pietism (John and Charles Wesley, George Whitefield, Nikolaus Ludwig Graf von Zinzendorf). Against the grain of the Enlightenment, it initiated the exploration of the unconscious in dreams and visions brought about by reveries in nocturnal churchyards, charnel houses, or decaying Gothic or dark neo-Gothic mansions (Walpole's Strawberry Hill and Beckford's Fonthill Abbey) and by natural or drug-induced sleep (Walpole, Beckford). The Enlightenment concept of \*nature, the rational design of a unified and finished *natura naturata* as promulgated by Isaac Newton and Pope, was gradually replaced by the concept of an ever dynamically growing, decaying, and self-regenerating *natura naturans*. This new concept of nature found expression in a cult of growth and decay opposed to Pope's "unchanged and universal light." It included literary \*fragments, a revival of Gothic against Palladian architecture (Walpole), the invention of the Eng. landscape garden (William Kent) ranking variety above unity, and the creation of other anticlassical styles suggesting natural variety and growth (\*rococo, Chippendale, chinoiserie). Gothic buildings breaking all cl. proportions were seen much as Sterne's *Tristram Shandy* (pub. in 9 v., 1760–67) was read: unfinished heterogeneous works of art *in statu nascendi*. With this revaluation of a freely growing nature hardly controlled by gardeners and a freely floating imagination hardly controlled by reason, cultural, chronological, and aesthetic \*primitivism was pitted against progressivism.

Neoclassical advocates of the cl. trad. satirized preromanticism's popular cult of "morbid" literary sensibility—demonstrated by the case of Thomas Chatterton. Such sensibility was widely promoted by the abolition of the perpetual copyright of booksellers in 1774 and by the introduction of a postal system in Britain. Neoclassicists also derided preromanticism's shift of emphasis from the cultural center of London to the rural margins of the British Isles, esp. Scotland and Wales, and later to the Lake District. James Macpherson's construction of a Scottish national past in his Ossianic forgeries (pub. 1760–62) with their lang. of sensibility imitated from OT Heb. poetry naturally provoked the enmity of Samuel Johnson, who went to Scotland and the Hebrides to prove the fraud and to deride such primitivism, in opposition to his Scottish companion James Boswell, whose account of the tour of 1773 differs sharply from Johnson's. Many Britons, who suspected the fraud, would yet believe in the poems' authenticity (John Home), and Ossianism became a Eur. literary fashion undercutting the Enlightenment and cl. trad. With its integrative egalitarian character, sensibility—as opposed to distinguishing reason—fostered a wave of women's liberation as well as abolition of slavery, promoted esp. by women (Hannah More, Ann Yearsley). The revaluation of OT poetry as lit. challenged the neoclassical concept of a universally valid Augustan norm of refinement by postulating the existence of other, equal or superior aesthetic values, even as it demolished the neoclassical concept of a chiefly formal distinction between prose and poetry, thus creating the rhythmic \*prose poem (Christopher Smart).

*See* ROMANTIC AND POSTROMANTIC POETRY AND POETICS, ROMANTICISM.

■ P. van Tieghem, *Le préromantisme* (1924–27); J. M. Longacre, *The Della Cruscans and William Gifford* (1924); K. Clark, *The Gothic Revival* (1928); H. N. Fairchild, *The Noble Savage* (1928); S. H. Monk, *The Sublime* (1935); A. B. Friedman, *The Ballad Revival* (1961); M. Roston, *Prophet and Poet* (1965); R. Kiely, *The Romantic Novel in England* (1972); M. Butler, *Jane Austen and the War of Ideas* (1975); G. Kelly, *The English Jacobin Novel* (1976); J. Engell, *The Creative Imagination* (1981); J. Sitter, *Literary Loneliness in Eighteenth-Century England* (1982); J. Mullan, *Sentiment and Sociability* (1988); R. Lessenich, *Aspects of English Preromanticism* (1989); M. Brown, *Preromanticism* (1991); M. Kilgour, *The Rise of the Gothic Novel* (1995); P. Baines, *The House of Forgery in Eighteenth-Century Britain* (1999); *Bluestocking Feminism*, ed. G. Kelly et al., 6 v. (1999–2006): D. E. White, *Early Romanticism and Religious Dissent* (2006); M. Faubert, *Rhyming Reason: The Poetry of Romantic-Era Psychologists* (2009); K. O'Brien, *Women and Enlightenment in Eighteenth-Century Britain* (2009).

R. LESSENICH

**PRESENCE.** Presence as expected and enjoyed by readers of poetry has a spatial more than a temporal dimension: it is related to the kind of presence we mean when we say that someone who enters a room "has presence"—a bodily reaction, a sudden feeling of immediacy with things that had been remote, even a desire to touch the world. Poetry can make things "present" not exclusively in the sense of bringing them back from a past into which they were receding but also "present from the future," in the sense of an anticipation, and "present," above all, suggesting that whatever has this quality can be touched and touches the reader.

Most likely, the indestructible, unavoidable, and today much overlooked presence of poetry comes from the same energy that premod. cultures drew on when they crafted prosodic lang. for prayers and \*charms. While the feeling of such presence has long been familiar to readers, critics began only recently to explain how presence originates in what we call poetic \*form or \*artifice, e.g., in \*lines, \*rhyme, \*stanzas, and \*rhythm. For instance, none of the analyses that characterize the past century of crit. concerning the work of Charles Baudelaire—neither Walter Benjamin, Roman Jakobson, Erich Auerbach, nor P. de Man—have paid attention to the presence dimension in poetry. To describe this dimension is still a precarious conceptual operation but nonetheless is worthwhile for the promise of answers to unresolved questions about the functions of poetic form.

As manifested on the syntactic level, poetic form often involves structures of highly symmetrical distribution and arrangement that we call *meter or *verse.* As a matter of *performance, poetic form is realized as rhythm and rhyme, phenomena that we can hear and feel as bodily experience organized into a pattern (and for present purposes, the difference between the effects of rhythm and those of rhyme are immaterial). From a certain level of complexity, *sound *repetition entails a conjuring and presence-producing function. Two properties of rhythm are decisive for this capacity to produce presence effects. In the first place, what we call *rhythm* can be a response to the challenge of how, phenomenologically speaking, temporal objects in the proper sense can have a form. Second, "rhythms" make up for one basic type of relation through which systems can be coupled to each other; rhythms are, in this sense and according to Luhmann, the consensual domain of "first-order couplings," couplings that are nonproductive because they leave unchanged the systems that they bring together. To illustrate the effects of presence as a dimension of poetry, this article follows the double—phenomenological and systems-theoretical—inspiration, in full awareness that it is one of several conceptual programs that can help in this project of poetic reflection.

Regarding the first of the above-mentioned properties of rhythm, why is it a problem at all for a time-object in the proper sense to have a form? We can define *form* as the simultaneity of self-reference and outside reference: a quadrangle, e.g., simultaneously points to itself and to the space outside itself. Once the shape that defines the quadrangle starts moving, however, it becomes a time-object and, thus (unless this movement is sheer expansion or contraction), it no longer has the stability of a form. But a moving form can acquire such stability on a higher level if the sequence of changes that it runs through is recurrent, returning to the quadrangular form, e.g., then departing from it again in the same way it departed before, and so on. Because of repetition, a rhythm suspends the open progression of change that belongs to time-objects without rhythm, incl. any kind of lang. without prosodic form.

It may well be this suspension of temporal progression and the constant change of prose lang., as a background, that accounts for the impression that rhythmic lang., e.g., the lang. of a charm, establishes a relationship of immediacy with—can "make present again"—discrete moments of the past: a relationship of epiphany, of divine intervention, of personal bliss. It is as if the temporal progression suspended and frozen through rhythm becomes a vacuum that tends to at-

tract and to absorb parts of the past. This conjuring power of prosodic lang., as lang. with form quality, may also explain its mnemonic function, i.e., the fact that we recall more easily any meaning that is cast into verse. The conjuring function of poetry, however, is not exclusively related to recovering things from the past. Any modification of what we consider the normal flow of time can be relevant here. In Gottfried Benn's probably most famous poem, "Asters" (1937), e.g., "incantation" and "spell" as functions of the poem are associated with an effect that Benn describes as "hesitation": "Asters, and days that smolder, / Old incantation, spell, / The gods hold the scales in balance / A hesitant moment still."

Second, rhythm is the medium, the "consensual domain" of two (or more) systems linked in a first-order coupling. First-order couplings are nonproductive, i.e., system (1) triggers a state in system (2) that triggers a different state in system (1) that triggers a different state in system (2) and so forth, until system (1) returns to its original state and both systems go through the same sequence again. What we call *languages*, by contrast, belongs to the level of second-order couplings. They demonstrate a different type of consensual domain, in which the interaction between systems is productive, i.e., it brings to the fore new, unprecedented states in both systems that, at a certain level of complexity, can become self-reflexive and, hence, self-descriptive. This is the reason that we always expect "language" to have a content, a meaning, semantics, a descriptive relationship to the world of which it is a part. Now, this view not only implies that meaning and rhythm are heteronomous and casts a skeptical light on all theories of poetry (like the theory of overdetermination) that have claimed prosody to "supplement" or "structure" content. Our insight indeed suggests that a tension exists between first-order and second-order couplings, between meaning and rhythm, between meaning effects and presence effects. Instead of bringing together meaning effects and presence effects into some kind of harmony, poetry always produces situations of oscillation between them. The listener or reader of poetry cannot be on both sides of this oscillation at the same time, on the presence side and on the meaning side, with equal *attention. Surprisingly, lit. crit. has never had much to say about this oscillation. Sympathetic descriptions tend to come from outside this narrow academic field, among them Paul Valéry's description of poetry as "hesitation between sound and sense" or H. G. Gadamer's insistence, toward the end of an intellectual life completely dedicated to the philosophical bases of meaning identification, that poetry was about not only "propositional content" but sound and *voice (Gadamer uses the Ger. word *Volumen* here).

In those moments when our predominant attention is on the presence side, words, verses, and stanzas function as sound material that touches our bodies. This is why poems are sometimes appealing as sound structures even to those who do not understand the lang. of which they are made. Empirically speaking, such foregrounding of the material side of lang. seems to have an affinity with the conjuring function of poetry. Charms can function independently of being understood by those who use them—as long as their words and verses are pronounced in what is considered to be the correct way. Names are often functionally equivalent to prosodic form, inasmuch as they establish a relation of immediacy with the—always individual—objects to which they refer. This functional equivalence probably explains why sound quality is particularly relevant for names. Rhythmic sound and names as conjuring devices come together in those OHG charms that give away (or hide) a secret name through which whoever recites the charm might sometimes gain power over supernatural beings.

Without any doubt, the presence effects and the presence functions of poetry have receded each time that its predominant modes of circulation and reception turned to script, print, and silent reading. Yet the conjuring *power* and the oscillations between meaning and presence never completely vanished from Western poetry. In this sense, it is remarkable that, as we know today, the historical transition to *prose poems and to *free verse during the 19th and 20th cs. did not become a threshold without return; the fact that poetic form long survived the historical transition from ms. to print, from *recitation to silent reading, suggests indeed that the conjuring power of poetry within the Western trad. never completely faded. This rigor of poetic form, far from having disappeared, seems to attract a renewed fascination today, in combination and coordination with music and through innovative forms of recitation. Because of the often exclusive concentration on the *hermeneutic level, i.e., the dominance of *interpretation as the attribution of meaning in the humanities, lit. crit. seems to have fallen behind such contemp. devels. in the production and reception of poetry. A return to recitation as an in-class practice might be a step back in the right direction.

*See* ÉCRITURE, SOUND POETRY.

■ C. Altieri, *Enlarging the Temple: New Directions in American Poetry during the 1960s* (1979), and *Self and Sensibility in Contemporary American Poetry* (1984); H. U. Gumbrecht, "Rhythmus und Sinn," *Materialität der Kommunikation*, ed. K. L. Pfeiffer (1988); H.-G. Gadamer, *Hermeneutik, Ästhetik, praktische Philosophie* (1993); N. Luhmann, *Social Systems*, trans. J. Bednard Jr. and D. Baecker (1995); H. U. Gumbrecht, *Production of Presence* (2003), and *Stimmungen lesen* (2011).

H. U. GUMBRECHT

**PRIAMEL** (Ger.; Lat. *praeambulum*, "prelude," "introduction"). The term was conceived to designate a subgenre of epigrammatic poems composed primarily in Germany from the 12th through the 16th cs. and characterized by a series of seemingly unrelated, often paradoxical statements cleverly brought together at the end, usually in the final verse. Numerous collections survive, but the author most noted in the genre

is the 15th-c. Nuremberg poet Hans Rosenplüt. The first scholars to study the priamel not as a form of the *Spruch* but as a separate genre were G. E. Lessing and J. G. Herder in the 18th c. The first to study the form of the priamel in world lit. was Bergmann, who, however, restricted his survey to didactic verse (e.g., *Proverbs* 30.21–23).

In cl. studies since the pioneering work of Dornseiff and the dissertation of his student Kröhling, the term *priamel* refers to a poetic (and rhetorical) form that occurs throughout Greco-Roman poetry but has received the most attention in connection with Pindar (Bundy) and Horace (Nisbet and Hubbard). As it is currently defined, the priamel consists of two basic parts: the foil and the climax. The function of the foil is to introduce and highlight the climactic term by enumerating or summarizing a number of other instances that then yield (with varying degrees of contrast or analogy) to the particular point of interest or importance. A brief example is Sappho, frag. 16.1–4: "Some say an array of cavalry, others of infantry, and others of ships is the most beautiful thing on the black earth, but I say it is whatever a person loves." Here various military arrays are foils to the real subject of the poem, "whatever a person loves." There are hundreds of examples in Gr. and Lat. poetry.

Recent studies refine our understanding of how the priamel functions differently according to genre: Davies shows how Euripides' *Cyclops* transforms the tragic topos into a comic tool; Compton-Engle notes that Aristophanes uses the priamel as a mock-tragic device in the *Acharnians*. Increasingly, scholars acknowledge and discuss the use of the priamel in mod. lit. Holzinger and Ramajo Caño trace the devel. of the priamel in Sp. Golden Age poetry. Race (2000) explores the use of the priamel in the work of two 20th-c. Am. poets, Richard Wilbur and Raymond Carver; a further study of Carver's use of the priamel is Kleppe. Other examples can be found in Shakespeare (sonnet 91), Charles Baudelaire ("Au Lecteur"), W. B. Yeats ("An Irish Airman Foresees his Death"), and W. H. Auden ("Law Like Love").

■ F. G. Bergmann, *La Priamèle dans les différentes littératures anciennes et modernes* (1868); W. Uhl, *Die deutsche Priamel und ihre Entstehung und Ausbildung* (1897); K. Euling, *Das Priamel bis Hans Rosenplüt* (1905); F. Dornseiff, *Pindars Stil* (1921); W. Kröhling, *Die Priamel (Beispielreihung) als Stilmittel in der griechisch-römischen Dichtung* (1935); E. L. Bundy, *Studia Pindarica* (1962); R.G.M. Nisbet and M. Hubbard, *A Commentary on Horace, Odes Book I* (1970); U. Schmid, *Die Priamel der Werte im Griechischen von Homer bis Paulus* (1964); W. H. Race, *The Classical Priamel from Homer to Boethius* (1982); H. Kiepe, *Die Nürnberger Priamel-Dichtung* (1984)—controversial; W. H. Race, *Classical Genres and English Poetry* (1988); M. Davies, "Comic Priamel and Hyperbole in Euripides, *Cyclops* 1–10," *CQ* 49 (1999); G. Compton-Eagle, "Mock-Tragic Priamels in Aristophanes' *Acharnians* and Euripides' *Cyclops*," *Hermes* 129.4 (2001); W. P.

Holzinger, *Priamel Structure in the Spanish Golden Age Sonnet* (1973); A. Ramajo Caño, "El carácter proemial de la Oda primera de Fray Luis (y un excurso sobre la priamel en la poesía de los Siglos de Oro)," *Romanische Forschungen* 106 (1994); W. H. Race, "Some Visual Priamels from Sappho to Richard Wilbur and Raymond Carver," *CML* 20 (2001); S. L. Kleppe, "Four More Priamels in the Poetry of Raymond Carver," *CML* 24 (2004).

W. H. RACE; C. DOAK

**PRIAPEA.** In Alexandrian Gr. and in Lat. poetry, short erotic poems honoring the god of fertility, Priapus. Euphronius of Chersonesus is traditionally said to be the inventor of the *priapeum*, but it was Leonidas of Tarentum who set the fashion in the 3d c. CE. Such poems use a distinctive meter called the Priapean, consisting of a *glyconic and a pherecratean separated by a *diaeresis. This was used by Anacreon and other Gr. erotic poets and is also found in dramatic poetry, esp. the chorus of satyr plays. In Lat., it is found in Catullus (e.g., 17.1) and in the anonymous *Priapea*, of which some 80 examples survive.

*See* EROTIC POETRY, ITHYPHALLIC.

■ M. Coulon, *La Poésie priapique dans l'antiquité et au moyen âge* (1932); V. Buchheit, *Studien zum Corpus Priapeorum* (1962); Koster; Crusius; Dales; Halporn et al.; West; A. Richlin, *The Garden of Priapus* (1983); *Priapea: Poems for a Phallic God*, trans. W. H. Parker (1988); R. Zipoli, *I Carmina priapea di Sûzanî* (1995)—on priapea in the Iranian trad.; L. C. Sandoz, "L'image de la femme dans les 'Priapea,'" *Museum Helveticum* 63 (2006).

P. S. COSTAS; T.V.F. BROGAN

**PRIMITIVISM.** The idealization of another culture, whether described as ancient, savage, premod., or wholly "other," that reflects writers' attitudes toward their own historical moment and their culture's relation to itself. Primitivism can be understood as a form of nostalgia: a desire for lost origins perceived as foundational for, or preferable to, the idealizing culture.

Primitivism is not particular to one period, region, or style but encompasses a number of contradictory tendencies: the primitive mind as nonrational (violently savage or innocently childlike); the space of nature (unruly threat or harmonious Eden); the primitive as feminine (seductively exotic or willingly passive); primitive society (debased origin of or redemptive cure for capitalist modernity). Many lits. celebrate or lament a distant past, e.g., the *topos of a golden age in cl. and Ren. poetry. However, the discourse of primitivism in its mod. usage originates in the 18th-c. Enlightenment and the attendant rise of Eur. colonialism, which enabled increasing contact with non-Western cultures in Africa, the Americas, and Oceania. Michel de Montaigne's "Des Cannibales" and Denis Diderot's *Supplément au voyage de Bougainville* are inspired by early accounts of Brazil and Tahiti. Jean-Jacques Rousseau speculated on "savage" state and the "noble

savage" in his two *Discours*, which influenced 18th- and early 19th-c. lit. Friedrich Schiller celebrated the "naïve" perfection of both childhood and Gr. poetry in "Über naive und sentimentalische Dichtung" (1795–96; see NAÏVE-SENTIMENTAL); J. W. Goethe's *Leiden des jungen Werthers* (1774) typifies *Sturm und Drang lit. (and Eng. *"sensibility") in its ascription of intuitive wisdom and a fuller emotional life to women, children, and peasants. William Wordsworth and S. T. Coleridge celebrated the "elementary" qualities of rustic life and lang. and "primal" emotional experience of rustics, children, and the mentally deranged (*Lyrical Ballads,* 1798, 1800, 1802). Primitivism accounts in large part for the romantic and Victorian poets' interest in the Middle Ages, in Gr. antiquity, in "Oriental" cultures and societies, and in the Am. Indian. In the 20th c., the rise of comparative anthropology (Franz Boas, J. G. Frazer) and mod. psychology (Sigmund Freud, C. G. Jung) gave primitivism renewed force as an instinctive, primal impulse in the individual and collective unconscious. Modernist poets (W. B. Yeats, Ezra Pound, T. S. Eliot, R. M. Rilke, W. C. Williams, D. H. Lawrence, H.D.) deployed primitivism to shatter earlier conventions of poetic beauty and refinement and to critique the pretenses of mod., bourgeois civilization. Poets affiliated with *surrealism and *Dada experimented with "automatic writing" and self-consciously primitive poetry. More recently, Brit., Ir., and Am. poets appeal to the notion of the artist as shaman (as in Ted Hughes, W. S. Merwin, Gary Snyder, and Seamus Heaney) and tap into deep ecology.

Primitivism's imperialist hist. has produced a range of responses among postcolonial and multiethnic poetries. In the early to mid-20th c., poets of the *Harlem Renaissance (Langston Hughes, Jean Toomer, Claude McKay) and *Negritude (Aimé Césaire, Léopold Sédar Senghor, Birago Diop) claimed the constitutive modernity of pan-Af. cultures and relocated imperial assumptions about race within the West. Primitivism has been further complicated by contemp. poetries informed by *postmodernism and *poststructuralism. Poets from the Caribbean (Louise Bennett, Derek Walcott, Kamau Brathwaite), the South Asian diaspora (A. K. Ramanujan, Daljit Nagra), Africa (Christopher Okigbo, Okot p'Bitek), Ireland (Eavan Boland, Paul Muldoon), and Native America (Leslie Marmon Silko, Joy Harjo, Sherman Alexie) wryly appropriate primitivist discourse by adopting *irony, *satire, *pastiche, and *parody both to mock primitivism and to question the artificial bases for separating the mod. from the primitive, West from non-West, masculine from feminine, self from other.

The endurance of primitivism registers the continuation of the notion of "modernity" (and with it the ideals of reason, technological progress, political freedom, diachronic time, and civilization itself) as it also undergoes transformation in its supposed origins, meaning, and historical and geographic reach. Like modernity, primitivism is a fundamentally discursive construction, produced primarily through a crisis in the time and location of its enunciation, and hence capable of taking on new meanings in shifting contexts.

See ANTHROPOLOGY AND POETRY, COLONIAL POETICS, CULTURAL CRITICISM, EXOTICISM, MODERNISM, POSTCOLONIAL POETICS, RELIGION AND POETRY.

■ I. Babbitt, *Rousseau and Romanticism* (1919); H. N. Fairchild, *The Noble Savage* (1928); L. Whitney, *Primitivism and the Idea of Progress* (1934); A. O. Lovejoy et al., *Primitivism and Related Ideas in Antiquity* (1935); E. A. Runge, *Primitivism and Related Ideas in Sturm und Drang Literature* (1946); G. Boas, *Essays on Primitivism and Related Ideas in the Middle Ages* (1948); D. Hoffman, *Barbarous Knowledge* (1967); G. Boas, "Primitivism," and A. O. Aldridge, "Primitivism in the 18th Century," *DHI*; M. Bell, *Primitivism* (1972); J. B. Vickery, *The Literary Impact of "The Golden Bough"* (1973); Welsh; J. R. Cooley, *Savages and Naturals* (1982); M. Torgovnick, *Gone Primitive: Savage Intellects, Modern Lives* (1991); C. Rhodes, *Primitivism and Modern Art* (1994); M. E. Novak, "Primitivism," *CHLC*, v. 4, ed. H. B. Nisbet and C. Rawson (1997); M. Torgovnick, *Primitive Passions: Men, Women, and the Quest for Ecstasy* (1998); J. K. Olupona, *Beyond Primitivism: Indigenous Religious Traditions and Modernity* (2003); S. Garrigan Mattar, *Primitivism, Science, and the Irish Revival* (2004); C. Bracken, *Magical Criticism: The Recourse of Savage Philosophy* (2007); G. Willmott, *Modernist Goods: Primitivism, the Market and the Gift* (2008).

A. RICHARDSON; O. HENA

**PROCEDURAL POETRY.** See ALEATORY POETICS; CONCEPTUAL POETRY; OULIPO.

**PROCELEUSMATIC** (Gr., "rousing to action beforehand"). In *classical prosody, a resolved *anapest, i.e., a metrical foot of four short syllables. It is found among the lyric anapests of Gr. drama and in Lat. drama, esp. comedy, as a resolution in *iambs and trochees as well, though with certain restrictions.

■ W. M. Lindsay, *Early Latin Verse* (1922); Crusius; D. Korzeniewski, *Griechische Metrik* (1968); West.

P. S. COSTAS

**PROEM,** Sp. *proemio*, Fr. *proème*. A poem or lines of poetry that introduce a longer poetic work, or sections of a long poem, often characterized by such gestures as invocation and dedication. Proems may be differentiated metrically or visually from what follows. The proem originates in cl. *epic and is typically associated with that genre but, from the 14th c., is often synonymous with *prologue* in Eng. and also denotes a prose preface to nonpoetic works. Petrarch's first *sonnet in the *Canzoniere* is perhaps the most famous and widely imitated proem in any Western vernacular; Philip Sidney's first sonnet in *Astrophil and Stella* (1591) is probably its counterpart in Eng.

■ S. Gilman, "The Proem to *La voz a ti debida*," *MLQ* 23 (1963)—on Pedro Salinas; U. Bosco, "The Proem to the *Paradiso*," *Forum for Modern Language Studies* 1 (1965); L. Brill, "Other Places, Other Times: The Sites of the Proems to *The Faerie Queene*," *SEL* 34 (1994); A. Miller, "The Proem to *The Faerie Queene*, Book II: Spenser, Pliny, and Undiscovered Worlds," *Classical and Modern Literature* 25 (2005); H. Peraki-Kyriakidou, "Antonomasia and Metonymy in the Proem to Virgil's *Georgics*," *What's in a Name?*, ed. J. Booth and R. Maltby (2006); N. G. Discenza, "Alfred the Great and the Anonymous Prose Proem to the *Boethius*," *JEGP* 107 (2008).

R. LEWIS

**PROJECTIVE VERSE.** The term derives from the title of Charles Olson's 1950 *manifesto, one of the most influential statements in Am. *poetics since World War II and widely reprinted as a starting point for innovative poetry in the period. Olson and his associates advanced an alternative to what they saw as the dominance of an unambitious and formally conventional poetry that ignored the creative possibilities opened up by the modernist experimentation of, among others, Ezra Pound, W. C. Williams, and Louis Zukofsky. Projectivism's organicist view of poetic form can be traced back to S. T. Coleridge's distinction between "Form as proceeding" and "Shape as superinduced," and in Am. poetry to R. W. Emerson's call for "not meters but a meter-making argument" and the claims of Walt Whitman's Preface to the first ed. of *Leaves of Grass*. (The masculine nature of the projective verse trad. has become one object of scholarly analysis.)

In Olson's essay, projective verse rests on a set of distinctions between a "closed" poetry, shaped by the dictates of page-based traditional forms, and an "open" or "projective" poetry, shaped by the individual poet's breath and physiology. Olson goes on to develop the "kinetics," "principle" and "process" of projective verse, or "composition by field." He uses "kinetics" as a metaphor for the poem as a "high energy-construct," a means for transferring the poem's originating energy from writer to reader. The central "principle" of projective verse as a poetics is the subsequently influential—though not, in itself, original—aphorism that "form is never more than an extension of content." The "process" by which this kinetic transfer occurs is that "one perception must immediately and directly lead to a further perception," in a mobile line and syntax through which the poem establishes its own form in the exploratory, unpredictable act of writing. The poet must be wary of *similes, adjectives, and description generally as slowing this process and be willing to break *syntax open, since it imposes restrictive logical conventions on thought. The implications of projective verse for *prosody include intensive attention to details of *sound (at the syllabic level) and to the *rhythm of the breath-based line. Olson extends his formal concerns into the epistemological realm in arguing that projective verse involves a "stance toward reality" that he labels "objectism": "getting rid of the lyrical interference of the individual as ego," an ethically antihumanist move to take poetry beyond mere self-expression into more culturally capacious realms of statement. A final, crucially influential component of Olson's essay emphasizes the opportunities afforded by the typewriter for experimenting with the space of the page, as an active formal element in the poem and as a score for *performance and an indicator of the poet's breath patterns.

Following Olson's essay, *projective verse* became a catchall term for a wide range of poetic practices extending into the 1970s (and in some cases, well beyond) that emphasized organic form, orality, breath and the body, and the poetics of process. Variations on these principles mark the poetics of many poets associated with the New American Poetry (the nexus of poets gathered in the Allen anthol. of the same name), and esp. those of the *Black Mountain school. Thus, the term played a central role in the so-called anthol. wars of the early 1960s, the poetic debates between the early postmodernists of the New American Poetry and their more stylistically and intellectually traditional contemporaries. At the same time, there is no definable group of poets that can be accurately referred to as the projectivist "school," despite some critics' use of that term.

The practice of projective verse among this postwar generation of experimental poets proved important for the Language poets, who were influenced by the formal adventurousness and cultural ambition of their predecessors but felt compelled to counter the oral emphasis within their work and its implications of unmediated *presence. *Language poetry moves away from the projective emphasis on voice and embodied presence toward a poetry that foregrounds the materiality of lang., of the written word rather than the oral; that sees poetic form as constructed rather than organic and expressive; that takes the poet's voice as more multiple and socially embedded than projectivism sometimes allows for; and that takes as a central subject questions of reference that projectivism often leaves unexamined. Thus, projective verse has left a powerful legacy not simply through its own practice but also in the questions it has provoked for later poets.

*See* AVANT-GARDE POETICS, COMPOSITION BY FIELD, OPEN FORM.

■ *The New American Poetry 1945–1960*, ed. D. Allen (1960); *Poetics of the New American Poetry*, ed. D. Allen and W. Tallman (1973)—for statements of poetics in the projectivist trad.; S. Paul, *Olson's Push* (1978); P. Christensen, *Charles Olson* (1979); J. Breslin, *From Modern to Contemporary* (1984); S. Fredman, *The Grounding of American Poetry* (1993); C. Olson, *Collected Prose*, ed. D. Allen and B. Friedlander (1997); J. Osborne, "Black Mountain and Projective Verse," *A Companion to Twentieth-Century Poetry*, ed. N. Roberts (2003); R. Blau DuPlessis, *Blue Studios* (2006)—for projective verse and gender.

E. BERRY; A. GOLDING

**PROMOTION.** Because of our tendency to perceive alternation in lines of metrical verse, a reader/performer will often sense that an unstressed word or syllable carries a *beat, or *ictus, thus fulfilling a metrical expectation ("this is pentameter" or "these are four-beat lines"). Such "promotion" of an unemphasized element

to one carrying a beat is experienced when two conditions exist. Derek Attridge describes the first condition in this way: "An unstressed syllable may realize a beat when it occurs between two unstressed syllables."

E.g., in William Wordsworth's tetrameter line "I wandered lonely as a cloud" the "as," between the unstressed syllables "-ly" and "a," remains unemphasized but is promoted to realize the expected meter. A prose expectation would likely produce only three emphases, on "wan-," "lone-," and "cloud," with "ly-as-a" run together. When Hamlet refers to "The slings and arrows of outrageous fortune," metrical expectation of a pentameter will promote "of" to a beat—though without a trace of added emphasis.

A second condition of the Attridge rule for promotion is this: "An unstressed syllable may realize a beat when it occurs with a line-boundary on one side and an unstressed syllable on the other." This kind of promotion is often noted at the endings of metrical lines, as when, in John Milton's *Paradise Lost*, Beelzebub finds himself "Here swallowed up in endless misery," with an unemphatic "-ry" completing the pentameter; or when Matthew Arnold concludes the first stanza of "Dover Beach" with a promoted "in," as the waves bring "The eternal note of sadness in."

Promotion thereby allows unemphasized syllables to help convey, within a familiar metrical pattern, Wordsworth's casual wandering, Hamlet's equal balancing of weapons and fate, and both a fallen angel's and Arnold's spiritless resignation.

■ Attridge, *Rhythms*; Carper and Attridge.

T. CARPER

**PRONUNCIATION** (Lat. *pronuntiatio*, "delivery"), one of the five *canons of cl. rhet. originating in Aristotle's *Rhetoric* and formalized in Roman treatises on rhet. Originally, *pronunciation* was distinct from *elocutio* (*style). *Pronunciation* treats the manner of vocal and physical execution: *pitch, *accent, volume, phrasing, posture, gesture, and countenance. Cl. categories in Ren. rhetorical and pedagogical theories were inherited largely from Cicero and Quintilian. Around the turn of the 13th c., Matthew of Vendôme in *Ars versificatoria* (ca. 1175) and Geoffrey of Vinsauf in *Poetria nova* (ca. 1210) applied Ciceronian rhetorical theories to poetry. Countenance, gesture, and voice conditioned med. audiences' reception of recited poetry, creating an experience of the literary text different from that of mod. readers (Rowland). In the early 16th c., *pronunciation* more frequently describes poetry's oral delivery; see Stephen Hawes's *The Pastime of Pleasure* (pub. 1509).

Despite theories of "proper" Eng. and other pronunciations since before the 15th c., pronunciation was unsystematically theorized as a rhetorical category through the Ren. In *The Book Named the Governor* (1531), Thomas Elyot remarks on Eng. neglect of the canons of elocution and pronunciation. By the middle of the 16th c., the study of physical delivery concentrates on the ling. physiology of pronunciation; Thomas Wilson in *The Art of Rhetoric* (1553) foregrounds the role of the "tongue, or voice" in audible and persuasive speaking.

Wilson recommends that youth, or those otherwise lacking a "strong" natural voice, imitate exemplary pronunciation to attain fluency in standard Eng. *The Art of Rhetoric* emphasizes pedagogical training and methods of remediating pathologies of pronunciation resulting from an accent, nonstandard articulation, or improper use of countenance or gesture. Another treatise on poetry in the Eng. vernacular, George Puttenham's *Arte of English Poesie* (1589), prescribes that Eng. be pronounced in the fashion of the court or within London and a 60-mile radius. The *Arte* instructs the courtier in counterfeiting, or dissembling in both speech and countenance, to obtain royal favor.

*Pronunciation* retains its cl. meaning in the *Defence of Poesy* (1595), where Philip Sidney uses it to denote the delivery of public oration. By the 17th c., however, *to pronounce* often means simply to speak, though it frequently refers to poetic utterance. The 17th c. sees the rise of orthoepy, the study of correct pronunciation; John Wilkins is a leading figure in this domain, as in other areas of early mod. ling. science. Elocution increasingly subsumes pronunciation, as Obadiah Walker's *Some Instructions Concerning the Art of Oratory* (1659) includes pronunciation, *recitation, and action under discussion of "elocution." Also in the 17th c., the study of gesture branches from that of oral delivery, though it still couches its analysis in the lang. of verbal pronunciation: see John Bulwer's *Chirologia: or, the Natural Language of the Hand* and *Chironomia: or, the Art of Manual Rhetoric* (1644). In the 18th c., pronunciation no longer designates a category of rhetorical delivery encompassing gesture but is limited to its mod. sense of "sounding of the words" (see Thomas Sheridan, *Lectures on Elocution*, 1762). Sheridan was a prominent figure of the 18th-c. elocutionary movement, so named because *pronunciation* had by then acquired specialized meaning in studies of orthoepy and phonation. The division between pronunciation and gesture holds in rhet. (see John Mason's *An Essay on Elocution: or, Pronunciation*, 1757), as well as dramatic performance: Charles Gildon's *The Life of Mr. Thomas Betterton* (1710) characterizes the complementarity of "pronunciation" or "utterance" and "gesture" or "action" as the actor's "eyes and hands" are the "Principal Helps of Pronunciation." John Walker's *Elements of Elocution* (1799) defines *pronunciation* "in its most limited sense" as the utterance of discrete words but, "in its largest sense," as words in "connection" with one another; thus, the domain of pronunciation overlaps with that of elocution or the sounding of sentences and longer discourse. (See also Walker's *Critical Pronouncing Dictionary* [1791], a genre that continues through the 20th c.) Early 20th-c. phonetic and phonological analyses of Eng. pronunciation intended for pedagogical training include Daniel Jones's *The Pronunciation of English* (1909), which uses phonetic transcription of literary examples to model the sounds of standard Eng. *Rhyme in poetry has also provided evidence of original vocal pronunciation in earlier periods (Wyld). For a historical phonology of Eng. in the 16th and 17th cs., see Dobson's two-volume study (1968).

*See* DICTION, INVENTION, LINGUISTICS AND POETICS, PROSODIC FEATURE ANALYSIS OF VERSE, PROSODY, RHETORIC AND POETRY, SOUND, STYLE.

■ H. Wyld, *Studies in English Rhymes from Surrey to Pope* (1923); D. Jones, *The Pronunciation of English*, 4th ed. (1963); E. J. Dobson, "Milton's Pronunciation," *Language and Style in Milton*, ed. R. D. Emma and J. T. Shawcross (1967); and *English Pronunciation, 1500–1700*, 2d ed., 2 v. (1968); B. Rowland, "*Pronuntiatio* and Its Effect on Chaucer's Audience," *Studies in the Age of Chaucer* 4 (1982); M. Moran, *Eighteenth-Century British and American Rhetorics and Rhetoricians* (1994); R. Cloud, "Shakespear Babel," *Reading Readings: Essays on Shakespeare Editing in the Eighteenth Century*, ed. J. Gondris (1998); C. Marimón Llorca, "La especificidad pragmática de la *pronuntiatio* y su incidencia en la construcción del discurso retórico," *Quintiliano: Historia y actualidad de la retórica, I–III*, ed. T. Albaladejo et al. (1998); A. Calvo Revilla, "Rasgos de oralidad en la *Poetria Nova* de Godofredo de Vinsauf: Un acercamiento a la memoria y a la *actio / pronuntiatio*," *Revista de teoría de la literatura y literatura comparada* 9–10 (1998–99); J. García Rodríguez, "Aproximación a la retórica del siglo XVII: Actio y pronuntiatio en el Epítome de la eloquencia española," *Alazet* 14 (2002); M. Worley, "Using the *Ormulum* to Redefine Vernacularity," *The Vulgar Tongue*, ed. F. Somerset and N. Watson (2003); T. Skouen, "The Vocal Wit of John Dryden," *Rhetorica* 24 (2006); G. E. Bentley Jr., "Blake's Pronunciation," *SP* 107 (2010).

R. LEWIS

**PROPHETIC POETRY.** The prophet-poet claims to be the conduit of supernatural *inspiration to a human audience. The source of this inspiration may be immediate (e.g., a direct message from some divine being) or the last link in a causal chain of inspiration that has passed through a series of prophets. Prophetic poetry need not be prescient but must appear as a kind of public quotation: it claims to be the utterance not of the poet but ultimately of some supernatural author.

Much of the mod. tendency to see poetry as an expression of "inspiration"—as "prophetic" in a broad sense—arises from the influence of Robert Lowth's examination of biblical metrical arrangement in *De sacra poesi Hebraeorum* (1753). Before Lowth, the Western poetic trad. had seen the essence of poetry as alternately mantic and nonvatic. Early Heb. commentators were often at pains to separate true prophecy from mere poetry: the two were distinct genera, with different social functions and often separate modes of graphic and metrical arrangement. However, Plato's *Ion* evidenced a strong view in ancient Greece that poetry arose only from inspiration and possession, a view embodied in the verse of the Pythian oracle and still evident at the time of Pindar (see FUROR POETICUS).

When the Gr. and Hebraic trads. filtered separately into Christianity and, ultimately, Eng.-lang. poetics, tension between the concepts of poetry and prophecy continued. If Philip Sidney could, in the *Defence of Poesy,* look to the Roman *vates and Gr. oracles as ideal poetic models, less than a century later Thomas Hobbes could see prophetic poetry as at best pagan pretension, a position countered by John Milton's expression of prophetic vocation in *Paradise Lost*. However, Lowth argued that biblical prophecy was, in effect, a species of poetry with principles of arrangement lost in antiquity; consequently, poetry and prophecy had "one common name, one common origin, one common author, the Holy Spirit." Lowth's identification of poetry and prophecy became firmly established in the Eng. poetic trad., contributing to the romantic conception (epitomized in William Blake) that all "true" poetry must be of inspired origin. This attitude has found sporadic expression in the 20th and 21st cs. in (e.g.) *surrealism, *Black Mountain poetry, and *Beat poetry, but these various influences have entailed Western *poetics with at least the vestigial notion that all poetry, even poetry not self-consciously invoking the prophetic trad., contains traces of the divine.

The Eng. poetic trad. is one of many that associate the social function of *poet and prophet. The Sanskrit *kavi* was a poet in contact with an unseen world, a conception also found in parts of ancient China. The Ar. *kuhhan* and *shu'ara* were poet-oracles of supernatural knowledge wielding an authority later expressed in the Qur'an's sura of "the Poets." India's *Bhakti* and Persia's *Sufi* poetry both self-consciously insert themselves into a prophetic trad., while Native Am., Polynesian, Af., Central Am., and Siberian cultures have also productively conflated the roles of poet and prophet at various times.

*See* AEOLIC; AFFLATUS; AFRICA, POETRY OF; ARABIC POETRY; CHINA, POETRY OF; CLASSICAL POETICS; GREEK POETRY; HEBREW POETRY; HEBREW PROSODY AND POETICS; INDIA, POETRY OF; INDIGENOUS AMERICAS, POETRY OF THE; INSPIRATION; MYTH; ROMANTICISM; SUBLIME.

■ N. K. Chadwick, *Poetry and Prophecy* (1942); J. Gonda, *The Vision of the Vedic Poets* (1963); M. Roston, *Prophet and Poet* (1965); E. M. Santí, *Pablo Neruda: The Poetics of Prophecy* (1982); *Poetic Prophecy in Western Literature*, ed. J. Wojcik and R.-J. Frontain (1984); G. Nagy, *Greek Mythology and Poetics* (1990); *Poetry and Prophecy*, ed. J. L. Kugel (1990); J. Halifax, *Shamanic Voices* (1991); *Poetry and Prophecy*, ed. J. Leavitt (1997); I. Balfour, *The Rhetoric of Romantic Prophecy* (2002); *Prophet Margins*, ed. E. L. Risden, K. Moranski, S. Yandell (2004).

M. BARR

**PROSE POEM.** The extreme conventions of 18th-c. Fr. neoclassicism, with its strict rules for the differentiation of poetry from prose, are to be blamed—or, depending on one's point of view, thanked—for the controversially hybrid and (aesthetically and politically) revolutionary genre of the prose poem. With its oxymoronic title and its form based on contradiction, the prose poem is suitable to an extraordinary range of perception and expression, from the ambivalent (in content as in form) to the mimetic and the narrative or anecdotal. Let's come down clearly on the side of gratefulness, since the prose poem occasions a rap-

idly increasing interest. Its principal characteristics are those that would ensure unity even in brevity and poetic quality even without the line breaks of *free verse: high patterning, rhythmic and figural repetition, sustained intensity, and compactness. The short form is a sure model here; otherwise, the prose poem merges with the essay.

Generally speaking, the prose poem represents a field of vision, only to be, on occasion, cut off abruptly. Emotion is contracted under the force of ellipsis, so deepened and made dense. The rhapsodic mode and what Charles Baudelaire called the "prickings of the unconscious" are, in the most interesting examples, combined with the metaphoric and the ontological. So the prose poem aims at knowing or finding out something not accessible under the more restrictive conventions of verse (Beaujour). It is frequently the manifestation of a willfully self-sufficient form characterized above all by its brevity. It is often spatially interesting (D. Scott). For some critics, it is necessarily intertextual (Riffaterre); for others, politically oriented (Monroe). It is, in any case, not necessarily "poetic" in the traditional sense of the *lyric and can even indulge in an engaging wit.

The prose poem is usually considered to date from Aloysius Bertrand's *Gaspard de la Nuit* (1842), though he was writing prose poems earlier, and to be marked by heavy traces of Fr. *symbolism and conditioned by the stringency of the Fr. separation of genres. Among its antecedents are the poeticized prose verses of the Bible (see VERSET), of cl. and folk lyrics, and of other foreign verse; the poeticized prose of such romantics as Chateaubriand and the prose passages of William Wordsworth's *Lyrical Ballads*; as well as the intermixtures of verse and prose in Maurice de Guérin's "Le Centaure," Ludwig Tieck's *Reisegedichte eines Kranken*, and Charles Augustin Sainte-Beuve's *Alexandrin familier*. Characteristically, it was the romantics who came to the defense of this hybrid form: Victor Hugo's plea for the *mélange des genres* (mixture of genres) in his preface to *Cromwell* is the natural counterpart to Jules-Amédée Barbey d'Aurevilly's apology for the prose poem. A case could be made for certain manifestos (see MANIFESTO) as the natural extension of the prose poem into a form fitted for display.

Perhaps the most celebrated example of the prose poem is Baudelaire's *Petits Poèmes en prose*, or *Le Spleen de Paris* (begun 1855, pub. 1869), in which he pays tribute to Bertrand for originating the genre. Baudelaire's texts can complicate *figuration to the point of "figuring us" as reader (Johnson, in Caws and Riffaterre). His "Thyrse" offers female poetic windings and arabesques around an upright male prose pole as the highly eroticized primary metaphor of mixing, while the *Petits poèmes* themselves are at once anecdotal and intimate, to the point of mixing the self with the subject. Arthur Rimbaud's *Illuminations* (written 1872–76) celebrate with extraordinary intensity the emergence of poems from less intimate matter, a newness dynamic in its instantaneity, yet the precursor of the aesthetic of suddenness practiced by Hugo von Hofmannsthal in his *Philosophie des Metaphorischen*—the speed of the metaphor is an "illumination in which, for just a moment, we catch a glimpse of the universal analogy"—and by imagists such as Ezra Pound. Rimbaldian confusion of first- and third-person perspective ("the lyric process of undergoing oneself and the more properly novelistic business of mapping out a behavior," according to C. Scott) sets up, together with his notational rapidity, a kind of vibratory instant. Stéphane Mallarmé's *Divagations* (begun 1864, pub. 1897) with their intricate inwindings of metaphor, Comte de Lautréamont's *Chants de Maldoror* (the first canto in 1868, the rest published posthumously in 1879), lush with a sort of fruity violence, André Gide's *Nourritures terrestres* (Earthy eats, 1897), and Paul Claudel's *Connaissance de l'est* (Knowing the East, 1900), nostalgic and suggestively pictorial, lead to Paul Valéry's *Alphabet* (1912), whose form has been compared to what Valéry later calls, speaking of the dual function of discourse, "the coming and going between two worlds" (Lawler).

Elsewhere, the prose poem flourishes with a different cast: early on, in Switzerland, with Salomon Gessner (*Idylls*, 1756); in Germany, with Novalis and Friedrich Hölderlin, then Stefan George, R. M. Rilke, Franz Kafka, Ernst Bloch, and recently, in former East Germany, Helga Novak; in Austria, Hofmannsthal, Peter Altenberg, and Alfred Polgar; in Belgium, Emile Verhaeren; in England, Thomas De Quincey, Thomas Lovell Beddoes, Oscar Wilde, and the imagists; in Russia, Ivan Turgeynev and the Rus. futurists, esp. Velimir Khlebnikov; in Italy, the cubo-futurists such as F. T. Marinetti (see FUTURISM); in Spain, Gustavo Adolfo Bécquer, Juan Ramón Jiménez, and Luis Cernuda; in Latin America, recently, Jorge Luis Borges, Pablo Neruda, and Octavio Paz; and in Denmark, J. B. Jacobsen.

Modernist writing as practiced in France after symbolism and postsymbolism increasingly problematized the genre; the so-called cubist poets Max Jacob, Pierre Reverdy, and Blaise Cendrars (see CUBISM) each gave a particular slant to the prose poem, emphasizing respectively its "situation," its strangely reticent irresolution, and its simultaneous perceptions. The Fr. surrealists Paul Éluard, André Breton, and Robert Desnos provide a rich nostalgia and revelatory illumination by means of a startling juxtaposition of images; Gertrude Stein's *Tender Buttons* reaches a height of the lyric and the everyday held in tension, taking its energy from the androgynous. Among recent 20th- and 21st-c. Fr. poets, René Char, Saint-John Perse, and Francis Ponge, and then Yves Bonnefoy, Jacques Dupin, and Michel Deguy prove the sustained vigor of the genre, proved equally in the U.S. (after Walt Whitman, of course), by such prose poets as James Wright, Robert Bly, W. S. Merwin, Russell Edson, John Ashbery, and John Hollander, and such Language poets (after Stein and W. C. Williams) as Charles Bernstein.

*See* RHYME-PROSE, VERS LIBRE, VERSE AND PROSE.

■ V. Clayton, *The Prose Poem in French Literature of the Eighteenth Century* (1936); G. Díaz-Plaja, *El poema en prosa en España* (1956); S. Bernard, *Le Poème en prose de Baudelaire jusqu'à nos jours* (1959); M. Par-

ent, *Saint-John Perse et quelques devanciers* (1960); U. Fülleborn, *Das deutsche Prosagedicht* (1970); D. Katz, "The Contemporary Prose Poem in French: An Anthology with English Translations and an Essay on the Prose Poem," *DAI* 31 (1970), 2921A; R. Edson, "The Prose Poem in America," *Parnassus* 5 (1976); U. Fülleborn, *Deutsche Prosagedichte des 20. Jahrhunderts* (1976); *The Prose Poem: An International Anthology*, ed. M. Benedikt (1976); C. Scott, "The Prose Poem and Free Verse," *Modernism*, ed. M. Bradbury and J. McFarlane (1976); D. Lehman, "The Marriage of Poetry and Prose," *DAI* 39, 8A (1979): 4938; K. Slott, "Poetics of the 19th-Century French Prose Poem," *DAI* 41, 3A (1980): 1075; J. Holden, "The Prose Lyric," *Ohio Review* 24 (1980); D. Keene, *The Modern Japanese Prose Poem* (1980); B. Johnson, *The Critical Difference* (1981), chap. 3; S. H. Miller, "The Poetics of the Postmodern American Prose Poem," *DAI* 42 (1981): 2132; R. E. Alexander, "The American Prose Poem, 1890–1980," *DAI* 44, 2A (1983): 489; *The Prose Poem in France: Theory and Practice*, ed. M. A. Caws and H. Riffaterre (1983)—13 essays on Fr. and Eng.; D. Scott, "La structure spatiale du poème en prose," *Poètique* 59 (1984); U. Fülleborn, *Deutsche Prosagedichte vom 18. Jahrhundert bis zur letzten Jahrhundertwende* (1985); S. H. Miller, "John Ashbery's Prose Poem," *American Poetry* 3 (1985); M. Perloff, *The Dance of the Intellect* (1985); D. Wesling, *The New Poetries* (1985), chap. 6; M. S. Murphy, "Genre as Subversion: The Prose Poem in England and America," *DAI* 46 (1986): 1932A; R. G. Cohn, *Mallarmé's Prose Poems* (1987); J. Kittay and W. Godzich, *The Emergence of Prose* (1987); J. Monroe, *A Poverty of Objects: The Prose Poem and the Politics of Genre* (1987); R. Silliman, *The New Sentence* (1987); J. Simon, *The Prose Poem as a Genre in 19th-Century European Literature* (1987); S. Fredman, *Poet's Prose*, 2nd ed. (1990); M. Delville, *The American Prose Poem: Poetic Form and the Boundaries of Genre* (1998); *Great American Prose Poems: From Poe to the Present*, ed. David Lehman (2003).

M. A. CAWS

## PROSE RHYTHM

I. Overview
II. Classical and Medieval
III. Modern

**I. Overview.** In the Western trad., and in the simplest and most general sense, all prose has *rhythm, at least insofar as lang. itself has shorter or longer rhythms of phonological, morphological, and syntactic structuring. Since *rhythm* etymologically means "flow," almost any prose that seems to flow may be said to be rhythmic. But if rhythm is taken to refer to grammatical elements—members of equal size or length—disposed at equal distances or delivered with equal or approximately equal timing, then *prose rhythm* refers to prose wherein rhythmic effect is deliberately sought. Such *ornament or *figuration has been cultivated in nearly all cultures with written records, some of these trads. being very extensive and of great antiquity.

Prose that cultivates rhythmical effects comes in two species: either the patterns are smaller and exact or else larger and inexact. Small and exact prose rhythm strictly controls the number of syllables and patterns of quantity or stress. This includes Gr. and Lat. prose, which is quantitative (see QUANTITY) and regulates the last few syllables of syntactic periods (known as the "terminal cadence" or "clausula"); med. Lat. *accentual verse apparently derived from these Gr. and Lat. accentual forms. Large and inexact "prose rhythm" includes most mod. forms of rhythmical prose, which employ syntactic *parallelism, *anaphora, and *amplification. Such prose has been referred to as periodic, balanced, or Attic style.

Cl. rhet.'s chief purpose was to give figuration to prose utterances in order to enhance recognition, persuasion, and memory. The resultant inventory of sound and syntactic shapes are the familiar rhetorical figures, variously classed as *scheme and *trope. Once a syntactic form was established, such as "reversal" in *chiasmus or "reiteration" in parallelism, it only remained to require an equal number of syllables in each member to make the sequence rhythmical, exactly as in verse. In the terminology of cl. rhet., syntactic phrases or clauses equal in shape or structure are treated under the figure parison; those equal in number of syllables and quantitative pattern are treated under *isocolon.

The most common method for identifying varieties of prose rhythm is by breaking down sentences or phrases into syllables, then analyzing quantitative or accentual patterns by poetic *scansion. Since the structure of any lang. generates rhythmic patterns, statistical analysis can take prosodic patterns as the ground against which to measure variation. Scholars have taken texts, portions of texts, and speech forms as possible grounds for analysis, with mixed results.

**II. Classical and Medieval.** Prose rhythm was an accepted part of ancient rhetorical theory. Major texts include Aristotle's *Rhetoric*, Demetrius's *On Style*, Dionysius's *On Literary Composition*, Quintilian's *Institutio oratoria*, and Cicero's *De oratore*. Aristotle conflates rhythm with periodic structure and treats the rhythm of the whole sentence with that of merely the sentence end or clausula. Neither of these issues is distinguished by subsequent theorists, though they emphasize variety and closely analyze sentence rhythm to produce few regularities other than the marked patterning of the closing syllables (the *cadence) of the syntactic period. Marking the end of the sentence with one of only a small class of fixed patterns is one of the most distinctive laws of rhythmical structure in prose.

The ancients believed the Sophist rhetorician Thrasymachus of Chalcedon (459–400 BCE) was the first to cultivate quantitative patterns in Gr. prose, as did Gorgias and Demosthenes later. Plato uses them in *Phaedrus* but also objects to and parodies them in the *Symposium*. After the shift from quantity to accent, Gr. and Byzantine writers cultivated accentual clausulae or cursus. Cicero took the Gr. quantitative system into Lat. and developed a clear system of preferences

for clausulae. His example provoked wide imitation by Seneca, Suetonius, Nepos, Quintilian, Pliny, and Tertullian. Cicero's clausulae also showed significant coincidences of accent and quantity. Purely accentual clausulae first appear in the work of the Afs. Minucius and Cyprian in the early 3d c. CE, and by the late 4th c. accentual clausulae supplanted quantitative clausulae altogether. In the 11th c., professional scribes of the Roman Curia took up cursus as an obligatory stylistic feature for papal correspondence. Cursus have three main types:

(1) *planus* or plain: ´— — ´—
(2) *tardus* or slow: ´— — ´— —
(3) *velox* or fast: ´ — — — —´—

which, despite their accentual form, continued to be described by their older quantitative terms: (a) *dactyl plus *spondee, (b) dactyl plus dactyl; (c) dactyl plus dispondee. The two features of cursus are Blass's Law (three or more short syllables in a row are not allowed) and Meyer's Law (the number of syllables between accents must be a multiple of two). Petrarch and Dante were familiar with the cursus, and it is used as evidence to deny Dante's authorship of a famous letter to Can Grande (prefixed to the *Paradiso* espousing the fourfold method of interpretation).

**III. Modern.** Strict or clausular prose rhythm did not survive the Middle Ages. Ren. interest in prose developed a full range of rhetorical figuration, as in euphemism and *mannerism, though strict or clausular prose rhythm was not practiced. The most influential rhythmical prose to emerge from the Ren. was that of the Authorized Version of the Bible (1611), which sought to import parallelism, the chief prosodic feature of Heb. verse, into Eng. prose. Deriving from this fountainhead is the trad. of 17th-c. devotional prose, as in John Donne's sermons and Thomas Browne's essays. Many writers after the Ren. employ prose rhythm to great effect, though there is no common critical model for its analysis. During the middle and late 19th c., when scholars were obsessed with defining and codifying cl. and med. prose rhythm, anglophone poets such as Alfred, Lord Tennyson, H. W. Longfellow, and Matthew Arnold experimented with cl. meters in Eng., and their results were often accused of sounding too much like prose. Examples of rhythmic phrases appear in much 19th-c. nonfictional and fictional prose (e.g., "the crystallizing feather-touch; it shook flirtation into love" from George Eliot's *Middlemarch*). Most scholarly accounts of 20th-c. prose rhythm focus on James Joyce's *Ulysses* and his engagement with the literary historian George Saintsbury, whose *History of Prose Rhythm* (1912) scanned prose according to cl. scansion, a practice imitated by contemp. scholars.

■ L. Havet, "La Prose métrique de Symmaque et les origines métriques du cursus," *Bibliothèque de l'École des Hautes Études* 94 (1892); T. Zielinski, *Das Clauselgesetz in Ciceros Reden* (1904); Meyer; H. Bornecque, *Les Clausules métriques latines* (1907); A. C.

Clark, *The Cursus in Medieval and Vulgar Latin* (1910); P. Fijn van Draat, *Rhythm in English Prose* (1910); C. Zander, *Eurhythmia* (1910–14); Saintsbury, *Prose*; A. C. Clark, *Prose Rhythm in English* (1913); T. Zielinski, *Der constructive Rhythmus in Ciceros Reden* (1914); P. Fijn van Draat, "Voluptas Aurium," *Englische Studien* 48 (1915); R. L. Poole, *Lectures on the History of the Papal Chancery* (1915); W. M. Patterson, *The Rhythm of Prose* (1916); M. W. Croll, "The Cadence of English Oratorical Prose," *SP* 16 (1919); H. D. Broadhead, *Latin Prose Rhythm* (1922); K. Polheim, *Die lateinische Reimprosa* (1925); A. W. De Groot, *La Prose métrique des anciens* (1926); L. Laurand, *Études sur le style des discours de Cicéron* (1928), and "Bibliographie du *cursus* latin," *REL* 6 (1928)—also 12 (1934); F. Novotny, "État actuel des recherches sur le rythme de la prose latine," *Eus supplementa* 5 (1929); M. G. Nicolau, *L'Origine du cursus rythmique et les débuts de l'accent d'intensité en latine* (1930); A. Schiaffini, "La tecnica della prosa rimata nel medio evo latino," *Studi romanzi* 21 (1931); N. Denholm-Young, "The Cursus in England," *Oxford Essays in Medieval History*, ed. F. M. Powicke (1934); D. Seckel, *Hölderlins Sprachrhythmus* (1937); F. Di Capua, *Il ritmo prosaico nelle lettere dei Papi nei documenti della cancellaria romanza dal IV al XIV secolo* (1937–46); A. Classé, *The Rhythm of English Prose* (1939); F. Di Capua, *Fonti ed esempi per lo studio dello "stilus curiae romanae" medioevale* (1941); M. Schlauch, "Chaucer's Prose Rhythms," *PMLA* 65 (1950); P. F. Baum, *The Other Harmony of Prose* (1952); M. M. Morgan, "A Treatise in Cadence," *MLR* 47 (1952); W. Schmid, *Über die klassische Theorie und Praxis des antiken Prosarhythmus* (1959); G. Lindholm, *Studien zum mittellateinischen Prosarhythmus* (1963); L. P. Wilkinson, *Golden Latin Artistry* (1963); A. Primmer, *Cicero Numerosus: Studien zum Antiken Prosarhythus* (1968); T. Janson, *Prose Rhythm in Medieval Latin from the Ninth to the Thirteenth Century* (1975); H. Aili, *The Prose Rhythm of Sallust and Livy* (1979); Morier, "Prose cadencée"; T. Habinek, *The Colometry of Latin Prose* (1985); S. M. Oberhelman, "History and Development of the *Cursus Mixtus* in Latin Literature," *CQ* 82 (1988); R. G. Hall and M. U. Sowell, "*Cursus* in the Can Grande Epistle: A Forger Shows His Hand?" *Lectura Dantis* 5 (1989); Lausberg; M. Gooch, "Saintsbury's Anglo-Saxon in Joyce's 'Oxen of the Sun,'" *Journal of Modern Literature* 22 (1999); R. Graff, "Prose versus Poetry in Early Greek Theories of Style," *Rhetorica* 23 (2005).

T.V.F. BROGAN; M. MARTIN

**PROSIMETRUM.** A text composed in alternating segments of prose and verse. The *prosimetrum* is widely attested in both Western and Eastern lits. and apparently appears worldwide. Typically, the verse portions serve as lyric, emotive, or personal insets within a philosophical or narrative frame, often with connectives between prose and verse sections; but, in fact, there are several varieties still not thoroughly understood: the definitive cross-cultural study remains to be written.

Formal variables include whether the sections alternate regularly or irregularly; whether the number and form of the sections are controlled by a larger architectonic structure (i.e., the principle of mixture); whether the one form is a paraphrase of the other and whether by the same author and whether at the same time; whether there is more than one narrator or, if two, whether both speak in both modes or are kept separate; whether the content of the two modes is similarly kept separate (e.g., philosophical versus lyric); whether differing subgenres (philosophy, fictional narratives, drama) differ categorically in structure; and whether variety of meters is required in the verse sections.

In Chinese, prosimetric form is manifested in the *fu* (*rhyme-prose; see CHINA, POETRY OF) and in some 10th-c. *bianwen* (narratives; see CHINA, POPULAR POETRY OF); in Japanese, it is used for the collection of mythical hist. known as the *Kojiki* (ca. 712 CE); and in Sanskrit, it is a major component of Vedic narrative poetry, as evidenced in the *Mahābhārata*, the long dynastic *epic containing the *Bhagavad-Gītā*, among many others. Indeed, some have seen the *lyric itself as emergent from these emotive or sung inserts in epic narratives.

In the West, the earliest exemplars are the satires of the Gr. writer Menippus (3d c. BCE.), from which developed the Lat. *satura* (later "satire," but originally "medley") and the *Satyricon* of Petronius; extant too are four Gr. texts in a ms. of the 2d c., two of which seem to be romances. Both *satire and the prose *romance retained long association with prosimetric form. But the central text that established the popularity of the prosimetrum for the Middle Ages was Boethius's *De consolatione philosophiae* (early 6th c.), five books of alternating, numbered segments called "Metrum" and "Prosa" and set within a larger numerological structure (see NUMEROLOGY). The *Consolation* moves from emotive complaint to metaphysical contemplation: the male prisoner-narrator and female personified Philosophy speak both the first two metra and the last prosa. Polymetry in the verse segments is emphasized (some two dozen meters). The influence of Boethius's prosimetrum on the later Middle Ages was extensive and prolonged, even though subsequent translators and imitators did not all retain the prosimetric format: the OE *Meters of Boethius* attributed to King Alfred, the OF trans. by Jean de Meun, and Chaucer's *Boece* are entirely in prose; the Occitan *Boëce* (11th c.), the Anglo-Norman *Roman de fortune*, and the one other surviving ME version are entirely in verse.

Also influential, though less so, was Martianus Capella's *De nuptiis philologiae et mercurii* (*The Marriage of Philology and Mercury*), an odd work in nine books wherein the Seven Liberal Arts become the bridesmaids at the wedding of Learning and Eloquence: here the verse insets are arranged irregularly. The prosimetrum was revived in the 12th c. in Lat.—as instanced in Bernardus Silvestris's *De universitate mundi* (ca. 1150) and *Cosmographia*, which return to regular alternation of segments and free use of both modes by all characters, and Alan of Lille's *De planctu naturae*, a complaint on sodomy—and then the vernaculars. Very similar in form are the Occitan *\*vidas* and *\*razos*, biographical story collections incl. poems meant to be sung; these, along with Boethius, influenced Dante. Dante's *Vita nuova* (1292–93), 31 poems introduced and connected with prose, and *Convivio* (1304–7), esp. interesting in that one narrator recounts all, the verse segments being, he says, from his own earlier writings. Giovanni Boccaccio's *Ameto* (1342) provides a frame story in which seven stories are told and seven songs sung, a structure leading directly to the *Decameron* and Chaucer, where the regular alternation of segments is lost. But it is retained in the pastoral romance, esp. Jacopo Sannazaro's *Arcadia* (1485; 12 prose segments and 12 verse) and Philip Sidney's *Arcadia* (1590, 1593), with its inset eclogues and experiments in Eng. quantitative verse (see QUANTITY).

Fr. also explored the prosimetrum: from the 13th c., there are 13 extant OF versions of Boethius, some of them prosimetric. The anonymous author of the 13th-c. *Aucassin et Nicolette* calls his text a *\*chante-fable* or song-story, showing that the verse segments had moved from lyric into song. This devel. made natural the extension of prosimetric form into med. drama, where inset songs, if occasional, provided relief from dialogue and narrative in prose. Other Fr. prosimetra include Jean Froissart's *Prison amoureuse* (ca. 1372) and Guillaume de Machaut's *Voir dit* (1361–65), where prose letters and love poems are set in a verse frame.

Other med. lits. knew the prosimetrum: the Ar. *maqāmāt*, which originated around 1000 CE; the Celtic epic *Taín*; some of the Icelandic sagas; and the Turkish epic known as *The Book of Dede Korkut*. Snorri Sturluson's *Edda* (ms. early 14th c.) is in prose but includes a 100-meter catalog of Icelandic verse forms. The relations of prose and verse in the Middle Ages were more fluid than today (Curtius); within the range of mixed forms, the prosimetrum is but one hybrid form among several, e.g., rhythmical prose (see PROSE RHYTHM) and rhyme prose. A related genre is the *opus geminatum* (twinned work), written once in prose and then versified or vice versa, the prose for recitation in church, the verse for private meditation. This takes its origin in the rhetorical doctrine of *conversio* or paraphrase and emerges in Caelius Sedulius's *Carmen paschale* and *Opus paschale* of the mid-5th c., followed by Aldhelm (*De virginitate*, 60 chs. of prose transformed into a *Carmen de virginitate* of 3,000 hexameters), Bede, and Alcuin among others.

■ H. R. Patch, *The Tradition of Boethius* (1935); Curtius; H. Scheible, *Die Gedichte in der "Consolatio philosophiae" des Boethius* (1972); E. Walter, *Opus geminatum* (1973); M. Dillon, *Celts and Aryans* (1975); D. Bartoňková, "Prosimetrum, The Mixed Style, in Ancient Literature," *Eirene* 14 (1976); R. A. Dwyer, *Boethian Fictions* (1976); P. Godman, "The Anglo-Latin *Opus geminatum*," *Medium Ævum* 50 (1981); C. D. Eckhardt, "The Medieval *Prosimetrum* Genre," *Genre* 16 (1983); Norden 2.755 ff.; J. Kittay and W. Godzich, *The Emergence of Prose* (1987), ch. 4; B. Pabst, *Prosimetrum* (1994); M. Witzel, "Sarama and the Panis: Origins of Prosimetric Exchange in Archaic India,"

*Prosimetrum*, ed. J. Harris and K. Reichl (1997); *Il prosimetro nella letteratura italiana*, ed. A. Comboni and A. Di Ricco (2000); E. Johnson, "Chaucer and the Consolation of *Prosimetrum*," *Chaucer Review* 43 (2009).

T.V.F. BROGAN

**PROSODIC FEATURE ANALYSIS OF VERSE.** A system of metrical analysis developed by Karl Magnuson and Frank G. Ryder in the late 1960s and early 1970s that applies the principles of Prague School distinctive-feature analysis in phonology to metered verse to identify those features that are prosodically (metrically) distinctive. In phonology, distinctive features represent minimal differences between sounds expressed as polar extremes of the same category or the presence or absence of a particular quality. Similarly, the identification of prosodic features is based on the occurrence or nonoccurrence of different types of two-syllable sequences relative to the underlying meter. If two prosodic word-types (e.g., *holding/behold*) occur in mutually exclusive environments, they are in complimentary distribution and differ in at least one prosodically distinctive feature. Magnuson and Ryder found that certain features occur most often in metrically prominent positions, others in nonprominent positions (labelled x and o, respectively, below). The former support or "affirm" the meter in prominent positions and disrupt or "disaffirm" it in nonprominent positions, the latter the reverse.

Magnuson and Ryder originally identified four prosodically distinctive features in Ger. verse and applied them to Eng. verse: *stress* (ST) and *word onset* (WO) affirm prominent positions of the meter, while *prestress* (PS), assigned to all syllables preceding a stressed syllable within the same orthographic word, and *weak* (WK) affirm nonprominent positions. The presence or absence of a feature is indicated by a + or − sign:

| | | o | x | o | x | o | | x | o | x | o | | x |
|---|---|---|---|---|---|---|---|---|---|---|---|---|---|
| | | Making a famine where abundance lies (Shakesp.) | | | | | | | | | | | |

| | | | | | | | | | | | | | |
|---|---|---|---|---|---|---|---|---|---|---|---|---|---|
| ST | + | − | − | + | + | − | | − | − | + | + | − | + |
| WO | + | − | + | + | − | | + | + | − | − | + |
| PS | − | − | − | − | − | | − | + | − | − |
| WK | − | + | + | − | + | | + | + | − | + | − |

Whereas the "weak" feature (later redefined by Chisholm in lexical terms) is redundant for Eng. (i.e., all +ST syllables are −WK and vice versa), it is distinctive for Ger. On the basis of these features, Magnuson and Ryder formulated prosodic rules that account for the presence or absence of all two-syllable sequences in Ger. and Eng. verse.

At the core of the theory is the concept of a binary relation between contiguous positions of the meter such that the poet's selection in the second position may be constrained as a result of his selection in the first. This principle of loss and recovery of metrical equilibrium places constraints on filling a metrical position when the feature filling the preceding position disrupts the meter. If, e.g., the ST feature occurs in a position that disrupts the meter, it must be followed by at least one feature (ST in the following examples) that "affirms" the meter in the immediately following position:

```
    o   x       o x o x o x   o    x
Thy youth's proud livery, so gazed on now
(Shakespeare)
```

```
    o   x     o x o   x o x o
Die Nacht schuf tausend Ungeheuer ( J. W. Goethe)
```

On the basis of prosodically distinctive features, Magnuson and Ryder demonstrate that the metrical relation x-o is more strictly constrained than the relation o-x in both Eng. and Ger.: words such as Eng. *holding* and (much less frequently) Ger. *dränge* can occur in the relation o-x, whereas words such as *behold* and *gedrängt* are prohibited from occurring in the relation x-o.

Prosodic distinctiveness varies in different langs.: because of the much higher frequency of monosyllables in Eng., WO is distinctive for Ger., but not for Eng. verse.

■ R. Jakobson, G. Fant, and M. Halle, *Preliminaries to Speech Analysis* (1965); N. S. Trubetzkoy, *Principles of Phonology*, trans. C. A. M. Baltaxe (1969); K. Magnuson and F. G. Ryder, "The Study of English Prosody," *CE* 31 (1970), and "Second Thoughts on English Prosody," *CE* 33 (1971); D. Chisholm, "Lexicality and German Derivational Suffixes," *Lang&S* 6 (1973); K. Magnuson, "On the Distinctiveness of the Word in German and English Prosody," *Husbanding the Golden Grain*, ed. L. Frank and E. George (1973); and "Rules and Observations in Prosody," *Poetics* 12 (1974); D. Chisholm, *Goethe's Knittelvers* (1975); R. Wakefield, *Nibelungen Prosody* (1976); D. Chisholm, "Generative Prosody and English Verse," *Poetics* 6 (1977); B. Bjorklund, *A Study in Comparative Prosody* (1978); C. Küper, *Sprache und Metrum* (1988); B. Bjorklund, "Iambic and Trochaic Verse: Major and Minor Keys?" *Phonetics and Phonology*, vol. 1, ed. P. Kiparsky and G. Youmans (1989); D. Chisholm, "Prosodic Aspects of German Hexameter Verse," *PoT* 16 (1995); and "Metrical Structures as Stylistic Features in German Literary Prose" *Meter, Rhythm and Performance*, ed. C. Küper (2002).

D. H. CHISHOLM

**PROSODY** (Gr. *prosodia*, originally the musical part of a song, "tune"; later, the marking of accents; Lat. *accentus*, "song added to speech").

I. Introduction
II. Elements, Structure, System
III. Analysis
IV. Prose and Free Verse
V. Linguistic Prosody and Literary Studies

**I. Introduction.** Traditionally, prosody is the study of measurable structures of *sound in language and in poetry. Linguistic prosody is concerned with describing and explaining the structure and function of the suprasegmentals in lang., those aspects—pitch, duration, loudness, and juncture—that produce the contoured streams of sound by which the *segments* are voiced.

Literary prosody was traditionally the study of *prose rhythm and *versification. From the 19th c., prosody began a slow expansion toward inclusion of other levels of organization, as verse experimentation, reactions to metricality, and the rise of *free verse shifted importance to qualitative sound (see below), which increasingly performed many of the binding functions of verse design formerly associated solely with *meter. In addition, the visual patterning of verse joined prosody, as the visible aspects of printed poems also performed prosodic functions (see TYPOGRAPHY, VISUAL POETRY). With generative and functional ling., prosody has now come to include the hierarchy of structures, up to the *stanza, built from nonphonological elements affected by the phonological system (see Ross 2008). Since poetry is a verbal design using linguistic material, literary prosody has benefited enormously from the concepts, categories, and analytic approaches of ling. An objective attention to the lang. object, detailed and overarching, enriches the literary critic's apprehension and understanding of aesthetic elements, forms, and processes that work with and on lang. and form.

**II. Elements, Structure, System.** Prosody belongs to the phonological system, the lowest order system interacting with and affecting the morphological, syntactical, and semantic systems. An influential theory, articulated by Paul Kiparsky (in Fabb et al.), regards prosody in all langs. as characterized by four interactive systems: (1) periodicity, or repetitive patterning in alternating stresses by a set of processes that maintains the periodic return; (2) constituency, or grouping of stresses into feet—strong/weak or weak/strong—depending on the lang.; (3) maximal articulation, or hierarchical grouping into several levels of larger groups, each comprised of smaller bundles, e.g., syllables into words, words into phrases, and (in poetry) feet into half lines, half lines into lines, lines into couplets, and so on; and (4) even distribution, or balancing the phrase or line, by regulating where heavy and light units may be positioned to maintain a sense of equal order (see Lerdahl and Jakendoff for an opposing theory based on a musical metaphor instead of on the constituency metaphor). These systems include the lang. of poetry. Ross (2008) has recently combined these four systems to yield two prosodic structuring systems: sectioning and arraying. The first includes the first three of Kiparsky's systems, and the second speaks to the fourth, wherein the entire system of a poem contains an array of prosodies (elements functioning in and as patterns) distributed in an organized fashion for aesthetic texture and effects. Recalling earlier critics' metaphor for poetic texture as woven tapestry, Ross includes the qualitative structures (segmentals) and sees them as a set of overlays the analyst can look at one by one, group by group, as he or she lays them down over others. Boundaries are then the intersections, the "cusps" of rhythmic shape where the features relevant to poetic meaning and effect are made prominent. These are the areas of density that rise into prominence in the reader's perception to become salient features for interpretation (see Ross).

In addition, Gil and Shoshany and others regard pragmatic and rhetorical features as part of the prosodic system at the higher hierarchical levels.

Sound is produced by the breathing and vocal apparatus of the physical body and is felt as vibration and resonance for semantic, emotive, and aesthetic effects. Temporal and measurable, sound is energy in the form of waves. It becomes meaningful in lang. when perceived by users as consisting of elements and structures of the phonological system. As temporal, the structural units (e.g., feet, phrases) have perceptual *isochrony (though not actual isochrony) and *rhythm. The more rhythmic a passage of lang., the greater the tendency toward isochrony, with metered verse bearing the closest perceptual equivalence among units and groupings of units. The tendency toward isochrony is a feature of lang., but in poetry, the more highly regular the recurrence of units from which a pattern is built, the closer the tendency toward approximation. While some theorists disagree that isochrony operates in lang. testing of perception by actual hearers gives evidence that perception counts as much as actual phonic measurement. What is important is the perception of isochrony, the felt equivalence of time, as in music. Similarly, with sound in written texts, what counts is the perceptual experience of sound "heard" by readers of poetry and rhythmic prose as an approximate equivalence of timing with which a performance's phrasing works as the baseline for expansive expression (Lehiste; Bolinger).

Segmentals are the smallest units of lang., the *phones* or actual sounds represented somewhat inaccurately in Eng. by the letters or *graphemes* (though the *graph* is important in some visual prosody). Phones are the important elements of the segmental patterns in poetry; they make up the figures of speech that are repetitions of sound for the sake of sound (e.g., *alliteration, *assonance, *rhyme), permitting a range of rhythmic expressivity. Suprasegmentals are the components that comprise the measurable production of sound, because they exist in time: loudness (intensity, volume), *duration (length), *pitch (tone or fundamental frequency), and juncture (markers of boundary and linkage among segments and groupings). They are the phonological components of lang., working together in various ways in the different langs. to give shape—contour, grouping, and boundary. They are said to be *over* (*supra*) the segments because they are the sound occurring when the various groupings of linguistic segments are spoken. They produce coherence, make meaningful distinctions, foreground information, and indicate where emotional interest lies. The three components of temporal sound—pitch, loudness, and duration—are most often found in combination, but in varying degrees in the different langs. and situations. One of these three components is characteristically dominant in a lang.: e.g., Japanese keeps syllabic length even and the pitch range narrow so as not to be an influence over the syllable, but tonic pitch, as in Chinese, may distinguish the words that otherwise sound and are written the same. By contrast in Eng. a different aspect of pitch—relative change in frequency—is meaningful. Sound prominence in langs. like Eng. is also called *accent or stress. Syllables in the nonprominent range are called *unaccented* or *unstressed*. Stress, still the term most frequently used in common parlance, is perhaps the least accurate because of its more general meaning as emphasis or prominence and because of its long association with loudness, which was mistakenly thought until 50 years ago to be the most important factor in realizing prominence. Instead, pitch change (not *a* pitch) is the most frequent and reliable indicator of prosodic prominence, occurring in 99 percent of cases of prominent syllables, with loudness and/or length also a factor though not always both (see Fry 1955; Ladefoged). Like musical notes, pitch change in lang. can be heard as rises and falls from the pitch level on which nonprominent syllables occur within the range of the specific speaking voice. Loudness and length also change relative to the nonprominent level of voicing, but these can be artificially produced in such a way as to throw the perception off, without a true change in prominence.

When distributed among nonprominent syllables, prominence shapes the sound of lang. The more regular the distribution of peaks, the more rhythmic the lang., with meter defining the extreme of greatest regularity. The suprasegmental system places some syllables into a nonprominent range and thrusts other syllables onto peaks, but a highly rhythmic system will tend to draw the linguistic prominence system into the overlaid poetic system, causing prominence peaks to be promoted or demoted in level (see PROMOTION and DEMOTION). This is the reason meter, which counts only two levels of prominence (strong and weak), and rhythm, which counts more, are distinguished by literary analysts. Most agree that there are four perceptual levels of stress in Eng.: primary, secondary, tertiary, and nonprominent (see RELATIVE STRESS PRINCIPLE; Chomsky and Halle; Halliday; see Bolinger on three-level perceptual system; Gates 1987 on why a three-level system is not always adequate). The prosodic shape that is spread over groupings is called either an accentual, a stress, a prominence, or an intonation *contour*, depending on what aspects of the prosodic system are under consideration. Chomsky and Halle termed the contour unit the *phonological phrase*, aligning it with the syntactic phrase, which they believed motivated prominence. The "phrase" is now often thought of as akin to the musical phrase, which distributes the tonal shape of an information unit (Halliday), or as a unit of emotional interest as recognized by the speaker (Bolinger). More recently, there is agreement that information is sectioned into "chunks" because the brain appears to process it that way, in both the making and receiving modes (Ross 2008). The chunks present the way the speaker is thinking about the information's importance as foreground and background. A chunk may have up to five or six prominence peaks, a number which appears to correspond to the brain's processing limit. This limit matches that noticed by Chomsky and Halle, and it matches the upper number of peaks in poetic lines in the world's langs.—besides the pentameter, the line has a strong tendency to group into three and three (*hexameter), three and four (*fourteener), etc. But in poetry, these chunked linguistic groupings coexist with the rhythmic groupings, working sometimes within, sometimes across the established rhythmical set of a poem. The cross-structuring creates potentials for vocal realizations that open up a multivalent, polysemantic verbal design. The dual systems' additional key functions are to indicate poetic *genre; give pleasure; provide cohesion; compose structure; and support, undercut, inflect, and reflect meaning (see ICONICITY, TONE).

The fourth suprasegmental—juncture—gives boundary to syllables, words, phrases, "chunks" and at the same time indicates how they are to be joined. Silence is the aspect of juncture most relevant to poetic analysis, emerging, for instance, in and around *caesura, line ending (pause, *enjambment), and word boundaries that cut across the perception of foot boundaries (e.g., *The form was steady*, in iambic pentameter, where *steady* crosses the fourth into the fifth iambic foot). In visual prosody, juncture is often the most prominent of the suprasegmentals, with spacing indicating silence, lack, drama; appearing instead of *punctuation; and functioning in all manner of expressive, rhetorical, and semantic ways.

Qualitative prosody refers to phonic (vs. phonemic) cohesion: e.g., repetition of consonantal sounds, vowel sounds, and groupings of sounds from two phones to syntactic units (e.g., *br, str, I saw the, out of the, down from the, Turning and turning*). Qualitative sound patterning is rhyming in its broadest sense (Kiparsky in Fabb, et al., for a componential view of rhyme). Whereas quantitative sound patterns are paralinguistic, operating to organize meaning for coherence *over* a segment of lang., qualitative sound patterns function to provide cohesion among units and groups *within* a text. Ross (1999) views these two types as "interpenetrating" prosodies. And while linguistic sound systems function largely to gather and focus meaning and tone for communication, when density of features is high enough to foreground lang. itself (Jakobson's *poetic function), rhythm works to restrain linear forward progression, thrusting the mind back on repetition, drawing the reader/auditor away from sense into the flow that is rhythm itself. It is the nature of poetic lang. to move against and counteract the semantic system, and it is the principal characteristic, function, and effect of poetry (Jakobson; Kristeva—both in Cook).

**III. Analysis.** What literary prosody keeps to the fore is the dialectic between rhythm and code (i.e., between semiotic and symbolic, felt and rational modes). When prosody is left out of poetic analysis and interpretation, what is left is impoverished as aesthetic crit.

The tension created by the pull of a lang. system's features and functions against the way a verbal artist uses, exploits, and pressures the system has been regarded for the past 100 years as the main subject of the study of literature *as literature*. Variety in prominence levels that pressures the ideal metrical pattern, along with other pressuring features, has been valued since *New Criticism and other varieties of *formalism described and privileged tensive forces in its valuations. While the theory wars and debates over the *canon in the postmod. period gave pause to aesthetic study in the U.S., cognitive stylistics, which studies the way poetic elements, structures, and functions are processed in the mind, has generated a body of research from data on actual readers' understanding that demonstrates how the tensions are created by the semantic associations that all words carry. Words with similar sound features and similar sets of semantic features will create convergence, while words with similar sound features and very different semantic features will create divergence, with a range of lower to higher between these extremes (Tsur). Tension results from aggregates of features that possess varying degrees of sound, semantic, and/or syntactic clash: e.g., in W. B. Yeats's "The Wild Swans at Coole" the rhyming words "rings" and "wings" converge in terms of their grammatical status as nouns, but the shapes of the two objects are divergent: rings are circular and stable, wings are blade-shaped and associated with motion. So there is a satisfaction of similarity in sound and grammar, but also an emotional intensity in the small dissimilarity of the initial phones and the greater clash of the two objects drawn into semantic relation. The lines are thereby texturally entwined, so that they produce an emotional intensity higher than the normative emotional interest a prominence word acquires in the normative intonation/information system of the Eng. lang. (Hollander on "mounting" prominence; Gates 1987 on "surmounting" prominence; Bolinger on the heightening of emotion when the normal pitch range is exceeded).

It could be said that Yeats is making "rings" (in two senses, phonic and semantic) of qualitative sound in end and internal rhymes:

> And scatter wheeling in great broken rings
> Upon their clamorous wings.

The -*ing* of *rings* circles back and also chimes with *wheeling*, and again with *wings*. *And, scat-,* and *clam-* make another cohesive pattern, and *Up-* and -*ous* yet another, holding the lines in close relation through assonance, creating the beauty and pleasure of ordering, as in music, while also, some might argue, imitating the repetitive circling of which the lines speak. There is, however, tension as well, in that only some of the syllables rhyme; and in the differing parts of speech drawn together in rhyme. The open vowels, *a* in *great* and *o* in *open* and *clamorous,* work contrastively, in tension, with the *e* and short *i* sounds to round and open out the sonorous quality of the lines, giving an expansiveness to accompany the repeated closing in of circularity. Morphological, syntactic, and semantic features brought into sound cohesion both unify and clash, initiating perceptual experiences that serve to signal the poetic function of play, of genre, of pleasure, of tension, of meaning (see Tsur; Ross 1999).

**IV. Prose and Free Verse.** Since lang. has prosody, prosody may be artistically shaped in prose as well as in verse (see VERSE AND PROSE). Ancient Gr. and Rom. orators elaborated at length on how to use rhythm for persuasion in grammar, music, and rhet. (Cicero, Quintilian, Augustine; Aristotle cautioned against too much rhythm; see RHETORIC AND POETRY). The marks of punctuation, capitalization, and paragraphing originated as a graphic system to mark writing for oral performance. Med. writers continued to develop prose rhythm as part of rhet. (e.g., *cursus in ars dictaminis* and *ars praedicandi*); rhetorical handbooks included prosody through the 19th c.; and prosodic patterning continues to be taught in some schools as part of prose composition, though without the elaborations of the earlier centuries. Mod. free verse makes use of prose rhythm, beginning with Walt Whitman's 1855 ed. of *Leaves of Grass*, which, according to one theory, marked breath pauses with dots in the manner recommended by 19th-c. rhetorical manuals (Hollis). In the eds. following the first, Whitman dropped the dot-marking system and used the standard system of punctuation to mark off rhythmic units (Gates 1985). Emily Dickinson used the dash for many junctures in lieu of standard punctuation early on. Stéphane Mallarmé, follower of Whitman's practice and an inventor of the *prose poem, declared that prose did not exist—"There is alphabet, and then there are verses which are more or less closely knit, more or less diffuse. So long as there is a straining toward style, there is versification." Some 20th-c. poets created systems of punctuation for distinctive prosodic styles, in some cases omitting it entirely (e.g., e. e. cummings, W. S. Merwin in some of his work). W. C. Williams wrote in a system of the prose unit he called at first the *variable foot, later revised to the relative measure, which produced cultural, social, and poetic meanings and effects (Cushman 1985; Steele; Gates). The prosodies of dramatists and fiction writers have also been examined as part of their prose styles (e.g., G. B. Shaw, Henry James, Ernest Hemingway, Thomas Wolfe, Annie Dillard). Varieties of free verse range from highly cadenced prose to mixed meters (the majority of free verse today) to prosodies made of the appearance or sounds of graphs and phonemes. The prose poem is without the highly regular prosody of meter, but its qualitative and rhythmic qualities provide the cohesion that meter and narrative give in other genres. The resources of mod. ling. make intensive analysis of these forms possible. As in poetry but in lesser degree, the regularity of prosodic styling in prose and free verse promotes *attention to the qualitative and quantitative sound systems, enhancing perceptual attention, heightening *emotion, and working the felt experience to some effect.

**V. Linguistic Prosody and Literary Studies.** Ling. continues to develop highly sophisticated understandings of prosody. The structuralists' failed attempt to discover a universal system has been recuperated by a somewhat different inquiry into the possibility of constructing a universal prosody in the form of a set of obligatory and optional rules for poetries in all langs. As with the structuralist project, the effort is yielding detailed knowledge about lang. and poetic systems, whether or not the end goal can be reached. While the literary historian and critic need not know ling. prosody theory, drawing from the systematic knowledge of linguists changes what can be analyzed, and so greatly assists interpretation. To ignore the functions and effects of the sound system is to risk less complete, less insightful understanding.

■ D. Fry, "Experiments in the Reception of Stress," and "Duration and Intensity as Physical Correlates," *Journal of the Acoustical Society of America* 28 (1955); P. Ladefoged, *Elements of Acoustic Phonetics* (1962); Chatman; Chomsky and Halle; M. K. Halliday, *Halliday: System and Function in Language*, ed. G. Kress (1976); I. Lehiste, "Isochrony Reconsidered," *Journal of Acoustics* 5 (1977); C. Hartman, *Free Verse: An Essay on Prosody* (1980); Attridge, *Rhythms*; C. Hollis, *Language and Style in "Leaves of Grass"* (1983); F. Lerdahl and R. Jackendoff, *A Generative Theory of Tonal Music* (1983); D. Gil and R. Shoshany, "On the Scope of Prosodic Theory," *Discussion Papers, Fifth International Phonology Meeting*, ed. W. Pfeiffer and J. Rennison (1984); Hollander; S. Cushman, *William Carlos Williams and the Meanings of Measure* (1985); R. Gates, "The Identity of American Free Verse: The Prosodic Study of Whitman's 'Lilacs'," *Lang&S* 18 (1985); D. Bolinger, *Intonation and Its Parts* (1986); *The Linguistics of Writing: Arguments between Language and Literature*, ed. N. Fabb, D. Attridge, A. Durant, C. MacCabe (1987); R. Gates, "Forging an American Poetry from Speech Rhythms: Williams after Whitman," *PoT* 8, nos. 3–4 (1987); T. Steele, *Missing Measures* (1990); R. Gates, "T.S. Eliot's Prosody and the Free Verse Tradition: Restricting Whitman's 'Free Growth of Metrical Laws'," *PoT* 11, no. 3 (1991); R. Tsur, *Toward a Theory of Cognitive Poetics* (1992); S. Cushman, *Fictions of Form in American Poetry* (1993); D. Gil, "'Il pleut doucement sur la ville': The Rhythm of a Metaphor," *PoT*, 14, no. 1 (1993); H. Gross, *Sound and Form in Modern Poetry*, 2d ed. (1996); G. Cooper, *Mysterious Music: Rhythm and Free Verse* (1998); C. Scott, *The Poetics of French Verse: Studies in Reading* (1998); J. Ross, "Beauty—How Hopkins Pied It," *Language Sciences* 21 (1999); V. Shemtov, "Metrical Hybridization: Prosodic Ambiguities As a Form of Social Dialogue," *PoT* 22, no. 1 (2001); J. Cook, *Poetry in Theory* (2004); T. Wharton and D. Wilson, "Relevance and Prosody," *Journal of Pragmatics* 38, no. 10 (2006); M. Hurley, "The Pragmatics of Prosody," *Style* 41, no. 1 (2007); J. Ross, "Structural Prosody," *Cognitive Poetics* 1, no. 2 (2008).

R. WINSLOW

**PROSOPOPOEIA** (Gr. *prosopon*, "face," "person," and *poiein* "to make"). The speech of an imaginary person.

A term still used for *personification—the attribution of human qualities to animals or inanimate objects—to which it is closely allied. Pierre Fontanier, however, argues, prosopopoeia "must not be confused with personification, apostrophe or dialogism . . . [since it] consists in staging, as it were, absent, dead, supernatural or even inanimate beings. These are made to act, speak, answer as is our wont" (Riffaterre 1985). As a means of making a speech "vivid" or lively, Fontanier's definition agrees with that of the Tudor rhetoricians, who placed prosopopoeia in the list of figures that included *prosopographia, characterismus, ethopoeia* (which together give us our notions of fictional portraiture); mimesis of gesture, pronunciation, and utterance; and *dialogismus* or *sermocinatio*, by which an imaginary person is given the ability to speak. In antiquity, *prosopopoeiae* were school exercises in which writers took on the persona of a famous historical or mythological figure in a composition with the end of exhibiting his character (cf. Quintilian 3.8.49). At times, however, both rhetorical and poetic theoreticians use prosopopoeia far more expansively to indicate the vivid presentation of something absent or imaginary before the eye and ear. The example given by Quintilian (9.3.89), "Avarice is the mother of cruelty," shows that prosopopoeia exists as a *trope at the basic levels of *metaphor or axiom. Likewise, P. de Man calls prosopopoeia "the master trope of poetic discourse" (1986), because it posits "voice or face by means of language" (1984). Thus, prosopopoeia operates like a mask and is analogous to any adoption of *persona. To address an imaginary person as if present engages the figure of *apostrophe; however, J. Douglas Kneale insists that prosopopoeia is the more appropriate term. Historically, apostrophe is defined as a "turning away" from the primary audience; thus, Kneale argues, unified addresses, such as William Blake's "The Sick Rose," P. B. Shelley's "Ode to the West Wind," and John Keats's "Ode on a Grecian Urn," are all prosopopoeiae because they infer the possibility of reply.

■ Fontanier; P. de Man, "Autobiography as De-Facement," *The Rhetoric of Romanticism* (1984); P. de Man, "Hypogram and Inscription," *The Resistance to Theory* (1986); M. Riffaterre, "Prosopopoeia," *YFS* 69 (1985); J. D. Kneale, "Romantic Aversions: Apostrophe Reconsidered," *ELH* 58 (1991).

T.V.F. BROGAN; A. W. HALSALL; J. S. SYCHTERZ

**PROTEST POETRY.** Like the protest song, protest poetry goes by many names: *social, revolutionary,* or *topical poetry,* or occasionally *poetry of commitment,* or a subgenre of political poetry. However, two things distinguish protest poetry from other poems with political content: a connection to a social movement and a direct and obvious pertinence to events in the immediate present. The 1960s folk singer Phil Ochs's comment that "a protest song is a song that's so specific that you cannot mistake it for bullshit" might easily be extended as a valid if minimal definition for protest poetry as well. Given its formal and geographic diversity, the genre requires this theoretical simplicity; protest poetry can take the form of avant-garde manifestos, testimony, *elegies, or *ballads and is as widespread as the resistance to power that it seeks to articulate. It is primarily a 20th- and even late 20th-c. form; the term *poetry of social protest* was used to describe Af. Am. poetry of the 1920s, but *protest poetry* did not reach wide usage and was not often applied to poetry outside the U.S. until the 1960s.

Protest poetry's insistence on topicality has often meant a reduction in its staying power or longevity; once the topics have changed, it may be difficult for later readers to reconstruct the poem's full power. One great exception to this seems to be poems protesting war, which may indeed be the preeminent examples of the genre. Poetry opposing the glamour or glorification of war has a long hist.; one critic roots the trad. in a speech in book 2 of the *Iliad* by the commoner Thersites, who defies Agamemnon and the Gr. army by ridiculing their insatiable lust for spoils. Most accounts of antiwar poetry, however, identify World War I as the first conflict that elicited strong and general poetic opposition, although most of the widely read poetry opposing the war was written by returning soldiers. Later wars—particularly, for Americans, the Vietnam War—would be protested mainly by civilian poets. In either case, poems opposing a war are among the most famous and long-lasting protest poems and serve, to some degree, as models for other causes.

Protest poets share a common political orientation: they are unambiguously critical of the status quo and the dominant forces in society, and they call for change. This directness has caused some critics to analyze protest poetry in strictly functional terms—isolating its didactic, persuasive, or hortatory elements from any aesthetic considerations. Many have even dismissed the genre as propaganda or agitation, its lack of ambiguity obviating any need for the elaborate formal analysis normally brought to bear on lyric poetry. Other critics, particularly those studying Af. Am. poetry of the 20th c. or the Am. counterculture of the 1960s, have emphasized how the overtly rhetorical elements of the poems frequently depend on complex aesthetic effects and strategies.

Furthermore, the directness required of protest poetry does not preclude *figuration or even *allegory; what is necessary is merely clarity of reference. Little directness is lost, for instance, in the Soviet dissident Osip Mandelstam's "Stalin Epigram" (1933), despite the mannered and somewhat surreal imagery employed: "the huge laughing cockroaches on his top lip, / the glitter of his boot-rims" (trans. W. S. Merwin).

In part, this clarity comes from protest poetry's necessary connection to a social movement, but as one can see from the example of Mandelstam, who died as a prisoner in 1938, this connection is obviously contingent on the degree to which a social movement is capable of forming and voicing its concerns publicly; this may be more difficult under repressive governments than in comparatively open societies. Yet what drives protest poems is the palpable sense of speaking collectively and of addressing a broad social concern, even if it is articulated through the lang. of individual experience or idiosyncratic vision. One might think here of the poem "Incident" (1925), by the *Harlem Renaissance poet Countee Cullen. Depicting a moment when, as a young boy, Cullen smiled at a white boy of similar age and was rebuffed with a racial slur, the connection to the national context of deep and unthinking prejudice needed no explicit invocation. Or one might think of Allen Ginsberg's comic *apostrophe to "America" (1956), a shambolic indictment of America's excesses, foibles, and sins. Through a disjointed slew of pop-culture references, semiparanoid questions that are not quite rhetorical ("Are you being sinister or is this some form of practical joke?"), and allusions to current events and to historical injustices, Ginsberg constantly defers any explicit or specific (realistic) recommendation or demand, emphasizing instead a diffuse personal disappointment, confusion, and frustration with Am. society. "There must be some other way to settle this argument," Ginsberg writes, but the poem withholds that kind of solution. As Ginsberg's poem shows, protest poetry can be only vaguely politically programmatic, diagnosing general social ills without proposing identifiable policies or actions. Many other protest poems however, can be quite direct, specifying discretely contextualized wrongs that can be redressed in an ostensibly straightforward manner—bring the troops home, end apartheid, and so on.

Many protest poems seek to achieve a balance between general or universal social problems and concrete injustices that give the poem immediacy and definition. Frequently, protest poems serve as elegies for the poet's actual or spiritual compatriots who have died in the service of the cause that the poem seeks to call attention to or defend. The Peruvian poet César Vallejo's "España, aparta de mí este calíz" ("Spain, Take This Cup from Me," 1937), for instance, laments the death of Pedro Rojas, a Republican soldier in the Sp. Civil War; Vallejo honors Rojas individually but also takes him as a symbol of the type of man who would give his life to fighting Fascism or any oppressive regime: "in his body a greater body, for / the soul of the world . . ." (trans. C. Eshleman and J. Rubia Barcia).

In recent years, the international success of *poetry slams has arguably renewed the vitality of protest poetry. While not all slam poetry is written or performed in protest, much of it is politicized, and the slams' competitive performance format has tended to encourage poets to express strong opinions and to draw in their audiences with topical references. Similarly, online communities have served to increase the circulation of poetry protesting the war in Iraq, environmental degradation, and other issues. Poetry also played a prominent role in the revolts of the Arab Spring of 2011, with many crowds using couplets from poets living and dead as rallying cries and street chants. Protest poetry's ability to fuse personal indignation with collective commitment and universal themes with highly specific events promises to keep the genre relevant and useful long into the future.

*See* AFRICAN AMERICAN POETRY; ASIAN AMERICAN POETRY; BEAT POETRY; BLACK ARTS MOVEMENT; CHANT; INDIGENOUS AMERICAS, POETRY OF THE; NUYORICAN POETRY; NUYORICAN POETS CAFÉ; OCCASIONAL VERSE; POLITICS AND POETRY; WAR POETRY.

■ **Anthologies:** *On Freedom's Side: An Anthology of American Poems of Protest,* ed. A. Kramer (1972); *Poetry from the Russian Underground: A Bilingual Anthology,* ed. J. Langland (1973); *Penguin Book of Spanish Civil War Verse,* ed. V. Cunningham (1980); *Poetry and Reform: Periodical Verse from the English Democratic Press, 1792–1824,* ed. M. Scrivener (1992); *The Wound and the Dream: Sixty Years of American Poems about the Spanish Civil War,* ed. C. Nelson (2002); *Poets against the War,* ed. S. Hamill (2003); *With an Iron Pen: Twenty Years of Hebrew Protest Poetry,* ed. T. Nitzan and R. T. Back (2009).

■ **Criticism and History:** J. Mersmann, *Out of the Vietnam Vortex:* (1974); *Soweto Poetry: Literary Perspectives,* ed. M. Chapman (1982); E. Wright, *Poetry of Protest under Franco* (1986); C. Nelson, *Repression and Recovery: Modern American Poetry and Cultural Memory, 1910–1945* (1989); F. Murray, *Aesthetics of Contemporary Spanish American Social Protest Poetry* (1990); B. Halker, *For Democracy, Workers, and God: Labor Song-Poems and Labor Protest, 1865–95* (1991); J. E. Smethurst, *The New Red Negro: The Literary Left and African American Poetry, 1930–1946* (1999); C. Nelson, *Revolutionary Memory: Recovering the Poetry of the American Left* (2001); M. A. Reid, *Black Protest Poetry: Polemics from the Harlem Renaissance and the Sixties* (2001); S. I. Morgan, *Rethinking Social Realism: African American Art and Literature, 1930–1953* (2004); J. E. Smethurst, *The Black Arts Movement: Literary Nationalism in the 1960s and 1970s* (2005); P. Metres, *Behind the Lines: War Resistance Poetry on the American Homefront since 1941* (2007); D. Loewen, *The Most Dangerous Art: Poetry, Politics, and Autobiography after the Russian Revolution* (2008); W. J. Miller, *Langston Hughes and American Lynching Culture* (2011).

A. SEAL

**PROVENÇAL POETRY.** *See* OCCITAN POETRY.

**PROVERB.** A traditional saying, pithily or wittily expressed. Proverbial expression is traditionally given to customs and legal and ethical maxims, *blasons populaires,* superstitions, weather and medical lore, prophecies, and other categories of conventional wisdom. Proverbs are among the oldest poetic expressions in Sanskrit, Heb., Germanic, and Scandinavian lits. "Learned" proverbs are those long current in lit., as distinct from "popular" trad. The former come into Western Eur. lit. both from the Bible and the Church fathers and from such cl. sources as Aristophanes, Theophrastus, Lucian, and Plautus. Erasmus's *Adagia* (1500) was instrumental in spreading cl. proverb lore among the Eur. vernaculars. The first Eng. collection was John Heywood's *Dialogue conteining . . . All the Proverbs in the English Language* (1546). But proverbs had been commonly used by OE and ME writers, particularly Chaucer. The Elizabethan delight in proverbs is evident in John Lyly's *Euphues* (1580) and in countless plays—as it is in Shakespeare. The genres of lit. in which proverbs frequently occur are the didactic (e.g., Chaucer's "Tale of Melibeus," Ben Franklin's *Way to Wealth*, and J. W. Goethe's "Sprichwörtliches"); the satirical (Alexander Pope); works depicting folk characters (Miguel de Cervantes's *Don Quixote*, J. R. Lowell's *The Biglow Papers*); works reproducing local or national characteristics (E. A. Robinson's "New England"); and literary tours de force (François Villon's "Ballade des proverbes").

What distinguishes proverbs from other figures such as idioms or *metaphors, Milner proposes, is their structure of "four quarters" in a "balanced relationship . . . both in their form and content." This configuration, evident in *Waste / not, / Want / not* or *Qui seme / le vent / Recolte / la tempete* (He who sows the wind shall reap the whirlwind), appears in ancient and non-Eur. as well as in mod. langs. Milner associates this balanced four-part form with Carl Jung's paradigm of the structure of the mind. Milner's analysis, however, is found inadequate by Dundes, who proposes the proverb as "a traditional propositional statement consisting of at least one descriptive element" that consists of "a topic and a comment." Proverbs that contain "a single descriptive element are non-oppositional," while those with two or more "may be either oppositional or non-oppositional." Dundes relates proverbial structures to that of *riddles; however, "proverbs only state problems in contrast to riddles which solve them." Dundes calls for empirical testing of his hypothesis with proverbs from various cultures.

*See* DIDACTIC POETRY, EPIGRAM, GNOMIC POETRY, PAROEMIAC, REFRÁN.

■ G. Bebermeyer, "Sprichwort," *Reallexikon* 4.132–51; W. Bonser and T. A. Stephens, *Proverb Literature: A Bibliography* (1930); A. Taylor, *The Proverb* (1931; reissued with index, 1962); B. J. Whiting, *Chaucer's Use of Proverbs* (1934); W. Gottschalk, *Sprichwörter des Romanen*, 3 v. (1935–38); G. Frank, "Proverbs in Medieval Literature," *MLN* 58 (1943); S. Singer, *Sprichwörter des Mittelalters*, 3 v. (1944–47); W. G. Smith and P. Harvey, *Oxford Dictionary of English Proverbs*, 2d ed., rev (1948); M. P. Tilley, *Dictionary of the Proverbs in England in the Sixteenth and Seventeenth Centuries* (1950); O.E.E. Moll, *Sprichwörterbibliographie* (1958); D. MacDonald, "Proverbs, *Sententiae*, and *Exempla* in Chaucer's Comic Tales," *Speculum* 41 (1966); H. Weinstock, *Die Funktion elisabethanischer Sprichwörter und Pseudosprichwörter bei Shakespeare* (1966); F. Seiler, *Deutsche Sprichwortkunde*, 2d ed. (1967); C. G. Smith, *Shakespeare's Proverb Lore*, 2d ed. (1968); G. B. Milner, "What Is a Proverb?" *New Society* (Feb. 6, 1969); and "De l'Armature des Locutions Proverbiales: Essai de Taxonomie Semantique," *L'Homme* 9 (1969); F. A. de Caro and W. K. McNeil, *American Proverb Literature: A Bibliography* (1970); *Oxford Classical Dictionary*, "Paroemiographers" (1970); M. I. Kuusi, *Towards an International Type-System of Proverbs* (1972); W. R. Herzenstiel, *Erziehungserfahrung im deutschen Sprichwort* (1973); P. Zumthor, "L'épiphonème proverbial," *Revue des sciences humaines* 163 (1976); A. Dundes, "On the Structure of the Proverb," *The Wisdom of Many: Essays on the Proverb*, ed. W. Mieder and A. Dundes (1981); R. W. Dent, *Shakespeare's Proverbial Language: An Index* (1981); W. Mieder, *International Proverb Scholarship: An Annotated Bibliography* (1982), *Supplement 1* (1990), *Supplement 2* (1992); R. W. Dent, *Proverbial Language in English Drama Exclusive of Shakespeare, 1495–1616: An Index* (1984); H. and A. Beyer, *Sprichwörterlexikon* (1985); *Prentice-Hall Encyclopedia of World Proverbs*, ed. W. Mieder (1986); W. Mieder, *American Proverbs: A Study of Texts and Contexts* (1989); B. J. Whiting, *Modern Proverbs and Proverbial Sayings* (1989); C. Cannon, "Proverbs and the Wisdom of Literature," *Textual Practice* 24 (2010).

D. HOFFMAN

**PSALM** (Gr. *psalmos*, "sacred song," "hymn"). A *psalm* is a sacred song or poem, conventionally describing the chapters of verse comprising the book of Psalms in the Heb. Bible. There are 150 psalms in the Heb. canon, with several more appearing in postbiblical sources such as the Dead Sea Scrolls. Several poems of the psalm type appear throughout the Bible, placed in the mouths of individual or collective prayers.

The poetic form of the psalm, at least as it has come down in the Western literary trad., is an invention of the ancient Near East. Often associated with ritual, the psalm was an important literary medium in Mesopotamia, Egypt, Hatti (Asia Minor), Ugarit (northern Syria), and, one may assume, despite the lack of surviving texts, in Canaan. The psalmists of ancient Israel took over forms from the surrounding cultures, adapting images, phrases, and even whole sequences of lines, but often with an evident polemical purpose: to attribute to the God of Israel those powers and beneficences that others claimed for their gods.

The book of Psalms as we have it is a product of the Second Temple (Hellenistic) period, when various, occasionally overlapping, collections of poems were assembled into a single anthol. The included psalms were composed over a period of several hundred years, the earliest going back to the beginning of the first millennium BCE. While certain diachronic shifts in lang. and poetics are discernible, far more striking are the continuities of *style and *convention. A parade example is the adaptation in Psalms 96 and 98 of an invocation of the "sons of the gods" to render homage to the Lord in the archaic Psalm 29: first, the mythological cohort is replaced by the peoples of the earth; then, the sacrifices they are bidden to offer are replaced by a musical fanfare.

The most common Heb. term for psalm—*mizmor*—denotes a song sung to musical accompaniment. The earliest Heb. name of the book is "The Book of Praisings," although the word for *praise—tehillah—*is used only intermittently and serves as the title of only one psalm. Other psalm headings ascribe the poem to King David, the legendary singer of Israelite trad., or to another figure; or they describe the occasion giving rise to the psalm; or they describe the musical mode in which the psalm is to be chanted. In spite of shared terminology, the psalter includes a wide variety of song types. The two predominant genres are praise and supplication, the latter of which features a complaint in need of remediation. Together these make up more than two-thirds of the book of Psalms. Many psalms, however, are of mixed genre and treat diverse situations. Even within one subgenre, there are striking differences in emphasis: a supplication may stress sin and contrition, the speaker's terror in a moment of acute distress, a reflective meditation on human transience, and much else. Among the other genres, such as wisdom meditations and historical reviews, most unusual are royal psalms, which are addressed not to the deity but to the king.

Some of the Heb. psalms are marked for liturgical performance on specified occasions or at specified moments in the temple rite. A view promulgated by Mowinckel and others holds that many psalms were used at an annual New Year festival, when the God YHWH was enthroned as king. There is both internal and external support for this hypothesis. Other psalms seem designed for individual recitation in moments of anguish or exaltation. The double nature of the psalms, alternately collective and personal, thankful and remonstrative, has been a source of their relevance both to the institutional and the individual lives of Jews and Christians ever since.

Poetically, the psalms exhibit a higher degree of convention, *cliché, and patterning than other genres of biblical poetry. A few psalms are cast as alphabetic *acrostics (see ABECEDARIUS). The reader encounters *refrains or refrain-like *repetitions, antiphonal voices, and *inclusio* or *envelope structures, in which the ending echoes *images, *motifs, or even whole phrases from the beginning (see RING COMPOSITION). The rich *imagery and other sophisticated tropes of Psalm 23 ("The Lord is my shepherd; / I shall not want" . . .) are not characteristic of the psalter as a whole.

Yet the beautifully arranged movements and the archetypal simplicity of style of the biblical psalms have made them a recurrent source of inspiration to later poets. With the resurgence of interest in the Bible after the Reformation, adaptations of psalms became widespread. In France, the versions of Clément Marot are particularly noteworthy. The apogee of psalmodic verse in Western langs. was reached in Ren. England, where the Bible in its new vernacular version became central to the culture. A variety of Eng. poets, from Thomas Wyatt and Philip Sidney to George Herbert and John Milton, tried their hand at metrical versions of psalms. In the signal instance of Herbert, the poet's original production owes something abiding in its diction, imagery, and sense of form to the model of the biblical psalms. Mod. Eng. poetry continues to evince a deep interest in psalms, as in the work of Dylan Thomas and in Donald Davie's *To Scorch or Freeze* (1988).

*See* HEBRAISM; HEBREW PROSODY AND POETICS; HYMN; LITURGICAL POETRY; PSALMS, METRICAL.

■ J. Julian, *A Dictionary of Hymnology* (1925); H. Smith, "English Metrical Psalms in the Sixteenth Century and Their Literary Significance," *Huntington Library Quarterly* 9 (1946); S. Mowinckel, *The Psalms in Israel's Worship*, trans. R. Ap-Thomas, 2 v. (1962); R. C. Culley, *Oral-Formulaic Language in the Biblical*

*Psalms* (1967); H. L. Ginsberg, "A Strand in the Cord of Hebraic Hymnody," *Eretz-Israel* 9 (1969); A. L. Strauss, *Bedarkhei hasifrut* (1970); C. Freer, *Music for a King* (1972)—Herbert and metrical psalms; L. Sabourin, *The Psalms*, rev. ed. (1974); C. Westermann, *Praise and Lament in the Psalms*, trans. K. R. Crim and R. N. Soulen (1981); C. Bloch, *Spelling the Word: George Herbert and the Bible* (1985); G. H. Wilson, *The Editing of the Hebrew Psalter* (1985); J. L. Kugel, "Topics in the History of the Spirituality of the Psalms," *Jewish Spirituality from the Bible through the Middle Ages*, ed. A. Green (1986); R. Alter, "Psalms," *Literary Guide to the Bible*, ed. R. Alter and F. Kermode (1987); E. L. Greenstein, "Psalms," *Encyclopedia of Religion*, ed. M. Eliade, v. 12 (1987); E. S. Gerstenberger, *Psalms, Part 1, with an Introduction to Cultic Poetry* (1988); W. L. Holladay, *The Psalms through Three Thousand Years* (1993); N. M. Sarna, *Songs of the Heart: An Introduction to the Book of Psalms* (1993); Y. Avishur, *Studies in Hebrew and Ugaritic Psalms* (1994); S. E. Gillingham, *The Poems and Psalms of the Hebrew Bible* (1994); P. D. Miller, *They Cried to the Lord: The Form and Theology of Biblical Prayer* (1994); B. Nitzan, *Qumran Prayer and Religious Poetry* (1994); H. J. Levine, *Sing unto God a New Song: A Contemporary Reading of the Psalms* (1995); S. Weitzman, *Song and Story in Biblical Narrative* (1997); H. Gunkel and J. Begrich, *An Introduction to the Psalms*, trans. J. D. Nogalski (1998); E. S. Gerstenberger, *Psalms, Part 2, and Lamentations* (2001); *The Book of Psalms: Composition and Reception*, ed. P. W. Flint and P. D. Miller (2005); K. L. Sparks, "Hymns, Prayers, and Laments," *Ancient Texts for the Study of the Hebrew Bible* (2005)—survey of extrabiblical parallels to Psalms with bibl.

R. ALTER; E. L. GREENSTEIN

**PSALMS, METRICAL.** The Heb. psalms were rendered into vernacular meters for two reasons, one participatory and the other prosodic, resulting in two trads. of metrical psalms.

Regarding participation, the regular rhythms and line lengths of metrical versions of the psalms promoted singing, whether in public worship or domestic devotions. Recognizing this, Martin Luther, John Calvin, and other Protestant reformers believed metrical psalms effective for spreading doctrine. Among Luther's first publications, metrical psalms quickly spread to France, the Netherlands, England, Hungary, Poland, and much of the rest of Europe. In Great Britain, psalms were translated into Welsh, Ir., Cornish, and Manx. Eng. Separatists emigrating to Am. colonies took metrical psalms along; *The Bay Psalm Book* (1640) was the first book printed in New England. Following Protestant practice, metrical psalms caught on later in Catholic countries, incl. Italy and Spain, though for private devotion rather than congregational singing. Ger. (Luther, Johann Walter), Dutch (Jan Utenhove), and esp. Fr. (Clément Marot, Théodore de Beza) metrical psalms used in churches were often written in sophisticated verse. In England, a simple *ballad meter (and close variants) became standard for singing-psalms, esp. following publication of the immensely popular psalter versified by Thomas Sternhold and John Hopkins (from 1562). George Sandys attempted a poetically more sophisticated metrical psalter (1648), but common meters dominated 17th-c. collections of metrical psalms, incl. the Scottish Psalter (1635) and that of Nahum Tate and Nicholas Brady (1696), which finally supplanted Sternhold and Hopkins in public worship. In the 18th c., Isaac Watts, Charles Wesley, William Cowper, and Christopher Smart transformed common- (now hymn-) meter psalms into fine poetry. Many functional but poetically bland metrical psalters were produced from the 18th to the 20th cs., and metrical psalms are still sung in Protestant churches, sometimes as *hymns.

Concerning *prosody, psalms were also translated into meter because of a misunderstanding about the nature of Heb. poetry. The defining technique of biblical *parallelism was not accurately described by Christian scholars until the 18th c.; but from the time of Jerome, psalms had been understood to be poems and (erroneously) the formal models for ancient Gr. and Roman poetry. Accordingly, poets felt the translated psalms should reflect such (notional) formal excellence, so turned them into "poems" according to the norms of their own langs. Early trans. of the psalms into OE verse may reflect this feeling, though the impact of humanist studies on biblical trans., along with poets' recognition that the biblical precedent justified vernacular poetry, made metrical psalms popular. Eng. poets were also inspired to compete with continental psalmodists such as Marot. Thomas Wyatt, the Earl of Surrey (Henry Howard), and George Gascoigne translated psalms into *terza rima, *blank verse, and other innovative meters; Richard Stanyhurst and Abraham Fraunce attempted psalms in quantitative verse (see QUANTITY). The psalter begun by Philip Sidney and completed by Mary Sidney Herbert, Countess of Pembroke, was the masterpiece of Eng. poetic psalm trans., containing psalms in most of the lyric forms then available (incl. *sonnets, terza rima and *ottava rima, *rhyme royal, *acrostics, heroic hexameters, and quantitative *sapphics). The Neo-Lat. metrical psalms of the Scot George Buchanan (from 1556) were internationally acclaimed. Metrical psalms continued to be popular across Europe: powerful poetic psalms were written by John Donne, Thomas Carew, Richard Crashaw, Henry Vaughan, and John Milton; Philippe Desportes, Guillaume du Vair, Jean de Sponde, and Jean-Antoine de Baïf; Luís de León, St. John of the Cross, and Jorge de Montemayor; Luís de Camões; Martin Opitz and Paul Fleming. The vogue waned after the 17th c., but some metrical psalms continued to be written by major poets, incl. in Eng. James Thomson, Robert Burns, Lord Byron, and John Clare. The biblical psalms have continued to attract mod. poets, incl. G. M. Hopkins, Bertholt Brecht, Paul Celan, Geoffrey Hill, and Yehuda Amichai, but they have preferred paraphrase, adaptation, or imitation to trans. proper.

See DEVOTIONAL POETRY, LITURGICAL POETRY, PENITENTIAL PSALMS, PSALM.

■ P. von Rohr-Sauer, *English Metrical Psalms from 1600 to 1660* (1938); H. Smith, "English Metrical Psalms in the Sixteenth Century and Their Literary Significance," *Huntington Library Quarterly* 9 (1946); M. Jeanneret, *Poésie et tradition biblique au XVI^e siècle* (1969); I. D. McFarlane, *Buchanan* (1981); R. Zim, *English Metrical Psalms* (1987); R. Todd, "'So Well Attyr'd Abroad': A Background to the Sidney-Pembroke Psalter and Its Implications for the Seventeenth-Century Religious Lyric," *TSLL* 29 (1987); I. Bach and H. Galle, *Deutsche Psalmdichtung vom 16. bis zum 20. Jahrhundert* (1989); R. Greene, "Sir Philip Sidney's Psalms, the Sixteenth-Century Psalter, and the Nature of Lyric," *SEL* 30 (1990); R. Leaver, *Goostly Psalms and Spiritual Songs* (1991); *The Psalms in English*, ed. D. Davie (1996); *The Place of the Psalms in the Intellectual Culture of the Middle Ages*, ed. N. Van Deusen (1999); M. P. Hannay, "'So May I With the Psalmist Truly Say': Early Modern English Women's Psalm Discourse," *Write or Be Written*, ed. B. Smith and U. Appelt (2001); L. Kaplis-Hohwald, *Translation of the Biblical Psalms in Golden Age Spain* (2003); M. P. Kuczynski, *Prophetic Song: The Psalms as Moral Discourse in Late Medieval England* (2004); H. Hamlin, *Psalm Culture and Early Modern English Literature* (2004); B. Quitslund, *Reformation in Rhyme: Sternhold, Hopkins, and the English Metrical Psalter* (2008)

H. HAMLIN

**PSEUDO-STATEMENT.** *Pseudo-statement* is used by the 20th-c. Brit. critic I. A. Richards in *Science and Poetry* (1926), where he describes the term: "A pseudo-statement is a form of words which is justified entirely by its effect in releasing or organizing our impulses and attitudes . . . ; a statement, on the other hand, is justified by its truth, i.e. its correspondence, in a highly technical sense, with the fact to which it points." Richards uses this distinction between propositional statements (which aim to express truth about the external world) and the "pseudo" statements of poetry (which do not) to posit a deeper opposition between poetic lang. (emotive) and scientific lang. (denotative). For him, an identical sequence of words or phrasing would be propositional in scientific lang. but emotive in poetic lang. The function of the poem is not to supply a repertoire of verifiable facts but to impart "a perfect emotive description of a state of mind." What separates the "truth" of poetic pseudo-statement from that of scientific statement is its special ability to organize experience in richly complicated and imaginatively stimulating ways. The whole of pseudo-statement is epitomized by this complex organization of feelings and impulses in the emotive utterance.

Pseudo-statement was debated in Britain and the United States in the 1930s and 1940s. Since the term is equivocal (Murry) and since it privileges the emotive over the cognitive, Richards's formulations did not find favor with a number of critics. Tate, e.g., made the point that poetic value is much more related to "the knowing mind" than to a "projection of feeling." Although Richards continued to be preoccupied with the question of belief and poetry, it appears that, in practice, he ceased to make use of the controversial term. Snow's influential lecture "The Two Cultures" (1959) about the unproductive effects of the separation of sciences and humanities, Northrop Frye's comments about the common structure of discourses in the final chapter of *Anatomy of Criticism* (1957), together with structuralist and poststructuralist thought in the 1960s and 1970s, all imply that a larger framework of discourse is more productive than the distinction between scientific and emotive lang. Generally speaking, pseudo-statement is best viewed as one of Richards's attempts to furnish crit. with adequate technical vocabulary and with systematic critical principles.

■ I. A. Richards, *Practical Criticism* (1929)—esp. 186–88; J. M. Murry, "Beauty if Truth," *Symposium* 1 (1930); A. Tate, "Literature as Knowledge," *Southern Review* 6 (1941); C. P. Snow, *The Two Cultures and a Second Look*, 2d ed. (1964); P. Wheelwright, *The Burning Fountain*, rev. ed. (1968); G. Graff, *Poetic Statement and Critical Dogma* (1970); J. P. Russo, *I. A. Richards* (1989); G. Ortolano, *The Two Cultures Controversy* (2009).

P. McCallum

## PSYCHOLOGY AND POETRY

I. Psychoanalytic Psychology
II. Archetypal Psychology
III. Other Psychologies

Among the disciplines most often applied to problems in lit., incl. poetry, psychology has been esp. resilient. Long before the formal establishment of the discipline of psychology in the 19th c., theorists and readers used insights about the emotions, the cognitive process, and other manifestations of what we now call *psychology* to analyze lit. Some would say that, when Plato speaks of poetry enfeebling the mind or composition as poetic madness, when Aristotle writes of *catharsis or S. T. Coleridge of *imagination, he is making psychological statements. By the 20th c., terms and assumptions from psychology were deeply embedded in literary reading, even for those readers whose critical method was (and is) not explicitly psychological.

Lit. both embodies the psychological conditions of its makers and is realized through the psychological premises of its interpreters. Even critics who posit an "objective" *text are making a psychological assumption, namely, that the perception of that text can be independent of the activities of the perceiver's mind. A single work may be read different ways according to psychology: a historical critic may explore early mod. notions of the mind to explicate a play of Shakespeare, while a psychoanalytic critic may apply mod. ideas about the unconscious or the Oedipus complex to the same play. Some mod. critics tend to leave their psychological assumptions tacit, deriving them from common sense or philosophy, not the discipline of psychology as such. Since the devel. of psychoanalysis, however, most critics make their psychological assumptions formal and explicit as a way of contributing to a common discourse.

Near the end of the 19th c., Sigmund Freud began to develop psychoanalytic psychology. At the same time, academic psychology was evolving from a branch of philosophy into a science. Psychological crit., properly so called, dates from the first efforts to use these now-separated experimental, clinical, or "scientific" psychologies instead of aesthetic or philosophical statements about the nature of the human. From that time to the present, psychological crit. has drawn esp. on three psychologies: psychoanalytic (Freudian), archetypal (analytic or Jungian), and cognitive. Psychologies, however, deal in the first instance not with poems but with persons. The application of any form of psychology to poetry will usually discuss the author, some member(s) of the author's audience, a character, or the lang. (usually meaning a character or some psychological process represented in the lang.).

**I. Psychoanalytic Psychology.** By far, the largest body of psychological crit. draws on psychoanalysis, perhaps because from the very beginning Freud was a kind of literary reader, concerned with the exact wording of a patient's free associations, a slip of the tongue, or the telling of a dream or joke. Hence, one can use psychoanalytic psychology to study details of poetic lang. Also, since the 1960s, psychoanalysis has become more and more a general psychology, as theorists have drawn on anthropology, experiments, neuroscience, and such mod. theories as *semiotics and information theory. Controversies that loomed large in the 1920s, such as Freud vs. Carl Jung, now seem small as psychoanalysis has become a psychology of the self.

One can think of psychoanalysis in three phases: a psychology of the unconscious (1897–1923), ego psychology (1923–), and a psychology of the self in its contexts (ca. 1950–), though the latter era has produced its own phases. The later phases build on and include the earlier, enlarging the field of human behavior that psychoanalysis attempts to explain. The most recent thinking in psychoanalysis incorporates and generalizes much of Freud's earliest work. One can define these phases by the polarity used to explain events: conscious and unconscious, ego and non-ego, or self and not-self.

The first stage grew directly from Freud's most fundamental discovery. If a patient free associates in connection with a symptom, i.e., says whatever comes to mind, sooner or later the patient will enunciate (over strongly felt resistance) a repressed thought or feeling that the symptom expresses. Similarly, if a patient free associates to a dream, the patient will become aware (also against resistance) of a previously unconscious wish—so too, Freud found, with slips of the tongue or pen, lapses of memory, forgettings, or jokes. In all these odd, marginal behaviors, free association reveals a resisted latent or unconscious content underneath the tolerated manifest or conscious behavior. Once Freud realized that this manifest-latent pattern occurred in many spheres of mental activity, he concluded that he had arrived at something fundamental to human nature itself, a general principle of psychological explanation, the struggle between the conscious and the unconscious.

In this "classical" phase, Freud thought of the conscious and the unconscious as opposed forces, as systems or even places. He and his first followers explained human behaviors as either repressions or expressions of unconscious material in which psychic energy shifted from one state to the other. The other major event of the first phase was their understanding of child devel. as having clear stages leading to adult life. In particular, adult character developed from the child's resolution of his or her Oedipus complex. That is, a style of adult relations to other persons grew out of how the child coped with its love and hate toward mother and father as the child grew into a world divided into male and female and parent and child. Even earlier, the child developed character from how it learned to adapt internally to adult concerns about the management of the child's body in feeding, defecating, urinating, walking, masturbating, and so on. Within this first framework, Freud developed highly general ideas about the working and structure of the mind, although psychoanalysis often focused primarily on special behaviors such as neurosis and dreams.

Lit. played a key role in Freud's discoveries. In the letter of October 15, 1897, in which he announced that he had found love of the mother and jealousy of the father in his self-analysis, he went on to identify this complex with the "gripping power" of Sophocles' *Oedipus Rex* and the unconscious forces behind Shakespeare's writing of *Hamlet*, as well as the latter protagonist's inability to act. Freud, thus, addressed all three of the persons of psychological crit., although in this first phase he confined his writings largely to author and character.

In "Creative Writers and Day-Dreaming" (1908), Freud developed a powerful model of the literary process. Stimulated by a present wish, the writer enriches it unconsciously with wishes from childhood and embodies it in a literary form that entices an audience (who, in its turn, takes the text as stimulus and elaborates it with its own unconscious wishes). Using this model, he wrote studies of Leonardo da Vinci and Fyodor Dostoyevsky and his longest literary analysis, an interpretation of the dreams in Wilhelm Jensen's novel *Gradiva*. He also analyzed a variety of literary characters: Hamlet, Macbeth and Lady Macbeth, Henrik Ibsen's Rebecca West, and Falstaff (see Strachey).

Freud's writings attracted other early psychoanalytic figures to lit. crit. Typical were Ernest Jones's study of *Hamlet*, Marie Bonaparte's of E. A. Poe, and Phyllis Greenacre's of Jonathan Swift and Lewis Carroll. Characteristically, these first-phase critics used only such early psychoanalytic concepts as unconscious content or the Oedipus complex or the phallic and anal stages of child devel. They relied heavily on Freud's lists of symbols in the 1914 additions to *The Interpretation of Dreams* or the first set of *Introductory Lectures* in 1915–17, a tactic that resulted in some bizarre crit. and a dubious reputation for psychoanalytic studies among conventional literary critics.

Perhaps because it was so novel, this earliest style, the search for latent content, set the image of psychoanalytic crit. in literary circles. Also, a number

of prominent literary critics of the 1930s, 1940s, and 1950s began to use this first-phase theory, esp. William Empson, Edmund Wilson, Lionel Trilling, Kenneth Burke, and Leslie Fiedler (see Phillips). Work continued in this vein into the 1960s and 1970s (Crews; Kaplan and Kloss). Some of this work remains highly effective precisely because of the simplicity of its theory. Harold Bloom's influential theory of poetic *influence, e.g., rests on Freud's early version of the Oedipus complex.

Freud himself, however, found that a quarter century of clinical experience required him to revise his first theories. In the second phase of his thought, Freud complicated the simple division of the mind into conscious and unconscious by mapping it onto the "structural" hypothesis of a mind whose workings consisted of the interaction of id, superego, reality, and repetition compulsion under the governance of a presiding ego. Id, one would define today as the psychic representation of biological drives; superego, the internalized commands of one's parents, both to do and not to do, violation of which leads to guilt or depression; repetition compulsion, the tendency to try old solutions even on new problems; the ego, the synthesizer and executive that chooses strategies and tactics that best balance these competing needs. Freud and his colleagues of the 1930s expanded their inventory of defense mechanisms from repression to other strategies such as reversing anger into kindness and projecting one's own impulses onto others. Although Freud had largely ceased writing on lit. by 1923, some of his earlier works illustrate what his second-phase writing might have been like: studies of jokes and humor, the legend of the Medusa's head, the theme of beauty's transience (an essay prompted by R. M. Rilke), or the "uncanny" in ghost stories. These writings all have less to do with author or character and more with the audience and an assumed collective response to a literary stimulus.

Second-phase psychoanalytic theory made possible a more powerful poetics. Kris and Mauron were able to integrate the new ego psychology of multiple defenses into studies of the writing process. Sharpe and Rogers showed how the new theories could explicate the psychological function of metaphors and poetic lang. Kris, Lesser, and Holland used ego psychology to study the response to literary texts. Reflecting the new complexity in the theory of defense, Kris approached lit. as "regression in the service of the ego." Lesser showed how lit. variously appeals to id, ego, and superego. Holland developed a model of lit. as a fantasy modified by poetic forms (analogous to psychological defenses) toward a meaning. Where first-phase critics felt that they could talk only about persons, second-phase critics could use the new theories to consider genres such as *lyric poetry. Thus, Matthew Arnold's "Dover Beach" denies a primal scene fantasy; W. B. Yeats's "The Second Coming" splits a fantasy of omnipotent rage. Psychoanalytic studies of writers could become more realistic with biographers such as Edel, Kaplan, Meyer, Fruman, or Wolff. The anthols. by Ruitenbeek, the Manheims, and Tennenhouse sample this phase.

The third phase took place largely after Freud's death in 1939. Psychoanalytic psychology went beyond the ego to address the self in the largest sense and, finally, all of human behavior. As early as 1930, in the first chapter of *Civilization and Its Discontents*, Freud ushered in this phase: "Originally the ego includes everything; later it separates off an external world from itself." Nazi persecutions forced the emigration of Freud and his circle from Vienna and spread second- and third-phase psychoanalysis all over the world.

Brit. theorists, during the 1940s and 1950s, replaced Freud's biological determinism from innate drives with learning based on interpersonal encounters between the child and its significant others ("object relations"). Concentration on these pre-Oedipal experiences led to a more comprehensive account of the themes in a child's devel. that persisted in the adult's style. The Oedipus complex was only one among several critical events; indeed, the child's first-year relation to the mother overshadowed what Freud had thought dominant, the relation to the father in the third year and after. In particular, both theory and observation indicated a crucial period early in life when the child felt he or she was not yet separate from the mother, and Holland (1968) showed how this early experience could explain "absorption" in lit. later in life. From this "object-relations school," theories of "potential space" and "transitional object" (Winnicott) had an important influence on literary theory (Schwartz, Hartman, Grolnick and Barkin), evidenced, e.g., in work on Shakespeare (Schwartz and Kahn). A number of literary critics built on the work of Melanie Klein, an important figure in object-relations theory who posited a dynamic picture of the psyche, and Karen Horney, who focused early on defensive patterns and object relations.

In France, under the influence of Jacques Lacan (after ca. 1965), psychoanalysis turned toward understanding conscious and unconscious experiences as an entry into a ling. culture. Lacan wrote in an arcane, metaphorical way, describing concerns of the third phase of psychoanalysis (object relations or personal style) in the lang. of the first phase (phallus, castration). Although much Lacanian critical writing simply explicates Lacan, he posited important psychoanalytic ideas on analyses of Poe's "The Purloined Letter" and *Hamlet*; and many critics turned to analyzing discrete works (see Bersani, Felman, and the Davis and Felman anthols.) In some versions, Lacanian psychoanalysis meshes with the work of such Fr. thinkers as Roland Barthes, Michel Foucault, and Jacques Derrida, who treated lang. as an active, autonomous system and the speaker as passive. Psychoanalytic psychology in this form is more widely read in literary circles (in the U.S., U.K., France, and South America) than earlier versions were, though, paradoxically, it reduces the importance of the actual methods such as free association on which psychoanalysis rests.

A particularly vigorous current in the 1980s was feminist psychoanalytic crit., this despite Freud's unsophisticated theories about women. Feminists sometimes reread Freud as if he were a literary text; sometimes they use Freud to understand a patriarchal society (Mitchell); sometimes they rewrite him into a more sophisticated psychology (Chodorow). Some feminist critics drew on Fr. theory (Irigaray; Marks and de Courtivron), others on Anglo-Am. ego psychology and object-relations theory (Gilbert and Gubar; Garner). All found in psychoanalytic psychology both a challenge and a resource.

Influential recent discussions of psychoanalysis in relation to poetry have often been wide-ranging instances of cultural and literary crit. rather than narrow applications of Freud, Lacan, and their successors. The Bulgarian theorist Julia Kristeva, in *La Révolution du langage poétique* (*Revolution in Poetic Language*, 1974) and other works, borrows from Freud and other psychoanalytic models to build "a theory of signification based on the subject, his formation, and his corporeal, ling., and social dialectic." The Brit. literary historian Jacqueline Rose in several books, notably *Sexuality in the Field of Vision* (1986) and *On Not Being Able to Sleep* (2003), reshapes Freudian insights into a set of adaptable tools for the analysis of a broad range of poems but also other kinds of phenomena such as the spectacle of Princess Diana. The French psychotherapist Félix Guattari published several powerful books expanding psychoanalytic concepts to address the making of subjectivity in society, modes of political resistance to fascism and capitalism, and the cultivation of an ecologically oriented philosophy; his most famous book, the collaboration with Gilles Deleuze called *Anti-Oedipus* (1972), proposes a "materialist psychiatry" that proceeds from a critique of Freud's Oedipus complex. The Israeli-born theorist Shoshana Felman has probed madness in psychiatric and literary contexts, trauma, and sexual difference. The Am. critic Barbara Johnson continued many of Felman's approaches, freely applying Freud and Lacan in important essays on Stéphane Mallarmé and Poe, among others. And in *The Sublime Object of Ideology* (1989), still his best book, the Slovenian philosopher Slavoj Žižek returned to Lacanian concepts, now braided with Hegelian dialectics, in a searching contribution to the theory of ideology.

**II. Archetypal Psychology.** Archetypal psychology was a significant force in critical theory from the 1920s to the 1960s. Its theoretical foundation derives from the work of the Swiss psychoanalyst Carl Jung, esp. his idea that archetypal structures are the primary factors organizing human personality. For Jung, the personal unconscious consists of memories and images (*imagos*) collected in the course of an individual life. The collective unconscious, on the other hand, is limited to the imposition of structural laws—*archetypes. The personal unconscious is like a lexicon where each of us accumulates a distinctive vocabulary; these lexical units, however, acquire value and significance only insofar as they are archetypally structured. If the unconscious activity of the psyche consists in imposing structures (archetypes) upon content (imagos) and if these structures are fundamentally the same for all personalities, then to understand and interpret a literary text it is necessary to analyze the unconscious structures underlying the text itself. This is the model used in traditional Jungian crit.

Jung published the first archetypal analysis of a literary text in 1912 in "Wandlungen und Symbole der Libido," an extensive treatment of the structures underlying H. W. Longfellow's "Hiawatha." Here Jung introduced his interpretive method know as *amplification*. Earlier, Freud had demonstrated the importance of free association for understanding the unconscious motivation and meaning of a person's dreams. Jung extended this idea not only to the personal associations of the dreamer but to intertextual associations within the dreamer's cultural canon and, in some cases, cross-cultural associations as well. By establishing a larger intertextual context for the dream image through philological, iconological, mythological, and historical research, Jung showed that the process of amplification deliteralizes the image, cultivating an attitude that psychologically questions the naïve, literal level of lang. and image in order to expose its more shadowy, metaphorical significance (see INTERTEXTUALITY).

Analysis of archetypal structures and the phenomenological amplification of images characterized archetypal crit. from the 1920s to the mid-1960s, esp. in the early work of Maud Bodkin, John Thorburn, Herbert Read, and Elizabeth Drew, through the later Kathleen Raine and Graham Hough, and culminating in the prodigious writings of Northrop Frye (see also MYTH).

In the 1970s, revolutionary changes in archetypal crit. came from two areas: (1) expansion of clinical analysis to a phenomenological study of *imagination and lang. and (2) study of the depth-psychological dimension of religion and lit. The most influential figure was the Jungian psychoanalyst James Hillman. To extend Jungian psychology beyond clinical practice to a study of Western imagination, Hillman called for a "postanalytic consciousness" committed to an articulation of the "poetic basis of mind." Hillman's phenomenological view of mind holds fantasy images to be the means by which consciousness and self-consciousness are possible and through which the world is imagined. Work with images, whether in therapeutic, cultural, or literary analysis, thus became a work as much on the process of seeing as on the object seen.

The shift from Jung to Hillman may be illustrated in their differing approaches to alchemy. Where Jung writes an "objective" and "empirical" psychology of alchemy, Hillman tries instead to provide an experiential closeness to the alchemical images and tropes themselves. In writing about "silver and the white earth," Hillman intends his writing, like a poem, to bear traces of "silver," to become a "silver mine," unearthing and performing the images' tropological structure. The metaphor of silver "author-izes" the actual style of writing and internal logic of the text. As a mode of psychological crit., Hillman's new archetypal psychology assumes that a literary work brings with it the very *hermeneutics (imagos and tropes) by which it can be interpreted. In the late 1970s, Paul Kugler further

developed the interrelation between alchemy and the poetic dimension of lang. by focusing on the interrelation among consciousness, lang. (texts), and imagos. Consciousness is continually being imagined (imaged, in-formed) by the metaphors in the very text it is writing or reading.

In its last burst of activity in the 1980s, archetypal crit. drew on the philosophy of the later Martin Heidegger, Derrida, and the notions of nothingness and emptiness from Zen Buddhism, to further deepen the imaginal hermeneutic toward semiotic and postmod. literary theory.

**III. Other Psychologies.** Except for I. A. Richards's and Morse Peckham's somewhat eclectic use of psychology, an occasional nod to a Gestalt psychologist like Kurt Koffka, or a mention of Jean Piaget's work on the devel. of play and symbolic thought in children, academic psychology did not attract the attention of theorists on poetics until the 1970s. After that, a number of literary theorists explored artificial intelligence, developmental and cognitive psychology, and other subfields of the cognitive sciences that deal with poems, stories, humor, metaphor, and general symbolic activities.

Evolutionary psychology—the study of psychological adaptations to environments by human populations, such as emotion, imitation, and lang.—has been an intriguing (though an eclectic and dispersed) method in recent work on poetics. Considering that many features of poetry (e.g., figurative lang., meter) are useless or even counterproductive to some human activities but deeply useful in others, the factors of environment and adaptation hold promise as an analytical context not available to other methodologies. The interpretive (as opposed to the speculative) value of an evolutionary approach remains to be seen.

*Metaphors We Live By*, a 1980 book by the cognitive linguist George Lakoff and the philosopher Mark Johnson, was a crossroads for research into psychology and poetics in that it demonstrated an approach that came to be called *cognitive poetics*—the study of poetic phenomena according to their relation to the processes of the human mind. Cognitive poetics fundamentally changes how poetics draws on psychology, based as it is on a constantly changing body of empirical research rather than endless reinterpretations of the psychoanalytic models of Freud, Lacan, and others. Following this empirical turn, and the absorption of insights from related fields such as discourse analysis, cognitive ling., and artificial intelligence, the study of psychology and poetry has acquired new dimensions that were hardly imaginable in the 1950s and 1960s.

■ **Overviews**: F. J. Hoffman, *Freudianism and the Literary Mind* (1957); J. Strachey, "List of Writings by Freud on Aesthetic Subjects," *Standard Edition of the Complete Psychological Works of Sigmund Freud*, ed. J. Strachey, v. 21 (1961); M. Grimaud, "Recent Trends in Psychoanalysis," *Sub-Stance* 13 (1976); N. N. Holland, "Literary Interpretation and Three Phases of Psychoanalysis," *Psychoanalysis, Creativity, and Literature*, ed. A. Roland (1978); D. Bleich et al., "The Psychological

Study of Language and Literature," *Style* 12 (1978)—bibl.; M. A. Skura, *The Literary Use of the Psychoanalytic Process* (1981); M. Grimaud, "Part Three: A Reader's Guide to Psychoanalysis," *Saint/Oedipus: Psychocritical Approaches to Flaubert's Art*, ed. W. J. Berg, M. Grimaud, G. Moskos (1982); E. Winner, *Invented Worlds* (1982); E. Wright, *Psychoanalytic Criticism* (1984); J. Ryan, *The Vanishing Subject: Early Psychology and Literary Modernism* (1991); S. A. Mitchell and M. J. Black, *Freud and Beyond: A History of Modern Psychoanalytic Thought* (1995); M. Edmundson, *Towards Reading Freud* (2007); M. Bell, *The German Tradition of Psychology in Literature and Thought, 1700–1840* (2009); M. S. Lindauer, *Psyche and the Literary Muses* (2009). ■ **Psychoanalytic Psychology.** *Freudian*: E. Wilson, *The Wound and the Bow* (1929); W. Empson, *Some Versions of Pastoral* (1935); K. Burke, *The Philosophy of Literary Form* (1941); E. Jones, *Hamlet and Oedipus* (1949); L. Trilling, "Freud and Literature" and "Art and Neurosis," *The Liberal Imagination* (1950); S. Freud, *Standard Edition of the Complete Psychological Works of Sigmund Freud*, ed. J. Strachey, 24 v. (1953–74, 1995); P. Greenacre, *Swift and Carroll* (1955); Wellek and Warren, ch. 8; *Art and Psychoanalysis*, ed. W. Phillips (1963); K. Burke, *Language as Symbolic Action* (1966); *Psychoanalysis and Literary Process*, ed. F. C. Crews (1970); M. Kaplan and R. Kloss, *The Unspoken Motive* (1973); H. Bloom, *The Anxiety of Influence* (1973); C. Bernheimer and C. Kahane, *In Dora's Case* (1990); *Cambridge Companion to Freud*, ed. J. Neu (1991); S.L. Gilman, *The Case of Sigmund Freud* (1994), and *Freud, Race, and Gender* (1995); *Freud 2000*, ed. A. Elliott (1998); G. Frankland, *Freud's Literary Culture* (2000); R. Gallo, *Freud's Mexico* (2010); A. I. Tauber, *Freud, The Reluctant Philosopher* (2010). **Second Phase**: E. F. Sharpe, *Collected Papers on Psycho-Analysis* (1950); E. Kris, *Psychoanalytic Explorations in Art* (1952); L. Edel, *Henry James* (1953–72); S. O. Lesser, *Fiction and the Unconscious* (1957); L. Edel, *Literary Biography* (1959); C. Mauron, *Des Métaphores obsédantes au mythe personnel* (1963); *Psychoanalysis and Literature*, ed. H. Ruitenbeek (1964); *Hidden Patterns*, ed. L. and E. Manheim (1966); J. Kaplan, *Mr. Clemens and Mark Twain* (1966); B. C. Meyer, *Joseph Conrad* (1967); N. N. Holland, *The Dynamics of Literary Response* (1968); N. Fruman, *Coleridge, the Damaged Archangel* (1971); B. C. Meyer, *Houdini* (1976); *The Practice of Psychoanalytic Criticism*, ed. L. Tennenhouse (1976); C. G. Wolff, *A Feast of Words* (1977); R. Rogers, *Metaphor* (1978); J. Kaplan, *Walt Whitman* (1980); C. G. Wolff, *Emily Dickinson* (1986); *Psychoanalytic Literary Criticism*, ed. M. Ellmann (1994). **Post-Freudian**: J. Lacan, *Le séminaire* (1953–75); K. Horney, *Collected Works*, 2 v. (1963); H. Kohut, *The Analysis of the Self* (1971); D. W. Winnicott, *Playing and Reality* (1971); "French Freud," *YFS* 48 (1972)—spec. iss. on "Structural Studies in Psychoanalysis"; N. N. Holland, *Poems in Persons* (1973), and *5 Readers Reading* (1975); M. Klein, *Writings*, 4 v. (1975); M. Schwartz, "Where is Literature?" *CE* 36 (1975); L. Bersani, *Baudelaire and Freud* (1977); F. Guattari with G. Deleuze, *Anti-Oedipus*, trans.

R. Hurley et al. (1977); *Literature and Psychoanalysis*, ed. S. Felman (1977); *Between Reality and Fantasy*, ed. S. A. Grolnick and L. Barkin (1978); N. Chodorow, *The Reproduction of Mothering* (1978); *Psychoanalysis and the Question of the Text*, ed. G. Hartman (1978); S. M. Gilbert and S. Gubar, *The Madwoman in the Attic* (1979); *New French Feminisms*, ed. E. Marks and I. de Courtivron (1980); B. Johnson, *The Critical Difference* (1980); "Psychology and Literature," *NLH* 12.1 (1980)—spec. iss.; *Representing Shakespeare*, ed. M. Schwartz and C. Kahn (1980); *The Fictional Father*, ed. R. Con Davis (1981); N. N. Holland, *Laughing* (1982); F. Guattari, *Molecular Revolution: Psychiatry and Politics*, trans. R. Sheed (1984); J. Kristeva, *Revolution in Poetic Language*, trans. M. Waller (1984); R. Silhol, *Le texte du désir: la critique après Lacan* (1984); N. Hertz, *The End of the Line: Essays on Psychoanalysis and the Sublime* (1985); L. Irigaray, *This Sex Which Is Not One*, trans. C. Porter and C. Burke (1985); *The (M)other Tongue*, ed. S. N. Garner et al. (1985); L. Bersani, *The Freudian Body* (1986); B. J. Paris, "Horney, Maslow, and the Third Force," *Third Force Psychology and the Study of Literature* (1986); *Narcissism and the Text*, ed. L. Layton and B. A. Schapiro (1986); J. Rose, *Sexuality in the Field of Vision* (1986); S. Felman, "The Case of Poe: Applications/Implications of Psychoanalysis," *Jacques Lacan and the Adventure of Insight* (1987); B. Johnson, *A World of Difference* (1987); S. M. Gilbert and S. Gubar, *No Man's Land* (1988); N. N. Holland, *The Brain of Robert Frost* (1988); J. Adelman, *Suffocating Mothers: Fantasies of Maternal Origin in Shakespeare's Plays, "Hamlet" to "The Tempest"* (1991); J. Rose, *The Haunting of Sylvia Plath* (1993), and *Why War: Psychoanalysis, Politics and the Return to Melanie Klein* (1993); H. Sussman, *Psyche and Text* (1993); F. Guattari, *Chaosmosis*, trans. P. Bains and J. Pefanis (1995); J. Mitchell, *Psychoanalysis and Feminism*, 2d ed. (2000); *Cambridge Companion to Lacan*, ed. J.-M. Rabate (2003); S. Felman, *Writing and Madness*, trans. M. N. Evans et al. (2003); J. Rose, *On Not Being Able to Sleep: Psychoanalysis and the Modern World* (2003); J. Lacan, *Écrits*, trans. B. Fink et al. (2006); E. K. Sedgwick, "Melanie Klein and the Difference Affect Makes," *South Atlantic Quarterly* 106 (2007); S. Žižek, *The Sublime Object of Ideology*, 2d ed. (2009). ■ **Archetypal Psychology**: M. J. Thorburn, *Art and the Unconscious* (1925); M. Bodkin, *Archetypal Patterns in Poetry* (1934); C. Jung, *Collected Works*, Bollingen Ser., 20 v. (1956–79); Frye; C. Jung, *The Structure and Dynamics of the Psyche* (1960); H. Read, *Poetry and Experience* (1967); K. Raine, "Poetic Dynamics as a Vehicle of Tradition," *Eranos Jahrbuch* (1970); G. Hough, "Poetry and the Anima," *Spring* (1973); J. Hillman, *Re-Visioning Psychology* (1975); P. Berry-Hillman, *Echo's Subtle Body* (1982); P. Kugler, *The Alchemy of Discourse* (1982); J. Hillman, *Archetypal Psychology* (1983); R. Avens, *The New Gnosis* (1984); B. L. Knapp, *A Jungian Approach to Literature* (1984); M. Adams, "Deconstructive Philosophy and Imaginal Psychology," *Journal of Literary Criticism* 2 (1985); B. L. Knapp, *Machine, Metaphor, and the Writer* (1989); *Jungian Literary Criti-*

*cism*, ed. R. P. Sugg (1992); J. Hillman, *The Soul's Code* (1997); *Cambridge Companion to Jung*, ed. P. Young-Eisendrath and T. Dawson (2008).

■ **Other Psychologies**: Richards; J. Piaget, "The Secondary Symbolism of Play," *Play, Dreams and Imitation in Childhood* (1962); M. Peckham, *Man's Rage for Chaos* (1965); C. Martindale, *Romantic Progression* (1975); *The Arts and Cognition*, ed. D. Perkins and B. Leondar (1977); T. van Dijk, "Advice on Theoretical Poetics," *Poetics* 8 (1979); J. Hobbs, "Metaphor Interpretation as Selective Inferencing," *Empirical Studies of the Arts* 1 (1983); E. Rosch, "Prototype Classification and Logical Classification," *New Trends in Conceptual Representation*, ed. E. K. Scholnick (1983); R. Brooke, "Three Models of Narrative Comprehension," *Empirical Studies of the Arts* 2 (1984); G. Lakoff, *Women, Fire, and Dangerous Things* (1987); G. Lakoff and M. Turner, *More Than Cool Reason* (1989); S. Pinker, *The Language Instinct* (1994); T. Deacon, *The Symbolic Species* (1997); G. Lakoff and M. Johnson, *Metaphors We Live By*, 2d ed. (2003); J. Carroll, *Literary Darwinism* (2004), and "An Evolutionary Paradigm for Literary Study," *Style* 42.2–3 (2008)—spec. double iss. with 35 responses;. Dutton, *The Art Instinct: Beauty, Pleasure, and Human Evolution* (2009); N. N. Holland, *Literature and the Brain* (2009); T. Karshan, "Evolutionary Criticism," *Essays in Criticism* 59 (2009); M. Austin, *Useful Fictions: Evolution, Anxiety, and the Origins of Literature* (2010); J. Carroll, *Reading Human Nature* (2011); J. D. Hall, "Materializing Meter: Physiology, Psychology, Prosody," *VP* 49 (2011).

N. H. Holland; P. K. Kugler;
M. Grimaud; R. Greene

**PUERTO RICO, POETRY OF.** *See* Caribbean, poetry of the.

**PUN.** *See* paronomasia.

**PUNCTUATION** (Lat. *punctus*, "point"). A system of nonalphabetical signs that express meaning through implied pauses, pitch shifts, and other intonational features. For prose, in western Europe, punctuation began as a pedagogical and scribal guide to reading aloud. It evolved to mark syntax for silent readers, as urged by Aldus Manutius in *Orthographiae ratio* (1566) and Ben Jonson in *The English Grammar* (ca. 1617, pub. 1640). For poetry, however, the diachronic shift from oral delivery to silent reading had less impact on comprehension because in poetry—whether its *sound is actual (heard) or virtual (read)—sound helps create sense.

Both pedagogy and *performance loom large in the hist. of punctuation. Speech seems continuous; thus, the earliest Gr. inscriptions do not separate words. Points occasionally separate longer phrases, and Aristotle mentions a horizontal line, the *paragraphos*, used to introduce a new topic. At the Museum in Alexandria, ca. 200 BCE, the librarian Aristophanes proposed terms and marks (not corresponding to their mod. counterparts) to distinguish a short section (*comma*)

from the longer and longest textual sections (*colon, periodos*). His terms survived via the Roman grammarians, notably Donatus in the 4th c. CE, and via early Christian teachers such as Jerome, who devised punctuation *per cola et commata* (by phrases) specifically to facilitate reading aloud of his new Vulgate trans. of the Bible. Over the next millennium, various writers developed systems of punctuation, adapting musical notation (neumes) to indicate *pitch shifts as well as pauses. Thus authorities long dead could continue to prescribe correct oral recitations of sacred texts.

For secular poetry, early printers (e.g., William Caxton) and theorists (e.g., George Puttenham) emphasized the practical functions of punctuation—esp. breath breaks—rather than syntax or prescriptive interpretation. During the 17th c., syntactic punctuation became the norm for imaginative as well as expository prose, whereas drama and poetry tended to retain sound-based flexibility. Before John Urry (1721), for instance, eds. preparing Chaucer for print punctuated ordinary line ends only sporadically. Similarly, readers of Shakespeare's plays as scripts for performance realized that no amount of enforced syntactic punctuation can hold to one set meaning Hamlet's "To die, to sleep / No more and by a sleep to say we end." During the 19th c., however, the study of the mod. langs. succumbed to the strictures of academic respectability. Teachers and eds. began using syntactic punctuation to prescribe their own imagined performances of secular poetry, just as clerics a millennium earlier had prescribed oral performances of sacred Lat. prose.

The illuminated works of William Blake provide striking examples of authorial punctuation as a guide to imagined performance, for Blake laboriously engraved each plate with letters, visual art, and other marks, incl. punctuation. In the first stanza of "London," nonsyntactic periods that close two lines help express the narrator's initial, but illusory, sense of control. Each stanza has progressively lighter punctuation, the second spilling with no end mark into the third, until—as ever more appalling images engulf the narrator—punctuation disappears altogether from the final stanza. The abyss yawns. Despite Blake's efforts, his 20th-c. ed. Geoffrey Keynes repunctuated "London" in accord with mod. canons of punctuation and sense, i.e., in accord with prose syntax, so that the poem in his ed. (though not in others) presents a detached narrator calmly cataloguing social problems.

Many eds. long considered standard have imposed syntactic prose punctuation on poetry. In the *Twickenham Edition* of Alexander Pope, e.g., each ed. records words that differ from the copy-text chosen, but each modernizes punctuation at will, despite Pope's letter telling a printer to "contrive the Capitals & evry [*sic*] thing exactly to correspond" with an earlier printing.

How do eds. justify changing authorial punctuation? In part, they are applying methodologies developed for cl. and med. mss., in which any punctuation that appears is based on a local scribal dialect that may bear little or no relationship to our present standardized system. In one ms. trad., a virgule (slash, solidus) might mark poetic *caesura, e.g.; in another trad., a virgule may mark the shortest of three pauses and in yet another, the longest of six divisions into sense units. The slanted line went nameless until 1837, when Henry Hallam adopted a zoological term to declare that virgules in Chaucer mss. always mark caesura—an assertion that, though dead wrong, was not definitively disproven until 1982.

In mss., other punctuation marks also vary from one region to another, even within the same decade. Med. dialects of neumes varied likewise, yet standardized musical notation is not now expected to explicate a set meaning for either readers or performers of a score. But eds. of cl. and med. poetry began to supply less experienced readers with syntactic punctuation suitable to explicative prose. Nearly all Chaucer eds. since 1835, e.g., have imposed the full range of mod. punctuation. Quotation marks, in particular, create demonstrable interpretive problems absent from mss. of Chaucer, wherein a given speech need not be assigned definitely to the narrator or to one or another character. By specifying punctuation absent from or altering punctuation present in mss., mod. eds. continue to prescribe their own silent performances of key poetic passages.

In cultures that have not undergone such a pronounced shift from religious to secular textual education, such as Ar. or Chinese, most punctuation still signals breath breaks and major new topics. Only occasionally does it indicate change in speaker or the many other vocal intonations commonly prescribed in the West by means of syntactic punctuation applied—or misapplied—to poetry.

*See* PERIOD.

■ P. Simpson, *Shakespearian Punctuation* (1911); W. J. Ong, "Historical Backgrounds of Elizabethan and Jacobean Punctuation Theory," *PMLA* 59 (1944); A. Pope, *The Rape of the Lock and Other Poems*, ed. G. Tillotson, 3d ed. (1962), "General Note"; M. Treip, *Milton's Punctuation and Changing English Usage, 1582–1676* (1970); E. O. Wingo, *Latin Punctuation in the Classical Age* (1972); L. D. Reynolds and N. G. Wilson, *Scribes and Scholars*, 2d ed. (1974)—discursive bibl. on current debates concerning Gr. and Lat. punctuation; N. Blake, "Punctuation Marks," *English Language in Medieval Literature* (1977); G. Killough, "Punctuation and Caesura in Chaucer," *SAC* 4 (1982); B. Bowden, *Chaucer Aloud* (1987), under "Punctuation" in index; V. Salmon, "English Punctuation Theory 1500–1800," *Anglia* 106 (1988); G. Nunberg, *The Linguistics of Punctuation* (1990); J. Lennard, *But I Digress* (1991); M. B. Parkes, *Pause and Effect: The History of Punctuation in the West* (1992); A. Graham-White, *Punctuation and its Dramatic Value in Shakespearean Drama* (1995); T. Suzuki, *Punctuation of "The Faerie Queene" Reconsidered* (1999); T. J. Brown, "Punctuation," under "Writing," *New Encyclopedia Britannica*, 15th ed. (2007).

B. BOWDEN

**PUNJABI POETRY.** Poetry has been written in the Punjabi lang. since around the 12th c. CE. The literary

devel. can be divided into roughly three overlapping periods: med. to early mod. Sufi and Sikh devotional writing (12th–18th cs.), epic romantic verse (17th–19th cs.), and the mod. period (1890–present). As Punjabi was historically a demotic rather than a literary lang., Punjabi poetry has been influenced by verse forms from Hindi, Urdu, and Persian, with heavy use of the *sloka,* a couplet-based form common in cl. Sanskrit, in med. and early mod. Punjabi, and forms such as the *ghazal* since the 18th c.

Poets historically have used two scripts when writing in Punjabi, Gurmukhi and Shahmukhi. Though the grammar and diction in the two scripts are identical, Shahmukhi script derives from Persian, while Gurmukhi bears some resemblance to the standard script used in Hindi, Devanagri, though Sekhon and Duggal suggest resemblances to Takri and Sharda scripts as well. Gurmukhi is also associated with the Sikh trad. since it is the script of the Sikh holy book, the *Gurū Granth Sāhib*, while Shahmukhi traditionally has been used by Muslim Punjabi speakers, a division intensified since the partition of the Indian subcontinent in 1947.

Scholars agree that the first major poetry written in Punjabi was composed by Fariduddin Ganj-i-shakar, commonly known as Sheikh Farid (ca. 1173–1265). Sheikh Farid was a Sufi mystic of the Chishti order, whose writings have had a deep and lasting impact on Punjabi speakers from the Muslim, Hindu, and Sikh communities (Chopra). Farid's *slokas* reflect Sufi philosophical precepts, esp. focused on the critique of institutional religious authority as well as material attachments: "Farīdā pankh parāhunī ḍunī suhāvā bāg / Naubat vajī subah sio chalaṇ kā kar sāj" (Farid says, the bird is a guest in the beautiful garden. / Morning bells are ringing, get ready to go).

The Sikh gurus wrote a considerable body of *devotional poetry in Punjabi from the 16th to the 18th cs. In his verses, Gurū Nānak (1469–1539) asserted an iconoclastic ethos under the influence of Sufis such as Farid as well as the Hindu *Bhakti* trad. Nanak worked with a variety of elements in his verses, many of them originating in Hindi poetry, incl. *padas* (stanzas) and *ashtapadis* (eight-stanza compositions), as well as *chhants, paharas, savayyas,* and slokas. The Sikh gurus also set their compositions in 31 different ragas, indicating how the verses were to be recited melodically. Beginning with Guru Arjan (1563–1606) and his contemporary Bhai Gurdas (1551–1636), Sikh devotional poets came to prefer Braj Bhasha (a historical literary lang. closer to Hindi) over demotic Punjabi, opening a window for further devel. of Sufi Punjabi poetry beginning in the 17th c. (Singh 1988).

The themes of Punjabi Sufi poetry from the early mod. period echo that of Sheikh Farid and Gurū Nānak, though the form preferred by these writers is called the *Kāfi*, a monorhyme stanzaic verse form usually set to music. One poet of particular note is Bulleh Shah (ca. 1680–1757), whose iconoclastic verses have been revived in Indian popular music, as in "Bulla ki jāna": "Nā mei momin vich masīt ān / Nā mei vich kufar diyan rīt ān / Nā mei pākān vich palīt ān / Nā mei mūsa nā pharaun." (Not I, a believer inside a mosque / Not I, an infidel doing rituals / Not I, pure amongst the wicked / Neither Moses nor Pharoah, am I) Other important Sufi Punjabi poets include Madhulal Hussain (also referred to as Shah Hussain, 1538–99), Sultan Bahu (1628–91), and Shah Sharaf (1640–1724).

Waris Shah (ca. 1722–98) is the most influential writer in the extended romantic lyric form known in Punjabi as the *qissa* (also spelled *kissa*), derived from the Ar. *\*qaṣīda*. Shah's most influential contribution is his version of the verse narrative *Heer-Ranjha* (1766), an archetypal tale of doomed lovers. The intense imagery and natural-sounding voices in *Heer* have made it a key text in the Punjabi trad. Related to the qissa is the epic heroic poem, known in Punjabi as the *vār*, which recounted wars and other historical events. The vār form was also used by Sikh gurus in the *Gurū Granth Sāhib* (see HINDI POETRY).

Punjabi poetry was marginalized under Brit. colonialism in India, as educational policies in the 19th c. favored national langs. such as Urdu over regional langs. However, a new phase of Punjabi poetry arose with the reformist Singh Sabha movement in the latter half of the 19th c. Bhai Vir Singh (1872–1957), a leading literary figure in the movement, was an active novelist and publisher, as well as a major poet. He is widely cited by critics (incl. the authors of the major reference works cited below) as the father of modern Punjabi poetry, perhaps because he instantiated the independent short poem in Punjabi; he was also likely one of the first Punjabi poets to distribute his poetry commercially in the form of printed books. Singh's influence on contemporaries is readily evident in the writing of Puran Singh (1881–1931), the latter being a poet also deeply influenced by both Japanese aesthetics and the Am. Walt Whitman. Puran Singh is likely the first Punjabi poet to use *free verse, though thematically his writing retains a lyric and devotional focus.

Self-consciously secular poetry in Punjabi emerges as part of the Progressive Writers' movement in South Asian lit. in the 1930s. While the movement is known for works in Hindi, Urdu, and Eng., it had a substantial influence on Punjabi writers such as Mohan Singh (1906–78), Sharif Kunjahi (1915–2007), Amrita Pritam (1919–2005), Prabhjot Kaur (b. 1924), and, slightly later, Shiv Kumar Batalvi (1936–73). As with the Progressive movement more broadly, a significant number of Punjabi Progressive writers were women, incl. Kaur and Pritam. Evidence of the continuing influence of writing from the qissa period is seen in Pritam's "Aj Ākhan Waris Shah Nū," a reflection on the partition of the subcontinent addressed apostrophically to Shah: "Aj ākhan Waris Shah nū kito qabra vicho bol / te aj kitāb-e-ishq da koi aglā varka phol" ("I say to Waris Shah today, speak from your grave / And add a new page to your book of love," trans. D. S. Maini).

*Modernism in Punjabi Indian poetry emerged roughly in tandem with modernism in Hindi, where it is referred to as the *Nayī Kavitā* (New Poetry). An experimental, modernist sensibility can be seen in the work of Jasbir Singh Ahluwalia (b. 1935), who published an anthol. of "experimental" (*Prayogashīl*) Punjabi poetry in 1962, which included his own verses as well as those of established poets, such as Pritam and Mohan Singh, associated with the previous generation. Despite the presence of self-conscious experimentalism since the 1960s and free verse since the 1920s, the dominant voices in Punjabi poetry after 1947 have continued to emphasize traditional rhyme (generally *monorhyme) associated with the *ghazal* and *Kāfi* forms, as well as traditional meters.

Crit. related to 20th-c. Punjabi poetry has been heavily constrained by the partition of 1947, which fractured literary communities in Punjabi along religious lines. Studies by Indian scholars tend to focus exclusively on mod. writers from Hindu and Sikh backgrounds (works by Sekhon and Duggal and by Malhotra and Arora are cases in point), while, in Pakistan, Javeid's study is framed as an explicitly nationalist project and exclusively invokes writers of a Muslim background. Rammah has explored the status of West Punjabi poetry, focusing on Kunjahi, Najm Hosain Syed (b. 1936), Munir Niazi (1928–2006), and Ahmed Rahi (ca. 1923–2002) as the leading voices in postpartition Punjabi poetry from Pakistan.

Finally, the growing body of Punjabi-lang. poetry by writers outside the Indian subcontinent should be noted. The best-known figure is Sadhu Binning (b. 1947, Canada), whose bilingual edition of *No More Watno Dur* (No More Distant Homeland, 1994) has been widely influential. Other frequently cited Punjabi poets in the diaspora include Ajmer Rode (b. 1940, Canada) and Amarjit Chandan (b. 1946, U.K.). Diasporic writing uses elements from traditional Punjabi poetry but adds themes associated with the diasporic experience, often with an infusion of transliterated Eng. vocabulary.

*See* INDIA, ENGLISH POETRY OF; INDIA, POETRY OF; INDIAN PROSODY; PERSIAN POETRY; RĀMĀYAṆA POETRY; URDU POETRY.

■ J. S. Ahluwalia, *Prayogashīl Punjabi Kavita* (1962); N. H. Syed, *Recurrent Patterns in Punjabi Poetry* (1968); D. S. Maini, *Studies in Punjabi Poetry* (1979); J. Bedi, *Modern Punjabi Poets and Their Vision* (1987); A. Singh, *Secularization of Modern Punjabi Poetry* (1988); S. S. Sekhon and K. S. Duggal, *A History of Punjabi Literature* (1992); I. H. Javeid, *Pakistan in Punjabi Literature* (1993); M. Singh, *Glimpses of Modern Punjabi Literature* (1994); T. Rahman, *Language and Politics in Pakistan* (1996); S. Mukherjee, *A Dictionary of Indian Literature, Vol. 1: Beginnings–1850* (1998); P. M. Chopra, *Great Sufi Poets of the Punjab* (1999); P. K. Singh, *Representing Women: Tradition, Legend and Panjabi Drama* (2000); *Encyclopaedic Dictionary of Punjabi Literature*, ed. R. P. Malhotra and K. Arora (2003); L. Sakata, "Kafi," *South Asian Folklore: An Encyclopedia: Afghanistan, Bangladesh, India, Nepal, Pakistan, Sri Lanka*, ed. P. Claus, S. Diamond, M. A. Mills (2003); P. Gopal, *Literary Radicalism in India: Gender, Nation, and the Transition to Independence* (2005); *Journal of Punjab Studies* 13.1–2 (2006)—Z. Ahmad, "Najm Hosain Syed: A Literary Profile"; T. S. Gill, "Reading Modern Punjabi Poetry from Bhai Vir Singh to Surjit Patar"; S. Rammah, "West Punjabi Poetry: From Ustad Daman to Najm Hosain Syed."

A. Singh

**PURE POETRY,** Fr. *poésie pure*; Ger. *absolute Dichtung*; Sp. *poesía pura*. This term refers to a doctrine derived from E. A. Poe by the Fr. symbolist poets—Charles Baudelaire, Stéphane Mallarmé, and Paul Valéry—and widely discussed in the late 19th and early 20th cs. The debate also extended to Spain, Mexico, and Cuba. In this context, *pure* is equivalent to *absolute* as in *absolute music*, i.e., the structuring of sound without ostensible semantic content, a significant analogy in that both the theory and practice of *symbolism was influenced by the relations of *music and poetry. The meanings of this term, however, vary considerably from poet to poet.

Poe articulated the basis of this doctrine in "The Poetic Principle" (1850). In that essay, he argued that poems should be short, because poetry is directly related to the *intensity of excitement the poem produces, a necessarily transient phenomenon. Thus, for Poe, the long poem was a "flat contradiction in terms." Moreover, poetry worthy of its name, Poe argued, is entirely independent of the intellect and moral sense, its only goal being "to attain a portion of that Loveliness whose very elements perhaps appertain to eternity alone." It is in music that humans best achieve the aim of creating "supernal beauty"; thus, Poe considered *meter, *rhythm, and *rhyme as "absolutely essential" and "the union of Poetry with Music" as "the widest field for the Poetic development."

In developing his ideas on pure poetry, Baudelaire drew heavily on Poe. Like Poe, he staunchly opposed moral or *didactic poetry, arguing that poetry had no other goal but beauty, and he adopted Poe's view of the *imagination as a quasi-divine faculty that allowed the poet to see the intimate and secret relations among things, the correspondences and analogies. Baudelaire also praised *concision, brevity, and "intensity of effect" as the true qualities of poetry, noting Poe's penchant for the short story, a genre in which he often achieved "purely poetic" results. Like Poe, Baudelaire acknowledged rhythm as the most useful tool in the devel. of the idea of beauty, the aim of pure poetry.

In varying degrees, the symbolists sought to confer *autonomy on poetry by subjecting the semantic properties of lang. to the phonetic properties of words, their sounds, kinship, and connotations. For Baudelaire, the autonomy of poetic lang. was incomplete in that meaning involved "correspondences" with an ultimate reality. Poe, in his reference to the "supernal beauty" that pure poetry was capable of achieving, had hinted at the possibility of a metaphysical or mystical significance in verbal music. Mallarmé's conception of pure poetry was of a point at which poetry would attain

complete ling. autonomy, the words themselves taking over the initiative and creating the meanings, liberating themselves from the semiotic tyranny of the lang. and the deliberate *intentions of the poet. With Mallarmé, subject matter is a function of an intense preoccupation with the medium.

Following Mallarmé, Valéry found the processes of poetic composition more interesting than the poetry itself. Valéry's contribution to the doctrine of pure poetry focused on the most fundamental yet ineluctable aspects of poetic lang., the relation of sound and sense. In his preface to a volume of verse by Lucien Fabré (*Connaissance de la déesse*, 1920), Valéry defines *pure poetry* as poetry that, like the chemical purification of an element, is isolated from everything but its essence. Poe's strictures on long poems and on the didactic motive are repeated. Pure poetry seeks to attain from lang. an effect comparable to that produced on the nervous system by music. An important debate began in 1925, when Henri Bremond, a Jesuit writer on mystical subjects eager to support Valéry's candidacy for the Fr. Academy, delivered an address entitled "Poésie Pure" at a meeting of the Institut de France. Although he agreed with Valéry's analogy between pure poetry and music, Bremond was more explicit in claiming a mystical value for pure poetry. This prompted Valéry to define his own views differently, rejecting any mystical connection. Without abandoning the doctrine, Valéry later denied the existence of pure poetry, deeming it instead a theoretical goal rarely attainable in view of the intimate ling. connections between sound and meaning.

The influence of Poe's ideas of pure poetry on Eng.-speaking critics and poets was negligible; the idea was mainly imported from France. *Imagism demanded the utmost precision in the rendering of the *image, which ran counter to the vagueness and suggestiveness espoused by Poe and the symbolists. In 1924, George Moore published an anthol. titled *Pure Poetry*. While he had absorbed the views of the symbolists, Moore's own conception returns to the earlier, plastic trad. of *Parnassianism. T. S. Eliot regarded pure poetry as the most original devel. in the aesthetic of verse made in the last century, characteristically mod. in its emphasis on the medium of verse and its indifference to content, yet also an event that decisively terminated with Valéry. Other critics, however, have continued to find the absolutist, sound-intensive, and antireferential mode in mod. poems such as Wallace Stevens's "Sea Surface Full of Clouds," as well as more radical experiments that followed *modernism in the *Beat poets, *Language poetry, "text-sound," and *sound poetry.

In Spain, from about 1916 on, Juan Ramón Jiménez had pursued a purification of poetic lang. similar to Mallarmé's. Jorge Guillén and Pedro Salinas, who were familiar with Valéry and Mallarmé, theorized and practiced pure poetry through abstraction and the relations between subjective and objective elements in poetry. In Spanish America in the 1920s, pure poetry was often pitted against social or national poetry. Cuban pure poetry followed the path of abstraction, in the work of Eugenio Florit, and of sound play known as *jitanjáforas*, in the work of Emilio Ballagas and, esp., of Mariano Brull, who lived and published in Europe in the 1920s. Around the same time, in Mexico, the poets of the review *Contemporáneos* intensely debated pure poetry in their essays. The poetry of Xavier Villaurrutia and José Gorostiza, in particular, exemplifies such a trend. If all poetry does indeed aspire to the condition of music, that aspiration will make itself manifest somewhere in the poetry of every age and culture.

*See* AESTHETICISM; AVANT-GARDE POETICS; FRANCE, POETRY OF; HERMETICISM; MEXICO, POETRY OF; RELIGION AND POETRY; SEMANTICS AND POETRY; SOUND; SPAIN, POETRY OF; SPANISH AMERICA, POETRY OF.

■ H. Bremond, *La Poésie pure* (1926); F. Porché, *Paul Valéry et la poésie pure* (1926); R. P. Warren, "Pure and Impure Poetry," *KR* 5 (1943); C. de Ste. M. Dion, *The Idea of "Pure Poetry" in English Criticism, 1900–1945* (1948); T. S. Eliot, "From Poe to Valéry," *HudR* 2 (1949); F. Scarfe, *The Art of Paul Valéry* (1954); H. W. Decker, *Pure Poetry, 1925–1930: Theory and Debate in France* (1962); J. O. Jiménez, "Hacia la poesía pura en Cuba," *Hispania* 45 (1962); D. J. Mossop, *Pure Poetry: Studies in French Poetic Theory and Practice 1746 to 1945* (1971); S. Hart, "*Poésie pure* in Three Spanish Poets," *Forum for Modern Language Studies* 20 (1984); R. Larraga, *Mariano Brull y la poesía pura en Cuba* (1994); A. Stanton, "Los Contemporáneos y el debate en torno a la 'poesía pura,'" *Las vanguardias literarias en México y la América Central*, ed. M. Forster (2001).

S. FISHMAN; T.V.F. BROGAN; O. CISNEROS

**PYRRHIC** (Gr., "used in the *pyrriche* or war dance"). In *classical prosody, a metrical foot of two short syllables. This may be said to have been the shortest metrical foot in Gr. and Lat. verse, although its admissibility was denied by the ancient *rhythmici* such as Aristoxenus (see METRICI AND RHYTHMICI), who felt that feet must be of at least three *chronoi* (temporal elements). In the mod. prosodies based on *accent, such as Eng., the existence of pyrrhic feet is disputed: several important metrists (e.g., J. B. Mayor, Robert Bridges, Joseph Malof, G. T. Wright) have recognized them as legitimate variations or substitutions in iambic verse; others deny them ( J. M. Schipper, George Saintsbury). The dispute between the two camps turns on the issue of whether gradations of stress in the line are to be treated relatively or absolutely.

In a line such as Andrew Marvell's "To a green thought in a green shade," the stress pattern (using notation of four levels of stress numbered 1 through 4, 1 being strongest, 4 weakest) might be said to be 3-4-2-1-3-4-2-1. Since Otto Jespersen's seminal 1903 article "Notes on Metre," many prosodists have accepted his claim that stress is perceived only in relation to its surroundings; and if one asks about each pair of syllables in the line from Marvell's "The Garden," 3s outweigh 4s, as 1s do 2s, so that the *scansion is properly trochee + iamb + trochee + iamb (see RELATIVE STRESS PRINCIPLE). There are, additionally, some theoretical grounds for thinking that feet composed of homogeneous members should not be recognized; for further discussion of this issue, with bibl., see FOOT and SPONDEE.

Other metrists, however, would say that, in Marvell's line, 2s and 1s are both stronger than 3s and 4s and that readerly distinctions of stressing are made in absolute terms, not relative—giving the scansion pyrrhic + spondee + pyrrhic + spondee. Absolutists thus view the pyrrhic as a foot of two weakly stressed syllables; precisely how weak the one syllable is in relation to the other is unimportant. Historically, this approach has appealed to classicizing metrists, and it has a certain direct appeal; Saintsbury is eccentric (here as in much else) in accepting spondees but not pyrrhics. The sequence weaker-weaker-stronger-stronger is reasonably common in Eng. iambic pentameter verse; Wright gives many examples from Shakespeare. What one calls it—some classicizing metrists once liked to call it an *ionic foot, while Attridge calls it "stress-final pairing"—is, however, less important than whether one hears relatively or absolutely.

■ Crusius; F. Pyle, "Pyrrhic and Spondee," *Hermathena* 107 (1968); J. Malof, *A Manual of English Meters* (1970); Attridge, *Rhythms*; West; G. T. Wright, *Shakespeare's Metrical Art* (1988).

T.V.F. BROGAN; R. J. GETTY

**PYTHIAMBIC.** A mod. term (*versus pythius* or Pythian verse = dactylic hexameter) for the strophic form of Horace's *Epodes* 14–15 (called First Pythiambic: hexameter + iambic dimeter; also found in Archilochus) and *Epode* 16 (Second Pythiambic: hexameter + iambic trimeter). There is no ancient authority for the term.

*See* HEXAMETER.

J. W. HALPORN

# Q

**QAṢĪDA.** A *monorhyme verse form that emerged in the oral Ar. poetry of the 6th c. as a composite *ode. It was adapted in the 10th and 11th cs. to Persian and Heb. poetry (along with other Ar. poetic conventions) and then spread to Turkish and other Middle Eastern, Af., and South and Southeast Asian lits. Basic formal features shared by qaṣīdas across these trads. include the following: all lines of the poem observe the same *meter and *rhyme (aa ba ca, etc.); each line divides in symmetrical *hemistichs, graphically arranged in two columns, often marking a syntactic *caesura, esp. in Persian; length varies, usually 20 to 100 lines, though longer qaṣīdas are not uncommon; it is consciously literary and epideictic, often a praise poem (see EPIDEICTIC POETRY), frequently intended for *performance in a ritual, ceremonial, or festive context. Anthols. of pre-Islamic qaṣīdas (e.g., the Muʿallaqāt) reveal a fluidity in theme and structure, but Ar. critics of the 9th and 10th cs. abstracted an idealized polythematic, tripartite qaṣīda as the generic model: the tribal Bedouin poet weeps over the beloved's abandoned campsite, falling into nostalgic, often erotic reverie (nasīb); he evokes scenes of his solitary trek through the desert on his she-camel (raḥīl); closing with praise of himself or his tribe (fakhr) or his patron (madīḥ). Earlier views of qaṣīda poetics as atomistic or "mere" *ekphrasis have given way to understanding the cl. tripartite qaṣīda as a complex sonata structure, rite of passage, Maussian gift exchange, and so on. In the highly literate courtly milieus of the Abbasid age, esp. after al-Mutanabbī, the qaṣīda dropped its raḥīl and generally adhered to a bipartite structure of nasīb (on amatory, bacchic, garden, or hunt themes), followed by madīḥ. Persian, Heb., Turkish, and Urdu generally followed this "secondary" bipartite model of the qaṣīda for *panegyric; but the qaṣīda was also dedicated to homiletic, ascetic, philosophical, and mystical themes (e.g., al-Būṣīrī's widely performed qaṣīda in praise of the Prophet Muhammad). The qaṣīda continued to thrive across the trads. in neoclassical form in the 19th c. and remained the prestige verse form in Ar. until the advent of *free verse ca. 1950.

See ARABIC POETRY, GHAZAL, HEBREW POETRY, PERSIAN POETRY, TURKISH POETRY, URDU POETRY.

■ A. J. Arberry, *The Seven Odes* (1957); "Ḳaṣīda," *Encyclopaedia of Islam*, ed. H.A.R. Gibb et al., 2d ed. (1960–2005); R. Jacobi, *Studien zur Poetik der altarabischen Qaside* (1971); A. Hamori, *On the Art of Medieval Arabic Literature* (1974); G. J. van Gelder, *Beyond the Line: Classical Arabic Critics on the Coherence and Unity of the Poem* (1982); *Cambridge History of Arabic Literature: Arabic Literature to the End of the Umayyad Period*, ed. A.F.L. Beeston et al. (1983); S. Sperl, *Mannerism in Arabic Poetry* (1989); J. Stetkevych, *The Zephyrs of Najd: The Poetics of Nostalgia in the Classical Arabic Nasib* (1993); S. Stetkevych, *The Mute Immor-tals Speak: Pre-Islamic Poetry and the Poetics of Ritual* (1993); *Qasida Poetry in Islamic Asia and Africa*, ed. S. Sperl and C. Shackle, 2 v. (1996); *Encyclopedia of Arabic Literature*, ed. J. S. Meisami and P. Starkey (1998); S. Stetkevych, *The Poetics of Islamic Legitimacy: Myth, Gender, and Ceremony in the Classical Arabic Ode* (2002); J. Meisami, *Structure and Meaning in Medieval Arabic and Persian Poetry* (2003); *General Introduction to Persian Literature*, ed. J.T.P. de Bruijn, v. 1 (2009).

F. D. LEWIS

**QIṬʿA.** A *monorhyme poetic form common to Ar., Persian, Turkish, Urdu, and other related lits. The name qiṭʿa means "fragment" or "piece" and originally served to distinguish this form from the *qaṣīda. Formally, the qiṭʿa typically lacks the *internal rhyme found between the *hemistichs in the first verse of the qaṣīda (and *ghazal) and is much shorter than the qaṣīda, containing at least two and normally no more than 20 verses. In contrast to the polythematic qaṣīda, the qiṭʿa is characterized by a unity of topic and mood. Despite its name, however, most qiṭʿa are not, in fact, *"fragments" of an original whole but constitute complete, self-standing poems. In pre-Islamic Ar. poetry, the qiṭʿa was most often employed for mourning the death of a warrior and calling for tribal vengeance. But with the rise of Islam and the establishment of a cosmopolitan empire in the 8th and 9th cs. CE, the thematic range of the qiṭʿa expanded tremendously. Since the prestige of the qasida genre made it the standard medium for political *panegyric and court ceremony, the qiṭʿa became a favorite vehicle for the devel. of *anacreontic, amatory, homiletic, and *nature poetry, addressed to an increasingly diversified urban audience; the simple expedient of removing the opening internal rhyme took the qiṭʿa out from under the weighty authority of the qaṣīda and opened the door to significant literary innovation. In Persian and later Islamicate trads., the themes of wine and love became the domain of the lyric ghazal, and the qiṭʿa took on a new role as the poetic form for ostensibly extemporaneous, *occasional poetry. Topics might include panegyric, requests for *patronage or payment, *invective, *elegy, social *satire, friendly correspondence, or philosophical or ethical meditation. After the 15th c., the qiṭʿa also became the typical form for the chronogram, a poem that disposes the numerical values of the letters in a memorable phrase to commemorate the year an event occurred. The *diction of the qiṭʿa normally requires neither the formality of the qaṣīda nor the *euphony of the ghazal and often tends toward the idiomatic or colloquial.

See ARABIC POETRY, PERSIAN POETRY.

■ J. Rypka, *History of Iranian Literature*, ed. K. Jahn (1968); A. A. Badawi, "Abbasid poetry and its antecedents," *Cambridge History of Arabic Literature: ʿAb-*

*basid Belles Lettres*, ed. J. Ashtiany et al. (1990); H.ʿAbbāspur, "qiṭʿa," *Dānishnāmah-i Adab-i Fārsī*, v. 2, *Farhangnāmah-i adab-i Fārsī*, ed. Ḥ Anūsha (1997); J. S. Meisami, "qiṭʿa," *Encyclopedia of Arabic Literature*, ed. J. S. Meisami and P. Starkey (1998); S. Aslam Bayk, *Qiṭʿa-sarāʾī dar adab-i Fārsī-i Shibh-i Qārra* (2007).

P. Losensky

## QUANTITY

I. Concepts Ancient and Modern
II. Linguistic Basis

**I. Concepts Ancient and Modern.** Quantity is a property of syllables and forms the basis of the metrical *prosody of some langs. Quantitative verse is contrasted with verse based on syllable count or on word accent. Terminology and concepts of quantity in Western poetics descend from practice and description in cl. Gr. and Lat. In ancient and in many mod. theories, quantity is closely connected with vowel length—also called vowel quantity—and the same terms, *long* and *short*, are used to describe both vowels and syllables. So, "durationalists" have assumed that the elapsed time of the entire syllable is the criterion of difference, and some have made a point of variation within the two categories (ancient *rhythmici*, unlike *metrici*, focused on the varied realizations of quantity in performance [see METRICI AND RHYTHMICI]). Most scholars now treat the distinction as an opposition of structures; W. S. Allen (1973) recommends following the ancient Indian trad. in calling syllables either "heavy" or "light" in weight.

A separate distinction, between "open" and "closed" syllables, is often part of the definition of quantity; open syllables end in a vowel, closed in a consonant. Gr. and Lat. syllabification rules allow closed syllables only when a vowel is followed by at least two consonants (VC-CV). Open syllables with a short vowel are short; closed syllables and syllables with a long vowel are long. So: *ar-mă vĭ-rŭm-quĕ* . . . (vowel quantity above the line, syllable quantity below; in *ar-* the actual vowel quantity is "hidden" since the internal closed syllable is necessarily long). A syllable is long "by nature" if it has a long vowel; if it has a short vowel but is closed, it is long "by position" (Gr. *thesei*; Lat. *positione*, meaning either "by convention" or "by placement"; the distinction reflects the confusion of vowel and syllable quantities). Since the combination of a plosive + liquid was sometimes treated as a single consonant (Gr. *pat-ros* vs. *pa-tros*), the preceding syllable was said to be "common"—long or short. Syllables were reckoned across a line of verse without regard to word end, although word-final syllables might be subject to special treatment (in particular, *elision). The details of practice, incl. interaction with word stress and the permissibility of ad hoc adjustments to quantity, varied between langs., over time, and with degree of stylization (*epic is freest, while comedy, in particular, respects spoken norms), but they do not affect the fundamental categorization of long and short syllables. In Eng., efforts to apply the cl. quantitative system to analysis or composition have foundered on the difficulty of defining long and short (Attridge; cf. Stone and various experiments by Robert Bridges).

The metrical patterns of quantitative poetry comprise long or short "elements" (Maas) or "positions" (West) in which a particular syllable quantity is required, but patterns often incorporate alternatives (the distinction between pattern and instance, never entirely absent, was formalized by Maas). An element where either a short or long may be used is *anceps (a postclassical term); the final element of a verse is always "indifferent" to short or long (anceps, "common," and "indifferent" have had multiple and overlapping usages; "neutralization" is the mod. technical term). By "contraction," one long may replace the positions for two short syllables, and by "resolution," two shorts replace a long syllable. Both are restricted in application. Contraction is very familiar from the epic dactylic; resolution is common in comic *iambic; much *lyric excludes both. But the 2:1 replacements (not unique to Gr. and Lat.) are understood in durational terms to mean that a long quantity temporally equals twice a short; the short is the minimal time unit, Gr., *chronos* or *sema*; Lat. and mod. technical term, *mora*. A "triseme" and "tetraseme" are each a further prolongation of a long syllable. Surviving Hellenistic and later musical settings incorporate these ratios. For most 19th- to mid-20th-c. scholars, anceps was identified with what ancient rhythmicians recognized as an *alogos* (irrational) duration, between long and short, and so was taken to require a third quantity whose intermediate length was satisfied by altered performance of either syllable structure (the possibility of a third quantity was refuted in Devine and Stephens [1975]).

Quantitative rhythm may inhere in a pattern, since most patterns require a long element after every anceps or one or two short ones; a sequence of more than two shorts is taken to imply underlying resolution and of two or more longs to involve anceps, contraction, or *syncopation (the omission of a short; never in this context for rhythmic reversal). Scholars differ on whether syncopation implies prolongation. Nonetheless, patterns have traditionally been analyzed into quantitative feet formed by combinations of long and short syllables, with *rhythm determined by the internal ratios and usually with allowed *substitutions among feet providing the variations in pattern. Some scholars have held that quantitative feet are only the verbal representation of nonverbal rhythms incorporating a metrical *ictus (i.e., stress) or a musical beat and ratios other than 2:1 between long and short; some durationalists even adjusted unequal feet to equal "bars." Quantitative feet have allowed more opportunity than syllable quantity to confound separate systems of prosody (so Lanier, Kitto).

**II. Linguistic Basis.** In phonology, quantity, also known as syllable weight, is measured in moras, also known as weight units (Hyman). A light (or short) syllable has one *mora, a heavy (or long) syllable has two moras, and a superheavy (or overlong) syllable has three moras. Quantity is a property of the *rhyme of a syllable (in phonology "rhyme" means the part of the syllable that excludes the onset); that is, initial consonants never count for weight (though see Gordon 2005 for possible exceptions). The quantity of a syllable is determined by how many moras constitute the rhyme of that syllable.

In a quantity-insensitive lang., coda consonants do not contribute to weight; rather they share a mora with the vowel. Such langs. also lack long vowels, by definition. Quantity-insensitive langs. include Fr. and Polish. In a typical quantity-sensitive lang., a syllable is heavy either by having a long vowel or being closed by a coda consonant—this is also called weight by position—or both. Eng., Lat., Sanskrit, and Ar. are examples of quantity-sensitive langs. Some quantity-sensitive langs. (e.g., Khalkha Mongolian) have nonmoraic codas, meaning that syllable weight is determined only by vowel length, not by the number of consonants. Still other langs. (e.g., Kwakw'ala [Gordon 2004]) show a pattern where sonorant consonants, such as *m*, *n*, *r*, and *l*, are moraic, while obstruent consonants such as *t*, *d*, *p*, and *k* are not. While it may seem arbitrary that a consonant may add weight in one lang. but not in another, recent work has shown that these patterns reflect subtle differences in the way these sounds are pronounced across langs. (Broselow, Chen, and Huffman).

The relationship between quantity sensitivity and quantitative verse is not a simple one. Quantity-sensitive langs. do not necessarily have quantitative verse. Lat. and It., e.g., are both quantity-sensitive, stress-accent langs.; yet Lat. verse is largely quantitative, while It. verse is based on stress and syllable count. Furthermore, the distinction between quantitative verse and *accentual verse is not black and white. There is a statistical tendency in both Lat. and Gr. verse to align word stress with metrical ictus (Allen 1965, 1968), while in several Eng. meters, the phenomenon of *resolution is sensitive to syllable weight (Kiparsky and Hanson; Kiparsky). Thus the sequence of vowels and consonants in a syllable does not automatically determine whether that syllable will count as light or heavy in verse; rather, this is a product of the interplay among the quantity sensitivity of the lang., metrical conventions, and ultimately the stylistic preferences of particular poets.

*See* CLASSICAL PROSODY, DURATION, FOOT.

■ **Concepts Ancient and Modern:** S. Lanier, *The Science of English Verse* (1880); W. J. Stone, *On the Use of Classical Metres in English* (1899)—describes, critiques and prescribes; H.D.F. Kitto, "Rhythm, Metre, and Black Magic," *Classical Review* 56 (1942); Maas, 1–25; W. S. Allen, *Accent and Rhythm* (1973); T. Georgiades, *Greek Music, Verse, and Dance*, trans. E. Benedict and M. L. Martinez (1973); D. Attridge, *Well-Weighed Syllables* (1974); A. M. Devine and L. D. Stephens, "Anceps," *Greek Roman and Byzantine Studies* 16: 197–215 (1975); West, 7–25—a compromise between durationalist and structuralist approaches; T. Cole, *Epiploke* (1988)—proposes

quantitative patterns as temporal designs; L. Pearson, *Aristoxenus: Elementa Rhythmica* (1990); A. M. Devine and L. D. Stephens, *The Prosody of Greek Speech* (1994), chap. 2.

■ **Linguistic Basis:** W. S. Allen, *Vox Latina* (1965), and *Vox Graeca* (1968); P. Kiparsky, "Sprung Rhythm," *Phonetics and Phonology, Volume 1: Rhythm and Meter* (1989); B. Hayes, *Metrical Stress Theory* (1995); K. Hanson and P. Kiparsky, "A Parametric Theory of Poetic Meter," *Lang* 72.2 (1996); E. Broselow, S. Chen, and M. Huffman, "Syllable Weight: Convergence of Phonology and Phonetics," *Phonology* 14 (1997); L. Hyman, *A Theory of Phonological Weight* ([1984] 2003); M. Gordon, "Syllable Weight," *Phonetic Bases for Phonological Markedness*, ed. B. Hayes, R. Kirchner, and D. Steriade (2004); M. Gordon, "A Perceptually-driven Account of Onset-sensitive Stress," *Natural Language and Linguistic Theory* 23 (2005); M. Gordon, *Syllable Weight* (2006).

J. LIDOV (ANCIENT/MODERN);
A. JAKER (LINGUISTICS)

**QUATORZAIN.** Any stanza or poem of 14 lines, incl. the *sonnet, though the term is now normally reserved for any 14-line poem other than the cl. Petrarchan (It.) or Shakespearean (Eng.) sonnet. The dispersion and success of the sonnet have tended to conceal from view other members of this class of stanzas. The assonantal *laisses* of OF epic poetry are usually quatorzains (see LAISSE), as are, in Rus. poetry, the nearly 400 stanzas of Alexander Pushkin's *Evgenij Onegin* (1825–32; see ONEGIN STANZA). In Eng. poetry, one can point to Capel Lofft's *Laura; or an Anthology of Sonnets . . . and Elegiac Quatorzains* (5 vols., 1813–14), and in mod. Am. poetry they have served as the vehicle of the verse-novel *The Golden Gate* by Vikram Seth (1986), with the rhyme scheme *ababccddeffegg*.

T.V.F. BROGAN

**QUATRAIN.** A stanza of four lines, usually rhymed. The quatrain, with its many variations, is the most common stanza form in Eur. poetry. Established as the meter of the *hymn in the 3d c. CE (after the Lat. iambic dimeter or two-foot line), it became a conventional meter in the Middle Ages as iambic tetrameter (alone or mixed with trimeter). These four- and three-foot lines correspond to the four-beat line, which is the basis for several forms of the *ballad meter, also a vernacular staple in the Middle Ages. Since then, the "four by four" (a quatrain with lines of four "feet" or "stresses") has been a common stanza for hymns, *ballads, and *nursery rhymes. The quatrain is the form of the Sp. *cópula*, the Rus. *chastushka*, the Georgian *shairi*, the Malay *pantun*, the Ger. *Schnaderhüpfel*, the Chinese and Japanese *shichigon-zekku*, the Iranian *rubā'ī*, and the Welsh *englyn*. In 1834, August Meineke argued that Horace's *Odes* exhibit quatrain structure.

Irrespective of length, most rhyming quatrains adhere to one of the following rhyme patterns: *abab* or *xbyb*, called *"cross rhyme" (in which *x* and *y* represent unrhymed lines), which includes ballad meter, the elegiac stanza, the heroic quatrain (as in Thomas Gray's "Elegy Written in a Country Churchyard") and is the rhyme scheme of most Fr. quatrains; *abba* called "envelope rhyme" or the *envelope stanza of which Alfred, Lord Tennyson's *In Memoriam stanza is a type. Theses two rhyme schemes have been the most popular forms in Western poetry since the 12th c., used primarily as a unit of composition in longer poems and forming the two components of the octave of the *sonnet. Other rhyme schemes include *aabb*, in which internal balance or *antithesis is achieved through opposed *couplets, as in P. B. Shelley's "The Sensitive Plant"; *aaaa* or *aaxa*, a monorhymed or nearly monorhymed stanza, such as Gottfried Keller's "Abendlied" or the *Rubaiyat* stanza. There are also interlinking rhyming quatrains that alternate *masculine and feminine rhymes, as in the most common Rus. stanza form (*AbAb* or *aBaB*, in which the capitals denote feminine rhymes). As a complete poem, the quatrain is often epigrammatic (see EPIGRAM). In hymn meter, common quatrain variations are common meter or common measure (alternating iambic tetrameter and trimeter rhyming *abab*), long meter (four iambic tetrameter lines, rhyming the second and fourth lines and sometimes the first and third), and short meter (two iambic trimeter lines, followed by a third line of iambic tetramter and ending with another trimeter line, rhyming the second and fourth lines and sometimes the first and third).

■ P. Martinon, *Les Strophes* (1912); Meyer; Carper and Attridge.

T.V.F. BROGAN; M. MARTIN

**QUEER POETRY.** A multivalent term whose meanings have all been articulated in the very recent past, most often it denotes the effect of poetry's representation of desire and eroticism on a reader. In such theoretical accounts, *queer poetry* is seen as distinct from the identity-based rubrics of *gay* or *lesbian poetry*. As many critics of queer theory (and several queer theorists themselves) note, the effort to disentangle the term *queerness* from *gayness* or *lesbianism* is never complete. Nonetheless, critics insist on *queer poetry*'s distinction insofar as queer texts challenge and deconstruct the identity-based logic of fixed social categorization whereby understandings of gender, sexuality, nationhood, race, ethnicity, religious culture, and other social categories are constructed.

In the early 1990s, U.S. scholars began to form the field of queer studies and queer theory as a disciplinary movement distinct from gay and lesbian studies. The first volume to articulate the field as such was Warner's edited volume *Fear of a Queer Planet* (1993). The contributors to this anthol. were inspired by two contemp. activist organizations: ACT UP (AIDS Coalition to Unleash Power) and Queer Nation. Founded in New York City in 1987 as a response to the Reagan administration's silence and inaction regarding the HIV/AIDS crisis, ACT UP challenged policies injurious to all people living with AIDS/HIV (PLWAs), incl. seropositive persons, loved ones, and caregivers. The

communities served by ACT UP and contributing to its activist base are, by definition, not limited to sexual minorities. Queer theorists and critics adopted this coalitional spirit and often investigated how cultural production by the entire spectrum of sexual and gender minorities might address the social needs or political issues of larger national, regional, or global populations. Although short-lived, Queer Nation (1990–ca. 1994) modeled forms of social disruption through demonstrations in urban centers in the U.S. and Canada. Queer Nation's confrontation of politicians and corporate retailers often involved public displays of affection intended to affirm that sexuality and eroticism need not always conform to heteronormative models. Queer theorists and activists often view the study of cultural productions—and sometimes their own performative critical projects—as the keys to general social transformation.

*Performativity* is a theoretical concept originating in *speech act theory and developed in poststructuralist philosophies. It describes how the *performance of a discourse affects and transforms a particular identity. Speaking, writing, and all lang. practices are limited by a subject's context; those limits, in turn, inform the subject's identity. However, every ling. performance also has the potential to challenge those contexts and their underlying ideologies. Hence, performative critique can also disrupt normative and seemingly "natural" categories of identity. Although queer theory draws on different philosophers (Jacques Lacan, Michel Foucault, Gilles Deleuze, Jacques Derrida, Luce Irigaray, Hélène Cixous, Julia Kristeva, Roland Barthes), the core idea of performativity depends on linguistically and socially inflected theorizations of *desire*. Prominent queer theorists such as Leo Bersani, Judith Butler, Tim Dean, and Lee Edelman generally maintain that desire is not simply object orientation. Rather, they understand *desire* as a force akin to Lacan's *Real* or Derrida's *supplement*. As such, *desire* is conceived as a part of the structure of lang., but it acts as the "unconscious" of lang. (Lacan) or is that part of lang. that interferes with clear communication (Derrida). Thus, desire lies outside acknowledged social systems of meaning that construct social categories, such as identity. When one finds traces of this destabilizing force in texts, as in *performative* lang. practices, one also finds disruptions of meaning and identity. Understanding the work of desire through performance, across both literary works and social acts, becomes a major preoccupation of queer theorists and critics.

Is queer poetry limited to the production of sexual or gender minorities? Scholars deploying the term are in a double bind owing to their fields' political origins. On the one hand, they claim that queer poetry, much like the activism of ACT UP, strives to build new collectives and social orders in a coalitional spirit. On the other hand, the performativity they associate with queer poetry, as in Queer Nation's actions, proceeds from nonheteronormative, often same-sex, eroticism. Given this contradictory situation, critics and even some contemp. poets still rely on definitions of *queer poetry* that refer to poetic production by anyone from a gender or sexual minority, even if the text is not explicitly politicized. Thus, as a category, *queer poetry* has become esp. useful for collating poetry representing same-sex desire, experiences, or cultures by sexual and gender minorities from eras or cultures in which the terms *gay* or *lesbian* are inappropriate. E.g., the term regularly denotes poets from other global cultures—particularly Africa, Southeast Asia, the Caribbean, and Latin America—to whom it is inappropriate to impose such categories as *gay* or *lesbian*, which connote conformity to U.S. and other Western industrialized nations' prevalent understandings of sexual minorities. The term has also sufficed to describe poetry written before the late 19th c. by poets who may have engaged or did engage in same-sex sexual activity before the social identities *gay* or *lesbian* had come into existence.

In addition to this usage, the rubric of *queer poetry* describes the potential of certain poetic texts—whether or not authored by a self-identified "queer" (or lesbian, gay, transgender) writer—somehow to transform existing social attitudes, discourses, or gender categories. For instance, while the Chicana feminist poet Gloria Anzaldúa described herself as a lesbian, her *Borderlands/ La Frontera* (1987) is a paradigmatic example of queer poetry. A bilingual project that hybridizes memoir, social commentary, and lyric poetry, Anzaldúa's book uses ling. experiments to render the text a corporeal extension of the author's own body, and thus as a desiring entity in its own right. The queerness of *Borderlands/ La Frontera* resides in its characterization of lang. as a kind of body that acts on and interacts with readers' consciousnesses, in an intimate and even erotic manner. The result, as Anzaldúa explicitly imagines it, is a coalitional community, suturing the North-South divide as well as redressing sexual, gender, racial, and other exclusions.

Queer theory postulates that the coalitional capacity of a text like *Borderlands/La Frontera* specifically derives from its "performative" nature and its consequential ability "to queer" (to deconstruct through the deployment of desire) all manner of social constructs and identity categories. Anzaldúa responds to the aforementioned tenet of queer theorists and other observers of performativity—that desire precedes lang. but is closely bound to ling. structures—by demonstrating that a rearrangement of *structure or *syntax, whether willfully through *style or unconsciously through *repetition, reintroduces an erotic difference into the ling. or representational order, and from there into culture and society. When emerging into a lang. system or practice, desire disrupts social codes and conventions. Thus, the ling. introduction of desire brings about discursive and social transformation. Such disruptions are often thought to affect discursive and even generic boundaries as well, thus causing the blurring of lines between poetry and fiction or other prose. Writers working during the era of *poststructuralism in the late 1960s through the 1980s, incl. the Cuban expatriate Severo Sarduy, the Brazilian Clarice Lispector, and the Quebecois Nicole Brossard, deliberately established

their poetry and poetic fiction as literary enactments of such theoretical principles. For this reason, their queer poetry doubles as a kind of queer theory.

Much of the effort to disengage the "queerness" of queer poetry from a poet's own sexual identification has concentrated on desire as a formal issue of lang.'s structure, syntax, or ethics (i.e., lang. as a vehicle enabling relations between authors and audiences or among groups of readers). The Jewish-Am. lesbian expatriate Gertrude Stein established an early 20th-c. precedent wherein erotic disruptions of poetic lang. intend to provoke the transformation of a subject's attitudes toward hist. and the social world, esp. since she envisioned subjects' relationships to reality as mediated materially by lang. itself. Stein's early work *Tender Buttons* (1914) links lesbian eroticism to experimental lang. practice in the interest of introducing readers to different general conceptual, ling., even social orders, inclusive of but not limited to prevailing heternormative understandings of gender and sexuality: "All this and not ordinary, not unordered in not resembling. The difference is spreading." In *Lectures in America* (1935), Stein directly links eroticism to poetic writing: "So as I say poetry is essentially the discovery, the love, the passion for the name of anything," and "it is a state of knowing and feeling a name." Her body of work experiments with lang., as a desiring form, in order to reconfigure perception and experience.

Stein's heirs in contemp. Am. poetry draw similar connections between experimental poetic practices and desire, furthering a politically progressive agenda to articulate poetry's socially and culturally transformative potential. Such heirs include the Am. homosexual anarchist poet Robert Duncan. Chapters of his *H.D. Book*, a prose project written and revised from 1961–ca. 1975 (pub. 2011), advance his own understanding of lang. as a socially queering mechanism, a vehicle introducing impersonal desire into the mainstream world order. Although a major portion of Duncan's project entailed a reimagining of gender and sexual norms (he was specifically interested in embracing, rather than disavowing, perceptions of poetry's "effeminacy" and "passivity"), he distanced his work from the categories of *gay* and *homosexual* in favor of having it read as *humanism*, intent on redressing imperialism, capitalism, and solipsism. The influence of Stein's linking of what now is called poetry's "queering" potential to a formalist understanding of the eroticism of nonnormative lang. practices has also been acknowledged by heterosexual Am. writers, such as the Language poets Lyn Hejinian and Leslie Scalapino, the Af. Am. Harryette Mullen, and the Korean Am. Theresa Hak Kyung Cha. In her poetic memoir *The Transformation* (2007), Juliana Spahr, another poet influenced by Stein, explicitly struggles with the term *queer* as an apt social category for describing her protagonists' unconventional relationship (one woman and two men committed to one another); yet Spahr's memoir and her other poetry are "queer" insofar as they evince her conviction of desire's ability to transform social situations through readers' interactions with self-described "avant-garde" poetic performance.

See AVANT-GARDE POETICS, GAY POETRY, LESBIAN POETRY.

■ G. Hocquenghem, *Homosexual Desire* (1972); T. de Lauretis, *Technologies of Gender: Essays on Theory, Film, and Fiction* (1987); L. Bersani, *The Culture of Redemption* (1990); J. Butler, *Gender Trouble: Feminism and the Subversion of Identity* (1990); E. K. Sedgwick, *Epistemology of the Closet* (1990); P. Quartermain, *Disjunctive Poetics: From Gertrude Stein and Louis Zukofsky to Susan Howe* (1992); J. Butler, "Critically Queer," *GLQ: A Journal of Lesbian and Gay Studies* 1 (1993); *Fear of a Queer Planet: Queer Politics and Social Theory*, ed. M. Warner (1993); L. Bersani, *Homos* (1994); L. Edelman, *Homographesis: Essays in Gay Literary and Cultural Theory* (1994); E. Grosz, *Volatile Bodies: Toward a Corporeal Feminism* (1994), and *Space, Time, and Perversion: Essays on the Politics of Bodies* (1995); J. Butler, *Excitable Speech: A Politics of the Performative* (1997); T. Dean, *Beyond Sexuality* (2000); J. E. Vincent, *Queer Lyrics: Difficulty and Closure in American Poetry* (2002); E. K. Sedgwick, *Touching Feeling: Affect, Pedagogy, Performativity* (2003); N. Sullivan, *A Critical Introduction to Queer Theory* (2003); L. Edelman, *No Future: Queer Theory and the Death Drive* (2004); E. A. Povinelli, *The Empire of Love: Toward a Theory of Intimacy, Genealogy, and Carnality* (2006); L. Bersani and A. Phillips, *Intimacies* (2008); M. D. Snediker, *Queer Optimism: Lyric Personhood and Other Felicitous Persuasions* (2008); L. Bersani, *The Death of Stéphane Mallarmé* (2009); E. Keenaghan, *Queering Cold War Poetry: Ethics of Vulnerability in Cuba and the United States* (2009).

E. KEENAGHAN

## QUERELLE DES ANCIENS ET DES MODERNES

(Battle of the Ancients and the Moderns). The most serious challenge to the Ren. doctrines of poetic *imitation and regularity, the *Querelle*, a dispute over the relative superiority of cl. or mod. lit., reflected an antiauthoritarian, rationalistic, progressivist trend that dated from René Descartes's *Discours de la méthode* (1637) and Blaise Pascal's *Traité du vide* (1647) and that reached its height from 1687 to ca. 1719.

In 1687, Charles Perrault asserted in *Le Siècle de Louis le Grand* that contemp. art outshone the achievements of the Augustan Age of Rome. Jean de La Fontaine replied for the ancients in his *Epître à Huet*, followed by Jean de La Bruyère in his *Caractères*. Bernard le Bovier de Fontenelle took up the mod. cause in *Digression sur les Anciens et les Modernes* (1688), and over the next four years, Perrault sharpened his arguments in the *Parallèles des Anciens et des Modernes* (1688, 1690, 1692). Nicolas Boileau then defended the ancients while attacking the moderns in his *Discours sur l'ode* (1693) and *Réflexions sur Longin* (1694). The opponents reconciled in the same year.

Perrault criticized the ancients for works he often found tiresome or confused and for physics that had been reduced to absurdity by the telescope and the microscope. Unquestioning admiration of ancient errors could only result, he argued, from a lack of critical spirit; with the advent of mod. thought, however, scientists began to study nature itself rather than the writings of Aristotle, Hippocrates, and Ptolemy. Mod. artists, too, must reclaim their freedom. Fontenelle, assuming the permanence of human nature, argued that, whereas the ancients invented everything, equally talented moderns would have done equally well had they come first. Adding the idea of progress, Perrault in his *Parellèles* likened the arts to the sciences, both of which had advanced in the 17th c.

Mainly practitioners rather than theoreticians, the ancients advanced arguments strongly influenced by their creative experiences. They first reaffirmed the cult of Greco-Roman lit. La Fontaine did not deny the merits of the moderns but reaffirmed Homer and Virgil, among others, as "the gods of Parnassus." Imitation was not to be slavish, however: La Fontaine subsumed it under reason and nature. Boileau emphasized that the rules, inferrable from masterpieces, must be used as a guide to rather than a blueprint for original composition, as well as a basis for sensible judgment. Boileau also appealed to the test of time: if antiquity is not a title of merit, long-standing and constant admiration must be, for the majority of readers do not err over the long term.

The moderns won the first battle. Although, in his *Lettre à Charles Perrault* (1694), Boileau denied that the mod. writers surpassed all the ancients, he freely admitted that the 17th c. was superior to any similar period of antiquity. Charles de Saint-Évremond, taking a more nuanced position, in *Sur les poèmes des anciens* (1685) anticipated both evolution and relativism: creative production must accommodate time and place—i.e., as religion, government, and manners change, so too must art.

In England, the Querelle focused somewhat less on poetry than on the relative merits of Scholasticism and its 17th-c. competition—free inquiry and induction as expounded by Francis Bacon, Robert Boyle, and Isaac Newton. Debate began with the "Essay on the Ancient and Modern Learning" in Sir William Temple's *Miscellanea* (1690). Temple was as reluctant to defend the ancients as he was to idolize the moderns. In 1694, William Wotton countered with *Reflections on Ancient and Modern Learning*, arguing for the artistic superiority of the ancients and the scientific preeminence of the moderns. The narrowly literary manifestations of the Querelle turned on the rules, known through trans. of René Rapin and Boileau, among others, and promoted by Thomas Rymer in a critique of Elizabethan drama, *The Tragedies of the Last Age Considered* (1678). John Dryden, a tentative defender of the rules in his *Essay of Dramatic Poesy* (1668), proved inconsistent in his critical views, admiring the ancients but keenly aware that they and the moderns inhabited very different worlds. This implies a skeptical posture toward the unthinking and systematic application of inherited frameworks.

Independent and antidogmatic, Jonathan Swift's "Battle of the Books" (written 1697, pub. 1704) burlesques the Querelle without arriving at a definitive conclusion.

The Fr. Querelle was reignited in 1714 when Antoine Houdard de la Motte published an embellished *Iliad* based on the accurate prose trans. by Anne Dacier (1711). Much that Mme. Dacier had found powerful, harmonious, and majestic in Homer was condemned by La Motte in his *Discours sur Homère* as contemptible and graceless by mod. standards. In his celebrated *Lettre à l'Académie* (1718), François Fénelon straddled the issue: whereas mod. writers need not idolize their forerunners, neither should they scorn them. The Abbé Dubos had the last word in his *Réflexions critiques sur la poésie et sur la peinture* (1719). First, he contended, the superiority of mod. to ancient science has more to do with the quantity and quality of available fact than with reason, a universal. Second, progress in poetry and painting depends less on a knowledge of past achievements than on *invention or natural *genius. Accordingly, Dubos rejected any evaluation of art tied to the hist. of science. Echoing Boileau, Dubos argued that the final test is that of time, though he identified sentiment rather than trad. or authority as the decisive factor in aesthetic judgment.

Subsequent attitudes toward the Querelle have varied. Like Thomas Macaulay in his 1878 essay on William Temple, who dismissed this "most idle and contemptible controversy," Van Tieghem pronounces the issues unimportant and its problems ill-defined. Saisselin finds in the plethora of treatises and broadsides the very germ of major 18th-c. literary theories. While the Querelle had little impact on applied poetics, it, nevertheless, remains a remarkable case study of critical ideas and methods in conflict and change.

*See* BAROQUE, CLASSICISM, NEOCLASSICAL POETICS, RENAISSANCE POETICS, SCIENCE AND POETRY.

■ H. Gillot, *La Querelle des anciens et des modernes en France* (1914); T. S. Eliot, "Tradition and the Individual Talent," *The Egoist* 6 (1919); R. F. Jones, *Ancients and Moderns* (1936); P. Van Tieghem, *Les Grandes Doctrines littéraires en France* (1946); L. Wencelius, "La Querelle des anciens et des modernes et l'Humanisme," *Bulletin de la Société d'Etude du XVII siècle* (1951); Curtius; A. O. Aldridge, "Ancients and Moderns in the 18th Century," *DHI*; G.F.A. Gadoffre, "Le *Discours de la méthode* et la querelle des anciens et des modernes," *Modern Miscellany Presented to Eugène Vinaver*, ed. T. E. Lawrenson et al. (1969); Saisselin; I. O. Wade, *Intellectual Origins of the French Enlightenment* (1971); G. S. Santangelo, *La Querelle des anciens et des modernes nella critica del' 900* (1975); Hollier, 364 ff.; J. M. Levine, *The Battle of the Books* (1991); J. de Jean, *Ancients against Moderns* (1997); J. M. Levine, *Between the Ancients and the Moderns: Baroque Culture in Restoration England* (1999); L. F. Norman, *The Shock of the Ancient: Literature and History in Early Modern France* (2011).

D. L. RUBIN

**QUINTAIN.** Sometimes called a *quintet* and most commonly known as a *cinquain*, this poem or stanza consists of five lines, sometimes with the same meter in each line but often with alternating meters and line lengths (e.g., the *limerick). The earliest Fr. poem, the 11th-c. *Vie de Saint Alexis,* is written in decasyllabic cinquains; in 1174, Guernes de Pont-Sainte-Maxence wrote cinquains in *alexandrines. The 19th-c. poet Victor Hugo wrote cinquains with alternating alexandrine and eight-syllable lines. In Eng., George Puttenham uses the term *quintain*. Examples include Philip Sidney (Psalms 4, 9, 20, 28; *Astrophil and Stella*, Song 9; *Old Arcadia*), John Donne ("Hymne to God my God"), Edmund Waller ("Go, lovely Rose"), William Wordsworth ("Peter Bell," "The Idiot Boy" in tetrameters), and E. A. Poe ("To Helen"). The Am. poet Adelaide Crapsey popularized unrhymed cinquains, inventing a syllabic form (built on the analogy to Japanese *tanka* [see JAPAN, MODERN POETRY OF] and influenced by *haiku) in her 1915 book *Verse*. Her five lines consisted of 2-4-6-8-2 syllables; and her poems were mostly iambic. Unlike Japanese tanka, Crapsey gave her cinquains titles, which often served as a sixth line. Twentieth-c. variations on Crapsey's form include the following (all syllabic): reverse (two, eight, six, four, and two syllables); mirror (a cinquain followed by a reverse cinquain); butterfly (a concrete, nine-line stanza with two, four, six, eight, two, eight, six, four, two syllables); crown (a sequence of five connected cinquains forming one poetic sequence); and garland (a series of six cinquains in which the sixth cinquain is formed from lines taken from the preceding five poems, line one from stanza one, two from two, etc.). Since the early 20th c., *cinquain* tends to refer specifically to Crapsey's original (two, four, six, eight, two) syllabic verse form, which has achieved specific popularity in Am. elementary classrooms as the "didactic" cinquain. The term *cinquain*, then, has supplanted the more general *quintain*, which describes only a poem or stanza of five lines rather than Crapsey's syllabic form. More specific rhyme schemes for the quintain are named the *English cinquain* (a poem in no specified measure with rhyme *abcba*), the *Sicilian quintain* (*ababa*), and the *pentastich* (no specified meter). Tetrameter quintains include the *Spanish cinquain* or *quintilla (*ababa*, *abbab*, *abaab*, *aabab*, and *aabba*).

■ Schipper, v. 2; A. Crapsey, *Verse* (1915); Lote, v. 2; Scott; A. Toleos, http:\\www.cinquain.org.

T.V.F. BROGAN; M. MARTIN

**QUINTILLA.** A Sp. stanza form formerly considered a type of *redondilla* and so called (Diego García Rengifo, *Arte poética española*, 1592), probably formed by the separation, in the 16th c., of the two parts of the nine- or ten-line *copla de arte menor* when it was embryonic (see ARTE MENOR). The *quintilla* is a five-line octosyllabic *strophe having the following restrictions: there may not be more than two rhymes or two consecutive rhymes, and the strophe may not end with a *couplet. The five possible rhyme combinations are, therefore, *ababa*, *abbab*, *abaab*, *aabab*, *aabba*. The last two combinations, which begin with a couplet, are generally avoided in the independent quintilla but frequently appear as the second half of the *copla real*. The quintilla probably ranks among the three or four most commonly used octosyllabic strophes in Castilian. N. Fernández de Moratín's famous *Fiesta de toros en Madrid* is written in quintillas employing four of the five possible rhyme schemes.

■ D. C. Clarke, "Sobre la quintilla," *Revista de Filología Española* 20 (1933); Navarro.

D. C. CLARKE

# R

**RĀMĀYAṆA POETRY.** Few if any works of world lit. have had as great an impact on the theorization and production of poetry as the monumental ancient Indian epic poem the *Rāmāyaṇa*, composed in Sanskrit, according to trad., by the legendary poet-seer Vālmīki sometime in the middle of the first millennium BCE.

First and foremost, the ancient and copious Indian lit. on poetry and poetics generally agrees that the *epic is the original example of the poetic genre in hist. The poem itself, as it has been transmitted, contains a prologue in the form of a celebrated metapoetical narrative that tells how the sage Vālmīki, moving through a sequence of transformative personal experiences, the first edifying, the second emotive, and the third inspirational, is able to fuse them into the production of a new medium of expression, the poetic. The incident is referred to many times in later poetic works and theoretical treatises on the nature of poetry. Thus, the work is often referred to as the *ādikāvya* (first poem), while its author is celebrated as the *ādikavi* (first poet).

Equally noteworthy is how the epic has served as the inspiration for countless poetic retellings of its central narrative in virtually all of the langs. of South and Southeast Asia and several langs. of West, Central, and East Asia as well. According to some traditional works, there are no fewer than one *crore* (10 million) extant in the world. Many langs. have more (sometimes many more) than one *Rāmāyaṇa* to their credit, and in many instances, like Vālmīki's influential work, these regional versions are regarded as standing at the head of their lit. trads. Several of these are among the most important and influential literary works in their respective langs.

In Sanskrit alone, the *Rāmāyaṇa* has inspired dozens, perhaps hundreds, of major poems and poetic dramas that highlight different aspects of the epic tale. Important literary examples, to name but a few, are Kālidāsa's major narrative poem, the *Raghuvaṃśa,* and Bhavabhūti's powerful poetic dramas, the *Mahāvīracarita* and the *Uttararāmacarita*. Many Jain versions in Prakrit, such as Vimalasūri's *Paumacariya*, were central to that religion's lit. hist. Important and highly influential med. and early mod. poetic *Rāmāyaṇas* in major regional langs. continue to be read and performed and exert tremendous cultural influence. Important examples are the Tamil poet Kamban's *Irāmāvatāram* (early 13th c.), Kṛttibās's Bengali version (early 15th c.), and the incomparably influential devotional poem the *Rāmcaritmānas* of the Avadhi (Old Hindi) poet-saint Tulsīdās (late 16th c.).

*See* ASSAMESE POETRY; BENGALI POETRY; GUJARATI POETRY; HINDI POETRY; INDIA, ENGLISH POETRY OF; KANNADA POETRY; KASHMIRI POETRY; MALAYALAM POETRY; MARATHI POETRY; NEPALI AND PAHARI POETRY; NEWAR POETRY; ORIYA POETRY; PUNJABI POETRY; SANSKRIT PO-

ETICS; SANSKRIT POETRY; TAMIL POETRY AND POETICS; TELUGU POETRY.

■ B. S. Miller, "The Original Poem: Vālmīki-Rāmāyaṇa and Indian Literary Values," *Literature East and West* 17 (1973); J. Brockington, *The Sanskrit Epics* (1998); *The Rāmāyaṇa of Vālmīki: An Epic of Ancient India*, ed. R. P. Goldman, 6 v. (1984–2009); R. P. Goldman, "The Ghost from the Anthill: Vālmīki and the Destiny of the *Rāmakathā* in South and Southeast Asia," *A Varied Optic: Contemporary Studies in the Rāmāyaṇa*, ed. M. Bose (2000); R. P. Goldman and S. J. Sutherland Goldman, "The Ramayana," *The Hindu World*, ed. S. Mittal and G. Thursby (2004).

R. P. GOLDMAN

**RAP.** *See* HIP-HOP POETICS.

**RAZO** (Lat. *ratio*, "reason," "explanation"). A brief Occitan prose narrative that tells the story leading up to the composition of a particular *troubadour song. *Razos* are often referred to jointly with the *vidas as the "biographies of the troubadours." Like the vidas, the razos probably originated with *jongleurs, who used them in their performances. Though typically somewhat longer than vidas, razos rarely exceed several paragraphs. Certain of the stories they recount are based on a literal interpretation of the imagery found in the poem that they purport to explain; others appear to draw from a fund of *fabliau-like episodes. The material for the razos, none of which postdates 1219, must have been collected by the primary biographer Uc de Saint Circ before he left southern France for Italy. The frequent Italianisms that they contain suggest that Uc did not write the razos immediately on his arrival in the Veneto. The razos for the *sirventes of Bertran de Born were produced before the other razos and always remained separate from them. The boundary between vida and razo was fluid in the Middle Ages: the extant corpus of troubadour biographies includes a number of hybrid texts bearing traits of both types.

*See* OCCITAN POETRY.

■ J. Boutière and A. H. Schutz, *Biographies des troubadours*, 2d ed. (1964); *Razos and Troubadour Songs*, trans. W. E. Burgwinkle (1990); E. W. Poe, "*Vidas* and *Razos*," *Handbook of the Troubadours*, ed. F.R.P. Akehurst and J. M. Davis (1995); W. E. Burgwinkle, *Love for Sale: Materialist Readings of the Troubadour Razo Corpus* (1997).

E. W. POE

**READER.** Poetry without readers is a contradiction in terms, but poets have long expected conflict between situations of production and reception, whether problems with addressed rulers, patrons, and other powerful figures who could be offended (e.g., the exiles of Ovid in 8 CE and Osip Mandelstam in 1934) or an inability to produce work appealing to a wide readership in a mass democracy. From the exclusion of poets in Plato's *Republic* to their dropping from publishers' lists through failing to generate sufficient sales, poets have hoped that they might a "fit audience find, though few," as John Milton put it in *Paradise Lost*. Such long-standing ambivalence about poetry's aim has resulted in theories and assumptions about the position and role of readers and of poets' responsibilities toward them. The range of these approaches, however theoretically elaborated, covers such duties as are outlined in Horace's *Ars poetica*, summarized in the phrase *ut doceat, ut moveat, ut delectet* (to teach, to move, to delight). Contemp. pressures include requirements to entertain or distract, to move for educative ends, or to disturb reader relations so as to effect cultural and political transformations.

During the romantic period, matching the poet's social isolation, readers were located in the margins—exemplified by John Stuart Mill's observation in "What Is Poetry?" (1833) that "eloquence is *heard*, poetry is *over*heard. Eloquence supposes an audience; the peculiarity of poetry appears to us to lie in the poet's utter unconsciousness of a listener. Poetry is feeling confessing itself to itself in moments of solitude." This notion best suited the poetry experiencing its heyday when Mill wrote: seemingly solitary meditation like William Wordsworth's and dramatic *monologues such as Alfred, Lord Tennyson's and Robert Browning's. In Wordsworth, even when (as in *The Prelude*) there is an interlocutor, the "Friend," a figure identified with S. T. Coleridge, it can still be argued that the reader, not being this friend, overhears the poem as an *apostrophe directed elsewhere. Browning's "Andrea del Sarto" appears to be an *address by its eponymous speaker to his silently departing wife. Mill's assertion protected poetry's special value as something other than propagandistic manipulation. Its influence shows in W. B. Yeats's oft-quoted 1918 aphorism that "[w]e make out of the quarrel with others rhetoric, but of the quarrel with ourselves, poetry."

Yet it may be one more defense, as in Philip Sidney's *Defence of Poesy*, that protects by haplessly diminishing poetry's social consequence. Would Mill's theory allow for the eloquent addresses and apostrophes of Walt Whitman's *Leaves of Grass* or Allen Ginsberg's *Howl*? Would Yeats's aphorism explain the many poems including the prepositions *to* and *for* in their titles or dedications? Counterarguments have it that the staging of the poem as a solitary meditation is its fictional dimension (see FICTION, POETRY AS). Dorothy Wordsworth's diary shows that the inspiring occasion of "Daffodils" did not find the poet "lonely" with his thoughts but traveling with his sister. Equally, an address to a named or unnamed interlocutor—let alone an implied character receiving the poem's address, as in Browning's "My Last Duchess"—is an enabling fiction for poetic speech, the true addressee being the reader,

who, far from "overhearing" what is said to a friend or projected interlocutor, receives what is obliquely directed, for instance, toward the "British Public" evoked in Browning's epic *The Ring and the Book*.

Such fictional dimensions of a poem's internal speaking relations were taken up by poststructuralist critics to assert a difference in kind between the empirical addressee of a letter and the fictive addressee of a poem, showing how poems containing apostrophes evoke absences, underlying the narcissistic or solipsistic spheres of the lyric, in which the poet's apostrophizing inanimate objects, *prosopopoeia, and persons (since poetry "makes nothing happen" in the words of W. H. Auden's *elegy for Yeats) constructs substitute hermetic events that survive as a "way of happening, a mouth." Yet such poetic happenings are activated in readers' lives, where things will happen, by those readers; and, despite its partiality, *reader-response theory did underline that the poem's meaning is not quite *in* its shaped words but in the enabling of those words through the learned and intersubjective activity of reading. Emphasizing the fictive dimension of lyric address underplayed functioning similarities between writing a love letter and a love poem and disabled enacted relationships between the reader and interlocutor or addressee of a poem—when, e.g., directed to a dedicatee of the poet's acquaintance, such as Elizabeth Bishop's "Invitation to Miss Marianne Moore." Could readers not activate an affiliation between the intimate address to a once-living person and the living person who is, at that moment, reading the poem? Such an account argues for imaginative links among interlocutors, dedicatees, addressees, and the poem's anonymous reader. This reader is not left to overhear the articulation of those relationships but invited into them by means of the poem's formal features, as an equally occasioning figure of the poem's written speech. Such reader relations have invited reflections on the pronouns *I* and *you*, as on other deictic words such as *here* and *now*, arguing against the assumption that, in poems, they have no referents (see DEIXIS). Such discussions of occasioned communication have contributed to current debates about poetry's addressing its culture with transitivity and commitment beyond the fictive through the necessary somatic response to poetry in the reader's body and nervous system.

A range of variously explicit attitudes to readers has, thus, developed from a highly conscious appeal to an assumed reader, the poet second-guessing what will please, which attitudes can be played up and which down, while at the other extreme are writers whose strategy is to address their materials and medium and to treat the reader as a figure that will be imagined into existence in the work of a genius who "creates the taste by which he shall be appreciated," in words from Thomas Noon Talfourd's 1837 campaign for the establishment of copyright. One widespread theory of modernist and experimental writing has it that, though not addressing the reader, nevertheless, its disturbances of *syntax, or unexpected *diction, are political engagements with consciousness and result in a "making of the reader."

Thus, there has been a struggle in poetry and poetics among the claims of poet, poem, reader, and interpreter. When on October 26, 1751, in the *Rambler* no. 168, Samuel Johnson writes of "the Force of Poetry," he places efficacy in a power of the text, put there by the poet, able to shape and change readers. Ezra Pound, writing in a postcard to Mary Barnard on February 23, 1934, of how the rhythm of a poem is "forced onto the voice" of the reader, founds his belief on poetry's efficacy as a constructed form with power over the reader's speech. Similar assumptions of poetry's power shape W. S. Graham's belief in his 1946 "Notes on a Poetry of Release" that the poem assists with "the reader's change." Yet, as Auden put it in his Yeats elegy, the poet's words are "modified in the guts of the living." The reader brings the poem to life in consciousness, in the voice and body (in silence or out loud) or in those listening to it, producing that Johnsonian force. The reader is coactive in the exchange that makes things happen.

In the light of such conflicted relations among the role of the poem, of the making poet, and of the freely responding reader, attempts have been made to articulate them as contractual, or quasi-contractual, prompting skepticism about such necessarily informal arrangements. The deconstructive crit. of Austin's performative utterances and Searle's *speech act theory underlined the banishing of the poetic to the realm of the parasitical, by arguing that lang. use is necessarily fictive (there are only parasites and no host). By contrast, its supporters have criticized that appeal to the imagined as a failure to identify how poetry may promise and affirm, if properly understood in its transactions with readers. They note that when, for instance, John Donne apparently urges us to "Go and catch a falling star," it would be mistaken to assume that he is really inciting such an action in his reader but equally wrong to suppose he does not have designs that must be realized by readers' collaborative enactment of the poem's shape and significance, a realizing that need not prevent a coming to conclusions or preferring to believe views about a woman's fidelity other than those of Donne's poem. The cultural action of poetry is as dependent on a readiness to be invited into, to engage with, and be changed by the poems we read, as it is by a capacity to evaluate, criticize, and resist them; and, to that end, let it not be forgotten, poets are first readers, too.

*See* ABSORPTION, APPRECIATION, CLOSE READING, EXPLICATION, EXPLICATION DE TEXTE, PERFORMANCE, RECITATION.

■ J. S. Mill, "Thoughts on Poetry and Its Varieties" [1833], *Dissertations and Discussions* (1859); J. L. Austin, *How to Do Things with Words* (1962); J. Searle, *Speech Acts* (1969); J. Culler, *The Pursuit of Signs* (1981); D. Trotter, *The Making of the Reader* (1984); G. Hill, "Our Word Is Our Bond," *The Lords of Limit* (1984); J. Derrida, *Limited Inc.*, trans. S. Weber and J. Mehlman (1988); J. Hillis Miller, *Speech Acts in Literature* (2001); P. Robinson, *Poetry, Poets, Readers: Making Things Happen* (2002); M. de Gaynesforde, "The Seriousness of Poetry," *Essays in Criticism* (2009).

P. ROBINSON

**READER RESPONSE.** An epithet applied to crit. that focuses on a *reader's or an audience's experience of a poem. In general, much more of crit. involves ideas of reader response than would appear at first glance. Any poetic theory that makes statements about how we feel as we read a poem, what poetry aims to do, how poetry affects us morally, or how we perceive the world described by the poet is making claims about reader response. Plato, in banning poets from his *Republic*, and those critics who assert against Plato the moral efficacy of poetry are both making assumptions about reader response. Aristotle's *catharsis, Longinus's *sublime, and mod. concepts such as Bertolt Brecht's alienation effect or the Rus. formalists' *defamiliarization all rest on reader-response claims. One could argue that poetic theory always involves a model of understanding lang., even if the model remains tacit.

More specifically, reader-response crit. refers to a group of critics who explicitly studied not a poem but readers reading a poem. This critical school emerged in the 1960s and 1970s in North America and Germany, in work by Stanley Fish, Wolfgang Iser, H. R. Jauss, and N. N. Holland. Important predecessors would include I. A. Richards, who in 1929 analyzed a group of Cambridge undergraduates' misreadings of poems, and Louise Rosenblatt, whose 1937 book insisted on the unique relationship of each reader to aesthetic texts. In opposition, W. K. Wimsatt and M. C. Beardsley in 1954 attacked the *"affective fallacy." To evaluate a poem in terms of its emotional effect, they argued, was to confuse the poem with its result. They thus assumed an "objective" text, separate from its reader but entailing certain appropriate responses. The affective fallacy became a theoretical cornerstone of the *New Criticism.

The reader-response critic holds exactly the opposite view. A poem involves a psychological or phenomenological process in which author and reader interact through a physical text. Therefore, one cannot isolate some objective poem that exists prior to readers' experience of it. Critics often claim "objectivity," but that is an illusion. In fact, one can only see a poem through our human processes of perception (and they are driven by our sense of the poem's relation to our feelings and values, incl. our ideas of how one ought to read a poem).

Within this general position, critics (primarily in Germany and the U.S.) developed differing versions of reader-response theory. Some sample the responses of actual readers, while others posit on theoretical grounds a response or (more usually) a reader (the narratee [Prince], the superreader [Riffaterre], the informed reader [Fish 1967], the reader implied or required by this poem [Iser], or simply "the" reader). Among those who consider actual readers, some seek "free" responses (Bleich, Holland), while others use questionnaires that structure response. Thus, some reader-response critics regard individual differences in response as important, while others prefer to consider response as common to a class or era.

There is a fundamental distinction between those

reader-response critics who envisage a largely uniform response to a poem (with unimportant personal variations) and those who see the reader in control at every point. The former say that which is common to different readers' readings results from the poem, while those who see the reader in control explain that which is common as resulting from common codes and *canons for reading that are individually applied by different readers. The most fundamental difference among reader-response critics is probably, then, between those who regard individual differences among readers' responses as important and those who do not. By and large, Ger. and other continental critics tend to use generic and theoretical concepts of the reader, Am. critics actual and individual.

E.g., Jauss's landmark paper (1967; trans. as "Literary History as a Challenge to Literary Theory") defined lit. as a dialectic process of production and reception. In reception, readers have a mental set that Jauss called a *horizon of expectations* (*Erwartungshorizont*), from which vantage point a reader, at a given moment in hist., reads. Lit. hist., then, becomes the charting of these horizons of expectations. Jauss, however, derives this horizon by reading literary works of the period, thus introducing a circularity in his theory. In subsequent writings, he dealt extensively with the kinds of pleasure we take in lit.

Iser also exemplified the Ger. tendency to theorize the reader. Drawing on the Polish aesthetician Roman Ingarden's idea of *Konkretisation*, Iser argues that a poem is not an object in itself but an effect to be explained. Nevertheless, he brackets the real reader and relies instead on an implied reader, the reader a given poem requires.

Among the Americans, David Bleich pioneered the study of the actual feelings and free associations of actual readers as early as 1967, and he applied his findings both theoretically, to model the reading process, and practically, to reform the classroom teaching of lit. Bleich has written extensively on particular teaching strategies using readers' responses.

In *Surprised by Sin* (1967), Fish provided the first reader-oriented study of a major literary work, John Milton's *Paradise Lost*. An appendix, "Literature in the Reader," used "the" reader to examine responses to complex sentences sequentially, word by word (such as "Nor did they not perceive the evil plight"). After the mid-1970s, however, Fish emphasized the real differences among real readers, focusing attention on the reading tactics endorsed by different critical schools and by the literary professoriate. Milton's "Lycidas" is *pastoral for one "interpretive community," a set of themes for another, and a fantasy defense for a third.

In recent years, the approach has been less a discrete method and more a widely adopted concern fused with other methods by critics who would not always accept the *reader-response* label. Much of the best work since 2000 has been in pedagogy; in aesthetic experiences (Felski) and affects (Ngai); and in the emotions produced in fiction (Keen).

Ethically, the reader-response critic's emphasis on the activity of the reader makes it possible to be precise about the effects of reading, e.g., self-effacement, refining one's moral criteria, learning to heed details, adding to one's knowledge, or discovering new strategies of *interpretation. In this vein, reader-response critics have often shared the concerns of critics writing from a feminist, queer, or postcolonial vantage. Such readers are likely to arrive at readings of a poem not available to a white, middle-class, Western male reader.

Socially, because reader-response critics pay attention to the strategies readers are taught to use, they have often become concerned with the teaching of reading and lit., with the profession of letters, and with the literary professoriate. What ways of reading are we teaching, and what do those ways show about our society and our values?

*See* SEMIOTICS AND POETRY, SPEECH ACT THEORY.

■ **Criticism and History**: I. A. Richards, *Practical Criticism* (1929); W. K. Wimsatt, and M. C. Beardsley, "The Affective Fallacy," *The Verbal Icon* (1954); N. N. Holland, *The Dynamics of Literary Response* (1968); G. Poulet, "Phenomenology of Reading," *NLH* 1 (1969); H. R. Jauss, *Literaturgeschichte als Provokation* (1970); W. Slatoff, *With Respect to Readers* (1970); W. Bauer et al., *Text und Rezeption* (1972); N. N. Holland, *Poems in Persons* (1973); G. Prince, "Introduction à l'étude du narrataire," *Poétique* 14 (1973); W. Iser, *The Implied Reader* (1974); D. Bleich, *Readings and Feelings* (1975); N. N. Holland, *5 Readers Reading* (1975); M. Schwartz, "Where Is Literature?" *CE* 36 (1975); *Basic Processes in Reading*, ed. D. Laberge and S. J. Samuels (1977); D. Bleich, *Literature and Self-Awareness* (1977); *Schooling and the Acquisition of Knowledge*, ed. R. C. Anderson et al. (1977); D. Bleich, *Subjective Criticism* (1978); W. Iser, *The Act of Reading* (1978); M. Riffaterre, *Semiotics of Poetry* (1978); Fish; *Theoretical Issues in Reading Comprehension*, ed. R. J. Spiro et al. (1980); H. R. Jauss, *Toward an Aesthetic of Reception*, trans. T. Bahti (1982); M. Meek, *Learning to Read* (1982); R. G. Crowder, *The Psychology of Reading* (1982); H. R. Jauss, *Aesthetic Experience and Literary Hermeneutics*, trans. M. Shaw (1982); *Discovering Reality*, ed. S. Harding and M. B. Hintikka (1983); E. Kintgen, *The Perception of Poetry* (1983); M. Meek, *Achieving Literacy* (1983); I. Taylor and M. M. Taylor, *The Psychology of Reading* (1983); D. Bordwell, *Narration in the Fiction Film* (1985); *Human Abilities*, ed. R. J. Sternberg (1985); *Opening Moves*, ed. M. Meek (1985); *Gender and Reading*, ed. E. A. Flynn and P. P. Schweickart (1986); N. N. Holland, "The Miller's Wife and the Professors," *NLH* 17 (1986); E. Freund, *Return of the Reader* (1987); A. N. Grant, *Young Readers Reading* (1987); D. Bleich, *The Double Perspective* (1988); V. B. Leitch, *American Literary Criticism from the Thirties to the Eighties* (1988), ch. 8; S. Noakes, *Timely Reading* (1988); S. Fish, *Doing What Comes Naturally* (1989); T. Rajan, *The Supplement of Reading* (1990); J, Oster, *Toward Robert Frost* (1991); T. Rajan, "Intertextuality and the Subject of

Reading/Writing," *Influence and Intertextuality in Literary History*, ed. J. Clayton and E. Rothstein (1991); *Readers in History*, ed. J. L. Machor (1993)—19th-c. Am. lit.; F. Smith, *Understanding Reading*, 5th ed. (1994); L. Rosenblatt, *Literature as Exploration*, 5th ed. (1995); C. Beach, *Poetic Culture: Contemporary American Poetry between Community and Institution* (1999); N. Cronk, "Aristotle, Horace, and Longinus: The Conception of Reader Response," *CHLC*, v. 3, ed. G. P. Norton (1999); *Reception Study*, ed. J. L. Machor and P. Goldstein (2001); J. Spahr, *Everybody's Autonomy: Connective Reading and Collective Identity* (2001); M. A. Caws, "Taking Textual Time," *Reimagining Textuality*, ed. E. B. Loizeaux and N. Fraistat (2002); *Reading Sites: Social Difference and Reader Response*, ed. E. A. Flynn and P. P. Schweickart (2004); S. Ngai, *Ugly Feelings* (2005); D. Bleich, "The Materiality of Reading," *NLH* 37 (2006); R. Felski, *The Uses of Literature* (2008); *New Directions in American Reception Study*, ed. P. Goldstein and J. L. Machor (2008); I. Yaron, "What Is a 'Difficult Poem'? Towards a Definition," *Journal of Literary Semantics* 37 (2008); Y. Ansel, "Pour une socio-politique de la reception," *Littérature* 157 (2010); K. Breen, *Imagining an English Reading Public, 1150–1400* (2010); S. Keen, *Empathy and the Novel* (2010); G. Steinberg, *Philip Larkin and His Audiences* (2010).

■ **Overviews**: A. C. Purves and R. Beach, *Literature and the Reader* (1972); R. T. Segers, "Readers, Text, and Author," *Yearbook of Comparative and General Literature* 24 (1975); *The Reader in the Text*, ed. S. R. Suleiman and I. Crosman (1980); *Reader-Response Criticism*, ed. J. P. Tompkins (1980); R. C. Holub, *Reception Theory* (1984)—distinguishes between Am. reader-response crit. and Ger. reception theory; T. F. Davis, *Formalist Criticism and Reader-Response Theory* (2004); M. Garber, *The Use and Abuse of Literature* (2011).

N. N. HOLLAND; R. GREENE

**REALISM.** The term *realism* denotes both a diversely practiced stylistic method and, esp. in the Ger. context, a heterogeneous period in lit. hist., during which poetry is at best of secondary importance. In either case, a succinct definition, even the speculative construction of an ideal type, of *realism* is made difficult by the semantic indeterminacy or multivalence of its underlying concept, reality. In principle, an understanding of what is "realistic" in an artistically created ("fictitious" or "fictional") world is based on the implicit agreement between reader and writer, differences in their subjective perceptions, purposes, and talents notwithstanding, that reality is constituted by the objective factuality of natural laws. These laws are accessible to empirical ("scientific") cognition. External events in human affairs, natural phenomena, and interpersonal experiences are determined by the logic and dynamics of cause and effect, of coherence and continuity, in their social, psychological, and material implications. This is a tenet of absolute veracity and validity. Hence, reality is identical with truth, and beauty exists objectively in real nature (and not merely in the eye of the beholder). Nature's poetic transformation into *das Kunstschöne* (beauty in art) can only serve the purpose of intensifying, i.e., of distilling into an aggregate of greater purity, what is already beautiful (*das Realschöne*, beauty in reality). Likewise, the empirical world is a meaningful entity that needs to be described in its multifarious ordinary details but not imaginatively invented or rearranged. Aesthetic theory must, therefore, uphold the fundamental conviction that reality by necessity is orderly and that it affords pleasurable experiences. Art itself is a distinctive mode of representing particular aspects of this essential structure of reality and of contributing to facilitate its sensory cognition. These widely accepted assertions, incl. their recourse to trads. of speculative idealism, established the dominance of narrative genres over all other forms of lit. in the second half of the 19th c., perhaps even preventing the emergence of a distinctly "realistic" poetry.

Critical discussions in continental Europe during the 1830s postulated realism as a school of writers and their style as arising from an aesthetic opposition to the continued authority of *classicism's *idéalisme*. As *réalisme romantique*, this realism is seen as constituting itself as a "natural" consequence of *romanticism rather than as an oppositional reaction against it, even where it follows a pointedly antipoetic orientation. The realists, in other words, appear as objective romanticists. These controversies started in the early 1820s in critical response to a style of painting that refused to transfigure the common aspects of life and hence was denounced as a distortion of reality. But they had lost much of their vehemence by 1855, when an exhibition of 40 paintings by Gustave Courbet in the pavilion "Le Réalisme" at the Paris World's Fair initiated a revaluation of critical standards.

In historical terms, by 1840, realism was concomitant with the full emergence of bourgeois culture—in France during the reign of Louis-Philippe, *le roi bourgeois*—even though the political and economic foundations of this culture were significantly different among the Eur. monarchies and in the U. S. In Germany esp., a mood of resignation became prevalent after the failure of the 1848 revolutions, which erased an upswell of public poetry that, with an agitating, satiric, and often antidynastic patriotic temper, had advocated republican ideals and decried the ubiquitous injustices and miseries (pauperism) inflicted on the populace. But even the rhetorical pathos of these poems seems driven by the realization that this era (the post-Napoleonic generation) is a time of shattered illusions that has, in fact, become a prosaic age. It defies any attempt to "idealize" it. Consequently, the difference between "reality" as the material of *poiēsis* and its ling. articulation has to be so inconspicuous as never to challenge readers' expectations of probability, i.e., their ability to recognize their own *Lebenswelt* (life-world) in its artistic representations.

As a result, realistic poetry projects normal rather than extraordinary perceptions of reality. It provides plausible rather than imaginative explanations. Its style reinforces rather than questions what is generally accepted as relevant and truthful. It prefers quotidian situations and average characters with modest experiences and simple emotions, renouncing rhetorical intensity or flourishes in the interest of descriptive verisimilitude. Consistently applied, these principles would, of course, bring about the desiccation of poetry, as they did in the immensely popular and genteel versification of Emanuel Geibel (1815–84), e.g., and in the sentimental imitations of the romantics in the late 19th-c. U.S. or late Victorianism.

The *Unlyrische*, for the poet-novelist Theodor Fontane (1819–98) the defining characteristic of his time, was only bypassed and not disproved in attempts to absorb it in such hybrid forms as the *ballad and the verse *epic and even in the revival of the vernacular. This is perhaps also true of the Rus. *poemy*, long narrative poems, usually depicting the lives of the poor in colloquial language (A. N. Maikov, 1821–97, and N. A. Nekrasov, 1821–77), in A. P. Barykova's (1839–93) and I. S. Nikitin's (1824–60) poetry of social protest, or in the populist idealization of the peasantry in the *narodnik* movement of the 1870s. A solution to this critical dilemma would be to avoid the designation *realistic* altogether, speak of "poetry in the age of realism" instead, and point out its "realistic" aspects. The alternative is to accept for poetry a paradigm shift that sees all reality as perspectivism and a construction. In this sense, it would be legitimate to include both "socialist" and "magic" realism in its basic definition.

■ V. da Sola Pinto, "Realism in English Poetry," *E&S* 25 (1939); R. Wellek, "The Concept of Realism in Literary Scholarship," *Concepts of Criticism* (1963); H. Schlaffer, *Lyrik im Realismus* (1966); A. Todorov, "Lyrik und Realismus in der Mitte des 19. Jahrhunderts," *Bürgerlicher Realismus*, ed. K.-D. Müller (1981); L. Völker, "Bürgerlicher Realismus," *Geschichte der deutschen Lyrik*, ed. W. Hinderer (1983); R. C. Cowen, *Der poetische Realismus* (1985); Terras—Rus.; R. Selbmann, *Die simulierte Wirklichkeit: Zur Lyrik des Realismus* (1999).

M. WINKLER

**RECEPTION THEORY.** *See* READER RESPONSE.

**RECITATION.** The act of repeating a written text from memory, often following conventions of elocution and dramatic representation, recitation has been central to the educational and social practices of many cultures. In Islam, for instance, Muslims are expected to memorize portions of the Qur'an, and recitation is a sophisticated art (one sense of the word *Qur'an* is "recitation"). In most Eur. cultures and esp. the Eng.-speaking world, the art of vernacular (as opposed to Lat.) recitation of poetry played an important role in the 18th, 19th, and early 20th cs.

The aesthetic and literary significance of recitation must be distinguished from the oral trad. In preliterate oral cultures (e.g., Homer's milieu) and in settings that draw on oral cultures (such as the Appalachian folk-ballad trad.), the *performance is* the text. The performer is expected to improvise and elaborate; his or her fundamental role is to participate in the creation of the poem and its meaning. Thus, the received poem is subordinate to, and dependent on, the performer (see ORAL POETRY). By contrast, recitation, while it has an interpretive element, is not additive or improvisational;

the point is to remember the written text accurately and to interpret it correctly. In other words, the performer is mostly subordinate to, and dependent on, the received text.

Before the 18th c., well-educated boys were compelled to recite Lat. poetry and prose. After the Enlightenment, however, schools shifted their focus to vernacular langs. as they opened their doors to a broader population. By the early 19th c., schools in the Eng.-speaking world were teaching children to recite from poets such as Shakespeare, William Cowper, and William Cullen Bryant. Wide literacy also meant that moderately prosperous people could enjoy poetry at home; on both sides of the Atlantic, Robert Burns rivaled Shakespeare as a favorite because his lyrics in dialect lent themselves to dramatic recitation in parlors (see DIALECT POETRY). During the 19th c., then, and in Europe and Latin America as well as Britain and the U.S., the recitation of poetry flourished in both the private and public spheres, reflecting and influencing the rise of the middle class. The Mexican critic Alfonso Reyes tells of such a family occasion, normally devoted to the declamation of romantic poetry, in which the Cuban poet Mariano Brull introduced the variety of *sound poetry he called the *jitanjáfora*.

In the romantic period and after, the art of recitation depended, in part, on the cult of the singular *poet. Poets became role models, and reciters not only mouthed their words but sometimes internalized their values (see ABSORPTION). This sense of identity through performance tended to favor poets whose work seemed to accord with conventional middle-class values: while it led to a backlash against figures like Lord Byron, others such as Alfred, Lord Tennyson and H. W. Longfellow ascended to secular sainthood. Recitations of poetry in schools, parlors, churches, union halls, and settlement houses were believed to have an elevating effect; to recite a poem was to express both ambition and subordination to established cultural authorities. Of course, cultural authority is never evenly distributed, and some poems passed quickly into the oral trad., becoming—like folk rhymes—subject to appropriation and improvisation; examples include Jane Taylor's "The Star" ("Twinkle, twinkle," 1806), or Elizabeth Akers Allen's "Rock Me to Sleep" (1860). But poems by "great men" remained the standard in a culture of recitation that supported established literary authorities and conventions.

The culture of recitation influenced the contract between poets and their readers, pressuring poets to write accessible lyric poems that sounded melodious when read aloud (see EUPHONY). During the 18th and 19th cs., the most widely read poets produced works that engaged the voice and the ear. Some poems even took recitation as a topic, such as David Everett's "The Boy Reciter" (1791): "You'd scarce expect one of my age / To speak in public on the stage / And if I chance to fall below / Demosthenes or Cicero / Don't view me with a critic's eye / But pass my imperfections by."

Elocution manuals stressed the value of both control and emotiveness as readers learned to speak in public while curbing their "imperfections." Speakers were taught to practice articulation, inflection, emphasis, modulation, and pauses; to control their breathing; and to position their feet and hands properly. The poem was a demonstration not only of literary merit but of the speaker's training. The link between recitation and bodily control has led Robson to link poetic meter with the experience of corporal punishment. From this perspective, recitation worked as a disciplinary measure that regulated young readers' bodies and hearts. Many popular recitation pieces thematized self-making or "character building." Rudyard Kipling's "If" (1910), e.g., promises: "If you can keep your head while all about you / Are losing theirs and blaming it on you," then, in the end, ". . . you'll be a Man, my son." To remember and recite such lines could be a way not merely to learn Kipling but to make Kipling's values part of the speaker's lived and voiced experience.

Recitation, however, was not only a social performance; it was a feat of memory. William Wordsworth's *The Prelude* implies that the self is literally made of memories; from a romantic perspective, then, memorized poems—like other memories—become integral to the speaker's selfhood. Although many recitation pieces stress character building, many more express and elicit a longing for the past, as in J. G. Whittier's "Barefoot Boy" (1855): "From my heart I give thee joy / I was once a barefoot boy!" In this poem, the act of repeating a *refrain is also an exercise in nostalgia—and in self-assertion. To repeat a poem learned in the past is to, in some sense, recover a past self. Moreover, the practice of recitation raised, and continues to raise, questions about the nature and functions of poetry generally. When a poem is recited, what precisely is being remembered? How much depends on the text, and how much depends on the speaker?

By the mid-20th c., the practice of Eng.-lang. recitation of poetry was in decline. Progressive 20th-c. educators sometimes called it "drill and kill," implying that rote memorization deadened both the poem and the reader's enthusiasm for poetry. However, there have been sporadic calls for a revival. In his intro. to the anthol. *Committed to Memory*, Hollander suggests that learning a poem by heart is still one of the best ways to understand it fully. He argues that, far from "killing" poetry, the act of recitation brings poems alive by engaging the voice, the ear, and the mind. In much of the world, this lesson remains fully understood.

*See* BALLAD, DIDACTIC POETRY, FIRESIDE POETS, PRESENCE, PRONUNCIATION.

■ Y. Winters, "The Audible Reading of Poetry," *HudR* 4 (1951), and *The Function of Criticism* (1957); P. Valéry, "On Speaking Verse" and "Letter to Madam C.," *The Art of Poetry*, trans. D. Bernard-Folliot (1958); A. Reyes, "Las jitanjáforas," *Obras completas*, v. 14 (1962); M. J. Carruthers, *The Book of Memory: A Study of Memory in Medieval Culture* (1990); J. Hollander, *Committed to Memory* (1996); M. Morrisson, "Performing the Pure Voice: Elocution, Verse Recitation, and Modernist Poetry in Prewar London," *Modernism/Modernity* 3 (1996); C. Robson, "Standing on the Burning Deck," *PMLA* 120 (2005); J. S.

Rubin, *Songs of Ourselves: The Uses of Poetry in America* (2007).

A. SORBY

**RECUSATIO** (Lat., "refusal"). A term applied by cl. scholars to a poem in which the speaker implicitly or explicitly "refuses" to write on a certain subject or in a particular style. A type of programmatic poetry, *recusationes* often dramatize the poet's rejection of one kind of poem and choice of another; he may claim to have been asked to compose a different kind of poem; he may even pretend to have tried to do so; he may claim to be reacting to crit.; a god may rebuke the poet or give his approval.

Although elements of the form can be found in Sappho, fragment 16 (which implicitly rejects martial *epic poetry for amatory lyric poetry; cf. *Anacreontea* 26, a later imitation that makes the *recusatio* explicit), recusatio flourishes in the Hellenistic period, beginning with the prologue of Callimachus's *Aetia* and the epilogue of his "Hymn to Apollo," in both of which Apollo approves of Callimachus's rejection of grand themes (compared to the sea and the Euphrates) in favor of highly refined treatment of small subjects (compared to pure drops of water from a spring), thus beginning a long trad. in Lat. poetry that includes Virgil (*Eclogues* 6), Horace (*Odes* 1.6, 2.12, 4.2, 4.15), Propertius (2.1, 3.1, 3.3, 3.9), and Ovid (*Amores* 1.1, 2.1, 3.1). In line with Callimachean aesthetics, these poets refuse grand-style treatments of epic themes in favor of shorter lyric and elegiac *love poetry. Roman satirists such as Horace (*Satires* 2.1), Persius (*Satires* 5), and Juvenal (*Satires* 1) also expressed their poetic programs in the recusatio.

The recusatio became popular again in the Ren., esp. in anti-Petrarchan *sonnets that purport to eschew learned allusions and dense styles for straightforward treatments employing direct lang. Prominent examples in sonnets include Joachim du Bellay, *Regrets* 4; Philip Sidney, *Astrophil and Stella* 1, 3, 6, 15, 28, 74; Samuel Daniel, *Delia* 46; and George Herbert's two "Jordan" poems. With the exception of Robert Burns's "Epistle to J. Lapraik," the recusatio was not popular among romantic poets, but beginning with A. E. Housman's "Terence, This Is Stupid Stuff," numerous examples appeared in the 20th c., incl. W. B. Yeats's "A Coat" and "On Being Asked for a War Poem," Wallace Stevens's "The Man on the Dump," W. H. Auden's "We Too Had Known Golden Hours," J. V. Cunningham's "For My Contemporaries," Czesław Miłosz's "No More," Zbigniew Herbert's "A Knocker," and John Hollander's *Powers of Thirteen*, sonnet 1.

*See* PALINODE.

■ W. Wimmel, *Kallimachos in Rom* (1960); W. Clausen, "Callimachus and Latin Poetry," *Greek, Roman, and Byzantine Studies* 5 (1964); G. Williams, *Tradition and Originality in Roman Poetry* (1968); *Horace, Odes, Book I* (1970) and *Book II*, ed. R.G.M. Nisbet and M. Hubbard (1978); J. V. Cody, *Horace and Callimachean Aesthetics* (1976); G. Davis, "The Disavowal of the Grand (*Recusatio*) in Two Poems by Wallace Stevens," *Pacific Coast Philology* 17 (1982); N. Hopkinson, *A Hellenistic Anthology* (1988); W. H. Race, *Classical Genres and English Poetry* (1988), ch. 1; S. L. James "The Economics of Roman Elegy," *AJP* 112 (2001).

W. H. Race

**REDERIJKERS.** Members of vernacular amateur literary confraternities called *kamers van retorica* (chambers of rhetoric), who had their heyday in the southern Netherlands, esp. in Flanders and Brabant, during the 15th and 16th cs. They also existed in the north, esp. in Zeeland and Holland. Many chambers evolved from urban confraternities such as neighborhood groups and religious brotherhoods, although analogous Fr. associations such as the *puys* also seem to have functioned as a model. Chambers were organized as guilds, with a name, patron saint, motto, and blason and generally designated a number of specific functions, such as the *prince* (patron), and the *factor* (principal author).

The activities of the chambers, whose membership consisted of male, mainly middle-class artisan urbanites, were characterized by a strong competitive element. The *rederijkers* held contests within the chamber, generally for poetry, as well as among chambers, mostly for drama (such as the Brabant *landjuweel*). They owed a considerable part of their prestige, as well as their official status, to their activities during urban public festivals, such as religious processions and joyous entries, where they performed literary texts and *tableaux vivants*. Individual rhetoricians, such as Jan Smeken from Brussels, were sometimes hired by city authorities to organize public festivals.

Typical genres practiced by the rederijkers are, in drama, the serious *spel van zinne* (morality play) and the comical *esbattement*; and in poetry, the *\*refrein*. Their compositions are often outspokenly didactic and moralizing, with an elaborate use of *\*allegory*, as well as formalist and complex, with frequent gallicisms and neologisms.

Well-known chambers are *De Fonteine* from Ghent, *De Heilige Geest* from Bruges, *De Violieren* from Antwerp (which was part of the local painters' guild of Saint Luke), and *De Eglantier* from Amsterdam. Many rederijker texts, such as the morality play *Elckerlijc* (probably the source for the Eng. *Everyman*) and the hybrid work, part prose novel and part verse drama, *Mariken van Nieumeghen*, came down to us anonymously. Nevertheless, a number of rhetoricians, like Anthonis de Roovere from Bruges, Matthijs de Castelein from Oudenaarde, Anna Bijns from Antwerp, and Louris Jansz from Haarlem seem to have enjoyed considerable renown in their own day.

*See* LOW COUNTRIES, POETRY OF THE; POETIC CONTESTS.
■ *Conformisten en rebellen*, ed. B. Ramakers (2003); H. Pleij, *Het gevleugelde woord* (2007); A. L. van Bruaene, *Om beters wille* (2008); *Met eigen ogen*, ed. D. Coigneau and S. Mareel (2009).

S. Mareel

**REDONDILLA.** A Sp. stanza form in octosyllabic quatrains, rhyming *abba* and sometimes called *redondilla*

*mayor, cuarteta, cuartilla*. Quatrains having the rhyme *abab* are occasionally called *redondillas* but generally use the name *serventesio*. The redondilla written in lines of fewer than eight syllables is called *redondilla menor*. The term formerly included the *\*quintilla* and was also applied to any octosyllabic *\*strophe* in which all verses rhymed. The redondilla apparently is the result of the breaking in two at the strophic *\*caesura* of the *copla de arte menor* (see ARTE MENOR). The separation was completed in the 16th c., and the redondilla has been one of the most commonly used octosyllabic strophes in Castilian ever since. Ezra Pound experimented with the form.
■ D. C. Clarke, "*Rendondilla* and *copla de arte menor*," *HR* 9 (1941); Le Gentil; Navarro; R. Strauss, "'External modernity,' or something of that sort: Ezra Pound's American 'Redondillas,'" *Paideuma* 39 (2012).

D. C. Clarke

**REFRAIN** (Ger. *Kehrreim*). A line, lines, or the final part of a line repeated verbatim within a poem, esp. at ends of stanzas; in song, a *\*burden or chorus (through the 16th c., also called *refreit*); a structurally significant repetend separated by at least one line of nonrepeating material (hence distinguished, in Eur. poetics, from rime riche, *\*anaphora*, and epistrophe). Refrains may be as short as one word or longer than the longest nonrepeated stanza. They may dispense with paraphrasable meaning entirely or become units of independent sense whose changing implications comment on the rest of a poem; most refrains fall somewhere in between.

A frequent (though by no means universal) feature of *\*oral poetry*, refrain may give a solo performer time to remember the next verse or encourage communal recitation. Refrains appear in sacred writings of antiquity, incl. the Egyptian *Book of the Dead*, the Heb. Psalms (e.g., 24, 67), and the *Rig Veda* (e.g., 10:121), as well as in early Gr. *\*pastoral poetry*, Lat. *\*epithalamia* of Catullus (61, 64), and the OE *Deor*.

Refrain and forms based on refrain take on unparalleled frequency and importance in med. Europe: refrains appear in med. Lat. hymnody and antiphonal responsion, in almost all ME *\*carols*, and in OF from ca. 1147. Refrains then become required components of such med. and Ren. forms as *\*ballade* and roundeau, ME *\*tail rhyme*, Dutch *refrein*, It. *ballata*, Sp. *\*villancico*, and Port. *\*cantiga*. Later poets (esp. in the 19th c.) can hence use refrain and forms requiring refrain to signal med. inheritance.

In ms. cultures and in oral transmission, otherwise differing poems may share a refrain, or the "same" poem may exist with various refrains. A refrain may separate itself on linguistic grounds from the rest of a poem, preserving other (almost always older) vocabulary and grammar or using another lang. altogether (e.g., Lat. refrain in ME and Ren. Eng.; Ar. refrain in Sp.; Mozarabic in 9th-c. Andalusian Heb. and Ar.). The text of a poem set down to be sung or recited often records a refrain only once: where performance trad. is lost or unclear, mod. scholars may remain unsure (as in Andalusian *muwashshaḥ*) whether or when a certain segment (in *muwashshaḥ*, the *\*kharja*) constitutes a refrain or stands apart in some other (non-repeated) way.

Analogous to refrain in Eur. and Eur.-derived poetics is the Persian and Persian-derived *radif*, a word or short phrase repeated at each line end after a given rhyme in Persian poetry from the 10th c. on, and in later poetry with Persian models, esp. Urdu and Turkish (but never Ar.). Persian and Persian-derived monorhymed forms *\*ghazal*, *\*qaṣīda*, and *\*rubāʿī* (quatrain) use the same radif (if any) throughout a given poem. The radif becomes most important (and most like refrain in Eur. poetry) in the ghazal from the 12th c. (e.g., in the Persian poet Sanāʾī) on, when the ghazal in Persian becomes a fixed form. Wholly apart from Persian-influenced forms, longer refrains (of full sentences or complete ideas) occur in postclassical poetry of the Indian subcontinent, incl. Kannada *vacanas* (from 10th to 12th c.) and the Hindi *Bhakti* poetry of, e.g., Kabīr (15th c.).

Refrains in Ren. and later written poems link them to oral trads., to "folk" poetry and to song, esp. to such popular or participatory sung genres as work songs, dance songs, *\*ballads*, *\*lullabies*, and children's games. A mod. poet's frequent recourse to refrain (as in W. B. Yeats or Okot p'Bitek) often pays homage to oral or "folk" culture generally. Some refrains with musical settings include *\*nonsense*, as in Shakespeare's songs, or consist entirely of it, as in Korean *Koryo sogyo* songs (11th c.), whose otherwise senseless refrain not only fits but imitates accompanying music.

Refrain promises regularity (even when the promise is violated or fulfilled in some nonliteral way) and implies a distinction (of speaker, *\*tone*, subject, or audience) between repeated and nonrepeated parts. Refrain risks monotony within a long work but can bind together a short one; most poems organized around refrains are relatively short, either narrative (as ballads) or lyric. Within long works, refrain may distinguish inset lyric or odic passages from the narrative or dramatic verse that surrounds them. In mod. poems not otherwise songlike, refrain can suggest self-division, haunting, or obsession, these mortality (E. A. Poe, "The Raven"; M.-L. Halpern, "Memento Mori") or else a congregation's call-and-response (Sterling Brown, "Old Lem"). Refrain in freestanding poems may also comment on the passage of time (Edmund Spenser, *Prothalamion*; Federico García Lorca, "Llanto por Ignacio Sánchez Mejía") or interrupt narrative and argument with the stronger emotion of song.

*See* BALLAD, REPETITION, SONG.

■ F. Gummere, *The Beginnings of Poetry* (1908) but also L. Pound, *Poetic Origins and the Ballad* (1921) and P. Gainer, *The Refrain in the English and Scottish Popular Ballads* (1933); N. van den Boogaard, *Rondeaux et refrains du XIIe au début de XIVe siècle* (1969); T. Newcombe, "The Refrain in Troubadour Lyric Poetry," *Nottingham Medieval Studies* 19 (1975); J. Hol-

lander, *The Figure of Echo* (1981), and *Melodious Guile* (1988), chap. 7; L. Magnus, *The Track of the Repetend* (1989); F. D. Lewis, "The Rise and Fall of a Persian Refrain," *Reorientations*, ed. S. P. Stetkevych (1994); L. A. Garner, "Contexts of Interpretation in the Burdens of Middle English Carols," *Neophilologus* 84 (2000); *Literature of Al-Andalus*, ed. M. R. Menocal and M. Sells (2000), chap. 7; J. M. Foley, *How to Read an Oral Poem* (2002); G. Alkon, "Refrain and the Limits of Poetic Power in Spenser, Herbert, Hardy and Stevens," *Western Humanities Review* 58 (2004).

S. BURT

**REFRÁN** (Sp., "proverb"). A short, pithy, popular saying in Sp. expressing advice based on wisdom gained through common experience or observation. It may deal with any subject, such as medicine, hygiene, agriculture, morals, or philosophy, to name but a few. It is often composed of two short phrases that rhyme or contain *\*alliteration* or employ *\*parallelism* or have some other sound device that makes them appeal to the ear and cling to the memory. The Sp. lang. is rich in this sort of expression, and collectors have been busy for at least half a millennium gathering them into *refraneros*. The first known collection is the mid-15th-c. *Refranes que dicen las viejas tras el fuego*, generally attributed to the Marqués de Santillana. Many thousands have been gathered by dozens of collectors since then. Some of the important collections are those of Hernán Núñez, Juan de Mal Lara, Gonzalo Correas, F. Rodríguez Marín, and J. Cejador y Frauca.

*See* PROVERB.

■ Le Gentil.

D. C. CLARKE

**REFREIN.** A poetic form typical of the *\*rederijkers* in the 15th and 16th c. Netherlands, derived from the French *\*ballade*. A *refrein* (or *referein*) generally consists of four *\*stanzas*. The first three have the same *\*rhyme* scheme and number of lines (13 to 17 on average); the last one, which is addressed to a prince, generally the patron of the chamber or a saint, is often shorter and has a different rhyme scheme. Each stanza ends with an identical line, called the *\*stock*.

On the basis of content, the rederijkers distinguished between *refreinen in t'zot* (comical), *in t'vroed* (religious, didactic, moralistic), and *in t'amoureus* (amatory). Refreinen were often written in the context of a competition, between the members of a chamber or between chambers (called *refreinfeest*). They had to integrate a given stock or provide an answer to a specific question. The poems were generally recited, in a lively, theatrical, yet always spoken manner but could also be posted in a public place.

Most of the well-known rhetoricians, such as Anthonis de Roovere, Matthijs de Castelein, Anna Bijns, and Eduard de Dene, left a significant number of refreinen. The majority of the extant specimens of the genre came down to us anonymously, however, e.g., in the refrein-collections by the rederijker Jan van Styevoort and by the printer Jan van Doesborch, although the name of the author is sometimes integrated into the poem in the form of an *acrostic.

■ A. van Elslander, *Het refrein in de Nederlanden tot 1600* (1953); D. Coigneau, *Refreinen in het zotte bij de rederijkers*, 3 v. (1980–83); and "Bedongen creativiteit: Over retoricale productieregeling," *Medioneerlandistiek*, ed. R. Jansen-Sieben (2000).

S. MAREEL

**REJET.** Part of the Fr. prosodic terminology for *enjambement* (see ENJAMBMENT) but equally applicable to other verse systems. *Rejet* refers to the word, or small word-group, *rejeté* by enjambment into a following line, so that the larger part of the syntactic unit interrupted by the line ending occurs in the preceding line, e.g., Victor Hugo: "C'est le sceau de l'état. Oui le grand sceau de cire/*Rouge*" (It is the seal of state. Yes, the great seal of red wax). A rejet can also occur line-internally (*rejet à l'hémistiche*), where there is syntactic overflow across the caesura, from the first hemistich to the second, e.g., Charles Baudelaire: "Pour qui? C'était hier//l'été; voici l'automne!" (For whom? It was summer yesterday; now autumn is here!). Correspondingly, *contre-rejet* refers to the word, or small word-group, *initiating* an enjambment, where the larger part of the syntactic unit interrupted by the line ending occupies the following line. *Contre-rejet* likewise has a line-internal equivalent (*contre-rejet à l'hémistiche*), where the caesura isolates the smaller part of the syntactic unit in the first hemistich, e.g., Hugo: "Le Sauveur a veillé pour tous les yeux, *pleuré*/Pour tous les pleurs, *saigné*// pour toutes les blessures" (The Saviour has watched for all eyes, wept/For all tears, bled//for all wounds).

■ H. Golomb, *Enjambment in Poetry* (1979); Scott; Mazaleyrat; Morier; M. Aquien, *La versification* (1990); B. Buffard-Moret, *Introduction à la versification* (1997).

C. SCOTT

**RELATIVE STRESS PRINCIPLE.** One of the most important theories in mod. metrics, the principle of relative stress asserts that the degree of stress of a syllable is determined in relation to the stress of the syllables adjacent to it. It was first articulated in a 1900 lecture by Otto Jespersen, who stated that relative stress results from "a natural tendency towards making a weak syllable follow after a strong one and inversely." E.g., the stress pattern of the word *uphill* differs in the phrases: "to walk uphill" and "an uphill walk." The stress shifts from "up*hill*" in the first instance, to "*up*hill" in the second: it is the position of the syllables relative to the strongly stressed syllable "walk" that causes this shift. "Thus," states Jespersen, "syllables which ought seemingly to be strong are weakened if occurring between strong syllables, and naturally weak syllables gain in strength if placed between weak syllables." This "effect of surroundings" is heard in the way that the phrase "when one" is pronounced in the following line: "I know when one is dead and when one lives." In the first instance, "one" receives the stronger stress; in the

second, "when" is stronger. Jespersen used four degrees of accent, rather than two, to scan relative stress. In this system, he accounted for metrical regularity in places where a traditional foot-based prosody might not. In foot-based scansion, the line "In the sweet pangs of it remember me" contains pyrrhic and spondaic substitution in the first two feet. However, Jespersen scans the first four syllables as four increasing degrees of stress. Thus, the syllables "in the" are iambic in relation to each other; likewise "sweet pangs." While foot-based prosody sees two variations of feet in this line, relative stress sees only one departure from an overall iambic pattern: the stress increase between the third and fourth syllable. Because relative stress places equal attention to such relationships occurring between metrical feet, the principle leads Jespersen to reject the notion of the foot.

*See* FOOT, PYRRHIC, SPONDEE.

■ O. Jespersen, "Notes on Metre," *Linguistica* (1933).

T.V.F. BROGAN; W. WENTHE

## RELIGION AND POETRY

  I. Introduction
  II. Ancient Works
  III. Medieval Works
  IV. Modern Works
  V. Modern Responses

**I. Introduction.** It has been said that all poetry is religious and just as firmly that poetry excludes religion. Those who affirm the former position sometimes argue that the earliest poetry arises from the celebration of fertility rites and that, although later poetry may distance itself from its religious origin, it never quite escapes it: religious motifs—inspiration, rebirth, the divided border between life and death—get reworked in secular poetry, taking on new significations rather than being eliminated altogether. Northrop Frye articulates a version of this view in his *Anatomy of Criticism* (1957), and in doing so, he draws on the work of the Cambridge School of Anthropology: J. G. Frazer, Jane Harrison, Francis Cornford, and Gilbert Murray, among others. Those who argue that poetry excludes religion tend to agree with the 18th-c. Eng. critic Samuel Johnson in his "Life of Waller" that poetry turns on *invention and that a revealed religion such as Christianity does not lend itself to invention, or they maintain with T. S. Eliot that poetry requires firsthand experience and that religion offers itself to us as secondhand experience at best. Religious poetry, Eliot argues, is mostly minor poetry; it invites the writer to pretend to feel things that he or she does not and restricts experience to a small range, too small to generate poems of wide appeal and lasting power.

Such large-gestured claims about religion and poetry are perhaps only to be expected when allowing two overdetermined concepts to engage one another without mediation. Although *religious poetry* does not specify either a genre or a mode, more clarity and precision may be found by examining the conjunction of religion and poetry from the perspectives of lit. hist., mode, and *genre. The line that divides ritual from secular space in poetry is seldom straight and continuous.

**II. Ancient Works.** The majestic Hindu narrative the *Rāmāyaṇa* may well be the oldest religious *epic; it is dated to 300 BCE, if not earlier. The poem consists of 24,000 verses arranged in seven books. It tells the story of Rāmā, the seventh incarnation of Viṣṇu, whose wife Sītā is taken by Ravana, emperor of the demons. The poem is less a literary work about a religious trad. (John Milton's *Paradise Lost*, e.g.) than an integral part of that trad. (see RĀMĀYAṆA POETRY). Rāmā is worshiped as a god, as well as revered as an epigone of male honor. Venerated in India as a work of great wisdom, the *Rāmāyaṇa* broods on ideal types (brother, king, servant, and wife) and on *dharma*, the righteous path that each person must take in life, one that requires different things of people at different times. A short version of the *Rāmāyaṇa*, known as the *Rāmopākhyāna*, in which Rāmā has no divine traits, may be found in the third *parva* of the *Mahābhārata*, the other vast religious epic of Hinduism and the longest epic poem in the world. Its beginnings in oral trad. may go back to the Vedic age, 8th c. BCE, although it reached its immense size only in the Gupta age in the 4th c. CE. The sixth parva, the Bishna Parva, contains the *Bhagavad-Gītā,* in which Kṛṣṇa (Krishna) speaks to Arjuna on the eve of battle and reveals himself as the god who destroys as well as creates. Older than even the *Rāmāyaṇa* are the Vedas, the most archaic texts of Hinduism, which range from *incantations and *charms to sacred *hymns. Orthodox believers hold them to be revealed texts; nonorthodox believers regard them as inspired poems.

The Finnish folk epic the *Kalevala* has its oldest stratum in ancient oral verse, which was sung to the accompaniment of the *kantele*, a sort of zither, also used to accompany the songs collected in the *Kanteletar*, incl. both pagan and Christian lyrics. "Prayer for Peace" is addressed to Ukko, the chief god of the Finnish pantheon (*ukko* in Finnish means "old man"). "The Ballad of the Virgin Mary" is strikingly at variance with the standard Christian teaching: Jesus is born after Mary swallows a berry. (A version of the same story is told at the very end of the *Kalevala*.) Both the *Kalevala* and the *Kanteletar* were late in being transcribed and edited; the process for the *Kalevala* began in the late 17th c., and the epic was given its final editorial shape of 22,795 lines by Elias Lönnrot only in 1849. The hero of the poem is Väinämöinen who, like all shamans, communicates with the spirit world. This is an epic rich in spells and magic, in demons and other spirits. (Shamanic poetry is not restricted to the West; it may be found in China—Qu Yuan's "Nine Songs" in the 4th-c. BCE *Chuci*, e.g.—and somewhat later in Korea.) The first Väinämöinen cycle of the *Kalevala* explains the origin of the earth: a traditional function of religion. The Judeo-Christian explanation of creation may be found in the writings of the priestly author in the sublime opening of Genesis, the first book of the Heb. Bible. For the Gr. Hesiod in his *Theogony* (ca. 700 BCE), there is no creation story but rather a genealogy of the gods. Quite different are the early song cycles of the Australian aborigines, for here the emphasis is not on a pantheon of gods but on the acts of the ancestors, the construction of sacred *nara* shade, the naming of holy trees and drinking holes, and singing the country into being. The Djanggawul cycle, for instance, consists of 188 songs that chart the Djanggawul people on their passage from Bralgu Island, home of the Bralgu Spirits, to Port Bradshaw, and their progressive establishment of sacred sites on the mainland.

Explanations of creation and sacred sites, along with stories of communicating with the spirit world, appear in some early narrative poems, though certainly not all. Homer's world is full of gods, and Odysseus speaks with the spirits of the mighty dead, but no explanation of the origin of life is given. Of course, the genre of the epic does not have a monopoly on religion in the ancient world. The plays of Sophocles and Aeschylus, poetry of the first order, are thoroughly religious in impulse, being concerned with the vexed relations between mortals and immortals, with hubris and guilt, and with the apparently feckless actions of the gods. Religious feelings, sometimes intertwined with myths and legends, are also to be found in *lyric poems in the ancient world. The Psalms, conventionally associated with King David, are among the most commanding religious poems ever composed. Not all religious lyrics are preserved in scriptural canons, however. Pindar's *odes, composed in the 5th c. BCE, praise the victors in athletic competitions; yet the very theme of success requires Pindar to sound darker notes of warning, for triumph comes only with the consent of the gods who, if they observe too much hubris, will punish it unflinchingly. The Olympic pantheon appears in the odes, along with other divine or semidivine beings, and, from time to time, an ode is consumed with religious thought: the second Olympian, for instance, dilates for many lines on the afterlife.

Long before Pindar and even Homer, poets were intoning charms, spells, and poems that name the sacred, examples of which have survived in Africa, the Americas, Asia, and Oceania. There were also hymns to the gods. Enheduanna, earliest of all known poets, who flourished about the year 2300 BCE, served as a high priestess in ancient Sumer. Her "Hymn to Inanna" praises the moon goddess for her might as well as for her beauty. Hymns served liturgical functions in the ancient cults, and Christianity absorbed this practice: the Eastern liturgy features several solemn hymns, incl. the "Cherubikon," which was inserted into the standard liturgy in the 6th c. The first important Christian poet, Prudentius (ca. 348–405) is remembered for the *Peristephanon*, 14 hymns celebrating the lives and acts of the martyrs, and for the *Cathemerinon*, 12 hymns that give a Christian inflection to everyday events such as waking, eating, and sleeping. Passages from Prudentius's hymns may be found in the Sp. Mozarabic Breviary.

**III. Medieval Works.** If we order world lit. according to the Western conception of the med. age, a long and varied period between the ancient world and modernity, we find a rich corpus of religious poetry. One finds *Bhakti* lyrics, poems of acute religious devotion, such as those Rābi'ah, an 8th-c. Sufi, a follower of the mystical strain of Islam. Of equal beauty are the lyrics of Ḥāfiz, a Sufi poet of the 14th c., and Kabīr whose work is claimed with equal zeal by Hindus, Muslims, and Sikhs. Widely regarded as the pinnacle of Islamic poetry is the *Masnavī* of Rūmī, a poem in about 26,000 couplets written in the 13th c. in Farsi and Arabic. How we pass from the material world to the divine world is Rūmī's high theme, which is explored also in many of his other lyrics. Verses of the Qur'an are folded into the *Masnavī*: the line between poetry and canonical scripture is hard to trace here.

In 10th-c. Hinduism, one finds an eruption of *vacanas*, intense religious lyrics in unmetered verse. Mahādēviyakka, a 12th-c. devotee of Śiva, speaks movingly to her "lord white as jasmine" about the sheer difficulty of living in this world while longing for the spiritual world. Yet it is Mīrābāī, a 16th-c. rather than a med. Bhakti poet, who has written the poems that most intimately resonate with mod. readers in the West. "All I was doing was being, and the Dancing Energy came by my house," she says: her candor and freshness are attractive. The Christian West features many beautiful lyrics, mostly anonymous, devoted to Mary and Jesus: e.g., "I sing of a maiden" and "Quia amore langueo," both from the early 15th c.

If we turn to China, we find poems informed by Taoism, Buddhism, and Confucianism, sometimes with traces of all three in the one piece. By the time of the T'ang dynasty, there are poems in which one discerns a Buddhist emphasis on rinsing the mind of attachment so as to see clearly. Liu Zongyuan's lyric "River Snow," dated to the late 8th or early 9th c., is a prime example of a religious attitude being delicately suggested rather than stated:

A thousand mountains. Flying birds vanish.
Ten thousand paths. Human traces erased.
One boat, bamboo hut, bark cape—an old man
Alone, angling in the cold river. Snow.
                              (trans. Barnstone and Ping)

Korean poetry of the same period is similarly inflected by Buddhist themes. The *hyangga* or native songs of Yi Kyu-bo in the 13th c. express Buddhist concern for the well-being of ordinary folk as well as for transcendence of this world. In Japan, the 8th-c. *Kojiki*, the earliest surviving book of the culture, gathers poems about many things, not only the imperial family and other important families but the creation and the gods, along with ritual songs used in the Shinto religion. Also compiled in the 8th c. is the massive *Man'yōshū*, which includes long and short poems, some of which go back to the 4th c. The earliest poems included show Confucian or Taoist influence, while later ones are almost all Buddhist in orientation, even though the number of poems dealing explicitly with Buddhist themes is small. In the 13th c., there is compiled the *Ogura Hyakunin*

*Isshu*, a survey of Japanese poetry from the 7th c. to the middle of the 12th: 100 poems by 100 poets. Many are love poems, but there are several in which Buddhism appears covertly or even overtly.

Looking forward, past the Western med. period but in the same poetic trad., we can glimpse the 17th-c. poet Bashō who, with winning subtlety, relates a spiritual as well as a physical journal in his *Narrow Road to the Interior*. Bashō's journey to Oku is, as the name itself suggests in Japanese, a passage away from civilization as well as to the place most deeply within oneself. The *haibun* that compose the work, prose interspersed with haiku (see RENGA), are marvels of a hard-won simplicity. Years of study of Zen, incl. the poems attributed to the 9th-c. Chinese Zen poet Hánshān (the *Cold Mountain* poems) resulted for Bashō in a poetry that is at once profound Zen and high art.

Religious dream poetry begins early in Britain: the Anglo-Saxon alliterative poem "The Dream of the Rood," about the Cross of Jesus, is preserved in a 10th-c. Vercelli Book. *Piers Plowman*, a long alliterative poem composed in the late 14th c. by William Langland, embodies the quest for the true Christian life; its mixture of *dream vision and *allegory, along with its caustic social satire, take us deeply into the Eng. Catholic mind in the Middle Ages. The same is true of Eng. play cycles, the most moving of which are the York Corpus Christi plays, which relate the entire story of salvation hist., from Creation to Eschaton, in lively verse. They were performed from the middle of the 14th c. until the middle of the 16th c. Dante's *Divine Comedy*, written in the 14th c., relates the solemn passage of the author through hell, purgatory, and paradise; it remains the summa of med. Christian self-understanding, the strongest poem ever written in *terza rima, and an inescapable work of the Western literary imagination.

The Middle Ages have bequeathed us Lat. as well as vernacular poetries. Some are anonymous hymns, such as the 7th or 8th c. "Ave maris stella" (Hail star of the sea) whose art is contained in its stark purity, and the "Veni, creator Spiritus" (Come creator spirit), trans. by, among others, John Dryden. Others are anonymous *carols, such as the 13th-c. "Cantet omnis creatura," or sequences in the Mass, such as the "Rosy Sequence," dated to the late 12th c. The "Dies irae," a sublime 13th-c. Lat. hymn, evokes the Day of Judgment and is incorporated in the requiem Mass. Sts. Ambrose, Bonaventure, Thomas Aquinas, and Hildegard of Bingen all wrote religious lyrics in Lat. Special mention should be made of Aquinas's "Pange, linguae, gloriosi corporis mysterium," still sung in trans. throughout Europe at the feast of Corpus Christi.

**IV. Modern Works.** Until modernity, poetry did not have to be devotional in order to be religious. Religion supplied an overarching imaginative structure within which writers worked. Secular poems were written and sung, but they were not informed by a comprehensive imaginative structure known as "modernity" in which science, rather than religion, is held to offer the better explanation of cosmic events. One does not think of

Chaucer as a religious poet, but the 14th-c. *Canterbury Tales* is deeply informed by Christian practices. Shakespeare is a more difficult writer to assess in this regard: whatever his personal beliefs may have been, his vision does not harmonize with Christian understandings of life and death. And yet it would be impossible to understand his plays without a working knowledge of Christianity. There is no one version of modernity, however: in the West, it comes in various waves (the age of the Alexandrian Library, the Carolingian age, the Ren., the Enlightenment); and outside the West, it comes more hesitantly. Orthodoxy resists modernity to some extent, while many Muslims deflect the encounter, at least with respect to the understanding of scripture.

Supreme among Eur. religious poets in the 16th c. is the Sp. Carmelite mystic St. John of the Cross, whose *Cántico espiritual* (*Spiritual Canticle*) resets motifs from the biblical Song of Songs: the soul searches for the heavenly Bridegroom, Christ. the *Dark Night of the Soul*, a lyric poem of exquisite beauty and imagistic richness, also tells of the soul's quest for a loving union with God. That the soul must suffer in its quest has become known in the Christian West as the experience of "the dark night." John's line-by-line commentary on his poem is itself a work of piercing spiritual insight.

In the 17th c., it was still possible to write a religious epic. In *Paradise Lost* (1667, 1674), Milton seeks "[t]o justify the ways of God to man," which he does by tracing the fall of the angels and then showing how Lucifer brings about the fall of humankind. The theology of *Paradise Lost* is far from orthodox, for Milton's God is not a trinity. William Blake was doubtless correct when he declared in *The Marriage of Heaven and Hell* (1790) that Milton wrote better of evil than good because he "was a true Poet and of the Devils party without knowing it." Milton's Lucifer is a romantic figure; his God is a tyrant. A wayward religious genius himself, Blake imitated biblical lang. while also developing a quasi-Christian mythological system in long poems such as *Vala, or The Four Zoas* (1797) and *Jerusalem* (1820). Many of his short lyrics, such as the preface to *Milton* (1808; "And did those feet in ancient times"), are among the most piercing religious poems of all time. The lyric is based on the legend that the young Jesus visited England. Unorthodox though the theology of the poem surely is, the lyric's setting by Hubert Parray in 1916 made it a much-loved hymn in Brit. churches.

Of Eng. religious lyricists in the 17th c. the major figures are George Herbert whose *The Temple* (1633) is a spiritual autobiography in exquisite lyrics, some of which are shaped ("The Altar" and "Easter Wings"), and John Donne whose *Holy Sonnets* and hymns are indexes of a passionate religious sensibility. If later poets such as Richard Crashaw, Henry Vaughan, and Thomas Traherne are less often discussed, it is only because of the poetic authority of the generation that preceded them. To find a Christian poet of comparable sway to Herbert, one must wait until the 19th c. when G. M. Hopkins's poems, incl. his great *ode "The Wreck of the Deutschland" (1876), were written. His *sonnets, whether of ecstatic praise or spiritual desolation, mark an intensity of religious feeling seldom reached in any lang. In America, many of Emily Dickinson's lyrics offer witness to a similar spiritual potency, although it is a religion affirmed on her own terms. Another Victorian, Matthew Arnold, serves as a counterweight to Hopkins's Ultramontane ode about a physical and a spiritual shipwreck. "Dover Beach" (1867) speaks of supernatural faith leaving the earth, so that the poet can almost hear "[i]ts melancholy, long, withdrawing roar."

The withdrawal of the Christian God is a theme sounded throughout Friedrich Hölderlin's odes and elegies, mostly written in the late 18th c. and the first years of the 19th c. When human beings turn away from God, God turns away from them. Yet this "default of God," as Hölderlin calls it, does not erase a sense of the sacred for the Ger. poet; on the contrary, for Hölderlin, it is the poet who keeps that sense alive: a theme that weaves its way through romantic poetry and that Heidegger intensifies in his elucidations of Hölderlin's poems. Whether the romantics preserve religion by way of the *sublime or hold it there to be unpicked by philosophers in the 20th c. is still debated (see ROMANTICISM). Certainly with the romantics and those who follow them, religious awareness is dissociated from doctrine. René Char, who writes in the wake of Hölderlin and alongside Heidegger, inflects this association of poetry and the sacred in his own way and combines a pre-Christian sense of the sacred with deep feeling for the landscape of his native Provence. His sequence "Lascaux" is a prime example. Even more compelling in its spiritual intensity is the poetry of R. M. Rilke, whose *Sonnets to Orpheus* (1923) and *Duino Elegies* (1923) both exude a strong religious disposition in which the poet crosses the border between this world and the next and in which Christianity and Judaism are pushed to the margins.

Charles Baudelaire, by contrast, adopts a distinctly anti-Christian attitude in his *Flowers of Evil* (1857). For all his celebration of evil, however, his prizing of the symbol in the sonnet "Correspondances" generates a displaced religiosity in poetry, one taken up ecstatically by Arthur Rimbaud, who saw himself as a mod. savant, and then was further folded in an intricate manner by the surrealists, and then unfolded in ultraorthodox Catholic terms by Paul Claudel. In Claudel's versets, esp. in his *Five Great Odes* (1907), one experiences a violent upsurge of baroque Catholic feeling. The influence of the Vulgate trans. of the Psalms is apparent. Lyrics influenced by his theological insight into Sophia or Wisdom were composed in Rus. by Vladímir Soloviev in the late 19th c.; of course, Rus. religious poetry has deep roots in the old oral trad. of *dukhovnye stikhi* or spiritual verses, some of which are still recited today. A longing for the infinite also pervades the emotionally charged lyricism of Anna Akhmatova and Osip Mandelstam. Alphonsus de Guimaraens and Augusto Frederico Schmidt, both 20th-c. Brazilians, also testify to a strong sense of mystery and the eternal in their lyrics. Getting to be better known in the West today is the astonishing 19th-c. Urdu poet Ghālib, whose *ghazals* express a strong personal religion of love, combined with a disdain for those he regarded as overly traditional in their Islamic faith.

T. S. Eliot's admirable poem of conversion *Ash Wednesday* (1930) and the more contemplative *Four Quartets* (1936–42) interlace lines from The Book of Common Prayer and med. Eng. mystical writings. Both poems seek to recover authentic religious feeling as the basis for traditional Christian teachings, and the *Quartets* in particular register a strong sense of "the darkness of God." With the early poems of Robert Lowell ("The Quaker Graveyard in Nantucket," 1946, e.g.) and the work of the Australian Francis Webb, we find more fervent Catholic verse. More nuanced in their Catholic imagery are the lyrics of the 20th-c. Korean poet Chŏng Chi-yong, whose poems have been touched by Blake's *Songs of Innocence* as well as by the landscape of his own childhood. W. H. Auden explores the world of Protestant thought and feeling, often with a strong ethical flavor: his sequence *Horae Canonicae* remains memorable. For works later in the century, we often need to talk of religiosity or spirituality rather than religion (as in poems that show awareness of a spirit or natural force: Robert Bly and Philippe Jaccottet are examples); or of poetry that diagnoses failed religious experience, such as Geoffrey Hill's *Tenebrae* (1978); or of poetry that regards itself as a stairway to a God who can no longer be believed in (Charles Wright, for instance), or of poetry marked by a Western understanding of Buddhism (Gary Snyder and Robert Gray, e.g.).

The horror of the Holocaust has generated more religious poetry among Jews than Christians. The Holocaust remains a religious issue for Christians, yet it has scarcely entered poetry in the mode of religious feeling or thought. Paul Celan's "Psalm" in his *The No-Man's-Rose* (1963) "praises" God as "No one" and walks the delicate border between Rhineland mysticism and mod. atheism. Edmond Jabès's *The Book of Questions* (1963–73) reflects in fragments, some lyrical, on the Shoah and generates pseudo-Talmudic commentaries on life in a world in which God is painfully absent. Yehuda Amichai's poems bear witness to a personal struggle with faith, and for him the word *God* means something different before and after the Shoah. An immense heritage of Jewish religious poetry precedes him, beginning with the Bible and incl., among many others, the oeuvre of Jehudah Halevi (ca. 1074–1141), many of whose poems associate the suffering of Israel with the hidden name of God and make use of the Song of Songs.

**V. Modern Responses.** Religious poetry has not attracted the detailed attention of the best-known mod. literary critics although specialists attend closely to many of the poets already named. Fairchild's six-volume *Religious Trends in English Poetry* remains a valuable reference; and individual studies by Buckley on the sacred in the poetry of Donne, Blake, and Eliot; Lynch on the theological imagination; and Scott on mod. poetry and "sacramental vision" are touchstones still for students,

as is Gardner's *Religion and Literature*. Perhaps the most irruptive works on poetry and religion are those of Heidegger (his essays on Rilke and Georg Trakl, as well as those on Hölderlin) and Bloom's Charles Eliot Norton Lectures gathered together as *Ruin the Sacred Truths*, a Gnostic interpretation of poetry from the Bible to the present day. Anthols. of religious poetry, generally understood, appeared in significant numbers in the late 20th c. Some emphasize the number of centuries poets have been writing religious poetry, what can plausibly count as religious poetry, and the different cultures in which such poetry has been written. Anthols. by Bly and Hirshfield are prominent examples of this trend and remind us that, in the East, the distinction between the secular and the sacred often works in quite different ways from how it does in the West.

*See* DEVOTIONAL POETRY, EXEGESIS, LITURGICAL POETRY, MYTH, PSALM.

■ *Religious Trends in English Poetry*, ed. H. N. Fairchild, 6 vols. (1939–68); Eliot, *Essays*, "Religion and Literature"; and "What Is Minor Poetry?," *On Poetry and Poets* (1957); V. Buckley, *Poetry and the Sacred* (1968); H. Gardner, *Religion and Literature* (1971); N. A. Scott, *The Wild Prayer of Longing: Poetry and the Sacred* (1971); *Speaking of Siva*, trans. A. K. Ramanujan (1973); A. Waley, *The Nine Songs: A Study of Shamanism in Ancient China* (1973); W. F. Lynch, *Christ and Apollo: The Dimensions of the Literary Imagination* (1975); H. Bloom, *Ruin the Sacred Truths: Poetry and Belief from the Bible to the Present* (1989); *Women in Praise of the Sacred: Forty-Three Centuries of Spiritual Poetry by Women*, ed. J. Hirshfield (1994); *The Soul Is Here for Its Own Joy: Sacred Poems from Many Cultures*, ed. R. Bly (1995); D. Acke, "Philippe Jaccottet et les ambiguités du religieux," *Courrier du Centre International d'Etudes Poétiques* 209–10 (1996); D. Smith, *The Dance of Siva: Religion, Art, and Poetry in South India* (1996); C. V. Caske, *Spenser and Biblical Poetics* (1999); M. Dickstein, "Is Religious Poetry Possible?" *Literary Imagination* 2 (2000); M. Heidegger, *Elucidations of Hölderlin's Poetry*, trans. K. Hoeller (2000); *The Columbia Anthology of Traditional Korean Poetry*, ed. P. H. Lee (2002); J. R. Barth, *Romanticism and Transcendence* (2003); B. Brown, "The Dark Wood of Postmodernity (Space, Faith, Allegory)," *PMLA* 120 (2005); *Ecstasy and Understanding: Religious Awareness in English Poetry from the Late Victorian to the Modern Period*, ed. A. Grafe (2008); A. C. Yu, *Comparative Journeys: Essays on Literature and Religion East and West* (2009).

K. HART

**REMATE.** A Sp. metrical term denoting a short stanza placed at the end of a poem and serving as a conclusion to the poem. The *remate* generally repeats the last rhymes of the preceding full-length *strophe. It is most commonly used at the end of the *canción. In it, the poet addresses himself to the canción, giving it a special message to bear to a particular person, "recognizing some flaw in the *canción,* or making an excuse for it, or telling it what it must answer if it should be found wanting in some respect" (Diego García Rengifo, *Arte poética española*, 1592). It has also been called *vuelta*, *commiato*, *despido*, *envío*, *ripressa*, *ritornelo* (*retornelo*), and *contera*.

See ENVOI.

■ E. Segura Covarsí, *La canción petrarquista en la lírica española del siglo de oro* (1949); Navarro.

D. C. CLARKE

## RENAISSANCE POETICS

I. Introduction
II. The Defense of Poetry
III. The Language of Poetry
IV. The Genres of Poetry
V. The Principle of Imitation
VI. Rhetoric and Poetics
VII. Conclusion

**I. Introduction.** Lit. crit. was first recognized as an independent form of lit. and the critic first accepted as a new kind of writer in the Ren.; indeed, nearly all mod. *poetics derives directly from ideas advanced in this period. Ren. crit. began in the struggle to defend imaginative lit. against attacks of immorality and frivolity and to put forward the tenets and practices of humanist education. In establishing a place for the writing and study of poetry, the use of the vernacular was debated (and also vindicated); genres were distinguished, each with its own conventions; the humanist movement instituted as the basis of poetics the practice of imitating cl. texts; and rhetoricians supplied a basic *technē* or set of rules on which poetic art could rely.

**II. The Defense of Poetry.** Giovanni Boccaccio in his *Genealogia deorum gentilium* (*Genealogy of the Gentile Gods*, 1360) and in his *Life of Dante* laid down the main lines for defending poetry against clerical and secular charges. He argues that *religion and poetry are not opposed; on the contrary, the Bible is poetry and teaches, as all poetry does, by means of *allegory, i.e., *metaphors with fixed and continuing referents. In addition, the poets were cast as the first theologians. Seemingly immoral pagan stories may thus be interpreted in wholly moral ways. For Boccaccio, even the story of Leda and the swan could be viewed allegorically as anticipating (or shadowing) the Virgin and the dove. Boccaccio also defended poetry against charges of frivolity, arguing that it had always been admired by the people, protected by their leaders and rulers, and supported by wealthy patrons. Moreover, the poet is a creator like God himself; there is, Boccaccio says, no higher vocation possible for the human.

Once these arguments were in place, they were copied, expanded, and developed in nearly all It., Fr., Sp., and Eng. defenses of poetry from the 14th through the 16th c. Meanwhile, much technical lore about cl. poetry was spread abroad through elaborately annotated eds. of Horace's *Ars poetica*, most esp. the popular ed. by Badius Ascensius first pub. in Paris in 1500. The result was summed up in It. crit. by Marco Girolamo Vida's *De arte poetica* (1527), a long verse treatise imitating

Horace but also incorporating much humanist theory about the moral purpose and genres of poetry and the function of the critic. As for theory relating specifically to vernacular poetic theory, the most important work of the early 16th c. is Giangiorgio Trissino's *La poetica* (books 1–4, 1529; books 5–6, 1563), an elaborate analysis of It. *versification and verse conventions.

A new factor was introduced into Eur. lit. crit. in 1508 with the publication by Aldus Manutius of a reliable Gr. text of Aristotle's *Poetics* and a Lat. trans. by Alessandro Pazzi in 1536. The *Poetics* was known in the Middle Ages only through a Lat. trans. of a paraphrase by the Arab philosopher Averröes and a badly flawed Lat. trans. by Lorenzo Valla that was published in the late 15th c. Pazzi's Lat. trans. was an immediate and powerful stimulus to critical thought. Detailed commentaries on the *Poetics* began to appear in the 1540s and continued to be produced in Italy throughout the rest of the century. In the earlier commentaries—e.g., those by Francesco Robortello (1548) and by Vincenzo Maggi and Bartolomeo Lombardi (1549)—Aristotle mixes theories derived from rhet. with didactic theories drawn from the humanist trad. and from Horace. In general, these treatises interpret *catharsis as purgation of wicked impulses, and *tragedy as a form providing examples of vices to avoid.

The most famous It. Ren. commentary on Aristotle is *Poetica d'Aristotele vulgarizzata e sposta* (1570, 1576) by Lodovico Castelvetro, which insists that tragedy is popular entertainment and that catharsis is insensitivity to suffering created by seeing it in plays. After 1540, most full-blown It. critical essays—e.g., Antonio Minturno's *De poeta* (1559), usually considered a source of Philip Sidney's *Defence of Poesy* (written ca. 1580, pub. 1595)—draw heavily on Aristotle. These texts usually treat lit. as a source of moral instruction through examples of virtue and vice. They regularly combine Aristotelian ideas with the Horatian trad. that poetry should "profit" morally, even as it "delights." More narrowly focused treatises—e.g., Giambattista Giraldi Cinthio's *Discorso intorno al comporre dei romanzi* (1554)—mix Aristotelian ideas with ideas drawn from theories of vernacular versification and trads. about popular vernacular genres such as romance.

Whatever the point of view, after 1540 few critical treatises were written in Italy that did not draw on the *Poetics*. That the Sp. followed the It. lead is illustrated by Alonso Pinciano's *Filosofía antigua poética* (1596), a commentary on the *Poetics* treating *imitation, verisimilitude, and wonder, among other topics. In northern Europe, conversely, the influence of Aristotle is not felt until the last quarter of the 16th c. Indeed, in northern Europe the most influential critical work was, for many years, the massive but derivative *Poetices libri septem* (1561) of J. C. Scaliger. Although Aristotle is often cited by northern Eur. critics in the last quarter of the 16th c., not until 1611 with the *De tragoediae constitutione* of Daniel Heinsius was a study of the *Poetics* produced comparable in scope and sophistication to its It. predecessors; but with Heinsius, we begin to move from Ren. to *neoclassical poetics.

Another critical position, deriving from Aristotle's

*Rhetoric*, appears in, e.g., Baltasar Gracián's *Agudeza y arte de ingenio* (*Cleverness and the Art of Wit*, 1648) in Spain and Emanuele Tesauro's *Il cannocchiale aristotelico* (The Aristotelian Telescope, 1654) in Italy. *Concettismo* (see CONCEIT, CONCEPTISMO), as it is called, is concerned neither with plot and character nor with moral uplift. Instead, it is concerned with the effect of brilliant *imagery, understood for the most part as pleasure and awe.

**III. The Language of Poetry.** It. theories about poetic lang. were much influenced by the revival of interest in cl. poetry that occurred in the 14th c. The humanist movement thus generated spent much of its early years interpreting—and in some cases recovering and perfecting through imitation—Gr. and Lat. mss., even though some of the best poets, such as Dante, Petrarch, and Boccaccio, were writing in the vernacular. Humanists assumed that the great texts of the past, in all genres, were best in the cl. langs., esp. Lat. The support of vernacular writing was further complicated in Italy because of the many dialects in the separate city-states: the country as yet had no national unification and no national lang. Hence, those interested in a vernacular body of work had first to defend a particular dialect for it (see ITALY, POETRY OF).

Dante's *De vulgari eloquentia* (ca. 1304) is the first and still the best argument for vernacular lit.; it has no worthy successor until Leon Battista Alberti's *Trattato del governo della famiglia* (1438), which contends that the vulgar (or common) tongue would become as polished as Lat. if patriotic writers gave it their attention. In *Prose della volgar lingua* (1525), Pietro Bembo claims that the Florentine dialect is as good as Lat., and even superior to it as a lang. for mod. subjects. Since Florentine was the one dialect with a strong literary trad., most Italians who wrote in the vernacular used it, yet some opposed it in favor of a truly national literary lang. they termed "Italian" or even "Courtier's Tongue." Il Calmeta and Baldassare Castiglione (esp. in his *Il Cortegiano*, 1528) were foremost among these proponents, although they took most of their arguments from Dante's earlier essay.

Nationalism also aided the cause of vernacular lit. in France. Joachim du Bellay's *La Deffence et illustration de la langue françoyse* (1549) is firmly nationalistic. Du Bellay took many of his arguments from the *Dialogo delle lingue* of Sperone Speroni (1542); he claims that the Fr. are as good as the Romans, so that it follows that their lang. is equally good. It is, therefore, the patriotic duty of all Fr. scholars and poets to write in Fr. and enrich the lang.; translators can also participate by enlarging the Fr. vocabulary with words "captured" from other langs. (see FRANCE, POETRY OF).

The Eng. were, if possible, even more nationalistic than the Fr., yet the widespread taste for Lat. produced by grammar-school education made the battle more difficult than it might otherwise have been. Roger Ascham writes in *Toxophilus* (1545), his defense of the use of the ancient longbow in battle, that "to have written this book either in Latin or Greek . . . had been more easier." Indeed, in the 17th c., Francis Bacon had some of his more important scientific works pub. in Lat.

because he feared that "these modern languages will at one time or other play bankrupt with books." On the other hand, Richard Mulcaster, a prominent educator, thought of Eng. as "the joyful title of our liberty and freedom, the Latin tongue remembering us of our thraldom and bondage." In this, he undoubtedly spoke for the majority of the Eng. people. Both in England and in northern Europe, the cause of national langs. and lits. was enhanced by the growing Reformist and Protestant movements, which insisted that the scriptures be translated and available for all believers to read for themselves.

But once the cause of vernacular poetry was established, the practice raised problems of its own. The initial problem was *meter: how could a vernacular lang. (lacking *quantity) imitate the (quantitative) meter natural to Gr. and Lat.? Claudio Tolomei in his *Versi et regole de la nuova poesia toscana* (1539) tried to show how It. poetry could be written so as to imitate the prosody of Lat. verse. He was followed in France by Jacques de la Taille, who writes in the preface to his *La Manière de faire des vers en françois, comme en grec et en latin* (1573) that the real issue is the yearnings of "ultraclassicists" to rival Virgil or Homer and argues for a new Fr. spelling and pronunciation that will permit the lang. to fit cl. meter. The Eng. were more tolerant still, and many Eng. poets in the later 16th c. came to write an Eng. quantitative verse in imitation of the Gr. and Lat. because the Eng. lang. seemed closer to the cl. langs., esp. Lat., than it did to It., with its greater percentage of rhyming words, or to Fr., with its more musical accent. For the Eng., meter superseded *rhyme, and in *The Scholemaster* (1570), Ascham, associating rhyme with med. scholastic verse, even calls rhyme "barbarian" (see CLASSICAL METERS IN MODERN LANGUAGES).

Later treatises by William Webbe (*Discourse of English Poetrie*, 1586) and George Puttenham (*The Arte of English Poesie*, 1589) provide an additional, Protestant argument by declaring that the past age, when rhyme was employed, was not only "gothic" but papist. Webbe recalls "this tinkerly verse which we call rime" and condemns monks for having invented "brutish Poetry." Puttenham speaks of rhyme as "the idle invention of Monastical men," supporting the superiority of Protestant classicists. Even Edmund Spenser briefly became part of the quantitative movement, and as late as 1602, Thomas Campion in his *Observations* questions "the childish titillation of riming." The positive outcomes of such complaints in Eng. were a notable increase in poetic experimentation and the devel. of a flexible and powerful medium for *dramatic poetry—*blank verse.

**IV. The Genres of Poetry.** Ren. concern with cl. verse forms was matched by interest in cl. distinctions of *genre, distinctions first worked out by the commentators on Horace and Aristotle and later codified by such critics as Minturno, Scaliger, and Sidney. In general, the commentators associated each of the major genres with a particular social stratum, with the nobility at the top and peasants and artisans at the bottom.

*Epic or *heroic verse was usually considered the

most important and noble of all genres, since its heroes were rulers and military leaders and were meant to represent a nation's best values. In Italy, Ludovico Ariosto, Giangiorgio Trissino, and Torquato Tasso attempted major national epics. Their efforts were paralleled by those of Luís de Camões in Portugal, Pierre de Ronsard in France, and Edmund Spenser and John Milton in England. But whether such mod. poetic narratives as *Orlando furioso* and *The Faerie Queene* could actually be considered epics was the cause of argument. Ariosto's *Orlando furioso* and Tasso's *Gerusalemme liberata* are popular romances, unlike the more classically oriented *L'Italia liberata dai Goti* of Trissino. Minturno attacks romances for lacking cl. *unity and for appealing to lower tastes, while Cinthio argues for the right of a new age to develop its own forms and to depart from the universal Ren. poetic principle of imitation.

Tragedy ranks highest among dramatic genres both because its heroes are rulers and because Aristotle himself ranked tragedy highest in the *Poetics*. Scaliger notes that tragic plots are based on the activities of kings—the affairs of state, fortress, and camp. Cinthio adds that we call the actions of tragedy illustrious not because they are virtuous but because the characters who enact them are of the highest rank. Tragedy calls for elevated style and, in Italy, for magnificent scenery in presentation as well.

*Comedy is complementary to tragedy. It treats middle- and lower-class characters, and it concentrates on situations that are amusing or ridiculous rather than pitiable and fearful. In *L'arte poetica* (1563), Minturno suggests that, while noble ladies appear in public, middle-class women do not do so until after marriage and that the poet will violate comic decorum if he counters this practice. Castelvetro writes that, while members of the strong-willed aristocracy constitute a law unto themselves, the middle class will run to magistrates with its difficulties and live under the law. Consequently, the comic plot must not involve vendettas or other inappropriate behavior but instead treat the commonplaces of bourgeois life in which characters speak an everyday lang. Farce concentrates on lower-class characters and situations; here the chief responsibility of the poet is keeping *decorum, since the action is broad and the speech colloquial.

Most Fr. and Eng. critics followed this threefold generic division, giving almost exactly the same definitions as the It. critics. Pierre de Laudun, for instance, in *L'art poétique françois* (1597), contends that "[t]he characters of tragedy are grave people of great rank and those of comedy are low and of small position. . . . The words of Tragedy are grave and those of Comedy are light. . . . The characters in Tragedy are sumptuously dressed and those of Comedy garbed in an ordinary way." Most Ren. dramatists, incl. Shakespeare, followed these principles or, as in the Prologue to *Henry V*, announce it conspicuously when they do not. In Spain, Félix Lope de Vega explained in *Arte nuevo de hacer comedias* (1609) that, while he admires Aristotle's theories, along with those of his Ren. interpreters, he has to

make a living, and pleasing the crowd requires violating most of the cl. rules, incl. those relating to the three unities.

Shakespeare's prologue speaks to the problem of unity—specifically, unity of place—as much as to social decorum, while Ben Jonson in *Sejanus* apologizes for not keeping to a unity of time (one 24-hour period). The unities of place and time were added by Ren. critics to the single unity of action (or *plot), which Aristotle argues in the *Poetics* is the basis for drama. The three unities were introduced for the first time in England through Sidney's *Defence*. They were never observed rigorously, however, by the Eng. popular dramatists. In France, they became critical dogma, and it was principally from France that they were reintroduced into Eng. crit. in the later 17th c.

The theory of genres was complicated by two developing dramatic and narrative forms in the Ren.—*tragicomedy and romance. For conservative critics, tragicomedy was by name and definition a "mongrel" form because it mingled kings and clowns, as Sidney puts it. However, Giovanni Battista Guarini, the author of *Il pastor fido* (1590), argued that, since the great and the lowly exist side by side in actual life, it is perfectly natural and correct to have both in a single drama. The response came from Jason DeNores (*Apologia*, 1590) when he remarked that comedy instructs citizens how to act, but a mixed genre, since it cannot instruct this way, is without any useful end; moreover, it gives no certain direction to the playwright as to appropriate behavior or lang. Guarini later published an extended reply, *Compendio della poesia tragicomica* (1601), in which he hinted that he writes to please rather than to follow "rules" or to instruct; and he adds that some of his shepherds are noble and some are not: hence his use of both tragedy and comedy. The best playwrights agreed, as we see in Shakespeare's late plays, *Cymbeline*, *Pericles*, *The Winter's Tale*, and *The Tempest*, all of which introduce wonder as a means of combining genres. In John Fletcher's prologue to *The Faithful Shepherdess*, "a God is as lawful in this as in a tragedy, and mean people as in a comedy."

**V. The Principle of Imitation.** The various strands of Ren. *imitatio* began with Plato, who notes in *The Sophist* (219a–c) two kinds of art he calls icastic and fantastic. *Icastic* or "likeness-making art" occurs "whenever anyone produces the imitation by following the proportions of the original in length, breadth, and depth, and giving, besides, the appropriate colors to each part" (235d)—when the artist records what he sees without any imaginative changes. Icastic art, thus, copies the original precisely. *Fantastic* art, on the other hand, either creates that which does not exist—Sidney suggests the Cyclops as an example—or else gives a disproportioned, inexact representation of the object being imitated: fantastic art, thus, "produces appearance," according to Plato, "but not likeness" (236c). While both kinds of art share the identical end, *representation, their means are opposed: one teaches by exact copying, the other persuades by asking the audience to accept what seems to be for what is. Since Plato uses sculpture and painting as his examples, his distinction is a distinction in poetics.

Beginning in the 14th c. with Petrarch, another kind of imitation—stylistic imitation of the ancients, esp. of Cicero and Virgil—became popular. This theory of imitation persisted throughout the Ren. and overlaps other, more philosophical theories. It was closely associated with Ren. education, since much of the grammar-school curriculum involved translating, paraphrasing, and imitating Lat. authors. Questions associated with it include whether one should imitate a single author or the best features of many; whether one should use cl. forms directly or seek vernacular equivalents of them; and how *originality and imitation can coexist. Two treatises that nicely illustrate Ren. understanding of imitation in this sense are the *Ciceronianus* of Erasmus (1528) and the second book of Ascham's *Scholemaster*.

The rediscovery of Aristotle's *Poetics* introduced yet another kind of imitation. Whatever Aristotle may have understood by *mimesis*, most Ren. writers understood it to mean either (a) the direct representation in lang. and dramatic action of the real world, or (b) the representation of typical (or "probable") aspects of the real world. The argument that mimesis should focus on the typical or probable rather than on the specific or topical justified departures in plots from strict historical fact. A very prominent thrust of the theory was the justification for reshaping hist. so that it conformed to the requirements of moral instruction. When interpreted in this way, the *Poetics* seemed entirely consistent with the traditional theory inherited from Horace that poetry mixes the morally useful with the aesthetically delightful. Thus, in *La poetica* (1536), Bernardino Daniello argues that the poet, unlike the historian, can mingle fiction with fact because he is held not to what is or was but rather to what ought to be. Robortello in his commentary on the *Poetics* likewise argues that the poet can add invented material in imitating reality, citing as exemplars Xenophon's ideal portrait of Cyrus and Cicero's ideal portrait of the orator; moreover, he adds, poets can invent matters that transcend nature so long as they can be logically inferred from what we know in nature: there is even room in the epic, he admits, for the marvelous. Girolamo Fracastoro similarly argues in the *Naugerius* (1555) that the poet, in depicting the simple and essential truth of things, should not simply reproduce it but clothe it in beauty that is formal, ethical, and aesthetic, keeping only to decorum, which is for him suggested by the idea the poet wishes to portray.

Tasso further complicates the question of imitation in his *Discorsi dell'arte poetica* (composed 1567–70, pub. 1587) when he seeks some balance between the claims of Christian and allegorical truth and poetic license and adornment: the naked truth, he claims, should be enhanced by novelty and surprise that will increase the sense of wonder. To some critics, the requirement that certain kinds of poetry present wonderful and marvel-

ous events and arouse admiration (*admiratio*), as well as teach moral lessons, seemed to be compatible with the *Poetics*; but to others, it contravened the dictum that the poet should represent the real world (or "nature"). The latter position is taken in the *Della poetica la deca disputata* (1586) of Francesco Patrizi, popularly known as the *Deca ammirabile*. For Patrizi, there are two forms of the marvelous: one is a quality of the poem itself, which springs from the divine inspiration or enthusiasm of the poet and suitably combines the credible and incredible, making the work admirable (*mirabile*); the other is the effect produced in the audience, the extrinsic end of poetry (*la maraviglia*).

While the theory of imitation was considerably more advanced in Italy than elsewhere in the 16th c., there was great interest in France, Spain, and England as well. Du Bellay's *Deffence* argues that Fr. poetry can only hope to attain perfection by imitating the classics and that, while the true poet is born, only education in the classics will protect his talent from being useless or ill-formed. But du Bellay does not distinguish one kind of imitation from another; he left that to Jacques Peletier, who says (not unlike Tasso) in his *Art poétique* (1555) that the poet's responsibility is to imitate old things by adding to them something new, something beautiful. Ronsard invokes the fundamental principle of *imitatio* both in his *Abrégé de l'art poétique françois* (1565) and in the 1572 preface to his incomplete epic *La Franciade*. While he urges the use of images that are inspiring (since he sees the end of poetry as moral edification), he rules out images that are fantastic, unnatural, or marvelous. But the sense of morality is strongest in the work of Jean Vauquelin de la Fresnaye, who prefers scriptural themes for poetry. Indeed, he notes in his *Art poétique* (1605) that if the Greeks had been Christian they too would have sung of the life and death of Christ.

**VI. Rhetoric and Poetics.** References to *ornament and to memory suggest that, for many of the major Ren. critics, Ren. poetics also grew directly out of Ren. rhet. Vida's *De arte poetica*, e.g., combines a Horatian discussion of the training of the poet and a defense of poetry (in book 1) with rhetorical treatises on invention and disposition (in book 2) and elocution (in book 3). Daniello's *La poetica* expands Horace around the same three rhetorical concerns; and even Minturno's *L'arte poetica* combines Horace and Aristotle's *Poetics* with the rhetorical writings of Cicero and Quintilian. In the 14th c., Coluccio Salutati had urged in *De nobilitate legum et medicinae* the practice of disputations, or *controversiae*, as a practical means to sharpen the mind, inspire further learning, and engender practical results in the life of early humanist students; in the 15th c., Fracastoro argues that the poet can persuade his reader by imitating natural things. Such an art of persuasion was at first the chief purpose not so much of poetry as of rhet., yet poets too needed to persuade readers to the basic truths of their poetry, whether it was deliberately verisimilitudinous or not. By the 15th c. in Italy and by the 16th c. in northern Europe, poetics frequently rested on the principles and practices of rhet. because that was the substance of education and, further, because both shared the common end of persuasion.

Extant syllabi and lectures from humanist schools of the 15th and 16th cs. illustrate the close alliance between rhet. and poetics. Humanist students were taught Lat. grammar and syntax followed by orations, imitating historical and imagined speeches; they also practiced fables, biographies, epistles, and descriptions. Regardless of form, such exercises promoted deliberative, judicial, and demonstrative speeches that would discuss an issue, argue a point, or award praise or blame; after this, students would move on to disputations and debates.

Indeed, the rhetorical technē taught in the humanist schools provided esp. imaginative ways to think, write, and speak, such as *prosopopoeia, the creation (or *feigning) of a fictive *persona; and *topographia*, the description (or creation) of places such as Utopia or Arcadia. The rhet. studied in humanist schools also taught the value and practice of ethos, or the feigned persona of the speaker, and pathos, the ways in which a speaker (or poet) puts his audience into a particular frame of mind. Such classroom lessons were easily transferred into poetic technique, esp. since Aristotle's chief rhetorical end, probability, was transformed into verisimilitude by Cicero (*De inventione* 1.21.29).

Rhet. also emphasized the centrality of the audience, pointing the need for interest, emotional connection, and learning. Shakespeare, e.g., addresses this in the Prologue to *Henry V* in which he instructs his audience concerning the limitations of stage performances, but it was the ongoing concern of *paragena*, dedicatory letters, and dramatic prologues such as the Introduction to Ben Jonson's *Bartholomew Fair* or the epilogues of Shakespeare's Puck or Rosalind. Constant interruptive addresses to the *reader are also a feature of François Rabelais's *Gargantua and Pantagruel*, Miguel de Cervantes's *Don Quixote*, Sidney's *Arcadia*, and Spenser's *Faerie Queene* (see RHETORIC AND POETRY).

**VII. Conclusion.** One of the important cl. texts for Ren. poetics is Epistle 45 of the Roman philosopher Seneca. According to Seneca, art is best understood as an imitation determined by the four causes of Aristotle's *Prior Analytics*. As Seneca applies them, the first cause is actual matter (such as the bronze of a bronze statue); the second cause is the agent (the artist or worker); the third is the form (the sense of the form and function of a statue); and the fourth is the purpose (money, reputation, religious devotion). What became crucial for Ren. poetics, however, is Seneca's own "fifth cause"—the model or original against which the new creation is made and to which it always, implicitly or explicitly, refers. The theory of models was consonant with the Ren. interest in turning away from the Middle Ages to Gr. and Roman texts for an understanding of form, genres, and techne, reinforcing both the understanding and practice of poetry. Cl. models lie behind

not only the epics of Ariosto, Tasso, Spenser, and Milton, but *The Praise of Folly* of Erasmus, such plays as Shakespeare's *Othello* and Ben Jonson's *Volpone*, and such prose fictions as Sidney's *Arcadia* and Cervantes's *Don Quixote*.

The It. Ren. critics and their Sp., Fr., and Eng. successors were the founders of mod. Eur. crit. and mod. Eur. lit. as well. The Dutch and Ger. critics of the Ren. added little that was new. The theories that were produced by Ren. critics were learned, sophisticated, and detailed, but they were often divorced from the realities of the literary marketplace. This was esp. true of theories of drama. Lope de Vega confessed that, of his 483 comedies, "all except six of them sin grievously against art." In other words, the only way he or anyone else prior to the collapse of the neoclassical spirit could talk about art was in the terms formulated and promulgated by Ren. poetics, and these terms were for the most part irrelevant to the kind of drama that Lope de Vega was writing.

*See* RENAISSANCE POETRY.

■ **Anthologies**: *English*: Smith—collects the major Ren. prosodists and critics; *Critical Essays of the Seventeenth Century*, ed. J. E. Spingarn, 3 v. (1907); *Literary Criticism of Seventeenth-Century England*, ed. E. W. Tayler (1967); *English Renaissance Literary Criticism*, ed. B. Vickers (1999). *French*: Patterson—while a hist., contains copious excerpts from Ren. essays; *Literary Criticism*, ed. A. Gilbert (1940)—a generous selection in trans.; *Critical Prefaces of the French Renaissance*, ed. B. Weinberg (1950); *Trattati di poetica e retorica del cinquecento*, 4 v. (1970–74); *Poetiken de Cinquecento*, ed. B. Fabian, 25 v. (1967–69); *Traités de poétique et de rhétorique de la Renaissance*, ed. F. Goyet (1990). *Italian*: U. Nisieli, *Proginnasmi poetici*, 2 v. (1639); Weinberg.

■ **Criticism and History**: K. Borinski, *Die Poetik der Renaissance* (1886); F. E. Schelling, *Poetic and Verse Criticism of the Reign of Elizabeth* (1891); W. H. Woodward, *Vittorino da Feltre and Other Humanist Educators* (1897); K. Vossler, *Poetische Theorien in der ital. Frühren* (1900); F. Padelford, *Select Translations from Scaliger's Poetics* (1905); I. Scott, *Controversies over Imitation of the Renaissance* (1910)—includes trans. of Erasmus's *Ciceronianus*; H. Charlton, *Castelvetro's Theory of Poetry* (1913); Félix Lope de Vega, *The New Art of Writing Plays*, trans. W. T. Brewster (1914); C. Trabalza, *La critica letteraria nel rinsaciamento* (1915); D. L. Clark, *Rhetoric and Poetic in the Renaissance* (1922); C. S. Baldwin, *Renaissance Literary Theory and Practice* (1939); M. T. Herrick, *The Poetics of Aristotle in England* (1930); T. W. Baldwin, *William Shakspere's Small Latine & Lesse Greeke*, 2 v. (1944); V. Hall Jr., *Renaissance Literary Criticism* (1945); H. Wilson and C. Forbes, *Gabriel Harvey's Ciceronianus* (1945)—facsimile of 1567 ed.; W. Lily, *A Shorte Introduction of Grammar*, ed. V. J. Flynn (1945)—facsimile of 1567 ed.; M. T. Herrick, *The Fusion of Horatian and Aristotelian Literary Criticism, 1531–1555* (1946); J.W.H. Atkins, *English Literary Criticism: The Renascence* (1947); V. Hall Jr., "Scaliger's Defense of Poetry," *PMLA* 63 (1948); J. Burckhardt, *The Civilization of the Renaissance in Italy*, trans. S.G.C. Middlemore (1950); M. T. Herrick, *Comic Theory in the Sixteenth Century* (1950); J. E. Spingarn, *A History of Literary Criticism in the Renaissance*, 2d ed. (1954); R. R. Bolgar, *The Classical Heritage and Its Beneficiaries* (1954); M. T. Herrick, *Tragicomedy* (1955); W. S. Howell, *Logic and Rhetoric in England, 1500–1700* (1956); W. Ong, *Ramus and the Decay of Dialogue* (1958); Weinberg; P. O. Kristeller, *Renaissance Thought*, 2 v. (1961, 1965); B. Hathaway, *The Age of Criticism: The Late Renaissance in Italy* (1962); O. B. Hardison Jr., *The Enduring Monument* (1962); A. García Berrio, *La formación de la teoría moderna* (1963); D. Bush, *Mythology and the Renaissance Tradition in English Poetry*, rev. ed. (1963); M. Vitale, *La Questione de la lingua* (1967); J. E. Seigel, *Rhetoric and Philosophy in Renaissance Humanism* (1968); R. Weiss, *The Renaissance Discovery of Classical Antiquity* (1969); A. Patterson, *Hermogenes and the Renaissance* (1970); F. G. Robinson, *The Shape of Things Known: Sidney's "Apology" in Its Philosophical Tradition* (1972); D. Attridge, *Well-Weighed Syllables* (1974); J. B. Altman, *The Tudor Play of Mind* (1978); W. J. Kennedy, *Rhetorical Norms in Renaissance Literature* (1978); A. Weiner, *Sir Philip Sidney and the Poetics of Protestantism* (1978); R. L. Montgomery, *The Reader's Eye: Studies in Didactic Literary Theory from Dante to Tasso* (1979); C. Greenfield, *Humanist and Scholastic Poetics, 1250–1500* (1981); L. Holtz, *Donat et la tradition de l'enseignement grammatical* (1981); I. Silver, *Ronsard and the Hellenic Renaissance*, 2 v. (1981); T. M. Greene, *The Light in Troy: Imitation and Discovery in Renaissance Poetry* (1982); M. W. Ferguson, *Trials of Desire: Renaissance Defenses of Poetry* (1983); *Jacopo Mazzoni's "On the Defense of the Comedy of Dante,"* trans. R. L. Montgomery (1983); W. Trimpi, *Muses of One Mind* (1983); *Englische Literaturtheorie von Sidney bis Johnson*, ed. B. Nugel (1984); J. H. Meter, *The Literary Theories of Daniel Heinsius* (1984); V. Kahn, *Rhetoric, Prudence, and Skepticism in the Renaissance* (1985); K. Eden, *Poetic and Legal Fiction in the Aristotelian Tradition* (1986); A. F. Kinney, *Humanist Poetics: Thought, Rhetoric, and Fiction in 16th-Century England* (1986); D. K. Shuger, *Sacred Rhetoric* (1988); *CHLC* v. 3, ed. G. P. Norton; O. B. Hardison Jr., *Prosody and Purpose in the English Renaissance* (1989); S. K. Heninger Jr., *Sidney and Spenser* (1989); A. F. Kinney, *Continental Humanist Poetics* (1989); Vickers; Vickers, *Defence*; J. P. Roach, *The Player's Passion* (1995), ch. 1; R. Bushnell, *A Culture of Teaching* (1996); J. Farrell, *Latin Language and Latin Culture* (2001); *Blackwell Companion to Rhetoric and Rhetorical Criticism*, ed. W. Jost and W. Olmstead (2004).

V. Hall; O. B. Hardison; A. F. Kinney

**RENAISSANCE POETRY.** The Ren. was the first period in postclassical Eur. lit. hist. to conceive itself as a period, in the spirit of Petrarch's designation of his age as a "rinascimento" (rebirth) of knowledge after what he supposed to be the intellectual obscurity of the Middle Ages. Beginning in Italy in the 15th c., the period opens unevenly across Europe from Portugal to Poland and Eur. outposts from Mexico City to Macau. In outline, the Ren. begins with the assimilation of Petrarch's thought and concludes with the rise of neoclassicism in the late 17th c.; but there are several divisions and reactions within the period proper—the *baroque is perhaps the most problematic of these—and many countries have their own period concepts within the larger age. The Ren. was made by humanism, which radiated outward from Petrarch and his It. successors—incl. thinkers such as Lorenzo de' Medici (1449–92), Giovanni Pico della Mirandola (1463–94), Pietro Bembo (1470–1547), and countless poets—who speculated on such topics as the nature of humanity, the intellectual and moral character of love, and the proper interactions between human beings and their world. Humanism had educational, philological, aesthetic, political, and other dimensions. It provided the intellectual atmosphere in which such technological and cultural inventions as movable type and linear perspective could be conceived and flourish; it was closely connected to the exaltation of the individual, the rise of the mod. state, and the devel. of imperialism.

The poetry of the Ren. began with the vernacular poetry of Petrarch (1304–74), whose *Rime sparse* or *Canzoniere* and *Trionfi* were in poetic terms as technologically revolutionary as printing and pictorial perspective. The facts that these poems were composed in the vernacular, that they represented the thoughts and emotional states of a single person over time, that they shunned obvious *allegory in favor of a rich attention to the textures of both lang. itself and immediate experience, and that they treated amatory love as the summa of human existence, as complete in its way as the devotional or philosophical life and in a sense containing those kinds of life within it—all these made Petrarch's work seem astonishingly mod. for the 15th and 16th cs. The absorption of Petrarch into other lits. meant that his work attained the status of a mod. classic, comparable to the poetry of Virgil or Horace: when the Venetian printer Aldus Manutius produced the first mod. eds. of the Gr. and Roman classics around 1500, he included Petrarch's *Canzionere* in that *canon. As *Petrarchism arrived in each Eur. culture, it was not so much a set of strict conventions as a model for mod. writing that could be adjusted to local conditions, and the acceptance of Petrarchism invariably meant that a new generation had appeared, ready to remake vernacular poetry in its own way.

The foundational monuments of Petrarchan poetry across Europe include Maurice Scève's (ca. 1511–64) *Délie* (1544) and the experiments in love poetry and other genres by the poets of the *Pléiade*, Pierre de Ronsard (1524–85), Joachim du Bellay (ca. 1522–60), and Jean-Antoine de Baïf (1532–89) in France, whose emergence was heralded by du Bellay's *La Deffence et illustration de la langue françoyse* (1549); the adaptations of Italianate and cl. forms such as the *sonnet, the *elegy, and the *eclogue into Sp. by Juan Boscán (ca. 1490–1542), Garcilaso de la Vega (1503–36), and their follower Fernando de Herrera (1534–97), and into Port. by Francisco Sá de Miranda (1481–1558); and the introduction of Petrarchism into Eng. by Thomas Wyatt (1503–42) and Henry Howard, the Earl of Surrey (1517–47). Nearly every Eur. culture has one or several of these poets, the transformational figures of their national poetries.

Of course, the picture is more complicated in each setting, and there are precursors, dissenters, and hybrids to take into account. Clément Marot (1496–1544), against whom the Pléiade defined itself, had absorbed many elements of Italianate poetics into his practice and had differentiated his work from that of his father, the *rhétoriqueur* Jean Marot (ca. 1450–1526); the reform represented by Ronsard and his brigade was perhaps as much about explicit declaration as about radical change. For that matter, Garcilaso's introduction of Petrarchism into Castilian had been anticipated by his grandfather's uncle, the 14th-c. poet the Marqués de Santillana (1398–1458); as in France, the difference was made by a highly visible publication, in this case *Las obras de Boscán con algunas de Garcilaso de la Vega* (1543). Each culture had its figures who defied the modernizing influence of Petrarchism, such as the Sp. poet Cristóbal de Castillejo (ca. 1490–1550), who favored national over imported resources. And no poet of significance was entirely converted to Petrarch's models: e.g., we remember Wyatt and Surrey as his agents in Eng. letters, but a substantial part of their poetry, esp. Wyatt's, remained closely involved with a nativist trad. known as the *plain style. Wyatt's and Surrey's posthumous publication occurred in a volume called *Songes and Sonettes, written by the ryght honorable Lorde Henry Haward late Earle of Surrey, and others*, now known as *Tottel's Miscellany* (1557). The import of this notional generation whose members were mostly born between 1500 and 1525 was not that they were literally the first in any category—Petrarchans, reformers, classicists—but that their work (in some cases pub. posthumously) emerged contemporaneously in the 1540s and 1550s with a burst of attention and self-awareness. They not only rehabilitated cl. genres but developed vernacular ones such as the sonnet and found in the *sonnet sequence an adaptable medium for fusing experiments in *diction and *figuration, mythological *allusion, and a vivid first-person *voice. This group's collective efforts made an apex for *love poetry; and, for several generations, the topic of love in poetry became a *metonymy for many other kinds of human endeavors. Hundreds of sonnet sequences were composed in Europe between 1550 and 1640, more than 60 in England during the period known as the "sonnet boom" (1580–1630), incl. such distinguished works as Philip Sidney's *Astrophil and Stella* (1591) and William Shakespeare's *Sonnets* (1609).

The influence of It. thought and letters on the rest of Europe extended well beyond lyric, however, esp. where Italy was seen to have a privileged relation to humanism and the classics. Like Petrarch, who had written an *epic titled *Africa* along with his voluminous work in other genres, many poets of the 16th c. strove to fashion epics that would revisit cl. and med. heroes in light of present-day dynastic and political concerns: these include the several epics conceived around an updated Roland (now called Orlando) such as Luigi Pulci's (1432–84) *Morgante maggiore* (1483), Matteo Maria Boiardo's (1441–94) *Orlando innamorato* (1495), and Ludovico Ariosto's (1474–1533) *Orlando furioso* (1516); Torquato Tasso's (1544–95) reimagining of Godfrey of Bouillon's exploits during the first crusade in *Gerusalemme liberata* (1581); and Edmund Spenser's (1552–99) configuration of the story of Arthur with that of his own monarch, Elizabeth I, in *The Faerie Queene* (1590, 1596). One should mention Ronsard's unfinished *Franciade*, which concerns the adventures of Francus, son of Hector.

While most of the period's epics accept this reinvestment in cl. and med. lit., the most notable example that falls outside the tendency is *The Lusiads* (1572) of Luís de Camões (1524–80), the Port. national epic of empire in which Vasco da Gama's exploration of India and Africa is portrayed as fulfilling the providential destiny of his nation. Mythological characters abound in *The Lusiads*, but they play a supporting role to the Port. themselves; instead of adapting a received story such as Orlando or Arthur to present-day realities, Camões boldly begins from those mod. circumstances and renders them as densely as any cl. or med. tale, with the stock motifs appearing ad hoc in service to his nationalist vision. Another striking revision of epic convention appears in the Basque Alonso de Ercilla's (1533–94) *La Araucana* (1569–89), an epic concerning the conquest of Chile, in which the narrator is a principal character who negotiates his way among Sp., indigenous, and cl. figures.

Like nearly all 16th-c. Eur. epics, *The Lusiads* and the *Araucana* honor the cl. trad. of Homer and Virgil while instilling an atmosphere of romance that those poets would not have entirely recognized. Romance was the mode of much med. and early mod. vernacular narrative: it offers heroes greater in degree than we are and more emotionally variegated than those of epic, a landscape and world that often reflect the geopolitical concerns of the audiences, and a supernatural ambience that does not violate but fulfills the terms of the fiction. The conflation of romance and epic values in early mod. epic—as in the *Faerie Queene*, for instance, where epic significance is attached to a plot and characters largely driven by romance—acknowledged how much narrative fiction and its readerships had changed over the long rise of the vernaculars. A romance ethos was one of the things that made 16th-c. epic seem mod. On the other hand, the modernity of one era becomes obsolescent in the next, and many of these epics were rendered quaint if not unseasonable with the coming of the novel in Miguel de Cervantes's (1547–1616) *Don Quixote* (1605, 1615), which explicitly satirized romance conventions. As a result, many Eur. and trans-Atlantic societies found their early mod. epics to be barren of descendants until much later, often when romantic poets discovered the distinctive early mod. fusion of fancy, heroism, and passion that populates the great narrative poems of the Ren. (see ROMANTICISM).

Petrarchan lyric was widely adapted but not universally absorbed; epics are few in number. While these genres set the agenda for much of what we retrospectively consider Ren. poetry, they were two threads in a fabric. What is often anthologized as representative of the period is not the entire cloth. One factor, diminished in strength since Petrarch's career but still important, was the continued vitality of Lat. A great deal of 16th- and 17th-c. poetry was written in Lat. within a comprehensive range of genres and modes. Some poets whom we know for their vernacular poetry, such as du Bellay in France and John Milton (1608–74) in England, wrote significant short poems in Lat.; other figures of considerable influence, such as the Sp.-It. poet Baptista Spagnuoli Mantuanus, known as Mantuan (1448–1516), and the Scottish George Buchanan (1506–82), wrote entirely in Lat. If Lat. and the vernaculars remained in close proximity throughout the period, so did amatory and *devotional poetry. Even as poets explored the possibilities of what we could consider secular poetry (on amatory, social, or *epideictic topics), many of them developed substantial corpora of devotional poetry. Trans. of the *Psalms were a common milestone because they put ambitious poets into direct contact with the work of David, who was conventionally seen as the supreme poet of the Judeo-Christian world; the challenge of rendering the Psalms into the vernaculars was a parallel to the humanist problem of how to relate contemp. writing to the classics, and the established doctrines of humanist poetics—Aristotelian *mimesis, Horatian *imitation, Ciceronian *invention—had a deeper meaning when the original work was scripture. Clément Marot, Wyatt, Surrey, Baïf, Philippe Desportes (1546–1606), Luis de León (1527–91), Camões, Buchanan, Philip Sidney (1554–86), Mary Sidney (1561–1621), Martin Opitz (1597–1639), John Donne (1572–1631), Richard Crashaw (1613–49), Milton—all confronted an opportunity braided with a problem, requiring not only convincing trans. of the poems but a legible position on the poetics. And this is to say nothing of the popular versions of the Psalms that, in Reformed countries, were often the most widely read, such as the Eng. psalter (1549) by Thomas Sternhold and John Hopkins and Ambrosius Lobwasser's adaptation of the Genevan Psalter into German (1573), both of which remained in use for centuries. The first book published in Brit. North America, *The Bay Psalm Book* (1640), was just such a popular psalter. Beyond the Psalms, of course, devotional and other kinds of religious poetry were among the most thoroughly developed modes of the period. Responses to scripture, meditations, *contrafacta that refashioned amatory verse, *narrative poems—notwithstanding the inattention of mod. readers, all these were prominent and were sometimes the work of the same poets (e.g., Scève and Tasso) whom we now read avidly for their poetry of love, adventure, or courtly life.

The penchant of many 16th- and 17th-c. poets for Lat. and divine poetry may appear remote from a mod. world that is predominantly demotic and secular. Likewise, to present-day urban culture, it can be hard to fathom the esteem for *pastoral poetry in the Ren.—

like devotional writing, a mode it may seem everyone attempted. Recent scholars generally agree that pastoral typically wears a shell of idealization around a hard kernel of social and political commentary and that the play between the literal and figurative levels—a relation not usually of allegory but of a less closed, more indeterminate kind of figuration—constitutes much of the mode's appeal to readers who were steeped in cl. and recent models as well as the contemporaneous persons and events under representation. While pastoral claimed a biblical antecedent in Psalm 23, the most powerful models for early mod. pastoral were found in the Hellenistic poets Theocritus, Moschus, and Bion and esp. the eclogues of Virgil; and closer to hand, in imitations of Virgil's eclogues by Dante, Petrarch, and Giovanni Boccaccio (1313–75), in Mantuan's Neo-Lat. eclogues, in the It. humanist Jacopo Sannazaro's (1458–1530) romance *Arcadia* (1502) and five *Eclogae piscatoriae* (written 1501–44), and in the Port. Jorge de Montemayor's (1520?–61) *Diana* (1559).

Once pastoral was revived in the 16th c., it became a widely understood perspective that could be assumed for the sake not of idealism or nostalgia—the ostensible values of its surface—but of saying difficult or harsh things cloudily, behind an unimpeachable convention. Moreover, while every pastoral has its own social, political, or religious polemic to make, at the same time all pastorals tell the same stories of singing contests, spurned lovers, and the daily lives of shepherds. Ren. readers must have found pleasure in this mix of consistency and difference, surface and depth, obvious fiction and truth-telling. Major instances of early mod. pastoral are too many to list, but every reader should know Boiardo's eclogues in Lat. and It., which prepare for his unfinished epic *Orlando innamorato*; Garcilaso's three eclogues that reflect the complexity of his career in the service of the absolutist regime of Charles V; Marot's two eclogues of the 1530s that articulate humanist values in the face of the court, the first ("Eglogue sur le Trespas de ma Dame Loyse de Savoye") an elegy for the mother of King Francis I, the second ("Eglogue au roy, soubz les noms de Pan & Robin") an address to the king that broaches the reciprocal obligations of poet and monarch; Spenser's *The Shepheardes Calender* (1579), a densely layered, polyvocal set of 12 eclogues that announced a new generation in Eng. letters and an avant-garde sensibility disguised within a scholarly attention to past works (for these qualities, it should be considered the *Waste Land* of its era); Sidney's prose romance *Arcadia* (1590, 1593), which includes a great deal of exquisite verse that honors but also galvanizes the conventions of pastoral lyric; Luis de Góngora's (1561–1627) two *Soledades* (composed 1613, the second unfinished), a recasting of pastoral motifs for a baroque world concerned with the legibility of verbal signs and the difficulty of reaching nature through any means but direct experience; and Milton's "Lycidas" (1637), an astonishing self-evocation that is perhaps the most famous pastoral elegy in the lang.

The shorter *genres such as the *epigram, the elegy, the *epyllion, the *satire, and the *hymn undergo a revival throughout the period, often coincident with the renewal of interest in the cl. figures who were their most visible exponents—such as Martial for the epigram, Juvenal for satire, and Ovid for the epyllion. Observers of poetry such as Sidney (*Defence of Poesy*, 1595) and George Puttenham (*The Arte of English Poesie*, 1589) often revel in the lists of available genres (Sidney: "heroic, lyric, tragic, comic, satiric, iambic, elegiac, pastoral") as though taking stock of how mod. poets have augmented the resources received from the classics. In many ways, the Ren. is a period of multiple genres, forms, and modes in productive collision with one another. It might be claimed that this was the first period in Eur. lit. in which the idea of genre became fully developed as both a theoretical and a practical matter.

After about 1600, this first, properly humanist phase of the Ren. drew to a close and another phase began, still humanist but in a different spirit. Intellectual life changed with the emergence of recognizably mod. disciplines such as astronomy, physics, and philosophy, and empirical discovery assumed a new value as a condition of knowledge; the absolutist political order across Europe was roiled by social and economic instability; and the Counter-Reformation produced new expressions of spirituality, as well as new forms of ecclesiastical intervention in cultural life. In poetry, the age is characterized by a poetics that revisits the established genres and forms of the past century with an augmented measure of *artifice, self-consciousness, and intellectual engagement, esp. in view of the highly charged advances in disciplinary knowledge. There are several names in circulation for this poetic turn, from the general—*mannerism and the baroque, which appear in the national poetries in various moments and guises—to the local, such as *Marinism in Italy, *conceptismo and *culteranismo* in Spain, and *metaphysical poetry in England and colonial New England. Conventional lit. hists. often treat these names as representing highly distinctive movements, autochthonous to the lang. or nation, and even (as in the case of conceptismo and culteranismo) ineluctably opposed to one another; but from the vantage of a common Eur. lit. hist., it must be noticed that these movements had in common the building of a poetic technology that was adapted to the state of knowledge in its time, as Petrarchism and other varieties of humanist poetry had been in the long era of their dominance.

The principal figures of 17th-c. poetry are innovators in this sense: they establish voices and values of their own in ways that even the most accomplished Petrarchans seldom do. Examples of the best of the period must include the Englishmen Donne and George Herbert (1593–1633), the latter probably the greatest devotional lyric poet in the lang.; and Góngora and Francisco de Quevedo (1580–1645) in Spain, ostensibly opposed to one another. Another category of intriguing figures—often disparaged, poorly understood (or too well understood), associated with other genres—might include the Germans Opitz, often didactic and descriptivist, and Andreas Gryphius (1616–64), who, like many poets of the century, evolved into a dramatist; in France, the fabulist Jean de La Fontaine (1621–95) and the early clas-

sicist François de Malherbe (1555–1628); the astonishingly prolific Sp. poet and dramatist Félix Lope de Vega (1562–1635), who wrote about 3,000 sonnets (nearly ten times Petrarch's *Canzoniere*) and 1,800 plays; and in England, the Catholic Crashaw and the *Cavaliers Thomas Carew (1595–1640) and John Suckling (1609–42). Still, there are stark differences between the generations of 17th-c. poetry—T. S. Eliot advanced a famous argument about the *dissociation of sensibility that he found between Donne's and Milton's eras—and over the middle and later decades, the influence of neoclassicism grew palpable and insistent, as though revisiting the discovery of the classics that inaugurated the Ren. more than 150 years earlier. The period sees many remarkable holdovers, foreshadowings, and coexistences. Looking back to the baroque as the source of their self-definition, some poets, theorists, and observers emphasize the powers of the poet in forming *conceits and analogies, as Baltasar Gracián (1601–58) does in his *Agudeza y arte de ingenio* (1648), one of the most influential Sp. treatises on poetics of the century; others look forward to the return of classicism by dwelling on the poet's restraints, as Nicolas Boileau (1636–1711) does in *L'Art poétique* (1674), the principal Fr. document in poetics of the later century. While Ben Jonson (1572–1637) was an early neoclassicist in England, his restrained poetry is impoverished by the label, embracing a rich array of cl. and vernacular models as well as a productive tension with Donne's poetics. On the other hand, Sor Juana Inés de la Cruz (ca. 1648–95) is a late baroque poet, writing into the 1690s, and a principal fount of Sp. Am. poetry. A generation apart, Jonson and Gracián inhabit different 17th-c. worlds, as do Boileau and Sor Juana—or the latter two and Milton, the natural heir of the 16th-c. epic poets such as Spenser and Camões.

*See* LATIN POETRY, NEOCLASSICAL POETICS, RENAISSANCE POETICS.

■ W. W. Greg, *Pastoral Poetry and Pastoral Drama* (1906); Schipper; J. M. Berdan, *Early Tudor Poetry* (1920); *The Love Poems of Joannes Secundus*, ed. and trans. F. A. Wright (1930)—with valuable essay on Neo-Lat. poetry; A. Scolari, *Ludovico Aristo* (1930); A. Meozzi, *Il Petrarchism europeo: Secolo XVI* (1934); Patterson; Lewis; C. Privitera, *La poesia e l'arte di Torquato Tasso* (1936); L. Bradner, *Musae Anglicanae: A History of Anglo-Latin Poetry, 1500–1925* (1940); P. Van Tieghem, *La littérature latine de la renaissance* (1944); M. Prior, *The Language of Tragedy* (1947); R. Tuve, *Elizabethan and Metaphysical Imagery* (1947); *Historia general de las literaturas hispánicas*, ed. G. Diaz-Plaja, 6 v. (1949–68); D. Alonso, *Poesia española* (1950); H. Smith, *Elizabethan Poetry* (1952); C. S. Lewis, *English Literature in the Sixteenth Century, Excluding Drama* (1954); L. L. Martz, *The Poetry of Meditation* (1954); E.M.W. Tillyard, *The English Epic and Its Background* (1954); B. Weinberg, *French Poetry of the Renaissance* (1954); L. B. Campbell, *Divine Poetry and Drama in Sixteenth-Century England* (1959); A. Kernan, *The Cankered Muse: Satire of the English Renaissance* (1959); G. Dickinson, *Du Bellay in Rome* (1960); J. Hollander, *The Untuning of the Sky: Ideas of Music in English Poetry, 1500–1700* (1961); I. Silver, *Ronsard and* the *Hellenic Renaissance in France*, 2 v. (1961, 1987); J. Thompson, *The Founding of English Metre* (1961); O. B. Hardison Jr. *The Enduring Monument* (1962); *Renaissance and Baroque Poetry of Spain*, ed. E. Rivers (1964); G. Castor, *Pléiade Poetics* (1964); P. Thomson, *Sir Thomas Wyatt and His Background* (1964); J. W. Lever, *The Elizabethan Love Sonnet*, 2d ed. (1965); W. L. Grant, *Neo-Latin Literature and the Pastoral* (1965); G. Mazzacurati, *Misure del classicismo rinascimentale* (1967); L. Forster, *The Icy Fire* (1969); S. Fish, *Surprised by Sin: The Reader in "Paradise Lost"* (1971); P. V. Marinelli, *Pastoral* (1971); B. W. Wardropper, *Spanish Poetry of the Golden Age* (1971); D. Attridge, *Well-Weighed Syllables* (1974); I. D. McFarlane, *Renaissance France, 1470–1589*, v. 2, *A Literary History of France*, ed. P. E. Charvet (1974); Wilkins; D. Javitch, *Poetry and Courtliness in Renaissance England* (1978); A. L. Prescott, *French Poets and the English Renaissance* (1978); B. K. Lewalski, *Protestant Poetics and the Seventeenth-Century Religious Lyric* (1979); S. Greenblatt, *Renaissance Self-Fashioning* (1980); C. Freer, *The Poetics of Jacobean Drama* (1981); G. Hibbard, *The Making of Shakespeare's Dramatic Poetry* (1981); R. Peterson, *Imitation and Praise in the Poetry of Ben Jonson* (1981); M. Donker and G. M. Muldrow, *Dictionary of Literary-Rhetorical Conventions of the English Renaissance* (1982); T. M. Greene, *The Light in Troy: Imitation and Discovery in Renaissance Poetry* (1982); J. Goldberg, *James I and the Politics of Literature: Jonson, Shakespeare, Donne, and Their Contemporaries* (1983); J. Guillory, *Poetic Authority: Spenser, Milton and Literary History* (1983); M. Quilligan, *Milton's Spenser: The Poetics of Reading* (1983); D. Quint, *Origin and Originality in Renaissance Literature* (1983); H. Dubrow, *Captive Victors: Shakespeare's Narrative Poems and Sonnets* (1987); A. Patterson, *Pastoral and Ideology: Virgil to Valéry* (1987); T. P. Roche Jr., *Petrarch and the English Sonnet Sequences* (1989); A. R. Jones, *The Currency of Eros: Women's Love Lyric in Europe, 1540–1620* (1990); R. Greene, *Post-Petrarchism* (1991); D. Quint, *Epic and Empire* (1993); I. Navarrete, *Orphans of Petrarch: Poetry and Theory in the Spanish Renaissance* (1994); P. Alpers, *What Is Pastoral?* (1996); *CHLC*, v. 3, ed. G. P. Norton (1999)—essays on several genres; R. Greene, *Unrequited Conquests* (1999); W. J. Kennedy, *Authorizing Petrarch* (1994), and *The Site of Petrarchism* (2003); H. Hamlin, *Psalm Culture and Early Modern English Literature* (2004); C. Warley, *Sonnet Sequences and Social Distinction in Renaissance England* (2005); C. Alduy, *Politique des "Amours": Poétique et genèse d'un genre français nouveau (1544–1560)* (2007); L. Middlebrook, *Imperial Lyric: New Poetry and New Subjects in Early Modern Spain* (2009).

R. Greene

**RENGA** is a once popular but now seldom practiced genre of Japanese poetry in which verses (*ku*) alternately of 17 and 14 morae (see MORA) are joined into long sequences according to rules (*shikimoku*) that govern how constituent images are to be employed. By the latter half of the med. era (1185–1600), orthodox linked verse (*ushin renga*) had become the most widely prac-

ticed form of Japanese poetry in the vernacular; vast numbers of hundred-verse sequences (*hyakuin*) survive, and some linked-verse practitioners rank among Japan's greatest poets. In the beginning of the early mod. (Tokugawa or Edo) period (1600–1868), ushin renga was eclipsed by unorthodox or comic *haikai* [*no*] *renga* (or *renku*, \**haikai* linked verse), which has far fewer restrictions on topics and vocabulary than the orthodox variety. The term *renga* usually refers to the orthodox form of the art, and that form will be the focus of the following discussion.

The practice of linking verses dates from the earliest recorded times; examples of protorenga are found in *Kojiki* (Record of Ancient Matters, 712 CE) and \**Man'yōshū* (late 8th c.). Renga composition was a leisure pursuit in the early med. period, but thereafter it developed into a serious art form; and while it never reached the canonical stature of the 31-morae \**waka* poem, the orthodox form of linked verse came to rank just beneath it, thanks in large part to the contributions of the court noble Nijō Yoshimoto (1320–88) and his commoner poetic advisor Kyūsei (or Gusai; ca. 1281–1376), who together compiled the first imperially authorized collection of linked verse, *Tsukubashū* (Anthology of the Way of Tsukuba, 1356–57); the first mature critical works (*rengaron*); and the first widely disseminated rules. The art reached its apogee in the linked verse of Shinkei (1406–75), Inō Sōgi (1421–1502), and many others of their era. Sōgi compiled the second imperially sanctioned renga collection, *Shinsen Tsukubashū* (Newly Selected Anthology of the Way of Tsukuba, 1495). Sequences linking Japanese verses and Chinese couplets (*wakan renku*) were popular as well, and there were also experiments that included employing one Sino-Japanese word in each stanza of otherwise pure native diction. The art remained vibrant during the time of Sōgi's disciples and up through the first years of the early mod. period, then become fossilized. Though ushin renga continued to be composed throughout the Tokugawa period and even thereafter, most linked-verse poets of those centuries turned to haikai [*no*] renga, which had also been enjoyed by previous generations of orthodox linked-verse poets in their lighter moments but which had not yet come to be seen as a poetic way of legitimacy and value in its own right.

Orthodox renga was usually composed orally by a group of poets, though solo sequences (*dokugin*) were often made as well. The first verse, the *hokku*, was the only one that could be prepared in advance, and it initially stood alone; it consists of 17 morae (divided into segments of 5, 7, and 5) and is the ancestor of the haiku (literally, "haikai verse"). A second poet would add a rejoinder of 14 morae (divided into two segments of 7), which related to the first while at the same time constituting an independent poetic statement. A third poet would then add another 17-morae verse, which by the rules could relate only to the verse immediately preceding it. Verses of 17 and 14 morae thus alternated until a hundred-link sequence was completed, a process that might take a full day or more. Every link after the introductory hokku, therefore, elicits three possible readings: as a verse in isolation, as a rejoinder to the previous verse, and as the inspiration for the following; and part of the artistry and pleasure of linked verse inheres in the way one poet's interpretation may be recast (*torinashi*) by the poet who follows. If any proffered verse in the sequence leapt over its immediate predecessor and referred to the specific subject of the penultimate link, it was rejected by the ranking renga poet (*sōshō*), who supervised the sequence, or by the scribe (*shuhitsu*). The renga lexicon was divided into various thematic categories, such as "spring" or "travel," which were adopted from waka usage, and lexical categories, such as "falling things" (e.g., rain or snow) or "flora" (e.g., grasses or trees). As each new verse was recited, the scribe would mentally check for infractions against the rules of repetition (how often a given poetic image could appear in a sequence), seriation (the minimum and maximum number of contiguous verses in which a thematic or lexical category could be employed), and intermission (how many verses had to separate the occurrences of an image or category). If a verse was satisfactory in terms both of rules and artistry, the scribe wrote it down. The final written record consisted of four sheets of paper (*kaishi*) folded lengthwise and inscribed both front and back, with eight verses on the front of the first page and the back of the last page, and 14 verses on the remaining sides. Ideally, the completed sequence would demonstrate a balance of linkage between each pair of verses (*tsukeai*) and overall thematic transition (*yukiyō*) through numerous verse worlds. A sequence was also expected to divide into an introduction (*jo*), devel. (*ha*), and swift conclusion (*kyū*), a formula renga shares with other cl. arts such as *gagaku* music and *nō* drama. In that each 17- or 14-morae verse by necessity constituted a complete statement, renga links could be even more condensed and elliptical than those of 31-morae waka, and every image deployed therein was energized by centuries of prior waka practice.

Linked verse responded to the contestatory spirit of the age, combining the high ideals and lexicon of the waka way with intense competition as each poet vied to be the first with the next link. While waka for most of its hist. had been dominated by courtier poets, many of the great renga masters (*rengashi*) were of modest or even humble origins, a fact that reflects the increasing social mobility of the violent late med. period. But linked-verse masters also composed waka and taught it, and the allied cl. literary trad., to students and wealthy patrons, contributing thereby to the establishment and dissemination of the Japanese literary canon. In that renga masters made their livings through their art (as opposed to earlier court poets, who were supported by emoluments), they have been called Japan's first professional literary figures. And because of the universal respect for the poetic way, rengashi could travel safely even through contiguous warrior domains that were in a state of conflict, and the records of their journeys, written in a blend of poetry and prose *prosimetrum*, constitute some of the most vivid examples of Japanese travel and diary writing (see JAPANESE POETIC DIARIES). Though renga verses did not generally become sources for later allusion as many waka poems did, some hundred-verse sequences, like *Minase sangin hyakuin* (One Hundred Verses by Three Poets at Minase, 1488) and *Yuyama sangin hyakuin* (One Hundred Verses by Three Poets at Yuyama, 1491), remain monuments of the Japanese poetic trad. Some critical writings on renga, like Shinkei's *Sasamegoto* (Murmured Conversations, 1463–64), likewise are models of Japanese poetic exegesis. In mod. times, the renga art has also inspired experiments in linked poetry in foreign langs.—notably the quadrilingual "chain of poems" by Octavio Paz, Jacques Roubaud, Edoardo Sanguineti, and Charles Tomlinson (pub. in Eng. as *Renga*, 1971).

■ **Anthologies**: *Rengashū* (Anthology of Linked Verse), ed. T. Ijichi, v. 39 of *Nihon koten bungaku taikei* (Great Compendium of Classical Japanese Literature, 1960); *Rengaronshū, haironshū* (Anthology of Linked-Verse and Haikai Criticism), ed. S. Kidō and N. Imoto, v. 66 of *Nihon koten bungaku taikei* (1961); *Rengashū, haikaishū* (Anthology of Linked Verse and Haikai), ed. K. Kaneko et al., v. 61 of *Shinpen Nihon koten bungaku zenshū* (Complete Collection of Classical Japanese Literature rev. ed., 2001); *Rengaronshū, nōgakuronshū, haironshū* (Anthology of Linked Verse, Nō, and Haikai Criticism), ed. I. Okuda et al., v. 88 of *Shinpen Nihon koten bungaku zenshū* (2001).

■ **Criticism and History**: J. Konishi, "The Art of Renga," trans. K. Brazell and L. Cook, *Journal of Japanese Studies* 2.1 (1975); E. Ramirez-Christensen, "The Essential Parameters of Linked Poetry," *HJAS* 41–42 (1983); K. Kaneko, *Rengaron no kenkyū* (Research in Linked-Verse Criticism, 1984); K. Kaneko, *Renga sōron* (Overview of Linked Verse, 1987); S. D. Carter, *The Road to Komatsubara: A Classical Reading of the Renga Hyakuin* (1987), and "Mixing Memories: Linked Verse and the Fragmentation of the Court Heritage," *HJAS* 48.1 (1988); H. M. Horton, "Renga Unbound: Performative Aspects of Japanese Linked Verse," *HJAS* 53.2 (1993); E. Ramirez-Christensen, "*Heart's Flower*": *The Life and Poetry of Shinkei* (1994); H. M. Horton, *Song in an Age of Discord*: "*The Journal of Sōchō" and Poetic Life in Late Medieval Japan* (2002); E. Ramirez-Christensen, *Emptiness and Temporality*: *Buddhism and Medieval Japanese Poetics* (2008).

■ **Translations**: "Linked Verse at Imashinmei Shrine: *Anegakoji Imashinmei Hyakuin*, 1447," trans. T. W. Hare, *Monumenta Nipponica* 34 (1979); "Highly Renowned" and "Three Poets at Yuyama," in *From the Country of Eight Islands*, trans. H. Sato and B. Watson (1981); *Three Poets at Yuyama*, trans. S. D. Carter (1983), and "Three Poets at Minase," in *Traditional Japanese Poetry*, trans. S. D. Carter (1991); *The Journal of Sōchō*, trans. H. M. Horton (2002); *Murmured Conversations*, trans. E. Ramirez-Christensen (2008).

H. M. HORTON

**REPETITION.** The structure of repetition underlies the majority of poetic devices, and it is possible to argue that repetition defines the poetic use of lang.

The effects of repetition are, however, multivalent and range from lending unity and coherence to exposing the fundamental difference between the repeated elements. Even as repetition may effect poetic closure and provide the poem with a regular pattern, exact repetition is impossible: the simple fact of temporal discontinuity between repeated elements leads to a difference in their functions, via the accumulation of significance and recontextualization (as demonstrated, e.g., by Edgar Allan Poe's "The Raven" in the radically unstable meaning of the repeated word "nevermore"). That is why Gertrude Stein, famous for her highly repetitive texts, claims "there is no repetition." At the same time, the poem's repetitions set up expectations and guide interpretation.

Repetition structures poetic forms at all levels, as in the repetition of sounds (*alliteration, *assonance, *consonance, *rhyme, homonym, or *paronomasia); repetition of syllables (*syllabic verse, *rich rhyme); repetition of words (*anaphora, *anadiplosis, parechesis, traductio, *ploce); *identical rhyme, repetend, *catalog, list, and the pattern of word repetitions in traditional *lyric forms, such as, e.g., the end words in a *sestina; repetition of lines (*refrain, *incremental repetition, *envelope stanza pattern, used also in verse forms such as *pantun and *villanelle); repetition of measure (*rhythm; *meter); repetition of syntactical patterns (*parallelism, *hypotaxis and parataxis); repetition of the line break (*free verse); semantic repetition (pleonasm, synonymy, and repetitions of figures, images, concepts, themes); and intertextual repetition (*allusion or *pastiche).

Repetition not only patterns (as the examples above demonstrate) but parallels and reinforces those poetic devices that distinguish verse from prose. Similarly to the line break, it disrupts the linearity of lang., creating a counterpoint rather than continuity of narrative logic. Repetition of the same element in different contexts may also perform a metaphorical function. As readers often observe, repetition draws attention to itself and tends to denaturalize lang.: the more repetitions there are in a poem, the more we are conscious of the poem's *artifice and the less able to come up with the poem's paraphrasable meaning. In fact, intense repetition may lead to the loss of meaning (the signifier entirely replaces the signified). It has been observed also that repetition marks the collective in lang., revealing a polyphony and taking poetic expression beyond a single voice.

A poem's various repetitions interact, creating a complex effect. E.g., in the final couplet of Shakespeare's sonnet 18, a pattern of alliteration, assonance, paronomasia, and syntactic parallelism creates a series of echoes: "So long as men can breathe, or eyes can see / So long lives this, and this gives life to thee." W. C. Williams's "To a Poor Old Woman" is an example of *free verse exploiting the counterpoint between syntax and line break. The sentence/line that begins the second stanza, "They taste good to her," is repeated twice but broken into three lines. Apart from revealing an ambiguity or plurality of meanings inherent in a simple sentence, because of the mismatch between syntax and lineation, the repetitions create a pronounced, syncopated rhythm.

In ritual poetries, repetition has a performative function and lends them illocutionary power. Prayers, mantras, Santería or voodoo rituals, and various liturgies all rely on verbal repetition that supplants logic with emotive effect. Repetition is the basis of prosody in the Heb. Bible; its syntactical parallelism has exerted an influence on Anglo-Am. poetry of such dissimilar poets as Christopher Smart (*Jubilate Agno*), William Blake ("The Garden of Love"), Walt Whitman ("Song of Myself"), and Allen Ginsberg (*Howl*).

Oral poems are repeated by being passed from generation to generation as well as structured by repetition that serves as a mnemonic device (see ORAL POETRY). Scholars of orality point to various degrees of balance between the repetition of formulas, themes and story patterns, and improvisation (see ORAL-FORMULAIC THEORY). Needless to say, the function of repetition in oral texts is different from that in written poetry, and oral trad. demonstrate a wide range of practices, thus varying among themselves in their use of repetition.

In Native Am. poetics, because of the traditional connection between the sacred and the verbal, often much importance has been placed on exact repetition of an oral text. Embedded in a specific occasion (where many other elements, such as music, dance, and gesture actively produce meaning, comparably to contemp. intermedia art) a *song, *chant, spell, prayer, or oration has a performative function and may be repeated several times, depending on the specificity of the event (e.g., a healing prayer repeated line by line after the shaman by the patient). Native Am. songs and chants employ repetition as a structural device (often said to echo natural cycles, as well as tribal inheritance), where grammatical and semantic repetition is said to increase the incantatory (as opposed to narrative) qualities of a given performance. Considering the Native Am. concept of authorship (and audience), a "poem" is always a type of repetition entailing a source larger than the speaker (communal, natural, or sacred), rather than an expression of a unique voice. Western poetics has less patience for repetition: ethnocentric critics reveal that Native Am. repetitions are often expurgated in trans. into Eng. because considered untranslatable, redundant, or meaningless.

Rhythm and repetition (sometimes engaged in chiastic reversals) are said to be the defining elements of black culture. James A. Snead juxtaposes this feature of black "non-progressive" culture with Western tendency (present in Eur. and Eurocentric cultures from the late 16th c. up until the modernist revolution in the 20th) to "cover up" its repetitions for the sake of the ideology of progress, realism, and faithful representation of reality in art. Repetition lies at the core of Af. verbal trad. (e.g., call-and-response patterns) that informs much of black art: it shapes Af. and Af. Am. music and its lyrics (slave songs, *spirituals, gospel, *blues, and rap); it grounds improvisation in jazz (which needs an established pattern to diverge from); it is a pronounced feature in black folk sermons. All of these models find their way into *African American poetry. Snead refers to the repeated beat as "social," i.e., available to be played with by new voices. *Signifying, defined by Henry Louis Gates Jr. as the "black trope of tropes," depends on repetition with a difference. As a play of signifiers, this "figure for black rhetorical figures" (Gates) consistently draws attention to its repetitions, a feature often explored by Af. Am. poets. Harryette Mullen's *Muse & Drudge* signifies, among others, on W.E.B. Du Bois's concept of "double consciousness" (Huehls); Michael Harper's "Dear John, Dear Coltrane" signifies on Coltrane's "Love Supreme"; Langston Hughes's *Ask Your Mama* is, according to Gates, the most representative Af. Am. poem based on signifying as a mode of discourse.

Repetition in poetry has been studied from a number of perspectives and with tools from various fields. Mod. philosophers (from Søren Kierkegaard and Friedrich Nietzsche to Gilles Deleuze and Jacques Derrida) make a distinction between two forms or competing effects of repetition that can be provisionally defined as repetition-as-unity and repetition-as-difference. The former, sometimes referred to as "Platonic repetition" or "recollection," is based on the principle of identity or original similitude that is recovered by repetition (e.g., by *mimesis); the latter is a disclosure or production of difference. This binary definition of repetition often extends to other binary oppositions, such as hierarchy vs. nonhierarchical difference; theological grounding vs. lack of ground; order vs. disorder; stasis vs. movement; habit vs. creativity; trad. vs. individual talent; codification vs. dissent; authority of the text vs. surrender of authorial control; and linearity vs. rupture. An example of the former model is found by Mircea Eliade in archaic societies' belief in the possibility of recovering an ideal past, of repeating the original act performed by the gods, heroes, or ancestors. Transformational grammar (Noam Chomsky) aims at recovering the "deep structure" of lang. from which all "surface structures" may be generated. The later model, of repetition without an original, is present, e.g., in Baudrillard's concept of the simulacrum. *Structuralism in anthropology (Claude Lévi-Strauss)—but also in ling. (Ferdinand de Saussure) and literary studies (Roman Jakobson); see the *poetic function as a type of repetition—posits the existence of a system that underlies all concrete manifestations of social (also linguistic) phenomena. (Were one to apply the Saussurean structuralist linguistic model directly to poetic repetition, repetition of the sign would be realized by repeated words and phrases; repetition of the signifier by rhyme and alliteration; repetition of the signified by, e.g., synonymy.) In a Freudian psychoanalytic definition of the repetition compulsion, repetition is seen as both symptom (mechanical reenactment of the repressed) and cure (repetition in the transferential context of therapy). The cure consists in the move from unconscious, mechanical reenactment to conscious remembering: paradoxically, one needs to remember in order to forget, i.e., to free oneself of the past. Some readers argue that, through its various

repetitions, poetry speaks to the irrational side of our brains (Finch). Conceptions of the historical (also in literary and poetic hist.) similarly rely on alternative uses of repetition. Edward Said's critique of Giambattista Vico's model of hist., e.g., works along the common binary: in place of the "filiative" or genealogical model of repetition embraced by Vico, Said proposes a model that is "affiliative." Said emphasizes those forces in hist. that counter generative continuity and are based on affiliation. Obviously, the very tendency to account for repetition via binary oppositions is itself structuralist in its provenance, and, arguably, the two types of repetition always coexist, one always calling up the other, even as the tendency of a text and/or interpretation leans toward one more than the other.

The multivalence of poetic repetition is reflected in the variety of theoretical approaches to it. Those, again, tend to fall into two recognizable types: a grounded repetition that recovers an original and an ungrounded repetition that reveals difference. Thus, e.g., the notion of *"organic form" in poetry is usually grounded in the first type of repetition (and tends to be less explicitly repetitive or "covers up" its repetitions), while highly crafted poetic forms seem more of a "mechanical" exercise in which form produces content. In literary theory, Harold Bloom's *Anxiety of Influence* uses the genealogical model of repetition (critiqued by Said) to set the stage for his theory of poetic influence. Barbara Johnson discusses two types of repetition used, respectively, by William Wordsworth and E. A. Poe, arguing that the distinction between the two gives the study of poetry the key to "articulating authenticity with conventionality, originality and continuity, freshness with what is recognizably 'fit' to be called poetic." Wordsworth's and Poe's models of poetic creativity may seem incompatible, as Wordsworth's is based on "emotion recollected in tranquility" and aims at the recovery of an original moment, while Poe's rests on mechanical repetition of words and sounds; one is based on the signified, the other on the signifier. Johnson, however, deconstructs the opposition demonstrating that the two types of repetition and, consequently, the two definitions of poetic lang. are inextricable, even if one is the text's explicit argument and the other its "subversive ghost" (see also J. Hillis Miller). The confusion between the two types of repetition, argues Johnson, is not an error but the condition of poetic lang. itself.

■ M. Eliade, *The Myth of the Eternal Return*, trans. W. R. Trask (1954); Jakobson, v. 3; B. H. Smith, *Poetic Closure* (1968); D. Tedlock, "Introduction," *Finding the Center* (1972); "Tradition and the Individual Talent," Eliot, *Essays*; E. Said, "On Repetition," *Literature of Fact* (1976); J. Hollander, *The Figure of Echo* (1981); J. A. Snead, "Repetition as a Figure of Black Culture," *Black American Literature Forum* 15 (1981); J. H. Miller, *Fiction and Repetition* (1982); S. Kierkegaard, *Fear and Trembling*, trans. H. V. Hong and E. H. Hong (1983); D. Fried, "Repetition, Refrain and Epitaph," *ELH* 53 (1986); H. L. Gates Jr., *The Signi-*

*fying Monkey* (1988); B. Johnson, *A World of Difference* (1989); J. Baudrillard, *Simulacra and Simulation*, trans. S. F. Glaser (1994); G. Deleuze, *Difference and Repetition*, trans. P. Patton (1994); G. Stein, "Portraits and Repetition," *Gertrude Stein: Writings 1932–1946* (1998); S. Freud, *The Complete Psychological Works of Sigmund Freud: Beyond the Pleasure Principle, Group Psychology and Other Works*, v. 18 (2001); M. Huehls, "Spun Puns (and Anagrams): Exchange Economies, Subjectivity and History in Harryette Mullen's *Muse & Drudge*," *Contemporary Literature* 44 (2004); A. Finch, *The Body of Poetry* (2005); K. Mazur, *Poetry and Repetition* (2005).

K. MAZUR

## REPRESENTATION

   I. Definition
  II. Classic and Romantic
 III. Saussure and Peirce
 IV. The Verbal Medium
  V. Translation
 VI. Design
VII. The Master Trope

**I. Definition.** Representation is the process by which lang. constructs and conveys meaning. One major component—perhaps *the* major component—of the process of representaton is *reference*: words (texts) refer, or create pointers to, the external world, to other words (other texts), to themselves, or to the process of referring; Linda Hutcheon (in Whiteside and Issacharoff) identifies these four types or directions of reference as, respectively, extratextual, intertextual, intratextual, and metatextual (see INTERTEXTUALITY). Reference concerns the ability of lang. to describe, capture, express, or convey—the verbs have often been interchangeable—the external world in symbols that the mind can manipulate.

Representation lies at the very heart of the nature of lang., i.e., speech as a system of communication for encoding information symbolically and transmitting it from speakers to auditors (for diagram, see Jakobson; see also Abrams). It is one of the most difficult problems in philosophy; the issues are central not merely to aesthetics, but to epistemology and metaphysics. The structures and limitations inherent in words presumably already constrain our ability to talk about lang. at all: there is no vantage point from which we can stand outside lang. so as to critique it. But, conversely, we do not know how severe these constraints are, and we do know that lang. is capable of both creativity and growth so as to convey new concepts. A priori, it would seem reasonable to explore the nature of hammers as a construction tool by hammering and the nature of paint as an aesthetic medium by painting: hence, the nature of lang. by engaging in verbal discourse.

One would think that it might be possible to escape representation altogether; and indeed experimental poetries such as *poésie pure* in the 19th c. (see PURE

POETRY) and *sound poetry in the 20th sought escape from denotation and reference. All art aspires, Walter Pater remarked, to the condition of music. But, in fact, representation is almost impossible to escape even in nonrealistic or nonreferential art: thus, Rudolf Arnheim, commenting on abstractionist painting, suggested that "even the simplest patterns point to the meaning of the objects to which they apply," so that ultimately "there is no form without representation." Whether abstract or realistic, art largely engages in representation.

Though Samuel Johnson disparaged "representative meter" in poetry and though the range of imitative prosodic effects in Alexander Pope's *Essay on Criticism* is limited, *mimesis extends much deeper, and the *desire* for it is embedded in the very fabric of poetic lang. John Crowe Ransom said that poetic lang. aspires to the condition of nature: it "induces the provision of icons among the symbols." In perfected poetic speech, every word would be motivated and wholly natural, appropriate in form to its meaning. When devices such as sound patterning and repetition are used for artistic purposes, the inert categories of ordinary grammar are energized and raised to a higher level of valency where order *is* naturalized: here words *become* natural experience. Representation is, thus, the desire for the motivated sign.

**II. Classic and Romantic.** The Greeks bequeathed to posterity not one conception of poetry but two. The first strain derives from Plato's theory of Forms; in it, the issue of mimesis as *imitation is central. In this theory, which survived until the late 18th c., verbal experience is characterized as secondary and derivative, a *re*-presentation of actual experience. For Plato, lit. offers only an *image of an image, a copy of a copy of the real, so it is suspect. By the 18th c., copying "Nature" meant something else (see CONVENTION), but "imitation" was still embraced as sound poetic praxis. In the 19th, Thomas Carlyle and Friedrich Nietzsche's announcements that God is dead sealed the fate of this theory forever by removing any possibility of a being apart from our experience of the world who would validate the accuracy of mimetic representation. In the absence of all such verification, only making remains. All 20th- and 21st-c. art, therefore, exists in a postmimetic mode; notice that the chief drive in late industrial technology is to devise machines of ferocious efficiency at *copying*, at creating facsimiles. Endless repetition becomes the postmod. condition.

The second strain derives from the Gr. conception of *poiēsis* as making, the creation of objects from formless matter. This strain eventuated in romantic poetics, where form is made over as internal and individual; in *organicism, every entity has a form that proceeds from a principle that is self-contained, even as the oak tree springs from the acorn. The advent of *romanticism effected a fundamental epistemological shift by reformulating lit. not as an *imitative* but as a *constitutive* art, presenting not external reality but a fuller, partly interior version of reality that includes the feeling subject.

Mimesis as imitation was thus supplanted in romantic poetics by the concept of creative *imagination, the faculty by which the poet envisions and creates realities never before seen and not a part of the external world.

The romantic (expressive) strain has roots in antiquity in Aristotle's argument that the *poet surpasses the historian because he or she is not tied to mere fact but provides a more accurate (if less "factual") account of reality. This is the line followed in the Ren. by J. C. Scaliger (*Poetices libri septem* 1.1) and Philip Sidney: since the poet as seer (see VATES) can envision a higher order of nature than the one known to ordinary mortals, he or she becomes not a slave to or a copier of reality but a creator. The poet, says Sidney, "doth grow in effect another nature." Since the poet does not make propositional statements about the external world directly ("nothing affirmeth"), the poet is not a fabricator of falsehoods ("never lieth"). The poet models "truth" at a deeper level, where recreating the sense of life as felt experience is largely not a matter of descriptive detail; nor is verisimilitude required in order to persuade a reader of the "reality" of the fiction.

**III. Saussure and Peirce.** The most extensive mod. theories of verbal representation are those of Ferdinand de Saussure, the publication of whose lecture notes subsequently created an entire school in poetics (see STRUCTURALISM), and Charles Sanders Peirce, whose semiotics has been, if more extensive and philosophically coherent, much less influential in Am. lit. crit. (see SEMIOTICS AND POETRY). Both theories place the activity of signification—i.e., symbolization, sign making and sign interpreting—at the center of human cognition and interaction with the external world. Saussure followed all Western thought about lang. since Plato in conceiving the nature of ling. signs to be arbitrary: since the words for the same referent in two different langs. normally differ, there cannot be any innate, natural, or "motivated" relation between the particular sound shape of a word (the signifier) and its referent in the external world (the signified; see SIGN, SIGNIFIED, SIGNIFIER). He departed from such trad., however, in assigning the locus of meaning to the *difference* between such signs and their referents, both between langs. and within a lang. (see SOUND). Since, for Saussure, the vast majority of words have no motivated form, meaning arises only in the interplay of signs: hence, it is polyvalent, unstable, and indeterminate (see INDETERMINACY, TEXTUALITY).

Peirce conceives the world as triadic: his ontology identifies Firstness (a thing that is without relation to any other thing), Secondness (a thing that has its being in relation to any one other thing), and Thirdness (a thing that brings into relation a First and a Second). Thirdness is the realm of signs. For Peirce, all thought is carried on in signs; hence, all representation, as thought, is mediate cognition. Things in this triadic world may be either objects, meanings, or signs: a sign mediates between an object and its meaning. Meaning exists a priori, apart from human cognition; what remains for us

is only to discover and know it in greater or lesser degree. Hence, meaning is entirely objective, existing on an ideal plane that Peirce makes clear is essentially Hegelian.

The relations of sign to object—i.e., the fundamental modes of representation—possible in Peirce are three: resemblance, producing an *icon* (see ICONICITY); physical contiguity or action, producing an *index*; and thought (cognition), producing a *symbol* or sign. Since all signifying activity for Peirce is mental and even idealist, the first two indicate resemblance or emotive meanings and may express possibilities that might obtain or actualities that do obtain in the world—but not necessary relations that must obtain logically. Such signs are, therefore, not genuine, though their very ambivalences and ambiguities guarantee that they will be used widely. Genuine signs, incl. lang., exist in the autonomous realm of interpretive thought, which is fundamentally symbolic in character.

The noncongruence of ontological and epistemological assumptions between Peirce and Saussure is stark. For Peirce, subjectivity is a minor issue; for Saussure, it is fundamental. For Peirce, meaning is always already existent; for Saussure, it is local, unstable, and evanescent. Saussure's account is binary and linear; meaning is endlessly deferred. All the other major philosophical systems are ternary and triangular: all of them—including ling., semantics, semiotics, psychology, and cognitive studies—take meaning as a *given*.

**IV. The Verbal Medium.** Lang., the 20th c. realized with a shock, is a modeling system based on a code: everything cast into verbal form is *encoded*. Like other systems of expression both natural (gestures) and artificial (ciphers, mathematics), the elements of the system and the rules for combining them are largely arbitrary. Fundamental to all representation, therefore—whether mimetic or not—is the nature of the medium. Every representation is a mediation; all representations are formalizations and symbolizations. The nature of a symbol demands that it be radically unlike that for which it stands.

It is of the very essence of art that the medium be different from that of its objects. But it is the peculiarity of verbal art that the medium is both physical and symbolic—hence, double, inextricably so. Words, besides having such physical characteristics as shape and length, bear meaning as part of their primary substance. In expository prose, the physicality of words is suppressed, whereas, in poetry, it is foregrounded. The *medium* is the *mediation*; lacking it, there is no *translation* of the expression into another form, for all art partakes of the condition of trans. Lang., like art, is a "secondary modeling system"; and though it is true that lang. is art-full, more deeply, one must say that lang. *is* art in its enabling conditions, processes, and achieved effects.

From the point of view of cognitive science and information theory, a representation is a type of modeling; our recognition that an artwork is an imitation of the external world is one species of pattern recognition.

But the re-presentation in every representation is also, more directly, a presentation itself. So every representation is re-present and re-presents as it represents. The relation of the verbal representation to the original sensory one is one of *analogy* or *resemblance*, which is very different. An analogy is a perceived congruity in structural relationships between two sets of phenomena. Now the difference in modality is foregrounded, and difference is accepted as an essential part of the process.

**V. Translation.** The nature of verbal representation may become clearer if we consider the case of trans. The translated poem is not a copy good or bad; it is a *version* enacted in another medium. The nature and quality of the trans. are controlled by the translator's skill but also by the resources offered by both the source and the target langs. All trans., i.e., is mediation, so that the aim of faithful representation is not to copy the original but to try to do the thing that the original did in its medium as well as that can be done in the new medium, insofar as the doing in the original is understood by the translator.

This account, which relates one verbal representation to another, can be extended to all representation in art and indeed to lang. itself as representation. All verbal representation *is* trans. by its very nature. A verbal representation is, in effect, a trans. target lang., except that the source lang. is not verbal; it is sensory. The point is not that direct comparison between the two modes of representation is impossible but simply that it is confounded by the radical differences between the representational media, which are very different codes.

**VI. Design.** Many recent commentators have seemed to think that the verbal representation of experience in lit. does not effect and instantiate any real presence. But it is odd to complain that lit. is an order of experience secondary to sense experience. We should ask, rather, whether a literary (poetic) artwork represents the same objects, in the same way as, and with the same resulting degree of credibility as, sense experience: if so, how and how much, and if not, why and what instead. Is verbal representation inferior to sensory representation? Plato answers in the affirmative; the romantics answer in the negative. Sense experience itself is, of course, a representation; the verbal artifact, however, during the process of reception—reading, hearing, or observing—presents itself directly to cognition, supplanting the external world. It blocks out normal sense data, replacing them with other data about sensation in a precoded form. "It is hard to write any piece of literature that corresponds to anything as such, whatever it be," says Viktor Shklovsky in *O teorii prozy* (*Theory of Prose*, 1925), because "art is not the shadow of a thing but the thing itself." The eye sees the words on the page, in prose, only to ignore them: they are transparent. Poetry, by contrast, is translucent if not opaque: meaning is still conveyed but now in words whose design arrests our *attention.

Fundamental to the nature of all art is that it achieves its effects by increase of order or design. Regardless of authorial intention, most artworks show themselves to be supercharged with design. It is traditional in Western poetics to think of the faculty or capacity of imagination, i.e., image making, as central to literary representation, This is indeed important, esp. for realistic representation and verisimilitude, but it cannot supplant the making, the craft, the shaping of the medium that evokes those images and, as it does so, binds their elements more tightly together by *form. In poetry, the shaping is of the sensory medium (sound) and carried out largely at the preverbal (phonological) level (*meter, *rhyme, sound patterning). In its heightened design, texture, and materiality, poetry does not compete with the external world as a species of representation: it offers additional resources and forms of order that are constitutive, not imitative: they enact a heightened form of representation that creates that heightened mode of consciousness that, since antiquity, has been called *poetic*.

Poetry aims to show that relationships exist among the things of the world that are not otherwise obvious; it accomplishes this by binding words together with the subtler cords of sound. These bindings, like the relations they enact, are formal. Ernest Fenollosa observed that "the relations between things are more important than the things which they relate." If mimesis is to occur at all, therefore—given the differences between the representational media—it must address formal rather than substantial features. As Ludwig Wittgenstein remarks, "What any picture of whatever form must have in common with reality, in order to be able to depict it . . . is logical form, i.e. the form of reality" (*Tractatus* 2.18). Hence, the problem of representation is not so much that of the elements of lang. as, again and ever, the problem of form (see PROSODY).

Even Aristotle supports this view: mimesis as "imitation" is only part of the account of art given in the *Poetics*. Aristotle certainly views imitation as a central human activity; nevertheless, he makes it clear that the chief criterion for drama is not spectacle, diction, credible character, or even verisimilitude but the making of a strong *plot, i.e. *structure*. As for poetry, the account of the means of imitation given in ch. 1 of the *Poetics* is truncated and somewhat garbled; but several modes are identified, and the manner of the imitation is by no means assumed to be direct or literal. The role attributed to imitation in the *Poetics* has distinct limits: only some arts are imitative. Indeed, Aristotle holds that the order of art need not be—and at least once he holds it must not be—the order of reality (else poetry would be inferior to hist.). On the whole, Aristotle goes to considerable lengths to differentiate the art object from the reality it imitates, and this almost entirely on account of aesthetic *design*. Both imitative and nonimitative arts share this feature, which suggests that, for Aristotle, it is design itself that distinguishes art from life. Even in realistic and referential art, where design is a signifier for the reality outside the artwork, the signifier is a presentational form. In all art, i.e., the artwork itself stands as an icon for signification itself.

**VII. The Master Trope.** There was much interest in the 20th c. in lang. as it manifests itself in psychology, philosophy, prose fiction, and culture. Sigmund Freud showed that words are often the keys to dream interpretation, because lang. itself writes the structure of the unconscious. And while the relation of signifier to signified is central in Saussure, much of Jacques Lacan's work explores processes based on links between signifier and signifier. René Girard has argued that desire itself derives from mimesis. In philosophy, Martin Heidegger conceived poetic lang. as presentational rather than representational, presenting Being itself, a framework built upon by H.-G. Gadamer. Reference and representation have been major subjects in the study of narrative fiction. It has been argued by cultural theorists that the study of representation must focus not only on the code but on the physical and cultural means of production of that code, since these forces undeniably affect both the nature of the code and the uses speakers put it to. All these inquiries bear directly and deeply on the fundamental issue of how lang. functions, which is to say, on what is possible in verbal representation. All of them take lang. as the master *trope for human mind and action.

*See* ARTIFACT, POETRY AS; CRITICISM; EMOTION; EXPRESSION; FICTION, POETRY AS; FIGURATION; IMITATION; INTERPRETATION; NATURE; ONOMATOPOEIA; POETICS; POETRY; SEMANTICS AND POETRY; SPEECH ACT THEORY; SYMBOL.

■ Abrams; R. Bernheimer, *The Nature of Representation* (1961); Jakobson, esp. "Linguistics and Poetics" and "Quest for the Essence of Language"; G. Hermeren, *Representation and Meaning in the Visual Arts* (1969); R. Rorty, *Philosophy and the Mirror of Nature* (1979); P. Ricoeur, "Mimesis and Representation," *Annals of Scholarship* 2 (1981); *On Referring in Literature*, ed. A. Whiteside and M. Issacharoff (1987); K. Mills-Courts, *Poetry as Epitaph: Representation and Poetic Language* (1990); J. N. Riddel, *The Turning Word: American Literary Modernism and Continental Theory*, ed. M. Bauerlein (2005); A. Grossman, *True-Love: Essays on Poetry and Valuing* (2009); *Beyond Representation: Philosophy and Poetic Imagination*, ed. R. Eldridge (2011).

T.V.F. BROGAN

## RESOLUTION

 I. Linguistic Basis
 II. Germanic Metrics

In Gr. and Lat. metrics, *resolution* refers to the admissibility of two short syllables where the basic pattern of the meter has one longum; it is generally distinguished from contraction or *substitution of two light syllables for a metrical breve or *anceps. Comparable phenomena can be found in the verse of many langs., such as the cl. Somali *gabay* genre and the Prakrit *arya* meter, which suggests that there is a basis for resolution in the phonology of ordinary speech. In Gr., resolution, always excluded from the last foot, is rare in the

iambic trimeter; and the trochaic tetrameter of the archaic iambographers, more frequent in *tragedy, grows rapidly over the course of Euripides' devel., is more frequent still in the satyr play, and is very frequent in *comedy. In comedy, substitution in iambic trimeters is very common, being excluded from only the last foot; in tragedy, however, it is restricted to the first foot, except for proper names. In general, the two light syllables of a resolution or substitution cannot be separated or followed by a word boundary.

**I. Linguistic Basis.** When Luganda poems and songs are accompanied on the drums, a single drumbeat is assigned to a light syllable (◡) and two to a heavy syllable (–). These drumbeats directly reflect the *mora count of ling. rhythm. The moraic equivalence of two light syllables to one heavy is attested in the ling. rules of many langs., even those not having long vowels. In Manam, a word ending in a heavy (closed) syllable reduplicates only that last syllable, but a word ending in two light syllables reduplicates both. Moraic equivalence explains why some verse systems allow a sequence of two light syllables to be mapped onto one rhythmically strong position in the foot (see ARSIS AND THESIS) when that position is preferentially occupied by a heavy syllable.

**II. Germanic Metrics.** In Germanic metrics, incl. OE, OHG, and ON, where *ictus is usually borne by a long syllable, resolution applies specifically to a short stressed syllable and the following syllable whether short or long. Metrical resolution is not to be confused with phonological *elision or contraction, which depends on certain sonorant patterns (esp. liquids and nasals) such that two syllables are either reduced or have the potential to be reduced to one. In resolution, the syllables must remain distinct, but they count as one ictus-bearing unit at the metrical level of abstraction (just as, in *Beowulf*, two or more unstressed syllables count as one nonictus-bearing unit, i.e., a dip).

■ **Linguisitic Basis**: A. N. Tucker, "The Syllable in Luganda," *Journal of African Languages* 1 (1962); Allen, 60, 255; F. Lichtenberk, *A Grammar of Manam* (1983).

■ **Germanic Metrics**: Sievers; A. J. Bliss, *The Metre of Beowulf*, rev. ed. (1967); B. E. Dresher, "The Germanic Foot: Metrical Coherence in Old English," *LingI* 22 (1991); B. H. Carroll Jr. "Metrical Resolution in Old English," *JEGP* 92 (1993); G. Russom, "Constraints on Resolution in *Beowulf*," *Prosody and Poetics in the Early Middle Ages*, ed. M. J. Toswell (1995); S. Suzuki, "Resolution and Mora Counting in Old English," *American Journal of Germanic Linguistics and Literatures* 7 (1995).

A. M. DEVINE, L. D. STEPHENS (LING. BASIS);
T. CABLE (GERMANIC METRICS)

**RESPONSION.** The relation of *equivalence that exists between two or more corresponding (i.e., metrically identical) sections of the same larger rhythmical whole. The term is ordinarily used in reference to the repeated stanzas or strophes of a piece of Gr. choral lyric (see MELIC POETRY, ODE) or to the shorter segments within such a *lyric. *Strophe and *antistrophe in a given poem are then said to be in responson to each other; every syllable in the one either has its responding counterpart in the other or else belongs to a pair of syllables that has such a counterpart (usually two shorts that respond, through resolution or contraction, to one long, though other possibilities do exist—"anaclastic" responsion between – ⌣ and ⌣ – [see ANACLASIS], e.g., or responsion between – ⌣ and –, found occasionally in the creto-paeonic verse of Gr. Old Comedy). "Exact" or strict responsion between single syllables of the same quantity is often contrasted with the "free" responsion that exists in pieces that allow *anceps resolution, contraction, and the like; and responsion between the principal subdivisions of a whole composition (the type to which the term usually refers) is occasionally distinguished, as "external" responsion, from the "internal" responsion of one foot or metron to the next that exists within such subdivisions. Since Maas, the concept of responsion has come to seem one of the principal compositional and structural strategies for one kind of strophic verse.

■ Maas, sect. 28 ff.; Dale, 62–66, 89–91; E. Wahlström, *Accentual Responsion in Greek Strophic Poetry* (1970); J. S. Klein, "Responsion in the Rigveda," *JAOS* 122 (2002); C. A. Faraone, *The Stanzaic Architecture of Early Greek Elegy* (2008).

A. T. COLE

**REVERDIE.** A dance song or poem, popular throughout Europe in the late Middle Ages, that celebrates the coming of spring—the new green of the woods and fields, the singing of the birds, the time of love. By a natural association, the *reverdie* began to welcome Easter as well as spring, and Ger., OF, Lat., and Occitan poets described how longing for spring leads to longing for heaven and praise of the Blessed Virgin. The form is usually that of the chanson of five or six stanzas without *refrain. A further variation was developed by the Occitan *troubadours, who extended their praise to other seasons of the year.

*See* NATUREINGANG.

■ J. Bédier, "Les Fêtes de mai et les commencements de la poésie lyrique au Moyen-Âge," *Revue des deux mondes* 135 (1896); Jeanroy, *Origines*; P. S. Diehl, *The Medieval European Religious Lyric* (1985).

U. T. HOLMES; R. L. HARRISON

**REVERSED CONSONANCE.** A stylistic device developed by the Filipino poet Jose Garcia Villa in which the first and last consonants of a word or the two consonants of the last syllable are reversed in the corresponding *rhyme. Thus, the corresponding rhyme of a word like *maiden* would either begin with the letter *n* and end with the letter *m* or begin with *n* and end with *d*. The two consonants reversed in the rhyming word do not need to retain the original pronunciation they had in the first word. E.g., the word *sing* may be rhymed with a word like *begins*, as the last syllable of *begins* involves a reversal of the two consonants, *s* and *g*. In the case of a word that has only one sounded consonant, the corresponding rhyme may be formed by reversing this consonant with the last

sounded consonant of the previous word. Garcia Villa developed this technique in the belief that it would provide a subtler, less obtrusive rhyme than what is conventional in Eng.

*See* CONSONANCE; PHILIPPINES, POETRY OF THE.

■ J. Garcia Villa, *Have Come, Am Here* (1942).

J. CRISOSTOMO

**REVERSE RHYME,** inverse rhyme. In full or true rhyme, the medial vowel and final consonant (or cluster) of the syllable are held constant, while the initial consonant is varied. In reverse rhyme, the first consonant and the vowel remain the same, and the final consonant changes, as in *bat/back, yum/yuck*. This is a rare form in Eng. poetry; indeed, many might deny that it qualifies as rhyme at all, since it thwarts rhyme's traditional structure of "begin differently, end same." Sometimes the term is also used for a kind of *chiasmus in which the first and last consonants of a word are switched, e.g., *rap/pair*.

■ W. Harmon, "Rhyme in English Verse: History, Structures, Functions," *SP* 84 (1987).

T.V.F. BROGAN; M. WEINSTEIN

**RHAPSODE** (Gr., "one who stitches songs" or, by false etymology, "one who sings while holding a staff [*rhabdos*]"). In early Greece, a singer who selected and "stitched together" his own poetry or that of others, originally a selection or a portion of *epic poetry, usually the *Iliad* or the *Odyssey*, partly extemporaneously or from memory. By the 6th c. BCE, with the establishment of what were regarded as authentic Homeric texts, the term labeled a professional class of performers who recited the Homeric poems in correct sequence, not merely selected extracts. *Rhapsodes* are to be distinguished from *citharodes* or *aulodes*, singers of lyric texts to the accompaniment of the cithara or flute. Subsequently, the term *rhapsody* came to denote any highly emotional utterance, a literary work informed by ecstasy and not by rational organization; it is also applied to a literary miscellany or a disconnected sequence of literary works.

*See* GREEK POETRY.

■ C. M. Bowra, *Tradition and Design in the "Iliad"* (1930); R. Sealey, "From Phemios to Jon," *Revue de études grecques* 70 (1957); G. F. Else, *The Origin and Early Form of Greek Tragedy* (1965); W. Salmen, *Geschichte der Rhapsodie* (1966); Parry; Michaelides; *CHLC*, v. 1, ed. G. A. Kennedy (1989), esp. ch. 3; K. Bartol, "Where Was Iambic Poetry Performed? Some Evidence from the Fourth Century B.C.," *CQ* 42 (1992); Lord.

R. A. HORNSBY; T.V.F. BROGAN

## RHETORIC AND POETRY

I. Interpretation
II. Composition

Traditionally, rhet. has been identified with the kind of public oratory in which speakers seek aims and effects ranging from (at one end) a persuasiveness that shapes and resolves an audience's belief or action regarding some relatively circumscribed problem, chiefly through argument, to (at the other end) an eloquence that transforms the listener by elevating the imagination or passions, or amplifying the emotions, and/or displaying impressive form and style. Yet any distinction between persuasion and eloquence must be held as tenuous at best, for theorists and critics have seen them sometimes as distinct, sometimes as interpenetrating and mutually constitutive. Aristotle understood style as contributing to argumentative proofs, and Cicero (and later even David Hume) understood that the eloquence of high style and raised passions can help to constitute the very arguments of law or politics. The art of oratory has typically identified three genres—the deliberative or political speech given before policy-determining bodies, the judicial or forensic before courts of law, and the epideictic or demonstrative before occasional assemblies. In addition, however, rhet. has periodically expanded to become not only a prominent but the overarching art of discourse, e.g., in the Roman Republic and throughout the Ren. in Europe. When this occurred, poetry itself was usually written and read by people for whom rhet. was not only the major craft of composition but the general intellectual context for interpreting *all* matters of thinking, feeling, and acting. At times, the similarity of poetry and rhet. has been stressed, e.g., as a *mimesis of persuasion (Philip Sidney's or Shakespeare's *sonnet sequences) and/or an intensification of social passion or *imagination (poetry is the "most prevailing eloquence," remarked Ben Jonson); and both have been thought of as modes of practical thought and action aimed at good judgment (Aristotle) and even practical wisdom (Gr. *phronesis*, Lat. *prudentia*), esp. when rhet. is conceived as architectonic. Pindar's odes, e.g., were performed as direct public interventions into the social matrix of his time and place, as was much Gr. lyric (Walker).

By contrast, at other times differences between poetry and rhet. were stressed, esp. in the last several centuries, as in John Stuart Mill's self-conscious pronouncement that "[p]oetry and eloquence are both alike the expression or utterance of feeling: but, if we may be excused the antithesis, we should say that eloquence is *heard*, poetry is *over*heard." In our own time, even if it is not rhet. as traditionally conceived (as one of the *ars disserendi* or arts of discourse), nevertheless, the traditional preoccupations of rhet. have become pervasive and for some architectonic, e.g., in much cultural crit. and the many varieties of ideology-critique, often under different names and guises and in complex interactions with more disciplinary pursuits, like economics or psychoanalysis (Bender and Wellbery). Poetry can always be interpreted rhetorically, but contemp. poetry in England and America and indeed throughout the world may be thought to consider itself rhetorical to the extent that it is seen to have absorbed and superseded "modernist" concerns with formal epiphanies (Langbaum) and is intent on evincing "postmodernist" orientations to communication and its difficulties (Altieri, Bernstein, Perloff), to social, public and/or political interventions (von Hallberg, Pinsky, Nelson,

Spiegelman), to representing variants of practical reason and ethics (Sloane, Booth 1983, Phelan, Vendler), or to enlarging the *sensus communis* as an "epideictic rationality" (Garver 2004, Walker, Jost).

The bearing of rhet. on poetry has always involved composition and interpretation, sometimes at elementary levels, as in many med. manuals, sometimes in quite sophisticated theories. Quintilian's influential *Institutio oratoria* (1st c. CE) offers one traditional attitude: skill in oratory is founded on "speaking correctly" and "interpreting poets" (1.4.2), and conflates the inventive processes of rhet. and poetry, otherwise often differentiated (see INVENTION). These differentiations have usually been impelled, like devels. and even revolutions in interpretation, by reactions against a perceived restrictiveness of rhetorical method. Because, over the last 100 years or so, interpretation in general and rhetorical interpretation of poetry in particular have undergone a more conscious revolution than has the art of composition, interpretation will be discussed first.

**I. Interpretation.** Rhetorical interpretation and crit. can take many forms, but generally speaking, they emphasize relationships among speaker, audience, text, purpose, situation, and occasion (Jost and Olmsted); more narrowly, they consider how any discourse can be understood as if it were a public address of some kind, whether persuasive or eloquent or both. Just as a speech act encompasses such extratextual elements as its speaker's delivery and the audience's response, so rhetorical theorists and critics have insisted that poetry too might be understood as intentionally addressed at a certain time, by someone, to someone else, for some purpose, and toward some effect (Phelan; see INTENTION, SPEECH ACT THEORY). Borrowing from Aristotle, one might inquire, e.g., how intention is secured through different "modes of proof" (Aristotle, *Rhetoric* 1.2) to help establish one's case, that is, through forms of argumentative and other persuasive appeals regarding the substantive issue(s), or *logos*, as well as through manipulation of the audience's perception of the speaker's moral character, or *ethos*, and through manipulation of the audience's emotion, or *pathos*. In the Middle Ages, the distinctiveness of rhet. was its search for identifiable causes of audience effects, closely related to but different from the enterprise of grammar, which was often both a search for the forms of "correctness" in speech and an intro. to the ancient *auctores*, and the enterprise of logic or dialectic, which included the study of validity in deduction and universals (Copeland). (Together, grammar, rhet., and dialectic constituted the *trivium* of the high med. liberal arts curriculum, distinguished both from the *quadrivium* of arithmetic, geometry, music, and astronomy, and from professional disciplines like medicine, law and theology.) On the one hand, rhetorically minded interpreters concerned with the three modes of proof are necessarily historicist and contextual, conceiving *all* poetry as a kind of social act or performance and even locating the rhetorical impulse in, e.g., romantic, symbolist, imagist, objectivist, or other modernist poetry, on its face often non- and even antirhetorical (Blasing, Altieri). On the other hand, rhetorical theorists and critics in our own time are often faulted for their privileging of authorial intention, that is, for their failure to view poetry *sui generis*.

Distinguishing poetry from rhet. and other arts or "powers" (Gr. *dynameis*) was the analytic project of Aristotle's *Poetics*. Aristotle made *mimesis* (the representation or *imitation of human action) the genus of poetry, with *mythos* (*plot) its species. By contrast, persuasion was the genus of rhet., audience differentiation in terms of judging (deliberative and forensic) or observing (epideictic) its species, and good judgment—*not* persuading at all costs—its internal end or *telos* (Garver 1995). Aristotle's analytic efforts to distinguish and arrange the arts and sciences "horizontally," so to speak, form a sharp contrast to Plato's efforts to synthesize the arts and arrange them hierarchically, all governed by the mode of disputation he called "dialectic," which subsumed the rhetorical.

Aristotle's analytic division was, however, lost sight of for more than a millennium, and Plato's was radically reformulated in the cl. world by Cicero's elevation of rhet. as an architectonic art of eloquent persuasion in all matters, and in the Middle Ages by Horace's *Ars poetica*, which similarly gives poetry the ends of rhet. The Horatian view, moreover, reaffirmed the Ciceronian position that "knowledge-qua-practical" should be the basis of all persuasion and extended that view to the notion that a poet's unique powers were (additionally) to delight. To teach, to delight, to move (*docere, delectare, movere*) were for a long time the ends of traditional rhet., understood as both persuasion and eloquence, and could be achieved by poetry. Thus, most med. manuals of poetry were often equally manuals of rhet., with only the sections on versification constituting any significant distinction between them.

After Aristotle's *Poetics* was rediscovered in the 15th c., its former analytic distinctiveness from rhet. slowly but gradually overcame the by then long-standing symbiosis of rhet. and poetry. At first, however, the temper of the Ren. continued to mute any such antagonism, for rhet. had again become architectonic in the culture and the curriculum, restored to something of its former centrality after having been displaced by logic and dialectic in the 12th c. *Renaissance poetics at first reaffirmed, then surpassed, the lesser didactic, Horatian qualities of the earlier Middle Ages: that is, a poem's utility—its proficiency at teaching or moving, so argued Antonio Minturno (1559), J. C. Scaliger (1561), and Sidney (1595)—was achieved through its unique capacity for delighting and esp. through (quasi-Aristotelian) "imitative" means. In these and similar apologetics, poetry became in effect a superior rhet., and Virgil and Horace were cited as the Ciceronian *perfectus orator*, eloquent by virtue of both persuasive and stylistic abilities to make wisdom practical, effective, and situated (Altman, Lanham 1976). Rhetorical *imitatio*, meaning here the composer's exercise of copying the work of others, became in interpretive theory the readerly role of imitating model behavior as represented in another text, historically a theoretical position ancient as Plato's *Republic,* and negatively sanctioned by the Puritan closing of the theaters in 1642. In this way, Ren. *imitatio* blunted later, more accurate and analytic rereadings of Aristotle's notion of mimesis, even while ostensibly encompassing it. In time, however, a new emphasis on form—on a poem's organization and on a playwright's use of the so-called "unities" of time, place, and action—began to sweep crit., increasingly relegating rhet. to matters of emotion and style only. Further stimulating this new emphasis was the revival, with Francesco Robortello's ed. of Longinus in 1554, of the thesis that the "sublimity" of poetry does not so much persuade as more nearly "transports" its audience (see SUBLIME). This concept also revived interest in a post-Hegelian "organic" theory of poetry compatible with Aristotelianism and echoed in the mod. insistence, extending through S. T. Coleridge into the 20th c., that poetry must be read as if its *form and content were fused (see ORGANICISM), further relegating argument and reason to nonpoetic discourse. This later insistence controverts the sometime rhetorical view, esp. prominent in the allegorical orientation of the earlier Middle Ages, that form is isolable, interchangeable, and strategic, while content is a manageable body of knowledge, truths, or arguments.

Although a certain, mainly Aristotelian formalism was inaugurated in the poetics of the late Eng. Ren., the movement did not reach its apotheosis until the 20th c., first with Joel Spingarn in 1910 and Benedetto Croce in 1933, both of whom called for a scrapping of all of the older, rhetorically infested terminologies; and then with the *New Criticism of the 1930s and the Chicago neo-Aristotelians (see CHICAGO SCHOOL), with their insistence that a poem constructs its own uses for otherwise referential discourse, adjacent to or beyond the parameters of ordinary communication. Poetry speaks a different lang., Richards theorized in 1929. Poetry does not communicate, Brooks insisted in 1947. Or if it does, Frye argued in 1957, it does so as a kind of "applied literature." Prophetically, Kenneth Burke offered a "counter-statement" to this increasingly dominant *formalism as early as 1931, calling for the restoration of a rhetorical perspective in which discursive form could again be seen as strategic and in which content could be seen as a complex fusion of the "motives" (causes and reasons) of speaker, intention, utterance, and audience.

The mod. restoration of rhet. to interpretation found three main emphases: the author's relation to the text and audience, the role of the reader in the communication, and style. The first distinguished two levels of speaking in the poem, the one in which the narrator of the poem is talking to himself or to another person (see VOICE), and the one in which the poet is speaking to us (Olson, Eliot, Booth 1983, Wright, Ong; see PERSONA). Increasingly, however, 20th-c. poetics pursued the second emphasis, focusing on the role of the reader—whether real-life, authorial or ideal, narrative, and either *of* or *in* the poem—whose interaction with the poem's structures gives it meaning or whose presence at least raises questions about the conditions of *textuality and communicability (Barthes, Holland, Culler, Iser, Fish, Suleiman and Crosman, Scholes, Phelan).

Whereas formalists, in their "organic" view of poetry, insist that poetry *means* what it *says*, postformalist critics argue that poetry means what it *does*. Nonetheless, these first two emphases involve at best a partial or fragmentary use of rhet. and often an antagonism toward its ends. But when the reader is a listener, as when poetry is performed in an oral culture (Errington, Connelly, Sweeney), or in a culture of "secondary orality" (Ong), or in a multicultural environment, the role of rhet. becomes much more extensive, at once more traditional and more Burkean, a general heuristic of communicative strategies, the study of whose scope is now beginning to reach beyond Western cultural confines (see ORAL POETRY).

For the specifically stylistic analysis of poetry, rhet. (here, amplification and ultimately eloquence) has traditionally supplied detailed taxonomies of figures, schemes, and tropes, ranging from such textual effects as *irony to such local effects as *alliteration. Style catalogs burgeoned particularly among med. and Ren. rhetoricians, for whom an embellished *style was the sum total of eloquence (in Peacham [1593] over 350 figures are described). Four tropes—*metaphor, *metonymy, *synecdoche, irony—were early conceived as master tropes (Fraunce [1588]) because they generate all figurative uses of lang., an idea reiterated by *inter alia* Kenneth Burke in the 1940s, the philosopher Stephen Pepper in the 1960s, the historian Hayden White in the 1970s, and others later. In 1956, Roman Jakobson found metaphor and metonymy to be attitudes the mind assumes in coping with degrees of similarity or contiguity between matters and thus began a movement to view tropes as inherent in intellection. Subsequently, the act of interpretation itself came to be seen as tropological, even in psychoanalysis (Genette, Nietzsche, Freud): figures, esp. the master tropes, map mental strategies or processes in the reader's work of unraveling the meaning of a text. The figures and tropes have supplied a taxonomy for anthropology, psychology, ling., and hist.; in mod. rhet., they serve as indicators of the inherent plasticity of lang. (Vickers, Quinn) or as cognitive templates (Turner). The plasticity and figurality of lang. have also become concerns of mod. deconstructionists (Derrida, de Man) in their rhetorical examination of the often indeterminate gap between what poetry says and what it ostensibly does (see INTERTEXTUALITY).

This brief review may suggest that the ultimate choice for contemp. interpretation is less to rhetoricize or not to rhetoricize than how or to what extent to do so: to consider poetry as persuasively audience-directed and stylistically eloquence-directed or both at once, even if viewing it as something other than a conventionally communicative act; to subsume all of rhet. or only those fragments thought to be applicable, in such mod. sciences as ling. or psychology; or even to rejuvenate rhet. as an architectonic productive art (McKeon). Some of the alternatives may be further clarified, and some of the gaps in our survey bridged, by shifting our attention to theories of composition that, by offering attitudes toward the use of lang., also speak to possibilities of interpretation.

**II. Composition.** Among extant Western handbooks of composition, Aristotle's *Rhetoric* is the oldest. His master stroke in the *Rhetoric*, one too easily overlooked or absorbed within other theories, is his doctrine that rhetorical practice embodies its own unique mode of thought. The orator discovers the available means of persuading his audience chiefly by consulting (having previously mentally absorbed and made second nature) the "common" and particularly the "special" "topics" (Gr. *topoi*; Lat. *loci*, *"commonplaces"). Topics are discursive "*re*-sources," esp. pairs of terms, useful for provisionally locating and organizing the relevant circumstances and facts and interpretive premises of an indeterminate case, a contingent matter susceptible to competing understandings. This part of practical reasoning, called "invention" in later theories, deals with probable rather than demonstrable matters: the orator weighs alternatives, substantiates his case with facts and value-premises, and chooses strategies that she or he believes will move (when properly employed) to good judgment. To establish the uniqueness of rhetorical invention to some collective audience, Aristotle advanced the *example* and the *enthymeme* as the counterparts, respectively, of logical induction (to a singular not to a generalization) and syllogism. The latter has two premises and a conclusion with clear canons of formal completeness and validity operating on expert subject matters (in dialectic) and on commonly held matters (in rhet.). The enthymeme, in other words, draws its major premise from the audience's beliefs (e.g., Had we but world enough and time, / This coyness, Lady, were no crime); its facts also draw from the audience's perceived situation (but we have not world enough and time); and its conclusion accordingly (therefore, this coyness, Lady, is a crime). Rhet. allows the audience silently to supply a condition, premise, and even a conclusion itself. Induction, or argument by example (*paradeigma*), works by analogy and has many forms. In either enthymeme or example, the audience, its knowledge and emotions, has a priority in rhet. that is otherwise held (generally speaking) by formal validity in logic, forms of correctness in grammar, and the "formal cause" or "plot" in poetry.

In one respect, rhetorical invention became poetic invention by default. Aristotle does not describe the latter and distinguishes the two largely by implication; his *Poetics* is not a handbook of composition but a theory of the nature and elements of poetry, developed in part by comparison with drama. One of those elements— "thought" (*dianoia*), or what is appropriate for a fictional character to say—Aristotle declines to discuss at length in the *Poetics* (6.16) because he had already treated it in the *Rhetoric*. That is, poetic invention (*heuresis*), where it does not depend upon plot, seems to arise from a certain natural plasticity (17), the poet's ability to visualize action and assume attitudes and arguments, which is Aristotle's way of avoiding ascribing poetic invention to either *inspiration or poetic madness as Plato did. Nevertheless, the Platonic alternatives have had their advocates through the centuries: the divine *furor* usually associated with Neoplatonism was expressed by Shakespeare in *A Midsummer Night's Dream* ("The lunatic, the lover, and the poet / Are of imagination all compact"), though Shakespeare himself was steeped in a rhetorical culture. The turn to inspiration reached its culmination in the romantic movement of the 19th c. (see ROMANTICISM). Still, in the larger historical view, it was rhet., esp. in its devels. after Aristotle, that remained the chief discipline by which writers and speakers learned their craft.

By the time of Cicero, whose Latinity was influential for centuries and whose theories of rhet. were to achieve enormous popularity among Ren. humanists, rhet. had become much more systematized and more intellectually architectonic. A unified process of composition implicit in Aristotle became divided into five discrete functions: thought (*inventio*), arrangement (*dispositio*), style (*elocutio*), memory (*memoria*), and delivery (*actio* or *pronuntiato*). Aristotelian rhetorical invention, the search for available means of persuasion, later became a pro-and-contra analysis of inventive topics regarding the substance of the speech, the credibility of the speaker, and the emotion of the audience; forensic oratory, as in Cicero, was the paradigm (Sloane 1997). Oratorical arrangement also became more prominent: where Aristotle had advised only two parts (statement and proof) but allowed for four (plus introd. and conclusion), Cicero advised six (exordium, background of the question, statement, proof, refutation, conclusion) but allowed seven (plus a digression). Although Cicero (himself a poet) may have found poetry limiting, the two were firmly joined in his extension of rhet. well beyond the genres of public oratory, not least through Horace's aims of teaching, pleasing, and moving in the *Ars poetica*. Rhet. became the art of persuasive eloquence governing all disciplines, a lang. whose stylistic force numbered among the formal means by which its content achieves persuasiveness. As such, rhet. was to cap the statesman's education and be, above all, the avenue through which the wisdom of philosophy would be made practical. To accomplish this last, Cicero in effect rhetoricized philosophy, extending Aristotle's teachings on rhetorical thought far beyond its carefully delimited boundaries. Ciceronian rhet. now became a kind of surrogate philosophy that still had great attraction for Ren. humanists 14 centuries later, a particularly self-reflexive example of which is the first sonnet in Sidney's sonnet series *Astrophil and Stella*. In fact, throughout the 16th c., Cicero's formalized rhet. and ideal of persuasive eloquence were ready tools to fill the practical and apologetic needs of critics and poets, ethical philosophers and lawyers, theologians, and even, in part, protoscientists like Francis Bacon (see CICERONIANISM).

In the Middle Ages, Cicero's youthful *De inventione* and the pseudo-Ciceronian *Rhetorica ad Herennium* never waned in popularity, though both were merely schematic catalogs offering little more than systematizing. Med. rhets. and poetics stressed *dispositio* and *elocutio*, as seen in Geoffrey of Vinsauf's *Poetria nova* (ca. 1210), which, like so many others, used rhetorical invention for interpretive ends. The most formalized functions of Ciceronian rhet., functions that directly pertain to the creation of plot (argument) and/or style, became the critical determinants of eloquence in either

art. A concern with rhetorical thought, or any intrusion of *inventio* into systematic philosophy, let alone poetics, was increasingly neglected, although much earlier Augustine's *De doctrina christiana* (426 CE) used rhetorical invention for hermeneutic purposes (Copeland).

It was precisely that concern with "thought" or invention that was revived in the Ren. The first pub. book in Italy was Cicero's masterpiece *De oratore*, a dialogue in which famous Roman statesmen and lawyers, engaged in a dialogue, give critical precedence not to *dispositio* and *elocutio* but to the strategies of *inventio* in moving others to action. The recovery of Quintilian and the rise to prominence of law as a secular profession gave added impetus to this "new" mode of thought and disputation, preeminent examples of which were Baldassare Castiglione's *The Book of the Courtier* (1528) and Niccolò Machiavelli's *The Prince* (1532). Ciceronian tactics drawn from judicial rhet. seemed to fire the poets' imaginations as well: arguing *in utramque partem*, on both sides of a question, though rigidified as a feature of med. scholastic disputation, became a kind of lawyerly embracing of contraries (*controversia*), reappearing in the argumentative and ostensibly irresolute fabric of Tudor poetry and drama; *qualis sit*, or individuating a phenomenon by setting it within a thesis-to-hypothesis (or definite-to-indefinite-question), suffuses Boccaccian fiction and Sidneyan crit.; *ethos* and *ethopoiesis*, the illusion of mind and of behavioral probability, pervade dialogues, mock encomia, and most discussions of courtliness. Schoolroom *imitatio*, incl. the formal requirements of the forensic oration (esp. the second part, the *narratio* or relevant background of the main issue), brought fictiveness itself well within rhetorical exercises.

Ultimately, however, it was just this Ciceronian *inventio*, incl. those vestiges within it of Aristotle's distinction between rhetorical and logical modes of thought, that suffered most in the reformations that accompanied the Ren. Rhet. eventually became utterly formalized far beyond anything Cicero imagined (in fact he warned against such formalization) or its allegorization in the Middle Ages. To mention but one of the influential books of the early Ren., *De Inventione dialectica* by Rudolphus Agricola (d. 1485): logic or dialectic, according to Agricola, is "to speak in a probable way on any matter"; grammar teaches correctness and clarity; rhet., style. Subsequently, the reformers known as Ramists (after Peter Ramus) bled rhet. of *inventio* and *dispositio* (these became solely functions of logic), reducing it to style and delivery (*memoria* was seen as a function of arrangement or *dispositio*). Though the Ramist reform did not last, rhet. was drastically dispersed among other arts and sciences, eventually submitting to further reformative efforts, scientific and philosophic, to restrict its scope. Thereafter, Cicero's public mind in search of probabilities has been more or less displaced by an isolated, psychologized, and meditative mind at odds with traditional *inventio*.

As *inventio* declined in prominence, style (*elocution*) rose, not only in the new rhets. of the 16th c. but in the new poetics. With the rise of the vernacular over Lat. as the lang. of lit., scholarship, and commerce, rhetorical theories burgeoned with discussions of style, further cutting across what few boundaries yet remained between rhet. and poetry, the former again reduced to merely the stylistic dimension of the latter. Although Thomas Wilson, who wrote the first Ciceronian rhet. in Eng. (1553), stayed within rhetorical genres for his examples, other traditional stylists, such as Richard Sherry, Henry Peacham, and Abraham Fraunce, treated *elocutio* by drawing virtually all of their examples from vernacular poetry. George Puttenham's *Arte of English Poesie* (1589) devotes much attention to style and is equally a work on rhetorical *elocutio*, involved as both arts are in what Puttenham regards as the courtly requirements of "dissembling."

Like many of the continental poetics of the time (Joachim du Bellay, Pierre de Ronsard, Jacques Peletier), Puttenham's book divides theory along the lines of the first three offices of traditional rhet.: *inventio, dispositio, elocutio*. But this rhetoricizing of poetics did little to salvage the rapidly disappearing uniqueness of rhetorical invention, incl. those poetics that had clear bearing on compositional matters. Geoffrey of Vinsauf's advice to med. poets, to invent merely by thinking of structure first, was seldom superseded. Similarly, Puttenham taught that invention was to be performed by the "phantasticall part of man," his imagination, and controlled by choice of *genre and by *decorum, not by discursive topics or places. Audience-anchored doctrines of rhetorical *invention*—whether the Aristotelian search for the means of persuasion via the probable or the Ciceronian pro-and-contra reasoning through a grid of topics toward eloquence—were, for all intents and purposes, dead. Nor did either of these doctrines play a significant role in the new literary theories fostered by the recovery of Aristotle's *Poetics*, such as those by the 16th-c. humanists Francesco Robortello and Lodovico Castelvetro, though the two terminologies coexisted. Throughout 17th- and 18th-c. poetics, Aristotelian plot ("fable"), character ("manners"), thought ("sentiments"), and diction continued to exist side by side with Ciceronian terminology ("passions," "propriety"). *Inventio* remained the creator's first responsibility, but its thought-content was relegated thereafter to logic and its considerations of audience relegated mainly to stylistic decorum. In the 18th c., the creative processes began to be scrutinized by the rising science of psychology and taught through whatever relicts of ancient rhet. were considered salvageable. Among those relicts, *elocutio*, or style, retained greatest prominence and for centuries constituted virtually the whole of rhet., only to become the scapegoat of conscious artifice in romantic and postromantic poetics before being revived as an important feature of mod. interpretation. In the 20th c., along with Kenneth Burke, William Empson was one of the few lamenting this situation: "It is a misfortune that the whole literary tradition of Symbolism has grown up so completely divorced from the tradition of fair public debate."

Two remaining offices of rhet. have received comparatively little attention over the centuries. *Actio*, claimed by Demosthenes as the *sine qua non* of persuasion, did achieve some vogue in the 18th and 19th cs. under the name of "elocution." An effort to scientize delivery, which began with John Bulwer in 1644, occupied the attention of 18th-c. lexicographers and actors (Thomas Sheridan, John Mason) in teaching graceful gesture and correct phonation (now called *"pronunciation"). With the teachings of Del Sartre in the 19th c., the movement had an impact, through mannered *recitations, on Eng. and Am. education, on styles of acting, and esp. on poetry written to be recited, the latter inviting a sentimental theatricalism against which the modernist poets rebelled. *Memoria*—the storehouse of wisdom as it was known in rhet. and the mother of the Muses (cf. W. H. Auden's "Homage to Clio")—was resistant to much theorizing outside medicine, where it was studied as a faculty of the soul (Yates). Rhyme was early considered not only a figure but a mnemonic device; so was the pithy form of eloquence known as *sententia*. When the two were combined (as in Edgar's speech closing *King Lear*: "The oldest hath borne most; we that are young / Shall never see so much, nor live so long"), a *terminus ad quem* was made memorable. The art of memory also became involved with the creation of fantastic images (the more fantastic, Quintilian advised, the easier to remember) and elaborate "memory theaters" for the rapid recall of complex, even encyclopedic knowledge.

In sum, whether one considers the interpretation or composition of poetry or rhet., shared interests in persuasion and eloquence, and in form and style, have always linked the two. The fragmentation of rhet. and its dispersal through various disciplines and critical approaches were steady devels. in Western culture after the Ren., particularly after the rise of science in the 16th c., of formalist crit. in the 17th c., and of romanticism in the 18th. At the present time, on the one hand, the uniqueness of poetry is arguably more fully understood than that of rhet. On the other hand, mod. efforts to reestablish rhetorical *inventio* (e.g., Perelman, Lanham, Booth 1983, Ulmer) may ultimately serve to reauthenticate rhet. as *sui generis* and to reinvigorate rhetorical thinking for crit. of all lit. in a digital age.

■ R. Sherry, *A Treatise of Schemes and Tropes* (1550); T. Wilson, *The Arte of Rhetorique* (1553); A. Minturno, *De poeta* (1559); J. C. Scaliger, *Poetices libri septem* (1561, 1581); A. Fraunce, *The Arcadian Rhetorike* (1588); P. Sidney, *Astrophil and Stella* (1591); H. Peacham, *The Garden of Eloquence*, 2d ed. (1593); P. Sidney, *An Apology for Poetrie* (1595); J. Bulwer, *Chironomia* (1644); J. Dryden, Preface to *Annus mirabilis* (1667); J. Mason, *An Essay on Elocution* (1748); T. Sheridan, *A Course of Lectures on Elocution* (1762); J. S. Mill, "Thoughts on Poetry and Its Varieties" [1833], *Dissertations and Discussions* (1859); P. Verlaine, "Art poétique" (1884); S. Freud, *The Interpretation of Dreams*, 3d ed., trans. A. A. Brill (1911); J. E. Spingarn, "The New Criticism" [1910], *Criticism and America* (1924); I. A. Richards,

*Practical Criticism* (1929); K. Burke, *Counter Statement* (1931); B. Croce, *The Defence of Poetry*, trans. E. F. Carritt (1933); E. Olson, "Rhetoric and the Appreciation of Pope," *MP* 37 (1939); K. Burke, *A Grammar of Motives* (1945); K. Burke, *A Rhetoric of Motives* (1950); T. S. Eliot, *The Three Voices of Poetry* (1953); Jakobson and Halle; Wellek and Warren; Frye; R. Langbaum, *The Poetry of Experience: The Dramatic Monologue in Modern Literary Tradition* (1957); S. Pepper, *World Hypotheses: A Study in Evidence* (1961); G. T. Wright, *The Poet in the Poem* (1962); C. Perelman and L. Olbrechts-Tyteca, *The New Rhetoric: A Treatise on Argumentation* (1969); F. Yates, *The Art of Memory* (1969); R. Barthes, *S/Z*, trans. R. Miller (1970); W. Ong, *Rhetoric, Romance, and Technology: Studies in the Interaction of Expression and Culture* (1971); W. C. Booth, *Modern Dogma and the Rhetoric of Assent* (1974); Culler; S. E. Errington, *A Study of Genre* (1975); N. Holland, *5 Readers Reading* (1975); H. White, *Metahistory* (1975); R. Lanham, *The Motives of Eloquence: Literary Rhetoric in the Renaissance* (1976); J. Altman, *Tudor Play of Mind: Rhetorical Inquiry and the Development of Elizabethan Drama* (1978); W. Iser, *The Act of Reading* (1978); R. Pinsky, *The Situation of Poetry* (1978); S. Fish, *Is There a Text in this Class?* (1980); *The Reader in the Text*, ed. S. R. Suleiman and I. Crosman (1980); J. Gage, *In the Arresting Eye* (1981); C. Perelman, *The Realm of Rhetoric* (1982); A. Quinn, *Figures of Speech: 60 Ways to Turn a Phrase* (1982); W. C. Booth, *The Rhetoric of Fiction*, 2d ed. (1983); P. de Man, *The Rhetoric of Romanticism* (1984); R. von Hallberg, *American Poetry and Culture, 1945–1980* (1985); T. Sloane, *Donne, Milton, and the End of Humanist Rhetoric* (1985); B. Connelly, *Arab Folk Epic and Identity* (1986); R. Scholes, *Textual Power: Literary Theory and the Teaching of English* (1986); W. Empson, *Argufying: Essays on Literature and Culture* (1987); A. Sweeney, *A Full Hearing* (1987); C. Bernstein, *Artifice of Absorption* (1988); M. K. Blasing, *American Poetry: The Rhetoric of Its Forms* (1989); C. Nelson, *Repression and Recovery: Modern American Poetry and the Politics of Cultural Memory, 1910–1945* (1989); M. Turner, *More Than Cool Reason: A Field Guide to Poetic Metaphor* (1989); Vickers; W. Spiegelman, *The Didactic Muse: Scenes of Instruction in Contemporary American Poetry* (1990); *The Ends of Rhetoric: Theory, History, Practice*, ed. J. Bender and D. Wellbery (1990); G. Genette, *Les figures du discours* (1993); R. McKeon, "The Uses of Rhetoric in a Technological Age: Architectonic Productive Arts," *Professing the New Rhetoric*, ed. T. Enos and S. C. Brown (1994); G. Ulmer, *Heuretics: The Logic of Invention* (1994); R. Copeland, *Rhetoric, Hermeneutics, and Translation in the Middle Ages: Academic Traditions and Vernacular Texts* (1995); E. Garver, *Aristotle's* Rhetoric: *An Art of Character* (1995); R. Lanham, *The Electronic Word: Democracy, Technology, and the Arts* (1995); A. Quinn, *Figures of Speech: 60 Ways to Turn a Phrase* (1995); M. Perloff, *The Dance of the Intellect: Studies in the Poetry of the Pound Tradition* (1996); J. Phelan, *Narrative as Rhetoric: Technique, Audiences,*

*Ethics, Ideology* (1996); T. O. Sloane, *On the Contrary: The Protocol of Traditional Rhetoric* (1997); Derrida; M. Turner, *The Literary Mind: The Origins of Thought and Language* (1998); J. Walker, *Rhetoric and Poetics in Antiquity* (2000); F. Yates, *The Art of Memory* (2001); *A Companion to Rhetoric and Rhetorical Criticism*, ed. W. Jost and W. Olmsted (2004); E. Garver, *For the Sake of Argument: Practical Reasoning, Character, and the Ethics of Belief* (2004); W. Jost, *Rhetorical Investigations: Studies in Ordinary Language Criticism* (2004); C. Altieri, *The Art of Twentieth-Century American Poetry: Modernism and After* (2006); H. Vendler, *Poets Thinking: Pope, Whitman, Dickinson, Yeats* (2006).

T. O. SLOANE; W. JOST

**RHÉTORIQUEURS, GRANDS.** A group of late med. or early Ren. courtly writers who wrote in the Fr. vernacular in very ornate style, both in verse and in prose, to celebrate the feats and virtues of the princes who employed them. The major figures include Jean Bouchet, George Chastelain, Guillaume Cretin, André de La Vigne, Jean Lemaire de Belges, Jean Marot, Jean Meschinot, Jean Molinet, Jean Robertet, and Octavien de Saint-Gelais. The phrase *grands rhétoriqueurs* was found in a satirical text by Guillaume Coquillart and mistakenly applied by 19th-c. scholars to a cluster of authors spanning almost a century (from the mid-15th to the mid-16th) and two main political entities (in addition to a number of lesser courts): the duchy of Burgundy, whose northern territories, from which many of these writers hailed, were incorporated in the Holy Roman Empire after the defeat and death of Duke Charles the Bold (1477); and the kingdom of France. The misnomer caught on and remains in use, perhaps because it summarizes three major characteristics of the Grands Rhétoriqueurs: while they never formed a "school," they praised one another as masters of their craft while working for powers that often fought one another; they understood their art to be a form of "rhetoric"—indeed, eloquence itself—organized around the task of praising and chronicling their patrons; and they had a "grand" notion of this task, signaled by the elaborate grandiloquence of their style and by the elevated position that, in spite of their bourgeois origins, they came to occupy, at least in the Burgundian court. On the other hand, the satirical connotations of the term *rhétoriqueur* reflected the contempt felt by late 19th-c. historians for writers who spouted propaganda and accumulated encomiastic hyperboles in bizarrely mixed forms (such as the *prosimetrum*), seemingly unable to distinguish between prose and verse, hist. and poetry, chronicle and fiction, extravagant praise and reasonable advice. The spectacular style of the Grands Rhétoriqueurs—notably their reliance on ultrarich rhymes and puns—became the focus of their rehabilitation during the course of the 20th c., at the hands first of surrealist poets, then of poeticians such as Zumthor, who suggested that such dazzling *elocutio* techniques subverted the monolithic political message that the rhétoriqueurs were paid to promote. In recent decades, a more balanced view has emerged, justifying the cohort's flamboyant figuration by connecting it with the requirements of epideictic *inventio* (see EPIDEICTIC POETRY). Building on a trad. initiated in the early 15th c. by Alain Chartier, the successive Indiciaires de Bourgogne (Chastelain, Molinet, Lemaire) and their Fr. imitators (La Vigne, Saint-Gelais, Cretin, Marot, Bouchet) indeed strove to combine (not confuse) the resources of "first" and "second" rhetoric (i.e., prose and verse: see SECONDE RHÉTORIQUE), as well as those of hist. and "poetry" (allegorical fiction), in order to illustrate, interpret, and justify the glory of the prince as exemplary ruler and image of God. Should the prince fail to live up to this standard, however, the rhétoriqueur could advise him to mend his ways, typically by giving voice to symbolic representatives of his people or to entities such as Counsel and Truth. This syncretic notion of political rhetoric as the noblest form of verbal art also allowed for some celebration of creative power, at least by peers, as the author himself invariably struck a humble pose in his own work. All this developed at first within the bounds of mss. composed for the prince's and the court's enjoyment and then entered into the larger stage of print (some rhétoriqueurs did not care to see their works printed; others, such as Lemaire, exploited the new technology with gusto). The holistic art of the Grands Rhétoriqueurs soon fragmented, however, as hist. and poetry began to separate again; it was the son of Jean Marot, Clément, who quietly gave up the historiographer's duties as well as the grand style's signature effects and thus reinvented Fr. poetry as an autonomous art, aesthetically exalted but, in a way, rhetorically diminished. Nevertheless, the grands rhétoriqueurs played a key role in the devel. of poetic forms and ideas in the early Fr. Ren.; conversely, many 16th-c. poets who touted their own sophistication while proclaiming that their art had nothing to do with hist. or immediate persuasion also retained a keen sense of what poetry had lost, in terms of rhetorical authority and social status, by renouncing the political calling of their "ignorant" predecessors.

■ P. Jodogne, *Jean Lemaire de Belges* (1972); P. Zumthor, *Le masque et la lumière* (1978); C. J. Brown, *The Shaping of History and Poetry in Late Medieval France* (1985); J. Britnell, *Jean Bouchet* (1986); F. Cornilliat, *Or ne mens* (1994); J. Devaux, *Jean Molinet, indiciaire bourguignon* (1996); M. Randall, *Building Resemblance* (1996); D. Cowling, *Building the Text* (1998); A. Armstrong, *Technique and Technology* (2000); E. Doudet, *Poétique de George Chastelain* (2005); V. Minet-Mahy, *L'automne des images* (2009).

F. CORNILLIAT

**RHOPALIC VERSE** (Gr., "clublike," i.e., thicker toward the end, from *rhopalon*, the club of Hercules). "Wedge verse," in which each word is a syllable longer than the one before it, e.g., *Iliad* 3.182, "o makar Atreide, moiregenes, olbiodaimon" which begins with a monosyllable and closes with a fifth word of five syllables, or Virgil's "Ex quibus insignis pulcherrima Deiopeia" or Richard Crashaw's "Wishes to His Supposed Mistress."

*See* CONSTRAINT.

■ Morier; T. Augarde, *Oxford Guide to Word Games*, 2d ed. (2003).

T.V.F. BROGAN

## RHYME

I. Origin and History of Rhyme in World Poetries
II. Rhyme in Western Poetries, Particularly in English

### I. Origin and History of Rhyme in World Poetries

**A. *Introduction.*** There have been two chief views on the origin and devel. of rhyme. The derivationist position is that rhyme originated in one locus and was disseminated to all others. Turner argued as early as 1808 that rhyme originated in Chinese or Sanskrit (but not Ar.; for Ren. arguments about the Ar. origin of rhyme, see Dainotto), whence it spread via the trade routes to Europe. Draper claimed China as the single point of origin (according to him, the earliest attested rhymes in Chinese date from ca. 1000 BCE; according to Kenner, 1200 BCE), from which it spread to ancient Iran by means of Mongol hordes and westward to Rome with Persian mystery cults; but, as McKie has argued, Draper's ambiguous evidence suggests dual sources in Iran and China. The alternate view, set forth as early as 1803 by Swift, is that rhyme does not take its origin exclusively in any one lang. but is a natural ling. structure that can arise in any lang. having the right set of features. The fact that rhyme originated once shows that it can originate at any time. It is a simple ling. fact that the number of sounds available in any lang. is limited, and it's many words must, therefore, be combinations of only a few sounds. There is considerable evidence that children manufacture rhymes spontaneously as one basic form of sound permutation; also conspicuous is rhyme in the *chants and *charms of many primitive cultures. Systematic rhyming has appeared in such widely separated langs. that its spontaneous devel. in more than one of them seems a reasonable assumption. We should not seek to find the ultimate "origin" of rhyme in Western poetry by tracing rhyme forms back through langs. to some common source. Still, it is a thundering fact that most of the world's 4,000 langs. lack or avoid rhyme in their poetries altogether (Whitehall).

In the hist. of the world's poetries, those cultures that have most extensively developed rhyme have been Chinese in the East and in the West, Ar., Ir., Occitan, Fr., Ger., Eng., and Rus. Note that rhyme is not originally native to any Eur. lang. or even IE. Regardless of whether rhyme had one source or several, it is indisputable that, both in ancient and med. lits., there are several discernible routes of transmission, the tracing of which is neither impossible nor unimportant, merely difficult. It is obvious that specific rhyme forms, like meters and stanzas, have been imported into langs. via trans. or imitation of famous poets and canonical works in another lang. (Homer, Virgil, Dante, Petrarch, Shakespeare), even where rhyme was already indigenous.

What can be said reliably at present about the earliest rhyme trads., Chinese and Ar., is as follows.

**B. Chinese.** Rhyme is an essential element of Chinese versification; it has been largely ignored by Western translators and readers because it cannot be fully reproduced in trans. Because Chinese is a tonal lang., not a stress-based lang., and because every Chinese character is pronounced as one syllable, Chinese rhymes more readily than most other langs. (though the distribution of tones may complicate the rhyme patterns). End rhyme occurs in all traditional verse, with rhyme schemes varying according to different forms of poetry. In the open-ended ancient-style verse (*gushi*), rhyme generally occurs at the end of each *couplet; and the rhyme, in either the level or the oblique tone, may change in the course of the poem. But in a more rigid form such as the eight-line regulated verse (*lushi*), the same rhyme should be used throughout the poem and is almost always in the level tone. This level-tone rhyme falls at the end of each couplet, but it is also permissible at the end of the first line of the poem. Compared to regulated verse, the *ci* (lyric) is relatively more complex and varied. In composing a song in ci style, the poet chooses a tune, out of some 825 tunes, and writes words for it. Each tune pattern determines the tonal category of the end rhyme and *internal rhymes, as well as the number of lines and the number of syllables per line. For the historical evolution of rhyme, see CHINA, POETRY OF.

**C. Arabic and Persian.** Until the 20th c., rhyme (*qāfiya*) was one of two primary features in the Ar. definition of poetry itself; in the famous dictum recorded by Qudāma ibn Jaʿfar (d. 934), the author of *Kitāb naqd al-shiʿr*, a manual on poetics, poetry is "discourse with rhyme and meter." The central position accorded rhyme in Ar. and Persian poetics leads to the devel. of a theoretical science of rhyme parallel to though separate from that of prosody, with the Basran scholar Al-Khalīl ibn Aḥmad (d. 791), as its alleged founder. In these trads., as indeed in most others, rhyme is based on *sound; there is no visual rhyme. Thus, it may be said that critical writing on rhyme in Ar. dates from the 8th or 9th c.; rhyme itself is already present in the first extant exemplars of Ar. poetry (6th c.), its origins lost in the unrecorded beginnings of oral trad. The question of whether rhyme exists in the Old Iranian Avesta (ca. 1500 BCE) is disputed.

In Ar., the essential part of rhyme is the word-final consonant called *al-rāwī*, which remains constant throughout the poem (this consonant will sometimes be preceded by a further consonant that is also part of the rhyme). Rhyme in Ar. can be of two sorts: fettered (*muqayyada*), i.e., ending with a consonant; or loose (*muṭlaqa*), i.e., ending with a vowel. While occasional examples of *assonance or *near rhyme are known in Middle Persian poetry, the intricate rules and conventions for rhyme in Islamic Persian were adapted from Ar. practice. Rhyme in Persian may comprise from one to four syllables, the last ending with the same consonant preceded by the same vowel, e.g., *bām / kām*; *sardam / mardam*; *revāyati / shekāyati*; *pāyandagān / āyandagān*. Some variation is allowed in the longer rhymes but no license.

The majority of cl. *qaṣīda* and *ghazal* poetry is composed of verses in *monorhyme, with the rhyme at the end of the second of two *hemistichs (*miṣrāʿ*). More often than not, the rhyme is called to the attention of the poem's audience by being used at the end of both hemistichs of the first line of the poem, a process called *taṣrīʿ*. A rhyme word should not be repeated except at distant intervals. A special feature of Persian rhyme is the *radīf*, a syllable, word, or phrase repeated verbatim following the rhyme, e.g., *yār dāram/khomār dāram*, where the rhyme is -*ār* and the *radīf* is *dāram*. Some typical rhyme schemes are the following: qaṣīda and ghazal, *aabaca*; quatrain, *aaaa* or *aaba*; *masnavi* or rhyming couplet, *aabbcc*, etc.; *qeṭa*, *bacada*. Strophic forms have more complicated schemes. This can be seen most notably in the Andalusian, *muwashshaḥ*, where, within a series of *strophes, one section (usually termed *ghuṣn*) will normally have an independent rhyme for each instance, while the other (termed *simṭ* or *qufl*) will retain the rhyme of the final segment of the poem, the *kharja* (see AL-ANDALUS, POETRY OF).

Since World War II, rhyme has lost its formerly privileged position and become but one of a number of features of poetic discourse as poets and critics have abandoned the dictates of cl. Ar. poetics in favor of new (and often imported) genres such as *free verse and the *prose poem. For more information, see ARABIC POETICS (CLASSICAL), ARABIC POETRY, ARABIC PROSODY.

**D. Western European.** In the West, while rhyme is rare in all cl. poetry, it is rarer in Gr. than in Lat.: still, it is not unknown in Homer (*Iliad* 2.87–88, 9.236–38) and the Gr. dramatists (Aristophanes' *Clouds* 709–15, *Wasps* 133–35, and *Acharians* 29–36); Euripides in the *Alcestis* has a drunk Hercules speak in rhyme (782–86), a passage clearly meant to be comic. Rhyme can be found in the Alexandrian poets and, among Lat. poets, in Ennius and Ovid (a fifth of the lines in the *Tristia* show *leonine rhyme), Virgil (*Aeneid* 1.625–26, 2.124–25, 2.456–57, 3.549, 3.656–57, 4.256–57, 8.620–21, 8.646–47, 9.182–83, 10.804–5), and Horace (*Ars poetica* 99–100).

The emergence of rhyme in the West had to await the devel. of accent (Clark remarks that "the history of the adoption of rhyme is almost exactly parallel to, and contemporaneous with, the history of the substitution of accent for quantity"); the shifting of word accent from the root syllable rightward; and, progressively, the transition from inflectional to positional syntax. But since rhyme obviously appears in inflected langs., we must say that, insofar as it is to be distinguished from *homoeoteleuton, it should be seen as arising in response to the decay of the inflectional system and, therefore, growing stronger only as like endings disappear (Whitehall). Langs. that retain inflections but use rhyme (e.g., Fr.) will, therefore, impose extensive constraints on rhyme forms so as to differentiate the two systems.

The earliest indigenous rhyme trad. in Europe was apparently Ir., and elaborate canons of rhyme have remained a central feature of *Celtic prosody up to the 20th c., though it is necessary to distinguish between Celtic vernacular and Ir.-Lat. verse (McKie). The Ir. missionaries apparently brought rhyme with them to the continent (the older view was that this influence worked in the opposite direction). Assonantal precursors of rhyme first appear in the Christian Lat. hymns of Hilary of Poitiers, Ambrose, and Augustine (late 3d through 4th cs.); and McKie calls arguments in favor of a Christian Lat. (incl. Ir.-Lat.) source of rhyme in OE "decisive." Meyer thought the source for this practice to be Semitic, a view not now followed. In Byzantium, Romanus and Synesius were exploiting its possibilities in hymnology by the 6th c.

Except for the intervention of med. Lat., the Eur. langs. would have developed their prosodies in opposing directions. The Germanic langs., with forestressing of words, developed structural *alliteration for their prosody, as in OHG and OE, less ornate than the elaborately interlaced sound patterns of the Celtic poetries, i.e., Ir. and Welsh, but more closely linked to meter (see Árnason for the argument that "in-rhyme" in ON could have developed inherently in ON lit., not as the result of Ir. influence). The Romance langs., in which word stress was weaker and phrase stress stronger, developed first assonance then rhyme; the great flowering of short-lined, rhymed stanzas in *Occitan poetry by the *troubadours directly influenced every other vernacular on the continent, and even med. Lat. *Goliardic verse. Occitan was itself influenced, perhaps strongly, by Ar. sources, though the nature and extent of this influence is still disputed.

Ger. early fell under the influence of med. Lat. versification, as Eng. did of Fr. after the Norman Conquest. Rhyme first appears in the Germanic vernaculars in the 9th c. in the work of Otfrid (*Evangelienbuch*, ca. 863–71), directly influenced by med. Lat. versification. There are also some vestiges of rhyme in OE as a result of Celtic influence, chiefly the "Rhyming Poem." *French prosody itself was an outgrowth of med. Lat. principles. Northern Fr. exerted enormous influence on ME from the 12th c. (*The Owl and the Nightingale*, the Harley lyrics) through Chaucer (who also knew Boccaccio) into the 15th c. The collapse of the OE inflectional system had left numbers of monosyllabic words in early ME, but the large number of Romance loan words imported, most of them polysyllabic and oxytonic or paroxytonic, readily encouraged rhyme: many of them kept their Romance end-stressing in ME and even influenced the stressing of other Eng. words. Chaucer takes advantage of a variable final *e*, which was in the process of disappearing during his own lifetime, for both meter and rhyme. After Chaucer, the loss of final *e* and the Great Vowel Shift in the 15th c. sounded the end of ME versification; mod. Eng. prosody was reinvented by Thomas Wyatt and by Henry Howard, the Earl of Sur-

rey, though even here on Romance principles of rhyme and stanza (e.g., the *sonnet).

Since the Ren., the emergence of standardized varieties of the mod. langs. has worked to restrict the canons for permissible rhyming in literary verse, but three other forces have exerted pressure against this trend: (1) oral and popular trads., along with literary imitations of them, esp. folk poetry such as the *ballad in the 18th c., have strongly influenced or, more recently, arisen to challenge literary verse, particularly in *romanticism (e.g., *Lyrical Ballads*); in the 19th-c. Ger. cult of the lit. of the Volk (see ORAL POETRY); in *dialect poetry, once extensive and important, as in Scottish, southern Ger., and It., but subsequently marginalized from literary verse even while it flourishes in oral trad.; and, beginning in the late 20th c. in the U.S., in many public performances of poetry (see, e.g., PERFORMANCE, POETRY SLAM, NUYORICAN POETS CAFÉ); (2) song lyrics, such as those of W. S. Gilbert in the 19th c. or Cole Porter, Ira Gershwin, and Stephen Sondheim in the 20th, and the lyrics of many hip-hop artists in the 20th and 21st cs. present vigorous, inventive, often comic challenges to the more limited rhyming of much literary verse (see SONG, HIP-HOP POETICS); and (3) in literary verse itself, the devel. of variant forms of rhyme in the 19th and 20th cs., such as near and *eye rhyme, continues to offer poets many possibilities.

## II. Rhyme in Western Poetries, Particularly in English

Philip Sidney in the *Defence of Poesy* calls rhyme "the chiefe life" of mod. versifying; indeed, so it must still seem, despite the advent of the great trad. of Eng. *blank verse from Shakespeare to Alfred, Lord Tennyson, and even the advent of the several free-verse prosodies after 1850: the first edition of the *Oxford Book of English Verse* (1900) contains 883 poems of which only 16 lack rhyme. And what is true of Eng. is even more true of Rus., where the trad. of rhyme is more extensively developed, and esp. Fr., where rhyme is truly fundamental to the whole system of versification. Rhyme is, as Oscar Wilde said, "the one chord we have added to the Greek lyre."

**A. Definition.** In the specific sense of the term as used in Eng., *rhyme* is the linkage in poetry of two syllables at line end (for internal rhyming, see below) that have identical stressed vowels and subsequent phonemes but differ in initial consonant(s) if any are present—syllables that, in short, begin differently and end alike. This is the paradigmatic case for Eng.; but in the half-dozen other langs. where rhyme has been developed as a major poetic device, many other varieties have been developed, resulting in more expansive definitions admitting any one of several kinds of sound echo in verse. More broadly, however, we must say that *rhyme* is the phonological correlation (see EQUIVALENCE) of differing semantic units at distinctive points in verse. It is essential that the definition not be framed solely in terms of sound, for that would exclude the cognitive function.

Rhyme calls into prominence simultaneously a complex set of responses based on identity and difference. On the phonic level, the likeness of the rhyming syllables (at their ends) points up their difference (at their beginnings). The phonic semblance (and difference) then points up semantic semblance or difference: the equivalence of the rhyme syllables or words on the phonic level implies a relation or likeness or difference on the semantic level. Rhyme in this sense, i.e., *end rhyme*, is, with *meter, a primary form of sound patterning in mod. verse and deploys sound similarity as the means to semantic and structural ends.

Crucial to these ends, as with all others in *prosody, is segmentation. As with the clausulae of late antique *prose rhythm, rhyme marks the ends of runs of syllables in speech and thereby segments the sound stream into equal or perceived-equal units or sections: this segmentation, in turn, establishes equivalence, which is essential to *repetition and the effects it is capable of. Lotman says that, if all equivalences in the poetic line are classed as either positional (rhythmic) or euphonic (sonal), then rhyme is created at the intersection of the two sets.

From the usual sense of the term *rhyme*—i.e., the sound common to two or more words or a word that echoes another word—other senses derive by *synecdoche, i.e., (1) a poem in rhymed verse or (2) rhymed verse in general; or by *metonymy, i.e., (3) any kind of sound echo between words (e.g., alliteration, assonance, *consonance) or (4) more generally, any kind of correspondence, congruence, or accord (cf. J. R. Lowell's "of which he was as unaware as the blue river is of its rhyme with the blue sky" from *The English Poets*, 1888).

The spelling *r-h-y-m-e* became common in Eng. in the 17th c.; the earlier Ren. and ME spelling, *r-i-m-e*, derives from OF *rime, ritme* (< Med Lat. *rithmi* < Lat. *rithmus, rhythmus* < Gr. *rhythmos*). The OF form gave the Occitan, Sp., Catalan, Port., and It. cognates *rima* and MHG, ON, and Old Icelandic *rim*, later *rima* (rhymed poem, ballad; see RÍMUR). This form of *rim* is not to be confused with (though it is related to) OHG, OE *rim* (number) or with OE, ON *hrim* (hoar-frost, rime-frost). The term *rim* in the mod. sense of *rhyme* first appears in an Anglo-Norman rhymed sermon of the early 12th c.; in this century, rhyme became a central feature of short-lined lyric poetry in Occitan and came to replace assonance in the *laisses* of the OF *chansons de geste*. In Eng., the spelling *r-i-m-e* / *r-y-m-e* for vernacular, accentual, rhymed verse was preserved to ca. 1560, when spelling reform based on the classics brought in *r-i-t-h-m-e* / *r-y-t-h-m-e* (pronounced to rhyme with *crime* and spelled *r-i-'-m-e* by Ben Jonson), current to 1700, after which time *r-h-y-t-h-m* became the spelling for that concept in the mod. sense. About 1600, however, *rhime/rhyme* appears, presumably to distinguish rhyming from rhythmical/metrical effects; *r-h-y-m-e* subsequently won out, though the (historically correct) spelling *r-i-m-e* has never entirely disappeared.

In med. Lat., *rithmus/rythmus* denotes *versus rithmici* (rhythmical verse), meaning verse whose meter is based on *accent, not *quantity (*versus metrici*) and that employs end-rhyme. Lat. rhythmical verse, appears as early as the 3d to 4th cs. CE and reaches its culmination in the 12th c., though verse written on quantitative principles continued to be written throughout the Middle Ages. This fact—two metrical systems side by side in med. Lat.—is responsible for the mod. phrase "without rhyme or reason," meaning neither *rhythmus* nor *ratio*, i.e., not any kind of verse at all. In short, the word for accentually based and rhymed verse in med. Lat. vacillated between an *i* and *y* spelling for its vowel; the Ren. distinguished these two criteria and, hence, terms for them. Ren. spelling reform affected the visual shapes of the words; pronunciation diverged later. *Rhythm* and *rhyme* are, thus, intimately related not only etymologically but conceptually.

There are two final points about definition. First, the definition of what counts as rhyme is conventional and cultural: it expands and contracts from one national poetry, age, verse trad., and genre to another. Hence, definition must shortly give way to a taxonomy of types (below). Second, there is the issue of positing rhyme at line end itself (see LINE). Žirmunskij, looking at rhyme as not only sound echo but the marker of line end, sees that function as having an effect on the rhythmic organization of the line. Indeed, it is commonly assumed that rhyme exerts a metrical function in marking the ends of the lines. But, of course, rhyme is not restricted to line end, suggesting that "any sound repetition that has an organizing function in the metrical composition of the poem should be included in the concept of rhyme" (1923). Further, as de Cornulier argues, rhyme does not exactly reside at line end: its positioning shapes the entire structure of the line, so that we should more accurately say that the rhyme resides in the entire line. Removing rhymes from lines does not merely render them rhymeless; it alters their lexical-semantic structure altogether.

**B. *Taxonomy.*** Rhyme correlates syllables by sound. We may describe the structure of the *syllable as initial consonant or consonant cluster (the so-called support or prop consonant [Fr. *consonne d'appui*]; this may be in the zero state, i.e., absent) + medial vowel (or diphthong) + final consonant (or cluster, if present), which we may schematize as CVC. If we ask which elements of a syllable can be repeated in a second syllable in correspondence with the first, letting underlining denote a sound repeated identically, then seven configurations are possible (the eighth possibility is null; these are simply the permutations of a set of three elements), having these forms and Eng. names:

1. C̲ V C alliteration (*bad / boy*)
2. C V̲ C assonance (*back / rat*)
3. C V C̲ consonance (*back / neck*)
4. C̲ V̲ C reverse rhyme (*back / bat*)
5. C̲ V C̲ [no standard term] frame rhyme, para-rhyme (*back / buck*)
6. C V̲ C̲ rhyme strictly speaking (*back / rack*)
7. C̲ V̲ C̲ Rich rhyme, rime riche, or identical rhyme (*bat* [wooden cylinder] / *bat* [flying creature])

This schema presumes that both syllables are identical in all other respects, i.e., their phonological and morphological characteristics—e.g., that both syllables are stressed monosyllables. But, of course, this is not usually the case, certainly not for Fr. or It. or Rus., not even for Eng. A more elaborate taxonomy would subsume all such variants. To date, no such inventory of rhyme structures has yet been given. When it is, it will explain a number of effects as yet unaccounted for, clarify relations between forms in the same or different langs. hitherto thought unrelated or remote, and provide a comprehensive and synthetic overview of the structure of the system, showing how rhyme processes function as an integral system. It will also, presumably, correlate with the schema of rhetorical figures and processes given by Group μ.

As a preliminary to such a taxonomy, we may distinguish 12 criteria for the analysis and categorization of rhyme types:

(1) By the *number of syllables* involved in the rhyme:

(a) single, monosyllabic, or masculine. This is the norm or zero state of rhyme, at least in Eng.—two stressed monosyllables, e.g., *Keats / beets* (John Crowe Ransom's examples from "Surveying Literature," here and below). Whether this is the norm in any given lang. depends on the morphological and syntactic structure of that lang., i.e., whether it is inflectional or positional or mixed. All other more complex forms of rhyme are generated by *extension*, either rightward into syllables following the rhyming syllable or leftward to the consonant or syllables preceding the vowel, esp. proclitics and separate words (Ger. *erweiterter Reim*).

(b) Double, disyllabic, or feminine (see MASCULINE AND FEMININE), e.g., *Shelley / jelly*. Two contiguous syllables that rhyme. In the paradigmatic case in Eng., both words are disyllables and have a trochaic word shape, and both rhyming syllables (the first in each word) are stressed and stand in the last metrical position (*ictus) of the line. The post-rhyming syllables are pronounced but not stressed and are identical; metrically, they do not count: they are *extrametrical*. (It is also possible for the second syllables themselves also to rhyme, e.g., *soreness / doorless*.) But these conditions do not apply in other langs., and even in Eng., many other complex and variant forms are possible. Indeed, Eng. is probably not a good norm: in It., nearly all rhymes are double or triple. Scherr usefully treats syllabic variance of the rhyming syllable in Rus. poetry under the rubric of "heterosyllabic" forms.

(c) Triple (Ger. *gleitender Reim*, "gliding"), also called compound and multiple, e.g., *Tennyson / venison*; two extra (identical and extrametrical) syllables after the rhyming syllable. Triple rhymes are, of course, rarer; usually they are *mosaic rhyme, since rhyming of more than two successive syllables is difficult in any lang. The effect in Eng. since Lord Byron has almost always been comic. See TRIPLE RHYME.

(2) By the *morphology* of the words that the rhyming syllables inhabit. The zero state is that the rhyming syllables are each monosyllabic words—i.e., that the rhymes do not breach a word boundary. In double and triple rhymes, the words being rhymed are normally di- or polysyllabic or a series of short words (*stayed with us / played with us*) or ends of words followed by one or more whole words (*beseech him / impeach him*),

but it is also possible to rhyme several short monosyllables with one polysyllable, known as mosaic rhyme in Eng. (*poet / know it*). In Welsh *cywydd couplets, one of the rhymes must be a monosyllable but the other a polysyllable. But if rhyme depends for its distinctive effects on the morphology of the particular words involved in the rhyme, it also, therefore, depends on the morphological structure of the lang. itself as the ground against which the pattern becomes visible.

Inflectional endings are, as it were, the antithesis or reflex of rhyme, though it is not accurate to say, as did Whitehall, that langs. in which like endings result automatically from inflection will never use rhyme as a structural device in verse. Rhyme is occasionally to be found, consciously used, in the lit. of the cl. langs. The notion of like endings (Gr. *homoeoteleuton*, Lat. *similiter desinens*) is discussed by the ancients—Aristotle (*Rhetoric* 3.9.9–11), Dionysius of Halicarnassus (23), and Quintilian (9.3.77)—under the rubric of "verbal resemblance" or sound correspondence between clauses (*paromoeosis*). Late antique *rhyme-prose continues this trad.; the *grammatical rhyme of the *Grands Rhétoriqueurs* (see RHÉTORIQUEURS, GRANDS) takes a different slant. But the two systems—case endings and rhyme—overwrite the same space and so in the main are mutually exclusive. And when, in any lang., rhyming is relatively easy, poets will tend to complicate it by employing forms of *rich or *identical rhyme (as in Fr.) or complex stanza forms (as in Occitan and Fr.) or both, or else by eschewing rhyme completely (as in *blank verse). Poets who choose to rhyme, in fact, walk a tightrope between ease and difficulty: too easy rhyming or too difficult rhyming eventually produce the same result—the poetic disuse of rhyme. In some verse systems, the rules in a prosody survive sometimes for centuries after the ling. facts on which they were originally based have disappeared. One of the chief instances of this process is the mute *e* suffix in Fr., which disappeared from pronunciation in the 15th c. but was preserved in a set of elaborate rhyme rules into the 19th.

Since Eng. dropped nearly all its inflectional suffixes about a thousand years ago, the sets of rhyming words in Eng. are smaller and different in character as well. How much smaller, however, is an interesting question, for it is often claimed that rhyme is much more difficult in Eng. than in other langs. But accurate statistical information about the relative poverty of rhyme in one lang. vs. another has yet to be assembled. Owing to the large number of ways in which Eng. words can terminate, the number of words that rhyme on a sound, on average, is certainly under three, but the distribution is extremely uneven. The number of words that rhyme strictly (in the manner of no. 6 in the taxonomy table above) with only one other word is large (*mountain / fountain, babe / astrolabe*), and those that cannot rhyme strictly is as large or larger—e.g., *orange* or *circle*, which one could "rhyme," by consonance (no. 3 in taxonomy table above) with *flange* (paired with the unstressed syllable of *orange*) or *snorkel*, respectively, (though not strictly with any one-word mate). But the rhymes on words like *day* are legion.

One other way of approaching this issue, however, is to point out that rhyme depends less on the structure of the lang. than on the semantic field presently relevant in the poem: only some of the available rhymes for a given word are possible candidates for use in a poem on a given subject. What this means, most generally, is that it is dangerous to discuss rhyme as an abstract entity divorced from the constraints imposed on it in each individual poem. The subject of morphology and rhyme is a large and complex one that still remains to be mapped out.

(3) By the *position of the stress* on the rhyming (and adjacent) syllables. Normally, single rhymes are ictic and stressed; double rhymes add an extra unstressed syllable. Rhyming masculine with feminine words, i.e., a stressed monosyllable with a disyllable the rhyming syllable of which is unstressed (e.g., *sing* / *loving*, *free* / *crazy*, *afraid* / *decade*) Tatlock called "hermaphrodite" rhyme (an odd term, since male mating with female in love would not be thought so). Others have called it "apocopated" or "stressed-unstressed" rhyme; it was popular in the 16th and 17th cs. and is used by John Donne and by Ezra Pound (*Hugh Selwyn Mauberley*). There is also "unstressed rhyme," where the rhyming syllables are both unstressed or weak: e.g., *honey* / *motley*, *mysteries* / *litanies*, *wretchedness* / *featureless*. But there is some question whether this constitutes rhyme at all. Scherr calls all such cases in Rus. poetry "heteroaccentual" forms and cites the taxonomy given by Markov.

A related type rhymes a stressed syllable with one bearing only secondary speech stress, which is promoted under metrical ictus, e.g., *sees* / *mysteries*. Many rhyme pairs of this sort formerly differed in pronunciation and were good rhymes in their time, though they are not now; others were not so, then as now. Rhymes like *eye* / *harmony*, *eye* / *symmetry* (William Blake), or *flies* / *mysteries* force the critic to call on the researches of historical phonology.

Perhaps the most interesting case of all is the pair *die* / *poetry*, common in the Ren. There is some evidence (e.g., Alexander Gill in *Logonomia Anglica*, 1620) that, for words like *poetry*, alternative pronunciations existed as late as the first quarter of the 17th c., one form pronounced as the word is today, to rhyme with *me*, the other to rhyme with *die*. If so, rhyme pairs like *poetry* / *die*—and others like *majesty* / *eye*, *crie* / *graciously*, and most others ending in *ty* or *ly*—may well have been good rhymes for Shakespeare and the Ren. sonneteers, as they were for John Milton. But the diphthongal ending apparently lost out, so that sometime after 1650 *poetry* and *die* ceased being a good rhyme and became merely conventional. They may well have continued to be used by poets but only on account of their having precedent. Whether poets after 1650 actually altered their pronunciation of *poetry*, in reading aloud their verses, so as to rhyme with *die*, is unknown; one may speculate that their acceptance of convention did not extend so far. If so, the reader would be expected to recognize such rhymes as poetic *convention, a kind of *poetic license admissible on the

grounds that they were so in a former state of the lang. A mod. instance appears in W. H. Auden's elegy on Yeats: "Let the Irish vessel lie / Emptied of its poetry." But the evidence is very complex and uncertain, and the number of cases where later poets knowingly reproduce such archaic rhymes must be few: far more important is the fact that, in earlier stages of the lang., they were apparently good rhymes.

(4) By the *lexical category* of the rhyming words. In much verse, the rhymes are commonly words of the same grammatical category, noun rhyming with noun, verb with verb. The phonic echo highlights semantic differences certainly, but not functional ones. More striking effects are to be had by extending the differentiation, so that the words not only mean different things but function differently as well. The predominance of substantives for rhymes creates a verse of a distinctive texture, whereas the use of function words gives a radically different texture and virtually demands *enjambment: thus, John Donne's "Love's not so pure and abstract as they used / To say who have no mistress but their Muse" ("Love's Growth"). Even within substantives, the use of nouns for rhymes gives a markedly different texture from the use of verbs, which, as the conveyors of action, energy, state, and change, take on even greater power when positioned at line end. Wimsatt in his classic 1944 essay discusses the importance of this strategy, but detailed data have only very recently begun to be collected. Cohen, e.g., reports that the 17th-c. Fr. classicists used different category rhymes only 19% of the time, the romantics 29%, and the symbolists 31% (1966); one would like to see Eng. data for comparison.

(5) By the *degree of closeness of the sound match* in the rhyme. The standard definition for "true" or "perfect" rhyme (the usual Eng. terms; cf. Ger. *reiner Reim*, Rus. *tochnaia rifma*) is relatively narrow, with the result that the other collateral forms—near rhyme and eye rhyme—are problematized. But in other verse trads., this is not the case: Rus., e.g., admits "inexact rhyme" as part of the standard definition of canonical rhyme (see Scherr). *Welsh poetry recognizes a very large category of "generic rhyme" in which sounds echo closely but not exactly. But it is misleading to frame the analysis in terms of "near" vs. "perfect" to begin with: exactness is not the only or even the most important criterion in some verse systems. As a number of critics (e.g., Burke, Small) have observed, sounds themselves are related to each other in phonology in categories; within these categories, individual sounds—such as voiced and voiceless fricatives—are interchangeable in some verse trads. To recognize this fact is to recognize that sounds come in "equivalence sets," e.g., nasals (*m*, *n*, and *ng*) or sibilants (*s*, *f*, *z*, *sh*, *zh*), that a poet may use to expand the range of rhyming. This approach should neutralize mechanistic attempts to assess the *"purity"* of rhyme (Ger. *Reinheit des reims*). In general, it may be said that the strictness of the definition of "true" rhyme in langs. varies in inverse ratio to the ease of rhyming in that lang., which is itself a function of morphology and syntactic rules: langs. in which rhym-

ing is relatively easy will impose additional constraints, such as the rules constraining the grammatical gender of rhymes in Fr.; langs. in which it is more difficult will admit wider variation.

(6) By the *relationship between the sonal figuration created in the rhyme and the semantic fields* of the words. Rhyme is a figure of sound; but, of cour\se, words in poetry, as in lang., bear sense, and both levels of information are delivered to the auditor or reader not separately but simultaneously: rhyme, therefore, figures meaning. This is how rhyme is able to increase the amount of *information carried in verse, despite the fact that the establishment of a *rhyme scheme leads to expectedness, normally reductive of information load.

Of such semantic figuration, there are two possibilities: either sound similarity can imply semantic similarity in words otherwise so unrelated that, in prose, no relation would have ever been noticed; or sound similarity can emphasize contrast in two words that echo. As Lotman puts it, "[P]honic coincidence only accentuates semantic difference." G. M. Hopkins held that the beauty of rhyme, for the Eng. reader at least, "is lessened by any likeness the words may have beyond that of sound" (*Note-books and Papers*). The "richness" or "sonority" of a rhyme is, therefore, not merely a function of the degree of phonic echo but of the semantic aspect as well (Lotman).

Wimsatt cites a classic example from Alexander Pope's *Rape of the Lock*: "Whether the nymph shall break Diana's law, / Or some frail China jar receive a flaw." Wimsatt remarks the rhyme prompts us to ask in what way breaking Diana's law is like marring a valuable vase. The answer we will be led to is that, in Belinda's refined society, losing one's virginity is simply an indiscretion, a clumsiness, equivalent to scarring a Ming porcelain—both signs of poor taste. In this way, study of the semantic effects of the phonic coupling in the rhyme augments the hermeneutic process, directing us toward a deeper and more powerful interpretation. Wimsatt calls rhyme, somewhat awkwardly, "alogical" and "counterlogical," by which he means not asemantic but simply bearing semantic import that runs in addition to, and sometimes counter to, the lexicosyntactic, denotative "logic" or sense of the words in the lines. However one chooses to describe it, this sense borne by the rhymes is supplemental to the import the words would have borne were they merely set as prose (see VERSE AND PROSE), showing thereby the additional expressive resources of verse form.

At the same time, several poets and critics have remarked that rhymes, particularly in a long work, come to form a system of their own that is the correlate of an idiolect or, if it be influential, a dialect in natural lang. Clark remarks that, "when a poet rhymes well," it is "as if he had invented a new lang., which has rhyme as one of its natural characteristics."

Rhyme semantics is a vast subject only beginning to be explored. It was first charted by the Rus. formalists, esp. Žirmunskij, but his book was not known in the West until the 1960s: in the Anglo-Am. world, it was Wimsatt's 1944 essay that paved the way, followed by Lotman's 1970 book (trans. 1977) on the

stratification of the artistic text (see also Nemoianu). Shapiro applies the Saussurean paradigm influenced by Peircean semiotics, i.e., markedness theory, under which distinctive features appear in pairs of binary opposites, one present, one absent, with the present one, therefore, marked: he shows by phonological analysis marked features that seemingly remote rhymes have in common.

Study of rhyme semantics must examine both the semantic fields available in the lang. and those chosen for the poem. As every rhyming poet knows, choice of one word for a rhyme immediately constrains the range of words available for its mate(s), hence for extension or completion of the sense. In the lang., the sound shape, orthographic form, and semantic fields of each word are determined by the historical interaction of complex sets of ling. processes and accidents of hist. (wars, migrations, customs). These constraints affect the field of meaning in a given poem and are, in turn, affected by choices made by the poet. Some semantic contrasts are already coded into the lang. as rhymes, e.g., *light / night, Gehalt / Gestalt*: these are pairs that must be actively avoided by serious poets. These are rhymes so outworn that the (semantic) life has gone out of them altogether. Pope satirizes *breeze / trees* in the *Essay on Criticism*, but others—*anguish / languish, length / strength, death / breath, tomb / womb*—are easy to name. The fault in all these is that they seem to let the rhyme too obviously dictate the sense. A whole semantic field is coded into some rhyme pairs, e.g., *mad / bad, stranger / danger*.

One other consequence of the preceding is the expectedness or surprise of the rhyme: a common or unprepossessing first rhyme word followed by a startling or shocking mate from a radically different lexical category is almost certain to be used for either comic or satiric effect. Rhymes can also be constructed from nonsense syllables and nonce words, as in Lewis Carroll.

(7) By the effects of *further complication of sound patterning* in the rhyme words themselves. More than one pattern may be figured in the rhyming words: typically assonance or consonance is mounted on top of the rhyme scheme, not as a reduction but as a complication. In Milton's sonnet "On the Late Massacre in Piedmont," e.g., the octave rhymes are *bones / cold / old / stones / groans / fold / rolled / moans*. The rhyme scheme is thus *abbaabba*, but the vowel is held constant, assonating *aaaaaaaa*. Milton's "On His Deceased Wife" rhymes *abbaabba cdcdcd* but assonates *aaaaaaaa bbbbbb*. "To the Lord General Cromwell" has for its octave rhymes *cloud / rude / fortitude / ploughed / proud / pursued / imbued / loud*, also *abbaabba*, but all eight lines are in consonance on final –*d*. Yeats achieves the same effect in "Among School Children," reiterating the final consonant of *images / those / reveries / repose / presences / knows / symbolize / enterprise*. This is rhyme yet more interwoven and complete.

(8) By *participation* of the rhymes *in sound patterning nearby*. Part of the perceived effect of the rhyme also depends on the density of sound patterning in the lines surrounding the rhyme words. Here we enter the

realm of those larger constellations of sound that schematize the entire poem, over and above, though not apart from, the rhyme scheme. Like rhyme, these too impose a surplus of design on the verbal material, binding words together, promoting salient words, underlining significant semantic parallels between otherwise disparate words, punctuating the seriatim flow of text processing by repetition of significant sounds recently heard and remembered, and marking the text as aesthetic through the increase of attention required—and rewarded—in reading.

(9) By the *position in the line* of the rhymes. Normally rhyme is presumed to be end rhyme, i.e., sound linkage of lines by marking their ends (it is known that ends of members in series have special cognitive "visibility"), but more complex forms rhyme the word at line end with other words line-internally or rhyme two line-internal words in the same or successive lines, or both, thus opening up a spectrum of new possibilities for more complex sound figuration. Further, even the end-rhyme word itself may be hyphenated or broken over the line end to effect the rhyme (see BROKEN RHYME).

(10) By the *interval* between the rhymes. Without the space or gap between the rhyme words, no rhyme is possible: hence, the distance is no less significant than the repetition. In fact, repetition requires distance, the absence enabling the presence. The variance of distancing and of repetitions, of course, yields the patterning of rhyme in the stanza, i.e., the rhyme scheme; more interestingly, it also enables the distinction between "nonrhymes" and "antirhymes." Abernathy points out that it is not sufficient to characterize some types of verse as "unrhymed," for this fails to distinguish between "rhymeless" verse, wherein rhyme is neither required nor prohibited but merely unspecified, and "antirhymed" verse, such as blank verse, where rhyme is specifically proscribed. Rhyme schemes reveal intervals not only between rhymes but between unrhymed lines; and in some unrhymed verse, passages of deliberate rhyme may even appear (T. S. Eliot). It is also worth noting that rhymes that are very widely separated *are not rhymes* because they are not *perceived* so. There are, in fact, some hundred-odd rhymes in *Paradise Lost*, despite Milton's strictures in his prefatory "Note" against "modern bondage" (his term for rhyme). But a rhyme not felt is not a rhyme.

(11) By the *order* or sequencing of the rhymes. The rhyme architectonics that is schematized in rhyme schemes binds lines into more complex stanza forms both *isometric and *heterometric. This is one of the chief pleasures of formal verse (see STANZA). Rhyme schemes also reveal links with identical kinds of order in other domains such as rhet. or meter. The scheme for the Petrarchan sonnet, e.g., is *abbaabba cdecde*, i.e., an octave of two sets of envelope rhyme followed by a sestet of two tercets whose rhyme is repeated seriatim. The orders here are *envelope—a scheme of repetition in reverse—and sequence—repetition in order.

Normally, rhymed stanzas contain rhymes that have at least one mate inside the same stanza; other less common but still important elements of order in rhyming are monorhyme, i.e., iteration of the same rhyme sound (as in OF assonance or triplets in couplet verse); lines whose rhyme is indeterminate or optional in the midst of other lines with obligatory participation in the rhyme scheme (marked with an *x* in the rhyme scheme); "isolated rhyme" or "thorn rhymes" (Occitan *rim estramp*, Ger. *Korn*—see CLAVIS); lines that have a mate only in following stanzas; and rhymeless lines without mates anywhere in the poem (Ger. *Waise*, "orphan" lines; more exploited in Rus.). All these devices structure the aesthetic space either by adding higher levels of order or by opening up spaces within the order for some amount of free play.

(12) By *sight versus sound*. In most poetry of all ages and langs., sound is the primary stratum, and rhymes are based on sound correspondence; strictly speaking, the spelling of words is irrelevant. Furthermore, spelling can mislead inattentive readers if they respond to the visual shape of the words instead of the aural. Still, this is a narrow view, and it is undeniable that literate poets of all ages have been aware to some degree of the visual dimension of poetry (Hollander's "poem in the eye"). The relations of sound to orthography in a given lang. are more manifold than is usually supposed, and these must be attended to. The first point is that fundamental processes of sound change in a lang., such as the Great Vowel Shift in Eng., have altered the pronunciation that some words formerly had, but since orthography tends to ossify—to change much more slowly than sound and via differing laws—some words that formerly rhymed and were spelled similarly now retain only the orthographic similarity. Some writers have called these "historical rhymes," but this is only to say that, in the original poem, they were authentic rhymes and should be so understood now. Conversely, orthography has itself exerted an influence on pronunciation at times, so that words spelled alike come to be pronounced alike despite former difference: this phenomenon is called "spelling pronunciation."

An important related issue is that of rhyming in dialect poetry and dialect rhymes in standard-dialect poetry. Orthography and time conceal some of these rhymes, such as Keats's Cockney rhymes, e.g., *thoughts / sorts* (with the *r* suppressed in Cockney slang; see COCKNEY SCHOOL), or the South Ger. dialect rhymes of J. W. Goethe, Friedrich Schiller, and others.

Some poets have exploited the visual forms of words to create visual analogues of aural rhyme: these maneuvers require rapid shifts in category recognition on the part of the reader to realize the nature of the sleight-of-hand. Finally, the invention of script and then printing has exerted so powerful an influence on mod. consciousness that poetry itself is now in effect a bivalent form wherein visuality comes to have, in the mod. world, equal legitimacy with sound as the mode of poetic form, leading to the several forms of pattern poetry, *concrete poetry, *lettrisme, *calligrammes, and *visual poetry.

C. *Terminology*. The terminologies for rhyme, its varieties, and its analogues in the several Western langs. derive from the 12th c.; they are unsystematic and inconsistent. In med. Lat., rhyme emerges from the

Christian hymn trad. into the elaborate forms of rhyming in the silver-age poetry of the Carolingian Ren. (see Raby). In the vernaculars, rhyming achieves its first flowering in Occitan poetry, where the troubadours exhibited in their verse perhaps the most sustained interest in rhyme ever seen in the West, before or since. From Occitan, it passed to all the other Eur. vernaculars, with later efflorescence in northern France in the poetry of the rhétoriqueurs in the late 15th–early 16th cs., influencing even, through Ger., the poetries of the Scandinavian countries. From this thumbnail hist., one would think that Fr. rhyme terminology would have dominated all others, incl. Eng. But since Eng. prosody developed out of 19th-c. Ger. philology, itself based on cl. philology, the 20th c. inherited a confused and confusing apparatus.

Further, given the conservatism of traditional prosodists, one would think that rhyme terminology would be relatively consistent from one lang. to another. But all langs. do not admit the various morphological forms of rhyme with equal facility and so tend to develop one or another rhyme form more extensively. The practice of a major poet also has great effect. Thus, simple trans. of a term from one lang. to another gives a misleading impression, for the effects of a given structure are not precisely the same in two different langs. This is a significant constraint on building cross-ling. taxonomies and terminologies. It is not a constraint, however, on the more immediate problems of making the reference of terms clear and precise or of eliminating confusion. To date, no full and systematic analysis of the terminologies in the major Western langs.—med. Lat, Occitan, OF, OE, ON, ME, MHG, and mod. Ger., Fr., Eng., Sp., and Rus.—much less in the major Asian langs.—Chinese and Japanese—has yet been given. Since the most influential mod. prosodies have been Fr. and Eng., a brief discussion of terminological issues therein will be instructive.

(1) *French.* In 19th- and early 20th-c. Fr. prosody, rhyme classification distinguished between phonemic material following the tonic (rhyming) vowel and phonemic material preceding it:

(a) rhyme of tonic vowel alone:
   *rime pauvre* or *faible*
(b) rhyme of vowel + following consonant(s):
   *rime suffisante*
(c) rhyme of vowel + preceding consonant(s):
   *rime riche*
(d) rhyme of vowel + preceding syllable(s):
   *rime léonine*

Under (c), the homophony of the rhyme words' *consonne d'appui* (the consonant immediately preceding the tonic vowel) was a condition of rime riche (see RICH RHYME). The incidence of rime riche increased with the romantic poets and became an important plank in the aesthetic platform of *Parnassianism: "Without the *consonne d'appui*, there is no rhyme and, consequently, no poetry" (Banville); but it should not be assumed that this increase in rime riche was designed to compensate for the concomitant increase in other metrical freedoms by shoring up the line end

(Cornulier). Among these poets, rime riche enriches the rhyming words, investing them with more resonance, color, and dramatic presence. To later 20th-c. analysts, however, this 19th-c. system of classification has seemed too crude, particularly in that it allows rhymes like *bonté / cité* to be rich, while denser accumulations of phonemes (e.g., *tordre / mordre, arche / marche*) are classed as merely suffisantes. Accordingly, a purely numerical approach to rhyme classification has been preferred, whereby the more identical phonemes there are, in whatever position, the richer the rhyme:

(1) *rime pauvre* or *faible*:
   identity of one element, the tonic vowel
   (*bossu / vu*)
(2) *rime suffisante*:
   identity of two elements, tonic vowel +
      consonant
   (*roc / bloc*) or consonant + tonic vowel
   (*main / carmin*)
(3) *rime riche*:
   identity of three or more elements in the tonic
      syllable
   (*s'abrite / s'effrite, tordu / perdu, charmes / larmes*)
(4) *rime léonine*:
   identity of two or more syllables, the tonic syl-
      lable + one or more syllables preceding it
   (*tamariniers / mariniers, désir, Idées / des iridées*).

But in the assessment of the degree or relative richness of rhyme, other factors also need to be taken into account, e.g. the "amplification" of the rhyme (identical phonemes in the rhyme words but not involved in the rhyme itself, e.g. *rivage / image; galopin / maroquin*) and correspondence of the number of syllables in the rhyme words or rhyme measures.

(2) *English.* Eng. has never succeeded in codifying its terminology for rhyme forms. Surveys of usage even show very little consistency of treatment. The most common terms for rhyme in Eng. have been *end rhyme, full rhyme, perfect rhyme,* and *true rhyme.* The first of these simply denotes line position and, while unsatisfactory, seems least problematic; the second corresponds to Fr. rime suffisante and would be useful were that all it were taken to mean, i.e., meeting the minimum criteria for rhyme. The last two, however, imply that the one form of sound echo denominated "rhyme" is somehow the ideal or epitome toward which all other forms strive (and fail), whereas, in fact, end rhyme is but one of several related configurations of sound correspondence. The terms *perfect* and *true* should be avoided as prejudicing a priori the status of other forms of rhyme, whose own terms (*off rhyme, near rhyme*) are also objectionable.

But again, it is essential to bear in mind that, even for rhyme types directly appropriated from the Romance langs. and for which the Eng. terms are simply direct trans., the effect is not the same: rhyme is a markedly different phenomenon in inflectional langs., where identity of word ending is pervasive and often must be actually avoided, than in positional langs., where inflectional endings are almost entirely absent and where sound similarity is more dependent on the historical evolution of the lexicon. Notwithstanding, this difference does not automatically make the Romance langs. rhyme "rich" and the Germanic langs. rhyme "poor," as has often been thought: it is not merely the quantity of like endings that is at issue.

**D. Analogues.** Inside poetry, there are a number of structures that have rhyme-like effects or functions or exceed the domain of rhyme, verging into repetition. The *sestina, e.g., repeats a sequence of whole words rather than rhyme sounds. Several rhetorical devices generate comparable effects to those of rhyme even in unrhymed verse: in the 10,000 lines of *Paradise Lost*, there are over 100 cases of epistrophe, nearly 100 of *anaphora, 60 of *anadiplosis, 50 of *epanalepsis, and 40 of epizeuxis, all of them, as Broadbent says, "iterative schemes tending to the effect of rhyme." Milton also weights words at line end (Broadbent calls this "anti-rhyme"), counterposing semantically heavy and contrastive terms at *Paradise Lost* 4.561–62, e.g.: "Tempt not the Lord thy God, he said and stood. / But Satan smitten with amazement fell"—an effect reinforced all the more by reiteration of these two terms via *ploce ten more times in the following 21 lines, and echoed thereafter at 4.590–91 (cf. 9.832–33). In *American Sign Language poetry, poets achieve rhyme-like effects using hand shapes.

Outside poetry, rhyme is commonly thought of as a "poetical" device, but, in fact, it is a broadly attested ling. structure used for marking the ends of important words and phrases to make them memorable. Rhyme is widely used not only for ludic and didactic purposes, as in rhymed and rhythmical calendrical mnemonics, children's counting-out and jump-rope rhymes, and jingles for ads (see Chasar) but for other types of memorable speech such as *proverbs, *epigrams, inscriptions, mottoes, *riddles, puns, and jokes (Brogan). Children seem to be able to manufacture rhymes not only spontaneously and happily but more readily than the other six forms cited at the top of section II.B above, suggesting that the closural or "final-fixed" structure that is rhyme is somehow more salient for cognitive processing (see Rayman and Zaidel), as the vast lit. on the role of rhyme in promoting children's phonemic awareness, lang. acquisition, and literacy suggests. Perhaps the most common form of rhyming in lang. is seen in mnemonic formulas, catch phrases that rhyme, e.g., *true blue, ill will, fender bender, double trouble, high and dry*. The list of such popular and proverbial phrases is astonishingly long, and the device is also used in poetry (Donne, "Song (Go and Catch a Falling Star"); Eliot, *Four Quartets*; see CLOSE RHYME).

In an important study, Bolinger has shown that in every lang., words that begin or end alike in sound come to be perceived as related even when they have no etymological connection. This sort of paradigmatic or synchronic associativity is even stronger than the historical kinship of words, which is often concealed by spelling and pronunciation changes, and is extended naturally into poetry as rhyme without any alteration of form or function. The inevitability of rhyme suggested by this study becomes harder to deny in light of evidence that rhyme-like structures apparently exist even in nonhuman langs., such as that of whales (Guinee and Payne), challenging those who think of rhyme as more artificial than natural to reconsider.

■ J. S. Schütze, *Versuch einer Theorie des Reims nach Inhalt und Form* (1802)—Kantian semantic theory; T. Swift, "Essay on the Rise and Progress of Rhime," *Transactions of the Royal Irish Academy* 9 (1803); S. Turner, "An Inquiry Respecting the Early Use of Rhyme," *Archaeologia* 14 (1808); A. Croke, *Essay on the Origin, Progress, and Decline of Rhyming Latin Verse* (1828); F. Wolf, *Über die Lais, Sequenzen, und Leiche* (1841), 161 ff.; W. Masing, *Über Ursprung und Verbreitung des Reims* (1866); T. de Banville, *Petit traité de poésie française* (1872); Schipper, 1.1.7, 1.4.1; E. Freymond, "Über den reichen Reim bei altfranzösischen Dichtern," *ZRP* 6 (1882); W. Grimm, "Zur Gesch. des Reims" (1852), rpt. in *Kleinere Schriften* (1887)—still the best Ger. survey; A. Ehrenfeld, *Studien zur Theorie des Reims*, 2 v. (1897–1904); P. Delaporte, *De la rime française* (1898); G. Mari, *Riassunto e dizionarietto di ritmica italiana* (1901); Kastner, ch. 3; Meyer, v. 1, ch. 2—med. Lat.; A. Gabrielson, *Rhyme as a Criterion of the Pronunciation of Spenser, Pope, Byron, and Swinburne* (1909); Schipper, *History* 270 ff.; Thieme, ch. 8 and 376, 379–80—full list of Fr. work to 1914; W. Braune, "Reim und Vers," *Sitzungsb. der Heidelberger Akad. der Wiss., phil.-hist. Klasse* (1916)—etymology; F. Zschech, *Die Kritik des Reims in England* (1917); O. Brik, "Zvukovie povtory," *Poetika* (1919); E. Sapir, "The Heuristic Value of Rhyme," *Queen's Quarterly* 27 (1920); B. de Selincourt, "Rhyme in English Poetry," *E&S* 7 (1921); H. C. Wyld, *Studies in English Rhymes from Surrey to Pope* (1923); V. M. Žirmunskij, *Rifma, ee istoriia i teoriia* (1923); W. B. Sedgwick, "The Origin of Rhyme," *Revue Benedictine* 36 (1924); Morris-Jones—Celtic; K. Wesle, *Frühmittelhochdeutsche Reimstudien* (1925); P. Habermann, "Reim," etc., *Reallexikon I* 3.25–44; J. W. Rankin, "Rime and Reason," *PMLA* 44 (1929); H. Lanz, *The Physical Basis of Rhyme* (1931); N. Törnqvist, "Zur Gesch. des Wortes Reim," *Humanistika Vetenskapssamfundet i Lund, Årsberättelse* (1934–35), v. 3—Celtic, Germanic, and Romance; Patterson—fullest source for the Rhétoriqueurs; K. Stryjewski, *Reimform und Reimfunktion* (1940)—near rhyme in Eng.; K. Burke, "On Musicality in Verse," *The Philosophy of Literary Form* (1941); F. W. Ness, *The Use of Rhyme in Shakespeare's Plays* (1941); U. Pretzel, *Frühgesch. des deutschen Reims* (1941); A. M. Clark, *Studies in Literary Modes* (1945); Le Gentil, v. 1, bk. 2; A. Oras, "Echoing Verse Endings in Paradise Lost," *South Atlantic Studies for S. E. Leavitt*, ed. S. A. Stoudemire (1953); Raby, *Christian*; W. K. Wimsatt, "One Relation of Rhyme to Reason" and "Rhetoric and Poems," *The Verbal Icon* (1954)—classic studies of semantics; J. W. Draper, "The Origin of Rhyme," *RLC* 31 (1957), 39 (1965); Beare—broad scope for Western; Raby, *Secular*; J. B. Broadbent, "Milton's Rhetoric," *MP* 56 (1959); Saintsbury, *Prosody*, v. 1, App. 8, and v. 3, App. 4; F. G. Ryder, "How Rhymed Is a Poem?" *Word* 19 (1963);

M. Masui, *The Structure of Chaucer's Rime Words* (1964); D. L. Bolinger, "Rime, Assonance, and Morpheme Analysis," *Forms of English* (1965); J. Cohen, *Structure du langage poétique* (1966); C. A. Owen Jr., "'Thy Drasty Ryming,'" *SP* 63 (1966)—Chaucer; R. Abernathy, "Rhymes, Non-Rhymes, and Antirhyme," *To Honor Roman Jakobson*, v. 1 (1967); E. J. Dobson, *English Pronunciation 1500–1700*, 2d ed., 2 v. (1968); H. Whitehall, "Rhyme: Sources and Diffusion," *Ibadan* 25 (1968); M. Perloff, *Rhyme and Meaning in the Poetry of Yeats* (1970); L. Pszczołowska, *Rym* (1970)—Polish; V. Nemoianu, "Levels of Study in the Semantics of Rhyme," *Style* 5 (1971); E. H. Guggenheimer, *Rhyme Effects and Rhyming Figures* (1972)—cl.; T. Eekman, *The Realm of Rhyme* (1974)—comparative Slavic; V. F. Markov, "V zaščitu raznoudarnoi rifmy (informativnyi obzor)," *Russian Poetics*, ed. T. Eekman and D. S. Worth (1975); L. P. Elwell-Sutton, *The Persian Metres* (1976), App. 1; M. Shapiro, *Asymmetry* (1976), ch. 4; *Die Genese der europäischen Endreimdichtung*, ed. U. Ernst and P.-E. Neuser (1977); J. M. Lotman, *The Structure of the Artistic Text*, trans. G. Lenhoff and R. Vroon (1977); D. S. Worth, "Roman Jakobson and the Study of Rhyme," *Roman Jakobson: Echoes of His Scholarship*, ed. D. Armstrong (1977); W. E. Rickert, "Rhyme Terms," *Style* 12 (1978); G. Schweikle, "Reim," etc., *Reallexikon II* 3.403–31; D. Wesling, *The Chances of Rhyme* (1980); Scott; Brogan, 77 ff.—full bibl. for Eng. to 1981, with coverage of other langs. in appendices, extended in *Verseform* (1989); B. de Cornulier, "La rime n'est pas une marque de fin de vers," *Poétique* 46 (1981); Group μ; Mazaleyrat; J. Molino and J. Tamine, "Des rimes, et quelques raisons," *Poétique* 52 (1982); D. S. Samoilov, *Kniga o russkoi rifme*, 2d ed. (1982)—fullest study of Rus.; R. Birkenhauer, *Reimpoetik am Beispiel Stefan Georges* (1983); B. de Cornulier, "Sur les groupements de vers classiques et la rime," *Cahiers de grammaire* 6 (1983); F. P. Memmo, *Dizionario di metrica italiana* (1983); Navarro—Sp.; Norden, 2.810 ff.; *The Old English Riming Poem*, ed. O. Macrae-Gibson (1983); D. Billy, "La nomenclature des rimes," *Poétique* 57 (1984); M. T. Ikegami, *Rhyme and Pronunciation* (1984)—ME; W. E. Rickert, "Semantic Consequences of Rhyme," *Literature in Performance* 4 (1984); Chambers—Occitan; "Rhyme and the True Calling of Words," in Hollander; W. E. Rickert, "B. de Cornulier, "Rime 'riche' et fonction de la rime," *Littérature* 59 (1985); B. Nagel, *Das Reimproblem in der deutschen Dichtung vom Otfridvers zum freien Vers* (1985); Scherr, ch. 4; W. Harmon, "Rhyme in English Verse: History, Structures, Functions," *SP* 84 (1987); L. M. Guinee and K. B. Payne, "Rhyme-Like Repetitions in Songs of Humpback Whales," *Ethology* 79 (1988); C. Scott, *The Riches of Rhyme* (1988); J. J. Small, *Positive as Sound* (1990); G. Stewart, *Reading Voices* (1990), ch. 2; B.M.H. Strang, "Language, General," *The Spenser Encyclopedia*, ed. A. C. Hamilton et al. (1990); L. Mugglestone, "The Fallacy of the Cockney Rhyme," *RES* 42 (1991); J. Rayman and E. Zaidel, "Rhyming and the Right Hemisphere," *Brain and Language* 40 (1991); Gasparov, *History*; M. McKie, "The Origins and Early Development of Rhyme in English Verse," *MLR* (1997); Morier; W. Flesch, "The Conjuror's Trick, or How to Rhyme," *Literary Imagination* 3 (2001); K. Hanson, "Vowel Variation in English Rhyme," *Studies in the History of the English Language*, ed. D. Minkova and R. Stockwell (2002); H. Kenner, "Rhyme: An Unfinished Monograph," *Common Knowledge* 10 (2004); R. Dainotto, "Of the Arab Origin of Modern Europe: Giammaria Barbieri, Juan Andrés, and the Origin of Rhyme," *CL* 58 (2006); J. P. Hunter, "Seven Reasons for Rhyme," *Ritual, Routine, and Regime*, ed. L. Clymer (2006); K. Árnason, "On the Principles of Nordic Rhyme and Alliteration," *Arkiv for Nordisk Filologi/Archives for Scandinavian Philology* 122 (2007); A. Bradley, *Book of Rhymes: The Poetics of Hip Hop* (2009); S. Stewart, "Rhyme and Freedom," *The Sound of Poetry/The Poetry of Sound*, ed. M. Perloff and C. Dworkin (2009); M. Chasar, "The Business of Rhyming: Burma-Shave Poetry and Popular Culture," *PMLA* 125 (2010).

■ **Chinese**: J.J.Y. Liu, *The Art of Chinese Poetry* (1962); H. Frankel, "Classical Chinese [Versification]," in Wimsatt.

■ **Arabic and Persian**: G. W. Freitag, *Darstellung der Arabischen Verskunst* (1830, rpt. 1968); H. Blochmann, *The Prosody of the Persians according to Saifi, Jami and Other Writers* (1872, rpt. 1970); W. Wright, *A Grammar of the Arabic Language* (1896–98); Shams al-dīn Moḥammad *Al-Moʿjam fīmaʿāyer ashʿār al-ʿajam* (1935); Al-Akhfash, *Kitāb al-qawāfi* (1970); L. P. Elwell-Sutton, *The Persian Metres* (1976); F. Thiesen, *A Manual of Classical Persian Prosody* (1982); S. Bonebakker, "Kāfiya," *Encyclopedia of Islam*, ed. H.A.R. Gibb, 2d ed., v. 4 (1990); D. Frolov, *Classical Arabic Verse* (2000).

T.V.F. Brogan, S. Cushman;
K. S. Chang (Chinese); R.M.A. Allen,
W. L. Hanaway (Arabic and Persian);
C. Scott (French)

**RHYME COUNTERPOINT.** A phenomenon noted by Hayes in the verse of John Donne, Henry Vaughan, and esp. George Herbert (e.g., "Denial"): the pattern of line lengths in a *heterometric poem is independent of the pattern of the rhymes. For example, a quatrain of lines of eight, seven, eight, and seven syllables has the metrical pattern *abab*, but the rhyme scheme is *abba*. Normally, rhymed verse is isometric (see ISOCHRONISM OR ISOCHRONY), and even in heterometric verse, lines bound together by rhyme are generally assumed to be isosyllabic. In the case of rhyme counterpoint, however, meter and rhyme are set in contrast, rather than in harmony, making the reader's expectations for both prosodic features act in concert. The distinctive and formally ambiguous effect of rhyme counterpoint is consonant with other features of *metaphysical poetry.

■ A. M. Hayes, "Counterpoint in Herbert," *SP* 35 (1938); R. Fowler, "'Prose Rhythm' and Metre," *Essays on Style and Language* (1966).

T.V.F. Brogan; M. Weinstein

# RHYME-PROSE

I. Latin
II. Arabic
III. Chinese

**I. Latin.** Ancient literary theory in the West posits a gradation from prose to poetry rather than a sharp distinction. In antiquity, a general class of prose was made artful by the application of artifice and *figuration (see ARTIFICE, POETIC); this includes rhythmical prose (see PROSE RHYTHM) and rhymed prose or what will be called here *rhyme-prose.* Such prose is divided into rhythmical units separated by pauses and end-marked by *rhyme. The largest units are *periods, full-sense units equivalent to mod. independent clauses or sentences; the next largest units are cola, i.e., phrases or subordinate clauses (see COLON); the smallest are commas. Prose has *rhythm; poetry has rhythm and adds *meter (Aristotle, *Rhetoric* 3.8.1408b30; cf. Augustine, *De musica*).

The so-called Gorgian figures introduced by Gorgias of Leontini (ca. 485–ca. 380 BCE) define sound effects created by control of rhythm through such strategies as *parallelism (*parisosis*), balance (*isocolon*), and *antithesis. According to Aristotle (*Rhetoric* 3.1.1404a25), the Gorgian figures were taken from the poets. They are reinforced in antiquity by two devices—terminal rhythms defining natural pauses (see CADENCE) and like sounds created by like endings (*homoeoteleuton* or "case rhyme"). Art prose that makes use of the Gorgian figures and related devices was called *rhetoricus sermo* or *eloquentiae prosa*. Formulas for the period and colon and for types of prose rhythm and homoeoteleuton are given in the *Rhetorica ad Herennium*, the earliest extant Lat. rhet., and in Cicero's *De oratore* and Quintilian's *Institutio oratoria*. During the Middle Ages, the quantitative terminal rhythms (cadences) of art prose were expressed in accentual forms (the *cursus*); the Vatican adopted certain of these for papal correspondence. As the use of prose rhythms became widespread, the use of homoeoteleuton was broadened and became full rhyme. The convergence of the two resulted in rhyme-prose. Here rhyme is typically used to mark the ends of periods and cola. Much of the rhyme is simple homoeoteleuton, but rhyme of two and three syllables is also found. Rhyme pairs, marking the ends of balanced parallel or antithetical elements, are usual; but practice varies, and *cross rhyme (*abab*) and bracket rhyme (*abba*) are common. Rhyme is also found within the period or colon, esp. to mark moments of thematic importance or emotional intensity.

Rhyme-prose was cultivated by Christian writers—e.g., Tertullian, Augustine, Lactantius, Fortunatus, and Hrabanus Maurus—and flourished most vigorously between the 10th and 14th cs. The significance of rhyme-prose is disputed. Norden argued that ancient rhyme-prose coupled with the accentual rhythms of the cursus is the source of rhyme in all Eur. vernacular poetry, but his theory is generally rejected. The more modest position (Polheim) is simply that rhyme-prose is an important med. Lat. form (see LATIN POETRY).

**II. Arabic.** In Ar., rhyming prose (known as *saj*[c], literally, the cooing of a dove) is found from the very beginnings of literary trad. The aphorisms of pre-Islamic soothsayers are couched in this style, in which a sequence of short utterances all end in the same rhyme and also show evidence of stress patterning (with possible implications for the origins of Ar. poetry itself). The text of the Qur'an itself is predominantly in this style, with a number of the earliest *suras* (chs.) showing its exclusive use. The most famous literary manifestation of this style occurs in the genre of *maqāmāt*, a combination of verbal virtuosity and picaresque social commentary apparently originated by Badī[c] al-zamān al-Hamadhānī (d. 1008) and exploited with great virtuosity by Al-Harīrī (d. 1120).

**III. Chinese.** *See* FU.

■ **Latin:** Meyer; K. Polheim, *Die lateinische Reimprosa* (1925); G. Schweikle, "Reimprosa," *Reallexikon II*; Morier; E. Norden, *Die Antike Kunstprosa*, 9th ed., 2 v. (1983), 2.760 ff.

■ **Arabic:** "Saj[c]," *Encyclopedia of Islam* (1913–34); Anīs al-Maqdisī, *Tatawwur al-asālīb al-nathariyya* (1968).

O. B. HARDISON (LAT.); R.M.A. ALLEN (AR.)

**RHYME ROYAL.** A seven-line *pentameter *stanza rhyming *ababbcc,* one of many complex stanzas developed in the late Middle Ages; sometimes called the Troilus stanza, after Chaucer's use of it in *Troilus and Criseyde.* The name has speculatively been associated with the stanzaic form of the Scottish King James I's "The Kingis Quair" (c. 1425) but is more likely to have emerged from late med. Fr. forms of ceremonial and festive addresses to royalty; these trads. underlie the vigor of rhyme royal in John Skelton's Eng. *Magnyfycence,* Thomas Sackville's induction to *A Mirror for Magistrates,* and other works of drama, pageantry, and rhetorical address in Eng.

Chaucer's devel. of rhyme royal emerges from his familiarity with Fr. courtly poetry, esp. the *ballade stanzas of Guillaume de Machaut and Eustache Deschamps, and with the *ottava rima* of Giovanni Boccaccio. Chaucer adapted and shortened by one line each of these forms while amplifying the stanza's syntactic spaciousness. He uses rhyme royal in a ballade-like way for reflection, philosophizing, and emotional expressiveness, as does his contemporary John Gower, who favors rhyme royal for philosophical love poetry. Chaucer also uses rhyme royal for narrative, a brilliant innovation, in the *Troilus* and *The Parliament of Fowls, Anelida and Arcite,* and certain *Canterbury Tales.* In the *Troilus,* it is agile and flexible: enjambed or end-stopped at any point, enjambing even across stanza breaks, it accommodates dialogue, action, or reflection; it moves swiftly or slowly, in tones exalted, rough, or colloquial. When Shakespeare used rhyme royal in *The Rape of Lucrece,* he tested its capacities for violent action and violent reflection at once.

The rhyme scheme of rhyme royal, with its medial *bb* *couplet, means that the first *quatrain, in alternating rhymes, ends with a line (line 4) which is also the first line of that medial couplet (lines 4–5). Readers might experience this overlap as a unifying ligature or as a gradual disruption or surprise in the move from quatrain to couplet; the third *b*-rhyme (line 5) as a dilation or amplification that slows narrative momentum. These potentialities create a sense of amplitude and openness within the stanza, lending it to delineation of elusive temporal experiences: reverie, dream, vision, thresholds between waking and sleeping, dawns and dusks. Chaucer explores rhyme royal's temporal capacities in the directions of dream vision and comedy in *The Parliament of Fowls*, in the direction of philosophical love narrative and tragedy in the *Troilus*. Thomas Wyatt develops temporal bemusement in other directions through rhyme royal in "They Flee from Me"; Edmund Spenser in "An Hymne of Heavenly Beauty"; John Milton in "On the Death of a Fair Infant Dying of a Cough" and in the proem of "On the Morning of Christ's Nativity." In this latter poem, the rhyme royal stanza has been expanded and its historical argument deepened by augmenting its seventh line to a Spenserian *alexandrine, a move that would influence the rhyme royal practices of Thomas Chatterton, S. T. Coleridge, and William Wordsworth when they revived med. forms and genres (e.g., Wordsworth's "Resolution and Independence"). In mod. times, the most powerful poem in this line is W. B. Yeats's "A Bronze Head."

The rhyme royal stanza has been decreed solemn at least since the 16th c., when George Gascoigne considered it "serving best for grave discourses"; this could fairly be said of some rhyme royal works by 15th- and early 16th-c. Chaucerians like John Lydgate, Thomas Hoccleve, William Dunbar, Robert Henryson, Stephen Hawes, and Alexander Barclay. But it could not be said of the range of Chaucerian work in the form, much less of W.H. Auden's use of it for tonal juxtapositions in the 1955 poem "The Shield of Achilles," or his 1937 tour de force *Letter to Lord Byron,* which impersonates a light poem by achieving a long rhyme royal poem with abundant feminine rhymes and a wittering air. It is a bravura, unique performance—as is Francis Kinaston's 1635 achievement of translating a full two books of Chaucer's *Troilus* into perfect Lat. rhyme royal stanzas, published as *Amorum Troili et Creseidae libri duo priores Anglico-Latini*.

*See* SEPTET.

T. KRIER

**RHYMERS' CLUB.** The Rhymers' Club was a loose association of late Victorian male poets, conventionally called *aesthetes* and *decadents*. They were characterized (much later) by their most famous member, W. B. Yeats, as "overwrought, unstable men," doomed to personal and poetic failure because of their dissipated, self-destructive personal lives. They met regularly from 1890 to 1895 at London's Cheshire Cheese pub and elsewhere, where they recited and discussed each other's poetry. These meetings, precursors of the mod. *poetry reading, were usually decorous and often dull. Yet as Yeats later observed, that the Rhymers read their poems out loud and thought that they could be so tested was a definition of their aims. A number of Rhymers besides Yeats—Ernest Dowson, Lionel Johnson, Arthur Symons—later became famous in their own right. And because many Rhymers were Celtic by birth, the club is sometimes seen as foreshadowing the Celtic Literary Revival. But in their own time, the Rhymers were distinguished by their collective voice, by their rejection of the high mission claimed for poetry by John Stuart Mill and Matthew Arnold, and by their rigorous refusal to sound notes of individual mastery or *genius.

When others were beginning to experiment with *free verse, the Rhymers delighted in speech, rhyme, and lyricism—in what Yeats called "song for the speaking voice"—and a number of their poems reflect self-consciously on their own spoken or *song-like condition. Their poetry is also significant for the seamlessness and care with which it was mediated into book form. In both *The Book of the Rhymers' Club* (1892) and *The Second Book of the Rhymers' Club* (1894), the poetic voice of the individual is woven artfully into the collective whole, making it difficult to read individual poems in isolation. The Rhymers themselves arranged the contents of the two collections. But the books' cohesiveness was due also to the artfulness with which they were published and printed. As their prosaic titles imply, the books of the Rhymers' Club really are *books* (see BOOK, POETIC)—and they played a small role in what has been termed the renaissance of printing that took place in the 1890s.

■ W. B. Yeats, "The Tragic Generation," *The Trembling of the Veil* (1922); J. G. Nelson, *The Early Nineties* (1970); B. Gardiner, *The Rhymers' Club* (1988); J. Gardner, *Yeats and the Rhymers' Club* (1989); J. J. McGann, "Introduction," *Black Riders: The Visible Language of Modernism* (1993) N. Alford, *The Rhymers' Club* (1997); *The Fin De Siècle Poem*, ed. J. Bristow (2005); N. Frankel, "The Books of the Rhymers' Club as Material Texts," *Masking The Text* (2009).

N. FRANKEL

**RHYME SCHEME** (Ger. *Reimfolge*). An ideal pattern of rhyme in strophic or stichic verse or the written representation of the same. Usually, the term *rhyme scheme* refers to end rhymes, but variants of the conventional representation can refer also to *internal rhyme. Poets may undertake significant departures from the model rhyme scheme suggested by a poem, and the variability of *rhyme itself leads to further variability of actual rhyme patterns. A standardized notation for rhyme scheme uses lowercase letters of the alphabet to represent patterns: the first rhyme sound is represented as *a* at its first and every subsequent occurrence, the second *b*, and so on, with *x* (and sometimes *y*, *z*, etc., in sequence) for lines that do not rhyme. Thus, *couplets rhyme *aa bb cc dd*, etc., *rhyme royal *ababbcc*, and the Shakespearean *sonnet *ababcdcdefefgg*. This system of notation was employed as early as the Ren., when

Antonio Minturno used it in his *L'arte Poetica* (1563). No standardized notation exists for the *refrains of forms in which entire words or lines are repeated, e.g., the *sestina, the *villanelle, and the *ghazal, but critics generally use the capital *R* or a superscript diacritical mark or number. Rhyme schemes bind constellations of sound and meaning as they link poems to formal trads. Just as the rhyme scheme of a Shakespearean sonnet divides the poem sonically into three quatrains and a couplet, e.g., the thought in the poem typically progresses in three parts toward the proposition of the closing couplet. Even as it binds internally, the rhyme scheme of a sonnet can connect it to the larger hist. of all sonnets and, by means of that connection, generate a range of figurative meanings. Not all rhyme schemes bind sound, meaning, and poetic trad. as tightly as the typical Shakespearean sonnet, however, and various rhyme schemes have greater and lesser degrees of complexity and bond force (Ger. *Reimzwang*).

*See* CLAVIS; STANZA.

▪ A. Minturno, *L'arte poetica* (1563); J. Hollander, *Melodious Guile* (1988), ch. 5—how particular sonnets allegorize their own rhyme schemes; S. Adams, *Poetic Designs* (1997); M. N. Carminati et al., "Readers' Responses to Sub-genre and Rhyme Scheme in Poetry," *Poetics* 34 (2006).

T.V.F. BROGAN; E. RETTBERG

# RHYTHM (Gr. *rhythmos*; Lat. *rhythmus*).

 I. Features of Rhythm
 II. Rhythm versus Meter
 III. Analysis of Rhythm

Although when it was first used in Eng., in the 16th and 17th cs., the word *rhythm* was not clearly distinguished from the word *rhyme* (both words being spelled in a variety of ways), by the 18th c. it was being consistently employed to refer to the durational qualities of poetry and music, and soon extended to analogous properties of the visual arts. In the 19th c., it was generalized to movement of a regular kind—most often the alternation of strong and weak elements—in any sphere, and appropriated by the physical sciences for periodicities and patterns in a range of natural phenomena. The word has retained throughout its hist. an aesthetic aspect, suggesting a movement or spatial arrangement that exhibits some degree of regularity without being mechanical. In poetry and music, it is often opposed to *meter, understood as a more precisely structured, quantifiable movement.

One cannot understand rhythm without considering its realization in human psychology and physiology; as readers of poetry, it is the *experience* of rhythm that is important to us, and this experience is both mental and bodily. At its most basic, rhythm is a patterning of energy, of tension and release, movement and countermovement that we both perceive and produce—or reproduce—in our own brains and muscles. The most powerful stimuli in producing a sense of rhythm are those that can be interpreted as bursts of energy, the drum being an obvious example. There is a distinction to be made between the noun *rhythm* and the adjective *rhythmic*: the latter usually implies a fairly strong regularity, so that we can say, "This is not a particularly rhythmic line," whereas the former can embrace both movements that are metronomic in character and those that are far from metronomic. In their use of rhythm, poetry and music are most closely allied—which does not mean that poetry can be adequately analyzed by means of musical notation (though the many attempts to do so are not without interest), but that both arts draw on the same human rhythmic faculty and thus can gain insights from one another.

Every spoken lang. has its own rhythm, which is to say a distinctive movement of sound, and the pulses of energy that produce it, in a temporal dimension. Linguistic rhythm is a product of the particular language's deployment of volume, duration, *timbre, and *pitch in reflecting lexical and syntactic structures as well as particular emphases. As the use of the term *rhythm* suggests, there is a degree of periodicity in this use of sound, although different langs. achieve it in different ways. The most common classification of langs. is threefold: stress-timed langs., such as Eng., Ger., and Dutch; syllable-timed langs., such as Fr., It., and Sp.; and mora-timed langs., such as Japanese and Tamil (where the speech rhythm is based on subsyllabic elements). This does not mean that in spoken Eng., e.g., the durations between stresses are objectively equal, nor that in spoken Fr., all syllables are of the same length. Phonetic evidence shows that *isochronism is not a matter of equal duration but of a tendency in this direction, evident, for instance, in the relative durations of vowels to consonants, which are proportionally higher in stress-timed languages (see Ramus et al.). Speakers of Eng. perceive stresses as the dominant element in the language's tendency toward regular rhythm, whereas the syllables—although they too play a part in creating the rhythmic quality of Eng. speech—are felt to be subsidiary. In Fr., by contrast, the syllables are felt to be the carriers of rhythm, with stress a secondary feature.

The characteristic verse forms of a lang. reflect its rhythm; thus, traditional Fr. verse is based on a syllable count, while traditional Eng. verse is based on the disposition of stresses. However, in Fr. and in Eng., the rhythmic subtlety of which metrical poetry is capable arises from the interplay between syllabic and stress rhythms, both of which are produced by the operation of the body's musculature in sequences of tension and release. In the most strongly regular verse, the different sources of rhythmic movement in a lang. are aligned, and the resulting movement conforms to the general properties of rhythmic organization.

*Free verse does not organize the features of the lang. in such a way as to produce a regular rhythm, but due to the inherently rhythmic character of every lang. and the structuring devices used by the poet (which can include lineation, syntactic arrangement, and rhyme), rhythm remains an important element in the reader's experience.

**I. Features of Rhythm.** Rhythm as a psycho-physiological phenomenon possesses certain properties, irrespective of the medium in which it is realized. Stable rhythms characteristically display five features: regularity, repetition, variety, hierarchy, and grouping.

**A.** *Regularity.* Rhythmic series consist of perceived signals occurring at intervals that are either regular or are close enough to being regular to create and constantly reinforce the expectation of regularity. In reading a text, the mind is continually making rapid predictions about what is likely to be perceived on the basis of what it has just perceived (and still holds in short-term memory); if the expected signal is delayed or missing, the mind will often supply it. An experience of rhythm will not arise if the time lapse between signals is too great; this, however, is not likely to happen in the case of poetry, except in a very unusual style of performance. When regularity is marked, and the expectation of regularity strong, the signals are perceived as *beats. (It has been argued, e.g. by Couper-Kuhlen, that this happens in spoken Eng. as well as in verse.)

**B.** *Repetition.* In order for a rhythm to be perceived, the successive stimuli must be experienced as *the same* stimulus occurring over and over again. In poetry, the rhythm is based on identifiable linguistic units: stressed syllables, syllables, or mora (irrespective of the phonetic differences that occur as these units are repeated). Again, expectation plays a large role in the perception of rhythmic stimuli: having heard a number of repeated signals, we are likely to interpret further stimuli as more of the same.

**C.** *Variation.* Exact repetition is usually felt to be monotonous, however, though the precise point at which pleasurable repetition becomes tedious is not easily specifiable. Variation is thus crucial to the enjoyment of rhythm, but if the signal varies too greatly from what is expected, the pattern will be perceived as unrhythmical—or as the beginning of a new rhythmic series.

**D.** *Hierarchy.* The repeated stimuli that create a regular rhythm are usually perceived as possessing some further organization, rather than being understood as a simple series. The fact that we hear a clock's "tick-tick-tick-tick" as "tick-tock-tick-tock" is one of the most familiar examples of this tendency: in this case, an exactly repeated stimulus is interpreted as an alternation between a stronger and weaker signal. This interpretation produces a hierarchy: over and above the rhythm of the repeated sounds, we hear a more widely spaced rhythm made up of the "stronger" sounds. If we were asked to tap on one out of every two sounds, we would find ourselves tapping on those we hear as "ticks" rather than those we hear as "tocks."

The hierarchical nature of regular rhythm is very clear in music, where the fundamental rhythmic units, the beats, are perceived in patterns of strong and weak, or strong, less strong, and weak, and so on. Thus a *measure of four beats will begin (according to convention) with the strongest beat, followed by a weak beat, then a somewhat strong beat, then another weak beat. Once this pattern is established (something that can be achieved in a number of ways, incl. variations in pitch, timbre, or loudness), it will continue to be heard unless an alternative organiza-

tion imposes itself on the hearer. In verse, a four-beat line will tend to follow the same pattern, although other factors such as emphasis and syntax can obscure it. The common stanza in *accentual-syllabic verse consisting of 4 four-beat, or *tetrameter, lines can be thought of as having an underlying rhythm in which the initial beats of the first and third lines are the strongest (the "highest" level of the hierarchy, where each unit is two lines), the next strongest beats are at the start of the second and last lines, then the third beats of each line, then the second and final beats of each line. The first stanza of William Blake's "London" will illustrate, using **B**, B, **b**, b to indicate beats of descending strength:

> I wander thro' each charter'd street.
> **B**      b      **b**      b
>
> Near where the charter'd Thames does flow
> B      b      **b**      b
>
> And mark in every face I meet
> **B**      b      **b**      b
>
> Marks of weakness, marks of woe
> B      b      **b**      b

This tendency is particularly marked in *dipodic verse, in which the lang. of the lines induces a strong alternation between the beats; alternatively, it can be obscured by the establishment of a contrary rhythm by the lang.

Rhythmic hierarchies are based on twos and threes; series of four or more are perceived as having stronger and weaker beats, and therefore a hierarchical structure. At the lowest level of the hierarchy, this gives rise to duple and triple rhythms; above this level, arrangements of threes are less common. By far the commonest rhythm is the duple rhythm, that is, one based on simple alternation between stronger and weaker stimuli, beat and offbeat; and in popular verse in many langs., this alternation is repeated at higher levels to produce the familiar four-beat rhythm—also a staple of med. verse, Lat. and vernacular, sacred and profane, and many trads. of art verse.

At a certain point in the hierarchy that cannot be defined precisely (and no doubt varies from reader to reader), rhythm fades, to be replaced by what might be called balance. Thus, the relation between 2 four-line tetrameter stanzas is unlikely to be perceived as a matter of rhythm—which is to say, it is unlikely to be registered somatically—though it may be intellectually understood as a strong-weak, or weak-strong, relation. Some analysts, however, incl. Cureton, use the word *rhythm* for relations over these much longer spans.

**E.** *Grouping.* As a result of rhythm's hierarchical nature, mora, syllables, or stresses (depending on the lang.) are perceived in groups of two or three or combinations thereof. Grouping is achieved not by the insertion of dividers between the groups, although the use of bar lines and foot divisions may seem to suggest this, but rather by a number of factors working together to encourage the perception of a closer link between some elements than between others. The use of a strict meter is one such factor: accentual-syllabic verse in a duple meter that begins regularly with an unstressed syllable or offbeat will encourage the perception of groups of two syllables, unstressed then stressed; this is *iambic meter, each unit of which is an iambic *foot. The reverse arrangement produces *trochaic feet. If, as in the former, weaker elements are grouped before stronger elements, the result is a rising rhythm; if, as in the latter, stronger elements are grouped before weaker elements, the result is a falling rhythm (see RISING AND FALLING RHYTHM). Tetrameter lines exhibit a tendency to divide into two groups of four syllables; in *pentameter lines, there is less pressure to fall into a regular grouping (though 4:6 and 6:4 are the most common groups). *Alexandrines most often fall into two groups of six syllables. However, word, phrase, clause, and sentence divisions may cut across these metrically induced groupings to produce a more complex, less clear-cut pattern of groups. And if the meter does not generate particular expectations of grouping—for instance, if the openings of lines vary freely between beats and offbeats—these linguistic divisions, together with line divisions, play the dominant role in determining the perception of groups.

**II. Rhythm versus Meter.** The distinction between rhythm and meter is old, dating to at least the 4th c. BCE. The disagreement between the *metrici and the rhythmici in ancient Greece reflected two approaches to verse, one strictly quantitative, the other musical, and the two terms have retained these connotations. Meter is that aspect of regular rhythm that can be labeled and counted. It is sometimes conceptualized as an abstract pattern coexisting with the actual, varied rhythm of the poem's lang., and most systems of *scansion are designed to provide a graphic representation of this pattern, though there is no psychological evidence for the simultaneous perception of two different levels in our apprehension of metrical verse. The evidence of Ren. attempts to write vernacular verse in cl. meters, however, suggests that the intellectual apprehension of complex metrical patterns can coexist with the aural appreciation of rhythm (see also CLASSICAL METERS IN MODERN LANGUAGES).

When the rhythm-bearing features of a lang. are arranged in such a way as to produce marked regularity, and thus the perception of beats, the basis for metrical organization exists. And when the series of beats and intervening offbeats are themselves organized into patterns, a meter is perceived, usually in conformity with a set of numerical constraints that has developed in the linguistic trad. in question. Meter can thus be understood as a particular form of rhythm, but it must be remembered that even the strictest metrical verse will retain some of the variety and unpredictability of the language's native rhythm. The establishment of a metrical pattern will also have an effect on the perception of rhythm, for instance, in the *promotion or *demotion of certain syllables. Any verse allows for a variety

of individual *performances, within the parameters set by the norms of the lang., and, in the case of regular verse, the demands of the meter.

**III. Analysis of Rhythm.** The task of rhythmic analysis is to reflect the movement of lang.—words, phrases, clauses, and sentences—in verse, as perceived by the reader. In free verse, this movement does not induce the experience of a regular pattern and its accompanying expectations, although with some free verse, it is appropriate to include an indication of its movement toward and away from such a pattern. In metrical verse, a full rhythmic analysis will include scrutiny of the movement that both creates and varies a metrical pattern.

One approach to rhythmic analysis is to examine phonetic records of performances of verse, using techniques developed for the phonetic analysis of speech (see, e.g., Chatman and Tsur, Poetic Rhythm). This approach is esp. useful for illuminating the different performance styles of different readers and periods, less useful in understanding the rhythmic properties common to a number of readings. The use of musical symbols to represent the rhythmic features of spoken lang. in verse, as proposed, for instance, by Joshua Steele in Prosodia Rationalis (1775) and Sidney Lanier in The Science of English Verse (1880), has proved less successful, since musical rhythm is determined by specified pitches and durations, whereas linguistic rhythm depends on relations among units.

Phonological investigations of lang. rhythms may utilize terminology that overlaps with that of poetic analysis, thanks to the close connection between natural speech rhythm and verse trad., thus providing tools for rhythmic analysis in poetry (see Hanson and Kiparsky; Hayes 1984 and 1989). Whereas earlier phonological accounts of stress in Eng. relied on the apportioning of numbered levels to syllables, often influencing studies of poetic rhythm, generative phonology and subsequent devels. in linguistic science have demonstrated the importance of lexical and syntactic structures, as well as the operation of general rules of rhythm, in establishing rhythmic hierarchies.

Another approach draws on studies of rhythm in music to scrutinize the complex hierarchies created by the phonological, morphological, and syntactic properties of the lang. used in verse. Cureton, for instance, exploits the influential theory of musical rhythm propounded by Lerdahl and Jackendoff (itself owing much to generative studies of lang.) to develop an account of rhythmic phrasing in verse (see also Attridge, Poetic Rhythm, chap. 8). Discussions of folk songs by Hayes and MacEachern and by Kiparsky using optimality theory have provided insights into the relation among the rhythm of the spoken lang., the rhythm established by the meter, and the rhythm of the musical setting. Approaches within the field of *cognitive poetics make use of studies of brain functions, such as the operation of short-term or working memory, and build on older studies of perception such as Gestalt theory (see Tsur 1977). There is still much that is not fully understood about the operation of rhythm in verse, and its relation to the rhythms of lang. and of music, and to rhythm itself as a perceptual phenomenon.

■ **Rhythm and Music:** D. Tovey, "Rhythm," *Encyclopaedia Britannica*, 11th ed. (1910–11); G. W. Cooper and L. B. Meyer, *The Rhythmic Structure of Music* (1960); F. Lerdahl and R. Jackendoff, *A Generative Theory of Tonal Music* (1983); J. London, "Rhythm," *Grove Music Online*, http://www.grovemusic.com/shared/views/article.html?from=az&section=music.45963.

■ **Rhythm and Speech:** K. L. Pike, *The Intonation of American English* (1945); D. Abercrombie, *Studies in Phonetics and Linguistics* (1965); D. L. Bolinger, *Forms of English* (1965); Chomsky and Halle; D. Crystal, *Prosodic Systems and Intonation in English* (1969); J. G. Martin, "Rhythmic (Hierarchical) versus Serial Structure in Speech and Other Behavior," *PsychologR* 79 (1972); Allen—Part I on general questions; G. D. Allen, "Speech Rhythm," *JPhon* 3 (1975); M. Liberman and A. Prince, "On Stress and Linguistic Rhythm," *LingI* 8 (1977); I. Lehiste, "Isochrony Reconsidered," *JPhon* 7 (1979); H. J. Giegerich, "On Stress-Timing in English Phonology," *Lingua* 51 (1980); B. Hayes, "The Phonology of Rhythm in English," *LingI* 15 (1984); E. Couper-Kuhlen, *English Speech Rhythm* (1993); F. Ramus, M. Nespor, and J. Mehler, "Correlates of Linguistic Rhythm in the Speech Signal," *Cognition* 73 (1999).

■ **Rhythm and Verse:** Chatman; M. W. Croll, *Style, Rhetoric and Rhythm*, ed. J. M. Patrick et al. (1966); W. Mohr, "Rhythmus," *Reallexikon II* v. 3 (1971); D. W. Harding, *Words into Rhythm* (1976); P. Kiparsky, "The Rhythmic Structure of English Verse," *LingI* 8 (1977); R. Tsur, *A Perception-Oriented Theory of Metre* (1977); T.V.F. Brogan, *English Versification, 1570–1980* (1981)—bibl.; Attridge, *Rhythms*; Scherr; C. Scott, *A Question of Syllables* (1986)—rhythm in Fr. verse; B. Hayes, "The Prosodic Hierarchy in Meter," *Phonetics and Phonology I*, ed. P. Kiparsky and G. Youmans (1989); Cureton; Attridge, *Poetic Rhythm*; K. Hanson and P. Kiparsky, "A Parametric Theory of Poetic Meter," *Lang* 72 (1996); B. Hayes and M. MacEachern, "Quatrain Form in English Folk Verse," *Lang* 74 (1998); R. Tsur, *Poetic Rhythm* (1998); E. Arndt and H. Fricke, "Rhythmus," *Reallexikon III*, v. 3 (2003); P. Kiparsky, "A Modular Metrics for Folk Verse," *Formal Approaches to Poetry*, ed. B. E. Dresher and N. Friedberg (2006).

D. ATTRIDGE

**RHYTHMIC FIGURES.** Metrical verse in Eng. is experienced as the regular alternation of *beats and offbeats, but very often these do not coincide with stressed and unstressed syllables. Such variations from the simplest realization of the meter frequently fall into one of a very small number of rhythmic figures (the phrase is borrowed from musical analysis). The five most common of these regularly encountered patterns can add expressive power, as well as variety, to the lines in which they occur.

The first figure involves three successive syllables in a metrical line that are all very lightly emphasized in pronunciation, although the middle syllable is felt as a beat, or *ictus, defining the metrical pattern (see PRO-

MOTION). In Shakespeare's opening line of sonnet 150, "How hea*vy* do *I* jour*ney* on *the* way," unemphatic beats on "do" and "on" fulfill the reader/performer's sense of a pentameter. The same figure is used in these lines by Alexander Pope and Emily Dickinson to satisfy five-, four-, and three-beat expectations: "The sound **must** seem **an** echo **to** the sense"; "I died for beau*ty*— but *was* scarce / Adjust*ed* in *the* tomb."

The second figure is the mirror image of the first, where three sequential syllables are all emphasized, though only the first and last syllables carry beats (see DEMOTION). In Thomas Hardy's trimeter "For **then,** *I,* **un**distressed," Robert Herrick's tetrameter "And **this same flower** that smiles today," and Emma Lazarus's pentameter "The **air-*bridged* har**bor that twin cities frame," the emphasized "I" and "same" and "bridged," although as prominent as the adjacent syllables, are not sensed as beats that define their poems' metrical schemes. A two-syllable version of this second figure is experienced at the beginnings of lines in countless instances, where only the second of equally emphasized syllables carries a beat, as with John Milton's "**Hence vain** deluding joys," or Lazarus's "**Send these,** the homeless, tempest tost to me."

Instances of both the first and the second rhythmic figures constitute almost the entirety of this single line by Pope: "The line too lab**ors, and** *the* words move slow" (figure one), and (figure two) "The **line** *too* la**b**ors, and the **words** *move* **slow**."

The third familiar rhythmic figure occurs frequently at the beginning of lines and is often labeled "initial inversion," which *foot-scansion prosodists explain as the substitution of a *trochee (/ u) for an expected *iamb (u /). But the four-syllable pattern of stressed and unstressed syllables (/ u u /) is so common and easily perceived that identifying it as a single metrical pattern both simplifies and clarifies the nature of the reader/performer's experience. Thus, the rhythmic figure can add energy to such lines as Dickinson's trimeter "**Men** *do* **not** sham Convulsion," Herrick's tetrameter "**Gather** *ye* **rose**buds while ye may," and Lord Byron's pentameter "**Nel**son *was* **once** Britannia's god of War."

This third rhythmic figure can also occur after a midline break in the rhythm, as in William Wordsworth's tetrameter "My horse moved on, **hoof** *after* **hoof**" or in Milton's pentameter "Others whose fruit, **burn**ished *with* **gold**en rind"—a line where one experiences the rhythmic pattern at the line's beginning as well: "**Others** *whose* **fruit,** burnished with golden rind."

The fourth rhythmic figure, less frequently experienced because more complex than the previous ones, is, like the third, formed by four syllables. Here two unstressed syllables, or offbeats, are followed by two stressed ones, or beats. This "u u / /" pattern is found in such trimeter lines as Wordsworth's "All ov*er* *the* **wide lea**," and Shakespeare's pentameter "When in disgrace with For**tune** *and* **men's eyes**."

The fifth rhythmic figure occasionally employed is the reverse of the previous one. Here the pattern of stresses, or beats, is / / u u, and can be experienced in this line from George Herbert's "Easter Wings": "Then shall the **fall** fur*ther* *the* flight in me." (Contrast this rhythm with the relative slackness of a rewritten "Then shall the fall extend the flight in me.") John Keats's "Ode on Melancholy" has consecutive lines that exemplify both the fourth and fifth rhythmic figures as the poet writes about a weeping cloud "That fos*ters the* **droop-head**ed flowers all, / And hides the **green hill** *in an* April shroud."

By taking these rhythmic figures into account when they occur and sensing their varying effects, the reader/performer may forgo an intellectual effort to discern conventional feet with their line segmentations, labels, and substitutions, and experience more immediately the pleasures that the figures add to the enjoyment of metrical poetry.

■ M. Tarlinskaja, "Rhythm and Meaning," *Style* 21 (1987); Attridge, *Poetic Rhythm*; Carper and Attridge (2003).

T. CARPER

**RICH RHYME** (Fr. *rime riche*, Ger. *reicher Reim*, It. *rima cara*). Definitions of "exact" or "true" rhyme tend to require a difference in sound along with the similarity: the final vowel and all following phonemes sound the same, but the preceding consonant or consonants differ, if any are present (e.g., *may/day*). In accentual langs. such as Eng., exact rhyme will entail the sameness of the final stressed vowel and all following phonemes (see RHYME). Rich rhyme extends sonic similarity back to the preceding consonant, e.g., *may/dismay* or even *may/May*.

The consonant-vowel-consonant likenesses of rich rhyme suggest three general possibilities. First, the rhymed terms may be homophones, with like sound but different spelling and meaning, e.g., *night/knight*, *foul/fowl*, *stare/stair*, or Fr. *violence/balance*. Homographs, with differing sound but like spelling, as in *read / read* (present tense, past tense) or *conflict/conflict* (verb, noun), have affinities with rich rhyme but can be more accurately labeled *eye rhyme since they feature differing vowel sounds. The most extreme case of rich rhyme is the homonym, in which both spelling and sound are alike but meaning significantly differs, e.g., Eng. *want/want* (lack, desire), *port/port* (harbor, wine) or Fr. *été/été* (summer, been).

The term *rich rhyme* derives from a Fr. spectrum of rhyming, from the poor rhyme of *assonance through sufficient and rich rhyme to the even richer *leonine rhyme, which extends rhyming backward over two full syllables (and must be distinguished from the homonymous med. verse form). The Fr. origin of the term suggests its frequency in the lang. The technique appears in quantity in the 15th c. as one of the devices of the *rhétoriqueurs, and Thomas Sébillet gave it the name *rime riche* in 1490. Pierre de Ronsard, Joachim du Bellay, and other poets of the *Pléiade allowed it in moderation. After 1600, rich rhyme fell out of favor in Fr. but was later revived by the romantics, particularly Victor Hugo. Championed subsequently by Théodore de Banville, it was used even more by the *Parnassians.

Chaucer and John Gower, whose Eng. owes much to Fr., employ rich rhyme regularly: *heere/heere* (here /

hear), e.g., and *herte/herte* (hurt/heart). However, since the Ren., in which Thomas Wyatt and Edmund Spenser used rich rhyme regularly, the practice has been quite rare. Many *prosody manuals insist that rich rhyme is impermissible in Eng., to the extent that some give rich rhyme the name "false rhyme." Hollander argues that rich rhyme in Eng. "always must fall ridiculously flat, underlined as the like syllables are by their stressed position. In English *rime très riche* is always in a sense, *rime pauvre*." Small has argued that Eng. resistance to rich rhyme arises more from convention than from actual qualities of the lang., and she finds a surprising prevalence of rich rhyme in Emily Dickinson's verse. Because of its rarity, rich rhyme in Eng. offers an element of surprise that can be used to accentuate semantic meaning. The two rhymed words may be alike in sound, but they can differ with respect to local meaning or usage while also contrasting with the more typical rhymes around them.

Rich rhyme occurs in many other lits., incl. It., Sp., and cl. Ar. *Identical rhyme extends the similitude of rich rhyme to the level of meaning, e.g., *may/may*, where both are the verb. The echo device (see ECHO VERSE) is one species of rich rhyme. Ger. *rührende Reim* is a type of mosaic rich or identical rhyme popular in MHG in which one of the rhyming words is a compound of the other, e.g., Ger. *zeigen/erzeigen*, Fr. *aroi/a roi*, Eng. *mortal/immortal* (see MOSAIC RHYME).

■ T. de Banville, *Petit traité de poésie française* (1872); P. Delaporte, *De la rime française* (1898); Kastner; Schipper, *History*, 273; C. von Kraus, "Der rührende Reim im Mittelhochdeutschen," *ZDA* 56 (1918); Patterson; M. Ito, *John Gower the Medieval Poet* (1976); C. Smith, "On Sound-Patterning in the *Poema de mio Cid*," *Hispanic Review* 44 (1976); Scott; Mazaleyrat; D. Billy, "La Nomenclature des Rimes," *Poétique* 15 (1984); B. de Cornulier, "Rime 'riche' et fonction de la rime," *Littérature* 59 (1985); Hollander; Scherr; C. Scott, *The Riches of Rhyme* (1988); J. J. Small, *Positive as Sound* (1990), ch. 4; G.J. van Gelder, "Rhyme in Maqāmāt," *Journal of Semitic Studies* 44 (1999).

T.V.F. BROGAN; E. RETTBERG

**RIDDLE.** Ancient and worldwide phenomena in both oral trad. (the "folk riddle") and written lit. (the "literary riddle"), riddles take the form of question and answer. Typically, an intentionally misleading question presents an enigma that can be resolved only by a clever "right" answer. The impulse to dismiss riddle as "a sort of trick question which, once answered, has no further interest—a silly puzzle which, once clarified, self-destructs" (Wilbur) has been refuted by a long trad. of scholarship that treats riddle as a site for central aspects of poetry and poetics, incl. *metaphor, wordplay, *paradox, and *imagery.

In a "true riddle," the question presents a description, which usually describes something in terms of something else, and a "block element," a contradiction or confusion that disrupts the initial description. E.g., the riddle "What plows and plows, but no furrow remains" first appears to describe a plow, then blocks that answer by eliminating the effect of a plow. The implicit answer to this riddle—a ship—arises only after the listener or reader suppresses the initial response and thinks of another object to which the verb *plow* might apply. Such riddles are essentially metaphors with one term concealed, pointing out both similarities and differences between the terms. Some metaphorical riddles leave the block element implicit: "Back of the village sit those who have donned white kerchiefs" (fence posts, each with a cap of snow). Other kinds of riddles rely on puns—"What turns without moving" (milk)—or on anomalies in the laws of nature—"I tremble at each breath of air, / And yet can heaviest burdens bear" (water).

The folk riddle tends to appear in structured social occasions, from children's games to adult rituals like courtship in tribal South Africa and funeral wakes in the West Indies. A number of other kinds of enigmatic questions associated with riddle also occur in social ritual: e.g., biblical riddles, which describe a character in the Bible; the joking questions known as "conundrums," e.g., "How is a duck like an icicle? Both grow down"; wisdom questions, as in a catechism; charades, which describe a word syllable by syllable; and parody forms such as the catch-riddle, which tricks the answerer into an embarrassing answer.

Literary riddle brings literary ambitions to the basic form of folk riddle, tending toward longer and more elaborate expression. In contrast to folk riddles, literary riddles may use abstractions as topics (e.g., creation, humility, death, wisdom), exploit the device of *prosopopoeia*, delight in obscene suggestions, and even give away the answer in the text or title.

The literary riddle has a long hist., appearing in Sanskrit, in which the cosmological riddles of the *Rig Veda* go back to the early first millennium BCE; in Heb., where a trad. of literary riddles runs from the OT and Talmud through the Heb. poetry of med. Spain, incl. the poetry of Dunash Ibn Labrat (10th c.) and Jehudah Halevi (ca. 1074–1141); in Gr., esp. in the *Greek Anthology* and in Byzantine lit.; in Ar., from the 10th c. to the present, the most famous Ar. riddlemaster being Al-Ḥarīrī (ca. 1050–1120); in Persian lit. extending from the 10th and 11th cs. through the 16th, incl. the epic *Shāhnāma* of Firdawsī (b. 940); and perhaps in Chinese, where evidence, though no discovered text, suggests literary riddling in the 12th and 13th cs. A rich med. trad. began in Europe with 100 Lat. riddles by Symphosius (5th c.). In England, Aldhelm (640–709) wrote 100 riddles in Anglo-Lat. hexameters (*Enigmata*), contributing to the genre of the etymological riddle, which uses the text of the riddle to explore the Lat. name of the answer. The riddles of the OE Exeter Book (ca. 10th c.), which feature involved riddling descriptions of everyday things, are exemplary and have been the focus of much critical consideration. The Ren. was another productive period for the literary riddle, particularly in Italy. Later writers attracted to riddles include Miguel de Cervantes, Jonathan Swift, Friedrich Schiller, Heinrich Heine, and Emily Dickinson.

These instances of the riddle genre can be distinguished from a pervasive literary mode of riddling at work in a bevy of other genres incl. "sacred writing, . . . tragedy, comedy, romance, lyric kinds, even the novel," as Cook has noted. Indeed, the conjunction and disjunction of implicitly compared terms in riddle suggest poetic *metaphor, as Aristotle argued in the *Rhetoric*: "metaphors imply riddles, and therefore a good riddle can furnish a good metaphor." Frye, in *Anatomy of Criticism*, associates riddle with visual imagery, arguing that "the radical of *opsis* in the lyric is *riddle*," and Welsh treats the visual imagery of riddles as the basis for a theory of the roots of *lyric poetry. Wilbur observes that the visual suggestions in the question of a riddle imprint themselves on readers' minds, a mental quirk that gives the metaphoric pairings of riddles more impact: "If someone says to me, *think of a white bird*, a white bird appears in my mind's eye; if I am then told to forget about the bird, I find that its image will not go away."

The dialogic structure of even literary riddle suggests social interaction, "a competition between the riddler and the riddlees" (Pagis). As such, a riddle holds in social and literary tension the meaning it conceals and the meaning it reveals. "The deliberate obscurity of riddles," Tiffany argues, "does not imply the absence of disclosure or sociability." The process of mental concentration and play that riddles demand, in fact, can instruct: children, e.g., explore the ling. and cognitive systems of their cultures through riddle contests (McDowell).

Riddles, in fact, model *defamiliarization, the poetic process of making the world strange that Viktor Shklovsky treated as central to the literary imagination. The first term of the question is made strange by the block element, and once an answer arrives, both terms are made strange in relation to each other. As Tiffany has argued, a riddle "withholds the name of a thing, so that the thing may appear as what it is not, in order to be revealed for what it is." The figurative operations of riddle, then, have suggested compressed instances of the operations of poetic imagery and wordplay. The task of discerning the connections and disjunctions of lang. and meaning that the interpreter of riddles undertakes, far from a passing triviality or a forgettable joke, mirrors the process of literary *interpretation itself.

*See* EMBLEM, KENNING, WIT.

■ *The Demaundes Joyous* (1511; rpt. 1971)—first mod. Eng. riddle book; J. B. Friedrich, *Geschichte des Räthsels* (1860); K. Ohlert, *Rätsel und Gesellschaftsspiel der alten Griechen*, 2d ed. (1886); W. Schultz, "Rätsel," Pauly-Wissowa; W. Schultz, *Rätsel aus dem hellenischen Kulturkreise* (1909–12); *The Riddles of Aldhelm*, trans. J. H. Pitman (1925); M. De Filippis, *The Literary Riddle in Italy to the End of the Sixteenth Century* (1948); A. Taylor, *The Literary Riddle before 1600* (1948), and *English Riddles from Oral Tradition* (1951); M. De Filippis, *The Literary Riddle in Italy in the Seventeenth Century* (1953); V. Hull and A. Taylor, *A Collection of Irish Riddles* (1955); Frye; K. Wagner, "Rätsel," *Reallexikon II*; J. F. Adams, "The Anglo-Saxon Riddle as Lyric Mode," *Criticism* 7 (1965); D. Bhagwat, *The Riddle in Indian Life, Lore and Literature* (1965); C. T. Scott, *Persian and Arabic Riddles* (1965); A. Hacikyan, *A Linguistic and Literary Analysis of Old English Riddles* (1966); M. De Filippis, *The Literary Riddle in Italy in the Eighteenth Century* (1967); D. D. Lucas, *Emily Dickinson and Riddle* (1969); C. T. Scott, "On Defining the Riddle," *Genre* 2 (1969); R. Finnegan, *Oral Literature in Africa* (1970), ch. 15; R. D. Abrahams and A. Dundes, "Riddles," *Folklore and Folklife*, ed. R. M. Dorson (1972); *Deutsches Rätselbuch*, ed. V. Schupp (1972); I. Basgöz and A. Tietze, *Bilmece: A Corpus of Turkish Riddles* (1973); J. Lindow, "Riddles, Kennings, and the Complexity of Skaldic Poetry," *Scandinavian Studies* 47 (1975); N. Frye, "Charms and Riddles," *Spiritus Mundi* (1976); *JAF* 89.352 (1976)—special iss. on riddles and riddling; *The Old English Riddles of the Exeter Book*, ed. C. Williamson (1977); Welsh; J. H. McDowell, *Children's Riddling* (1979); C. Williamson, *A Feast of Creatures* (1982); *Riddles Ancient and Modern*, ed. M. Bryant (1983); W. J. Pepicello and T. A. Green, *The Language of Riddles* (1984); D. Sadovnikov, *Riddles of the Russian People* (1986); R. Wilbur, "The Persistence of Riddles," *Yale Review* 78 (1989); D. Pagis, "Toward a Theory of the Literary Riddle," *Untying the Knot*, ed. G. Hasan-Rokem and D. Shulman (1996)—useful ed. collection; R. Wehlau, *The Riddle of Creation* (1997); E. Cook, *Engimas and Riddles in Literature* (2006); D. Tiffany, *Infidel Poetics* (2009).

A. WELSH; E. RETTBERG

**RIME RICHE.** *See* IDENTICAL RHYME; RHYME; RICH RHYME.

**RÍMUR** (pl.; sing. *ríma*). A form of stanzaic narrative poetry, cognate with the ME *rime*, surviving from the mid-14th c. *Rímur* are Icelandic poems in multiple fits, a *ríma* having only one. More than a thousand such poems survive, most still unpub. The four-line Lat. *hymn stanza was adapted to include *alliteration and the complicated poetic vocabulary of *kenning and *heiti* borrowed from skaldic poetry. While the most popular meter was *ferskeytt* ("squared meter," four lines; the first and third lines have seven syllables, and the second and fourth have six, rhyming *abab*), 22 different varieties developed, and it became traditional that no two consecutive fits should be in the same meter. Two- and three-line stanzas appeared, and internal rhymes became increasingly intricate, as did the complex technical vocabulary associated with rímur metrics. Subject matter was wide-ranging, but adaptations of stories set in ancient Scandinavia (*fornaldarsögur*) or adaptations of chivalric romances (*riddarasögur*) were esp. favored. Emphasis was on action and adventure, and the rímur were never popular with the ecclesiastical and intellectual elite. Among the most prolific rímur poets were Guðmundur Bergþórsson (1657–1705; 14 rímnaflokkar, "sets of rímur," incl. *Olgeirs rímur danska*, 60 fits, pub. 1948 in two v.) and Sigurður Breiðfjörð (1798–1846; 27 rímnaflokkar). Steinunn Finnsdóttir (ca. 1641–1710) is the earliest known woman rímur poet. Rímur were the most popular literary form in Iceland until well into the 19th c., being performed esp. during the rural evening work period (*kvöldvaka*) and in the win-

ter fishing camps (*verbúðir*). They were chanted, not read, and a good *kvæðamaður* (chanter of rímur) was always in demand. The *chant melodies (*stemmur*) reentered popular music thanks to the efforts of Sveinbjörn Beinteinsson (1924–1993), followed by Steindór Andersen (b. 1954) and the band Sigur Rós.

*See* ICELAND, POETRY OF.

■ *Sýnisbók íslenzkra rímna*, ed. W. A. Craigie, 3 v. (1952)—a sampling from all periods but no apparatus.
■ **Rímur before 1600**: *Riddararímur*, ed. T. Wisén (1881); *Rímnasafn*, ed F. Jónsson, 2 v. (1905–21) with *Ordbog* (1926–28); *Íslenzkar miðaldarímur*, ed. Ó. Halldórsson, 4 v. (1973–75); *Skíðaríma*, ed. T. Homan (1975).
■ **Rímur after 1600**: H. Sigurðsson, *Safn til bragfræði íslenzkra rímna* (1891)—metrical terms and meters; B. K. Þórólfsson, *Rímur fyrir 1600* (1934)—the standard study; *Rit Rímnafélagsins*, ed. B. K. Þórólfsson et al., 11 v. (1948–76), S. Breiðfjörð, *Rímnasafn*, 6 v. (1971–73)—15 of his rímnaflokkar). F. Sigmundsson, *Rímnatal I–II* (1966)—catalog of poems and poets; S.F.D. Hughes, "Report on Rímur," *JEGP* 79 (1980) and "Rímur," *Dictionary of the Middle Ages*, ed. J. R. Strayer, v. 10 (1989)—intros. in Eng.; G. Ólafsson, *Silfurplötur Iðunnar* (2004)—stemmur collected 1930–36 (incl. four CDs).

S.F.D. HUGHES

**RING COMPOSITION.** A structural principle or rhetorical device in which an element or series of elements is repeated at the beginning and at the end of a poem or narrative unit, thus comprising a "ring" framing a nonannular core. Van Otterlo, the pioneer in this branch of literary study, distinguished between simple framing structures, in which a single repeating element encloses the core material in the pattern *a-x-a*, and annular systems, in which the core material is set off by two or more concentric rings, e.g., *a-b-c-x-c-b-a*. The repeating elements in an annular system are chiastically ordered. Thus, ring composition provides a mechanism for configuring circles into the production and reception of linear narratives. The terms *ring structure*, *envelope pattern* (see ENVELOPE), *framing*, and *chiasmus* often refer to the same figure.

Ring composition operates on several scales. Sometimes lexical repetition encapsulates a passage comprising a few lines, a stanza, a fit, or a short poem; longer episodes or digressions are usually marked off by annular patterns of greater complexity. In their most expanded and intricate forms, ring systems can organize entire *epic poems, as Whitman has argued for the *Iliad* and Niles for *Beowulf*. Rings can be made up of repeating material of various sorts—individual words or word roots, themes, images, *motifs, or even elaborate narrative sequences. To function successfully as a ring marker, however, the convention of repetition must be sufficiently recognizable within the trad. or the repeating element sufficiently developed within the poem to enable listeners or readers to recognize the recurrence.

Ring composition possibly arose in response to mnemonic necessity: it provided oral poets with a powerful compositional technique and aural audiences with a means of keeping track of the movement of the story. Structurally, it can function in two ways: (1) to connect the ring-encapsulated passage or episode with the larger story or (2) to create coherence within such a passage. Yet its usefulness can be exaggerated, since the particular pattern that ring composition imposes cannot easily accommodate nonpaired repetitions, linear plot progressions, and other nonsymmetrical movements. A perspicuous lit. hist. of ring composition cannot yet be written, as its incidence has been thoroughly examined in relatively few genres and historical periods, although this list has been rapidly expanding. The governing scholarly assumption has been that ring composition serves the intellectual and stylistic economies of oral-based composition. This assumption has been validated by the high incidence of the device in the oral or oral-derived poetries (particularly epic and narrative) of the ancient Greeks and Anglo-Saxons. In these two fields, research into ring composition under varying rubrics originated independently during the 1930s and 1940s. On the other hand, it had long been known among Celtic scholars that ancient Ir. and Welsh poets made extensive use of a ring device called *dúnad(h)*, which requires that a poem begin and end with the same word. From the latter part of the 20th c. on, the device has been documented in other works and trads. arising out of close association with an oral background, such as the OF *chanson de geste*, the MHG *Nibelungenlied*, 20th-c. Yugoslav oral epic, Scottish balladry, the Zoroastrian Avesta, cl. Ar. poetry, the Gospels, Paul's epistles, and the Heb. Tanakh. Increasingly, ring composition has been found in various texts from a wide range of lit. trads.

The discovery of ring composition in Laurence Sterne's *Tristram Shandy*, Ezra Pound's *Cantos*, and other mod. and highly literate works has suggested that it might fill more uses over a broader literary spectrum than had been hitherto suspected. Some scholars have hypothesized that the use of such an intricate structure as ring composition might in fact suggest the later reorganization of earlier oral material, rather than simply being a remnant of oral-based composition. Douglas has argued that mod. readers are so accustomed to the assumption of linear composition that ring composition poses a serious obstacle to comprehension. According to this argument, ring composition is associated with a fundamentally different method of constructing and extracting meaning.

*See* CONCATENATION, CORONA, ORAL POETRY.

■ A. C. Bartlett, *The Larger Rhetorical Patterns in Anglo-Saxon Poetry* (1935); W. van Otterlo, *De Ringcompositie als Opbouwprincipe in de epische Gedichten van Homerus* (1948); C. Whitman, *Homer and the Heroic Tradition* (1958); P. L. Henry, "A Celtic-English Prosodic Feature," *ZCP* 29 (1962–64); J. Gaisser, "A Structural Analysis of the Digressions in the *Iliad* and the *Odyssey*," *Harvard Studies in Classical Philology* 73 (1969); D. Buchan, *The Ballad and the Folk* (1972); J. D. Niles, *Beowulf* (1983); B. Fenik, *Homer and the "Nibelungenlied"* (1986); A. B. Lord, "The Merging of Two Worlds," *Oral Tradition in Literature*, ed. J. M. Foley (1986); W. Parks, "Ring Structure and Narrative Embedding in Homer and Beowulf," *NM* 89 (1988); K. Stanley, *The Shield of Homer: Narrative Structure in the "Iliad"* (1993); C. G. Thomas and E. K. Webb, "From Orality to Rhetoric: An Intellectual Transformation," *Persuasion: Greek Rhetoric in Action*, ed. I. Worthington (1994); J. D. Harvey, *Listening to the Text: Oral Patterning in Paul's Letters* (1998); M. Douglas, *Thinking in Circles: An Essay on Ring Composition* (2007).

W. W. PARKS; S. S. BILL

**RISING AND FALLING RHYTHM.** *Rising rhythm* typically refers to groups of syllables or words in which the relative stress or the general stress contour moves from lighter to heavier, and *falling rhythm* designates the opposite movement, or directionality, from heavier to lighter syllables. In traditional Eng. prosody, *iambs and *anapests indicate a rising pattern, while *trochees and *dactyls indicate a falling one. *Rising rhythm* and *falling rhythm* are sometimes used as if they were synonymous with iambic and trochaic meters and trads., respectively, but directionality of meter does not necessarily define directionality of rhythm in a given passage or poem.

Historically, the interest in rhythmical directionality emerged, in fact, partly out of dissatisfaction with *foot analysis itself (see Hopkins). In poetic practice, rising and falling rhythms often move against the patterns of the feet, as occurs in "inversions" and other metrically allowed substitutions; but, more important, word or phrase rhythms may cut across foot boundaries and thus create rhythmic ambiguity or neutrality even within a metrical context. A polysyllabic word with a final falling rhythm, e.g., may straddle two iambs in a line, or a phrase with a rising rhythm may spread across the boundaries of several trochaic feet. The abundance of such rhythmic ambiguities within regular metrical lines from all periods—one writer claims as much as 45 percent of the *accentual-syllabic trad. cannot be clearly classified as rising or falling rhythm (Stewart)—may thus argue against the foot being the most important unit of perceived rhythm (Creek). Headless or *catalectic lines are also prone to ambiguous directionality in their meter, since schematically the only difference between a headless iambic line and a catalectic trochaic line is where foot boundaries are drawn.

In spite of these ambiguities, it has been almost universally acknowledged since at least the 16th c. that verse in rising meters differs in important and perceptible ways from that in falling meters. Most characterize the rhythm of poetry in iambic meter, at any rate, as more subtle, complex, and variable than that of poetry in trochaic meter, which has been described as more heavily stressed, insistent, inflexible, and even strained, unnatural, or against the grain of the lang. Some have noted that these qualities of verse in falling meters closely resemble those of the accentual trad. in popular verse. Mod. empirical studies have pointed to measurable differences between rising and falling rhythms, suggesting that the ratio of duration between stressed and unstressed syllables in groupings with a falling rhythm is close to 1:1, while that for syllables in a rising rhythm is approximately twice that, 2:1. In metrical terms, this means that tro-chees are perceived as shorter than iambs and have less variety of syllable length, but while stress in rising rhythms is thus tied to greater stress length, in fall-ing rhythm stress is tied to perceived greater intensity (see Chatman and Newton). Accordingly, the mere perception of a longer stressed syllable seems to en-courage perceptual grouping of that syllable with pre-ceding ones, while a perception of greater intensity in a stressed syllable encourages perceptual grouping of that syllable with ones that follow it (Woodrow), making the stresses in falling rhythms intrinsically tied to perceived intensity of stress. Also, beat inter-vals in falling rhythm, like those in accentual verse, seem to tend toward perceptual, if not actual, *iso-chronism, whereas beat intervals in rising rhythms are less regular and more modulated (see Woodrow and Newton). While not entirely uncontested, such studies seem at the very least to corroborate the sense that there is a significant difference between the two rhythms.

But is rising meter somehow more "natural" to the lang., as common opinion and the great predominance in Eng. of the iambic meter over all other alternatives seem to suggest? The linguistic evidence is mixed. Ris-ing rhythm seems to be the fundamental tendency in Eng. *phrase* construction, with the greatest phonologi-cal prominence ordinarily falling on the final stressed syllable of a phrase or syntactical unit. Falling rhythms, however, are far more common than rising ones in polysyllabic Eng. *words*, esp. disyllables. The play of lexical rhythms (generally falling) within and across phrasal rhythms (generally rising) does, in short, seem to be a part of the rhythmic texture of Eng., and, owing to the language's analytic character, in which phrase is more fundamental than inflected word, the rising, phrasal tendency might reasonably be thought to offer a natural base for meter. On the other hand, if falling rhythms are somehow akin to accentual verse, with its roots in the early hist. of the lang. and the continu-ing trad. of popular poetry, it might be argued that the iambic trad., adapted from continental syllabism and cl. meters, is less native to the origins of Eng., though perhaps equally as natural to its post-Norman, hybrid character (see Tarlinskaja).

In any case, skillful interweaving of the rising and falling rhythmic strands intrinsic to the language's mod. texture is surely in part responsible for the complexity and nuance that most attribute to sophis-ticated art verse. Much of the directional ambiguity of many lines in the trad. should thus be appreciated as carefully modulated, balanced, or *counterpointed rhythm. Tabulations of verse in the trad. suggest that verse written in rising rhythms really has tended to exhibit more variations and contrasting internal rhythms such as initial and mid-line inversions as well as countermetrical rhythmic groupings falling across foot boundaries than trochaic and dactylic verse (Has-call, Halpern, Newton). Some reasons for this might be found in the intrinsic linguistic and perceptual dif-ferences discussed above. Even so, poets such as Rob-ert Browning and P. B. Shelley have written varied

and complex verse in falling meters (Kiparsky), and the relatively less modulated quality of verse in fall-ing meters in the metrical trad. may owe as much to conventional preconceptions about the character of the two kinds of rhythm as to properties inherent in them.

*See* ACCENTUAL VERSE, COUNTERPOINT, DURATION, IAMBIC, METER, RHYTHM, TROCHAIC.

■ H. Woodrow, *Quantitative Study of Rhythm* (1909); H. L. Creek, "Rising and Falling Rhythm in English Verse," *PMLA* 35 (1920); G. R. Stewart, *The Technique of English Verse* (1930); G. M. Hopkins, "Author's Preface," *Poems and* Prose, ed. W. H. Gardner (1953); M. Halpern, "On the Two Chief Metrical Modes in English," *PMLA* 77 (1962); Chatman; Chomsky and Halle; D. L. Hascall, "Trochaic Meter," *CE* 33 (1971); P. Kiparsky, "Stress, Syntax, and Meter," *Lang* 51 (1975); R. Newton, "Trochaic and Iambic," *Lang & S* 8 (1975); Attridge, *Rhythms*; M. Tarlinskaja, *Shakespeare's Verse* (1987).

P. WHITE

**RISPETTO.** An It. stanza of variable length, usually ranging from 6 to 12 lines in *hendecasyllables, but most commonly an octave rhyming *ababbcc*, and for this reason often confused with the *Sicilian octave (*abababab*) and the Tuscan variety of the *strambotto*. Some variation in the form occurs in the last four verses or *ripresa*, which came to have two rhyming *couplets of different rhymes, giving *ababccdd*. Originally a form of Tuscan popular poetry, the *rispetto* came to be used throughout Italy. The content is generally amatory hence the name, "respect," i.e., honor paid the be-loved woman. In the 15th c., Leonardo Giustiniani, Angelo Poliziano (Politian), and Lorenzo de' Medici wrote series of *rispetti*; in mod. times, Giosuè Carducci composed many, and Giovanni Pascoli included a number of them in his *Myricae*. The possible connec-tion of the rispetto to the Fr. *respit* is not likely, given the difference in subject matter, generally amatory in the former and didactic in the latter.

*See* OTTAVA RIMA.

■ H. Schuchardt, *Ritornell und Terzine* (1875); G. Lega, *Rispetti antichi pubblicati da un codice magliabechiano* (1905); M. Barbi, *Poesia popolare italiana* (1939); *Ris-petti e strambotti del Quattrocento*, ed. R. Spongano (1971); Spongano; Wilkins; F. P. Memmo, *Dizionario di metrica italiana* (1983); Elwert, *Italienische*, sect. 98; S. Orlando, *Manuale di metrica italiana* (1994).

L. H. GORDON; C. KLEINHENZ

**RITORNELLO** (also *ripresa*). A group of lines (from one to four or more) in a variety of meters (*quinario* through *endecasillabo*) that introduce an It. *ballata* and that are repeated as a *refrain at the end of each stanza. The last line (sometimes the last two lines) of each stanza is linked through rhyme to the *ritornello*, thereby providing a sort of metrical "return" to the refrain. The ritornello may have begun as a *ritornello intercalare*, an exclamation from the congregation in response to the priest who was reading a psalm or se-quence. In most instances, the ritornello expresses in concise terms either an emotional response to or the essence of the idea or action treated in the stanza or the poem as a whole. Since the ritornello serves as the refrain of a ballata, the number of lines in the ritornello determines the name applied to each variety of this lyric form: one-line ritornello, *ballata piccola*; two-line, *ballata minore*; three-line, *ballata mezzana*; four-line, *ballata grande* (the most common form); five-line (or more), *ballata stravagante*.

*See* ITALIAN PROSODY, LAUDA.

■ H. Schuchardt, *Ritornell und Terzine* (1875); F. Flamini, *Notizia storica dei versi e metri italiani* (1919); L. Castelnuovo, *La metrica italiana* (1979); F. P. Memmo, *Dizionario di metrica italiana* (1983); S. Orlando, *Manuale di metrica italiana* (1994).

L. H. GORDON; C. KLEINHENZ

**ROCOCO.** Taken from art hist., *rococo* was invented by the engraver Charles-Nicolas Cochin *fils* in the mid-18th c. to designate pejoratively the *style rocaille* in Louis XV furniture and interior decoration. Although poets composed rococo works as early as 1660, the heyday of the style extends from 1685 to 1770. Thematically, rococo poetry celebrates seduction and inconstancy (Guillaume Amfrye de Chaulieu, Alexis Piron, John Gay, Paolo Rolli, J.W.L. Gleim), anacreontic conviviality (Friedrich von Hagedorn, Voltaire, Giuseppe Parini, William Congreve, Carlo Frugoni), and frivolity (C. M. Wieland, Jean Dorat, Matthew Prior). Rather than honoring grand passion, e.g., rococo poets immortalize luxury items such as snuff boxes and tiny objets d' art, pet birds and lap dogs, tobacco and coffee. In *tone, rococo writing is often humorous but opts for a smile rather than laughter. Rococo writers explicitly avoid seriousness and mortality while concentrating on entertainment in the here and now. Formally, monotony is avoided by keeping the poems short or employing seemingly negligent *variation (use of the *genre mêlé* [e.g., mixing poetry and prose in the same piece] and verse with irregular *rhyme schemes and line lengths; mixing formal *diction with colloquialism). Although rococo poetry has been termed "feminine" because of its charm, grace, delicacy, and refinement, on a deeper level it is often misogynistic and even misanthropic. Not only are rococo poets overwhelmingly male, but women are depicted in ways consonant with the *querelle des femmes* (quarrel of women, the med. and early mod. dispute between critics and defenders of women): as frivolous, chatty, inconstant, erotic, passive, and even inanimate sex objects (see, e.g., Stanislas, Chevalier de Boufflers's poem "La Bergère"). Typically, women are undressed coquettes, while men are silk-clad beaux. The style also includes *mock-heroic poems such as Jean-Baptiste Gresset's *Ver-Vert* and Alexander Pope's *Rape of the Lock*.

*See* BAROQUE, PREROMANTICISM.

■ W. Sypher, *Rococo to Cubism in Art and Literature* (1960); S. Atkins, "Zeitalter der Aufklärung," *Fischer-Lexicon: Literatur*, ed. W.-H. Friedrich and W. Willy, v. 2 (1965); A. Anger, *Literarisches Rococo*, 2d ed. (1968), "Rokokodichtung," *Reallexikon II*, v. 3; H. Hatzfeld, *The Rococo: Eroticism, Wit, and Elegance in European Lit-*erature (1972); H. Zeman, *Die deutsche anakreontische Dichtung* (1972); I. Magnani, "Premesse allo studio del Rococò letterario in Italia," *Studi e Problemi di Critica Testuale* 15 (1977); H. Hatzfeld, "L'Esprit rococo dans la poésie du XVIIIe siècle," *Mélanges à la mémoire de Franco Simone*, v. 2, ed. H. Gaston Hall (1981); P. Brady, *Rococo Poetry in English, French, German, Italian* (1992); S. D. Nell, "Looks Can Be Deceiving: The *Trompe-l'Oeil* Poetics of French Rococo Style," *L'Esprit Créateur* 33 (1993); *Visual and Transient Love: An Anthology of Rococo Poetry in English, French, German, Italian*, ed. P. Brady (1995); S. D. Nell, "The Last Laugh: Carnivalizing the Feminine in Piron's 'La Puce,'" *Carnivalizing Difference*, ed. P. Barta et al. (2001); P. Chézaud, "Baroque et sensualisme: Le Rococo et la pensée anglaise au XVIIIe siècle," *Bulletin de la Société d'Etudes Anglo-Américaines des XVIIe et XVIIIe Siècles* 54 (2002); D. T. Gies, "Más sobre el erotismo rococó en la poesía española del XVIII," *Actas del XIV Congreso de la Asociación Internacional de Hispanistas III*, ed. A. Alonso, I. Lerner, R. Nival (2004); K. Ireland, *Cythera Regained? The Rococo Revival in European Literature and the Arts, 1830–1910* (2006).

S. D. NELL

**ROMANCE** (Sp., *ballad). The *romance* is the simplest and most common fixed form in Sp. poetry. It is usually written in octosyllabic verse in which the even lines assonate alike and the odd-numbered are left free. In the *romance doble*, the odd-numbered lines have one *assonance and the even-numbered another. Other variations of the basic form (even some having a periodic *refrain) have at times been popular. The learned and the semilearned—and probably even the illiterate—produce these ballads wherever Sp. is spoken, and scholars collect them by the hundreds. They reflect almost every phase of Sp. life. Since many of them are anonymous and have been transmitted largely in oral form, their origin and complete hist. cannot be traced. The earliest known written romances date from the early 15th c. In the early 16th c., *romanceros* (collections devoted exclusively to ballads) began to appear, the first (1545–50?) being the famous *Cancionero de romances*—often called the *Cancionero sin año* because it bears no date of publication—by Martin Nucio in Antwerp. The most convenient classification of romances—that summarized by S. G. Morley and adapted from those of Agustin Durán, Ferdinand Wolf and Conrad Hofmann, and Manuel Milà i Fontanals—covers the period from the 15th through the 17th c. It corresponds, with the exception of the *romances vulgares*, to three periods of creation—traditional, erudite, and artistic: (1) the anonymous *romances viejos*, primitive or traditional ballads, usually on historical themes and thought to be among the earliest; (2) the 15th- and early 16th-c. *romances juglarescos*, minstrel ballads, "longer and more personal, but still supported by tradition"; (3) *romances eruditos*, erudite ballads, written by known authors after 1550 and based on old chronicles; (4) *romances artisticos*, artistic ballads, usually lyric, on varied themes, and written by known poets from the late 15th c. through the 17th c.; and (5) the crude *romances vulgares*, blind beggar ballads, from about 1600 on. Large numbers of orally transmitted romances were collected in the Americas and abroad by such scholars as Samuel G. Armistead and Joseph Silverman (Sephardic), Manuel da Costa Fontes (Port.), and others. A strong impulse to romance composition emerged in the early 20th c. with Federico García Lorca, who used the form for expressing complex emotions.

The *romance heroico*, also called *romance endecasílabo* or *romance real*, is a romance in Italianate *hendecasyllables. A romance in lines of fewer than eight syllables is called *romancillo*. One variation of the romance is the *corrido* (ballad with guitar accompaniment), esp. popular in Mexico. The *jácara* is a romance in which the activities of ruffians are recounted, usually in a boisterous manner.

■ E. Mérimée and S. G. Morley, *A History of Spanish Literature* (1930); E. Honig, *García Lorca* (1944); S. G. Morley, "Chronological List of Early Spanish Ballads," *HR* 13 (1945); A. Barea, *Lorca: The Poet and His People* (1949); Le Gentil; R. Menéndez Pidal, *Romancero hispánico*, 2 v. (1953); *Romancero y poesía oral*, v. 4: *El romancero hoy: Historia, comparatismo, bibliografía crítica*, ed. S. G. Armistead et al. (1979); Navarro; L. Mirrer, "The Characteristic Patterning of 'Romancero' Language," *HR* 55 (1987); *Spanish Ballads*, trans. R. Wright (1987); F. G. Lorca, *Romancero Gitano* and *Lorca's "Romancero Gitano": Eighteen Commentaries*, both ed. H. Ramsden (1988); W. H. González, "La dicción formularia en el corrido," *Oral Tradition and Hispanic Literature*, ed. M. M. Caspi (1995); J. Gornall, "Assonance in the Hispanic Romance: Precept and Practice," *MLR* 90 (1995); A. González, "El romance: transmisión oral y transmisión escrita," *Acta Poética* 26 (2005); R. Marrero-Fente, "Romances y coplas relacionados con la conquista de México," *Poesía satírica y burlesca en la Hispanoamérica colonial*, ed. I Arellano and A. Lorente Medina (2009).

D. C. CLARKE

**ROMANIA, POETRY OF.** Poetry is one of the few areas of Romanian culture in which one notices a kind of organic continuity over the centuries. The earliest surviving texts of Romanian poetry date from the 17th c. In the 17th and 18th cs., Romanian poetry is chiefly of three kinds. The first is religious poetry, esp. verse trans. of biblical books. Thus, Dosoftei, a learned Moldavian clergyman, translated the Psalms (1673) in rhymed *couplets of variable length that indicate equally the influence of Romanian oral folk verse and of classicist Polish poetry (see POLAND, POETRY OF). The second is *occasional verse following Western models—*elegies, *odes, pattern poetry, and *epigrams. The most prominent example is by the historian and statesman Miron Costin (1633–91), whose *Viața lumii* (The World's Life, ca. 1672) is a meditation on the vanity of life and the mutability of fortune, written in rhymed couplets of 12 or 13 syllables in irregular meter. The third kind is represented by a wide variety of historical chronicles in verse that flourished in the 18th c. in the southern principality of Wallachia. These

are often polemical, always picturesque, and undoubtedly circulated orally.

The 18th c. also witnessed the culmination of oral folk verse, references to and quotations from which are found already in the 15th and 16th cs. They express in a variety of genres the existential horizon and emotional universe of a stable agrarian society. While steeped in a religiosity that combines a simplified Christianity and a broad pantheistic sacrality, this poetry also preserves some traces of a pre-Roman pagan mythology. Heroic trads. are rendered not in epics but rather in short *ballads. The bulk of folk poetry consists of *doinas*, lyrical expressions of love, loneliness, grief, and yearning, or, less often, glee, carousal, or revolt. Broader visions are provided by the myth of the master-builder Manole, who sacrificed his and his wife's lives to the achievement of a unique building, and particularly by *Miorița*, which is often said to embody a Romanian folk philosophy. It tells the story of a migrant shepherd who, on hearing his companions' plot to murder him, does not defend himself but rather turns the occasion into a grand reconciliation with nature, the stars, and the animals. The popularity of folk poetry declined toward the end of the 19th c., and it had virtually disappeared by the middle of the 20th.

The end of early Romanian lit. was marked by Anton Pann (1796?–1854), who synthesized the oral, didactic, and mythical-historical modes in a mock-naïve style. The decisive turn of Romanian poetry toward Western values and forms occurred in the last two decades of the 18th c. The Wallachian nobleman Ienache Văcărescu (1740?–93) and his two sons wrote gracious and erotic *anacreontic verse on Gr., It., and Fr. models. At almost the same time, in Transylvania, Ion Budai-Deleanu (1760?–1820) wrote a satirical *mock epic of the medieval struggle against the Ottoman Empire.

The first half of the 19th c. in Romanian poetry is characterized by the simultaneous assimilation of Enlightenment, neoclassical, romantic, and *Biedermeier forms and ideas, which led to a number of interesting combinations (see NEOCLASSICAL POETICS, ROMANTIC AND POSTROMANTIC POETRY AND POETICS). Dimitrie Bolintineanu (1819–72) and Grigore Alexandrescu (1814–85) wrote historical ballads, *satires, *fables, and elegies much influenced by Alphonse de Lamartine and Lord Byron. Vasile Alecsandri (1821–90) combined the fervent struggle for democratic reform and national unity common to the generation inspired by the ideals of 1848 radicalism with poetic serenity, a smiling Epicureanism, and a search for cl. balance. He excelled in patriotic verse, natural description, poetic drama, and adaptations of the newly recovered oral trad.

The greatest 19th-c. Romanian poet was Mihai Eminescu (1850–89), who was influenced by the Ger. romantics and by the philosophies of Immanuel Kant and Arthur Schopenhauer. Unfortunate love, social marginality, intense nationalism, mental illness, and early death no less than his towering poetic achievement soon turned Eminescu into a mythic figure. He gave to Romanian poetry the mod. form of its poetic lang. Eminescu's poetry (melancholy meditations on hist., society, sentimental love, and allegory) is founded on a deeper level of mythical cosmology, irrational vision, and subjective pantheism. Eminescu's unpublished work contains huge fragmentary epics that describe the universe as emerging out of the lamentations of universal or divine self-consciousness; he also evoked the pre-Roman society of the Dacians as a pristine, luxuriant, and crystalline world of which later hist. is but a series of deformed copies. Eminescu's radical conservatism was the wellspring for all later forms of nationalism in Romania.

For three decades after Eminescu's death, two poetic schools vied for primacy. One was *symbolism, which appeared largely under Fr. influence; its most important representative was Alexandru Macedonski (1854–1920), a flamboyant artist who believed fervently in aesthetic perfection; his poetry abounds in images of precious stones, fabulous mirages, and morbid obsessions. Ion Minulescu (1881–1944), an able manipulator of grandiloquent images and sentimental intimations, continued the movement. The other school was the populist and idyllic movement mainly advocated by the jour. *Semănătorul*. Its proponents emphasized the use of simple lang. and drew their inspiration from national trads. and local themes. The best poets in this trad. were George Coşbuc (1866–1918), who also produced a superb trans. of Dante's *Divine Comedy*; Octavian Goga (1881–1938), whose best verse expresses a kind of primeval suffering; and Stefan O. Iosif (1875–1913).

The unification of all Romanian provinces following World War I and the beginnings of capitalist democracy favored an unparalleled growth of poetic diversity and power. The Romanian high modernists strove to combine trad. and innovation; the influence of Ger. *expressionism and of Fr. modernists such as Stéphane Mallarmé and Paul Valéry can often be recognized in them. George Bacovia (1881–1957) expressed a universal hopelessness through his austere and obsessive verse, full of images of rain, mud, illness, and provincial dreariness. His poems, inspired by Moldavian towns, evoked a symbolic universe of humidity and putrefaction. Ion Barbu (1895–1961), a mathematician, wrote obscure, semantically packed, tightly structured verse exploring philosophical propositions; for him, the formal order of poetry outlined "a purer, secondary game." In other poems, Barbu indulged his voluptuous pleasure in the verbal thickness of a lush and lurid Balkan world, with its jesters, whores, and sages. Lucian Blaga (1895–1961), philosopher, diplomat, and professor, inquired poetically into the connections between natural reality and transcendent mystery; he evolved from Dionysian rhapsodic tones to praise of the agrarian order as a suggestion of cosmic harmony. Tudor Arghezi (1880–1967) renewed the discourse of Romanian poetry by mixing metaphysics and realism. He is particularly impressive for his astounding thematic range, from pamphleteering virulence, coarse violence, and sexuality to the worlds of children and of wrestling with religious faith and doubt.

In the same generation, there were able traditionalists such as the cultivated neoclassicist Ion Pillat (1891–1945); the natural mystic Vasile Voiculescu (1884–1963); Adrian Maniu (1891–1968), who clothed a decadent weariness in the mock simplicity of folk iconography; and the late neoromantic Alexandru Philippide (1900–79), whose poems abound in cosmic visions and historical nightmares. Among the many nationalist poets of the age, the most prominent was Aron Cotruş (1891–1957), whose messianic thunderings were couched in rolling *free verse and a racy, sonorous vocabulary.

At least as vital and effective was the group of experimentalists, surrealists, and avant-garde radicals who eventually came to influence even Western Eur. poetry. Best known among them was the founder of *Dada, Tristan Tzara (1896–1963), but of comparable distinction were Benjamin Fondane (1898–1944), Ilarie Voronca (1903–46), and Gherasim Luca (1913–1994), all of whom emigrated to France. Gellu Naum (1915–2001) and Saşa Pană (1902–81) were among the chief animators of poetic anarchism, which they aligned with leftist political attitudes. Camil Baltazar (1902–77), with his fluid and melodious verse and his morbid yearning for paradisal innocence, as well as Ion Vinea (1895–1964), with his jazzy rhythms and strident prose inserts, strove to bring experimental poetry closer to the mainstream and to endow it with more finished forms.

The poets who emerged in the later 1930s and 1940s had to suffer the trauma of war and of repeated political upheavals. Some chose exile. Others had to accept long periods of silence. They can be roughly grouped into the Bucharest and the Sibiu schools. The former is exemplified by Ion Caraion (1923–86), Geo Dumitrescu (1920–2004), Dimitrie Stelaru (1917–71), and Constant Tonegaru (1919–52), all ironic pessimists who clamored for adventurous vitality and the demolition of philistine prejudices. Among them Caraion is remarkable for the unrelenting and ferocious darkness of his images. The Sibiu group, exemplified by Radu Stanca (1920–62), the abstractionist Ion Negoiţescu (1921–1993), and above all Stefan Aug Doinaş (1922–2002), eloquently pleaded for the autonomy of culture and the humanizing role of aesthetic production. Doinaş is a consummate craftsman in a wide range of genres and forms, an admirable translator of poetry (e.g., *Faust*), a poet of intense metaphoric creativity, and the author of ethical satire and Neoplatonic visionary evocations.

The establishment of a communist regime in 1947 that suppressed artistic freedoms led to more than a decade of poetic barrenness. Only the more liberal 1960s brought a revival of poetry. Nichita Stănescu (1933–83) became the standard-bearer of a generation devoted to experiment and to a metaphorical version of reality free from ideological interference. Ioan Alexandru's (1941–2000) best verse moved from the cruelty of tragic naturalism toward a kind of religious harmony. Ion Gheorghe (b. 1935) manages to alternate crass primitivism and oracular obscurities with sophisticated lang. games. Mircea Ivănescu (1931–2011) wrote self-analytic elegies in which stream-of-consciousness techniques are applied with lucid irony. Marin Sorescu (1936–1997) dealt in *parody and in the jocular debunking of habit. Leonid Dimov (1926–1987) inaugurated an "oneiric" movement based on dream imagery and associations of verbal music. Despite adverse political pressures, the feeling that the maintenance of high aesthetic standards is crucial for national survival encouraged the continuation of these efforts, either in the direction of lyrical purity, as in the poems of Sorin Mărculescu (b. 1936) and Ana Blandiana (b. 1942), or in the more open discontent and ethical rage of Ileana Mălăncioiu (b. 1940), Mircea Dinescu (b. 1950), and the dissident Dorin Tudoran (b. 1945). Many of these poets were in the forefront of the 1989 anti-Communist revolution. A new generation emerged soon thereafter, led by the postmodernist Mircea Cărtărescu (b. 1955); the cynical, street-wise Florin Iaru (b. 1955); the elegant religious poet Eugen Dorcescu (b. 1942); and Ion Stratan (1955–2005).

Two things should be added. One is that poetic and aesthetic values occupied a much more prominent place in Romanian culture than in the West: lit. was a respected mode of conveying wisdom and social values. The greater poets and movements were flanked for two centuries by hundreds of minor authors, and only an awareness of these can suggest the thick texture of Romanian poetry. The other is that the Romanian territory was hospitable to lit. written by numerous ethnic groups—Hungarian, Serbian, Saxon Ger., Bukowina Jewish, and others. Important literary figures such as Nikolaus Lenau (1802–50) and Paul Celan (1920–70), besides others mentioned above, originated here and can thus round off our understanding of the landscape of Romanian poetry.

■ **Anthologies**: *Rumanian Prose and Verse*, ed. E. D. Tappe (1956); *Anthology of Contemporary Romanian Poetry*, ed. R. McGregor-Hastie (1969); *46 Romanian Poets in English*, ed. and trans. S. Avădanei and D. Eulert (1973); *Antologia poeziei românești*, ed. Z. D. Bușulenga (1974); *Petite anthologie de poésie roumaine moderne*, ed. V. Rusu (1975); *Poezia româna clasică*, ed. A. Piru, 3 v. (1976); *Modern Romanian Poetry*, ed. N. Catanoy (1977); *Poezia romena d'avanguardia: Testi e manifesti da Urmuz a Ion Caraion*, ed. M. Cugno and M. Mincu (1980); *An Anthology of Contemporary Romanian Poetry*, ed. B. Walker and A. Deletant (1984); *Born in Utopia: An Anthology of Modern and Contemporary Romanian Poetry*, ed. C. Firan (2006).

■ **Criticism and History:** E. Lovinescu, *Istoria literaturii române moderne* (1937); B. Munteano, *Modern Romanian Literature* (1939); G. Caliněscu, *Istoria literaturii române* (1940); G. Lupi, *Storia della letteratura romena* (1955); V. Ierunca, "Littérature roumaine," *Histoire des littératures*, ed. R. Queneau, v. 2 (1956); K. H. Schroeder, *Einführung in das Studium des Rumänischen* (1967); C. Ciopraga, *La Personnalité de le littérature roumaine* (1975); *Scriitori români*, ed. M. Zaciu (1978); V. Nemoianu, "The Real Romanian Revolution," *The World and I 6* (1991); I. Negoițescu, *Istoria literaturii române, 1800–1945* (1991), *Scriitori contemporani* (1994); M. Popa, *Istoria literaturii române*

*de azi pe mîine* (2001); A. Stefănescu, *Istoria literaturii române contemporane, 1941–2000* (2005); I. Rotaru, *O istorie a literaturii române de la origini pîna în prezent* (2006); N. Manolescu, *Istoria critică a literaturii române* (2008).

V. P. Nemoianu

**ROMANI POETRY.** The ancestors of today's Roma (Gypsies) left northern India ca. 1000 CE and migrated to Europe and later to other parts of the world. Although traditionally regarded as nomadic, many Roma have been sedentary for generations. Persecution, exclusion, injustice, and poverty have characterized much of Romani hist. and find expression in Romani poetry. Romani, a lang. of Indo-Aryan origin, is spoken by numerous Roma, although many also or only speak the dominant tongue of their surroundings. There is no standard literary form of Romani, but there are many spoken dialects. Romani is the vehicle of both oral and written lit., but Roma also compose poetry in non-Romani langs.

Oral traditional poetry, both ritual and lyric, was the only Romani poetry until the mid-20th c. Ritual wedding songs express joy and bittersweet sorrow, while funeral laments articulate the grief of separation. In this Hungarian-Romani lament, the voice of the deceased cries out in the first two stanzas, while the mourner speaks in the third; a tragic sense of the Romani plight is pervasive:

> To die, to die, one has to die.
> I have to leave my family behind.
> Unfortunate as I am,
> I must perish this way.
>
> I am wandering and cannot find a place
> Where I can put my head down.
> I put my head on the soil
> Look how much I am suffering!
>
> I live, I live, but for what?
> When I do not have a single happy day?
> Oh, my God, it is so bad for me.
> My life is full of mourning.
>
> (Kertész-Wilkinson)

Oral lyric songs at times celebrate the pleasures of family life, but many more tell of hardship, sorrow, and heartache. Roma proverbially claim that a "Gypsy song is a song that expresses pain and suffering."

In the late 1920s and 1930s, with the founding of Romani jours. in the USSR, Romania, and Yugoslavia, Roma began to voice their concerns in written lit. Literary poetry emerged after World War II. It is primarily *lyric, inspired by oral poetry in both form and content; like Romani song, it overwhelmingly expresses pain. The collective anguish of being Romani in a cruel world permeates the poetry, as do metaphors of traveling and forced migration. The Romani soul is often portrayed as finding solace and shelter in nature.

Bronisława Wajs (1910–87) from Poland, known as Papusza (doll), is considered the mother of Romani poetry. She was discovered in the late 1940s by the poet

Jerzy Ficowski, who translated her verse for publication from Romani to Polish. Papusza's "Tears of Blood" is a moving account of how she and fellow Roma suffered in hiding under Ger. occupation in the 1940s. Her most famous poem, "O Land, I am Your Daughter," also autobiographical, evokes nostalgia and her own sense of being Romani and connecting with nature:

Oh land, mine and afforested,
I am she, your daughter.
The woodlands and plains are singing.
The river and I combine our notes
into one Gypsy hymn.
I will go into the mountains
in a beautiful swinging skirt
made of flower petals.
I shall cry out with all my strength . . .

(Hancock et al.)

Because of her association with Ficowski, who became linked to the Polish government's program to settle Roma after the war, Papusza was ostracized in the mid-1950s by the local Romani community and pressured to lay down her pen. A contemporary of Papusza (known primarily for his prose), Mateo Maximoff (1917–99), was a well-known Rus.-Romani author living in France who wrote poetry in both Fr. and Romani.

A new generation of Romani poets emerged in the 1960s and 1970s. In Western Europe, Sandra Jayat (b. 1938) published Fr. verse starting in 1961. José Heredia Maya (1947–2010) was a prominent Romani poet, essayist, and playwright, whose poems in Sp. have appeared since the 1970s. Romani has developed as a written lang.—although with numerous dialects—and is employed esp. by poets from Eastern Europe. One of the best-known cultural figures of this generation was Leksa Manuš (1942–97) of Latvia. He viewed the migrations and constant struggles of his people with wearied, longing eyes, as in his "Roads of the Roma":

Each night, my God, as I close my eyes,
I see before me the roads of the Roma.
But where, my God, is the long-lost road,
the one true road, the one first-traveled?

(Hancock et al.)

Dezider Banga (b. 1939), from Slovakia, published his first volume of lyric poetry in 1964 in Slovak; he has also written in Romani. Rajko Djurić (b. 1947), from Serbia, is a poet and journalist. Writing in Serbian and Romani, he focuses on the hist. and culture of the Roma and depicts the Holocaust and injustices meted out to Roma, often conveying anger and futility in his poems. Originally from Slovakia but presently residing in Belgium, Margita Reiznerová (b. 1945) evokes the burden of persecution in her Romani verse. From Belarus, Valdemar Kalinin (b. 1946) now dwells in England where he writes poetry in Romani and advocates its standardization to unify Roma globally. In Macedonia, where radio and periodicals foster Romani lang. and culture, a circle of poets developed. Šaban Iljaz (b. 1955), from Skopje, is one of

the best known of this group; his verse includes bitter meditations on Romani suffering and forced migration.

Romani authors of the 1980s and 1990s were increasingly involved in social causes, e.g., Béla Osztojkán, from Hungary (b. 1948), a prolific poet (and prose writer) who began publishing verse in 1981. Djura Makhotin (b. 1951), a poet, journalist, and musician from Russia, is also a Romani activist. From Romania, Luminiţa Cioabă (b. 1957) writes in both Romani and Romanian as she embraces the ethnic communities of her world. Among a more recent generation of bards, Alexian Santino Spinelli (b. 1964), a poet, essayist, and musician from Italy, is involved in advancing Romani lang., lit., and music worldwide. Nicolás Jiménes González (b. 1968), from Spain, writes poetry (in Sp.) to promote Romani culture.

While hampered by the lack of a standardized written lang., Romani poets are at the same time part of the wider Eur. trad. and vital instruments in the devel. of genuine Romani culture.

■ **Anthologies**: *Stimme des Romani PEN*, ed. R. Djurić and R. Gilsenbach (1996–); *Littérature*, spec. iss. of *Études Tsiganes* n.s. 9 (1997); *The Roads of the Roma*, ed. I. Hancock, S. Dowd, and R. Djurić (1998).
■ **Criticism and History**: J. Ficowski, *Gypsies in Poland* (1989); N. B. Tomašević et al., *Gypsies of the World* (1990); I. Kertész-Wilkinson, "Song Performance: A Model for Social Interaction among Vlach Gypsies in Southeastern Hungary," *Romani Culture and Gypsy Identity*, ed. T. Acton and G. Mundy (1997); *What is the Romani language?*, ed. P. Bakker and H. Kyuchukov (2001); G. Kurth, *Identitäten zwischen Ethnos und Kosmos* (2008).
■ **Journals**: *Romani Studies* (*Journal of the Gypsy Lore Society*): http://www.gypsyloresociety.org/journal.htm; *Études Tsiganes:* http://www.etudestsiganes.asso.fr/; *Lacio Drom*; *Patrin*: http://reocities.com/Paris/5121/; *Roma*.
■ **Poetry**: B. Osztojkán, *Halak a fekete citeràban* (1981); J. Heredia Maya, *Charol* (1983); S. Jayat, *Nomad Moons*, trans. Ruth Partington (1995); D. Banga, *Slnečný vánok* (1999).

M. H. BEISSINGER

**ROMANSH POETRY.** *See* SWITZERLAND, POETRY OF.

**ROMANTIC AND POSTROMANTIC POETRY AND POETICS**

I. Romantic Poetry and Poetics in the 18th Century
II. 19th-Century Romanticism and Postromanticism

Romantic poetry is a chronologically shifting category whose conception differs not only from nation to nation but often within national trads. The tendency of romantic poetry to elude fixed determination is already apparent in the first explicit definition of its object: "Romantic poetry is a progressive universal poetry" (K.W.F. Schlegel, 1798). Rather than characterizing its aims, content, or style, Schlegel predicates romantic poetry in specifically nonprescriptive terms. Unlike the thrust of his inaugural dictum, Schlegel was, of course, a historically situated critical thinker, whose recognition of *romanticism arose in the wake of pivotal reconceptions of the poetic in the second half of the 18th c.

While the writing of "poetics" in a formulaic or neo-Aristotelian sense had waned by the mid-1700s, theoretical reflection on the fundamental nature and role of poetry became a touchstone for the major philosophical and political, as well as aesthetic, writings of the time. Following the experimental methods advanced in philosophy, natural science, and mathematics by René Descartes, Francis Bacon, Blaise Pascal, G. W. Leibniz, and Isaac Newton, speculation on the "natural" rather than divine origin of humankind's ling. abilities led to a consideration of the essential part played by poetic lang. in human experience and thinking.

## I. Romantic Poetry and Poetics in the 18th Century

A. *France.* An early theory of romantic poetry resulted from the joint investigation of the origins of knowledge and lang. by l'Abée (Etienne Bonnot) de Condillac (1715–80) in the *Essai sur l'origine des connoissances humaines* (1746). Following John Locke's argument against the theory of innate ideas in the *Essay concerning Human Understanding* (1689–90), Condillac argued that ideas themselves stem from perceptions and are known through what Locke called "the signs of our ideas," "words." Yet unlike Locke, who maintained a distinction between signs and ideas of things and submitted that one may dispense with signs in contemplating "the reality of things," Condillac argued that signs are "absolutely necessary" to the primary act of reason, the formation of relations between ideas. The relating of ideas (*la liaison des idées*) through *imagination and reflection is the "single principle" named in the subtitle of the *Essai* as the source of all understanding; thus, Condillac's inquiry into the origin of knowledge necessarily became an inquiry into the origin of the ling. signs by which ideas are related and knowledge is formed. Part Two of the *Essai*, on the "origin and progress of language," sketches a hist. in which "natural signs," or "cries of passion," are slowly replaced by "instituted signs" or "articulate sounds." Music, gesture, and dance all refer back to the natural signs of the passions; *metaphor refers forward to articulate sounds in its attempt to "paint" the passions in words. Situating figurative lang. at the crossroads of articulate sound and natural sensory expression, Condillac's poetic theory (v. 2, ch. 8) hypothesizes that all ling. "style" was originally poetic and that poetry and music, articulated in tandem, formed the passionate lang. in which ancient societies first instituted religion and law.

The influence of Condillac's speculations on the poetic origin of lang. appears most prominently in the romantic poetics formulated by Jean-Jacques Rousseau (1712–78) and Denis Diderot (1713–84). In his *Discours sur l'origine de l'inégalité parmi les hommes* (1754), Rousseau supported Condillac's thesis that the first lang. was one of natural cries and gestures, for which articulate sounds and instituted signs were eventually substituted. The first words, however, are not viewed synesthetically by Rousseau as paintings or copies of gesture and pure sound (see SYNAESTHESIA). Words by nature, Rousseau argued, exist only by common con-

sent and thus paradoxically would already be necessary to the social process by which they are created. On this point, Rousseau took issue with Condillac, whose historical account of the formation of lang. presupposes a kind of preverbal society from which lang. springs.

The link among social relations, lang., and poetics is also established in the *Essai sur l'origine des langues* (written 1750s), in which Rousseau makes the important theoretical distinction between gestures and words. Gestures are viewed in the *Essai* as the products of physical "needs," while words are considered the offspring of "passions" or "moral needs." Lang. owes its origin not to "reasoning" (based on needs) but to "feeling," and the langs. of "the first men" were "the languages of poets." With this consideration, romantic poetry achieves one of its first full formulations: poetry does not follow a prior lang. of natural cries and gestures but is itself identical with lang. in its origin. Man's "first expressions were tropes," a "figurative language" that preceded dispassionate or "proper meanings."

The romantic poetry formulated by Diderot also conjoins the theory of the origin of lang. to questions of natural sentiment and theatricality. In the *Lettre sur les sourds et les müets* (1751), Diderot elaborates an understanding of poetry that pervades his diverse writings, incl. treatises on the technical and natural sciences (primarily in the *Encyclopédie*, 1751–66), lit. crit., aesthetic crit., and philosophy, and works of drama and fiction. Following Condillac, whom he praised and debated in his earlier *Lettre sur les aveugles* (1749), Diderot distinguishes between natural and institutional aspects of lang. In order to exemplify a "natural order of ideas" hypothetically correlative with lang. at its origin, Diderot appeals to the gestures employed by deaf mutes. Rather than speculating that gesture preceded articulate sounds, as argued by Condillac and, in part, by Rousseau, Diderot regards such gestures as ongoing evidence of the natural workings of the soul. These he then relates specifically to poetry. Poetry is closer to gesture and the origin of lang. because it combines many simultaneous ideas. His conception of gesture as an "animal language" lacking any form of subordination leads Diderot to a theory of poetry opposed to the basic successivity of lang. as such. Poetry, he argues, is less a discursive than a synchronous medium; fusing movement and simultaneity, it appeals "all at once" (*toute à la fois*) to the senses, to understanding, and to imagination; rather than rendering verbal, it "paints" the "moving tableau" of "the soul." Diderot describes the combination of movement and stasis in poetry as "a tissue of hieroglyphs superimposed upon each other," a form of lang. that is "emblematic" in the visual sense (see EMBLEM).

B. *Germany.* Like Diderot, G. E. Lessing (1729–81) understood poetry to be naturally dynamic. Yet his landmark theoretical work *Laokoön* (1766) definitively distinguishes plastic from verbal art by the same criteria that Diderot's conceptions of poetry had combined, namely, simultaneity and successivity. Gesture, *hieroglyph, painting, emblem, tableau—the pictorial or plastic terms of Diderotian poetry—are for Lessing spatial metaphors that cloud rather than clarify our understanding of poetry. Departing from an observation regarding the recently rediscovered Laocoön statue made by the cl. scholar and archaeologist J. J. Winckelmann (1717–68), in his widely influential *Gedanken über die Nachahmung der griechischen Werke in der Malerei und Bildhauerkunst* (1755)—to wit, "Laocoön suffers as Sophocles' Philoctetes suffers"—Lessing's *Laokoön* argues why, in actual artistic terms, this can never be the case. For Winckelmann, the statue presents additional evidence of the "noble simplicity and silent greatness" of all Gr. artworks, aesthetic reflections of the supposed balance and serenity of the Gr. soul. By equating the suffering of an apparently self-composed Laocoön with that of Sophocles' dramatic figure, Winckelmann, Lessing argues, overlooks the philological fact that Sophocles devotes whole lines of text to his character's exclamations of anger and groans of pain. The Laocoön statue itself, Lessing reasons further, appears noble solely because its plight is rendered in marble. Winckelmann has taken the effect of the statue's expression for its cause, mistaking a general technical requirement of the plastic arts for a specific psychic reality and failing thereby to distinguish not only between matters of *technē* and *psyche* but between the distinct material realities of the different art forms.

Lessing's argument is directed against not so much Winckelmann nor, certainly, antiquity, but the misleading notion commonly underlying aesthetic theory that "painting is mute poetry, and poetry, speaking painting." Effectively refuting (neoclassical) equations of aesthetic media under the aegis of *ut pictura poesis*, Lessing's technical distinctions between the arts in *Laokoön* provide a first theoretical foundation for a fundamental proposition of romantic poetry, namely, the unequaled power of poetry, at not one but any moment, to free the mind of synchronic representational constraints by setting its "imagination" into motion.

Theory of the origin of lang. was pursued in the *Abhandlung über den Ursprung der Sprache* (1770) of J. G. Herder (1744–1803), who argues equally against divine and mechanistic views of the origin of lang. by asserting that, while humans originally shared the lang. of animals, the inarticulate sounds of pain and passions that, by "natural law" could not be contained within the sufferer, specifically human lang. was formed of a person's unique ability for "reflection," already active within his or her soul even while the person was "mute."

Yet even while disputing his naturalistic account of ling. devel., the *Abhandlung* remains deeply indebted to Condillac's double epistemological emphasis on the function of "reflection" in lang. formation and thus of lang. itself in thought. Herder considers lang. tantamount to reason in its ability to make "distinctions" and recommends that, rather than developing "hypotheses" of its genesis, students of lang. would do better to collect ling. "data" from every age and domain of human life. This comparative and empirical approach to lang. study is later taken up by Wilhelm von Humboldt (1767–1855), one of the early advocates of comparative ling., lit., and anthropology, whose "Einleitung" to *Über die Kawisprache auf der Insel Java* (1836) first proposed what we now call the "Sapir-Whorf" hypothesis, namely, that thinking is largely linguistically determined and that individual langs. constitute distinct mental frameworks for thought. In the *Kawi-Einleitung*, Humboldt also links poetry to music and speculates, like Rousseau before him and G.W.F. Hegel to come, that the "free reign of the spirit" in poetry probably preceded and provoked the "intellectual" institution of prose.

Although he identified ling. competence with reason rather than passion, Herder's interest in poetic lang. was unequivocally romantic, a split commonly attributed to his association with both Immanuel Kant (his professor in Königsberg) and J. G. Hamann (his friend and mentor). Under Hamann's influence, he began to formulate a theory of hist. as progressive revelation (in *Auch eine Philosophie der Geschichte zur Bildung der Menschheit*, 1774, and *Briefe zur Beförderung der Humanität*, 1793–97) that would be developed later by Hegel and to study the romantic literary models he would share with the young J. W. Goethe (in Strassburg, 1771), such as the OT, Homer, the purported ballads of the 3d-c. Celtic bard Ossian (James Macpherson, pub. 1760–63), folk and popular poetry, and Shakespeare. Like Lessing, he opposed Shakespeare to neoclassical dramatists, praising "the new Sophocles" as an author of "universal nature" whose plays were, in the romantic sense, "historic" rather than generic in conception. His views, pub. in *Shakespear* (1773), exerted a formative influence on the romantic dramas of the *Sturm und Drang* and were reflected in Goethe's *Rede zum Shakespeares-Tag* (1771). Herder's collection of *Volkslieder* (1774; 1778–79), suggested by Thomas Percy's *Reliques of Ancient English Poetry* (1765), called for a return to native med. poetry and contributed to a contemp. revival of the *ballad, incl. Goethe's and Friedrich Schiller's later collaborative efforts (1797). His argument for the affinity of Ger. and Eng. lit. (*Über die Ähnlichkeit der mittleren englischen und deutschen Dichtkunst*, 1776) was borne out by the return to indigenous forms and themes linking the poetic to common lang. in the romantic poetry of both nations.

**C. England.** The single figure to dominate discussion of poetry in the second half of the century was Samuel Johnson (1709–84), whose critical writings elaborated not so much a poetics as the achievements and deficiencies of poets. Still, some fundamental criteria remained constants of judgment in Johnson's mind: that all great poetry consists in the new expression of universal or general truths; that these truths are gathered in the observation of *"nature" rather than through poetic *imitation; and (the Horatian dictum) that poetry must provide moral instruction through pleasure—principles Johnson articulated most clearly in Imlac's "Dissertation upon Poetry," ch. 10 of *Rasselas* (1759); in the "Preface to Shakespeare" (1765); and in the *Lives of the Poets* (1779–81).

On this basis, Johnson famously faults the *metaphysicals (in the *Life of Cowley*) for shattering mimetic illusion with a *\*discordia concors* of unnatural *wit and Shakespeare, too, for occasionally composing "swelling figures" in which "the equality of words to things is very often neglected" and being "more careful to please than to instruct." John Milton, on the other hand, sacrifices pleasure to instruction in *Paradise Lost*, which, while second only to Homer as *epic, lacks "human interest" and is "a duty rather than a pleasure" to read. Johnson's concern in the *Dictionary* to make "signs" "permanent" reflects his esteem for "the common intercourse of life" as that "style which never becomes obsolete" ("Preface to Shakespeare"), a romantic tenet that achieves greatest prominence in the poetics of William Wordsworth and S. T. Coleridge.

Edmund Burke (1729–97), in *A Philosophical Enquiry into the Origin of Our Ideas of the Sublime and the Beautiful* (1757), examines the psychophysiological composition of the feelings of the *sublime and the beautiful, i.e., which "affections of the mind produce certain emotions of the body" and, reciprocally, what bodily "feelings" produce certain "passions in the mind." On the basis of this view of beauty experienced in independence of reason and rational proportion, Burke criticizes the formal garden in particular for falsely imposed architectural principles on nature (and thus turning "trees into pillars, pyramids, and obelisks"), thereby pointing to the aesthetic domain first called "romantic" in England, landscaping. But it is the sublime, in its power to suggest "ideas of eternity and infinity," that is most closely allied to poetics. In the final part of the *Enquiry*, Burke argues that the effect of words cannot be explained by way of the sensory, physiological model he has hitherto employed: poetic lang. is not "imitative" of nonlinguistic sensations in that there is no "resemblance" between words and "the ideas for which they stand." Burke's *Enquiry* thus develops Locke's principle of the arbitrary relations between signs and ideas into a central problematic of romantic poetry. Hypothesizing (as will Wordsworth) that "unpolished people" are given to more "passionate" or sublime expression, he views lang. as a special repository of the sublime because it can join ideas unrelatable by any other medium (citing the example of Milton's "universe of death" as a "union of ideas" "amazing beyond conception," i.e., beyond concrete description). In contrast to the secondary, mimetic status ascribed to tragedy at the outset of the *Enquiry*, the words of poetry are argued to affect us "sometimes much more strongly" than "the things they represent." Thus, the principle of a necessary equivalence between word and thing that underlies Johnson's crit. of extravagant imagery is superseded in Burke's analysis by the romantic consideration of the disproportionate way in which lang. functions and affects us generally.

**D. Italy.** The functions of lang. are identified with a theory of hist. in *Scienza nuova* (1725; rev. ed., 1744) of Giambattista Vico (1668–1744). Rather than hypothesizing a historical origin of lang., Vico finds in lang., its "tropes" and "poetic logic," the origin and

devel. of human hist.: his "new science" unites poetry and reality in an essentially romantic poetic. The "fantastic speech" of humankind's "first lang." yielded four fundamental *tropes, or "corollaries of poetic logic," corresponding to distinct phases in the recurrent hist. of human consciousness. Metaphor is identified by Vico with the divine pagan or poetic phase; *metonymy, with the aristocratic or (Homeric) heroic; *synecdoche, with the lawfully democratic or human; *irony, with the period of reflection leading to the dissolution of civil bodies and reemergence of barbarism, followed in turn by the divine, heroic, and human phases of Christianity. Poetic lang. is not the "ingenious inventions of writers" but the "common sense of the human race" and key to the structure of "ideal, eternal history." A more conventional view of poetics characterized the transition to romanticism in the field of It. crit. While Saverio Bettinelli (1718–1808) and Giuseppe Baretti (1719–89) exhorted It. authors to break with cl. norms, the period saw a broad assimilation of diverse literary models in trans. of works extending from the ancients to the Eng. and Fr. "moderns," incl. the pseudoancient Ossian, trans. by philologist and philosopher of lang. Melchiorre Cesarotti (1730–1808).

**E. Spain.** After the Golden Age of Luis de Góngora and Pedro Calderón de la Barca, poetics, like poetry, suffered an eclipse throughout the 18th c., as a new wave of *classicism arose in response to mannered imitations of the *baroque masters. The major poetic treatise of the century was the Aristotelian *Poética* (1737) of Ignacio de Luzán (1702–54).

## II. 19th-Century Romanticism and Postromanticism

**A. Germany.** The distinctively rapid devel. of romantic poetry and the flowering of postromanticism owed to two enormously influential and not entirely compatible strains of crit.: the critical theory of Friedrich Schlegel (1772–1829) and the critical epistemology of Immanuel Kant (1724–1804). Kant's restriction of the field of knowledge to "representations" of experience countered, on the one hand, the insistence on the random nature of experience theorized by David Hume, and, on the other, the antiexperiential dogmatic idealism of George Berkeley and Christian Wolff. Kant's critical philosophy—consisting of the *Kritik der reinen Vernunft* (1781), its summation in the *Prolegomena zu einer jeden künftigen Metaphysik, die als Wissenschaft wird auftreten können* (1783), the *Kritik der praktischen Vernunft* (1788), and the *Kritik der Urteilskraft* (1790)—argues, in opposition to idealism, that all knowledge must be related to sensory objects and, in opposition to skepticism, that our experience of objects is not arbitrary but rather structured a priori by mental forms (e.g., time and space) and relational categories (e.g., causality). Our knowledge of experience is thus not of an object as it is "in itself" (as "noumenon") but of its "representation," the "phenomenon" that our minds construct in the very act of experience. This hypothesis of the phenomenal limits of knowledge in the *First Critique* is countered by the deduction of a single, necessarily nonphenomenal object of knowledge, the concept of (practical or moral) "freedom," in the *Second Critique*. Moral freedom, the freedom to act without respect to the welfare of one's own phenomenal being, is the one hypothetical noumenal object of knowledge in Kant's critical system, for without "freedom," all actions would be confined to the causal chain of mentally formed phenomena; thus, no real ground for *moral* action could exist, nor would there be any "real knowledge" to which we could lay claim, not even that of the phenomenal limits of cognitive reason. At once central to Kant's entire philosophical system and foundational for romantic poetics, the "bridge" (*Übergang*) between the real freedom of "practical reason" and the limited phenomenal cognitions of "pure reason" occurs in acts of *aesthetic* judgment; without the mediating power of judgment, Kant stipulates, the entire *Critique* would collapse into two irreconcilable spheres. Never before had aesthetic experience been considered so essential (rather than detrimental or distracting) to the potency of the mind; the unparalleled position Kant accords aesthetics relates acts of judgment to the separate reasons of knowledge and practical action by way of the distinct categories of the beautiful and the sublime. In the first place, the *Third Critique* criticizes the loose identification of aesthetics with personal *"taste" in order to prove that aesthetic *judgments*, no less than phenomenal cognitions and moral actions, are based on universal mental operations. Judgments, however, are neither cognitive nor active but contemplative; aesthetic objects please freely because they are "purposive" forms without practical "purpose" (*Zweckmüssigkeit ohne Zweck*). In the experience of the beautiful, "imagination and understanding" come together in a state of mutual "free play" (*freies Spiel der Einbildungskraft und des Verstandes*), while the experience of the sublime brings imagination and *reason* into conflict. Such conflict arises when the mind encounters an object of which it can make no adequate sensory image but which reason can nonetheless "think": objects that are "absolutely large," that suggest an insuperable "power" in nature or, as does poetic lang., a nonrepresentational power of the mind. This freedom of reason evoked by the sublime links aesthetic judgment to the moral freedom and to such nonimageable "ideas" as totality and infinity. Its analysis of the sublime as the unique juncture between moral action and scientific knowledge made the *Kritik der Urteilskraft* the seminal articulation of a romantic poetry that would locate the bridge to the sublime itself within poetry.

Friedrich Schiller (1759–1805), Kant's first major proponent in the field of poetics, translates Kant's distinction between phenomenon and noumenon into analogous conceptual categories ("matter" and "form," "the physical" and "the moral," etc.) deriving from the opposing "drives" of sensory experience and reason mediated, as in Kant, by aesthetic experience. In *Über das Pathetische* (1795) and *Über das Erhabene* (ca. 1795), and *Ästhetische Erziehung des Menschen* (1795), Schiller effectively dispenses with Kant's *Second Critique* by identifying moral freedom wholly with aesthetic

experience. "Aesthetic freedom" becomes the locus of moral action for Schiller, who, while indebted to Kant, departs significantly from the *Critique* in defining beauty as the sensory means of making freedom "visible" (*Über das Pathetische*). His *Über Naïve und sentimentalische Dichtung* (1795), which names Kant as the source of its theoretical oppositions between "being" and "seeking" nature (the ancients versus mod. admiration for antiquity) and between "feeling" nature and "reflecting" on feeling (*naïve versus sentimental), was credited by K.W.F. Schlegel with altering his appraisal of mod. poetics. While openly disdainful of the systematic nature of Kant's philosophy, Schlegel, once an avatar of classicism (see *Über das Studium der griechischen Poesie*, 1795), owed his conversion to romantic poetics to the Kantian Schiller and to Kant's devoted follower J. G. Fichte (1762–1814). In his early writings, Schlegel had opposed the harmony of cl. beauty to the "interesting," irregular, and aesthetically unsatisfying creations of "romantic poetry," by which he meant all med. and mod. lit., from chivalric romances through the works of Christoph Martin Wieland. For Schlegel, *romantic* is no longer a generic or historical category but the name for poetry perpetually in a "state of becoming" that, like irony, "no theory can exhaust," while "other kinds of poetry are finished" and can be "fully analyzed" (*Athenäum* no. 116). What is romantic is what is "poetry itself," whether written in verse or prose, whether ancient or mod., and what is poetry is "infinite" by dint of its own eternal self-crit. (*Athenäum* no. 51). As Schlegel defines them, the poles of irony informing all romantic poetry are recognizable from Fichte's *Wissenschaftslehre* (1794). Intending to "complete" Kant's project, Fichte overreached the essential limits of the *Critique* by identifying the thing-in-itself with a thinking self or ego capable of positing both itself and all that it perceives as not itself, the material world. But whereas Fichte saw the self-positing ego as freely containing contradiction within it (a self that recognizes the not-self must first be itself), Schlegel's conception of *poetic* irony never rests on a principle of self-certainty. This is made clearest in the essay written for the last issue of the controversial *Athenäum*, "Über die Unverständlichkeit" (1800), in which Schlegel describes "the irony of irony" as a "tiring" of irony from which one nonetheless cannot "disentangle oneself," since to speak about irony either nonironically *or* ironically is still to be caught in irony and thus (as in this "essay on incomprehensibility") not to comprehend fully one's own speech.

Schlegel's conception of perpetual self-crit. takes the form of "infinite" textual interpretation in the works of Friedrich Schleiermacher (1768–1834), an early friend of Schlegel and the author of *Vertraute Briefe über Schlegels Lucinde* (1800). In his *Lectures on Hermeneutics* (*Vorlesungen über die Hermeneutik*, 1819), Schleiermacher described textual *interpretation (see HERMENEUTICS) as a properly philosophical endeavor whose endless "task" is to comprehend texts in terms both of the past and of futurity.

Schlegel's views were popularized by his brother

A. W. Schlegel (1767–1845), cofounder of *Athenäum* and author of the broadly historical *Vorlesungen über dramatische Kunst und Literatur* (1808), and reproduced by such contemporaries as J.P.F. Richter (1763–1825), who in his *Vorschule der Ästhetik* (1804) speculates that metaphors preceded denotative expressions in lang. formation. Karl Solger (1780–1819), in *Erwin: Vier Gespräche über das Schöne und die Kunst* (1815), a work commended by Søren Kierkegaard in his *Concept of Irony* (1841), describes "the true realm of art" as the passing of the idea into the particular, that moment of creation and destruction that "we call irony." Schlegel's and Solger's theories of romantic irony are reflected in the critical work of Ludwig Tieck (1773–1853), incl. several volumes devoted to Shakespeare (1811, 1826, 1838, 1920), and the "Fragmente" (*Athenäum*, 1798) and *Dialogen* (1798) of Friedrich von Hardenberg (Novalis; 1772–1801). The self-reflexivity of romantic irony is dramatized in supernatural mirrorings of the natural in stories by E.T.A. Hoffmann (1776–1822) and by the absolute absence or absolutely paralyzing presence of self-consciousness in stories and dramas by Heinrich von Kleist (1777–1811).

While the romantic poetry derived from Kant and Schlegel is predominantly synchronic in conception, an essentially diachronic understanding of poetry is developed in the poetry and theoretical essays of Friedrich Hölderlin (1770–1843) and in the philosophy and aesthetics of G.W.F. Hegel (1770–1831). The concern with antiquity pervading Hölderlin's works owes not to a neoclassical idealization of the purported harmony of Gr. art but to a conception of the temporal nature of experience exemplified in ancient poetry and mythological hist. In early lyrics (1801–3), the dramatic fragments of *Der Tod des Empedokles* (1798–1800), the essays on *Empedokles*, and the essay *Werden im Vergehen* (ca. 1799), Hölderlin focuses on the moment of passage, of present becoming past, which, fatal for the individual, at once represents the life of the world and is represented in turn by the signs of lang. Poetry both retells this passage in poetic narrative and embodies its occurrence in the creation of poetic lang. until, in Hölderlin's fragments (1803–6), these two ling. means of representing transience are divided, and signs replace story as the elliptical vehicles of narratives whose own poetic possibility is already past.

The anteriority of art is the overarching theme of Hegel's *Vorlesungen über die Ästhetik* (1820–29, pub. 1835, 1842), in which the famous statement that "in its highest determination, art for us is that which is past," speaks cryptically for Hegel's entire philosophy of the dialectical becoming of spirit over time. In the *Ästhetik*, Hegel correlates the epochs of human hist. with different kinds of art distinguished by their structural relationship of intellectual content to form; the dialectical transformation of this relationship signifies the progress of spirit toward ultimate freedom from all relation at the end of time. In keeping with this progressive conception of aesthetics, Schlegel's concept of irony is condemned by Hegel. Departing from Fichte's proposition that all existence is posted by an ego that

can also destroy it, Schlegel's irony, Hegel argues, views the artist as a divine *genius who can create and annihilate at will and thus for whom all moral and social relations conducted in reality are also viewed ironically as a "nullity." Hegel praises Solger, whom he distinguishes from Schlegel's followers, for recognizing the negativity of irony as a "dialectical moment of the idea," which, itself negated, reinstates the "general and infinite in the particular." The ironic, Hegel emphasizes, is "only a moment" (in the progress of the idea or spirit) and, as such, pertains to the diachronic dialectic between human hist. and the universal spirit rather than the Fichtean principle of absolute subjectivity.

Arthur Schopenhauer (1788–1860) rejected Hegel's philosophy of spirit entirely and based his *Welt als Wille und Vorstellung* (1819) on Kant's *Critique*, which he, like Fichte, claimed to complete. For Schopenhauer, the thing-in-itself is not the Fichtean self but the will, represented in all temporally and spatially structured appearances. Reducing Kant's categories to the mechanism of causality, Schopenhauer argues that only disinterested artistic genius is freed from the causal chain of willed representations. The highest forms of art are poetry and music, the latter being a pure reflection, rather than worldly representation, of the will. In *Parerga* (1819), Schopenhauer discusses general aspects of poetics and literary style, observing that the best authors write "objectively" by employing the "concrete" means of everyday lang., using "common words to say uncommon things." Misjudged for this reason in their own lifetimes, their genius comes to inform the life of the "whole species."

Schopenhauer's philosophy of will influenced Friedrich Nietzsche (1844–1900), whose writings effectively transferred romanticism into the 20th c. In *Die Geburt der Tragödie* (1872), Nietzsche rewrites the cl. conception of Gr. antiquity by arguing that combative tendencies underlie its poetry: the Dionysian spirit of music and the Apollonian spirit of imaging. The Dionysian, prompting man's "highest symbolic faculties," is a state of intoxication that destroys the individual as it expresses "the essence of Nature," while the Apollonian imagines a world of "beautiful appearances" delimited by the scale of the individual. Nietzsche commends Schiller, among the Ger. "classicists," for recognizing "the musical mood" that precedes the act of poetic imaging and analyzes the figure of the tragic hero as an image meant to turn us, through the experience of compassion, from the Dionysian to the individual. Nietzsche does not suggest that poetry is ever entirely Dionysian, i.e., *is* the music from which it originates, but rather that, within tragedy, the Dionysian and Apollonian are eventually compelled to speak "each other's language" and that, in this exchange, the "highest aim of tragedy and of art in general is reached." The thesis that music is the essential romantic art form appears repeatedly in the late *Der Wille zur Macht* (1901), in which romantic art is also equated with "a makeshift substitute for defective 'reality,'" and Gustave Flaubert is called a "postromantic" for having translated the "romantic faith in love and the future" into "the desire for nothing." Thus, Nietzsche already sees romantic *art* as postromantic or self-retrospective (not unlike Hegel), while distinguishing it from *romanticism*, whose "most fundamental form" he identifies as "German Philosophy as a whole" (Leibniz through Schopenhauer).

Nietzsche's contemporary Wilhelm Dilthey (1833–1911) pursued the psychological strain in interpretation Schleiermacher had proposed. In *Das Leben Schleiermachers* (1870), *Die Entstehung der Hermeneutik* (1900), and *Das Erlebnis und die Dichtung* (1905), Dilthey argued that an author's life could be "reconstructed," by methods as demonstrable as those of the natural sciences, into a larger theory of historical knowledge. While his grounding of the "human sciences" in psychology limited his hermeneutics to individual hists., Dilthey's attention to the temporal basis of poetry proved influential on the philosophy of Martin Heidegger (1889–1976), a characteristic (perhaps the only one) he shared with Nietzsche.

**B. England.** William Wordsworth (1770–1850) and S. T. Coleridge (1772–1834) considered incl. a critical intro. to the 2d ed. of their joint poems; the ensuing Preface to the *Lyrical Ballads* (1800), written by Wordsworth, may be the single most important document of Eng. romantic poetry. The immediate aim of the Preface was to describe that aspect of the *Lyrical Ballads* that made them "so materially different" from the poetry of the day: their lang. The *Lyrical Ballads*, Wordsworth states, relate "common life" in the "real language of men," the properly "philosophical" lang. he opposes to conventional "poetic diction." First arguing that the presence of *meter alone distinguishes poetry from prose, he then states that only "matter of Fact, or Science" is meaningfully distinguished from "Poetry," since meter also enters "naturally" into the composition of prose. Meter maintains "something regular" in the reading of "words" that, "in themselves powerful," "produce" "an unusual and irregular state of the mind": those who use it merely to "accompan[y]" "colours of style" "greatly underrate the power of metre in itself." Similarly, when used as mere "mechanical devices," such rhetorical "colours" are a deadening substitute for the "figures" that arise naturally in our impassioned interaction with the "objects" around us. Recalling Rousseau, Wordsworth regards unmannered, rustic lang. as a more "permanent" and "philosophical" lang. than that of authors intent only on feeding "fickle appetites of their own creation." This view may have led to his mischaracterization as a sentimentalist and the commonplace abbreviation of the definition of poetry that, in its truncated version, has become the best-known phrase in the Preface ("all good poetry is the spontaneous overflow of powerful feelings"), but that, as Wordsworth in fact composed it, continues past a full colon to oppose "feelings" to the equally powerful, and more valuable, basis of poetry in long-term "thought" (". . . feelings: and though this be true, Poems to which any value can be attached were never produced . . . but by a man who . . . had also thought long and deeply").

Other definitions in the Preface—such as "Poetry is the first and last of all knowledge"; "Poetry is the most philosophic writing" (following Aristotle) in that its "object" is "general and operative" rather than "individual and local" "truth"; and "the Poet binds together by passion and knowledge the vast empire of human society"—clearly indicate a poetics that, instead of substituting feeling for knowledge, finds its only true relation in poetry, a view Wordsworth extends beyond his own or other contemp. poetry to the "judgment" of "the greatest Poets both ancient and modern." In the "Appendix" to the Preface, Wordsworth elaborates his crit. of "poetic diction," underscoring that, with regard to "works of imagination and sentiment," a single lang. is used for both verse and prose. His introduction of the historical argument, familiar from 18th-c. romantic poetry, that the "figurative" lang. of the "earliest poets" was the "language of men" animated by "passion," links Wordsworth to Condillac, Vico, Diderot, and Rousseau, among others.

Coleridge's *Biographia Literaria* (1817), a mixture of biographical narrative, crit., speculation, and trans. and summary (esp. of Schelling, Fichte, and Kant), draws a distinction (ch. 12) between imagination, the "shaping or modifying power," and *fancy, the "aggregative and associative power," thereby disagreeing with Wordsworth, who held that the imagination shared these latter powers but used them differently to more permanent ends (1815 Preface). Coleridge criticized Wordsworth's view of the lasting value of the lang. of rustic life, arguing that such lang. itself varies "in every county" and that whatever is invariable and universal in lang. should not be identified with any particular class (ch. 17). Echoing the distinction drawn by Schiller between the "naïve" and "sentimental," Coleridge indicated the existence of a "secondary," recreative "echo" of the "primary" imagination (ch. 13), while defining poetry generally as the joining in imagination of good sense, fancy, and motion (ch. 14).

In the letters of John Keats (1795–1821), the identification of truth with beauty (already ambiguously evoked in the context of "Ode on a Grecian Urn" [1819]) is questioned in intensely speculative formulations relating beauty to the "passions" while truth to dispassionate "abstraction" while comparing the truth of imagination to an earthly "dream." Keats's contrast between the "delights" of sensation and the desire for truth opposes pure sensation, described as "falling" through "space" and "being blown up again" "continually," to sensations experienced "with knowledge" and "without fear." *"Negative capability," the capacity for "being in uncertainties" that Keats attributed not to himself but to Shakespeare, contrasts sharply with the either/or constructions that often propel his own poems.

P. B. Shelley (1792–1822), an early admirer of Keats, asserts a poetics that surely would have struck Keats as post-Wordsworthian, in that it admits no rival creative power to poetry at all. His *Defence of Poetry* (1821) ascribes to imaginative poetic works the ethical character of civilization itself, placing the greatest poets (Dante through Milton) above philosophers (Locke through Rousseau) in their influence on "the moral nature of man." Shelley's sweeping overview of the part played by poetry in the hist. of civilization responds to Thomas Love Peacock's thesis, in *The Four Ages of Poetry* (1820), that, as civilization develops, poetry must decline. Shelley argues that civilization is, rather, the result of poetry and that poetry produces humanity's "moral improvement" not by teaching moral doctrine but by enlarging the power of imagination by which people put themselves "in the place of another." Poetry alone exerts this power over "the internal world," whereas the "external" progress of the empirical sciences incurs human beings' "enslavement." Like Burke in the *Enquiry (*and, later, Hegel in his *Aesthetics*), Shelley considers lang. to be more "plastic" than the plastic arts since it is "arbitrarily produced by the imagination" and so relates "to thoughts alone." Recalling lang. theorists on the continent, Shelley also equates "language itself" with "poetry," asserting that, at the beginning of hist., all authors were poets and that lang. at its origin resembled "the chaos of a cyclical poem." At the same time, because poetry stimulates moral speculation, poets also originally authored all "laws" and "civil society" and, the *Defence* concludes, remain "the unacknowledged legislators of the world."

Following the self-romanticizing identification of poetics with personality in the life and poetry of Lord Byron (1788–1824), Eng. romanticism yields to a series of postromantic attempts to overreach, or retreat from, its poetics. Poetic thought after romanticism divides between doctrinal classicism and pictorially based aestheticism, and works of prose crit. that take on a poetic life of their own. In *Sartor Resartus* (1833–34), the first major postromantic critic, Thomas Carlyle (1795–1881) presents a Philosophy of Clothes (espoused by one Diogenes Teufelsdröckh, professor of Things in General at the University of Weissnichtwo [I-Don't-Know-Where]), that defines clothing as "whatsoever represents Spirit to Spirit." From all the "garments," the imagination "weaves" to reveal the otherwise invisible creations of reason, Carlyle distinguishes "language," understood instead as "the Body of thought," whose "muscles and tissue" are the old and new "Metaphors" of which lang. is composed.

A postromantic emphasis on the essentially poetic nature of prose is the theme of John Ruskin (1819–1900) in *Sesame and Lilies* (1865), a series of lectures aimed at answering the question "Why to read?," that contrasts the literal act of reading "syllable by syllable—nay, letter by letter," with all more or less accidental or associative forms of verbal communication. In *Modern Painters* (2 v., 1846), he distinguishes "Poetical" from "historical" Painting, the former being "imaginative," the latter, a relation of "plain facts," and coins the phrase *"pathetic fallacy" to describe self-projecting metaphoric lang. that, while betraying an ungoverned "weakness of character," may be true to the emotion expressed.

Matthew Arnold (1822–88), a neoromantic poet who disavowed romanticism in the Preface to his collected *Poems* (1853) and the first layman to be made professor of poetry at Oxford (1857), reintroduced a Johnsonian strain into crit. Arnold defines the terms *classic, classical* as meaning of "the class of the very best" (*The Study of Poetry*, 1880) and broadly describes the function of crit. of the classics so defined as "a disinterested endeavour to learn and propagate the best that is known and thought in the world" (*The Function of Criticism at the Present Time*, 1864; intro. to *Essays in Criticism*, 1865). Arnold's advocacy of "disinterested" crit. and the greatness of the classics proffers the one in support of the other without specifying what constitutes either, or, for that matter, poetics generally; in order to recognize "the best," he suggests in circular fashion, one need only memorize *"touchstone" lines from recognized masters. His praise of stylistic simplicity in the Preface recalls Johnson, while his exclusion of Chaucer, commended for a "sound representation of things," from the ranks of the classics, owes, Arnold asserts, to that poet's lack of "high seriousness."

The *Pre-Raphaelite Brotherhood of W. H. Hunt (1827–1910), D. G. Rossetti (1828–82), W. M. Rossetti (1829–1919), and J. E. Millais (1829–96) proposed a postromantic return to *naturalism in a renewed cooperation of painting and verse replacing academic rules of composition (conventional since Raphael) by highly detailed representation: in imitation of the med. allegorical trad., etchings accompanied poems in the Pre-Raphaelite journal *The Germ* (1850). Even while laying claim to med. "sincerity," the return of the ut pictura poesis topos informing the Pre-Raphaelite "return to nature" *after* romanticism yielded not naturalism but *aestheticism. The movement was rapidly adopted by Walter Pater (1839–94), who, in his review of *Poems by William Morris* (1868), famously commended "the love of art for art's sake." Pater's singular emphasis on beauty as an immediate sensuous experience based in "a certain kind of temperament" (*The Renaissance*, 1873) gave way inevitably to the fetishism of feeling associated with *decadence.

Crit. reflection emerged with a new vigor, however, in the writings of Oscar Wilde (1854–1900). *The Decay of Lying* (1889) brings the nature of the relationship between art and lived experience again into question by provocatively asserting that life imitates art and that the "ages" of the human spirit (by a turn on Hegel) symbolize aesthetic devels. rather than the other way around. Neatly reversing the mimetic principle by arguing that "facts" attempt to "reproduce fiction," Wilde moves beyond the limits of purely sensuous aesthetic criteria by returning, albeit in radically polemical form, to the romantic problem of mental perception. Wilde's ultimate conclusion that, like human life, nature too imitates the lit. that "anticipates" it, is based on the distinction he draws between mechanically "looking at a thing" and "seeing" it. Nature is only *seen* when its beauty is perceived, and that perception, like cognition itself, is not immediate but always mediated by "the Arts that have influenced us:" "we do not know anything" about nature until aesthetic detours permit us to "see" it. Closely related to perception, in "The Critic as Artist" (1890), is crit. Like the misconceived notion of "unimaginative realism" (exemplified for Wilde by

Émile Zola), crit. does not imitate but reveal: it is not aimed at "discovering" the "real intention" of the artist, whose capacity to "judge" is limited by his creative ability. Crit. instead "leads us" to the future creations suggested by the work of art as the critic "sees" it; "new" art works are thus already old with regard to the crit. that foresees them. As if to demonstrate, in the manner Wilde describes, this critical proposition, the poetry of his own age lagged behind his notion of crit. Bombastic neoromantic styles, such as that of A. C. Swinburne (1837–1909), were countered in part by the spare dramatic *monologue developed by Robert Browning (1812–89) and the recasting of Shakespearean love poetry in the *Sonnets from the Portuguese* (1850) by Elizabeth Barrett Browning (1806–61), whose critically successful "novel-poem," *Aurora Leigh* (1856), influenced by Mme. De Staël's *Corinne* (1807), was praised again by Virginia Woolf (*Times Literary Supplement,* 1931; see NARRATIVE POETRY). The dynamic poems of G. M. Hopkins (1844–89), whose posthumous publication in 1918 contributed to their classification as modernist, combined dense, sensuous lang. with the contrapuntal tension of Hopkins's own *"sprung rhythm," described in the Author's Preface as suggesting "two or more strains of tune going on together." Closer to romanticism than the ensuing postromanticisms of their time, Hopkins's poems recall the phrase by Wilde that most aptly describes the age: "Life goes faster than realism, but romanticism is always in front of life" (*The Decay of Lying*).

**C. United States.** The convergence of romanticism with liberal Protestantism produced a new movement that began in 1836 with the meetings of four active or one-time Unitarian ministers, most famous among them R. W. Emerson (1803–82). The movement took the name Transcendentalism, borrowing the term *transcendental* from Kant, whom Emerson and others understood, often imperfectly, through the mediation of Coleridge (see TRANSCENDENTALISTS). The most condensed statement of Transcendentalist poetics is Emerson's essay "The Poet" (1844), in which he describes poets as "liberating gods," who by means of tropes enable readers of poetry to recognize in the natural world correspondences with the supernatural. (Like Blake, Emerson was influenced by Emanuel Swedenborg's notion of correspondence.) Emerson's exalted notion of the poet anticipated the visions of Walt Whitman (1819–92) in *Leaves of Grass,* esp. in the Preface to the 1st ed. of 1855 and in "Song of Myself," and Emily Dickinson (1830–86), whose poems and letters brim with romantic images, both explicit and cryptic, of the poet, lang., nature, and desire. The romantic poetry of E. A. Poe (1809–49) anticipated, while it differed from, Pater's "art for art's sake" credo by stating that, while the "poem [is] written solely for the poem's sake" and poetry is "the rhythmical creation of Beauty" ("The Poetic Principle," 1850), the melancholic mood of beauty could only be achieved through analytic craft ("The Philosophy of Composition," 1846), ideas that,

furthered by Poe's Fr. translator and advocate Charles Baudelaire, exerted singular influence on romantic and modernist poetics in France.

**D. France.** Romanticism arrived late in France and was disrupted early and long. Just as the Fr. Revolution was linked to the romanticism of Rousseau, ensuing political upheavals and displacements played a major role in the fractious hist. of Fr. romantic poetry. This is most evident in the writings of François René de Chateaubriand (1768–1848), whose crit. of Shakespearean drama for its untempered representation of nature, in *Essai sur la littérature anglaise* (1801) and concurrently his romantic novel *Atala,* were followed by *Le Génie du Christianisme* (1802), whose assimilation of romanticism to religion, favored by Napoleon, was expanded into an identification of Christianity with human liberty in *Memoires d'Outre Tombe* (1848–50). By contrast, the romanticism of Mme. De Staël (1766–1817) linked the devel. of lit. with political freedom rather than religious belief; her *De l'Allemagne,* advocating the importance of Ger. romantic philosophy and lit. for France, was suppressed by Napoleon (1811; pub. in London, 1813). In *Racine et Shakespeare* (1823), Stendhal (Marie Henri Beyle, 1783–1842) transposed the Fr. debate between cl. and romantic poetry from contemp. political (proroyalist, or "ultra," versus liberal) into larger temporal terms, arguing that any new literary form is "romantic" in its time, while Victor Hugo (1802–85) unequivocally identified romantic drama with contemp. liberalism in his "Préface de *Cromwell*" (1827).

In addition to the political allegiances dividing proponents of classicism from those of romanticism in 19th-c. France, a division also developed, unlike any in Germany or England, between poets and critics. C. A. Sainte-Beuve (1804–69) stressed a psychological and personality-oriented approach to authors in his *Portraits littéraires* (1862–64) and *Portraits contemporains* (1869–71), a view expanded into the conception of lit. as a function of documentable social factors by Hippolyte Taine (1828–93) and as grounded in empirical scientific methods by Émile Zola (1840–1902). Yet while different forms of positivism informed the poetry advocated critically, nothing could be less positivistic in outlook than the poetry written during this period. While differing in style and temperament, the first significant poets of the century, Alphonse Marie Louis de Lamartine (1790–1869), (Comte) Alfred Victor de Vigny (1797–1863), Hugo, and Alfred de Musset (1810–57), were all romantic in their turn from conventional cl. themes and strict *alexandrine meter to the more malleable prosody of emotive verse. Still, the lyrics of the poet viewed posthumously as the greatest of the century, Charles Baudelaire (1821–67), indicate the endurance of a dialectic between classicism and romanticism within Fr. poetry. Focusing on the mundane and the abstract, sounding high themes and low, the cl. rigor of his *Fleurs du mal* (1857, 1861, 1868) gave lived reality the quality of dreamed or perpetually receding meaning and identified allegory and myth with the contemp. landscape of the city. Just as his *Peintre de la vie moderne* (1863) defines the fleeting "present" aesthetically by its already dated "representation," Baudelaire's romanticism rejects from the outset any possibility of naturalism; in "Correspondances," his most famous lyric, "nature" is immediately equated with a meaningful construct, "a temple," and "forests" are composed of "symbols." Baudelaire's imagistic precision, graceful versification, and unsurpassed control of Fr. poetic diction made him one of the early *Parnassians, a group that rejected undisciplined effusions for a new romantic decorum.

Paul Verlaine (1844–96) was more neoromantic than Parnassian in his emphasis on the suggestive quality of poetry. His views proved influential for the poets of *vers libre* but were later retracted by Verlaine on the grounds that the new poetry, lacking all rhythm, bordered too closely on prose. Arthur Rimbaud (1854–91) described his poetics as a form of self-induced vision, arguing that poets must make themselves *voyants* through a purposeful "disordering of the senses." For Rimbaud, all romantic poets, but above all Baudelaire, have been voyants. Like "critics," he states however, "romantics" themselves have never been able properly to "judge romanticism," from which follows the famous agrammatical dictum "car Je est un autre" (for *I* is another), by which the self, identified by being "disordered" with what is not the self, acquires the double (creative and reflective) vision of the voyant. Although Rimbaud probably wrote his last poetry at the age of 19, the influence by the end of the century of his already repudiated *Illuminations* (1886) was matched only by the work of the poet least like him in life, Stéphane Mallarmé (1842–98).

Mallarmé, who was employed as a lycée teacher until his retirement at 51, worked at eliminating the visual from poetic lang. in any sense but that of the graphic display of letters on the page, as in the late *Un coup de dés* (*A Throw of the Dice*, 1897), the prototype of modernist *concrete poetry. His formal manipulation of the rule of syntax and immediate power of sound in the composition of grammatical and semantic labyrinths defying image-based interpretation seems to invest lang. itself with a density outweighing any particular sense made of it. Just as, in "Le Tombeau d'Edgar Poe" (1877), "eternity" alone "changes" "the poet" "into himself," so Mallarmé's compressed poetic lang. seems to acquire inexhaustible substance by severing itself from all worldly service, an extreme version of the negative factor of temporality informing the trad. of romantic poetry within which it remains.

**E. *Italy*.** Romanticism was at first a distinctly political movement focused on the "revolutionary" figure of Napoleon; the *Ultime lettere di Jacopo Ortis* (1802) of Niccolò Foscolo (1778–1827) added the motive of political disillusion to the suicide of its Wertherian hero. The downfall of Napoleon and the treaty of Vienna (1815) contributed to a new affiliation of liberal thinking with romanticism whose major literary forum was the jour-

nal *Il Conciliatore* (1818–19). The poetry of Giacomo Leopardi (1798–1837), the most important of the 19th c., involved a romantic tension of aspiration and deception that was not directly political in nature. With the achievement of national unity after decades of struggle incl. the imprisonment or exile of many authors in the romantic movement, It. romanticism began to wane. Giosuè Carducci (1835–1907) wrote lyrics of renewed cl. vigor reflecting an antireligious, realist spirit most reminiscent of the Fr. *philosophes*. The formulation of a philosophical approach to lit. crit. first appeared in the essays and *Storia della letteratura italiana* (1870–71) of Francesco de Sanctis (1818–83), which aimed at establishing critical practices uninfluenced by particularities of politics, religion, or taste. Gabriele D'Annunzio (1863–1938), poet, novelist, playwright, and the single most significant It. literary figure of the latter 19th c., was also one of the most internationally informed; his literary "decadence" was greatly influenced by the Fr. postromantic poets and Nietzsche.

Earlier Ger. idealism, by contrast, shaped the *Filosofia dello spirito: estetica come scienza dell'espressione e linguistica generale* (1902) of Benedetto Croce (1866–1952). Equating art with instinctive, as opposed to conceptual, knowledge, Croce's *Filosofia* subordinated hist. to aesthetics. It argued that classicism and romanticism represent not historical categories but rather views of the artistic *symbol as either extrinsic or intrinsic to the content of art. Reviving 18th-c. origin-of-lang. debates, Croce suggested that lang. itself is art in a state of "perpetual creation." Reaction against Croce's own idealism soon inspired the It. futurists (see FUTURISM).

**F. *Russia*.** Classicism in the Western Eur. sense had never been a fully integrated literary force, while the 18th-c. lit. of sensibility exerted a considerable influence. Romanticism was identified most strongly with Lord Byron and the circle surrounding Alexander Pushkin (1799–1837), whose unsentimental portrayal of a jaded Byronic hero in *Evgenij Onegin* (1825–32) used realism to reveal the dramatic insufficiency of high romantic narrative style. A jaded Satan in love with a mortal woman is the doubly alienated Byronic hero of the long poem *The Demon* (1829–40) by M. Y. Lermontov (1814–41), whose mod. syntax and complex first-person narrative, contrasting sharply with Pushkin's classically harmonious verse, are forerunners of the symbolist movement at the close of the century. Influenced by Schopenhauer, Nietzsche, and Rus. mysticism, the symbolists discounted traditional poetics. Foremost among them were Konstantin Bal'mont (1867–1943), whose crystalline sonnets recall Baudelaire; Valery Bryusov (1873–1924), whose experimental meters and imagery introduced an exotic effect; Andrei Bely (Boris Bugayev; 1880–1934), known for his devel. of the *prose poem; and Alexander Blok (1880–1921), whose symbolism was linked to mysticism. The exhaustion of *symbolism in Russia and a renewed concern with cl. lit. as revelatory of the historical and temporal dimension of poetry inform the lyrics of the imprisoned Osip

Mandelstam (1892–1938). Mandelstam's attention to compositional perfection, characteristic of Rus. *ac-meism, recalls the Fr. postromantic Parnassians.

**G.  Spain.** The return of exiled liberal writers after the death of Ferdinand VII in 1833 led to a belated experimentation with Byronesque romanticism in the works of José de Espronceda (1808–42) and José Zorrilla (1817–93). The most popular romantic Sp. drama, *Don Álvaro* (1835) by Ángel de Saavedra (Duke of Rivas, 1791–1865), echoed the *succès fou* of its Fr. model, Hugo's *Hernani* (1830). The most important critical documents were the *Discurso sobre el influyo que ha tenido la crítica moderna en la decadencia del teatro antiguo español* (1830) of Agustín Durán (1793–1862), which praised native med. Sp. lit. as truly romantic, and *El clasicismo y romantismo* (1838) of Juan Donoso Cortés (1809–53). The first Sp. romantic poetry devoid of Byronism, the *Rimas* (*El libro de los gorriones*, 1868) of Gustavo Adolfo Bécquer (1836–70), later praised by such critics as Dámaso Alonso as the starting point of all mod. Sp. poetry, combined relatively simple poetic lang. with great economy of diction. Bécquer was probably influenced by newly collected Andalusian folk poetry, as Galician folk songs were to influence the *Cantares gallegos* (1863) of Rosalía Castro (1837–85), who wrote in Galician rather than Castilian (see GALICIA, POETRY OF). The most important Sp. critic of the 19th c., Marcelino Menéndez y Pelayo (1856–1912), is generally credited with single-handedly creating a critical and historical framework for the study of Sp. lit. His scholarly renewal of Sp. literary culture, in such works as *Historia de las ideas estéticas en España* (1833–91), *Antología de poetas líricos castellanos* (1890–1908), and *Ensayos de crítica filosófica* (1892), contributed to the liberal and nationally oriented Generation of 1898, which included Miguel de Unamuno (1864–1937), the individualist philosopher, and José Ortega y Gasset (1883–1955), whose studies in Germany (of Kant in particular) influenced his philosophical critique of art (*La dehumanización del arte*, 1925). Finally, Spain's greatest 20th-c. poet, Federico García Lorca (1898–1936), is also its greatest romantic. His *Romancero Gitano* (1928), a collection of poems modeled on Andalusian ballads, elevated native poetic forms to the level of the Ren. and baroque masters. In the dramatic trilogy of *Bodas de Sangre* (1933), *Yerma* (1934), and *La Casa de Bernarda Alba* (1936); in elegies such as *Llanto por Ignacio Sanchez Mejías* (1935); and in his short lyrics, García Lorca's impassioned imagery, rhythmic sonority, and limpid diction may be compared with Wordsworth's *Lyrical Ballads* and Baudelaire's *Fleurs du mal* in the impact they exerted on an entire national literary trad., already marking this poet as Spain's most significant mod. romantic at the time of his murder by a Falangist firing squad during the Sp. Civil War.

*See* PREROMANTICISM.

■ **Comparative and General:** A. O. Lovejoy, *Essays in the History of Ideas* (1948); Wellek, v. 1–4; H. Peyre, *Qu'est-ce que le romantisme?* (1971); H. Dieckmann, *Diderot und die Aufklärung* (1972); H. Friedrich, *The*

*Structure of Modern Poetry*, trans. J. Neugroschel (1974); P. de Man, *Allegories of Reading* (1979); J. Derrida, *Dissemination*, trans. B. Johnson (1981); H. Aarsleff, *From Locke to Saussure* (1982); H. R. Jauss, *Aesthetic Experience and Literary Hermeneutics* (1977), trans. M. Shaw (1982); de Man; E. Auerbach, *Scenes from the Drama of European Literature*, 2d ed. (1984); P. de Man, *The Rhetoric of Romanticism* (1984), *Critical Writings, 1953–1978* (1989), and *Romanticism and Contemporary Criticism*, ed. E. S. Burt, K. Newmark, and A. Warminski (1993).

■ **England:** G.A.C. Bradley, *Oxford Lectures on Poetry* (1909); Brooks; W. K. Wimsatt, *Philosophic Words* (1948); Abrams; W. Empson, *The Structure of Complex Words* (1954); H. Bloom, *Shelley's Mythmaking* (1959), and *The Visionary Company* (1961); C. C. Clarke, *The Romantic Paradox* (1962); L. Spitzer, *Essays on English and American Literature* (1962); G. H. Hartman, *Wordsworth's Poetry* (1964); K. Burke, *Language as Symbolic Action* (1966); R. J. Onorato, *The Character of the Poet: Wordsworth in "The Prelude"* (1971); T. Weiskel, *The Romantic Sublime* (1976); H. Aarsleff, *The Study of Language in England, 1780–1860* (1979); H. Vendler, *The Odes of John Keats* (1983); S. Wolfson, *The Questioning Presence* (1986); S. Schmid, *Shelley's German Afterlives* (2007); A.-L. François, *Open Secrets* (2008); C. Brodsky, "The Poetic Structure of Complexity: Wordsworth's Sublime and 'Something Regular'," *Wordsworth's Poetic Theory*, ed. S. Hoesel-Uhlig and A. Regier (2009).

■ **France:** A. Béguin, *L'Ame romantique et le rêve* (1939); F. Venturi, *Jeunesse de Diderot* (1939); B. Guetti, "The Double Voice of Nature in Rousseau's *Essai sur l'origine des langues*," *MLN* 84 (1969); H. Peyre, *Qu'est-ce que le romantisme?* (1971); H. Dieckmann, *Diderot und die Aufklärung* (1972); J. Chouillet, *L'Esthétique des lumiéres* (1974); W. Benjamin, *Charles Baudelaire* (1977); Y. Bonnefoy, "The Poetics of Mallarmé," *YFS* 54 (1977); R. Chambers, "Baudelaire et l'espace poétique," *Le Lieu de la formule* (1978); P. de Man, *Allegories of Reading* (1979); H. Aarsleff, *From Locke to Saussure* (1982); R. Chambers, *Mélancolie et opposition* (1987); C. Brodsky, "Convention Theory and Romanticism," *Rules and Conventions*, ed. M. Hjort (1992), and "Whatever Moves You: 'Experimental Philosophy' and the Literature of Experience in Diderot and Kleist," *Traditions of Experiment from the Enlightenment to the Present*, ed. N. Kaiser and D. Wellbery (1992); S. Blood, *Baudelaire and the Aesthetics of Bad Faith* (1997).

■ **Germany:** F. O. Nolte, *Lessing's Laokoön* (1940); M. Kommerell, *Lessing und Aristoteles* (1944); H.-G. Gadamer, "Hölderlin und das Zukünftige," *Beiträge zur geistigen Überlieferung* (1947); G. Lukács, *Goethe und seine Zeit* (1947); R. Brinkmann, "Romantische Dichtungstheorie in Friedrich Schlegels Frühschriften und Schillers Begriffe der Naiven und Sentimentalischen," *Deutsche Vierteljahrsschrift für Literaturwissenschaft und Geistesgeschichte* 32 (1950); P. Szondi, "Friedrich Schlegel und die romantische Ironie," *Euphorion* 48 (1954); H. Eichner, "F. Schlegel's Theory of Romantic Poetry," *PMLA* 71 (1956); T. W. Adorno, "Parataxis. Zur Späten Lyrik Hölderlins," *Die Neue Rundschau* 75 (1964);

P. Szondi, *Poetik und Geschichtsphilosophie*, 2 v. (1974), and *Schriften*, 2 v. (1978); K. S. Guthke, *G. E. Lessing*, 3d ed. rev. (1979); C. Brodsky, "Lessing and the Drama of the Theory of Tragedy," *MLN* (1983); *Geschichte der deutschen Literaturkritik (1730–1980)*, ed. P. Hohendahl (1985); A. Warminski, *Readings in Interpretation* (1987); T. Pfau, "Critical Introduction," *Friedrich Hölderlin: Essays and Letters on Theory* (1988); C. Brodsky, "Contemporary Pictorialism and Aesthetics and Epistemology from Lessing to Kant," *CL* 45 (1993); A. Cascardi, *Consequences of Enlightenment* (1999); C. Brodsky, "Housing the Spirit in Hegel: From the Pyramids to Romantic Poetry," *Rereading Romanticism*, ed. M. Helfer (2000).
■ **Russia**: A. Stender-Petersen, *Gesch. der russischen Literatur* (1978); V. Erlich, *Russian Formalism: History–Doctrine*, 3d ed. (1981).
■ **Spain**: F. García Lorca, *Conferencias y lecturas*, in *Obras completas*, ed. A. del Hoyo (1954); *Historia y antología de la poesía española en la lengua castellana*, ed. F. C. Sainz de Robles, 2 v. (1967); G. A. Bécquer, *Crítica literaria*, in *Obras completas* (1995).
C. BRODSKY

# ROMANTICISM

I. European
II. British and American

**I. European.** Romanticism (Ger. *Romantik*, Fr. *romantisme*, Rus. *romantizm*) was the leading aesthetic and intellectual trend in the first half of the 19th c. Its most important common denominators were the emphasis on individual consciousness in its tense relationship with the material and social environment and cultivation of loosely structured artistic forms rife with fragmentation, discontinuities, and stylistic and emotional contrasts. The hist. of romanticism can be divided into three periods: early (mid-1790s–1800s), when the philosophical foundations of romantic consciousness were formulated; middle or "high" (1810s–40s), when romanticism spread throughout Europe; and late (after 1848), when vestiges of its heritage maintained their presence in a postromantic world.

Romanticism had numerous predecessors in the 18th c., from the critique of rationalism by J. G. Herder, Jean-Jacques Rousseau, and J. G. Fichte, to preromantic literary practices (sentimentalism, *Sturm und Drang*; see PREROMANTICISM) conceptualized by Friedrich Schiller as "sentimental poetry." The romantic movement proper emerged in the mid-1790s in Jena in writings of the *Athenaeum*, a jour. whose chief contributors were the Schlegel brothers, Friedrich (1772–1829) and August Wilhelm (1767–1845); Novalis (1772–1801); Friedrich Schleiermacher (1768–1834); and Ludwig Tieck (1773–1853). Outside the *Athenaeum* circle, similar philosophical views and features of poetics were developed by Friedrich Hölderlin (1770–1843).

Romanticism sprang to life in response to Immanuel Kant's (1724–1804) critique of pure reason, out of the sense of metaphysical anxiety caused by Kant's exposure of the contingency of cognition, which left consciousness confined in a priori categories and thereby cut off the infiniteness of the "world in itself" transcendent to those categories. Early romantics rejected the remedy offered by Idealist philosophy (Fichte), which consisted in proclaiming the absoluteness of subjective consciousness, thus making it the noncontingent anchor of cognition. The romantics strove to approach the transcendent world without losing sight of its objective existence independent of consciousness. The early romantic solution to this dilemma consisted in making Kantian pure reason "impure" by invading it with free-flowing fantasy. An emphasis on the free, creative fantasy as an inexorable component of reflection stood behind the choice of the provocative term *romantic*, a word traditionally associated with overblown fantasies carried to the point of being ridiculous and bizarre. The notion of "romantic poetry," introduced by K.W.F. Schlegel in the collective series of "Athenaeum Fragments" (1798), signified a dynamic mode of creativity driven by an unceasing pursuit of an unreachable yet anticipated ideal. Fragmentation and discontinuity, brought to reflection by the uncontrollable and unpredictable creative element, "potentialized" all phenomena (Novalis, "Blütenstaub" [Grains of Pollen]), setting their cognition into a "progressive" (i.e., unceasingly evolving) commotion, in which they ever approximate yet never achieve the absolute. A "marriage" of rational thought and untamed fantasy turns metaphysical reflection into an open-ended narrative of the "philosophical years of learning" (from the title of K.W.F. Schlegel's work), while products of free creativity emerge illuminated by romantic *irony— a concept of key importance understood as exposing, by means of metareflection, the relative and transient character of any artistic and intellectual achievement.

Among early literary examples of romantic philosophical doctrine were Novalis's *Heinrich von Ofterdinger* (posthumously pub., 1802) and Hölderlin's *Hyperion* (1797–99), works that introduced fragmentary novelistic narrative, and K.W.F. Schlegel's novel *Lucinde* (1799), whose discourse comprised freely juxtaposed third-person narrative, philosophical dialogues, and embedded stories. Although J. W. Goethe did not belong to the romantic movement and later condemned its penchant for disorder as "sick," some of his works showed a kinship with romantic ideology and aesthetics. In particular, *Faust* (1st pt., 1808) explored quintessential features of the romantic hero: the sense of being imprisoned in his subjectivity and the yearning for the "real" world, resulting in perpetual restlessness and never-satisfied longings. An important role in the *Athenaeum* heritage belonged to trans. (Shakespeare's plays by A. W. Schlegel, Cervantes's *Don Quixote* by Tieck), which contributed to the eventual "globalization" of Eur. lit. under the auspices of romanticism.

Principles of Ger. romanticism found an early resonance in England and France. William Wordsworth (1770–1850), in the Preface to his and S. T. Coleridge's (1772–1834) *Lyrical Ballads* (1798–1802), advocated a poetic lang. devoid of any conventional rhetorical flourish and argued for the importance of ordinary life experiences as catalysts of reflection. Wordsworth's idea of "spots of time" (*The Prelude*, 1805, pub. 1850) designated revelational moments that punctuate the incremental process of personal devel. François René de Chateaubriand (1768–1848), in his short novels *Atala* (1801) and *René* (1802), carried the never-satisfied quest of the Faustian romantic character to an exotic locus: having fled civilization, René seeks harmony in the world of the Am. Indians, whom he initially perceives as being blissfully united with *nature. Yet the meeting of the world of nature and the world of self-conscious civilization leads to nothing but a series of catastrophes, in which all the protagonists are eventually destroyed.

With the advent of high romanticism, principles of romantic art, alongside features of "romantic" consciousness and behavior, spread across ling. barriers, cultural trads., and artistic media. In this process, romanticism largely abandoned the relativizing critique that was central for the early romantics in favor of utopian or mystical dreams of an all-encompassing organic synthesis, typically under the auspices of the national collectivity. These trends drew strong crit. from authors who otherwise were not alien to romantic psychological insights and aesthetic innovations. Heinrich Heine's (1797–1856) polemical essay *Die romantische Schule* (*The Romantic School*, 1833–35) was particularly influential in shaping the image of romanticism as a regressive movement that retreats from modernity into mystical otherworldliness and the idealized national past. Yet the high romantic exalted vision of the messianic role of art resulted in high and manifold aesthetic achievements.

In France, high romanticism opened with the polemic between "classics" and "romantics," which rapidly spread to many other lands. The advent of the "new school" was proclaimed in numerous *manifestos, most notably Stendhal's (1783–1842) *Racine and Shakespeare* (1823) and Victor Hugo's (1802–85) preface to *Hernani* (1830). They declared a revolt against the neoclassical "rules" of Nicolas Boileau's (1636–1711) poetics, and ultimately, against any conventional constraints, claiming the sole responsibility of an artist to be the exploration of all the complexities and contradictions of the human soul by any artistic means at his or her disposal. The Parisian cultural scene at large presented itself as a romantic discontinuous narrative of a kind, with a flamboyant variety and incessant commotion of personalities, events, and ideas.

In Germany, the romantic metaphysics received a new ground in Friedrich Schelling's (1775–1854) *Systeme des transzendentalen Idealismus* (*System of Transcendental Idealism*, 1800). Schelling cast the central romantic concept of duality of the world of spirit and the world of nature into complementary polarities that are longing to meet, with the spirit perpetually exerting itself in a pursuit of the organic unity of the world of nature, while nature languishes in its inability to reflect on and express itself. The synthesis is to be achieved by a philosopher or an artist of *genius, whose work emerges as an act of free, creative will yet possesses the organic harmony of nature. The romantic cult of the "absolute" genius—Goethe, Pushkin, Shakespeare, Dante, Mozart—ensued from this idea. With its long-

ing for the absolute, high romanticism gave rise to revelatory utopian visions, either mystical (William Blake's *Jerusalem*, 1804–20) or revolutionary (P. B. Shelley's *Prometheus Unbound*, 1820).

High romantic *organicism awakened interest in folklore and "primitive" cultures, the prehistoric past, and the collective ling. consciousness as domains in which vestiges of primordial harmony withstood the fragmentation of mod. civilization. Wilhelm von Humboldt (1767–1835) spoke of lang. as the vessel of the collective memory of a nation, whose forms bear an imprint of its "character" and historical destiny. Achim von Arnim (1781–1831) and Clemens Brentano's (1778–1842) collection of folk poems, *Des Knaben Wunderhorn* (The Youth's Magic Horn, 3 v., 1805–8), alerted Germany and eventually all Europe to the treasures of folk consciousness and artistry. Particularly in smaller Eur. nations, the rising national self-consciousness and national lang. tended to be focused on a single figure of the "national" poet: Karel Mácha (1810–36) in Czech, Mihai Eminescu (1850–89) in Romanian, Sándor Petöfi (1823–49) in Hungarian, Taras Shevchenko (1814–61) in Ukrainian lit. The view of folklore and lang. as the embodiment of national self-consciousness gave rise to messianic efforts to reclaim the "soul" of a nation from the primordial depths of its folk poetry—a trend most spectacularly manifested in Elias Lönnrot's (1802–84) composition of the Finnish national *epic *Kalevala* (1835–49) out of authentic Karelian and Finnish epic folk songs.

Nevertheless, the early romantic emphasis on fragmentariness persisted in artistic practices, even though their philosophical background was largely forgotten. The polymorphous novel, initiated by K.W.F. Schlegel and Hölderlin, reached its climax in the oeuvre of E.T.A. Hoffmann (1776–1822), whose tales featured instant shifts of narrative voices and a constant vacillation between the real and the fantastic. In a similar way, the polymorphous composition in verse comprising different styles and forms loosely attached to each other in a manifold composition, a genre introduced by Goethe's *Faust*, was maintained in some major poetic works of the time, notably Adam Mickiewicz's (1798–1855) *Dziady* (*Forefathers' Eve*, 1821–32).

The metaphysical anxiety of early romanticism was now reinterpreted as the psychological malaise of the mod. age, whose carriers felt themselves condemned to inaction and perpetual doubt because of the contradictory nature of the soul. Benjamin Constant's (1767–1830) *Adolphe* (1816), Alfred de Musset's (1810–57) *Confession d'un enfant du ciècle* (*Confession of a Child of the Century*, 1836), and Mikhail Lermontov's (1814–41) *Geroi nashego vremeni* (*A Hero of Our Time*, 1840) explored this predicament of mod. consciousness. In a parallel devel., earlier depictions of the "eternal feminine" as the passively harmonious counterpart to the Faustian male hero gave way to the heroines of Germaine de Staël (1766–1817), Charlotte Brontë (1816–55), and George Sand (1804–76) with a complex character and rich inner life. Lord Byron's (1788–1824) oeuvre and personality epitomized the perpetual vacillation between degrading sarcasm and lofty exaltation grounded in the self-destructive restlessness of romantic consciousness. Heroes of Byron's poems and dramas (*Childe Harold's Pilgrimage*, 1812–19; *The Prisoner of Chillon*, 1816; *Manfred*, 1817; *The Deformed Transformed*, 1824) feel their spirit imprisoned in the physical and social world, and ultimately, within their own body—a sense that condemns them to wanderings and the self-imposed ejection from the "normal" life. Byron and Byronism signified the advent of a phenomenon that Rus. modernists would later call "life-creation," whereby the artist's oeuvre transparently refers to his life and personality, while his life path acquires dimensions of an artistic "work."

The romantic principle of existential-spiritual duality received compelling representations in music and painting. In canvases by Caspar David Friedrich (1774–1840), crippled fragmentariness of the phenomenal world paraded itself as a hint at a mystical truth behind it. The works by Hector Berlioz (1803–69), particularly his *Symphonie fantastique* (1830), offered a poignant musical expression of the "romantic character" in all its burning contradictions. In Franz Schubert's (1797–1828) vocal cycles, the overt naïveté of the folklore element, predicated on the highest artistic ingenuity, achieved a poignantly transcendental effect. Romantic music (Schubert, Robert Schumann, 1810–56; Frédéric Chopin, 1810–49) cultivated free-flowing, quasi-improvisational piano miniatures; the piano, its timbre and dynamic register greatly expanded because of technical innovations, became the favored instrument whose potential for contrasting effects and multiplicity of voices ideally fitted the task of expressing "dialectics" of the human soul.

The favorite mode of expression in lyric poetry of the time can be called elegiac. Its free poetic form and the easiness with which poetic thought could establish symbolic "correspondences" between contrasting phenomena—between past and present, nature and human soul, this and the other world, passion and its ironic subversion—made *elegy or quasi-elegy the dominant poetic genre. Its mood perpetually wandered from sweetly beautiful, radiant depictions (Joseph Eichendorff, 1788–1857; Musset) to passionate and bitter effusions (Giacomo Leopardi, 1798–1832) to somber introspection (Evgenii Baratynsky, 1800–44) to mystical meditation (Alphonse de Lamartine, 1790–1869) to, finally, a precarious balance between passion and self-irony (Alexander Pushkin, 1799–1837; Heine). At the same time, some strictly shaped poetic genres thrived as well, for instance, the *sonnet (Mickiewicz, Wordsworth), whose chiseled shape symbolically represented, as it were, the organic harmony of the world.

The romantics' acute awareness of an abyss between the inner dreamlike world of the soul and a hard existential reality sought remedy in retreating into the fairy-tale and mystical element, a mood that struck a powerful chord in the spiritual climate of the age of the Bourbon restoration. The dreamlike ballade thrived in Germany (Ludwig Uhland, 1787–1862) and consequently in Russia (Vasily Zhukovsky, 1783–1852). The romantic penchant for otherworldliness expressed itself in eruptions of the Gothic element (Hoffmann; E. A. Poe, 1809–49).

On the other side of the spectrum of genres catalyzed by the duality of romantic consciousness, exploration of the conflict between the inner and the phenomenal world gave rise to the social novel, in which the focus on heroes' complex psychological motivations came hand in hand with detailed and precise depictions of the material and social conditions under which they acted. Early examples of the genre in works of Jane Austen (1775–1817), Stendhal, Honoré de Balzac (1799–1850), Charles Dickens (1812–70), Alessandro Manzoni (1785–1873), and Lermontov, which portend the rise of the realist novel, owed their emergence not to a small extent to the romantic longing for reaching out to reality. Finally, from general interest in hist. arose the historical novel, pioneered by Walter Scott (1771–1832) and championed by such authors as Hugo, Alfred de Vigny (1797–1863), and Edward Bulwer-Lytton (1803–73).

During its first two decades (from 1810 through the '20s), Rus. romantics, while intensely exploring various romantic genres and modes of expression, remained largely unconcerned with romanticism's roots in metaphysics, the philosophy of hist., and the philosophy of lang. Pushkin's *Kavkazskii plennik* (*The Prisoner of the Caucasus*, 1821), Baratynsky's *Eda* (1824), and Lermontov's *A Hero of Our Time* carried romantic exoticism à la Chateaubriand to the loci of Rus. imperial conquest, paradoxically coupling the restlessness of the romantic character with the vicissitudes of military duty. The Rus. elegy of the 1820s exploited a volatile state of the Rus. lang. of the time for creating a dynamic discourse, rife with ambiguities and rapid mood shifts. Lermontov's poetic persona in the 1830s presented arguably the most compelling embodiment of Byronism on the Eur. scene. In his Ukrainian stories (1831–32), Nikolai Gogol (1809–52) presented the ethnographic element in an artful mixture of naïve exuberance and irony. Most important, Pushkin's *Evgenij Onegin* (written 1825–32, first full ed. 1833) became one of the foremost achievements of the prerealist novelistic narrative strategy, with its ellipses and evasions, its reliance on an implied meaning, and its ironic unreliability of the authorial voice.

It was only in the 1830s and particularly in the 1840s, partly because of an overwhelming influence of Schelling and Hegel, that Rus. lit. turned to early philosophical values of romanticism, reinterpreting artistic forms as a means for representing metaphysical reflection. Pushkin's poetic works in the 1830s often pose as a metareflection on themes and genres he had mastered in the previous decade. Gogol's novel *Dead Souls* (1st pt., 1841) combined an episodic and ironic travelogue-like narrative with an effort (doomed to remain unaccomplished) to carry out a moral message of cosmic and mystical proportions. Another example of philosophically charged prose was Vladimir Odoevsky's (1803–69) *Russkie nochi* (*Russian Nights*, 1844), whose polymorphous narrative, comprising philosophical discussions, Hoffmanesque phantasmagoria, and embedded novellas, embodied the key romantic idea of the multiplicity of alternative representations through which the absolute can be indirectly accessed.

In a way, the hist. of Rus. romanticism directly counters the course of romanticism's evolution in western Europe, a paradox that may explain the flowering of "metaphysical poetry" (late Baratynsky, Fyodor Tiutchev, 1803–73; Afanasy Fet, 1820–92) in the 1840s–'70s, which arguably constituted the highest literary achievement of late romanticism at the time when its literary tides were ebbing elsewhere. Particularly striking is the total symbolization that is the central feature of Tiutchev's poetics. Echoing motifs, through which the world of the spiritual absolute let itself be anticipated in material forms of being, reverberate in Tiutchev's poetry, recalling Charles Baudelaire's (1821–67) poetics of "correspondences," yet Tiutchev's total symbolization remains distinctly "romantic" in that it does not have characteristically modernist sharp dissonances of Baudelaire's *imagery.

One domain in which late romanticism continued to thrive was music. Richard Wagner (1813–83), Johannes Brahms (1833–87), and Franz Liszt (1811–86) in Germany and Austria; Pyotr Tchaikovsky (1840–93) and Nicolai Rimsky-Korsakov (1844–1908) in Russia; Georges Bizet (1838–75) in France; and Giuseppe Verdi (1813–1901) in Italy explored such central domains of romantic consciousness and aesthetics as the dialectics of characters, the quest for the primordial, and the penchant for the fantastic and the exotic. Literary and musical late romanticism directly influenced *symbolism, *impressionism, and *expressionism, whose eventual appearance signified the emergence of modernist aesthetics (see MODERNISM). In this sense, the romantic element continued its subliminal presence in mod. Eur. culture.

**II. British and American.** The romantic movement was both self-critical and self-conscious from its inception and also the product of waves of like-minded thought over a number of decades, rather than a single intellectual and artistic entity. From an aesthetic standpoint, romanticism is clearly a reactive concept, and poetic self-consciousness is central to it. Much of its greatest lit. is about the act of writing as it develops from the work of the *imagination (e.g., John Keats's *Fall of Hyperion* [written 1819, pub. 1856], Coleridge's "Kubla Khan" [1797, pub. 1816], Wordsworth's *The Prelude* [1805, pub. 1850]). Many romantic poems are at least in part about stripping bare the creative process in disarmingly personal ways, and this, in turn, often contributed to their authors' initial reluctance to make them public. In contrast to the public nature of much of the writing of the 18th c., that of romanticism is often deeply private and personal, circulating among close groups of friends and fellow writers for some time before publication. Indeed, the matter of romantic writing is often autobiographical—the closely observed personal experience of the writers themselves, even or esp. that which is intangible, half-remembered, or known through altered states, both waking and sleeping (e.g., Byron's *Childe Harold's Pilgrimage*, pt. 3 [1816]; Shelley's "Triumph of Life" [written 1822; pub. 1824]; Blake's *Marriage of Heaven and Hell* [1790]; Keats's "Ode to a Nightingale" [1819; pub. 1820]; Coleridge's *conversation poems [1796–98]). A related phenomenon is an extraordinary outpouring of reflection on the essence of lit. (e.g., Keats's letters; Shelley's *Defence of Poetry* [written 1821; pub. 1840]; Coleridge's *Biographia Literaria* [1817]) and also a related body of transformational lit. crit. (e.g., the Shakespeare crit. of William Hazlitt, Coleridge, and Charles Lamb).

Broadly understood, romanticism in Britain can be taken to describe the group of artistic ideas emerging between two key political events: the revolution in France of 1789 and the Reform Act of 1832. Together, these are transformational moments in Brit. hist. Many writers assumed the first of these events to be the greatest moment of historical calamity since the fall of the Roman Empire; it shook up the geopolitical order of western Europe and ushered in a period of great uncertainty. Although outside the realm, it caught a mood in political thought at home that recognized the need for reforms providing for increased suffrage and greater individual liberty in a rapidly industrializing nation expanding its imperial boundaries into foreign lands as it built itself into a serious international power. The second episode enacted many of these desires for reform by redesigning the political landscape, ushering in a period when the Crown, church and aristocracy had reduced power. In between the two events, other key devels. had an impact on life in Britain. One was the ongoing war with postrevolutionary France (1799–1815), which generated considerable social change; another was the emancipation of Catholics (1829), which presented challenges to the role of the established church. Both cast doubts on the existing structures of power and forced progressive governments to reconsider the ways in which the country was ruled. Writers in the romantic period reflected these concerns widely. They also took their aesthetic ambitions from a cultural environment concerned with social improvement and individual liberty but aware at the same time of the strictures placed on these by the changing state of Britain. The period saw the abolition of slavery and advancements in gender equality but also terrible privations brought on by the war and periods of political repression (all of which are reflected in the work of the poet Anna Laetitia Barbauld, 1743–1825, for instance). Equally, industrialization brought new wealth to the middle class and generated enlightened discussion of workers' rights while contributing to rural poverty and urban squalor.

A particular paradox surrounds romanticism in America. While it clearly takes its lead, in intellectual and artistic terms, from Britain, a central theme is the challenge of matching an independent cultural response to a new nation with its unique landscape and demography. The movement, moreover, has more fluid dates than its Brit. counterpart. Romantic elements are visible in the writing of the first generation that followed the Revolutionary War (1775–83) and may be traced throughout the lit. of antebellum America (pre-1861). During this period, Am. artists looked to instantiate myths of independent origins, often by appealing to the extraordinary power of the landscape, but also inevitably nodding to Brit. cultural priority. Many writers of the first half of the 19th c. had close links to Britain: Washington Irving (1783–1859) and George Ticknor (1791–1871) knew Byron, while W. C. Bryant (1794–1878) and R. W. Emerson (1803–82) visited Wordsworth. Coleridge, largely because of his philosophical and religious writings, had a greater following in America than he did at home. Nevertheless, by 1842, confidence in the national *canon was sufficient to encourage the publication of an anthol. of Am. poetry. Dedicated to the Harvard-educated painter Washington Allston (a friend of Coleridge), some of those included retain their reputation as important writers in the romantic trad. such as Poe and Bryant; others such as H. W. Longfellow (1807–82), Richard Dana Sr. (1787–79), and C. F. Hoffman (1806–84) may have looked to the Am. wilderness for their subject, but their poetics are conventionally Victorian.

America's most interesting contribution to romanticism grew out of the intellectual movement associated with opposition to the Unitarianism of the Harvard Divinity School. *Transcendentalism*, as it came to be known, draws together many of the most important figures in Am. culture: Emerson, H. D. Thoreau (1817–62), and Margaret Fuller (1810–50). As a reaction to nonconformism, further analogies may be drawn with Britain, where a number of important writers developed their ideas from unconventional religious convictions, incl. Blake, Coleridge, Hazlitt, and Leigh Hunt (1784–59). Transcendentalism also built on the romantic interest in the subject-centered philosophy of idealism, made popular in Britain by Coleridge after his reading of Kant, and it sought to connect this with a celebration of Am. nature in all its vastness. Much of the great writing of the mid-century (in particular that of Walt Whitman; Herman Melville, 1819–91; and Nathaniel Hawthorne, 1804–64) embraces these two themes and attempts in form as well as subject matter to develop a voice that is distinctly Am. Still, there remains a related body of lit. constituting a trans-Atlantic romanticism by writers with a place in both trads., or those concerned with negotiating America's place in the Atlantic World, such as Melville in his great whaling novels or Hannah More (1745–1843), Harriet Martineau (1802–76), and Olaudah Equiano (1745–97), whose various writings form part of the vast lit. related to slavery and abolitionism.

Complex contradictions beset efforts to define *romanticism* as a critical term; in his highly influential 1923 lecture to the Modern Language Association, Lovejoy argued that any coherent appraisal of it is impossible. Nevertheless, to such Victorian commentators as Thomas Carlyle (1795–81), Matthew Arnold (1822–88), and George Eliot (1819–80), it was clear that parallels could be drawn between the artistic trends of the previous generation in the Eng.-speaking world and Eur. ideas, which had themselves exerted a steadily increasing influence on a number of key figures during the period itself. *Romantic* may have been a term im-

ported from abroad; but the word had already begun to take on its mod. meaning in Britain during the 18th c., when the impulses of the movement were first felt. Thomas Warton (1728–90) distinguished between cl. and romantic elements in Dante as early as 1774, and the word had connotations of medievalism from the 17th c. An unsettling "deep romantic chasm" lies at the heart of Coleridge's visionary masterpiece "Kubla Khan," suggesting that the word was charged for him with more meaning than it has in its conventional amatory guise, and both there and in Walter Scott's preface to his first novel, *Waverley* (1814), it is related to a nostalgia for an archaic world of fantastic romance that is not obedient to the laws of mod. rationalism. Romantic thought more widely betrays an obsession with the past, and one of its key tenets, expressed in Carlyle's important essay of 1830, "On History," is that the knowledge of a people's spiritual nature is only arrived at through an understanding of their historical past. If 18th-c. historians are characterized in the imagination of romantic writers as suspicious of the primitive past, then the later generation falls in line with one of its most important thinkers, Edmund Burke (1729–97), whose account of the Fr. Revolution takes it to be the last and most barbaric act of the Enlightenment, which cares nothing for hist.: "people will not look forward to posterity who never look back to their ancestors," he warned in "Reflections on the Revolution in France" (1790).

The recovery and indeed invention of national mythology are both fundamental to romanticism in Britain and America. Antiquarianism, the earlier fashion for recovering artifacts relevant to Britain's distant past, fed into a more literary preoccupation with the recording of popular poetic trads. and the creation of a national canon independent of the classics. Shakespeare became established in romantic crit. as the quintessentially Eng. genius, all the better for his ignorance of the rules of neoclassicism. Meanwhile, the other pinnacle of Eng. poetry, John Milton (1608–74), exerted an influence in more testing ways. All the major poets of the period display a debt to Milton; for Keats (1795–1821) and Blake (1757–1827), esp., this runs over into an antagonistic struggle to escape from his shadow. The desire to create a literary work that is epic in scope but mod. in form, and hence different from *Paradise Lost*, haunts romanticism; and it may be said to have been achieved only insofar as writers made themselves the subject of their work either directly, as in Wordsworth's *Prelude* or Whitman's "Song of Myself," or indirectly, as in Byron's *Don Juan* or Melville's *Moby Dick*.

One set of works that obsessed many writers in the period, in both Britain and America, was that of the supposedly ancient Scots bard Ossian. This collection of poems, apparently drawn from local highland sources and then translated by James Macpherson (1736–96) in the 1760s, was widely and rightly contested as a hoax, but it satisfied the longing for a northern Eur. epic and was popular with Thomas Jefferson and Goethe. *Fingal* (1761), purporting to be an ancient epic poem trans. from Gaelic, invoked distant Celtic hist. and thus contributed to the kind of myth of origins sought by romanticism, with its local, nationalistic leanings. The historical novels of Scott, rooted in the very events out of which Brit. national mythology was made but invoking a romanticized vision of highland life, are one product of this impulse; another is the pompous epic *Columbiad* (1807) by Joel Barlow (1784–1812), the Connecticut poet, first written in the aftermath of the Am. Revolution, which tells of the founding of the nation.

Part of the attraction of Ossian's poetry was no doubt its setting at the farthest reaches of Scotland, beyond the limits of the civilized world as traditionally conceived. Romantic artists were, in fact, fascinated by the ancient cl. past and in particular the ruins of its empires (e.g., Shelley's "Ozymandias" [1817]; Keats's "Ode on a Grecian Urn" [1819]; Byron's *The Curse of Minerva* [written 1811, pub. 1813]), but the locus classicus for the romantic imagination remains the sublime natural landscape, untamed by human interference. Wordsworth climbing Snowdon, Shelley before Mont Blanc, Whitman by blue Ontario's shore, or the artist J.M.W. Turner observing the eruption of Vesuvius are all expressions of the romantic preoccupation with a sublime nature that stretches human imagination to its very limits and threatens to destroy civilized human life. Frequently, expressions of the *sublime reveal connections to the nation and its hist. Scott's highlanders, bound by ancient, elemental codes of honor, are inseparable from their wild environment; and Wordsworth's subjects are often unpolished but heroic members of a rural poor, whom he describes as though they had emerged from the landscape itself. One of the most memorable is the leech gatherer described in the poem "Resolution and Independence" (1807), in which Wordsworth reflects on the madness that afflicts many poets. Shelley puts this well in a poem about Lord Byron: "Most wretched men / Are cradled into poetry by wrong, / They learn in suffering what they teach in song." A familiar *topos, this romantic fixation also relies on the sublime, only here it is internalized as a figure for the vast, unknowable quality of the human mind.

Wordsworth had Thomas Chatterton (1752–70) in mind in "Resolution and Independence." While still a teenager, "the marvellous Boy" had forged a number of pseudomedieval poems, trying to pass them off as originals before committing suicide, and his unhappy story contributed to the cult of the untrained genius that fed the reputation of supposedly uneducated, natural poets from the rural laboring class: Robert Burns (1759–96), James Hogg (1770–1835), Robert Bloomfield (1766–1823), and John Clare (1793–1864) in particular. Traditional poems, *ballads and folk songs from rural communities were popular with early romantic readers, the most dedicated collector of these being Thomas Percy (1728–1811), whose *Reliques of Ancient English Poetry* (1765) was aimed at an audience like that which appreciated Ossian. These trends combined with political and aesthetic concerns in one of the most important aspects of romantic poetics: the radical transformation of the lang. of poetry itself. Undoubtedly,

the most significant publications in this regard are the first two eds. of *Lyrical Ballads* (1798, 1800). Some of the greatest poems in this collection—Coleridge's "The Nightingale" and *The Rime of the Ancient Mariner* or Wordsworth's "Tintern Abbey," "Michael," and "The Brothers"—have little to do with the traditional ballad form and certainly do not employ the "language really used by men," as the Preface of 1800 claimed. Nevertheless, the poems clearly inaugurate a trad. of writing that makes a radical break with 18th-c. poetics. There are dark, disturbing elements in many of the poems in *Lyrical Ballads* and the influence of popular Ger. ballads, such as G. A. Bürger's "Lenore" (1773), with their gothic mixture of the macabre and the mystical, is apparent throughout the period. In fact, the gothic pervades many romantic genres (poems, plays, novels), and it appealed both to a popular taste for ghoulish tales of the supernatural and also to an intellectual milieu that was fascinated by aspects of experience that had not already been explained away by enlightened science. Isaac Newton (1643–1727) and John Locke (1632–1704), the great heroes of the Eng. empirical trad., are frequent whipping boys in the period; Keats attacked the former in a famous phrase from "Lamia": "Philosophy will clip an angel's wings." Romanticism certainly does not dismiss science (indeed, some writers, incl. Coleridge and Shelley, studied devels. in contemp. science very closely), but many of its greatest works suggest strongly that the powerful truths of human life cannot be found in the empirical analysis of the immanent alone. Rather, as in the moments of idealist transport that accompany the tough intellectualism of Wordsworth's "Tintern Abbey," they are uncovered through a subjective intuition of transcendence that comes from within.

■ **I. European**: R. Haym, *Die romantische Schule* (1870); G. Lukács, *Die Zerstörung der Vernunft: Der Weg des Irrationalismus von Schelling zu Hitler* (1954); A. Huyssen, *Die frühromantische Konzeption von Übersetzung und Aneignung* (1969); J. Körner, *Romantiker und Klassiker: Die Brüder Schlegel in ihren Beziehungen zu Schiller und Goethe* (1971); R. Bourgeois, *L'ironie romantique* (1974); M. Crouzet, *Essay sur la genèse du romantisme, 1. La poétique de Stendhal* (1983); G. Gusdorf, *L'homme romantique* (1984); S. Pratt, *Russian Metaphysical Romanticism: The Poetry of Tiutchev and Boratynskii* (1984); W. M. Todd III, *Fiction and Society in the Age of Pushkin* (1986); A. Kuzniar, *Delayed Endings: Nonclosure in Novalis und Hölderlin* (1987); P. Lacoue-Labarthes and J.-L. Nancy, *Literary Absolute: The Theory of Literature in German Romanticism*, trans. P. Barnard and C. Lester (1988); E. Behler, *Studien zur Romantik und zur idealistischen Philosophie*, 2 v. (1988–93); M. Frank, *Einführung in die frühromantische Ästhetik* (1989); T. Ziolkowski, *German Romanticism and Its Institutions* (1990); E. Ostermann, *Das Fragment: Geschichte einer ästhetischen Idee* (1991); A. Seyhan, *Representation and Its Discontents: The Critical Legacy of German Romanticism* (1992); E. Behler, *German Romantic Literary Theory* (1993);

M. Greenleaf, *Pushkin and Romantic Fashion: Fragment, Elegy, Orient, Irony* (1994); *Romantik-Handbuch*, ed. H. Schanze (1994); W. Benjamin, "The Concept of Criticism in German Romanticism" (1920), *Selected Writings*, ed. M. P. Bullock et al., v. 1 (1996); D. E. Wellbery, *The Specular Moment: Goethe's Early Lyric and the Beginnings of Romanticism* (1996); M. Frank, *"Unendliche Annäherung": Die Anfänge der philosophischen Frühromantik* (1997); *Salons der Romantik*, ed. H. Schultz (1997); L. Pikulik, *Frühromantik: Epoche—Werke—Wirkung*, 2d ed. (2000); M. Götze, *Ironie und absolute Darstellung: Philosophie und Poesie in der Frühromantik* (2001); F. C. Beiser, *The Romantic Imperative: The Concept of Early German Romanticism* (2003); H. Ram, *Imperial Sublime: A Russian Poetics of Empire* (2003); B. Gasparov, "Pushkin and Romanticism," *Pushkin Handbook*, ed. D. M. Bethea (2005); A. Kubik, *Die Symboltheorie bei Novalis: Eine ideengeschichtliche Studie in ästhetischer und theologischer Absicht* (2006); C. Dahlhaus and N. Miller, *Europäische Romantik in Musik*, 2 v. (2007); B. Frischmann, *Das neue Licht der Frühromantik* (2009).
■ **II. British and American**: A. O. Lovejoy, "On the Discrimination of Romanticisms," *Essays in the History of Ideas* (1948); H. Bloom, *Shelley's Mythmaking* (1959); Abrams; K. Kroeber, *Romantic Narrative Art* (1960); H. Bloom, *The Visionary Company* (1961); R. Wellek, "The Concept of 'Romanticism' in Literary History," *Concepts of Criticism*, ed. S. G. Nichols Jr. (1963); G. H. Hartman, *Wordsworth's Poetry, 1787–1814* (1964); M. H. Abrams, *Natural Supernaturalism: Tradition and Revolution in Romantic Literature* (1971), and *English Romantic Poets: Modern Essays in Criticism* (1975); L. Furst, *Romanticism*, rev. ed. (1976); H. Honour, *Romanticism* (1979); H. G. Schenk, *The Mind of the European Romantics* (1979); M. Butler, *Romantics, Rebels and Reactionaries: English Literature and its Background, 1760–1830* (1981); J. J. McGann, *The Romantic Ideology* (1983); P. de Man, *The Rhetoric of Romanticism* (1984); *English and German Romanticism: Cross-Currents and Controversies*, ed. J. Pipkin (1985); M. Kipperman, *Beyond Enchantment: German Idealism and English Romantic Poetry* (1986); M. Levinson, *The Romantic Fragment Poem: A Critique of a Form* (1986); L. Chai, *The Romantic Foundations of the American Renaissance* (1987); D. Morse, *American Romanticism*, 2 v. (1987); *Romanticism in National Context*, ed. R. Porter and M. Teich (1988); C. H. Siskin, *The Historicity of Romantic Discourse* (1988); R. Weisbuch, *Atlantic Double-Cross: American Literature and British Influence in the Age of Emerson* (1988); N. V. Riasanovsky, *The Emergence of Romanticism* (1992); M. Cranston, *The Romantic Movement* (1994); C. Rosen, *The Romantic Generation* (1996); R. Gravil, *Romantic Dialogues: Anglo-American Continuities, 1776–1862* (2000); R. Eldridge, *The Persistence of Romanticism* (2002); C. Armstrong, *Romantic Organicism: From Idealist Origins to Ambivalent Afterlife* (2003); *Transatlantic Romanticism: An Anthology of British, American, and Canadian Literature, 1767–1876*, ed. L. Newman et al. (2006); R. Holmes, *The Age of Wonder: How the Romantic Generation Discovered the Beauty and Terror of Science* (2008); T. Blanning, *The Romantic Revolution* (2010).

B. Gasparov (Eur.); M. Scott (Brit. and Am.)

**RONDEAU.** Originally the generic term for all Fr. forms derived from dance-rounds (*rondes* or *rondels*) with singing accompaniment (see RONDEL, TRIOLET): the refrain was sung by the chorus—the general body of dancers—and the variable section by the leader. The written forebears of the rondeau are generally thought to be the *rondets* or *rondets de carole* from 13th-c. romances (see CAROL).

The form by which we know the rondeau today emerged in the 15th c. and by the beginning of the 16th c. had displaced all competitors. The poem is constructed on two rhymes only with lines of eight or ten syllables, and the first word or phrase of the first line is used as a *refrain; this curtailed, repeating line, called the *rentrement*, usually does not rhyme. As a type of truncated refrain, the *rentrement* may have derived from copyists' habits of abbreviation, common in the Middle Ages. In Fr. prosody, *rentrements* are usually associated with the rondeau, but whenever the refrains of any poem are an abbreviated version of the first line either of the poem or of each stanza (e.g., Thomas Wyatt, "In *aeternum*," "Forget not yet," " *Quondam* was I"), then the term *rentrement* can be justifiably applied.

Traditional lengths for the rondeau are 12 or 15 lines (if the two brief *rentrements* are not considered lines, 10 or 13) printed in two or three stanzas. In the 15th c., both lengths appear: François Villon's "Mort, j'appelle de ta rigueur" is 12 lines in length, while Clément Marot's "Au bon vieulx temps" is 15, and both poems have been lineated with two and three stanzas. If we let *R* stand for the *rentrement*, the 12-line rondeau is *abbaabR abbaR* in two stanzas or *abba abR abbaR* in three, while the 15-line rondeau is *aabbaaabR aabbaR* in two stanzas or *aabba aabR aabbaR* in three.

During the course of the 16th c., the rondeau gradually disappeared. It was restored to fashion at the beginning of the 17th c. by the *précieux* poets, esp. Vincent Voiture, on whose 15-line example Théodore de Banville based his 19th-c. revival of the form. Although Alfred de Musset had experimented with the form earlier in the 19th c., taking some liberties with the rhymes, it was Banville's practice that provided the model for the later 19th- and 20th-c. explorations of the form. In England, aside from 16th-c. examples (Wyatt in particular), the rondeau did not really flourish until the end of the 19th c., when under Banville's influence, Fr. forms attracted the enthusiasm of *light verse poets such as Austin Dobson, Edmund Gosse, W. E. Henley, Ernest Dowson, Thomas Hardy, and Robert Bridges. Their influence was felt in America: the Af. Am. poet Paul Laurence Dunbar's most well-known poem may be the 1896 rondeau "We Wear the Mask," whose title is also its *rentrement*. In Germany, where it has also been called *Ringelgedicht, Ringelreim*, and *Rundreim*, the rondeau was used by Georg Rudolf Weckherlin, Johann Nikolaus Götz, Johann Fischart, and later Otto Eric Hartleben.

In the 20th c., an immensely famous rondeau was Canadian doctor John McCrae's "In Flanders Fields" (1915), a poem frequently recited and reprinted both during and long after World War I. "In Flanders fields the poppies blow," begins the lyric, ending with a stern call to the public to "keep faith" with the battlefield dead. Through the efforts of the Royal Legion of Canada, the YMCA, the National American Legion, the American and French Childrens' League, and the British Legion, McCrae's Flanders poppy became an instantly recognizable symbol worn in Canada and Britain annually on November 11, Remembrance Day, to commemorate the Great War dead. When the poem first appeared, few of these literal legions may have recognized its form: even the best-selling posthumous collection of McCrae's poetry published in 1919 referred to it as a highly original kind of *sonnet. In 2001, the first stanza of "In Flanders Fields" was printed on the Canadian ten-dollar bill.

The management of the *rentrement* is the key to the rondeau's expressive capabilities. Banville says that the *rentrement* is "both more and less than a line, for it plays the major role in the rondeau's overall design. It is at once the rondeau's subject, its *raison d'être* and its means of expression." Fr. poets, wishing to keep the *rentrement* unrhymed, yet fatally drawn to rhyme, found a solution in the punning *rentrement*, which rhymes with itself rather than merely repeating itself (e.g., "son or," "sonore," "s'honore"). Consequently, in the Fr. rondeau, the *rentrement* tends to remain unassimilated, full of wit, buoyancy, and semantic fireworks. The Eng. poets, on the other hand, sought to integrate the *rentrement* more fully, both by frequently allowing it to rhyme with either the *a* or *b* lines, thus pushing the rondeau in the direction of that exclusively Eng. form, the *roundel, and by exploiting its metrical continuity with the rest of the stanza. The Eng. *rentrement* is also usually longer than the Fr., four syllables rather than one or two. In short, the Eng. rondeau is altogether graver and more meditative than the Fr., its *rentrement* more clearly a lyric destination, a focus of self-recollection, intimate knowledge, and haunting memory.

The *rondeau redoublé*, similar in form, was rare even at the time of Jean Marot, who is known to have composed one in 1526. In the 17th c., a few isolated examples occur in the works of Mme. Deshoulières and Jean de La Fontaine; Banville uses the form in the 19th c. Marot's *rondeau redoublé*, 24 lines in six *quatrains plus the *rentrement*, may be schematized as follows (R signifying the *rentrement* and capitals and primes denoting whole-line refrains): *ABA'B' babA abaB babA' abaB' babaR*. Each line of stanza 1 is employed in turn as the last line of each of the following four stanzas, which thus serve to develop the content of stanza 1; the final stanza then makes a comment or summation. Dorothy Parker's "Rondeau Redoublé (And Scarcely Worth the Trouble, At That)" of 1926 follows the four-century-old scheme of Marot exactly.

■ T. de Banville, *Petit traité de poésie française* (1872); Patterson; M. Françon, "La pratique et la théorie du rondeau et du rondel chez Théodore de Banville," *MLN* 52 (1937); F. Gennrich, "Deutsche Rondeaux," *BGDSL(H)* 72 (1950), and *Das altfranzösische Rondeau und Virelai im 12. und 13. Jahrhundert* (1963); N.H.J. van den Boogaard, *Rondeaux et Refrains du XIIe siècle au début du XIVe* (1969)—prints all known rondeaux ca. 1228–1332, but must be used with caution; F. Deloffre, *Le Vers français* (1969); M. Françon, "Wyatt et le rondeau," *RQ* 24 (1971); F. M. Tierney, "The Causes of the Revival of the Rondeau," *Revue de l'Université d'Ottawa* 43 (1973); Elwert; C. Scott, "The Revival of the Rondeau in France and England 1860–1920," *RLC* 213 (1980), and *French Verse-Art* (1980); Morier; J. Britnell, "'Clore et rentrer': The Decline of the Rondeau," *FS* 37 (1983); J.F.W. Vance, *Death So Noble* (1997).

C. Scott; T.V.F. Brogan; A. L. French

**RONDEL.** Like the terms *roundel and *rondeau, the term *rondel* did not apply in the Middle Ages to one rigidly fixed poetic form but to a "round" song with a *refrain or to any of several similar two-rhyme patterns for such a song's lyrics. Eustache Deschamps gave five separate schemes for the rondel in his *L'Art de dictier* (1392), one of which would later be renamed the *triolet. Poems by 15th-c. poets Christine de Pisan, Jean Froissart, Octavien de Saint-Gelais, and Charles d'Orléans designated as rondels are schematically distinct. In the 19th c., Théodore de Banville's popular handbook *Petit traité de poésie française* (1872) took a rondel by d'Orléans as a model for and example of the rondel form. Banville's first ed. printed the d'Orléans poem with 14 lines, but upon discovering that transcribers who habitually indicated refrains with "etc." had confused him, Banville corrected the example in later eds. to 13 lines. Banville and other *Parnassians adhered to the 13-line scheme, but the Eng. Aesthetes as often chose the more *sonnet-like 14-line scheme. The rondel can therefore be defined as a form with two rhymes, three stanzas, and a two-line refrain that repeats either two and a half or three times: *ABba abAB abbaA(B)*.

■ Kastner; M. Françon, "La pratique et la théorie du rondeau et du rondel chez Théodore de Banville," *MLN* 52 (1937); J. M. Cocking, "The 'Invention' of the Rondel," *French Studies* 5 (1951); C. Scott, "The Revival of the Rondeau in France and England, 1860–1920," *RLC* 213 (1980); C. Scott, "Poetry and the Fixed," *The Poetics of French Verse* (1998).

A. L. French

**ROTA VIRGILIANA** (Lat., "Virgilian wheel"). The term illustrates the division of Virgil's major works into a hierarchical triad. Authors of late antiquity recognized the generic progression from the *pastoral *Eclogues to the didactic *Georgics to the *epic *Aeneid* as reflecting the developing complexity of Virgil's writing style and life station. In his grammar *Parisiana poetria* (ca. 1220), John of Garland introduces the rota virgiliana as a mnemonic device that portrays the works' stylistic differences and their corresponding occupations and imagery in a schema of concentric circles divided by three spokes.

The "low" style of the *Eclogues*, the "middle" style of the *Georgics*, and the "high" style of the *Aeneid* correspond to the occupations of "leisurely shepherd," farmer, and soldier or governor, respectively. Each style and occupation has its own representatives (Tityrus and Melibeus; Triptolemus and Ceres; Hector and Ajax), animal (sheep, cow, horse), implement (crook, plow, sword), locale (pasture, field, camp, or city), and tree (beech; apple and pear tree; laurel and cedar).

The rota virgiliana had great influence during the burgeoning nationalism of the Eng. Ren. Poets, notably Edmund Spenser and John Milton, fashioned themselves as national laureate poets in the manner of Virgil by following his career pattern, first composing works in the pastoral genre before tackling the weighty matters of the epic.

*See* BUCOLIC, DIDACTIC POETRY, POET LAUREATE.

■ Curtius; John of Garland, *The "Parisiana Poetria" of John of Garland,* ed. and trans. T. Lawler (1974); R. Neuse, "Milton and Spenser: The Virgilian Triad Revisited," *ELH* 45 (1978); P. Cheney, *Spenser's Famous Flight* (1993); Donatus, Aelius, *Life of Virgil,* trans. D. Wilson-Okamura, http://www.virgil.org/vitae/a-donatus.htm (1996, rev. 2008); *The Virgilian Tradition,* ed. J. M. Ziolkowski and M.C.J. Putnam (2008); *Classical Literary Careers and Their Reception,* ed. P. Hardie and H. Moore (2010).

K. CLELAND

**ROTROUENGE.** OF stanza form of uncertain origin (perhaps originally "song of Rotrou") and of indeterminate form. The *rotrouenge* perhaps derived from adaptation to lyric use of the epic *laisse*, with its characteristic sequence of isometric lines sung to one repeated musical phrase, but this structure may well have undergone early modification. Adapted into Occitan as *retroensa* or *retroncha*, the term was applied to strophic songs having a two-line *refrain* (whence the verb *retronchar*, to repeat in the manner of a refrain).

■ F. Gennrich, *Die altfranzösische Rotrouenge* (1925); Bec; Chambers; P. Uhl, "Oez com je sui bestornez (Rayn. 919): Rotrouenge ou no-sai-que-s'es?" *Studia Neophilologica* 65 (1993); P. Davies, "Rotrouenge," *The New Oxford Companion to Literature in French,* ed. P. France (1995).

J. H. MARSHALL

**ROUNDEL.** In the Middle Ages, this term was simply a synonym for the *rondeau* or the *rondel*—e.g., Chaucer, "Knight's Tale" (1529). But in its mod. sense, the term usually refers to the variant form introduced by A. C. Swinburne in his *A Century of Roundels* (1883). The Swinburne roundel is a three-stanza, two-rhyme poem of 11 lines on the pattern *abaR bab abaR* where *R* stands for the *rentrement*. The *rentrement,* as in the rondeau, is a shortened line—a word or phrase—that repeats in the manner of a *refrain*; in the Swinburne roundel, the *rentrement* normally rhymes with the *b* lines of the poem. The few other poets who have written Swinburne roundels include John Davidson, Ernest

Dowson, and Sara Teasdale; Christina Rossetti drafted but never published a self-referential Swinburne roundel in which the word *roundel* rhymes with such words as *scoundrel* and *groundswell.*

■ R. Rooksby, "Swinburne in Miniature," *Victorian Poetry* 23 (1985).

T.V.F. BROGAN; A. L. FRENCH

**RUBĀĪ** (pl. *rubāʿīyāt,* Ar., "four-parter"). A *monorhyme *quatrain originating in the Persian trad. and subsequently adapted into other Islamicate lits. The term *rubāʿī* refers to the four *hemistichs (*miṣrāʿ*) that comprise the quatrain. In Ar. and Persian versification, every line (*bayt*) of verse consists of a symmetrical pair of miṣrāʿ, graphically arranged in two columns and separated by a visual *caesura. The quatrain can thus be parsed both as a four-line poem (rubāʿī) by counting miṣrāʿs and as a two-line form (*du-baytī*) by counting bayts:

1st miṣrāʿ . . . . . a | 2d miṣrāʿ . . . . . a || (= *bayt* 1)
3d miṣrāʿ . . . . . . x | 4th miṣrāʿ . . . . a || (= *bayt* 2)

The terms *rubāʿī* and *du-baytī* are not, however, interchangeable. Rubāʿī quatrains conform to a unique meter not used for other verse forms, its 20 *morae usu. resolving as a 13-syllable pattern, either

$$- - \cup - - - \cup \cup - - -$$

or $- - \cup \cup - \cup - \cup - - \cup \cup -$ . But since one long may replace two consecutive breves, possible permutations allow as few as 10 syllables. The du-baytī quatrain, by contrast, is composed in a canonical Persian meter, usually *hazaj,* in a shorter 11-syllable (19-morae) pattern: $\cup - - - | \cup - - - | \cup - -$. The rhyme scheme for all rubāʿī and du-baytī quatrains is *aaxa* and often, esp. in the early period, *aaaa.* In Persian, Turkish, and Urdu rubāʿīs, the rhyme may occur before the end of each miṣrāʿ, to be followed by a uniform refrain (*radīf*).

The Persian quatrain is an epigrammatic genre, tersely developing an image, thought, or problem that is then wittily or forcefully resolved in the final line, ideally with an aphorism, didactic maxim, or philosophical/mystical aperçu. Each quatrain treats a single theme, but the genre's topical scope is broad: love, wine, homily, mysticism, praise, politics, or satire. It emerged from folk poetry, often in regional dialect, more often sung than written (in music, a separate term, *tarāna,* is applied to sung quatrains). Oral circulation of rubāʿīs in this popular performance milieu led to frequent misattribution, with many so-called wandering quatrains attributed to multiple authors. The cl. rubāʿī is amply attested in both courtly and Sufi milieus in the 10th c., and by the 11th–12th cs., legendary vitas had built up around some quatrain composers or reciters, e.g., Mahsatī, renowned for her amorous and sometimes bawdy rubāʿīs; the "naked" dervish Bābā Ṭāhir with his dialect du-baytīs of love and devotion; and Abū Saʿīd-i Abi al-Khayr, who in his sermons regularly recited rubāʿīs composed by others for mystical inspiration. At court, an impromptu rubāʿī might receive rich reward for particular wit or elegance; a 14th-c. anthol., *Nuzhat al-majālis,* compiles 4,000 rubāʿīs by some 300 poets, topically organized in 17 chapters for the shah's amusement at court.

While living, 'Umar Khayyām (d. 1122) was not known as a poet; a trickle of rubāʿīs were attributed to him in scattered 13th-c. sources, about 25 in total by the year 1330. His corpus then began to grow, reaching well over 500 rubāʿīs by the mid-15th c., attesting to a growing vogue for the philosophically skeptical Khayyamesque rubāʿī. The astounding success of Edward FitzGerald's trans. of the *Rubáiyát of Omar Khayyám* (anonymously pub. in 1859, with subsequent revisions and expansions, 1868, 1872, and 1879) led to the creation of Khayyām societies in most anglophone capitals, to numerous parodies (e.g., the rubaiyat of golf, rubaiyat of a Persian kitten, etc.), and to trans. in most other world langs. FitzGerald's command of Persian was good, though his trans. style was free. Subsequent scholars and poets (e.g., Robert Graves, John Heath-Stubbs) have been unable to displace FitzGerald's rubāʿīs, which follow Eng. prosody (iambic pentameter) but retain the *aaba* rhyme scheme and a cynical epicurean outlook, while rearranging the Khayyamesque corpus into a quasi-narrative sequence, "something of an Eclogue." In the mid-20th c., forgeries purporting to be early mss. of Khayyām's rubāʿīs were foisted on scholars; in Amin Maalouf's novel *Samarcande* (1998), an apocryphal early ms. of Khayyām's rubāʿīs plays a central fictional role.

We may question Khayyām's authorship, but most canonical Persian poets did compose rubāʿīs, some in great quantity: about 1,900 by Jalāl al-Dīn Rūmī (ca. 1207–73), incl. several in Ar. ʿAṭṭār (ca. 1145–1221) tells us he composed 6,000 rubāʿīs, of which he preserved 2,000 in his *Mukhtār-nāma*, on amatory, Khayyamesque, and mystical themes, topically arranged to illustrate a subtle theosophy of love. The Persian rubāʿī remained a vibrant form, practiced by most poets from the 11th to 19th cs.; even after cl. forms gave way to *free verse in the mid-20th c., poets such as Nīmā Yūshīj (1896–1960) and Saeed Yousef continue to innovate in this form.

The rubāʿī form and meter were introduced to Ar. under the Persian name du-baytī, probably by 11th-c. bilingual Persian-Ar. poets composing *macaronic rubāʿīs for musical performance. It became popular among Ar. poets of the 13th–14th cs. as far west as Iberia, with some one thousand examples surviving, sometimes experimentally embedded in other forms, such as the *qaṣīda and muwashshaḥ. Though not in the rubāʿī meter of cl. convention, the quatrain form in other meters remains popular in mod. Ar. lit. (e.g., Jamīl Ṣidqī al-Zahāwī [1863–1936], Maḥmūd Darwīsh [1941–2008]). Despite the presence of a four-line strophic form (*dörtlük*) attested in eastern Turkic from the 11th c., the cl. rubāʿī was borrowed by Turkic lits. from Persian models, adopted in eastern Anatolia by Kadī Burhaneddin (1344–98), in Azerbayjan by Nesimi (ca. 1369–1417), and in Central Asia by ʿAlī-Shīr Navāʾī (d. 1501), though Azmi-zade Haleti (1570–1631) is considered the master of the Turkish rubāʿī and the Khayyām of Anatolia. Ottoman Turkish

poets continued to produce rubāʿī through the 19th c.; even the communist poet Nazim Hikmet (1902–63) produced a small volume of quatrains inspired by the rubāʿī form in 1945–46.

*See* ARABIC POETICS, ARABIC POETRY, EPIGRAM, GHAZAL, PERSIAN POETRY, TURKIC POETRY, TURKISH POETRY, URDU POETRY.

■ V. Zhukovsky, "Umar Khayyām and the 'Wandering' Quatrains," *Journal of the Royal Asiatic Society* 30, trans. E. D. Ross (1898); A. Christensen, *Critical Studies in the Rubāʿiyāt of ʿUmar-i-Khayyām* (1927); H. Ritter, "Zur Frage der Echtheit der Vierzeiler ʿOmar Chajjāms," *Orientalistische Literaturzeitung* 32 (1929); H. H. Schaeder, "Der geschichtliche und der mythische Omar Chajjam," *Zeitschrift der Deutschen Morgenländischen Gesellschaft* 88 (1934); Ṣ. Hidāyat, *Tarānah'hā-yi Khayyām* (1934); A. Bausani, "La Quartina," *Storia della letteratura persiana*, ed. A. Pagliaro and A. Bausani (1960); F. Meier, *Die Schöne Mahsati: Ein Beitrag zur Geschichte des Persischen Vierzeilers* (1963); W. Eilers, "Vierzeilerdichtung, persisch und ausserpersisch," *Wiener Zeitschrift für die Kunde des Morgenlandes* 62 (1969); A Dashti, *In Search of Omar Khayyam*, trans. L. P. Elwell-Sutton (1971); J. Yohannan, "The Fin de Siècle Cult of FitzGerald's *Rubaiyat of Omar Khayyam*," *Review of National Literatures* 2 (1971); L. P. Elwell-Sutton, "The 'Rubāʿī' in Early Persian Literature," and J. A. Boyle, "ʿUmar Khayyam: Astronomer, Mathematician and Poet," *The Cambridge History of Iran*, ed. W. B. Fisher et al., v. 4 (1975); M. A. Isani, "The Vogue of Omar Khayyám in America," *Comparative Literature Studies* 14 (1977); V.-M. D'Ambrosio, *Eliot Possessed: T. S. Eliot and FitzGerald's Rubáiyát* (1989); S. Shamīsā, *Sayr-i rubāʿī* (1995); E. FitzGerald, *Rubáiyát of Omar Khayyám*, ed. C. Decker (1997); J.T.P. de Bruijn, *Persian Sufi Poetry* (1997); W. Stoetzer, "Du baytī," *Encyclopedia of Arabic Literature*, ed. J. S. Meisami and P. Starkey (1998); O. Davidson, "Genre and Occasion in the Rubāʿiyyāt of ʿUmar Khayyām: The Rubāʿī, Literary History, and Courtly Literature," *Writers and Rulers: Perspectives on Their Relationships from Abbasid to Safavid Times*, ed. B. Gruendler and L. Marlow (2004); J. Biegstraaten, "Parodies in Books on FitzGerald's Rubáiyát of Omar Khayyám," *Persica* 20 (2004–5); A. Razavi, *The Wine of Wisdom: The Life, Poetry and Philosophy of Umar Khayyam* (2005); Sunil Sharma, "Wandering Quatrains and Women Poets," *The Treasury of Tabriz: The Great Il-Khanid Compendium*, ed. A. Seyed-Gohrab and S. McGlinn (2007); I. Gamard and R. Farhadi, *The Quatrains of Rūmī* (2008); B. Utas, "Prosody, Meter and Rhyme," *General Introduction to Persian Literature*, ed. J.T.P. de Bruijn (2009); A. Tafaẓẓoli, "Fahlavīyāt," *Encyclopedia Iranica*, http://www.iranicaonline.org/articles/fahlaviyat.

F. D. LEWIS

**RUNE.** A character of the Old Germanic alphabet (called the *futhorc* from its first characters), probably derived from Gr., Lat., and related scripts. From about the 4th c. CE, runes were widely inscribed on such objects as coins, memorial stones, weapons, and other personal objects. Notable poetic inscriptions include those on the 5th-c. Horn of Gallehus (now lost), and the 8th-c. Ruthwell Cross and Auzon Casket. Two runes (named *thorn* and *wyn*) were used in the OE adaptation of the Lat. alphabet, and *thorn* was also used in ON. Runes are sometimes found in OE poetic mss., where the rune names (e.g., *epel*, "home" and *sigel*, "sun") must be substituted for the characters. In the OE riddles, runes sometimes provide clues or spell out solutions. The OE poet Cynewulf wove his runic signature into his works. The OE "Husband's Message" is spoken by a cryptic rune staff; and poetic collections of gnomes organized around the *futhorc* are found in both OE and ON.

■ R. Derolez, *Runica Manuscripta* (1954); R. I. Page, *An Introduction to English Runes*, 2d ed. (1999); R.W.V. Elliott, *Runes: An Introduction*, 2d ed. (1989).

J. B. Bessinger; T.V.F. Brogan; P. S. Baker

**RUNNING RHYTHM** (common rhythm). A term coined by G. M. Hopkins to denote the standard rhythms of Eng. *accentual-syllabic verse measured, in traditional prosody, by feet of two or three syllables. The rhythm is said to be rising if the stress falls at the end of the foot (*iamb, *anapaest), falling if the stress occurs on the first syllable of the foot (*trochee, *dactyl; see RISING AND FALLING RHYTHM). If the stress occurs between two unstressed or "slack" syllables (*amphibrach), Hopkins calls it "rocking rhythm." However, running rhythm employed with too much regularity becomes "same and tame." Poets have counteracted this tendency by resorting to reversed feet and reversed or *counterpoint rhythm, which Hopkins dubs "that irregularity which all natural growth and motion shews."

■ G. M. Hopkins, "Author's Preface on Rhythm," *The Poetical Works of Gerard Manley Hopkins*, ed. N. H. Mackenzie (1992).

C. Scott

## RUSSIA, POETRY OF

I. 17th and 18th Centuries
II. 19th Century
III. 20th Century and Beyond

Four interrelated tendencies characterize the hist. of Rus. poetry from its origins in the 17th c. until the early 21st c. The first concerns the incremental growth of the versification system. While writers and readers have valued strict-form verse, every period has produced innovation in the prosodic resources of Rus. verse in response to movements such as *classicism, *romanticism, and *modernism. The second direction relates to openness to foreign poets, trads., and aesthetic movements through adaptation, imitation, and trans. The third pattern concerns the pervasive intra- and intergenerational affiliations that poetic texts express through subtextual and intertextual allusion. Rus. poets acquire with their education almost complete access to the entire trad., with the result that

poets and readers are highly attuned to the connotative and associative connections triggered by the poetic, as opposed to prosaic, word. The fourth characteristic is the continuous regulation of Rus. poetry by political authorities. While the severity of censorship varied under both the imperial and Soviet regimes (as did the self-censorship practiced by writers), periods of complete freedom of expression were curtailed, leading on occasion to poetry of outright dissidence, as well as encouraging subtle techniques of satire and ironic suggestion.

**I. 17th and 18th Centuries.** From the mid-17th c. until the early 1760s, poetry was restricted to centers of learning, the bureaucracy, and court. The roots of early mod. Rus. literary culture lie in the Lat. and Scholastic orientation of 17th-c. Kyivan literary culture and its transfer to Moscow. The earliest writers to produce a corpus of poems were the literate functionaries collectively known as the Chancery school (*Prikaznaya shkola*). Their activity in the mid-17th c. demonstrates the relation between lit. and the court, personal ideals and state service as expressed in verse dedications, epistolary petitions, *acrostic dedications, and rebus poems. At court, the major figure was the erudite Simeon Polotsky (1629–80), who displayed his mastery of the *baroque poetics of Polish, Ukrainian, and Neo-Lat. lit. in two massive collections of verse, the *Rifmologion* (Rhymology) and the *Vertograd mnogotsvetnyi* (Variegated Vine). Backed by Tsar Aleksei Mikhailovich, whose policies of secular enlightenment anticipated those of his son, Peter the Great, Polotsky and his followers Silvester Medvedev (1641–91) and Karion Istomin (1650–1717) introduced the idea that poetry has an autonomous role in culture. Cast in the baroque form of the allegorical garden, Polotsky's two enormous poetic cycles, which contain a verbal labyrinth and *emblem poem in the shape of a heart, invite the reader into a morally pure world of Christian virtue. Polotsky is the first in a long series of Horatian imitators in Russia, extending all the way to Joseph Brodsky in the 20th c., who maintain that the purpose of poetry, as Polotsky thought, "is to teach, please and move by means of connected speech."

In this respect, his successor, and the great innovator of the next generation, is Prince Antiokh Kantemir (1709–44). A diplomat posted in Paris and London, Kantemir defined his ambitions for poetry and Rus. culture by adopting Fr. neoclassicism as a progressive model. Kantemir saw *satire as an efficient didactic mode in which to take a stand on cultural politics in support of Peter's reforms. Based on contemp. speeches of Peter's chief propagandist Feofan Prokopovich, the *Petriada*, Kantemir's epic fragment, celebrates the physical splendor of the city (more illusion than reality before the 1740s) and the speed of its creation. Kantemir's juxtaposition of civilization and nature anticipates a recurrent theme in the Petersburg myth. His *Satires* drew on the techniques of irony and caricature from a wide range of Eur. exemplary satirists, from Horace to Nicolas Boileau to Voltaire to Jonathan

Swift. The poems project a Eur. sophistication well beyond the competence of all but the smallest readership in Russia at the time. Kantemir, whose work was published first in London and circulated in ms. in Russia before printed Rus. eds. appeared from the 1740s, received due recognition only after 1762, when Catherine the Great espoused Peter the Great's more secular vision of culture.

Debates about genre, imitation, and innovation, and ling. and prosodic norms engaged with neoclassical theory and progressed by trial and error from the late 1730s into the first decades of the 19th c. There were no official court poets during the reigns of Peter the Great or his successors, and a culture of literary patronage is more notional than material during Catherine's reign. The prominent poets and theoreticians were Vasily Trediakovsky (1703–69), Mikhail Lomonosov (1711–65), and Alexander Sumarokov (1718–77). Despite personal rivalry, their common purpose was to prescribe the ling., syntactic, and prosodic system that would enable Rus. poets to domesticate Western genres and create a native trad. Trediakovsky and Lomonosov argued in their treatises (respectively, "New and Brief Method for Composing Russian Verse," 1735; "Epistle on the Rules of Russian Versification," 1739) that the syllabotonic system was the appropriate basis for mod. Rus. versification. Lomonosov applied his rules with panache in his "Ode on the Capture of Chocim" (1739). This spelled the end for *syllabic verse as the basis of versification. Sensitive to the relation between form and affect, each theorist attributed to the selection of feet a fundamental role in the creation of poetry's emotional capacity. Trediakovsky advocated the trochee as the basic metrical foot, whereas Lomonosov promoted the *iamb. In the event, Lomonosov prevailed. Trediakovsky had devised such complex rules of syntax for verse that his system became unworkable (though it is displayed with great ingenuity in *Tilemakhida* [1766], his transposition into verse of François Fénelon's *Télémaque*). The transition to the syllabotonic system has been attributed to numerous factors: statistical analysis of syllabic verse, in fact, suggests that tonicization was under way and that these theoretical pronouncements reflected a transition rather than a dislocation. These discussions yielded a new repertory of varied stanza forms and modes, incl. epic, song, *epitaph, *verse epistle and *elegy, from which two subsequent generations drew heavily.

In the newly secular culture of the mid-18th c., dozens of poets, some dilettantish nobles, some translators, and some figures of lasting achievement created a substantial poetic *canon. The composition of poetry among the educated elite, who absorbed the lessons of native and foreign handbooks and enthusiastically formed literary associations, enjoyed prestige as a demonstration of civility and cultivation. The most important poets were the scientist Lomonosov and statesman Gavrila Derzhavin (1743–1816), who enjoyed early acclaim and earned lasting renown. Their biographies—each was from a remote part of Russia and reached a high rank at court—conferred an aura of genius, lending stature when they addressed the monarch. Both

Lomonosov and Derzhavin took the notion of a poetic persona to new heights. The *ode is the definitive high genre of 18th-c. Rus. poetry, a showcase for ling. experimentation as well as a mirror to the image of the monarch. Lomonosov's solemn odes, relentlessly paced by iambic tetrameter and alternating *masculine and feminine rhyme, reveled in Pindaric chains of metaphors contained by the signature ten-line stanza. Rhetorically, these occasional poems restored poetry to its ceremonial place at court in the trad. of Polotsky. The turgidity of the Lomonosovian ode derives from a propensity to create semantic clusters, usually through etymologic play or tropes, such as *zeugma. Lomonosov made Enlightenment progress (from the uses of glass to the advantages of Western dress) the subject of his verse. He evoked cl. *allegory in celebration of Russia's triumphs of the 1750s and 1760s, advised on cultural policy, declared the arrival of a utopian age, encouraged imperial expansion, and promoted the political economy of a mercantile nation. The authority of the poet derives less from vatic inspiration, which turns out to be rational rather than visionary in the display of loyalty and practical wisdom. Lomonosov speculates in verse on the nature of the universe, but in the famous evening and morning meditations written in 1743, he becomes the first Rus. poet to capture a sublime appreciation of nature.

This view of poetry as a mode of inquiry into the universe, society, and man finds its most eloquent spokesman in Derzhavin at his peak in the 1780s. Famed as a rule-breaker both in his poetic style—his idiosyncratic attitude to rhyme would look particularly clumsy to later generations—and subject matter, Derzhavin is a philosophical poet imbued with an Enlightenment belief in self-examination, rational skepticism, and empiricism. A spirit of cosmic enquiry inspires Derzhavin's remarkable meditation "God" (1784), a text that employs the discourse of natural philosophy (with some debt to G. W. Leibniz) as well as contemp. optics. Derzhavin is, above all, an eloquent poet who experiences metaphysical problems with pictorial vividness.

Derzhavin's poems often proceed by counterpointing reason and emotion and abstraction with realistic detail. His aim in mixing high and low, elevated diction and colloquialism, is to show that the genre system, with its rules about form and diction, is subordinate to the style of the poet's mind. Thanks to this force of personality and stylistic liberty, poems fold the sheer matter of everyday life into their argumentative structure. As a statesman, Derzhavin, like Horace, wrote in a civic mode with a view to instructing the ruler on the theory of natural law, good governance, and progress, all mainline Enlightenment topics. Whereas Lomonosov remained the respectful courtier, the senatorial Derzhavin in the late 1770s and 1780s showed greater boldness in mixing flattery with irony and dressing up topical discussion in thinly veiled allegory. In poems of statecraft, read and sometimes appreciated by Catherine the Great, he put the ruler and poet on virtually equal footing. He is the first Rus. poet to use the lang. of natural law in reminding the ruler of limits to autocracy. Derzhavin's choice of philosophical and political subjects conferred gravitas on the figure of the poet.

Yet not all is high seriousness in the period. Numerous poets from the 1730s to the 1770s were adept at song as well as verse tragedy and comedy. Light verse of an ephemeral nature enjoyed a vogue. Alexander Sumarokov (1717–1777), the director of the Imperial Theatre (and dubbed the Rus. Boileau), preferred pastoral themes. Parody and burlesque reached sparkling heights in the mock epic *Dushen'ka* (a transposition into poetry of Jean de La Fontaine's *Les Amours de Psyche et Cupidon* [1669]), which brought Ippolit Bogdanovich (1744–1803) admirers well into the 1820s.

## II. 19th Century.
This rapid experimentation with styles and genres laid the ground for the first generation of classic Rus. poets of the 1810s. In the roughly 25 years before Alexander Pushkin published his first poem in 1815, the poetic norms established during Catherine's reign persisted. Most lyric poetry earlier in the period continued to circulate among a small coterie of amateur men of letters. Before the mid-1820s, public and private readerships were identical, since national literacy rates remained low and there was no system of distribution to bookshops. No one could aspire to be a professional poet much before the early 1820s. Lomonosov's poems had been published at court in tiny print-runs. Derzhavin's poetry circulated mostly in handsome ms. copies, but he lived long enough to see the transition toward printed eds., overseeing the publication of his own collected verse in 1814.

The devel. of smaller lyric forms proved to be a boon when sentimentalism reached Russia in the 1780s. Much more than prose in the period, which tended to emulate archaic models, Rus. poetry remained up to date in its openness to other national trends and movements, esp. from France. The lang. of *sensibility developed in the 1790s by Nikolai Karamzin (1766–1826) and his acolytes Mikhail Muravev (1757–1807) and Ivan Dmitriev (1760–1837), all accomplished writers of *poèsie fugitive*, attracted the poets of early romanticism. Vasily Zhukovsky (1783–1852), a writer and translator of *ballads, opened new conduits to Eur. currents as a smooth and idiomatic translator. His 1802 version of Thomas Gray's "Elegy Written in a Country Churchyard" (1750) was considered a masterpiece of the art of trans. in Russia and marked the inception of early romanticism. Older-generation canonical figures include the classicists Alexei Merzliakov, a translator of Virgil and professor of rhet.; Nikolai Gnedich (1784–1833), famed for his 1831 trans. of the *Iliad* into heroic hexameter; and Konstantin Batiushkov (1787–1855), an imitator of the musicality and sensibility of Tibullus and Torquato Tasso. Batiushkov exercised a formative influence on Pushkin and his contemporaries. The elegiac speakers of the 18th c., drawn from tragedy, proved archaic after sentimentalism, which cultivated the expression of feeling. From the 1800s, the lyric landscape utilized manifold props and techniques of *preromanticism, incl. ruins, *pathetic fallacy, epigraphs, and wanderers. Poets employed a wider repertory of verse forms, turning out epistles in iambic trimeter, narratives in trochaic tetrameter with dactylic rhyme, and verse fables in mixed iambs, with notable success, e.g., in the fables of Ivan Krylov (1769–1844). For the next generation, working in the 1820s and 1830s, versification roughly adhered to the norms developed at this time: the default narrative meter was the iambic tetrameter (in more than 40% of works written in the 1820s), blank verse rather than *alexandrines or iambic hexameter was employed in tragedy with Shakespearean overtones, and exact rhyme gradually became the norm. However, stanza boundaries, which a generation earlier had adhered to strophic forms like the eight- and ten-line ode, were relaxed as the romantics preferred openness and continuity in their lyric forms.

The greatest poet of the 19th c. is Alexander Pushkin, whose body of lyric and narrative verse was unprecedented in its variety and standard of accomplishment. From the 20th c. on, he has also been widely considered Russia's national poet. A discussion of Pushkin's unparalleled standing in the Rus. poetic trad. necessarily has three components: his intrinsic creative qualities, his contribution to the growth of the professional status of the writer in Russia, and finally the symbolic position he occupies in aesthetic debates, literary politics, and national identity from the time of his death through the Soviet period up to the present day. His idiom flows from the lang. that Karamzin and others refined, and he deploys it with unfailing elegance and deeper psychological nuance. His command of the genres is impeccable, yet his mastery of *parody and *pastiche are one source of delight, most esp. in *Evgenij Onegin*, his novel in verse that appeared in installments from 1825–32. Dubbed by the influential critic Vissarion Belinsky an "encyclopedia of Rus. life," it is also an encyclopedia of Rus. lit., packed with quotation and allusion. It is highly sophisticated in its narrative voice, creation of time frames, deconstruction of realism, and metatextual play. If Pushkin's metrical profile tends to the standard iambic tetrameter and his stanza forms are traditional, numerous examples demonstrate his aptitude for verse forms that match the mobility of his thought. Emotional transparency, conveyed in cultivated and conversational diction, characterizes his lyric corpus of nearly 700 poems in which he sloughs off poetic *cliché—or uses it to devastating effect. The publication of his lyric poetry as a collection in 1826 was a landmark, following on the critical and financial success of early romantic narratives on Byronic themes. Lyric poetry had been the preserve of the amateur elite; few poets previously had courted a readership for their verse. The step was decisive in establishing the preeminence of lyric poetry in the 1820s and Pushkin's superiority among practitioners. He took a conservative approach to organizing the poems chronologically and according to genre, as was the custom among Fr. poets. By contrast, his highly esteemed contemporary Evgenii Baratynsky (1800–44) would later arrange the poems of his landmark collection *Sumerki* (*Twilight*, 1842) thematically, creating an impression of psychological coherence and implied linkages. This approach anticipated the thematic structure of the poetic book that many later poets, esp. the symbolists in the 1890s, would develop. Lapidary diction and pace characterize Pushkin's eight narrative poems, which move from Byronic themes to the greatest Rus. poetic meditation on hist., *The Bronze Horseman* (1834), while his fairy-tales have the vitality of folk idiom and considerable humor. His famed clarity does not negate a capacity to use polyphony, intertextual allusion, and form to suggest depth and dialogue with the trad. In his hands, for instance, *blank verse rather than the alexandrine becomes an ideal medium for dramatic soliloquy in the Shakespearean historical tragedy *Boris Godunov*.

Poetry for Pushkin was certainly a calling, but he also called it "my trade, a branch of honest industry, which provides me with food and domestic independence." Bedeviled by censorship and goaded by his precarious critical reception, Pushkin was acutely aware that financial independence was a risk for aristocratic writers unable to live on revenues from their estates and reluctant to serve in the bureaucracy. Yet Pushkin braved different types of self-assertion in promulgating the authority of the *poet. In "The Prophet" (1826), which may well be the most famous of all Rus. poems, he asserted the twin principles of the divine basis for the poet's genius and a duty of public enlightenment. The first claim grew out of Pushkin's appropriation of the romantic discourse of genius, rather than from any clear belief in a divine mission, and the second reflected his hopes that a poet of his talent, intelligence, and noble ancestry could advise the tsar. It is doubtful whether Pushkin subscribed to P. B. Shelley's view that poets were the legislators of humankind, but his exalted image of the poet fit in well with the younger generation of Moscow-based Schellingians like Dmitrii Venevitinov (1805–27) and found favor among the intelligentsia in the late 19th c., esp. symbolist writers, who adopted a hieratic notion of the poet.

The slump in Pushkin's critical reputation and his death in a duel created the perception that he was the victim of a repressive government and society hostile to poetic genius—suppositions in which there is some grain of truth, although these were not the immediate causes of the debacle. In "The Death of the Poet" (1837), the younger Mikhail Lermontov (1814–41) railed against an unworthy society, positioning the martyred poet as the upholder of cultural and moral values. Read as an attack on the government, it earned Lermontov a term of exile that bolstered his pose as a "Pushkin" to the younger generation. In his final years, Lermontov, who was also the victim of a duel, extended Pushkin's theme of the poet's aloofness from the debased crowd. His mature verse—and virtually all the poems written in 1841 are anthologized masterpieces—embraces a persona of alienation and despair, partly as a romantic reflex of Rus. Byronism, partly as a response to the constraints of life in Russia under Nicholas I. His narrative poetry explored topics such as the interrelation of consciousness and nature, jealousy and love, while his lyrics project a poet-figure afflicted by a sense of solitude and fate. His view of the poetic calling as a lonely destiny reverberated in the work of later poets facing hostile imperial and Soviet regimes.

Alongside Pushkin and Lermontov, the two outstanding poets of the period were Baratynsky and Fyodor Tiutchev (1803–73). They are often paired because of their philosophical themes and their common debt to Ger. idealist thought on hist. and nature. Baratynsky's gift is for compressing material of different logical kinds—observation, meditation, simile, satire—into a syntactically varied but metrically stable pattern that proves adaptable for the searching tones of his voice, which slips suddenly into bitter regret, then rises in metaphysical exaltation; and in his last poetry, achieves a distance from the world that is sublime. Both are poets of nature, the first imbued with a sense of awe and reason akin to J. W. Goethe, the second informed by F.W.J. Schelling and later Arthur Schopenhauer's pessimism. Both are among the most powerful love poets in Rus., expert at portraying an unrequited longing that corrodes hope and breeds disillusion. Baratynsky treated the relationship of poetry to hist. in one of the greatest lyrics of the century, "Poslednii poet" ("The Last Poet," 1835). Inspired by Viconian theories about the evolutionary cycles of culture, Baratynsky surveyed the progress of poetry from Homer to Pushkin, which for him marked the beginning of an Iron Age pitting prose against poetry, industrialization against creativity, capital against intangible genius. Like Lermontov's theme of the wanderer poet, this vision of an age governed by commercialism, positivist intellectual values, and mechanization would strike a chord with later poets.

The generation following Pushkin and his younger contemporaries, which includes now-forgotten but then-celebrated poets like Alexander Polezhaev (ca. 1805–38), saw itself as the possessor of a ready-made poetic lang. and a substantial trad. Nonetheless, there is a widespread perception that, from the 1840s to the 1890s, the rise of the novel eclipsed Rus. poetry. This judgment, which reflects some critical distaste for the breakdown of thematic boundaries between prose and poetry, is simplistic. Even in the supposedly fallow decades leading up to the rise of the next major movement, *symbolism, poetry was highly productive and widely printed from the 1850s. If anything, the cultural status of poetry became increasingly an issue for debate, polarizing factions according to their position on an ideological spectrum between, at one end, Afanasy Fet (1820–92), Tiutchev, and others, who combined conservative nationalism with a commitment to Pushkinian values of art and craft; and, at the other extreme, the gifted democratic and radical Nikolai Nekrasov (1821–78). Along with lesser writers like Aleksei Khomiakov (1804–60) who used verse as a vehicle for a Slavophile ideology, it was Fet and Tiutchev who perfected the capacity of the Rus. lyric to create speakers of psychological depth and to distill entire areas of thought about nationalism, politics, and, above all, nature as a pantheistic force.

From the 1840s, the literary field was transformed by the rapid growth in literacy, demographic shifts toward cities, the improvement in print technology and the publishing infrastructure, and the crumbling of both class and gender barriers. Few notable women poets were active during Rus. classicism, although the early 19th c. poets Anna Bunina (1774–1829) and Anna Volkova (1781–1834) were treated respectfully by literary societies. Over the next decades, Bunina, an amateur, would be followed by female poets like the formidable Evdokiia Rostpochina (1811–58), Elizaveta Shakhova (1822–99) and, above all, Karolina Pavlova (1807–93), who published substantial collections to positive critical and public response. Pavlova is a pioneer of poetry as a type of emotional diary and devoted lyric cycles to her affairs with Adam Mickiewicz and Boris Utin, while also departing from ostensibly "feminine" themes in more polemical verse about Russia and the mission of the poet.

The growth of an educated nongentry class, from which teachers, university professors, translators, and writers emerged, led to an expansion of the number of jours. in which poetry was featured. While the Rus. reading public consumed prose fiction above all, poetry sold and circulated in quantities that would have struck Pushkin as fabulous. Aesthetic debates current in Western Europe about the social function of lit. and "art for art's sake" reached Russia in the 1860s and 1870s. Yet in the "thick journals" that treated the famous "accursed questions" of Rus. politics and hist., the radical critics contested the worth of Pushkin and "pure" poets to a country experiencing severe social tensions because of agrarian reform and industrialization. Poets declaimed with prosaic explicitness in defense of the downtrodden and urban poor.

Pushkin's status as an object of attack from the Left, veneration from the Right, and adoration from the nonpolitical middle classes in itself gives evidence of the unusual importance accorded to poetry in ideological debates about the purpose of art. Some regarded him as irrelevant because he had failed to produce a positive hero who would be a model of political activism: *Onegin for Our Times* (1865) by Dmitrii Minaev (1835–89) fought fire with fire by parodying Pushkin's novel-in-verse. For the so-called radical critics, Pushkin's name was largely a byword for effete aestheticism. The vehement critic Dmitrii Pisarev (1840–68) derided Pushkin and Zhukovsky as "parodies of poets" and Lermontov as the author of "absurdities." In fact, Pushkin's reputation was a moving target since the true nature of his legacy was only then becoming known in Russia through radical émigré publications. There is an irony that attacks from radicals on Pushkin coincided with the first publication in the émigré press of some of his most radical poetry, which had been banned in Russia, incl. the pornographic burlesque *Gabrieliad* (1821), which mocked church dogma, and the lyric "Sower of the seed in the desert" (1823). By the time Fyodor Dostoevsky, in his famous speech on the opening of the Pushkin monument in Moscow (1880), elevated him as the embodiment of the Rus. soul, Pushkin had been claimed by all camps from radicals to pan-Slavists.

Readers continued to respond personally to Pushkin's lyric poetry. A large (and predominantly female) section of the now-substantial readership turned to poets as soul mates who intuited reader's private feelings. These included second-tier masters like A. K. Tolstoy (1817–75) and Konstantin Sluchevsky (1837–

1904). Apollon Grigoriev (1822–64), Yakov Polonsky (1819–98), and Aleksei Apukhtin (1840–93) enjoyed particular favor thanks to their autumnal landscapes, moonlit-night settings, and emotional vagueness, often adapted in song.

Nonetheless, these melodists were out of step with an age gripped by questions of political and social change. The best of the "naturalists" is Nekrasov, ed. of the leading liberal jour. *The Contemporary*, who believed that all the prose of life could be made the subject of poetry. To the service of this credo, Nekrasov, nicknamed the Poet-Citizen, applied a formal mastery and an acute ear for popular idiom and dialect. The characters of his narrative poems are drawn from the world of the peasantry and new urban underclass.

The publication of *Poems* (1856) was a historic populist call. It unites the virtues of craft and irony that Nekrasov esteemed in Pushkin and Baratynsky with a forthrightness and cynicism seen earlier only in Derzhavin and Krylov. If any poem speaks for Nekrasov's generation, and for his aspirations for poetry, it is that collection's explicitly anti-Pushkinian and programmatic "Muse," which begins by repudiating "a Muse who sings gently and beautifully," but whose inspiration is imbued with a spirit of revenge that will sustain the poet across the "dark abysses of despair and evil." Nekrasov further expressed this ethos with verse portraits of radical critics such as Nikolai Chernyshevsky (1828–89), whose views on lit. would later become precepts of Marxist-Leninist aesthetics in Soviet lit. crit.

The culmination of Nekrasov's career was the cycle of lyric and narrative poems united under the title *Komu na Rusi zhit' khorosho'* (*Who Lives Well in Russia?*, 1863–78), which applies a satirical eye to all facets of the Rus. empire. Nekrasov's ability to orchestrate polyphony and different modes makes him the true contemporary of Dostoevsky, while his eye for detail owes much to populist movements in the visual arts. Like Pushkin's lyric hero who spoke in the tones and manner of his social class, Nekrasov fashioned a speaker in the social image of his reader, thereby creating an intense emotional bond between him and a larger, socially engaged readership of urban professionals, incl. writers, students, and doctors, who made up the "mixed estates." Nekrasov's funeral became a mass demonstration at which Dostoevsky (in the company of the young Marxist philosopher Georgii Plekhanov) proclaimed him the legitimate heir of Pushkin and Lermontov.

Poets of Nekrasov's generation had engaged intensely with the so-called accursed questions, adding women's rights, poverty, and political freedoms. The assassination of Alexander III in 1881 and a period of reaction led to a gradual national subsidence into relative torpor until the first Rus. Revolution of 1905. The most popular poets of the 1870s were hackneyed imitators of Nekrasov, their politics expressed in often crudely sloganizing verse. By the late 1880s, Rus. poetry regained some measure of sophistication, deploying longer verse lines and ternary meters and, as in the poetry of the highly popular Semen Nadson (1862–87), even altering the rhythmic balance of iambic tetrameter. In the

1880s, Fet broke his 20-year silence with his final collection, *Vechernie ogni* (*Evening Flames*, 1891). His exquisite mastery of short forms combined subtle shifts in rhythm, verbal inventiveness, and sound play to mirror the febrile moods of his subjects. It came as a timely reminder of the lyric trad.'s marvelous fusion of music and psychology, inspiring the next two generations of poets to concentrate on smaller forms and personal subjects.

**III. 20th Century and Beyond.** These tentative stirrings in the 1880s anticipated the burst of formal daring shown by both generations of symbolist poets who were great enlargers of the tonal and rhythmic palette of Rus. verse. From the start, the Europeanness of Rus. symbolism is reflected in its culture of trans. Trans. and imitations of numerous other authors, incl. Arthur Rimbaud, Stéphane Mallarmé, Maurice Maeterlinck, E. A. Poe, as well as Pre-Raphaelite critics such as Walter Pater and John Ruskin, steered the symbolists away from civic topics toward personal themes expressed for an intimate circle of readers (see PRE-RAPHAELITISM). Cross-currents in the aesthetic affiliations and philosophies of poets made the entire period highly dynamic and rich. First-generation symbolists, incl. Dmitrii Merezhkovsky (1865–1941), the febrile Zinaida Gippius (1869–1945), and the hugely popular Konstantin Bal'mont, shared the decadent preoccupation with death together with a yearning for an unattainable fullness of life, the belief in art for art's sake, self-obsession, and a tendency to conflate art and life. With hypnotic musicality, Fyodor Sologub (1863–1927) created a poetic dream-world of secret gardens and imagined realms in which symbolist hopes for cosmic renewal vied with Schopenhauerian pessimism about a decadent world. We are back in the world of coterie poetry. Valerii Briusov (1873–1924) and Georgy Ivanov (1894–1958), for instance, indicated their exclusivity by assigning Lat. titles to their collections, e.g., Briusov's *Me eum esse* (1898) and *Tertia Vigilia* (1901). Lyric, rather than narrative, was the dominant form. Poetic collections presented complex cycles. The degree to which poets become known to readers through the book of poems rather than miscellaneous publications is striking. It would be possible to write a hist. of Rus. poetry starting at this juncture by following a series of such titles. Some poets arranged their collections according to hidden feelings that obscurely moved the reader like a musical impulse. Others viewed the collection as a lyric diary, attaching dates to create a chronological progression. The first poetic collection to represent his spirit of pessimism and despair is Bal'mont's *Pod severnym nebom* (Under a Northern Sky, 1894). Unlike Bal'mont, who emphasized the musical expressivity of the word over its sense, Innokenty Annenskii (1856–1909), an older symbolist whose first collection was not published until 1908, conveyed a sense of existential unease and ennui through oblique images and periphrastic diction, the music of his verse stored up in the intonation of its questioning phrases rather than in sound orchestration. The poetry of Annenskii casts a hypnotic musicality over his dream world of secret gardens and imagined

realms pervaded by corrupted innocence and the devil, emanations of his Schopenhauerian pessimism. Briusov occupied a unique position as critic, scholar, and publisher and was a leading arbiter of taste until after the revolution. While his eclecticism may now look more affected than genuine, younger writers respected his formal virtuosity, fell under the spell of his versatile poetic persona, and were dazzled by his aptitude in adapting mod. Fr. verse, whether Charles Baudelaire's misanthropic brilliance or the coldness and exoticism of the *Parnassians.

Both Alexander Blok (1880–1921) and Andrei Bely (1880–1934) conveyed the symbolist belief that the concrete world is only a damaged reflection of the world of eternal essences and that poetry captures the movement of the spirit from *realia ad realiora*. Blok's poetry, which shares Fet's plangent sound structure, mesmerized contemporaries with the new rhythmic capacities he revealed by using the *dol'nik, rather than the iamb, to give his lines an accentual (and more speech-like) beat. This flexibility of rhythm, adapted to the intonation and changing mood of each line, and exemplified in the *Verses on the Beautiful Woman* (*Stikhi o prekrasnoi dame*, 1903), became widely imitated over the 20th c. Blok's *Collected Verse* (1911–1912) united his first five collections and reordered the poems according to chronology, thereby creating an autobiographical narrative about the growth of the poet from a Baudelairean *poète maudit* under the spell of the Eternal Feminine into a visionary attuned to the elemental music of hist. Blok was a phenomenon because the individual personality and voice of his lyric speaker was patently autobiographical to a greater degree than any other poet since Baratynsky. The interrelation of life and art and the symbolist project of perfecting life through art inform the poet's spiritual presentation throughout his collections. In the heady aestheticism of the prerevolutionary period, writers from the next generation like Anna Akhmatova (1889–1966) and Marina Tsvetaeva (1892–1941) fell under Blok's spell, dedicated youthful cycles to him, and emulated him by giving biographical detail and psychological continuity to their lyric cycles. Arguably, Blok did more than any previous writer to give thematic cohesion and a sense of psychological devel. to the unitary poetic collection, and while he enjoys much less popularity in the post-Soviet period, his status and influence were once towering.

Blok felt that the poet possessed an acute sense of hist. that came with an obligation, in the trad. of Pushkin's Prophet, to teach the nation. Clearly, some members of the intelligentsia, esp. in St. Petersburg, subscribed to these pretensions, but it is hard to substantiate the persistent claim that the mass of readers generally endowed their poets with mystical charisma. Even before the revolution of 1917 elevated proletarian art, a host of factors had already enlarged the popular base for poetry. There is clear evidence that, like the cinema, poetry readings were enjoyed as a type of elevated entertainment and a conduit for popular expression. Both Blok and Bely caught the turbulence of their revolutionary age at an early stage. In his 1905 collection *Pepel'* (Ashes), Bely shed his learned style and assumed a more popular persona under the inspiration of Nekrasov. Anxiety about Russia's future pervades Blok's prose in which he warned his readers about the "music of history"—and perhaps for the last time in the hist. of Rus. poetry, he invoked the authority of the poet in making such national pronouncements. When the October Revolution occurred, Blok captured the actual violence of the revolution in *Dvenadtsat'* (*The Twelve*, 1918), which tells the story of a marauding band of soldiers let loose on Petrograd. This cycle fuses the symbolic lang. of Blok's philosophy of hist. with a polyphonic narrative of upheaval at street level. Blok punctuates whole sections with onomatopoeic, non-verbal explosions of sound effects to convey rifle fire. Class distinctions mark the speech of characters, and Blok makes extensive use of *accentual verse to characterize peasant speech. All the great 20th-c. narrative poems, incl. Tsvetaeva's *Krysolov* (*Ratcatcher*, 1925), Mikhail Kuzmin's *Forel' razbivaet led'* (*The Trout Breaks the Ice*, 1929) and Akhmatova's *Rekviem* (*Requiem*, written 1935, pub. 1963) follow his example in forging a sequence out of highly varied metrical structures.

In the years between the revolutions of 1905 and 1917, symbolism made way for the most remarkable concentration of great poets since the Pushkin period. Poetic groups across a spectrum of artistic philosophies came together and by dint of sometimes marginal differences splintered into numerous subgroups. One common denominator across the Silver Age (as it was retrospectively called) was the cult of Pushkin, who appears in many guises as a ghostly interlocutor for Annenskii, a haunting friend for Akhmatova, a poetic sun for Osip Mandelstam (1892–1938), and a dandy for Mikhail Kuzmin (1872–1936). In her prerevolutionary collections, Akhmatova, whose understatement and irony communicated this poetic kinship, freed erotic psychology from the frenzy and melodrama of the decadents. Voiced in cl. binary meters, these short lyrics present subdued dramas of emotional reckoning. The very different characterizations of Pushkin in the work of Akhmatova and Tsvetaeva show how malleable his reception and image continued to be and help crystallize the differences in their poetics (Akhmatova was clearly cl., while Tsvetaeva was an iconoclast in idiom and sentiment). Tsvetaeva, one of the great formal innovators of Rus. poetry, celebrated Pushkin as the "scourge of tsars," a poet of Af. ancestry whose protean genius and aptitude set the standard in many genres. If Akhmatova's attention to the emotions finds its natural form of expression in short poems, Tsvetaeva required the expansiveness of confessional, autobiographical modes practiced with devastating candor in poems written after her emigration in 1922 such as the "Poema gory" ("Poem of the Mountain," 1924) and at a metaphysical level in her ethereal *Novogodnee* (*New Year Letter*, 1927) to R. M. Rilke, works that blur generic boundaries by expanding the introspection and dense imagery associated with the lyric on a narrative scale.

Literary *futurism was officially inaugurated in 1913 when Vladimir Mayakovsky (1893–1930) established its antiestablishment credentials by repudiating Pushkin as an aesthetic standard. Certain slogans ("A slap in the face of public taste," "Throw Pushkin overboard") together with deliberate outrageousness in public displaced the listless symbolist persona with the bad-boy image cultivated by Mayakovsky. The graphic appearance of futurist poetry, with its jagged lines and use of the verse ladder (*lesenka*), gives a visceral sense of the distance it puts between itself and cl. poetry (see TYPOGRAPHY, VISUAL POETRY). While futurism is best known by representatives such as Mayakovsky, the term is a portmanteau word for a range of subgroups responsible for the doctrine of cubofuturism, and the imaginists (made up of thirteen poets incl. Anatoly Mariengof [1897–1962] and Vladimir Shershenevich [1893–1942]), as well as the later Left Front in Art (LEF). Individual poets and factions were heavily implicated in producing and applying the lessons of post-Saussurean ling. theory elaborated across a wide spectrum of thinkers from A. A. Potebnya to members of the formalist movement whose theories of the literary device, the literary system, and the dynamic literary word galvanized poets to exploit poetic lang. in all its semantic, phonetic, and even visual complexity and to assume that the poetic word has a special density of expressivity that exceeds its denotative function as a signifier. The poetic avant-garde experimented with form and lang. as the means to defamiliarize reality for new readers in a mod. age (see AVANT-GARDE POETICS, DEFAMILIARIZATION). This common impulse, shared by all groups, animates some of the most daring formal innovation in Rus. poetry, whether expressed in the trans-sense lang. that the imagist-futurist poet Velimir Khlebnikov (1885–1922) coined or in Mayakovsky's attention to poetic lang. as a nearly material substance (*faktura stikha*) that delivers the shock of the new through neologism, unusual rhymes, explosive intonation, rapid syntax, and unusual verse forms.

Mayakovsky remains one of the great iconoclasts of Rus. verse, a magnetic civic poet, and in the cycle *Pro eto* (*About That*, 1923) a moving writer of love poetry. By setting out his revolutionary rhet. in lines of unprecedented metrical variety over extensive monologues, he maximized intonational variety and rhythmic flexibility. But Mayakovsky is hardly alone in taking metrical sophistication to new lengths. Readers appreciated the skillful *amphibrach in Boris Pasternak's second collection, just as they esteemed the dexterity with which Tsvetaeva (in the trad. of Bal'mont) mastered Gr.-style logoaedic meters in her verse tragedies. Boris Pasternak (1890–1960) initially participated in futurist groups before going his own way. Like Tsvetaeva, he refracted the observation of contemp. historical events, such as the Kronstadt rebellion and the October Revolution, through a lyric optic. His second book *Sestra moia zhizn'* (*My Sister Life*, 1917), a lyric diary of emotional upheaval during a year of revolution, remains one of the great collections of Rus. poetry, remarkable as a phenomenological transcription of consciousness. The subject is the poet's emotional and intellectual hist. when his ardent openness to the sensual experience of life merges with utopian excitement. Like Tiutchev and

Fet, Pasternak presents nature as a Schellingian force, imbued with subjectivity and spirit. His landscapes, defamiliarized through metonymy and metaphor, reflect his common heritage with the futurists.

Like the imagists, the acmeist poet—and here Mandelstam excelled in his first collection *Kamen'* (*Stone*, 1913)—creates out of the verbal texture of the poem an image of an object that seems real in material terms (thus, opposing the Platonic ideal of symbolist poetry; see ACMEISM). Many of the poems in *Stone* weave together a tissue of allusions to Eur. poets and themes, creating a concentrated sense of culture in a manner similar to T. S. Eliot's high *modernism. Great buildings like Notre Dame and Hagia Sophia are emblems of the syncretism of religions and civilizations and communicate a modernist conviction that culture can be remade from its own past. The collections Mandelstam published in his lifetime are touchstones of Rus. poetry, not least because they seem to sum up their historical moment. In their focus on memory and beauty, strategies of poetic identity and the interrelation of painting, poetry, and music, *Stone* managed to be a timeless example of lyric perfection while also being steeped in the mood and idioms of fin de siècle Europe.

Mandelstam's next collections, *Tristia* (1923) and *New Verse* (1928), have a formal inventiveness and a range of reference and allusion that consciously distance them from the proletariat poetry sanctioned by the regime. Haunted by Lermontov's image of the poet as an outcast, Mandelstam reacted to the historical turmoil of "War Communism," the emergency economic measures Lenin imposed between 1918 and 1921, by introducing a new type of complexity into Rus. poetry characterized by layered *allusion, metaphorical density, and the trans. of the contemporary into mythic *archetypes. Poetic composition for Mandelstam (as well as for Mayakovsky), was an exercise in multiplying the self and describing its tension points within a tumultuous political and literary context. His later poems, most of which were written from exile in Voronezh in the 1930s, have a Mallarmé-like poise in considering the relation between music and silence and explore consciousness and an intersubjective perception of time and space.

As the Bolsheviks established state-run literary organizations and publishing houses, poets of all schools were mobilized for propagandistic purposes in building the "dictatorship of the proletariat." The poetic landscape changed in direct measure as the new Soviet state progressed in the 1920s through the next stages of civil war and War Communism to the establishment of the New Economic Policy (NEP) and finally its demise in 1929. Much ephemeral poetry (now collected in historical anthols.), often expressed in the form of versified slogans or songs, captured public jubilation during the October Revolution. Poems by the thousand were written in a utilitarian style to mark technological achievements of the new state, to celebrate workers, and to vilify counterrevolutionaries. Professional writers were not immune to such propaganda. Numerous poetic narratives sympathetic to the Bolsheviks, like *Glavnaia ulitsa* (Main Street, 1922) by the proletarian

poet Demian Bednyi (1883–1945), depicted—and approved—the violence inflicted on the peasantry.

A qualitative difference, however, surely marks out masterpieces of Communist poetry from hackwork. Like the constructivists who sought to move art out into the public realm by applying it to mass-produced textiles and household goods, poets of the stature of Mayakovsky, Nikolai Aseev (1889–1963), and the young Nikolai Tikhonov (1896–1979) tried to create a new revolutionary art by joining poetry and agitprop. Nothing was too prosaic to be turned into easily memorizable verse, incl. the endless decrees produced in the new jargon of the regime. The same poets also projected their utopian vision of revolutionary reality by mythologizing the new state and its leaders. Just as he rallied workers to the socialist cause, so did Mayakovsky (whose style was far too modernist for the conservative Vladimir Lenin) in his narrative poems cast the revolution in cosmic terms.

Meanwhile, poets of the so-called neo-peasant school, which included the wildly popular Sergei Esenin (1895–1925) and the Old Believer Nikolai Kliuev (1887–1937), were focused on the countryside: their writings during War Communism caught the hardship of the times in popular folk idiom. Contrary to the image of official propaganda, the neo-peasants frankly depicted the devastated landscapes of Russia during its civil war. Even as the Bolsheviks purged institutions of perceived enemies, the restored free-market economy of the 1920s (known as NEP) led to wild bursts of prosperity. The cityscape that Nikolai Zabolotsky (1903–1958) created in *Stolbtsy* (Columns, 1929) combines cinematic montage with Gogolian grotesque, presenting an expressionist portrait of city life. The poets grouped as OBERIU, incl. Daniil Kharms (1905–42), Nikolai Oleinikov (1898–1942), and Konstantin Vaginov (1899–1934), in the years before their arrest and suppression in the early 1930s, created a new style of absurdist poetry that expressed their alienation from a menacing Soviet context by contrasting the grammatical logic of propositions with their sometimes violent content.

By the end of the 1920s, the regime's strong preference for conservative form and lang. in poetry had forcefully curtailed proletarian groups, demoralized the futurists (Mayakovsky committed suicide in 1930), hounded Akhmatova into silence, and marginalized Mandelstam (in whose fate Stalin took a personal interest). Literary institutions, under instruction from Stalin, began to orchestrate the cult of Pushkin as a national poet, culminating in a series of mass events and publications that made this elite poet into a household name, a proverbial byword, and a comrade. The Soviet literary establishment systematically inculcated respect for poetry by pedagogical means, by cultivating a rich children's lit. written in verse and, perhaps above all, by publishing in large print-runs the Soviet equivalent of the Fr. Pléiade editions, the Biblioteka Poeta series founded by Maksim Gor'ky (1868–1936). The 250-plus titles published over the entire lifetime of the Soviet Union signified official acceptance and canonical status for individual poets and poetic movements.

The official requirement that writers adhere to socialist realism, together with Josef Stalin's terror, created a sorry record for Rus. poetry as pub. from the 1930s until the 1960s. Socialist realism required lit. to deliver a positive message confirming the achievement of socialism and the party's ideals. Form and lang. were to be simple, and all traces of irony and ambivalence were expunged by the censors or preempted through self-censorship. Poetic anthols. devoted to national anniversaries show how quickly poetry fossilized into fixed tropes and ideological clichés; unsurprisingly, the formal blandness and thematic repetitiveness blighted poetry during the Stalinist period.

While the official picture was superficially one of monolithic conformity, unofficial channels led poetry in more creative directions from the end of the 1950s. In the post-Stalin period, and esp. the thaw of the early 1960s, innumerable talented poets were associated with dozens of separate, and often ephemeral, poetic groups that tested official limits. Three misleading perceptions about Soviet lit. in the post-Stalin thaw and subsequent stagnation under the regime of Leonid Brezhnev have arisen: first, that Joseph Brodsky (1940–1996) was the only significant poet at this time; second, that the gulf between official and unofficial lit. was unbridgeable; and finally, that the description "practitioner of unofficial lit." during these years is coterminous with "political dissident." The truer picture is one of interrelated backgrounds and artistic formations joining many major and minor Leningrad poets of the time with officially sanctioned literary groups.

While censorship persisted, the state's efforts to turn out talented poets unwittingly encouraged new directions. Poets trained in a quasi-official literary group like Gleb Semenov's famous LITO (Literary Society) also broadened their horizons by meeting other young poets and sharing unorthodox views and copies of both foreign and Rus. poetry that had been smuggled from abroad. A whole new generation of poets came of age in the 1960s. Akhmatova, who survived official denunciation in the 1940s, was a beacon to younger poets like Brodsky, Evgenii Rein (b. 1935), Dmitrii Bobyshev (b. 1936), and Viktor Sosnora (b. 1937), known after Akhmatova's death as her "orphans." Similarly, another survivor of a legendary era, Pasternak inspired a younger generation in Moscow, and his Zhivago poems remain one of the high points of his oeuvre. Both older writers treated the moral standing of the poet in works that could only be published abroad, such as *Requiem*, published in Munich in 1963, the cycle in which Akhmatova reacted to the Stalinist terror by articulating her grief as a victim and mother and as spokesman for the traumatized people of Leningrad.

For every poet like Evgenii Evtushenko (b. 1933), who moderated his political message for advantage, numerous others followed an anti-Soviet direction. This is the case with Alexander Galich (1918–1977), a master of dissident song, and the subtle strict-form lyric poet Vladimir Ufliand (1937–2007). Many other poets in both metropolitan Russia and provincial cities ignored the transparency and prosaic sense demanded by socialist realism. In this diversity and wealth of talent, we might cite the minimalism of Aleksei Khvo-

stenko (1940–2004); the delightful illogic of the Muscovite Evgenii Kharitonov (1941–1981), which harks back to the techniques and absurdist outlook of Kharms; Igor Holin (1920–1999), who in the mid-1960s applied the jingle-type rhymes of the *chastushka* to questions about identity and ontology; and Genrikh Sapgir (1928–1999), a member of the Lianosovo group of painters and poets, whose ironical vignettes and epigrammatic brilliance have a moral force. Much poetry circulated unofficially in ms., in samizdat publication in Russia and abroad in "tamizdat" anthols. like *The Blue Lagoon* (1980–86).

In the 1960s, the "guitar poets" or bards Vladimir Vysotsky (1938–1980) and Bulat Okudzhava (1924–1997) achieved popularity as lyric poets and balladeers; their poetic songs eschewed official lang. and were much closer to people's daily lives and concerns, while also expressing subversive countercultural and sometimes implicitly anti-Soviet views. Brodsky's first collection, *Ostanovka v pustyne* (*A Halt in the Wilderness*, 1970), which contained a formally startling tribute to John Donne and poignant elegy for T. S. Eliot, caused a sensation when published abroad and galvanized the literary underground in Leningrad. Mannerisms and innovations that would become unmistakable appear, incl. his extensive relaxation of verse line through *enjambment, intricate stanza forms (a striking contrast with the iambic tetrameter quatrain sanctioned by Soviet practice), aphorism and paradox, religious themes (again, a provocation), and his obsession with time and space. Brodsky voiced a degree of self-irony shared by many if not all his contemporaries, an irony that stripped away the residual mystical status of the poet as spiritual guide and prophet that was a legacy of the trad. from the romantics to Blok. The generation of the 1960s sought wit, novelty, and individuality of voice. A lack of explicit interest in Pushkin is a striking feature among poets from both Leningrad/St. Petersburg and Moscow, reflecting fatigue with his Soviet-sponsored familiarity.

The hist. of 20th-c. Rus. poetry contains many chronological displacements due to censorship. Much poetry written from the 1930s until the 1960s would not officially see the light in Russia before perestroika. Poets who had fallen into disfavor were rarely granted posthumous publication. Tsvetaeva was at the height of her creative powers after leaving Russia, and her unique body of metrically startling narrative and vivid autobiographical lyrics were known clandestinely in Russia to a small readership. During the thaw, while noteworthy eds. were published abroad, the Soviet rehabilitation of figures like Mandelstam and Tsvetaeva was uneven; their work was subject to distortion through censorship and unreliable editing. Their legacy remained more legendary than real until the 1980s.

The same period also saw significant geographical displacement. We should not leave 20th-c. poetry without mentioning the possibly unique phenomenon of Rus. poetry abroad, a stunning and essential chapter in its hist. The degree to which poetry written in Rus. from the diaspora is separate from and even in counterpoint to devels. in Soviet Russia is hard to assess. The poets of the first wave of emigration in the 1920s who achieved lasting distinction had already started writing in imperial Russia or the Soviet Union. The experience of revolution and emigration deeply marked Vladislav Khodasevich (1886–1939), author of two exquisite collections full of bitter self-irony and truculence about the immediate past who sought refuge in nostalgia for the Pushkinian trad. By contrast, Georgy Ivanov (1894–1958), whose Rus. collections had taken up fashionable decadent themes, became increasingly experimentalist and surreal in emigration, while Boris Poplavsky (1903–35) quickly assimilated the program of André Breton and his followers. Despite the large numbers of poets in the diaspora from the 1930s (incl. Vladimir Nabokov [1899–1977], who was a prolific writer of lyric poems), it is not until the third wave of emigration in the 1970s that a generation of truly significant poets, incl. Brodsky, Lev Loseff (1937–2009), and Rein emerges. All came of age in Soviet Russia and took up residence either in the U.S. or Europe. Their poetry was often first appreciated in the West before becoming known to readers in Russia through underground distribution and subsequently in print from the inception of perestroika.

In post-Soviet Russia, poetry quickly regained formal innovativeness, acquired an edge of political unorthodoxy, and reveled in the shock of the new. While many gifted poets born in the 1930s no longer lived in Russia, a generation of young poets born in the late 1940s and 1950s included outstanding lyric talents, among them Oleg Chukhontsev (b. 1938), Elena Shvarts (b. 1948), Ol'ga Sedakova (b. 1949), and Yunna Morits (b. 1937), whose individual voices spoke with uncommon interiority and religious feeling long before the collapse of the Soviet Union. In the post-Soviet period, their poetry continues to develop in familiar directions. Among Moscow poets who bridged the Soviet and post-Soviet division, Aleksei Tsvetkov (b. 1947) and Sergei Gandlevskii (b. 1952) write in the elegiac trad. about core existential questions. While their poems evoke great reaches of the Rus. trad., their grandeur is offset by irony, mordant humor, and highly inventive rhyme. The experience of unfettered freedom in the Boris Yeltsin years lent rampant experimental exuberance to the poet's task in the 1990s. Avant-garde poetic movements reflected the outlook and methods of deconstruction and *postmodernism. The act of writing, which in recent memory had carried extreme personal risk, became an act of ling. and philosophical daring for many poets. This is nowhere better seen than in the work of the "metametaphorist" Alexei Parshchikov (1954–2009), as well as the "conceptualists" Lev Rubinshtein (b. 1947) and Dmitrii Prigov (1940–2007) and the "postconceptualists," incl. Timur Kibirov (b. 1955), all of whom were originally based in Moscow. Like the futurists, these poets flaunted their colorful personalities and exploited ling. resources to the full, reconnecting with the trad. of Khlebnikov and *Dada while also displaying the assimilative powers of Rus. verse by domesticating foreign writers like the *Beat poets. Each in his highly individual fashion combines verbal energy with sarcasm and affected in-

nocence. For many readers, the cleverness with which these writers dismantled the Soviet experience and its made-to-order art remains the most memorable feature of their works. Interestingly, Pushkin's stock rose once again in the 1990s, as post-Soviet avant-garde groups claimed him as a fellow postmodernist.

*See* BINARY AND TERNARY.

■ **Anthologies**: *Na Zapade*, ed. J. P. Ivask (1953); *Anthologie de la poésie russe*, ed. K. Granoff (1961); *Poety 1820–1930-kh godov*, ed. L. Ia. Ginzburg (1961); *The Heritage of Russian Verse*, ed. D. Obolensky (1965); *Modern Russian Poetry*, ed. V. Markov and M. Sparks (1966); *The New Russian Poets 1953–1968*, ed. G. Reavey (1968); *Fifty Soviet Poets*, ed. V. Ognev and D. Rottenberg (1969); *Russkaia sillabicheskaia poeziia XVII–XVIII vv.*, ed. A. Panchenko (1970); *The Silver Age of Russian Culture*, ed. C. and E. Proffer (1971); *Poety XVIII veka*, ed. G. Makognenko and I. Z. Serman (1972); *Russkaia poeziia XVIII-ogo veka*, ed. G. Makogonenko (1972); *Poeziia 1917–1920 godov*, ed. A. Mikhailov (1975); *The Blue Lagoon*, ed. K. K. Kuzminsky and G. L. Kovalev, 5 v. (1980–86); *Third Wave*, ed. K. Johnson and S. M. Ashby (1992); *Contemporary Russian Poetry*, ed. G. S. Smith (1993); *Russkaia poeziia serebrianogo veka, 1890–1917*, ed. M. L. Gasparov (1993); *In the Grip of Strange Thoughts*, ed. J. Kates (1999); *The Garnett Book of Russian Verse*, ed. D. Rayfield (2000); *Sto odna poetessa serebrianogo veka*, ed. M. L. Gasparov, O. B. Kushlina, T. L. Nikol'saia (2000); *Contemporary Russian Poetry*, ed. E. Bunimovich and J. Kates (2008).

■ **Criticism and History**: A. Sinyavsky and A. Menshutin, *Poeziia pervykh let revoliutsii, 1917–1920* (1964); *Istoriia russkoi poezii*, ed. B. P. Gorodeckii, 2 v. (1968–69); R. Silbajoris, *Russian Versification* (1968); V. Zhirmunskii, *Teoriia stixa* (1968); B. Eikhenbaum, *O poezii* (1969); V. Markov, *Russian Futurism* (1969); A. M. Panchenko, *Russkaia stikhotvornaia kul'tura XVII-ogo veka* (1973); L. Ginzburg, *O lirike*, 2d ed. (1974); J. M. Lotman, *Analysis of the Poetic Text*, ed. and trans. D. B. Johnson (1976); *Modern Russian Poets on Poetry*, ed. C. R. Proffer (1976); J. M. Lotman, *The Structure of the Artistic Text*, trans. G. Lenhoff and R. Vroon (1977); P. France, *Poets of Modern Russia* (1983); G. Struve, *Russkaia literatura v. izgnanii*, 2d ed. (1984); G. S. Smith, *Songs to Seven Strings* (1984); P. Steiner, *Russian Formalism* (1984); S. Pratt, *Russian Metaphysical Romanticism* (1984); M. Altshuller and E. Dryzhakova, *Put' otreniia: Russkaia literatura 1953–68* (1985); Terras—see "Bylina," "Poema," "Versification, Historical Survey"; W. M. Todd III, *Fiction and Society in the Age of Pushkin* (1986); Scherr; D. Lowe, *Russian Writing since 1953* (1987); E. Beaujour, *Alien Tongues* (1989)—writers of the first emigration; R. Jakobson, *Language in Literature* (1990; includes "On the Generation That Squandered Its Poets"); J. Doherty, *The Acmeist Movement in Russian Poetry* (1995); M. Epshtein, *After the Future* (1995); M .L. Gasparov, *Izbrannye stat'i* (1995); K. Hodgson, *Written with Bayonet* (1996)—Soviet poetry of WWII; M. L. Gasparov, *Izbrannye trudy* (1997); D. S. Mirsky, *Stikhotvoreniia; Stat'i o russkoi poezii*, ed. G. K.

Perkins and G. S. Smith (1997); R. Polonsky, *English Literature and the Russian Aesthetic Renaissance* (1998); M. Wachtel, *The Development of Russian Verse* (1998); M. L. Gasparov, *Metr i smysl* (1999); *Rereading Russian Poetry*, ed. S. Sandler (1999); S. Küpper, *Autostrategien im Moskauer Konzeptualismus* (2000); G. S. Smith, *Vzgliad izvne* (2002); Emily Lygo, *Leningrad Poetry 1953–1975: The Thaw Generation* (2010).

■ **Web Sites**: Russkaia poeziia 1960-kh godov, http://ruthenia.ru/60s/poets/index.htm; Vavilon, Sovremennaia russkaia literatura, http//www.vavilon.ru/.

■ **Works on Individual Writers**: L. Ginzburg, *Tvorcheskii put' Lermontova* (1940); R. A. Gregg, *Fedor Tiutchev* (1965); R. F. Gustafson, *Imagination of Spring* (1966)—on Afanasy Fet; I. Z. Serman, *Derzhavin* (1967); S. S. Birkenmeyer, *Nikolai Nekrasov* (1968); C. Brown, *Mandelstam* (1973); E. Brown, *Mayakovsky* (1973); G. Khetso, *Evgenii Baratynskii* (1973); S. Hackel, *The Poet and the Revolution* (1975)—on Blok's *The Twelve*; G. McVay, *Esenin* (1976); A. Pyman, *The Life of Aleksandr Blok*, 2 v. (1979–80); B. M. Eikhenbaum, *Lermontov* (1981); D. M. Bethea, *Khodasevich* (1983); V. Terras, *Vladimir Mayakovsky* (1983); R. Vroon, *Velimir Xlebnikov's Shorter Poems* (1983); J. D. Clayton, *Ice and Flame* (1985)—on *Eugene Onegin*; J. D. Grossman, *Valery Bryusov and the Riddle of Russian Decadence* (1985); S. Karlinsky, *Marina Tsvetaeva* (1985); G. Freidin, *A Coat of Many Colors* (1987)—on Osip Mandelstam; K. O'Connor, *Boris Pasternak's "My Sister-Life"* (1988); I. Z. Serman, *Mikhail Lomonosov* (1988); D. A. Sloane, *Alexander Blok and the Dynamics of the Lyric Cycle* (1988); S. Sandler, *Distant Pleasures* (1989)—on Pushkin; L. Fleishman, *Boris Pasternak* (1990); S. Amert, *In a Shattered Mirror: The Later Poetry of Anna Akhmatova* (1992); M. Makin, *Marina Tsvetaeva* (1993); C. Cavanagh, *Osip Mandelstam and the Modernist Creation of Tradition* (1995); A. Kahn, *Pushkin's "Bronze Horseman"* (1998); *Joseph Brodsky*, ed. L. Loseff and V. Polukhina (1999); J. E. Malmstad, *Mikhail Kuzmin* (1999); O. Proskurin, *Poeziia Pushkina, ili Podvizhnyi palimpsest* (1999); S. Sandler, *Commemorating Pushkin* (2004); N. Skatov, *Nekrasov* (2004); C. Ciepiela, *The Same Solitude: Boris Pasternak and Marina Tsvetaeva* (2006); L. Losev, *Iosif Brodskii* (2006); A. Kahn, *Pushkin's Lyric Intelligence* (2008).

A. KAHN

# RUSSIAN FORMALISM

**I. Doctrine and Historical Position**
**II. Competition with Marxism and Later Resonance**

A school of literary studies that emerged in the mid-1910s and peaked by the early 1920s; its formal end was marked by an article of enforced self-crit. by Viktor Shklovsky, "Monument to a Scholarly Error" (1930). Formalism originated in the study of lang. dialects and folklore at the Moscow Linguistic Circle, established in 1915, and in the work of the Petrograd Society for the Study of Poetic Language (Opoyaz), founded in 1916, although the earliest important text to be associated with the school, Shklovsky's "The Resurrection of the

Word," dates to 1914. The most prominent exponents of Rus. formalism were Shklovsky (1893–1984), Roman Jakobson (1896–1982), Yuri Tynianov (1894–1943), Boris Eikhenbaum (1886–1959), Osip Brik (1888–1945), and Boris Tomashevsky (1890–1957). Vladimir Propp (1895–1970) and Pyotr Bogatyrev (1893–1971) developed the ideas of the formalists in the 1920s in the study of folklore; a group of "young Formalists" (*mladoformalisty*) was active in Leningrad in the late 1920s (Lidiya Ginzburg, 1902–90, being the most prominent) but gradually moved away from its teachers and their methodology.

**I. Doctrine and Historical Position.** Rus. formalism laid the foundations of mod. literary theory. The formalists were the first to see lit. as an autonomous domain of theoretical inquiry, steering away from aesthetics, sociology, psychology, and hist. and seeking support in ling. In Germany, there had been earlier attempts to apply a similarly autonomous approach to music and the visual arts. Heinrich Wölfflin's (1864–1945) dream of a hist. of art without names was echoed in Brik's belief that, had Alexander Pushkin never been born, *Evgenij Onegin* would still have been written. Breaking with a long trad. of thinking about lit. in terms of subjectivity and individual creativity, the Rus. formalists discussed the literary work of art in terms of "literariness" (*literaturnost'*), a quality they believed had to be explained before the uniqueness of lit. in relation to other discourses could be located. Uncontrolled by, and irreducible to, ethics, religion, or politics, lit. was now shaped not by individual imagination and authorial will but by a repertoire of devices, motifs, and rules, the exploration of which stimulated the formalists' interest in rhyme, rhythm, sound patterns and repetition, plot structure, and narrative frames.

Although the formalists actively studied prose and film (but not drama), poetry occupied pride of place in their work. Rus. formalism considered poetry to be the product of a specific use of lang. that highlights and draws attention to the act of expression itself. Hence the central notion of self-referentiality, capturing the essential distinction between the lang. of lit. (epitomized by poetry) and everyday lang.: "Poetry, which is simply an utterance orientated toward the mode of expression, is governed by immanent laws" (Jakobson, "Noveishaia russkaia poeziia," 1921; partial Eng. trans., "Modern Russian Poetry: Velimir Khlebnikov," 1973). Poetry is thus the best example of the self-referentiality of the literary text, which—unlike the texts generated by everyday lang.—does not focus on transmitting a message or prompting action but seeks instead to arrest the reader's attention and to direct it onto the act of expression itself. The purpose behind this redirection of attention was never unambiguously formulated. For Jakobson, this was a mechanism of "deautomatizing" the reader's perception of the text; or as Eikhenbaum wrote, "[T]he aim of poetry is to make perceptible the texture of the word" (*Lermontov*, 1924; Eng. trans., 1981). For Shklovsky, it was more than that. In his version, art is called on to deliver "estrangement," which he employs as a synonym for *deautomatization*, while extending its powers: not only is our perception of form deautomatized, so that we can shed the ballast of conventions acquired through previous experiences of reading lit., but the objects themselves also regain freshness and substance in the process. In Shklovsky's famous dictum, estrangement makes the stone "stonier."

Early on, formalism conceived of the literary work of art as a "sum of devices," but this static notion was later abandoned in favor of a more dynamic view of the literary text as a system of features and functions, in whose interaction one feature or function plays the dominant role at any one time. Jakobson usually referred to that feature by using a substantive: *dominanta*. This impulse was carried forward by Tynianov in an attempt to understand and describe literary evolution as systemic change that reshuffles and rejuvenates the genre repertoire of lit. In Tynianov's account, lit. grows by the margins: it incorporates previously nonliterary discursive domains populated by hitherto marginal genres. Literary forms are not born and do not disappear, but they change their status and place on the literary map: "In the epoch of the decomposition of a certain genre, it moves from the centre to the periphery, while from the trivialities of literature, from its backyard and lowlands, a new phenomenon emerges in its place" (Tynianov, *Arkhaisty i novatory* [Archaists and Innovators]).

The exceptional significance of Rus. formalism as the first school to assert lit. as an autonomous object of theoretical analysis has obscured its background and complex position among other intellectual formations at the end of the 19th and the start of the 20th c. Formalism was a phenomenon and offspring of late modernity, epistemologically related to positivism, psychoanalysis, and Marxism. Formalism was as technical, precise, meticulous, and cold as positivism itself, but it differed from positivism in that it abandoned trust in encyclopedic scholarship and the genetic explanations inherited from the Enlightenment trad. of attention to climate, environment, race, and the historical "moment." Formalism sought to reconcile the exactitude of positivism with its own insistence on the independence of lit. from various "extra-literary series." Scientific soundness (*nauchnost'*) remained a paramount value for both positivism and formalism, and the formalists proved this by their rigorous concentration on the quantifiable aspects of verse (Jakobson, Brik, Tomashevsky). Leon Trotsky (1879–1940) characterized formalist analysis, somewhat vulgarly but not far off the mark, as "essentially descriptive and semi-statistical."

There is also an important proximity to cl. psychoanalysis. Sigmund Freud was adamant that we are not altogether masters of our own inner lives. Dreams, jokes, and verbal slippages all come to denote the inevitable manifestation and validation of laws that operate independently of us but are nevertheless knowable; we cannot govern our own psychic lives, although we can hope to know what governs them. Similarly, formalism wanted to demonstrate that writers are unseated from their writing desks by forces that are beyond their control (most important, the structural characteristics of lang.) but that are, nevertheless, entirely amenable to scientific study and rationalization. This new understanding of human agency makes formalism much more than a school in literary studies and highlights its importance as an integral part of 20th-c. intellectual hist.

**II. Competition with Marxism and Later Resonance.** The formalists were active at a time when, in the Soviet Union, the intellectual scene was increasingly dominated by Marxism. Karl Marx's belief that hist. unfolds according to inexorable objective patterns, much as *Evgenij Onegin* would have been written, in Brik's account, even without Pushkin, made formalism and Marxism bitter competitors in the field of rational inquiry into the objective laws governing social life and creativity. After the October Revolution (1917), both movements strove to embody the ideals and values of scientism in a society that had succumbed to the lures of rapid modernization. In this sense, Marxism and formalism were competing on the same ground. It was no accident that Eikhenbaum was irritated when Lev Pumpiansky (1891–1940), in their conversations, thought the formalists close to the Marxists (Ustinov). This hidden competition never amounted to true dialogue, however, mainly because of one fundamental asymmetry characterizing the relationship between formalism and Marxism. Unlike Marxism, formalism never became a prescriptive discourse. Discovering the patterns of form, rhyme, and rhythm never amounted to formulating recipes for writing good prose or poetry. Thus, instead of a seminal dialogue, the two competitors were involved in a number of polemics usually initiated as attacks on formalism by Marxist ideologues. The first and most important example is Leon Trotsky's critique of formalism in *Literatura i revoliutsiia* (1923; Eng. trans., *Literature and Revolution*, 1925), followed much later by a prominent dispute in Leningrad (1927), in which Eikhenbaum, Tomashevsky, Tynianov, and Shklovsky represented the formalists, against Nikolai Derzhavin (1877–1953), Georgii Gorbachev, Mikhail Yakovlev, and the writer Lidiya Seifullina (1889–1954) as proponents of Marxism. Trotsky was not against the formal method as such. On the contrary, he welcomed it precisely because of its scientific potential to explain form. He objected to extending the sphere of the method's application too far: "The methods of Formalism, *if confined within legitimate limits*, may help to clarify the artistic and psychological peculiarities of literary form" (*Literature and Revolution*; italics added). This appeal for restraint and confinement suggests the nature of the emerging turf war between formalism and Marxism, waged not least with a view to securing a larger share of public attention and credit.

Formalism was not indifferent to power, nor was it driven to gestures of political significance solely as a means of survival. In 1924, the formalists published a number of interconnected articles devoted to Vladimir Lenin's style; some of the formalists were seriously engaged with *constructivism, the "literature of fact" (*literatura fakta*), and other devels. in leftist art. Formalism was thus not estranged from the processes of constructing a new culture and a new political identity after 1917. Of particular importance were Jakobson's and Brik's close association with Vladimir Mayakovsky (1893–1930) and the various phases of Rus. futurism, as well as the gravitation of some of the most distinguished formalists to LEF (Levyi Front Iskusstv [Left Front of the Arts]) and its jours. *Lef* and *Novyi Lef*. Eikhenbaum's desire to see "the revolution and philology" as mutually supportive entities indicated the determination with which the formalists were trying to inscribe themselves in the new social order.

By the mid-1920s, the formalists reached the recognition that neither formalism nor Marxist sociology of lit. could work in isolation and without some form of mediation. This new turn in Rus. formalism signaled fresh interest in literary circles and in the sociology of literary production, publishing, and reading. The idea of the "literary everyday" (*literaturnyi byt*), a porous notion that was summoned to capture the social situatedness of literary production, gained prominence. Eikhenbaum, in particular, engaged in the study of extraliterary "series" (*riady*). However, the Marxists took this not as a serious sign of natural scholarly evolution but as an admission of weakness or even past guilt. Medvedev's 1928 critique of formalism remains a rare example of a more sophisticated Marxist objection to its methodology.

The fate of formalism in the Soviet Union after 1930 was marked by wholesale rejection; formalism became a label of condemnation widely applied to stigmatize any interest in the formal aspects of lit. and art, as opposed to the "healthy" preoccupation with "content" (ideas). While the representatives of semantic paleontology (Olga Freidenberg, 1890–1955, and Izrail Frank-Kamenetsky, 1880–1937), the most interesting leftist movement in literary studies in the 1930s, were highly critical of formalism, Mikhail Bakhtin (1895–1975) safeguarded and continued its attention to marginal discursive forms. His theory of the novel draws on Tynianov's account of the evolution of "junior genres." As the *ode was for Tynianov, the novel is, in Bakhtin's account, an underdog before coming to prominence as a major genre; its life, according to Bakhtin, can be captured in the words Tynianov uses in *Arkhaisty i novatory* to describe the ode: "it existed not so much as a finished, self-enclosed genre, but as a certain constructional tendency." In Bakhtin's theory of the novel, one detects the same vision of not-yet-ready literary forms that present a dynamic discursive direction (*ustanovka*) rather than a finished product. Bakhtin's claim that the novel holds a unique position among other genres, guaranteed by its refusal to ossify into a fixed *canon, is foreshadowed by Shklovsky's judgment: "the canon of the novel as genre is perhaps more often than any other [canon] capable of parodying and modifying itself" (*O teorii prozy*, 1925–1929; Eng. trans., *Theory of Prose*, 1990).

When the Moscow-Tartu School (see STRUCTURALISM) came to prominence in the late 1960s, the revival of formalism was rather selective. While interest in the verifiable, quantitative aspects of the literary text was welcome and endorsed by Jurij Lotman, estrangement, a central category of early formalism, was cast aside as less productive. The "young formalists," esp. Ginzburg, who had seemed like mere traitors to their teachers, were now admitted to the wider canon of literary studies that had evolved since (and to some extent also from) formalism. Outside the Soviet Union, scholars of lit. in Poland and Czechoslovakia showed considerable appreciation of formalism, and some followed in its tracks during the 1930s. Of particular significance was the work in the late 1920s and throughout the 1930s of the Prague Linguistic Circle, in which Jakobson played a major role. In the West, the initial reaction, notably among Rus. émigré literary critics (e.g., Georgy Adamovich, 1894–1972, and Vladislav Khodasevich, 1886–1939), was negative; it was felt that formalism contradicted a long Rus. trad. of uncovering and asserting the moral values of lit. Speculations that a conversation between Sergei Tretyakov (1892–1937) and Bertolt Brecht (1898–1956) in 1935 led to the latter's adopting (and adapting) Shklovsky's *ostranenie* (see DEFAMILIARIZATION) as a cornerstone of his own method of *Verfremdung* have not been fully substantiated (cf. Tihanov 2005). Thus, it was not until the 1960s that Rus. formalism began to enjoy a notable presence in the West. An early influential selection of articles by the Rus. formalists, ed. by Todorov and prefaced by Jakobson, was published in France in 1965, arousing Herbert Marcuse's interest. The enduring legacy of formalism, enriched with the insights of the Prague Circle, was a significant factor in the growth of structuralism and narratology in the West in the 1960s and 1970s. Comparisons between Rus. formalism and Am. *New Criticism, on the other hand, while grounded in their shared predilection for *"close reading" and sustained focus on the structure of the poetic text, are less productive in establishing direct influence by the formalists. The arrival of *poststructuralism and deconstruction signaled the dominance, throughout the closing decades of the 20th c., of a new agenda, in which Rus. formalism has been present under erasure: recognized for its resistance to traditional notions of subjectivity and creative autonomy and, at the same time, disregarded for its insistence on poetic and everyday lang. being qualitatively different and on the literary work of art presenting a meaningfully structured whole.

*See* CRITICISM, FORMALISM, INTERPRETATION, LINGUISTICS AND POETICS.

■ *Poetika: Sborniki po teorii poeticheskogo iazyka* (1919); L. Trotsky, *Literature and Revolution*, trans. R. Strunsky (1925); Y. Tynianov, *Arkhaisty i novatory* (1929); *Théorie de la Littérature: Textes des formalistes russes*, ed. and trans. T. Todorov (1965); K. Pomorska, *Russian Formalist Theory and Its Poetic Ambiance* (1968); *Texte der Russischen Formalisten*, ed. J. Striedter and W.-D. Stempel, 2 v. (1969–72); E. M. Thompson, *Russian Formalism and Anglo-American New Criticism* (1971); F. Jameson, *The Prison-House of Language* (1972); *Formalist Theory*, ed. A. Shukman and L. M. O'Toole (1977); R. H. Stacy, *Defamiliarization in Language and Literature* (1977); *Formalism: History, Comparison, Genre*, ed.

A. Shukman (1978); A. Hansen-Löve, *Der Russische Formalismus* (1978); P. N. Medvedev and M. M. Bahktin, *The Formal Method in Literary Scholarship*, trans. A. J. Wehrle (1978); B. M. Eikhenbaum, *Lermontov: A Study in Literary-Historical Evaluation*, trans. R. Parrott and H. Weber (1981); V. Erlich, *Russian Formalism: History–Doctrine*, 3d ed. (1981); P. Steiner, *Russian Formalism: A Metapoetics* (1984); *Russian Formalism: A Retrospective Glance*, ed. R. L. Jackson and S. Rudy (1985); R. Jakobson, *Language in Literature*, ed. K. Pomorska and S. Rudy (1987); J. Striedter, *Literary Structure, Evolution, and Value: Russian Formalism and Czech Structuralism* (1989); V. Shklovsky, *Theory of Prose*, trans. B. Sher (1990); D. Ustinov, "Materialy disputa 'Marksizm i formal'nyi metod' 6 marta 1927 g.," *Novoe literaturnoe obozrenie* 50 (2001); A. Karcz, *The Polish Formalist School and Russian Formalism* (2002); G. Tihanov, "Why Did Modern Literary Theory Originate in Central and Eastern Europe? (And Why Is It Now Dead?)," *Common Knowledge* 10 (2004); I. Svetlikova, *Istoki russkogo formalizma* (2005); G. Tihanov, "The Politics of Estrangement: The Case of the Early Shklovsky," *PoT* 26 (2005); D. Robinson, *Estrangement and the Somatics of Literature* (2008); C. Depretto, *Le Formalisme en Russie* (2009); R. Jakobson, *Formal'naia shkola i sovremennoe russkoe literaturovedenie*, ed. T. Glanc (2011).

G. Tihanov

**SAGA.** The word is borrowed into Eng. (and other langs.) from Icelandic. Through its Germanic root, *saga* is related to the Eng. *say, saying*; exact cognates are OE *sagu* and mod. Eng. (*old*) *saw*. At core, Old Icelandic *saga* signified an event that was spoken about, hence (1) the significant event itself, i.e., hist., story; or (2) the prose literary work in which it is realized—thus, roughly *histoire* and *discours*. For the extended Eng. senses, see the *OED*. In Old Icelandic lit., various types of sagas are recognized, among them: Icelandic family sagas (e.g., *Njáls saga*); kings' sagas (e.g., *Heimskringla*); mythic-heroic sagas (e.g., *Völsunga saga*); contemp. sagas (with several subgroups, e.g., *Sturlunga saga*); and Eur. romances in prose adaptation (*riddarasögur*). The "saga literature" as a whole comprises a huge corpus of narrative prose from med. Iceland (and Norway), whether native or adapted from continental models. The most renowned as lit., the 40-odd family sagas written mainly in the 13th c., center on conflicts among the settlers of the new land c. 930–1030 and are closely bound up with social, legal, historical, and cultural realities; they have been compared to historical novels, but the comparison does not do justice to the dialectic between oral trad. and written creativity in the genre's evolution. The chaste saga style, with invisible narrator and realistic drama, is justly famous; its prose poetics is largely a poetics of human behavior viewed through an apparently clear glass: the saga itself. Prose surface is broken by quoted poems in many sagas, creating a prosimetrical counterpoint between sobriety and passion.

*See* NORSE POETRY, PROSIMETRUM.

■ J. Kristjánsson, *Eddas and Sagas* (1988); V. Hreinsson, ed., *The Complete Sagas of Icelanders*, 5 vols. (1997)—in trans.; V. Ólason, "Family Sagas," *A Companion to Old Norse-Icelandic Literature and Culture*, ed. R. McTurk (2005, 2007)—see also other relevant chapters; G. Sigurðsson, *The Medieval Icelandic Saga and Oral Tradition* (2004).

J. HARRIS

**SAN FRANCISCO RENAISSANCE.** On October 13, 1955, a poetry reading by five poets at the Six Gallery in San Francisco—Allen Ginsberg, Philip Lamantia, Michael McClure, Gary Snyder, and Philip Whalen—began what came to be known as the San Francisco Renaissance. The principal event of that reading and the following years was the emergence of *Beat poetry, manifested on this occasion by Ginsberg's *Howl*; but even at the reading, Beat poetics (*confessional, incantatory, and profane) was only one section of a literary environment that grew to embrace precursors, contemporaries, and dissenters incl. Kenneth Rexroth, Lawrence Ferlinghetti, Robert Duncan, Jack Spicer,

Joanne Kyger, and William Everson. As one of the early episodes of *postmodernism in Am. poetry, the San Francisco Renaissance joined several vivid tendencies of postwar poetic culture (*nature poetry, *jazz poetry, *performance) with the indigenous character of the city's dispersed literary scene, an alternative to long-dominant centers such as New York and Boston. The San Franciscan "poetics of place" paid particular homage to the city's unique landscape and culture, as well as its political and social radicalism. Moreover, since at least the 1940s, many Bay Area poets had identified with a *canon of influences, such as *surrealism and the extreme lang. play of Gertrude Stein and the later James Joyce, that set them apart from the conversation among Am. poets elsewhere. Its best historian, Michael Davidson, has characterized the San Francisco Renaissance as held together by an expressivist poetics that was fundamentally neoromantic in ideology and performative in ethos.

Like the *New York school of the 1960s, the San Francisco Renaissance expressed a place and a moment together but also launched a number of careers that outlasted it. Most observers agree that the renaissance was over by the late 1960s. It was quickly succeeded and overwritten by several renaissances, some that carried forward its central preoccupations with exploring subjective expression (now by such poets as Robert Hass, Robert Pinsky, and Denise Levertov), but others reacting to the idealisms and omissions of the renaissance poets by foregrounding collective voices (as did several poets of color of the 1970s and after, notably Lorna Dee Cervantes and Victor Hernández Cruz); or in the case of the *Language poets of the Bay Area such as Ron Silliman, Leslie Scalapino, and Lyn Hejinian (the Western cohort of a movement that originated concurrently in New York), disclosing the complicity of lang. in social discourses that create the very subjects who purport to speak directly through poems by Ginsberg or Snyder. In this second phase from 1970 to the turn of the 21st c., no position lacks a model or a forerunner in the multifarious generation of poets who made the San Francisco Renaissance, but, at the same time, no assumption of that earlier group goes unmodified or uncontradicted by its diverse successors.

*See* UNITED STATES, POETRY OF THE.

■ M. Davidson, *The San Francisco Renaissance* (1989); D. Wakoski, "The Birth of the San Francisco Renaissance: Something Now Called the Whitman Tradition," and L. Hamalian, "The Genesis of the San Francisco Renaissance: Literary and Political Currents, 1945–1955," *Literary Review* 32 (1988); L. Hamalian, "Regionalism Makes Good: The San Francisco Renaissance," *Reading the West*, ed. M. Kowalewski (1996);

L. Ellingham, *Poet Be Like God: Jack Spicer and the San Francisco Renaissance* (1998).

R. Greene, A. Slessarev

## SANSKRIT POETICS

I. Early History
II. Middle Period: Sanskrit Poetics in Kashmir and Beyond
III. New Poetics in Early Modernity

Sanskrit poetics is an intellectual discipline that accompanied literary production in the highly prestigious medium of Sanskrit for nearly two millennia. The discipline had its roots in the early centuries of the first millennium CE and continued uninterrupted into the early mod. era. It formed an important component of the education of Sanskrit literati and of writers, scholars, and artists in other langs. and media.

Indeed, while Sanskrit poetics tended to ignore local langs. in the vast area stretching from present-day Afghanistan in the west to the Indonesian archipelago in the east, it had a profound impact on lit. and culture in these regions. Works on Sanskrit poetics traveled throughout this world and were translated into many of its langs. A prominent example is Daṇḍin's *Kāvyādarśa* (Mirror of Poetry, ca. 700 CE), a work that was transmitted to southeast Asia, if not to China, and translated into Tamil and Kannada in the south of the Indian peninsula, Pali and Sinhalese in Sri Lanka, and Tibetan (see TIBET, TRADITIONAL POETRY AND POETICS OF) far to the north. Poets, intellectuals, and artists in the Indian subcontinent proper constantly kept up to date with Sanskrit poetics. A case in point is Bhānudatta (fl. ca. 1500), whose treatises on aesthetics inspired early mod. literati in Telugu and Hindi, as well as miniature painters in various Indian locations in the 17th and 18th cs.

The achievements of this long-standing and sophisticated discipline include an unparalleled analysis of figurative lang., as in the investigation of the formal, logical, semantic, and pragmatic aspects of *simile and its numerous sister *tropes; a complex and overarching theory of readers' emotional response to lit. (see AFFECT, EMOTION); and a highly complex semantic-cognitive analysis of denotation (see CONNOTATION AND DENOTATION), *metaphor, and suggestion, ling. capacities identified as enabling the readers' emotional and aesthetic responses.

We can divide the hist. of Sanskrit poetics into three phases: first, an early stage, from the discipline's mostly lost origins in the first centuries of the Common Era to about the 8th c., during which it was primarily concerned with imparting the prescriptions of poetry. A second stage, from the 9th c. to the 15th c., was marked by repeated attempts to turn the early discussion into a respectable, coherent theory, on a par with Sanskrit's other branches of thought, and by an increasing focus on reading rather than writing poetry. During a third phase, which lasted until the early colonial era, Sanskrit poetics reinvented itself as a prestigious theory that attracted thinkers from other disciplines and provided space and tools for philosophical and theological issues

outside poetics proper. While this tripartite division is crude and while earlier disciplinary strands continued to thrive concurrently with the new ones, it may help to frame the important voices, topics, and tensions in the long hist. of Sanskrit poetics.

**I. Early History.** Sanskrit poetics must have evolved late relative to the poetry itself. The first extant works of this discipline are Bhāmaha's *Kāvyālaṃkāra* (Ornamenting Poetry), written in the 6th or 7th c. CE, and Daṇḍin's *Kāvyādarśa*. These works lag behind Sanskrit's first surviving narrative poems and plays by Aśvaghoṣa (fl. 2d c. CE) and Kālidāsa (fl. 4th c.), even though the poetry assumes some codified knowledge about it. It is also clear that Bhāmaha and Daṇḍin follow predecessors whom they occasionally name, and fragments of this earlier discussion are traceable. But it is telling that later authors hardly ever refer to ancient sources: in the eyes of posterity, Bhāmaha and Daṇḍin are the discipline's founding fathers.

Indeed, Bhāmaha and Daṇḍin were deeply influenced by ideas and analytical tools that were first formulated in separate, more established knowledge systems. These include the authoritative Veda-related trads. of grammar, which devised a highly complex descriptive tool kit and a metalinguistic idiom for the analysis of vast ling. phenomena; *Mīmāṃsā* (Vedic hermeneutics), which developed a sophisticated philosophy of lang. for the purpose of clarifying Vedic statements and countering the Buddhist critique of the Veda; and *Nyāya* (logic), which produced, among other things, a comprehensive theory of inference, oral testimony, and verbal debate with the aim of examining the validity of Vedic utterances. Another corollary of Vedic scripture worth mentioning here is the separate science of *prosody, which Daṇḍin dubs a "raft for those who sail the sea of poetry." Common to all these disciplines was their focus on lang., a trajectory shared by the nascent poetics. A major question of Sanskrit poetics was what distinguishes the lang. of poetry from other "things made of language," as Daṇḍin put it. In a way, Bhāmaha's and Daṇḍin's works are generative grammars for poetic lang.; Bhāmaha's even has a chapter dedicated to grammatical issues per se.

In addition to the Veda-related knowledge systems, Sanskrit poetics was also influenced by practical and artistic discourses that had a ling. dimension to them. Particularly important in this connection is dramaturgy (*Nāṭyaśāstra*), where aspects of stage plays, incl. plot construction, character types, and various poetic qualities of the script have already been theorized. Although Sanskrit did not develop an independent discipline of rhet., practical knowledge regarding eloquent and persuasive speech, accumulated in South Asian courts and chanceries and preserved in inscriptional *panegyrics, also influenced Sanskrit poetics. The latter strand of knowledge, like the poetry it accompanied, was closely associated with the royal court.

These varied influences are apparent in the discipline's early phase, when theoreticians were busy documenting the charming elements of poetry, whether euphonic, syntactic, or semantic, in an approach reminiscent of grammar's description of all elements of the lang. from the level of phonemes on. The key category in this investigation was the \*alaṃkāra or \*ornament (to the body of a poem), a highly flexible concept allowing for a wide variety of aesthetic effects and analyses. Under this heading, the quintessential literary devices of simile (\*upamā) and metaphor (rūpaka) were defined and analyzed according to their propositional structure (A is like B; A is B) and the logical relationship they entail (semblance, identity). The method and lang. for analyzing such figures were borrowed originally from grammar, where both figures were described as occurring in normal nominal compounds (as in snow-white or moon-face). A second group of alaṃkāras allowed for the intimation of similarity through propositions of "doubt" (saṃśaya: "is this a lotus, or is it your face?") and its "resolution" (nirṇaya: "The luster of the lotus simply cannot shame the moon. / For, after all, the moon has it soundly defeated. / This therefore must be nothing but your face."). These were modeled after steps in the logicians' syllogism. A third group of ornaments, defined by their emotional content (e.g., rasavat, "flavorful"), reflected the insights of theorists of drama, who analyzed a play's ability to evoke certain emotional "flavors" or rasas. Other ornaments mimicked courtly speech behaviors, such as the elegant pretext (paryāyokta), veiled critique (aprastutapraśaṃsā), and artful praise (vyājastuti); and still others involved auditory effects, such as \*alliteration (anuprāsa) and twinning (yamaka).

In addition to ornaments, two other early categories need mention here: Bhāmaha and Daṇḍin defined a set of literary qualities (guṇas) such as lucidity (prasāda) and intensity (ojas), and explained how these combine in regional poetic dialects (although these were idealtype dialects that poets could adopt regardless of their region), and flaws (doṣas) that hinder the success of poetry (anything from nongrammaticality and loose construction to obscenity). The early works also include a cursory mapping of literary genres (both in verse and prose) and of literary langs. of the cosmopolitan variety (which, in addition to Sanskrit, included a few Middle Indic langs. collectively known as Prakrits). But there is no attempt to present anything like a rigorous conceptual framework that incorporates all the different elements of analysis. The early trad. was not invested in developing a universal theory of poetics or aesthetics, but rather in cataloging, defining, and illustrating the various figurative and ornamental devices, typically exemplified on the level of single verses created ad hoc for the purpose of discussion and primarily under the catchall category of alaṃkāra.

Nonetheless, the discussion was not entirely particularistic or atheoretical. General aesthetic (and socioaesthetic) criteria were occasionally invoked in debating the value of certain devices. E.g., Bhāmaha did not endorse factuality (svabhāvokti) in the description of (typically natural) entities, whereas Daṇḍin believed that such portrayals, although more typical of scientific idiom, are welcome in poetry as well, if the entities

in question are pretty in and of themselves. Still, both agreed that a certain type of "crookedness" or indirection (vakrokti) is the defining characteristic of poetic expressivity. Precious little is said about this crookedness. Bhāmaha mentions it in the context of poetic intensification or \*hyperbole (atiśayokti). His example concerns the dita tree: so white is its blossom that it becomes entirely invisible in moonlight, when its presence can only be inferred by the humming of bees. This is not the most straightforward way of describing the tree, but it is precisely the circuitous highlighting of its ties with moonlight, which replicates the hue of its flowers, and with the melodious bees, which call to mind its fragrance, that, according to Bhāmaha, allows the poet to capture its unworldly beauty. For Daṇḍin, a key to poetic crookedness is the poet's exploitation of \*polysemy and other ling. accidents to create additional layers of signification. This "embrace" (\*śleṣa) of extra signification into the text, a phenomenon far wider in scope than \*paronomasia and \*allegory combined, emerged as a serious theoretical problem in Sanskrit poetics, partly because of its capacity to inhabit and replicate the entire spectrum of tropes. Bhāmaha was at pains to contain śleṣa and present it as an encapsulated form of \*figuration, but for Daṇḍin, it is coterminous with crooked expressivity.

Indeed, Daṇḍin's work offers a subtle but holistic framework, wherein a self-reflexive interplay exists between a host of ornamental devices that liken, intentionally confuse, or blatantly identify entities from the poem's here and now (say, a woman's face) and those of a figurative realm (the moon), and those that playfully question or sever the ties between the two realms: from "distinction" (vyatireka), where the face is said to excel the moon; to "dissimilarity" (viṣama), where the two are said to be worlds apart; and "incongruity" (ananvaya), where the very notion that the beloved's face can have a parallel is effectively denied by comparing it to itself. Daṇḍin's inventory of ornamental devices hints at the relations between such unions and separations and indicates how ling. doubling can heighten the coexistence of these contradictory trajectories every step of the way.

**II. Middle Period: Sanskrit Poetics in Kashmir and Beyond.** Starting in the last decades of the 8th c., the Himalayan kingdom of Kashmir strove to turn itself into the center of Sanskrit learning and arts. Here, thinkers first ventured to make Sanskrit poetics an independent and respectable science (śāstra). Several tendencies typify the long-standing and highly influential discussion on poetics in Kashmir. First was the push for systematization: This trend is first illustrated by Vāmana, who worked at the court of Kashmir's King Jayāpīḍa (r. 779–813) and whose treatise on poetics deliberately mimics Pāṇini's aphorisms on grammar. Among his theoretical innovations, Vāmana demonstrated that the highly heterogeneous alaṃkāras are analyzable within a single and coherent paradigm, as variations on the basic formula of the simile. But while many later thinkers agreed that simile was the core of Sanskrit's figuration, the subjecting of all tropes to a single analysis acquired little following. This failure indicates the danger in oversystematization, when the discipline's multifaceted conceptual insights are put in a formal straitjacket.

A second dominant trend was the large-scale incorporation of semantic theories. An early example is in the work of Udbhaṭa, Vāmana's colleague at the same court. Udbhaṭa sought to move from a formal/logical analysis of tropes to grounding them in specific semantic capacities and cognitive scenarios. Consider Udbhaṭa's own illustration of metaphor: "Pouring moonlight-spray / from their lunar jars, / the night-maidens watered the heavens, / that garden whose blossoms are stars." Earlier writers dubbed the metaphorical identification at play here "forming" (rūpaka), since of the two entities, one—namely, gardeners—lends its form (rūpa) to the other—namely, moonrise. Udbhaṭa, however, explained this process not by the proposition of identification or the notion of form lending but by a secondary ling. capacity (guṇavṛtti) it necessitates: the primary denotative function of a word such as "spray," as soon as it is equated with "moonlight," is blocked and gets replaced by qualities that are only metaphorically associated with "spray," such as purity and coolness. Rudraṭa, who followed Udbhaṭa by several decades, showed similar tendencies in his innovative analysis of "embrace" or manufactured *polysemy (*śleṣa). Whereas earlier writers dealt with the tendency of polysemy to inhabit the propositional structures of simile, metaphor, and other tropes, Rudraṭa was interested in exploring the cognitive interplays between the two sets of meaning (supplanting, supplementing, etc.) in a śleṣa and their charms.

A third important tendency was the gradual assimilation of a separate discussion, much of which was also taking place in Kashmir, concerning theatrical performance and the spectators' response to it. Unlike Aristotle's notions of *mimesis and *catharsis, this debate highlighted a fixed set of eight or nine emotional states on the part of the depicted character and/or actor and the dramatic conditions that allowed the spectator to experience, or "taste," them in a special aesthetic form. Kashmiri theorists were increasingly drawn to discussing such emotional "flavors" (rasas) in poetry as well. Thus, in addition to writing on tropology, Udbhaṭa composed a (now lost) commentary on the ancient treatise on dramaturgy, and Rudraṭa divided his work on poetics proper between alaṃkāras and rasas, although still without a theoretical framework combining the two types of concepts.

All these trends are combined masterfully in the *Dhvanyāloka* (Light on Suggestion) of Ānandavardhana, one of the trad.'s seminal figures, who worked at the court of Kashmir's King Avantivarman (r. 855–83). Ānandavardhana merged the aesthetic theory of drama, which highlights the evocation of rasas, with a teleological hermeneutic model derived from the discipline of scriptural analysis (*Mīmāṃsā*), according to which all the elements of a text are seen as subordinate to the production of a single overriding import (a dictum, in the case of the Veda). For him, the overriding telos of poetry is inducing rasa. This goal cannot, of course, in lit., be achieved by means of artistic performance, as on stage. It comes about instead through suggestion, a semantic capacity beyond denotation and metaphor that, as he points out, none of his predecessors had recognized. This newly discovered ling. power is potentially informative (*vastu-dhvani*) when facts are intimated, or figurative (*alaṃkāra-dhvani*), when tropes are implied; but, in poetry, these analytically separable types of insinuation ultimately culminate in the suggestion of an emotional flavor (*rasa-dhvani*). Indeed, Ānandavardhana subordinated all the other elements his predecessors had identified—and in particular the poetic ornaments—to emotive suggestion, which he identified as poetry's "soul." Ānandavardhana, thus, cleverly inverted his discipline's old root metaphor to support his new theory: literary ornaments, he said, just like bracelets and necklaces, can embellish an already beautiful body, but they cannot explain its intrinsic charm.

Consider a verse by Kālidāsa (fl. 4th c.) describing the god Śiva when awakened from deep meditation by the beautiful Umā: "Śiva, his calm somewhat disturbed, / like the ocean when the moon begins to rise, / cast his eyes on Umā's face / with its balsam pear of a lip" (trans. adapted from McCrea). Umā's lip is identified here with the red balsam pear, and Śiva's disturbed composure is likened to the ocean's turbulence during moonrise, implying that Umā's face *is* the moon. Earlier theorists would have analyzed this verse using the categories of metaphor and simile. But for Ānandavardhana, its poetic effect rests on its emotional content, namely, Śiva's budding love for Umā, which these literary ornaments serve only to enhance. Śiva's falling in love, argues Ānandavardhana, is neither denoted nor brought about through metaphorical usage. Rather, it is *suggested* by the poet's depiction of Śiva's loss of composure and gazing at Umā's beautiful face. Actors on stage evoke emotional states through bodily gestures, and sensitive spectators can "taste" the flavor of the depicted love. But Ānandavardhana argued that responsive readers too can enjoy the same flavor, thanks to Kālidāsa's skilful use of suggestion. Indeed, he demonstrated that his new semantic-aesthetic theory empowered Sanskrit literati to engage, perhaps for the first time, in serious lit. crit.: he identified the chief emotional components in the great epics, judged some classics by their success in producing a good balance among the different "flavors," and maintained that it is only *dhvani* that explains both the genius of masters such as Kālidāsa and the possibility of meaningful innovation in poetry.

Initially stirring a heated debate, Ānandavardhana's thesis was adopted by all Kashmiri thinkers after 1100 CE. With dhvani as its centerpiece, the Kashmiri strand of Sanskrit poetics emerged as a unified, hierarchical, and powerful theory. The highly influential *Kāvyaprakāśa* (Light on Poetry, ca. 1100) by Mammaṭa, yet another illustrious Kashmiri thinker, provided a definitive synthesis of Kashmiri poetics following Ānandavardhana's intellectual revolution.

Mammaṭa used the different capacities of lang. as described by Ānandavardhana—denotation, metaphorical usage, and suggestion—to explain the existence of different grades of poetry. It is at its best when dominated by suggestion that leads to the tasting of emotions (dhvani); ranking second is "ancillary suggestion" (guṇībhūtavyaṅgya), poetry whose suggested content is subordinate, aesthetically or otherwise, to what is directly or metaphorically expressed; finally, "flashy" (citra) poetry is devoid of suggestion and based only on other ling. capacities. Within this gradation, the discipline's different analytical categories were put to use: suggestive processes and emotional flavors were crucial for the analysis of dhvani, while the charm of "flashy" poetry was analyzed using the alaṃkāra tool kit, which Mammaṭa revisited at length. If Ānandavardhana led a "paradigm shift" in Sanskrit poetics, Mammaṭa signaled the resumption of "normal science." The overall framework he provided invited new studies on alaṃkāras, rasa-related matters (in poetry or dramaturgy), semantics, and cognition, either in independent treatises or commentaries on older works (Mammaṭa's own work in particular). "Normal science" also meant that the new theory was now used in the analyses of poems by leading literati and commentators such as Arjunavarmadeva (fl. 13th c.) and Mallinātha (fl. 14th c.), both of whom lived outside Kashmir.

And yet the discipline's paradigm shift was never complete, as the new paradigm was ridden by several irresolvable tensions. The subsequent discussion was, thus, never entirely "normal" and was primarily driven by these frictions. One important friction was between the new theoretical framework with dhvani at its center and the earlier conceptual apparatus, in particular the alaṃkāras. Note that, despite the rather marginal role Ānandavardhana assigned these devices, he was unwilling to dispose of them altogether. At the same time, his theory, for all its universality, did not really explain the aesthetic effects of individual alaṃkāras, esp. in poetry that was not oriented toward the suggestion of emotional flavors, and this problem found no real solution in Mammaṭa's synthesis. After Mammaṭa, the discipline increasingly regravitated toward the analysis of the expressivity, structure of, and interrelations among the many "ornaments" of poetry. This analysis was carried out outside the dhvani framework and often resisted any overriding scheme. A clear indication of this tension is that Sanskrit poetics, now claiming dhvani as its greatest theoretical achievement, nonetheless came to be called the Science of Literary Ornaments (alaṃkāras), or Alaṃkāraśāstra.

Another problem was the location of rasa and how readers accessed it. Ānandavardhana left out of his discussion the mysterious process by which readers "savor" the emotions of depicted characters while avoiding the complications of sharing the love of others or the potential unsavoriness of emotions such as grief or fear. Another pair of seminal Kashmiri thinkers, Bhaṭṭa Nāyaka (fl. ca. 900) and Abhinavagupta (fl. ca. 1000), tried to fill this lacuna by producing yet another semantic theory of literary lang. modeled after Mīmāṃsā, one that came with a groundbreaking aesthetic psychology. Both argued that, just as a Vedic passage that describes a sacrificial act has the *pragmatic* effect of producing a desire to take similar action in the faithful, so lit. has a special kind of "illocutionary" power (bhāvanā) to produce an aesthetic experience in readers. This experience, they argued, is necessarily pleasurable because lit. abstracts characters of their individuality, precisely by identifying Umā's face with the moon and similar "alienating" features of literary lang.; it thus enables readers to "taste" love for no one in particular or to experience fear that is stripped of any frightening cause. Rasa is, thus, the experience of emotions in the pure state, outside the boundaries of subject and object, self and other, an experience that leads to a rapturous state that both Bhaṭṭa Nāyaka and Abhinavagupta compared to the religious ecstasy of self-transcendence. In the case of Abhinavagupta, this comparison was further colored by his nondualist metaphysics, according to which the rasa experience resulted from the temporary removal of a veil covering the ultimate self (ātman). But whereas Ānandavardhana's theory became a consensus, those of Bhaṭṭa Nāyaka and Abhinavagupta were not: the location and experience of rasa remained an unresolved question. There were even those who postulated that rasa was overrated. As early as the late 10th c., a Kashmiri thinker named Kuntaka cataloged a large variety of aesthetically pleasing elements. These included both "ornaments" and "flavors" but also many other aspects of poetry—from the name of a work to its strategies of *intertextuality—all of which he viewed as part of an expanded but very loosely defined catalog of poetry's "crooked" nature. Many of the items on Kuntaka's vast catalog could not find a place in a rasa-dominated theory.

This rasa-centered tension is related to another friction, between Kashmir and the rest of the subcontinent. The centuries-long intellectual hegemony of the small northern vale notwithstanding, work of literary thinkers elsewhere was not suspended. These thinkers paid close attention to the discussion in Kashmir but often had their own ideas about where the discipline should go. Particularly worthy of mention here are King Bhoja of Dhār (r. 1011–55) and the Jain mendicant Hemacandra (fl. 11th c., Gujarat). Both these highly prolific writers composed encyclopedic texts on poetics, and both attempted their own syntheses of the field. Like Kuntaka, both combined the theories coming from Kashmir with a vast variety of other materials, incl., in the case of Hemacandra, ideas about how poets should work and lead their lives. While the syntheses of Bhoja and Hemacandra never proved as influential as Mammaṭa's, they did produce innovative arguments and followers, esp. with respect to the question of rasa. Bhoja saw the Kashmiri discussion as obsessed with the reader, where in fact, he believed, rasa was located in the depicted character. This character-centered model of rasa is crucial to the socially normative function of lit. as understood by Bhoja, for whom the emotional experience of characters such as Rāma functions *didactically* as a model for emulation. As for Hemacandra, two of his direct students, Rāmacandra and Guṇacandra, boldly challenged the Kashmiri theory that the experience of rasa is necessarily pleasant, even when the underlying emotions are not. Rather, they believed, the aesthetic flavor of the emotion is not very different from the emotion itself (i.e., grief is the "flavor" of grief), even if the spectator/reader can intellectually appreciate, and thus enjoy, the skill involved in evoking it. These views reflect an undying resentment against the powerful rasa theory of Abhinavagupta and also, in the case of these Jain thinkers, to its specific theological inflection.

Another noteworthy tension pertains to Sanskrit poetics' constant borrowing from older and prestigious knowledge systems while attempting to establish itself as an independent discipline. A clear manifestation of this tension is in Ānandavardhana's crowning of the hierarchical semantic model, which he borrowed wholesale from Mīmāṃsā, with a ling. capacity not recognized in the discipline of Mīmāṃsā or, for that matter, in any South Asian philosophical school. Indeed, most of Ānandavardhana's immediate critics attacked his postulating the ling. capacity of suggestion for the evocation of rasa. Even after this argument subsided, the need for respectability for Sanskrit poetics and independence as a branch of thought continued to be felt in the subsequent discussion.

**III. New Poetics in Early Modernity.** The clearest indication that something fresh was happening in Sanskrit poetics starting around the 1500s is that the literary theorists themselves began to label in profusion particular views and viewers as new. Researchers have only started to explore this trend, found across Sanskrit knowledge systems around this time, and identify what, in fact, was novel in the last active period of Sanskrit poetics. Here we will mention several areas of innovation, using two of the discipline's last towering figures as our primary reference point: Appayya Dīkṣita (1520–93), who was associated with several minor courts in South India, and Jagannātha Paṇḍitarāja, so-called King of Pundits at the Mughal court of Shāh Jahān (r. 1628–58) in the north.

Newness in this era consists, first, of a new engagement with the old topics. Early mod. writers approached the received categories with an acute historical awareness of a sort the discipline had never before seen. They tended to write in a pioneering essay style, where the product, in the form of refined answers to older, unresolved questions, was often subjugated to the process: an exercise in the hist. of ideas. An example is Appayya Dīkṣita's essay on *simile in his incomplete magnum opus *Citramīmāṃsā* (Investigation of Figuration). While the essay does provide a new definition for one of the discipline's quintessential tropes, it focuses more on previous formulations and the difficulties facing any attempt to capture simile accurately.

Historical awareness is tied to a new methodology, partly related to the procedures and jargon of Sanskrit's Navyanyāya (New School of Logic), of applying unprecedentedly demanding standards of intellectual rigor, consistency, parsimony, and clarity in dealing with the disciplinary issues. This methodology emboldened explorations about which earlier generations had seemed hesitant. Appayya Dīkṣita, e.g., described *suggestion* as a process involving attention to subtle clues and the systematic elimination of alternative conclusions that is not unlike *deduction*. This rather subversive view of dhvani forced Sanskrit literati to revisit a position that had been emphatically rejected many centuries before, namely, Mahimabhaṭṭa's (ca. 1050) critique of Ānandavardhana's "suggestion" as another name for *inference*.

Jagannātha, who wholeheartedly opposed Appayya's views on dhvani, was nonetheless receptive to other bold suggestions inspired by the same rigorous method. Consider, e.g., his breathtaking survey of the views on rasa in his encyclopedic *Rasagaṅgādhara* (Ocean of Rasa), another example of the discipline's new historicity. Here Jagannātha reports not unfavorably that the new view on the rasa experience is that it is based on a temporary identification with a fictive character, made possible by the reader's sensitivity, which is theoretically analyzed as a form of a cognitive defect. It is this "defect" that allows the reader to feel, while the illusion lasts, the character's emotion, such as Rāma's love for Sītā. This novel view, as presented by Jagannātha, audaciously inverts Abhinvagupta's cl. metaphor. For Abhinavagupta, the rasa experience results from the temporary removal of a veil covering the self, but, for Jagannātha's contemporaries, it results from the imposition of a veil. Thus, in this case, the new position moves away from mysticism and metaphysics to a logical stance and a mundanely oriented psychology. The same is true with respect to the joyousness of the experience. For Abhinavagupta, the question receives an automatic and extreme answer in the mystical doctrine of the inherently blissful nature of the self, which needs only to be unveiled to shine forth. But the new position allows for the possibility that the identification with a suffering character may produce a mixture of pleasure and pain, even if pleasure is more dominant.

Another novelty is in the status of Sanskrit poetics, which finally comes to enjoy considerable cross-disciplinary prestige and asserts its autonomy from other branches of learning. Several trends are indicative of this change. First, poetics suddenly began to attract scholars in the authoritative fields of grammar, logic, Mīmāṃsā, and Vedānta, who composed in profusion treatises or commentaries in poetics (Appayya himself is a writer on Mīmāṃsā and Vedānta who took to poetics). Second, reversing the pattern characterizing the previous millennium, concepts and terminology from Sanskrit poetics were now widely applied to other philosophical, theological, and sectarian discussions. The most famous example of this is in the works of Rūpa Goswamin and his followers, who made a new "devotional" (*Bhakti*) rasa the centerpiece of a soteriology, wherein acting in Kṛṣṇa's cosmic play led to tasting his essence. Both Appayya and Jagannātha reject the "devotional rasa," but Appayya himself applies the poetical toolkit to a sectarian debate concerning the theological message of the *Rāmāyaṇa*. Arguing against attempts by followers of Viṣṇu to appropriate this epic poem (and also against Ānandavardhana's claim that its main suggested content is the flavor of compassion), Appayya used his subversive notion of dhvani to assert that the *Rāmāyaṇa* is scattered with subtle clues about the power of the god Śiva and is, therefore, carefully designed to suggest his supremacy. Third, late thinkers such as Jagannātha constantly maintain that the stances of poetics are independent of those of all other knowledge systems. Indeed, at the heart of this "new poetics" is an appeal to the taste and sensibilities of the expert reader as the only authority in a discipline that had a rather turbulent hist. and never possessed a core (*sūtra*) treatise of unchallenged command. This stance is both the source of a new confidence in early mod. poetics and a cause of anxiety when, as in the case of Jagannātha's critique of Appayya, the reader's judgment is thoroughly contested.

Anxiety may also be understood in the context of new external challenges. For centuries, Sanskrit literary culture maintained a largely stable set of conventions, characters, and scenarios; and the basic tool kit of Sanskrit poetics did not significantly change since the introduction of dhvani. But in the second half of the second millennium CE, this long-standing trad. found itself in a radically new political context and facing increasing competition from a series of fully formed and confident literary cultures: regional lits. in Telugu, Hindi, and a host of other South Asian literary langs.; Persian, the prestige lang. of India's Muslim courts, incl. the mighty Mughals; and finally Eng., the lang. of colonial power. The extent to which Sanskrit literary culture reacted to these new challenges is still open to debate. In poetics, to be sure, one can detect the presence of new realities. Appayya Dīkṣita invents a pair of poetic ornaments for the reworking of *proverbs, and one of his examples is explicitly presented as translating a popular Telugu saying. Then, there is the "new" position famously reported by Jagannātha, namely, that out of Mammaṭa's three "conditions" for composing poetry—talent, learning, and training—only the first was essential. It has been argued that this stance reflects the new ideal of spontaneity claimed by Hindi's devotional poets. It has also been suggested that Jagannātha's ideas and poetry bear traces of Persian lit., in which he was well versed. These traces, however, are peripheral to the main current of Sanskrit poetics in early modernity. Despite the fact that every writer on alaṃkāra and rasa was fluent in at least one regional lang. and although the regional literary cultures constantly engaged with Sanskrit's cosmopolitan model, Sanskrit poetics remained largely oblivious to devels. in the vernaculars. The discipline likewise ignored Persian, even as many literati received patronage from Muslim rulers and even though some Sanskrit poets undertook daring experiments of incorporation and trans. In the 19th c., when Eng. gradually became the lang. of power, education, and lit. in South Asia, the discipline of Sanskrit poetics, not unlike other Sanskrit knowledge systems, dwindled and came to be studied more as an object of mod. intellectual and cultural hist. than practiced as the living and ever-innovative trad. that it once was.

*See* HINDI POETRY; INDIA, POETRY OF; KANNADA POETRY; PERSIAN POETRY; RĀMĀYAṆA POETRY; SANSKRIT POETRY; SEMANTICS AND POETRY; TAMIL POETRY AND POETICS; TELUGU POETRY; UTPREKṢĀ.

■ **Introduction and Early History:** E. Gerow, *A Glossary of Indian Figures of Speech* (1971), and *History of Indian Poetics* (1977)—the former for looking up the different tropes, the latter for a historical overview; V. Raghavan, *Bhoja's Śṛṅgāra* Prakāśa (1978)—excellent overview of *guṇas*; I. Peterson, "Playing with Universes," *Shastric Tradition in the Indian Arts*, ed. A. L. Dallapiccola (1989)—interplay between objective and figurative; S. Pollock, *The Language of the Gods in the World of Men* (2006)—Sanskrit's cosmopolitan space and vision; H. Tieken, "Aśoka's Fourteenth Rock Edict and the Guṇa *mādhurya* of the Kāvya Poetical Tradition," *Zeitschrift der Deutschen Morgenländischen Gesellschaft* 156 (2006)—poetics and chanceries; S. Pollock, *Bouquet of Rasa and River of Rasa* (2009)—on Bhānudatta; Y. Bronner, *Extreme Poetry* (2010)—esp. ch. 7 on Daṇḍin.

■ **Middle Period:** R. Gnoli, *The Aesthetic Experience according to Abhinavagupta* (1968); K. K. Raja, *Indian Theories of Meaning* (1969); D.H.H. Ingalls, J. M. Masson, M. V. Patwardhan, *The Dhvanyāloka of Ānandavardhana with the Locana of Abhinavagupta* (1990)—annotated trans. of Ānandavardhana's treatise and Abhinavagupta's commentary; S. Pollock, "Bhoja's Śṛṅgāraprakāśa and the Problem of *Rasa*," *Asiatische Studien/Études asiatiques* 70 (1998); G. Tubb, "Hemacandra and Sanskrit Poetics," *Open Boundaries*, ed. J. Court (1998); D. Mellins, "Unraveling the *Kāvyaprakāśa*," *Journal of Indian Philosophy* 35 (2007)—discusses Mammaṭa; Y. Bronner and G. Tubb, "Blaming the Messenger," *Bulletin of the School of Oriental and African Studies* 71 (2008)—frictions in Sanskrit poetics; L. McCrea, *The Teleology of Poetics in Medieval Kashmir* (2008)—main source for this section; S. Pollock, "What Was Bhaṭṭa Nāyaka Saying?," *Epic and Argument in Sanskrit Literary History*, ed. S. Pollock (2010).

■ **Early Modernity:** D. Haberman, *Acting as a Way of Salvation* (1988)—devotional rasa; S. Pollock, "The New Intellectuals in Seventeenth-Century India," *Indian Economic and Social History Review* 38 (2001); Y. Bronner, "What Is New and What Is Navya?," *Journal of Indian Philosophy* 30 (2002); and "Back to the Future," *Weiner Zeitschrift für die Kunde des Südasiens* 48 (2004); S. Pollock, *The Ends of Men at the End of Premodernity* (2005)—influence of vernacular literary culture and Persian on Sanskrit poetics; D. Shulman, "Illumination, Imagination,

Creativity," *Journal of Indian Philosophy* 36 (2008); G. Tubb and Y. Bronner, "Vastutas tu," *Journal of Indian Philosophy* 36 (2008)—methodology of new poetics.

Y. Bronner

## SANSKRIT POETRY

**I. The Origins of Kāvya.** Lit. in India—and in particular poetry in an early form of the Sanskrit (*Saṃskṛtam*) lang.—has a hist. of least 3,500 years, from roughly the second millennium BCE to the present. An IE (Indo-Aryan) lang. spoken and used primarily by social and cultural elites in early and med. India, Sanskrit continues to serve as a medium of creative expression in mod. India as well. At some point in the early centuries of the Common Era, the descriptive designation *Sanskrit* becomes synonymous with what was previously conceived of as only a sophisticated register of lang. (*bhāṣa*) itself. The word *Sanskrit* connotes sophistication, a lang. that has been "processed," "crafted," and "refined." While ordinarily it is the notion of lang. processed by grammar that is intended in the appellation *Sanskrit*, poetry in Sanskrit—esp. "classical" belles lettres—also bears the qualities of refinement, sophistication, and high levels of craftsmanship.

In the interest of precision and concision, the focus of this entry is on Sanskrit poetry understood as belles lettres *(kāvya, vānmaya, sāhitya)*, whose origins may be fixed around the several centuries prior to the beginning of the Common Era and whose cl. period culminates around the 12th c. CE; Sanskrit poetry more or less in the cl. style, however, continues to be written and received to the present day. The existing corpus from these centuries alone is, at a conservative estimate, at least 1,000 times larger than what has survived in cl. Gr. While certainly relevant to a broader discussion of Sanskrit lit., this entry excludes any elaboration on the multiple genres of Sanskrit poetic lit. that precede, prefigure, and inform what ultimately comes to be called kāvya—lit. (largely in verse and written, though with a strong emphasis on recitation and oral transmission) consciously crafted as an art form that is predominantly secular and humanist in scope. While kāvya can be written in numerous langs.—at least 40, incl. the various regional langs. of premod. South Asia (Prakrit) and the several Jain langs. called the *Apabhraṃśa*—the preponderance of extant poems are in Sanskrit. Kāvya subsumes most poetic forms (*lyric, *narrative, *dramatic, *panegyric, etc.), but its significance as "imaginative literature" excludes (for the Sanskrit intellectual trad.) sacred scripture (*āgama*), such as the versified collection of ancient hymns to Vedic gods and poems of Vedic life (*Rig Veda*), e.g., or the flashes of poetry in the early Buddhist Pali *canon known as the *Tripiṭaka* (Three Baskets). While often regarded as the "longest poem in the world" (seven times the length of the *Iliad* and the *Odyssey* together) and replete with elements of kāvya, the great *epic *Mahābhārata* (The Great Story of Bharata's Descendants) technically falls out of the purview of kāvya since it is regarded as a work of received "history" or "tradition" (*itihāsa*) and also a discourse on ethics and morality (*dharmaśāstra*), likewise the store of versified myths and legends known as *purāṇa*.

Since the *Mahābhārata* sometimes refers to itself as a kāvya, however, and contains within it the widely translated *Bhagavad-Gītā* (The Song of the Lord)—a lyrically charged philosophical poem regarded both as lit. and scripture—many plausibly consider it as among the earliest Sanskrit poems. The other "historical" epic of the ancient period that complements the *Mahābhārata* certainly fits the category of kāvya by all emic estimations: in fact, the *Rāmāyaṇa* (Rāma's Journey) is considered to be the first poem (*ādi-kāvya*) in Sanskrit and its author Vālmīki the first poet (*ādi-kavi*). Both epics (assuming some semblance of a final form sometime around the beginning of the Common Era) take in a wide scope, subsuming Vedic India's social, political, moral, spiritual, and aesthetic imagination. The *Mahābhārata* creatively details the dynastic struggles and ultimate destruction of early Indian royalty (the self-styled lunar dynasty) centered on Yamuna river settlements north of mod. Delhi. A dramatically tragic and gloomy work—punctuated with moments of romance, comedy, *riddles, and *hymns, prosaic moralizing, and the epiphanic grandeur of divine revelation (Kṛṣṇa as God)—the *Mahābhārata* has been the single greatest source for later Sanskrit poetry's narrative themes. The poetry of the *Mahābhārata* is often described as a rough diamond, with frequent irregularities in terms of standard grammatical practice (magnificently described and codified sometime in the 4th or 5th c. BCE by the grammarian Pāṇini) and loaded with oral formulas of stock *epithets and *similes; in contrast are the later *mahākāvyas* (great courtly epic poems) and *muktaka*s (loose *stanzas and *epigrams), written in pristine cl. Sanskrit and fancied as chiseled diamonds with favored angles and cuts. Unlike the confused status of the *Mahābhārata* as kāvya, the *Rāmāyaṇa* prefigures the major elements (through a narrative of poetry's origins embedded in the story itself) that will come to define Sanskrit kāvya for at least two millennia: a self-conscious literariness that contains complex *tropes (of sound and sense) and is composed in the most popular Sanskrit meter (that can be sung, recited, with or without musical instrumentation); a consistent narrative trajectory with choice interludes; and the devel. of the all-important aesthetic concept of *rasa*, or taste (treated below). The structure of the *Rāmāyaṇa* is akin to a classic fairy tale with important culture-specific twists and turns (prince meets princess, evil demon abducts princess, prince defeats demon and saves princess, prince and princess live happily ever after) or of a picaresque novel (hero-prince is initiated into manhood through a series of adventures and misfortunes while exiled from his kingdom). The *Rāmāyaṇa*, reflecting a seminal moment in the dynastic hist. of the kings of the "solar dynasty" clustered around a tributary of the great river Gaṅgā, simultaneously functions as a great devotional text, with the hero Rāma as an avatar of Lord Viṣṇu. Like the *Mahābhārata*, the *Rāmāyaṇa* has been an immensely important source text for later Sanskrit poets.

**II. Elements of Sanskrit Poetry.** While, according to many proverbial formulations in Sanskrit, the poet is not beholden to any rules, literary theorists over the centuries have observed and marked essential presuppositions for the production and appreciation of Sanskrit poetry. Recent commentators on Sanskrit poetry have emphasized its "impersonal" stamp, its oscillation between explicit frankness and understated sublimity, and its occasionally impassioned or disturbing lyricism. Another aspect of much of Sanskrit poetry is its frequent didactic, proverbial, but generally nonmoralizing tone. Med. literary critics continually emphasize that kāvya teaches softly and indirectly like a lover, whereas other genres teach like a master (*śāstra*) or a friend (*itihāsa-purāṇa*). Ubiquitous also is the notion that the purpose of kāvya is to delight and to create an uplifting (*maṅgala*) atmosphere; to bring pleasure, solace, scholarly and worldly erudition, as well as indirect moral instruction to the audience; and to shower the poet with fame and wealth.

Kāvya is characterized by a polished and self-conscious use of poetic lang. that crosses seamlessly over such generic formulations as lyric or epigram (*padya*), epic (*itihāsa*), drama (*nāṭya*), lyrical prose (*gadya*), extended hymn (*stotra*), and prose narrative (*ākhyāna*, *ākhyāyikā*, *kathā*). Whereas the practice of lit. crit. on individual poems (as well as on prose, drama, etc.) is scanty before mod. times, analysis of the lang. of poetry and the study of its effects have been given ample attention in Sanskrit poetics. Some argue that kāvya presupposes "kāvya theory" and, in essence, they are mutually constitutive, the full appreciation of which (like cl. music) requires some measure of theoretical familiarity and training. The great masters of Sanskrit poetics (from the 6th c. CE onward) draw many of their ideas from earlier texts like the *Nāṭyaśāstra* (A Treatise on Drama), the foundational text on dramaturgy, and the encyclopedic *Agnipurāṇa* (Ancient Lore of Agni, Lord of Fire). For nearly a thousand years, they debate a variety of definitions for *kāvya* and its broader significance. Kāvya can be recited and visualized in performance (*dṛśya*) as in drama, or it can be solely recited and aurally received (*śravya*). Kāvya can be further divided along three formal and three evaluative axes. Formally, it can be prose (*gadya*), verse (*padya*), or a mixture of prose and verse (*miśra*) known as *campu-kāvya*. It can be judged as either a superior composition (*uttama*), a mediocre one (*madhyama*), or an inferior composition (*adhama*). The values on which to judge superiority, mediocrity, or inferiority are themselves multiple, one of the most common being the extent to which a poem suggests meaning rather than explicitly delivering it.

The unique creations of Sanskrit poetry are ultimately informed by the lang. Sanskrit's particular ling.

characteristics (case inflection, variable syntax and word order, euphonic coalescence of sound sequences, limitless potential to compound words to create specific meaning, etc.) render a body of poetry that is at once flexible and restrained: flexible in that poets are free to create complex syntax patterns and inscribe within them hosts of simultaneous literary effects, incl. extremely complex and subtle rhythms of *assonance and *alliteration alongside expressions within the same word or compound unit carrying multiple meanings. Even double narrative poems are possible and common in Sanskrit, where entire texts are read in two or more senses. A long parade of more or less interchangeable synonyms for commonly occurring entities goes a long way in providing Sanskrit poets with the freedom to match the sonic with the semantic in ways that are unique, e.g., from what is available to poets of other cl. or mod. Indian langs.

Synonyms also enable the Sanskrit poet to function within the extraordinary restraints placed on him or her by metrical considerations. Since the metered hymns of the earliest Vedic poets, Sanskrit poetry has marked itself—like poetry in other cl. langs.—by strict adherence to metrical principles. Thus, the most common meters consist of four feet with a defined number of syllables (or syllabic instants) allowed within each foot. These meters are governed by certain defined principles (a short or long syllable preceding a conjunct consonant or a diphthong, e.g., is considered metrically long). *Caesuras are present, though optional or variable for many meters. Sanskrit poets also work within a circumscribed world of signifying conventions (*kavi-samaya*), although they frequently reinvent these *conceits in the service of creating novel images and meanings. Nevertheless, unlike other literary trads. in South Asia, Sanskrit poetry reveals a consistent conformity to the notion that *inspiration and *imagination flow free so long as they violate neither convention nor a factual precision within that conventionalized world that could stand the test of critical analysis.

While all genres of imaginative lit. fall more or less under the scope of kāvya, the two major divisions of Sanskrit poetry are *mahākāvya* and *laghukāvya*. The mahākāvya are grand, multicantoed entertainments employing multiple meters and telling a story or a part of a story from one of the great epics or narrative cycles. Laghukāvya, on the other hand, take various forms that reflect such genres as the epigram, short lyrics about seasons, *love poetry and erotica, extended devotional poems to gods and goddesses, hymns to nature, reflective philosophical poems, and loose collections of verses on all of the above topics and also such common themes as adolescence and old age, eulogies to kings and patrons, emotional states such as greed and anger, scenes of village and field, and works about all the social groups that comprise the Sanskrit *imaginaire*. These poems may be in any one of multiple meters (or combinations thereof)—easily recitable and memorizable in a variety of tunes and bearing names such as the *vasanta-tilaka* (mark of spring) and *sārdūlavikrīḍitam* (tiger's play). Many Sanskrit poets place as much effort on producing dazzling sound effects as they do on producing profound sense. Often Sanskrit verses are at once compact of form and broad in expression. *Imagery is refined, exacting, and concrete, assuming visceral and emotional semiotic codes whose suggestive qualities need to be elucidated by a trained reader. Frequently, Sanskrit poets compose playful verse, fully taking advantage of the extensive punning available to them in the lang. Sometimes, however, kāvya verses can be dreamy or impassioned.

### III. The Production and Appreciation of Sanskrit Poetry.

According to literary critics, the competent Sanskrit poet must possess, in addition to inborn imaginative power (śakti, pratibhā), a broad cultural education about the world and its ways (vyutpatti). Once the poet has married these two qualities and embarked on his profession as a poet, he must then uninterruptedly practice (abhyāsa) his art. Being the creator in the "boundless world of poetry," as the 9th-c. literary theorist Ānandavardhana puts it, the Sanskrit poet could in principle treat any subject he desires. Sanskrit poetry reveals the breadth of the Sanskrit poet's erudition and training. Part of the standard curricula of a Sanskrit poet included such subjects as erotics and scripture, logic and the arts, political science and the natural world, and, of course, Pāṇinian grammar. The able poet could describe with equal facility scenes of city and forest, things royal and rustic, the psychic world of lovers and ascetics, the abstruse details of philosophy and the earthy charms of drunken revelry. In essence, all four of the traditionally formulated Vedic "ends of human life" (puruṣārtha) were open to the poet's explorations: virtue (dharma), power (artha), pleasure (kāma), and spiritual freedom (mokṣa). While the poet is rarely a moralist (in the way authors of philosophical, religious, or legal treatises could be), Sanskrit poetry is filled with moral aphorisms (subhāṣita) that often encapsulate in pithy form the spirit of entire passages composed in prose.

According to Sanskrit literary critics throughout hist., one who would appreciate Sanskrit poetry essentially has to have a modicum of the cultural training, sensibility, and experience of the poet in order to be one who can "be of one mind and heart" (sahṛdaya) with the poetry. Another way theorists understand the appreciator of Sanskrit poetry is as a rasika—one who can "taste" in aesthetic terms the flavors of poetic composition (rasa). The "theory of rasa" stands as the most important discourse of Indian poetics and essentially comprises an entire knowledge system of the modes, mechanics, and psychology of art production and art reception. The eight rasas roughly correspond to the major genres of popular cinema: the romantic comedy (śṛṅgāra), the sad story evoking pity (karuṇā), the uplifting heroic drama (vīra), the action film (raudra), gore (bibhatsā), horror (bhayānaka), the slapstick comedy (hāsya), and science-fiction fantasy (adbhuta). A more subtle, not universally accepted, and heavily theorized "ninth rasa" is known as śānta, or the rasa of contemplative peace that one associates with medita-

tion practice. Alongside these eight (or nine) chief rasas are differently numbered sets of transient aesthetic experiences, such as envy, anxious tension, shame, pride, excitement, depression, confusion, and indignation. Any short or long Sanskrit poem, according to theorists who observe poetry in practice, should have one predominant rasa and perhaps other secondary ones. These same theorists variously characterize the rasa experience of drama and of poetry as either utterly similar, utterly different, or somewhere in between.

### IV. A Summary History of Sanskrit Poems and Poets.

The early hist. of cl. Sanskrit poetry (distinct from the epic poetry of the Mahābhārata and the Rāmāyaṇa) ranges from kāvya royal *panegyrics (praśasti) on stone inscriptions (the earliest one in Sanskrit being the famous Junāgaḍh inscription of Rudradāman from the 2th c. CE) to free-floating, Indian miniature paintinglike stanzas (muktaka) collected later into anthols. (kośa) such as the 10th-c. Subhāṣitaratnakośa (Treasury of Well-Spoken Verse), collected by a Buddhist monk named Vidyākara, or the 12th-c. Saduktikarṇāmṛta (Nectar for the Ears in the Form of Good Verse). Many aphorisms in these collections also come from fable and literary-folkloric texts such as the Pañcatantra (Five Strategies for Worldly Success), Hitopadeśa (Fables Offering Good Advice), and Kathāsaritsāgara (The Ocean of Rivers of Stories). In terms of Sanskrit poetry understood as kāvya, however, most commented upon are the lengthy, canto-bound court poems (mahākāvya, sargabandha) of Aśvaghoṣa and Kālidāsa, both flourishing one after the other sometime (dates are debated) between the last century before the Common Era and the early centuries of the Common Era. Aśvaghoṣa's two poems describe the early life and awakening of Prince Siddhartha Gautama (Buddhacarita) and the Buddha's leading his half-brother Nanda from worldly society to the monastery (Saundarānanda).

Kālidāsa—hailed as the greatest of all Sanskrit poets—left two surviving mahākāvya in addition to two dramas and two laghukāvya. The two mahākāvyas treat the regal dynastic hist. of the Raghu clan (Raghuvaṃśa), of which Rāma is the best-known king, and the lyrical retelling of the courtship and marriage of Lord Śiva and goddess Pārvatī, culminating in the birth of their son, the god of war Kumāra (Kumārasambhava). Kālidāsa's plays include Mālavikāgnimitra (The Story of Mālavikā and Agnimitra), a "middle-class" love story; the Vikramorvaśiya (The Story of Urvaśī Won through Valor), whose theme is drawn from the legendary romance of Pururavas and Urvaśī; and the world-famous Abhijñānaśākuntala (Recognition of Śakuntalā), about the romance and tribulations of lovers Śakuntalā and King Duṣyanta. Kālidāsa's Meghadūta (The Cloud Messenger), a long lyric poem of about 100 connected verses composed in the same meter (khaṇḍakāvya), is celebrated as one of the most refined pieces of poetry ever composed in Sanskrit. Most well-known of the "messenger" genre (sandeśakāvya), the poem personifies a cloud bringing a comforting message between separated lovers across a vast span of natural and urban landscape, perceptively commenting on the scenes of life below along the way. Another poem attributed to Kālidāsa is the short "Ṛtusaṃhāra" (On the Various Seasons).

After Kālidāsa, there are at least 300 surviving specimens of mahākāvya and numerous laghukāvya. Although there are multiple canons of Sanskrit poetry within which traditional Sanskrit audiences have immortalized significant works, the five model poems of the mahākāvya genre are composed by Kālidāsa, Bhāravi (early 7th c. CE), Māgha (late 7th c. CE), and Śrīharṣa (mid-to-late 12th c. CE). Kālidāsa's two mahākāvya works have already been discussed above. The other three draw the subject matter of their plots strictly from the *Mahābhārata*: Bhāravi's *Kirātārjunīya* (Arjuna and the Kirāṭa), Māgha's *Śiśupālavadha* (Śiśupāla's Slaying), and Śrīharṣa's *Naiṣadhīyacarita* (The Life of Nala). The *Kirātārjunīya* inaugurates a poetic trad. that proudly incorporates the considerable weight of a Sanskrit intellectual's learning with the delicate craftsmanship of a wordsmith skilled in shaping meter, trope, and thought into refined stanzas. The other two poems, by Māgha and Śrīharṣa, have for centuries been studied, commented on, and emulated by Sanskrit intellectuals and poets. Other well-received poems include works by 7th-c. mahākavis Kumāradāsa (*Jānakīharaṇa* [The Abduction of Sītā]) and Bhaṭṭi (*Rāvaṇavadha* [Rāvaṇa's Slaying], aka *Bhaṭṭikāvya*). This latter work artfully tells the story of the *Rāmāyaṇa* while simultaneously exemplifying the aphorisms of Pāṇini's *Aṣṭādhyāyī*, a masterpiece of descriptive grammar from the 4th c. BCE. The *Bhaṭṭikāvya* eventually becomes the major source for the devel. of both an indigenous Javanese *Rāmāyaṇa* trad. and a broader interest in kāvya culture. From the 9th and 10th cs., important works include the *Haravijaya* (Victory of Śiva) by Ratnākara and *Kapphiṇābhyudaya* (The Rise of Kapphiṇa) by Śivasvāmin. The 11th c. produced several notable mahākāvyas, incl. Bilhaṇa's *Vikramāṅkadevacarita* (The Life of His Majesty King Vikramāṅka) and Padmagupta's *Navasāhasāṅkacarita* (The Life of King Navasāhasāṅka).

Many of the great prose and short poems of Sanskrit lit. were written in the 7th c. Among works of epigrammatic poetry, the most famous is Bhartṛhari's *Śatakatrayi* (Three Sets of One Hundred Verses) on love, life, and world-weariness. Bāṇa's (or Bāṇabhaṭṭa's) romance narrative *Kādambarī* (named after the heroine), Subandhu's *Vāsavadattā* (also named after the heroine), and Daṇḍin's *Daśa-kumāra-carita* (The Tale of Ten Young Princes) rank among the great prose works of Sanskrit lit. Bāṇa's *Caṇḍīśataka* (One Hundred Verses to the Goddess Caṇḍī) and Mayūra's *Sūryaśataka* (One Hundred Verses to the Sun) represent two of the finest examples of intricate kāvya panegyrics structured around a "century" of verses. The most famous lyric on love's various forms also appears around this time in the oft-anthologized collection of verses known as the *Amaruśataka* (One Hundred Verses of King Amaru), a work that treats the entire spectrum of moods associated with courtship, romance, and

consummation in specific social contexts—from the longing for love, its loss and recovery, to specific reactions of elation and depression experienced by lovers at different stages of a passionate relationship. Also from this period are well-known literary dramas, incl. Bāṇa's historical play *Harṣacarita* (The Story of King Harṣa), Harṣa's *Ratnāvalī* (Princess Ratnāvalī), and Bhaṭṭanārāyaṇa's *Veṇisaṃhāra* (The Tying Up of the Braid). The 8th c. produced one of the great literary dramatists of Sanskrit lit. in Bhavabhūti, whose three plays *Mahāvīracarita* (The Life of the Great Hero Rāma), *Mālatīmādhava* (The Romance of Mālatī and Mādhava), and *Uttararāmacarita* (The Later Life of Rāma) have drawn much comment over the centuries. The last work, a sensitive exploration of the inner conflicts and psychic trauma that torment the characters of the *Rāmāyaṇa*, has been hailed by many over the centuries as the finest specimen of Sanskrit drama. A notable laghukāvya from the 11th c. includes Bilhaṇa's *Caurasuratapañcāsika* or *Caurapañcāsika* (Fifty Verses on Secret Love or Fifty Verses of the Love Thief). From the 12th c., there is the unique and much-translated work *Gītagovinda* (*Love Songs of Rādhā and Kṛṣṇa*) by the poet Jayadeva; this poem, about Kṛṣṇa and Rādhā's love, has the structure of a mahākāvya but is essentially a collection of lyrics that fuses devotional passion and erotic love in ways much emulated and explored by succeeding trads. of lit., music, dance, and painting.

In a hist. so varied and long, many other kāvya works bear mentioning, not the least of which are the difficult-to-date dramas of the very early playwright Bhāsa, incl. *Svapnavāsavadatta* (The Vision of Princess Vāsavadatta) and the vastly popular *Mṛcchakaṭika* (Little Clay Cart) by Śūdraka. Essentially an offbeat romantic comedy—at the center of which is a financially strapped hero, an intelligent courtesan as his romantic interest, and a sociopathic villain and his entourage—this latter play has been adapted numerous times over the centuries on the stage, in books, and in film. Also important to mention are influential works in Māhārāṣṭrī Prakrit such as Hāla's *Sattasaī* (Seven Hundred Poems)—the oldest collection of lyric poetry in any Indian lang.—and Pravarasena's *Setubandha* (Building the Bridge), both of which preceded and served often as intertexts with kāvya composed in Sanskrit. Govardhana's 12th-c. *Āryasaptaśati* is an especially well-known collection of erotically charged lyric stanzas, modeled on Hāla's Prakrit work and, in turn, profoundly influential for similarly themed works that emerge later in regional langs. like Bihārī's *Sattsai* in Hindi. Prior to but esp. after the 12th c., in the form of genres of Sanskrit poetry already detailed and in newer creative formats, there are hosts of poems and poets that deserve attention. These poems range from the cl. mahākāvya to the historical mahākāvya; messenger poems in the style of the *Meghadūta*; Sanskrit collections of similar works earlier produced in Prakrit; adaptations of popular works; and hosts of erotic, hagiographic, and religious poems (covering the vast spectrum of India's religions, incl. Hindu, Buddhist, Jain, Islamic, and Christian themes). The reader is directed to the 20th-c. lit. hists. of Sanskrit lit. cited at the end of this entry for detailed information about the numerous Sanskrit poems composed between the 13th and 20th cs.

Since the first centuries of the Common Era, kāvya and poetry in the style of Sanskrit kāvya have also been composed and chiseled in the archaeological record of what today are the nation-states of Myanmar, Thailand, Cambodia, Indonesia, Malaysia, and Singapore. Though deserving, Sanskrit poetry from the 19th to 21st cs. has thus far received little sustained scholarly attention. However, poets, scholars, and Indian governmental bodies such as the Rashtriya Sanskrit Sansthan (National Institute of Sanskrit) are promoting the continuing production and study of mod. Sanskrit lit. through various scholarly projects and programs. In contemp. India, Sanskrit poetry continues to be written, performed, and published alongside lit. in the 20 or so other Indian langs. Numerous magazines and jours. (such *as Saṃskṛta Vimarśaḥ* and *Saṃskṛta Sāhitya Pariṣat*) publish the work of Sanskrit poets working in contemp. India, and "gatherings of poets" (*kavisammelana*) continue to recite and share their work in centers of Sanskrit learning and diverse public spaces. Since the 1970s, a biannual gathering of international scholars of Sanskrit known as the World Sanskrit Conference has also provided a forum for poets from all over the world to share their literary compositions with each other.

*See* DEVOTIONAL POETRY; INDIA, POETRY OF; PRAKRIT POETRY: RĀMĀYAṆA POETRY; SANSKRIT POETICS; TASTE.

■ D.H.H. Ingalls, "Introduction," *Sanskrit Poetry from Vidyakara's Treasury*, trans. D.H.H. Ingalls (1968); A. K. Warder, *Indian Kāvya Literature*, 6 v. (1972–92); S. Lienhard, *A History of Classical Poetry: Sanskrit, Pali, Prakrit* (1984).

D. M. PATEL

**SAPPHIC.** In early Gr. poetry, an important \*aeolic verse form named after Sappho, a Gr. poet from the island of Lesbos of the 7th–6th c. BCE. Prosodically, this form has been of interest to poets throughout most of the hist. of Western poetry; generically, it has evoked ever-increasing interest in the subjects of gender and love vis-à-vis poetry (see GENDER AND POETRY), most recently poetry written by women.

The term *sapphic* refers to both a meter and a stanza form. The sapphic line, called the *lesser sapphic*, is a \*hendecasyllable of the pattern $- \cup - x - \cup \cup - \cup - -$. The sapphic stanza consists of two lesser sapphic lines followed by a 16-syllable line that is an extended form of the other two: $- \cup - x - \cup \cup - \cup - x + - \cup \cup - -$. This latter has been analyzed in several ways; one traditional account sees the last \*colon as an \*adonic colon $(- \cup \cup - -)$ and treats it as a separate line, giving the sapphic stanza four lines in all. Sappho's contemporary Alcaeus also used the stanza and may have been its inventor. Catullus composed two \*odes in sapphics (11 and 51), the second of which is a trans. and adaptation of Sappho frag. 31 (Lobel-Page); with these poems, he probably introduced the sapphic into Lat. poetry, but it is not certain. It is Horace, however, who provided the sapphic model for subsequent Roman and Eur. poets; in his *Odes*, he uses the form 27 times, second in frequency only to \*alcaics. Horace also makes a single use (*Odes* 1.8) of the greater sapphic \*strophe, i.e., an Aristophaneus $(- \cup \cup - \cup - -)$ followed by a greater sapphic line of 15 syllables $(- \cup - - - | \cup \cup - | - \cup \cup - \cup - -)$, which can be analyzed as a sapphic hendecasyllable with an inserted \*choriamb. His treatment of the sapphic as a four-line stanza canonized that form for posterity. Seneca sometimes uses the separate elements in a different order, e.g., by arranging a continuous series of longer lines with an adonic clausula.

In the Middle Ages, the sapphic acquired rhyme and was instrumental in the transition from metrical (quantitative) to rhythmical (accentual) meter (Norberg). After the hexameter and the iambic dimeter quatrain (for \*hymns), it is the most popular verse form of the med. period: there are 127 examples in *Analecta hymnica* (Selected Hymns). In the Ren. and after, accentual versions of the sapphic became three lines of 11 syllables followed by a fourth line of five, the whole in trochees and \*dactyls. The fourth line instances the phenomenon of tailing or end shortening well attested in other stanza forms (see TAIL RHYME).

The revival of Horatian influence on poetics evoked wide interest in the sapphic stanza among poets and prosodists in Italy, France, Germany, England, and Spain. Leonardo Dati used it for the first time in It. (1441), followed by Galeotto del Carretto, Claudio Tolomei, and others; in the 19th c., experiments were made by Felice Cavallotti and by Giosuè Carducci (*Odi barbare*). Estéban de Villegas is the chief practitioner in Spain. In the 18th-c. Ger. revival of interest in quantitative verse, F. G. Klopstock varied an unrhymed stanza with regular positional changes of the trisyllabic foot in the lesser sapphic lines; later, August von Platen and others essayed the strict Horatian form. In Eng., sapphics have been written by Philip Sidney (*Old Arcadia*; *Certain Sonnets* 25); Isaac Watts (*Horae lyricae*); Alexander Pope ("Ode on Solitude"); William Cowper ("Lines under the Influence of Delirium"); Robert Southey ("The Widow"); Alfred, Lord Tennyson; A. C. Swinburne (*Poems and Ballads*); Thomas Hardy (the first poem in *Wessex Poems*); Ezra Pound ("Apparuit"), and John Frederick Nims (*Sappho to Valéry*, 2d ed., 1990). The sapphic has been the longest lived of the cl. lyric strophes in the West. But full studies of its hist. in several vernaculars still remain to be written.

*See* CLASSICAL METERS IN MODERN LANGUAGES, LOVE POETRY.

■ G. Mazzoni, "Per la storia della saffica in Italia," *Atti dell'Acc. Scienze lett. arti* 10 (1894); E. Hjaerne, "Das sapfiska strofen i svensk verskonst," *Sprak och Stil* 13 (1913); Pauly-Wissowa, Supp., 11.1222 ff.; Hardie, pt. 2, ch. 3; Omond; H. Rüdiger, *Geschichte der deutschen Sappho-Übersetzungen* (1934); D. L. Page, *Sappho and Alcaeus* (1955); Norberg; Bowra; W. Bennett, *German Verse in Classical Metres* (1963); L. P. Wilkinson, *Golden Latin Artistry* (1963); Koster; H. Kenner, "The Muse in Tatters," *Agenda* 6 (1968); N. A. Bonavia-Hunt, *Horace the Minstrel* (1969); R.G.M. Nisbet and M. Hubbard, *A Commentary on Horace, Odes Book 1* (1970); R. Paulin,

"Six Sapphic Odes 1753–1934," *Seminar* 10 (1974); E. Schäfer, *Deutscher Horaz* (1976); E. Weber, "Prosodie verbale et prosodie musicale: La Strophe sapphique au Moyen Age et à la Renaissance," *Le Moyen Français* 5 (1979); Halporn et al.; P. Stotz, *Sonderformen der sapphischen Dichtung* (1982); Navarro; West, 32 ff.; J. Crawford, "Sidney's Sapphics and the Role of Interpretive Communities," *ELH* 69 (2002).

R. A. SWANSON; T.V.F. BROGAN; J. W. HALPORN

**SATANIC SCHOOL.** Derogatory term coined by Robert Southey in his preface to *A Vision of Judgement* (1821) for those poets "of diseased hearts and depraved imaginations" whose works exude "a Satanic spirit of pride and audacious impiety." While Southey mentioned no names, the preface clearly targeted Lord Byron, with whom Southey had been quarreling for some years; the critique probably extends to P. B. Shelley and Thomas Moore as well. Southey warned, "[T]his evil is political as well as moral" and ominously prophesied "where the manners of a people are generally corrupted, there the government cannot long subsist." Byron retaliated with his own parodic vision of judgment; he mocked Southey for his transformation from a youthful republican to a staunchly conservative poet laureate. A few 19th-c. critics used Southey's term, contrasting the Satanic school with the Lake school, but the term never gained widespread acceptance. More enduring is the concept of the Satanic hero, understood as a cursed Cain figure doomed to self-destruction, as in Byron's *Manfred* (1817). This figure draws on John Milton's *Paradise Lost* and J. W. Goethe's *Faust* and prefigures the *\*poète maudit* as developed later by Charles Baudelaire and his successors.

■ M. Praz, *The Romantic Agony*, 2d ed. (1951); L. Madden, *Robert Southey: The Critical Heritage* (1972); J. J. McGann, *Byron and Romanticism* (2002); *Romanticism*, 3d ed., ed. D. Wu (2006).

L. METZGER; C. DOAK

**SATIRE.** Satire is both a mode and a genre of verse and prose lit. that adopts a critical attitude toward its target with the goal of censuring human folly. Satire is an eminently versatile form whose structure, style, tone, and subjects vary across a wide spectrum, but generally intends, as Jonathan Swift states, "to mend the world" ("A Vindication of Mr. Gay and *The Beggar's Opera*").

In terms of its purpose, satire is polemical, contentiously attacking its victims with the hope of dissuading readers from vice and persuading them (to greater and lesser degrees) toward virtue. In terms of structure, satire is primarily a borrower of literary and rhetorical forms, using other genres to support its didactic agenda (see Guilhamet). As Paulson describes it, satire explores the lowest range of potential human actions within a framework or fiction that best serves its ridiculing function (*Fictions of Satire*). Some of satire's favorite housing fictions include diatribe (the outraged declamations of Lucilius and Juvenal);

Socratic-style dialogue (the *sermones* or conversations of Horace and the more cynical dialogues of Lucian); epic (Lucian's *True History*, which parodies the works of Homer and Herodotus; Nicolas Boileau's *\*mock epic* *Le Lutrin* and Alexander Pope's *The Dunciad* and *The Rape of the Lock*, which parody the works of Virgil and John Milton); romance (Petronius's *Satyricon*, Voltaire's *Candide*, Samuel Butler's *Hudibras*, Lord Byron's *Don Juan*); burlesque (e.g., the ridiculing of Homer in the *Battle of the Frogs and Mice*); the *\*encomium* (the ironic praises of Erasmus's *Praise of Folly* and John Dryden's "MacFlecknoe"); beast fable (Apuleius's *The Golden Ass* [or *Metamorphoses*], the med. tales of Reynard the Fox, Edmund Spenser's "Mother Hubberds Tale"); epistle (Pope's "To a Lady" and "To Dr. Arbuthnot"; Mary Wortley Montagu's "An Epistle from Mrs. Yonge to Her Husband"); religious complaint (cf. the parodies of the med. Goliard poets; the *\*dream vision* of William Langland's *Piers Plowman*, Chaucer's "Pardoner's Tale," T. S. Eliot's "The Hippopotamus"); *\*pastoral* (Aphra Behn's "The Disappointment," Swift's "A Description of the Morning" and "A Pastoral Dialogue"); civic poetry (Samuel Johnson's *London*, W. H. Auden's "The Unknown Citizen, e. e. cummings's "next to of course god america"); treatise (Swift's deeply ironic *A Modest Proposal* and *A Tale of a Tub*, and Pope's *Peri Bathous*); travel narrative (e.g., Swift's *Gulliver's Travels*); and drama (the Gr. Old Comedy of Aristophanes, the humor plays of Ben Jonson, John Gay's *The Beggar's Opera*). In fact, there are few if any genres that the satiric mode cannot adopt with effects that range from the richly comic to the devastatingly tragic. Similarly, there are few if any media that satire cannot inhabit, including mod. favorites such as film (*Dr. Strangelove*), television, and the Internet. Since the focus of the present article is on poetry and poetics, many major artistic, dramatic, and novelistic satires are beyond its scope, such as the paintings of William Hogarth; select dramas of Molière, Henry Fielding, William Congreve, W. S. Gilbert, G. B. Shaw, Oscar Wilde, and Caryl Churchill; the novels of George Orwell (*Animal Farm*, *1984*), Charlotte Gilman (*Herland*), and Joseph Heller (*Catch-22*); the satiric writings of Mark Twain and Ambrose Bierce; the satiric cartoons and essays of the magazine *Punch*; and so on.

Although satire can call upon a long hist. of formal conventions and rhetorical tropes such as *\*irony*, *\*personification*, and *\*hyperbole*, satire is distinctive for its overt engagement (at varying levels of critical distance) with its immediate historical context ("all the things which men do . . . is the hodge-podge of my little book"; Juvenal, *Satires* 1.85–86), a fact that often makes the colloquial lang. and topical subjects of satiric verse obscure. Because satire criticizes the contemp. world, the satirist is frequently compelled to employ an array of self-protective structures, including a range of personae, apology, *\*allegory*, and claims of innocent comedic intent; however, such gestures are belied by the satirist's bold assertion that his work alone offers "antidotes to [the] pestilential sins" of a morally diseased society (Everard Guilpin's *Skialetheia*, Prelud. 70). The satirist serves as self-appointed prosecutor, judge, and jury, exposing and condemning the worst excesses of human behavior, sometimes, like Horace, with the intention of improving the wicked through humorous moral instruction, and sometimes, like Juvenal, with the object of provoking the wicked to guilt, shame, rage, and tears (Horace, *Satires* 1.4.103–29 and Juvenal, *Satires* 1.166–68). Despite satire's standard defensive claim to employ only "feigned [i.e., fictitious] private names to note general vices" (John Marston's "To Him"; *The Scourge of Villanie* 8–9), the perception of libelous lampoons in satire has often drawn the attention of the authorities and has frequently provoked censorship, from the Roman Twelve Tables outlawing libelous verses (Cicero, *De republica* 4.12; Horace, *Epistles* 2.1.152–54) to Emperor Augustus's edict against "defamatory little books" (in Suetonius, *Life of Augustus* 55) to England's 1599 prohibition against the publication of satire, as well as the Theatrical Licensing Act of 1737.

As described by Kernan in *The Cankered Muse*, satire demonstrates a tension between the comic and the tragic strains; however, satire employs both as strategies in the service of its didactic and apotropaic agendas. Horace prefers his ironic mode of satire "to speak the truth with a laugh" (*Satires* 1.1.24), and Persius admires the comic ability of the "sly rogue" Horace to "touch every fault while his friend stands and laughs" (*Satires* 1.116–17). Anderson (1982) characterizes the Horatian comic mode as not merely witty but socially "constructive" and "humane" (39), and many Ren., Restoration, and Augustan-era imitators have been drawn to Horace's apparent benevolence and erudition. In his prefatory epistle to *The Praise of Folly*, Erasmus states his preference for the Horatian principle of delightful instruction and his dislike of Juvenal's "cesspool of secret vice"; in *The Defence of Poesy* (1595), Sir Philip Sidney, citing Persius's praise of Horace, says satire "sportingly never leaveth until he make a man laugh at folly"; and in *An Essay on Criticism*, Pope writes that Horace "charms with graceful Negligence, / And without method, talks us into sense" (653–54). The Juvenalian approach is more severe, denouncing the crimes rather than mocking the follies of a society where depravity is the norm. Anderson (1982) identifies the "tragic" character of the Juvenalian mode in its symbolic depiction of Roman degeneracy. Milton claims that true satire is "borne out of a Tragedy, so ought to resemble his parentage, to strike high" (*An Apology* 6.12–13), a vision shared by the banned group of Eng. Ren. satirists who preferred the Juvenalian tragic mode as a means to expose the moral excesses common at the end of the reign of Elizabeth I: "Satire hath a nobler vein / He's a Strappado, rack, and some such pain / To base lewd vice" (Guilpin). Where the comic satiric strategy employs fools as types of ridiculous behavior that are more instructive than threatening (like "the terrible people" of Ogden Nash's comic poem), the tragic strategy presents a hopeless world inhabited entirely by the wicked, which often includes the satiric speaker himself.

Although both the etymology of the word *satire* and the historical origin of the concept are equivocal, many of satire's defining characteristics can be traced back to a number of related trads. The word itself is derived from the Latin *satura*, meaning a "mixture," and is related to the Lat. *satur*, meaning "full." The Lat. grammarian Diomedes (late 4th c. CE) contends that *satura* may have derived from the *satura lanx*, the ritual plate overflowing with offerings to the gods; or from the word for a kind of stuffing made from various ingredients; or from the *lex satura*, a single legal proposition composed of a number of smaller issues. Diomedes links these separate roots: all, in one way or another, refer to the structure of satire as a miscellany poem, an array of different kinds of verse united by their common intent to ridicule a range of subjects, such as the miscellanies produced by the Roman poets Ennius and Pacuvius (see Keil). As an individual poetic genre, the Roman grammarian Quintilian (ca. 35–100 CE) claimed verse satire as a wholly Roman invention devoid of Gr. influence, with Lucilius as the first Roman to advance the genre (*Institutio oratoria* 10.1.96–97).

While it is true that the etymology of the word *satire* is not related to the Gr. word for satyrs (σατυρος; Lat. *satyrus*), as demonstrated by Isaac Causabon in 1605 (see *De satyrica Graecorum poesi et Romanorum satira*), the form and style of Roman verse satire owe much to the trad. of Gr. *invective poetry; Dryden explains in his 1693 work "A Discourse Concerning the Original and Progress of Satire," "And thus far 'tis allowed that the Grecians had such poems; but that they were wholly different *in specie* from that to which the Romans gave the name of Satire." Horace himself admits to the complementary nature of Gr. and Roman invective poetry, noting that Lucilius modeled his keen and witty satiric style on the Gr. playwrights of Old Comedy, Aristophanes, Eupolis, and Cratinus, changing only their meter while maintaining their freedom to assault the vicious in society by name (*Satires* 1.4.1–8). Diomedes' position is similar, claiming that Roman verse satire may have been named for the goat-legged companions of Dionysus because Roman satire discusses the same kind of laughable and shameful behaviors practiced by the Gr. satyrs. This idea of complementary stylistic trads. continued well into the Ren., as suggested by the conscious conflation of the two trads. in the spelling of the word as *Satyre*. Thomas Drant's 1566 definition of satire, e.g., claims that it was named either for the Satyrs or for the "waspish" god, Saturn. Intriguingly, Drant also wonders if the word might have the same origin as the Ar. word for "spear," referring to the satirist's method of skewering his targets. Similarly, Elliott claims the satiric poems of ancient Arabia (the *hija'*) as an early example of satire's conventional use as a magical weapon intended to destroy one's enemies.

Other ancient rituals cited by Elliott as conceptual influences on satire include the Gr. phallic songs (*iambic verses intended to cleanse society as part of the fertility rites), the invective poetic curses of Archilochus (7th c. BCE), and the *glám dícind* satiric poems used by ancient Ir. bards to bring infamy and death upon those who displeased them. Dryden mentions two other influential Gr. trads.: the parody-rich *silloi* poems, perhaps derived from Silenus, foster-father of Dionysus, and the Gr. satyr play (the only remaining example of which is Euripides' *Cyclops*), a play performed after three tragedies in which satyrs act as chorus in order to mock issues taken seriously in the preceding plays. Horace describes one other decidedly Roman poetic trad. underlying the conception of satire: the Fescennine ritual. As part of the harvest festivals, participants would hurl humorous rustic abuse at each other in alternating verses. Such liberal verbal freedom was made illegal, states Horace, only after its "cruel tooth" offended honorable families (*Epistles* 2.1.139–56).

Philosophically, cl. satire owes much to the Cynic and Stoic schools. Much of Juvenal's style is cynical in its iconoclastic perspective, angry tone, and declamatory rhet. Other cynic satirists of note include Menippus and his Roman imitator Varro, as well as Petronius, Lucian, John Marston, and John Wilmot, the Earl of Rochester. Shakespeare's railing satirists Thersites (*Troilus and Cressida*) and Apemantus (*Timon of Athens*) exemplify the Cynic trad. with their incessant barking at fools and hypocrites. Elements of Stoic philosophy, a softened version of Cynicism, are present in the satires of Persius and Juvenal, as when, e.g., Juvenal asserts in Satire 10 the virtues of wishing for a "healthy mind in a healthy body" (356) or as Johnson writes in his imitation titled *The Vanity of Human Wishes* (1749), "Pour forth thy fervors for a healthful mind, / Obedient passions, and a will resign'd" (359–60). However, one should not confuse a satirist's engagement with the institutions of his era with adherence to them; Highet (*Juvenal*, 93) argues that Juvenal rejected Stoic teachings (as suggested in Satire 13.120–24), a position supported by Coffey. Satirists conventionally present themselves as staunch individualists, the lone voice of reason driven to mock or to decry the wealth of abuses that surround them. With so much evil in the world, writes Juvenal, "it is difficult *not* to write satire" (1.30).

Structurally, the kind of Roman verse satire practiced by Lucilius, Horace, Juvenal, and later imitators such as John Donne and Pope, has elements in common with dramatic forms such as Gr. Old Comedy and Roman New Comedy. Roman verse satire is often framed as a rhetorical/dramatic debate between the satirist's speaking persona and an adversary, the former taking the position of *vituperatio* (blame) and the latter taking the position of *laus* (praise). The vice in question is then, as Randolph describes it, thoroughly examined in the first sect. of the poem, and the opposing virtue is recommended in the final sect. However, even within the confines of this generic structure, formal verse satire is rarely a stable form, flowing easily into congenial genres such as comedy, beast fable, and prose narrative. Horace, e.g., inserts the Aesopian beast fable of the town mouse and the country mouse into bk. 2, Satire 6, and Juvenal inserts an allegorical tale of a giant fish into satire 4.

In addition to formal verse satire, Quintilian mentions another "older type of satire" practiced by Menippus's Roman imitator Varro in which verse satire is mixed with prose (10.1.95–96). Dryden also mentions the influence of the cynical satires of Menippus and

their manner of mixing several sorts of verse with prose, as well as their paradoxical tone of *spoudogeloioi*, or serious-laughter (64–67). In this category, Dryden places the works of Petronius, Apuleius, and Lucian, as well as John Barclay's picaresque novel *Euphormionis Satyricon* and his own *Absalom and Achitophel* and "MacFlecknoe." Given their cynical and unorthodox perspectives and despite their heavy reliance on prose, one could also place works such as Thomas More's *Utopia*, Miguel de Cervantes's *Don Quixote*, and Aldous Huxley's *Brave New World* under the Menippean umbrella.

The critical hist. of satire in the 20th and early 21st cs. is an uneasy stalemate between formalist and historicist perspectives. From the mid-1950s through the 1960s, the formalist or New Critical methodology recommended a mode of inquiry that rejected the historicists' concerns with literary origins in favor of exploring the conscious "artifice" of the poetry, i.e., the recurrent rhetorical and dramatic conventions of satire (see FORMALISM, HISTORICISM, NEW CRITICISM). One particularly innovative formalist study of the period is Frye's *Anatomy of Criticism*, in which satire is categorized among the four interrelated pregeneric *mythoi* (specifically, the mythos of winter). Frye argues that satire is a kind of "militant irony" whose structural scheme is the ironic application of romantic conventions to realistic contents. Some half-century later, the debate over the "historicity" of satire, meaning the nature and extent of satire's contact with its social context, continued, with scholars such as Bogel, Griffin, and Knight attempting to find a balance between historical conditions and formal traditions. In this context, the sociolinguistic theories of Mikhail Bakhtin are especially relevant for their ability to reconcile the dialogue between form and context in satire. Bakhtin argues that cl. "serio-comical" lit., which includes both formal verse and Menippean satire, is a precursor to the mod. novel, a form intended to provoke "the permanent corrective of laughter" that familiarizes and debases the loftier genres. Another of Bakhtin's contributions is his conception of "carnivalistic literature," a humorously profane remnant of folk culture and ritual that is deliberately contrasted against the usual hierarchical relationships of everyday life; another is his exploration of the ideological nature of Menippean satire as a carnivalized genre that combines topical and fantastic situations in order to test conventional truths, the effect of which is a challenge to all forms of orthodoxy.

*See* BEAST EPIC, HUMORS, GOLIARDIC VERSE, PARODY.

■ **Anthologies**: *A Treasury of Satire*, ed. E. Johnson (1945); *Poems on Affairs of State*, ed. G. deF. Lord et al., 7 v. (1963–75)—Eng. satirical verse, 1660–1714; *English Poetic Satire*, ed. G. Rousseau and N. Rudenstine (1972); *Oxford Book of Satirical Verse*, ed. G. Grigson (1980); *An Anthology of 18th-Century Satire*, ed. P. Heaney (1994); *The Malcontents*, ed. J. Queenan (2002).
■ **Criticism and History**: J. Dryden, "A Discourse concerning the Original and Progress of Satire" (1693); *Essays of John Dryden*, ed. W. P. Kerr, 2 v. (1926); M. C. Randolph, "The Structural Design of the Formal Verse

Satire," *PQ* 21 (1942); M. Mack, "The Muse of Satire," *Yale Review* 41 (1951); I. Jack, *Augustan Satire* (1952); G. Highet, *Juvenal the Satirist* (1954); J. Peter, *Complaint and Satire in Early English Literature* (1956); Frye; A. Kernan, *The Cankered Muse* (1959); R. Elliott, *The Power of Satire* (1960); G. Highet, *The Anatomy of Satire* (1962); J. P. Sullivan, *Satire* (1963)—Roman lit.; W. S. Anderson, *Anger in Juvenal and Seneca* (1964); A. Kernan, *The Plot of Satire* (1965); R. Paulson, *The Fictions of Satire* (1967), and *Satire and the Novel in 18th-Century England* (1967); H. D. Weinbrot, *The Formal Strain* (1969); *Tudor Verse Satire*, ed. K. W. Gransden (1970); R. Paulson, *Satire* (1971); W. Booth, *A Rhetoric of Irony* (1974); R. Seldon, *English Verse Satire 1590–1767* (1978); E. A. Bloom and L. D. Bloom, *Satire's Persuasive Voice* (1979); T. Lockwood, *Post-Augustan Satire* (1979); M. Seidel, *The Satiric Inheritance* (1979); M. M. Bakhtin, *The Dialogic Imagination*, ed. M. Holquist, trans. C. Emerson and M. Holquist (1981); W. S. Anderson, *Essays on Roman Satire* (1982); N. Rudd, *The Satires of Horace*, 2d ed. (1982); H. D. Weinbrot, *Alexander Pope and the Traditions of Formal Verse Satire* (1982); V. Carretta, *The Snarling Muse* (1983); M. M. Bakhtin, *Problems of Dostoevsky's Poetics*, ed. and trans. C. Emerson (1984), and *Rabelais and His World*, trans. H. Iswolsky (1984); F. Nussbaum, *The Brink of All We Hate: English Satires on Women, 1660–1750* (1984); L. Hutcheon, *A Theory of Parody* (1985); E. Pollack, *The Poetics of Sexual Myth* (1985)—Swift and Pope; L. Guilhamet, *Satire and the Transformation of Genre* (1987); H. Javadi, *Satire in Persian Literature* (1988); *Eighteenth-Century Satire*, ed. H. D. Weinbrot (1988); K. Freudenburg, *The Walking Muse* (1992); *Horace Made New*, ed. C. Martindale and D. Hopkins (1993); J. Relihan, *Ancient Menippean Satire* (1993); D. Griffin, *Satire* (1994); L. Hutcheon, *Irony's Edge* (1994); C. Rawson, *Satire and Sentiment 1660–1830* (1994); M. Wood, *Radical Satire and Print Culture, 1790–1822* (1994); *Cutting Edges*, ed. J. Gill (1995)—postmod. crit. on 18th-c. satire; R. Zimbardo, *At Zero Point* (1998); F. Bogel, *The Difference Satire Makes* (2001)—from Jonson to Byron; K. Freudenburg, *Satires of Rome* (2001); J. Ogborn and P. Buckroyd, *Satire* (2001); C. Knight, *The Literature of Satire* (2004); *The Cambridge Companion to Roman Satire*, ed. K. Freudenburg (2005); J. Scott, *Satire* (2005); H. D. Weinbrot, *Menippean Satire Reconsidered* (2005); C. Keane, *Figuring Genre in Roman Satire* (2006); R. Rosen, *Making Mockery* (2007).

W. R. Jones

**SATURNIAN** (Lat. *saturnius*, "belonging or pertaining to the reign of Saturn"). The verse form used in the two earliest Lat. *epics, the trans. of the *Odyssey* by Livius Andronicus (ca. 280–200 BCE) and the *Bellum Punicum* of Naevius (ca. 270–201 BCE), and also of scattered *epitaphs, dedications, *proverbs, and *incantations composed or committed to writing in the 3d and 2d cs. BCE. Fewer than 200 instances survive; the example of Ennius (239–169 BCE) turned Lat. prosody to imitating Gr. quantitative meters, with the result that the saturnian was soon rejected in favor of the *hexameter for epic and the *elegiac distich and iambic *senarius for epitaphs and dedications. Horace's description of the *horridus numerus Saturnius* as a "grave virus" is an example of later taste in regard to it. Structure and origin are accordingly obscure—least so, perhaps, in those verses, roughly a third of the total, which show a 4-3-3-3 grouping of syllables into words or word groups, with a strong central break and *parallelism between groups or subgroups, reinforced by frequent *alliteration and *assonance: *virum mihi, camena, insece versutum* (Livius); im*mortales mortales siforet fasf lere* (Naevius epitaph).

The regularities here are too numerous and conspicuous to be accidental. Moreover, the structural principle is so unlike anything found in Gr. poetry and so similar to that attested in the balanced alliterative and assonantal dicola and tricola of early Lat. ritual formulas that the theory espoused by some metrists, both ancient and mod., of direct derivation from Gr. models is highly unlikely. One is left with two possibilities: either (as the name itself would suggest) a native Italic form (perhaps distantly related to the Old Ir. heptasyllable) or some early Gr. import domiciled in Italy for several centuries and thereby radically transformed by the time Livius and Naevius tried to give it literary status. Almost everything beyond this is highly problematic. Verses longer than those cited above can always be regarded as resolved versions of the 13-syllable "model," which might suggest the operation of quantitative principles; but there is no one quantitative scheme to which all or even a large majority of extant examples conform, and there exist shorter half lines with 4-2, 3-2 and 2-3 groupings of syllables that are equally hard to reconcile with a quantitative analysis. Explanations that posit the working of two or more different rhythmical principles (quantitative, syllabic, accentual) are, on the whole, more plausible than those that involve a single one. It is possible, e.g., that a quadripartite line originally based on grouping of syllables by 4s, 3s, and 2s evolved, under the influence of Gr. models, into a 13-syllable line with the same groupings but a generally iambo-trochaic movement, similar to that found in Macaulay's accentual imitation: "The quéen was ín her párlour, éating bréad and hóney." While such theories may resolve the quantitative irregularity of the verse form, the origins of the saturnian nevertheless remain conjecture.

■ F. Leo, *Der Saturnische Vers* (1905); G. Pasquali, *Preistoria della poesia latina* (1936); M. Barchiesi, *Nevio epico* (1962); T. Cole, "The Saturnian Verse," *Yale Classical Studies* 21 (1969); J. Starobinski, *Les Mots sous les mots* (1971); J. Parsons, "A New Approach to the Saturnian Verse and Its Relation to Latin Prosody," *TAPA* 129 (1999); A. O. Mercado, "Towards Proto-Indo-European Metrics: The Italic Saturnian Reinterpreted," *Langue poétique indo-européenne*, ed. G.-J. Pinault and D. Petit (2003), "A New Approach to Old Latin and Umbrian Poetic Meter," *Proceedings of the Fourteenth Annual UCLA Indo-European Conference*, ed. K. Jones-

Bley et al. (2003), and "The Latin Saturnian and Italic Verse," *DAI* (2007).

A. T. COLE

**SAUDOSISMO.** A literary-poetic movement in Portugal founded by the Port. Renaissance (1912) group in Porto, whose best-known proponent was the poet Teixeira de Pascoaes (1877–1952). Based on *saudade*, or nostalgic yearning, a mainstay of Port. lit. since the Middle Ages, *saudosismo* was both a literary and a political-social doctrine, a resurgence of nationalistic sentiment prompted by the proclamation of the Port. Republic (1910) that attempted to capture the "national soul." Through articles in *A Águia*, Pascoaes and his contemporaries raised saudade above the status of national affect to a theory of humankind, a development of 19th-c. mystical-nationalist thought that would chart the future of the "Lusitanian Race" and would be revealed by poets. It was a religion, a philosophy, and a political credo. Fernando Pessoa (1888–1935) wrote about saudosismo but eventually abandoned it because of its traditional, neo-romantic leanings. As a movement of national renewal, saudosismo recalls Sebastianism or the earlier belief in the prophetic return of the lost King Sebastião (d. 1578) who was to deliver Portugal from the yoke of Sp. rule, which occurred between 1580 and 1640.

*See* PORTUGAL, POETRY OF.

■ J. P. Coelho, "Saudosismo," *Dicionário de literatura*, ed. J. P. Coelho, v. 4 (1985).

J. BLACKMORE

# SCANSION

 I. Definition and History
 II. Notation
 III. Meter, Rhythm, and Scansion
 IV. Pros and Cons of Scansion

**I. Definition and History.** Scansion describes the structure of verse lines by breaking them down into their component feet and identifying the metrical character of the individual syllables. The word comes from the Latin *scandere*, "to climb," and *scansio*, "a climbing." Charlton T. Lewis and Charles Short, in their *Latin Dictionary*, suggest that figurative uses of the verb in Roman poetry (e.g., Lucretius's comment that living things climb step by step to maturity [*On the Universe* 2.1123] and Horace's remark that care climbs aboard a ship with the restless traveler [*Odes* 2.16.21]) led Late Lat. grammarians to adopt the idiom *scandere versus*—"to climb up, i.e., *to measure* or *read* [verse] by its feet." Other authorities (e.g., *The American Heritage Dictionary of the English Language*, 4th ed., and *The New Oxford American Dictionary*, 2d ed.) speculate that the term originates in the custom of lifting and lowering the foot to keep time with a piece of music or poetry. Both hypotheses associate the human foot with the metrical foot (Gr. *pous*, Lat. *pes*) and involve the concept of verse as measure or count (Gr. *metron*, Lat. *numerus*). Terentianus Maurus, who toward the end of the 2nd c. CE composed a verse essay about metrics, appears to be one of the earliest writers to speak of scanning poetry (*On Letters, Syllables, and Meters* 547, 1753). Though one might suspect that *scansion* etymologically connects with *scan* in the sense of "examine closely," this latter denotation does not appear until the 16th c. and is an extension of the prosodic usage rather than an influence upon it.

Scansion and metrical analysis are almost as old as poetry. No sooner do poets start composing in meter than they begin exploring ways in which it can enhance meaning. When, for instance, at *Iliad* 23.221, Achilles is "calling to the spirit of poor Patroclus" and pouring out wine to the gods in honor of his dead friend, Homer contracts all the *dactyls of the *hexameter into *spondees, which create a solemn, heavy movement appropriate to his hero's act. Indeed, in Greek, *sponde* means "libation," and the prosodic spondee (*spondeios*) is so named because the foot, consisting of two long syllables, suits the slow rhythms of libational songs and chants. Further, the wine that mortals present the gods is unwatered—Homer himself speaks at *Iliad* 2.341 and 4.159 of the "unmixed libations," *spondai akretoi*, that conclude a truce or treaty—and this purely spondaic line about Achilles' devotions not only suggests their ceremonial gravity but also perhaps points to the undiluted nature of his offering and his grief:

ψυχην κικλησκων Πατροκληος δειλοιο

‒ ‒  ‒ ‒  ‒ ‒  ‒ ‒  ‒ ‒  ‒ ‒

psuchen | kikles | kon Pat | rokle | os dei | loio

(Ancient poets always treat the final syllable of the hexameter as long, even when it is short, as it is here, where it consists simply of an omicron—the theory being that the pause at the line end compensates for the syllable's brevity.)

By the cl. age, metrical analysis has become a subject of general literary interest and study, as we can infer from the amusing scene in Aristophanes' *Clouds* in which Socrates proposes to teach the ignorant farmer Strepsiades about trimeters and tetrameters and the dactyl. The very nature of the jokes—Strepsiades mistakes the meters for measures of commercial exchange and can understand *daktulos* only with respect to its common meaning of "finger," as in giving somebody the finger—indicates that the playwright trusts that his large and miscellaneous audience knows something about versification and the vocabulary employed to discuss it. By the same token, Gr. and Lat. writers on rhet., incl. Isocrates, Aristotle, Cicero, and Quintilian, discuss rhythmical arrangement in terms of short (Gr. *brachus*, Lat. *brevis*) and long (Gr. *makros*, Lat. *longus*) syllables and consider various prosodic topics as they relate to the composition of both verse and prose.

Metrical analysis, moreover, plays a critical role in the trad. of textual scholarship inaugurated in the Hellenistic period at the library in Alexandria. Prior to this time, Gr. lyric poetry seems to have been written out consecutively in the manner of prose; but Aristophanes of Byzantium (3rd–2nd c. BCE), in his eds. of lyric writers, divides their poems into metrical *cola* in order to clarify the poems' linear and strophic structures (see COLON). Similarly, in part to facilitate the accurate reading of poems and the understanding of their meters, Hellenistic scholars develop various diacritical and punctuation marks; and as M. L. West indicates, the macron and breve signs we still use in scanning cl. verse appear as early as the 2nd c. BCE in papyri of scholarly copies of the poets "over vowels about whose quantity the reader might be uncertain because the words or forms were archaic or poetic." In addition, in Hephaestion's *Guide to Meter* (mid-2nd c. CE), we have a prototype of the student manual of prosody that lists different feet and rhythms and illustrates them with apposite passages of poetry.

Yet, as the word's relatively late appearance suggests, scansion seems most notably to reflect or respond to the linguistic conditions and educational needs of the postclassical world. In late antiquity, accent replaces length as the central prosodic element in Gr. and Lat.; and in the Middle Ages, Gr. falls into disuse throughout much of Europe, while the vernaculars supplant Lat. in everyday speech. Though Lat. remains, in the Middle Ages and beyond, a lingua franca for the intellectual community, it is no longer native to those who use it, nor do they speak it as the ancients did. Knowledge of metrics is essential for those wishing to comprehend the lang. and its lit. This situation grows even more critical during the revival of ancient learning in the Ren., when the humanists make the study of cl. Lat. the basis of elementary education and when the composition of quantitative Lat. verse becomes both a measure of scholastic achievement and a serious pursuit for many major poets from Petrarch to John Milton.

Scansion figures throughout Eng. lit. crit., which adopts the exercise from cl. studies. Both George Gascoigne, in his pioneering "Certain Notes of Instruction concerning the Making of Verse or Rhyme in English" (1575), and George Puttenham, in his *Arte of English Poesie* (1589), refer to scanning by name and supply sample scansions to illustrate their ideas about Eng. metrical structure. (Gascoigne uses an acute accent to register what we would call metrically accented syllables and a grave accent to mark metrically unaccented ones, while Puttenham scans with breves and macrons.) In the 17th, 18th, and 19th cs., the study of Eng. prosody is advanced by, among others, Ben Jonson, John Dryden, Thomas Warton, Thomas Sheridan, Samuel Johnson, Thomas Jefferson (whose underappreciated "Thoughts on English Prosody" anticipates, in its differentiation of degrees of accent, approaches to scansion adopted by 20th-c. linguists like Otto Jespersen), William Wordsworth, S. T. Coleridge, and Edwin Guest. Further, beginning with Nicholas Rowe, Shakespeare's editors apply metrical analysis to the texts of his plays, with a view to correcting mislineations in the folio eds. These mislineations had occurred for various reasons, including the practice, among the original compositors, of splitting verse lines in two, or of breaking up a prose passage into shorter lines as if it were verse, when there was too little text to fill a column or page. (Conversely, when the compositors needed to conserve space, they sometimes ran verse lines together in prose fashion.) During this time, metrical analysis also continues to figure in cl. scholarship, as is shown by Richard Bentley's celebrated discovery of the digamma. Bentley postulates that this consonant existed in archaic Gr. but had disappeared by the cl. age, when he realizes that its absence explains many apparent metrical glitches in the eds. of Homer from the Alexandrian period forward—particularly those cases where a word-ending short vowel followed by a word beginning with a vowel still receives full metrical value rather than being elided. Gr. verse generally avoids such hiatuses, and Bentley perceives that their occurrences in Homer often reflect the loss of the digamma that originally began the second word and separated the two vowels. Scansion becomes even more prominent in Eng. literary studies in the second half of the 19th c., when Eng. lit. enters school curricula as a formal discipline. This period launches a vogue for handbooks on Eng. meter that has continued ever since.

This period also witnesses the beginning of what will eventually become a widespread misapprehension that to write in a meter is to limit oneself to a single, rigid formula rather than to adopt a general pattern susceptible to various internal modulations; and several developments in scansion contribute to this misapprehension. For one thing, in the second half of the 19th c., Eng. prosodists increasingly use, in scanning, vertical bars to separate feet from one another, a practice relatively rare prior to this time. Since Eng. meters customarily entail a succession of metrically identical feet, the practice gives scanned lines a strong visual impression of uniformity that deflects attention from the rhythmical shadings the lines may possess when spoken. (Foot division does not produce this effect so markedly in cl. verse because its quantitative metric allows that a long syllable may at points replace two short syllables and that two shorts may replace one long. Hence, though the hexameters of Homer and Virgil, to take two obvious cases, are strictly isosyllabic in a durational sense, they usually contain a mix of dactyls and spondees.)

Another practice that emerges in this period and that emphasizes the structural regularity of metrical poetry at the expense of its tonal variety is the schoolroom exercise of having students verbally scan verse by sing-songing it in unison:

> I *wan*dered *lone*ly *as* a *cloud*

or

> *This* is the *for*est pri*mev*al. The *mur*muring *pines*
> and the *hem*locks

Though this exercise highlights basic prosodic structures, it drains metered verse of its human inflections and natural rhythms.

A final and related factor that focuses awareness on the simplicity of metrical description and slights the complexity of metrical practice is Sidney Lanier's *Science of English Verse* (1880). In this work, which exerts considerable influence on prosodic thinking in the late 19th and early 20th cs., Lanier suggests that iambic verse is written in 3/8 time, involves an alternation of verbal eighth notes and quarter notes, and follows the sequence of tick-*tack*, tick-*tack*. This theory contributes to the notion, in Ezra Pound and others, that the rhythms of traditional versification are those of the metronome, itself an invention of the 19th c.

Overall, these developments serve as a warning that scansion and metrical analysis may, if misunderstood or misapplied, muddle the subject they aim to illuminate.

**II. Notation.** Most literary cultures devise notation to register the rhythmic or phonological properties of their lang. and poetry, and students of Eng. verse have explored many systems of scansion, incl. those involving letters, musical notes, numbers, and graphic representations. However, a simple group of symbols has generally held sway. Prior to the 20th c., Eng. prosodists usually signify metrically unaccented syllables with the breve ( ⌣ ) cl. prosodists use to register short syllables. When signifying metrically accented syllables, they employ the macron ( – ) cl. prosodists apply to long ones. During the 20th c., the breve and macron give way to an x for metrically unaccented syllables and an acute accent ( ´ ) for metrically accented ones. This shift reflects a growing consensus that xs and acute accents better indicate that Eng. metric weighs syllabic stress and not, as the breve and macron might suggest, syllabic length. (Be it noted, however, that breves and macrons persist in some discussions of Eng. versification; and in other discussions, the two systems mix—the most common blend assigning breves to metrically unaccented syllables and acute accents to metrically accented ones.)

Another mark that often figures in scansion (esp., as has been noted, in the last century and a half) is a vertical bar to divide the individual feet of the line from one another; and here it is important to remember two points. First, scansion treats verse lines merely as rows of syllables. *It concerns units of rhythm, not units of sense.* Hence, as the line already cited from Homer demonstrates—and as some of the lines cited below testify—divisions between feet do not necessarily correspond to divisions between words, phrases, and clauses. Second, in scanning Eng. verse, we determine whether a syllable is metrically accented solely by comparing it with the other syllable or syllables of the foot in which it appears. We do not weigh it against all the other syllables in the line or poem. Nor do we concern ourselves with whether the foot's accented syllable is much heavier than its unaccented syllable or syllables or only a little heavier. Though such nuances will affect and enliven the specific rhythm of the spoken line, scansion cannot, with its simple descriptive tools, register their continual and shifting complexities.

With regard to more specialized aspects of notation, there exist wide and confusing variations of practice—sadly, no metrical Moses has ever climbed Parnassus and received an authoritative Ten Commandments of Scansion from Apollo—yet several devices appear with some frequency. In particular, when prosodists mark a feminine ending (i.e., an extra, metrically unaccented syllable at the end of a line), most place the x in parentheses to indicate that the syllable is, literally, "hypermetrical"—beyond the measure and having no effect on its identity (see HYPERMETRIC). For the same reason, they usually do not place, in front of the syllable, a vertical foot-division bar, a procedure that might mislead the casual observer into thinking that the syllable comprised an additional foot.

Conventional notation, then, renders as follows these lines from E. A. Robinson's "Eros Turannos" and Louise Bogan's "Cassandra." (Bogan's line has a feminine ending.)

> x / x / x / x /
> Tra di | tion, touch | ing all | he sees
> x / x / x / x / x / (x)
> To me, | one sil | ly task | is like | another

Scansion thus demonstrates that Robinson's line is an iambic tetrameter, a line consisting of four iambic feet, and that Bogan's line an iambic pentameter, a line consisting of five iambic feet. Moreover, since any type of foot can be "substituted" for another, as long as such substitutions are not so frequent or so placed as to dissolve the meter, scansion can enable us to locate metrical variants and appreciate their effect in those cases where they serve an expressive purpose.

Occasionally, feet admit of different scansions, as is illustrated by the famous line from Shakespeare's *Hamlet*:

> To be, or not to be: | that is | the question

Probably, most actors treat the fourth foot as trochaic: *that* is the question. Such a reading stresses the crux of Hamlet's situation: should he live and suffer the corruption he sees about him, or should he oppose it and thereby almost surely bring on his death? Yet an actor might speak the fourth foot as an iamb—that *is* the question—to emphasize the immediacy of Hamlet's predicament and the urgency of resolving it. (Either reading is metrically conventional. Historically, along with the feminine ending, the most common variants in Eng. iambic verse are a trochaic substitution at the beginning of the line and a trochaic substitution after a midline pause.)

**III. Meter, Rhythm, and Scansion.** One can steer clear of the confusions that sometimes plague scansion by bearing in mind that versification involves the concurrent but distinguishable phenomena of meter and rhythm. A meter is an analytic abstraction, a norm or basic pattern. For instance, the norm of the iambic pentameter is

> weak *strong*, weak *strong*, weak *strong*, weak *strong*, weak *strong*

Rhythm, on the other hand, concerns the realization of this pattern in living speech.

On rare occasions, as in this line from Thomas Traherne's "The Salutation," the poet's rhythm may replicate the normative pattern and consist of five successive two-syllable, rear-stressed phrases or words:

The earth, the seas, the light, the day, the skies

More frequently, the rhythm may entail an alternation of weak and strong syllables that tracks the norm fairly closely, as in this line from John Keats's "To Autumn":

And touch the stubble-plains with rosy hue

However, most iambic pentameters do not feature uniform fluctuation. Rather, the alternation between weak and strong syllables will be relatively emphatic at some points and less so at others. Poets compose not only in feet but also in larger words, phrases, clauses, and sentences whose tones are not limited to minimal and maximal accent but incorporate innumerable gradations of stress.

In this respect, we might compare iambic pentameters to mountain ranges. Valleys and peaks alternate. But not every peak is an Everest, nor is every valley a Grand Canyon. For example, this line from Thom Gunn's "In Santa Maria del Popolo" features two peaks that are not very high:

Resisting, by embracing, nothingness

And this line from Wallace Stevens's "Sunday Morning" has a valley that is not very deep:

She causes boys to pile new plums and pears

Further, because the iambic line requires only the maintenance of the lighter-to-heavier fluctuation—and because the only requirement of an iamb is that its second syllable be weightier than its first—a metrically unaccented syllable at one point in the line may carry more speech stress than a metrically accented syllable at another point. This occurs in this line from Philip Larkin's "Vers de Société":

Beyond the light stand failure and remorse

"Stand" (the metrically unaccented syllable of foot three) has more speech stress than "and" (the metrically accented syllable of foot four). Even so, the line maintains the fluctuation of lighter to heavier syllables and scans conventionally:

| x | / | x | / | x | / | x | / | x | / |
|---|---|---|---|---|---|---|---|---|---|

Beyond | the light | stand fail | ure and | remorse

Sometimes, a poet follows an iamb of two relatively light syllables with an iamb of two relatively heavy

ones. When this occurs, the fluctuation in stress is suspended in favor of an ascent over four syllables. Philip Sidney, in the opening line of his sonnet to the moon, employs this scheme to reinforce sonically the image he presents:

With how sad steps, O moon, thou climb'st the sky

Some authorities scan feet like "new plums," "stand fail-," and "sad steps" as spondees and feet like "-ing by," "-ure and," and "With how" as *pyrrhics, in the belief that such feet are analogous to ancient spondees, which, as we observed earlier, consist of two long syllables, and ancient pyrrhics, which consist of two short ones. However, it is doubtful whether pyrrhics and spondees are generally helpful or necessary to the analysis of Eng. verse. Ancient metrics measure syllabic quantity, and long and short syllables can be identified by phonetic rules; hence, cl. pyrrhics and spondees are immediately recognizable metrical phenomena. In contrast, mod. Eng. meter measures syllabic stress, and this cannot be consistently determined by external principle but is often affected by verbal environment, grammatical function, rhetorical sense, or some combination of these factors. In particular, any of the lang.'s many monosyllabic words can serve, given the right context, as metrically accented or unaccented. Because of such variabilities and because successive syllables in Eng. rarely feature equal degrees of stress, Eng. pyrrhics and spondees are not so much objective metrical facts as rhythmical effects, the perception and identification of which must be to some extent subjective. Each reader must decide for him- or herself when two syllables are close enough in their stress properties to be treated as equal. More specifically, introducing routinely spondees and pyrrhics into the scansion of Eng. iambic verse misconstrues its nature, insofar as the practice implies that feet whose syllables are relatively close in weight are metrical variants, whereas such feet occur all the time in any naturally and competently written iambic poem.

**IV. Pros and Cons of Scansion.** Because scansion has at times contributed to confusions of metrical description with metrical practice, some have wondered whether we should scrap the exercise in favor of prosodic studies that more broadly address ways in which meters cooperate with the lexical and syntactical elements of lang. Might it be wiser, some have asked, to direct attention to phrasal and clausal arrangements in verse lines rather than focusing on little two- and three-syllable units? As Cunningham puts it, we might be better off "regarding a meter, not as a schematic diagram of scansions, but as a collection of syllabic-syntactic types . . . [for] this is the way we perceive meter when we read without hesitation or analysis, that is, poetically. We do not hear diagrams."

The approach Cunningham suggests merits the most serious consideration, holding out the prospect of engaging the actual process by which poets compose

SCHEME 1263

poems and readers experience them; still, there remains a strong case for retaining traditional scansion. To be sure, it construes words, phrases, and clauses merely as abstract feet, and this procedure sometimes appears peculiar and unnatural. Yet we should remember, again, that scansion concerns rhythmical organization, not verbal sense. And it is only reasonable, when discussing a type of rhythm, to speak of its most fundamental component, such as (in the case of iambic rhythm) a weak syllable followed by a strong one. Moreover, scansion provides a compact and comprehensive method for examining metrical structure. And though we would in theory benefit greatly from an account of all the syllabic-syntactic types relevant to a particular meter, compiling such a compendium would probably prove in many cases a practical impossibility. The Eng. pentameter, even when self-contained and end-stopped, can accommodate any number of syntactical forms. If we add arrangements that involve run-over lines— arrangements that traverse as well as interact with metrical units—the possibilities seem boundless.

Further, scansion does not exclude other kinds of analysis. Scanning by feet does not prevent our considering ways in which grammar and meter cooperate, any more than it precludes our appreciation of how the stress a syllable carries may be influenced by its verbal environment, grammatical function, or rhetorical sense. Ultimately, negative feelings about scansion mostly result from misunderstandings of it. And instead of jettisoning a system that has, whatever its quirks and deficiencies, fruitfully served centuries of poets and readers, we should try, as patiently as possible, to correct the misunderstandings. More specifically, whenever we discuss prosody, we should be careful to distinguish between meter and rhythm— between the comprehensive pattern of the norm and the many particular ways it can be realized in living speech.

Scansion and metrical analysis have served literary scholarship and education in the past and can continue to do so in the future. They may also encourage and support versification in an age when much imaginative lit. has gravitated to prose or to forms of free verse that, though valuable and interesting in themselves, explore concepts and cadences outside the registers of traditional metrics. Perhaps most important of all, metrical analysis and scansion may help us keep poetry, even as we acknowledge its grandeurs and mysteries, connected with the modest but nourishing disciplines of rhet., grammar, logic, and phonetics.

See CLASSICAL PROSODY, ENGLISH PROSODY, METER, RELATIVE STRESS PRINCIPLE, RHYTHM, VERSE AND PROSE.

■ **History:** Bridges; G. L. Trager and H. L. Smith Jr., *An Outline of English Structure* (1951); Saintsbury, *Prosody*; Chomsky and Halle; R. Pfeiffer, *History of Classical Scholarship from the Beginnings to the End of the Hellenistic Age* (1968); Brogan; West; P. Werstine, "Line Division in Shakespeare's Dramatic Verse: An Editorial Problem," *Analytical and Enumerative Bibliography* 8 (1984); S. Woods, *Natural Emphasis* (1985); G. T. Wright, *Shakespeare's Metrical Art* (1988); J. Thompson, *The Founding of English Metre*, 2d ed. (1989); T. Cable, *The English Alliterative Tradition* (1991); L. D. Reynolds and N. G. Wilson,

*Scribes and Scholars*, 3d ed. (1991); B. O'Donnell, *The Passion of Meter* (1995); *English Historical Metrics*, ed. C. B. McCully and J. J. Anderson (1996); *Twentieth-Century American Poetics*, D. Gioia, D. Mason, and M. Schoerke, with D. C. Stone (2004).

■ **Criticism:** O. Jespersen, "Notes on Metre," *Linguistica* (1933); E. Pound, "A Retrospect," *Literary Essays of Ezra Pound*, ed. T. S. Eliot (1954); Y. Winters, "The Audible Reading of Poetry," *The Function of Criticism* (1957); M. Halpern, "On the Two Chief Metrical Modes in English," *PMLA* 77 (1962); V. Nabokov, *Notes on Prosody* (1964); W. K. Wimsatt and M. C. Beardsley, "The Concept of Meter," *Hateful Contraries* (1965); J. McAuley, *Versification* (1966); R. A. Hornsby, *Reading Latin Poetry* (1967); J. V. Cunningham, "How Shall the Poem Be Written?" *Collected Essays* (1976); *The Structure of Verse*, rev. ed., ed. H. Gross (1979); P. Fussell, *Poetic Meter and Poetic Form*, rev. ed. (1979); Attridge, *Rhythms*; T. Jefferson, "Thoughts on English Prosody," *Writings*, ed. M. D. Peterson (1984); J. Hollander, *Rhyme's Reason*, 2d ed. (1989); *Rhythm and Meter*, ed. P. Kiparsky and G. Youmans (1989); *Meter in English*, ed. D. Baker (1996); A. Corn, *The Poem's Heartbeat* (1997); R. Pinsky, *The Sounds of Poetry* (1998); T. Steele, *All the Fun's in How You Say a Thing* (1999); Finch and Varnes; S. Fry, *The Ode Less Travelled* (2005); D. Caplan, *Poetic Form* (2007); R. Frost, "The Figure a Poem Makes," *The Collected Prose of Robert Frost*, ed. M. Richardson (2007); M. D. Hurley, "The Pragmatics of Prosody," *Style* 41 (2007).

T. STEELE

**SCHEME.** A technical term from the cl. art of rhet., a *scheme* is a general category of figurative lang. that includes any artful deviation from the ordinary arrangement of words. Unlike *tropes, which work on the signification of words, schemes involve only their arrangement, as in this *chiasmus: "I do not live to eat, but eat to live." This syntactical rearrangement may take a variety of forms, incl. changes in word order (anastrophe), the omission or repetition of words (*asyndeton, *antimetabole), or the use of parallel or antithetical grammatical structures (*isocolon, *antithesis). The term derives from *schēma*, one of many Gr. words for outward "form" or "shape," which was used to name a general concept of perceptible form in the arts of rhet., grammar, logic, mathematics, and music (Auerbach). In antiquity, schemes were often divided into schemes of words and of thought (*schēmata lexeos* and *dianoias*), although rhetors rarely agreed on a list of schemes that alter verbal expression without altering thought as well. Cicero (*De oratore*) and the anonymous *Rhetorica ad Herennium* use *schēmata* to refer to the three levels of *style (grand, middle, simple), while Quintilian translates the term as *figura*, meaning "a configuration of language distinct from the common and immediately obvious form" (*Institutio oratoria*). In Lat. and vernacular rhets. after Quintilian, *scheme* becomes differentiated from its Lat. trans. (figura), becoming instead the term for a *kind* of rhetorical figure. Along with its counterpart *trope*, *scheme* persists as a subclassification of *figure* well into the 17th c., when it begins to fade from regular use in writing on rhet. and lit. Although structuralist ling. and deconstruction resuscitated rhet. as a hermeneutical code in the 20th c., *scheme* was not restored to regular use as a term of art, and it is now rarely used to speak about figurative lang. in rhet. or lit.

In distinguishing schēma from trope, Quintilian calls it "a purposeful deviation in sense or language from the ordinary simple form; the analogy is now with sitting, bending forwards, or looking back" (*Institutio oratoria*). Later analogies reinforce this distinction between inward meaning and outward form by comparing schemes to costume, clothing, and ornament. Cl. definitions of *scheme* thus rely on an idea of ordinary (naked, natural, or plain) speech that is then clothed by the figures of rhet. The discursive force of such *ornament varies throughout rhet.'s long hist., with schemes swelling in number and acquiring greater currency in courtly cultures that emphasize fashion, performance, or external show as constitutive of identity. In theories of rhet. and poetics informed by mod. ling., there is considerable skepticism toward the notion that there exists an "ordinary" lang. to be ornamented by figures of speech. Such theory concludes that rhetorical figures are not supplementary decorations but rather fundamental structures of lang. and thought (Jakobson, Derrida, de Man). Although this theory of figures as constitutive of, and coextensive with, lang. makes its exemplary arguments with reference to tropes such as *metaphor and *metonymy, it has resulted in a generalized critical method inclined to discover substantive meaning in the lexical patterns and shapes of what used to be called rhetorical schemes.

*See* FIGURATION, LINGUISTICS AND POETICS, RHETORIC AND POETRY.

■ Jakobson and Halle, "Two Aspects of Language and Two Types of Aphasic Disturbances"; E. Auerbach, "Figura," trans. R. Manheim, *Scenes from the Drama of European Literature* (1959); O. Ducrot and T. Todorov, *Encyclopedic Dictionary of the Sciences of Language*, trans. C. Porter (1979); G. Genette, *Figures of Literary Discourse*, trans. A. Sheridan (1981); T. Todorov, *Introduction to Poetics*, trans. R. Howard (1981); de Man, "The Rhetoric of Temporality" and "The Rhetoric of Blindness"; P. de Man, "Anthropomorphism and Trope in the Lyric," *The Rhetoric of Romanticism* (1984), and "Hypogram and Inscription" and "The Resistance to Theory," *The Resistance to Theory* (1986); J. Derrida, "White Mythology," *Margins of Philosophy*, trans. A. Bass (1986); Vickers, *Defence*; B. Dupriez, *A Dictionary of Literary Devices* (1991); Lanham; *Renaissance Figures of Speech*, ed. G. Alexander, S. Anderson, and K. Ettenhuber (2007); G. Burton, "Silva Rhetoricae," http://rhetoric. byu.edu.

J. C. MANN

**SCHOOL OF SPENSER.** A group of Eng. poets of the earlier 17th c., strongly under the influence of Edmund Spenser (1552–99). Their work is sharply distinguished from the more radical poetic movements of the time, epitomized by the *classicism of Ben Jonson and the *metaphysical style of John Donne. The principal poets of the Spenserian school—William Browne of Tavistock, Michael Drayton, George Wither, Giles and Phineas Fletcher, and the Scottish poets William Drummond of Hawthornden and Sir William Alexander—show the influence of Spenser in their sensuous imagery, smooth meter, archaic *diction, and fondness for narrative and *pastoral modes of expression. They also owe to Spenser their allegorical and moral tendencies. Such ambitious narrative poems as Giles Fletcher's *Christ's Victory and Triumph* and Phineas Fletcher's *The Apollyonists* suggest Spenser's *Faerie Queene* in their pictorial quality and their stanza forms (modified *Spenserian stanzas); they also anticipate John Milton, who, occasionally echoing the Fletchers, followed them in the use of Christian material for epic purposes and who himself acknowledged his indebtedness to Spenser, whom he called *master*.

■ H. E. Cory, *Spenser, the School of the Fletchers, and Milton* (1912); D. Bush, *English Literature in the Earlier Seventeenth Century, 1600–1660*, 2d ed. (1962); J. Grundy, *The Spenserian Poets* (1969); *The English Spenserians*, ed. W. B. Hunter Jr. (1977)—anthol.; P. J. Finkelpearl, "John Fletcher as Spenserian Playwright: *The Faithful Shepherdess* and *The Island Princess*," *SEL* 27 (1987); M. Quilligan, *Milton's Spenser* (1987); G. M. Bouchard, "Phineas Fletcher: The Piscatory Link between Spenserian and Miltonic Pastoral," *SP* 89 (1992).

A. PREMINGER; F. J. WARNKE

**SCHÜTTELREIM.** In Ger. verse, a rhyme, usually in a single line or couplet, that achieves witty and memorable effect by transposing the initial consonants of two words or syllables (in Ger., *schütteln* means "to shake"). Schüttelreim has existed since the 13th c. and was once considered a serious poetic form. Since the 19th c., however, it has been used as a comic verse form often of a lewd or suggestive nature. The sudden sound reversal lends itself well to humorous and satirical ends in Ger., e.g., "Als Gottes Atem leiser ging, schuf er den Grafen Keyserling" (attributed to Friedrich Gundolf), while it can also be found in proverbs. Among the shortest known schüttelreims are "Du bist Buddhist," and "Wo bist, Bovist?" Regine Mirsky-Tauber (*Schüttelreime*, 1904) and Anton Kippenberg have written entire cycles of *light verse in this form. The nearest equivalent in Eng. is the spoonerism, e.g., "You have hissed my mystery lecture; in fact, you have tasted a whole worm."

■ B. Papentrigk (pseud. of A. Kippenberg), *Schüttelreime* (1939); M. Hanke, *Die Schüttelreimer* (1968); *Franz Mittler: Gesammelte Schüttelreime*, ed. F. Torberg (1998).

T.V.F. BROGAN; U. K. GOLDSMITH; I. D. COPESTAKE

**SCIENCE AND POETRY**

   I. Science and Literary Theory
  II. The History of Science and Poetry
 III. Poetry versus Science

Poetry has had many different connections with science: mod. literary theories have defined themselves in terms of poetry's relation to science; poems have treated science and its social consequences as a theme for wonder, critique, or didactic transmission; science has made possible machines for writing and circulating poems, as well as medicine to alter the poet's mind and body; poetry has been used by many different theories to represent forms of thought contrasted both favorably and unfavorably with science; poets have protested the encroachment of natural and social sciences that assume exclusive rights to authoritative knowledge over domains where poetry formerly flourished; poetry has aspired to be the site of quasi-scientific inquiry; practicing scientists have written poetry and crit. of poetry; and enterprising poets and scientists have proposed scientific studies of poetry. These broad categories are not exhaustive. Levine cautions anyone trying to understand the hist. of science and lit. to recognize "the variousness and incompleteness of writers' and scientists' interrelations." One reason for this incompleteness is that poets are rarely scientists, nor do they have direct access to the nontextual hinterland of science that Hilary Putnam calls "unformalizable practical knowledge" (*Meaning and the Moral Sciences*, 1978). The singular noun *science* itself can be misleading because science is far from a unity, comprised as it is of a changing array of heterogeneous sciences. Its hist. stretches back at least 4,000 years, according to recent historians of science; it has roots in India, China, and Persia, as well as cl. civilization and Europe; and what counts as a science changes over time. Astrology was considered scientific in Isaac Newton's time, and race science was still being published in *Scientific American* in the 1960s. There have even been recurrent attempts to establish sciences of poetry; Roman Jakobson argues that structuralist poetics is part of the science of ling. (see LINGUISTICS AND POETICS).

While science claims epistemological priority over other forms of knowledge and methods for acquiring it, poetry has almost always been sharply limited in its epistemological and expressive scope, if not by science then by religion, society, or custom. Douglas Bush's study *Science and English Poetry* (1950) triangulates this hist. as poetry's struggle to decide between loyalty to imagination's spiritual values and acknowledgment of the truths produced by sciences that increasingly negated such values with their pictures of an animal humanity and a mechanistic universe. Later scholarship has confirmed and extended Bush's identification of a long hist. of poetic engagement with science, while revealing that the connections between science and theology have been extremely diverse and complex. Negotiating around the epistemic authority of science entails more than simply bearing witness to science's dominance. The emergence of positivism and other scientific transformations of formerly humanistic modes of inquiry has created even more complexity. Science's epistemological authority has presented poets with a range of choices: they can follow in a long trad. of verse that includes Persian botanical poets, the astronomical poets of India and China, and Lat. medical poetry and report the prior findings of science using poetic technique to make the knowledge memorable;

they can welcome the reception of scientific ideas and work for their cultural assimilation, as did the poets who celebrated Newton's achievement in the 18th c. and reconciled his insights with praise of the Creator who instigated these scientific laws; they can ally themselves with alternative worldviews against science, as Amiri Baraka does in his poem "Ka 'Ba" (1969), where Af. Americans are seen to be "defying physics in the stream of their will" by recovering the "magic" of their Af. heritage; they can directly resist the claims of science to universal knowledge; or they can lay claim to a poetic form of what Hejinian calls a "language of inquiry" and insist that poetry retains a valid cognitive capacity for research capable of standing up to the sciences. Poets faced with the authority of science can be synthesizers, cultural brokers, advocates of sheer imagination, or even researchers. What is hard to do is ignore science.

**I. Science and Literary Theory.** The ever-growing cultural centrality of science has meant that its relation to poetry is a significant part of the DNA of mod. literary theory. Many of our ideas can be traced back to the work of the Eng. rhetorician I. A. Richards and his attempts to reconcile literary crit. with logical positivism. His *Science and Poetry* (1926) offered a powerful summary of the apparent marginality of poetry in a scientific culture, arguing that it would appear that, in contrast to what Matthew Arnold believed, "the future of poetry is *nil*." Richards was an ambitious synthesizer who combined literary critical principles with Charles Sherrington's physiology of the impulses in the nervous system and the emerging philosophy of logical positivism, which equated the meaning of a statement with its method of verification. Poems, Richards concluded, can offer only simulacra of propositions or *"pseudostatements," "pseudo" because the truth of these statements depends not on verification but merely on "acceptability *by* some attitude." Scientific propositions require rigorous testing; poetic utterances require merely an emotional response.

The idea that science and poetry are inevitably in conflict was foundational for the *New Criticism. For the New Critics, poetry was built both on expressive *ironies that put the propositions in quotation marks and on structures of *affect that supplanted reasoning and, therefore, sidestepped any confrontation with the sciences. Cleanth Brooks announced in *Modern Poetry and the Tradition* (1939) that "all poetry since the middle of the seventeenth century has been characterized by the impingement of science upon the poet's world." This view became so widespread that even Crane, who attacked the New Criticism, agreed that the key question was how poetry could continue to justify itself in the face of science: "How, with science everywhere dominant and the method of science universally accepted as the one road to truth, can poetry still be made to seem a valuable and respectable form of mental activity, rather than merely a survival of prescientific modes of thought destined to disappear in the future?" (see CHICAGO SCHOOL). New Critical orthodoxy on this question was established by John

Crowe Ransom in *The World's Body* (1938) and *The New Criticism* (1941), where he argues (against Richards) that, far from being merely affective, the statements made in poetry are ontologically distinct from those of science. Poetry "treats an order of existence, a grade of objectivity, which cannot be treated in scientific discourse." He goes on: "[W]e live in a world which must be distinguished from the world, or the worlds, for there are many of them, which we treat in our scientific discourses. They are its reduced, emasculated, and docile versions. Poetry intends to recover the denser and more refractory original world which we know loosely through our perceptions and memories. By this supposition it is a kind of knowledge which is radically or ontologically distinct." The final chapter of *The New Criticism*, titled "Wanted: An Ontological Critic," posits a critic who would mount a thoroughgoing defense of poetic knowledge as different in nature from scientific knowledge. Mod. science gives us a logical structure for the world; poetry departs from, defers, and diffuses that structure, which "testifies to a diffuseness in the constitution of the world which we are undertaking to know." Ransom's doctrine made its way into the opening sentence of the next ed. of the most influential textbook for the teaching of poetry, Cleanth Brooks and Robert Penn Warren's *Understanding Poetry* (1960), which announced that "poetry gives us knowledge" (see KNOWLEDGE, POETRY AS).

The New Criticism drew a sharp line between science and poetry. Why should a more ambitious literary theory not develop its own science? *Structuralism offered this hope. Jakobson, in his key essay "Linguistics and Poetics," writes that "poetics deals with problems of verbal structure," and "since linguistics is the global science of verbal structure, poetics may be regarded as an integral part of linguistics." Poetics is a science, and major poets can be called scientists: G. M. Hopkins, for instance, is "an outstanding searcher in the science of poetic language." On the other hand, as structuralism begat *poststructuralism, Jakobson's confidence in poetics as a science gave way to a decentered view of knowledge that construed science as a kind of poetry. In practice, this meant that the natural sciences, and their appeals to truth, reality, and fact, could be treated as socially constructed discourses. Here was a new twist to Richards's idea that poetic propositions are pseudo-statements; now even scientific propositions were revealed as pseudo-statements. Thomas Kuhn's theory of scientific revolutions and the more radical stance of science studies were often enlisted to support this view, as was the apparent subjectivism of key ideas in physics such as Werner Heisenberg's uncertainty principle or Niels Bohr's theory of complementarity. A recent essay on Victorian science and poetry by Dawson and Shuttleworth, for instance, argues that science "is intrinsically and inextricably textual, and relies on the same rhetorical structures and tropes found in all other forms of writing, including poetry, as well as being subject to a corresponding instability of meaning." Can science be said to be *intrinsically* the same as poetry? Others contend that such claims create a gulf between

literary studies and most sciences, which are predicated on the belief that scientific knowledge offers a reliable account of a reality existing independently of observers and their lang. Levine believes the "science/literature dichotomy has got to be reimagined" so that we are not left treating either all science as poetry or all poetry as (bad) science.

**II. The History of Science and Poetry.** Cl. poets from Hesiod to Lucretius wrote extensively about subjects that would later become fields of scientific inquiry, such as medicine, astronomy, matter, and botany. Recent scholarship traces similar hists. of poetry in ancient and med. China, India, and the Middle East. Poetry was an effective form both for recording and transmitting knowledge; for learned writers such as Avicenna, it could be as appropriate for recording their own investigations as the short scientific essay is for scientists today. Christine van Ruymbeke introduces her account of *Science and Poetry in Medieval Persia* (2007) with an epigraph from the 12th-c. Ar. poet Niẓāmī that could be applied to many of these poets: the poet "must be well versed in many sciences and quick to pick up information from his environment; because, as much as poetry is of advantage in every science, so is every science of advantage in poetry." Dante and Chaucer both display considerable knowledge of contemp. sciences, notably astronomy. In Dante's *Paradiso*, the narrator sees different perspectives of the heavens, such as the "quattro cerchi giugne con tre croci" (1:39), the four great circles of the celestial sphere with three crosses formed by intersections of one circle with the others in the ninth Ptolemaic sphere. Cornish summarizes Dante's attitude: "the best kind of verse deserving the best language should also convey the best concepts arrived at through acquired knowledge (*scientia*) and innate genius (*ingenium*)."

Pierre Duhem claimed that mod. science began with Étienne Tempier's condemnation of Aristotelian doctrines in Paris in 1277, but its beginnings are more usually located in such events as the publication in one year, 1543, of both Nicolaus Copernicus's theory in *De revolutionibus orbis coelestium* that the earth orbited the sun and Andreas Vesalius's anatomy based on dissection. Copernicus's theory could be read as an adjustment of Ptolemaic astronomy, but the work of Johannes Kepler, Tycho Brahe (whose report on his astronomical observation of a supernova concluded with a poem in Lat., "Elegy to Urania"), and Galileo Galilei proved the validity of Copernican astronomy as a new cosmology. The power of the mechanical model to explain many features of the world and human life became increasingly evident. René Descartes' *Discourse on Method* (1637) presented a mechanical, corpuscular theory of the universe, incl. human bodies, though he thought the human capacity to talk and reason distinguished people from machines. William Harvey, trained in the Paduan trad., explained the circulation of the blood as a mechanical system in *An Anatomical Study of the Motion of the Heart and of the Blood in Animals* (1628). These new scientific texts did not appear antipoetic.

John Donne's poetry brilliantly conveys the excitement, confusion, and suspicion generated by the new natural philosophy. The "First Anniversarie" (1611) laments that "new philosophy calls all in doubt" and the cosmos is "crumbled out again to his atomies," while in the "Second Anniversarie" (1612), Donne begins to doubt the scope of the new knowledge: "Why grass is green, or why our blood is red / Are mysteries which none have reach'd unto." Like many 17th-c. poets, he recognizes the significance of the new sciences but maintains extensive references to older knowledges such as alchemy, astrology, magic, and Ptolemaic astronomy. Like Donne, John Milton hedges his bets, managing to balance the demands of competing Ptolemaic and Copernican alternatives. Still, Milton is generally up to date; his interest in color echoes the contemp. researches of Robert Boyle and others.

Early in the 17th c., Francis Bacon set out the necessary conditions for experimental science, ideas that eventually led to the founding of the Royal Society. Although he is often portrayed as an opponent of poetry, Bacon did find a niche for it within the production of knowledge even if it was "not tied to the laws of matter." In book two of *The Advancement of Learning* (1605), Bacon asserts that "the parts of human learning have reference to three parts of man's understanding, which is the seat of learning: history to his memory, poesy to his imagination and philosophy to his reason," conceding to poets their own role as part of a wider intellectual enterprise. The poet that Milton most admired after Edmund Spenser and Shakespeare, Abraham Cowley, was a founder of the Royal Society and wrote poems celebrating it; he thought poetry itself was a "divine science." The poets John Denham, John Dryden, and Edmund Waller were also members, although tensions between poetry and science were already evident. Jones notes that Thomas Sprat warned poets "that their interest is united with that of the Royal Society; and that if they shall decry the promoting of experiments they will deprive themselves of the most fertile subjects of fancy." Cowley's own poetry reveals the strain of trying not to be surprised by science. His comparing love to magnetism in *Davideis* (1656) is likely to strike mod. readers as demonstrating an inability to achieve a synthesis of poetry and science: "How is the *Loadstone*, Natures subtle pride, / By the rude *Iron* woo'd, and made a *Bride?*"

The establishment of the Royal Society and Newton's *Mathematical Principles of Natural Philosophy* (1687) were major devels. in the hist. of science. Newton offered mathematically formulated laws of gravitation and motion, giving natural philosophy seemingly unshakable foundations and showing incontrovertibly that science dealt with intangibles beyond the realm of the senses. His influence was enormous; he himself emblematized the new natural philosophy, and his ideas—about astronomy, motion, optics, electrical phenomena, and plant respiration—fascinated poets. Newton's physics became a favorite topic of poets incl. John Reynolds ("Death's Vision," 1709), Richard Blackmore ("The Creation," 1712), and James

Thomson, whose poem *The Seasons* (1730) has often been considered the great Eng. scientific poem of the 18th c. He describes a rainbow in Newtonian terms as the "showery Prism" shining out of "The various twine of light, by thee disclos'd / From the white mingling Maze" ("Spring," 2.209–12). Poets read Newton, however, scarcely more than most poets today have read Albert Einstein's mathematical accounts of relativity or Heisenberg's scientific papers. Poets learned their science from popularizers, and the great majority of these early in the century wrote from a religious standpoint. Typical was William Derham, whose "Physicotheology" gave a name to this praise of science for revealing the wonderful complexities of a world created by a benevolent God.

Women found it esp. difficult to gain access to scientific training, and Mary Leapor ended "The Enquiry" (pub. posthumously in 1748) by saying that a poet trying to follow natural philosophy and hist. "has need of Judgment better taught than mine" (2.84–7). Her honesty about difficulties understanding the new natural philosophy is a reminder that 18th-c. poets rarely had firsthand expertise. This may partly be why poets had little to say about a science central to the Enlightenment, chemistry, and such crucial steps as the discovery of oxygen and the overthrow of the phlogiston theory by Antoine Lavoisier and others. Chemistry was hard to grasp without direct experience of experimental practice and perhaps offered fewer figures for human experience than Newtonian physics or biology. Not all poets found science relevant. Samuel Johnson speaks for many poets (and critics) before and since when he insists in his "Life of Milton" (1779) that learning about science is not worth the effort: "the truth is that the knowledge of external nature, and the sciences which that knowledge requires or includes, are not the great or the frequent business of the human mind. . . . [W]e are perpetually moralists, but we are geometricians only by chance."

Natural hist. gradually replaced the Newtonian sublime of astronomy and theology in poetry from mid-century on. Poems such as George Ritson's "Kew Gardens" (1763), Henry Jones's "Kew Garden" (1767), and John Dalton's "A Descriptive Poem, addressed to Two Ladies at their Return from Viewing the Mines near Whitehaven" (1755) offered extensive observations on plants and the natural landscape (see LANDSCAPE POEM). Erasmus Darwin's long poem "The Temple of Nature" (1803) aims to explain "how rose from elemental strife / Organic forms" in a theory of evolution, set out in rhymed *couplets, that helped inspire his grandson Charles Darwin.

A long trad. defines *romanticism as utterly opposed to science. An instance would be William Blake's prophetic vision of science as a partner to tyranny in the form of Urizen forming universal laws "in books formed of metals" and Blake's famous picture of Newton turning his back on the beauty of the world to measure with compasses. Perhaps the most cited response to science written by any poet appears in William Wordsworth's "The Tables Turned" (1798): "Sweet is the lore which Nature brings / Our meddling intellect / Misshapes the beauteous forms of things:—/ We murder to dissect." Recent historians have convincingly shown that this is a one-sided view; the romantic poets were broadly receptive to the sciences of their day, and, when they were critical of science, it was often technology that elicited hostility. Anna Barbauld watched many of Joseph Priestley's laboratory experiments; Lord Byron tested William Herschel's telescope for himself and met Humphry Davy several times; Davy wrote competent poetry and discussed connections between science and poetry with his early friend Robert Southey; and S. T. Coleridge, also a close friend of Davy, attended the meeting of the British Association for the Advancement of Science when the term *scientist* was first used to replace the older designation *natural philosopher* ("by analogy with *artist*," according to its proposer William Whewell). In the second ed. of *Lyrical Ballads* (1800), Wordsworth made a famous declaration that comes much closer to the romantics' attitude toward science than his idea of the "meddling intellect" (though the dissonance between these statements is a reminder of how complex their reactions were):

> If the labours of men of science should ever create any material revolution, direct or indirect, in our condition, and in the impressions which we habitually receive, the poet will sleep then no more than at present; he will be ready to follow the steps of the man of science, not only in those general indirect effects, but he will be at his side, carrying sensation into the midst of the objects of science itself. The remotest discoveries of the chemist, the botanist, or mineralogist, will be as proper objects of the poet's art as any upon which it can be employed.

Wordsworth's poetry bears out his belief in many informed references to contemp. researches.

P. B. Shelley was a keen amateur scientist, and an atheist, whose poems such as *Prometheus Unbound* (1820) draw on chemistry and astronomy. Inspired by the discoveries of the astronomer Herschel, he argues in notes to "Queen Mab" (1813) that the "indefinite immensity of the universe" made it impossible to believe in a Christianity based on events local to one tiny planet, and in "Essay on a Future State" (1819), he uses scientific knowledge to dismiss the idea of resurrection. None of the Eng. poets went as far, however, as the Ger. poet and scientist J. W. Goethe, who believed that science had developed from poetry and who saw himself as much a scientist—interested in morphology, optics, theory of color, geology, mineralogy, and meteorology—as a poet. He was committed to the view that humanity was embedded in the natural world and that knowledge and experience formed a totality, a belief articulated in "Die Metamorphose der Pflanzen": "Alle Gestalten sind ähnlich, und keine gleichet der andern; / Und so deutet das Chor auf ein geheimes Gesetz, / Auf ein heiliges Rätsel. Oh könnt' ich dir, liebliche Freundin, / Überliefern sogleich glücklich das lösende

Wort!" (All forms are alike but not identical, and thus they point to a secret law, a sacred mystery. If only I could pass it on to you, sweet friend, the crucial word that solves it [1790]). But even Goethe could not manage to become both a great scientist and a great poet and, though friendly with scientists of his time, was not treated as a scientist of the same rank as he was a poet, partly because of his belief in such ideas as the ur-plant.

Science expanded enormously in the 19th c., as chemistry provided bountiful opportunities for new industries and as physics, guided by J. C. Maxwell, Hermann von Helmholtz, Ernst Mach, and Michael Faraday, made it possible to control the energies of electricity, magnetism, and heat to the extent that human and animal labor would cease to be the main source of power. Charles Baudelaire's famous remark in a letter to Alphonse Toussenel in 1856 calling the *imagination "that most scientific of faculties" is as much a tacit acknowledgment of these changes as of any residual belief in the preeminence of poetry. Charles Darwin's theory of evolution demonstrated how powerful the scientific imagination had become, providing new and powerful metaphors of life and death that challenged religious certainties and constructed foundations for biology that would prove as durable as Newton's contribution to physics. Alfred, Lord Tennyson's poetry decisively registers the end of the natural theology characteristic of the later 18th c. and still prevalent in romantic poetry. *In Memoriam* (1850) makes extensive reference to the sciences of his time, incl. Charles Lyell's uniformitarian geology, Pierre-Simon Laplace's nebular hypothesis, and Robert Chambers's precursory theory of evolution; but the poem's strongest sentiment about science is pessimistic. If science thinks it can prove that humans are merely "clay," then "What matters Science unto men / At least to me?" (120.5–8). Instead of the uplifting visions seen by 18th-c. poets, Nature now reveals fossils that show its true colors: "A thousand types are gone: / I care for nothing, all shall go" (56.1–8).

G. M. Hopkins was one of the last Eng. poets able to work out a reconciliation of science, poetry, and religion. At the university, he was exposed to new scientific discoveries, incl. the energy physics of John Tyndall and the chemistry of the atmosphere. Clouds and sunlight form a heat engine in "nature's bonfire" in the sonnet "That Nature Is a Heraclitean Fire and of the Comfort of the Resurrection" (1888), and Beer (1992) aptly describes the poet as "beset by entropy and azure, delighted by optics and acoustics, and roused to combat and to embrace caprice." Signs of the future for poetry and science are evident in Thomas Hardy, whose melancholic vision of the natural world as a scene of struggle for survival yields no consolation to poetry.

The very name *modernist* underlines one of the most striking yet paradoxical features of 20th-c. poetry's relations with science. To be mod. was in part to be scientific. The very first thing that Ezra Pound tells his readers in his poetry textbook *The ABC of Reading* (1934) is that this is an "age of science"; In "A Collect of Philosophy" (1951) Wallace Stevens looks back over his career and tells his audience that the physicist Max Planck, the founder of quantum theory, is a "truer symbol of ourselves" than a philosopher or a poet; T. S. Eliot espouses impersonality in poetry because "it is in this depersonalization that art may be said to approach the condition of science." Walter Pater thought all art strove to achieve the pure form of music. Now some poets take for granted that science is the true model for poetry, and scholars such as Whitworth, Albright, and Tiffany have shown how readily modernist poets used scientific metaphors and models as a lang. for their poetics. Yet despite brave statements about the importance of science in their essays, these poets did not have so much to say explicitly in their poetry: Pound mentions only two mod. scientists, the Curies, and then somewhat dismissively; and Stevens's own poetic landscapes are filled with unscientifically conceived plants, animals, trees, and winds, nor is there any sign of the laboratories or technologies that might evoke the spirit of Planck. In "Cape Hatteras" from his *long poem *The Bridge* (1930), Hart Crane manages to ask explicitly whether the products of science will "carve us / Wounds that we wrap with theorems sharp as hail" and poses a question that touches on the broad issue of how science changes the life-world: he asks, "tell me, Walt Whitman, if infinity / Be still the same as when you walked the beach." The answer to this rhetorical question would have been no: Georg Cantor's mathematics had revealed new infinities. Many poets wrote about Einstein (W. C. Williams jokingly called him Saint Einstein) the way predecessors wrote about Newton. What is probably the best of these, Archibald MacLeish's poem "Einstein" (1929), imagines the scientist's own inner-world picture of life in a space-time comprised of nothing but the new forces and particles. As a poetic solution to the problem of how to represent the new science of relativity and quantum theory, the poem faces the same difficulties as Crane's. Whitman cannot know whether infinity has changed, nor can the surreal visions experienced by the Einstein of MacLeish's poem tell us anything authoritative about the theory of relativity. Neither poem knows how to engage with the methods, ontologies, and epistemological claims of the new sciences, other than by imagining a suffering subjectivity. Stevens is arguably more successful, because he follows out rigorously the implications of living in a world without teleology, a world of nothing more than matter in space and time, where imagination's subjective coloring needs to be erased in the attempt to "find the real" ("Notes Toward A Supreme Fiction," 1942).

Instead of trying imaginatively to inhabit the new world of the scientist as their predecessors might have done, some mod. poets step sideways and think of poetry as a possible scene of investigation similar to science. Science may be too complex and elusive to picture directly, but surely some of its methods and aims may be borrowed. Perhaps the poet can perform experiments? Eliot talks of the poet's mind as similar to the platinum in a test tube of oxygen and sulfur dioxide, Pound likens the critical comparison of pas-

sages of verse to the scientist's comparing microscope slides, and critics have thought that Gertrude Stein was scientific in the way she treated writing as a space for experiment. John Dewey gave credence to this idea in *Art as Experience* (1934), saying that the artist is an experimenter who is "as unsatisfied with what is established as is a geographic explorer or a scientific inquirer." Mina Loy's poem "Gertrude Stein" (written 1924) calls her "Curie / of the laboratory / of vocabulary" investigating the "radium of the word" (Gottfried Benn also spoke of the "Laboratorium für Worte"). Experiment could also lead to broader models of inquiry in which poets might observe the natural world (D. H. Lawrence's *Birds, Beasts, and Flowers*, 1923), inquire into past models of government and ethics (Pound's *Cantos*, 1925–72), or test verbal etymologies for their psychological insight (H.D.'s *Trilogy*, 1944–46). As these examples suggest, the forms of poetic inquiry involved, while they were influenced by the example of the success of the natural sciences, might diverge from the construction of testable hypotheses that characterizes natural science, though affinities with the social sciences may be more evident.

Over the course of the century, poets became increasingly engaged in writing directly about science for many reasons: the world wars, better scientific education, and a more sophisticated philosophical and historical understanding of science. World War II and its nuclear technology compelled poets opposed to nuclear deterrence to learn more about science. Scientific jours. aimed at the intelligent reader became more widely available, and controversies among scientists, whether over cloning, Darwinism, or climate change, have become staples of very public debate. The scientific rhet. of Charles Olson's essay *"Projective Verse" (1950) and the manifestos of *Language poetry only accelerated the trend.

Other Western lits. have had active mod. trads. of interrelations between science and poetry that can be mentioned only briefly here. The Fr. poet Paul Valéry had a lifelong interest in science and mathematics and even applied his understanding of group theory to his concepts of the aesthetic object. In Ger., Paul Celan extensively mined discursive connections between geology and physiology in his metaphors as in the poems "Schliere" ("Streaks," 1959) or "Entwurf einer Landschaft" ("Projection of a Landscape," 1958). This type of engagement then became a live question among a number of late 20th-c. Ger. poets such as Raoul Schrott, Hans Magnus Enzensberger, Thomas Kling, Ulrike Draesner, Brigitte Oleschinski, Durs Grünbein, and others. Enzensberger published the essay "Die Poesie der Wissenschaft" ("The Poetry of Science," 2002), claiming that supposed connections between the aims of science and the imagination of poetry were just *Zufallsbekanntschaften* (chance acquaintances), while others such as Schrott believe this consonance a sign of a *Wahlverwandtschaft* (echoing Goethe's idea of elective affinities or chemical bonds). Similar preoccupations can be found in Sp.-lang. poetry, notably the Nicaraguan Ernesto Cardenal's *Cántico cósmico* (*Cosmic Can-*

*ticle*, 1989). The Scottish poet Robert Garioch ("The Muir," 1955), the Brit. poet J. H. Prynne (*Wound Response*, 1974), and the Am. Jena Osman ("The Periodic Table as Assembled by Dr Zhivago, Oculist," 1999) have all written poems that question scientific nationalisms, expose the values in scientific discourse, or work directly with scientific lit. Westerners are now "geometricians of nature," and images of the universe largely come from science rather than religion: nuclear particles and forces construct our world, genes encode our bodies, and we are encouraged to think of ourselves as mites on a small sphere in a huge cosmos. The Brit. poet Allen Fisher, author of *Brixton Fractals* (1985), probably overstates the case when he says that "a poet's attitude and understanding of quantum field theory will affect the poet's experience of gravity, drawing, and reading," but he is surely right that, for most poets writing in the 21st c., scientifically derived beliefs about the universe increasingly direct poetic vision.

**III. Poetry versus Science.** This hist. of poetic treatments of science raises many issues. Should poetry's relation to technology be considered an integral part of this hist.? Why has poetry been treated by philosophers and scientists as an abstraction representing a type of cognition variously to be praised or derided, and how has this treatment affected poetry and poetics? Many 20th-c. poets have responded to the encroachments of the natural and social sciences by emulating features of scientific inquiry. How valid are these attempts, and do they have antecedents in earlier poetry? Besides these questions, the hist. of poetic accounts of science often leaves out two further issues of importance. The scientific study of poetry, ranging from dubious rationalizations of *prosody to highly respectable empirical experiments on the brains of poetry readers, has a long and culturally significant hist. both inside and outside literary studies. And the hist. of poetry excludes as marginal most of the poetry and poetry crit. written by scientists themselves, although this activity is part of the cultural-historical relations of science and poetry.

Should we treat poems about technology, such as a poem by W. C. Williams about the then relatively new experience of driving, as scientific poems? This remains a contentious issue among philosophers, historians, and scientists themselves. In an essay on "Contemporary Science and the Poets" pub. in *Science* in 1954, J. Z. Fullmer, a chemist, dismissed mod. poems that mistakenly "equate the products of applied science with science itself" in favor of poems by Eliot, MacLeish, Robert Frost, and Marianne Moore that address pure science as "an attitude, a method, a point of view." When Williams (a doctor and, therefore, one of the very few scientifically trained poets) in his preface to *The Wedge* (1944) calls the poem a "small (or large) *machine* made of words," he asserts that the poem is a technology and, therefore, scientific (emphasis added). Tichi argues that Williams's poems "are unmistakably occasioned by the machine age in which acceleration in the pace of living had become a cultural commonplace and the machine a constant presence in everyday life," making an assumption about the close connection between poetry and technology that could be extrapolated to earlier and later lit. hists. If, therefore, we consider technology to be an inalienable element of the hist. of science, then the rich trad. of poems about optic glasses, satanic mills, loaded guns, express trains, the Titanic, big cars, the "hydrogen jukebox," and triodes are part of the story of science and poetry.

Another feature of the story is the long hist. of treating poetry and science as contraries. F.W.J. Schelling called the universe a poem and so implicitly treated science as a branch of poetry. Such optimism has been the exception; poetry is more usually treated as the antithesis of science and often as a shorthand for this opposition in a manner that has significant consequences for the self-image of poetry and poetics. Newton called poetry "ingenious nonsense"; the quantum physicist Erwin Schrödinger (who also wrote poetry, though the poet Stefan Zweig told him that he hoped his physics was better than his poetry) compared poetic imagination unfavorably with the sober clarity of scientific thought. Such comments have circulated widely and take a toll on the status of poetry. Even the geneticist and poet Miroslav Holub, who values poetry highly and writes with great clarity about science and poetry, still treats them as antithetical: "the scientific theme implies as much light as possible, the poetic one as many shadows as possible" (*The Dimension of the Present Moment*, 1990). The contrast of light and shadow implies a familiar negative hierarchy. The philosopher of science Wesley Salmon expresses the now-conventional view of science as almost the negation of poetry: "what makes a scientific world-picture superior to a mythic or religious or poetic world-view" is that "we have much better reason to regard that world-view as true" ("Scientific Explanation," 1990). W. H. Auden memorably expressed the effects of such disdain in *The Dyer's Hand* (1962): "When I find myself in the company of scientists, I feel like a shabby curate who has strayed by mistake into a drawing room full of dukes."

However, not all poets and thinkers grant intellectual authority to science. Martin Heidegger argues that mod. science forgets Being and insists that we have to look to poetry as the place where "language speaks" and Being can still manifest itself. In *Science and Poetry* (2001), the philosopher Mary Midgley calls for the imaginative vision of poetry to counterbalance the "over-exaltation of science," and her insistence that science is not "a central government under which both poetry and philosophy are minor agencies" has affinities with Richard Rorty's call for our "scientized" culture to be "poeticized" (*Contingency, Irony, and Solidarity*, 1989). Midgley has almost nothing to say about actual poems and poets; poetry functions as a place-holder for a general mode of being, as it does in much of the metadiscourse of science.

Since at least the 17th c., poets have feared the encroachment of science, and although this perceived threat has taken many forms, three stand out: science's indifference to human values, science's failure to recognize the truths of poetic imagination, and science's claims to exclusive methodological access to truth. The first two were recurrent themes in the hist. of science and poetry discussed earlier. What are the consequences of science's claims to exclusive access to the methods of producing reliable knowledge? The Am. poet and philosopher Emily Grosholz argues in Kurt Brown's collection *The Measured Word* (2001) that poetry risks handing "the discursive, systematic, and objective over to science" and retreating into a zone "that is relentlessly subjective, hermetic, and fragmentary." One strategy of resistance to science's expansionism is to insist on poetry's own rights to inquiry.

Explicitly epistemological preoccupations with the natural world, anthropology, government, and cultural memory inspire *invention in many poets, and increasingly so in the 20th c. Charles Bernstein writes in his poetic essay "Artifice of Absorption" (1987) that poetry must recognize its capacity for "epistemological inquiry," because otherwise it will "cede meaning" to what he calls "the hegemony of restricted / epistemological economies." This implies that poets could aspire to work on more equal terms with science. The art critic Stephen Wilson explains in *Information Arts* (2002) what it might mean for visual artists, arguing that if they are prepared to learn the science, artists can "explore technological and scientific frontiers" and even explore regions scientists are not able to study, tracing out "different inquiry pathways, conceptual frameworks, and cultural associations than those investigated by scientists and engineers." What might this mean for poets?

The Am. poet Alice Fulton offers a possible strategy: "I often lift scientific language for my own wayward purposes. That isn't to say I play fast and loose with denoted meanings. I'm as true to the intentions of science as my knowledge allows. But my appropriations from science are entwined with other discourses, other ideas" (*Feeling as a Foreign Language*, 1999). Many poets have done this. Muriel Rukeyser's *The Life of Poetry* (1949), which offers one of the most original mod. accounts of the interdependence of science and poetry, argues that this strategy of appropriation can be self-limiting if not informed by an understanding of the science behind the rhet. Poets trying to respond adequately to new scientific conceptions face a "trap . . . the use of the discoveries of science instead of the methods of science." Exhibiting scientific lang. and discoveries in poems can be restrictive; poets ought to try to develop forms of investigation informed by current scientific practices. One strategy adopted by poets has been to draw out the implications of scientific metaphors. In *Open Fields*, Beer eloquently justifies this process of linguistically focused inquiry: "new scientific and technical knowledge allows the poet to contemplate with fresh intensity intransigent questions which grip language in all generations." Support for poetry comes from philosophers of science such as Ernan McMullin, who share this belief that *metaphor is central to innovation and draw parallels between poetic metaphors and the use of models in scientific theory. A productive model of the object of scientific study is one that hints at possible improvements to the theory; similarly, a complex poetic metaphor also helps us begin to grasp new facets of something not yet well understood.

Metaphor is only one mode that scientifically aware poetic inquiry takes. As we saw in the case of *modernism, experiment is another. Reports of sustained, rigorous observation of self, nature, lang., and society are another. Denise Levertov offers one of the best statements of this in her poem "O Taste and See" (1964), where her remedy for estrangement, the sense that "The world is / not with us enough," is heightened sensory and cognitive attention represented by metaphors of ingestion. This poem, with its enveloping trad. of observation reaching back to the 18th c., is a rejoinder to the authoritative claims by physics to know that the world is made of invisible and intangible atomic particles. To sum up, the challenge for poets and critics is to understand the diversity of methods in the sciences without treating them as exhausting the possibilities of a poetics of inquiry.

The inverse of emulation is *parody. Implicit in the discussion so far is a certain respect toward science, usually a mix of awe, wonder, and critique. Ridicule is relatively rare because of the authority of science (Jonathan Swift's cucumbers are unusual), but one intermittent 20th-c. literary movement turned mockery into a full-scale genre of its own. 'Pataphysics originated with the Fr. writer Alfred Jarry, who proposed that 'pataphysics extended "as far beyond metaphysics as the latter extends beyond physics"; in Christian Bök's words, 'pataphysics questions the authority of science "by becoming its hyperbolic extreme." Its most prominent mod. exponent was probably the Fr. poet Raymond Queneau (*Petite cosmogonie portative*, 1950), but it continues to influence new generations of poets. The literary group *Oulipo, known for generative formulas (such as *acrostics and *lipograms) used in a spirit of ludic investigation, has roots in 'pataphysics, as does the work of other poets such as the Brazilian Eduardo Kac, and of artworks that merge science and aesthetics. 'Pataphysics may abandon all pretense that poetry can make a serious contribution to knowledge the way science does, but it then manages to reveal new possibilities for investigation that hint that this too may be an extrapolated mode of inquiry.

Scientists themselves have also been critics, readers, writers, and even experimental researchers of poetry. Darwin found poetry difficult but owed a conceptual as well as stylistic debt to his reading of Milton and Shakespeare. Such cross-pollination in mod. science is still an under-researched area of the mod. hist. of science. The poet, chemist, and Nobel laureate Roald Hoffmann strikingly attributes his insights into the geometry of protein folding to his love of the arts: "I have no problem doing (or trying to do) both science and poetry. Both emerge from my attempt to understand the universe around me" ("How I Work as Poet and Scientist," 1988). Scientists have rarely been significant poets in their own right: Goethe, Davy, and Holub are exceptions. But success as a poet is not necessarily the most important measure of the contribution of scientists to poetry; the mere involvement of scientists in poetry has contributed to its hist. Literary jours. have a long hist. of publishing essays by scientists aimed at the literary world. Less recognized is that scientific jours. also have a long trad. of publishing essays about poetry. In the 1930s, for instance, *The Scientific Monthly* offered articles on color and insects in poetry, followed later in the decade by others on "Poetry of the Rocks" and "Poetry and Astronomy."

The Ger. philosopher and historian Wilhelm Dilthey famously talked of a *science* of poetry. Many attempts have been made to provide a science based in mathematics or the natural sciences. In 1845, a "poetry-making machine" called Eureka that could generate sequences of randomly chosen words to form poetic lines was exhibited in London, an early popular manifestation (according to Hall) of a would-be "prosodic science," exemplified by Sidney Lanier's unabashedly titled *Science of English Verse* (1880). Scientists have used a changing array of mathematics, kymographs, machines for graphing vocal frequency, MRI scanners, cognitive science, and computer spectrography to investigate the material effects of reading poetry. Douglas Oliver is one of the few poets to have written extensively about the use of sonic analysis to study oral prosody, though he is revealingly coy about crediting the technology with authority when employing it to challenge F. R. Leavis's claim that Milton treats "language as a kind of musical medium outside himself": "A passage of *Paradise Lost*, examined by machine, can show that the music is by no metaphorical stretch 'outside' Milton, nor lacking in the most subtle currents of feeling and sensation. This time again, the machinery is being used only as objective evidence of my personal interpretation of the verse music."

The hist. of science and poetry presents a fast-changing picture. Louis Zukofsky's claim that poets are not in the least surprised by science encapsulates much of the hist. of the relation between poetry and science. Science continues to develop, surprise, and confirm prejudices among poets. New scientific insights also act retroactively on our understanding of the past. Sociology, hist., and philosophy of science are also rapidly evolving and indirectly helping reveal new aspects of the complex interrelations of science and poetry. Poets appear to be immersing themselves in science more than ever, and they too are changing our sense of the hist. and possibilities in science and poetry.

*See* COGNITIVE POETICS; FRACTAL VERSE; KNOWLEDGE, POETRY AS; NATURE; PHILOSOPHY AND POETRY; TECHNOLOGY AND POETRY.

■ **Anthologies, Bibliographies, and Reference Works**: *Imagination's Other Place: Poems of Science and Mathematics*, ed. Helen Plotz (1955); *Poems of Science*, ed. J. Heath-Stubbs and P. Salman (1984); R. S. Scholnick, "Bibliography: American Literature and Science through 1989," *American Literature and Science*, ed. R. S. Scholnick (1992); *A Quark for Mister Mark: 101 Poems about Science*, ed. M. Riordan and J. Turney (2000); *Encyclopedia of Literature and Science*, ed. P. Gossin (2002); British Council, "Hunting Down the Universe" (science and literature bibliography, 2003), downloadable from www.britishcouncil.org/revisedhunting_down_the_universe1.doc; *Signs and Humours: The Poetry of Medicine*, ed. L. Greenlaw (2007); *Dark Matter: Poems of Space*, ed. M. Riordan and J. B. Burnell (2008).

■ **Criticism, History, and Theory**: C. A. Fusil, *La Poésie scientifique de 1750 à nos jours* (1917); G. R. Stewart Jr., "Color in Science and Poetry," *Scientific Monthly* 30 (1930); R. Crum, *Scientific Thought in Poetry* (1931); L. Stevenson, *Darwin among the Poets* (1932); A. M. Schmidt, *La Poésie scientifique en France au 16e siècle* (1938); A. Gode, *Natural Science in German Romanticism* (1941); C. H. Waddington, *The Scientific Attitude* (1941); S. I. Hayakawa, "Poetry and Science," *English Institute Annual—1942* (1943); J. B. Conant, "The Advancement of Learning in the United States in the Post-War World," *Science* 2562 (1944); M. H. Nicolson, *Newton Demands the Muse* (1946); R. S. Crane, "Cleanth Brooks: Or, the Bankruptcy of Critical Monism," *MP* 45 (1948); N. H. Pearson, "The American Poet in Relation to Science," *American Quarterly* 1 (1949); H. H. Waggoner, *The Heel of Elohim* (1950); H. Levy and H. Spalding, *Literature for an Age of Science* (1952); E. Larrabee, "Science, Poetry, and Politics," *Science* 3042 (1953); B. I. Evans, *Literature and Science* (1954); W. C. Williams, "The Poem as a Field of Action," *Selected Essays* (1954); K. Svendsen, *Milton and Science* (1956); *The New American Poetry 1945–1960*, ed. D. Allen (1960); W. Curry, *Chaucer and the Medieval Sciences* (1960); P. Ginestier, *The Poet and the Machine*, trans. M. Friedman (1961); G. E. McSpadden, "New Light on Speech Rhythms from Jorge Guillén's Reading of His Poem *Gran Silencio* (Based on Measurements of Sound Spectrograms)," *HR* 30 (1962); D. Davie, *The Language of Science and the Language of Literature* (1963); W. P. Jones, *The Rhetoric of Science* (1966); H. R. Jauss, "Paradigmawechsel in der Literaturwissenschaft," *Linguistische Berichte* 1 (1969); *Mathematik und Dichtung*, ed. H. Kreutzer and R. Gunzenhauser, 4th ed. (1971); K. Richter, *Literatur und Naturwissenschaft* (1972); D. Ault, *Visionary Physics* (1974); I.F.A. Bell, *Critic as Scientist* (1981); Jakobson; N. K. Hayles, *The Cosmic Web* (1984); D. Oliver, *Poetry and Narrative in Performance* (1989); J. Roubaud, "Mathematics in the Method of Raymond Queneau," *Oulipo* (1986); F. Turner, "Space and Time in Chinese Verse," *Time, Science, and Society in China and the West*, ed. J. T. Fraser, N. Lawrence, F. C. Haber (1986); *In the American Tree*, ed. R. Silliman (1986); L. M. Steinman, *Made in America* (1987); C. Tichi, *Shifting Gears* (1987); R. Hoffman, "How I Work as Poet and Scientist," *The Scientist* (March 21, 1988); W. Lepenies and B. Harshav, "Between Social Science and Poetry in Germany," *PoT* 9 (1988); S. M. Fallon, *Milton among the Philosophers* (1991); E. Lamadrid, "The Quantum Poetics of Ernesto Cardenal," *Ometeca* 2 (1991); G. Beer, "Helmholtz, Tyndall, Gerard Manley Hopkins," *Comparative Criticism* 13 (1992); H. T. Crawford, *Modernism, Medicine, and William Carlos Williams* (1993); D. Albright, *Quantum Poetics* (1997); D. Brown, *Hopkins' Idealism: Philosophy, Physics, Poetry* (1997); J. Alder, "The Aesthetics of Magnetisation: Science, Philosophy, and Poetry in the Dialogue Between Goethe and Schelling," *The Third Culture: Literature and Science*, ed. E. S. Shaffer (1998); C. Altieri, "The Concept of Force as Modernist Response to the Authority of Science," *Modernism/Modernity* 5 (1998); T. Armstrong, *Modernism, Technology, and the Body* (1998); S. Peterfreund, *William Blake in a Newtonian World* (1998); J. Rogers, *The Matter of Revolution: Science, Poetry, and Politics in the Age of Milton* (1998); C. Andrews, *Poetry and Cosmology* (1999); S. Carter, *Bearing Across* (1999); K. L. Edwards, *Milton and the Natural World* (1999); A. Fisher, "The Poetics of the Complexity Manifold," *Boundary 2* 26 (1999); H. Groth, "Victorian Women's Poetry and Scientific Narratives," *Gender and Genre*, ed. I. Armstrong and V. Blain (1999); D. Brown, "Victorian Poetry and Science," *The Cambridge Companion to Victorian Poetry*, ed. J. Bristow (2000); A. Cornish, *Reading Dante's Stars* (2000); L. Hejinian, *The Language of Inquiry* (2000); M. N. McLane, *Romanticism and the Human Sciences* (2000); D. Tiffany, *Toy Medium* (2000); K. Brown, *The Measured Word* (2001); S. Meyer, *Irresistible Dictation: Gertrude Stein and the Correlations of Writing and Science* (2001); R. J. Owen, "Science in Contemporary Poetry," *German Life and Letters* 54 (2001); R. Sobel and G. Elata, "The Problems of Seeing and Saying in Medicine and Poetry," *Perspectives in Biology and Medicine* 44 (2001); M. H. Whitworth, *Einstein's Wake* (2001); C. Bök, '*Pataphysics* (2002); *From Energy to Information*, ed. B. Clarke and L. D. Henderson (2002); L. Irigaray, *To Speak Is Never Neutral*, trans. G. Schwab (2002); T. Rajan, *Deconstruction and the Remainders of Phenomenology* (2002); C. J. Cavanaugh, "Reading Lorca through the Microscope," *Hispania* 86 (2003); G. Dawson and S. Shuttleworth, "Introduction: Science and Victorian Poetry," *VP* 41.1 (2003)—spec. iss.; C. Gruber, *Literatur, Kultur, Quanten* (2003); E. G. Wilson, *The Spiritual History of Ice* (2003); *Science and Literature in Italian Culture*, ed. P. Antonello and S. A. Gilson (2004); F. De Bruyn, "Reading Virgil's Georgics as a Scientific Text," *ELH* 71 (2004); G. P. Nabhan, *Cross-Pollinations* (2004); S. P. Sondrup, "Against Two Cultures: Östen Sjöstrand and the Poetry of QED," *Cybernetic Ghosts*, ed. D. M. Figueira (2004); M. Brady, "Galileo in Action: The 'Telescope' in *Paradise Lost*," *Milton Studies* 44 (2005); R. Richards, *The Romantic Conception of Life* (2004); N. Roberts, "The Science of the Subjective: An Interview with Peter Redgrove," http://www.liv.ac.uk/poetryandscience/essays/science-subjective.htm (2005); K. Blair, *Victorian Poetry and the Culture of the Heart* (2006); R. Crawford, *Contemporary Poetry and Contemporary Science* (2006); E. E. Langley, "Anatomizing the early-modern eye," *Renaissance Studies* 20 (2006); R. Tobias, *The Discourse of Nature in the Poetry of Paul Celan* (2006); P. Coleman, *On Literature and Science* (2007); J. Gillies, "Space and Place in *Paradise Lost*," *ELH* 74 (2007); M. Golston, *Rhythm and Race in Modernist Poetry and Science* (2007); J. D. Hall, "Popular Prosody: Spectacle and the Politics of Victorian Versification," *Nineteenth-Century Literature* 62 (2007); G. Levine, "Why Science Isn't Literature," *Realism, Ethics, and Secularism* (2007); A. M. Paliyenko, "Illuminating the Poetic Turn to Science," *Romance Studies* 26 (2008); Y. Haskell, "Latin Poet-Doctors of the Eighteenth Century," *Intellectual History Review* 18 (2008); M. M. Mahood, *The Poet as Botanist* (2008); R. O'Connor, *The Earth on Show* (2008); S. Faulkner, *Poetry as Method* (2009); J. Holmes, *Darwin's Bards* (2009); B. Gold, *ThermoPoetics* (2010); L. Vetter, *Modernist Writings and Religio-Scientific Discourse* (2010); N. Jackson, *Science and Sensation in Romantic Poetry* (2011).

P. MIDDLETON

**SCOP.** The most common OE word for "poet": others include *leopwyrhta* (song-maker) and *gleoman* (glee-man). *Scop* is attested as late as the 13th c. (in Layamon's *Brut*); it is drawn from the same Germanic root as mod. *shape* and cognates with the same meaning are found in OHG (*scof*) and Old Saxon (*scop*). *Gleoman* continued in use throughout the ME period. Both *scop* and *gleoman* are used in *Beowulf* of oral poets reciting heroic lays, no doubt in traditional meter. Two OE poems are in the voice of such poets: *Deor* is the lament of a court poet who has lost his lord's favor, and *Widsith* is a catalog of names and places by a scop who claims to have traveled widely in space and time. But *scop* and other words are freely applied in both prose and poetry to poets of all kinds, incl. Homer and Boethius. The work of most OE *scopas* is anonymous, but a few can be named: Cædmon, whose miraculous gift of song is described by Bede; Cynewulf, who wove his signature into his works in *runes; King Alfred, who trans. the metrical portions of Boethius's *Consolation of Philosophy* into prose, then verse. The 7th-c. bishop Aldhelm is described in an OE poem as a scop, presumably because he wrote Lat. poetry; but he is reputed to have recited OE poetry so as to attract audiences for his sermons. The existence of a word *gleomæden* (glee-maiden) suggests that the scop may sometimes have been a woman. Though *Beowulf* depicts the scop as an important figure in the royal court (even the Danish king Hrothgar performs), he was not always held in high esteem: *scop*, *gleoman*, and related words are also used of low and scurrilous entertainers and productions; and as if rebuking Aldhelm, a rule for priests reads, "If a priest loves excessive drunkenness or becomes a glee-man or ale-*scop*, let him do penance for that."
■ I. M. Hollowell, "*Scop* and *woðbora* in OE Poetry," *JEGP* 77 (1978): 317–29; J. Opland, *Anglo-Saxon Oral Poetry* (1980).

P. S. BAKER

# SCOTLAND, POETRY OF

I. Scots and English
II. Gaelic

**I. Scots and English.** Scottish poetry has been written in Welsh, Lat., Gaelic, Lallans (Scots), and Eng.; in this section, the concern is for the last two and their admixture. Because Lallans from Northumbrian Anglian is undeveloped, it has steadily lost ground to Eng. (of the 1,200 separate poems submitted to *New Writing Scotland* 5 [1987], e.g., "a bare sprinkling" is in Lallans); nevertheless, just how much freshness, range, color, and memorability it can still command is clear in *Sterts & Stobies*, the Scots poems of Crawford and Herbert, as well as in the poetic prose of W. Lorimer's brilliant trans. of *The New Testament in Scots*.

The main sources of early Scottish poetry are three 16th-c. mss.: Asloan, Bannatyne, and Maitland Folio; however, Andrew of Wyntoun's (ca. 1350–ca. 1423) rhymed *Cronykil* (1424) is the source for what is possibly the oldest surviving fragment (ca. 1286)—eight octosyllabic lines rhyming *abababab*, of which the last three have now epitomized Scotland's hist. for 700 years: "Crist, borne in virgynyte, / Succoure Scotland, and ramede, / That is stade in perplexitie." Several unskilled romances such as *Sir Tristrem* followed these verses before 1374–75, when John Barbour (ca. 1320–95) composed *The Bruce,* Scotland's first literary achievement. A superb story of freedom, this "factional" romance, based on the Fr. *medieval romance,* introduces a new subject matter: Scotland. Barbour, the poet-chronicler, seldom slackens his pace through 20 books of octosyllabic *couplets; when he does, it is often to show that he is remembered in Scotland because he himself remembers his countrymen's "hardyment," with such lines as "And led thair lyff in gret trawaill, / And oft, in hard stour of bataill, / Wan eycht gret price off chewalry, / And was woydyt off cowardy."

In 1424, Scotland crowned James Stewart after his 18-year imprisonment in London. As James I (1394–1437), he described Chaucer and John Gower to his court as "Superlative poetis laureate" and under their influence composed "The Kingis Quair." Here *rhyme royal, conventional *allegory of lover and rose, matter from Boethius, and ME all suggest that this James is the first and last *Scottish Chaucerian. The mid-15th c. claims Sir Richard Holland's (ca. 1415–82) *The Buke of the Howlat,* an ingenious *beast epic examining Scotland's court life. The late 15th c. claims Blind Harry's (ca. 1440–92) extravagant *The Wallace,* an epic romance in *heroic couplets extending Barbour's nationalism; *Cockelbie's Sow,* an anonymous country tale with alliterative play in irregular three- and five-beat couplets; and the anonymous, amusing *Rauf Coilyear,* a satiric antiromance on the theme of a king (Charlemagne) among unaware rustics. The 13-line stanza of *Rauf* (nine long and four short lines of black letter) parodies the old alliterative stanza of *Sir Gawain and the Green Knight.* Last, the anonymous descriptive pieces "Christ's Kirk on the Green" and "Peblis to the Play" start a trad. of rustic brawl that finds new life in the 20th-c. merrymaking of Robert Garioch's "Embro to the Ploy." Other poems in this trad., like Robert Fergusson's "Leith Races" and Robert Burns's "Holy Fair," adapt the "Christ's Kirk" stanza of ten lines, 4-3-4-3-4-3-4-3-1-3 rhyming *abababbcd,* the last as *refrain.

Nowhere are the post–World War II advances in Scottish studies more apparent than with respect to Scottish poetry of the 15th c., the Aureate Age, the high creativity of the Scottish Chaucerians or *makars.* Influences on these superior poets are today known to have been not only Eng. but directly Fr. and It., as well as native. At the forefront were Robert Henryson and William Dunbar.

Robert Henryson (ca. 1425–1505?) drew on several med. literary forms (*lyric, *ballad, *pastoral) for his delightful "Robene and Makyne," arguing "The man that will nocht quhen he may, / Sall haif nocht quhen he wald." "The Annunciation" is unusual as religious verse of the Middle Ages in that its appeal is to intellect through paradox; "Orpheus and Eurydice," the most famous of the shorter love poems, masterfully illustrates cl. narration of romance material under Fr. and It. influences. The 13 beast fables after Aesop and Pierre de Saint Cloude are uncompromisingly Scottish. Skillfully, Henryson reveals personality by gesture and remark; delicately, he controls narrative rhythm in a blend of entertaining story and central moral. Political questions within the allegory (e.g., "The Tale of the Lion and the Mouse") present the poet as a democrat in the line of David Lindsay, Fergusson, and Burns. The fable "The Preiching of the Swallow" and *The Testament of Cresseid,* both in rhyme royal, are Henryson's two finest poems, full of charity, humanity, and high-mindedness. Central to the *Testament* is the question of why men made in the image of God become "beistis Irrational."

William Dunbar (ca. 1460–1513) was priest and poet at the court of James IV. Strong Fr. and Occitan influences on a variety of lyric forms are apparent in his 80-odd poems, never long. The temperament is Eur.; the craftsmanship superb in its intricacies, ling. virtuosity, and harmony of sound and sense; the tone variously personal, witty, exuberant, eccentric, blasphemous, and manic-depressive: "Now dansand mery, now like to dee." Dunbar's favorite subjects are himself, his milieu, woman (dame, widow, Madonna), and Catholic Christianity. Some poems, like "The Goldyn Targe," a dream allegory, and "Ane Ballat of Our Lady," belong to the poetry of rhet. and the court; thus, they are replete with the favorite phrase "me thocht," *internal rhyme, and *aureate diction. Other poems, such as "The Flyting of Dunbar and Kennedie" (see FLYTING) and "The Tretis of the Twa Mariit Wemen and the Wedo" (the first *blank verse in Scots, strongly alliterative), belong to the poetry of ribald speech.

Bishop Gavin Douglas (1475?–1522) and Sir David Lindsay (1490?–1555?) complete the makars' roll. More learned than either Henryson or Dunbar, Douglas focused his *dream vision *The Palice of Honour* on the nature of virtue and honor in educating a young poet and, therewith, acknowledged indebtedness to such It. humanists as Gian Francesco Poggio Braccilini and Petrarch. Douglas's magnum opus is his trans. of the *Aeneid,* also in heroic couplets, the first trans. of a classic into Scots and a major source for Henry Howard, the Earl of Surrey's *Aeneid,* the first Eng. blank verse. Its prologues, notably that to book 7, reveal an individual voice, a wealth of lang., and the typical Scots poet's eye for nature and weather. Sir David, Lyon King-at-Arms, promoter of John Knox, intellectual revolutionary, and early defender of writing for "Iok" and "Thome"—i.e., the common people—in the maternal lang., made his reputation as the most popular Scots poet before Burns primarily on *Ane Pleasant Satire of the Thrie Estaitis*, a morality play or propaganda drama with Lady Sensuality and Flattery as the leads. Blending comedy and common sense, Lindsay gives answer to "What is good government?" in sophisticated verse forms: *bob and wheel, eight-line stanzas of iambic pentameter in linking rhyme for formal speeches, and exchange of single lines in couplets of *stichomythia.

With Robert Wedderburns's (ca. 1510–57) *Gude and Godlie Ballatis*, (assisted by his brothers John and James) and the songs of Alexander Scott (1520?–1583?), national Scotland approached the death of the Eng. queen, Elizabeth I (d. 1603), the Union of the Crowns (James VI of Scotland crowned James I of England), and the loss of court and courtly lang. Such loss, together with the King James Bible, the splendor of Edmund Spenser and Shakespeare, and the victories of Covenanting Puritans, makes it impossible to name one Scots poet of high distinction during the entire 17th c., not excluding Alexander Montgomerie (1555?–97?), poet of *The Cherry and the Slae*, dream vision and allegory; any other member of King James's "Castalian band"; or William Drummond of Hawthornden (1585–1649), who showed with some success what a Scotsman could compose in Eng. No longer a court lang., Scots lived on as the vernacular of folk lit.: ballad and song.

Scottish ballads represent an oral trad. (see Buchan 1972) of anonymous narrative songs arising in the late Middle Ages to flourish in the 16th and 17th cs. and to be collected in the later 19th c. by F. J. Child. Chief subjects are violent hist. ("Oterborne"), tragic romance ("Clerk Saunders"), and the supernatural ("Tam Lin"). The vernacular is simple and stark, grimly realistic and fatalistic. The vividly dramatic story unfolds through unity of action, characterization, and the relentless pace of the *ballad meter. *Formula, *epithet, *incremental repetition, refrain, *alliteration, and question and answer also advance the plot. Colors are primary; images are violent ("The curse of hell frae me sall ye beir / Mither, mither"), tender ("O waly, waly! but love be bony / A little time, while it is new"), eerie ("The channerin worm doth chide"), and beautiful ("And she has snooded her yellow hair / A little aboon her bree").

The period from 1603 to World War I produced many poets who began to choose literary Eng. as their medium because they thought it was impossible to use Lallans and be taken seriously. So, James Thomson (1700–48), poet of *The Seasons*; Robert Blair (1699–1746); and James Beattie (1735–1803) used standard Eng. for their remembered works. Sir Walter Scott (1771–1832) retained the vernacular of the ballads he collected and improved for his *Minstrelsy* but chose Eng. for his long poems (*The Lady of the Lake*) and for the excellent songs in his novels ("Proud Maisie"). Lord Byron (1728–1824) and Thomas Campbell (1777–

1844) used Eng. and later poets such as Bysshe Vanolis (pseud. of James Thomson, 1834–82) and Robert Louis Stevenson (1850–94) again chose Eng. for *City of Dreadful Night* and *A Child's Garden of Verses*, respectively. Published poetry in Lallans, however, had been kept alive—just barely—until it experienced a significant revival when the 1707 Union of Parliaments had seemed to reduce Scotland to a "region" of Great Britain.

James Watson's *Choice Collection* in two vols. (1706–9) includes Robert Sempill the Younger's (ca. 1595–1663) mock elegy "The Life and Death of Habbie Simpson" (ca. 1650) in a stanza that gives name to the "standard Habbie," better known as the *Burns stanza; William Hamilton of Gilbertfield's (?1665–1751) "Bonny Heck" has the same stanza for the last words of a dying greyhound, anticipating Burns's "Poor Mailie's Elegy." These poems are in Lallans. So, too, are such works of Allan Ramsay (1685–1758) as are his invention of the *verse epistle (usually in tetrameters), his burlesque elegy on a church treasurer who could smell out a bawd, his poetic drama *The Gentle Shepherd*, many of the songs in his *The Tea Table Miscellany*, and all of the older Scots poems published in his *The Ever Green*. Ramsay's prosody becomes Robert Fergusson's (1750–74); Fergusson's becomes Burns's. Within the vernacular revival, these three poets compose their satires, genre poems, epistles, and comic narratives, principally in six verse forms: *ballad meter, octosyllabic couplets, heroic couplets, the standard Habbie, "Christ's Kirk," and "Cherrie and the Slee." Among Fergusson's poems in Lallans is his masterpiece "Auld Reekie," realistically describing everyday life in Edinburgh, "Whare couthy chiels at e'ening meet / Their bizzin craigs and mou's to weet."

More and more, the measure of Robert Burns's (1759–96) high accomplishment has become the satires like "Holy Willie's Prayer," *The Jolly Beggars*, the narrative "Tam o' Shanter," and the hundreds of songs. The cantata *The Jolly Beggars* has his characteristic merits of description, narration, dramatic effect, metrical diversity, energy, and sensitivity to the beauties inherent in Scottish words and music. Otherwise, hearing a song like "Scots wha hae" or "Ca' the Yowes," each showing masterful skill at uniting words and music, will unforgettably illustrate this genius. To Burns under the Scottish Enlightenment we owe the perpetuation of Scottish folk song. How rich this heritage is has been the further study of those like Cecil Sharp, James Bruce Duncan, and Gavin Greig in the 19th c. and Hamish Henderson and others at the School of Scottish Studies in the 20th. By contrast, literary songs from the 18th c. to the 20th c. tend toward sentimentalism, such as Jean Elliot's (1727–1805) "Flowers o' the Forest" or Carolina Oliphant, Lady Nairne's (1766–1845) "Caller Herrin."

Seldom does 19th-c. Scottish poetry better James Hogg's (1770–1835) idiosyncratic verse. Slavish imitations of Burns strike low, nor rise by the *Whistle-Binkie* (fiddler's seat at merrymakings) anthol. or the couthy (sociable) sentimentality of Kailyard (a type of fiction from about 1880 of rural life, dialect, and sentiment; see James M. Barrie's *A Window in Thrums* or Ian Maclaren's [pseud. of Rev. John Watson] verse epigraph).

Industrialization and the Calvinist ethic of profitability and genteel respectability bring poets to their knees. At century's close, however, Stevenson composes poems like "The Spaewife" in a literary Scots, the precision of which opposes the Kailyard; "blood and guts" John Davidson (1857–1909) experiments in Eng. with new myths, symbols of science's dethroning religion; and the founder of the Scottish renaissance grows as a lad in Langholm.

Christopher Murray Grieve (1892–1978) initiates the revival of cultural and creative confidence in the 1920s, throwing off Victorian sentimentalism with the war cry "Back to Dunbar!" Abandoning his early Eng. verse, he took the pseud. Hugh MacDiarmid to produce two collections of lyrics in a revived form of lowland Scots (Lallans). The audacious images of love and death in these poems combine expressionist intensity with a fine melodic power and balladlike structures in settings that are both domestic and cosmic:

> Mars is braw in crammasy,
> Venus in a green silk goun,
> The auld mune shak's her gowden feathers,
> Their starry talk's a wheen o' blethers,
> Nane for thee a thochtie sparin',
> Earth, thou bonnie broukit bairn!
> —*But greet, an' in your tears ye'll droun*
> *The haill clanjamfrie!*
>
> ("The Bonnie Broukit Bairn")

Such verses recall and indeed surpass the lyrical concentration and estrangement of early *imagism. MacDiarmid coined another slogan, "Not Traditions—Precedents!," to catch the energy of his masterpiece *A Drunk Man Looks at the Thistle* (1926). This long poem sequence in different verse forms is Whitmanesque in scale, and as a romantic celebration of ever-changing and contradictory modes and moods, it is also modernist, invoking flux and crisis to match what the poet took to be the glorious instability of life itself, not to mention the parlous condition of mod. Scotland.

Taking their cue from MacDiarmid, poets (and poetry) play a leading part in the early years of the Scottish literary renaissance, with William Soutar (1898–1943) aiming to revive Lallans by way of "whigmaleeries" and "bairn rhymes" to capture a young audience. Soutar looked back to the ballad trad., as did Violet Jacob (1863–1946) and Marion Angus (1866–1946), whose eerie Scots lyrics (not without sentiment) anticipated and supported MacDiarmid's early work. In the 1930s, MacDiarmid returns to Eng. for an overtly socialist verse, followed by the *free verse and intermittent rhymes of "On a Raised Beach" (1934), one of the finest long philosophical poems in mod. lit. His late work seeks a unifying vision of scientific materialism and world lang. in a densely prosaic "poetry of fact," epic in scale and (rather like Ezra Pound's *Cantos*) finally unfinished or unfinishable. The Eng. lyrics of Edwin Muir (1887–1959) are the antithesis of MacDiarmid's materialistic optimism, as Muir is haunted by a sense of loss, going back to his idyllic childhood in Orkney and the family's traumatic move to Glasgow in 1901. Muir did not support MacDiarmid's program for the revival of Scots lang. and culture ("Burns and Scott, sham bards of a sham nation": "Scotland 1941"), and the two leading poets of the day fell out with each other. Images of frozen time and Edenic expulsion characterize Muir's often symbolic and melancholy verse ("Childhood," "One Foot in Eden," "The Labyrinth"). He and his wife, Willa, were the first to translate Franz Kafka into Eng. ("The Interrogation").

Notable work was done in Scots by Sydney Goodsir Smith (1915–75) whose poetic *persona harks back to the rambunctious Edinburgh of Fergusson. *Under the Eildon Tree* (1948) is his masterpiece, as 24 elegies on legendary lovers lead him to confront mortality and desire. The Scots poems of Robert Garioch (1909–81) are closer to contemp. urban speech, whether he is translating the 19th-c. Roman dialect *sonnets of Giuseppe Belli or casting a wry and often humorously satirical eye on the pretensions of his fellow citizens in the "Edinburgh Sonnets" or striking a more personal note on the constraints of everyday living in "The Percipient Swan." The verses of Tom Scott (1918–95) and Alexander Scott (1920–89) have a forceful and combative wit, and their commitment to the medium of Scots was taken up in later years by William Neill (1922–2010), who also wrote in Gaelic, and by the tender and understated plainness that is the characteristic Scottish voice of Alastair Mackie (1925–95) and his publisher, the editor and poet Duncan Glen (1933–2008).

Some of the best poetry of World War II was produced in Eng. by Hamish Henderson (1919–2002), most notably his sequence *Elegies for the Dead in Cyrenaica* (1948); by G. S. Fraser (1915–80); and by the Gaelic poets Sorley MacLean (1911–96) and George Campbell Hay (1915–84). A founder member of the School of Scottish Studies, Henderson wrote his own ballads and was an influential scholar of the folk-song revival in the 1950s and 1960s.

The leading lyric poets of what has been called the second generation of the literary renaissance are Norman MacCaig (1910–96) and George Mackay Brown (1921–96), who wrote only in Eng.; Iain Crichton Smith (1928–98), who also wrote in Gaelic; and MacLean, who wrote exclusively in Gaelic. The urbane poet and broadcaster Maurice Lindsay (1918–2009) was a tireless proponent of the cultural revival, editing its first anthol., *Modern Scottish Poetry*, in 1946. MacCaig's first poems were in the syntactically dense and quasi-surreal mode of the New Apocalypse group, two of whose leading members, J. F. Hendry (1912–86) and Fraser, were also Scottish; but the hundreds of short lyrics he went on to write, first in formal verse and later in a succinct free verse, are characterized by clarity, compassion, and an unsentimental delight in the natural world. These factors, along with his gift for memorable and witty images and a dryly humorous reading style, made him Scotland's most popular poet for over 30 years. Brought up in Lewis and indelibly marked by his Free Kirk background, Crichton Smith's poetry can achieve a piercing lyrical beauty ("Old Woman") with an undercurrent of loneliness and existential unease. Never quite "confessional" (see CONFESSIONAL POETRY), his later work was influenced nevertheless by Robert Lowell, with elliptical poems that reflect on exile and on the concept of the island as both a literal and metaphysical place ("Australia").

The "island" for Brown was undoubtedly his native Orkney. Unlike Muir, Brown spent almost all his life in Orkney, creating an impersonally spare free verse modeled on the sagas and the cryptic understatement of OE and ON verse. In collections such as *Fishermen with Ploughs* (1971), the cyclic patterns of farming and fishing are merged with the rituals of Catholic faith and carried across time to invoke archetypes of meaning and value that he could not find in the mod. world. George Bruce (1909–2002) had his own roots in the fishing communities of the northeast of Scotland. His Eng. verse also takes spareness as a virtue, but his vision is extravert and enthusiastic. After an early flirtation with the New Apocalypse and *The Nightfishing* (1955), a long poem that linked net fishing with the creative struggle, W. S. Graham (1918–86) spent most of his life in Cornwall reflecting on the nature of lang. and meaning. Poems such as "What Is the Language Using Us For" and "Malcolm Mooney's Land" show his finely nuanced, meditative, and subtly cerebral lines at their best.

Ian Hamilton Finlay (1925–2006) was also haunted by boats and nets, and the early poems of *The Dancers Inherit the Party* (1960) were influenced by the prosody of Robert Creeley. They offer *minimalism, gentle humor, and a Zen-like inconsequence as an antidote to what he saw as MacDiarmid's nationalist stridency and the grandiose ambitions of Anglo-Am. *modernism. Finlay matured to become an internationally recognized exponent of *concrete poetry, though he was less well appreciated in his home country. The 1960s and 1970s see what might be termed a third generation of poets, such as Finlay, who looked to America or Europe and were less interested in, or even hostile to, the cultural nationalism of the original renaissance. As a correspondent for *The New Yorker* and a major verse translator of Jorge Luis Borges and Pablo Neruda, Alastair Reid (b. 1926) stands outside to reflect on both lang. and place in a poetry that stems from his life in Scotland, Spain, and the U.S. The poetry of Kenneth White (b. 1936) is marked by the *Black Mountain school; his long engagement with Fr. academic culture marks the discipline he has called "geopoetics" and his interest in the value of marginal and in-between states. In the 1970s, D. M. Black (b. 1941) created surreal narratives with echoes of Kafkaesque absurdity, while the hip Blakean rage of Alan Jackson (b. 1938) caught the youth culture of the times with street-wise, protopunk *performance poems satirizing consumerism, bourgeois hypocrisy—and Scottishness.

The year 1968 saw the publication of *The Second Life* by Edwin Morgan (1920–2010). Although Morgan had published poems (and a verse trans. of *Beowulf*) beginning in the 1950s, *The Second Life*, followed by *From Glasgow to Saturn* (1973), marked his arrival as Scotland's most innovative, influential, and popular poet for decades to come, writing concrete poetry, *sound poetry, and "science fiction" poetry, as well as stark reflections on urban deprivation in his native Glasgow ("Glasgow Green"). Looking to Europe, America, and the cosmos rather than to England, experimental and eclectic, Morgan sees Scotland in even wider perspectives of space and time than MacDiarmid ever envisaged (*Sonnets from Scotland*, 1984), and not least in the discreet and finely tender love poems that speak for the poet's homosexuality ("One Cigarette," "Absence," the late sequence "Love and a Life"). Equally adept as a playwright, essayist, and translator, Morgan was appointed Scotland's first national makar in 2004, the year he composed a poem for the opening of the new parliament building.

Scottish writing gained renewed energy in the last 30 years of the 20th c., and poetry was no exception. The finely measured work of Douglas Dunn (b. 1942) comes to terms with class and national identity ("Washing the Coins") in formally structured poems, offering reflective commentaries on the world around him (*Barbarians*, 1979; *St Kilda's Parliament*, 1981; *Northlight*, 1988). The collection *Elegies* (1985) offers an almost unbearably powerful set of poems on the death by cancer of his first wife. At odds with Dunn's almost Georgian decorum, the poetry of Tom Leonard (b. 1944) uses the demotic Scots accent of the Glasgow streets to challenge all preconceptions of what poetry is or can be, along with the conventions of spelling and every social discrimination against those whose voices do not "fit": "if / a toktaboot / thi truth / lik wanna yoo / scruff yi / widny thingk / it wuz troo" (*Intimate Voices*, 1984). Less concerned with MacDiarmid's case for Lallans and the nation, these younger writers are much more engaged with issues of class, identity, and gender. Liz Lochhead (b. 1947) draws on the demotic energy of common lives and voices, in poems infused with subtle speech dynamics, colored by an ironic ear for rhyme, clichés, and puns, and marked by a sharp eye for the female condition in the masculinist culture of her native Glasgow. Lochhead is only the first of the women to have transformed contemp. Scottish writing in prose and poetry. Kathleen Jamie (b. 1962) came to interrogate her Scottish roots starting with the title poem of *The Queen of Sheba* (1994), which throws a wry and energizing light on the stifling of female aspiration in her home village and Scotland at large. Jackie Kay (b. 1961) draws on her own experience as an adopted black child in a working-class Glasgow family, to write beautiful poems transfused with compassion and energy, even as they recognize the pains of sexual and racial difference. Carol Ann Duffy (b. 1955) and Kate Clanchy (b. 1965) found themselves living in England from their early years, but their first sense of transition and ling. difference informs their work and their reflections on sexism in all its forms. Tessa Ransford (b. 1938) is more conventionally lyrical, while the poems of Valerie Gillies (b. 1948) are deeply engaged with ecology and the landscape. Sheena Blackhall (b. 1947) writes in broad northeastern Scots, while Magi Gibson (b. 1953), Dilys Rose (b. 1954), and Angela McSeveney (b. 1964) use Eng.

Lang. and identity are still an issue in the witty Eng. poems of Robert Crawford (b. 1959) who fondly reimagines Scotland's past and present through every kind of eclectic metaphor. He is joined in this by W. N. Herbert (b. 1961). They shared a volume (*Sterts & Stobies*) that revisited and supercharged the "artificial Scots" of MacDiarmid's lyrics to hilarious effect, but Herbert's muse is wilder still, simultaneously intellectual and playful, dense with arcane information and popular culture. Fellow Dundonian Don Paterson (b. 1963) shares something of this esoteric breadth. His work is self-aware, rooted in the real but ironically alert to literature, contingency, and mortality (*God's Gift to Women*, 1997). David Kinloch (b. 1959) reflects tellingly on sexuality and identity, while the long free-verse sequences of Frank Kuppner (b. 1951) generate a unique voice that is formal, even pedantically distanced, low-key, and ultimately strangely moving. The poetry of John Burnside (b. 1955) is much more conventionally lyrical, nuanced by his own Catholic faith, his fine landscapes, and interiors that often seem existentially numinous. The humane verse of Stewart Conn (b. 1936) has been steadily engaged with the interface between personal hist. and culture over many years, while Ron Butlin (b. 1949), Tom Pow (b. 1950), Brian McCabe (b. 1951), Andrew Greig (b. 1951), Donny O' Rourke (b. 1959), Gerry Cambridge (b. 1959), Richard Price (b. 1966), and Robin Robertson (b. 1955) have all made significant contributions to the richness that is the contemp. scene.

## II. Gaelic

**A. *The "Classical" Tradition.*** The origins of written Scottish Gaelic poetry are closely entwined with those of the poetry of Ireland, a commonality evidenced in the shared "classical" trad. of the professional court poets, formalized in Ireland in the 12th c. and sustained by a hereditary caste of learned males who had undergone arduous training in established bardic schools (see IRELAND, POETRY OF; BARD). Cl. poetry in its strictest form continued to be composed without significant regional variation across Ireland and Gaelic Scotland into the early mod. period (as late as the 18th c. in Scotland), written in a shared literary supradialect, using identical heroic diction and identical meters (based on syllable count rather than the stress patterns of Gaelic speech), with an identical attention to complex rules of ornamentation. Poems of identifiably Scottish provenance are preserved in mss. of the 16th to 18th c. but are many fewer in number than their Ir. counterparts.

The excellence of bardic verse lies in its highly developed lang., its sophisticated allusive style, and above all in the elaborate, subtly modulated music of its intricate metrical patterns. Its limitations inhere neither in subject matter nor technique, but rather in a formalism of conventions inseparable from the office of the professional poet, that of public panegyrist to the great men of his society (see PANEGYRIC). *Syllabic verse that uses an easier, modified technique and makes concessions to vernacular speech is fairly common too, whether written by professionals or by aristocrats—male and female—who had at least some facility for composing competent verse. All these features of style are displayed in the earliest and principal collection of cl. verse surviving in Scotland: the book of the Dean of Lismore, compiled 1512–42, with the bulk of the Scottish poetic content composed from 1400 to ca. 1520. This ms. provides a surprisingly eclectic sample of the range and thematic variety of syllabic verse: as well as the predictable *encomia of court poets for their patrons, we find *satire, religious poetry, heroic "ballads" of Fionn and Oisein, moral and didactic verse, and poetry in the Eur. *courtly love trad., much of this *occasional verse composed by nonprofessionals. A prominent interest in the "argument about women" and the morals of the clergy further links the compilation to Lowland-Scots, Eng., and continental literary cultures. While much of the impetus and early leadership for cl. Gaelic culture came from Ireland, it is clear from the dean's book and other sources that, by the later med. and early Ren. period, some of the Scottish Gaelic literati were as engaged with their multilingual Scottish environment as with the pan-Gaelic world, not least in their preference for a Lowland-Scots-based orthography in "secretary hand" over the *corra litir* script of the bardic schools.

**B. *Vernacular Panegyric.*** The culture of the cl. poets was by definition literate, but oral song trads. (equally old or, conceivably, older) existed alongside the high-prestige bardic productions. The late survival of heroic clan society and the siege mentality brought about by the balkanization of the Gaelic polity in early mod. Scotland stimulated the devel. of a vernacular court panegyric praising the caste of aristocratic warrior-hunters who protected and rewarded their people. Panegyric—organized in sets of conventional images or formulas that work as a semiotic code—is a pervasive style, particularly in the period ca. 1600–1800, with its workings and reflexes traceable even in contemp. poetry. The vernacular bards were not, on the whole, literate, and their work was captured in writing only by 18th-c. or later collectors. Yet, too much can be made of the literacy-orality disjunction, since vernacular poetry continued to express many of the attitudes of cl. poetry and employ many of its *tropes, and irregularly stressed meters derived from syllabic versification survived demotically.

Among regularly stressed meters, one of the most distinctive is the so-called strophic meter, closely associated with vernacular panegyric—minimally, an asymmetrical verse of two short lines and a longer line, to which musical symmetry is restored through repetition either of the unit or of the final line. A particularly interesting variant, deployed for occasions of high solemnity, allows the poet to stretch the run of short lines from anything between 4 and 14 lines within the same song, creating dramatic crescendos of musical and lyrical tension. The two great early practitioners of strophic forms whose work has survived, Mairi Nighean Alasdair Ruaidh (Mary Macleod, ca. 1615–1707) and Iain Lom (John MacDonald, ca. 1620–1710), are not, as was once claimed, innovators: although MacDonald is exercised by national issues, both are clan poets composing in a strong panegyric trad., and both clearly have the security of established practice behind them—perhaps even extending to before the introduction of Lat. learning.

C. *The Female Tradition.* Both Macleod and MacDonald also used meters associated with the subliterary trad. of generally anonymous female composition (typically marked by short verses and more complex *refrains and often used for *laments). Largely ignored by 18th- and 19th-c. collectors, this "folk-song" corpus has been hailed in more recent times as one of the glories of Gaelic lit., exceptional in its emotional intensity, its rhythmic subtleties, and its apparent lack of artifice. It ceased as an active creative trad. in the course of the 18th c. (in tandem with the demise of clan society), but a large static repertoire was preserved and transmitted well into the 20th c.

D. *The Eighteenth to Twenty-first Centuries.* In the dominant male *canon, fresh dimensions were added in the 18th c. to the scope and expressiveness of Gaelic poetry, particularly by Alastair mac Mhaighstir Alastair (Alexander MacDonald, 1700–70), the nationalist bard of the 1745 Jacobite uprising, and by the hunter-poet Donnchadh Bàn (Duncan Ban Macintyre, 1724–1812). A highly educated and daringly innovative poet who drew on all the resources of Gaelic, MacDonald is the outstanding literary figure of his age. Along with the controlled, detailed naturalism of Macintyre's "Praise of Ben Dorain," much of MacDonald's work embodies an audacious movement away from clan poetry and aristocratic panegyric. Rob Donn (Robert Mackay, 1714–78), like Macintyre a completely oral poet, is the most subtle satirist in Gaelic lit., while the poetry of Uilleam Ros (William Ross, 1762–90) manifests a wider sensibility—particularly in his anguished love songs—which certainly owes something to his learning in Eng. and the cl. langs.

In contrast to the innovative glories of the 18th c., 19th-c. verse has tended to be judged harshly as the nadir of Gaelic lit., the weak and sentimental expression of a trad. debilitated by the social upheaval of land clearance and mass emigration, the encroachment of Eng., and the nostalgic conservatism of émigré Gaelic communities. But more recent scholarship has highlighted the thematic breadth of songs of the period and their engagement with the technological and sociopolitical changes of their era. Certainly, while the devel. of a mod. Gaelic prose will continue to be seen as the period's greatest literary achievement, an appreciable body of vigorous oral poetry continued to be composed, notably against the background of land politics. The best work of Màiri Mhòr nan Òran (Mary Macpherson, 1821–98) is memorable for its delicate lyricism and its political commitment, while from the university-educated Seonaidh Phàdraig Iarsiadair (John Smith, 1848–81) came powerful, radical indictments of an immoral social order.

After World War I, the oral poetic trad. entered an era of terminal decline: it suffered irremediably from the ling.-cultural shift toward Eng. (in the wake of the 1872 Education Act) and from the loss of its organic context (communal orality centered around the *cèilidh* house) as mod. media and population change fundamentally altered Gaelic society. It showed astonishing resilience in its decline, however, its practice skillfully upheld into the later 20th c. by aging and increasingly isolated song makers. The most formidable of these was the stonemason Dòmhnall Ruadh Phàislig (Donald Macintyre, 1889–1964), who displayed the technical range and mastery of the best 18th-c. practitioners while addressing the issues of his own era. But the dependence of the oral bardic trad. on high-level ling. dexterity and density of diction and its attachment to traditional modes of thought and transmission placed it beyond the reach or tastes of most younger poets following World War II, so that the dominant devels. in poetic practice since the 1940s have been in written mod. poetry, typically by university graduates, and increasingly composed in freer metrics, though with not infrequent reference to the sung oral trad. (Songwriters, meanwhile, increasingly gravitated towards folk, country, and rock idioms.) The poetry of Somhairle MacGill-Eain (1911–96) in particular marked a point of no return, in its extraordinary fusion of traditional and modernist (see MODERNISM), Gaelic and non-Gaelic sensibilities; George Campbell Hay (1915–84) rehabilitated the subtle movement of older meters and opened up a vast creative space through his multilingual, multicultural adventurism; Ruaraidh MacThòmais (Derick S. Thomson, 1921–2012) decisively developed *vers libre*, a departure of great interest in Gaelic metrics and of irreversible impact in Gaelic poetic practice. Iain Mac a' Ghobhainn (Iain Crichton Smith, 1928–98) and Dòmhnall MacAmhlaigh (1926–89) gave the modernist push further impetus.

The influence of MacGill-Eain and MacThòmais on younger poets has been liberating rather than shackling, and interestingly varied voices came to prominence in the last decades of the 20th c. (incl. those of nonnative Gaelic speakers), some of them startling in their detachment from Gaelic trad. Of these, a good number have gone on to develop an important body of work, e.g., Aonghas MacNeacail (b. 1942), Maoilios Caimbeul (b. 1944), Crìsdean Whyte (b. 1952), Meg Bateman (b. 1959), and Rody Gorman (b. 1960). In the 21st c., new voices have been sparser, with few signs of a wave of poets to rival the exuberant creativity of the 1980s and 1990s, a lull perhaps attributable to the remarkable florescence in fiction writing (supported by substantial public funding) in the first decade of the new millennium.

■ **Anthologies and Primary Texts.** *Scots and English*: *The Scots Musical Museum*, ed. J. Johnson, 6 v. (1786–1803); *Bishop Percy's Folio Manuscript*, ed. J. Hales and F. Furnivall, 3 v. (1867–68); *English and Scottish Popular*

*Ballads*, ed. F. J. Child, 5 v. (1883–98); *The Bruce*, ed. W. W. Skeat, 2 v. (1894); *Scott's Minstrelsy of the Scottish Border*, ed. T. Henderson, 4 v. (1902); *Traditional Tunes of the Child Ballads*, ed. B. Bronson, 4 v. (1959–72); *Oxford Book of Scottish Verse*, ed. J. MacQueen and T. Scott (1966); *Contemporary Scottish Verse*, ed. N. Mac-Caig and A. Scott (1970); *A Scottish Ballad Book*, ed. D. Buchan (1973); *Made in Scotland*, ed. R. Garioch (1974); *Collected Poems of S. G. Smith* (1975); *Voices of Our Kind: An Anthology of Modern Scottish Poetry*, ed. A. Scott, 3d. ed. (1975); *Poetry of Northeast Scotland*, ed. J. Alison (1976); *Modern Scottish Verse, 1922–77*, ed. A. Scott (1978); *Choice of Scottish Verse, 1560–1660*, ed. R.D.S. Jack (1978); *Akros Verse, 1965–82*, ed. D. Glen (1982); *Twelve More Modern Scottish Poets*, ed. C. King and I. C. Smith (1986); A. Mackie, *Ingaitherins: Selected Poems* (1987); D. Dunn, *Northlight* (1988); *The Best of Scottish Poetry: Contemporary Scottish Verse*, ed. R. Bell (1989); D. Lindsay, *Ane Satyre of the Thrie Estaitis*, ed. R. Lyall (1989); *Radical Renfrew: Poetry from the French Revolution to the First World War*, ed. T. Leonard (1990); *An Anthology of Scottish Women Poets*, ed. C. Kerrigan (1991); *The New Makars: Contemporary Poetry in Scots*, ed. T. Hubbard (1991); *The Faber Book of Twentieth-Century Scottish Poetry*, ed. D. Dunn (1993); *Scottish Ballads*, ed. E. Lyle (1994); *The Poetry of Scotland, Gaelic Scots and English, 1380–1980*, ed. R. Watson (1995); *The Christis Kirk Tradition: Scots Poems of Folk Festivity*, ed. A. MacLaine (1996); *Scottish Literature: An Anthology*, ed. D. McCordick, 3 v. (1996); J. Barbour, *The Bruce*, ed. A. Duncan (1997); *The Mercat Anthology of Early Scottish Literature, 1375–1707*, ed. R.D.S. Jack and P.A.T. Rozendaal (1998); *The Triumph Tree: Scotland's Earliest Poetry, AD 530–1350*, ed. T. Clancy (1998); *The Makars: The Poetry of Henryson, Dunbar and Douglas*, ed. J. A. Tasioulas (1999); *The New Penguin Book of Scottish Verse*, ed. R. Crawford and M. Imlah (2000); *Scottish Religious Poetry: An Anthology*, ed. M. Bateman and R. Crawford (2000); *Before Burns: Eighteenth-Century Scottish Poetry*, ed. C. MacLachlan (2002); *Dream State: The New Scottish Poets*, ed. D. O'Rourke, 2d ed. (2002); *Scottish Literature in the Twentieth Century: An Anthology*, ed. D. McCordick (2002); Blind Harry, *The Wallace*, ed. A. McKim (2003); *The Canongate Burns*, ed. A. Noble and P. S. Hogg, rev. ed. (2003); *Modern Scottish Women Poets*, ed. D. McMillan (2003). **Gaelic**: *Gàir nan Clàrsach / The Harps' Cry*, ed. C. Ó Baoill, trans. M. Bateman (1994)—17th-c. verse; *An Tuil*, ed. R. Black (1999)—20th-c. verse; *An Lasair*, ed. R. Black (2001)—18th-c. verse; *Caran an t-Saoghail / The Wiles of the World*, ed. D. E. Meek (2003)—19th-c. verse; *Duanaire na Sracaire / Songbook of the Pillagers*, ed M. Bateman and W. McLeod (2007)—verse to 1600.

■ **Criticism and History.** *Scots and English*: T. F. Henderson, *Scottish Vernacular Literature* (1900); J. H. Millar, *A Literary History of Scotland* (1903); G. G. Smith, *Scottish Literature, Character and Influence* (1919); A. Mackenzie, *Historical Survey of Scottish Lit-*

*erature to 1714* (1933); J. Speirs, *The Scots Literary Tradition* (1940); *Scottish Poetry*, ed. J. Kingsley (1955); K. Wittig, *The Scottish Tradition in Literature* (1958); T. Crawford, *Burns: A Study of the Poems and Songs* (1960); D. Craig, *Scottish Literature and the Scottish People* (1961); K. Buthlay, *Hugh MacDiarmid* (1964); D. Daiches, *The Paradox of Scottish Culture* (1964); D. Glen, *Hugh MacDiarmid and the Scottish Renaissance* (1964); F. Collinson, *Tradition and National Music of Scotland* (1966); T. Scott, *Dunbar* (1966); J. MacQueen, *Robert Henryson: A Study of the Major Narrative Poems* (1967); T. C. Smout, A *History of the Scottish People, 1560–1830* (1969); H. M. Shire, *Song, Dance and Poetry of the Court of Scotland under King James VI* (1969); A. M. Kinghorn, *Middle Scots Poets* (1970); D. Buchan, *The Ballad and the Folk* (1972); *Hugh MacDiarmid: A Critical Survey*, ed. D. Glen (1972); R.D.S. Jack, *The Italian Influence in Scottish Literature* (1972); *Robert Burns*, ed. D. Low (1974); R. Fulton, *Contemporary Scottish Poetry* (1974); A. Bold, *The Ballad (Critical Idiom)* (1979); R. Knight, *Edwin Muir* (1980)—best study; G. Kratzmann, *Anglo-Scottish Literary Relations, 1430–1550* (1980); W. R. Aitken, *Scottish Literature in English and Scots* (1982)—excellent bibl.; D. Daiches, *Literature and Gentility in Scotland* (1982); C. Kerrigan, *Whaur Extremes Meet* (1983)—study of MacDiarmid's work; J. MacQueen, *Progress and Poetry, 1650–1800* (1982); *Scotch Passion*, ed. A. Scott (1982)—erotic poetry; *The New Testament in Scots*, trans. W. L. Lorimer (1983); *Concise Scots Dictionary*, ed. M. Robinson (1985)—intro. is Aitken's excellent "History of Scots"; R.D.S. Jack, *Scottish Literature's Debt to Italy* (1986); W. Scheps and J. A. Looney, *The Middle Scots Poets: A Reference Guide* (1986); T. C. Smout, A *Century of the Scottish People, 1830–1950* (1986); *The History of Scottish Literature*, ed. C. Craig, 4 v. (1987–88); A. Bold, *MacDiarmid: A Critical Biography* (1988); T. Lopez, *The Poetry of W. S. Graham* (1989); F. Stafford, *The Sublime Savage: James Macpherson and the Poems of Ossian* (1989); *About Edwin Morgan*, ed. R. Crawford and H. Whyte (1990); E. Morgan, *Nothing Not Giving Messages: Reflections on His Life and Work*, ed. H. Whyte (1990); *N. MacCaig: Critical Essays*, ed. J. Hendry and R. Ross (1990); P. Bawcutt, *Dunbar the Makar* (1992); *Iain Crichton Smith: Critical Essays*, ed. C. Nicholson (1992); M. Lindsay, *History of Scottish Literature*, 2d ed. (1992); C. Nicholson, *Poem, Purpose, Place: Shaping Identity in Modern Scottish Verse* (1992); *Hugh MacDiarmid: Man and Poet*, ed. N. K. Gish (1993); *Liz Lochhead's Voices*, ed. R. Crawford and A. Varty (1993); T. Royle, *The Mainstream Companion to Scottish Literature* (1993); *Wood Notes Wild, Essays on the Poetry and Art of Ian Hamilton Finlay*, ed. A. Finlay (1995); M. Walker, *Scottish Literature since 1707* (1996); J. Corbett, *Language and Scottish Literature* (1997); *A History of Scottish Women's Writing*, ed. D. Gifford and D. McMillan (1997); *Contemporary Scottish Women Writers*, ed. A. Christianson and A. Lumsden (2000); J. D. McClure, *Language, Poetry and Nationhood: 1887 to the Present* (2000); L. McIlvanney, *Burns the Radical: Politics and*

*Poetry in Late Eighteenth-Century Scotland* (2002); *Scottish Literature in English and Scots*, ed. D. Gifford, S. Dunnigan, A. MacGillivray (2002); J. Sheeler and A. Lawson, *Little Sparta: The Garden of Ian Hamilton Finlay* (2003); *Modernism and Nationalism: Source Documents for the Scottish Renaissance*, ed. M. McCulloch (2004); C. White, *Modern Scottish Poetry* (2004); M. Fergusson, *George Mackay Brown: The Life* (2006); B. Kay, *Scots: The Mither Tongue* (2006); R. Crawford, *Scotland's Books* (2007); *The Edinburgh History of Scottish Literature*, ed. I. Brown, 3 v. (2007); R. Watson, *Literature of Scotland*, 2d ed., 2 v. (2007); *The Edinburgh Companion to Contemporary Scottish Poetry*, ed. M. McGuire and C. Nicholson (2009); *The Edinburgh Companion to Twentieth-Century Scottish Literature*, ed. I. Brown and A. Riach (2009). *Gaelic*: See the intros. to the anthols. above; J. MacInnes, "The Panegyric Code in Gaelic Poetry and Its Historical Background," *Transactions of the Gaelic Society of Inverness* 50 (1979); D. S. Thomson, "Gaelic Poetry in the Eighteenth Century: The Breaking of the Mould," *The History of Scottish Literature, Vol. 2*, ed. A. Hook (1987); W. Gillies, "Gaelic: The Classical Tradition," *The History of Scottish Literature, Vol. 1*, ed. R.D.S. Jack (1988); J. MacInnes, "Gaelic Poetry in the Nineteenth Century," *The History of Scottish Literature, Vol. 3*, ed. D. Gifford (1988); D. Thomson, *An Introduction to Gaelic Poetry*, 2d ed. (1989); W. Gillies, "Traditional Gaelic Women's Songs," *Alba Literaria*, ed. M. Fazzini (2005), and "Gaelic Literature in the Later Middle Ages: *The Book of the Dean* and Beyond," *The Edinburgh History of Scottish Literature, Vol. 1*, ed. T. O. Clancy et al. (2007); T. A. McKean, "Tradition and Modernity: Gaelic Bards in the Twentieth Century," *The Edinburgh History of Scottish Literature, Vol. 3*, ed. I. Brown et al. (2007); D. E. Meek, "Gaelic Literature in the Nineteenth Century," *The Edinburgh History of Scottish Literature, Vol. 2*, ed. S. Manning et al. (2007).

R. D. Thornton, R. Watson (Scots and Eng.); J. MacInnes, M. Byrne (Gaelic)

## SCOTTISH CHAUCERIANS OR MAKARS.

A name applied to a group of Scottish poets of the 15th and 16th cs. whose work, although the freshest and most original Eng. poetry of the period, shows a common indebtedness to the example of Chaucer. The most important Scottish Chaucerians were King James I of Scotland, Robert Henryson, William Dunbar, Gavin Douglas, and Sir David Lindsay; of these Henryson and Dunbar were poets of major importance. Henryson is remembered for "Robene and Makyne," a superb *pastoral, and for *The Testament of Cresseid*, a profound and moving elaboration and continuation of Chaucer's *Troilus and Criseyde*. Dunbar, a poet of wider range, wrote elaborate *occasional verse, biting *satires, and such memorable short poems as his famous elegiac "Lament for the Makaris." In formal terms, the Scottish Chaucerians continued the vogue of the seven-line stanza

introduced into Eng. poetry by Chaucer; indeed, the name for this form, *rhyme royal*, was once thought to have been derived from its use by King James in his poem "The Kingis Quair."

*See* COURTLY MAKERS; SCOTLAND, POETRY OF.

■ H. S. Bennett, *Chaucer and the Fifteenth Century* (1947); G. G. Smith, "The Scottish Chaucerians," *CHEL* 2 (1949); C. S. Lewis, *English Literature in the Sixteenth Century, Excluding Drama* (1954); D. Fox, "The Scottish Chaucerians," *Chaucer and Chaucerians*, ed. D. S. Brewer (1966); A. M. Kinghorn, *Middle Scots Poets* (1970); G. Kratzmann, *Anglo-Scottish Literary Relations, 1430–1550* (1980); W. Scheps and J. A. Looney, *The Middle Scots Poets: A Reference Guide* (1986); L. A. Ebin, *Illuminator, Makar, Vates* (1988); A. S. Tomko, "William Dunbar's Poetics: A Reconsideration of the Chaucerian in a Scottish Maker," *DAI* 56 (1996).

R. D. Thornton

## SCOTTISH GAELIC POETRY. *See* SCOTLAND, POETRY OF.

## SECONDE RHÉTORIQUE.

In late med. Fr. poetic treatises, a distinction came to be made between the art of persuasion or oratory as applied in prose—i.e., rhet., the figures and *tropes—and the art of persuasion in verse—i.e., *versification or *prosody; the former came to be called *first rhetoric* and the latter *second rhetoric*. Patterson dates these treatises on the art of verse from 1370 to 1539; they form the link between the few Occitan and OF treatises and the *Arts poétiques* of the *Pléiade in the Ren.

How prosody came to be allied with rhet. is one of the chapters of *medieval poetics. In med. Lat., prosody was treated primarily as a branch of grammar, being either included in grammars as a chapter called "Prosodia" or else written as a separate manual, e.g., Bede's *De arte metrica* (both types are collected in Keil). Rhet. took a parallel but distinguishable course except in encyclopedic works such as Isidore of Seville's *Etymologiae* (7th c.; prosody and rhet. are the subjects of the first two chapters). Alternatively, some theorists viewed prosody as a branch of music (e.g., Augustine); these two trads. devolve from the *metrici and rhythmici of the ancients. In the 12th and 13th cs. emerged the treatises known as *artes poeticae*; such works, following the inspiration of Horace, treated both rhet. and prosody together. These are instanced in John of Garland's *Parisiana poetria* (much on prosody), Matthew of Vendôme's *Ars versificatoria* (virtually nothing), Geoffrey of Vinsauf's *Poetria nova*, Alexander of Ville Dei's *Doctrinale*, and Eberhard the German's *Laborintus* (collected in Faral). Dante's unfinished essay on poetry, *De vulgari eloquentia* (ca. 1304), which treats chiefly *diction and prosody, provides the transition to the vernaculars. By the 15th c., in France, manuals distinguish not between rhet. and prosody but between prose and verse, and since prosody treats of precisely those devices that are the differentia of verse form, it became a "second rhetoric"; *pleine rhétoriques* treated both. Langlois collects seven principal texts by Jacques Le Grand, Baudet Herenc, Jean Molinet, and four anonymous authors, but the most influential was Eustache Deschamps' *L'Art de dictier* (1392).

*See* RHÉTORIQUEURS, GRANDS.

■ Keil; E. Langlois, *Recueil d'arts de seconde rhétorique* (1902)—long intro.; Faral; Patterson; H. Lubienski-Bodenham, "The Origins of the Fifteenth-Century View of Poetry as 'Seconde Rhétorique,'" *MLR* 74 (1979); Hollier; E. Mechoulan, "La musique du vulgaire: Arts de seconde rhétorique et constitution de la littérature" *Études littéraires* 22 (1989–90); A. M. Finoli, "La ricezione della mitologia negli 'Arts de seconde rhétorique,'" *Studi di Letteratura Francese* 16 (1990); A.T.B. Butterfield, "Arts de seconde rhétorique," *Medieval France: An Encyclopedia*, ed. W. W. Kibler et al. (1995); C. Thiry, "Prospections et prospectives sur la Rhétorique seconde," *Moyen Français* 46–47 (2000); *Poétiques en transition: entre Moyen Age et Renaissance*, ed. J.-C. Mühlethaler and J. Cerquiglini-Toulet (2002).

T.V.F. BROGAN

**SEGUIDILLA.** A Sp. poetic form of popular origin. It probably originated as a dance song and was popular, at least in the underworld, early in the 17th c. In the beginning, it was probably a four-line *strophe of alternating long (usually seven- or eight-syllable) and short (five- or six-syllable) lines, the short (even-numbered) lines assonating (called *seguidilla simple* or *seguidilla para cantar*). Later, probably in the 17th c., a second, semi-independent part of three lines—short, long, short—was added, the short lines having a new *assonance. Eventually, the strophe became regularized as a literary form to lines of 7-5-7-5: 5-7-5 (the colon denotes a pause in thought), lines two and four having one assonance, lines five and seven another (called *seguidilla compuesta* or *seguidilla para bailar*), often found in 18th-c. poetry. Sometimes the rhythm has been used only in lines of seven plus five syllables, as by Rubén Darío in his *Elogio de la seguidilla*. The seguidilla favors all paroxytonic verses except when six-syllable oxytones are substituted for the five-syllable (paroxytonic) lines. The seguidilla sometimes serves as a conclusion (*estribillo) to another song.

The *seguidilla gitana* (Gypsy seguidilla), also called *flamenca* or *playera*, is usually a five-line strophe of 6, 6, 5, 6, 6 syllables, lines two and five assonating. Lines three and four may be written together as one line of from ten to twelve syllables.

■ F. Hanssen, "La seguidilla," *Anales de la Universidad de Chile* 125 (1909); F. Rodríguez Marín, *La copla* (1910); P. Henríquez Ureña, *La versificación irregular en la poesía castellana*, 2d ed. (1933); D. C. Clarke, "The Early Seguidilla," *HR* 12 (1944); José Mercado, *La seguidilla gitana* (1982); Navarro; L. Pastor Pérez, "La seguidilla: Trayectoria histórica de una forma poética popular," *Lírica popular/lírica tradicional*, ed. P. Piñero Ramírez (1998); R. E. González, "y arriba iré . . . Acerca

de la seguidilla folclórica de México," *Anuario de letras* 39 (2001); J. M. Pedrosa, "Seguidillas sefardíes de Marruecos: Diacronía, poética y comparatismo," *Revista de literaturas populares* 2 (2002).

D. C. CLARKE

## SEMANTICS AND POETRY

I. Development of Semantics as Science of Meaning
II. Poetic Language: A Challenge to Semantics

**I. Development of Semantics as Science of Meaning.** The term *semantics* (Gr. *sēmantikos*, "significant") is of fairly recent origin compared with its field of interest. The ponderings on the nature of meaning have their roots in Aristotelian logic, poetics, and rhet., as well as in a long trad. of philosophy and such areas of study as grammar, philology, literary theory, and *stylistics. Around 1825, Karl Reisig introduced the term *semasiology* to describe a subdivision of grammar focused on the study of meaning. In 1897, Michel Bréal proposed *sémantique* to denote the "science of meaning." Both Reisig and Bréal regarded semantics as a diachronic study, occupied mostly with historical changes of words and, at most, phrases. Thus, this initial stage can be called the philologically oriented *lexical semantics*. In 1909, Charles Bally presented his treatise on stylistics. In turn, Ferdinand de Saussure's structural way of thinking about lang. brought to the semanticists' attention the importance of such intralinguistic sense relations as synonymy, antonymy (oppositeness), hyperonymy (class inclusion), and *ambiguity. This view of lang. was complemented by the study of semantic fields by Ger. scholars (Trier, Weisgerber) and later broadened by the invocation of stylistic fields, scrutinized by statistical stylistics.

In the Am. behaviorist trad., Charles Morris (1946, 1971), inspired by Charles S. Peirce's works, proposed the tripartite subdivision of ling. into syntactics, semantics, and pragmatics. The first was supposed to deal with the internal relations of signs within lang., the second with the signification of signs (incl. reference to reality), the third with the relation between signs and their users in a specific context (see SIGN, SIGNIFIED, SIGNIFIER). It is owing to philosophers and logicians that ling. semantics, by making recourse to formal semantics, acquired its scientific shape and became *sentence semantics*. Considerable influence was also exerted by logical positivists, particularly the early Ludwig Wittgenstein (1921) and Rudolf Carnap; the Am. behaviorists Leonard Bloomfield and Willard v. O. Quine; the Am. analytical philosophers Saul Kripke, Donald Davidson (1972, 1975, 1978), and Nicholas Rescher; and the Oxford school of ling. philosophy, incl. the late Wittgenstein (1953), Gilbert Ryle (see crit. in Gellner), and John L. Austin (1961).

Semantics gradually broadened its scope to accommodate various functional aspects of lang. Apart from its leading representative function (communication of ideas), Karl Bühler specified the expressive and the vocative functions, both conspicuous in poetic lang. Further elaborations of the functional taxonomy (Ogden and Richards—emotive meaning; Jakobson 1960—*poetic function; Halliday—textual and imaginative function; Lyons—expressive function) prove the unfailing concern of semantics to accommodate within its scope all types of discourse marked with the feature of subjectivity, emotionality, and poeticity. Roman Jakobson implemented the ideas of *Russian formalism and artistic semiotics (Shklovsky; Lotman, cf. Shukman) in the description of poetic lang. Jakobson was also the first to introduce the concept of the large textual strategy by postulating *metaphor and *metonymy as two basic modes of ling. and semiotic construal and interpretation of artistic texts.

The philosophical contribution of ordinary lang. philosophers and the subsequent devel. of ling., along the lines laid most notably by the late Wittgenstein and carried on by Austin (1962) and John R. Searle within *speech act theory, have demonstrated that semantics and pragmatics ought to be treated as closely interrelated fields of research concerned with the felicitous functioning of human lang. in diverse contexts.

In America, the late 1960s and 1970s brought a devel. in formal semantics for natural lang. Within this trend, Davidson (1975) propagated the truth-functional model of semantics (based on the evaluation of sentences as true or false) and proposed a peculiar theory, according to which metaphorical constructions are meant literally and are either obviously true or patently false. Of much greater import was the devel. of modal logic and possible-worlds semantics. The former deals with such notions as, among others, necessity, (im)possibility, obligation, prohibition, knowledge, belief, doubt, wish, hope, beauty vs. ugliness, and goodness vs. evil. The latter allows us to extend these ideas to alternative worlds of imagination (Hintikka 1969, Kripke, Rescher). Such concepts as *text worlds* and *discourse worlds* of contemp. literary semantics are the adaptations of a formal logical construct called *possible world* to the analysis of fictional discourse. The issue of the ontological status of fictional discourse and fictional individuals, so important for all literary genres, has been tackled by John Woods, Searle (1975), Richard Rorty, and Umberto Eco (1990), among others.

The school of transformational-generative (TG) grammarians (Noam Chomsky and his followers), though focusing on the creative potential of human ling. competence, at first refused to accept semantics as a part of their model. Under the influence of Jerrold J. Katz and Jerry A. Fodor's semantic theory, Chomsky introduced some semantic considerations into his Standard Theory (1965). Yet poetic lang. under this system turned out to be either syntactically ill formed or semantically deviant. The Extended Standard Model of Chomsky allowed for a separate semantic component, called *interpretative semantics* (Jackendoff). The inability of the consecutive variants of TG grammar to deal with syntactically and semantically marked (anomalous) structures added to the emergence of generative semantics at the turn of the 1960s (McCawley, Lakoff). McCawley was also the first to use the term *mental picture of the universe* to explain how metaphors

refer to imaginary situations. Indeed, he can be seen as a precursor of the possible-worlds thinking later applied to metaphoric lang. (Levin 1988, Hintikka and Sandu). Metaphor was perceived, then, as a violation of certain presuppositions conventionally cherished about reality (the actual world). *Generative poetics* also used Uriel Weinreich's idea about the need to recategorize syntactically deviant structures abundant in literary lang. The accompanying notion of a *semantic calculator* was meant to evaluate the degree of semantic oddity.

The 1970s saw an important devel. in ling. semantics. The semantico-pragmatic description (a combination of intra- and extralinguistic factors of meaning) crossed the boundaries of a single sentence and turned its attention to texts interpreted in various contexts by various interpreters (discourses). In Europe, Teun van Dijk's as well as Robert de Beaugrande's and Wolfgang U. Dressler's seminal works on text grammars enlarged the scope of semantic description to all kinds of texts. In the U.S., the functional approach of M.A.K. Halliday recognized the textual dimension of lang. already in 1973.

In turn, game-theoretic semantics revitalized the Wittgensteinian concept of language games. Though initially concerned only with sentences (propositions), with time it broadened its application to discourse, esp. in Lauri Carlson's *Dialogue Games* (1983). The semantics and pragmatics based on the conception of game, applicable to conversational exchanges, can also be extended to the study of literary texts, where authors and readers embark on semantic and pragmatic games of text production and text reception, respectively (Chrzanowska-Kluczewska 2004).

One of the most conspicuous paradigmatic shifts in ling. was the birth of cognitive grammar in the 1980s and its steady growth over the consecutive two decades. The cognitive approach to lang., which stresses the importance of conceptual metaphor and its pervasiveness in lang. (Lakoff and Johnson), has made poetic lang. a focus of interest for semanticists. In Europe, cognitive theory has caught on in several academic centers, as shown in Paul Werth's work on extended metaphor (1994) and later on text and discourse worlds (1999); Elena Semino's studies (1997, 2008, Semino and Short 2004) on various literary and nonliterary discourses, amply exemplified by poetic metaphor and supported by the quantitative findings of corpus stylistics (computer-assisted statistical analysis of style-related phenomena); Reuven Tsur's (1992, 2003) and Peter Stockwell's cognitive approach to poetics; the contribution of Zoltán Kövecses to metaphor studies and of Elżbieta Tabakowska to trans. studies in the light of cognitive poetics.

**II. Poetic Language: A Challenge to Semantics.** A gradual devel. of mod. semantic theories, as sketched above, from word-oriented to text-centered, provides a framework for the ling. investigation of literary texts, whether prose or poetry. Yet poetic lang., with its unbounded creativity and innovation, has proven a conundrum for all semantic theories. Not without reason did Philip Wheelwright (1974) postulate a separate poeto-semantics to deal specifically with literary texts.

The problems semantics has faced when applied to literary lang., which is predominantly fictional, are as follows.

(1) Poetic lang. has often been classified as logically deviant on two interrelated grounds: (a) reference failure and (b) problems with the assignment of truth values (true, false). For these reasons, already Gottlob Frege (in Schmidt 1976) proposed to distinguish between scientific and literary texts, while Richards referred to literary assertions as *"pseudo-statements." The introduction of the notion of possible worlds, text worlds, and discourse worlds alleviates such problems, for now fictional expressions can denote individuals and objects that exist not within the real world but within a specific imaginary world. For those unwilling to accept such a solution, the Russellian treatment of imaginary entities as purely ling. objects, existing as mere names, remains open and the concepts of metaphorical truth, truth in fiction, or truth by convention has to be invoked (Levin 1988). A steady devel. of nonclassical logical systems has offered solutions to the problems of non-denoting terms or truth assignment, such as free and neutral logics, both admitting of nondenoting terms in their domains of *interpretation. Many-valued logics offer either the indeterminate value I or a truth-value gap (neither true nor false) for fictional statements, whereas logics of inconsistency tolerate paradoxes in the system, where contradictory propositions can obtain simultaneously (cf. Haack 1974, Rescher and Brandom, Chrzanowska-Kluczewska 2010 for more details). The theories of nonstandard possible worlds that such logical systems are capable of supporting could be of interest to transrealistic genres of prose (e.g., fantasy, science fiction) and of poetry (e.g., *nonsense verse).

(2) Semino's work on the creation of poetic worlds (1997), invoking Marie-Laure Ryan's typology of fictional worlds, proves that poetic text worlds yield themselves not only to this type of description but also to the analysis within the alternative schema theory (with origins in cognitive psychology and artificial intelligence; cf. Schank and Abelson 1977), where *schema* stands for a mental structure in which our knowledge of the world is stored. The reader's interpretation and overall reception of a text world will depend on the way in which such schemata are activated and challenged (esp. in the case of more demanding, sophisticated or densely figurative texts, to which poetry obviously belongs).

(3) Within the theory of speech acts (which has a mixed semantico-pragmatic foundation), Austin (1962) described speech acts in poetry as parasitic upon real-world talk. In a similar vein, Richard Ohmann referred to fictional statements as "quasi-speech acts" or impaired and incomplete illocutions whose function is mimetic of real speech acts. Searle (1975) qualified them as nondeceptive pseudoperformance (but not lies, as in Plato's evaluation of literary statements). In a friendlier frame of mind, Levin (1976) proposes a covert performative prefix "I imagine this world and invite you to enter it" appended to every fictional work,

thus formally capturing S. T. Coleridge's famed "willing suspension of disbelief," i.e., poetic faith.

(4) *Figuration* is of utmost importance for poetry, where the density (clustering) of stylistic and rhetorical devices by far exceeds the one found in prose. The concern with figuration in mod. Anglo-Am. trad. runs from Richards (1936) and Max Black, the supporters of the theory of metaphor funded by the tension between its two elements *vehicle* and *tenor* (renamed *source* and *target domain* in cognitive ling.), in which both similarity and difference can be appropriately highlighted (also Nowottny). Wheelwright (1974) calls due attention to the strong symbolic undercurrent in poetry, often archetypal and mythical in nature, analyzed also by Ernst Cassirer. The realization that figuration structures not only poetic lang. but also human conceptual makeup is well visible in Kenneth Burke's study of four *master tropes* (metaphor, metonymy, *synecdoche, *irony), grounded in neoclassical rhet. and Giambattista Vico's thought. Master tropes, as "styles of thinking" are, thus, powerful text-organizing strategies (cf. Werth 1994, 1999 on *megametaphors*).

The rhetorical impact and ubiquity of figuration, described already in the poststructuralist writings of Roland Barthes, the philosophical concern with discourse and the limits of poetic lang. voiced by Michel Foucault, and the deconstructionist claims about the all-pervasive and even destructive play of ling. signs, coupled with the assumption of the ineradicable metaphoricity of lang. as propounded by Jacques Derrida, were all recognized in the works of Am. postmodernist and deconstructionist crit. Most noticeable were here the works of Paul de Man (1974, 1984), Geoffrey Hartman, and J. Hillis Miller. Tropology was also developed successfully by Harold Bloom's innovative treatment of figural intricacies present in poetry and of poetic influence, the latter apparently also regulated by figurative schemas of great generality. This preoccupation with the tacit, underlying level of figuration is an extension of the prolonged discussion on the double layering/coding/symbolization of literary and poetic lang. in particular (cf. Eco 2002). The idea of an inherent and pervasive presence of metaphor in human thought and lang. has found a sturdy continuation within the Lakoffian framework of cognitive studies devoted to conceptual metaphor, conventional and nonconventional alike. Its elaboration in Eur. thought has shaped cognitively oriented considerations of the poetic potential of human lang., esp. in metaphorical creativity (Werth 1994; Tsur 1992, 2003; Semino 2008). The cognitive paradigm runs parallel to a long-established classic ling. stylistics as practiced by Geoffrey Leech (1969, 2008) and Mick Short, which has focused on such aspects of poetic lang. as deviation (limits of *poetic license), deception, semantic indeterminacy, and stylistic foregrounding realized through figuration. Likewise, Michael Toolan (1990) in his literary-ling. approach proposes that the ling. and critical aspects of literary studies should be treated as complementary rather than competing.

The above-mentioned problems a semanticist faces while trying to analyze the highly unpredictable lang.

of poetry are accompanied by the phenomenon that Wheelwright (1968, 1974) called "plurisignation." A poetic artwork will never be adequately interpreted and evaluated if it is not taken as a complex object, endowed with several levels of signification. Such "integral" (holistic) meaning, according to Wheelwright, has to be additionally supported by the phonetics (*versification, *rhythm, sound effects; in a word, the poem's peculiar orchestration) and, at times, graphic effects (as in pattern poetry, *concrete poetry, *lettrisme, etc.). Literary semantics/stylistics/poetics also calls for the complementary investigation of interpretative strategies (Ingarden 1931, 1973, Iser 1978) and cognitive mechanisms of reading (Miall 2005). The fact that the relevance theory, developed by Dan Sperber and Deirdre Wilson (1986), has taken up the issue of figuration, esp. of irony and metaphor (Pilkington 2000), indicates that contemp. semantic thinking about poeticity is linked to psycho- and sociolinguistic considerations. Thus, the directions of future research on poetic lang. seem to be clearly laid out, incl. the philosophy of lang., for which the problematic of figuration remains an open question (Lycan 2000).

See LINGUISTICS AND POETICS, SEMIOTICS AND POETRY.

■ **Linguistics**: M. Bréal, *Essai de sémantique* (1897); F. de Saussure, *Cours de linguistique générale* (1916); C. K. Ogden and I. A. Richards, *The Meaning of Meaning* (1923); L. Bloomfield, *Language* (1933); K. Bühler, *Sprachtheorie* (1934); J. Trier, "Das sprachliche Feld. Eine Auseinandersetzung," *Neue Jahrbücher für Wissenschaft und Jugendbildung* 10 (1934); I. A. Richards, *The Philosophy of Rhetoric* (1936); C. Bally, *Traité de stylistique française* [1909], 3d ed. (1951); L. Weisgerber, "Die Sprachfelder der geistigen Erschliessung der Welt," *Festschrift für J. Trier* (1954); R. Jakobson, "Two Aspects of Language and Two Types of Linguistic Disturbances," Jakobson and Halle; N. Chomsky, *Syntactic Structures* (1957); R. Jakobson, "Linguistics and Poetics," *Style in Language*, ed. T. A. Sebeok (1960); M. Black, *Models and Metaphors* (1962); S. Ullmann, *Semantics* (1962); J. J. Katz and J. A. Fodor, "The Structure of a Semantic Theory," *Language* 39 (1963); N. Chomsky, *Aspects of the Theory of Syntax* (1965); U. Weinreich, "Explorations in Semantic Theory," *Current Trends in Linguistics*, ed. T. A. Sebeok, v. 3 (1966); J. D. McCawley, "The Role of Semantics in Grammar," *Universals in Linguistic Theory*, ed. E. Bach and R. T. Harms (1968); G. Lakoff, "On Generative Semantics," *Semantics*, ed. D. D. Steinberg and L. A. Jakobovits (1969); G. N. Leech, *A Linguistic Guide to English Poetry* (1969); J. R. Searle, *Speech Acts* (1969); R. Ohmann, "Speech Acts and the Definition of Literature," *Philosophy and Rhetoric* 4 (1971); T. van Dijk, *Some Aspects of Text Grammars* (1972); R. Jackendoff, *Semantic Interpretation in Generative Grammar* (1972); M.A.K. Halliday, *Explorations in the Functions of Language* (1973); J. Hintikka, *Logic, Language-Games and Information* (1973); J. R. Searle, "The Logical Status of Fictional Discourse," *NLH* 6 (1975); S. R. Levin, "What Kind of Speech Act a Poem Is?" and S. J. Schmidt, "A Pragmatic Interpretation of Fictionality," *Pragmatics of Language and Literature*, ed. T. van Dijk (1976); J. Lyons, *Semantics*, 2 v. (1977); G. Lakoff and M. Johnson, *Metaphors We Live By* (1980); D. Sperber and D. Wilson, "Irony and the Use-Mention Distinction," *Radical Pragmatics*, ed. P. Cole (1981); J. Hintikka and J. Kulas, *The Game of Language* (1983); D. Sperber and D. Wilson, *Relevance* (1986); S. Levin, *Metaphoric Worlds* (1988); G. Lakoff and M. Turner, *More Than Cool Reason* (1989); R.-A. de Beaugrande and W. U. Dressler, *Introduction to Text Linguistics* (1990); M. Toolan, *The Stylistics of Fiction: A Literary-Linguistic Approach* (1990); M.-L. Ryan, *Possible Worlds, Artificial Intelligence and Narrative Theory* (1991); R. Tsur, *Toward a Theory of Cognitive Poetics* (1992); E. Tabakowska, *Cognitive Linguistics and Poetics of Translation* (1993); J. Hintikka and G. Sandu, "Metaphor and Other Kinds of Non-Literal Meaning," *Aspects of Metaphor*, ed. J. Hintikka (1994); P. Werth, "Extended Metaphor," *Language and Literature* 3 (1994); M. Short, *Exploring the Language of Poems, Plays and Prose* (1996); E. Semino, *Language and World Creation in Poems and Other Texts* (1997); P. Werth, *Text Worlds* (1999); A. Pilkington, *Poetic Effects* (2000); Z. Kövecses, *Metaphor* (2002); P. Stockwell, *Cognitive Poetics: An Introduction* (2002); R. Tsur, *On the Shore of Nothingness* (2003); E. Chrzanowska-Kluczewska, *Language-Games: Pro and Against* (2004); E. Semino and M. Short, *Corpus Stylistics* (2004); D. S. Miall, "Beyond Interpretation," *Cognition and Literary Interpretation in Practice*, ed. H. Veivo, B. Pettersson, M. Polvinen (2005); G. Leech, *Language in Literature. Style and Foregrounding* (2008); E. Semino, *Metaphor in Discourse* (2008); D. Sperber and D. Wilson, "A Deflationary Account of Metaphor," *The Cambridge Handbook of Metaphor and Thought*, ed. R. Gibbs (2008); E. Chrzanowska-Kluczewska, "An Unresolved Issue: Nonsense in Natural Language and Non-Classical Logical and Semantic Systems," *Philosophy of Language and Linguistics*, ed. P. Stalmaszczyk (2010).

■ **Literary Criticism**: K. Burke, *A Grammar of Motives* (1962); W. Nowottny, *The Language Poets Use* (1962); P. Wheelwright, *The Burning Fountain* (1968); R. Ingarden, *The Literary Work of Art*, trans. G. G. Grabowicz (1973); P. Wheelwright, "Semantics and Poetry," *Princeton Encyclopedia of Poetry and Poetics*, ed. A. Preminger (1974); R. Barthes, *S/Z*, trans. R. Miller (1975); H. Bloom, *A Map of Misreading* (1975); A. Shukman, *Literature and Semiotics: A Study of the Writings of Yu. M. Lotman* (1977); W. Iser, *The Act of Reading* (1978); P. de Man, *Allegories of Reading* (1979), and *The Rhetoric of Romanticism* (1984); G. Hartman, *Easy Pieces* (1985); J. Hillis Miller, "On Edge," *Romanticism and Contemporary Criticism*, ed. M. Eaves and M. Fischer (1986); V. Shklovsky, "Art as Technique" (1917), *Contemporary Literary Criticism*, ed. R. C. Davis and R. Schleifer (1986); U. Eco, *The Limits of Interpretation* (1990), and *On Literature* (2002), trans. M. McLaughlin (2004).

■ **Philosophy**: L. Wittgenstein, *Tractatus Logico-Philosophicus* (1921); E. Cassirer, *Language and Myth*, trans. S. Langer (1946); C. W. Morris, *Signs, Language and Behavior* (1946); R. Carnap, *Meaning and Necessity* (1947); L. Wittgenstein, *Philosophical Investiga-

*tions*, trans. G.E.M. Anscombe (1953); G. Ryle, *The Revolution in Philosophy* (1956); E. Gellner, *Words and Things* (1959); W. V. Quine, *Word and Object* (1960); J. L. Austin, *Philosophical Papers* (1961), and *How to Do Things with Words* (1962); M. Foucault, *Raymond Roussel* (1963); J. Hintikka, *Models for Modalities* (1969); M. Foucault, *The Order of Things* (1970); C. W. Morris, "Foundations of the Theory of Signs," *Writings on the General Theory of Signs* (1971); S. Kripke, *Naming and Necessity* (1972); *Semantics of Natural Language*, ed. D. Davidson and G. Harman (1972); S. Haack, *Deviant Logic, Fuzzy Logic* (1974); J. Woods, *The Logic of Fiction* (1974); D. Davidson, "Semantics for Natural Language," *The Logic of Grammar*, ed. D. Davidson and G. Harman (1975); N. Rescher, *A Theory of Possibility* (1975); R. C. Schank and R. Abelson, *Scripts, Plans, Goals and Understanding* (1977); D. Davidson, "What Metaphors Mean," *Inquiries into Truth and Interpretation* (1978); N. Rescher and R. Brandom, *The Logic of Inconsistency* (1979); R. Rorty, *Consequences of Pragmatism* (1982); G. Vico, *The New Science of Giambattista Vico*, trans. T. G. Bergin and M. H. Fisch (1984); Derrida; W. G. Lycan, *Philosophy of Language* (2000).

E. Chrzanowska-Kluczewska

**SEMIOTICS AND POETRY.** The mod. usage of the term *semiotics* is attributed to John Locke, who appropriated the Gr. *semeiotiké* to designate the *doctrine of signs*, "the business whereof is to consider the nature of signs the mind makes use of *for the understanding of things*, or conveying its knowledge to others." The study of *signs, however, has ancient roots. In speculating on the origin of lang., the Platonic dialogue *Cratylus* describes the linkage between ling. *sound and meaning as motivated by either nature or convention (*physei* versus *thesei*), thus establishing one of the basic dichotomies for all subsequent discussions. Aristotle's *On Interpretation* and *Rhetoric* and St. Augustine's *De doctrina christiana* (*On Christian Doctrine*) and *The Teacher* are other important ancient treatises on the subject, and various Scholastics continue the line of inquiry through the Middle Ages. The major mod. figures, besides Locke, are the philosophers and linguists G. W. Leibniz, Johann Heinrich Lambert, Étienne Bonnot de Condillac, Wilhelm von Humboldt, and Bernhard Bolzano. Contemp. semiotic studies are a combination of several intellectual trads. stemming from the turn of the 20th c. Three schools of thought esp. stimulate the application of sign theory to poetics: Peircean pragmatism, Husserlian phenomenology, and Saussurean structuralism.

The most comprehensive program for the general science of signs was charted by the Am. philosopher Charles Sanders Peirce. According to Peirce, "a sign or *representamen* is something which stands to somebody for something in some respect or capacity." Hence, every sign process (or *semiosis*) is the correlation of three components: the sign itself, the object represented, and the interpretant. The relationship between the sign and its object (as the above definition suggests) implies a certain inadequacy between the two. The sign does not stand for the object in its entirety but merely for some of its aspects. Peirce claimed that there are three basic modes in which the sign can represent something else and, hence, three types of signs. A sign that resembles its object (such as a model or a map) is an *icon*; a sign that is factually linked to its object (such as a weathercock or a pointer) is an *index*; a sign conventionally associated with its object (such as words or traffic signals) is a *symbol*. To interpret the word *table*, one can resort to an icon (by drawing its picture), an index (by pointing to an actual table), or a symbol (by supplying a synonym). In short, the process of *interpretation is nothing but the substitution of certain signs for others. From this perspective, then, thought or knowledge is a web of interconnected signs capable of unlimited self-generation.

In contrast to the Am. pragmatist Peirce, who considered the semiotics domain in its entirety, continental thinkers focused on lang. as the most important human signifying mechanism. The Ger. phenomenologist Edmund Husserl was concerned with verbal signs as vehicles of logical thought capable of embodying truth. For him, only a repeatable sign that retains its essential self-sameness under all circumstances can fulfill this role. In his quest for a universal semiotics, Husserl divided all signs into two categories: the self-identical *expression* (*Ausdruck*) and the vacillating *indication* (*Anzeichen*). To explain why expressions can remain unaffected by the context of the significatory act, Husserl analyzed the internal structure of the word to isolate a factor resistant to contextual change. "In the case of the name," he wrote, "we distinguish between what it 'shows forth' (i.e. a mental state) and what it means. And again between what it means (the sense or 'content' of its naming presentation) and what it names (the object of that presentation)." Both the "showing forth" and the "naming" are contingent on empirical reality (whether mental or physical) and, thus, cannot retain their sameness in repetition. Only the "content of an expression's naming presentation," the "meaning" (*Bedeutung*), is independent of the phenomenal context. It is, therefore, this lexical meaning inherent in the word prior to its representing other entities that endows the expression with its identity and distinguishes it from the indication.

The nature of verbal signs was also the central concern of another pioneer of mod. semiotics, the Swiss linguist Ferdinand de Saussure. Saussure focused exclusively on the system of ling. conventions (*langue*) that makes actual utterances (*parole*) understandable to lang. users. He considered langue a purely formal set of relations that (in the absence of other motivations) arbitrarily conjoin the two components of the ling. *sign*—the sensory *signifier* and the intelligible *signified*. Accordingly, the study of the signifier was to yield a set of oppositions (i.e., the phonological system) that provides sonorous substance (the continuum of the sound stream) with ling. form by articulating it into a limited inventory of *phonemes*, the minimal sound units capable of differentiating words of unlike meaning in a given lang. (e.g., the voiceless voiced bilabial stops *p* and *b* in *pit* and *bit*, sounds that would be identical except for the one "distinctive feature" of voicing, or vibration of the vocal cords, which feature alone creates, for speakers of Eng., two words, two meanings). The study of the signified, on the other hand, would be concerned with the semantic grid that segments extralinguistic reality into meaningful ling. units (words). The semantic value of every particular signified would be derived solely from its opposition to other signifieds coexisting within the grid, hence, creating a parallel matrix of distinctive oppositions. The Eng. *mutton* differs from Fr. *mouton* precisely because the meaning of the former is circumscribed by the word *sheep*, which has no equivalent in the Fr. vocabulary.

Another set of relations obtains in lang. through the combination of ling. elements into more complex units. If concatenated into a sequence, the value of each segment is determined both by its juxtaposition to all the actual components in the sequence that precede or follow it and by the presence or absence of all the potential elements of langue in some respect similar to it and capable of taking its place. The first of these, the aspect of the *continuity* of elements in sequence, which gives lang. its "horizontal dimension," Saussure termed the *syntagmatic* aspect of lang.; the latter, the "vertical dimension" in which one word that fills a slot in the syntactic string could be replaced, potentially, by others, Saussure termed the *associative* (in later usage, *paradigmatic*) aspect of lang. It remained for Roman Jakobson to give the equation relating the one to the other in verse via *equivalence as the "poetic principle." As Saussure persuasively argued, these two functions are operative at all three ling. levels: phonological, morphological, and syntactic. In the example above, the *p* in *pit* is opposed to the *i* that follows it as consonant to vowel, and at the same time, it is opposed to the absent *b* that could have been substituted for it (giving *bit*) as voiceless phoneme to voiced. The words *pits*, *pitted*, *pitting*, and *bits* that combine the same or different stems and affixes illustrate the same dual linkage at the morphological level as, mutatis mutandis, the lexical collocations *drilling bit*, *drilling pit*, and *orchestra pit* do at the syntactic level.

The first systematic attempts to apply the theory of signs to lit. date from the 1920s. The devel. of this critical method has to a large extent been linked to the worldwide interest in the structuralist paradigm over the past 60 years (see STRUCTURALISM). The cultural heterogeneity of this paradigm and its historical diversity have prevented semiotically inclined critics from reaching full agreement about the epistemological underpinnings of their enterprise, its scope and limits, or even common methodologies. What binds such critics together is merely the general explanatory model that regards lit. as a specific mode of signifying practice governed by conventions that are distinct from all other uses of verbal signs. In the practical application of this

model, each school or critic focuses on different facets of literary semiosis, defines in separate terms the conventions governing it, and accounts for its distinctness accordingly.

Though critics have always been aware that the special manipulation of lang. is one of the indispensable properties of poetry, only the antimimetic revolt of modernist art at the turn of the 20th c. led them to scrutinize and schematize the ways in which the ling. medium can be used to achieve poetic effects (see MODERNISM). Keeping in step with Archibald MacLeish's celebrated dictum that "a poem should not mean / But be," the most radical theorists of the day denied verbal art any referential quality at all, rather identifying its *telos* with the striking orchestration of the ling. sound devoid of meaning. Semiotic poetics came about as a partial corrective to the one-sidedness of such *formalism. Without rejecting the salience of phonic devices for poetry, it attributed to them a value only insofar as they participate in poetic semantics.

This stance was first formulated by Jakobson, perhaps the most seminal figure of this critical trend, in his 1921 booklet on the Rus. futurist poet Velimir Khlebnikov. He based his argument on the two earlier theories of the ling. sign by Saussure and Husserl. Drawing particularly on the phonological insights of Saussure, Jakobson rejected the possibility of separating sound from meaning in lang. *Phoné*, as the signifier's substance, is always semanticized because its chief function is to distinguish among different signifieds. If poetry were to succeed in voiding the semantic charge from its sonorous substance, it would inevitably lose its verbal nature and turn into a kind of vocal music. Moreover, Jakobson made the semiotic orientation of his poetics explicit by anchoring it in Husserl's concept of expression. It is the "set (*Einstellung*) toward expression itself," Jakobson claimed, that designates it "as the only factor essential for poetry" and that imparts to verbal art its "thorough-going symbolic, multiplex, polysemantic essence." Jakobson also drew attention to the associative principles that underlie the two fundamental ling. operations of selection and combination. Selection substitutes one element for another on the basis of their partial lexical similarity, in the same way as does the rhetorical trope of *metaphor. Combination links elements that are spatially or temporally contiguous, very much as does the trope of *metonymy. The synthetic power of ling. consciousness stems from its capacity to create an interplay between the metaphoric and metonymic poles. Each concrete utterance strikes its own balance between the two, depending on the overall function it serves. Since a self-centered poetic message tends to establish as many equations among its constitutive elements as possible, assimilating them into coherent structures of *repetition and *parallelism at every level, poetry, in Jakobson's opinion, gravitates clearly toward the metaphoric extreme.

Jakobson's revision of Saussurean *sémiologie* rekindled interest in the most ancient issue of sign theory: how ling. sound is linked to its meaning. Saussure always insisted that, in most instances, the relation between the signifier and the signified is wholly conventional, wholly arbitrary. For him, compound words such as *nineteen*, whose signification is motivated through paradigmatic and syntagmatic relations with other words comprised of its constituent morphemes (*nine*, *-teen*), impose certain limits on this arbitrariness but do not invalidate it. For Jakobson, however, the signification of a poetic sign challenges Saussure's assumption. The meaning of a poem is above all a function of its ling. texture, and the very makeup of the signifier determines the signified. Hence, their relation is always motivated. In the 1960s, Jakobson turned to the semiotics of Peirce to support this claim and, in particular, to this concept of the icon.

The icon can be regarded as a motivated sign, since, according to Peirce, it "stands for something merely because it resembles it." This representational likeness, however, can have a variety of grounds, of which only two are directly relevant to the present discussion. An icon may resemble an object by sharing simple physical qualities with it (color, shape, etc.), in which case it is what Peirce termed an *image*. Or it might resemble an object by containing within itself the same intelligible relations as the object (the ratio of parts to whole, structural homology, etc.) in which case it is what Peirce called a *diagram*. It is the latter type of *iconicity that intrigued Jakobson. Traditional accounts of ling. *mimesis usually neglected this motivation and focused on words whose sound imitates a nonlinguistic sound, i.e., the process traditionally called *onomatopoeia. Given the paucity and marginality of such words in most langs., however, this argument obviously did not carry much weight. In contrast, Jakobson located the iconicity of lang. not in its sonorous matter but in the deep-seated diagrammatic likeness or homology of the signifier to the signified embodied in the sign's phonological, morphological, and syntactic structures. E.g., Caesar's dictum *veni, vidi, vici*, Jakobson insisted, is a motivated sign because the sequence of verbs repeats the sequence of reported events. However, in a nonreferential poetic utterance, the direction of motivation is reversed. Here the relational properties of the signifier, the interactions among its partial signs, create the structure of the signified, the poem's semantic universe.

Jakobson's fusion of previously separate doctrines of the sign into a coherent disciplinary matrix represents a stage in the hist. of semiotic poetics that reached its apogee in the late 1960s. In subsequent years, this theoretical model and the entire structuralist trad. it epitomizes were subjected to thoroughgoing scrutiny. The Fr. philosopher Jacques Derrida and the deconstructionist critics whom he inspired rejected the entire semiotic project *tout court*. It was marred from its inception, they argued, by adherence to "the Western metaphysics of presence," a tendency inimical to the very process of representation because of its drive to obliterate the essential precondition of this process—the radical difference or gap between the sign and what it stands for. Those critics who retained the concept of the sign in their discourse revised it in a number of ways. To schematize their dissent from Jakobsonian semiotics, we may group all these new devels. under three headings, the three charges most commonly leveled against the structuralist heritage: *linguistic imperialism*, *semantic determinism*, and *monologism*.

*Linguistic imperialism* is the reduction of poetic (and other) structures to ling. data. Structuralism might be right in seeing poetry as a purposive manipulation of lang., but not all patterns that a ling. analysis discovers in a text need be aesthetically effective or even perceived. "Stylistic facts," Riffaterre writes in *Semiotics of Poetry*, "must have a specific character, since otherwise they could not be distinguished from linguistic facts." In other words, the ling. code alone is an insufficient tool for reading a poem qua poem. It must be supplemented by additional codes, literary conventions that are extralinguistic. Thus, Culler (1981) claims that an adequate response to lyric poetry is predicated on the following set of conventional expectations that transcend lang.: (1) distance and *deixis (the text is detached from its originator and the speech situation); (2) coherence (it presents a unified whole); (3) significance (it contains a moment of epiphany); (4) resistance and recuperation (it can be processed despite its surface opacity). The semiotic analysis of poetry, however, need not stop at the subject of literary conventions. Soviet scholars from the Moscow-Tartu school (Viacheslav Ivanov, Jurij Lotman, Boris Uspenskij) conceive of verbal art as a "secondary modeling system," i.e., a code superimposed on lang. (the "primary system"), yet closely linked with other secondary systems (the arts, science, religion, etc.) within the overarching cultural system of a period. Thus, literary norms are the product of a complex interaction among all the semiotic codes and must be studied in conjunction with them. From this perspective, *poetics turns into a branch of the semiotics of culture, the general discipline concerned with the "collected nonhereditary information accumulated, preserved, and handed on by the various groups of human society."

As for *semantic determinism*, the patterning of the poetic signifier establishes the total range for the constitution of the signified. This assumption has been challenged on a number of grounds. Within the Prague School, a literary historian, Felix Vodička, drew attention to the temporal rupture between the literary sign and the set of conventions against which it is read. This hist. of literary reception furnishes copious examples of works reconstituted according to codes that did not exist at their inception, thus assuming new and unpredictable semiotic identities. Besides the vicissitudes of hist., the very organization of texts can make them resistant to a totalizing interpretation. Such are, in Eco's parlance, the "open works" that employ indeterminacy as their structuring principle. Their ambiguity may stem from the fact that they are simultaneously liable to incompatible codes or that they invite the reader to project them against the exigencies of an uncoded context. Roland Barthes's concept of a "writerly text" celebrates the infinite free play of signification in a work that is "a galaxy of signifiers, not a structure of signifieds," because "the codes it mobilizes extend *as far as the eye can reach*" and "are indeterminable (meaning here is never subject to a principle of determination, unless by throwing dice)." Julia Kristeva blames the deterministic tenor of structuralist semiotics on its neglect of the speaking subject as a psychobiological being. Poetic lang., she believes, is not just a system-governed activity but, above all, a system-transgressing creativity corresponding to a subject's capacity for enjoyment ( *jouissance*). Rather than the smooth matching of a discrete signified to its proper signifier based on some logical isomorphism, literary discourse is a violent irruption of a subject's semiotic dispositions (e.g., libidinal drives) into preexisting symbolic systems. Hence its liberating force: it has the ability to dissolve the customary ling. grids and establish new networks of signifying possibilities.

With respect to *monologism*, the sign is studied only in relation to an abstract system (langue), apart from the communicative situation. This issue was raised in the late 1920s by the Rus. scholars around M. M. Bakhtin (P. N. Medvedev, V. N. Vološinov), but it gained wide currency only some 40 years later. For the Bakhtinians, lang. exists only in communication. In this process, the intersubjective ling. forms (hypostasized by Saussure as langue) serve merely as an auxiliary mechanism for the transmission of contents unique and particular to each interlocutor. Our understanding of the other speaker does not reside in a passive recognition of self-identical signs but in their active appropriation, the trans. of an alien word into our own tongue. Accordingly, every lang. use is a dialogue—a response to a word by a word—and the structure of the verbal parcel reflects this. The word is not a static entity with a fixed meaning but a locus of action, a cross-section of different and often clashing points of view. In literary discourse, it is the genre of the novel, the Bakhtinians claim, that best embodies this dialogic principle. Bakhtin's insights were subsequently used by Kristeva, who coined the term *intertextuality* to designate the polyphonic nature of poetic lang., with its tendency to transpose one system of signs over another. Riffaterre employed the notion of intertextuality for his analyses of 19th- and 20th-c. Fr. poetry. In his view, poetic texts depend on what he terms *hypograms*—*clichés, quotations, or sayings, the *loci communes* of the given period—and they make sense only if related to the verbal background they engender. The successful interpretation of a poem, therefore, requires the discovery of an appropriate hypogram, the semiotic key that locks disparate textual elements into a unified whole.

As a general theory of signs, semiotics extends beyond the field of poetics. Instrumental for this interdisciplinary diffusion of semiotics was the rise, in the early 1960s, of structuralism, which emphasized the analysis of semiotic codes governing such disparate phenomena as prose narrative (Gérard Genette, Cesare Segre, Tzvetan Todorov), mythical thought (Claude Lévi-Strauss), the unconscious (Jacques Lacan), fashion (Roland Barthes), and film (Jurij Lotman, Christian Metz). Semiotics also branched out into various behav-

ioral sciences and new fields of inquiry that began to be charted: *kinesics* (gestures and body movements as conduits of information), *proxemics* (the meaning of spatial organization of the human environment), and animal communication (for which Thomas Sebeok coined the label of *zoosemiotics*).

*See* ANAGRAM, HISTORICISM, INTERTEXTUALITY, LINGUISTICS AND POETICS, SEMANTICS AND POETRY.

■ E. Husserl, *Logische Untersuchungen* (1900); E. Cassirer, *Philosophie der Symbolischen Formen* (1923–29); V. N. Vološinov, *Marksizm i filosofija jazyka* (1929); C. S. Peirce, *Collected Papers*, ed. C. Hartshorne and P. Weiss, 8 v. (1931–58)—esp. v. 2, 8; C. Morris, *Foundations of the Theory of Signs* (1938); J. Mukařovskij, *Kapitoly z české poetiky* (1941); L. Hjelmslev, *Omkring sprogteoriens grundlaeggelse* (1943); M. Bense, *Theorie der Texte* (1962); Jakobson—esp. v. 3; J. Derrida, *De la grammatologie* (1967); U. Eco, *La struttura assente* (1968); J. M. [Y.] Lotman, *Struktura chudožestvennogo teksta* (1970); R. Barthes, *S/Z*, trans. R. Miller (1970); *Essais de sémiotique poétique*, ed. A. J. Greimas (1972); C. Segre, *Semiotics and Literary Criticism*, trans. J. Meddemmen (1973); J. Kristeva, *La Révolution du langage poétique* (1974); R. Mayenova, *Poetyka teoretyczna* (1974); Culler—esp. ch. 3; U. Eco, *A Theory of Semiotics* (1976); M. Riffaterre, *Semiotics of Poetry* (1978); J. Culler, *The Pursuit of Signs* (1981); T. Todorov, *Theories of the Symbol*, trans. C. Porter (1982); M. Riffaterre, *Text Production*, trans. T. Lyons (1983); H. Baran, "Structuralism and Semiotics," Terras; J. Culler, *Ferdinand de Saussure*, 2d ed. (1986); *Encyclopedic Dictionary of Semiotics*, ed. T. A. Sebeok (1986); R. Jakobson, *Language in Literature*, trans. K. Pomorska and S. Rudy (1987); F. de Saussure, *Course in General Linguistics*, ed. C. Bally and A. Sechehaye (1989), trans. W. Baskin [1974]; J. K. Sheriff, *The Fate of Meaning* (1989); W. Nöth, *Handbook of Semiotics* (1990); T. Sebeok, *Global Semiotics* (2001).

P. STEINER; H. SMITH RICHMOND

**SENARIUS** (Lat., "of six each"). The Lat. equivalent of the Gr. iambic trimeter, the *senarius* (x – x – x – x – x – ᴗ –) is the common dialogue meter of Roman *comedy. This Lat. version is organized by feet rather than metra, as in the Gr., and all odd positions are *anceps except the eleventh position, which is always a pure short. So-called split *anapests are generally avoided; i.e., a resolved anceps (x – ᴗ ᴗ –) may not be followed or split in the middle by the end of a word spilling over from the preceding *foot. Avoidance of linc cnds ᴗ – | ᴗ – and – ᴗ – | ᴗ – was made so strict in Seneca and Petronius that an iambic word or word end cannot fill the fifth foot in their verses; the ninth position in Seneca's senarii is almost invariably a long even when a four-syllable word fills the last two feet. Though writers from the 1st c. BCE on adhere to the Gr. practice of allowing short syllables in the third and seventh positions, late Lat. archaizing poets, incl. Hilary of Poitiers and Ausonius, return to the senarius in its original Lat. form.

*See* CANTICUM AND DIVERBIUM, SEPTENARIUS.

■ Hardie, pt. 1, ch. 5; W. M. Lindsay, *Early Latin Verse* (1922); Norberg; Crusius; C. Questa, *Introduzione alla metrica di Plauto* (1967); Halporn et al.; J. Soubiran, *Essai sur la versification dramatique des romains: Senaire iambique et septenaire trochaique* (1988).

J. W. HALPORN

**SENHAL.** A fanciful name (My Magnet, Tristan, Good Hope) used in Occitan poems to address a lady, patron, or friend. A few of the persons so addressed have been identified with some certainty, but for the most part, they remain either completely unknown or the objects of more or less probable conjectures.

*See* OCCITAN POETRY, TROUBADOUR.

■ M. Delbouille, "Les senhals désignant Raimbaut d'Orange et le chronologie de ces témoignanges," *Cultura Neolatina* 17 (1957); S. Gutiérrez García, "Le senhal occitan et le secret de la dame en galicien-portugais," *Revue des langues romanes* 107 (2003); O. Scarpati, "I senhals nella poesia catalana medievale," *Cultura Neolatina* 65 (2005).

F. M. CHAMBERS

**SENSIBILITY.** A Eur. and Am. cultural phenomenon beginning in the late 17th c. that emphasized passionate experience and linked materialist concepts of body and mind to a moral system based on sympathy. Sensibility crossed all genres, from those now called literary to works of natural and moral philosophy, divinity, political economy, and medicine, and ideas of sensibility were a key influence for the Gothic and for *romanticism. The focus of sensibility on the human body and its passions promoted radical ideas of equality for many writers and readers, as it emphasized a universal basis for subjective experience. Sensibility thus played an important role in evolving ideals of individual liberty (William Godwin) and abolition (Harriet Beecher Stowe). Sensibility is closely related to its cognate, *sentimentality, though sentimentality increasingly takes on negative connotations from the 19th c. forward.

Sensibility engages two categories of sensory experiences: sensations that might be called external, coming from the five senses; and internal sensations, coming from the passions (*emotion* generally does not find its mod. usage until the 19th c.). The origins of sensibility are in the rise of materialism and empiricism in the 17th and 18th cs. Mod. empiricism privileged sensory experience; John Locke argued that "all ideas come from sensation or reflection" (*Essay Concerning Human Understanding*, 1689), and David Hume went on to argue that the basis of all experience is either impressions (which include "sensations, passions, and emotions") or ideas ("the faint images of [impressions] in thinking and reasoning"; *Treatise of Human Nature*, 1739–40). While some thinkers did not care to speculate on the physical processes by which such ideas or impressions were formed, materialists argued that the physical bases of subjective experience were discoverable: for some, what mattered was the vibration of nerves (Isaac Newton), for others, the circulation of animal spirits (René Descartes, Thomas Willis) or the vibration of individual particles (Pierre Gassendi

and later David Hartley). Eighteenth-c. devels. in associationist psychology and physiology helped drive scientific interest in sensation, but shifts in religious discourse, from Methodism to natural theology, also placed increased emphasis on the body, perceptual experience, and the passions. In Britain, a Pietist version of sensibility was dominant, but by the late century, particularly in France, sensibility was increasingly divorced from a lang. of faith or moralism and became a foundational part of a mechanist view of body and mind (Paul-Henri Thiry, Baron D'Holbach; Julien Offray de La Mettrie). The mechanist version of sensibility, which saw the body as a sensory machine bound by laws of causation—and nothing more—found its extreme form in the work of Donatien Alphonse François, Marquis de Sade.

There are several intellectual routes by which contemporaries understood the moral implications of the relations between mind and body posed by proponents of sensibility. In antiquity, the passions were seen to be interconnected; theories of such interrelations (Aristotle, Zeno of Critium, et al.) offered a way of understanding human motivations and implied rules for modifying thought and behavior, as the connections between passions might lead to good or ill. With early mod. theories of sensibility, the need for regulation pertained not only to the vehement passions (jealousy, fear, hatred, avarice, etc.) but to calm passions as well (benevolence, amity, pity, and, for Hume, even reason itself): e.g., if pity could lead to love, it might be a dangerous emotion for a young woman lacking parental guidance. Religious zeal, known as *enthusiasm*, was seen by many as highly communicable and, hence, particularly dangerous; writers such as John Dennis saw such enthusiasm as one of the contributing factors in the horrors of the Eng. Civil War.

One key strain of sensibility, however, can be traced to the aftermath of the Eng. Civil War. In part as a response to Thomas Hobbes's vision of a debased human nature, Ralph Cudworth, Henry More, Benjamin Whichcote, and others, known as the Cambridge Platonists, argued for the essential goodness of the human heart. In *Leviathan* (1651), Hobbes had argued that, in the state of nature, humankind would be dominated by the darker passions and would exist in a "war of all against all." Only the monarch's government could save his subjects from lives that would at best be "nasty, brutish, and short." The Cambridge Platonists argued that the social passions (particularly sympathy, benevolence, and love) were innate and just as active as their more violent counterparts. In their view, cultivation of those passions was as necessary to human happiness as was good government.

This line of reasoning was developed by so-called moral sense theorists such as Anthony Ashley Cooper, the third Earl of Shaftesbury, and Francis Hutcheson, who argued that we perceive beauty and virtue by a single, internal sense: susceptibility to beauty was also sensibility to virtue. Such theories of moral sensibility were key to the rise of aesthetics and placed increased critical and authorial focus on the affective components of art and on the affective potential of beauty, the picturesque, and the *sublime (see AFFECT). Links between morality and aesthetic sensibility also helped define and promote *taste as a marker of class privilege and gender identity for both men and women.

Adam Smith's *Theory of Moral Sentiments* (1759) offered a crucial paradigm for understanding the unique contribution of the arts to moral sensibility. Smith argued that the basis for social cohesion was the impulse toward sympathy, one of the "original passions of human nature," and that sympathy could come only from the *imagination. With Smith and his followers, the special place of some of the belles lettres in the cultivation of sensibility was reinforced because the imagination was understood to be the functional organ of sympathy; arts that best spoke to the imagination took on increased value. In this respect, the emergence of sensibility is closely linked to the emergence of the mod. idea of lit. from the concept of the belles lettres.

The lit. of sensibility is primarily associated with the celebration of *pathos, but as its affective range grew, it opened new themes and perspectives, offering new approaches to landscape, as well as a new focus on animals, slaves, madness, servants, mothers, children, the poor, and the so-called primitive. *Landscape poetry thrived, encompassing ekphrastic, painterly writing (see EKPHRASIS) as well as inquiry into natural philosophy (James Thomson's *The Seasons*, 1730; Erasmus Darwin's *Loves of the Plants*, 1791). In the late 18th c., Della Crucian poetry painted nature as itself sentient: "every flower / Enjoys the air it breathes" (Robert Merry, "Monody Addressed to Mr. Tickell," 1788). Stephen Duck's "Threasher's Labor" (1730) opened up the subjective experience of labor to poetic view, and he was imitated by many, incl. Ann Yearsley and Mary Leapor. The many poetic versions of the tale of Inkle and Yarico (Frances Seymour, William Pattison, John Winstanley, et al.) brought into Brit. popular culture the story of betrayal of a woman into slavery by her white lover. Elsewhere (in John Dyer's *The Fleece*, 1757; William Cowper's *The Task*, 1785; or Frank Sayers's "Dying African," ca. 1804), the horrors of slavery and the slave trade were represented with sympathetic intensity. Christopher Smart and Cowper explored madness as a state that opened one up to religious and poetic *inspiration and to prophecy (see PROPHETIC POETRY, VATES). Thomas Gray's "Ode on a Distant Prospect of Eton College" (1747) is a major work in the sentimental revaluation of childhood, a revaluation that led to the romantic vision of childhood innocence; and Hannah More, Anna Laetitia Barbauld, Felicia Hemans, William Blake, et al. explore the emotions of motherhood and images of maternity. In its celebration of the truth of the passions, the culture of sensibility also gave new value to "primitive" poetry, fostering interest in reclaimed oral trad. and in the ancient poetry of the British Isles. The Gothic, in part an outgrowth of sensibility, opened up a new emotional register, as well. Relying on the aesthetics of the picturesque and the increasing antiquarian interest in Eur. vernacular hist., the Gothic explored the darker side of sensibility. The passions of curiosity, fear, delight, lust, anger, envy, avarice, love, and benevolence were often combined with stories of (sometimes doomed) romance and were staples of Gothic poetry (e.g., Thomas Chatterton, Anne Radcliffe, and P. B. Shelley).

Some poetic genres were particularly important to the lit. of sensibility. The heroic epistle (letters written by abandoned women to their betrayers, a genre invented by Ovid) became a key locus for representing women's romantic passions and was adapted by Aphra Behn, Alexander Pope, and others. The greater (Pindaric) *ode was one of the dominant forms of the period, and it was seen as the most appropriate of the cl. forms for the representation of grand passions (Abraham Cowley, Mark Akenside, William Collins, and Gray). *Narrative poems were important as well, offering the freedom to develop numerous characters and vignettes of sympathetic interest (Thomson, Cowper, George Crabbe). The *hymn was a major poetic form, and the focus on the passions in Charles Wesley's hymns was part of a broad revaluation of religious enthusiasm. Landscape emerged as a locus for patriotic passions but also for the pleasures of grief, love, and aesthetic and religious contemplation in Thomson's *Seasons* or Edward Young's *Night Thoughts* (1742). *Pastoral and *georgic were rewritten to accommodate new understandings of how human sensation shapes our physical world (concepts stemming from devels. in natural philosophy by Newton, George Berkeley, and others), as well as the new promise and problems of human interconnection within and across mod. nations (first in Great Britain and later in Germany, France, and America). In the late 18th c., *sonnets were used increasingly for landscape meditations (W. L. Bowles, Charlotte Smith). Particular poets offered important models for *imitation as well. John Milton's "L'Allegro" (1645) was widely imitated, and his melancholy "Penseroso" (1645) was followed by a long series of poems about nocturnal wanderers, from Anne Finch through *graveyard poetry to Cowper, Smith, and William Wordsworth.

One of the most significant poetic subgenres focused on the poet's own sensibility (Gray, Collins, Helen Maria Williams, Frances Greville, et al.). There were multiple models in these poems for describing poetic inspiration, incl. the ancient *bards (Gray), the Aeolian harp (S. T. Coleridge), the associative and creative imagination (Akenside), and a range of personified passions, from Fear to Pity and Peace (Collins; see PERSONIFICATION). Sensibility, with its focus on subjective experience, contributed to the redefinition of poetry as something other than metrical writing: it was becoming linked to particular acts of heightened perception. This position is nascent in Gray's "Elegy Written in a Country Churchyard" (1750) with its "mute inglorious Miltons," and it progresses through the meditative poems of Collins, Cowper, and Smith. The concept of poetic sensibility is foundational to Wordsworth's poetry, beginning with his first pub. poem, "Sonnet, on seeing Miss Helen Maria Williams weep at a Tale of Distress" (1787). Women's sensibility to painful emotion was a central theme in the lit. and culture of sensibility, but such emotion is a *topos not entirely or fundamentally gendered feminine: as Cowper writes in *The Task*: "I was born of woman, and drew milk, / As sweet as charity, from human breasts. / I think, articulate, I laugh and weep, / And exercise all functions of a man."

It is difficult and in some cases improper to isolate the poetry of sensibility from drama and novels (indeed, drama is the first genre to engage the rubrics of sensibility). Much of the lit. of sensibility is self-consciously experimental. Some of it is sui generis (Young's *Night Thoughts*), some deliberate in its manipulation of genre (georgic in Dyer's *Fleece*, Thomson's *Seasons*, or Cowper's *Task*). Such generic experimentation could blur boundaries between poetry and prose. The Gothic novel combined prose with poetry (M. G. Lewis's *The Monk*, the novels of Radcliffe). The popularity of the literary *fragment (a piece designed to seem unfinished, often carrying the fiction of being a discovery from ancient times), driven by both antiquarianism and the appeal of the Gothic, also meant that poetry, drama, and prose narrative could be mixed in interesting ways (e.g., the poetry of Ossian, or James Macpherson). Bishop Thomas Percy rewrote many Brit. *ballads in accord with the taste of the age of sensibility, and he drew on novels as well as drama for the revisions. In France, Jean-Jacques Rousseau's prose *Les reveries du promeneur solitaire* (1782) combined philosophical musings with lyric expressivity and meditation on nature and the passions.

The lit. and culture of sensibility were subject to sharp critique. Some objected to the publication of voices that had previously been silent. Female authorship and the representation of women's inner lives at times violated established rules of *decorum. The poetry of labor and of slavery carried political and social threats to established interests, and the Jacobin novel explored the potential of sensibility and its focus on the passions to foster radical social critique (Godwin, et al.). However, many—not least Immanuel Kant—questioned the validity of a moral system based on sympathy, contending that sympathetic identification was incomplete and idiosyncratic and was no substitute for moral precept. For radical thinkers as well, sympathy could not be an end in itself, even for those who owed an intellectual debt to theories of sensibility. Mary Wollstonecraft, e.g., saw the emphasis on women's sensibility as prejudicial to proper valuation of women's intellect and felt that it was dangerously sexualizing. The erotic potential of a cultivated sensibility made it subject to critique by religious thinkers, and the morality of the passions was also at times opposed to Christian revisions of Stoicism, which held that the regulation of the passions and the search for moderation and temperance were paramount for both sexes (see Greville's "A Prayer for Indifference," 1759). For critics thus influenced, reading and writing might be of moral use, helping to properly regulate the passions by exercising them, showing the relations between them (how envy, lust, and anger or how pity, benevolence, and joy are connected) or teaching how to avoid dangerous passions and their fruits. However,

perceived excesses of sensibility were particularly problematic, and debased sensibility was scorned as mere sensation seeking by some and by others as effeminate and corrupting. The materialist underpinnings of sensibility were also subject to critique, esp. the more radical deistic or atheistic versions that came largely from France (D'Holbach, de la Mettrie, et al.). Reactions by conservatives to the Fr. Revolution also came to include denunciation of sensibility.

Critics took the dangers of sensibility to heart in their discussions of literary form, as well. Gothic writing, e.g., was often understood to undertake illegitimate, dangerous manipulation of the passions, leading its unwary readers astray. The Della Crucians were widely mocked and became a touchpoint for Wordsworth's revisions of poetic lang. (McGann). The focus on subjective experience was also at odds with cultural pressures that made first-person expression seem self-indulgent, indecorous, or solipsistic; first-person poetic forms were accordingly used less frequently throughout most of the 18th c. than second-person (particularly the hymn, invitation, and epistle) or third-person (generally narrative) poetic forms. It is not until the romantic period that first-person representations of sensibility become more widely accepted, though still subject to charges of solipsism and self-indulgence.

In the 19th c., sensibility does not die. Melodrama and Victorian sentimental lit. retained popularity through the late century. However, sensibility increasingly marked a fault line between high and low culture, esp. in the 20th c. High modernist poets found the emphasis on sympathetic emotion anathema to many of their poetic goals, and they largely abandoned that part of the ethos of sensibility (see MODERNISM). Nonetheless, sensibility still had resonance. While much of the celebration of pathos and sympathy as its own end disappeared, poetic subjects introduced or cultivated by the poets of sensibility persisted. The interest in domestic life continued, in new tenor, with Robert Frost, Anne Sexton, or Dylan Thomas, and, crucially, the idea of the *poet as a person of heightened sensibility has never quite been lost.

*See* FUROR POETICUS, LANDSCAPE POEM, PREROMANTICISM.

■ Eliot, "The Metaphysical Poets," *Essays*; A. Sherbo, *English Sentimental Drama* (1957); *From Sensibility to Romanticism*, ed. F. W. Hilles (1970); J. Hagstrum, *Sex and Sensibility* (1980); R. Williams, *Keywords*, 2d ed. (1983); J. Todd, *Sensibility* (1986); C. J. Barker-Benfield, *The Culture of Sensibility* (1992); J. J. McGann, *The Poetics of Sensibility* (1996); M. Doody, "Sensuousness in the Poetry of Eighteenth-Century Women Poets," *Women's Poetry in the Enlightenment*, ed. I. Armstrong and V. Blain (1999); S. Kaul, *Poems of Nation, Anthems of Empire* (2000); D. Griffin, *Patriotism and Poetry in Eighteenth-Century Britain* (2002); K. Goodman, *Georgic Modernity* (2004); G. G. Starr, *Lyric Generations* (2004).

G. G. STARR

**SENTIMENTALITY.** In poetry, *sentimentality*—along with the related forms *sentimental* and *sentimentalism*—often carries negative connotations, but some historical and critical uses of the term have also served a more neutral, descriptive function.

While *sentimentality* may simply refer to the quality of possessing *emotion or feeling, in calling poetry *sentimental*, a reader may mean to identify and condemn an emotional treatment in excess of its object, a false or contrived response that is not convincingly suited to an occasion. Candidates for such dismissal are poems that lament the suffering of another at a safe distance (H. W. Longfellow's "The Slave in the Dismal Swamp") and poems on the death of small animals (H. M. Williams's "Elegy on a Young Thrush"). William Cowper's lines to his pet rabbit in *The Task* exemplify the traits of sentimental poetry that easily fall prey to ridicule: "If I survive thee I will dig thy grave; / And when I place thee in it, sighing say, / I knew at least one hare that had a friend." Such scenarios are at least ostensibly intended to invoke pity or sympathy for suffering while demonstrating the exquisite feeling—and, therefore, humanity—of the poet. If the emotional expression is found to be insincere, however, an accusation of false feeling rebounds on the speaker, and the poem is understood as an indulgence in pleasure and self-congratulation at the expense of another's pain. Literary critics employ *sentimentality* in this condemnatory sense when they want to dismiss a work out of hand. But such condemnation often does little except to indicate the taste of the particular critic, for one person's sentimentality may be another's sincere expression of authentic emotion.

Though *sentimentality* carries a burden of negative judgment, it also refers to a strain of lit. that privileges the expression of feeling over intellect or reason. In this sense, sentimentality has a long and complex hist. that brings together philosophy, morality, and aesthetics, at least since the 18th c. Following in the wake of Anthony Ashley Cooper, third Earl of Shaftesbury, the Scottish moral philosophers Francis Hutcheson, David Hume, and Adam Smith located morality in the cultivation of "right feeling." Reason was not sufficient to forge constructive social bonds between people. Benevolent social relations might be arrived at through subordinating selfish feelings to emotions such as sympathy and pity, interpersonal feelings that enable caring for and helping others. In this historical sense, sentimentality is closely linked to *sensibility. As this project of social improvement increasingly fell under criticism and out of favor, sentimental poetic practices lost purpose and prestige, and *sentimentality* increasingly became a term of censure. Recently, however, scholarly interest in the emotions, as well as a general understanding that all social behaviors and feelings are at least in part socially constructed, has generated increased interest in and respect for the term, even to the point where, esp. in the study of 18th- and 19th-c. Am. lit., sentimentalism has been championed as an alternative feminine aesthetic and an effective mode of social reform.

Sentimentality spans all genres. Novelists in the sentimental trad. include Laurence Sterne and Samuel Richardson in the 18th c. and Charles Dickens and Harriet Beecher Stowe in the 19th. The initiation of the poetic trad. is commonly located between the Augustan and romantic periods, during what Northrop Frye designated the Age of Sensibility. Poets of that period include Thomas Gray, Cowper, Charlotte Smith, William Blake, Mary Robinson, Robert Burns, and Williams. William Wordsworth, Lydia Sigourney, Felicia Hemans, John Keats, and Longfellow are some of the 19th-c. inheritors of the trad. Recent critics, notably McGann and Pinch, have focused on the cultural and formal operations of sentimental poetry, analyzing rather than condemning them. Pinch argues that sentimentality in poetry renders legible the ways that emotions are both external and internal to the individual. Sentimental poetry exposes the way that feeling "constructs and mediates between the categories of literary convention and personal experience. . . . [T]he concept of sentimentality may be defined precisely as a confrontation between the personal and the conventional."

*See* AFFECT, EXPRESSION.

■ N. Frye, "Towards Defining an Age of Sensibility," *ELH* 23 (1956); J. Todd, *Sensibility* (1986); F. Kaplan, *Sacred Tears: Sentimentality in Victorian Literature* (1987); J. J. McGann, *The Poetics of Sensibility* (1996); A. Pinch, *Strange Fits of Passion* (1996); A. Douglas, *The Feminization of American Culture* (1998); J. Howard, "What Is Sentimentality?" *American Literary History* 11 (1999); J. Keith, "Poetry, Sentiment, and Sensibility," *Companion to Eighteenth-Century Poetry*, ed. C. Gerrard (2006).

E. RICHARDS

**SEPHARDIC POETRY.** *See* JUDEO-SPANISH POETRY.

**SEPTENARIUS** (Lat., "of seven each"). The Lat. equivalent of the Gr. trochaic tetrameter catalectic ($- \times - \times$ $- \times - \times - \times - \cup -$). The Gr. form is scanned as composed of four metra (see METRON), but the Lat. version has seven feet and an additional syllable. It is the common recitative meter of Roman comedy. All the even positions except the last are *anceps in the septenarius; the 12th position is thus always a pure short. Generally, there is a *diaeresis after the eighth position. "Split dactyls" are generally avoided; i.e., a resolved anceps ($- \times -$ $\cup \cup$) may not be followed or split in the middle by the end of a word spilling over from the preceding foot. There is the same avoidance of line ends $\cup - | \cup -$ and $\cup - \cup | \cup -$ as in the *senarius. The septenarius also appears as the *versus quadratus* (see CLASSICAL PROSODY) of soldiers' songs and satires, as well as in late Lat. and med. Lat. hymns. Schipper uses the Latinate term *septenary* to refer to the iambic 14-syllable line in ME, based on an assumed derivation of the vernacular line directly from med. Lat., but this derivation glosses over significant problems of structure and transmission, and as such is but one instance of the appropriation of terminology from one verse system into another without due consideration of the fundamental differences between the two.

*See* CANTICUM AND DIVERBIUM.

■ Schipper; Hardie, pt. 1, chap. 7; W. M. Lindsay, *Early Latin Verse* (1922); E. Fraenkel, "Die Vorgeschichte des *versus quadratus*," *Hermes* 62 (1927); Beare; Norberg; Crusius; C. Questa, *Introduzione alla metrica di*

*Plauto* (1967); Halporn et al.; J. Soubiran, *Essai sur la versification dramatique des Romains: Sénaire iambique et séptenaire trochaique* (1988).

J. W. Halporn; T.V.F. Brogan

**SEPTET.** A seven-line stanza in one of a large number of metrical and *rhyme schemes. Isometric forms include the Sicilian septet, rhyming *ababab*, and the Sp. septet or septilla, traditionally octosyllabic, presently octosyllabic or pentameter and rhyming *aabccba* or *abbacca*. Heterometric forms include the roundelet, a med. Fr. seven-line stanza with *refrain, in which lines 1, 3, and 7 are identical, and with syllable counts of 4-8-4-8-8-8-4. These tight forms are marked by the play of a strict two-rhyme pattern and/or verbal repetitions; these schemes are adapted freely in ambitious poems like Eustache Deschamps' "Vous qui vivez à présent en ce monde" (14th c.), and, earlier, in *troubadour song. Septets are found in the poetries of Eur., East Asian, and West Asian lang. families. In Eng., septets are developed with subtlety and syntactic expansiveness by Mary Sidney Herbert in her dedicatory poem to her brother, "To the Angel Spirit of the Most Excellent Philip Sidney" in 13 stanzas of *iambic *pentameter septets; by John Donne in "The Good-morrow," and by John Milton in "On the Death of a Fair Infant Dying of a Cough," both of whom end their septets with an *alexandrine in the Spenserian mode. The richest septet form in Eng. is *rhyme royal, developed brilliantly by Chaucer and used as well by John Gower, Thomas Wyatt, Milton, and W. H. Auden.

■ Le Gentil.

T. Krier

**SERBIAN POETRY.** The earliest Serbian poetry dates from the period of the Nemanjići dynasty (12th–14th c.) and is of an ecclesiastical nature influenced by the Byzantine trad. The liturgical verse mostly originated from Gr. sources and was rendered in the Serbian recension of Old Church Slavonic, written in the Cyrillic alphabet. From the 14th c. comes a laudatory poem by Siluan (dates unknown) in honor of St. Sava, who established the Serbian monastery Hilandar on Mt. Athos and was a pivotal figure in reinforcing the Christian Orthodox faith among the Serbs. A prose poem by Stefan Lazarević (1377–1427), *Slovo ljubve* (Of Love, 1404 or 1409), is among the most lyrical texts of the period, as are two elegies by the nun Jefimija (ca. 1349–after 1405), wife of the despot Uglješa Mrnjavčević, one on the loss of her infant, the other in praise of Prince Lazar. The vibrant med. culture of the powerful Serbian state was brought to its knees by the invasion of the Ottomans, who ruled the region until the 19th c. Owing to these politically unfavorable conditions, the Serbian literary scene returned to life only during the Enlightenment. Even during the Ottoman period, however, traditional folk poetry continued to flourish, commemorating important historical events and preserving an awareness of national identity. Although *lyric and *ballad genres prospered as well, the most famous works are decasyllabic *epic songs, in particular one cycle dealing with Kraljević Marko and another with the battle of Kosovo, an event that marked the decline of the med. Serbian state.

Reduced literary activity led to closer ties with Russia and the introduction of the Rus. version of Church Slavonic. The two principal authors of the 18th c. were Jovan Rajić (1726–1801), who composed an allegorical-historical epic *Boj zmaja s orlovi* (The Battle of the Dragon with the Eagles, 1791), and Zaharije Orfelin (1726–85; *Plač Serbii* [Serbia's Lament, 1761]). Both wrote in the archaic lang. of the intellectual elite, which differed significantly from the vernacular. The Enlightenment introduced a note of individualism, as in the poetry of Lukijan Mušicki (1777–1837), which is dominated by a didactic orientation and cl. motifs.

While the romantic period saw folk poetry used throughout Europe as a way of encouraging greater national awareness, this was particularly true of Serbia. Vuk S. Karadžić (1787–1864) not only systematically collected a vast body of oral songs but proposed the lang. reform based on the vernacular lang. of folk songs and tales that became the foundation of contemp. Serbian. One of the most prominent singers in his collections is Filip Višnjić (1767–1834). Also influenced by both the romantic spirit and folk trad. is Sima Milutinović (1791–1847), best known for his long epic *Serbijanka* (1826), a chronicle of the Serbian uprising against the Turks. His student, the Prince-Bishop of Montenegro Petar Petrović Njegoš (1813–51), wrote work resembling oral epic poetry but using clearer, more refined lang. His most famous works are *Luča mikrokozma* (The Torch of the Microcosm, 1845), a philosophical epic poem in the manner of John Milton; and *Gorski vijenac* (Mountain Wreath, 1847), an epic that offers a vivid picture of Montenegrin life and hist.

A new orientation in Serbian poetry was introduced by Branko Radičević (1824–53), who built on the more diverse rhythms of folk lyric songs but also gradually departed from the folk idiom in favor of the more mod. expression typical of the Eur. scene. Lyric poetry and the romantic spirit remained staples of literary life for decades to come and produced some of the most important Serbian writers of the 19th c.: Jovan Jovanović Zmaj (1833–1904), known for his moving personal lyrics as well as his commentaries on contemp. society; Đura Jakšić (1832–78), who oscillated between elegiac personal verses (e.g., *Na Liparu* [In the Linden-Grove, 1866]) and patriotic poems; and Laza Kostić (1841–1910), a trans. of Shakespeare and author of numerous lyric poems.

The epoch of *realism is reflected in the descriptive poetry of Vojislav Ilić (1862–94), who also raised the formal and aesthetic bar for later modernist authors. Aleksa Šantić (1868–1924) and Jovan Dučić (1874–1943), two poets from Herzegovina, both continued the legacy of Ilić, the former remaining more of a traditionalist with a focus on a range of themes from love to patriotism and social justice, and the latter very much a follower of *Parnassianism with an exceptional feel for the nuances of lang. and form. Milan Rakić (1876–1938) was an intellectually minded poet whose formally impeccable verses, influenced by Fr. poetic schools, are imbued with pessimism and irony. Dark motifs dominate the poetry of another symbolist, Sima Pandurović (1883–1960), for whom love is inevitably tied to the theme of dying. The collection *Utopljene duše* (The Drowned Souls, 1911) by Vladislav Petković-Dis (1880–1917) not only announced a new modernist era but eerily foreshadowed the author's tragic death by drowning. Unlike the more measured poets of his time, Dis often embarked on a journey in his verses, capturing the irrational quality of dreamlike states. Veljko Petrović (1884–1967) was a poet from Pannonia whose poems are filled with mythical motifs of fertile soil.

Although *modernism brought with it a number of different orientations, it was *expressionism—with its quest for vital immediacy, its merging of the unexpected and irrational, and its pursuit of cosmic heights—that left the deepest imprint. Poetry was liberated from formal requirements, and *free verse became predominant. Stanislav Vinaver (1891–1955) took this approach to an extreme by placing exclusive emphasis on sound while rejecting the importance of the semantic level.

Although better known for his prose works, Miloš Crnjanski's (1893–1977) elegiac verses about love and his homeland (*Stražilovo*, 1921) are some of the finest from this period. Other important authors include Momčilo Nastasijević (1894–1938), a poet of folkloric impressionism and conciseness; Rastko Petrović (1898–1949), who oscillates between Slavic paganism and dark expressionist moods; and the pacifist Dušan Vasiljev (1900–1924). The poems of Rade Drainac (1899–1943), a neoromantic who soon showed a kinship with the surrealist school (see SURREALISM), reflect in their imagery the technological advancement of his time but also provide powerful emotional landscapes. The prolific surrealist Oskar Davičo (1909–89) is best known for his early poetry bursting with emotion and unusual metaphors. One of a limited number of women poets, Desanka Maksimović (1898–1993), marked a whole era with her lyrical poetry of exceptional clarity and fluidity. Vasko Popa (1922–91), one of the finest Serbian authors, abandoned the surrealist model and treated poetry as a rational process in which one has to be cognizant of the form. His poems typically form part of a larger cycle. Miodrag Pavlović (b. 1928) is a contemplative poet who often employs images from Serbia's mythical past, while Stevan Raičković (1928–2007) was a melancholic nature-oriented lyricist.

Despite Branko Miljković's (1934–61) premature death, he left a deep mark on the Serbian poetic scene, particularly with his first collection, *Uzalud je budim* (I Am Waking Her in Vain, 1957), a symbiosis of mod. imagery and a heightened sensitivity for lang. Ivan V. Lalić (1931–96) was a neoclassicist of refined expression whose works include a vivid visual component, while Ljubomir Simović (b. 1935) turns toward rustic Serbia for his inspiration. Aleksandar Ristović (1933–94)

was a neosymbolist poet of the quotidian, while Jovan Hristić (1933–2002) captured in his measured expression both the elegiac and resilient aspects of life. Belonging to the same generation but representing a host of poetic styles are Borislav Radović (b. 1935), Aleksandar Petrov (b. 1938), Matija Bećković (b. 1939), Rajko Petrov Nogo (b. 1945), Stevan Tontić (b. 1946), Novica Tadić (b. 1949), and Radmila Lazić (b. 1949).

■ **Anthologies**: *Srpske narodne pjesme*, ed. V. Karadžić, 4 v. (1958–64); *Antologija srpskog pesništva*, ed. M. Pavlović (1964); *Antologija novije srpske lirike*, ed. B. Popović, 12th ed. (1968); *Srpske pesnikinje od Jefimije do danas*, ed. S. Radovanović and S. Radaković (1972); *Marko the Prince: Serbo-Croat Heroic Songs*, ed. and trans. A. Pennington and P. Levi (1984); *Anthology of Serbian Poetry: The Golden Age*, ed. M. Dordevic (1984); *Mediaeval and Renaissance Serbian Poetry*, ed. P. R. Dragić Kijuk (1987); *Serbian Poetry from the Beginnings to the Present*, ed. M. Holton and V. D. Mihailovich (1988); *Staro srpsko pesništvo: IX–XVIII vek*, ed. Đ. S. Radojičić (1988); *The Horse Has Six Legs: An Anthology of Serbian Poetry*, ed. and trans. C. Simic (1992); *Songs of the Serbian People: From the Collections of Vuk Karadžić*, ed. and trans. M. Holton and V. D. Mihailovich (1997); *Antologija moderne srpske lirike (1920–1995)*, ed. M. Šutić (2002); *The Serbian Epic Ballads: An Anthology*, trans. G.N.W. Locke (2002); *Places We Love: An Anthology of Contemporary Serbian Poetry*, ed. G. Božović (2006); *An Anthology of Serbian Literature*, ed. V. D. Mihailovich and B. Mikasinovich (2007); *Jutro misleno: Nemanjićko doba: Zbornik srednjovekovne srpske poezije*, ed. V. Popa (2008).

■ **Criticism and History**: A. Kadić, *Contemporary Serbian Literature* (1964); M. P. Coote and M. Kašanin, *Srpska književnost u srednjem veku* (1975); M. P. Coote, "Serbocroatian Heroic Songs," *Heroic Epic and Saga*, ed. F. J. Oinas (1978); S. Koljević, *The Epic in the Making* (1980); C. Hawkesworth, *Voices in the Shadows: Women and Verbal Art in Serbia and Bosnia* (2000); J. Deretić, *Istorija srpske književnosti*, rev. ed. (2002); D. Andrejević, *Srpska poezija XX veka* (2005).

A. VIDAN

**SERIAL FORM.** Serial form has a literary-historical provenance that distinguishes it from other critical terms used to describe the variety of long-poem forms that emerged during the 20th c. (see EPIC, LYRIC SEQUENCE, LONG POEM). Jack Spicer was the first to use the term to designate a distinct compositional method informing his poetry along with that of his *San Francisco Renaissance peers. In *Admonitions* (1958), Spicer credits Robert Duncan with helping him view the book as the central unit of composition, where individual poems become less important than the resonances and energies they generate through accumulation. Offering a more explicit definition in his 1965 Vancouver lectures, Spicer stresses the importance of openness, contiguity, and dictation.

Evolving from these early formulations—and learning from artistic production in other media incl. musical serialism, filmic montage, and cubist painting—serial form has assumed certain core attributes. Serial poems tend to be open rather than closed, prospective rather than introspective, and driven by empirical reality rather than internal necessity. They value process over product. Resisting thematic or narrative strictures, serial poems tend to be discontinuous, elliptical, and open to recombination and extension. While not present in every serial poem, these traits—more like malleable, informing concepts than strict formal prescriptions—distinguish the series from the mod. poetic sequence.

Though some have suggested Philip Sidney's *Arcadia* and the *carmen perpetuum* (perpetual song) of Ovid's *Metamorphoses* as early examples, poets and critics tend to cite more recent influences on a formal practice that achieved poetic currency only in the latter half of the 20th c. The idiosyncratic ordering of the poems in Emily Dickinson's fascicles suggest a prescient serial logic, while Walt Whitman's extended catalogs and his life's work as a whole, represented in multiple eds. of *Leaves of Grass*, exhibit dynamic variation and extension as they figure the adaptive capacities of serial form. Gertrude Stein's *Tender Buttons* (1912), W. C. Williams's *Spring and All* (1923), Jean Toomer's *Cane* (1923), and Langston Hughes's *Montage of a Dream Deferred* (1951), all of which abandon the integrity of the isolated lyric as they seek a more integrated, book-length serial structure, provide significant modernist touchstones. In works that served as a model for a socially engaged serialism, the objectivists (see OBJECTIVISM) developed an extensive body of serial work, incl. Charles Reznikoff's *Rhythms* (1918), George Oppen's *Discrete Series* (1934), Lorine Niedecker's *New Goose* (1946), and Louis Zukofsky's *Anew* (1946).

Since the 1960s, serial form has become a dominant long-poem form, whether it constitutes a short series, a book-length project, or an ongoing series. The trad. extends from Duncan's *Passages* (1968–87), Oppen's "Of Being Numerous" (1968), and Robert Creeley's *Pieces* (1968) to Rachel Blau DuPlessis's *Drafts* (1986–), Nathaniel Mackey's "Song of the Andoumboulou" (1985–), Michael Palmer's "Baudelaire Series" (1988), and beyond. Though serial poetics is most pronounced in Am. poetry, other national lits. also have pursued some version of the mode, most prominently in France, where Stéphane Mallarmé's *Un coup de dés* (1897) and his unfinished *Igitur* (1869) were models for subsequent work such as Edmond Jabès's *Le Livre des Questions* (1963–73) and Claude Royet-Journoud's *Tetralogy* (1972–97), among others.

*See* AVANT GARDE POETICS; BOOK, POETIC.

■ R. Blaser, "The Fire," *Poetics of the New American Poetry*, ed. D Allen and W. Tallman (1973); A. Golding, "George Oppen's Serial Poems," *Contemporary Literature* 29.2 (1988); J. Conte, *Unending Design* (1991); L. Keller, *Forms of Expansion* (1995); J. Spicer, *The House That Jack Built* (1998); C. Bernstein, "Reznikoff's Nearness," *My Way* (1999); B. Edwards, "Notes on Poetics regarding Mackey's *Song, Callaloo* 23.2 (2000); S. Marijnissen, "'Made Things': Serial Form in Modern Poetry from Taiwan," *Modern Chinese Literature and Culture* 13.2 (2001).

A. VANDER ZEE

**SERRANILLA.** A Sp. poem composed in any short meter, but esp. in the *\*arte mayor* half line, and dealing lightly with the subject of the meeting of a gentleman and a pretty country girl. The *serranilla* was particularly characteristic of the late med. period. The most famous are those of the archpriest of Hita (1283?–1350?), and esp. those of the Marqués de Santillana (1398–1458); the latter may have been influenced by the "great volume of Portuguese and Galician *cantigas, serranas,* and *decires*" to which he says he had access in his youth.

*See* PASTOURELLE.

■ Le Gentil; B. W. Wardropper, "Góngora and the Serranilla," *MLN* 77 (1962); A. Swan, "Santillana's *Serranillas*: A Poetic Genre of Their Own," *Neophilologus* 63 (1979); Navarro; J. Dagenais, "*Cantigas d'escarnho* and *serranillas*: The Allegory of Careless Love," *BHS* 68 (1991); L. R. Bass, "Crossing Borders: Gender, Geography, and Class Relations in Three Serranillas of the Marqués de Santillana," *La Corónica* 25 (1996); M. García, "La 'serrana' castellana, ¿género paródico?" *La Corónica* 38 (2009).

D. C. CLARKE

**SESTET** (It. *sestette, sestetto*). According to the *OED,* the term first appeared in Eng. in 1867, when Leigh Hunt and S. Adams Lee used it to signify the minor division or last six lines of a *\*sonnet, preceded by an *\*octave. Sometimes the octave states a proposition or situation and the sestet a conclusion, but no fast rules for content can be formulated. The rhyme scheme of the sestet varies: in an It. sonnet, it is usually *cdecde,* in an Eng., *efefgg,* but there are others. The term *sestet* is not generally used for a six-line stanza apart from a sonnet. The older term *\*sexain* is still used for such stanzas, which may be patterned in various ways.

■ *The Book of the Sonnet,* ed. L. Hunt and S. Adams Lee, 1:10–11 (1867).

R. O. EVANS; S. CUSHMAN

**SESTINA** (It. *sestine, sesta rima*). The most complicated of the verse forms initiated by the *\*troubadours, the sestina is composed of six stanzas of six lines each, followed by an *\*envoi of three lines, all of which are unrhymed, and all decasyllabic (Eng.), hendecasyllabic (It.), or *\*alexandrine (Fr.). The same six end words occur in each stanza, but in a shifting order that follows a fixed pattern: each successive stanza takes its pattern from a reversed (bottom-up) pairing of the lines of the preceding stanza (i.e., last and first, then next to last and second, then third from last and third). If we let the numbers 1 through 6 stand for the end words, we may schematize the pattern as follows:

| | | |
|---|---|---|
| stanza 1 | : | 123456 |
| stanza 2 | : | 615243 |
| stanza 3 | : | 364125 |
| stanza 4 | : | 532614 |
| stanza 5 | : | 451362 |
| stanza 6 | : | 246531 |
| envoi | : | 531 or 135 |

More commonly, the envoi, or *\*tornada, is further complicated by the fact that the remaining three end words,

246, must also occur in the course of its three lines, so that it gathers up all six together.

The invention of the sestina is usually attributed to Arnaut Daniel (fl. 1180–95), and the form was widely cultivated both by his Occitan followers and by poets in Italy (Dante, Petrarch, Gaspara Stampa), Spain, and Portugal (Luís de Camões, Bernardim Ribeiro). A rhymed version (*abcbca* in the first stanza) was introduced into France by Pontus de Tyard (*Erreurs amoureuses*, 1549), a member of the *Pléiade*; Philip Sidney dispenses with rhyme for "Ye Goatherd Gods," a double sestina in the *Arcadia* (1590, 1593). In Germany, the poets of the 17th c. were attracted to the sestina (Martin Opitz, Andreas Gryphius, G. R. Weckherlin). In France and England, the sestina enjoyed a revival in the 19th c., thanks to the Comte de Gramont and to A. C. Swinburne, both of whom developed rhymed versions, Gramont's all on the same two-rhyme model (*abaabb* in the first stanza), Swinburne's not surprisingly more variable, given that he also composed a double sestina of twelve 12-line stanzas ("The Complaint of Lisa"). Gramont prefaced his collection with a hist. of the sestina, in which he describes it as "a reverie in which the same ideas, the same objects, occur to the mind in a succession of different aspects, which nonetheless resemble one another, fluid and changing shape like the clouds in the sky." The sestina interested the Fr. and Eng. *Parnassians less than the other romance fixed forms, but it has enjoyed a growing popularity in the 20th and 21st cs. Ezra Pound called the sestina "a form like a thin sheet of flame, folding and infolding upon itself," and his "Sestina: Altaforte" and "Sestina for Isolt" reintroduced the form to readers. Following W. H. Auden's "Paysage moralisé" and Louis Zukofsky's "Mantis," Am. poets have shown a remarkable interest in the form. Anthony Hecht's "The Book of Yolek," Elizabeth Bishop's "Sestina" and "A Miracle for Breakfast," and John Ashbery's "Farm Implements and Rutabagas in a Landscape" suggest the form's flexibility, as the repetitions evoke states as different as uncanny menace, claustrophobic containment, and comic playfulness. Indeed, from the mid-20th c. to the present, the sestina has enjoyed a great popularity in Am. poetry, at least partly because it serves the poetic culture's needs. A favorite exercise in creative writing classes, it allows poets to demonstrate a professional skill while exploring its limits. The form's repetitions also inspire poets interested in word games, as lang. forms the material of composition.

■ F. de Gramont, *Sestines, précédés de l'histoire de la sextine* (1872); Kastner; F. Davidson, "The Origin of Sestina," *MLN* 25 (1910); A. Jeanroy, "La 'sestina doppia' de Dante et les origines de la sestine," *Romania* 42 (1912); H. L. Cohen, *Lyric Forms from France* (1922); E. Pound, *The Spirit of Romance* (1952); L. Fiedler, "Green Thoughts in a Green Shade," *KR* 18 (1956); J. Riesz, *Die Sestine* (1971); I. Baldelli, "Sestina," *Enciclopedia Dantesca*, ed. G. Petrocchi et al., 5 vols. (1970–78); M. Shapiro, *Hieroglyph of Time: The Petrarchan Sestina* (1980); Morier; A. Roncaglia, "L'invenzione della sestina," *Metrica* 2 (1981); Elwert, *Italienische*, sect. 82; J. F. Nims, *A Local Habitation* (1985); D. Caplan, *Questions of Possibility: Contemporary Poetry and Poetic Form* (2004); S. Burt, "Sestina! or, The Fate of the Idea of Form," *MP* 105 (2007).

A. PREMINGER; C. SCOTT; D. CAPLAN

**SEXAIN,** sixain, sextain, sextet, sestet, hexastich. Names used for various stanza patterns of six lines. The term *sestet* is normally restricted to the final six lines of a *sonnet, esp. an It. sonnet, in distinction to the term *octave, or first eight lines. The other terms are applied indiscriminately to all six-line stanzas, only some of which have distinctive names. The best-known varieties of sexains in Eng. poetry are the following: (1) *ababcc*, in iambic pentameter, i.e., a heroic *quatrain capped by a *couplet, the so-called *Venus and Adonis stanza from its use by Shakespeare, common for Ren. *epyllia and *complaints and one of Matthew Arnold's favorite forms; (2) *ababcc*, in iambic tetrameter (e.g., William Wordsworth's "I Wandered Lonely as a Cloud"), very popular in Ger. poetry; (3) *tail rhyme, *aa4b3cc4b3*, sometimes called *Romance-six*, which is an extension of *ballad meter, popular in OF and ME verse, often used by 16th-c. dramatists, found in religious and secular poems up to George Herbert and evidenced as late as Thomas Hardy ("The Sigh") and Robert Bridges ("Nightingales"); (4) the *Burns stanza, *aaa4b2a4b2*, which may go back to Occitan models of the 11th c. and is found also in *medieval romances and miracle plays; (5) *xayaza*, e.g., D. G. Rossetti's "Blessed Damozel"; and (6) *abcabc*, popular in Eng. poetry since A. C. Swinburne, e.g., in W. B. Yeats, John Berryman, Dylan Thomas, Richard Wilbur, and Thom Gunn. In Sp., the octosyllabic sexain rhyming *aabccb* or *ababcc* is called a *sextilla. One of the earliest extant texts of Fr. verse, the *Vie de Saint Leger*, is set in 129 sexains rhyming in couplets and the *rhétoriqueurs termed a poem of three short-line sexains *plate rime brisée* (see CROSS RHYME). The most famous and most spectacular poetic form in sexains, the *sestina, uses elaborate patterns of repeated words. Six-line stanzas occur almost as often as quatrains and couplets and more frequently than five-line stanzas.

■ Schipper, *History*; Morier, "Sextine."

A. PREMINGER; E. HAÜBLEIN

**SEXTILLA.** A Sp. stanza form of six octosyllabic or shorter lines. In the classic period, the usual rhyme schemes were *abbaab, ababba, ababab, abbaba, aabbab*, and *abaabb*; mod. definitions often call for *aabccb* or *ababcc* (sometimes this last is called *sestina*) and occasionally stipulate that the *b* lines be oxytones and the others paroxytones. *Sextillas* have been pointed out in the prologue to the Galician-Port. *Cantigas de Santa Maria* (13th c.) of King Alfonso X *el Sabio* (the Wise) and in the *Libro de buen amor* (14th c.):

> ¡Ventura astrosa,
> cruel, enojosa,
> captiva, mequina!
> ¿Por qué eres sañosa,
> contra mí tan dañosa,
> e falsa vesina?

■ D. G. Rengifo, *Arte poética española* (1592); A. de Trueba, *Arte de hacer versos* (1905); Navarro.

D. C. CLARKE

**SHI** (or *shih*, in Wade-Giles romanization).

**I. Early History of Shi.** The term *shi*, most frequently used to denote "poetry" in traditional China and translated as "lyric poetry," originally referred to the lyrics of a song (as opposed to the song's musical aspects or performance). However, by the Springs and Autumns period (770–476 BCE), the term would be used almost exclusively to denote a particular corpus of poems—the *Shijing* (*Classic of Poetry*, also known as the *Book of Songs*). The *Shijing* primarily used a tetrasyllabic line; four-syllable lines were so strongly associated with the collection that later tetrasyllabic poetry was thought to evoke the *Shijing*'s archaic simplicity. The assoc. of the *Shijing* with Confucius, as well as comments attributed to Confucius about the importance of learning the collection, has played a significant role in locating shi within a trad. of literary didacticism. In the Han dynasty (206 BCE–220 CE), a version of the early hermeneutical formula *shi yan zhi*, or "poetry articulates aims," would be invoked in a commentary to the *Shijing*. This formula would wield great influence on later poetics, essentially defining the poem as the literary expression of what was on the speaker's mind. To understand the poem, therefore, meant understanding the speaker's autobiographical occasion and historical situation—i.e., the critical trad. construed the poem as a work of factual statement, rather than of the fictive imagination. These critical assumptions could result in unconvincing allegorical readings of simple love songs, particularly where the *Shijing* was concerned.

Also important to the early history of shi was the *Chuci* or *Lyrics of Chu*. This was an early anthol. associated with the semi-independent southern kingdom of Chu. The *Chuci* made striking use of a caesura-marker particle *xi*, which divided lines into hemistichs. In this anthol. was the "Jiu ge" ("Nine Songs"), a group of actually 11 songs attributed to the late Warring States figure Qu Yuan (c. 340–278 BCE) that recast Chu religious rites in poetic form. The "Nine Songs" were the precursor to the subgenre of "Chu songs," which were popular among Chu aristocracy and Han emperors. The Chu songs were the earliest surviving poetic compositions from the Western Han (206 BCE–9 CE), and the longer meter of the Chu song line has been identified as contributing to the rise of the heptasyllabic shi line in later centuries.

**II. From the Han to Jin Dynasties.** Though the Han has often been credited with the emergence of penta-syllabic shi poetry, it was only at the end of the dynasty that one finds much evidence of this. For much of the Han (and indeed in the two centuries after the Han), rhapsodic composition and tetrasyllabic poetry were still the dominant forms. There are examples of Western Han pentasyllabic shi poems, but these are generally problematic, as in the case of poems attributed to Su Wu (140–60 BCE) and Li Ling (d. 74 BCE). These were poems supposedly written between friends, one of whom was a Western Han general who had surrendered to the Xiongnu confederacy and the other a Han envoy to the Xiongnu. It is likely that the Su Wu-Li Ling corpus was actually composed near the end of the Eastern Han (25–220) and was part of a larger anonymous corpus known as *gushi* or "old poems." The most famous of these were a set of poems called the "Gushi shijiu shou" ("Nineteen Old Poems"). These pentasyllabic poems took up themes of *carpe diem*, insomnia, separation, and displacement. As a number of scholars have noted, these anonymous shi were closely associated with *yuefu* (music bureau) poetry and indeed cannot always be clearly distinguished from them.

The historian Ban Gu (32–92) is identified as the first known historical author of a pentasyllabic shi, but it was during the Jian'an era (196–220) that pentasyllablic poetry truly came into its own. This period was dominated by the warlord Cao Cao (155–220), a talented writer of tetrasyllabic and pentasyllabic yuefu poetry. His heir Cao Pi (186–226) was also a fine poet, but the younger son Cao Zhi (192–232) was the major poet of the age. Cao Zhi composed with a confidence and inventiveness that neither his elder brother nor his father commanded. The Cao clan served as patrons to the so-called Seven Masters of the Jian'an, a group of writers that included the important poet Wang Can (177–217). Few poems survive from this period; but in those that remain, one can see how the pentasyllabic line emerged out of the tetrasyllabic line through the addition of a literary particle or an adjective. In addition to poems on gushi topics, Jian'an era poets composed in poetic subgenres such as *youxian shi* (poems on wandering with immortals) and *gongyan shi* (poems on the lord's feast). In the decades following Cao Pi's founding of the Wei (220–65), there was Ruan Ji (210–63), who composed 82 poems (mostly pentasyllabic), all entitled "Yong huai" ("Singing of My Cares"). Ruan Ji's poems are rather obscure, and they are almost always interpreted through the model of *shi yan zhi* and thought to contain veiled criticism of politics during the age.

Many shi poets during the subsequent Western Jin dynasty (265–316) elaborated upon Eastern Han and Jian'an period themes and styles. *Ni gushi* (poems in imitation of the old poems) were composed by leading writers such as Lu Ji (261–303). However, traditional critics have often complained that Western Jin poetry lacked vigor and suffered from a surfeit of rhetorical ornament. After the northern heartland was lost to ethnic non-Han Chinese tribes, the Jin relocated itself south of the Yangtze River. The most important poet of this age (though not celebrated as such during his own life) was Tao Qian (365–427), also known as Tao Yuanming. Tao Qian composed in a strongly autobiographical mode, describing his rejection of official life for a return to a life of farming. Although such *tianyuan shi* (farmland poetry) are often thought to idealize the agrarian life, Tao Qian's poems also describe the difficulties and hardships that he and his family faced. His imitations of gushi were in a more straightforward style than the Western Jin poets. Closely associated with Tao Qian was the poet Xie Lingyun (385–433), who is often identified as being the first great writer of *shanshui shi* (landscape poetry).

**III. Shi of the Southern Dynasties.** During the Southern Dynasties (420–579), increasing attention was paid to prosody, which was codified as the *sisheng babing* (four tones and eight faults) during the Yongming era (483–94). The "four tones" were the level, rising, departing, and entering tones; these differ from the current four tones of standard mod. Chinese. The "eight faults" stipulated the avoidance of using the same tones, initial consonants, and rhyme sounds in certain positions of each line or couplet. The practitioners of the new style championed the pentasyllabic line and worked in shi of eight lines, with strong grammatical *parallelism in the middle two couplets. They also composed in quatrains, which were called *xiaoshi* (little poems), or later, *jueju*, (cut-off lines.) The heptasyllabic line was also used, particularly in poems that drew on anonymous southern yuefu topics or styles. Leading poets of this period belonged to literary coteries and princely courts where normative competence was as important as individual brilliance. The poetic subgenre of *yongwu shi* (poems on things) was popular, allowing poets to display their verbal wit and elegance through riddling descriptions of objects at banquets. During the Liang dynasty, the *Wen xuan* (*Selections of Refined Literature*) was compiled by the crown prince Xiao Tong (501–31). This would become the major pre-Tang source for all genres, including shi. The poems contained here represent an orthodox view of lit., excluding *yongwu* poetry and erotic pieces. The counter-anthol. to the *Wen xuan* was the *Yutai xinyong* (*New Songs from Jade Terrace*), an anthol. devoted to love poems and supposedly aimed at a female readership. The *Yutai xinyong* is identified with *gongti shi* (palace-style poems), intricately crafted poems that thematized the leisure of palace life and women's longings in boudoirs.

**IV. Medieval Shi Prosody.** After the founding of the Tang dynasty, the Yongming prosodic rules would be both simplified and normalized. This new form would be known either as *lüshi* (regulated poetry) or as *jinti shi* (recent-style poetry), in contrast to the more relaxed form of *guti shi* (ancient-style poetry), which did not insist upon strict tonal balance or parallelism (though these were often employed). The Tang poets simplified the four tonal divisions by reducing them to

two categories: level and deflected. The basic prosodic rules for regulated verse are as follows: (1) meters of either five or seven syllables; (2) poem lengths of four or eight lines; (3) a single rhyme in the level tone that falls on the last syllable of even-numbered lines (the last syllable of the first line might also rhyme); (4) a more or less fixed pattern of tonal balance. There are two patterns for the distribution of tones in regulated pentasyllabic verse. These are shown below, with "–" marking a level tone and " \ " marking a deflected tone (patterns are determined by the tone of the second syllable of the first line):

**A. *Deflected Tone Opening***

```
    \ \ – – \
2   – – \ \ –
    – – – \ \
4   \ \ \ – –
    \ \ – – \
6   – – \ \ –
    – – – \ \
8   \ \ \ – –
```

**B. *Level Tone Opening***

```
    – – – \ \
2   \ \ \ – –
    \ \ – – \
4   – – \ \ –
    – – – \ \
6   \ \ \ – –
    \ \ – – \
8   – – \ \ –
```

Moreover, within each line, there were also strictly regulated tone positions and variable tone positions. The second, fourth, and fifth positions were "fixed," while the other positions were not. Thus, in practice, the actual pentasyllabic couplet would appear as one of the following (with "x" marking variable tone positions):

```
x \ x –\
x – x \ –

x – x \ \
x \ x – –
```

Regulated heptasyllabic poems simply add two deflected tones or two level tones to the beginnings of what would otherwise be a pentasyllabic line. Again, there are fixed and unfixed tone positions, which are the second, fourth, sixth, and seventh syllables. As patterns, the couplets would appear as follows (along with the fixed position tonal distribution):

**A. *Deflected Tone Opening***

```
\ \ – – – \ \      x \ x – x \ \
– – \ \ \ – –      x – x \ x – –
```

**B. *Level Tone Opening***

```
– – \ \ – – \      x – x \ x – \
\ \ – – \ \ –      x \ x – x \ –
```

The heptasyllabic poem would then alternate these two couplet patterns to fill out its eight lines, whereas regulated quatrains, whether five- or seven-syllable, would simply consist of half of an eight-line poem.

**V. Shi of the Tang Dynasty.** The Tang is often called the golden age of shi poetry. Later literary scholars have divided the Tang into four distinct periods, based both on literary trends and political circumstances: the Early Tang, the High Tang, the Mid-Tang, and the Late Tang. Court poetry dominated much of the Early Tang period, though the most distinctive of poets in this age, such as Wang Ji (590–644), wrote outside the courtly circles and on topics far removed from the occasional verse of the court. It is the High Tang that most readers think of when discussing Tang shi. The poets Wang Wei (701–61), Li Bo (701–ca. 762), and Du Fu (712–70) were active during this time, along with a number of other famed poets. Wang Wei was a member of an important clan and served in the court during the long reign of Emperor Xuanzong (712–56). However, his poems often represent him in a Tao Qian-like mode of pastoral retirement. Particularly famous is his "Wangchuan ji" ("Wangchuan Collection"), a set of poems written about sites on his sizable estate. In contrast to the metropolitan Wang Wei, Li Bo was born in the western regions of China and was likely of mixed Central Asian background. An outsider in many ways, his route to the court was through his literary talent and his outlandish personality. Li Bo is best known for his imaginative and often extravagant yuefu poems, which transformed poetic conventions into astonishing visions of hyperbole. He is also known for a series of poems titled "Gufeng" ("Ancient Airs") and for his Daoist-inflected poems. Du Fu, arguably the greatest of the three great Tang poets, is remembered now for his powerful moral vision and his role as poetic witness to the An Shi Rebellion, which shook the Tang empire to its core. In many of his poems, one finds sympathy for the suffering of commoners, a sense of duty to the polity, and a ruthless sense of irony. This is the case with "Zi jing fu Fengxian yonghuai wubaizi" ("Singing of My Cares While Going from the Capital to Fengxian"). As he leaves the capital, Du Fu juxtaposes the pleasures of the wealthy with the frozen corpses of the poor but finds that he is himself implicated in this neglect, arriving home to discover that a young son has died in his absence.

Poets of the Mid-Tang often seem more self-conscious than those of the High Tang, looking back to figures such as Du Fu and Li Bo. Poets like Han Yu (768–824) and Liu Zongyuan (773–819) were associated with the archaist (*fugu*) literary circles, prizing a kind of awkwardness and rejecting the high sheen of court poetry. Others, like Bo Juyi (772–846), were famed for socially conscious "new yuefu" poems, which satirized inequalities of wealth and injustice. Li He (790–816) was a poet of real strangeness who invoked ghostly imagery and cryptically ominous scenes, outdoing even Li Bo's rhetorical extravagance. In the Late Tang, poets such as Du Mu (803–52), Li

Shangyin (ca. 811–58), and Wen Tingyun (ca. 813–70) combined a sense of glamorous decadence with the use of historical allusions. A number of their poems looked back to the Southern Dynasties and to the Sui (581–617), evoking a sense of dynastic decline and belatedness.

**VI. Poetry of the Song to Qing Dynasties.** The composition of shi poetry was central to the ideal of the literatus (*wenren*) during the Song dynasty (960–1279). Major writers like Ouyang Xiu (1007–72) and Mei Yaochen (1002–60) reaffirmed the connection between poetry and Confucian moral transformation. Mei Yaochen is also responsible for one of the lasting critical judgments of Song poetry, describing it as *pingdan* (bland). Certainly, there was a kind of discursive quality to many of the famous Song poems, a willingness to engage in philosophical speculation. There was also an interest in the ordinariness of daily life, which had been introduced by Du Fu. The greatest poet of the Song was Su Shi (1037–1101), known also as Su Dongpo, whose poems reveal attention to subjective perception and a feel for particular details, bringing together Song philosophical abstraction with beautifully honed imagery. His poem "Zhouzhong yeqi" ("Standing Up on a Boat at Evening") plays with misperceptions of sensory evidence and the flickering sense of a lyric moment that passes quickly from a framed aesthetic scene back into the ordinary realm of noise. Wang Anshi (1021–86), remembered now as the architect of the "New Policies," was also an important poet and famed for his regulated quatrains. During the Southern Song, major poets included Yang Wanli (1124–1206), Lu You (1125–1210), and Fan Chengda (1126–93), who all knew one another and exchanged poems. At the end of the Song, there was Wen Tianxiang (1246–82), a poet famed for his patriotism to the Song, who indeed was martyred by order of Khubilai Khan (1215–1368), the founder of the Yuan dynasty (1279–1368).

During the Yuan, Ming (1368–1644), and Qing (1644–1911) dynasties, the Song ideal of wenren poetry gave way to poets of other social classes and groups. The sheer amount of shi poetry written and collected after the Song is staggering, with poetry writing becoming an increasingly popular activity for commoners, i.e., those born not of aristocratic or official families. Gao Qi (1336–74), who is often considered the greatest Ming poet (though most of his life was lived during the Yuan), was common-born but rose to renown in significant measure because of his literary talents. In his early poem "Qingqiuzi ge" ("Song of the Man of the Green Hill"), he constructs a pseudoautobiographical statement of his devotion to poetry through evocations of Li Bo and *Chuci*-influenced ascension lit. Gao Qi is also sometimes seen as a precursor to the Ming archaist poets, such as Li Mengyang (1473–1529), who were active in the middle period of the Ming dynasty and who insisted that the High Tang should be taken as the model for all good verse. That this period also saw a number of important compilations of earlier poetry and works of poetry crit. was a likely reason for the resurgence in archaist sentiment. The Qing conquest spurred loyalist passions in poets like Chen Zilong (1608–47) and the female poet Liu Shi (1618–64). The two poets were romantically linked, but she later married another famed poet, Qian Qianyi (1582–1664), who left his wife for her. Chen Zilong would achieve political martyrdom by committing suicide rather than be captured by Qing troops.

**VII. Shi Composed by Women.** The relationship between male and female poets would become more complex in the late imperial period. It has been speculated that Liu Shi was responsible (though uncredited) for the sections on women poets and the annotations in Qian Qianyi's anthol. of Ming poets, the *Liechao shiji* (Poetry Collections from the Arrayed Reigns [of the Ming]). It is also worth noting that the number of poetry collections by women increased in the late imperial period. There had always been women who composed shi, though in earlier periods, these were mostly court ladies, high-born daughters in aristocratic households, nuns, and courtesans—i.e., women who had a certain amount of freedom in their interactions with educated men. The Tang poets Xue Tao (770–830) and Yu Xuanji (840–68) socialized with leading Tang writers; significant portions of their poetry have been preserved. Yu Xuanji's poetry is particularly notable for the bitter awareness of how sex was a limit that talent could not overcome. During the Song, there was Li Qingzhao (1084–ca. 1151), though she was better known for her *ci, and Zhu Shuzhen (fl. 1100), whose poem "Zi ze" ("Reprimanding Myself") was a self-conscious critique of how women were not supposed to engage in literary pursuits. Beginning in the Ming, one finds female literary circles that were formed within family and social networks. One of the most famous of these was the Banana Garden Poetry Club, formed in the early days of the Qing. The male poet Yuan Mei (1716–98) also taught female students and published a volume collecting their poems.

**VIII. Modern Shi.** In more mod. times, cl.-lang. shi has made room for poetry written in mod. vernacular Chinese. Writers associated with the May Fourth Movement were interested in experimenting with Western-style *free verse. However, cl.-lang. shi continued to be written by poets like Lu Xun (1881–1936) and Mao Zedong (1893–1976) and indeed is still practiced by many poets today. However, the term *shi* in the contemp. literary context now refers to a general notion of "poetry," rather than to the specific cl. genre that is distinct from other cl. poetic genres.

*See* CHINA, POETRY OF; CHINA, POPULAR POETRY OF; CHINESE POETICS; CHINESE POETRY IN JAPAN.

■ **Anthologies:** *The Jade Mountain*, trans. W. Bynner (1929); *Poems of the Late T'ang*, trans. A. Graham (1965); *Anthology of Chinese Verse*, ed. and trans. J. Frodsham with C. Hsi (1967); *Sunflower Splendor*, ed. W. Liu and I. Lo (1975); H. Stimson, *Fifty-five T'ang Poems* (1976); *New Songs from a Jade Terrace*, trans. A. Birrell (1982);

*Columbia Book of Chinese Poetry*, ed. and trans. B. Watson (1984); *Columbia Book of Later Chinese Poetry*, ed. and trans. J. Chaves (1986); *Waiting for the Unicorn*, ed. I. Lo and W. Schultz (1986); *The Red Azalea*, ed. E. Morin (1990); *Anthology of Modern Chinese Poetry*, ed. and trans. M. Yeh (1992); *Columbia Anthology of Traditional Chinese Literature*, ed. V. Mair (1994); *Songs of the Immortals*, trans. Y. Xu (1994); *Anthology of Chinese Literature*, ed. and trans. S. Owen (1996); *Women Writers of Traditional China*, ed. K. Chang and H. Saussy (1999); *Classical Chinese Literature*, ed. J. Minford and J. Lau (2000); W. Idema and B. Grant, *The Red Brush* (2004); *The Anchor Book of Chinese Poetry*, ed. T. Barnstone and P. Chou (2005); *Classical Chinese Poetry*, ed. and trans. D. Hinton (2008); *Transparante tranen*, ed. and trans. W. Idema (2008).

■ **Criticism and History:** W. Hung, *Tu Fu*, 2 v. (1952); J.J.Y. Liu, *Art of Chinese Poetry* (1962); J. Diény, *Les dix-neuf poèmes anciens* (1963); K. Yoshikawa, *Introduction to Sung Poetry* (1967); J. Diény, *Aux origines de la poésie classique en Chine* (1968); J.J.Y. Liu, *The Poetry of Li Shang-yin* (1969); J. Hightower, *The Poetry of T'ao Ch'ien* (1970); A. Davis, *Tu Fu* (1971); B. Watson, *Chinese Lyricism* (1971); J. Lin, *Modern Chinese Poetry* (1972); S. Owen, *Poetry of Meng Chiao and Han Yü* (1975); J. Chaves, *Mei Yao-ch'en and the Development of Early Sung Poetry* (1976); H. Frankel, *The Flowering Plum and the Palace Lady* (1976); D. Holzman, *Poetry and Politics* (1976); M. Duke, *Lu You* (1977); S. Owen, *Poetry of the Early T'ang* (1977); P. Yu, *The Poetry of Wang Wei* (1980); S. Owen, *Great Age of Chinese Poetry* (1981); F. Cheng, *Chinese Poetic Writing* (1982); R. Miao, *Early Medieval Chinese Poetry* (1982); A. Davis, *T'ao Yüan-ming*, 2 v. (1983); R. Egan, *The Literary Works of Ou-yang Hsiu* (1984); R. Lynn, *Guide to Chinese Poetry and Drama*, 2d ed. (1984); S. Owen, *Traditional Chinese Poetry and Poetics* (1985); R. Bodman and S. Wong, "Shih"; and C. Hartman, "Poetry," *Indiana Companion to Traditional Chinese Literature*, ed. W. H. Nienhauser Jr., rev. ed. (1986); K. Chang, *Six Dynasties Poetry* (1986); C. Hartman, *Han Yü and the T'ang Search for Unity* (1986); P. Kroll, "Li Po's Transcendent Diction," *JAOS* (1986); *Vitality of the Lyric Voice*, ed. S. Lin and S. Owen (1986); P. Yu, *The Reading of Imagery in the Chinese Poetic Tradition* (1987); R. Mather, *The Poet Shen Yüeh* (1988); K. Yoshikawa, *Five Hundred Years of Chinese Poetry, 1150–1650*, ed. J. T. Wixted (1989); M. Fuller, *The Road to East Slope* (1990); K. Chang, *The Late-Ming Poet Ch'en Tzu-lung* (1991); S. Van Zoeren, *Poetry and Personality* (1991); M. Yeh, *Modern Chinese Poetry* (1991); J. D. Schmidt, *Stone Lake* (1992); P. Rouzer, *Writing Another's Dream* (1993); R. Egan, *Word, Image, and Deed in the Life of Su Shi* (1994); E. Chou, *Reconsidering Tu Fu* (1995); J. Kowallis, *The Lyrical Lu Xun* (1996); J. Hightower and F. Yeh, *Studies in Chinese Poetry* (1998); J. Diény, *Les poèmes de Cao Cao* (2000); *Columbia History of Chinese Literature*, ed. V. Mair (2001); P. Kroll and D. Knechtges, *Studies in Early Medieval Chinese Literature and Cultural History* (2003); P. Varsano, *Tracking the Banished Immortal*

(2003); D. Warner, *A Wild Deer amid Soaring Phoenixes* (2003); X. Tian, *Tao Yuanming and Manuscript Culture* (2005); S. Owen, *The Late Tang* and *Making of Early Chinese Poetry* (both 2006); G. Sanders, *Words Well Put* (2006); *How to Read Chinese Poetry*, ed. Z. Cai (2007); X. Tian, *Beacon Fire and Shooting Star* (2007); D. Bryant, *The Great Recreation: Ho Ching-ming (1483–1521) and His World* (2008); W. Swartz, *Reading Tao Yuanming* (2008).

J. Chen

**SHIJING.** The Chinese poetic trad. begins spectacularly with the *Shijing* (*Classic of Poetry*, also known as *Book of Songs*), usually dated ca. 1000–600 BCE. This places the formation of the text during the rule of the Zhou royal kingdom, a time long associated with the foundations of early Chinese culture. Although the anthol.'s origin is shrouded in mystery and legend, its materials must have passed through a long period of oral transmission before becoming recorded and fixed. Even after being written down, the poems no doubt circulated primarily in a culture of secondary orality: recited, quoted, and heard but not often read. Our earliest example of this circulation is in quotations from the *Zuo zhuan* where a poem, or a few lines, is applied freely to the political or rhetorical situation at hand—the *Zuo zhuan* is a collection of historical narratives from the 8th–5th c. BCE, although its compilation dates from somewhat later. Thus, not only is there no sense of authorship to these poems, but, at this early date, even their meanings were contingent on their application.

Judging from textual and archaeological evidence, the *Shijing* that we now have appears to represent the text as known in the late cl. period—the greatest variations were in the written forms of the individual words. Thus, although there are many issues with interpretation of the poems, the poem texts themselves appear to have been stable at least since the 3d c. BCE. This collection eventually became one of the five Confucian classics and set the bedrock of cl. Chinese poetry.

The 305 poems (*shi*) that form the anthol. are clearly of one cloth in terms of lang. and *prosody: composed mostly in four-syllable lines with regular end rhyme and sharing lang. and *tropes throughout. Yet within the "three hundred poems," as the collection was traditionally called, there is represented a wide variety of voices, themes, forms, and settings. The collection presents no grand narrative or overarching political or religious vision, but rather offers materials that intersect with numerous cultural practices, personae, and social sites. We find liturgical hymns to the early kings, narratives of dynastic legends, poems of feasting, agricultural calendars, and most famously, ballads of love and hardship from across the feudal states. As a sample of that range consider these two short poems. The first is a brief prayer (perhaps a fragment) to the founding Zhou king, written in solemn, austere lang.:

Pure and luminous
Are the laws of King Wen,

Founding the rites
That now still triumph,
These auspicious omens of the Zhou.

(268)

Compare this to a rural ballad of lost friendship played out in two short stanzas built entirely of *incremental repetitions:

If along the wide road
I catch hold of your sleeve,
Do not hate me for it.
Be not hasty with old friends.
If along the wide road
I catch hold of your hand,
Do not be mad at me.
Be not hasty with loved ones.

(81)

Between these extremes of prayers from the hallowed halls of the Zhou ancestral temple and songs along the dirt roads in the state of Zheng are embedded many poetic strata. Those strata are first clearly announced by shape of the anthol., which orders and labels three separate sections: the "Airs" (*feng*), the "Odes" (*ya*), and the "Hymns" (*song*). These sections are then subdivided into 15 sets of airs by feudal state (poems 1–160); two sections of the odes, called "Minor" and "Major" (161–234, 235–65, respectively); and the hymns (266–305) are divided between two royal houses and the state of Lu. This general shape is attested as early as 6th c. BCE; the specific order of the individual poems has been set at least since the 1st c. CE. Both traditional and mod. scholars have also detected here a chronological layering, with the airs being the latest addition to the collection and the hymns, esp. those associated with the Zhou royal house, the oldest.

The *Shijing* has long been associated with Confucius and his school of thought. In fact, in the 1st-c. BCE general history, *Shiji* by Sima Qian, Confucius is claimed to have been the editor of the text; he is said to have worked with 3,000 poems, from which he "eliminated the duplicates and selected texts that could be used with ritual propriety," extracting the 305 (Allen). While the shape of the collection clearly results from the effort of an editorial hand, it is far from clear it was actually that of Confucius. Nonetheless, he and his school held the "three hundred poems" in very high regard, both as pedagogical tools and as moral models. The orthodox hermeneutical trad. that emerged in the 1st c. CE, the so-called Mao school, developed readings of the poems along these lines, interpreting them as commentaries on the moral and political conditions during the Zhou feudal period. These readings are now often criticized as patent fabrications, but they dominated understanding of the poems up until the 12th c., when more social and literary interpretations came to the fore. Late imperial scholarship focused on the philological aspects of the text. In the 20th and 21st cs., readings of the poems, in both China and abroad, typically pursue these literary, philological, or anthropological understandings of the anthol. The *Shijing* is seen as a literary masterpiece and as a window onto ancient Chinese ling. and material culture.

*See* CHINA, POETRY OF.

■ **Anthologies:** *The She King or the Book of Poetry*, trans. J. Legge (1871); *The Book of Odes*, trans. B. Karlgren (1950); *The Confucian Odes*, trans. E. Pound (1954); *The Book of Songs*, trans. A. Waley and J. Allen (1996).

■ **Criticism:** M. Granet, *Festivals and Songs of Ancient China*, trans. E. Edwards (1932); W. Dobson, "Linguistic Evidence and the Dating of the *Book of Songs*," *T'oung Pao* 51 (1964); C. H. Wang, *The Bell and the Drum* (1974); P. Yu, "Allegory, Allegoresis, and the *Classic of Poetry*," *HJAS* 43 (1983); C. H. Wang, *From Ritual to Allegory* (1988); S. Van Zoeren, *Poetry and Personality* (1991); H. Saussy, *The Problem of a Chinese Aesthetic* (1993); J. Allen, "A Literary History of the *Shi jing*," *The Book of Songs*, ed. S. Allen (1996); E. Shaughnessy, *Before Confucius* (1997); S. Owen, "Reproduction in the *Shijing* (Classic of Poetry)," *HJAS* 61 (2001); *Text and Ritual in Early China*, ed. M. Kern (2005); L. Zhang, *Allegoresis: Reading Canonical Literature East and West* (2005).

J. ALLEN

**SHINKOKINSHŪ.** *Shinkokinshū*, a work of 1,978 poems divided into multiple books, was commissioned by the retired Japanese emperor Go-Toba and formally submitted in 1205, though poems continued to be added at least through 1208. The copy on which the text used today is based was completed in 1216.

Go-Toba had begun laying the groundwork in 1200. Over the next several years, he sponsored a series of poetry events (contests, hundred-poem sequences, etc.; see POETIC CONTESTS), often with themes, that yielded many poems for the collection. In 1201, he revived the Wakadokoro (Bureau of Poetry), which had been dormant for about 250 years, to provide a locus for poetic activity and research and editing of the anthol. From the outset, Go-Toba was determined to balance the two major factions (the Rokujō and Mikohidari houses) and to promote the careers of young poets who had no ties to either faction (e.g., Asukai Masatsune, Kunaikyō, etc.). The most dramatic example of this is the *Sengohyakuban uta-awase* (Poetry Contest in 1500 Rounds), in which 30 poets representing all the major poetic schools and political factions were invited to submit 100-poem sequences (*hyakushu no uta*) following a set pattern. Go-Toba then configured these 3,000 poems into a series of one-on-one matchups and farmed them out in sections to be judged by eight prominent poetscholars, incl. Fujiwara Teika himself and his allies and rivals. He thus, in effect, picked the brains of the top literary talents of his age, and 90 poems from this contest ended up anthologized in *Shinkokinshū*.

Go-Toba's orchestration of not only the anthol. but of the many events connected to it was an early step in his attempt to revive the centrality of the imperial house in relation to the aristocratic families in Kyoto and to the growing influence of the Kamakura Bakufu.

(His effort came to a head in the Jōkyū War of 1221, in which he was defeated and sent into exile for the remainder of his life.)

The title of the collection—"New *\*Kokinshū*"—suggests a neoclassical program, and in fact, the collection is well known for the use in many of its poems of the techniques of *honkadori*, an allusive practice that borrows a phrase or line from an earlier poem but places it in a new, reconfigured context; and *honzetsu*, where the allusion is to an earlier prose work. Teika, his father, Fujiwara Shunzei, and many other poets in *Shinkokinshū*, drew particularly from the prose classics of the mid-Heian period, esp. *Genji monogatari* (*Tale of Genji*). In so doing, they were staking out new territory in competition with the other major poetic school of their day, the Rokujō house, which prided itself as expert in the 8th c. *\*Man'yōshū* poetry collection and the older, strictly poetic trads. So part of what made *Shinkokinshū* "new" was its intertextual relationship with Heian prose, with particular attention to the courtship narrative that leads inevitably to separation, frustration, and loss. The poem below simultaneously alludes to a *Kokinshū* poem, a Chinese legend, and the final chapter of the *Tale of Genji*:

> Haru no yo no
> Yume no ukihashi
> Todae shite
> Mine ni wakururu
> Yokogumo no sora
>
> (On a spring night
> The floating bridge of dreams
> Is interrupted—
> Trailing across the sky
> Clouds parted by the mountain peak.)

(Fujiwara Teika, *Shinkokinshū* 38)

The structural relationship of *Shinkokinshū* to *Kokinshū* is readily apparent, with a similar focus on the three major types of poetry: Seasonal, Love, and Occasional (e.g., poems of celebration, parting, and so on). However, with *Shinkokinshū*, the distinctions between these categories begin to be blurred, with Teika himself stating that the best poems combine the elements from more than one category. Thus, from *Shinkokinshū* onward, the category known as *Miscellaneous* takes on ever greater significance.

*Shinkokinshū* has enjoyed high esteem in the post-Meiji *\*canon of cl. Japanese lit. but was less esteemed in its time. One mark against it was its association with a disgraced emperor (Go-Toba), whose fall was so complete that neither he nor his son Juntoku, who aided him in his restoration efforts and who was similarly exiled, has a single poem in the final version of the next imperial anthol. (*Shinchokusenshū*). (In fact, neither Go-Toba nor Juntoku was allowed to be buried in Kyoto—their tombs stand together in the village of Ohara north of the capital.) Teika's own descendants, who dominated the world of poetry for the next several centuries, also shunned *Shinkokinshū*, presumably because it was compiled by a committee rather than by

Teika alone. On the other hand, scholars and readers from the Meiji period onward have valued its innovative approach, the layers of meaning achieved through *allusion and overlapping syntactical phrasing, and its relatively sad, lonely tone that suits subsequent devels. in Japanese arts and aesthetics, as exemplified by, e.g., the tea ceremony.

*See* JAPANESE POETICS, WAKA.

■ R. Bundy, "The Uses of Literary Tradition: The Poetry and Poetics of the *Shinkokinshū*," *DAI* 45 (1984); A. Hirota, "Ex-Emperor Go-Toba: A Study in Personality, Politics and Poetry," *DAI* 51 (1989); D. Bialock, "Voice, Text, and the Question of Poetic Borrowing in Late Classical Poetry," *HJAS* 54 (1994); R. Bundy, "*Santai waka*: Six Poems in Three Modes," *Monumenta Nipponica* 49, 2 pts. (1994); E. Kamens, *"Utamakura," Allusion, and Intertextuality in Traditional Japanese Poetry* (1997); R. Huey, *The Making of Shinkokinshū* (2002).

R. HUEY

**SIAMESE POETRY.** *See* THAILAND, POETRY OF.

**SICILIAN OCTAVE** (*ottava siciliana* or *napoletana*). An eight-line It. stanza rhyming *abababab* and composed of *hendecasyllables. It was generally used for amatory topics of a popular nature. The origin of this type of octave is unclear. According to some scholars, it existed early in the 13th c. in southern Italy and Sicily and influenced the invention of the *sonnet by serving as the model for its *octave, appearing in Tuscany (*ottava toscana*) only toward the end of that century. Others tend to place its origin in Tuscany and consider it, conversely, a derivation from the octave of the sonnet. The Sicilian octave never had the success that *ottava rima* enjoyed, although it remained in popular use through the 15th c., when it was replaced by the *madrigal.

*See* STRAMBOTTO.

■ Spongano; Wilkins; A. Balduino, "Pater semper incertus. Ancora sulle origini dell'ottava rima," *Metrica* 3 (1982); F. P. Memmo, *Dizionario di metrica italiana* (1983); Elwert, *Italienische*; P. G. Beltrami, *La metrica italiana* (2002).

L. H. GORDON; C. KLEINHENZ

**SICILIAN SCHOOL.** A loosely organized group of poets writing in the vernacular who were active at the court of the Hohenstaufen monarchs in Sicily during the first half of the 13th c. They flourished particularly under Frederick II and his son Manfred. Some 30 poets are associated with the Sicilian school; the majority of them were Sicilians, but a fair proportion came from the It. mainland, some from as far north as Tuscany. The major importance of the Sicilian poets is that they established It. as a literary lang. They show familiarity with the work of the Occitan *troubadours, the northern Fr. *trouvères, and the Ger. *Minnesänger* (see MINNESANG). The primarily amatory content of their work is derived from troubadour models, but unlike their northern It. contemporaries, they abandoned Oc-

citan, the traditional lang. of the love *lyric, and wrote in their own tongue. Of almost equal importance is their formal achievement: they invented the *sonnet, and they developed from Occitan, Fr., and Ger. models the distinctive structure of the *canzone*, the two most important lyric forms of It. poetry. The sonnet of the Sicilian school, as written by its presumed inventor Giacomo da Lentini and others, shows in some instances what would become the characteristic feature of the form, the distinctive separation into octave and *sestet. The octave always rhymes *abababab*, and the sestet is either *cdecde* or *cdcdcd*.

These first It. poets exerted a powerful effect on all subsequent It. lyric verse through their influence, both formal and thematic, on the Tuscan poets of the 13th and 14th cs., Guittone d'Arezzo, Guido Guinizzelli, Dante, and Petrarch. Indeed, their influence was ling. as well as literary: the occurrence of typically southern locutions in the Tuscan dialect, which became the standard literary lang. of Italy, may be traced to their example. The best of the Sicilian poets, in addition to da Lentini, are Guido delle Colonne, Pier delle Vigne, Giacomino Pugliese, and Rinaldo d'Aquino.

*See* CANSO; ITALIAN PROSODY; ITALY, POETRY OF; SESTINA; SICILIAN OCTAVE.

■ G. A. Cesareo, *Le origini della poesia lirica e la poesia siciliana sotto gli Svevi*, 2d ed. (1924); V. de Bartholomaeis, *Primordi della lirica d'arte in Italia* (1943); W. T. Elwert, *Per una valutazione stilistica dell'elemento provenzale nel linguaggio della scuola poetica siciliana* (1955); E. Kantorowicz, *Frederick the Second, 1194–1250* (1957); E. H. Wilkins, *The Invention of the Sonnet and Other Studies* (1959); *Poeti del Duecento*, ed. G. Contini, 2 v. (1960); D. Mattalia, "La Scuola siciliana," *I Minori* (1961); *Le Rime della scuola siciliana*, ed. B. Panvini, 2 v. (1962–64); G. Folena, "Cultura e poesia dei siciliani," *Le Origini e il Duecento*, ed. E. Cecchi and N. Sapegno (1965); W. Pagani, *Repertorio tematico della scuola poetica siciliana* (1968); A. Fiorino, *Metri e temi della scuola poetica siciliana* (1969); E. Pasquini and A. E. Quaglio, *Le origini e la scuola siciliana* (1971); T. C. Van Cleve, *The Emperor Frederick II of Hohenstaufen* (1972); Wilkins; M. Marti, "Siciliana, scuola," *Enciclopedia dantesca*, ed. U. Bosco, v. 5 (1978); R. Antonelli, *Repertorio metrico della scuola siciliana* (1984); C. Kleinhenz, *The Early Italian Sonnet* (1986); *The Poetry of the Sicilian School*, ed. and trans. F. Jensen (1986); *Poeti alla corte di Federico II*, ed. C. Ruta (2001); K. Mallette, *The Kingdom of Sicily, 1100–1250* (2005); *I poeti della scuola siciliana: v. 1. Giacomo da Lentini*, ed. R. Antonelli; v. 2. *Poeti della corte di Federico II*, ed. C. Di Girolamo (2008).

A. PREMINGER; T.V.F. BROGAN; C. KLEINHENZ

**SIGN, SIGNIFIED, SIGNIFIER.** This triad originated in a series of lectures Ferdinand de Saussure (1857–1913) gave at the University of Geneva from 1906 to 1911. These were compiled by colleagues on the basis of student notes and published in 1916 under the title *Cours de linguistique générale*. The phrase *sign, signified, signifier* encapsulates one of Saussure's core insights, namely, that the ling. sign (*signe*) consists of two interdependent and necessary elements: a concept or "signified" (*signifié*) and an "acoustic image" or "signifier" (*signifiant*).

At the turn of the 20th c., ling. involved above all the gathering of data for comparative historical research, most notably into the origins of IE lang. According to Saussure, this paradigm impeded the study of "Language" (*langage*), an "instrument of thought" involving social, physiological, psychological, and other factors, and of "language" (*langue*), a socially determined system of signs. Saussure set aside inquiries into "Language," too heterogeneous to lend itself to scientific analysis, and into *parole*, a term that is usually translated as "speech" and that refers to the potentially infinite number of individual ling. utterances. He investigated "language" instead, a distinct and homogeneous system better suited to scientific inquiry. In particular, he focused on *synchronic* lings., namely, the systematic study of lang. at a particular moment in time, thereby breaking with the prevailing, data-driven *diachronic* or historical model. Saussure further disallowed what he saw as the Western privileging of writing over speech. Describing writing as a mere representation of spoken lang., he defined lang. as sequences of phonemes, which are the smallest units of sound that a lang. can use in permutation to create meaning. (The list of phonemes varies from lang. to lang.: Eng., but not Fr., includes /θ/, as in "thaw," while Fr., but not Eng., includes the phoneme /œ/, as in *œuf*, Fr. for "egg.")

Saussure's decisions allowed him to disentangle a paradox at the heart of the Western view of lang., divided between the Adamic ideal of a lang. characterized by a perfect correspondence between words and things and the realization that no necessary relationship obtains between words and extralinguistic objects. Traces of the Adamic model can be found in our initial surprise when we learn that a familiar term does not have an equivalent in a foreign lang.: "What do you mean, there is no word for 'dating'?" This reaction betrays a deep-seated tendency to think of lang. as a *nomenclature*, a list of words that are one-to-one matches to something extralinguistic. And yet, as anyone who has learned a foreign lang. knows, the relationship between word and thing is arbitrary. Both Eng. and Fr., e.g., have words that signify a substance made of milk curd: *cheese* and *fromage*. Clearly, nothing in the foodstuff in question demands that it be called "cheese" or "fromage."

Saussure was hardly first in noticing the arbitrariness of the sign, but he took this observation several steps further and made it a centerpiece of his theory. First, he noted that signs are *always* arbitrary, even in the case of *onomatopoeias—Eng. "cock-a-doodle-doo" and Fr. "cocorico" represent very distinct phonetic sequences—and "spontaneous" exclamations such as Engl. "ouch!" and Fr. "aïe!" Second, recognizing the arbitrary nature of the sign led him to define lang. as a set of conventions imposed on individual speakers. Specifically, meaning is possible only because lang. is a closed system of interdependent elements that have "linguistic value." Eng., for instance, grants ling. value to the sounds /θ/, /ð/, and /t/ since they permit speakers to distinguish between "thaw" and "though," "theme," and "team." Fr., by contrast, assigns no ling. value to either /θ/ or /ð/ but does, unlike Eng., include the phoneme /œ/, thereby making possible the difference between /œf/ ("oeuf") and /uf/ (*ouf*, "phew"). In short, signifiers only signify within a particular ling. system of differences: *theme* equals "not team," and vice versa, while "oeuf" equals "not *ouf*," and vice versa.

Ling. value also operates at the level of the signified. Consider, to use one of Saussure's examples, the Eng. *sheep* and *mutton* and the Fr. *mouton*. The signified <sheep> equals <not other farm animals> plus <not dead meat>. <Mutton> equals <not other kinds of meat>. <Mouton>, on the other hand, equals <not other farm animals and not other kinds of meat>. In other words, *mouton* can mean "sheep" but does not have the same value as <sheep>, in part because it does not have a differential relationship with another signified that parallels the difference between *sheep* and *mutton*. In short, lang. is an arbitrary system of agreed upon and recognizable differential values. These and only these generate meaning, or, as Saussure famously claimed, "[I]n language, there are only differences."

The impact of Saussure's work has extended far beyond the field of lings. It put semiotics at the heart of 20th-c. poetics. Along with *Russian formalism, it laid the groundwork for *structuralism and *poststructuralism. Finally, it accounts for the "linguistic turn" that dominated Western thought of the last decades of the 20th c. Indeed, as the bibliography indicates, Saussure's triad has crossed over into a wide array of areas of inquiry, from literary theory, philosophy, anthropology, and psychoanalysis to art hist., sociology, law, and economics.

*See* ÉCRITURE, ICONOLOGY, POSTMODERNISM, SEMANTICS AND POETRY, SEMIOTICS AND POETRY, TEXT.

■ **Criticism:** J. Culler, *Ferdinand de Saussure* (1976); P. J. Thibault, *Re-reading Saussure* (1996); *The Cambridge Companion to Saussure*, ed. C. Sanders (2004).
■ **Saussure's Legacy:** C. Lévi-Strauss, *Structural Anthropology* (1958), trans. C. Jacobson and B. G. Schoepf (1963); R. Barthes, *Writing Degree Zero*, trans. A. Lavers and C. Smith (1967); F. Jameson, *The Prison-House of Language* (1972); U. Eco, *A Theory of Semiotics* (1976); J. Derrida, *Of Grammatology*, trans. G. C. Spivak (1974), and *Writing and Difference* (1967), trans. A. Bass (1978); J. Kristeva, *Desire in Language*, trans. T. Gora, A. Jardine, and L. S. Roudiez (1980); T. Todorov, *Introduction to Poetics*, trans. R. Howard (1981); J. Baudrillard, *For a Critique of the Political Economy of the Sign*, trans. C. Levin (1981); J. Derrida, *Margins of Philosophy*, trans. A. Bass (1982); M. Foucault, *This Is Not a Pipe*, trans. J. Harkness (1983); P. Bourdieu, *Distinction*, trans. R. Nice (1984); A. J. Greimas, *Structural Semantics,* trans. D. McDowell, R. Schleifer, and A. Velie (1984), and *On Meaning*, trans. P. Perron and F. Collins (1987); R. Posner, *Law and Literature* (1988); J.-J. Goux, *Symbolic Economies,*

trans. G. C. Gage (1990); M. Bal and N. Bryson, "Semiotics and Art History," *Art Bulletin* 73 (1991); *Economics and Language*, ed. W. Henderson, T. Dudley-Evans, and R. Backhouse (1993); L. Irigaray, *To Speak Is Never Neutral*, trans. G. Schwab (2002); J. Lacan, *Écrits*, trans. B. Fink (2006).

C. LABIO

**SIGNIFYING** is a dominant satiric form in Af. Am. verbal expression that provides a basis for both poetry and literary reception, a procedure for speakers and poets and a program by which Af. Am. writers read and interpret one another (Gates). Signifying subsumes many other tropes (e.g., *metaphor, *metonymy, *catachresis) and has many tones, often ironic. It was nurtured significantly in Af. Am. vernacular poetic forms such as *toasts, *sagas, and *blues. There is a toast trad. known specifically as the *signifying monkey poem*, which treats all kinds of subjects satirically. Among the sagas, "Titanic Shine" is perhaps the best known. The blues is replete with signifying lines such as "Ain't a baker in town / Can bake a sweet jelly roll like mine" and "Take this hammer and carry it to my captain: / Tell him I'm gone." Although not restricted to poetry, the use of the signifying trad. in Af. Am. writing can be traced from the earliest poets such as Jupiter Hammon (b. 1711) through Paul Laurence Dunbar (1872–1906), Langston Hughes (1902–67), then to poets of the 1960s and after such as Haki Madhubuti (Don L. Lee; b. 1942), Sonia Sanchez (b. 1934), Nikki Giovanni (b. 1943), and June Jordan (1936–2002).

*See* AFRICAN AMERICAN POETRY, SATIRE.

■ C. Mitchell-Kernan, "Signifying," *Motherwit from the Laughing Barrel: Readings in the Interpretation of Afro-American Folklore*, ed. A. Dundes (1973); G. Smitherman, *Talkin and Testifyin* (1977); H. L. Gates Jr., "The Blackness of Blackness: A Critique on the Sign and the Signifying Monkey," *Figures in Black* (1987), and *The Signifying Monkey* (1988); K. Euell, "Signifyin(g) Ritual: Subverting Stereotypes, Salvaging Icons," *African American Review* 31 (1997); M. Marrouchi, *Signifying with a Vengeance* (2002)—postcolonial culture; A. Smith, "Blues, Criticism, and the Signifying Trickster," *Popular Music* 24 (2005).

E. A. PETERS

**SILLOI** (Gr., "squint-eyed pieces," i.e., satirical verses). Title of a *hexameter poem in three books by Timon of Philus (fl. ca. 250 BCE) satirizing dogmatic philosophers. Such satirical verse had earlier been written, and perhaps invented, by Xenophanes of Colophon (ca. 570–475 BCE), the philosopher-poet who founded Eliatic philosophy. By late antiquity, five books of *silloi* had been credited to him, but only fragments survive. Both poets used to be referred to as sillographers. Silloi parodied not personalities but the doctrines of philosophers or their schools.

■ Pauly-Wissowa; C. Wachsmuth, *Sillographi graeci* (1885); Schmid and Stählin; *CHCL*, v. 1.

T.V.F. BROGAN

**SILVA.** A Sp. poem in Italianate *hendecasyllables and *heptasyllables in which the poet makes strophic divisions at will, usually in unequal lengths, and rhymes most of the lines without set pattern, sometimes leaving a few lines unrhymed. Other meters may be used. The *silva*, introduced in the 16th c., is sometimes considered a form of Italianate *canción* and called *canción libre*. Morley and Bruerton distinguish four types in Lope de Vega's silvas, which are also the types generally used by other poets: (1) "*silva de consonantes*, *aAbBcCdD*, etc.," which "could be called *pareados* [couplets] de 7 y 11"; (2) "sevens and elevens mixed irregularly, no fixed order of length or rime, some unrimed lines"; (3) "all elevens, the majority . . . rimed, not counting the final couplet, no fixed order, mostly pairs," some *abab* and *abba*; these "may approximate to *sueltos* [free-riming lines] or *pareados* [couplets] de 11"; (4) "sevens and elevens mixed irregularly, all rimes in pairs."

■ S. G. Morley and C. Bruerton, *The Chronology of Lope de Vega's "Comedias"* (1940); Navarro; C. J. Pagnotta, "La silva y su proyección en la escritura dramática de Lope de Vega," *Actas del XVI Congreso de la Asociación Internacional de Hispanistas*, ed. P. Civil and F. Crémoux (2007); L. Fernández Guillermo, "La silva en la tragedia del Siglo de Oro," *Hacia la tragedia áurea*, ed. F. de Armas et al. (2008); R. Cacho Casal, "The Memory of Ruins: Quevedo's Silva to 'Roma Antigua y moderna,'" *RQ* 62 (2009).

D. C. CLARKE

**SIMILE.** A figure of speech most conservatively defined as an explicit comparison using *like* or *as*—e.g., "black, naked women with necks / wound round and round with wire / like the necks of light bulbs" (Elizabeth Bishop, "In the Waiting Room"). The function of the comparison is to reveal an unexpected likeness between two seemingly disparate things—in this case, the necks of tribal women and light bulbs. Simile is probably the "oldest readily identifiable poetic artifice in European literature" (Holoka), stretching back through Homer and Mycenaean epic poetry to Sumerian, Sanskrit, and Chinese.

Critics and theorists disagree over what distinguishes simile from factual comparisons on the one hand and *metaphor on the other. While some theorists argue that factual comparisons ("My eyes are like yours") and similes (such as Chaucer's "hir eyen greye as glas") differ only in degree, others argue that they differ in kind (a confusion that William Wordsworth successfully exploits in "Tintern Abbey" when he follows the "wreaths of smoke / Sent up, in silence" with "as might seem / Of vagrant dwellers in the houseless woods"). Similarly, some critics adhere to the traditional view that metaphor is a compressed simile, distinguishable from simile only in being an implicit rather than an explicit comparison (Miller), whereas others conclude that not all metaphors and similes are interchangeable, that metaphor is a "use of language," whereas comparison itself is a "psychological process" (Ortony). These questions have entered the domain of ling., where at least one theorist has argued in favor of a single "deep structure" of comparison, variously realized as either simile or metaphor, that is capable of distinguishing both similes from factual comparisons and also metaphors from mere copulative equations such as "My car is a Ford" (Mack). The latter solution supports a growing sense that simile may be marked not only by *like* or *as* but also by many other comparative markers, incl. verbs such as *resemble*, *echo*, and *seem*; connectives such as *as if* and *as though*; and phrases such as *the way that* (Darian). From this perspective, it seems likely that simile encompasses analogy, rather than being a discrete form of comparison. At the very least, the current exploration into the range of simile suggests that it may be a far more pervasive aspect of both lang. and perception than has previously been thought.

In Western culture, there has been a traditional prejudice against simile in favor of metaphor. Wheelwright suggests that this trad. begins with Aristotle, who judges simile inferior for two reasons: since it is longer than metaphor, it is "less pleasing" and since simile "does not affirm that this *is* that, the mind does not inquire into the matter" (*Rhetoric* 3.4.1406b). As Derrida has noted, "[T]here is no more classical theory of metaphor than treating it as an 'economical' way of avoiding 'extended explanations': and . . . of avoiding simile." The 20th c. was esp. rigid in privileging metaphor over simile. At least prior to poststructuralist crit., many 20th-c. critics and theorists heralded metaphor as a model for understanding lang., thought, and philosophy. Frye, e.g., regards simile as a "displaced" metaphor, which, for him, corresponds to the displacement of mythic identity into *naturalism. Only recently have a few critics begun to regard simile not just as "literary embellishment" but as "a tool for serious thinking, scientific and otherwise" that "transcribes a paradigm of the creative act itself, whether in poetry or physics" (Darian).

Despite the long denigration of simile by critics, poets have consistently used the simile. The earliest recorded Western lit., Sumerian, uses similes in virtually every genre (Kramer). Among them are similes that seem uncannily familiar, such as "as wide as the earth" and "as everlasting as the earth." Similes are used throughout the *Rig Veda*—e.g., "In the East the brilliant dawns have stood / Like posts set up at sacrifices" (Cook). Certainly, Homer uses similes, though his nearly formulaic ones (such as Thetis's rising out of the sea like a mist) hover somewhere between *epithet and metaphor; and in this regard, it is provocative that Aristotle allies "proportional metaphor, which contains an epithet" with comparisons (McCall). As Green has pointed out, Virgil's "characteristic trope" is the simile. Chaucer frequently turns to simile, esp. for humor, as when describing "hende Nicholas" as being "as sweete as is the roote / Of lycorys, or any cetewale." Shakespeare achieves *irony by negating conventional similes in "My mistress' eyes are nothing like the sun."

Despite the prevailing 19th-c. emphasis on the *symbol, P. B. Shelley habitually turns to simile. In the "Hymn to Intellectual Beauty," the "unseen Power" visits

with as inconstant wing
As summer winds that creep from
    flower to flower,—
Like moonbeams that behind some
    piny mountain shower,
It visits with inconstant glance
Each human heart and countenance;
Like hues and harmonies of evening,—
Like clouds in starlight widely
    spread,—
Like memory of music fled—

Equally curious—given the early 20th-c. bias in favor of *imagism that followed Ezra Pound's injunction to "use no unnecessary word" (and that encouraged the excision of similes)—is Wallace Stevens's increasing use of the simile in key passages of his poetry. He concludes his *Collected Poems* with "It was like / A new knowledge of reality," a simile that calls attention to the problematic relation between poetry and what it represents.

The most revered form of simile is the epic simile, a lengthy comparison between two highly complex objects, actions, or relations. Homer is credited with inaugurating the epic simile, there being no known simile before the *Iliad* of such length or sophistication as the following:

As is the generation of leaves, so is that of
    humanity.
The wind scatters the leaves on the ground, but
    the live timber
burgeons with leaves again in the season of spring
    returning.
So one generation of men will grow while another
dies.

While the epic simile may be used by Homer for contrast, digression, or thematic amplification, subsequent poets such as Virgil, Dante, Ludovico Ariosto, Edmund Spenser, and John Milton refine the device, making it integral to the structure of the epic. Later poets frequently resuscitate specific Homeric similes (Holoka), as does Virgil when comparing the "whole crowd" to the "forest leaves that flutter down / at the first autumn frost" (*Aeneid* 6.305–10), or as does Milton when describing Lucifer's "Legions" that "lay-intrans't / Thick as Autumnal Leaves that strow the Brooks / In *Vallombrosa*" (*Paradise Lost* 1.301–3).

*See* UPAMĀ.

■ H. Fränkel, *Die homerischen Gleichnisse* (1921); W. P. Ker, *Form and Style in Poetry* (1928); C. M. Bowra, *Tradition and Design in the "Iliad"* (1930); J. Whaler, "The Miltonic Simile," *PMLA* 46 (1931); Z. E. Green, "Observations on the Epic Simile in the *Faerie Queene*," *PQ* 14 (1935); Frye; K. Widmer, "The Iconography of Renunciation: The Miltonic Simile," *ELH* 25 (1958); C. S. Lewis, "Dante's Simile," *Nottingham Medieval Studies* 9 (1965); P. Wheelwright, *The Burning Fountain*, rev. ed. (1968); M. H. McCall, *Ancient Rhetorical Theories of Simile and Comparison* (1969); S. N. Kramer, "Sumerian Simile," *JAOS* 89 (1969); S. G. Darian, "Simile and the Creative Process," *Lang&S* 6 (1973);

D. Mack, "Metaphoring as Speech Act," *Poetics* 4 (1975); J. Derrida, "White Mythology," *NLH* 6 (1975); J. P. Holoka, "'Thick as Autumnal Leaves,'" *Milton Quarterly* 10 (1976); R. H. Lansing, *From Image to Idea: The Simile in Dante's "Divine Comedy"* (1977); G. A. Miller, "Images and Models, Simile and Metaphors," and A. Ortony, "The Role of Similarity in Simile and Metaphors," *Metaphor and Thought*, ed. A. Ortony (1979); J. N. Swift, "Simile of Disguise and the Reader of *Paradise Lost*," *South Atlantic Quarterly* 79 (1980); K. O. Murtaugh, *Ariosto and the Classical Simile* (1980); A. Cook, *Figural Choice in Poetry and Art* (1985); J. V. Brogan, *Stevens and Simile: A Theory of Language* (1986); S. A. Nimis, *Narrative Semiotics in the Epic Tradition: The Simile* (1987); S. J. Wolfson, "'Comparing Power': Coleridge and Simile," *Coleridge's Theory of Imagination Today*, ed. C. Gallant (1989); W. Prunty, *Fallen from the Symboled World* (1989); S. Glucksberg, *Understanding Figurative Language* (2001).

J. V. BROGAN; H. SMITH RICHMOND

**SINCERITY.** Derived from Lat. *sincerus* (clean or pure), the word *sincerity* entered Eng. in the early 16th c. and briefly retained the meaning of its cognate, so that, e.g., "sincere wine" denoted wine that was undiluted. But William Shakespeare uses sincerity exclusively to indicate the absence of duplicity or dissimulation, and by 1600, the term had assumed its mod. connotations. It was not until the end of the 18th c. that sincerity became a valued literary commodity. For William Wordsworth and the romantics, sincerity was an indication of literary excellence since it emphasized the necessity of a congruence between the poet's emotion and his utterance. Matthew Arnold ambitiously expanded the concept, adding to it a moral dimension, when he claimed that the *touchstone of great poetry was "the high seriousness which comes from absolute sincerity."

Much poetry and crit. of the 20th c., however, has questioned the fundamental values implied by the term. Donald Davie has suggested that W. B. Yeats's mask, Ezra Pound's persona, and T. S. Eliot's view of the poem as an impersonal, essentially dramatic structure rendered the question of the poet's sincerity "impertinent and illegitimate." Roughly contemporaneous with the high modernists, the New Critics in America propounded a methodology that emphasized the formalist analysis of textual features such as *imagery, structure, *meter, and *rhyme (see NEW CRITICISM). These formal concerns, which foreground the verbal artistry and design of the work, were inimical to a concern with the poet and, hence, with the concept of sincerity; and during the first half of the 20th c., the term fell into disuse.

Henri Peyre, however, has suggested that sincerity involves far more than a mere "transposing of autobiographical data," and he accords the longevity of Jean-Jacques Rousseau's writings, particularly the *Confessions*, to his singleminded devotion to sincerity. Yet even literary cultures less obviously attracted by the ideals of sincerity are considered by Peyre to have confronted and resolved the issue.

For the 16th-c. Fr. poets Joachim du Bellay, Pierre de Ronsard, Philippe Desportes, as well as for the Eng. poets the Earl of Surrey (Henry Howard), Philip Sidney, and Edmund Spenser, the critical issue involves not so much whether the poet *achieves* sincerity as how forcefully the poet, deploying the various conventions of the *sonnet sequence, *gives the impression* of sincerity. And Eliot's interest in John Donne's verse, which eschewed several ornamentations that had encumbered Elizabethan poetry, resulted simply from the tendency "to read more sincerity in wit than in pathos, in impudence than in adoration."

Much contemp. literary theory, however, has called into question even such an accommodating definition of the term. Deconstructive theories emphasize the perpetual *indeterminacy of meaning, in which scheme sincerity, which depends upon the congruency of feeling and avowal, has no value. *Reader-response crit. finds that there is *unity not "in the text but in the mind of the reader" (Holland) and that the question of meaning involves analysis of the reading process (see READER). For both types of critics, and for much of the linguistically oriented crit. of the late 20th c., the most pressing engagement available for critical discussion is the one between reader and text, not the one between author and text; and sincerity, which concerns the latter relation, is not a fundamental concern of these methodologies. But there is no reason to assume that crit. might not return to its earlier interest. The recognition of sincerity depends upon the reader's ability to evaluate the successful fulfillment within the work of the author's *intention, and E. D. Hirsch's seminal work, *Validity in Interpretation*, still represents one of the most formidable attempts in the latter half of the 20th c. to reestablish authorial intention as the guideline for accurate interpretation.

Although recent appearances of the term have tended to follow the traditional lines discussed above, commentators concerned with ethnography and race have used sincerity in opposition to the term "authenticity." In *Real Black*, e.g., John L. Jackson states that "sincerity and authenticity have very different ways of imagining the real . . . and so racial sincerity, which should not be confused with racial authenticity, exemplifies an epistemologically distinct rendering of race, identity, solidarity, and reality." These different renderings vary among cultures, races, and ethnicities, but the binary oppositions often associated with ethnographic description (objectivity vs. subjectivity, collectivities vs. individuals, e.g.) elucidate the opposition between sincerity and authenticity, where the former is often complicit with traditional power structures, while the latter often opposes and deconstructs them.

■ G. H. Lewes, "The Principle of Sincerity," *The Principles of Success in Literature* (1865); I. A. Richards, *Practical Criticism* (1929); H. Peyre, *Literature and Sincerity* (1963); P. M. Ball, "Sincerity: The Rise and Fall of a Critical Term," *MLR* 59 (1964); D. Perkins, *Wordsworth and the Poetry of Sincerity* (1964); E. D. Hirsch Jr., *Validity in Interpretation* (1967); D. Davie,

"On Sincerity: From Wordsworth to Ginsberg," *Encounter* (1968); P. M. Spacks, "In Search of Sincerity," *CE* 29 (1968); H. Read, *The Cult of Sincerity* (1969); J. Derrida, "Structure, Sign, and Play in the Discourse of the Human Sciences," *The Structuralist Controversy*, ed. R. Macksey and E. Donato (1972); L. Trilling, *Sincerity and Authenticity* (1972); L. Guilhamet, *The Sincere Ideal* (1974); N. Holland, "Recovering 'The Purloined Letter,'" *The Reader in the Text*, ed. S. Suleiman and I. Crosman (1980); J. P. Russo, *I. A. Richards* (1989), chap. 15; J. L. Jackson, *Real Black: Adventures in Racial Sincerity* (2005).

S. Burris

**SINDHI POETRY.** *See* INDIA, POETRY OF.

**SINHALESE POETRY.** *See* SRI LANKA, POETRY OF.

**SIRVENTES.** A poem in med. Occitan that is strophic in form but is not a *canso* or *love poem. The main themes are politics and current events, incl. war and the Crusades, ad hominem attacks or (occasionally) praise, social and literary satire, or moralizing on the decline of society and standards of behavior. The tone is mostly satiric, and gross vituperation is common. In form, the *sirventes* came to be seen as a subservient, less original genre than the love song, and it became common practice to borrow the tune, meter, and even rhyme sounds of an existing canso for a new sirventes. (Paden explains the name sirventes as reflecting the fact that the genre is often the "servant" of the canso.) Later med. poetic treatises foreground this imitative dimension, although it is very unlikely that the poets themselves saw it as essential to the genre. The popularity of the sirventes increased from the end of the 12th c. as the formal and thematic dynamism of the love song declined.

*See* OCCITAN POETRY, TROUBADOUR.

■ D. Rieger, *Gattungen und Gattungsbezeichnungen der Trobadorlyrik* (1976); S. Thiolier-Méjean, *Les Poésies satiriques et morales des troubadours du XIIe siècle à la fin du XIIIe siècle* (1978); Chambers; M. Aurell, *La Vielle et l'épée: Troubadours et politique en Provence au XIIIe siècle* (1989); G. Gouiran, "Un genre à la jonction de l'histoire et de la littérature: Les sirventés (à partir de textes de Bertran de Born)," *Histoire et littérature au Moyen Age*, ed. D. Buschinger (1991); E. M. Ghil, "The Triumph of the *Sirventes* in Thirteenth-Century Troubadour Poetry," *Medieval Perspectives* 9 (1994); S. Thiolier-Méjean, *La poétique des troubadours: Trois études sur le sirventes* (1994); W. D. Paden, "Sirventes," *Medieval France: An Encyclopedia*, ed. W. W. Kibler (1995); C. Léglu, *Between Sequence and Sirventes: Aspects of Parody in the Troubadour Lyric* (2000).

F. M. Chambers; R. Harvey

**SKELTONIC.** A kind of poem named after its originator, the Eng. *poet laureate John Skelton (ca. 1460–1529). Skeltonic poems are distinguished by short lines and long stretches of *monorhyme, called *leashes*. End *rhymes are not crossed. Lines have between two and five stresses, although three-stress lines occur most fre-

quently. *Alliteration abounds, and although he writes primarily in Eng., Skelton includes scraps of Lat. and Fr. occasionally as well (see MACARONIC, XENOGLOSSIA). The rhymes continue "as long as the resources of the language hold out," in Lewis's phrase; rhyme, rather than meaning, seems to drive the poems forward.

A vigorous vernacular form, Skeltonics served Skelton primarily for his *satires, which ranged in *tone from the lighter humor of *The Book of Philip Sparrow* to the fierce misogyny of *The Tunning of Elinor Rumming* to the moral strains of *Colin Clout* to the vicious ad hominem attacks of *Why Come Ye Not to Court?*, to name the works most pub. in the 16th c. and most anthologized now. Although involved in the courts of both Henry VII and VIII; laureated by Oxford, Cambridge, and Louvain; and a Catholic priest, Skelton was long linked with popular or even vulgar verse. George Puttenham in *The Arte of English Poesie* (1589) dismissed him as a "rude rayling rimer," part of which critique is in reaction to his use of "short distances and short measures, pleasing only the popular ear."

Scholars have not yet achieved a consensus on the origin of Skeltonics: they have been seen as deriving from various med. trads., incl. Lat. verse, Lat. rhyming prose, and the Catholic liturgy, among others. Scholars and critics since Skelton's time also dispute the value of the Skeltonic. Many, following Puttenham, have seen it simply as *doggerel. Mod. poets such as Robert Graves and W. H. Auden held the Skeltonic in higher esteem. Among mod. critics, Lewis sees it as fitting only when representing "immature or disorganized states of consciousness," while Fish sees it as a choice of blunt moral content over false eloquence.

Other than Skelton himself, poets have rarely used Skeltonics, although some Protestant reformers employed them soon after his death. Although Skelton was a Catholic priest hired by Cardinal Thomas Wolsey to write an anti-Protestant propaganda poem (*Replycacion*), his attacks on the Church made his poetry easily assimilable to the Protestant cause, and several Protestant satires were written in Skeltonics, incl. *The Image of Hypocrisy* (1534) and *Vox Populi Vox Dei* (1547).

*See* ENGLAND, POETRY OF; RENAISSANCE POETRY.

■ W. Nelson, *John Skelton, Laureate* (1939); C. S. Lewis, *English Literature in the Sixteenth Century, Excluding Drama* (1954); S. Fish, *John Skelton's Poetry* (1965); A. Kinney, *John Skelton: Priest as Poet* (1987); G. Walker, *John Skelton and the Politics of the 1520s* (1988); J. Griffiths, *John Skelton and Poetic Authority* (2006).

R. Kaplan

**SKOLION.** A type of early Gr. lyric poetry, a drinking song. The etymology of the term is uncertain but perhaps derives from Gr. *skolios* (crooked): the guests at a symposium would sing in sequence, each holding a myrtle branch, then passing it to another at random—"crookedly." Trad. ascribes its origin to Terpander (fl. mid-7th c. BCE), who was the first to give it artistic form. *Skolia* could be purely extemporized pieces, excerpts from lyric poetry, or even selections from Homer. Its stanzas were composed of two *phalaeceans, a *colon of the form ∪ ∪ − ∪ − − ∪ ∪ − and another with – ◡ ◡ – ◡ – repeated. The skolion was accompanied by the lyre or flute and dealt with historical events, expressed deep personal feeling, or made a trenchant comment on daily life. In the course of the 5th c., it was considerably simplified.

■ R. Reitzenstein, *Epigramm und Skolion* (1893); W. Aly, "Skolion," Pauly-Wissowa, 2.5.558–66; Schmid and Stählin; Maas; A. M. Dale, *Collected Papers* (1969); Michaelides; West; G. Lambin, "L'origine du skolion," *Eranos* 91 (1993); V. Liapis, "Double Entendres in *Skolia:* The Etymology of *Skolion*," *Eranos* 94 (1996).

P. S. Costas; T.V.F. Brogan

**SLAM, POETRY.** *See* POETRY SLAM.

**SLANG.** *See* DICTION.

**SLAVIC POETICS.** *See* BOSNIAN POETRY; CROATIAN POETRY; CZECH POETRY; POLAND, POETRY OF; RUSSIA, POETRY OF; SERBIAN POETRY; SLOVENIAN POETRY.

**ŚLEṢA** (Sanskrit, "embrace"). Technically speaking, *śleṣa* is a literary device or *"ornament" (*alaṃkāra*), one of many in the poet's tool kit. Authorities on Sanskrit poetics define it as a case of two sets of meanings (or two sets of signifiers, each with its own meaning) in "embrace," yielding a single, simultaneous utterance. Consider an illustration by the poet and theorist Daṇḍin (fl. 700 CE): "Here's a king who has risen to the top. / He's radiant, his surrounding circle glows, / and the people love him for his levies, / which are light." This verse depicts moonrise as a king's rise to power, by juxtaposing homonyms that lend themselves to the portrayal of both (e.g., *kara* denotes both "rays" and "taxes"). This sort of śleṣa is potentially translatable, if similar homonyms are found in the target lang. But Sanskrit poets developed a far more sophisticated repertoire of ling. embraces that can be reproduced only by a mere pair of parallel "translations." These include exploiting phonetic, morphological, and syntactic *ambiguities to create *oronyms*: strings of sounds that can be differently segmented into words. A simple example is *nakṣatra*, which can be taken as a single word (meaning "planet") or carved into two (*na* = "no," and *kṣatra* = "warrior"). Thus, this short utterance supports another simultaneous depiction of the moon (which "resides among the planets") and a king (who "fails to follow the warrior's path") by Daṇḍin.

This technical definition, however, ignores śleṣa's central role in defining a large and self-conscious literary movement in South Asia. Starting around the 6th c. CE, Sanskrit authors began to experiment extensively with simultaneity, using śleṣa to describe kings and gods concurrently (in royal eulogies), estrange poetic protocols by linguistically "embracing" unconventional pairs (as in Subandhu's 6th-c. *Vāsavadattā*), depict both the hidden and apparent sides of disguised characters (as in Nītivarman's *Kīcakavadha*, ca. 600), and conarrate India's major epics, the *Rāmāyaṇa* and the *Mahābhārata*, in a manner that highlights their meaningful ties (as in a lost work by Daṇḍin, ca. 700, and Dhanañjaya's *Dvisandhānakāvya*, ca. 800).

This literary movement boomed in the first centuries of the second millennium CE: prominent examples include Kavirāja's conarration of the epics in his *Rāghavapāṇḍavīya* and the concurrent depiction of Nala and the divinities impersonating him in Śrīharṣa's *Naiṣadhacarita*, both composed in the 12th c. The boom coincided with the extensive production of special lexicons and guidebooks catering to the needs of śleṣa poets and readers. Starting around the 1600s, this movement carried over to India's regional langs., most prominently Telugu and Tamil (see TELUGU POETRY, TAMIL POETRY AND POETICS). Śleṣa also existed in other artistic media, such as sculpted narrative panels. Even in Sanskrit poetics proper, śleṣa resisted being encapsulated as a mere device, and Daṇḍin himself argued that it replicates—and in that sense defines—the entire spectrum of poetic expressivity.

*See* POLYSEMY, SANSKRIT POETICS, SANSKRIT POETRY.

■ Y. Bronner, *Extreme Poetry: The South Asian Movement of Simultaneous Narration* (2010).

Y. Bronner

**SLOVAKIA, POETRY OF.** Poetry in Slovakia has evolved amid overlapping lang. trads., incl. Lat., Hungarian, Czech, and Ger. Since the reign of St. Stephen (977–1038), Upper Hungary—today's Slovakia—has been within the orbit of the Western Church. Czech and Slovak speech forms are very closely related, and earlier Slovak writing adhered in general to broadly Czech-derived ling. norms.

Earlier surviving compositions include Lat. humanist works, vernacular *ballads of love and war, and much *devotional poetry. From 1526 until the later 17th c., the Turks occupied much of Hungary. Some anonymous Slovak *love poetry recorded in 1604 is linked by affinity to the Hungarian poet Bálint Balassi (1554–94). Vernacular hymnography is represented esp. by *Tranoscius* (1636), named for its Lutheran Czech compiler, Jiří Třanovský (1592–1637). Love poems include "Obraz pani krásnej, perem malovaný" (Picture of a Beautiful Lady, Painted by the Pen, 1701), by a law student, Štefan Selecký (fl. 1700). A long moralizing cycle of 17,000 lines, *Valašská škola—mravov stodola* (Wallachian School—Garner of Morals, 1755) was composed by the Franciscan Hugolín Gavlovič (1712–87). Traditional song and balladry abounded, and the story of Juraj Jánošík, a Robin Hood-like bandit figure in 1711–13, captured, and hung from one of his ribs, became a favorite national theme.

A standardized West Slovak produced under the modernizing Hapsburg emperor Joseph II (1780–90) by the Catholic priest Anton Bernolák (1762–1813) was short lived. Its outstanding poet, the father of mod. Slovak poetry, was another priest, Ján Hollý (1785–1849), who translated Virgil's *Aeneid* (1828) and composed, in quantitative *hexameters, some cl.-style historical *epics, most notably *Svatopluk* (1833). His Theocritan *pastoral verse produces a fresh fusion of cl. and vernacular idiom. As a writer in Czech, Jan Kollár (1793–1852), a Protestant pastor and proponent of pan-Slavism, produced a celebrated and monumental *sonnet cycle *Slávy dcera* (Daughter of Slavia, 1824, 1832), with a sonorous prologue in quantitative elegiac *couplets, lamenting past oppression. The poet's beloved Mína metamorphoses into a Slav goddess's daughter; a pilgrimage traverses the Slav lands, then goes, Dante-style, into a Slavic Lethe and Acheron. Kollár's sonnets (and most later Slovak poetry) use stress-based meters. (Slovak has first-syllable word stress, like Czech, though premod. verse was generally syllabic.)

In the 1840s, Lutherans led by Ľudovít Štúr (1815–56) derived a new standard Slovak from central dialects, fundamentally today's variety (Kollár was antagonistic). Like Herder, Štúr stressed native originality. Poetry, the highest product of the spirit, should take folk song as a starting point, not its goal. Štúr's group energized Slovak poetry. In the revolutionary year of 1848, Janko Kráľ (1822–76) exhorted the villagers to overthrow their landowners. Incarcerated briefly, he then involved himself with pro-Hapsburg volunteers, entered government service after 1849, and virtually ceased writing. In his best work (sharply analyzed by Jakobson), folk idiom combined with a solitary central figure, *divný* Janko (weird Janko)—aspiring eagle-like to soar to freedom but relapsing into suicidal melancholy. Pastor Andrej Sládkovič (1820–72) wrote his lyrical-narrative masterpiece *Marína* (1846) in ten-line, sonnet-like stanzas, inspired by unhappy love. Where, for Kollár, erotic and patriotic love are divided, here they harmonize. Love is no mere sensual adventure of youth: it is a divine gift, enabling Hegelian transcendence, harmonizing body and mind, embracing truth through beauty. Ján Botto (1827–76) is most celebrated for his balladic *Smrť Jánošíkova* (Jánošík's Death, 1862). Tension between fairy-tale-like, messianic visions, and gloomy near-realism places freedom's ideals apart from the human world—where a chasm divides the bandit's dream world from the impassive peasantry.

Post-1867 Hungarian autonomy closed some Slovak high schools, giving the Hungarian lang. preference in education. Pavol Országh Hviezdoslav (1849–1921), a lawyer, became a prolific, preeminent poet. In *Hájnikova žena* (The Gamekeeper's Wife, 1884–86), Hanka kills her would-be rapist, a corrupted aristocrat. The life of the seasons blends with the life of the forest—fetching water, felling trees, picking raspberries, hunting deer, looking at the night stars, the woodland torrent crashing like chains, "which however does not bind, does not fetter legs, or spirit, does not confine in its circle the spirit which flew like an eagle in between the hills, to sate itself with freedom, and feel that it is spirit." Hviezdoslav's Parnassian diction pursues dense textures (see PARNASSIANISM). His *Krvavé sonety* (Sonnets of Blood, 1919) laments the madness of war, doubting divine justice, ending with hope. Svetozár Hurban-Vajanský (1847–1916), another lawyer and twice-imprisoned newspaper ed., combines realistic and nationalistic notes in his collection *Tatry a more* (The Tatras and the Sea, 1879). The pre-1914 *Moderna* group, close to *symbolism, had, as its major poet, Ivan Krasko (1876–1958), with two collections, *Nox et solitudo* (1909) and *Verše* (1912), of musically refined, often ostensibly simple (but enigmatic) lyricism, evok-

ing landscapes of loneliness, melancholy, pessimism, hesitation, in mistily defined (often erotic) situations; Christianity functions here nostalgically, evoking trad. or collapsed values.

The Slovak lang. dominated after Czechoslovakia's creation in 1918. Emil Boleslav Lukáč (1900–79), pastor and parliamentary deputy, evolved from home-and-abroad meditations into tersely agonized erotic and reflective verse and castigatory treatment of social themes. Ján Smrek (1898–1982) established himself as a vitalist and deftly lyrical eroticist. Valentin Beniak (1894–1973) was a more enigmatic word spinner. His topics involve rural hardship, trad. and beauty, existential disharmony, artistic themes of France and Italy, apocalyptic war, with stimuli from symbolism, Czech poetism, *surrealism, and folklore. Ladislav Novomeský (1904–76), a communist of the DAV (Throng) group, although skeptical about poetry's public role, wrote associative, playful, gently melancholy, reminiscing, social, and personal avant-garde verses, loosely related to Czech poetism. Later, he recalled his 1952 incarceration as a "bourgeois nationalist" (rehabilitated 1962) but reaffirmed his socialism. Surrealism's chief voice was Rudolf Fabry (1915–82), with arresting imagery and phrases, e.g., in *Vodné hodiny piesočné* (Water Sandglass, 1938). Slovak *Nadrealismus* (suprarealism) also espoused antifascism.

Leading post-1945 and post-Stalinist names include Miroslav Válek (1927–91) and Milan Rúfus (1928–2009). Women have now become more prominent: Maša Haľamová (1908–95), the intimate Viera Prokešová (b. 1957), the sexually provocative Tatjana Lehenová (b. 1961), and the complex, psychologically probing Mila Haugová (b. 1942). In the bilingual volume *Six Slovak Poets* (2010), Haugová is placed alongside Ján Buzássy (b. 1935), Ivan Štrpka (b. 1941), Peter Repka (b. 1944), and Kamil Peteraj (b. 1945)—poets all variously meditative, inward, complex, elusive, or cryptic—as well as the younger Daniel Hevier (b. 1955), representing a more humorous poetic streak.

■ **Anthologies and Translations**: J. Botto, *The Death of Jánošík*, trans. I. J. Kramoris (1944); *Anthology of Slovak Poetry*, trans. I. J. Kramoris (1947); *The Linden Tree*, ed. M. Otruba and Z. Pešat (1963); P. O. Hviezdoslav, *A Song of Blood: Krvavé sonety*, trans. J. Vajda (1972); *Janko Kráľ 1822–1972*, trans. J. Vajda (1972); *Anthology of Slovak Literature*, ed. A. Cincura (1976); *Not Waiting for Miracles: Seventeen Contemporary Slovak Poets*, trans. J. Sutherland-Smith, V. Sutherland-Smith, Š. Allen (1993); M. Válek, *The Ground beneath Our Feet*, trans. E. Osers (1996); J. Buzássy, *Melancholy Hunter*, trans. J. Sutherland-Smith and V. Sutherland-Smith (2001); M. Haugová, *Scent of the Unseen*, trans. J. Sutherland-Smith and V. Sutherland-Smith (2003); *In Search of Beauty: An Anthology of Contemporary Slovak Poetry in English*, trans. J. Sutherland-Smith and J. Bajánek (2003); L. Novomeský, *Slovak Spring*, trans. J. Minahane (2004); M. Rúfus, *And That's the Truth*, trans. E. Osers, J. Sutherland-Smith, V. Sutherland-Smith (2006); *Six Slovak Poets*, trans. J. Minahane (2010).

■ **Criticism and History**: R. Jakobson, "The Grammatical Structure of Janko Král's Verses," *Sborník filozofickej fakulty Univerzity Komenského* 16 (1964); S. Šmatlák, *Hviezdoslav: A National and World Poet* (1969); P. Brock, *The Slovak National Awakening* (1976); G. J. Kovtun, *Czech and Slovak Literature in English: A Bibliography*, 2d ed. (1988); *The Everyman Companion to East European Literature*, ed. R. Pynsent and S. Kanikova (1993); *Traveller's Literary Companion to Eastern and Central Europe*, ed. J. Naughton (1995); P. Petro, *History of Slovak Literature* (1996); V. Petrík, *Slovakia and Its Literature* (2001).

J. NAUGHTON

**SLOVENIAN POETRY.** *Brižinski spomeniki* (Monuments of Freising, ca. 10th c.), a semipoetic trans. of three religious texts into Slovenian, are the oldest recorded documents in the Lat. alphabet in any mod. Slavic lang. Not until the Protestant era many centuries later was the first poem proper written in Slovenian. Primož Trubar (1508–86) paved the way for the Slovene literary lang. with his composition of several original religious poems.

The first to write poetry of artistic value was the Franciscan friar Valentin Vodnik (1758–1819). But during the romantic period, France Prežeren (1800–49) developed Slovenian to as yet unequalled artistic heights. He is still considered the greatest Slovenian poet; he played an important role in establishing the Slovenian nation and is the author of the Slovene *anthem.

The poetry of Simon Jenko (1835–69) marks the transition from late romantic poetry to the work of four modernist poets of the late 19th c.: Oton Župančič (1878–1949), Josip Murn (1879–1901), Dragottin Kette (1876–99), and Ivan Cankar (1876–1918), who later become the leading Slovenian writer.

*Expressionism became the leading influence in the early 20th c., giving rise to revolutionary poetry during World War II. Numerous poets, incl. the apocalyptic Miran Jarc (1900–42), Edvard Kocbek (1904–81), Božo Vodušek (1905–78), and Lojze Krakar (1926–95), later joined by the revolutionary poets Matej Bor (1913–93) and Karel Destovnik Kajuh (1922–44), became strong social critics, while France Balantič (1921–43), a devout Catholic, died battling the partisan resistance.

The two leading 20th-c. Slovenian poets are Srečko Kosovel (1904–26) and Edvard Kocbek. Kosovel reached the peak of his short but creative life in his avant-garde constructivist poetry, published over 40 years after his death in 1926 (see CONSTRUCTIVISM). Kocbek suffered under the post-World War II regime because of his dissident views, but his poetry of cosmic energy and vision never voiced complaints.

Postwar poets faced the political suppression of free speech. The work of such poets as Jože Udovič (1912–86), Dane Zajc (1929–2008), Gregor Strniša (1930–70), Kajetan Kovič (b. 1931), Veno Taufer (b. 1933), Saša Vegri (1934–2010), Niko Grafenauer (b. 1940), and Svetlana Makarovič (b. 1939) became intimate, full of double meanings, and surrealistic imagery (see SURREALISM).

The next generation of poets—incl. Franci Zagoričnik (1933–97), Tomaž Šalamun (b. 1941), Iztok Geister (b. 1945), Andrej Brvar (b. 1945), Aleš Kernmauner (1946–66), Andrej Medved (b. 1947), Matjaž Hanžek (b. 1949), and Ivo Volarič-Feo (1948–2010)—deconstructed the semantic use of the word and turned it into a graphic or textual element. This poetic transformation paralleled political changes that allowed poets to explore their newly discovered freedom of expression. The new formalists Milan Dekleva (b. 1946), Ivo Svetina (b. 1948), Milan Jesih (b. 1950), and Boris A. Novak (b. 1953) went back to cl. poetic forms, while the generation of Vojko Gorjan (1949–75), Marjan Strojan (b. 1949), Jure Detela (1951–92), Iztok Osojnik (b. 1951), and Vladimir Memon (1953–80) clung to *free verse, insisting rather on a radical ethical stance.

Since the 1980s, there have been two poetic trends: the postmodernists Tone Škrjanec (b. 1953), Aldo Žerjal (b. 1957), Brane Mozetič (b. 1958), Aleš Debeljak (b. 1961), Alojz Ihan (b. 1961), Uroš Zupan (b. 1963), Peter Semolič (b. 1967), Primož Čučnik (b. 1971), Miklavž Komelj (b. 1973), Aleš Šteger (b. 1973), and Gregor Podlogar (b. 1974); and a group of women poets representing the strongest creative force in contemp. Slovene poetry, incl. Meta Kušar (b. 1952), Maja Vidmar (b. 1961), Tatjana Soldo (1962–92), Barbara Korun (b. 1963), Taja Kramberger (b. 1970), and Lucija Stupica (b. 1971).

■ **Anthologies**: *Iz roda v rod duh išče pot*, ed. J. Menart (1962); *Afterwards Slovenian Writing, 1945–1995*, ed. A. Zawacki (1999); *The Imagination of Terra Incognita*, ed. A. Debeljak (1999); *Nova slovenska lirika*, ed. R. Dabo (2002); "Unlocking the Aquarium: Contemporary Writing from Slovenia," ed. F. Sampson, A. Jelnikar, I. Osojnik, *Orient Express* 5 (2004)—special iss.; *Nevihta sladkih rož, Antologija slovenske poezije 20. stoletja*, ed. P. Kolšek (2006).

■ **Criticism and History**: B. Paternu, *Od ekspresionizma do postmoderne* (1965); *Slovenska književnost, Leksikon Cankarjeve založbe*, ed. K. Dolinar et al. (1982); J. Pogačnik, *Twentieth-Century Slovene Literature*, trans. A. Čeh (1989); B. A. Novak, "Poetry in the Slovene Language," trans. A. McDonell Duf, *Left Curve* 22 (1997), http://www.leftcurve.org/LC22WebPages/slovene.html; *Slovenska književnost I, II, III*, ed. J. Pogačnik and F. Zadravec (1998–2000); M. Mitrovič, *Geschichte der slowenischen Literatur* (2001); D. Poniž, *Beseda se vzdiguje v dim, stoletje slovenske lirike 1900–2000* (2000); I. Popov Novak, *Sprehodi po slovenski književnosti* (2003).

■ **Web Sites**: *Slovenia, Poetry International Web*, http://slovenia.poetryinternationalweb.org/piw_cms/cms/cms_module/index.php?obj_id=23.

I. OSOJNIK

**SMITHY POETS** (Rus. *Kuznitsa*). A group of proletarian writers in the Soviet Union (1920–31) that published the jours. *Kuznitsa* (The Smithy, 1920–22) and *Rabochii zhurnal* (Workers Journal, 1924–25). Their poetry depicted collective labor, mechanization, and industrialization; they eschewed traditional rhythms and forms. The prevailing view considers their work crude and naïve. The group's prominent poets included Vasilii Aleksandrovskii, Vasilii Kazin, Vladimir Kirillov, Grigorii Sannikov, and Sergei Obradovich, among others. From the mid-1920s, the group was dominated by prose writers.

■ G. Z. Patrick, *Popular Poetry in Soviet Russia* (1929); A. Voronskii, "Prozaiki i poety Kuznitsy," *Literaturno-kriticheskie stat'i* (1963); E. J. Brown, *The Proletarian Episode in Russian Literature 1928–1932* (1971); Terras; N. N. Skatov, *Russkaia literatura XX veka: slovar'* (2005).

W. E. HARKINS; C. DOAK

**SOMALI POETRY.** Poetry is at the core of Somali expressive culture and, until relatively recently, was composed, memorized, and disseminated in purely oral form. There are many genres, some folkloric in nature, such as work songs that accompany rural activities like watering camels, weaving mats, or loading camels. These songs may be widespread, but the original composer is no longer known. They are short and are often performed in sequence; furthermore, they may be changed by anyone who wishes to do so. They may also be composed to convey messages allusively to people within earshot to whom the performer might not be able to present his or her thoughts directly. Of the dance-song genres, such as *dhaanto* and *wiglo,* some are specific to certain areas of the Somali-speaking territories. These may be composed during the performance of a dance, and traditionally light-hearted competition in poetry between young men and women in such dances may occur. The generic term used for the work and dance songs is *hees,* although this term is now mostly used for mod. songs performed to musical accompaniment. Other genres, which are regarded as more prestigious, are those belonging to the classification sometimes referred to in Somali as *maanso.* These are poetic works of which the composer is known and of which, following the original recitation by the poet, the goal is to memorize them verbatim, which means that for each such poem there is a definitive text. Traditionally, all forms were performed to a particular type of tune (*luuq*), although this is much less common for maanso genres such as *gabay* and *geeraar.* One genre known as *buraambur* is used exclusively by women in a variety of contexts.

The earliest known Somali poems date from the middle of the 19th c. Some of the most famous are those of Raage Ugaas Warfaa, who is regarded as one of the greatest Somali poets and who composed on a range of subjects, such as the famous "Alleyl Dumay" (Night Has Fallen), a lament after the poet's fiancée married another. In the early 20th c., Sayid Maxamed Cabdille Xasan, the leader of the Dervish movement that fought the imperial powers in the northern areas, used poetry as a powerful tool for influence and propaganda. The use of poetry in the sociopolitical domain remained important. Some time after the defeat of the Sayid in 1921, a poet named Cali Dhuux composed an *invective poem addressing a particular lineage, which was replied to by a poet from that lineage, Qammaan Bulxan. Others then also joined in, and a poetic chain (*silsila*) ensued known as *Guba,* which became widely known. Such chains still occur every so often; some have been conducted via the Internet.

During the 1940s, a new form, the *heello,* developed out of another form known as *belwo.* Initially these were predominantly love poems and were also the first to be performed to musical accompaniment after Cabdullaahi Qarshe introduced the oud, a stringed instrument, to Somali culture and became one of the most important composers, not just of the music but of the poems. The heello subsequently developed into an important vehicle for nationalist poetry as part of the Somali struggle for independence, which was assisted by the introduction of radio as a further means of dissemination to a wider audience. It was at this time that theater began in Somalia. Plays were based on poetic texts composed by the playwright and then memorized by the actors, who would improvise the connecting parts in prose. Some parts of plays were sung to musical accompaniment as songs and became popular in their own right. After Somalia became independent in 1960, the heello developed into the mod. hees, which became the dominant form during the 1970s, a time when a number of famous young poets pioneered further devels., such as the use of traditional work song and children's song metrical patterns in serious poetry. Poetry became important politically both in support of and in opposition to the military regime that came to power in a coup in 1969.

All Somali poetry conforms to two stylistic requirements: *meter and *alliteration. The pattern of alliteration is such that every line in a poem, or every half line in certain genres, must contain a word beginning with the same sound, as in this extract from "Beledweyne" by Maxamed Ibraahim Warsame 'Hadraawi' (nicknames are widely used in Somali and are given throughout this entry in single quotation marks), in which the alliterative sounds are in italics: "webigoo *b*utaacoo / *b*eeraha waraabshoo / dhulka *b*aadku jiifshoo / dhirta ubaxu *b*uuxshoo" (as the river overflowed / watering the farms / the pasture lay on the ground / the flowers filled the trees). The alliterative sound is always the word's initial, and just the one sound is used throughout the poem. A poem may also alliterate in *alif,* which means that there must be a word beginning with a vowel in each line; any vowel may be used, in the short or long pronunciation. Alliteration is so important that it is used in naming characters in plays, in proverbs, even occasionally in naming children. In chain poems, mentioned above, the alliteration of each poem within the chain is most often the same; the *Siinley* chain of the early 1970s and *Deelley* of 1979–80 (both important chains of political poems) were named after the alliterative sound used in the poems. Certain sounds are considered more difficult than others depending on the number of words that begin with that sound; *alif, b,* or *d* are regarded as easier to compose in than *n* or *j,* with *y* probably the most difficult and recognized as such.

Meter in Somali poetry is quantitative and based on the patterning of long and short vowel syllables and syllable final consonants, which was first written about by the poet and scholar Maxamed Xaashi Dhamac 'Gaarriye' in 1976. The *jiifto* meter is the one most commonly used in mod. hees poetry, and its metrical patterning is presented here as an example of how the system works. In the basic pattern, ⏙ is a metrical position in which either one long or two short vowel syllables may occur, and ⏑ indicates an obligatory short vowel syllable:

(⏑) ⏙ (⏑) ⏙ ⏑ ⏙ ⏙

A short optional vowel syllable might be found at the beginning of the line or after the first metrical position when the following syllable has a long vowel (only one optional syllable is allowed). Syllable final consonants can occur at the end of metrical positions; but when a position of the type ⏙ is realized as two short vowel syllables, then the first of these syllables may contain a final consonant only in the first metrical position. E.g., the word *dhulka* (the earth, ground) may be found in the first metrical position, as in *dhulka baad ku jiifshoo,* but not in the other three positions of the shape ⏙. The position in which a syllable final consonant may occur is also the only position in which a word break may occur and, hence, where the alliteration also occurs. Geminate or doubled consonants are always analyzed as heterosyllabic, so these also may only occur in these positions as do the consonants *sh, s, f, t, k, j, w,* and *y,* which behave in the meter as geminate consonants. A large number of metrical patterns are associated with particular genres of poetry. *Free verse never emerged in Somali, although some Somali poetry, particularly that of Cabdi Muxumed Aamiin, seems to use patterning that does not follow the accepted meters; this poetry was composed to be sung to musical accompaniment, however. The demands of meter and alliteration are used artistically by good poets as extra raw material with which to enhance their poems aesthetically, a characteristic that brings value to poetry in the mind of the audience.

■ B. W. Andrzejewski and I. M. Lewis, *Somali Poetry: An Introduction* (1964); J. C. Ciise, *Diwaanka Gabayadii Sayid Maxamed Cabdulle Xasan* (1974); J. W. Johnson, *Heellooy Heelleellooy: The Development of the Genre Heello in Modern Somali Poetry* (1974); S. S. Samatar, *Oral Poetry and Somali Nationalism* (1982); *Literature in African Languages,* ed. B. W. Andrzejewski et al. (1985); *Poesia orale somala: storia di una nazione,* ed. F. Antinucci and A. F. Cali 'Idaajaa' (1986); A. C. Abokor, *Somali Pastoral Work Songs* (1993); *An Anthology of Somali Poetry,* trans. B. W. Andrzejewski with S. Andrzejewski (1993); G. Banti and F. Giannattasio, "Music and Metre in Somali Poetry," and J. Johnson, "Musico-Moro-Syllabic Relationships in the Scansion of Somali Oral Poetry," *Voice and Power: The Culture of Language in North East Africa,* ed. R. J. Hayward and I. M. Lewis (1996); M. Orwin, "On Consonants in Somali Metrics," *Afrikanistische Arbeitspapiere* 65 (2001), and "On the Concept of 'Definitive Text' in Somali Poetry," *Bulletin of the School of Oriental and African Studies* 63 (2003); *War and Peace: An Anthology of Somali Literature,* ed. R. S. Cabdillaahi 'Gadhweyne' (2009); "Night Has Fallen," trans. M. Orwin, http://pacoarts.com/PoetLangSite/flashpaper/raagel.swf.

M. ORWIN

**SONG** (Lat. *carmen,* Fr. *chanson,* Ger. *Lied*). Song refers broadly to the combined effect of music and words in a composition meant to be heard as music rather than read silently. Music, in addition to being the vehicle of transmission, frequently reinforces or enhances the emotional force of the text as perceived by the composer of the musical setting. While some songs are dramatic, song is distinguished from extended compositions involving music and text (such as opera) by its relative brevity. Since most songs are poems set to music, by extension any poem that is suitable for combination with music or is expressive in ways that might be construed as musical may also be referred to as song, and occasionally *song* is used to designate a strictly musical composition without text, deemed "poetic" in its expressivity or featuring markedly "vocal" melodic writing for instruments. From the musical standpoint, *song* has been restricted almost exclusively to musical settings of verse; experiments in setting prose have been very limited. Further, *song* has usually been reserved for compositions for solo voice or a small group of voices (typically one or two voices to a part) rather than a full choir and for voice(s) alone or in combination with one or two instruments rather than a full orchestra. In any case, the resulting balance, favoring the audibility of the text and thus appreciation of the nuances of its combination with music, is a defining characteristic of the genre; for literary purposes, these characteristics have also fostered perception of *song* as personal utterance projecting a limited emotional stance experienced by a single *persona.

As a literary term, *song* is related to *lyric, originally a text or poem sung to the accompaniment of the lyre and eventually used in lit. in divergent senses to refer, on the one hand, to any poem actually set or intended to be set to music (*ditty), and, on the other, to any poem focusing on the arousal of *emotion as would be characteristic of the kind of poem typically sung to the lyre (or to any other musical accompaniment) as song. *Lyric,* however, has attained much wider currency than has *song* and is the commonly accepted term today for both these meanings, whereas *song,* as a literary term, means an utterance partaking in some way of the condition of music. The musicality of a poem may be thought of in relation to the ways a text might be interpreted by a musical setting. Some songs correspond closely to the formal properties of the text (incl. metrical, linear, and strophic form), while others emphasize the semantic properties (rendering the meaning of individual words or phrases or expressing the tone or mood of the poem). They need not, of course, exclude each other; indeed, it is frequently difficult if not impossible to separate what may be a metrical rendering from its expressive function. The distinction is useful, however, as some songs favor one or the other, in turn influencing what are considered song-like elements or effects in poetry. The association of poetry with music in the songs of the late Ren. in England offers examples of both types of correspondence. In some (as in songs by Thomas Campion, who wrote both words and music), the rendering of the formal dimensions of poetry is precise: musical meter is aligned with poetic *meter, lines of verse are of uniform length and set to musical phrases of the same length (words are not repeated or extended by musical means), and the strophic *repetition of the poem is rendered through repetition of music (as in traditional hymn singing). Poetry that lends itself to settings of this sort is typically predictable in all these dimensions; hence, such a poem may be designated *song*. In the *madrigal and in some lute songs, by contrast, such formal properties are likely to be ignored and musical devices instead correlated with individual words to enhance meaning. This might mean repetition of words of special poignancy ("weep, weep") or highlighting of such words through exaggerated duration or unusually high or low *pitch; frequently such representation is accomplished through a technique called *word-painting*, which aligns individual words with musical figures that can be said to depict their meaning (a descending scale for the word *down*; a *dissonance for the word *grief*). Such practices also lead to predictability, in this case, in *diction. In the poetic miscellanies of the period, *song* and *sonnet* sometimes seem to be used interchangeably and often refer to poems with one or more of these characteristics. At worst, they are poems filled with *cliché and cloyingly regular in formal properties; at best, they achieve a delicate balance between the demands of successful musical rendition and fresh invention.

Songs featuring more general expressivity of mood or tone in music appear less frequently in this period, although the lutenist-composer John Dowland achieved some remarkable successes in this mode. Perhaps most famous is his "Lachrimae," which existed as an instrumental composition before being provided with its now-famous text, "Flow, my tears." The pervasively doleful mood of the piece is created musically in the accompaniment through its preponderance of descending melodic lines, its minor harmonies, its low register, and the slow, deliberate pace of its phrasing; the poem seems, in effect, to make verbal what the musical rhet. of emotion suggests. The role of music, then, in this type of song is less specifically text-dependent than in other types, and the required balance between music and poetry depends to a greater extent on the availability of appropriate instrumental resources to combine with the voice.

The *lied of 19th-c. Ger. lit. best exemplifies the fully developed expressive setting. In the hands of Franz Schubert, and to a great extent of those who followed him (Robert Schumann, Johannes Brahms, Hugo Wolf), the role of the accompanying instrument was enhanced to create a highly emotional song evocative of the overall tone or mood of the poem. Many give credit to the devel. of the mod. grand piano for the success of the lied. Although the notion of expressive setting was not new, as the role of the instrumental accompaniment in Claudio Monteverdi's "Combattimento di Tancredi e Clorinda" demonstrates, such pieces violated the required intimacy of voice and single instrument characteristic of song, and it was not until the devel. of a single instrument with the expressive range of the piano that this mode of song could flourish. The genre also depended on—and stimulated—a poetry that provided the appropriate moods, expressed in terms that could be adequately mimicked by music. This is found in the poetry of Ger. *romanticism, with its frequent evocation of nature or of ordinary human activity as the locus of emotion. For Schubert, the presence in the poem of a running brook or a woman spinning wool as the background to an emotion-filled reverie provided a means for music to enhance what the poem could only suggest. In this context, poetry can be said to be song-like if it presents an intense, sustained, clear, emotional stance, called forth by an activity that takes place in time. Typically, such poems feature only one such stance or a decided shift from one to another; striking *ambiguity or *paradox is less song-like insofar as these conditions are less readily imitated in music.

Curiously, poems that depend extensively on the so-called musicality of words (e.g., Edith Sitwell's "abstract poetry" and the later experiments in *sound poetry) are not necessarily song-like, because the sounds of the words draw attention to themselves and thereby detract from the poem's ability to evoke an emotional state.

The most extended use of *song* to refer to a kind of poetry takes the connection well beyond any mechanical representation or concurrence to questions of intent or of the relation to strains of creativity. Thus, Maritain uses *song* to designate the entire genre of lyric poetry, as distinct from narrative or dramatic, referring to "the Poem or the Song as the poetry of internal music . . . the immediate expression of creative intuition, the meaning whose intentional content is purely a recess of the subjectivity awakened to itself and things—perceived through an obscure, simple, and totally nonconceptual apperception." Such conceptions of the nature of song center on the ability of music to tap some source of understanding or sympathy that is not touched by lang. Kramer speaks of "the mythical union of a lower reality embodied in language and a higher one embodied in music," stating that "through song, usually the song of a disincarnate voice or of a figure touched by divinity, lang. is represented as broaching the ineffable"; this is the sense implied in the use of music to evoke the supernatural, whether through strictly instrumental means or through *charms, as is common in drama. Music has traditionally been associated with magic and with religious experience (despite the objections at various times of both Catholic and Puritan), and it is commonly thought of as the lang. of love. The fusion, therefore, of music and poetry in song has been thought to bring about the most perfect communication possible, combining the ineffable expressivity of music with the rational capabilities of words. And by derivation, poems that are perceived as visionary, conjuring some understanding beyond the normal capacities of words, may be called songs. Edmund Spenser's *Epithalamion* and *Prothalamion*, William Blake's *Songs of Innocence and Experience*, and Walt Whitman's "Song of Myself" come to mind.

Scholarship on song as music and text frequently focuses on function and social context. Vernacular song and folk song, for instance, have generated a huge independent lit. (not represented in the biblio. below). Although the distinctions between these and the many types of so-called art song are not always clear, the popular genres are less likely to have strong literary connections. Similarly, the literary connection is clearest with secular song, though the relations between music and text in sacred song run the same gamut as in secular. All song types, however, lend themselves well to critical methodologies of recent prominence (such as feminism or *New Historicism) and a growing number of comparative explorations of song lit. of other cultures has emerged.

*Song* has also come to designate certain purely musical compositions, presumably those, like poems called "song," that partake in some measure of the shared experience of music and poetry. Most frequent in this usage are such 19th-c. compositions as Felix Mendelssohn's "Songs without Words" for piano—short, expressive pieces, typically with a striking, singable melody and the sense that one could describe in words a suitable emotional frame of reference. Their proximity to the lied is probably not coincidence; *song*, or *lied*, in that context describes that combination of words and music producing a compressed and intense expression of the rhet. of emotion, and if words are merely implied, the effect is nevertheless present and the composition known as "song."

Several specialized types of song, established by use, have similarly given their names to poetic types, esp. *elegy, *lament, *hymn, lay or **lai*, *ballad, *carol, *rondeau, and canzonet.

*See* AIR, ALBA, BLUES, CACOPHONY, CANSO, CARMEN, CHANT, DESCORT, GESELLSCHAFTSLIED, JAZZ POETRY, MUSIC AND POETRY, RHYTHM, SOUND, SPIRITUAL, TAGELIED.

■ **Song as Music**: F. Gennrich, *Grundriss einer Formenlehre des mittelalterlichen Liedes* (1932); J. Maritain, *Creative Intuition in Art and Poetry* (1953); R. Lebègue, "Ronsard et la musique," *Musique et poésie au XVI siècle* (1954); G. Müller and G. Reichert, "Lied," *Reallexikon II* 2.42–62; D. Cooke, *The Language of Music* (1959); A. Sydow, *Das Lied* (1962); C. M. Bowra, *Primitive Song* (1962); R. H. Thomas, *Poetry and Song in the German Baroque* (1963); *The Penguin Book of Lieder*, ed. S. S. Prawer (1964); R. Taylor, *The Art of the Minnesinger* (1968); B. H. Bronson, *The Ballad as Song* (1969); D. Ivey, *Song* (1970)—on musical settings of Eng., Fr., Ger., and It. poetry, 17th–20th cs.; E. Brody and R. A. Fowkes, *The German Lied and Its Poetry* (1971); J. M. Stein, *Poem and Music in the German Lied* (1971); M. C. Beardsley, "Verse and Music," Wimsatt; H. van der Werf, *The Chansons of the Troubadours and Trouvères* (1972); D. Fischer-Dieskau, *Schubert's Songs: A Biographical Study* (1977); *Medieval English Songs*, ed. E. J. Dobson and F. Ll. Harrison (1979); "Song" and "Lied," *New Grove*; M. Booth, *The Experience of Songs* (1981); R. C. Friedberg, *American Art Song and American Poetry*, 2 v. (1981); S. Ratcliffe, *Campion: On Song* (1981); J. A. Winn, *Unsuspected Eloquence: A History of the Relations between Poetry and Music* (1981); E. B. Jorgens, *The Well-Tun'd Word: Musical Interpretations of English Poetry, 1597–1651* (1982); L. Kramer, *Music and Poetry: The Nineteenth Century and After* (1984); S. Banfield, *Sensibility and English Song: Critical Studies of the Early Twentieth Century*, 2 v. (1985); M. M. Stoljar, *Poetry and Song in Late Eighteenth-Century Germany* (1985); E. Doughtie, *English Renaissance Song* (1986); W. Maynard, *Elizabethan Lyric Poetry and Its Music* (1986); J. Stevens, *Words and Music in the Middle Ages* (1986); D. Seaton, *The Art Song: A Research and Information Guide* (1987)—esp. "Aesthetics, Analysis, Criticism"; J. W. Smeed, *German Song and Its Poetry, 1740–1900* (1987); D. M. Hertz, *The Tuning of the Word* (1988); *Lyrics of the Middle Ages*, ed. J. J. Wilhelm (1990); L. E. Auld, "Text as Pre-Text: French Court Airs and Their Ditties," *Literature and the Other Arts* (1993); S. Hart, "Masking the Violence in Melody: Songs of World War II," *The Image of Violence in Literature, the Media, and Society*, ed. W. Wright and S. Kaplan (1995); M. L. Switten, *Music and Poetry in the Middle Ages* (1995); S. Zheng, "Female Heroes and Moonish Lovers: Women's Paradoxical Identities in Modern Chinese Songs," *Journal of Women's History* 8 (1997); D. Fischlin, *In Small Proportions: A Poetics of the English Ayre, 1596–1622* (1998); D. Schaberg, "Song and the Historical Imagination in Early China," *HJAS* 59 (1999); P. Coren, "Singing and Silence: Female Personae in the English Ayre," *Renaissance Studies* 16 (2002).

■ **Song in Literature**: T. S. Eliot, *The Music of Poetry* (1942); W. R. Bowden, *The English Dramatic Lyric, 1603–42* (1951); J. Hollander, *The Untuning of the Sky: Ideas of Music in English Poetry, 1500–1700* (1961); P. J. Seng, *The Vocal Songs in the Plays of Shakespeare* (1967); E. Garke, *The Use of Songs in Elizabethan Prose Fiction* (1972); J. H. Long, *Shakespeare's Use of Music* (1972); C. Ericson-Roos, *The Songs of Robert Burns* (1977); B. H. Fairchild, *Such Holy Song: Music as Idea, Form, and Image in the Poetry of William Blake* (1980); W. R. Johnson, *The Idea of Lyric* (1982); L. Schleiner, *The Living Lyre in English Verse from Elizabeth through the Restoration* (1984); E. H. Winkler, *The Function of Song in Contemporary British Drama* (1990).

E. B. Jorgens

**SONGBOOK.** A multiauthored *lyric *anthology in a ms. codex volume of parchment leaves bound as a book, or printed book that displays an intention to gather and organize discrete (usually vernacular) lyric texts into a collection. Songbooks range from anthols. occupying only a few folios within a larger volume to large compilations coextensive with an entire codex. Given that all short med. texts are transmitted either in miscellanies (ranging from haphazard or practical incorporation to collections assembled on commission or speculation by a patron) or anthols. (items brought together according to some intelligible governing principle), the songbooks considered precursors to mod. eds. are the collections of individual nonnarrative poems in stanzaic form rather than single-author anthols., narrative anthols. in octosyllabic *couplets (such as the OF romance or *dit), or prose works that share thematic similarities with the *courtly love song. In the devel. of Western poetry, the most significant songbooks in terms of their typical qualities are the monumental mss. of the continental trad. compiled from the 13th c. on, such as the *chansonniers* of *troubadour and *trouvère poetry and *Liederhandschriften* of Ger. *Minnesänger*. These scribally compiled, multiauthored anthols. preserve and memorialize a lyric production that had been mostly transmitted orally since the beginning of the 12th c. They are among the earliest collections of secular lyric poetry in the Eur. vernaculars, and they organize lyric texts written out in prose by *genre (*cansos, *sirventes, *tensos; later *formes fixes* such as the motet and *canción*) and by *poet. While some contain musical notation, many songbooks of the Eur. vernaculars such as the Occitan chansonniers and MHG Liederhandschriften transmit only lyrics. In this way, these trads. differ notably from the Fr. chansonniers, which tend to preserve melodies and lyrics. Even when songbooks group nonlyric texts such as the biographies of poets in Occitan chansonniers (*vidas*) or prose commentaries (*razos*) with lyrics to memorialize a trad. or collate heterogeneous elements of genre or lang. (long, moralizing texts with *chansons, Occitan and Fr.), they were compiled to manifest a deliberate coherence in their reading programs as a single entity while maintaining a variety of discrete pieces of poetry. As Huot has shown, the compilations often demonstrate a narrative or thematic coherence while emphasizing individual authors. In addition to being carefully organized under genre and author, songbooks often contain rubricated initials and miniatures, such as distinctive portraits of troubadours or more typical ones of aristocrats, clergy, or knights. In their comprehensive plans for rubrication—in particular, the importance of the figure of the poet—and attention to lit. hist., they are cultural objects in their own right while also serving as a vehicle for preserving poetry. They reflect a new consciousness of vernacular lyric as an object of study and codification. While the continental Eur. songbook trad. generally emphasizes authorial expression in contrast to the ME anthols. of mostly anonymous lyrics collated with other kinds of writing (such as prayers and hagiographies in the early 14th-c. Harley 2253 ms.), songbooks express an aesthetic motivation or design of a whole greater than the sum of its parts. Thus, even as the term *songbook* may be a misnomer as assigned to a compilation of nonlyric and lyric texts or to an anthol. contained within a section of a ms. rather than the entire codex, one may perceive a songbook as both compiling lyric poems and exhibiting the presence of artificial principles by which a reader may interpret those poems. As Nichols (1990) and Lerer have argued, such principles may be perceived in a ms.'s performance—through or despite the physical "manuscript matrix" of dissimilar materials from various points of time—or when the "idea of the anthology," the social, historical or literary purposes of a collection, become clear whether by textual disposition, organization, rubrication, or illustration.

Despite attempts in the 19th c. to establish stemmata of written sources that make a songbook, the mod. scholarly consensus is that the earliest vernacular songbooks are a combination of both oral and written transmission, as generally we lack early exemplars or song sheets; the textual variability of lyric texts in the mss. attests to an early stage of oral transmission and the performance of these lyrics as remembered improvisation (Holmes, Paden 1995, Van Vleck). While songbooks would have been assembled from different sources, incl. both local and circulating ur-models used for multiple collections, their compilation greatly contributed to the stabilization of the lyric trad. and the devel. of single-authored compilations of lyric cycles (Holmes). Older mss. such as the OF ms. U (Huot) show an earlier stage of lyric anthols. in that the lyrics are anonymous, are more randomly organized, and lack the illumination and generic organization that codify a lyric trad. Despite this range of editorial intention, songbooks differ from the earliest instances of vernacular lyric that contain these texts in the margins and flyleaves of ecclesiastical or legal codices (see Occitan lyrics in Paden and Paden; ms. 201, folio 89 verso and vernacular lyric in England in Thomson and Gullick) or include them in heterogeneous vernacular miscellanies based primarily on principles such as subject matter or practical considerations of accessibility. Songbooks may also be seen as contiguous with the trad. of middle Lat. songbooks incorporating vernacular texts, such as the *Carmina Burana* and the earlier Carolingian *flores auctorum*. Nichols (1996) believes the pandect, since the 6th c. a term for compilations of laws and later sacred writings, also provided a model for songbooks.

With the rise of vernacular literacy in western Europe during the 13th c., songbooks became a symbol of cultural prestige, as patrons and composers of lyric poetry in It., Iberian, and Ger. courts looked to associate themselves with a courtly mythology of poetic trad. In general, songbooks not only catalog lyrics but document and archive the social and cultural context from which the lyrics arose through their rubrication and commentary (Burgwinkle). In the case of troubadour chansonniers compiled in Italy, these mss. reflect the desire of It. aristocrats to establish a written trad. of a lyric poetry even as it was still orally transmitted in Occitan-speaking areas of southern France and northern Spain. Codices of the 14th c. and after, such as the large Heidelberg ms. of the MHG trad. known as the *Codex Manesse* and the 15th-c. Castilian *cancioneros*, establish the songbook as a literary genre. Songbooks became a means of cultural self-justification for aristocrats and lettered men with social ambitions: the composition *and* publication of poetry in songbooks (mss. and then printed codices—see Dutton and Krogstad's bibl.) constituted an important courtly pastime. The individual songbook often represented a poetic coterie or particular court as was the case in the 15th- and 16th-c. Castilian cancioneros (see Gerli and Weiss, Dutton and Krogstad). Further, the codices of the troubadour trad. served as models for later It. lyric collections and for poets such as Dante and Petrarch (see PETRARCHISM).

Many scholars have noted that, as visual representations of oral poems and musical performances, songbooks show codicological practices and cultural agendas that have much to do with the formation of lyric trads. The arrangement of vernacular poetry in anthols. was an impetus for the idea of the author as the foundation of a literary *canon*; it also affected the evolution of lyric genres, from the priority of the aristocratic chanson to *formes fixes*. The idea of the songbook belongs to the mod. reevaluation of so-called canonical works, as songbooks represent how much a canon and lit. itself are material and social products of times and places, and a category such as poet a social construction that reflects different lyric audiences (Hanna, Guillory). Thus, a discrete single literary work must be seen in relation to its mode of transmission and to other works in an assembly of works such as a songbook. In the mod. era, songbooks came to represent a culture of lyric poetry that could reinforce a geographical or ling. identity, such as the Galician-Port. cancioneiros for the Iberian trad. or Liederhandschriften for Ger.-speaking people. In this sense, during the 19th c., songbooks were implicated in the romantic search for ling. and national identity, as they reflected the desire to justify cultural or regional origins through ling. artifacts (Kendrick).

Whether determined by scribe, patron, or poet, the songbook—and by extension the textual crit. of songbooks—reflects cultural preoccupations governing the interpretation of poetry and its social role in different historical periods.

*See* LYRIC SEQUENCE, MINNESANG, SONNET SEQUENCE.

■ G. Gröber, "Die Liedersammlungen der Troubadours," *Romanische Studien* 2 (1875–77); D. S. Avalle, *La letteratura medievale in lingua d'oc nella sua tradizione manoscritta* (1961); A. Parédes, *A Texas-Mexican Cancionero* (1976); *Codex Manesse: Die Grosse Heidelberger Liederhandschrift*, Facsimile of Codex Palatinus Germanicus 848 of the Universitätsbibliothek Heidelberg, with "Interimstexten" from I. F. Walther (1975–78), commentary, ed. W. Koschorreck and W. Werner (1981); E. Poe, *From Poetry to Prose in Old Provençal: The Emergence of the "Vidas," the "Razos," and the*

*"Razos de trobar"* (1984); J. Boffey, *Manuscripts of Early Courtly Love Lyrics in the Later Middle Ages* (1985); J. Guillory, "Canonical and Non-Canonical: A Critique of the Debate," *ELH* 54 (1987); S. Huot, *From Song to Book: The Poetics of Writing in Old French Lyric and Lyrical Narrative Poetry* (1987); S. G. Nichols, "Introduction: Philology in a Manuscript Culture," *Speculum* 65 (1990); *El cancionero del siglo XV, c. 1360–1520*, ed. B. Dutton and J. Krogstad, 7 v. (1990–91); T. Stemmler, "Miscellany or Anthology: The Structure of Medieval Manuscripts, MS Harley 2253, for Example," *Zeitschrift für Anglistik und Amerikanistik* 39 (1991); rev. in Fein (2000); A. Roncaglia, "Rétrospectives et perspectives dans l'étude des chansonniers d'oc," *Lyrique romane médiévale: La tradition des chansonniers: Actes du Colloque du Liège, 1989*, ed. M. Tyssens (1991); A. E. Van Vleck, *Memory and Re-Creation in Troubadour Lyric* (1991); W. D. Paden, "Manuscripts," *A Handbook of the Troubadours*, ed. F.R.P. Akehurst and J. M. Davis (1995); *The Whole Book: Cultural Perspectives on the Medieval Miscellany*, ed. S. G. Nichols and S. Wenzel (1996)—esp. Nichols, "'Art' and 'Nature': Looking for (Medieval) Principles of Order in Occitan *Chansonnier* N (Morgan 819)"; R. Hanna III, *Pursuing History: Middle English Manuscripts and Their Texts* (1996); *Medievalism and the Modernist Temper*, ed. R. H. Bloch and S. G. Nichols (1996)—esp. L. Kendrick, "The Science of Imposture and the Professionalization of Medieval Occitan Literary Studies"; *Poetry at Court in Trastamaran Spain: From the "Cancionero de Baena" to the "Cancionero General,"* ed. E. M. Gerli and J. Weiss (1998); W. Burgwinkle, "The *Chansonniers* as Books," *The Troubadours: An Introduction*, ed. S. Gaunt and S. Kay (1999); O. Holmes, *Assembling the Lyric Self: Authorship from Troubadour Song to Italian Poetry Book* (2000); *Studies in the Harley Manuscript*, ed. S. Fein (2000); R. M. Thomson and M. Gullick, *A Descriptive Catalogue of the Medieval Manuscripts in Worcester Cathedral Library* (2001); S. Lerer, "Medieval English Literature and the Idea of the Anthology," *PMLA* 118 (2003); J.H.M. Taylor, *The Making of Poetry: Late-Medieval French Poetic Anthologies* (2007); *Troubadour Poems from the South of France*, ed. W. D. Paden and F. F. Paden (2007); G. Kornrumpf, *Vom Codex Manesse zur Kolmarer Liederhandschrift: Aspekte der Überlieferung, Formtraditionen, Texte* (2008); M. Galvez, *Songbook: How Lyrics Became Poetry in Medieval Europe* (2012).

M. GALVEZ

**SONNET** (from It. *sonetto*, "a little sound or song"). A 14-line line poem normally in *hendecasyllables* (It.), iambic pentameter (Eng.), or *alexandrines* (Fr.), whose rhyme scheme varies despite the assumption that the sonnet form is fixed. The three most widely recognized versions of the sonnet, with their traditional rhyme schemes, are the It. or Petrarchan (octave: *abbaabba*; sestet: *cdecde* or *cdcdcd* or a similar combination that avoids the closing couplet), the Spenserian (*ababbcbc cdcdee*), and the Eng. or Shakespearean (*ababcdcdefef gg*). Weeks showed in a sample of just under 6,000

Eng. sonnets that 60% used the *abbaabba* pattern for the octaves and 22% *ababcdcd*.

The It. pattern (the most widely used) invites a two-part division of thought: the octave's unified pattern leads to the *volta or "turn" in the more varied sestet. The *abbaabba* octave is a blend of three brace-rhyme quatrains: the middle four lines, whose sounds overlap the others, reiterate the identical envelope pattern but with the sounds reversed, i.e., *baab*. The sestet, with its element of unpredictability, its usually more intense rhyme activity (three rhymes in six lines coming after two in eight), and the structural interdependence of the tercets, implies acceleration in thought and feeling.

The Spenserian and Shakespearean patterns offer relief to the difficulty of rhyming in Eng. and invite a division of thought into three quatrains and a closing or summarizing couplet; even though such arbitrary divisions are frequently ignored by the poet, the more open rhyme schemes tend to impress the fourfold structure on the reader's ear and to suggest a stepped progression toward the closing couplet.

Most deviations from the foregoing patterns have resulted from liberties taken in rhyming, but a few innovations of the sonnet are the following: *alternating*, where the tercets alternate with the quatrains (Catulle Mendès); *caudate*, with "tails" of added lines (G. M. Hopkins, Albert Samain, R. M. Rilke); *chained* or *linked*, each line beginning with the last word of the previous line; *continuous, iterating*, or *monorhymed* on one or two rhyme sounds throughout (Giacomo da Lentini, Stéphane Mallarmé, Edmund Gosse); *corona*, a series joined together by theme (It.) or rhyme or repeated lines (Sp. and Eng., e.g., John Donne) for *panegyric; *curtal*, a sonnet of ten lines with a halfline tailpiece, divided 6 + 4½ (Hopkins); *dialogue*, a sonnet distributed between two speakers and usually *pastoral in inspiration (Cecco Angiolieri, Austin Dobson); *double*, a sonnet of 28 lines (Monte Andrea); *enclosed*, in which the tercets are sandwiched between the quatrains (Charles Baudelaire, Jean Pierre Rambosson); *interwoven*, with medial as well as end rhyme; *retrograde*, reading the same backward as forward; *reversed* (also called *sonettessa*), in which the sestet precedes the octave (Baudelaire, Paul Verlaine, Ricarda Huch)—for a reversed Shakespearean sonnet, see Rupert Brooke's "Sonnet Reversed"; *rinterzato*, a sonnet with eight short lines interspersed, making a whole of 22 lines (Guittone d'Arezzo); *terza rima*, with the linked-tercets *aba bcb* rhyme scheme; *unrhymed*, where the division into quatrains and tercets is still observed, but the lines are blank (Joachim du Bellay, J. R. Becher). In Eng., the 16-line poems of George Meredith's sequence *Modern Love* (1862) are clearly related to the sonnet in their themes and *abbacddceffeghhg* rhyme scheme.

Historically, the sonnet began as some variant of the It. pattern; it is probable that the form resulted either from the addition of a double refrain of six lines (two tercets) to the two-quatrain Sicilian *strambotto or from conscious modeling on the form of the *canzone. The current form of the sonnet originated in the Sicilian court of Frederick II (1205–50), with 60 of the Sicilian

school's sonnets in existence today. The sonnets of Giacomo da Lentini (fl. 1215–33) were followed by those of Guido Guinizzelli and Guido Cavalcanti. Although others of Lentini's contemporaries (the Abbot of Tivoli, Jacopo Mostacci, Pier delle Vigne, Rinaldo d'Aquino) used the form and established the octave-sestet divisions (with quatrain-tercet subdivisions), it remained for d'Arezzo (1230–94) to invent the *abbaabba* octave, which became traditional through its use by Dante (*Vita nuova, Rime*) and Petrarch (*Canzoniere*); Antonio da Tempo, in his *Summa artis rithmici* (1332), is the first to enunciate theoretical discussion of the sonnet as a type. The sonnets of Dante to Beatrice and of Petrarch to Laura normally opened with a strong statement that was then developed; but they were not unmarked by the artificiality of treatment that stemmed from variations on the Platonic love themes, an artificiality that was to be exported with the form in the 15th and 16th cs. as the sonnet moved to Spain, Portugal, the Netherlands, Poland, and England, and later to Germany, Scandinavia, and Russia, until its use was pan-Eur. and the number of poets not attempting it negligible. The sonnet entered the Heb. lang. (in hendecasyllables) in Italy and Spain, as a primary form in which rhyme entered its poetry, esp. in sonnets by Immanuel of Rome at the end of the 13th to the beginning of the 14th c. Following Petrarch, there was in Italy some diminution of dignity in use of the form (as in Serafino dall'Aquila [1466–1500]), but with the work of Michelangelo, Pietro Bembo, Baldassare Castiglione, Gaspara Stampa, Vittoria Colonna, and Torquato Tasso, the sonnet was reaffirmed as a structure admirably suited to the expression of emotion in lyrical mood, adaptable to a wide range of subject matter (e.g., love, politics, religion), and employed with skill by many writers in the centuries to follow (Vittorio Alfieri, Ugo Foscolo, Giosuè Carducci, Gabriele D'Annunzio).

It was the Marqués de Santillana (1398–1458), who introduced the sonnet form (in hendecasyllables, even) to Spain, although it was not established there until the 16th c., the time of Juan Boscán (ca. 1490–1542) and esp. Garcilaso de la Vega (1503–36), Félix Lope de Vega (1562–1635), and other dramatists of the *siglo de oro*. Francisco Sá de Miranda (1481–1558) and his disciple António Ferreira brought the sonnet to Portugal, where it is better known in the *Rimas* of Luís de Camões (1524–80) and in the exquisite work of Antero de Quental (1842–91). Clément Marot (1496–1544) and Mellin de Saint Gelais (1491–1558) introduced it to France, but du Bellay (ca. 1522–60) was most active, writing (in the Petrarchan pattern) the first non-Italian cycle, *L'Olive*, as well as *Les Regrets* and *Les Antiquités de Rome* (trans. by Edmund Spenser as *The Ruins of Rome*, a source for Shakespeare's sonnets). Pierre de Ronsard (1524–85), who experimented with the form in alexandrines, Philippe Desportes (1546–1606), and Louise Labé (1522–66) wrote many sonnets, while François de Malherbe (1555–1628) put his authority behind the *abbaabbaccdede* pattern in alexandrines, which became the accepted line length. After an era of decline in Europe in the 18th c., Théophile Gautier

(1811–72), Gérard de Nerval (1808–55), and Baudelaire (1821–67) revived the form, as did Verlaine, Mallarmé, Arthur Rimbaud, J.-M. de Heredia (1842–1905), and Paul Valéry (1871–1945). Germany received the form relatively late, in the writings of G. R. Weckherlin (1584–1653) and, esp. insofar as creative achievement is concerned, Andreas Gryphius (1616–64). A period of disuse followed until Gottfried Bürger (1747–94) revived the form and anticipated its use by A. W. Schlegel, J. F. Eichendorff, Ludwig Tieck, and other romantic writers. The sonnets of August Graf von Platen (1796–1835), *Sonette aus Venedig*, rank among the best in mod. times, while in more recent years the mystical sequence *Sonette an Orpheus* (1923) of Rilke and the writings of R. A. Schröder have brought the Ger. sonnet to another high point.

The sonnet arrived in England from Italy via Thomas Wyatt (1503–42), who preferred the sestet's closing couplet. Wyatt adhered to the Petrarchan octave; Henry Howard, the Earl of Surrey (1517–47), established the *ababcdcdefefgg* rhyme scheme, a pattern more congenial to the comparatively rhyme-poor Eng. lang. in that it filled the 14 lines by seven rhymes, not five. This pattern was popular in the Ren. Wide variation existed in rhyme schemes and line lengths; Shakespeare was its best practitioner. A rhyme scheme more attractive to Spenser (and in its first nine lines paralleling his *Spenserian stanza) was *ababbcbccdcdee*, a compromise between It. and Eng. patterns. The period also saw many *sonnet sequences, including those of Philip Sidney (*Astrophil and Stella*, pub. 1591), Samuel Daniel (*Delia*), Michael Drayton (*Idea*), Spenser (*Amoretti*), Lady Mary Wroth (*Pamphilia to Amphilanthus*), and Shakespeare. It remained for John Milton to introduce the true It. pattern, to break from sequences to occasional sonnets, to have a wider sense of content, to give greater unity to the form by frequently permitting octave to run into sestet (the "Miltonic" sonnet anticipated by the Elizabethans), and to give a greater richness to the texture by employing *enjambment. And sonnet-like structures of 14 lines have even been discerned in the stichic verse of *Paradise Lost*, a practice later echoed by William Wordsworth and Thomas Hardy (Johnson 1982). Milton's was the strongest influence when, after a century of disuse, the sonnet was revived in the late 18th c. by Thomas Gray, Thomas Warton, William Cowper, and William Lisle Bowles and reestablished in the early 19th by Wordsworth (who eased rhyme demands by use of an *abbaacca* octave in nearly half of his more than 500 sonnets), by Anna Seward, and by John Keats, whose frequent use of the Shakespearean pattern reaffirmed its worthiness. By this time, the scope of sonnet themes had broadened widely; in Leigh Hunt and Keats, it even embraced an unaccustomed humor. Sonnet theory was also developing tentatively during this period (as in Hunt's "Essay on the Sonnet") to eventuate in an unrealistic purism in T.W.H. Crosland's *The English Sonnet* (1917) before it was later more temperately approached. Since the impetus of the romantic revival, the form has had a continuing and at times distin-

guished use, as in D. G. Rossetti (*The House of Life*), Christina Rossetti, Elizabeth Barrett Browning (*Sonnets from the Portuguese*), and A. C. Swinburne. Few poets of the 20th c. (W. H. Auden, Dylan Thomas, Geoffrey Hill, and Seamus Heaney might be named) matched the consistent level of production found in the earlier work, although an occasional single sonnet, such as W. B. Yeats's "Leda and the Swan," has rare beauty.

While sonnets were ubiquitous in the colonial Americas, the form did not appear in New England until the last quarter of the 18th c., in the work of Col. David Humphreys, but once introduced, the form spread rapidly if not distinctively until H. W. Longfellow (1807–82), using the It. pattern, lifted it in dignity and lyric tone (esp. in the *Divina commedia* sequence) to a level easily equal to its counterpart in England. Subsequently, E. A. Robinson, Robert Frost, Claude McKay (born in Jamaica), Edna St. Vincent Millay, e. e. cummings, and Robert Lowell, among others, produced memorable sonnets, as have more recent Am. and Eng.-lang. poets such as Ted Berrigan, James K. Baxter (New Zealand), Rafael Campo, Anne Carson (Canada), Tony Harrison (England), Marilyn Hacker, John Hollander, Edwin Morgan (Scotland), and Bernadette Mayer.

In the 20th and early 21st cs., sonnets have continued to broaden to include almost any subject and mood. Structurally, even within the traditional patterns, the sonnet has reflected the principal influences evident in mod. poetry as a whole: *free-verse innovations have frequently led to less metronomic movement within the iambic norm; alternatives to exact rhymes have replenished the stock of rhyme pairs and have sophisticated acoustic relationships; and a more natural idiom has removed much of a burdensome artificiality. Such adaptability suggests continued interest in and use of the form.

*See* ONEGIN STANZA, PETRARCHISM, QUATORZAIN.

■ H. Welti, *Gesch. des Sonettes in der deutschen Dichtung* (1884); Schipper, 2.835 ff; L. Biadene, *Morfologia del sonetto nei secoli XIII e XIV* (1889); *Sonnets on the Sonnet*, ed. M. Russell (1898); M. Jasinski, *Histoire du sonnet en France* (1903); L. T. Weeks, "The Order of Rimes of the English Sonnet," *MLN* 25 (1910)—data; Thieme, 381 ff—lists 17 Fr. works, 1548–1903; F. Villey, "Marot et le premier sonnet français," *Revue d'Histoire Littéraire de la France* 20 (1920); R. D. Havens, *The Influence of Milton on English Poetry* (1922)—surveys 18th- and 19th-c. Eng. sonnets; W. L. Bullock, "The Genesis of the English Sonnet Form," *PMLA* 38 (1923); L. G. Sterner, *The Sonnet in American Literature* (1930); L. Zillman, *John Keats and the Sonnet Tradition* (1939); W. Mönch, *Das Sonett* (1955)—most comprehensive study to date, with extended bibl.; E. Rivers, "Certain Formal Characteristics of the Primitive Love Sonnet," *Speculum* 33 (1958); E. H. Wilkins, *The Invention of the Sonnet and Other Studies in Italian Literature* (1959); E. Núñez Mata, *Historia y origen del soneto* (1967); S. Booth, *An Essay on Shakespeare's Sonnets* (1969); *Das deutsche Sonett*, ed.

J. U. Fechner (1969); J. Levy, "The Development of Rhyme-Scheme and of Syntactic Pattern in the English Renaissance Sonnet," "On the Relations of Language and Stanza Pattern in the English Sonnet," rpt. in his *Paralipomena* (1971); M. Françon, "L'Introduction du sonnet en France," *RPh* 26 (1972); J. Fuller, *The Sonnet* (1972); L. M. Johnson, *Wordsworth and the Sonnet* (1973); F. Jost, "The Sonnet in its European Context," *Introduction to Comparative Literature* (1974); Wilkins; R. L. Colie, *Shakespeare's Living Art* (1974); C. Scott, "The Limits of the Sonnet," *RLC* 50 (1976); F. Kimmich, "Sonnets before Opitz," *German Quarterly* 49 (1976); D. H. Scott, *Sonnet Theory and Practice in Nineteenth-Century France* (1977); H.-J. Schlütter, *Sonett* (1979); S. Hornsby and J. R. Bennett, "The Sonnet: An Annotated Bibliography from 1940 to the Present," *Style* 13 (1979); J. Geninasca, "Forme fixe et forme discursive dans quelques sonnets de Baudelaire," *Cahiers de l'Association internationale des études françaises* 32 (1980); Brogan, 455 ff.; Fowler; L. M. Johnson, *Wordsworth's Metaphysical Verse* (1982)—blank-verse sonnets; *Russkij sonet*, ed. B. Romanov, and *Russkij sonet*, ed. V. S. Sovalin (both 1983)—anthols.; Elwert, *Italienische*, sect. 83; F. Rigolot, "Qu'est-ce qu'un sonnet?" *Revue d'Histoire Littéraire de la France* 84 (1984) C. Kleinhenz, *The Early Italian Sonnet* (1986); Hollier; S. L. Bermann, *The Sonnet over Time* (1989)—Petrarch, Shakespeare, and Baudelaire; P. Oppenheimer, *The Birth of the Modern Mind* (1989); G. Warkentin, "Sonnet, Sonnet Sequence," *The Spenser Encyclopedia*, ed. A. C. Hamilton et al. (1990); A. L. Martin, *Cervantes and the Burlesque Sonnet* (1991); *Six Masters of the Spanish Sonnet*, ed. and trans. W. Barnstone (1992); M.R.G. Spiller, *The Development of the Sonnet* (1992); D. Bregman, *The Golden Way* (1995)—Heb. sonnet; Moirer; H. Vendler, *The Art of Shakespeare's Sonnets* (1998); *The Oxford Book of Sonnets*, ed. J. Fuller (2000); *Penguin Book of the Sonnet*, ed. P. Levin (2001); *The Making of a Sonnet*, ed. E. Boland and E. Hirsch (2008); *The Reality Street Book of Sonnets*, ed. J. Hilson (2009); S. Burt and D. Mikics, *The Art of the Sonnet* (2010); *The Cambridge Companion to the Sonnet*, ed. P. Howarth (2010).

T.V.F. BROGAN; L. J. ZILLMAN; C. SCOTT; J. LEWIN

**SONNET SEQUENCE.** A subset of the *lyric sequence consisting of a series of *sonnets, of any number, that may be organized according to some fictional or intellectual order. The sequence made entirely of sonnets is rarer than readers often suppose and seldom holds an author's or a culture's attention for long before deliberate variations emerge. The rise of the sonnet sequence in most Eur. langs. coincides with that of *Petrarchism: because Petrarch's late 14th-c. *Canzoniere* is made largely but not exclusively of sonnets (317 of 366 poems), many of its imitators and adapters in Fr., Eng., Port., and Sp. saw their roles as involving the domestication of his sonnet form; hence, the first Petrarchans in the vernaculars (e.g., Thomas Wyatt and Henry Howard, the Earl of Surrey, in Eng.) are often the first sonneteers in their langs. as well (e.g., Joachim du Bellay

and Pierre de Ronsard in Fr., Francisco Sá de Miranda and Luís de Camões in Port., Juan Boscán and Garcilaso de la Vega in Sp.). The most extreme vogue for sonnet sequences was that of Eng. poets in the later 16th c.: examples include Thomas Watson's *Hekatompathia* of 18-line sonnets (1582); Philip Sidney's *Astrophil and Stella* (written early 1580s, pub. 1591); Edmund Spenser's *Ruins of Rome* (1591—an adaptation of du Bellay's *Antiquités de Rome* [1558] and drawn upon by Shakespeare) and *Amoretti* (with its completing *Epithalamion* [1595]); Henry Constable's *Diana* (1592); Samuel Daniel's *Delia* (1592); Michael Drayton's much revised *Idea* (1593); and Shakespeare's *Sonnets* (written 1590s, pub. 1609). In the 17th c., while poets such as the Spaniard Francisco de Quevedo, Sidney's niece Mary Wroth, and the Mexican nun Sor Juana Inés de la Cruz continue to extend the reach of the amatory and philosophical sonnet sequence, the orientation of the sequence at large (like that of the lyric sequence) turns toward *devotional poetry. Aside from Quevedo and John Donne, notable religious sonneteers incl. the Ger. Andreas Gryphius, the It. Tommaso Campanella, the Dutchman Constantijn Huygens, and the Frenchman Jean de La Ceppède.

In the early mod. period generally, the sonnet sequence is often thought to have a special, almost automatic claim to overall integrity—whether topical (as in du Bellay's *Les Regrets* [1558]), meditative (as in the *"corona" used by Donne and others), or vaguely chronological (as in the common usage of the Eng. word *century* for 100 sonnets). As scholars such as Warley and Alduy have demonstrated, the sonnet sequence can be as much a political and economic as a literary construction—an arena or marketplace for the working out of collective interests; earlier scholars have dwelt on its character as a ritual experience, a type of public space, and an art form with analogues in painting, religion, and architecture, among other disciplines. The job of cultural mediation enacted by the sonnet sequence perhaps indicates why poetic amateurs of note—such as the It. sculptor and painter Michelangelo Buonarroti in the 1530s and 1540s, the Eng. Puritan polemicist Henry Lock in the 1590s, or the Am. philosopher George Santayana in the 1890s—are drawn to this form as a uniquely deprivileged space: it enables them to think through emotional, philosophical, or religious issues in a formally determined, publicly accessible medium. In fact, the first sonnet sequence in Eng.—Anne Lock's *Meditation of a Penitent Sinner* (1560), inspired by the Scottish Puritan John Knox—is the ideologically charged work of a poetic amateur, intervening in contemp. religious debates in the mode of a deeply personal meditation (Roche).

Like the lyric sequence, the sonnet sequence seems to have had few important instances in the 18th c. but became a major romantic and postromantic vehicle. Notable examples incl. William Wordworth's several sonnet sequences.; E. B. Browning's *Sonnets from the Portuguese* (1850); George Meredith's narrative *Modern Love* (1862), in which the "sonnets" have 16 lines; D. G. Rossetti's *House of Life* (1881); Rubén Darío's "sonetos" and "medallones" in *Azul . . .* (1888), the book that impelled Sp.-Am. *modernismo*, which had a recurrent fascination with the sonnet in loosely organized collocations; Fernando Pessoa's *35 Sonnets* in Eng. (1918); R. M. Rilke's *Sonette an Orpheus* (1923); and e. e. cummings's several sonnet sequences in his early volumes *Tulips and Chimneys* (1923), *&* (1925), and *XLI Poems* (1925). With the 20th c. and *modernism came another hiatus, followed by a renewed sense of the sonnet sequence's potential for organizing experience, esp. love, though, in the later 20th c., it was perhaps impossible for the sonnet sequence to occur without formal irony, cultural critique, or anachronistic pathos. Thus, Nicolás Guillén's political volumes are founded on his early experiments as a sonneteer, a role to which he returns for ironic effect (as in "El abuelo" in *West Indies, Ltd.* [1934]); and John Berryman's adulterous *Sonnets* (written 1940s, pub. 1968) seek out a self-conscious Petrarchism (esp. 15, an adaptation of *Canzoniere* 189). Robert Lowell became all but exclusively a sonneteer in late career: his experiments in recasting the sonnet sequence *Notebook 1967–68* as *Notebook* (1970), *History* (1973), and *For Lizzie and Harriet* (1973) might be considered the climax of his work, culminating in *The Dolphin* (1973) and *Day by Day* (1977). Among late-century adaptations in Eng. are Seamus Heaney's ten "Glanmore Sonnets" (in *Field Work*, 1979) and his eight-sonnet elegy "Clearances" (in *The Haw Lantern*, 1987); Tony Harrison's dissonant rewriting of the formal trad. in *Continuous: 50 Sonnets from the School of Eloquence* (1982); Marilyn Hacker's amatory *Love, Death, and the Changing of the Seasons* (1986), incl. an updated crown of sonnets; and Bill Knott's cultural polemic in *Outremer* (1989).

■ *Elizabethan Sonnet-Cycles*, ed. M. F. Crow (1896); L. C. John, *The English Sonnet Sequences* (1938); W. Mönch, *Das Sonett: Gestalt und Geschichte* (1955); *European Metaphysical Poetry*, ed. F. J. Warnke (1961); D. Stone, *Ronsard's Sonnet Cycles* (1966); B. Stirling, *The Shakespeare Sonnet Order* (1968); S. Booth, *An Essay on Shakespeare's Sonnets* (1969); T. Cave, *Devotional Poetry in France 1570–1613* (1969); essays on Ronsard, Scève, and du Bellay in *YFS* 47 (1972); T. Cave, *The Cornucopian Text* (1979); J. de La Ceppède, *From the Theorems*, trans. K. Bosley (1983); R. A. Katz, *The Ordered Text* (1985)—du Bellay's sonnet sequences; J. Fineman, *Shakespeare's Perjured Eye* (1986); Hollier; T. P. Roche Jr., *Petrarch and the English Sonnet Sequences* (1989); G. Warkentin, "Sonnet Sequence," *The Spenser Encyclopedia*, ed. A. C. Hamilton et al. (1990); W. C. Johnson, *Spenser's "Amoretti"* (1990); A. R. Jones, *The Currency of Eros: Women's Love Lyric in Europe, 1540–1620* (1990); R. Greene, *Post-Petrarchism* (1991); E. Hanson, "Boredom and Whoredom: Reading Renaissance Women's Sonnet Sequences," *Yale Journal of Criticism* 10 (1997); R. Kuin, *Chamber Music: Elizabethan Sonnet Sequences and the Pleasure of Criticism* (1998); J. Holmes, *Dante Gabriel Rossetti and the Late Victorian Sonnet Sequence* (2005); C. Warley, *Sonnet Sequences and Social Distinction in Renaissance England*

(2005); C. Alduy, *Politique des "Amours" (1544–1560)* (2007), and "Lyric Economies: Manufacturing Values in French Petrarchan Collections," *RQ* 63 (2010).

R. Greene

**SOTADEAN.** In cl. poetry, a type of stichic verse usually analyzed as a succession of three complete major ionic metra ( – – ◡ ◡ ) followed by a doubly shortened (brachycatalectic) concluding one ( – – ). *Resolution and contraction are possible in any metron but the last, as is the substitution of – ◡ – ◡ or, in freer forms of composition, certain other tetrasyllabic variants. The meter was associated with obscene or satiric verse. Most examples are from the late Hellenistic or imperial period, the earliest Gr. ones being by Sotades himself, an Alexandrian poet (3d c. bce). The sotadean was introduced to Lat. by Ennius, but while it can be found in Plautus, Accius, Varro (*Menippean Satires*), Petronius (twice), and Martial (3.29), it was never extensively used in Lat. poetry.

■ F. Koch, *Ionicorum a maiore historia* (1926); Crusius; Halporn et al; West.

A. T. Cole

# SOUND

I. Theoretical Overview
II. Articulation, Acoustics, and Cognition
III. Recent Approaches to Sound
IV. Expressivity
V. Sound Effects and Sound Patterning in Poetry
VI. Conclusion

**I. Theoretical Overview.** This synthetic account of sound in poetry will recognize important devels. in poetry, poetics, literary theory and crit., ling., acoustics, and cognitive science without attempting to privilege one kind of knowledge over another. The topic of sound in poetry often raises an unresolvable theoretical controversy about the nature of poetry, namely, where the *poem exists: concretely on the page, temporally as a spoken verbal utterance, or liminally between the two. If a poem simply exists on the page, then what do its auditory qualities mean? If, as Paul Valéry argued, the poem should be approached as a musical score to be performed aloud, what happens to the poem when it is closed in a book and ceases to be read? The recent profusion of poetry in electronic and recorded media, which seems to present a new medium, a new type of *textuality, or what Ong has called a "secondary orality," nevertheless falls into the same two categories of visual representation on a screen or as hypertext and as oral performance recorded or streamed live. For present purposes, this philosophical antinomy may be resolved pragmatically: the poem exists in tension between the extremes of audible speech and silent reading.

The prosodies of different langs. focus on different qualities of sound (see PROSODY), and *meter typically focuses on one phonological element of lang.—stress, *pitch, or length (i.e., *quantity)—reducing the varying levels of such elements to a binary of more or less prominence. Some meters incorporate a second element in subsidiary patterns. This process, at work in every lang. and developed over time, is not subject to the whims of a poet since the element is intrinsic to the lang. Attempts by poets to select a different marker for the lang. (e.g., Eng. Ren. poets writing in *syllabic verse or quantitative meters) are generally academic exercises, because the lang.'s phonological features will, as Fussell has shown, overrun the intended metrical effect. While such attempts have played a constitutive role in the evolution of poetry and while poets consistently experiment with the limits of a given lang., nevertheless, the phonological limitations on the metrical resources of a lang. will dictate a native speaker's *performance of a poem or experience of one. In short, the rhythm of Eng. will trump syllabic length. Thus, the phonology of a lang. not only decides the meter but also typically locks the poet into the inherited trad.

## II. Articulation, Acoustics, and Cognition

**A.** *Articulation.* The place and manner of articulation of vowels in the mouth are often graphically represented by a trapezoid broken into nine sections, high to low and front to back. Consonants are created by impeding, through the use of the tongue, lips, and palate, the flow of air at different positions of articulation.

**B.** *Acoustics.* According to the science of acoustics, sounds are waves passing through a medium. In the case of voiced poetry, that medium is air (with the Fr. lettrist group of the 1950s, the It. poet Arrigo Lora-Totino experimented with vocalizing poetry through water; see SOUND POETRY). A wave from one crest to another is a single cycle, while the number of cycles per second is the *frequency* of a sound and is measured in Hertz (Hz). Although the human voice ranges from 100 to 200 Hz, the ear can perceive a range from 20 to 20,000 Hz. Middle C is 261 Hz. The higher the *frequency*, the higher the *pitch*. The intensity of the sound, known as *stress*, is measured in decibels, i.e., amplitude or a sound's overall power (the height and depth of a wave's crests and peaks). *Quantity* refers to the *duration of a sound. Meter is at stake when these phenomena are applied to syllabic lang. and patterned in accordance—or in opposition to—its rules.

**C.** *Cognition.* Contemp. cognitive science holds that the hemispheres of the brain process sound in different ways or to different degrees. While the left hemisphere, which possesses logical and analytical functions, interprets ling. sounds for meaning, the right hemisphere processes ambient sounds and music. Simultaneous words and music, as in song, are analyzed by both hemispheres of the brain at once. For poetry, both hemispheres function in the apprehension and analysis of ling. and aesthetic sounds. The left hemisphere processes speech rhythm and lexical-semantic sounds, while the right analyzes poetic sound patterning and the aesthetics of poetry (Turner attempts to show the relation of cognition to meter). Thus, poetry, using both hemispheres at once, makes use of both ling. sound and poetic sound, mapping both lexical pat-

tern and designed aesthetic patterns. In brain functions themselves exists the dichotomy of the sensuous and the semantic, of sound and sense.

## III. Recent Approaches to Sound.

The ascendancy of deconstruction during the late 20th c. largely relegated scholarship on sound to linguists and prosodists. Deconstruction's privileging of writing over speech left sound as a large gap in the analysis of poetry. The difference between langs. suggests that words are determined differentially. The difference in a single lang. between words like *bit* and *bat*, *puck* and *puke*, *lock* and *lick* suggested to Saussure that lang. was grounded through differentials, not the presence of word features. As Saussure himself observed, however, the etymological trad. does solidify meaning in practice (see also the discussion of *onomatopoeia below). Meaning depends on both the nature of signifiers and their hist. (see SIGN, SIGNIFIED, SIGNIFIER). Change clearly occurs through time, and the various forces of historical ling. are always at work (e.g., Grimm's law, vowel shifts). Transubstantiated as *textualité*, speech generally becomes a nonissue for deconstructionists and those who read poetry as they do, whether knowingly or not. L'écriture (writing; see ÉCRITURE) trumps lecture (speech) every time for Jacques Derrida; sound becomes a secondary matter in lang., if it matters at all.

However, beyond the meanings that may or may not be produced through the opposition of signifier and signified, lang. can also mean obliquely through *metaphor. Typically, when there is not a word for something, we do not feel the need to invent one, since no one else would know what it means. Rather, metaphor, *simile, and analogy generate meaning where there was none before (see Ricoeur). Metaphorical truth moves beyond arbitrary word-truth and encapsulates a role of poetry. It concedes or ignores the truth of the arbitrary signifier and moves in the opposite direction. While meaning can be perceived as just as unstable within metaphor as in lang., metaphor transcends the sign (sound-image and concept), and meaning emerges at the edge of lang. The meaning of the tenor and the meaning of the vehicle, when combined, produce something that was not in the originals when they were separate, namely, a poetic meaning (see TENOR AND VEHICLE). Poetic lang. revels in words, while their representational function is diminished. Poets give primary importance to phonological patterning and sound effects. When lang. is transformed into poetry, when pattern is made through sound, and when poetic effects are produced by sound, words construct meaning through their effects on each other and the reader. The following W. B. Yeats line (from "The Lake Isle of Innisfree") aggregates meanings through sound juxtapositions that did not inhere individually in words like *lap*, *lake*, *low*, *sound*, *shore*, *hear*: "I hear lake water lapping with low sounds by the shore." Meaning, constructed and resilient through sound, is produced in poetry outside the signifier-signified dichotomy.

In *La révolution du langage poétique* (1974), Julia Kristeva gives poetic lang. a sexually charged, prerational, and bodily importance. Essentially, she agrees with both Ezra Pound, i.e., that poetry is lang. charged with meaning to the highest degree (see "How to Read," *Literary Essays*, 1968), and Jakobson, i.e., that poetic lang. represents standard lang. charged with its infinite possibilities—its study comprehends the becoming of signification, i.e., meaning. She divides the semiotic (i.e., nonverbal signifying systems) from the symbolic but insists that both are inseparable from the signifying process. Kristeva privileges the semiotic as preverbal, libidinal, and corporeal, in opposition to Alexander Pope's rational sound symbolism, as expressed in his *Essay on Criticism* (1711). The semiotic, however, includes rhythm (its effect on the body) in a variation on Mallarméan poetic mystery and power. According to Kristeva, the communication of libidinal subjectivity is the ultimate object of poetic lang. The sounds of words become their expressive desire and expressive meaning. Thus, they do not echo sense in a rational way but rather echo an individual's unconscious, chthonic drives. Where Pope locates the importance of sound in the mimetic imitation of the meaning of a line, Kristeva finds that poetic sound vibrates deeply in the core of one's being, ultimately agreeing with Roethke and complementing Turner's discussion of poetic rhythm and the brain.

It is also important to recognize the emergence of a poetry that is concerned almost exclusively with the sound of words and not, or at least not primarily, with their meaning. Twentieth-c. devels. in *sound poetry and later *Language poetry exploit the disjunction between signifier and signified, transforming signs into mere sounds divorced from semantic content. The *Dada poems of Hugo Ball or Kurt Schwitters are among the many important forerunners of this line of poetic inquiry. Similarly, Bernstein (1992) has questioned when it is that noise becomes semantically meaningful. There are all varieties of meanings composed at the subsemantic or sublexical units of lang. production (i.e., onomatopoeia, grunts, groans, nonlexical voicings of dissent and agreement, etc.). Where Bernstein disappointingly finds meaning self-embodied by the whole poem, he does provide a starting point for the discussion of nonlexical elements, though not always sound based, within a poem. Such questions find a predecessor in early 20th-c. avant-garde music and the futurist noise-art of Luigi Russolo (see FUTURISM).

Slam poetry, on the other hand, is to a far greater degree concerned with semantic meaning, often a poem's political or moral message (see POETRY SLAM). Such poetry, frequently memorized, is located almost exclusively as an oral phenomenon and later disseminated in textual transcription or recorded performance. Emerging from the convergence of a textual avant-garde, popular music, and the poetry reading, slam poetry created its own oral trad. with its clearest analogues in the 1950s *Beat poets. Its sonic qualities are most typically *alliteration, *assonance, *anaphora, and paromoiosis; thus, its difference from traditional poetry lies mostly in locale.

**IV. Expressivity.** One debate about sound and poetry, dating to Plato's *Cratylus*, concerns the inherent meaning in sound; i.e., does sound express meaning? The answer is no, but with numerous qualifications that have fascinated poets. Meaning can clearly be evoked or connoted by sounds as in onomatopoeia (see also the concept of the ideophone in Tedlock), but this kind of meaning in large part corresponds to a historical train of significance. If words are signifying abstractions, onomatopoetic effects seem to express a generalized meaning based on natural phenomena such as animal sounds or water. Ultimately, however, when we examine the written words that langs. have for the sounds animals make, the *trope descends almost to the arbitrariness of most words, e.g., the Eng. *woof* and the Fr. *ouah ouah* for the sounds of a dog; likewise, the Gr. *barbaros* for *barbarians* was derived from the sounds the Greeks ascribed to other langs. While such words stem etymologically from sound imitation, their meanings are virtually as arbitrary as those of any other signifier, given their subsequent devel.

*Iconicity, the concept that there is an analogy or resemblance between a word and the object to which it refers, was propagated by C. S. Peirce. Mimetic sound effects accordingly become central to the representational system of lang. Subsequent research in the 20th c. demonstrated its existence in all langs. and at every level of ling. structure. For Peirce, the icon, one of three types of *representation, is a sign that resembles its object, however inexactly (*pop, hiss, murmur*—the names of sounds tend to be onomatopoetic). The *phonestheme (a term coined by J. R. Firth) is a phoneme that has a recognizable semantic association because it appears in numerous words with similar meanings and sounds. Such words seem to have a familiar, natural force on a reader and seem mimetically expressive. In "Vowel and Consonant Patterns in Poetry," Masson has observed this phenomenon in the different connotations of the word for *night* across langs. Wellek and Warren use the term *orchestration* for such morphemic echoing in poetry. Perhaps more useful to poetry is kinesthetics, which associates the sound produced or being produced with a semantic meaning (i.e., traditional sound symbolism). Richards (1929) and Ransom (1936) demonstrated, through a dummy version of stanza 15 of John Milton's "On the Morning of Christ's Nativity" and a *parody of Alfred, Lord Tennyson's "Come Down, O Maid," respectively, that the same sounds and the same rhythm, when divorced from original meaning, lose their expressivity. (For an approach to sound expressiveness via pragmatic theory and relevance theory, see Pilkington.)

**V. Sound Effects and Sound Patterning in Poetry.** However arbitrary sound expressivity may be, readers may often experience an echo of sense in the sound of lines like Homer's "para thina poluphloisboio thalasses" (*Iliad* 1.34) and Matthew Arnold's "roar / Of pebbles which the waves draw back, and fling, . . . / Begin, and cease, and then again begin" ("Dover

Beach," 9–10, 12), both purporting to imitate the actual sound of waves. Likewise, Milton's fricatives also accentuate meaning, as in "Out of my sight, thou Serpent, that name best / Befits thee with him leagu'd, thyself as false / And hateful" (*Paradise Lost*, 10.867–69). Any attempt to ascribe meaning to sound, however, should heed the warning proferred by Ransom's parody. Tennyson's "The moan of doves in immemorial elms, / The murmuring of innumerable bees" (30–31) becomes "The murdering of innumerable beeves," which demonstrates that, while sound may well echo sense, the same sounds in different words do not generate the same meanings. Sound as mimetic representation, thus, clearly entails a reader's recognition of the meaning of a line before the meaning of a sound pattern.

There are certain associations made with particular sounds, though there are invariably exceptions. High vowels tend toward brightness, highness, vivacity, sharpness (see COGNITIVE POETICS). P. B. Shelley's "To a Skylark" begins on a shrieking fever pitch of the four highest vowels, "Hail to thee, blithe spirit," setting the tone for the poem. In John Keats's "Ode to a Nightingale," the poet addresses the nightingale in appropriately high vowels in response to the bird's high-pitched song: "light-wingèd Dryad of the trees." By contrast, low vowels tend to convey wholeness, roundness, downness, heaviness, or darkness. Milton's "On the Late Massacre in Piedmont," e.g., is full of low vowels. In the final lines of the *sonnet, Milton's curse on the It. fields is set low, and the last line presents a steady descent "that from these may grow / A hundredfold, who having learnt thy way / Early may fly the Babylonian woe." Keats's ode similarly begins with low vowels of tubercular sleep before it ascends with the prospect of the nightingale—"drowsy numbness," the hemlock "drunk," the "dull opiate," and the speaker Lethe-ward "sunk." The final line of the first stanza alternates high and mid vowels, without low ones, before a striking ascent in the line's last syllable, "Singest of summer in full-throated ease." These associations are not, strictly speaking, meanings of sounds or abstractions but rather connotations that poets have traditionally embraced.

Consonants, too, have their feelings. Liquids, nasals, fricatives, and plosives produce their own peculiar sound effects and are often combined with alliteration. Yeats's famous lapping lake water illustrates sufficiently. The liquid consonants, *l* and *r* and sometimes *w*, are soft and melodic, giving the impression of water and smoothness, as in the famous Yeats line, or, in Keats's *Endymion*, "Wild thyme, and valley-lilies whiter still / Than Leda's love, and cresses from the rill" (1.157–58), which conveys languor and softness.

Nasals *m*, *n*, and *ng* (as in si*ng*) divert the flow of air into the nasal passage. Tennyson's murmuring bees imitate the insects with the string of nasals. Fricatives include *f*, *th* (both in *th*in and *th*en), *s*, *sh*, *h*, *v*, *z*, and the sound in the middle of the word "mea*s*ure." Milton consistently plays on fricatives; in *Paradise Lost*, book 10, Satan addresses the fallen angels as they turn into serpents: "On all sides, from innumerable tongues / A dismal universal hiss, the sound / Of public scorn[.] . . . punisht in the shape he sinn'd, / According to his doom: he would have spoke, / But hiss for hiss return'd . . . to Serpents all as accessories" (507–9, 516–18, 520).

The affricates *ch*, and *j* (as in "*j*udge") begin as plosives or stops and then, like the fricatives, rasp through a friction upon airflow. *J* is voiced, which means the vocal cords vibrate in its pronunciation. Philomel, her tongue cut out, throatily cries "jug, jug."

Plosives or stops—*b*, *d*, *g*, *p*, *t*, *k*—are the harshest consonants and are probably those the most often used to emphasize sense through sound. Yeats's "King Billy bomb balls" ("Lapis Lazuli") explodes in the speaker's mouth, while Pope twice uses plosives to imply constipation: in the *Essay on Criticism*, poets "Ev'n to the Dregs and *Squeezings* of the *Brain*; / Strain out the last, dull droppings of their Sense, / And Rhyme with all the *Rage* of *Impotence*" (607–9); and in the "Epistle to Dr. Arbuthnot" regarding Ambrose Philips, who "Just writes to make his barrenness appear, / And strains from hardbound brains eight lines a year" (181–82).

In *The Expression of the Emotions in Man and Animal* (1872), Charles Darwin used photographs to examine the facial expressions that occur with particular sounds. While Darwin did not concern himself so much with the actual sounds, Nims uses the photographs to analyze consonant clusters. Darwin reproduced a photograph by Oscar Gustave Rejlander of a woman sneering and exposing part of a canine tooth. Nims observes that most words beginning with the consonant cluster *sn* are as unpleasant as the expression of the woman in the photograph—*sneer* itself, *snitch*, *snob*, *snaggle*, *snort*, and *snarl*. The short *u* can be *ugsome* as in *ugh* and *upchuck*, *slut*, *sludge*, and *pus*, and in a photograph of Rejlander himself hamming an expression as he says the word *disgusted*. Such sounds can, as Nims says, physicalize a poem's meaning.

The use by poets of vowels and consonants to underline meaning in the line is often conjoined with alliteration or other nonfixed sound patterns to emphasize and underline the designed effect. These examples illustrate that, despite the popping of plosives, the mellifluousness of liquids, or the sliding of glides (semivowels *w*, *y*, and sometimes *j*), there is no inherent meaning within the sounds. The issue of sound expressivity or mimetic sound, while not a tenable theoretical position, provides an enactment of meaning or a gesture toward it. Poets dramatically associate sounds with the meaning of a word or line for emphasis or effect.

The archetypical demonstration of auditory pyrotechnics in Pope's *Essay on Criticism* delivers, as does the poem in its entirety, both the argument and evidence for the claim that "The *Sound* must seem an *Echo* to the *Sense*" (365). A soft wind must be demonstrated by a soft line, as Pope both says and shows through the repetition of the letter *s* (366–67). The loud, hoarse lines (368–69) likewise enact his own dictum as it roars. However, Pope alliterates with the same *s* sound, though the line is tempered by consonant clusters and heavy with monosyllables. Pope also envelops the two harsh, roaring *couplets (368–71) between the two soft couplets (366–67 and 372–73). The final two couplets of the passage (370–73), while spectacular for mostly metrical reasons, deserve analysis as well:

> When *Ajax* strives, some Rock's vast Weight to throw,
> The Line too *labors*, and the Words move *slow*;
> Not so, when swift *Camilla* scours the Plain,
> Flies o'er th'unbending Corn, and skims along the Main.

Ajax's slow, heavy lines are both loaded with monosyllables and consonants (even the typically mellifluous liquids are overpowered as they shudder and heave into the middle of the third foot). The first line of the Camilla couplet again repeats the alliterating *s* sounds, before moving into the fastest line in the Eng. lang. Line 373 sports more words beginning with vowels than the sole two in the previous Ajax couplet. The *elision and light vowels give the impression of speed. Lines 356–57 before this passage had castigated poets for using needless *alexandrines that are "languishingly slow," but Pope the metrical genius makes his speedy line 373 itself an alexandrine.

Sound pattern, like alliteration, assonance, paromoiosis (the *parallelism between the sounds of words in adjacent clauses or lines), *consonance, and onomatopoeia, can function to tag words of special importance. Sound patterning can then be used to underline the semantic import or key words of a line. Sound schemes are sometimes used to produce a demonstrable pattern on a higher level of design than simple repetition. Masson ("Vowel and Consonant Patterning") observed sequence (*abcabc*) and *chiasmus (*abccba*) at work in sound patterning and found them to be in consistent usage. *Envelope (*abba*) and simpler alternation (*abab*) of sound can also have broad application, although analysis of such patterns and their complications deserves further study. Consider, e.g., the Yeats line referenced throughout: "lake water lapping with low." The *l*s and *w*'s alternate *abab* at the beginning of each word. Such sound patterns can be used alongside rhythm to coincide or *counterpoint, just as, in Latin prosody, it has been suggested that stress was often patterned to coincide with long syllables in the fixed final feet of dactylic *hexameter.

All such sound-patterning shapes order and intensifies meaning and is, thus, essential to the analysis of a poem. *Rhyme is perhaps the most familiar sound patterning in poetry. According to Levý and others (Wimsatt, Hollander), rhyme, which binds two words that would normally not be connected in a prose sentence, produces secondary semantic effects, incl. ironical contrasts with humorous potential. Lord Byron is a master of this technique ("even when he prayed / He turned from grisly saints, and martyrs hairy, / To the sweet portraits of the Virgin Mary" [*Don Juan*, 2. 149.

6–8]), having learned it from Pope ("But thousands die without or this or that, / Die, and endow a College, or a Cat" ["Epistle to Bathurst," 97–98]). Or as Hopkins said, condensing this matter, "There are two elements in the beauty rhyme has to the mind, the likeness or sameness of sound and the unlikeness or difference of meaning."

**VI. Conclusion.** Sound, the foundation of lang., ultimately comprises the form and craft of poetry, subsuming meter; the schemes of alliteration, assonance, and rhyme; and the segmental phonemes of vowels and consonants. Such elements of sound have been analyzed with varying degrees of comprehensiveness. (See the only extensive bibl. in Brogan 1981.) There is no appropriate term for sound patterning as there is for *rhythm. Thus, *prosody* is frequently used to incorporate both metrical and segmental sound patterning.

Some have argued that there is a norm or experiential core behind the varying realizations of a single poem. Correct *scansion and recognition of rhyme depend on historical context. The study of recorded readings seems generally to assume this position by tracking the variety and range of differences. This approach ultimately proves, however, that there is no definitive performance of a poem. While there are a certain number of sounds that a speaker must get right to give a correct reading—the core or norm of the reading of a given poem—there are numerous ling. and nonphonemic differences that can vary from reader to reader while still constituting a perfectly acceptable reading of the poem, as one can discern clearly in the strange-to-modern-ears recordings by Yeats and what can be heard of Tennyson's. This wavering style of recitation, now out of favor, was "author-approved." An analysis of recorded readings should not, of course, be in any way seen as a foray into the realm of authorial *voice or the *intentional fallacy, in that the rightness of a sound is a matter of (1) historical devel. (2) an understanding of poetics, and (3) a recognition of design in a poem that is demonstrably patterned. Effects on a reader might vary, but the fact remains that designed effects occur.

Jakobson believes that every verbal element in a line of verse is transformed into an element of poetry or poetic speech. Though Jakobson's argument cannot be falsified, it is noteworthy in that it reminds a reader that both levels of lang., sound and meaning, intersect at all times in any poem and necessitate a synthetic analysis, treating neither in isolation from the other. At the same time, a systematic analysis of every element of sound, meaning, and their nexus at work is daunting. The interplay of sounds between themselves and on meaning fully expresses and accomplishes the craft of verse, as in T. S. Eliot's concept of the auditory imagination. Poetic lang. constitutes the poem and is creative action.

According to Wallace Stevens, the sound of words is their importance in poetry; sound is the principal business of poetry. The poet harnesses reality and makes a reader's or listener's first response an aesthetic one. As

Stevens says, "A poet's words are of things that do not exist without the words." We attempt through words to express the truth of our existence, our thoughts, and feelings. And we respond to these words not only with analysis but with our physical senses, as in the case of William Blake's mellifluous phrasing in "To the Evening Star," "to wash the dusk with silver."

■ F. de Saussure, *Cours de linguistique générale* (1916); I. A. Richards, *Practical Criticism* (1929); J. C. Ransom, *The World's Body* (1938); D. I. Masson, "Patterns of Vowel and Consonant in a Rilkean Sonnet," *MLR* 46 (1951); W. Stevens, "The Noble Rider and the Sound of Words," *The Necessary Angel* (1951); D. I. Masson, "Vowel and Consonant Patterns in Poetry," *JAAC* 12 (1953); "Word and Sound in Yeats's 'Byzantium,'" *ELH* 20 (1953); and "Free Phonetic Patterns in Shakespeare's Sonnets," *Neophilologus* 38 (1954); W. K. Wimsatt, "One Relation of Rhyme to Reason," *The Verbal Icon* (1954); J. Hollander, "The Music of Poetry," *JAAC* 15 (1956); Wellek and Warren; P. Valéry, "Poésie et pensée abstraite," *Oeuvres*, ed. J. Hytier, v. 1 (1957); *The Journals and Papers of Gerard Manley Hopkins*, ed. H. House and G. Storey (1959); D. H. Hymes, "Phonological Aspects of Style," Sebeok; D. I. Masson, "Thematic Analysis of Sound in Poetry," *Proceedings of the Leeds Philosophical and Literary Society-Literary and Historical Section* 9 (1960); C. S. Peirce, "The Icon, Index, and Symbol," *Collected Papers of C. S. Peirce*, v. 2, *Elements of Logic*, ed. C. Hartshorne and P. Weiss (1960); J. Hollander, *The Untuning of the Sky* (1961); D. I. Masson, "Sound Repetition Terms," *Poetics—Poetyka—Poetika*, ed. D. Davie et al. (1961); J. R. Firth, *The Tongues of Men and Speech* (1964); T. Roethke, "Some Remarks on Rhythm," *On the Poet and His Craft* (1965); A. A. Hill, "A Phonological Description of Poetic Ornaments," *L&S* 2 (1969); D. I. Masson, "The Keatsian Incantation," *John Keats*, ed. K. Muir (1969); J. Levý, "The Meanings of Form and the Forms of Meaning," *Paralipomena* (1971); J. C. Ransom, "Positive and Near-Positive Aesthetics," *Beating the Bushes* (1972); T. S. Eliot, "Milton I," *Selected Prose*, ed. F. Kermode (1975); A. A. Hill, "Analogies, Icons, and Images," and "Two Views of Poetic Language and Meaning," *Constituent and Pattern in Poetry* (1976); D. I. Masson, "Poetic Sound-Patterning Reconsidered," *Proceedings of the Leeds Philosophical and Literary Society-Literary and Historical Section* 16 (1976)—Masson's sonal summa and survey of eight national lits.; W. K. Wimsatt, "In Search of Verbal Mimesis," *The Day of the Leopards* (1976); J. M. Lotman, *The Structure of the Artistic Text*, trans. G. Lenhoff and R. Vroon (1977); P. Ricoeur, *The Rule of Metaphor*, trans. R. Czerny (1977); P. Fussell, *Poetic Meter and Poetic Form*, rev. ed. (1979); B. Hrushovski, "The Meaning of Sound Patterns in Poetry," *PoT* 2 (1980); Brogan; W. J. Ong, *Orality and Literacy* (1982); R. Chapman, *The Treatment of Sounds in Language and Literature* (1984); Hollander, "The Poem in the Ear"; F. Turner, "The Neural Lyre," *Natural Classicism* (1985); G. Stewart, *Reading Voices* (1990); C. Bernstein, "Arti-fice of Absorption," *A Poetics* (1992); J. F. Nims, *Western Wind*, rev. ed. (1992); R. Tsur, *What Makes Sound Patterns Expressive?* (1992); H. Gross and R. McDowell, *Sound and Form in Modern Poetry*, rev. ed. (1996); *Close Listening*, ed. C. Bernstein (1998); R. Tsur, *Poetic Rhythm* (1998); A. Pilkington, *Poetic Effects* (2000); D. Tedlock, "Ideophone," *Key Terms in Language and Culture*, ed. A. Duranti (2001); N. Fabb, *Language and Literary Structure* (2002); A. Hecht, "The Music of Forms," *Melodies Unheard* (2003); C. Noland, "Phonic Matters," *PMLA* 120 (2005); L. Wheeler, *Voicing American Poetry* (2008); *The Sound of Poetry / The Poetry of Sound*, ed. M. Perloff and C. Dworkin (2009); "Wallace Stevens and 'The Less Legible Meanings of Sound,'" *The Wallace Stevens Journal* 33.1 (2009)—spec. iss; R. Tsur, "The Poetic Function and Aesthetic Qualities: Cognitive Poetics and the Jakobsonian Model," *Acta Linguistica Hafniensia* 42.1 (2010)—spec. iss.

D. WOOD

**SOUND POETRY.** If poetry is the verbal art in which *sound and sense are arranged in ideal tension, sound poetry (also "sonorist rhythms," "phonetic poetry," or *poesie sonore*) alters this relationship by multiplying, reducing, or denying semantic reference, while amplifying the phonetic and aural properties of lang. Some sound poems attempt to generate natural signifying relationships between sound and meaning through phonetic symbolism; others use sound as antagonistic or indifferent toward meaning. Sound poems challenge the limits of natural langs. and produce the illusion of lang. before, beyond, or after meaning, from the Adamic to the utopian.

Surveys of sound poetry often furnish it with a long genealogy encompassing all ancient and mod. uses of preverbal speech codes such as *onomatopoeia, *glossolalia, the *incantations of *oral poetry, *nonsense verse like Lewis Carroll's "Jabberwocky," and Stéphane Mallarmé's formulation of *inanité sonore*. While these codes are among sound poetry's principal resources and precedents, the practice of sound poetry has fairly distinct origins in an extensive, international network of avant-garde poets from the late 19th c. into the 1930s, and it has been extended and theorized by neo–avant-garde poets from the 1940s to the present (see AVANT-GARDE POETICS).

In Europe, nearly all the historical avant-garde movements practiced a version of sound poetry. In the pamphlet *Declaration of the Word as Such* (1913), the Rus. futurist Aleksei Kruchenykh coined the neologism *zaum' (transrational or beyonsense) to describe poems he had written "in their own language," of which the most notorious example is "Dyr bul schyl," though Velimir Khlebnikov's 1910 "Zaklyatie smekhom" ("Incantation by Laughter") also anticipated this tendency. While Kruchenykh's poems deploy nonce words or write through source texts via lipogrammatic removals of all consonants (see LIPOGRAM) in the attempt to "destroy language" and install referential indeterminacy, more ambitious zaum' poems, such as

Khlebnikov's "Zangezi," dramatize a universal lang. of the future that fixes references at varying planes of psychic evolution, purporting to vocalize the speech of gods, birds, and other nonhuman phenomena. The Chilean poet Vicente Huidobro's *Altazor* (1931), the voyage of a poet-parachutist ejecting himself from the lang. system into what Octavio Paz calls a "post-Babelic" fantasy of ling. reunification, bears comparison (see CREATIONISM).

Experiments contemporaneous to zaum' in Italy include Aldo Palazzeschi's examples of a *poetica del divertimento*, playful poems in which infantile stutters and syllabic refrains are a refuge for the crepuscular poet discarded by the culture of modernity. Although he was briefly associated with It. *futurism, Palazzeschi's ludic sound has little in common with F. T. Marinetti's *parole in libertà* (words in freedom), a poetry that attempts to enact a synthetic *mimesis of the city or mod. warfare, most often through martial onomatopoeias such as *Zang Tumb Tuum* (1912). Guillaume Apollinaire voiced a familiar objection in his remark that this scientific notation of machine noise could be faulted as "gags" or *trompe-oreilles*.

In the germanophone context, *Dada sound poetry built on examples of nonsense poetry like that of Christian Morgenstern. Most often cited among the many varieties of sound poetry produced by the Dadaists, Hugo Ball's "gadji beri bimba," a cycle of five *lautgedichte* (noise poems) or *verse ohne worte* (wordless verses), posited a primitive refounding of the word in reaction to the commodification of lang. Performed at the Zurich Cabaret Voltaire in 1916, these poems offer a prophetic authority for sound poetry based on a magical "innermost alchemy" of antiquated words and a liturgical performance register, while also suggesting the babbling repetitions of a traumatized soldier. Other Dada sound poetry, such as Kurt Schwitters's lengthy *Ursonata*, established musical protocols and structuring devices for sound poetry, and Raoul Housmann's "optophonetic poetry" pioneered typographical notation systems for performance volume, tempo, and duration. Tristan Tzara and Richard Hülsenbeck employed the ethnographic imitation of Af. sounds, which North has identified as a ling. form of racial masquerade. Dada had a poorly documented but marked impact on the vanguard poets of the Sp. Caribbean, such as Luis Palés Matos, yet the misappropriation of pseudo-African vocables by Dada *chantes negres* must be sharply distinguished from the sound motifs characteristic of *negrismo* poetry of the late 1920s and 1930s such as that of Nicolás Guillén, who is also identified with the use of the *jitanjáfora inaugurated by the Cuban poet Mariano Brull's "Leyenda" (1928).

Despite the increasingly self-aware, international proliferation of sound poetry as a genre—esp. from 1910 to 1930—no poetry advertised itself as such in the Anglo-Am. trad. at that time. Sound play in the work of James Joyce and Gertrude Stein was instrumental to the late modernist notion of "the revolution of the word," and even Louis Armstrong's scat has been proposed as a cousin to sound poetry. However, the emer-gent orthodoxies of New Critical *formalism (see NEW CRITICISM) make T. S. Eliot's 1942 remark a mainstay of the anglophone view well into the postwar period: "We can be deeply stirred by hearing the recitation of a poem in a language of which we understand no word; but if we are then told that the poem is gibberish and has no meaning, we shall consider that we have been deluded—this was no poem, it was merely an imitation of instrumental music." As if anticipating and flounting such objections, Dada *bruitisme* and Rus. zaum' persistently employ *xenoglossia as a device. Indeed, the deliberate use of incomprehensible foreign langs. is a primary asemantic speech code in which sound poetry traffics, often in open response to the diasporic displacements of global cultures. Performed in the langs. of three warring nations at once, Tzara's 1916 "Simultaneist" poem "L'amiral cherche une maison à louer" (The Admiral Searches for a House to Rent) dilates this technique.

While even its staunchest proponents, such as Jolas, considered sound poetry to be a limited ling. strategy in the wake of World War II, the genre has a rich postwar life in Fr. *lettrisme, esp. in the work of Isidore Isou (1925–2007) and Henri Chopin (1922–2008), as well as in that of Bob Cobbing (1920–2002) in England, Ernst Jandl (1925–2000) in Austria, Jackson Mac Low (1922–2004) in the U.S., and later bpNichol (1944–88) and Steve McCaffery (b. 1947) in Canada. McCaffery, alongside Chopin and Fluxus artist Dick Higgins (1938–98), have been instrumental to the validation of sound poetry as a historical genre and performance practice. The U.S. Language poets emergent in the 1970s bear out that influence, as in Bernstein's remark in "Artifice of Absorption" that "there is no fixed / threshold at which noise becomes phonically / significant; the further back this threshold is / pushed, the greater the resonance at the cutting / edge" (see LANGUAGE POETRY). With some exceptions, Chopin's distinction holds that sound poetry before World War II is phonetic poetry, preserving an attachment to words and syllables as compositional units, while, after the war, lettrisme arbitrarily assigns phonic values to letters, moving sound poetry toward performance scores for "sub-phonemic" levels of noise. Postwar practitioners have placed greater emphasis on nontextual performance and recording media, often disseminating poems by tape recorder as in the works of François Dufrêne and stressing ambitious research programs over ludic play. Still, much *concrete poetry includes an active sound component, and the long *visual poetry trad. runs in tandem with that of sound poetry, as typographical innovations often enhance or dictate performance standards (see TYPOGRAPHY).

*Voice has become a major theoretical issue for sound poetry. Antonin Artaud's scream poems and Michael McClure's "beast language" offer an affiliation to sound poetry that reconnects the voice to biological priorities, while McCaffery has rethought the voice as a "paleotechnic" instrument in a wider media ecology. A third critical view, exemplified by the philosopher Giorgio Agamben, holds that written, asemantic speech codes are the textual figuration of embodied voice, opening poetry to an "unheard dimension sustained in the pure breath of the voice, in mere *vox* as insignificant will to signify." A countertendency could be located in a group of sound collagists and aleators working in the trad. of John Cage, for whom the approximation of lang. to noise often eschews the voice as a unifying performance principle in favor of random and found materials (see ALEATORY POETICS and CONSTRAINT).

Sound poetry has a complex but coherent status in the hist. of poetic forms, but it should be stressed that sound poetry also belongs to a hist. of dissonance and noise in 20th-c. cinema, music, phonographic reproduction, and radio, and emerges not by coincidence in a transformative historical period for auditory technologies. The generation of sound poets now reaching maturity, such as the Canadian poet Christian Bök (b. 1966), has suggested that the "theurgical," antitechnological reaction of early sound poets such as Hugo Ball is untenable for contemp. poets who may be the first "who can reasonably expect in our lifetime to write poems for a machinic audience." Bök's work in progress *The Cyborg Opera* refigures the sound poetry inheritance for an "undreamt poetics of electronica" or a "spoken techno" that he allies with the technical virtuosity of beatboxers such as Razael. Bök reimagines sound poems as participants in a "growing digital culture," as in his lettristic drum kit notation systems ("Bhm--T-Nsh--tpt'Bhm--T--Nsh [thsss]"), and he also systematically plumbs vernacular phonetic patterns: "my tongue muttering / an unsung lettering."

■ A. Reyes, "Las jitanjáforas," in *La experiencia literaria* (1942); I. Isou, *Introduction à une Nouvelle Poésie et une Nouvelle Musique* (1947); E. Jolas, "From the Jabberwocky to Lettrisme," *Transition* 1 (1948); G. Apollinaire, "The New Spirit and the Poets," *Selected Writings*, trans. R. Shattuck (1950); T. S. Eliot, "The Music of Poetry," *Selected Prose,* ed. F. Kermode (1975); H. Chopin, *Poésie Sonore Internationale* (1979); *Sound Poetry,* ed. S. McCaffery and bpNichol (1979); J. Schnapp, "Politics and Poetics in F. T. Marinetti's *Zang Tumb Tuuum*," *Stanford Italian Review* 5.1 (1985); O. Paz, *Convergences,* trans. H. Lane (1987); C. Bernstein, "Artifice of Absorption," *A Poetics* (1992); G. Janecek, *Zaum* (1996); M. North, *The Dialect of Modernism* (1997); G. Agamben, "Pascoli and the Thought of the Voice," *The End of the Poem,* trans. D. Heller-Roazen (1999); D. Kahn, *Noise, Water, Meat: A History of Sound in the Arts* (1999); S. McCaffery, *Prior to Meaning* (2001); T. J. Demos, "Circulations: In and Around Zurich Dada," *October* 105 (2003); C. Dworkin, "To Destroy Language," *Textual Practice* 18 (2004); *The Sound of Poetry / The Poetry of Sound,* ed. M. Perloff and C. Dworkin (2009).

■ **Discography/Web Resources**: *Text Sound Compositions,* RELP 1049, 1054, 1072–74, 1102–03 (1968–70)—seven records of the Stockholm festivals of sound poetry (partly available on UbuWeb); *Futura: Poesia Sonora,* ed. A. Lora-Totino, Cramps 5206-301–307 (1978)—six-record international anthol., available on

UbuWeb, http://www.ubu.com (best audio resource on sound poetry).

■ **Periodicals**: *Ou,* ed. H. Chopin (1963–68); *Stereo Headphones,* ed. N. Zurbrugg (1969–)—most issues include records.

H. FEINSOD

## SOUTH AFRICA, POETRY OF

I. Afrikaans
II. English

**I. Afrikaans.** The first examples of poetry in Afrikaans date from the late 19th c. and formed part of efforts to raise the political consciousness of Afrikaner people by elevating the status of the spoken lang. Afrikaans—derived from the 17th-c. Dutch spoken by the first colonizers of the Cape of Good Hope and influenced by Malay, Creole-Port., Ger., Fr., southern Nguni langs., and Eng.—to the status of a written lang. with its own lit. Because of the racially divided nature of South Af. society, this process partly excluded Afrikaans speakers of mixed racial descent who played a significant role in the devel. of the lang. The primary aims of the early Afrikaans poets were to inspire readers to fight for the official recognition of their lang., to educate, and to entertain. To do this, they focused on the lives of ordinary burghers, their folklore, South Africa as fatherland, religion, and topical events, also using humor in poems that contained elements of the surreal or absurd. The style was mostly rhetorical rather than original, naïve rather than sophisticated.

After the Anglo-Boer War (1899–1902), attempts to standardize Afrikaans and produce a body of lit. in that lang. gathered renewed impetus; Afrikaans gained official status only in 1925. This process gained credibility through the greater sophistication and literary sensibility displayed by poets of the "first generation": Jan F. E. Celliers (1865–1940), Totius (pseud. of J. D. du Toit, 1877–1953), and C. Louis Leipoldt (1880–1947). Their early volumes show the effects of the war, but their work included other subjects (the landscape, religion, historical themes, political matters), as well as a variety of poetic techniques and styles, incl. *free verse and the dramatic *monologue.

The following generation added new elements to the repertoire of Afrikaans poetry, such as greater individualism, eroticism, and cl. allusions; but it did not make the same impact as its predecessors. Toon van den Heever (1894–1956) can be regarded as the most important of the new poets, while older poets like Eugène Marais (1871–1936) and A. G. Visser (1878–1929) also published distinctive work in the 1920s. Marais explored new terrain in the volume *Dwaalstories en ander vertellings* (*Rain Bull and Other Tales from the San,* 1927), a small collection of stories and poems based on the oral trad. of the San tribe.

The early 1930s brought an important renewal in Afrikaans poetry with the emergence of a group of poets (N. P. van Wyk Louw [1906–70], W.E.G. Louw [1913–80], Uys Krige [1910–87], Elisabeth Eybers [1915–2007]) who consciously reflected on their vocation as artists. They argued for a lit. that would adhere to the highest possible aesthetic and artistic standards, taking the best in Dutch, Ger., Eng., Fr., and Sp. lit. as their benchmark. Their poetry was known for its confessional nature and explorations of inner life but also turned to topics such as hist., religion, philosophy, and politics. All these poets built important oeuvres in the subsequent decades; van Wyk Louw achieved the highest status with works such as the epic poem *Raka* (1942) and the volume *Tristia* (1962). Eybers dealt with female experience in poems of great sobriety and technical refinement in an oeuvre that spanned nearly 60 years.

The poets who made their debut in the late 1940s (D. J. Opperman [1914–85], Ernst van Heerden [1916–97], S. V. Petersen [1914–87], Olga Kirsch [1924–97], G. A. Watermeyer [1917-72]) reflected the reality of a modernizing, urban, postwar world in the themes, imagery, and formal attributes of their work. The most important poet of this generation was Opperman, whose poetry distinguished itself through its concrete imagery, symbolic layering, and verbal economy as well as its portrayal of racial tension in South Af. society. High points are the epic poem *Joernaal van Jorik* (Jorik's Journal, 1949) and the volume *Blom en baaierd* (Flower and Chaos, 1956).

The 1960s brought revolutionary change to Afrikaans lit., signaling the beginning of a strong antihegemonic strain in Afrikaans. This was preceded by the work of certain poets in the late 1950s. The immigrant Peter Blum (1925–90) published only two volumes before leaving South Africa in the early 1960s but remains acclaimed for the sophisticated, satirical, and challenging nature of his work. Ingrid Jonker's (1933–65) poetry is known for its surreal imagery and spontaneous musicality. She became an iconic figure after her early suicide and is esp. remembered for her poem "Die kind" (The Child) about the shooting of a child during political unrest in 1960. In this period, political verse was also written by Barend Toerien (1921–2009) and Adam Small (b. 1936), who used the Cape vernacular in his volume *Kitaar my kruis* (Guitar My Cross, 1961). The most radical departure from the existing trad. came with the work of Breyten Breytenbach (b. 1939), who made his debut in 1964. Under the influence of the Fr. surrealists and the Dutch experimental poets of the 1950s (see SURREALISM; LOW COUNTRIES, POETRY OF THE), Breytenbach wrote powerfully original free verse that transgressed boundaries through its use of every available register of lang. and the inclusion of startling imagery, explicit erotic content, and political commentary. Breytenbach's poetry also introduced Zen Buddhism to the largely Protestant Afrikaans trad.

The 1970s saw the emergence of several strong women poets. The most important of these were Sheila Cussons (1922–2004), who brought Catholic mysticism to Afrikaans poetry; Wilma Stockenström (b. 1933), who probed human insignificance within the vast theater of the Af. landscape; and Antjie Krog (b. 1952), who explored the compromised position of the creative woman in a patriarchal and racist society.

Although there were a number of new poets in the 1970s and 1980s who addressed existential issues in the traditional mode (Lina Spies [b. 1939], I. L. de Villiers [1936–2009], Petra Müller [b. 1935], T. T. Cloete [b. 1924]), this period also brought the introduction of poetry that openly explored gay sexuality (Lucas Malan [1946–2010], Johann de Lange [b. 1959], Joan Hambidge [b. 1956]), as well as "struggle poetry," written by mixed-race poets (Peter Snyders [b. 1939], Clinton V. du Plessis [b. 1963], Patrick Petersen [1951–97], Marius Titus [b. 1946]) in protest against the apartheid regime.

After the first democratic election in South Africa in 1994, new themes emerged under the pressure of the changing political and social landscape. Apart from exploring existing themes, poets focused on identity issues (Krog, Ronelda Kamfer [b. 1981]), ownership of the land (Krog, Bernard Odendaal [b. 1955]), ecological questions (Johann Lodewyk Marais [b. 1956], Martjie Bosman [b. 1954]), the position of Afrikaans in a multilingual society (Breytenbach, Diana Ferrus [b. 1953], Spies), and the new South Africa as a dystopia plagued by poverty, crime, and corruption (Toerien, Louis Esterhuizen [b. 1955]). In recent years Afrikaans poetry has seen a narrative turn, with poets using narrative elements, a parlando style, and a more accessible manner of writing in reaction to the existing trad. of hermetic poetry.

Although doubts were expressed about the sustainability of Afrikaans poetry around the change of the millennium, it regained its vigor and vitality by the end of the new century's first decade, showing an increase in the number of volumes pub. since 2005, as well as a lively interest in the *Versindaba* Web site (http://versindaba.co.za/) established to promote Afrikaans poetry.

**II. English.** South Africa first appears in Eng. poetry in the work of John Donne, John Milton, and John Dryden, in the wake of the Port. Luís de Camões, who creates in his epic *The Lusiads* (1572) the vivid mythological character Adamastor to stand for the dangers of the Cape of Good Hope. Anonymous Brit. visitors to South Africa, wintering from service in India, brought poetry to its shores, which, in 1820, became substantially colonized by Eng. speakers. The first South Af. Eng. poet as such, Thomas Pringle (1789–1834), emigrated from Scotland to the Eastern Frontier and adapted Scottish border *ballads and the Wordsworthian reverie for lyrics such as the widely anthologized "Afar in the Desert." Pringle also established *The South African Literary Journal* in 1824.

In 19th-c. South Africa, the violent conflict among Dutch speakers, indigenous blacks, and the Brit. gave rise to an alternate popular trad. of antiemancipationist verse in the person of Andrew Geddes Bain (1797–1863), who in the Victorian era used his polyglot resources for humorous purposes. His successor, Albert Brodrick (1830–1908), wrote of the diamond fields, the goldfields, and the early process of industrialization.

The Anglo-Boer War, which became a media event

(incl. the first newsreels), was the first major occasion of 20th-c. *war poetry that extended into World War I. Rudyard Kipling on the jingo side advocated imperial progress; Thomas Hardy mourned the losses due to the imperial war in poems such as "Drummer Hodge" and "The Man He Killed." Meanwhile, Beatrice Hastings (1879–1943), born in London and raised in South Africa, defended home rule through her writings for the jour. *New Age* (1909–14). Black poets, particularly in multilingual newspapers, began a trad. of protest against deprivation of human rights, which persists to the present day.

After the Union of South Africa was established in 1910, Natal produced two major poets whose careers developed around the cultural magazine *Voorslag* in the 1920s: Roy Campbell (1901–57) and William Plomer (1903–73). Both eventually settled in Europe to pursue right-wing and left-wing politics, respectively. Campbell's early *The Flaming Terrapin* (1924) combined influences from *imagism and *symbolism to assert a futuristic Af. life force, while Plomer's successive volumes of 1927 maintained a democratic, satirical view of the segregated south.

After World War II, many returning soldier-poets, such as Anthony Delius (1916–89) and Guy Butler (1918–2001), asserted a "stranger-to-Europe" view of their local culture with a white Af. sense of belonging in the subcontinent. This, in turn, produced the jours., societies, and academic disciplines that constructed South Af. Eng. poetry as at least somewhat independent of the Brit. mainstream.

With the accession to power of the Afrikaner apartheid government in 1948, Eng. as a cultural medium moved into an oppositional role that has produced a lit. of resistance written by blacks and whites alike. The banning or forcing into exile of many poets in the 1960s, such as Dennis Brutus (1924–2009) and Mazisi Kunene (1930–2006), further fragmented the poetry into an international diaspora whose links to the internal scene were sometimes tenuous. But in 1971, with *Sounds of a Cowhide Drum* by Oswald Mtshali (b. 1940), a period of intense internal publication commenced and gave rise to the Black Consciousness movement, notably in the work of Sipho Sepamla (b. 1932), Keroapetse Kgositsile (b. 1938), and Mongane Serote (b. 1944), sometimes known (after the June 1976 uprising) as "Soweto poets."

The struggle over the end of apartheid, from the 1980s to the 1990s, led poets to question the role and importance of poetry in resisting continuing effects of colonialism and reimagining the newly democratic nation after 1994. Important poets of the 1980s include Douglas Livingstone (1932–96), Lionel Abrahams (1928–2004), Stephen Gray (b. 1941), Jeni Couzyn (b. 1942), Christopher Hope (b. 1944), and Jeremy Cronin (b. 1949). With the transition to democracy, South Af. poetry—like other postcolonial poetries in Eng.—has become increasingly transnational and global in thematic content and cross-cultural formal experimentation. Writing in traditional Eng. forms, Ingrid de Kok (b. 1951) borrows from Brit., Ir., Am.,

and Caribbean poetic trads. Born in South Africa but living in New York, Yvette Christiansë (b. 1954) writes of overlapping Af. Am. and South Af. hists. of racism and diaspora. Although many South Africans vigorously promoted the antiapartheid struggle, they have also been sharply critical of the ineffectiveness of South Africa's postapartheid governments in transforming the social order. *Performance poetry by Gcina Mhlophe (b. 1959), Lesego Rampolokeng (b. 1965), and Vonani Bila (b. 1972), among others, has been a powerful venue for making black South Af. experiences seen and heard, both at home and abroad. A younger generation of poets includes Seitlhamo Motsapi (b. 1966), Rustum Kozain (b. 1966), Mxolisi Nyezwa (b. 1967), Gabeba Baderoon (b. 1969), and Isobel Dixon (b. 1969). Jours. as diverse as *Botsotso*, *Carapace*, *New Coin*, and *Timbila*; the publishing houses Snail Press and Deep South; and online resources such as *Poetry International* have published an abundance of South Af. poems. South Af. poetry is marked by its ling. and ethnic hybridity: poets of many ethnic backgrounds borrow from indigenous and foreign cultural resources to embody the diversity of South Africa, whether their work concerns violence and poverty, HIV/AIDS and economic globalization, race and sexuality, the domestic and the everyday, or poetry itself.

*See* AFRICA, POETRY OF; COLONIAL POETICS; POSTCOLONIAL POETICS; XHOSA POETRY; ZULU POETRY.

■ **Afrikaans.** *Anthologies*: *Afrikaans Poems with English Translations*, ed. A. P. Grové and C.J.D. Harvey (1962); *The New Century of South African Poetry*, ed. M. Chapman (2002); *Groot verseboek Deel 1–3*, ed. A. Brink (2008). **Criticism and History**: *Perspektief en Profiel Deel 1–3*, ed. H. P. van Coller (1998, 1999, 2006); J. C. Kannemeyer, *Geskiedenis van die Afrikaanse literatuur 1652–2004* (2005).

■ **English.** *Anthologies*: *Centenary Book of South African Verse*, ed. F. C. Slater, 2d ed. (1945); *A Book of South African Verse*, ed. G. Butler (1959); *Penguin Book of South African Verse*, ed. J. Cope and U. Krige (1968); *Return of the Amasi Bird: Black South African Poetry (1891–1981)*, ed. T. Couzens and E. Patel (1982); *Soweto Poetry*, ed. M. Chapman (1982); *Modern South African Poetry*, ed. S. Gray (1984); *Paperbook of South African English Poetry*, ed. M. Chapman (1986); *Penguin Book of Southern African Verse*, ed. S. Gray (1988); *Breaking the Silence: A Century of South African Women's Poetry*, ed. C. Lockett (1990); *Essential Things: An Anthology of New South African Poetry*, ed. A. W. Oliphant (1992); *The Heart in Exile: South African Poetry in English*, 1990–95, ed. L. de Kock and I. Tromp (1996); *The Lava of This Land: South African Poetry, 1960–1996*, ed. D. Hirson (1997); *Ten South African Poets*, ed. A. Schwartzman (1999); *The New Century of South African Poetry*, ed. M. Chapman (2002); *It All Begins: Poems from Postliberation South Africa*, ed. R. Berold and K. Sole (2003); *Botsotso: An Anthology of Contemporary South African Poetry*, ed. A. K. Horwitz and K. Edwards (2009). **Criticism and History**: G. M. Miller and H. Sergeant, *A Critical Survey of South African Poetry in English* (1957); M. van Wyk Smith,

*Drummer Hodge: The Poetry of the Anglo-Boer War* (1978); M. Chapman, *South African English Poetry* (1984); *Companion to South African English Literature*, ed. D. Adey et al. (1986); M. Van Wyk Smith, *Grounds of Contest: A Survey of South African English Literature* (1989); *Writing South Africa: Literature, Apartheid, Democracy, 1970–1995*, ed. D. Attridge and R. Jolly (1998); S. Nuttall, *Entanglement: Literary and Cultural Reflections on Post-Apartheid* (2000); A. O'Brien, *Against Normalization: Writing Radical Democracy in South Africa* (2001); D. Attwell, *Rewriting Modernity: Studies in Black South African Literary History* (2006); S. Graham, *South African Literature after the Truth Commission* (2009).

L. VILJOEN (AFRIKAANS); S. GRAY, O. HENA (ENG.).

**SOUTH AMERICA, POETRY OF.** *See* ARGENTINA, POETRY OF; BOLIVIA, POETRY OF; BRAZIL, POETRY OF; CHILE, POETRY OF; COLOMBIA, POETRY OF; ECUADOR, POETRY OF; GAUCHO POETRY; GUARANÍ POETRY; INDIGENOUS AMERICAS, POETRY OF THE; MAPUCHE POETRY; PERU, POETRY OF; URUGUAY, POETRY OF; VENEZUELA, POETRY OF.

**SPACE, POETIC.** Changing concepts of geographical relationships and accelerating processes of globalization, sometimes referred to as the *spatial turn* in cultural and social theory, can be identified in mod. and contemp. poetic practice. Lefebvre, in *The Production of Space*, explains that space is produced by human activity, rather than that activity occurring in an already existing space. The *free-verse poem can also be characterized as producing its own space, spreading over the page in unpredictable ways and ungoverned by any quantitative or qualitative regularity. Critics also have consistently questioned the idea of "place," a staple of romantic and postromantic poetry. Place becomes more than a bounded area within space and the accumulation of its own hists.; for Massey (1994, 2005) and other geographers, it is characterized as much by its interconnectedness as its exclusiveness. A "sense of place" becomes relational and its scale global. While national and regional poetries often use an idea of place to authenticate national identity or as unified places of resistance to colonial or imperial power through collapsing hist. into geography (see Gillian Clarke and R. S. Thomas in Wales, e.g., or Seamus Heaney in Ireland), other more experimental poets (Charles Olson in the U.S. or Roy Fisher or Lee Harwood in the U.K.) draw on a broader range of information to demonstrate the incoherent nature of places and their intersections. *Language poetry, a politicized movement from the U.S. that began in the 1970s, emphasized structuralist and synchronic ling. relationships within poetry to demonstrate the ways that lang. asserted and maintained structures of cultural and social power and control. As a consequence, the Language poets produced work that often lacked any relationship with an identifiable place in the material world. If there is a place in Language poetry, then it might be the specific poem itself, while space is that of the general lang. system. More recent poetry in the U.K. and U.S. has reintegrated a sense of place (and voice), while avoiding the more reductive or exclusive claims of earlier place-based work. It has developed elusive geographies and produced identities that reflect the process of the production of places and meanings that slip away or recombine into new meanings as perspectives and spatial configurations change.

The poem, in the process of its construction, also produces the space of the page. If, in an oral culture, poetry is distinguished by *rhythm and *rhyme (and Ezra Pound described rhythm as a form cut into time), then in page-based work, the visual design of the work becomes a poetic characteristic. A *sonnet, e.g., may be identified by its shape, and the regularity of the rhythm and rhyme of a poem such as E. A. Poe's "The Raven" may be guessed at by the regularity of the space it produces on the page. Free-verse poetry—the poem "All Fours," pub. in the 1990s by the Brit. poet Tom Raworth, is one example—often uses the visual appearance of the poem as part of the overall meaning. In "All Fours," the title foreshadows the four-line stanzas, their regularity accentuated not by patterns of stress or syllabic count but by a broadly similar line length, an absence of punctuation marks and capital letters, and the four walls of the house that features in the poem and a human figure that is on "all fours." Other work, ranging from Stéphane Mallarmé's *Un coup de dés* (*A Throw of the Dice*) to Eugen Gomringer's "silencio," uses the space the poem produces on the page to challenge the reading process itself. Mallarmé's text is characterized by the distribution of lines in a variety of fonts across the page in such a way that no single order to the lines or words is paramount and that different readings might produce new combinations. Gomringer's "silencio" baffles in a different way; its design suggests both reading the word from left to right, with a pause in the center, and a response that might itself be silence. Later poems by Brit. poet Bob Cobbing often have no text at all or occasional broken or fragmented words, and their performance often consists of subverbal sounds and gestures, giving a "time" to the space of the page. More contemp. poets have a range of digital tools with which to combine the spatial aspects of *concrete poetry with the time-based aspects of its performance.

A number of spatial concepts have been used to describe poetic form: the constellation (particularly in concrete or *visual poetry), the *collage in modernist experimental work, mapping as a process of making meaning, the rhizomatic as a description of ling. relationships in a poem, the nomadic as a process of inhabiting space without controlling it, and the situationist *derive* as a process of composition. Poets and critics often speak of the "architecture" of the poem and the ling. material as building blocks, as if the poem had three-dimensional form. The poetry resulting from these concepts tends to be governed by a logic of coincidence and contiguity. Things happen to be next to each other at the same time. Rather than the logic of cause and effect or a poem constructed from a single lyric voice that gives the "truth" of moments or relationships, such poems tend to produce multiple perspectives that destabilize any movement toward a single meaning. It is a distinction that may be exemplified by the shift in Frank O'Hara's work from the voice-driven "I do this, I do that" poems that apparently record O'Hara's walks through New York to the multivoiced "t.v." poems in "The End of the Far West" sequence that he wrote at the end of his life, where he combines voices from various sources on a fragmented ling. surface with a shifting left-hand margin. The rhizomatic, a concept taken from Deleuze and Guattari, describes a system without a center and without coordinates. It cannot be plotted. If collagist aesthetics and those of the *fragment are largely structuralist and synchronic, then the rhizome is poststructuralist and diachronic and concerned with simultaneously deconstructing space as it produces it. It has direction but also always has motion or flow and has no beginning or ending. These spatial concepts are descriptions of processes of composition but also support readings of a variety of "postmodern" and contemp. poems, in working with texts that seem stubbornly to resist closure and support varieties of competing meanings.

See COMPOSITION BY FIELD, CONCEPTUAL POETRY, TOPOS.

■ **Anthologies and Primary Texts**: *An Anthology of Concrete Poetry*, ed. E. Williams (1967); *Poems for the Millennium*, ed. J. Rothenberg, P. Joris, J. Robinson, 3 v. (1995–2009).

■ **Criticism and Theory**: G. Bachelard, *The Poetics of Space*, trans. M. Jolas (1964); G. Deleuze and F. Guattari, *Anti-Oedipus: Capitalism and Schizophrenia*, trans. R. Hurley et al. (1977); *The L=A=N=G=U=A=G=E Book*, ed. B. Andrews and C. Bernstein (1984); D. Harvey, *The Condition of Postmodernity* (1990); H. Lefebvre, *The Production of Space* (1991); D. Massey, *Space, Place and Gender* (1994); M. Davidson, *Ghostlier Demarcations* (1997); P. Barry, *Contemporary Poetry and the City* (2000); D. Massey, *For Space* (2005); I. Davidson, *Ideas of Space in Contemporary Poetry* (2007), and *Radical Spaces of Poetry* (2010).

I. DAVIDSON

## SPAIN, POETRY OF

I. To 1700
II. 1700 to the Present

### I. To 1700

**A. Early Romance Orality.** The origins of poetry in Spain are neither national nor exclusively Sp. Poetry flourished with many arts and sciences in med. Iberia under Muslim rule (711–1492). Thriving poetic communities in Ar. and Heb. antedate the earliest record (ca. 1042) of verse in Sp. (then called *romance* or Romance), in turn a century later than the first extant prose example. First recovered in 1948 by S. M. Stern, the *kharjas*, fragments in Mozarabic Romance (the

lang. spoken by Christians living in Muslim territory) or vernacular Ar., serve as lyric codas to *panegyric and erotic poems written in cl. Ar. and Heb. Used in *Al-Andalus (Muslim Spain) during the cultural flowering of the 10th and 11th cs., these brief single-rhymed *refrains stand in marked contrast to the longer *muwashshah*. Yet the separate parts are yoked in perfect symbiosis: the young girl's love-longing serves as a figure for a male speaker's formal expressions of humility, gratitude, or expectation to a political superior. Kharjas and muwashshahāt were invented and cultivated by leading Andalusian poets of the 11th–13th cs., incl. King al-Mutamid, Ibn Quzmān (1078–1160), Jehudah Halevi (ca. 1074–1141), Moses Ibn Ezra (1055–1135), and Todros Abulafia (1247–after 1300). Both forms speak eloquently of med. cultural interaction among Arabs, Christians, and Jews.

The vernacular refrains point to the existence of an oral Romance trad. of love lyrics in the feminine voice. The Galician-Port. *cantiga de amigo* (a girl's song for her beloved), dating to the late 12th c., launches the collaborative poetic trad. known as *lírica de tipo popular* (lyric of the popular type). Its earliest forms, refrain-based, are the *zéjel or zajal (another peninsular innovation in Ar.), *villancico, and *cossante. Codified, colloquial female-voiced poetry forms one of the strongest strands of Sp. *lyric. Its direct eroticism, set in the natural fertility of agrarian life, is heard in contrast with the tortured male-voiced codes of Occitan and Sp. courtly poetry and the tendentious voices of *epic and philosophical and didactic verse.

*Cantiga forms, intermingled with Occitan themes and song types, are also found in male-voiced lyric, most famously in the *Cantigas de Santa María* of Alfonso X *el Sábio* (the Wise; 13th c.), who offers himself as Mary's "troubadour," promising to abandon objects of idolatrous devotion. The 420 cantigas fuse praise and petitions with testimonials to Mary's intervention on behalf of efforts to return southern Spain to Christian control. Its text and musical notation, preserved in a ms. richly illuminated with scenes from the Toledan court and the frontier with Islam, constitute an invaluable resource for studying the intertwining of art and life in 13th-c. Spain.

It is telling that the first instances of Iberian Romance lyric should perform poetic crossings of lines of gender, race, lang., and class. In kharjas, muwashshahāt, and cantigas is foreshadowed the complex coexistence of multiple codes and compositional forms, each bearing traces of different national and ling. origins, that is a hallmark of Sp. poetry. In the later med. and early mod. periods, the interweaving of motifs and langs. shapes voices, works, genres, movements, and literary polemics. The strength of early oral lyric also works to extend poetry's ties with music well into the early mod. period.

**B. Medieval Epic and Religious Verse.** Epic trads. germinated in the conflicted political and social world of the so-called *Reconquista* (Reconquest). The *Poema del Cid*, saga of the life and deeds of Rodrigo Díaz de Vivar, is the most complete *cantar de gesta* (see CAN-

TAR, CHANSON DE GESTE), composed in the 12th c. and extant in a 1207 copy by the cleric Per Abat (Peter Abbott). Like other poems of the *minstrel school (*mester de juglaría*) lost and only partially reconstructed (*Poema de Fernán González, Los siete Infantes de Lara*), Abbott's version of the *Poema del Cid* draws on hist. and legend for its two plots, the hero's exile and his daughters' unfortunate marriages, stories connected through King Alfonso VI and his vassal's shared quest to restore Rodrigo's honor. The rise of Castile to political leadership and the emergence of Castilian as the dominant Iberian vernacular are both reflected and enabled by this remarkable poem, laced with appeals to a communal audience to endorse standards of vassalage, Christian soldiery, familial devotion, and personal honor. Among the poem's vividly rendered voices are Rodrigo weeping as he goes into exile, his men and wife Ximena, the young girl who defies the king's order to shun Rodrigo, hoodwinked Jewish moneylenders, and Moors calling on a Christian to rescue them from their rulers.

The broad popularity of minstrel sagas becomes clear in succeeding centuries with the emergence of the *romance* (*ballad), the most uniquely Sp. of poetic forms. Early ballads adapt epic into octosyllabic verses with a single assonant rhyme on even lines and no strophic division, creating a model still standard in the 21st c. Like the cantares de gesta, the anonymous ballads of the *Romancero Viejo* (Old Balladry) were *performance art, acted and sung for audiences before being transcribed and provided with musical scores beginning in the 14th c. Ballad families include tales from national hist. and legend (King Rodrigo, blamed for Muslim dominance, and celebrated in epic episodes), frontier encounters (Reconquest sieges, intrigues involving Christians, Moors, and half-castes), Carolingian chivalric material, and "novelesque" songs about faithful wives, adulterers, incest, prisoners, and sentimental treason (as in the famous "Fontefrida" [Cooling Fount]). As a group, according to Gilman, ballads speak a distinct poetic lang., used to conjure a shared past and a communal present. Ballad speeches often become proverbial, repeatedly cited by figures like Don Quixote and in colloquial usage. The trad. has offered poets of many centuries the lang. of conservatism on the one hand and of protest and popular empowerment on the other. Med. Sp. balladry has enjoyed a long life in peninsular orality and in Sephardic and other Sp.-speaking communities around the world, giving rise to later ballad genres such as the Mexican *corrido*.

Med. religious poetry reflects the larger contexts of two strikingly different centuries. The 13th c., under Fernando III *el Santo* (the Holy) and Alfonso X *el Sábio*, saw unification of Castile and León and dramatic Christian advances into southern Andalusia, while Aragon conquered Mallorca. With these successes, Castilian monasteries expanded their local influence and royal courts enjoyed a cultural flowering of the arts reflecting Alfonso's cosmopolitan cultural vision. Early works like *Vida de Santa María Egipcíaca* (Life of St. Mary the Egyptian) and the Catalan *Libre dels tres reys d'Orient* (Book of the Three Kings of the Orient) reflect Fr. influence. As the clerical style (*mester de clerecía*) coalesces in the form known as *cuaderna vía* (*monorhyme quatrains of 14-syllable lines divided at the *hemistich), poems such as the *Libro de Aleixandre* on the life of Alexander the Great and the *Libro de Apolonio* on Apollonius of Tyre, anticipate the work of the century's most important poet, the Rioja native Gonzalo de Berceo (ca. 1196–ca. 1264). Berceo wrote four saints' lives in verse (two associated with local Benedictine monasteries: Santo Domingo de Silos and San Millán de la Cogolla) and a number of devotional poems to the Virgin Mary (*Duelo de la Virgen* [The Virgin's Lament], *Loores de Nuestra Señora* [A Eulogy on Our Lady], *Milagros de Nuestra Señora* [Miracles of Our Lady]), all preserved in 14th-c. copies. His poetic lang.—learned, yet intimate and gracefully colloquial—reveals ties to the mester de juglaría, the cantiga trad., and *troubadour lyric. His *Milagros* show Berceo's familiarity with Marian lore popularized by Gautier de Coincy (1177–1236). The 13th c. also nurtured a lively trad. of poetic debates on religious and philosophical issues, notably *Disputa del alma y el cuerpo* (Debate between the Body and the Soul) and *Elena y María*. Another remarkable debate poem, made famous by the 20th-c. poet Pedro Salinas, is *Razón de amor con los Denuestos del Agua y el Vino* (Poem of Love with the Dispute between Water and Wine), which frames its debate with the dream of a young scholar whose beloved appears to him, speaking the lang. of female desire of the cantigas.

Three major figures and a pair of works reflect the 14th c.'s dynastic struggles, growing cities, and intellectual and religious ferment. Little is known of Juan Ruiz (ca. 1284–1351) other than what he reports in the celebrated *Libro de buen amor* (Book of Good Love, 1330–43), where he styles himself simultaneously as a wayward priest in search of erotic fulfillment and a penitent sinner bent on teaching "Good Love" to his fellow men. Framed with prayers to Christ and the Virgin, Aristotelian discourses on natural sexuality, and Ovidian lessons in lovemaking, his sentimental adventures move through social and literary worlds of unprecedented variety, evoked in multiple prosodic forms (cuaderna vía, traditional lyric, *serranilla*) and narrative types (notably the Oriental *alcahueta* or procuress motif). Ruiz's mirror of cultural diversity, the piquancy and freshness of his lang., and his own ironic and ambivalent authorial figure ensure the book's enduring popularity and influence. More recognized in his own day was the great Heb. poet Sem Tob ibn Ardutiel ben Isaac (ca. 1290–1369), known as Santob de Carrión. The dark vision of his only work in Sp., *Proverbios morales* (ca. 1350), whose text also circulated in Heb. characters, spoke powerfully from trads. of Jewish scripture and thought, using Ar., Lat., and Castilian sources, to communities in impending religious crisis. Two other texts at the intersection of three cultures are cuaderna vía poems about Joseph in Egypt: the early 14th-c. *Coplas de Yosef*, composed in Sp. in Heb. script, and the later Aragonese *Poema de Yúçuf*, in *aljamiado* or Sp. in Ar. script. A third figure from the public sphere, the chancellor of Castile Pero López de Ayala (1332–1407), anthologized his religious, moral, and didactic poems, with some Marian lyrics, in the *Rimado de Palacio*.

**C. Poetry of Fourteenth- and Fifteenth-Century Courts.** The reigns of Castilian monarchs Juan I (1379–90), Enrique III (1390–1406), and Juan II (1406–54) witnessed factional strife over royal succession, eventually resolved in favor of the Catholic Queen Isabel I (1479–1504), whose marriage in 1469 to Fernando of Aragon ultimately brought political unity with the taking of Granada in 1492. The period also saw widespread anti-Jewish riots in 1391 and a subsequent wave of conversions, ominous signs of the high human and cultural price that would be paid for national unification. But thriving courts, urban centers, and increased trade prompted a cultural renewal that Lida de Malkiel called a "Spanish pre-Renaissance."

Poetry of the 15th c. boasts its share of giants. Juan de Mena (1411–56) studied in his native Córdoba and in Salamanca and Rome before entering the service of Juan II as royal chronicler and Lat. secretary. Author of short love lyrics and political and moral verses, Mena owes his exalted place in lit. hist. to the long poem titled *Laberinto de Fortuna* (1444). Merging the goddess Fortune with the figure of the labyrinth, the poet creates an *allegory for his time that is at once political, philosophical, theological, and aesthetic. Alternating examples contrast Fortune's followers with those of a personified Providence, who ultimately points the way out of the maze. Politically, the *Laberinto* puts forward Juan II and the controversial constable of Castile Álvaro de Luna as instruments of Providence. Composed in *arte mayor* (regularly accented 12-syllable lines), the poem itself constitutes a maze of Latinate lexicon and syntax, cl. *allusions, and imitations that earned the scholar-poet the admiration of 16th- and 17th-c. apostles of learned poetry.

Another giant is Mena's friend, Íñigo López de Mendoza, the Marqués de Santillana (1398–1458), author of allegorical *decires, a poetic tribute to a Catalan poet contemporary (*Coronación de Mossén Jordi di Sant Jordi*), a *Triumphete de Amor* inspired by Petrarch, and the political poems *Comedieta de Ponza* and *Bías contra Fortuna*. Noted for his 42 *Sonetos fechos al Itálico modo* (Sonnets in the Italian Style), which anticipate the 16th-c. Italianate mode, and a *Carta-Prohemio* (Letter-Preface) on the aristocratic practice of poetry, Santillana is perhaps most admired for his eight serranillas, lighthearted, rustically erotic *pastorelas* (see PASTOURELLE). A third singular voice is that of the soldier-courtier Jorge Manrique (1440–79), known for fine *courtly love lyrics and a celebrated elegiac poem dedicated to his father, Rodrigo Manrique. In these *Coplas por la muerte de su padre* (Verses on the Death of His Father, ca. 1476–79) Manrique meditates on the transitory nature of mortal existence, celebrates his father's devotion to family and society, and imagines Death knocking at Don Rodrigo's door, received with "free and cheerful will" as a messenger of God's omniscience. The poem musters literary devices such as the *ubi sunt*

(where are they?) *topos and cl. heroic examples, biblical lang., and the med. trad. of the *danza de la muerte* (dance of death), intertwining them with simple imagery (the soul waking from mortal sleep, life as a delta of rivers flowing to the sea), simple axioms, and direct, intimate address of the ethical and metaphysical dimensions of life and death. Unique in med. poetry, this elegant fusion of elevated and colloquial registers, of popular and learned discourses, has earned the *Coplas* their firm place in the memory of Sp. speakers. A fourth figure deserving of special mention is the great Catalan lyric poet Ausiàs March (1397–1459), inheritor of Fr. and It. lyric trads., whose arresting psychological portrayals inspired numerous 16th-c. Castilian poets.

The *arte menor (short Castilian meters) production of the late 14th and 15th cs. is found in the period's numerous *cancioneros, which anthologize compositions representing decades of poetic activity. Chief among these are the Castilian and Aragonese *Cancionero de Palacio* (ca. 1400), the *Cancionero de Baena* (1445–54), the Navarrese *Cancionero de Herberay des Essarts* and contemp. Neapolitan *Cancionero de Stúñiga* (ca. 1460–63), Hernando del Castillo's *Cancionero general* (1511), and the *Cancionero Musical de Palacio* (1505–20). The cancioneros' aristocratic and chivalric conception of poetry as science, lettered ally of arms, suasory discourse, sister art of music—formulated in the poetics of Juan Alfonso de Baena (1406–54), Santillana, and Juan del Encina (ca. 1468–1529 or 30)—grows out of a courtly and urban context. Among cancionero poets and their audiences, there was considerable diversity of region, class, education, occupation, religion, and ethnic identity. Eclectic in content, *anthologies embraced many poetic kinds (political poems and panegyrics, *satires, religious verse, *love poetry) and verse and compositional types (see SONGBOOK).

Whether sacred or profane, elevated or colloquial, cancionero favor the code known as *conceptismo, which features a tightly controlled lexicon, witty wordplay, and a taste for *antithesis, *paradox, and contradiction. Their figurative lang. draws on social and bodily experience (wars, castles, prisons, cathedrals, servitude, wounds, plagues, death) rather than on nature. Courtly love poems represent the psychic anguish of individual subjects in the mirror (often inverted) of social and political order. Paradigms of frustration, defeat, and morbidity enact rhetorically willed subjection of the (usually male) body and soul. Like med. balladry, cancionero poetry and its *conceptista* lang. have a long afterlife in the polyphonic world of Ren. and *baroque poetry.

**D. Renaissance Reinvention of the Lyric.** The hist. of Sp. poetry took a striking turn early in the reign of the Hapsburg king and Holy Roman emperor Charles V (1516–58), as It. prosodic and compositional types brought the themes and practices of Ren. humanism fully into courtly verse, revising the traditional hierarchy of poetic codes. Spearheading the Italianizing movement were the Catalan Juan Boscán (ca. 1490–1542) and the Toledan Garcilaso de la Vega (1503–36).

Italianate modes held understandable appeal for these well-placed courtiers and imperial soldiers, who collaborated (Boscán as trans., Garcilaso as prologuist) in bringing out Baldassare Castiglione's *Book of the Courtier* in Sp. (1534). The two friends' works were published together (1543) following Boscán's death. The latter's poems feature Petrarchan *sonnets of frustrated love, a striking *verse epistle on the joys of married life, and a version of the *fable of Hero and Leander (see PETRARCHISM).

Strictly speaking, the Italianate revolution had begun a century or more earlier, with Santillana's experimental sonnets and with imitations of Petrarch by Mossén Jordi di Sant Jordi (ca. 1400–24) and March. But it was with Garcilaso's works that It. forms and the imitation of cl. authors were naturalized into the Castilian lang., altering it permanently. Running to a handful of villancicos, 40 sonnets, two *elegies, a verse epistle, and three *eclogues, the slim corpus won the young poet, killed in battle in Provence at 33, instant recognition; a host of imitators; a series of learned commentaries of the sort devoted to Virgil, Dante, and Petrarch; and the title Prince of Spanish Poets. Eclectic by contrast with the It. giants and dispensing with their Christian itinerary of sin, guilty penance, and the journey toward salvation, the Toledan chooses entirely secular subjects set against the competing backdrops of *pastoral's *locus amoenus* and the military campaigns and the imperial geography of his aristocratic experience. New to Sp. vernacular verse is his attention to idealized nature, human beauty, Neoplatonic love, and unchristianized cl. mythology. While continuing to draw on 15th-c. poets such as March and Garci Sánchez de Badajoz (ca. 1460–1526), particularly in sonnets and canciones, Garcilaso demonstrates familiarity with Lat. authors and It. models encountered during imperial service.

Most of his sonnets are love sonnets. Although often startling in their movement between the stark *conceits and insistent redundancy of cancionero codes and the copious sensuous imagery of Lat. and Italianate material, they nonetheless achieve unprecedented collaboration among these trads. Garcilaso experiments with the flexible structure of the *canción*, inventing a new type, subsequently much used, the *lira*, in the "Oda ad florem Gnidi" ("Ode to the Flower of Gnido [Naples]"). The solitary deserts and allegorical dramas of *Canciones* 1, 2, and 4 stand in dramatic contrast to the verdant island setting and political subtext of the third song and to the discursive coyness and mythological figures of the fifth.

Their choice of subject anticipated in turn-of-the-century pastoral dramas of Encina, Garcilaso's eclogues display the poet's extraordinary range. The three poems share themes, characters (Salicio, Nemoroso, Elisa), and the device of *ekphrasis*. The first prefaces two freestanding, symmetrical monologues of shepherds with a dedication to the viceroy of Naples, whom Garcilaso served from 1532 to 1536. The second, longest and most challenging, is divided into two parts, posing a pastoral drama about the shepherd Albanio's love madness against the river spirit Severo, whose ekphrastic description of an urn depicting exploits of the House of Alba is offered as a cure for lovesickness. In the third, an invisible poet describes four nymphs who spin from the sands of the Tagus river tapestries representing tragic love stories. Three of their stories come from ancient fable (Orpheus and Eurydice, Daphne and Apollo, Venus and Adonis); the last and most elaborate creates the mod. myth of Elisa and Nemoroso. The poem, whose Orphic dedication gave Pedro Salinas the title for his volume *La voz a ti debida*, also features an eclogue within an eclogue, as the poet catches strains of the exchanged songs of living shepherds, whose approach sends the weaver nymphs back into the waves.

In the *Eclogues*, the poet's figure occupies the center of Garcilaso's self-mirroring and self-monumentalizing creation, acting as protagonist, in parallel with military and political figures such as the emperor or the Duke of Alba, in campaigns of cultural conquest acted out not on a placeless allegorical landscape but on real geography (the rivers Tagus and Tormes, the Mediterranean, North African outposts, and shores of the Danube) as the poetic project of emulative imitation of ancient Rome coincides with Hapsburg imperialism. Garcilaso's use of Virgil's homoerotic shepherds and the *Aeneid*'s Dido as prototypes for tragic subjectivity, projected against ancient and mod. contexts, opens new avenues of expression for male lyric subjects.

Firmly established for succeeding generations of poets is the Ren. aesthetic of *imitation and the practice of syncretic appropriation from multiple models. Garcilaso borrows not only from Petrarch but from Dante, Jacopo Sannazaro, Pietro Bembo, and Luigi Tansillo; not only from Virgil, Ovid, and Horace but also from Lucretius, Seneca, Tibullus, and more. In the area of style, Garcilaso embraces the *hendecasyllable (11-syllable line—impossible to divide into hemistichs), melodious *cadences, subtle *enjambments, cultivated (though not obscure) Latinate lexicon and allusion, luxurious near-synonyms, narrative *pathos, and plastic idealization of human and natural beauty. Key to the success of Italianization was Garcilaso's demonstration that rich *conceits and melodic *syntax could be fused, elegantly and seamlessly, with the stark imagery, terse wit, emphatic *rhythms, and insistent *repetition of Castilian codes.

Success in courtly circles did not guarantee the Italianate coup universal acceptance. Cristóbal de Castillejo (ca. 1490–1550) called the new poetry and its jarringly new lang. to account in mock-inquisitorial proceedings against the suspect foreigners and heretics, charges that would resonate throughout 16th- and 17th-c. polemics. If some traditionalists rejected alien forms and diction, most 16th-c. poets opted for ambidextrous alternation between native and imported styles. Period anthols. and prosimetric pastoral *romances* like the Port. Jorge de Montemayor's *Diana* collect diverse examples of both kinds. The new poetics spread through educated, cosmopolitan circles, where humanistic imitation of It. and Roman culture was an article of personal pride and Sp. imperial ambition, refashioning cultivated Sp. to a degree comparable with Petrarch's reinvention of Tuscan It.

Among the first to adopt Italianate poetics were three other soldier-poets: Diego Hurtado de Mendoza (1503–75), historian, satirist, imperial ambassador to Rome and Venice, and author of sonnets on paradoxes of sentiment and *Fábula de Adonis*; Gutierre de Cetina (ca. 1510–54), native of Seville, soldier in Europe and Mexico, best known for the sweetness of his verse and for his *madrigal "Ojos claros, serenos" (Eyes So Bright and Serene), who (like Garcilaso) uses the ruins of empire as a figure for erotic anguish; and Hernando de Acuña (ca. 1520–80), friend of the emperor, author of sonnets and *Fábula de Narciso*, best known as author of the emblematic imperial sonnet, "Ya se acerca, señor, o es ya llegada" (Now approaches, sire, or has already arrived). In the next generation, a Castilian school of soldier-poets, incl. Francisco de la Torre (1534?–94?), Francisco de Figueroa (1536–1617), and Francisco de Aldana (1537–75), who died with King Sebastian of Portugal in Africa, contributed to the growing body of Sp. sonnets, canciones, eclogues, elegies, and epistles. A Salamanca school of contemplative, Christian humanist poets took shape around the figure of the university professor, biblical scholar, and Inquisition target Luis de León (1527–91), who translated into Sp. the Song of Songs and the book of Job, as well as Virgil and Horace. The Augustinian's Neoplatonic odes—notably "Vida retirada," "A Francisco de Salinas" (organist at Salamanca's cathedral), and "Noche serena"—set the standard for elegant clarity favored by Francisco de Quevedo (1580–64), who published León's poems with those of Torre in 1631 as a poetic manifesto against Gongorism.

To the south, a Sevillian school of Andalusian poets headed by Fernando de Herrera (1534–97) included Baltasar del Alcázar (1534–78), Juan de Arguijo (1567–1623), Andrés Fernández de Andrada (1575–1648, probable author of "Epístola moral a Fabio"), Rodrigo Caro (1573–1647), known for his "Canción a las ruinas de Itálica"), and Pedro Espinosa (1578–1650), who published an influential anthol., *Flor de poetas ilustres* (Flower of Illustrious Poets, 1605), and *Fábula de Genil*. The densely figured diction of Herrera's Pindaric odes (commemorating the Christian naval victory at Lepanto and King Sebastian's ill-fated Af. campaign), Petrarchan sonnets dedicated to the Countess of Gelves ("Luz"), canciones, and eclogues, representing the height of Sp. *mannerism, earned him the epithet *El Divino* and the role of ling. innovator, forerunner of Luis de Góngora. Fittingly, the schools of Salamanca and Seville produced the first erudite commentaries on Garcilaso's verse: the restrained notes to the ed. (1574) of Francisco Sánchez de las Brozas (1523–1600), known as *El Brocense*, and Herrera's encyclopedic *Anotaciones* (1580), which offer lengthy treatment of imitation, *metaphor, vernaculars, the passions, and Sp. national character. Enunciating a heroic poetics of Sp. cultural supremacy, the Andalusian scholar-poet champions learned *difficulty and figurative abundance but pronounces against *obscurity, thereby standing both as

a forerunner of the baroque and a rhetorical conservative who will be invoked in the battle over Góngora.

Throughout the 16th c., religious themes attract poets like Montemayor (1520?–1561), much of whose verse uses traditional Sp. meters. In 1575, Sebastián de Córdoba's (1545–1604) Christian adaptation "*a lo divino*" of love poems by Boscán and Garcilaso ushers in a vogue of Petrarchan sonnets addressed to Jesus and Mary (see CONTRAFACTUM). Partly prompted by these forgettable verses come the extraordinary mystical poems of Juan of Yepes or St. John of the Cross (1542–91), the Carmelite friar tied to Salamanca and, like Luis de León, imprisoned by the Inquisition. Using Garcilaso's five-line lira stanza, John's three most celebrated poems—*Cántico espiritual* (*Spiritual Canticle*, ca. 1584), *Noche oscura del alma* (*Dark Night of the Soul*, ca. 1578) and "Llama de amor viva" ("Living Flame of Love," ca. 1584)—draw deeply on León's trans. of the Song of Songs, traditional feminine-voiced lyric, cancionero conceits, and Garcilaso's own verses to evoke the erotic torment and rapture of the Bride (Soul) searching for union with God. The poet and his fellow Carmelite Teresa of Ávila (1515–82) use Castilian meters and the cancionero code to ponder the mystical paradoxes of learned ignorance and death in life.

**E. Imperial Epic and the New Balladry.** The Italianate turn also led to the reinvention of epic, from midcentury on composed mainly in tercets and octaves, dressed in *diction elevated by Latinate vocabulary and cl. learning. Imitators of Homer, Virgil, Lucan, Ludovico Ariosto, Luís de Camões, Torquato Tasso, and others could draw on a wave of prose and verse trans. into Sp., widely disseminated by printing. There they found Virgilian *similes, heroic orations, sea battles and shipwrecks, dramas of exile and discovery, fables of dynastic foundation, and philosophical and ideological lessons germane to national and imperial projects. Publication statistics put their broad appeal beyond dispute: Pierce finds some 150 Sp. epic poems in print from 1550 to 1700, often reprinted and extended. The largest number treat Christian themes (lives of Mary, Jesus, OT figures; saints' lives, crusades, miracles, and conversions). Notable among these are Félix Lope de Vega's (1562–1635) *El Isidro* (1599), a life of Madrid's farmer patron composed in Castilian *quintillas; his voluminous Tasso imitation *La Jerusalén conquistada* (1609); Cristóbal de Virués's (1550–1614) *El Montserrate* (1587); and Diego de Hojeda's (1570–1615) *La Christiada* (1611). Luis Barahona de Soto (ca. 1548–95) and Lope, among others, produce Ariosto spinoffs featuring the elusive Angelica. Celebrating Sp. hist. and legend are works such as Juan de la Cueva's (ca. 1550–1610) *Conquista de la Bética* (1603), Juan Rufo Gutiérrez's (1547–1620) *La Austríada* (1584, about the emperor's son and Lepanto commander Juan de Austria), and Bernardo de Balbuena's (1561–1627) *El Bernardo* (1624). Among New World verse epics are Alonso de Ercilla's (1533–94) influential *La Araucana* (1569–89), Gabriel Lobo Lasso de la Vega's (1555–1615)

*Mexicana* (1594), Juan de Castellanos's (1522–1607) *Elegías de Varones Ilustres de Indias* (Eulogies of Illustrious Men of the Indies, 1589), the Chilean Pedro de Oña's (ca. 1570–1643) *Arauco domado* (Arauco Tamed, 1596), and Lope's saga of Francis Drake, *La Dragontea* (1598). The 17th c. sees the creation of burlesque epics such as Miguel de Cervantes's (1547–1616) *Viaje del Parnaso* (Journey to Parnassus, 1614) on the *mock-heroic quest of Sp. poets and Lope's feline epic *La Gatomaquia* (War of the Cats, 1634).

Popularity of cultivated epic is matched by a new vogue of balladry, visible in the proliferation of anthols. of med. ballads such as the 1547–48 *Cancionero de romances*, the 1561 *Silva de varios romances*, and the 1600 *Romancero general*. This most accessible and easily improvised form is pressed into the service of news making, self-promotion, scandal-mongering, political manipulation, and mockery. Seventeenth-c. poetic giants gravitated toward the ballad. Lope de Vega, who styled himself in pastoral and Moorish ballads as the rustic Belardo and the sentimental Moor Zaide, also published a *Romancero espiritual* (1619). Luis de Góngora (1561–1627), who launches the captive's ballad, uses the form to appropriate Ariosto's Angelica and Medoro in intensely erotic verses and to subject cl. myths (Hero and Leander, Pyramus and Thisbe) to parodic deformation. Quevedo's caustic ballads send up cl., chivalric, and national myths; his most original contribution are picaresque ballads called *jácaras*, whose protagonists, the convict Escarramán and his concubine La Méndez, trade missives about their low-life adventures.

Bardic narrative, dialogue, and performative lyric are among the resources that make ballads the bedrock of poetic dramatization in the theater, where they play the leading prosodic role in the polymetric *Comedia Nueva* (New Comedy). Many plays spin out stories from traditional *romances viejos*. As ballads came to be written in a vast range of poetic and rhetorical codes, from the religious and aesthetic sublime to the obscene, they serve as sites for the intermingling of learned and popular (*culto* and *popular*), native and foreign, that spills over into other forms.

**F. Horizons of Baroque Poetry.** The mannerist transition toward baroque poetics begins to appear in the last decades of the 16th c., in the poetry of figures such as Herrera and the equally learned Aragonese brothers Lupercio and Bartolomé Leonardo de Argensola (1559–1613 and 1562–1631, respectively), in anthols. like Espinosa's, and in early compositions by Cervantes, Góngora, Lope de Vega, and Quevedo. The overwhelming majority of 17th-c. poets are literary polyglots, fluent in a variety of poetic idioms, rhetorical registers, and tones, and increasingly inclined to mix them. Heirs to Petrarch, Garcilaso, and earlier generations of their imitators, most poets were from the start avid sonneteers, though not—or not long—to the exclusion of other types. Many, as we have just seen, wrote ballads, along with other traditional Sp. forms like the villancico and the *letrilla. Italianate canción varieties continued in

frequent use; *tercets were a popular choice for verse epistles, solemn and satiric, and other long poems. In addition to heroic *octaves, poets gravitated toward the more open, irregular patterning of the *silva, famously used by Góngora in his meandering *Soledades* (Solitudes, 1613) and by Lope de Vega in his feline epic.

New thematic and formal preferences emerge. One is the long mythological poem, whose larger-than-life protagonists provide allegorical mirrors for dramas of *affect (love, jealousy, melancholy) and art. Among poems of this kind, Góngora's sensational *Fábula de Polifemo and Galatea* (1613), which adopts Polyphemus as a prototype of erotic frustration and his tortured song as the standard-bearer for the Cordoban's controversial new poetics, enjoys pride of place as the period's most original mythography. Along with Góngora's fable and Lope's *Filomena* (1621) and *Circe* (1624) came others: an earlier *Polifemo* by Luis Carrillo de Sotomayor (1585–1616), *Phaeton*s and an *Adonis* by Juan de Tassis y Peralta, Count of Villamediana (1582–1622) and Pedro Soto de Rojas (1584–1658), a *Hero and Leander* by Gabriel Bocángel (1603–58), and many mythological dramas by Pedro Calderón de la Barca (1601–81) and others, incl. the Mexican nun Sor Juana Inés de la Cruz (ca. 1648–95).

The choice of outsized allegorical *personifications of the poet went along with flamboyant self-fashioning and complex poetic *personas made up of contradictory extremes. Two cases in point are Lope de Vega, whose Petrarchan *Rimas* (1602) are transmuted *a lo divino* into histrionic confessionals and penance in his *Rimas sacras* (1614) and later subjected to a festive send-up in the *Rimas humanas y divinas* (1634) of his alter ego, the Licenciado Tomé de Burguillos. Quevedo's verse spans perhaps the most extreme range of moods and tastes, running from the spiritual sublime of *Un Heráclito cristiano* (1613) and the erotic sublime of love lyrics to biting satire sonnets and taste for the grotesque, obscene, and scatological. Affinity for extreme contrasts generates ubiquitous antitheses and the baroque *coincidentia oppositorum* of the conceit.

Publication hist. in this period tells its own story. Many poets did not gather their own work in pub. volumes but instead circulated it in ms., recited it in *poetic contests and meetings of literary academies, or contributed it to collections. Many published discrete works separately, as Lope de Vega did often. Cervantes left his lyrics scattered throughout his prose works; Góngora circulated his major poems in ms. only; and Quevedo, like his Andalusian rival, left most of his poetry to be collected after his death. In this age of inflated opulence and class-enforced leisure, poetry was a social practice and a widespread one at that. Many complained that there were far too many aspiring poets; others could rejoice that practicing poets included women like María de Zayas y Sotomayor (1590–1669?) and Catalina Clara Ramírez de Guzmán (1611–70?).

Poetry's popularity meant that its form and matter could become burning questions for society. The central issue for early 17th-c. Spain was the proper nature of poetic lang. and the purpose (moral, social, episte-mological) of poetry itself. Tensions over competition between Sp. and Italianate styles boiled over in reaction to the ms. circulation (1613–14) of Góngora's *Polifemo* and the unfinished *Soledades*. Enthusiasts of the poems' layered *artifice seized on this new New Poetry, which would earn the poet posthumous epithets such as the Sp. Homer and the Andalusian Pindar, as heroic cultural triumph. But critics including Juan de Jáuregui (1583–1641) and Francisco Cascales (1564–1642) decried their prohibitive difficulty as the mask of heresy (the pejorative term *culteranismo*, used to caricature Góngora's style, is modeled on *Luteranismo* or Lutheranism) or atheistic nihilism, designed to bring down the edifice of Poetry and Culture. The poet, once hailed as Prince of Light, became a Luciferine Prince of Darkness. Lope and Quevedo joined the traditionalist assault claiming that Góngora's multiple metaphors, Latinate lang., and cl. allusions were anti-Sp. They proposed native conceptismo, based on *agudeza or *wit—which Baltasar Gracián (1601–58) would honor as the quintessential Sp. attribute in his *Agudeza y arte de ingenio* (*Cleverness and the Art of Wit*, 1642, rev. ed. 1648)—rather than on *ornament, as the intellectually and politically respectable choice. Over critics' objections, many poets imitated Góngora eagerly; most were influenced by his verse. Indeed, while partisan rhet. made culteranismo and conceptismo appear to be worlds apart, it is not easy to find clear examples of one or the other. Superficially imitated in the 18th c. and discredited in the 19th, this baroque giant would be resurrected by the Generation of 1927 as artistic patron of a poetics centered on the *image and on ling. freedom.

Debts to Counter-Reformation theology are implicit in the contradictory baroque aesthetic, which embraces corporeal beauty, opulence, and artifice, only—or the better—to represent their disintegration, disappearance, and annihilation. Among the period's most exquisite poems are sonnets by Góngora ("Mientras por competir con tu cabello" [As long as, to compete with your hair], "Ilustre y hermosísima María" [Illustrious and Beautiful Maria], "Menos solicitó veloz saeta" [Less swiftly did the arrow seek]) and Quevedo ("Cerrar podrá mis ojos" [My eyes may be closed], "¡Ah de la vida!" [Is any life home?], "Miré los muros de la patria mía" [I gazed upon my walls]) that reflect acute consciousness of the imminence of death. Frequent effects of ling. and sensory trickery (*hyperbaton, *paronomasia, *catachresis, paradox, *trompe-l'oeil*, dreams) set up dramas in which illusion is ritually succeeded by disillusion, the baroque *desengaño*. These interests give poetry strong ties to comedies of trickery such as Tirso de Molina's (1584–1648) *El burlador de Sevilla* (*The Trickster of Seville*, 1630), philosophical plays such as Calderón's *La vida es sueño* (*Life Is a Dream*, 1635–36), allegorical and liturgical drama, painting, architecture, ekphrasis, *emblems, and public ceremonials.

The relevance of Spain's trans-Atlantic experience to the evolution of baroque poetry is generally acknowledged, though the nature of that relation remains unclear. It is often said that the peninsular baroque was exported to *Spanish America, where it did some of its most exuberant flowering. But there is considerable evidence to suggest that the baroque style may be as much a response to awareness of that New World as a cultural gift to it. Words, proper names, and poetic rhythms in Lope; Góngora's gold, silver, and gems; Quevedo's obsession with Sp. greed, alchemy, the perils of navigation, and nouveau riche intruders—such references work to make the New World the invisible backdrop against which dramas of desire, identity, and cultural values are played out.

## II. 1700 to the Present

**A. *The Eighteenth Century.*** The death in 1681 of Calderón, the last major author of the Sp. baroque, marked the end of an epoch. The 1737 *Poética* of Ignacio de Luzán (1702–54)—heavily indebted to It. sources and somewhat less to Nicolas Boileau—denounced the excesses of baroque poetry, esp. Góngora and his followers, but did not lead immediately to a vital Sp. neoclassicism (see NEOCLASSICAL POETICS). The canonical poets of the 18th c., in fact, are clustered in the last third of the century. Sp. lit. of this period is still the object of a great deal of condescension. In the standard view, the turn away from the achievements of the Sp. baroque, together with the emulation of Fr. neoclassical poetics, led to an epoch of dutifully mediocre verse. Not coincidentally, other genres of imaginative writing suffered a similar fate during this period. The theater fared better than prose fiction, but provided little that might be compared to the achievements of the *siglo de oro* (Golden Age) of Lope de Vega and Calderón.

Some critics continue to value the poetry of the 18th c. only to the extent that it is preromantic (see PREROMANTICISM)—as though the neoclassical aesthetic itself were inherently devoid of interest. From the perspective of intellectual hist., however, we can see this period as one in which prominent Enlightenment figures, *ilustrados*, used the medium of verse along with that of prose, and for similar ends. Eighteenth-c. writers held a Horatian idea of verse as a medium suited to a wide variety of purposes, incl. satire, epistle, and moral instruction. Many significant intellectuals of the Sp. Enlightenment left behind a significant body of verse along with their prose writings. The result is a healthy diversity of genres, metrical forms, and poetic subjects.

The most prominent poet of the century was Juan Meléndez Valdés (1754–1817), who imitated Alexander Pope's *Essay on Man* and participated in the vogue for *anacreontic odes. This genre, practiced by many other poets of the period, incl. others in Meléndez Valdés's circle such as José Cadalso (1741–82), was devoted to the celebration of the pleasures of life. The animal fables in verse of Tomás de Iriarte (1750–91) and Félix María de Samaniego (1745–1801) are also worthy of note, although Iriarte is now better regarded than Samaniego. Neither is as significant as Jean de La

Fontaine is for Fr. lit. Nicolás Fernández de Moratín (1737–80) practiced a Horatian aesthetic of instructing and delighting, devoting poems to bullfighting and prostitution. Gaspar Melchor de Jovellanos (1744–1811), the most prominent thinker of his time, also left behind a significant number of poems. He is perhaps the best model of the *ilustrado* whose works of literary creation form part of a larger intellectual project but who does not conform to the postromantic ideal of the literary creator.

Cadalso's preromantic anguish is more in tune with later taste, although, in this case, the poetic prose of *Noches lúgubres* (Lugubrious Nights, 1798) remains somewhat better known than the verse of *Ocios de mi juventud* (Leisures of my Youth, 1781).

**B. *The Nineteenth Century.*** Sp. *romanticism has been disparaged, in much the same way Sp. neoclassicism was, as belated, lacking in first-rate poets, and overly derivative of foreign models. The failure of neoclassical poetics, in this conventional view, derives from a weak and imitative Sp. Enlightenment, whereas the weakness of Sp. romanticism parallels the political failure of liberalism, repressed by the regime of Fernando VII (1813–33).

The historical *romances* of Ángel de Saavedra, Duke of Rivas (1791–1865) are of interest mostly to specialists, though they kept alive the ballad trad. that had always been a part of Sp. popular culture. This trad. had persisted in the anonymous *romances de ciego* (blind man's ballads) of the 17th and 18th cs.—a genre often disparaged by Enlightenment intellectuals. José Zorrilla (1817–93), whose most famous work was the play *Don Juan Tenorio* (1844), originally made his name with a funeral oration in verse read at the funeral of José de Larra, the prominent essayist who committed suicide in 1837. Like Larra, the Byronic José de Espronceda (1808–42) died young. His long poem, *El estudiante de Salamanca* (1840), reprises the Don Juan myth. He wrote two other long poems, *El diablo mundo* (1841) and *Canto a Teresa* (1837), preserving some of the generic diversity of the neoclassical period.

The Sevillian Gustavo Adolfo Bécquer (1836–70) wrote romantic poetry long after the heyday of Eur. romanticism. His adaptation of some features of the oral trad., such as assonant rhyme, makes him a favorite of 20th-c. poet Luis Cernuda. Most other 19th-c. Sp. poets, in contrast, are given to overblown rhet. Rosalía de Castro (1837–85), one of the most interesting figures of the period, wrote poetry both in Sp. and in Galician and is often compared to Bécquer. Her major work in Sp. was *En las orillas del Sar* (On the Banks of the Sar, 1884). Castro was not the only female poet of the century: Carolina Coronado (1821–1911) and Gertrudis Gómez de Avellaneda (1814–73) were more or less conventional romantic poets who enjoyed some popularity.

While not a poet himself, the Sp. folklorist Antonio Machado y Álvarez (1848–93) collected the lyrics of the *cante jondo in two major anthols., anticipating the neopopularist movement of the early 20th c.

and the work of his own sons, Antonio and Manuel Machado. The latter part of the century also saw the satirical *Humoradas* of Ramón del Campoamor (1817–1901) and the patriotic verse of Gaspar Núñez de Arce (1834–1903). Something of the 18th-c. impulse toward generic diversity and moral edification persists in the work of these poets, who otherwise have little to offer. The residence in Spain of the Nicaraguan poet Rubén Darío, beginning in 1898, introduced *modernismo to the peninsula, a welcome antidote to the prosaic poetic *realism of Campoamor.

**C. *The Twentieth Century and Beyond.*** Two influential poets stand at the beginning of the 20th c.: Antonio Machado (1875–1939) and Juan Ramón Jiménez (1881–1958). Both come to reject the perceived excesses of modernismo, with its ornamental conception of verse. Machado, following Bécquer, purified his style in the neosymbolist *Soledades, Galerías y otros poemas* (Solitudes, Passageways, and Other Poems, 1907). *Campos de Castilla* (Fields of Castile, 1912) is another emblematic book, bringing the consciousness of Sp. *decadence characteristic of other writers of the so-called Generation of 1898. Machado famously defined himself as "good, in the good sense of the word" and denounced the decadence of a Castilian culture that "despises all that it does not know." Such phrases have become touchstones for subsequent Sp. poets and intellectuals.

Jiménez, like Machado, rejected modernismo but did so in order to pursue an even more rigorous stylistic perfection. In so doing, he became the sponsor of high modernist projects like those of José Ángel Valente. He has often been disparaged for developing a kind of narcissistic poetics, even as he was admired for his devotion to his craft. Jorge Guillén (1893–1984) and Pedro Salinas (1891–1951) began as neosymbolist poets influenced by Jiménez's *pure poetry. Salinas is known mostly for the rather abstract love poetry of *La voz a ti debida* (My Voice Because of You, 1936). Guillén, while a close friend of Salinas, is ultimately a different sort of poet: he devised a formally elaborate discourse to express a jubilant vision of a reality subjected to the poet's ordering imagination. The second ed. of *Cántico*, pub. in 1936, collected his most enduring poetry.

The most celebrated poet of the 1920s and 1930s is Federico García Lorca (1898–1936). In Spain, Lorca is known mostly as a neopopularist poet, somewhat akin to the virtuosic Rafael Alberti (1902–99). Internationally, he is the sponsor of the *duende* and the quasi-surrealist author of *Poeta en Nueva York* (Poet in New York), which was not published until 1940. His most popular work in his own lifetime was the 1928 *Primer romancero gitano* (First Gypsy Ballad Book). His most significant influence has been on the poetry of the U.S., where Af. Am. and gay poets took up his cause. Lorca is known in the Eng.-speaking world primarily as a "Spanish surrealist," but he was not, in fact, affiliated with *surrealism. The surrealist-influenced poetry of Vicente Aleixandre (1898–1984) and Luis Cernuda (1902–63), along with analogous works by the Chilean poet Pablo Neruda (who resided in Spain in the 1930s), has had an enthusiastic reception in the Eng.-speaking world; but, in reality, most Sp. poetry of this period was not surrealist.

The period from about 1918 to 1936 is a fertile one, with a profusion of styles arising in rapid succession: the pure poetry of Jiménez, Guillén, and Salinas; *ultraísm, an avant-garde movement derived from Vicente Huidobro's Chilean *creationism; neopopularism; some short-lived experiments in a neobaroque aesthetic (Alberti's *Cal y canto* [1929], e.g.); neoclassicism; and the quasi-surrealist mode seen in some books of Aleixandre and Cernuda. In many cases, a single poet might experiment with two or three of these styles with no sense of contradiction. Alberti and Gerardo Diego (1896–1987) were poets of great flexibility and virtuosity.

During the Sp. Civil War (1936–39), poets affiliated with both sides wrote ballads to be sung on the front lines. Miguel Hernández (1910–42), who died of tuberculosis in a Francoist prison, composed the heart-wrenching "Nanas de la cebolla" (Lullaby of the Onion) lamenting that his young son had only onions to eat. His *Romancero y cancionero de ausencias* (Ballads and Songs of Absence, 1958), to which this poem belongs, turns away from the neobaroque style of his prewar work as well as from the propagandistic rhet. of his war poetry. Poets on the right included Luis Rosales (1910–92), Luis Felipe Vivanco (1907–75), and Manuel Machado (1874–1947), the latter an erstwhile follower of Darío's modernismo. Many poets who initially supported the military rebellion became dissidents during the ensuing Franco dictatorship, experiencing a kind of "inner exile."

The assassination of Lorca at the beginning of the war, the death of Antonio Machado in 1939 as he was fleeing to France, and the exile of numerous other significant figures (Salinas, Guillén, Cernuda, Alberti) left a void in Sp. poetry of the postwar period. Prominent poets who remained behind in Spain included Diego, Dámaso Alonso (1898–1990), and Aleixandre. Aleixandre became a mentor to young poets of successive generations within Spain and would go on to win the Nobel Prize in 1984. Major works written by exile poets include Salinas's *El contemplado* (The Contemplated One, 1946), a set of formally virtuosic variations on a single theme, the contemplation of the sea, and Jiménez's densely metaphysical *Dios deseado y deseante* (God Desired and Desiring, 1949). Jiménez won the Nobel Prize in 1956. Cernuda's dramatic *monologues, collected in successive editions of *La realidad y el deseo* (Reality and Desire, 1936) were more influential on subsequent Sp. poets than any other comparable figure. His final work, *Desolación de la quimera* (Desolation of the Chimera, 1962), contains vitriolic attacks on figures of his own generation such as Salinas and Alonso.

The *Garcilasismo* of José García Nieto (1914–2001), emphasizing traditional forms and patriotic content, enjoyed a brief vogue in the 1940s. This movement was a carryover from the neoclassical trend of the years immediately before the war. The major movement in

postwar poetry, however, was the social poetry of Blas de Otero (1916–79) and José Hierro (1922–2002). These poets are both masters of traditional verse. Otero began with the existentialist anguish typical of the 1950s and moved toward a more sharply defined political stance. Hierro's groundbreaking *Libro de las alucinaciones* (Book of Hallucinations, 1964) presented a phantasmagoric vision of reality. Gabriel Celaya (1911–91) wrote poetry of social protest in a more bombastic and verbose mode. At the margins of major trends was a belated avant-garde movement: *postismo*, led by Carlos Edmundo de Ory (1923–2010). The use of the label *postismo* for this avant-garde movement indicates its anachronism, but, in some respects, Ory was ahead of his time, anticipating the neo-avant garde of the 1970s and 1980s.

Claudio Rodríguez (1934–99), a visionary poet, inaugurated a new era with *Don de la ebriedad* (Gift of Drunkenness, 1954), heralding the decline of social poetry in the following decade. Rodríguez, the most naturally gifted Sp. poet since Lorca, is linked to other contemporaries in the so-called Generation of the 1950s. These poets practiced a more ironic mode of social poetry or, like Francisco Brines (b. 1932), wrote in a meditative mode at the margins of political engagement. Jaime Gil de Biedma (1929–90), influenced by W. H. Auden, founded the School of Barcelona along with his friends Carlos Barral (1928–89) and José Agustín Goytisolo (1928–99). Some poets of this cohort who lived in neither Madrid nor Barcelona emerged into view somewhat later, in the 1970s and 1980s: María Victoria Atencia (b. 1931) in Málaga, and Antonio Gamoneda (b. 1931) in León. The cultural decentralization of the post-Franco period led to a greater recognition of these peripheral figures.

The anthol. *Nueve novísimos poetas españoles* (Nine Very New Spanish Poets, ed. J. Castellet), pub. in 1970, brought to the foreground a group of younger poets who rejected what they felt was the drab realism of social poetry, drawing inspiration instead from the poetic *modernism of Sp. poetry of Lorca's generation, from the international avant-garde of the period between the two world wars, and from popular culture, esp. the movies. These poets practiced an exuberantly allusive, though sometimes melancholic, "culturalism." Of the nine poets included in the anthol., José María Álvarez (b. 1942), Pere Gimferrer (b. 1945), Guillermo Carnero (b. 1947), and Leopoldo María Panero (b. 1948) best illustrated the prototype of *novísmo* poetry. Gimferrer produced his early work in Sp. before turning to his native Catalan. *La muerte en Beverly Hills* (Death in Beverly Hills, 1968) is dreamlike *collage of images from classic Hollywood movies. Carnero's 1967 *Dibujo de la muerte* (Sketch of Death) reflects the aestheticism of this era, while the hyperrationalism of *Variaciones y figuras sobre un tema de La Bruyère* (Variations and Figures on a Theme by La Bruyère, 1974) connects him to neoclassical lit. The poetry of Panero, the son of the prominent right-wing poet of the 1940s Leopoldo Panero (1909–62), self-consciously reflects on the discourse of schizophrenia. Other poets emerging in this period, like Aníbal Núñez (1944–87), Jenaro Talens (b. 1946), José-Miguel Ullán (b. 1944), and Jaime Siles (b. 1951), who were not included in this anthol., may ultimately turn out to be as significant as the novísimos themselves.

Sp. poetry after 1980 witnesses three major devels.: (1) The emergence of a new movement of women poets, incl. Ana Rossetti (b. 1950), Isla Correyero (b. 1957), Blanca Andreu (b. 1959), and Amalia Iglesias (b. 1962), who use a neo-avant-garde style to write freely about issues of gender identity and sexuality; (2) a neorealist reaction against the perceived excesses of the novísmo aesthetic, spearheaded by a group of mostly Andalusian poets, among them Luis García Montero (b. 1958), Felipe Benítez Reyes (b. 1960), and Aurora Luque (b. 1962); and (3) the persistence of a "late modernist" aesthetic in the work of two major figures, José Ángel Valente (1929–2000) and Gamoneda, and in the work of many younger poets, incl. Miguel Casado (b. 1954), Chantal Maillard (b. 1951), and Juan Carlos Mestre (b. 1956). Valente was a somewhat imperious presence, championing an austere aesthetic rooted in the trads. of Sp. mysticism. Gamoneda takes inspiration from mod. Fr. poetry (René Char, Saint-John Perse) in *Libro del frío* (Book of the Cold, 1992). In *Libro de los venenos* (Book of Poisons, 1997), a multilayered commentary on a Ren. trans. of an ancient treatise on poisons and their remedies, Gamoneda breaks down the barrier between poetry and prose.

Because proponents of both the neo-avant garde and of Valente's high modernism tend to disparage García Montero's "poetry of experience," and vice versa, there is as yet no universally accepted *canon for the poetry of this period. During the 1990s, it seemed as though García Montero's approach, in the trad. of the dramatic monologues of Cernuda and the ironic social poetry of Gil de Biedma and Ángel González (1925–2008), was the most significant tendency in contemp. Sp. poetry. In the first decade of the 21st c., however, Gamoneda has emerged as a significant elder statesman. His mature work, beginning with his 1977 *Descripción de la mentira* (Description of the Lie), strongly resonates with the contemp. concern for the recuperation of the historical memory of the Civil War and the political repression of the Franco regime. Poets who are more or less in Gamoneda's orbit practice a wide variety of styles. They are linked only by a certain seriousness of purpose and by a rejection of facile aesthetic solutions. Olvido García Valdés (b. 1950) writes an extremely subtle poetry of sharp syntactic and prosodic ruptures, working through cinematic montage. Jorge Riechmann (b. 1962), influenced by Char and by the intellectual trad. of Marxism, writes out of a deep social and environmental consciousness.

The dominance of an artificial canon of male poets, perpetuated by institutional sclerosis, by the "generational" method of literary historiography, and by the ghettoization of women's writing, persists even in post-1975, democratic Spain. Two significant anthols. of poetry written by women have made an impact on this situation. The 1985 *Las Diosas Blancas* (The White Goddesses), ed. by Ramón Buenaventura, presented poetry written by women through the anthologist's sexualized filter: while celebrating the genuine novelty of this body of work, Buenavantura tended to highlight its more sensationalistic aspects. *Ellas tienen la palabra* (They Have the Word, ed. N. Benegas and J. Munáriz), pub. in 1998, presents a more inclusive and measured view. The critical introduction frames the work of women poets born after 1950 in the context of a trad. in women's poetry from the romantic movement to midcentury precursors such as Gloria Fuertes (1917–98) and Ángela Figuera (1902–84). Significant poets represented in this anthol. are too numerous to list by name. Standouts include Julia Otxoa (b. 1953), who experiments with the *prose poem and laments the violent hist. of her native Basque country; Concha García (b. 1956), who explores the tedium of everyday life in a *neobaroque style; Lola Velasco (b. 1961), who writes long sequences with a subtle interplay among poetic voices; and Luisa Castro (b.1966), with her unsparing vision of a semisavage childhood.

*See* AUTO SACRAMENTAL; AVANT-GARDE POETICS; BASQUE COUNTRY, POETRY OF THE; CATALAN POETRY; GALICIA, POETRY OF; ITALIAN PROSODY; ITALY, POETRY OF; JUDEO-SPANISH POETRY; MEDIEVAL POETICS; MEDIEVAL POETRY; RENAISSANCE POETICS; RENAISSANCE POETRY; ROMANTIC AND POSTROMANTIC POETRY AND POETICS; SPANISH AMERICA, POETRY OF; SPANISH PROSODY.

■ **I. To 1700.** *Anthologies, Bilingual Editions, and Translations*: *Spanish Poetry of the Golden Age*, ed. B. W. Wardropper (1971); *Garcilaso de la Vega y sus comentaristas*, ed. A. Gallego Morell et al., 2d. ed. (1972); *Renaissance and Baroque Poetry of Spain*, ed. E. L. Rivers (1972)—Sp. texts with Eng. paraphrase; *The Spanish Traditional Lyric*, ed. J. G. Cummins (1977); J. Ruiz, *Libro de Buen Amor/ The Book of True Love*, ed. A. N. Zahareas, trans. S. R. Daly (1978); *Poesía de la Edad de Oro, vol. I, Renacimiento, vol. II, Barroco*, ed. J. M. Blecua (1984); *Corpus de la antigua lírica popular hispánica (siglos XV a XVII)*, ed. M. Frenk (1987); *Poesía de cancionero*, ed. A. Alonso (1995); Alfonso X, el Sabio, *Cantigas de Loor*, ed. by M. G. Cunningham (2000)—Sp. and Eng. texts with musical score; St. John of the Cross, *The Poems*, trans. R. Campbell (2000); *The Golden Age: Poems of the Spanish Renaissance*, trans. E. Grossman (2006); *The Dream of the Poem: Hebrew Poetry from Muslim and Christian Spain, 950–1492*, ed. and trans. P. Cole (2007); *Selected Poems of Góngora*, trans. J. Dent-Young (2007); *Spanish Ballads*, trans. W. S. Merwin (2008); *Selected Poems of Garcilaso de la Vega*, trans. J. Dent-Young (2009); *Selected Poems of Francisco de Quevedo*, trans. C. D. Johnson (2009). ***Criticism and History***: P. Salinas, *Reality and the Poet in Spanish Poetry* (1940); M. R. Lida de Malkiel, *Juan de Mena, poeta del Prerrenacimiento español* (1950); R. Menéndez Pidal, D. Catalán, J. Galmés, *Cómo vive un romance* (1954); T. Navarro Tomás, *Métrica española* (1956); R. Lapesa, *La obra literaria del Marqués de Santillana* (1957); B. W. Wardropper, *Historia de la poesía lírica a lo divino en la cristiandad occidental* (1958); D. Alonso, *Estudios y ensayos gongorinos*

(1960); O. H. Green, *Spain and the Western Tradition*, 4 v. (1963–66); R. Menéndez Pidal, *En torno al Poema del Cid* (1963); C. F. Fraker, *Studies on the "Cancionero de Baena"* (1966); A. Collard, *Nueva poesía: conceptismo, culteranismo en la crítica española* (1967); P. Bénichou, *Creación poética en el romancero tradicional* (1968); F. Pierce, *Poesía épica del Siglo de Oro*, 2d. ed. (1968); R. Lapesa, *La trayectoria poética de Garcilaso*, enlarged ed. (1968); S. Reckert, *Style and Symbol in Iberian Traditional Verse* (1970); A. D. Deyermond, *A Literary History of Spain: The Middle Ages* (1971); M. Frenk, *Entre folklore y literatura: lírica hispánica antigua* (1971); R. O. Jones, *A Literary History of Spain. The Golden Age: Prose and Poetry* (1971); S. A. Gilman, "On *Romancero* as a Poetic Language," *Homenaje a Casalduero*, ed. R. Pincus Sigele et al. (1972); F. Márquez Villanueva, *Investigaciones sobre Juan Álvarez Gato*, 2d ed. (1974); E. de Chasca, *The Poem of the Cid* (1976); M. Molho, *Semántica y poética: Góngora, Quevedo* (1977); A. Martínez Arancón, *La batalla en torno a Góngora* (1978); E. L. Bergmann, *Art Inscribed: Essays on "Ekphrasis" in Spanish Golden Age Poetry* (1979); J. Beverley, *Aspects of Góngora's "Soledades"* (1980); *Quevedo in Perspective*, ed. J. Iffland (1982); C. Smith, *The Making of the "Poema de Mío Cid"* (1983); L. S. Lerner, *Metáfora y sátira en la obra de Quevedo* (1984); F. López Estrada, *Las poéticas castellanas de la Edad Media* (1984); L. López Baralt, *San Juan de la Cruz y el Islam* (1985); J. A. Maravall, *Culture of the Baroque*, trans. T. Cochran (1986); M. E. Barnard, *The Myth of Apollo and Daphne from Ovid to Quevedo* (1987); M. P. Manero Sorolla, *Introducción al estudio del Petrarquismo en España* (1987); F. Márquez Villanueva, *Lope: vida y valores* (1988); P. J. Smith, *Writing in the Margin* (1988); A. Egido, *Fronteras de la poesía en el Barroco*. B. López-Bueno, *Templada lira: Estudios sobre la poesía del Siglo de Oro* (1990); A. L. Martin, *Cervantes and the Burlesque Sonnet* (1991); A. Terry, *Seventeenth-Century Spanish Poetry: The Power of Artifice* (1993); I. E. Navarrete, *Orphans of Petrarch: Poetry and Theory in the Spanish Renaissance* (1994); R. Greene, *Unrequited Conquests* (1999); E. B. Davis, *Myth and Identity in the Epic of Early Modern Spain* (2000); "Poetry of Medieval Spain," "Renaissance Poetry," "Making of Baroque Poetry," *The Cambridge History of Spanish Literature*, ed. D. T. Gies (2004); L. M. Girón-Negrón, "El laberinto y sus 'reveses' en Juan de Mena, *Medioevo Romano* 28 (2004); R. Padrón, *The Spacious Word* (2004); R. Helgerson, *A Sonnet from Carthage: Garcilaso de la Vega and the New Poetry of Sixteenth-Century Europe* (2007); C. Chemris, *Góngora's "Soledades" and the Problem of Modernity* (2008); J. Dodds, M. R. Menocal, A. K. Balbale, *Arts of Intimacy: Christians, Jews, and Muslims in the Making of Castilian Culture* (2008); L. Middlebrook, *Imperial Lyric: New Poetry and New Subjects in Early Modern Spain* (2009); *Studies on Women's Poetry of the Golden Age*, ed. J. Olivares (2009); C. D. Johnson, *Hyperboles: The Rhetoric of Excess in Baroque Literature and Thought* (2010).

■ **II. 1700 to the Present.** *Anthologies*: *Poesía española*, ed. G. Diego (1932); *Veinte años de poesía española*, ed.

J. M. Castellet (1962); *Nueve novísimos poetas españoles*, ed. J. M. Castellet (1970); *Roots and Wings*, ed. H. St. Martin (1976); *Las diosas blancas*, ed. R. Buenaventura (1985); *Ellas tienen la palabra*, ed. N. Benegas and J. Munáriz (1998); *Feroces*, ed. I. Correyero (1998). **Criticism and History**: D. Alonso, *Poetas españoles contemporáneos* (1952); J. Guillén, *Language and Poetry* (1961); J. A. Valente, *Las palabras de la tribu* (1971); C. B. Morris, *Surrealism and Spain* (1972); G. Siebenmann, *Los estilos poéticos en España desde 1900* (1973); A. P. Debicki, *Poetry of Discovery* (1982); S. Daydí-Tolson, *The Post–Civil War Spanish Social Poets* (1983); G. Carnero, *La cara oscura del siglo de las luces* (1983); P. Silver, *La casa de Anteo* (1985); C. Soufas, *Conflict of Light and Wind* (1989); S. Kirkpatrick, *Las románticas* (1989); C. Soufas, *Conflict of Light and Wind* (1989); *Novísimos, postnovísimos, clásicos*, ed. B. Ciplijauskaité (1990); J. Mayhew, *The Poetics of Self-Consciousness* (1994); A. P. Debicki, *Twentieth-Century Spanish Poetry* (1994); J. Wilcox, *Women Poets of Spain* (1997); M. Persin, *Getting the Picture* (1997); P. Silver, *Ruin and Restitution* (1997); J. Mayhew, *Apocryphal Lorca* (2008), and *The Twilight of the Avant-Garde* (2008).

M. M. GAYLORD (TO 1700); J. MAYHEW (1700 TO PRESENT)

**SPANISH AMERICA, POETRY OF.** At the time of the first Sp. conquests in the Americas (notably Mexico in 1519–21 and Peru in 1532), the poetry of Castilian-speaking Spain was being transformed by Italianate and Petrarchan forms (see PETRARCHISM), Greco-Roman mythology, and cl. models. Spain's first viceroyalties, New Spain and then Peru, established court societies and monasteries in which poetry played a significant role. While the *romance* (*ballad), based on the *octosyllable, continued to flourish as the basis of popular poetry (Rio Plate gauchesque, Chilean *lira*, Mexican *corrido*), the *hendecasyllable became the standard for lettered verse, two strands that continued until the 20th c., when *free verse became dominant. Poetry's strength was perhaps enhanced by the fact that prose romances and, later, novels were nominally banned in the colonies from 1531.

Naturally, the first Sp. Am. poets were Spaniards who had settled in the New World. Alonso de Ercilla y Zúñiga (1533–94) is the author of *La Araucana* (1569, 1578, and 1589), a verse *epic in *ottava rima* that both celebrates the Sp. conquest in Chile and praises the enemy. Particularly moving are the scenes of Araucanian women seeking to bury their dead and of vivid battle. Recognized as the best epic poem in Sp., it was followed by Pedro de Oña's (1570–1643?) *Arauco domado* (1596).

*Baroque practice took hold in Sp. America toward the end of the 16th c. Conventions of cl. mythology, strange and wonderful phenomena, and a highly wrought lang. are signs of the *Barroco de Indias* (Baroque of the Indies). Just as architecture adapted elements from indigenous cultures, so lit. recorded Am. wonders and marvels. Bernardo de Balbuena's (Spain,

1561–1627) *Grandeza Mexicana* (1604) extols Mexico City's riches. Later, Rafael Landívar (Guatemala, 1731–93) wrote an extensive poem in Lat. celebrating Am. landscapes, *Rusticatio Americana* (1781). This celebration of America's distinctive bounty will recur throughout 18th- and 20th-c. poetry, from Andrés Bello's *silvas* to Pablo Neruda's *Canto general.*

*Satire was prominent in colonial poetry, inevitable where fortunes were quickly made and lost, circumstances of birth were reinvented, and viceregal courts dazzled in stark contrast to surrounding native realities. Juan del Valle Caviedes's (Peru, 1652–97) *Diente del Parnaso* (The Tooth of Parnassus, 1689) attacks doctors; its coarse lang. and physical emphasis present a counterpoint to religious or courtly verse. Also in Lima, Mateo Rosas de Oquendo (b. 1559?) published a scatological romance of over 2,000 lines, "Sátira . . . a las cosas que pasan en el Perú" (Satire of Events in Peru) in 1598.

The place of honor in colonial letters is occupied by a poet at the close of the baroque period, the Mexican nun Sor Juana Inés de la Cruz (ca. 1648–95), who exhibited a genius for all forms of poetry and theater, as well as her famous epistle in defense of her intellectual ambitions. Showing the cultural fluidity of the times, she wrote *villancicos in Nahuatl, the Aztec lang., as well as in Sp. Her masterwork is the *Primero sueño* (First Dream, 1692), an exploration of the mind's coming into consciousness.

Like Sor Juana, poets wrote in other langs. and translated from native langs. to Sp. In Perú, the Andean chronicler Felipe Guáman Poma de Ayala (ca. 1535–1616) includes poems in Quechua in his *El primer nueva corónica y buen gobierno* (*First New Chronicle and Good Government*, ca. 1615). The Peruvian mestizo historian known as El Inca Garcilaso de la Vega (1539–1616), a cousin of the Sp. poet of the same name, dedicated a chapter of the *Comentarios reales de los Incas* (*Royal Commentaries of the Incas*, 1609, 1617)—book 2, chap. 27—to a description of Incan poetry.

Enlightenment ideals came late to Sp. America, brought in part by scientists such as Alexander von Humboldt. These intellectual values had to struggle against the vestiges of the Counter-Reformation, which had attempted to silence Sor Juana and frustrated ideals of liberty and scientific experiment. The Jesuits, teachers of cl. langs. and scholars of native langs., were expelled in 1767. The ideal of liberty, important for 18th-c. revolutions and for the Haitian Revolution of 1802, was seen as dangerous by both church and crown.

In the 18th and 19th cs., periodical publications took on greater importance, and the long poem (whether *narrative, *dramatic, or *lyric), unwieldy for the aims of journalism and popular debate, ceded importance to shorter forms. The introduction of photography in the 19th c. shifted the notion of representation itself, just as the introduction of film at the turn of the 20th c. was to change the dynamics of represented movement.

Early 19th-c. poetry was involved in the revolutionary struggles, with countless *odes to military heroes and statesmen. Anthols. collected these poems and distributed them throughout the Americas, helping to establish national literary trads. in the nascent republics (except for Cuba and Puerto Rico, which remained colonies of Spain until the Sp.-Am. War of 1898). The period witnessed an intense interest in the space of Sp. America—its landscape, its indigenous civilizations (particularly ruins), and patriotic fervor. Mariano Melgar (Peru, 1790–1815) adapted the Quechua song form, the *yaraví*, to Sp. poetry.

Andrés Bello (Venezuela, 1781–1865) was an architect of Latin Am. independence. Sent to England in 1810 by the revolutionaries, he had been exposed to Eng. and Continental philosophy and poetics, as well as to the Industrial Revolution. His "Alocución a la poesía" (Discourse to Poetry, 1823) proclaimed the future to be Am., not Eur. His *Silvas americanas* (1823), which include "A la agricultura de la zona tórrida" (The Agriculture of the Torrid Zone), set forth an ideal, bucolic society to heal the ravages of the revolutionary wars. Bello replaces cl. allusions with Am. ones; he is important as a translator of Lord Byron, Alphonse de Lamartine, and Victor Hugo. (Neruda will return to the *Silvas* as one of his primary sources for *Canto general.*)

The Cuban José María Heredia (1803–39) presents, contemporaneously with Bello's neoclassical stance, a *romanticism tinged with melancholy, evoking his exile from Cuba. "En el teocalli de Cholula" (On the Pyramid of Cholula, 1820), a meditation on the Aztec past, and "A Niágara" (To Niagara, 1824) embody romanticism's divided self and the *sublime. His focus on exile will be repeated by other poets.

Gertrudis Gómez de Avellaneda (Cuba, 1814–73) was a poet, dramatist, and novelist tutored by Heredia. While she lived most of her adult life in Spain, America, esp. Cuba, is a central topic of her poetry, which involved experimentation with metrics. "Al partir" (On Leaving, 1836), dedicated to Cuba, is her most famous *sonnet.

José Joaquín de Olmedo (Ecuador, 1780–1847) contributed the best-known ode to the wars of independence. His "Victoria de Junín: Canto a Bolívar" (1825), modeled on Virgil, incorporated the Incan past as a ghost who prophesies Simón Bolívar's victory and acclaims the revolutionaries as scourges of the Sp. Although Bolívar himself noted the paradox of an Indian figure applauding the Spaniards' descendants, the Indian in 19th-c. poetry often appears as a prophetic *muse or a doomed hero.

Esteban Echeverría (Argentina, 1805–51) was sent to Paris, where he was initiated into romantic doctrines. Because of his publications, he was forced into exile in Uruguay in 1840. His masterwork in poetry is the long narrative poem "La cautiva" (The Captive, 1837), which relates the story of a white woman captured by Indians, a common topic in 19th-c. lit.

Bartolomé Hidalgo (Uruguay, 1788–1823) brought to print culture the oral trad. of the *gauchos* (see GAUCHO POETRY), whose singing contests had roots in the med. romance. Hidalgo, with the *cielito* (little heaven) and the *diálogo*, initiates a lettered trad. that reaches its height with the Argentinian epic *Martín Fierro* (1872) by José Hernández (1834–86). *Martín Fierro* recounts the story of the outcast gaucho as deserter soldier in the eyes of the government, an enemy as seen by the Indians. The *Vuelta de Martín Fierro* (The Return of Martín Fierro, 1879) reconciles the gaucho with his past and with the law. As shown by Ludmer, the passage to print culture parallels the government's militarization of the gaucho (wanderer, delinquent) during the wars of independence; thus, his body is used by the army and his voice by print culture. Comic and parodic possibilities of the gauchesque are exploited in Estanislao del Campo's (Argentina, 1834–80) *Fausto*.

The rise of *modernismo* begins with the publication of Rubén Darío's (1867–1916) *Azul . . .* (1888); the movement is often thought to end with his death in 1916. Yet by the 1880s, there was already poetry in the new spirit. Manuel Gutiérrez Nájera (Mexico, 1859–95), José Martí (Cuba, 1853–95), Julián del Casal (Cuba, 1863–93), and José Asunción Silva (Colombia, 1865–96) were innovative poets who explored outside Sp. trad. Unquestionably the poet of his century, Darío transformed poetry in Spain as well as in Sp. America. For the first time, the leadership of an influential literary movement in a Eur. lang. emerged from the New World, not from Europe.

Modernismo appeared in a Sp. America on the threshold of modernity, esp. in its largest cities. The central premise of the *modernistas* was innovation, and they reacted against emergent capitalism, positivism, and 19th-c. canons of propriety. Their models were Charles Baudelaire, Paul Verlaine, Walt Whitman, and E. A. Poe, as well as visual sources such as the *Pre-Raphaelite Brotherhood and art nouveau. The modernistas introduced to poetry a new technical vigor, a cosmopolitanism (their orientalism is notable), and a new *syntax. Modernismo rediscovered the musical harmonies of poetry, and Darío himself reached back into med. Sp. trad., Fr. *Parnassianism, and *symbolism for his inspiration. He reintroduced the *alexandrine into Sp. and experimented rhythmically as well as metrically. Besides *Azul . . .*, his central volumes are *Prosas profanas* (1896) and *Cantos de vida y esperanza* (1905), where he addresses political themes, particularly the domination by the U.S. after the Sp.-Am. War.

Born of mixed ancestry in Nicaragua, Darío ventured first to Chile, where he published *Azul . . .*, and then to Buenos Aires. Like many modernistas, he supported himself through journalism. Darío's taste for the exotic, his explicit eroticism, and his direct, often intimate tone shocked many who disparaged him and his followers as *modernistas*, a title they soon embraced.

Martí was very different from Darío but is important as an innovator. His *Ismaelillo* (1886) and *Versos sencillos* (Simple Verses, 1891, in *redondillas based on the octosyllable) reintroduced into lettered culture traditional and popular rhythms. His posthumous *Versos libres* (Free Verse, 1913) are more hermetic, with reflections on exile, mod. urban life (he spent a great deal of his life in New York), and internal strife.

Gutiérrez Nájera was known for his natural scenes and lively verse such as the poem "La Duquesa Job" (Duchess Job, 1884). A journalist, he specialized in short, contemp. accounts called *crónicas* (chronicles). In Mexico, the modernistas grouped around the *Revista Moderna* (1894–96) and the *Revista Azul* (1892–1915), whose art and poetry emphasized *decadence and eroticism. Del Casal produced a series of sonnets based on paintings by Gustave Moreau. His "impure love of the city" shifts the scene from the natural world to an urban one. His younger compatriot and friend Juana Borrero (1877–96) excelled at both painting and poetry until her early death.

In Argentina, the primary modernist was Leopoldo Lugones (1874–1938). His *Lunario sentimental* (Sentimental Moon Calendar, 1909) introduced verse free of conventional meter, and its parody of the moon and introduction of the colloquial signaled a fissure in the aesthetics of modernismo. Jorge Luis Borges acknowledged Lugones as an antecedent to *ultraism. The careers of Lugones and Julio Herrera y Reissig (Uruguay, 1875–1910) converge in their early works, since both were influenced by the Fr. symbolist Albert Samain. They are also counterparts in pushing poetic systems to the limit, as in Herrera y Reissig's "Tertulia lunática" (Lunatic Gathering, 1911) where shocking wordplay presaged vanguardist energies.

One of the most striking voices of modernismo was the Uruguayan Delmira Agustini (1886–1914). She is the most sexually explicit, introducing female sexuality into modernista currents, and was the starting point for a new generation of female poets, incl. the Argentinian Alfonsina Storni (1892–1938) and the Chilean Gabriela Mistral (1889–1957).

Other modernistas include Ricardo Jaimes Freyre (Bolivia, 1868–1933), who explored Nordic mythology, and Enrique González Martínez (Mexico, 1871–1952), whose 1912 poem on wringing the neck of the swan complains about striving for eloquence. José Santos Chocano (Peru, 1875–1934) introduced a new thematics into modernista poetry called *mundonovismo* (New Worldism) that exalted America's indigenous past. Amado Nervo (Mexico, 1870–1919) was the most read poet of his generation. José Juan Tablada (Mexico, 1871–1945) experimented with *haiku and ideographic forms incl. the *calligramme. Ramón López Velarde's (Mexico, 1888–1921) poetry has gained increased critical attention. His "Suave patria" (The Gentle Homeland, 1921) is a tribute to a gentler Mexico of the provinces. His work (e.g., "Mi prima Agueda" [My Cousin Agueda], 1916) wrestles with eroticism but also the speech of daily life.

Octavio Paz writes that, after modernismo, there are two directions in Sp. Am. poetry: that of Lugones in *Lunario sentimental* and that of Darío; and that mod. poetry follows the path of Lugones. This is true in the sense of poetic form, since vanguardist poets and their followers will largely dispense with rhyme and meter, while another trad. will employ the forms of previous centuries. This second trad. is also tied to the declamation of poetry, a *performance practice important in public events in Latin America until the mid-20th c. (see RECITATION).

Closely following the modernistas was a new generation eager to clear the way for a different kind of lit. Vanguardist movements sprang up in all Latin America—e.g., *estridentismo* in Mexico, *ultraísmo* in Argentina, *indigenismo* in Peru, *diepalismo* in Puerto Rico, *\*antropofagia* in Brazil—as did little magazines such as *Prisma* (Argentina 1921–22), *Martín Fierro* (1924), *Proa* (1922–25), *Elipse* (Chile, 1922), *Irradiador* (Mexico, 1923), *Vórtice* (Puerto Rico, 1922), *Revista de Avance* (Cuba, 1927–30), and *Contemporáneos* (Mexico, 1928–31). In Peru, the vanguard is often linked to the indigenous question, most famously in José Carlos Mariátegui's jour. *Amauta* (1926–30), but also in *Boletín Titikaka* (based in Puno) with poets such as Gamaliel Churata (1897–1969).

The vanguard sought to strip poetry of its excess, to reduce it to essentials. They dispensed with meter, rhyme, and extended patterns of imagery in favor of free verse of high visual and aural impact. With film now widespread, poets sought ways to incorporate new techniques of perception. In the *estridentistas*, the influence of It. \*futurism and the fascination with technology was strong; the *ultraísta* movement in Buenos Aires, led by Borges (Argentina, 1899–1986), sought to reduce poetry to its basic element, the \*metaphor. Borges adopted the orthography of colloquial speech in his books dedicated to Buenos Aires: *Fervor de Buenos Aires* (1923), *Luna de enfrente* (Moon across the Way, 1925), and *Cuaderno San Martín* (San Martín Notebook, 1929). Over time, he returned to conventional forms, disavowing his vanguardist past.

What distinguishes the vanguards of Sp. America from those of Europe and the U.S. are the political and ethnic issues involved. Yet this presented a dilemma: how is vanguard poetry to be meaningful socially? Many believed, like Vicente Huidobro (Chile, 1893–1948), that changing lang. was itself revolutionary. Huidobro called his aesthetic *creacionismo* (\*creationism) and was, with César Vallejo, the most radical innovator of his generation. Interested in \*cubism, he collaborated with artists such as Juan Gris in poem-paintings. His *Altazor* (1931) is a verse epic of a journey through the spheres in the aftermath of destruction. As the poem evolves, lang. loses its representational character, becoming only dispersed sounds.

In Peru, César Vallejo (1892–1938), from a provincial background, became, with Neruda, the most influential Sp. Am. poet of the 20th c. His *Heraldos negros* (*The Black Heralds*, 1919) has echoes of modernismo but shows the earthiness of his stripped down lang. and a loss of faith in overarching systems, esp. Christianity. *Trilce* (1922) is hermetic and baffling, destroying syntax and confounding meaning. Its visceral appeal has inspired generations of poets, as has the posthumous political poetry collected in *Poemas humanos* (1939).

In Chile, Pablo Neruda (pseud. of Ricardo Neftalí Reyes Basoalto) (1904–73) gained notice first as the author of *Veinte poemas de amor y una canción desesperada* (*Twenty Love Poems and a Song of Despair*, 1924). As a diplomat in Asia, he continued work on the

*Residencia en la tierra* (*Residence on Earth*, 1933–47), which expressed inner turmoil in relation to the natural and material world. In 1937, he published *España en el corazón* (*Spain in Our Hearts*) in solidarity with the Republicans in the Sp. Civil War. *Canto general* (*General Song*, 1950) is a vast epic of the Americas. Originally inspired by Bello's *Silvas americanas* (1823), Neruda traces Am. origins from primitive vegetal and animal states to the cold-war realities of the 1940s. He recounts hist.—esp. conquest and independence heroes, along with sections devoted to rivers, birds, the common man and woman ("La tierra se llama Juan"). The most famous section is "Alturas de Macchu Picchu," which evokes the Incan past out of its slumber within the stones of the ruined city. Neruda went on to break new ground in his *Odas elementales* (*Elemental Odes*, 1954), celebrating the natural and the everyday in short verses, with odes to artichokes, socks, and dictionaries.

Nicolás Guillén's (Cuba, 1902–89) long writing career gave voice to Afro-Cuban aesthetics and a new political urgency. His early publications, *Motivos de son* (Son Motifs, 1930) and *Songoro cosongo* (1931), develop the possibilities of an Afro-Cuban music and dance in the form of the *son*, a rhythmic pattern with roots in African slave culture of the colonial period. Guillén reproduces vernacular \*diction and dialect (see DIALECT POETRY) in these works, asserting the legitimacy of Afro-Cuban speech and affirming the beauty of the black woman, taking her from racist cliché to personhood. Guillén joined Fidel Castro's revolution and became a cultural symbol and the head of the writers' union in Cuba.

Not all poets cast off formal restraints. Mistral and Storni, both teachers of modest origins, were traditionalists in form. Mistral, who favored the nine-syllable line, paid special attention to themes of motherhood, children, and the natural world, and generations of children in Sp. America have learned to recite her poems. *Desolación* (1922), *Tala* (Clearcut, 1938), and *Lagar* (Winepress, 1954) are her principal poetic works; the latter volume introduces a new \*hermeticism, and *Poema de Chile* (1967) presents a puzzling antiepic of a journey through the homeland. Mistral received the Nobel Prize in 1945, the first Latin Am. to be so honored. Storni presents a sharper edge to the female voice in poetry. She is faithful to poetic form until her final works but shatters convention by expressing rage and sorrow at the female condition in a male-dominated society as in her most anthologized poems, "Tú me quieres blanca"(You Want Me White, 1918) and "Hombre pequeñito" (Little Man, 1919). Her urban poems capture the dislocations brought about by immigration. After a prolonged illness, she committed suicide in 1938 in a dramatic and self-publicized way. Her contemp. Juana de Ibarbourou (Uruguay, 1895–1979) was extremely well known in her time, fitting more easily into the conventions for women. Her lyric poetry includes themes of nature and of love.

The Mexican Revolution (1910–20) brought visibility to indigenous and mestizo issues in a range of arts, incl. the murals of Diego Rivera, David Alfaro

Siqueiros, and José Clemente Orozco and the later paintings of Frida Kahlo. Nonetheless, a group of poets, *Los Contemporáneos* (named for their magazine), ignored postrevolutionary politics and devoted themselves to interiority, as in Xavier Villaurrutia's (1903–50) beautiful and sometimes homoerotic *Nocturnos* (1933), José Gorostiza's (1901–73) *Muerte sin fin* (Death without End, 1939), and Carlos Pellicer's (1897–1977) tropical landscapes. Salvador Novo (1904–74) is also associated with this group.

The impact of *surrealism continued well into the century, esp. with Octavio Paz (Mexico, 1914–98). In addition to being the leading poet of his era (he won the Nobel Prize in 1990), Paz was a commanding voice on poetics and lit. hist. The books of criticism *El arco y la lira* (*The Bow and the Lyre*, 1956) and *Los hijos del limo* (*Children of the Mire*, 1974) have shaped our understanding of poetry in theory and act. His poetic work ranges widely, with roots in pre-Columbian and Asian cosmologies, eroticism, and Mexican realities.

Conversational style became increasingly important around mid-century with Nicanor Parra's (Chile, b. 1914) "anti-poetry" (*Poemas y antipoemas*, 1954) and the work of Roque Dalton (El Salvador, 1935–75). Dalton's colloquial style became associated with Central Am. liberation movements and the poetry of political denunciation throughout Latin America. A special mention should be made of Violeta Parra (Chile, 1917–67) and her incorporation of oral culture into written poetry. Basing her work on the octosyllable, she wrote and performed her *décimas* throughout Chile and in Europe, bringing full circle a trad. as old as the conquest.

Military conflicts and dictatorships of the 1970s and 1980s provided poets such as Juan Gelman (Argentina, b. 1930), Ernesto Cardenal (Nicaragua, b. 1925), Claribel Alegría (El Salvador, b. 1924), Juan Luis Martínez (Chile, 1942–93), and Raúl Zurita (Chile, b. 1950) material for some of their most notable poetry.

Gonzalo Rojas (Chile, 1917–2011), Blanca Varela (Peru, 1926–2009), José Emilio Pacheco (Mexico, b. 1939), and Alejandra Pizarnik (Argentina, 1936–72) are central to recent decades.

Also important is a group of *neobaroque poets inspired by the Cuban José Lezama Lima (1910–76), incl. the Argentine Néstor Perlongher (1949–92), the Cuban José Kozer (b. 1940), and the Argentine Diana Bellessi (b. 1946), among others. A renewal of pan-indigenous movements in the Americas has sparked new interest in indigenous langs. and topics.

See ARGENTINA, POETRY OF; AVANT-GARDE POETICS; BOLIVIA, POETRY OF; CARIBBEAN, POETRY OF THE; CHILE, POETRY OF; EL SALVADOR, POETRY OF; GUATEMALA, POETRY OF THE; INDIGENOUS AMERICAS, POETRY OF THE; MEXICO, POETRY OF; NICARAGUA, POETRY OF; PERU, POETRY OF; SPAIN, POETRY OF; URUGUAY, POETRY OF; VENEZUELA, POETRY OF.

■ G. Brotherston, *Latin American Poetry: Origins and Presence* (1975); A. Rama, *Las máscaras democráticas del modernismo* (1985); O. Rivera-Rodas, *La poesía hispanoamericana del siglo XIX (Del romanticismo al modernismo)* (1988); *Las vanguardias latinoamericanas:*

*textos programáticos y críticos*, ed. J. Schwartz (1991); O. Paz, *Children of the Mire: Modern Poetry from Romanticism to the Avant-Garde*, trans. R. Phillips (1991); V. Unruh, *Latin American Vanguards: The Art of Contentious Encounters* (1994); *The Cambridge History of Latin American Literature*, ed. R. González-Echeverarría and E. Pupo-Walker, 2 v. (1996); C. Jrade, *Modernismo, Modernity, and the Development of Spanish American Literature* (1998); W. Rowe, *Poets of Contemporary Latin America: History and Inner Life* (2000); A. Bush, *The Routes of Modernity: Spanish American Poetry from the Early Eighteenth to the Mid-Nineteenth Century* (2002); M. González and D. Treece, *The Gathering of Voices: The Twentieth-Century Poetry of Latin America* (2002); J. Ludmer, *The Gaucho Genre: A Treatise on the Motherland*, trans. M. Weigel (2002); S. Yurkiévich, *Fundadores de la nueva poesía latinoamericana: Vallejo, Huidobro, Borges, Girondo, Neruda, Paz, Lezama Lima* (2002); *Encyclopedia of Twentieth-Century Latin American and Caribbean Literature, 1900–2003*, ed. D. Balderston and M. González (2004); J. Kuhnheim, *Spanish American Poetry at the End of the Twentieth Century: Textual Disruptions* (2004); *Literary Cultures of Latin America: A Comparative History*, ed. M. J. Valdés and D. Kadir, 3 v. (2004); *Compromiso e hibridez: Aproximaciones a la poesía hispánica escrita por mujeres*, ed. T. Escaja (2007); A. González, *A Companion to Spanish American "Modernismo"* (2007).

G. KIRKPATRICK

**SPANISH PROSODY.** Until the advent of *free verse and aside from time-measured song form (*verso lírico medieval*) and the chanted epic verse (*verso épico, mester de juglaría*), Sp. verse measure was based on syllable count, involving the principles of *hiatus, *synaloepha, *synaeresis, and *diaeresis. Syllables per line are counted to the last stressed syllable, plus one count. In the earliest period, hiatus was obligatory in syllable counting, but by the late 14th c., synaloepha in court poetry prevailed. *Hemistichs are metrically independent.

One of the earliest and most durable of Sp. verse forms is the *octosyllable or *romance (Sp. ballad) meter. The earliest *strophe is probably the *couplet (*pareado*; see SEXTILLA). Med. two-part verse of the *mester de juglaría* (minstrel verse) dating from or before the 12th c. is the earliest known long-form measure, found primarily in the *cantar de gesta* (popular epic; see CANTAR). The hemistichic lines vary in length from about 10 to 20 syllables. The more sophisticated *mester de clerecía* (clerical verse) poems composed in *cuaderna vía* stanzas, whose seven + seven syllable *alejandrino* lines were probably in imitation of the Fr. *alexandrine, date from ca. 1200 (see COPLA, SERRANILLA, ZÉJEL). The all-purpose *copla de arte menor*, a stanza of any moderate length in octosyllabic or shorter verse, and its variation, the *copla de pie quebrado*, became popular. In verse, the favored long lines, all with *caesuras creating metrically independent hemistichs, were 12, 14, or 16 syllables in length, each with its optional *quebrado*.

While these forms, along with other less prominent strophic arrangements (e.g., *villancico), were being developed for both didactic purpose and popular entertainment, the courtly and learned poets of the 14th and 15th cs. were often composing in Galician-Port., which had been used in the 13th c. by King Alfonso X *el Sábio* (the Wise), e.g., in his *Cantigas de Santa María*, and was still lingering in the early 15th c., when most poets were favoring Castilian. The couplet (*pareado, pareja*), the *tercet (*terceto*) in any rhyme scheme, various types of *eco* (see ECHO VERSE), and some experimental forms are found. Poetic license was tolerated, e.g., accent shift in a word, *syncope, haplology, disregard of the penult of a proparoxytone, and acoustic *equivalence for true rhyme (see ARTE MAYOR, ARTE MENOR, DÉCIMA, ENDECHA, ESTRIBILLO, FINIDA, GAITA GALLEGA, GLOSA, LETRILLA, MOTE, PREGUNTA, REFRÁN, REMATE).

The 16th and 17th cs. in Spain firmly established Italianate verse and stanza forms. The *sáfico* (see SAPPHIC) soon appeared. Old forms were regularized (e.g., the alejandrino, the *seguidilla*). The *pentasílabo* (pentasyllable) served occasionally as hemistich of the hendecasyllable and was also used with the *adónico* (pentasyllabic paroxytonic verse) to form the sáfico adónico strophe (three sáficos plus one adónico), also known as the *oda sáfica*. Italianate importations incl. the *soneto, *terza rima, octava rima, or heroico or real* octave (see OTTAVA RIMA), *verso suelto* (unrhymed verse, usually hendecasyllabic, sometimes combined with seven- or five-syllable verse; cf. VERSI SCIOLTI). The hendecasyllabic *romance heroico* (or *endecasilábico* or *real*), the *lira* variations, and the *silva* are among the new. The *redondilla, *quintilla, seguidilla, and their relatives became popular, as did irregular meters and such minor stanza forms as the *ensalada, *espinela, and *folia*.

Publication of Ignacio de Luzán's *Poética* (1737) coincides approximately with the beginning of Sp. neoclassicism, when poets resurrected, restored, and regularized the old and borrowed (mainly from Fr.) or created new variations on old verse and stanza forms (see NEOCLASSICAL POETICS). Experimentation was common. From the alejandrino and *verso de arte mayor* to the *trisílabo* (three-syllable verse), every verse length, often with set rhythmic pattern, can be found. Decasyllabic patterns included (1) $\cup \cup - \cup \cup \cup - (\cup)$; (2) $- \cup \cup - \cup | - \cup \cup - (\cup)$; (3) $\cup \cup \cup - \cup | \cup - \cup - (\cup)$; (4) the double adonic (*adónico doblado* or *asclepiadeo*); and (5) the *libre*, without fixed pattern. The nine-syllable line includes the *eneasílabo iriartino* (predominantly $\cup \cup - \cup \cup - \cup - [\cup]$), the *esproncedaico* ($\cup - \cup \cup \cup - [\cup]$), the *eneasílabo de canción* ($\cup \cup \cup - \cup \cup \cup - [\cup]$), the *eneasílabo laverdaico* or *brachycatalecto* ($\cup - \cup \cup \cup - \cup - [\cup]$), and the *eneasílabo libre* or *polirrítmico* (no set pattern). Occasionally, an octosyllabic poem has stress consistently on the third syllable, simulating *pie quebrado. A fixed rhythm, esp. *iambic, sometimes appears in heptasyllabic compositions; the *hexasílabo*, usually with fluctuating inner stress patterns, is occasionally *trochaic. The seldom independent pentasyllabic adónico, generally in combination with the hendecasyllabic sáfico, may have fluctuating inner stress.

Romantic nostalgia was reflected in the use of the *verso de arte mayor*, the alejandrino, and their quebrados but did not slow the process of innovation:

the *alcaico* (five + five syllable line), the nine-syllable *laverdaico*, and the anapestic 13-syllable were added to the repertory. Within a poem, random *assonance could replace true rhyme, and rhythm mixing served a purpose. Essentially ad hoc strophes were common; free verse was in the offing. In the mod. period, poets continued reaching for the new while clinging to the old, further loosening the rules without releasing them completely. The major advance was the full acceptance of *verso libre*, a natural outgrowth of centuries of change. Metrical structure no longer dominates or restricts verse but serves it flexibly as the background instrumental accompaniment to the words.

*See* CATALAN POETRY; GALICIA, POETRY OF; SPAIN, POETRY OF.

■ J. Vicuña Cifuentes, *Estudios de métrica española* (1929); P. Henríquez Ureña, *Versificación irregular en la poesía castellana*, 2d ed. (1933); D. C. Clarke, *Una bibliografía de versificación española* (1937); E. Díez Echarri, *Teorías métricas del siglo de oro* (1949); D. C. Clarke, *Chronological Sketch of Castilian Versification* (1952); Navarro; J. Domínguez Caparrós, *Diccionario de métrica española* (1985); A. Quilis, *Métrica española*, 3d ed. (1986); *Issues in the Phonology and Morphology of the Major Iberian Languages*, ed. F. Martínez-Gil and A. Morales-Front (1997); G. A. Toledo, "Jerarquías prosódicas en español," *Revista Española de Lingüística* 29 (1999); J. Domínguez Caparrós, *Métrica española*, 2d ed. (2000).

D. C. CLARKE

**SPASMODIC SCHOOL.** A term applied by contemp. critics (generally negatively) to a loosely affiliated group of mid-Victorian poets. Heavily influenced by Lord Byron and P. B. Shelley and also to a high degree by the early works of Alfred, Lord Tennyson and Robert Browning, "spasmodic" poets tended to produce poems characterized by extravagant lang. and imagery and varying verse forms, often centered on a tormented poet-hero musing at length on his cosmic ambitions and failings. The best-known examples of the genre are Alexander Smith's *A Life-Drama* (1853) and Sydney Dobell's *Balder* (1854), both of which were championed by the critic George Gilfillan and achieved short-lived but intense critical acclaim and popular success. Other minor poets associated with spasmodic writing include P. J. Bailey (author of *Festus*), J. Stanyan Bigg, J. Westland Marston, Ebenezer Jones, and Gerald Massey. Several of these writers came from working-class backgrounds, and the radical political, religious, and social beliefs of some spasmodic writers can be perceived in the energies of their verse and its often sensational plotlines. After the publication of a superb parody by W. A. Aytoun, *Firmilian* (1854), spasmodism became a subject of ridicule. Yet it lingered on as a critical concept, and its influence on canonical Victorian poetry was considerable: Matthew Arnold's 1853 Preface was partly aimed at the spasmodics, while Tennyson's *Maud*, Elizabeth Barrett Browning's *Aurora Leigh*, and A. C. Swinburne's *Poems and Ballads* have been read in terms of their spasmodic tendencies.

■ J. H. Buckley, *The Victorian Temper* (1951); M. A.

Weinstein, *W. E. Aytoun and the Spasmodic Controversy* (1968); "Spasmodic Poetry and Poetics," spec. iss. of *VP* 42:4, ed. J. Rudy and C. Laporte (2004).

K. BLAIR

**SPATIAL FORM.** A concept describing various structures revealed when a text is apprehended as a simultaneous whole rather than as a sequence unfolding in time. Constituted by patterns of repetition and self-reflexive reference, such structures are said to contribute a sense of internal coherence and unity to literary works. The mod. use of the term originates in Frank's influential essay "Spatial Form in Modern Literature" (1945), which argues that mod. poets and novelists such as T. S. Eliot, James Joyce, and Djuna Barnes resist temporal succession in order to create atemporal patterns of simultaneity in their work. Challenging G. E. Lessing's distinction between the temporal character of poetry and the spatiality of the plastic arts, Frank suggests that mod. lit. resists the tendencies of its own medium so as to produce forms of unity in defiance of the vicissitudes of passing time. Following from Eliot's "mythic method," these forms are also understood as an attempt to replace the perceived chaos of hist. with the timeless certainties of myth. Critics generally acknowledge that spatial form is only a metaphor. It is spatial, for instance, only in the sense that its patterns are understood to be perceived simultaneously. Many critics have also questioned Frank's suggestion that spatial form is a particular feature of *modernism, arguing that the reading of any text produces synchronic structural patterns. Some of the most severe crits. of the concept, however, accept its validity as a formal description of modernist texts but link its celebration of myth and its attempt to impose order to a vision of modernism defined by its extremist politics.

■ J. Frank, "Spatial Form in Modern Literature," *The Widening Gyre* (1963); F. Kermode, *The Sense of an Ending* (1967); M. Krieger, "Ekphrasis and the Still Movement of Poetry, or *Laokoön* Revisited," *The Poet as Critic*, ed. P. W. McDowell (1967); W.J.T. Mitchell, "Spatial Form in Literature," *The Language of Images*, ed. W.J.T. Mitchell (1980); J. Frank, *The Idea of Spatial Form* (1991).

B. GLAVEY

**SPEAKER.** *See* PERSONA; VOICE.

**SPEECH ACT THEORY.** A pragmatic theory of lang. first articulated by J. L. Austin and elaborated by H. P. Grice and John Searle, and compatible in many respects with the philosophy of the later Ludwig Wittgenstein, speech act theory defines lang. in terms not of formal structure but of use. When people speak, they assume a complex system of rules that give meanings to particular utterances according to the context in which they are performed. For speech act theorists, the minimal ling. unit is, therefore, not the symbol, word, or sentence but "the production or issuance of the symbol or word or sentence in the performance of [a] speech act" (Searle 1969).

This understanding led Austin to recognize a little-examined aspect of speech that he called "illocution-ary action." Even a declarative sentence, he argues, is more than a proposition (locution) expressing truth or falsehood insofar as it implies the speaker's stance toward the utterance. Searle classifies illocutionary acts into five categories: representatives (e.g., claiming, predicting, suggesting); directives (e.g., requesting, commanding, inviting); commissives (e.g., promising, threatening, vowing); expressives (e.g., congratulating, thanking, welcoming); and declarations (e.g., blessing, baptizing, firing). While all illocutionary acts are performative in the sense that they function as social action, a declaration actually brings about the state of affairs it predicates.

Austin calls an illocution "felicitous" when it successfully evokes the conditions conventionally attached to the particular speech act. In ordinary circumstances, e.g., "Your dress is ugly" would not constitute a compliment, and "I marry you" would be infelicitous if the speaker were already married to someone else. This approach locates *intention not in a psychological or moral state but in the evocation of conventions, incl. the convention that an illocutionary act will be sincere. Speech acts "properly" accomplished should generate "perlocutionary effects": e.g., the act of asking will conventionally produce an answer; the act of firing will cause an employee to recognize that she has been dismissed.

Since illocutionary action relies on complex rules and assumptions about sociocultural behavior and lang. use, the meaning of an illocutionary act depends less on its precise verbal form than on the conventions of its performance. "That stove is hot" might be an assertion, a warning, a complaint, or even a compliment. Conversely, a warning about the stove might be expressed in any number of sentences. As Grice observes, communicators draw on contextual assumptions to make inferences; the sentence "I have an aspirin," said in response to "I have a headache," can constitute an offer even though no explicit words of offering have been expressed. Speech act theory thus suggests that context limits the potential of lang. for *ambiguity and free play. However, such rules of inference assume shared understandings that may not be operating in a given speech act, a particular problem for written discourse given its detachment from the site of its production.

The most direct avenue speech act theory opens for lit. concerns the study of textual speakers and characters, as, e.g., in Fish's reading of the double banishment in Shakespeare's *Coriolanus*, Altieri's analysis of W. C. Williams's "This is Just to Say," or, more recently, Nolan-Grant's take on Austen's "language-based society," all of which consider aspects of discourse that formal analysis overlooks. But Austin complicated the application of speech act theory to lit. by considering speech acts to be "hollow or void if said by an actor on the stage, or if introduced in a poem, or spoken in soliloquy." On this basis, he identified fictional speech as "not serious" and "parasitic." This exclusion, along with disagreements about lang., meaning, and subjectivity, generated extensive debate between speech act theory and deconstruction beginning with a famous exchange between Searle and Derrida in *Glyph* 1 (1977).

Some theorists argue that lit. is itself a context rather than a detachment from context. Searle, Wolfgang Iser, Richard Ohmann, and Mary Louise Pratt have all understood fictional speech acts to carry a particular kind of illocutionary force. Using Grice's work on "implicature," which postulates maxims that govern ordinary conversation, Pratt evolved characteristics for the specific speech situations of lit. Searle has employed speech act theory to analyze such "literary" tropes as *irony and *metaphor. Speech act theory has attracted scholars with interests ranging from law to the Bible, some of whom also attempt to ameliorate speech act theory's tendency to abstract speaking subjects and conventions of speech from historical and cultural contexts. Hillis Miller has framed literary speech acts as forms of ethical conduct underwriting the formation of social communities. Petrey has usefully shifted literary inquiry from intention to effect, though Gorman charges Petrey with misapprehensions of speech act theory that he also attributes to nearly all literary theorists and scholars who have engaged with Austin's work.

Esp. because speech act theory understands speech as performance, it has also influenced important trends in postmod. thought. Felman's analysis of the seductive false promises of Don Juan (*Le Scandale du corps parlant*, 1980) synthesized Lacanian psychoanalysis with Austin's ideas in ways that both critique and revalue speech act theory as a lens for understanding the precarious performativity of promises, the embodied theatricality of speech, and the play of transgression that destabilizes pragmatic approaches to lang. In Felman's wake, Butler argues (1993) for the performativity of gender relations and exposes the "binding power" of authoritative speech acts such as marrying, while showing how performance can destabilize that power. In *Excitable Speech*, Butler maintains "that speech is always in some ways out of control" and stresses the temporal gaps and social differences that intervene between performance and consequence. Through such fruitful conversations with a wide range of theories, texts, and performative settings, speech act theory continues both to influence the study of lang. and lit. and to rethink its own formulations.

■ J. L. Austin, *How To Do Things with Words* (1962); J. Searle, *Speech Acts* (1969); R. Ohmann, "Literature as Act," *Approaches to Poetics*, ed. S. Chatman (1973); H. P. Grice, "Logic and Conversation," *Syntax and Semantics*, ed. P. Cole and J. Morgan, v. 3 (1975); *Glyph* 1 (1977); M. L. Pratt, *Toward a Speech Act Theory of Literary Discourse* (1977); T. Van Dijk, *Text and Context* (1977); W. Iser, *The Act of Reading* (1978); J. Searle, *Expression and Meaning* (1979); S. Fish, *Is There a Text in This Class?* (1980); C. Altieri, *Act and Quality* (1981); S. Lanser, *The Narrative Act* (1981); S. Felman, *The Literary Speech Act*, trans. C. Porter (1983); D. Sperber and D. Wilson, *Relevance* (1986); "Speech Act Theory and Biblical Criticism," special iss. of *Semeia* 41, ed. H. White (1988); H. P. Grice, *Studies in the Way of Words* (1989); S. Petrey, *Speech Acts and Literary Theory* (1990); J. Butler, *Bodies That Matter* (1993) and *Excitable Speech: A Politics of the Performative* (1997); D. Gorman, "The Use and Abuse of Speech Act Theory in Criticism," *PoT* 20 (1999); J. H. Miller, *Literature as Conduct: Speech Acts in Henry James* (2005); C. Nolan-Grant, "Jane Austen's Speech Acts and Language-Based Societies," *SEL* (2009).

S. S. LANSER

**SPENSERIAN STANZA.** The Spenserian stanza has been taken up by poets from Robert Burns to John Keats to Alfred, Lord Tennyson; but as its name suggests, it has never escaped association with its inventor, Edmund Spenser (1552–99). Its combination of versatility and idiosyncrasy may be unmatched: nine lines long, with a mix of alternating rhyme and *couplets (*ababbcbcc*), it proceeds in strict *pentameter up to its concluding *alexandrine. Spenser's principal sources were doubtless the Chaucerian *rhyme-royal stanza, which shifts, like his, to couplets at the fifth line (*ababbcc*), and the *ottava rima of It. epic (*abababcc*). The stanza is also shaped by the manifold narrative, imagistic, argumentative, and visionary uses to which *The Faerie Queene* puts it.

The first jolt the stanza gives its reader is that unexpected couplet. At the beginning of book 1, we learn that Red Cross's armor bears "The cruell markes of many a bloudy fielde," and in the next breath, "Yet armes till that time did he neuer wield" (1.1.1). It is the first of many double takes. That fifth line can also usher in a new stage of argument or a new event; it can drive a point home with double force; it can offer a resting place in the middle of the stanza. Any rest, however, is provisional at best, for the alternating rhymes promptly resume.

Some version of the same effect happens at the stanza's end, but this time, the line that completes the couplet has an extra foot. Length gives a sense of finality, and the alexandrine makes a good home for the poem's frequently sententious pronouncements ("That blisse may not abide in state of mortal men" [1.13.44]). There is authority in the nod to epic *hexameter and in the evenhandedness of the usual medial *caesura. That split down the middle, however, can also have a contrary effect, introducing, with the help of an unstated *beat at the joint, the native jounce and narrative carry of *ballad meter ("She turnd her bote about, and from them rowed quite" [2.12.16]).

Spenser uses this peculiar stanza to think with, and it suits his epic's self-critical habits of mind: sometimes careening but more often pausing to doubt, to declare, and then to doubt again. Other poets have variously adapted these potentials. James Thomson's *Castle of Indolence* is full of Spenserian stops and starts; Keats's "Eve of St. Agnes" is more apt to swoon through the middle of the stanza without taking a breath, as Tennyson does in "The Lotus Eaters." Some of the stanza's inheritors conjure Spenser's resuscitated medievalism, some his dreamy storytelling; all of them conjure Spenser, who can never be cast out of the strange room he built.

■ Empson; P. Alpers, *The Poetry of "The Faerie Queene"* (1967); J. Dolven, "The Method of Spenser's Stanza," *Spenser Studies* 21 (2004).

J. DOLVEN

**SPIRITUAL.** Although blues singers often say "all of our music came out of the church," the spiritual and the *blues are quite different. Originating probably in the 18th c., the spiritual is a religious folk song distinct from the *hymn, the *psalm, and other sacred songs of a biblical or ecclesiastical character. Originally called *jubilee*, the spiritual was centered in the daily lives and concerns of Af. slaves and driven by the Protestant revivals of the 18th and 19th cs. Arna Bontemps observed the earthiness of the blues in contrast to the heavenly aspirations of the spiritual. In addition, the spiritual is communal and choral, whereas the blues is often individualistic and even idiosyncratic.

Epstein and Lovell discuss the devel. of the Af. Am. spiritual in historical perspective and discuss the reactions of 19th- and 20th-c. observers. Tribute to the deeply moving music may be found in accounts by James Weldon Johnson, W.E.B. Du Bois, Thomas W. Higginson, and others. Higginson repeatedly refers to the texts of the songs as poetry, a description often used by others who heard the music. The influence of Af. musical and verbal forms as well as the nature of the spiritual's transformation of camp-meeting hymns (popular with white Protestants of the 19th c.) is a topic of perennial discussion. But there is no doubt that the Af. Am. spiritual is a distinctive fusion of Eur. and Af. models, Am. frontier Christianity, and the experience of slavery. The best of the songs, in Johnson's words, "sang a race from wood and stone to Christ."

*See* AFRICAN AMERICAN POETRY, DEVOTIONAL POETRY.

■ T. W. Higginson, *Army Life in a Black Regiment* (1870); W.E.B. Du Bois, *The Souls of Black Folks* (1903); G. P. Jackson, *White Spirituals in the Southern Uplands* (1933); J. W. Johnson and J. R. Johnson, *The Books of American Negro Spirituals* (1940); G. P. Jackson, *White and Negro Spirituals* (1943); A. Bontemps, "Introduction," *The Book of Negro Folklore*, ed. L. Hughes and A. Bontemps (1958); J. Lovell Jr., *Black Song* (1974); D. J. Epstein, *Sinful Tunes and Spirituals* (1977); A. J. Raboteau, *Slave Religion* (1978); W. T. Walker, *"Somebody's Calling My Name": Black Sacred Music and Social Change* (1979); E. J. Lorenz, *Glory Hallelujah! The Story of the Camp-Meeting Spiritual* (1980); D. J. Epstein, "A White Origin for the Black Spiritual? An Invalid Theory and How It Grew," *American Music* 1 (1983); E. Peters, "The Poetics of the Afro-American Spiritual," *Black American Literature Forum* 23 (1989), and *Lyrics of the Afro-American Spiritual* (1991); W. F. Pitts, *Old Ship of Zion: The Afro-Baptist Ritual in the African Diaspora* (1993).

S. E. HENDERSON

**SPLIT LINES.** Originating in cl. drama, split lines are metrically complete lines shared by two or more speakers, often producing an effect of rapidity in the exchange between them. Examples include exchanges between Oedipus and Creon in Sophocles' *Oedipus Rex* and between Medea and her nurse in Seneca's *Medea*. In his essay on Senecan tragedy in Elizabethan trans., T. S. Eliot quotes the latter, calling the split lines "minimum antiphonal units." Split lines became a feature of Elizabethan drama, with Thomas Kyd, Christopher Marlowe, John Webster, and Ben Jonson among those using them, in addition to Shakespeare, whose plays show a steady increase in the percentage of split lines over his career—the late plays contain from 15 to almost 20%, peaking in *Antony and Cleopatra* and *Coriolanus*—as the point of breaking in the line steadily moves to the right. Whereas the First Folio of Shakespeare's plays does not distinguish split lines visually, they appear with a distinct visual format—the second part of the line indented beyond the end of the first after an intervening strophic boundary—in William Wordsworth's "Tintern Abbey," in which the visible break signals some transition in the speaker's thought or feeling, rather than an exchange between two speakers. Among the modernists, visible split lines appear in the poems of Robert Frost (his two-speaker dramatic poems), Wallace Stevens, Ezra Pound, W. C. Williams, and Eliot, among others. But often in the case of Williams or Pound, a question arises: in verse without a metrical norm, how can one distinguish between, on the one hand, two or more parts of a single line and, on the other, two or more lines with visual formatting that uses indentation? In the later 20th c., Charles Wright made split lines his signature technique (as in *Halflife*, 1988), speaking of the "dropped line" or "low rider" and signaling the intralinear status of his breaks by capitalizing the first words of left-justified lines.

■ T. S. Eliot, *Elizabethan Dramatists* (1963); M. G. Tarlinskaja, *Shakespeare's Verse* (1987), ch. 4; G. T. Wright, *Shakespeare's Metrical Art* (1988), ch. 8.

T.V.F. BROGAN; G. BRADEN; S. CUSHMAN

**SPOKEN WORD.** *See* PERFORMANCE, POETRY SLAM.

**SPONDEE** (Gr., "used at a libation," i.e., poured to the accompaniment of the two long notes). In *classical prosody, a metrical unit consisting of two long syllables; in the mod. accentually based prosodies, a *foot of two stressed syllables. Cl. meters entirely composed of spondees—*versus spondaicus* (spondaic verse)—are rare but do occur (West). But normally, as in the dactylic hexameter, the spondee is an optional substitution for a *dactyl in the first five feet and obligatory in the last (metrical marking of closure is a widely attested phenomenon). Allen, therefore, thinks the spondee "can hardly be termed a 'foot' in its own right," since it does not manifest internal opposition or contrast of members, and cites Pohlsander, who holds that the spondee "has no real existence of its own . . . but must always be considered the contracted form of some other metrical unit."

In the prosodies of the mod. Germanic langs.,

which have been traditionally scanned in feet, the existence of spondaic feet is disputed. Several knowledgable and sensible mod. metrists (J. B. Mayor, George Saintsbury, Fitzroy Pyle, Clive Scott, G. T. Wright) have long held that the foot of two heavy syllables is a legitimate variation in iambic verse: they point to examples such as the last two syllables of the following lines: "The dove pursues the griffon, the mild hind" (Shakespeare, *A Midsummer Night's Dream* 2.1.232), or "The long day wanes, the slow moon climbs" (Alfred, Lord Tennyson, "Ulysses"), or "Silence, ye troubl'd waves, and thou Deep, peace" (John Milton, *Paradise Lost* 7.216), or the third and fourth syllables of "That in one speech two negatives affirm" (Philip Sidney, *Astrophil and Stella* 63.14). Absolutists, these metrists hold that, if two contiguous odd-even stresses in a line are both strong—perhaps not perfectly equal in strength (though that is certainly possible) but nearly so—then they should both be counted as strong, and the foot is, thus, a spondee. That is, if both stresses are, on a scale of four degrees of stress (1 strongest, 4 weakest), 1s or 2s (i.e., either the sequence 1-2 or 2-1), then *scansion should reflect the fact that these levels are both above 3 and 4. As in the examples from Tennyson and Milton, such alleged instances of spondees are often made possible by two adjacent monosyllables or, more clearly, by a major syntactic juncture within the foot.

Other mod. metrists (e.g., Edwin Guest, W. W. Skeat, Jakob Schipper, Derek Attridge, Susanne Woods), esp. those who base their theories on ling., deny the existence of the spondee and *pyrrhic in mod. verse, either on the basis of their definition of the foot itself as an element of metrical theory or else on the basis of Otto Jespersen's Relative Stress Principle (RSP), which explicitly prohibits absolute weighting of stress (hence, two heavy syllables within one foot). Jespersen's relativity principle assumed the existence of metrical feet and amounted to the claim that stress matters only in relation to immediately contiguous syllables, esp. the one syllable preceding. Hence, for him, the sequence "and thou Deep, peace" amounts to two iambs—unequal ones, perhaps, but iambs. The RSP yielded, for many metrists, elegant and subtle scansions that preserved both extensive metrical conformity (it allowed only iambs and trochees, in effect) and expressive readings. But it did this at the expense of variety in feet and of, some felt, due recognition of weighting in the line. Pyle rightly identifies the underlying issue at stake as being the question of "how far does the metre actually influence our rendering of stress as we read?" Readers and metrists who grant a strong influence will deny the existence of spondees (McAuley), those a weak influence, affirm (Pyle). Relativist scansion more accurately tracks the shape of line movement; absolutist scansion more accurately takes account of which syllables are heavy and which not.

It is evident that, in certain contexts where full syllable realization is granted every syllable, spondaic words can occur (Fussell gives the example of "Amen"), but these may represent an unusual performance mode and

so be exceptions. In any event, the normal processes of stress alternation and reduction operate so systematically in Eng. phonology that, in compound words or in phrases of any length, spondees are difficult at best. Still, absolutists in scansion can produce strong examples, as Wright does from Shakespeare. Of course, mod. imitations of cl. meters such as the *hexameter attempt to reproduce spondees either accentually or by some theory of quantities.

*See* CLASSICAL METERS IN MODERN LANGUAGES.

■ P. Fussell, *Poetic Meter and Poetic Form* (1965); J. McAuley, *Versification* (1966); F. Pyle, "Pyrrhic and Spondee," *Hermathena* 107 (1968); Allen; West; Scott; Attridge, *Rhythms*; G. T. Wright, *Shakespeare's Metrical Art* (1988); *Meter in English: A Critical Engagement*, ed. D. Baker (1996); C. Addison, "Stress Felt, Stroke Dealt: The Spondee, the Text, and the Reader," *Style* 39 (2005).

T.V.F. BROGAN

**SPONTANEITY.** A key term in romantic poetics, *spontaneity* falls at one end of the perennial debate over whether great art results from craft or *inspiration. Although Horace allows for *invention, he claims that technique and moral sense are "the source and font of proper writing" (*Ars poetica* 309). This position influenced the poetics of the Ren. In *Certayne Notes of Instruction* (1575), George Gascoigne recommends that the poet "stand most upon the excellencie of [his] Invention, & sticke not to studie deeply for some fine devise" but emphasizes the necessity of tempering invention with technical precision. Likewise, although Philip Sidney's *Defence of Poesy* (1595) refers to the poet being "lifted up with the vigour of his own inventions," Sidney ultimately prioritizes moral instruction as the task of true poetry. Seventeenth-c. empirical philosophy, notably in Thomas Hobbes and John Locke, opposes the innateness of emotional awareness to acquired knowledge and skill, stressing the need to control *wit and invention through reason and judgment. Given the influence of these ideas on the Enlightenment, spontaneity was not esp. prized in the 18th c.; witness Alexander Pope's poetry and Samuel Johnson's crit.

The Eng. romantics, who connected spontaneity with *sincerity and *naturalism, make the strongest claims. William Wordsworth's Preface to the 2d ed. of *Lyrical Ballads* proclaims "good poetry" the "spontaneous overflow of powerful feelings." P. B. Shelley's *Defence of Poetry* (1821; pub. 1840) distinguishes poetry from reasoning, "a power . . . exerted according to the determination of the will," insisting that "[a] man cannot say 'I will compose poetry.'" In "The Two Kinds of Poetry" (1833), John Stuart Mill states that "the poetry of a [natural poetic mind] is Feeling itself, employing Thought only as the medium of its utterance." Mill's account parallels Friedrich Schiller's notion of *naive Dichtung*—itself based on Immanuel Kant's characterization of how poetry "expands the mind . . . by letting it feel its faculty—free, spontaneous, and independent of determination" (3d *Critique* § 53). Other 19th-c.

writers, incl. Thomas Carlyle and R. W. Emerson, emphasize the lyrical nature of the poet's sentiments; in "The Poet," Emerson counsels, "Doubt not, O poet, but persist. Say 'It is in me, and shall out.'"

Fin de siècle poetics valued the subjective immediacy of spontaneity as a vehicle for conveying instantaneous feelings; consider Walter Pater's aesthetics and the Fr. symbolists (see SYMBOLISM). Modernist movements, esp. *Dada, inherited this interest in subjective immediacy, as evinced in the *sound poetry of Hugo Ball, Tristan Tzara, and Richard Huelsenbeck. Spontaneity also proved particularly important for the automatic techniques of *surrealism in the expression of imagination and emotion without deliberate control. Drawing on elements of late surrealism and socialist realism, 20th-c. Lat.-Am. avant-garde poetry advanced a new conception of the relationship between spontaneity and method; witness Pablo Neruda's notion of *espontaneidad dirigida* (directed spontaneity) and Octavio Paz's insistence that poetry is born out of the "struggle" or "embrace" between spontaneity and "conscious lucidity." After World War II, the *Beat poets, with their loose structures and spontaneous prosody, furnish other good examples—as does, more recently, the work of *performance and spoken-word poets, such as Hedwig Gorsky, Cid Corman, David Antin, and Lemn Sissay.

*See* INTENTION.

■ Abrams; W. J. Bate, *The Burden of the Past and the English Poet* (1970); J. Engell, *The Creative Imagination: Enlightenment to Romanticism* (1981); W. Fox, *Immediacy: A Poetic Stance from the Romantics to the Contemporaries* (1981); D. Belgrad, *The Culture of Spontaneity: Improvisation and the Arts in Postwar America* (1999); L. Wheeler, *Voicing American Poetry: Sound and Performance from the 1920s to the Present* (2008).

J. L. MAHONEY; C. DONALDSON

**SPRUCHDICHTUNG.** The term *Spruchdichtung* is used in med. studies to denote two predominantly didactically oriented text types in Ger. lit. of the 12th to 15th cs. and partly of the 16th, which, however, are genetically unconnected. These text types—involving, on the one hand, spoken poems of short or medium length in four-beat rhyming *couplets (*Reimsprüche, Reden*) and, on the other, sung stanzas (*Sangsprüche*) composed in more or less complicated forms—are not directly related to *didactic poetry in Lat. or in the Romance-speaking areas. The term *Spruch* for spoken texts was already common in the Middle Ages, while the term *Spruch* or *Sangspruch* for sung stanzas was not coined until the 19th c.

The text type, Sangspruch, is found from the 12th c. alongside other forms of the med. Ger. song (*Minnelied*, the spiritual and secular leich, and other spiritual songs). Sangspruch texts incorporate elaborations on all kinds of teaching about religion, morals, and social class; positions taken on political events and their protagonists; learned nature studies; praise of poets; and polemics between poets. Until the middle of the 14th c., the monostanzaic principle prevailed: each stanza was in principle an independent entity, though several single stanzas could combine to form more or less loose groupings. This principle constituted an important formal difference between the Sangspruch and the Minnelied, in which several stanzas were the rule. From the middle of the 14th c., the polystanzaic principle became the rule in Spruchdichtung. It is characteristic that the stanzaic forms and melodies the authors used were for the most part not employed only once (as was the case with *Minnesang*), but the individual poets also had at their disposal a definite, if small, repertoire of *Töne* (sing. *Ton*), which they employed repeatedly for texts of the most varied contents. *Ton* is understood to be the combination of stanzaic form (metrical and rhyme scheme) and melody. From the period around 1200, the tripartite form was prescribed for the Töne, consisting of two metrically and melodically identical parts (AA = *Aufgesang*, upsong) and a divergent third part (B = *Abgesang*, downsong) or a variant of this.

The Sangspruch poets were predominantly professional authors who gained their livelihood for the most part as traveling poets writing on commission. They were often in competition with one another as well as with other entertainers. They drew on a well-developed awareness of their own art and trad. Their typical role was that of the knowledgeable teacher, which explains the then-customary designation as *meister*, i.e., *magister*, a title that emphasized their authority.

The traceable hist. of Spruchdichtung begins with two authors of the late 12th c. whose texts have been passed down under the single name Spervogel (sparrow). The text type reaches its high point around 1200 with Walther von der Vogelweide (who was at the same time the most important Ger. *Minnesinger*). Through the high quality of Walther's poetry and his integration of political themes, Spruchdichtung became the second most important genre of med. Ger. song. Between Walther's time and about 1475, some 60 Sangspruch poets are known. Other famous poets include Frauenlob (d. 1318), Heinrich von Mügeln (d. ca. 1370), and Michel Beheim (d. ca. 1472 or 1479). From ca. 1400, Spruchdichtung was imitated and continued by the urban mastersingers down to the 18th c.

The Reimspruch lasted from the early 13th c. to the 16th. The authors of this formally less demanding art were professional poets or dilettantes. Religious and secular teaching of all kinds, politics, and, at times, entertainment were also involved here. Three poets of particular note in this connection are, in the 13th c., Freidank, author of a widely circulated collection of poems with short texts of a didactic and contemp. character, and der Stricker, author of, among others, spiritual, secular-didactic, and political Spruchdichtung; in the 14th c., Heinrich der Teichner. From the 15th c. on, poetry-writing artisans in towns made particular use of this form, which in the 16th c. underwent a further revival, thanks to Hans Sachs.

■ **Criticism and History:** E. Lämmert, *Reimsprecherkunst im Spätmittelalter* (1970); B. Wachinger, *Sängerkrieg* (1973); H. Brunner, *Die alten Meister* (1975); F.

Schanze, *Meisterliche Liedkunst*, 2 v. (1983–84); *Repertorium der Sangsprüche und Meisterlieder des 12. bis 18. Jhs.*, ed. H. Brunner and B. Wachinger, 16 v. (1986–2009); *Sangspruchdichtung*, ed. D. Klein et al. (2007). ■ **Primary Texts**: *Reinmar von Zweter*, ed. G. Roethe (1887); *Heinrich der Teichner*, ed. H. Niewöhner, 3 v. (1953–56); *Heinrich von Mügeln*, ed. K. Stackmann, 3 v. (1959); *Michel Beheim*, ed. H. Gille and I. Spriewald, 3 v. (1968–1972); *Frauenlob*, ed. K. Stackmann and K. Bertau, 2 v. (1981); *Walther von der Vogelweide*, ed. K. Lachmann and C. Cormeau (1996).

H. BRUNNER

**SPRUNG RHYTHM.** G. M. Hopkins coined the term *sprung rhythm* to characterize the poetic rhythm that he used first in his great ode "The Wreck of the Deutschland" and in numerous subsequent poems, incl. most of his best known. Hopkins describes the rhythm most valuably in his Author's Preface, composed for the later poems, "Deutschland" and after, and in a long letter to his poet-friend, Canon Richard Watson Dixon (October 5, 1878). He tells Dixon the "echo" of the rhythm long "haunted" his ear before he "realized [it] on paper" in the ode. To explain how poetic rhythm may be "sprung," he instances the work of John Milton, "the great standard in the use of counterpoint." *Counterpoint is prominent in *Paradise Lost* and *Paradise Regain'd*, and then Milton carries it much further in the choruses of *Samson Agonistes*, which are "counterpointed throughout" so that each line "has two different coexisting scansions. But when you reach that point the secondary or 'mounted rhythm,' which is necessarily a sprung rhythm, overpowers the original or conventional one and then this becomes superfluous." Sprung rhythm, as Hopkins points out, cannot be counterpointed.

Hopkins tells Dixon that sprung rhythm "consists in scanning by accents or stresses alone . . . so that a foot may be one strong syllable or it may be many light and one strong." His imprecision does not mean, however, that the foot patterns are in his mind arbitrary or of no importance, as his explanation in his Author's Preface shows. Except for "particular effect," the sprung-rhythm foot will have one to four syllables. The nuclear stress may come at any point in the foot, but "it is a great convenience to follow the example of music and take the stress always first," producing "four sorts of feet, a monosyllable and the so-called accentual Trochee, Dactyl, and the First Paeon [four syllables ('xxx)]. And there will be four corresponding natural rhythms." However, labeling a poem's rhythm accordingly, as, for instance, the poet's headnote identifying "The Windhover" as "falling paeonic," seems of minimal practical help for *scansion. It is more useful to consider the effect that the poet aims for with sprung rhythm.

Hopkins wants his poetry to be "logaoedic," to combine the advantages of prose and verse. Writing to Robert Bridges (August 21, 1877), he states he uses sprung rhythm "because it is the nearest to the rhythm of prose, that is the native and natural rhythm of speech, the least forced, the most rhetorical and emphatic of all possible rhythms, combining, as it seems to me, opposite and, one wd. have thought, incompatible excellences, markedness of rhythm—that is rhythm's self—and naturalness of expression." In sprung rhythm, two kinds of verbal music happily intersect: on the one hand, it has marked rhythm, requiring a clearly defined recurrence of stress; on the other hand, it has naturalness, the stress pattern of natural speech. The *paeon is of particular interest to Hopkins. In his lecture notes on "Rhythm and Other Structural Parts of Rhetoric," he observes that the foot patterns that Aristotle prescribes for oratory are the first and fourth paeon, neither of which can make "meters" (verse lines) in the common ("running") rhythms. Sprung rhythm, however, makes the metrical paeon possible.

The naturalness of sprung rhythm results importantly from its free mixing of foot types, producing both adjacent and widely separated stress, thereby obscuring the underlying regularity of the rhythm. Hopkins emphasizes that his rhythm does not result from laxity in timing, but rather is carefully planned. He contrasts his rhythm with Walt Whitman's, whose verse he admired: Whitman's verses verge on "decomposition into common prose," while his own are "very highly wrought. . . . Everything is weighed and timed in them" (letter to Bridges, Oct. 18, 1882). "The native and natural rhythm of speech" that Hopkins aims for with sprung rhythm, then, does not arise from imitating ordinary linguistic intonation. Instead, it comes from an artful reconstitution of it. He tells his brother Everard in a late letter (Nov. 5, 1885), "Sprung rhythm makes verse stressy; it purges it to an emphasis as much brighter, livelier, more lustrous than the regular emphasis of common rhythm as poetry in general is brighter than common speech." A reading of sprung rhythm verse will be "poetical" rather than rhetorical; in his Author's Preface, he instructs the reader of sprung rhythm "strongly to mark the beats of the measure . . . not disguising the rhythm and the rhyme, as some readers do, who treat poetry as if it were prose fantastically written to rule . . . , but laying on the beat too much stress rather than too little." He declares to Bridges (May 21, 1878), "Stress is the life of it."

■ *Correspondence of Gerard Manley Hopkins and R. W. Dixon,* ed. C. C. Abbott (1935); *Letters of Gerard Manley Hopkins to Robert Bridges,* ed. C. C. Abbott (1935); M. Holloway, *Prosodic Theory of Gerard Manley Hopkins* (1947); W. Ong, "Hopkins' Sprung Rhythm and the Life of English Poetry," *Immortal Diamond,* ed. N. Weyand (1949); *Journals and Papers of Gerard Manley Hopkins,* ed. H. House and G. Storey (1959); E. Schneider, *Dragon in the Gate* (1968); C. Scott, *A Question of Syllables* (1986), chap. 5; P. Kiparsky, "Sprung Rhythm," *Rhythm and Meter,* ed. P. Kiparsky and G. Youmans (1989); N. MacKenzie, "Metrical Marks," *Poetical Works of Gerard Manley Hopkins,* 5th ed. (1990); J. I. Wimsatt, "Alliteration and Hopkins's Sprung Rhythm," *PoT* 19 (1998), and *Hopkins's Poetics of Speech Sound* (2006).

J. I. WIMSATT

# SRI LANKA, POETRY OF

I. Sinhala
II. Tamil
III. English

Sri Lankan poetry covers work in three langs.: Sinhala, which dates to the 1st c. CE; Tamil, which developed a distinctly Sri Lankan identity in the 20th c.; and Eng., of which a small but significant body of work now exists, dating mainly from the mid-20th c.

I. Sinhala. The Sinhala lang. has been used almost exclusively in Sri Lanka, but the contours of Sinhala's poetic heritage resonate with those generally found elsewhere in South Asia. These contours include two key features of literary cultures in premod. South Asia: the restriction of the production of poetry to a limited number of langs., such as Sanskrit and various literary Prakrits, and the recourse to multiple langs. by authors within a single literary culture. These two features have left a profound imprint on Sinhala poetry writing across the centuries, first, in terms of a continuing sense of Sinhala's intrinsic exceptionalism in poetry and, second, in terms of how Sinhala poetry was often inflected by values and conventions that originated in poetry written in other langs.

The most striking feature of exceptionalism in Sinhala literary cultures is in the very fact of the use of Sinhala as a vehicle for poetry. Along with Tamil, Sinhala was among the first local langs. used for poetry in South Asia, with significant examples of poetry and poetic crit. surviving from at least the 7th c. CE. Sinhala poets seem remarkably early to have considered the Sinhala lang. as equal to Sanskrit in its capacity to be a vehicle for poetry, and, ironically, they displayed this confidence in their poems at about the same time that theorization about poetry in Sanskrit explicitly denied that local langs. like Sinhala were capable of poetry. If Sinhala provides some of the earliest evidence for a literary culture in South Asia using a local lang. for poetry, it also provides evidence that this choice must have involved self-consciousness on the part of poets about not being bound by at least some of the conventions that defined literary works and persons in Sanskrit literary culture, even though it was generally normative in premod. South Asia.

Sinhala also provides evidence that the transformation of a lang. used for everyday interaction into one capable of poetry occurred through a standardization and theorization of lang. in grammar and poetics. The processes that transformed Sinhala into a lang. of poetry, however, were often the result of interaction with thinking about poetry found in other langs. The 9th-c. *Siyabaslakara* (Poetics of One's Own Language), one of the earliest extant scholarly works in Sinhala, is a handbook on poetics that turned to Sanskrit texts such as Daṇḍin's *Kāvyādarśa* for models of thinking about poetics, while the cl. *Sidatsangarava* (Compilation of Methods), a work of both grammar and poetics, seems related to a similar text in Tamil, the 11th-c. *Viracoliyam*. Moreover, in view of this exceptionalism, Sinhala

poets were quite self-conscious about their literary heritage, and they took a variety of steps to ensure the continuity of the lang. used in Sinhala poetry. Their success in this is evident in the gulf between the lang. commonly used in poetry and that used in other written expressions and in speech.

The generative interaction between Sinhala literary cultures and the poetry and poetics produced in other langs. has resulted in a composite Sinhala poetic heritage, one with distinct strands that display their origin in the interaction of Sinhala poets with other literary langs., esp. with Sanskrit, Tamil, and Eng. Another distinct strand within the Sinhala poetic heritage comes from interaction with various forms of folk poetry in Sri Lanka, whether in the form that shades into secular songs or in the form that shades into religious rituals. Folk poetry, whether closer to *song or to ritual expression, is marked by the absence of identifiable poets. A case could be made that the trads. of folk poetry continually nourished and sustained the poetic heritage of Sinhala literary cultures but that, in a stricter sense, those cultures were concerned with the production of poets, as identifiable figures, as much as with the production of poems.

The earliest extant examples of poetry in Sinhala are found at Sigiriya, a ruined palace complex in central Sri Lanka. A body of poems about representations of women in paintings found at these ruins was inscribed by visitors at Sigiriya between the 7th and 9th cs., and the poetic conventions found in these graffiti are clearly continuous with the lang. and form of Sinhala poetry written between the 10th and 15th cs. While there are meters used in the poems that seem to be unique to Sinhala poetry, there also seems to be a sophisticated awareness of *Sanskrit poetry and poetics.

Beginning around the 11th or 12th c., Sinhala poets began to adapt more of the conventions of Sanskrit poetry, esp. in ornate poems (*mahākāvya*) that recounted the stories of the previous lives of the Buddha. The content of these poems often seems subordinate to the conventions of the genre in Sanskrit, such as the descriptions of a set number of topics, but they also preserved the formal qualities of Sinhala poetry in meter and style. The greatest of these poems perhaps is *Kavsilumina* (The Crest Gem of Poetry), which continues to occupy a central place in the canon of Sinhala poetry.

This adaptation of models from Sanskrit for Sinhala poetry continued throughout the med. period, esp. in the genre of messenger poems (*sandēśa*), which took Kālidāsa's *Meghadhūta* as a model. The Sinhala poems produced in this genre, such as the *Sälalihini sandēśa*, share distinctive features with poems composed on the same model across southern South Asia—in Sanskrit, *Malayalam, and *Tamil—in the same period.

In the early mod. period, Sinhala poets adapted more from Tamil poetry than seems to have been the case earlier, as can be seen in *internal rhyming patterns and literary *allusions, but at the same time, Sinhala poets of this era expanded the scope of appropriate subjects for poetry writing beyond the set topics that had characterized earlier poetry. As a result, these poets, writing in the colonized southern coastal regions of the island, introduced a greater sense of personal emotion into the heritage of Sinhala poetry. New forms of adaptation from other poetic models occurred in the 20th c., when nationalist movements stimulated literary activity, much of it Buddhist, classicist, revivalist, and didactic. The 20th c. also saw the growth of a secular poetry, nationalist in theme and traditional in form. By the 1930s, Munidasa Kumaranatunge (1887–1944) had begun a movement for lang. reform termed *Hela*, to rid Sinhala of Sanskrit influences. Kumaranatunge's critical writings had considerable impact, and his poems for children introduced a new simplicity into Sinhala poetry.

The major breakthrough came with the introduction of *nisandäs kavi* (*free verse). G. B. Senanayake (1913–85) had experimented with unrhymed verse forms as early as 1945 in his poems in *Paligänima* (Revenge). However, it was Siri Gunasinghe (b. 1925) in *Mas Le Näti Äta* (Bones without Flesh or Blood, 1956), *Abhinikmana* (Renunciation, 1958), and *Ratu Käkulu* (Red Buds, 1962) who established and popularized the form. Gunasinghe together with others such as Gunadasa Amerasekera (b. 1929) and Wimal Dissanayake, who were part of the literary world of the University of Peradeniya in the 1950s, became known as the Peradeniya poets. Influenced by the literary theories of Am. *New Criticism, they were at first criticized as Westernized ivory-tower aesthetes, but their work soon gained acceptance. Their writings gave a new vitality and flexibility to the lang. Ediriweera Sarachcharanda (1914–96), the foremost critic and theorist of the group, also revolutionized the theater with his poetic dramas *Maname* (1956) and *Simhabahu* (1958).

The 1970s saw a fresh burst of poetic activity by writers whose works reflected a strong social concern. However, their evocative use of lang. and the confidence with which they drew on cl. and folk as well as foreign lits. gave their work an energy that overrode the didacticism. Mahagama Sekera's (1929–76) *Heta Irak Payayi* (Tomorrow a Sun Will Rise, 1971), *Nomiyami* (I Will Not Die, 1973), and *Prabuddha* (1976); Parakrama Kodituwakku's *Akikaru Putrayakuge Lokayak* (The World of a Disobedient Son, 1974) and *Alut Minihesk Ävit* (A New Man Has Come, 1976); and Monica Ruwanpathirana's (1945–2004) *Tahanam Desayakin* (From a Forbidden World, 1972) and *Obe Yeheliya Äya Gähäniya* (Your Friend, She Is Woman, 1975) are some of the important works of this group.

The dynamic energy of the 1970s slackens perceptibly by the 1980s. The civil war, disturbing and demoralizing but strangely distant because it was fought in the north, left hardly any mark on the poetry. The creative impetus seems to shift away from poetry to drama. However, the 21st c. has seen the resurgence of a vibrant poetic idiom in the work of Liyanage Amarakeerthi. He draws from life in rural Sri Lanka in conflict with political and social change in his collection *Ekamatha Eka Pita Rataka* (2005).

**II. Tamil.** While the Tamil presence in Sri Lanka goes back to very early times, Tamil lit. gained a distinct Sri Lankan identity only much later. The earliest reference to a Sri Lankan Tamil poet is in the Sangam lit. of the 3d c. CE, where verses attributed to Putatevanar with the prefix *Elathu* (Lanka) appear. In 1310 CE, *Caracotimalai* by Pocaraca Panditar was presented in the court of the Sinhala king Parakramabahu III at Dambadeniya. These are the only references for the early period.

The flourishing Tamil kingdom in the Jaffna peninsula (14th–17th c.) gave rise to several poetical works. The best known was *Rakuvamcam* by Aracakecari, the *poet laureate. Under colonial rule, the proselytizing activities of Christian missionaries spawned a genre of religious poetry that was given further impetus by the introduction of printing.

Early Sri Lankan Tamil poetry had traditionally been seen merely as an extension of Indian Tamil writing; but by the 1940s, a renaissance occurred, when many young poets began to emphasize their Sri Lankan identity. A distinctly different Tamil poetry soon evolved. Nantaran, Kantacami, and Mahakavi are important poets of this period. Simplicity, colloquial meters, and concrete visual images are the hallmarks of this Lankan Tamil poetry.

When Sinhala was made the official lang. in 1956, a new political consciousness evolved among the Tamils. Three schools of poetry emerged. The first was nationalist, in support of a Tamil federal state. The second group called themselves *Progressives*, was influenced by left-wing ideologies, and advocated a radical transformation of Sri Lankan society, both Sinhala and Tamil. The third refused to be identified with either group and wrote a very individualized poetry. Mod. forms such as free verse were introduced, and poets and poetry proliferated.

By the 1970s, Tamil political aspirations for a separate state led to guerrilla war. Thereafter, the experience for Sri Lankan Tamil poets was blood, tears, violence, battle, exile, death, and life amid death. The new *war poetry reflected these realities. Sri Lankan Tamil poetry now charts its own course and is entirely different from Indian Tamil writing unexposed to such experiences. During the second half of the war, from the mid-1990s, poetry became the foremost choice as the medium of literary expression. The major poets of the time are Jeyapalan, Ceran, Ceyan, Yecuraca, Vicayentran, Puthuvai Rathnadurai, and Vilvaratinam.

Love and war had been the basic themes of early Sangam lit. Once Tamil military exploits ceased after colonial conquest, war poetry died out. It is notable that Tamil-speaking writers of different regions in Sri Lanka have used the medium of poetry to express their lives in time of war and interethnic conflict. The Muslim writers in Tamil from the eastern region, such as Vedanti, Natchathiran Sevvinthiyan, N. Atma, Deva Abira, and Aswagosh have written about their distinct experience of displacement during the Tamil-Muslim conflict in the north and their experience as a Tamil-speaking community separate from the ethnically Tamil community of Sri Lanka. There are also the writers of the Tamil diaspora based in countries such as Canada, the U.K., France, and Germany who are using the poetic medium to express their experience of the Sri Lankan conflict and their private experience within the context of exile. Jeyapalan, Vijayendran, and Aravinthan use imagery at times that is a part of their migrant lives but new to *Tamil poetry.

**III. English.** English poetry in Sri Lanka developed its own identity in the mid-20th c. Lakkdasa Wickremasinghe in his pioneering work boldly experimented with the rhythms of Lankan Eng. *Lustre Poems* (1965) has a dynamic energy, while later works such as *The Grasshopper Gleaming* (1976) show his growing control of his medium. Yasmine Gooneratne's (b. 1935) *Word, Bird and Motif* (1971) and *Lizard's Cry* (1972) reveal her flair for the satiric mode, where her control of tone and sensitivity to the nuances of words have full play. Anne Ranasinghe's (b. 1925) *Poems* (1971) and *Plead Mercy* (1975) provide sharp insights into a range of personal experiences that bridge two worlds. Ranasinghe's works draw from her experiences as a Holocaust survivor and a child growing up in Europe during World War II and later as a resident in Sri Lanka by marriage. In works such as *July 1983* (1983), she comments from the inside with the perspective of the outsider, drawing parallels between historic events of extreme violence and cruelty in Europe and South Asia. Basil Fernando (b. 1944) in *A New Era to Emerge* (1973) and Jean Arasanayagam (b. 1931) in *Apocalypse* (1983) and *A Colonial Inheritance* (1985) write movingly of the realities of Sri Lankan life. Several new voices emerged at the beginning of the 21st c.: Vivimarie VanderPoorten (b. 1967), *Nothing Prepares You* (2007) and *Stitch Your Eyelids Shut* (2010); Ramya Chamalie Jirasinghe (b. 1971), *There's an Island in the Bone* (2010); and Malinda Seneviratne (b. 1965), *Threads* (2007). VanderPoorten uses sparse lang. to capture the experiences of violence, war, and exclusion, while Jirasinghe employs local *metaphor and vivid *imagery to write about personal narratives of identity and belonging against larger political and social structures. There are also a few of poets and writers of Sri Lankan origin who reside overseas, such as Rienzi Crusz (b. 1925) in Canada. They have appropriated a poetic lang. heavy with desire and longing to write about the experience of displacement, as Crusz does in *Love Where the Nights Are Green* (2008). The readership for Eng. poetry in Sri Lanka is small but influential, with the potential of international importance.

*See* ORAL POETRY, SANSKRIT POETICS.

■ **Anthologies**: *Poetry from the Sinhalese*, trans. G. Keyt (1939); *Sigiri Graffiti*, ed. and trans. S. Paranavitarne (1955); *An Anthology of Classical Sinhalese Literature*, ed. C. Reynolds (1970); "Poetry of Sri Lanka," *Journal of South Asian Literature* 12.1 (1976)—spec. iss.; *Modern Writing in Sinhala*, ed. R. Obeyesekere and C. Fernando (1978); "Sinhala and Tamil Writing from Sri Lanka," *Journal of South Asian Literature* 22.2 (1987)—spec. iss.; *Twelve Centuries of Sinhala Poetry*, trans. L. de Silva (2004); *The Penguin Book of Tamil Poetry: The Rapids of a Great River*, ed. and trans. L. Holstrom (2009); *Kaleidoscope 2: An Anthology of Sri Lankan English Literature*, ed. D.C.R.A. Goonetilleke (2010).

■ **Criticism and History**: C. E. Godakumbura, *Sinhalese Literature* (1955); K. S. Sivakumaran, *Tamil Writing in Sri Lanka* (1964); R. Obeyesekere, *Sinhalese Writing and the New Critics* (1974); K. Sivathamby, *Tamil Literature in Eelam* (1978); *The Sri Lanka Reader: History, Culture and Poetics*, ed. J. C. Holt (2011).

C. HALLISEY, R. OBEYESEKERE (SINHALESE);
D.B.S. JEYARAJ (TAMIL); R. OBEYESEKERE,
R. C. JIRASINGHE (ENG.)

**STANCES.** A Fr. verse form that is, on the one hand, synonymous with the *strophes of the *ode and, on the other hand, often confused with strophes, from which stances appear to differ by their restriction to lyrical themes and, in conformity with the etymology (Lat. *stantia*, "pause"; It. *stanze*, "stopping places"), by a more definite pause at the end of each division. Introduced into France from Italy in the second half of the 16th c., stances continued in use until well into the 19th c. (e.g., Alfred de Musset, F.R.A. Sully-Prudhomme). In early 17th-c. theater, esp. *tragedy, they were used as highly organized lyric *monologues: their thematic density, varied meters, and complex *rhyme schemes contrasted vividly with the *alexandrine couplets of dialogue. In the first half of the 18th c., stances were banished from the theater in the name of verisimilitude: that characters should possess such poetic skill when in the throes of violent emotion was no longer considered logical.

*See* FRENCH PROSODY.

■ P. Martinon, *Les Strophes* (1912), App. 2; J. Scherer, *La Dramaturgie classique en France* (1950), pt. 2, ch. 6; D. Janik, *Geschichte der Ode und der "Stances" vom Ronsard bis Boileau* (1968); M-F. Hilgar, *La Mode des stances dans le théâtre tragique français 1610–1687* (1974); B. de Cornulier, *Art poétique: Notions et problèmes de métrique* (1995).

A. E. EUSTIS; C. KLEINHENZ

**STANZA.** A unit of poetic lines organized by a specific principle or set of principles. The possibilities include *alliteration, *syntax, lineation, *meter, arc of thought, although most familiarly in Eng., the end rhyme fashions a stanza. Stanzas are sequential: they are identified as such by the intervals and by the other units of lines (often isomorphic with the first stanza) before and after them. They are periodic, guiding the reader alternately through a sojourn in their organized lines, then through the suspensions of stanzaic intervals. Traditionally, they are partitioned from each other by techniques of closure, e.g., a tag in another lang., *couplet or strong rhyme, *refrain or *envoi, *proverb or aphorism, *dialogue, lengthened or shortened line, or *tail rhyme. Longer, nonisomorphic groups of lines are sometimes referred to as *strophes.

Stanzas are found in poetic cultures both written and oral. They may emerge from a *song tradition in which words are composed to accompany a preexisting melody—an origin asserted in poetics from George Puttenham to Ezra Pound and manifest in the practice of poets like Thomas Campion and George Herbert. Stanzas arise also within the widespread professional cultures of compositional virtuosity like the *bardic and skaldic guilds of northwest Europe, the *troubadour culture of southern Europe, or late med. clerical and courtly milieux; these are often stanzas of technical intricacy. Stanza forms are also continually developed by major poet-thinkers of form (e.g., in Eng., the *Gawain/Pearl*-poet, Chaucer, Edmund Spenser, Ben Jonson, the John Keats of the odes, Thomas Hardy, Langston Hughes, A. R. Ammons, and Jorie Graham). In Eng., end rhyme has been the chief means of binding the massed lines of a stanza for more than 600 years, though poetries in other langs., as well as earlier alliterative work in OE and modernist and postmod. practice, manifest other ways of conceiving stanzaic form. Stanzas may hew to a simple pattern, three or four lines with one or two rhyme sounds, e.g., the *blues stanza or the *ballad stanza; a stanza may have identical or varying line lengths within a single stanza (*isometric or *heterometric, respectively); Eng. line lengths themselves may be as brief as one or two syllables, as long as a William Blake or a C.K. Williams can extend them. In spacious stanza forms—e.g., *ballade and pseudo-ballade, long-line alliterative stanzas, *ottava rima, *rhyme royal, the more ambitious tail-rhyme stanzas, *Spenserian stanza—rhyme patterns and groupings of line create dynamic complexities of internal movement. Such complexity is also evident in terse stanzas like the skaldic eight-line form *drottkvaett* or the Eng. common meter in the hands of Emily Dickinson. Syntax threads pathwise through the enclosed space of the stanza; the flexible play of syntax in relation to rhyme and line creates variety and movement through sequences of stanzas, while metrical structure maintained and repeated through sequences creates stability.

The relationship between the stanza and its interval offers flexible resources for shaping the stanza's *closure and the reader's temporal experience of periodicity; stanzas often deploy verb forms, tense, mood, and aspect as means to slow, to quicken, to close off, or to open upon the interval. (The Spenserian stanzas of P. B. Shelley and Lord Byron are swift-moving and climactic; the Spenserian stanzas of Keats are weightier and noun-based; those of Spenser himself are characterized by verbs of temporal extensivity, marking actions habitual, sustained, or repeated.)

Most descriptive and taxonomic work on Eur. stanza forms focuses on the stanza as an object or chunk of matter, a box-like unit, a "room" of poetic discourse in which aural elements governed by rules are lodged and fixed. Apropos of Eng. stanzas, this tendency to take the stanza as object or structure is intensified by defining stanzas chiefly in relation to their rhyme scheme. Stanzas have thus been evaluated by the degree to which they demonstrate internal coherence or integrity, in terms of form, syntax, content, and *figuration. Readers who require this sense of stanzaic

integrity are often disappointed with stanzaic devels. in the 20th and 21st cs., when aesthetics and philosophy articulate an opposition to the spatialization of time in preference to process and duration; when *organicism inherited from romantic poetics, *free verse, and field poetics challenge set forms; and when Western poets' encounters in the first half of the 20th c. with Chinese poetry and poetics (see CHINESE POETICS) give them access to a syntactic freedom and spareness that releases them from their sense of Eur. stanzaic traditions' enervation. But in light of early med., modernist, and postmod. practice as well as research in *ethnopoetics, no account of stanzas can be limited to the single story of form versus freedom; a global account would include multiple stories of stanzas' changeful work in mediating temporal experience.

Specific stanza forms arise and thrive in specific moments and cultures. They are always being embroiled in debates about form and freedom. But the political and ideological implications of specific stanza forms are never intrinsic, nor their future life predictable. The rigid form of the *sestina, which had pretty well disappeared from Eur. poetries after two decades of popularity in the 16th c., was revitalized in 20th-c. Am. poetry; the Persian *ghazal* with its single rhyme and its couplets has come into Eng. in the late 20th and 21st cs.; traditional Eng. poetry and free verse have shaken up 20th-c. Chinese poetry just as cl. Chinese poetry did Eng. modernism; Alexander Pushkin's *Onegin stanza now does interesting work in verse and novel all over the world; the engagements of Af. Am. and Caribbean writers with Eng. stanza trads. demonstrate the shifting and generative work of stanzaic form.

■ Schipper, *History*; P. Martinon, *Les Strophes: Études historiques et critiques sur les formes de la poésie lyrique on France depuis la Renaissance* (1912); I. Frank, *Répertoire métrique de la poésie des troubadours*, 2 vols. (1953–57); Maas; W. Pfrommer, *Grundzüge der Strophenentwicklung in derfranzösischen Lyric von Baudelaire zu Apollinaire*, diss., Tübingen (1963); Koster; T. Navarro, *Repertorio de estrofas españolas* (1968); U. Mölk and F. Wolfzettel, *Répertoire métrique de la poésie lyrique française des origines à 1350* (1972); F. Schlawe, *Die deutsche Strophenformen: Systematisch-chronologische Register zur deutschen Lyrik 1600–1950* (1972); Wimsatt; S. Ranawake, *Höfische Strophenkunst: Vergleichende Untersuchungen zur Formen-typologie von Minnesang und Trouverelied an der Wende zum Spatmittelalter* (1976); Tarlinskaja; E. Häublein, *The Stanza* (1978); H. J. Frank, *Handbuch der deutsche Strophenformen* (1980); A. Solimena, *Repertorio metrico dello Stil novo* (1980); T.V.F. Brogan, *English Versification, 1570–1980: A Reference Guide with Global Appendix* (1981); F. P. Memmo, *Dizionario di metrica italiana* (1983); G. S. Smith, "The Stanza Typology of Russian Poetry 1735–1816: A General Survey," *Russian Literature* 13, no. 2 (1983); T.V.F. Brogan, *Verseform: A Comparative Bibliography* (1989); Gasparov, *History*; P. Seital, *The Power of Genre: Interpreting Haya Oral Literature* (1999); A. Addison, "Little Boxes: The Effects of the Stanza on Poetic Narrative," *Style* 37, no. 2 (2003);

D. Hymes, *Now I Know Only So Far: Essays in Eth-nopoetics* (2003); J. Boffey and A.S.G. Edwards, *A New Index of Middle English Verse* (2005).

T. KRIER

**STASIMON** (Gr., "stationary song"). In Gr. drama, an *ode sung by the *chorus after it has taken its position in the orchestra. Aristotle distinguishes the *stasimon* from the *parodos*, the entrance ode of the chorus (in anapestic meter) as it marches into the orchestra, and defines it as "a song of the chorus without anapests or trochees" (*Poetics* 1452b). The stasima alternate with the episodes, the dialogue passages delivered by the actors; their number in *tragedy varies between three and five. Originally, and during the greater part of the 5th c. BCE, the stasima were intimately connected with the subject matter of the episodes. However, this connection gradually became tenuous until finally Agathon (ca. 447–400 BCE) replaced them by the *embolima*, intercalary pieces, mere choral interludes that could be introduced into any play (*Poetics* 1456a).
■ W. Aly, "Stasimon," Pauly-Wissowa; W. Kranz, *Stasimon* (1933); W.J.W. Koster, "De metris stasimi I and II Electrae Euripidis," *Mélanges Emile Boisacq*, v. 3 (1938); A. M. Dale, *Collected Papers* (1969)—esp. ch. 3; Michaelides.

P. S. COSTAS

**STAVE,** a back-formation from the pl. *staves*, of *staff*. (1) The old term for a group of lines or a stanza of a poem or song, particularly a hymn or drinking song, both of which often use *refrains. The term was perhaps derived from the musical staff and once was restricted to poems intended to be sung. (2) The initial *alliteration (sound) in a line of Old Germanic or OE verse. This sense of the term comes from Ger. *Stab* (staff)—hence, the Ger. terms *Stabreim* for alliteration and *stabreimender Vers* or *Stabreimvers* for alliterative verse.
*See* GERMANIC PROSODY, ENGLISH PROSODY, MUSIC AND POETRY.

R. O. EVANS

**STICHOMYTHIA** (Gr., "line-speech"). Refers to a highly formalized kind of *dialogue in Gr. and Lat. drama in which each speech is confined to a single metrical line. Equally formalized are two related phenomena: *distichomythia*, in which the exchanges are each exactly two lines long, and repartee in *split lines (the split line being called *antilabé*) in which one of two speakers gets the beginning of a line and the other gets the end (we might call this *hemistichomythia*). Every one of the 33 extant Gr. tragedies makes use of stichomythia (50, 75, or 100 lines of stichomythia occur), and many use the other two kinds as well. Long passages of stichomythia or distichomythia are not characteristic of Aristophanes or of Menander, who likes to start speeches midline. This naturalism was passed on to the Roman comic poets, who make no use of stichomythia. The fragments of the Roman tragic poets before Seneca show no traces of it. It was revived by Seneca, who uses

it in most of his plays, though the long runs of stichomythia characteristic of Gr. tragedy are rare.

Seneca's use of stichomythia and antilabé for repartee influenced William Shakespeare (e.g., *Richard III* 4.4 and *Hamlet* 3.4) and Molière. J. W. Goethe uses stichomythia in *Iphigenia auf Tauris*. An adaptation of stichomythia to another genre is the amoebean verse contest in *pastoral poetry (e.g. Theocritus, *Idyll* 5, and John Milton, *Comus*). There is a hilarious parody of tragic stichomythia and distichomythia in A. E. Housman's "Fragment of a Tragedy" (Burnett).
■ A. Gross, *Die Stichomythie in der griechischen Tragödie und Komödie* (1905); J. L. Hancock, *Studies in Stichomythia* (1917); J. Myres, *The Structure of Stichomythia in Attic Tragedy* (1950); W. Jens, *Die Stichomythie in der frühen griechischen Tragödie* (1955); E.-R. Schwinge, *Die Verwendung der Stichomythie in den Dramen des Euripides* (1968); B. Seidensticker, *Die Gesprächsverdichtung in den Tragödien Senecas* (1968), and "Die Stichomythie," *Die Bauformen der griechischen Tragödie*, ed. W. Jens (1971); S. Ireland, "Stichomythia in Aeschylus," *Hermes* 102 (1974); D. J. Mastronarde, *Contact and Discontinuity* (1979), chaps. 3 and 4; *The Poems of A. E. Housman*, ed. A. Burnett (1997).

W. H. RACE; D. KOVACS

**STICHOS,** Gr., "row," "line"; pl. *stichoi*. In cl. prosody, the term for a line of verse. A single line (or a poem one line long) is, therefore, called a *monostich, a couplet a *distich, a half line a *hemistich, etc. Outside of cl. prosody, the noun form now used is *line*, though the adjective *stichic* is still common. Stichic verse—e.g., *narrative poetry—is that which is written *kata stichon*, i.e., in a continuous run of *isometric lines, whereas in stanzaic verse—e.g., the *lyric—a small number of lines or cola (usually fewer than ten but often four or multiples of four) are grouped together by structures such as *rhyme into integral units. Stichic arrangement is the norm for recited verse (see RECITATION)—in antiquity, the dactylic hexameter for *epic and the iambic trimeter for drama—whereas song verse (incl. the lyric) is normally stanzaic. It is not exactly true, as Maas points out, that verse forms are either stichic or strophic: there are some intermediary or transitional forms, and some of the same principles of construction apply to both types.
*See* ALLÆOSTROPHA, STANZA, STROPHE.
■ J. W. White, *The Verse of Greek Comedy* (1912); Maas; A. M. Dale, "Stichos and Stanza," *Collected Papers* (1969).

T.V.F. BROGAN; R. J. GETTY

**STOCK** (also called *sto(c)kreg(h)el, reg(h)el, sluutvers*). The refrain that concludes each stanza of the Dutch *refrein* and that expresses the theme of the poem. The stock is borrowed from the Fr. *ballade* and is generally a single line, although occasionally it is a half line, one-and-a-half-lines, or even two lines. The refrein was popularized in the 15th c. by the Rhetoricians (*rederijkers*). The ling. borrowing and neologisms that characterized the poetry and drama of the Rhetoricians are manifest in the stock, as many of the loan words were used to achieve rhymes. McTaggart argues that the stock fulfilled a more structural or musical function than the refrain in the ballade, which often had greater semantic import.

*See* LOW COUNTRIES, POETRY OF THE.

■ A. Borguet, "De 'stok' van het Referein," *Revue des langues vivantes* 12 (1946); A. van Elslander, *Het refrein in de Nederlanden tot 1600* (1953); W. Waterschoot, "Marot or Ronsard? New French Poetics among Dutch Rhetoricians in the Second Half of the Sixteenth Century," *Rhetoric–Rhétoriqueurs–Rederijkers*, ed. J. Koopmans et al. (1995); T. Susato, *Musyck boexken: Dutch Songs for Four Voices*, ed. T. McTaggart (1997); E. M. Kavaler, "Renaissance Gothic in the Netherlands: The Uses of Ornament," *Art Bulletin* 82 (2000); B. Parsons and B. Jongenelen, "The Refrein and the Chambers of Rhetoric in the Early Modern Low Countries," *European Medieval Drama* 12 (2008).

R. F. LISSENS; D. J. ROTHMAN

**STORNELLO** (sometimes called *fiore*). A short It. folk verse form whose name (perhaps from Occitan *estorn*, "struggle") suggests the manner in which it was sung—responsively—as well as the sort of popular *poetic contests that measure the improvisational talents of the competitors. While the earliest examples date from the 15th c., the *stornello* flourished in Tuscany in the 17th c. and from there spread throughout central and southern Italy. The stornello has three principal forms: (1) a rhymed *couplet of *hendecasyllables, the oldest form and a type now common in Sicily, which may trace its origin to rhymed proverbs; (2) a tercet of hendecasyllables, the first and third rhyming and the second in *assonance or *consonance with them; and (3) a couplet of hendecasyllables prefixed by a five-syllable (*quinario*) or a seven-syllable verse (*aBB, aBA*), which often consists of an invocation to a flower or plant (hence, the alternate name, *fiore*) or an exclamatory or vocative phrase.

*See* HEPTASYLLABLE, TENSO.

■ V. Santoli, *I Canti popolari italiani* (1940); Spongano; L. Castelnuovo, *La metrica italiana* (1979); A. Falassi, *Per forza e per amore* (1980); F. P. Memmo, *Dizionario di metrica italiana* (1983); Elwert, *Italienische*, sect. 99; A. M. Cirese, *Ragioni metriche* (1988); S. Orlando, *Manuale di metrica italiana* (1994); G. Sica, *Scrivere in versi* (2003).

J. G. FUCILLA; C. KLEINHENZ

**STRAMBOTTO.** A monostrophic It. composition generally of eight or six *hendecasyllables (less commonly of four or ten). One of the oldest of It. verse forms, the *strambotto* has uncertain but popular origins. The term derives from Fr. *estrabot* (Occitan *estribot*), but whereas the French used it to apply to satirical compositions, the Italians have restricted it to rhymes that are sentimental and amatory in content. The number of its verses and the characteristic rhyme scheme vary from region to region: the so-called Sicilian strambotto has the pattern *abababab*, and the Tuscan variety (*ottava toscana* or *rispetto*) has several: *ababababcc, ababccdd,*

*aabbccdd, ababcc, ababab,* and *aabbcc.* In its Sicilian form, the strambotto may have influenced the devel. of the *sonnet by serving as the model for the *octave. The form has been employed by many poets over the centuries, from the 15th c. (Leonardo Giustiniani, Angelo Poliziano, Lorenzo de' Medici, Francesco Galeota) to the 19th (Giosuè Carducci, Giovanni Pascoli).

*See* OTTAVA RIMA, SICILIAN OCTAVE.

■ H. R. Lang, "The Spanish *estribote, estrambote* and Related Poetic Forms," *Romania* 45 (1918–19); E. Li Gotti, "Precisazioni sullo strambotto," *Convivium* 5 (1949); G. D'Aronco, *Guida bibliografica allo studio dello strambotto* (1951); Spongano; Wilkins; L. Castelnuovo, *La metrica italiana* (1979); F. P. Memmo, *Dizionario di metrica italiana* (1983); Elwert, *Italienische*, sect. 98; A. M. Cirese, *Ragioni metriche* (1988); S. Orlando, *Manuale di metrica italiana* (1994); G. Sica, *Scrivere in versi* (2003).

J. G. FUCILLA; C. KLEINHENZ

**STROPHE.** From the Gr. for *turn* or *bend,* a defined unit of movement with song performed in ancient Gr. drama by the *chorus as it turned now one way (strophe), then another (*antistrophe), then stood (*epode). Strophe and antistrophe were of identical metrical and musical structure, with the epode of a different structure. In cl. antiquity and later poetry modeled on it, the term came to refer to a structural unit of a poem, like a *stanza, with varying line-length, notably in *odes with their expansive strophes (e.g., Pindar, Horace, Ben Jonson, Thomas Gray, John Keats). But a strophe could be brief, as with the two-line dactylic *distich or the four-line *sapphic strophe; other cl. forms included the elegiac strophe, the *alcaic strophe, and the *asclepiadean strophe. In all of these, a crucial feature is the repetition, at least once, of the first strophe's metrical pattern. In analysis of song and poetry derived from song, a strophe is one of a metrically and melodically identical set of stanzas; thus, popular song, *troubadour song, Ger. lieder, *blues stanzas, verse-and-refrain forms like the muwashshah and the *zéjel proceed by adding new strophes to the melody of the first strophe. In contemp. usage about Eng.-lang. poetries, *strophe* is sometimes used for long, nonisomorphic units, *stanza* for more regular ones. Biblical scholars speak of several strophes gathered together into a single stanza, but the unit definitions are not airtight. Discourses about Gr. and Lat. drama and poetics, about Ar. and Andalusian med. song and performance practice, about Semitic poetries, about music forms, and ethnopoetic studies in sub-Saharan Af. poetries often use *strophe* for its flexibility in discussing poetic performance with music, gesture, dance, and breath. In either case, *stanza* carries a long-standing implication of fixed "rooms" or boxes of verse; "strophe" implies movement of speakers/singers, currents, alternation of speakers, shared or exchanged parts.

*See* ARABIC POETRY, DACTYL, ELEGIAC DISTICH, STICHOS.

■ F. M. Warren, "The Troubadour *canso* and Latin Lyric Poetry," *MP* 9 (1912); D. C. Clarke, "Miscellaneous Strophe Forms in the Fifteenth-Century Court Lyric,"

*Hispanic Review* 16, no. 2 (1948); G. Rouget, "African Traditional Non-Prose Forms: Reciting, Declaiming, Singing, and Strophic Structure," *Proceedings of a Conference on African Languages and Literatures*, ed. J. Berry, R. P. Armstrong, and J. Povey (1966); R. H. Finnegan, *Oral Literature in Africa* (1970); S. M. Stern, *Hispano-Arabic Strophic Poetry: Studies,* ed. L. P. Harvey (1974); Halporn et al; *A Handbook of the Troubadours,* ed. F.R.P. Akehurst and J. M. Davis (1995); J. P. Fokkelman, *Reading Biblical Poetry: An Introductory Guide*, trans. Ineke Smit (2001); H. Heijkoop and O. Zwartjes, *Muwassah, Zajal, Kharja: Bibliography of Strophic Poetry and Music from al-Andalus and Their Influence in East and West* (2004).

T. KRIER

# STRUCTURALISM

I. Prague School
II. Moscow-Tartu School
III. French and American Schools

**I. Prague School.** The Prague school (P. S.) is an established label for the international group of scholars in ling., lit., theater, folklore, and general aesthetics that was organized as the Prague Linguistic Circle from 1926 to 1948. Initially, the P. S. was partly indebted to *Russian formalism, esp. the Moscow Linguistic Circle (see below), whose institutional name it echoed, sharing both some of its members (Pyotr Bogatyrev, Roman Jakobson) and also the concept of lit. as the art of lang. At the same time, the P. S. borrowed from the Czech trad. of 19th-c. Herbartian formalism (Josef Durdík, Otakar Hostinský), which conceived of the artistic work as a set of formal relations, and also certain post-Herbartian devels. in poetics and theater (Otakar Zich). Among other schools of thought, the P. S. was influenced by Saussurean ling., Edmund Husserl's phenomenology, and Gestalt psychology. Such intellectual affinities were welcomed by the members of the P. S., since they perceived their enterprise as the crystallization of a new scholarly paradigm for the humanities and social sciences, which, in 1929, they christened *structuralism*—the term was coined by Jakobson.

The hist. of the P. S. can be divided into three periods. The first begins with the establishment of the Circle in 1926 and continues until 1934. During this period, the research of the Prague structuralists focused on the internal organization of poetic works, esp. their sound stratum. Jakobson's and Jan Mukařovský's hists. of old and mod. Czech metrics are the most representative works of this phase. The subsequent period, 1934–38, opens with Mukařovský's study of a little-known Czech poet of the early 19th c., Milota Zdirad Polák, and ends with the Circle's collective volume devoted to the leading Czech romantic, Karel Hynek Mácha. In this period, the P. S. began to study verbal art in relation to other social phenomena. The earlier preoccupation with poetic sound was supplemented with a concern for how literary works signify extralinguistic reality. The last period, dating roughly from 1938 to 1948, is delimited by external interventions. The Ger. invasion forced some members of the P. S. (Bogatyrev, Jakobson, René Wellek) to leave Czechoslovakia; the communist takeover ten years later effectively banned the structuralist study of art and eventually led to the disbanding of the Circle. During this final period, the research of the P. S. shifted to the study of the human dimension of the artistic process, both author and perceivers. Felix Vodička's systematic attempt at elaborating the hist. of literary reception belongs among the most promising devels. of this period.

In the postwar years, the intellectual heritage of the P. S. was disseminated throughout the world by those members who left Prague. The structuralist revolution of the 1960s in France and the United States (see below) was largely stimulated by Jakobson, who in the 1940s helped establish the Linguistic Circle of New York, of which the Fr. anthropologist Claude Lévi-Strauss was a member. Bogatyrev, who returned to his native land after the outbreak of the war, performed a similar role in the Soviet Union. A group of young literary scholars (Miroslav Červenka, Lubomír Doležel, Mojmír Grygar, Milan Jankovič) attempted to resurrect the P. S. in Czechoslovakia in the 1960s, but the Soviet invasion of 1968 dealt a final blow to structuralism in that country.

For the P. S., structuralism was a dialectical synthesis of the two global paradigms dominating Eur. thought in the 19th c.: *romanticism and positivism. The former sacrificed empirical data to universal philosophical schemes; the latter tipped the scales in the opposite direction. Structuralism, the Prague scholars argued, would avoid the onesidedness of its predecessors by being neither a philosophical system nor a concrete science but an epistemological stance negotiating between the general and the specific. What characterizes the Prague version of structuralism in particular is a conceptual frame of reference formed by the interplay of three complementary notions: structure, function, and sign.

The concept of *structure* requires special attention. For the P. S., it referred to two distinct entities. On the one hand, it denoted the holistic organization of a single work as a hierarchical system of dominant and subordinate elements. But just as Ferdinand de Saussure recognized that every concrete utterance (*parole*) is meaningful only against the background of the collectively shared ling. code (*langue*), the Prague scholars saw every individual artwork as an implementation of a particular aesthetic code—the set of artistic norms. These they also termed a *structure*. Unlike Saussure, however, the P. S. did not believe that any code exists in and of itself. Rather, these sets of norms together comprise a higher structure—the cultural system valid for a given society at a particular stage in its historical devel.

The second key concept, *function*, was the trademark of P. S. It served the circle's members as a criterion for differentiating among discrete cultural codes. Functionally speaking, such codes are nothing but hierarchies of norms regulating the attainment of socially sanctioned values. The dominance of the symbolic function, e.g., distinguishes the symbolic code from the aesthetic and theoretical codes. Particular artifacts embody these immaterial structures, and their material organization implements the hierarchy of functions they serve. However, artifacts not only carry out their functions, but signify them: hence, the importance of the third element of the P. S. frame of reference, the *sign*. As a conjunction of the material vehicle and immaterial meaning, the sign reiterates the dual nature of the concept of structure—its mental, socially shared existence and its physical embodiment in individual artifacts. From the semiotic point of view, culture appears as a complex interaction of signs mediating among the members of a given collectivity (see SEMIOTICS AND POETRY).

In the field of poetics, the P. S. pioneered the ling. approach to verbal art. Its members conceived of lit. as a particular mode of using lang.: a functional dialect. In contrast to other such dialects (e.g., the emotive, the practical), which focus on the extralinguistic components of the speech act (the speaker, the referent), poetic lang. foregrounds the very medium of discourse, the ling. sign itself. This "set toward the message" has important consequences for the structure of poetic signs and the way they signify. The sound stratum of poetic lang. is organized according to the code peculiar to this dialect. Consequently, the P. S. investigated problems of sound orchestration, intonation, and *prosody in poetic compositions. The distinctive feature of these inquiries was their phonological basis. For the Prague structuralists, only those phonic elements of lang. capable of differentiating cognitive meanings could be exploited poetically. The P. S. regarded the sound configurations permeating the poetic work not as mere formal constructs but as partial semantic structures comprising the overall meaning of the text. The unusual arrangement of poetic sounds in the literary sign disrupts the conventional link between the signifier and the signified, and the meaning of the work becomes a function of its internal organization rather than of the reality outside it. Hence, the *poetic* designation refers only obliquely, and its truth value cannot be tested. By problematizing the process of verbal representation, poetic lang., according to the P. S., performs a signal role in the ling. system. Whereas other functional dialects stress the adequacy of signs to what they stand for, poetic lang. underscores the reciprocal inadequacy of the two, their deep-seated nonidentity. In this way the *poetic function promulgates ling. self-awareness, enabling us to renew our semiotic grasp of reality and revealing lang. as the most versatile tool of human cognition and communication.

**II. Moscow-Tartu School.** (M.-T. S.). This term designates a broad research effort in semiotics and such related disciplines as structural poetics, verse theory, cultural theory, folklore, and mythology that began in 1960 and was since carried on by a number of Soviet scholars, principally at the Academy of Sciences in Moscow (Viacheslav Ivanov, Vladimir Toporov, Mikhail Gasparov, Eliazar Meletinskij) and at Tartu University in Estonia (Jurij Lotman, Zara Minc, Igor Chernov). The M.-T. S. originated in the relatively

liberal atmosphere of the Khrushchev period and represented both a rejection of official Marxist-Leninist scholarship and a return to the strong Rus. philological trad. of the early 20th c. Initially, it drew on the critical heritage of Rus. formalism and P. S. structuralism, esp. the work of Yuri Tynianov and Jakobson. This theoretical legacy was enriched by perspectives offered by general ling., semiotics, information theory, and cybernetics; by comparative IE and Asian studies; by the study of versification, reconstituted in the late 1950s after lying in abeyance for decades; and by the intellectual heritage of a number of major Rus. thinkers, some of them reclaimed from obscurity by the efforts of the M.-T. S.: e.g., Mikhail Bakhtin, Ol'ga Frejdenberg, Pavel Florenskij, Gustav Shpet, Vladimir Propp, and Bogatyrev. As important as the many publications of the M.-T. S., esp. the celebrated Tartu series *Trudy po znakovym sistemam* (Works on Semiotics, 1967–92), were its summer schools (which ended in the mid-1970s), noted for their effervescent and interdisciplinary atmosphere.

During the 1970s and early 1980s, several key figures of the M.-T. S. emigrated to the West (Aleksandr Pjatigorskij, Boris Ogibenin, Boris Gasparov, Dmitrij Segal), yet the movement remained the focus of intensive scholarly and cultural activity by younger scholars.

In its early phase (until the mid-1970s), the methodology of the M.-T. S. was based primarily on the model provided by structural ling. (esp. Saussure, Nicolai Trubetzkoy, and Jakobson), the central concepts of which—e.g., *langue/parole* (code/message), *synchrony/diachrony*, and *marked/unmarked*—were broadly applied. Lit., folklore, myth, film, and other fields of human cultural activity where *signs* play a central role were described as *secondary modeling systems* or *languages*: these were regarded as built upon the basis of natural lang., hence analyzable in similar terms. Thus, for each system, one could establish both a *lexicon* (a set of signs and their associated meanings) and a *grammar* (combinatorial rules). A number of studies from this period offer descriptions of simple semiotic systems such as the system of road signs, the rules for cartomancy, or the paremiological genres in folklore (G. Permjakov, *Ot pogovorki do skazki* [1970], and other works): behind these efforts lay a broad assumption that describing more complex objects, such as the novel or lit. as a whole, would be a more difficult yet fundamentally similar task. The initial optimism faded in the 1970s, however, when the methodology of much of the M.-T. S. work shifted away from the ling. model. While their terminology remained the same, many of the scholars focused on the *text* rather than the *code*, turning from simple systems describable by means of formalized metalangs. toward complex semiotic objects, each of which involved far more than an implementation of a particular set of rules. Culture, regarded as a complex mechanism of interrelated, often conflicting codes, became the principal focus of the M.-T. S., while the role of neurolinguistic and sociological factors in its creation, preservation, and transformation received special attention.

Poetry and poetics were areas of major interest for the M.-T. S., because of the influence of the Rus. trad. of the ling. study of the poetic text (Lev Shcherba, Jakobson), the role of verse theory in formalist and early structuralist endeavors, and the special situation of post-Stalinist Russia, where entire layers of early 20th-c. culture, esp. lit., had to be brought out of the oblivion to which they had been officially consigned.

In poetics, two main research trends have characterized the activities of the M.-T. S. The first, structuralist in the traditional sense, has involved the study of the discrete text, regarded as a hierarchy of levels (phonic, rhythmical, grammatical) that may be studied separately or as a totality. This approach, discussed extensively in Lotman's early monographs (1976, 1977) and at the core of his structuralist poetics, owes much to Jakobson, esp. his classic article "Linguistics and Poetics" (1960) and his many studies of the "grammar of poetry," as well as to Tynianov's classic work on poetic semantics. Lotman emphasizes the notion that the poetic function establishes hierarchically organized networks of *equivalence (parallelisms) throughout the poetic work, and he traces the effect of such relationships (absent in ordinary discourse) on both the *paradigmatic* and the *syntagmatic* planes, seeking to identify the underlying semantic opposition(s) from which the work as a whole may be seen as deriving. In addition to studying the semantic effects resulting from lang. operating within the horizontal (intralinear) and vertical (interlinear, interstrophic) dimensions of the poem, Lotman and his colleagues focused on the structural role of extratextual factors, esp. on the aesthetic results of the poem's relationship to various contexts (a poetic cycle, a collection, an author's oeuvre, the work of a poetic school); here they relied on a semiotic conception of the text that emphasizes the flexibility of its boundaries and its mutually reinforcing relationship with different cultural codes.

The other trend in M.-T. S. poetics involved research on three broad classes of phenomena:

**A. *Verse Rhythm*,** studied by means of the linguostatistical model developed by Boris Tomashevsky, expanded by Kiril Taranovsky in the 1950s, and reformulated by the mathematician Andrej Kolmogorov and his students. Major work, in some cases applying newer ling. methodologies to problems of versification (e.g., generative theory), has also been carried out by such scholars as P. A. Rudnev, V. S. Baevskij, and Mikhail Lotman (son of Jurij). Subsequently, major interest turned to the hist. of Rus. verse, incl. mapping the metrical repertoires of individual poets and poetic movements. Gasparov and others were also increasingly drawn to the relationship between metrical forms and semantics, i.e., toward the hist. of associations between certain meters and specific themes.

**B. *Poetic Lexicon*,** the study of which attracted a number of scholars in the early period of the M.-T. S. Establishing the specific vocabulary used by a poet in a single work, a collection, a period, or an oeuvre has been seen as a way of objectively analyzing the shifts

lang. undergoes in the process of poetic creation and of pinpointing the difficult, often highly displaced meanings of images and motifs in the work of mod. poets.

**C. *Intertextual Relations*,** which came into the purview of the Soviet structuralists in the early 1970s in connection with their research into *acmeism. Much research also has been devoted to intertextual elements of works by symbolist authors, esp. Alexander Blok, Andrei Bely, and Fyodor Sologub (see SYMBOLISM), and by other major Silver Age figures (Mikhail Kuzmin, Aleksej Remizov). Minc is the author of the conception of the *polygenetic* nature of symbolist (modernist) subtexts: in many cases, a cited element may derive from several different sources, which themselves may enter into complex, potentially conflicting relationships with each other (see her "Funkcija reminiscencij v poetike A. Bloka," *Trudy po znakovym systemam* 6 [1973]). The shift toward the text as a principal focus of M.-T. S. research brought an increased emphasis on *intertextuality, with the concept being extended to other areas of semiotic activity such as film.

**III. French and American Schools.** Inspired by devels. in structural ling. and structural anthropology, structuralism as a method of analysis and a theory of lit. reached its height in France in the 1960s, in the work of Roland Barthes, Gérard Genette, A. J. Greimas, Jakobson, and Tzvetan Todorov, whence it was transported to Am. crit. Structuralism is difficult to delimit because structuralist work swiftly became assimilated to so-called *poststructuralism, a movement often defined in opposition to structuralism but that, in fact, carried on many of its projects.

Structuralism can be opposed to all atomistic theories that attempt to explain phenomena individually. Saussure, the founder of mod. ling., distinguishes concrete speech acts (*parole*) from the underlying system of the lang. (*langue*), a formal entity whose elements have no positive or inherent qualities but are defined solely in relational terms. *Synchronic* study, treating lang. as a formal system of interrelated elements functioning at a particular time, takes precedence over *diachronic* study tracing the hist. of individual elements. Lévi-Strauss, the central figure of structuralism, adopted this perspective in anthropology and rejected attempts to explain social and cultural phenomena in piecemeal fashion, treating them instead as manifestations of underlying formal systems. For Lévi-Strauss, the codes by which myths operate are sets of binary oppositions drawn from different areas of experience that can be used to express a variety of contrasts; they thus bear striking resemblance to those operative in poetic discourse. Structuralist analysis of this logic of the concrete is related to semiology, the study of sign systems. The two fundamental insights on which structuralism is based are (1) that social and cultural phenomena do not have essences but are defined both by their internal structures and by their place in the structures of the relevant social and cultural systems and (2) that social and cultural phenomena are signs: not physical events only, but events with meaning. The most successful structural analyses isolate those structures that permit phenomena to function as signs.

Structuralism in lit. crit. began as a revolt against the lit. hist. and biographical crit. that dominated the Fr. university orthodoxy. Structuralism sought to return to the text, but, unlike Anglo-Am. *New Criticism, it assumed that one could not study a text without preconceptions and that, in order to discover structures, one required an objective methodological model. The goal of structuralism was not the interpretation of texts but the elaboration, through particular texts, of an account of the modes of literary discourse and their operation. Barthes distinguished *criticism*, which places the text in a particular context and assigns it meaning, from a science of lit. or *poetics*, which studies the conditions of meaning, the formal structures that organize a text and make possible a range of meanings. Trans. of the Rus. formalists in the late 1960s gave structuralists analogues to their own work and stimulated the study of lit. as an autonomous institution. Two versions of structuralism can be distinguished by their different uses of ling.: as a technique applied directly to the description of the lang. of texts or as the model for a poetics that would stand to lit. as ling. stands to lang.

The first strain involves study of the patterns formed by the distribution in the text of elements defined by phonological and syntactic theory. Jakobson's characterization of the poetic function of lang. as "the projection of the principle of equivalence from the axis of selection into the axis of combination" led to study of the ways in which items that are paradigmatically equivalent (related by membership of a grammatical, lexical, or phonological class) are distributed in ling. sequences (on the axis of combination). Jakobson's analyses of poems focus on symmetrical and asymmetrical patterns of distribution that unify the text and throw certain elements into relief. It has been claimed that many patterns he discovers are irrelevant to the reader's experience and thus to the meaning of the poem, but the issue is a difficult one, since appeal to the reader's experience is scarcely decisive—patterns may work subliminally—and formal patterns need not contribute to meaning to have a unifying effect.

Structuralist poetics is founded on the presumption that, while lit. uses lang., it is also itself *like* a lang.; its meanings are made possible by systems of convention that serve readers as models for interpretation. The work of Genette, Riffaterre, and esp. Barthes has contributed to a metalang. that serves both as a theory of lit. and as the outline of an analytical method.

Within the literary system, ling. signs become second-order signifiers whose signifieds are their special meaning in the literary discourse. The conventions that give sentences additional meanings and functions are those of what Barthes calls an *écriture*: a particular mode of writing involving an implicit contract between author and reader. The system or institution of lit. is made up of a series of écritures that constitute its historical or generic moments. In reading a sentence in a lyric differently from a sentence in a newspaper report, one is implicitly recognizing and employing the conventions of a particular lyric écriture.

According to structuralism, cultures tend to *naturalize* their signs, to motivate the connection between signifier and signified so that meanings seem natural and not the result of convention; lit. may, therefore, be described according to the ways in which it resists or complies with this process. *Interpretation is itself a mode of *naturalization* or *recuperation*, the attempt to bring the text within a logical discursive order by making it the expression of a meaning. We read texts in accordance with a series of *codes* that provide, on the one hand, models of human behavior (coherence and incoherence of personality, plausible and implausible relations between action and motive, logical and illogical chains of events) and, on the other hand, models of literary intelligibility (coherence and incoherence, plausible and implausible symbolic extrapolations, significance and insignificance) that enable us to make sense of texts by organizing their elements into coherent series. These codes are models of the *vraisemblable*, in the broad sense in which structuralists use the term—models of the natural and intelligible; and a work that lends itself to this process of recuperation is *lisible* (readable), whereas one that is unintelligible in terms of our traditional models is *scriptible* (writable): it can be written but not read, except in a kind of vicarious writing. A structuralist analysis of a work aims at examining the ways in which it responds to the reader's attempts to make it unified and coherent. The critic attends to a play of signifiers that defer meaning by offering materials that exceed meanings that can be assigned them—e.g., meter, rhyme, and sound patterns in poetry, all instances of the surplus of the signifier. The play of the signifier is the productivity of the text because it forces the reader to become the active producer of meaning and the participant in the exploration of possible modes of order.

This series of concepts leads to a stress on the text as ling. surface. The play of lang. is valued insofar as it leads to a questioning of the relationship between lang. and experience; hence, critics attend to effects of *intertextuality*: the interaction within a text of various modes of discourse or of langs. drawn from other literary texts and from other discourse about the world. Whereas the Rus. formalists saw the text as a way of "making strange" ordinary objects or activities (see DEFAMILIARIZATION), structuralists emphasize the "making strange" of discourses that order the world and that the work puts on display.

Structuralist work on poetry may be grouped under several headings. (1) The reconstruction of poetic codes or systems: Genette has described *baroque imagery as a system of interrelated items defined less by individual connotation than by oppositions and has analyzed images of day and night as a poetic code; Zumthor has reconstructed the codes of med. poetry, from the generic types of discourse to systems of *topoi* (see TOPOS), rhythmical formulas, descriptive schemata, and conventionalized knowledge. (2) The correlation of particular structures with the interpretive operations they require: Riffaterre has analyzed a variety of poetic devices, from the revitalized *cliché to the extended metaphor of surrealist poetry, and describes lyrics as periphrastic transformations of clichés or prior literary formulas; Levin's theory of "couplings" shows how phonological or grammatical equivalence affects semantic interpretation. Greimas and his followers have attempted to show how a level of coherence or *isotopie* is attained in the interpretation of poetic sequences. (3) The rehabilitation of rhet.: Genette, Group μ, and others have redefined rhetorical figures in ling. terms and opened the way to a theory that would treat the figures as instructions for symbolic reading, as sets of conventional operations that readers may perform on poetic texts. (4) The reinvention of poetic *artifice: Julia Kristeva and poets of the *Tel Quel* school (Marcelin Pleynet, Denis Roche) have undertaken readings of poets designed to show how they undermine by their formal invention the traditional operations of the sign and have emphasized the need for contemp. poets to question and write against the codes and implicit contracts of poetry.

See CULTURAL CRITICISM; INFLUENCE; LINGUISTICS AND POETICS; SIGN, SIGNIFIED, SIGNIFIER; STRUCTURE; TEXTUALITY.

■ **Prague School**: Jakobson, esp. v. 3, 5, 6; *A Prague School Reader on Esthetics, Literary Structure, and Style*, ed. P. L. Garvin (1964); J. Vachek, *The Linguistic School of Prague* (1966); R. Wellek, *The Literary Theory and Aesthetics of the Prague School* (1969); *Semiotics of Art: The Prague School Contribution*, ed. I. R. Titunik and L. Matejka (1976); S. Rudy, "Jakobson's Inquiry into Verse and the Emergence of Structural Poetics," *Sound, Sign, and Meaning*, ed. L. Matejka (1976); J. Mukařovský, *Structure, Sign, and Function* (1977); and *The Word and Verbal Art* (1978), both ed. and trans. J. Burbank and P. Steiner; *The Prague School: Selected Writings, 1929–1948*, ed. P. Steiner (1982); F. W. Galan, *Historic Structures: The Prague School Project, 1928–1946* (1985); J. G. Merquior, *From Paris to Prague: A Critique of Structuralist and Post-Structuralist Thought* (1986); J. Striedter, *Literary Structure, Evolution, and Value* (1989); J. Toman, *The Magic of a Common Language: Jakobson, Mathesius, Trubetzkoy, and the Prague Linguistic Circle* (1995); *Jan Mukařovský and the Prague School*, ed. V. Macura and H. Schmid (1999); L. Doležel, "Structuralism of the Prague School," *CHLC*, v. 8, ed. R. Selden (2005); *Structuralism(s) Today*, ed. V. Ambros, R. Le Huenen, A. Perez-Simon (2009); *Roman Jakobson: Themes in His Science of Language*, ed. K. I. Yamanaka and E. Asazuma (2010).

■ **Moscow-Tartu School**: *Anthologies*: *Texte des sowjetischen literaturwissenschaftlichen Strukturalismus*, ed. K. Eimermacher (1971); *Semiotics and Structuralism: Readings from the Soviet Union*, ed. H. Baran (1976); *Soviet Semiotics*, ed. and trans. D. P. Lucid (1977); *Readings in Soviet Semiotics*, ed. L. Matejka et al. (1977); *Russian Poetics in Translation*, ed. L. M. O'Toole and A. Shukman, 10 v. (1975–83). *Bibliography*: K. Eimermacher and S. Shishkoff, *Subject Bibliography of Soviet Semiotics: The Moscow-Tartu School*

(1977). *Criticism and History*: E. M. Meletinskii and D. M. Segal, "Structuralism and Semiotics in the USSR," *Diogenes* 73 (1971); D. M. Segal, *Aspects of Structuralism in Soviet Philology* (1974); V. V. Ivanov, *Ocherki po istorii semiotiki v SSSR* (1976); J. M. Lotman, *Analysis of the Poetic Text*, ed. and trans. D. B. Johnson (1976); and *Structure of the Artistic Text*, trans. G. Lenhoff and R. Vroon (1977); A. Shukman, *Literature and Semiotics: A Study of the Writings of Ju. M. Lotman* (1977); Y. Tyianov, *The Problem of Verse Language*, trans. M. Sosa and B. Harvey (1981); H. Baran, "Structuralism and Semiotics," Terras; E. Bojtár, *Slavic Structuralism*, trans. H. Thomas (1985); S. Rudy, "Semiotics in the USSR," *The Semiotic Sphere*, ed. T. Sebeok and J. Umiker-Sebeok (1986); H. Baran, "Ob itogax i problemax semioticheskix issledovanij," *Trudy po znakovym sistemam* 20 (1987); B. A. Uspenskij, "K probleme genezisa tartusko-moskovskoj semioticheskoj shkoly," *Trudy po znakovym systemam* 20 (1987); P. A. Rudnev, *Vvedenie v nauku u russkom stixe. Vyp. 1* (1989); B. M. Gasparov, "Tartuskaja shkola 1960-x godov kak semioticheskij fenomen," *Wiener Slawistischer Almanach* 29 (1989); *Moskovsko-tartuskaja semiotičeskaja škola*, ed. S. Nekliudova (1998); *Conceptual Dictionary of the Tartu-Moscow Semiotic School*, ed. J. Levchenko (1999); *Lotman and Cultural Studies: Encounters and Extensions*, ed. A. Schoenle (2006).

■ **French and American Schools**: *General*: J. Harari, *Structuralists and Structuralisms* (1971); Culler; J. M. Miller, *French Structuralism: A Multidisciplinary Bibliography* (1981); S. Freedman and C. Taylor, *Roland Barthes* (1983). *Criticism and History*: R. Barthes, *Le Degré zéro de l'écriture* (1953); M. Titzmann, "Struktur, Strukturalismus," and G. Martens, "Text," *Reallexikon II* 4.256–78, 403–17; Jakobson, esp. v. 3, 5; C. Lévi-Strauss, *La Pensée sauvage* (1962); S. Levin, *Linguistic Structures in Poetry* (1962); R. Barthes, *Essais critiques* (1964); C. Lévi-Strauss, *Le Cru et le cuit* (1964); M. Pleynet, *Comme* (1965); R. Barthes, *Critique et vérité* (1966); and "Introduction á l'analyse structurale des récits," *Communications* 8 (1966); G. Genette, *Figures of Literary Discourse*, trans. A. Sheridan, 3 v. (1981); A. J. Greimas, *Sémantique structurale* (1966); M. Foucault, *Les Mots et les choses* (1966); "Structuralism," *YFS* 36–37 (1966)—special iss.; J. Derrida, *L'Écriture et la différence* (1967); "Structuralism: Idéologie et méthode," *Esprit* 35.360 (1967)—special iss.; P. Caws, "Structuralism," *DHI*; U. Eco, *La struttura assente* (1968); *Qu'est-ce que le structuralisme?* ed. F. Wahl (1968); D. Roche, *Eros énergumène* (1968); P. Sollers, *Logiques* (1968); J. Kristeva, *Semeiotikè* (1969); S. Booth, *An Essay on Shakespeare's Sonnets* (1969); G. Deleuze, *Proust et les signes* (1970); A. J. Greimas, *Du Sens* (1970); T. Todorov, *La Littérature fantastique* (1970); J. Geninasca, *Analyse structurale des Chiméres de Nerval* (1971); *Essais de sémiotique poétique*, ed. A. J. Greimas (1971); M. Riffaterre, *Essais de stylistique structurale* (1971); J. Derrida, *La Dissémination* (1972); F. Jameson, *The Prison-House of Language* (1972); N. Ruwet, *Langage, musique, poésie* (1972); *The Structuralist Controversy*, ed. R. Macksey and E. Donato (1972); P. Zumthor, *Essai de poétique médiévale* (1972); R. Jakobson, *Questions de poétique* (1973); J. Broekman, *Structuralism: Moscow, Prague, Paris* (1974); R. Scholes, *Structuralism in Literature* (1974); E. Stankiewicz, "Structural Poetics and Linguistics," *Current Trends in Linguistics, XII*, ed. T. A. Sebeok (1974); R. Barthes, *S/Z*, trans. R. Miller (1975); Culler; A. J. Greimas, *Maupassant* (1976); *Sound, Sign and Meaning*, ed. L. Matejka (1976); Group μ, *Rhétorique de la poésie* (1977); T. Hawkes, *Structuralism and Semiotics* (1977); V. Forrest-Thomson, *Poetic Artifice* (1978); M. Riffaterre, *Semiotics of Poetry* (1978); and *La Production du texte* (1979); Group μ; J. Culler, *Roland Barthes* (1983); A. J. Greimas, *Du Sens II* (1983); D. Rice and P. Schofer, *Rhetorical Poetics* (1983); F. de Saussure, *Cours de linguistique générale*, ed. R. Engler [1967–68], trans. R. Harris (1983); K. Silverman, *The Subject of Semiotics* (1983); J. Fekete, *The Structural Allegory* (1984); J. Culler, *Ferdinand de Saussure*, 2d ed. (1986); J. G. Merquior, *From Prague to Paris* (1986); R. Harland, *Superstructuralism* (1987); R. Jakobson, *Language in Literature*, ed. K. Pomorska and S. Rudy (1987); P. Caws, *Structuralism: The Art of the Intelligible* (1988); V. B. Leitch, *American Literary Criticism from the Thirties to the Eighties* (1988), ch. 9; T. G. Pavel, *The Feud of Language* (1989); D. Holdcroft, *Saussure* (1991); F. Dosse, *History of Structuralism* (1991).

P. STEINER (P.S.); H. BARAN, C. KLAMANN (M.-T. S.); J. CULLER (FR. AND AM.)

**STRUCTURE** (Ger. *Aufbau*). Structure is an important interpretive and methodological concept for critics who are more interested in the internal dynamics of a literary work (the interrelationships that comprise a literary system) than in its relation to hist., its thematic content, or its genetic origins. Emphasis on structure allows the literary work to be conceived as an autonomous object (see AUTONOMY) and to be characterized in terms of its structural or internal relations. One early example of a focus on structure is Aristotle's claim in the *Poetics* to analyze "poetry in itself and of its various kinds." This approach has certain affinities with important 20th-c. understandings of structure (though Aristotle ultimately relegates the formal character of poetic structure to the periphery in favor of such psychological issues as *catharsis*).

Some of the most crucial aspects of the concept of structure may be seen in the difference between two dominant theoretical models: the generic and the organic. *Genre crit. stresses the relationship between the whole (the overall generic code that articulates the structural rules, formal characteristics, or subcategories of the class) and the part (the discrete poem that deviates merely in details). This formulation of the relationship of part to whole is unlike that of organic theories of poetry that assume that each discrete poem, each poetic structure, is unique. In the organic model, the structure of the poem has priority over generic rules, and its identification (the structure of its logical argument or its figurative patterns) is the object of study.

The distinction between the internal structure of the poem and its extraliterary or contextual references is set forth clearly in Am. *New Criticism and esp. Cleanth Brooks's influential study *The Well Wrought Urn* (1947), subtitled *Studies in the Structure of Poetry*. Brooks is not concerned with a conventional analysis of content; rather, he endeavors to work out a systematic theory of *poetics. In Brooks's conception, what is essential is the inner, paradoxical structure of the poem, with its tensions and contradictions. As he writes, the structural "principle is not one which involves the arrangement of the various elements into homogeneous groupings, pairing like with like. It unites the like with the unlike." These inner tensions and paradoxes uniting "like with unlike" define poetic structure. Far from seeking to establish some homogeneous grouping (common themes, period styles, recurring images), Brooks seeks to isolate the "pattern of resolved stresses" that comprises the completed structure of the poem. John Crowe Ransom, too, in "Criticism as Pure Speculation" (1941) directs the critic's attention away from extralinguistic references toward the inner form and verbal autonomy of the poetic structure itself. Ransom differs from Brooks in that the logical structure of the poem is bound up with its local *texture, which he articulates in an architectural conceit: poetic structure corresponds to the walls, beams, and supports of a house; texture to the paint, wallpaper, and surface decoration. For Ransom, poetic structure is bound up with texture's sensuous immediacy and vital concreteness. Ransom's distinction was taken up by M. C. Beardsley (*Aesthetics*, 1958), who extended it to the plastic arts, music, and narrative.

The separation of the formal poetic structure from the object of reference formed an important assumption in Eur. structuralist crit. from the 1950s to the 1980s. In contrast to the usage of the term in New Criticism, Eur. thinking about structure discards an organic model for a ling. paradigm. What is important in *structuralism is the primacy of the signifier itself (the sounds or letters that are meaningful in a given lang. system (see SIGN, SIGNIFIED, SIGNIFIER). This displacement brackets the object of reference. As a result, the fundamental locus becomes the complex differential relationships of the signifiers within the boundaries of a ling. system, not the relation of the signifier to the external world. Drawing on work of the Swiss linguist Ferdinand de Saussure with his crucial distinction between *langue* (the ling. possibilities that make up a total lang. system) and *parole* (the local and contingent speech acts that are performed by individuals), a critic attempts to restore to the object of study the hidden and unarticulated rules of its synchronic functioning (or dysfunctioning). As Roland Barthes notes in "The Structuralist Activity," "[S]tructure is therefore actually a *simulacrum* of the object, but a directed, *interested* simulacrum, since the imitated object makes something appear which remained invisible or, if one prefers, unintelligible in the natural object."

Such a construct of a synchronic system allows Roman Jakobson and Claude Lévi-Strauss to delineate a basic poetic structure in Charles Baudelaire's "Les

Chats" ("Cats") In particular, the emphasis on synchronic structure makes visible the tensions between two sets of symmetrical/asymmetrical relations. This decoding device foregrounds "a division of the poem into two sestets separated by a distich whose structure contrast[s] vigorously with the rest." In the first, real cats occupy an important place; in the second, an unexpected reversal opens an imaginary space beyond the factual and physical world where surreal cats stand out. Structural analysis highlights how these intentional ambiguities combine to produce a new utterance: the sensual and external world of the first *sestet is maintained at the same time that it is transferred to the intellectual and internal world of the second. There is no doubt that Jakobson and Lévi-Strauss's reading of "Les Chats" is a paradigmatic example of analysis based on structure. Yet it should be noted that other critics have contested their decipherment of the formal features in question. Riffaterre, e.g., suggests that the structure of the sonnet is "a sequence of synonymous images, all of them variations on the symbolism of the cat as representative of the contemplative life."

The same application of a ling. or synchronic model to poetry is to be found in the poetics of Tzvetan Todorov, where the task of the critic is the discovery and description of an overall "structure of significations whose relations can be apprehended." For Todorov, like Jakobson and Lévi-Strauss, the speech act is reconstituted as a signifying system or set of ling. relations so that the content of a poem becomes lang. itself. E.g., in his analysis of the *Odyssey,* the emphasis is on events of lang. (speeches, the songs of the Sirens, and prophecies) rather than Odysseus's adventures.

In the late 1970s and 1980s, structure was reconceived with an emphasis on its formal gaps or breaks. Gérard Genette's *Figures in Literary Discourse* emphasizes the spaces and gaps inscribed within the poetic text, distinguishing his microscopic analyses of poetic structure from Todorov's more general theoretical propositions about poetic lang. According to Genette, "[P]oetry finds its place and its function *where language falls short,* in precisely those shortcomings that constitute it." For Genette, poetic structure is the particular space that disconnects two or more forms. Yet poetic structure is also a negation of the gap, for it projects a utopia of lang. in which the gap between signifier and signified would be effaced. Poetry, Genette writes is "gap from the gap, negation, rejection, oblivion, effacement of the gap, of the gap that *makes* language; illusion, dream, the necessary and absurd utopia of language without gap, without hiatus—without shortcomings." At the same time, it should be noted that Genette's theory of poetics is unmistakably linked with that of Todorov, in that both critics attempt to define the formal properties of poetic structures.

The question of structure is taken up by the poststructuralist thinker Jacques Derrida and other theorists (most notably the *Tel Quel* group and, in particular, Julia Kristeva). This group of writers undertakes the deconstruction of those structures that fix a poem conceptually as a centered structure or a transcendental signified. Such hypostasized structures—

Derrida sees them as metaphysical substances or mythical plenitudes—derive from a nostalgia for origins, a longing for a metaphysic of absolute presence. Derrida attempts to escape the closure of such a centered structure by emphasizing the free play of the signifier. This *indeterminacy of the heterogeneous text is intimately connected with what he has called *différence,* a term that implies both difference and deferral: an interminable temporal movement of signification that cannot be arrested in an absolute presence or closure of "meaning." However, it must be recognized that Derrida's ultimate emphasis on the free play of the signifier is still tied to the way the question of structure is posed within the ling. premises and traditional logic of Western metaphysics. The decoding of poetic script, the textual decipherment of poetry's specific structures, can be achieved in the first place only in terms of the older modes of lang. and thought that Derrida sets out to deconstruct—i.e., in terms of what he called the "always-already-written" (the *trace*). This suggests that Derrida's deconstructionist readings and analyses remain somehow structural, in spite of his effort to avoid the metaphysical closure of centered structure or absolute presence.

*Poststructuralism's emphasis on the free play of the signifier inspired poets to think of structure in a less restrained way. Alan Davies, associated with Am. *Language poetry, writes a series of short aphorisms about structure, sometimes contradictory, all without an attempt to create a logical *argument. In the 21st c., the Prague critic Louis Armand situates structural analysis within the new technologies of computing and artificial intelligence, a strategy that conceives structure in a mobile, dynamic form. "For discourse, for possibility to be what it is," he writes, "it must risk everything in its openness to what structures and underwrites the very concept of the limit." This openness puts in question the coherence of an organic model of structure and the finite combinations of lang. models. At the same time, an awareness of limit suggests the continued significance of structure.

■ Crane—important critique of Brooks; R. S. Crane, *The Languages of Criticism and the Structure of Poetry* (1953); S. Fishman, "Meaning and Structure in Poetry," *JAAC* 14 (1956); *Sens et usage du terme structure,* ed. R. Bastide (1962); H. Meyer, "Über der Begriff Struktur in der Dichtung," *Neue Deutsche Hefte* 10 (1963); R. Wellek, "Concepts of Form and Structure in Twentieth-Century Criticism," *Concepts of Criticism* (1963); M. Riffaterre, "Describing Poetic Structures," *Structuralism,* ed. J. Ehrmann (1970); R. Barthes, "The Structuralist Activity," *Critical Essays,* trans. R. Howard (1972); R. Jakobson and C. Lévi-Strauss, "Charles Baudelaire's 'Les Chats,'" *The Structuralists,* ed. R. DeGeorge and F. DeGeorge (1972); F. Jameson, *The Prison-House of Language* (1972); D. Wunderlich, "Terminologie des Strukturbegriffs," *Literaturwissenschaft und Linguistik,* ed. J. Ihwe, v. 1 (1972); F. Martínez-Bonati, "Die logische Struktur der Dichtung," *Deutsche Vierteljahrsschrift für Literaturwissenschaft und Geistesgeschichte* 47 (1973); Culler; T. Hawkes, *Structuralism and Semiotics* (1977); J. M. Lotman, *The Struc-*

*ture of the Artistic Text*, trans. G. Lenhoff and R. Vroon (1977); T. Todorov, *The Poetics of Prose*, trans. R. Howard (1977); T. D. Young, "Ransom's Critical Theories: Structure and Texture," *Mississippi Quarterly* 30 (1977); J. Derrida, "Structure, Sign and Play," *Writing and Difference*, trans. A. Bass (1978); and "Living on: *Border Lines*," H. Bloom, P. de Man, J. Derrida, G. Hartman, and J. H. Miller, *Deconstruction and Criticism* (1979); G. Genette, *Figures of Literary Discourse*, trans. A. Sheridan (1982); R. Williams, "Structural," *Keywords*, 2nd ed. (1983); J. Kristeva, *Revolution in Poetic Language*, trans. M. Waller (1984); *The L=A=N=G=U=A=G=E Book*, ed. B. Andrews and C. Bernstein (1984); J. C. Rowe, "Structure," *Critical Terms for Literary Study*, ed. F. Lentricchia and T. McLaughlin, 2d ed. (1995); L. Armand, *Literate Technologies: Language, Cognition, Technology* (2006).

P. McCallum

**STURM UND DRANG** (Ger., "storm and stress"). The term refers to a revolutionary literary movement that flourished in Germany from the late 1760s to the early 1780s. Because most of its representatives ceased to be radicals with advancing years, the term frequently denotes a brief period of youthful exuberance or maladjustment, although the *hendiadys originally meant the impulse to give violent expression to one's individuality. It also refers to the second title of a wildly bombastic play (1776) by F. M. Klinger. Participants in the movement were often called *Originalgenies* (original geniuses); thus, *Geniezeit* (genius epoch or time) is an earlier term for *Sturm und Drang*.

Hostile to neoclassicism as exemplified in Fr. lit. and hence often deliberately indecorous in theme and lang., *Sturm und Drang* was greatly influenced by Fr. and Eng. *preromanticism, the latter esp. important in that, since the 1740s, Eng. lit. had been regarded as particularly congenial to the Ger. national character. A general repudiation of normative aesthetics based itself on (1) the new sense of historical relativism and the importance attributed to environmental differences, (2) the revaluation of the primitive and of early national lit. and art, and (3) the cult of original *genius, which J. G. Herder, like Adam Ferguson, conceived as dynamic.

Sturm und Drang developed as the optimism of 18th-c. rationalists began to seem unwarranted in light of what the Enlightenment had actually achieved. Herder and his theologically less liberal teacher J. G. Hamann were both centrally concerned with religious issues, and many Sturm und Drang writers subscribed to a Herderian pantheism in which elements of Baruch Spinoza and G. W. Leibniz were sometimes fused with pietistic subjectivism. With nature felt to be a demonic force not entirely accessible to reason, a deliberate cult of the irrational—and of *myth as opposed to *allegory—became widespread.

For drama, Shakespeare, as formally unconventional, and Denis Diderot and Louis-Sébastien Mercier, as socially realistic, were inspirations and models. The *lyric

was permanently enriched with folk song elements (new structural freedom, simpler and more direct lang.) and forceful Pindaric directness (esp. in J. W. Goethe), although the *ode after F. G. Klopstock was still cultivated, esp. by members of the Göttingen Dichterbund. Yet despite new, almost expressionistic technical experiments in drama and lyric, the movement was abortive. Repudiation of despotic absolutism was perhaps the only sociopolitical attitude shared by all Sturm und Drang writers, whose apparent concern with contemp. social issues often reflects only the choice of unconventionally naturalistic themes. As Sturm und Drang writers' primary interests were private rather than social, Sturm und Drang could not realize its vision of a broadly popular national lit. in a complex and sophisticated age. Analogous features of Sturm und Drang have been discerned in some other 18th-c. lits. (Swedish, Eng.), but only in Germany was Sturm und Drang a self-conscious movement. Though strongly secular and limitedly cosmopolitan, by radically undermining traditional conceptions of poetry, Sturm und Drang undoubtedly hastened the first flowering of a conscious *romanticism, that of Germany in the 1790s.

■ **Anthologies**: *Sturm und Drang: Kritische Schriften*, ed. E. Loewenthal (1949); *Sturm und Drang: Dramatische Schriften*, ed. E. Loewenthal, 2 v. (1959); *Sturm und Drang*, ed. R. Strasser, 3 v. (1966); *Sturm und Drang: Dichtungen und theoretische Texte*, ed. H. Nicolai, 2 v. (1971); *Sturm und Drang und Empfindsamkeit*, ed. U. Karthaus (1978); *Sturm und Drang: Weltanschauliche und Ästhetische Schriften*, ed. P. Müller, 2 v. (1978); *Sturm und Drang*, ed. A. Leidner (1992); *Klassische Schullektüre, Sturm und Drang: Bilder, Texte, Materialien zu einer Epoche*, ed. D. Lüttgens (1994); *Gedichte des Sturm und Drang und der Klassik*, ed. G. Malsch (1997).

■ **Criticism and History**: K. Wais, *Das antiphilosophische Weltbild des französischen Sturm und Drang* (1934); E. A. Runge, *Primitivism and Related Ideas in Sturm und Drang Literature* (1946); H. B. Garland, *Storm and Stress* (1952); F. S. Schneider, *Die deutsche Dichtung der Geniezeit* (1952); R. Pascal, *The German Sturm und Drang* (1953); Wellek, v. 1.9; E. Blackall, "The Language of Sturm und Drang," *Stil- und Formprobleme in der Literatur*, ed. P. Böckmann (1959); S. Atkins, "Zeitalter der Aufklärung," *Fischer-Lexikon: Literatur*, v. 2 (1965); W. Kliess, *Sturm und Drang* (1966); H. A. Korff, *Geist der Goethezeit*, 8th ed., v. 2 (1966); A. Heuyssen, *Drama des Sturm und Drang* (1980); H. Thomke, "Sturm und Drang," *Reallexikon II* 4.278–96; Kollektiv für Literaturgeschichte, *Sturm und Drang*, 6th ed. (1983); B. Kieffer, *The Storm and Stress of Language* (1986); E. McInnes, *Ein Ungeheures Theater: The Drama of the Sturm und Drang* (1987); A. Leidner, *The Impatient Muse: Germany and the Sturm und Drang* (1994); M. Luserke, *Sturm und Drang Autoren, Texte, Themen* (1997); B. Duncan, *Lovers, Parricides, and Highwaymen: Aspects of Sturm und Drang Drama* (1999); G. W. Bertram, *Philosophie des Sturm und Drang* (2000); U. Karthaus, *Sturm und Drang*

(2000); S. Frank, *Kunst-Konzepte des Sturm und Drang* (2002); *Literature of the Sturm und Drang*, ed. D. Hill (2002); G. Kaiser, *Aufklärung, Empfindsamkeit, Sturm und Drang* (2007); S. Frank, *Kunst-Konzepte des Sturm und Drang* (2008); *Sturm und Drang Junge Autoren blicken auf eine Epoche*, ed. H.-G. Koch (2009).

S. ATKINS; K. BOWERS

**STYLE.** *Style* is the way something is done or made: not the what, but the how; not the method, but the manner. This rudimentary definition has been current for millennia, but the word commands interest not least for its contradictions. It has been used to define the distinctive voice of an individual and also the common features that identify the works of particular places, times, groups, or schools; for the holistic charisma of first impressions and the scrupling analyses of *stylistics; for the highest artistic achievement (having a style) and the season's passing fashions. That range is a challenge for theory and suggests (as such contradictions do) how much cultural work *style* does, defining how we recognize likeness and difference, community and individuality, present and past in our works and in one another.

In the Western trad., style was treated first as a department of rhet. *Style* for Aristotle consists of those aspects of lang.—*syntax, *diction, *figuration—that can be adapted to suit a persuasive occasion. He bequeathed this emphasis on decorum to Cicero, whose *Orator* codifies the flexibility of style in three *genera dicendi*, or kinds of speech: high, middle, and low. The high style, "forceful, versatile, copious and grave," suits affairs of state; the low, "refined, concise [and] stripped of ornament," is "clear rather than impressive" and serves for explanation and familiar talk. The middle is a compromise (never as clearly defined as its neighbors, in Cicero or in the trad. that followed him). This tripartite scheme offers a set of rhetorical strategies that may be taught to anyone, and though variations were proposed (like Hermogenes's 2d-c. *Seven Types of Style*), it remained central to rhetorical instruction through the Middle Ages and into the Ren. Its flexibility encourages a conceptual distinction between manner and matter, as though a single subject could be dressed (a common metaphor) in a variety of styles. Similarly persistent was the promise of a normative or best style: Cicero himself held that role for many Ren. humanists, and it was the characteristic aim of 18th-c. rhetorical manuals.

Cicero might also be said to be the source of a rival strand of the trad. His *De oratore*, written ten years before the *Orator*, asks, "Do you not expect that we shall find almost as many styles of oratory as orators?" Here is style as the mark of an individual, a signature (to take up the metaphor implicit in the Latin *stilus*, or pen). The idea of individual style, cultivated or innate, was a persistent undercurrent in Eur. letters through the 18th c. and became a critical preoccupation in the 19th. Style simultaneously developed into a central category for historical understanding. Ren. *historicism arguably began in the recognition of stylistic difference, as

eds. of cl. texts learned to date them (and to unmask forgeries) by changes in lang. over time. Art historians of the 18th and 19th cs. elaborated taxonomies of style to define periods and schools. Indeed, style, understood as the recognition of origins, might be said to be the most vivid way that historical stratification is present in daily life (Ginzburg): we are surrounded by things that look like the time and place they were made or pretend to have been made.

In the 20th c., ling. and technology transformed the study of style for literary analysis. The revolution of Noam Chomsky's generative grammar gave rise to a subdiscipline of stylistics that considers stylistic variation in relation to deep structure. Computers permitted ambitious statistical portraits of texts, providing evidence for dating and even attribution to individuals. In breaking texts down into features (like relative letter frequency) that no reader could be expected to notice, much less quantify, computer-assisted stylometrics has moved far away from the immediate power of style. That extension from total impression to incidental, telltale element has been a provocation to theorists, and philosophical thinking of the last 50 years has centered around a few recurring questions. Do texts, objects, or people have specifically stylistic features? This question is a version of the matter and manner problem: can we separate the subject of a poem, say, or its form, from what defines its style? Mod. opinion has tended to reject any a priori distinction—saying in advance what features of a text can and cannot count as stylistic—but there have been many attempts to set criteria. Stylistic features may be those, e.g., that express or solicit an affective response (Bally) or that express the psychology of the maker (Wollheim, Gilmore) or that convey the way something was made (Walton). Another common question is whether style requires a choice among possible alternatives. Would style be intelligible if there were only one style; is having a style necessarily a conscious choice? Other theorists have treated stylistic difference as the deviation from a norm, so that style, choice or no, is necessarily supplementary to the usual or the merely useful (Barthes, Todorov). The unity of style has attracted comment, too, much of it engaging the work of Spitzer. If a novel has a style, is that style necessarily present in each of its details? Is unity—which the critic discovers by traveling Spitzer's hermeneutic circle, moving from detail to whole and around again—the criterion of style?

Such theoretical questions coexist with a popular conversation about style that makes its social aspects particularly obvious. Style defines communities of people who dress similarly and read similar books, as well as communities that make similar poems. Having a style affords all of them a certain ease or at least a way of knowing what to do or how to do it. That goes for membership in a group as well as for individual style, insofar as a poet with a recognizable style can be said to imitate himself or herself. (The word's adaptability both to singling out and to collecting allows for delicate calibrations of affiliation and independence, in art and life.) In a social context, it becomes clear that the affiliations we perceive when we recognize a style are more than merely formal. We also register something like charisma: style impresses us when we see not only a way of proceeding but how someone might want to act or dress or make something that way (whether we ourselves would want to or not). Much of our life with works of art involves such negotiations of imitative desire, as we map the stylistic variety of our world, its communities and its hist., and define the boundaries of *taste within which we will live.

For all this attention and interest, the concept of style, still vital in art hist. and musicology, has been relatively peripheral to lit. crit. of the last 50 years. The *New Criticism often treated stylistic description as a distraction from the interpretive challenges of the particular text. Neither *poststructuralism nor historicism found terms for reviving its currency. But the bearing toward the world that style names is perdurably important to literary experience, and reading for the style—for who wrote the text, where it comes from, but also for what the writer's life might be like and what it might offer our own—is arguably far more widespread than formal *interpretation. Style has great promise for contemp. crit. as a neglected connection among form, society, and hist.

*See* ESTILISTICA.

■ W. Pater, "Style," *Appreciations* (1889); L. Spitzer, *Linguistics and Literary History* (1948); C. Bally, *Traité de stylistique française*, 3d ed. (1951); S. Ullman, *Language and Style* (1964); S. Sontag, "On Style," *Against Interpretation* (1966); E. Gombrich, "Style," *International Encyclopedia of the Social Sciences*, ed. D. L. Sills (1968); G. Hough, *Style and Stylistics* (1969); *Literary Style: A Symposium*, ed. S. Chatman (1971)—see esp. R. Barthes, "Style and Its Image," and T. Todorov, "The Place of Style in the Structure of the Text"; R. Lanham, *Style: An Anti-Textbook* (1974); N. Goodman, "The Status of Style," *CritI* 1 (1975); D. Russell, "Theories of Style," *Criticism in Antiquity* (1981); W. Sauerländer, "From Stilus to Style," *Art History* 6 (1983); *The Concept of Style*, ed. B. Lang, rev. ed. (1987)—see esp. K. Walton, "Style and the Products and Processes of Art," and R. Wollheim, "Pictorial Style: Two Views"; G. Genette, *Fiction and Diction*, trans. C. Porter (1993); C. Ginzburg, "Style as Inclusion, Style as Exclusion," *Picturing Science, Producing Art*, ed. P. Gallison and C. A. Jones (1998); J. Gilmore, *The Life of a Style* (2000).

J. DOLVEN

**STYLISTICS.** In its broadest sense, the study of style. In literary studies, stylistics most often refers to approaches that use mod. ling. to analyze and interpret the lang. of literary art. Ling. stylistics is the study of style in all genres, treating style as *register*, lang. associated with social uses and meanings, defined by M.A.K. Halliday as comprising field, tenor, and mode (semantic domain, relationship of communicative participants, and speech or writing). Mod. ling. has transformed stylistics so thoroughly that stylistics is regarded by many as the application of the concepts and tools of ling. to the study of style in lit.

The goals of literary stylistics include investigating the style of a particular author, period, genre, or national style; attributing authorship and dates; describing and analyzing an author's or group's "mind style" or habitual thought (psychological, philosophical, political, etc.); theorizing how lang. features are selected from among options (theoretical stylistics); analyzing socially constructed lang. of groups and genres (feminist stylistics, critical stylistics, functional stylistics). In the past four decades, stylistics has branched in several directions, each investigating style using a different field or more often a combination of fields: functional ling., feminist studies, critical studies, pragmatics, philosophy of lang., discourse analysis, reception theory, reader-response theory, performance theory, psycholinguistics, sociolinguistics, cognitive ling., cognitive psychology, semiotics, and *cognitive poetics. These branches share the problem of defining what style is and locating whatever it is in specific texts. Of the many definitions of style that have been put forth, style as "choice" is the most accurate and widely used (see also Wales). "Choice" distinguishes the "way" content is expressed in a specific instance of lang. (*parole*) as selected from among the available options in a lang. (*langue*). The objects for study are elements of style, called *stylistic features*, as they are structured and function in actual verbal instances. All the levels of the linguistic system are investigated and interrelated: phonological, syntactic, lexical, and semantic. Structures with functions above the sentence level, such as point of view, frames, and social interaction codes, are excluded except insofar as the elements of style affect the large structures. And since the small elements are always the actual lang., the large structures are said to contain, stylistics is relevant to the interpretations made by discourse analysts. Nevertheless, little work combining discourse-level analysis and stylistic analysis has been done. A small minority of stylistic studies include discourse studies, e.g., narratology (for discussions and opposing views, see Shen; Fludernik and Margolin). To examine style as choice is necessarily to view it as something separable from content, as something that includes both conscious and unconscious selection of features and structures, and as something individual as well as shared e.g., characteristic of a group, era, nation, genre). Actual separation between the "way" (style) and the "what" (content) of lang. elements, known as *dualism*, has been strenuously debated, and the dichotomy does not hold up in all senses and situations, esp. in poetry. Stylistic monists consider the substitution theory advanced by Roman Jakobson (in Sebeok and in Weber) to be inaccurate and insist that selection involves differences in meaning, however minute (e.g., the *New Critics were monists in theory; see Levin). A middle ground is sensibly used in actual analytic practice: a cline gives a more accurate way to regard lang. options, a slide from most similar to least similar options (see Ross on grammar clines); but stylistics analysis cannot proceed without the assumption of some degree of form/content divide. The problem of an assumed norm against which a style can be measured plagued early stylistics because there is no actual norm; instead, scholars must use their impression of a norm of use, or they must gather data on examples of writing comparable to the texts under investigation. Comparative studies require large-corpus data analysis, arduously compiled before computer programs by pioneers like Josephine Miles in the 1950s and 1960s, and Marina Tarlinskaja in the 1970s and 1980s. Miles researched continuity and change over 500 years of Eng. poetry, using representative sampling of a small set of features for analysis from a large representative sampling. Tarlinskaja examined a similar corpus of poetry, and later the corpus of Shakespeare's verse drama, for a full picture of metrical characteristics. Now data can be gathered and partially analyzed with the aid of increasingly powerful computer programs (see Semino, Short, and Culpepper for methodology and for results on Henry James's style; for computer applications, see Hoover et al.; Siemens and Schreibman). Large comparative data sets greatly assist the analyst in determining norms, but the analyst still has to exert good intuitive insight into which features stand out as salient—distinctive and significant to the functioning of a particular text or group of texts.

Mod. stylistics has direct roots in the Ren. version of cl. rhet., when rhet. was largely style (see RHETORIC AND POETRY): in Fr. *stylistique*, which extended cl. ideas and further reduced style to ethos in the 18th c., famously in Buffon's declaration, "Style is the man" (*Le style c'est l'homme*); and in Ger. *Stilforschung*, which examined style as expressiveness of authorial attitudes, a viewpoint that reigned in stylistics in the mid-20th c. and manifests in cognitive stylistics as "mind style" at present. From ancient Gr. into the 20th c., with few exceptions, stylistics was prescriptive, concerned with propriety of lang. usage or effective style. Stylistics relied on rhetorical analysis for concepts and categories, from the Sophists through the practical crit. of I. A. Richards and the New Critics, but turned descriptive and analytic in the 1920s with Richards in the U.S. and with *Rus. formalism and structural ling. in Europe (in Great Britain with T. E. Hulme in 1908; see Hulme in Cook). The Indiana Conference on Style of 1958 brought practical crit. and *structuralism together in an attempt at reaching agreement, but the aims and methods of the two were substantially different. Though both orientations investigated formal elements, practical crit. (U.S. and Great Britain) was interested in analyzing and evaluating individual poems, while the Eur. schools had as their goal building a systematic view of lang. and literary code. The conference launched ling.-based stylistics in the U.S. as poetics, a field that at the time was limited to the stylistic investigation of structural elements of poetry and their function (see Jakobson's closing statement in "Linguistics and Poetics" in Sebeok and in Cook). Since then, practical crit. and stylistics have continued uneasily side by side in the U.S., with stylistics developing analytic rigor and the more impressionistic practical crit. sometimes employing linguistic concepts and approaches, although sometimes not. Helen Vendler is the foremost defender of the view that the stylistics of the individual critic is superior to the objectivity of linguistic approaches (in Cook).

The 1980s saw stylistics about to become the central literary analytic method; in fact, stylistics did thrive in Britain and Europe, but it suffered a decline in the U.S. because of the combined influence of deconstruction, *poststructuralism, culture and canon wars, and the privileging of narrative over poetry. Subsequently, the U.S. has become the world center for narratology, and Great Britain has risen to the fore in stylistics, powered by Halliday's devel. of functional ling., which provided a detailed communicative framework that could be used for differentiating, analyzing, interpreting, and integrating aspects of lang. within all genres (see Birch and O'Toole). Germany is foremost in combining narratology and stylistics, as both are required courses of study in university curricula (see Fludernick and Margolin). Continuing its long interest in speaker/author, Fr. stylistics is distinguished by its continued focus on subjectivity. Fr. stylistics is divided, as is its U.S. counterpart, on the issue of whether using ling. is the best avenue; like Great Britain, Fr. stylistics takes for study all genres and has branched in several directions, with special interest, like Brit. functional stylistics and discourse stylistics, in styles of professional, political, and social genres (Rotge). In line with these interests, Fr. stylistics prefers cognitive stylistics, as do the cognitive poetics centers in the Netherlands (see the jour. *Poetics*) and Israel (see Tsur). Across the globe, Chinese stylistics has continued a trad. of objective investigation drawing from mod. Western ling., focusing on text elements as they affect discourse-level structures (see Shen).

The burgeoning of the ling.-based stylistics has not meant that insightful studies have not continued along the lines of older literary-historical and critical models. Excellent research in stylistics has continued with traditional topics and methods while incorporating some aspects of linguisitics: e.g., Marie Borroff's work on various poets' styles and Emerson Marks's study of period stylistics. The alliance of lit. hist. and crit. with ling. has yielded greater objectivity, systematization, and explanatory power because meaning and affect can be located in the functions of lang. as shared knowledge. Impressionistic practices, to the extent that they depend on individual assessments of meaning and affect, have lost much of their former authoritative power.

The next territories to be explored appear to be the continued expansion of cognitive stylistics and the intersections of stylistics with pragmatics and narratology: intensive investigation into how the mind makes, receives, and reconstructs lang. features; how lang. features affect the large extralinguistic structures, their functions, and meanings (see Leech and Short; Short; Turner; Birch; Downes; Semino and Culpepper; and Dan). Until the 1960s, the near-exclusive investigation in stylistics was on the lang. of poetry, much of it on *prosody, since sound structure was viewed as the defining aspect of literary art (see essays in Sebeok; and in Chatman and Levin). The first stylistics collection on prose, published in 1966, applied practical crit. to fiction (Lodge). The seminal work on linguistic approaches to fiction appeared in 1981 (Leech and Short). Reactions in the 1960s to the code as an objective entity without consideration for how texts come to be and how they are understood have progressed from various pragmatic, *speech-act, and reader-based theories to the current keen interest in cognitive studies, sparked by such influential studies as George Lakoff's on conceptual metaphor. Tropes have long been a principal area of investigation in stylistics, since Freud and Jakobson based their theories of lang. on *metaphor and *metonymy. The study of metaphor in lit., however, is, as yet, excessively constrained by most of the cognitive linguistic work, which seeks determinate meanings (e.g., see essays in Barcelona), whereas literary artists seek to "raid the inarticulate"—to indicate new worlds, new thought, new ways of indicating experience that is not adequately expressible in the ordinary shared lang. that ling. studies (see Ricoeur; Tracy and Ricoeur in Sacks; Levin; Ross 1972 and 1984; Tsur 2003; and Winslow). While cognitive studies have been centrally concerned with shared stylistic indicators (e.g., lexical) and mental processing for shared gestalts and frames (e.g., Lakoff; Turner), what is needed is more investigation into how literary texts defamiliarize by leaving gaps and creating blocks in the shared frames to promote new thought and world views.

*See* ESTILISTICA, LINGUISTICS AND POETICS, NEW CRITICISM, STYLE.

■ Richards; L. Spitzer, *Linguistics and Literary History* (1948); H. A. Hatzfeld, *A Critical Bibliography of the New Stylistics Applied to Romance Literatures* (1953); J. Miles, *Eras and Modes in English Poetry* (1957); Sebeok; S. Levin, *Linguistic Structures in Poetry* (1962); D. Lodge, *Language of Fiction* (1966); S. Chatman and S. Levin, *Essays on the Language of Literature* (1967); S. Chatman, ed., *Literary Style, A Symposium* (1971); J. Ross, "Squishing," *Canadian Journal of Linguistics*, 17.2 (1972); and "Parallels in Phonological and Semantic Organization," *Papers from the Parasession on Functionalism*, ed. J. Kavanagh and J. Cutting (1975); M.A.K. Halliday, *Halliday: System and Function in Language*, ed. G. Kress (1976); P. Ricoeur, *The Rule of Language* (1976); Tarlinskaja; H. White, *Tropics of Discourse* (1978); M. Borroff, *Language and the Poet* (1979); S. Sacks, ed., *On Metaphor* (1979); S. Fish, *Is There a Text in This Class?* (1980); G. Lakoff and M. Johnson, *Metaphors We Live By* (1980); G. N. Leech and M. H. Short, *Style in Fiction* (1981; 2d ed., 2007); J. Ross, "Speaking the Unspeakable," *The Counterfeit Ark*, ed. J. Leaning and L. Keyes (1984); J. Bennett, *Bibliography of Stylistics and Related Criticism, 1967–83* (1986); N. Fabb, D. Attridge, A. Durant, and C. MacCabe, *The Linguistics of Writing* (1987); M. Tarlinskaja, *Shakespeare's Verse* (1987); D. Birch and M. O'Toole, *Functions of Style* (1988); S. Levin: *Metaphoric Worlds*

(1988); R. Tsur, *Toward a Theory of Cognitive Poetics* (1992); H. Widdowson, *Practical Stylistics* (1992); G. Cook, *Discourse and Literature: The Interplay of Form and Mind* (1994); D. Birch, *Context and Language: A Functional Theory of Register* (1995); J. Mills, *Feminist Stylistics* (1995); R. Fowler, *Linguistic Criticism* (1996); M. Turner, *The Literary Mind: The Origins of Language and Thought* (1996); J. Weber, ed., *The Stylistics Reader: From Roman Jakobson to the Present* (1996); D. Crystal, *Language Play* (1998); W. Downes, *Language and Society* (1998); E. Marks, *Taming the Chaos: English Poetic Diction Theory Since the Renaissance* (1998); A. Barcelona, ed., *Metaphor and Metonymy at the Crossroads: A Cognitive Perspective* (2000); K. Wales, *A Dictionary of Stylistics* (2000); M. Toolan, *Narrative: A Critical Linguistic Introduction*, 2d ed. (2001); *Cognitive Stylistics: Language and Cognition in Text Analysis*, ed. E. Semino and J. Culpepper (2002); R. Tsur, *On the Shore of Nothingness* (2003); J. Cook, *Poetry in Theory* (2004); M. Fludernik and U. Margolin, "Introduction," *Style*: Special Issue on German Stylistics 38.3 (Fall 2004); W. Rotge, "Stylistics in France Today," *Style* 38.4 (Winter 2004); E. Semino, M. Short, and J. Culpepper, *A Corpus-Based Study of Speech, Thought and Writing in a Corpus of English Writing* (2004); R. Winslow, "Troping Trauma: Conceiving (of) Experiences of Speechless Trauma," *JAC* (2004); D. Shen, "How Stylisticians Draw on Narratology: Approaches, Advantages and Disadvantages," *Style* 39:4 (Winter 2005); E. Black, *Pragmatic Stylistics* (2006); D. Hoover, J. Culpepper, B. Louw, and M. Wynne, *Approaches to Corpus Stylistics* (2007); R. Siemens and S. Schreibman, *Blackwell Companion to Digital Literary Studies* (2007); M. Lambrou and P. Stockwell, *Contemporary Stylistics* (2008).

R. WINSLOW

# SUBLIME

I. Classical
II. Enlightenment to Modern

**I. Classical.** Sublime (Lat. *sublimis*, "[on] high, lofty, elevated") owes its currency as a critical and aesthetic term to the anonymous Gr. treatise *Peri hypsous* (*On the Sublime*; *hypsos*, "height, elevation") once ascribed to the rhetorician Longinus of the 3d c. CE but now generally agreed to belong to the 1st c., perhaps around 50 CE. Whatever his name and origin, its author was certainly a rhetorician and a teacher of the art, but one of uncommon mold. His treatise, with its intimacy of tone (it is addressed to a favorite pupil, a young Roman) and breadth of spirit, stands more or less isolated in its own time but has had a recurrent fascination for the mod. mind since the 17th c.

The idea of sublimity had its roots in the rhetorical distinction, well established before Longinus, of three levels of *style—high, middle, and low. His achievement was to draw it out of the technical sphere, where it had to do primarily with style, and to associate it with the general phenomenon of greatness in lit., prose and poetry alike. The author regards sublimity above all as a thing of the spirit, a spark that leaps from the soul of the writer to the soul of his reader and only secondarily as a matter of technique and expression. "Sublimity is the echo of greatness of spirit." Being of the soul, it may pervade a whole work (speech, hist., or poem: the author pays little attention to generic distinctions), or it may flash out at particular moments. "Father Zeus, kill us if thou wilt, but kill us in the light." "God said, 'Let there be light,' and there was light." In such quotations as these, Longinus shows among other things his sharp eye for the particular passage and his capacity for empathy with the actual work, qualities that are, in fact, rare in ancient crit. and that presage the mod. spirit.

The distinguishing mark of sublimity for this ancient author is a certain quality of feeling. But he will not allow it to be identified simply with *emotion, for not all emotions are true or noble. Only art can guard against exaggerated or misplaced feeling. Nevertheless, art is subordinated to *genius in his thinking. He enumerates five sources of the sublime: great thoughts, noble feeling, lofty figures, *diction, and arrangement. The first two, the crucial ones, are the gift of nature, not art. He even prefers the faults of a great spirit, a Homer, a Plato, or a Demosthenes, to the faultless mediocrity that is achieved by following rules.

In later antiquity and the Middle Ages, the treatise remained unknown, or at least exercised little influence. In the Ren., it was first published by Francesco Robortello in 1554, then translated into Lat. in 1572 and into Eng. in 1652 by John Hall. But it made no great impression until the late 17th c. Paradoxically enough, it was Nicolas Boileau, the high priest of Fr. neoclassicism, who launched the *Peri hypsous* on its great mod. career and thus helped to prepare the ultimate downfall of *classicism. His trans. (1674) had immense reverberation, esp. in England. The English, always restive under the so-called Fr. rules, instinctively welcomed Longinus as an ally. As neoclassicism advanced and subjectivity became increasingly central to Eng. thinking, not only about lit. but about art in general, the sublime became a key concept in the rise of *romanticism in poetry and the concurrent establishment of aesthetics as a new, separate branch of philosophy.

**II. Enlightenment to Modern.** In the 18th c., the sublime represented merely one type of experience that could be described under the general philosophical rubric of sensationism (see NEOCLASSICAL POETICS). For a host of writers producing everything from aesthetic treatises to Gothic novels, it was synonymous with irresistible forces that produced overwhelming sensations. In the 18th and 19th cs., *sublime* came increasingly to be a term of aesthetic approbation, as attested by the interest in both sublime landscapes and paintings of sublime landscapes. In the popular view, the term amounted to a description: it represented primarily a subject matter, the wild and desolate natural scene (see NATURE) or the natural force that dwarfed the individual human figure. Its effect was simultaneously to make one conscious of one's own comparative weakness in the face of natural might and to produce a sense of the strength of one's own faculties. As John Baillie put it in his *Essay on the Sublime* (1747), "Vast Objects occasion vast Sensations, and vast Sensations give the Mind a higher Idea of her own Powers."

Along with the increasing currency of the term in the 18th c., two particularly strong arguments about the place of the sublime and sublime nature emerged: Edmund Burke's *Philosophical Enquiry into the Origin of Our Ideas of the Sublime and the Beautiful* (1757) and Immanuel Kant's *Critique of Judgment* (1790; commonly referred to as his Third Critique, after the *Critique of Pure Reason* [1781] and *Critique of Practical Reason* [1788]). In the hist. of what we now call *aesthetics*, these two works were esp. important for according significance to pleasure in objects that were not, strictly speaking, beautiful. Burke developed the sensationist position into an affectivism that continually connected the sublime with the issue of an individual's relationship to society, and Kant made his discussion of the sublime a cornerstone of a formalist account of aesthetics (see INTUITION).

Burke's *Enquiry* sets out the affectivist position on the sublime in an argument that emphasizes the power of experience. In the "Introduction on Taste" added to the 2d ed. (1759), Burke made two claims for the importance of *taste. First, his emphasis on the regular operation of the senses makes taste as meaningful and as generalizable as reason: "as the conformation of their organs are nearly, or altogether the same in all men, so the manner of perceiving external objects is in all men the same, or with little difference." Second, his emphasis on the origin of the passions treats taste as a field of determinate knowledge in which the "remembrance of the original natural causes of pleasure" can be distinguished from the acquired tastes that fashion and habit promote. People, he observes, are not likely to be mistaken in their reactions to sensation even though they may often be confused in their reasoning about them.

Burke traced the attractions of the beautiful and the sublime to human impulses that are ultimately utilitarian. The beautiful he saw as a manifestation of the human instinct toward sociability, with sociability, in turn, serving the purpose of the continuation of the species. The sublime he treated as a manifestation of the instinct for self-preservation, the response of terror that "anticipates our reasonings, and hurries us on by an irresistible force." The beautiful represents what we love (and love specifically for submitting to us and flattering our sense of our own power); the sublime represents all that we fear for being greater and more powerful than we are.

If the notion of sympathy (see EMPATHY AND SYMPATHY) had for writers like Adam Smith suggested how persons might identify with the interests of others, Burke's discussion of the sublime and the beautiful emphasizes relations between individuals and objects far more than intersubjective relations. Yet Burke argues for the social utility of our feelings of the sublime and beautiful. He increasingly aligns the beautiful not merely with the sociable and pleasing but with a relaxation of the bodily functions that eventually becomes disabling. The sublime, by contrast, presents difficulties that require "exercise or labour" to be overcome. Although the sublime feelings of astonishment or awe may resemble pain, the excitation and exertion that they produce yield a very real pleasure—a consciousness of one's own powers and even a physical exercise that keeps the various organs of sensation in tone. Burke's account may be empiricist in suggesting that objects have regular and predictable operations on the senses, but it ultimately deemphasizes knowledge of the external world and stresses instead the uses of objects in gratifying and challenging the individual human organism.

Kant, in his *Critical Observations on the Feeling of the Beautiful and Sublime* (1784), does not depart strikingly from the Burkean position. He identifies the beautiful and the sublime as terms under which contrasting kinds of objects of experience might be subsumed; and he sees the enjoyment or displeasure in these objects as having essentially a psychological dimension. In this, his remarks are consistent with the familiar critical view that shifted discussions of pleasure in art and nature from an emphasis on production—what the artist must do to achieve certain effects—to an emphasis on reception—how the response to certain objects raises questions of a viewer's or reader's psychology.

With the Third Critique, however, Kant reoriented aesthetic discussion. Burke and other writers (incl. the Kant of the *Observations*) had described the sublime and the beautiful in terms of both natural and human-made objects; Homeric and Miltonic poetry could serve as examples of sublimity as well as the seemingly infinite expanse of the ocean or a powerful animal in whom "the terrible and sublime blaze out together." Kant reduced the metaphorical reach of the term *sublime* and identified it exclusively with natural objects. The effect of this reduction was to enable him to argue that the sublime is not—or not particularly—important for establishing human inferiority relative to natural might. Rather, the pleasure that one takes in sublime nature reveals a pleasure in judging objects that are not the vehicles of a message and not expressions of anyone's intentions. If a poem or a statue cannot exist without the intentional action of its maker, natural sublimity appeals to human viewers in a fashion that stands outside such communication of *intention.

Kant's claim for sublime intentionlessness obviously opposes itself to the "argument from design," which reads the book of nature as revealing divine intention. Its primary significance, however, is not so much to argue against belief in divinity as to identify aesthetic judgment as a faculty that is, in interesting ways, unable to ground itself in claims about the prior value of external objects. The sublime becomes the primary vehicle for the Kantian argument about the importance of "purposiveness without purpose" in aesthetic objects. While natural beauty might appear to have been formed by design (echoing Joseph Addison's sense

of the mutually enhancing relationship of art and nature to one another), the sublime, lacking the form of beautiful nature, bespeaks pleasure in an object that is without bounds not merely in appearing infinite but in having no form. The aesthetic judgment, i.e., does not respond to the intrinsic beauty of an object in appreciating natural sublimity, but neither does it merely provide a screen on which individual psychology is projected. Rather, the sublime in its intentionlessness and formlessness makes visible the judgment's role as a form-giving faculty.

In the 1970s and after, the sublime gained prominence in *poststructuralism, rhetorical crit., and continental philosophy. In the work of Jacques Derrida, for instance, it figured in his challenge to Kantian formalism. Indeed, for many critics it came to represent something like an inversion of the Kantian claim about it: namely, the view that the sublime represents an "excess" in lang. that keeps it from ever assuming any fixed form or meaning. More recently, the Fr. philosopher Jean-François Lyotard revisited the Kantian sublime as an Enlightenment anticipation of the epistemological complexity associated with *postmodernism, while the Slovenian philosopher Slavoj Žižek has argued that political regimes depend on extrapolitical "sublime objects" (such as the state or religion) to frame their subjects' worldview. Meanwhile, many literary scholars have been concerned to develop the material, psychological, and transhistorical dimensions of the sublime.

*See* BATHOS, DESCRIPTIVE POETRY, HEBRAISM, IMAGINATION, JE NE SAIS QUOI, ROMANTIC AND POSTROMANTIC POETRY AND POETICS.

■ T. R. Henn, *Longinus and English Criticism* (1934); S. H. Monk, *The Sublime: A Study of Critical Theories in XVIII-Century England* (1935); B. Weinberg, "Translations and Commentaries on Longinus to 1600, A Bibliography," *MP* 47 (1949–50); F. Wehrli, "Der erhabene und der schlichte Stil in der poetisch-rhetorischen Theorie der Antike," *Phylobolia fauur P. von der Mauuhll* (1946); E. Olson, "The Argument of Longinus' *On the Sublime*," Crane; Wimsatt and Brooks, esp. chs. 6, 14; W. J. Hipple, *The Beautiful, The Sublime, and the Picturesque* (1957); J. Brody, *Boileau and Longinus* (1958); M. H. Nicolson, *Mountain Gloom and Mountain Glory* (1959); E. Tuveson, *The Imagination as a Means of Grace* (1960); M. Price, "The Sublime Poem," *Yale Review* 58 (1969); Saisselin; A. Litman, *Le Sublime en France, 1666–1714* (1971); D. B. Morris, *The Religious Sublime* (1972); T.E.B. Wood, *The Word "Sublime" and Its Context, 1650–1760* (1972); A. O. Wlecke, *Wordsworth and the Sublime* (1973); W. P. Albrecht, *The Sublime Pleasures of Tragedy* (1975); T. Weiskel, *The Romantic Sublime* (1976); J. Derrida, "Economimesis," trans. R. Klein, *Diacritics* 11 (1981); P. H. Fry, *The Reach of Criticism* (1983); P. de Man, "Hegel on the Sublime," *Displacement*, ed. M. Krupnick (1983); A. Leighton, *Shelley and the Sublime* (1984); N. Hertz, *The End of the Line* (1985); E. Escoubas, "Kant ou la simplicité du sublime," *Poésie* 32 (1985); S. Knapp, *Personification and the Sublime: Milton to Coleridge* (1985); "The Sublime and the Beautiful: Reconsiderations," *NLH* 16.2 (1985)—spec. iss.; *The American Sublime*, ed. M. Arensberg (1986); P. Lacoue-Labarthe, "La Verité sublime," *Poésie* 38 (1986); L. W. Marvick, *Mallarmé and the Sublime* (1986); J. Derrida, *The Truth in Painting*, trans. G. Bennington and I. McLeod (1987); *La Via al Sublime*, ed. M. Brown et al. (1987); T. M. Kelley, *Wordsworth's Revisionary Aesthetics* (1988); P. Boitani, *The Tragic and the Sublime in Medieval Literature* (1989); P. Crowther, *The Kantian Sublime* (1989); *Das Erhabene*, ed. C. Pries (1989); J.-F. Lyotard, *The Differend*, trans. G. Van Den Abbeele (1988); and "The Sublime and the Avant-Garde," *The Lyotard Reader*, ed. A. Benjamin (1989); J. Ramazani, "Yeats: Tragic Joy and the Sublime," *PMLA* 104 (1989); S. Guerlac, *The Impersonal Sublime* (1990); R. Wilson, *American Sublime* (1991); V. A. De Luca, *Words of Eternity: Blake and the Poetics of the Sublime* (1991); F. Ferguson, *Solitude and the Sublime* (1992); N. A. Halmi, "From Hierarchy to Opposition: Allegory and the Sublime," *CL* 44 (1992); J.-L. Nancy, "The Sublime Offering," *Of the Sublime*, trans. J. S. Librett (1993); *Eighteenth-Century Studies* 28.1 (1994)—several essays on the sublime in France and Germany; M. Lollini, *Le muse, le maschere e il sublime* (1994); J.-F. Lyotard, *Lessons on the Analytic of the Sublime*, trans. E. Rottenberg (1994); *Beauty and the Critic*, ed. J. Soderholm (1997); D. Bromwich, "The Sublime before Aesthetics and Politics," *Raritan* 16 (1997); E. Baker, "Fables of the Sublime: Kant, Schiller, Kleist," *MLN* 113 (1998); S. Budick, *The Western Theory of Tradition* (2000); M. Donougho, "Stages of the Sublime in North America," *MLN* 115 (2000); J. Turner, "Wordsworth and the Psychogenesis of the Sublime," *Romanticism* 6 (2000); R. Gasché, "The Sublime, Ontologically Speaking," *YFS* 99 (2001); I. Balfour, "The Sublime between History and Theory: Hegel, de Man, and Beyond," *After Poststructuralism*, ed. T. Rajan and M. J. O'Driscoll (2002), and "The Sublime Sonnet in European Romanticism," *Romantic Poetry*, ed. A. Esterhammer (2002); M. Blackwell, "The Sublimity of Taste in Edmund Burke's *A Philosophical Enquiry into the Origin of Our Ideas of the Sublime and Beautiful*," *PQ* 82 (2003); H. Ram, *The Imperial Sublime: A Russian Poetics of Empire* (2003); *Georgia Review* 58.2 (2004)—symposium on the poetic sublime; C. Duffy, *Shelley and the Revolutionary Sublime* (2005); *Phrasis* 46.1 (2005)—several essays on the sublime; I. Balfour, "Torso: (The) Sublime Sex, Beautiful Bodies, and the Matter of the Text," *Eighteenth-Century Studies* 39 (2006); A. J. Cascardi, "The Genealogy of the Sublime in the Aesthetics of the Spanish Baroque," *Reason and Its Others*, ed. D. Castillo and M. Lollini (2006); B. Kim, "Generating a National Sublime: Wordsworth's *The River Duddon* and *The Guide to the Lakes*," *SIR* 45 (2006); C. Battersby, *The Sublime, Terror and Human Difference* (2007); R. Rothman, "Modernism, Postmodernism, and the Two Sublimes of Surrealism," *Modernism and Theory*, ed. S. Ross (2009); S. Žižek, *The Sublime Object of Ideology*, 2d ed. (2009); R. A. Barney, "The Splenetic Sublime: Anne Finch, Melancholic Psychology, and Post/Modernity," *Studies in Eighteenth-Century Culture* 39 (2010); A. Richardson,

*The Neural Sublime* (2010); C. Stokes, *Coleridge, Language, and the Sublime* (2011).

G. F. Else, T.V.F. Brogan (cl.); F. Ferguson, R. Greene (mod.)

**SUBSTITUTION.** According to traditional Eng. versification, one of several ways of explaining why a particular line departs from the meter of a poem. The idea is that poets need not strictly adhere to a meter: one kind of foot can be substituted for another. E.g., in 1906, Saintsbury argued that George Chapman shows artistry in his trans. of the *Iliad* by substituting an *anapest (*-ible cave*) where the reader expects an *iamb: "From bréasts heróic; sént them fár, to thát invísible cáve."

Substitution fully entered Eng. prosodic thinking only in the mid-19th c. Attridge (1974), Fussell, and Taylor have explained that, in the 17th and 18th cs., prosodists paid little attention to departures from the meter. Typically, they described meter only by counting the number of syllables. When they did discuss stress, they argued that the pattern must be regular and that departures were flaws.

In proposing the idea of substitution, Victorian prosodists imported a concept from *classical prosody. As Gasparov explains, when the notion of the *foot appeared in Gr. verse sometime between 1000 and 750 BCE, the concept of substitution arose at the same time: where the line called for a long syllable, two short syllables could be substituted instead.

In the 20th c., linguists rejected substitution for failing to explain how many and what kinds of substitution a line could bear before another meter emerged or the meter collapsed entirely. E.g., each of these lines has only two iambs, but Robert Browning's is heard as iambic pentameter ("Your búsiness is nót to cátch mén with shów"; "Fra Lippo Lippi") while Hollander's is not ("Withóut ány arrángement of dównbeats"). Linguists responded to such problems by trying to articulate the unspoken rules of meter; and in 1966, Halle and Keyser founded *generative metrics when they replaced the concepts of foot and substitution with the concept of position.

The work of Halle and Keyser and of their successors has largely gone unnoticed by literary scholars, who have tended to follow the lead of Wimsatt and Beardsley, who, in 1959, famously rejected linguistic efforts, believing that substitution creates a *counterpoint between the abstract grid of meter and the actual *rhythm of each line. In 1962, Halperin argued that iambic meters accommodate substitution more easily than other meters; but in 1996, Finch and Wallace countered that substitution appears frequently in noniambic meters as well, a claim disputed by Steele.

The success of Wimsatt and Beardsley has led to a continuing divide between the understanding of meter found in poetry handbooks, poetry classes, and most literary scholarship, on the one hand, and the understanding of meter explored by linguists, on the other. In 1982, Attridge tried to bridge the gap between literary and linguistic approaches.

*See* LINGUISTICS AND POETICS, METER, RHYTHM.

■ Saintsbury, *Prosody*; Wimsatt and Beardsley; M. Halperin, "On the Two Chief Metrical Modes in English," *PMLA* 77 (1962); P. Fussell, *Theory of Prosody in Eighteenth-Century England* (1966); M. Halle and S. J. Keyser, "Chaucer and the Study of Prosody," *CE* 33 (1966); D. Attridge, *Well-Weighed Syllables* (1974); Attridge, *Rhythms*; D. Taylor, *Hardy's Metres and Victorian Prosody* (1988); D. Baker, *Meter in English* (1996)—see essays by Finch, Wallace, and Steele; Gasparov, *History*; J. Hollander, *Rhyme's Reason* (2001).

M. L. MANSON

**SUMERIAN POETRY.** A corpus of more than 100 compositions in the Sumerian lang. written out on clay tablets in verse form, ranging from short lyric pieces to narrative *epics of over 700 lines. Uncertainty about Sumerian phonetics hinders appreciation of how Sumerian poetry sounded. The earliest Sumerian poetry dates to the mid-3d millennium BCE. Most manuscripts date approximately to the 18th c. BCE, when Sumerian was a cultural rather than a spoken lang.; the latest date to the Achaemenid and Hellenistic periods. Native rubrics suggest that Sumerian poetry was closely associated with performance, by singers individually or in chorus, accompanied by drums, winds, and harps.

Although lines of Sumerian poetry often show a loose rhythm of syllables or words, no strict meter has been detected. *Simile, *metaphor, wordplay, and *chiasmus are highly cultivated. Some genres, such as *laments, make extensive use of *refrains, *repetition, and simple replacive *parallelism. More complex parallelism is developed in *love poetry and epic narratives. *Assonance and *alliteration are rare but striking when they occur, as in magic spells, which also use *concatenation and *chain rhyme. Political and historical *allegory have been alleged but disputed.

Religious poetry includes *hymns of praise to deities and temples and laments. Frequently compared to mountains, temples are described as linking heaven and earth, their glory radiating throughout the land. Hymns to major deities, such as Enlil, Utu, Nanna, and Inanna, praise their transcendent powers, support of justice and order, beauty, and valor. Some of the earliest known religious hymns of praise were written cryptographically, but this practice disappeared thereafter. Laments over the destruction of cities and the land of Sumer range from 300 to 500 lines, divided into units called *kirugus*. These depict social disorder, violence, invasion, famine, and destruction, followed by restoration at the command of the gods. Although they contain historical references, their lang. tends to be stereotypical. Ritual laments to appease the anger of the gods are known as late as the Hellenistic period. They were performed in a special Sumerian dialect called "thin," characterized by major phonetic changes (e.g., *zeb* for *dug*, sweet).

Mythological narratives relate the deeds of deities, among them creation stories and etiologies. They include a group about the hero-god Ninurta, in one of which he defeats a volcano and assigns destiny to stones; a group about the chief god on earth, Enlil, and his sanctuary at Nippur; a group about Enki, god of wisdom, in one of which he organizes the world; and a group about Inanna, goddess of love and procreation.

Court poetry includes epic tales of kings of the remote past, praises of living kings, and *poetic contests. Four epics celebrate the victories of two legendary kings of Uruk—Enmerkar and Lugalbanda—over the lord of the city of Aratta in Iran. These trials of valor, rhet., and ingenuity provide vehicles for fanciful and entertaining narratives. A cycle of poems about the hero-king Gilgamesh includes episodes incorporated into the later Mesopotamian *Epic of Gilgamesh*, such as an expedition to cut cedar trees and a battle with the bull of heaven; but others not in the later epic, notably the death and burial of Gilgamesh, in the later epic are transformed into the death and burial of Gilgamesh's companion Enkidu.

Hymns in praise of kings of the dynasty of Ur (late 3d millennium BCE), in the case of Shulgi redolent of a personality cult, praise their bravery, athleticism, musical and linguistic skills, and other courtly attainments, and in some cases refer to important events of their reigns. These were imitated in the successor state of Isin, the best known focusing on the king's role in the *hieros gamos*, or ritual wedding with a goddess, but disappear thereafter.

Poetic contests pit against each other elements of Sumerian civilization, such as sheep and grain; tools, such as plow and pickaxe; seasons, such as summer and winter; animals, such as bird and fish; and materials, such as silver and gold and tree and reed, disputing their relative usefulness to the human race. At the end, a winner is declared. Like the court epics, these are witty, elegant, and amusing, but they offer penetrating analyses of Sumerian culture. Other poetic dialogues include literary abuse and school debates between masters and students.

More than 25 love songs deal with the courtship and marriage of the deities Inanna and Dumuzi (Tammuz), portrayed as young lovers. These too have been associated with the hieros gamos. Related to these are mythological narratives dealing with Dumuzi's death, such as *Dumuzi's Dream* and *The Descent of Inanna to the Netherworld*, and laments about Dumuzi's death.

Miscellaneous Sumerian poetry includes short drinking, work, and love songs; *elegies; and even a royal lullaby.

Much Sumerian poetry was copied and composed in an Akkadian-speaking environment (see ASSYRIA AND BABYLONIA, POETRY OF) and some was transmitted in bilingual versions, but mutual literary influences have not yet been explored in depth.

The native term *sher* (song) comes closest to the mod. term *poetry*. There is no word for "poet" but only for performers of poetry (*nar*, singer; *gala*, singer of ritual laments). There are no native treatises or remarks on poetics. Most Sumerian poetry is anonymous, with the major exception of a group of compositions ascribed in antiquity and mod. times to Enheduanna, daughter of King Sargon of Akkad (ca. 2300 BCE). These are noteworthy for their original style and subject matter, difficult diction, autobiographical content, remarks on the creative process, and intense feeling, so invite consideration as the first identifiable oeuvre of an individual poet in world lit.

■ **Anthologies:** *The Harps That Once*, trans. T. Jacobsen (1987); *The Literature of Ancient Sumer*, trans. J. Black (2009); *Love Songs in Sumerian Literature*, ed. Y. Sefati (1998).

■ **Criticism:** C. Wilcke, "Formale Gesichtspunkte," *Assyriological Studies* 20 (1976); W. Heimpel, "Mythologie" [in Eng.], *Reallexikon der Assyriologie* (1993, 1997); A. Zgoll, *Rechtsfall der En-hedu-Ana* (1997); G. Rubio, "Sumerian Literature," *From an Antique Land*, ed. C. Ehrlich (2009).

B. FOSTER

# SURREALISM

I. Overview
II. Definitions
III. History

**I. Overview.** One of the principal experimental movements of the 20th c., surrealism grew from a Paris-based group of young poets and artists to a broadly international intellectual phenomenon, gaining adherents and fellow travelers throughout the world from the 1920s through the late 1960s. The word *surrealism* designates two major poetic inclinations. It refers, first, to the active, organized network of friends and collaborators who contributed to surrealist periodicals, met regularly in cafés, and signed the group's political tracts. At the same time, *surrealism* also signifies a more general tendency in poetry, plastic arts, and thought associated with experimental techniques such as automatic writing, *collage, the game of "exquisite corpse," and the analysis of dreams.

For André Breton (1896–1966), a leading poet and principal theorist of the movement, the distinction between a committed surrealist practice and a generalized surrealism hinged less on the use of formal techniques than on a commitment to fusing the group's poetic ambitions with a liberatory political imperative. As Breton put it in a 1934 speech, "What Is Surrealism," the movement evolved according to an unceasing aversion to belles lettres, a wish "at all costs to avoid considering a system of thought as a refuge." Surrealism pursued instead a wide-ranging set of investigations that contributed to the intellectual as well as literary life of the 20th c. Pioneering the Fr. reception of G.W.F. Hegel and Sigmund Freud after World War I, surrealism was instrumental to mod. devels. in psychoanalysis, philosophy, and aesthetics. Surrealist poets and artists likewise participated in contemp. thinking about gender and subjectivity, as well as in the fields of ethnography and political philosophy. In spite of its predominantly Fr. origins, active surrealist groups developed—and, in some cases, continue to exist today—throughout Eastern and Western Europe, Latin America, the Caribbean, and North Africa, as well as in the U.S. and Japan. Moreover, as a major intellectual movement between and after the world wars, surrealism offered both an influence and a target for later experimental groups,

incl. *Negritude, existentialism, *lettrisme, *Oulipo, Fluxus, situationism, magical realism, the theorists of *Tel Quel, and, more broadly, the feminist and anticolonial movements of the post-World War II era.

This broad yet heterodox set of resonances owes much to the availability of surrealism as a freestanding set of creative activities beyond the organized movement. Surrealism's hist. is rife with debates about the consequences of abstracting its poetic devices and creative processes from the group's political imperatives. All the same, a large number of so-called excommunicated, marginal, and dissident figures claimed to practice no less viable forms of surrealism. Other poets and artists have engaged with surrealism more obliquely, based on their interest in surrealist poets or techniques or their pursuit of the movement at a geographical or historical remove.

**II. Definitions.** In the words of literary critic Chénieux-Gendron, surrealism presents itself less as a concept or literary-historical school than as "a machine for integration." Refusing the divisions on which Enlightenment reason is founded—between *genius and hack, art and nonart, private experience and public politics, truth and falsehood—surrealism sought to mingle imagination, expression, and desire in ways that involved all the institutions and social forms that affected mod. life.

Breton, in his first *Manifeste du surréalisme* (*Manifesto of Surrealism*, 1924), gave two provisional definitions of surrealism: the first describes a creative process, the second a philosophy of mind. Both announced a fundamental break with existing modes of communication and the conventional manner in which one perceives and accepts the exterior world. The first definition promotes the practice of "psychic automatism," the work of disclosing repressed activities of the mind through oral, written ("automatic writing"), or other means. The second definition, called "encyclopedic" by Breton, expands on the first; it describes the epistemological and social effects of the "actual functioning of thought" outlined in the first definition. According to Breton, surrealism forges an alternative network of signs and meanings capable of replacing the existing systems we take for granted; it proposes the "superior reality" of discomfiting associations, powerful dream states, sexual desire, and the disinterested play of thought.

Throughout the movement's hist., the surrealists developed numerous experimental artistic and critical strategies. In addition to automatic writing, surrealist practices included the creation of collage poems and multimedia *poèmes-objets*; the exploration of cities according to the dictates of chance; the collection of found objects ("readymades" and *trouvailles*) and *found poetry; the simulation of hysterical and psychotic states; and collaborative poetic exercises such as the "exquisite corpse" game, in which hybrid phrases or images are composed by participants unaware of what the other contributions look like. More than the sum of its poetic devices, surrealism describes the project of using these and other techniques toward a renewal of the *imagination and an application "to the principal problems of life." Poetry in this context becomes a means and not an end: "Lyricism is the development of a protest," declared Breton and his colleague Paul Éluard (1895–1952) in *Notes sur la poésie* (1936).

**III. History.** Surrealism began in the same manner as it persisted for more than 50 years: through a series of encounters and upheavals that first took place in the aftermath of World War I. The young Fr. poets Breton and Louis Aragon (1897–1982), who both trained as medical students during the war, met Philippe Soupault (1897–1990), himself a war veteran, through Guillaume Apollinaire (1880–1918). After publishing early poems in avant-garde jours., they founded their own jour., *Littérature*, in 1919. This ironically titled periodical, whose early issues featured poems by Paul Valéry, André Gide, Pierre Réverdy, Léon-Paul Fargue, Max Jacob, and other older modernists, along with unpublished texts by Stéphane Mallarmé, Apollinaire, and Arthur Rimbaud, soon became the flagship jour. for the Parisian incarnation of *Dada. With the arrival of Tristan Tzara (1896–1963) from Zurich in 1919, Parisian Dada became the gathering place for a contentious group of young poets galvanized by their contempt for France's postwar efforts to return to bourgeois normality and in particular for the resurgence of nationalism and xenophobia in Europe.

Over the next several years, the Paris Dada group expanded to include the poets Éluard, Benjamin Péret (1899–1959), and Robert Desnos (1900–45), as well as the artists Max Ernst, Joan Miró, Man Ray, and Francis Picabia. After collaborating on the first extended work of automatic writing, *Les Champs Magnétiques* (The Magnetic Fields, 1919), Breton and Soupault assumed editorial control of *Littérature*, which became increasingly attentive to literary hist. The jour., which launched a "new series" in 1922, fused its Dada iconoclasm with surveys about the group's literary preferences. As their ranks expanded, the group began to scandalize canonical Fr. cultural figures, while championing an alternative genealogy of literary precursors excluded from official Fr. culture. This latter group included—along with the largely Germanic Dada movement itself—Ger. romantics such as Novalis, Gérard de Nerval, Achim von Arnim, and Hegel, as well as Freudian psychoanalysis; the ideologically unsettling work of the Marquis de Sade; and symbolist poets such as Charles Baudelaire, Germain Nouveau, and Rimbaud. Of particular significance to the young protosurrealists was the virtually unknown Comte de Lautréamont (pseud. of Isidore Ducasse, 1846–70), whose elaborate *metaphors would deeply inform surrealist poetics, most notably the line from *Les Chants de Maldoror* (1869), "as beautiful as the chance encounter of an umbrella and a sewing machine on a dissecting table."

This increased historical self-consciousness had much to do with the protosurrealist group's break with Dada and its subsequent emergence, in 1924, as the surrealist movement. The genealogy of visionary and subversive figures assembled by the *Littérature* group would form the conceptual basis for surrealist thinking

and the common ground for subsequent articulations of surrealist poetics. These "precursors" were notable for the extent to which they reoriented the arts from the aesthetic to the epistemological, replacing the contemplation of beauty with an investigation into "the marvelous," defined by Aragon in 1924 as "the contradiction that reveals itself within the real."

Apollinaire himself had used the word *surréaliste* to qualify his satirical play *Les Mamelles de Tirésias* (The Breasts of Tirésias), first staged in 1917. In separating themselves rhetorically and ideologically from Dada, the surrealist group appropriated the term for the masthead of its flagship jour. *La Révolution surréaliste* (1924–29) and redefined it in texts such as Breton's *manifesto and Aragon's "Une Vague de rêves" (A Wave of Dreams, 1924). The surrealist coalition thus formed consisted of both poets and artists incl., along with Breton, Soupault, and others, the writers Antonin Artaud, René Crevel, Michel Leiris, Raymond Queneau, Roger Vitrac, and eventually a rehabilitated Tzara. A number of artists joined forces with them—incl. Ernst, Miró, Salvador Dalí, Luis Buñuel, Yves Tanguy, and André Masson—along with a largely autonomous group of Belgian surrealists that included René Magritte, E.L.T. Mesens, and Paul Nougé. Under the leadership of Breton, there emerged a laboratory atmosphere probing lang., human relationships, objects, and sites in the contexts of psychoanalysis, ling., ethnography, alchemy, and the laws of probability. Much of the theoretical writing, poetry, accounts of experiments, and surrealist games appeared in the series of jours. that began with *La Révolution Surréaliste* and continued with *Le Surréalisme au service de la Révolution* (1930–33) and *Minotaure* (1933–39), as well as later jours. around the world, incl. *The London Bulletin* (1938–40), *Tropiques* (1941–45), *VVV* (1942–44), *NEON* (1948–49), *Médium* (1953–55), *Les Lèvres nues* (1954–58), and *Le Surréalisme, meme* (1955–57), among others.

In 1924, the surrealist group marked the death of the novelist Anatole France with a defamatory pamphlet "A Corpse," which brought them into contact with a group of young Marxist intellectuals from the jour. *Clarté* who had similarly expressed their critique of jingoistic Fr. tributes to the late novelist. The ensuing collaboration would lead to a foray into organized leftist politics, stemming from the combined group's protest against Fr. colonial activity in Morocco during the Rif War (1920–26). Their increasing political involvement led to numerous disagreements and exclusions, which have often characterized accounts of this period. From 1925 through 1939, the surrealists would continually struggle to maintain their political thrust in the face of an increasingly orthodox Communist Party, as well as a gradual rightward turn in Fr. culture during the 1930s. During this period, the surrealists sought to uphold not only the subversive quality of their work but the imperative for an experimental poetics of the revolutionary Left as well. Resisting the enshrinement of socialist realism as Stalinism's official revolutionary style, the surrealists advocated for a fundamental upheaval in human consciousness that drew as much from collective poetic activity, psychoanalysis, and the unruliness of sexual desire as from Communist militancy. A second generation of active surrealists included René Char (1907–88), Aimé Césaire (1913–2008), Jules Monnerot (1909–95), A. Pieyre de Mandriargues (1909–91), Lise Deharme (1898–1980), Jehan Mayoux (1904–75), Gisèle Prassinos (b. 1920), Georges Hugnet (1906–74), Vítězslav Nezval (1900–58); and the artists Hans Bellmer, Claude Cahun, Leonora Carrington, Jindřich Štyrský, Toyen, Meret Oppenheim, and Victor Brauner.

During the 1930s and 1940s, surrealist groups emerged in other cities threatened by fascism—particularly Prague, Bucharest, Tokyo, and London. As the Nazi occupation of France forced the Parisian surrealists to disperse, the older surrealists also extended their internationalism, with Breton and others visiting and working with intellectuals in Martinique, Haiti, Mexico, Quebec, and New York. After the war, Breton's return to Paris and a major international surrealist exhibition in 1947 marked a renewal of the movement's activity in France, while incurring increasing pressure from younger intellectual movements on the Left, such as existentialism. The Breton-centered group would continue its activities with an anti-Stalinist and anticolonial emphasis, becoming particularly active in its support of Algerian independence in the 1950s. Later incarnations of the movement emphasized unconventional modes of political leftism based on ideas of collectivity derived from thinkers other than Karl Marx, such as Charles Fourier, as well as from a revised genealogy of indigenous and hermetic "precursors" from around the world. After Breton's death in 1966, the Parisian movement continued for three years before officially disbanding in 1969, though some participants contested this decision.

Alternative modes of surrealist activity continue to permeate the arts throughout Europe and Latin America, particularly in countries previously under authoritarian regimes. With a particular focus on anticolonial struggle and independence movements, the various incarnations of surrealism have remained committed to a political poetics: as Breton famously put it, "Beauty will be convulsive or it will not be." Figures in the broader surrealist diaspora include the Latin and South Am. poets César Moro (1903–56), Octavio Paz (1914–98), Aldo Pellegrini (1903–73), Braulio Arenas (1913–88), Enrique Molina (1910–97), and Enrique Gomez-Correa (1915–95); the Franco-Egyptian poets Joyce Mansour (1928–86) and Georges Henein (1914–73); the Romanian poets Gherasim Luca (1913–94), Paul Celan (1920–70), and Gellu Naum (1915–2001); the U.S. writers Franklin Rosemont (1943–2009), Penelope Rosemont (b. 1942), Mary Low (1912–2007), and Ted Joans (1928–2003); the Fr. writers José Pierre (1927–99), Jean Schuster (1929–95), Nora Mitrani (1921–61), Gerard Legrand (1927–99), and Julien Gracq (1910–2007); and artists such as Alexander Calder, Arshile Gorky, Matta, Wifredo Lam, Dorothea Tanning, Remedios Varo, Mimi Parent, Nelly Kaplan, Maya Deren, and Jan Švankmajer.

Since 1965, there has been extensive research on surrealism, particularly in France, the U.K., and the U.S. Much scholarly documentation has been collected in archives such as the Bibliothèque Littéraire Jacques Doucet in Paris and at research forums such as the Centre de Recherche sur le Surréalisme, and disseminated in its jour. *Mélusine*. In the U.S., major holdings include the collections at the Museum of Modern Art, the Philadelphia Museum of Fine Art, the Getty Research Institute, the Menil Collection, and the Harry Ransom Center, as well as at the Universities of Iowa and Michigan.

*See* AVANT-GARDE POETICS; FRANCE, POETRY OF; MODERNISM.

■ M. Raymond, *De Baudelaire au surréalisme* (1933); D. Gascogne, *A Short Survey of Surréalisme* (1935); G. Lemaître, *From Cubism to Surrealism in French Literature* (1941); M. Nadeau, *Histoire du surréalisme* (1945); and *Documents surréalistes* (1946); A. Balakian, *Literary Origins of Surrealism* (1947); J. Gracq, *André Breton* (1948); C. Mauriac, *André Breton* (1949); A. Bosquet, *Surréalismus* (1950); W. Fowlie, *Age of Surrealism* (1950); A. Kyrou, *Le Surréalisme au cinéma* (1952); J. Hardré, "Present State of Studies on Literary Surrealism," *Yearbook of Comparative and General Literature* 9 (1960); F. Alquié, *The Philosophy of Surrealism*, trans. B. Waldrop (1965); J. H. Matthews, *Introduction to Surrealism* (1965); R. Short, "The Politics of Surrealism," *The Left-Wing Intellectuals between the Wars, 1919–1939*, ed. W. Laqueur and G. Mosse (1966); R. Champigny, *Pour une esthétique de l'essai: "Une Définition du Surréalisme"* (1967); P. Ilie, *The Surrealist Mode in Spanish Literature* (1968); M. A. Caws, *The Poetry of Dada and Surrealism* (1970), and *André Breton* (1971); A. Balakian, *André Breton* (1971); X. Gauthier, *Surréalisme et sexualité* (1971); J. H. Matthews, *Surrealism and Film* (1971); P. Ray, *The Surrealist Movement in England* (1971); S. Alexandrian, *Le Surréalisme et le rêve* (1974); M. Carrouges, *André Breton and the Basic Concepts of Surrealism*, trans. M. Prendergast (1974); H. Gershman, *The Surrealist Revolution in France* (1974); *The Poetry of Surrealism*, ed. M. Benedikt (1974); M. Riffaterre, "Semantic Incompatibilities in Automatic Writing," *About French Poetry*, ed. M. A. Caws (1974); L. Binni, *Il movimiento surrealista* (1975); M. Bonnet, *André Breton: Naissance de l'aventure surréaliste* (1975); J. H. Matthews, *The Custom-House of Desire* (1975); G. Legrand, *Breton en son temps* (1976); J. H. Matthews, *Toward the Poetics of Surrealism* (1976); M. Bonnet, *Le Surréalisme dans le texte* (1978); A. Breton, *What Is Surrealism?* ed. F. Rosemont (1978); G. Legrand, *Breton* (1978); P. Hammond, *The Shadow and Its Shadow* (1978); H. Finkelstein, *Surrealism and the Crisis of the Object* (1979); *The Autobiography of Surrealism*, ed. M. Jean (1980); *Tracts surréalistes et déclarations collectives (1922–1969)*, ed. J. Pierre (1980); M. A. Caws, *A Metapoetics of the Passage* (1981); M. Fauré, *Histoire du surréalisme sous l'occupation* (1982); J. H. Matthews, *Surrealism, Insanity, and Poetry* (1982); J. Chénieux-Gendron, *Le Roman surréaliste* (1983); D. Desanti, *Les Clés d'Elsa* (1983); M. Foucault, *This Is Not a Pipe*, ed. and trans. J. Harkness (1983); J. Pierre, *Surréalisme et l'anarchie* (1983);

A. Balakian, *Surrealism: The Road to the Absolute* (1986); J. H. Matthews, *Languages of Surrealism* (1986); R. Riese, *Surrealism and the Book* (1987); H. Lewis, *The Politics of Surrealism* (1988); *André Breton Today*, ed. A. Balakian and R. Kuenzli (1989); J. Chénieux-Gendron, *Surrealism*, trans. V. Folkenflik (1990); S. Suleiman, *Subversive Intent* (1991); G. Bataille, *The Absence of Myth*, ed. and trans. M. Richardson (1994); K. Conley, *Automatic Woman* (1996); *Refusal of the Shadow*, ed. and trans M. Richardson and K. Fijalkowski (1996); M. A. Caws, *The Surrealist Look* (1997); E. Adamowicz, *Surrealist Collage in Text and Image* (1998); C. Reynaud-Paligot, *Parcours politique des surréalists (1919–1969)* (1998); *Surrealist Women*, ed. P. Rosemont (1998); *Surrealism against the Current*, ed. and trans. M. Richardson and K. Fijalkowski (2001); R. Vaneigem, *A Cavalier History of Surrealism*, trans. D. Nicholson-Smith (2001); G. Durozoi, *History of the Surrealist Movement*, trans. A. Anderson (2002); S. Harris, *Surrealist Art and Thought in the 1930s* (2004); M. A. Caws, *Surrealism* (2006); *Undercover Surrealism*, ed. D. Ades and S. Baker (2006); *Surréalisme et politique-Politique du surréalisme*, ed. W. Asholt and H. Siepe (2007); J. Eburne, *Surrealism and the Art of Crime* (2008); *Black, Brown & Beige*, ed. F. Rosemont and R. Kelley (2009); E.-A. Hubert, *Circonstances de la poésie* (2009); M. Sanouillet, *Dada in Paris*, rev. and enl. A. Sanouillet, trans. S. Ganguly (2009).

J. P. Eburne

## SWAHILI POETRY

I. Swahili Prosody
II. History of Swahili Poetry

Swahili lit. occupies a distinctive place among lits. in Af. langs., having a trad. that dates to the 18th or even the 17th c. All the old mss., written in Ar. script, were of poetic texts, composed predominantly in the dialects of the islands of Pate (Kipate) and Lamu (Kiamu), and from the 19th c. onward also in the dialect of Mombasa (Kimvita); mss. in prose appear only in the 19th c. (chronicles of the coastal Swahili towns).

**I. Swahili Prosody.** Most Swahili poetry is metrical and meant to be sung or chanted. Swahili prosody is based on counting syllables (sing. and pl. *mizani*) and involves a monosyllabic rhyme (*kina*, pl. *vina*) at the end of metrical units. The shortest independent metrical unit is called *kipande* (pl. *vipande*), of three, four, five, six, or eight mizani. The arrangement of vipande in a stanza (*ubeti*, pl. *beti*) characterizes the individual poetic forms. Vipande are written down in lines (*mstari*, pl. *mistari*, or *mshororo*, pl. *mishororo*).

The most common poetic forms are *utenzi* and *shairi*. Utenzi (or *utendi*, pl. *tenzi/tendi*) is the form used for long epic descriptions (tenzi frequently have hundreds, even thousands, of stanzas), but also for religious instruction. It has four vipande per stanza, and each kipande has eight (rarely six) mizani. The three first vipande rhyme with one another, and the last kip-ande has a rhyme that goes throughout the entire poem (*aaax*).

Shairi (pl. *mashairi*) is a form used for witty elaborations of moral and philosophical concepts. Typically, it has four lines with two eight-syllable vipande per line. The first vipande of the first three lines rhyme, as do the second vipande of these lines. The last line may only consist of one kipande, rhyming with the last vipande of the first lines, or a second kipande rhyming with the first vipande of the first lines (*ab/ab/ab/ba*); sometimes this last kipande does not rhyme with anything, or it has a rhyme going through the whole poem (*ab/ab/ab/bx*). The last line may also be the same in every stanza in the shairi, making a *refrain (*ab/ab/ab/xy*).

Other forms include *wimbo* (three 12-syllable lines per stanza), *kisarambe* (four 11-syllable lines per stanza), or *ukawafi* (two, four, or five 15-syllable lines per stanza).

**II. History of Swahili Poetry.** The dating of Swahili mss. or the compositions themselves is often controversial. It relies on available historical sources (e.g., information known about the events or the poets), coupled with a relative chronology based on ling. criteria. Although some of the poems include a poetic colophon—the last stanza or stanzas naming the poet and the year of composition—it does not always provide reliable information to date the ms. The dates may contain unclear words or illegible figures and, depending on the interpretation of these, the dating can differ by as much as a century.

Ancient Swahili compositions were mostly religious in content, such as *qaṣīda (praise poems to the Prophet Muhammad and his family) and *maghazi* (descriptions of fights between the early Muslims and their enemies). A famous example of the former is *Hamziya* (literally, "a poem rhyming in [the Ar. character of] *hamza*"; the Swahili poem is a trans. from the Ar.; in Swahili, the poem rhymes in *-ma*), composed by Sayyid Aidarus bin Athman. The ms. is dated by Knappert (1968) to 1062 AH (1651/52 CE), but Hichens (1934) dates it to 1162 AH (1748/49 CE), a discrepancy derived from different readings of one word in the colophon. The poem, an ukawafi in two-line stanzas, describes the extraordinary qualities of the Prophet Muhammad. An example of early maghazi lit. is *Utendi wa Tambuka* (Utenzi of [the battle of] Tabuk), also called *Chuo cha Herkali* (Book of Herakleios), by Mwengo bin Athuman. It is dated to 1141 AH (1728/29 CE) by Knappert (1979), but 1241 AH (1825/26 CE) by Zhukov. This utenzi describes the miraculous victory of Muslims led by Muhammad over the army of the Byzantine emperor Herakleios.

A secular trad. in old Swahili poetry is represented by the half-legendary hero Fumo Liyongo. While the lifetime of the warrior and poet is disputed, the dates suggested by researchers range from the 9th c. (Ahmed Nabhany, Joseph Mbele, cited in Mulokozi 1999) to the 1700s (Neville Chittick, cited in Knappert 1983). Fumo Liyongo is the possible author of the ancient *Takhmis ya Liyongo*, a praise poem to himself. The composition is usually attributed to Sayyid Abdallah bin Ali bin Nasir, who lived in Pate sometime between 1720 and 1820 and who is also the author of the renowned *Al-Inkishafi* (see below), but convincing arguments have been presented by Carl Meinhof that the poem may have double authorship: the last two lines of this five-line ukawafi appear to be more ancient (the lang. is older and contains fewer Arabisms, and the imagery is more vivid), and the first three lines may have been added by a later poet.

The early 19th c. produced some of the most remarkable compositions in Swahili. *Al-Inkishafi* (literally "it is revealed," also translated as "the soul's awakening" or "self-examination") describes the fall of the once powerful and rich Pate sultanate. Built on the commonplaces of the vanity of earthly delights and the illusory nature of worldly fame and riches and presenting plastic descriptions of downfall and decay, the poem admonishes the soul to turn to religion, the way to avoid the punishment for sins in hell and a source of true happiness.

The secular trad. continues in the poems of the Mombasan poet Muyaka bin Haji bin Ghassaniy (ca. 1776–1840) and his contemporaries in Lamu, who employed the shairi form in dialogic political poetry. Muyaka's poems are characterized by great wit and ingenious use of lang., typically playing with the many meanings of homonymous words.

A famous composition from the second half of the 19th c. is *Utendi wa Mwana Kupona*, composed by Mwana Kupona binti Mshamu (ca. 1810–1860) in 1858 for her 17-year-old daughter. Within the framework of Islam, the poet tells her child how a Swahili woman is expected to behave in society and in the domestic sphere, how to treat her husband, how to keep herself and her home clean and appealing for the husband, and how to observe religious duties.

The period of the early colonization of the Swahili territory by the Brit. and the Germans (ca. 1890–1930) has produced a vast historiographic lit., mostly in utenzi or shairi form. The most notable poets of this era came from the family of poets from Tanga, el Buhriy. In 1930, the Inter-Territorial Language Committee of the East African Dependencies decided the standard form of Swahili (*Kiswahili Sanifu*), based on the dialect of Zanzibar Town (Kiunguja). Among the ardent devotees of Standard Swahili was Shaaban Robert (1909–62), who introduced new genres (such as the novel) and topics into Swahili lit. while remaining true to the existing trad. of Swahili poetry in form and spirit.

In the first decades after independence, poetry developed in different ways in Tanzania and Kenya. Kenyan poets, who mostly originated from the coastal area, often rejected Standard Swahili and continued writing in their native dialects (Kimvita, Kiamu, etc.). The most prominent among them are the Mombasan half-brothers Ahmad Nassir Juma Bhalo (b. 1936), the prolific author of several poetry collections and innumerable lyrics for *taarab* songs, and Abdilatif Abdalla (b. 1946), who became famous for poetry he wrote during his imprisonment for opposing the Kenyatta regime (1969–72), *Sauti ya Dhiki* (The Voice of Agony, 1973).

Tanzanian poetry after independence was much less traditionalist, possibly because of revolutionary spirit of the policy of *ujamaa* (Tanzanian socialism). Standard Swahili, used in all areas of life, became the medium of expression of many authors whose ethnic background was not Swahili. Poetry was often used for the propagation of ujamaa. Mathias Mnyampala revived a type of dialogic poetry called *ngonjera* and employed it for political education of the masses. A true revolution in Swahili poetry took place at the University of Dar es Salaam in the late 1960s and early 1970s. A group of students rejected the traditional prosodic rules and started writing poetry in *free verse, inspired both by oral poetry in their native langs. and by Eng. poetry. Euphrase Kezilahabi (b. 1944), one of the best Swahili novelists, is the author of three collections: *Kichomi* (Sharp Pain, 1974), *Karibu ndani* (Welcome Inside, 1988), and *Dhifa* (Banquet, 2008). As in his novels, Kezilahabi uses a simple, everyday lang. in his poems to elaborate highly complex philosophical topics.

Since the 1990s, the literary devels. of Tanzania and Kenya have converged, with Kenya gradually gaining the upper hand in publishing and on the book market. In both countries, metrical poetry continues to be highly popular (daily newspapers have a poetry page with circumstantial commentaries in verse). A number of young poets are convinced "traditionalists," producing poetry that is metrical in form and conservative in tone, such as the poet and novelist Omar Babu (b. 1967). On the other hand, many authors do not feel obliged to subscribe to either metrical or free-verse poetry and write in both ways or in a mixture of styles. This is the case of the nestor of Swahili lit., Said Ahmed Mohamed (b. 1947) from Zanzibar, and the versatile Kenyan poet, novelist, and literary theorist Kyallo Wadi Wamitila (b. 1965).

■ **Anthologies:** "Das Lied des Liongo" (Liongo's Song), ed. and trans. C. Meinhof, *Zeitschrift für Eingeborenen-Sprachen* 15 (1924–25); *The Advice of Mwana Kupona upon the Wifely Duty*, ed. and trans. A. Werner and W. Hichens (1934); *Al-Inkishafi: The Soul's Awakening*, ed. and trans. W. Hichens (1939); *Swahili Poetry*, ed. and trans. L. Harries (1962); *Poems from Kenya: Gnomic Verses in Swahili by Ahmad Nassir bin Juma Bhalo*, ed. and trans. L. Harries (1966); *Traditional Swahili Poetry*, ed. and trans. J. Knappert (1967); "The Hamziya Deciphered," ed. and trans. J. Knappert, *African Language Studies* 9 (1968), *Swahili Islamic Poetry*, ed. and trans. J. Knappert, 3 v. (1971); *Tendi*, ed. and trans. J.W.T. Allen (1971); *Al-Inkishafi: Catechism of a Soul*, ed. and trans. J. de V. Allen (1977); *Muyaka: Nineteenth-Century Swahili Popular Poetry*, ed. and trans. M. H. Abdulaziz (1979); *Four Centuries of Swahili Verse*, ed. and trans. J. Knappert (1979); *Epic Poetry in Swahili and Other African Languages*, ed. and trans. J. Knappert (1983); *Tenzi Tatu za Kale (Fumo Liyongo, Al-Inkishafi, Mwanakupona)* (Three Ancient Tenzi; Fumo Liyongo, Al-Inkishafi, Mwanakupona), ed. M. M. Mulokozi (1999); *Kala Shairi: German*

*East Africa in Swahili Poems*, ed. and trans. G. Miehe, K. Bromber, S. Khamis, R. Grosserhode (2002); *Liyongo Songs: Poems Attributed to Fumo Liyongo*, ed. and trans. G. Miehe et al. (2004).

■ **Criticism and History:** F. Topan, "Modern Swahili Poetry," *Bulletin of the School of Oriental and African Studies* 37 (1974); G. Miehe, "Die Perioden der Swahililiteratur und ihre sprachliche Form," *Paideuma* 36 (1990); A. A. Zhukov, "The Dating of Old Swahili Manuscripts: Towards Swahili Paleography," *Swahili Language and Society. Notes and News* 9 (1992); M. M. Mulokozi and T.S.Y. Sengo, *History of Kiswahili Poetry (AD 1000–2000)* (1995); A. Biersteker, *Kujibizana: Questions of Language and Power in Nineteenth- and Twentieth-Century Poetry in Kiswahili* (1996).

■ **Swahili Prosody:** K. A. Abedi, *Sheria za Kutunga Mashairi na Diwani ya Amri* (Rules of Composing Poetry and Amri's Collection, 1954); J. Knappert, "Swahili Metre," *African Language Studies* 12 (1971); I. N. Shariff, *Tungo Zetu* (Our Compositions, 1988).

A. Rettová

**SWEDEN, POETRY OF.** While runic inscriptions show the existence of a lost heroic poetry, the oldest preserved poems in Sweden date from the beginning of the 14th c., in the form of trans. of three Fr. verse novels. The anonymous versified chronicle *Erikskrönikan* was written a few decades later. The many folk *ballads are a significant feature of the poetry of the Swedish Middle Ages. They exist only in late records from the end of the 16th c. and onward. Most likely, the majority of them were created in the 14th and 15th cs. and then transmitted orally until they were written down.

All the ballads are anonymous. With a few exceptions, it is not until the 17th c. that we find poets identified, most important, Georg Stiernhielm (1598–1672). His *Hercules* (1658) is a long allegorical and didactic poem written in *hexameters where the *quantity of cl. poetry was replaced by accentuation. Ascending rhythm, however, soon became the rule, and the most common verse form is the *alexandrine. This is the case both in the pseudonymous Skogekär Bergbo's collection of *sonnets (1680) and in Gunno Dahlstierna's (1661–1709) long poem in *ottava rima written for the funeral of King Karl XI. More appreciated by mod. readers are the poems of Lars Wivallius (1605–69), Lars Johansson Lucidor (1638–74), and Johan Runius (1679–1713).

In the 18th c., the strong Ger. influence on Swedish poetry was replaced by Fr. and, later, Eng. models. Olof von Dalin (1708–63) was most important as a prose writer, but he also developed most genres of poetry. His writing was a step away from the *baroque style of the previous century and a step closer to Fr. neoclassicists like Nicolas Boileau and Voltaire.

An even more crucial contribution was made around 1760, when Hedvig Charlotta Nordenflycht (1718–63), Gustaf Fredrik Gyllenborg (1731–1808), and Gustaf Philip Creutz (1731–85) published their best poems. Nordenflycht stood out as early as the 1740s as a pioneer for a subjective, emotional poetry, which has been compared to Eng. *preromanticism, and Creutz is the

author of a minor classic, the long *pastoral poem *Atis och Camilla* (1761).

The breakthrough of Fr. neoclassical taste came during the reign of Gustav III (1771–92), a time that saw a great rise in cultural life. In 1786, the Swedish Academy was established, and over the following hundred years, the academy would influence literary life in various ways. The most important author and critic during this period was Johan Henrik Kellgren (1751–95), who wrote both satires in Voltaire's spirit and lyrical poems influenced by Eng. and Ger. preromantics. The leading Swedish preromantics, however, were Thomas Thorild (1759–1808) and Bengt Lidner (1757–93), while Fr. neoclassicism was represented by Johan Gabriel Oxenstierna (1750–1818) and Carl Gustaf Leopold (1756–1829). Anna-Maria Lenngren's (1754–1817) witty satires, written in a simple, informal style and with a keen eye for realistic details, still have their dedicated readers.

The most important Swedish poet of the 18th c. is Carl Michael Bellman (1740–95). His poetry is deeply original but indebted nonetheless to the songs of Lucidor, Runius, and Dalin. Most of his poems are songs, which is one explanation for their enormous success. *Fredmans epistlar* (Fredman's Epistles, 1790), published with an enthusiastic foreword by Kellgren, is regarded by many as the most important of all Swedish poetry collections. Fredman is an apostle of Bacchus, and the songs are letters to his faithful group of followers, worshipers of the gods of wine and love.

The poetry collection most read in the 18th and 19th c. was the hymnbook, legalized by the state and the Lutheran Church. The ed. of 1695, where the most important poets were Jesper Svedberg (1653–1735) and Haquin Spegel (1645–1714), was used until 1819, when a new edition was published, in which Johan Olof Wallin (1779–1839) and Frans Michael Franzén (1772–1847) made the greatest contributions.

In the 1810s and 1820s, Swedish poetry moved toward *romanticism. The Fr. influence became weaker, and the models now were Eng. and Ger. Fr. Enlightenment ideas made room for Ger. romanticism and philosophical idealism. Med. material—mainly from ON—was often used. The interest in the Vikings had its center in Götiska Förbundet (The Gothic Society), whose leading poet was Erik Gustaf Geijer (1783–1847).

The greatest poet of the period was Esaias Tegnér (1782–1846). His poems connect to Ger. neoclassicism in both form and ideas. Tegnér is the author of some of the greatest occasional poems in Swedish lit. but also of subjective lyrical poems. His best-known work is *Frithiofs saga* (1824), a formally brilliant cycle of 24 romances in different meters, with a story based on an Old Icelandic saga. This work with its synthesis of cl., ON, and romantic motifs and forms became the foremost Swedish poetic classic for the following hundred years.

The central figure in Swedish romanticism, both as a poet and a critic, was Per Daniel Amadeus Atterbom (1790–1855). Several of his shorter poems have worn well, but his largest poetical work *Lycksalighetens ö* (The Isle of Bliss, 1824–27), an extensive drama, formally and ideologically highly interesting, has not been much read by posterity. The case of Erik Johan Stagnelius (1793–1823) is quite different. He was little noticed by his contemporaries but has been more appreciated by succeeding generations. His formally perfect poems, cl. in form but romantic in motifs, are influenced by Neoplatonic ideas. Thematically, they often express the opposition between mysticism and erotic passion.

Tegnér's metaphor-laden, rhetorical style was infectious for his many imitators over the 19th c., and the reaction was not late in coming. Carl Jonas Love Almqvist's (1793–1866) poems *Songes,* written in the 1830s and 1840s, are distinguished by a simplicity free from both metaphors and rhetorical patterns, which must have been seen as a powerful deviation from Tegnér's poetry. And as early as 1830, Johan Ludvig Runeberg (1804–77) made his debut with a collection of poems that, with a simple style and few metaphors, also strongly contrasted to Tegnér's poetry. Runeberg lived in Finland but was hailed by many contemporaries as the greatest poet in the Swedish lang. He was a master both in lyric poetry and in narratives in hexameter, in which he portrays the life of the Finnish people. In other poems, he uses ancient Nordic and cl. motifs. The most important of his works is *Fänrik Ståls sägner* (The Tales of Ensign Stål, 1848), a series of poems portraying characters from the war with Russia (1808–9), in which Sweden lost Finland and thereby its position as a great political power. A second part of the tales was published in 1860.

Among the poets from the 1860s and 1870s, Carl Snoilsky (1841–1903) stands out with his formal virtuosity. His *Svenska bilder* (Swedish Pictures, 1894), a series of poems with motifs from Swedish hist., was for a long time a classic reader in Swedish schools. Viktor Rydberg (1828–95) continued the idealistic line from the romantics and from Tegnér. Many of his poems were written as early as the 1870s, but his two collections of poems were published relatively late, in 1882 and 1891.

The most important genres in the 1880s were the drama and the novel, with August Strindberg (1849–1912) as the main representative of both. He was, however, important as a poet as well. *Dikter* (Poems, 1883) and *Sömngångarnätter på vakna dagar* (Sleepwalking Nights on Wide-Awake Days, 1884) are both connected to Strindberg's general critique of society and to his programmatic anti-idealism. In *Ordalek och småkonst* (*Word Play and Minor Art*, 1905), which includes some of his best poems, Strindberg is not far from Fr. and Ger. *symbolism.

The poets from the end of the 19th c. who are closest to symbolism are Ola Hansson (1860–1926) and Oscar Levertin (1862–1906). Verner von Heidenstam (1859–1940) stood for a more romantic, national—if not provincial—direction. His mix of orientalism, decadence, the cult of beauty, and national activism were features typical of the end of the century, but they have led to a diminished interest in his poems by posterity. He is at his best in the short format. His last collection, *Nya dikter* (New Poems, 1915), is marked by simplicity and a strong expression.

Erik Axel Karlfeldt (1864–1931) and Gustaf Fröding (1860–1911) both derived motifs from their native provinces, Karlfeldt from Dalarna and Fröding from Värmland. Karlfeldt is formally masterful but impersonal in his poetry, whereas Fröding does not shy away from depicting his broodings and his loneliness in deeply personal poems. With Fröding's five collections of poems from the 1890s, traditional verse reaches its culmination in Swedish poetry. He is probably the most popular of all Swedish poets. Formally, he has never been surpassed. After him, Swedish poetry would be forced to find new ways.

A new direction was pointed out by Vilhelm Ekelund (1880–1949). In the first decade of the 20th c., he published seven collections of poems, in which he gradually approaches a *free verse without rhyme, mainly built on rhythm. The starting point is Fr. symbolism, but gradually patterns from antiquity and Ger. neoclassicism emerge. His poems became important both formally and thematically for a growing modernist poetry over the following decades.

The first attempts at *modernism came in the 1910s. In 1916, Pär Lagerkvist (1891–1974) published a collection of poems with a title typical of its time: *Ångest* (Anguish). In the same year, Edith Södergran (1892–1923) made her debut with a volume *Dikter* (Poems). Södergran belonged to the Swedish-speaking minority in Finland. She had studied in St. Petersburg and had read both Rus. and Ger. contemp. poetry. Her four collections of poems are among the highlights in Swedish 20th c. lit., and they constitute the prelude to Finland-Swedish modernism in the interwar period. During this time, Elmer Diktonius (1896–1961), Gunnar Björling (1887–1960), and Rabbe Enckell (1903–1974) would become leading names.

Both Södergran and Lagerkvist could be called expressionists (see EXPRESSIONISM). Birger Sjöberg (1885–1929) started his writing with very popular songs—*Fridas bok* (Frida's Book, 1922)—that he also performed. A few years later, he surprised his audience with the expressionistic *Kriser och kransar* (Crises and Wreaths, 1926), the most remarkable of all Swedish collections of poems in the 1920s. It would gradually gain great importance, esp. for poets during the 1940s and 1950s.

Bo Bergman (1869–1967), Anders Österling (1884–1981), and Hjalmar Gullberg (1898–1961) are more traditional. Gullberg was the most praised poet of the 1930s. He was a virtuoso with a simple, often ironic style of expression. In his last collections of poems from the 1950s, he approached modernism without ever neglecting formal demands. Johannes Edfelt (1904–97), who was close to Gullberg stylistically and thematically, positioned himself between traditional verse and modernism, as did Karin Boye (1900–41) and Nils Ferlin (1898–1961), who was one of the most original and also most popular poets of the period.

Three writers most prominently represented poetic modernism in the 1930s: Artur Lundkvist (1906–91),

Harry Martinson (1904–78), and Gunnar Ekelöf (1907–68). For four decades, Lundkvist was the most influential Swede in introducing foreign modernist poetry, primarily as a critic but also as a translator. While Lundkvist's poems are expansive, a never-ending torrent of images, many of Martinson's best poems are highly compressed. He is a master of form, creating exquisite nature poems with precise observations of reality. But he is also a committed poet of ideas, strongly critical of mod. technical civilization. The various themes in his poetry join together in his most famous work, the space epic *Aniara* (1956), pub. at the beginning of the space age.

Ekelöf occupies the main position in Swedish 20th-c. poetry. In his two first collections of poetry (from 1932 and 1934), he introduces *surrealism—in style, in theme, and in the ideas presented. In *Färjesång* (Ferry Song, 1941), the influence of T. S. Eliot can be detected. These three collections of poetry would have considerable influence in the 1940s. *Non serviam* (I will not serve, 1945) and *Om hösten* (In Autumn, 1951) include several of Ekelöf's best-known poems. *Strountes* (Trifles, 1955) marked a new phase in his career, one that would have great significance for Swedish poetry in the 1960s. His three last collections of poems from 1965 to 1967 form a trilogy distinguished by formal simplicity, Byzantine motifs, and an attitude to life close to mysticism. Its intensity is unmatched in 20th-c. Swedish lit.

The real breakthrough for lyric modernism came in the 1940s. Erik Lindegren's (1910–68) *mannen utan väg* (the man without a way, 1942) is the most important collection of poems of that decade, both formally and thematically. More accessible are the poems in his two subsequent collections, *Sviter* (Suites, 1947) and *Vinteroffer* (Winter Rites, 1954).

While Lindegren is linked with symbolism and surrealism, Karl Vennberg (1910–95) was most influenced by Eliot. For decades, Vennberg would be a leading critic and poet; he personified better than anyone the lyric modernism of the 1940s with its demand for a poetry that is ideologically aware, covers essential and preferably universal themes, and is written in a trad. of experimentation.

Werner Aspenström's (1918–97) style is clear and simple, and his motifs are often concrete and close to reality. His nature miniatures sometimes resemble the poetry of Martinson. Ragnar Thoursie (1919–2010) has a place of his own. His poetic technique was of great importance for the poets of the 1950s and 1960s. Elsa Grave (1918–2003) and Rut Hillarp (1914–2003) have motherhood and love as their leading themes.

The 1950s was a harvest time for Swedish poetry, a decade when many poets from the 1930s and 1940s published their best works. The lyrical modernism in Swedish lit. would reach its peak with Lindegren's and Ekelöf's late poems. Among the new poets that would appear in the 1950s, Lars Forssell (1928–2008) is of special interest. In his poetry, the links to the modernism of the 1940s are quite clear. Formally, he is a virtuoso

in several genres, high and low, serious and humorous. However, the Nobel laureate Tomas Tranströmer (b. 1931) is the key figure continuing the modernist legacy and the most important Swedish poet of the latter half of the 20th c. His works are not extensive, however. The poems are often short, strongly compressed, and rich in ingenious and innovative metaphors. More than any other Swedish poet, he has reached an international audience. Among the other poets of the 1950s, Östen Sjöstrand (1925–2006), Göran Printz-Påhlson (1931–2006), Majken Johansson (1930–93), Lennart Sjögren (b. 1930), and Kjell Espmark (b. 1930) should be mentioned.

A reaction against lyrical modernism, or perhaps rather against its symbolist variant, came in the early 1960s. The reaction was twofold, through a poetic lang. that approached spoken lang. and dealt with everyday motifs (the so-called neosimplicity) and through a sort of neo-avant-gardism (the so-called *concrete poetry). Concrete poetry would prove to be a poetic cul-de-sac. The most important of the movement's representatives, Bengt Emil Johnson (1936–2010), would soon abandon it and develop into a tranquil poet of nature.

Neosimplicity was more successful, at least when it came to its most prominent representatives. Sonja Åkesson (1926–77) is one of the truly important poets of the period. Her style is often ironic, and the poems deal with everyday experiences and women's lives. She has a successor in Kristina Lugn (b. 1948), whose poems are not formalistically innovative but use a subtle self-irony. Göran Palm (b. 1931), in his capacity as both critic and writer, led the attack on symbolism. Consequently, he turns his back on the whole of modernism in his main work *Sverige En vintersaga* (Sweden: A Winter Tale, 1984–2005), an extensive and genre-transcending poem written in blank verse (see BLANK VERSE).

Göran Sonnevi (b. 1939), on the other hand, would remain faithful to modernism. He was one of the first in the 1960s to write poetry with political themes. His collections of poems are often extensive, filled with what could be described as torrents of images and reflections. Because of this, he is in many ways the opposite of Tranströmer. The same can be said about Lars Norén (b. 1944), who in the beginning of the 21st c. was the most celebrated playwright in Sweden but who from his debut in 1963 and in the following two decades published poetry almost exclusively (15 collections of poems in various styles over 18 years).

Lars Gustafsson (b. 1936) has since the early 1960s established a place of his own. His poems have a distinctly intellectual mark. They often have philosophical content and use images and motifs from technical and scientific hist. This intellectual line in poetry is continued by, among others, Jesper Svenbro (b. 1944) and Ulf Eriksson (b. 1958).

Among the poets who had their breakthrough in the 1970s, Tobias Berggren (b. 1940), Gunnar Harding (b. 1940), and Bruno K. Öijer (b. 1951) attracted the most attention. In the last decades of the 20th c., female dominance was striking in Swedish poetry. Eva Ström (b. 1947), Eva Runefelt (b. 1953), and Birgitta Lillpers (b. 1958) have all been noticed for their personal style and their existential themes.

In the 1980s, modernism returned, now as *postmodernism, and with Stig Larsson (b. 1955) as its leading poet. The most important poets at the end of the 20th c. were Katarina Frostenson (b. 1953), who works with a fragmented poetical lang. with great power of suggestion, and Ann Jäderlund (b. 1955), whose poetry is based on rhythmic patterns and merges simplicity with complexity. At the beginning of the 21st c., Swedish poetry shows great variation, both formally and thematically.

■ **Anthologies**: *Svensk dikt från trollformler till Lars Norén*, ed. L. Gustafsson (1987); *Svensk lyrik från medeltid till nutid*, ed. G. Lindström et al. (1993); *De bästa svenska dikterna: från Stiernhielm till Aspenström*, ed. J.-O. Ullén (2007).
■ **Criticism and History**: A. Gustafson, *A History of Swedish Literature* (1961); E. H. Linder, *Fem decennier av 1900-talet*, 2 v. (1965–66); *Ny illustrerad svensk litteraturhistoria*, ed. E. N. Tigerstedt, 2d ed., 4 v. (1967); G. Brandell and J. Stenkvist, *Svensk litteratur 1870–1970*, 3 v. (1974–75); I. Algulin, *A History of Swedish Literature*, trans. J. Weinstock (1989); I. Algulin and B. Olsson, *Litteraturens historia i Sverige* (1995); *A History of Swedish Literature*, ed. L. G. Warme (1996); *Aspects of Modern Swedish Literature*, ed. I. Scobbie (1999); *Den svenska litteraturen*, ed. L. Lönnroth et al., 2d ed., 3 v. (1999); *Finlands svenska litteraturhistoria*, ed. J. Wrede and C. Zilliacus, 2 v. (1999–2000); S. Bergsten, *Den svenska poesins historia* (2007).

S. Göransson

## SWITZERLAND, POETRY OF

I. German
II. French
III. Italian
IV. Romansh

Although Switzerland officially defines itself as a multilingual country, each lang. group forms a geographically separate and—with few exceptions—monolingual area. Ger. is the dominant lang.; with approximately 64% of the speakers in 2002, it largely outnumbers Fr. (20%), It. (6.5%), and Romansh-speaking (0.5%) Swiss. The question of whether lit. from Switzerland should be considered a single entity constitutes a matter of debate. Official cultural institutions such as Pro Helvetia uphold a national perspective by supporting interaction among the four lang. groups. Attempts by Swiss intellectuals to promote a truly national lit., linked to a privileged role for Switzerland as mediator between Latin and Germanic cultures in Europe—the *Helvetia Mediatrix* idea—proved to be utopian. In reality, each lang. group forms a separate literary entity. For this reason, they are presented here discretely.

In a country with only 7.8 million inhabitants, writers largely depend on sales outside Switzerland. Most authors reject the label "Swiss writer" because of the fear of appearing provincial and choose instead to be grouped with writers from other countries who write in the same lang. A constitutive element in all Swiss lits. is the perception of belonging to a minority. Even Ger.-Swiss writers, who form the majority in Switzerland, constitute a small minority within Ger. lit. Another important characteristic of Swiss intellectual life is the tension between internationalism and localism in the definition of identity. Migration is a recurrent topic; several of the most important Swiss authors lived abroad and incorporated this foreign experience in their work. In addition, the influx of refugees during times of international crisis made neutral Switzerland a temporary intellectual center of Eur. importance. Examples include the foundation of the *Dada movement in Zurich during World War I and the Zurich *Schauspielhaus*, the major anti-Fascist theater in Ger.-speaking Europe during World War II. However, Switzerland's multilingual conception of national identity and its international orientation stand in sharp contrast to its tendency toward political isolation and intellectual "narrowness." *Heidi*, the country's famous literary creation by Johanna Spyri (1827–1901), symbolizes the glorification of alpine, "typically Swiss" virtues in combination with a strong distrust of potentially dangerous urban and foreign influences. This tendency was reinforced in the late 1930s with the promotion of Swiss patriotism in order to combat aggressive Fascist and Nazi propaganda from neighboring countries. Lit. played a key role in this "spiritual defense" of Switzerland.

**I. German.** During the Middle Ages, present-day Switzerland was officially part of the Holy Roman Empire of the Ger. nation. Lat. was the written lang. in Ger.-speaking Europe, but religious centers such as the abbey of Saint Gall aided the devel. of *med. poetry in the Ger. vernacular. In the mid-14th c., a rich collection of songs by *Minnesingers*, the Codex Manesse, was compiled in Zurich (see MINNESANG). The military victories against Hapsburg in the 14th c. and the expansion of the Swiss Confederacy until 1515 created an awareness of cultural singularity within Ger.-speaking Europe. This perception reflected itself in the production of heroic verse about battles and mythical figures such as William Tell. Switzerland's separate evolution from Germany was reinforced by the Reformation, which stimulated the use of the vernacular in militantly Protestant religious poetry.

The birth of a consciously distinctive Swiss lit. is traditionally linked to the publication, in 1732, of *Die Alpen* (The Alps), a long poem by the famous naturalist Albrecht von Haller (1708–77). Haller idealized the alpine people as the true successors of the heroic Confederates who had guaranteed Swiss freedom against foreign aggressors. Haller himself lived in the city of Berne and used the Alps as a contrast to the decadent lifestyle of the Bernese upper class. With his poems, he created the basis of the alpine myth that strongly influenced both the national and international image of Switzerland. A similar utopian vision of harmony and purity characterized the internationally famous *Idyllen* (Idylls, 1756) by Salomon Gessner (1730–88). The trad. of patriotic lit. was continued by the physiognomist Johann Caspar Lavater (1741–1801) in his collection of *Schweizerlieder* (Swiss Songs) in 1767.

In the 19th c., lit. from Switzerland achieved a prominent position in Ger.-speaking lit. with the novelists Jeremias Gotthelf (1797–1854), Gottfried Keller (1819–90), and Conrad Ferdinand Meyer (1825–98). Keller and Meyer also wrote poetry. Many of Keller's poems reflect his commitment to the foundation of the liberal Swiss Federal State in 1848. The words of his poem *O mein Heimatland!* (Oh My Fatherland) acquired the popularity of a national *anthem. Meyer's poetic work is apolitical and characterized by an aesthetic symbolism. He excels in the evocation of landscapes and city life, most famously those of Venice and Rome. His description of a Roman fountain in *Der Römische Brunnen* is considered a perfect *Dinggedicht*. Heinrich Leuthold (1827–79) is one of the few Swiss authors who dedicated himself almost exclusively to poetry. His work is strongly aesthetic, though considerably less expressive than that of Meyer.

The work of Nobel Prize winner Carl Spitteler (1845–1924) has almost completely fallen into obscurity, incl. his allegoric-epic poem *Olympischer Frühling* (Olympic Spring, 1905). The opposite can be said about his contemp. Robert Walser (1878–1956), whose short stories, novels, and poems were rediscovered in the 1970s as important writings of literary *modernism. Hans Morgenthaler (1890–1928) also made his reputation posthumously. He worked as a geologist in Asia and attempted to transcend exoticism in his literary work, incl. poems. The poetic work of the Ger. Nobel Prize winner Hermann Hesse (1877–1962), who in 1923 became a naturalized Swiss, is characterized by its introspection and Buddhist influence. Despite the presence in Zurich of prominent Ger. Dadaists such as Hugo Ball (1886–1927), Emmy Hennings (1885–1948), and Hans (Jean) Arp (1887–1966), the impact of *expressionism and the avant garde was weak among Swiss poets (see AVANT-GARDE POETICS). These new currents did, nevertheless, influence the work of the graphologist Max Pulver (1889–1952), the melancholic poetry of Albin Zollinger (1895–1941), the politically committed, urbane work of Albert Ehrismann (1908–98), and the surrealistic poems of the famous artist Meret Oppenheim (1913–85).

As Switzerland had remained neutral during World War II, there was no immediate need for a break with the past. The division of Berlin and consequent loss of a dominant Ger. cultural center increased the importance of Swiss cities such as Zurich and Basel that could compete as equals with Frankfurt, Munich, Hamburg, Cologne, and Vienna. The Swiss novelists and playwrights Max Frisch (1911–91) and Friedrich Dürrenmatt (1921–90) achieved leading positions in Ger.-speaking lit. In postwar poetry, traditional forms continued with the aesthetic work of Werner Zemp

(1906–59), the melancholic poems of the gardener Rainer Brambach (1917–83), and most prominently with Gerhard Meier (1917–2008) and Erika Burkart (1922–2010), whose poems on the splendor of nature, the discovery of beauty in small things, and the lost innocence of childhood transcend nostalgic romanticizing.

A different path was chosen by Alexander Xaver Gwerder (1923–52), who vehemently opposed the bourgeois mentality in his cynical poetry. Gwerder's lifelong search for a poetic form that suited his rebellious character ended in resignation and suicide. An important formal innovation was achieved by Eugen Gomringer (b. 1925), the father of *concrete poetry. Gomringer originally worked as secretary of the architect and designer Max Bill (1908–94), whose ideas on concrete art he applied to poetry.

The poetic work of Kurt Marti (b. 1921) combines the ideas of two leading Swiss intellectuals: formally, Marti was influenced by Gomringer, and intellectually, he followed the trad. of political commitment set out by the theologian Karl Barth. Commitment is also a key word in Dürrenmatt's (few) poems as well as in the *protest poetry of investigative journalist Niklaus Meienberg (1940–93).

While poetry in the 1950s and 1960s was a hotbed of literary innovation, this has changed since the 1970s. Poets such as Herbert Meier (b. 1928) and Jörg Steiner (b. 1930) turned to prose, and younger writers such as Klaus Merz (b. 1945), who started with poetry, favored prose as soon as their talent was discovered. Prominent authors such as Hugo Loetscher (1929–2009), Jürg Federspiel (1931–2007), Franz Hohler (b. 1943), and Thomas Hürlimann (b. 1950) published important poetic work but remained primarily focused on prose. Poetry has become a niche market for devotees yet continues to surprise with the beautifully illustrated broadsheets of Beat Brechbühl (b. 1939), for instance, or the musical poetry of Raphael Urweider (b. 1974), influenced by the lively Swiss hip-hop scene.

Although local dialects can be found all over Ger.-speaking Europe, nowhere do they have a higher social standing and a greater common usage than in Switzerland. There exists an important Swiss *dialect poetry. The trad. began at the end of the 18th c., when Switzerland's autonomy was threatened by France. For a long time, patriotism was an important characteristic of this poetry. With Josef Reinhart (1875–1957) and Meinrad Lienert (1865–1933), dialect poetry achieved a status almost comparable to standard Ger. During the "spiritual defense" in the 1930s, the use of dialect was encouraged in order to distinguish the Swiss from their Ger. neighbors. In protest against this overly patriotic policy, the famous dialect writer Carl Albert Loosli (1877–1959) provocatively switched to standard Ger. and restricted his use of dialect to poetry. In the 1960s, dialect poetry went through a revival with singer-songwriter Mani Matter (1936–72), who had a great influence on the lively Swiss dialect music scene. Prominent authors have also used colloquial dialect for their poetry, as was the case with Gomringer, Marti, and Kuno Raeber

(1922–92), who developed his unique poetic lang. on the basis of the Lucerne dialect.

**II. French.** The unique identity of lit. from Fr.-speaking Switzerland (Romandy) is primarily the result of the Reformation (in opposition to Catholic France). The teachings of John Calvin stimulated the use of the vernacular in poetry supporting the Protestant cause. Fr. refugees, driven by religious persecution, stimulated intellectual life in Romandy. In the mid-18th c., Geneva temporarily became a Eur. intellectual center with the presence of the philosophers Voltaire (1694–1778) and Jean-Jacques Rousseau (1712–78), whose introspection and celebration of natural purity had a long-lasting influence on Romand lit.

For centuries, poetry in Romandy remained moralizing and didactic. Although the general mood was patriotic, poets such as Juste Olivier (1807–76) slavishly imitated Fr. patterns. With Charles Ferdinand Ramuz (1878–1947), a radical break took place. On his return from Paris in 1914, Ramuz rejected all moralization and provocatively identified himself no longer with France, Switzerland, or Romandy, but only with his rural canton Vaud. He abandoned the artificial Fr. he had been using and invented his own syntax in combination with an expressive, polyphonic lang. that he applied in lyrical novels and poems. In *Le Petit Village* (The Little Village, 1903), he experimented with *free verse. Ramuz's literary journal *Cahiers vaudois* (Journal from Vaud) generated new talents, among them the deeply solitary poet Gustave Roud (1897–1976) and Pierre-Louis Matthey (1893–1970), whose strongly musical and baroque poetry achieved mythological dimensions. The journalist and poet Edmond-Henri Crisinel (1897–1948) represents a singular case. Crisinel's poetry, in cl. prosodic forms, reflects his paranoia, which resulted in long periods of institutionalization.

Whereas Ramuz was a confirmed regionalist, albeit in a metaphysical, tragic, and cosmic dimension, Blaise Cendrars (1887–1961) was a quintessential cosmopolite. In 1904, he left Switzerland and later became a naturalized Fr. citizen. Inspired by the modernity of New York, Cendrars wrote *Les Pâques à New York* (Easter in New York, 1912), which became a landmark in the devel. of mod. poetry. His strongly rhythmic, utterly mod. and wholly unconventional style in free verse had a strong influence on the surrealist Guillaume Apollinaire and Brazilian modernism.

The dominant figure in postwar Romand poetry is Philippe Jaccottet (b. 1925), who analyzes poetry from different angles: in his theoretical works, his literary trans., and his own poetic production. Jaccottet, who left Switzerland at young age and has lived in France ever since, writes introspective poetry in which light and darkness, nature and the trauma of war play an essential role. Introspection also characterizes the work of Anne Perrier (b. 1922), Pierre Chappuis (b. 1930), and Pierre-Alain Tâche (b. 1940). Alexandre Voisard (b. 1930) placed much of his poetry at the service of the secessionist movement in the (Fr.-speaking and Catholic) Jura in opposition to the (primarily Ger.-speaking

and Protestant) canton Bern. The work of Maurice Chappaz (1916–2009) and Jacques Chessex (b. 1934) combines regionalism with baroque magniloquence. Chappaz's poetry reveals concern about the environment in his canton Valais. His struggle with Calvinist morality led to an unrestrained celebration of sensuality. In 1973, he was the first Swiss to win the prestigious Fr. Prix Goncourt award. Ágota Kristóf (b. 1935), who came to Switzerland as a refugee from Hungary, made her literary debut in Fr. with poetry. Her later prose work on topics such as war and destruction, love and loneliness, remained characterized by a strongly lyrical lang.

Romand poets of a younger generation such as Pierre Voélin (b. 1949), Frédéric Wandelère (b. 1949), and José-Flore Tappy (b. 1954) found themselves confronted by the cultural centralism of Paris. In the wake of trends toward regionalization, however, Romandy has undoubtedly gained a sharper profile against Fr. cultural domination.

**III. Italian.** Theoretically, It.-speaking Switzerland is limited to some 300,000 people in the (traditionally Catholic) canton Ticino and some valleys in the (traditionally Protestant) canton Grisons. Because of immigration from Italy, however, there are some 200,000 It.-speaking Swiss in other parts of the country. Nevertheless, It. remains a tiny minority lang. in Switzerland, and the cultural attraction of Italy and its nearby metropolis Milan is immense.

The first Swiss-It. writer of Eur. importance is Francesco Chiesa (1871–1973), who, because of his long life, remained the dominant literary personality in Ticino for almost a century. Chiesa was a traditionalist, who celebrated an idyllic and slightly moralistic, though not humorless, vision of his region in poems and novels.

After the war, a new generation of writers took over Chiesa's dominant position. Among them was Giorgio Orelli (b. 1921), whose strongly rhythmical poetry, characterized by an ironic ambiguity, made him famous beyond the borders of Switzerland. With Remo Fasani (1922–2011), whose poetry reflects a deep concern about the environment, the It.-speaking Grisons transcended its literary provincialism. Alberto Nessi (b. 1940) writes poetry primarily about outsiders: people stricken by illness, poverty, and physical decay.

The youngest generation of Swiss-It. poets increasingly manifests itself in close collaboration with colleagues from the northern It. Lombardy region. Many of them combine their literary activities with teaching, journalism, and trans. work. One example is Fabio Pusterla (b. 1957), who played an essential role in the dissemination of Jaccottet's poetry in Italy.

**IV. Romansh.** With approximately 40,000 speakers, Romansh is one of the smallest langs. in the world. Its official status, achieved in 1938, should be seen in the context of Switzerland's "spiritual defense" and emphasis on a multilingual, democratic Swiss identity in opposition to Nazi Germany and Fascist Italy.

Romansh is a generic term for several langs. that were only (artificially) standardized in 1982. Despite considerable government support, its chances of survival in the predominantly Ger.-speaking canton Grisons are uncertain.

The emergence of Romansh as a literary lang. is generally dated to the mid-16th c. when the Reformation stimulated the use of the local vernacular. Cultural awareness became stronger in the 19th c. in opposition to both an attempted Germanization of the region and to It. irredentism that considered Romansh an It. dialect. Much of the poetry by Gion Antoni Huonder (1824–67), Giacun Hasper Muoth (1844–1906), and Peider Lansel (1863–1943) reflects this concern about a proper Romansh identity.

After World War II, poetry became less political and more concerned with aesthetics, most notably in the case of Andri Peer (1921–85), Hendri Spescha (1928–82), and Luisa Famos (1930–74). The youngest generation of poets increasingly publishes bilingual (Romansh-Ger.) work, in which both langs. appear separately or in a mixed form.

*See* AUSTRIA, POETRY OF; FRANCE, POETRY OF; GERMAN POETRY; ITALY, POETRY OF.

■ **Swiss Poetry, General:** M. Gsteiger, "Comparative Literature in Switzerland," *Yearbook of Comparative and General Literature* 30 (1981); H. Loetscher, *How Many Languages Does Man Need?* (1982); *Anthology of Modern Swiss Literature*, ed. H. M. Waidson (1984); *Modern Swiss Literature*, ed. J. L. Flood (1985); *The Four Literatures of Switzerland*, ed. B. Stocker et al. (1996); *Images of Switzerland*, ed. J. Charnley and M. Pender (1998); H. Loetscher, *Lesen statt klettern* (2003); *Nationale Literaturen heute*, ed. C. Caduff and R. Sorg (2004); *Schweizer Literaturgeschichte*, ed. P. Rusterholz and A. Solbach (2007); *From the Margins to the Centre*, ed. P. Studer and S. Egger (2007).
■ **In German:** *Geschichte der deutschsprachigen Schweizer Literatur im 20. Jahrhundert*, ed. K. Pezold (1991); P. von Matt, *Die tintenblauen Eidgenossen* (2001); P. von Matt and D. Vaihinger, *Die schönsten Gedichte der Schweiz* (2002); "Young Swiss Writers," *Dimension 2*, ed. R. Sabalius and M. Wutz (2007).
■ **In French:** J. Monnier, *Contemporary French-Swiss Literature* (1975); D. Maggetti, *L'Invention de la littérature romande* (1995); *Histoire de la littérature en Suisse romande*, ed. R. Francillon, 3 v. (1996–99); *Dictionnaire de poésie*, ed. M. Jarrety (2001); *La poésie en Suisse Romande depuis Blaise Cendrars*, ed. M. Graf and J. F. Tappy (2005); *L'anthologie de la poésie romande hier et aujourd'hui*, ed. J. Küpfer and C. Delafontaine-Küpfer (2007).
■ **In Italian:** G. Calgari, *Storia delle quattro letterature della Svizzera* (1959); *Svizzera italiana*, ed. G. Orelli (1986); *Lingua e letterature italiana in Svizzera*, ed. A. Stäuble (1989); A. Stäuble and M. Stäuble, *Scrittori del Grigioni Italiano* (1998).
■ **In Romansh:** *The Curly-Horned Cow*, ed. R. R. Bezzola (1971); I. Camartin, *Rätoromanische Gegenwartsliteratur in Graubünden* (1976); D. B. Gregor, *Romontsch Language and Literature* (1982); C. Riatsch,

*Mehrsprachigkeit und Sprachmischung in der neueren bündnerromanischen Literatur* (1998).

J. DEWULF

## SYLLABIC VERSE

I. System of Versification
II. English

**I. System of Versification.** Syllabic verse is one of the earliest and most widespread modes of versifying: it is evidenced in Old Iranian, Sanskrit, ancient Gr., and the earliest Chinese and Japanese poems. Its defining feature is that the lines match (or, more rarely, contrast) only in the number of syllables they contain. The syllabic line's rhythm is termed a *simple primary rhythm* because a single type of *event*, a syllable, is repeated. A passage of syllabic verse is, thus, a series of fours, sixes, or eights or whatever line length the poet chooses.

Versifying by counting syllables alone has serious drawbacks, the first of which is that some syllables have no consonant at their boundary with the next, and the result may be pronounced as one syllable or two. This has largely been left to fashion: in cl. verse, such adjacent vowels counted as one syllable (by *elision or *synaloepha); in med. Lat., they counted as two (by *hiatus); and in mod. romance verse, they almost always count as one.

The other drawbacks of syllabic verse are more fundamental. One reflects the psychological limits to human counting: we can learn to recognize a series of threes, sixes, or even eights intuitively, but a series of tens or fifteens is beyond us. For that reason, syllabic meters must be either short (up to eight syllables) or compound (made up of regular subunits each with no more than eight syllables). The second drawback is that the syllables of most langs. have properties that are more obvious than their number, such as length (see DURATION), stress (see ACCENT), and *pitch. The moment poets begin to regularize any of these, the verse is no longer simply syllabic, and for this reason, most syllabic meters have developed into something rather more complex.

Gr., Sanskrit, and Chinese poets soon departed from strictly syllabic verse and introduced patterns in the duration or the pitch of their syllables. Japanese poets introduced the refinement of recognizing long vowels as two syllables. Lat. poets seem at first to have counted words, not syllables; but by the 2d c. BCE, they had adopted the Gr. system with its contrasts between long and short syllables. By the 3d c. CE, most Lat. speakers had lost any intuitive sense of the difference between long and short vowels, and for several centuries, some Lat. poets composed in the old meters but with the wrong length given to some of their syllables. Most Lat. poets, however, followed the example of the composers of popular hymns and wrote syllabic verse.

There were also new forces influencing versification: *assonance and *rhyme, which were occasional devices in cl. Lat., became mandatory in the new syllabic meters; and stress, which had played a minor role in cl. Lat. meters, became a vital element. The essence of systematic assonance and rhyme is stress: thus, rhymes are either oxytonic (*cat/mat*) or paroxytonic (*horses/courses*), depending on whether a posttonic syllable follows the stressed, rhymed syllable.

Much med. Lat. verse is syllabic, although some poets clearly favored certain positions in their lines for stress, esp. between 1100 and 1500. And in the 11th c., Fr. verse became syllabic: from then on, only the final stresses of lines and *hemistichs had metrical significance. Syllabic verse fits well the mod. Fr. lang., where only phrasal stress has survived.

When poets of other langs. tried to adopt Fr. syllabic metrics, they faced the problem of word stresses in midline, which interfered with the reader's perception of the syllabic pattern. Hispanic and It. poets used these midline stresses to produce a variety of rhythms in their lines, but Eng. poets used them to create regular patterns—that is, *accentual-syllabic verse.

Rhyme and syllable count entered Eng. verse after the Norman Conquest, but in England, something happened to strict syllable count. It began in Anglo-Norman (the official lang. from 1066 to 1363), where the ubiquitous *octosyllabe* was often a syllable short or in excess (see OCTOSYLLABLE). Eng. audiences had always counted stresses, not syllables, and many poets and scribes in this period tolerated lines with approximately eight syllables, providing they had four stresses. Eng. poets never really accepted syllabic verse in their own lang., having incorporated stress patterns from the very first.

These two distinctions have remained: most Eng. verse is *accentual-syllabic, most Fr. syllabic. Mod. Fr. metrists argue that the syllable-timed delivery of their lang. means that syllabic lines occupy equal time in performance and that such equal-time units are the essence of Fr. verse rhythm. Eng. with its stress-timing offers no such *isochrony, and the prevalence of *syncope in the lang. leaves the syllabification of many words ambiguous (thus, *mystery* may be two syllables or three). But this has not prevented mod. Eng.-lang. poets from attempting syllabic meters, incl. W. B. Yeats, W. H. Auden, and Marianne Moore.

**II. English.** In many poetries, including Japanese and those of the Romance languages, meter is organized around the counting of syllables, known as syllabism (see METER, I.B.). The prevalence of this principle, however, is qualified by the fact that purely syllabic meters are uncommon. Traditional Japanese prosody, which depends on the regulation of syllables or *morae in the line and favors five- and seven-syllable lines as in the 31-syllable *tanka, is perhaps the most thoroughly syllabic of any major lang.

As Martin Duffell observes, "in the verse traditions of most languages syllabism came to be compounded or replaced by the regulation of some other suprasegmental feature, such as duration/weight (as in Sanskrit and Ancient Greek), pitch (as in Chinese), or stress (as in Iranian, Greek, Romance, and the Slavonic languages), and some evidence of such regulation is often present in the earliest surviving texts in these lan-

guages." Duffell notes that purely syllabic meters are "fragile," and that syllable counts alone are not "obvious" enough for readers and listeners. Even med. Lat. verse, where syllabism arose after 300 CE in the ruins of quantitative prosody, often depends on stress patterning and rhyme to support the less perceptible syllable count. OF versification took note of the regulation of word stress in med. Lat., and came to include the principle that the final position in each line (and in longer lines, the final position in each hemistich) must contain a stress. While the location of the stress itself is regulated by the syllable count (e.g. in an *octosyllable* it must occur in the last of eight positions), it also in turn defines the end of the line for metrical purposes; where additional syllables occur after the stress, they are not counted, and therefore the syllabic line is negotiated rather than strictly empirical. "This metre," Duffell writes, "although it regulates phrasal stress, is termed syllabic in traditional French metrics"; its phrasal-stress versification became the basis for syllabism in many languages "from Italian and Spanish in the South to Polish and Russian in the North." The devel. of particular syllabic meters often involved further negotiations with local conditions, especially an accommodation of word stress in those languages where it was phonologically prominent.

In Eng., syllabic verse is not so much a metrical program as an experiment or even a curiosity. Many poets and scholars have doubted that verse lines in Eng. regulated by nothing more than identity of numbers of syllables would be perceived by auditors as verse, for there would be nothing to mark them as such except for end-of-line pauses in performance, if that (though Robert Beum argues otherwise). Paul Fussell and others have questioned whether syllabic versification accords with the accentual nature of Eng. Notwithstanding such skepticism on the part of prosodists troubled by the auditory elusiveness of syllabic verse, the number of syllabic poems in Eng., already considerable, continues to grow.

Aside from some debatable Ren. examples, the practice is a mod. one, pioneered by Robert Bridges in the late 19th and early 20th cs. Bridges wrote nearly 5,000 lines of syllabic *alexandrines, esp. for *New Verse* (1925) and *The Testament of Beauty* (1929), the longest syllabic-verse poem in the lang. In the 1910s, Adelaide Crapsey invented the cinquain. Beginning in the same decade, Marianne Moore, the Am. poet best known for the practice, wrote poems in elaborate syllabic stanzas featuring wide variations in line length, complex patterns of rhyme or half rhyme, and conspicuous use of prose rhythms. This last point, highlighted by Roy Fuller and others, suggests that Moore's version of syllabic verse has affinities with the *verset and the *prose poem. From the mid-20th c. on, notable syllabic poems have been written by Elizabeth Daryush, Dylan Thomas, W. H. Auden, Donald Justice, Thom Gunn, Richard Howard, Robert Wells, and others. Some have used haiku as stanzas; Richard Wilbur in doing so rhymes the first and third lines of each. As Steele notes, most poets working in syllabic verse in Eng. attempt to avoid sustained regular (particularly iambic) rhythms, although, for expressive purposes, these may be admitted. Syllabic verse can, in fact, be so accommodating to audible patterns that it can be mistaken for other forms: some of Daryush's syllabic poems can be read as accentual-syllabic with minor variations, and Justice's "For the Suicides," in seven-syllable lines, can be read as an accentual poem because the three beats in each line, though variably placed, are invariably prominent. That which makes syllabic verse conceptually dubious to some prosodists has made it artistically inviting to a widening array of poets, some of whom view it as a half measure between traditional meter and *free verse, and all of whom exploit its paradoxical combination of constraint (in the strict syllable count) and freedom (in the possibility of shifting rhythms at will within the syllabic matrix). The term *syllabic verse* used in relation to Ir. and Welsh prosody is not a categorically exclusive designation, since in these systems, the syllable count of a line is but one of a number of required prosodic features.

*See* CHINESE PROSODY, FRENCH PROSODY, ITALIAN PROSODY, JAPANESE PROSODY, SPANISH PROSODY.

■ **Versification:** G. B. Pighi, *Studi di ritmica e metrica* (1970); M. L. West, "Greek Poetry 2000–700 BC," *CQ* 23 (1973), and "Indo-European Metre," *Glotta* 51 (1973); S. Oliva, *Mètrica catalana* (1980); P. M. Bertinetto, *Strutture prosodiche dell' italiano* (1981); P. G. Beltrami, *La metrica italiana* (1991); B. de Cornulier, *Art poëtique* (1995); M. L. Gasparov, *A History of European Versification*, trans. and ed. G. S. Smith, M. Tarlinskaja, and L. Holford-Strevens (1996); R. Pensom, *Accent and Metre in French, 1100–1900* (1998); J. Domínguez Caparrós, *Métrica española*, 2d ed. (2000); M. J. Duffell, "French Symmetry, Germanic Rhythm, and Spanish Metre," *Chaucer and the Challenges of Medievalism*, ed. D. Minkova and T. Tinkle (2003); *Syllable and Accent: Studies on Medieval Hispanic Metrics* (2007); and Duffell.

■ **English:** R. Bridges, "New Verse: Explanation of the Prosody of My Late Syllabic 'Free Verse'," *Collected Essays*, vol. 2 (1933); E. C. Wright, *Metaphor, Sound and Meaning in Bridges' "Testament of Beauty"* (1951); R. Beum, "Syllabic Verse in English," *Prairie Schooner* 31 (1957); R. Beloof, "Prosody and Tone," *KR* 20 (1958); Sr. M. G. Berg, *The Prosodic Structure of Robert Bridges' "Neo-Miltonic Syllabics"* (1962); R. Fuller, "An Artifice of Versification," *Owls and Artificers* (1971); E. Daryush, "Note on Syllabic Metres," *Collected Poems* (1976); P. Fussell Jr., *Poetic Meter and Poetic Form*, rev. ed. (1979); Brogan; T. Steele, *All the Fun's in How You Say a Thing* (1999); M. Holley, "Syllabics: Sweeter Melodies," Finch and Varnes; M. J. Duffell, "The Metric Cleansing of Hispanic Verse," *BHS* 76 (1999); Duffell; Gasparov, *History*; R. H. Brower, "Japanese," A. B. Giamatti, "Italian," L. Nelson, Jr., "Spanish," and J. Flescher, "French"—all in Wimsatt.

M. J. DUFFELL (VERSIFICATION); T.V.F. BROGAN; R. B. SHAW (ENG.)

**SYLLABLE.** The syllable is at once a traditional element of grammatical analysis handed down since antiquity and one of the most elusive concepts of 21st-c. ling. The sound stream that is speech is segmented by junctures (pauses) into sentences, sentences into phrases, and phrases into words. These can be identified with digital instrumentation. But the analysis of words into syllables is not so easily determined. The rules for syllabification of words in a lang. such as Eng. are far from consistent or exact.

From the point of view of articulatory phonetics, the syllable has been conceived as (1) one separate respiratory movement (R. H. Stetson's "chest pulse"), (2) one opening and closing of the vocal tract aperture (Ferdinand de Saussure), (3) one peak of sonority in the sound stream (Otto Jespersen), and (4) simply a fiction (Scripture); but no one phonetic criterion or definition has proven sufficient. In any event, the definition must be posed at the phonemic level, not the phonetic, since rules of syllabification are, in part, conventional and lang. specific. Thus, a speaker of Tamil may hear a certain sound sequence as one syllable, while a speaker of Eng. will hear it as two; this follows from differences in the phonemic structure of the two langs.

In general, however, it is possible to develop a structure that will describe the syllable in most langs. Specific terms vary, but the syllable can be said to have three parts, "onset," "nucleus" or "peak," and "coda." The nucleus most often corresponds to a vowel; the onset and coda are consonants or consonant clusters. The syllable is thus commonly schematized as consonant + vowel + consonant, or CVC. Syllables are also differentiated as to whether "closed" or "open" (the coda may be absent); the rules of syllabic *quantity in Gr. and Lat. prosody depend on whether the vowel is long and whether the syllable is closed. This CVC schema also proves remarkably useful for analyzing varieties of sound patterning in poetry such as *alliteration and *rhyme.

When lang. is submitted to the system of phonological organization in poetry that is meter, the syllable is made equivalent to the metrical "position," normally one syllable but under some conditions two. Thus, iambic pentameter has ten positions, and the normal line of such verse will have ten syllables. The relation of syllable to position can take only three forms: one to one, many to one, or one to many; metrical theory specifies which forms are allowed and then gives "correspondence rules" for the mapping of syllables onto positions in the line. These vary somewhat from age to age as usage and conventions for pronunciation (and spelling) change, and our ability to read earlier poetry correctly thus depends on evidence obtained from research in historical phonology. Such questions carry more prosodic weight in some langs. than in others; e.g., the syllable carries more weight as a unit of meter in Fr. and Japanese poetry, where accentual considerations play a minimal role. For further discussion of the handling of syllabification in metrics, see ELISION.

In ling., the problem of syllable boundaries is an issue that becomes a question of whether the syllable is to be taken as running from onset to onset or peak to peak. This makes a difference but can be bypassed in the phonemic model; it has been suggested that statistical probabilities of the various consonant combinations permitted in a given lang. should determine structure. Early in the 20th c., a good deal of effort was invested in trying to apply research in acoustics directly to metrics (for references, see Brogan, 226 ff.), incl. the question of syllable boundaries. At mid-century, Roman Jakobson treated sound in poetry as phonemic not phonetic, rendering boundaries irrelevant to metrics by taking syllables as given in any ordinary dict. For those less willing to rely on phonemic abstractions, the issue remains context-dependent, and therefore much thornier. What is most important for metrics is, more simply, the issue of how many syllables there are in a line, i.e., whether syllables were elided in contemporaneous pronunciation or pronounced in full. In some periods, syllabification is fairly carefully coded into orthography ("heav'n" is monosyllabic, while "heaven" is disyllabic), in others not. There is a presumption that *scansion and possibly also *performance should conform to the usage of the time.

■ E. W. Scripture, *Elements of Experimental Phonetics* (1902); E. Hermann, *Silbenbildung im Griechischen und in den anderen indogermanischen Sprachen* (1923); K. L. Pike, *Phonemics* (1947); E. Haugen, "The Syllable in Linguistic Description," *For Roman Jakobson* (1956); B. Hala, "La syllabe, sa nature, son origine et ses transformations," *Orbis* 9 (1961)—full review of the older theories; Chatman, chap. 3; E. Pulgram, *Syllable, Word, Nexus, Cursus* (1970); R. A. Zirin, *The Phonological Basis of Latin Prosody* (1970), chap. 1; Allen, esp. chap. 3; E. O. Selkirk, "The Syllable," *The Structure of Phonological Representations II*, ed. H. van der Hulst and N. Smith (1978); *Syllables and Segments*, ed. A. Bell and J. B. Hooper (1978); Scott; Brogan; Morier, under "Syllabe"; E. O. Selkirk, *Phonology and Syntax* (1984), 22 ff.; J. A. Goldsmith, *Autosegmental and Metrical Phonology* (1990), esp. 103 ff.; D. Minkova, "Syllable Weight, Prosody, and Meter in Old English," *Diachronica* (1994).

T.V.F. BROGAN; J. M. COCOLA

**SYLLEPSIS** (Gr., "taking together"). A figure closely related to and probably one species of *zeugma, i.e., constructions in which one word serves two others (typically a verb and a compound object); in zeugma, the "yoking" word agrees grammatically or semantically with both its objects or subjects, but in syllepsis, it agrees with only one. (Since both grammar and sense are involved, technically one could make a fourfold distinction.) The one word, then, bears two differing senses, the first one asserted, the second one only implied—hence, the surprise. Herodian, the Gr. rhetorician of the 2d c. CE, gives an example from Homer (*Iliad* 9.5): "The north wind and the west wind that blow from Thrace" (true only of the north wind; the verb is the predicate of a compound subject). And Virgil (*Aeneid* 5.508) has: "alta petens, pariterque oculos telumque tetendit" (he looked up [at the target, a pi-

geon] with gaze and arrow alike extended). Syllepsis is rare in the It. and Fr. sonneteers, but Shakespeare makes it a major verbal device for double entendre both witty and serious, as at *Othello* 4.1.34 ff., where Iago plays on the senses of "lie," in order to inflame Othello, and all by implication. Alexander Pope uses syllepsis frequently: "Here thou, great Anna! whom three realms obey, / Dost sometimes counsel take—and sometimes tea"; "Or stain her honour, or her new brocade"; "Or lose her heart, or necklace, at a ball" (*The Rape of the Lock*). All three of these instances agree grammatically but not semantically ("brocade" being stained literally, but honor abstractly). The effect, which is striking, depends on the sudden reinterpretation of the sentence as the reader realizes the shift in meaning. As such syllepsis seems one form of *paronomasia or pun; some have also seen it as an effect of *ambiguity, though there it would seem that an element of doubt is introduced that the Pope examples do not evince. Riffaterre, following Jacques Derrida, who uses *syllepsis* in the sense of pun to point to the binding together of opposite senses in a word, even as one coin has two sides, distinguishes three roles for syllepsis and hence three types of *intertextuality; he sees the two ways we understand the word as its "contextual meaning" versus its "intertextual meaning" and thus views syllepsis as "the literary sign par excellence." For further bibliography, see ZEUGMA.

■ M. Riffaterre, "Syllepsis," *CritI* 6 (1980); J. M. Molesworth, "Syllepsis, Mimesis, Simulacrum: The Monk and the Grammar of Authenticity," *Criticism* 51 (2009); K. Puckett, "Some Versions of Syllepsis," *Partial Answers* 9 (2011).

T.V.F. BROGAN

## SYMBOL

I. In Culture
II. In Poetry

In literary studies, the term *symbol* (Gr. verb *symballein*, "to put together," and the related noun *symbolon*, "mark," "token," or "sign," referring to the half coin carried away as a pledge by each of the two parties to an agreement) has had a broad range of applications and interpretations. In the study of lang., e.g., words are symbols of what they stand for, but the more common ling. terminology after Ferdinand de Saussure (see STRUCTURALISM; SIGN, SIGNIFIED, SIGNIFIER) is sign, which joins a signifier and a signified. *Sign* generally refers to a relatively specific representation of one thing by another—a red traffic light, e.g., means "stop"—while *symbol* refers to a more polysemous *representation of one thing by another—as when the sea, e.g., is used to stand for such different feelings as the danger of being overwhelmed (by analogy with drowning) or the excitement and anxiety of making a transition (as in a journey) or the power and fulfillment of strength (as in mighty), and so on.

For the present purpose, however, the meanings and uses of *symbolism* can be analyzed in terms of two main categories: on the one hand is the study of the symbol in such larger contexts as lang. and the interpretation of lang. (philology, rhet., ling., semantics, *semiotics, *hermeneutics), of philosophy (metaphysics, epistemology, aesthetics), of social science (sociology, anthropology, psychology), and of hist. and religion; on the other hand is the study of the symbol in its discrete contexts as an aspect of art, of literary theory and crit., and of poetry (Wimsatt 1965, Hayes).

**I. In Culture.** Historically as well as logically, the larger field comes first. Where people once tended habitually to see the physical world in terms of emotional and spiritual values, they now tend to separate their values from the world. It has become one of the clichés of mod. crit. that, due to the anti-imagistic crusade of the Protestant Reformation (see IMAGERY), the growth of science and its search for "objective" knowledge, the changes in focus from sacred to secular gradually effected in school curricula, and the mere passage of time, many traditional symbols have been rendered meaningless to poets and readers alike. Thus, received symbolism was called in the 20th c. the "lost" or "forgotten" lang. (Bayley, Fromm).

It may be said, then, that the evolution of symbolism began with the evolution of primitive humanity. It was not until the med. period, however, that symbols and the interpretation of symbols became a branch of learning. The patristic trad. of biblical *exegesis, heavily under the influence of the Platonic and Neoplatonic schools of thought, developed standards and procedures for the doctrinal interpretation of scripture according to four levels of meaning—literal, allegorical, moral and tropological, and anagogic. The purpose was twofold: to reconcile the OT with the NT and to reconcile various difficult portions of each with Catholic teaching. Thus, e.g., while the Song of Songs is a mildly erotic wedding poem on the literal level, its true meaning on the allegorical level is the "marriage" of Christ and the Church.

This exegetical trad. evolved during the 16th c. into Ren. nature philosophy and, under the influence of the mysticism of the Ger. Jakob Boehme (1575–1624) and the Swede Emanuel Swedenborg (1688–1772), into the doctrine of correspondences, which viewed the external world as a system of symbols revealing the spiritual world in material form. By the romantic period, the view that nature is the visual lang. of God or spirit became established as one of the mainstays of poetry, but two fundamental shifts had occurred: the material and spiritual worlds were seen as merged rather than related simply as representation to the thing represented; and, as a result, the meaning of symbols became less fixed and more ambiguous (Seward, Sewell, Hirst, Wimsatt, Todorov, and Adams).

Out of this romantic trad. grew a large and influential 20th-c. movement that tried to reunite what the Reformation and science ostensibly had sundered. Following the lead of such writers as Urban, Cassirer, Langer, and Wheelwright, mod. philosophers and critics developed a set of concepts whereby the lang. of symbols can be regarded as having as much epistemo-logical status as—if not more than—the lang. of fact and reason. The question, therefore, is as follows: if the latter refers to the "real" or "objective" world, and is subject to test and verification, what does the former refer to, and does it too have analogous evaluative procedures?

The answers range along a spectrum: at the one extreme are the positivists, who say that the lang. of fact and science is the only true lang. and, therefore, that all other langs. are nonsense; at the other end are the mystics, who claim that the lang. of fact and science is trivial and that the only true lang. is that of symbols. Northrop Frye, in *Anatomy of Criticism*, however, falls off the spectrum altogether: neither world for him, at least as literary critic, exists. He simply postulates that there is an "order" of lit., that this order has an objective existence in the totality of literary texts, and that it is based on the fundamental seasonal monomyth of death and rebirth (see ARCHETYPE).

Closer to the center are two other positions that seek either to balance this subject-object split or to reconcile it. The first is exemplified by I. A. Richards, who accepted the distinction between scientific and poetic lang. but then proceeded to accord to the latter a status and value of its own. Thus, he distinguished between "referential" lang., the lang. of fact and science, and "emotive" lang., the lang. of poetry. The status and value of the latter were found in its ability to arouse and organize our emotions, thus giving poetry some sort of psychological and therapeutic if not metaphysical "truth." The *New Criticism, not entirely satisfied with this distinction, claimed further that poetry gives us another and "higher" kind of truth, a truth of human existence that is more complex and profound than that of mere fact and science.

The reconcilers, exemplified chiefly by Cassirer and Langer and their followers, claim that *all* langs., whether of science or poetry, or of any in between, are various ways in which the human mind constructs reality for itself and, therefore, that all our knowledges give *pictures* of reality rather than reality *itself*. For this school, humanity has not "lost" or "forgotten" the lang. of symbols; it has merely come to prefer one kind of symbolic lang. to another.

Such is the process of hist., however, that this ambitious theory itself has been turned inside out, and later movements have claimed that, since all our langs. are equally symbolic, they are all equally meaningless—at least insofar as the quest for "objective" truth is concerned. Thus, we find the theory of "paradigms" in the philosophy of science (Kuhn, Rorty; see SCIENCE AND POETRY), which says that scientific hypotheses are merely arbitrary constructs that may appear true in one era but are supplanted by other hypotheses in another era— "truth" being more a matter of cultural convenience, mental set, and consensus than of objective verifiability. And we find the theory of deconstruction in ling. and lit. theory and crit. (Culler), which claims that, since the relation between signifier and signified is arbitrary, lang. itself carries multiple meanings.

Another and somewhat more "rational" approach,

represented by Wimsatt (1954), Kermode, and Fingesten, and anticipated by Whitehead, is that symbols, since they come between ourselves and reality, can be the agents of distortion and error as well as of knowledge and insight. Thus, they urge that the subjective be balanced by the objective.

**II. In Poetry.** To the reader considering how to recognize and interpret symbols in poetry, these philosophical disputes may seem not only bewildering but irrelevant. However, one's practical approach to symbols will be governed in large part by one's theory, for a critic's use of any given term is determined by the assumptions he or she makes about lit., lang., and reality, and by the kind of knowledge sought.

Olson (in Crane), e.g., as a neo-Aristotelian, is primarily concerned with literary works in their aspect as artistic wholes of certain kinds; therefore, he regards symbolism as a device that is sometimes used in the service of the work's artistic effect—to aid in the expression of remote ideas, to vivify what otherwise would be faint, to aid in framing the reader's emotional reactions, and the like. Yeats, by contrast, is primarily interested in the suggestive powers of poetry, so he extends his definition of *symbolism* to include not only images, *metaphors, and *myths, but all the "musical relations" of a poem—*rhythm, *diction, *rhyme, *sound. Or again, Wheelwright, Langer, Cassirer, and Urban, as antipositivists, are concerned to defend poetry as having epistemological status, so they stress symbolism's powers of bodying forth nondiscursive meaning, truth, or vision. Burke, as a student of lang. in terms of human motives, deduces the form of a literary work from speculations as to how it functions in relation to the poet's inner life, so he emphasizes how various elements of that work symbolize an enactment of the poet's psychological tensions.

But the simplest way to begin interpretation is to regard symbols, although they may derive from literal or figurative images or both, as a kind of figurative lang. in which what is shown (normally referring to something material) means, by virtue of some sort of resemblance, suggestion, or association, something *more* or something else (normally immaterial).

**A.** *Identification.* When interpreting symbols in a poem, it is helpful to begin by identifying its *figuration—incl. metaphor, *metonymy, and *synecdoche—and analyzing the source of those figures in experience, whether from the natural world, the human body, human-made artifacts, or so on. We then proceed to ask how the figures in question are something other than literal. A figure may present itself as figurative in several ways, notably (1) it may be presented as if it were literal, but as it develops we see that it is, rather, a dream, a vision, a fantasy, or an imaginary action and, hence, must be understood entirely on a symbolic level, as is the case in W. B. Yeats's "Sailing to Byzantium," where the speaker talks about crossing the sea and coming to the holy city, which seems literally improbable; (2) there is a literal action and situation, but certain metaphors and *similes are presented in relation to one another and to the literal action so as to produce an additional level of meaning—by way of expanded, recurring, or clustered figures (Burke, Brower).

Thus, symbolism resembles figures of speech in having a basic doubleness of meaning between what is meant and what is said (*tenor and vehicle, but it differs in that what is said is *also* what is meant. The "vehicle" is also a "tenor," so a symbolism may be said to be a metaphor in reverse, where the vehicle has been expanded and put in place of the tenor, while the tenor has been left to implication [cf. Bartel]). And this applies even to recurring figures within a literal action, because such figures are embedded in a context of more complex relationships within the work as a whole rather than occurring simply as figures per se.

Similarly, symbolism resembles allegory. Technically, *allegory* refers to the use of personified abstractions in a literary work. Edmund Spenser's *The Faerie Queene* is a standard example: the Redcrosse Knight represents the Christian soul, Duessa the duplicity of temptation, Una the true Church, and so on. Not only the characters may be allegorical, however; the setting and actions may follow suit. Thus, the work in its entirety may be allegorical. The difference between this form and symbolic works is that allegory begins with the tenor, the vehicle being constructed to fit, while symbol begins with the vehicle and the tenor is discovered, elicited, or evoked from it. Beginning with J. W. Goethe and S. T. Coleridge, this distinction was turned into a value judgment, with allegory being condemned as didactic and artificial and symbol being praised as natural and organic. This judgment became a commonplace of romantic and mod. crit., until a line of defense was established for allegory by more recent critics such as Honig, Fletcher, Hayes, de Man, Brett, Bloomfield, Todorov, and Adams. De Man, in particular, developed a detailed contrast between symbol and allegory as modes of representation distinguished by their avoidance and acknowledgment, respectively, of temporality in human existence; he proceeded from this contrast to build a critique of romantic ideology, esp. the romantics' celebration of symbol over allegory.

**B.** *Interpretation.* Once we know that something in the figurative inventory of a poem is symbolic, we need to see how it became so and, therefore, what it means. As a final practical suggestion, we will inquire into the various ways in which links may be established between a figure and an idea to form a symbol.

(1) The connection, as in metaphor and simile, may be based on resemblance, as mentioned above. A great many natural and universal symbols arise in this way: accomplishing something is like climbing a mountain, making a transition in life is like a journey to a new land, and so on. Examples are to be found everywhere in poetry (Bevan, Kimpel, Frye, Douglas, Embler), as well as in everyday usage.

(2) The link may evolve into an associative connection by virtue of repetition, as when a metaphor or simile is repeated so often, either in the work of a

single author or in literary trad., that the vehicle can be used alone to summon up the tenor to which it was usually attached, somewhat in the manner of a code. An example is found by comparing Stéphane Mallarmé's swan imagery in "Le Vierge, le vivace et le bel aujourd'hui" with Yeats's in "Leda and the Swan" and "Among School Children."

(3) The connection may be based on the internal relationships that obtain among the elements of a given work, whereby one thing becomes associated with another by virtue of structural emphasis, arrangement, position, or devel. (which is, of course, true to some degree in all works containing symbols). Examples are the wall as division between the primitive and civilized in Robert Frost, the guitar and the color blue as the aesthetic imagination in Wallace Stevens, and the island as complacency and the sea as courage in W. H. Auden.

(4) The connection may be based on primitive and magical associations, as when the loss of a man's hair symbolizes the loss of strength (Samson) or the rejection of worldly desires (monastic and ascetic practice), not because of any resemblance between them but rather because a mythic and ritualistic relationship has been established among secondary sex characteristics, virility, and desire. The underlying sterility/fertility symbolism in T. S. Eliot's *The Waste Land* is a conspicuous example.

(5) The connection may be derived from a particular historical convention, such as the transmutation of lead to gold as redemption, the lily as chastity and the rose as passion, or the fish as Christ (Hirst). A noted poetic instance is Yeats's use of the Rosy Cross, derived from Rosicrucianism, to symbolize the joining of flesh and spirit.

(6) The connection may derive from some private system invented by the poet—e.g., the phases of the moon as the cycles of hist. combined with the psychology of individuals in Yeats, or embalmment as an obstacle that cannot be overcome in the attempt to resurrect the spirit in Dylan Thomas (Olson 1954).

Critics rightly warn that symbolic associations should be neither too explicit nor too fixed, for implications of this sort are better felt than explained and they vary from work to work depending on the individual context (see, e.g., Carlson, Mischel, Cary, Wimsatt 1965, and Todorov).

*See* CONNOTATION AND DENOTATION, CONVENTION, POLYSEMY.

■ W. B. Yeats, "The Symbolism of Poetry," *Ideas of Good and Evil* (1903); H. Bayley, *The Lost Language of Symbolism*, 2 v. (1912); D. A. Mackenzie, *The Migration of Symbols* (1926); I. A. Richards, *Science and Poetry* (1926); A. N. Whitehead, *Symbolism* (1927); H. F. Dunbar, *Symbolism in Medieval Thought* (1929); E. Bevan, *Symbolism and Belief* (1938); W. M. Urban, *Language and Reality* (1939); K. Burke, *The Philosophy of Literary Form* (1941); S. K. Langer, *Philosophy in a New Key* (1942); C. M. Bowra, *The Heritage of Symbolism* (1943); E. Cassirer, *An Essay on Man* (1944), and *Language and Myth*, trans. S. Langer (1946); E. W. Carlson, "The Range of Symbolism in Poetry," *South Atlantic Quarterly* 48 (1949); M. Foss, *Symbol and Metaphor in Human Experience* (1949); R. Hertz, *Chance and Symbol* (1949); R. A. Brower, *The Fields of Light* (1951); E. Fromm, *The Forgotten Language* (1951); T. Mischel, "The Meanings of 'Symbol' in Literature," *Arizona Quarterly* 8 (1952); E. Olson, "A Dialogue on Symbolism," Crane; "Symbol and Symbolism," spec. iss., *YFS* 9 (1952); H. D. Duncan, *Language and Literature in Society* (1953); C. Feidelson Jr., *Symbolism in American Literature* (1953); "Symbolism," spec. iss., *JAAC* 12 (1953); E. Cassirer, *The Philosophy of Symbolic Forms*, trans. R. Manheim, 3 v. (1953–57); B. Kimpel, *The Symbols of Religious Faith* (1954); E. Olson, *The Poetry of Dylan Thomas* (1954); P. Wheelwright, *The Burning Fountain* (1954); W. K. Wimsatt, *The Verbal Icon* (1954); *Symbols and Values* (1954) and *Symbols and Society* (1955), both ed. L. Bryson et al.; F. F. Nesbit, *Language, Meaning and Reality* (1955); W. Y. Tindall, *The Literary Symbol* (1955); Wellek and Warren, ch. 15; Frye; F. Kermode, *Romantic Image* (1957); S. K. Langer, *Problems of Art* (1957); J. Cary, *Art and Reality* (1958); E. Honig, *Dark Conceit* (1959); J. W. Beach, *Obsessive Images* (1960); *Literary Symbolism*, ed. M. Beebe (1960); *Metaphor and Symbolism*, ed. L. C. Knights and B. Cottle (1960); B. Seward, *The Symbolic Rose* (1960); *Symbolism in Religion and Literature*, ed. R. May (1960); H. Musurillo, *Symbol and Myth in Ancient Poetry* (1961); E. Sewell, *The Orphic Voice* (1961); T. J. Kuhn, *The Structure of Scientific Revolutions* (1962); R. Ross, *Symbols and Civilization* (1962); *Truth, Myth, and Symbol*, ed. T.J.J. Altizer et al. (1962); P. Wheelwright, *Metaphor and Reality* (1962); *Myth and Symbol*, ed. B. Slote (1963); A. Fletcher, *Allegory* (1964); D. Hirst, *Hidden Riches* (1964); E. Sewell, *The Human Metaphor* (1964); *Literary Symbolism*, ed. H. Rehder (1965); W. K. Wimsatt, *Hateful Contraries* (1965); K. Burke, *Language as Symbolic Action* (1966); W. Embler, *Metaphor and Meaning* (1966); G. Hough, *An Essay on Criticism* (1966); N. Goodman, *Languages of Art* (1968); *Perspectives on Literary Symbolism*, ed. J. P. Strelka (1968); R. Wellek, "Symbol and Symbolism in Literature," *DHI*; R. L. Brett, *Fancy and Imagination* (1969); H. D. Duncan, *Symbols and Social Theory* (1969); C. Hayes, "Symbol and Allegory," *Germanic Review* 44 (1969); *Interpretation*, ed. C. S. Singleton (1969); M. Douglas, *Natural Symbols* (1970); P. Fingesten, *The Eclipse of Symbolism* (1970); C. Chadwick, *Symbolism* (1971); J. R. Barth, *The Symbolic Imagination* (1977); R. Rorty, *Philosophy and the Mirror of Nature* (1979); *Symbol, Myth, and Culture*, ed. D. P. Verene (1979); *Literature, Criticism and Myth*, ed. J. P. Strelka (1980); *Allegory, Myth, and Symbol*, ed. M. Bloomfield (1981); J. D. Culler, *On Deconstruction* (1982); T. Todorov, *Theories of the Symbol*, and *Symbolism and Interpretation*, both trans. C. Porter (1982); H. Adams, *Philosophy of the Literary Symbolic* (1983); R. Bartel, *Metaphors and Symbols* (1983); de Man, "The Rhetoric of Temporality"; J. Whitman, "From the Textual to the Temporal: Early Christian 'Allegory' and Early Romantic 'Symbol,'" *NLH* 22 (1991); Morier; D. Fried, "The Politics of the Coleridgean Symbol," *SEL* 46 (2006); N. Halmi, *The Genesis of the Romantic*

*Symbol* (2007); R. E. Innis, "The Making of the Literary Symbol: Taking Note of Langer," *Semiotica* 165 (2007).

N. FRIEDMAN

## SYMBOLISM

I. Origins and Characteristics
II. History and Evolution
III. Criticism

A major artistic movement of the late 19th and early 20th cs., which included lit. (esp. poetry, but also drama and prose), visual arts, and music. Like many "-isms," it is impossible to define precisely; some of its leading practitioners avoided the term entirely, while others embraced it but construed it idiosyncratically. It is often associated with other labels—*decadence, *aestheticism, neoromanticism, *hermeticism, *modernismo, and *imagism. As a self-conscious "school," symbolism had its greatest flowering in France and, somewhat later, in Russia; however, it was a truly pan-Eur. phenomenon, in one way or another influencing major figures in most national lit. trads., e.g., R. M. Rilke and Stefan George in Germany; Hugo von Hofmannsthal in Austria; Federico García Lorca in Spain; Gabriele D'Annunzio in Italy; and W. B. Yeats, T. S. Eliot, and Ezra Pound in the Eng.-speaking world. Fr. symbolism also left an indelible mark on South America (esp. in the seminal work of Rubén Darío) and in Asia, both in Japan, where Ueda Bin's trans. of Fr. poetry had an enormous impact on subsequent poets, and in China, notably in the work of Lin Jinfa and Dai Wangshu.

**I. Origins and Characteristics.** The word *symbol* goes back to the Greek noun *symbolon* (sign, token), suggesting things that are split in two and need to be rejoined to obtain their full value. Since the concept of the *symbol is found in virtually all cultures, it can hardly be seen as the distinctive feature of the symbolist movement. What distinguishes the symbolists is not their reliance on symbols, but rather their understanding of the term, which drew on Ger. aesthetic thought of the 18th and early 19th cs. As part of this trad., J. W. Goethe praised "symbol" at the expense of "*allegory," the former being dynamic, the latter schematic. According to his argument, a symbol does not function as a standard *metaphor (naming one thing by another), but rather as a *synecdoche, using a specific instance to designate a general principle or abstract concept. Goethe intimated (and the symbolists developed this line of thinking) that the symbol offered—if only fleetingly—a means of reaching beyond a physical phenomenon to the otherwise inexpressible realm of the eternal. Neither Goethe nor the symbolists recognized a fixed one-to-one correspondence between the physical and the metaphysical; few poems attempt to spell out a specific "meaning" of the symbol. Charles Baudelaire's sonnet "Correspondances," often seen as a seminal text of symbolism, features a typically elusive exploration of nature's "forests of symbols." To the symbolist, symbols are multivalent, allowing broad interpretive possibilities. As Yeats wrote in an essay on P. B. Shelley: "It is only by symbols that have numberless meanings . . . that any highly subjective art can escape from the barrenness and shallowness of a too conscious arrangement, into the abundance and depth of nature." According to such a conception, the rose is not simply a symbol of love or of death but a combination of all the significations it has possessed in countless cultures through the ages.

In contrast to decadence and naturalism, both of which denied the existence of a world beyond the quotidian, symbolism considered physical reality either a distorted reflection or a too-faint echo of the world of essences. The paradigm of the former would be Plato's cave allegory, of the latter the mystical *Tabula smaragdina* (emerald tablet) of Hermes Trismegistus, according to which "things below are copies." Establishing a connection to a higher, spiritual reality was a symbolist preoccupation. However, there was little consensus on how to achieve this goal. One finds a range of possibilities within symbolism, at times within the work of a single poet: (1) a theory of discovery, whereby maximum receptivity (contemplation of the natural world) leads directly to a visionary moment; (2) a theory of invention, requiring a heroic act of will to transform the phenomenal world; (3) a recognition of an inability to achieve true transcendence, hence a focus on the moment of anticipation that precedes it. A fourth position, which disregards the very possibility of transcendence and luxuriates in the world's imminent demise, should be labeled as decadent, not symbolist; but it can be found with some frequency in the works of the symbolists, whether as a pose or as a conviction (Paul Verlaine's "Je suis l'Empire à la fin de la décadence," Valerii Briusov's "Griadushchie gunny" [Coming Huns]).

The Rus. symbolist Viacheslav Ivanov formulated the symbolist program with the slogan *a realibus ad realiora* (from the real to the more real). To receive access to the "more real" demanded a special type of visionary poet and poetic technique. Symbolists were open to virtually any means of encountering this mysterious "other" world—from erudite studies of philosophy (Plato and the Neoplatonists), religion (orgiastic cults of antiquity, med. mystics), lit., and myth (of all nations) to immersion in hermeticism (magic, astrology, alchemy, the occult), and experiments in personal life with séances, alcohol, and mind-altering drugs. Symbolist perception reflected what Stéphane Mallarmé called "changes in our basic mental disposition." It was apt to mix the senses—hence the centrality of *synaesthesia from Baudelaire's "Correspondances" to Arthur Rimbaud's "Voyelles," where each vowel is assigned a color, to the composer Alexander Scriabin, who assigned specific colors to musical keys and chords.

Musicality is arguably a part of all poetry, but the extent to which the symbolists turned to music was unprecedented. Ger. aesthetic thought prepared the way: Arthur Schopenhauer had granted music the highest status of the arts. Richard Wagner's operas exemplified the marriage of text and music, and his notion of the *Gesamtkunstwerk* encouraged a wide range of theories about the synthesis of the arts. The first Fr. symbolist journal was called *La Revue Wagnerienne*, and the vogue for Wagner can be traced through the Rus. periodical lit. as well. Music frequently enters symbolist poetry as a theme but also as an ideal. In his programmatic "Art poétique," Verlaine insisted on the nature of poetry as "Music above all else" ("De la musique avant toute chose"); the very title of his book *Romances sans paroles* (Songs without Words) underlines this musical orientation. In Russia, Andrei Bely (pseud. of Boris Bugayev) initiated his career by writing "symphonies," rhythmic prose works divided into "movements" and using numbered leitmotifs. Another way to create a musical quality in poetry was technical, based on a high degree of *assonance or *alliteration that produced an effect of incantation, e.g., Verlaine's "Chanson d'automne" or Konstantin Bal'mont's "Pesnia bez slov" (Song without Words). Often the symbolist poet chooses words on the strength of their sound rather than their sense or, put another way, believes that specific sounds supply a priori meanings. The most abstract of the arts, music was praised for its suggestivity, a means of hinting at something without actually naming it. The creation of a mood, rather than a precise subject, aligned symbolist poetry with music, and it made new demands on the reader.

The interest in music led to increased attention to formal questions of verse. René Ghil sought to determine a scientific basis for the correlation between instrumental sound and sound combinations in poetic lang. Other Fr. symbolists (e.g., Gustave Kahn) argued for a return to med. verse forms and irregular line length. Some of the most important work of Baudelaire and Rimbaud is in the form of prose poems, a genre that takes the immediacy and musicality of poetry without its formal constraints. The Rus. symbolists likewise extended the technical possibilities of verse; they domesticated *accentual verse, esp. the *dol'nik, which was introduced by Zinaida Gippius and canonized by Alexander Blok, and intricate Eur. models, ranging from sapphic stanzas to *terza rima. They initiated a *sonnet renaissance, including such tours de force as the crown of sonnets and the *sonetto di risposta* (a sonnet written in response to another, using the same rhymes).

Though inspiration could not be taught—and the symbolists believed in the Poet with the capital letter, the seer—they also believed in craft. E. A. Poe's "The Philosophy of Composition" was a key precursor text. In both France and Russia, poetry circles were formed around a venerable figure. The Tuesday meetings led by Mallarmé had their counterpart a decade later in the Wednesday symposia at Ivanov's Tower in St. Petersburg. Stefan George, who had visited Mallarmé's gatherings, created a similar circle in Germany. These meetings had a major impact on their respective national cultures, serving as both a training ground for young poets and a locus for open philosophical colloquy.

The themes of symbolism are perhaps its least distinctive feature. The Fr. symbolist landscape is marked by repeated images: gray skies; a variety of birds and flying creatures such as fireflies and bees; a topography of wastelands, glaciers, stagnant pools, frozen parks, fossilized and shining stones. These melancholy vistas suggest an end-of-the-world lassitude, a notion of festering beauty, a general sense of mortality, but also the possibility of an encounter with the absolute. Themes of Rus. symbolism range from "decadent" ennui, demonism (often in specifically Rus. variants), and urban debauchery (influenced by Baudelaire) to the eternal feminine (originating in Goethe but refracted through Rus. Sophiology) and Russia herself as a force of mystical renewal.

Though lyric poetry was the central genre of symbolism, drama was by no means neglected. Many of the major symbolist poets turned to the theater; but few of their plays were successful, and virtually none has entered the permanent repertoire. This drama tended to eschew conflict between characters in favor of dream or reflection. Psychology—in terms of standard human motivations (greed, revenge, power)—is often entirely absent. Even love is on a purely spiritual plane, hence the absence of traditional love plots. The characters, faceless or masked, exist in a mythical or undefined place with little resemblance to the contemp. world. The lang. is hieratic, often in verse, consciously avoiding the vernacular. Symbolist theater mystified an audience accustomed to realist drama, yet it left a significant legacy to the 20th c. in terms of acting, directing, and *mise en scène*. Its static quality (repetition of action, of key words, and even of entire phrases) and spiritual nature forced directors to think about presentation, about redefining the relationship of actor and audience. This theater aspired to music; it is noteworthy that Maurice Maeterlinck's drama *Pelléas et Mélisande* is now known only as the source of the libretto for Claude Debussy's opera. It is likewise revealing that Vsevelod Meyerhold, the great innovator of "antirealist" modernist theater, was a champion of Rus. symbolist drama, directing and playing the lead role in Blok's *Balaganchik* (*The Puppet Booth*). Meyerhold applauded and tried to implement Ivanov's idea that the theater should remove the physical and spiritual boundaries that separate audience and actor, uniting them in the spirit of religious rites of antiquity.

In France, the concept of the novel with its centrality of narrative was generally viewed as inimical to symbolism (J.-K. Huysmans's work, e.g., is not considered symbolist, but rather decadent.) However, the Rus. symbolists produced any number of plot-oriented novels, the best of which were admired in their own time and are now canonical. Fyodor Sologub's *Melkii bes* (*The Petty Demon*), at once an homage and a parody of the great Rus. 19th-c. novelistic trad., gives an unforgettable picture of the madness of a sadistic provincial schoolteacher. While Sologub grounds his style in the prose of his realist predecessors, Bely produced a true symbolist prose, unique and immediately recognizable in its syntax, punctuation, repetitions of words and phrases, sound orchestration, and protocubist portrayals of people and scenes. *Serebrianyi golub'* (*The Silver*

*Dove*) revolves around a poet's encounter with an orgiastic cult of provincial sectarians, while the urban *Petersburg* concerns the revolutionary events of 1905 as reflected in the family of a high-ranking civil servant.

Both personally and spiritually, the symbolists had close ties to visual art. Virtually all the significant Fr. artists of the period (e.g., the Nabis and the Pont Aven school, as well as Georges Seurat and Paul Gauguin) were in one way or another connected to symbolism. Some of Verlaine's most celebrated poems (*Fêtes galantes*) were inspired by Antoine Watteau. The impressionist Edouard Manet, a close friend of Mallarmé, illustrated the poet's "L'Après-midi d'un faune" as well as his prose trans. of Poe's "The Raven." Leading Fr. symbolist artists include Pierre Puvis de Chavannes and Odilon Redon; the latter produced lithographs for Mallarmé's *Un coup de dés*. Redon was acquainted with a number of Rus. symbolists as well, and his work was featured in an issue of the Rus. symbolist journal *Libra*. Though Mikhail Vrubel's dreamlike canvases were the fullest visual expression of the Rus. symbolist spirit, the symbolists themselves were more closely affiliated with members of the Petersburg *Mir isskustva* (World of Art) movement, noted esp. for its interest in "prerealist" depictions of earlier, more stylized epochs.

## II. History and Evolution.

Scholars of Fr. lit. usually distinguish between the small group of minor poets who consciously called themselves symbolists and the truly major poets who either predated the term (Baudelaire and to a considerable extent Mallarmé, who had written most of his work before the movement existed) or were simply not eager to accept this appellation (Verlaine, Rimbaud). The term *symbolism* was coined in 1885 by Jean Moréas (pseud. of Jean Papadiamantopoulos, a Gr. by nationality, living in Paris), who used it in contradistinction to *decadence*. Moréas was soon forgotten, and he himself rejected the movement within a few years. However, the name caught on and came to be associated with all Fr. poetry of the period and subsequently with kindred souls such as Paul Valéry and Paul Claudel. Symbolism was less a Fr. phenomenon than a Parisian one, which is to say that Paris, as the cultural capital of Europe, attracted aspiring poets from all over the world and turned them into symbolists. Hence, the "Fr." symbolists include Belgians (Emile Verhaeren, Maeterlinck), Grs. like Moréas, and Ams. (Francis Viélé-Griffin and Stuart Merrill). The fact that Rilke, George, Hofmannsthal, Yeats, J. M. Synge, Miguel de Unamuno, and D'Annunzio gravitated to Paris by the end of the century ensured that the innovations of Fr. poetry would be widely disseminated.

In Russia, the first inklings of symbolism occurred in the early 1890s. Dimitri Merezhkovsky praised it as a method in an 1892 essay; a book of his poetry called *Symbols* appeared that same year. A year later Briusov published the first of three miscellanies called *Russian Symbolists*. The second, "younger" generation—so-called not because of their age but because of their later appearance on the cultural scene—includes Ivanov, Blok, and Bely, the movement's greatest theoretician, poet, and prose writer, respectively. This generation viewed the Fr. influence as superficial; they traced their inspiration to Rus. sources—esp. the romantic poet Fyodor Tiutchev, the "realist" novelist Fyodor Dostoevsky, the mystic philosopher Vladimir Soloviev—and to Germany (Goethe, Novalis, Friedrich Nietzsche, Wagner). Since both generations often collaborated, the distinction is largely heuristic, indicating tendencies subject to exception. However, the younger symbolists were more overtly philosophical and religious. They had a more ambitious program; in their thinking, symbolism is a worldview, a means for cognizing, changing and—in Bely's conception—even creating reality.

## III. Criticism.

Fr. critics consider the label *symbolist* applicable to poets in the 15-year period of 1885–1900. Non-Fr. critics go back to Baudelaire and include Verlaine, Mallarmé, and Rimbaud. Although Rimbaud coexisted with the symbolists, his theories about the poet as "seer" emerged in his "*voyant*" letter (see SURREALISM) published posthumously in 1912. Edmund Wilson's *Axel's Castle* (1931; the title refers to a play by Auguste Villiers de l'Isle-Adam) popularized the symbolist movement in America, as did Arthur Symons's *The Symbolist Movement in Literature* (1899, rev. 1919)—dedicated to and admired by Yeats—in England and Ireland. Though symbolism dominated Rus. cultural life in the first decade of the 20th c., its hegemony was forcefully challenged by other movements (e.g., *acmeism and *futurism) and its legacy distorted by political events. With the exception of Blok (whose ambiguous poem *The Twelve* was read as a canonic Soviet text), the Rus. symbolists were rarely republished or studied in the USSR.

*See* FRANCE, POETRY OF; IMAGERY; POÈTE MAUDIT; PURE POETRY; ROMANTIC AND POSTROMANTIC POETRY AND POETICS; RUSSIA, POETRY OF.

■ **Bibliographies:** H. Krawitz, *A Post-Symbolist Bibliography* (1973); D. L. Anderson, *Symbolism: A Bibliography* (1975). P. Davidson, *Viacheslav Ivanov: A Reference Guide* (1996).

■ **Criticism:** A. Symons, *The Symbolist Movement in Literature* (1899, rev. ed. 1919); R. Taupin, *L'Influence du symbolisme français sur la poésie américaine (de 1910 À 1920)*, rev., trans., and ed. W. Pratt ([1929] 1985); E. Wilson, *Axel's Castle* (1931); M. Raymond, *De Baudelaire au surréalisme* (1933); P. Valéry, *Existence du Symbolisme* (1939); S. Johansen, *Le Symbolisme* (1945); G. Michaud, *Message poétique du symbolisme*, 3 v. (1947), and *Documents* (1947); T. S. Eliot, *From Poe to Valéry* (1948); A. G. Lehman, *The Symbolist Aesthetic in France (1885–95)* (1950); K. Cornell, *The Symbolist Movement* (1951); *Index du vocabulaire du symbolisme*, ed. P. Guiraud, (1953–60); *RR* 46.3 (1955)—spec. iss.; K. Cornell, *The Post-Symbolist Period* (1958); G. Donchin, *The Influence of French Symbolism on Russian Poetry* (1958); H. M. Block, *Mallarmé and the Symbolist Drama* (1963); P. Ricoeur, "Le Symbolisme et l'explication structurale," *Cahiers Internationaux du Symbolisme* 4 (1964); A. Balakian, *The Symbolist Movement* (1967);

R. Wellek, "The Term and Concept of Symbolism in Literary History," *Discriminations* (1970); T. Todorov, *Théories du symbole* (1977), trans. C. Porter (1982); J. P. Houston, *French Symbolism and the Modernist Movement* (1980); *An Anthology of French Symbolist Poetry*, ed. J. P. Houston and M. T. Houston (1980); *Symbolism*, ed. T. G. West (1980); K. Tu, "The Introduction of French Symbolism into Modern Chinese and Japanese Poetry," *Tamkang Review* 10 (1980); *The Symbolist Movement in the Literature of European Languages*, ed. A. Balakian (1982); P. Florence, *Mallarmé, Manet and Rodin* (1986); *Andrey Bely*, ed. J. E. Malmstad (1987); D. M. Hertz, *The Tuning of the Word* (1987); P. Hoffmann, *Symbolismus* (1987); J. Kearns, *Symbolist Landscapes* (1989); W. Fowlie, *Poem and Symbol* (1990); K. Newmark, *Beyond Symbolism* (1991); A. Pyman, *A History of Russian Symbolism* (1994); *Creating Life: The Aesthetic Utopia of Russian Modernism*, ed. J. Grossman and I. Paperno (1994); R. Keys, *The Reluctant Modernist: Bely and Russian Fiction* (1996); A. Wanner, *Baudelaire in Russia* (1996); S. Morrison, *Russian Opera and the Symbolist Movement* (2002); O. Matich, *Erotic Utopia* (2005); J. Acquisto, *French Symbolist Poetry and the Idea of Music* (2006).

M. WACHTEL

**SYNAERESIS** (Gr., "drawing together"). The coalescing of two contiguous vowels within a word, usually for metrical purposes, e.g., *theoi* for *thĕoï* (*Iliad* 1.18) or *Thĕudŏsĭŭs* for *Thĕŏdŏsĭŭs*. Strictly speaking, synaeresis in Gr. denotes coalescing, where the second vowel is iota or upsilon, in order to form a diphthong. This is indicated in Gr. by the cornois mark (equivalent to smooth breathing). The term is often confused with or synonymous with synizesis, *syncope*, and *synaloepha*. An Eng. example would be "seest" for "seëst." In the opening line of *Paradise Lost*, "Of Man's First Disobedience, and the Fruit," the *ie* in "Disobedience" changes to what is called a "y-glide," reducing the word from five syllables to four. But to some degree, synaeresis is simply a normal linguistic process frequently carried on in ordinary speech, of which the poet takes advantage for writing verse with regulated syllable count: several words have syllabically alternative forms, e.g., "heaven" as both disyllable and monosyllable. Coalescing of vowels across a word boundary (end of one word, beginning of next) is synaloepha.

*See* ELISION.

■ Allen; Morier; West.

T.V.F. BROGAN; R. A. HORNSBY; J. W. HALPORN

**SYNAESTHESIA.** The phenomenon in which one sense is felt, perceived, or described in terms of another, e.g., describing a voice as velvety or sweet or a trumpet blast as scarlet ("To the bugle," says Emily Dickinson, "every color is red"). In poetics, it is usually considered a species of *metaphor. Evidence for synaesthesia in lit. is ancient and cross-cultural; its critical conceptualization in the West, however, dates from the 18th c., and a specific term for it appeared only in 1891 (*Century Dictionary*). In the literary sense, it seems to have been first employed by Jules Millet in 1892. Synaesthesia

was popularized by two *sonnets, Charles Baudelaire's "Correspondances" (1857) and Arthur Rimbaud's "Voyelles" (1871), as well as by J.-K. Huysmans's novel *À rebours* (1884); from these sources, it became one of the central tenets of *symbolism. The device had been widely employed earlier in Ger. and Eng. romantic poetry, and it also can be found in some of the earliest lit. of the West (in the *Iliad* 3.152, the voices of the old Trojans are likened to the "lily-like" voices of cicadas; in the *Iliad* 3.222, Odysseus's words fall like winter snowflakes; and in the *Odyssey* 12.187, in the "honeyvoice" of the Sirens). In Aeschylus's *Persians* (395), "the trumpet set all the shores ablaze with its sound." In the Bible, Heb. 6.5 and Rev. 1.12 refer to "tasting" the word of God and "seeing" a voice. Dante refers to a place "where the sun is silent" (*Inferno* 1.60). John Donne mentions a "loud perfume," Richard Crashaw a "sparkling noyse." P. B. Shelley refers to the fragrance of the hyacinth as "music," Heinrich Heine to words "sweet as moonlight and delicate as the scent of the rose."

Synaesthesia as the expression of intersense analogues has been exploited in lit. for a variety of effects, particularly increase of textural richness, complication, and unification. It is evident that other kinds of metaphor, esp. in the *tenor and vehicle model, and *simile can also approximate the same kinds of suggestion, albeit in looser and more taxonomic forms. Shelley, one of the first Eng. poets to use synaesthesia extensively, employs it particularly in connection with visionary and mystical states of transcendental union ("Alastor," "Epipsychidion," "The Triumph of Life"); in these, synaesthesia suggests not only a greater "refinement and complexity of sensuous experience" but a "harmony or synthesis of all sensations" and a kind of "supersensuous unity" (O'Malley 1964). Cf. Baudelaire's "métamorphose mystique / De tous mes sens fondus en un" ("Toute Entière").

Because of its susceptibility to modify "inappropriate" objects (Meltzer), color has a long hist. of metaphorical richness, and the critical lit. has paid particular attention to it. One important species of synaesthesia is *audition colorée*, in which sound (or even silence) is described in terms of colors. Silence is "perfumed" (Rimbaud), "black" (Pindar, Peretz Markish), "dark" (James Macpherson, *Ossian*), "green" (Giosuè Carducci, Georg Trakl), "silver" (Oscar Wilde), "blue" (Gabriele D'Annunzio), "purple" (David Fogel), "chill" (Edith Sitwell), "green water" (Louis Aragon). Perhaps the most famous example of the use of synaesthesia in poetry is Rimbaud's sonnet "Voyelles" (Vowels) beginning "A noir, E blanc, I rouge, U vert, O bleu, voyelles . . ." Such terms as "golden voice," *coloratura soprano*, "chromatic scale," Ger. *Klangfarbe* (sound-color; see TIMBRE) show the assimilation of audition colorée into both common and scholarly usage. More important still is the "light–dark" opposition in vowels first demonstrated by Köhler in 1910 and subsequently shown to exist in many of the world's langs.: Köhler argued that this opposition is not merely metaphorical but, in fact, a feature of all the senses resulting from some "central physiological perceptual correlate."

The related term *synaesthesis* appears in the late 19th c. in the course of evolving psychological theories of beauty to mean a wholeness in perception or anti-atomism in epistemology. I. A. Richards takes up this term for his psychological theory of crit. as part of his neurologically derived account of literary value (*Principles of Literary Criticism*, 1925): he too uses it in the sense of "wholeness" to refer to the synergistic nature of sense-experience, wherein wholes, "sensation-complexes," are greater than the sum of their parts (see UNITY).

The increasing interest in synaesthesia not only in psychology but in neuroscience, ling., and other fields has enhanced the interest in, and study of, literary synaesthesia. Literary critics have begun looking at various kinds of pseudosynaesthesia or "conceptual synaesthesia" (Sacks)—i.e., the use of concepts or other nonsensory objects as sensory data—to understand better the metaphorical relationships between the senses and how this metaphorical resource is used in the construction of poetic discourses.

*See* COGNITIVE POETICS, PSYCHOLOGY AND POETICS.

■ **Criticism, General**: W. Köhler, "Akustische Untersuchungen," *Zeits. für Psychologie* 54–72 (1910–15); J. E. Downey, "Literary Synesthesia," *Journal of Philosophy, Psychology and Scientific Methods* 9 (1912); A. Wellek, "Das Doppelempfinden im abendländischen Altertum und Mittelalter," and "Zur Geschichte und Kritik des Synästhesie-Forschung," *Archiv für die gesamte Psychologie* 79–80 (1931); W. B. Stanford, *Greek Metaphor* (1936) and "Synaesthetic Metaphor," *Comparative Literature Studies* 6–7 (1942); A. G. Engstrom, "In Defense of Synaesthesia in Literature," *PQ* 25 (1946); S. Ullmann, *The Principles of Semantics* (1951); G. O'Malley, "Literary Synesthesia," *JAAC* 15 (1957); L. Schrader, *Sinne und Sinnesverknüpfungen* (1969)—synaesthesia in It., Sp., and Fr.; P. Ostwald, *The Semiotics of Human Sound* (1973); P. E. Dombi, "Synaesthesia and Poetry," *Poetics* 3 (1974); L. Vinge, *The Five Senses* (1975); S. Sandbank, *Shtei Breikhot Ba-ya'ar* (Two Pools in the Wood, 1976); L. E. Marks, *The Unity of the Senses* (1978); D. Johnson, "The Role of Synaesthesia in Jakobson's Theory of Language," *International Journal of Slavic Linguistics and Poetics* 25–26 (1982); L. E. Marks, "Synesthetic Perception and Poetic Metaphor," *Journal of Experimental Psychology: Human Perception and Performance* 8 (1982); L. E. Marks, "Synesthetic and the Arts," *Advances in Psychology* 19 (1984); J. H. Ryalls, "Synaesthesia," *Semiotica* 58 (1986); J. P. Russo, *I. A. Richards* (1989); R. Tsur, "Literary Synaesthesia," *Hebrew Linguistics* 28–30 (1990); J. Harrison and S. Baron-Cohen, "Synaesthesia," *Leonardo* 27 (1994); R. Tsur, "Picture Poetry, Mannerism, and Sign Relationships," *PoT* 21 (2000); A. Motoyoshi, "Sensibility and Synaesthesia," *Journal of Arabic Literature* 32 (2001); R. E. Cytowic, *Synesthesia* (2002); O. Sacks, *Musicophilia* (2008).

■ **Criticism, Poets**: W. Silz, "Heine's Synaesthesia," *PMLA* 57 (1942); E. Noulet, *Le premier visage de Rimbaud* (1953); C. F. Roeding, "Baudelaire and Synaesthesia," *Kentucky Foreign Language Quarterly* 5 (1958); G. Guder, "The Meaning of Colour in Else

Lasker-Schüler's Poetry," *German Life and Letters* 14 (1961); R. H. Fogle, "Synaesthetic Imagery in Keats," *Keats*, ed. W. J. Bate (1964); G. O'Malley, *Shelley and Synaesthesia* (1964); R. Étiemble, *Le Sonnet des voyelles* (1968); G. Cambon, "Synaesthesia in the *Divine Comedy*," *Dante Studies with the Annual Report of the Dante Society* 88 (1970); N. Ruddick, "Synaesthesia in Emily Dickinson's Poetry," *PoT* 5 (1984); J. Finkin, "Markish, Trakl, and the Temporaesthetic," *Modernism/Modernity* 15 (2008).

■ **Criticism, Senses and Movements**: J. Millet, *Audition colorée* (1892); V. Ségalen, "Les synesthésies et l'école symboliste," *Mercure de France* 42 (1902); I. Babbitt, *The New Laokoön* (1910)—attacks synaesthesia as decadent; E. von Erhardt-Siebold, "Synäksthesien in der englischen Dichtung des 19. Jahrhunderts," *Englische Studien* 53 (1919–20); A. Argelander, *Das Farbenhören und der synästhetische Faktor der Wahrnehmung* (1927); E. von Erhardt-Siebold, "Harmony of the Senses in English, German, and French Romanticism," *PMLA* 47 (1932); S. de Ullmann, "Romanticism and Synaesthesia," *PMLA* 60 (1945); A. H. Whitney, "Synaesthesia in Twentieth-Century Hungarian Poetry," *Slavonic and East European Review* 30 (1952); K. Mautz, "Dir Farbensprache der expressionistischen Lyrik," *Deutsche Vierteljahrschrift für Literaturwissenschaft und Geistesgeschichte* 31 (1957); M. Chastaing, "Audition colorée," *Vie et langage* 105, 112 (1960, 1961); F. Meltzer, "Color Cognition in Symbolist Verse," *CritI* 5 (1978).

T.V.F. BROGAN; A. G. ENGSTROM; J. FINKIN

**SYNALOEPHA**, synalepha, synalephe (Gr., "coalescing"). In *classical prosody, the term for all forms of elision in which two syllables are reduced to one. In mod. usage, it tends to be restricted to the coalescing of a vowel at the end of one word with one that begins the next word. *Crasis* (Gr., "mixture," "combination") is a synonymous term sometimes used for the fusion of a vowel or diphthong with another that follows, e.g., *haner* for *ho aner*, *kago* for *kai ego*, *onax* for *o anax*, and *mentan* for *mentoi an*. Synaloepha is not allowed in *French prosody—a final mute *e* followed by a vowel is simply elided—but is used liberally in It. In Sp., it is used moderately and generally unobtrusively. In Eng., it is a conspicuous feature of 17th- and 18th-cs. prosody, e.g., in works by John Milton and Alexander Pope, where it is used to maintain the syllabic conformity of lines. In metrical theory, therefore, synaloepha is the important mechanism affecting situations where the relation of metrical position to syllable is one to many, acting to reduce an excess of syllables. By contrast, *diaeresis affects the situation position : syllable = many:one. Coalescing of contiguous vowels within a word is *synaeresis.

*See* ELISION.

■ Koster; Allen (1973); West.

T.V.F. BROGAN; R. J. GETTY

**SYNAPHEIA** (Gr., "fastening together"). In cl. verse, prosodic continuity between any two syllables or syllable sequences that follow each other in delivery without interruption, as part of the same flow of sound. As a general rule, synapheia exists between all contiguous syllables that do not constitute the beginning and ending of separate, independent rhythmical sequences such as *stichos or *strophe. Even sequences in contrasting rhythms—the components of most *asynartete verses—could be "in synapheia" provided that neither one, taken by itself, constituted an autonomous rhythmical whole. Break in synapheia involved some sort of pause in delivery at word end—a pause long enough to legitimize juxtapositions of a final vowel or diphthong with a succeeding initial one that ordinarily count as objectionable instances of *hiatus and to lengthen a final syllable that would have been short under other circumstances (*brevis in longo* or final *anceps). The occurrence of either hiatus or *brevis in longo* in a poetic text is thus an indication that synapheia has been broken. Their absence, however, need not indicate that synapheia has been maintained: a break may simply have occurred at a point where there are no short syllables or contiguous vowels to reveal its presence—hence, some of the uncertainties that plague mod. eds. of Gr. lyric texts. In the absence of identifiable breaks in synapheia, it can be difficult to know where one basic rhythmical unit ends and another begins.

*See* PERIOD, SYSTEM.

■ L. E. Rossi, "La sinafia," *Studi in onore di Anthos Ardizzoni* (1978).

A. T. COLE

**SYNCOPATION.** In mod. discussions of Gr. prosody, *syncopation* is a common way of referring to what musicians would call a "hold" or "rest," i.e., the suppression (*syncope*) of one syllable in a metrical pattern and the supplying of its time value either by a pause (usually notated by a dot or caret) or by protraction of an adjoining long syllable so that it becomes the durational equivalent of three or four shorts rather than two. These two phenomena are the "empty time length" (*kenos chronos*) and the "trisemic" ( ⏑__| ) or "tetrasemic" ( |__| ) longs of ancient metrical theory. Both have been regarded on occasion as peculiar to late—i.e., Hellenistic or post-Hellenistic—stages of Gr. versification, but their occurrence in the lyrics of Gr. drama—frequently where the rhythm is iambic or trochaic, sporadically elsewhere—is now widely accepted. It provides a plausible explanation for certain restrictions on the use of *resolution that all the dramatic poets observe when composing in those meters. In discussions of mod. prosody, however, the term *syncopation* is used only by those who hold that time, or particularly musical time, is the basis of metrical organization; and these theories are not widely accepted by post-19th c. theoreticians.

*See* LOGAOEDIC, ISOCHRONISM OR ISOCHRONY.

■ J. D. Denniston, "Lyric Iambics in Greek Drama," *Greek Poetry and Life, Essays Presented to Gilbert Murray* (1936); Dale, "Iambic, Trochaic and Iambo-Trochaic"; West, "Drama: Song," sect. IIIC; J. B. Lidov, "Alternating Rhythm in Archaic Greek Poetry," *Transactions of the American Philological Association* 119 (1989); E. C.

Kopff, "Diggle's Critique of Dale's Canon of Iambic Resolution," *La colometria antica dei testi poetici greci*, ed. B. Gentili and F. Perusino (1999).

A. T. COLE

**SYNCOPE** (Gr., "a cutting up"). The omission of a letter, syllable, or a sound from the middle of a word, related to *aphaeresis (initial omission) or *apocope (final omission). Punctuation is often used ("e'er" for "ever," "giv'n" for "given") to indicate syncope. Shakespeare's double syncope of "overtaken" removes excess syllables and exposes a rhyme: "She might have been o'erta'en; and yet she writes,/Pursuit would be but vain" (*All's Well That Ends Well,* 3.4). It may be used solely to approximate the sounds of speech. Paul Laurence Dunbar's "A Warm Day in Winter" offers both: "Missis gone a-drivin',/Mastah gone to shoot;/Ev'ry da'ky lazin'/In de sun to boot," where "Ev'ry" is shortened for either metrical rhythm or speed of dialect, but "da'ky" (for "darky") is strictly dialect.

*See* ELISION.

K. McFADDEN

**SYNECDOCHE** (Gr., "act of taking together," "understanding one thing with another"). A *trope (change of meaning) in which part is substituted for whole (hired "hands" for hired men); species for genus (live by the "sword" for weapons) or vice versa; or individual for group (the "Romans" won for the Roman army). Lausberg and Group μ, discussed below, would limit synecdoche to these types. In cl. rhet., synecdoche also includes material for the object made of it ("steel" for sword) and abstract quality for its possessor ("pride" for the person displaying it).

In 20th-c. attempts to organize the terminology inherited from rhet., one group of critics held that there are four basic tropes, and another claimed that there are only two. For discussion of these views, see METAPHOR and METONYMY. Definitions of synecdoche and metonymy have always overlapped. Both entail a material, factual, or conceptual connection to the literal meaning evoked. Genette and Eco show that the name of the trope can depend on how the example is interpreted.

Ruwet and Le Guern argue that most examples of synecdoche are not figurative: they either are part of ordinary usage or can be understood literally. The use of "tree" or "oak" for oak tree or "weapon" for pistol need not be considered synecdoche since the generic name can be applied literally to the species. Linguists find that purported instances of synecdoche often result from *ellipsis—deletion of a phrase that, if included, would be redundant. "A herd of thirty head" does not require "of cattle." "The animal that laughs" (man) and "the gods of blood and salt" (Mars and Neptune) can be classified as *periphrasis rather than as synecdoche with qualification. Thus, synecdoche can often be viewed as a stylistic phenomenon, its effect being dependent on whether it is expected in its context (Klinkenberg).

Todorov and Group μ reawakened interest in synecdoche with their claim that it is the fundamental figure, based on an increase or decrease of a word's semes (lexical features), from which metaphor and metonymy are derived. They found four possible changes of meaning in synecdoche: generalizing or particularizing, and material (part-whole) or conceptual (species-genus). "The enemy," meaning the enemies, is particularizing; the cl. example of part for whole is "sail" for ship; "mortal" for man is species for the genus.

Attempting to draw a clear distinction between metonymy and synecdoche, Sato and Seto suggest that synecdoche be limited to semantic or conceptual relations, with all material connections, such as part–whole, being assigned to metonymy. Meyer (1985) would limit the latter to contextual or accidental connections, synecdoche being a more abstract relation. Others see synecdoche as a figure of integration, metonymy representing fragmentation or reduction. Each of these views has something to recommend it, but evidence and logic do not show that any of them is correct. In popular usage and handbooks, "metonymy" usually includes all tropes that have been called synecdoche. This is especially true in ling. and fields such as conceptual metaphor theory and cognitive ling.

Synecdoche does remain important in one area of literary study. Like Burke, practitioners of *New Historicism show how lit. and life produce events representing the social structure as a whole. Burke's examples of the importance of synecdoche range from the traditional idea of microcosm and macrocosm to crucial issues of political representation. A character named Synecdoche in a Restoration play says, "By me a single Monarch makes himself a multitude . . . a whole Kingdome fits in Parliament at once." By the absolute ruler, as Thomas Hobbes said, "a multitude of men are made one person" (Christiansen, Baldo). Further examples of such representations appear in studies of synecdoche in Shakespeare's plays. The trope remains important in both sociology and anthropology (Parsons, Fernandez). Attempts to assign part-whole and species-genus relations to either metonymy or synecdoche eliminate the crucial space of their interaction, which is ideology. This is clear in anthropological studies, where synecdoche mediates between groups in the social structure and the species and genera found in nature. Analogous situations appear today. Synecdoche has become a crucial trope in arguments between environmentalists and commercial interests (Moore). Often appearing as a particular example representing the norm or ideal of the genus, synecdoche remains important in poetics, rhet., and other disciplines.

■ K. Burke, "Four Master Tropes," *A Grammar of Motives* (1945); T. Todorov, "Synecdoques," *Communications* 16 (1970); M. Le Guern, *Sémantique de la métaphore et de la métonymie* (1973); N. Ruwet, "Synecdoques et métonymies," *Poétique* 6 (1975); A. Parsons, "Interpretive Sociology," *Human Studies* 1 (1978); N. Sato, "Synecdoque, un trope suspect," *Revue d'esthétique* 1 (1979); B. Meyer, "Synecdoques du genre?" *Poétique* 57 (1980); Group μ; G. Genette, "Rhetoric Restrained," *Figures of Literary Discourse*, trans. A. Sheridan, 2d ed. (1982); J. Klinkenberg,

D. Bouverot, B. Meyer, G. Silingardi, J.-P. Schmitz in *Le Français moderne* 51 (1983); B. Meyer, "La synecdoque d'espèce," *Langues et Littératures* 3 (1983); U. Eco, "Metaphor, Dictionary, and Encyclopedia," *NLH* 15 (1984); B. Meyer, "Sous les pavés, la plage: Autour de la synecdoque du tout," *Poétique* 62 (1985); *Beyond Metaphor*, ed. J. Fernandez (1991); M. Moore, "Constructing Irreconcilable Conflict," *Communication Monographs* 60 (1993); J. Baldo, "Ophelia's Rhetoric, or Partial to Synecdoche," *Criticism* 37 (1995); Lausberg; K. Seto, "Distinguishing Metonymy from Synecdoche," *Metonymy in Language and Thought*, ed. K.-U. Panther and G. Radden (1999); N. Christiansen, "Synecdoche, Tropic Violence and Shakespeare's *Imitatio* in *Titus Andronicus*," *Style* 34 (2000); K. Acheson, "Hamlet, Synecdoche and History," *College Literature* 31 (2004).

W. Martin

**SYNTAX, POETIC** (Gr., *syntaxis*, "a putting together in order"). All oral and written lang. uses that fall under culturally specific definitions of poetry have *syntax*, if that term is defined as a meaning-making arrangement of words in a sequence. But not all poetries, oral or written, are distinguished from other discourses in ways that would allow us to say that they have poetic syntax, as opposed to syntax in general; nor is there scholarly consensus about what that former (poetic syntax) phrase might mean across different times, places, and langs. Mod. linguists have, for instance, noted parallels among ancient Gr., Ar., and Indian (Sanskrit) concepts of the *proposition* or *sentence*, a unit that Aristotle defined in his *Rhetoric* as expressing a "complete" thought and that has been foundational to many theories of syntax. But cross-cultural generalizations about syntax are difficult: problems of trans. arise not only between what linguists call *natural* langs. but also between competing professional metalanguages for describing syntactic features in relation to sometimes overlapping ones assigned to related areas such as grammar, morphology, phonemics, *semantics, and *rhetoric, with its many rules aimed at classifying and controlling the use of *tropes. Tropes in some taxonomic systems include a specific category of syntactic figures (figures of speech) recognized as such by virtue of their alleged deviation from what is thought to be ordinary or normal lang. use.

As a term that denotes both an object and a field of study, *syntax* has been decisively marked by the origins of the word itself in ancient Greece. The earliest uses of *syntaxis* have to do not with words or mathematical symbols but with soldiers. But many scholars have seen issues of hierarchy, governance, and obedience as no less critical to the workings of ling. syntax than they are to the workings of armies and of the societies that armies are thought to serve. Deutscher compares sentences to military maneuvers; in both, "chaos would prevail" without a chain of command subordinating some elements to others through rules that can be specified.

Metaphysically and socially charged debates about order are at the center of a Greco-Eur.-Eng. trad. of thinking about syntax in relation to poetry, a trad. that this article constructs provisionally and, of necessity, by relying in part on a terminology for syntax that some mod. theorists have critiqued as fundamentally inadequate to the understanding of ling. phenomena. The critiques come chiefly from those associated with the structuralist movement in ling. led by Ferdinand de Saussure (see STRUCTURALISM); this movement turns away—in conjunction with similar turns in many areas of modernist thought—from a mimetic or "substantialist" theory of lang. inscribed into the very notion of the noun as a "substantive." Structuralism directs us to a view of lang. as a fluid system constituted by differential relations among various elements. Acknowledging the philosophical problems in the substantialist trad. but acknowledging at the same time the continuing importance of that trad. for those who write, read, recite, hear, and reflect on poetry, this entry attempts a dialectical approach to the topic. The differential relations of "poetic syntax" are here considered as arising not only from a system of discourse that can be analyzed synchronically in terms of key binary oppositions (between "ordinary" and "extraordinary" word order, or poetry and prose, or poetry and science, or poetry and "not poetry"); the relations also arise along vectors of time, space, and trans. among some of the world's more than 6,000 (now extant) langs. We cannot know in how many of these langs. "syntax" and "poetry" exist as loci of historical influence, current practice, and reflection. The present entry assumes that what linguists call a "natural" lang. is not a unified entity; differently positioned and differently educated practitioners within a certain lang. field have construed and indeed encountered poetic syntax differently.

In the Greco-Eur.-Eng. trad. discussed here, "appropriate" syntactic arrangements have typically been seen as imitating an order given by nature or by logic. The latter is sometimes conceived as a subset of the former, but sometimes these two key strands of a "mimetic" trad. diverge, with interesting consequences for views of syntax (see MIMESIS). Those who see syntax primarily as reflecting an external reality have tended to focus on an *iconic* dimension of syntax, i.e., on ways in which the placement of words, phrases, clauses, and other units can be interpreted as imitating—and indeed as being determined by—a real sequence of events in "Nature" or in hist. Deutscher invokes Caesar's famous series of parallel clauses, *veni, vidi, vici* (I came, I saw, I conquered), to illustrate the principle that "the order in which events are expressed in language mirrors the order in which they occur in reality." (For Deutscher, it is only a joke, not a threat to Caesar's principle, that the first clause, in Lat. or in Eng., has a bawdy figurative meaning that allows the premise of a single natural order to expand into nine possibilities for ostensibly mimetic clause arrangement.)

A second major mimetic principle of syntax has been adduced—also debatably—to explain why grammatical subjects precede verbs and objects in a "majority" of the world's langs. (Dirven and Verspoor, Deutscher). A natural hierarchy in which the human actor and particularly the self are of supreme importance is said to be recognized by "most" speakers' preferences for arrangements in which the subject precedes the verb and object; linguists writing in Eng. term these SVO or SOV patterns and find them predominating in all but a handful of langs. Deutscher mentions Welsh, biblical Heb., and Maori as exceptions to this rule of (human) subject-first. But many other exceptions can be and have been adduced in ways that do not accept the premise of exceptionality. Some scholars of written Ar. consider a "verb-subject-object" pattern typical, for instance, while other scholars see case endings as more important than word order for understanding this lang. Peled observes that, among students of written Ar., sentence types and word order have been a focus for debate since med. times. Inflected langs. such as Lat., Ger., and Gr. do not exhibit a clear tendency toward subject-first syntactic arrangements in declarative sentences, at least if one considers the partial evidence about lang. use provided by the written record. A sentence pattern that puts the "object" or predicate first, followed by a subject and verb—which may well be expressed in one rather than two words—is clearly familiar to poets working in many langs.; it was known to poets writing in Eng. for centuries from their grammar-school study of Lat. classics, incl. Virgil's *Aeneid*, which begins, "Arma virumque cano" (arms and the man I sing). We need not accept foundationalist claims for the relation between syntax and the world to recognize that many poets have experimented with syntactic patterns in ways that might be called "mimetic" but that might also be called "thematic": interpreters have found syntactic patterns mimicking both natural spaces (dells, for instance) and culturally charged objects (Christ's cross can be evoked by a "chiastic" pattern in a line or couplet; see CHIASMUS).

Poetic theories and practices also cluster around a second major strand of thought about mimetic syntax that stretches back to the ancient Greeks: this is the theory that sees syntax "following" logic or reason (the Gr. term *logos*, which becomes central to Christian theological discourses). On this view, syntax illuminates the workings of a rational order assumed to precede lang. and to have universal qualities. Although this line of thought is sometimes expressed as a corollary to the first, the two strands of the mimetic theory at times diverge in consequential ways. Both Land and Cohen have traced one historical instance of divergence in 17th- and 18th-c. Eng. writing about lang., a movement from a "grammar of things" focused on relations among signs and their referents to a "grammar of the mind" focused on "bundles" of words and on those parts of speech that have no obvious analogues in the world. John Locke illustrates this tendency in his *Essay Concerning Human Understanding* (1690), which holds that knowledge "consists in propositions." For Locke, as for the Port-Royal group of lang. philosophers in 17th-c. Paris, the verb takes priority over the noun because it is seen as critical to acts of judgment; moreover, there is a marked interest in the "syntax of connectives" (Cohen). Locke argues that the humble particle has been unjustly neglected; he approaches syntactic relations as windows into the way in which the mind pursues "connexion, restriction, distinction, opposition, emphasis, etc." (*Essay* 3.7.2). A number of scholars have found a significant correlation between such a philosophical view of syntax and features of neoclassical poetry, particularly the use of parallel and antithetical clauses in the rhymed *couplets of John Dryden, Jean Racine, Pierre Corneille, and Alexander Pope (see NEOCLASSICAL POETICS).

For the major strands of Occidental speculation that conceive of syntax as imitating a corresponding order of reality, tropes are anomalous; paradoxically, they are also typical of poetry perceived as a form of discourse granted "license" to deviate from ordinary lang. "Aside from figurative speech," as Chomsky states the central idea of the Port-Royal grammarians, "the sequence of words follows an 'ordre naturel,' which conforms "à l'expression naturelle de nos pensées' [to the natural expression of our thoughts]." It can be argued, however, that poetic syntax, which stresses questions of figurative lang., is constitutive of, rather than marginal to, syntax as an object of multicultural knowledge with Gr. roots. This is so partly because theorists from Aristotle on define the basic units of syntax as phenomena that, when correctly performed in speech or writing, reflect reality in ways that reveal both completeness of thought (*dianoia*) and elegance of expression (*lexis*, sometimes trans. as *"diction"). Moreover, as Basset has shown, when Aristotle discusses syntactic units such as the *colon or the *period in terms of such qualities as elegance and completeness, it is hard to know whether he is judging such units for their rhythmic, grammatical, or logical properties, or for a combination of these in which "appropriateness" of tropes plays a role.

By the 1st c. BCE, *syntaxis* began to be used by Gr. grammarians and philosophers in ways that encompassed discussions of "parts" of speech and relations of "agreement" among forms of words signaling such concepts as gender, tense, mood, number, and grammatical case. The first extant Gr. treatise on syntax, *Peri Syntaxeôs* (2d c. CE), sees syntactic irregularities as corruptions of a rule that reflects reason and that can be traced back to a pristine natural past. Written by Apollonios Dyskolos (the "surly"), who worked as a teacher of grammar in Alexandria, the treatise analyzes examples of "ungrammaticality" (*akatallēlia*) drawn both from ordinary usage and from poetry, esp. the Homeric epics. As Blank shows, Apollonios oscillates between correcting errors and explaining them (away) when they occur in Homer. Deeply influenced by Stoic logic, which distinguished between "complete" and "deficient" propositions and which saw the former as demonstrating an ethical ideal of self-sufficiency (*autoteleia*), Apollonios repeatedly discusses syntactic issues by contrasting arrangements of words that are morphologically, syntactically, and semantically akin.

The subject of syntax as Apollonios constructs it is dependent on comparative judgments; it becomes even more complexly comparative when Gr. discourses on syntax are appropriated by Roman poets and educa-

tors and, subsequently, by later Eur. and Eng. writers extensively educated in Lat. grammar, poetry, and rhet. In treatises that variously transliterate the Gr. word *syntaxis* into Roman letters or render it in the Lat. words *constructio*, *dispositio*, or *ordinatio*, the subject of syntax retains its focus on the illustration and discussion of errors in lang., whether these occur in single words or in larger signifying units. Though the names for these errors are legion and the category distinctions among them are often perplexing—esp. as the examples begin to appear in both Gr. and Lat. forms—there is considerable continuity in this discursive trad. focused on right and wrong syntax. The trad. mingles poetical examples with pedagogical and philosophical precepts. Priscian, whose influential 6th-c. CE discussion of syntax in the final two books of his *Institutionem Grammaticorum* appropriates many points from Apollonios, repeatedly asks his readers "whether a phrase is right or wrong" ("recta sit an non," 17:14). Prisician's analysis of "irregularities" (*incongruae* or *inconcinnae*), however, conceives lang. as a phenomenon with a past. This may complicate present judgments of correct usage. Priscian cites many poetic lines illustrating "uncommon" usages that are, he acknowledges, "preferred by old communities" (2:122). His use of ancient Gr. examples along with his awareness of ling. "preferences" among old Lat.-speaking communities highlights how hist. impinges on a theory or practice of syntax considered primarily as a set of rules.

Moreover, Priscian's *Institutio* contributes to a continuing question about the place of syntax in a course of study: is it a subset of grammar, as Joseph Aiken indicated in his *British Grammar* (1693), where the subject is divided into orthography, prosody, etymology, and syntax? Or is syntax a step above grammar in a hierarchy that points further up toward the study of poetry or *bonae literae* (good letters, a humanist ideal) in Lat. and in those vernacular langs. lexically and syntactically indebted to Lat.? In many 16th-c. Eng. grammar schools, syntax was studied by boys in the third form after basic Lat. grammar and before poetry approached as a matter to be translated from Lat. to Eng. and back again. According to the *OED*, as late as the 19th c., the term *syntax* denoted a school subject below poetry and above grammar.

Wherever syntax is placed in school curricula, it has often been viewed as a surly and difficult subject. This perception derives in part from the fact that syntactic analysis requires a historical education in several taxonomic schemes and in multilingual terminologies for rhetorical tropes involving varying perceptions of "transgressive" behavior in the construction of sentences. The figure of *hyperbaton, for instance, denoting "various forms of departure from ordinary word order" (Lanham), is called *transgressio* in Lat. and "the trespasser" by George Puttenham in *The Arte of English Poesie* (1589). Despite or perhaps because of the fact that there is no stable or single concept of ordinary (or common or natural) syntax that crosses from Gr. to Lat. to the Eur. vernaculars, the notion of difficult syntax—as a written and later a printed phenomenon that members of an educated elite can appreciate as something different from "vulgar" speech—has been valued by writers such as Torquato Tasso, Giovanni della Casa, Luis de Góngora, Sor Juana Inés de la Cruz, Maurice Scève, and John Milton, as well as by mod. poets such as Stéphane Mallarmé, Giuseppe Ungaretti (see HERMETICISM), R. M. Rilke, e. e. cummings, and Ezra Pound. Different instances of a poetic syntax designed to deviate conspicuously from vernacular usages may, of course, refract quite different political and philosophical views about ordinary lang. and the people who are thought to speak it.

In his *Institutio oratoria* (1st c. CE), Quintilian suggests that a "difficult" style might appropriately be described as "Virgilian" or even as "rhythmical"—the latter quality presented in a way that admits of no clear division between admirable poetry and artistically crafted prose. The best way we have of making our speech (*sermonem*) rhythmical (*numerosum*), writes Quintilian, is by "opportune change[s] of [word] order" (8.6. 64–65). Such changes clearly raise questions about the appropriate limits of poetic license both for the writer and the reader. Quintilian avers that "language would very often be rough, harsh, limp, or disjointed if the words were constrained as their natural order demands" (*si ad necessitate ordinis sui verba redigantur*; 8.6.62); however, he also insists that the freedom exhibited in hyperbaton and related syntactic figures would not be allowed in *oratio* (rendered as "prose" by one Eng. translator at 8.6.66). *Oratio*, however, can also be translated as "speech," and Quintilian in the same passage praises Plato for trying out many different patterns of word order in his prose sentences (8.6.64). Worrying that errors may arise from *hyperbata* that are too long, Quintilian does not say exactly how long is too long; nor does he distinguish clearly between aesthetic and moral dimensions of appropriate and inappropriate syntax. Finally, he relies on tropes to explain what counts as "good" syntax: "Words," he writes, are to be "moved from one place to another so as to join where they fit best, just as, in constructions made of unhewn stones, the irregularity itself (*ipsa enormitas*) suggests the right stones which each piece can fit or rest upon" (9.4.27).

Many poems in various langs. create effects of "irregularity" in ways that call attention to poetic form while asking the reader or listener to reflect on what often began as his or her subconscious knowledge of verbal regularity in a given lang. Such calling attention to the medium is central to what Jakobson defines as the *poetic function of lang. The writer's or linguist's or literary critic's educated perspective on what constitutes regular and irregular patterns in a given evidentiary field makes poetic syntax into an object of study but seldom warrants generalizations about it across cultures. An exception might be in those cases where we can hypothesize a foreign influence on an Eng. poetic construction that can be observed in numerous examples from a certain era. An example is the "absolute participial" construction that occurs with some frequency in med. and early mod. Eng. lit.—in this line

of *Hamlet*, for instance: "The passion ending, doth the purpose lose" (3.2.185). Some linguists have explained the apparent irregularity of this line—what is its grammatical subject and how does that "agree" with the verb form?—as a sign of the significant influence of Lat. or Fr. syntax on Eng. poetry.

In a famous letter, John Keats deplored the "gallicisms" of Chaucer's poetry and found Milton's *Paradise Lost* a "corruption" of the Eng. lang. But Keats himself had been criticized for "bad" writing, and many of his lines imitate Milton's in syntax and diction. For poets and their interpreters, the distinction between proper and improper usages is fluid and usually open to testing, as is the distinction between native and foreign. Inversions of word order, so critical to Quintilian's understanding of what makes an admirable high style like Virgil's, occur as often in Pope's poetry as in Milton's, according to Brogan; and such "inversions" also occur in poems by those who explicitly reject a high style. S. T. Coleridge described one of his *conversation poems, for instance—"Reflections on Having Left a Place of Retirement"—as a "poem which affects not to be Poetry"; he elaborates the paradox in that phrase with his first line, which conspicuously departs from what many feel is the usual word order of Eng.: "Low was our pretty Cot!" In versions printed after 1797, moreover, Coleridge's poem begins with a Lat. epigraph: "Sermoni propriora." Charles Lamb jokingly translated this as "properer for a sermon," whereas others—more seriously but not necessarily more correctly—have rendered it "more suitable for conversation/prose." The adjective in its original context, however (Horace's *Satire* 4) is spelled differently: *propiora*, which is usually translated into Eng. as "nearer." Coleridge plays with the meaning of the Eng. word *proper* as "one's own." Is a low style, nearer to prose, more properly Eng. than a high style? Like many other poets, Coleridge poses the question without providing a definitive answer.

As this story of trans. indicates, matters of poetic syntax invite analysis in relation to other aspects of a poem or the culture where it was produced and where it continues to be interpreted. Chomsky proclaimed the existence of an "autonomous syntax principle" and of a phenomenon he named ling. "competence" and defined as an "innate" knowledge of syntactic and grammatical rules possessed by every speaker of a natural lang. His theory, frequently revised, is important because it calls attention to the issue of constraints on syntax without moralizing them—but also without considering them in relation to educational institutions or to the entire domain of what Chomsky called "performance" and defined as a set of specific utterances produced by *native* speakers. Chomsky's "performance," which some critics have allied with Saussure's "parole," is conceived without reference to the institution of the theater or to some cultures' trads. of oral poetic performances (see ORAL POETRY). For poetic syntax considered in a comparative context, there is no "autonomous" principle of syntax, ontological or hermeneutic. There is, however, a useful heuristic notion (also a spatial metaphor) proffered by structuralist theorists in the 20th c.: the notion of the "syntagmatic" and "paradigmatic" axes of lang. Formulated by Saussure for the field of semiotics and elaborated for poetry by Jakobson, Jameson, Silverman, Culler, and others, this interpretive schema relies on Gr. terms but departs from Gr. presuppositions concerning syntax as mimesis and tropes as instances of both culpable and admirable erring. The notion of the two axes—often visually represented as a horizontal (syntagmatic) line crossed by numerous vertical (paradigmatic) ones—allows Saussure to explain how ling. meaning arises from two kinds of difference: that which we might provisionally see as occurring in a syntactic unit (a clause or a sentence) as extended in the time of speech or the space/time of the text; and that which arises in the reader's or hearer's mind from the relations between a sign and other elements in its "system." The vertical axis, which Saussure called "associative," works with the syntagmatic axis to create sequences of various degrees of complexity. The paradigmatic axis may include case endings or parts of speech other than the ones actualized in the words of a given sentence or clause; the paradigmatic axis is more commonly thought of as "supplying" the missing terms of a *metaphor or alternate sounds or letters of a rhyme or a pun. Any word, *line, couplet, or *stanza of poetry can be analyzed with reference to these axes, with syntactic elements now construed as aspects of lang. working in concert (via forms of *parallelism incl. tropes such as *isocolon) but also in tension with other elements of the poetic line and/or with other signifying units.

Many syntactic units are, of course, smaller or larger than the sentence; and many poets have worked against as well as with the traditional idea, inherited from Aristotle and the Stoics in many elegantly circular forms, that a *proper* sentence or clause "reflects" a *complete* thought. One could indeed say that the enigmatic idea of a proper sentence (as memory or expectation or pedagogical rule) exists on the paradigmatic axis created jointly by many Eng. poems and their readers and hearers; consider, for instance Pound's "In a Station of the Metro," which consists of two syntagms (incl. the title) that traditional Western grammarians would call *sentence fragments*. Inspired in part by Japanese and Chinese poems, Pound uses the fragment to present a new reality; in one of his *manifestos for *imagism, he contrasts poetic "presenting" with painterly "describing" ("A Retrospect," 1913). But his *fragment poem relies on the reader's knowledge of what counts as a complete sentence, as do many poems that delay a main verb in long invocations of a *muse who figures *inspiration.

An approach to poetic syntax that is at once structuralist (synchronic) and historical (diachronic) is difficult, as Jameson observes in his *Prison-House of Language* (1972); but attempting it allows us to construct a paradigmatic axis that extends over time and space to encompass a recurring contrast between theories and practices of "difficult" syntax and those devoted to a style that aspires to plainness and that presents features of colloquial, even dialectal, speech, the vulgar or

"mother" tongue (see PLAIN STYLE). Under a different figure, this is what William Wordsworth, in the Preface to the 2d ed. of *Lyrical Ballads* (1800), called lang. "really spoken by men." But which lang. is that? And does it exist except as it has been historically (re)constructed in relation to a poetic lang. marked by "irregularities" such as *elision and inverted word order?

Elision and inversion are perennially interesting and conceptually difficult for a comparative approach to poetic syntax or to syntax in general. Lacking evidence of normal speech patterns for many past cultures and some present ones, we cannot securely distinguish between approved omissions of words (elisions) and ones that are classified as errors (*vitia*) in the Occidental written record, often under such Gr. terms as *barbarism* and *solecism*. Like children, foreigners, and jokesters, poets often use lang. in ways that have been deemed transgressive; but for past cultures, even in the West, we do not know who would have judged a transgression playful, enigmatic (because the sign of textual corruption), or inept. Some forms of elision have been named, noticed, and generally approved as achieving effects of *wit. Elision combines with complex *figuration in *zeugma or *syllepsis: consider, e.g., Pope's famous couplet comparing, contrasting, and compressing the idiomatic Eng. phrases "take counsel" and "take tea" (*The Rape of the Lock*, 1714). Other forms of elision arise from syntactic arrangements extending over many lines and often creating instances of double syntax: a syntagm that starts by inviting one interpretation but grows to invite a second reading that conceptually revises the first; see, e.g., the first four lines of cummings's "since feeling is first" or the transition between stanzas 3 and 4 of Emily Dickinson's "A bird came down the walk" (Empson, Ferguson). Elisions of main-clause verbs in Eng. and Am. poetry have sometimes accompanied semantic inquiries into domination and subordination, disobedience and obedience to rules, and the relation of parts to putative wholes. An example is W. C. Williams's "The Young Sycamore," which uses ambiguous syntax to explore whether a sapling is an independent entity or is not (yet). The rhetorical figures of anapodoton (omitting a main clause from a conditional sentence) and *aposiopesis (breaking off suddenly in the middle of speaking) are important to poems that explore and dramatize relations between syntax and a fictional speaker's emotional states; Virgil, for instance, illustrates the sea god Neptune's anger— and his ability to control it—in a famous aposiopesis in the *Aeneid*: "quos ego—! sed motos praestat componere fluctus" (whom I—! But better it is to calm the troubled waves [1.135]). Milton combines anapodoton and aposiopesis in Satan's opening address to Beelzebub in *Paradise Lost* ("If thou beest he; But oh how falln, how changed / From him . . .). The initial subordinate conditional clause breaks off, and Satan (as represented by the narrator) seems to forget his conventional obligation to complete his thought with a main clause.

Like Milton's Satan, many poets have conspicuously failed to obey the rules of the "well-formed" sentence, and sometimes they have done so by following the incompletely codified and imperfectly translated rules of tropes. Sometimes, however, poets transgress in ways that strain even the cl. notion of *poetic license, which relies on hypotheses about the poet's *intention and about the poem's ultimate intelligibility. In "Adonais" (51–53), P. B. Shelley, for instance, often writes sentences that are "almost impenetrable" (Austin 1993):

Thy extreme hope, the loveliest and the last,
The bloom, whose petals nipped before they blew
Died on the promise of the fruit, is waste.

What rules of (Eng.) syntax is Shelley breaking or bending here? How are historically variable conventions of printing and punctuation (here, the absence of the expected "closing" comma after "blew") implicated in our perceptions of what is and is not an intelligible sentence? Shelley's sentence appears to illustrate Chomsky's argument that a "well-formed" sentence, one operating correctly by a recursive rule of sentence formation, may nonetheless be "unacceptable." Indeed, Shelley's sentence appears to illustrate the phenomenon of "center-embedding" that Chomsky uses to explain the distinction between grammaticality and acceptability; an example is "The man who the boys who the students recognized pointed out is a friend of mine." Such a sentence fails to be acceptable to an Eng. speaker, Chomsky suggests, because of a problem in the domain of performance, not competence. In MacCabe's paraphrase of Chomsky, "the body is simply unable to store the necessary bits of information to decode the sentence although it does have the necessary decoding mechanisms." Shelley's lines, however, like the prose passage by James Joyce that MacCabe analyzes to show "center-embedding" at work, challenge us to think recursively, testing the human memory encountering something like a sentence in the medium of print. Shelley's lines counter common assumptions about lang. as communication while suggesting the social value of puzzles and *riddles, traditionally close kin to certain experiments in extreme syntax.

Poetic syntax, like unmodified syntax, has seemed a surly subject to many school children taught to attend to lang. through syntactic categories. But poets shaped by multilingual educational theories and practices have been in constant conversation with philosophers, teachers, and linguists on the question of what is a proper sentence—in the senses both of being correct and of belonging to one's own ling. trad. Chomsky generated a mod. chapter in this conversation when, in his *Syntactic Structures* (1957), he gave an example of a syntactically correct sentence that is "unacceptable" because it makes no sense: "Colorless green ideas sleep furiously." A number of writers, incl. Chinese linguist Yuen Ren Chao and Am. poets John Hollander and Clive James, have contested Chomsky's point by using figuration and recontextualization to make his string of words legible after all, if not necessarily on first glance. In so doing, such writers participate in a long-enduring and multicultural game that exploits the resources of syntax and tropes—the "colors" of rhet.—to test the boundaries between sense and nonsense, figurative

and proper meanings, practices and theories of lang., and last but not least, between prose and poetry. Hollander's poem makes Chomsky's sentence into a subordinate clause in a larger syntactic unit titled "Coiled Alizarine." The title serves as an apt concluding emblem for the transformational powers of poetic syntax. "Coiled" like a snake, with the potential for fuller extensions in the future, poetic syntax has metamorphic powers like those of alizarine: an organic dye used in the past, and still used today, to change the colors of various paints and inks.

*See* ELLIPSIS, HYPOTAXIS AND PARATAXIS, LINGUISTICS AND POETICS.

■ E. Pound, "A Few Don'ts by an Imagiste," *Poetry* 1 (1913); and *ABC of Reading* (1934); F. T. Prince, *The Italian Element in Milton's Verse* (1953); Empson; D. Davie, *Articulate Energy* (1955); J. Miles, *Eras and Modes in English Poetry* (1957); C. Brooke-Rose, *A Grammar of Metaphor* (1958); F. Perry, *Poet's Grammar* (1958); E. Wasserman, *The Subtler Language* (1959); S. Levin, *Linguistic Structures in Poetry* (1962); W. Nowottny, *The Language Poets Use* (1962); C. Ricks, *Milton's Grand Style* (1963); N. Chomsky, *Aspects of a Theory of Syntax* (1965); R. Levin, "Internal and External Deviation in Poetry," *Word* 21 (1965); F. T. Visser, *An Historical Syntax of the English Language* (1966); W. Baker, *Syntax in English Poetry, 1879–1930* (1967); W. N. Francis, "Syntax and Literary Interpretation," *Essays in the Language of Literature*, ed. S. Chatman and S. Levin (1967); J.-C. Chevalier, *Histoire de la syntaxe . . . (1530–1750)* (1968); B. H. Smith, *Poetic Closure* (1968); R. Mitchell, "Toward a System of Grammatical Scansion," *Lang&S* 3 (1970); I. Michael, *English Grammatical Categories and the Tradition to 1800* (1971); F. Jameson, *Prison-House of Language* (1972); J. M. Sinclair, "Lines and 'Lines,'" *Current Trends in Stylistics*, ed. B. Kachru and H.F.W. Stahlke (1972); J. S. Borck, "Blake's 'The Lamb': The Punctuation of Innocence," *TSL* 19 (1974); S. K. Land, *From Signs to Propositions* (1974); Culler; G. Dillon, "Inversions and Deletions in English Poetry," *Lang&S* 8 (1975); and "Literary Transformations and Poetic Word Order," *Poetics* 5 (1976); I. Fairley, *E. E. Cummings and Ungrammar* (1975); D. C. Freeman, "Iconic Syntax in Poetry: A Note on Blake's 'Ah! Sun-Flower,'" *University of Massachusetts Occasional Papers in Linguistics* 2 (1976); J. M. Lipski, "Poetic Deviance and Generative Grammar," *PTL* 2 (1977); J. M. Lotman, *The Structure of the Artistic Text*, trans. G. Lenhoff and R. Vroon (1977); E. Kintgen, "Perceiving Poetic Syntax," *CE* 40 (1978); M. Borroff, *The Language and the Poet* (1979); M. Cohen, *Sensible Words: Linguistic Practice in England, 1640–1785* (1979); R. Cureton, "e. e. cummings: A Study of the Poetic Use of Deviant Morphology," *PoT* 1 (1979); H. Golomb, *Enjambment in Poetry* (1979); D. Simpson, *Irony and Authority in Romantic Poetry* (1979); R. Cureton, "'He danced his did': An Analysis," *JL* 16 (1980); and "Poetic Syntax and Aesthetic Form," *Style* 14 (1980); Brogan; R. Cureton, "e. e. cummings: A Case Study of Iconic Syntax," *Lang&S* 14 (1981); R. Jakobson, "The Poetry of Grammar and Grammar of

Poetry," Jakobson, v. 3; J. Moulton and G. M. Robinson, *The Organization of Language* (1981); G. Roscow, *Syntax and Style in Chaucer's Poetry* (1981); D. Blank, *Ancient Philosophy and Grammar* (1982); A. Easthope, *Poetry as Discourse* (1983); K. Silverman, *The Subject of Semiotics* (1983); M. Sirridge, "Socrates' Hood: Lexical Meaning and Syntax in Jordanus and Kilwardby," *Cahiers de l'Institut du Moyen-Âge Grec et Latin* 44 (1983); T. R. Austin, *Language Crafted* (1984); V. Bers, *Greek Poetic Syntax in the Classical Age* (1984); D. Donoghue, *Style in Old English Poetry* (1984); M. Tarlinskaja, "Rhythm–morphology–syntax–rhythm," *Style* 18 (1984); R. Cureton, "Poetry, Grammar, and Epistemology: The Order of Prenominal Modifiers in the Poetry of e. e. cummings," *Lang&S* 18 (1985); M.A.K. Halliday, *An Introduction to Functional Grammar* (1985); R. Hasan, *Linguistics, Language, and Verbal Art* (1985); Hollander; C. Miller, *Emily Dickinson: A Poet's Grammar* (1987); J. P. Houston, *Shakespearean Sentences* (1988); A. Kaster, *Guardians of Language* (1988); R. M. Baratin, *La naissance de la syntaxe à Rome* (1989); H. Pinkster, *Latin Syntax and Semantics* (1990); D. Lateiner, "Mimetic Syntax: Metaphor from Word Order, Especially in Ovid," *AJP* 3 (1990); Lanham; R. Cureton, *Rhythmic Phrasing in English Verse* (1992); T. R. Austin, "Syntax, Poetic," *The New Princeton Encyclopedia of Poetry and Poetics*, ed. A. Preminger and T.V.F. Brogan (1993); R. Cureton, "Poetry, Language, and Literary Study: The Unfinished Tasks of Stylistics," *Language and Literature* 21 (1996); T. J. Taylor and M. Toolan, "Recent Trends in Stylistics," *The Stylistics Reader*, ed. J. J. Weber (1996); R. Cureton, "Linguistics, Stylistics, and Poetics," *Language and Literature* 22 (1997); and "Toward a Temporal Theory of Language," *Journal of English Linguistics* 25 (1997); F. J. Newmeyer, *Language Form and Language Function* (1998); M. Collins, "On Syntax in Poetry," *Field* (1999); R. Dirven and M. Verspoor, *Cognitive Explorations in Language and Linguistics* (1999); R. Cribiore, *Gymnastics of the Mind* (2001); M. De Grazia, "Shakespeare and the Craft of Language," *The Cambridge Companion to Shakespeare*, ed. M. de Grazia and S. Wells (2001); *Cambridge Grammar of the English Language*, ed. R. Huddleston and G. K. Pullum et al. (2002); C. MacCabe, *James Joyce and the Revolution of the Word*, 2d ed. (2003); Z. Pickard, "Milton's Latinisms" (2003): http://www.chass.utoronto.ca/˜cpercy/courses/6362Pickard1.htm; *Syntax in Antiquity*, ed. P. Swiggers and A. Wouters (2003)—see esp. L. Basset, "Aristote et la Syntaxe";

A. Luhtala, "Syntax and Dialectic in Late Antiquity"; P. Swiggers and A. Wouters, "Réflexions à propos de (l'absence de?) la syntaxe dans la grammaire Gréco-Latine"; and T. Viljamaa, "Colon and Comma. Dionysius of Halicarnassus on the Sentence Structure"; G. Deutscher, *The Unfolding of Language* (2005); M. Ferguson, "Poetic Syntax," *The Norton Anthology of Poetry*, ed. M. Ferguson, M. J. Salter, J. Stallworthy, 5th ed. (2005); A. Luhtala, *Grammar and Philosophy in Late Antiquity* (2005); A. M. Devine and L. D. Stephens, *Latin Word Order* (2006); Y. Peled, *Sentence Types and Word-Order Patterns in Written Arabic* (2009).

M. W. Ferguson

**SYSTEM** (Gr. *systema*). In Gr. metrics, a *period composed of a sequence of either similar cola in *synapheia with each other or identical metra (also in synapheia), whether or not grouped into cola. In this (mod.) sense, a system is a special kind of period; ancient metrists tend to use it as a term for any sequence of cola in synapheia that exceeds a certain length, whether or not the cola are identical. When sequences of identical metra resist grouping into cola, the usual term is *hypermeter*, coined on the analogy of *trimeter, *tetrameter, *hexameter, etc., to designate a structure that differs from those forms only in that it goes over (*hyper*) the customary limit on the maximum number of metra a single line may contain. Hypermeters are a characteristic feature of comic versification, and the longest attested examples appear in the comic poets of the 4th c. BCE.

*See* COLON, METRON.

■ J. W. White, "Analysis of Systematic Periods," *The Verse of Greek Comedy* (1912); Dale, "Strophic Construction"; West, "Iambic and Trochaic Runs," sec. IIIB.

A. T. Cole

**SYZYGY** (Gr. *syzygos*, "yoked together"). In *classical prosody, an older term for fusion, combination: so the *hexameter is by some metrists said to be a syzygy of two (hemistichic) metrical cola. In the 19th c., *phonetic syzygy* is a term coined apparently by Sylvester and adopted by Lanier to describe types of sound patterns and *elision, but this usage is eccentric and never found acceptance.

■ J. J. Sylvester, *Laws of Verse* (1870); S. Lanier, *The Science of English Verse* (1880).

T.V.F. Brogan

# T

**TACHTIGERS** (Dutch, "'80ers," "Movement of the 1880s"). A group of young Dutch poets and prose writers active during the last two decades of the 19th c. who were united by a shared aversion toward the then-dominant sentimentalism, didacticism, and domesticity of Dutch poetry. Many of the poems and prose works of the Tachtigers, as well as an important body of lit. crit., first appeared in the periodical *De Nieuwe Gids* (The New Guide, first issue 1885), ed. by the poets Willem Kloos, Albert Verwey, and Frederik van Eeden. Other prominent members of the movement were Jacques Perk and Herman Gorter, whose long poem *Mei* (May) may be considered one of the finest products of the Tachtigers. The most famous descriptions of the poetics of the Tachtigers—with doctrines of *impressionism, *aestheticism, and a strongly individualistic and passionate vision of the *poet, elevated above everyday reality and influenced by Eng. *romanticism and Fr. art for art's sake—were written by Kloos. Other Tachtigers, esp. van Eeden, were closer to Fr. *naturalism and defended a more socially engaged kind of authorship. This opposition between a more ethical and a more aesthetically oriented vision of artistry marked the decline of the movement after 1890. Despite its brief duration and its lack of a coherent poetic program, the Tachtigers represent a high point in the hist. of Dutch poetry.

*See* LOW COUNTRIES, POETRY OF THE.

■ H. Brandt Corstius, *Het poëtisch programma van Tachtig* (1968); W. van den Berg and P. Couttenier, *Alles is taal geworden* (2009).

F. J. WARNKE; S. MAREEL

**TAGELIED** (Ger. *Tageliet, tagewîse*, "dawnsong"). A subgenre of *Minnesang, 13th–16th c., probably influenced by the Romance *alba; often a *dialogue. While Minnesang precludes sexuality, the *tagelied* presupposes (and often describes) a situation when lovers have to separate in the morning. If the new light of the day is celebrated in religious and profane poetry of most lits., as Hatto suggests, the tagelied complains of its threat to secret love; in this regard, the tagelied shares the social values of Minnesang and its mode of *klage* (*lament), but unlike the Minnesang, it can imagine the sensuality of mutual attraction. After the end of the 12th c., the tagelied accompanies the courtly *Minnekanzone* (Dietmar von Aist, Heinrich von Morungen, Walther von der Vogelweide). It also can be the foil of an unfulfilled love (Reinmar von Hagenau's antidawn song). Wolfram von Eschenbach's tagelied particularly focus on the danger and the fear of being discovered, the grief of separation, and the last passionate embrace; one tagelied praises marriage as the happier alternative to *helde minne* (secret love). Wolfram introduces the role of the *wechter* (watchman), the knight's faithful servant,

warning the lovers. Later, the tagelied could become a matter of parody, as in the poetry of Steinmar, the repertoire of roles involved could be expanded (Ulrich von Liechtenstein), and the social characteristics of the lovers (knight and lady) and the inherent social conflict could be abandoned. In this broader sense, by the late Middle Ages, every lyric complaining of the separation of lovers at dawn can be called "tagelied" (Oswald von Wolkenstein, Hans Folz, anonymous songbooks). So, the borderlines between *Gesellschafts-* and *Volkslied* (folk song) are blurred (see GESELLSCHAFTSLIED). There are allusions to tagelied in other genres, even epic and dramatic (*Romeo and Juliet*).

■ *Eos: An Enquiry into the Theme of Lovers' Meetings and Partings at Dawn in Poetry*, ed. A. T. Hatto (1965); U. Knoop, *Das mittelhochdeutsche Tagelied* (1976); A. Wolf, *Variation und Integration: Beobachtungen zu hochmittelalterlichen Tageliedern* (1979); *Deutsche Tagelieder von den Anfängen der Überlieferung bis zum 15. Jahrhundert*, ed. S. Freund (1983); *Owe, do taget ez: Tagelieder und motivverwandte Texte*, ed. R. Hausner, v. 1 (1983); H. Fromm, *Der deutsche Minnesang*, 2 v. (1985); C. Cormeau, "Zur Stellung des Tagelieds im Minnesang" and G. Hahn, "'Es ruft ein wachter faste' oder 'Verachtet mir die Meister nicht!': Beobachtungen zum geistlichen Tagelied des Hans Sachs," *Festschrift Walter Haug und Burkhard Wachinger*, ed. J. Janota et al., 2 v. (1992); *Tagelieder des deutschen Mittelalters*, ed. M. Backes (1992); H.-J. Behr, "Die Inflation einer Gattung: Das Tagelied nach Wolfram" *Lied im deutschen Mittelalter*, ed. C. Edwards (1996); U. Ruberg, "Gattungsgeschichtliche Probleme des geistlichen Tagelieds. Dominanz der Wächter- und Weckmotivik bis zu Hans Sachs" *Traditionen der Lyrik: Festschrift für Hans-Henrik Krummacher*, ed. W. Düsing (1997); A. Schnyder, *Das geistliche Tagelied des späten Mittelalters und der frühen Neuzeit* (2004).

J.-D. MÜLLER

**TAIL RHYME** (Med. Lat. *versus tripertiti caudate*; Fr. *rime couée*; ME *rime couwee*; Ger. *Schweifreim*; rarely, caudate rhyme). A stanza of six or 12 lines in which a rhyming couplet is followed by a shorter tail line, the rhyme of which unites the stanza, i.e., *aabccb* or *aabaab*, or *aabccbddbeeb* or *aabaabaabaab*. "At once jubilant and stately," tail rhyme can be seen as an extension of the ballad stanza, made by doubling the first and third lines (Hamer), and indeed both William Wordsworth ("Three Years She Grew") and W. H. Auden ("A Summer Evening") have made tail rhyme serve as a kind of ballad stanza. Tail rhyme appears in med. Lat. and OF verse, from which it was transmitted to ME, where it flourished in the 14th c. In ME, the six-line form, or "Romance six," came to be associated with the *lyric and the 12-line form with romance; half of the

70 extant metrical romances use this form, which enjoyed a vogue in East Anglia in the 14th c. (Trounce). The Fr. *douzaine* (*aabaabbbabba* in octosyllables) is similar to tail rhyme, but the *b* line is of the same length as the *a*.

In med. Lat., tail rhyme is used almost exclusively for religious lyric (not at all for narrative verse); in Eng., however, tail rhyme appears in a wide variety of verse genres. Although Chaucer's parody of tail rhyme in "Tale of Sir Thopas" has sometimes been considered the death knell of the form, the tail-rhyme stanza continued to be used after 1500 to lend an old-fashioned, rustic air to dialogue. Erler notes that pastoral dialogues in tail rhyme were popular in the 16th c., beginning with trans. of Clément Marot and Théodore de Beza that found their way to Mary Sidney, whose shepherds Thenot and Piers converse in tail rhyme. Edmund Spenser, in the March *eclogue from *The Shepheardes Calender*, has two of his shepherds speak to each other in tail rhyme. Tail rhyme can be seen more generally as an index of character. The 15th-c. morality play *The Castle of Perseverance*, e.g., uses the tail-rhyme stanza to mark the three lowest vices (Virtue, meanwhile, appears in *rhyme royal); Edward Taylor employs a tail-rhyme stanza for Christ's reply to the Soul in *Gods Determinations* (Wright). There are many later examples of tail rhyme in Michael Drayton ("Nymphidia"), Thomas Gray ("Ode on the Death of a Favorite Cat"), William Collins ("Ode to Pity"), Christopher Smart (*A Song to David*), Alfred, Lord Tennyson ("The Lady of Shalott"), Robert Burns ("To a Mouse"), and Paul Laurence Dunbar, who uses tail rhyme in his 1898 poem "The Conquerors," written for black Am. soldiers in the Sp.-Am. War. A particularly clever instance of tail rhyme comes from Lewis Carroll, whose lines extend sinuously down the page in the shape of a tail ("The Mouse's Tale"—see CALLIGRAMME).

*See* BOB AND WHEEL, CAUDA, CAUDATE SONNET.

■ Schipper; Meyer, v. 1; C. Strong, "History and Relations of the Tail Rhyme Strophe in Latin, French, and English," *PMLA* 22 (1907); A. McI. Trounce, "The English Tail-Rhyme Romances," *Medium Aevum* 1–3 (1932–34); N. Wright, "The Morality Tradition in the Poetry of Edward Taylor," *AL* 18 (1946); E. Hamer, *The Metres of English Poetry* (1954); U. Dürmüller, *Narrative Possibilities of the Tail-Rime Romance* (1975); A. T. Gaylord, "Chaucer's Dainty 'Dogerel,'" *SAC* 1 (1979); J. R. Payne, "Afro-American Literature of the Spanish-American War," *MELUS* (1983); M. Erler, "Davies's *Astraea* and Other Contexts of the Countess of Pembroke's 'A Dialogue,'" *SEL* 30 (1990); T. Steele, *All the Fun's in How You Say a Thing* (1999); M. Tajiri, *Studies in the Middle English Didactic Tail-Rhyme Romances* (2002).

T.V.F. BROGAN; W. HUNTER

**TAMIL POETRY AND POETICS.** The Tamil lang., the earliest attested member of the Dravidian lang. family, is India's only mod., living lang. with a lit. trad. reaching back over 2,000 years. Tamil is spoken by about 65 million people in the South Indian state of Tamil Nadu but also in Sri Lanka, Malaysia, Singapore, Mauritius, and diasporic communities around the world, notably in Europe, Canada, and the United States. Premod. or cl. Tamil lit., i.e., the lit. composed before roughly the second half of the 19th c., is almost entirely written in verse. Narrative prose lit. (such as novels and short stories) did not emerge before the colonial period. Tamil developed its own *prosody based on different combinations of various elements: letters/syllables (*eḻuttu*), metrical syllables (*acai*), feet (*cīr*), linkage between feet (*taḷai*), metrical lines (*aṭi*), and ornamentation or tropes (*toṭai*) such as *alliteration (*mōṉai*), initial rhyme (*etukai*), and others. The earliest extant Tamil texts, datable to the beginning of the common era, are known today collectively as *Caṅkam* lit., since a legend tells us that they were composed by academies of poets (*caṅkams*). This lit. consists of approximately 2,400 poems ranging in length from four to about 800 lines that are collected in two books, each containing several anthols. of poems: the *Eṭṭuttokai* (Eight Anthologies), which includes the famous collections *Kuṟuntokai* (Anthology of Short [Poems]) and *Puṟanāṉūṟu* (Four Hundred [Poems on] *Puṟam*), and the *Pattuppāṭṭu* (Ten Poems). The theoretical framework required to understand the highly refined and sophisticated poetics underlying Caṅkam lit. is detailed in the *Tolkāppiyam*, the oldest known treatise on Tamil grammar and poetics (considered to be contemporaneous with the Caṅkam poems but probably altered variously until perhaps the 5th c. CE). The *Tolkāppiyam* divides the poems into two distinct genres: *akam* (interior), love poetry, and *puṟam* (exterior), poems on war, kings, or social and historical circumstances. Both akam and puṟam poems derive much of their beauty from a complex system of nature imagery that draws on a taxonomy of five poetic Tamil landscapes (hill, seashore, forest and pasture, countryside, wasteland), providing repertoires of flora, fauna, and other elements deployed to evoke specific feelings. In the akam poems, these landscapes are linked metaphorically to different phases of love, the times of day, and the seasons appropriate for these phases. Thus, the hillside is the landscape of (first) union, at night, during the cool season; forest and pasture provide the landscape of the woman's patient waiting for her lover and of domestic togetherness, late in the evening and during the rainy season, and so on.

Between ca. 400 and 900 CE, there developed a trad. of *epic poetry, notably with the two thematically interlinked poems *Cilappatikāram* (Talc of an Anklet, 5th c.?) and *Maṇimēkalai* (The Jewel Belt, ca. 500). The *Cilappatikāram*, combining great poetic beauty with a gripping narrative, tells the story of a young merchant who is unjustly executed by the king of Madurai for a crime he did not commit and of his faithful wife who takes revenge, destroys the city of Madurai, and turns into a goddess of chastity. While the *Maṇimēkalai*, which continues the story of the *Cilappatikāram*, is clearly influenced by Buddhism, the *Cīvakacintāmaṇi* (9th c.?), which describes the many love conquests of prince Cīvakaṉ, is considered a Jain text. Jain influence is also found in the *Tirukkuṟaḷ* (ca. 5th c.), a comprehensive manual on ethics, polity, and love in 1,330 pithy *couplets and a book that remained highly popular through the ages as a repository of ancient Tamil wisdom and a symbol of Tamil culture.

After about the 6th c., some of the poetic strategies of Caṅkam poetry were absorbed by a corpus of religious hymns extolling the Hindu gods Śiva and Viṣṇu through the expression of intense personal devotion (*Bhakti*). The earliest Tamil Bhakti poets were devotees of Śiva known as *nāyaṉmār* (lords). This group included the female poet Kāraikkāl Ammaiyār and the three poets whose verses are collected in the *Tēvāram*, Appar and Campantar (both 7th c.) and Cuntarar (8th c.), known as the "harsh devotee." The 9th-c. Śaivite poet-saint Māṇikkavācakar is known for his collection of hymns *Tiruvācakam* and his poem *Tirukkōvaiyār*. The latter explicitly redeploys akam amatory poetics for religious purposes and weaves the discrete vignettes of the Caṅkam poems into a narrative. Among the devotees of Viṣṇu, known as Āḻvār, were the female poet Āṇṭāḷ (8th c.) and Nammāḻvār (9th c.). Their works and the works of the other Vaiṣṇava saint-poets were collected during the 10th or 11th c. as the *Nālāyirativviyappirapantam* (Four Thousand Divine Works), the Vaiṣṇava canon.

The period between the 11th and 14th cs. saw the flourishing of the great courtly culture of the med. Cōḻa (Chola) dynasty that led to the production of new literary texts, such as the most famous Tamil version of the pan-Indian *Rāmāyaṇa* story, the *Kamparāmāyaṇam*, and the authoritative hagiography of Śaivite *nāyaṉmār* saints, the *Periyapurāṇam* (Great History [of the Holy Servants of Lord Śiva]). At the same time, a process of "philologization" led to new perspectives on Tamil grammar and poetics, crystallizing in the heavily Sanskrit-influenced treatises *Vīracōḻiyam* and *Taṇṭiyalaṅkāram*, and later the *Naṉṉūl*, which remained the standard Tamil grammar for several centuries. Iḷampūraṇar's commentary on the *Tolkāppiyam*, written during this period, may have been part of this new surge of interest in and revision of Tamil lit. and grammar, as were the works of the other three great commentators on the *Tolkāppiyam*, Cēṉāvaraiyar, Pēraciriyar, and Nacciṉārkkiṉiyar, all of which belong to the period between the 11th and 14th cs. and which are some of the few examples of premod. Tamil prose. The extant Chola court poems stand out as tokens of refined literary sensibilities and courtly culture, e.g., the court poet Oṭṭakkūttar's *Mūvarulā* (Procession Poems on the Three [Kings]), which portray how women of various ages are entranced by seeing the Chola king, a paragon of virtue and beauty, ride by in his glamorous royal procession (*ulā*); or Cayaṅkoṇṭār's *panegyric *Kaliṅkattupparaṇi* (1113–18), which not only celebrates the victory of the Cholas in the second Kaliṅga war but is a masterful *satire with terrifying and macabre imagery in its descriptions of the fierce goddess Kāḷi and her demons feasting on corpses on the battlefield. The ulā and the *paraṇi* were new poetic genres that, together with a number of others, became known as *pi-*

*rapantam*s (compositions). The term *pirapantam* (from Sanskrit *prabandha-*) subsumes a motley group of traditionally 96 different genres in verse form as described in the so-called *pāṭṭiyal* grammars (the nature [*iyal*] of poetry [*pāṭṭu*]), which were written from about the 10th c. until the end of the 19th c. with a view toward theorizing the characteristics of pirapantam poems. Some of these genres may be defined by their form (especially stanzaic structure), e.g., *antāti* or *iraṭṭaimaṇimālai*, some by their content, e.g., ulā (poems about the king in procession), *kātal* (courtly love poems), or paraṇi (poems on war and the battlefield); and some by a combination of both content and form, e.g., *piḷḷaittamiḻ* (poems in praise of the childhoods of gods or human characters), *tūtu* (messenger poems), *kōvai* (narrative "garlands" of love or devotional poems), or *kuṟavañci* (fortune-teller dramas). Their length varies, and some of them are older than others. This relative diversity, however, has not prevented Tamil poetological trad. from grouping all of them together under the single term *pirapantam* or under the term *ciṟṟilakkiyam* (small or minor lit.).

Despite its name, this "minor literature" came to play an increasingly important part in the literary production from the late med. period on. The two most important locales of literary production and circulation were the courts of local kings and princes and religious institutions, such as monasteries and temples. Many poets depended entirely on the patronage of kings and religious authorities and wrote all their verses as commissioned works. Some of the better-known poetic works during this period include the religious poetry of Aruṇakirinātar (15th c.) and Tāyumāṉavar (17th c.); the 16th-c. epic *Naiṭatam*, which elaborates the love story between prince Nala and princess Damayantī from the *Mahābhārata*; and the *Tirukkuṟṟālakkuṟavañci* (ca. 1718), a play on Lord Śiva in Kuṟṟālam. This period also saw the rise of the great Tamil temple myths (*talapurāṇam*s), verse narratives relating the myths and legends around the foundation of a Śiva temple, as well as the oldest fully extant Muslim poem in Tamil, Vaṇṇapparimaḷap Pulavar's *Āyiramacalā* (One Thousand Questions, 1572). The widespread system of late med. literary patronage gradually fell apart during the latter half of the 19th c., when the many transformations of a colonial society also affected literary production and reception. While the advances of the printing press meant that more texts reached more people than ever before, prose became valued over poetry as the vehicle of mod. thought and expression.

Mod. Tamil poetry begins for many critics with the works of the famous patriot-poet and social reformer C. Cuppiramaṇiya Pārati (1882–1921), better known simply as Bharati and perhaps the most important voice of 20th-c. Tamil lit. But while Bharati certainly is much better known, a case can also be made for Māyūram Vētanāyakam Piḷḷai (1826–89), remembered chiefly as the first Tamil novelist, to have been the first mod. poet, since his *Nītinūl* (Book of Moral Conduct), pub. in 1859, purposely deviated from the traditional learned poetics of his time in order to create something that was both formally and thematically new. Though Bharati died young, his more than 250 poems cover a wide range of themes, such as love, nature, mythology, philosophical and religious speculation, and political ideas. His candid patriotism is important, as is his experimentation with what he called prose poetry, an ancestor of Tamil *free verse or what was later referred to as *putukkavitai* (new poetry). Bharati's poetic innovations and experimentations were continued in the 1930s and 1940s by a number of writers associated with the avant-garde literary magazine *Maṇikkoṭi* (The Jewel Banner), notably N. Pitchamurthy (1900–77), who was inspired by Walt Whitman's *Leaves of Grass* (1855), and K. P. Rajagopalan (1902–44), who wrote about love and village life. Kanaka Subburatnam (1891–1964) called himself Bharatidasan (Bharati's slave) and continued to write patriotic and nature poetry following but also modifying Bharati's style. Another literary magazine, C. S. Chellappa's *Eḻuttu* (Writing) founded in 1959, gave further impetus to the develop. of mod. poetry or *putukkavitai*. In 1962, editor Chellappa published his milestone anthol. *Putukkuralkaḷ* (New Voices), featuring some of the now canonical mod. poets: Nakulan (pseud. of T. K. Doraiswamy, 1922–2007), Sundara Ramaswamy (1931–2005), S. Vaidheeswaran (b. 1935), S. Mani (1936–2009), and Pramil (pseud. of Dharmu Sivaram, 1939–97).

In the 21st c., Tamil poetry is a multifaceted global phenomenon, with Tamil poets and their audiences living in many different countries. Some of the most exciting contemp. poetry is written by South Indian Dalit poets, such as Ravikumar (b. 1960), Vizhi. Pa. Idayavendhan (b. 1962), Adhavan Deetchanya (b. 1964), and N. T. Rajkumar (b. 1968), calling for a renegotiation of the role of Dalits in society, as well as by female, often feminist, poets. Candid poems about women's roles in society and the female body by poets such as Salma (b. 1968), Kutti Revathi (b. 1974), Malathi Maitri (b. 1968), and Sukirtharani (b. 1973) have caused considerable controversy. Poets of Sri Lanka such as S. Sivasegaram (b. 1942), M. A. Nuhman (b. 1944), V.I.S. Jayapalan (b. 1944), S. Vilvaratnam (1950–2006), Solaikkili (b. 1957), R. Cheran (b. 1960), and S. Sivaramani (1968–1991) have focused—among other themes—on the atrocities of the Sri Lankan civil war and the new modes of life found in the diaspora. Malaysian hip-hop artists, such as Yogi B. (b. 1974) and Dr. Burn (b. 1981), continue to explore new poetic modes and possibilities of doing things with Tamil words.

*See* INDIA, POETRY OF; SRI LANKA, POETRY OF.

■ **Anthologies and Translations:** *The Interior Landscape*, trans. A. K. Ramanujan (1967); *Hymns for the Drowning: Poems for Viṣṇu by Nammāḷvār*, trans. A. K. Ramanujan (1981); *Poems of Love and War*, trans. A. K. Ramanujan (1985); *Modern Tamil Poetry*, trans. M. S. Ramaswami (1988); *Bharathi Patalkal*, ed. T. N. Ramachandran (1989); *Songs of the Harsh Devotee: The Tēvāram of Cuntaramūrttināyanār*, trans. D. Shulman (1990); *Tiruvalluvar: The Kural*, trans. P. S. Sundaram (1990); *The Tale of an An-*

*klet*, trans. R. Parthasarathy (1993); *The Four Hundred Songs of War and Wisdom (Puṟanāṉūṟu)*, trans. G. L. Hart and H. Heifetz (1999); "Ancient Tamil Literature," *Ancient Indian Literature*, ed. T.R.S. Sharma (2000); "Tamil," *Medieval Indian Literature*, ed. K. Ayyappa Paniker (2000); *Lutesong and Lament: Tamil Writing from Sri Lanka*, ed. C.Kanaganayakam(2001); *The Kamba Ramayana*, trans. P. S. Sundaram (2002); *Cīvakacintāmaṇi: The Hero Cīvakaṉ, the Gem That Fulfills All Wishes*, v. 1, trans. J. D. Ryan (2005); *Tamil New Poetry*, trans. K. S. Subramanian (2005); *The History of the Holy Servants of the Lord Siva: A Translation of the Periya Purāṇam of Cēkkiḻār*, trans. A. McGlashan (2006); *The Rapids of a Great River: The Penguin Book of Tamil Poetry*, ed. L. Holmström, S. Krishnaswamy, and K. Srilata (2009).

■ **Criticism and History:** K. Zvelebil, *The Smile of Murugan* (1973); K. Zvelebil, *Tamil Literature* (1974); G. L. Hart, *The Poems of Ancient Tamil* (1975); K. Zvelebil, *Tamil Literature* (1975); D. Shulman, *Tamil Temple Myths* (1980); Vallikkaṇṇaṉ, *Putukavitaiyiṉ tōṟṟamum vaḷarcciyum* (The Emergence and History of New Poetry), 2d ed. (1980); F. Hardy, *Viraha Bhakti: The Early History of Kṛṣṇa Devotion in South India* (1983); U. Niklas, "Introduction to Tamil Prosody," *Bulletin de l'École Française d'Extrême-Orient* 77 (1988); I. V. Peterson, *Poems to Śiva: The Hymns of the Tamil Saints* (1989); K. Zvelebil, *Lexicon of Tamil Literature* (1995); M. Muilwijk, *The Divine Kuṟa Tribe: Kuṟavañci and Other Prabandhams* (1996); I. Manuel, *Literary Theories in Tamil* (1997); P. Richman, *Extraordinary Child* (1997)—on the piḷḷaittamiḻ genre; E. Wilden, *Literary Techniques in Old Tamil Caṅkam Poetry* (2006); S. Ebeling, *Colonizing the Realm of Words: The Transformation of Tamil Literature in Nineteenth-Century South India* (2010).

S. EBELING

**TASTE.** The term *taste* first emerged in early mod. Europe as a *metaphor for aesthetic appreciation. For the ancients, taste and smell ranked low on the philosophical hierarchy of the senses because they were associated with bodily pleasure rather than cognition. Whereas sight and hearing were thought to allow for a proper representative distance from the object of contemplation (hence, the regulating principles of consciousness and morality), taste was bound up with the physical whims of the body. It appealed, therefore, to bodily instinct and pleasure, which Aristotle maintained was *not* the objective of art. While the exertion of the "higher" senses theoretically led to more mind, taste led through the chemical physiology of the body to the "lower" corporeal realm of appetites and aversions. The neck physically separated the head from the body as the seat of all the passions, which stemmed from the stomach and ruled human behavior without reference to shared principles or ideals. Whereas sight and hearing came to be known as "objective" senses, taste and smell were clumped together as suspiciously "subjective." (Touch wavered somewhere between these two extremes and was sometimes demoted to the bottom of the sensation hierarchy.) Traditionally thought to be less mentally reflective than the "distal" senses, taste was associated with sensuousness and overindulgence.

In Enlightenment Europe, however, *taste* became the dominant metaphor for a disinterested appreciation of the arts—and more generally beauty. Precisely when the metaphorical usage of *taste* was first adopted to indicate mental discernment is up for debate. Townsend traces it to the Ren. polymath Leon Battista Alberti (1404–72) and Saisselin to a later generation of It. humanists (Michelangelo, Ludovico Ariosto, and Benvenuto Cellini, among others). In the aristocratic world of neoclassical France, the *je ne sais quoi* tied to the inexplicable quality of gustatory preference came to stand in for the rhetorical irreducibility of aesthetic experience. The 18th-c. trad. of Brit. taste philosophy follows Joseph Addison's 1711 *Spectator* essay on taste (no. 409), which credits the Sp. *baroque author Baltasar Gracián (1601–58) with the application of the gustatory metaphor to mental discernment. Like the "sensitive taste" of the tongue, the "mental taste" of the critic was defined by Addison as "that faculty of the soul, which discerns the beauties of an author with pleasure, and the imperfections with dislike." His analogy between the art connoisseur and the tea taster, who could distinguish blindly among different blends of tea, informed the Enlightenment concept of taste as an ideal of cultured refinement, grounded in natural sensibility.

The paradox characterizing the so-called Man of Taste was this tension between subjective response and objective principles. Even Immanuel Kant, who dismissed empiricist sensation psychology as philosophically unsound, began his reflections on taste in *Anthropology from a Pragmatic Point of View* (1772–73) as a rumination on the physicality of the metaphor: "How might it have happened," he asked, "that the modern languages particularly have chosen to name the aesthetic faculty of judgement with an expression (*gustus, sapor*) which merely refers to a certain sense-organ" and that mental discrimination as well as physical preference should be determined by it. What Kant faced was the difficulty of proceeding logically, according to a priori logic, when aesthetic-taste experience was stubbornly somatic. The difficulty plagued most taste theorists who sought principles on which to found legitimate judgments of taste.

Bodily taste may be dependent on the fleshy organ of the tongue with its sensory "tentacles" or papillae, but mental taste conceived of as a feeling or sentiment of beauty must entail more than physical sensation. It had to involve an element of necessity, or there could be no meaning ascribed to it—no standard, no principles, nothing beyond physical instinct. In addition to David Hume ("Of the Standard of Taste," 1757), empiricist philosophers of taste included John Gilbert Cooper (*Letters concerning Taste*, 1757), Edmund Burke (*A Philosophical Enquiry into the Origin of Our Ideas of the Sublime and the Beautiful*, 1757), Hugh Blair (*Lectures on Rhetoric and Belles Lettres*, 1783), Thomas Reid

(*Essays on the Intellectual Powers of Man*, 1785), and Archibald Alison, *Essays on the Nature and Principle of Taste*, 1790). Yet the dilemma continued in philosophical discourse of the early 19th c.

In his Preface to the 2d ed. of *Lyrical Ballads* (1800), William Wordsworth disapproved of those "who will converse with us gravely about a taste for poetry, as they express it, as if it were a thing as indifferent as a taste for rope-dancing, or Frontiniac or Sherry." Along similar lines, S. T. Coleridge remarked disapprovingly in his *Philosophical Lectures* of 1819 on the gustatory metaphor: "One man may say I delight in Milton and Shakespeare more than Turtle or Venison another man that is not my case for myself I think a good dish of turtle and a good bottle of port afterwards give me much more delight than I receive from Milton and Shakespeare you must not dispute about tastes." There may be no disputing physical-taste preference, but the extensive amount of disputation about aesthetic taste suggests that the maxim *de gustibus non est disputandum* did not apply philosophically. Like the moral-sense theorists (e.g., Anthony Ashley Cooper, the third Earl of Shaftesbury, *Characteristics* [1711] and Francis Hutcheson, *An Inquiry into the Origin of Our Ideas* [1725]), Kant drew on the idea of an "inner sense" capable of apperception to characterize taste as an innate. Nevertheless, his *Critique of Judgment* (1790) continued to be preoccupied with the analogy as a stumbling block to a coherent aesthetics: "a man may recount to me all the ingredients of a dish, and observe of each and every one of them that it is just what I like," yet I must "try the dish with *my own* tongue and palate" in order to "pass judgement according to their verdict (not according to universal principles)."

Beauty was the object of aesthetic taste, and empiricists like Hume believed that certain qualities that could excite a sentiment of aesthetic pleasure (or its converse, disgust) must exist "out there" in the object, waiting to be perceived correctly. Such logic dictated that to judge correctly was to judge without interest from a condition of subjective transparency—hence, universality or "disinterest." (As Eagleton notes, the rhetoric of taste had always been juridical.) The critic's job was to discriminate among undigested material, like the famous wine tasters of Sancho Panza's anecdote retold by Hume in "Of the Standard of Taste." These men, who could detect beauties as well as defects, e.g., an old key tied to a leathern thong at the bottom of a hogshead of wine, were emblems of refinement no less than the tea connoisseur cited by Addison. Voltaire's article on taste (*Goût*), begun by Montesquieu for Denis Diderot and Jean d'Alembert's *Encyclopédie*, also highlights the analogy: "just as the gourmet immediately perceives and recognizes a mixture of two liqueurs, so the man of taste, the connoisseur, will discern in a rapid glance any mixture of styles. He will perceive a flaw next to an embellishment." In addition to being "cleared of all prejudice," therefore, the ideal critic must achieve (as Hume puts it) a "perfect serenity of mind."

Backing the 18th-c. philosophical idealism that aesthetic-taste experience could be shared was a political optimism: taste is a "social quality" uniting all citizens in a *sensus communis* or political body from which all idiosyncrasies of birth, habit, prejudice, and circumstance have been cleared. The requisite for aesthetic experience, i.e., personal objectivity or disinterestedness, also promised social cohesion through a "standard of taste." Starting out from the assumption that taste could be shared, Hume (like Burke [*Philosophical Enquiry*], Alexander Gerard [*Essay on Taste*, 1759], and Lord Kames [*Elements of Criticism*, 1762]), believed that when "men vary in their judgments, some defect or perversion in the faculties may commonly be perceived." For these men in "the Century of Taste" (Dickie's phrase), the standard of taste amounted to the collective opinion of a group of ideal critics with acute natural sensibilities, improved by years of practice, and experience with the best models of what has been thought and done in any given culture. Recent challenges to canonical formulations of "the best," however, remind us that the serene and dispassionate, hegemonic Man of Taste was a cultural construct often involving privilege (the leisure and means to gain experience and exposure) and unequal power relations. One name for the aesthetic arena of taste is Jürgen Habermas's "public sphere," another the Enlightenment "Republic of Letters."

In many ways, the Enlightenment concept of taste was a reaction to the Hobbesian view of society as a brutish state of nature, or clash of individual appetites. What Elias has identified as "the civilizing process" represented a trajectory away from instinctual desire toward cultured refinement. As the middle classes grew in importance economically, individuals were taught to regulate themselves and their motivating appetites from within—in part through the aesthetic ideology of 18th-c. taste philosophy, in part through the cultural barrage of conduct manuals, painting and dancing masters, and other practical guides to culture and etiquette. Taste was a middle-class mode of producing subjects, and the consumer was to attain social distinction by navigating the fine line between aesthetic appreciation and material desire. The shift in the nature of that subject from amateur (or lover of the arts) to professional followed the shift from taste to aesthetics.

■ W. J. Bate, *From Classic to Romantic* (1946); E. Cassirer, *The Philosophy of the Enlightenment,* trans. F.C.A. Koeblu and J. P. Pettegrove (1951); I. Kant, *Critique of Judgment,* ed. and trans. J. C. Meredith (1952); R. G. Saisselin, *Taste in Eighteenth-Century France* (1965); N. Elias, *The Civilizing Process: The History of Manners,* trans. E. Jephcott (1978); P. Bourdieu, *Distinction: A Social Critique of the Judgment of Taste,* trans. R. Nice (1984); H. Caygill, *Art of Judgement* (1989); T. Eagleton, *The Ideology of the Aesthetic* (1990); L. Ferry, *Homo Aestheticus: The Invention of Taste in the Democratic Age,* trans. R. de Loaiza (1993); G. Dickie, *The Century of Taste* (1996); I. Kant, *Anthropology from a Pragmatic Point of View,* ed. and trans. V. L. Dowdell (1996); D. Townsend, "Taste: Early History," *Encyclopedia of Aesthetics,* ed. M. Kelly (1998); C. Korsmeyer, *Making Sense of Taste: Food and Philosophy* (1999); D. Gigante, *Taste: A Literary History* (2005).

D. GIGANTE

**TECHNOLOGY AND POETRY.** Poetry has long maintained relations with technology, ranging from the concrete and practical to the philosophical and theoretical. Poets have employed multiple technologies in the composition of their works, and a hist. of these technologies is relevant to an understanding of poetry's own hist. However, the philosophical trad. has often obscured these interrelations, attempting to separate poetry from technology in order to assert poetry's privileged access either to nature or divine truth. In the Platonic dialogues, for instance, *\*poiēsis*, the Gr. root of *poetry*, is carefully distinguished from *technē*, the Gr. root of *technology*, often meaning "craft" or "knowledge." As a consequence, a tension emerges between poetic making and mechanical fabrication. This tension has shaped discourses on poetry throughout the ages, producing a paradoxical situation in which the poetic genre identifies itself in opposition to the very means on which it relies and through which it evolves.

Socrates (via Plato) frequently defines *technē* as type of knowledge that is practically oriented: a technē is a craft, such as building a ship, healing a body, or playing the harp. In the *Republic,* Plato makes a further distinction between higher and lower forms of craft or making. The highest craft, that of statesmanship, involves a deep knowledge, an understanding of the Forms; it is an *epistemē* to be distinguished from the lower form of making, *poiēsis* (from *poiein,* both to make and to compose poetry). In book 10, Plato argues further that the *\*poet* (*poiētēs*), like the painter, imitates Forms at a third remove. The demise of poetry as a form of *\*knowledge,* and the beginning of its conflict with other types of craft (techniques and technology), is established here. In the *Symposium,* poiēsis appears somewhat differently: as a generative force responsible for everything from sexual procreation to the cultivation of the soul. But such associations cannot save poetry per se from being considered by Plato to be a craft of persuasion grounded in neither morality nor truth.

Martin Heidegger makes the next crucial step in the philosophical understanding of poetry's relation to technology, and he does so by standing Plato on his head. In opposition to the argument advanced in the *Republic,* Heidegger's essays of the 1950s submit that it is poetry, rather than discourses based on reason and mathematical calculation, that enjoys a privileged relation to truth. For Heidegger, poetry is the most elevated of all the *technai,* and its elevation consists precisely in its distance from crafts implicated in the blind pragmatics of mod. industrialization. Heidegger introduces a new distinction between technē as damaging, "enframing" technology and technē as the poetic revelation of truth. In "The Origin of the Work of Art" (1950), Heidegger posits that poetry, as the highest form of lang., "brings what is, as something that is, into the Open for the first time." Thus, instead of being elided with the imitation—at three removes—of Forms, poetry reveals the very truth of being. Poetry remains a kind of technē, but only, Heidegger underscores, insofar as we understand technē to be "a mode of knowing," a "bringing out of beings." By imposing a strict distinction between *technē* as poetic "revealing" (poiēsis) and *technē* as "enframing" (*Gestellung*), Heidegger produces a clean break between poetry and technology or, more specifically, between the two types of lang. counterposed during his own generation: poetic writing and technologically mediated radiophonic speech.

Anticipating Heidegger, the Brit. romantics conceived of poetry as singularly capable of providing human beings with alternatives to technologically mediated forms of contact with the world (see ROMANTICISM). William Blake's ambivalence toward rapid industrialization set the tone for the reception of new technologies during the romantic period. The "dark satanic mills" of Blake's *Songs of Innocence and Experience* (1794) underscored the threat of technology, even as their author innovated in the printing technique of etching. William Wordsworth perfected the negative posture toward mod. industrialization (and thus, as a corollary, technology and science): in *The Prelude* (pub. posthumously in 1850) even "skill" is placed under suspicion, whereas seeing with "a heart / That watches and receives" is praised. Other famous expressions of poetry's epistemological (and moral) superiority over technē may be found in S. T. Coleridge's *The Rime of the Ancient Mariner* (1798) and "The Eolian Harp" (1795). P. B. Shelley's "Letter to Maria Gisborne" (1820) displays an ambivalent attitude toward technology (in the form of a steam engine), while John Keats's "Isabella" (1820) laments the inevitable implication of technology in the pursuit of capital. Romantic poetry's most powerful reflections on technē revolve around the figure of Prometheus (Shelley's *Prometheus Unbound* [1820] and Lord Byron's "Prometheus" [1816]). Here, the Enlightenment emblem of progress returns in romantic verse as simultaneously demon and hero, reflecting the poet's ambivalent attitude toward the tangible consequences of technology and its industrial exploitation.

The encroachment of technology into everyday life only increased during England's Victorian age. As Picker argues, mod. technologies not only suggested thematic material but also imposed alterations on the poet's sensorium. The invention of the microphone in 1827 and other means of acoustic amplification changed the very experience of sound and, thus, writing, reading, and listening practices. Poets from the Victorian age onward began to integrate at the level of composition the technologies of their age in a manner that was both self-aware and purposeful. What Heidegger fears in ". . . Poetically Man Dwells . . ." (1951) was thus actualized in a curious way: it turned out that accommodating and even imitating "radiophonic" and other forms of technologically mediated speech were not incompatible with the unfolding of poetry's own potential as a form of reflection and critique.

It is ironic, then, that Heidegger sought to distinguish poetry from the discourse of broadcasting ("radiophonic speech") at the very moment that many poets were exploring the potential of radio and other new media to disseminate and produce poetry. Heidegger's recoil from such "fallen," technologically mediated speech was arguably a perverse reaction to the poets' own enthusiastic embrace of the same. The response of many poets to technology was curiosity, not disdain. Alfred, Lord Tennyson, for one, excitedly recorded parts of *The Princess* (1847) on a phonograph presented to him by Thomas Edison himself. And in France, poets rarely hesitated to adopt recording technologies for their own use. (Radio became widely accessible when transmissions from the Eiffel Tower were standardized in 1921.) Blaise Cendrars, Jean Cocteau, and Robert Desnos all performed on the radio; the latter worked with Paul Deharme, Alejo Carpentier, and Jean-Louis Barrault to produce radio shows throughout the 1930s. Bertolt Brecht ("Radiotheorie" [1927]) and Theodor W. Adorno (see his unfinished writings on radio collected in *Current of Music: Elements of a Radio Theory*, 2009) remained skeptical because of radio's implication in the advertising world. However, Paul Deharme (*Pour un art radiophonique* [1930]), Walter Benjamin ("Reflections on Radio" [1931]), and Rudolf Arnheim (*Radio* [1936]) all discerned the avant-garde potential of the radiophonic medium, as did Velimir Khlebnikov, F. T. Marinetti, Gertrude Stein, and Ezra Pound. Some major poetic works were conceived specifically *for* the radio, such as Antonin Artaud's *Pour en finir avec le jugement de Dieu* (1947) and Francis Ponge's *Le Savon* (1965), to mention just a few.

The interest these poets exhibited in the radio was only the most recent instance of poetry's enduring fascination with—and appropriation of—technological means. The story often told is that the invention of radiophonic, phonographic, cinematic, and televisual technologies signaled the demise of the voice, and with it, the subjective *lyric genre. However, hist. shows the reverse to be true. Echoing Heidegger, Kittler has insisted that once the voice could be recorded, poetry was no longer required. *Rhythm and *rhyme suddenly became "superfluous," writes Kittler, as "technology triumphs over mnemotechnology. And the death bell tolls for poetry, which for long had been the love of so many." While typical, this account ignores that, for many poets, the possibility of registering the voice—first with the phonograph, then with the tape recorder—was seen as an opportunity, not a threat. The phonograph itself was invented by a poet, Charles Cros, in 1877, at roughly the same time it was conceived by Thomas Edison, who had the means to put the invention into production. Although some poets lacked access to technology, they still expressed their enthusiasm by imitating the sounds and rhythms of various machines: Blaise Cendrars's and Sonia Delaunay's *La Prose du Transsibérien et de la petite Jehanne de France* (1913) reproduces the rhythm of the train and the seriality of film; F. T. Marinetti's *Zang Tumb Tuuum* (1914) copies the sounds of machine guns; Guillaume Apollinaire's "Lettre-Océan" (1914) portrays the concentric circles of TSF (*Télégraphe sans fil*) transmission; Jean Cocteau's *Parade* (1917) integrates the sound of typewriting, while *La Voix humaine* (1930) features telephones; Pierre Reverdy emulates cinematic montage in *Les ardoises du toit* (1918); and André Breton borrows "automatic writing" from electronic modes of sound recording (*Le Manifeste du surréalisme*, 1924).

As the 20th c. dawned, industrialists joined forces with inventors to make recording technologies more available to the general public. The entrepreneurial Émile Pathé provided financial support for the first phonographic recording of poems by Apollinaire, Emile Verhaeren, and René Ghil in 1913. Their daring act paved the way for Marinetti, who published the first bona fide poetry record, "La Battaglia di Andrianopoli," in 1924. Marinetti was followed by Kurt Schwitters, who recorded parts of *Ursonate* in 1925 and Joyce Joyce, who recorded "Anna Livia Plurabelle" in London in 1929. Writing in 1917, Apollinaire made it clear that poets sought from phonographic technologies not an accurate registration of the lyric voice (*pace* Kittler) but rather a revelation of sounds not formerly considered poetic. He and others hoped to amplify the aural matter at the heart of poetic expression, thereby uncovering a kind of auditory unconscious that would rival the "optical unconscious" described by Walter Benjamin in "The Work of Art in the Age of Mechanical Reproduction" (1936). Representing the early 20th-c. avant-garde, Apollinaire exclaimed in "La Victoire" (1917): "We want new sounds new sounds new sounds." Phonographic technologies were embraced because they offered the opportunity to record a vast array of aural phenomena, from glottal and labial vocalizations such as the licking, sucking, and gulping introduced into lyric circulation by Christian Morgenstern in his *Fisches Nachtgesang* (1905) to nonhuman sounds such as the breaking dishes and sleigh bells Apollinaire employed in his soundscape for *Les Mamelles de Tirésias* (1917). Arguably, the most significant contribution to poetry was the avant-garde's intuition that diverse elements of the aural universe could become poetic materials in their own right. In the 1950s, the same logic would inspire poets in both France and the United States to experiment with the most advanced audio technology of their own generation, the tape recorder. Elaborating on the techniques of *Dada and *surrealism, William Burroughs and Brion Gysin produced "cut-ups" by manipulating magnetic tape, which had been introduced into wide circulation during the post–World War II era. In France, François Dufrêne inaugurated the movement known as *poésie sonore* (*sound poetry) with his *Crirythmes* (1953). Extending the work of Hugo Ball, Antonin Artaud, and Luigi Russolo, Dufrêne reimagined poetry as an electroacoustic vocal improvisation, a sequence emerging from both amplified human sounds (groans, coughs, nasalizations) and the microphone itself (invented in 1925). Bernard Heidsieck and Henri Chopin soon followed suit, composing written scores with phonetic and semantic content in the first instance, and exploring the expressive possibilities of amplifiers, microphones, and the body's own internal organs in the second. In this way, technological means originally invented for military use were placed at the service of poetic experiment.

Far from proving that advanced technologies ring the death knell for poetry, hist. shows that poets frequently celebrate—and even anticipate—the possibilities they offer. The phonetic babble of Ball, the *simultanéisme* of Henri Martin Barzun, and the *zaum' poetry of Velimir Khlebnikov and Aleksei Kruchenykh were all forms that called for technologies still to come. "The history of every art form shows critical epochs in which a certain art form aspires to effects which could be fully obtained only with a changed technical standard," Benjamin wrote in 1936. Funkhouser makes a similar observation with regard to digital poetry, arguing that the foundations of the new genre existed conceptually decades before personal computers became available. The proleptic quality of poetic experiment is a historical constant. Although recording devices from the magnetic to the digital permit poets to disseminate their works to a larger audience, the true aesthetic entailments of mod. audio technologies have been creative rather than reproductive.

The same thing could be said for printing methods. Well before George Herbert's canonical *technopaegnion "Easter Wings" (1633), poets began to exploit the possibilities of movable type. Invented in the Western hemisphere in 1450 by Johannes Gutenberg (in China, in 1040), movable type placed visual emphasis on the isolated letter, the graphemic rather than the phonic content of words. During the 19th c., typographic layout became a focal point for creative innovation. Kittler has argued that Stéphane Mallarmé turned his attention to the letter (and to *textuality per se) as a defense against the phonographic registration of the voice. However, it is more likely that Mallarmé's interest in the spatial and pictorial dimensions of the page grew in tandem with devels. in publishing and cinematographic media. Mallarmé's meditation on the paper medium was part of a generational concern with the evocative and semantic potentials of *typography, which reached its apotheosis in late 19th-c. newspaper and advertising graphics. Whereas radio, cinema, and television would become the mass media technologies of the 20th c., print was the quintessential mass media technology of Mallarmé's time. When Richard March Hoe increased the rapidity of print processing with his lithographic rotary press in 1843 and Ottmar Mergenthaler introduced linotype in 1884, the presence of printed text and graphics in daily life became inescapable. However, as Drucker has observed, devels. in the use of print were governed less by the invention of new technologies than by larger social changes, such as the emergence in England, France, and the U.S. of a strong industrial core, the formation of a literate bourgeoisie, and the weakening of the *patronage and academy systems in the domain of high art.

Mallarmé's typographic experiment of 1897, *Un coup de dés*, was the most daring appropriation of print technologies for the use of poetic composition to date. Sensitive to the way mod. readers approached typographic display as a spectacle for the eye, Mallarmé replaced the temporality of prosody with the simultaneity of spatial organization, imposing the constraint of the two-page spread as a frame in which to arrange words or phrases. In the first print version (in the jour. *Cosmopolis*, 1897), he suppressed all punctuation and references to the hand, voice, or breath of the writer that had existed in the drafts. Anticipating Albert Lord's argument in *The Singer of Tales* (1960) concerning the transition from oral to written poetry, Mallarmé approached writing not as secondary, a dictation subordinated to speech, but rather as an originary medium producing uncontrollable *ambiguities realized through acts of reading. Mallarmé also claimed that cinema played a crucial role in his experimental practice; he advanced a parallel between the *déroulement* (unfolding) of filmic projection and the processual format of *Un coup de dés*. Mallarmé's insight was prescient: in the 20th c., achieving a poetic rendering of cinematic phenomenality would become one of poetry's central preoccupations. As Ortel (*La littérature à l'ère de la photographie* [2002]), North (*Camera Works* [2005]), and Wall-Romana (*Cinepoetry* [2012]) have cogently argued, visual media such as photography and film transformed the very way poets conceive of the word in space.

The visual possibilities of letters were exploited further by 20th-c. poets such as Apollinaire (*Calligrammes*, 1918), the Rus. constructivists (see CONSTRUCTIVISM); the Lettristes, e. e. cummings, Ezra Pound, and Wyndham Lewis; the Brazilian concrete poets Augusto and Haroldo de Campos (see NOIGANDRES); and Eugen Gomringer, Ian Hamilton Finlay, and Pierre Garnier. Another important inheritor of Mallarmé's spatial poetics is Charles Olson, who experimented in the American context with *composition by field. If Mallarmé's major sources of inspiration were print graphics and the cinema, Olson's poetry was profoundly shaped by the mechanics of the typewriter. Invented simultaneously in Denmark by Rasmus Malling-Hansen and in the U.S. by Christopher Latham, the typewriter was introduced into mass production by the arms manufacturing company Remington in the 1860s. By the time Olson began writing after World War II, the typewriter was a ubiquitous tool. Whereas Heidegger lamented that the typewriter tears composition from the hand, degrading the written word by separating it further from human speech, Olson believed, on the contrary, that typewriting reverses the momentum of Gutenberg's revolution. "It is the advantage of the typewriter," he wrote in *"Projective Verse" (1950), that "it can, for a poet, indicate exactly the breath, the pauses, the suspensions even of syllables, the juxtapositions even of parts of phrases, which he intends." The visual arrangements on the page (or field) can thus allude to aural and corporeal phenomena; further, they can be perceived as a map forming semantically charged patterns in plastic space.

Creating patterns with letters and words is not original to Olson, Apollinaire, or even Mallarmé. Scholars point to examples found in ancient Greece (2d and 3d cs. BCE) as well as George Herbert. Dick Higgins, an artist associated with the Fluxus movement and one of the early theorists of computer-generated texts, observes that pattern poetry becomes possible as soon as writing appears, i.e., as soon as the word, to paraphrase Ong, is committed to space. In a similar vein, Derrida theorizes that writing (as *écriture* or spacing) is the exemplary technology, the originary corruption of an immediate *phusis* (nature) by an artificial technē that brings nature into consciousness of itself. Without écriture, there would be no storing of experience, he reasons, no self-reflexivity and, thus, no apprehension of the difference between *poiēsis* and *technē* in the first place. Opposing Heidegger, Derrida asserts not only that speech is a variety of writing but that the subjective immediacy of lyric is made possible through the impersonal mediation of a technics—whether that technics be conceived as *rhetoric, *prosody, *convention, or lang. itself. Writing during the same period, Adorno approaches the issue from a more historical perspective, insisting that relations and means of technological production dominant during any given era inflect the procedures employed by the artist. Technai, or modes of spacing, vary according to generation; thus, a true understanding of poetry's relation to technology can be attained only when historically specific modes of production are identified and their influence deeply probed. Adorno points out that technological means and their aesthetic entailments always permeate cultural environments; to refuse technological means is not to escape them but merely to remain blind to the way they already inform the poetic *imagination at work.

Adorno's praise is awarded to poets who, like Arthur Rimbaud, openly acknowledge that lyric subjectivity is far from immediate and that it belongs to a discursive "apparatus" (for Michel Foucault, a *dispositif*) generated by a particular technology-based medium in a particular medialogical, or socioeconomic, context. This historicized notion of écriture as apparatus is a useful tool for approaching the intensified relations between poetry and technology in the 21st c. Today's poets are mobilizing computer word-processing systems, animation software, digital cameras, and even mobile phones to produce poems combining kinetic, graphic, and verbal elements. The pioneers of digital poetry—incl. Max Bense, Theo Lutz, Pedro Barbosa, Philippe Bootz, Jackson Mac Low, and Alan Sondheim—expanded the experimental use of computer technologies for the creation, and not simply dissemination, of poems. Members of early 21st c. movements such as *Flarf and Conceptual ("Uncreative") Writing (see CONCEPTUAL POETRY) maintain that the internet has provided the possibility for appropriative and permutational procedures that redefine not only what constitutes poetry but also *what constitutes poiēsis itself*. Hayles (2005) argues that human subjectivity is now so thoroughly mediated by digitality that the expressivity supposedly at the root of poetic writing is no more than an epiphenomenon of a hybrid consciousness constantly interfacing with code. As ever, poetry finds itself in the thick of debates on what constitutes the human being. Through its relations with technology across time, poetry offers a laboratory for exploring the ever-changing nature of what we are.

See ALEATORY POETICS; AVANT-GARDE POETICS; BOOK, POETIC; CODEWORK; COMPUTATIONAL POETRY; CONCRETE POETRY; CYBERTEXT; ELECTRONIC POETRY; PHILOSOPHY AND POETRY; VISUAL POETRY.

■ C. Olson, *Selected Writings of Charles Olson*, ed. R. Creeley (1950); G. Apollinaire, *Oeuvres complètes*, ed. M. Adéma and M. Décaudin (1959); Lord; W. Benjamin, *Illuminations*, ed. H. Arendt, trans. H. Zohn (1969); M. Heidegger, *Poetry, Language, Thought*, trans. A. Hofstadter (1971); M. Carrouges, *Les Machines célibataires* (1976); W. Ong, *Orality and Literacy: The Technologizing of the Word* (1982); R. Debray, *Cours de médiologie générale* (1991); J. Drucker, *The Visible Word: Experimental Typography and Modern Art, 1909–1923* (1994); *Wireless Imagination: Sound, Radio, and the Avant-Garde*, ed. D. Kahn and G. Whitehead (1994); T. W. Adorno, *Aesthetic Theory*, ed. and trans. R. Hullot-Kentor (1997); Derrida; F. A. Kittler, *Gramophone, Film, Typewriter*, trans. G. Winthrop-Young and M. Wutz (1999); C. Noland, *Poetry at Stake: Lyric Aesthetics and the Challenge of Technology* (1999); P. Ortel, *La Littérature à l'ère de la photographie: enquête sur une révolution invisible* (2002); J. M. Picker, *Victorian Soundscapes* (2003); M. North, *Camera Works: Photography and the Twentieth-Century Word* (2005); N. K. Hayles, *My Mother Was a Computer: Digital Subjects and Literary Texts* (2005); C. T. Funkhouser, *Prehistoric Digital Poetry: An Archaeology of Forms, 1959–1995* (2007); J.-P. Bobillot, *Poésie Sonore: Éléments de typologie historique* (2009); M. Perloff, *Unoriginal Genius: Poetry by Other Means in the New Century* (2010); C. Wall-Romana, *Cinepoetics: Imaginary Cinemas in French Poetry* (2012).

C. NOLAND

**TECHNOPAEGNION** (Gr., "shaped poetry," pl. *technopaegnia*, Lat. *carmina figurata*). A poem in which the letters, words, or lines are arrayed visually to form recognizable shapes, usually the gross forms of natural objects. While the origins of *technopaegnia* in the West are unknown (a Cretan piece dating from ca. 1700 BCE and some Egyptian pieces dating from 700 BCE are debated examples), there are six surviving poems by Gr. *bucolic poets, shaped as an axe, an egg, wings, two altars, and a syrinx. In late cl. Lat., there is a panegyric cycle by P. Optatianus Porphyrius (fl. 325 CE) praising the emperor Constantine the Great, for whom he was court poet. These poems are for the most part rectilinear or square, with "intexts" woven into or cancelled out from the main text (hence, their names *carmina, quadrata*, and *carmina cancellata*). This subgenre, revived at the Merovingian court by Fortunatus, was also popular in the Carolingian renaissance (Boniface, Alcuin, Josephus Scotus) and was the dominant form of visual poetry through the Middle Ages and into the 12th c., when the popularity of the mode waned. Extant intexts are shaped as a galley with oars (Optatian) and a crucified Christ (Hrabanus Maurus

[ca. 784–856]; texts in Migne, *PL*, 107.133 ff.); about 70 late cl. and med. pieces are known.

A second and larger wave of technopaegnia began in the 16th c., at first written mainly in Lat. and Gr. by learned poets in imitation of the *Greek Anthology*, but, later, in virtually all the vernaculars of Europe as well as Heb. and Lat., in such new shapes as suns, circles, pyramids, and columns, and in dozens of less common shapes (Puttenham, book 2, ch. 12). By the 17th c., shaped poems had become associated with occasional verse, though in Eng. George Herbert (1593–1633) and Robert Herrick (1591–1674) wrote serious instances; Herbert's "The Altar" and "Easter Wings" are widely anthologized. While from this period nearly 2,000 pieces are known, a reaction against *visual poetry set in with the spread of *neoclassical poetics in the late 17th c. Caustic comments were heaped on shaped poems in the 18th and early 19th cs., e.g., by Joseph Addison in *Spectator* no. 58. When the technopaegnion was accepted at all, it was taken as suitable only for comic verse, e.g., "The Mouse's Tale" in *Alice in Wonderland*.

But late in the 19th c., visual poetry in an expanded sense reemerged as an innovative technique, notably in Stéphane Mallarmé's *Un coup de dés* (1897) and Guillaume Apollinaire's *Calligrammes* (1918), which proved inspirational to *Dadaism and later the *concrete poetry movement germinating in Brazil, greater Latin America, and Ger.-speaking Europe in the mid-20th c. Dylan Thomas's "Vision and Prayer" is comprised of stanzas arranged in geometric forms in spatial dialogue with the verse itself, a trait also consistent in John Hollander's *Types of Shape* (1969). The Fluxus figure Dick Higgins (see ALEATORY POETICS) was a tireless collector of what he called pattern poetry. Most recently, David Daniels's *The Gates of Paradise* (2000) stands as the longest pub. volume of visual poetry, at over 400 pages.

Close analogues to technopaegnia exist in many non-Western poetries, such as *hüi-wen* in Chinese (from the late Han, 2d c. CE, up to mod. times), *ashide-e* in Japanese (esp. in the early Tokugawa, 16th c.), and *citra-kāvyas* in Sanskrit (from the 7th c. CE on) and other langs. of the Indian subcontinent. Like Western technopaegnia, these latter are composed in traditional shapes and classified by these into *bandhas*, with each bandha having its own associations and trads.

See CALLIGRAMME, VISUAL POETRY.

■ *Bucoli graeci*, ed. A.S.F. Gow, 2 v. (1958)—the *Greek Anthology*; Curtius; K. Jhā, *Figurative Poetry in Sanskrit Literature* (1975); "Die Entwicklung der optischen Poesie in Antike, Mittelalter und Neuzeit," *Germanisch-Romanische Monatsschrift* 26 (1976); C. Doria, "Visual Writing Forms in Antiquity: The *Versus intexti*," *Visual Literature Criticism*, ed. R. Kostelanetz (1979); G. Pozzi, *La Parola depinta* (1981); D. W. Seaman, *Concrete Poetry in France* (1981); J. Adler, "Technopaegnia, carmina figurata and Bilder-reime," *Yearbook of Comparative Criticism* 4 (1982); U. Ernst, "Europäische Figurengedichte in Pyramidenform aus dem 16. und 17. Jahrhundert," *Euphorion* 76 (1982); W. Levitan, "Dancing at the End of the Rope," *TAPA* 115 (1985); Hollander, esp., "The

Poem in the Eye," and *Types of Shape*, 2d ed. (1991); E. Cook, *Seeing through Words* (1986); *Pattern Poetry*, ed. D. Higgins, spec. iss. of *Visible Language* 20.1 (1986); D. Higgins, *Pattern Poetry: Guide to an Unknown Literature* (1987); R. Greene, "The Concrete Historical," *Harvard Library Bulletin* NS 3.2 (1992); D. Colón, "Embodying the Ideogram: Orientalism and the Visual Aesthetic in Modernist Poetry," diss., Stanford University (2004); Puttenham.

D. A. COLÓN

**TELESILLEUM,** telesillean. In cl. prosody, the technical term for the metrical sequence – ◡ ◡ – ◡ ◡ –, which is one of the *aeolic cola (an *acephalous glyconic), though its use is not confined to the Aeolic poets. It is named after Telesilla, a poetess of Argos of the early 5th c. BCE, who used it for stichic verse. It also occurs in Gr. choral lyric and in the choruses of Gr. drama. The catalectic form of the telesilleum, i.e. the sequence x – ◡ ◡ – –, is sometimes called the Reizianum, so named by the early 19th-c. cl. scholar Hermann after his teacher Reiz (1733–90). In Lat. the Reizianum has a slightly different form and occurs both as a colon (in Plautus it has the form x – x – –) and as part of an *asynarteton, i.e., a verse composed of two differing cola, known as the *versus Reizianus* and having the pattern x – x – x – ◡ – | x – x – –.

*See* COLON.

■ L. Havet, "Le Distique (dit 'vers') de Reiz," *REL* 19 (1941); J. W. Halporn, "Reizianum (2)," *Lexikon der alten Welt* (1965), 2572; Koster; Dale; Snell; West.

J. W. HALPORN

**TEL QUEL.** *Tel Quel* was a Fr. quarterly literary jour. that ran from 1960 to 1982 and was the platform for many of the radical and avant-garde critical and creative practices in France during that period. The jour. and the writers who produced it (principally Philippe Sollers, Marcelin Pleynet, Julia Kristeva, and Denis Roche) were associated with a highly theoretical approach to lit., drawing on the work of Louis Althusser, Jacques Lacan, and Roland Barthes. However, the specifically theoretical moment in the jour.'s hist. (1965–71) should not obscure its long advocacy of lit., esp. poetic lang., as exceptional with regard to social and psychological norms and its challenge to readers to question the epistemological assumptions on which they rest. While the political affiliations of the review, specifically Marxism and Maoism, charted the attempts to weld the radical affirmation of lit.'s exceptional status to social and political revolution, the more lasting legacy of *Tel Quel* is twofold. First, the review consistently proposed a revalorization of the hist. of lit., disseminating new material, new trans., and new critical readings of major figures of the past. In the field of poetry and poetic lang., *Tel Quel* featured extensive renewals and reconfigurations of the work of Dante, Stéphane Mallarmé, Friedrich Hölderlin, James Joyce, Ezra Pound, the Comte de Lautréamont, Arthur Rimbaud, Antonin Artaud, Georges Bataille, and the surrealists (of whom *Tel Quel* was severely critical;

see SURREALISM). As this chain of names suggests, the poetry affirmed by *Tel Quel* tended to feature exceptional rather than conventional figures, and there was an orientation toward poetic prose rather than verse poetry, although this was not explicit. The theory of poetic lang. proposed by Kristeva (the principal theorist associated with the jour., e.g., in *La Révolution du langage poétique*, 1974), held that it has the capacity to reorganize the signifying system on which meaning as such is based; this system also incl. the social and historical framework of the *work and the *poet. In the critical work of Sollers, the permanent and directive presence behind *Tel Quel*, the hist. of lit. is punctuated with certain "limit texts," which express an exceptional logic and puncture the illusions of collective social life. Dante, the Marquis de Sade, Mallarmé, Joyce, Louis-Ferdinand Céline, and an increasing host constitute this chorus of moral revolt. The second aspect of *Tel Quel*'s contribution to the hist. of poetry and poetics was the publication of contemp. poetry in the jour. itself. Associated in its early years with the rhetorically innovative work of Francis Ponge, the poets associated with the review began in the 1960s to develop a style of poetry that eschewed lyricism and subjective poetry (Lautréamont), favored the incorporation of "foreign" elements (newspaper clippings, Chinese characters, Etruscan runes, the *I Ching*), but, significantly, tended over time toward a destructive critique of poetry as such. Thus, Roche's *Le Mécrit* (1972) was announced as a destruction of "poetry" and included texts written in undecipherable characters. Marcelin Pleynet's poetic oeuvre (*Stanze*, 1973; *Rime*, 1981) tends increasingly toward the *fragment, the residue of an aggressivity directed against lang. In terms both of its challenge to the critical trad. and its affirmation of lit. and of the poetic as such, *Tel Quel* is a crucial point of reference.

*See* AVANT-GARDE POETICS; FRANCE, POETRY OF; POST-STRUCTURALISM.

■ *Tel Quel*, 94 v. (1960–82); P. Sollers, *Writing and the Experience of Limits*, ed. D. Hayman, trans. P. Bernard and D. Hayman (1983); J. Kristeva, *Revolution in Poetic Language*, trans. M. Waller (1984); P. ffrench, *The Time of Theory: A History of "Tel Quel"* (1996).

P. FFRENCH

**TELUGU POETRY.** Telugu, a Dravidian lang. spoken by about 70 million people who live mostly in the south Indian state of Andhra Pradesh, has a thousand years of continuous literary production in various separate but interrelated trads.

The earliest extant text in Telugu is the first two and a half volumes of a Telugu rendering of the Sanskrit *Mahābhārata*, by the 11th-c. Nannaya, who is called the *ādi kavi*, the first poet. Nannaya was associated with the court of the Calukya king Rājarāja, who ruled from Rājamahendri, the present day Rajahmundry, on the banks of the river Godavari. Though Rājarāja's kingdom was short-lived, he commissioned a poem that survived to create lasting conventions of courtly poetry in Telugu. The poem begins with a prayer to the gods; goes on to describe its royal patron; describes in some detail the court scene where the king praises the poet, his scholarship, and his literary skills; expresses his interest in the particular book he wants composed; and commissions the poet to write it. The poet reverently accepts the commission and prepares to compose the poem, wishing continued good luck to his patron. The chapters are addressed to the patron as they open and end with eulogizing vocatives. The colophon includes the poet's name and titles.

This template, which Nannaya established, lasted for almost a thousand years with minor changes to the end of the 19th c. Nannaya's choice of meters selected from Sanskritic and Dravidian sources, along with a judicious combination of verses with heightened prose, also lasted as long. However, Nannaya's storytelling style, his economy of words with deep meaning that make the character come alive in the narrative, and his talent of combining words to create controlled and balanced sonic effects were never replicated in a thousand years. Nannaya's narrative requires a trained performer to present it for an educated audience, the performer adding his own commentary to make it immediately accessible. Nannaya's discrete verses captivate the attention of listeners, who memorize them for their mantric quality of sound. Such qualities make Nannaya the "first poet" for Telugu in a sense other than the chronological accident of his being the earliest. He mapped the literary path for all later generations. His followers, Tikkana (13th c.) and Errāpragaḍa (14th c.), who completed the Telugu rendering of the *Mahābhārata* Nannaya had begun, firmly established the path Nannaya had created.

The trad. Nannaya created does not, however, indicate a singularity of literary production. In less than two centuries after Nannaya's achievement, Pālkuriki Somanātha voices a protest calling for a countertrad. in a meter not derived from Sanskrit. This meter, called *dvipada* (a unit of two lines that can be combined to narrate a long story or a series of stories) and amenable to being sung collectively, closes the distance between the reader and the listener, which Nannaya's work requires, and promotes instead absorption into a collective identity. Pālkuriki Somanātha wrote two major works in dvipada—*Basavapurāṇa* and *Paṇḍitārādhya caritra*—to celebrate the two 12th-c. leaders of the *Vīra Śaivas*, militant worshippers of the god Śiva—Basaveśvara and Mallikārjuna Paṇḍitārādhya—who propagated an antiestablishment religion that demanded that its adherents reject their caste in favor of an egalitarian ethic and treat all members of their cult equally, even if they were untouchables and other low castes. In time, this movement gave way to its own caste hierarchy. The literary trad. of this group gradually waned for lack of *patronage.

Meanwhile, the dominant literary trad. continued to flourish with poets such as Nācana Somanātha and Śrīnātha of the 14th and 15th cs., respectively. Śrīnātha, who was called *kavisārvabhauma* (the emperor of poets), was a prolific author who traveled across the length and breadth of the Telugu-speaking area. His legendary biography speaks of his conquest

of a certain Diṇḍima Bhaṭṭu in the court of the Karṇāṭa king Devarāya II. Diṇḍima, the legend says, carried a bronze drum to exhibit his superiority over other poets. Śrīnātha, who defeated him in a literary debate, had the drum smashed in public and was, in the end, rewarded by the emperor with a shower of gold. Śrīnātha's works include *Śṛṅgāranaiṣadhamu,* a Telugu rendering of Śrīharsha's *Naiṣadhīyacarita,* which tells the love story of Nala and Damayanti and which is celebrated as the most erudite poem in Sanskrit. Śrīnātha was the first poet to imagine an Andhra land and a Telugu literary empire of which he was the unchallenged ruler.

The 16th c. is generally called the golden age of Telugu poetry. During this period, court poets of the Vijayanagara emperor Krishnadevarāya (r. 1509–29) wrote superbly imagined and exquisitely descriptive poems called *mahā-prabandha*. Among them, Peddana excels with his justly famous *Svārociṣamanusambhavamu,* popularly called *Manucaritramu*. This is ostensibly the story of the birth of the first man Manu but famously includes the celebrated love story of the heavenly Gandharva woman Varūdhini, who falls in love with a brahmin man called Pravara.

The poets of the mahā-prabandha broadly follow the narrative structure Nannaya initiated but entirely transform the quality of the poetic lang. with descriptions of events and things in minute detail—a richly imagined world. Characters in their psychological nature are exquisitely presented, and extensive, detailed descriptions intensify the narrative. The ornate diction deliberately maintains a ling. distance but surprisingly brings the poem's evocative quality closer to real-life experience. The mahā-prabandhas of this period, at least the best of them, can be classed among the classics of any great lit. produced by the world's great civilizations.

The emperor Krishnadevarāya himself wrote one of the masterworks of this period, *Āmukatamālyada* (The Girl Who Gave the Garland She Had Worn to God), perhaps the most remarkable poem in Telugu. A long narrative of human-divine love loosely combined with several other narratives, descriptions of seasons and lives of common people and kings, and an argument concerning the policy a king should adopt in ruling his kingdom, in verses that range from lyrical to ornate, realistic to fantastic, in simple Telugu words and jaw-breaking Sanskrit compounds, this long poem remains a high literary achievement.

This period includes another great poet, Bhaṭṭumūrti, also known as Ramarājabhūṣaṇuḍu, who wrote *Vasucaritramu* (The Story of Vasu). This is an artful poem of semantically dense verses that are nonetheless lyrical and musical, creating inexhaustible new worlds in every reading.

During the late 16th and early 17th cs., Telugu poetry underwent a significant shift in the works of Piṅgali Sūranna, who flourished in the second half of the 16th c. His two verse narratives, *Kaḷāpūrṇodayamu* (Birth of Kaḷāpūrṇa) and *Prabhāvatī Pradyumnamu* (The Story of Prabhāvatī and Pradyumna), might be called the earliest novels in Telugu. These poems follow the psychological devel. of the characters through their inner conflicts, with unpredictable surprises.

While the mahā-prabandha genre continued in a courtly style, an entirely different line of poetry flourished, composed by poets who were devoted to a deity associated with temples. Potana (14th c.) wrote the *Bhāgavatamu*, which told stories of Viṣṇu and his avatars, chiefly Kṛṣṇa, and of his devotees. Prahlāda, the demon king Bali, the elephant Gajendra, Rukmiṇi who eloped with Kṛṣṇa, and the *gopi* cowherd girls who fell in love with him, became household names in Telugu primarily because of Potana.

Among the temple poets, Annamayya or Annamācārya (15th c.), who served the god Venkaṭeśvara in Tirupati, a temple town in southern Andhra Pradesh, stands out as a composer of songs. His songs, known as *padams*, number into the several thousands—Annamayya's grandson gives a symbolic number, 32,000. The songs, editorially classified into two groups, *śṛṅgāra* (erotic) and *adhyātma* (metaphysical), were inscribed on copper plates even during the life of Annamayya and are now preserved in the temple museum.

Later padam writers who followed Annamayya include Kṣetrayya and Sāraṅgapāṇi. The erotic lyrics that Kṣetrayya wrote were objectionable to Eng.-educated, Victorianized new literati but came to be preserved when new interpretations of the songs emerged, reading spiritual meanings into them. Earlier, these songs had been sung by courtesans to their customers. The practice ended when, in the mid-20th c., the occupation of the courtesan was prohibited as immoral.

During the 17th and 18th cs., Telugu poets moved south to Tanjavur and Madurai (presently in Tamil-Nadu), under the patronage of Nayaka kings and later Maratha kings who ruled the area. During this period, women who were courtesans flourished as poets, such as Rangājamma and Muddupaḷani. Muddupaḷani's *Rādhikāsvāntanamu* was condemned by 20th-c. male critics as obscene in that a female poet wrote explicitly about Kṛṣṇa and his beloved Rādhā making love; however, the poem received better treatment among feminist critics. The 17th c. is also the period in which new classes of literati, who mostly served as scribes and accountants for landowners but acquired a social status of their own, composed poems that they attributed to famous poets and kings of the past such as Pĕddana and Krishnadevarāya. Stories told about Tenāli Rāmaliṅgaḍu, a fictitious poet said to be in the court of Krishnadevarāya, belong in this trad. These verses and stories were and continue to be quoted orally in conversations among literate communities. Such verses, known as *cāṭus*, number in the hundreds and suggest a public literary culture unrelated to any king or his court. Themes in these verses represent a subtle social crit. of irresponsible kings and bad poets and demonstrate a community with a good taste for poetry.

A genre called *śataka*, comprising about 100 independent verses loosely connected with one vocative addressing a deity in a local temple, became popular in the late 16th c. and after. Several of these śatakas are known for their social crit. and protest, and were written by poets frustrated by the behavior of degenerate kings or those who could not accept the many radical changes occurring in society around them. Among such śatakas, Dhūrjaṭi's *Kālahastīśvara śatakamu* is noteworthy for the quality of poetry and for the courage of the poet. It is partly confessional in nature, and its agonizing subjectivity and emotional intensity appeal to any reader who recognizes the pain of living in a troubled world.

By and large, the period of the 17th and 18th cs. ushers in what might be called an indigenous modernity in Telugu poetry, with its depiction of a new subjectivity, a cultivation of interiority, a psychologized personhood, and a representation of personal privacy and social mobility.

The 19th and 20th cs. bring about yet another radical shift in Telugu lit. with the opening of new ideas and sensibilities from the introduction of Eng. into colonial schools and colleges. Gurajada Apparao is often credited as the leading figure of modernity during this period, and his play *Kanyāśulkam* is regarded as the first mod. play in Telugu. A movement called *Bhāvakavitvam* (Poetry of Feeling) follows Apparao. Poets of Bhāvakavitvam sing of romantic love and celebrate nature. They depict woman not as an object of desire but as a person to be loved and adored. Poets such as Devulapalli Krishna Sastri and Rayaprolu Subbarao set the tone for the poetry of this period, with their delicate and carefully chiseled verses speaking of the meeting of hearts and dreamlike images of the beloved. Poets of this period rebelled against the excessively eroticized descriptions of women in the prabandha poetry, rejecting conventional pundits who tried to control poetry with their outdated grammar and fossilized poetics.

Within decades, Bhavākavitvam was rejected by a group of poets influenced by an international wave of Marxism. Led by Srirangam Srinivasa Rao, better known as Sri Sri, a large number of young poets, who called themselves *abhyudaya* (progressive) poets, wrote about the poor and the downtrodden working class, calling for them to reject the dominance of the wealthy. Rapid changes in Telugu poetry such as these brought about a rejection of what was considered to be the misguided and derivative modernity of the colonial period in favor of the imported revolutionary fervor of the progressive poets, with an invitation to celebrate India's indigenous literary and cultural strength, which had suffered under colonialism. Viswanatha Satyanarayana led this move with his six-volume *Rāmāyaṇa Kalpavṛkṣamu* (Ramayana, the Wish-Giving Tree) and his magnum opus *Veyipaḍagalu* (Thousand Hoods).

More recent devels. include feminist poems by women against male dominance, by Dalits (former untouchables) against the injustices done to them by the upper castes, and by Muslims about their oppression as minorities. Muslim women and Dalit women write about the double injustice done to them by men of upper castes, as well as their own community. Telangana writers also demand recognition of their identity separate from Andhra.

The hist. of Telugu poetry of the past thousand years

presents a conspectus of the historical and cultural devels. in Andhra. At the same time, the corpus transcends time and place to appeal to literary connoisseurs across langs.

See ASSAMESE POETRY; BENGALI POETRY; GUJARATI POETRY; HINDI POETRY; INDIA, POETRY OF; INDIA, ENGLISH POETRY OF; RĀMĀYAŅA POETRY; SANSKRIT POETICS; SANSKRIT POETRY.

■ *Siva's Warriors: Basava Purāna of Pālkuriki Somanātha*, trans. V. Narayana Rao (1990); *When God Is a Customer: Telugu Courtesan Songs by Ksetrayya and Others*, ed. A. K. Ramanujan, V. Narayana Rao, D. Shulman (1994); *A Poem at the Right Moment: Remembered Verses from Premodern South India* (1998), and *Classical Telugu Poetry: An Anthology* (2002), both ed. V. Narayana Rao and D. Shulman; V. Vallabharaya, *A Lover's Guide to Warrangal: Vallabharaya's Kridabhiramamu*, trans. V. Narayana Rao and D. Shulman (2002); *Hibiscus on the Lake: Twentieth-Century Telugu Poetry from India*, ed. and trans. V. Narayana Rao (2003); P. Sūranna, *Sound of the Kiss, or the Story That Must Never Be Told*, trans. V. Narayana Rao and D. Shulman (2003); Annamayya, *God on the Hill: Temple Songs from Tirupati*, trans. V. Narayana Rao and D. Shulman (2005); P. Sūranna, *The Demon's Daughter: A Love Story*, trans. V. Narayana Rao and D. Shulman (2006); G. Apparao, *Girls for Sale: Kanyasulkam. A Play from Colonial India*, trans. V. Narayana Rao (2007).

V. NARAYANA RAO

**TENOR AND VEHICLE.** Because he was dissatisfied with the traditional grammatical and rhetorical account of *metaphor, which he believed emphasized its merely decorative and embellishing powers, I. A. Richards in 1936 reintroduced this pair of terms—already reflected, as Engell points out, in the 18th c. in Samuel Johnson's *Dictionary* (1755) and used by such later Augustan rhetoricians as George Campbell and Hugh Blair—with the notion of "a borrowing between and intercourse of thoughts." Since any metaphor at its simplest gives two parts, the thing meant and the thing said, Richards used *tenor* to refer to the thing meant—purport, underlying meaning, or main subject of the metaphor—and *vehicle* to mean the thing said—that which serves to carry or embody the tenor as the analogy brought to the subject.

But Richards intended more than simply to reintroduce this terminology for existing concepts; rather, he intended to develop a mod. concept not just of metaphor but of the nature of *poetry itself. Having traced out tenor and vehicle as the elements of metaphor, he (and the critics who followed him) went on to distinguish between *poetic* metaphor and other kinds. In attempting to show that true poetic metaphor is never merely decorative, logical, explanatory, or illustrative, he claimed that the "transaction" it establishes between tenor and vehicle "results in a meaning (to be clearly distinguished from the tenor) which is not attainable without their interaction"—which is, in effect, not attainable by direct and literal prose statement. The

vehicle, he continued, "is not normally mere embellishment of a tenor which is otherwise unchanged by it but . . . vehicle and tenor in cooperation give a meaning of more varied powers than can be ascribed to either."

These special powers of poetic metaphor Richards credited to the way the vehicle brings with it, because it derives from an aspect of experience outside or different from the literal experience in the poem, a host of implicit associations that, although circumscribed by the tenor, are never quite shut out entirely. This unsuppressible range of connotations closely resembles what John Crowe Ransom later called "irrelevant texture," which he (and other mod. critics) valued as the very essence of poetry. Such an approach to poetry presumed special qualities for poetic lang.—*ambiguity, *irony, *paradox, and so on—which found their cause in the tension set up between the tenor in a poetic metaphor and the emotional, sensory, or conceptual connotations brought into the poem by the vehicle. This approach goes beyond simply attributing emotional and imaginative powers to metaphor to claim for it special cognitive powers as well. Thus, e.g., Hawkes sees metaphor as embodying in little the larger relation between lang. and reality: there is the world (tenor), and there are the terms in which we see it (vehicle); Ricoeur finds an interesting similarity between metaphor and the psychoanalytic concept of transference, where an adult tends to see the world of the present (tenor) via the habits of mind he or she learned from the parents as a child (vehicle).

Other critics, however, have found the tenor-and-vehicle distinction unclear, inconsistent, or inaccurate. Black develops the boundaries of four distinct theories of metaphor—the comparison, integration, interaction, and substitution theories—as a way of placing Richards's concept in a fuller context. While most critics (Wimsatt, Shibles, Gerhart, and Russell) agree that the tension of difference and interaction between tenor and vehicle is central, Empson and Brooke-Rose, e.g., emphasize the presence of the necessary basic similarity and fusion. Still others, such as Wheelwright, try to coin new definitions for *tenor* and *vehicle*.

However this may be, two main points should be kept in mind. First, metaphor depends, as Aristotle said, on the perception of the similarity in dissimilars. It is true that the vehicle must be logically different from the tenor, but it is also true that the basic effect depends on seeing the similarities between two things that at first appear to be different. It is true, moreover, that a third and new meaning is created between tenor and vehicle that is not the same as the tenor, but this effect depends not so much on the "irrelevancies" or differences imported by the vehicle as on the surprising fullness of appropriate meanings it brings to the tenor There are, thus, two additional parts to a metaphor: the point or points of contact or similarity between tenor and vehicle, often called the *ground*, and the role played by the consequent differences. The second and related point is that the interpretation must be limited and controlled by the poetic context.

In the well-known "stiff twin compasses" figure in John Donne's "A Valediction: Forbidding Mourning," the tenor (two lovers about to part) and the vehicle (a piece of mechanical drawing equipment) seem particularly remote, even incongruous. But closer inspection will reveal the similarity or point of contact: the lovers will remain connected in separation even as the legs of the compass remain attached at the top when pushed apart at the bottom. And there are the obvious differences, esp. if we consider the range of connotations: a compass is a scientific measuring device, is cold and impersonal, and is stiff and unbending, while the lovers are passionate, yearning, and fearful. Interpretation could emphasize difference by pointing up the complexity of the speaker's mind, uniting thought and feeling, aware of the subtle contradictions of love; or it could remain within the poem's context and show how the analogy is appropriate to the speaker's effort to console his lady about their impending separation: he is trying to cool their passion, arguing that a separation will not be a threat to their love. The "irrelevant texture" is relevant after all, and the third and new meaning, which arises out of the interaction between "lovers parting and needing to be consoled" as tenor and "compasses which remain connected at the top even when their feet are separated" as vehicle, is that there is a strong and precise mental and spiritual bond between true lovers that unites them when they must part physically. The meanings brought into the tenor by the vehicle have mainly to do paradoxically with making "material" the bond that is on its deepest level mental and spiritual: the compass, i.e., while denoting unity in separation, connotes the qualities of accuracy and firmness, and it does this in terms of a sharp and clear image. These meanings and their interplay create a complex of meanings that could not be conveyed by a direct and literal prose statement—exemplified by the present interpretation of "A Valediction"—because a large part of what is being conveyed is thought and feeling in-situation. This contextual reality could be "explained" in prose, but it could not very well be *felt*, and that is the function of poetic metaphor.

■ H. W. Wells, *Poetic Imagery* (1924); K. Burke, *Permanence and Change* (1935); I. A. Richards, *The Philosophy of Rhetoric* (1936); C. Brooks, *Modern Poetry and the Tradition* (1939); J. C. Ransom, *The New Criticism* (1941); W. Empson, *The Structure of Complex Words* (1951); W. K. Wimsatt, *The Verbal Icon* (1954); Wellek and Warren; C. Brooke-Rose, *The Grammar of Metaphor* (1958); M. Black, *Models and Metaphors* (1962); P. Wheelwright, *Metaphor and Reality* (1962); W. Embler, *Metaphor and Meaning* (1966); K. K. Ruthven, *The Conceit* (1969); M. Peckham, "Metaphor," *The Triumph of Romanticism* (1970); W. A. Shibles, *An Analysis of Metaphor in the Light of W. M. Urban's Theories* (1971); M. C. Beardsley, "The Metaphorical Twist," *Essays on Metaphor*, ed. W. A. Shibles (1972); T. Hawkes, *Metaphor* (1972); D. Lodge, *The Modes of Modern Writing* (1977); P. Ricoeur, *The Rule of Metaphor*, trans. R. Czerny (1977); *Metaphor*, ed. D. S. Miall (1982); M. Gerhart and A. M. Russell, *Metaphoric Process*

(1984); E. R. MacCormac, *A Cognitive Theory of Metaphor* (1985); D. E. Cooper, *Metaphor* (1986); J. Engell, "The New Rhetoricians," *Psychology and Literature in the Eighteenth Century*, ed. C. Fox (1987); R. J. Fogelin, *Figuratively Speaking* (1988); S. Glucksberg and B. Keysar, "Understanding Metaphorical Comparisons: Beyond Similarity," *Psychological Review* 97 (1990); K. Walton, *Mimesis as Make Believe* (1990); S. Glucksberg and B. Keysar, "How Metaphors Work," *Metaphor and Thought*, ed. A. Ortony, 2d ed. (1993), and "Metaphor and Communication," *PoT* 13 (1993); K. Walton, "Metaphor and Prop-Oriented Make-Believe," *European Journal of Philosophy* 1 (1993); D. Hills, "Aptness and Truth in Verbal Metaphor," *Philosophical Topics* 25 (1997).

N. FRIEDMAN

**TENSO** (Occitan, also *tençon*; It. *tenzone*). A type of poetic composition that matured in Provence early in the 12th c., *tenso* consists of a verbal exchange largely in the form of *invective expressed through the medium of *sirventes* or *coblas*. The earliest example seems to be by Cercamon and Guilhelmi. Later it developed into the *partimen* or *joc partit*, an exchange minus the personal element, and was applied to moral, literary, and political problems. In many cases, the subject matter is imaginary, and often the original argument and the exchange are by the same person. The *troubadours carried the device into Italy, where we find Lanzia Marques and Alberto Malaspina making use of it in Occitan compositions. In Sicily, the feigned tenso in *canzone*-form called *contrasto* was quite popular (e.g., Cielo d'Alcamo, Giacomino Pugliese). In Italy, however, a tenso (*tenzone*) generally assumes the form of an exchange of *sonnets between two (or more) poets on a specific topic. One general characteristic of the tenzone is the practice of responding *per le rime*, i.e., in the answering sonnet the poet would adopt the same rhymes used in the initial sonnet. An early tenzone of the *Sicilian school treats of the nature of love and contains sonnets by Jacopo Mostacci, Pier delle Vigne, and Giacomo da Lentini. In Tuscany, the tenzone was also adopted for discussion of political, literary, and moral topics. The example of Guittone d'Arezzo was extremely influential in making it common among his followers (the *guittoniani*) and the poets of the *Dolce stil nuovo*, incl. Dante and Cino da Pistoia.

*See* ITALY, POETRY OF; OCCITAN POETRY.

■ P. E. Guarnerio, *Manuale di versificazione italiana* (1893); H. Stiefel, *Die italienische Tenzone des XII Jahrhunderts und ihr Verhältnis zur provenzalischen Tenzone* (1914); S. Santangelo, *Le tenzoni poetiche nella letteratura italiana delle origini* (1928); D. J. Jones, *La Tenson provençale*(1934); E. Köhler, *GRLMA*, v. 2.1.B.3; Elwert, *Italienische*; S. Orlando, *Manuale di metrica italiana* (1994); *Il genere "tenzone" nelle letterature romanze delle origini*, ed. M. Pedroni and A. Stäuble (1999); P. Bec, *La Joute poétique* (2000); C. Giunta, *Due saggi sulla tenzone* (2002), and *Versi a un destinatario* (2002).

J. G. FUCILLA; C. KLEINHENZ

**TERCET.** A verse unit of three lines, usually rhymed, most often employed as a stanzaic form. It was first developed systematically in It. poetry (*terzina*): Dante chose the tercet with interlocking rhymes (*terza rima*) for the stanza of the *Divine Comedy*, whence it spread to the other vernacular poetries. In those versions of the *sonnet derived from It., the *sestet is made up of two tercets rhyming (often) *cdecde*. Eng. users of tercets or terza rima include Thomas Wyatt, John Donne, Robert Herrick ("Whenas in Silks my Julia Goes") and P. B. Shelley ("Ode to the West Wind," "The Triumph of Life"). The tercet became the major form of the mature Wallace Stevens: fully half of the poems in his last three books of poetry use it, incl. nearly all of the major poems ("Notes toward a Supreme Fiction," "Auroras of Autumn," "Sea Surface Full of Clouds"). W. C. Williams uses a variant "triadic stanza" as his staple form. Monorhymed tercets in stichic verse are *triplets. Though three-line stanzas are less common in the poetries of the world than *quatrain, they are important nonetheless: the Fr. *villanelle comprises five tercets and a quatrain, and two forms of Welsh *englynion are in tercets, incl. most of the work of Llywarch Hen (6th c.; see ENGLYN). Western adaptations of the Japanese *haiku (see RENGA) normally set it as a tercet of five-, seven-, and five-syllable lines, unrhymed.
■ E. Berry, "W. C. Williams' Triadic-Line Verse," *Twentieth-Century Literature* 35 (1989).

T.V.F. BROGAN

**TERZA RIMA.** It. verse form consisting of interlinked *tercets, in which the second line of each tercet rhymes with the first and third lines of the one following, *aba bcb cdc,* etc. The sequence of tercets formed in this way may be of any length and is usually brought to a conclusion by a single final line, which rhymes with the second line of the tercet preceding it, *aba a.* Terza rima has a powerful forward momentum, while the concatenated rhymes provide a reassuring structure of woven continuity, which may on occasion, however, imprison the poet in a movement of cyclical repression or driven mindlessness (Alfred de Vigny, "Les Destinées"; Hugo von Hofmannsthal, "Ballade des äusseren Lebens"). In all its realizations, terza rima suggests processes without beginning or end, an irresistible *perpetuum mobile*.

Terza rima (in *hendecasyllables) was introduced by Dante as an appropriate stanza form for his *Divina commedia*. Its symbolic reference to the Holy Trinity, its other numerological implications, and the overtones of tireless quest and of the interconnectedness of things were particularly apposite. Most probably Dante developed terza rima from the tercets of the *sirventes, but whatever the origin of the form, it found immediate popularity with Giovanni Boccaccio, who used it in his uncompleted *Amorosa visione*, and with Petrarch (*I Trionfi*). After Dante, terza rima became the preferred verse form for allegorical and didactic poems such as Fazio degli Uberti's *Dittamondo* and Federico Frezzi's *Quadriregio*. But its implicit difficulty discouraged its widespread use after the 14th c., although Vincenzo

Monti in the late 18th c. and Ugo Foscolo in the early 19th c. had recourse to it.

In France, terza rima first appeared in the work of Jean Lemaire de Belges ("Le Temple d'honneur et de vertus," 1503; "La Concorde des deux langages," 1511) and was taken up by poets of the *Pléiade—Pontus de Tyard, Étienne Jodelle, Jean-Antoine de Baïf. The *decasyllable almost invariably used by these 16th-c. poets yielded to the *alexandrine in the form's 19th-c. revival, which was subscribed to by *Parnassians (Théodore de Banville, Charles-Marie Leconte de Lisle) and symbolists alike (see SYMBOLISM).

The form makes even greater demands on poets who write in a lang. less rich in rhymes than It. or Fr. Chaucer first experimented with terza rima in Eng. for parts of his early "Complaint to His Lady," but its first significant use is by Thomas Wyatt, followed by Philip Sidney and Samuel Daniel. The romantics experimented with it, Lord Byron for "The Prophecy of Dante" and P. B. Shelley for "Prince Athanase" and "The Triumph of Life." Shelley's "Ode to the West Wind" is composed of five sections, each rhyming *aba bcb cdc ded ee* (see TERZA RIMA SONNET). Since the romantics, it has been used, sometimes with variation of line length and looser rhymes, by Thomas Hardy, W. B. Yeats, T. S. Eliot, W. H. Auden ("The Sea and the Mirror"), Roy Fuller ("Centaurs"; "To my Brother"), and Archibald MacLeish ("Conquistador"). More recently, in Derek Walcott's *Omeros* (1990), an almost free-rhyming terza rima ("Dantesque design") is combined with a polymorphous *hexameter (Homer); in this "undone" state, terza rima supports a thematics of woundedness and of the difficult curing of the present by the past, but still manages to embody the poem's final line: "When he left the beach the sea was still going on."

*See* ITALIAN PROSODY.
■ L. E. Kastner, "A History of the Terza Rima in France," *ZFSL* 26 (1904); J.S.P. Tatlock, "Dante's Terza Rima," *PMLA* 51 (1936); L. Binyon, "Terza Rima in English Poetry," *English* 3 (1940); J. Wain, "Terza Rima," *Rivista di Letterature Moderne* 1 (1950); R. Bernheim, *Die Terzine in der deutschen Dichtung* (1954); M. Fubini, "La Terzina della *Commedia*," *DDJ* 43 (1965); P. Boyde, *Dante's Style in His Lyric Poetry* (1971); J. D. Bone, "On 'Influence' and on Byron and Shelley's Use of Terza Rima in 1819," *KSMB* 32 (1982); J. Freccero, "The Significance of Terza Rima," *Dante, Petrarch, Boccaccio*, ed. A. S. Bernardo and A. L. Pellegrini (1983); P. Breslin, "Epic Amnesia: Healing and Memory in *Omeros*," *Nobody's Nation: Reading Derek Walcott* (2001); M. Hurley, "Interpreting Dante's *Terza Rima*," *FMLS* 41 (2005).

L. J. ZILLMAN; C. SCOTT

**TERZA RIMA SONNET.** A term used to describe a quatorzain whose rhyme scheme has four *tercets in the interweaving pattern characteristic of terza rima (*aba bcbcdcded*), followed by a closing *couplet (*ee*). It has sometimes been suggested that this pattern, of which P. B. Shelley's "Ode to the West Wind" provides the most celebrated cycle of examples, resembles the Spenserian sonnet with its couplet ending (*ababbcbc cdcdee*). But the connection is tenuous: the *quatrains of the Spenserian sonnet are a sequence of overlapping, alternating rhyme pairs rather than a series of interlinked tercets; and its final couplet does not function as a *refrain or invocation or exhortation as those in Shelley's cycle do. On the other hand, it should be noted that the Sicilian sonnet has been proposed as the source of terza rima. In any event, this hybrid form (cf. the terzanelle) has not been lost from sight: Robert Frost's "Acquainted with the Night" (in an *envelope pattern) is a splendid mod. example.

■ H. Haworth, "'Ode to the West Wind' and the Sonnet Form," *Keats–Shelley Journal* 20 (1971).

C. Scott

## TETRAMETER (Gr., "of four measures").

I. Classical
II. Modern

**I. Classical.** In Gr. and Lat., the basic meter for recitation forms is the trochaic tetrameter catalectic, i.e., four trochaic metra (units of measurement; see METRON): $- \cup - x \mid - \cup - x \mid - \cup - x \mid - \cup - x$ where x = *anceps (a syllable that, independently of its real metrical value, can be counted as long or short, according to the requirements of the meter), with truncation (see CATALEXIS) of the final anceps. There is a *diaeresis (coincidence of a word ending with the end of a metrical unit) after the second anceps, which in comedy is sometimes replaced by a *caesura before it or, more rarely, the third breve. In Gr. drama, this meter is often associated with scenes of excitement. Several prosodic phenomena, such as (1) the occasional *responsion of $- \cup \cup \cup$ with a trochaic metron in Aristophanes; (2) the fact that even in the strict versification of Solon, Havet's *bridge in his tetrameters is slightly less stringent than Porson's bridge in his trimeters; and (3) the lower rate of the substitution of $\cup \cup$ for $\cup$ or x as compared to the *trimeter suggest that the trochaic tetrameter was less constrained in its access to the rhythms of Gr. speech than some other meters. Ancient trad. (e.g., Aristotle, *Rhetoric* 1407; Marius Victorinus 4.44) considered the trochaic tetrameter a faster meter than the iambic trimeter. At any rate, the greater speed of the tetrameter is probably more than a matter of conventional performance tempo and may reflect a universal feature of falling rhythm in ordinary speech. The trochaic tetrameter catalectic was employed by the archaic iambographers (writers of *iambs); Aristotle (*Poetics* 1449a2) states that it was used in tragedy before the iambic trimeter, but in extant drama, it is much less frequent than the latter.

Besides its use in trochaic, the tetrameter length was also used in antiquity with anapestic and iambic metra. The anapestic tetrameter catalectic is used in comic dialogue. It is characterized by metron diaeresis as well as regular median diaeresis, frequent contraction of all but the last pair of *brevia*, and resolution of *longa*. The iambic tetrameter catalectic was used by Hipponax and is fairly frequent in comedy for the entrance and exits

of choruses and for contest scenes. Diaeresis after the second metron is preferred but caesura after the third anceps is common; resolution and substitution are frequent. The *acatalectic iambic tetrameter is used only by Sophocles in the *Ichneutai* and in Ion's satyr-play *Omphale*.

The Lat. adaptation of the Gr. trochaic tetrameter catalectic is the trochaic *septenarius*, used commonly for comic dialogue and favored by Plautus. It stands in the same relation to its Gr. model as does the *senarius*, showing the same regard for linguistic stress. The absence of polysyllabic oxytones (words whose last syllable is stressed) and infrequency of proparoxytones (words stressed on the antepenultimate syllable) in Lat. means that the frequent trochaic closes of paroxytonic words (stressed on the penultimate syllable) will effect a prevailingly trochaic rhythm. As a popular form, it is known as the *versus quadratus*. Beare summarizes the long-held view that it was this meter, widely used for popular verse forms such as the marching songs of Caesar's legions, and common in late antiquity, that became the basis for much of med. Lat. versification. It is the meter of the *Pervigilium veneris* and a number of Christian *hymns, notably Venantius Fortunatus' *Pange lingua*, and was surpassed only by the iambic dimeter hymn quatrain (itself octosyllabic when regular) and the sequence as the most popular meter of the Middle Ages.

**II. Modern.** In mod. langs., the tetrameter is based on feet rather than metra; hence, it is but half as long as the cl. type. The mod. vernacular tetrameter, strictly speaking, is a verse line of four regular metrical feet; with freer metrical patterning, it is simply an *octosyllable as in Fr. and Sp. versification, or else stress verse, as in *ballad meter and hymn meter. The Fr. *tétramètre*, however, is a 12-syllable line with four divisions. In Eng. poetry, the tetrameter is second only to iambic pentameter in wideness of use; it is employed frequently in popular verse, *nursery rhymes, songs, *hymns, and *ballads, as well as literary verse. Eng. tetrameters are chiefly in iambic rhythm, although trochaic tetrameters are also common. Eng. and Scottish traditional ballads usually consist of four-line stanzas that alternate iambic tetrameter and trimeter. Considerably less common than iambic and trochaic tetrameters, anapestic and dactylic tetrameters were popular during the romantic period; the most famous example is Lord Byron's "The Destruction of Sennacherib," in anapestic rhythm. Eng. tetrameter is almost always rhymed: in a famous footnote to his 1933 Leslie Stephen lecture, A. E. Housman singles out as one of the mysteries of versification "why, while blank verse can be written in lines of ten or six syllables, a series of octosyllables ceases to be verse if they are not rhymed." Well-known examples of iambic tetrameter verse in Eng. include one (only) of William Shakespeare's sonnets (145), John Donne's "The Extasie," Andrew Marvell's "To His Coy Mistress," William Wordsworth's "I Wandered Lonely as a Cloud," Alfred, Lord Tennyson's *In Memoriam*, and Robert Frost's "Stopping by Woods on a Snowy Evening." Something of a literary curiosity,

Herman Melville's *Clarel: A Poem and Pilgrimage in the Holy Land* (1876), at nearly 18,000 lines the longest poem in Am. lit., is composed (except for its epilogue) in iambic tetrameter.

Rus. poetry features iambic tetrameter most famously and successfully in the work of Alexander Pushkin, who wrote nearly 22,000 tetrameters, over half his entire output, for *The Bronze Horseman* (1833) and *Evgenij Onegin* (1825–32).

Trochaic tetrameters are almost as common in Eng. as iambic, a fact of interest because trochaic pentameters, e.g., are almost nonexistent (see PENTAMETER). One of the more notorious and frequently parodied instances of mod. trochaic tetrameter is H. W. Longfellow's "Song of Hiawatha" (1855). Eng. poems in trochaic tetrameter frequently employ catalexis, truncating the second syllable of the line's last foot. Examples include Thomas Carew's "A Prayer to the Wind" and W. H. Auden's "Lullaby." Other famous poems in tetrameter combine iambic and trochaic feet along with catalexis: John Milton's "L'Allegro" and "Il Penseroso" and P. B. Shelley's "Lines Written among the Euganean Hills."

■ **Classical:** J. Rumpel, "Der trochäische Tetrameter bei den griechischen Lyrikern und Dramatikern," *Philologus* 28 (1869); H. J. Kanz, *De tetrametro trochaico* (1913); Beare; F. Crusius, *Römische Metrik*, 2d ed. (1955); F. Perusino, *Il tetrametro giambico catalettico nella commedia greca* (1968); West; A. M. Devine and L. D. Stephens, *Language and Metre* (1984).

■ **Modern:** Schipper, *History*; W. L. Schramm, "Time and Intensity in English Tetrameter Verse," *PQ* 13 (1934); P. Habermann, "Tetrameter," *Reallexikon I*; V. Nabokov, *Notes on Prosody* (1964); J. Bailey, *Toward a Statistical Analysis of English Verse* (1975); Attridge, *Rhythms*; M. Tarlinskaja, "Meter and Meaning: The Semantic 'Halo' of Verse Form in English Romantic Lyrical Poems (Iambic and Trochaic Tetrameter)," *AJS* 4 (1986); Morier.

A. M. Devine, L. D. Stephens (Classical); T.V.F. Brogan, E. T. Johnston (Modern)

**TÉTRAMÈTRE.** A term used to denote the metrical structure of the regular 12-syllable Fr. *alexandrine and so distinguish it sharply from the less common *trimètre structure. Strictly speaking, the regular alexandrine has only two fixed accents, on the sixth and twelfth syllables, i.e., at the *caesura and at the line ending, marking off each *hemistich. It is usual, however, for the alexandrine to have two further "secondary" accents, of no fixed position, one in each hemistich, making a total of four in the line—hence, *tétramètre*. Jean Racine's *Phèdre* affords a famous example: "C'est Vénus / tout entière // à sa proie / attachée" (1.3.306).

A regular tétramètre may, therefore, contain two accents only, e.g., in Charles Baudelaire: "Elle se développe // avec indifférence" (six-six); or three, e.g., in Guillaume Apollinaire: "Une chanson d'amour // et d'infidélité" (four-two-six); or four, e.g., in Alfred de Vigny: "La Nature t'attend // dans un silence austère" (three-three-four-two); but four is the conventional number. The optionality and mobility of the two

secondary accents furnish the tétramètre with 36 different rhythmic configurations. The trimètre, by contrast, which has three measures and no caesura, is indelibly ternary in structure; even when the tétramètre has three accents, its medial caesura still preserves its essentially binary character. The tétramètre, whose roots go back at least to *Le Pèlerinage de Charlemagne* (12th c.), was shaped in the cl. age by the strict rules of François de Malherbe into the form championed by Nicolas Boileau and brought to perfection in the tragedies of Pierre Corneille and Racine.

■ Kastner; Elwert; Mazaleyrat; Scott; C. Scott, *A Question of Syllables* (1986); H. Morier, "L'Alexandrin classique était bien un tétramètre," *Langue, littérature du XVIIe et du XVIIIe siècle*, ed. R. Lathuillère (1990).

A. G. Engstrom; C. Scott

**TEXT.** *Text* belongs to a way of designating writing associated with certain values and emphases, a way of thinking about writing and lit. The usage arose in France in the 1960s and in the decades following as part of the general tendency toward a more scientific or more formalized approach to lit. It was associated with an approach to lit. that has been called *antihumanist*, and this label is accurate insofar as the term and the way of thinking it represents sought in different ways to displace the authority of the human agent (i.e., author or *poet) supposedly "behind" the writing and to valorize the writing itself.

The term *text* is used and emphasized differently, however, by various schools of thought and now may have entered into the common critical currency to such a degree that the values with which it was associated are taken for granted. It is evident, nevertheless, that a *text* is not the same as a *book*, a *work*, or a *poem*, and that it cuts across generic boundaries. It is less easy to identify and circumscribe the values that the word carries, but they can be more or less precisely situated historically and epistemologically.

Historically, *text* and *textuality* came to the fore in the 1960s in France primarily in the wake of the so-called structuralist controversy that had displaced the dominant philosophical program of Sartean existentialism. *Formalism, *semiotics, and *structuralism shifted the focus from the psychology of the intentional subject to the *form of the work or its signifying structure. Textuality, however, emphasized the *written* aspect of the object, the act of writing that produced it, and the act of reading that reproduces it. This stress on writing emerges as a key focus in the work of Roland Barthes, Julia Kristeva, and Jacques Derrida. With important distinctions, all three propose the text as a quite new object of study. From this basis, and with the significant advocacy of the group of writers associated with the jour. *Tel Quel*, textuality expands beyond its initially Fr. context and enters into the vocabulary and ethos of scholars and practicing writers around the world.

Textuality is associated on the one hand with a negative, critical moment in the hist. of lit. crit.: the displacement of the figure of the author (as, e.g., in Barthes's "Death of the Author," 1967), or of the notion of a reality external to the writing that it purports to represent. A text has a *scriptor*, or more plainly, a writer, rather than an *author*. Texts are not primarily representative but exist independently of their referents. An important element in the thought behind the notion of the text, in other words, is the *autonomy of writing. Textual crit. thus sought to liberate the study of lit. and of written documents more generally from the apparent constraints of psychological or metaphysical worldviews. *Text*, however, also carries positive values. Liberated from its referent, a text consists of meaning, of sense. The term *text* is closely connected to the semiological perspective that sees lang. as a network of signs (see SIGN, SIGNIFIED, SIGNIFIER). As a signifying entity, the text is necessarily plural. It is a network, system, or structure of signs or signifiers, susceptible to an analysis that will disassemble it. But if semiology produces the austerity of Roman Jakobson and Claude Lévi-Strauss's "technical" analysis of Charles Baudelaire's "Les Chats," e.g., the more ludic textual approach emphasizes the plurality of meanings in the text or that the text produces. It sees the text as a field or volume of meanings produced in the act of reading, imagines the writing as a woven texture of lines of sense, and allows a certain freedom to the reader in the creation of these strands. Barthes's book *S/Z* (1970) proposed a reading of Honoré de Balzac's novella *Sarrasine* (1830) according to the elements of sense that were scattered across the text "like gold dust," suggesting with the felicitous term "parsimonious plural" that Balzac's "classical" text nevertheless contained elements of a mod., plural, and heterogeneous philosophy of writing, or at least could be read as such.

For Barthes, the text is a utopia or a horizon. In the useful article "From Work to Text" (1971), he emphasizes that a text is not an "accountable object." In other words, *text* means a way of thinking about writing that foregrounds those elements that liberate us from the *doxa* (or commonly unquestioned beliefs), from ideological determination, from human psychology. *Text* denotes a utopia of writing that paradoxically carries something of an existential drive—a liberation of meaning from established and stereotypical values, or more simply, a freeing of meaning, as a present participle, from fixed *meanings* (whence the Fr. term *signifiance* often associated with the text or Kristeva's notion of the text as a "signifying practice"). Text as essentially a space for the "free play" of meaning also represents—and this is very palpable in the work of Barthes—a space of freedom and pleasure for the subject, reader, or writer who engages with it.

The *plurality* of a text is closely associated with its connectedness to other texts. The term *intertextuality* designates the flow of meaning from text to text; texts are engaged with other texts in explicit or implicit processes of rewriting, but intertextuality, an important element of textual thinking, also suggests on the one hand that a piece of writing is potentially engaged with the entirety of the "anterior textual corpus" (Kristeva). Innovative or "limit texts" are those that displace this previous textual body. On the other hand, however, the notion of intertextuality and the generalized notion of text propose a far more radical view that "everything is a text." If the term *text* connotes the weaving together of strands, like Penelope by day, there is the suggestion that the human subject, too, is a textual entity, that hist. consists of a plurality of meanings and is, therefore, a text (which can be rewritten), that the everyday real we perceive is a text that we are constantly in the process of reading, rereading, writing, and rewriting.

*See* BOOK, POETIC; ÉCRITURE; POSTSTRUCTURALISM.

■ *The Structuralist Controversy*, ed. R. Macksey and E. Donato (1970); R. Barthes, *S/Z*, trans. R. Miller (1974); and "Death of the Author" and "From Work to Text," *Image-Music-Text*, trans. S. Heath (1977); J. Derrida, *Writing and Difference*, trans. A. Bass (1978); J. Kristeva, *Desire in Language*, trans. T. Gora et al. (1980); J. Derrida, *Dissemination*, trans. B. Johnson (1981); S. Gavronsky, *Toward a New Poetics: Contemporary Writing in France* (1994); C. Belsey, *Critical Practice* (2002).

P. FFRENCH

**TEXTUAL CRITICISM** is the term traditionally used to refer to the scholarly activity of analyzing the relationships among the surviving texts of a work so as to assess their relative authority and accuracy. It is also often taken, more broadly, to encompass scholarly editing, in which the conclusions drawn from such examination are embodied in the texts and annotation of a new ed. (printed or electronic). Textual criticism is a historical undertaking, for its aim is to elucidate the textual hist. of individual works and to attempt to reconstruct the precise forms taken by their texts at particular past moments. Like all other efforts to recover the past, it depends on judgment at every turn, and the word *criticism is therefore an appropriate element in the standard name for this endeavor. Nevertheless, there has been a widespread misconception of textual crit. as somehow mechanical or objective, and one often encounters the view that textual criticism precedes lit. crit.—that the textual critic merely establishes the text for the literary critic to interpret. But in fact, the text constructed by a textual critic is inevitably a product of lit. crit.: a textual critic's decisions (about what words and visual features—such as *punctuation, indentation, and *stanza breaks—should constitute the text of a given work) will reflect, whether consciously or not, some point of view toward lit. in general, some assumptions about the nature of poetic production, and some interpretation of the work in question and its constituent passages. It is consequently as inappropriate to call a scholarly ed. containing a critically edited text *definitive* as it is to apply that adjective to a critical essay. Conceivably, the apparatus in such an ed. can be definitive, if it accurately reports all known relevant evidence; but the text itself can never be, for the conclusions it embodies cannot be declared the only reasonable ones that can ever emerge from an assessment of that evidence.

Textual crit. and lit. crit. are therefore not separable activities: questioning the makeup of the text is an essential element in the act of reading, and any conclusions about it reflect a critical position. Paradoxically, however, many literary critics (esp. from the mid-20th c. onward) have used terms like *textual analysis* or *textual criticism* to refer to their activities, without having this point in mind. They have generally been led into this usage by thinking of *text* and *work* as synonyms. Yet distinguishing texts and works—or, more precisely, distinguishing the texts of documents from the texts of works—is fundamental to all discussion of lit. (or any other verbal communication) and goes to the heart of why textual crit. is necessary. A text is a specific arrangement of elements; a literary work—a verbal construct—does consist of a text (or succession of texts), but its text cannot be assumed to coincide with any written or printed text purporting to be the text of that work. The medium of lit. is lang., which is intangible, not paper and ink, which merely serve as one vehicle for transmitting lang. Therefore works of lit. do not exist on paper, and the texts that appear there are only the texts of physical documents, which may be relatively successful or unsuccessful in representing the texts of works. This point is not inconsistent with the fact that some writers, particularly poets, incorporate visual features into their works; they are not thereby changing the ontology of lang. but rather creating mixed-media works. Similarly, the effect of a literary work on a reader is sometimes linked to the physical features of the document in which the work is read; but those features were not necessarily part of the work as conceived by any of its producers and might not be present in other documentary appearances of it.

Determining the accuracy (according to one standard or another) of documentary texts is a matter of judgment, and we can never know with certainty how accurate any of them, or any editorial reconstruction, is. But if we are interested in works rather than documents, all we can do is continually to attempt the recreation of works by critically assessing the evidences of those works that we find in the extant printed or ms. texts at our disposal. Most readers understand that typographical errors and slips of the pen can occur, and many readers occasionally detect and correct such errors. But few seem to be aware that by this elementary action they are recognizing a basic truth about the nature of lit.—that the effort to read the texts of literary works requires a questioning of the texts of the documents that attempt to convey those works. This problem is equally central in poetry and in prose, in the texts of med. mss. and in those of mod. printed books: it is the unavoidable consequence of the intangibility of the medium of lit. (Similar points could be made about oral texts or the texts of other arts, like music, that employ intangible media.)

There is thus no such thing as a literary work that does not pose a textual problem, if *work* is taken to mean a communication from the past. Readers may, of course, choose not to approach lit. historically, and there are various schools of lit. crit. founded on that premise. For such readers and critics, texts are not links to the past but found objects existing in the present. Any text they encounter can serve as the subject of analysis, and textual crit. is therefore largely irrelevant to their concerns—unless they make historical connections between texts, such as saying that two texts are from the same period or by the same author. Even if all surviving texts of a work were found to be identical, the historical scholar would still have to examine that single text critically with a view to detecting errors in it. But texts of a work usually differ, and not only because of scribes' and printers' errors (which are almost inevitable whenever a text is copied or reset in type). Authors may revise their works—sometimes repeatedly—and textual variants may reflect shifting authorial intentions at different points in the author's life. Variants may also result from alterations made by other persons involved in bringing a work to the public, as when a publishing-house ed. imposes a house style or tones down an expression of opinion that might give offense. Readers who wish to approach a work as a communication from the past need to know the variants that have appeared in its documentary texts and the errors that former readers have postulated, so that they are not at the mercy of the idiosyncrasies of particular documents.

Investigating the textual hist. of a work involves the identification and examination of the documents (both ms. and printed) containing texts of it, along with any relevant associated documents, such as letters, notebooks, diaries, books that served as the author's sources, and publishers' records. Just which of the documentary texts of a work are relevant depends on one's historical focus: if one is interested in the author's intentions (whether early or late), e.g., the group of documents to be considered might be different from those that would be relevant if one's concern were with the texts that were available to readers at a given time. Once the potentially relevant documentary texts are located, they must be collated (compared word by word, punctuation mark by punctuation mark) and any differences in them recorded. The variant readings are then analyzed in an effort to determine the relationships among the texts, identifying which are direct ancestors or descendants of others, which represent collateral lines of descent, and which result from conflation of different lines. Several methods have been advanced over the years for performing this analysis, such as the classic "genealogical method," as codified by Paul Maas (*Textual Criticism*, 1958), and quasi-mathematical ones, like Vinton A. Dearing's (*A Primer of Textual Geometry*, 2005). All these efforts strive for objectivity, but each reaches a point where critical judgment is required.

The problem of determining relationships among the extant texts of a work is most acute for ancient writings, which are generally represented by mss.—sometimes in great number—produced long after the authors' deaths. But the problem also exists for later writings, published during their authors' lifetimes in printed eds., because the text of each successive ed. is not always based on that of the immediately preceding ed. It is a fundamental truth of textual crit. that the chronology of mss. and printed eds. (if it can be established) does not necessarily coincide with the genealogy of the texts contained in those documents. Nevertheless, the analysis of the physical evidence present in documents is essential for understanding how the production hist. of documents affects the texts they contain. Much work of this kind on printed material was accomplished in the 20th c., using the methods illustrated in R. B. McKerrow's *An Introduction to Bibliography for Literary Students* (1927), Fredson Bowers's *Principles of Bibliographical Description* (1949) and *Bibliography and Textual Criticism* (1964), and G. T. Tanselle's *Bibliographical Analysis* (2009); some of the necessary background in printing hist. for this kind of work has been provided in Philip Gaskell's *A New Introduction to Bibliography* (1972).

What use eds. make of a hypothesized genealogy of the texts of a work depends principally on their view of two questions, the first of which is the role of judgment in historical inquiry. One position on this matter is that editorial judgment should be kept to a minimum and that the most valuable editorial activity is the accurate transcription or reprinting of individual documents. Judgment is nevertheless involved here in deciding (in the light of the genealogy) which documents to focus on and—in the case of handwritten material—deciphering the script; but beyond that the editor's judgment is not allowed to operate. In contrast, one may believe that the textual accidents embodied in individual documents make the texts of those documents a less reliable guide to past intentions than eclectic texts, which aim—through editorial choices among variant readings (*recensio* in cl. textual crit.) and editorial emendations of perceived errors (*emendatio*)—to restore texts to the states that existed or were intended at times in the past. Thus every text presented by an ed. is either *documentary*, attempting to reproduce without alteration what appears in a particular document, or *critical*, embodying critical judgments regarding choices among variant readings and the incorporation of further corrections.

The other major influence on editors' approaches to their task is their assumptions about the nature of literary works—indeed, of all works made of words—and their consequent preference for one stage rather than another in the hist. of individual works. Even a facsimile ed. is affected by the critical predisposition of its ed.: e.g., eds. who believe that literary works are essentially the products of writers working alone might choose an author's final ms. for reproduction rather than the published ed. based on it, whereas eds. who feel that literary works are social products, resulting from the interaction of authors and other persons involved in the publishing process, would be inclined to choose the printed ed. Most discussion of this issue, however, has occurred in connection with critical eds.; and over the centuries, most of the thinking about such eds. has assumed that the aim of making alterations in documentary texts was to bring them closer to what their authors intended. This aim has not necessarily meant that authors were regarded as having had single intentions: in some cases, such as William Wordsworth's *The*

*Prelude* or Walt Whitman's *Leaves of Grass*, an author's changed intentions at different times have been recognized as producing discrete versions that are deserving of separate eds. The advent of electronic eds., with their unlimited space, has enabled eds. more easily to present multiple texts, both documentary and critical, rather than choosing a single one; but it has not eliminated the necessity for eds. to think through all the issues they have always dealt with.

In the second half of the 20th c., the traditional focus on authorial intention was repeatedly challenged. The debate in the Eng.-speaking world centered on the rationale of W. W. Greg and Fredson Bowers, who argued that, in the absence of contrary evidence, final authorial intention could be best reconstructed by incorporating into an early "copy-text" any later variants judged to be authorial. One class of objections came from those who advocated a more "social," and less author-centered, view, such as Jerome J. McGann (who regarded published works as inevitably collaborative) and D. F. McKenzie (who believed that the visual features of printed texts, such as typography and layout, deserve more editorial attention as part of the social context that influences readers' responses). Another view focused on the study of textual growth and change, as in the work of Almuth Grésillon and the Fr. school of *critique génétique*. Arguments for particular approaches have frequently been offered as if their acceptance entails the rejection of other approaches; but there is no exclusively valid approach to the past. An interest in authors' intentions (or their revisions) and an interest in the public texts that were made available to readers do not invalidate one another: each focuses on a different aspect of textual hist., and each therefore tells one part of a larger story. Textual crit., like other forms of hist., can never tell the whole story, nor can it reconstruct any part of it with certainty; but we must make the attempt to uncover the story whenever we wish to read works as communications from the past.

■ For extensive listings of relevant material, see G. T. Tanselle, *Introduction to Scholarly Editing*, 2d ed. (2002), http://www.rarebookschool.org/tanselle.

F. Bowers, *Textual and Literary Criticism* (1959); W. W. Greg, "The Rationale of Copy-Text" [1950], *Collected Papers*, ed. J. C. Maxwell (1966); E. J. Kenney, *The Classical Text* (1974); F. Bowers, *Essays in Bibliography, Text, and Editing* (1975); J. J. McGann, *A Critique of Modern Textual Criticism* (1983); A. E. Housman, "The Application of Thought to Textual Criticism" [1921], *Collected Poems and Selected Prose*, ed. C. Ricks (1988); G. T. Tanselle, *A Rationale of Textual Criticism* (1989), and *Textual Criticism and Scholarly Editing* (1990); L. D. Reynolds and N. G. Wilson, *Scribes and Scholars*, 3d ed. (1991); D. C. Greetham, *Textual Scholarship* (1992); A. Grésillon, *Éléments de critique génétique* (1994); G. T. Tanselle, "Editing without a Copy-Text" [1994], *Literature and Artifacts* (1998); *Scholarly Editing*, ed. D. C. Greetham (1995)—incl. G. T. Tanselle, "The Varieties of Scholarly Editing"; P. Shillingsburg, *Scholarly Editing in the Computer Age*, 3d ed. (1996), and *Resisting Texts* (1997); D. F. McKenzie, *Bibliography and the Sociology of Texts* (1999); G. T. Tanselle, *Textual Criticism Since Greg* (2005).

G. T. Tanselle

**TEXTUALITY.** A key concept in *poststructuralism that enabled that movement's way of understanding writing, reading, and the relations between them. It was meant to stand in opposition to the idea of the *work, its unity, and its humanistic underpinnings and thus underwrote an attack on the metaphysical presuppositions of the traditional conception of lit. in the West.

According to the assumptions that precede a poststructuralist approach to lit., the concept of the *work* entails meaning, *unity, and the authority of a transcendent source. A work is complete, it exists in space, and it is wrought by the creative power of the artist. On the other hand, a **text* in the particular lexicon of poststructuralism—distinct from the term as used, for instance, in *textual criticism—inhabits and is inhabited by lang., without a privileged outside, an origin or source, to guarantee or authorize its meaning. The source of each text is always another text, but there is always another text before that. No text lies outside the endless play of lang., and no text is complete: each exhibits traces or "sediments" of some other text in an endless repetition of originary lack. To humanistic ("logocentric") assertions of a transcendent referent (the transcendental signified) that organizes human experience and renders lang. meaningful, textuality opposes the notion that, at the origin, there is "always already" lang., writing, a trace of some other text. The terms *trace, supplement,* and *writing* indicate an absence in the text, its impossibility of self-presence. Each text is haunted by this absence, which opens it up to an entangled web of relations with every other text and which permits the articulation of a "subtext." The subtext is not that which is "meant" or "expressed" but rather that which tends to "dissimulate or forbid" and which it nonetheless makes evident at certain points of stress or conflict. The subtext functions as a text's unconscious—what it does not know it knows—and indicates a reading against the grain.

The subtext was not always conceived as a strategic dismantling of the text. In the view of *Russian formalism and early *structuralism, the subtext was one of the visible components of the text, one of the parts that fitted into the whole. The stable ling. that gave rise to structuralism perceived the subtext as a partially hidden segment of the text, elucidation of which would provide a synchronic view of the whole. Later views of textuality, which perceived the text diachronically rather than synchronically, in terms of what is missing or absent rather than merely hidden from view, think of the subtext as a destabilizing element in the play of significations. The subtext is not assimilable to the text; it works against and undermines a text's potential meaning.

Textuality is thus fraught with dissonance. Each text is a locus of conflict that cannot be decided without repression. In a further phase of its application, textuality became associated with questions of power: the power not only between text and subtext but of the competing claims and ideologies that make themselves evident in a text. The major effect of textuality is to problematize the question of knowledge—the relation between *what* we know and *how* we know. Textuality assumes the impossibility of thought without lang., thus effectively subsuming knowledge within lang. itself. Disciplinary knowledge, like the work, also lacks a transcendental signified and is not authorized by any epistemological high ground. Each discipline constitutes itself as a discipline by repressing its ling., rhetorical nature, but textuality disrupts this movement of repression, highlights it, and focuses on what a field of knowledge tends to "dissimulate" or "forbid." Textuality assumes the "textuality" of all disciplines and thus the tropological (rhetorical) nature of all knowledge.

*See* ALLUSION, INTERTEXTUALITY, ORGANICISM.

■ M. Foucault, *The Archaeology of Knowledge and the Discourse on Language,* trans. A. M. Sheridan Smith (1972); R. Barthes, *Le plaisir du texte* (1973); and "De l'oeuvre au texte," *Revue d'esthétique* (1974); E. Said, "Abecedarium Culturae," *Beginnings* (1975); J. Derrida, *Of Grammatology,* trans. G. C. Spivak (1976)—essential preface by Spivak; E. Said, "The Problem of Textuality: Two Exemplary Positions," *CritI* 4 (1978); *Textual Strategies,* ed. J. Harari (1979)—excellent intro., bibl.; M. Foucault *Power/Knowledge,* ed. and trans C. Gordon (1980); *Untying the Text,* ed. R. Young (1981); G. Bruns, *Inventions: Writing, Textuality, and Understanding Literary History* (1982); J. Culler, *On Deconstruction* (1982); J. Derrida, "Signature, Event, Context," *Margins of Philosophy,* trans. A. Bass (1982); *The Question of Textuality,* ed. W. Spanos and P. Bové (1982); M. Riffaterre, *Text Production,* trans. T. Lyons (1983); H. Baran, "Subtext," Terras; J. MacCannell, "The Temporality of Textuality: Bakhtin and Derrida," *MLN* 100 (1985); *Demarcating the Disciplines,* ed. S. Weber (1986); *Textual Analysis,* ed. M. A. Caws (1986); *Unnam'd Forms: Blake and Textuality,* ed. N. Hilton and T. A. Vogler (1986); G. Harpham, *The Ascetic Imperative in Culture and Criticism* (1987); C. Norris, *Derrida* (1987); S. Weber, *Institution and Interpretation* (1987); G. Jay, "Paul de Man: Being in Question," *America the Scrivener* (1990); R. Scholes, "Canonicity and Textuality," *Introduction to Scholarship in Modern Languages and Literatures,* ed. J. Gibaldi (1992); C. Norris, "Textuality, Difference, and Cultural Otherness: Deconstruction v. Postmodernism," *Common Knowledge* 3.3 (1994); *Texts and Textuality: Textual Instability, Theory, and Interpretation,* ed. P. Cohen (1997); J. McGann, *Radiant Textuality: Literature after the World Wide Web* (2001); J. Drucker, "Theory as Praxis: The Poetics of Electronic Textuality," *Modernism/Modernity* 9 (2002); *Reimagining Textuality: Textual Studies in the Late Age of Print,* ed. E. B. Loizeaux (2002); J. Mowitt, "What Is a Text Today?," *PMLA* 117 (2002); J. A. Walker, "Why Performance? Why Now? Textuality and the Rearticulation of Human Presence," *Yale Journal of Criticism* 16 (2003); N. K. Hayles, *My Mother Was a Computer:*

*Digital Subjects and Literary Texts* (2005); "Textual Materialism," *PMLA* 125.1 (2010)—spec. section.

H. R. ELAM; R. GREENE

**TEXTURE.** *Texture* signifies the palpable, tangible details inscribed in the poetic text. It refers to the distinguishing elements in a poem that are separate and independent of its structure, the elements that persist when the argument of a poem has been rendered into a prose paraphrase (see PARAPHRASE, HERESY OF). The term has close affinities with the concept of surface detail in painting and sculpture. Such a conception is designed to solve the difficulties posed by schematic and overgeneralized theories of *poetics. A poem has texture to the degree that the phonetic and ling. characteristics of its surface promote stylistic density. At one level, texture involves the familiar poetic techniques of *assonance and *alliteration; at another level, it assumes the form of sensory intensities and tactile association (harshness or softness). It is to these surface qualities that texture corresponds and is made more complex by metrical patterns.

Texture was of crucial importance to Am. *New Criticism, esp. to John Crowe Ransom. For Ransom, the texture of the poem is specifically related to "a sense of the real density and contingency of the world" ("Criticism as Pure Speculation"). By definition, then, texture is intended to correct the exaggerations of "logic" in poetry that cause colorful local details to disappear into the grayness of systematized abstraction. Thus, in his formulation, poetic texture is characterized by its "sensuous richness," by its "fullness of presentation," by its "immediacy," and by its "concreteness." Such an emphasis is quite distinct from what Ransom saw as the prominence of structure for Cleanth Brooks. In Ransom's view, the function of the concrete detail is not to authorize the abstract generality of structure (as, e.g., in Brooks's claim that paradoxical structure underpins all poetry from the *Odyssey* to *The Waste Land*). For Ransom, the detail becomes formally and explicitly disjoined from the structure when the poet chooses words, metaphors, images, and other devices. This reversal of Brooks's emphasis on structure serves to reimmerse poetics in the immediate and sensory experience of contingent reality (something Ransom felt Brooks's paradoxically abstract poetics could not address). From such a viewpoint, it follows that one important function of detail is precisely to *impede* the argument of the poem. A poet's accommodation of the details to the demands of *meter and *euphony affords unexpected insights that then become themselves the most prominent feature of texture and generate a set of unforeseen and unique meanings out of the reach of structure.

In avant-garde experimental *concrete poetry and *sound poetry of the late 20th c., texture takes on material forms: voice, intonation, even grunts and shrieks, constitute the poetry, a flow of breath through lungs and throat. To be sure, poetry has been sung, recited, and chanted since its beginnings. Both sound and concrete poetry, however, mobilize modernist concepts of *"defamiliarization" or "making strange," together with psychoanalytical and psychological theories of repression and release. As poet and critic Steve McCaffery writes, "When considering text-sound it is energy, not semantically shaped meaning that constitutes the essence of communicated data." The texture of sound poetry releases "forces of libido" caught in "the overcoded structure of grammar." Other forms of concrete texture include overprinted columns of text, poetry incised into wood or stone, or the use of materials to interact with the words of the poem. In the Scottish poet Ian Hamilton Finlay's "Wave-rock," e.g., letters are etched into colored glass so that their arrangement suggests the texture of water and shore. The Brazilian avant-garde *Noigandres group (see, e.g., the poetry of Augusto de Campos) produces poetry whose visual combinations of lines and curves create fabriclike texture. Poet and critic Scobie points out that skills in reading visual images are crucial for interpreting these new constructions of texture in poetry.

*See* ARTIFICE, FORM.

■ J. C. Ransom, *The World's Body* (1932); and "The Inorganic Muses," *KR* 5 (1943); Brooks; Wimsatt and Brooks; M. C. Beardsley, *Aesthetics* (1958); J. E. Magner, *John Crowe Ransom: Critical Principles and Preoccupations* (1971); T. D. Young, "Ransom's Critical Theories: Structure and Texture." *Mississippi Quarterly* 30 (1977); S. McCaffery, *Sound Poetry: A Catalogue* (1978); Ransom, "Criticism as Pure Speculation" and "Wanted: An Ontological Critic"; N. Masselink, "Apparition Head versus Body Bush: The Prosodical Theory and Practice of John Crowe Ransom," *Southern Quarterly* 29 (1991); M. Perloff, *Radical Artifice: Writing Poetry in the Age of Media* (1991); M. Jancovich, *The Cultural Politics of the New Criticism* (1992); S. Scobie, *Earthquakes and Explorations: Language and Painting from Cubism to Concrete Poetry* (1997)—esp. ch. 9.

P. MCCALLUM

**THAILAND, POETRY OF.** Poetry dominated Thai lit. until the early 20th c., when prose also became widespread. Noted for rhyme and sound play, Thai poetry is written in syllabic meters in five major verse forms: *rāi, khlōng, kāp, chan,* and *klǫn.* The Thai (Siamese) lang. presently has five tones that also form part of the metrical requirements. The king and court poets used these forms nearly exclusively until 1932, though in many cases the works are anonymous.

The earliest verse appeared during the Sukhothai period (ca. 1240–1438). Sukhothai reached a high level of civilization, but extant poems are few; the only significant extant text is *Suphāsit phra ruang,* a series of moral maxims written in rāi and credited to King Ramkhamhaeng (ca. 1279–98). These stanzas have an indefinite number of five-syllable lines linked by rhyme. Melodious and concise phrases, suggestive of poetry, also appear in inscriptions from the period.

The Ayutthaya period (1351–1767) saw the rise of classics in rāi, khlōng, kāp, and chan. Khlōng, like rāi, originally appeared when Thai had only three tones. Khlōng consists of five-syllable lines grouped into stanzas of two lines (*khlōng sǫng*), three (*khlōng sām*), and four (*khlōng sī*). The kāp stanzas, probably borrowed from Khmer, include *yānī* with two 11-syllable lines, *surāngkhanāng* with seven four-syllable lines, and *chabang* with one four-syllable line between two six-syllable lines. Indic in origin, the chan meters were adapted from meters found in *Sanskrit and Pali poetry during this period.

One of the earliest and most difficult Ayutthayan works is *ōngkān chāeng nam* (the Water Oath), a composition used by officials to reaffirm their loyalty to the king. Throughout the era, Buddhist themes dominate many compositions. In 1482, King Traylokkhanat (1448–88) commissioned a royal version of the *Vessantara Jataka*, the Buddha's life prior to his last birth on earth. This version, the *Mahāchāt kham luang*, consists of passages in Pali followed by Thai trans. into rāī, khlōng, and chan. Important compositions with historical themes began with *Lilit yuan phāī* (ca. 1475). Written anonymously in *lilit*, a combination of rāī and khlōng, this poem describes the victories of King Traylokkhanat. The popular *nirāt* genre, in which the poet compares his lover's features to the beauties of nature, also developed about this time. During the reign of King Narai (1656–88), the court became a major center of poetry production, and the era came to be known as the Golden Age of Thai lit. Probably the most famous of Narai's court poets was Sri Prat. In and out of favor with the king because of his sharp wit, he composed the famous *Kamsuan sī prāt*, a nirāt describing his journey into exile. The chan meters gained prominence with the adaptation of Buddhist birth stories into verse such as the *Samutthakhōt kham chan* and *Sua khō kham chan*. The most famous work from this period, although some scholars date it in the reign of King Traylokkhanat, is the lilit classic *Phra lọ*, the tragic romance of Prince Phra Lọ and two princesses from a neighboring kingdom. Literary output declined after Narai, however, because of war and internal strife. Notable works from the end of the Ayutthaya period include a collection of boating songs in kāp, *Kāp hāē rua*, and a description in chan of the king's journey to a Buddhist shrine, *Bunnōwāt kham chan*. In 1767 the Burmese destroyed Ayutthaya.

The establishment of the new capital at Bangkok in 1782 revived literary production at court, this time primarily in *klọn*, which probably first appeared during the Thonburi period (1767–82). Since then it has been the favored Thai verse form, with two types used regularly: *klọn hok* with six syllables per line and *klọn pāēt* with eight. The four-line klọn stanzas are famous for rhyme schemes and rhyme links that often continue for thousands of stanzas. Hoping to recreate lost works, Rama I, Phra Phutthayotfa (1782–1809), the first king at Bangkok, organized a royal composition committee that produced the *Rāmakian* (the Thai version of the Indian classic, the *Rāmāyaṇa*) and parts of *Inau* and *Dālang* (romances based on the Javanese Panji cycle introduced through Malaysia). Rama II, Phra Phutthaloetla (1809–24), continued the literary revival with another version of the *Rāmakian* and a complete version of *Inau*, which, it is thought, he composed much of himself. Sunthorn Phu (1786–1856), arguably Thailand's greatest poet, used klọn for many nirāt poems and for the long imaginative romance *Phra aphaimanī*. Probably written down as a complete poem after the

founding of Bangkok with parts attributed to Rama II and Sunthorn Phu, *Khun Chāng Khun Phāēn* relates the lifelong competition between two friends for the love of a village beauty, who also happens to be their childhood friend. Originally composed by wandering poets in the late Ayutthaya period, the poem is famous for its depiction of customs, trads., and lifeways of ordinary people. Prince Paramanuchit (1790–1853), monk, poet, and Indic classicist, contributed textbooks on the chan meters, the final part of *Samutthakhōt kham chan*, and *Lilit talēng phāī*, a glorification of the battles of King Naresuan. Khun Phum (1815–80), the leading woman poet of the 19th c., produced satirical poems of biting wit in her famous literary salons. Traditional narrative poetry continued into the 20th c. in compositions by Prince Bidyalongkarana (1876–1945): one of his most noted works is *Sām krung*, a hist. of the three Thai capital cities, Ayutthaya, Thonburi, and Bangkok.

The 1932 revolution gave Thailand a constitutional monarchy, and court-dominated poetry thereafter ceased. Post-1932 poetry differed from cl. works in its brevity, its lyricism, and its emphasis upon crit. and instruction in the ongoing social world. Many of these changes resulted from the efforts of Chao Phraya Thammasakdimontri, known as Khru Thep (1876–1943), a journalist-poet. Later, in the 1940s and 1950s, Assani Phonlachan (1918–1987) sought to deemphasize the importance of rhyme and sound in Thai poetry. At the same time, Chit Phumisak (1932–66), a left-wing political idealist, helped launch the Art for Life's Sake movement, which attacked individuals and even whole political systems; Phumisak criticized cl. Thai poetry for not meeting the needs of the people. Other poets such as Prakin Xumsai, writing as Ujjeni (b. 1919), and later Naowarat Pongpaiboon (b. 1940) emphasized nature, love, and emotion along with social crit. The 1960s saw much experimentation with verse forms, incl. free verse (*klọn plāu*). During this time, the poet-painter Angkarn Kalayanapongse (b. 1926), probably the most respected of contemp. poets, developed his themes and style. Often described as a nature poet, he finds expressions of universal messages in Buddhism, nature, art, and the past. The fluid political climate of the early 1970s revived protest and socialist themes. The student uprising of October 14, 1973; the return to democracy; and the subsequent suppression on October 6, 1976, have provided the themes for much of Thai poetry up to the present. Naowarat Pongpaiboon (b. 1940) has emerged as the most eloquent chronicler of these events. Women's issues, along with moral, political, and social concerns, remain major themes in contemp. poetry. Paramount among these themes is the lament for the loss of the environment and traditional Thai culture and values because of Western influences and globalization. Important poets working with these themes include Sujit Wongthet (b. 1945), Saksiri Meesomsueb (Krittisak, b. 1957), Chiranan Pitpreecha (b. 1955), Rewat Phanpipat (b. 1966), and Montri Sriyong (b. 1968). The emergence of regional lit., esp. from northeastern Thailand, can be found in the poetry of Paiwarin Khaongam (b. 1961) and in Tossa's

1990 study of a northeastern folk epic. Political and social crit. provides major themes of Thai poetry today, and poets continue to use both cl. and a variety of experimental verse forms.

■ **Anthologies and Translations**: P. na Nakh o n, *Prawat wannakhadī Thai* (History of Thai Literature, 1964); R. Jones and R. Mendiones, *Introduction to Thai Literature* (1970); *Sang Thong*, trans. F. S. Ingersoll (1973); *Ramakien*, trans. J. M. Cadet (1982); *Mere Movement*, trans. N. Pongpaiboon (1984); *Thai P.E.N. Anthology*, ed. N. Masavisut and F. S. Jose (1984); *A Premier Book of Contemporary Thai Verse*, ed. M. Umavijani et al. (1985); *Phādāēng Nāng Ai: A Thai-Isan Folk Epic in Verse*, trans. W. Tossa (1990); *Sunthorn Phu*, ed. M. Umavijani (1990); T. J. Hudak, *The Tale of Samuttakote* (1993); P. Khaongam, *Banana Tree Horse and Other Poems*, trans. B. Kasemsri (1995); *The S.E.A. Write Anthology of Thai Short Stories and Poems*, ed. N. Masavisut and M. Grose (1996); S. Chongstitvatana, "Love Poems in Modern Thai Nirat," *Journal of the Siam Society* 88 (2000); *ASEAN Short Stories and Poems by S.E.A. Write Awardees, 1999*, ed. S. Poolthupya (2001); C. Baker and P. Phongpaichit, "Phlai Kaeo Ordains as a Novice: A Chapter from *Khun Chang Khun Phaen*," *Journal of the Siam Society* 95 (2007); C. Baker and P. Phongpaichit, "The Career of *Khun Chang Khun Phaen*," *Journal of the Siam Society* 97 (2009).

■ **Criticism and History**: H. H. Prince Bidyalankarana, "The Pastime of Rhyme-making and Singing in Rural Siam," *Journal of the Siam Society* 20 (1926); P. Schweisguth, *Étude sur la littérature siamoise* (1951); J. N. Mosel, *A Survey of Classical Thai Poetry* (1959), and *Trends and Structure in Contemporary Thai Poetry* (1961); M. Chitakasem, "The Emergence and Development of the Nirat Genre in Thai Poetry," *Journal of Siam Society* 60 (1972); T. H. Bofman, *The Poetics of the Ramakian* (1984); K. Wenk, *Sunthon Phū—ein Thai Literat* (1985); C. Nagavajara, "Literary Historiography and Socio-cultural Transformation: The Case of Thailand," *Journal of the Siam Society* 73 (1985); H. P. Phillips, *Modern Thai Literature with an Ethnographic Interpretation* (1987); W. J. Gedney, "Siamese Verse Forms in Historical Perspective," *Selected Papers on Comparative Tai Studies*, ed. R. J. Bickner et al. (1989); T. J. Hudak, *The Indigenization of Pali Meters in Thai Poetry* (1990); R. J. Bickner, *An Introduction to the Thai Poem "Lilit Phra Law"* (1991); *Thai Literary Traditions*, ed. M. Chitakasem (1995); N. Eoseewong, *Pen & Sail*, ed. C. Baker and B. Anderson (2005); T. J. Hudak, "Tai Aesthetics," *The Tai-Kadai Languages*, ed. A.V.N. Diller et al. (2008).

T. J. Hudak

**THEMATICS.** The study of patterns (repetitions of *imagery, codes, rhetorical figures, etc.) in lit. In general, the evolution of thematics has paralleled that of *topoi or topics (Ger. *Toposforschung*, Curtius 1948) and *stylistics/*explication du texte*, developing into various strains of text-immanent and intertextual (paradigmatic, syntagmatic) interpretation. Critics such as Armstrong have cited an interaction between the poetic "world"—divided into dialogical or oppositional fields reflecting differing degrees of abstractness and concreteness—and thematics. The existence of an objective "structure" distinct from social forces or intentional consciousness remains open to debate.

According to Zholkovsky (1984), generic themes reveal their invariability through structural patterns; thematic analysis furnishes essential information for typological modeling. Bachelard (1943, 1957), the so-called *Geneva school, Raymond, Richard (1954, 1961, 1979), Poulet, Béguin, and Starobinski have made important contributions to the discourse of thematics, using tools of psychology and phenomenology (with a debt to *surrealism in the case of Bachelard). Text-immanentist *New Criticism, beginning with I. A. Richards and enjoying a vogue from roughly 1940 to 1970, focuses on repetition and *irony as major features of thematics.

The study of genetic paradigms in thematics begins with Shklovsky, founder of the Society for the Study of Poetic Language, on the "resurrected word" (1917), *defamiliarization (1917), and the canonization of subgenres (1925). In *Paris in the Nineteenth Century*, Benjamin explores, e. g., the motif of the crowd in Charles Baudelaire, examining the literary-historical sequence from the minutest particular to the universal. Studies using thematics in conjunction with other disciplines include Williams, sociology; Wardley, sociology and gender studies; Langan, history of ideas (freedom) and *Toposforschung*; Komar, character refiguration in mod. lit. and media, gender studies; Turner, cultural hist.; Rickels and Ronell, psychoanalysis; de Baecque, art and political hist.; and Zholkovsky (1984, 1994), lit. hist. and poetics. While *poststructuralism has called into question its metatextual status, thematics remains useful in fields of research (concerning gender, race, multiculturalism) surpassing an exclusively literary *epistemē*, requiring judgment and evaluation of distinct yet comparable sign-systems (Todorov). T. Ziolkowski has traced character transfiguration during specific historical periods.

The study of motivation, not to be confused with Burkean motive, addresses compositional technique, sequencing, scaling, modeling, projection, and perspectivization, drawing connections among lit., anthropology, and sociology. The aesthetic function of motivation is to create an illusion of reality for the audience/reader (*aut prodesse . . . aut delectare*) according to a horizon of expectations. *Russian formalism distinguishes *fable*, a temporal sequence of events assigning cause, from *sujet*, which brings the fable into sharper, more complex focus through stylization. In the sujet, a lit. text takes on spatial or temporal contours in order to shape readerly experience. The fable, on the other hand, is nothing more than the sum of motivic elements. Jakobson; Barthes (1966, 1970), using methods adapted from Alexander von Humboldt's studies of J. W. Goethe and the Rus. formalists; Genette; and Greimas (1966) have developed sophisticated theoretical instruments, such as semiotics (see

SEMIOTICS AND POETRY), to analyze fable and sujet not as static but rather as dynamic elements or actants.

In folklore studies, beginning with the categorization of tale types by Aarne, fable has assumed central importance. Thompson assigned ling. labels (e.g., "Snow White," "The Brave Tailor") and type numbers. Both Propp and Dundes took motivic indexing to task for inattention to narrative structure. Propp's classification emphasizes function, isolating seven fundamental character types in Rus. fairytales (*skaz*). Dundes has criticized the ambiguity of the term *motif*, inasmuch as it can be applied to "actors, items, or incidents" while calling for a reinvigorated study of the meaning of the tale. Daemmrich and Daemmrich understand motivic and thematic patternings in literary texts as centripetal or centrifugal but also link the study of thematics and motivation to period codes. Hybridizing Shklovsky and Tynianov, Bakhtin valorizes *intertextuality (dialogism in Rabelais, Dostoevsky, stylization of antecedent texts, the carnivalesque, polyphony). Among his most important discoveries is the notion of "genre memory" ("semantic halos" associated with meters). The studies of Girard (1977, 1978, 1982), constituting a critical oeuvre, stand among anthropological crit., the study of motifs, and thematics; their rigorously polemical approach to received ideas in anthropology and lit. crit., provocative readings of the Bible, and analyses of violence and sacrifice address fundamental issues of social being, lit., and religion.

By widening its epistemic horizon and challenging its own reading practices, thematics has evolved from a literary typology transcending national lits. to the evaluation of period themes and cultural codes uncovered by such disparate methodologies as *New Historicism (shaming, surveillance, confession, the "social presence to the world" of the lit. text and of that world in the text; see Greenblatt 1980, 1987), and the philosophy of knowledge (skepticism, fanaticism; see Cavell) in the context of the Ren.

*See* RHETORIC AND POETRY.

■ A. Aarne, *Verzeichnis der Märchentypen* (1910); L. Spitzer, *Studien zu Henri Barbusse* (1920); B. Tomashevsky, *Russkoe stikhoslozhenie* (1923); V. Zhirmunsky, *Rifma* (1923; rpt. 1970); L. Spitzer, "Der Unanismus Jules Romains im Spiegel seiner Sprache," *Archivum Romanicum* 8 (1924); V. Zhirmunsky, *Baïron i Pushkin* (Byron and Pushkin, 1924); W. Benjamin, *Arcades Project*, ed. R. Tiedemann, trans. H. Eiland and K. McLaughlin (2002); B. Tomashevsky, *Literary Theory* (1928); M. Raymond, *De Baudelaire au surrealisme* (1933); A. Béguin, *L'âme romantique et le rêve* (1937); R. Jakobson, "The Statue in Pushkin's Poetic Mythology," *Slovo a slovesnost* 3 (1937); J. Honti, "Märchenmorphologie und Märchentypologie," *Folkliv* 3 (1939); G. Bachelard, *L'eau et les rêves* (1943); V. Propp, *Istoricheskie korni volshebnoĭ skazki* (Historical Roots of the Magic Tale, 1946); S. Thompson, *The Folktale* (1946); Curtius; J.-P. Richard, *Littérature et sensation* (1954); S. Thompson, *Motif-Index of Folk Literature*, rev. ed. (1955–58); J.-P. Richard, *L'univers imaginaire de Mallarmé* (1961); L. Spitzer, "Zu Charles Péguy's Stil," *Stilstudien* 5 (1961); V. Shklovsky, "Art as Technique," *Russian Formalist Criticism: Four Essays*, trans. L. T. Lemon and M. J. Reis (1965); E. Frenzel, *Stoff-, Motiv- und Symbolforschung* (1966); G. Genette, *Figures of Literary Discourse,* trans. A. Sheridan (1981); G. Poulet, *Metamorphoses of the Circle*, trans. C. Dawson and E. Coleman (1966); V. Propp, *Morphology of the Folk-Tale*, trans. L. Scott [1958], ed. L. A. Wagner, 2d ed. (1968); T. Todorov, "Motif," *Encyclopedic Dictionary of the Sciences of Language*, ed. O. Ducrot and T. Todorov, trans. C. Porter (1979); T. Ziolkowski, *Fictional Transfigurations of Jesus* (1972); V. Shklovsky, "The Resurrection of the Word," trans. R. Sherwood, *Russian Formalism: A Collection of Articles and Texts in Translation*, ed. S. Bann and J. Bowlt (1973); R. Williams, *The Country and the City* (1973); R. Barthes, *S/Z*, trans. R. Miller (1974), and "Introduction to the Structural Analysis of Narrative," *NLH* 6 (1975); J. Honti, *Studies in Oral Epic Tradition*, trans. Eva Róna (1975); E. Frenzel, *Motive der Weltliteratur* (1976); R. Girard, *Violence and the Sacred*, trans. P. Gregory (1977); Y. Tynianov, "Dostoevsky and Gogol (On the Theory of Parody)," *Poetika: istoriya literatury kino* (1977); T. Ziolkowski, *Disenchanted Images* (1977); R. Girard, *Things Hidden since the Foundation of the World*, trans. S. Bann and M. Metteer (1978), and *"To Double Business Bound": Essays on Literature, Mimesis, and Anthropology* (1978); P. N. Medvedev and M. M. Bakhtin, *The Formal Method in Literary Scholarship*, trans. A. J. Wehrle (1978); Y. Tynianov and R. Jakobson, "Problems in the Study of Literature and Language," *Readings in Russian Poetics, Formalist and Structuralist Views*, ed. and trans. L. Matejka and K. Pomorska (1978); J.-P. Richard, *Microlectures* (1979); S. Greenblatt, *Renaissance Self-Fashioning* (1980); "Thematologie," *Vergleichende Literaturwissenschaft*, ed. M. Schmeling (1981); R. Girard, *The Scapegoat*, trans. Y. Freccero (1982); E. Frenzel, *Stoffe der Weltliteratur* (1983); A. Greimas, *Structural Semantics: An Attempt at Method*, trans. D. McDowell, R. Schleifer, A. Velie (1983); T. Ziolkowski, *Varieties of Literary Thematics* (1983); M. M. Bakhtin, *Problems of Dostoevsky's Poetics*, ed. and trans. C. Emerson (1984); A. Zholkovsky, *Themes and Texts: Towards a Poetics of Expressiveness*, trans. K. Parthé (1984); S. Cavell, *Disowning Knowledge in Six Plays of Shakespeare* (1987); H. S. Daemmrich and I. Daemmrich, *Themes and Motifs in Western Literature: A Handbook* (1987); J. Starobinski, *Jean-Jacques Rousseau: Transparency and Obstacle*, trans. A. Goldhammer (1988); *Gattungsinnovation und Motivstruktur*, ed. T. Wolpers, v. 1 (1989); S. J. Greenblatt, "Towards a Poetics of Culture," *The New Historicism*, ed. H. A. Veeser (1989); L. Doležel, *Occidental Poetics: Tradition and Progress* (1990); V. Shklovsky, *Theory of Prose*, trans. B. Sher (1990), and *Gender at the Crossroads of Knowledge*, ed. M. di Leonardo (1991); N. Armstrong, "A Brief Genealogy of Theme," *Harvard English Studies* 18 (1993); *The Return of Thematic Criticism*, ed. W. Sollors (1993); G. Bachelard, *The Poetics of Space*, trans. M. Jolas (1994); A. Zholkovsky, *Text Counter Text: Rereadings in Russian Literary History* (1994); *Thematics Reconsidered*, ed. T. Ziolkowski and F. Trommler (1995); A. Dundes, "The Motif Index and the Tale-Type Index: A Critique," *Journal of Folklore Research* 34 (1997); A.

de Baecque, *The Glory and the Terror*, trans. C. Mandell (2001); A. Ronell, *Stupidity* (2002); J. G. Turner, *Libertines and Radicals in Early Modern London* (2002); K. Komar, *Reclaiming Klytemnestra: Revenge and Reconciliation* (2003); T. Ziolkowski, *The Hesitant Hero* (2004).

R. G. Eisenhauer

## THERAPY AND POETRY

I. Historical and Theoretical Foundations
II. Application

The use of poetry and of a variety of poetic methods (e.g., *metaphors, jour. writing, letter writing, and ceremonies) in health and mental-health disciplines has been widely reported in the professional lit. *Poetry therapy* is defined as the use of lang., symbol, and story in therapeutic, educational, and community-building capacities. The purview of poetry therapy includes bibliotherapy, narrative therapy, and jour. therapy. The field of poetry therapy is interdisciplinary, drawing from helping disciplines (e.g., psychology, social work, and medicine), literary and creative arts (poets/writers), and education (elementary through university level). Central to understanding the connection between literary and therapeutic viewpoints are the professional boundaries and perspectives that each discipline brings to poetry therapy. A poet, e.g., may be invited into a hospital, runaway shelter, hospice, or prison to teach or read poetry to the patients or residents. The purpose for the poet is to provide support and enrichment, not therapy, but there are therapeutic qualities inherent in writing or listening to poetry. For the therapist, however, the writing of, listening to, or reading of poetry could serve to validate feelings, provide a method to express feelings, serve a means for communication, or restore some sense of order and control. Thus, while there are inherent therapeutic and educational qualities involved in the process of poetry therapy, its use must be consistent with the individual's professional background and role.

The healing and empowering aspects of the lang. arts can be found in the spontaneous outpouring of poetry, lyrics, letters, and stories resulting from shootings on high-school and college campuses and the terrorist attacks of September 11, 2001. Poetic response to social, psychological, and health concerns include writing programs for inmates, runaway teenagers, battered women, and the terminally ill. Like music in many ways, poetry and other literary genres have the power to evoke, validate, and universalize powerful personal feelings. The popularity of performance poetry (e.g., *poetry slams) is a recent example of the therapeutic and social value of poetry.

**I. Historical and Theoretical Foundations.** The starting point for poetry therapy has been traced to ancient Gr. mythology and Apollo, the god of both poetry and medicine (Leedy 1969). The potential for *catharsis to effect an emotional cure and contribute to insight and recognition of universal truths has also been attributed to Aristotle's *Poetics*. Blinderman traced the use of poetry for promoting health to preliterate times and the use of *incantations and invocations. The power of ritual could be seen in the use of the chanted word to bring about change in oneself, in others, or in one's environment.

Poetry and other literary genres have been used both formally and informally in healing capacities in the U.S. since the early 19th c., when psychiatric patients wrote poems for the Pennsylvania Hospital newspaper *The Illuminator* (Jones). Prescott, a professor of Eng. noted the therapeutic value of poetry for troubled individuals in its capacity to provide an emotional outlet in his 1922 work; and in 1925, Robert Haven Schauffler wrote *The Poetry Cure: A Pocket Medicine Chest of Verse*.

Many mental-health professionals have long recognized the potential healing power of poetry. Through the work of Jack J. Leedy, M.D., poetry therapy was formally recognized in 1969 with the establishment of the Association for Poetry Therapy and, in 1981, became institutionalized as The National Association for Poetry Therapy (NAPT). NAPT holds annual conferences at various sites across the United States, has developed standards for practice, and is part of the National Coalition of Arts Therapies Association (NCATA). Membership in NAPT is interdisciplinary and international. Contributors to the scholarly and practice base of poetry therapy include Leedy, Arthur Lerner, Arleen McCarty Hynes, and Nicholas Mazza.

The *Journal of Poetry Therapy: The Interdisciplinary Journal of Practice, Theory, Research, and Education* is the leading jour. in this field, having been established in 1987. A review of the lit. indicates a wide use of poetic methods across populations (along developmental markers, culture, and socioeconomic status), problem areas (e.g., trauma, depression, stress, anxiety, cancer, AIDS, homelessness, and physical disabilities), and institutions (e.g., mental-health centers, hospice, family-service agencies, hospitals, and counseling centers).

**II. Application.** Mazza's (2003) multidimensional poetry-therapy practice model encompasses the complete range of poetry-therapy methods through its three primary domains: *(1) Receptive/Prescriptive*—introducing existing poems (or other forms of lit.) in a therapeutic capacity to validate a feeling, promote self-expression, or advance group process; *(2) Expressive/Creative*—the use of written expression (e.g., poetry, letters, jours., and stories) for clinical/health purposes; and *(3) Symbolic/Ceremonial*—the use of metaphors, rituals, symbols, storytelling, and *performance (e.g., dance and movement) to deal with life transitions.

This tripartite system is a synthesis of the major poetry-therapy methods that may be applied in an independent or integrated manner. Consider, e.g., the role of poetic material in dealing with death. Grieving individuals often use creative writing to release powerful feelings, create meaning, and honor the memory of a loved one. Writing a letter to the deceased loved one and engaging in a ceremonial act, such as burning or burying it, is one example. Reading or listening to a poem often provides a measure of comfort, insight, and strength. Of course, experiencing a poem or song can also bring up powerful emotions that might overwhelm the individual. The power of poetry is clearly evident, and the place of poetry as a healing tool is in the early stages of systematic empirical investigation.

Poetry therapy and the therapeutics of poetry will continue to develop through interdisciplinary study, practice, and evaluation. The promise of the poetic in the classroom, clinic, or larger community will be best served through the complementarity of art and science.
■ F. C. Prescott, *The Poetic Mind* (1922); *Poetry Therapy*, ed. J. J. Leedy (1969), esp. R. E. Jones, "Treatment of a Psychotic Patient by Poetry Therapy"; A. Blinderman, *Shamans, Witch Doctors, Medicine Men and Poetry, Poetry the Healer*, ed. J. J. Leedy (1973); *Poetry in the Therapeutic Experience*, ed. A. Lerner (1978); A. M. Hynes and M. Hynes-Berry, *Biblio/Poetry Therapy: The Interactive Process: A Handbook* (1986); J. V. Knapp, *Striking at the Joints: Contemporary Psychology and Literary Criticism* (1996); N. Mazza, *Poetry Therapy* (2003); and "Twenty Years of Scholarship in the *Journal of Poetry Therapy*: The Collected Abstracts," *Journal of Poetry Therapy* 21 (2008); C. J. Maddalena, "The Resolution of Internal Conflict through Performing Poetry," *The Arts in Psychotherapy* 36 (2009); http://www.poetry therapy.org.

N. F. MAZZA

**TIBET, CONTEMPORARY POETRY OF.** From the adoption of Indian *kāvya* poetic codes in the 13th c. until the 1950s, Tibetan poetic production was tremendous, but poets demonstrated limited interest for innovation. One late exception was the iconoclastic genius Gendun Choephel (1903–51), who brought in a new tone and contemp. themes, while in some pieces rehabilitating pre-kāvya versification (mainly *hexameters) and ancient historical themes. He may be considered a key figure in the transition from the Indian-inspired cl. Tibetan poetry to the new Tibetan poetry.

With the Chinese occupation starting in 1950, the Tibetan literary scene saw the emergence of a "monastic vanguard" (Hartley 2008), consisting of traditionally trained Buddhist clerics co-opted by the Chinese Communist Party, to eulogize the new regime and its platforms, as well as material progress. The clerics' poetic works, communist in content, remained strongly reminiscent of their traditional, Indian-influenced literary training. From the mid-1950s onward, strong resistance to radical communist reforms led to a virtual halt in original Tibetan literary production, as many intellectuals and educated people were excluded from official circles, imprisoned, or even killed. The Cultural Revolution (1966–76) further ostracized the intellectual elite. As a consequence, between the late 1950s and the late 1970s, hardly any poetic innovation, or even writing, is to be noted in the Tibetan lang.

Within a few years of Mao's death in 1976, a new era dawned: Tibetan-lang. literary and cultural jours., supported and controlled by the Chinese state, started to appear. A turning point in contemp. Tibetan lit. occurred in 1983 when the poem *Lang-tsho'i rbab-chu* (Waterfall of Youth) was published. This long poem, written by the short-lived prodigy Dondrupgyal (1953–85), is considered the very first *free-verse work in Tibetan, although rare instances of verse irregularity can be found in earlier writings. The irregular structure of *Lang-tsho'i rbab-chu* encouraged people not trained in the cl. Tibetan *canon to compose poetry according to their own terms, without restraint or arduous training in the subtleties of traditional poetics. The result was a sudden and long-lasting surge in poetic composition among Tibetan lay youth, whereas poetic composition had been for centuries a quasi-monopoly of clerics.

The next evolution came with Jangbu (pseud. of Dorje Tsering, b. 1963), who was inspired both by Dondrupgyal and by Chinese "obscure poetry" (Chinese *menglong shi*, Tibetan *rab-rib kyi snyan-ngag*). An obscurity of meaning, a chaotic flow of clauses, and total irregularity in form became marks of this new genre. A small coterie of Tibetan authors, trained in the mod. educational system, familiar with Chinese, and possessing a strong connection to Tibetan folk culture, led this movement. Like Dondrupgyal, they were frowned upon by traditionalists, who despaired at finding neither meaning nor Tibetan flavor in these enigmatic and personal works. But the new, lay intellectual elite, eager to be in tune with literary modernity in the rest of the world, was enthusiastic.

The year 2005 marked the latest turning point, with the first privately organized poetry festival in Tibet, also titled "Waterfall of Youth." The festival has since been held in 2007, 2009, and 2011. Under Jangbu's leadership, it has brought together eminent poets to discuss and recite their poetry and to meet students in local schools. Also in 2005, led by Kyabchen Dedröl (b. 1977), the poetic circle *mi-rabs gsum-pa* (Third Generation, a name inspired by Chinese artistic circles) was formed, a group of about 20 poets and intellectuals in their 30s and 40s who write either in Tibetan or Chinese, who are free from any trend or current, and whose generation follows that of Dondrupgyal and Ju Kälzang (b. 1960). Members of the group do not profess a particular style, nor any political stance. Their specificity lies not so much in their style or content as in their close friendship and openness to world lit.

Although it is difficult to summarize the wealth of themes that inform Tibetan poems today, religion is no longer the dominant theme. Instead, frequent themes include individual moods, with an emphasis on sadness and solitude; a sense of commonality among Tibetans; and dismay toward an uncertain future, with nature offering convenient and discreet parallels to political concerns too sensitive to be expressed openly. Social concerns and everyday life also have become prominent topics.

A common feature of Tibetan poets is their relatively young age: very few manage to develop a literary career in the long term. Only a handful have become lasting and prolific: Jangbu, Ju Kälzang, and, in the younger generation, Kyabchen Dedröl, Chän Metak (b. 1968), and Gangzhün (pseud. of Sangye Gyatso, b. 1969). Among them, only Jangbu has achieved international fame and is published in Eng. Women poets also lack visibility, with the exception of Palmo (b. 1968) and Dekyi Drolma (b. 1966), who have earned well-deserved recognition in the otherwise male-dominated Tibetan poetic scene.

While there are six million Tibetans, only half of whom are literate, about 100 Tibetan-lang. magazines are currently being published in China, half of them state sponsored. Most are either literary or cultural, and they always include poems, sometimes to the exclusion of other literary genres, as is the case for *Ganggyän Metok* (Snow Flower). In addition, Web sites in the Tibetan lang. have gradually begun to appear since 2005, and many offer a daily delivery of online poems.

With the occupation of Tibet, a number of highly educated Tibetans have gained mastery in the Chinese lang. and have begun writing poetry in Chinese. First came Yidam Tsering (1933–2004), whose poetry is informed by a good knowledge of Chinese and Tibetan culture. His often nationalistic tone endeared him to Tibetans, and a selection of his works has been translated into Tibetan. Tsering Woeser (b. 1966) has also published a number of poetic works, some of which have been translated into Eng. Tsobu Gade, born in the late 1980s and a member of the third-generation group, won two all-China literary prizes in 2009.

Regarding the exile Tibetans after the Chinese occupation, poetic creation temporarily came to a halt in the first years after the settlement in India (1959), although some poems did appear in *Shecha* (Knowledge), the first magazine founded by the Tibetan government-in-exile. The new generation educated in India started *Young Tibet* (later changed to *Lotus Fields*) in 1977, the first exile Tibetan literary magazine, which published only poems written in Eng. Poetic writing in the Tibetan lang. gained vitality and renewal only after the second wave of refugees, fleeing Tibet from the mid-1980s onward, brought with them the concept of literary magazines written in Tibetan and free-verse poetry. The launching of *Jangshön* (Young Shoot) in December 1990, a magazine dedicated to old and new Tibetan-lang. poetry and fiction, heralded a new era. From then onward, more and more magazines began to be published, usually at the initiative of recently arrived exiles with a poor knowledge of Eng. but good mastery of Tibetan script. There are currently over 30 jours. and magazines in Tibetan pub. in exile, most of which include poetry. A Guild of Tibetan Writers was created in India in 1999 and joined the PEN Club in 2003, becoming the Tibetan Writers Abroad PEN Center. It is headed by the acclaimed writer and Tibetan lit. expert Chabdak Lhamokyab (b. 1963).

Finally, a number of exile Tibetans now write poetry in Eng., such as Tenzin Tsundue (living in India, b. ca. 1975) and Bhuchung Sonam (India, b. ca. 1972). Their work is often political, with a strong presence of Tibet- and exile-related themes. Tsering Wangmo Dhompa (U.S., b. 1969) stands out as an acclaimed award-winning woman poet whose work is highly personal and creative.

*See* CHINA, MODERN POETRY OF; TIBET, TRADITIONAL POETRY AND POETICS OF.

■ **Anthologies and Primary Texts**: *The Blighted Flower and Other Stories*, ed. R. Virtanen (2000); *Manoa 12: Song of the Snow Lion*, ed. F. Stewart, H. J. Batt, T. Shakya (2000); *Muses in Exile: An Anthology of Tibetan Poetry*, ed. B. D. Sonam (2005); T. Woeser, *Tibet's True Heart: Selected Poems*, trans. A. E. Clarke (2009); Jangbu, *The Nine-eyed Agate: Stories and Poems*, trans. H. Stoddard (2010).

■ **Criticism and History**: L. R. Hartley, "Themes of Tradition and Change in Modern Tibetan Literature," *Lungta* 12 (1999); *Contemporary Tibetan Literary Studies. PIATS 2003: Proceedings of the Tenth Seminar of the International Association for Tibetan Studies, Oxford, 2003*, ed. S. J. Venturino (2007); *Modern Tibetan Literature and Social Change*, ed. L. R. Hartley and P. Schiaffini-Vedani (2008)—esp. L. R. Hartley, "Heterodox Views and the New Orthodox Poems: Tibetan Writers in the Early and Mid-Twentieth Century"; Y. Dhondup, "Roar of the Snow Lion: Tibetan Poetry in Chinese"; P. Bhum, "'Heartbeat of a New Generation': A Discussion of the New Poetry," and "'Heartbeat of a New Generation' Revisited"; S. Gyatso (Gangzhün), "Modern Tibetan Literature and the Rise of Writer Coteries"; H. Jigme, "Tibetan Literature in the Diaspora."

■ **Electronic Sources**: The Lamp (in Tibetan), www.tibetcm.com; *Where Tibetans Write* (in Eng.), www.tibetwrites.org.

F. ROBIN

## TIBET, TRADITIONAL POETRY AND POETICS OF.

The Tibetan formal term for poetry is *snyan-ngag* (Sanskrit, *kāvya*), "ornamental language," and its author is the *snyan-ngag-mkhan* (Sanskrit, *kavi*). *Snyan-ngag* is characterized by the use of rhetorical ornament (*don-rgyan*, Sanskrit, *arthālaṃkāra*) and phonetic ornament (*sgra-rgyan*, Sanskrit, *śabdālaṃkāra*). It may be either verse or prose, and there is little deliberate use of rhyme. Colloquially, however, Tibetans speak of *rtsom*, literally "composition," to refer to poetic verse in particular. Tibetan verse typically consists of *quatrains, with lines of 5, 6, 7, 8, 9, 11, 13, or 15 syllables, and sometimes more in very ornate verse. The use of shorter lines is characteristic of archaic and folk poetry, while trans. of Sanskrit verse and poetry influenced by Sanskrit models use lines of seven or more syllables. The lines forming a single verse most often are metrically regular, generally in trochaic feet, with the addition of a final stressed syllable when the line consists of an odd number of syllables, though meters not according with this scheme are also known. Parallel syntax is often employed, one or more syllables being repeated at the beginning, middle, or end of each line, or with repetitions of the same syllable within a single line. *Tropes include various sorts of *simile (*dpe-rgyan*) and *metaphor (*gzugs-rgyan*), and the use of elegant literary synonyms (*mngon-brjod*).

The indigenous Tibetan poetic genres, little influenced by translated lit., include folk songs (*glu*, songs of varied meter, and *gzhas*, dance songs of four six-syllable lines), *epic and bardic verse (*sgrung-glu*), and versified folk oratory (*tshig-dpe/mol-ba*). Traditionally, these were generally unwritten but have informed Tibetan lit. in many respects, beginning with the earliest known Tibetan poetic works, dating to the early 9th c. and discovered at Dunhuang. In later times, the inspiration of folk song permeates the poems of the Sixth Dalai Lama (1683–1706), as in this example, in the characteristic trochaic trimeter of the dance song (using accents to mark the stressed syllables):

Mdzángs ma'i thúgs dang bstún na
Tshé 'di chós skal chád 'gro
Dbén pa'i rí khrod 'gríms na
bú mo'i thúgs dang 'gál 'gro.

(If I follow my girl friend's heart,
Life's religious wealth will run out;
If I adhere to single retreat,
I'll be running against my girl's heart.)

The subject matter of Tibetan folk song may include love and courtship; politics; grief; nature; or activities such as grazing, sowing, and harvesting; construction work; or picnicking. Literary redactions of Tibet's epic and bardic trads. are represented by ms. and printed versions of the popular tales of King Gesar (*ge-sar sgrung*). Folk oratory, on the other hand, was seldom recorded before recent times, though its colorful rhetoric occasionally punctuates Tibetan yogic songs and biographical lit., particularly in the writings of authors from the nomadic regions of Tibet's far eastern provinces, Khams and Amdo.

The Tibetan script and literary lang. developed in the 7th c. CE, an early literary effort incl. very extensive trans., particularly of Indian Buddhist lit. During the 13th c., this translated lit. was canonized in the form of two great collections: the Kanjur (literally "translated pronouncements") in roughly 100 volumes, consisting of the discourses attributed to the Buddha, and the Tanjur (literally "translated treatises") in roughly 200 volumes, consisting mostly of the writings of later Indian scholars and sages. These include much verse, providing enduring examples for Tibetan writers. The latter collection also includes trans. of Sanskrit treatises on the "language sciences" (*sgra-rig*, Sanskrit *śabdavidyā*)—grammar, synonymics, poetics (above all the *Kāvyādarśa* [Mirror of Poetry], by the Indian poet Daṇḍin, ca. 700), metrics, dramaturgy—the basis for all later Tibetan literary education. Following are notes on some of the major genres of Indian-influenced Tibetan poetic composition, with the names of a few prominent authors and works in each field. (For reasons of space, a given author is mentioned only once, even though he may have contributed to several of the genres mentioned.)

As in India, verse was often the vehicle for works on philosophy and dogmatics (*lta-ba/grub-mtha'*). While highly technical works were versified for mnemonic reasons, poetic elaboration of Buddhist doctrine employed scriptural figures of speech, as in this example, from the work of Klong-chen Rab-'byams-pa (1308–64):

Life is impermanent like clouds of autumn,
Youth is impermanent like flowers of spring,
The body is impermanent like borrowed property,
Wealth is impermanent like dew on the grass.

Many of Tibet's major religious writers, incl. Karma-pa III Rang-byung-rdo-rje (1287–1339), Tsong-kha-pa (1357–1419), and 'Jigs-med Gling-pa (1729–98), composed outstanding doctrinal verse.

*Gnomic poetry (*legs-bshad*, Sanskrit *subhāṣita*) modeled on aphorisms from Indian books of polity (*nītiśāstra*) found their greatest exponent in Sa-skya Paṇḍita (1181–1252), whose *Legs-bshad rin-po-che'i gter* (*Treasury of Aphoristic Gems*) is cited proverbially. Other famed aphoristic collections are those of Paṇ-chen Bsod-nams grags-pa (1478–1554), Gung-thang Bstan-pa'i sgron-me (1762–1823), and Mi-pham rnam-rgyal (1846–1912). Ethical and spiritual instructions (*zhal-gdams*) may closely adhere to doctrinal models or to the conventions of gnomic verse, but they may also make powerful use of colloquialisms and elements of folk song, as do the *Ding-ri brgya-rtsa* (Hundred Admonitions to the People of Ding-ri) attributed to Pha-dam-pa Sangs-rgyas (12th c.), by origins an Indian yogin, and the *Rgyal-sras lag-len so-bdun-ma* (Thirty-seven Skills of the Bodhisattva) by Rgyal-sras Thogs-med bzang-po (1295–1369).

The intricate ritualization of Tibetan religion encouraged the devel. of ritual and devotional verse (*cho-ga, gsol-'debs*). Accomplished academic poets, such as Paṇ-chen Blo-bzang chos-rgyan (1570–1662), author of a popular *Bla-ma mchod-pa* (Worship of the Guru), have contributed here, as have inspired "treasure-discoverers" (*gter-ston*), whose visionary verses are chanted daily by devout Buddhists throughout Tibet.

Drama (*zlos-gar*) often included vivid poetic passages and was represented above all by the popular "Tibetan opera" (*lha-mo*), usually based on religious legends. Indian dramaturgy also inspired some Tibetan poems, though these were not, despite their titles, actually plays. An example is the much admired *Lha-chos-dang mthun-pa'i gtam Padma'i tshal-gyi zlos-gar* (Drama of Padma-tshal: A Divine Discourse) by O-rgyan 'Jigs-med chos-kyi dbang-po (1808–87).

Verse narratives (*rtogs-brjod*) embrace fables and legends, as well as hists. and biographies (*rnam-thar*), incl. autobiographies. Among them are works that are sometimes reminiscent of Indian Puranic texts, as is the *Padma bka'-thang* (Testament of Padmasambhava), redacted by O-rgyan Gling-pa (b. 1323), or ornate poems modeled on refined Sanskrit kāvya, as are the *Mi-dbang rtogs-brjod* (Narrative of the Lord of Men) and other writings by Mdo-mkhar Tshe-ring dbang-rgyal (1697–1763).

Drawing thematic inspiration from the Apabhraṃ-śa songs of the Indian Buddhist tantric masters and imagistic and metrical resources from indigenous bardic and popular verse, the Buddhist yogins of Tibet created an entirely distinctive family of verse forms, collectively known as *mgur* (yogic songs). The greatest author of mgur was the inspired sage Mi-la-ras-pa (1040–1123), who is virtually famed as Tibet's national poet. Here he sings of his foremost disciple, Ras-chung (1085–1161):

> He's gone off riding a fine steed:
> Others' steeds are skittish,
> But Ras-chung's steed doesn't shy.
> On the stallion of thought's vital wind,
> My son Ras-chung, he's gone riding off.

The poetry *anthology was not a well-developed form in Tibet, perhaps owing to the emphasis placed on the collected works (*gsung-'bum*) of single authors and the collected songs (*mgur-'bum*) of individual yogins, above all. Commentarial treatises on Buddhist doctrine often make such extensive use of quotations that they amount to anthols. in any case. Nonetheless, mention must be made of the extraordinary *Bka'-brgyud mgur-mtsho* (Ocean of Songs of the Bka'-brgyud School), originally compiled by the eighth Karma-pa hierarch, Mi-bskyod rdo-rje (1507–54), an anthol. of masterpieces of the mgur genre.

Indian erotic lore was known primarily through tantric Buddhist lit., and frankly erotic imagery is often used symbolically in religious verse, less frequently in secular verse. A mod. author, Dge-'dun chos-'phel (1894–1951), composed an original and highly amusing *'dod-pa'i bstan-bcos* (Treatise on Love), inspired primarily by the *Kāma Sūtra* but in some respects reminiscent of Ovid's *Ars amatoria*.

Owing to the stability of the Tibetan cl. literary lang., the form and lexicon of Tibetan poetic composition until very recently differed little from models dating back a millennium. The secularizing and colloquializing tendencies of contemp. Tibetan writing in general have influenced recent Tibetan poetry, however, as has exposure to contemp. poetry from outside of Tibet. These devels. are addressed in the entry TIBET, CONTEMPORARY POETRY OF.

■ **Criticism and History**: P. Poucha, "Le vers tibetain," *Archiv Orientalni* 18 (1950) and 22 (1954); J. Vekerdi, "Some Remarks on Tibetan Prosody," *Acta Orientalia* 2 (1952); K. Chang, "On Tibetan Poetry," *Central Asiatic Journal* 2 (1956); R. Stein, *Tibetan Civilization* (1972); *Tibetan Literature: Studies in Genre*, ed. J. Cabezón and R. Jackson (1995); M. Kapstein, "The Indian Literary Identity in Tibet," *Literary Cultures in History: Perspectives from South Asia,* ed. S. Pollock (2003).

■ **Folk Verse and Bardic Traditions**: R. Stein, *L'épopée tibétaine de Gesar dans sa version lamaïque de Ling* (1955), and *Recherches sur l'épopée et le barde au Tibet* (1959); G. Tucci, *Tibetan Folk Songs*, 2d ed. (1966); N. N. Dewang, "Musical Tradition of the Tibetan People: Songs in Dance Measure," *Orientalia Romana: Essays and Lectures, II*, ed. V. S. Agrawala (1967); M. Helffer, *Les chants dans l'épopée tibétaine de Ge-sar d'après le livre de la Course de cheval* (1978); B. Aziz, "On Translating Oral Traditions: Ceremonial Wedding Poetry from Dingri," *Soundings in Tibetan Civilization*, ed. B. N. Aziz and M. T. Kapstein (1982).

■ **Translations**: *Three Tibetan Mysteries*, trans. J. Bacot (1924); *Le Dict de Padma*, trans. G. Toussaint (1933); *The Buddha's Law among the Birds*, trans. E. Conze (1955); *The Hundred Thousand Songs of Milarepa*, trans. G. Chang (1962); *A Treasury of Aphoristic Jewels*, trans. J. Bosson (1969); *Vie et Chants de 'Brug-pa Kun-legs le Yogin*, trans. R. Stein (1972); *The Rain of Wisdom*, trans. Nalanda Translation Committee (1980); *Songs of the Sixth Dalai Lama*, trans. K. Dhondup (1981); *Visionary Journey: The Story of Wildwood Delights and the Story of Mount Potala Delights*, trans. H. Guenther (1989); *The Life of Shabkar: The Autobiography of a Tibetan Yogin*, trans. M. Ricard et al. (1994); *The Tale of the Incomparable Prince*, trans. B. Newman (1996); *Songs of Spiritual Experience*, trans. T. Jinpa and J. Elsner, (2000); *In the Forest of Faded Wisdom: 104 Poems by Gendun Chopel*, trans. D. Lopez Jr. (2009).

T. T. RINPOCHE; M. T. KAPSTEIN

**TIMBRE,** tone color, sound color (Ger. *Klangfarbe*). There is no generally accepted term. *Timbre* derives from low Lat., then Fr. terms for a drum, a bell, the sound of a bell. *Timbre* now denotes the sonorous quality of a *sound, as opposed to its length (duration) or loudness or pitch or accent. (Note that the quality of a color, its tint or shade, is called its *tone*.) Technically, timbre is changed by increasing the intensity of one or another set of harmonics of formants comprising the sound. Formants may be roughly defined as pitch zones in which voice overtones are strengthened, owing to the voice-cavity configuration. In music and speech, *timbre* is the characteristic auditory quality of a musical instrument or voice producing a sound and, by extension, the kinesthetic "feel" of the sound to the listener. Common adjectives for the description of sound deriving from sight, touch, and taste include *heavy*, *light*, *dark*, *soft*, *rough*, *crisp*, *salty*, *sweet*, *sharp*, *dim*, *long*, *shallow*, and *blunt*: these are the province of the phenomenon known in Eng. as *synaesthesia*.

Beyond synaesthesia, how might timbre be identified in poetry? Two possibilities suggest themselves: (1) *place of articulation* and (2) *distinctive features*. It is necessary first to distinguish between articulatory phenomena (manner and place of production of the sound), acoustic phenomena (the inherent characteristics of the sound itself, as measured with instruments in acoustics experiments), and perceptual (auditory) phenomena (the way sounds are classed by hearers). Concerning place of articulation—i.e., high-mid-low and front-mid-back on the standard phonetic chart of articulatory points in the mouth cavity—there is evidence that auditors make category distinctions between groups of sounds, e.g., all vowels that are high versus low or front versus back. This could be subject to patterning in poetry, as could the several sets of binary pairs of distinctive acoustic features of sounds, as classified by mod. linguists such as Morris Halle and Roman Jakobson. Distinctive feature analysis is a system of metrical analysis developed by Karl Magnuson and

Frank Ryder in the late 1960s to identify those features that are prosodically (metrically) distinctive. Whether and how the sounds of poems have been patterned on the basis of such features remain to be shown—as do, indeed, the full relations of this class of human sound response to the other two major classes, *mimesis (see ONOMATOPOEIA) and association.

■ K. Bühler, *Sprachtheorie* (1934); K. Hevner, "An Experimental Study of the Affective Value of Sounds in Poetry," *American Journal of Psychology* 49 (1937); M. M. Macdermott, *Vowel Sounds in Poetry* (1940); P. Delattre, "The Physiological Interpretation of Sound Spectrograms," *PMLA* 66 (1951); F. Lockemann, *Das Gedicht und seine Klanggestalt* (1952); P. Delbouille, *Poésie et sonorités*, 2 v. (1961, 1984); R. Jakobson, G. Fant, M. Halle, *Preliminaries to Speech Analysis* (1965); N. S. Trubetzkoy, *Principles of Phonology*, trans. C.A.M. Baltaxe (1969); K. Magnuson and F. G. Ryder, "The Study of English Prosody," *CE* 31 (1970), and "Second Thoughts on English Prosody," *CE* 33 (1971); D. Chisholm, "Lexicality and German Derivational Suffixes," *Lang&S* 6 (1973); K. Magnuson, "Rules and Observations in Prosody," *Poetics* 12 (1974); D. Chisholm, *Goethe's Knittelvers* (1975), and "Generative Prosody and English Verse," *Poetics* 6 (1977); R. Cogan, "Tone Color," *Sonus* 1 (1980); W. Slawson, *Sound Color* (1985); J. D. Puterbaugh, "Between Location and Place: A View of Timbre through Auditory Models and Sonopoietic Space," *DAI* 60 (1999); K. Bergeron, "A Bugle, a Bell, a Stroke of the Tongue: Rethinking Music in Modern French Verse," *Representations* 86 (2004); G. Olwage, "The Class and Colour of Tone," *Ethnomusicology Forum* 13 (2004); W. Everett, "Painting Their Room in a Colorful Way: The Beatles' Exploration of Timbre," *Reading the Beatles*, ed. K. Womack and T. F. Davis (2006).

T.V.F. BROGAN

**TISH** was a Canadian little magazine (subtitled *a poetry newsletter*) pub. in Vancouver from 1961 to 1969. Used more broadly, the term refers to the poetry and poetics associated with the eds. of the magazine, whose work came to represent the first wave of *postmodernism in Canadian poetry. The name, an anagram for *shit*, is in part indicative of the group's poetics, which eschewed the finely crafted *lyric in favor of an intense, embodied, and improvised immediacy. TISH was significant as a literary movement in a national lit. often lacking such collective formations.

Inspired by the introduction to the *anthology *The New American Poetry 1945–1960*, ed. by Donald Allen (1960), and by lectures given in the summer of 1961 by the Am. poet Robert Duncan (1919–88) in the Vancouver home of the poetry scholar Warren Tallman, the first (of three) editorial collectives, consisting at first of George Bowering (b. 1935), Frank Davey (b. 1940), David Dawson (1942–2008), Jamie Reid (b. 1941), and Fred Wah (b. 1939), brought out 19 consecutive monthly eds. of the magazine until disbanding after the Vancouver Poetry Conference in the summer of 1963. *TISH* the magazine was modeled on underground

Am. magazines such as the *Black Mountain Review* and *Floating Bear*. As a vanguard movement in an aesthetically conservative and soundly postcolonial country, TISH pointed the way to a more engaged practice, enabling later devels. such as the Toronto avant-garde that formed around bpNichol and Steve McCaffery, as well as Vancouver's *Kootenay School of Writing.

Participants in TISH have produced some of the most innovative and significant Canadian lit. in the past 40 years. Through the 1970s and 1980s, Bowering produced numerous serial poems, from his anti-imperialist *At War with the US* (1974) to his transformations of R. M. Rilke across time and space in *Kerrisdale Elegies* (1984). Like many TISH poets, Daphne Marlatt (b. 1942) has explored the significance of place and hist. in her book-length poem *Steveston* (1974), as well as her evolving sexuality in such groundbreaking *lesbian poems as "Booking Passage" (1991). Wah, winner of the Governor General's Award for *Waiting for Saskatchewan* (1985), has published several volumes of his lifelong prose poem *Music at the Heart of Thinking* (beginning in 1987). Davey, while continuing to publish poetry, has become one of the most influential critics of his generation.

*See* AVANT-GARDE POETICS; CANADA, POETRY OF.

■ *TISH: 1–19*, ed. Frank Davey (1975)—an anthol.; *The Writing Life: Historical and Critical Views of the Tish Movement*, ed. C. H. Gervais (1976); *Beyond TISH*, ed. D. Barbour (1991); P. Butling and S. Rudy, *Writing in our Time: Canada's Radical Poetries in English, 1957–2003* (2005).

S. COLLIS

**TLACUILOLLI** (Nahuatl, "painting" or "writing"). *Tlacuilolli* is a pictorial script with classic period (250–1000 CE) antecedents that flourished during the postclassic period (1000–1521 CE ) in Central Mexico and regions to the southeast of Central Mexico. This script remained in use during the early colonial period, immediately following the Sp. conquest (1519–21).

Pre-Columbian tlacuilolli script was painted onto cotton sheets or screen-fold books and rolls made of deerskin or native bark paper, or carved into stone and painted on pottery and murals. Largely because of the ravages of conquest and the early colonial period, there are a limited number of extant pre-Columbian painted books, sheets, and rolls. Scholars include at least 12 works in this category. A larger number of tlacuilolli writings survive in which Eur. stylistic influence is slight or debatable.

The surviving examples of pre-Columbian painted books are either historical or ritual in nature. Native and Eur. sources from Mexico's early colonial period describe additional genres of tlacuilolli writings, incl. lineage books, books of divinities, dream books, *songbooks, maps, and administrative documents.

Tlacuilolli script integrates *ideograms and pictographs with numerical and symbolic information. Pictographs depict persons, objects, or information in a way that recognizably corresponds to their fundamental form or qualities. The concept *mountain,* e.g., is painted as a stylized mountain, and the year *two rabbit* is depicted with two dots beside a stylized rabbit. Ideograms convey more abstract concepts. Speech scrolls emerging from the mouths of human beings or animals represent voice and song. Similarly, footprint trails indicate human directional movement or reading direction. Tlacuilolli script uses color to render meaning symbolically and, to a very limited degree, represents sounds. An example of phonetic information in tlacuilolli works by Nahuatl speakers is the image of teeth (*tlantli*), to represent the homonymous suffix *tlan* (at or place of; next to or below).

Tlacuilolli script continued to be produced decades after the conquest, albeit transformed through contact with Eur. artistic conventions and scriptural technologies. Tlacuilolli writings of this period were frequently produced on Eur. paper, employed Eur. artistic perspective, or incorporated alphabetic glosses and Christian dates. By the end of the 16th c., however, tlacuilolli script had largely been replaced by alphabetic writing.

*See* COLONIAL POETICS; INDIGENOUS AMERICAS, POETRY OF THE; MEXICO, POETRY OF.

■ M. León-Portilla, *Pre-Columbian Literatures of Mexico,* trans. G. Lobanov and M. León-Portilla (1969); G. Brotherston, *Book of the Fourth World* (1992); J. Lockhart, *The Nahuas after the Conquest* (1992); M. León-Portilla, "Have We Really Translated the Mesoamerican 'Ancient Word'?" *On the Translation of Native American Literatures,* ed. B. Swann (1992); J.M.D. Pohl, "Mexican Codices, Maps, and Lienzos as Social Contracts," *Writing without Words: Alternative Literacies in Mesoamerica and the Andes,* ed. E. H. Boone and W. D. Mignolo (1994); D. Robertson, *Mexican Manuscript Painting of the Early Colonial Period* (1994); G. Brotherston, *Painted Books from Mexico* (1995); E. H. Boone, "Pictorial Documents and Visual Thinking in Postconquest Mexico," and F. E. Karttunen, "Indigenous Writing as a Vehicle of Postconquest Continuity and Change in Mesoamerica," *Native Traditions in the Postconquest World,* ed. E. H. Boone and T. Cummins (1998); E. H. Boone, *Stories in Red and Black: Pictorial Histories of the Aztecs and Mixtecs* (2000); M. León-Portilla, *Códices: Los Antiguos Libros del Nuevo Mundo* (2003); G. Brotherston, *Feather Crown: The Eighteen Feasts of the Mexican Year* (2005); K. A. Nowotny, *Tlacuilolli: Style and Contents of the Mexican Pictorial Manuscripts with a Catalog of the Borgia Group,* ed. and trans. G. A. Everett Jr. and E. B. Sisson (2005).

S. SCHMIDT

**TMESIS** (Gr., "a cutting"); also *diacope.* Insertion of a word within another word or phrase. Addition of a mere syllable (sometimes for metrical purposes) is *epenthesis.* Group μ defines *tmesis* to include "all the cases where two morphemes or syntagms that grammatical usage ties together strictly are separated by the insertion of additional elements." Earlier rhetoricians

traditionally separated such syntactical permutations into two forms of tmesis according to whether a single word or a sentence was divided by an intercalated element. In Gr. syntax, *tmesis* means the separation of a preposition from its verb to which, in postepic lang., it was completely joined. In Attic Gr. poetry, the two elements were separated by unimportant words for the sake of emphasis. Lat. poetry does the same thing, e.g., *seque gregari* for *segregarique.* Eng. allows the breaking up of any compound word, e.g., "that Man—how dearly ever parted" (Chaucer, *Troilus and Criseyde* 3.3.96); "See his wind—lilycocks—laced" (G. M. Hopkins, "Harry Ploughman"). By far the most extensive mod. practitioner of tmesis in Eng.-lang. poetry is e. e. cummings, who makes it virtually a constitutive principle of poetic form in his verse. Mod. ling. describes one form of this process in colloquial speech as "expletive insertion," commonly scissoring words such as *outstanding* by a profanity. An example of syntagmatic interpolation is "Lay your sleeping head, my love, / Human on my faithless arm" (W. H. Auden, "Lullaby").

■ F. Amory, "Tmesis in Medieval Latin, Old Norse, and Old Irish Poetry," *Arkiv für Nordisk Filologi* 94 (1979); Group μ; Lausberg; Morier; E. R. Anderson, *A Grammar of Iconism* (1999).

R. A. HORNSBY; A. W. HALSALL; T.V.F. BROGAN

**TOAST.** A long poetic tale or saga of salute or tribute (hence, the term), a form of street and prison poetry found in the Af. Am. community. The toast, like the *dozens,* is characteristically a recited poetry generally created and performed by males. The origin of the form dates to the second half of the 19th c. in celebrations of bad men, bandits, and tricksters and possibly back to the praise poem trad. that is pervasive in Africa. Some toasts are related to and derived from the narrative trad. of the Wild West. The oral form has been appropriated into written lit. by writers such as Nikki Giovanni and Julius Lester. The raconteur may open or close the performance with a tribute or salute to the celebrant, e.g., "Here's to Shine!" The subject of the toast is generally secular and its lang. witty, satiric, bawdy, and profane, told mostly in *couplets or in *ballad meter (*xbyb* in alternating four- and three-stress lines). There may be internal rhyme, off-rhyme, and triplet rhymes as well. Through its adventurous narrative, the toast may provide astute commentary on any number of subjects from human vanity to politics. It is episodic, lengthy, and detailed. Because it is improvised, the toast requires of its composer tremendous verbal ingenuity and dexterity for creating wit and excitement, for controlling the rhyme and the frequently irregular rhythm, and for maintaining a high level of spontaneity. The dominant tone of the toast is braggadocio. Typical of the disposition of the speaker are the lines: "I've got a tombstone disposition, graveyard mind, / I know I'm bad motherfucker, that's why I don't mind dying" (Levine).

*See* EPIDEICTIC POETRY, POETIC CONTESTS.

■ R. D. Abrahams, *Deep Down in the Jungle* (1970); B. Jackson, *Get Your Ass in the Water and Swim like Me* (1974); L. W. Levine, *Black Culture and Black Consciousness* (1977); G. Smitherman, *Talkin and Testifyin* (1977); A. M. Reynolds, "Les Toasts de 'zonards' noirs de Los Angeles," *Cahiers de littérature orale* 31 (1992).

E. A. PETERS

**TONE** (Gr. *tonos,* Lat. *tonus,* "stretching"). *Tone* primarily refers to the perceptible quality (*pitch, intensity or loudness, and inflection) of *sound, particularly of the spoken or sung human voice. While all langs. use tone to convey meaning, phonetics distinguishes nontonal langs., in which it is primarily a syntactical determinant, from tonal langs., such as Mandarin Chinese, in which tone is also an essential feature of the meaning of individual words (lexical tone). While the notion of a literary tone is relatively recent, it has important precedents in cl. Gr. and Lat. rhet. and philosophy.

Cl. treatments of tone in rhet. are informed by the view that the tone of the human voice naturally expresses the emotions and attitudes of the speaker. Aristotle in the *Rhetoric* complains that earlier rhetoricians had not paid sufficient attention to the "delivery" of their oration, which is "a matter of voice, as to the mode in which it should be used for each particular emotion; when it should be loud, when low, when intermediate; and how the tones (*tonoi*), i.e., shrill, deep, and intermediate, should be used" (1403b). Aristotle's discussion relies on the notion that the tone of the human voice should be in tune with human emotion, an idea indebted to the Pythagorean-Platonist philosophy that uses a mathematical model of music to interpret the universe and the human being in terms of harmony (Spitzer). The notion that the human voice, and indeed the body, is a musical instrument that expresses the emotions tonally becomes, after Aristotle, a crucial aspect of the third and final part of rhet. (*pronunciatio* or *actio*). The mathematical-musical model is reflected in Cicero's discussion of delivery, which he finds "the dominant factor in oratory" in *De oratore*: "nature has assigned to every emotion a particular look and tone of voice and bearing of its own; and the whole of a person's frame and every look on his face and utterance of his voice are like the strings of a harp, and sound according as they are struck by each successive emotion" (3.212, 216). The sense that the tone of the human voice expresses the emotional state of the speaker is carried by the first vernacular variations of the word (12th c. in Fr., 14th c. in Eng.), and it is reflected by the psychological descriptors often used with the word. Although cl. rhet. discusses the significance of sound in oratory, treatments of tone are largely restrained to the literal sense of *tone* as the material quality of the human voice, and as such they remain part of the third and final part of rhet. (Vega Ramos).

While in the cl. rhetorical trad. discussions of the tone of the voice belong to delivery, mod. literary discourse has applied the term to written texts. From the perspective of cl. rhet., this may be considered a category mistake, and it certainly leads to complications in the mod. use of the concept. In both tonal and nontonal langs., the tone of the voice may be used to enhance and complement the semantic content of the utterance, as well as to add to, modify, or even reverse it (as in the case of *irony). While some uses of vocal tone support meaning that may be grammatically codified and may appear in script (from sentence types to emphases), the mod. literary use of *tone* usually refers precisely to those aspects of written lang. that are neither lexical nor syntactical, but that appear, at least at first, somewhat intangibly, as a quality of the text as a whole, or of a significant part of it.

This mod. usage of *tone* is often considered a metaphorical use of the original concept, but it also goes back to the original meaning of the Gr. *tonos* as "stretching" and "tension." Indeed, the Pythagorean-Platonist concept of the human being as instrument was not restrained to the human voice or even to sound in general, and the notion that nonaural phenomena may have tone is central in Stoic philosophy, where *tone* is used to describe a tensile force that holds together inimical elements at both cosmological and psychological levels. This sense of *tone* as a cohesive force and harmony is evident in cl. and Christian philosophy through the Middle Ages and the Ren. (Spitzer).

In the 17th c., some Eur. vernaculars began to use *tone* to refer to a person's character, style, and manners, as well as to the air and mood of a phenomenon or a person. Parallel with this devel., the concept was also applied to written text, often in the same sense as an expression of the author's personality, manners, or mood; Madame Sévigné wrote, in 1691, that "[mes lettres] ont des tons, et ne sont pas supportables quand elles sont ânnonées" (my letters have tones, and they are intolerable when read monotonously). This application of *tone* to written texts implies a shift in what may be called the rhet. of tone: while in cl. rhet., the tone of the voice belongs to the actual vocal delivery of the oration, the mod. literary sense of *tone* belongs to what cl. rhet. discussed under the category of style (*elocutio*).

Within this trad. that takes tone as a feature of the written text, we may distinguish two distinct views. In the first, tone is associated with the mood or general atmosphere of the written text. This view is esp. prominent within the Ger. trad. after J. W. Goethe, and its most important and controversial proponent is the romantic poet Friedrich Hölderlin, who in a series of difficult theoretical writings produced a theory of poetry as tonal movement (the so-called *Tönewechsel* doctrine). In Hölderlin's theory, the three "basic" tones of poetry correspond to the three basic genres: the heroic tone to the tragic genre, the idealist tone to the lyric genre, and the naïve tone to the epic genre. Hölderlin uses the Ger. word *Ton* (tone, sound) essentially synonymously with the word *Stimmung* (mood, attunement), a word crucial to both the poetics and the philosophy of the postromantic era.

The other trad., by contrast, tends to associate the tone of the written text with a personal attitude, whether that of the author or of an implied speaker within the text. The most influential theorist of this position in Eng. lit. crit. is Richards, who in *Practical Criticism* identified tone as one of the "Four Kinds of Meanings." Besides sense, feeling, and intention, Richards codified the term *tone* to refer to that aspect of the utterance that "reflects [the speaker's] awareness of [his] relation [to his listener], his sense of how he stands toward those he is addressing." Richards's definition is remarkable in its profound debt to cl. rhet.: tone in *Practical Criticism* refers to that aspect of the poem that reflects the author's awareness of how an audience might receive his discourse. While Richards's definition thus conflates the Aristotelian notions of *ethos* (the orator's character constructed in the oratorical performance) and *pathos* (the emotional response that the orator tries to obtain from an audience), it essentially identifies the tone of the text with the style of the text. Indeed, it is as such an index of authorial self-awareness that Richards considers tone to be one of the most important and most difficult aspects of poetry: "many of the secrets of 'style' could, I believe, be shown to be matters of tone, of the perfect recognition of the writer's relation to the reader in view of what is being said and their joint feelings about it." Finally, this also implies that Richards can locate the cl. rhetorical notion of propriety in the tone of the text; tone can be proper or improper, and "faults of tone are much more than mere superficial blemishes. They may indicate a very deep disorder."

While Richards's attempt to codify the literary meaning of *tone* had an enormous influence on *New Criticism, in more recent lit. crit. the concept has received considerably less attention, partly because of the psychological assumptions that support it in Richards's definition. Attempts have been made to sever the concept from Richards's psychological framework; thus, Ngai theorizes a notion of tone that allows one "to generalize, totalize, and abstract the 'world' of the literary object, in a way that seems particularly conducive to the analysis of ideology." Yet in an essay on treatments of lyric poetry after the New Critics, Culler has argued that, even for a critic like Smith, to interpret the poem is to "identify the concerns to which the speaker is responding and the tone of the response." If lyric poems are fictional representations of personal utterances, Culler states, "the methodological heritage of the New Critics encourages us to focus above all on the complexities of the speaker's attitude revealed over the course of the overheard utterance, and on the culmination of the poem in what Cleanth Brooks calls the 'total and governing attitude.'" He goes on to suggest that, while continental theorists were instrumental in the shift from the New Critical interest in poetic tone to a structuralist investment in narrative voice and mood (Genette), the post-New Critical era has not produced a general theory of the lyric.

The recent reluctance to use *tone* as an analytical concept is probably due to difficulties implied in the application of the term for written lang.: most conspicuous in Richards's definition of *tone* as an expression of the author's attitude to an audience is the fact that the tone of a written text is identified not in particular textual features but by its alleged effect on the reader. On the other hand, the hist. of the concept shows that tone began to be used for written texts precisely in order to refer to that intangible quality of the text that cannot be immediately accessed through an analysis of individual textual features; it is, rather, a holistic quality, something that belongs to the text as such. Indeed, the New Critics's concept of tone was never an analytical tool for poetry only; rather, *tone* in their sense might be characterized as a rhetorical effect common to all ling. utterances. A more accurately poetic concept of tone is implied in Stewart's discussion of sound. She asserts that, in the case of written texts, to speak about sound is to speak about the recollection of sound that the written text evokes from the reader. Stewart goes on to discuss G. M. Hopkins's theoretical writings, which define the poem as "the figure of spoken sound" and which ultimately suggest that "emotional intonation" is produced in the poem by the tension between the rhythms of speech and the poetic meter. Although this method of rhythmic *dissonance has been analyzed in the works of many other poets, it has rarely been considered as the "tone" of the poem, even though it would be a proper recycling of the term's connotation as "stretching" and "tension" for the purposes of poetics.

■ I. A. Richards, *Practical Criticism* (1929); G. M. Hopkins, "Rhythm and the Other Structural Parts of Rhetoric—Verse," *The Journals and Papers of Gerard Manley Hopkins*, ed. H. House (1959); L. Spitzer, *Classical and Christian Ideas of World Harmony: Prolegomena to an Interpretation of the Word "Stimmung"* (1963); G. Genette, *Figures of Literary Discourse,* trans. A. Sheridan (1981); B. H. Smith, *On the Margins of Discourse* (1981); J. Culler, "Changes in the Study of the Lyric," *Lyric Poetry: Beyond New Criticism,* ed. C. Hošek and P. Parker (1985); S. Stewart, "Letter on Sound," *Close Listening: Poetry and the Performed World,* ed. C. Bernstein (1998); "Tone," *A Dictionary of Linguistics and Phonetics,* ed. D. Crystal (1992); "Tönerhetorik," *Historisches Wörterbuch der Rhetorik,* ed. G. Ueding (1992–); M. J. Vega Ramos, *El secreto artificio* (1992); "Tone Languages" *The Encyclopedia of Language and Linguistics,* ed. R. E. Asher (1994); D. Wellbery, "Stimmung," *Ästhetische Grundbegriffe,* ed. K. Barck (2003); S. Ngai, *Ugly Feelings* (2005); "Ton," *Le dictionnaire culturel en langue française,* ed. A. Rey (2005).

D. MARNO

**TOPOS** (Gr., literally, "place, region"; pl. *topoi*). A conventionalized expression or passage in a text that comes to be used as a resource for the composition of subsequent texts. The term is first used in a technical sense in cl. rhet., where it is treated under *invention and refers to a standard line of argument based on generally accepted logical probabilities such as "possible or impossible" or "greater or lesser" or "post hoc ergo propter hoc" or "a fortiori," as when it is argued, e.g., that, since Achilles gave in to wrath, it is not surprising that ordinary citizens sometimes do so too. Topoi can be specific to a certain type of discourse—demonstrative, legal, or epideictic—or common to all types. The former are *eide*; the latter are *koinoi topoi* (Lat. *loci communi*), which translates literally as *commonplaces. This calls attention to the enlargement of meaning of the term to include standard metaphors and "topics" such as the invocation of the Muse or the description of the ideal "pleasant place" (*locus amoenus*)—e.g., Eden—by poets and writers of narrative. Originally, topoi were presumably not formulas but spontaneous creations, and even in their schematized form, they are activated out of a distinct aesthetic feeling.

Topos in the sense of a standard topic is central to the approach to lit. taken by Curtius. In his system, topoi are established schemes of thought, extended *metaphors, standardized passages of description, and the like that recur in the lit. of Western Europe from Homer to the mod. age, most strikingly during the Lat. Middle Ages and the Ren. The topos constitutes a principal unifying element in this lit. Among the examples related by Curtius are the "inexpressability" topos, in which the poet describes his inability to do his subject justice (see ADYNATON); the "world upside-down" topoi (*mundus inversus*), in which the world's disorder is shown by fish in trees, children ruling parents, and the like; and set pieces like the *locus amoenus* topos. The opposite of the *locus amoenus* topos is the wasteland topos, which was adapted from med. sources in T. S. Eliot's poem *The Waste Land*. Among metaphors considered topoi by followers of Curtius are "the world as a stage," "the Book of Nature," and the "cosmic dance." Generalized in this way, the use of topoi is closely related to *imitation, and there is a legitimate sense in which many of the standard motifs of any well-established med. or early mod. genre—for instance, the Petrarchan *sonnet sequence (see PETRARCHISM) can be called *topoi*).

Although certain kinds of topoi are related to certain literary forms or genres, the forms and genres are not themselves topoi, since the term refers to a standardized matter rather than a structure or a regular sequence of events. Thus, the literary consolation (*consolatio*) has a definite shape created by its use of a selection from among a number of consolatory topoi (e.g., "all must die," "he is gone to a better world," "his memory will be eternal," "his example will lead many to virtue") but is not, itself, a topos. A perfect example of a poem that is almost a collage of such topoi plus many others from different trads. such as *pastoral is John Milton's lament for the death of his friend Edward King, "Lycidas." The remarkable vitality of topoi over centuries is illustrated by independent use of many of the same ones found in "Lycidas" over two centuries later by Matthew Arnold in "Thyrsis" and by Walt Whitman in "When Lilacs Last in the Dooryard Bloom'd."

Later critics (e.g., H. G. Gadamer, Theodor Adorno) have taken Curtius as a point of departure for a critique of ideas of cultural unity and continuous trad. Others (e.g., Antonio Garcia-Berrio) have pointed out that the very existence of a well-defined set of topoi and conventions such as those found in the Petrarchan sonnet

gives the poet a means of expressing individuality by variations on expected norms.

*See* COMMONPLACE, MOTIF.

■ Curtius; J. M. Lechner, *Renaissance Conceptions of the Commonplaces* (1962); B. Emrich, "Topik und Topoi," *Deutschunterricht* 18 (1966); A. R. Evans Jr., "E. R. Curtius," *Four Modern Humanists*, ed. A. R. Evans Jr. (1970); *Topik-Forschung: Eine Dokumentation*, ed. P. Jehn (1972); *Topik-Forschung*, ed. M. L. Baeumer (1973); *Topik: Beiträge zur interdisziplinären Diskussion*, ed. D. Breuer and H. Schanze (1981); F. J. D'Angelo, "The Evolution of the Analytic Topoi: A Speculative Inquiry," *Classical Rhetoric and Modern Discourse*, ed. R. J. Connors et al. (1984); L. Bornscheuer, "Topik," *Reallexikon II*; R. Wellek, "Ernst Robert Curtius als Literarkritik," *Französische Literatur des zwanzigsten Jahrhunderts* (1986); R. J. Goebel, "Curtius, Gadamer, Adorno: Probleme literarische Tradition," *Monatshefte* (1986); E.P.J. Corbett, "The Topoi Revisited," *Rhetoric and Praxis*, ed. J. D. Moss (1986); *The Return of Thematic Criticism*, ed. W. Sollors (1993); E. U. Grosse, "Curtius et les *Topoi*," *Ernst Robert Curtius et l'idée d'Europe*, ed. J. Bem and A. Guyaux (1995); G. Prince, "Notes on the Categories 'Topos' and 'Disnarrated,'" *Thematics Reconsidered*, ed. F. Trommler (1995); C. Landauer, "Ernst Robert Curtius and the Topos of the Literary Critic," *Medievalism and the Modernist Temper*, ed. R. H. Bloch and S. G. Nichols (1996); R. Ceserani and C. Meiner, "Le défi de la topologie littéraire," *Revue Romane* 42 (2007).

O. B. HARDISON; E. H. BEHLER

**TORNADA.** A final short stanza, comparable to the Fr. *envoi, added to many Occitan poems as a kind of dedication to a patron or friend. In form, the *tornada* usually reproduces the metrical structure and the rhymes of the last part of the preceding stanza. Some poems have two or even three tornadas, addressed to different persons.

*See* OCCITAN POETRY.

■ U. Mölk, "Deux remarques sur la tornade," *Metrica* 3 (1982); Chambers.

F. M. CHAMBERS

**TOTTEL'S MISCELLANY** was an anthol. of Eng. poetry compiled by the printer Richard Tottel, to which he gave the title *Songes and Sonettes*. The first ed. was published in June 1557; an amplified second ed. appeared at the end of July. Tottel's main distinction was to offer to the public the poetry of two famous members of the court of Henry VIII, the Earl of Surrey (Henry Howard), whose name is on the title page, and Thomas Wyatt; their poems together (97 by Wyatt and 40 by Surrey) make up about half of the 271 poems in the collection. (Another 40 belong to Nicholas Grimald, and 94 are by "uncertain authors.") Surrey's and Wyatt's poems include the first known *sonnets in Eng.; Surrey's set the *rhyme scheme (*ababcdcdefefgg*) that comes to be known as the Eng. or Shakespearean sonnet. The importation of the sonnet comes as part of the first sustained attention in Eng. *lyric poetry to

Petrarch's *Canzoniere*, a sequence that, in the course of the 16th c., exercises a strong influence on the devel. of vernacular lyric throughout western Europe. Surrey and Wyatt translate a number of Petrarch's poems and imitate his distinctive manner throughout their work. Collectively that work, first composed and circulated in ms. within elite circles, sets a new course for Eng. lyricism; Tottel's collection made it generally available at a propitious moment, 18 months before the accession of Elizabeth I; in its popularity, it became one of the foundational texts for Elizabethan lit. It was regularly reprinted during Elizabeth's reign; there are at least nine eds. by the end of the century, and it served as a model for a run of similar anthols. that were a major route by which Elizabethan poetry reached its readership. Tottel's collection is mentioned in Shakespeare's *Merry Wives of Windsor* (1.1.198–99) as a valued practical asset in courtship and seduction.

The avant-garde Am. poet Ron Silliman published a jour. called *Tottel's* from 1970 to 1981, implicitly making (but also ironically disavowing) for *Language poetry what the original Tottel's was for Eng. Ren. verse, a *canon-defining event.

*See* ENGLAND, POETRY OF; PETRARCHISM; RENAISSANCE POETRY.

■ *Tottel's Miscellany*, ed. H. E. Rollins (1966); *Richard Tottel's Songes and Sonettes*, ed. P. A. Marquis (2007).

G. BRADEN

**TOUCHSTONES.** Matthew Arnold's term for "short passages, even single lines" of poetry that serve as an "infallible" resource "for detecting the presence or absence of high poetic quality and also the degree of this quality, in all other poetry which we may place beside them." The examples given in "The Study of Poetry" (1880, rpt. 1888 in Arnold's *Essays in Criticism*, 2d ser.) are 11 lines, three each from Homer, Dante, and Milton, and two from Shakespeare, most based on *similes. Arnold's criteria for inclusion were impersonality, "truth and seriousness," along with a commensurate "diction" and "rapid movement." Chaucer ("not one of the great classics") was excluded as lacking in "high seriousness."

Reference to such passages, according to Arnold, permits a "real estimate" rather than a merely "historic" or "personal estimate" of poetic value. Objective excellence, he believed, needed simple means of defense against historicist and impressionist critics, for whom all terms of *taste were relative. Arnold feared that democracy and consumerism would encourage, as "a vast and profitable industry," the production of a "charlatan" lit. His touchstones were to slow that devel. by making excellence accessible in anthols.

Neither the problem as Arnold formulated it nor his much-belittled solution has disappeared with time. As late as 1987, Hirsch introduced a related approach to pedagogy that was popular with those unhappy with a choice between theory-based and context-based literary study. An academic consensus, however, still rejects Arnold's solution for its ahistoricism. As Kermode put it in 2004, touchstones "cannot, for all time and for ev-

erybody, bear the broad cultural significance [Arnold] claims for them."

The method of commenting on individual lines of poetry is ancient (Longinus) and was in vogue in the 18th c. (Denis Diderot, Joseph Addison, John Dennis, Joseph Warton); but in Arnold's case, lines are cited more for their aesthetic than their moral value. His method may be closer to that of Chinese "poetry-talk" crit. (*shih-hua tz'u-hua*), in which, beginning in the 11th c., lines were selected for purely aesthetic appreciation, out of context.

■ J. Eels, *The Touchstones of Matthew Arnold* (1955); Wellek, v. 4, ch. 7; E. D. Hirsch, *Cultural Literacy* (1987); M. Schneider, *Poetry in the Age of Democracy* (1989); P. Rose, "Getting and Spending: Nostalgia for the Old Way of Reading Poetry," *American Scholar* 70 (2001); D. Kline, " 'Unhackneyed Thoughts and Winged Words': Arnold, Locke, and the Similes of Sohrab and Rustum," *VP* 41 (2003); F. Kermode, *Pleasure and Change* (2004); J. Caufield, " 'Most Free from Personality': Arnold's Touchstones of Ethics," *Cambridge Quarterly* 38 (2009).

J. M. PERL

**TRADITION**

I. Literary or Written
II. Oral

**I. Literary or Written.** *Tradition* is a term used routinely to name a line of literary works falling under a particular description, which may be generic ("the epic tradition"), historical ("the Augustan tradition"), thematic ("the modern tradition"), or composed of any combination of features ("the tradition of 19th-c. African American women's writing"). More generally, *tradition* has been defined as "the body of texts and interpretations current among a group of writers at a given time and place" (Cunningham)—a definition suggestive of the degree of contingency most contemp. critics ascribe to the concept. These usages seem neutral and commonsensical, but trad. is a concept implicated in almost every aspect of the crit. of poetry, and it acquired in the 20th c. a good deal of polemical baggage.

An emphasis on the traditional character of successful poetry has been a feature of crit. since Aristotle's *Poetics*. This emphasis reflects the premise that lit. is a highly conventional activity; that new writers develop, differently but not necessarily progressively, the forms and themes of their predecessors; that we learn to understand and to evaluate a poem by placing it first in the context of the "tradition," meaning the whole of the lit. we know, and then in the more restricted context of the trad. or trads. (e.g., "epic," "romantic") to which we judge it to belong. This contextualization may produce analyses that are structural, emphasizing formal similarities and differences, or genetic, emphasizing sources and influences, or both. Avant-garde or experimental writing is, on this view, still writing that can be understood only in terms of the trad. from which it deviates; and such writing once widely practiced may be regarded as constituting a trad. of its own.

How a poem fits into the trad., which trad. or trads. it is best understood in the context of, whether its mix of conformity and difference constitutes a "strong" or a "weak" response to the trad.—these questions are at the heart of much crit. of poetry, both scholarly and appreciative. They bear as well on the consideration of a number of central literary values, issues, and techniques: *imitation, *influence, *originality, *textuality, authority, belatedness, *allusion, appropriation, and intentionality (see INTENTION). For most of the mod. era, trads. were conceived of along national (Brit. poetry) or ling. lines (anglophone poetry). Recent crit. tends to emphasize transnational and hybrid trads. as contexts for understanding individual writers and texts.

Since the 1920s, the term has been strongly associated with Anglo-Am. modernist poetry (see MODERNISM), particularly with W. B. Yeats, Ezra Pound, and T. S. Eliot, who make prominent mention of "the" trad., referring sometimes to the whole of the literary past, more often to a single line of poetry (and other, sometimes nonliterary, writing) that the poet regards as central to the civilization and within which his own work is designed to fit. Eliot's "Tradition and the Individual Talent" (1919) remains the classic theoretical expression of the modernist idea. New work acquires its significance from its relation to the preexisting trad.: "For order to persist after the supervention of novelty, the whole existing order must be, if ever so slightly, altered, and so the relations, proportions, values of each work of art toward the whole are readjusted; and this is conformity between the old and the new." Eliot may have been responding to a book containing attacks on Pound's poetry and his own, Waugh's *Tradition and Change* (1919); "Tradition and the Individual Talent" was an attempt (hugely successful) to legitimate modernist formal innovation as "traditional" in the true sense and to condemn apparently traditional writing, e.g., the poetry of the Brit. Georgians, as merely conventional.

That the appropriation of the term by poets who seemed to many contemp. observers to be *breaking* with trad. was a tactical coup was made clear by essays such as Eliot's "The Metaphysical Poets" (1921), which championed 17th-c. *metaphysical poetry by arguing that it belonged to "the direct current of English poetry," with the suggestion that most Eng. poetry of the 19th c. did not. The defense of modernist poetry in the name of a continuity that leapfrogged a century or more of Eng. lit. became standard among modernism's academic champions, notably Brooks and Leavis. Eliot's insistence that poetry be judged "as poetry" was echoed by 20th-c. critics in other fields, notably Greenberg in his defense of abstract painting, "Avant-Garde and Kitsch" (1939).

In the later crit. of Eliot and in the writings of some of the New Critics, *tradition* and its synonyms became a homogeneous culture of Western Christendom that liberalism and secularism were accused of destroying. And even when *tradition* is intended in a neutral descriptive sense, connotations of orthodoxy and exclusion are difficult to avoid. Since the 1950s, the idea of "the tradition" has become clouded by the suspicion that, as Frye argued, the criteria for inclusion always involve, tacitly, extraliterary values. Crit. since the 1960s has, consequently, sometimes explicitly in reaction to Eliot and the *New Criticism, taken an interest in the politics of literary trad. making (or, more commonly, "canon-formation"; see CANON). The received trad., it has been argued, reflects the interests of a dominant culture whose ostensibly purely literary criteria in fact exclude minority or deviating voices—hence, the construction by some critics of alternative canons, defined sometimes as cohesive in their own right, sometimes as subverting the dominant trad. The interest, since the 1970s esp., in lit. by women as a discrete category of writing is the most prominent instance of this widespread trend. Motivated by different concerns, Bloom (1973) proposed a theoretical model of the relations between trad. and the individual talent to replace Eliot's. Bloom stressed the efforts of the new poet to escape the oppressive influence of his precursors—by, among other rhetorical strategies, misreading their work to make his own possible. This theory tends to support a trad. composed principally of writers, such the Brit. romantic poets, largely written out of the modernist and New Critical canon.

Crit. that uses the concept of a literary trad. as the basis of analysis is formalist: it treats lit. as an autonomous practice in which poems can be understood primarily "as poems" and in the context of other poems. On such claims are academic lit. departments founded. But (as Eliot understood) the assertion of a transhistorical trad. in a social formation—modernity—characterized by discontinuity and change is a means of claiming legitimacy. Groups in mod. societies "invent" trads. (Hobsbawm and Ranger), much as Eliot and Pound can be said to have invented theirs, and trads. also function, in such societies, as forms of social memory (Nora). The provisional and historically determined character of any so-called trad. is now widely accepted, but the basic hermeneutical issue—how to understand the relations between what is new and what is already there—remains. That question is addressed significantly in the work of Gadamer, which emphasizes the impossibility of stepping outside the interpretive matrix of one's own trad., but the general issue has absorbed the attention of critics from a variety of philosophical persuasions.

**II. Oral.** The 20th c. has also witnessed the rediscovery of oral poetic trads., both defunct and continuing, in cultures all over the world. With the classicist Parry, his coworker Lord, and the advent of the *oral-formulaic theory, scholars became aware of the oral traditional roots of Homer and dozens of other trads. This school of "literary anthropology" has shown how oral poets eschew the original in favor of the traditional and how they use not only a repertoire of repeated "formulas" to compose metrical lines in performance but also an array of stock narrative patterns ("themes") to move the story forward. *Tradition* in this sense is the sum total of all the oral performances by all the poets who practice in the culture and, thus, comes also to refer both to what lies behind the texts that are written down and to the transitional poems that derive from oral trads.

■ A. Waugh, *Tradition and Change* (1919); G. Murray, *The Classical Tradition in Poetry* (1927); J. L. Lowes, *Convention and Revolt* (1930); F. R. Leavis, *Revaluation* (1936); C. Brooks, *Modern Poetry and the Tradition* (1939); A. Tate, *Reason in Madness* (1941); G. Highet, *The Classical Tradition* (1949); T. S. Eliot, "Tradition and the Individual Talent" [1919] and "The Metaphysical Poets" [1921], *Essays* (1950); Frye; H. Rosenberg, *The Tradition of the New* (1959); J. V. Cunningham, *Tradition and Poetic Structure* (1960); H. Bloom, *The Visionary Company* (1961); C. Greenberg, "Avant-Garde and Kitsch," *Art and Culture* (1961); E.M.W. Tillyard, *The English Epic Tradition* (1969); W. J. Bate, *The Burden of the Past and the English Poet* (1970); H. Bloom, *The Anxiety of Influence* (1973); H.-G. Gadamer, *Truth and Method*, ed. and trans. G. Barden and J. Cumming (1975); R. K. Martin, *The Homosexual Tradition in American Poetry* (1979); H. Bloom, *The Breaking of the Vessels* (1982); E. Hobsbawm and T. Ranger, *Inventing Tradition* (1983); Parry; J. Foley, *Oral Formulaic Theory and Research* (1985); *Oral Tradition* (1986–)—jour.; L. Menand, *Discovering Modernism* (1987); S. Gilbert and S. Gubar, *No Man's Land*, 2 v. (1987–89); L. Keller, *Remaking It New: Contemporary American Poetry and the Modernist Tradition* (1987); J. Foley, *The Theory of Oral Composition* (1988); *Les Lieux de mémoire*, ed. P. Nora, trans. as *Realms of Memory*, ed. L. Kritzman, trans. A. Goldhammer (1996–98); Lord; C. Ricks, *Allusion to the Poets* (2002); *T. S. Eliot and the Concept of Tradition* (2007), ed. G. Cianci and J. Harding.

L. Menand (written); J. M. Foley (oral)

# TRAGEDY

I. Origins, Early History, and Concept
II. Performances

**I. Origins, Early History, and Concept.** Tragedy was invented in Greece in the 6th–5th c. BCE, its heyday and reputedly greatest poets—Aeschylus, Sophocles, and Euripides—spanning Athens's 5th c. Scholars have speculated ever since on its derivation from a putative "tragico-lyrical chorus," the *dithyramb, or sacrifice and ritual violence: the Gr. root of the word for tragedy refers to goats. Its rites would mark a spring regenerative cycle (Murray), a break between a "Dionysiac" gloving of humans in a natural world and their rational "Apollonian" split from it (Nietzsche), or a path from inhuman asocial chaos to ordered society and culture (Girard). The tragic protagonist would be a scapegoat whose death or rejection rejuvenates, cleanses, even makes civil society. Besides being tautological, drawn from (very few) tragedies, such speculations require a purely Western idea of reason as defeating a prior absent or "savage" reason. Let us just say that tragedies

act out a hardship of human effort before a determining process (fate, gods, social compulsion) that humans know imperfectly—though the very action of tragedies posits knowledge, showing and working through this condition. Tragedies insist that humans live essentially in a world of scission and rupture: human from divine, reason from unreason or emotion, written from spoken, culture from barbarism, us from others. This seems a defining facet of Western cultures, as of their judgment of other cultures. It may be why tragedy first appeared in Greece and was long limited to Western cultures. Perhaps tragedy helps defeat those ruptures. Certainly, doing so often defines mod. non-Western tragedy.

What we know of ancient tragedy draws on 33 plays from among hundreds (or thousands), a few material facts, Plato's censure, and Aristotle's *Poetics*. Yet the usual critical claim has been that tragedy was constant and largely homogeneous from between 536 and 533 BCE when Thespis of Athens performed a so-called tragedy at his city's Greater Dionysia. This article's first section doubts the claim and the broad speculations dependent on it. Ninety-nine percent of tragedies from the earliest centuries are lost. Facts are a dubious few. For what likely began as a duet of poet-protagonist and *chorus, Aristotle tells that Thespis invented the tragic mask: face paint, then cloth, later clay. Arion of Corinth may have developed the dithyramb. Cleisthenes, tyrant of Sicyon, perhaps dedicated to Dionysus the tragic choruses. At Phleius, Pratinas perhaps wrote the first satyr plays, whose genre then often ended an eventual set of four plays each by rival tragic poets who probably competed with one another from the start. Aeschylus is said to have been first to compose such a thematic tetralogy. He also introduced a second actor, Sophocles a third—said Aristotle a century later.

By the early 5th c., performances of the Dionysia occurred in a wooden structure built on stone footings at the southern base of the Acropolis. This and other impermanent buildings have left little trace. The first stone structure dates from the late 4th c. BCE. The theater of Dionysus visible today is a much later structure on a site that has seen many buildings. Vase paintings, reliefs, figurines, and mosaics offer glimpses of performers and performance, masks, clothing, and stage apparatus—but all "had their own plots to weave" (Hart). To draw clear dramatic facts from art forms with their own conventions is very delicate, even as they signal theater's weight in Gr. life (Hart, Taplin 2007). The chorus danced before a raised stage, accompanied by a musician (*auletes*) playing a double pipe. (Later, the stage was lifted higher.) The chorus was composed of citizens from one *deme*; actors were semi-professional. All were male. Stage machinery included cranes, multisided revolving "flats," and other devices.

Dearth of plays is another bar to speculation on tragedy's origins and meaning. Though we have myriad fragments of 5th–4th-c. BCE tragedies, a handful survive in full: 7 each by Aeschylus and Sophocles, 18 by Euripides (plus one doubtful, *Rhesus*). One of the earliest poets, Phrynichos, like Choirilos, was said to have written 160 tragedies; Astydamas II, from the 4th c. BCE, 240. Aeschylus and Euripides both composed 70 to 90 plays, Sophocles 120 to 130. These are only 6 of many. Some 60 authors are known from the Hellenistic era, and records survive of competitions late into the 1st c. BCE. This implies thousands of plays. The extant corpus is tiny. Furthermore, its survival is due to far later Alexandrian anthologists, whose aims were not literary or dramatic but philological, grammatical, and rhetorical.

Finally, we have Plato and Aristotle. While the first rejected tragedy as menacing the city's good order by raising violent emotions, the second contradicted him, defining tragedy and its benefits, among them that tragedy, in fact, *calmed* such emotions. Aristotle stated that tragedy had six basic parts: *plot, character, *diction (poetic *style and order), thought, spectacle, and music. The first two were supreme. Later critics, scholars, and dramatists agreed that this gives tragedy's rules, its models of actual performance coming from the Greeks and Seneca. They affirmed that its aim was that of *catharsis taken vaguely as a "purging" of the spectator's emotions of pity and terror, a "medical" reduction of their force, or a "religious" emotional purification making the spectator wiser and more tolerant. Catharsis, said Aristotle, occurred through *mimesis or *representation, enabled by tragedy's structure as a linear "plot" or mythos, leading the spectator from a beginning *in medias res through a confused middle with at least one "change of fortune" (peripeteia) to an end that embodied "recognition" (anagnorisis) of earlier ignorance and new understanding. Tragedy's main protagonist was a person of high estate, neither wholly good nor bad, who suffered this experience because of a "tragic flaw" (hamartia).

Unfortunately, battles have been continual over the meaning of even these fundamentals. *Catharsis* has been the single most disputed term, yet it occurs but once in the *Poetics*. *Mimesis* has posed similar problems, though it is now generally agreed that it does not mean representational copying but rather depiction of what is essential to human action, enabling specific instances to be generalized as in some way typical. *Mythos* denotes the form of such depiction. *Hamartia* has also proved provocative. From the Ren. until quite lately, *hamartia* was interpreted as a trait close to *hubris*, an overweening pride, whose exemplary Ren. figures were Christopher Marlowe's Tamburlaine and Faustus: indeed, this interpretation works well when applied to the growing stress on individualism and psychological "self-understanding" increasingly depicted in late Ren. and Enlightenment tragedy. The term was then interpreted in a fundamentally ethical sense, as a moral failure for which the protagonist was personally responsible. This has now been shown not to work for Gr. drama, with its wholly different view of subject and character, and to be an erroneous interpretation of Aristotle (Vernant and Vidal-Naquet). Closer analysis of the *Poetics* has shown that the term is connected not

so much with lack of will (though it can imply that) as with *unwittingness*. Indeed, Halliwell shows that it ranges from willful evil (but is *that* then a "failure"?) to plain lack of knowledge. We can then say that ha-martia, the so-called "tragic flaw," simply named the apparent single cause of *any* failure by the protagonist to act or to know, offered as such to the spectators' understanding.

Finding a generalizable ancient meaning for these terms is impossible. It would lie in the huge lost corpus. But that trying to do so can affect judgment and consideration of *facts* is shown by argument for a view of tragedy that is quite un-Greek, though used to assert tragedy's mod. "death," also a clearly inexact perception. As Steiner writes, "[A]ny realistic notion of tragic drama must start from the fact of catastrophe. Tragedies end badly." From the early Ren. to now, many have held this view. But for the Greeks, *catastrophe* was a technical device that did not have to end a tragedy, as we see in some plays (e.g., *Eumenides, Philoctetes, Oedipus at Colonus,* or *Helen*) and learn from Aristotle, who preferred fortunate endings. To see final catastrophe as defining tragedy means "we must either exclude a very large part of extant Greek tragedy or redefine *tragedy* or *badly*" (Reiss, 1980). Nor does the caveat apply only to Gr. tragedy. Were Pierre Corneille's *Le Cid* or *Horace* tragedies? What of Jean Racine's *Bérénice* or Nahum Tate's *King Lear*? Certainly, the first two *contain* catastrophe, but it would be a nice critic who could define their endings as unambiguous in that regard. As for *Bérénice,* does it even contain a catastrophe? (Does Euripides' *Alcestis*?) And while a contemp. reader might think Tate's *Lear* an absurd botching of a glorious predecessor, neither late 17th- nor 18th-c. audiences thought so: they preferred it.

The *Poetics* instituted a trad.; mod. philology, fresh discoveries, contextual awareness, all enjoin us to take it warily. Let us give separate due to authors and audiences of the Gr. 5th c. BCE, the Sp., Fr., and Eng. 16th–17th cs., the Ger. and Scandinavian 19th c., and those of a 20th c. running from Georg Büchner to Gerhart Hauptmann to Bertolt Brecht, Aimé Césaire, Wole Soyinka, Ola Rotimi, and Zulu Sofola; to J. P. Clark-Bekederemo, Athol Fugard, and Efua Sutherland, Ebrahim Hussein, Silvain Bemba, Maryse Condé, August Wilson, and Femi Osofisan; to the mod. Japanese film and theater trad. represented by Akira Kurosawa, Tadashi Suzuki, and Yukio Ninagawa; or to earlier Indian reuses of Shakespeare. This pell-mell list signals not just the global contemp. wealth of tragedy (clearly not "dead") but that, despite differences of hist., society, and culture, people have yet been able to believe, if not in the identity of tragedy through time and place, surely in sufficient similarity and above all utility of function or meaning. We can explore that similarity precisely by emphasizing those very historical and cultural differences. Indeed, only by so doing can we get a clear idea of what tragedy has actually done, of what has been the cultural function of tragedies in the environments where they have really existed. For it is manifest that a dramatic form called *tragedy* persistently recurred at times in the Western trad., and now many others, since the Greeks.

Much disputation may be avoided if we understand that Aristotle's descriptive terms had their origin in his effort to comprehend how tragedy functioned in his own time and place. For if a few facts further to those named at the start do exist in papyri, occasional remarks (e.g., by Herodotus), and vase paintings, our main source remains the *Poetics*, written in the mid-4th c. BCE, a century and a half later. His stated goal was to analyze tragedy's structure and function, comparing it to *epic and *comedy—the part on comedy is lost—but evidence is that he used his account of tragedy's hist. for political and ideological ends (Jones). Of the vast body of plays he knew, he stressed his favorites. One of these retains pride of place: *Oedipus Rex* exemplified tragedy, telling a serious, complete, and unique human action (introduced in medias res), showing its typicality and its limitation, involving people of high rank and issues vital to the whole polis, depicting characters not wholly good or bad passing through changes of fortune, recognition, and catastrophe. The play embodied tragedy's six essential parts, ending with music and spectacle.

The importance of the last two is certain. Trad. tells us that, in 5th-c. Athens, performances first occurred in the agora (marketplace), which we have no reason to doubt, the less so since we know that the tragedies of Félix Lope de Vega, Pedro Calderón de la Barca, Tirso de Molina, or Francisco de Rojas Zorrilla were played in the inn yards of Golden Age Spain, those of Marlowe, Shakespeare, Thomas Middleton, and their fellows in open-air Eng. theaters, while those of many of the African dramatists named earlier also occur in public spaces. There were, too, the Caribbean and Aztec *areitos*, widely reported by 16th-c. Europeans, performed by "three and at times four thousand and more men [and women]" who intriguingly "represented an image of their deeds in the manner of comedy or tragedy," said Francisco Hernández, ca. 1575 (1986). Probably, he meant dramatic performance. Be that as it may, via music and spectacle, Aristotle further stressed, beside the aesthetic and emotional, the *public* reality of tragedy performance, its role in the polis as political and historical debate.

That Aristotle politicized aesthetic goals is no surprise. Through the 5th c. BCE, Athens (and Greece as a whole) suffered anxious political conflict. Tragedies and their authors were vitally involved from the start. In 500, the Ionian cities of Asia Minor provoked the Persian Wars. Their revolt ended in 494 with the fall of Miletos. Serious threat ended in 480–79, but war dragged on until 449. Others soon lit up. Aeschylus and Sophocles were much involved: the first fought at Marathon and Salamis. Sophocles was *strategos* with Pericles in the Samian war of 441–39 and again in 428; often used as an ambassador, he was a member of the ruling council after 413. Political and military events are clearly not irrelevant to the devel. of tragic drama: they give the context essential to any understanding of tragedy's role in Athenian society, and they still play such a role, offering no little explanation as to why tragedy has gone dramatically global over the last half century. Tragedies were a deeply serious forum to address political and religious issues. In 472, e.g., Aeschylus's *Persians* targeted Greece's war, as had Phrynichos's *Capture of Miletos* (performed 493–92, just a year after the fall of that city). One of the usual interpretations of Aeschylus's *Oresteia* (the only extant trilogy) has been that it shows passage from a society dominated by divine justice to one relying on human justice in a city the authority for whose status remains divine. (The goddess Athena finally exonerates Orestes as she simultaneously institutes a new governing order.) No one, surely, doubted the political significance of tragedies.

This draws immediate attention to a notable fact about tragedy: besides "tragedy" itself, two things are common to its several historical occurrences.

First, tragedy has occurred in eras of precarious social and political consolidation, which soon proved times of transition from one sort of society to another. In Greece, the heyday of Aeschylus, Sophocles, and Euripides fell right between the Persian and Peloponnesian wars. The first war signaled a turn from archaic Gr. society toward city-state consolidation; the second marked decay of those conflict-prone states before Macedonian hegemony and advent of a "Hellenistic world." Similarly, in the Eur. 16th and 17th cs., the great age of tragedy was also an age of warfare, incl. revolts against the Hapsburgs of Spain and of the Holy Roman Empire, religious wars in France, the Thirty Years' War, the Eng. Civil War, and the Frondes. It was an age navigating between dying feudalism and strengthening capitalism. In Germany, the age between the mid-18th and mid-19th cs. (from G. E. Lessing, Friedrich Schiller, and J. W. Goethe to Heinrich von Kleist, Friedrich Hölderlin, and Franz Grillparzer) saw transformation from the 18th-c. feuding statelets to the Prussian Customs Union of 1830, into eventual unification and empire under Otto von Bismarck. Similarly fraught places and times certainly include the Germany of two world wars and Brecht; the postwar Japan of Kurosawa's *Throne of Blood* (*Macbeth*) and *Ran* (*Lear*), and equally arresting *nō-bunraku-* and *kabuki*-inflected workings of *Medea*, *Oedipus Rex*, *The Bacchae*, *Troiades*, and others by Ninagawa and Suzuki; the era of Caribbean and African independence struggles and their aftermath; the postwar U.S. civil rights and militaristic decades, all with their outpourings of tragedies. Tragedy again offers ways to manifest political dilemmas at times of profound social crisis and, as important, to ponder and analyze them.

Second, tragedy has in every case been followed by the consolidation of a political theory of extraordinary power: Plato and Aristotle, Thomas Hobbes and John Locke, G.W.F. Hegel and Karl Marx. Whether such will follow the tragedies of the 20th c.'s second half, it is too soon to know; but it is as if tragedy had found in its confused environment, and then related, a new conceptual and discursive process enabling certain doubts to be overcome, clearing up the incomprehensions inherent in earlier political and social decay and dissolution and facilitating instauration of a new order of rationality (Quayson, Scott). Many recent analysts have observed just how much Gr. tragedy focused on "lack of security and misplaced certainty in and about lang." (Goldhill 1986; cf. Segal 1981, 1986). The same is true of Ren. tragedy in Fr. and Eng. (Reiss 1980) and Ger. (Benjamin). Within those limits, what links tragedies is their presentation of protagonists whose will to reach some goal seems inevitably to confront limits against which they are powerless, cut off, ruptured from that objective. The limits may be self-created, imposed from without (by gods, people, or some social force), or even an inability to establish any exact sense of what is at stake (as is usual in the Ren. tragedies of George Buchanan, for instance). The result is an impasse for the protagonist—defeat, humiliation, often death. Whatever particular interpretation we may make of this, in general such drama signals a tense process in a transitional time after collapse of a stable order and before establishment of another.

**II. Performances.** Throughout the 5th c. BCE, tragedy had remained deeply caught up in issues both of the internal political order of an Athens whose form of government and power relations were a constant matter of debate and conflict and of external relations whose instability climaxed in the war with Sparta in 431. Final defeat came in 404. But the entire period was one of political and military struggle in which the Athenians had mounted various offensives. Among these was tragedy: Aeschylus produced his first play in 499, losing to Thespis, and took his first victory in 484, four years before Salamis. Phrynichos did a play on the fall of Miletos in 493–92, while Aeschylus won with his *Persians* in 472 and again with his war tragedy *Seven against Thebes* in 467. His *Oresteia* trilogy of 458 is generally seen to concern the inception of the well-ordered patriarchal city-state, even as *Eumenides*, its last play, can be read as a plea for concord in a city rent by factionalism. Sophocles' *Antigone*, a tragedy naturally read in political terms as a conflict between two perceptions of what laws rightly guide human behavior in civil society, was likely first played in the same decade or soon after. *Oedipus Rex* and *Ajax*, plays targeting right rule and the grief and madness of war, were probably produced shortly after outbreak of war with Sparta. We know that *Philoctetes*, a tragedy on war, betrayal, disloyalty, and dejected hope, was staged in 409. *Oedipus at Colonus*, apparently Sophocles' last play, was staged in 401, after Athens's defeat in 404, projecting a last plea for his city. Euripides also saw tragedy as tied to his century's political and military upheavals, seeing in them reflection of the decay and loss of trust in divine support for the city—or indeed for human life more broadly.

Contrary to what is often claimed, tragedy has less demonstrated human incapacity in face of a powerful or incomprehensible event than explained, or at least shown, what might otherwise be unintelligible. It has traced why, even how, a given group or person failed or was defeated in given conditions. The Athenians

sought to build a new, trustworthy political and epistemological order. To do that, in addition to real practice, they had to create some ordered conceptual process to "enclose" whatever might elude that knowledge and order (any conceptual or political process requires selection and exclusion) and set it outside their new system. They had to find a way either to show that nothing eluded such order or to assert that it explained and understood events that did escape it. Tragedy was one of those ways, and the audience had thus to understand it. It performed order in a theater where semiprofessional actors, a representative chorus of the deme, and the citizen body gathered together on the slopes of the Acropolis within shouting distance of the Pnyx, the everyday arena of political debate (Else 1965).

As Athens neared defeat in 404 BCE (a process violently figured in Euripides' *Bacchae*, where state order yields to a dissolution forced by Dionysus himself, divine warrant of Gr. tragedy), tragedy became quite direct. The *Bacchae* and *Oedipus at Colonus* were performed posthumously during Athens's final defeat. They mark the end of the great age of Gr. tragedy (and Athens). The "classics" began to be played again after 385, but, in that era of "revival," tragedy was the work of itinerant professional troupes and no longer central to any city's political and cultural fabric. Never again in antiquity would it recover that role. Perhaps the lack of cultural centrality explains why from the 500 years between 5th-c. Athens and Nero's Rome, when Seneca wrote tragedies the nature of whose performances (if any) remains disputed, there survive little but fragments and titles of tragedies and their authors' names.

Tragedy was "rediscovered" by Italy, France, Spain, England, and the Netherlands in the 16th–17th cs. Seneca was the major influence, esp. in his bombastic style, but Sophocles and Euripides had mild impact. Initially, a school exercise in rhetorical composition and performance, a way to amend vernaculars and reproduce antiquity's political and ethical commonplaces, Ren. humanist tragedy rapidly took on an aura of national political commentary. It also helped create vernaculars able to rival Gr. and Lat. in expressive quality and enabled writers to forge an elite literary genre whose perfection would contribute to making the new Eur. cultures equal to those of antiquity (see RENAISSANCE POETICS). At the same time, esp. in France, tragedies became tools in real political battles: Protestant and Catholic hostilities occurred on stage as well as on the battlefield. Théodore de Beza's 1550 *Abraham sacrifiant* was thus answered by Étienne Jodelle's 1552 *Cléopâtre captive*, praising Henri II and equating him with Octavian. In Spain, the tragedies of honor by dramatists such as Lope de Vega and Calderón reflected both the glory of imperial Spain and the worries of growing internal instability and external threats. In England, the hubristic individualist tragedies of Marlowe and Shakespearean tragedies that seem to place their protagonists up against conflicts they cannot resolve gave way to the darkening tones and violence of Jacobean revenge tragedy, as if preparing for the political and military struggles to come. In France, humanist tragedy was replaced by that of the elder Corneille, Jean Mairet, Georges de Scudéry, Pierre du Ryer, François Tristan l'Hermite, and Jean Rotrou. In Corneille esp., one can follow that era's confrontations between feudal nobility and central monarchical authority, between conspiratorial conflict and state stability. That trad. was continued (in his own way) by Racine, whose tragedies are easily interpreted as a set of experiments performed on different political situations and conditions. At the same time, these plays show how individuals and circumstances threatening to social stability were overcome and removed.

Among many tragic writers of the age, Shakespeare is preeminent. Writing in *blank verse on subjects drawn from hist. or legend, he draws characters ranged against obstacles frequently not simply of their own choosing but not even of their own making: *Hamlet* and *Macbeth* introduce supernatural elements, to be sure, but these do not gravely affect the instance of choice. Richard II glories in his eloquent railing but fails by mistaking his place in a now-altered divine order. *King Lear* may be the most terrifying tragedy of all, in that Lear himself seems responsible for setting the heavens against him, visiting disaster on innocent and guilty victims alike in a general collapse of the realm. In France, the debate was always between the opulent elder Corneille and Racine, whose clarity of diction, paucity of display, and tautness of *alexandrine, were all unique. All three created the mod. psychological tragic figure, as Friedrich Schlegel and A. W. Schlegel and other Ger. romantic critics claimed Lope de Vega and Calderón did in Spain (though recent work suggests otherwise) and, less familiarly, the Dutch Shakespeare, Joost van den Vondel, whose 1556 *Lucifer* was a source of Milton's epic and a possible precursor of Goethe's *Faust*.

In 18th-c. Europe, tragedy became a dry effort to recover that earlier active tragedy and tended to be a pale reflection of the political and conceptual order in whose creation earlier tragedy had shared. Some work was interesting, but most offered moralistic support for an accepted order of Enlightenment rationality and political organization. Only in Germany from the mid-18th c. does tragedy attain the sort of constructive process seen in 5th-c. BCE Athens or the 16th- to 17th-c. authors just named. Lessing was the first to launch this creative tragedy, and the process culminated in Schiller, Goethe, Kleist, and Hölderlin. After 1850, Henrik Ibsen and August Strindberg are the best candidates for consideration as writers of tragedy. Yet here, characters do not really *compose* a realm of knowledge and action but rather address systematic truths that preexist their activities—much as did 18th-c. protagonists. Among mod. Eur. dramatists of tragedy maybe in Federico García Lorca into the Spanish Civil War and mostly in Brecht, the questions haunting the great ages of tragedy are again "constitutive." In his theatrical practice, Brecht rediscovered tragedy as a place to reflect a new systematic process in an era marked by overthrow of cultural and political order. He denied that he wrote tragedies because he accepted the still-usual critical trad. holding tragedies to show human

incomprehension to be ineluctable, so he saw them as elite tools of ideological mystification. But in showing his protagonists striving to grasp a historical process they themselves make—and must make—meaningful, even as they are made by it, he adopts a *practice* of tragedy like that described here. In Brecht, tragedy again becomes creative of a new order and a new understanding of the social and political action enabled by such order.

But most of the provocative, productive, and even socially and politically constitutive tragedies of mod. times surely come from other parts of the world and most notably from peoples whom Europeans have one way or another oppressed. Their use of tragedy has often been to express forms of that oppression and ways to break it. In the U.S., if Lee Breuer's famed 1980s *Gospel at Colonus*, tying Sophocles and African American Christian gospel trads., yielded a praise song to post-civil rights comity, perhaps the most powerful U.S. tragedy from this or any other decade is August Wilson's *Ma Rainey's Black Bottom*, in which racist oppression and sentiment enforce the victims' self-immolation. In the 1990s, Rita Dove's *The Darker Face of the Earth* reworked *Oedipus Rex* to explore slavery, miscegenation, and a bleak aftermath of violently harmful exploitation, while in the same decade, Rhodessa Jones, rethinking *Medea* in prison performance, forged it into an ongoing project to free incarcerated women literally but also, through continuing self-made performances, from the social and political torments that prison iterates, exacerbates, and represents metaphorically (Fraden). In the last two decades in fact, *Medea* has proven to be a rich medium for new expression, esp. in Europe, Japan, and South Africa.

We have mentioned postwar Japanese reworkings of Gr. and Shakespearean tragedy in film and theater, hinting that they too have turned to tragedy as a way to reflect and analyze fraught social and political times. Long before, in the late 19th c., writers and publics in Bengal (notably) had used Shakespearean tragedy to analogous ends: to cope with inequities of colonialism, certainly, but more complicatedly with their sense both of the inferiority of their much older culture and of its already being deeply inflected by Brit. culture. Today, many Asian theaters look to Gr. tragedy, not always, sadly, for such locally driven reasons, as Diamond observes, criticizing a Malay-lang. production, the Beijing Opera, and Taiwan's Contemporary Legend Theatre for what she sees as "multicultural" performances of *The Bacchae* and *Oresteia* aimed less at a local spirit of place than at a global, chiefly Eur. audience. This may, of course, have a less "kitsch" future in an ever more globalizing world and, in that changing context, come to speak constructively and constitutively. That remains to be seen, as does the future of the mod. Arab theater's striking use of *Oedipus* (Carlson; Decreus and Kolk) and, again, reworkings of Shakespeare.

Soyinka (1994) has fun with this, suggesting that Shakespeare got *Romeo and Juliet*, at least, from the Arabs, even as he notes how much Arab poets and dramatists translated or adapted Shakespeare from the late

19th c. on. Soyinka is himself among those who have done much to transfer tragedy between cultures. His *The Bacchae of Euripides* (1973) makes that play a reflection on colonialism and performance of a "communion rite" that rethinks a decolonizing culture and society, defeating ruptures of slavery and rule, belief and disbelief, freedom and force, while *Death and the King's Horseman* (1975) reflects from inside Yoruba hist. on the violent distortions inherent in unequal conflicts of different cultures. Here, too, hope for a future community is held. Katrak remarks that "the goal of Yoruba tragedy is to energize the community at the conclusion; therefore, the need for calamitous endings is eliminated. The resolution lies not in the protagonist's death but in his bringing new strength into the communal life-blood." This is true of much other African tragedy and is one of the ways that African tragedies in particular reply to Western tragedy.

Soyinka is one among many African dramatists who use tragedy to meditate on conditions of violently stressed change. Sometimes they again adapt the Greeks, sometimes they use reminders of Gr. tragedy as elements in a plot otherwise entirely locally based, but sometimes no direct reference outside African culture is apparent. Of the first, one could mention Sutherland's *Edufa* (*Alcestis*), Osofisan's *Tegonni* (*Antigone*) and *Women of Owu* (*The Trojan Women*), Rotimi's *The Gods Are Not to Blame* (*Oedipus*), Soyinka's *Bacchae*, and many others. Of the second, Fugard's *The Island* (*Antigone*), Bemba's *Noces posthumes de Santigone*, and Clark-Bekederemo's *Song of a Goat* are good examples; of the third, Ama Ata Aidoo's *Anowa*, Hussein's *Kinjeketile*, Ngũgĩ wa Thiong'o and Micere Mugo's *Trial of Dedan Kimathi*, and Sony Labou Tansi's *La parenthèse de sang* (Parentheses of Blood).

Their political probings tend to be focused via four overlapping narratives. One involves colonization and its horrors; a second, conflicts that enfeebled cultures before colonial onslaught; a third, current struggles of cultural values, often entailing failures of combative will and act; a fourth, neocolonialism and its elites' crimes and corruptions. All mean to inform and enable political action. Rotimi's *Ovonramwen Nogbaisi* (1974) typifies the first (Rotimi said it also did the fourth), exploring the ruin of the Empire of Benin by an Eng. army: death of a culture, end of an era, loss of values. A noted case of this narrative is the Swahili dramatist Hussein's *Kinjeketile* (1970), relating the 1906 Maji Maji uprising against Ger. colonizers in southern Tanganyika. Aidoo's *Anowa* (1970) tells this narrative otherwise, showing how Kofi Ako's collusion with the colonists in the 1870s enriches but crushes him, his wife Anowa, and trad. Rotimi's *Kurunmi* (1971) epitomizes the second narrative, telling of a precolonial war to uphold traditional against new deforming values. Sofola's *Old Wines Are Tasty* (1981) portrays the third, its strife between trad. and neocolonialism baldly direct, ending in the death of the latter's misguided delegate. Césaire's *Une saison au Congo* exemplifies the fourth, notably in its final version (1973), which ends not with its sanza player's optimistic banter toward a new future

but with the tyrant Mokutu publicly rehabilitating the Lumumba he has murdered yet, enraged by the crowd's joy, ordering his guards to shoot, killing many, including the sanza player. Similarly, Rotimi's 1979 *If* acidly shows the poverty, the abuse of the people, and "the tragedy of the ruled" and savagely damns the corrupt wealth and misused power of neocolonial elites. Labou Tansi's "tragic farce" *La parenthèse de sang*, also from 1979, condemns equally ferociously the dictatorial corruption rampant in Zaire, ending with a stage covered in blood (as the play's title implies).

Not a few of these plays echo Soyinka's *Bacchae* in offering hope and a new community. *Kinjeketile*'s eponymous hero dies, but in doing so offers a path to collective unity and power to resist. Bemba's *Santigone* (1988), a tragedy of neocolonial corruption inspired by Sophocles' *Antigone*, turns that play against its trad., damning division and the agony it depends on: Melissa Yadé, Antigone, will die in the end in a plane crash, but she and her death will live in people's memory to inspire them to a new future. Much the same is true of Rotimi's *The Gods Are Not to Blame* (1968), which ends with Odewale, Oedipus but also Ogun, walking off with his children at the end, leaving a reformed village community behind but taking to the road again (like the god he represents), always with the hope of forging another new community. Many of these plays, too, incorporate debate about the uses and force of tragedy in their very structure and dialogue: this is esp. the case in Clark-Bekederemo's *Song of a Goat* (1961), from its title to its characters to its dialogue a self-conscious working of Gr. tragedy to capture a local collective reality.

Much such tragedy, we saw, has no Gr. reference. Rotimi's *Ozidi* (1966) takes local trads., song, dance, and dialogue. Played a year before the outbreak of the Biafran War as tensions grew to a peak, it also pleads to be read as reflecting those events, as Rotimi's *Gods* was during them and Soyinka's *Bacchae* after. Labou Tansi's *Parenthèse* uses a healing ceremony, *kingizila*, as the basis for its tragic ridiculing of neocolonial doublespeak and violence. Nor does tragedy in Africa always make colonization, its forerunners and aftermath, its focus—or it may do so only obliquely. Sofola's *Wedlock of the Gods* (1972) is a kind of Romeo and Juliet story, concerned with how a series of breached taboos ensuant on greed for wealth ends in disaster not only for the two main protagonists, whose death ties them in a "wedlock of the gods," but for entire families and the community—community being usually, one way or another, a major concern of these tragedies.

A similarly enormous wealth of explorations in tragedy has occurred in the Caribbean. Best known, no doubt, are Césaire's *Saison* and *La tragédie du roi Christophe*, which focus on the Haitian revolution and, not unlike *Kinjeketile* and others, hold hope for a new future community. This is poles apart from Derek Walcott's earlier *Henri Christophe* (1949), which tells of a revolt whose leadership is awash in self-interest and the venalities of power. One could also mention Condé's 1972 *Dieu nous l'a donné* and 1973 *Mort d'Oluwémi d'Ajumako*, whose first follows the failures and pettiness of Caribbean colonialism into disaster, but whose second shows how the appropriation of death can be turned into a claim for the power of a threatened culture. Kamau Brathwaite's *Odale's Choice* again uses *Antigone*. Many Caribbean playwrights have turned to Gr. tragedy to forge local commentary: the Haitian Félix Morisseau-LeRoy's *Antigone en creole* (1953); the Cuban Antón Arrufat's prize-winning *Los siete contra Tebas* (1968), which was, however, banned from the Cuban stage as being a censure of the revolution (which it was not, though it certainly criticized aspects of what the revolution had become ten years later); the Puerto Rican Luis Rafael Sánchez's *La pasión según Antigona Pérez* (1968).

All this just scratches the surface. Tragedy is alive and well in part because, as Quayson observes, it gives an ordered way to set "real-life events . . . in the emotionally and philosophically charged discourse of literary tragedy." He risks the example that to see Sani Abacha's murder of Ken Saro-Wiwa (who wrote of his Ogoni people's genocide as a "tragedy") in this tragic prism "arouse[s] a silent people into engagement with their history." Similarly, Scott argues from a rereading of C.L.R. James's hist. of the Haitian Revolution, which he shows between its first and second ed. transformed its narrative from one of romance to one of tragedy, that tragedy allows its spectators (or readers) to apply a particular sort of plot to historical events, a particular order that lets them become actors envisaging, planning for, avoiding, and changing outcomes. This is, of course, why from the start, tragedies marked transitional times in societies in transformation, always (so far) being followed by powerful analytic political theories producing actual polities and real-life consequences and outcomes. Whether these mod. tragedies will entail such theories (or have already done so), they certainly play the same reflective role.

*See* CLASSICAL POETICS, DRAMATIC POETRY, GENRE, GREEK POETRY, TRAGICOMEDY.

■ F. Nietzsche, *Die Geburt der Tragödie* (*The Birth of Tragedy*, 1872); A. C. Bradley, *Shakespearean Tragedy* (1904); C. J. Sisson, *Shakespeare in India* (1926); A. Pickard-Cambridge, *Dithyramb, Tragedy and Comedy* (1927); G. Murray, *Aeschylus, the Creator of Tragedy* (1940); G. F. Else, *Aristotle's Poetics* (1959); H.D.F. Kitto, *Greek Tragedy*, 3d ed. (1961); E. Olson, *Tragedy and the Theory of Drama* (1961); G. Steiner, *The Death of Tragedy* (1961); J.H.F. Jones, *On Aristotle and Greek Tragedy* (1962); G. F. Else, *The Origin and Early Form of Greek Tragedy* (1965); A. Lesky, *Greek Tragedy* (1965); R. Williams, *Modern Tragedy* (1966); B. M. Knox, *The Heroic Temper: Studies in Sophoclean Tragedy* (1966); N. Frye, *Fools of Time: Studies in Shakespearean Tragedy* (1967); C. Leech, *Tragedy* (1969); R. Girard, *La violence et le sacré* (1972); B. Vickers, *Towards Greek Tragedy* (1973); W. Soyinka, *Myth, Literature and the African World* (1976); W. Benjamin, *The Origin of German Tragic Drama*, trans. J. Osborne (1977); G.W.F. Hegel, *Hegel on Tragedy*, ed. A. Paolucci and H. Paolucci (1978); O. Taplin, *Greek Tragedy in Action* (1978); B. M. Knox, *Word and Action* (1979); R. B. Sewall, *The Vision of Tragedy*,

2d ed. (1980); T. J. Reiss, *Tragedy and Truth* (1980); J. Orr, *Tragic Drama and Modern Society* (1981); M. S. Silk and J. P. Stern, *Nietzsche on Tragedy* (1981); C. Segal, *Tragedy and Civilization* (1981); J. Dollimore, *Radical Tragedy* (1984); G. Steiner, *Antigones* (1984); C. Belsey, *The Subject of Tragedy* (1985); H. P. Foley, *Ritual Irony: Poetry and Sacrifice in Euripides* (1985); G. F. Else, *Plato and Aristotle on Poetry* (1986); S. Goldhill, *Reading Greek Tragedy* (1986); *Greek Tragedy and Political Theory*, ed. J. P. Euben (1986); S. Halliwell, *Aristotle's Poetics* (1986); F. Hernández, *Antigüedades de la Nueva España* (1986); K. H. Katrak, *Wole Soyinka and Modern Tragedy* (1986); M. C. Nussbaum, *The Fragility of Goodness: Luck and Ethics in Greek Tragedy and Philosophy* (1986); C. Segal, *Interpreting Greek Tragedy* (1986); N. Loraux, *Tragic Ways of Killing a Woman* (1987); J.-P. Vernant and P. Vidal-Naquet, *Myth and Tragedy in Ancient Greece*, trans. J. Lloyd, rev. ed. (1988); E. Hall, *Inventing the Barbarian: Greek Self-Definition through Tragedy* (1989); *Nothing to Do with Dionysos: Athenian Drama in Its Social Context*, ed. J. J. Winkler and F. I. Zeitlin (1989); M. J. Smethurst, *The Artistry of Aeschylus and Zeami: A Comparative Study of Greek Tragedy and Nō* (1989); J. P. Euben, *The Tragedy of Political Theory* (1990); M. McDonald, *Ancient Sun, Modern Light: Greek Drama on the Modern Stage* (1992); C. Meier, *The Political Art of Greek Tragedy* (1993); F. Macintosh, *Dying Acts: Death in Ancient Greece and Modern Irish Tragic Drama* (1994); W. Soyinka, *Art, Dialogue, and Outrage: Essays on Literature and Culture*, 2d ed. (1994); T. Olaniyan, *Scars of Conquest, Masks of Resistance: The Invention of Cultural Identities in African, African-American and Caribbean Drama* (1995); *The Cambridge Companion to Greek Tragedy*, ed. P. E. Easterling (1997); J. Drakakis and N. C. Liebler, *Tragedy* (1998); L. A. Johnson, *Shakespeare in Africa (and Other Venues): Import and the Appropriation of Culture* (1998); C. Diamond, "The Floating World of Nouveau Chinoiserie: Asian Orientalist Productions of Greek Tragedy," *New Theater Quarterly* 15 (1999); *(Dis)Placing Classical Greek Theatre*, ed. S. Patsalidis and E. Sakellaridou (1999); D. A. Shankar, *Appropriating Shakespeare (A Study of Shakespeare's Plays Rendered into Kannada between 1895–1932)* (1999); *Shakespeare in Indian Languages*, ed. D. A. Shankar (1999); *Medea in Performance, 1500–2000*, ed. E. Hall, F. Macintosh, O. Taplin (2000); R. Fraden, *Imagining Medea: Rhodessa Jones and Theater for Incarcerated Women* (2001); A. D. Nuttall, *Why Does Tragedy Give Pleasure?* (2001); *Amid Our Troubles: Irish Versions of Greek Tragedy*, ed. M. McDonald and J. M. Walton (2002); T. J. Reiss, "The Law, the Tragic and Cultures of Dissonance," *Against Autonomy: Global Dialectics of Cultural Exchange* (2002); K. J. Wetmore Jr., *The Athenian Sun in an African Sky: Modern African Adaptations of Classical Greek Tragedy* (2002), and *Black Dionysus: Greek Tragedy and African American Theatre* (2003); T. Eagleton, *Sweet Violence: The Idea of the Tragic* (2003); M. McDonald, The *Living Art of Greek Tragedy* (2003); A. Quayson,

*Calibrations* (2003); *Dionysus since 69: Greek Tragedy at the Dawn of the Third Millennium*, ed. E. Hall, F. Macintosh, A. Wrigley (2004); *Rereading Classics in "East" and "West": Post-Colonial Perspectives on the Tragic*, ed. F. Decreus and M. Kolk (2004); D. Scott, *Conscripts of Modernity: The Tragedy of Colonial Enlightenment* (2004); *A Companion to Tragedy*, ed. R. Bushnell (2005)—esp. T. J. Reiss, "Using Tragedy against Its Makers: Some African and Caribbean Instances"; *The Arab Oedipus: Four Plays*, ed. M. Carlson (2005); V. Lambropoulos, *The Tragic Idea* (2006); B. Goff and M. Simpson, *Crossroads in the Black Aegean: Oedipus, Antigone, and Dramas of the African Diaspora* (2007); O. Taplin, *Pots and Plays: Reflections of Tragedy and Comedy in Greek Painted Pottery of the Fourth Century B.C.* (2007); *Rethinking Tragedy*, ed. R. Felski (2008); A.C.Y. Huang, *Chinese Shakespeares* (2009); *Sophocles and the Greek Tragic Tradition*, ed. S. Goldhill and E. Hall (2009); E. Hall, *Greek Tragedy: Suffering under the Sun* (2010); *The Art of Ancient Greek Theater*, ed. M. L. Hart (2010).

T. J. Reiss

**TRAGICOMEDY.** A term that refers to *tragedies, melodrama, and ironic drama that contain comic scenes or characters. The earliest plays mixing such elements are those of Euripides (ca. 480–406 bce), e.g., *Alcestis*; Aristotle remarks on a public taste for plays in which bad characters came to a bad end and good characters survived happily (*Poetics* 13). Plautus (ca. 254–184 bce) coined the term *tragicomedy*, applying it to his *Amphitruo*, a play anomalous in its time for mixing noble and humble characters as well as serious and comic action. However, Plautus established no clear generic form (Herrick), and the forms of liturgical drama in the Middle Ages precluded tragicomedy. It began to emerge only in the Ren., when both Neo-Lat. and vernacular plays adapted cl. Lat. comic forms to the dramatization of biblical narrative. A number of them, such as George Gascoigne's (1534–77) *Glass of Government*, mix melancholy material with endings that avoid catastrophe and include explicit moral lessons.

Secular tragicomedy became firmly established in Italy in the plays of Giambattista Giraldi Cinthio (1504–73), though he is careful to avoid commitment to the idea of a separate genre. His essay *Discorso intorno al comporre dei romanzi* (Discourse on the Composition of Romances, 1554) identifies two kinds of tragedy, one ending in sorrow, the other in happiness. Cinthio prefers the second: "Plots that are terrible because they end unhappily (if it appears the spirits of the spectators abhor them) can serve for closet dramas; those that end happily for the stage" (Gilbert, Herrick).

What Cinthio calls a type of tragedy, Giovanni Battista Guarini (1538–1612), the most important Ren. partisan, openly and extensively defends as tragicomedy. In his *Compendium of Tragicomic Poetry* (1601), Guarini's argument, like that of Cinthio, places its main theoretical emphasis on audience response, but more than a happy ending is involved. He regards tragedy, as Aristotle defines it, as less likely to settle the troubled passions of the audience than tragicomedy. He proposes, therefore, to retain compassion and forgo horror. Hence, his definition of *tragicomedy* as a mean between affective extremes: "the mingling of tragic and comic pleasure, which does not allow hearers to fall into excessive tragic melancholy or comic relaxation" (Gilbert).

Guarini's aim is to produce a balanced and harmonized state in the soul of the spectator by means of tightly plotted comic intrigues moving from potential disaster to a happy conclusion. Guarini would retain elevated or distinguished protagonists but situate them in private, domestic experience. More important perhaps is the paradigm he establishes for character devel.: in his *Il pastor fido* (*The Faithful Shepherd*, 1590) he employs for his protagonist Silvio the *topos of inner transformation from scorning to acceptance of love, "a natural metaphor for his conception of tragicomedy as a genre that functions as a medicine to purge the human temperament of excesses and so bring men, like Silvio, to a happier balance" (Cope).

One of the chief inheritors of both the romantic plots of Cinthio and the pattern of inner change formulated by Guarini was Shakespeare, though, with the exception of *The Tempest*, he inclined to a much greater looseness of plot and everywhere mingled levels of character and incongruous subjects in successful defiance of neoclassical principles of *decorum. An indifference to rules of structure or decorum was standard in Eng. Ren. drama, and the habit of mixing the serious and the farcical, even in plays nominally identified as tragic, such as *Dr. Faustus* or *King Lear*, seriously undermined neoclassical concepts of *genre. In Shakespeare's later plays and in some of the work of Francis Beaumont and John Fletcher, the presence of tragicomedy is evident in the encouragement of paradoxical responses through the mixture of fantastic event and moral redemption. In *The Winter's Tale*, there is repeated stress on artifice, as in Hermione's long survival as a statue, where adherence to the rules would require verisimilitude.

Fr. theater of the 17th c. tended to a more rigorous observance of imposed standards and, hence, to less theoretical tolerance of tragicomedy, though Pierre Corneille's *Le Cid* is a tragedy with a happy ending, and his self-justifying "Discourse on Tragedy" (1660) argues, as Guarini had, that the catastrophic ending was not the best kind. Hence, his tragedies can be viewed as tragicomic under a different name, and *Le Cid* as "the supreme flowering of neoclassical tragicomic romance" (Hirst; see Lancaster for discussion of tragicomedy as a dominant genre in 16th- and early 17th-c. France). There are elements of tragicomedy in the work of Molière as well, as in *Le Misanthrope*. In Eng., the 17th and early 18th c. witnessed radically opposed opinions on tragicomedy. John Milton decries the "error of intermixing Comic stuff with Tragic sadness and gravity" (Preface to *Samson Agonistes*), a view echoed by Joseph Addison (*Spectator* no. 40). But John Dryden in his *Essay of Dramatic Poesy* (1668) approves of tragicomedy as more natural and indeed wrote several plays in that mode. Samuel Johnson's judgment is prophetic of more recent views: "Is it not certain that the tragic and comic affections have been moved alternately with equal force and that no plays have oftener filled the eye with tears and the breast with palpitation than those which are ariegated with interludes of mirth?" (*Rambler* no. 156).

With the decline of verse drama and the relaxing of firm generic standards, tragicomedy becomes associated with 19th-c. popular melodrama and the more cerebral plays of G. B. Shaw and Anton Chekhov (Hirst). Two formal patterns can be identified in the 19th c.: one largely involves the rescue of sympathetic victims at the last minute, continuing the emphasis on careful and suspenseful plotting established by Guarini; the other is more a matter of tone, a mixing of attitudes toward character and event that tends toward a drama of ironies. Thus, the critical and theoretical terms for discussion of tragicomedy emphasize audience response over formal or generic contexts or patterns of character change. Twentieth-c. drama ignored such considerations as the social status of characters, consistency in levels of lang., and decorum in subject matter, deliberately mixing tragic and comic elements without any attempt at the harmony and balance advocated by Guarini. As in T. S. Eliot's *Murder in the Cathedral*, the audience may be encouraged simultaneously to tragic empathy and comic detachment; and complexity of tone and, hence, of response become common features of mod. dramas as diverse as those by Shaw and Chekhov and the writers of the Theater of the Absurd.

*See* COMEDY, DRAMATIC POETRY.

■ H. C. Lancaster, *The French Tragicomedy* (1907); H. Corbach, "Tragikomödie," *Reallexikon I*, v. 4; K. S. Guthke, *Geschichte und Poetik der deutschen Tragikomödie* (1961); M. T. Herrick, *Tragicomedy* (1962); G. Guarini, *The Compendium of Tragicomic Poetry*, excerpted in *Literary Criticism Plato to Dryden*, ed. A. Gilbert (1962); J. L. Styan, *The Dark Comedy* (1962); C. Hoy, *The Hyacinth Room* (1964); K. Guthke, *Modern Tragicomedy* (1966); J. Hartwig, *Shakespeare's Tragicomic Vision* (1972); J. Cope, *The Theater and the Dream* (1973); M. Esslin, *Theatre of the Absurd*, 3d ed. (1980); B. J. Bono, *Literary Transvaluation from Vergilian Epic to Shakespearean Tragicomedy* (1984); M. Carlson, *Theories of the Theatre* (1984); D. L. Hirst, *Tragicomedy* (1984); P. Hernadi, *Interpreting Events* (1985); R. Dutton, *Modern Tragicomedy and the British Tradition* (1986); J. Orr, *Tragicomedy and Contemporary Culture* (1990); *The Politics of Tragicomedy: Shakespeare and After*, ed. G. McMullan (1992); L. Cabranes-Grant, "La resistencia a la tragicomedia: Giraldi Cintio y una polemica sobre 'Celestina,'" *Celestinesca* 22 (1998); R. Barker, "Tragical-Comical-Historical Hotspur," *ShQ* 54 (2003); V. A. Foster, *The Name and Nature of Tragicomedy* (2004); T. Miller, "Ridiculously Modern Marsden: Tragicomic Form and Queer Modernity," *Modernist Cultures* 2 (2006); Z. Lesser, "Tragical-Comical-Pastoral-Colonial: Economic Sovereignty, Globalization, and the Form of Tragicomedy," *ELH* 74 (2007); V. Forman, *Tragicomic Redemptions* (2008); T. Pollard, "Romancing the Greeks: Cymbeline's Genres and Models," *How to Do Things with Shakespeare*, ed. L. Maguire (2008); C. Nocentelli, "Spice Race: *The Island Princess* and the Politics of Transnational Appropriation," *PMLA* 125 (2010).

R. L. MONTGOMERY; R. GREENE

**TRANSCENDENTALISTS.** Am. transcendentalist poets and cultural theorists were part of a loosely organized mid-19th-c. intellectual movement centered in New England (primarily Concord, Massachusetts, and the Boston area). The term *transcendentalists* derives from the unsystematic connection of their thought to the idealist philosophy of Immanuel Kant, as they emphasize attributes of reality that in part transcend sensual perception. The transcendentalists served as the most important conduit of Eur. *romanticism to America. Leading figures include R. W. Emerson (1803–82), H. D. Thoreau (1817–62), and Sarah Margaret Fuller (1810–50). Members of the circle met periodically, sometimes as the Transcendental Club, and produced *The Dial* (1840–44) under the editorship of Fuller, then Emerson. *The Dial* published a significant number of their texts. Although better known for their prose—Emerson's addresses, lectures, and essays; Fuller's *Woman in the Nineteenth-Century* (1845); and Thoreau's "Resistance to Civil Government" (or "Civil Disobedience," 1849) and *Walden* (1854)—the transcendentalists wrote much pub. and unpub. verse and accorded poetry a primary cultural role. Their theories of poetry, esp. those of Emerson, are indispensable to Am. romanticism and much subsequent Am. poetry.

For all their differences, shared tendencies of their poetry are clear. Notions of divinity are particularly important to the poets, but they depart from traditional theism to locate divinity not within conventional religious figures, institutions, and texts but within humankind, nonhuman nature, life itself, and a wide diversity of writings. Unlike Unitarianism, from which most transcendentalists emerged, transcendentalism celebrates enthusiasm, *emotion, *imagination, and *intuition over moderation, cognition, and tuition. Key terms, derived from Emerson, include *self-reliance* and *nonconformity*, by which he means not hyperindividuality but reliance on oneself instead of on dominant social structures or popular opinion for one's beliefs. The transcendentalists stress both the infinite value and potential of all individuals and social reform. Their faith in a definitive interconnection among beauty, truth, goodness, joy, and action led to their involvement in such political and social issues as abolition, women's rights, poverty, and the Italian Revolution; and the formation of two communes, Brook Farm and Fruitlands. Seeking revolutionary ways of thinking and writing, they address a wide range of topics, incl. philosophy, national cultures, education, and science. Through their interest in J. W. Goethe, William Wordsworth, S. T. Coleridge, and Asian literary and religious texts, the transcendentalists paradoxically aspire to create uniquely Am. voices but also broadly to affirm global culture.

Transcendentalist poetry treats the beauty and sacredness of bucolic nature, self-actualization, the power of poetry and of the imagination, and political reform. Formally, the transcendentalists emphasize matter over manner; Emerson famously claims in his essay "The Poet," "It is not metres, but a metre-making argument, that makes a poem." Their forms are relatively conventional, but they engage in considerable experimentation within them. Often, their poetry contains compressed orphic utterances—epigrammatic proverbs or assertions—sometimes in interpolated voices. Heavily influenced by 17th-c. Brit. poets, esp. George Herbert and John Milton, they consider Shakespeare the quintessential poet in Eng. even as they emphasize the need for distance from him.

The most important transcendentalist poet is Emerson, who played a central role in encouraging other transcendentalist poets, as well as Walt Whitman. Emerson published over 200 poems and trans. (often from Ger. versions of *Persian poets, esp. Ḥāfiz), many of them collected in his two main books of poetry, *Poems* (1847) and *May-Day and Other Pieces* (1867). *Poems*, the more groundbreaking volume, includes most of Emerson's best-known pieces, among them, "The Sphinx," "The Rhodora," "The Snow-Storm," "Hamatreya," "Bacchus," "Uriel," "Concord Hymn," and the elegy for Emerson's young son, "Threnody." *May-Day* is best read with Herman Melville's *Battle-Pieces* and Whitman's *Drum-Taps* as a response to the Am. Civil War. The volume represents poetry as a call to justice, a reminder of natural beauty, and a balm to heal suffering after the conflict. Among its best poems are "Brahma," "Boston Hymn," "Voluntaries," "Days," "Two Rivers," "Waldeinsamkeit," and "Terminus."

Thoreau wrote a great deal of poetry early in his life, then turned his primary attention to prose. Esp. prolific as a poet from 1839 to 1843, Thoreau produced over 200 poems and published 85 in some form, many in his prose work *A Week on the Concord and Merrimack Rivers* (1849). Some poems treat his youthful sense of inadequacy ("*Sic Vita*"), but most celebrate nature. The few poems that Fuller published appear in her nonfiction prose, esp. *Summer on the Lakes* (1843) and *Woman in the Nineteenth Century*. Yet she wrote a significant amount of poetry, esp. in the mid-1840s. Some of her best poems—"Double Triangle, Serpent and Rays," "Sistrum," "Winged Sphynx," and "Raphael's Deposition from the Cross"—employ mythic female emblems to depict feminist self-actualization through the attainment of combined power and equilibrium.

Although he wrote poetry much of his life, Jones Very (1813–60) is remembered for his ecstatic, visionary religious sonnets. Written from 1838 to 1849, the poems appear in sometimes mingled voices of the godhead and the poet himself. Although Very was for a time psychologically unmoored and briefly incarcerated in an asylum, Emerson encouraged him, editing the one book Very published in his lifetime, *Essays and Poems* (1839).

Among the other transcendentalist poets, Christopher Pearse Cranch (1813–92), poet, painter, caricaturist, is the strongest, with such poems as "Enosis" and "Correspondences" that versify transcendentalist philosophy. William Ellery Channing (the Younger, 1817–1901) was the most prolific, publishing periodical verse and eight books of poetry from 1843 to 1886 that treat nature, solitude, and poetic aspiration, and furnish portraits of other transcendentalists. He was also the most criticized, famously by E. A. Poe, for technical flaws and incoherence; Emerson and Fuller almost alone defended him. Ellen Sturgis Hooper (1812–48) and her sister Caroline Sturgis Tappan (1818–88) also published poems in *The Dial*. Bronson Alcott (1799–1888), father of Louisa May Alcott, published verse in periodicals and within his prose volumes in the period 1860–80, as well as producing the autobiographical *New Connecticut* (1881) and *Sonnets and Canzonets* (1882).

The influence of the transcendentalists remains disproportionate to the small size and brief duration of the initial movement. Whitman and Emily Dickinson, their most direct descendants, reflect close thematic similarities. Tonally and formally, Whitman's poetry tends to resemble Emerson's prose, and Dickinson's poetry often resembles Emerson's poetry (one of her anonymously pub. poems was attributed to him). Transcendentalist influence has also spanned the globe. Thoreau and Emerson were important to Gandhi and Martin Luther King Jr., and Fuller promoted internationalism by serving as a foreign correspondent. In his essay "Emerson," the Cuban revolutionary and poet José Martí calls Emerson's poems "the only polemic verse to sanctify the great struggle on this earth." Some 20th-c. poets wrote of their indebtedness to Emerson's prose and poetry, among them Robert Frost, A. R. Ammons, and Mary Oliver, while other poets acknowledged their admiration for Thoreau and Fuller. In some senses, much U.S. postromantic, ecopolitical, and social-reform poetries continue and sometimes contest the transcendentalist trads.

See GERMAN POETRY; ROMANTIC AND POSTROMANTIC POETRY AND POETICS; ROMANTICISM; UNITED STATES, POETRY OF THE.

■ **Anthologies and Primary Texts:** *The American Transcendentalists* (1957) and *The Transcendentalists*, both ed. P. Miller (1958); *The Dial*, 4 vs., rpt. (1961); H. D. Thoreau, *Collected Poems*, enl. ed., ed. C. Bode (1964); W. E. Channing II, *Collected Poems*, ed. W. Harding (1967); C. P. Cranch, *Collected Poems*, ed. J. M. DeFalco (1971); M. Fuller, *The Essential Margaret Fuller*, ed. J. Steele (1992); *American Poetry: The Nineteenth Century*, Vol. I, ed. J. Hollander (1993); J. Very, *Complete Poems*, ed. H. R. Deese (1993); *Ralph Waldo Emerson: Collected Poems and Translations*, ed. H. Bloom and P. Kane (1994); *Transcendentalism*, ed. J. Myerson (2000); H. D. Thoreau, *Henry David Thoreau: Collected Essays and Poems*, ed. E. H. Witherell (2001); *The American Transcendentalists*, ed. L. Buell (2006).

■ **Criticism:** O. B. Frothingham, *Transcendentalism in America* (1876); L. Buell, *Literary Transcendentalism* (1974); H. H. Waggoner, *Emerson as Poet* (1974); D. Porter, *Emerson and Literary Change* (1978); R. A.

Yoder, *Emerson and the Orphic Poet in America* (1978); *The Transcendentalists*, ed. J. Myerson (1984)—esp. essays by R. E. Burkholder and Myerson (Emerson), F. C. Dahlstrand (Alcott), F. B. Dedmond (Channing), R. N. Hudspeth (Fuller), M. Meyer (Thoreau), D. Robinson (Cranch and Very); L. Buell, "The American Transcendentalist Poets," *Columbia History of American Poetry*, ed. J. Parini (1993); *Encyclopedia of American Poetry: The Nineteenth Century*, ed. E. L. Haralson (1998)—esp. H. R. Deese (Very), L. Honaker (Cranch), P. T. Kane (Emerson), J. Steele (Fuller), K. Walter (Channing), E. H. Witherell (Thoreau), G. R. Woodall (Alcott); S. Morris, " 'Metre-Making' Arguments: Emerson's Poems," *Cambridge Companion to Ralph Waldo Emerson*, ed. J. Porte and S. Morris (1999); B. Packer, "The Transcendentalists," *Cambridge History of American Literature*, ed. S. Bercovitch, v. 4 (2004); *The Oxford Handbook of Transcendentalism*, ed. J. Myerson, S. H. Petrulionis, and L. D. Walls (2010), esp. S. Morris, "Twentieth-Century Poetry."

■ **Websites**: The Emerson Society: http://www.cas.sc.edu/engl/emerson/; The Margaret Fuller Society: http://mendota.english.wisc.edu/~jsteele/index.html/; The Ralph Waldo Emerson Institute: http://www.rwe.org/; The Thoreau Society: http://www.thoreausociety.org/; The Web of American Transcendentalism: http://www.vcu.edu/engweb/transcendentalism/.

S. MORRIS

**TRANSLATION.** "Till I heard Homer speak out loud and bold": many readers know that the eighth line of John Keats's famous sonnet "On First Looking into Chapman's Homer" (1817) does not read this way. Why not? The legendary Gr. name fits the iambic beat as neatly as the less venerable "Chapman" that takes its place. Through this unexpected substitution, Keats calls attention to the key role that trans. plays in the transmission and creation of poetic culture. By relying on a trans., Keats admits that he cannot read the original Gr., as his university-educated precursors and contemporaries might have. He also flaunts his unorthodox taste by spurning Alexander Pope's then-standard trans. in favor of George Chapman's less favored Ren. version. He raises, moreover, the vexed issue of the translator's relationship to his or her poetic source: the poem's climactic moment comes when the speaker hears not Homer's voice but that of his latter-day translator.

The two Homers Keats presumably knew suggest other questions of poetic trans. Both Pope and Chapman employ *rhyme and *meter in transmitting the Gr. text. Chapman uses the epic *fourteener, while Pope draws on a tidier iambic *pentameter with tightly rhymed neoclassical *couplets: neither aims to reproduce the dactylic *hexameter of the original. Would the results have been more faithful if they had? Though Eng.-lang. *versification derives from cl. sources, the ling. structure of Eng. can only approximate, through *accents, the long- and short-vowel alternation that shapes ancient Gr. *prosody. The very verse structure of Eng. is, thus, an imperfect trans. of its early model:

the iambs and trochees of anglophone verse would be unrecognizable to those who first used the terms.

The form Keats employs, moreover, likewise derives from foreign sources, as its Italianate name suggests: without the 14th-c. Petrarchan *sonetto*, there would be no 19th-c. Eng. *sonnet celebrating a 17th-c. trans. from the ancient Gr. Indeed, the plethora of prosodic terms, in Eng. and other langs., that owe their existence to trans., ancient and mod., points to the constant "crossbreeding and hybridization" (Osip Mandelstam) that shape the Western poetic trad. Trans. not only sustain the cultural "afterlife" of poetic works, as Walter Benjamin states in "The Task of the Translator"; they generate future incarnations: "I want Ovid . . . and Catullus to live once more and I am not satisfied with the historical Ovid . . and Catullus," Mandelstam insists in "The Word and Culture."

Translating poetry is, the adage runs, impossible. It is also, so Keats's sonnet suggests, imperative. Keats's mod. poem springs from a work available to him only through the ling. mediation of others, and such mediation, when successful, provides the immediate shock of the new that catalyzes further poetic creation. This paradox is key not just to the hist. of verse trans. but to its analysis and reception. Various theorists and practitioners have seen poetic trans. as dominated by one of three guiding principles. The translator may aspire to (1) semantic accuracy or (2) prosodic accuracy; or he or she may aim instead for the kind of (3) "creative transposition" (Jakobson), "raid" (Heaney), or "imitation" (Lowell) that relies on "the muse of translation" (Young) to generate new inspiration.

"The clumsiest literal translation is a thousand times more useful than the prettiest paraphrase," Vladimir Nabokov insists in the intro. to his notoriously clunky trans. of Alexander Pushkin's *Evgenij Onegin*. His fellow exile and self-translator Joseph Brodsky was equally adamant on the need for "prosodic verisimilitude": the translator must endeavor to reproduce, above all, the rhyme and meter of the original poem. Robert Lowell, whose Rus. "imitations" Nabokov abhorred, freely "dropped lines, moved lines, moved stanzas and altered meter and intent" in his efforts to avoid translatorly "taxidermy." Which approach is correct? None, or all of the above. Poetic trans. can be no more "pure" than the various trads. it shapes and is shaped by: "There is no answer, there are only the choices people make," Heaney remarks pragmatically. Much discussion of poetic trans. focuses on the problems inherent in each of these three emphases and on the continuous negotiation among them that constitutes so much translatorly practice.

What is a literal trans.? Nabokov curtails all debates with brusque efficiency: "The term 'literal translation' is tautological since anything but that is not truly a translation." Poets from Pope to Paul Valéry have seen things differently. Pope deplores "servile, dull adherence to the letter" ("Preface to the *Iliad* of Homer"), while Valéry upends the old cliché (itself translated from the It.) about translators as traitors: "Where poetry is concerned, fidelity to meaning alone is a kind of betrayal" ("Variations on the *Eclogues*"). In "The Poetry of Grammar and the Grammar of Poetry," Jakobson insists on the inseparability of meaning and form—in both its ling. and prosodic embodiments—that marks poetic speech. "Sense in its poetic significance is not limited to meaning," as Benjamin comments. Poetic lang. transforms the very notion of literal meaning by activating semantic possibilities in places we do not ordinarily think to look for them. If one goal of poetic lang. is to shake the reader loose from the fetters of literal mindedness, then a literal rendering of a poetic text, such as Nabokov's *Onegin*, runs the risk of violating more than just the spirit in its fidelity to the letter. What is poetic lang. deprived of poetry?

It follows from Jakobson's argument that too strict a reverence for poetic form poses its own dangers. Brodsky's insistently structured trans. of his own poems often do violence not just to the virtuosic forms he borrowed in many cases from adoptive Eng. forebears from John Donne to W. H. Auden but also to the extraordinary Rus. originals. Moreover, metrical structures carry different semantic charges from lang. to lang. and culture to culture. Czesław Miłosz takes his inspiration, metrical and otherwise, from Auden's *New Year Letter* for his own—still untranslated— "Traktat moralny" (Treatise on Morals, 1947). But the familiar rhythms of Auden's iambic *tetrameter come as a shock when translated into a lang. where fixed penultimate stress lends itself far more readily to trochees.

Miłosz's acerbic take on postwar Polish intellectual life gains an additional measure of ironic distance through his use of a borrowed metrical structure, esp. when combined with his wittily polonized revamping of Auden's couplets and slant rhymes. Miłosz's prosodic virtuosity in his native Polish goes virtually unseen in the Eng. trans. he shepherded into being with the help of various cotranslators, though. Here he stood opposed to Brodsky: "good enough" was "good enough for him," since, as he told his long-time collaborator Robert Hass, "it is after all a poem in Polish, not a poem in English." His most metrically intricate work—often inspired by Anglo-Am. models—remains largely untranslated or has been translated, at Miłosz's insistence, into *free verse.

Are all poetic trans. either doomed to marginal success at best or destined for the dubious distinction of becoming "stand-alone" poems that make only passing reference to their purported originals? Are we left only with multiple embalmments, desecrations, and "Lowellizations"? Of course not. Every poem, as many critics have noted, is a complex, shifting system participating in numerous other systems—literary, ling., social, historical, political, and so on. Poetic trans. must likewise remain in constant motion if it is to do justice to each poem's distinctive "mode of signification" (Benjamin). When Valéry speaks of "the labor of approximation, with its little successes, its regrets, its conquests, and its resignations," he describes both poetic creation and its subsequent trans.

Holmes describes the translator as a decoder and reencoder of the "hierarchy of correspondences" governing the individual poetic work. The Polish poet and translator Stanisław Barańczak suggests something similar in his notion of the "semantic dominant": "The translator's decision process can be described precisely as the process of realizing what in the 'poetry' of the original is the most characteristic, important and irreplaceable; in other words, it is the process of forming for oneself a system of priorities, one valid solely within the precincts of this and not another poem."

Barańczak's own practice as translator and poet suggests ways in which creative fidelity to the forms of meaning and the meaning of forms can lead in turn to the "form creation" that Mandelstam sees as activating poetic speech. Elizabeth Bishop's famous poem "One Art" (1975) marks a creative revision of yet another poetic transplant, the *villanelle. Barańczak's Polish version retains both the original's intricate structure and, to a startling degree, the sense that this structure embodies. He cannot salvage the seemingly crucial rhyme of "master" / "disaster"; nor can he duplicate the eloquent series of rhymes and half rhymes that Bishop builds around this pairing. And it is a loss, but it is not a disaster. Even the literal meaning of the movingly imperfect rhymes he employs in the stanzas' second lines shows how closely he keeps to the original poem's sense: "foreboding," "keys," "to flee," "pang," "won't return," "in art." Most important, he sustains the villanelle's structuring patterns of continuity and slippage, repetition and change: the perfect analogue to its concern with what is lost through time and what survives.

Barańczak later took inspiration from Bishop's poem and his own trans. to create one of the most moving love lyrics in the Polish trad. In "Płakała w nocy" (She Cried at Night), he follows Bishop's lead in psychologizing the villanelle form, as repetition, recognition, and resistance intertwine to dramatize the psyche's efforts both to evade and to accept knowledge almost past bearing. The poem's power was perceived immediately by Polish critics and readers. But they took the form to be Barańczak's own invention: there is no villanelle trad. in Poland. Or rather, there was no such trad. before Barańczak's poem: the form has subsequently been taken up by a number of younger Polish writers.

"Poetry is what is lost in translation," Robert Frost infamously—and perhaps apocryphally—proclaimed. Bishop's villanelle suggests ways in which poetry itself may be conceived as "the art of losing," a mode clearly akin to "the art of loss" (Felstiner) that is poetic trans. "You can't translate a poem," Yves Bonnefoy insists in "Translating Poetry." Yet there is likewise "no poetry but that which is impossible," he comments in the same essay, and this is its bond with trans., which is "merely poetry re-begun." "Translation and creation are twin processes," Octavio Paz observes ("Translation: Literature and Letters").

Loss, impossibility, trans., and new creation: let us return in this context to mod. imaginings of ancient epics. "We have no satisfactory translation of any Greek author," Ezra Pound proclaims in "How to

Read": "Chapman and Pope have left *Iliads* that are of interest [only] to specialists." Keats may celebrate trans. as immediate discovery, but Pound takes his reader on a different kind of voyage some hundred years later, as he journeys through layers of lang. and hist. in a work that is simultaneously a trans., a meditation on trans., and the magnificent poem that launches his lifework, the *Cantos*:

> And then went down to the ship,
> Set keel on the swart breakers, forth on the godly
>     sea, and
> We set up mast and sail on that swart ship,
> Bore sheep aboard her, and our bodies also
> Heavy with weeping. . . .

Pound's trans. from book 11 of the *Odyssey* comes mediated through his own earlier rendition of the Eng. med. poem "The Seafarer"; Anglo-Saxon *alliteration and monosyllables shape the story of the ancient Gr. wayfarer. Pound tips his hand still further as the canto concludes:

> Lie quiet Divus. I mean that is Andreas Divus,
> In officina Wecheli, 1538, out of Homer.

Pound's Lat. was stronger than his Gr., and he relied on Andreas Divus's 16th-c. Lat. *Odyssey* in composing his own trans. cum poem. This poem does not open to the unexplored expanses uncovered by Keats's Cortez; nor does it lead him home, with the wandering Odysseus. It draws him instead into the dense, interlingual web of culture and hist. represented in the poem by trans. The romantic Keats converts mediation into immediacy, while the modernist Pound makes a virtue of inescapable mediation. Both poets point, though, to the symbiotic relationship between those two "impossibilities," poetry and poetic trans., that has shaped the Western trad.

■ E. Pound, *ABC of Reading* (1951); E. Pound, "How to Read" [1929], *Literary Essays of Ezra Pound*, ed. T. S. Eliot (1954); R. Lowell, Introduction, *Imitations* (1961); J. Holmes, "Describing Literary Translations: Models and Methods," *Literature and Translation*, ed. J. Holmes, J. Lambert, R. van den Broek (1978); R. Jakobson, "Poetry of Grammar and Grammar of Poetry," *Verbal Art, Verbal Sign, Verbal Time*, ed. R. Jakobson, K. Pomorska, S. Rudy (1985); S. Heaney, "The Impact of Translation," *The Government of the Tongue* (1988); B. Raffel, *The Art of Translating Poetry* (1988); *The Art of Translation: Voices from the Field*, ed. R. Warren (1989); *Translating Poetry: The Double Labyrinth*, ed. D. Weissbort (1989); S. Barańczak, *Ocalone w tłumaczeniu* (1992), and "Saved in Translation . . . : Well, Part of It," *Harvard Review* 1 (1992); *Theories of Translation: An Anthology of Essays from Dryden to Derrida*, ed. R. Schulte and J. Biguenet (1992)—essays by Benjamin, Mandelstam, Nabokov, Valéry, Bonnefoy, Paz; J. Felstiner, *Paul Celan: Poet, Survivor, Jew* (1995); M. Friedberg, *Literary Translation in Russia: A Cultural History* (1997); S. Bassnett, "Transplanting the Seed: Poetry and Translation," *Constructing Cultures: Essays on Literary Translation*, ed. S. Bassnett and A. Lefevre

(1998); S. Heaney and R. Hass, *Sounding Lines: The Art of Translating Poetry* (2000); *Translation Studies Reader*, ed. L. Venuti (2000); D. Davis, "All My Soul Is There: Verse Translation and the Rhetoric of English Poetry," *Yale Review* 90 (2002); C. Cavanagh, "The Art of Losing: Polish Poetry and Translation," *Partisan Review* 70 (2003); *Oxford History of Literary Translation in English, Volume 3: 1660–1790*, ed. S. Gillespie and D. Hopkins, (2005); *Translation: Theory and Practice: A Historical Reader*, ed. D. Weissbort and A. Eysteinson (2006); V. Nabokov, *Verses and Versions: Three Centuries of Russian Poetry*, ed. B. Boyd and S. Shvabrin (2008); *Oxford History of Literary Translation in English, Volume 1: To 1550*, ed. R. Ellis (2008); L. Venuti, *The Translator's Invisibility: A History of Translation* (2008); S. Weber, *Benjamin's Abilities* (2008); P. Robinson, *Poetry and Translation: The Art of the Impossible* (2010); *Oxford History of Literary Translation in English, Volume 2: 1550–1660*, ed. G. Braden, R. Cummings, S. Gillespie (2011); E. M. Young, *The Mediated Muse: Catullan Lyricism and Roman Translation* (2012).

C. CAVANAGH; Y. LORMAN

**TRIBRACH.** In Gr. and Lat. verse, a sequence of three short syllables, almost always a resolved iamb or trochee rather than an independent *foot (see RESOLUTION). The *ictus falls on the second syllable if it replaces an iamb and on the first if it replaces a trochee.
■ Koster; West.

P. S. COSTAS

**TRILOGY.** In Gr. drama, a group of three *tragedies that treat a single myth. At the annual Great Dionysia in Athens, three poets competed, each offering three tragedies plus a satyr play, a *parody of the tragic form that employed a *chorus of satyrs; if this satyr play also deals with the same myth, then the whole is called a *tetralogy*. The origin of the custom requiring three tragedies is unknown; the addition of the satyr play occurred around 500 BCE. Aeschylus is believed to have been the first playwright to connect the plays in one year's offering into a trilogy or tetralogy. In the *Oresteia*, the only extant trilogy, Aeschylus traces the problem of blood-guilt through successive generations of Agamemnon's family; *Seven against Thebes*, the final tragedy in a trilogy on the House of Laius, exhibits a similar concern with a family curse. Yet the outcomes are very different: the Theban trilogy ends in the ruin of the royal house, while *Eumenides*, which concludes the *Oresteia*, dramatizes a resolution of the guilt and the foundation of a new order of justice. The Danaid trilogy, of which the first play, *Suppliant Women*, survives, evidently climaxed in a similar celebration of the sanctity of marriage. Yet this trilogy differs in that its three tragedies dramatized a single, tightly knit event spanning only a few days rather than events separated by many years. The fragmentary evidence of other Aeschylean trilogies suggests that such *unity of plot was not uncommon. After Aeschylus, the trilogy as a genre fell into disuse. Sophocles abandoned it (the composition of his three

Theban plays spanned 40 years, so that one refers to the Oedipus cycle as a trilogy only in a loose sense), and Euripides apparently only once offered three tragedies connected in subject matter: his *Trojan Women* is the third play in a series on the Trojan War. The terms *trilogy* and *tetralogy* were not current in 5th-c. Athens, nor does Aristotle use them; they first appear in Alexandrian commentaries. A mod. sequence of plays consciously based on the ancient model is the trilogy by Eugene O'Neill, *Mourning Becomes Electra*.

It was uncommon in the Ren. to link tragedies, but sequences of two plays were written occasionally, e.g., Christopher Marlowe's *Tamburlaine* (pts. 1 and 2), Shakespeare's *Henry IV* (pts. 1 and 2), and George Chapman's *Bussy D'Ambois* and *The Revenge of Bussy D'Ambois*. Shakespeare's *Henry VI* is in three parts, and he wrote two series of four hist. plays that mod. scholars (but no Elizabethans) sometimes call *tetralogies*. These are the four plays extending from *Henry VI*, pt. 1, to *Richard III* (the first historical "tetralogy" to be written, though the later of the two tetralogies chronologically) and the four plays extending from *Richard II* to *Henry V*. In mod. usage, the terms refer to dramatic or literary works written in three or four parts.

■ G. F. Else, *The Origin and Early Form of Greek Tragedy* (1967); A. Lesky, *Die tragischen Dichtung der Hellenen*, 3d ed. (1972); A. W. Pickard-Cambridge, *The Dramatic Festivals of Athens*, 2d ed. (1989).

V. Pedrick; O. B. Hardison

**TRIMETER** (Gr., "of three measures"). Aristotle (*Poetics* 1449a24, *Rhetoric* 1408b33) regards the iambic trimeter as the most speech-like of Gr. meters (see IAMBIC). It is first employed mixed with dactylic hexameters in the *Margites* ascribed to Homer, though some scholars regard the first line of the "Nestor's cup" inscription, ca. 750–700 BCE, as a trimeter. Despite ancient trad. (e.g., Pseudo-Plutarch, *De musica* 28), Archilochus (fl. 650 BCE) is not its inventor, although he was the first to use the word *iamb* and developed the trimeter as a medium for personal *invective, a practice in which he was followed by Semonides. The Athenian lawgiver Solon used the trimeter for political poetry. The trimeter is the basic dialogue meter of Gr. tragedy, satyr-play, and comedy. It consists of three iambic metra (units of measurement; see METRON) (x represents *anceps [a syllable which, independently of its real metrical value, can be counted as long or short, according to the requirements of the meter]): x – ◡ – | x – ◡ – | x – ◡ –. The penthemimeral *caesura (after the fifth position [second anceps]) is much more frequent than the hephthemimeral (after the seventh position [second breve]); median *diaeresis (coincidence of a word ending with the end of a metrical unit) is permitted occasionally in tragedy, though in Euripides only when accompanied by *elision (omission or blurring of a final unstressed vowel followed by a vowel or mute consonant). *Resolution of a *longum* (long syllable) is permitted at differing rates in all feet but the last. The final element may be short (*brevis in longo*). Most of these departures from the basic iambic pattern

are subject to a complex of finely graded phonological, lexical, and syntactic constraints that form a hierarchy of strictness that decreases from the archaic iambographers (writers of iambs) through early tragedy and later Euripides to satyr-play and finally comedy. The trimeter is subject to a number of *bridges, the strictness of which follows the same generic and stylistic hierarchy.

The Lat. adaptation of the Gr. trimeter is the *senarius, first used by Livius Andronicus. The senarius is a common dialogue meter of early Lat. drama and was frequently used in funerary inscriptions. This version of the trimeter, however, is organized as six feet rather than three metra. The most striking departure from the Gr. trimeter is the permissibility of *spondees in the second and fourth feet. This variation and many differing constraints on word boundaries are motivated by the differing nature of the Lat. stress accent. Iambic-shaped words, even those of the type not regularly subject to *iambic shortening, are severely restricted in the interior of the line, since otherwise they would produce conflict of accent with metrical *ictus. Spondee-shaped (or -ending) words, however, could be permitted in trochaic segments of the verse, since their stress pattern would preserve the iambic rhythm. In contrast to the senarius, the Lat. lyric poets, such as Catullus and Horace, and Seneca in his dramas, follow the pattern of the Gr. trimeter more closely, excluding spondees in even feet, restricting resolution and substitution, and not admitting iambic shortening.

The prosodies of the mod. vernacular followed the Lat. metrical practice of scanning in feet rather than metra, so that the trimeter of the Germanic langs. (incl. Eng.) of the later Middle Ages, Ren., and mod. period is most often a very short line of three binary feet or six syllables—too short to be capable of sustained effects in *narrative or *dramatic verse, but very suitable for song and for humor or *satire. Literary examples include a dozen songs by Thomas Wyatt ("I will and yet I may not," "Me list no more to sing"); Henry Howard, the Earl of Surrey; Ben Jonson's "Dedication of the King's New Cellar" (with feminine rhymes); Elizabeth Barrett Browning's "The Mourning Mother"; a dozen poems by P. B. Shelley (incl. "When the Lamp Is Shattered," and another of them, "To a Skylark," trochaic trimeter with an *alexandrine close), and Theodore Roethke's "My Papa's Waltz" (with occasional extra syllables at the ends of lines). In *French prosody, the line now called the *trimètre is not a trimeter in this sense: it is an alexandrine of 12 syllables divided into three rhythmical phrases and made its appearance only with the advent of *romanticism.

■ Schipper, *History*; F. Lang, *Platen's Trimeter* (1924); J. Descroix, *Le Trimètre iambique* (1931); G. Rosenthal, *Der Trimeter als deutsche Versmasse* (1934); P. W. Harsh, *Iambic Words and Regard for Accent in Plautus* (1949); Maas; D. S. Raven, *Latin Metre* (1965); C. Questa, *Introduzione alla metrica di Plauto* (1967); Allen; S. L. Schein, *The Iambic Trimeter in Aeschylus and Sophocles* (1979); West; A. M. Devine and L. D. Stephens, *Language and Metre* (1984); M. Lotman, "The Ancient Iambic Trimeters: A Disbalanced Harmony," *Formal Approaches to Poetry*, ed. B. E. Dresher and N. Friedberg (2006).

A. M. Devine; L. D. Stephens;
T.V.F. Brogan; E. T. Johnston

**TRIMÈTRE.** In *French prosody, a variation on the *té-tramètre;* an *alexandrine of three *measures rather than four. It is an extension of the rhythmic and expressive range of the tétramètre, not an alternative form, since no poems have been written exclusively in *trimètre.* Examples of trimètre are to be found in the freer alexandrines of the *Pléiade* poets and in the less punctilious genres of the 17th and 18th cs. (*comedy, *fable). It was with the romantics, and with Victor Hugo in particular, that it achieved an ideological status and a subversive intention, hence, another of its names, the *alexandrin romantique* (it is also called the *alexandrin ternaire*). Care should be taken to distinguish between different degrees of trimètre. The romantics and the poets who preceded them maintained the possibility of an accent on the sixth syllable, even though, in the event, it was not accented; in other words, the *caesura still enjoyed a spectral existence despite being effaced by the greater syntactic and rhythmic claims of ternary structure; the romantic trimètre is thus quite easy to envisage as a tétramètre with *enjambment at the caesura, e.g., in Hugo: "Nous demandons, vivants // douteux qu'un linceul couvre" (4-4-4). The romantic trimètre usually has this regular 4-4-4 pattern, though it may occasionally explore other combinations, e.g., 3-5-4. The Parnassians and symbolists (see PARNASSIANISM, SYMBOLISM) developed extremer forms of the trimètre, by frequently erasing the caesura completely, e.g., in Théodore de Banville: "Où je filais pensivement la blanche laine" (4-4-4), and by multiplying asymmetrical combinations of measures, e.g., in Stéphane Mallarmé: "Une ruine, par mille écumes bénie" (4-5-3). In these more radical forms, the trimètre became a central feature of *vers libéré.*

■ Kastner; G. Aae, *Le Trimètre de Victor Hugo* (1909); J. Mazaleyrat, "Élan verbal et rythme ternaire dans l'alexandrin,"*Français Moderne* 40 (1972); Elwert; M. Grimaud, "Trimètre et rôle poétique de la cesure chez Victor Hugo," *RR* 70 (1979); Scott; Mazaleyrat.

C. Scott

**TRIOLET.** A Fr. fixed form with eight lines, two rhymes, and two *refrain lines, patterned *ABaAabAB.* It may be split into two *quatrains or employed as a *stanza form, although poems of one *strophe are typical. Line length and meter are not fixed.

In the 13th c., it was not considered a poetic form unto itself, but merely a common variant of the *rondel; today, it is considered the *Urform* of the entire *rondeau family. Descended from popular round dance (*ronde*) songs, not the courtly *trouvère tradition, it was sung to two musical strains, A and B, that matched its poetic structure. Examples can be found in the *Cléomades* by Adenez le Roi, "King of the Minstrels." Lyric poets incl. Guillaume d'Amiens, Adam

de la Halle, and Jean Froissart produced poems in the form, usually on the subject of love. In his 1392 *L'Art de dictier,* Eustache Deschamps tagged the form the *rondel sangle* or "simple rondel."

The name *triolet* emerged in the 15th c. While Paul Marcotte links the term to the three "A" lines and Helen Cohen to three-part song, Leo Spitzer suggests that it may be a corruption of *kyrie eleison,* reflecting the Christian religious lyrics that had been put to many of the old refrain songs. Jean Regnier; Octavien de Saint-Gelais; and Clotilde de Surville, a woman, wrote 15th-c. specimens.

The *Pléiade* poets succeeded in driving the triolet and other med. poetic genres out of fashion during the last half of the 16th c. But with the Fronde uprisings of the 17th c., the triolet was put to political use. Both sides generated "attack triolets," which could be sung to popular tunes. Marc-Antoine Girard de Saint-Amant, produced a collection of *Nobles Triolets.* Eng. poet Patrick Carey, studying for a time in France, encountered the form and harnessed it for religious poems.

Although Alexis Piron in France and several Ger. poets produced triolets during the years that the *heroic couplet, then romantic nonce-forms, were ascendant, the triolet fell into dormancy until being revived by Fr. poet Théodore de Banville in the 1840s. Arthur Rimbaud, Stéphane Mallarmé, Maurice Rollinat, and Alphonse Daudet were among 19th-c. Fr. poets using the form, usually as a stanza form and with feminine "b" rhymes. Banville's fixed-forms revival spread to England in the 1870s, with Robert Bridges being the first to publish a triolet. *Vers de société* poets such as Austin Dobson and Edmund Gosse chose to foreground the triolet's artifice in their examples, reflecting Gosse's view of the form as a "tiny trill of epigrammatic melody, turning so simply on its own innocent axis." But Thomas Hardy achieved dramatic intensity within its confines, although G. M. Hopkins was less successful in using it to "gloss" quoted lines of text. In America, writers incl. H. C. Bunner and Clinton Scollard produced triolets.

By the mid-20th c., the triolet seemed relegated to *Saturday Evening Post* *light verse or the juvenilia of poets such as Dylan Thomas and Sylvia Plath. But with the rise of *New Formalism, new life was breathed into the eight-line pattern once again. Sandra McPherson, Wendy Cope, and A. E. Stallings have produced memorable poems in the form, while Marilyn Nelson's "Triolets for Triolet" is an eight-poem sequence that approaches the range of *epic.

■ T. de Banville, *Petit traité de poésie française* (1872); E. Gosse, "A Plea for Certain Exotic Forms of Verse," *Cornhill Magazine* 36 (1877); G. White, *Ballades and Rondeaus* (1887); Kastner; P. C. Standing, "Triolets and Their Makers," *The English Illustrated Magazine* 32 (1904/05); H. L. Cohen, *Lyric Forms from France* (1922); P. Champion, *Histoire poétique du XV siècle,* 2 vols. (1923); M. Françon, "La pratique et la théorie du rondeau et du rondel chez Théodore de Banville," *MLN* 52 (1937); L. Spitzer, "Triolet," *RR* 39 (1948);

J. M. Cocking, "The 'Invention' of the Rondel," *FS* 5 (1951); P. J. Marcotte, "An Introduction to the Triolet," *Inscape* 5 (1966); A. Thomas, "G. M. Hopkins: An Unpublished Triolet," *MLR* 61 (1966); P. J. Marcotte, "A Victorian Trio of Triolet Turners" and "More Late-Victorian Triolet Makers," *Inscape* 6 (1968); C. Scott, "The 19th-Century Triolet: French and English," *OL* 35 (1980); Morier; K. West, "Triolet: Trippingly on the Tongue," Finch and Varnes.

A. PREMINGER; C. SCOTT; J. KANE

**TRIPLE RHYME.** Three consecutive syllables at the end of two or more lines that rhyme. Rhyming more than two syllables in sequence is difficult in Eng., hence relatively rare. In Eng. Ren. verse, double and triple rhymes are more common than is usually supposed, however. These are almost always the result of deliberate imitation of It. models; since *sdrucciolo* (proparoxytonic) endings on words are more frequent in It. than in the other Romance langs. (see VERSO SDRUCCIOLO), compound rhymes of two, three, or more syllables are an important component of It. versification. Philip Sidney mentions triple rhyme in the *Defence of Poesy* and has virtuoso examples of it in the *Arcadia*. Since Lord Byron (*Don Juan, Beppo*, etc.), however, most examples have been comic and deliberately exhibitionist: thus, Byron has "gymnastical / ecclesiastical" (*Beppo*) and "intellectual / hen-peck'd you all" (virtually quadruple, if *-te-* in *intellectual* is elided; cf. *meticulous / ridiculous*). In the 20th c., good examples are to be found in Ogden Nash.

In the most common form of triple rhyme, only the first syllable of the three is stressed, the other two being extrametrical—e.g., *glaringly / sparingly*. The word shape is *dactylic, which is sometimes used as an alternate term for triple rhyme, as is *double feminine*. But all three syllables might be metrical if the third syllable bears secondary stress (*cretic word shape) and falls under the final *ictus in the line. Since in Eng. it is more difficult to rhyme two polysyllabic words than a phrase of monosyllables, most triple rhymes (e.g., the second Byron example) are mosaic—i.e., several short words rhyming with one long one (see MOSAIC RHYME). Triple rhyme is to be distinguished from the *tercet, a rhymed stanza of three lines, and the *triplet, a run of three rhymes in couplet verse.

*See* RHYME.

T.V.F. BROGAN

**TRIPLET** (Ger. *Dreireim*). In Eng. Restoration and 18th-c. verse written in *heroic couplets, a run of three lines rhymed together. Often these are marked visually as well by a brace in the margin. John Dryden says that he employs them "frequently" because they "bound the sense"; he makes the third line an *alexandrine ("Dedication to the *Aeneis*"). Triplets are familiar in Dryden and (less so) in Alexander Pope; John Donne wrote most of his *verse epistles in monorhymed iambic triplets. Schipper shows other examples in the *fourteeners and *pentameters of George Chapman and Robert Browning. John Keats follows Dryden for their use in "Lamia."

■ Schipper; C. A. Balliet, "The History and Rhetoric of the Triplet," *PMLA* 80 (1965).

T.V.F. BROGAN

**TROBAIRITZ.** Feminine form of *troubador*, found in a 13th-c. grammar and the Occitan romance *Flamenca*. Twenty named trobairitz were active between 1170 and 1260, a period of relative power for aristocratic women in Occitan society. They composed songs in the style of the *troubadours, whose already well-established poetic system they manipulated with the same inventive shifts, reversals, repetitions, and variations as male poets, though in general with less virtuosic formal play in rhyme schemes. The *vidas and *razos included in some *chansonniers* (song mss.) name 13 trobairitz, five with short biographies. Tibors, Comtessa de Dia, Azalais de Porcairagues, Castelloza, and Lombarda are represented with the same qualities as their male counterparts: they are noble, agreeable, educated, courteous, and knowledgeable in composing songs. Their poems as well as documented historical evidence show that trobairitz participated fully in the social network of troubadour song as patrons and friends, subjects as well as objects of love, sisters, daughters, and wives of troubadours. Maria de Ventadorn, the wife of Eble V (the grandson of Eble III, patron and rival of Bernart de Ventadorn), became the patron of many troubadours. Named in numerous poems, she initiated a *tenso with Gui d'Ussel, who according to a razo sang his love for her. Formal analysis shows the Comtessa de Dia (possibly Beatrice, wife of William II of Poitiers) in poetic correspondence with Raimbaut d'Aurenga, Bernart de Ventadorn, and Azalais, who sent a *planh for Raimbaut to Ermengarde of Narbonne.

Though small, this remarkable repertoire of some 40 songs brings onstage a rare group of med. women poets (cf. Ar. women poets of Al-Andalus and women *trouvères of northern France). Trobairitz poems are scarce in northern mss., somewhat better represented in important Occitan collections, and most numerous in Catalan and It. chansonniers, where they are sometimes gathered together. The corpus remains difficult to determine exactly, given questionable attributions, unnamed poets, and female speakers invented by male poets. Among mod. scholars, disagreements abound over whether anonymous or even certain named poets represent fictions or refer to real women.

The trobairitz composed mostly *cansos and tensos but also participated in other lyric genres: *sirventes, *salut d'amor* (love letter), *planh*, *alba, and *balada. Only Comtessa de Dia (four cansos, incl. the single extant melody) and Castelloza (three or four cansos) are assigned more than one song; all the others have one each (the typical troubadour oeuvre is three to four poems).

The voices of trobairitz are most distinctive in their choice and mixing of different personae. The self-effacing Castelloza performs a double reversal of male/

female roles by taking for herself the feminized stance of poet-lover as humble servant, while Comtessa de Dia retains the pride typically invested in the troubadour's lady, now combined with the verbal power of the troubadour's poetic first person and modulated through the *persona of a sensuous, desiring woman conventional to women's song. Trobairitz who engage in dialogue about love with male poets, like Guilielma de Rosers and Lombarda, playfully demonstrate their wit and innuendo; others keep the conversation on the distaff side to exchange views on more unexpected topics (childbirth and sagging breasts or the deprivations of sumptuary laws). All the trobairitz call our attention to what may happen when the silent lady of the troubadours begins to speak for herself within the conventionalized world of troubadour lyric.

*See* OCCITAN POETRY, DIVAN.

■ **Anthologies**: *Biographies des troubadours*, ed. J. Boutière and A. H. Schutz (1973); *Trobairitz*, ed. A. Rieger (1991); *Chants d'amour des femmes-troubadours*, ed. P. Bec (1995); *Songs of the Women Troubadours*, ed. M. Bruckner et al. (2000).
■ **Criticism**: P. Bec, "'Trobairitz' et chansons de femme: Contribution à la connaissance du lyrisme féminin au moyen âge," *Cahiers de Civilisation Médiévale* 22 (1979); T. Garulo, *Dīwān de las poetisas de Al-Andalus* (1986); *The Voice of the Trobairitz*, ed. W. D. Paden (1989); M. Bruckner, "Fictions of the Female Voice: The Women Troubadours," *Speculum* 67 (1992); K. Gravdal, "Metaphor, Metonymy, and the Medieval Women Trobairitz," *RR* 83 (1992); M.-A. Bossy and N. Jones, "Gender and Compilational Patterns in Troubadour Lyric: The Case of Manuscript *N*," *French Forum* 21 (1996); E. W. Poe, "*Cantairitz e trobairitz*: A Forgotten Attestation of Old Provençal Trobairitz," *Romanische Forschungen* 114 (2002).

M. T. BRUCKNER

**TROBAR CLUS, TROBAR LEU.** Controversy between *troubadours defending the *trobar clus* (enclosed, hermetic poetry) and those extolling the *trobar leu* (light or easy poetry) is found ca. 1160–1210, with later echoes, and seems to have centered on some poets' desire to write for a select audience of connoisseurs. The clus manner is characteristically allusive, oblique, and recherché in vocabulary and rhymes (e.g., Raimbaut d'Orange), though similar features occur in earlier troubadours who make no claim to be clus (e.g., Marcabru). Though the trobar leu ultimately prevailed, the trobar clus influenced a manner often called *trobar ric* (rich, i.e., elaborate poetry) involving verbal and metrical acrobatics without much of the profundity of thought claimed by clus poets. All three categories concerned poetic aims rather than specific stylistic traits and were never mutually exclusive: Guiraut de Bornelh, notably, claimed to excel in trobar clus and trobar leu alike. The terminology itself was far from fixed: *trobar car* (dear) and *trobar prim* (delicate, subtle) seem to refer to much the same manner as *trobar ric*, while *trobar plan* (smooth) is a synonym of *trobar leu*.

*See* OCCITAN POETRY.

■ U. Mölk, *Trobar clus, trobar leu* (1968); A. Roncaglia, "Trobar clus: discussione aperta," *Cultura Neolatina* 29 (1969); L. M. Paterson, *Troubadours and Eloquence* (1975); M. A. Bossy, "The *trobar clus* of Raimbaut Aurenga, Giraut de Bornelh and Arnaut Daniel," *Mediaevalia* 19 (1996).

J. H. MARSHALL

**TROCHAIC** (Gr., *trochee*, *choree*, respectively, "running," "belonging to the dance"). A term used for both metrical units and whole *meters having the rhythm "marked–unmarked" in series. In the mod. accentual meters, a *trochee* is a *foot comprising a stressed syllable followed by an unstressed; in the quantitative meters of the cl. langs., however, the elements were long and short. In Lat., the trochaic foot comprised one long syllable followed by one short, whereas in Gr., the unit was the trochaic *metron, – ᴗ – x (x denotes *anceps). Trochaic measures were used in archaic Gr. poetry at least from the time of Archilochus; and in Gr. *tragedy and *comedy, they appear in both choral lyric and spoken dialogue. In Lat. comedy, the trochaic seems to have lent itself esp. well to rapid movement and dancing; the most common meter of Plautus and Terence is the trochaic tetrameter catalectic or *septenarius. This is the meter also used by Caesar's legions for marching songs (Beare). In all these registers, it seems to maintain close ties with popular speech and popular verse genres.

In mod. verse, trochaic meter used for entire poems is far less common than *iambic and does not appear until the Ren.: the first clearly accentual trochaics in Eng. are by Philip Sidney (*Certain Sonnets* 7, 26, 27), followed by Nicholas Breton. From Sidney's example, they became more popular in the 1590s, though still mainly in *tetrameters. King Lear's "Never, never, never, never, never" is an exception meant to reaffirm the iambic rule. On the other hand, trochaic meters are quite common in many *songs and *chants; in idioms, formulaic expressions, *proverbs, *riddles, slogans, *jingles, and cheers; and in much popular and folk verse. In short, trochaic verse is rare in literary poetry but common in popular. The most obvious explanation for this difference would be that most of these forms have some close relation to song. They are either sung to music, recited in a singsong chant, or originally derived from song. In music, trochaic rhythm is structural since a stress begins every bar. It is presumed that the use of trochaic meters for text simplifies the fitting of the words to music.

Some metrists (e.g., Boris Tomashevsky, V. E. Xolsevnikov) have denied that there is any difference between iambic and trochaic meters except for the first syllable (see ANACRUSIS). But, in fact, poets make it very clear that they perceive a radical distinction between the two meters. Whole poems in trochaic meter are relatively rare in any mod. verse trad. (Saintsbury, 3.529; Gasparov 1974), and trochaic meter is clearly associated with only certain kinds of genres, subjects, and rhythmic movements. The distribution of line forms is also quite different; trochaic pentameter is almost unheard of, while trochaic tetrameters are as common as iambic, if not more so. Poems where metrical code switching between iambic and trochaic is systematic are rare (in Marina Tsvetaeva in Rus.; in the verse known as "8s and 7s" in Eng.). And internal line dynamics differ radically: first-foot stress reversals are four times more common in iambic verse (12%) than in trochaic (3%) in Eng. and 30 times more common in Rus. There is a widespread perception among poets and prosodists that trochaic meters are in some way more rigid, more brittle, "more difficult to maintain" (Hascall) than iambic ones.

In Eng., there is a mixed iambo-trochaic form known as "8s and 7s," instanced most famously in John Milton's "L'Allegro" and "Il Penseroso," which seems to mix iambic and trochaic lines seamlessly or else to mix normal iambic lines with *acephalous ones that only *seem* to be trochaic (see RISING AND FALLING RHYTHM). This problem points up the importance of distinguishing between trochaic *meters* and trochaic *rhythms* in iambic meters. Traditional Eng. metrics would say that an iambic pentameter line such as "And quickly jumping backward, raised his shield," although in iambic meter, has a "falling rhythm" that is the result of trochaic word shapes. While meter organizes lang. on the phonological level, it nevertheless affects, and is affected by, morphology as well.

There is some evidence that trochaic rhythms predominate in certain speech contexts, esp. children's speech, and that trochaic rhythms are easier both to produce and to perceive. But it is disputed whether Eng. as a lang. is essentially iambic or trochaic in character. Comprehensive data on word shapes in the lexicon (i.e., how many are monosyllabic, disyllabic iambic, disyllabic trochaic, trisyllabic, polysyllabic) and the frequencies of these words in ordinary speech versus poetry (many words in the dictionary will never appear in poetry), along with comparable data on the shapes of Eng. phrases and their frequencies, are difficult to come by; even for one lang. Gil makes a global distinction between iambic and trochaic langs.: iambic "are characterized by subject-verb-object (SVO) word order, simple syllable structures, high consonant-vowel ratios, and the absence of phonemic tones," while trochaic have SOV, complex syllable structures, low C-V ratios, and phonemic tone.

Several efforts have been made to analyze the frequency of word types both in iambic versus trochaic verse and in these as set against the norm of the lang. to try to discover significant statistical deviations (e.g., Jones; Tarlinskaja, following Gasparov). Some striking statistics have emerged. But the very idea of a ling. "norm" against which poetic lang. "deviates" is an approach now viewed as suspect. Lexical selection is not the only or even perhaps the central issue; certainly, poets think in terms of significant words, but more generally these must be woven into the fabric in syntactically predetermined ways. Analyzing word-shape rhythms in relation to line rhythms misses the crucial point that lines are not formed by stringing words together but, rather, mainly by putting phrases together: most words come in packaged phrasal containers of relatively fixed rhythmic shape—prepositional phrases, noun phrases, compound verbs. And once a poet selects a word in a line, the range of relevant words for that or even following lines is constrained by the chosen semantic field. It is precisely the power of iambic verse, e.g., that an iambic line may comprise two monosyllables and four trochaic words. Word shapes are the elements, and, certainly, these vary in significant ways; but it is the stitching that counts.

*See* BINARY AND TERNARY, PYRRHIC, SENARIUS, SPONDEE.

■ Schipper 2.375–98; W. Brown, *Time in English Verse Rhythm* (1908); H. Woodrow, *A Quantitative Study of Rhythm* (1909); Schipper, *History*, chs. 13, 14.2; J.E.W. Wallin, "Experimental Studies of Rhythm and Time," *Psychology Review* 18 (1911), 19 (1912); J. W. White, *The Verse of Greek Comedy* (1912); Wilamowitz, pt. 2, ch. 5; K. Taranovski, *Ruski dvodelni ritmovi* (1953); P. Fraisse, *Les Structures rythmiques* (1956); Beare; Norberg, 73 ff.; C. L. Drage, "Trochaic Metres in Early Russian Syllabo-Tonic Poetry," *Slavonic and Eastern European Review* 38 (1960); Saintsbury, *Prosody*; P. Fraisse, *The Psychology of Time*, trans. J. Leith (1963); Koster, ch. 6; C. Questa, *Introduzione alla metrica di Plauto* (1967); Dale; G. Faure, *Les Éléments du rythme poétique en anglaise moderne* (1970); D. L. Hascall, "Trochaic Meter," *CE* 33 (1971); P. Fraisse, *Psychologie du rythme* (1974); M. L. Gasparov, *Sovremennyj russkij stix* (1974); R. P. Newton, "Trochaic and Iambic," *Lang&S* 8 (1975); Tarlinskaja; D. Laferrière, "Iambic versus Trochaic: The Case of Russian," *International Review of Slavic Linguistics* 4 (1979); R. G. Jones, "Linguistic and Metrical Constraints in Verse," *Linguistic and Literary Studies in Honor of A. A. Hill*, ed. M. ali Jazayery et al., v. 4 (1979); Halporn et al.; Snell; West; D. Gil, "A Prosodic Typology of Language," *Folia Linguistica* 20 (1986); G. T. Wright, *Shakespeare's Metrical Art* (1988), ch. 13; B. Bjorklund, "Iambic and Trochaic Verse," *Rhythm and Meter*, ed. P. Kiparsky and G. Youmans (1989); *CHCL*, v.1.5; M. L. Gasparov, "The Semantic Halo of the Russian Trochaic Pentameter: Thirty Years of the Problem," *Elementa* 2 (1996); D. Zec, "The Prosodic Word as a Unit in Poetic Meter," *The Nature of the Word*, ed. K. Hanson and S. Inkelas (2009).

T.V.F. BROGAN

**TROPE** (Gr., "turn"). In its most restricted definition, a *trope* is a figure of speech that uses a word or phrase in a sense other than what is proper to it. Cl. rhetoricians describe this change in meaning as a movement: the artful deviation of a word from its ordinary signification, a deviation that usually involves the substitution of one word or concept for another. As devices of rhetorical *style, tropes give lang. what Aristotle calls a "foreign air" (*xénos*), using strange words to refer to familiar concepts or assigning novel meaning to ordinary words (*Rhetoric*). Quintilian distinguishes tropes from other figures of speech by defining them as stylistic deviations that affect only a word or a small group of words (*Institutio oratoria*). According to this understanding, tropes such as "the Lord is my shepherd" (*metaphor), "from the cradle to the grave" (*metonymy), and "the face that launched a thousand ships" (*synecdoche) operate by changing the signification of the words "shepherd," "cradle," "grave," and "face." Tropes allow lang. to mean *more* or *something other*, leading to Richards's position that a metaphor allows two or more ideas to be carried by a single word or expression (the vehicle), its meaning (the tenor) resulting from their "interaction" on the basis of a relation (the ground).

In order to define *trope* as a figure of speech, cl. rhet. naturalizes ordinary locutions as the basic norms of lang., as when Quintilian identifies *trope* as "language transferred from its natural and principal meaning to another for the sake of embellishment" (*Institutio oratoria*). This depiction of *figuration as movement from a fixed location recurs in definitions of *trope* from antiquity forward, as tropes "transport" words from their normal, familiar habitat. As Barthes observes, the distinction between proper and figured lang. frequently becomes expressed as a distinction between the native and the foreign or the normal and the strange. Definitions of *trope* are thus themselves inescapably metaphorical, that is, relying on an idea of "home" (*oikos*) to theorize the ling. transports of figures of speech, as when César Chesneau Dumarsais defines *metaphor* as occupying a "borrowed home" (*Traité des Tropes*, 1730).

The cl. definition of *trope* as deviation from a ling. norm (variously defined as the ordinary, proper, or familiar) has repeatedly been challenged in the mod. era, first by romantic critics (Johann Georg Hamann, Jean-Jacques Rousseau, and Friedrich Nietzsche), and still more aggressively by linguistically oriented literary theorists (Jakobson, Barthes, Genette, Todorov, Derrida, de Man). While cl. rhet. presumes the existence of two langs., one proper and one figured, mod. literary theory identifies *trope* as a fundamental structure of a single ling. system, rather than an exception or deviation from a prior norm. From the romantic point of view, tropes such as metaphor comprise our most basic mechanisms of thought and expression: we have no way of understanding "the Lord" except through the application of metaphors such as "shepherd." From a deconstructive perspective, "the Lord" does not exist prior to the "shepherd" metaphor; rather, the trope confers an illusory presence on what it signifies (its signified). The argument that trope is *the* principle of thought and verbal organization leads to the claim that lit. is a privileged vehicle for access to the problems that lang. poses for understanding (de Man).

*See* CATACHRESIS, LINGUISTICS AND POETICS, ORNAMENT, RHETORIC AND POETRY, SCHEME, TENOR AND VEHICLE.

■ I. A. Richards, *The Philosophy of Rhetoric* (1936); K. Burke, "Four Master Tropes," *A Grammar of Motives* (1945); Jakobson and Halle, "Two Aspects of Language and Two Types of Aphasic Disturbances"; E. Auerbach, "Figura," trans. R. Manheim, *Scenes from the Drama of European Literature* (1959); J. L. Austin, "The Meaning of a Word," *Philosophical Papers* (1961); O. Ducrot and T. Todorov, *Encyclopedic Dictionary of the Sciences of Language*, trans. C. Porter (1979); G. Genette, *Figures of Literary Discourse*, trans. A. Sheridan, 3 v. (1981); P. Ricoeur, *The Rule of Metaphor*, trans. R. Czerny et al. (1981); P. de Man, "The Rhetoric of Temporality," "The Rhetoric of Blindness," *Blindness and Insight*; and "Anthropomorphism and Trope in the Lyric," *The Rhetoric of Romanticism* (1984); and "Hypogram and Inscription" and "The Resistance to Theory," *The Resistance to Theory* (1986); J. Derrida, "White Mythology," *Margins of Philosophy*, trans. A. Bass (1986); Vickers, *Defence*; R. Barthes, "The Old Rhetoric," *The Semiotic Challenge*, trans. R. Howard (1988); P. Parker, "Metaphor and Catachresis," *The Ends of Rhetoric*, ed. J. Bender and D. Wellbery (1990); Lanham; *Tropical Truth(s): The Epistemology of Metaphor and Other Tropes*, ed. A. Burkhardt and B. Nerlich (2010).

T. BAHTI; J. C. MANN

**TROUBADOUR.** Med. Occitan lyric poet. The term expresses the agent of the verb *trobar* (to find, invent, compose verse); the etymon of *trobar* may have been hypothetical med. Lat. *tropare* (to compose a trope, a liturgical embellishment, Gr. *tropos*) or hypothetical Sp. Arabic *trob* (song) from cl. Ar. *ṭarab* (to sing) or Lat. *turbare* (to disturb, stir up). These proposed etyma correspond to theories of the origin of *courtly love in med. Lat., Ar., or cl. Lat.

Extant troubadour production dates from ca. 1100 to ca. 1300, beginning with William IX, Duke of Aquitaine and Count of Poitiers (1071–1126) alternately bawdy and courtly, and continuing with Jaufré Rudel (fl. 1125–48), whose distant love tantalizingly blends secular and religious qualities; the biting moralist Marcabru (fl. 1130–49); the love poet Bernart de Ventadorn (fl. 1147–70); the witty Peire Vidal (fl. 1183–1204); the political satirist and war poet Bertran de Born (ca. 1150–1215); and the jolly, worldly Monk of Montaudon (fl. 1193–1210). Composition in a difficult style or *trobar clus* is associated with the names of Peire d'Alvernhe (fl. 1149–68), Raimbaut d'Aurenga (ca. 1144–1173), and Arnaut Daniel (fl. 1180–95); Giraut de Bornelh (fl. 1162–99), "the master of the troubadours," practiced both *trobar clus* and *trobar leu*, or the easy style. In the early 13th c. appear the *trobairitz or women troubadours, incl. the moody Castelloza and the vivacious Comtessa de Dia, who left several songs apiece. Peire Cardenal (fl. 1205–72) followed the satirical trad. of Marcabru and Bertran de Born but was more concerned with religious issues in the period of the Albigensian Crusade; late in the century, Guiraut Riquier (fl. 1254–92) lamented that he was among the last of the troubadours. In the 14th to 15th cs., Occitan poetry became an academic prolongation of the earlier trad.; those who wrote it are not called troubadours but poets. We know some 360 troubadours by name.

Though we have the melodies of only one-tenth of the extant troubadour poems, it is generally assumed that most of them were set to music. The troubadour wrote both text and melody, which were performed by the *joglar* (see JONGLEUR), who served as the messenger for a particular troubadour by singing his song before its addressee. We have circumstantial information about 101 individual troubadours in the prose *vidas* and *razos* that accompany the poems in some mss. This information is reliable in objective matters, such as the troubadour's place of birth, place of death, and social class, but not in regard to amorous adventures, which were largely invented by the prose writers on the basis of what they read in the poems. The outstanding example of such imaginative biography is the vida of Jaufré Rudel, which has him perish of love in the arms of his beloved, the countess of Tripoli.

The troubadours exerted influence on the Fr. *trouvères* as early as the 12th c. and in the 13th c. on poets writing in Galicia and in Ger. (see MINNESANG). In Italy, their influence was felt in the *Sicilian school presided over by Frederick II Hohenstaufen and then by Dante and his friends, who created the *Dolce stil nuovo*. Through Petrarch, who acknowledged his debt to them, they affected the develop. of poetry of the Ren. and beyond.

See OCCITAN POETRY, SONGBOOK.

■ M. R. Menocal, "The Etymology of Old Provençal *trobar, trobador*: A Return to the 'Third Solution,'" *RPh* 36 (1982); J.-C. Huchet, *L'amour discourtois* (1987); P. Bec, *Écrits sur les troubadours et la lyrique médiévale* (1992); M. L. Meneghetti, *Il pubblico dei trovatori* (1992); *Handbook of the Troubadours,* ed. F.R.P. Akehurst and J. Davis (1995); *Songs of the Troubadours and Trouvères,* ed. S. N. Rosenberg et al. (1998); *Troubadours,* ed. S. Gaunt and S. Kay (1999); *Troubadour Poems from the South of France,* trans. W. D. Paden and F. F. Paden (2007).

W. D. PADEN

**TROUVÈRE.** Med. lyric poet of northern France. The term corresponds to Occitan (of southern France) *troubadour*; it is commonly applied to northern Fr. lyric poets who composed in the troubadour manner, but not to distinctively Fr. lyric poets such as Rutebeuf or the authors of OF narrative. We know over 300 troubadours by name and over 200 *trouvères*. Troubadour lyrics were written ca. 1100–1300 and waned with the decline of the Occitan lang.; extant trouvère production began somewhat later, ca. 1190, and continued until ca. 1300, when Fr. poetry evolved into new forms. The lyric corpus in the two langs. is comparable in size (about 2,500 songs); the trouvères cultivated esp. the genres of the courtly *chanson* or love song, religious verse, and the *pastourelle*, while avoiding the *sirventes* or satire. Genres in the popular style, better preserved in Fr. than in Occitan, include the *mal mariée*, the *chanson de toile*, and dance songs such as the *rondet de carole*, the *balete*, and the *estampie* (see ESTAMPIDA). We have the melodies for only one-tenth of troubadour poems, but for three-quarters of those of the trouvères.

See FRANCE, POETRY OF; OCCITAN POETRY.

■ **Anthologies:** *The Medieval Lyric*, ed. M. Switten et al., 3 v. (1987–88); *The Anglo-Norman Lyric*, ed. D. L. Jeffrey and B. J. Levy (1990); *Chansons des trouvères*, ed. S. N. Rosenberg (1995); *'Prions en chantant': Devotional Songs of the Trouvères*, ed. M. J. Epstein (1997); *Songs of the Women Trouvères*, ed. E. Doss-Quinby et al. (2001).

■ **Bibliographies:** H. Spanke, *G. Raynauds Bibliographie des altfranzösischen Liedes neu bearbeitet und ergänzt* (1955); N.H.J. van den Boogaard, *Rondeaux et refrains du XIIe siècle au début du XIVe* (1969); R. W. Linker, *Bibliography of Old French Lyrics* (1979); E. Doss-Quinby, *The Lyrics of the Trouvères: A Research Guide (1970–1990)* (1994); M. L. Switten, *Music and Poetry in the Middle Ages: A Guide to Research on French and Occitan Song, 1100–1400* (1995).

■ **Criticism and History:** J. Frappier, *La Poésie lyrique française aux XIIe et XIIIe siècles* (1954); R. Dragonetti, *La Technique poétique des trouvères dans la chanson courtoise* (1960); R. Guiette, *D'une poésie formelle en France au moyen âge* (1972); P. Zumthor, *Essai de poétique médiévale* (1972); Bec—study with texts; W. Pfeffer, "Constant Sorrow: Emotions and the Women Trouvères," *The Representation of Women's Emotions in Medieval and Early Modern Culture,* ed. L. Perfetti (2005); M. O'Neill, *Courtly Love Songs of Medieval France* (2006); M. G. Grossel, "'J'ai trové qui m'amera': Chansons de femmes et 'troveresses' dans la lyrique d'oïl," *Chançon legiere a chanter,* ed. K. Fresco and W. Pfeffer (2007); H. Dell, *Desire by Gender and Genre in Trouvère Song* (2008).

■ **Versification and Music:** U. Mölk and F. Wolfzettel, *Répertoire métrique de la poésie lyrique française des origines à 1350* (1972); H. van der Werf, *The Chansons of the Troubadours and Trouvères* (1972); J. Stevens, *Words and Music in the Middle Ages* (1986); C. Page, *The Owl and the Nightingale: Musical Life and Ideas in France, 1100–1300* (1989).

W. D. PADEN

**TUMBLING VERSE.** A phrase used by King James VI of Scotland in his *Reulis and Cautelis* (1584) for making Scottish verse to characterize lines that in mod. terminology we would say are loosely anapestic or else in falling rhythm and four-stress *accentual verse. James distinguishes "tumbling" verse from "flowing" (text in Smith, 1.218–19, 223, 407n); the latter clearly means "regular," so the former may simply mean *doggerel, i.e., irregular, rough. He also terms it "rouncefallis" (*OED,* "rouncival") and associates it with *flyting. In Eng. poetry, the example of tumbling verse usually pointed to is Thomas Tusser's very popular *Five Hundred Points of Good Husbandry* (1557 et seq.), which is in *anapests and other meters. Schipper thought that tumbling verse was the descendant of the ME alliterative line, a view now abandoned. Ker relates it to the four-stress lines of popular song, *ballad meter, and Sp. *arte mayor. Tumbling verse* seems more likely crude terminology than any distinct species of verse.

■ Schipper, 2.223–25; Smith; Schipper, *History*, 89–90; Saintsbury, *Prosody*, 1.326–28, 408; W. P. Ker, *Form and Style in Poetry* (1928); C. S. Lewis, *English Literature in the Sixteenth Century, Excluding Drama* (1954)—discusses Tusser; D. Parkinson, "Alexander Montgomerie, James VI, and 'Tumbling Verse,'" *Loyal Letters*, ed. L.A.J.R. Houwen and A. A. MacDonald (1994).

T.V.F. Brogan

## TURKIC POETRY

I. Oral Poets in Central Asian Nomadic Turkic Society
II. Pre-Islamic Poetry
III. Islamic Poetry
IV. The Modern Period

**I. Oral Poets in Central Asian Nomadic Turkic Society.** The term *Central Asia* is here understood as the region of the newly independent Turkic republics of Kazakhstan, Kyrgyzstan, Uzbekistan, and Turkmenistan. After Russia had concluded its conquest of the region (1864–89), it became known as Rus. Turkistan, which also included Tajikistan. Under Soviet rule (1917–91), the territory was referred to as Kazakhstan and Central Asia. The following is an overview of common devels. in Kazakh, Kyrgyz, Uzbek, and Turkmen poetry and prosody.

The Kazakhs, Kyrgyz, Turkmens, and the so-called Kypchak Uzbeks led a nomadic or seminomadic life until the beginning of the 1930s, when Soviet policies forced them to become sedentary. Nomads in general honored oral poets called *aqïn, jïrchï/ïrchï* (Kaz., Kyr.), *jïrau* (Kaz.), *bagshï/baxshi* (Trkm., Uzb.), or *dostonchi, shoir* (Uzb.) who were the historians of their tribes and tribal groups, accompanying themselves on the *dombïra* (Kaz.) or the *dutar/dutor* (Trkm., Uzb.), a two-stringed lute, or the *qobïz/komuz* (Kaz., Kyr.), *qopuz* (Trkm.), a two- or three-stringed fiddle. These poets sang heroic and romantic-lyrical epic songs and competed in singing contests of improvised poetry in which women too participated.

The oral poets enjoyed a high status in Turkic nomadic society. Well-known Kazakh aqïn/jïrau would serve as advisors to khans, as, e.g., Bûxar jïrau (ca. 1693–1787) served Khan Ablay (1711–81), himself a gifted singer and *küychi* (composer of melodies). Kazakh singer/poets were also known as leaders of the many uprisings the Kazakhs staged against the Rus. conquerors. Famous is the aqïn Maxambet Ütemisûlï (1804–46), who together with his friend Isatay Taymanûlï led an uprising in 1837–38. He composed several fiery songs against some of the khans who had collaborated with the Russians. In one of them, he sings,

Xan emessiñ—qasqïrsïñ.
Qara albastï basqïrsïñ.
Dostarïñ kelip tabalap,
Dûspanïñ seni basqa ursïn!

(You are not a khan—you are a wolf.
You are an evil spirit, an oppressor.

May your friends scorn you,
May your enemy hit you on the head!)

Maxambet's outspokenness was much admired. He inspired generations of Kazakh poets before and after the establishment of Soviet colonial rule in 1917. His continuing influence can be seen in a collection of poems about him written by 98 Kazakh poets between 1963 and 2003 ( *Jïr arqauï—Maxambet* [The Power of the Song—Maxambet], 2003).

## II. Pre-Islamic Poetry

**A. *Orkhon Turkic Poetry*.** All Turkic peoples consider the funeral inscriptions of the 8th c., written in the Turkic runic alphabet and known as the Orkhon Inscriptions, their common heritage. Although the texts were written in prose, certain lines have always stood out as lines of poetry. A good example is the Kül Tegin Inscription, inscribed on a stele erected in 732 for Prince (Tegin) Kül, the younger brother of Bilgä Kaghan, "the Wise Kaghan" (d. 734). Bilgä Kaghan himself eloquently commemorates in the second part of the inscription the life story of his brother Kül, relating his accomplishments and campaigns until his death: *inim kül tegin kärgäk boltï* (My younger brother Kül passed away). At this point, Bilgä Kaghan is overcome by grief:

Özim saqïntïm.
Körir közim körmäz täg boltï
Bilir bilgim bilmäz täg boltï
Özim saqïntïm.

(I mourned deeply.
My eyes, always seeing, became like not-seeing.
My mind, always knowing, became like
    not-knowing.
So much I mourned.)

By arranging the above lines, written as prose in the original text, into consecutive lines, we have before us the original, pre-Islamic metrical scheme of Turkic poetry characterized by a fixed number of syllables in each line expressing one complete idea. The internal *alliteration in the second and third verse lines is remarkable. The end rhyme occurs as the result of *repetition and *parallelism. By repeating the same sentence structure, the same one-syllabic suffix will appear at the end of each verse line, creating a simple grammatical end rhyme.

Poetical lines like those cited above prompted Stebleva (1965) and Joldasbekov (1986) to rearrange the prose texts, particularly those of the Kül Tegin and the Tonyuquq Inscriptions into verses and to translate them into Rus. and Kazakh, respectively. In doing so, both scholars paid attention to the close connection between the poetic style of the inscriptions and the memorial songs and *laments recorded much later, considered to be the foundation of the Turkic heroic epic (Joldasbekov, Winner). The Orkhon Inscriptions present the first written examples of Turkic oral poetry.

**B. *Old Uighur Poetry and the Syllabic Meter/Initial Alliteration*.** Written Old Uighur poetry that has come down to us dating from the 8th to the 13th c. can be considered a continuation of the Orkhon Turkic poetry with one additional distinctive feature: initial alliteration. The written Manichaean and Buddhist Old Uighur poetry (Arat) displays the fully developed features of the syllabic meter that became known as *barmak* (finger) meter (ttü. *parmak hesabi*, finger counting). On the basis of the examples given by Arat, one can characterize the barmak as follows: (1) restricted number of syllables in each verse line, the preferred number being seven or eight, but extension to 11 or 14 syllables is also possible; (2) initial alliteration, whereby the initial word of two or more consecutive verse lines must start with the same syllable, consisting either of a vowel or a consonant and a vowel (the vowels *u* and *o* and *ö* and *ü* are equivalent in alliteration).

The syllabic meter with mostly seven or eight syllables, combined with initial alliteration, has been considered the traditional meter of Central Asian Turkic oral lit., particularly of the epic songs such as the Kyrgyz heroic epic *Manas*. Most likely because of the influence of the singers of *Manas*, many of today's Kyrgyz poets continue to use initial alliteration with the barmak meter. The situation is different in Kazakhstan. Texts of heroic epic songs recorded in the second half of the 19th c. rarely show lines with initial alliteration, although they use syllabic meter. However, some Kazakh oral poets like Maxambet employed initial alliteration in their songs, as in the example above. Kazakh-writing poets of the crucial period before and after the establishment of Soviet rule, like Maġjan Jumabayûlï (1893–1938), seemed to have revived the initial alliteration in some of their patriotic songs. In Uzbek, as in Ottoman Turkish poetry, initial alliteration seems to be less known, though the barmak meter is widely employed in oral as well as written poetry (Andrews). The strongest use of initial alliteration in combination with the seven- or eight-syllabic meter is to be found in Mongolian oral poetry, notably in epic songs (Poppe). It survived in mod. Mongolian written poetry (Wickham-Smith and Shagdarsüren). The prevalence of initial alliteration in conjunction with the syllabic seven or eight meter among the Altai Turks and the Tuvans (Taube) is probably due to Mongolian influence (Doerfer).

### III. Islamic Poetry

A. *Arabo-Persian Aruz Meter.* With the acceptance of Islam, the knowledge of Ar. and Persian became fashionable among the intellectuals of the sedentary and later the nomadic groups of the Turkic world. Soon Arabo-Persian rules and trads. were introduced, regardless of the fact that they did not fit the Turkic lang. The prosodic system of the Arabo-Persian *'aruz* distinguishes between short and long vowels (see DURATION, QUANTITY), a distinction that does not exist in Turkic (Andrews).

B. *Karluk-Karakhanid Poetry.* The first Turkic poetical work displaying the influence of Arabo-Persian prosody is the *Qutadgu Bilig* (The Knowledge of How to Become Happy, 1069–70) by Yusuf Hass Hajib, who wrote the work in Karakhanid Turkic or Middle Turkic, based on Old Turkic, i.e., Orkhon Turkic and Old Uighur. In his choice of verse pattern, the poet was influenced by Firdawsī's (940–1025) use of the Arabo-Persian *mutaqārib* in the *Shah-nameh* (Dankoff).

C. *Chagatay Turkic Poetry.* Like in the *Qutadgu Bilig*, a sense of urgency of writing down one's life experiences as a lesson for future generations can also be detected in Mir Alisher Navā'ī's (1441–1501) last work *Mahbub-ul-qulub* (The Beloved of the Hearts, composed its 1500). The work consists of three parts. The first two present a crit. of society, whereas the third part, *Tanbihlar* (Admonitions), consists of authoritative advice in the oral style of *proverbs. Indeed, Navā'ī's words were soon accepted as proverbs, cited by Uzbek elders even today, as, e.g., *tilga ihtiyorsiz, elga e'tiborsiz* (Disrespect for one's language is disregard for one's people). Navā'ī wrote mostly in Chagatay Turkic and has been revered as the promoter of the Chagatay Turkic literary lang. However, his extensive use of Persian and Ar. words cannot be overlooked. He also favored exclusively the Arabo-Persian meter and poetical forms, as, e.g., the *ghazal. The 15th c., esp. the second half, has been called the golden period of Chagatay Turkic poetry. Because of Navā'ī's *Majālis un-nafā'is* (Meeting of the Finest, 1492), a collection of short biographies of over 400 poets with citations of their works, we are well informed about the poets of that time.

### IV. The Modern Period

A. *From Oral to Written Poetry.* Among the forerunners of the mod. period was the much revered Turkmen poet Makhtumqulï (Trkm. Magtïmgulï, 1733–98). Like Navā'ī, Makhtumqulï was a Sufi. His poems express mystical-religious messages, wisdom, and advice like those of the Sufi saint Ahmad Yasawï (d. 1166). Concerned with the political situation of the Turkmen tribes, he also composed patriotic songs calling on the Turkmens to unite in the face of attempts by Persia, Chiwa, and Bukhara to occupy their territory. Makhtumqulï is considered the first Turkmen poet to write his verses; his counterparts in the other Turkic regions are the Kazakh oral poet Abay (1845–1904) and the Kyrgyz Moldo Kilich (1868–1917). Like Makhtumqulï, Abay received his first education in Muslim schools (*maktab, madrasa*), learned Persian and Ar., and became acquainted with cl. Persian-Ar. lit. Later, he studied Rus. and translated many Rus. poets into Kazakh. His greatest concern was the survival of the Kazakh trads., lang., and culture after the Rus. conquest of the Kazakh steppe. Kilich composed his poetry in such a pure Kyrgyz that it was suggested that his lang. be made a model for a common literary lang. for all Turkic people, one of the goals of the reformer Ismail Gaspirali/Gasprinskiy (1851–1914). Kyrgyz scholars termed his poems *ghazals* (Kyr. kazal) without commenting on his frequent initial alliteration, short lines of seven or eight syllables, and the lack of strophic arrangements. In 1910, he composed a long poem, *Zilzala*, about an earthquake which had occurred in the same year in northern Kyrgyzstan. He describes in this poem the earthquake itself and predicts that in five or six years more calamities will strike the Kyrgyz. These lines have been interpreted as a forecast of the great uprising of 1916, when the Central Asian Turkic people revolted against Rus. colonialism.

**B.** *Poetry of the Jadids/Reformers, 1905–38.* Meanwhile in the region of the Kazakhs, Abay's concern about the future of his people was soon taken up by other Kazakh intellectuals. Their voices were echoed in the neighboring Turkic regions as well, becoming stronger and stronger after 1905, the year of Russia's defeat in its war against Japan, demonstrating to the Central Asians that Russia was not invincible. In all Central Asian Turkic regions intellectuals (*Jadids*) established schools according to the methods (*usul-i jadid*) of the Crimean Tatar Gaspirali/Gasprinskiy. While they cared about their native langs. and the education and status of girls and women, their ultimate concern was freedom from Rus. and Soviet colonial oppression. The Jadids' preferred medium for reaching out to the public was poetry. The Kazakh Jadids, by some called *enlighteners*, Baytursïnûlï (1873–1937), Älixan Bökeyxanûlï (1870–1937), and others, though originally not known for their poetry, trained themselves as poets. Writing or composing poetry was expected of any educated Central Asian, and only poetry was considered lit. Moreover, the high regard for the oral poet as a leader and teacher had been transferred to the writing poet. In the Central Asian Turkic regions, written poems, if well received, would become songs (Kaz. *öleń*), thus reaching a wider audience.

The voices from Uzbekistan were equally powerful, reminding the people of their hist. and invoking the spirits of their ancestors. Abdurauf Fitrat (1886–1938), a scholar and educator who had spent several years in Istanbul, appealed in his poems to the spirit of Amir Temur (1336–1405) to help the Turkic people gain their freedom. His poetry is written in a free style or in the *barmak* (Uzbek *barmoq*) meter. He was against the use of the 'aruz meter and urged his contemporaries to write in the syllabic barmoq, which he called "our national meter." Next to Fitrat, the most influential and courageous poet of the period was Abdulhamid Sulayman (1898–1938), known as Cholpon (the Morning Star). Like Fitrat and other Jadids, he felt obligated as a poet to be a spokesperson for his people, disregarding any dangers. His poetic style shows many variations, with no preference for Arabo-Persian prosody. To some of his poems, he would give the title *qo'shiq* (folk song), or he would even indicate the melody for a given poem, as if he were striving to become an oral poet through the combined power of word and sound. A few lines from one of his most frequently sung and cited poems will show the intensity of his words:

Men va Boshqalar
Kulgan boshqalar, yig'lagan menman
O'ynagan boshqalar, yigragan menman,

Erk ertaklarini eshitgan boshqa.
Qulluq qo'shig'ini tinglagan menman. . .
Erkin boshqalardir, kamalgan menman,
Hayvon qatorida sanalgan menman. (1921)

(I and the Others
Others are laughing, but I am weeping,
Others are playing, but I am wailing,
Others are hearing tales of freedom,
Only I listen to words of slavery.
Others are free, only I am a prisoner,
Only I am treated like an animal.)

As a subtitle to this poem, Cholpon added the words "From the Mouth of an Uzbek Girl," prompting many readers to interpret it as a reflection of the restricted life of women living behind the walls of the traditional homes in Uzbekistan. It is more likely, however, that Cholpon is describing here life in general and his own life under Soviet rule. He voices similar sentiments in other poems pub. in 1922 in a collection titled *Uyg'onish* (Awakening), e.g., in *Vijdon erki* (Freedom of Conscience), where he concludes "faqat, erkin vijdonlarga / ege bo'lmoq munkin emes" ([Tyrants] can never control free consciences).

In 1937–38, all Jadids mentioned above and countless more were shot on the orders of Josef Stalin. During these years, Kazakhstan alone lost about 60,000 intellectuals. The Uzbek losses may have been even higher. Stalin's purges affected not only individuals but their families, who were also sent to concentration camps. Generally, poets and writers could be grouped in two: the silent or silenced ones and those who carried out the directives of the Communist Party. All this changed with the death of Stalin in March 1953, when the terror was lifted.

**C.** *The Generation of the 1960s: Heralds of Independence.* With the new Soviet leader Nikita Khrushchev's denunciation of Stalin's crimes in 1956, a period of relaxation began, called the *Thaw*. Censorship became less strict, and Stalin's victims who were still alive were released from the gulags. Those who had perished were posthumously acquitted. A young generation of poets and writers, who were between 20 and 30 years of age at the beginning of the 1960s, became known as the Generation of the 1960s. Their first task was to challenge the restrictive Soviet doctrine of "Socialist Realism." Next, they took up the question the Jadids had asked: "Who were we, who are we now?" Like the much admired Kyrgyz writer Chingiz Aitmatov (1928–2008), who raised this question in all his works, poets reminded their compatriots to honor the spirits of their ancestors and to respect their traditions and values. Some wrote patriotic poems about their own motherland and their own people. Others wrote about historical personalities. The Uzbek poet Muhammad Ali (b. 1942), e.g., composed a lengthy poem (*doston*) about Amir Temur in 1967 and in 1979 a doston centered on Dukchi Eshon, the leader of the 1898 uprising against the Russian colonizers. During the years of Gorbachev's glasnost and perestroika (1985–91) Central Asian

Turkic poets and writers of the generation of the 1960s became fully engaged in the struggle for independence, which they helped to achieve in 1991.

*See* ARABIC POETRY, ORAL POETRY, PERSIAN POETRY.

■ **General Introductions**: B. Hayit, "Die Sowjetisierung Turkistans," *Turkestan im XX. Jahrhundert* (1956); A. Adamovich, "The Non-Russians," *Soviet Literature in the Sixties*, ed. M. Hayward and E. I. Crowley (1964); E. Allworth, "The Changing Intellectual and Literary Community" and "The Focus on Literature," *Central Asia: 130 Years of Russian Dominance, A Historical Overview*, ed. E. Allworth (1994).

■ **Pre-Islamic Literature**: R. R. Arat, *Eski Türk Şiiri* (1965); A. Bombaci, "The Turkic Literatures: Introductory Notes on the History and Style"; and G. Doerfer, "Die Literatur der Türken Südsibiriens," *Philologiae Turcicae Fundamenta*, ed. J. Deny and L. Bazin, v. 2 (1965); I. V. Stebleva, *Poetika Drevnetyurkskoy Literatury i ee Transformatsiya v Ranne-Klassiceskiy Period* (1976); N. Poppe, *The Heroic Epic of the Khalkha Mongols*, trans. J. Krueger, D. Montgomery, M. Walter (1979); A. von Gabain, "Zentralasiatische türkische Literaturen I: Nichtislamische alt-türkische Literatur," *Handbuch der Orientalistik*, ed. H. Altenmüller et al. (1982); M. Joldasbekov, *Asil Arnalar* (1986); K. Reichl, *Turkic Oral Epic Poetry: Tradition, Form, Poetic Structure* (1992).

■ **Islamic Period**: J. Eckmann, "Die Tschagataische Literatur"; and M. F. Köprülü, "La Metrique 'Aruz Dans la Poesie Turque, *Philologiae Turcicae Fundamenta*, ed. J. Deny and L. Bazin, v. 2 (1965); Z. V. Togan, "Zentralasiatische Türkische Literaturen II: Die Islamische Zeit," *Handbuch der Orientalistik, Turkologie*, ed. H. Altenmüller et al. (1982); W. G. Andrews, *Poetry's Voice, Society's Song* (1985); O. Nosirov, "Aruz va O'zbek xalq og'zaki ijodi," *Xalq ijodi xazinasi*, ed. O. Nosirov and O. Sobirov (1986).

■ **Regions**. *Kazakh*: T. G. Winner, *The Oral Art and Literature of the Kazakhs of Russian Central Asia* (1958); *Qazaq Poeziyasindaği Dästür Ülasuï*, ed. A. Narïmbetov et al. (1981)—trad. in Kazakh poetry; *XV–XVIII Ġasïrdaġï Qazaq Poeziyasï*, ed. A. Derbiselin et al. (1982); *XIX: Ġasïrdaġï Qazaq Poeziyasï*, ed. A. Derbiselin, B. Aqmuqanova et al. (1985)—anthol. of 19th-c. lit; *Bes Ġasïr jïrlaydï. 15. Ġasïrdan 20. ġasïrdïñ bas kezine deyingi qazaq aqïn-jïraularnïñ shiġarmalarï*, ed. M. Maġauïn and M. Baydildaev (1989); M. Dulatûlï, *Oyan Qazaq* (1991); *Qazaqtïñ XVIII–XIX Ġasïrdaġï ädebiyetiniñ tarixïnan oçerkter*, ed. S. Muqanov (2002)—hist. of 18th and 19th-c. lit. *Kyrgyz*: M. Kïlïç, *Kazaldar*, ed. Sooronov (1991)—ghazals; Z. Bektenov and T. Bayjiev, *Kïrgïz adabiyatï* (1993); *Manas: Kïrgiz elinin baatïrdik eposu. Sagïmbay Orozbakovdun variantï boyuncha akademiyalik basïlïshï*, 3 v. (1995)—*Manas*, Kyrgyz national epic; "Kïrgïz Ruxu—*Manas*," *Ala-Too* (1995)—spec. iss. on *Manas*. *Turkmen*: *Türkmen Poeziyasïnïñ Antologiyasï* (1958)—anthol.; J. Benzing, "Die Türkmenische Literatur," *Philologiae Turcicae Fundamenta*, ed. J. Deny and L. Bazin, v. 2 (1965); *Mahtumkulu Divani*, ed. H. Biray (1992)—divan of Makhtumquli; W. Feldman,

"Interpreting the Poetry of Makhtumquli," *Muslims in Central Asia: Expressions of Identity and Change*, ed. J.-A. Gross (1992); *Songs from the Steppes of Central Asia: The Collected Poems of Makhtumkuli, Eighteenth Century Poet-Hero of Turkmenistan*, ed. B. Aldiss, trans. Y. Azemoun (1995); S. Zeranska-Kominek and Arnold Lebeuf, *The Tale of Crazy Harman*, trans. J. Ossowski (1997). *Uzbek*: E. Vohidov, *Muhabbat: Saylanma*, 2 v. (1986)—poetry; E. Allworth, *The Modern Uzbeks: From the Fourteenth Century to the Present: A Cultural History* (1990); T. Kocaoglu, "Özbekler ve Özbek Edebiyati," *Türk Dili ve Edebiyati Ansiklopedisi* 7 (1990); B. Orak, "Modern Özbek Edebiyati va Erkin Vohidov," *Erkin Vohidov: Seçme Şiirler*, ed. B. Orak (1991); M. Ali, *Saylanma* (1997)—poetry; A. Oripov, *Tanlangan Asarlar*, 4 v. (2000).

■ **Translations**: T. Tekin, *A Grammar of Orkhon Turkic* (1968); *Tuwinische Lieder: Volksdichtungen aus der Westmongolei*, ed. and trans. E. Taube (1980)—oral poetry from western Mongolia; Y. K. Hajib, *Wisdom of Royal Glory (Kutadgu Bilig): A Turko-Islamic Mirror of Princes*, trans. R. Dankoff (1983); *Rawshan: Ein Usbekisches Mündliches Epos*, trans. K. Reichl (1985)—oral epic *Ravshan*; S. Cabbar, *Kurtulush Yolïnda: A Work on Central Asian Literature in a Turkish-Uzbek Mixed Language* (2000)—Jadid period poetry; *Das usbekische Heldenepos Alpomish: Einführung, Text, Übersetzung*, trans. K. Reichl (2001)—epic *Alpomish*; *Ancient Splendor: The Best of Mongolian Poetry*, ed. and trans. S. Wickham-Smith and T. Shagdarsüren (2006); *The Semetey of Kenja Kara: A Kirghiz Epic Performance on Phonograph with Musical Score and AC*, ed. and trans. D. Prior (2006).

I. LAUDE-CIRTAUTAS

## TURKISH POETRY

I. Early Poetry: Prosody, Form, Content
II. The History of Ottoman/Azeri Poetry
III. The Tanzimat and the Dawn of Modernism
IV. Modern Turkish and Azeri Poetry
V. Modern Azeri Poetry

The poetry of the major western Turkic dialects, Azeri, and Ottoman Turkish are the heirs of two quite different trads.: that of Turkic peoples with roots in Central Asia and an adopted Perso-Ar. Islamicate high-culture trad. (Here and below, *Islamicate* and *Persianate* refer to the fact that not all "Islamic" style poetry was written by Muslims and not all "Persian" poetry was written by Persians.) When Turkic peoples began to enter the central Middle East in large numbers as invaders or settlers in the 11th c., they encountered a highly developed Persian literary trad. dominated by poetry. At the courts of Turkic rulers and among the intellectual and literary elites in Asia Minor, the early tendency was to adopt Persian as the lang. of poetry, together with its verse forms, style, and poetic sensibility. At the same time, village and nomadic Turks generally retained their native forms and lang., which had gradually absorbed themes and some vocabulary from the Islamicate trad. since as early as the 9th c. in Central Asia. The tensions, divisions, and junctions between these two distinct formal and ling. trads. and their reflections of class and status ground nearly all general discussions of Turkish poetry of all periods.

**I. Early Poetry: Prosody, Form, Content.** The Turkish lang. does not recognize vowel qualities (vowel length and brevity, or accent) as rhythmic elements, so the traditional prosody of the Turkic dialects—called *parmak hesabı* (finger counting) or *hece vezni* (syllable meter)—was based on the number of syllables in a line and on repeated groups of syllables separated by *caesuras (+). E.g., an 11-syllable line might scan as 11 unbroken syllables and repeat itself in that form throughout a poem. However, each 11-syllable line in another poem might be broken by caesuras into groups of 4+4+3 syllables or, in yet another poem, 5+6 syllables. There are many possible syllable counts for a poetic line and many possible groupings, and each verse form has its own preferred line lengths and groupings. E.g., the following is one 4+3 stanza of a verse form called *mani*, in which the four-line stanzas rhyme *aaba ccda*:

> Kız saçların + örmezler
> Seni bana + vermezler
> Sen bu gece + bana kaç
> Ay karanlık + görmezler

> (Girl they'll never + braid thy hair
> Let us live as + wedded pair
> So tonight run + off to me
> Moonless dark will + hide us there)

Turkish poetry—written, oral, and sung—in this trad. has continued to be popular from the earliest days of the Turkish presence in the western Middle East to the present. Although the popular trad. is generally oral and anonymous, even the devel. of a high-culture Turkish poetry in the Persian style was strongly influenced by mystical love (*aşk, ışk*) poetry in popular Turkish forms with which Sufi missionaries began to spread Muslim mysticism among Turkish and non-Turkish villagers and nomads at least as early as the 12th c. Perhaps the most widely known poet from this period is Yunus Emre (late 13th, early 14th cs.), whose nondoctrinal mystical verses hover between Persianate and Turkic forms as in the following excerpt in four-line stanzas with a *refrain and eight-syllable lines (4+ 4×2) rhyming *aaab cccb*:

> Ben yürürem + yana yana // aşk boyadı + beni kana
> Ne âkilem + ne divane // gel gör beni + aşk neyledi

> Geh eserim yiller gibi geh tozarım yollar gibi
> Geh akarım seller gibi gel gör beni aşk neyledi

> (I go and as + I go I cry // love's painted me + with bloody dye
> Nor wise nor wit + less now am I // come see what love + has made of me

> Now just like the winds do I blow, then like the roads all dusty grow

Now like the torrents do I flow, come see what love has made of me)

Following the Mongol invasions of the mid-13th c., the Seljuk dynasty of Rum (Asia Minor) lost control of large areas that were dominated culturally and intellectually by Persian and Ar. This, combined with the need to express the Islamic cultural heritage in a lang. that they and their supporters could understand, inclined Turkic rulers to begin demanding and patronizing Turkish poetry in the Persian style.

The Turkish version of the Perso-Ar. trad. employs the traditional Islamic verse forms: the *gazel* (Ar. *\*ghazal*), a more or less sonnet-length lyric love poem; the *kaside* (Ar. *\*qaṣīda*), a longer *panegyric or occasional poem; the *mesnevi* (Ar. *mathnavī*), an extended narrative poem in rhyming *couplets, *rubā'ī* (quatrain), and an assortment of stanzaic forms incl. some (*şarkı, türkü, tuyug*) that closely resemble popular Turkic forms. The basic building block of these forms is the couplet (*beyt*) and all, except the mesnevi and some stanzaic forms, are monorhyming, most often with a rhyming first couplet. Serious poets collected their poems in volumes called *\*divans* and this type of Ottoman-Azeri poetry is often referred to as *divan poetry*.

The prosodic system, which the Turks called *aruz*, is a further adaptation of the Persian adaptation of the formal rhythms of Ar. In all three cases, rhythm is created by the alternation of "long" syllables (cV: consonant + long vowel) or cvc (consonant + short vowel + consonant) and "short" syllables (cv) grouped into "feet" of various lengths (e. g., short [u] + long [−] + long [u−−] or long+short+long+long [−u−−]), which are combined in standardized rhythmic lines (*miṣra'*). In Ar., the feet have some syllables that can be lengthened or shortened. In Persian, the feet are fixed, with a few minor exceptions, and flexibility is achieved by permitting certain vowels (e.g., the vowel of the *izafet* [the adjectival/genitive connector] and the "vocalic h = a/e") to be read as either long or short and by using "shortened" versions of some common words (e. g., *māh* = > *meh* [moon]). Ottoman Turkish poets, who copiously adopted Persian and Ar. vocabulary and even some syntax, created their own adaptation of Persian prosody and its flexibility, much as the Persians had adapted Ar. Because there are no long vowels in Turkish, only "closed" (cvc), syllables are naturally long according to Perso-Ar. prosody, and words with extended strings of short (cv) syllables are quite common. However, unlike Ar. and Persian, there was no fixed spelling of Turkish words in the Ar.-Ottoman script, so it was always possible, although frowned on to some extent, to spell Turkish words using some Ar.-Ottoman script long vowels and at times to consider such vowels as long for purposes of rhythm. The following is the initial couplet, with an indication of scansion and rhyme, of a five-couplet gazel by Zātā (1471–1546), an elite Ottoman poet of the early 16th c.:

> u−−  −/u −−−  /u −−−/u −−  −
> Garībem gur/bete düşdüm/ gönül āvā/re yār*um yok*
> Benüm āh etdügüm 'ayb etmen kim ihtiyār*um yok*

(I'm a stranger, plunged into exile, my heart a
   vagabond, no beloved do I have
Do not find fault with me, when I go around
   sighing, for no choice do I have)

In these lines, the rhyme is in *ār* (*underlined*) with a
repeated postrhyme element called *redif* (originally the
name for a warrior who rides on the back of another's
saddle).

Poetry that adapted the Perso-Ar. trad. was hugely
popular among western Turkish speakers during the
Ottoman period, from the 14th c. through the early
20th. Hundreds upon hundreds of recognized poets
from rulers, high officials, and courtiers to soldiers,
shopkeepers, and mendicant dervishes are recorded in
the collections of biographies of poets of every era and
were said to be only the visible members of a vast po-
etic population. Although poems were written about
almost everything, the core of Ottoman and Azeri elite
poetry, whether lyric, narrative, or panegyric, was the
emotional content of a love, most commonly homo-
erotic love, which often carried with it a burden, large
or small, of mystical passion. In a context where pub-
lic expressions of heterosexual love were disapproved,
love poetry commonly had as its object young men,
some of whom became quite famous. The presumed
occasion of this poetry was a gathering of friends
(often transmuted into mystical [dervish] ceremonial
gatherings) that in many ways resembled the Gr. *sym-
posion*, in which food, drink (often alcoholic), witty
conversation, love, music, and, above all, poetry were
the primary ingredients. Its setting was an idealized
garden—reflected everywhere in Ottoman art and
decoration—wherein every natural phenomenon was
a potential metaphor for some feature of the lover, the
beloved, and the gathering.

**II. The History of Ottoman-Azeri Poetry.** The peri-
odization of Ottoman-Azeri poetry is a controversial
topic. However, it is possible to sketch some broad
tendencies and trends. The rise of the Ottomans as
the dominant power in western Anatolia and East-
ern Europe, which began in the second quarter of
the 14th c., initiated a gradual consolidation of lit-
erary *patronage affirmed by an Ottoman literary
historical view that adopted, as Ottoman precur-
sors, famous early poets such as Şeyhi (d. ca. 1431),
a court poet whose primary patron was the prince of
the independent province of Germiyan, and Nesimi
(d. ca. 1404), an Eastern Anatolian-Syrian Azeri mys-
tical poet.

The centralization of Ottoman Islamic poetic pro-
duction escalated with the conquest of Constanti-
nople in 1453. The patronage of poetry burgeoned in
the court of Mehmet the Conqueror. His grand vizier
and court poet Ahmet Pasha (d. 1469) is said to have
raised the level of Ottoman poetry to compete with
Persian, in part by translating some Chagatai (Eastern
Turkic) gazels by Mir Ali Shir Neva'i (1441–1501) sent
from the court of the Timurid ruler Huseyn Baykara
in Herat. At much the same time, the other acknowl-
edged foundational poet, known by the pseud. Necati
(1451?–1509), rose from slave status to wealth and

fame with verses such as the following that reflect his
skill at combining folk wisdom with the most refined
themes:

The whole world is ignited by your beauty from
   the tip of your locks
When they happen by night, fires cause the
   populace great loss

Is it any wonder that my heart moans as you give
   me advice
You should know, if they sprinkle water on it, the
   fire cries out

By the late 15th c., the stage had been set for the
great Ottoman renaissance of Islamic culture that
would take place in the 16th c. At the cultural pinnacle,
Turkish incorporated the vocabularies of Persian and
Ar. to create a ling. tool capable of astounding flights of
rhetorical fancy, which adorned expressions of intense
emotional power. From the Anatolian courts of Otto-
man princes and cultural centers in Eastern Europe,
poets flocked to the capital, competing to join the
literary salons of the rich and powerful. The princely
court of Amasya in the east produced Mihri Hatun (d.
ca. 1512), the most famous Ottoman woman poet. The
courtly-mystical poet Hayali (d. 1557) came from Var-
dar Yeniçesi in Bosnia, Zātī from the town of Balıkesir.
From the time of Mehmet the Conqueror to the mid-
16th c., hundreds of poets received annual stipends
from the royal treasury.

During this time, Lami'i (1472–1532) adapted sev-
eral masterpieces of Persian narrative verse to Turkish,
and Ca'fer Chelebi (ca. 1463–1515), a powerful official,
composed a unique narrative describing a love affair
with a married woman during a spring camping trip
to a popular park. Zātī made a living solely on gifts
given in exchange for panegyrics and love poems. Even
the rulers of the age participated in poetry. Shah Ismail
Safavi (1487–1524), founder of the Safavid dynasty of
Persia, composed Azeri mystical love poetry in both
the Islamicate and popular Turkic trads., which helped
rally the Turkmen tribes to his Sufi vision of Shi'ite
Islam:

Go now, go now, go . . . let Him be yours
Let a fully committed beloved be yours

If you launch yourself into the air and fly high
Let the sky reaching up from all the earth be yours

Suleyman the Magnificent (r. 1520–66) too was an
avid poet and patron of poets. He writes of his beloved
wife Hurrem:

My solitude, my everything, my beloved, my
   gleaming moon
My companion, intimate, my all, lord of beauties,
   my sultan

My life's essence and span, my sip from the river of
   Paradise, my Eden
My springtime, my bright joy, my secret, my idol,
   my laughing rose

In Suleyman's intimate circle was the master poet of the century, Baki (1526–1600), who rose to the second highest canon-law position in the empire and dominated the period with verses, such as the first and last couplets of his famed meditation on old age:

> The time of spring has suffered
> loss of fame and loss of face
> The leaves of trees have fallen
> in the meadow far from grace
> . . .
> On this meadow-earth, the leaves
> of books and trees are torn, Baki
> It seems they have a true complaint
> against the winds of time and fate

The Iraqi poet Fuzuli (d. 1556), who compiled divans in Ar., Persian, and Azeri Turkish, is much beloved by the Turks and is considered an Ottoman poet, which has more to do with the conquest of Iraq in 1534 than his actual lang. and culture. He composed exquisite love poetry often in a mystical mode and produced a retelling of the mystical love story of Leyla and Mecnun in Azeri Turkish. The following is an example of his passionate mystical verses:

> My heart blooms joyous when it sees your tousled
> locks
> I lose the power to speak, when I see your rosebud
> laughing
>
> I look at you, blood spatters from my eyes
> When our glances meet, eyelash arrows pierce my
> heart

By the 17th c., the regularization of bureaucratic and intellectual institutions combined with a decline in patronage reduced opportunities for aspiring poets, many of whom then found their inspiration in dervish lodges rather than in the gatherings of the powerful. Nonetheless, one of the most brilliant poets of the age, Nef 'i (d. 1635), was best known as a court panegyrist (and lampooner of rivals and stingy patrons). His most famous panegyric begins with a paean to spring initiated by the following couplet (with a supererogatory internal rhyme reminiscent of popular quatrains):

> As the springtime breezes blew, at morn the roses
> bloomed anew
> Oh let our hearts be blooming too, please, saki,
> pass the cup of Djem

Perhaps the most striking elite poetic movement during this period was the introduction of an adaptation of the Persian "Indian Style" (named for the style perfected in the Mughal courts of India). Complex and often formidably obscure, this style was esp. suitable for mystical verse, as the following by Na'ili (d. 1666) exemplifies:

> Who thirsts with dry lips for the stream of desire,
> slips onto paths of rejection

> Who rushes in haste after his desire, ever wanders
> the waste of distraction

The 17th-c. decline in opportunity for poets at the elite level is balanced by the burgeoning of more popular poetry. The *saz* (long lute) poets and wandering *aşıks* (lovers) like the famed Aşık Ömer (d. ca. 1707), who also dabbled in elite-style verses, provided a link between elite and common, village and city with their verses most often set to music. E.g., from Aşık Ömer,

> I'm a lover, alas, alack
> Bewitched by you, don't burn me black
> Keep that dog of a rival back
> One soul has tight embraced another

In the early 18th c., an era of peace and the rise of a prosperous merchant class led to a period of exuberant cultural production called the Tulip Period (1718–30) after the tulip craze that swept the Ottoman Empire and Europe. In an atmosphere of lavish spending on parties, pleasure gardens, and parks, poetry flourished, typified by the poems of Nedim (d. 1730), many of which echoed the lang., forms, and topical themes of popular verse, as in this example:

> Saki, let my soul rejoin my body, come to the
> gathering
> To that goblet sacrifice all promises and all
> repenting
> Have a care where you set your foot, my monarch
> and my king
> There may be wine spilt here and too the broken
> bottles of the drunks

The latter years of the century were marked by the poetic genius of Şeyh Galip (1757–99), who while still young became the master of a prestigious Mevlevi dervish lodge, the confidant of a reformist sultan, and the author of an original narrative poem entitled "Beauty and Love" that represents an allegorical summing up in the Indian style of the mystical trad. descended from Rūmī and the last great masterpiece of Ottoman narrative poetry.

**III. The Tanzimat and the Dawn of Modernism.** By the 19th c., the impetus for political, social, and even cultural reform gradually became overwhelming. The reformers were energized, but adherents of the old cultural order despaired, as is poignantly expressed in the following couplet by 'İzzet Molla (1786–1829):

> We have reached a season of spring
> in this world
> When the bulbul is silent, the pool empty
> and the rose-bed is in ruins

The bulbul, one of the central metaphors of cl. poetry, would soon be relegated to the footnotes of lit. hist. by advocates of literary modernization. Namık Kemal (1840–88), one of the major proponents of constitutionalist reform, subverted the mystical subtext of the ageless *topos and evoked an encaged nightingale crying out for freedom, a direct reference to the liberal inclinations of the Young Ottomans. The new focus of poetry was on the here and now. In the wake of the westernizing *Tanzimat* reforms of 1839, reformist intellectuals, paying little heed to the high levels of illiteracy, domesticated Fr. literary models and focused on the need to develop an engaged lit. that would enlighten the people and support even more wide-ranging changes. They argued that the metaphorical nature of cl. lit. was unsuited to that purpose. The lang. issue became central. Writers explored ways to bridge the gap between the learned literary lang. and ordinary speech. Though poets, such as İbrahim Şinasi (1826–71), Ziya Paşa (1825–80), and Kemal explored a great variety of new themes, poetry was the least affected by change. Traditional high-culture poetry, its prosody, and its major genres were maintained. This relative conservatism was not surprising since the reformists' main endeavor was the appropriation of new literary genres such as the novel, short story, and drama. Nonetheless, huge controversies raged over the origins, sources of inspiration, and role of poetry.

**IV. Modern Turkish and Azeri Poetry.** In the light of conflicting influences ranging from Fr. *romanticism to *Parnassianism, poets such as Abdülhak Hamit (1852–1937) and Recaizade Mahmud Ekrem (1847–1914) questioned the instrumentalization of poetry and introduced new aesthetic concerns together with a more confessional dimension. In particular, Ekrem's theoretical writings had a lasting impact on the neo-Parnassian poets of the *Edebiyat-ı Cedide* (New Literature) group who advocated an elitist art-for-art's-sake approach. Muallim Naci (1850–93) defended ideas that were quite close to those of Ekrem, his nemesis; but as he was closer to intellectual circles linked to the authoritarian regime of Sultan Abdülhamid II, he is unjustly seen as an advocate of literary conservatism by historians. The neo-Parnassian poets' elaborate and sometimes artificial lang. was the source of much crit. by the nationalist proponents of neofolk poetry, who supported the use of the syllabic folk meter and the Istanbul vernacular. The publication of *Türkçe Şiirler* (Poems in Turkish) in 1899 by Mehmed Emin (1869–1944) was the starting point of a long-lasting and often ruthless battle of words between elitist neo-Parnassians and populists. After the relative liberalization following the promulgation of the second constitution in 1908, the ephemeral jour. *Genç Kalemler* (1911) played a major role in the promotion of the neofolk movement. With the blessings of the Union and Progress government and later the early republican authorities, nationalist versifiers, such as the Five Syllabists, influenced by the writings of Ziya Gökalp (1867–1915), the father of Turkish nationalism, developed a discourse on the supposed foreignness of the traditional aruz prosody and its inappropriateness for the Turkish lang. Nonetheless, four late masters of the aruz had a major impact on the devel. of Turkish poetry even after the foundation of the republic in 1923: Tevfik Fikret's (1867–1915) engaged humanism, Mehmet

Akif's (1873–1936) mod. Islamicist verse, Ahmet Haşim's (1884–1933) Ottoman symbolism, and Yahya Kemal's (1884–1958) neoclassicism. Fikret's, Akif's and Haşim's experiments with *free verse ( *şir-i müstezad* ) that broke up the traditional couplet into lines with changing numbers of aruz rhythmic feet were a precursor of truly mod. free verse. This devel took place partly under the influence of Fr. *vers libre*, but it was also partly in response to a perceived need to integrate the spoken lang. into poetry. A new generation of syllabists emerged, marrying the symbolist quest for musical perfection with nationalist endeavors. Among them, Fazıl Hüsnü Dağlarca (1914–2008) deserves particular notice as he lived through the century, unaffected by changing fashions, and left behind works that delved into themes ranging from mysticism to anticolonialism and remained popular for generations.

Syllabism, however, was outflanked by younger poets such as Ercüment Behzad Lav (1903–84), who discovered Ger. *expressionism, and Nazım Hikmet (1901–63), who explored Rus. *futurism. A new divide appeared between the mainly left-wing advocates of free verse and the mostly conservative and nationalist proponents of folk prosody.

Relentlessly hounded by the Kemalist state, Hikmet nonetheless revolutionized Turkish poetry. After a short-lived futurist period, he worked, while imprisoned in Bursa in the 1930s, toward a fusion of futurist, folk, and cl. elements while developing a novel form of subjective *realism. Heavy censorship made it difficult for socialist poets to explore Hikmet's new endeavors, which explains why they, with some exceptions, espoused a rather rigid interpretation of socialist realism. Only after the military coup of 1960 and the ensuing democratic reforms did Hikmet's poetry become easily available and hugely influential for a new generation of socialist poets, such as Ataol Behramoğlu (b. 1942).

Toward the end of the 1930s, a group of young poets, Orhan Veli (1914–50), Melih Cevdet Anday (1915–2002), and Oktay Rifat (1914–88) launched the *Garip* movement. They combined subjective realism and *surrealism and finally published a groundbreaking *manifesto in 1941. The movement caused a huge upheaval during the 1940s, even though its perceived apolitical stance was often the subject of reproach. Influenced by independent poets, such as Asaf Halet Çelebi (1907–58) and Behçet Necatigil (1916–79), who explored correspondences between modernist verse and the cl. trad., a new generation of poets who were later to be known as the *İkinci Yeni* (Second Renewal) questioned the downgrading of poetry by the prolific offspring of the Garip generation and developed a more individualist, and to a certain extent opaque, poetry that explored even the darkest realms of human experience and consciousness. Some of the original advocates of this new trend, among them Turgut Uyar (1927–85), Edip Cansever (1928–96), Cemal Süreya (1931–90), Gülten Akın (b. 1933), and Hilmi Yavuz (b. 1936), proved to have a profound influence on a new generation of poets who rediscovered their works in the

1990s, in the context of wide-ranging debates about the role of the Ottoman trad. in mod. Turkish poetry.

Reclaiming and subverting the heritage of Akif and Necip Fazıl Kısakürek (1905–83), a modernist Islamicist poetry movement surfaced. It was championed by Sezai Karakoç (b. 1933) and Cahit Zarifoğlu (1940–87) and gained strength during the 1970s. Though political, in particular socialist, poetry was much in vogue during that decade, the years following the 1980 military coup were characterized by the depoliticization of the literary field and saw the devel. of elitist concerns ranging from neoimagism to modernist appropriations of Ottoman elite lit. Nonetheless, two major new devels. testified to the transformations affecting Turkish society and poetry. One was the growing number of women poets published during the 1980s. Some of them, such as Gülseli İnal (b. 1947), Lale Müldür (b. 1956), and Nilgün Marmara (1958–87), were hugely influential. Though their works bore the marks of post-1980 poetry, they consciously subverted the male-dominated poetry trad. with a novel lang. and daring images. The other was a group of young Kurdish poets who published both in niche magazines and mainstream literary jours. They introduced original features such as proclaiming their Kurdishness in Turkish through a deconstruction of Turkish syntax and the transposition of Kurdish expressions into Turkish, as well as by focusing on the Kurdish experience.

**V. Modern Azeri Poetry.** In Azeri-speaking regions during the 18th and 19th cs., cl. trends survived. The Rus.-Iranian wars of 1813–28 and subsequent treaties dividing Azeri-speaking populations on both sides of the Araxes River did not impede cultural and social interactions. Poets such as Molla Panah Vagif (1717–97), Mirza Shafi Vazeh (1792–1852), Seyyid Azim Shirvani (1835–88), and Ali Agha Vahid (1896–1965) continued to write love poems, many glorifying earthly love in cl. aruz meters, and achieved fame throughout the area with poems often set to music. The 20th c. saw the rise of a realistic trend that became more pronounced after the workers' uprising in Russia (1905) and the Iranian constitutional revolution (1906). Ali Akbar Sabir (1862–1911) and Mo'juz of Shabustar (1872–1932), e.g., devoted themselves to poetic socialist realism, condemning illiteracy, injustice, and the plight of women. In the second half of the century, poets wrote a wide variety of poetry in both aruz and free-verse forms, among them Shahriyar (pseud. of Mohammad-Hoseyn Behjat-Tabrizi, 1907–86), Suleyman Rustam (1906–89), and Bakhtiyar Vahabzada (1925–2009).

■ **Anthologies**: *English*: *Ottoman Literature: The Poets and Poetry of Turkey*, trans. E.J.W. Gibb (1901); *The Penguin Book of Turkish Verse*, ed. N. Menemencioğlu (1978); *Modern Turkish Poetry*, ed. F. Kayacan Fergar (1982); *An Anthology of Turkish Literature*, ed. K. Silay (1996); *Eda: An Anthology of Contemporary Turkish Literature*, ed. M. Nemet-Nejat (2004); *Translation Review: Turkish Literature and Its Translation* 68 (2004)—trans., biblio., articles; *A Brave New Quest: 100 Modern Turkish Poets*, ed. T. S. Halman (2006); *Ottoman Lyric Poetry: An Anthology*, ed. and trans. W. G. Andrews, N. Black, and M. Kalpakli, rev. ed. (2006). *French*: *Anthologie de la Poésie Turque Contemporaine*, ed. J. Pinquié and Y. Levent (1991); *Anthologie de la poésie turque XVIIIè–XXè siècle*, ed. N. Arzik (1994). *German*: *Aus dem Goldenen Becher: Türkische Gedichte aus Sieben Jahrhunderten*, ed. A. Schimmel (1993).

■ **Criticism and History**: *Modern Azeri Poetry*: *Azerbaijan Poetry: Classic, Modern, Traditional*, ed. M. Ibrahimov (1976); S. Berengian, *Azeri and Persian Literary Works in the Twentieth Century Iranian Azerbaijan* (1988); H. Sultan-Qurraie, *Modern Azeri Literature: Identity, Gender and Politics in the Poetry of Mo'juz* (2003). *Ottoman Poetry*: E.J.W. Gibb, *A History of Ottoman Poetry*, 6 v. (1900–09)—copious information, but unacceptable racist and orientalist critique; W. G. Andrews, *Introduction to Ottoman Poetry* (1976), and *Poetry's Voice, Society's Song* (1985); V. Holbrook, *The Unreadable Shores of Love* (1994); W. G. Andrews and M. Kalpakli, *The Age of Beloveds* (2005). *Post-Tanzimat Poetry*: T. S. Halman, "Poetry and Society: The Turkish Experience" *Modern Near East: Literature and Society*, ed. C. M. Kortepeter (1971); M. Fuat, "Giriş," *Çağdaş Türk Şiiri Antolojisi* (1985); G. Turan, "The Adventure of Modernism in Turkish Poetry," *Agenda* 38.3–4 (2002).

W. G. Andrews; L. Mignon

**TYPOGRAPHY.** Typography is the act of setting text with regularly formed, repeatable letters made with metal, film, digitally generated output, or other mechanical means. Typographic formats usually conform to conventions of linearity and quadrature established by the constraints of hot-metal type. While linearity is a feature of writing practices almost since their invention over 5,000 years ago, quadrature is a specific feature of metal casting and the mechanical process of creating letters on the square or rectangular bodies required for composition. Typographic production contrasts strikingly with calligraphic writing, in which the expressive gesture of the hand leaves an affective trace. Calligraphic methods are largely production techniques resulting in one copy at a time from a single hand. Each copy is distinct and unique, even when many are produced simultaneously. Typographic methods are reproductive in nature and lend themselves to editioned works in which the copies are more similar than different. These distinctions between productive/calligraphic and reproductive/typographic modes are easily blurred, particularly in more recent technologies.

While conventional typesetting was codified by Johannes Gutenberg's invention in the 15th c., other possibilities for reproduction have expanded the range of typography. Photographic methods treat the image on film as information and can manipulate the original source image in a variety of ways, stretching, resizing, scaling, and distorting it. Digital media treat all information as data and are capable of taking keyboarded input and typographic notation and transforming them into any output format available. Digital media allow for all manner of calligraphic marks to be output in multiple formats, manipulated in photographic and algorithmic manner, and created without the same constraints of material that were inherent in the production of letterforms using trad. methods. Given the fluidity of current methods of writing production, the distinction between calligraphic and typographic methods is no longer absolutely clear.

The earliest technologies of writing include both productive and reproductive techniques. Incising, scratching, marking, painting, and drawing are ways of making unique written marks, while seals and stamps were used for repeating signs. Successive inventions expanded the range of possibilities rather than replacing earlier methods. In commercial industries, economic pressures sometimes cause certain technologies to be abandoned or discarded (e.g., early versions of phototypesetting or digital production have become obsolete as more advantageous innovations have appeared). New technologies do not necessarily find their aesthetic potential immediately. No technological obstacles prevented Gutenberg's type from being set at a diagonal or in a circle, but the idea of using type in this way, or in any manner that freed it from the constraints of linear setting in the rationalized grid of letterpress, simply did not occur. Older models for such formats are embodied in med. decorative techniques, esp. in designs of micrographia, but did not transfer easily into metal type.

Technological means of producing texts do not determine aesthetic values, and poetical forms do not stand in a fixed relation to material modes of expression. But every visual form of writing has certain inherent tendencies that dispose it to certain graphic arrangements over others. For instance, while handwriting is hard to discipline into regular square rows of even-shaped letters, hot-metal type can only be set in a free form flow with great difficulty, and neon signage has never been used for extended presentation of verse. The techniques of typography carry cultural and historical associations in their material and are integral to poetic composition.

While a poem carved in stone has a different presence from one scribbled on a sheet of notepaper, the effect of different production techniques on the semantic value of a poem is difficult to calculate. All written texts are material instantiations that call forth associations. They are also indexes of production, signaling the state of a culture and its ideological beliefs (what counts as official poetry or intimate verse is often indicated by the material of expression). At its most formal, written lang. carries the authority of the state, church, or other ruling body; at its most ephemeral, it is the trace of human life, brief and transient. Most written forms of poetic expression lie somewhere between the monumental and the ephemeral, clustered around the vast middle ground of conventional formats on semipermanent materials.

No direct relationship exists between media of writing and lineation or other graphical encoding of verse forms. The oldest extant example of poetic composition is a cuneiform tablet of a work by Enheduanna, the daughter of the Akkadian ruler Sargon, composed some time about 2300 BCE. The two-column format of the tablet and the distinct act of lineation in this work reinforce its identity as a song. Many examples of ancient writing did not contain spaces between words, no matter what the means of production, and were written in tightly packed lines, or using *boustrophedon (in which the direction of alternate lines is reversed, as is the direction of the letters). Expectations about the function of writing and its ability to connect metrical and graphical forms of poetic expression took time to develop. Evidence for constructing a hist. of these visual conventions is fragmentary. Early scribal culture combined economic motivation with lineation, maximizing the space used on the surface of parchment while making standard line lengths a metric for setting fees for transcription. Verse forms were not standardized in Western mss. until the later Middle Ages, around 1000–1100. Even then, conventions varied according to the familiarity of the scribe with the lang. of the work and assumptions this carried about the relation of sound to graphic forms or verse lines. Lines with standard metrics closer to the scribe's tongue (and ear) were more likely to be lineated, for instance, than those whose rhymes and meter the writer could not understand or "hear" (see LINE).

Typographic conventions for the presentation of verse become steadily more fixed across the hist. of printing. Verse forms and graphical structures come to share an identity (e.g., the couplet comes to be seen as a graphical unit as well as a metrical one). The typographic features of line breaks, indentation, capitalization, *punctuation, spacing, and so on become conventions capable of being manipulated and violated. But the technical underpinnings of typographic form—linearity and quadrature—remain intact once they migrate from ms. notation into metal type. Exceptions are remarkable and notable, such as shaped or pattern poems (see CARMINA FIGURATA). On close examination, most such works created with metal type turn out to have a format consistent with the linearity of its technology (type has to be set in a solid form in order to be printed), since deviations are time consuming and difficult to print.

Between the 15th and the 19th cs., the methods for reproducing writing (aside from letterpress printing) included relief impressions from the surface of wood or metal or intaglio impressions from engraved plates. Neither of these is an efficient means of producing large amounts of text. Each involves drawing and/or carving each individual letter, rather than taking advantage of the considerable efficiencies of reusable metal type. Interesting tensions in the cultural authority of typographic methods show in the efforts of writing masters to demonstrate the virtues of their methods through engraved reproductions. Engravers and carvers had considerable license to deviate from strict linear formats, but in so doing, they marked their writing as a different order of notation. Competition for business was particularly keen in the 18th c., and one remarkable artifact, the volumes of Brit. engraver John Pine's *Horace* (issued in 1733–37), was printed from plates engraved to resemble metal type.

Display fonts, those typographic forms created to compete for attention in the commercial marketplace, had been developed extensively in the 19th c. (in hot metal, in wood, and in lithographic poster design). The graphical imagination of floriated, shadowed, textured, and otherwise decorative and decorated letters brought a staggering number of new visual letterforms into being, almost none of which was considered acceptable for literary purposes. Late 19th-c. improvements that automated setting, namely, the monotype and linotype machines, inscribed linear characteristics even more absolutely because of their methods of casting type in lines. Not until the early 20th c. were the regular linear patterns of hot metal disturbed for poetic purposes. Even Stéphane Mallarmé's landmark 1897 work *Un coup de dés* (*A Throw of the Dice*) kept horizontal and vertical axes intact. In the 1910s, Guillaume Apollinaire's *Calligrammes*, some set using dental plaster to hold the metal type in place, and F. T. Marinetti's *Zang Tumb Tuuum,* along with the work of many Dada and futurist poets, broke the stranglehold of letterpress convention on poetic forms. Mixing font sizes and faces, disposing their work in arrangements that resembled advertising, they pushed typography to exploit its unruly potential rather than its capacity for well-governed behavior.

Two very different innovations extended typographic potential in the 19th c.: stone lithography, whose receptive surfaces allowed for hand-drawn letterforms of any imaginative invention to be reproduced, and the typewriter, a device whose mechanisms disciplined the hand and body to its own requirements. The typewriter is a writing machine, a means of authorial expression and formalization that relies on a single operator. Though designed for business, its characteristic alignments allowed for the grid of vertical and horizontal relations to be activated as part of a semantic field. The mechanical regularity of the typewriter was perceived as an asset by many graphically inclined poets who used it inventively to create figurative and imaginative visual works, esp. in the 20th c.

Photographic methods of type production became the industry standard in the mid-20th c. These replaced hot metal with images produced in a camera using filmstrips and photo-sensitive paper. Poets in the Fr. group known as the Lettrists began to play with the distorting possibilities of film in the 1950s, curling and cutting the negatives to create dimensional illusions in the printed versions of their texts. This technique added a new spatial quality to the appearance of texts on the page that often justified the diminishment of legibility in favor of effect.

Press type, a plastic film that was produced in sheets meant to be transferred to paper or other surface by burnishing, became a commercially viable product in the 1960s. The flexibility offered by having a sheet one could lay anywhere on a surface, wall, page, or image allowed for layering and overlap not possible in a letterpress approach. Press type changed conventions for spacing and put commercial display fonts into the hands of poets and writers. Press type could be used in a clean studio, on a desktop or kitchen table, to assemble works with elaborately complex shapes, like the circular pieces of Ferdinand Kriwet. But press type was expensive, difficult to align, and both tedious and time consuming to use.

In the 1970s, the first digital devices for phototypesetting appeared. These quickly expanded their capabilities and improved in quality. They output a sheet of photo paper that could be readily collaged into inventive layouts. In phototype, letterform designs did not have to follow the conventions of traditional type. Imaginative fonts like Baby Teeth and Jitter figured the letters in imaginative ways or fractured their once-solid forms in modes unthinkable in an era of metal and wood that worked well in the photo-mechanical techniques of offset printing.

The arrival of desktop capabilities for digital type production and font design radically altered the field of typography. Letters could be programmed and so could texts. Their sizes and shapes could be altered through software designed to stretch or distort them. Their forms could be generated with algorithmic protocols that conceived of letters as a rasterized object, a pixilated image, or a set of instructions for drawing. The integration of text and image in Photoshop and drawing programs blurred boundaries with vertiginous results for experimentation in poetry of all kinds. The use of programs for animation introduced movement and temporality into poetic expression. The idea of poetry as an animated medium spawned poetic experiments. Letters and texts could be generated through procedural means that had been slow in a mechanical or even photographic world, impossible in an analogue universe where the sheer mass of calculations involved in their production would have made such work impossible. Whether digital means will expand the capacities of poetic production in any substantive way remains to be seen (see ELECTRONIC POETRY).

■ D. B. Updike, *Printing Types: Their History, Forms and Use* (1962); M. Parkes, *Pause and Effect: A History of Punctuation in the West* (1992); C. Perfect and J. Austen, *The Complete Typographer* (1992); J. McGann, *The Black Riders* (1993); E. Lupton and A. Miller, *Design Writing Research* (1996); R. Huisman, *The Written Poem: Semiotic Conventions from Old to Modern* (1998); A.-M. Christin, *The History of Writing* (2002); *Rhetoric Before and Beyond the Greeks*, ed. C. Lipson and R. Binkley (2003); J. Drucker and E. McVarish, *Graphic Design History: A Critical Guide* (2009).

J. DRUCKER

**UKRAINE, POETRY OF.** The hist. of Ukrainian poetry can be divided into three major periods, made all the more distinct by sharp discontinuities among them. Underlying and producing these discontinuities are profound shifts in Ukrainian society; not only do basic political and social structures disappear, to be replaced by entirely new ones, but, at least until the mod. period, Ukrainian literary and historical consciousness does not succeed in bridging these changes.

The first period, from the 10th–11th cs. to roughly the 14th c., coincides largely with the lit. of Kyivan Rus', which is taken as the common patrimony of the East Slavs—the Ukrainians, Belarusians, and Russians. The second, middle period, late 16th to the late 18th cs., reflects primarily the poetics of the *baroque; and the third period, beginning 19th c. to the present, coincides with the birth of the mod. Ukrainian nation and the emergence of literary Ukrainian based on the vernacular.

One can speak of poetry in Old Ukrainian (Kyivan) lit. in terms of (1) the oral trad., (2) trans. and "borrowed" lit., and (3) verse elements in the original lit. Old Ukrainian oral lit. is often identified with folklore, but this lit., while oral, was probably a product of a court or "high" trad., which over the centuries "sank" into the repertoire of folklore. Whether the epic cycle of *byliny* (in Ukrainian *staryny*; see BYLINA) that depict the Kyivan context but were preserved in the northern Rus. territories or the gamut of ritual poetry related to the agricultural cycle and pagan rites, the actual texts date only from the 18th–19th cs., conclusions about the range and function of oral lit. in this earliest period remain speculative.

Verse as such is found in the various trans. and adaptations of Byzantine liturgical lit., particularly hymnography (see BYZANTINE POETRY). These *hymns influenced contemp. Kyivan texts and had an impact on the bookish versification of the 16th to 18th cs. The major poetic work of this period is the *Slovo o polku Ihorevi* (Tale of Ihor's Campaign) describing an unsuccessful military campaign of 1185. Written in the early 13th c., it was discovered and published at the turn of the 19th c. Its sonorous, vivid lang. and imagery, its deft narrative of rhythmic prose, have made the *Slovo* for all the mod. East Slavic lits. the quintessential poetic correlative of Kyivan Rus'.

In the middle period, sometime in the 16th c., a new form of oral poetry emerged, the *duma* (pl. *dumy*), which supplanted the older staryny and was to have a strong impact on much of subsequent Ukrainian poetry. The dumy, sung by wandering, often blind singers, were not a narrowly folkloric genre—its perspective encompassed all Ukrainian society. These "sacred songs," conveying profound social and historical experiences like wars with the Turks and Tatars or wars of liberation from Poland, reflected elements of heroic *epic, *ballad, and *elegy.

At the end of the 16th c., Ukrainian society and culture underwent a remarkable revitalization, which culminated in the mid-17th c. with an autonomous Cossack state that was to last more than a century. A characteristic feature of Middle Ukrainian lit. is its bilingualism: in the 17th and early 18th cs., it is Ukrainian or Polish, depending on theme, genre, or projected audience; by the mid-18th c., it is Ukrainian-Rus. In both cases, the choice of the other lang. reflects not a hedging of the writer's Ukrainian identity but rather the conventions of the literary system.

The earliest poetry of this period, beginning from the 1580s and 1590s, is syllabic in meter; in genre, emblematic and heraldic. Throughout the first part of the 17th c., Ukrainian poetry is represented mainly by *panegyric, historical, and *didactic poetry; by the second half of the 17th c., it shows a relatively broad range of forms and a differentiation into "high" genres (reflecting *baroque poetics) and popular genres. In the former, such important poets as Lazar Baranovych (1616–93) and esp. Ioan Velychkovs'ky (ca. 1640–1701), writing in both bookish Ukrainian and Polish and reflecting religious themes, give a new depth to national self-expression. The popular genres—*fables, *satires, and Christmas and Easter verse—are mostly anonymous and close to the vernacular.

The early 18th c. witnesses the maturation of Ukrainian school drama. Feofan Prokopovich's (1681–1736) tragicomedy *Vladymir* (1705) exemplifies the didactic poetics of this genre, as the historical theme—the Christianization of Kyivan Rus'—becomes a vehicle for political satire and for the apotheosis of the Ukrainian *hetman* (leader) Ivan Mazepa. At the end of the 18th c., there appears the most significant talent of premod. Ukrainian lit.: the peripatetic philosopher and poet Hryhorii Skovoroda (1722–94). His book of devotional poetry, *The Garden of Divine Songs*, synthesizing cl. and biblical, mystical and folk elements, remains the high point of 18th-c. Ukrainian poetry.

Mod. Ukrainian poetry is traditionally dated with the appearance of Ivan Kotliarevs'ky's *Eneida* of 1798, a travesty of Virgil's *Aeneid*. Finding its analogue to the fall of Troy in the destruction of the last Cossack stronghold (the Zaporozhian Sich), marking the end of Ukrainian autonomy in the 18th c., *Eneida* focuses on the wanderings of a band of Cossacks and provides an encyclopedic and loving account of Ukrainian provincial life and customs. Mixing an energetic optimism, satire, and nostalgia for the past with broad humor, the poem became a rallying point for a new Ukrainian lit. in the vernacular. Kotliarevs'ky (1769–1838) drew on a wide range of comic and burlesque devices characteristic of 18th-c. Ukrainian poetry, and this burlesque mode was adopted by other poets, Petro Hulak-Artemovs'ky (1790–1865) among them.

Beginning with the 1820s, Ukrainian *romanticism introduced an entirely new poetics: the focus of this poetry fell on the turbulent Cossack past and on the wealth of Ukrainian folklore. Early romantic poets, like Levko Borovykovys'ky (1806–89), Amvrosii Metlyns'ky (1814–70), and esp. Mykola Kostomarov (1817–85), and clergymen-poets in western Ukraine, then under Austria-Hungary, the so-called Ruthenian Trinity (Markiian Shashkevych [1811–43], Ivan Vahylevych [1811–66], and Yakiv Holovats'ky [1814–88]), sought to legitimize the vernacular lang., to rediscover historical and ethnic roots, and to advance cultural and national autonomy.

Taras Shevchenko (1814–61), born a serf and freed at the age of 24, came to be lionized by both Ukrainian and Rus. society as a uniquely powerful and inspired romantic poet. Arrested in 1847 in connection with the secret society the Brotherhood of Saints Cyril and Methodius and exiled for ten years, he returned in ill health but with poetic powers unimpaired. Seen as a martyr and bard even in his lifetime, Shevchenko became on his death the animating spirit of the Ukrainian national movement and remains a popular cult figure to this day. Shevchenko's poetry, traditionally called *Kobzar* (the Minstrel) after his first collection of 1840, divides along the lines of intimate *lyric poetry; political poetry, with powerful excoriations of social and national oppression, particularly by tsarist authority; and narrative poems, incl. historical poems and *ballads. All these modes are unified and guided by structures of mythical thought, which project a movement from the present state of victimization to a redeemed and purified humanity.

Panteleimon Kulish (1819–97)—friend, critic, and rival of Shevchenko—significantly broadened the range of Ukrainian poetry by new historical themes and expanded formal concerns and by renderings of the Bible, Shakespeare, Lord Byron, and other Western poets. Shevchenko's successors tended either to emulate him, like the western Ukrainian poet Yuri Fed'kovych (1834–88), or to resist the pull of the bard's model, like Stepan Rudans'ky (1834–73) and Yakiv Shchoholiv (1823–98), two poets on the borderline of romanticism and *realism.

Ukrainian poetry in the second half of the 19th c. was strained by the weight of perceived realist obligations and by official Rus. edicts of 1863 and 1876 banning the publication and importation of Ukrainian books. A poet who exemplifies both the call of national civic duty and the thrust of an authentic personal poetry is the western Ukrainian Ivan Franko (1856–1916). A renaissance man of indefatigable energy, Franko covers a broad gamut of genre and styles—historical, satiric, lyrical, and confessional, the last by far the most successful.

Throughout much of the 20th c., Ukrainian lit. was dominated by two competing aesthetic views: *modernism with its call for innovation and artistic freedom and its Eur. orientation vs. the populism

that morphed into socialist realism under Soviet rule. Another important classification of Ukrainian literary production that resulted from the failure to establish a Ukrainian state after World War I and that remained valid until independence is the split of lit. into Soviet and émigré. This political divergence influenced aesthetic approaches and resulted in different literary models.

The period of early modernism, generally from the 1890s to World War I, witnessed the differentiation of the Ukrainian literary marketplace and the emergence of poetry for a more select public. One of the first to turn to Eur. and universal historical and philosophical themes was Lesia Ukrainka (1872–1913); her poetic drama also presents a powerful vehicle for gender concerns. A call for modernization and a rejection of utilitarian obligations were at the heart of the *Moloda muza* (The Young Muse) poetic group's activity, whose oeuvre betrays decadent and neoromantic inclinations.

On the eve of World War I, there appeared the symbolist poetry of Mykola Vorony (1871–1942), Mykola Filians'ky (1873–1938), and Oleksandr Oles' (1878–1944), anticipating the outstanding poet of the 20th c.: Pavlo Tychyna (1891–1967) (see SYMBOLISM). At first a symbolist and spirited supporter of the Ukrainian national revolution and at the end of his life an orthodox spokesman for the Soviet system, Tychyna underwent a complex evolution; but in his early and mature poetry, he remains the most innovative and influential poetic voice of his time.

In the 1920s, with the establishment of Soviet rule in Ukraine and the official policy of "Ukrainization," Ukrainian lit. experienced a spectacular revival, as manifested in the proliferation of separate modernist and avant-garde movements, mainly neoclassicism, with such outstanding poets as Maksym Ryl's'ky (1895–1969) and Mykola Zerov (1890–1937); and *futurism, with Mykhail Semenko (1892–1937) and Mykola Bazhan (1904–83), who began as a futurist but quickly shifted to become the second most important Ukrainian Soviet poet of the century. Other notable poets from this period include Yevhen Pluzhnyk (1898–1936) and Volodymyr Svidzins'ky (1885–1941).

By the 1930s, the Stalinist terror had crushed the national and cultural revival, and hundreds of writers perished in camps. The poetic scene shifted to western Ukraine, then under Poland, and farther abroad. The most significant émigré poetic group that emerged in the interwar period was the so-called Prague school. Such poets as Yevhen Malaniuk (1897–1968), Oleksa Stefanovych (1899–1970), and Oksana Liaturyns'ka (1902–70) evinced patriotic fervor without sacrificing high standards of poetic craft. But the greatest poet of that period in western Ukraine was Bohdan Ihor Antonych (1909–37), known for his novel imagery and formal experimentation. In his mature poetry, he attained an expressive power and metaphysical and symbolic complexity that put him in the forefront of 20th-c. Eur. poetry.

In the postwar period, the high point of Ukrainian émigré poetry was the New York Group that originated in the mid-1950s and continued its activity into the 1990s. Such poets as Bohdan Boychuk (b. 1927), Yuriy Tarnawsky (b. 1934), Bohdan Rubchak (b. 1935), and Emma Andijewska (b. 1931), all born in the interwar period, eagerly experimented with poetic forms privileging *vers libre* and *metaphor and embraced such fashionable artistic and philosophical trends as *surrealism and existentialism. Gravitating toward the group were two poets of a slightly older generation, Oleh Zuievs'ky (1920–96) and Vasyl Barka (1908–2003), whose oeuvre manifested hermetic difficulty in its search for purity.

Soviet Ukrainian poetry experienced a major revival in the early 1960s with the appearance of such poets as Lina Kostenko (b. 1930), Mykola Vinhranovs'ky (1936–2004), and Ivan Drach (b. 1936). Known as the Generation of the Sixties, they strove for authenticity and liberalization. Their works, imbued with lyric intensity, centered on ethical and historical concerns but did not overtly experiment with poetic forms. More innovative and experimental were the poets of the Kyiv school who had their literary debuts also in the 1960s, though they were not encouraged by the state. Nonconformists and aesthetes, Vasyl Holoborod'ko (b. 1945), Mykola Vorobiov (b. 1941), Viktor Kordun (1946–2005), and Mykhailo Hryhoriv (b. 1947) published most of their oeuvre in the 1980s and 1990s, having a limited impact on the literary process of the 1960s. This is also true of such cerebral dissident poets as Vasyl Stus (1938–85) and Ihor Kalynets' (b. 1939). Their contribution was fully acknowledged only after 1991.

Beginning with the 1980s, a new generation of poets emerged. With the advent of Mikhail Gorbachev's *perestroika*, this generation no longer faced the prospects of harsh censorship. They focused on aesthetic freedom and on constructing a new cultural identity. The poetry of Ihor Rymaruk (1958–2008) and Vasyl Herasym'iuk (b. 1956) offers a dense, metaphoric language, biblical and regional motifs, and contemplates creativity as such. Other poets of the same generation reacted differently to the Soviet legacy. The period immediately preceding independence in 1991 witnessed the formation of many poetic groupings in Lviv, Kyiv, Kharkiv, and other cities, all finding distinctive ways to resist the symptoms of Sovietization. The most prominent among them, the Bu-Ba-Bu group, founded in the mid-1980s by Yuri Andrukhovych (b. 1960), Viktor Neborak (b. 1961), and Oleksandr Irvanets' (b. 1961), professed poetry as *performance and employed postmodernist devices such as *parody, *pastiche, and self-reference. Mocking the seriousness of their predecessors and debunking Soviet and nationalistic taboos became Bu-Ba-Bu's favorite pastime.

Ukrainian poetry of the postindependence period is dynamic and stylistically diverse. There is a strong undercurrent of female poetic voices, from the fiercely feminist and intellectual oeuvre of Oksana Zabuzhko (b. 1960) to more gender-balanced approaches of the younger Mar'iana Savka (b. 1973) and Marianna Kiianovs'ka (b. 1973). While the performative and playful manner of the Bu-Ba-Bu poetics appealed to some younger poets, with Serhii Zhadan (b. 1974) as the most talented, others rejected the group's carnivalesque spirit in favor of a more intellectual, ironic, and even metaphysical approach. Among the latter, Kostiantyn Moskalets' (b. 1963) and esp. Vasyl Makhno (b. 1964) deserve recognition. The youngest generation of Ukrainian poets, entering the poetic scene in the 2000s, displays a wide range of attitudes, from an offhand colloquiality to existential reflection. Unlike the poets of the 1980s, this generation does not need to assert its artistic freedom: these young poets just live it.

■ **Anthologies**: *The Ukrainian Poets*, ed. and trans. C. H. Andrusyshen and W. Kirkconnell (1963); *Khrestomatiia davn'oi ukrains'koi literatury*, ed. O. I. Bilets'kyi (1967); *Koordynaty*, ed. B. Boychuk and B. T. Rubchak (1969); *Antolohiia ukrains'koi liryky*, ed. O. Zilyns'kyi (1978); *Ukrains'ka literatura XVIII st.*, ed. O. V. Myshanych; (1983); *Antolohiia ukrains'koi poezii*, ed. M. P. Bazhan et al. (1984); *Visimdesiatnyky*, ed. I. Rymaruk (1990); *Poza tradytsii*, ed. B. Boychuk et al. (1993); *From Three Worlds: New Ukrainian Writing*, ed. E. Hogan et al. (1996); *A Hundred Years of Youth: A Bilingual Anthology of Twentieth-Century Ukrainian Poetry*, ed. O. Luchuk and M. M. Naydan (2000); *Pivstolittia napivtyshi*, ed. M. G. Rewakowicz (2005); *Dvi tonny naikrashchoi molodoi poezii*, ed. B.-O. Horobchuk and O. Romanenko (2007); *Dyvoovyd*, ed. I. Luchuk (2007); *In a Different Light: A Bilingual Anthology of Ukrainian Literature*, ed. O. Luchuk (2008); *Ukrains'ki literaturni shkoly ta hrupy 60–90 rr. XX st.*, ed. V. Gabor (2009).

■ **Criticism and History**: G. Luckyj, *Literary Politics in the Soviet Ukraine 1917–1933* (1956); *Istoriia ukrains'koi literatury*, ed. IE. P. Kyryliuk et al. (1967–71); D. Čyževs'kyj, *A History of Ukrainian Literature* (1975); G. Grabowicz, *Toward a History of Ukrainian Literature* (1981); G. Grabowicz, *The Poet as Mythmaker* (1982); O. S. Ilnytzkyj, *Ukrainian Futurism* (1997).

G. G. GRABOWICZ; M. G. REWAKOWICZ

**ULTRAISM.** An iconoclastic Sp. movement that first appeared in 1919 and had virtually disappeared by 1923. Spain's answer to the Eur. avant-garde, ultraism proposed to merge advanced contemp. artistic tendencies. The Argentinian Jorge Luis Borges, who was in Spain in 1918, contributed to the origins of ultraism and took its theories to Buenos Aires in 1921. A founder and major theoretician of the group was the critic Guillermo de Torre, author of the *Manifiesto Vertical*. Rafael Cansinos-Assens, writer and intellectual figure of the postwar period, also had much to do with the promotion of the new aesthetic, and Ramón Gómez de la Serna deserves his place as a significant antecedent. Both led important *tertulias* such as the one in the Café Colonia, and the latter writer was the first to publish F. T. Marinetti's futurist *manifesto in Sp. (see FUTURISM). Ultraism was a youthful revolt against outworn, secondhand *modernismo*; it fiercely opposed routine and inertia. The ultraists welcomed mod. life and were guided by subversive postwar attitudes. Above all, they sought to rehabilitate the poem by daring imagery; their most characteristic poems were generally formed by a series of unconnected images, the more original the better. The poets of ultraism rejected narrative and anecdotal matter as well as sentimentality, ornamentality—a reference to the style of Rubén Darío—and rhetorical effusion, preferring to cultivate a humor and playfulness reminiscent of futurism. They advocated *free verse and the elimination of rhyme and punctuation, and they strove to give visual form to their images by typographical techniques. Although rebelling against modernismo, they were, in fact, influenced by *symbolism and *Parnassianism.

It has been said that ultraism had no great poet, nor did it produce lasting works; hence, to some extent it has been disregarded by literary historians. Nevertheless, many jours. of the time published ultraist poems by such writers as Gerardo Diego and Juan Larrea. Lucía Sánchez Saornil was one of the few women ultraists. Others of the ultraism movement were Isaac del Vando-Villar, Pedro Grafias (Spain), Raúl González Tuñón, F. L. Bernárdez, R. Güiraldes, and E. González Lanuza (Argentina).

Diego's *Manual de espumas* (1924) is usually cited as the best ultraist book, although images modeled on the same aesthetic precepts can be found in a number of poets. Moreover, ultraism promoted creative freedom and experimentation concomitant with what was taking place in other countries, esp. in Latin America, as evidenced by the journal *Proa* (1924–26), and it opened new avenues for the future.

*See* AVANT-GARDE POETICS; SPAIN, POETRY OF.

■ M. de la Peña, *El ultraísmo en España* (1925); G. de Torre, *Literaturas europeas de vanguardia* (1925); R. Cansinos-Assens, *La nueva literatura* (1927); G. Videla, *El ultraísmo* (1963); G. de Torre, *Historia de las literaturas de vanguardia* (1965); J. G. Manrique de Lara, *Gerardo Diego* (1970); M. Scrimaglo, *Literatura argentina de vanguardia (1920–1930)* (1974); *Los vanguardismos en la América Latina*, ed. O. Collazos (1977); J. Cano Ballesta, *Literatura y tecnología. Las letras españolas ante la revolución industrial: 1900–1933* (1981); W. Bohn, *The Aesthetics of Visual Poetry, 1914–1928* (1986); H. Wentzlaff-Eggebert and D. Wansch, *Las vanguardias literarias en España: Bibliografía y antología crítica* (1999); H. Martínez Ferro, *Ultraism, Creacionismo, Surrealismo: Análisis textual* (1999); P. Rocca, "Las orillas del Ultraismo," *Hispamérica* 31 (2002); *Las vanguardias literarias en Argentina, Uruguay y Paraguay*, ed. C. García (2004); R. M. Silverman, "Questioning the Territory of Modernism: Ultraism and the Aesthetic of the First Spanish Avant-Garde," *RR* 97 (2006).

A. W. PHILLIPS; K. N. MARCH; R. GREENE

## UNITED STATES, POETRY OF THE

### I. English

**A. *Beginnings to 1900*.** A hist. of poetry in the U.S. "from the beginning" must begin by acknowledging that "the beginning" has always been a matter of debate. "Where to begin?" is the critical question, and the common answer has been to begin again in the present. The earliest anthol. to use *American poetry* as an organizing concept was Elihu Hubbard Smith's (1771–98) *American Poetry, Selected and Original* (1793), which heavily emphasized the poems of Smith's fellow *Connecticut Wits (1770s–90s) while ignoring the poetry of the 17th c. Later *canon-makers followed the same strategy by excising the 18th c. to endorse the 19th. Rufus Wilmot Griswold's (1815–57) anthols. of the 1840s, *The Poets and Poetry of America* (1842) and *Female Poets of America* (1848), centered on the work of New York poets affiliated with the Young America movement (1840s); and Edmund Clarence Stedman's (1833–1908) *Poets of America* (1885), an influential collection of essays, grounded Am. poetry in the work of the *Fireside poets (1870s–80s). All these efforts were overturned in the 20th c., which reinvented two minor poets of the previous century, Walt Whitman (1819–92) and Emily Dickinson (1830–86), as the only legitimate claimants to the beginnings of a poetic trad. that could genuinely be called *American*. Thus, the poetic hist. of the U.S. has often been conditioned by the effort to find a usable beginning that leads to the present.

Perhaps the major problem is that Am. poetry seems always to have begun somewhere else. The Am. hemisphere, depicted as an Edenic paradise of noble savages and natural abundance or as a howling wilderness of pagan devilry, was a rich source of imagery and inspiration for a number of Eur. poets who wrote from a distance, such as Shakespeare, Luís de Camões, or Joost van den Vondel, as well as others who envisioned and settled North Am. colonies, including George Sandys (1577–1644), Walter Ralegh (1552–1618), and George Berkeley (1685–1753), whose "Verses on the Prospect of Planting Arts and Learning in America" (written 1726, pub. 1752), prompted by a sojourn in Rhode Island, coined the line "Westward the Course of Empire takes its Way," which encapsulated a key motif for New World poetics.

Early poetry on America was generally published in Europe and tended to adopt cl. themes, meters, and styles. It also participated overtly in the imperial contests between Eur. powers. While elite authors took from New World materials to furnish poems for a Eur. readership, the process also worked in reverse: Port., Dutch, Sp., Fr., and Eng. settlers in New World plantations brought *songs with them. These popular *ballads, sea chanteys, work songs, and bawdy lyrics often adapted the Native Am. and Af. song trads. with which Eur. settlers came into contact. While primarily oral and improvisational, such songs were also based on established trads. of versification mediated by cheap print. New words could readily be fitted to old tunes, making it easy for songs to comment on current, local events in modes familiar to audiences that need not have been literate to enjoy them.

Like such popular lyrics, religious *hymns and *psalms also circulated widely, usually with the consent of colonial authorities. *The Bay Psalm Book* (1640, known in its day as *The New England Psalter*), a metrical trans. of the Psalms, is considered the first book of poems printed in colonial North America. The Puritan apostle John Eliot (ca. 1604–90) also published verse trans. of the Psalms in the Massachusett lang., to aid in converting the Native Am. peoples in the New England colonies.

Although these song and hymn trads. ranged across North America, the earliest printing press was licensed in Cambridge, in the Massachusetts Bay colony, in 1638, and printing penetrated most deeply in New England (no other press was licensed until 1686, in Philadelphia); thus, the Eng. Puritans have tended to dominate the hist. of 17th-c. colonial poetry. Anne Bradstreet (1612?–72) is perhaps the best-known Puritan poet; her volume *The Tenth Muse Lately Sprung Up in America* (1650) employed the *conceits and elaborate *similes of the *metaphysical poets on religious, political, and domestic subjects. Other popular New England poets included Michael Wigglesworth (1631–1705), whose best-selling poem on the Last Judgment, *The Day of Doom* (1662), popularized a style of *quatrain with internal rhymes on the first and third lines; and Benjamin Tompson (1642–1714), author of *New England's Crisis* (1676), a providential epic recounting King Philip's War. This sort of text was both poetry and also information about the conflict for highly interested audiences around the Atlantic (see INFORMATION, POETRY AS). Such work indicates the multiple functions poetry served in early Am. culture.

It is important to note that, with the exception of the rhyming *abecedarius *The New England Primer* (1690), possibly the best-selling book of the 18th c., books of poems were published in London (as were most books for the Am. market) and remained unavailable to all but the wealthiest colonial readers. Aside from psalters and primers, the most common type of poetry printed in North America was the *elegy, which was typically written by one minister for another (or a person of wealth and standing), as illustrated by Urian Oakes's (1631–81) elaborately titled "An Elegie Upon that Reverend, Learned, Eminently Pious, and Singularly Accomplished Divine, my ever Honoured Brother, Mr. Thomas Shepard" (1677). While they circulated freely, usually as broadsides, such texts also extolled the ministry as the proper guardians of public discourse. Elegies were performed as part of Puritan mourning rituals and were reproduced in *commonplace books, weavings, and tombstones, among other locations, underwriting a culture of mourning that would be satirized by Benjamin Franklin and Mark Twain.

Like the Puritan elegy, almost every early Am. poem printed in North America appeared in the cheapest possible formats: single-sheet broadsides, stitched pamphlets, almanacs, newspapers (after 1720 or so), and magazines (after 1760 or so); typical genres included ballads, *satires, squibs, pasquinades, execution songs, tavern songs, and versified sermons, which were usually anonymous, set to a familiar tune (such as "Chevy Chace") and sold for a penny or two. "The Poor Unhappy Transported Felon's Sorrowful Account of His Fourteen Years Transportation at Virginia" (ca. 1670s), by the possibly apocryphal author James Revel (1659–80), is an example of a broadside narrative derived from a long trad. of scaffold verse. Its opening stanza indicates the mixed mediation characteristic of so much 17th-c. verse:

> My loving countrymen pray lend an ear,
> To this relation that I bring you here,
> My present sufferings at large I will unfold,
> Altho' its strange, 'tis true as e'er was told.

We can imagine a ballad monger singing these lines in a London street, gathering an audience that would indeed lend an ear to the story and possibly buy a sheet to take home. This poem about the hardships of Virginia was published in London for an Eng. audience; it is hard to overstate the degree to which colonial poetry was oriented toward London, the cosmopolitan metropole of the anglophone world. Only from the retrospective vantage point of U.S. nationalism does such an orientation seem a problem; early Americans located themselves within the world system of Eur. colonialism. Colonial literary rivalries, such as that between the Tory wits Joseph Green (1706–80) and Mather Byles (1707–88), were triangulated through Brit. periodicals like the *London Magazine*, where Green placed two poems in 1733. Metropolitan jours. carried greater weight in Boston than the local *New-England Weekly Journal*, where Byles's popular "Proteus Echo" series had appeared, and colonial authors often wrote with a trans-Atlantic audience in mind.

Yet despite the prestige that certain publications offered, the vast majority of early Am. poets did not publish in print but circulated their works in ms., often to a small coterie of friends, but sometimes to a much more extended audience. The circulation of ms. poems through competing coffeehouses fueled most of the conflict between Byles and Green. The now-famous works of the Massachusetts minister Edward Taylor (1642–1729), *Preparatory Meditations* and *Gods Determinations* (1680s–1720s), known only to a few contemporaries, were not published until 1939. Unlike the worldly wit of Byles and Green, which was meant to dazzle and win prestige, Taylor used complex *syntax and elaborate metaphysical conceits to make his poems a form of spiritual exercise, as in a meditation on 1 Cor. 3.22:

> Thy Grace, Dear Lord's my golden Wrack, I finde
> Screwing my Phancy into ragged Rhimes,
> Tuning thy Praises in my feeble minde
> Untill I come to strike them on my Chimes.

While Taylor intended his poems for private devotional use, many colonial poets chose ms. circulation as the polite alternative to print. Literary circles like the Annapolis-based Tuesday Club (1745–56) sprang up across the colonies in emulation of London counterparts. Their purpose was to cultivate members' sentiments and sensibilities through belles lettres and polite conversation. *Epigrams, *acrostics, *riddles, *anagrams, and *dialogues were some of the favored poetic vehicles for the display of *wit and learning among members.

"Publishing" poems through the circulation of mss. was esp. common for early Am. women poets, whose access to print was highly limited. Even an elite woman like Annis Boudinot Stockton (1736–1801), who wrote more than 100 poems, published only about 20, all anonymously. Instead of print publication, most women poets participated in coteries. One prominent circle of elite Quaker women living in the Delaware Valley included poets Milcah Martha Moore (1740–1829), Hannah Griffitts (1727–1817), Susanna Wright (1697–1784), and Elizabeth Graeme Fergusson (1737–1801). They gathered to read and discuss poems, commented on them in letters and diaries, and wrote poems in response to each other on a wide variety of topics. Another circle living around Boston promoted the ms. poetry of Phillis Wheatley (1753–84) before the publication in London of her volume *Poems on Various Subjects, Religious and Moral* (1773). Wheatley, known as the "the sable prodigy" and "the Ethiopian Poetess," had been kidnapped as a child from the Gambian coast and, as a slave, became a literary celebrity in prerevolutionary Boston. These coterie poems tended to adopt neoclassical styles (authors often signed in *pastoral pseuds. like "Aminta") and discussed matters of both domestic and political interest. Poetry was a key vehicle for debating gender roles and the place of women in colonial society (a discussion known as the *battle of the sexes*), but such debates mostly occurred within the constraints of politeness—in ms., in parlors, and among fellow elites—rather than in the emerging realm of printed discourse.

That printed discourse was often hurly-burly. The dismantling of Stuart absolutism that followed the Glorious Revolution in England (1688), esp. the end of prepublication state censorship in 1695, created the conditions for a market-oriented print world. The Whig ascendancy after the Hanoverian succession (1714) forced a generation of Tory authors, thrown out of power and with no hope of state *patronage, to write for money. Concentrated in an impoverished district surrounding London's Grub Street, these "hacks," as they became known, developed a combative poetic idiom that sought to expose the corruptions of the new social and economic order through scurrilous, personalized attacks on figures of authority. The Grub Street ethic translated easily to 18th-c. colonial entrepôts such as Boston, Philadelphia, and New York City, where perennial conflicts among colonial governors (appointed by the Crown), assemblies (elected by the local population), and various local factions ensured a steady market for political controversy. In these "paper wars," stinging, catchy ballads (passed in song, ms., and print) proved esp. useful. In Philadelphia, Henry Brooke (1678–1736), an Oxford-educated scion, led a riotous campaign against the Quaker authorities, particularly their crackdown on public drinking. Brooke's mastery of impromptu compositions, esp. epigrams, combined the Georgian ideal of belletristic wit with tavern culture's masculine ethos and led to instantly popular satirical portraits of officials such as William Penn. The reign of Jonathan Belcher (1730–41) in Massachusetts provoked another such war, in which anonymous pasquinades against the governor were nailed to doors, copied into commonplace books, and passed around in taverns. In New York, Cadwallader Colden (1688–1776), James Alexander (1691–1756), and Lewis Morris Sr. (1671–1746) used an extensive arsenal of poems to further the political aims of their Country

Party in endless machinations against the Merchant Party of Governor William Cosby. Morris's verse *fable "The Mock Monarchy; or, the Kingdom of the Apes" (1730) circulated in ms. throughout the colony and in England. Morris also used the press to attack his political enemies, who retaliated by publicly burning two Country Party ballads denouncing Cosby. Meeting fire with fire, Cosby hired Archibald Home (1705–44) to circulate anti-Morris songs and poems. So impressed was Morris by his rival's literary flair that he recruited Home to his side.

Home later moved to New Jersey, where he presided over a polite literary circle in Trenton. His example shows how the rowdy culture of the tavern, the coffeehouse, and the press developed in tandem with the polite realm of the coterie, the parlor, and the tea table. Benjamin Franklin (1706–90) memorably described the masculine culture of the printing houses in Boston, Philadelphia, and London, where hard words, hard work, and hard drinking went together. However, Franklin's rise was driven by his facility with both the vituperative discourse of print and the polite conversation of civility. As a boy, he wrote several successful broadside poems, which he described as "wretched Stuff, in the Grubstreet Ballad Style," as well as an Aesopian fable against Governor Jonathan Belcher, "The Rats and the Cheese" (1730), and throughout his career he capitalized on his mastery of print controversy. But access to the library of his patron Matthew Adams (d. 1753) familiarized Franklin early with key works in the discourse of civility (famously, *The Spectator*), and this familiarity with the rhet. of politeness helped him flourish in the sociable world of 18th-c. mercantilism. Some of Franklin's closest associates were fellow belletrists, such as the poets Aquila Rose (1695–1723) and Joseph Breintnall (1695–1746), an inaugural member of the Junto, the literary circle Franklin founded in 1727.

Breintnall's elegy "To the Memory of Aquila Rose, Deceas'd" (1740) addressed a trans-Atlantic circle of friends in the terms of poetic sociability:

> Ye *Rose's* Friends, that in *Britannia* dwell
> Who knew his Worth, and best the Loss can tell:
> As I transmit such mournful News to you,
> Do you the tuneful sad Account pursue.
> And ye bright Youths, that meet at *Bendall's*
>   Board,
> An Elegy his hov'ring Shade afford:
> Had one of you deceas'd, and he surviv'd,
> His Memory by him had been reliv'd.

The transmission of poetry grounded communities locally (in Boston, Philadelphia, or London) and across long distances, and the spaces opened by death could be filled, at least in part, by the circulation of "tuneful sad Accounts" or elegies, which secured the bonds of fellowship.

While Britain's victory in the Seven Years' War (1756–63) secured Eng. hegemony in North America, it also drove the Crown to seek ever greater control over the economy and governance of the colonies. The resulting imperial crisis was mediated through institutions of oratory (club, tavern, pulpit) and print (broadsides, pamphlets, newspapers), and poetry worked through all the media of debate. Popular songs such as "Yankee Doodle" ostentatiously appropriated well-known Brit. tunes for patriot purposes. Poets such as Wheatley petitioned key figures such as the Earl of Dartmouth and George Washington in verse. A leading circle of revolutionary-era poets, the Connecticut Wits, incl. Joel Barlow (1754–1812), Timothy Dwight (1752–1817), John Trumbull (1750–1831), and David Humphreys (1752–1818), made recourse to poetry in support of the colonies. Trumbull's mock epic *M'Fingal* (1775, 1782), e.g., was a ubiquitous piece of revolutionary rhet. Philip Freneau (1752–1832), Ann Eliza Bleecker (1752–83), Lemuel Haynes (1753–1833), and Mercy Otis Warren (1728–1814) all produced patriotic verse supporting Am. independence. Sung in homes, taverns, and battlefields; recited during sermons and orations; or circulated in mss., broadsides, and newspapers, this poetry underwrote the discourse of liberty that authorized revolution.

After the revolution, however, poetry was circuited into the partisanship of the Federalist era. Humphreys, Barlow, Trumbull, and Lemuel Hopkins (1750–1801) collaborated on *The Anarchiad* (1786–87), a *mock epic satirizing social disorder in the wake of Shays's Rebellion; Dwight wrote one *epic attacking deism (*The Triumph of Infidelity*, 1788) and another supporting Federalist orthodoxy (*Greenfield Hill*, 1794). Barlow switched sides to Paineite democracy (*The Conspiracy of Kings*, 1792), and Jeffersonian republicanism (*The Columbiad*, 1808). These epics and mock epics featured neoclassical balance, *periphrasis, and an immensely complex set of references that can be difficult for mod. readers to parse without extensive footnotes. But their rhet. of satirical declension, ideological unmasking, and civic renewal was well known to contemporaries through the popularity of Augustan authors such as Alexander Pope, Jonathan Swift, and James Thomson.

The Boston wit Robert Treat Paine Jr. (1773–1811) expressed Federalist ambitions for the U.S. amid the welter of Eur. revolutions and Barbary Coast warfare in a 1798 song, "Adams and Liberty":

> In a clime, whose rich vales feed the marts of the
>     world,
> Whose shores are unshaken by Europe's
>     commotion,
> The trident of Commerce should never be hurled,
> To incense the legitimate powers of the ocean.
> But should pirates invade,
> Though in thunder arrayed,
> Let your cannon declare the free charter of trade.

(Incidentally, Paine's anthem of Federalist pieties borrowed the tune of "To Anacreon in Heaven," a ribald drinking song that Francis Scott Key's (1779–1843) "The Defense of Fort McHenry"—later "The Star-Spangled Banner"—also adopted). In reality, the U.S. population in 1798 was young, rural, agrarian, and poor. Literacy rates were increasing, but the rise was uneven, with the Northeast outpacing the South and the trans-Appalachian West. Limited roads and

bridges made transportation and communication between regions difficult. Consequently, there was no national market for books, periodicals, or newspapers; and chronically undercapitalized printers preferred steady sellers to risky new imaginative works. Coastal ports and, later, river and canal boomtowns were distinct literary capitals with a flourishing business reprinting popular Eng. authors. The existence of parallel domestic markets and the absence of an international copyright meant that Am. readers were more likely than Eng. to read books such as William Wordsworth and S. T. Coleridge's *Lyrical Ballads* (1798) or Walter Scott's *The Lay of the Last Minstrel* (1805). The literary nationalist James Kirke Paulding (1778–1860) expressed his frustrations about the Am. scene in an 1818 epic, *The Backwoodsman*:

> Neglected Muse! of this our western clime,
> How long in servile, imitative rhyme,
> Wilt thou thy stifled energies impart,
> And miss the path that leads to every heart? . . .
> Thrice happy he who first shall strike the lyre,
> With homebred feeling, and with homebred fire.

Paulding's call for "homebred" materials would be echoed by the Young America movement of the 1840s and the International Copyright League of the 1890s. Yet while an Am. poetry did not gain a stable institutional form until after the Civil War, Am. citizens, *pace* Paulding, were writing, reading, singing, circulating, and performing all kinds of poems. The Marylander Francis Scott Key published "The Defense of Fort McHenry" (the first stanza of which became the national *anthem in 1916) in a Baltimore newspaper in 1814; William Cullen Bryant (1794–1878), who had written an anti-Jeffersonian satire, "The Embargo," as a 13-year-old, published the instant classic "Thanatopsis" (1817) in *The North American Review*, a Boston jour. founded in 1815 to foster Am. letters; and "A Visit from St. Nicholas," by Clement Moore (1779–1863), was published anonymously in a Troy, New York, newspaper in 1822. All these poems were wildly popular across the entire country.

However, the most influential poet of early 19th-c. America was Lydia Huntley Sigourney (1791–1865). Sigourney commanded national acclaim and attention in poems on all possible topics, from child elegies ("dead-baby poems") and domestic instruction to Indian removal and slavery. Following the model of the Eng. poet Felicia Hemans, Sigourney deployed the *persona of the *Poetess, a gendered form of literary authority that spoke in nationalist, even imperialist cadences through the voice of sentimental domesticity. Her best work, like "To a Shred of Linen" (1838), demonstrated the centrality of women's labor to the hist. of the nation. Many, although not all, women poets gained access to public representation through the privatized figure of the Poetess: these included Elizabeth Oakes Smith (1806–93), Sarah Helen Whitman (1803–78), Maria Brooks (Maria del Occidente, 1794–1845), and the Ojibwe poet Jane Johnston Schoolcraft (Bamewawagezhikaquay, 1800–42).

As a figure for popular verse, the Poetess also influenced mid-century male authors. Two of the most prominent, E. A. Poe (1809–49) and H. W. Longfellow (1807–82), followed dramatically opposed trajectories in the literary world. By the 1830s, improved material conditions in the U.S. (a larger reading public, greater economic capitalization, and better internal communication), had made a literary career possible; but economic instability (exemplified by the Panic of 1837) made it a tenuous occupation, at best. Hundreds of newspapers and periodicals were founded in the 1830s, but the average one lasted less than a year before closing. Poe tried unsuccessfully to make his way in this literary climate, editing magazines in Richmond, Baltimore, Philadelphia, and New York, but always seeming to fail on the brink of success. His work was very popular—"The Raven" (1845) was one of the most reprinted and parodied poems in Am. lit.—but it could not earn him a living, and he died in poverty.

Poe's Gothic work cannily adopted many of the Eur. themes and motifs that abounded in antebellum magazine culture. "Lenore" (1843), "Ulalume" (1847), and "Annabel Lee" (1849) evoke a dreamy state of unreality, like the Am. Republic of Letters Poe imagined but could not realize. Poe was eccentric to the circles of literary authority that existed in his lifetime, and he reserved particular wrath for the literary culture of Boston ("Frogpondia" to him): the *Transcendentalist circle associated with R. W. Emerson (1803–82); and the group of Harvard-based poets that included O. W. Holmes (1809–94), J. R. Lowell (1819–91), and, esp., Longfellow.

Longfellow was the most successful poet of the mid-19th c. In long poems such as *Evangeline* (1847), *Hiawatha* (1855), and *Tales of a Wayside Inn* (1863), he fused North Am. themes such as Native Am. lore and the Revolution with cl. and Eur. meters and the narrative structures of poems like the *Canterbury Tales* and the *Divine Comedy* (which Longfellow, a scholar of the Romance langs., translated in the 1860s). *Hiawatha* combined Ojibwe stories (based on the ethnography of H. R. Schoolcraft) with the *trochaic tetrameter of the Finnish epic the *Kalevala*, while *Evangeline* was one of the most successful (and controversial) experiments with Eng. *hexameters:

This is the forest primeval. The murmuring pines
 and the hemlocks,
Bearded with moss, and in garments green, indis-
 tinct in the twilight,
Stand like Druids of eld, with voices sad and
 prophetic,
Stand like harpers hoar, with beards that rest on
 their bosoms.

The syncretism of this work (Poe called it "plagiarism") aspired to an ideal of comparative lit. that Longfellow, the Smith Professor of Modern Languages at Harvard, sought to forge in the image of J. W. Goethe's *Weltliteratur*. From his position at Harvard and by way of his close alliances with Boston's publishers, Longfellow enjoyed unprecedented cultural prestige and business success (he became the first author to own the stereotype plates of his work, e.g.). *Hiawatha* was a runaway best seller in 1855, the same year a relatively obscure newspaperman in New York City issued *Leaves of Grass*.

Although its eccentricity to the orbit of antebellum letters was greatly exaggerated in the 20th c., *Leaves of Grass* was an unusual book (mostly because it lacked the organizing structures that mid-century readers had come to expect: a table of contents, titles for poems, line numbers, and, esp., a named poet). In lieu of a name (which appeared unexpectedly within the poems), the frontispiece showed the image of a typical workingman, with open collar and hand on hip, eyes staring boldly into the reader's. This sort of assertive yet anonymous intimacy also marked the poems. The long lines, mostly lacking a recognizable meter or rhyme pattern, conformed to the space of the page, thus incorporating print materiality into the poems' structure, while the loosely organized *strophes encouraged readers to create their own ways of reading the work. "I celebrate myself, / And what I assume you shall assume," it began, and, throughout the long poem later known as "Song of Myself," Walt Whitman pursued a leveling strategy for the reading of poetry: "Have you practiced so long to learn to read? / Have you felt so proud to get at the meaning of poems? / Stop this day and night with me and you shall possess the origin of all poems, / You shall possess the good of the earth and sun." *Interpretation was very much subordinated to intimacy in Whitman's poetics: reading, for him, should be like sex.

This project of intimacy thrust *Leaves of Grass* into the fraught and violent politics of the 1850s: not only did Whitman (who 13 years earlier had written a temperance novel) seek to check the growing stigmatization of the body in reform discourses like the temperance movement ("Welcome is every organ and attribute of me, and of any man hearty and clean, / Not an inch nor a particle of an inch is vile"), he sought to establish a poetic basis for collective experience, which the political system of the era had resoundingly failed to provide. Thus, the poems were filled with the daily experiences of ordinary people in lengthy *catalogs (the most aesthetically controversial aspects of the poems, then and now; see INFORMATION, POETRY AS). Whitman piled incident atop humdrum incident in an effort to make working life poetic, to extend the circle of democratic belonging further and further outward. We could all find ourselves in these poems, he suggested, and no one would assume priority over anyone else.

Whitman's faith in Am. democracy was shaken by the Civil War and the assassination of Abraham Lincoln (who, incidentally, also wrote poetry). But by way of his elegies to Lincoln, "When Lilacs Last in the Dooryard Bloom'd" (1865) and "O Captain! My Captain!" (1865), his most popular poem, he gradually reached wide appreciation in the 1880s, with devoted readers (known as *Whitmaniacs*) making pilgrimages to his small home in Camden, New Jersey.

Between 1882 and 1894, all the major poets of the mid-19th c. died. The culture felt a palpable sense of loss. Where would poetry go? In the last decade of the century, the first eds. of Emily Dickinson's poems produced an unexpected publishing sensation. Dickinson had died in 1886, but for almost 30 years before her death she had been known to her familiar correspondents as a poet (though no one knew how extensive her collection of ms. poetry had grown until after her death). Some of those correspondents were important in the public sphere, so 11 of Dickinson's poems appeared in print during her lifetime by their hands. But in the elaborately ed. volume *Poems* (1890), her editor's description of Dickinson's verse as "something produced absolutely without the thought of publication, and solely by expression of the writer's own mind" became a model of *lyric expression protected from what one review called "the mass of popular print." Somewhat ironically, the poet whose writing life participated intimately and actively in so many of the reading and writing practices we have traced in Am. poetry (hymnal meter, the figure of the Poetess, familiar circulation followed by publication in print) became representative of a poetry held apart from the spirit of its age.

This myth about Dickinson has been so persistent that she and Whitman are still often mischaracterized as the first mod. Am. *lyric poets, but it is important to note that, at the end of the 19th c., Dickinson and Whitman were not the only examples of poets produced in expensive print eds. and made to look like exceptions to earlier rules. In 1896, Paul Laurence Dunbar's (1872–1906) *Lyrics of Lowly Life* was introduced as if it were an innocent version of black culture removed from the realities of the last decade of the 19th c. If Dickinson became a lyric representative by being characterized as isolated from the public in which her lyrics would circulate, Dunbar became another representative made to personify a culture imagined as less mod. than the rest of America. The framing of Dickinson and Dunbar as throwbacks, as poets too pure for the modernity that welcomed them, speaks to the ways that the 20th c. would begin to think of poems as expressions of individual alienation and as dramatic versions of fictional speakers. Before 1900, poetry in America was much more often thought of as the expression of a group and, after the late 18th c., as the expression of a nation. The era after 1900 would seek to elevate poetry through an ever-increasing complexity of lyric expression, thus closing a period when all kinds of verse circulated as the most popular genres of literary production in the U.S.

B. *Modernist Poetry, 1900–1945.* The "word of the modern, the word En-Masse" that Whitman celebrates describes the dynamic modernity of an emerging mercantile America—a dynamism that many modernists deplored. Dickinson's formal innovations were effaced by early eds. who limited her canon to more conventional poems on love and nature. The two most important poets of the late 19th c. had to wait for their *modernism to be born.

Poetry in the United States entered the 20th c. as a conservative retrenchment. Edwin Arlington Robinson (1869–1935), Edgar Lee Masters (1868–1950), Robert Frost (1874–1963), and John Crowe Ransom (1888–1974) form a transitional group that confronted the period's secularization and materialism by vaunting a rural, regional ethos. Building on the model of Robert Browning, several of these poets developed dramatic *monologues and poetic dialogues, often in the voices of rural speakers who epitomized the virtues of small-town values against cosmopolitan malaise.

Masters's *Spoon River Anthology* (1915) offers an example of these tendencies, chronicling the diverse population of his western Illinois small-town heritage. His portraits earned him a wide reputation, even though he often satirized the limits and provincialism of his readers. Perhaps speaking for the limits of poets of his generation, Petit, the poet, ruefully regrets his blindness to the heroic potential of his rural life composing "Triolets, villanelles, rondels, rondeaus, / Seeds in a dry pod, tick, tick, tick . . . what little iambics, / While Homer and Whitman roared in the pines?"

Robinson *did* write *villanelles and *rondeaux, chronicling the varied life of rural America based on his native town, Gardiner, Maine. Robinson's preference for complex stanzaic forms, regular rhyme schemes, and conventional meters contrasts with the psychological *realism and dramatic *voice of his characters. His persistent exploration of the unfulfilled life anticipates T. S. Eliot.

Frost offers the closest bridge between the Emersonian trad. of New England and his modernist peers. Like Masters and Robinson, Frost chronicled rural life through dramatic monologues. Often regarded as a New England moralist, Frost is a considerably more complex figure whose poems often present irreconcilable ethical choices for people often ill equipped to confront the implications of their acts. "Mending Wall" (1914) is usually seen as a warning against the building of barriers ("Something there is that doesn't love a wall, / That sends the frozen-ground-swell under it"), yet as its farmer-philosopher speaker demonstrates, the act of seasonal rebuilding of a rustic wall brings neighbors together to cement a taciturn yet resilient community. Frost's repudiation of *free verse made him a reluctant modernist, yet his mastery of *blank verse offered "a momentary stay against confusion."

Frost's preference for rural life looks back to Wordsworth, and it was perhaps this retrospective quality to much U.S. poetry that prompted the Brit. poet and critic George Barker to observe in his 1948 essay "Fat Lady at the Circus" that "American poetry is a very easy subject to discuss for the simple reason that it does not exist." W. C. Williams (1883–1963) saw this as Am. poetry's great advantage—the possibility of a new, perhaps violent beginning. In *Paterson* (1946–58), Williams posed the question that animated the work of many of his generation:

How to begin to find a shape—to begin to begin
   again,
turning the inside out: . . .

For Williams, son of a Brit. father and a Puerto
Rican mother, the question was how "American" was
Am. poetry when written by ex-slaves, Rus. Jewish im-
migrants, Native Americans, and the sons and daugh-
ters of Mexican Californios?

Poets responded to the claim that the U.S. lacked a
unitary culture in a variety of ways. Some, such as T. S.
Eliot (1888–1965), H.D. (1886–1961), Gertrude Stein
(1874–1946), and Ezra Pound (1885–1972), expatriated
to Europe in order to "make it new" amid older, more
established cultural trads. Others, including Frost, Hart
Crane (1899–1932), Wallace Stevens (1879–1948),
Marianne Moore (1887–1972), and Williams hoped to
"find a shape" on native soil and in the Am. idiom.
Af. Am. poets who migrated to Harlem following
World War I negotiated what it meant to be both black
and a bard in Jim Crow America. A number of these
writers—Langston Hughes (1902–67), Richard Wright
(1908–60), Claude McKay (1890–1948)—also traveled
abroad, living for periods of time in Europe and the
Soviet Union.

Of the expatriate group, Pound offered the most
sustained diagnosis of what was wrong with contemp.
verse. He felt poetry needed to rid itself of *sentimen-
tality, platitudes, and "emotional slither" by means out-
lined in the March 1913 issue of *Poetry*:

1. Direct treatment of the "thing" whether subjec-
   tive or objective.
2. To use absolutely no word that does not contrib-
   ute to the presentation.
3. As regarding rhythm: to compose in the se-
   quence of the musical phrase, not in sequence
   of a metronome.

These axioms, the basis of *imagism, provided an al-
ternative to Victorian rhet. and romantic excess by their
advocacy of clear, concrete images. Pound's third axiom
proposed a more flexible metric tied to emotive and
acoustic properties in each line. In defining the *image,
Pound fused a symbolist poetics of the autonomous
aesthetic object (see SYMBOLISM) with a psychologist's
model of integrated consciousness, "an intellectual and
emotional complex in an instant of time." His own
imagist experiments reflected the influence of Chinese
and Japanese precedents. "In a Station of the Metro"
(1913) reflects the influence of Japanese haiku:

The apparition of these faces in the crowd,
   Petals on a wet, black, bough.

Imagism was only one component in Pound's early
attempt to master all forms and idioms of poetry. His
early "masks of the self" constituted a poetic appren-
ticeship on his way to writing an epic poem. The most
important transitional poem, in this respect, is *Hugh
Selwyn Mauberley* (1920), which provided Pound
with a method of collating different voices to mark a
historical epoch, a method already being tested in the
early sections of *The Cantos*, upon which he worked for
the rest of his life.

*The Cantos* (1925–72) attempted to tell the "tale
of the tribe," to create a cultural hieroglyph of values,
both Eastern and Western, that would awaken soci-
ety from its collective sleep. Mythological references,
trans. from cl. sources and Romance langs., quotations
from historical chronicles, catalogs of historical figures,
personal conversations, and moments of great lyrical
beauty create a dense, often incomprehensible cultural
*collage. Rather than link these fragmentary materials
via editorial or rhetorical commentary, Pound left them
as "luminous details" to constellate a larger cultural
edifice. Unfortunately, that edifice increasingly took
the form of a totalitarian ethos. Pound's support for
Mussolini and the Axis powers during World War II
led to his incarceration near Pisa and then in a
Washington, D.C., mental hospital for 13 years after
the liberation. While he was incarcerated after the war,
he published in 1948 *The Pisan Cantos* (Cantos 74–84),
which, amid controversy, won the Bollingen Prize
sponsored by the Library of Congress. Pound contin-
ued to work on *The Cantos* until his death, publishing
*Rock Drill* (Cantos 85–95) in 1955 and *Thrones* (Cantos
96–109) in 1959. In the poem's last segments, *Drafts
and Fragments* (1969), Pound seemed to feel that his
poem would itself resemble one of the ruins depicted
in his poem: "Tho' my errors and wrecks lie about me. /
And I am not a demigod, / I cannot make it cohere."

In the January 1913 "Imagist" number of *Poetry*,
Pound presented as his exemplary case the work of
Hilda Doolittle (who took the pen name H.D.), whose
early poetry (*Sea Garden* [1916], *Heliodora* [1924]) pro-
vided a model of spareness that fused the economy
and clarity of the *Greek Anthology* with streamlined
modernity, as in her "Oread" (1914):

Whirl up, sea—
   whirl your pointed pines,
splash your great pines
   on our rocks,
hurl your green over us,
   cover us with your pools of fir.

H.D.'s early poetry drew from the cl. lyric and
drama (she translated Euripides's *Ion*). Her first books
of poetry refined a short, epigrammatic lyric, often
spoken from the standpoint of a nymph or nature god.
The poems in *Sea Garden* contested the usual romantic
association of women with flowers by creating poems
about violent natural forces, gods of the harvest, and
tough, resilient plants that survive against the ele-
ments. In her later, longer poems, she expanded her
critique of patriarchal authority by rewriting masculine
stories—stories of war and violence often legitimated
by reference to deceptive female figures such as Helen
of Troy or Eve or Pandora. In place of masculinist sto-
ries of deceptive or dangerous women, H.D. posited
priestesses and worshippers of Isis. Much of her work
was indebted to readings in hermetic trads., Neoplatonic
philosophy, and pre-Christian myth. *Helen in Egypt*
(1961) has been seen as a pointed riposte to many of

her male colleagues who see the Trojan War from the standpoint of its putative cause.

T. S. Eliot also benefited from Pound's support and tutelage, most famously through the latter's editing of *The Waste Land* (1922), which turned a *pastiche of Popean satire, Browningesque monologues, and Pre-Raphaelite imitations into one of the most important poems of the era. Born in St. Louis, Missouri, Eliot completed most of his Ph.D. in philosophy at Harvard, then moved to London, where he lived for the rest of his life. His early poems, collected in *Prufrock and Other Observations* (1917), were influenced by the Fr. symbolists as well as Browning's dramatic monologues. "The Love Song of J. Alfred Prufrock" (1915) summarizes a mood of claustrophobia and solipsism that typified his early verse, and other poems—"Preludes" (1910–11), "Portrait of a Lady" (1917), and "Gerontion" (1920)—provided psychological portraits of the era.

Eliot's "impersonal theory of art," as he developed it in the essays "Tradition and the Individual Talent" (1919), "Hamlet and His Problems" (1919), and "The Metaphysical Poets" (1921), constitutes one of the most important components of modernist poetics, providing much of the theoretical armature for the *New Criticism of the 1940s and 1950s. At the core of his poetics is an abiding desire to recover what he calls "the historical sense," which can be achieved only if the poet transcends his or her particular psychological state and creates a "general emotion" to which all readers throughout time could respond. Eliot's advocacy of impersonality was by no means strictly literary; it bespoke his own psychological condition, an instability that led to several stays at sanitaria and a disastrous early marriage.

Eliot's most important work, *The Waste Land*, chronicles in five sections the mod. era's malaise and spiritual vacuity through a series of vivid images of sterility:

> April is the cruellest month, breeding
> Lilacs out of the dead land, mixing
> Memory and desire, stirring
> Dull roots with spring rain.

The poem represents a series of disembodied voices that narrate the fall of empires, the despoliation of nature, and the debasement of sexuality and reproduction. Underlying these instances of contemp. violation lie subterranean references to Arthurian legend, pre-Christian vegetation myth, and Eastern religion. Precedent for this layering of cultural materials, past and present, had been provided by the "mythic method" that Eliot saw in James Joyce's novel *Ulysses* (1922). Although Eliot provided no single narrator for his poem, he adapted the cl. figure of the blind Theban prophet Tiresias into a "spectator" to the events of the poem.

Eliot found doctrinal solution to this dehumanized landscape by converting to Anglo-Catholicism in 1927, following which the poems became increasingly concerned with theological questions of faith, incarnation, and belief. *Ash Wednesday* (1930), the inaugural poem of this period, coincided with his new religion and Brit. citizenship. Later poems such as *The Four Quartets* (1936–42) and his plays were attempts to give vertical authority to temporal progress, seeking, as he said, "the still point of the turning world" and a kind of incarnation of the word in silence. This synthesis of religious incarnation with aesthetic perfection is the hallmark of Eliot's contribution to many poets of the 1940s seeking an organic fusion of local particulars and universals in a secular age.

Eliot's impact on subsequent poets was substantial, but not everyone appreciated his example. Williams spent much of his career in a one-way debate with the poet of *The Waste Land*, feeling that, by adopting Eurocentric values and conservative political and religious views, Eliot had turned his back on the possibility of a vibrant U.S. trad. *The Waste Land*, Williams wrote in his *Autobiography* (1951), "set me back twenty years." Eliot's cultural elitism provided Williams with a much-needed foil for his own home-grown avant-garde response. Instead of living the bohemian life in Europe, Williams went to medical school and served as a general practitioner for the rest of his life in Rutherford, New Jersey. He maintained contact with Am. abstract painters such as Marsden Hartley, Charles Sheeler, and Charles Demuth and supported vanguard publications such as *Broom* and *Others* that forged alliances between new poetry and Eur. movements such as *Dada and *surrealism.

Williams's early poetry in *Al Que Quiere!* (1917), *Sour Grapes* (1921), and *Spring and All* (1923) celebrates the quotidian and the ordinary:

> so much depends
> upon
>
> a red wheel
> barrow
>
> glazed with rain
> water
>
> beside the white
> chickens

This focus on the unadorned reality of things—what he and others later called *objectivism*—stressed not only the value of the ordinary object but the power of the imagination to bring the object into view. The wheelbarrow upon which "so much depends" is framed in a specific landscape, "glazed with rain / water // beside the white / chickens," and the alternating three- and one-word lines reinforce the material creation of that landscape in words.

Williams's frontal attack on trad., manners, and received opinion are characteristic of his work, culminating in his epic poem *Paterson*. Unlike Pound's *Cantos* with its sources in Eur. and Chinese hist., *Paterson* is based on the author's New Jersey hometown as a *metonymy for the possibility of renewal. Like William Blake's archetypal Albion, Paterson is a sleeping giant, waiting to be reborn, while Dr. Paterson, the local poet-doctor tries to piece him together. In this sense, Williams continued Whitman's hope for an epic grounded in his native country and Am. speech. Williams identified his doctor-hero with the city itself, its hist. merging with the poet's own hist. In book 2, he begins to deploy a new kind of lineation, a triadic, stepped stanza that became the model for much of his later verse. In *The Desert Music* (1954) and *Pictures from Breughel* (1962), he experimented further with what he called this *variable foot*, which he linked with the possibilities of a specifically Am. idiom.

Stevens is Williams's counterpart in his desire to ground the poem in a reality that does not exist without the imagination. But whereas Williams stakes everything on the object (incl. the poem), Stevens is interested in the subjective apprehension of the object, the constant oscillation of imaginative self and bare reality. In the absence of sustaining myths and transcendental options, "Poetry / exceeding music must take the place / Of empty heaven and its hymns." This may sound like a latter-day version of symbolist escapism, yet Stevens felt that, through poetry, one would be returned to an earth one had forgotten how to see. Like Williams, Stevens had a professional career, working as an insurance lawyer in the firm of Hartford Accident and Indemnity Company. It was not until he was 44 that he published his first book, *Harmonium* (1923), in whose lyrics and satires Stevens wrote dazzling, often witty monologues on philosophical matters, often in vivid, color-drenched imagery. In subsequent work, he increasingly dramatized the mind in its speculative acts. Later long poems such as "Notes toward a Supreme Fiction" (1942), "Esthetique du Mal" (1945), "The Auroras of Autumn" (1947), and "An Ordinary Evening in New Haven" (1950) are less a departure from his early, symbolist-influenced lyrics than a logical evolution of problems advanced in them. "Notes toward a Supreme Fiction" speculates over 31 sections on how the "first idea" or "supreme fiction" is incarnated in the poem. But the "supreme fiction" must be discovered in the propositional logic of the poem itself; it cannot be imposed, as Stevens's Canon Aspirin supposes: "He imposes orders as he thinks of them, . . . But to impose is not / To discover." Stevens rejects imposition in favor of immanent discovery, marking a crucial link with earlier romantics and looking ahead to the immanent poetics of postmod. poets.

If poetry for Stevens offers a "supreme fiction" for a skeptical age, poetry for Moore offers *"sincerity" in a mendacious age, "a magnetism, an ardor, a refusal to be false." Semantic approximations of *sincerity*, such as *authenticity*, *integrity*, and *genuine*, appear throughout her poetry, but one never encounters the kinds of moral imperatives that such terms imply. Sincerity in "Poetry" (1919) is hard won:

> I, too, dislike it: there are things that are important
>     beyond all this fiddle.
>   Reading it, however, with a perfect contempt for
>     it, one discovers in
>   it after all, a place for the genuine.

Moore's poetry seeks the genuine in a wild menagerie of flora and fauna—jerboas, steam rollers, pangolins,

elephants, and wood weasels. An inveterate fan of the Brooklyn Dodgers and hired for a time to name a new Ford automobile (her suggestions were rejected in favor of the name *Edsel*), Moore was often portrayed as a kind of spinster crank; yet her tightly controlled *syllabic lines, extensive *allusions to literary and scientific texts, and wry, spare *irony show her work to be a good deal more complicated. Moore's longtime affection for mythological beasts, sea creatures, armored animals, and curious insects is more than a naturalist's curiosity but an *objective correlative for psychological and affective states. She often begins a poem with a minute description of an animal but then becomes distracted by other associations. In "The Pangolin" (1936), Moore seems to remark in her opening lines on the persistence of these figures and, perhaps, on herself: "Armor seems extra," yet like her tightly controlled syllabics, armor offers a shield that is both decorative and protective at the same time.

If Moore conducted her critique of lang. by quoting works of natural hist. and H.D. by revising cl. myth, Stein conducted hers by a radical deformation of lang. itself. There are no vegetation gods or cl. sources behind her works; nor, in fact, are there symbols attached to them. For Stein, words are returned to their grammatical, phonemic, and morphemic elements, as if to ground writing in the sheer materiality of words on the page. Her early psychological experiments while a student of William James at Radcliffe College convinced her that patterns of verbal repetition are a marker of character or "bottom nature" by which each person could be recognized. Although she applied such theories in her early prose works such as "Melanctha" (1905) or *The Making of Americans* (1911), she deployed *repetition extensively in her poems as well, particularly those that she called "portraits" of objects and people. Her theory of repetition was also influenced strongly by Eur. modernist painters, particularly Henri Matisse, Pablo Picasso, and Georges Braque, whom she and her brother Leo befriended in Paris. In her most sustained comment on poetry, "Poetry and Grammar" (1934), she notes that the function of poetry is with "using with abusing, with losing with wanting, with denying with avoiding with adoring with replacing the noun." Nowhere is this practice of uncovering the noun more pronounced than in *Tender Buttons* (1914), a series of prose meditations on ordinary objects, rooms, and food, in discontinuous sentences often generated by *paronomasia, verbal associations, and rhymes.

Stein, Moore, Stevens, and Williams all in some way attempted to return, as Stevens said, to the "basic slate" of a given locale, to deal with a godless world and to find immanent potential in ordinary things. For their younger contemporary Hart Crane, the Brooklyn Bridge, which serves as the centerpiece of his epic poem, stands as a complex symbol for Am. potentiality, space, and psychic resonance. The bridge "lends a myth to God" and gives form to a hist. from which we have become alien. Crane, like Eliot, imbibed the spirit of symbolism through Arthur Symons's *The Symbolist Movement in Literature* (1899) and, throughout his short career, attempted to follow what he called a "logic of metaphor" to map unconscious associations between things. The son of a candy manufacturer, Crane worked in his early years for his father's business while imbibing A. C. Swinburne, Ernest Dowson, and Oscar Wilde, the decadent lit. of the fin de siècle. His early poems were modeled on the Victorian poetry of Swinburne and Alfred, Lord Tennyson, and he never quite lost his taste for sensuous, alliterative textures in lang. His first book, *White Buildings* (1926), reflects his reading of other modernist peers via pastiches of Eliot, Pound, Stevens, Williams, and others.

Crane's magnum opus, *The Bridge* (1930), attempts an epic survey of United States hist., from Columbus's first landing through the Civil War, westward expansion, and Indian Wars to mod. technologies (rail, electricity, telephones, subways). *The Bridge* features multiple voices, from its rhapsodic opening ("O Sleepless as the river under thee . . .") to the jazz rhythms of "The River" ("Stick your patent name on a signboard / brother–all over–going west–young man / Tintex–Japalac–Certain-teed Overalls ads . . .") to the ecstatic finale of "Atlantis." Throughout, Crane is conscious of prior epic trads.—from Homer to Dante to Whitman—and self-consciously places himself as their Am. heir. As much as *The Bridge* is a celebration of Am. hist. and accomplishment, it is often a poem of the *isolato*, in Crane's case, the homosexual poet whose solitude is flanked by the bustling crowds, tall buildings, and racing conveyances of the mod. metropole.

Crane's optimistic belief in the mythic potential of the Am. city was not shared by Af. Am. poets, who had yet to achieve anything like social or economic equality. The first real flowering of an Af. Am. intellectual and artistic renaissance could be seen in the *Harlem Renaissance of the 1920s. Alain Locke (1885–1954) provided the seminal call to arms through his anthol. of writings by black intellectuals *The New Negro* (1925), whose introduction observed that the Negro had been more of a formula than an expression of human complexity and that the time had come for a change in black self-expression through music, painting, lit., and debate. Among black poets, this change took the form of a debate over lang. Should Af. Am. poetry be based, as Langston Hughes believed, in the vernacular, oral trad. of black people, influenced by jazz rhythms and speech rhythms—or should it be based, as Countee Cullen (1903–46) and Claude McKay demonstrated, in traditional meters and stanzaic forms? Dunbar, the early James Weldon Johnson (1871–1938), and McKay had written significant black *dialect poetry, and among Harlem Renaissance poets, a number, incl. Hughes and Sterling Brown (1901–89), drew on the rich heritage of the black vernacular. Writing in reaction to Cullen's tendency to write in traditional *sonnets and versification, Hughes argued in "The Negro Artist and Racial Mountain" (1926) that the use of such models reflected the hegemony of whiteness—the "racial mountain" by which black writers configured their work around white models. In "The Weary Blues" (1926), Hughes quotes a *blues lyric within the larger

poem, thereby creating a double-voiced representation of the black experience.

Cullen and McKay's ballads and sonnets often asserted race-conscious themes, in a sense "blackening" the white canon just as white poets had attempted, through Uncle Remus tales and popular music, to "whiten" black culture. McKay's "If We Must Die" (1919) is written in the form of an Elizabethan sonnet, yet its content concerns black resistance to racism and lynching:

> If we must die, let it not be like hogs
> Hunted and penned in an inglorious spot, . . .

Harlem Renaissance women writers such as Georgia Douglas Johnson (1880–1966), Anne Spencer (1882–1975), Angelina Weld Grimké (1880–1958), and Alice Dunbar-Nelson (1875–1935) also wrote in traditional meters and stanzaic patterns yet filled these forms with issues relating directly to the politics of an emerging black community, as well as to matters of gender and domesticity.

The 1930s and the Popular Front produced another version of modernism, galvanized by the Depression and fueled by political activism. Prominent poets of the period—Muriel Rukeyser (1930–80), Edwin Rolfe (1909–54), and Edna St. Vincent Millay (1892–1950)—rejected avant-garde formal strategies of the earlier modernists and subjected poetic form to political ends. "Not Sappho, Sacco," Rukeyser advised other poets, speaking of the need to turn from modernists' appropriation of cl. models to contemp. events such as the trial of accused anarchists Ferdinando Nicola Sacco and Bartolomeo Vanzetti. Rukeyser adapted Eliot's mythic method in her own *documentary poem "Book of the Dead" (1938), which chronicles a mining workplace disaster in West Virginia and the congressional hearings into corporate malfeasance that led to the deaths of miners from silicosis. Millay, in "Justice Denied in Massachusetts" (1927), attacked the legal malfeasance surrounding the Sacco and Vanzetti trial in 1920, and in "Say That We Saw Spain Die" (1938) responded to the defeat of the Sp. Republic by Franco's fascists.

One group of poets who came to prominence during the Popular Front era and combined modernist aesthetics and politics were the objectivists (see OBJECTIVISM): Louis Zukofsky (1904–78), George Oppen (1908–84), Charles Reznikoff (1894–1976), Carl Rakosi (1903–2007), and Lorine Niedecker (1903–70). Although they resisted defining themselves as a movement, they nevertheless built upon the examples of Pound and Williams in creating a poetry of direct presentation and economy. Zukofsky's essay "An Objective" (1930–31) stresses the unity of seeing eye and object: "*An Objective: (Optics)—The lens bringing the rays from an object to a focus. That which is aimed at. (use extended to poetry)—Desire for what is objectively perfect . . .*" Such perfection implies not fidelity to nature but sincerity or honesty in "thinking with the things as they exist." Zukofsky's involvement in Left politics can be felt in his long poem *"A,"* composed throughout the poet's life between 1927 and 1978, where, in several instances, he quotes directly from Karl Marx's *Das Kapital* and relates the labor of writing to other forms of social materiality. Similarly, his colleague Oppen in *Discrete Series* (1934) creates short lyrics that attack capitalism and its excrescences: "Closed car–closed in glass– / At the curb, / Unapplied and empty: / A thing among others: . . ." The bare-bones style of such poems offers lang. unadorned, its surfaces and grammatical structure returning a degree of use value to lang., a quality that would become important to poets of the *Black Mountain school and *Language poetry movement.

More conservative poets of the period felt that ideological concerns of the Popular Front were irrelevant to art. In the wake of modernist excesses and experimentation, what was needed was a return to the poem as aesthetic *artifact, detached from its historical conditions or its author's psychology. Poets and critics who formed around John Crowe Ransom at Vanderbilt University, known as the *Fugitives, included Allen Tate (1899–1979) and Robert Penn Warren (1905–89). Their agrarian *manifesto *I'll Take My Stand* (1930) endorsed Southern rural values and the cl. curriculum against forms of collectivism and cosmopolitanism. They staked their aesthetics on Eliot's crit., with its emphasis on the impersonality of the poet, the devel. of the objective correlative, and the formally closed text. Their poems used traditional meters and complex metaphors and, in many cases, were based on southern hist. Tate's "Ode to the Confederate Dead" (1928) is an elegy for universal ideals and moral authority that he associates with the defeated South. The subject of the poem is twofold: the crisis of mod. solipsism and the death of heroic possibilities in a secular society. The narrator, speaking on an autumn afternoon in a Confederate military cemetery, muses on his alienation from the heroic dead but also senses his inability to rectify the "fragmentary cosmos," as Tate calls it in an essay on the poem ("Narcissus on Narcissus," 1938), of contemp. reality. To this extent, Tate echoes Eliot's warnings against solipsism in poems like "Prufrock" and *The Waste Land*, except that in his *ode, Tate locates the crisis of inaction against a specific U.S. historical moment.

Warren, Tate, and Ransom, along with fellow Fugitive Cleanth Brooks (1906–94), were perhaps better known as literary critics whose New Criticism offered a technical, even scientific alternative to the often impressionistic, biographical crit. of the era. Ransom's crit., esp. "Poetry: A Note in Ontology" (1934), repudiated what he called "Platonic poetry" (the poetry of ideas) and "Physical Poetry" (imagism and the various forms of objectivism) in favor of what he called "Metaphysical Poetry," which created a "miraculist" fusion of universal ideas and concrete particulars. The religious implications of miraculism suggest the ways that the New Critics sought a secular version of Christian incarnation through the aesthetic. Such ideas, when institutionalized in Brooks and Warren's influential teaching anthol. *Understanding Poetry* (1938), exerted an enormous influence on literary pedagogy for generations to come.

C. *Postwar Poetry, 1945–2010.* World War II produced its own poetry. Perhaps the most representative poem of the period was Randall Jarrell's (1914–65) "The Death of the Ball Turret Gunner" (1945), written from the standpoint of an Air Force gunner, "hunched" in the belly of an airplane like an animal and who, when killed, is "washed . . . out of the turret with a hose." This bleak vision of the hopelessness of war is matched by the sequence of 12 sonnets by Gwendolyn Brooks (1917–2000), "Gay Chaps at the Bar" (1945), based on letters from black soldiers in the then-segregated army that chronicles the difficult tension between learning "white speech" and knowing black alienation. Finally, there are poems by those who opposed the war, incl. Pound, William Everson (1912–94), Robert Lowell (1917–77), William Stafford (1914–93), and Robert Duncan (1919–88), who, whether as conscientious objectors or, in the case of Pound, war criminals, were incarcerated for periods during the war. One might add to this list many poets and intellectuals on the Left who were disaffected by the pact between Hitler and Stalin at the war's outset.

Poets who came of age in the period immediately after World War II found themselves in a difficult relation to their modernist predecessors. On the one hand, the work of Eliot, Pound, Stevens, Frost, Moore, and Crane had provided younger poets with an extraordinary range of formal and thematic resources; at the same time, this variety also proved a stumbling block to further experimentation. It seemed to Jarrell that modernism, "the most successful and influential body of poetry of this century—is dead." Such an elegiac assessment of the era masked a desire felt by many poets of this generation to have a clean slate. Innovative works such as Williams's *Spring and All*, Pound's *Cantos*, Stein's *Stanzas in Meditation*, or Eliot's *The Waste Land* had challenged the structure of traditional verse, and now it was time for a stock-taking that would seize upon the liberating advantages of Fr. *vers libre and the derived Anglo-Am. free verse while curbing their excesses.

Writers born in the first two decades of the 20th c.—Theodore Roethke (1908–63), Elizabeth Bishop (1911–79), John Berryman (1914–72), Jarrell, Lowell, Howard Nemerov (1920–91), and Richard Wilbur (b. 1921)—turned away from free verse and developed a technically complex, rhetorically difficult poetry modeled on the values of the New Critics, esp. the work of metaphysical poets such as John Donne and George Herbert. Where poets of the first generation capped their careers by writing long epic or dramatic poems, postwar poets perfected a kind of reflective, ironic lyric that would become the formal model for the two decades following World War II.

Eliot's lit. crit. provided a major impetus for many of these tendencies, and his cultural crit. introduced a religio-ethical frame within which poetry could be assessed. The characteristic voice in poems written during this period is arch and ironic, cautious of bardic pronouncements yet assured in its mastery of complexity and contradiction. Irony now implies more than saying one thing while meaning another; it signals that the artist is in control, able to moderate feeling by transforming it into rhet. In a paradox that seemed quite normal to the age, Wilbur spoke of irony as being the "source . . . of what richness and honesty we may sense in a poem," as illustrated by his own example from *The Beautiful Changes* (1947):

> Does sense so stale that it must needs derange
> The world to know it?

Wilbur's "Praise in Summer" (1947), with its careful management of ironic tension, richly embroidered *figuration, and steady iambic meters, seems destined less for sensual *appreciation than for *explication. As Jarrell conceded, it was an "age of criticism" in which the techniques of *close reading and scientific analysis were perfected in ways that ultimately affected how poems were written. The postwar years saw colleges and universities expanding their enrollments with students on the G.I. Bill, and the curriculum needed practical critical methodologies to accommodate this influx. For the first time in hist., poets in increasing numbers became teachers, and creative writing became part of the literary curriculum. Whereas for the first generation of modernists, poetry emerged within bohemian enclaves and expatriate communities, it now became a province of the university quarterly and the English Department classroom.

Arguably, the three poets who most typify—but at the same time challenge—the conservative tenor of the times were Lowell, Berryman, and Bishop. Lowell's first two books, *Land of Unlikeness* (1944) and *Lord Weary's Castle* (1946), exhibit the effects of his close relationship to his New Critical mentors, Ransom and Tate. In these works, Lowell takes the metaphysical mode to an extreme, employing a gnarled, convoluted syntax and *alliteration to represent issues of incarnation and existential doubt. With *Life Studies* (1959), Lowell shocked his teachers and friends by dropping his metaphysical style and speaking in a more personal voice about his ambivalent relationship to his patrician New England family, troubled marriages, mental breakdowns, and theological anxieties. Despite Lowell's new personalism, he still maintained the formal *diction and iambic *cadences of his earlier work:

> These are the tranquilized *Fifties*,
> and I am forty. Ought I to regret my seedtime?

Lowell's rather archaic diction and heavy alliterations temper his *confessional poetry with a need to contain feeling within definite formal boundaries. In later volumes (*History, For Lizzie and Harriet*, and *The Dolphin*, all 1973) he returned to a more traditional verse, working extensively in unrhymed, blank-verse sonnets.

Berryman began by writing in the style of W. H. Auden and W. B. Yeats, but with "Homage to Mistress Bradstreet" (1956) and even more powerfully in *77*

*Dream Songs* (1964), he developed an idiosyncratic use of persona that permitted him a wide range of voices to dramatize various sides of his rather volatile personality. In the former poem, he collapses his own voice into that of America's first poet, speaking of his own existential malaise through Anne Bradstreet's confessions of spiritual doubt. His major work, *The Dream Songs* (1969), confronts the poet's own biography in a long sequence of lyrics, each built on three six-line stanzas, written from 1955 until the time of his death in 1972. Despite its autobiographical content, *The Dream Songs* offers a complex series of personae in which mocking accusation merges with ironic self-deprecation:

> Life, friends, is boring. We must not say so.
> After all, the sky flashes, the great sea yearns.

("Dream Song 14")

Bishop, though less rhetorically explosive than either Lowell or Berryman, combined flexible meters with microscopically sharp observations to achieve a broken, tense lyricism, reminiscent of Moore. She describes the skin of a fish as

> . . . like wallpaper:
> shapes like full-blown roses
> stained and lost through age.

("The Fish")

In such lines, lang. isolates and refines the image until it loses its conventional associations and becomes something exotic and even heroic. Without moralizing commentary, Bishop sees a world of vivid particulars that gain luster by her patient, at times obsessive, enumerations. In Bishop, as in her two poetic peers, formal mastery implies less the creation of seamless artifice than it does a charged ling. and rhetorical field in which cognitive acts may be tested. Lowell's and Berryman's harsh, crabbed lang. and Bishop's enjambed, condensed lines represent a *formalism impatient with its own limits, dramatizing by sheer verbal energy areas of psychological intensity that cannot yet be expressed.

Lowell's poetry after *Life Studies* made an indelible mark on a number of writers, incl. Sylvia Plath (1932–63), Anne Sexton (1928–75), W. D. Snodgrass (1926–2009), and, to a lesser extent, Berryman. Despite their emphasis on charged psychic materials, these poets reflect a much more carefully modulated response to their personal content. The strength of Plath's vehement attack in "Daddy" (1962) comes not from its specific address to her actual father, Otto Plath, who died when she was a child, but from its conscious and careful manipulation of conflicting discursive modes (childhood rhymes, holocaust imagery, obsessive repetitions) that form an objective correlative to her psychological condition. Confessional poetry, as M. L. Rosenthal pointed out in his inaugural essay on that movement ("Poetry as Confession," 1959), should be considered not as a prescriptive formula held by any one group but as a general permission felt by most poets of the period to treat personal experience, even in its most intimate and painful aspects.

If Eliot, Auden, and Frost exerted a pervasive

influence on the dominant trad. of the 1950s, Pound and Williams began to exert a like effect on an emerging experimental trad. Pound's *Cantos* had provided a model for a historical, "open" poetry, and Williams's hard, objectivist lyrics had encouraged a poetics of visual clarity and metrical experimentation. Charles Olson's (1910–70) essay on *"projective verse" (1950) extended their ideas with a special emphasis on the poetic line as a register of physiological and emotional contours. He sought to reinvigorate poetic lang. by what he called *composition by field*, in which poetic form extends directly from subject matter and in which the line is a register of momentary perceptions. He explored this stance in his *Maximus Poems* (written 1950–70, pub. 1960–75), which dwells on the separation of the individual from his or her locale because of the ill effects of entrepreneurial capitalism. Early portions of *The Maximus Poems* engage the hist. of Olson's hometown, Gloucester, Massachusetts; but in later sections, his interests extend outward to Asia, Africa, and the Americas and back to the Pleistocene period.

Although "projective verse" had few adherents when it first appeared, it was a harbinger of things to come, as poets sought a loosening of poetic forms and an alternative to New Critical strictures. The most public announcement of a change came from Allen Ginsberg (1926–97), whose long poem *Howl* (1956) revived romanticism in its most vatic form and with Whitman-esque enthusiasm made the poet's specific, personal voice the center of concern:

> I saw the best minds of my generation destroyed
>     by madness, starving hysterical naked,
> dragging themselves through the negro streets at
>     dawn, looking for an angry fix

Ginsberg's protest against institutional mind control and McCarthy-era paranoia was made in what he called his "Hebraic-Melvillian bardic breath" and in a lang. as direct and explicit as Wilbur's or Lowell's was oblique. The carefully nuanced ironies of the period were jettisoned in favor of a tone alternately funny, frank, and self-protective. *Howl* received its first major critical forum in the San Francisco Municipal Court when its publisher, City Lights Books, went on trial for pornography, adding new meaning to the poem's social indictment and bringing a mass readership to the work of other Beat generation writers (see BEAT POETRY). Many of Ginsberg's colleagues—Jack Kerouac (1922–69), Lawrence Ferlinghetti (b. 1920), LeRoi Jones (b. 1934, now known as Amiri Baraka), Gregory Corso (1930–2001), Michael McClure (b. 1932)—provided their own critique of the era, reviving a demotic, populist poetics inspired by Whitman and Williams as well as the romantic, visionary work of William Blake and P. B. Shelley. Performing their poetry in jazz clubs or coffeehouses, occasionally accompanied by jazz, the Beat poets made the *poetry reading a primary fact of postwar literary life.

The Beat movement is the most public face of a general romantic revival during the late 1950s and 1960s. Whether through Olson's notion of composition by

field, Robert Bly's (b. 1926) ideas of the psychological *deep-image, or Frank O'Hara's (1926–66) personism, poets began to think of the poem not as an imitation of experience but as an experience itself, a map of moment-to-moment perceptions whose value is measured by immediacy and sincerity rather than artistic unity. As Duncan said, "[T]he order man may contrive upon the things about him . . . is trivial beside the divine order or natural order he may discover in them." Duncan's remark reinvests John Keats's *negative capability with sacramental implications: the poet relinquishes order that he may discover an order prior to and immanent within experience.

In the late 1950s, these general tendencies could be seen in little magazines such as *Origin, The Black Mountain Review, Yugen, The Fifties, Evergreen Review*, and, most important, in Donald Allen's 1960 anthol. *The New American Poetry 1945–1960*, which first divided the experimental tendencies of Am. poetry into five groups. One group consisted of the poets associated with Black Mountain College in North Carolina, incl. Olson, Robert Creeley (1926–2005), Duncan, Denise Levertov (1923–1997), and Edward Dorn (1929–99). Another group, the *New York school, incl. O'Hara, John Ashbery (b. 1927), Kenneth Koch (1925–2002), and James Schuyler (1923–91), was closely associated with painters and musicians. The *San Francisco Renaissance was represented by poets such as Jack Spicer (1925–65), Robin Blaser (1925–2009), Brother Antoninus (the aforementioned William Everson), and Philip Lamantia (1927–2005). A fourth category included other West Coast writers such as Gary Snyder (b. 1930), Philip Whalen (1923–2002), and David Meltzer (b. 1937). Along with the Beats, these groups shared less a common aesthetic than a spirit of bohemian exuberance and antiestablishment camaraderie.

In a similar vein but coming from different sources, Bly, James Wright (1927–80), W. S. Merwin (b. 1927), Galway Kinnell (b. 1927), Mark Strand (b. 1934), and others were developing a poetics of the "deep-image." Using Sp. and Fr. surrealism as a source, they experimented with associative techniques that would circumvent discursive thought and tap into unconscious realms. Among Deep Image poets, one can draw a distinction between those who create discontinuous "leaps" within a minimal, denuded landscape and those for whom the "leap" implies access to a world of numinous presence. Strand and Merwin would be examples of the first sort, creating poems in which lang. has been reduced to a bare minimum. In Wright's or Bly's poetry, conversely, the deep image serves to join quotidian, unreflective experience with realms of spiritual or natural value. Taking a walk, mailing a letter, or wasting time becomes an initiatory rite of passage into archetypal experiences. In Bly's "Snowfall in the Afternoon," (1962), a snowstorm transforms a barn into a "hulk blown toward us in a storm at sea; / All the sailors on deck have been blind for many years." Waking in the morning "is like a harbor at dawn; / We know that our master has left us for the day" ("Waking from Sleep," 1962).

The Eur. avant-garde provided a common ground

for another group that was initially associated with Bly and Wright but ultimately moved in a very different direction. David Antin (b. 1932), Jackson Mac Low (1922–2004), Jerome Rothenberg (b. 1931), and Armand Schwerner (1927–99) merged a strong interest in Dada and surrealism with the poetics of Stein, the aesthetic theories of Marcel Duchamp and John Cage, and the theatrical "happenings" movement. In a desire to find aesthetic models that exist outside of Western trad. (or marginalized within it), many of these poets turned to oral and nonliterate cultures, creating along the way an *ethnopoetics that stresses cultural and social sources of poetry.

The identity politics of the 1960s brought new constituencies into the poetry world, assisted by access to cheap, offset printing technologies and art venues. Af. Am., gay and lesbian, Asian Am., Native Am., and Chicana/o poets drew on alternative cultural models to challenge the canon of anglocentric, male models. Poet and playwright LeRoi Jones threw off his previous Black Mountain and Beat affiliations and adopted the name Imamu Amiri Baraka to signal his alliance with the Black Nationalist movement. The *Black Arts movement with which Baraka was associated created an angry, frontal poetry that addressed racism, drawing on Afrocentric cultural trads., free jazz improvisation (see JAZZ POETRY). and street vernacular. Other poets not directly tied to the Black Arts movement—David Henderson (b. 1942), Audre Lorde (1934–92), June Jordan (1936–2002), and Michael S. Harper (b. 1938)—also worked to foreground black cultural experience and lang. Although alternate cultural sources became important allies in this endeavor (the use of jazz rhythms in black writing, the use of oral chant in Native Am. poetry, bilingualism in *Chicana/o poetry), the primary formal imperatives came from the more populist, oral styles of the Beats and other new poetry movements.

Coinciding with the growth of literary communities among ethnic minorities, women writers began to write out of the social and political context of the feminist movement. Presses, reading spaces, distribution services, and anthols. provided a range of new resources for women writers, many of whom—like Adrienne Rich (1929–2012)—began their careers within the predominantly male literary community. Although "women's poetry" defines less a set of stylistic features than a spectrum of gendered concerns, many women writers agreed with the necessity for revision as defined by Rich: "the act of looking back, of seeing with fresh eyes, of entering an old text from a new critical direction." Many of Rich's poems are just such revisions of previous texts as she sorts through the "book of myths" ("Diving into the Wreck," 1972) to find moments in which women have been marginalized—or ignored outright. Although she began by writing poems very much in the formalist mode of the 1950s, Rich's style gradually loosened to admit her own changing awareness of women's oppression and to express her anger at patriarchal authority.

The proliferation of poetic styles during the 1970s and 1980s repeated many of the tendencies of the modernist period, with subtle refinements. Poets rejected the more bardic and expressive gestures—what Stanley Plumly (b. 1939) calls "experience in capital letters"—of the 1960s in favor of a discursive, even chatty surface that belies more complex social and psychological issues. The dominant mode of the 1970s and 1980s is a reflective lyricism in which technical skill is everywhere evident but nowhere obtrusive. The overtly romantic stance of 1960s poetry, with its emphasis on participation, orality, and energy, gave way to quiet speculation.

One can identify three general areas of practice among mainstream writers of the 1970s and 1980s linked by a shared concern with *voice and *tone. Among the first group, A. R. Ammons (1926–2001), Ashbery, Robert Pinsky (b. 1940), Louise Glück (b. 1943), Sandra McPherson (b. 1943), and Robert Hass (b. 1941) merge the philosophical skepticism of Stevens with the ethical, cultural concerns of Yvor Winters (1900–68) or Warren. Ashbery's poetry, perhaps the most sophisticated and complex of the group, manifests what he calls "the swarm effect" of lang., vacillating between opposing lures of what he calls "leaving out" or "putting in." His long, desultory lyrics such as "The Skaters" (1966), *Self-Portrait in a Convex Mirror* (1975), and the prose trilogy *Three Poems* (1972) record the fluctuating patterns of a disjunct consciousness. Unable to believe either in a supreme fiction or in a self-sufficient ego, Ashbery leaves "the bitter impression of absence" in lines that are often hilariously funny even as they are self-deprecating. Ammons's poetry, while similar to that of Stevens in its treatment of philosophical issues, builds upon Frost's naturalism and his concern for the morality of "place." For Ammons, "small branches can / loosen heavy postures" ("Essay on Poetics," 1970), and he conducted a quiet campaign for the restorative effects of weather, seasonal change, animal life, and horticulture as they interact with the speculative intellect. Hass's poetry continues Ammons's naturalist concerns—Frost and Kenneth Rexroth (1905–82) are important sources as well—but builds upon subtle shifts of voice and tone. Philosophical speculation alternates with epiphanic moments.

A second group, closely aligned with the first but extending more directly out of the deep-image aesthetic of Bly and Merwin, would include poets such as C. K. Williams (b. 1936), Marvin Bell (b. 1937), Philip Levine (b. 1928), Tess Gallagher (b. 1943), Charles Wright (b. 1935), Plumly, and Carolyn Forché (b. 1950). In their work surrealist juxtaposition combines with a spare, sometimes minimalist style to expose unconscious or atavistic resonances in everyday events. Less inclined toward the ecstatic "leaps" of Bly and James Wright, these poets prefer a more narrative progression and an elaborate use of analogy that allows the poet to achieve some kind of transcendence or political clarity amid mundane particulars.

A third variation on the dominant mode, what von Hallberg characterizes as "the Cosmopolitan Style," is represented by John Hollander (b. 1929), Richard Howard (b. 1929), James Merrill (1926–95), and Anthony Hecht (1923–2004). In this work, discursiveness becomes a foil for strategies of self-preservation and effacement. At the same time, a tendency toward conversation conflicts with the use of formal meters and complex *internal and terminal rhymes. This tension can be felt in the work of Merrill, which often uses its own aesthetic virtuosity to mock aesthetic solutions. His poems are willfully bookish, his tone, derived to some extent from Auden, arch and urbane. Merrill's reticence and detachment are calculated frames for viewing a conflicted personal hist., a condition given fullest treatment in his trilogy, *The Changing Light at Sandover* (1980). In this long poem, the poet's personal ardors, his "divine comedies," are subjected to an extraordinary anthol. of literary forms, from sonnets and verse dramas to blank-verse paragraphs, all subsumed under the pose of having been received during Ouija board séances. Like many of his earlier poems, *The Changing Light at Sandover* is a poem about writing, a celebration of the "surprise and pleasure [of] its working-out," that offers an elaborate allegory about erotic and spiritual love in an increasingly secularized society.

Merrill is usually regarded as a principal influence on a movement known as the *New Formalism, which would include Alfred Corn (b. 1943), Marilyn Hacker (b. 1942), Brad Leithauser (b. 1953), Katha Pollitt (b. 1949), and Gjertrud Schnackenberg (b. 1953). Their renewed interest in traditional forms (as well as the possibilities of *narrative poetry) has been undertaken less as a rear-guard attack on debased culture than as a recovery of the liberating potential of limits. New Formalists stress that writing in traditional forms aims to rebalance scales that had tipped too strongly in the direction of free verse since the 1960s, leading, as a result, to a rather amorphous autobiographical lyricism in which open form became an excuse for sloppy practice. The challenge for New Formalists has been to hide or at least diminish pattern through the use of slant rhyme, nonce forms, syllabic rhythms, and expressive variants on repeated meters. At the same time, poets attempt to combine their use of regular meters and rhyme with diction drawn from contemp. life, using the idiom of urban experience, technology, and advertising to blur the usual association of traditional forms with "high" or nonstandard diction.

All these tendencies could be linked by their resistance to the more autobiographical and vatic modes of the 1960s. The most frontal critique of such tendencies has come from writers associated with *Language poetry. The work of Lyn Hejinian (b. 1941), Bruce Andrews (b. 1948), Rae Armantrout (b. 1947), Carla Harryman (b. 1952), Charles Bernstein (b. 1950), Ron Silliman (b. 1946), Bob Perelman (b. 1947), and Barrett Watten (b. 1948) explores the degree to which the "self" and "experience" are constructs, enmeshed in social discourse. Deriving from Black Mountain, *futurism, and objectivism, these writers foreground lang. as signifying system (see SIGN, SIGNIFIED, SIGNIFIER). Fragmentation and non sequitur open up new realms of play and semantic complexity that invite (or cajole) the reader into cocreation of the poem. Language poets' interest in the *prose poem and nonlinear sentencing challenges the generic boundaries of lined verse. That

interest can be taken as a marker of a certain *crise de vers* that haunts recent poetry in general. If "a word is a bottomless pit" (Hejinian), a lang.-oriented poetry joins poet and reader in an agency by which that pit shall be explored, and postmod. poets have taken this realization as a generative fact.

By the end of the 20th c., many of the techniques associated with language writing (non sequitur, collage, decentered point of view) became standard features of much mainstream verse, leading the Marxist critic Fredric Jameson to feel that avant-garde innovation was the cultural dominant, as evident in advertising or fashion as in experimental art. At the same time, the increased importance of creative-writing programs and the MFA in college curricula has produced a generic "workshop poem" that, as Altieri explains, "appears spoken in a natural voice [with] a sense of urgency and immediacy to this 'affected naturalness' so as to make it appear that one is re-experiencing the original event." Such "studied artlessness" has itself become a kind of formula, leading some academic critics to wonder if poetry can survive its own institutionalization. Books and articles with titles like *After the Death of Poetry* (V. L. Shetley, 1993) and *Can Poetry Matter?* (D. Gioia, 1992) bemoan the domestication of poetry through creative-writing programs and the detachment of poetry from public life. This elegiac response to an increasing professionalization on the one hand and to the increasing fragmentation of traditional poetic values on the other is premised on the illusion that there was an earlier, more vibrant moment in which poetry mattered in public life.

These elegiac remarks conflict with the historic upsurge of *performance poetry in coffeehouses, art spaces, and bars. Often distant from academic venues, slams, stand-up, and spoken-word events have brought poetry back to the public arena, merging formal rhymes and patterned rhythm with *hip-hop and rap music. The *Nuyorican Poets Café, founded by Miguel Algarín (b. 1941) in 1973 in New York, featured a multicultural mix of spoken-word poetry, open mike, and performance events. *Poetry slams involve poets competing for the best improvised poem on a given theme (see POETIC CONTESTS). Although the spirit of spoken-word poetry has precedents in Dada performance as well as Beat poetry readings, its strongly community-based, democratic ethos contrasts with coterie or school-based poetry movements.

If the "little magazine" revolution of the 1960s was a poetry of the page in which *typography and lineation represented expressive intent, the digital revolution of the 1990s and after inaugurated new forms of digital poetry (see ELECTRONIC POETRY) in which the word is released to cyberspace. In some cases, poets adapted the computer to *aleatory (chance-generated) composition. In other cases such as *Flarf, poems are created out of Web searches and databases. This new media also made poetry available in ways unimaginable in an era of tape recorders and offset printing. Sites such as the Buffalo Electronic Poetry Center (EPC), Ubuweb, Pennsound, and online magazines such as *Jacket* and *Big Bridge* allow readers around the world to hear live poetry readings and interviews and even to participate in the composition of new work.

The collaborative potential of digital poetry problematizes the expressivist basis of much previous poetry. The natures of *presence, voice, orality, and identity are rendered esp. complex in hypertext, where different links may provide multiple narrative roads for the reader to follow or where multiple readers may interact with the text. Issues of beginnings and closure, the page and scoring no longer have the same relevance in the age of the scrolling screen. Claims for the democratization of poetry through digital media have led to a renewed consideration of new forms of public address. Flarf practitioners use open-source software principles to access free information on the Web that is then modified, redistributeds, and deformed.

It seems clear that the emergent poetry of the 21st c. no longer can be described by binaries such as "raw and cooked" (Robert Lowell's description of his contemporaries in 1960), experimental and formalist, symbolist and immanent, speech-based and text-based. In a digital and postidentity age, collective labels (Black Mountain, Deep Image) and categories of identity seem both limiting and beside the point. The strong lyric tendency of poetry of the 1970s and 1980s is now matched by an equally strong commitment to narrative, prose poetry, performance, and satiric verse. To adapt the title of a recent anthol., we live in an age of the Am. hybrid, linking formalists and experimentalists, proceduralists and stand-up poets. The outlines of a 21st-c. U.S. poetry are still difficult to see, but the resilient spirit of Emerson's "metre-making argument" endures.

## II. Spanish.
See CARIBBEAN POETRY (SPANISH), CHICANA/O POETRY, NUYORICAN POETRY.

## III. French.
See FRANCOPHONE POETS OF THE U.S.

## IV. Indigenous Language.
See INDIGENOUS AMERICAS, POETRY OF THE; INUIT POETRY; NAVAJO POETRY.

*See* AFRICAN AMERICAN POETRY, AMERICAN SIGN LANGUAGE POETRY, ASIAN AMERICAN POETRY.

■ **To 1900.** *Anthologies*: *African-American Poetry of the Nineteenth Century*, ed. J. R. Sherman (1992); *American Poetry: The Nineteenth Century*, ed. J. Hollander, 2 v. (1993); *American Women Poets of the Nineteenth Century*, ed. C. Walker (1995); *American Poetry: The Seventeenth and Eighteenth Centuries*, ed. D. S. Shields (2007). **Criticism and History**: F. O. Matthiessen, *American Renaissance* (1941); R. H. Pearce, *The Continuity of American Poetry* (1961); A. Gelpi, *The Tenth Muse: The Psyche of the American Poet* (1975); S. Cameron, *Lyric Time: Dickinson and the Limits of Genre* (1979); W. Dowling, *Poetry and Ideology in Revolutionary Connecticut* (1990); D. S. Shields, *Oracles of Empire: Poetry, Politics, and Commerce in British America* (1990); S. Cameron, *Choosing Not Choosing: Dickinson's Fascicles* (1992); *Breaking Bounds: Whitman and American Cultural Studies*, ed. B. Erkkila and J. Grossman (1996); D. S. Shields, *Civil Tongues and Polite Letters in British America* (1997); M. P. Brown, "'BOSTON/

SOB NOT': Elegiac Performance in Early New England and Materialist Studies of the Book," *American Quarterly* 50 (1998); M. L. Kete, *Sentimental Collaborations: Mourning and Middle-Class Identity in Nineteenth-Century America* (2000); C. Wells, *The Devil and Doctor Dwight: Satire and Theology in the Early American Republic* (2002); P. B. Bennett, *Poets in the Public Sphere: The Emancipatory Project of American Women's Poetry, 1800–1900* (2003); C. C. Calhoun, *Longfellow: A Rediscovered Life* (2004); M. Loeffelholz, *From School to Salon: Reading Nineteenth-Century American Women's Poetry* (2004); E. Richards, *Gender and the Poetics of Reception in Poe's Circle* (2004); M. Warner, "Introduction," *The Portable Walt Whitman* (2004); V. Jackson, *Dickinson's Misery: A Theory of Lyric Reading* (2005); M. Cavitch, *American Elegy: The Poetry of Mourning from the Puritans to Whitman* (2007); *The Traffic in Poems: Nineteenth-Century Poetry and Transatlantic Exchange*, ed. M. McGill (2008); M. C. Cohen, "Contraband Singing: Poems and Songs in Circulation during the Civil War," *AL* 82 (2010); J. van der Woude, "The Migration of the Muses: Translation and the Origins of American Poetry," *Early American Literature* 45 (2010).

■ **1900–2010.** *Anthologies*: *The Book of American Negro Poetry*, ed. J. W. Johnson (1931); *An "Objectivists" Anthology*, ed. L. Zukofsky (1932); *The Morrow Anthology of Younger American Poets*, ed. D. Smith and D. Bottoms (1985); *Shadowed Dreams: Women's Poetry of the Harlem Renaissance*, ed. M. Honey (1989); *The Oxford Anthology of Modern American Poetry*, ed. C. Nelson (2000); *In the American Tree*, ed. R. Silliman (2002); *American Hybrid: A Norton Anthology of New Poetry*, ed. C. Swensen and D. St. John (2009); *Against Expression: An Anthology of Conceptual Writing*, ed. C. Dworkin and K. Goldsmith (2011). **Criticism and History**: J. H. Miller, *Poets of Reality: Six Twentieth-Century Writers* (1965); H. Kenner, *The Pound Era* (1971); C. Altieri, *Enlarging the Temple: New Directions in American Poetry during the 1960s* (1979), and *Self and Sensibility in Contemporary American Poetry* (1984); M. Perloff, *The Dance of the Intellect: Studies in the Poetry of the Pound Tradition* (1985); R. von Hallberg, *American Poetry and Culture, 1945–1980* (1985); H. A. Baker Jr., *Afro-American Poetics: Revisions of Harlem and the Black Aesthetic* (1988); M. Levenson, *A Genealogy of Modernism: A Study of English Literary Doctrine, 1908–1922* (1989); C. Nelson, *Repression and Recovery: Modern American Poetry and the Poetics of Cultural Memory, 1910–1945* (1989); R. Pérez-Torres, *Movements in Chicano Poetry: Against Myths, Against Margins* (1995); A. Nielsen, *Black Chant: Languages of African-American Postmodernism* (1997); *The Objectivist Nexus: Essays in Cultural Poetics*, ed. R. B. DuPlessis and P. Quartermain (1999); R. B. DuPlessis, *Genders, Races and Religious Cultures in Modern American Poetry* (2001); *New Media Poetics: Contexts, Technotexts, and Theories*, ed. A. Morris and T. Swiss (2006); T. Yu, *Race and the Avant-Garde: Experimental and Asia American Poetry since 1965* (2009); M. Davidson, *On the Outskirts of Form: Practicing Cultural Poetics* (2011).

M. COHEN (TO 1900); M. DAVIDSON (MODERNIST, POSTWAR)

**UNITY.** A fundamental—quite possibly *the* funda-
mental—aesthetic criterion, akin to harmony, integ-
rity, and coherence. In the *Phaedrus*, Plato holds that
an oration should have unity analogous to the organic
unity of a living creature; in the *Symposium*, he sug-
gests, in connection with the musical scale, that unity
is a reconciliation of opposites or discords. The first
full-blown Western theory of dramatic unity emerges
in Aristotle's *Poetics*. Unity of plot is dramatic in that it
expresses unity of action (the only unity Aristotle actu-
ally sponsors). Tragedy is held to be superior to *epic
because of its tighter internal relations (5.23–24). The
ideal tragedy is an imitation of a unified action, large
enough to be clear while small enough to be com-
prehensible. Aristotle's conception of unity is closely
related to his artistic requirements of probability and
necessity as they constitute the criteria for the connec-
tion of parts (6–9).

Aristotle is concerned only with dramatic unity;
Horace has a looser but broader conception of unity
that refers not only to action but, even more, to *dic-
tion. He thinks of it as an effect of harmony obtained
by skillful "order and arrangement," analogous either
to music or, more significantly, to the blending of col-
ors, light, and shadow in painting (*ut pictura poesis*).
*Peri hypsous* (*On the Sublime*), the late cl. text long as-
cribed to Longinus, includes an analysis of an ode by
Sappho in which intensity of feeling is seen to produce
an organic unity that manifests itself as a reconciliation
of opposing elements, a view that has obvious affinities
to both Plato and Horace.

With the rediscovery of the text of Aristotle's *Po-
etics* and its trans. and commentary by Lodovico
Castelvetro in the Ren. (*Poetica d'Aristotele vulgariz-
zata e sposta*; 1570, 1576), Aristotle's argument for unity of
action gradually became doctrine, then ossified into a
prescription, one of the poetic "rules" of Fr. *classicism,
the three unities—of action, time, and place. Aristotle
had remarked that tragedies confined themselves to the
events of a single day, but it was J. C. Scaliger who first
established the tendency to identify the duration of the
action represented with the duration of the represen-
tation. This was done in the name of verisimilitude;
Philip Sidney thought it was common reason (i.e., con-
cern for *verisimilitude) as well as Aristotle's precept
that the stage should always represent only one place
and the events of one day. Yet, as formal criteria, the
three unities rather challenge the artist to concentrate
on the autonomy of his or her work. In the heyday of
the unities, in the drama of 17th-c. Fr. classicism, Jean
Racine clearly drew strength from them, while Pierre
Corneille strained against them—his play *Le Cid* oc-
casioned a great controversy over the unities.

The three unities were never fully adopted in En-
gland, and John Dryden assessed the reasons in the
*Essay of Dramatic Poesy* (1668), justifying the Eng. pref-
erence for subplot. Samuel Johnson's "Preface to Shake-
speare" (1765) showed, with great humor, how such
mistaken scruples as to verisimilitude were given the lie
by the very nature of dramatic illusion. The audience
manages a shift of scene from Rome to Alexandria with
the same ease it accepts the original setting as Rome.

At the same time, the artifice of strictly observing the
unities enhances the dramatic illusion wherever the
concentration is psychologically compelling. Eng. crit-
ics since Dryden, particularly John Dennis, had gone
back to Aristotle for a deeper grasp of the principle of
dramatic unity in its interdependence with probability
and necessity as felt by the audience. The three uni-
ties were, thus, not central to the more general concern
with dramatic unity but merely a subset of it.

From antiquity up to the mid-18th c., theories of
unity had been mainly theories of dramatic unity. But
18th-c. theories of unity dealt with other genres be-
sides drama, as René Le Bossu's *Traité du Poëme épique*
(1675) and Joseph Addison's *Spectator* papers on *Para-
dise Lost* show. And the rise of psychological aesthetics
in the 18th c. opened the way to more adequate ideas
of the role of unity in lyric poetry as well. New and en-
larged conceptions of the creative *imagination and the
shift from a mechanistic to a vitalist worldview led to
the romantic emphasis on organic unity. This appeared
variously as unity of feeling, unity as an imitation of
the poet's mind in the act of creation, and imagina-
tive unity, with the imagination being the shaping,
unifying ("esemplastic"), and reconciling power (S. T.
Coleridge, *Biographia Literaria*, ch. 14).

The conception of poetic unity fostered by the
*New Criticism of the mid-20th c. was directed against
*romanticism but remained romantic nonetheless.
Organic unity was also a mainstay of the subsequent
schools of formalist, psychological, and myth crit.,
both as a standard of judgment and as a method of ex-
position. Thus, even beyond the explicitly Aristotelian
emphasis of the *Chicago school, poetic unity was ex-
plained by Richards as a reconciliation of impulses; by
Brooks as a reconciliation of thought and feeling mani-
fested in the interaction of theme with lang. and meta-
phor; by the surrealists as a unifying of the total mind
through freeing of the unconscious; by the Freudians
through poetic analogues of the "dream-work" follow-
ing associations of symbols; and by the Jungians in the
replication of archetypal motifs.

At the same time, the principle of unity was
variously questioned and even made problematic by
some of these same movements, just as some romantics
had developed an aesthetic of the *fragment. Indeed,
such a reversal may be implicit in the sophistication
of the sense of unity, which drew it away from formal
constraints. The structuralist and poststructuralist
tendencies that followed in the wake of New Criti-
cism may outwardly have resembled it in its attention
to the complexities and tensions that articulate a given
work as a whole; but, in effect, they showed its unity
to be contingent, relative, and superficial. The text
is a meeting place for myriad relations that have no
common objective form; real unity is either that of the
underlying systems or an illusion, the lure held out by
the surface of the work. The poetic gesture of imposing
or inducing unity is just a jar in Tennessee (as Wallace
Stevens might say), as poetry itself turns against that
pretension. Yet the will to form may always have to
express itself in art by breaking with accustomed modes
of unity, and one sort of crit. will find its task in show-

ing that, where a work is experienced as art, some manner of unity has been created and communicated. For further discussion of modes of unity and the postmodernist reaction thereto, see ORGANICISM.

■ H. Breitinger, *Les Unités d'Aristote avant le Cid de Corneille* (1895); H. B. Charlton, *Castelvetro's Theory of Poetry* (1913); Richards; J.W.H. Atkins, *Literary Criticism in Antiquity*, 2 v. (1934); M. Bodkin, *Archetypal Patterns in Poetry* (1934); Brooks; Crane; Abrams; Wellek; Wellek and Warren; G. F. Else, *Aristotle's Poetics* (1957); Frye; Wimsatt and Brooks; G.M.A. Grube, *The Greek and Roman Critics* (1965); *Aristotle's Poetics*, trans. L. Golden, with commentary by O. B. Hardison Jr. (1968); D. W. Lucas, *The Poetics* (1968); Culler; G.J.H. van Gelder, *Beyond the Line* (1982)—Ar. poetry; de Man; L. Castelvetro, *Castelvetro on the Art of Poetry*, ed. and trans. A. Bongiorno (1984); M. F. Heath, *Unity in Greek Poetics* (1989). G. C. Carrington Jr., *The Dramatic Unity of "Huckleberry Finn"* (1976); S. Halliwell, *Aristotle's Poetics* (1986) and *The Poetics of Aristotle*, trans. and with commentary by S. Halliwell (1987); M. Davis, *Aristotle's Poetics* (1992); *Aristotle's Poetics*, ed. J. Baxter and J. P. Atherton, trans. G. Whalley (1997).

R. H. FOGLE; J. BARNOUW

**UPAMĀ.** Since similarity is the basis of many poetic figures, *upamā* is regarded in Sanskrit poetics as the most important kind of *arthālamkāra* or semantic poetic figure. When two different objects are compared on the basis of some resemblance, it is an instance of upamā. Usage of upamā involves four elements: (1) *upameya* (the object to be compared with something), (2) *upamāna* (the something with which it is compared), (3) the point of comparison, and (4) the word used to suggest the comparison. In the sentence "kamalaiba mukham sundaram" (The face is beautiful like a lotus), e.g., "mukham" (face) is the upameya, "kamalam" (lotus) is the upamāna, and "iba" (like) is the word suggesting comparison. Upamā can be broadly divided into two categories: *purṇopamā*, where all four elements are manifested, and *luptopamā*, where not all the elements appear. E.g., in the expression "mukhaminduryathā" (the moonlike face) we have the upameya (the face) and the upamāna (the moon). We have also the word *iba* (like), suggesting resemblance, but the point of resemblance (beauty) is not mentioned. It is *lupta* (lost/hidden/understood), so it is called *luptopamā*. Both purṇopamā, and luptopamā have many subdivisions depending on the different kinds of grammatical form used such as verbal root, compounds, and syntactic structures. Vāmana puts great emphasis on upamā and propounds that upamā or comparison lies at the root of all poetic figures, which is given the collective name of *upamā-prapañca*.

*See* SANSKRIT POETICS, SANSKRIT POETRY, SEMANTICS AND POETRY, SIMILE.

■ Daṇḍin, *Kāvyādarśa* (1924); Vāmana, *Kāvyālam kārasūtra* (1928); Bharata, *Nāṭyaśāstra* (1950); P. V. Kane, *Sāhityadarpaṇa: Paricchedas* I, II, X *Arthālam kāra with Exhaustive Notes* (1965); Rudraṇa, *Kāvyālam kāra* (1965); Ruyyaka, *Alam-kārasarvásva* (1965); R. Mukherji, *Literary Criticism in Ancient India* (1966); Bhāmaha, *Kāvyālamkāra* (1970); *Dhvanyāloka* of Ānandavardhana, ed. K. Krishnamoorthy (1974); S. K. De, *History of Sanskrit Poetics* (1976); K. Kapoor, *Literary Theory: Indian Conceptual Framework* (1998); B. Pal, *Alamkāra-Vicintā* (2007).

M. K. RAY

**URDU POETRY.** Urdu, the mother tongue of more than 60 million people in India and Pakistan, is read or understood by many more millions across South Asia and around the world. In the past, most Urdu poets were better known by their *takhallus*, pen names either derived from the poet's actual name or words reflective of the poet's sense of himself. The practice is much less common now. (Below, takhallus are given within quotation marks at the end of a name.)

Urdu's earliest poetic texts appeared chiefly at two Muslim courts in South India, Bijapur and Golconda, where rulers of the Adil Shahi (1490–1685) and Qutub Shahi (1518–1687) dynasties patronized major poets and often practiced the art. Much of that sizable poetry—now linguistically remote—consists of *ghazals* (lyrics) and substantially long *masnawī* (or *masnavī* in Ar., narrative poetry). The latter are either historical accounts or indigenous and foreign love stories, enjoyable both as secular romances and tales of Sufi quests.

When in the second half of the 17th c. the Mughals destroyed the two courts, the center of *patronage for Urdu poetry moved northward, eventually to Delhi. A shift in literary taste also occurred. While the ghazal remained greatly popular, the masnawī seemingly lost appeal. Two other significant devels. took place at Delhi. First, poetry became an art that one learned by becoming the pupil (*shāgird*) of some master poet (*ustād*). The master explained the intricacies of poetics to the pupil, corrected his verse for grammar and idiom, and defended him if the pupils of another master criticized him at frequently held assemblies of poets called *mushā'ira*. Second, more poets began to compile books, called *tazkira*, containing very brief biographies of their peers and earlier poets, together with a selection of their verses, frequently interspersed with evaluative comments—commonly regarded as the first examples of lit. crit. in Urdu.

As the Mughals grew weaker in the 18th c., various invaders plundered Delhi, and the city's ability to provide patronage rapidly declined. By the 1780s, Delhi was steadily losing its best poets to such regional courts as Lucknow and Hyderabad. At Lucknow, Shi'a rulers and nobility provided particular patronage to the poets who excelled at writing religious elegies known as *marsiya*. Also at Lucknow, some poets popularized a kind of verse called *rekhtī*. Written exclusively by men, it used vocabulary, idioms, and themes that were intimately feminine. Originally merely entertaining, rekhtī is now invaluable for its unusual lexical richness.

After the Brit. took Delhi from the Marathas and the Fr. in 1803, peace and prosperity gradually returned to the city. Talented people stopped emigrating, and before long Delhi again had its share of notable poets. Meanwhile, Urdu poetry continued to flourish at Lucknow, Patna, Hyderabad, and other places, leading to much rivalry among poets on the basis of their affiliation to an ustād or a place. The introduction of lithography in the 1840s revolutionized book production in Urdu and made possible newspapers and literary jours. that enabled poets to gain readership far beyond local audiences.

After the failed rebellion of 1857, Brit. control over North India became absolute. Earlier, in 1837, the Brit. had replaced Persian with Urdu in official use, and now they gave the lang. further prominence by making it a part of school curricula. Through their tight control of public education, colonial authorities encouraged lit. that would, in their view, be "useful" and "moral." Their ideas found immediate favor with the emerging Muslim middle class and its reform-oriented leaders, who scorned traditional poetry for its elaborate *conceits, *hyperbole, and frank descriptions of love. Invoking the prestige of poetry in Urdu culture, the reformists called for a new poetry that could lift Muslim youth into worldly success. Two influential poet-critics, Muhammad Husain "Āzād" (1830–1910) and Altāf Husain "Hālī" (1837–1914), set out to create an Urdu poetry that was "simple" and "natural," thus also "moral" and "useful." They quickly found many followers. These ideas remained dominant until the 1920s, when a rehabilitation of Urdu's poetic heritage began, partly as a generational reaction but mostly inspired by a better understanding of Western, Persian, and Indian poetries. Though the Nationalist movement and Marxist Progressivism briefly reinforced the notion that poetry must serve some good cause, a more balanced literary view has prevailed since the 1950s.

Until the 1880s, Urdu poetics was fundamentally what Urdu poets had adopted from Persian and Ar. The primary unit of expression in that poetics was *bait*—two metrically identical lines, each line generally a syntactic whole. The bait was then used as the chief building block to construct poems in various genres. Even a *quatrain, e.g., used a binary logic. Previously, the most significant genres had been *qaṣīda*, masnawī, marsiya, and ghazal; in the 20th c., a fifth—*nazm*—became equally important.

A *qaṣīda is a poem of substantial length in high diction, consisting of *couplets, with the rhyme scheme *aa ba ca da ea*. In Urdu, it is usually a *panegyric, praising some religious figure or the poet's actual or prospective patron and seeking some spiritual or worldly gain. The opening section of a qaṣīda, called *tashbīb*, can itself be an *ode-like poem on any theme, in which the poet can display his prowess with words and thought. Some powerful *satires and literary polemics also exist in this form. The famous names in qaṣīda are Muhammad Nusrat "Nusratī" (d. 1674), Muhammad Rafiʿ "Saudā" (1713–80)—he is also Urdu's fiercest satirist—Inshaʾallah Khan "Inshā" (1756–1817), Shāh Nasīr "Nasīr" (d. 1838), Muhammad Ibrāhīm "Zauq" (1788–1854), and Asadullah Khan "Ghālib" (1797–1869).

In a masnawī, both lines of every couplet rhyme, but the rhyme itself changes from couplet to couplet. Its relative freedom makes masnawī the preferred genre for narratives that demand linear progression, such as romances, hists., ethical discourses, and topical or anecdotal verse. It flourished more in South India, where several poems of epic length were composed. While those poets mostly treated popular romances as narratives of mystical passion, the practice became rare at Delhi and disappeared completely at Lucknow. The best masnawī writers in Urdu were Nusratī, Asadullah "Wajahī" (d. 1659), and Sirājuddin "Sirāj" (1714–63) in the Deccan; Muhammad Taqī "Mīr" (1722–1810) at Delhi; and Mīr Hasan "Hasan" (1727–86), Dayāshankar "Nasīm" (1811–43), and Nawāb Mirzā "Shauq" (1773–1871) at Lucknow.

*Marsiya* literally means *"elegy," but in Urdu lit. hist. it chiefly refers to poems that honor the martyrdom of Imam Husain—a grandson of the Prophet Muhammad—and his companions in the battle of Karbala (680 CE). These elegies form an integral part of the ritual of public mourning during certain months for the Shiʿa Muslims of South Asia. Initially, a marsiya could be written in any form. But in the early 19th c., both the writing of a marsiya and its public declamation—often accompanied with hand gestures and facial expressions—became profound arts at the hands of several masters, who exclusively used the six-line stanza form called *musaddas* (*aaaabb*). A marisya ultimately seeks to produce a cathartic effect in its listeners. It is never exclusively lachrymose; it makes an effort to exhilarate the devout by presenting, at various moments, descriptions of natural beauty, amusing details of familial relationships, and awe-inspiring battle scenes. Two outstanding practitioners of this genre at Lucknow were Babar Alī "Anīs" (1802–74) and Salāmat Alī "Dabīr" (1803–75), whose family members and pupils further enriched the trad. The religious elegies of Anīs and Dabīr elevated musaddas to such high esteem that several later poets chose the form for their own secular poems on social and political themes. Hālī's *Madd-o-Jazr-i-Islām* (The Tide and Ebb of Islam)—a poem of unique significance in the cultural hist. of South Asian Muslims—is a musaddas, as are "Shikwa" (Complaint) and "Jawāb-i-Shikwa" (Reply to the Complaint)—an exchange with God—by Muhammad Iqbāl "Iqbāl" (1877–1938).

Formally identical to the qaṣīda, the ghazal is shorter in length but more discursive thematically. Also, in almost every ghazal, each couplet demands that it be experienced as a discrete little poem in itself. That perhaps came about because Urdu poetry was more heard than read, and two lines were easier to hold in attention and savor than five or six. Even now, as in the past, Urdu speakers regularly experience poetry at gatherings called *mushāʾira*, where poets present their verses—predominantly ghazals—to large audiences over several hours. The audience, in turn, interacts with the poets, responding to each couplet as it is presented, praising or criticizing it. Further, ghazal couplets are quite casually quoted in common discourse in Urdu—from ordinary conversations to newspaper columns—and deemed to possess the same quality of truth or wisdom as a *proverb or an *epigram.

The ghazal, in essence, is poetry of relationships, be they cosmic, human, elemental, verbal, or graphic. Images in a ghazal couplet come bundled with other images, and *metaphors open into other metaphors—if the rose reminds the poet of his beloved and makes him think of himself as a nightingale, it also recalls for him the garden that bloomed in spring but was ravaged in autumn, and where a hunter lurked to catch the nightingale, or lightning crashed down from a gladdening rain cloud and destroyed the bird's meager nest. So it is also with the words: they link up with each other on the basis of phonetics, etymology, or calligraphic features; through conventional binary oppositions; or in some other manner. At its best, a traditional ghazal couplet lays down a "net of awareness," woven out of different strands, that grabs the reader's attention with tantalizing multiple readings. The list of great ghazal poets is long, but two names tower above everyone: Mīr and Ghālib—the first for a simplicity of diction that belies perceptive explorations of human emotions and the second for a deliberate intellectuality that is rich with *wit while profound in thought. Other major names are Sirāj, Saudā, Ghulām Hamdānī "Mushafī" (1750–1824), and Khwaja Haidar Alī "Ātish" (1778–1846) among the elders. Iqbāl and Wājid Ali "Yagāna" (1822–87) dominated the 20th c. in ghazal, followed by Shād Arifi (1900–64), Faiz Ahmed "Faiz" (1911–84), and Asrārul Hasan Khan "Majrūh" (1919–2000) in setting the trends for other poets. In the 1950s, there began a new phase in Urdu ghazal's hist. when poets such as Nāsir Kāzmī (1925–72), Munīr Niyāzī (1928–2006), Ahmed Mushtāq (b. 1929), Zafar Iqbāl (b. 1933), and Parvīn Shākir (1952–94) further pushed the possibilities in the form.

*Nazm* first meant "poetry" but in the late 19th c. also came to indicate "poem." From then through the 1930s, the word identified any poem that carried a title or had a single definable topic. Ever since *blank verse and *free verse took firm hold in Urdu in the 1930s, *nazm* has come to mean a poem that is constructed with lines, not couplets, and has an irrevocable linear progression that gives the poem completeness and is itself not bound to some traditional genre convention. Topical poems were always popular in Urdu. Walī Muhammad "Nazīr" of Agra (1735–1830) excelled at the nazm, and his poems on festivals and market scenes are still read with pleasure. But nazm gained much greater currency under the impetus of the sociopolitical movements mentioned above. Earlier poets had used various traditional forms; those who followed employed stanzaic poems of several kinds. Now blank and free verse are the preferred forms.

In popularity with Urdu poets, nazm is second only to the ghazal. Iqbāl's profound explorations of myriad issues—philosophical, political, and existential—were done in nazm. Shabbīr Hasan Khān "Josh" (1898–1982) wrote on nature and politics in this genre. Faiz and two of his contemporaries, Nūn Mīm Rāshid (1910–75) and Sana'ullah Dār "Mīrājī" (1912–49), created separate distinct contours of thought and diction that still attract imitators. Other major poets of that generation were

Asrārul Haq Majāz (1909–55), Majīd Amjad (1914–74), and Akhtarul Īmān (1915–96). Since the 1960s, many more distinct voices have established themselves, the most noteworthy being Wazīr Āghā (1922–2010), Shafiq Fātima Shi'rā (b. 1937), Muhammad Alvī (b. 1927), Munīr Niyāzī, Sāqī Fārūqī (b. 1936), Kishwar Nāhīd (b. 1940), Fahmīda Riyāz (b. 1946), Afzāl Ahmad Sayyad (b. 1946), and Azrā Abbās (b. 1950).

*See* ARABIC PROSODY; GHAZAL; INDIA, POETRY OF; PERSIAN POETRY.

■ **Anthologies**: *The Golden Tradition*, ed. and trans. A. Ali (1973)—premod. poetry; *We Sinful Women*, ed. and trans. R. Ahmad (1990)—feminist poets; *An Evening of Caged Birds*, ed. and trans. F. Pritchett and A. Farrukhi (1999)—postmodernist poets; *An Anthology of Modern Urdu Poetry*, ed. and trans. R. Habib (2003); *The Oxford Anthology of Modern Urdu Literature*, ed. M. A. Farooqi, 2 v. (2008); *Pakistani Urdu Verse: An Anthology*, ed. and trans. Y. Hameed (2010).

■ **Criticism and History**: R. Russell and K. Islam, *Three Mughal Poets* (1968); *Studies in the Urdu Ghazal and Prose Fiction*, ed. M. U. Memon (1979); M. Sadiq, *A History of Urdu Literature* (1984); R. Russell, *The Pursuit of Urdu Literature* (1992); A. J. Zaidi, *A History of Urdu Literature* (1993); F. Pritchett, *Nets of Awareness* (1994)—premod. poetry and its critics; C. M. Naim, *Urdu Texts and Contexts* (2004); S. R. Faruqi, *The Flower-Lit Road* (2005)—premod. and mod. poetics; S. A. Hyder, *Reliving Karbala* (2006)—the marsiya; A. H. Mir and R. Mir, *Anthems of Resistance* (2006)—Marxist "progressive" poetry.

C. M. NAIM

**URUGUAY, POETRY OF.** There is no documentary evidence of an indigenous oral poetic trad. within the territory now called Uruguay, whose genesis is the product of imperialist disputes among the Sp., Port., and Brit. empires and among the centralist aspirations of Montevideo and Buenos Aires. Generally speaking, in the 18th and 19th cs., poets were either Hispanic or descendants of Sp. families settled in the River Plate region. Literary tendencies were, thus, mostly rooted in Hispanic foundations. Poetic production attests to the conflict between the city, as an image of cosmopolitanism but also of dependence, and the countryside as an image of freedom and telluric nationality. This conflict is evidenced in the works of Bartolomé Hidalgo (1788–1822) and Francisco Acuña de Figueroa (1791–1862), whose extensive oeuvre encompassed all poetic trends and tendencies manifest in Sp.-Am. cultural centers until the advent of *romanticism. The latter movement was considered as a national project by the *epic poem *Tabaré* (1886) by Juan Zorrilla de San Martín (1855–1931). In the 20th c., the dialectic between urban and rural life resurfaced in diverse quarrels among different poetic schools and found a synthesis in the works of Juan Cunha (1919–85) and Washington Benavídes (b. 1930).

The hist. of Uruguayan poetry in the 20th c. is often considered by starting with the works of Julio Herrera y Reissig (1875–1910) and Delmira Agustini (1886–1914), two poets who contributed in a fundamental way to the devel. of Latin Am. and Sp. *modernismo. Among the late flourishing of *avant-garde movements, the work of Alfredo Mario Ferreiro (1899–1959), a response to It. *futurism, is the most important. The poets who subverted and undermined that trad. include Álvaro Figueredo (1907–66), who developed a highly personal and critical use of received forms—esp. the *sonnet—that stood out against the more conventional formalist approach of the established Uruguayan poetic writing in the first half of the century. After 1945, the Generation of '45 or Critical Generation—as the critic Angel Rama named it—showed a new appraisal of everyday reality and the poet's social and political commitment to the problems of his or her times. One of the foremost figures of this period was the poet and translator Idea Vilariño (1929–2009), for decades a highly visible intellectual presence; the most complex counterfigure of the era was Juana de Ibarbourou (1895–1979), whose work is often strongly telluric and erotic.

The military dictatorship (1973–85) favored silence and exile for poets; therefore, poetry arose from the countercultural margins, whether it was overtly opposed to the values of the established culture (as was the group that formed around the publishing house Ediciones de Uno) or symbolically so, as expressed in the brief and intense work of Julio Inverso (1963–99). It also brought about a reapprochement among poets of the Southern Cone, such as the hermeneutic project of the *Neobarroso*, a southern reaction of the 1980s—partly mediated through Brazilian *antropofagia—to the Latin Am. *Neobarroco* or *neobaroque, the name first applied by critics of Caribbean origins. (Since *barroso* is a neologism, the term *Neobarroso* is untranslatable into Eng.) Exile as a poetic *trope also inspired new readings of the works of Uruguayan poets writing in Fr., such as Isidore Ducasse (1846–70; pub. as the Comte de Lautréamont) and Jules Supervielle (1884–1960). Among the poets who work in exile, Eduardo Milán (b. 1952) is worthy of mention, while among those who did so in *insile*, Marosa Di Giorgio (1932–2004) was one of the most original and influential. Two of the foremost names of the 20th c. are Melisa Machado (b. 1966) and Aldo Mazzucchelli (b. 1961).

At the beginning of the 21st c., Uruguayan poetic production is highly dispersed. Revisionist currents producing different readings of social and gendered poetic trads. and readings of *postmodernism coexist—more or less aligned with the poetic productions of Argentina and Chile. In addition, there is also strong evidence of attempts to revitalize traditional verse forms and hybridized versions of popular *song and refined poetry forged in performative spaces and *visual poetry, whose most important local exponents are Clemente Padín (b. 1939) and Jorge Caraballo (b. 1941).

*See* SPANISH AMERICA, POETRY OF.

■ **Anthologies and Primary Texts**: *Poesía uruguaya siglo XX*, ed. W. Rela (1994); *Antología Plural de la poesía uruguaya siglo XX*, ed. W. Benavides, S. Lago,

R. Courtoisie—20th-c. poetry (1996); *Medusario*, ed. R. Echavarren et al. (1996)—Neobarroso poems; *Orientales*, ed. A. Hamed (1996)—20th-c. poetry.

■ **Criticism and History**: A. Zum Felde, *Proceso Intelectual del Uruguay y Crítica de su Literatura* (1930); Á. Rama, *180 años de literatura: Enciclopedia uruguaya II* (1968); C. Maggi, C. Martínez Moreno, C. Real de Azúa, *Capítulo oriental:* (1968–69); *Nuevo Diccionario de Literatura Uruguaya*, ed. A. Oreggioni and P. Rocca (2001).

F. TOMSICH

**UT PICTURA POESIS.** In Horace's *Ars poetica*, the phrase *ut pictura poesis* (as is painting, so is poetry) offers an analogy to painting to describe the effects of poetry. Some texts, Horace argues, reveal their value when scrutinized more closely than others; some please on one encounter, while others bear repeated examination. This comparison of painting and poetry has precedents, as in Simonides' formulation that "painting is mute poetry and poetry a speaking picture." Over time, however, Horace's dictum has moved from designating a comparison, to outlining a contest between the arts, and then to functioning prescriptively rather than descriptively, commanding that poetry and painting resemble each other. It has also faced questions about the validity of the initial analogy and participated in theories of representation that blur the boundaries between different categories of signs.

The relationship between painting and poetry underwent various early forms of examination, such as Dion of Prusa (Chrysostom)'s statement that a poem develops in time, unlike a painting. (The dichotomy of space and time would continue to inform discussions of ut pictura poesis throughout its hist.) During the Middle Ages, orthodox Christian culture asserted the text's superiority over the image, mistrusting the latter's potential falsity. At the same time, poetry continued to interact with visual art, as in Petrarch's reference to Homer as a painter. In the Ren., Leonardo da Vinci's *paragone* made the competition between the two arts explicit. Reasoning that sight is the most direct sense and that the sequentiality of writing divides up the experience of the beautiful, da Vinci argued for painting's superiority. The Ren. also explored *emblems as a means of approaching the goal of ut pictura poesis, offering poetry that functioned in visually "hieroglyphic" ways (Hagstrum—see HIEROGLYPH). Early mod. and *baroque painters seemed to use the terms of poetics to legitimize and ennoble their tasks, Nicolas Poussin being esp. renowned for his learning and his interartistic approach to theorizing painting. But, according to Lee, painters' work was often more deeply informed by earlier visual trads. G. E. Lessing's *Laokoön* (1766), an important critique of ut pictura poesis, disapproved of the use of painting as a metaphor for poetry. For Lessing, the more a poem tries to be visually descriptive, the more it shows how it cannot be—if short, it lacks sufficient detail; if long, it becomes too sequential. But rebuttals to Lessing followed, such as J. G. Herder's contention that poetry, not describing action, lacks sequentiality. During the romantic period, according to Steiner, the importance of the painting-poetry analogy waned, and discussions of these arts focused less than they had earlier on either's connections to empirical reality. In the mod. and postmod. periods, the work of art's self-conscious materiality encouraged reexamination of the interartistic comparison. Multimedia artistic objects have also complicated such comparisons. Even if, in these cases as well, one form ultimately dominates the other (Wimsatt), such art develops Friedrich Schlegel's and others' earlier interest in relations of accompaniment and simultaneity between the arts, rather than analogical comparison.

Throughout this hist., analogy and metaphor surface as important but problematic terms. Lessing's misgivings about critical attempts to literalize artistic metaphor through ut pictura poesis. These are revisited in contemp. critiques of the vagueness of metaphors comparing different arts. Analogical and metaphorical comparisons between the arts, Wellek and Warren note, cannot trace patterns of *influence and devel. At the same time, ut pictura poesis has consistently wielded power in discussions of poetics. For Krieger, metaphors of space and visuality "inevitably" inflect the critic's lang. for describing poetic *form. And while arguments of analogy and *metaphor impose certain limits on investigations of the interaction between painting and poetry, they also suggest a provocative challenge to transcend the analogy itself in the examination of the "sister arts."

Interartistic crit. and practice move beyond analogy in part by providing a forum to discuss representation and signs. Plato's writings on poetry and painting regarded representation itself as a tool of analysis; to Plato, painting's and poetry's capacity as representational arts also exposed their deceptiveness. Rather than critiquing *mimesis, Aristotle sought in each art the achievement of a form with its own unity (energeia) through, for instance, plot in drama or design in painting. Plutarch privileged the vividness of imitation (*enargeia) available to painting and poetry, holding up painting as the art form with the closest relationship to reality. For Joshua Reynolds, a painting's representation of reality was a "sign," like the signs used in poetry; but in separate ways, each art should activate an encompassing imagination, rising above the specular faculty. Markiewicz asserts that, while Lessing emphasized the material differences between poetry's and painting's respective signs, he also saw the potential for arbitrary signs to become natural signs, particularly in drama. For Mitchell, the Blakean "art of both language and vision" addresses the contrast wherein the signs of writing signify through difference and absence, whereas the visual image does so through similitude and presence.

These visually oriented issues surrounding ut pictura poesis suggest further questions about the nature of the image and the imagination. E.g., how do we define the images that painting and poetry each produce? One approach to the image appears in Hagstrum's "literary pictorialism," the relationship between a poem's evocation of a visual *image and its overall structure. Rich-

ards, however, points out that different readers perceive the images in a literary work differently; thus, a poetic image cannot be evaluated for its pictorial potential. Ut pictura poesis potentially asserts the image-making quality of lit. (explored in Marxist studies), yet it also exposes questions about the possibility of mental images. Assessing the mental image requires a turn to the beholder, another topic preoccupying interartistic discourse. Horace's dictum has been called a species of reception theory by Gadoin, with Trimpi asserting that its terms reveal a mistrust of "excessive scrupulosity" as an analytical method. For some, e.g., Gombrich and Faust, the intersection of the arts demands attention to the role of the viewer's imagination in constructing visual or verbal objects. Ut pictura poesis involves a specifically visual imagination (as distinct from the romantic imagination) and a need to investigate and transcend its own analogy. In response, we might conceive of an interdisciplinary poetics: art speaking about poetic representation in its own visual terms (Davidson, Chaganti), rather than having its visual features converted through the verbal machinery of metaphor.

■ I. Babbitt, *The New Laokoön* (1910); I. A. Richards, *Principles of Literary Criticism* (1924); R. Wellek and A. Warren, "Literature and the Other Arts," *Theory of Literature* (1949); J. H. Hagstrum, *The Sister Arts* (1958); R. W. Lee, *Ut Pictura Poesis* (1967); H. D. Goldstein, "*Ut Poesis Pictura*: Reynolds on Imitation and Imagination," *Eighteenth-Century Studies* 1 (1968); M. Krieger, "Ekphrasis and the Still Movement of Poetry: or, *Laokoön* Revisited," *Perspectives on Poetry*, ed. J. L. Calderwood and H. E. Toliver (1968); E. Panofsky, *Idea*, trans. J. S. Peake (1968); W. K. Wimsatt, *Day of the Leopards* (1976)—esp. "Laokoön: An Oracle Reconsulted" and "In Search of Verbal Mimesis"; W. Trimpi, "Horace's 'Ut Pictura Poesis': The Argument for Stylistic Decorum," *Traditio* 34 (1978); J.-M. Croisille, *Poésie et art figuré de Néron aux Flaviens* (1982), and rev. in *Journal of Roman Studies* 73 (1983); R. A. Goodrich, "Plato on Poetry and Painting," *BJA* 22 (1982); W. Steiner, *The Colors of Rhetoric* (1982); M. Davidson, "Ekphrasis and the Postmodern Painter Poem," *JAAC* 42 (1983); D. E. Wellbery, *Lessing's "Laocoön"* (1984); N. Bryson, "Intertextuality and Visual Poetics," *Style* 22 (1988); H. Markiewicz, "*Ut pictura poesis*: A History of the Topos and the Problem," *NLH* 18 (1987); G. E. Lessing, *Laocoön*, trans. E. A. McCormick (1989); W.J.T. Mitchell, *Picture Theory* (1994); E. H. Gombrich, *Art and Illusion*, 3d ed. (2000); I. Gadoin, "Re-reading Lessing's *Laocoön*," *Études Britannique Contemporaines* 31 (2006); J. Faust, "Blurring the Boundaries: *Ut pictura poesis* and Marvell's Liminal Mower," *SP* 104 (2007); S. Chaganti, *The Medieval Poetics of the Reliquary* (2008).

S. CHAGANTI

**UTPREKŞĀ.** *Utprekşā*, or poetical fancy, is a term in *Sanskrit poetics for imagining an object as almost identical with something else. The imagining, however, must be deliberate, not the effect of an illusion. The 17th-c. philosopher Viṣvanātha follows the *Alaṃkārasarvasva* of the 12th-c. poetic theorist Ruyyaka in the division of utprekṣā into *vācyā* (expressed) and *pratīyamānā* (implied). Vācyā, or the expressed utprekṣā, occurs when particles like *iba*, "like," are employed; and pratīyamānā, or the implied, occurs when such particles are not employed. Vācyā, then, is further subdivided into 56 varieties and pratīyamānā into 16.

Since both the terms *\*upamā* (\*simile) and utprekṣā are based on similarity, how can one distinguish an utprekṣā from an upamā? When the upamāna is taken from ordinary life, the poetic figure is upamā. The word *iba* then indicates the similarity. But when the upamāna is not taken from ordinary life but is a figment of the poet's fancy, then the figure is utprekṣā. The word *iba* then is used in the sense of "probably identical." When *iba* is employed in utprekṣā, the poet purposely represents one thing as almost identical with another. In upamā, on the other hand, the only object

of using *iba* is to indicate the similarity between the two objects.

Therefore, the essence of utprekṣā is that the upameya must be represented as probably identical with the upamāna drawn not from ordinary life but from fancy and that this representation, being an *\*alaṃkāra*, must be charming and based on implied resemblance.

*See* SANSKRIT POETICS, SANSKRIT POETRY.

■ Daṇḍin, *Kāvyādarṣa* (1924); Vāmana, *Kāvyālaṃkārasūtra* (1928); Bharata, *Nāṭyaṣāstra* (1950); P. V. Kane, *Sāhityadarpaṇa: Paricchedas* I, II, X *Arthālaṃkāra with Exhaustive Notes* (1965); Rudraṭa, *Kāvyālaṃkāra* (1965); Ruyyaka, *Alaṃkārasarvaṣva* (1965); R. Mukherji, *Literary Criticism in Ancient India* (1966); Bhāmaha, *Kāvyālaṃkāra* (1970); *Dhvanyāloka of Ānandavardhana*, ed. K. Krishnamoorthy (1974); S. K. De, *History of Sanskrit Poetics* (1976); K. Kapoor, *Literary Theory: Indian Conceptual Framework* (1998); B. Pal, *Alaṃkāra-Vicintā* (2007).

M. K. RAY

# V

**VARIABLE FOOT.** A term associated with W. C. Williams, who first used it to explain the triadic stanzas of his *Paterson* 2.3 (1948), later reprinted separately as "The Descent." Claiming that the concept of the foot had to be altered to suit a newly relativistic world, Williams insisted that the variable foot allowed both order and variability in so-called *free verse, which he claimed could never be truly free. The variable foot, he asserted, supplanted the fixed foot of traditional Eng. prosody in order to represent more accurately the speech rhythms of the mod. Am. idiom. Attempting to demonstrate his measurement of the variable foot, Williams explained that he counted "a single beat" for each line of his three-line stanzas so as to regulate the "musical pace" of his verse, though, in fact, his lines contain varying numbers of stresses and syllables. But, as his nine-poem sequence "Some Simple Measures in the American Idiom and the Variable Foot" (1959) shows, Williams did not always identify the variable foot with the triadic stanza form. Because his own explanations of the device often lack precision and consistency, subsequent critics have questioned the legitimacy of the concept of the variable foot, one remarking that the variable foot in verse is as impossible as a variable inch on a yardstick; an alternative approach to Williams's prosody lies in treating it as primarily visual (see VISUAL POETRY). E. A. Poe had used the term to describe the *caesura; for Poe, the caesura was "a perfect foot," the length of which would vary in accordance with the time it takes to pronounce other feet in the line. Williams read Poe's essays on prosody, which apparently influenced his conception of verse structure.

■ E. A. Poe, "The Rationale of Verse," *Complete Works*, ed. J. A. Harrison, vol. 14 (1902); W. C. Williams, Letter to R. Eberhart (May 23, 1954), *Selected Letters*, (1957); *I Wanted to Write a Poem*, ed. E. Heal (1958); "The American Idiom," *Interviews with W. C. Williams*, ed. L. Wagner (1976); H. M. Sayre, *The Visual Text of W. C. Williams* (1983); S. Cushman, *W. C. Williams and the Meanings of Measure* (1985); R. Gates, "Forging an American Poetry from Speech Rhythms: Williams after Whitman," *PoT* 8 (1987); E. Berry, "W. C. Williams' Triadic-Line Verse," *Twentieth Century Literature* (Autumn 1989); R. Bradford, *The Look of It* (1993); N. Gerber, "Getting the 'Squiggly Tunes Down' on the Page: Williams's Triadic-Line Verse and American Intonation," *Rigor of Beauty,* ed. I. Copestake (2004).

S. CUSHMAN

**VARIATION** is used in several senses in the study of poetry. In OE, the term refers to a technique of poetic composition by which the metrical pattern of half lines is deliberately not repeated from the first half line to the second. Variation seems to have been a deliberate attempt to avoid monotony in line construction. Metrical variation is often cited as an explanation for the fact that many actual lines of poetry do not entirely match the pattern of the *meter they are said to be written in. Variation is also integral to the basic structure of the classic *blues lyric, whereby the second line of a three-line stanza is a variation on the first, to be countered in the concluding line. More generally, variation is often held to be a desirable characteristic of structure that sustains readers' interest. Critics who see literary works as developing, exploring, or asserting themes (see THEMATICS) sometimes adapt the analogy of "theme and variation" from music, as in the construction of a symphony, where variation is recognized as one of only a few compositional strategies open to any composer. Auditors' and readers' recognition of a variation as in some respects different from but in others conforming to a prior theme is simply one form of pattern recognition, a fundamental cognitive process applicable across media.

■ C. P. Smith, *Pattern and Variation in Poetry* (1932); W. K. Wimsatt, "When Is Variation 'Elegant?'" *The Verbal Icon* (1954); K. Pomorska, *Themes and Variations in Pasternak's "Poetics"* (1975); C. S. Brown, "Theme and Variations as a Literary Form," *Yearbook of Comparative and General Literature* 27 (1978); S. L. Tarán, *The Art of Variation in the Hellenistic Epigram* (1979); F. C. Robinson, *"Beowulf" and the Appositive Style* (1985).

T.V.F. BROGAN; K. M. CAMPBELL

**VATES.** Two concepts of the *poet—as craftsman (maker) and as inspired seer or quasi-priest—are already established in early Gr. lit. In Pindar, they coexist, but Plato (notably in the *Ion*) exaggerates the notion of poetic "mania" (see FUROR POETICUS) to devalue the poet's claim to rational knowledge of truth. Lat. lit. adopted the Gr. term *poeta* in the sense of craftsman; accordingly, Ennius, followed by Lucretius, attacked the native *vates*, soothsayer and oracle-monger, as uncouth and ignorant. But under the influence of the Stoic philosopher Posidonius and of Varro Reatinus, the Augustans revived the term *vates*, suitable to their notion of the genuinely Roman poet voicing the moral reforms inspired by the new regime. This vatic ideal is esp. advanced in Horace's *Ars poetica* (391–407), where Orpheus is hailed as the original *vates*, though poets are also exhorted to tireless improvement of their lines by the "labor of the file." Virgil claimed to be a *vates* (*Aeneid* 7.41), but after his death in 19 BCE, enthusiasm for the *vates* waned even in Horace; and Ovid pokes open fun at his claims. But later poets like Manilius and Lucan are more respectful, and even in Tacitus's *Dialogus*, some memory of the Augustan status of the poet as seer persists. Eventually, in Longinus's treatise

**1503**

*On the Sublime*, the concept of the inspired poet took on fresh and influential life. Although the term *vates* is culturally specific, parallels of the underlying concept are prevalent around the world.

See CLASSICAL POETICS, INSPIRATION, LATIN POETRY.

■ T. Carlyle, *Heroes and Hero-Worship* (1841), lecture 3; J. K. Newman, *The Concept of Vates in Augustan Poetry* (1967); C. O. Brink, *Horace on Poetry, The "Ars Poetica"* (1971).

J. K. NEWMAN

**VEDIC POETRY.** See INDIA, POETRY OF.

**VENEZUELA, POETRY OF.** Venezuela first acquired geopolitical status in 1777, when the Sp. colonial power issued a *real cédula* (royal decree) by which seven provinces were united in the Capitanía General (General Captaincy) of Venezuela. Its politically independent status, however, was reached in a series of steps: first, the Declaration of the Republic in 1811; then, the War of Independence, which ended in 1821; and, finally, the definitive secession from Gran Colombia in 1830. Venezuelan poetry is considered to begin in the early stages of the republic, from the 1820s on.

Nineteenth-c. poetry in Venezuela is conventionally organized by the same categories as Fr. lit.: neoclassicism (see NEOCLASSICAL POETICS), *romanticism, and *Parnassianism. The founding figure of Venezuelan poetry is Andrés Bello (1781–1865), whose voluminous oeuvre spanned philological and literary studies, speeches, political essays, trans., and poetry. His best-known poems are the *silvas* "Alocución a la poesía" (Address to Poetry, 1823) and "A la agricultura de la zona tórrida" (Agriculture of the Torrid Zone, 1826). Both texts, neoclassical in style and intention, undertake a distinctly Americanist project: to create poetry inspired by the themes and the landscape of the New World. This neoclassical Americanism inspired the poetry of the humanist *bellistas*, incl. Fermín Toro (1806–65), Rafael María Baralt (1810–60), and Cecilio Acosta (1818–81).

Perhaps because he translated Victor Hugo's poetry, Bello's *diction demonstrated recognizable romantic influence, heralding a new generation of romantic Venezuelan poets: José Antonio Maitín (1804–74), Abigaíl Lozano (1821–66), José Ramón Yepes (1822–81), José Antonio Calcaño (1827–97), and Juan Antonio Pérez Bonalde (1846–92). Although Maitín and Lozano were no doubt consequential, the most prominent figure of the group is Pérez Bonalde, whose writing evokes a life besieged by loss and haunted by existential doubts. His two most significant poems are "Vuelta a la patria" (Return to the Homeland), included in his first book of poems, *Estrofas* (Stanzas, 1876), and "Poema del Niágara" (Poem on Niagara Falls), pub. in his second book of poems, *Ritmos* (Rhythms, 1880).

The *poetas parnasianos* were inspired by the precepts and rhet. of the Fr. Parnassian movement. The group included, among others, Jacinto Gutiérrez Coll (1845–1901), Miguel Sánchez Pesquera (1851–1920), Gabriel E. Muñoz (1863–1908), and Andrés Mata (1870–1931).

They adopted without reserve the characteristic traits of Parnassian poetry: exotic and cl. subject matter along with highly crafted composition. Nowadays, however, they are considered rather marginal or transitional figures.

At the end of the century, Venezuelan literary historiography began to deviate from the Fr. model. The Sp.-Am. literary movement *modernismo, which evolved from Eur. *symbolism, had a small following in Venezuela; however, few of its adherents achieved international renown. Rufino Blanco Fombona (1874–1944), Alfredo Arvelo Larriva (1883–1934), José Tadeo Arreaza Calatrava (1882–1970), and Ismael Urdaneta (1885–1928), among others, influenced by the Nicaraguan *modernista* Rubén Darío, opened the spectrum of lyric subject matter and diction: the politics of contemp. Venezuela, eroticism, military life, mining, and the emergence of modernity appear in their poetry presented in a variety of forms.

In 1901, Francisco Lazo Martí (1869–1909) published his "Silva criolla" (Creole Silva), a poem that revived the regionalist trend inaugurated by Bello. This interest in regionalism, labeled *criollismo* (creolism) or *nativismo* (nativism), emphasized the themes and motifs of Venezuelan rural life and landscape.

Perhaps because of the ironclad dictatorship (1908–36) of Juan Vicente Gómez, the *avant-garde movement was almost unsubstantial in Venezuela, although Salustio González Rincones (1886–1933) is sometimes considered an early adherent. His "Carta de Salustio para su mamá que estaba en Nueva York" (Letter from Salustio to his Mother, Who Was in New York [1907]), which combines colloquialism, humor, and self-referentiality, has no precedent in Venezuelan poetry. José Antonio Ramos Sucre (1890–1930) and Antonio Arráiz (1903–62) are also counted as defining authors of Venezuelan avant-garde poetry. Arráiz's book *Áspero* (Rough, 1924), which explored native Venezuelan themes, is usually considered the point of inception of the avant-garde; Ramos Sucre, on the other hand, wrote *prose poems of an extreme verbal austerity and precision.

Twentieth-c. Venezuelan lit. is typically organized either in terms of generations or by the literary magazines that gave cohesion to groups of writers. Two generations emerged during Gómez's dictatorship: the Generation of 1918 and the Generation of 1928, although only the first one was distinctly artistic and literary. The *Semana del estudiante* (Week of the Student) of February 6–12, 1928, characterized by a series of student protests and political editorials, gave name to the second, but it is unclear what produced the first appellation. The Generación del 18 was made up by the poets Enrique Planchart (1894–1953), Fernando Paz Castillo (1893–1981), Andrés Eloy Blanco (1897–1955), Luis Enrique Mármol (1897–1926), and Jacinto Fombona Pachano (1901–51). Paz Castillo wrote highly reflective, metaphysical poetry; Planchart, Mármol, and Fombona Pachano explored sober forms of expression, interiorizing the landscape, while Blanco wrote poetry with a decidedly popular slant.

In 1936, a collective of writers founded the literary group *Viernes* (Friday), which would later become a literary magazine and press of the same name. This magazine responded to the new political aperture with a cosmopolitan agenda, publishing trans. and reviews of world lit. alongside texts by contemporaneous Venezuelan writers. The group included Luis Fernando Álvarez (1901–52), Vicente Gerbasi (1913–91), Otto de Sola (1908–75), José Ramón Heredia (1900–87), Ángel Miguel Queremel (1899–1939), Miguel Ramón Utrera (1909–93), and Pablo Rojas Guardia (1909–78). Álvarez adopted the prose poem and a kind of surrealist lang. to explore the inner anxiety of urban life. Gerbasi's work, on the other hand, exhibited a balanced mixture of *surrealism, metaphysics, magical transfiguration of landscape, and exuberant versification. His book-length poem *Mi padre, el inmigrante* (My Father, the Immigrant, 1945) is considered his masterpiece, along with his next book, *Los espacios cálidos* (Balmy Spaces, 1952).

Not all poets, however, can be categorized by generations or literary magazines. While the poets of *Viernes* were publishing their first books, three women poets published theirs independently: Enriqueta Arvelo Larriva (1886–1962), Luisa del Valle Silva (1902–62), and María Calcaño (1906–56). These three poets were the founders of a women's literary movement that would not consciously develop until the late 20th c. In their works, they explored motifs of immediacy, intimacy, and reflection, sometimes in a gender-defined, body-conscious erotic poetry.

In the 1940s, a heterogeneous group of poets reacted against the cosmopolitanism of *Viernes* and proposed a return to conservative aspects of the Sp. poetic trad. This reactionary movement is mostly identifiable in isolated figures rather than a single group. Ida Gramcko (1924–94), Luz Machado (1916–99), and Ana Enriqueta Terán (b. 1918) rigorously explored complex rhythmic and rhyme patterns in a thematically idiosyncratic poetry, while reinforcing the growing trad. of women's poetry in the country. Juan Liscano (1915–2001), a markedly productive and versatile poet who explored a variety of subjects (eroticism, metaphysics, Americanism, etc.), was to become as well a prolific essayist and one of the most dedicated critics and promoters of Venezuelan lit.

José Ramón Medina (1921–2010) was the most relevant figure of the literary magazine *Contrapunto* (Counterpoint, 1948–50). He was not only one of Venezuela's main poets but a devoted historian and anthologist of its lit. Among the founders of the literary magazine *Cantaclaro* (Chanticleer, one issue in 1950) were Rafael José Muñoz (1928–81), Jesús Sanoja Hernández (b. 1930), and Miguel García Mackle (b. 1927). Muñoz was the first avant-garde Venezuelan poet in the strict sense of the term, and his book *El círculo de los tres soles* (The Three-Sun Circle, 1968) displayed a gamut of invented langs., *nonsense, neologisms, and mathematical speculations.

A herald of the *Generación de los 60* (Generation of the 1960s), Juan Sánchez Peláez (1922–2003) is considered the most revolutionary, complex, and stimulating Venezuelan poet of the 20th c. His poetry bore some thematic resemblance to previous poets (Ramos Sucre, Gerbasi) but distinguished itself by a revolutionary lang. that combined the grammatical transgressions of the avant-garde with a singular and tender intimacy, recognizable even in his first book *Elena y los elementos* (Elena and the Elements, 1952). The publication of his *Animal de costumbre* (The Usual Animal, 1958)—notably, in the same year as the downfall of dictator Marcos Pérez Jiménez—marked the beginning of a new era of poetic experimentation. The Generación de los 60 enjoyed the newfound creative liberty enabled by Sánchez Peláez. Arnaldo Acosta Bello (1927–96), Rafael Cadenas (b. 1930), Francisco Pérez Perdomo (b. 1930), Juan Calzadilla (b. 1931), Alfredo Silva Estrada (1933–2009), Guillermo Sucre (b. 1933), and Ramón Palomares (b. 1935) constituted the most remarkable series of poets in the hist. of Venezuelan poetry. Each of these writers created highly idiosyncratic forms of poetry; Palomares renewed and complicated the *nativista* trad. by infusing it with a new lang. simultaneously regional and surrealistic; Silva Estrada adopted a constructivist poetics (a unique case in Venezuelan poetry; see CONSTRUCTIVISM) marked by rigorous experiment with classic forms applied in the trad. of abstract poetry; Calzadilla explored short forms (*epigrams, aphorisms) to make a resolutely urban poetry; and Cadenas created a multifarious oeuvre—beginning with existential and hallucinatory situations à la Rimbaud, and (influenced by Ramos Sucre), he later wrote a concentrated, reflexive, almost aphoristic poetry with a philosophical slant.

The subsequent group of authors is sometimes classified with the Generación de los 60, although they are usually considered a transitional group because of their attempts to undermine the tenets of that generation. This group included Victor Valera Mora (1935–84), Caupolicán Ovalles (1936–2001), Ludovico Silva (1937–88), Miyó Vestrini (1938–91), Gustavo Pereira (b. 1940), Eugenio Montejo (1938–2008), Luis Alberto Crespo (b. 1941), José Barroeta (1942–2006), Reinaldo Pérez So (b. 1945), Julio Miranda (1945–98), Hanni Ossott (1946–2002), Márgara Russotto (b. 1946), William Osuna (b. 1948), Ramón Ordaz (b. 1949), and Alejandro Oliveros (b. 1949). Vestrini and Russotto reinforced the women's poetry movement with new forms of verbal exploration; Crespo and Barroeta revitalized the movement of regional poetry through their oneiric and even abstract perspective; Valera Mora and Ovalles, in the trad. of avant-garde poetry, combined lang. experimentation and political positioning; Ossott created an intensely personal and hermetic poetry in which abstract elements were supplemented with motifs from the philosophical trad.; Osuna inscribed himself in the trad. of urban poetry; Oliveros adopted an objectivist form of poetry (see OBJECTIVISM); and, finally, Montejo—along with Cadenas, the most internationally renowned Venezuelan poet—left behind a complex oeuvre, published under several *heteronyms. His verbal explorations ranged from quasi-vanguardist experimentation to playful engagement with cl. formality, sometimes with a whiff of irony. Under the name Montejo (also a pseud.) he wrote poetry in which remembrance and presence are woven through an artisanal attention to lang.

The last discernible cohort is the *Generación de los 80*. These poets were divided into two literary groups: *Tráfico* (Traffic) and *Guaire*, the name of the river that runs through Caracas. Both groups reacted bitterly against what they considered the deviations of previous poetry. Theirs was to be the poetry of reality—a poetry that would put an end to the outdated metaphysical, hermetic, escapist writing of the recent past, with Caracas (the "real" city) as its background. This generation included, among others, Armando Rojas Guardia (b. 1949), Igor Barreto (b. 1952), Yolanda Pantin (b. 1954), Miguel Márquez (b. 1955), Rafael Arráiz Lucca (b. 1959), Rafael Castillo Zapata (b. 1959), and Luis Pérez Oramas (b. 1960). After their early confrontational phase, most of these poets would go on to produce personal works that would become integrated into the poetic trad. they originally challenged.

The poets of the last decade of the 20th c. generally assembled in groups with no explicit creative agendas. However, a strongly growing trend is that of women's poetry, led by María Auxiliadora Álvarez (b. 1956), Laura Cracco (b. 1959), Martha Kornblith (1959–97), María Antonieta Flores (b. 1960), Patricia Guzmán (b. 1960), Claudia Sierich (b. 1963), Gabriela Kizer (b. 1964), Jacqueline Goldberg (b. 1966), Carmen Verde Arocha (b. 1967), and Eleonora Requena (b. 1968). Three poets—Arturo Gutiérrez (b. 1963), Luis Moreno Villamediana (b. 1966), and Luis Enrique Belmonte (b. 1971)—won international awards at the turn of the century and, along with Alexis Romero (b. 1966), already have a consolidated oeuvre. Each of these figures exhibits a heightened awareness of the trad. of Venezuelan poetry. They renew and rewrite it, combining a reflexive attention to the details of the surrounding world with the complex use of a number of verbal registers. The future, therefore, seems open to a widening spectrum of possibilities.

*See* INDIGENOUS AMERICAS, POETRY OF THE; SPAIN, POETRY OF; SPANISH AMERICA, POETRY OF.

■ **Anthologies**: *Las cien mejores poesías líricas venezolanas*, ed. P. P. Barnola (1935); *Las mejores poesías venezolanas*, ed. G. Sucre (1958); *La nueva poesía venezolana*, ed. J. R. Medina (1959); *Antología venezolana. Verso*, ed. J. R. Medina (1962); *La antigua y la moderna literatura venezolana*, ed. P. Díaz Seijas (1966); *Antología general de la poesía venezolana*, ed. J. A. Escalona-Escalona (1966); *Poesía de Venezuela: Románticos y modernistas*, ed. J. R. Medina (1966); *Orígenes de la poesía colonial venezolana*, ed. M. Páez Pumar (1979); *Antología actual de la poesía venezolana*, ed. J. A. Escalona-Escalona, 2 v. (1981); *Antología dispersa de la poesía venezolana*, ed. E. R. Pérez (1981); *Poetas parnasianos de Venezuela*, ed. P. A. Vásquez (1982); *Contemporary Venezuelan Poetry*, ed. J. Tello (1983); *Antología de la moderna poesía venezolana*, ed. O. D'Sola, 2 v., 2d ed. (1984); *Antología de la poesía venezolana*, ed. D. Palma (1987); *Los poetas de 1942*, ed. L. Pastori (1988); *Poetas parnasianos y modernistas*, ed. L. León,

2d ed. (1988); *Antología comentada de la poesía venezolana*, ed. A. Salas (1989); *Cuarenta poetas se balancean*, ed. J. Lasarte (1990); *Poesía en el espejo*, ed. J. Miranda (1995); *Antología de la poesía venezolana*, ed. R. Arráiz Lucca (1997); *Veinte poetas venezolanos del siglo XX*, ed. R. Arráiz Lucca (1998); *Diez poetas venezolanos del siglo XIX*, ed. R. Arráiz Lucca (2001); *Antología histórica de la poesía venezolana del siglo XX (1907–1996)*, ed. J. Miranda (2001); *Navegación de tres siglos (antología básica de la poesía venezolana 1826/2002)*, ed. J. Marta Sosa (2003); *Antología. La poesía del siglo XX en Venezuela*, ed. R. Arráiz Lucca (2005); *Conversación con la intemperie*, ed. G. Guerrero (2008); *En-obra*, ed. G. Saraceni (2008).

■ **Criticism and History**: P. Venegas Filardo, *Estudios sobre poetas venezolanos* (1941); E. Crema, *Interpretaciones críticas de la literatura venezolana* (1955); F. Paz Castillo, *Reflexiones de atardecer*, 3 v. (1964); P. Díaz Seijas, *La antigua y la moderna literatura venezolana* (1966); D. Miliani, *Vísperas del modernismo en la poesía venezolana* (1968); F. Paz Castillo, *De la época modernista* (1968); R. Agudo Freites, *Pío Tamayo y la vanguardia* (1969); P. P. Barnola, *Estudios crítico-literarios* (1971); U. Leo, *Interpretaciones estilísticas* (1972); G. Picón Febres, *La literatura venezolana en el siglo XIX*, 3d ed. (1972); V. Vargas, *El devenir de la palabra poética* (1980); J. Liscano, *Panorama de la literatura venezolana actual*, 2d ed. (1984); and *Lectura de poetas y poesía* (1985); N. Osorio, *La formación de la vanguardia literaria en Venezuela* (1985); M. Picón Salas, *Formación y proceso de la literatura venezolana*, 5th ed. (1984); G. Sucre, *La máscara, la transparencia*, rev. ed. (1985); E. Vera, *Flor y canto: 25 años de poesía venezolana* (1985); *Diccionario general de la literatura venezolana*, ed. L. Cardozo and J. Pintó, 2 v. (1987); P. Venegas Filardo, *53 nombres de poetas venezolanos* (1990); J. R. Medina, *Noventa años de literatura venezolana* (1992); J. Miranda, *Poesía, paisaje y política* (1992); G. Zambrano, *Los verbos plurales* (1993); J. Miranda, "Generaciones, movimientos, grupos, tendencias, manifiestos y postulados de la poesía venezolana del siglo XX," *Antología histórica de la poesía venezolana del siglo XX (1907–1996)*, ed. J. Miranda (2001); E. Nichols, *Rediscovering the Language of the Tribe in Modern Venezuelan Poetry* (2002); Jorge Romero, *La sociedad de los poemas muertos* (2002); R. Arráiz Lucca, *El coro de las voces solitarias* (2003); *Nación y literatura*, ed. L. Barrera, C. Pacheco, B. González (2006).

■ **Electronic Resources**: Poetas Venezolanos (in Sp.), http://poetasvenezolanos.blogspot.com; Veneopoetics (in Eng.), http://venepoetics.blogspot.com/; El Salmon, http://revistadepoesiaelsalmon.blogspot.com.

L. M. ISAVA

**VENUS AND ADONIS STANZA.** The most popular *sexain, consisting of a heroic quatrain and couplet rhyming *ababcc* in iambic pentameter. Its name derives from Shakespeare's verse epic *Venus and Adonis*, although it was used before Shakespeare by the Earl of Surrey, Philip Sidney, Edmund Spenser ( January and December eclogues of the *Shepheardes Calender*), John Donne ("The Expiration"), and other Ren. poets for solemn lyrics as well as for shorter amatory and longer narrative poems: it is particularly common for *complaints and epyllia (see EPYLLION). Shakespeare used it again in *Romeo and Juliet*, *Love's Labour's Lost*, and other plays. Many 18-line poems of the 16th c. contain three Venus and Adonis stanzas; some of them (many of the 100 sonnet-related poems in Thomas Watson's *Hekatompathia*; Sidney's *Old Arcadia* 46, *Certain Sonnets* 19; Lodge's *Scillaes Metamorphoses*) seem to be larger structural imitations of the stanza form itself: two corresponding or analogous stanzas are followed by a third departing from the analogy and concluding the poem succinctly. This AA/B pattern is descended from the *canzone and *canso*. The Shakespearean sonnet clearly resembles such poems in that it ends with a couplet having the same closural function. The Venus and Adonis stanza has been one of the most popular and superbly handled forms in Eng. and Am. poetry up to our time (seven poems by William Wordsworth; John Wain, "Time Was"; Theodore Roethke, "Four for John Davies"; Thom Gunn, "Mirror for Poets"; Robert Lowell, "April Birthday at Sea").

E. HAÜBLEIN; T.V.F. BROGAN

**VERISIMILITUDE.** *See* MIMESIS.

**VERS.** (1) In Occitan, a term used by the early *troubadours to designate any song, incl. the love song, later called *canso* or *chanso*. The term derives from med. Lat. *versus*. Distinctions between canso and vers were discussed by some troubadours ca. 1200, when it was becoming an outmoded term. During the 13th c., it was revived to denote songs on moral, political, or satirical subjects (see SIRVENTES) rather than amatory ones. The vers is apt to have short and uncomplicated stanzas. (2) In mod. Fr., the principal term for both the discrete line of verse and verse taken generically, as a form or mode of expression.

■ Jeanroy, v. 2; J. Chailley, "Les Premiers Troubadours et le versus de l'école d'Aquitaine," *Romania* 76 (1955); J. H. Marshall, "Le Vers au XIIe siècle: Genre poétique?" *Revue de langue et littérature d'Oc* 12–13 (1965); Chambers; E. Köhler, "'Vers' und Kanzone," *GRLMA* 2.1.3 (1987); and "Zum Verhaltnis von vers und canso bei den Trobadors," *Etudes de philologie romane et d'histoire litteraire offerts a Jules Horrent*, ed. J. M. D'Heur et al. (1980).

F. M. CHAMBERS; J. H. MARSHALL; C. SCOTT

## VERSE AND PROSE

   I. Definitions and Background
   II. History of Verse and Prose
   III. Collaborations between Verse and Prose
   IV. Transformations by Paraphrase or Translation
   V. Free Verse and Prose Poetry
   VI. Conclusions

**I. Definitions and Background.** The term *verse* derives from the Lat. *versus*, which originally denotes "a turning" of a plough at the end of a furrow or the furrow

itself. By analogy, the word means "a row" or "a line of writing," esp. a line a poet composes in making a poem. Etymologically, *versus* may recall the *boustrophedon or "turning-ox" style of writing we find in some Etruscan and early Roman inscriptions, in which the lines travel, like an ox drawing a plough back and forth on a field, alternately from right to left and left to right. The Gr. equivalent of *versus* is *metron*, "meter" or "measure," which conveys the same suggestions of length and regularity.

The ancients lack a specific noun for *prose*, a circumstance to which we will return below. Their nearest equivalents, the Gr. *logos* and the Lat. *oratio*, carry a wide range of denotations, incl. "word," "language," "speech," "story," "conversation," "oration," "discourse," "argument," "opinion," and "account." To indicate "prose," particularly in terms of its literary practice, Roman writers often attach an adjective to *oratio*. The most common of the resulting phrases is *oratio soluta*, "speech loosened [from meter]," but we also encounter (e.g., Quintilian, *Institutio oratoria* 1.5.18) *prosa oratio*, "straightforward speech." *Versus* is related to *vertere*, "to turn," and *prosus* to *provertere*, "to turn forward"; and this morphological connection between *versus* and *prosus* and their sharply contrastive characters—the first word signifying recurrence to a previously established course or pattern, the second indicating continuous movement in one direction—could explain why, in late antiquity and the Middle Ages, *prosa oratio*, in the ultimately contracted form of *prosa*, establishes itself as our noun.

In addition to its primary meaning, the term *verse* serves, esp. in the U.K., as a synonym for "stanza." *Verses* also refer to those numbered divisions of the chapters of the Bible that became standard after the scholar and printer Robert Estienne introduced them into his ed. of the Gr. NT of 1551. Of the secondary meanings of *prose*, the most notable may be that which applies to the texts of the *melismas*, or "sequences," of the med. mass. Since the *melismas* required performers to chant complicated musical phrases to a single syllable, young singers esp. had difficulty remembering them. To make the melodies easier to recall, writers started, in the 9th c., to set words to them. Because these texts were initially in prose, they took that name, though *prosae* were gradually elaborated and, by the 11th c., were composed in rhymed accentual verse.

Writers and readers commonly regard verse and prose as distinct from or even opposite to one another. Verse involves *measure—it organizes speech into units of a specific length and rhythmical character—whereas prose flows more freely at the discretion of the writer or speaker employing it. Verse is, as the *OED* puts it, "metrical composition, form, or structure; language or literary work written or spoken in metre; poetry, esp. with reference to metrical form. Opposed to *prose*." Prose is, in contrast, "the ordinary form of written or spoken language, without metrical structure: esp. as a species or division of literature. Opposed to *poetry*, *verse*, *rime*, or *metre*."

In one respect, we exhaust the subject by noting the difference between verse with its rhythmical organization and prose with its rhythmical freedom; yet in other respects, many factors complicate the relationship of the two media and blur the boundary between them. Throughout lit. hist., verse writers and prose writers share stylistic concerns and rhetorical strategies, and their methods of composition overlap in fascinating ways. Further, the relative status of verse and of prose shifts over time. Whereas from antiquity through the Ren., verse is preeminently the vehicle for imaginative lit., thereafter prose genres like the novel enjoy increasing prominence. Moreover, the expressive theories of lit. that arise during the romantic period call into question the efficacy of artifice, and many writers come to believe that verse, with its regulated rhythm, is unduly mechanical and that prose, with its freer rhythms, possesses greater organic authenticity. Such convictions contribute, in the 20th c., to the devel. and widespread adoption of *free verse, many of whose modes blend into verse elements of composition formerly associated with prose. And despite what dicts. say, some might argue that the opposition between the media has ceased to obtain and that, as W. C. Williams urges in a letter in 1948 to Horace Gregory, "there's an *identity* between prose and verse, not an antithesis."

## II. History of Verse and Prose.
As a literary medium, verse develops earlier than prose. Archaeological evidence indicates that music, dance, and *song played critical roles in the lives of our prehistoric ancestors. Our earliest surviving poetic texts, which date from 19th and 18th c. BCE and which appear on clay tablets from Sumer and papyri in Egypt, already employ such devices as syllabic and grammatical *parallelism, *antithesis, and *refrains. By the middle of the first millennium BCE, poets have worked out sophisticated prosodies and have produced verse of the highest order in, to cite three notable instances, China, India, and Greece. Ancient peoples also practice prose, using it to document commercial transactions, to record legal statutes and religious customs, and, as in the Heb. Bible and in Herodotus's *Histories*, to chronicle legends and events that have shaped their world. Yet most of the central early texts—e.g., the *Epic of Gilgamesh*, *The Tale of Sinuhe*, the Vedic poems, the *Iliad* and *Odyssey*, and the *Shih Ching*—are in verse. And this pattern repeats in later communities. Verse writers such as Abolqasem Ferdowsi, Dante and Chaucer are the first to explore and demonstrate the literary resources of their langs.

The mnemonic appeal of verse is the chief reason for its primacy. Because verse is rhythmically organized, we remember it more readily than prose. For much of our hist., literacy is rare and book production laborious, and the survival of texts depends to a great extent on oral transmission. People naturally favor verse as a means of articulating and preserving those stories and experiences that most deeply express their humanity. By the same token, insofar as people share an instinct for rhythm, verse suits public ritual and ceremony, as the folk songs and hymns of many cultures testify. The repetitive harmonies of verse give

the body in general, and the ear in particular, a purchase on meaning and significance. So, too, when a lang. is young or in a state of transition, metrical constraints help writers focus its grammar and explore its idioms and vocabulary, with the result that poets and their verse forms exercise a permanent influence on subsequent linguistic evolution. Mod. Eng., for example, would not have developed quite in the way it has, nor would we speak and think in quite the ways we do, if the iambic pentameter and William Shakespeare had never existed.

When literary prose does arise, its writers often begin by imitating verse, as can be seen in the Eur. trad. When in the 5th c. BCE, Gorgias establishes oratory as an independent art, his effort involves nothing less than importing into prose devices suggestive of verse, incl., according to Diodorus Siculus (*Library of History* 12.53.2-5), *isocolon (clauses of similar length), *parison* (balanced clauses) and *homoeoteuleton (flectional rhyme). More specifically, Gorgias's revolutionary periodic style (*lexis periodos*) aims to make, as Demetrius remarks (*On Style* 12), "the periods succeed one another with no less regularity than the hexameters in the poetry of Homer" (trans. Loeb Library ed.). Similarly, when Gorgias's student Isocrates starts systematically to cultivate prose rhythm, his motive is to attract to prose the attention people devote to verse. As Cicero later reports (*Orator* 174), "When [Isocrates] observed that people listened to orators with solemn attention, but to poets with pleasure, he is said to have sought for rhythms to use in prose as well" (trans. Loeb Library ed.). From this follows the preoccupation with *prose rhythm that we encounter among writers on rhet. from Aristotle forward (see RHETORIC AND POETRY). Indeed, this preoccupation is one reason that Roman prose writers, in speaking of their medium, characterize it not simply as *oratio* but by an adjective like *solutus, prosus, numerosus* ("rhythmical, melodius"), or *compositus* ("orderly, well-knit") to suggest its degree of rhythmical arrangement.

In the Middle Ages, the rhythmical basis of Eur. speech changes. The perception of syllabic length declines, and its place is supplied, both in Lat. and the emerging vernaculars, by syllabic accent. Yet the practice of prose rhythm persists, even to the extent that as the use of rhyme increases in med. Lat. verse, so it also increases in med. Lat. prose. (Trads. of rhymed prose also appear in Chinese lit. of the Han period and in cl. Ar. lit.) More to the point, verse remains the primary art, as is illustrated by Dante's *De vulgari eloquentia*, the earliest sustained study of poetics directed toward a mod. Eur. lang. In the first paragraph of the second book of this treatise, Dante proposes to demonstrate that It. is as "equally fit for use [for literature] in prose (*prosaice*) and in verse (*metrice*)" and then explains why he will treat verse first: "Because prose writers rather get this language from poets, and because poetry seems to remain a pattern to prose writers, and not the converse, which things appear to confer a certain supremacy, let us first disentangle this language as to its use in meter (*metricum*)" (trans. A.G.F. Howell, *Medieval Literary Criticism*, 1974). Further, just as most of the great imaginative writers of cl. times employ verse, it is the main instrument of expression for such med. and Ren. authors as Dante, Petrarch, François Villon, Ludovico Ariosto, Shakespeare, Lope de Vega, and Jean Racine.

During the Ren., however, the relation between verse and prose begins to alter. One factor in this process is Johannes Gutenburg's devel. in the 1450s of the printing press. This facilitates the production and distribution of books and makes memory less essential to textual preservation and transmission. Another factor is the entrance of Aristotle's long-lost *Poetics* into wide circulation in the 16th c. In the wake of this event, the study of poetry focuses increasingly on the nature and theory of the art per se and draws away from its historical associations with rhet. In the rhetorical trad., verse is the essence of poetry, in that verse is what distinguishes poetry from that other art of persuasive speech, oratory. Aristotle himself reflects this view when, in his *Rhetoric* (3.8.3), he identifies prose oratory with *rhythm and poetry with *meter: "Prose (*logon*) must be rhythmical (*rhythmon*), but not metrical (*metron*), otherwise it will be a poem (*poiēma*)" (trans. Loeb Library ed.). However, in his *Poetics*, which considers poetry in comparison not to oratory but to all forms of discourse, Aristotle rejects this identification, arguing instead (*Poetics* 1447b9–12; 1451b1–12) that a poem is first and foremost an imitation (*mimesis*) of human action embodied in a story or plot (*mythos*). Aristotle acknowledges that people customarily identify poets with their meter (*metron*) and treat both Homer and Empedocles as epic poets because they both write in dactylic hexameter; but he insists that only Homer imitates and deserves the name of poet (*poiētēs*), whereas Empedocles should be termed a physics writer (*physiologos*). And this mimesis-centered (or substance-not-style-centered) analysis of poetry gives rise to the view, which will strengthen over time, that verse embellishes rather than defines poetry and that poetry can be written just as well without verse as with it. As Philip Sidney puts it in his *Defence of Poesy* (1595), "Poesie therefore is an art of imitation, for so Aristotle termeth it in his word *Mimesis* . . . verse being but an ornament and no cause to Poetry, sith there have been many most excellent Poets that never versified [Sidney alludes here to ancient authors of prose romances like Xenophon and Heliodorus], and now swarm many versifiers that need never answer to the name of Poets."

No less significant is the rise of the mod. physical sciences. These give the mod. world an intellectual triumph comparable to that achieved by the ancients in the arts; and insofar as science is associated with prose—with, as Thomas Sprat puts in his *History of the Royal Society* (1667), "a close, naked, natural way of speaking, positive expressions, clear senses, a native easiness, bringing all things as near the Mathematical plainness as they can"—prose comes to be seen as more reliable and accurate than verse, which is increasingly connected with *fancy, sentiment, and caprice.

In addition, in the 18th and 19th cs., the prose novel rises to challenge and dislodge verse as the principal vehicle for imaginative writing. The very novelty of the novel attracts gifted authors like Gustave Flaubert, who writes to Louise Colet in 1852, "Prose was born yesterday. . . . Verse is the form par excellence of ancient lits. All possible prosodic variations have been discovered; but that is far from being the case with prose." So fresh and impressive are the achievements of 19th-c. novelists like Jane Austen, Stendhal, Honoré de Balzac, Ivan Turgenev, Flaubert, Leo Tolstoy, George Eliot, and Henry James that, early in the 20th c., we find Ford Madox Ford repeatedly instructing younger authors like Ezra Pound that, as Ford puts it in *Thus to Revisit*, "Verse must be at least as well written as prose if it is to be poetry." Though Ford's position makes perfect sense in light of the literary conditions of his day, his dictum also reflects that prose has taken over verse's traditional status as the leading form for imaginative lit.

Finally, *romanticism, with its emphasis on spontaneity and naturalness, undermines the traditional idea that prosodic rules assist the poet and sets in its place the belief that the structures of verse hinder self-expression. More specifically, meter becomes associated with mechanical sterility and freer rhythm with organic richness. Martin Tupper terms his *Proverbial Philosophy* (first series, 1837), an early popular work in what we might now call free verse, "Rhythmics"; and in his long scriptural line, and in Walt Whitman's subsequent transformation of it, we see beginnings of what George Saintsbury calls, writing of Tupper in *The Cambridge Companion to English Literature*, "the revolt of rhythm against metre." Moreover, many late 19th- and early 20th c. poets come to identify metrical composition itself with the dated idioms and stale subjects of Victorian poetry and, as a result, believe that to get rid of those idioms and subjects, they also need to dismantle the structures of verse. And the second and third decades of the 20th c. witness an explosion of poetic styles that forgo traditional metrical arrangement. If by the end of the 18th c., the prose novel has supplanted the verse epic—and if by the end of the 19th, drama has gone over to prose—by the end of the 20th, the *lyric has largely abandoned verse as historically understood. Whereas an ancient critic like Quintilian worries (9.4.53–57) that students of oratory may, in their concern for rhythm, turn prose into quasi-verse, mod. readers sometimes worry that poets are too little attentive to rhythmical arrangement and that the ascendance of prose has reduced verse to, in Edmund Wilson's famous phrase, "a dying technique."

**III. Collaborations between Verse and Prose.** Though often distinguished from one another, verse and prose collaborate in several literary genres. Chief among these is the *prosimetrum, an extended work of prose into which, at more or less regular intervals, the author inserts poems or passages of verse. First coined to designate those mixed-mode Eur. med. works, of which Boethius's *Consolation of Philosophy* and Dante's *Vita nuova* are the masterpieces, the term has since been expanded to include texts that, from other times and cultures, also feature prose with verse inserts. Within this enlarged category fall such ancient works as the Upanishads and Petronius's *Satyricon*; such med. works as the popular texts from the T'ang dynasty in China that dramatize and illustrate Buddhist teachings (*pien-wen*), Sadi's *Rosegarden* from Persia, and the Fr. folk tale *Aucassin et Nicollette* (which its anonymous author calls a *chantefable*, a "song-story"); and such Ren. and mod. works as François Rabelais's *Gargantua and Pantagruel*, the *Arcadias* of Jacopo Sannazaro and Sidney, the *hai-bun (prose-and-haiku style) writings of Bashō, H. D. Thoreau's *Week on the Concord and Merrimack Rivers*, Lewis Carroll's "Alice" books, Jean Toomer's *Cane*, and Vladimir Nabokov's *The Gift*.

It is difficult to generalize about prosimetra since they run the gamut from the somber moralizing treatises of Boethius and Sadi to the racy Menippean satires of Petronius and Rabelais to the contemplative travelogues of Bashō and Thoreau. Also, while in some instances (e.g., Sadi and Dante) the poetic inserts are entirely by the author of the overarching prose text, in others (e.g., Bashō and Thoreau) authors introduce not only their own verse but also verse by friends or by poets of the past. Nevertheless, one pattern recurs throughout the genre: the prose passages tend to be devoted to narrative or argument, whereas the verse is reserved for moments of lyric intensity or summary reflection. This practice appears to confirm the widely held belief that prose is best suited to discursive modes and moods, whereas verse is better adapted to concentrated expressions of thought and feeling. Further, because prosimetra appear in so many times and places and in such a variety of literary trads., it seems reasonable to infer that the genre expresses an almost universal curiosity, among people who relish lang., about the different tonal qualities of verse and prose and about the ways these qualities can be brought into effective contrast or balance.

Other works that mix verse and prose include certain Elizabethan and Jacobean dramas, in which the different media signal the social or political status of the dramatis personae. In his "Renaissance in England," J. V. Cunningham observes, "In *A Midsummer Night's Dream* . . . the heads of state speak a dignified blank verse, the wellborn lovers blank verse and couplets; the rude mechanicals speak rudely in prose; and the extra-human characters have their class distinction: they may use lyric measures." The mixed mode also occurs when a prose commentary is attached to a poem. Since this process usually involves two writers working separately—a poet composing the poem first and a scholar composing the commentary afterward—the result is, as a rule, not truly or uniformly prosimetric. However, in Nabokov's *Pale Fire*, a single author creates both the verse text and prose commentary and does so in such a way that the two run parallel to each other and tell intertwining stories. An analogous situation transpires when a writer plays the dual role of poet and scholiast, as S. T. Coleridge does in his *The Rime of the Ancient Mariner*, writing both the verses of his poem and the marginal prose glosses on it. A version

of the mixed mode also arises, in an oral context, when poets, in public presentations of their work, pass back and forth between reading poems and supplying anecdotal background about their genesis or meaning.

**IV. Transformations by Paraphrase or Translation.** If prosimetric forms demonstrate that verse and prose can collaborate, paraphrase and trans. suggest that the border between the two media is open and permits free passage between them.

In mod. parlance, paraphrase means restating, at length and for purposes of clarity, a piece of writing that presents some difficulty of interpretation; but from antiquity through the Ren., *paraphrasis* entails the more challenging exercise of turning verse passages and texts into prose and turning prose passages and texts into verse. Paraphrase is part of the curricula of the Roman schools of rhet., as it is in schools in the Middle Ages; and it contributes to literary practice in a number of ways.

Paraphrase in this sense has two basic forms. One involves a writer's taking a source work from another writer and turning it into verse if the source is in prose or prose if it is in verse. The second involves writers' creating their own prototypes in verse or prose and then rewriting them in the other medium. An instance of the first type of paraphrase occurs when Socrates, awaiting execution in prison and wishing to make poetry (*poiesanta poiemata*) before he dies, versifies (*enteinas*) some of Aesop's prose fables (*Aisopou logous*). Anticipating the theme that Aristotle will develop in the *Poetics*, Socrates explains that he believes that writing poetry entails not only versification but composing stories (*poiein mythous*); and because he is not a maker of stories (*mythologikos*), he avails himself of Aesop's (*Phaedo* 60D–61B). Another example of this type of paraphrase is provided by Chaucer's "Clerk's Tale": this presents, in elegant ME *rhyme royal verse, the tale of Patient Griselda, closely tracking in the process Petrarch's Lat. prose version of the story (which, in turn, is an adaptation of the final novella of Giovanni Boccaccio's It. prose *Decameron*). Shakespeare not only adopts plots from prose sources but on occasion metrifies passages from them. A case in point is Enobarbus's description (*Antony and Cleopatra* 2.2.198ff.) of the sensational appearance Cleopatra makes on her barge when she arrives in Cicilia and first meets Antony: Shakespeare skillfully cuts, pastes, and compresses, into iambic pentameter, much of Thomas North's trans. of Plutarch's account of the scene. Many poems of the Christian church are verse paraphrases of biblical prose. This trad. extends from the late-ancient paraphrases into Lat. hexameters of various OT and NT texts down to hymn collections like the Scottish church's *Translations and Paraphrases in Verse of Several Passages of Sacred Scripture* (1781). Well-known instances in Am. lit. of verse-to-prose paraphrases appear in Nathaniel Hawthorne's *Wonder Book*, some of the stories of which retell, in prose for young readers, verse tales from antiquity, such as Ovid's account of Midas and the golden touch.

Of those paraphrasers who work from their own prototypes, Virgil is the best known. Having learned to paraphrase during his studies of law and rhet., he writes the *Aeneid* in prose before turning it into meter (Donatus, *Life of Virgil*, 23). (He uses the prose version chiefly to keep in mind the epic's general structure while pursuing his unusual compositional technique of working, as the mood strikes him, on bk. 3 one day, bk. 7 the next, bk. 2 the day after that, and so on.) Ironically, the *Aeneid* becomes upon publication an instant classic, and generations of students are set the exercise of paraphrasing it back into prose; Augustine informs us (*Confessions* 1.17.27) that he won a prize at school for turning into prose (*solutis verbis*) those verses (*versibus*) in bk. 1 in which Juno rages about her inability to exterminate the small band of Aeneus-led Trojans who escaped the sack of their city.

Other paraphrasers working from their own prototypes include Bede, who writes his *Life of Cuthbert* in verse in 716 and then produces an expanded prose version five years later, and Ben Jonson, who tells William Drummond (*Conversations*, 15) that "he wrote all his [verses] first in prose, for so his master Camden [i.e., William Camden, the great scholar and antiquarian who was Jonson's teacher at Westminster School] had learned him." It is also interesting that E. A. Robinson's "Captain Craig," a poem about a down-and-out philosopher manqué, derives from an earlier prose sketch of its subject, while John Updike first creates and examines, in a poem titled "Ex-Basketball Player," a figure who in time will morph, after a brief stop as a character in the short story "Ace in the Hole," into the protagonist of his *Rabbit* novels.

As different as these examples are, they all suggest that verse and prose can be related interchangeably and that subjects and ideas expressed in one medium can sometimes be usefully transferred to the other. Not for nothing do Cleanth Brooks and the New Critics condemn paraphrase as "heresy." Form and content are always, in fine writing, vitally connected and mutually supportive; but effective paraphrase would seem to dispute the New Critical doctrine that they are inseparable (see NEW CRITICISM).

Like paraphrase, trans. sometimes has the effect of placing verse and prose in interchangeable relation rather than setting them in opposition to one another. This is esp. true of trans., in the Ren. and after, in which a poetic text from cl. Gr. or Lat. appears on one page while the facing page features a trans. version in a vernacular lang. (or sometimes in Lat. if the original is Gr.). Often, the trans. versions are in prose, with the result that the parallel texts and media seem equivalent.

An important and related case involves trans. that do not feature the original text but lay out on the page a literal line-by-line trans. of it, with line numbers given in the margin so that the reader can refer back and forth between it and a copy of the original text with an ease that would not be possible were the trans. written out as prose. Corresponding literally and linearly to the original poem but lacking its meter, such trans. produce an impression of free verse several centuries before its time; and in fact Pound begins his largely free-verse epic *The Cantos,* by rendering into Eng. a passage from just such a trans., Andreas Divus's 1538 Lat. trot of the *Odyssey*. As the poet and trans. Robert Wells once observed in conversation, Divus's stripped-down, lineated Lat. prose version of Homer appears to anticipate Pound's technique—evident in his earlier poems and trans., but esp. striking in *The Cantos*—of breaking up traditional verse rhythm and cutting away poetic ornament to drive directly at his subjects. (Pound, in his essay "Translations of Greek: Early Translators of Homer," praises Divus's Lat. for its "constant suggestions of the poetic motion.")

During the second half of the 20th c., trans. at times not only blurs the boundary between verse and prose but obscures the role verse has played in lit. hist. Fewer and fewer translators have the inclination or training to render earlier foreign-lang. poetry into native meter, and free trans. of metrical poems of the past become very common. Unlike earlier nonmetered trans., which usually present themselves simply as aids to study (or as prose), these later trans. often make claims to independent poetic merit. In many respects, these claims are justified. However, collectively such trans. leave some readers—esp. those who experience foreign lang. and lit. mainly or only through trans.—with a version of lit. hist. in which authors like Homer, Virgil, Horace, and Dante cease to write conventional verse and appear instead as practitioners of the looser rhythmical styles of mod. poetry. Such trans. tend, that is, to diminish the sense that verse is a medium with a long trad. distinguishable from other media and trads.

**V. Free Verse and Prose Poetry.** In addition to prosimetric forms—and in addition to paraphrastic or trans. works that transpose verse to prose or prose to verse—certain types of composition blend or fuse the two media.

Free verse is probably the preeminent form in this category. Because so many kinds of free verse exist, it is impossible to summarize it neatly. But many of its varieties occupy the area that lies, as Ford notes in his defense of *vers libre in *Thus to Revisit*, "between the entrenched lines of Prosaists and Versificators . . . the territory of Neither-Prose-Nor-Verse." In certain esp. impressive free-verse poems, such as Wallace Stevens's gravely cadenced "The Snow Man" and Williams's haunting "Widow's Lament in Springtime," one feels that the poet is exploring rhythms beyond the register of traditional meter, while at the same time retaining—mainly by means of repetitions of phrases and syntactical patterns—a feeling of the structural concentration of verse. In less sensitively organized forms, such as we find in the poetry of Edgar Lee Masters and Carl Sandburg, vers libre appears closer to prose than to verse, though it retains a connection to the latter, thanks to the mod. typographer's configuring its lines on the page in ways that visually suggest metrical or stanzaic arrangement.

If certain sorts of free verse achieve their effects by moving verse in the direction of prose, the mod. *prose poem accomplishes something comparable by moving prose in the direction of verse. The idea of prose poetry is ancient. The Elder Seneca describes (*Controversiae* 2.2.8) Ovid's student exercises in declamation as *solutum carmen*, which means "loose song" or "loose poem" but which also echoes the common phrase for prose, *oratio soluta*. (Seneca suggests that Ovid's speeches were, in their stylistic panache, poetry made of prose; and Ovid himself relates, in *Tristia*, 4.10.23–26, that even when, as a young man, he tried to write prose, it came out as verse.) Lucian, too, speaks (*How to Write History* 8) of "prosaic poetry" (*peze poietike*) when he discusses hist. and notes that it has a story-telling affinity to poetry without, however, employing the meters, fictions, and figurative ornaments that poets use. Yet the mod. prose poem, as it emerges in France in the 19th c., has a more specific character and aim than anything the ancients discuss. The mod. prose poem attempts to bring into prose the memorable rhythm and sensitivity of verse. This objective is well articulated by Charles Baudelaire when he writes in the preface to his own *Little Poems in Prose*, "Who among us has not, in his ambitious moments, dreamed of the miracle of a poetic prose, musical without rhythm and without rhyme, sufficiently subtle and sufficiently abrupt, to adapt to the lyrical movements of the soul, to the waves of reverie, to the tremblings of consciousness?"

Related mod. efforts to create a poetic prose include Amy Lowell's experiments with "polyphonic prose" and some of Gertrude Stein's work. (Wyndham Lewis, in *Time and Western Man*, characterizes Stein's *Three Lives* with a phrase—"prose-song"—very like that which the Elder Seneca applies to Ovid's declamations.) James Joyce also sometimes cultivates a species of prose poetry, as when he begins the Sirens episode in *Ulysses* with a burst of disjointed phrases rich in rhyme and alliteration.

Free verse and prose poetry remind us that, though verse and prose may be distinct, a continuous spectrum of rhythm connects the two. Just as we can slide around a color wheel from red to green by way of shades of orange and yellow and then back to red via shades of blue and violet, so we can pass by degrees from the loosest prose through increasingly organized speech to metrical arrangement and back again to prose. This continuity of rhythm is perhaps most strongly borne home to us when we hear speakers or writers of prose ascend unconsciously, because of strong feeling or pressing circumstances, into highly rhythmical utterance. George Bernard Shaw captures this phenomenon in that early scene in *Pygmalion* when Higgins demands to know why Doolittle has called on him but so bullies the dustman that he cannot get a word of explanation in edgewise until he forcibly asserts, "I'm willing to tell you. I'm wanting to tell you. I'm waiting to tell you." Another instance is supplied by Charles Dickens, who often drifts into blank verse when stirred by thoughts about death or love. Below, for instance, lineated as unrhymed iambic pentameter, is the final paragraph of *David Copperfield*, in which the hero, alone at his writing table late at night, apostrophizes his second wife and speaks of the inspiration she has given him to compose the book he has just finished. The third line

breaks awkwardly in the middle of a word—indeed, the enjambment it produces suggests a parody of John Milton's use of that device—but the iambic tread of the passage is unmistakable. (If the passage were an actual poem, we would call its final syllable "a feminine ending.")

> O Agnes, O my soul, so may thy face
> be by me when I close my life indeed;
> so may I, when realities are melt-
> ing from me, like the shadows which I now
> dismiss, still find thee near me, pointing upward!

**VI. Conclusions.** Because verse plays such a diminished role, vis-à-vis prose, in imaginative lit. in recent centuries, we might well concur with Wilson's assessment that it is a dying technique. Since human communities most notably embrace verse in their earlier stages and turn increasingly to prose as their technologies and institutions grow more complex, perhaps it is only natural that verse should have declined and perhaps it is inevitable that it will die. In "The Nature of Verse and Its Consequences for the Mixed Form," Kristin Hanson and Paul Kiparsky, discussing the manner in which prose narrative has replaced verse narrative in Eur. lit., comment generally, "Once the shift has taken place [in a tradition of writing], verse is never restored to the function of narrative within that trad., and may even be eventually eclipsed in all its functions by prose."

Nevertheless, even in a technological age, memory remains crucial to our species. It preserves us from the brutal and brutalizing conception of existence as an irreversible succession of moments with no depth beneath them and no dimension beyond them. Verse is an art of memory. More than any other literary form, we can take it into mind and heart. Lines of verse can return to us unbidden in times of grief to illuminate and make them bearable; and it is often with verse that we celebrate the joys of friendship and love and mark the occasion of a marriage or a birth. It is not just the ear or eye that pauses and turns back at the end of the line. The psyche, too, turns back, recovering and renewing a measure of being larger than itself and, at the same time, moving forward into its own mysterious future.

Finally, though the world seems always and confusingly in flux, human evolution occurs slowly, and we mod. peoples differ little, in our genetic and biochemical constitution, from our ancestors who, in Sumer, Egypt, China, Greece, and India, first started composing verse. Just as they responded to lang. and to its rhythms, symmetries, and surprises, so do we. For this reason alone, verse will likely endure in our culture, alongside of prose and among all the other media of imaginative lit. that serve and honor poetry.

*See* CHANTE-FABLE, RHYME-PROSE, SCANSION, VERSIFICATION.

■ **Historical Works:** G. Saintsbury, *A History of English Prose Rhythm* (1912); F. M. Ford, *Thus to Revisit* (1921); P. F. Baum, *The Other Harmony of Prose* (1952);

Abrams; Auerbach; Curtius; G. F. Else, *Aristotle's "Poetics"* (1957); I. Watt, *The Rise of the Novel* (1957); J. Greenway, *Literature among the Primitives* (1964); H. N. Schneidau, "Imagism as Discipline: Hueffer and the Prose Tradition," *Ezra Pound* (1969); H. Kenner, *The Pound Era* (1971); J. V. Cunningham, *The Collected Essays of J. V. Cunningham* (1976); West; Norden; W. Trimpi, *Muses of One Mind* (1983); M. Roberts, *Biblical Epic and Rhetorical Paraphrase in Late Antiquity* (1985); P. O. Kristeller, "The Modern System of the Arts" and "Afterword, 'Creativity' and 'Tradition,'" *Renaissance Thought and the Arts*, exp. ed. (1990); T. Steele, *Missing Measures* (1990); M. Kinzie, *The Cure of Poetry in an Age of Prose* (1993); A. Finch, *The Ghost of Meter* (1993); P. Dronke, *Verse with Prose from Petronius to Dante* (1994); G. A. Kennedy, *A New History of Classical Rhetoric* (1994); H. Bloom, *Shakespeare* (1999); M. E. Fassler, "Sequence," *The Harvard Dictionary of Music*, 4th ed. (2003); R. B. Shaw, *Blank Verse* (2007).

■ **Criticism:** A. Quiller-Couch, "On the Difference between Verse and Prose," *On the Art of Writing* (1916); A. E. Housman, *The Name and Nature of Poetry* (1933); E. Wilson, "Is Verse a Dying Technique?" *The Triple Thinkers* (1938); Brooks; Y. Winters, "The Influence of Meter on Poetic Convention," *In Defense of Reason* (1947); E. Pound, *Literary Essays of Ezra Pound*, ed. T. S. Eliot (1954); *The Selected Letters of William Carlos Williams*, ed. J. C. Thirlwall (1957); P. Valéry, "Concerning *Adonis*," *The Art of Poetry*, trans. J. Mathews (1958); W. C. Booth, *The Rhetoric of Fiction* (1961); T. S. Eliot, "Reflections on Vers Libre," *To Criticize the Critic* (1965); C. Baudelaire, *Oeuvres Complètes*, ed. C. Pichois (1975); I. A. Richards, *Verse versus Prose* (1978); C. O. Hartman, *Free Verse* (1980); *The Letters of Gustave Flaubert: 1830–1857*, trans. F. Steegmuller (1980); S. Cushman, *William Carlos Williams and the Meanings of Measure* (1985); Hollander; P. Levi, "Rhyming on the Counterattack," *The Mirror Maker*, trans. R. Rosenthal (1990); K. Hanson and P. Kiparsky, "The Nature of Verse and Its Consequences for the Mixed Form," *Prosimetrum*, ed. J. Harris and K. Reichl (1997); D. Davis, "All My Soul Is There: Verse Translation and the Rhetoric of English Poetry," *Yale Review* 90 (2002); A. Bradley, *Book of Rhymes* (2008).

T. STEELE

**VERSE DRAMA.** *See* DRAMATIC POETRY.

**VERSE EPISTLE** (Gr. *epistole*, Lat. *epistula*). A poem addressed to a friend, lover, or patron, written in familiar style and in *hexameters (cl.) or their mod. equivalents. Two types of verse epistles exist: the one on moral and philosophical subjects, which stems from Horace's *Epistles*, and the other on romantic and sentimental subjects, which stems from Ovid's *Heroides*. Though the verse epistle may be found as early as 146 BCE (L. Mummius Achaicus's letters from Corinth and some of the satires of Lucullus), Horace perfected the form,

employing common *diction, personal details, and a *plain style to lend familiarity to his philosophical subjects. His letters to the Lucius Calpurnius Piso and his sons (ca. 10 BCE) on the art of poetry, known since Quintilian as the *Ars poetica*, became a standard genre of the Middle Ages and after. Ovid used the same style for his *Tristia* and *Ex Ponto* but developed the sentimental epistle in his *Heroides*, which are fictional letters from the legendary women of antiquity—e.g., Helen, Medea, Dido—to their lovers. Throughout the Middle Ages, the latter seems to have been the more popular type, for it had an influence on the poets of *courtly love and subsequently inspired Samuel Daniel to introduce the form into Eng., e.g., his "Letter from Octavia to Marcus Antonius." Such also was the source for John Donne's large body of memorable verse epistles ("Sir, more than Kisses, letters mingle souls") and Alexander Pope's "Eloisa to Abelard."

But it was the Horatian epistle that had the greater effect on Ren. and mod. poetry. Petrarch, the first humanist to know Horace, wrote his influential *Epistulae metricae* in Lat. Subsequently, Ludovico Ariosto's *Satires* in *terza rima* employed the form in vernacular It. In all these epistles, Christian sentiment made itself felt. In Spain, Garcilaso de la Vega's "Epístola a Boscán" (1543) in *blank verse and the "Epístola moral a Fabio" in terza rima introduced and perfected the form. Fr. writers esp. cultivated it for its "graceful precision and dignified familiarity"; Nicolas Boileau's 12 epistles in couplets (1668–95) are considered the finest examples. Ben Jonson began the Eng. use of the Horatian form (*The Forest*, 1616) and was followed by others, e.g. Henry Vaughan, John Dryden, and William Congreve. But the finest examples in Eng. are Pope's *Moral Essays* and the "Epistle to Dr. Arbuthnot" in *heroic couplets. The romantics did not value the verse epistle, though P. B. Shelley, John Keats, and W. S. Landor on occasion wrote them. Examples in the 20th c. incl. W. H. Auden's *New Year Letter* and Auden and Louis MacNeice's *Letters from Iceland*.

■ H. Peter, *Der Brief in der römische Litteratur* (1901); J. Vianey, *Les Epéitres de Marot* (1935); W. Grenzmann, "Briefgedicht," *Reallexikon II*; J. A. Levine, "The Status of the Verse Epistle before Pope," *SP* 59 (1962); W. Trimpi, *Ben Jonson's Poems* (1962); J. Norton-Smith, "Chaucer's Epistolary Style," *Essays on Style and Language*, ed. R. Fowler (1966); *John Donne: The Satires, Epigrams and Verse Letters,* ed. W. Milgate (1967); N. C. de Nagy, *Michael Drayton's "England's Heroical Epistles"* (1968); R. S. Matteson, "English Verse Epistles, 1660–1758," *DAI* 28 (1968); D. J. Palmer, "The Verse Epistle," *Metaphysical Poetry*, ed. M. Bradbury and D. Palmer (1970); M. Motsch, *Die poetische Epistel* (1974); A. B. Cameron, "Donne's Deliberative Verse Epistles," *English Literary Renaissance* 6 (1976); M. R. Sperberg-McQueen, "Martin Opitz and the Tradition of the Renaissance Poetic Epistle," *Daphnis* 11 (1982); J. E. Brown, "The Verse Epistles of A. S. Pushkin," *DAI* 45 (1984); C. Guillén, "Notes toward the Study of the Renaissance Letter," *Renaissance Genres*, ed. B. K. Lewalski (1986); M. Camargo, *The Middle English*

*Verse Love Epistle* (1991); W. C. Dowling, *The Episto-lary Moment* (1991)—on the 18th c.; D. Aers, "'Darke Texts Need Notes': Versions of Self in Donne's Verse Epistles," *Critical Essays on John Donne*, ed. A. Marotti (1994); B. Overton, "Aphra Behn and the Verse Epistle," *Women's Writing* 16 (2009).

R. A. HORNSBY; T.V.F. BROGAN

**VERSE NOVEL.** *See* NARRATIVE POETRY.

**VERSE PARAGRAPH.** If a paragraph is defined as one or more sentences unified by a dominant mood or thought, then poetry, like prose, can be seen as moving forward in units that could be called paragraphs. Typically, the term *verse paragraph* is used to designate a group of lines that lacks regular stanzaic form and contains a nonstandardized number of lines and that is separated from the other verse paragraphs of a poem through indentation or blank space. Rhymed verse paragraphs do occur (e.g., the irregular *canzoni* of John Milton's "Lycidas" or the indented sections of varying numbers of couplets within the subdivisions of Alexander Pope's *Essay on Man*), but the term is used most frequently in relation to *blank verse. Lacking the somewhat arbitrary organization provided by an established *rhyme scheme, blank verse must provide units supporting the organization of idea such that the narration, description, or exposition unfolds in a series of stages felt as justly proportioned. In this sense, the verse paragraph is a syntactic period, frequently a single complex or periodic sentence, deployed in enjambed *stichic verse so that the beginnings and ends of the syntactic frames conspicuously do not coincide with those of the metrical frames (the lines), with the result that meter and syntax are in counterpoint or tension.

The verse paragraph is a common feature of Old Germanic heroic poetry and is an important element in Eng. poetry as early as *Beowulf*, where sentences often begin at the *caesura. But by general consent, the greatest master of the verse paragraph is Milton, who, in writing *Paradise Lost*, needed "to devise a formal unit not regularly rhymed, not necessarily brief, sufficiently coherent but sufficiently flexible, intermediate between the line and the book" (Weismiller 189). Many of the most characteristic effects of *Paradise Lost*—its majesty, its epic sweep, its rich counterpoint of line and sentence rhythms—are produced or enhanced by Milton's verse paragraphs. Certain shorter poems in Eng., such as William Wordsworth's "Tintern Abbey," also make use of the verse paragraph. In addition, many *free-verse poems, such as Walt Whitman's "Out of the Cradle Endlessly Rocking," which operate without a rhyme scheme or other regular structural organization, can be described as being composed of verse paragraphs.

■ G. Hübner, *Die stilistische Spannung in Milton's Paradise Lost* (1913); R. D. Havens, *The Influence of Milton on English Poetry* (1922); J. Whaler, *Counterpoint and Symbol* (1956); E. Weismiller, "Blank Verse," *A Milton Encyclopedia*, ed. W. B. Hunter Jr., et al. (1978); W. H. Beale, "Rhetoric in the OE Verse Paragraph," *NM* 80

(1979); J. Hollander, "'Sense Variously Drawn Out'" in Hollander; J. K. Hale, *Milton's Languages* (1997).

A. PREMINGER; E. R. WEISMILLER;
T.V.F. BROGAN; P. KLINE

**VERSE SYSTEMS.** *See* METER.

**VERSET.** This term is derived from the short "verses" of the Bible (cf. *versicle*) and etymologically refers to short lines (Occitan and OF); in Eng., it has been so used, esp. to refer to the lines of Heb. and biblical verse trans. However, in Fr., it refers to lines longer than standard meters in the later 19th-c. symbolist prosodies of poets such as Paul Claudel. In this sense, it denotes a Blakean or Whitmanesque line of variable but most often long length, neither rhymed nor metrical but organized by rhythmic and phrasal cadences. The influence of Walt Whitman on late 19th- and early 20th-c. Fr. verse ensured that the Fr. *verset* was rhythmically oriented more toward verse than prose, however multiform its realizations. Traditionally, three kinds of verset have been distinguished. In the *verset métrique*, such as Paul Fort's *Ballades françaises* (1898–1958), metrical forms remain perceptible, dividing the verset into smaller units. In the lyrical *verset cadencé*, such as Claudel's *Cinq grandes odes* (1910), the verset becomes a hybrid; "line" and "paragraph" are indistinguishable, except that the verset is clearly a rhythmic whole. The movement between degrees of rhythmicity allows an ascension from rhapsodic involvement with the world's primary elements, from a cataloguing "connaissance" to a less differentiated realm of omniscient "conscience." In the *verset amorphe* of Blaise Cendrars, fragmented syntax and disrupted discursivity result from the juxtaposition of short and long units of sense. Even where, as in Charles Péguy's verse (*Les Mystères*, 1910–13), the verset emerges from prose, lineation provides those variations in accentual prominence, length of *measure, and markedness of juncture that bespeak the modalities of inspiration and response: prose is transcended by the poised and expanded consciousness of verse. In Saint-John Perse's work (*Anabase*, 1924), the verset confronts the reader with challenging decisions about segmentation and association: the verset is a journey punctuated by a variety of rhythmic thresholds and boundaries. If accounts of the structure of the verset veer between ones that find in it a larger agglomeration of recognizably traditional rhythmic and metrical units and ones that locate its rhythm in the movements of enunciation in a periodicity founded on acoustic echoing and syntactic patterning, it is perhaps because the form is inclusive enough to tolerate their coexistence.

*See* VERSE AND PROSE.

■ P. Fort, Préface, *Le Roman de Louis XI* (1898); P. Claudel, "Réflexions et propositions sur le vers français," *Positions et propositions*, 2 v. (1928); L. Spitzer, "Zu Charles Péguys Stil," *Stilstudien*, 2 v. (1928); Y. Bozon-Scalzitti, "Le Verset claudélien," *Archives des Lettres Modernes* (1965): P. van Rutten, *Le Langage poétique de*

*St.-John Perse* (1975); F. Moreau, *Six études de métrique* (1987); C. Scott, *Vers libre* (1990).

T.V.F. Brogan; C. Scott; D. Evans

**VERSIFICATION.** Versification refers to the making of verse or verse craft. Derived from the Lat. *versificatio,* a form combining *versus* (turning a plow at the ends of successive furrows, which, by analogy, suggest lines of writing; see BOUSTROPHEDON) and *facio* (make), *versification* for a long time meant making lines. With the advent of mod. *free verse, esp. of *composition by open field, the original sense of versification as making lines according to some *measure, or *meter (Gr. *metron,* OE *mete*) has expanded to include all aspects of making poetry, from the smallest aspects of *sound to *stanzas to whole-poem forms and genres.

Versification is still sometimes defined and used as synonymous with *prosody (Gr. *prosodia,* the song accompaniment to words, pitch variation as spoken; Lat., *prosodia,* the marking of accent on a syllable). Prosody has referred to the sound patterns of lang. since the early Ren. and with verse practice since the mid-Ren. (*OED*). With the Ren., experiments with Romance models spurred close attention to rules for making lines and stanzas. By the late Ren., when poetry followed the taste for strict versions of metrical conformity, *prosodie* referred to both the practice of marking accents and to the rules for duration in pronunciation (*OED*). The marking of accents in making meters was a primary and necessary part of making verse, so the two terms served equally in discussing verse and became conflated. To the present, the two terms are sometimes interchangeable. W. K. Wimsatt (in 1972), e.g., was still using versification to mean the craft of making metrical poetry, even while John Hollander (in 1981) was distinguishing verse, as metered lines, from a mod. sense of poetry, as requiring the making of new metaphors.

With energetic Ren. experiments in adapting duration-based cl., It., and Fr. forms to the pitch-based prosody of Eng. (see CLASSICAL METERS IN MODERN LANGUAGES), versification was often a matter both of counting syllables and, in some cases, of determining their lengths as either "short" or "long"; thus, a versifier was largely occupied with prosodic considerations. Med. and Ren. grammars regarded prosody as pronunciation and often placed verse within the province of prosody. Because verse was an oral as well as a written art, pronunciation was a central concern.

With the expansion of styles and forms over the past century, individual poets and critics may use versification to refer to various aspects of poetry, incl. rhetorical structure (see RHETORIC AND POETRY), point of view, *figuration, *diction, *syntax, fixed forms (such as the *sonnet), and the use of a particular lyric *genre or mode (such as *ode, *elegy, dramatic monologue), as well as sound patterning (e.g., *rhythm, *meter, *assonance, *consonance, *rhyme), visual patterning (see VISUAL POETRY), or the blending of the auditory and the visual, as in the case of *line or stanza integrity.

The historical emergence of free verse, along with the expanded construing of *poetry* to signify many kinds of linguistic *poesis,* has largely rendered *versification* outmoded as a term in its original sense.

Contributing to the declining value and significance of the term *versification* are the ongoing reconsiderations of some of the basic terms associated with the craft of verse. The traditional metered line came under attack during *modernism, when a wave of experimentation with verse broke the consistency of meters, loosened them, or attempted to define and use new measures. Unlike Ren. innovations, modernism exploited the prosodic potentials in the lang. medium; the importation of foreign-lang. forms accounted for but a small portion of new line and verse forms (e.g., from OE and ME, Japanese, and Chinese). The line as it had been conceived until 1910 was exploded, freeing it to be redefined as metrical, nonmetrical, visual, or newly defined, as in W. C. Williams's poetry. The breakdown of the traditional meters, with the *prose poem and *concrete poetry being the extreme forms, spurred a reactive need to redefine the line and assert its priority as the most distinguishing marker of poetry. Accordingly, James Longenbach and others have argued for discarding the term *line breaks* for the more accurate *fulfillment,* since a line is not "broken"; it simply ends before another begins. The value placed on line integrity requires that a line be "fulfilled," i.e., that it have reason for being a piece of meaning, affect, and sound, as opposed to a randomly sliced bit of chopped prose. Similarly, a stanza (It. for "room") needs to be organized as a room of its own at the same time that it contributes to the whole. For Hollander and others, a verbal work must achieve the figurative level of metaphor to be a poem. These aspects of poetry point more clearly to the qualitative ends of verse craft: principles, assumptions, rules, guidelines, etc., exist for the writing of *good* poetry. When poetry was largely synonymous with *verse* and *verse* meant *metered lines,* versification pertained mostly to descriptions of craft. Now that boundaries between verse and prose have become less distinct and poetry, for many, serves as a general term for artful lang., discussions of versification have necessarily become more prescriptive, as they advance particular views of what poetry is or should be.

■ Wimsatt; P. Fussell, *Poetic Meter and Poetic Form,* rev. ed. (1979); J. Hollander, *Figure of Echo* (1981), and *Rhyme's Reason: A Guide to English Verse* (1981); Attridge, *Rhythms; The Line in Postmodern Poetry,* ed. R. J. Frank and H. M. Sayre (1988); G. T. Wright, *Shakespeare's Metrical Art* (1988); J. McCorkle, ed., *Conversant Essays, Contemporary Poets on Poetry* (1990); T. Steele, *Missing Measures: Modern Poetry and the Revolt against Meter* (1990); S. Cushman, *Fictions of Form in American Poetry* (1993); Gasparov, *History;* H. Gross, *Sound and Form in Modern Poetry,* 2d ed. (1996); Finch and Varnes; R. Abbott, "T. S. Eliot's Ghostly Footfalls: The Versification of 'Four Quartets,'" *Cambridge Quarterly* 4 (2005): 365–85; *Radiant Lyre: Essays on Lyric Poetry,* ed. D. Baker and

A. Townsend (2007); J. Longenbach, *The Art of the Poetic Line* (2008).

R. WINSLOW

**VERSI SCIOLTI** (It., *versi sciolti da rima*, "verses freed from rhyme"). In *Italian prosody, verses (generally *hendecasyllables, i.e., *endecasillabi sciolti*) not bound together by *rhyme or grouped in regular *strophes. *Versi sciolti* appear late in the 13th c. in the anonymous satire the *Mare amoroso* but were first cultivated during the Ren. as the It. equivalent of the cl. *epic meter, the *hexameter. Giangiorgio Trissino used them in his tragedy *Sophonisba* (1524; cf. his treatise *La poetica*, 1529) and in his epic *L'Italia liberata dai Goti* (begun 1528, pub. 1547), as did Torquato Tasso in his *Le Sette giornate del mondo creato* sophonisba (1594). They quickly became the preferred meter for It. trans. of cl. epics (e.g., Annibale Caro's *Eneide*, 1581). Despite Trissino's lack of success, however, a controversy arose between the advocates of cl. austerity and the advocates of rhyme. In the 16th c., rhyme won the day, but in the 18th c. and thereafter, versi sciolti were used with great success, particularly by Giuseppe Parini (*Il Giorno*, 1763–1801), Ugo Foscolo (*I Sepolcri*, 1807), Giacomo Leopardi (some of *I Canti*, 1831), and Alessandro Manzoni (*Urania*, 1807). Vittorio Alfieri almost single-handedly made them the standard meter for *tragedy. In the 20th c., the dramatist Sem Benelli used them, as did Giovanni Pascoli in his *Poemi Conviviali* (1904) and, to a lesser extent, Guido Gozzano, Umberto Saba, Giuseppe Ungaretti, and Franco Fortini. *Endecasillabi sciolti* are equivalent to *blank verse and were an important influence on the devel. of that form in Eng.

■ J. M. Steadman, "Verse Without Rime: Sixteenth-Century Defenses of Versi Sciolti," *Italica* 41 (1964); Wimsatt; F. Caliri, *Tecnica e poesia* (1974); L. Castelnuovo, *La metrica italiana* (1979); Elwert, *Italienische*, sect. 72, 57, 119; O. B. Hardison Jr., *Prosody and Purpose in the English Renaissance* (1989); A. Menichetti, *Metrica italiana: Fondamenti metrici, prosodia, rima* (1993); S. Orlando, *Manuale di metrica italiana* (1994).

L. H. GORDON; C. KLEINHENZ

**VERS LIBÉRÉ.** Not to be confused with either *vers libre*, i.e., 19th-c. Fr. *free verse proper, or with the *vers libres classiques* of the 17th and 18th cs., i.e., regular lines irregularly disposed, *vers libéré* is Fr. verse "liberated" from many of the traditional rules concerning *meter, *caesura, and end-stopping but still observing the principles of isosyllabism and regularly patterned rhyme. The beginnings of this process are to be found among the romantic poets, who employed *enjambment and the *trimètre with less inhibition than their forebears. However, as Cornulier and others have argued, while this was presented and interpreted as a liberation, the underlying 6 + 6 metrical pattern of the cl. *alexandrine was not forgotten, and vers libéré drew powerful expressive effect from the tensions between meter and *syntax at the caesura and line end. As Paul Verlaine observed, Charles Baudelaire was the first to place an unaccentu-

able word before the caesura, as in "Les Petites Vieilles": "Pour entendre un de *ces* // concerts riches de cuivre, Exaspéré comme *un* // ivrogne qui voit double." Arthur Rimbaud, Verlaine, Stéphane Mallarmé, and Jules Laforgue took this to extremes, often placing a word over the caesura, e.g., Verlaine in "Madrigal": "Du bout fin de la que // notte de ton souris" (3 + 4 + 5). The trimètre and enjambment thus became radical in the latter half of the 19th c., the line-terminal word often being no more than a particle, the trimètre assuming ever more asymmetrical configurations (5 + 3 + 4, 3 + 6 + 3, 4 + 3 + 5, etc.) The poets of vers libéré also cultivated the *vers impair* and the expressive, but rhythmically disruptive, effects of the *coupe lyrique* (see COUPE). All this contributed to the rhythmic destabilization of the line and undermined its cl. integrity. Metrical verse lost its firm contours and, consequently, its aptitude for eloquent and oratorical utterance; instead, it acquired a certain looseness, fluidity, and indeterminacy that favored the intimate, the prosaic, the impromptu, the *fantaisiste*. Similarly, Verlaine's fondness for poems in exclusively feminine rhymes is part of a wider tendency to disregard the rule prescribing the alternation of *masculine and feminine rhymes, a tendency whose origins lie in Baudelaire's "Ciel brouillé" (Cloudy sky) and "A une mendiante rousse" (To a begging redhead) (both 1857) and in Théodore de Banville's "Erinna" and "L'Enamourée" (both 1866). Other rules of rhyming were also infringed: masculine words rhyme with feminine ones (Banville's "Élégie," 1846; Verlaine's "Ariettes oubliées VI," (Forgotten Ariettas) 1874), singulars with plurals (Laforgue). Thus, even though rhyme was still felt to be indispensable to Fr. verse, poets sought to reduce its privileged status, both by treating it carelessly and by smudging the line ending. Some poets, however—Mallarmé and Banville, in particular—worked with inordinately rich rhymes, not only to subvert rhyme by comic excess but to activate larger acoustic fields. The step from vers libéré to vers libre was a short one; it was a step taken by Rimbaud ("Marine" and "Mouvement," both 1873) and by Laforgue (*Derniers Vers*, 1890); but Rimbaud also developed in a more radical prosodic direction (the *prose poem), as did Mallarmé, whose *Un coup de dés* (A Throw of the Dice) in 1897 already exploits most of the resources of *visual poetry.

*See* FRENCH PROSODY.

■ L. Guichard, *Jules Laforgue et ses poésies* (1950); M. Grammont, *Le Vers français*, rev. ed. (1961); Elwert; Mazaleyrat; B. de Cornulier, *Théorie du vers* (1982); C. Scott, *Vers Libre* (1990)—esp. ch. 2; B. de Cornulier, *Art poëtique* (1995); J.-M. Gouvard, *La Versification* (1999), and *Critique du vers* (2000); *Le Vers français: Histoire, théorie, esthétique*, ed. M. Murat (2000); D. Evans, *Rhythm, Illusion and the Poetic Idea* (2004); A. English, *Verlaine, poète de l'indécidable* (2005).

C. SCOTT; D. EVANS

**VERS LIBRE.** Because of its prosodic relatedness to *vers libres classiques* and *vers libéré*, this term is best reserved for 19th-c. Fr. *free verse and those modernist free-verse prosodies that acknowledge a debt to it (e.g., It. *futurism; the Anglo-Am. *vers libristes* Ezra Pound and T. S. Eliot; and *imagism). The directions mapped out by the vers libristes of the late 19th c., mostly advocates of the fashionable aesthetic of *symbolism with its emphasis on musicality, were variously explored and adapted by 20th-c. practitioners such as Guillaume Apollinaire, Blaise Cendrars, Pierre-Jean Jouve, Pierre Reverdy, Paul Éluard, Robert Desnos, René Char, Yves Bonnefoy, and Michel Deguy.

The emergence of vers libre is specifically datable to 1886, the year in which the review *La Vogue*, ed. by Gustave Kahn, published, in rapid succession, Arthur Rimbaud's free-verse *Illuminations*, "Marine," and "Mouvement" (possibly written in May 1873); trans. of some of Walt Whitman's *Leaves of Grass* by Jules Laforgue; Kahn's series of poems titled "Intermède" (to become part of his *Les Palais nomades*, 1887); ten of Laforgue's own free-verse poems (later collected in his posthumous *Derniers Vers* (Last verses), 1890); and further examples by Paul Adam and Jean Moréas. To this list of initiators, Jean Ajalbert, Édouard Dujardin, Albert Mockel, Francis Vielé-Griffin, Émile Verhaeren, Adolphe Retté, Maurice Maeterlinck, Camille Mauclair, and Stuart Merrill added their names in the years immediately following. Vers libre caused either considerable enthusiasm or anxiety, since its rejection of a traditional metrical order in favor of unbridled individuality appeared highly subversive in the context of Third Republican efforts to eradicate difference and create a stable, unified national identity; Mauclair, in F. T. Marinetti's *Enquête internationale sur le vers libre* (*International survey on free verse*, 1909), writes, "There are as many kinds of free verse as there are poets," while Laforgue claims, "My keyboard is constantly changing, and there is no other identical to mine. All keyboards are legitimate" (*Mélanges posthumes*, 1903). The conservative Catulle Mendès, however, in his governmentally commissioned *Rapport sur le mouvement poétique français 1867–1900* (Report on the French Poetic Movement, 1902) blames such rampant anarchy on the influence of foreigners and women, such as the Peruvian exile Della Rocca de Vergalo (*Poétique nouvelle*, 1880) and the Polish Jew Marie Krysinska (*Rythmes pittoresques*, 1890).

One might believe that the relative freedoms of vers libres classiques combined with those of vers libéré would produce the absolute freedom of vers libre, but this is not quite so. Certainly, vers libre is *heterometric and rhymes freely, and its lines are rhythmically unstable. But it goes further still; it rejects the indispensability of *rhyme with its line-demarcative function and instead relates lineation not to number of syllables but to the coincidence of units of meaning and units of rhythm or to integral impulses of utterance or else simply to the optimal expressive disposition of its textual raw materials. And indeed, the vers-libristes seek to abandon the principle of syllabism itself, by making the number of syllables in a line either irrelevant or indeterminable or both (see SYLLABIC VERSE). The undermining of the syllabic system is fa-

cilitated by the ambiguous syllabic status of the *eatone* (mute *e*)—should it be counted when unelided?—and by doubts about the syllabic value of contiguous vowels. Laforgue summarizes the *tabula rasa* of vers libre in a letter to Kahn of July 1886: "I forget to rhyme, I forget about the number of syllables, I forget about stanzaic structure."

Paradoxically, however, syllabic amorphousness produces rhythmic polymorphousness and *polysemy; in other words, a single line of vers libre is potentially several lines, each with its own inherited modalities. In addition, because of its heterometricity, vers libre can maximize rhythmic shifts between lines, creating a verse texture of multiplied tonalities. Within this paradox lies another fruitful contradiction. One of the original justifications for vers libre was its inimitability, its resistance to abstraction and systemization; thus, it could theoretically mold itself to the uniqueness of a personality, a psyche, a mood. Again Kahn: "For a long time I had been seeking to discover in myself a personal rhythm capable of communicating my lyric impulses with the cadence and music which I judged indispensable to them" (Préface to *Premiers Poèmes*, 1897). Yet, vers libre equally proposes a range of rhythmic possibilities that the reader is left to resolve into any one of a number of specific recitations. Given the significance of typographical arrangement in vers libre, this contradiction might be reformulated as a polarization of the visual and the oral, of the ling. and the paralinguistic, of the text as text, demanding to be read on its own terms, and the text as script, a set of incomplete instructions to the reader's *voice. One further contradiction might be mentioned: for all vers libre's ambiguation of syllabic number, with its transference of focus from syllable to accent, from number of syllables to number of measures, many free-verse poems are constructed on a "constante rythmique" (rhythmic constant), an intermittently recurrent measure that can be defined only syllabically.

Two broad currents of devel. can be distinguished in vers libre: one derives its rhythmic purchase from its varying approximation to, and distance from, recognizably regular lines and often cultivates ironic modes of utterance; the other seeks to undermine the primacy of the line by promoting rhythmic units larger than the line—the *verset* or the *stanza—or smaller than the line—the individual *measure; this latter strain is often informed by a rhapsodic voice. But in both currents, the line's role as guardian of metrical authority and guarantor of verse as ritual and self-transcendence is removed.

In both currents, too, the stanza finds itself without pedigree, infinitely elastic, ensuring no structural continuity. The stanza of vers libre ends not in conformity with some visible structural imperative—though who may say what invisible imperatives operate—but because a movement of utterance comes to an end and because only by ending can a sequence of lines define its own field of structural and prosodic activity. The stanzas of vers libre are a pursuit of unique kinds of formality constantly renewed, not the repeated confirmation of a certain stanzaic blueprint.

Vers libre can claim, with some justification, to have "psychologized" verse structure, to have made the act of writing apparently simultaneous with the changing movements of mind: "a poem is not a feeling communicated just as it was conceived before the act of writing. Let us acknowledge the small felicities of rhyme, and the deviations caused by the chances of invention, the whole unforeseen symphony which comes to accompany the subject" (Laforgue, *Mélanges posthumes*). By allowing the aleatory and the improvised to inhabit verse (see ALEATORY POETICS), by exploiting the psychological layering produced by variable rhyme interval and variable margin, by locating verse at the intersection of multiplied coordinates (rhyme, rhymelessness, *repetition, the metrical, the nonmetrical), by using ling. structures to attract and activate paralinguistic features (tempo, *pause, *tone, accentual variation, emotional coloring), vers libre establishes its affinities with the stream of consciousness of contemp. fiction and proffers a stream of consciousness of poetic reading.

■ Thieme 386; T. M. Dondo, *Vers Libre: A Logical Development of French Verse* (1922); E. Dujardin, *Les Premiers Poètes du vers libre* (1922); J. Hytier, *Les Techniques modernes du vers français* (1923); Patterson; L.-P. Thomas, *Le Vers moderne: ses moyens d'expression, son esthétique* (1943); H. Morier, *Le Rythme du vers libre symboliste*, 3 v. (1944); P. M. Jones, *The Background of Modern French Poetry* (1951), pt. 2; Z. Czerny, "Le Vers libre français et son art structural," *Poetics, Poetyka, Poetika*, ed. D. Davie et al. (1961); T. S. Eliot, "Reflections on *Vers Libre*" (1917), *To Criticize the Critic* (1965); *Le Vers français au 20e siècle*, ed. M. Parent (1967); F. Carmody, "La Doctrine du vers libre de Gustave Kahn," *Cahiers de l'Association Internationale des Etudes Françaises* 21 (1969); J. Mazaleyrat, "Problèmes de scansion du vers libre," *Philologische Studien für Joseph M. Piel* (1969); J. Filliolet, "Problématique du vers libre," *Poétique du vers français*, ed. H. Meschonnic (1974); Elwert; Scott; Mazaleyrat; D. Grojnowski, "Poétique du vers libre: *Derniers Vers* de Jules Laforgue (1886)," *Revue d'histoire littéraire de la France* 84 (1984); C. Scott, *A Question of Syllables* (1986), *Vers Libre: The Emergence of Free Verse in France* (1990), and *Reading the Rhythm: The Poetics of French Free Verse 1910–1930* (1993); Morier; M. Murat, *Le Vers libre* (2008).

C. SCOTT; D. EVANS

**VERS MESURÉS À L'ANTIQUE.** Imitations of the quantitative meters of cl. versification in Fr. verse mainly of the 16th c. Given the emphasis, during the Ren., on the imitation of cl. models, it is not surprising that poets of the *Pléiade such as Pierre de Ronsard, Jean-Antoine de Baïf, and Étienne Jodelle and their contemporaries. Étienne Pasquier and Jacques de la Taille wanted to transfer to poetry in the vernacular the metrical principles that had given rise to the august *canon of cl. poetry: how to attain similar ends but by similar means? The impulse was particularly strong where direct trans. was involved. These attempts usually entailed a rigid and quite arbitrary specification of quantitative values (long or short) for Fr. syllables,

from which any functional distinction between long and short vowels had all but disappeared (see SYLLABIC VERSE). Of the 16th-c. quantitative poets, Baïf was perhaps the most celebrated and most prolific (e.g., *Étrènes de poézie fransoèze au vers mesurés*, 1574, which contains *hexameters, iambic trimeters, sapphics, *alcaics, and other cl. meters). Even though reactions to Baïf's experiments were at best skeptical and at worst mockingly incredulous, others followed in his footsteps, notably Nicholas Rapin and Agrippa d'Aubigné. After a prolonged absence, *vers mesurés* reappeared in the 18th c., championed by l'Abbé d'Olivet and A.R.J. Turgot. Vers mesurés work best when supported by rhyme—a most unclassical device but long perceived as an essential rhythmic *point de repère* for the Fr. ear—and when patterns of accented and unaccented vowels are made to correspond to cl. patterns of long and short (i.e., accentual imitations of quantitative verse). But even where this latter equivalence is practiced, the gradual weakening of the Fr. accent, with its consequent shift from word to word group, has left fewer accents at the Fr. poet's disposal than there are long syllables in the cl. meter being imitated. The greater frequency of accents in Eng. and Ger. is one reason that verse based on cl. meters has had a longer hist. in these two poetries.

*See* ACCENT, CLASSICAL METERS IN MODERN LANGUAGES, METER, QUANTITY.

■ L. Bellanger, *Études historiques et philologiques sur la rime française* (1876); Kastner; Patterson; F. Deloffre, *Le vers français*, 2d ed. (1973); Elwert; B. E. Bullock, "Quantitative Verse in a Quantity-Insensitive Language: Baïf's *Vers mesurés*," *Journal of French Language Studies* 7 (1997); J. Vignes, "Brève histoire de vers mesurés français au XVIe siècle," *Albineana* 17 (2005).

C. SCOTT

**VERSO PIANO.** In It. prosody, any line that has the principal accent on the penultimate syllable, making the line ending paroxytonic; It. line forms are named on this basis. Thus, an *endecasillabo piano* is a line of 11 syllables with the principal accent on the tenth (e.g., Dante, *Inferno* 1.1: "Nel mezzo del cammin di nostra vita"); a *settenario piano* is a line of seven syllables with the principal accent on the sixth (e.g., Petrarch, *Canzoniere* 71.1: "Perché la vita è breve"). The *verso piano* is the most common line form in It.

*See* HENDECASYLLABLE, HEPTASYLLABLE, ITALIAN PROSODY, VERSO SDRUCCIOLO, VERSO TRONCO.

■ Wimsatt; Elwert, *Italienische*; F. P. Memmo, *Dizionario di metrica italiana* (1983); A. Menichetti, *Metrica italiana* (1993).

L. H. GORDON; C. KLEINHENZ

**VERSO SDRUCCIOLO.** In It. prosody, any line that ends in a *parola sdrucciola*, a word with the principal accent on the antepenultimate syllable, making the line ending proparoxytonic. Thus, an *endecasillabo sdrucciolo* has 12 syllables with the principal accent on the tenth (e.g., Dante, *Inferno* 15.1: "O-ra cen por-ta l'un de' du-ri *mar*-gi-ni"). A *settenario sdrucciolo* has eight syllables, retaining the principal accent on the sixth (e.g., Cielo d'Alcamo: "Ro-sa fre-sca au-len-*tis*-si-ma"). The endecasillabo sdrucciolo was cultivated in the 16th c. instead of the Lat. iambic *trimeter: Ludovico Ariosto used it in his comedies to imitate that meter in the theater of Plautus and Terence; Vincenzo Monti used it later in the *Canto d'Apollo* and in his *Prometeo*; Giosuè Carducci used it still later in his *Canto di Marzo*, wherein he tried to reproduce even the accents and pauses of the iambic trimeter.

*See* HENDECASYLLABLE, HEPTASYLLABLE, ITALIAN PROSODY, VERSO PIANO, VERSO TRONCO.

■ Wimsatt; Spongano; Elwert, *Italienische*; F. P. Memmo, *Dizionario di metrica italiana* (1983); A. Menichetti, *Metrica italiana* (1993).

L. H. GORDON; C. KLEINHENZ

**VERSO TRONCO.** In It. prosody, any line ending with an accented syllable, i.e., oxytonic. In particular, an *endecasillabo tronco* is a line with the principal accent on the tenth, because the final unstressed syllable has been dropped (*tronco*, from *troncato*, cut off ), giving the line ten rather than the usual 11 syllables (e.g., Dante, *Inferno* 4.60: "E con Rachele, per cui tanto *fé*"). In the generation after Dante, Antonio Pucci began a sonnet with a *verso tronco* ("Caro sonetto mio, con gran pietà") and used *versi tronchi* throughout the octave of another ("Maestro mio, deh non mi mandar più"). The *caccia frequently presents examples of *versi tronchi*. Later poets occasionally employed such lines for special metrical effects (e.g., Alessandro Manzoni and Aldo Palazzeschi).

*See* HENDECASYLLABLE, HEPTASYLLABLE, ITALIAN PROSODY, VERSO PIANO, VERSO SDRUCCIOLO.

■ Wimsatt; Elwert, *Italienische*; F. P. Memmo, *Dizionario di metrica italiana* (1983); A. Menichetti, *Metrica italiana* (1993).

L. H. GORDON; C. KLEINHENZ

**VIDA** (Occitan, "life"; from Lat. *vita*). A brief Occitan prose biography, rarely more than a few sentences long, that precedes a set of poems by a *troubadour in certain of the late 13th- and 14th-c. *chansonniers*, or anthols. of lyric verse. Using simple, highly formulaic lang., *vidas* situate the troubadour geographically and socially and often provide a general commentary on the quality of his or her verse. They frequently name the troubadour's patron and the person celebrated in the songs. Vidas, many of which occur in more than one ms., survive for approximately 100 troubadours. Although they undoubtedly originated with *jongleurs*, who invented them for performance purposes, they were collected by troubadour-scholars (notably Uc de Saint Circ and Miquel de la Tor), who cast them in their present written form.

*See* OCCITAN POETRY, RAZO.

■ J. Boutière and A. H. Schutz, *Biographies des troubadours*, 2d ed. (1964); *The Vidas of the Troubadours*, trans. M. Egan (1984); E. W. Poe, *From Poetry to Prose in Old Provençal* (1984), and "*Vidas* and *Razos*,"

*Handbook of the Troubadours*, ed. F.R.P. Akehurst and J. M. Davis (1995).

E. W. POE

**VIETNAM, POETRY OF.** Poetry permeates all aspects of Vietnamese life and became the most important medium of expression in Vietnamese society. Vietnamese *lyric poetry is indebted to both the poetic and cultural trads. and vernacular, or the spoken lang. At the same time, the cl. or formal trad. was modeled on poetic trads. from China (see CHINA, POETRY OF). The commitment to Confucian orthodoxy affixed poetry as a principal mode of literary production using Chinese script among the scholar gentry. Because of the tonal lang., the folk poetic trad.—meant to be sung—gave birth to a variety of verse forms and poetic genres.

Vietnamese independence, established in 939 CE, combined with nation-building, provided the textual trad. of different poetic forms. By the late 15th c., the canonical poetic trad. in Vietnam developed in ways that differed significantly from the folk trads. both in content and form. From the time of Vietnamese independence, *thơ Đường luật* (*lüshi*; see SHI) became the ideal literary form within the intelligentsia's textual trad. and was required as part of civil-service exams. The *thất ngôn bát cú*, seven syllables and eight lines styled after the lüshi form, became the preferred poetic pattern until the *thơ mới* period at the beginning of the 20th c. Borrowed from 9th-c. Tang Dynasty poetry, this form was modified by poets to fit Vietnamese ling. features and taste. There were also the *song thất lục bát*, a hybrid form combining the seven-syllable Tang lüshi form and the indigenous Vietnamese *lục bát* or six-eight *couplet, with a structure of the two seven-syllable lines and six eight-syllable lines; *ngũ ngôn* (five-syllable), and *tứ tuyệt* (a four-line poem with either four, five, or seven syllables per line). Cl. poetry dealt with the Confucian view of the world and the relationship between the individual and society; topics included moral cultivation, filial piety, neo-Confucian ideologies, heaven and earth, humanity and nature, love, fate, leisure, and beauty.

Poet-scholars adopted both the more formal lüshi as well as *lục bát* (six-eight), a more open, freer, indigenous Vietnamese form originally propagated orally. Most folk poems are written in lục bát. A lục bát poem in its smallest unit consists of a six-eight couplet. There is no limit to the number of couplets in a lục bát poem, though it must end in an even number. The Vietnamese lang. uses six tones divided into two main groups: low and high. The letter *S* (sharp or *trắc*) indicates an accented syllable, and the letter *F* (flat or *bằng*) indicates an unaccented syllable or tone. The odd numbered positions in a line can either be flat (bằng) or sharp (trắc) and is symbolized as *O*. The second, sixth, and eighth syllables are flat (F), while the fourth syllable is sharp (S). As a rule, the last syllable of the first line (FR1) rhymes with the sixth syllable of the second line (the eight-syllable line, FR1). If a poem has four lines (two couplets), the eighth syllable of the second line (FR2) rhymes with the sixth syllable of the third line (FR2). The rhyme scheme continues with the same pattern—i.e., the sixth syllable of the third line (FR2) rhymes with the sixth syllable (FR2) of the fourth line:

|          | 1 | 2 | 3 | 4 | 5 | 6   | 7 | 8   |
|----------|---|---|---|---|---|-----|---|-----|
| 1st line | O | F | O | S | O | FR1 |   |     |
| 2d line  | O | F | O | S | O | FR1 | O | FR2 |
| 3d line  | O | F | O | S | O | FR2 |   |     |
| 4th line | O | F | O | S | O | FR2 | O | FR3 |
| 5th line | O | F | O | S | O | FR3 |   |     |
| 6th line | O | F | O | S | O | FR3 | O | FR4 |

From the 11th to the 16th cs., the Buddhist trad. predominated under the Lý and Trần kings. Poets became more familiar with Buddhist concepts during this period. *Thơ Văn Lý Trần* (A Collection of the Poetry of Lý and Trần Dynasties), esp. the *Thiền Uyển Tập Anh* in Chinese script, provided reputable matter (Nguyen 1997). Buddhist notions of delusion, temporality, enlightenment, nirvana, and Buddha nature are distinctive characteristics of Lý Trần Zen poetry. Most of the poems are composed using the five-syllable quatrain characteristic of Tang style.

The vernacular lang. played a significant role in the emergence of nationalism and modernity in Vietnam. During the Trần Dynasty (13th c.), the devel. and standardization of the *nôm* script, modified Chinese characters used to record Vietnamese phonetics and vernacular lang., transformed and demarcated a distinctive Vietnamese literary trad. With the devel. of the nôm script, Vietnamese poetry arose as the preferred form to express the Vietnamese psyche, experience, and identity. Nôm script also prepared the way for the creation of the romanized writing system in the 17th c. The great Vietnamese poet Nguyễn Trái (1380–1442) is noted for his *Quốc Âm Thi Tập* (Anthology of Verse in the National Language). The *Hồng Đức Quốc Âm Thi Tập* (Hồng Đức's Anthology of Verse in the National Language), a collection of cl. Vietnamese poetry composed by King Lê Thánh Tông (1442–97) and members of his Tao Đàn Academy, was also compiled in the 16th c.

The reestablishment of national unity, expansion, and order under the Nguyễn Dynasty (1802–1945) ushered in social and political conditions conducive to the formulation of a new literati aesthetic. Bà Huyện Thanh Quan (b. 1800?), often writing in nôm script in the lüshi form and thất ngôn bát cú, skillfully captured natural images and sceneries with the intention of conveying the psychological states of the individual. Her poems can be read as autobiographical narratives. Hồ Xuân Hương (1772–1822) championed an indigenous and feminine perspective by using poetry as a critique of Confucian morality, esp. attitudes toward sexuality. She skillfully used the vernacular lang. and lüshi forms, as well as Confucian philosophical *tropes. She often masterfully used wordplay, esp. a form of Vietnamese secret lang. called *nói lái* (inverted speech). Many of her poems are designed to be read in two wholly different manners; thus, a reader may

find her poems beautiful while remaining oblivious to the hidden meaning. Using inverted speech, her poems are also playful and full of sexual innuendoes alluding to and depicting sexually obscene images and sex acts. She frequently challenged the unconditional acceptance of norms—namely, the rights and privileges bestowed on male scholars—and ridiculed the oppression of women.

During this period, scholars became disillusioned and apathetic toward sociopolitical affairs and more focused on personal expression. New poet-scholars emerged, most notably Nguyễn Du (1765–1820), the author of *Truyện Kiều* or *The Tale of Kieu*. This novel in verse, considered to be the masterpiece of Vietnamese poetry, is composed in both verse and the vernacular using the lục bát form in 1627 couplets. Nguyễn Du used romantic love as an allegory for political affiliation and suffering, simultaneously negotiating loyalty and its multiple obligations. Less concerned with the sociopolitical realm, 19th-c. poets such as Nguyễn Công Trứ, Cao Bá Quát, and Nguyễn Khuyến composed poems focused on personal experiences.

It took more than 300 years for the Vietnamese to embrace and adopt *chữ Quốc ngữ*, or the Roman alphabet writing system, after it was introduced to Vietnam by Eur. missionaries, specifically Alexander de Rhode (1591–1660). Poet Tản Đà Nguyễn Khắc Hiếu (1889–1939) delineated the sharp transition from the cl. trad. to the thơ mới movement, allowing countless others to follow suit. Phan Khôi experimented with the new form in "Tình Già" (Old Love) and was credited with using the first *free verse in romanized Vietnamese writing. As the Western writing system became more readily accepted, significant transformations in the aesthetic and content of poetry occurred, and a new crop of poets burgeoned: Thế Lữ, Lưu Trọng Lư, Huy Cận, Tố Hữu, Nguyễn Bính, Chế Lan Viên, Hàn Mạc Tử (who died of leprosy), and Xuân Diệu (who advocated art for art's sake). The form of the new poetry movement preserved many aspects of the lüshi form but was freer in rhyme patterns. These prewar poets (*thi nhân tiền chiến*) sought to cut Vietnamese poetry off from past conventions by incorporating Fr. poetic styles and *metaphors.

Poetry at the second half of the 20th c. was profoundly influenced by war. Leading prewar poets like Huy Cận, Xuân Diệu, Chế Lan Viên, and esp. Tố Hữu (who later served as minister of culture under the Social Democratic government of Vietnam) chose to join the Việt Minh and were committed to writing political poetry. Other poets of the thơ mới movement either emigrated to the South or remained invisible in the North throughout the war. On the emergence of a relatively free land in the South, a new poetic movement in the Republic of South Vietnam (RSVN) evolved. Vũ Hoàng Chương, Tô Thùy Yên, Tương Phố, Nguyên Sa, Đông Hồ, and Bùi Giáng, to name a few, brought the movement to new heights. Bùi Giáng used poetic tropes to play with meaning. He often used the lục bát style and is considered the most prolific poet for his ability to create poetry extemporaneously; he is famous for having written a hundred couplets in a day. While the war in the North generated a more radical tendency, poets such as Trần Dần, Phùng Quán, Hoàng Cầm, Lê Đạt, and others distanced themselves from political involvement and used free verse to experiment with form. Poetry in the postwar period followed a number of paths. Young female poets such as Vi Thùy Linh and Ly Hoàng Ly defied poetic conventions and male-dominant sexual politics by exploring female sexualities. However, their works were subject to censure and unfavorable crit.

■ **Criticism and History**: M. Durand and T. Nguyen, *An Introduction to Vietnamese Literature* (1985); D. H. Nguyen, *Vietnamese Literature: A Brief Survey* (1994); C. T. Nguyen, *Zen in Medieval Vietnam: A Study and Translation of Thiền Uyển Tập Anh* (1997); E. Pastreich, "Reception of Chinese Literature in Vietnam," *Columbia History of Chinese Literature*, ed. V. H. Mair (2001).
■ **Translations**: N. B. Nguyen et al., *A Thousand Years of Vietnamese Poetry* (1975); *The Heritage of Vietnamese Poetry*, trans. S. T. Huynh (1979); D. Nguyễn, *The Tale of Kieu*, trans. S. T. Huynh (1983); *An Anthology of Vietnamese Poems*, trans. S. T. Huynh (1996); X. H. Ho, *Spring Essence*, ed. and trans. J. Balaban (2000); *Black Dog, Black Night: Contemporary Vietnamese Poetry*, trans. D. Nguyen and P. Hoover (2008).

Q. Phu Van

**VILLANCICO.** A Sp. poem, often on a religious or popular theme and usually composed in a short meter, to be sung as a *carol. The introductory stanza (*cabeza, estribillo, repetición*, or *retornelo*), typically brief, sets forth the theme to be glossed in the body of the poem and frequently serves, in whole or in part, as the *refrain (*estribillo*). The body (*pies*) of the poem, composed of a few (usually about six) *strophes, each of about six lines plus the *chorus, develops the theme, often repeating verbatim phrases or lines from the introduction.
■ D. G. Rengifo, *Arte poética española* (1592); P. Henríquez Ureña, *Versificación irregular en la poesía castellana*, 2d ed. (1933); Le Gentil; P. Le Gentil, *Le Virelai et le villancico: Le problème des origines arabes* (1954); A. Sánchez Romeralo, *El Villancico* (1969); Navarro; M. Moraña, "Poder, raza, y lengua: La construcción étnica del Otyro en los villancicos de Sor Juana," *Colonial Latin American Review* 4 (1995); J. Martínez Gómez, "'Plebe humana y angelica nobleza': Los villancicos de Sor Juana Inés de la Cruz," *Cuadernos hispanoamericanos* supp. 16 (1995); M. Lilia Tenorio, *Los villancicos de Sor Juana* (1999); S. Armistead, "Kharjas and Villancicos," *Journal of Arabic Literature* 34 (2003).

D. C. Clarke

**VILLANELLE** (from It. *villanella*, a rustic song, *villano*, a peasant). As known today, a 19-line poem with two rhymes and two *refrain lines, in the form $A_1bA_2$ $abA_1$ $abA_2$ $abA_1$ $abA_2$ $abA_1$ $A_2$, where capital letters indicate refrains. Fr. poet Théodore de Banville compared the interweaving *a, b,* and refrain lines to "a braid of

silver and gold threads, crossed with a third thread the color of a rose." Also distinctive is the *quatrain occurring at the end of a series of *tercets, the extra line in the last stanza furnishing a sense of closure to the repetitive pattern with a conclusive *couplet. In the 16th c., however, the villanelle had no set form other than the presence of a refrain after each verse. When Fr. poets such as Joachim du Bellay and Philippe Desportes began writing lyric poems in the spirit of the *villanella*—a trendy It. style of song that imitated rustic dance tunes from the oral trad., although its composers were courtly and literate—the rhyme schemes varied widely, the refrain could be one to five lines in length, and there could be any number of verses, although four was the most common in both the musical and poetic versions. Many of the 16th-c. poetic villanelles were set to music by composers of the time, and references to the villanelle through the 17th c. portray it as a musical and not poetic genre.

Throughout the 18th c., the same single example of the villanelle was frequently cited: Jean Passerat's 19-line alternating-refrain "Villanelle" ("J'ay perdu ma Tourterelle"), first pub. in 1606. Most 18th-c. texts defined the villanelle simply as a "peasant song," but an obscure 1722 Fr. grammar by Denis Gaullyer asserted that the villanelle required the first and last lines of the first verse to alternate as refrains. A similar claim in Pierre-Charles Berthelin's 1751 rev. ed. of Pierre Richelet's authoritative rhyming dictionary and prosody manual probably had more influence. Nineteenth-c. Fr. dictionaries, grammars, encyclopedias, and handbooks subsequently defined the villanelle as a traditional schematic poetic form, but Passerat's form was one of a kind until Banville's "Villanelle de Buloz" of 1845. Significantly fortified by Banville's popular handbook *Petit traité de poésie française*, the mistaken belief that the villanelle was an antique form persisted tenaciously throughout the 19th and 20th cs.

Enthusiasm for med. and Ren. forms in the 19th c. also helped establish the villanelle among authentic antique Fr. forms such as the *triolet, *rondeau, and *ballade. French Parnassian poets (see PARNASSIANISM) believed that a villanelle might be any length (like a poem written in *terza rima*); but in 1878, Joseph Boulmier published an entire volume of 19-line villanelles on the Passerat template, arguing in an intro. that this was the best length. Boulmier also pointed out that the villanelle was not a poetic form in the Ren., but this correction went largely unnoticed. Eng. *aestheticism also admired archaic forms, and in the 1870s, Edmund Gosse helped make the villanelle a staple of *light verse. Poets such as Oscar Wilde, Andrew Lang, and (in America) E. A. Robinson wrote 19-line villanelles, which established that length as a rule.

Hardly any Fr. poets wrote villanelles after the 19th c., but the form gradually became surprisingly important in Eng.—though Eng. writers continued to refer to the villanelle as a "French form." James Joyce's 1916 *Portrait of the Artist as a Young Man* included a scene about the composition of a villanelle in which Joyce's mod. stream-of-consciousness prose contrasts starkly with the outdated fin de siècle theme and form of his hero's poem. But William Empson's "Villanelle" ("It is the pain, it is the pain endures") of 1928 was highly mod.; and when W. H. Auden adopted the form, his villanelles, like Empson's, were *pentameter: almost all earlier Eng. villanelles are *tetrameter or *trimeter. Dylan Thomas's first villanelle was a 1942 *parody of Empson titled "Request to Leda," but it was Thomas's 1951 "Do not go gentle into that good night" that ensured the villanelle's survival and status in Eng. poetry. Throughout the 1950s, 1960s, and 1970s, major poets occasionally wrote villanelles.

Elizabeth Bishop's 1976 villanelle "One Art," along with the emergence of *New Formalism, introduced what might be called the postmodern villanelle. In the last quarter of the 20th c., poet after poet adopted the villanelle, often making use of a new license to use *near rhyme and near refrain and overtly obeying or challenging to the supposedly strict, traditional rules of the form. Poets also began to invent similar forms, most unique but some not: the prose villanelle, the *terzanelle* (a hybrid with terza rima), and, most notably, a ludicrously repetitive form invented by Billy Collins. The *paradelle*, which Collins claimed was a langue d'oc form of the 11th c., is a "parody villanelle" whose origin story is only slightly falser than the one commonly told of the "real" villanelle.

■ J. Passerat, *Recueil des oeuvres poétiques* (1606); D. Gaullyer, *Abregé de la grammaire françoise* (1722); P. Richelet, *Dictionnaire des rimes,* ed. P. C. Berthelin (1751); T. de Banville, *Petit traité de poésie française* (1872); E. Gosse, "A Plea for Certain Exotic Forms of Verse," *Cornhill Magazine* 36 (1877); J. Boulmier, *Villanelles* (1878); C. Scott, *French Verse-Art* (1980); D. G. Cardamone, *The Canzone Villanesa alla Napolitana and Related Forms, 1537–1570* (1981); R. F. McFarland, *The Villanelle* (1987); J. Kane, "The Myth of the Fixed-Form Villanelle," *MLQ* 64 (2003); *The Paradelle,* ed. T. W. Welford (2006); A. L. French, "Edmund Gosse and the Stubborn Villanelle Blunder," *VP* 48 (2010).

J. KANE; A. L. FRENCH

**VIRELAI** (also called *chanson baladée* and *vireli*). Originally a variant of the common dance song with refrain, of which the *rondeau is the most prominent type, this med. Fr. lyric form developed in the 13th c. and at first may have been performed by one or more leading voices and a *chorus. It begins with a *refrain, followed by a stanza of four lines of which the first two have a musical line (repeated) different from that of the refrain. The last two lines of the stanza return to the music of the refrain. The opening refrain, words and music, is then sung again. The *virelai* usually continues with two more stanzas presented in this same way. A virelai with only one stanza would be a *bergerette*. In Italy, the 13th-c. *lauda* and, in Spain, the *cantiga, follow the same form. The syllables *vireli* and *virelai* were probably nonsense refrains that later came to designate the type.

The large number of variations and optional elements both in the *lai and in the virelai (as practiced by Guillaume de Machaut, Jean Froissart, Christine de Pisan, and Eustache Deschamps) produced much uncertainty among recent prosodists about how both forms should be defined, so that one must approach any mod. definition with great caution. Most recent commentators follow Théodore de Banville (*Petit traité de poésie française,* 1872), who, relying on the authority of the 17th-c. prosodist le Père Mourgues (*Traité de la poésie française,* 1685), tried to settle matters by defining the lai as a poem in which each stanza is a combination of three-line groups, two longer lines followed by a shorter one, with the longer lines sharing one rhyme sound and the shorter lines another (*aabaabaab ccdccdccd,* etc.). Then, calling on a false etymology of *virelai*—from *virer* (to turn) and *lai*—he defined the virelai as a lai in which the rhyme sounds are "turned" from stanza to stanza; i.e., the rhyme of the shorter lines becomes the rhyme of the longer lines in the following stanza (*aabaabaab, bbcbbcbbc,* etc.). Calling the virelai thus defined the *virelai ancien,* Banville goes on to describe the *virelai nouveau,* which bears no relation to the virelai ancien and is, if anything, more like the *villanelle. The virelai nouveau opens with a refrain, whose two lines then recur separately and alternately as the refrains of the stanzas following, reappearing together again only at the end of the final stanza, but with their order reversed. The stanzas of the virelai nouveau may be of any length and employ any rhyme scheme, but the poem is limited to two rhyme sounds only. Here again, Banville merely follows le Père Mourgues, whose "Le Rimeur rebuté" is used as an illustration. John Payne's "Spring Sadness" (virelai ancien) and Austin Dobson's "July" (virelai nouveau) are the only evidence that these two forms have excited any interest.

■ E. Gosse, "A Plea for Certain Exotic Forms of Verse," *Cornhill Magazine* 36 (1877); G. White, *Ballades and Rondeaus* (1887); Kastner; H. L. Cohen, *Lyric Forms from France* (1922); Le Gentil; P. Le Gentil, *Le Virelai et le villancico* (1954); M. Françon, "On the Nature of the Virelai," *Symposium* 9 (1955); G. Reaney, "The Development of the Rondeau, Virelai, and Ballade," *Festschrift Karl Gustav Fellerer* (1962); F. Gennrich, *Das altfranzösische Rondeau und V. im 12. und 13. Jahrhundert* (1963); F. Gennrich and G. Reaney, "Virelai," *MGG* 13.1802–11; N. Wilkins, "Virelai," *New Grove*; Morier; R. Mullally, "Vireli, Virelai," *Neuphilologische Mitteilungen* 101 (2000); J.-F. Kosta-Théfaine, "Les Virelais de Christine de Pizan," *Moyen Français* 48 (2001).

U. T. HOLMES; C. SCOTT

**VISUAL ARTS AND POETRY.** *See* CARMINA FIGURATA; CONCRETE POETRY; EKPHRASIS; PAINTING AND POETRY; UT PICTURA POESIS; VISUAL POETRY.

**VISUAL POETRY**

I. Forms
II. Functions
III. Development

## IV. Free Verse
## V. Mixed and Electronic Media

Visual poetry is poetry composed for the eye as well as, or more than, for the ear. All written and printed poetry is visual poetry in a broad sense, in that, when we read the poem, the visual form affects how we read it and so contributes to our experience of its sound, movement, and meaning. The overwhelming majority of lyric poems are meant to fit on a codex page, hence, to meet the reader's eye as a simultaneously apprehensible whole. As Mooij points out, "written poetry allows for devices of foregrounding not available to oral poetry." Among these devices are lineation, line length, line grouping, indentation, intra- and interlinear white space, punctuation, capitalization, and size and style of type. In traditional verse, however, the written text serves mainly a notational role, and its visual aspects are subordinate to the oral form they represent. In visual poetry in the strict sense, the visual form of the text becomes an object for apprehension in its own right. In some visual poetry, text is combined with nontextual graphic elements.

**I. Forms.** In general, the visual form of a poem may be figurative or nonfigurative; if figurative, it may be mimetic or abstract. In cl. and Ren. pattern poetry, we find figurative visual form that is mimetic, the printed text taking the shape of objects (see TECHNOPAEGNION); the best-known examples are two poems by George Herbert, "The Altar" and "Easter Wings." There are also 20th-c. examples of mimetic visual form, among them the *calligrammes of Guillaume Apollinaire and some *concrete poetry. Poems in the shape of geometric figures such as circles and lozenges, another kind of pattern poetry, realize the possibility of figurative visual form that is abstract: in the Ren., 15 such forms are enumerated by George Puttenham. Less rigidly geometric forms are not uncommon in conventional poetry (Ranta).

The visual form of most poems is nonfigurative: such poems are isometrical or heterometrical, hence, consist of regular or irregular blocks of long and/or short lines. Open arrangements of lines in the page space are usually also nonfigurative. Such nonfigurative visual form may contribute significantly to the effect of the poem. In the case of short poems, the shape of the whole poem is apprehended immediately as open or dense, balanced or imbalanced, even or uneven, simple or intricate. In stanzaic poems, the regular partitioning of the text may convey a sense of order and control and generate an expectation of regular closure. Further, the individual stanzas themselves are apprehensible visual units. Stanzas in symmetrical shapes may suggest stability or stillness, while asymmetrical shapes may suggest instability or movement in a direction. Stanzas of complex shape may convey a sense of elaborate artifice. Stanzas where lines of different lengths, or with different rhymes, are indented by different amounts, as in John Donne's *Songs and Sonnets*, may appear esp. highly ordered. For the reader steeped in poetry, the visual forms of stanzas may also recall antecedent poems written in stanzas of similar shape. The basic shape of the *sapphic stanza, e.g., is recognizable even in extreme variations.

**II. Functions.** The viability of visual poetry as a literary mode depends directly on the functions that can be served by visual form. These fall into two classes: (a) those that reinforce the sense of the poem's unity and autonomy and (b) those that point up its *intertextuality. In group (a), we can enumerate six integrative functions: (1) to lend prominence to phonological, syntactic, or rhetorical structures in the text (this would include scoring for performance and the use of white space to express emotion, invite contemplation, or signal closure); (2) to indicate juxtapositions of images and ideas; (3) to signal shifts in topic, tone, or perspective; (4) to render iconically the subject of the poem or an object referred to in it (incl. the use of white space as an icon of space, whiteness, distance, void, or duration); (5) to present the reader with an abstract shape of energy; and (6) to help foreground the text as an aesthetic object. In group (b), we can identify six dispersive functions: (1) to signal a general or particular relation to poetic trad.; (2) to allude to various other genres of printed texts; (3) to engage and sustain reader attention by creating interest and texture; (4) to cross-cut other textual structures, producing counterpoint between two or more structures occupying the same words; (5) to heighten the reader's awareness of the reading process; and (6) to draw attention to particular features of the text and, more generally, to defamiliarize aspects of lang., writing, and *textuality. The visual form of a given poem may realize several different functions, even ones from the two opposed classes, at once.

**III. Development.** Historically, "all poetry is originally oral, and the earliest inscriptions of it were clearly ways of preserving material after the tradition of recitation had changed or been lost" (Hollander). Subsequently, "the development has been from . . . visual organization of phonological data . . . to a visual organization that carries meaning without reference to the phonological" (Cummings and Simmons). "[O]nce the inscribed text was firmly established as a standard . . . end-product of literary art and typical object of literary appreciation, it was only natural that the literary artist would exploit the rich aesthetic possibilities offered by the inscribed medium" (Shusterman). From ca. 300 BCE, visual effects have been exploited in various modes of visual poetry and in mixed-media works.

Perhaps the best known of the modes of visual poetry is what is anachronistically called pattern poetry, a mode used by Western poets from the 4th c. BCE to the present. Less familiar than poems in figurative or geometric shapes are *versus intexti*, also called *carmina cancellata*, a subgenre of pattern poetry. Such poems were composed on a grid, 35 squares by 35, each square containing a letter, with type size and, later, color and outlining used to distinguish visual images from the background of the rest of the text. First composed in the 4th c., they reached their fullest devel. in the work of Hrabanus Maurus (9th c.). Another ancient visual genre, the *acrostic, subverts the convention of reading from left to right and from top to bottom. Inscriptions, originally cut in stone with no regard for the appearance of the text, acquired beautiful lettering in Roman monumental art, which was reproduced and imitated in the Ren. In the 16th and 17th cs., esp. in northern Italy, they flourished briefly as a literary genre in printed books (Sparrow). The form, used mainly for religious and political eulogy, was really lineated prose—prose composed and printed in centered lines of uneven lengths, with the line divisions supporting the sense. A mixed-media genre, the *emblem, flourished during the Ren. Typically, it comprised a short motto, a picture, and an explanatory, moralizing poem.

The 20th c. saw a diverse abundance of highly visual works. These were heralded, just before the turn of the century by Stéphane Mallarmé's late work *Un coup de dés,* a visual composition with text in various type sizes arranged in the space of two-page spreads. It was followed, early in the century, by Apollinaire's calligrammes, in which lettering (often handwriting) of different sizes typically sketches the shape of an object, e.g., a cigar with smoke. The typographical experiments of *futurism and *Dada, the typewriter compositions of the Am. poet e. e. cummings, and concrete poetry all use visual form in ways that counteract the transparency of the written medium.

**IV. Free Verse.** Visual form plays a more important role in the prosody of *free verse than in that of metrical verse. One distinguishing feature of much modernist free verse—the eschewal of line-initial capitals—is a purely visual feature. On the one hand, besides serving to label the verse as nonmetrical, the use of lower-case letters at the beginnings of lines (unless they are also beginnings of sentences) may have the effect of reducing the visual prominence of the line as a unit. On the other hand, where lineation and line grouping are not determined by meter and rhyme, lines and line groups may be constitutively visual units. Even where lines are phonological, syntactical, and/or semantic units as well, their visual aspect may be important to their effect.

In most cases, visual form in free verse assumes a subservient, pattern-marking role. E.g., lineation, in its visual aspect, may serve to juxtapose images, as in Ezra Pound's classic imagist poem "In a Station of the Metro." Lineation, layout, and other visual features may serve to score the text for oral performance. Charles Olson, in his 1950 essay *"Projective Verse," claimed that there should be a direct relationship between the amount of white space and the length of pause. Regardless of whether it signals pause, intra- or interlinear white space can work mimetically, expressively, and rhetorically. Many free-verse poets exploit these possibilities through arrangement of text in the page space, as does Denise Levertov in this passage from "The Five-Day Rain":

Sequence broken, tension
of sunlight broken.

So light a rain
fine shreds
pending above the rigid leaves.

Less commonly, the visual form takes on a privileged, pattern-making role. Where lines do not coincide with units of the text's linguistic structure, they may, esp. in the case of short lines, set up a counterpoint to it. Free-verse poets, notably W. C. Williams, sometimes arrange their lines in "sight-stanzas," perceptible as stanzas only by virtue of having equal numbers of lines and creating iterated visual patterns. Here, the visual order of the stanzas may compensate aesthetically for considerable density or sprawl in syntax or argument. In other free-verse poems, white space serves to defamiliarize split or isolated textual elements, as in these lines from the Canadian poet bpNichol's *The Martyrology*:

hand

the h &
what else

**V. Mixed and Electronic Media.** Besides exploiting the visual elements of written lang. for various effects, experimental poets occasionally incorporate pictorial elements in their texts. Some poets compose, or collaborate with visual artists in composing, works that combine visual art and text. Asian poetry has a long trad. of such work. William Blake's illuminated books are a major Western example. The artist's book, a mode developed by visual artists, has been used by some contemp. experimental poets to explore the visual properties of texts. Along the continuum from purely literary art to purely visual, there are many possibilities for visual poetry with a dual aesthetic appeal—even for poetry without words. Other lines of poetic experimentation also offer visual possibilities; thus, scores for *sound poetry have been treated as a type of visual poetry.

In recent decades, the wide availability of the computer has given poets a means of text production and presentation that opens new possibilities for visual poetry. For the visually oriented poet, its value lies not in its allowing automated generation of text (see ELECTRONIC POETRY), but in its facilitating creation of spatial form, integration of graphic elements with text, use of color, and, esp., control of the pace of appearance and disappearance of segments of text (see TYPOGRAPHY). This control allows poets to incorporate temporal rhythms into visual form.

*See* LETTRISME.

■ G. Puttenham, *The Arte of English Poesie* (1589), rpt. in Smith; J. Sparrow, *Visible Words* (1969); R. Massin, *La Lettre et l'image,* 2d ed. (1973); *Speaking Pictures,* ed. M. Klonsky (1975)—anthol.; J.J.A. Mooij, "On the 'Foregrounding' of Graphic Elements in Poetry," *Comparative Poetics,* ed. D. W. Fokkema et al. (1976); J. Ranta, "Geometry, Vision, and Poetic Form," *CE* 39 (1978); *Visual Literature Criticism,* ed. R. Kostelanetz (1979); R. Kostelanetz, *The Old Poetries and the New* (1981); Morier, under "Blanchissement," "Vide"; R. Shusterman, "Aesthetic Blindness to Textual Visuality," *JAAC* 41 (1982); M. Cummings and R. Simmons, "Graphology," *The Language of Literature* (1983); H. M. Sayre, *The Visual Text of W. C. Williams* (1983); S. Cushman, *W. C. Williams and the Meanings of Measure* (1985), chap. 2; C. Taylor, *A Poetics of Seeing* (1985); Hollander; W. Bohn, *The Aesthetics of Visual Poetry, 1914–1928* (1986); R. Cureton, "Visual Form in e. e. cummings' *No Thanks*," *Word & Image* 2 (1986); J. Adler and U. Ernst, *Text als Figur* (1987); *The Line in Postmodern Poetry*, ed. R. Frank and H. Sayre (1988); "Material Poetry of the Renaissance / The Renaissance of Material Poetry," ed. R. Greene, *Harvard Library Bulletin* NS 3.2 (1992); *Experimental—Visual—Concrete*, ed. K. D Jackson et al. (1996); *Visuelle Poesie*, ed. H. L. Arnold and H. Korte (1997); J. Drucker, *Figuring the Word* (1998); *New Media Poetics*, ed. A. Morris and T. Swiss (2006).

E. BERRY

**VISUAL RHYME.** *See* EYE RHYME.

**VOICE.** To define *voice* in written poetry immediately poses a problem, for there is no literal voice in the poem: voice is an oral *metaphor employed in the description and analysis of the written word. It is not just any metaphor, however, but one that foregrounds fundamental distinctions underpinning Western culture: orality and literacy, speaking and writing. Regardless of how much one insists that writing is not speaking and that voice is not literally present in the poem, literary critics have persistently relied on metaphors of voice to analyze writing; it is difficult to imagine how one would go about discussing poetry in particular if we were forbidden to use the terms *voice, speaker,* and other vocal terms like *monologue* or *song, to give a few examples. Teachers, students, and scholars regularly say that poetry "speaks" and readers "listen." The hist. of lit. crit. is saturated with more or less self-conscious uses of oral and aural terms for poetry. Though there are theories of narrative "voice"—see the work of Bakhtin and Genette, e.g.—poetry is regularly imagined to be the privileged site of vocal *presence; those who seek to demystify that presence work to dislodge or trouble oral metaphors that cleave far closer to poetry than to fiction, nonfiction, or perhaps even drama.

Studies of orality offer one approach to explaining why voice is so closely affiliated with poetry. These studies tend to agree that poetry is a crucial vehicle for the transmission of information in oral cultures. The repetitive sound structures that define poetry—*rhythm, *rhyme, *refrain, *alliteration, *assonance, *parallelism, *anaphora—are a central technology of cultural memory and historical transmission. In the absence of written documentation, sound patterns form a lang. system that enables recollection and recitation. Though oral cultures are certainly not extinct and though oral practices coexist alongside written practices in literate cultures, there is an abundance of work on the historical transition from orality to literacy in Western culture. Havelock, e.g., offers a theory of the "literate revolution" in Greece in the 7th to 4th cs. BCE that accounts for the saturation of vocal and aural

figures in Gr. lit. During that time, oral strategies—singing, *recitation, memorization—were not simply supplanted by a literate culture's documentary practices; instead, the two modes entered into "competition and collision." The jostling of literacy by the traces of orality never ended: "the Muse never became the discarded mistress of Greece. She learned to write and read while she continued to sing." Metaphors of orality continue to inhabit, unsettle, and complicate the textual realm to the present day. The earlier, crucial functions of poetry, however, have been replaced by more peripheral, optional practices. Rather than a warehouse for a culture's knowledge, poetry now serves, e.g., as an entertaining pastime, a form of individualized or collective aesthetic expression, or a tool in commercial marketing.

The profound if conflicted affiliation between orality and literacy is the subject of numerous investigations of textual communication that take voice as the central operative term. In his work on orality and literacy, Ong posits writing as an extension of speaking and, thus, uses the term *voice* to refer to both. As temporal rather than spatial practices, both writing and speech permit access to interiority—they exteriorize thoughts and feelings in human expression—and, therefore, enable communication. As Ong has it, spatial practices objectify, but temporal practices enable intersubjective exchange. While writing has spatial, objective qualities (see BOOK, POETIC; VISUAL POETRY), it is first and foremost temporal and communicative. For Ong, as for many other theorists, poetry's operations are the ideal example of literary communication. In the *lyric poem, the author masks his or her expression by speaking through an objectified figure of voice. In this way, the "poem . . . advertises the distance and remoteness which, paradoxically, are part of every human attempt to communicate, and it does this in so far as it is under one aspect 'objective,' . . . which is to say, non-vocal." But under another aspect, it is not objective, since it is trying to communicate; in this sense, the poem has a voice. That voice is not simply individual but compound, however, since the speaker anticipates the listener and vice versa. They meet in the poem.

A number of landmark romantic and postromantic studies place voice, and particularly what has come to be known as *lyric voice*—a figure that closely associates the poem's "speaker" with the author's perspective—at their centers, without commenting explicitly on their use of oral and aural metaphors to define written practices. William Wordsworth's Preface to the 2d ed. of *Lyrical Ballads* (1800) defined "the poet" as "a man speaking to men" in "a selection of the language really spoken by men." Here the spoken word is clearly the inspiration for Wordsworth's thoughts about writing poetry; he seems to mean that the *poet should try to write after the manner of everyday conversation. Distinguishing between *poetry* and *eloquence* in "What Is Poetry?" (1833), John Stuart Mill famously asserted that "eloquence is *heard*; poetry is *over*heard. Eloquence supposes an audience. The peculiarity of poetry appears to us to lie in the poet's utter unconsciousness of a listener." Here again, Mill uses oral terms to describe written practices without remarking on a difference of which he was surely aware. Mill's metaphors for poetry primarily come from the stage rather than from, as with Wordsworth, the street or other locations of everyday life. Mill likens poetry to soliloquy, the actor's monologue to himself onstage that puts the audience in the position of unperceived listeners. Mill also summons the oral art of song. Both theater and song are vocal and embodied, a persistent poetic ideal. The elision between speaking and writing is typical in treatises on poetry of the romantic period, which set the terms for the ways many critics write about poetry to the present day.

In his essay "The Three Voices of Poetry" (1954), T. S. Eliot extends Mill's argument by articulating distinctions among three kinds of poetic voice that lie along a dramatic spectrum. These are ideas or ideals, never found in their pure form; all poems tend in their expression one way or another, but all poems are combinatory. The "first voice is the voice of the poet talking to himself—or to nobody. The second is the voice of the poet addressing an audience. The third is the voice of the poet when he attempts to create a dramatic character speaking in verse." For Eliot, the third voice is the most difficult to accomplish because it requires the most complete self-concealment and imaginative *empathy on the part of the writer; Shakespeare's plays are the most memorable achievement in this mode. Eliot himself wrote verse dramas and discussed in this essay the difficulty of creating autonomous characters. Eliot's second voice is more commonly known as dramatic *monologue, though he insists that the dramatic *persona is merely a mask for the poet; in this way, he collapses dramatic monologue back into lyric. Eliot's interest in the dramatic and the impersonal is indicative of a larger transition "from lyrically expressive to dramatically objective norms for reading" consolidated by the *New Criticism, according to Tucker. The New Critics insisted on assuming "always that the speaker is someone other than the poet himself," even or esp. when reading lyric poetry. As Tucker observes, this attempt to move away from subjectivity actually reinforces it, precisely through the insistence on the orality of poetry: the emphasis on voice continues to invoke an isolated, "overheard" lyric subjectivity, now the speaker's rather than the poet's.

Tucker diagnoses this persistent tendency to think of poetry as oral and, therefore, rooted in the interior of a speaking subject who seeks to communicate with another as an "anxiety of textuality." It betrays the fear that the reader will be lost in a sea of unmotivated verbiage if he or she cannot organize reading experiences around a familiar model of individualized psychology: "What is poetry? Textuality a speaker owns." The insights of deconstruction, however, have made it increasingly impossible to overlook the *textuality of poetry, so that reading poems as if one were hearing them seems increasingly fantastical and inadequate. On the other hand, "the abysmal disfigurements of a deconstruction that would convert poetry's most beautiful illusion—the speaking presence—into a uniform textuality" is equally shortsighted.

The unsettling insights of deconstruction are articulated most compellingly in the work of Jacques Derrida, whose formulations inaugurated a new strain of lit. crit. that seeks to disrupt and show the limits of the oral/aural understanding of poetic textuality. In *Of Grammatology* (1967, trans. into Eng. 1976), Derrida decries the tyranny of voice that underpins and justifies an ethnocentrism rooted in what he calls "logocentrism." Logocentrism "is also a phonocentrism: absolute proximity of voice and being, of voice and the meaning of being, of voice and the ideality of meaning." He reads the Western philosophical trad., from Aristotle to Jean-Jacques Rousseau to Ferdinand de Saussure, as profoundly privileging the spoken word, which, in turn, privileges self-presence. The mind communing with itself speaks a kind of interior, universal lang. that vocal expression most closely approximates. For Derrida, this is the founding principle of metaphysics, which dichotomizes body and soul or spirit, presence and absence, speaking and writing. Writing in this system is derivative and discredited, a copy of a copy, "mediation of mediation"; it signifies "a fall into the exteriority of meaning." Its signs are arbitrary and bear no enchanted proximity to the inner workings of the mind. In the beginning was the spoken word, and it brought a worldview into being that Derrida seeks to overturn. His proposed grammatology, as opposed to *linguistics, which operates according to the vocal privilege, would be a way to begin to interrogate and dismantle the tyranny of voice.

Focusing a deconstructive lens on poetry (and esp. Charles Baudelaire's poetry) in "Anthropomorphism and Trope in Lyric" (1984), Paul de Man condemns the tendency to read voice into lyric as "delusional." That delusion emerges from a "terror" of modernity and a retreat into escapist nostalgia: terror calls lyric voice into being. Lyric reading practices that hear voices where there are only words anthropomorphize at their own peril (though de Man never specifies what precisely the danger is).

Critics after Derrida and de Man, for the most part, begin from two mutually incompatible premises: either they continue to assert that hearing voices in poetry is not delusional but rather an integral component of that literary experience, or they seek ways to grant the written or textual qualities of poetry a power independent of, or at least not subordinated within, an oral/aural framework. An example of the former approach is William Waters's sophisticated treatment of vocal and sensual metaphor in his study of *apostrophe, *Poetry's Touch* (2003). Acknowledging that writing cannot literally speak or touch, Waters nonetheless goes on to explore a persistent tendency of poetry to try to speak and gesture beyond the limits of the word, to communicate physically in a disembodied medium. Susan Stewart, in *Poetry and the Fate of the Senses* (2002), also acknowledges the fictive and sometimes clichéd deployment of vocal metaphors in the study and practice of poetry; nevertheless, she offers a valuable exploration of why we love certain voices and how poetry serves as a vehicle for the beloved voice. That voice is not singular, even though it emerges from an individual; it is imprinted by other voices, possessed by the hist. of those voices that have been heard by the speaker. Our voices carry and are composed of the voices of others. Poetry is the medium for these possessed voices.

The critical work that questions rather than embraces the oral/aural framework for reading poetry often draws on media hist., thinking through the ways technologies that transmit the word, written or spoken, might change the ways that people think, speak, and write. Because there were powerful media revolutions in the Ren. and the 19th c., much of this work is grounded in those periods—for instance, Mazzio's argument that the Ren. voice does not always coincide with eloquence and Griffiths's exploration of the written, textual, and specifically "printed" properties of the Victorian poetic voice.

*See* ADDRESS, DRAMATIC POETRY, EXPRESSION, ORAL POETRY.

■ T. S. Eliot, *On Poetry and Poets* (1957); F. Berry, *Poetry and the Physical Voice* (1962); W. J. Ong, *The Barbarian Within* (1962); M. M. Bakhtin, *The Dialogic Imagination*, ed. M. Holquist, trans. C. Emerson and M. Holquist (1981); W. R. Johnson, *The Idea of Lyric* (1982); G. Genette, *Narrative Discourse*, trans. J. E. Lewin (1983); P. de Man, *The Rhetoric of Romanticism* (1984); H. Tucker, "Dramatic Monologue and the Overhearing of Lyric," *Lyric Poetry: Beyond New Criticism*, ed. C. Hošek and P. Parker (1985); J. Goldberg, *Voice Terminal Echo: Postmodernism and English Renaissance Texts* (1986); E. Havelock, *The Muse Learns to Write: Reflections on Orality and Literacy from Antiquity to the Present* (1986); E. Griffiths, *The Printed Voice of Victorian Poetry* (1989); F. A. Kittler, *Discourse Networks 1800/1900*, trans. M. Metteer (1990); P. Zumthor, *Oral Poetry*, trans. K. Murphy-Judy (1990); B. R. Smith, *The Acoustic World of Early Modern England* (1999); Y. Prins, "Voice Inverse," *VP* 42 (2004); C. Mazzio, *The Inarticulate Renaissance* (2008); J. A. Peraino, *Giving Voice to Love: Song and Self-Expression from the Troubadours to Guillaume de Machaut* (2011).

E. RICHARDS

**VOLTA,** *volte* (It., "turn"). A musical and prosodic term for a turn, particularly the transition point between the *octave and *sestet of the *sonnet, which, in its It. form, usually rhymes *abbaabba cdecde*: the *volta* is significant because both the particular rhymes unifying the two quatrains of the octave and also the *envelope scheme are abandoned simultaneously, regardless of whether this break is further reinforced syntactically by a full stop at the end of the octave (though usually it is), creating a decisive "turn in thought." By extension, the term is applied to the gap or break at line nine of any sonnet type, though in the Shakespearean form, e.g., the type of rhyming (*cross rhyme) is not abandoned at that point.

T.V.F. BROGAN

**VORTICISM.** Vorticism was an Eng. avant-garde movement in the visual arts, primarily sculpture and painting. It is also important to literary modernism because of the guiding roles of Ezra Pound and Wyndham Lewis. Vorticism's literary corpus is small (largely restricted to the short-lived journal *Blast*, 1914–15), but the documents and debates surrounding the movement's brief flourishing remain historically significant. Given the general absence of other *manifesto-based groups in Eng. literary modernism, vorticism's direct engagement with *cubism, *expressionism, and, above all, *futurism provides a valuable record of Eng. modernism's relationship to the aesthetic practices and key ideas of the international avant-garde. Like these avant-gardes, vorticism explicitly explores the relationship between modernity in lit. and in the other arts, thus contributing to Eng.-lang. modernist aesthetics more generally. Because of Pound's and Lewis's extensive connections, other major modernists who were not themselves vorticists (e.g., F. M. Ford, T. S. Eliot, Rebecca West, and T. E. Hulme) are linked to the movement either historically or in subsequent crit.

The vorticist aesthetic seeks a charged synthesis of dynamism and stasis. In the visual arts, this involved a critique of both cubism's alleged stasis and of the futurist worship of speed and motion. In lit., this meant an effort to move beyond the static character of the image that now, for Pound, defined the imagist movement with which he had previously been associated (see IMAGISM). Pound describes the vortex as "a radiant node or cluster . . . from which, and through which, and into which ideas are constantly rushing." Poetic vorticism's program combined epigrammatic intensity with dynamism and movement; thus, it concisely formulates a central problem of modernist poetics.

The movement's politics remain a subject of controversy. Long held to be close in spirit and style to It. futurism, vorticism's violent rhet. often reinforces this interpretation, as do the later sympathies of both Lewis and Pound for radical right-wing politics. Particularly with Lewis, however, vorticist aggression is often mixed with humor and elements of self-critique largely lacking in futurism, to say nothing of fascism. Similarly, while vorticism does self-consciously represent a style specific to the machine age and its wars, it cannot be said to offer a straightforward celebration.

*See* AVANT-GARDE POETICS, MODERNISM.

■ *BLAST* 1–2 (1914–15, rpt. 1982); E. Pound, *Gaudier-Brzeska: A Memoir* (1916); W. Lewis, *Wyndham Lewis on Art*, ed. W. Michel and C. J. Fox (1969); H. Kenner, *The Pound Era* (1971); W. C. Wees, *Vorticism and the English Avant-Garde* (1972); F. Jameson, *Fables of Aggression* (1979); E. Pound and W. Lewis, *Pound/Lewis*, ed. T. Materer (1985)—letters; R. W. Dasenbrock, *The Literary Vorticism of Ezra Pound and Wyndham Lewis* (1985); M. Perloff, *The Futurist Moment* (1987); P. Peppis, *Literature, Politics, and the English Avant-Garde* (2000).

C. BUSH

**WAKA.** *Waka,* also referred to at times as *yamato uta* (Japanese verse) or simply *uta* (verse), is the oldest form of poetry in continuous use in Japan. The term is often taken to mean cl. poetry in Japanese, in distinction from poetry written in Chinese (*kanshi;* see CHINESE POETRY IN JAPAN). In this broad sense, waka encompass four of the earliest Japanese verse forms: *chōka, tanka, sedōka,* and *bussokuseki-ka.* Of these, only chōka (long verse) and tanka (short verse) survived past the 8th c. Although the chōka were used sporadically after this point, the overwhelming majority of waka were tanka, consisting of 31 syllables in five measures, with occasional allowance for additional syllables (*ji-amari*) or fewer (*ji-tarazu*) in each measure. This entry uses the narrowest definition of waka as tanka composed from the 8th c., when they first appear in texts, until the onset of westernization in the mid-19th c.

Early waka were exchanged between members of the court at banquets and royal rituals, as well as in more informal settings. By the 10th c., they had also become a means for legitimating political power through poetry matches (*uta-awase*) and anthols. By the end of the 12th c., waka had become a cl. lang. acquired through the formal study of archaic texts. Proficiency in this highly codified lang. was dependent on instruction by hereditary households of aristocratic poet-scholars. Competition between these households and educated commoners in the 17th c. stimulated growth in the fields of poetics and philology, culminating in the devel. of *kokugaku* (natavist learning), which viewed the earliest waka poetry as the expression of an eternal Japanese sensibility uncontaminated by continental culture.

In fact, waka's distinctive prosody arose from a complex interplay between the cl. East Asian ideal of symmetry on the one hand and a desire for its complementary opposite in the form of an asymmetric (and therefore indigenous) structure on the other. The pentasyllabic and heptasyllabic measures common to all waka were derived from *shi poetry. Unlike its Chinese counterpart, however, which amplified its trademark *parallelisms by consistently using one measure in any given verse, each waka poem alternated in an irregular pattern of 5-7-5-7-7 between both measures. At the same time, waka often reflected the yin-yang binary structures informing traditional East Asian notions of self, society, and the world. In particular poems, this binary could take the shape of a dialogue between two parties, a question and answer, or a sentence split by a concessive, causal, or hypothetical construction. Just like shi poems, in which the basic unit of meaning was the couplet, waka often consisted of an "upper line" (*kami no ku*) in the first three measures and a "lower line" (*shimo no ku*) in the last two. This tendency toward a binary structure spurred on the devel. of *renga

("linked verse"), in which the upper and lower lines of a waka became separate poems.

One reason for waka's ubiquity in Japanese court culture was its inherent interconnectedness with other texts and media. The word first appears in *Man'yōshū* poem prefaces, where it refers to verses that responded to earlier ones. Many of the earliest 31-syllable verses in that anthol. are *hanka* (envoi verses) that capped a longer chōka in the same manner as shorter Chinese poems might follow a lengthy *fu (prose rhapsody). By the end of the 8th c., prefaces written in literary Chinese replaced chōka, initiating a trad. of narrative contextualization that would drive waka's subsequent hist. Henceforth, waka would accompany prose passages that ranged in size from terse notes on a poem's topic in an anthol. to extended narratives in vernacular tales (*monogatari*) and memoirs (*nikki*; see JAPANESE POETIC DIARIES).

Even after the word *waka* came to mean primarily "Japanese verse," it continued to operate on some level as a response to a particular topic and social context, fictional or otherwise. The dialogic aspect of waka extended to its relations with other media: poems were often paired with shi couplets, decorated paper, paintings, plants, or dioramas. In their most common textual forms, waka were also typically paired with other waka. Careful integration of poems into associative and progressive sequences meant that any individual verse gained significance in relation to preceding ones. These sequencing techniques spurred on the devel. of elaborately organized imperial anthols. like the *Kokinshū* and *Shinkokinshū,* as well as tightly integrated, miniaturized versions known as *hyakushu* (hundred-verse sequences). Poetry collections also contributed to the categorization of poems according to particular seasonal, social, and religious topics (*dai*), each of which possessed a tightly defined set of connotations.

As a form of uta (song), waka were often recited with melodic flourishes and rhythmic pauses. *Euphony can be inferred in some poems from their arrangement of consonants and vowels into recognizable patterns. Canonical poetics, however, usually criticized the phonetic repetitions associated with rhyme and assonance. Instead, waka prosody has focused on syllabic meter (see SYLLABIC VERSE). Unlike traditional forms of Eng. meter, each syllable in a waka is given equal stress as a distinct *mora. The resulting metronome beat may explain why the chief verb for composition (*yomu*) also denoted counting and percussive rhythm. Metrical rhythm in waka is conventionally determined by the placement of the *caesura at different points between the poem's five measures. The earliest waka favor a tripartite structure using a 5-7 rhythm, with the caesura after the second and fourth measures (5-7, 5-7, 7) or after the second and third ones (5-7, 5, 7-7). From the 9th c., a 7-5 rhythm became increasingly common, with the caesura at the first and third measures (5, 7-5, 7-7) or, esp. in later waka, only after the third measure (5-7-5, 7-7). Individual letters in written poems could also make up *acrostics (*oriku*), *palindromes (*kaimon*), and elaborate *kutsu-kamuri* (shoe-and-cap) configurations, in which the first and last letters in a group of poems made up other poems. Such forms of word play often ignored the distinctions between voiced and unvoiced consonants observed in mod. Japanese orthography.

The rhetorical devel. of waka can be charted through the shifting emphasis placed on *kokoro* (mind) and *mono* (things). These two elements corresponded to distinct grammatical registers as well as phenomenological ones. Kokoro referred to emotions, sensations, perceptions, reasoning, and actions. In the agglutinative structure of Japanese, it was conveyed through verbs and adjectives that inflected to indicate tense, aspect, and mood. Mono, on the other hand, were concrete nouns indicating phenomena apprehended by the senses in the external world. Initially, emphasis was laid on mono, which were often sweeping depictions of landscapes whose epithet-laden names functioned as *synecdoches encapsulating mythic narratives and regional trads. By the 9th c., poetic depictions of landscape had become more generic, as they shifted focus inward toward the paintings and gardens of aristocratic urban mansions. During this period, kokoro came to occupy a growing proportion of the poem, and the vocabulary for expressing it expanded significantly. Greater emphasis on kokoro led in turn to greater interest in its narrative contextualization in tales and memoirs. By the 12th c., however, there was a growing countermovement away from kokoro and toward more noun-heavy poems, in which every object was infused with emotions through its intertextual links to earlier poems and narratives. Further innovations in the 13th c. involved strictly segregating mono and kokoro content into separate poems, which were then scrutinized through the lens of minute temporal or spatial distinctions.

Many waka tropes consist of different methods for configuring the mono and kokoro elements in a poem. Early verses typically opened with a poetic toponym (*utamakura*), preceded by a five-syllable epithet (*makurakotoba*) or embedded in a larger prefatory phrase (*jokotoba*). At the end would come a relatively brief and conventional expression of kokoro. In such cases, scene and sentiment could be linked by implicit metaphor, metonymy, or sound repetition. The most distinctive means of binding mono to kokoro were *kakekotoba* (pivot words), a form of *zeugma in which a cluster of syllables simultaneously signified both elements. Because kakekotoba also pivoted between separate syntactic registers, they could splice together distinct sentences with maximum economy. A related form of rhet. was *mitate* (double vision) in which objects that were normally temporally or spatially discrete overlapped visually. In the 12th c., the consolidation of waka as a written trad., along with heightened inter-

est in using intertextuality to infuse landscape scenes with human sentiments, led to the codification of such techniques as *honkadori* (literally "taking from an original poem") and *honzetsu* (allusion to a cl. prose narrative). Another rhetorical figure, *engo* (linked words), studded related lexemes throughout a poem, creating metonymic connections that crosscut syntactic divisions. The devel. of engo in turn contributed to such med. literary forms as renga poetry and *nō drama. Taken as a whole, waka tropes influenced virtually every other vernacular literary genre in premod. Japan.

Within the court society that claimed it as its own distinctive lang., diction and social decorum defined waka as much as its formal prosody. In many ways, the brevity of waka offers an extreme example of the general predisposition in Japanese toward heavily context-dependent utterances. Unlike their prose equivalents, however, waka even omitted the honorifics through which addresser and addressee were traditionally specified. Coupled with the lang.'s general tendency to omit grammatical number, person, and gender, this meant that any given poem could accommodate multiple speakers and contexts irrespective of gender or social status. The resulting semantic fluidity allowed waka to function as a common lang. binding together an otherwise intensely hierarchical court community through the expression of sentiments regulated by a sense of decorum that was finely attuned to seasonal and social rhythms.

At the same time, lexical restrictions in waka increasingly came to distinguish the court community from other social groups. By the 11th c., *utakotoba* (poetic diction) was limited to the roughly 2,000 words used in the first three imperial anthols. Subsequent poetry matches and collections adjudicated disputes over the precise boundaries of this lexicon, which expanded incrementally over time, esp. when waka interacted with the informal renga poetry adopted by townspeople and warriors in the 15th c. Beginning in the 17th c., these commoners also developed a parodic form of waka, known as *kyōka* (mad verse), which inverted distinctions between utakotoba and contemp. forms of lang. Unlike its "unorthodox" (*haikai) partner, which used bodily functions and popular culture as comic material, courtly waka strove to be "serious" (*ushin*), avoiding most Chinese loan-words, colloquial syntax, and inelegant diction in the process. The chief source for innovation was the *Man'yōshū*, whose antiquity guaranteed its legitimacy. With the introduction of Western lit. crit. at the end of the 19th c., traditional diction was repudiated wholesale, and waka were reincarnated as mod. tanka (see JAPAN, MODERN POETRY OF).

The narrow strictures on meter, diction, and decorum that governed the composition of waka for over a millennium endowed it with ritual qualities. Throughout premod. Japanese hist., waka were seen as a suprahuman form of lang. shared with native spirits and Buddhist deities. Supernatural beings could address mortals in verse, and humans could use poems to entreat them in turn. Insofar as the court aristocracy in general (and members of the imperial family in particular) claimed divine descent, they too were often the subject of waka. Perhaps the prime examples of waka's sacral authority are the imperial anthols. that were compiled between the 10th and 15th cs. to legitimate the court's leaders. From a mod. critical perspective that values intensely individual or innovative forms of expression, such qualities have sometimes made waka seem little more than a fossilized art form for most of its long history. Regardless, they have also enabled it to play a distinguished role in articulating both aesthetic values and notions of community in Japan right up to the present, when tanka are composed at the imperial palace on New Year's Day.

*See* JAPANESE POETICS, KOKINSHŪ, MAN'YŌSHŪ, SHINKOKINSHŪ.

■ **Anthologies and Translations**: *Nihon kagaku taikei* (Japanese Poetics Series), 13 v. (1956–64); *Shinpen kokka taikan* (New Compendium of Japanese Poetry), 10 v. in 20 (1983–92); *Waiting for the Wind*, trans. and intro. S. Carter (1989); *An Anthology of Traditional Japanese Poetry Competitions*, comp. and trans. S. Ito (1991); *A Waka Anthology*, trans. E. Cranston, 2 v. (1993, 2006); *Traditional Japanese Poetry*, trans. and intro. S. Carter (1993).

■ **Criticism and History**: A. Waley, *Japanese Poetry* (1919, rpt. 1976); J. Konishi, "Association and Progression," *HJAS* 21 (1958); R. Brower and E. Miner, *Japanese Court Poetry* (1961); P. Harries, "Personal Poetry Collections," *Monumenta Nipponica* 35.3 (1980); S. Carter, "Waka in the Age of Renga," *Monumenta Nipponica* 36.4 (1981); S. Ito, "The Muse in Competition," *Monumenta Nipponica* 37.7 (1982); H. McCullough, *Brocade by Night* (1985); M. Morris, "Waka and Form, Waka and History," *HJAS* 46.2 (1986); H. Sato and B. Watson, *From the Country of Eight Islands* (1987); R. Huey, *Kyōgoku Tamekane* (1989); S. Hideo, *Kodai waka shiron* (A History of Early Waka, 1990); E. Miner, "Waka," *HJAS* 50.2 (1990); P. Nosco, *Remembering Paradise* (1990); J. Mostow, *Pictures of the Heart* (1996); E. Kamens, *Utamakura, Allusion, and Intertextuality in Traditional Japanese Poetry* (1997); R. Thomas, "Macroscopic vs. Microscopic," *HJAS* 58 (1998); K. Kawamoto, *The Poetics of Japanese Verse* (2000); T. LaMarre, *Uncovering Heian Japan* (2000); R. Huey, *The Making of Shinkokinshū* (2002); S. Carter, *Householders* (2007); G. Heldt, *The Pursuit of Harmony* (2008).

G. HELDT

## WAR POETRY

I. Early Period
II. Middle Period
III. Modern Period

**I. Early Period.** War poetry, incl. depictions of battle, celebrations of victory, lamentations over defeat and captivity, and meditations on confronting death, has existed since the birth of lit. Although what binds an army has always been a concern, in early lit. poets probed the loyalty of men dominated by a vertical rather than a lateral or fraternal relation, usually expressed as the bond of the fighter to his ruler or ruling deity. In the Heb. Ps. 44:5, written sometime between the 10th and the 6th cs. BCE, the psalmist cried out to his God, "Through thee will we push down our enemies: through thy name will we tread them under that rise up against us." In the Sanskrit *Bhagavad-Gītā* of the 1st c. BCE, Arjuna labors to serve Krishna. Even as the epic opens with his exclamation about facing an imminent civil war, "I see no good in killing my kinsmen in battle," Arjuna closes in exalted obedience to Krishna and enters battle with unquestioning devotion toward the divine source of his strength and in serene defiance of death. While loyalties to multiple and quarreling deities are subject to destructive fraternal pressure in Homer's 8th-c. BCE epic, the *Iliad*, the fidelity to hierarchical authority is similar: petty, vindictive, or unjust as the Gr. gods may seem, they shape the hero's destiny, and war remains the necessary platform of that destiny.

But in this long period of fatalistic acceptances, ancient texts looked clearly enough at war's tragic consequences to suggest their resistance to war as masculine fate and human inevitability. The 12th-c. BCE Hebrew text of the song of Deborah and Barak in Judg. 5 offers striking views of women that deny the customary all-male cast of warfare. A male sensibility more typically owns the emotional field of the 10th-c. Anglo-Saxon "The Battle of Maldon," in which a grim exaltation rules the performance of right action: "When the shield breaks, the corselet sings a terrible song." The Maldon poet describes a battlefield loyalty and bravery in which an *amor fati* binds men; there is a joy in dying "by the side of my lord, by the man so dearly loved." In a variant of that intense love of men for men, the possibly preexilic lamentation of David for the deaths of Saul and Jonathan in 2 Sam. 1:25–26 offers another time-melting flash: "O Jonathan, thou wast slain in thine high places . . . thy love to me was wonderful, passing the love of women." But in the *Trojan Women*, the 5th-c. BCE Gr. dramatist Euripides shifts the coverage of grief away from the familiar battle glory and extends it to war's devastating impact on civilians. Other early fragments from Gr. poets, such as the 7th-c. BCE poet Archilochus, subvert the authority of heroic bonding and anticipate further antiheroic themes. Two 8th-c. Chinese poems, Tu Fu's "Song of the War-Carts" and Li Po's "War South of the Great Wall," represent a remarkable devel. away from the detail-parched space of other war poems toward a world of weather, plants, and animals, one notably occupied by humble foot soldiers.

**II. Middle Period.** The next millennium of war poetry expanded in range and depth. Chaucer's 1386 prologue to the *Canterbury Tales* introduces the "verray parfit gentil knighte" who will lead us to the mythical world of the dueling protagonists of "The Knight's Tale." But the premise of warfare as the making and testing of masculine character is undercut by a persistently dry comic wit and by the ironies of a detailed survey of the glories of the temple of Mars in which Mars presides over a world of horrifyingly savage and discordant fatality. At some distance from Chaucer's fantastic realism, George Gascoigne in "The Fruites of Warre" (1575) urges the perspective of the warrior morally and physically bruised by conquest, pillage, and captivity. He laments bitterly: "Search all thy bookes, and thou shalt finde therein, / That honour is more harde to holde than winne." A larger, more nuanced version of war poetry occurs within William Shakespeare's tragedy *Macbeth* and in historical plays like *Julius Caesar* and the Henry cycle. In these plays, thickening details of circumstance and character signal a literary advance in which many-faceted portraits of men and women caught up in armed conflict stress more than battleground, siege, and skirmish. A set piece from *Henry V* (3.1.1–34) affirms traditional martial strengths and loyalties, yet this play puts an array of rogues into battle alongside its heroes, as Shakespeare details the cowardice and venal betrayal attending war with an angle of attention unknown to the Anglo-Saxon bards. Political intrigue and power control but do not obliterate the vivid selves of those trapped between love and honor in *Antony and Cleopatra*, while the aggressive, state-switching pursuit of death and glory in *Coriolanus* offers a sustained investigation of the ethical imagination of the military hero.

In the ensuing centuries, as nation-states arise from feudal communities, Eng. war poetry, still largely written by literate observers rather than principals, both decries and praises war. Cannon mouths and rifle barrels increasingly displace slings, arrows, and muskets, with a ramifying sense of national pride, as well as a thorough despair at war's waste. "I hate that drum's discordant sound," says John Scott of Amwell in 1782, "To me it talks of ravaged plains, / And burning towns and ruined swains, / And mangled limbs, and dying groans, / And widows' tears and orphans' moans[.]" The spectacle of Napoleonic warfare, prelude to the global wars that would sweep the 20th c., stirred poets across Europe. S. T. Coleridge in "Fears in Solitude" urges repentance for misguided violence. In 1812, the Am. poet Joel Barlow's "Advice to a Raven in Russia" tells "the black fool" who cannot tear flesh from the frozen corpses littering the retreat from Moscow to wait further afield: his class is the only one Napoleon will never disappoint. Heinrich Heine's "Die Grenadiere" takes from the same piled bodies evidence of heroic loyalty. By 1853, Victor Hugo's "L'Expiation" describes the snow-covered retreat this way: "On ne connaissant plus les chefs ni le drapeau. / Hier la grande armée, et maintenant troupeau" ("You can't make out officers or flag. / Yesterday the Grand Army, today a herd"). An even more appalled view of battle suffuses Thomas Hardy's *The Dynasts* (1903–7). Confronting the devastation wrought at Waterloo, Hardy's "Spirit Ironic" cries out: "Warfare mere, / Plied by the Managed for the Managers." A centuries-old contempt for the common soldier (termed the "scum of the earth" by the Duke of Wellington) gradually yielded to concern for wounded soldiers and their after-service lives, prompting poems like E. B. Browning's "The Forced Recruit." Arthur Rimbaud's "Le Dormeur du Val" offers an even starker

image of hapless innocence. In 1865, Am. war poetry came of age with the color and high tenderness of Walt Whitman's *Drum-Taps*. A year later, Herman Melville in "A Utilitarian View of the Monitor's Fight" presciently saw how the increasing mechanization of war nullifies the individual's code of honor—a motif of increasing importance in subsequent decades.

**III. Modern Period.** From the Khyber Hills to Ypres, Rudyard Kipling's thumping rhyme, unforgiving of weak command but committed to imperial conquest, urged the dignity of the common soldier. Poets of World War I moved even more markedly to write poetry from an egalitarian perspective. Still, in 1907, the erotic tinge of R. M. Rilke's nostalgia for aristocratic gallantry in poems like "Der Fahnenträger" ("The Flag-bearer") and "Letzter Abend" ("The Last Evening") was followed by wildly popular poems espousing similar codes of honor and country by Rupert Brooke and Julian Grenfell, who died early in World War I. Staggered by mass casualties, medics like Georg Trakl, writing in Ger., and Giuseppe Ungaretti, in It., emphasized instead the mechanized butchery, as did soldier-poets like Wilfred Owen, Siegfried Sassoon, and Isaac Rosenberg. Occasionally, as these poets let glory fade from the generals, a kind of haggard reverse glory enfolded the lower ranks. Edmund Blunden, Robert Graves, Rosenberg, Owen, and Sassoon all register how the old disciplinary order needed to stiffen a conscript army broke down in the bloody stalemate of trench warfare. Machine-gun fire had supplanted the cavalry rush of Alfred, Lord Tennyson's "The Charge of the Light Brigade," and a paternalistic vertical loyalty receded before the lateral strength of the fraternal bond between soldiers, a bond strengthened by the perceived incomprehension of the home front. In "Dulce et Decorum Est," Wilfred Owen says that if a home-front supporter had seen a gas attack, "you would not tell with such high zest / To children ardent for some desperate glory, / The old Lie: Dulce et decorum est / Pro patria mori." Owen remained ambivalent about pacifism but returned to action and to poems portraying the numbing brutality that emerges from "the cess of war." Rosenberg and Owen were killed in action. Sassoon, after having his objections to the war's conduct read aloud in the House of Commons, rejoined his regiment, was wounded, and continued to write antiwar poems like "On Passing the New Menin Gate"; eventually, he advocated armed resistance against Nazism. In the decades succeeding 1914–18, Owen and Sassoon came to stand as the preeminent voices of antiwar feeling.

In "Spain 1937," W. H. Auden supported the Sp. loyalists but still saw "The conscious acceptance of guilt in the necessary murder[.]" Auden begins "September 1, 1939" by saying, "I sit . . . Uncertain and afraid / As the clever hopes expire / Of a low dishonest decade"; yet at poem's end, the speaker, "Beleaguered by . . . Negation and despair" must "Show an affirming flame." War guilt continued to travel in a direct line from hapless soldiers to impotent or war-mongering civilians, while the poets who succeeded Auden—Keith Douglas, Alun

Lewis, Henry Reed, and Roy Fuller—were burdened by a sense of belatedness. Soldier-poets moved faster across a wider geographical canvas and, unlike their World War I predecessors, shared with the civilian an overview of war by means of the ubiquitous camera. R. N. Currey remarked, "This is a civilization in which a man, too squeamish to empty a slop pail or skin a rabbit, can press a button that exposes the entrails of cities." In World War II, poets moved from the gaunt, mud-splattered soldiers of the trenches in World War I to survey scenes that the Czech poet Jaroslav Seifert described in "Never Again" as "A hundred houses . . . in ruins, / nearly a thousand . . . damaged / by aerial bombs" (trans. Ewald Osers).

Immense changes in war poetry had occurred when the professional soldier gave way to the literate conscript or volunteer. War poets not only introduced fresh meditations on the abrupt transit of living flesh to dead matter in tune with a prior generation's fixation on the crisis of mutability but turned more conspicuously to the ethics of killing. Terms like *antiwar poetry* should be used with care, since the frightfulness of war may be told as fully by those committed to violent resolution of conflict as by those opposed to it; yet poets have undeniably moved from the glory of killing to the glory of being killed and then to the doubt and shame of killing, the latter articulated in poems like Keith Douglas's "How to Kill" and Herbert Read's "The Happy Warrior," which updated William Wordsworth's poem of the same name. The novelty of an antiheroic verse may have lessened after World War I; but as the end of World War II merged seamlessly into the cold war, the contours defining war as heroic business, or its outcome as definitive victory or defeat, continued to crumble. In poems like Howard Nemerov's "Redeployment," Am. war poets resisted the training of soldiers into machines for perpetual war. Randall Jarrell turned the misery of the ball turret gunner in a bomber's crew into passive infantilism; "The Death of the Ball Turret Gunner" begins: "From my mother's womb I fell into the State, / And I hunched in its belly till my wet fur froze." It ends, "When I died they washed me out of the turret with a hose."

When war poets registered how technology was expanding the work of war into civilian factories and rear-echelon administration, refugees, forced labor, war prisoners, and concentration camp inmates began to displace battle as subjects. War poems gave way to poems about resistance and occupation, and lines between civilians and combatants blurred, as in the work of Polish poets Tadeusz Różewicz and Zbigniew Herbert. Anna Akhmatova's *Requiem* details the agony of Stalinist war, while in 1946, the searing poems of the Hungarian Holocaust victim Miklós Radnóti were unearthed at a newly exposed burial site. Postwar poems by Lee Roripaugh and Lawson Inada describe victims of the atom bomb and consider the lives of interned Japanese Americans. 20th-c. war poets explore psychological injury: James Dickey's "The Firebombing," about Am. use of napalm over Japan, showed the toll of aerial attacks on civilian and pilot. The Vietnam War,

like the Korean War, sparked many poems about aftermath by refugees who in the postwar period settled in the U.S.

In the wake of both Asian wars, many Am. soldier-poets began to see the soldier not simply as victim but as perpetrator of war's atrocities. In the 1972 anthol. of poems from the Vietnam War, *Winning Hearts and Minds,* ed. Larry Rottmann, Jan Barry, and Basil Paquet wrote, "What distinguishes the voices in this volume is their active identification of themselves as agents of pain and war—as 'agent-victims' of their own atrocities." Many poems by combat veterans like Bruce Weigl, Yusef Komunyakaa, W. D. Ehrhart, and Doug Anderson bear out this conclusion. Civilian protests by W. S. Merwin, Robert Bly, Denise Levertov, Hayden Carruth, and Galway Kinnell convey a national sense of shame and political impotence. Most of these poems mined colloquial and official diction for satiric effect and experimented with narrative technique from cinema and prose fiction. Prompted by the era's personal candor and increased awareness of the mental disorders bred by war, Vietnam War poetry included friendly fire, civilian casualties, and sexual relations. Yet the brotherhood of soldiers still preoccupied these poets, even when that bond was negatively inflected by class, race, and nation.

As global politics changed the nature, mobility, and visibility of war waged in countries such as Nicaragua, Bosnia, and Iraq, poems like Adrienne Rich's "The School among the Ruins" tell what happens to children, as teachers "sang them to naps told stories [and] washed human debris off boots and coats[.]" As the boundaries between home and battle front eroded, as gender assignments loosened, and as the cold war moved America and its allies into an endless war alert, war poetry absorbed these factors into its aesthetic. In *Klaonica, Poems for Bosnia* (1993), the Eng. poet Jon Silkin writes, "We, bitter heat-seeking / animals must make conscience. But touching / whose pain?" In the spreading wars of the 20th and 21st cs., civilians, soldiers, and men and women of all ethnic groups now readily blend their urge to witness into journalism, memoir, and fiction, as well as poetry. But as total war and ceaseless low-intensity imperial conflict have pitched the balance of suffering overwhelmingly toward civilians, war poetry, too, springs from ever-more diverse sites and circumstances.

■ **Anthologies:** *The War Poets,* ed. O. Williams (1945); *Winning Hearts and Minds,* ed. L. Rottmann, J. Barry, and B. Paquet (1972); R. N. Currey, *Poets of the 1939–1945 War* (1960); *The Penguin Book of First World War Poetry,* ed. J. Silkin (1981); *The Oxford Book of War Poetry,* ed. J. Stallworthy (1984, 1987); *Carrying the Darkness,* ed. W. D. Ehrhart (1989)—the Vietnam War; *Holocaust Poetry,* ed. H. Schiff (1995); *The Faber Book of War Poetry,* ed. K. Baker (1996); *Poetry of the Second World War,* ed. D. Graham (1998); *The Wound and the Dream,* ed. C. Nelson (2002)—the Spanish Civil War; *Poets against the War,* ed. S. Hamill (2003); *Poets of World War II,* ed. H. Shapiro (2003); *101 Poems against War,* ed. P. Keegan and M. Hollis (2003); *Amer-*

*ican War Poetry*, ed. L. Goldensohn (2004); *Poems of the Second World War*, ed. H. Haughton (2004); *Poets of the Civil War*, ed. J. D. McClatchy (2005).

■ **Criticism and History:** P. Fussell, *The Great War and Modern Memory* (1975); V. Scannell, *Not Without Glory* (1976)—poets and WWII; E. Longley, *Poetry in the Wars* (1986); S. Schweik, *A Gulf So Deeply Cut* (1991)—women poets and WWII; M. Bibby, *Hearts and Minds* (1996)—Vietnam era; S. Chatterji, *Memories of a Lost War* (2001)—Vietnam era; L. Goldensohn, *Dismantling Glory* (2003)—soldiers in the 20th c.; *The Oxford Handbook of British and Irish War Poetry*, ed. T. Kendall (2007); J. A. Winn, *The Poetry of War* (2008).

L. GOLDENSOHN

**WARTBURGKRIEG** (Ger., "Wartburg contest," *Sängerkrieg*, "minstrel's contest"). A corpus of strophic poems dating between the 13th and 15th cs. that treat a *poetic contest supposedly held at the castle Wartburg by the Count Hermann I of Thuringia in the early 13th c. Johannes Rothe designated the term as a collective title in the 15th c. It is misleading because the castle is not necessarily the scene of events in all cases (see Weigelt). The *Wartburgkrieg* occurs in two different *Töne* (a *Ton* being a verse form together with its melody): the *Thüringer-Fürsten-Ton* and the *Schwarzer Ton* (see GERMANIC PROSODY, MEISTERSINGER). The participants in the contest involve poets known from other sources as composers of *Minnesang* and *Sangspruch* (political poetry) such as Walther von der Vogelweide, Wolfram von Eschenbach, and fictional figures such as the necromancer Klingsor von Ungerlant derived from Wolfram's *Parzival* and various spirits. The loosely linked corpus of *strophes was composed in different stages over time, and the earliest ms. dates from around 1300. The corpus is transmitted in three mss., The Grosse Heidelberger (Manessische) Manuscript, the Jenaer Manuscript, and the Kolmarer Manuscript. The most important episodes of the contest date from the 13th c. The older account in *Schwarzer Ton* transmits the *Rätselspiel* (puzzle game) episode, in which a poetic duel takes place between Wolfram and the Hungarian sorcerer Klingsor. In the *riddle contest, Wolfram proves his pious learning against Klingsor's heathen knowledge by solving riddles with spiritual meaning. The *Fürstenlob* (praise of lords) episode in *Thüringer-Fürsten-Ton* treats a contest among six poets before Count Hermann and his wife: Heinrich von Ofterdingen, Walther von der Vogelweide, Biterolfe, Reinmar von Zweter, Wolfram von Eschenbach, and the Tugendhafte Schreiber. The poets compete on how best to sing praises of a prince, a set piece motif of *Sangspruchdichtung*, choosing different patrons for praise. Walther defeats Heinrich by a ruse, but the latter calls on Klingsor to arbitrate; this episode is regarded as a prequel to the *Rätselspiel*. Mod. interest in the Wartburgkrieg may be seen in Novalis's *Heinrich von Ofterdingen* (1802) and Richard Wagner's adaptation of the story for his opera *Tannhäuser* (1845). Moritz von Schwind's frescoes of the Wartburgkrieg on the occa-

sion of the restoration of the Wartburg castle (1854–56) and the oil sketch by Karl Theodor von Piloty for his painting of the contest hanging in the Conference Room of the Bavarian State Parliament in Munich attest to the Wartburgkrieg as a Ger. cultural symbol.

*See* GERMAN POETRY.

■ **Criticism and History**: B. Wachinger, *Sängerkrieg: Untersuchungen zur Spruchdichtung des 13. Jahrhunderts* (1973); H. Wolf, "Zum Wartburgkrieg: Uberlieferungsverhaltnisse, Inhalts-und Gestaltungswandel der Dichtersage," *Festschrift für Walter Schlesinger*, ed. H. Beumann et al. (1973); S. Weigelt, "Johannes Rothes Darstellung der Sage vom Sängerkrieg und ihre Quellen," *Deutsche Sprache und Literatur in Mittelalter and früher Neuzeit*, ed. H. Endermann and R. Bentzinger (1989); B. Wachinger, "Wartburgkrieg," *Verfasserlexikon*, ed. W. Stammler (1999); F. Wenzel, "Textkoharenz und Erzahlprinzip: Beobachtungen zu narrativen Sangspruchen an einem Beispiel aus dem 'Wartburgkrieg'-Komplex," *Zeitschrift für Deutsche Philologie* 124 (2005); B. Kellner and P. Strohschneider, "Poetik des Krieges: Eine Skizze zum *Wartburgkrieg*-Komplex," *Das fremde Schöne: Dimensionen des Ästhetischen in der Literatur des Mittelalters*, ed. M. Braun and C. Young (2007); A. Matthews, "Literary Lives in Medieval Germany: The Wartburg Song Contest in Three Hagiographical Narratives," *Deutsche Vierteljahrsschrift für Literaturwissenschaft und Geistesgeschichte* 84 (2010).

■ **Editions**: *Der Wartburgkrieg*, ed. Karl Simrock (1858); *Der Wartburgkrieg*, ed. T.A. Rompelman (1939); *Parodie and Polemik in mittelhochdeutscher Dichtung: 123 Texte von Kürenberg bis Frauenlob samt dem Wartburgkrieg nach der Großen Heidelberger Liederhandschrift C*, ed. G. Schweikle (1986); *Repertorium der Sangsprüche und Meisterlieder des 12. bis 18. Jahrhunderts*, ed. H. Brunner and B. Wachinger (1986–)—list of mss. and details of strophe transmission.

M. GALVEZ

**WELSH POETRY** has a hist. spanning 15 centuries, from the odes of Taliesin and Aneirin to the odes of the poets who now compete for the chair every year at the Royal National *Eisteddfod of Wales. From Gildas's diatribe on the bards of Maelgwn, king of Gwynedd (d. ca. 547 CE), who used their gift to glorify their king rather than God, we can deduce that theirs was a trad., derived through the Celts from IE peoples, that accorded bards a special role in relation to their rulers because of the magical powers attributed to them. They were expected to call into being and to praise in those rulers the qualities most needed to fulfill their functions, esp. prowess and valor in battle. In short, bards were assigned a sacral role in the life of their people.

While the earliest known Welsh poetry is attributed to poets who flourished in the 6th c., the oldest surviving texts of these poems date from the 13th c., and these necessarily reflect a long hist. of oral transmission and adaptation by generations of reciters and scribes. Poetry composed from the beginning of the

Welsh lang. to the end of the 11th c. is usually called *Yr Hengerdd* (the Old Song), and its composers are called *Y Cynfeirdd* (the Early Bards). Nennius's *Historia Brittonum* (9th c.) records the names of five 6th-c. Cynfeirdd: Talhaearn (known as *Tad Awen*, "Father of the Muse"), Neirin (or Aneirin), Taliesin, Blwchfardd, and Cian (known as *Gwenith Gwawd*, "Wheat of Song"). Of these, only two—Taliesin and Aneirin—have left works that survive to the present day. Most of the extant poetry written before the death of the last Welsh princes in 1282–83 is preserved in the *Black Book of Carmarthen*, *The Book of Aneirin*, *The Book of Taliesin*, *The Hendregadredd Manuscript*, and the *Red Book of Hergest*, ms. v. written between ca. 1250 and ca. 1400.

*The Book of Taliesin*, written in the first half of the 14th c., purports to contain the poems of Taliesin, but it is obvious from linguistic and thematic features that several of these works are of later date and relate to a different Taliesin: a legendary figure loosely connected with the 6th-c. poet, who, like Myrddin (Merlin), was credited with magical and prophetic powers by med. Welsh writers. While this mystical and mythological poetry represents a later accretion to the Taliesin corpus, there remains a core of twelve poems, mainly *panegyrics, that have been accepted by scholars as the work of the historical Taliesin. Most of these poems are addressed to Urien, who ruled ca. 575 over Rheged, a realm incl. parts of mod. Galloway and Cumbria.

*The Book of Aneirin* (ca. 1265) opens with the statement in Welsh, "This is the *Gododdin*. Aneirin sang it." The *Gododdin*, originally the name of a people in northeast England and southeast Scotland, is a long poem celebrating the bravery of a war band sent to recapture a stronghold from the English about the year 600 CE, although the date lacks any archaeological backing. The warriors fought and died almost to a man, gloriously but unsuccessfully. Aneirin eulogizes them for the most part individually, so that the poem comprises a series of elegies. The *Book of Aneirin* contains two versions of the *Gododdin*, one (the A text) roughly contemporaneous in lang. with the date of the ms., and the other (the B text) datable on ling. grounds to the 9th or 10th c.; both presumably derive from an older oral trad. that may extend back to the 7th c.

While these earliest works of the Cynfeirdd may have been composed outside Wales, there is a considerable degree of continuity between the poetic trad. of the Britons of southern Scotland and the Britons of Wales, which enabled the Welsh in later centuries to appropriate the poetry of Taliesin and Aneirin as their own. Like later Welsh verse, this poetry was sung to exalt the rulers on whose heroic qualities the survival of the people depended, and it used the same types of poetic embellishments: end rhyme to link lines and, within the line, the repetition of consonant or vowel sounds, a kind of incipient *cynghanedd* (see ODL, RHYME). In any case, there is very little linguistically to distinguish the earliest poetry produced in Wales from that of ancient northern England and southern Scotland, since at such an early date the differences between the various Brit. dialects were not great.

By the middle of the 9th c., Powys, the kingdom adjoining Gwynedd in north Wales, was hard pressed by the Eng. Its struggle is reflected in the work of a bard or school of bards who composed series of linked *englynion* (see ENGLYN) woven round the 6th-c. figure of Llywarch Hen (Llywarch the Old) and the 7th-c. princess Heledd, sister of Cynddylan, prince of Powys. While the narrative voices in these poems are those of Llywarch and Heledd and the events recounted are set in the 6th and 7th cs., the works themselves date from a later period and reflect the emotions aroused by contemp. events on the borders of Powys. These poems are often referred to as the *saga englynion*, since it has been theorized that they represent verse passages extracted from longer prose epics—now lost—that told the tales of Llywarch and Heledd. Such examples of *prosimetra (prose tales with verse inserted at moments of strong emotion or heightened tension) are typical of early Ir. lit., but there is no clear evidence for the existence of comparable sagas in early Welsh lit., and the figures described in these englynion would likely have been familiar to 9th-c. poets and their audiences even if the poems were presented without an epic narrative framework.

The med. Welsh kingdoms found themselves in a state of endemic warfare not only against the Eng. but among themselves. Since they were slow to accept primogeniture inheritance, internecine dynastic feuds were frequent, and in their function as praise poets for the princes, Welsh bards could not fail to be propagandists. Some of them claimed powers of vision and prognostication; in times of dire distress, these took on the role of prophesying victory against the Eng. foe. The most remarkable Welsh prophetic poem, *Armes Prydain* (The Prophecy of Britain), composed about 930 CE, foretold that the Welsh would be joined by the Cornishmen, the Bretons, the Britons of Strathclyde, and the Irish, incl. the men of Dublin (the Danes), to overthrow the Eng. and banish them across the sea whence they had come. Although in the Welsh trad. the legendary Taliesin and the equally legendary Myrddin were the seers par excellence and as such were credited with many anonymous prophecies, internal evidence suggests that *Armes Prydain* was composed by a monk in one of the religious houses of south Wales. Vaticinatory poems appear throughout the Middle Ages and were esp. numerous in the form of *cywyddau* (pl. of *cywydd*; sometimes referred to as *cywyddau brud*, prophetic cywyddau) during the Wars of the Roses.

At one time, it appeared that the Normans would conquer Wales as easily as they had conquered England, but the Welsh rallied and preserved their independence more or less intact until 1282–83. The national revival that secured the survival of the Welsh under their princes manifested itself also in a fresh flowering of poetry. The *Beirdd y Tywysogion* (the Poets of the Princes), sometimes called the *Gogynfeirdd* (the "not-so-early" bards, to distinguish them from their predecessors the Cynfeirdd) sang in much the same way

Taliesin had sung, but they were not content simply to imitate their predecessors; they developed a much more complex poetic style and a more sophisticated system of cynghanedd, sometimes called *cynghanedd rydd* ("free" cynghanedd, to distinguish it from the codified *cynghanedd gaeth* or "strict" cynghanedd that the bards of the nobility later evolved). The meters of the traditional Welsh verse forms also became more fixed and regularly syllabic during this period. The increased attention paid to structure and ornament in the poetry of the Gogynfeirdd reflects the likelihood that they formed a kind of order in which the *pencerdd*, the master craftsman who had won his position in competition, taught one or more apprentices in a school of *ars poetica*. According to some accounts, the function of the pencerdd was to sing the praise of God and the king. Next in order of rank stood the *bardd teulu*, originally the bard of the king's household troops; apparently he was expected to sing to these troops before they set off for battle, but he could also be called to sing to the queen in her chamber. At the bottom of the scale and not accepted as full members of the poetic class were the *cerddorion* or "minstrels," also known as the *clêr*: low-class performers who lacked the bards' professional training and were sometimes criticized for their ribald or satirical verses.

Among the foremost of these Gogynfeirdd were Gwalchmai (ca. 1140–80), Cynddelw (ca. 1155–1200), Llywarch ap Llywelyn (ca. 1173–1220), and Dafydd Benfras (ca. 1220–57). Their range of themes was not large, and their poetry dazzles by the intricacies of its cynghanedd, the superb command of lang., and by the wealth of literary and historical references rather than by any great individuality of thought. If the Gogynfeirdd borrowed their themes and much of their technique from the Cynfeirdd, they succeeded by their ingenuity in elaborating the former and refining the latter, producing poems remarkable for their subtlety of expression. After the defeat of the Welsh princes who were their patrons, they were saved from extinction partly by the resilience of their guild, though mostly by patronage from the newly emergent nobility. It is thus appropriate that the Welsh poets after 1282 are known as the Poets of the Nobility, *Beirdd yr Uchelwyr*.

In the reorganization following 1282, Welsh society finally had to shed its heroic-age features: no wars were allowed, and martial prowess and valor ceased to have their old value. The poets as well as the nobility had to reassess their function, the former becoming more of a craft guild than an order. The *cywydd deuair hirion* superseded the various forms of *awdl* (ode; pl. *awdlau*) as the favorite meter, "strict" cynghanedd took the place of "free" cynghanedd, and entertaining the nobility became more important than exalting it. The effects of foreign influences were mediated mainly by the new religious orders and by a few *clerici curiales*, esp. Einion Offeiriad, whose "bardic grammar" sought not only to impose order on the practice of the poets but to give it a new intellectual framework. Einion's is the earliest extant attempt at a metrical analysis of Welsh poetry. His division of "meters" into the three

categories of awdl, cywydd, and englyn—subject to the modifications by Dafydd ab Edmwnd, who in 1450 arranged the traditional "24 meters" of Welsh poetry into these three classes—remains a fundamental feature of "strict-meter" poetry to this day.

Dafydd ap Gwilym (fl. 1320–50) perhaps owes a great deal of his indisputable brilliance as a poet to the fact that he had inherited the poetic craft of the Gogynfeirdd and was able to adapt it to popularize the new poetic forms of the 14th c. He wrote awdlau in the old style, but by grafting the embellishments associated with them, the system of cynghanedd, on a lower-order verse form, the *traethodl*, he made the resulting *cywydd deuair hirion* into a meter that the new poets of the nobility took pride and delight in using and that won the favor and patronage of the nobility. Because of the popularity of the cywydd form in the 14th to 16th cs., Dafydd and his followers are collectively referred to as the *Cywyddwyr* (cywydd poets). Dafydd addressed cywyddau to his patron Ifor ap Llywelyn (fl. 1340–60), celebrating Ifor's generosity so much that he became renowned as Ifor *Hael* (the generous), henceforth the exemplar of all bardic patrons. But Dafydd's fame rests ultimately on his cywyddau to women and his masterly expression in them of his love of women and of nature.

Dafydd must have recited or sung these cywyddau to small audiences for their entertainment. One of his favorite strategies is to picture himself in a false or undignified situation, making himself the butt of his audience's laughter. Thus, he describes in a cywydd how one night in an inn he tried to make his way in the dark to the bed of a girl whose favor he had obtained by wining and dining her, only to strike his leg against a stool and his head against a trestle table, knocking over a huge brass pan in the process, and creating such a din that the household woke up and began to search for him as an intruder. It was only through the grace of the Lord Jesus and the intercession of the saints, he tells us, presumably with tongue in cheek, that he escaped detection, and he begs God for forgiveness. But Dafydd describes such situations with such wit, invention, verbal dexterity, and technical skill that one must conclude that the audience's enjoyment of the theme was secondary to its enjoyment of the expression and that the poet's extensive use of *\*dyfalu* (hyperbolic metaphor), *sangiadau* (poetic asides), and other complex ornamentation presumes a high degree of literary appreciation on the part of his listeners.

It was inevitable that Dafydd ap Gwilym should set the stamp of his poetry on that of his younger contemporaries and immediate successors and that, once the shock of his originality and exuberance had been absorbed, the trad. should reassert itself, albeit in modified form. The poets retained their guild organization, their way of transmitting knowledge of the poetic craft, and sundry privileges. But they and their patrons had become aware of the world outside Wales—the influences of the Hundred Years' War must not be underestimated—and some at least had become conscious that the eulogies that Welsh poets produced for their patrons could be interpreted as sycophancy. A poet of strong conscience, such as Siôn Cent in the first quarter of the 15th c., could not fail to feel this tension, and his vivid pessimism and gloomy *Weltanschauung* made him condemn the traditional Welsh muse as deceitful and proclaim his own as the "true" or Christian muse. But Siôn Cent had few followers. The bardic institution was strong enough to withstand his influence, as well as the disastrous effects of the Owain Glyndŵr Rebellion and the Black Death.

Indeed, there is evidence that, contrary to expectation, Wales shared, albeit to a lesser extent, the prosperity that England enjoyed in the 15th c. The Black Death seems to have put greater wealth in the hands of fewer people, and the poets shared in the new prosperity of their patrons. The result is that the century 1435–1535, the *grand siècle* of Welsh poetry, is remarkable not only for its large number of poets but for the very high standard achieved by many of them. The poets were sufficiently self-confident to assemble in eisteddfodau—first in Carmarthen (about 1450) and then in Caerwys (1523)—to make improvements in the rules of meter and cynghanedd. Dafydd ab Edmwnd is the poet esp. associated with the first eisteddfod, and Tudur Aled with the second, but other great names are not lacking: Dafydd Nanmor, Guto'r Glyn, Lewis Glyn Cothi, and Gutun Owain. Such poets (and the work of many has survived) broadened the themes of praise to include the more domestic and civilized: dynastic marriages, well-built mansions with gardens, excellent table fare, and material as well as cultural wealth. Although Middle Welsh strict-meter poetry was almost exclusively a male domain, at least one female poet, Gwerful Mechain (fl. 1462–ca. 1500), left a significant corpus of verse and participated in *ymrysonau* (poetic debates, conducted in verse) with her male colleagues (see YMRYSON).

After 1282, perhaps the most important date for Welsh poetry is 1485, the year Henry VII acceded to the throne of England, though the implications of that event became apparent only gradually. Under the Tudor dynasty, the Welsh nobility found greater opportunities for advancement in England, so that many of them abandoned their role as patrons of the Welsh muse. And there were a number of others whose contact with the Reformation and the Ren. made them eager to bring their native culture into line with that of England and the continent. This meant that Welsh poets should abandon their guild organization, make the secrets of their craft accessible to the general public, and, more important still, assimilate the new learning proffered by the recently invented printing press, esp. knowledge of the art of rhet. Above all, a purpose other than praise, particularly unwarranted praise, had to be found for the Welsh muse.

Most of these points were raised in the famous *ymryson farddol* (poetic debate) of 1580–87 between Archdeacon Edmwnd Prys and the poet Wiliam Cynwal and in an open letter that Siôn Dafydd Rhys addressed to the poets in 1597. Some efforts were indeed made to help the Welsh poets adjust to the new circumstances:

descriptions of the Welsh poetic art and handbooks of rhet. were published. Of special interest is the description of the poetic art published by Dr. Gruffydd Robert of Milan, a Roman Catholic in exile: he advocated a relaxing of the rules of "strict" cynghanedd and the adoption of the "free" accentual meters for epic poetry. But it was extremely difficult to abandon a poetic trad. and practice that had endured for a thousand years, and very few Welsh poets found it possible to take up the new learning. Deprived of patrons, the poets found themselves devoid of incentive either to teach or to learn the art that hitherto had been handed down from generation to generation. Grufydd Phylip of Ardudwy, who died in 1666, was the last of the "old" or professional poets. Henceforth their art was to be kept alive by amateurs drawn from the clergy or the ranks of the gentry. By the end of the first quarter of the 18th c., the old poetic trad. seemed dead.

In some mss. written after 1550, poems in free accentual meters began to appear side by side with poems in the strict (syllabic) meters. There is no reason to suppose that the free accentual meters had not previously been used; however, it would seem that they were not at first considered worthy enough to be copied into ms. collections with the more professional strict-meter poems. Their presence in increasing numbers implies that they were becoming more esteemed. It is usual to distinguish two kinds of free accentual meters, one old and native, the other new and borrowed, although some of the embellishments of the strict meters were added to both. The newly borrowed accentual meters were based on those of Eng. songs set to popular airs. There is, for instance, a Welsh ballad dated 1571 to be sung to the tune "Adew my Pretie Pussie." The practice of composing Welsh lyrics to musical airs, native and borrowed, continued throughout the 18th and 19th cs. and persists to this day.

In the quatrains of the *hen benillion* (literally, "old verses" or "old stanzas") that have been preserved orally and are sung to the accompaniment of the harp, we may find traces of a more indigenous trad. of Welsh verse in free meters. Sometimes several stanzas are strung together and deal with one theme, but generally the hen benillion consist of single verses. Some are strongly didactic, functioning as verse proverbs; most give expression to familiar feelings with varying degrees of literary artifice. Of anonymous authorship, they have been kept alive for their didactic and entertainment value and have been collected and preserved since the 16th c. The best-known collection is T. H. Parry-Williams's *Hen Benillion* (1940), and Glyn Jones has produced many fine Eng. trans. Dafydd Johnston notes that many of the hen benillion "project a female point of view" and suggests that this verse form may have provided an outlet for women poets excluded from the "male-dominated" world of Welsh strict-meter poetry.

Wales experienced two revivals in the 18th c.: one religious, the other literary. The religious or Methodist revival is important in the hist. of Welsh poetry, indirectly because it helped to extend literacy among the people by encouraging Bible reading and directly because it gave an impetus to the composition of hymns and hence to other kinds of poetry as well. William Williams, "Pantycelyn" (1717–91), wrote a long poem, *Theomemphus*, in which he describes the spiritual experiences of a soul caught up in the Methodist revival, as well as hundreds of hymns. Pantycelyn has every right to be regarded as the father of the mod. Welsh lyric. A later hymn-writer, Ann Griffiths (1776–1805), rivals him in the emotional intensity of her expression, if not in the extent of her poetic output. Unlike Pantycelyn, Griffiths never published any of her hymns during her lifetime, and most of her surviving work consists of verses reconstructed from memory by Ruth Evans, a maidservant who heard Ann sing them.

The literary revival is associated with the "Morrisian" circle, whose leading members—Lewis Morris (1701–65), Goronwy Owen (1723–69), and Evan Evans ("Ieuan Fardd," 1731–88)—were not only poets but scholars and, as such, drew much of their inspiration from the contemp. Eng. literary scene. The Ossianic productions of the Scot James Macpherson had stimulated general interest in the ancient popular lits., and the Morrisian circle was eager to demonstrate the antiquity of the Welsh poetic trad. Evans, their finest scholar, searched for material in the libraries of the landed gentry. Though most of the material he collected remained unpublished, his *Specimens of the Poetry of the Antient Welsh Bards* (1764) marked an important milestone in the rediscovery of the Welsh poetic trad. It also anticipated the publication of the *Myvyrian Archaiology of Wales* in three volumes, of which volume 1 (1801) was until mod. times the only printed source for the texts of the work of the Cynfeirdd and the Gogynfeirdd.

Goronwy Owen, the Morrisian circle's most accomplished poet, was so enamored with the Welsh strict-meter trad. that he could not bring himself to call anything else poetry. He was prepared to accord every praise to John Milton's compositions, but since they were not written in cynghanedd, he could not call them poetry. Yet at the same time he was too much of a cl. scholar not to accept that the most significant poetic genre was the heroic epic. Much to his disappointment, the Welsh poetic trad. could not boast a heroic epic in strict meter. This deficiency he attempted to supply by writing *Cywydd y Farn Fawr* (The Cywydd of the Great Judgment); he also left a legacy of critical ideas, esp. the principles that poetry should follow strict rules of composition and that it could be judged according to criteria derived therefrom.

Edward Williams (1747–1826), a stonemason from the *Morgannwg* (Glamorgan) region in southern Wales, better known by his bardic name "Iolo Morgannwg," was another of the chief architects of the Welsh revival of the 18th and early 19th cs. Although today he is largely remembered as a forger and a laudanum addict, Iolo was also a prolific writer and an autodidact who had gained an encyclopedic knowledge of the bardic trad. and Welsh strict-meter poetry from studying the great ms. collections of 18th-c. Wales. He contributed

to the production of the first published ed. of Dafydd ap Gwilym's poetry, *Barddoniaeth Dafydd ap Gwilym* (1789), and was one of the eds. of the *Myvyrian Archaiology*. Unfortunately—much like Macpherson with his Ossian cycle—Iolo was unable to resist inventing material to fill in the gaps in the Welsh bardic trad.: both *Bardd. Dafydd ap Gwilym* and the *M. Arch.* contain numerous forgeries fabricated by Iolo. Determined to prove the primacy of his native Glamorgan in the hist. of Welsh versification, he even concocted an entire system of *mesurau Morgannwg* (Glamorgan measures), which he claimed were older than the 24 cl. meters standardized by the eisteddfod of 1450. Iolo's mastery of Welsh literary forms enabled some of his forgeries to remain undetected for many years after his death, and some 19th-c. Welsh poets even composed verse in his "Glamorgan measures," believing them to be authentic.

The eisteddfodau of the early 19th c. were meetings at which small groups of poets delivered themselves of impromptu verses to test their skill and to entertain a few bystanders. The eisteddfod has since developed in several ways, but even as the range of the competitions held has been extended to include music and the other arts, one feature has remained constant: the highest honor (the "chair") is still awarded to the poet who can produce the best long poem in strict meters. When Goronwy Owen's view that poetry without strict meters was impossible could no longer be maintained, the second highest honor (the "crown") was added to reward the poet who could produce the best *pryddest*, a long poem in the free accentual meters or even in free verse. However, the presupposition for all these poetic competitions remained Owen's tenet that poetry is composed according to certain rules, so that success in following these rules can be measured and judged. On the whole, poems in the strict meters lent themselves better than those in the free accentual meters to this kind of competition: indeed, the two categories invited different kinds of crit. Still, both sorts of poems tend to have common characteristics: they are predominantly objective, impersonal, descriptive, formal in structure, and stylized in diction.

Although Welsh literary culture in the 19th c. had remarkable achievements to its credit, incl. the work of Evan Evans ("Ieuan Glan Geirionydd," 1795–1855), John Blackwell ("Alun," 1707–1840), and Robert Williams ("Robert ap Gwilym Ddu," 1766–1850), it had no firm base in a well established educational system. Schooling did not become compulsory until the end of the century, and even then only scant attention was paid to the Welsh lang. One of the results was a curious lack of self-confidence shown even by the most talented poets: an inability to recognize what they could do best and a failure to persevere and develop it when they achieved success. This is true of Ebenezer Thomas ("Eben Fardd," 1802–63), who wrote the best eisteddfodic awdl of the century in strict meter, *Dinystr Jerusalem* (The Fall of Jerusalem) for the Welshpool Eisteddfod of 1824 and then, dissatisfied with his success in the strict meters, wrote a long mediocre poem on the Resurrection (*Yr Adgyfodiad*) in the free accentual meters.

As a poet, critic, and ed., William Thomas ("Islwyn," 1832–78) concentrated in his mature years on poetry in the strict meters, but his major contribution to Welsh poetry was made as a young man, when he wrote two long poems entitled *Y Storm* (The Storm). They show a young poet struggling to express thoughts and emotions vaguely understood in words only rarely adequate, but they leave the reader with a feeling that, in better circumstances and with more persistence, he could have developed into a finer poet. Islwyn was claimed as the "father" of a group of poets who called themselves the New Poets. They believed that they were breathing new life into the Welsh poetic trad. by eschewing the strict meters in favor of the free accentual meters for long philosophical poems. But the nebulous nature of their thought is betrayed in their equally nebulous lang., which is often extremely bombastic.

John Morris-Jones (1864–1929) had a clearer vision than the "New Poets" of what was needed and undertook the task of restoring the literary standards of cl. Welsh. By emphasizing the entire span of the Welsh poetic trad. from its beginnings, he was able to reveal its greatness and to uncover some of the forgotten secrets of the prosody underlying that greatness. As a professor and author of both the standard grammar of the lang. and the definitive description of its prosody, his authority was unassailable; but he was also a successful poet in both strict and free meters and, hence, a constant adjudicator at the national eisteddfodau of his time. He took the Welsh nation to school. And he was fortunate in his brilliant disciples, some even more generously gifted at poetry than he. His influence is most obvious in the work of T. Gwynn Jones, W. J. Gruffydd, and R. Williams Parry. The next generation of poets—T. H. Parry-Williams, D. Gwenallt Jones, Waldo Williams, and Saunders Lewis—also benefited from his work on the lang. but developed their own ideas of poetic diction and form. Although many mastered the art of the strict meters, their most outstanding contributions have been in the free accentual meters. Some, notably Euros Bowen, have developed *vers libre in which a form of cynghanedd is almost essential. Euros Bowen, Bobi Jones (R. M. Jones), and Gwyn Thomas are among the most prolific, most diverse, and most significant poets of their generation.

Under the leadership of strict-meter poets like Alan Llwyd, Dic Jones, T. Arfon Williams, and Gerallt Lloyd Owen, the period since 1970 has witnessed a remarkable increase in the popularity of traditional verse forms among the younger generation of Welsh poets. This is perhaps because television and radio have provided a platform for poetry as entertainment. Teams drawn from the Welsh counties compete with each other in composing poems in the strict meters, the cywydd, the englyn, as well as lyrics in the free accentual meters; their meetings are recorded for broadcast, and successful teams compete again at the National Eisteddfod in *Y Babell Lên*, the Literary Pavilion. Such has been the success of these meetings that a Strict Meter Society

(*Cymdeithas Cerdd Dafod*) has been established with more than a thousand members, publishing a periodical called *Barddas* as well as volumes of poetry and lit. crit. As a revitalized strict-meter poetry reaches a growing and receptive audience in Wales, poets like Menna Elfyn and Einir Jones continue to expand the horizons of Welsh lit. with innovative works in free meters and vers libre, while other writers like Iwan Llwyd successfully cross back and forth between the two trads.

*See* BRETON POETRY; CELTIC PROSODY; IRELAND, POETRY OF; POETIC CONTESTS.

■ **General:** C. Donahue, "Medieval Celtic Literature" in Fisher; R. Bromwich, *Medieval Celtic Literature* (1974); *Llyfryddiaeth Llenyddiaeth Gymraeg*, ed. T. Parry and M. Morgan (1976); G. O. Watts, "Llyfryddiaeth Llenyddiaeth Gymraeg," *BBCS* 30 (1983).

■ **Anthologies:** *Poems from the Welsh* (1913), *Welsh Poems of the 20th Century* (1925), both ed. H. I. Bell and C. C. Bell; *The Burning Tree* (1956), *Presenting Welsh Poetry* (1959), both ed. G. Williams; *Oxford Book of Welsh Poetry*, ed. T. Parry (1962); *Medieval Welsh Lyrics* (1965), ed. J. P. Clancy; *The Gododdin*, ed. K. H. Jackson (1969); *The Earliest Welsh Poetry*, ed. J. P. Clancy (1970); *The Poetry of Llywarch Hen*, trans. P. K. Ford (1974); *Dafydd ap Gwilym: A Selection of Poems*, ed. R. Bromwich (1982); *Dafydd ap Gwilym*, trans. R. M. Loomis (1982); *20th-Century Welsh Poems*, ed. J. P. Clancy (1983); *Welsh Verse*, ed. T. Conran, 2nd ed. (1986)—long intro. and useful appendices; *Cyfres Beirdd y Tywysogion*, 7 vols., ed. R. G. Gruffudd et al. (1989–96); *Early Welsh Saga Poetry*, ed. J. Rowland (1990); *Cyfres Beirdd yr Uchelwyr*, 36 vols., ed. A. P. Owen et al. (1994–2007); *A People's Poetry: Hen Benillion*, trans. Glyn Jones (1997); *The Bloodaxe Book of Modern Welsh Poetry*, ed. M. Elfyn and J. Rowland (2003); *Welsh Women's Poetry 1460–2001*, ed. K. Gramich and C. Brennan (2003); *Legendary Poems from the Book of Taliesin*, ed. and trans. M. Haycock (2007).

■ **Criticism and History:** H. I. Bell, *The Development of Welsh Poetry* (1936); G. Williams, *An Introduction to Welsh Poetry* (1953); Parry, *History*; R. Bromwich, *Aspects of the Poetry of Dafydd ap Gwilym* (1986); B. Jones and G. Thomas, *The Dragon's Pen* (1986); H. Fulton, *Dafydd ap Gwilym and the European Context* (1989); *The New Companion to the Literature of Wales*, ed. M. Stephens (1998); *A Guide to Welsh Literature*, 7 vols., ed. O. H. Jarman, G. R. Hughes, R. G. Gruffydd et al. (1992–2003).

■ **Prosody:** J. Loth, *La métrique galloise*, 2 vols. (1900–2), but see the rev. by Morris-Jones in *ZCP* 4 (1903), 106–42; Morris-Jones—still useful, indexed by G. Bowen, *Mynegai i Cerdd Dafod* (1947); E. I. Rowlands, "Introduction" to *Poems of the Cywyddwyr* (1976); R. M. Jones, "Mesurau'r canu rhydd cynnar," *BBCS* 28 (1979); A.T.E. Matonis, "The Welsh Bardic Grammars and the Western Grammatical Tradition," *MP* 79 (1981); "Appendix on Metres," *Welsh Verse*, 2nd ed. (1986); *The New Companion to the Literature of Wales*, ed. M. Stephens (1998); M. ap Dafydd, *Clywed Cynghanedd* (2003); A. Llwyd, *Anghenion y Gynghanedd* (2007).

J.E.C. WILLIAMS; B. BRUCH

**WELSH PROSODY.** *See* CELTIC PROSODY.

**WEST INDIAN POETRY.** *See* CARIBBEAN, POETRY OF THE.

**WHEEL.** *See* BOB AND WHEEL.

**WIT.** *Wit* first entered the Eng. lang. via the Anglo-Saxon *ge-witan* (to know), although its original derivation (from the IE *wid-*) suggests a provenance of far greater antiquity. From before *Beowulf* until after Chaucer, *wit* or *wits* referred to the rational faculties: intelligence, consciousness, wisdom. In the 16th c., however, cl. learning and humanism designated a new definition for the word: *wit* indicated not simply the ability to know something but, more precisely, the kind of thing that was known: i.e., it came to specify a particularly *literary* skill, the verbal dexterity that characterized the "good wit" of the Shakespearean clown. In their Lat. puns and learned wordplay, Erasmus and Thomas More exemplified the Ciceronian skill of winning an audience over by means of an intelligent and well-placed joke, so that, when 16th-c. translators and commentators praised their "wit," it referred not simply to their knowledge but to their jesting expression. This verbal play, moreover, had a profound philosophical rationale, for it followed the method of Socratic *irony whereby the very errors of the human mind were used to access the truth that was presumed to lie behind them. Puns and double meanings might appear to show the inefficiency of human lang., but the joke that came of putting two apparently unrelated homophones together (e.g., More and *Encomium Moriae*, *The Praise of Folly*) suggested an underlying semantic connectedness. However far lang. might have fallen from an originally ideal state, every word was understood to refer, ultimately, to a foundational truth or God-given *Logos*. Thus, the name play, multilingual puns, and folk etymologies in *The Faerie Queene* demonstrate what Craig called the "secret wit" of Edmund Spenser's lang.: the belief that such apparently fortuitous ling. coincidences were in fact redeemed by the deeper meaning that their interconnectedness revealed. What Philip Sidney called our "erected wit" represented all that was godlike in the human being—the spark that inspired Neoplatonists to divine the mystical secrets that lay behind the surface of the universe. Equally, however, such wit was inseparable from our "infected will," so that the same quality that vaulted human beings heavenward threatened to make connections that were at bottom illusory or false.

These alternatively positive and negative estimations of *wit* persisted but, in the 17th and 18th cs., the force of the contrast increased dramatically. This was a direct consequence of the great epistemological revolution during which knowledge—formerly perceived as something God-given and presupposed—came to be reconceived as a field of possibility and probability to be deduced empirically and proved scientifically. In Foucauldian terms, the period marked a shift in *epistemē* from the age of similitudes to an age of signs (see SIGN, SIGNIFIED, SIGNIFIER). The old sense that meaning had inhered within the universe as a transcendental presence to be patiently uncovered gradually gave way to a sense that words were mere representations. What followed was an extraordinary devel. in the understanding of *wit*: an explosion of new meanings, definitions, confusions, and redundancies, in response to which Alexander Pope's plaintive question—"What is this Wit, which must our cares employ?"—could be taken as indicative. The 17th and 18th cs. are often designated the Age of Wit, not because this now key word then stabilized but rather because, bearing the brunt of the period's great paradigm shift, *wit* was in crisis.

Allowing for obvious areas of overlap, the history of *wit* during this crucial period reveals that the word responded to this shift in three broadly different ways. The first of these was an initial resistance to change. In the first half of the 17th c., a renewed emphasis on mystical similitudes became evident in the devel. of the retrospectively but aptly named "metaphysical" wit (see METAPHYSICAL POETRY). Treatises by Counter-Reformation Jesuits such as Baltasar Gracián and Emanuele Tesauro and poems by the so-called metaphysicals strove to perpetuate the belief that wit constituted the apprehension of divine truths. This understanding of *wit* remained essentially a poetics of the Word, for, albeit in different ways, each of these writers conceived of the universe as the supremely witty production of a poetic Creator. The sometimes bizarre or outlandish comparisons that the metaphysicals were later accused of producing—the result of their determination to see similitudes in dissimilar things—could be argued to reflect the strain of trying to keep alive an intellectual paradigm that was already on its way out.

The second response to the new epistemology was a readiness to accept its potentially radical implications but only under essentially conservative conditions. On the one hand, lang. was effectively being liberated from the old order of similitudes, which, in the light of empirical science, were beginning to look increasingly antiquated, quaint, and (to use Samuel Johnson's word) "occult." On the other, if lang. was no longer presumed to be grounded in some prior truth, what was there to guarantee its meaning? Unmoored from Logos, the verbal connections that lang. randomly threw up threatened to be arbitrary indeed, and wit ran the risk of being mere surface play. The response to this dilemma was an attempt to have it both ways: to enjoy the newly liberated power of wit (still prized as the supreme exercise of human creativity and as the enemy of its dreaded opposite, dullness) while at the same time strictly to regulate and monitor that power, subjecting it to the scrutiny of a second, more sober agency. This uneasy compromise—heir to earlier 16th-c. anxieties—found its classic expression in the period's most famous debate: wit vs. judgment. John Locke spoke for many when he declared that, while wit made connections "wherein can be found any resemblance or congruity," judgment lay "quite on the other side, in separating carefully, one from another, ideas . . . thereby to avoid being misled by similitude."

The third response followed on logically from the second but developed an altogether more pessimistic assessment that was to have serious consequences for the future history of *wit*. It began to be acknowledged that, if lang. was an arbitrary system of reference, verbal connections could still be made, regardless of whether they made sense or had any truth-value. Whatever steps "judgment" might take to try to ward off the danger, wit was still capable of escaping its containment. The result was an attempt to come down on the term more heavily than before. An increasingly moralized narrative developed in which *wit* came to be characterized negatively as a rogue element that badly needed to be quarantined, condemned, and if necessary declassified altogether. Thus, the kind of wit that persisted in making trivial and purely external connections was said not to be wit at all but, rather, "false wit," a low form that, in Joseph Addison's famous distinction, evoked merely "the similitude in Words." "True wit," by contrast, was worthy of the name because it preserved the sense that lang. was a vehicle for truth and thereby promised to rescue meaning from the abyss.

For *wit* to remain "proper" and "true" in this period, it increasingly had to be linked to judgment, the result being (somewhat ironically) that it ceased to be wit at all. Thus, by the 19th c., the apprehension of presence, of the *sublime, of a divine order of things (what had been wit in the 16th and early 17th cs.) became, for the romantics, judgment. Meanwhile "mere wit" could be reduced—as it was, e.g., by William Hazlitt—to "some casual and partial coincidence which has nothing to do . . . with the nature of things."

*Wit* would have remained languishing in this depleted condition had it not been for the radical movements in philosophy and aesthetics that developed toward the end of the 19th c. Nothing less than the death of God, a dedicated assault on "inner" truth, and a profound scepticism toward the powers of the rational mind would be capable of lifting *wit* up from the depths to which it had sunk. The future of *wit* lay with Friedrich Nietzsche's philosophy, with Oscar Wilde's cult of insincerity, and with Sigmund Freud's book on jokes. However, it was not until the age of Fr. deconstruction and *différance*, when Saussurean ling. asserted that signification was predicated not on presence but on absence and difference, that the potential liberation first glimpsed by 17th c. epistemology came to be realized fully. This is why the revival of interest in the wit of metaphysical poetry in the 1920s turned out to be a false lead, for the attempt to resuscitate the Logos was no less of a dead end then than it had been in the 17th c. Instead, *wit*'s future lay with the thorough discrediting of such logocentric theology, for, with Samuel Beckett's pronouncement in *Murphy* that "In the beginning was the pun," the old reverential poetics of the Word came definitively to an end. No longer bound by the pseudoethical belief that lang. served the higher purposes of communicating a prior, God-given meaning, writers (of philosophy, as well as of fiction) found themselves free to follow what Culler styles "the call of the phoneme": able to revel in new verbal connections. Never before had wordplay so manifestly been word

*play* as such: something that could be enjoyed for its own sake; that, no longer bearing the weight of ulterior motive, could afford to be unbearably light; and that could induce, at its best, an intoxicating joy, a Nietzschean gaiety or the (more typically Fr.) "pleasure of the text." With *postmodernism, *wit* enjoyed more license than it ever had before. If any period has claims to be an "age of wit," then perhaps it is this.

*See* AGUDEZA, BAROQUE, INVENTION, RENAISSANCE POETICS.

■ W. G. Crane, *Wit and Rhetoric in the Renaissance* (1937); W. Empson, *The Structure of Complex Words* (1951); M. A. Goldberg, "Wit and the Imagination in Eighteenth-century Aesthetics," *JAAC* 16 (1957); C. S. Lewis, *Studies in Words* (1960); A. Stein, "On Elizabethan Wit," *SEL* 1 (1961); G. Williamson, *The Proper Wit of Poetry* (1961); J. B. Leishman, *The Monarch of Wit* (1966); D. Milburn, *The Age of Wit 1650–1750* (1966); M. Craig, "The Secret Wit of Spenser's Language," *Elizabethan Poetry*, ed. P. Alpers (1967); M. Kundera, *The Joke* (1967), trans. M. H. Heim (1982); M. Roston, *The Soul of Wit: A Study of John Donne* (1974); E. Gilman, *The Curious Perspective: Literary and Pictorial Wit in the Seventeenth Century* (1978); *On Puns*, ed. J. Culler (1988); A. J. Smith, *Metaphysical Wit* (1992); J. Sitter, *Arguments of Augustan Wit* (1992); C. Hill, *The Soul of Wit: Joke Theory from Grimm to Freud* (1993); N. Saccamano, "Wit's Breaks," *Body and Text in the Eighteenth Century*, ed. V. Kelly and D. von Mücke (1994); C. Bates, *Play in a Godless World: The Theory and Practice of Play in Shakespeare, Nietzsche, and Freud* (1999); B. Michelson, *Literary Wit* (2000); R. Lund, "Infectious Wit: Metaphor, Atheism, and the Plague in Eighteenth-century London," *Literature and Medicine* 22 (2003), and "Wit, Judgement, and the Misprisions of Similitude," *Journal of the History of Ideas* 65 (2004).

C. BATES

**WORD-COUNT.** In the 1960s, the Am. poet Robert Francis wrote several poems in a verse form to which he gave the name *word-count*. In his autobiography, Francis later claimed to be the originator of the form. A word-count poem, as he explained it, is one in which every line has the same number of words. This is the only stipulation of the form: the number of syllables or of stresses in any line may vary greatly, depending on what words the poet has chosen. Although Francis usually arranged his word-count poems in stanzas, the form does not appear to require this. When Francis's lines are longer, as in "Dolphins," the form is not easy for readers to identify; in a shorter-lined poem like his "Icicles," it is more visually apparent.

Since the 1960s, other Am. poets have occasionally experimented with word-count. Whether they borrowed the concept from Francis or happened upon it independently is uncertain. Examples, generally brief, may be found in the work of May Swenson ("Four-Word Lines"), A. R. Ammons ("Chasm," "Mirrorment," and others), and Jonathan Williams (the sequence "Meta-Fours"). Extending Francis's strategy, a word-count poem featuring a recurring pattern of longer and shorter lines is eminently possible. "The Red Wheelbarrow," by W. C. Williams, written decades before Francis's pieces, is such a poem (each of its stanzas has three words in its first line and one in its second). A sustained rhythm may occur in a word-count poem, as it notably does in Louise Bogan's "Train Tune"; but since any such effect is not requisite to the form, it seems best to categorize word-count as a type of *free verse, albeit one displaying an unusual degree of visibly calculated shaping.

■ R. Francis, *The Trouble with Francis* (1971); P. Hoover, "Counted Verse: Upper Limit Music," in Finch and Varnes; J. Williams, note to "Meta-Fours," *Jubilant Thicket* (2005).

R. B. SHAW

**WORK** (Lat. *opus*, Fr. *oeuvre*, Ger. *werk*, It. *opera*, Sp. *obra*). A literary composition viewed as the product of its author or the entire production of a writer (as in "Eliot's work"), though, in most langs., the plural *works* (e.g., *werke*, *opere*, *obras*) is used to suggest collected writings. The term *work* connotes a composition appreciated by educated readers for its superior quality and is often used to enforce a distinction from popular writings. Counterintuitively, for much of lit. hist., the literary work is distinguished from textual productions more obviously marked by labor and the marketplace (i.e., a "work" is not produced to meet popular demand, nor does the artist toil primarily for remuneration)— though this usage changes as professional writers come to dominate literary production.

First used ca. 1300 to signify textual productions, the term *work* became associated with the rise of print culture after 1450. (Only in the 16th c. is the word *work* applied to a painting, sculpture, or other production in the fine arts.) The Venetian publisher Aldus Manutius issued Virgil's *Opera* as his first octavo volume in 1501, and thereafter the poems of Dante and other vernacular poets were often designated as *opere*. Often, in early mod. usage, *work* suggests a literary product resulting from the use or fashioning of a particular material. In one sense, a work may involve lang. being wrought into some desired shape; more often, it suggests the creative adaptation of earlier models (as in Michel de Montaigne, trans. by John Florio, in "Of the Institution and Education of Children"): "So of peeces borrowed of others, he may lawfully alter, transforme, and confound them, to shape out of them a perfect peece of worke [Fr. "ouvrage"], altogether his owne").

Perhaps through its association with the classics and with sacred texts, *work* came to signify a text both learned and timeless (e.g., in Edmund Spenser's *Shepheardes Calender*: "workes of learned wits and monuments of Poetry abide for euer"). As a *work* requires learning and guarantees immortality, accordingly it becomes associated with poetic ambition. One who embodies such "great ambition" is Ben Jonson, whose *The Workes of Benjamin Jonson* (1616) was the first folio in Eng. to contain stage plays. For his audacity, Jonson was targeted in an *epigram: "Pray tell me Ben, where doth the mystery lurk, / What others call a play, you call a work." A friend of Jonson answered: "Bens playes are works, when others works are plays." Here, *work*

signifies what is serious and permanent, with a trace of professionalism. Collecting John Marston's plays into a single volume, William Sheares defends the publication: "I cannot perceive wherein they should appear so vile and abominable, that they should be so vehemently inveighed against. Is it because they are Plays? The name, it seems, somewhat offends them; whereas, if they were styled WORKS, they might have their approbation also." Here, the appellation *work* for a literary production confers cultural stature.

With the rise of the professional writer in the 18th c., *work* changed connotations and came to mean a specimen of lit. produced by labor for pay. Fitting the ironic tone of the era, *work* often was used satirically, as in Henry Fielding's numerous references to "this prodigious work" and "this mighty work" in *Tom Jones*. By the romantic era, however, the elevated sense of the literary work as a kind of secular scripture effaced the term's brief association with commerce. Moreover, the developing esteem for the *originality of the product contributed to a sense of *work* distinct from its earlier association with adaptation. Thus, the mod. sense of *work* contains an expectation of a text more wholly original.

A related, useful term from bibliographic studies is *superwork*, which includes all manifestations and treatments of an original work (incl. performances, adaptations, trans., eds., etc.) along with all texts derived from it (e.g., crit., biblios., etc.).

*See* ARTIFACT, POETRY AS; CANON; POEM; TEXT; TEXTUALITY.

■ G. George, "The 'Work-of-Artness' of a Work of Art," *Queen's Quarterly* 77 (1967); M. Heidegger, "The Origin of the Work of Art," *Poetry, Language, Thought*, trans. A. Hofstadter (1971); R. Poirier, *Robert Frost: The Work of Knowing* (1977); U. Eco, *The Open Work*, trans. A. Cancogni (1989); G. Genette, *The Work of Art*, trans. G. M. Goshgarian (1997); J. Hollander, *The Work of Poetry* (1997); A. Wernick, "The Work of Art as Gift and Commodity," *Experiencing Material Culture in the Western World*, ed. S. M. Pearce (1997); D. E. Palmer, "Heidegger and the Ontological Significance of the Work of Art," *BJA* 38 (1998); W.J.T. Mitchell, "The Work of Art in the Age of Biocybernetic Reproduction," *Modernism/Modernity* 10 (2003); W. Benjamin, "The Work of Art in the Age of Its Technological Reproducibility," trans. E. Jephcott and H. Zohn, *The Work of Art in the Age of Its Technological Reproducibility and Other Writings on Media*, ed. M. W. Jennings et al. (2008); D. H. Hick, "When Is a Work of Art Finished?" *JAAC* 66 (2008)—theories of M. C. Beardsley; see reply by P. Livingston in the same v.; D. Attridge, "On Knowing Works of Art," *Inside Knowledge*, ed. C. Birdsall et al. (2009).

M. TAYLOR

**WRENCHED ACCENT.** The forcing of an accent onto a syllable that is not accented, in order to conform to a meter. The term seems to have been first used by Parsons in his manual *English Versification*. As the name suggests, it is generally considered a sign of faulty technique, as seen in a relatively inexperienced John

Keats's attempt in *Endymion* to wrench "purplish" into rhyming accentually as well as phonetically with "fish." Because wrenched accent would override the standard stress pattern of a word (pur*plish* instead of *pur*plish), wrenched accent asks the reader to let the metrical scheme override the rhythmic impulse of variation, in an extreme way, therefore calling attention to the artifice of the meter. The effect is common in ballads in order to accommodate a melody, as in "Sir Patrick Spens":

> Sir Patrick Spens is the best sailór
> That ever sailed the sea.

However, in premod. poems, what appears to be a wrenched accent may be an older pronunciation of a word. Thus, S. T. Coleridge, rhyming "countree" with "see" in *The Rime of the Ancient Mariner*, harks back to the original pronunciation of "country," which placed the accent on the second syllable. Whether read as wrenched accent or older pronunciation, the technique lends to the effect of the poem's imitation of an archaic folk ballad. Wrenched accent has also been used for ironic or comic purpose, as in the anapestic lines of T. Hardy's "The Ruined Maid," where his exaggerated wrenchings of "la-dy" and "prosperi-ty" characterize the affected manners of the country girl turned kept woman.

*See* ACCENT, METER, SCANSION, SCHEME.

■ J. C. Parsons, *English Versification* (1891); J. B. Esenwein and M. E. Roberts, *The Art of Versification* (1913); E. Smith, *Principles of English Metre* (1922).

W. WENTHE

**XENOGLOSSIA,** also *xenoglossy.* Denotes the intelligible use, through speech, aural comprehension, reading, or writing, of a natural lang. one has not learned formally and/or does not know. It derives from the Gr. *xenos* (foreign or strange), and *glossa,* which, since the time of Aristotle, has referred to speech foreign to the lang. of use or obscure terminology whose meaning is not understood; Quintilian, in *Institutio oratoria,* speaks of "glossemata" as particularly unusual sounds belonging to the "more mysterious language, which the Greeks call *glossas*" *(lingua secretior, quam Graeci glossas vocant),* thereby setting such "glosses" apart from nonsense. *Xenoglossia* and *xenolalia* (Gr., "foreign speaking/babbling"), or the faculty of speaking in human langs. unknown to the speaker, are to be distinguished from *\*glossolalia* (Gr. "speaking, babbling in tongues, glosses"), which refers to the production of lexically noncommunicative utterances, as found in a range of cultural and historical contexts.

The first appearance of xenoglossia in print dates to 1905, when the Fr. physiologist Charles Richet used *xénoglossie* to define the inexplicable experiences of a Madame X, who reputedly wrote long sentences in Gr. while in a trance, without having learned the lang. However, the canonical narrative of xenoglossia in Western lit. reaches back to the Acts 2:4ff., wherein, on the day of Pentecost, the Holy Spirit is said to have descended upon the Apostles of Christ, bestowing on them suddenly the ability to speak in langs. previously alien to them and effectively remedying the confusion of tongues meted out as divine punishment for construction of the Tower of Babel in Gen. 11:5–8. In 1 Cor. 1:12–14, Paul warns that speaking divine mysteries in an unknown tongue requires an accompanying act of \*interpretation, lest speaker and listener be rendered barbarians to one another, making infantile understanding of prophesy. Whether these key biblical passages describe instances of semantically intelligible speech (xenoglossia) or incomprehensible speech (glossolalia) has been the subject of extensive scholarly debate; however, theologians from the time of Augustine onward generally agree that the Pentecostal narrative describes a xenoglossic miracle that would serve as a vehicle for spreading the Christian faith by facilitating the conversion of foreign populations, whereas the polemic of Paul has been understood as a critique of charismatic glossolalia. The ambiguity or traffic between lexical intelligibility and unintelligibility continues to characterize examples and discussions of xenoglossia to this day, setting the practice apart from more syncretic, fluent strains of polylingualism: as Agamben writes, "Glossolalia and xenoglossia are the ciphers of the death of language: they represent language's departure from its semantic dimension and its return to the original sphere of the pure intention to signify."

Later narratives of Pentecostal inspiration such as those contained in the 14th-c. *Actus Beati Francisci et Sociorum Eius* (trans. and adapted into Tuscan It. as *I fioretti di San Francesco d'Assisi*) describe holy men and women who reconcile ling. difference by means of a "marvelous" eloquence in preaching comprehended by listeners of different native tongues. The oral/aural nature of xenoglossia expands to include miraculous literacy in works such as *The Book of Margery Kempe* (ca. 1438), where the ill-written transcription of the protagonist's revelations in a mongrel blend of Eng. and Ger. is miraculously understood and eventually translated into Lat. Such tales of miraculous trans. are thought to evince a yearning for the promise of correspondence between langs., and thereby of erased cultural difference, at moments when literary and scriptural trans. between Lat. and a range of vernaculars was on the rise. Xenoglossia is, in the domain of spiritual experience, what \*macaronic verse is in the domain of satire. Dante's *De vulgari eloquentia* (ca. 1304), which argues (through the medium of Lat.) for an illustrious vernacular in a context of vast ling. confusion, is an early example of a search for the origins of distinct common idioms in an Adamic tongue.

While these historical examples present narratives of xenoglossy, the spontaneous or strategic deployment of unknown tongues becomes a material component of modernist poetries that register the sudden, unruly copresence of previously remote langs. in an environment of increased mobility, mass communication, and urbanization at the turn of the 20th c. The cross-ling. research and contamination pervading \*avant-garde poetries—from \*Dada and \*sound poetry, which appropriated Af., South Pacific, and other "tribal" lyrics, to Rus. \*zaum', with its "transrational" investigation of a lost aboriginal tongue in common, and surrealist automatism (see SURREALISM)—may be read as xenoglossic as opposed to glossolalic insofar as these poetries integrate more or less submerged fragments of human langs., ultimately locating meaning in an elsewhere beyond the conventions of any single dominant idiom, as opposed to negating it. Examples of the literal transposition of tongues unlearned or unknown to a "native" textual fabric range from the mimetic broken Eng. of illiterate immigrants in the poems of Giovanni Pascoli (see, e.g., "Italy—Sacro all'Italia raminga" and "The Hammerless Gun") through the highly orchestrated cosmopolitan montages of Ezra Pound's *Cantos.*

More recently, the term *xenoglossia* has been used to describe the plurilingual, creolistic, and translational strategies of \*postcolonial poetics and poetries of migration and exile. No longer restricted to the domain of the paranormal, irrational, or exotic, the term *xenoglossia* encompasses ling. phenomena increasingly prevalent as texts reflect the incomplete weaving of unlearned or alien langs. into national or "mother" tongues, exemplifying an age of global networking, transit, and dislocation.

■ **Criticism and History**: C. Richet, "Xénoglossie: L'écriture automatique en langues étrangères," *Proceedings of the Society for Psychical Research* 19 (1905-07); E. Bozzano, *Polyglot Mediumship (Xenoglossy)*, trans. I. Emerson (1932); F. H. Wood, *This Egyptian Miracle; or, The Restoration of the Lost Speech of Ancient Egypt by Supernormal Means* (1939); I. Stevenson, *Xenoglossy: A Review and Report of a Case* (1974), and *Unlearned Language: New Studies in Xenoglossy* (1984); É. Glissant, *Poetics of Relation*, trans. B. Wing (1990); G. Agamben, *The End of the Poem*, trans. D. Heller-Roazen (1996); S. McCaffery, *Prior to Meaning: The Protosemantic and Poetics* (2001); M. K. Blasing, *Lyric Poetry: The Pain and the Pleasure of Words* (2006); C. F. Cooper-Rompato, *The Gift of Tongues: Women's Xenoglossia in the Later Middle Ages* (2010).

■ **Primary Texts**: T. Tzara, *Poèmes nègres* (1916); V. Khlebnikov, *Zangezi* (1922); J. Joyce, *Finnegans Wake* (1939); E. Villa, *17 variazioni su temi proposti per una pura ideologia fonetica* (1955); E. Adnan, *L'Apocalypse arabe* (1980); T. H. K. Cha, *Dictee* (1982); Y. Tawada, *Nur da wo du du bist da is nichts/Anata no iru tokoro dake nani mo nai* (1987); E. Torres, *The PoPedology of an Ambient Language* (2007); M. NourbeSe Philip, *Zong!* (2008); C. Bergvall, *Meddle English: New and Selected Texts* (2010).

J. Scappettone

**XHOSA POETRY.** Xhosa is the lang. spoken by a group of peoples who settled along the southeastern coast of South Africa. It is a member of the Bantu family of langs. widely distributed throughout the southern continent and is closely related to neighboring Nguni langs. such as Zulu, Swazi, and Ndebele. Poetry in Xhosa is principally transmitted through the spoken word and the printed word in books and newspapers.

Xhosa oral poetry (*izibongo*) is of one kind: it is praise poetry, commonly found in Africa in forms such as the Yoruba *oríkì*, Bahima *ekyevugo*, or Shona *nhétémbo*. It consists essentially of a set of names that can be expanded into a line or a variable number of lines. The names that form the core of these verses and stanzas can be *metaphors (often drawn from the animal kingdom) or compound names such as Stamps while Fighting (*Lwaganda*) or Watch the Red Dawn (*Jongumsobomvu*) or the names of relatives or ancestors. Nelson Mandela, e.g., is known by the praise name of one of his royal forebears, Madiba, a name that is expanded into the praise verse *uMadiba owadib' iindonga* (Filler who filled gullies), because the original Madiba united the estranged factions of his people. The core praise names, which may be used as alternative names in ordinary discourse, commemorate poetically physical features, actions, or attributes. These units—praise names, verses, and stanzas—are the "praises" that constitute a "praise poem."

Praises may be composed about domestic animals such as dogs, cattle, or horses or about inanimate objects such as motor cars; traditional praise poems about birds once formed a common stock. At various times, praises may be composed by any member of the community about him- or herself or by his or her associates and assembled to form a personal praise poem; there are also traditional poems about clans, which consist of the names and praises of the clan ancestors. Izibongo may be uttered to encourage animals or people, to express pride or gratitude. The clan praises, or the praises of ancestors, may be cited as invocations in ritual contexts. The order of the praises varies from one performance to the next: izibongo are not linear in structure, but are unified in presenting facets, not always flattering, of the subject of the poem. Nor are izibongo explicitly narrative. The elliptical *allusions, often cryptic in their compression, may be clarified by narrative if explanations are sought, but not in the poetry itself: izibongo are a set of shorthand references that encapsulate a person's evolving career or defining qualities or establish his or her relation to others. They are expressions of individual and communal identity.

Izibongo of members of the royal family are performed by men who present themselves as praise poets (*iimbongi*, sing. *imbongi*). They undergo no formal training in poetry, any more than ordinary members of the public do: they appear on ceremonial occasions and are tacitly absorbed into the royal entourage. They are poets of the chiefdom, not appointees of the chief. They wear hats and cloaks of animal skin and carry two spears or clubs. Through their poetry they mold social cohesion, uphold social norms, criticize excess or injustice, and mediate between ruler and ruled. The presence of iimbongi at royal courts is attested by visiting missionaries as early as 1825 and can be documented throughout the 19th and early 20th cs. The greatest of all iimbongi is widely acknowledged to be Samuel Edward Krune Mqhayi (1875–1945), who produced an izibongo in honor of the Prince of Wales on his visit to South Africa in May 1925. During the apartheid period, when many chiefs were co-opted under the government's homeland policy, many iimbongi declined to celebrate illegitimate rulers; but since 1994, the trad. has undergone a resurgence and national recognition, with iimbongi performing at the inauguration of Nelson Mandela as president and appearing in television commercials. Women, formerly barred as iimbongi, now perform poetry in public. An ed. and trans. of the oral poetry of the imbongi Bongani Sitole (1937–2003) was published in 1996, and a biography of the imbongi D.L.P. Yali-Manisi (1926–99), with trans. of his poetry, was published in 2005.

Christian missionaries transcribed and printed the Xhosa lang. for the first time in 1823. In the first decade of the 20th c., they began publishing original works of creative lit., but these books were mainly designed for use in schools. Submissions to mission presses that did not conform to Christian ideology or were considered too political were rejected or bowdlerized. Later commercial publishers were also constrained to satisfy the requirements of government departments, since there was a limited readership for Xhosa books outside educational institutions. Xhosa authors, obliged to censor themselves, were further disadvantaged when the spelling system was revised in 1936 and submissions that did not conform to the new orthography were rejected; this unpopular orthography was revised yet again in 1955. Xhosa lit. in published books is thus skewed, restricted in content and directed at students. It encouraged Western genres such as drama, which does not exist in Xhosa oral trad., and Western forms of poetry. Lyric poetry was solicited for early anthols. and narrative poetry for junior classes; poetry in Western stanzaic structures and rhyme, alien to Xhosa trad., was favored.

The earliest volumes of poetry published under such restrictions were John Solilo's *Izala* (A rubbish heap, 1925) and Mqhayi's *Imihobe nemibongo* (Songs and lullabies, 1927). To bypass the ideological control of the press, eds. and poets occasionally paid for the printing of their own books: W. B. Rubusana (1858–1936) paid for the printing and distribution of his pioneering anthol. *Zemk'inkomo magwalandini* (There go your cattle, you cowards!, 1911), which included the earliest collection of traditional izibongo, now long out of print and available only in an abridged ed. that excludes the poetry; D.L.P Yali-Manisi paid for the printing of his second volume of poetry, *Inguqu* (A return to the attack, 1954), which includes the earliest poem in praise of Nelson Mandela, then under banning orders.

Perhaps the most successful early poet who wrote in a Western mode was J.J.R. Jolobe (1902–76), who published two volumes of poetry, *Umyezo* (The orchard, 1936) and *Ilitha* (The sunbeam, 1959), as well as a volume of poetry for younger children (1952). The dominant poet who wrote largely in the style of traditional izibongo remains Mqhayi. In addition to *Imihobe nemibongo*, he wrote a set of poems about the king Hintsa (1937) and *Inzuzo* (Reward, 1942); his novel *Ityala lamawele* (The trial of the twins, 1914) includes more of his poetry. Michael S. Huna published two epic poems, on the cattle sickness (1966) and on the prophet Ntsikana (1973), while in recent years Peter T. Mtuze has been prominent as an ed. and poet. Poets are now free to adopt Western or traditional style.

Newspapers and jours. in Xhosa were issued by mission presses as of 1837. They sought to encourage contributions from readers but initially accepted poetry only in Western form. This restriction lapsed after 1884, with the appearance of secular newspapers under black editorial control, which served as major vehicles for lit. until the middle of the 20th c. A large proportion of this literary output was in poetry, written by adults for adult readers, free of ideological restrictions. Many poets who contributed to newspapers never subsequently published books; some of the poetry that appeared in newspapers was later included in published books; the vast majority of the newspaper poetry awaits collecting and publication. But it is to this medium that one must turn to find the unrestricted voice of the Xhosa poet in print.

The first generation of poets whose reputations were made in newspapers included M. K. Mtakati (fl. 1880s); Isaac Williams Wauchope (1852–1917); Jonas Ntsiko (d. 1918), who wrote under the pseud. Uhadi waseluhlangeni (Harp of the Nation); and William Wellington Gqoba (1840–88), all of whom adopted Western form. As ed. of the newspaper *Isigidimi samaXosa* (The Xhosa messenger), Gqoba published obituary poems, as well as two long serial poems that for many years remained the most sustained poetic achievements in Xhosa. Presented in octosyllabics as formal debates on education and on Christianity, they included strong expressions of social crit.

As of 1897, Mqhayi began contributing poetry to newspapers, mostly in traditional form, under a variety of pseuds. He is the most prolific Xhosa poet in this medium, publishing poetry regularly until 1944, the year before his death. Hundreds of his poems await republication, though a start has been made with an ed. and trans. of his historical and biographical articles (2009), many of which include poems about people. From 1920 to 1929, Nontsizi Mgqwetho published nearly a hundred poems in a Johannesburg newspaper, the first woman to write Xhosa poetry on a considerable scale. Her poetry is highly critical of ineffective black political leadership and immoral behavior among urban blacks; of white territorial dispossession, political control, and economic exploitation; and of male dominance over women. As a woman, she could not function as an imbongi, nor would her poetry have been suitable for publication in book form; but the medium of the newspaper empowered her and gave her access to her public. Her poetry was collected, translated, and republished in 2007.

■ *Zemk'inkomo magwalandini*, 2d ed., ed. W. B. Rubusana (1911); J. Opland, *Xhosa Oral Poetry* (1983); *Qhiwu-u-la!! Return to the Fold!! A Collection of Bongani Sitole's Xhosa Oral Poetry*, ed. and trans. R. H. Kaschula and M. C. Matyumza (1996); J. Opland, *Xhosa Poets and Poetry* (1998); R. H. Kaschula, *The Bones of the Ancestors Are Shaking: Xhosa Oral Poetry in Context* (2002); J. Opland, *The Dassie and the Hunter* (2005); N. Mgqwetho, *The Nation's Bounty*, ed. and trans. J. Opland (2007); S.E.K. Mqhayi, *Abantu besizwe* (People of the country), ed. and trans. J. Opland (2009).

J. OPLAND

**XUL.** A literary jour., *XUL* began publication in 1981 during the second half of the most repressive era in the hist. of Argentina. The magazine was founded during the military government (1976–83) that resulted in thousands of disappearances and exiles. A challenge to official censorship, the magazine was committed primarily to exploring the poetics and politics of formal experimentation. As Jorge Santiago Perednik, one of the founding editors, wrote in 1982: "*XUL*'s engagement with reality is found in its commitment to language: to again make legible that which has been used for coercion and deception."

The jour. owed its name to Xul Solar, the experimental painter, poet, and philosopher who influenced

Jorge Luis Borges during his formative years. Organized against the backdrop of the colloquial poetry of the 1970s, the jour., published intermittently over the course of 11 issues, shared many of the interests found in the U.S.-based $L=A=N=G=U=A=G=E$ jour. (see LANGUAGE POETRY). There was, however, no direct contact between the contributors of both jours. until the mid-1990s. *XUL* dedicated several issues to displaying a variety of new poets (Arturo Carrera, Roberto Cignoni, Perednik, Néstor Perlongher, and Susana Pujol, among others) and poetics that in many cases were informed by a strong interest in literary theory. The last issue of the jour. was published in 1997.

*See* ARGENTINA, POETRY OF.

■ *The XUL Reader*, ed. E. Livon-Grosman—for a facsimile and archival edit. of all issues, see http://www.bc.edu/research/XUL/index.html.

E. LIVON-GROSMAN

# YIDDISH POETRY

I. Pre-nineteenth-century Verse
II. The Nineteenth Century
III. The Twentieth Century

Yiddish is the lang. of Eastern Eur. Jewry and that culture's offshoots the world over. It is commonly believed to date back at least a thousand years, with its roots in Western Europe. Mod. Yiddish poetry exhibits every subject and technique known in the lits. of Europe and America and derives an extra measure of cosmopolitanism from a readership distributed over five continents. But out of its combined prehist. and hist. of nearly a millennium, only two or three generations have witnessed this unrestricted flourishing. In traditional Ashkenazic culture, it was rather study—the continuous interpretation of basic Talmudic law in the light of changing conditions of life—that absorbed the creative passions of the society. Literary expression in the Western sense was unimportant, and Jewish poetry of the premod. period (both Yiddish and Heb.) is marked, for all its diversity, by a generally ancillary character.

Then, with the revolutionary upheavals in Eastern Eur. Jewry in the late 19th and 20th cs.—urbanization, industrialization, internal migration and emigration, political organization, and eventual civic emancipation, attended by widespread secularization and "Europeanization" of Jewish culture—Jewish poetry in both langs. was lifted to the very top of the cultural values of Jewish culture. It attracted a body of talent that, in previous centuries, would have been otherwise engaged; and, in accordance with the increased receptivity of its writers and readers to outside influences, it quickly managed to catch up with common Eur. accomplishments. Yiddish poetry "in one grand leap landed in the general 20th century" (Harshav and Harshav 1986). Even in its treatment of specifically Jewish themes in an imagery full of traditional allusions, Yiddish poetry became avowedly and factually part and parcel of mod. Eur. and Am. poetic culture.

**I. Pre-nineteenth-century Verse.** The origins of Yiddish lit. have been lost, but early contemp. references to it, as well as the developed poetic technique of the oldest dated works so far discovered (1382), indicate a prehist. antedating the extant evidence. Prior to the 19th c., Yiddish lit., the bulk of which is in verse, was written in an idiom based predominantly on Western Yiddish dialects, a standardized lang. that functioned without interruption until it fell into disuse in Western Europe about 1800 and was superseded by a rapidly evolving new standard based on Eastern Eur. Yiddish dialects. In the premod. period, the influence of med.

Ger., its poetic trads., and a stylistic irradiation from intentionally literal Bible trans. caused the literary Yiddish to be highly stylized, thereby offering only a weak reflection of contemp. colloquial speech.

*Epic poems both of the general Eur. repertoire (King Arthur, Gudrun, etc., with specifically Christian references deleted) and OT themes (e.g., Samuel or the sacrifice of Isaac) are extant in 14th- and 15th-c. recensions that show relatively strict meters and, generally, "long-line" stanza structure of the type *xaxa xbxb*. Scholars originally theorized that much of this verse was meant for oral *performance by professional *minstrels or laymen, esp. since, even after the intro. of printing, the tune was often specified at the beginning or end of a work. More recently, however, strong arguments have been advanced against the so-called *shpilman* theory, positing that the Eur. epics are transcriptions or trans. of Ger. originals, while the works based on Jewish themes (Bible and Midrash) were authored by scribes or other well-educated writers (Shmeruk 1988). This critical revision, however, still awaits further research. In the "post-epic" period (at least since the 17th c.), there is a case to be made for the direct association of Yiddish poetic creativity with contemporaneous modes of public entertainment and performances at weddings or on holy days.

Two 16th-c. verse novels, *Bove Bukh* (1541) and *Pariz un Viene* (1556), strikingly bridge the gap between original Jewish works and borrowed secular ones. The first was composed by Elye Bokher (Elia Levita, 1469–1549) in 1507, and the second either by him or his unidentified disciple. Using It. sources, these works created novels in ostensibly superior versions in which the primary material has been reworked and Jewish elements freely integrated. In addition, Elye Bokher introduced *ottava rima into Yiddish well over a century before it was attempted in Ger. poetry, and he seems to have been the first to use accentual iambs in any Eur. poetry.

The metrical structures of epic poetry were not carried forth elsewhere in Yiddish verse. This is evident in collections of 16th- and 17th-c. popular songs (which reflect a convergence of traditional with current Ger. models), in religious lyrics, in the many verse chronicles and *dirges describing historical events, and in satirical or moralizing *occasional verse, where the meters decrease in regularity until the number of syllables per measure of music varies widely and sometimes grows quite high. Yiddish poetry of early mod. times thus corresponds in its free-accentual basis to most contemp. Ger. verse. Drawing on the Heb. liturgical trad., Yiddish verse sometimes made use of the *acrostic and ornamental extravagances such as making all lines of a reasonably long poem end in the same syllable.

**II. The Nineteenth Century.** Through most of the 19th c., the folk song flourished, and the recitative improvisation, the narrative (on biblical subjects), and the moralizing poem remained productive genres. the Meanwhile, Yiddish lit. made a new beginning, centered this time in Eastern Europe and carried by the emigrations toward the end of the century to England, the U. S., and the far corners of the globe. The new writers were stimulated mostly by the *Haskalah* (Enlightenment) movement, which encouraged familiarity with Eur. (esp. Ger. and Rus.) lit. and made Jewish writers increasingly self-conscious about the underdeveloped state of their langs., Yiddish and Heb., for the purposes of social crit., philosophy, and secular education.

While Heb. lit. toyed with a biblical manner, Yiddish writers explored the cultural framework offered by the folk song, which was noticed at last after a "submerged" existence spanning centuries, during which it was neither recorded nor reflected in lit. The Yiddish folk song favored an *xaxa* stanza and a free-accentual meter (usually four stresses per line) in which, compared with Ger. folk song, the use of unstressed syllables to fill the musical measures was increased, probably as a result of the Slavicized prosodic structure of the lang. However, more Eur. standards of song construction and phrasing introduced more elaborate rhyme schemes (*abab* and *aabccb* became widespread), and strict syllabotonic meters became de rigueur in the theater and in quasi-theatrical songs. The rising labor movement furnished a new public for song verse but also for declamatory verse—an additional factor conducive to regular syllabotonic meters.

In the 1890s, Yiddish poetry hit its stride at last. Though it lagged noticeably behind the devel. of prose—particularly the shorter forms—it now became the vehicle of truly lyrical expression, as exemplified by Shimen Frug (1860–1916, widely credited with introducing syllabotonic prosody into mod. Yiddish poetry), I. L. Peretz (1852–1915), and Morris Rosenfeld (1862–1923). These authors, who had all complained about the lexical and stylistic inadequacy of Yiddish, now laid the foundations of mod. Yiddish poetry by efforts to master a lyrical viewpoint and experiments with a variety of imagery and structural patterns.

**III. The Twentieth Century.** The existence of a new intelligentsia with secular education, some of it acquired in Yiddish-lang. schools, cast Yiddish poetry in this period of its culmination into the mainstream of contemp. world trends. Yiddish lit. now showed itself more sensitive than ever to devels. in other lits. with which it was in contact. Writers had the interest and the formal means to attempt *modernism along Am., Ger., and Rus. lines. At the same time, in the Yiddish poetic culture, there appeared genuine internal responses to innovation. In Russia, Dovid Hofshteyn (1889–1952) introduced some decisive innovations in meter and strophic structures. In America, the group *Di Yunge* (Young Ones, e.g., M.-L. Halpern [1886–1932], Mani Leib [1883–1953], and Zisha Landau

[1889–1937]) early in the century reacted to the political tendentiousness and rhet. of the labor poets by trying to write poetry that would be "more poetic" in diction and subject matter and more individuated in its sentiments.

Dedicated to art for art's sake, the poets of Di Yunge emphasized the expression of aesthetic experience even while supporting themselves as laborers: "Thank goodness I'm not a cobbler who writes poems, / But a poet who makes shoes" (Mani Leib). Di Yunge cherished a vision of Yiddish lit. in which a monolingual reader could be a well-educated world citizen. To this end, they turned some of their energies to trans. and to introducing "exotic" themes, such as Christianity and sexuality, into Yiddish poetry.

Di Yunge called forth the protest of *In zikh* (the Introspectivists), a group (Aaron Leyeles [1889–1966], Jacob Glatstein [1896–1971], and N. B. Minkoff [1893–1958], among others) which, avowedly inspired by Yehoyosh (1872–1927), and influenced by contemp. Eng. and Am. poetry, denied in principle a distinction between the intellectual and the emotional and opened wide the door of its poetry to all themes, all words, all rhythms, no matter how free or regular, so long as they embodied the personal experience of the poet. As expressed in its *manifesto of 1920, the In zikh poets saw no theoretical reason to identify themselves as Jewish artists other than that they were Jews and wrote Yiddish. Moreover, although they accepted syllabotonic meters as a possibility, they were, in fact, convinced that free rhythms were the surest vehicle for achieving poetic truth. Finally, they had no fear of exposing their deepest psychic realities, embracing free association as their chief poetic method.

As the cumulative effect of a growing corpus of poetry made itself felt, the demands for *originality pushed Yiddish poets onto new paths. *Assonance as a substitute for rhyme was explored (e.g., by Alter Katzizne [1885–1941] and Peretz Markish [1895–1952]). *Sonnet sequences and works in the more difficult Romance fixed forms were successfully created (e.g., by Mani Leib). Syntactic *parallelism, etymological figures, and *consonance were mobilized to recreate biblical Heb. effects in a new Jewish medium. Epic poems, verse novels, and verse drama (esp. by H. Leivick [1888–1962]) were produced and acclaimed. Interest in Old Yiddish poetry was awakened, and several writers attempted new works in 16th-c. lang. The poems of Solomon Etinger (1800–56), a forgotten modernist, were published posthumously. The folk song reappeared, but this time in subtly stylized forms (e.g., by Halpern and Itzik Manger [1901–69]).

Post-World War I regional constellations such as the expressionist group *Di Khalyastre* (the Gang) in Warsaw (U. Z. Greenberg [1896–1981], Melech Ravitch [1893–1976], and others) and *Yung-Vilne* (Young Vilna) in Vilna (notably Chaim Grade [1910–82] and Abraham Sutzkever [1913–2010]) set themselves specialized tasks against a common literary background. The sweet awareness of a poetic trad. being formed was reflected in poetic allusions to well-known poems. A standardized literary lang. came into use in which dialectal rhymes became often restricted for conspicuously emotive mood.

In this period, the "discovery of the mother tongue," now emancipated in its functions, was completed. Poets by the scores, following the major writers of the late 19th c., learned to use the Yiddish lang. to its full extent. Yiddish prosodic structure, Germanic but largely reconfigured along Slavic lines (concomitant with mod. Rus. poetry), was employed to create easy triple and even paeonic meters (see PAEON). The refreshing syntax of conversational folk Yiddish was channeled into poetry (notably by Eliezer Shteynbarg, 1880–1932). The pernicious etymologizing approach of the past was dead: words were used according to their precise Yiddish phonology and semantics, without reference to—and sometimes in defiance of—their form and meaning in the stock langs. Sound frequencies typical of a particular component of Yiddish were forged into a new poetic device, making it possible, for instance, to suggest "Slavicness," and hence village earthiness, by an accumulation of $z$ and $c$ sounds (thus, Moshe Kulbak, 1896–1940), or "Germanness" by emphasizing $a$ and final $e$ sounds (e.g., Glatstein).

At the same time, the idiom of traditional Jewish study was annexed to the mod. literary lang.; it found use not only when required by the subject (as in the poetry of Menahem Boreisho [1888–1949], Aaron Zeitlin [1899–1974], or Grade), but in thematically unspecialized writing, where it functions simply as a flexible abstract vocabulary. Above all, the many derivational patterns of Yiddish grammar were exploited for the enrichment of the lang. New coinages abounded, and some, like *umkum* (violent death) and *vogl* (restless wandering), have become common elements of the lang. The poetry of Glatstein and Sutzkever is particularly rich in novel derivations.

With the genocide of six million Jews by Germany and her Axis collaborators, Jewish cultural life in most of Eastern Europe was virtually destroyed; what was left received a second devastating blow through Stalin's ban of Yiddish culture and the elimination of Yiddish writers in the USSR after 1949, culminating in the August 12, 1952, murder of the Yiddish poets Peretz Markish, Dovid Hofshteyn, Leib Kvitko (b. ca. 1890), and Itzik Fefer (b. 1900), among others. The Holocaust of the war years naturally became the central theme of Yiddish lit., not only in the Nazi-made ghettos but globally. After 1948, however, the rebirth of a Jewish state in Israel opened new vistas, descriptive, psychological, existential, and ethical, to Yiddish poetry. Soon, an active Yiddish cultural life rapidly developed in Israel, incl. publication of *Di goldene keyt* (The Golden Chain), the premier Yiddish literary jour. (1949–95), and the establishment of a few Yiddish publishing houses in the late 1950s. Major postwar centers of Yiddish poetry were also in North America, Europe (esp. in France and, until the late 1960s, Poland), and post-Stalin Soviet Union (since the 1960s).

The technical brilliance of Yiddish poetry did not diminish in the postwar period. In its rhythmic features, however, postwar writing seems to have retreated from the experimentation of the previous period. As Leyeles put it, "When there are no bounds to suffering, create, through pain, a ritual fence [i.e., a preventive measure] of rigorously restrained patterning."

What might be called the second generation since the catastrophic events of the Holocaust and Stalinism reveals a shift in the balance of Yiddish verse. Whereas actual poetic production is shrinking, scholarship has reached new levels of sophistication and intensity. This phenomenon is directly related to the decline of the Yiddish-speaking community and, hence, the number of native speakers of Yiddish. Those poets who remained in the final decades of the 20th c., such as Yonia Fain (b. 1914), Rivka Basman Ben-Haim (b. 1925), and Alexander Spiegelblatt (b. 1927) had to contend with the problem of creating in a lang. whose future as a vibrant medium of mod. poetry was at best, uncertain: "During daytime a funeral, at night a concert / And inevitably, I go to both" (Sutzkever). Scholarly research, by contrast, became increasingly active and undertaken more and more by those who are not native speakers of Yiddish. Their work, encompassing a wide variety of perspectives, e.g., historical, social, feminist, psychoanalytic, and comparative, highlights the tremendous vitality of the poetic corpus, even if the number of living poets is small. Among the major outcomes of late 20th-c. studies and anthols. were the greater recognition and appreciation of Yiddish women poets, as well as poets whose work had been ignored out of earlier political considerations.

The turn of the 21st c. witnessed the steep decline of secular Yiddish lit. Since the 1990s, however, a new postwar generation has begun to make its mark, albeit on a substantially reduced scale and often in estranged surroundings. It consists of a drastically smaller and geographically dispersed group of poets born between the 1950s and the 1980s. Their work continues to be published in contemp. Yiddish periodicals, e.g., *Di tsukunft* (New York), *Gilgulim* (Paris), and *Yerusholaymer Almanakh* (Jerusalem).

*See* HEBREW POETRY.

■ **Anthologies:** *Di yidishe muze*, ed. J. Fichman (1911); *Antologye: finf hundert yor yidishe poezye*, ed. M. Bassin, 2 v. (1917); *Yidishe dikhterins*, ed. E. Korman (1928); *Naye yidishe dikhtung*, ed. Y. Paner and E. Frenkl (1946); *Dos lid iz geblibn*, ed. B. Heller (1951); *Mivhar shirat yidish*, trans. M. Basuk (1963)—Hebrew; *A shpigl af a shteyn*, ed. K. Shmeruk (1964)—works of murdered Soviet Yiddish writers; *A Treasury of Yiddish Poetry*, ed. I. Howe and E. Greenberg (1969); *Selected Poems of Jacob Glatstein*, trans. R. Whitman (1972); *Perl fun der yidisher poezye*, ed. J. Mlotek and E. Mlotek (1974); M.-L. Halpern, *In New York: A Selection*, ed. and trans. K. Hellerstein (1982); *American Yiddish Poetry: A Bilingual Anthology*, ed. B. Harshav and B. Harshav (1986); *Penguin Book of Modern Yiddish Verse*, ed. I. Howe et al. (1987)—Yiddish and Eng.; *Early Yiddish Texts, 1100–1750, With Introduction and Commentary*, ed. J. Frakes (2004)—Yiddish; *Proletpen: America's Rebel Yiddish Poets*, ed. A. Glaser and D. Weintraub, trans. A. Glaser

(2005)—Yiddish and Eng.; *Sing, Stranger: A Century of American Yiddish Poetry: A Historical Anthology*, ed. B. Harshav and B. Harshav (2006); *Step by Step: Contemporary Yiddish Poetry*, ed. E. Bemporad and M. Pascucci (2009)—Yiddish and Eng.; *With Everything We've Got: A Personal Anthology of Yiddish Poetry*, ed. and trans. R. Fein (2009)—Yiddish and Eng.

■ **Criticism and History**: L. Wiener, *History of Yiddish Literature in the Nineteenth Century* (1899); M. Erik, *Di geshikhte fun der yidisher literatur* (1928); D. Hofshteyn and F. Shames, *Literatur-kentenish (poetik)*, 2 v. (1928); and *Teorye fun literatur: Poetik* (1930); Z. Reyzen, *Leksikon fun der yidisher literatur*, 4 v. (1928); M. Weinreich, *Bilder fun der yidisher literatur-geshikhte* (1928); Y. Tsinberg, *Di geshikhte fun der literatur bay yidn*, v. 6 (1935); N. B. Minkoff, *Yidishe klasiker poetn*, 2d ed. (1939); Y. Mark, "Yiddish Literature," *The Jews*, ed. L. Finkelstein, v. 2 (1949); N. B. Minkoff and J. A. Joffe, "Old Yiddish Literature," and S. Niger, "Yiddish Literature of the Past 200 Years," *The Jewish People Past and Present*, v. 3 (1952); B. Hrushovski [Harshav], "On Free Rhythms in Modern Yiddish Poetry," *The Field of Yiddish*, ed. U. Weinreich, v. 1 (1954); *Leksikon fun der nayer yidisher literatur*, 8 v. (1956–81); Y. Tsinberg, *Pyonern fun yidisher poezye in amerike*, 3 v. (1956); U. Weinreich, "On the Cultural History of Yiddish Rime," *Essays on Jewish Life and Thought*, ed. J. L. Blau (1959); B. Hrushovski, "The Creation of Accentual Iambs," *For Max Weinreich on his Seventieth Birthday* (1964); S. Liptzin, *The Flowering of Yiddish Literature* (1964); and *The Maturing of Yiddish Literature* (1970); I. Howe, *World of Our Fathers* (1976), ch. 13; J. Hadda, *Yankev Glatshteyn* (1980); D. Goldberg, "The Juncture of Dialect and Rhyme in Yiddish Poetry," *Ha-Sifrut* (1986)—in Heb.; K. Shmeruk, *Prokim fun der yidisher literaturgeshikhte* (1988); R. Wisse, *A Little Love in Big Manhattan* (1988); F. W. Aaron, *Bearing the Unbearable: Yiddish and Polish Poetry in the Ghettos and Concentration Camps* (1990); B. Hrushovski, *The Meaning of Yiddish* (1990); A. Spiegelblatt, *Bloe vinklen, Itsik Manger—lebn, lid un balade* (2002); K. Hellerstein, "Gender and the Anthological Tradition in Modern Yiddish Poetry," and J. Shandler, "Anthologizing the Vernacular: Collections of Yiddish Literature in English Translations," *The Anthology in Jewish Literature*, ed. D. Stern (2004); M. Lev, *Literarishe portretn* (2007).

U. WEINRICH; J. HADDA; D.-B. KERLER

**YMRYSON.** The Welsh noun *ymryson* (pl. *ymrysonau*) is used to describe poetic debates or bardic contests. Most extant med. examples are in the strict-metre *cywydd* form (pl. *cywyddau*), with the longest being the 14th-c. ymryson between Dafydd ap Gwilym and Gruffudd Gryg (containing a total of eight *cywyddau*, four by each poet). The 16th-c. ymryson between Edmwnd Prys and Wiliam Cynwal ran to a total of 54 *cywyddau*. While the origins of the trad. might stem in part from competitions for patronage, little is known about the exact social context(s) in which the med. *ymrysonau* were composed and performed. A legendary dimension is provided by poems attributed to the character Taliesin, an all-knowing supernatural poet whose vic-

tory over Maelgwn Gwynedd's court poets is described in the 16th-c. narrative *Ystoria Taliesin*. Some extant *ymrysonau* contain discussions of aesthetics and bardic learning; e.g., while starting ostensibly as an argument over a broken promise, the ymryson between Prys and Cynwal became a forum for pitting the merits of the new humanist learning against the traditional values of the Welsh bardic profession. However, most med. and early mod. *ymrysonau* are also characterized by—and at times completely dominated by—boasting, belligerent posturing and ad hominem attacks of a bawdy and scatological nature. Parallels can be found in other literary trads., incl. the Scots *flyting and Occitan *tenso*. The term *ymryson* has continued in use during the 20th and 21st cs., and since the middle of the 20th c., it has been applied to Welsh-lang. poetic contests held on radio, television and the field of the National *Eisteddfod*.

*See* EISTEDDFOD, POETIC CONTESTS, WELSH POETRY.

■ A. Matonis, "Barddoneg a Rhai Ymrysonau Barddol Cymraeg yr Oesoedd Canol Diwedd," *Ysgrifau Beirniadol* 12 (1982); *Ymryson Edmwnd Prys a Wiliam Cynwal*, ed. G. A. Williams (1986); *Ystoria Taliesin*, ed. P. K. Ford (1992); M. Davies, "'Aed i'r coed i dorri cof': Dafydd ap Gwilym and the Metaphorics of Carpentry," *Cambridge Medieval Celtic Studies* 30 (Winter 1995); J. Hunter, "Cyd-destunoli Ymrysonau'r Cywyddwyr: Cipolwg ar 'Yr Ysbaddiad Barddol'," *Dwned* 3 (1997): 33–52; D. Johnston, *Llên yr Uchelwyr: Hanes Beirniadol Llenyddiaeth Gymraeg 1300–1525* (2005), esp. 375–400.

J. HUNTER

**YORUBA POETRY.** *See* AFRICA, POETRY OF.

**YUEFU.** The term *yuefu* is not a poetic genre but a label that has been applied retrospectively and inconsistently to a bewildering array of poetic texts related to musical performance over many centuries of Chinese hist. It first appears in the Former Han dynasty as the name of a music bureau, consolidated by Emperor Wu (156–87 BCE) to collect songs from his subjects, compose songs by imperial command, and perform music for court functions. Apart from some ritual hymns and a few pieces of dubious attribution to members of the Han court cited in the *Han shu* (*The History of the Former Han Dynasty*), it is unlikely that any text from this time has survived.

The literate ruling class continued to compose and perform song lyrics under a repertoire of melody titles through the dissolution of the Han and into the Wei and Jin dynasties, from the 1st to the early 4th c. CE. Many of these songs supposedly were performed at banquets by rulers such as Cao Cao (155–220) and his sons, Cao Pi (187–226) and Cao Zhi (192–232), while others are attributed to a group of scholars known as the *Jian'an qi zi* (Seven Masters of Jian'an), which included Wang Can (177–217). Other notable figures were Fu Xuan (217–278), Zhang Hua (232–300), and Lu Ji (261–303). These attributed song texts and a larger corpus of unattributed texts share a repertoire of melody titles and are usually in an irregular meter tending toward a five-syllable line. They overlap significantly with a corpus of attributed and unattributed *gushi* (old poems) in a regular five-syllable line not associated with specific music. Common elements among the corpora suggest that there was a shared repertoire of poetic resources (themes, adopted voices, topics, images, diction, grammar, sequence) that literate people would draw on to compose and perform poetry as the occasion demanded. The song texts from this era are referred to as "northern" and are characterized as having a masculine or martial air with a sense of urgency and an occasional satirical edge.

The Jin dynasty moved its capital to south of the Yangtze river in 317 CE, which led to the succession of the Southern Dynasties lasting to 589. The ruling class came into contact with an indigenous southeastern song trad., *Wusheng ge* (Songs of Wu), performed by singing girls in urban entertainment quarters. These slightly risqué, entertaining songs were brought into the repertoire of the elite, spawning a new wave of song texts, usually in five-syllable quatrain form, composed by men in the voices of women. While some texts are attributed directly to singing girls, such as the "Ziye ge" (Girl of the Night Songs), internal evidence suggests that extant texts were court compositions playing with informal registers. Rulers such as Xiao Yan (464–549) practiced this song form, while his younger son, Xiao Gang (503–51), sponsored *Yutai xinyong* (*New Songs from a Jade Terrace*), a collection incl. hundreds of song texts in this "southern" trad., which is characterized as being feminine and ornate. Some figures, such as Bao Zhao (d. 466), continued writing song texts in imitation of the earlier Han and Wei masculine style, even though the accompanying music had long been lost.

Two imperial anthols. of the 6th c.—the aforementioned *Recent Songs* and *Wenxuan* (Literary Selections), sponsored by Xiao Tong (501–31)—along with works of lit. crit.—such as "Yue zhi" (Treatise on Music) by Shen Yue (441–513) and *Wenxin diaolong* (*The Literary Mind and the Carving of Dragons*) by Liu Xie (465?–532?)—treated the trad. of song texts from the 1st through 6th cs. as a distinct corpus, giving it the label *yuefu* as a loose bibliographical term for a wide range of texts related to musical performance. The anthols. served to fix a lit. hist. for these fluid texts and to fashion a canon of northern and southern yuefu distinct from "old poems." The corpus of yuefu poetry continued to grow, though the term remained highly elastic and of inconsistent application, into the Tang dynasty (618–907), which saw Li Bai (701–62) take the adopted voices of yuefu to hyperbolic heights, and Bai Juyi (772–846) self-consciously fashion "Xin Yuefu" (New Yuefu) as a vehicle for social critique.

The evolution of the term *yuefu* reached its endpoint in the late Northern Song dynasty (960–1127) when Guo Maoqian (12th c.) compiled a collection of 5,500 song texts titled *Yuefu shiji* (Compendium of Yuefu Poetry), in which he attempted to preserve all received yuefu texts from earliest times to his day, grouping them into early folk pieces and later literary imitations, which constitute 80% of the collection. Guo had no direct access to the music, and many of his textual sources are lost or of unknown provenance. Recent scholarship suggests that many of the "original" folk pieces he cites are unattributed song texts by literati attempting to simulate the vitality of song performances that they imputed to earlier times. During the Northern Song, the composition of words to music passed to the more recently established form of poetry known as "lyrics" (*ci*), although the term *yuefu* was still used occasionally. *See* SHI.

■ **Anthologies:** *New Songs from a Jade Terrace*, trans. A. Birrell (1982); *Columbia Book of Chinese Poetry*, ed. and trans. B. Watson (1984); *An Anthology of Chinese Literature: Beginnings to 1911*, ed. and trans. S. Owen (1996).

■ **Criticism and History:** J. Allen, *In the Voice of Others: Chinese Music Bureau Poetry* (1992); C. Egan, "Were Yëeh-fu Ever Folk Songs? Reconsidering the Relevance of Oral Theory and Balladry Analogies," *Chinese Literature: Essays, Articles, Reviews* 22 (2000); R. Cutter, "Poetry from 200 B.C.E. to 600 C.E.," *Columbia History of Chinese Literature*, ed. V. Mair (2001); S. Owen, *Making of Early Chinese Poetry* (2006).

G. SANDERS

**ZAUM'.** A coinage by Rus. futurist poets Velimir Khlebnikov and Aleksei Kruchenykh based on the Rus. adjective *zaumnyi* (beyond comprehension, too complicated to understand) and used by them to name their nonstandard poetic lang. A synonym of *zaumnyi iazyk* (transrational, transsense, metalogical lang., "beyonsense"), *zaum'*, with its soft *m'* (indicated by an apostrophe), was a feminine, more compact nominal neologism covering the concept with a touch of greater abstraction (*za* beyond, outside; *um*, mind, reason, intellect). This poetic lang. was not intended to be meaningless or nonsense; rather, its meaning was indefinite or yet to be established. Kruchenykh adhered more closely to the former idea, while Khlebnikov sought to create new words that would ideally be used to name new and future phenomena with perfect iconic clarity. Before 1913, Khlebnikov had written poems that qualify as zaum' (e.g., "Bobeobi pelis' guby" ["Bobeobi sang the lips"] and "Zakliatie smekhom" ["Incantation by Laughter"], both 1909); but in that year, two of the most famous early examples of zaum' appeared: in March, Kruchenykh's three-part poem "dyr bul shchyl" (untranslatable zaum'; see below) in the collection "Pomada" (Pomade), and in December, the futurist opera *Pobeda nad solntsem* (*Victory over the Sun*), with text by Kruchenykh, prologue by Khlebnikov, and set and costume designs by Kazimir Malevich. Both of these works are considered to be preeminent examples of Rus. cubo-futurism, as distinct from It. *futurism, in which transrational lang. did not figure significantly. Zaum' was further developed by Kruchenykh and Il'ja Zdanevič in Tiflis (present-day Tbilisi) in 1917–21.

Zaum' can be classified by type, depending on the ling. level in which it deviates from norms of the given lang. For instance, semantic zaum' would use standard words in standard forms but combine them in such a way that the meaning is indefinite or absurd; morphological zaum' would use recognizable roots, prefixes, and suffixes in new combinations (Khlebnikov's "Incantation by Laughter" is of this sort, with many neologisms based on the root *smekh* (laughter); phonetic zaum' would use combinations of letters and sounds in which it would be difficult to identify familiar word components. Combinations and borderline cases are common. E.g., "dyr bul shchyl" begins with three monosyllables that have only hints of meaning (*dyr* [hole?]; *bul* [*bulka*, bun]?; *shchyl* [*shchel'*, crevice?]), while the second line, *ubeshchur*, is a combination of three possible interpretants (*ubeshchat'* [to promise]; *ubezhdat'* [to convince]; *chur* [fain, mum]). The third line, *skum*, also has several possibilities (see *scomber* [a fish]), while the final two lines of the first part trail off into syllables and discrete sounds (*vy so bu / r l ez*). The second part talks more clearly about the black tongue of love, while the final part returns to phonetic and

morphological zaum' but, in contrast to the harsh consonant clusters of the first part, is focused mainly on soft, liquid sounds, suggesting that there is an erotic subtext to the work. Nevertheless, the meaning is kept at a level of *indeterminacy akin to abstract art, in which the colors and shapes have an indefinite relationship to the natural world.

Zaum' in the sense of indefinite lang. can be found in the poetry of various eras and peoples, esp. in folklore and children's verse.

*See* NONSENSE VERSE; RUSSIA, POETRY OF; SOUND POETRY.

■ E. Beaujour, "Zaum'," *Dada/Surrealism* 2 (1972); R. Vroon, *Velimir Xlebnikov's Shorter Poems: A Key to the Coinages* (1983); D. Mickiewicz, "Semantic Functions in Zaum'," *Russian Literature* 15 (1984); V. Shklovsky, "On Poetry and Trans-Sense Language" (1916), *October* 34 (1985); G. Janecek, "A Zaum' Classification," *Canadian-American Slavic Studies* 30 (1986); N. Gourianova, "Suprematism and Transrational Poetry," *Elementa* 1 (1994); G. Janecek, *ZAUM'* (1996); N. Firtich, "Rejecting 'The Sun of Cheap Appearances': Journey Beyond 'Zero' with Kručenych, Malevič, Belyj, Jakobson and Jean-Luc Godard," *Russian Literature* 65 (2009).

G. J. JANECEK

**ZÉJEL** (Ar. *zajal*, Fr. *zadjal*). A Sp. poem consisting of an introductory *strophe (known as the *cabeza*), presenting the theme to be developed and followed by strophes each patterned as follows: a monorhymed *tercet, called the *mudanza*, followed by the *vuelta* (repetition) of one line or more rhyming with the introductory stanza. The simplest form of this strophe is the quatrain rhyming *aaab cccb* and so on, the *b* rhyme remaining constant throughout the poem. Multiple variations of this basic form are found. The octosyllable is a frequent line length, though others are also used. The problem of the zéjel's origins is the subject of scholarly debate: colloquial Hispano-Romance, med., Lat., and Hispano-Ar. poetry each have their advocates.

*See* AL-ANDALUS, POETRY OF.

■ P. Le Gentil, "A propos de la 'strophe zéjelesque,'" *Revue des langues romanes* 70 (1949); and *Le Virelai et le villancico* (1954); M. Frenk, *Estudios sobre lírica antigua* (1978), esp. 309–26; E. C. Minkarah, "The Zéjel in Fifteenth-Century Castile," *Fifteenth-Century Studies* 6 (1983); Navarro; V. Beltrán Pepió, "De zéjeles y *dansas*: Orígenes y formación de la estrofa con vuelta," *Revista de Filología Española* 64 (1984); J. T. Monroe, "Poetic Quotation in the Muwassaha and Its Implications: Andalusian Strophic Poetry as Song," *La Corónica* 14 (1986); M. Morras, "¿Zéjeles o formas zejelescas?," *La corónica* 17 (1988); J. T. Monroe, "Which Came First, the Zajal or the Muwaššaḥa? Some Evidence for the

Oral Origins of Hispano-Arabic Strophic Poetry," *Oral Tradition* 4 (1989).

D. C. CLARKE

**ZEUGMA** (Gr., "means of binding"; cf. Gr. *zeugos,* "yoke"). Form of brachylogy in which multiple clauses are governed by a single word, most often a noun or verb. According to Quintilian (*Institutio oratoria* 9.3.62), who calls the figure *synezeugmenon,* the governing word is always a verb (e.g., "Lust conquered shame, audacity fear, madness reason"). The *Rhetorica ad Herennium* (4, 27:37–38) allows for noun governance as well, a construction it labels *diazeugmenon* (e.g., "The Roman people destroyed Numantia, razed Carthage, and overthrew Fregellae").

Later rhetoricians extended the definition of zeugma to the "yoking" together of any two parts of speech by means of any other. Following Quintilian, George Puttenham (*The Arte of English Poesie* [1589], bk. 3, chap. 12) and other Ren. rhetoricians (e.g., Johannes Susenbrotus, *Epitome troporum ac schematum* [1541], and Henry Peacham, *The Garden of Eloquence* [1577]) distinguished three zeugmatic constructions according to whether the governing word precedes the words it governs (*prozeugma*); stands between them (*mesozeugma,* e.g., "Much he the place admired, the person more"—Milton, *Paradise Lost* 9.444); or follows them (*hypozeugma*).

There is little consensus regarding the distinction between zeugma and \*syllepsis. Puttenham argues that, whereas in zeugma the governing word agrees grammatically with each of the governed clauses, in syllepsis, it agrees with only one, thus producing what he calls the "double supply," a semantic sleight-of-hand. What seems clear is that zeugma, unlike syllepsis, requires an ellipsis. Peacham and others (e.g., A. Quinn, *Figures of Speech* [1982], 98) thus view zeugma as the opposite of *hypozeuxis,* in which the governing words are repeated in each clause (e.g., Winston Churchill's "We shall fight on the beaches, we shall fight on the landing grounds, we shall fight in the fields and in the streets. . . ."). Considered in relation to hypozeuxis, zeugma can be seen as an efficient means of emphasis (i.e., it lacks iteration).

Alexander Pope favors the figure, and he frequently employs mixed zeugmas (e.g., "See Pan with flocks, with fruit Pomona crowned" [*Windsor Forest,* 37], which relies on both hypozeugma and prozeugma to produce a \*chiasmus).

■ C. Walz, *Rhetores Graeci,* 9 vols. (1832–36), 8.474, 686, 709; M. Joseph, *Shakespeare's Use of the Arts of Language* (1947); L. A. Sonnino, *Handbook to 16th-Century Rhetoric* (1968); Lausberg, sect. 702–7; Vickers.

C. H. MOORE

## ZULU POETRY

Zulu (*isiZulu*) poetry has developed from oral to written form. Traditional Zulu poetic genres consist of oral praise poems called *izibongo,* the most important and influential of the traditional forms, which include clan praises (*izithakazelo*), lullabies (*imilolozelo*), and folk songs (*amaculo*).

Characteristics retained in mod. Zulu poetry reflect the influence of the praise poem. Compositional techniques can be divided into external and internal. External characteristics refer to sentences, e.g., oppositions and patterns of repetition; and to stanza construction, e.g., two lines, three lines, or more than three lines. Internal characteristics refer to the content, esp. to the various figures of speech (*izifengqo*) and imagery.

**I. Verse Structure.** Traditional Zulu poets could not have had any idea of verses. Their poetry knew no structural appearance of poetry as we know it today. The division into verse structure was introduced by the mod. poet when he or she tried to commit the oral poem to paper, and the idea of the length of each line must have been based on formulas (see ORAL-FORMULAIC THEORY, ORAL POETRY). This loose style of the praise poem generally has been referred to as poetry composed in lines without patterns of rhyme and meter.

Zulu traditional poems, esp. praise poems, are composed in lines that are based on the stresses resulting from the meaning of the line and its natural and punctuated pauses. Intonation is important in Zulu praise poems because Zulu is a tonal lang., like most Af. langs., and it is difficult to apply Eng. structural patterns to it. Various types of repetitions are characteristic of Zulu poetry. Rhythm in Zulu results from a particular patterning of the sounds of words in a line that reflects the poet's use of emphasis and tempo as well as stressed and unstressed syllables. Some elements of verse structure are:

(1) *Apostrophe, or honorific address.* E.g., in *UMenzi kaNdaba!* (He is Menzi [the Doer]), son of Ndaba!), King Senzangakhona, father of King Shaka, is praised as a descendant of King Ndaba and also as a member of the royal family. An \*apostrophe is often formulated in relationship to someone else, esp. important members of the family.

(2) *Simile and Metaphor.* \**Simile* involves using comparative words, such as *njenga* (like), *nganga* (as), *kuna* (than):

> UBhid' elimathetha ngezinyembezi
> Linjeng' elikaPhik' eBulawini
> (Variegation like a multicolored animal
> Like that of Phiko at Bulawini)

\*Metaphors are often poetic exaggerations.

(3) *Description.* Description is often couched in metaphoric lang.:

> Ibhicongo elimzimba buthaka
> Ozithebe zihle uMjokwane
> Ozithebe zihle zidlel' amancasakazi

(Tree with a fragile trunk
Whose eating mats are beautiful
Whose beautiful eating mats are eaten from by
  the womenfolk)

This means that King Senzangakhona was pop-
ular with women.

(4) *Parallelism (Impindamqondo)*. In *parallelism*,
related (similar or contrasting) ideas are linked
by using similar constructions or words in suc-
cessive lines. The following lines from the prais-
es of King Ndaba show perfect parallelism:

Obeyalala wangangemifula,
Obeyavuka wangangezintaba.
(Who when he lay down was the size of rivers,
Who when he got up was the size of
  mountains.)

Normally, parallelism by final linking involves
repetition of a noun, as in King Shaka's praises,
where the term *uhlanya* joins the following two
lines (see ANADIPLOSIS):

UMahlom'ehlathini onjengohlanya,
Uhlanya olusemehlwen' amadoda.
(He who armed in the forest, who is like a
  madman,
The madman who is in full view of the men.)

**II. Early Zulu Poets.** B. W. Vilakazi is the pioneer of
Zulu poetry. In his first book, *Inkondlo kaZulu* (Zulu
Poems, 1935), Vilakazi experimented with rhyme. Ac-
cording to Nyembezi (1961), Vilakazi's eminence can be
attributed to the fact that "he was mainly responsible
for developing poetry whose form departed radically
from the Izibongo (or praises). Instead of adapting the
style and pattern of the Izibongo, he experimented with
Eur. form." Ten years later, in 1945, Vilakazi's second
book of poems appeared under the title *Amal'Ezulu*
(Zulu Horizons); he apparently was not happy with the
results of his Eur. experiment because, in *Amal' Ezulu*,
he discarded rhyme almost completely.

The most important poet to appear in the 1950s was
J. C. Dlamini. His first volume, *Inzululwane* (Dizzi-
ness), was published in 1959. Cope remarks, "In his
volume of verse he shows a return to the traditional
model of the praise poem, with a completely different
sort of content. Dlamini uses the technique of the tra-
ditional praise-poem to express his philosophical and
psychological problems . . . often obscure but con-
stantly strong and deep."

The 1980s can justifiably be regarded as the "decade
of poetry" in Zulu. More volumes of poetry in Zulu
were published than at any previous time. Poets who
published at least four titles include L.B.Z. Buthelezi,
L.T.L. Mabuya, and C. T. Msimang. Msimang's *Iziziba
Zothukela* (Deep Pools of the Thukela River, 1980) con-
tains both praise poems and mod. poems. Like their
predecessors, these poets manage to produce a synthe-
sis of traditional and mod. styles, composing many
poems in the style of the typical oral praise poem. The
most outstanding book, however, is Z.L.M. Khumalo's
voluminous work *Amabhosho* (Bullets, 1989); in this
work, Khumalo composed mod. praise poems and
used parallelism, linking, refrains, and repetitions that
are characteristic of Zulu poetry.

**III. Post-Apartheid Era.** The beginning of the 1990s
saw many political changes in South Africa, particu-
larly the coming of democracy in 1994. The new era
brought its own difficulties and challenges, incl. rec-
onciling the various factions formed under apartheid,
dealing with the past, building a cohesive nation, and
fighting crime, drugs, and HIV/AIDS. These chal-
lenges demanded the focus and energy of the Zulu
poets to respond to the situation with their poetry.

The 21st c. saw the emergence of many female Zulu
poets. An anthol. of women's poetry, *Izimbali Ze-
sizwe* (Flowers of the Nation), was published in 2005;
*Ithunga Lenkosazana* (The Lady's Milking Pail) in
2007; *Izintombi Zengcugce* (Maidens of Ingcugce Regi-
ment) in 2008. The poet Lungile Bengani published
*Kwenzekeni Bazali Bami?* (What Has Happened, My
Parents?) in 2008. These titles do not provide any sig-
nificant description; the poet chooses any title for his
or her book.

Traditional oral Zulu poetry was characterized by
simplicity of form. Mod. Zulu poets have since tried
their hand at more sophisticated Western forms, with
a certain measure of success. In these attempts, they
have also realized the necessity of retaining some of the
simpler elements found in traditional poetry so that
their work may retain a distinct form, a typical Zulu
character that cannot be achieved by following Western
standards in all respects.

■ C.L.S. Nyembezi, *A Review of Zulu Literature*
(1961); *Izibongo, Zulu Praise-Poems*, ed. T. Cope (1968);
D.B.Z. Ntuli and C. F. Swanepoel, *South African Lit-
erature in African Languages* (1993); N. Canonici, *Zulu
Oral Poetry* (1994); C.L.S. Nyembezi, *A Catalogue of
Literature* (2007).

A. M. MAPHUMULO

# Index

Page numbers in **boldface** indicate article titles.

Otsuni, Iwama, 594
ottava rima, 200, 498, 730, 736, 913,
 **986–87**; rhyme royal, 1193; Yiddish
 poetry, 1547
Ottoman-Azeri poetry, 1471–72
Ó Tuama, Seán, 727
Otway, Thomas, 478
Otxoa, Julia, 1342
*Ouchitelno evangelie* (Preslavski), 167
Ouellette, Fernand, 183
Oulipo, 32, 288, 501, 503, 516, 626,
 **987–88**, 1096, 1271; constraint,
 301; morale élémentaire, 900; origi-
 nality, 983; palindrome, 993
*Oulipoems* (Niss), 288
"Our Cities Face the Sea" (Wright),
 943
"Out, Out—" (Frost), 650–51
"Out of the Cradle Endlessly Rock-
 ing" (Whitman), 398, 1514
Ouyang Xiu, 248, 1300
Ovando, Sor Leonor de, 200
Overbury, Thomas, 224
Ovid, 13, 35, 53, 87, 123, 190, 207,
 262, 264, 311, 444, 454, 532, 541,
 723, 897, 913; beast epic, 128;
 calendrical poetry, 175; catalog, 214;
 complaint, 287; description, 350,
 393; didactic poetry, 362; distich,
 624; elegy, 397; epic, 912; epitaph,
 451; epyllion, 416, 1166; erotic
 poetry, 456; heroic epistle, 1291;
 hexameter, 628; imitation, 677,
 678, 679; inspiration, 709; intertex-
 tuality, 717, 718; Latin poetry, 786,
 788, 789; love poetry, 396, 817;
 medieval poetics, 852, 854, 857;
 palinode, 993; paraclausithyron,
 996; poetic calling, 1050; poetic
 madness, 1058; recusatio, 1150;
 rhyme, 1183; translations of, 148,
 153, 504; verse and prose, 1512;
 verse epistle, 1513
Oviedo, José Miguel, 1027
Owen, Gerallt Lloyd, 1538
Owen, Goronwy, 329, 1537
Owen, Jan, 102
Owen, Wilfred, 42, 300, 359, 424,
 650, 914, 925, 973, 1039, 1531
*Owl and the Nightingale, The*, 412,
 790, 1054, 1184
Oxenstierna, Johan Gabriel, 1382
oxymoron, 59, 122, **988–89**, 996
*Ozidi* (Rotimi), 1451
"Ozymandias" (Shelley), 87, 1124

Paaltjens, Piet (pseud. of François
 HaverSchmidt), 821
"Pace non trovo e non ho da far
 guerra" (Petrarch), 9
Pacheco, Francisco, 363
Pacheco, José Emilio, 280, 437, 882,
 1347
Pachín (Francisco Gonzalo Marín), 201
Pacuvius, 1256
Padgett, Ron, 940
Padilla, Herberto, 205
Padín, Clemente, 1500

*Padmāvat* (Jāyasī), 630
paean, **990**
paeon, **990**
Page, Geoff, 102
Page, P. K., 179
Pagis, Dan, 608, 615
Pahari poetry. *See* Nepali and Pahari
 poetry
Paine, Robert Treat, Jr., 1483
"Painter of Modern Life, The" (Baude-
 laire), 107
painting and poetry, 891, **990–93**,
 1061; baroque, 121, 122, 125; im-
 pressionism, 680–81; Pre-Raphael-
 ites, 1102, 1103; romanticism, 1221;
 surrealism, 1378, 1379; symbolism,
 1397. *See also* ut pictura poesis;
 visual poetry
"Pair of Tricksters, A" (Sapir), 57
Pak Il-lo, 777
"Pak Utih" (Usman), 841
Palacký, František, 331
Palamas, Kostis, 583, 584
*Palatine Anthology,* 53, 449, 575
Palau i Fabre, Josep, 213
Palazzeschi, Aldo, 534, 746, 747,
 1328, 1519
*Pale Fire* (Nabokov), 1510
Palencia, Arturo, 588
Palés Matos, Luis, 203–4, 336, 1328
Palestinian poetry, 70, 280
Palgrave, Francis, 54
palindrome, 48, 225, **993**; boustro-
 phedon vs., 159
palinode, **993–94**
Pali poetry, 176–77, 1431
Pālkuriki Somanātha, 1419
Pallais, Azarías H., 946
Pallarés, Pilar, 539
"Pallone Frenato Turco" (Marinetti), 533
Pallotini, Renata, 163
Palm, Göran, 149, 1384
Palma, Ricardo, 1028
Palmer, Michael, 506, 1038, 1296
Palmo, 1436
Palomares, Ramón, 1505
Paludan-Müller, Frederik, 346
Pàmias, Jordi, 213
Paṃpa, 767
Pamperis, Ambrose, 993
*Pamphilia to Amphilanthus* (Wroth),
 418, 545, 1031, 1320
Pana, Saşa, 1206
Panaetius, 341
"Panama ou les aventures de mes sept
 oncles, Le" (Cendrars), 504
*Panchatantra,* 128, 476, 684
Paṇ-chen Blo-bzang chos-rgyan, 1437
Pandit, Waman, 846
Pandurović, Sima, 1295
Pane, Sanusi, 701
panegyric, 28, 122, 171–72, 409, 978,
 **994–95**, 1022
*Paneles del infierno* (Coronel Urtecho),
 946
Panero, Leopoldo (father), 1341
Panero, Leopoldo María (son),
 1341–42

"Pangolin, The" (Moore), 1488
Pāṇini, 983, 1245, 1250, 1253
Pann, Anton, 1205
Pannonius, Janus (pseud. of János
 Csezmiczei), 641, 792
Panofsky, E., 656–57
Panormita (pseud. of Antonio Bec-
 cadelli), 791
Pansaers, Clément, 131
*Pan Tadeusz* (Mickiewicz), 1074
pantun, 650, 701, 840–41, **995**
"Pantycelyn" (Williams), 1537
Pan Yue, 530
Paollo, Rosella de, 1030
Paparrhegopoulos, Demetrios, 583
Papusza (Bronisława Wajs), 1207–8
"Papyrus" (Pound), 506
*Pâques à New York, Les* (Cendrars), 1387
Paquet, Basil, 1532
parabasis, **995–96**
*Paracelsus* (Browning), 270
paraclausithyron, 452–53, 929, **996**
*Paradise Lost* (Milton), 12, 41, 42, 48,
 52, 98, 146, 147, 214, 225, 307,
 351, 365, 393, 417, 419, 433, 442,
 486, 498, 533, 563, 669, 703, 708,
 718, 762, 897, 902, 909, 913, 914,
 922, 959, 982, 1004, 1050, 1110,
 1112, 1255, 1325, 1354, 1450, 1553;
 Christian Hebraism, 600; epic con-
 ventions, 441, 442, 443, 444, 446,
 456, 1002; gendered elements, 544;
 landscape, 782; narrative, 914–15;
 oxymoron, 988; reader-response
 study of, 1147; rhymes, 1189, 1191;
 romantic poetics, 1223; stichos,
 1320; synaeresis, 1398; theology of,
 1156; translations of, 148, 511; verse
 paragraph, 1514
*Paradise Regain'd* (Milton), 146, 351,
 446, 958
*Paradiso* (Dante), 264, 365, 441, 444,
 469, 720, 739, 773, 1036, 1266
*Paradiso* (Lezama Lima), 125, 204, 927
paradox, 122, 936, 988, **996–97**
paralipsis, 997; aposiopesis vs., 61
parallelism, 455, 734, 804, **997–99**;
 free verse, 524; Hebraism, 598, 602,
 603, 611, 1114, 1125, 1169; syntax,
 807
paraphrase, heresy of, **999–1000**,
 1456, 1510–11
pararhyme, 299, 924–25, 973
Paraschos, Achilleas, 583
parataxis. *See* hypotaxis and parataxis
Parcerisas, Francesc, 213
Pardo y Aliaga, Felipe, 1028
Paredes, Americo, 227–28
parenthesis, **1000–1001**
Parini, Giuseppe, 363, 736, 743, 744,
 1204, 1516
parison. *See* isocolon and parison
*Pariz un Viene* (Bokher attrib.), 1547
Park, Josephine Nock-Hee, 93
Parker, Dorothy, 420, 1226
Parker, Pat, 798
Parker, Patricia, 1060
Parkes, Frank Kobina, 15